2010 U.S. Religion Census:

Religious Congregations & Membership Study

An Enumeration by Nation, State and County
Based on Data Reported for 236 Religious Groups

Clifford Grammich
Kirk Hadaway
Richard Houseal
Dale E. Jones
Alexei Krindatch
Richie Stanley
Richard H. Taylor

Association of Statisticians of American Religious Bodies (ASARB)

International Standard Book Number: 978-0-615-62344-3
Library of Congress Card Number: 2012936587

Printed and distributed by Nazarene Publishing House, Kansas City, Missouri
Cover design and interior layout by Richard Houseal

Suggested citation: Clifford Grammich, Kirk Hadaway, Richard Houseal, Dale E. Jones, Alexei Krindatch, Richie Stanley, and Richard H. Taylor. 2012. ***2010 U.S. Religion Census: Religious Congregations & Membership Study.*** Association of Statisticians of American Religious Bodies.

Published by the Association of Statisticians of American Religious Bodies. Web: www.ASARB.org.
Book includes fold-out map, ***Major Religious Families by Counties of the United States: 2010,*** published by Glenmary Research Center, Fairfield, Ohio. Map is also available separately at www.glenmary.org.

This page intentionally left blank.

Preface

This report contains statistics for 236 religious bodies or groups, providing information on the number of their congregations within each state and county of the United States. Where available, it also includes actual membership figures (as defined by the religious body), total adherents, and average attendance.

The Association of Statisticians of American Religious Bodies (ASARB) conducted this research. The permanent members of the Religious Congregations & Membership Study Operations Committee, as well as the president and secretary-treasurer of ASARB, served as authors of this book. Clifford Grammich, Glenmary Research Center (Catholic), served as chairman of the Operations Committee. Richard Houseal, Church of the Nazarene, served as Operations Committee Liaison. Richie Stanley, Southern Baptist Convention, served as president of ASARB during this study, and Dale E. Jones, Church of the Nazarene, served as secretary-treasurer. Other members of the committee were Kirk Hadaway, Episcopal Church, Alexei Krindatch, Assembly of Canonical Orthodox Bishops of North and Central America, and Richard H. Taylor, United Church of Christ.

Several persons provided special assistance in gathering data for this report. Jonathan Ament and Steven M. Cohen at Synagogue 3000 provided data on Jewish synagogues, members, adherents, and attendance. Alexei Krindatch collected data for Orthodox Christian Churches. Scott Thumma of Hartford Theological Seminary provided data on independent churches. Joseph Donnermeyer of The Ohio State University compiled data on Amish settlements, and Cory Anderson compiled data on Amish-Mennonite communities. Richard H. Taylor helped collect and compile data for several groups. Ihsan Bagby of the University of Kentucky once again provided data on Muslim congregations, adherents, and attendance. J. Gordon Melton of Baylor University collected data on congregations and adherents for 215 different Buddhist religious bodies in the United States, providing the most comprehensive-ever enumeration of these populations. Similarly, Constance Jones of the California Institute of Integral Studies collected data on congregations and adherents for 127 different Hindu bodies in the United States, providing the most comprehensive-ever enumeration of these populations. June Pasco of the Institute for the Study of American Religion helped contact non-responsive groups in the later stages of this research. Darrin J. Rodgers of the Flower Pentecostal Heritage Center helped to contact a number of Pentecostal groups.

Thanks also go to Roger Finke, Chris Bader, and the American Religion Data Archive (ARDA) for providing reports and maps of this data on their website, theARDA.com, in addition to those available at USReligionCensus.org.

We hope that this report, despite its limitations, will stimulate ecumenical awareness at the judicatory and county levels, aid in denominational planning, and contribute to the study of long-range religious trends in the United States of America.

This page intentionally left blank.

Contents

This page intentionally left blank.

Acknowledgments

The authors gratefully acknowledge the generous grant from **LILLY ENDOWMENT, INC.**, of Indianapolis, Indiana.

Funding for the Buddhist and Hindu counts was provided by the **JOHN TEMPLETON FOUNDATION**, West Conshohocken, Pennsylvania.

We also acknowledge the generous financial contributions of the Evangelical Lutheran Church in America and of the North American Mission Board of the Southern Baptist Convention to this work.

Special thanks are due to Research Services of the Church of the Nazarene Global Ministry Center in Lenexa, Kansas. Research Services made members of their staff available for correspondence, distributing the survey instruments, collecting the data, and preparing the data for publication. Their availability and interest allowed us to coordinate this large task, and their continued support has been invaluable.

Introduction

SCOPE OF THE STUDY

This publication presents data reported for the 236 religious bodies that participated in a study sponsored by the Association of Statisticians of American Religious Bodies (ASARB). Participants included 217 Christian denominations, associations, or communions (including Latter-day Saints, Messianic Jews, and Unitarian/Universalist groups); counts of Jain, Shinto, Sikh, Tao, and National Spiritualist Association congregations, and counts of congregations and individuals for Bahá'í, three Buddhist groupings, four Hindu groupings, four Jewish groupings, Muslims, and Zoroastrians.

The sponsors invited all religious bodies that could be identified as having congregations in the United States to participate. We also made several special efforts to identify and include data from several religious bodies which have not traditionally participated or been underrepresented in similar past studies. The 236 groups for which we report data have 344,894 congregations and 150,686,156 adherents.[1]

The present study is related to five previous studies.[2] The first reported 1952 statistics and was sponsored and published by the National Council of Churches of Christ in the U.S.A. in a series of bulletins between 1956 and 1958. The second reported 1971 statistics and was sponsored by the Office of Research, Evaluation and Planning of the National Council of Churches of Christ in the U.S.A., the Department of Research and Statistics of the Lutheran Church—Missouri Synod, and the Glenmary Research Center. It was published in 1974 by the Glenmary Research Center. The third reported 1980 statistics and was sponsored by the Department of Records and Research of the African Methodist Episcopal Zion Church, the Research Services Department of the Sunday School Board of the Southern Baptist Convention, the Office of Research, Evaluation and Planning of the National Council of the Churches of Christ in the U.S.A., the Lutheran Council in the U.S.A., and the Glenmary Research Center. The fourth reported 1990 statistics and was sponsored by the Association of Statisticians of American Religious Bodies (ASARB). The fifth reported 2000 statistics and was also sponsored by ASARB.

1: For purposes of this study, adherents were defined as "all members, including full members, their children and the estimated number of other regular participants who are not considered as communicant, confirmed or full members; for example, the 'baptized,' 'not confirmed,' 'those not eligible for communion,' and the like." See "Defining Membership," below.

2: Lauris B. Whitman and Glen W. Trimble, 1956-1958, *Churches and Church Membership in the United States: An Enumeration and Analysis by Counties, States, and Regions* (80 bulletins), New York, New York: National Council of the Churches of Christ in the U.S.A.; Douglas Johnson, Paul R. Picard and Bernard Quinn, 1974, *Churches and Church Membership in the United States 1971: An Enumeration by Region, State, and County*, Washington, D.C.: Glenmary Research Center; Bernard Quinn, Herman Anderson, Martin Bradley, Paul Goetting and Peggy Shriver, 1982, *Churches and Church Membership in the United States 1980: An Enumeration by Region, State, and County Based on Data Reported by 111 Religious Bodies*, Atlanta: Glenmary Research Center; Martin B. Bradley, Norman M. Green, Jr., Dale E. Jones, Mac Lynn and Lou McNeil, 1992, *Churches and Church Membership in the United States 1990: An Enumeration by Region, State and County Based on Data Reported for 133 Church Groupings*, Atlanta: Glenmary Research Center; and Dale E. Jones, Sherri Doty, Clifford Grammich, James E. Horsch, Richard Houseal, Mac Lynn, John P. Marcum, Kenneth M. Sanchagrin, and Richard H. Taylor, *Religious Congregations & Membership in the United States 2000: An Enumeration by Region, State and County Based on Data Reported for 149 Religious Bodies*, Nashville, Tenn.: Glenmary Research Center.

PARTICIPATING RELIGIOUS BODIES

The 19 religious groupings with at least one million adherents account for 89.4 percent of the reported adherents. The 42 groupings with 100,000 to 999,999 adherents account for an additional 9.4 percent. The 91 other groupings reporting adherents account for 1.2 percent. Congregations but not adherents are reported for an additional 84 groupings.

The following groups are included in this 2010 study. The number of counties in which the groups report congregations or adherents will provide a general idea of their geographic extension. (At the time of the study, there were 3,143 counties or county-equivalents in the United States.)

Groups with 1,000,000 or More Adherents	Counties with a Presence
African Methodist Episcopal Church	1,044
American Baptist Churches in the USA	1,051
Assemblies of God	2,563
Catholic Church	2,960
Christian Churches and Churches of Christ	1,580
Church of God (Cleveland, Tennessee)	1,598
Church of Jesus Christ of Latter-day Saints	1,873
Churches of Christ	2,427
Episcopal Church	2,049
Evangelical Lutheran Church in America	1,739
Lutheran Church—Missouri Synod	1,804
Muslim Estimate	592
National Baptist Convention, USA, Inc.	722
Non-denominational Christian Churches	2,665
Presbyterian Church (U.S.A.)	2,358
Seventh-day Adventist Church	1,827
Southern Baptist Convention	2,702
United Church of Christ	1,168
United Methodist Church	2,991

Groups with 100,000 to 999,999 Adherents	Counties with a Presence
African Methodist Episcopal Zion Church	442
American Baptist Association	497
Amish Groups, undifferentiated	363
Bahá'í	2,532
Christian and Missionary Alliance	696
Christian Church (Disciples of Christ)	1,278
Christian Methodist Episcopal Church	516
Christian Reformed Church in North America	248
Church of God (Anderson, Indiana)	929
Church of God in Christ	777

Groups Not Reporting Adherents — **Counties with a Presence**

PARTICIPATION IN 2000 AND 2010 COMPARED

There are 111 groups that participated in both studies, 125 groups that participated in 2010 but not 2000, 25 that participated in 2000 but not 2010, and 13 that participated in 2000 but are grouped differently in 2010.

Participants in both 2000 and 2010 studies include:

Antiochian Orthodox Christian Archdiocese of North America;
Albanian Orthodox Diocese of America
Allegheny Wesleyan Methodist Connection
American Baptist Association
American Baptist Churches in the USA
American Carpatho-Russian Orthodox Diocese
Apostolic Christian Church of America, Inc.
Armenian Apostolic Church of America (Catholicosate of Cilicia)
Armenian Church of North America (Catholicosate of Etchmiadzin)
Assemblies of God
Associate Reformed Presbyterian Church
Association of Free Lutheran Congregations
Bahá'í
Beachy Amish-Mennonite Churches
Brethren Church (Ashland, Ohio)
Brethren in Christ Church
Bruderhof Communities, Inc.
Bulgarian Eastern Orthodox Diocese of the USA, Canada and Australia
Calvary Chapel Fellowship Churches
Catholic Church
Christian and Missionary Alliance
Christian Church (Disciples of Christ)
Christian Churches and Churches of Christ
Christian Reformed Church in North America
Christian Union
Church of God (Anderson, Indiana)
Church of God (Cleveland, Tennessee)
Church of God General Conference
Church of God in Christ, Mennonite
Church of God of Prophecy
Church of Jesus Christ of Latter-day Saints
Church of the Brethren
Church of the Nazarene
Churches of Christ
Churches of God, General Conference
Community of Christ
Congregational Christian Churches, Additional (not part of any national CCC body)
Conservative Baptist Association of America
Conservative Congregational Christian Conference
Conservative Mennonite Conference
Convention of Original Free Will Baptists
Converge Worldwide/Baptist General Conference
Coptic Orthodox Church
Cumberland Presbyterian Church
Enterprise Baptists Association
Episcopal Church
Evangelical Covenant Church
Evangelical Free Church of America
Evangelical Lutheran Church in America
Evangelical Presbyterian Church
Fellowship of Evangelical Bible Churches
Fellowship of Evangelical Churches
Foursquare Gospel, International Church of the
Free Methodist Church of North America
Free Will Baptists, National Association of
General Association of Regular Baptist Churches
Greek Orthodox Archdiocese of America
Holy Orthodox Church in North America
Hutterian Brethren
International Churches of Christ
International Council of Community Churches
International Pentecostal Church of Christ
International Pentecostal Holiness Church
Jain
Lutheran Church—Missouri Synod
Macedonian Orthodox Church: American Diocese
Malankara Archdiocese of the Syrian Orthodox Church in North America
Malankara Orthodox Syrian Church
Mennonite Church USA
Metropolitan Community Churches, Universal Fellowship of

Midwest Congregational Christian Fellowship
Missionary Church
Moravian Church in America—Alaska Province
Moravian Church in America—Northern Province
Moravian Church in America—Southern Province
Muslim Estimate
National Association of Congregational Christian Churches
North American Baptist Conference
Old Order River Brethren
Orthodox Church in America
Orthodox Presbyterian Church
Patriarchal Parishes of the Russian Orthodox Church in the USA
Pentecostal Church of God
Presbyterian Church (U.S.A.)
Presbyterian Church in America
Primitive Baptists, Eastern District Association of
Primitive Methodist Church in the USA
Protestant Reformed Churches in America
Reformed Baptist Churches
Reformed Church in America
Reformed Church in the United States
Reformed Mennonite Church
Romanian Orthodox Archdiocese in Americas
Russian Orthodox Church Outside of Russia
Salvation Army
Serbian Orthodox Church in North America
Seventh-day Adventist Church
Sikh
Southern Baptist Convention
Syriac Orthodox Church of Antioch
Tao
U.S. Mennonite Brethren
Ukrainian Orthodox Church of the USA
Unitarian Universalist Association of Congregations
United Church of Christ
United Methodist Church
United Reformed Churches in North America
Vineyard Usa
Wesleyan Church
Wisconsin Evangelical Lutheran Synod
Zoroastrian

Participants in the 2010 study but not the 2000 study include:

African Methodist Episcopal Church
African Methodist Episcopal Zion Church
Alliance of Baptists
Amana Church Society
Ambassadors Amish-Mennonite
American Association of Lutheran Churches
American Presbyterian Church
Amish Groups, undifferentiated
Anglican Church in North America
Apostolic Faith Mission of Portland, OR
Apostolic Lutheran Church of America
Armenian Evangelical Churches (Additional)
Assemblies of God International Fellowship
Association of Messianic Congregations
Association of Reformed Baptist Churches of America
Berea Amish-Mennonite
Bible Fellowship Church
Bible Presbyterian Church (General Synod)
Canadian and American Reformed Churches
Central Yearly Meeting of Friends
Christian Brethren
Christian Methodist Episcopal Church
Church of Christ (Holiness), U.S.A.
Church of Christ, Scientist
Church of God (Seventh Day)
Church of God by Faith, Inc.
Church of God in Christ
Church of God of the Apostolic Faith, Inc.
Church of God, Mountain Assembly, Inc.
Church of Our Lord Jesus Christ of the Apostolic Faith, Inc.
Church of the Lutheran Brethren of America
Church of the Lutheran Confession
Church of the United Brethren in Christ
Churches of Christ in Christian Union
Communion of Reformed Evangelical Churches
Congregational Holiness Church
Congregational Methodist Church
Conservative Judaism
Conservative Lutheran Association
Conservative Yearly Meetings of Friends
Covenant Reformed Presbyterian Church
Cumberland Presbyterian Church in America
Elim Fellowship
Eritrean Orthodox
Ethiopian Orthodox
Evangelical Association of Reformed, and Congregational Christian Churches
Evangelical Church
Evangelical Congregational Church
Evangelical Friends Church International
Evangelical Lutheran Synod
Evangelical Methodist Church
Federation of Reformed Churches
Free Church of Scotland (Continuing)
Free Presbyterian Church of North America
Free Reformed Church of North America
Friends General Conference

Friends General Conference and Friends United Meeting, dually aligned meetings
Friends United Meeting
Full Gospel Baptist Church Fellowship
Fundamental Baptist Fellowship
Georgian Orthodox Parishes in the United States
Grace Brethren Churches, Fellowship of
Grace Gospel Fellowship
Heritage Reformed Churches
Hindu Post Renaissance
Hindu Renaissance
Hungarian Reformed Churches (Additional)
Independent Baptist Fellowship International
Independent Fundamental Churches of America
Independent Yearly Meetings of Friends
Indian-American Hindu Temple Associations
International Fellowship of Bible Churches
International Fellowship of Christian Assemblies
Jehovah's Witnesses
Korean Presbyterian Church Abroad
Korean Presbyterian Church in America
Korean-American Presbyterian Church
Lutheran Congregations in Mission for Christ
Mahayana Buddhism
Maranatha Amish-Mennonite
Mennonite Christian Fellowship
Midwest Beachy Amish-Mennonite
National Baptist Convention of America, Inc.
National Baptist Convention, USA, Inc.
National Missionary Baptist Convention, Inc.
National Spiritualist Association of Churches
New Apostolic Church of North America, National Organization of the
New Testament Association of Independent Baptist Churches
Non-denominational Christian Churches
North American Lutheran Church
Open Bible Standard Churches, Inc.
(Original) Church of God
Orthodox Judaism
Pentecostal Fire-Baptized Holiness Church
Pentecostal Free Will Baptist Church, Inc.
Pillar of Fire
Polish National Catholic Church
Presbyterian Reformed Church
Progressive National Baptist Convention, Inc.
Reconstructionist Judaism
Reform Judaism
Reformed Presbyterian Church General Assembly
Reformed Presbyterian Church Hanover Presbytery
Reformed Presbyterian Church in the United States
Reformed Presbyterian Church of North America
Schwenkfelder Church
Seventh Day Baptist General Conference, USA and Canada
Shinto
Southern Methodist Church
Swedenborgian Church
Tampico Amish-Mennonite
Theravada Buddhism
Traditional Hindu Temples
Unaffiliated Conservative Amish-Mennonite Church
Unaffiliated Friends Meetings
Union of Messianic Jewish Congregations
United Catholic Church, Inc.
United Holy Church of America, Inc.
United Pentecostal Church International
United Pentecostal Council of the Assemblies of God
United Zion Church
Unity Churches, Association of
Unity of the Brethren
Vajrayana Buddhism
Vicariate for the Palestinian/Jordanian Orthodox Christian Communities

Participants in the 2000 study but not the 2010 study include:

Apostolic Christian Church (Nazarean)
Baptist Missionary Association of America
Duck River And Kindred Baptists Associations
Eastern Pennsylvania Mennonite Church
Fundamental Methodist Church, Inc.
General Six Principle Baptists
Greek Orthodox Archdiocese of Vasiloupulis
Holy Apostolic Catholic Assyrian Church of the East
Independent Free Will Baptists Associations
Interstate & Foreign Landmark Missionary Baptists Association
Jasper And Pleasant Valley Baptists
Landmark Missionary Baptists, Independent Associations And Unaffiliated Churches
Mennonite, Other Groups
National Primitive Baptist Convention, USA
Netherlands Reformed Congregations
New Hope Baptist Association
New Testament Association of Independent Baptist Churches and Other Fundamental Baptist Associations/Fellowships
Old Order Mennonite Church
"Old" Missionary Baptists Association
Primitive Baptist Churches—Old Line
Progressive Primitive Baptists
Separate Baptists in Christ
Southwide Baptist Fellowship
Strict Baptists
Two-Seed-in-the-Spirit Predestinarian Baptists
Wayne Trail Missionary Baptists Association

Participants in 2000 counted with a different group in 2010 include:

Buddhist congregation counts from 2000, which have been replaced by adherent groupings for Mahayana Buddhism, Theravada Buddhism , and Vajrayana Buddhism.

Friends, which were reported as a single group in 2000 but are now reported as eight separate groups: Central Yearly Meeting of Friends, Conservative Yearly Meetings of Friends, Evangelical Friends Church International, Friends General Conference, Friends General Conference and Friends United Meeting (dually aligned meetings), Friends United Meeting, Independent Yearly Meetings of Friends, and Unaffiliated Friends Meetings.

Hindu congregation counts from 2000, which have been replaced by adherent groupings for Hindu Post Renaissance, Hindu Renaissance, Indian-American Hindu Temple Associations, and Traditional Hindu Temples.

Independent, Charismatic Churches and Independent, Non-Charismatic Churches, which are now reported in the new Non-denominational Christian Churches category.

Jewish Estimate from 2000, which has been replaced by separate enumerations for Conservative Judaism, Orthodox Judaism, Reconstructionist Judaism, and Reform Judaism.

Old Order Amish Church and Amish, Other Groups, now reported with Amish Groups, undifferentiated.

Orthodox Church in America: Albanian Orthdox Archdiocese; Orthodox Church in America: Territorial Dioceses; Orthodox Church in America: Bulgarian Diocese; Orthodox Church in America: Romanian Orthodox Episcopate, are now reported as one single church body—Orthodox Church in America.

Serbian Orthodox Church in the USA (New Gracanica Metropolitanate), now reported with the Serbian Orthodox Church in America.

The 26 groups that participated in 2000 but not in 2010 reported a little more than 740,000 adherents in 2000, with most of those being in two groups, New Testament Association of Independent Baptist Churches and Other Fundamental Baptist Associations/Fellowships, and the Baptist Missionary Association of America.

INCLUSIVENESS OF THE STUDY

The study identified, at county-level, nearly 320,000 congregations and more than 150 million adherents in 152 groups. It also identified more than 25,000 congregations of another 84 groupings for whom adherent data was unavailable. Thirty-seven of the 84 groups reporting only congregations have an estimated total membership of 4.3 million. (See individual entries in Appendix A.) Because the total number of religious congregations and adherents in the United States is not known, we do not know what percent of total religious adherents and congregations in the nation this represents.

National polls regularly report that at least 80 percent of Americans claim a religious preference. For instance, the 2010 General Social Survey (GSS) of the National Opinion Research Center indicates that 82 percent of respondents identify with a religious group.[3] The figures in this book, however, reflect affiliation with a specific congregation rather than self-identification.

For instance, the GSS for 2010 indicates that 25.2 percent of the population claims to be Catholic, but that only 20.2 percent of the population claims both to be Catholic and to attend religious services at least once yearly, and that only 15.4 percent claims both to be Catholic and to attend religious services several times (or more frequently) each year. Put another way, the GSS indicates that there is a U.S. Catholic population of nearly 78 million, but a U.S. Catholic population that goes to church at least once yearly of 62 million, and one that goes to church several times (or more frequently) each year of nearly 48 million. Our count of Catholics associated with an individual church was nearly 59 million.

Similarly, many Protestants may identify with a specific tradition but not with a specific denomination, much less individual congregation. For example, the GSS for 2010 indicates that 3.8 percent of the population identifies as Lutheran, while 3.3 percent of the population identifies as Lutheran and reports attending religious services at least once yearly, and 1.5 percent of the population identifies with a specific Lutheran body (e.g., Evangelical Lutheran Church in America) and attends religious services at least once yearly. Put another way, the GSS indicates that there is a Lutheran population of 12 million, a Lutheran population that attends church at least once annually of 10 million, and a population that is able to identify with a specific Lutheran body and attends religious services at least once yearly of 5 million. Our count of Lutherans associated with a specific religious body is more than 7 million.

Several religious bodies merit special discussion regarding inclusiveness.

First, there are independent and community churches, religious movements, and associations whose memberships are not reported to the *Yearbook of American and Canadian Churches* or other compilers. As a result, the total membership of these groups is unknown, and there is no way to determine what proportion of their membership has been included in this study. Nevertheless, for this study, Scott Thumma of Hartford Theological Seminary compiled statistics for 35,496 independent Christian congregations with 12,241,329 adherents not known to be affiliated with any other Christian body. See Appendix J for further details.

Second, Jonathan Ament and Steven M. Cohen at Synagogue 3000 provided congregational-level counts for Jewish synagogues, members, adherents, and attendance. These differ from counts provided in 1990 and 2000 in that they are of synagogues affiliated with a particular tradition and of persons affiliated with a particular synagogue. As such, they are not comparable to the "Jewish Estimate" counts provided in 1990 and 2000 versions of this work. See Appendix H for more details.

Third, we made several major efforts to enlist the participation of historically African American denominations. Using mailing lists and on-line church location systems, we made some estimates for the eight largest African

3: Tom W. Smith, Peter Marsden, Michael Hout, and Jibum Kim, serial, *General Social Surveys*, Chicago: National Opinion Research Center.

American denominations. See Appendix C for more details and explanations of likely undercounts.

Fourth, we divide twenty-three Orthodox Christian church bodies into two families, Eastern Orthodox and Oriental Orthodox Churches, accounting for 1,056,535 adherents total. Alexei Krindatch of the Assembly of Canonical Orthodox Bishops of North and Central America, collected the data on Orthodox Christian groups. Adherent counts for these groups were obtained from the local Orthodox parishes (congregations).

Finally, several other groups received special attention for this study. Further details on Buddhist groupings are in Appendix E, and those on Hindu groupings are in Appendix G. Joseph F. Donnermeyer of Ohio State University provided the most extensive count of Amish groups and adherents ever presented in this series; Cory Anderson of Newcomerstown, Ohio, provided the same for Amish-Mennonite groups; details on their methods are in Appendix D. Appendix F presents details of our gathering of data for Friends groupings, collected by Richard H. Taylor. Appendix I presents further details of Muslim data gathering by Ihsan Bagby. Appendix K provides details of our use of on-line listings to gather information on congregations for some bodies.

Non-participating Groups: The study made efforts to contact and invite at least 89 other religious groups, found either in the *Yearbook* or by referrals from interested individuals. Not all of the groups had size information in the *Yearbook*, but thirty-one of them combined reported just over 6,000 churches and 1.6 million members.

There are four non-participating religious bodies that reported more than 100,000 members to the *Yearbook of American and Canadian Churches: 2010*[4]:

Baptist Missionary Association of America
Christian Congregation, Inc.
Full Gospel Fellowship of Churches and Ministers International
Pentecostal Assemblies of the World, Inc.

These four groups reported a combined membership of 1.5 million in the *Yearbook*.

PROBLEMS

Defining Membership: Our most critical problem is defining membership. Because there is no generally acceptable definition of membership applicable across bodies, we left the designation of members to the religious bodies themselves. Many comment on their definition in Appendix A.

In an effort to achieve comparability of data, we established two major categories for individuals affiliated with a religious body:

MEMBERS: all individuals with full membership status; and

TOTAL ADHERENTS: all members, including full members, their children and the estimated number of other participants who are not considered members; for example, the "baptized," "those not confirmed," "those not eligible for communion," "those regularly attending services," and the like.

Of the 236 reporting groups, 49 reported members and adherents; 37 reported adherents only; 63 reported members only; four suggested a method for estimating adherents without reporting members; and 83 reported only congregation locations. Of the 63 that reported members only, 4 suggested their own adherent estimating processes, which we used to calculate adherents for them. We estimated total adherents for the 59 remaining groups reporting members only, using a formula we discuss below.

Estimating Total Adherents: We use the total adherent figure to compute the population percentage for each group. For those 59 groups that reported members but did not report adherents nor suggest a method for computing them, we estimated total adherents for each county by dividing membership by the population at least 14 years of age then applying this percentage to the Census 2010 100-percent count for the county. For example, the Southern Baptist Convention reported 204,332 full members in Dallas County, Texas. This represents 11.03% of the 14-and-over population of Dallas County. Applying the same percentage to the entire population yields a total adherent count of 261,216. An asterisk at the right end of the line in the Abbreviations Table indicates that total adherents were estimated through this procedure.

We asked the 49 groups for whom we estimated total adherents in this way to comment on the procedure. Their comments are in Appendix A.

Locating Members by County: Membership statistics are generally reported for the county in which the congregation itself is located, rather than for the county in which the member resides. We assume the county of residence will correspond to the county of the congregation in most cases, although modern mobility patterns suggest caution in accepting this assumption in every case. Especially in large urban areas, combining counties into standard metropolitan areas might be wiser when citing membership proportions.

Membership or Adherents without Congregations: In nearly all cases, members and adherents were reported for congregations. Exceptions include American Baptist Association (1 county); Amish Groups, undifferentiated (40); Associate Reformed Presbyterian Church (1); Bahá'í (2,064); Church of the Brethren (3); Church of the Nazarene (1); Conservative Judaism (9); International Churches of Christ (26); Orthodox Judaism (1); Reconstructionist Judaism (2); Reform Judaism (7); and Zoroastrian (266). A few groups count as members some individuals whose congregations have not met or no longer meet the criteria for official recognition as congregations. The International Churches of Christ have off-campus ministry sites in many major metropolitan areas, with adherents estimated for those off-site locations. For the Bahá'í and Zoroastrian groups, there are independent records for the location of adherents. More than 96 percent of adherent-without-congregation situations are accounted for by just the Bahá'í and the Zoroastrians.

4: Eileen W. Lindner. 2010. *Yearbook of American and Canadian Churches: 2010.* Nashville, Tennessee: Abingdon Press.

Average Attendance: Each group that provided average attendance figures was asked to define these. Their explanations are in Appendix A.

County Listings: The *2010 U.S. Religion Census: Religious Congregations & Membership Study* uses the same 3,143 counties or county-equivalents as the 2010 U.S. Census. These include census areas in Alaska, the District of Columbia, civil parishes in Louisiana, and independent cities, most prevalent in Virginia. These areas can change over time; readers wishing to understand how these have changed in the course of this series may wish to consult the Census Bureau listing of Substantial Changes to Counties and County-Equivalent Entities since 1970 at http://www.census.gov/geo/www/tiger/ctychng.html.

Reporting Date: We sought statistics comparable to the April 1, 2010, U.S. Census. Accordingly, we asked participants to provide data for their reporting year ending within calendar year 2010.

Accuracy of Reporting Procedures: Most large Protestant denominations maintain national offices that receive statistical reports from their individual congregations; we used these reports to provide county membership figures for this study. Many smaller groups, as well as those in which local congregations have a great deal of autonomy, only request and do not require such reports. This means that data for several groups is not as complete and current as might be desired.

We asked groups furnishing data to comment on the accuracy of their reporting procedures and to furnish copies of the forms they used to collect the data. Those forms that were received are in the data collection office at the Church of the Nazarene Global Ministry Center. We reproduce comments on accuracy in Appendix A.

Dual Affiliation: We also asked each group, "Do any local congregations of your denomination maintain affiliation with another denomination as well?" Comments we received on dual affiliation are in Appendix A.

Membership Greater Than Population: There are 31 counties or equivalents for which the number of reported adherents exceeds the total population in 2010. These are COLORADO: Kiowa; GEORGIA: Schley; IDAHO: Madison; KENTUCKY: Hickman; MISSISSIPPI: Yalobusha; MONTANA: Sheridan; NEW MEXICO: Harding; NORTH DAKOTA: Adams, Bowman, Burke, Dunn, Emmons, Foster, Rolette; OKLAHOMA: Choctaw, Harmon; SOUTH DAKOTA: Grant, Hyde; TEXAS: Collingsworth, Dimmit, Foard, Haskell, King, Lavaca, Terrell; VIRGINIA: Colonial Heights city, Covington city, Fairfax city, Falls Church city, Fredericksburg city, Manassas city.

Reasons for the discrepancy will differ from county to county, but the most plausible would include U.S. Census undercount, church membership overcount, and county of residence differing from county of membership. This is especially likely in Virginia, where many cities have been separated from their adjoining counties.

DATA PRESENTATION

This report consists of four tables, thirty-two pages of maps and charts, and a fold-out map insert.

In all the tables, we abbreviate group names. We list abbreviations on the pages immediately preceding Table 1.

Table 1, "Religious Congregations by Group for the United States: 2010," presents for each group the number of congregations; the number of communicant, confirmed, or full members; the average attendance (if any) reported by the group; and the total adherents the group has throughout the entire United States. It also indicates what percent of the U.S. population and what percent of the total reported adherents each group comprises. Population figures used for these calculations are from the 2010 U.S. Census.

Table 2, "Religious Congregations by State and Group: 2010," presents group totals for each state (and the District of Columbia): the total of congregations; communicant, confirmed, or full members; average attendance; and adherents. Also shown are the percent of state population and of total state adherents that each group has. States are arranged alphabetically.

Table 3, "Religious Congregations by County and Group: 2010," provides detailed data on which the totals in Tables 1, 2, and 4 are based. It presents for each county or county equivalent the numbers of congregations; communicant, confirmed, or full members; average attendance; and adherents; as well as the percent of the county population and of total county adherents that each group has.

Table 4, "Religious Congregations by Metropolitan Status and Group: 2010," presents for each group the proportion of its adherents in different-sized metropolitan areas. Also shown is the proportion of congregations within each group located outside metropolitan areas. For comparison, the proportion of the total U.S. population in each metropolitan category is shown on the first line of the table; and the proportion of total adherents within each category is shown on the second line.

Sizes are based on the four size categories of metropolitan areas, with additional categories for "Micropolitan counties" and for "Non-metropolitan counties" included for comparison. The metropolitan and micropolitan definitions are those of the Office of Management and the Budget as of April 1, 2010, with population figures from the 2010 census. Size categories for metropolitan areas were "At least 5,000,000 people," "Between 1,000,000 and 4,999,999 people," "Between 250,000 and 999,999 people," and "Metros with fewer than 250,000 people."

Maps Included in the Book: The color map section begins with 20 groups reporting at least one million adherents or groups reporting adherents with congregations present in at least 50% of U.S. counties. These maps show the proportion of the population of each county that is claimed by the group. The same scale is used on each map to make comparisons easier. Similarly, the next three maps show the proportion of each counties' population claimed by the Jewish, Eastern Orthodox, and Oriental Orthodox family groups.

The next maps show the largest group in each county or equivalent. The first of these shows the participating Eastern Religion group with the largest number of adherents. The second shows the largest participating group of any religious background. The third shows the largest participating Protestant group.

The Religious Diversity Map shows the Simpson Diversity Index for each county based upon the relative size of six religious groups: Catholic, Mormon, Protestant, Other Christian (primarily Orthodox), Muslim, Jewish, and Eastern Religions. The greater the index number, the more likely it is that two randomly selected individuals in that county belong to different religious groups.

The next four pages display some of the other maps and charts available at USReligionCensus.org for the various groups participating in the study.

The final map shows the population penetration of the total religious adherents in each county equivalent.

Wall Map: Accompanying this report is a color map, 25" x 38", entitled "Major Religious Families of the United States: 2010." A color code on this map indicates, for each county, the participating group that predominates. Based primarily upon family groupings found in the *Yearbook* and classifications in previous years, the various Anglican/Episcopal, Baptist, Brethren, Buddhist, Christian, Churches of God, Congregational, Friends, Hindu, Jewish, Latter-day Saints, Lutheran, Mennonite, Messianic Jewish, Methodist, Moravian, Old Catholic, Eastern Orthodox, Oriental Orthodox, Pentecostal, Presbyterian, and Reformed bodies were grouped into families. Other groups, such as the Catholics, Muslims, and United Church of Christ were not grouped into families but were treated as separate units.

In the table listings, religious bodies are grouped by these families, indicated by ANG/EPIS, BAPT, BRETH, etc., preceding the group abbreviation.

The number of counties in which the above-mentioned families or units predominate is as follows:

Baptist	1,249
Catholic	1,117
Lutheran	263
Methodist	248
Latter-day Saints	107
Christian	57
Non-denominational Christian Churches	46
Pentecostal	15
Mennonite	12
Eastern Orthodox	7
Reformed	7
United Church of Christ	3
Anglican/Episcopal	2
Brethren	2
Presbyterian	2
Christian and Missionary Alliance	1
Church of the Nazarene	1
Congregational Christian	1
Friends	1
Muslim	1
Seventh-day Adventist	1

A solid color on the map or upper-case coding indicates that a group has 50 percent of more of the total adherents in that county, as reported in the present study. When no group has 50 percent, striped shading or lower-case coding indicates the largest group with 25 to 49 percent of adherents in a county. The 193 counties where no group has 25 percent of adherents are left blank. The percentages on which the map is based can be found in Table 3, column 7 of this report.

METHODOLOGY

The Church of the Nazarene Global Ministry Center in Lenexa, Kansas, carried out the actual data collection. Richard Houseal, Research Services Manager, oversaw the data collection.

In 2009, we sent an invitation to participate in the study to every U.S. religious body listed in the *Yearbook of American and Canadian Churches*.[5] We also sent additional invitations to contacts suggested by the Advisory Committee and by members of the ASARB. Following the initial written invitation, we sent two additional general mailings. Those not responding to these received still additional special letters, personal contacts, e-mails, and phone calls. Altogether, we invited 296 groups to participate; of which 236 are included in the study, seven groups intended to participate but did not, four declined to participate, and 49 did not respond in any way.

Groups agreeing to participate were asked to appoint a contact person. We sent two forms to the contact person: instructions for reporting data; and a transmittal sheet to be signed and sent with the data collected. When asked, we provided a state-county form for listing the statistics. Contact persons could provide the data electronically, in printout, or using the state-county listing provided by the Church of the Nazarene Research Services staff.

The process put the major burden of work on the offices of the various religious groups, since they were asked to compile data by county for all their congregations. In some cases, however, groups were able to furnish information only in the form of yearbooks or other sources. Transferring yearbook information into county data then became the responsibility of the Church of the Nazarene Research Services staff. In a few cases, the groups instructed the staff to estimate congregational membership according to some formula, and approved the result. In all instances, the contact person was asked to review the statistics.

The Research Services staff employed standard procedures for checking the accuracy of data submitted. This included checking state and national totals against county data and adjusting discrepancies (reviewing adjustments with the contact person) and, when appropriate, applying the estimating procedure for adherents. We prepared several items for review by the contact person. These included a spreadsheet of the data that

5: Eileen W. Lindner. 2008. *Yearbook of American and Canadian Churches: 2008*. Nashville, Tennessee: Abingdon Press.

compared 2000 figures to 2010 figures for each county and state, as well as a series of maps comparing 2000 and 2010 presence by county, and, for 2010, location of congregations, ratio of adherents to each county's population, and number of adherents by county. Only after all problems raised by both the staff and the contact person were resolved were the statistics considered ready for publication.

The final step was to run a series of computer edit tests to check for errors. Finding incorrect county codes and locating records with no data were the most common corrections at that step. After this, the Church of the Nazarene Research Services staff produced the printouts of tables and maps for this document.

This page intentionally left blank.

Abbreviations

Code	Abbreviation	Full Group Name	Statistical Reporting Methods: Source	Level	Adherents
015	Amana Ch Soc	Amana Church Society	Faith Group	Congregation	Estimate*
033	ANG/EPIS–Anglican NA	Anglican Church in North America	Web	NR	NR
193	ANG/EPIS–Episcopal	Episcopal Church	Faith Group	Congregation	Supplied
040	Ap Chr Ch-Amer	Apostolic Christian Church of America, Inc.	Web	Congregation	Supplied
056	Bahá'í	Bahá'í	Faith Group	Congregation	Supplied
012	BAPT–Alliance Bapt	Alliance of Baptists	Web	NR	NR
017	BAPT–Amer Bapt Assn	American Baptist Association	Faith Group	Congregation	Estimate*
019	BAPT–Amer Bapt USA	American Baptist Churches in the USA	Faith Group	Congregation	Estimate*
047	BAPT–Asc Ref Bap Ch Am	Association of Reformed Baptist Churches of America	Directories	NR	NR
179	BAPT–Consrv Bapt	Conservative Baptist Association of America	Directories	NR	NR
057	BAPT–Converge/BGC	Converge Worldwide/Baptist General Conference	Faith Group	Congregation	Estimate
191	BAPT–Enterprise Bapt Assoc	Enterprise Baptists Association	Web	NR	NR
223	BAPT–Free Will Bapt	Free Will Baptists, National Association of	Faith Group	Allocated	Estimate*
228	BAPT–Fund Bapt Flwsp	Fundamental Baptist Fellowship	Directories	NR	NR
261	BAPT–Ind Bapt Flwsp Intl	Independent Baptist Fellowship International	Directories	NR	NR
313	BAPT–N Am Bapt Conf	North American Baptist Conference	Directories	Congregation	Estimate*
302	BAPT–Natl Mis Bapt Conv	National Missionary Baptist Convention, Inc.	Address Lists	Allocated	Estimate*
301	BAPT–NBC Amer	National Baptist Convention of America, Inc.	Address Lists	Allocated	Estimate*
300	BAPT–NBC USA	National Baptist Convention, USA, Inc.	Address Lists	Allocated	Estimate*
308	BAPT–NT Ind Bapt	New Testament Association of Independent Baptist Churches	Directories	NR	NR
336	BAPT–Orig Free Will Bapt	Convention of Original Free Will Baptists	Faith Group	Allocated	Estimate*
362	BAPT–Prim Bapt E Dst	Primitive Baptists, Eastern District Association of	Web	Allocated	Estimate*
364	BAPT–Prog NBC	Progressive National Baptist Convention, Inc.	Address Lists	Allocated	Estimate*
370	BAPT–Ref Bapt Ch	Reformed Baptist Churches	Web	NR	NR
388	BAPT–Reg Bapt Gen As	General Association of Regular Baptist Churches	Directories	NR	NR
415	BAPT–S-D Baptist Gen Con	Seventh Day Baptist General Conference, USA and Canada	Faith Group	Congregation	Estimate*
419	BAPT–So Bapt Conv	Southern Baptist Convention	Faith Group	Congregation	Estimate*
075	BRETH–Breth in Chr	Brethren In Christ Church	Web	NR	NR
071	BRETH–Brethren (Ash)	Brethren Church (Ashland, Ohio)	Faith Group	Allocated	Estimate*
157	BRETH–Ch of Brethren	Church of the Brethren	Faith Group	Congregation	Estimate*
244	BRETH–Grace Breth	Grace Brethren Churches, Fellowship of	Web	NR	NR
324	BRETH–Old Ord Rvr Br	Old Order River Brethren	Faith Group	Congregation	Supplied
459	BRETH–United Zion Ch	United Zion Church	Faith Group	Congregation	Estimate*
890**	BUDD–Mahayana	Mahayana Buddhism	Special Study	Allocated	Supplied
891**	BUDD–Theravada	Theravada Buddhism	Special Study	Allocated	Supplied
892**	BUDD–Vajrayana	Vajrayana Buddhism	Special Study	Allocated	Supplied
084	Calv Chpl	Calvary Chapel Fellowship Churches	Web	NR	NR
081	Catholic	Catholic Church	Faith Group	Congregation	Supplied
123	CGOD–Ch God (Ander)	Church of God (Anderson, Indiana)	Faith Group	Congregation	Supplied

* Total adherents estimated from known number of communicant, confirmed, full members.

** 127 Hindu groups and 215 Buddhist groups have been combined into four broad families for this report. Individual group data and codes are available on-line.

Abbreviations

Code	Abbreviation	Full Group Name	Statistical Reporting Methods: Source	Level	Adherents
171	CGOD–Ches God-Gen Con	Churches of God, General Conference	Faith Group	Congregation	Estimate*
168	Ch Christ Chr Union	Churches of Christ in Christian Union	Web	NR	NR
111	Ch Cr, Scientst	Church of Christ, Scientist	Faith Group	NR	NR
133	Ch God (7th Day)	Church of God (Seventh Day)	Faith Group	NR	NR
110	Ch of Chr (Hol)	Church of Christ (Holiness), U.S.A.	Web	NR	NR
121	Ch of God Gen Conf	Church of God General Conference	Faith Group	Congregation	Estimate*
165	Ch of Nazarene	Church of the Nazarene	Faith Group	Congregation	Supplied
089	Chr & Miss Al	Christian and Missionary Alliance	Faith Group	Congregation	Supplied
093	CHR–Chr Ch (Disc)	Christian Church (Disciples of Christ)	Faith Group	Congregation	Estimate*
097	CHR–Chr Chs & Chs Cr	Christian Churches and Churches of Christ	Faith Group	Congregation	Estimate*
167	CHR–Chs of Christ	Churches of Christ	Faith Group	Congregation	Supplied
264	CHR–Int Chs of Christ	International Churches of Christ	Faith Group	Congregation	Estimate*
353	Christian Brethren	Christian Brethren	Web	NR	NR
107	Christian Un	Christian Union	Faith Group	NR	NR
051	CONG–Armen Evang Add'l	Armenian Evangelical Churches (Additional)	Special Study	NR	NR
176	CONG–Cong Chr Add'l	Congregational Christian Churches, Additional (not part of any national CCC body)	Special Study	Congregation	Estimate*
175	CONG–Cong Chr, NA	National Association of Congregational Christian Churches	Special Study	Congregation	Estimate*
181	CONG–Consrv Cong Chr	Conservative Congregational Christian Conference	Special Study	Congregation	Estimate*
296	CONG–Midw Cong Chr Fel	Midwest Congregational Christian Fellowship	Directories	Congregation	Estimate*
198	Evan Assoc RCC	Evangelical Association of Reformed, and Congregational Christian Churches	Web	NR	NR
197	Evan Ch	Evangelical Church	Web	NR	NR
199	Evan Cong Ch	Evangelical Congregational Church	Special Study	Congregation	Estimate*
201	Evan Cov Ch	Evangelical Covenant Church	Faith Group	Congregation	Supplied
203	Evan Free Ch	Evangelical Free Church of America	Faith Group	Congregation	Supplied
085	FRND–Central Yr Mtg	Central Yearly Meeting of Friends	Special Study	Congregation	Estimate*
390	FRND–Consrv Yr Mtgs	Conservative Yearly Meetings of Friends	Special Study	Congregation	Estimate*
328	FRND–Evan Fr Ch Intl	Evangelical Friends Church International	Special Study	Congregation	Estimate*
391	FRND–Fr Gen Cf	Friends General Conference	Special Study	Congregation	Estimate*
393	FRND–Fr Gen Cf & Un Mtg	Friends General Conference and Friends United Meeting (dually aligned meetings)	Special Study	Congregation	Estimate*
225	FRND–Fr Un Mtg	Friends United Meeting	Special Study	Congregation	Estimate*
338	FRND–Indep Yr Mtgs	Independent Yearly Meetings of Friends	Special Study	Congregation	Estimate*
389	FRND–Unaffl Mtgs	Unaffiliated Friends Meetings	Special Study	NR	NR
243	Grace Gosp Fel	Grace Gospel Fellowship	Faith Group	NR	NR
643**	HINDU–I/A Temples	Indian-American Hindu Temple Associations	Special Study	Allocated	Supplied
641**	HINDU–Post Ren	Hindu Post Renaissance	Special Study	Allocated	Supplied
642**	HINDU–Renaiss	Hindu Renaissance	Special Study	Allocated	Supplied
644**	HINDU–Trad Temples	Traditional Hindu Temples	Special Study	Allocated	Supplied
259	Ind Fund Churches	Independent Fundamental Churches of America	Faith Group	NR	NR

* Total adherents estimated from known number of communicant, confirmed, full members.

** 127 Hindu groups and 215 Buddhist groups have been combined into four broad families for this report. Individual group data and codes are available on-line.

Code	Abbreviation	Full Group Name	Statistical Reporting Methods: Source	Level	Adherents
262	Int Cou Comm Ch	International Council of Community Churches	Faith Group	NR	NR
256	Intl Fell Bible Ch	International Fellowship of Bible Churches	Web	NR	NR
268	Jain	Jain	Web	NR	NR
272	Jehovah's Witness	Jehovah's Witnesses	Address Lists	NR	NR
270	JUD–Conserv	Conservative Judaism	Special Study	Congregation	Supplied
276	JUD–Orth	Orthodox Judaism	Special Study	Congregation	Supplied
275	JUD–Reconst	Reconstructionist Judaism	Special Study	Congregation	Supplied
271	JUD–Reform	Reform Judaism	Special Study	Congregation	Supplied
173	LDS–Comm of Christ	Community of Christ	Faith Group	Allocated	Supplied
151	LDS–L-D Saints	Church of Jesus Christ of Latter-day Saints	Faith Group	Congregation	Supplied
045	LUTH–Apostolic Luth	Apostolic Lutheran Church of America	Web	NR	NR
220	LUTH–Assoc Free Luth	Association of Free Lutheran Congregations	Web	NR	NR
164	LUTH–Ch Luth Conf	Church of the Lutheran Confession	Web	NR	NR
163	LUTH–Ch of Luth Br	Church of the Lutheran Brethren of America	Faith Group	Congregation	Supplied
182	LUTH–Cons Luth Assn	Conservative Lutheran Association	Web	NR	NR
207	LUTH–E.L.C.A.	Evangelical Lutheran Church in America	Faith Group	Congregation	Supplied
209	LUTH–Evan Luth Syn	Evangelical Lutheran Synod	Faith Group	Congregation	Supplied
284	LUTH–Luth Ch-Am Asc	American Association of Lutheran Churches	Web	NR	NR
255	LUTH–Luth Cong Msn Chr	Lutheran Congregations in Mission for Christ	Web	Congregation	Estimate*
283	LUTH–Luth–MO Synod	Lutheran Church–Missouri Synod	Faith Group	Congregation	Supplied
314	LUTH–Nor Amer Luth C	North American Lutheran Church	Web	NR	NR
469	LUTH–Wisc Ev Luth Syn	Wisconsin Evangelical Lutheran Synod	Faith Group	Congregation	Supplied
016	MENN–Amb Amish Menn	Ambassadors Amish-Mennonite	Special Study	Congregation	Supplied
031	MENN–Amish Undif	Amish Groups, undifferentiated	Special Study	Congregation	Supplied
061	MENN–Beachy Amish Menn	Beachy Amish-Mennonite Churches	Special Study	Congregation	Supplied
062	MENN–Ber Amish Menn	Berea Amish-Mennonite	Special Study	Congregation	Supplied
073	MENN–Bible Flwshp	Bible Fellowship Church	Faith Group	Congregation	Estimate
070	MENN–Bruderhof Comm	Bruderhof Communities, Inc.	Faith Group	Congregation	Supplied
143	MENN–CG in Cr (Menn)	Church of God in Christ, Mennonite	Faith Group	Congregation	Estimate*
183	MENN–Cons Menn Conf	Conservative Mennonite Conference	Faith Group	Congregation	Estimate*
211	MENN–Fel Evg Bib Ch	Fellowship of Evangelical Bible Churches	Faith Group	Congregation	Supplied
213	MENN–Fel Evg Ch	Fellowship of Evangelical Churches	Faith Group	Congregation	Estimate*
257	MENN–Hutt Breth	Hutterian Brethren	Web	NR	NR
278	MENN–Mara Amish Menn	Maranatha Amish-Mennonite	Special Study	Congregation	Supplied
237	MENN–Menn Br US Conf	U.S. Mennonite Brethren	Faith Group	Congregation	Estimate*
282	MENN–Menn Chr Fell	Mennonite Christian Fellowship	Special Study	Congregation	Supplied
288	MENN–Mennonite USA	Mennonite Church USA	Faith Group	Congregation	Estimate*
310	MENN–Midw Bchy Am Menn	Midwest Beachy Amish-Mennonite	Special Study	Congregation	Supplied
379	MENN–Ref Mennonite	Reformed Mennonite Church	Faith Group	Congregation	Supplied
424	MENN–Tamp Amish Menn	Tampico Amish-Mennonite	Special Study	Congregation	Supplied
432	MENN–Unaffil Amish Menn	Unaffiliated Conservative Amish-Mennonite Church	Faith Group	Congregation	Supplied
011	METH–A.W.M.C.	Allegheny Wesleyan Methodist Connection	Faith Group	Congregation	Supplied

* Total adherents estimated from known number of communicant, confirmed, full members.

Abbreviations

Code	Abbreviation	Full Group Name	Statistical Reporting Methods — Source	Level	Adherents
003	METH–AME	African Methodist Episcopal Church	Web/Address List	Allocated	Estimate*
005	METH–AME Zion	African Methodist Episcopal Zion Church	Web/Address List	Allocated	Estimate*
101	METH–C.M.E.	Christian Methodist Episcopal Church	Web/Address List	Allocated	Estimate*
180	METH–Cong Meth	Congregational Methodist Church	Faith Group	Congregation	Estimate*
215	METH–Evan Meth Ch	Evangelical Methodist Church	Web	NR	NR
221	METH–Free Methodist	Free Methodist Church of North America	Faith Group	Congregation	Supplied
363	METH–Prim Meth Ch	Primitive Methodist Church in the USA	Web	NR	NR
421	METH–So Methodist	Southern Methodist Church	Faith Group	NR	NR
449	METH–Un Methodist	United Methodist Church	Faith Group	Congregation	Supplied
467	METH–Wesleyan	Wesleyan Church	Faith Group	Congregation	Estimate
290	Metro Comm Ch	Metropolitan Community Churches, Universal Fellowship of	Faith Group	Congregation	Estimate
291	Missionary Ch	Missionary Church	Faith Group	Congregation	Supplied
058	MJEW–Assoc Mes Cong	Association of Messianic Congregations	Web	NR	NR
437	MJEW–Union Mes Cong	Union of Messianic Jewish Congregations	Web	NR	NR
292	MORAV–Morav Ch-AK	Moravian Church in America–Alaska Province	Faith Group	Congregation	Estimate*
293	MORAV–Morav Ch-North	Moravian Church in America–Northern Province	Faith Group	Congregation	Supplied
295	MORAV–Morav Ch-South	Moravian Church in America–Southern Province	Faith Group	Congregation	Supplied
461	MORAV–Unity Of Breth	Unity of the Brethren	Web	NR	NR
267	Muslim Est	Muslim Estimate	Special Study	Allocated	Supplied
303	Nat Spirit Asso	National Spiritualist Association of Churches	Web	NR	NR
309	New Apost Ch	New Apostolic Church of North America, National Organization of the	Faith Group	NR	NR
500	Non-denom Chr Chs	Non-denominational Christian Churches	Special Study	Congregation	Estimate
352	OCATH–Pol Natl Cath	Polish National Catholic Church	Web	NR	NR
439	OCATH–Un Cath Ch	United Catholic Church, Inc.	Web	Allocated	Estimate
009	ORTHE–Alban Orth Dio	Albanian Orthodox Diocese of America	Special Study	Congregation	Supplied
034	ORTHE–Ant Orth of NA	Antiochian Orthodox Christian Archdiocese of North America	Special Study	Congregation	Supplied
078	ORTHE–Bulgar Orth USA	Bulgarian Eastern Orthodox Diocese of the USA, Canada and Australia	Special Study	Congregation	Supplied
022	ORTHE–Carp Rus Orth	American Carpatho-Russian Orthodox Diocese	Special Study	Congregation	Supplied
242	ORTHE–Georgian Orth	Georgian Orthodox Parishes in the United States	Special Study	Congregation	Supplied
246	ORTHE–Greek Orthodox	Greek Orthodox Archdiocese of America	Special Study	Congregation	Supplied
251	ORTHE–Holy Orth in NA	Holy Orthodox Church in North America	Special Study	Congregation	Supplied
330	ORTHE–Macedonian Orth	Macedonian Orthodox Church: American Diocese	Special Study	Congregation	Supplied
331	ORTHE–Orth Ch in Amer	Orthodox Church in America	Special Study	Congregation	Supplied
337	ORTHE–Pal/Jor Orth	Vicariate for the Palestinian/Jordanian Orthodox Christian Communities	Special Study	Congregation	Supplied
395	ORTHE–Romania Orth Ar	Romanian Orthodox Archdiocese in Americas	Special Study	Congregation	Supplied
401	ORTHE–Rus Orth Abroad	Russian Orthodox Church Outside of Russia	Special Study	Congregation	Supplied
400	ORTHE–Rus Orth Moscow	Patriarchal Parishes of the Russian Orthodox Church in the USA	Special Study	Congregation	Supplied

* Total adherents estimated from known number of communicant, confirmed, full members.

Code	Abbreviation	Full Group Name	Statistical Reporting Methods: Source	Level	Adherents
410	ORTHE–Serb Orth USA	Serbian Orthodox Church in North America	Special Study	Congregation	Supplied
431	ORTHE–Ukrainian Orth	Ukrainian Orthodox Church of the USA	Special Study	Congregation	Supplied
049	ORTHO–Armen Ap Cilic	Armenian Apostolic Church of America (Catholicosate of Cilicia)	Special Study	Congregation	Supplied
050	ORTHO–Armen Ap Etchm	Armenian Church of North America (Catholicosate of Etchmiadzin)	Special Study	Congregation	Supplied
186	ORTHO–Coptic Orth Ch	Coptic Orthodox Church	Special Study	Congregation	Supplied
202	ORTHO–Eritrean Orth	Eritrean Orthodox	Special Study	Congregation	Supplied
204	ORTHO–Ethiopian Orth	Ethiopian Orthodox	Special Study	NR	NR
333	ORTHO–Malan Dioc Am	Malankara Orthodox Syrian Church	Special Study	Congregation	Supplied
334	ORTHO–Malan Syr Orth	Malankara Archdiocese of the Syrian Orthodox Church in North America	Special Study	Congregation	Supplied
423	ORTHO–Syrian Orth Ch	Syriac Orthodox Church of Antioch	Special Study	Congregation	Supplied
042	PENT–Apos Faith Msn	Apostolic Faith Mission of Portland, OR	Faith Group	Allocated	Estimate*
053	PENT–Assemb of God	Assemblies of God	Faith Group	Congregation	Supplied
044	PENT–Assm God Intl F	Assemblies of God International Fellowship	Web	NR	NR
127	PENT–Ch God (Cleve)	Church of God (Cleveland, Tennessee)	Faith Group	Congregation	Estimate*
120	PENT–Ch God Apos Fth	Church of God of the Apostolic Faith, Inc.	Web	NR	NR
146	PENT–Ch God Mtn Asm	Church of God, Mountain Assembly, Inc.	Faith Group	NR	NR
155	PENT–Ch Lord Jesus Apos	Church of Our Lord Jesus Christ of the Apostolic Faith, Inc.	Web	NR	NR
122	PENT–Ch of God by Faith	Church of God by Faith, Inc.	Web	NR	NR
145	PENT–Ch of God Proph	Church of God of Prophecy	Faith Group	Congregation	Estimate*
141	PENT–COGIC	Church of God in Christ	Address Lists	Allocated	Estimate*
177	PENT–Cong Hol Ch	Congregational Holiness Church	Faith Group	Allocated	Estimate*
190	PENT–Elim	Elim Fellowship	Web	NR	NR
346	PENT–Fire Bapt Hol Ch	Pentecostal Fire-Baptized Holiness Church	Web	NR	NR
232	PENT–Full Gosp Bapt	Full Gospel Baptist Church Fellowship	Web	NR	NR
260	PENT–I F Chr Assmbl	International Fellowship of Christian Assemblies	Faith Group	NR	NR
263	PENT–Int Foursq Gos	Foursquare Gospel, International Church of the	Faith Group	Congregation	Estimate*
265	PENT–Int Pent C Chr	International Pentecostal Church of Christ	Faith Group	Congregation	Supplied
349	PENT–Intl Pent Holiness	International Pentecostal Holiness Church	Faith Group	Congregation	Estimate*
329	PENT–Open Bible Std	Open Bible Standard Churches, Inc.	Faith Group	Congregation	Supplied
326	PENT–Orig Ch of God	(Original) Church of God	Web	NR	NR
339	PENT–Pent Ch of God	Pentecostal Church of God	Faith Group	Allocated	Estimate
347	PENT–Pent FW Bapt	Pentecostal Free Will Baptist Church, Inc.	Web	NR	NR
456	PENT–Un Pent Asbl God	United Pentecostal Council of the Assemblies of God	Web	NR	NR
454	PENT–Un Pent Ch Intl	United Pentecostal Church International	Web	NR	NR
445	PENT–United Holy Ch	United Holy Church of America, Inc.	Web	NR	NR
463	PENT–Vineyard	Vineyard USA	Faith Group	Congregation	Estimate*
350	Pillar of Fire	Pillar of Fire	Faith Group	Congregation	Supplied
030	PRES–AmPres	American Presbyterian Church	Web	NR	NR
055	PRES–As Ref Pres Ch	Associate Reformed Presbyterian Church	Faith Group	Congregation	Estimate*

* Total adherents estimated from known number of communicant, confirmed, full members.

Abbreviations

Code	Abbreviation	Full Group Name	Statistical Reporting Methods — Source	Level	Adherents
069	PRES–Bible Pres	Bible Presbyterian Church (General Synod)	Web	NR	NR
184	PRES–Cov Ref Pres	Covenant Reformed Presbyterian Church	Web	NR	NR
187	PRES–Cum Pres Am	Cumberland Presbyterian Church in America	Web	NR	NR
185	PRES–Cumber Presb	Cumberland Presbyterian Church	Faith Group	Congregation	Supplied
216	PRES–Evan Presby Ch	Evangelical Presbyterian Church	Faith Group	Congregation	Estimate*
224	PRES–Free Ch Scot	Free Church of Scotland (Continuing)	Web	NR	NR
222	PRES–Free Pres NA	Free Presbyterian Church of North America	Web	NR	NR
366	PRES–Kor Pres Abroad	Korean Presbyterian Church Abroad	Web	NR	NR
048	PRES–Korean Amer Pres	Korean-American Presbyterian Church	Faith Group	NR	NR
052	PRES–Korean Pres Amer	Korean Presbyterian Church in America	Directory	NR	NR
335	PRES–Orth Pres Ch	Orthodox Presbyterian Church	Faith Group	Congregation	Supplied
354	PRES–Pres Ref	Presbyterian Reformed Church	Web	NR	NR
355	PRES–Presb Ch (USA)	Presbyterian Church (U.S.A.)	Faith Group	Congregation	Estimate*
356	PRES–Presb Ch Amer	Presbyterian Church in America	Faith Group	Congregation	Supplied
380	PRES–Ref Pres GA	Reformed Presbyterian Church General Assembly	Web	NR	NR
382	PRES–Ref Pres Han	Reformed Presbyterian Church Hanover Presbytery	Web	NR	NR
383	PRES–Ref Pres of NA	Reformed Presbyterian Church of North America	Faith Group	Congregation	Supplied
385	PRES–Ref Pres US	Reformed Presbyterian Church in the United States	Web	NR	NR
086	REF–Can Amer Ref	Canadian and American Reformed Churches	Web	NR	NR
105	REF–Christian Ref	Christian Reformed Church in North America	Faith Group	Congregation	Estimate*
172	REF–Comm Ref Evan	Communion of Reformed Evangelical Churches	Web	NR	NR
210	REF–Fed Ref Ch	Federation of Reformed Churches	Web	NR	NR
227	REF–Free Ref NA	Free Reformed Church of North America	Web	NR	NR
248	REF–Heritage Ref	Heritage Reformed Churches	Faith Group	Congregation	Estimate*
254	REF–Hung Ref Add'l	Hungarian Reformed Churches (Additional)	Special Study	NR	NR
369	REF–Prot Ref Chs	Protestant Reformed Churches in America	Faith Group	Congregation	Supplied
371	REF–Ref Ch in Am	Reformed Church in America	Faith Group	Congregation	Supplied
373	REF–Ref Ch in U.S.	Reformed Church in the United States	Faith Group	Congregation	Supplied
455	REF–Un Ref Chs N.A.	United Reformed Churches in North America	Web	NR	NR
403	Salvation Army	Salvation Army	Faith Group	Congregation	Supplied
405	Schwenkfelder	Schwenkfelder Church	Faith Group	Congregation	Estimate*
413	Sev Day Adv	Seventh-day Adventist Church	Faith Group	Congregation	Supplied
408	Shinto	Shinto	Web	NR	NR
416	Sikh	Sikh	Web	NR	NR
239	Swedenborgian	Swedenborgian Church	Web	NR	NR
425	Tao	Tao	Web	NR	NR
438	Un Breth in Cr	Church of the United Brethren in Christ	Faith Group	Congregation	Estimate
443	Un C of Christ	United Church of Christ	Faith Group	Congregation	Estimate*
435	Unit Univ	Unitarian Universalist Association of Congregations	Faith Group	Congregation	Supplied
124	Unity Ch	Unity Churches, Association of	Faith Group	NR	NR
490	Zoroastrian	Zoroastrian	Web	Congregation	Supplied

* Total adherents estimated from known number of communicant, confirmed, full members.

Table 1: Religious Congregations by Group for the United States: 2010

Religious Group	Number of Congregations (Churches, Mosques, Synagogues, Temples, etc.)	Number of Attendees	Number of Communicant, Confirmed, Full Members	Adherents		
				Number of Adherents	% of Total Population	% of Total Adherents
THE NATION	**344,894**	**34,670,173**	**61,523,376**	**150,686,156**	**48.8**	**100.0**
Amana Ch Soc	1	NR	355	433	0.0	0.0
ANG/EPIS–Anglican NA	913	NR	NR	NR	-	-
ANG/EPIS–Episcopal	6,794	657,831	1,576,721	1,951,907	0.6	1.3
Ap Chr Ch-Amer	88	23,309	12,806	23,309	0.0	0.0
Bahá'í	1,130	NR	170,580	171,449	0.1	0.1
BAPT–Alliance Bapt	124	NR	NR	NR	-	-
BAPT–Amer Bapt Assn	1,368	NR	165,150	203,374	0.1	0.1
BAPT–Amer Bapt USA	5,243	713,135	1,286,457	1,560,572	0.5	1.0
BAPT–Asc Ref Bap Ch Am	67	NR	NR	NR	-	-
BAPT–Consrv Bapt	1,141	NR	NR	NR	-	-
BAPT–Converge/BGC	1,092	216,750	NR	260,100	0.1	0.2
BAPT–Enterprise Bapt Assoc	55	NR	NR	NR	-	-
BAPT–Free Will Bapt	2,285	NR	178,168	217,560	0.1	0.1
BAPT–Fund Bapt Flwsp	24	NR	NR	NR	-	-
BAPT–Ind Bapt Flwsp Intl	588	NR	NR	NR	-	-
BAPT–N Am Bapt Conf	285	NR	46,592	57,219	0.0	0.0
BAPT–Natl Mis Bapt Conv*	1,283	37,610	213,275	261,873	0.1	0.2
BAPT–NBC Amer*	575	110,524	246,044	304,414	0.1	0.2
BAPT–NBC USA*	3,536	634,802	1,535,087	1,881,341	0.6	1.2
BAPT–NT Ind Bapt	120	NR	NR	NR	-	-
BAPT–Orig Free Will Bapt	244	21,960	30,000	36,823	0.0	0.0
BAPT–Prim Bapt E Dst	57	1,425	5,065	6,046	0.0	0.0
BAPT–Prog NBC*	390	79,083	167,286	203,732	0.1	0.1
BAPT–Ref Bapt Ch	353	NR	NR	NR	-	-
BAPT–Reg Bapt Gen As	1,285	NR	NR	NR	-	-
BAPT–S-D Baptist Gen Con	96	2,817	4,244	5,168	0.0	0.0
BAPT–So Bapt Conv	50,816	6,263,277	16,132,444	19,896,975	6.4	13.2
BRETH–Breth in Chr	256	NR	NR	NR	-	-
BRETH–Brethren (Ash)	113	NR	10,890	13,260	0.0	0.0
BRETH–Ch of Brethren	1,032	56,943	120,781	146,588	0.0	0.1
BRETH–Grace Breth	266	NR	NR	NR	-	-
BRETH–Old Ord Rvr Br	6	NR	354	619	0.0	0.0
BRETH–United Zion Ch	12	NR	585	721	0.0	0.0
BUDD–Mahayana	1,836	NR	NR	732,783	0.2	0.5

* Incomplete totals; see Appendix C for African American Bodies and Appendix B for Jehovah's Witnesses NR–Not Reported - Represents no adherents reported. Percentages may not total 100 due to rounding.

Table 1: Religious Congregations by Group for the United States: 2010

Religious Group	Number of Congregations (Churches, Mosques, Synagogues, Temples, etc.)	Number of Attendees	Number of Communicant, Confirmed, Full Members	Adherents		
				Number of Adherents	% of Total Population	% of Total Adherents
BUDD–Theravada	422	NR	NR	203,900	0.1	0.1
BUDD–Vajrayana	596	NR	NR	55,000	0.0	0.0
Calv Chpl	1,136	NR	NR	NR	-	-
Catholic	20,589	NR	NR	58,928,987	19.1	39.1
CGOD–Ch God (Ander)	2,125	225,753	NR	225,753	0.1	0.1
CGOD–Ches God-Gen Con	330	27,272	32,486	39,331	0.0	0.0
Ch Christ Chr Union	194	NR	NR	NR	-	-
Ch Cr, Scientst	1,153	NR	NR	NR	-	-
Ch God (7th Day)	220	NR	NR	NR	-	-
Ch of Chr (Hol)	172	NR	NR	NR	-	-
Ch of God Gen Conf	84	NR	3,110	3,842	0.0	0.0
Ch of Nazarene	5,056	502,765	640,944	893,649	0.3	0.6
Chr & Miss Al	1,978	276,769	193,490	428,721	0.1	0.3
CHR–Chr Ch (Disc)	3,625	200,782	639,551	785,776	0.3	0.5
CHR–Chr Chs & Chs Cr	5,293	NR	1,183,535	1,453,160	0.5	1.0
CHR–Chs of Christ	12,584	1,210,228	1,228,988	1,584,162	0.5	1.1
CHR–Int Chs of Christ	126	NR	34,458	42,106	0.0	0.0
Christian Brethren	183	NR	NR	NR	-	-
Christian Un	104	NR	NR	NR	-	-
CONG–Armen Evang Add'l	12	NR	NR	NR	-	-
CONG–Cong Chr Add'l	63	NR	7,028	8,410	0.0	0.0
CONG–Cong Chr, NA	400	NR	54,928	66,749	0.0	0.0
CONG–Consrv Cong Chr	297	34,230	41,731	50,707	0.0	0.0
CONG–Midw Cong Chr Fel	25	1,143	987	1,213	0.0	0.0
Evan Assoc RCC	67	NR	NR	NR	-	-
Evan Ch	128	NR	NR	NR	-	-
Evan Cong Ch	132	NR	16,997	20,592	0.0	0.0
Evan Cov Ch	816	175,662	126,687	228,365	0.1	0.2
Evan Free Ch	1,470	357,186	NR	357,186	0.1	0.2
FRND–Central Yr Mtg	8	268	231	290	0.0	0.0
FRND–Consrv Yr Mtgs	40	NR	1,626	1,976	0.0	0.0
FRND–Evan Fr Ch Intl	306	37,690	28,002	34,565	0.0	0.0
FRND–Fr Gen Cf	382	NR	18,253	22,192	0.0	0.0
FRND–Fr Gen Cf & Un Mtg	240	NR	12,856	15,436	0.0	0.0
FRND–Fr Un Mtg	258	NR	20,236	24,826	0.0	0.0
FRND–Indep Yr Mtgs	95	NR	2,363	2,850	0.0	0.0

* Incomplete totals; see Appendix C for African American Bodies and Appendix B for Jehovah's Witnesses NR–Not Reported - Represents no adherents reported. Percentages may not total 100 due to rounding.

Table 1: Religious Congregations by Group for the United States: 2010

Religious Group	Number of Congregations (Churches, Mosques, Synagogues, Temples, etc.)	Number of Attendees	Number of Communicant, Confirmed, Full Members	Adherents		
				Number of Adherents	% of Total Population	% of Total Adherents
FRND–Unaffl Mtgs	26	NR	NR	NR	-	-
Grace Gosp Fel	120	NR	NR	NR	-	-
HINDU–I/A Temples	399	NR	NR	304,150	0.1	0.2
HINDU–Post Ren	820	NR	NR	36,720	0.0	0.0
HINDU–Renaiss	150	NR	NR	24,202	0.0	0.0
HINDU–Trad Temples	256	NR	NR	276,114	0.1	0.2
Ind Fund Churches	601	NR	NR	NR	-	-
Int Cou Comm Ch	157	NR	NR	NR	-	-
Intl Fell Bible Ch	27	NR	NR	NR	-	-
Jain	71	NR	NR	NR	-	-
Jehovah's Witness	5,769	NR	NR	NR	-	-
JUD–Conserv	592	165,591	186,713	501,776	0.2	0.3
JUD–Orth	1,932	681,285	253,218	947,020	0.3	0.6
JUD–Reconst	95	12,013	15,414	41,436	0.0	0.0
JUD–Reform	845	160,934	284,442	766,352	0.2	0.5
LDS–Comm of Christ	792	NR	123,189	123,189	0.0	0.1
LDS–L-D Saints	13,601	NR	NR	6,144,582	2.0	4.1
LUTH–Apostolic Luth	52	NR	NR	NR	-	-
LUTH–Assoc Free Luth	276	NR	NR	NR	-	-
LUTH–Ch Luth Conf	79	NR	NR	NR	-	-
LUTH–Ch of Luth Br	105	11,865	8,362	26,695	0.0	0.0
LUTH–Cons Luth Assn	4	NR	NR	NR	-	-
LUTH–E.L.C.A.	9,846	1,159,499	3,159,327	4,181,219	1.4	2.8
LUTH–Evan Luth Syn	129	8,625	15,224	19,291	0.0	0.0
LUTH–Luth Ch-Am Asc	70	NR	NR	NR	-	-
LUTH–Luth Cong Msn Chr	673	96,450	251,971	310,185	0.1	0.2
LUTH–Luth-MO Synod	6,040	821,282	1,758,195	2,270,921	0.7	1.5
LUTH–Nor Amer Luth C	305	NR	NR	NR	-	-
LUTH–Wisc Ev Luth Syn	1,269	164,154	303,786	382,883	0.1	0.3
MENN–Amb Amish-Menn	6	677	329	677	0.0	0.0
MENN–Amish Undif	1,755	NR	101,321	241,356	0.1	0.2
MENN–Beachy Amish-Menn	97	12,311	7,396	12,311	0.0	0.0
MENN–Ber Amish-Menn	11	914	501	914	0.0	0.0
MENN–Bible Flwshp	62	10,112	NR	13,653	0.0	0.0
MENN–Bruderhof Comm	13	2,253	1,003	1,813	0.0	0.0
MENN–CG in Cr (Menn)	153	NR	14,814	18,440	0.0	0.0

* Incomplete totals; see Appendix C for African American Bodies and Appendix B for Jehovah's Witnesses NR–Not Reported - Represents no adherents reported. Percentages may not total 100 due to rounding.

Table 1: Religious Congregations by Group for the United States: 2010

Religious Group	Number of Congregations (Churches, Mosques, Synagogues, Temples, etc.)	Number of Attendees	Number of Communicant, Confirmed, Full Members	Adherents		
				Number of Adherents	% of Total Population	% of Total Adherents
MENN–Cons Menn Conf	105	13,738	11,571	14,284	0.0	0.0
MENN–Fel Evg Bib Ch	19	2,121	1,785	2,121	0.0	0.0
MENN–Fel Evg Ch	46	13,059	7,428	9,193	0.0	0.0
MENN–Hutt Breth	135	NR	NR	NR	-	-
MENN–Mara Amish-Menn	12	1,548	789	1,548	0.0	0.0
MENN–Menn Br US Conf	190	NR	33,493	41,928	0.0	0.0
MENN–Menn Chr Fell	24	2,629	1,277	2,629	0.0	0.0
MENN–Mennonite USA	919	83,610	103,527	127,363	0.0	0.1
MENN–Midw Bchy Am-Menn	6	747	366	747	0.0	0.0
MENN–Ref Mennonite	9	NR	250	275	0.0	0.0
MENN–Tamp Amish-Menn	16	3,342	1,870	3,342	0.0	0.0
MENN–Unaffil Amish-Menn	33	3,224	1,813	3,224	0.0	0.0
METH–A.W.M.C.	99	3,219	1,296	4,031	0.0	0.0
METH–AME*	4,256	233,640	827,663	1,009,682	0.3	0.7
METH–AME Zion*	1,657	51,245	246,285	301,005	0.1	0.2
METH–C.M.E.*	1,462	46,852	236,242	290,601	0.1	0.2
METH–Cong Meth	153	NR	12,079	14,837	0.0	0.0
METH–Evan Meth Ch	97	NR	NR	NR	-	-
METH–Free Methodist	950	101,206	71,756	107,271	0.0	0.1
METH–Prim Meth Ch	67	NR	NR	NR	-	-
METH–So Methodist	100	NR	NR	NR	-	-
METH–Un Methodist	33,323	3,052,409	7,567,707	9,948,221	3.2	6.6
METH–Wesleyan	1,614	192,260	114,956	250,051	0.1	0.2
Metro Comm Ch	150	11,932	14,315	17,600	0.0	0.0
Missionary Ch	423	60,546	34,880	63,775	0.0	0.0
MJEW–Assoc Mes Cong	12	NR	NR	NR	-	-
MJEW–Union Mes Cong	65	NR	NR	NR	-	-
MORAV–Morav Ch-AK	23	NR	1,904	2,649	0.0	0.0
MORAV–Morav Ch-North	84	7,174	16,265	20,286	0.0	0.0
MORAV–Morav Ch-South	56	6,615	13,096	15,737	0.0	0.0
MORAV–Unity Of Breth	27	NR	NR	NR	-	-
Muslim Est	2,106	743,488	NR	2,600,082	0.8	1.7
Nat Spirit Asso	84	NR	NR	NR	-	-
New Apost Ch	296	NR	NR	NR	-	-
Non-denom Chr Chs	35,496	8,621,258	10,883,968	12,241,329	4.0	8.1
OCATH–Pol Natl Cath	119	NR	NR	NR	-	-

* Incomplete totals; see Appendix C for African American Bodies and Appendix B for Jehovah's Witnesses NR–Not Reported - Represents no adherents reported. Percentages may not total 100 due to rounding.

Table 1: Religious Congregations by Group for the United States: 2010

Religious Group	Number of Congregations (Churches, Mosques, Synagogues, Temples, etc.)	Number of Attendees	Number of Communicant, Confirmed, Full Members	Adherents		
				Number of Adherents	% of Total Population	% of Total Adherents
OCATH–Un Cath Ch	10	NR	NR	7,019	0.0	0.0
ORTHE–Alban Orth Dio	2	185	NR	700	0.0	0.0
ORTHE–Ant Orth of NA	249	27,256	NR	74,527	0.0	0.0
ORTHE–Bulgar Orth USA	22	989	NR	2,212	0.0	0.0
ORTHE–Carp Rus Orth	79	4,936	NR	10,457	0.0	0.0
ORTHE–Georgian Orth	7	345	NR	920	0.0	0.0
ORTHE–Greek Orthodox	545	107,289	NR	476,878	0.2	0.3
ORTHE–Holy Orth in NA	34	1,703	NR	2,212	0.0	0.0
ORTHE–Macedonian Orth	20	1,696	NR	15,513	0.0	0.0
ORTHE–Orth Ch in Amer	571	33,797	NR	84,928	0.0	0.1
ORTHE–Pal/Jor Orth	9	815	NR	6,775	0.0	0.0
ORTHE–Romania Orth Ar	32	2,158	NR	11,203	0.0	0.0
ORTHE–Rus Orth Abroad	146	8,864	NR	27,677	0.0	0.0
ORTHE–Rus Orth Moscow	32	1,952	NR	12,377	0.0	0.0
ORTHE–Serb Orth USA	135	15,331	NR	68,760	0.0	0.0
ORTHE–Ukrainian Orth	101	6,857	NR	22,362	0.0	0.0
ORTHO–Armen Ap Cilic	37	7,710	NR	30,530	0.0	0.0
ORTHO–Armen Ap Etchm	94	8,752	NR	64,545	0.0	0.0
ORTHO–Coptic Orth Ch	174	46,963	NR	92,191	0.0	0.1
ORTHO–Eritrean Orth	39	6,350	NR	12,685	0.0	0.0
ORTHO–Ethiopian Orth	58	NR	NR	NR	-	-
ORTHO–Malan Dioc Am	92	9,039	NR	16,952	0.0	0.0
ORTHO–Malan Syr Orth	41	3,395	NR	6,426	0.0	0.0
ORTHO–Syrian Orth Ch	32	4,213	NR	15,705	0.0	0.0
PENT–Apos Faith Msn	51	NR	2,565	3,119	0.0	0.0
PENT–Assemb of God	12,258	1,830,473	1,150,332	2,944,887	1.0	2.0
PENT–Assm God Intl F	18	NR	NR	NR	-	-
PENT–Ch God (Cleve)	6,100	556,996	905,929	1,109,992	0.4	0.7
PENT–Ch God Apos Fth	55	NR	NR	NR	-	-
PENT–Ch God Mtn Asm	101	NR	NR	NR	-	-
PENT–Ch Lord Jesus Apos	454	NR	NR	NR	-	-
PENT–Ch of God by Faith	162	NR	NR	NR	-	-
PENT–Ch of God Proph	1,743	NR	80,195	98,407	0.0	0.1
PENT–COGIC*	2,966	185,861	506,106	624,419	0.2	0.4
PENT–Cong Hol Ch	254	13,481	12,268	15,193	0.0	0.0
PENT–Elim	103	NR	NR	NR	-	-

* Incomplete totals; see Appendix C for African American Bodies and Appendix B for Jehovah's Witnesses NR–Not Reported - Represents no adherents reported. Percentages may not total 100 due to rounding.

Table 1: Religious Congregations by Group for the United States: 2010

Religious Group	Number of Congregations (Churches, Mosques, Synagogues, Temples, etc.)	Number of Attendees	Number of Communicant, Confirmed, Full Members	Adherents		
				Number of Adherents	% of Total Population	% of Total Adherents
PENT–Fire Bapt Hol Ch	216	NR	NR	NR	-	-
PENT–Full Gosp Bapt	699	NR	NR	NR	-	-
PENT–I F Chr Assmbl	80	NR	NR	NR	-	-
PENT–Int Foursq Gos	1,823	255,463	261,974	321,763	0.1	0.2
PENT–Int Pent C Chr	62	1,842	1,161	3,756	0.0	0.0
PENT–Intl Pent Holiness	1,995	189,382	236,095	289,475	0.1	0.2
PENT–Open Bible Std	261	22,659	NR	22,659	0.0	0.0
PENT–Orig Ch of God	13	NR	NR	NR	-	-
PENT–Pent Ch of God	1,101	80,460	NR	125,030	0.0	0.1
PENT–Pent FW Bapt	148	NR	NR	NR	-	-
PENT–Un Pent Asbl God	25	NR	NR	NR	-	-
PENT–Un Pent Ch Intl	4,062	NR	NR	NR	-	-
PENT–United Holy Ch	369	NR	NR	NR	-	-
PENT–Vineyard	552	132,175	180,079	220,941	0.1	0.1
Pillar of Fire	6	NR	2,100	2,100	0.0	0.0
PRES–AmPres	3	NR	NR	NR	-	-
PRES–As Ref Pres Ch	289	NR	26,155	31,978	0.0	0.0
PRES–Bible Pres	20	NR	NR	NR	-	-
PRES–Cov Ref Pres	3	NR	NR	NR	-	-
PRES–Cum Pres Am	107	NR	NR	NR	-	-
PRES–Cumber Presb	660	NR	40,029	66,960	0.0	0.0
PRES–Evan Presby Ch	291	NR	105,042	129,636	0.0	0.1
PRES–Free Ch Scot	5	NR	NR	NR	-	-
PRES–Free Pres NA	14	NR	NR	NR	-	-
PRES–Kor Pres Abroad	193	NR	NR	NR	-	-
PRES–Korean Amer Pres	210	NR	NR	NR	-	-
PRES–Korean Pres Amer	387	NR	NR	NR	-	-
PRES–Orth Pres Ch	319	22,940	21,080	28,559	0.0	0.0
PRES–Pres Ref	4	NR	NR	NR	-	-
PRES–Presb Ch (USA)	10,487	920,669	2,007,877	2,451,980	0.8	1.6
PRES–Presb Ch Amer	1,730	236,604	271,582	341,431	0.1	0.2
PRES–Ref Pres GA	9	NR	NR	NR	-	-
PRES–Ref Pres Han	8	NR	NR	NR	-	-
PRES–Ref Pres of NA	77	5,022	4,339	5,983	0.0	0.0
PRES–Ref Pres US	9	NR	NR	NR	-	-
REF–Can Amer Ref	4	NR	NR	NR	-	-

* Incomplete totals; see Appendix C for African American Bodies and Appendix B for Jehovah's Witnesses NR–Not Reported - Represents no adherents reported. Percentages may not total 100 due to rounding.

Table 1: Religious Congregations by Group for the United States: 2010

Religious Group	Number of Congregations (Churches, Mosques, Synagogues, Temples, etc.)	Number of Attendees	Number of Communicant, Confirmed, Full Members	Adherents		
				Number of Adherents	% of Total Population	% of Total Adherents
REF–Christian Ref	805	143,019	180,565	224,003	0.1	0.1
REF–Comm Ref Evan	73	NR	NR	NR	-	-
REF–Fed Ref Ch	7	NR	NR	NR	-	-
REF–Free Ref NA	2	NR	NR	NR	-	-
REF–Heritage Ref	5	NR	643	804	0.0	0.0
REF–Hung Ref Add'l	29	NR	NR	NR	-	-
REF–Prot Ref Chs	28	6,532	4,318	7,323	0.0	0.0
REF–Ref Ch in Am	864	145,410	244,387	295,120	0.1	0.2
REF–Ref Ch in U.S.	43	NR	3,052	3,923	0.0	0.0
REF–Un Ref Chs N.A.	74	NR	NR	NR	-	-
Salvation Army	1,234	74,158	119,089	379,031	0.1	0.3
Schwenkfelder	4	NR	2,227	2,695	0.0	0.0
Sev Day Adv	5,665	597,488	1,039,005	1,194,996	0.4	0.8
Shinto	5	NR	NR	NR	-	-
Sikh	246	NR	NR	NR	-	-
Swedenborgian	34	NR	NR	NR	-	-
Tao	43	NR	NR	NR	-	-
Un Breth in Cr	178	21,391	16,335	18,259	0.0	0.0
Un C of Christ	5,225	395,487	1,057,938	1,284,296	0.4	0.9
Unit Univ	1,022	99,025	157,752	211,606	0.1	0.1
Unity Ch	594	NR	NR	NR	-	-
Zoroastrian	33	NR	NR	6,558	0.0	0.0

* Incomplete totals; see Appendix C for African American Bodies and Appendix B for Jehovah's Witnesses NR–Not Reported - Represents no adherents reported. Percentages may not total 100 due to rounding.

This page intentionally left blank.

Table 2: Religious Congregations by State and Group: 2010

Religious Group	Number of Congregations	Number of Attendees	Number of Communicant, Confirmed, or Full Members	Adherents		
				Number of Adherents	% of Total Pop.	% of Total Adh.
ALABAMA	**10,514**	**1,003,980**	**2,251,695**	**3,007,553**	**62.9**	**100.0**
ANG/EPIS–Anglican NA	17	NR	NR	NR	-	-
ANG/EPIS–Episcopal	126	13,879	37,858	43,697	0.9	1.5
Ap Chr Ch-Amer	1	55	33	55	0.0	0.0
Bahá'í	8	NR	1,441	1,441	0.0	0.0
BAPT–Alliance Bapt	4	NR	NR	NR	-	-
BAPT–Amer Bapt Assn	32	NR	4,451	5,451	0.1	0.2
BAPT–Amer Bapt USA	4	3,049	6,622	8,157	0.2	0.3
BAPT–Free Will Bapt	140	NR	14,467	17,568	0.4	0.6
BAPT–Fund Bapt Flwsp	1	NR	NR	NR	-	-
BAPT–Ind Bapt Flwsp Intl	8	NR	NR	NR	-	-
BAPT–Natl Mis Bapt Conv	76	404	11,327	13,810	0.3	0.5
BAPT–NBC Amer	19	4,800	11,211	13,740	0.3	0.5
BAPT–NBC USA	382	51,215	143,172	175,176	3.7	5.8
BAPT–Prog NBC	9	2,235	5,686	6,936	0.1	0.2
BAPT–Ref Bapt Ch	7	NR	NR	NR	-	-
BAPT–S-D Baptist Gen Con	2	41	71	85	0.0	0.0
BAPT–So Bapt Conv	3,324	392,530	1,139,469	1,392,363	29.1	46.3
BRETH–Ch of Brethren	3	40	186	230	0.0	0.0
BUDD–Mahayana	7	NR	NR	921	0.0	0.0
BUDD–Theravada	2	NR	NR	410	0.0	0.0
BUDD–Vajrayana	1	NR	NR	53	0.0	0.0
Calv Chpl	6	NR	NR	NR	-	-
Catholic	169	NR	NR	200,657	4.2	6.7
CGOD–Ch God (Ander)	65	3,355	NR	3,355	0.1	0.1
Ch Cr, Scientst	9	NR	NR	NR	-	-
Ch God (7th Day)	1	NR	NR	NR	-	-
Ch of Chr (Hol)	4	NR	NR	NR	-	-
Ch of Nazarene	116	7,044	10,614	13,006	0.3	0.4
Chr & Miss Al	17	964	665	1,265	0.0	0.0
CHR–Chr Ch (Disc)	56	2,609	6,842	8,370	0.2	0.3
CHR–Chr Chs & Chs Cr	26	NR	2,682	3,280	0.1	0.1
CHR–Chs of Christ	867	91,327	89,042	114,015	2.4	3.8
CHR–Int Chs of Christ	2	NR	84	102	0.0	0.0
Christian Brethren	3	NR	NR	NR	-	-
Christian Un	2	NR	NR	NR	-	-
CONG–Cong Chr, NA	5	NR	280	342	0.0	0.0
Evan Assoc RCC	1	NR	NR	NR	-	-
Evan Cov Ch	4	164	368	212	0.0	0.0
Evan Free Ch	2	500	NR	500	0.0	0.0
FRND–Fr Gen Cf	5	NR	43	52	0.0	0.0
FRND–Fr Un Mtg	1	NR	0	0	0.0	0.0
Grace Gosp Fel	6	NR	NR	NR	-	-
HINDU–I/A Temples	2	NR	NR	129	0.0	0.0
HINDU–Post Ren	5	NR	NR	150	0.0	0.0
HINDU–Trad Temples	2	NR	NR	1,100	0.0	0.0
Ind Fund Churches	3	NR	NR	NR	-	-
Int Cou Comm Ch	8	NR	NR	NR	-	-
Intl Fell Bible Ch	1	NR	NR	NR	-	-
Jehovah's Witness	108	NR	NR	NR	-	-
JUD–Conserv	4	938	1,053	2,843	0.1	0.1
JUD–Orth	2	266	135	375	0.0	0.0
JUD–Reform	9	856	1,512	4,082	0.1	0.1
LDS–Comm of Christ	16	NR	2,471	2,471	0.1	0.1
LDS–L-D Saints	73	NR	NR	34,349	0.7	1.1
LUTH–Assoc Free Luth	1	NR	NR	NR	-	-
LUTH–E.L.C.A.	19	1,796	3,057	4,066	0.1	0.1
LUTH–Luth Cong Msn Chr	4	380	816	996	0.0	0.0
LUTH–Luth-MO Synod	62	4,713	8,282	10,290	0.2	0.3
LUTH–Wisc Ev Luth Syn	3	208	242	343	0.0	0.0
MENN–Beachy Amish-Menn	2	139	78	139	0.0	0.0
MENN–CG in Cr (Menn)	3	NR	361	438	0.0	0.0
MENN–Mennonite USA	1	58	45	55	0.0	0.0
MENN–Unaffil Amish-Menn	1	54	33	54	0.0	0.0
METH–AME	294	4,728	39,781	48,639	1.0	1.6
METH–AME Zion	189	2,208	24,018	29,300	0.6	1.0
METH–C.M.E.	183	2,783	22,697	27,620	0.6	0.9
METH–Cong Meth	23	NR	1,883	2,300	0.0	0.1
METH–Evan Meth Ch	1	NR	NR	NR	-	-
METH–Free Methodist	2	57	53	62	0.0	0.0
METH–So Methodist	4	NR	NR	NR	-	-
METH–Un Methodist	1,274	116,330	244,640	295,636	6.2	9.8
METH–Wesleyan	11	1,385	1,535	1,801	0.0	0.1
Metro Comm Ch	3	102	165	204	0.0	0.0
Missionary Ch	1	24	0	24	0.0	0.0
Muslim Est	31	4,464	NR	10,258	0.2	0.3
New Apost Ch	2	NR	NR	NR	-	-
Non-denom Chr Chs	875	157,084	203,199	220,938	4.6	7.3
ORTHE–Ant Orth of NA	2	46	NR	98	0.0	0.0
ORTHE–Greek Orthodox	5	675	NR	2,355	0.0	0.1
ORTHE–Orth Ch in Amer	3	185	NR	340	0.0	0.0
ORTHE–Rus Orth Moscow	1	30	NR	70	0.0	0.0
ORTHE–Serb Orth USA	1	45	NR	60	0.0	0.0
ORTHO–Coptic Orth Ch	2	35	NR	78	0.0	0.0
PENT–Apos Faith Msn	4	NR	140	172	0.0	0.0
PENT–Assemb of God	359	37,304	26,684	54,821	1.1	1.8
PENT–Ch God (Cleve)	387	39,283	70,342	86,003	1.8	2.9
PENT–Ch God Mtn Asm	1	NR	NR	NR	-	-
PENT–Ch Lord Jesus Apos	27	NR	NR	NR	-	-
PENT–Ch of God by Faith	11	NR	NR	NR	-	-
PENT–Ch of God Proph	77	NR	3,561	4,341	0.1	0.1
PENT–COGIC	91	7,510	25,514	31,298	0.7	1.0
PENT–Cong Hol Ch	43	1,596	1,358	1,647	0.0	0.1
PENT–Fire Bapt Hol Ch	4	NR	NR	NR	-	-
PENT–Full Gosp Bapt	17	NR	NR	NR	-	-
PENT–Int Foursq Gos	3	408	717	872	0.0	0.0
PENT–Intl Pent Holiness	51	4,620	8,747	10,791	0.2	0.4
PENT–Orig Ch of God	1	NR	NR	NR	-	-
PENT–Pent Ch of God	8	560	NR	871	0.0	0.0
PENT–Un Pent Ch Intl	98	NR	NR	NR	-	-
PENT–Vineyard	7	972	1,403	1,724	0.0	0.1
PRES–As Ref Pres Ch	9	NR	231	283	0.0	0.0
PRES–Cum Pres Am	50	NR	NR	NR	-	-
PRES–Cumber Presb	59	NR	3,600	5,874	0.1	0.2
PRES–Evan Presby Ch	5	NR	577	704	0.0	0.0
PRES–Free Pres NA	1	NR	NR	NR	-	-
PRES–Korean Pres Amer	1	NR	NR	NR	-	-
PRES–Orth Pres Ch	3	133	76	110	0.0	0.0
PRES–Presb Ch (USA)	147	8,891	21,580	26,347	0.6	0.9
PRES–Presb Ch Amer	108	15,866	22,311	28,009	0.6	0.9
PRES–Ref Pres of NA	1	37	37	47	0.0	0.0
REF–Comm Ref Evan	2	NR	NR	NR	-	-
REF–Fed Ref Ch	2	NR	NR	NR	-	-
Salvation Army	14	962	1,247	2,481	0.1	0.1
Sev Day Adv	115	10,890	18,929	21,771	0.5	0.7
Sikh	1	NR	NR	NR	-	-
Un C of Christ	15	587	1,129	1,381	0.0	0.0
Unit Univ	9	561	842	1,079	0.0	0.0
Unity Ch	7	NR	NR	NR	-	-
Zoroastrian	0	NR	NR	15	0.0	0.0
ALASKA	**1,246**	**71,303**	**97,674**	**240,833**	**33.9**	**100.0**
ANG/EPIS–Episcopal	50	1,777	5,476	7,234	1.0	3.0
Bahá'í	15	NR	1,353	1,353	0.2	0.6
BAPT–Amer Bapt USA	13	1,001	1,708	2,146	0.3	0.9
BAPT–Consrv Bapt	5	NR	NR	NR	-	-
BAPT–Converge/BGC	4	300	NR	360	0.1	0.1
BAPT–Free Will Bapt	1	NR	73	92	0.0	0.0
BAPT–Fund Bapt Flwsp	1	NR	NR	NR	-	-
BAPT–Ind Bapt Flwsp Intl	7	NR	NR	NR	-	-
BAPT–Natl Mis Bapt Conv	4	0	600	757	0.1	0.3
BAPT–NBC USA	1	0	0	0	0.0	0.0
BAPT–Reg Bapt Gen As	5	NR	NR	NR	-	-
BAPT–S-D Baptist Gen Con	2	13	NR	NR	-	-
BAPT–So Bapt Conv	102	7,269	15,863	19,891	2.8	8.3
BRETH–Grace Breth	4	NR	NR	NR	-	-
BUDD–Mahayana	6	NR	NR	986	0.1	0.4
BUDD–Theravada	4	NR	NR	3,405	0.5	1.4
BUDD–Vajrayana	2	NR	NR	73	0.0	0.0
Calv Chpl	2	NR	NR	NR	-	-
Catholic	104	NR	NR	50,866	7.2	21.1
CGOD–Ch God (Ander)	7	892	NR	892	0.1	0.4
Ch Cr, Scientst	5	NR	NR	NR	-	-
Ch of Nazarene	26	1,664	1,986	3,175	0.4	1.3
Chr & Miss Al	16	1,492	912	1,691	0.2	0.7
CHR–Chr Ch (Disc)	1	0	155	194	0.0	0.1
CHR–Chr Chs & Chs Cr	11	NR	2,870	3,586	0.5	1.5
CHR–Chs of Christ	26	1,799	1,726	2,451	0.3	1.0

NR–Not Reported   - Represents no adherents reported.   Percentages may not total 100 due to rounding.

Table 2: Religious Congregations by State and Group: 2010

Religious Group	Number of Congrega-tions	Number of Attendees	Number of Communicant, Confirmed, or Full Members	Adherents: Number of Adherents	Adherents: % of Total Pop.	Adherents: % of Total Adh.
CHR–Int Chs of Christ	1	NR	105	132	0.0	0.1
Christian Brethren	3	NR	NR	NR	-	-
CONG–Cong Chr, NA	3	NR	252	316	0.0	0.1
Evan Cov Ch	20	1,913	1,244	2,489	0.4	1.0
Evan Free Ch	1	30	NR	30	0.0	0.0
FRND–Evan Fr Ch Intl	12	661	1,000	1,387	0.2	0.6
FRND–Fr Gen Cf	8	NR	185	230	0.0	0.1
HINDU–Post Ren	4	NR	NR	76	0.0	0.0
HINDU–Renaiss	1	NR	NR	12	0.0	0.0
HINDU–Trad Temples	1	NR	NR	160	0.0	0.1
Ind Fund Churches	2	NR	NR	NR	-	-
Jehovah's Witness	22	NR	NR	NR	-	-
JUD–Orth	1	83	50	60	0.0	0.0
JUD–Reform	4	158	279	754	0.1	0.3
LDS–Comm of Christ	3	NR	501	501	0.1	0.2
LDS–L-D Saints	80	NR	NR	32,170	4.5	13.4
LUTH–Ch Luth Conf	3	NR	NR	NR	-	-
LUTH–E.L.C.A.	35	2,387	6,819	9,642	1.4	4.0
LUTH–Luth Cong Msn Chr	2	93	270	347	0.0	0.1
LUTH–Luth-MO Synod	14	1,589	2,747	3,665	0.5	1.5
LUTH–Wisc Ev Luth Syn	9	564	779	1,012	0.1	0.4
MENN–CG in Cr (Menn)	1	NR	4	5	0.0	0.0
MENN–Mennonite USA	1	40	40	50	0.0	0.0
METH–AME	1	15	20	25	0.0	0.0
METH–AME Zion	3	115	250	313	0.0	0.1
METH–C.M.E.	3	0	350	439	0.1	0.2
METH–Free Methodist	2	120	91	120	0.0	0.0
METH–Un Methodist	28	2,177	3,598	5,585	0.8	2.3
METH–Wesleyan	3	176	28	229	0.0	0.1
Metro Comm Ch	1	7	14	18	0.0	0.0
MORAV–Morav Ch-AK	23	NR	1,904	2,649	0.4	1.1
Muslim Est	3	402	NR	924	0.1	0.4
New Apost Ch	1	NR	NR	NR	-	-
Non-denom Chr Chs	157	27,738	28,974	38,070	5.4	15.8
ORTHE–Ant Orth of NA	3	313	NR	522	0.1	0.2
ORTHE–Bulgar Orth USA	1	25	NR	25	0.0	0.0
ORTHE–Greek Orthodox	1	86	NR	234	0.0	0.1
ORTHE–Orth Ch in Amer	86	2,498	NR	12,652	1.8	5.3
ORTHE–Serb Orth USA	3	37	NR	47	0.0	0.0
PENT–Assemb of God	87	6,309	2,961	10,261	1.4	4.3
PENT–Ch God (Cleve)	22	1,244	2,326	2,921	0.4	1.2
PENT–Ch of God Proph	4	NR	104	131	0.0	0.1
PENT–COGIC	4	215	355	442	0.1	0.2
PENT–Int Foursq Gos	7	219	259	321	0.0	0.1
PENT–Intl Pent Holiness	8	377	330	425	0.1	0.2
PENT–Open Bible Std	1	47	NR	47	0.0	0.0
PENT–Pent Ch of God	4	280	NR	436	0.1	0.2
PENT–Un Pent Ch Intl	26	NR	NR	NR	-	-
PRES–Kor Pres Abroad	1	NR	NR	NR	-	-
PRES–Korean Pres Amer	2	NR	NR	NR	-	-
PRES–Orth Pres Ch	1	70	61	79	0.0	0.0
PRES–Presb Ch (USA)	38	1,708	3,579	4,460	0.6	1.9
PRES–Presb Ch Amer	1	90	51	72	0.0	0.0
REF–Christian Ref	3	259	211	264	0.0	0.1
REF–Comm Ref Evan	1	NR	NR	NR	-	-
Salvation Army	17	540	994	1,968	0.3	0.8
Sev Day Adv	33	2,179	3,791	4,361	0.6	1.8
Sikh	2	NR	NR	NR	-	-
Un C of Christ	2	80	61	76	0.0	0.0
Unit Univ	6	252	365	527	0.1	0.2
Unity Ch	2	NR	NR	NR	-	-
ARIZONA	**4,673**	**506,056**	**708,851**	**2,379,928**	**37.2**	**100.0**
ANG/EPIS–Anglican NA	13	NR	NR	NR	-	-
ANG/EPIS–Episcopal	66	8,807	19,979	24,853	0.4	1.0
Ap Chr Ch-Amer	3	338	189	338	0.0	0.0
Bahá'í	34	NR	7,659	7,659	0.1	0.3
BAPT–Amer Bapt Assn	11	NR	1,065	1,320	0.0	0.1
BAPT–Amer Bapt USA	26	3,390	5,728	7,204	0.1	0.3
BAPT–Asc Ref Bap Ch Am	4	NR	NR	NR	-	-
BAPT–Consrv Bapt	98	NR	NR	NR	-	-
BAPT–Converge/BGC	22	6,075	NR	7,290	0.1	0.3
BAPT–Free Will Bapt	9	NR	369	461	0.0	0.0
BAPT–Fund Bapt Flwsp	3	NR	NR	NR	-	-

Religious Group	Number of Congrega-tions	Number of Attendees	Number of Communicant, Confirmed, or Full Members	Adherents: Number of Adherents	Adherents: % of Total Pop.	Adherents: % of Total Adh.
BAPT–Ind Bapt Flwsp Intl	15	NR	NR	NR	-	-
BAPT–Natl Mis Bapt Conv	2	0	150	189	0.0	0.0
BAPT–NBC Amer	4	920	1,500	1,853	0.0	0.1
BAPT–NBC USA	9	1,345	2,530	3,098	0.0	0.1
BAPT–NT Ind Bapt	3	NR	NR	NR	-	-
BAPT–Ref Bapt Ch	6	NR	NR	NR	-	-
BAPT–Reg Bapt Gen As	13	NR	NR	NR	-	-
BAPT–So Bapt Conv	404	47,338	101,835	126,830	2.0	5.3
BRETH–Brethren (Ash)	3	NR	240	296	0.0	0.0
BRETH–Ch of Brethren	3	154	174	219	0.0	0.0
BRETH–Grace Breth	1	NR	NR	NR	-	-
BUDD–Mahayana	40	NR	NR	14,089	0.2	0.6
BUDD–Theravada	5	NR	NR	3,715	0.1	0.2
BUDD–Vajrayana	15	NR	NR	1,457	0.0	0.1
Calv Chpl	47	NR	NR	NR	-	-
Catholic	277	NR	NR	930,001	14.5	39.1
CGOD–Ch God (Ander)	26	3,845	NR	3,845	0.1	0.2
CGOD–Ches God-Gen Con	1	60	0	0	0.0	0.0
Ch Christ Chr Union	3	NR	NR	NR	-	-
Ch Cr, Scientst	24	NR	NR	NR	-	-
Ch God (7th Day)	5	NR	NR	NR	-	-
Ch of God Gen Conf	1	NR	62	78	0.0	0.0
Ch of Nazarene	106	10,864	12,510	16,991	0.3	0.7
Chr & Miss Al	22	1,931	897	2,860	0.0	0.1
CHR–Chr Ch (Disc)	30	2,304	3,685	4,590	0.1	0.2
CHR–Chr Chs & Chs Cr	62	NR	38,641	48,386	0.8	2.0
CHR–Chs of Christ	137	10,994	11,069	14,151	0.2	0.6
CHR–Int Chs of Christ	1	NR	556	701	0.0	0.0
Christian Brethren	1	NR	NR	NR	-	-
CONG–Cong Chr, NA	3	NR	549	690	0.0	0.0
CONG–Consrv Cong Chr	1	0	0	0	0.0	0.0
Evan Cov Ch	10	1,794	1,134	2,332	0.0	0.1
Evan Free Ch	34	8,738	NR	8,738	0.1	0.4
FRND–Evan Fr Ch Intl	9	247	157	195	0.0	0.0
FRND–Fr Gen Cf	6	NR	199	246	0.0	0.0
Grace Gosp Fel	3	NR	NR	NR	-	-
HINDU–I/A Temples	9	NR	NR	7,775	0.1	0.3
HINDU–Post Ren	18	NR	NR	540	0.0	0.0
HINDU–Renaiss	4	NR	NR	13,072	0.2	0.5
HINDU–Trad Temples	4	NR	NR	11,500	0.2	0.5
Ind Fund Churches	10	NR	NR	NR	-	-
Int Cou Comm Ch	5	NR	NR	NR	-	-
Jain	1	NR	NR	NR	-	-
Jehovah's Witness	98	NR	NR	NR	-	-
JUD–Conserv	6	1,511	1,695	4,577	0.1	0.2
JUD–Orth	16	1,925	800	2,710	0.0	0.1
JUD–Reform	16	2,756	4,858	13,117	0.2	0.6
LDS–Comm of Christ	9	NR	1,926	1,926	0.0	0.1
LDS–L-D Saints	811	NR	NR	392,918	6.1	16.5
LUTH–Apostolic Luth	1	NR	NR	NR	-	-
LUTH–Assoc Free Luth	4	NR	NR	NR	-	-
LUTH–Ch Luth Conf	1	NR	NR	NR	-	-
LUTH–Ch of Luth Br	4	346	150	591	0.0	0.0
LUTH–E.L.C.A.	84	21,060	33,628	42,944	0.7	1.8
LUTH–Evan Luth Syn	3	213	276	349	0.0	0.0
LUTH–Luth Ch-Am Asc	3	NR	NR	NR	-	-
LUTH–Luth Cong Msn Chr	19	5,272	11,485	14,350	0.2	0.6
LUTH–Luth-MO Synod	72	14,103	21,218	26,322	0.4	1.1
LUTH–Nor Amer Luth C	1	NR	NR	NR	-	-
LUTH–Wisc Ev Luth Syn	54	6,313	8,999	12,760	0.2	0.5
MENN–CG in Cr (Menn)	5	NR	220	275	0.0	0.0
MENN–Cons Menn Conf	4	210	133	168	0.0	0.0
MENN–Menn Br US Conf	4	NR	24	30	0.0	0.0
MENN–Mennonite USA	7	676	743	933	0.0	0.0
METH–A.W.M.C.	1	18	0	20	0.0	0.0
METH–AME	9	830	2,250	2,814	0.0	0.1
METH–AME Zion	1	60	100	126	0.0	0.0
METH–C.M.E.	4	88	475	592	0.0	0.0
METH–Evan Meth Ch	7	NR	NR	NR	-	-
METH–Free Methodist	12	1,127	838	1,177	0.0	0.0
METH–Un Methodist	122	22,773	34,266	54,977	0.9	2.3
METH–Wesleyan	20	1,477	898	1,922	0.0	0.1
Metro Comm Ch	2	136	164	202	0.0	0.0
Missionary Ch	5	135	60	135	0.0	0.0

NR–Not Reported - Represents no adherents reported. Percentages may not total 100 due to rounding.

Table 2: Religious Congregations by State and Group: 2010

Religious Group	Number of Congrega-tions	Number of Attendees	Number of Communicant, Confirmed, or Full Members	Adherents		
				Number of Adherents	% of Total Pop.	% of Total Adh.
MJEW–Assoc Mes Cong	1	NR	NR	NR	-	-
Muslim Est	29	3,831	NR	8,557	0.1	0.4
Nat Spirit Asso	1	NR	NR	NR	-	-
New Apost Ch	4	NR	NR	NR	-	-
Non-denom Chr Chs	574	197,736	252,097	281,105	4.4	11.8
OCATH–Un Cath Ch	1	NR	NR	701	0.0	0.0
ORTHE–Ant Orth of NA	3	580	NR	1,320	0.0	0.1
ORTHE–Bulgar Orth USA	1	25	NR	150	0.0	0.0
ORTHE–Greek Orthodox	8	1,745	NR	8,100	0.1	0.3
ORTHE–Holy Orth in NA	1	15	NR	20	0.0	0.0
ORTHE–Macedonian Orth	1	50	NR	150	0.0	0.0
ORTHE–Orth Ch in Amer	6	383	NR	750	0.0	0.0
ORTHE–Rus Orth Abroad	2	35	NR	85	0.0	0.0
ORTHE–Serb Orth USA	3	150	NR	780	0.0	0.0
ORTHE–Ukrainian Orth	1	20	NR	40	0.0	0.0
ORTHO–Armen Ap Etchm	1	125	NR	3,600	0.1	0.2
ORTHO–Coptic Orth Ch	4	319	NR	608	0.0	0.0
ORTHO–Eritrean Orth	1	325	NR	150	0.0	0.0
ORTHO–Ethiopian Orth	1	NR	NR	NR	-	-
ORTHO–Malan Dioc Am	1	20	NR	60	0.0	0.0
ORTHO–Malan Syr Orth	1	95	NR	180	0.0	0.0
ORTHO–Syrian Orth Ch	1	125	NR	240	0.0	0.0
PENT–Assemb of God	285	55,964	39,488	123,713	1.9	5.2
PENT–Ch God (Cleve)	73	5,391	5,774	7,228	0.1	0.3
PENT–Ch Lord Jesus Apos	1	NR	NR	NR	-	-
PENT–Ch of God Proph	26	NR	1,327	1,672	0.0	0.1
PENT–COGIC	30	1,002	3,046	3,801	0.1	0.2
PENT–Cong Hol Ch	2	78	70	87	0.0	0.0
PENT–Full Gosp Bapt	16	NR	NR	NR	-	-
PENT–Int Foursq Gos	32	3,944	3,832	4,731	0.1	0.2
PENT–Int Pent C Chr	1	0	NR	35	0.0	0.0
PENT–Intl Pent Holiness	18	1,786	1,609	2,014	0.0	0.1
PENT–Open Bible Std	2	263	NR	263	0.0	0.0
PENT–Pent Ch of God	42	2,940	NR	4,569	0.1	0.2
PENT–Un Pent Ch Intl	42	NR	NR	NR	-	-
PENT–United Holy Ch	1	NR	NR	NR	-	-
PENT–Vineyard	18	5,764	10,432	13,114	0.2	0.6
PRES–As Ref Pres Ch	1	NR	25	32	0.0	0.0
PRES–Cumber Presb	1	NR	24	24	0.0	0.0
PRES–Evan Presby Ch	2	NR	236	297	0.0	0.0
PRES–Free Pres NA	1	NR	NR	NR	-	-
PRES–Kor Pres Abroad	7	NR	NR	NR	-	-
PRES–Korean Amer Pres	2	NR	NR	NR	-	-
PRES–Korean Pres Amer	5	NR	NR	NR	-	-
PRES–Orth Pres Ch	5	225	224	302	0.0	0.0
PRES–Presb Ch (USA)	97	11,577	20,958	26,078	0.4	1.1
PRES–Presb Ch Amer	16	2,429	2,412	2,601	0.0	0.1
PRES–Ref Pres of NA	1	48	23	40	0.0	0.0
REF–Christian Ref	9	528	747	950	0.0	0.0
REF–Comm Ref Evan	1	NR	NR	NR	-	-
REF–Hung Ref Add'l	1	NR	NR	NR	-	-
REF–Ref Ch in Am	8	1,238	1,208	1,618	0.0	0.1
REF–Un Ref Chs N.A.	1	NR	NR	NR	-	-
Salvation Army	28	1,716	2,164	4,612	0.1	0.2
Sev Day Adv	100	10,461	18,192	20,924	0.3	0.9
Sikh	6	NR	NR	NR	-	-
Tao	1	NR	NR	NR	-	-
Un Breth in Cr	1	0	0	0	0.0	0.0
Un C of Christ	33	3,566	6,735	8,390	0.1	0.4
Unit Univ	13	1,384	2,145	2,606	0.0	0.1
Unity Ch	20	NR	NR	NR	-	-
Zoroastrian	1	NR	NR	134	0.0	0.0
ARKANSAS	**6,697**	**515,358**	**1,155,819**	**1,614,357**	**55.4**	**100.0**
ANG/EPIS–Anglican NA	9	NR	NR	NR	-	-
ANG/EPIS–Episcopal	57	4,656	11,578	13,469	0.5	0.8
Bahá'í	5	NR	1,266	1,266	0.0	0.1
BAPT–Alliance Bapt	1	NR	NR	NR	-	-
BAPT–Amer Bapt Assn	463	NR	65,993	80,814	2.8	5.0
BAPT–Amer Bapt USA	1	43	88	113	0.0	0.0
BAPT–Free Will Bapt	193	NR	17,727	21,803	0.7	1.4
BAPT–Ind Bapt Flwsp Intl	6	NR	NR	NR	-	-
BAPT–Natl Mis Bapt Conv	49	465	6,956	8,569	0.3	0.5
BAPT–NBC Amer	9	595	1,250	1,559	0.1	0.1

Religious Group	Number of Congrega-tions	Number of Attendees	Number of Communicant, Confirmed, or Full Members	Adherents		
				Number of Adherents	% of Total Pop.	% of Total Adh.
BAPT–NBC USA	105	11,904	31,277	38,559	1.3	2.4
BAPT–NT Ind Bapt	1	NR	NR	NR	-	-
BAPT–Prog NBC	1	0	150	185	0.0	0.0
BAPT–Ref Bapt Ch	4	NR	NR	NR	-	-
BAPT–Reg Bapt Gen As	7	NR	NR	NR	-	-
BAPT–S-D Baptist Gen Con	2	24	131	162	0.0	0.0
BAPT–So Bapt Conv	1,515	174,514	535,924	661,382	22.7	41.0
BRETH–Ch of Brethren	1	10	29	37	0.0	0.0
BUDD–Mahayana	7	NR	NR	652	0.0	0.0
BUDD–Theravada	6	NR	NR	1,304	0.0	0.1
Calv Chpl	8	NR	NR	NR	-	-
Catholic	126	NR	NR	122,662	4.2	7.6
CGOD–Ch God (Ander)	30	2,397	NR	2,397	0.1	0.1
CGOD–Ches God-Gen Con	2	24	14	18	0.0	0.0
Ch Cr, Scientist	11	NR	NR	NR	-	-
Ch God (7th Day)	4	NR	NR	NR	-	-
Ch of Chr (Hol)	7	NR	NR	NR	-	-
Ch of God Gen Conf	5	NR	109	135	0.0	0.0
Ch of Nazarene	108	7,748	12,636	16,291	0.6	1.0
Chr & Miss Al	7	312	275	422	0.0	0.0
CHR–Chr Ch (Disc)	50	2,646	6,340	7,847	0.3	0.5
CHR–Chr Chs & Chs Cr	57	NR	7,216	8,974	0.3	0.6
CHR–Chs of Christ	721	66,438	66,604	84,635	2.9	5.2
CHR–Int Chs of Christ	1	NR	33	41	0.0	0.0
Christian Un	4	NR	NR	NR	-	-
Evan Ch	1	NR	NR	NR	-	-
Evan Free Ch	5	944	NR	944	0.0	0.1
FRND–Central Yr Mtg	1	11	8	10	0.0	0.0
FRND–Fr Gen Cf	2	NR	86	107	0.0	0.0
Grace Gosp Fel	2	NR	NR	NR	-	-
HINDU–I/A Temples	2	NR	NR	1,992	0.1	0.1
HINDU–Post Ren	4	NR	NR	128	0.0	0.0
HINDU–Trad Temples	1	NR	NR	400	0.0	0.0
Ind Fund Churches	4	NR	NR	NR	-	-
Int Cou Comm Ch	2	NR	NR	NR	-	-
Intl Fell Bible Ch	1	NR	NR	NR	-	-
Jehovah's Witness	88	NR	NR	NR	-	-
JUD–Orth	1	43	50	60	0.0	0.0
JUD–Reform	7	313	551	1,487	0.1	0.1
LDS–Comm of Christ	17	NR	2,046	2,046	0.1	0.1
LDS–L-D Saints	62	NR	NR	27,559	0.9	1.7
LUTH–E.L.C.A.	21	1,947	3,837	4,450	0.2	0.3
LUTH–Luth Cong Msn Chr	1	44	56	72	0.0	0.0
LUTH–Luth–MO Synod	66	5,690	9,819	11,843	0.4	0.7
LUTH–Wisc Ev Luth Syn	6	333	435	587	0.0	0.0
MENN–Amish Undif	2	NR	48	130	0.0	0.0
MENN–Beachy Amish-Menn	4	431	213	431	0.0	0.0
MENN–Ber Amish-Menn	1	107	63	107	0.0	0.0
MENN–CG in Cr (Menn)	4	NR	397	499	0.0	0.0
MENN–Cons Menn Conf	2	44	65	79	0.0	0.0
MENN–Menn Br US Conf	1	NR	53	63	0.0	0.0
MENN–Mennonite USA	2	44	60	72	0.0	0.0
MENN–Tamp Amish-Menn	6	883	497	883	0.0	0.1
METH–AME	184	1,530	22,874	27,991	1.0	1.7
METH–AME Zion	14	115	1,459	1,787	0.1	0.1
METH–C.M.E.	79	710	9,062	11,199	0.4	0.7
METH–Cong Meth	1	NR	12	15	0.0	0.0
METH–Free Methodist	1	48	10	48	0.0	0.0
METH–So Methodist	1	NR	NR	NR	-	-
METH–Un Methodist	691	54,008	135,733	158,574	5.4	9.8
METH–Wesleyan	9	345	408	449	0.0	0.0
Missionary Ch	1	15	15	15	0.0	0.0
Muslim Est	13	1,643	NR	3,746	0.1	0.2
New Apost Ch	3	NR	NR	NR	-	-
Non-denom Chr Chs	497	94,027	118,034	129,638	4.4	8.0
ORTHE–Ant Orth of NA	3	120	NR	420	0.0	0.0
ORTHE–Greek Orthodox	2	165	NR	330	0.0	0.0
ORTHE–Orth Ch in Amer	1	30	NR	60	0.0	0.0
ORTHE–Rus Orth Abroad	1	14	NR	51	0.0	0.0
ORTHE–Serb Orth USA	2	55	NR	321	0.0	0.0
ORTHO–Coptic Orth Ch	1	14	NR	18	0.0	0.0
PENT–Apos Faith Msn	1	NR	35	44	0.0	0.0
PENT–Assemb of God	436	46,008	29,271	68,946	2.4	4.3
PENT–Ch God (Cleve)	87	4,895	8,084	9,996	0.3	0.6

NR–Not Reported - Represents no adherents reported. Percentages may not total 100 due to rounding.

Table 2: Religious Congregations by State and Group: 2010

Religious Group	Number of Congrega-tions	Number of Attendees	Number of Communicant, Confirmed, or Full Members	Adherents		
				Number of Adherents	% of Total Pop.	% of Total Adh.
PENT–Ch God Apos Fth	12	NR	NR	NR	-	-
PENT–Ch of God Proph	27	NR	819	1,014	0.0	0.1
PENT–COGIC	103	4,046	14,109	17,353	0.6	1.1
PENT–Full Gosp Bapt	3	NR	NR	NR	-	-
PENT–Int Foursq Gos	8	573	757	927	0.0	0.1
PENT–Intl Pent Holiness	15	933	913	1,146	0.0	0.1
PENT–Open Bible Std	2	192	NR	192	0.0	0.0
PENT–Orig Ch of God	5	NR	NR	NR	-	-
PENT–Pent Ch of God	131	9,170	NR	14,247	0.5	0.9
PENT–Un Pent Ch Intl	160	NR	NR	NR	-	-
PENT–Vineyard	1	140	165	206	0.0	0.0
PRES–As Ref Pres Ch	5	NR	125	152	0.0	0.0
PRES–Cumber Presb	61	NR	2,108	3,592	0.1	0.2
PRES–Evan Presby Ch	2	NR	107	134	0.0	0.0
PRES–Korean Pres Amer	1	NR	NR	NR	-	-
PRES–Presb Ch (USA)	111	6,759	16,653	20,536	0.7	1.3
PRES–Presb Ch Amer	9	757	686	928	0.0	0.1
REF–Comm Ref Evan	3	NR	NR	NR	-	-
REF–Heritage Ref	1	NR	18	22	0.0	0.0
REF–Ref Ch in U.S.	1	NR	18	20	0.0	0.0
Salvation Army	14	1,060	1,055	2,089	0.1	0.1
Sev Day Adv	77	4,981	8,663	9,960	0.3	0.6
Tao	1	NR	NR	NR	-	-
Un C of Christ	3	13	189	236	0.0	0.0
Unit Univ	7	382	557	710	0.0	0.0
Unity Ch	7	NR	NR	NR	-	-
CALIFORNIA	**23,558**	**2,840,602**	**3,642,008**	**16,765,751**	**45.0**	**100.0**
ANG/EPIS–Anglican NA	83	NR	NR	NR	-	-
ANG/EPIS–Episcopal	409	45,014	104,221	130,709	0.4	0.8
Ap Chr Ch-Amer	2	138	89	138	0.0	0.0
Bahá'í	217	NR	29,638	29,638	0.1	0.2
BAPT–Alliance Bapt	5	NR	NR	NR	-	-
BAPT–Amer Bapt Assn	85	NR	6,890	8,658	0.0	0.1
BAPT–Amer Bapt USA	458	83,727	93,175	114,797	0.3	0.7
BAPT–Asc Ref Bap Ch Am	8	NR	NR	NR	-	-
BAPT–Consrv Bapt	226	NR	NR	NR	-	-
BAPT–Converge/BGC	151	30,600	NR	36,720	0.1	0.2
BAPT–Free Will Bapt	52	NR	2,392	3,035	0.0	0.0
BAPT–Fund Bapt Flwsp	2	NR	NR	NR	-	-
BAPT–Ind Bapt Flwsp Intl	3	NR	NR	NR	-	-
BAPT–N Am Bapt Conf	55	NR	14,232	17,780	0.0	0.1
BAPT–Natl Mis Bapt Conv	79	2,412	11,228	13,746	0.0	0.1
BAPT–NBC Amer	45	8,532	15,922	19,490	0.1	0.1
BAPT–NBC USA	113	15,960	47,590	57,968	0.2	0.3
BAPT–NT Ind Bapt	1	NR	NR	NR	-	-
BAPT–Prog NBC	19	1,635	4,657	5,757	0.0	0.0
BAPT–Ref Bapt Ch	23	NR	NR	NR	-	-
BAPT–Reg Bapt Gen As	100	NR	NR	NR	-	-
BAPT–S-D Baptist Gen Con	7	181	362	456	0.0	0.0
BAPT–So Bapt Conv	2,147	247,855	394,528	489,953	1.3	2.9
BRETH–Breth in Chr	18	NR	NR	NR	-	-
BRETH–Brethren (Ash)	5	NR	400	505	0.0	0.0
BRETH–Ch of Brethren	24	1,105	2,026	2,534	0.0	0.0
BRETH–Grace Breth	31	NR	NR	NR	-	-
BUDD–Mahayana	498	NR	NR	250,945	0.7	1.5
BUDD–Theravada	109	NR	NR	65,463	0.2	0.4
BUDD–Vajrayana	126	NR	NR	10,532	0.0	0.1
Calv Chpl	331	NR	NR	NR	-	-
Catholic	1,315	NR	NR	10,233,334	27.5	61.0
CGOD–Ch God (Ander)	122	20,634	NR	20,634	0.1	0.1
CGOD–Ches God-Gen Con	8	326	414	525	0.0	0.0
Ch Cr, Scientst	181	NR	NR	NR	-	-
Ch God (7th Day)	31	NR	NR	NR	-	-
Ch of Chr (Hol)	38	NR	NR	NR	-	-
Ch of God Gen Conf	2	NR	38	47	0.0	0.0
Ch of Nazarene	435	52,841	60,676	86,715	0.2	0.5
Chr & Miss Al	230	40,821	35,895	61,456	0.2	0.4
CHR–Chr Ch (Disc)	202	8,512	18,622	22,978	0.1	0.1
CHR–Chr Chs & Chs Cr	212	NR	66,765	82,719	0.2	0.5
CHR–Chs of Christ	632	55,663	56,631	73,405	0.2	0.4
CHR–Int Chs of Christ	7	NR	7,282	8,960	0.0	0.1
Christian Brethren	14	NR	NR	NR	-	-
CONG–Armen Evang Add'l	10	NR	NR	NR	-	-

Religious Group	Number of Congrega-tions	Number of Attendees	Number of Communicant, Confirmed, or Full Members	Adherents		
				Number of Adherents	% of Total Pop.	% of Total Adh.
CONG–Cong Chr, NA	29	NR	5,462	6,799	0.0	0.0
CONG–Consrv Cong Chr	9	4,265	4,685	5,755	0.0	0.0
Evan Assoc RCC	1	NR	NR	NR	-	-
Evan Cov Ch	148	41,525	27,012	53,984	0.1	0.3
Evan Free Ch	180	59,607	NR	59,607	0.2	0.4
FRND–Evan Fr Ch Intl	41	10,770	4,620	5,686	0.0	0.0
FRND–Fr Gen Cf	2	NR	92	113	0.0	0.0
FRND–Fr Un Mtg	3	NR	378	464	0.0	0.0
FRND–Indep Yr Mtgs	41	NR	1,323	1,603	0.0	0.0
Grace Gosp Fel	6	NR	NR	NR	-	-
HINDU–I/A Temples	63	NR	NR	45,234	0.1	0.3
HINDU–Post Ren	156	NR	NR	6,130	0.0	0.0
HINDU–Renaiss	45	NR	NR	5,142	0.0	0.0
HINDU–Trad Temples	34	NR	NR	55,626	0.1	0.3
Ind Fund Churches	71	NR	NR	NR	-	-
Int Cou Comm Ch	12	NR	NR	NR	-	-
Jain	5	NR	NR	NR	-	-
Jehovah's Witness	611	NR	NR	NR	-	-
JUD–Conserv	62	17,075	19,163	51,738	0.1	0.3
JUD–Orth	229	38,789	16,700	54,625	0.1	0.3
JUD–Reconst	10	1,964	2,508	6,771	0.0	0.0
JUD–Reform	95	21,478	37,878	102,270	0.3	0.6
LDS–Comm of Christ	41	NR	6,619	6,619	0.0	0.0
LDS–L-D Saints	1,362	NR	NR	763,818	2.1	4.6
LUTH–Apostolic Luth	2	NR	NR	NR	-	-
LUTH–Assoc Free Luth	7	NR	NR	NR	-	-
LUTH–Ch Luth Conf	4	NR	NR	NR	-	-
LUTH–Ch of Luth Br	3	263	181	670	0.0	0.0
LUTH–Cons Luth Assn	3	NR	NR	NR	-	-
LUTH–E.L.C.A.	446	48,836	94,165	123,908	0.3	0.7
LUTH–Evan Luth Syn	6	189	242	253	0.0	0.0
LUTH–Luth Ch-Am Asc	7	NR	NR	NR	-	-
LUTH–Luth Cong Msn Chr	41	8,273	19,841	24,525	0.1	0.1
LUTH–Luth–MO Synod	392	46,523	81,902	105,084	0.3	0.6
LUTH–Nor Amer Luth C	7	NR	NR	NR	-	-
LUTH–Wisc Ev Luth Syn	48	4,229	6,424	7,996	0.0	0.0
MENN–CG in Cr (Menn)	7	NR	829	1,078	0.0	0.0
MENN–Cons Menn Conf	1	0	65	80	0.0	0.0
MENN–Menn Br US Conf	70	NR	11,057	14,167	0.0	0.1
MENN–Menn Chr Fell	2	92	44	92	0.0	0.0
MENN–Mennonite USA	36	2,007	2,531	3,130	0.0	0.0
MENN–Unaffil Amish-Menn	1	114	53	114	0.0	0.0
METH–A.W.M.C.	1	96	18	151	0.0	0.0
METH–AME	98	24,999	50,039	61,557	0.2	0.4
METH–AME Zion	35	840	4,234	5,225	0.0	0.0
METH–C.M.E.	53	3,205	10,462	12,952	0.0	0.1
METH–Evan Meth Ch	6	NR	NR	NR	-	-
METH–Free Methodist	91	11,758	8,270	12,575	0.0	0.1
METH–Un Methodist	667	77,991	148,469	232,399	0.6	1.4
METH–Wesleyan	83	10,401	9,717	13,529	0.0	0.1
Metro Comm Ch	16	1,350	1,564	1,892	0.0	0.0
Missionary Ch	41	8,784	6,837	9,662	0.0	0.1
MJEW–Assoc Mes Cong	1	NR	NR	NR	-	-
MJEW–Union Mes Cong	8	NR	NR	NR	-	-
MORAV–Morav Ch-North	2	94	246	341	0.0	0.0
Muslim Est	246	84,870	NR	272,814	0.7	1.6
Nat Spirit Asso	11	NR	NR	NR	-	-
New Apost Ch	25	NR	NR	NR	-	-
Non-denom Chr Chs	2,964	968,709	1,287,792	1,420,908	3.8	8.5
OCATH–Pol Natl Cath	1	NR	NR	NR	-	-
OCATH–Un Cath Ch	1	NR	NR	702	0.0	0.0
ORTHE–Ant Orth of NA	29	3,606	NR	10,066	0.0	0.1
ORTHE–Bulgar Orth USA	2	65	NR	110	0.0	0.0
ORTHE–Georgian Orth	2	75	NR	250	0.0	0.0
ORTHE–Greek Orthodox	42	9,260	NR	38,463	0.1	0.2
ORTHE–Holy Orth in NA	3	146	NR	190	0.0	0.0
ORTHE–Macedonian Orth	1	45	NR	300	0.0	0.0
ORTHE–Orth Ch in Amer	43	2,253	NR	5,819	0.0	0.0
ORTHE–Pal/Jor Orth	8	785	NR	6,650	0.0	0.0
ORTHE–Romania Orth Ar	5	260	NR	1,550	0.0	0.0
ORTHE–Rus Orth Abroad	23	1,901	NR	7,354	0.0	0.0
ORTHE–Rus Orth Moscow	2	85	NR	890	0.0	0.0
ORTHE–Serb Orth USA	18	1,402	NR	8,646	0.0	0.1
ORTHE–Ukrainian Orth	4	190	NR	560	0.0	0.0

NR–Not Reported - Represents no adherents reported. Percentages may not total 100 due to rounding.

Table 2: Religious Congregations by State and Group: 2010

Religious Group	Number of Congrega-tions	Number of Attendees	Number of Communicant, Confirmed, or Full Members	Adherents		
				Number of Adherents	% of Total Pop.	% of Total Adh.
ORTHO–Armen Ap Cilic	11	1,365	NR	5,460	0.0	0.0
ORTHO–Armen Ap Etchm	23	3,285	NR	32,900	0.1	0.2
ORTHO–Coptic Orth Ch	38	17,026	NR	24,208	0.1	0.1
ORTHO–Eritrean Orth	6	700	NR	2,550	0.0	0.0
ORTHO–Ethiopian Orth	10	NR	NR	NR	-	-
ORTHO–Malan Dioc Am	5	255	NR	765	0.0	0.0
ORTHO–Malan Syr Orth	2	190	NR	360	0.0	0.0
ORTHO–Syrian Orth Ch	7	1,345	NR	7,240	0.0	0.0
PENT–Apos Faith Msn	6	NR	210	264	0.0	0.0
PENT–Assemb of God	1,260	230,876	145,010	348,747	0.9	2.1
PENT–Assm God Intl F	3	NR	NR	NR	-	-
PENT–Ch God (Cleve)	222	19,189	20,565	25,547	0.1	0.2
PENT–Ch God Apos Fth	1	NR	NR	NR	-	-
PENT–Ch Lord Jesus Apos	13	NR	NR	NR	-	-
PENT–Ch of God Proph	116	NR	5,212	6,503	0.0	0.0
PENT–COGIC	301	20,511	58,323	72,496	0.2	0.4
PENT–Fire Bapt Hol Ch	1	NR	NR	NR	-	-
PENT–Full Gosp Bapt	54	NR	NR	NR	-	-
PENT–Int Foursq Gos	586	81,211	84,883	105,086	0.3	0.6
PENT–Intl Pent Holiness	106	13,682	10,868	13,572	0.0	0.1
PENT–Open Bible Std	33	3,059	NR	3,059	0.0	0.0
PENT–Pent Ch of God	226	18,080	NR	28,084	0.1	0.2
PENT–Pent FW Bapt	2	NR	NR	NR	-	-
PENT–Un Pent Ch Intl	261	NR	NR	NR	-	-
PENT–United Holy Ch	5	NR	NR	NR	-	-
PENT–Vineyard	81	18,038	24,849	30,428	0.1	0.2
Pillar of Fire	2	NR	275	275	0.0	0.0
PRES–As Ref Pres Ch	17	NR	428	525	0.0	0.0
PRES–Cumber Presb	5	NR	910	952	0.0	0.0
PRES–Evan Presby Ch	18	NR	7,266	9,108	0.0	0.1
PRES–Kor Pres Abroad	69	NR	NR	NR	-	-
PRES–Korean Amer Pres	88	NR	NR	NR	-	-
PRES–Korean Pres Amer	131	NR	NR	NR	-	-
PRES–Orth Pres Ch	34	2,621	2,395	3,108	0.0	0.0
PRES–Presb Ch (USA)	553	84,066	138,918	170,641	0.5	1.0
PRES–Presb Ch Amer	106	10,337	9,560	11,352	0.0	0.1
PRES–Ref Pres of NA	3	183	148	200	0.0	0.0
REF–Christian Ref	141	21,015	21,544	26,922	0.1	0.2
REF–Comm Ref Evan	3	NR	NR	NR	-	-
REF–Hung Ref Add'l	4	NR	NR	NR	-	-
REF–Prot Ref Chs	1	221	155	239	0.0	0.0
REF–Ref Ch in Am	47	17,772	18,704	31,940	0.1	0.2
REF–Ref Ch in U.S.	14	NR	752	1,001	0.0	0.0
REF–Un Ref Chs N.A.	15	NR	NR	NR	-	-
Salvation Army	104	8,475	12,374	39,338	0.1	0.2
Sev Day Adv	613	107,317	186,625	214,635	0.6	1.3
Sikh	60	NR	NR	NR	-	-
Swedenborgian	4	NR	NR	NR	-	-
Tao	16	NR	NR	NR	-	-
Un Breth in Cr	1	22	30	19	0.0	0.0
Un C of Christ	234	16,060	34,626	42,397	0.1	0.3
Unit Univ	71	8,576	12,283	15,760	0.0	0.1
Unity Ch	75	NR	NR	NR	-	-
Zoroastrian	8	NR	NR	1,837	0.0	0.0
COLORADO	**4,188**	**472,288**	**654,157**	**1,902,282**	**37.8**	**100.0**
ANG/EPIS–Anglican NA	28	NR	NR	NR	-	-
ANG/EPIS–Episcopal	102	10,320	22,903	26,683	0.5	1.4
Ap Chr Ch-Amer	1	81	44	81	0.0	0.0
Bahá'í	32	NR	2,856	2,856	0.1	0.2
BAPT–Amer Bapt Assn	10	NR	728	907	0.0	0.0
BAPT–Amer Bapt USA	64	9,351	16,426	20,030	0.4	1.1
BAPT–Asc Ref Bap Ch Am	1	NR	NR	NR	-	-
BAPT–Consrv Bapt	45	NR	NR	NR	-	-
BAPT–Converge/BGC	35	7,700	NR	9,240	0.2	0.5
BAPT–Free Will Bapt	6	NR	60	75	0.0	0.0
BAPT–Fund Bapt Flwsp	2	NR	NR	NR	-	-
BAPT–Ind Bapt Flwsp Intl	3	NR	NR	NR	-	-
BAPT–N Am Bapt Conf	4	NR	351	448	0.0	0.0
BAPT–Natl Mis Bapt Conv	4	150	600	733	0.0	0.0
BAPT–NBC Amer	2	200	475	588	0.0	0.0
BAPT–NBC USA	10	2,453	4,737	5,795	0.1	0.3
BAPT–NT Ind Bapt	21	NR	NR	NR	-	-
BAPT–Ref Bapt Ch	4	NR	NR	NR	-	-
BAPT–Reg Bapt Gen As	14	NR	NR	NR	-	-
BAPT–S-D Baptist Gen Con	3	145	154	193	0.0	0.0
BAPT–So Bapt Conv	382	35,029	57,819	71,166	1.4	3.7
BRETH–Breth in Chr	1	NR	NR	NR	-	-
BRETH–Ch of Brethren	9	164	580	717	0.0	0.0
BRETH–Grace Breth	1	NR	NR	NR	-	-
BUDD–Mahayana	36	NR	NR	16,230	0.3	0.9
BUDD–Theravada	6	NR	NR	4,087	0.1	0.2
BUDD–Vajrayana	27	NR	NR	3,603	0.1	0.2
Calv Chpl	33	NR	NR	NR	-	-
Catholic	303	NR	NR	811,630	16.1	42.7
CGOD–Ch God (Ander)	19	1,045	NR	1,045	0.0	0.1
Ch Cr, Scientst	29	NR	NR	NR	-	-
Ch God (7th Day)	3	NR	NR	NR	-	-
Ch of Chr (Hol)	1	NR	NR	NR	-	-
Ch of God Gen Conf	1	NR	5	6	0.0	0.0
Ch of Nazarene	79	9,933	11,042	15,096	0.3	0.8
Chr & Miss Al	15	2,374	1,908	3,571	0.1	0.2
CHR–Chr Ch (Disc)	39	3,975	9,227	11,291	0.2	0.6
CHR–Chr Chs & Chs Cr	78	NR	21,127	26,461	0.5	1.4
CHR–Chs of Christ	146	12,821	12,166	15,760	0.3	0.8
CHR–Int Chs of Christ	3	NR	829	1,011	0.0	0.1
Christian Brethren	2	NR	NR	NR	-	-
CONG–Cong Chr Add'l	1	NR	0	0	0.0	0.0
CONG–Cong Chr, NA	1	NR	31	37	0.0	0.0
CONG–Consrv Cong Chr	11	601	1,312	1,663	0.0	0.1
Evan Cov Ch	23	7,821	4,273	10,165	0.2	0.5
Evan Free Ch	65	16,637	NR	16,637	0.3	0.9
FRND–Consrv Yr Mtgs	1	NR	0	0	0.0	0.0
FRND–Evan Fr Ch Intl	13	778	1,154	1,390	0.0	0.1
FRND–Fr Gen Cf	9	NR	430	518	0.0	0.0
Grace Gosp Fel	11	NR	NR	NR	-	-
HINDU–I/A Temples	2	NR	NR	1,812	0.0	0.1
HINDU–Post Ren	29	NR	NR	1,177	0.0	0.1
HINDU–Renaiss	4	NR	NR	48	0.0	0.0
HINDU–Trad Temples	1	NR	NR	2,000	0.0	0.1
Ind Fund Churches	22	NR	NR	NR	-	-
Jain	1	NR	NR	NR	-	-
Jehovah's Witness	100	NR	NR	NR	-	-
JUD–Conserv	3	1,357	1,523	4,112	0.1	0.2
JUD–Orth	14	1,546	1,000	2,175	0.0	0.1
JUD–Reconst	2	366	467	1,261	0.0	0.1
JUD–Reform	14	2,624	4,625	12,488	0.2	0.7
LDS–Comm of Christ	20	NR	2,560	2,560	0.1	0.1
LDS–L-D Saints	289	NR	NR	142,473	2.8	7.5
LUTH–Assoc Free Luth	1	NR	NR	NR	-	-
LUTH–Ch Luth Conf	3	NR	NR	NR	-	-
LUTH–Ch of Luth Br	4	222	169	391	0.0	0.0
LUTH–E.L.C.A.	114	18,141	41,526	55,573	1.1	2.9
LUTH–Luth Ch-Am Asc	2	NR	NR	NR	-	-
LUTH–Luth Cong Msn Chr	9	1,593	3,731	4,634	0.1	0.2
LUTH–Luth-MO Synod	122	16,819	32,465	42,353	0.8	2.2
LUTH–Nor Amer Luth C	4	NR	NR	NR	-	-
LUTH–Wisc Ev Luth Syn	26	2,329	3,459	4,558	0.1	0.2
MENN–Amish Undif	4	NR	118	330	0.0	0.0
MENN–CG in Cr (Menn)	3	NR	192	236	0.0	0.0
MENN–Menn Br US Conf	5	NR	705	875	0.0	0.0
MENN–Mennonite USA	19	1,130	1,605	1,976	0.0	0.1
MENN–Tamp Amish-Menn	1	70	38	70	0.0	0.0
METH–AME	6	1,170	1,891	2,313	0.0	0.1
METH–AME Zion	2	0	200	243	0.0	0.0
METH–C.M.E.	2	260	760	922	0.0	0.0
METH–Free Methodist	10	1,448	1,125	1,461	0.0	0.1
METH–Un Methodist	212	26,355	55,543	78,881	1.6	4.1
METH–Wesleyan	12	2,332	1,085	3,031	0.1	0.2
Metro Comm Ch	4	356	433	529	0.0	0.0
Missionary Ch	5	880	500	880	0.0	0.0
MJEW–Union Mes Cong	1	NR	NR	NR	-	-
Muslim Est	17	5,084	NR	16,738	0.3	0.9
Nat Spirit Asso	1	NR	NR	NR	-	-
New Apost Ch	4	NR	NR	NR	-	-
Non-denom Chr Chs	476	166,817	202,961	229,981	4.6	12.1
OCATH–Pol Natl Cath	2	NR	NR	NR	-	-
ORTHE–Ant Orth of NA	7	704	NR	1,278	0.0	0.1

NR–Not Reported - Represents no adherents reported. Percentages may not total 100 due to rounding.

Table 2: Religious Congregations by State and Group: 2010

Religious Group	Number of Congregations	Number of Attendees	Number of Communicant, Confirmed, or Full Members	Adherents: Number of Adherents	Adherents: % of Total Pop.	Adherents: % of Total Adh.
ORTHE–Greek Orthodox	9	1,409	NR	6,395	0.1	0.3
ORTHE–Orth Ch in Amer	9	782	NR	975	0.0	0.1
ORTHE–Rus Orth Abroad	1	130	NR	600	0.0	0.0
ORTHE–Serb Orth USA	2	60	NR	765	0.0	0.0
ORTHO–Armen Ap Cilic	1	45	NR	180	0.0	0.0
ORTHO–Coptic Orth Ch	1	150	NR	400	0.0	0.0
ORTHO–Eritrean Orth	1	75	NR	500	0.0	0.0
ORTHO–Ethiopian Orth	4	NR	NR	NR	-	-
ORTHO–Malan Dioc Am	1	10	NR	30	0.0	0.0
ORTHO–Malan Syr Orth	1	50	NR	90	0.0	0.0
PENT–Assemb of God	176	32,228	14,159	50,633	1.0	2.7
PENT–Ch God (Cleve)	28	2,727	2,832	3,506	0.1	0.2
PENT–Ch of God Proph	12	NR	354	442	0.0	0.0
PENT–COGIC	16	928	1,950	2,425	0.0	0.1
PENT–Full Gosp Bapt	2	NR	NR	NR	-	-
PENT–Int Foursq Gos	63	6,745	6,451	8,080	0.2	0.4
PENT–Intl Pent Holiness	33	2,600	2,359	2,958	0.1	0.2
PENT–Open Bible Std	3	43	NR	43	0.0	0.0
PENT–Pent Ch of God	10	700	NR	1,087	0.0	0.1
PENT–Un Pent Ch Intl	45	NR	NR	NR	-	-
PENT–Vineyard	16	8,187	11,871	14,383	0.3	0.8
Pillar of Fire	2	NR	200	200	0.0	0.0
PRES–As Ref Pres Ch	1	NR	0	0	0.0	0.0
PRES–Evan Presby Ch	18	NR	11,469	14,733	0.3	0.8
PRES–Kor Pres Abroad	1	NR	NR	NR	-	-
PRES–Korean Amer Pres	1	NR	NR	NR	-	-
PRES–Korean Pres Amer	5	NR	NR	NR	-	-
PRES–Orth Pres Ch	6	598	470	625	0.0	0.0
PRES–Presb Ch (USA)	125	14,431	29,266	35,957	0.7	1.9
PRES–Presb Ch Amer	22	3,043	2,902	3,899	0.1	0.2
PRES–Ref Pres of NA	3	263	216	329	0.0	0.0
REF–Can Amer Ref	1	NR	NR	NR	-	-
REF–Christian Ref	17	4,484	3,707	4,605	0.1	0.2
REF–Comm Ref Evan	3	NR	NR	NR	-	-
REF–Hung Ref Add'l	1	NR	NR	NR	-	-
REF–Prot Ref Chs	1	243	160	273	0.0	0.0
REF–Ref Ch in Am	10	1,250	1,757	2,267	0.0	0.1
REF–Ref Ch in U.S.	3	NR	144	210	0.0	0.0
REF–Un Ref Chs N.A.	2	NR	NR	NR	-	-
Salvation Army	13	704	1,220	9,139	0.2	0.5
Sev Day Adv	102	9,726	16,918	19,456	0.4	1.0
Sikh	4	NR	NR	NR	-	-
Tao	3	NR	NR	NR	-	-
Un C of Christ	59	4,979	12,127	14,940	0.3	0.8
Unit Univ	18	2,517	3,707	5,072	0.1	0.3
Unity Ch	14	NR	NR	NR	-	-
Zoroastrian	1	NR	NR	13	0.0	0.0
CONNECTICUT	**2,597**	**214,657**	**383,701**	**1,830,862**	**51.2**	**100.0**
ANG/EPIS–Anglican NA	7	NR	NR	NR	-	-
ANG/EPIS–Episcopal	171	17,767	47,101	59,261	1.7	3.2
Ap Chr Ch-Amer	1	575	360	575	0.0	0.0
Bahá'í	8	NR	1,014	1,014	0.0	0.1
BAPT–Alliance Bapt	1	NR	NR	NR	-	-
BAPT–Amer Bapt USA	122	13,343	33,570	40,672	1.1	2.2
BAPT–Asc Ref Bap Ch Am	1	NR	NR	NR	-	-
BAPT–Consrv Bapt	14	NR	NR	NR	-	-
BAPT–Converge/BGC	17	4,175	NR	5,010	0.1	0.3
BAPT–N Am Bapt Conf	1	NR	NR	NR	-	-
BAPT–Natl Mis Bapt Conv	4	55	600	727	0.0	0.0
BAPT–NBC Amer	3	1,300	2,300	2,774	0.1	0.2
BAPT–NBC USA	5	1,290	2,377	2,858	0.1	0.2
BAPT–Prog NBC	1	125	200	241	0.0	0.0
BAPT–Ref Bapt Ch	2	NR	NR	NR	-	-
BAPT–Reg Bapt Gen As	3	NR	NR	NR	-	-
BAPT–S-D Baptist Gen Con	3	49	48	58	0.0	0.0
BAPT–So Bapt Conv	52	4,678	5,996	7,271	0.2	0.4
BRETH–Grace Breth	1	NR	NR	NR	-	-
BUDD–Mahayana	23	NR	NR	5,297	0.1	0.3
BUDD–Theravada	4	NR	NR	1,296	0.0	0.1
BUDD–Vajrayana	10	NR	NR	917	0.0	0.1
Calv Chpl	2	NR	NR	NR	-	-
Catholic	399	NR	NR	1,252,936	35.1	68.4
CGOD–Ch God (Ander)	2	100	NR	100	0.0	0.0

Religious Group	Number of Congregations	Number of Attendees	Number of Communicant, Confirmed, or Full Members	Adherents: Number of Adherents	Adherents: % of Total Pop.	Adherents: % of Total Adh.
Ch Cr, Scientst	18	NR	NR	NR	-	-
Ch God (7th Day)	2	NR	NR	NR	-	-
Ch of Nazarene	20	1,310	1,379	2,007	0.1	0.1
Chr & Miss Al	19	1,617	1,530	2,601	0.1	0.1
CHR–Chr Ch (Disc)	8	37	136	168	0.0	0.0
CHR–Chr Chs & Chs Cr	6	NR	579	699	0.0	0.0
CHR–Chs of Christ	23	1,952	1,850	2,618	0.1	0.1
CHR–Int Chs of Christ	3	NR	513	621	0.0	0.0
Christian Brethren	5	NR	NR	NR	-	-
CONG–Cong Chr Add'l	4	NR	551	657	0.0	0.0
CONG–Cong Chr, NA	25	NR	2,851	3,412	0.1	0.2
CONG–Consrv Cong Chr	8	423	474	573	0.0	0.0
Evan Cov Ch	14	2,033	2,592	2,644	0.1	0.1
Evan Free Ch	23	3,666	NR	3,666	0.1	0.2
FRND–Fr Gen Cf & Un Mtg	10	NR	521	628	0.0	0.0
FRND–Unaffl Mtgs	1	NR	NR	NR	-	-
HINDU–I/A Temples	6	NR	NR	3,890	0.1	0.2
HINDU–Post Ren	21	NR	NR	686	0.0	0.0
HINDU–Trad Temples	2	NR	NR	1,883	0.1	0.1
Int Cou Comm Ch	3	NR	NR	NR	-	-
Jain	2	NR	NR	NR	-	-
Jehovah's Witness	55	NR	NR	NR	-	-
JUD–Conserv	27	6,165	6,919	18,681	0.5	1.0
JUD–Orth	35	5,876	2,425	8,160	0.2	0.4
JUD–Reconst	1	125	160	432	0.0	0.0
JUD–Reform	22	4,276	7,543	20,366	0.6	1.1
LDS–Comm of Christ	3	NR	365	365	0.0	0.0
LDS–L-D Saints	32	NR	NR	14,990	0.4	0.8
LUTH–Ch of Luth Br	2	330	234	599	0.0	0.0
LUTH–E.L.C.A.	73	6,745	19,239	24,736	0.7	1.4
LUTH–Luth Cong Msn Chr	2	50	110	131	0.0	0.0
LUTH–Luth–MO Synod	37	3,622	7,559	9,785	0.3	0.5
LUTH–Wisc Ev Luth Syn	2	141	200	243	0.0	0.0
MENN–Bible Flwshp	1	32	NR	43	0.0	0.0
MENN–CG in Cr (Menn)	1	NR	0	0	0.0	0.0
METH–AME	14	1,395	3,684	4,474	0.1	0.2
METH–AME Zion	24	1,122	4,858	5,845	0.2	0.3
METH–C.M.E.	7	1,000	1,800	2,180	0.1	0.1
METH–Free Methodist	6	930	898	974	0.0	0.1
METH–Un Methodist	124	9,921	36,193	47,627	1.3	2.6
METH–Wesleyan	4	138	101	179	0.0	0.0
Metro Comm Ch	2	73	105	127	0.0	0.0
MJEW–Union Mes Cong	2	NR	NR	NR	-	-
Muslim Est	36	5,084	NR	13,418	0.4	0.7
Nat Spirit Asso	6	NR	NR	NR	-	-
New Apost Ch	4	NR	NR	NR	-	-
Non-denom Chr Chs	276	49,494	64,884	72,863	2.0	4.0
OCATH–Pol Natl Cath	11	NR	NR	NR	-	-
OCATH–Un Cath Ch	2	NR	NR	1,404	0.0	0.1
ORTHE–Ant Orth of NA	2	335	NR	1,061	0.0	0.1
ORTHE–Carp Rus Orth	4	317	NR	1,003	0.0	0.1
ORTHE–Greek Orthodox	17	2,840	NR	11,727	0.3	0.6
ORTHE–Orth Ch in Amer	18	1,185	NR	3,086	0.1	0.2
ORTHE–Rus Orth Abroad	4	150	NR	340	0.0	0.0
ORTHE–Ukrainian Orth	5	227	NR	525	0.0	0.0
ORTHO–Armen Ap Cilic	1	60	NR	500	0.0	0.0
ORTHO–Armen Ap Etchm	3	205	NR	1,000	0.0	0.1
ORTHO–Coptic Orth Ch	1	275	NR	390	0.0	0.0
PENT–Assemb of God	89	12,933	7,394	17,947	0.5	1.0
PENT–Ch God (Cleve)	63	6,113	7,713	9,379	0.3	0.5
PENT–Ch Lord Jesus Apos	12	NR	NR	NR	-	-
PENT–Ch of God Proph	8	NR	948	1,149	0.0	0.1
PENT–COGIC	27	1,120	3,192	3,870	0.1	0.2
PENT–Elim	4	NR	NR	NR	-	-
PENT–Fire Bapt Hol Ch	5	NR	NR	NR	-	-
PENT–Full Gosp Bapt	3	NR	NR	NR	-	-
PENT–I F Chr Assmbl	3	NR	NR	NR	-	-
PENT–Int Foursq Gos	6	189	242	292	0.0	0.0
PENT–Int Pent C Chr	1	0	NR	75	0.0	0.0
PENT–Intl Pent Holiness	1	111	123	152	0.0	0.0
PENT–Open Bible Std	1	29	NR	29	0.0	0.0
PENT–Pent Ch of God	3	210	NR	327	0.0	0.0
PENT–Un Pent Asbl God	1	NR	NR	NR	-	-
PENT–Un Pent Ch Intl	27	NR	NR	NR	-	-

NR–Not Reported   - Represents no adherents reported.   Percentages may not total 100 due to rounding.

Table 2: Religious Congregations by State and Group: 2010

Religious Group	Number of Congrega-tions	Number of Attendees	Number of Communicant, Confirmed, or Full Members	Adherents		
				Number of Adherents	% of Total Pop.	% of Total Adh.
PENT–United Holy Ch	6	NR	NR	NR	-	-
PENT–Vineyard	3	251	392	471	0.0	0.0
PRES–Evan Presby Ch	1	NR	152	184	0.0	0.0
PRES–Korean Pres Amer	4	NR	NR	NR	-	-
PRES–Orth Pres Ch	2	109	82	132	0.0	0.0
PRES–Presb Ch (USA)	19	2,404	6,026	7,380	0.2	0.4
PRES–Presb Ch Amer	12	1,041	793	1,105	0.0	0.1
REF–Christian Ref	1	146	203	245	0.0	0.0
Salvation Army	22	981	2,112	3,840	0.1	0.2
Sev Day Adv	55	4,375	7,604	8,749	0.2	0.5
Sikh	2	NR	NR	NR	-	-
Tao	2	NR	NR	NR	-	-
Un C of Christ	242	26,033	80,008	96,506	2.7	5.3
Unit Univ	19	2,004	2,898	3,928	0.1	0.2
Unity Ch	7	NR	NR	NR	-	-
Zoroastrian	0	NR	NR	88	0.0	0.0
DELAWARE	**831**	**75,229**	**129,616**	**374,917**	**41.8**	**100.0**
ANG/EPIS–Anglican NA	1	NR	NR	NR	-	-
ANG/EPIS–Episcopal	35	3,686	8,819	10,808	1.2	2.9
Bahá'í	6	NR	279	279	0.0	0.1
BAPT–Amer Bapt Assn	1	NR	85	105	0.0	0.0
BAPT–Amer Bapt USA	16	2,049	3,854	4,699	0.5	1.3
BAPT–Asc Ref Bap Ch Am	1	NR	NR	NR	-	-
BAPT–Consrv Bapt	1	NR	NR	NR	-	-
BAPT–Converge/BGC	2	875	NR	1,050	0.1	0.3
BAPT–Free Will Bapt	2	NR	90	109	0.0	0.0
BAPT–Natl Mis Bapt Conv	1	0	150	182	0.0	0.0
BAPT–NBC Amer	1	0	0	0	0.0	0.0
BAPT–NBC USA	10	605	1,684	2,050	0.2	0.5
BAPT–Reg Bapt Gen As	5	NR	NR	NR	-	-
BAPT–So Bapt Conv	33	3,594	6,082	7,387	0.8	2.0
BRETH–Breth in Chr	1	NR	NR	NR	-	-
BRETH–Brethren (Ash)	1	NR	80	95	0.0	0.0
BRETH–Ch of Brethren	2	58	219	269	0.0	0.1
BUDD–Mahayana	4	NR	NR	421	0.0	0.1
BUDD–Vajrayana	1	NR	NR	13	0.0	0.0
Calv Chpl	1	NR	NR	NR	-	-
Catholic	45	NR	NR	182,532	20.3	48.7
CGOD–Ch God (Ander)	5	315	NR	315	0.0	0.1
CGOD–Ches God-Gen Con	1	0	0	0	0.0	0.0
Ch Cr, Scientst	4	NR	NR	NR	-	-
Ch of Chr (Hol)	1	NR	NR	NR	-	-
Ch of Nazarene	15	1,330	1,315	1,703	0.2	0.5
Chr & Miss Al	8	583	457	987	0.1	0.3
CHR–Chr Ch (Disc)	2	47	90	107	0.0	0.0
CHR–Chr Chs & Chs Cr	9	NR	1,070	1,281	0.1	0.3
CHR–Chs of Christ	12	882	1,044	1,306	0.1	0.3
CHR–Int Chs of Christ	1	NR	52	63	0.0	0.0
Christian Brethren	1	NR	NR	NR	-	-
Evan Free Ch	5	835	NR	835	0.1	0.2
FRND–Fr Gen Cf	8	NR	494	602	0.1	0.2
HINDU–I/A Temples	1	NR	NR	1,742	0.2	0.5
HINDU–Post Ren	3	NR	NR	51	0.0	0.0
HINDU–Renaiss	1	NR	NR	12	0.0	0.0
HINDU–Trad Temples	1	NR	NR	6,000	0.7	1.6
Ind Fund Churches	1	NR	NR	NR	-	-
Jehovah's Witness	14	NR	NR	NR	-	-
JUD–Conserv	2	414	464	1,253	0.1	0.3
JUD–Orth	1	43	50	60	0.0	0.0
JUD–Reconst	1	217	277	748	0.1	0.2
JUD–Reform	1	380	671	1,812	0.2	0.5
LDS–Comm of Christ	2	NR	322	322	0.0	0.1
LDS–L-D Saints	12	NR	NR	4,832	0.5	1.3
LUTH–E.L.C.A.	14	1,798	4,299	6,512	0.7	1.7
LUTH–Luth-MO Synod	7	881	1,691	2,133	0.2	0.6
LUTH–Wisc Ev Luth Syn	1	92	151	187	0.0	0.0
MENN–Amish Undif	9	NR	610	1,424	0.2	0.4
MENN–Bible Flwshp	3	559	NR	755	0.1	0.2
MENN–Cons Menn Conf	3	471	428	510	0.1	0.1
MENN–Mennonite USA	6	268	244	292	0.0	0.1
METH–AME	39	2,005	7,703	9,364	1.0	2.5
METH–AME Zion	7	120	730	876	0.1	0.2
METH–Un Methodist	158	16,871	42,352	53,656	6.0	14.3

Religious Group	Number of Congrega-tions	Number of Attendees	Number of Communicant, Confirmed, or Full Members	Adherents		
				Number of Adherents	% of Total Pop.	% of Total Adh.
METH–Wesleyan	16	2,209	1,473	2,872	0.3	0.8
Metro Comm Ch	1	28	35	42	0.0	0.0
Muslim Est	5	1,402	NR	7,124	0.8	1.9
Non-denom Chr Chs	106	16,977	19,763	22,973	2.6	6.1
ORTHE–Ant Orth of NA	2	62	NR	131	0.0	0.0
ORTHE–Greek Orthodox	1	280	NR	550	0.1	0.1
ORTHE–Orth Ch in Amer	2	150	NR	320	0.0	0.1
ORTHE–Ukrainian Orth	2	145	NR	275	0.0	0.1
ORTHO–Coptic Orth Ch	1	95	NR	210	0.0	0.1
PENT–Assemb of God	16	3,598	1,995	5,720	0.6	1.5
PENT–Ch God (Cleve)	20	1,825	3,399	4,054	0.5	1.1
PENT–Ch Lord Jesus Apos	3	NR	NR	NR	-	-
PENT–Ch of God Proph	8	NR	465	560	0.1	0.1
PENT–COGIC	5	385	740	899	0.1	0.2
PENT–Elim	2	NR	NR	NR	-	-
PENT–Fire Bapt Hol Ch	3	NR	NR	NR	-	-
PENT–Full Gosp Bapt	5	NR	NR	NR	-	-
PENT–Intl Pent Holiness	2	144	199	242	0.0	0.1
PENT–Pent Ch of God	1	70	NR	109	0.0	0.0
PENT–Un Pent Ch Intl	9	NR	NR	NR	-	-
PENT–United Holy Ch	4	NR	NR	NR	-	-
PRES–Kor Pres Abroad	1	NR	NR	NR	-	-
PRES–Orth Pres Ch	2	187	218	268	0.0	0.1
PRES–Presb Ch (USA)	36	3,272	8,168	9,907	1.1	2.6
PRES–Presb Ch Amer	12	2,852	2,589	3,159	0.4	0.8
Salvation Army	4	172	472	571	0.1	0.2
Sev Day Adv	22	1,645	2,861	3,291	0.4	0.9
Sikh	1	NR	NR	NR	-	-
Swedenborgian	1	NR	NR	NR	-	-
Un C of Christ	3	178	428	525	0.1	0.1
Unit Univ	5	575	955	1,331	0.1	0.4
Unity Ch	1	NR	NR	NR	-	-
Zoroastrian	0	NR	NR	45	0.0	0.0
DISTRICT OF COLUMBIA	**609**	**92,261**	**188,990**	**332,342**	**55.2**	**100.0**
ANG/EPIS–Anglican NA	4	NR	NR	NR	-	-
ANG/EPIS–Episcopal	32	7,313	15,029	18,551	3.1	5.6
Bahá'í	1	NR	521	521	0.1	0.2
BAPT–Alliance Bapt	3	NR	NR	NR	-	-
BAPT–Amer Bapt USA	63	15,077	32,493	37,379	6.2	11.2
BAPT–Consrv Bapt	1	NR	NR	NR	-	-
BAPT–Natl Mis Bapt Conv	4	140	350	403	0.1	0.1
BAPT–NBC USA	30	3,625	19,645	22,599	3.8	6.8
BAPT–Prog NBC	22	6,107	13,090	15,059	2.5	4.5
BAPT–S-D Baptist Gen Con	1	49	51	59	0.0	0.0
BAPT–So Bapt Conv	63	8,825	23,123	26,600	4.4	8.0
BRETH–Brethren (Ash)	1	NR	80	92	0.0	0.0
BRETH–Ch of Brethren	1	15	135	155	0.0	0.0
BRETH–Grace Breth	2	NR	NR	NR	-	-
BUDD–Mahayana	10	NR	NR	4,391	0.7	1.3
BUDD–Theravada	1	NR	NR	1,007	0.2	0.3
BUDD–Vajrayana	3	NR	NR	523	0.1	0.2
Catholic	45	NR	NR	75,948	12.6	22.9
CGOD–Ch God (Ander)	6	446	NR	446	0.1	0.1
Ch Cr, Scientst	6	NR	NR	NR	-	-
Ch of Chr (Hol)	1	NR	NR	NR	-	-
Ch of Nazarene	5	282	602	669	0.1	0.2
Chr & Miss Al	2	240	190	375	0.1	0.1
CHR–Chr Ch (Disc)	4	490	1,395	1,605	0.3	0.5
CHR–Chs of Christ	4	492	543	620	0.1	0.2
CONG–Armen Evang Add'l	1	NR	NR	NR	-	-
Evan Cov Ch	1	29	0	38	0.0	0.0
Evan Free Ch	1	20	NR	20	0.0	0.0
FRND–Fr Gen Cf & Un Mtg	3	NR	432	497	0.1	0.1
FRND–Unaffl Mtgs	1	NR	NR	NR	-	-
HINDU–I/A Temples	5	NR	NR	3,853	0.6	1.2
HINDU–Post Ren	4	NR	NR	60	0.0	0.0
Int Cou Comm Ch	3	NR	NR	NR	-	-
Jehovah's Witness	4	NR	NR	NR	-	-
JUD–Conserv	2	1,553	1,743	4,706	0.8	1.4
JUD–Orth	3	864	600	1,200	0.2	0.4
JUD–Reform	3	2,469	4,355	11,758	2.0	3.5
LDS–Comm of Christ	1	NR	137	137	0.0	0.0
LDS–L-D Saints	1	NR	NR	420	0.1	0.1

NR–Not Reported   - Represents no adherents reported.   Percentages may not total 100 due to rounding.

Table 2: Religious Congregations by State and Group: 2010

Religious Group	Number of Congregations	Number of Attendees	Number of Communicant, Confirmed, or Full Members	Adherents: Number of Adherents	Adherents: % of Total Pop.	Adherents: % of Total Adh.
LUTH–E.L.C.A.	13	1,322	2,002	3,305	0.5	1.0
LUTH–Luth–MO Synod	2	223	373	821	0.1	0.2
LUTH–Nor Amer Luth C	1	NR	NR	NR	-	-
MENN–Mennonite USA	3	205	110	127	0.0	0.0
MENN–Unaffil Amish-Menn	1	10	5	10	0.0	0.0
METH–AME	13	1,762	4,751	5,465	0.9	1.6
METH–AME Zion	14	1,132	2,741	3,153	0.5	0.9
METH–C.M.E.	5	950	2,110	2,427	0.4	0.7
METH–Free Methodist	1	25	56	56	0.0	0.0
METH–Un Methodist	29	3,683	8,960	10,664	1.8	3.2
METH–Wesleyan	1	54	107	70	0.0	0.0
Metro Comm Ch	1	242	358	412	0.1	0.1
MJEW–Union Mes Cong	1	NR	NR	NR	-	-
MORAV–Morav Ch-North	1	91	108	143	0.0	0.0
Muslim Est	7	1,586	NR	4,032	0.7	1.2
Nat Spirit Asso	1	NR	NR	NR	-	-
Non-denom Chr Chs	61	18,224	33,785	34,292	5.7	10.3
ORTHE–Ant Orth of NA	2	65	NR	100	0.0	0.0
ORTHE–Greek Orthodox	2	1,500	NR	9,500	1.6	2.9
ORTHE–Orth Ch in Amer	1	300	NR	1,500	0.2	0.5
ORTHE–Rus Orth Abroad	1	350	NR	800	0.1	0.2
ORTHO–Armen Ap Etchm	1	150	NR	1,000	0.2	0.3
ORTHO–Eritrean Orth	2	400	NR	1,150	0.2	0.3
ORTHO–Ethiopian Orth	3	NR	NR	NR	-	-
PENT–Apos Faith Msn	1	NR	35	40	0.0	0.0
PENT–Assemb of God	7	3,619	2,170	4,033	0.7	1.2
PENT–Ch God (Cleve)	3	87	168	193	0.0	0.1
PENT–Ch Lord Jesus Apos	4	NR	NR	NR	-	-
PENT–Ch of God Proph	4	NR	303	349	0.1	0.1
PENT–COGIC	9	650	1,300	1,496	0.2	0.5
PENT–Fire Bapt Hol Ch	3	NR	NR	NR	-	-
PENT–Full Gosp Bapt	4	NR	NR	NR	-	-
PENT–Int Foursq Gos	1	11	13	15	0.0	0.0
PENT–Un Pent Ch Intl	2	NR	NR	NR	-	-
PENT–United Holy Ch	4	NR	NR	NR	-	-
PRES–Presb Ch (USA)	16	2,436	5,594	6,435	1.1	1.9
PRES–Presb Ch Amer	1	495	433	494	0.1	0.1
REF–Christian Ref	1	100	136	156	0.0	0.0
REF–Hung Ref Add'l	1	NR	NR	NR	-	-
REF–Un Ref Chs N.A.	1	NR	NR	NR	-	-
Salvation Army	3	168	288	357	0.1	0.1
Sev Day Adv	11	2,610	4,537	5,219	0.9	1.6
Sikh	1	NR	NR	NR	-	-
Swedenborgian	1	NR	NR	NR	-	-
Tao	1	NR	NR	NR	-	-
Un C of Christ	9	992	2,953	3,397	0.6	1.0
Unit Univ	3	783	1,080	1,426	0.2	0.4
Unity Ch	2	NR	NR	NR	-	-
Zoroastrian	1	NR	NR	14	0.0	0.0
FLORIDA	**15,611**	**2,142,198**	**3,457,120**	**7,357,588**	**39.1**	**100.0**
ANG/EPIS–Anglican NA	60	NR	NR	NR	-	-
ANG/EPIS–Episcopal	334	51,684	109,239	129,482	0.7	1.8
Ap Chr Ch-Amer	3	170	108	170	0.0	0.0
Bahá'í	76	NR	9,110	9,110	0.0	0.1
BAPT–Alliance Bapt	1	NR	NR	NR	-	-
BAPT–Amer Bapt Assn	78	NR	9,036	10,868	0.1	0.1
BAPT–Amer Bapt USA	24	6,493	15,727	18,948	0.1	0.3
BAPT–Consrv Bapt	6	NR	NR	NR	-	-
BAPT–Converge/BGC	60	7,175	NR	8,610	0.0	0.1
BAPT–Free Will Bapt	60	NR	5,324	6,371	0.0	0.1
BAPT–Ind Bapt Flwsp Intl	32	NR	NR	NR	-	-
BAPT–N Am Bapt Conf	9	NR	950	1,125	0.0	0.0
BAPT–Natl Mis Bapt Conv	119	5,625	22,407	26,877	0.1	0.4
BAPT–NBC Amer	55	10,184	27,599	33,439	0.2	0.5
BAPT–NBC USA	172	47,487	102,432	122,811	0.7	1.7
BAPT–NT Ind Bapt	1	NR	NR	NR	-	-
BAPT–Prog NBC	6	250	1,225	1,485	0.0	0.0
BAPT–Ref Bapt Ch	27	NR	NR	NR	-	-
BAPT–Reg Bapt Gen As	44	NR	NR	NR	-	-
BAPT–S-D Baptist Gen Con	8	257	313	371	0.0	0.0
BAPT–So Bapt Conv	2,965	479,933	1,038,276	1,247,345	6.6	17.0
BRETH–Breth in Chr	54	NR	NR	NR	-	-
BRETH–Brethren (Ash)	4	NR	320	371	0.0	0.0
BRETH–Ch of Brethren	19	366	1,450	1,734	0.0	0.0
BRETH–Grace Breth	15	NR	NR	NR	-	-
BUDD–Mahayana	80	NR	NR	27,940	0.1	0.4
BUDD–Theravada	16	NR	NR	9,120	0.0	0.1
BUDD–Vajrayana	45	NR	NR	5,040	0.0	0.1
Calv Chpl	56	NR	NR	NR	-	-
Catholic	547	NR	NR	2,513,839	13.4	34.2
CGOD–Ch God (Ander)	107	15,832	NR	15,832	0.1	0.2
CGOD–Ches God-Gen Con	2	48	53	65	0.0	0.0
Ch Christ Chr Union	3	NR	NR	NR	-	-
Ch Cr, Scientst	72	NR	NR	NR	-	-
Ch God (7th Day)	13	NR	NR	NR	-	-
Ch of Chr (Hol)	1	NR	NR	NR	-	-
Ch of Nazarene	235	28,425	38,510	44,889	0.2	0.6
Chr & Miss Al	150	16,863	11,124	23,687	0.1	0.3
CHR–Chr Ch (Disc)	116	8,504	15,866	18,976	0.1	0.3
CHR–Chr Chs & Chs Cr	195	NR	44,647	53,140	0.3	0.7
CHR–Chs of Christ	500	53,524	55,732	70,094	0.4	1.0
CHR–Int Chs of Christ	9	NR	3,001	3,593	0.0	0.0
Christian Brethren	9	NR	NR	NR	-	-
CONG–Cong Chr, NA	14	NR	3,472	4,087	0.0	0.1
Evan Cov Ch	24	2,260	2,839	2,935	0.0	0.0
Evan Free Ch	32	6,268	NR	6,268	0.0	0.1
FRND–Evan Fr Ch Intl	4	2,029	680	821	0.0	0.0
FRND–Fr Gen Cf	20	NR	487	576	0.0	0.0
FRND–Fr Un Mtg	1	NR	0	0	0.0	0.0
Grace Gosp Fel	7	NR	NR	NR	-	-
HINDU–I/A Temples	25	NR	NR	19,044	0.1	0.3
HINDU–Post Ren	47	NR	NR	1,962	0.0	0.0
HINDU–Renaiss	12	NR	NR	243	0.0	0.0
HINDU–Trad Temples	21	NR	NR	15,816	0.1	0.2
Ind Fund Churches	7	NR	NR	NR	-	-
Int Cou Comm Ch	17	NR	NR	NR	-	-
Intl Fell Bible Ch	2	NR	NR	NR	-	-
Jain	8	NR	NR	NR	-	-
Jehovah's Witness	315	NR	NR	NR	-	-
JUD–Conserv	47	13,925	15,627	42,193	0.2	0.6
JUD–Orth	139	18,577	11,330	25,805	0.1	0.4
JUD–Reconst	5	231	296	800	0.0	0.0
JUD–Reform	57	12,507	22,056	59,550	0.3	0.8
LDS–Comm of Christ	32	NR	4,007	4,007	0.0	0.1
LDS–L-D Saints	235	NR	NR	136,925	0.7	1.9
LUTH–Apostolic Luth	1	NR	NR	NR	-	-
LUTH–Assoc Free Luth	2	NR	NR	NR	-	-
LUTH–Ch Luth Conf	3	NR	NR	NR	-	-
LUTH–Ch of Luth Br	3	287	173	471	0.0	0.0
LUTH–E.L.C.A.	194	30,359	53,636	68,140	0.4	0.9
LUTH–Evan Luth Syn	9	709	881	1,060	0.0	0.0
LUTH–Luth Ch-Am Asc	2	NR	NR	NR	-	-
LUTH–Luth Cong Msn Chr	14	1,748	3,322	3,978	0.0	0.1
LUTH–Luth–MO Synod	180	30,517	52,350	65,448	0.3	0.9
LUTH–Nor Amer Luth C	5	NR	NR	NR	-	-
LUTH–Wisc Ev Luth Syn	39	3,830	4,899	6,222	0.0	0.1
MENN–Amish Undif	1	NR	111	125	0.0	0.0
MENN–Beachy Amish-Menn	2	171	97	171	0.0	0.0
MENN–Bruderhof Comm	1	37	11	22	0.0	0.0
MENN–CG in Cr (Menn)	4	NR	199	239	0.0	0.0
MENN–Cons Menn Conf	4	949	605	688	0.0	0.0
MENN–Mennonite USA	27	3,184	2,558	2,975	0.0	0.0
METH–A.W.M.C.	1	13	0	16	0.0	0.0
METH–AME	453	22,585	92,727	111,300	0.6	1.5
METH–AME Zion	30	448	3,672	4,410	0.0	0.1
METH–C.M.E.	52	2,580	8,897	10,693	0.1	0.1
METH–Cong Meth	8	NR	292	351	0.0	0.0
METH–Free Methodist	33	3,158	3,102	3,605	0.0	0.0
METH–Prim Meth Ch	4	NR	NR	NR	-	-
METH–So Methodist	5	NR	NR	NR	-	-
METH–Un Methodist	768	157,721	328,035	468,080	2.5	6.4
METH–Wesleyan	41	2,902	2,071	3,774	0.0	0.1
Metro Comm Ch	20	2,363	2,488	3,046	0.0	0.0
Missionary Ch	11	548	283	553	0.0	0.0
MJEW–Union Mes Cong	6	NR	NR	NR	-	-
MORAV–Morav Ch-South	5	512	666	942	0.0	0.0
MORAV–Unity Of Breth	1	NR	NR	NR	-	-

NR–Not Reported   - Represents no adherents reported.   Percentages may not total 100 due to rounding.

Table 2: Religious Congregations by State and Group: 2010

Religious Group	Number of Congregations	Number of Attendees	Number of Communicant, Confirmed, or Full Members	Adherents: Number of Adherents	Adherents: % of Total Pop.	Adherents: % of Total Adh.
Muslim Est	118	47,908	NR	164,846	0.9	2.2
Nat Spirit Asso	2	NR	NR	NR	-	-
New Apost Ch	24	NR	NR	NR	-	-
Non-denom Chr Chs	2,387	603,151	793,855	868,527	4.6	11.8
OCATH–Pol Natl Cath	3	NR	NR	NR	-	-
OCATH–Un Cath Ch	2	NR	NR	1,404	0.0	0.0
ORTHE–Ant Orth of NA	14	1,392	NR	4,090	0.0	0.1
ORTHE–Carp Rus Orth	3	93	NR	177	0.0	0.0
ORTHE–Greek Orthodox	34	6,233	NR	32,587	0.2	0.4
ORTHE–Holy Orth in NA	1	15	NR	20	0.0	0.0
ORTHE–Macedonian Orth	2	135	NR	1,160	0.0	0.0
ORTHE–Orth Ch in Amer	26	1,461	NR	3,641	0.0	0.0
ORTHE–Romania Orth Ar	1	20	NR	100	0.0	0.0
ORTHE–Rus Orth Abroad	7	240	NR	2,550	0.0	0.0
ORTHE–Rus Orth Moscow	1	25	NR	80	0.0	0.0
ORTHE–Serb Orth USA	6	655	NR	4,525	0.0	0.1
ORTHE–Ukrainian Orth	3	145	NR	315	0.0	0.0
ORTHO–Armen Ap Cilic	2	130	NR	230	0.0	0.0
ORTHO–Armen Ap Etchm	7	490	NR	2,810	0.0	0.0
ORTHO–Coptic Orth Ch	19	3,493	NR	5,603	0.0	0.1
ORTHO–Eritrean Orth	1	300	NR	200	0.0	0.0
ORTHO–Ethiopian Orth	2	NR	NR	NR	-	-
ORTHO–Malan Dioc Am	7	148	NR	444	0.0	0.0
ORTHO–Malan Syr Orth	2	150	NR	288	0.0	0.0
ORTHO–Syrian Orth Ch	4	425	NR	1,350	0.0	0.0
PENT–Apos Faith Msn	4	NR	140	170	0.0	0.0
PENT–Assemb of God	688	146,442	88,372	246,270	1.3	3.3
PENT–Ch God (Cleve)	613	59,588	91,397	109,332	0.6	1.5
PENT–Ch God Apos Fth	1	NR	NR	NR	-	-
PENT–Ch God Mtn Asm	7	NR	NR	NR	-	-
PENT–Ch Lord Jesus Apos	48	NR	NR	NR	-	-
PENT–Ch of God by Faith	90	NR	NR	NR	-	-
PENT–Ch of God Proph	146	NR	6,994	8,377	0.0	0.1
PENT–COGIC	144	4,875	18,675	22,375	0.1	0.3
PENT–Cong Hol Ch	18	604	548	669	0.0	0.0
PENT–Elim	2	NR	NR	NR	-	-
PENT–Fire Bapt Hol Ch	10	NR	NR	NR	-	-
PENT–Full Gosp Bapt	28	NR	NR	NR	-	-
PENT–I F Chr Assmbl	3	NR	NR	NR	-	-
PENT–Int Foursq Gos	53	2,824	3,259	3,927	0.0	0.1
PENT–Int Pent C Chr	1	0	NR	40	0.0	0.0
PENT–Intl Pent Holiness	174	20,208	23,216	27,660	0.1	0.4
PENT–Open Bible Std	32	2,779	NR	2,779	0.0	0.0
PENT–Pent Ch of God	24	1,680	NR	2,612	0.0	0.0
PENT–Pent FW Bapt	5	NR	NR	NR	-	-
PENT–Un Pent Asbl God	2	NR	NR	NR	-	-
PENT–Un Pent Ch Intl	135	NR	NR	NR	-	-
PENT–Vineyard	27	6,778	9,027	10,766	0.1	0.1
PRES–As Ref Pres Ch	21	NR	3,596	4,290	0.0	0.1
PRES–Bible Pres	4	NR	NR	NR	-	-
PRES–Cov Ref Pres	1	NR	NR	NR	-	-
PRES–Cumber Presb	5	NR	399	459	0.0	0.0
PRES–Evan Presby Ch	10	NR	2,573	3,058	0.0	0.0
PRES–Free Pres NA	1	NR	NR	NR	-	-
PRES–Kor Pres Abroad	5	NR	NR	NR	-	-
PRES–Korean Amer Pres	1	NR	NR	NR	-	-
PRES–Korean Pres Amer	2	NR	NR	NR	-	-
PRES–Orth Pres Ch	14	896	713	892	0.0	0.0
PRES–Presb Ch (USA)	351	63,107	107,136	127,670	0.7	1.7
PRES–Presb Ch Amer	150	26,757	29,558	36,595	0.2	0.5
PRES–Ref Pres GA	3	NR	NR	NR	-	-
PRES–Ref Pres of NA	1	55	81	106	0.0	0.0
REF–Christian Ref	19	1,636	1,993	2,384	0.0	0.0
REF–Comm Ref Evan	3	NR	NR	NR	-	-
REF–Hung Ref Add'l	1	NR	NR	NR	-	-
REF–Ref Ch in Am	12	991	892	1,430	0.0	0.0
REF–Un Ref Chs N.A.	1	NR	NR	NR	-	-
Salvation Army	49	4,721	6,519	12,977	0.1	0.2
Sev Day Adv	405	59,602	103,651	119,209	0.6	1.6
Sikh	8	NR	NR	NR	-	-
Swedenborgian	2	NR	NR	NR	-	-
Tao	1	NR	NR	NR	-	-
Un Breth in Cr	3	513	114	438	0.0	0.0
Un C of Christ	101	15,022	25,116	29,582	0.2	0.4
Unit Univ	45	3,273	4,978	5,784	0.0	0.1
Unity Ch	68	NR	NR	NR	-	-
Zoroastrian	3	NR	NR	117	0.0	0.0
GEORGIA	**12,292**	**1,569,696**	**3,333,256**	**4,924,398**	**50.8**	**100.0**
ANG/EPIS–Anglican NA	30	NR	NR	NR	-	-
ANG/EPIS–Episcopal	166	22,981	56,897	68,812	0.7	1.4
Ap Chr Ch-Amer	1	41	22	41	0.0	0.0
Bahá'í	33	NR	7,690	7,690	0.1	0.2
BAPT–Alliance Bapt	6	NR	NR	NR	-	-
BAPT–Amer Bapt Assn	20	NR	2,707	3,379	0.0	0.1
BAPT–Amer Bapt USA	19	4,214	11,343	13,978	0.1	0.3
BAPT–Asc Ref Bap Ch Am	7	NR	NR	NR	-	-
BAPT–Converge/BGC	3	225	NR	270	0.0	0.0
BAPT–Free Will Bapt	114	NR	8,322	10,301	0.1	0.2
BAPT–Fund Bapt Flwsp	1	NR	NR	NR	-	-
BAPT–Ind Bapt Flwsp Intl	7	NR	NR	NR	-	-
BAPT–N Am Bapt Conf	1	NR	87	107	0.0	0.0
BAPT–Natl Mis Bapt Conv	68	1,090	11,658	14,390	0.1	0.3
BAPT–NBC Amer	8	1,465	3,748	4,650	0.0	0.1
BAPT–NBC USA	272	56,262	139,585	172,982	1.8	3.5
BAPT–Orig Free Will Bapt	4	360	492	610	0.0	0.0
BAPT–Prog NBC	18	4,125	6,805	8,373	0.1	0.2
BAPT–Ref Bapt Ch	19	NR	NR	NR	-	-
BAPT–Reg Bapt Gen As	2	NR	NR	NR	-	-
BAPT–S-D Baptist Gen Con	4	74	81	105	0.0	0.0
BAPT–So Bapt Conv	3,613	543,758	1,408,061	1,759,339	18.2	35.7
BRETH–Breth in Chr	1	NR	NR	NR	-	-
BRETH–Grace Breth	1	NR	NR	NR	-	-
BUDD–Mahayana	27	NR	NR	10,698	0.1	0.2
BUDD–Theravada	10	NR	NR	4,365	0.0	0.1
BUDD–Vajrayana	5	NR	NR	602	0.0	0.0
Calv Chpl	16	NR	NR	NR	-	-
Catholic	185	NR	NR	596,384	6.2	12.1
CGOD–Ch God (Ander)	49	3,000	NR	3,000	0.0	0.1
Ch Cr, Scientst	18	NR	NR	NR	-	-
Ch God (7th Day)	2	NR	NR	NR	-	-
Ch of Chr (Hol)	4	NR	NR	NR	-	-
Ch of God Gen Conf	3	NR	128	164	0.0	0.0
Ch of Nazarene	93	6,306	9,502	11,292	0.1	0.2
Chr & Miss Al	51	5,222	4,740	7,238	0.1	0.1
CHR–Chr Ch (Disc)	68	4,269	16,940	20,989	0.2	0.4
CHR–Chr Chs & Chs Cr	163	NR	34,561	43,168	0.4	0.9
CHR–Chs of Christ	417	41,561	42,456	55,105	0.6	1.1
CHR–Int Chs of Christ	6	NR	1,845	2,275	0.0	0.0
Christian Brethren	5	NR	NR	NR	-	-
CONG–Cong Chr, NA	5	NR	216	270	0.0	0.0
Evan Ch	1	NR	NR	NR	-	-
Evan Cov Ch	5	1,304	313	1,696	0.0	0.0
Evan Free Ch	5	305	NR	305	0.0	0.0
FRND–Consrv Yr Mtgs	1	NR	0	0	0.0	0.0
FRND–Fr Gen Cf	5	NR	149	183	0.0	0.0
FRND–Unaffl Mtgs	1	NR	NR	NR	-	-
Grace Gosp Fel	1	NR	NR	NR	-	-
HINDU–I/A Temples	18	NR	NR	15,911	0.2	0.3
HINDU–Post Ren	17	NR	NR	634	0.0	0.0
HINDU–Renaiss	3	NR	NR	1,474	0.0	0.0
HINDU–Trad Temples	7	NR	NR	10,907	0.1	0.2
Ind Fund Churches	3	NR	NR	NR	-	-
Int Cou Comm Ch	2	NR	NR	NR	-	-
Jain	3	NR	NR	NR	-	-
Jehovah's Witness	173	NR	NR	NR	-	-
JUD–Conserv	11	3,663	4,111	11,100	0.1	0.2
JUD–Orth	18	5,335	2,200	7,410	0.1	0.2
JUD–Reconst	1	157	201	543	0.0	0.0
JUD–Reform	18	3,610	6,367	17,191	0.2	0.3
LDS–Comm of Christ	5	NR	590	590	0.0	0.0
LDS–L-D Saints	150	NR	NR	77,587	0.8	1.6
LUTH–Ch Luth Conf	1	NR	NR	NR	-	-
LUTH–E.L.C.A.	84	10,335	23,213	29,076	0.3	0.6
LUTH–Luth Cong Msn Chr	10	706	1,314	1,663	0.0	0.0
LUTH–Luth-MO Synod	44	4,873	8,202	9,975	0.1	0.2
LUTH–Nor Amer Luth C	4	NR	NR	NR	-	-
LUTH–Wisc Ev Luth Syn	9	1,178	1,653	2,133	0.0	0.0

NR–Not Reported - Represents no adherents reported. Percentages may not total 100 due to rounding.

Table 2: Religious Congregations by State and Group: 2010

Religious Group	Number of Congrega-tions	Number of Attendees	Number of Communicant, Confirmed, or Full Members	Adherents: Number of Adherents	Adherents: % of Total Pop.	Adherents: % of Total Adh.
MENN–Beachy Amish-Menn	3	477	283	477	0.0	0.0
MENN–CG in Cr (Menn)	3	NR	396	489	0.0	0.0
MENN–Cons Menn Conf	1	15	11	13	0.0	0.0
MENN–Menn Br US Conf	1	NR	0	0	0.0	0.0
MENN–Mennonite USA	4	125	101	126	0.0	0.0
MENN–Unaffil Amish-Menn	1	94	55	94	0.0	0.0
METH–AME	540	23,243	94,948	117,271	1.2	2.4
METH–AME Zion	28	655	3,873	4,825	0.0	0.1
METH–C.M.E.	144	6,981	26,667	32,695	0.3	0.7
METH–Cong Meth	16	NR	4,939	5,946	0.1	0.1
METH–Evan Meth Ch	7	NR	NR	NR	-	-
METH–Free Methodist	4	756	402	761	0.0	0.0
METH–So Methodist	8	NR	NR	NR	-	-
METH–Un Methodist	1,550	178,821	490,331	619,394	6.4	12.6
METH–Wesleyan	27	10,597	1,425	13,778	0.1	0.3
Metro Comm Ch	5	334	528	648	0.0	0.0
Missionary Ch	8	910	350	950	0.0	0.0
MJEW–Union Mes Cong	1	NR	NR	NR	-	-
MORAV–Morav Ch-South	1	53	124	154	0.0	0.0
Muslim Est	69	18,630	NR	52,578	0.5	1.1
New Apost Ch	3	NR	NR	NR	-	-
Non-denom Chr Chs	1,449	379,741	523,121	566,782	5.9	11.5
ORTHE–Ant Orth of NA	2	265	NR	610	0.0	0.0
ORTHE–Carp Rus Orth	1	38	NR	60	0.0	0.0
ORTHE–Greek Orthodox	10	1,695	NR	6,265	0.1	0.1
ORTHE–Holy Orth in NA	1	15	NR	20	0.0	0.0
ORTHE–Orth Ch in Amer	7	460	NR	1,225	0.0	0.0
ORTHE–Romania Orth Ar	2	200	NR	1,040	0.0	0.0
ORTHE–Rus Orth Abroad	2	260	NR	875	0.0	0.0
ORTHE–Serb Orth USA	1	250	NR	1,600	0.0	0.0
ORTHE–Ukrainian Orth	1	39	NR	200	0.0	0.0
ORTHO–Armen Ap Cilic	1	70	NR	150	0.0	0.0
ORTHO–Armen Ap Etchm	1	125	NR	450	0.0	0.0
ORTHO–Coptic Orth Ch	4	720	NR	1,029	0.0	0.0
ORTHO–Eritrean Orth	2	625	NR	1,050	0.0	0.0
ORTHO–Ethiopian Orth	3	NR	NR	NR	-	-
ORTHO–Malan Dioc Am	2	108	NR	324	0.0	0.0
ORTHO–Malan Syr Orth	4	200	NR	378	0.0	0.0
ORTHO–Syrian Orth Ch	1	50	NR	100	0.0	0.0
PENT–Apos Faith Msn	2	NR	70	87	0.0	0.0
PENT–Assemb of God	253	35,215	27,214	56,268	0.6	1.1
PENT–Ch God (Cleve)	532	70,104	140,362	175,184	1.8	3.6
PENT–Ch God Mtn Asm	3	NR	NR	NR	-	-
PENT–Ch Lord Jesus Apos	22	NR	NR	NR	-	-
PENT–Ch of God by Faith	27	NR	NR	NR	-	-
PENT–Ch of God Proph	115	NR	5,751	7,187	0.1	0.1
PENT–COGIC	116	8,206	21,158	26,235	0.3	0.5
PENT–Cong Hol Ch	104	7,257	6,804	8,461	0.1	0.2
PENT–Fire Bapt Hol Ch	22	NR	NR	NR	-	-
PENT–Full Gosp Bapt	35	NR	NR	NR	-	-
PENT–Int Foursq Gos	22	1,171	1,408	1,773	0.0	0.0
PENT–Int Pent C Chr	3	121	115	260	0.0	0.0
PENT–Intl Pent Holiness	72	5,503	7,574	9,320	0.1	0.2
PENT–Open Bible Std	1	0	NR	0	0.0	0.0
PENT–Pent Ch of God	8	560	NR	871	0.0	0.0
PENT–Un Pent Ch Intl	94	NR	NR	NR	-	-
PENT–United Holy Ch	5	NR	NR	NR	-	-
PENT–Vineyard	16	2,436	3,279	4,081	0.0	0.1
PRES–As Ref Pres Ch	14	NR	1,084	1,379	0.0	0.0
PRES–Cumber Presb	6	NR	454	571	0.0	0.0
PRES–Evan Presby Ch	5	NR	1,395	1,734	0.0	0.0
PRES–Free Ch Scot	1	NR	NR	NR	-	-
PRES–Free Pres NA	1	NR	NR	NR	-	-
PRES–Kor Pres Abroad	6	NR	NR	NR	-	-
PRES–Korean Amer Pres	5	NR	NR	NR	-	-
PRES–Korean Pres Amer	8	NR	NR	NR	-	-
PRES–Orth Pres Ch	3	288	276	376	0.0	0.0
PRES–Presb Ch (USA)	296	33,155	74,409	92,436	1.0	1.9
PRES–Presb Ch Amer	139	21,756	25,040	31,991	0.3	0.6
PRES–Ref Pres of NA	1	28	27	35	0.0	0.0
PRES–Ref Pres US	4	NR	NR	NR	-	-
REF–Christian Ref	3	151	189	234	0.0	0.0
REF–Comm Ref Evan	2	NR	NR	NR	-	-
REF–Ref Ch in Am	2	147	264	282	0.0	0.0
Salvation Army	26	2,159	3,286	6,208	0.1	0.1
Sev Day Adv	197	22,885	39,794	45,780	0.5	0.9
Shinto	1	NR	NR	NR	-	-
Sikh	5	NR	NR	NR	-	-
Tao	1	NR	NR	NR	-	-
Un C of Christ	19	3,896	7,327	9,037	0.1	0.2
Unit Univ	17	1,687	2,223	3,139	0.0	0.1
Unity Ch	14	NR	NR	NR	-	-
Zoroastrian	1	NR	NR	157	0.0	0.0
HAWAII	**1,314**	**111,265**	**129,406**	**561,980**	**41.3**	**100.0**
ANG/EPIS–Anglican NA	1	NR	NR	NR	-	-
ANG/EPIS–Episcopal	34	3,056	5,702	6,932	0.5	1.2
Bahá'í	26	NR	NR	869	0.1	0.2
BAPT–Amer Bapt Assn	3	NR	165	199	0.0	0.0
BAPT–Amer Bapt USA	3	399	545	658	0.0	0.1
BAPT–Consrv Bapt	1	NR	NR	NR	-	-
BAPT–Converge/BGC	3	225	NR	270	0.0	0.0
BAPT–Free Will Bapt	1	NR	33	40	0.0	0.0
BAPT–Ref Bapt Ch	2	NR	NR	NR	-	-
BAPT–Reg Bapt Gen As	2	NR	NR	NR	-	-
BAPT–So Bapt Conv	108	7,839	15,318	18,520	1.4	3.3
BRETH–Grace Breth	2	NR	NR	NR	-	-
BUDD–Mahayana	127	NR	NR	61,727	4.5	11.0
BUDD–Theravada	5	NR	NR	3,692	0.3	0.7
BUDD–Vajrayana	8	NR	NR	340	0.0	0.1
Calv Chpl	23	NR	NR	NR	-	-
Catholic	93	NR	NR	249,619	18.4	44.4
CGOD–Ch God (Ander)	1	24	NR	24	0.0	0.0
Ch Cr, Scientst	7	NR	NR	NR	-	-
Ch of Nazarene	25	1,850	2,447	3,935	0.3	0.7
Chr & Miss Al	9	1,194	856	1,591	0.1	0.3
CHR–Chr Ch (Disc)	4	102	179	216	0.0	0.0
CHR–Chr Chs & Chs Cr	11	NR	1,445	1,745	0.1	0.3
CHR–Chs of Christ	14	817	711	911	0.1	0.2
CHR–Int Chs of Christ	3	NR	337	407	0.0	0.1
CONG–Cong Chr Add'l	5	NR	397	483	0.0	0.1
CONG–Consrv Cong Chr	1	50	20	24	0.0	0.0
Evan Cov Ch	2	412	463	535	0.0	0.1
Evan Free Ch	7	1,340	NR	1,340	0.1	0.2
FRND–Indep Yr Mtgs	5	NR	96	116	0.0	0.0
HINDU–I/A Temples	4	NR	NR	2,312	0.2	0.4
HINDU–Post Ren	9	NR	NR	455	0.0	0.1
HINDU–Renaiss	2	NR	NR	24	0.0	0.0
Jehovah's Witness	36	NR	NR	NR	-	-
JUD–Conserv	1	36	40	108	0.0	0.0
JUD–Orth	2	86	100	120	0.0	0.0
JUD–Reform	1	128	226	610	0.0	0.1
LDS–L-D Saints	134	NR	NR	69,872	5.1	12.4
LUTH–E.L.C.A.	11	1,504	1,918	2,573	0.2	0.5
LUTH–Luth–MO Synod	9	899	1,179	1,504	0.1	0.3
LUTH–Wisc Ev Luth Syn	1	63	80	103	0.0	0.0
MENN–Mennonite USA	2	23	28	34	0.0	0.0
METH–Un Methodist	31	4,637	6,686	8,304	0.6	1.5
Metro Comm Ch	1	30	33	40	0.0	0.0
Missionary Ch	16	1,704	988	1,712	0.1	0.3
Muslim Est	2	268	NR	616	0.0	0.1
New Apost Ch	2	NR	NR	NR	-	-
Non-denom Chr Chs	128	23,060	27,617	32,315	2.4	5.8
ORTHE–Greek Orthodox	2	121	NR	190	0.0	0.0
ORTHE–Orth Ch in Amer	1	25	NR	25	0.0	0.0
ORTHE–Rus Orth Abroad	1	10	NR	25	0.0	0.0
ORTHE–Serb Orth USA	1	30	NR	50	0.0	0.0
ORTHO–Coptic Orth Ch	1	40	NR	50	0.0	0.0
PENT–Assemb of God	83	16,744	9,346	22,543	1.7	4.0
PENT–Ch God (Cleve)	29	947	1,857	2,250	0.2	0.4
PENT–Ch of God Proph	3	NR	162	196	0.0	0.0
PENT–Int Foursq Gos	45	26,877	24,566	29,677	2.2	5.3
PENT–Intl Pent Holiness	5	418	488	590	0.0	0.1
PENT–Pent Ch of God	1	70	NR	109	0.0	0.0
PENT–Un Pent Ch Intl	19	NR	NR	NR	-	-
PENT–Vineyard	2	101	143	173	0.0	0.0
PRES–Kor Pres Abroad	1	NR	NR	NR	-	-
PRES–Korean Amer Pres	4	NR	NR	NR	-	-

NR–Not Reported   - Represents no adherents reported.   Percentages may not total 100 due to rounding.

Table 2: Religious Congregations by State and Group: 2010

Religious Group	Number of Congrega-tions	Number of Attendees	Number of Communicant, Confirmed, or Full Members	Adherents		
				Number of Adherents	% of Total Pop.	% of Total Adh.
PRES–Korean Pres Amer	6	NR	NR	NR	-	-
PRES–Orth Pres Ch	1	40	23	34	0.0	0.0
PRES–Presb Ch (USA)	6	1,454	1,507	1,827	0.1	0.3
PRES–Presb Ch Amer	3	324	202	287	0.0	0.1
REF–Christian Ref	1	25	41	50	0.0	0.0
REF–Hung Ref Add'l	1	NR	NR	NR	-	-
REF–Un Ref Chs N.A.	1	NR	NR	NR	-	-
Salvation Army	12	830	1,240	2,458	0.2	0.4
Sev Day Adv	33	3,344	5,815	6,689	0.5	1.2
Shinto	2	NR	NR	NR	-	-
Sikh	1	NR	NR	NR	-	-
Un C of Christ	115	10,007	16,275	19,684	1.4	3.5
Unit Univ	1	112	132	174	0.0	0.0
Unity Ch	5	NR	NR	NR	-	-
Zoroastrian	0	NR	NR	4	0.0	0.0
IDAHO	**2,427**	**124,582**	**173,097**	**801,655**	**51.1**	**100.0**
ANG/EPIS–Anglican NA	2	NR	NR	NR	-	-
ANG/EPIS–Episcopal	36	2,087	5,121	5,887	0.4	0.7
Bahá'í	10	NR	814	814	0.1	0.1
BAPT–Amer Bapt Assn	5	NR	274	345	0.0	0.0
BAPT–Amer Bapt USA	36	3,542	5,749	7,363	0.5	0.9
BAPT–Asc Ref Bap Ch Am	1	NR	NR	NR	-	-
BAPT–Consrv Bapt	10	NR	NR	NR	-	-
BAPT–Converge/BGC	1	75	NR	90	0.0	0.0
BAPT–Free Will Bapt	6	NR	252	326	0.0	0.0
BAPT–Ind Bapt Flwsp Intl	1	NR	NR	NR	-	-
BAPT–N Am Bapt Conf	2	NR	198	256	0.0	0.0
BAPT–Ref Bapt Ch	2	NR	NR	NR	-	-
BAPT–Reg Bapt Gen As	13	NR	NR	NR	-	-
BAPT–So Bapt Conv	95	5,522	10,216	13,037	0.8	1.6
BRETH–Ch of Brethren	6	104	580	757	0.0	0.1
BUDD–Mahayana	8	NR	NR	1,514	0.1	0.2
BUDD–Theravada	2	NR	NR	566	0.0	0.1
BUDD–Vajrayana	3	NR	NR	106	0.0	0.0
Calv Chpl	29	NR	NR	NR	-	-
Catholic	108	NR	NR	123,400	7.9	15.4
CGOD–Ch God (Ander)	8	1,329	NR	1,329	0.1	0.2
Ch Cr, Scientst	8	NR	NR	NR	-	-
Ch God (7th Day)	1	NR	NR	NR	-	-
Ch of Nazarene	53	11,145	12,307	17,967	1.1	2.2
Chr & Miss Al	8	1,345	602	1,573	0.1	0.2
CHR–Chr Ch (Disc)	16	923	2,551	3,261	0.2	0.4
CHR–Chr Chs & Chs Cr	27	NR	16,154	20,145	1.3	2.5
CHR–Chs of Christ	43	2,579	2,526	3,267	0.2	0.4
CHR–Int Chs of Christ	1	NR	71	90	0.0	0.0
Christian Brethren	1	NR	NR	NR	-	-
CONG–Consrv Cong Chr	3	255	248	309	0.0	0.0
Evan Cov Ch	1	61	44	79	0.0	0.0
Evan Free Ch	8	1,095	NR	1,095	0.1	0.1
FRND–Evan Fr Ch Intl	15	1,490	1,792	2,296	0.1	0.3
FRND–Fr Gen Cf	1	NR	0	0	0.0	0.0
FRND–Indep Yr Mtgs	3	NR	27	35	0.0	0.0
Grace Gosp Fel	1	NR	NR	NR	-	-
HINDU–I/A Temples	1	NR	NR	1,562	0.1	0.2
HINDU–Post Ren	2	NR	NR	31	0.0	0.0
Ind Fund Churches	10	NR	NR	NR	-	-
Jehovah's Witness	43	NR	NR	NR	-	-
JUD–Orth	1	43	50	60	0.0	0.0
JUD–Reform	1	121	213	575	0.0	0.1
LDS–Comm of Christ	8	NR	1,024	1,024	0.1	0.1
LDS–L-D Saints	1,067	NR	NR	409,265	26.1	51.1
LUTH–Ch Luth Conf	1	NR	NR	NR	-	-
LUTH–Ch of Luth Br	1	120	105	435	0.0	0.1
LUTH–E.L.C.A.	35	3,013	6,407	8,337	0.5	1.0
LUTH–Luth Cong Msn Chr	8	558	1,524	1,931	0.1	0.2
LUTH–Luth-MO Synod	43	4,050	7,880	9,863	0.6	1.2
LUTH–Nor Amer Luth C	1	NR	NR	NR	-	-
LUTH–Wisc Ev Luth Syn	3	476	554	781	0.0	0.1
MENN–CG in Cr (Menn)	8	NR	936	1,183	0.1	0.1
MENN–Fel Evg Ch	1	218	83	111	0.0	0.0
MENN–Mennonite USA	5	231	421	556	0.0	0.1
METH–C.M.E.	2	0	200	252	0.0	0.0
METH–Evan Meth Ch	2	NR	NR	NR	-	-

Religious Group	Number of Congrega-tions	Number of Attendees	Number of Communicant, Confirmed, or Full Members	Adherents		
				Number of Adherents	% of Total Pop.	% of Total Adh.
METH–Free Methodist	9	1,614	813	1,614	0.1	0.2
METH–Un Methodist	61	5,312	10,920	21,315	1.4	2.7
METH–Wesleyan	3	133	56	173	0.0	0.0
Metro Comm Ch	1	14	19	24	0.0	0.0
Muslim Est	6	686	NR	1,732	0.1	0.2
New Apost Ch	2	NR	NR	NR	-	-
Non-denom Chr Chs	193	46,982	53,111	62,637	4.0	7.8
ORTHE–Ant Orth of NA	4	193	NR	363	0.0	0.0
ORTHE–Greek Orthodox	2	125	NR	215	0.0	0.0
ORTHE–Rus Orth Abroad	1	35	NR	100	0.0	0.0
ORTHE–Serb Orth USA	1	60	NR	140	0.0	0.0
PENT–Assemb of God	89	12,399	5,365	22,183	1.4	2.8
PENT–Ch God (Cleve)	12	491	596	750	0.0	0.1
PENT–Ch of God Proph	11	NR	364	473	0.0	0.1
PENT–COGIC	3	100	440	570	0.0	0.1
PENT–Int Foursq Gos	25	1,534	1,260	1,606	0.1	0.2
PENT–Intl Pent Holiness	1	28	18	24	0.0	0.0
PENT–Open Bible Std	1	13	NR	13	0.0	0.0
PENT–Pent Ch of God	7	490	NR	763	0.0	0.1
PENT–Un Pent Ch Intl	15	NR	NR	NR	-	-
PENT–Vineyard	6	2,244	2,995	3,793	0.2	0.5
PRES–Bible Pres	1	NR	NR	NR	-	-
PRES–Korean Pres Amer	1	NR	NR	NR	-	-
PRES–Orth Pres Ch	3	103	105	142	0.0	0.0
PRES–Presb Ch (USA)	50	3,775	5,922	7,510	0.5	0.9
PRES–Presb Ch Amer	1	160	137	182	0.0	0.0
REF–Christian Ref	1	25	28	33	0.0	0.0
REF–Comm Ref Evan	4	NR	NR	NR	-	-
REF–Ref Ch in Am	3	1,069	1,273	2,069	0.1	0.3
REF–Un Ref Chs N.A.	3	NR	NR	NR	-	-
Salvation Army	7	356	405	19,269	1.2	2.4
Sev Day Adv	60	5,022	8,737	10,047	0.6	1.3
Tao	1	NR	NR	NR	-	-
Un Breth in Cr	2	26	24	23	0.0	0.0
Un C of Christ	11	749	1,003	1,255	0.1	0.2
Unit Univ	6	462	583	755	0.0	0.1
Unity Ch	3	NR	NR	NR	-	-
Zoroastrian	0	NR	NR	9	0.0	0.0
ILLINOIS	**12,453**	**1,344,758**	**2,204,117**	**7,094,832**	**55.3**	**100.0**
ANG/EPIS–Anglican NA	40	NR	NR	NR	-	-
ANG/EPIS–Episcopal	165	15,249	34,377	42,623	0.3	0.6
Ap Chr Ch-Amer	19	9,478	5,365	9,478	0.1	0.1
Bahá'í	41	NR	5,715	5,715	0.0	0.1
BAPT–Alliance Bapt	2	NR	NR	NR	-	-
BAPT–Amer Bapt Assn	15	NR	725	888	0.0	0.0
BAPT–Amer Bapt USA	274	28,426	56,947	69,456	0.5	1.0
BAPT–Asc Ref Bap Ch Am	2	NR	NR	NR	-	-
BAPT–Consrv Bapt	33	NR	NR	NR	-	-
BAPT–Converge/BGC	99	14,700	NR	17,640	0.1	0.2
BAPT–Free Will Bapt	41	NR	3,526	4,304	0.0	0.1
BAPT–Fund Bapt Flwsp	1	NR	NR	NR	-	-
BAPT–Ind Bapt Flwsp Intl	4	NR	NR	NR	-	-
BAPT–N Am Bapt Conf	12	NR	1,453	1,787	0.0	0.0
BAPT–Natl Mis Bapt Conv	65	3,958	15,784	19,317	0.2	0.3
BAPT–NBC Amer	26	5,265	8,105	9,898	0.1	0.1
BAPT–NBC USA	155	36,216	84,244	103,542	0.8	1.5
BAPT–NT Ind Bapt	9	NR	NR	NR	-	-
BAPT–Prog NBC	43	5,343	12,891	15,788	0.1	0.2
BAPT–Ref Bapt Ch	9	NR	NR	NR	-	-
BAPT–Reg Bapt Gen As	64	NR	NR	NR	-	-
BAPT–S-D Baptist Gen Con	2	30	58	70	0.0	0.0
BAPT–So Bapt Conv	1,059	92,208	233,446	283,519	2.2	4.0
BRETH–Breth in Chr	3	NR	NR	NR	-	-
BRETH–Brethren (Ash)	3	NR	240	287	0.0	0.0
BRETH–Ch of Brethren	38	1,342	3,577	4,370	0.0	0.1
BUDD–Mahayana	50	NR	NR	21,202	0.2	0.3
BUDD–Theravada	23	NR	NR	8,805	0.1	0.1
BUDD–Vajrayana	13	NR	NR	1,270	0.0	0.0
Calv Chpl	14	NR	NR	NR	-	-
Catholic	1,082	NR	NR	3,648,907	28.4	51.4
CGOD–Ch God (Ander)	100	8,196	NR	8,196	0.1	0.1
CGOD–Ches God-Gen Con	26	2,664	3,410	4,102	0.0	0.1
Ch Cr, Scientst	59	NR	NR	NR	-	-

NR–Not Reported - Represents no adherents reported. Percentages may not total 100 due to rounding.

Table 2: Religious Congregations by State and Group: 2010

Religious Group	Number of Congregations	Number of Attendees	Number of Communicant, Confirmed, or Full Members	Adherents: Number of Adherents	Adherents: % of Total Pop.	Adherents: % of Total Adh.
Ch God (7th Day)	7	NR	NR	NR	-	-
Ch of Chr (Hol)	6	NR	NR	NR	-	-
Ch of God Gen Conf	11	NR	499	609	0.0	0.0
Ch of Nazarene	223	19,595	24,671	34,303	0.3	0.5
Chr & Miss Al	53	5,195	4,027	7,258	0.1	0.1
CHR–Chr Ch (Disc)	153	9,291	33,929	41,052	0.3	0.6
CHR–Chr Chs & Chs Cr	482	NR	108,697	131,926	1.0	1.9
CHR–Chs of Christ	275	20,108	20,400	26,427	0.2	0.4
CHR–Int Chs of Christ	4	NR	2,172	2,648	0.0	0.0
Christian Brethren	10	NR	NR	NR	-	-
CONG–Cong Chr, NA	24	NR	2,517	3,096	0.0	0.0
CONG–Consrv Cong Chr	14	1,230	2,134	2,621	0.0	0.0
Evan Assoc RCC	2	NR	NR	NR	-	-
Evan Ch	3	NR	NR	NR	-	-
Evan Cong Ch	10	NR	555	672	0.0	0.0
Evan Cov Ch	78	10,522	13,881	13,680	0.1	0.2
Evan Free Ch	108	27,188	NR	27,188	0.2	0.4
FRND–Evan Fr Ch Intl	1	55	17	21	0.0	0.0
FRND–Fr Gen Cf	13	NR	603	736	0.0	0.0
FRND–Fr Gen Cf & Un Mtg	2	NR	244	299	0.0	0.0
FRND–Fr Un Mtg	4	NR	264	324	0.0	0.0
FRND–Unaffl Mtgs	2	NR	NR	NR	-	-
Grace Gosp Fel	5	NR	NR	NR	-	-
HINDU–I/A Temples	24	NR	NR	10,441	0.1	0.1
HINDU–Post Ren	30	NR	NR	1,010	0.0	0.0
HINDU–Renaiss	5	NR	NR	661	0.0	0.0
HINDU–Trad Temples	8	NR	NR	8,300	0.1	0.1
Ind Fund Churches	50	NR	NR	NR	-	-
Int Cou Comm Ch	13	NR	NR	NR	-	-
Intl Fell Bible Ch	3	NR	NR	NR	-	-
Jain	1	NR	NR	NR	-	-
Jehovah's Witness	197	NR	NR	NR	-	-
JUD–Conserv	21	6,707	7,528	20,325	0.2	0.3
JUD–Orth	63	12,031	4,600	16,710	0.1	0.2
JUD–Reconst	2	676	863	2,330	0.0	0.0
JUD–Reform	41	8,570	15,111	40,803	0.3	0.6
LDS–Comm of Christ	53	NR	5,334	5,334	0.0	0.1
LDS–L-D Saints	128	NR	NR	55,750	0.4	0.8
LUTH–Assoc Free Luth	22	NR	NR	NR	-	-
LUTH–Ch Luth Conf	2	NR	NR	NR	-	-
LUTH–Ch of Luth Br	1	100	67	260	0.0	0.0
LUTH–E.L.C.A.	497	63,062	169,318	222,698	1.7	3.1
LUTH–Evan Luth Syn	1	67	130	166	0.0	0.0
LUTH–Luth Ch-Am Asc	1	NR	NR	NR	-	-
LUTH–Luth Cong Msn Chr	23	3,343	10,012	12,415	0.1	0.2
LUTH–Luth-MO Synod	503	80,533	188,081	243,192	1.9	3.4
LUTH–Nor Amer Luth C	15	NR	NR	NR	-	-
LUTH–Wisc Ev Luth Syn	38	4,079	7,240	9,143	0.1	0.1
MENN–Amish Undif	47	NR	2,693	6,267	0.0	0.1
MENN–Beachy Amish-Menn	2	360	186	360	0.0	0.0
MENN–Ber Amish-Menn	1	197	84	197	0.0	0.0
MENN–CG in Cr (Menn)	1	NR	76	95	0.0	0.0
MENN–Cons Menn Conf	1	135	113	142	0.0	0.0
MENN–Fel Evg Ch	14	5,467	2,810	3,448	0.0	0.0
MENN–Mennonite USA	52	5,394	6,203	7,587	0.1	0.1
MENN–Midw Bchy Am-Menn	3	391	188	391	0.0	0.0
MENN–Ref Mennonite	1	NR	39	42	0.0	0.0
MENN–Tamp Amish-Menn	1	378	223	378	0.0	0.0
MENN–Unaffil Amish-Menn	3	180	129	180	0.0	0.0
METH–AME	109	5,620	19,543	23,924	0.2	0.3
METH–AME Zion	18	1,045	3,199	3,905	0.0	0.1
METH–C.M.E.	37	2,337	10,036	12,269	0.1	0.2
METH–Evan Meth Ch	2	NR	NR	NR	-	-
METH–Free Methodist	57	5,245	4,151	5,580	0.0	0.1
METH–Prim Meth Ch	1	NR	NR	NR	-	-
METH–Un Methodist	1,245	104,613	236,715	314,461	2.5	4.4
METH–Wesleyan	25	4,050	1,225	5,266	0.0	0.1
Metro Comm Ch	4	142	169	208	0.0	0.0
Missionary Ch	23	2,877	1,621	2,923	0.0	0.0
MJEW–Union Mes Cong	5	NR	NR	NR	-	-
MORAV–Morav Ch-North	1	96	228	274	0.0	0.0
Muslim Est	108	98,972	NR	359,264	2.8	5.1
Nat Spirit Asso	8	NR	NR	NR	-	-
New Apost Ch	14	NR	NR	NR	-	-

Religious Group	Number of Congregations	Number of Attendees	Number of Communicant, Confirmed, or Full Members	Adherents: Number of Adherents	Adherents: % of Total Pop.	Adherents: % of Total Adh.
Non-denom Chr Chs	1,443	374,691	471,491	533,464	4.2	7.5
OCATH–Pol Natl Cath	7	NR	NR	NR	-	-
ORTHE–Alban Orth Dio	1	150	NR	350	0.0	0.0
ORTHE–Ant Orth of NA	7	1,165	NR	4,521	0.0	0.1
ORTHE–Bulgar Orth USA	2	250	NR	425	0.0	0.0
ORTHE–Carp Rus Orth	3	197	NR	593	0.0	0.0
ORTHE–Georgian Orth	1	75	NR	150	0.0	0.0
ORTHE–Greek Orthodox	35	9,620	NR	41,364	0.3	0.6
ORTHE–Holy Orth in NA	1	42	NR	55	0.0	0.0
ORTHE–Macedonian Orth	2	190	NR	1,400	0.0	0.0
ORTHE–Orth Ch in Amer	19	1,872	NR	4,469	0.0	0.1
ORTHE–Romania Orth Ar	2	230	NR	740	0.0	0.0
ORTHE–Rus Orth Abroad	3	260	NR	595	0.0	0.0
ORTHE–Rus Orth Moscow	1	15	NR	40	0.0	0.0
ORTHE–Serb Orth USA	13	2,821	NR	9,284	0.1	0.1
ORTHE–Ukrainian Orth	5	565	NR	2,290	0.0	0.0
ORTHO–Armen Ap Cilic	3	245	NR	2,000	0.0	0.0
ORTHO–Armen Ap Etchm	5	235	NR	2,850	0.0	0.0
ORTHO–Coptic Orth Ch	3	1,210	NR	2,600	0.0	0.0
ORTHO–Eritrean Orth	2	410	NR	610	0.0	0.0
ORTHO–Ethiopian Orth	1	NR	NR	NR	-	-
ORTHO–Malan Dioc Am	4	240	NR	720	0.0	0.0
ORTHO–Malan Syr Orth	3	275	NR	522	0.0	0.0
ORTHO–Syrian Orth Ch	2	165	NR	560	0.0	0.0
PENT–Apos Faith Msn	1	NR	35	43	0.0	0.0
PENT–Assemb of God	320	72,163	40,821	119,747	0.9	1.7
PENT–Assm God Intl F	1	NR	NR	NR	-	-
PENT–Ch God (Cleve)	134	8,088	13,643	16,656	0.1	0.2
PENT–Ch Lord Jesus Apos	5	NR	NR	NR	-	-
PENT–Ch of God Proph	18	NR	849	1,047	0.0	0.0
PENT–COGIC	163	9,735	25,922	31,792	0.2	0.4
PENT–Elim	2	NR	NR	NR	-	-
PENT–Fire Bapt Hol Ch	3	NR	NR	NR	-	-
PENT–Full Gosp Bapt	39	NR	NR	NR	-	-
PENT–Int Foursq Gos	43	3,601	5,613	6,823	0.1	0.1
PENT–Intl Pent Holiness	5	161	159	198	0.0	0.0
PENT–Open Bible Std	15	1,336	NR	1,336	0.0	0.0
PENT–Pent Ch of God	19	1,330	NR	2,068	0.0	0.0
PENT–Un Pent Asbl God	6	NR	NR	NR	-	-
PENT–Un Pent Ch Intl	190	NR	NR	NR	-	-
PENT–United Holy Ch	6	NR	NR	NR	-	-
PENT–Vineyard	22	5,772	7,068	8,568	0.1	0.1
PRES–Cum Pres Am	2	NR	NR	NR	-	-
PRES–Cumber Presb	37	NR	1,389	2,724	0.0	0.0
PRES–Evan Presby Ch	7	NR	1,837	2,294	0.0	0.0
PRES–Kor Pres Abroad	8	NR	NR	NR	-	-
PRES–Korean Amer Pres	7	NR	NR	NR	-	-
PRES–Korean Pres Amer	12	NR	NR	NR	-	-
PRES–Orth Pres Ch	14	1,007	836	1,144	0.0	0.0
PRES–Presb Ch (USA)	422	34,720	82,740	101,312	0.8	1.4
PRES–Presb Ch Amer	45	5,509	6,012	7,293	0.1	0.1
PRES–Ref Pres of NA	2	58	54	79	0.0	0.0
REF–Christian Ref	47	9,452	13,268	16,337	0.1	0.2
REF–Comm Ref Evan	2	NR	NR	NR	-	-
REF–Hung Ref Add'l	1	NR	NR	NR	-	-
REF–Prot Ref Chs	3	662	433	747	0.0	0.0
REF–Ref Ch in Am	43	6,501	11,197	12,753	0.1	0.2
REF–Un Ref Chs N.A.	4	NR	NR	NR	-	-
Salvation Army	51	4,018	4,846	18,379	0.1	0.3
Sev Day Adv	158	15,183	26,410	30,370	0.2	0.4
Sikh	4	NR	NR	NR	-	-
Swedenborgian	2	NR	NR	NR	-	-
Tao	1	NR	NR	NR	-	-
Un Breth in Cr	3	67	93	59	0.0	0.0
Un C of Christ	351	34,185	101,159	124,398	1.0	1.8
Unit Univ	36	3,361	5,854	8,111	0.1	0.1
Unity Ch	24	NR	NR	NR	-	-
Zoroastrian	1	NR	NR	229	0.0	0.0
INDIANA	**9,061**	**875,783**	**1,470,855**	**2,874,144**	**44.3**	**100.0**
ANG/EPIS–Anglican NA	21	NR	NR	NR	-	-
ANG/EPIS–Episcopal	83	6,419	13,346	14,998	0.2	0.5
Ap Chr Ch-Amer	12	3,617	2,326	3,617	0.1	0.1
Bahá'í	8	NR	1,319	1,319	0.0	0.0

NR–Not Reported - Represents no adherents reported. Percentages may not total 100 due to rounding.

Table 2: Religious Congregations by State and Group: 2010

Religious Group	Number of Congregations	Number of Attendees	Number of Communicant, Confirmed, or Full Members	Adherents		
				Number of Adherents	% of Total Pop.	% of Total Adh.
BAPT–Alliance Bapt	1	NR	NR	NR	-	-
BAPT–Amer Bapt Assn	22	NR	1,792	2,204	0.0	0.1
BAPT–Amer Bapt USA	338	34,352	76,577	94,067	1.5	3.3
BAPT–Asc Ref Bap Ch Am	1	NR	NR	NR	-	-
BAPT–Consrv Bapt	1	NR	NR	NR	-	-
BAPT–Converge/BGC	11	3,800	NR	4,560	0.1	0.2
BAPT–Free Will Bapt	25	NR	1,387	1,718	0.0	0.1
BAPT–Ind Bapt Flwsp Intl	5	NR	NR	NR	-	-
BAPT–N Am Bapt Conf	2	NR	128	158	0.0	0.0
BAPT–Natl Mis Bapt Conv	28	1,160	3,945	4,856	0.1	0.2
BAPT–NBC Amer	24	4,490	9,740	12,008	0.2	0.4
BAPT–NBC USA	62	11,265	31,239	38,955	0.6	1.4
BAPT–NT Ind Bapt	1	NR	NR	NR	-	-
BAPT–Prog NBC	10	2,234	4,430	5,513	0.1	0.2
BAPT–Ref Bapt Ch	11	NR	NR	NR	-	-
BAPT–Reg Bapt Gen As	95	NR	NR	NR	-	-
BAPT–S-D Baptist Gen Con	1	15	22	27	0.0	0.0
BAPT–So Bapt Conv	424	38,845	91,241	112,064	1.7	3.9
BRETH–Breth in Chr	4	NR	NR	NR	-	-
BRETH–Brethren (Ash)	30	NR	3,140	3,882	0.1	0.1
BRETH–Ch of Brethren	91	4,975	9,795	12,250	0.2	0.4
BRETH–Grace Breth	14	NR	NR	NR	-	-
BUDD–Mahayana	20	NR	NR	3,502	0.1	0.1
BUDD–Theravada	5	NR	NR	350	0.0	0.0
BUDD–Vajrayana	2	NR	NR	156	0.0	0.0
Calv Chpl	19	NR	NR	NR	-	-
Catholic	449	NR	NR	747,706	11.5	26.0
CGOD–Ch God (Ander)	143	20,618	NR	20,618	0.3	0.7
CGOD–Ches God-Gen Con	25	3,435	3,993	4,902	0.1	0.2
Ch Christ Chr Union	12	NR	NR	NR	-	-
Ch Cr, Scientst	26	NR	NR	NR	-	-
Ch God (7th Day)	1	NR	NR	NR	-	-
Ch of Chr (Hol)	4	NR	NR	NR	-	-
Ch of God Gen Conf	10	NR	252	313	0.0	0.0
Ch of Nazarene	269	31,127	38,739	55,725	0.9	1.9
Chr & Miss Al	31	4,245	2,257	5,679	0.1	0.2
CHR–Chr Ch (Disc)	185	15,957	53,905	66,307	1.0	2.3
CHR–Chr Chs & Chs Cr	568	NR	160,912	199,088	3.1	6.9
CHR–Chs of Christ	334	26,788	26,750	34,152	0.5	1.2
CHR–Int Chs of Christ	2	NR	358	447	0.0	0.0
Christian Un	7	NR	NR	NR	-	-
CONG–Cong Chr Add'l	1	NR	104	124	0.0	0.0
CONG–Cong Chr, NA	9	NR	754	926	0.0	0.0
CONG–Consrv Cong Chr	3	343	465	557	0.0	0.0
CONG–Midw Cong Chr Fel	14	780	582	708	0.0	0.0
Evan Assoc RCC	3	NR	NR	NR	-	-
Evan Ch	8	NR	NR	NR	-	-
Evan Cov Ch	7	1,018	1,121	1,324	0.0	0.0
Evan Free Ch	24	11,783	NR	11,783	0.2	0.4
FRND–Central Yr Mtg	6	232	223	280	0.0	0.0
FRND–Fr Gen Cf	10	NR	338	407	0.0	0.0
FRND–Fr Gen Cf & Un Mtg	1	NR	8	10	0.0	0.0
FRND–Fr Un Mtg	94	NR	7,018	8,631	0.1	0.3
FRND–Unaffl Mtgs	4	NR	NR	NR	-	-
Grace Gosp Fel	5	NR	NR	NR	-	-
HINDU–I/A Temples	3	NR	NR	2,230	0.0	0.1
HINDU–Post Ren	14	NR	NR	428	0.0	0.0
HINDU–Trad Temples	1	NR	NR	400	0.0	0.0
Ind Fund Churches	33	NR	NR	NR	-	-
Int Cou Comm Ch	6	NR	NR	NR	-	-
Intl Fell Bible Ch	3	NR	NR	NR	-	-
Jehovah's Witness	107	NR	NR	NR	-	-
JUD–Conserv	4	980	1,100	2,968	0.0	0.1
JUD–Orth	4	900	360	1,250	0.0	0.0
JUD–Reconst	0	397	508	1,370	0.0	0.0
JUD–Reform	16	1,349	2,377	6,419	0.1	0.2
LDS–Comm of Christ	12	NR	1,318	1,318	0.0	0.0
LDS–L-D Saints	99	NR	NR	41,290	0.6	1.4
LUTH–Assoc Free Luth	2	NR	NR	NR	-	-
LUTH–E.L.C.A.	171	17,777	42,786	57,417	0.9	2.0
LUTH–Evan Luth Syn	3	219	315	403	0.0	0.0
LUTH–Luth Cong Msn Chr	10	769	1,855	2,311	0.0	0.1
LUTH–Luth-MO Synod	224	38,796	82,324	107,846	1.7	3.8
LUTH–Nor Amer Luth C	10	NR	NR	NR	-	-
LUTH–Wisc Ev Luth Syn	11	636	1,026	1,327	0.0	0.0
MENN–Amb Amish-Menn	1	127	57	127	0.0	0.0
MENN–Amish Undif	300	NR	19,199	45,144	0.7	1.6
MENN–Beachy Amish-Menn	11	1,428	912	1,428	0.0	0.0
MENN–Ber Amish-Menn	2	55	40	55	0.0	0.0
MENN–CG in Cr (Menn)	2	NR	149	185	0.0	0.0
MENN–Cons Menn Conf	9	1,991	1,787	2,287	0.0	0.1
MENN–Fel Evg Ch	8	3,067	1,523	1,905	0.0	0.1
MENN–Mennonite USA	61	7,841	10,080	13,010	0.2	0.5
MENN–Unaffil Amish-Menn	8	1,020	541	1,020	0.0	0.0
METH–A.W.M.C.	1	26	7	26	0.0	0.0
METH–AME	54	3,035	9,739	12,011	0.2	0.4
METH–AME Zion	15	610	2,540	3,157	0.0	0.1
METH–C.M.E.	18	1,542	5,209	6,476	0.1	0.2
METH–Evan Meth Ch	7	NR	NR	NR	-	-
METH–Free Methodist	44	3,995	3,549	4,190	0.1	0.1
METH–Un Methodist	1,183	117,509	200,486	355,043	5.5	12.4
METH–Wesleyan	217	18,367	12,528	23,891	0.4	0.8
Metro Comm Ch	2	435	423	526	0.0	0.0
Missionary Ch	87	23,139	9,928	23,420	0.4	0.8
MJEW–Assoc Mes Cong	1	NR	NR	NR	-	-
MORAV–Morav Ch-North	1	167	355	487	0.0	0.0
Muslim Est	33	5,240	NR	14,573	0.2	0.5
Nat Spirit Asso	4	NR	NR	NR	-	-
New Apost Ch	5	NR	NR	NR	-	-
Non-denom Chr Chs	1,179	281,057	347,500	396,576	6.1	13.8
OCATH–Pol Natl Cath	4	NR	NR	NR	-	-
ORTHE–Ant Orth of NA	7	653	NR	1,492	0.0	0.1
ORTHE–Bulgar Orth USA	3	75	NR	105	0.0	0.0
ORTHE–Carp Rus Orth	4	187	NR	315	0.0	0.0
ORTHE–Greek Orthodox	8	1,885	NR	10,791	0.2	0.4
ORTHE–Macedonian Orth	1	150	NR	3,500	0.1	0.1
ORTHE–Orth Ch in Amer	8	651	NR	1,530	0.0	0.1
ORTHE–Romania Orth Ar	1	25	NR	30	0.0	0.0
ORTHE–Rus Orth Abroad	3	57	NR	211	0.0	0.0
ORTHE–Serb Orth USA	8	1,334	NR	3,734	0.1	0.1
ORTHE–Ukrainian Orth	3	110	NR	220	0.0	0.0
ORTHO–Coptic Orth Ch	1	270	NR	455	0.0	0.0
ORTHO–Eritrean Orth	2	275	NR	500	0.0	0.0
ORTHO–Ethiopian Orth	1	NR	NR	NR	-	-
PENT–Assemb of God	257	36,145	21,577	54,710	0.8	1.9
PENT–Ch God (Cleve)	111	6,950	13,540	16,698	0.3	0.6
PENT–Ch God Mtn Asm	10	NR	NR	NR	-	-
PENT–Ch Lord Jesus Apos	5	NR	NR	NR	-	-
PENT–Ch of God Proph	29	NR	998	1,232	0.0	0.0
PENT–COGIC	77	3,338	9,463	11,729	0.2	0.4
PENT–Elim	1	NR	NR	NR	-	-
PENT–Fire Bapt Hol Ch	1	NR	NR	NR	-	-
PENT–Full Gosp Bapt	23	NR	NR	NR	-	-
PENT–Int Foursq Gos	27	3,002	3,763	4,563	0.1	0.2
PENT–Int Pent C Chr	1	25	NR	40	0.0	0.0
PENT–Intl Pent Holiness	7	203	296	369	0.0	0.0
PENT–Open Bible Std	2	106	NR	106	0.0	0.0
PENT–Pent Ch of God	26	1,820	NR	2,827	0.0	0.1
PENT–Un Pent Ch Intl	151	NR	NR	NR	-	-
PENT–Vineyard	17	5,765	6,842	8,511	0.1	0.3
PRES–Cumber Presb	6	NR	218	543	0.0	0.0
PRES–Evan Presby Ch	12	NR	4,261	5,248	0.1	0.2
PRES–Free Pres NA	1	NR	NR	NR	-	-
PRES–Korean Amer Pres	1	NR	NR	NR	-	-
PRES–Korean Pres Amer	2	NR	NR	NR	-	-
PRES–Orth Pres Ch	3	253	248	340	0.0	0.0
PRES–Pres Ref	1	NR	NR	NR	-	-
PRES–Presb Ch (USA)	237	16,034	39,568	48,969	0.8	1.7
PRES–Presb Ch Amer	19	2,605	2,256	2,949	0.0	0.1
PRES–Ref Pres of NA	10	1,050	789	1,174	0.0	0.0
REF–Christian Ref	18	3,738	4,927	6,092	0.1	0.2
REF–Comm Ref Evan	1	NR	NR	NR	-	-
REF–Hung Ref Add'l	1	NR	NR	NR	-	-
REF–Prot Ref Chs	1	108	74	119	0.0	0.0
REF–Ref Ch in Am	11	4,527	7,295	9,487	0.1	0.3
REF–Un Ref Chs N.A.	3	NR	NR	NR	-	-
Salvation Army	36	1,525	2,982	13,744	0.2	0.5
Sev Day Adv	99	7,076	12,298	14,147	0.2	0.5

NR–Not Reported - Represents no adherents reported. Percentages may not total 100 due to rounding.

Table 2: Religious Congregations by State and Group: 2010

Religious Group	Number of Congrega-tions	Number of Attendees	Number of Communicant, Confirmed, or Full Members	Adherents		
				Number of Adherents	% of Total Pop.	% of Total Adh.
Sikh	2	NR	NR	NR	-	-
Swedenborgian	1	NR	NR	NR	-	-
Un Breth in Cr	26	4,147	1,999	3,535	0.1	0.1
Un C of Christ	132	10,085	26,373	32,503	0.5	1.1
Unit Univ	17	1,637	2,361	3,192	0.0	0.1
Unity Ch	10	NR	NR	NR	-	-
Zoroastrian	0	NR	NR	29	0.0	0.0
IOWA	**5,107**	**399,246**	**826,253**	**1,642,344**	**53.9**	**100.0**
Amana Ch Soc	1	NR	355	433	0.0	0.0
ANG/EPIS–Anglican NA	1	NR	NR	NR	-	-
ANG/EPIS–Episcopal	61	2,929	7,130	9,060	0.3	0.6
Ap Chr Ch-Amer	8	1,989	898	1,989	0.1	0.1
Bahá'í	8	NR	1,019	1,019	0.0	0.1
BAPT–Amer Bapt USA	102	6,678	14,046	17,165	0.6	1.0
BAPT–Asc Ref Bap Ch Am	1	NR	NR	NR	-	-
BAPT–Consrv Bapt	14	NR	NR	NR	-	-
BAPT–Converge/BGC	41	4,125	NR	4,950	0.2	0.3
BAPT–Free Will Bapt	2	NR	76	94	0.0	0.0
BAPT–Ind Bapt Flwsp Intl	7	NR	NR	NR	-	-
BAPT–N Am Bapt Conf	15	NR	1,724	2,113	0.1	0.1
BAPT–Natl Mis Bapt Conv	2	400	800	992	0.0	0.1
BAPT–NBC USA	19	7,840	10,870	13,265	0.4	0.8
BAPT–NT Ind Bapt	3	NR	NR	NR	-	-
BAPT–Ref Bapt Ch	1	NR	NR	NR	-	-
BAPT–Reg Bapt Gen As	99	NR	NR	NR	-	-
BAPT–So Bapt Conv	106	10,256	13,367	16,466	0.5	1.0
BRETH–Breth in Chr	1	NR	NR	NR	-	-
BRETH–Brethren (Ash)	1	NR	80	96	0.0	0.0
BRETH–Ch of Brethren	25	666	2,057	2,536	0.1	0.2
BRETH–Grace Breth	6	NR	NR	NR	-	-
BRETH–Old Ord Rvr Br	1	NR	44	76	0.0	0.0
BUDD–Mahayana	4	NR	NR	561	0.0	0.0
BUDD–Theravada	5	NR	NR	739	0.0	0.0
BUDD–Vajrayana	2	NR	NR	493	0.0	0.0
Calv Chpl	7	NR	NR	NR	-	-
Catholic	454	NR	NR	503,080	16.5	30.6
CGOD–Ch God (Ander)	9	287	NR	287	0.0	0.0
CGOD–Ches God-Gen Con	8	188	291	355	0.0	0.0
Ch Cr, Scientst	13	NR	NR	NR	-	-
Ch God (7th Day)	2	NR	NR	NR	-	-
Ch of God Gen Conf	3	NR	64	79	0.0	0.0
Ch of Nazarene	75	4,276	6,254	10,173	0.3	0.6
Chr & Miss Al	20	3,379	1,927	5,199	0.2	0.3
CHR–Chr Ch (Disc)	136	8,100	31,366	38,654	1.3	2.4
CHR–Chr Chs & Chs Cr	122	NR	19,273	23,591	0.8	1.4
CHR–Chs of Christ	71	3,506	3,222	4,260	0.1	0.3
CHR–Int Chs of Christ	1	NR	31	38	0.0	0.0
Christian Brethren	8	NR	NR	NR	-	-
Christian Un	7	NR	NR	NR	-	-
CONG–Cong Chr Add'l	3	NR	231	281	0.0	0.0
CONG–Cong Chr, NA	10	NR	1,342	1,636	0.1	0.1
CONG–Consrv Cong Chr	9	855	1,528	1,859	0.1	0.1
Evan Ch	6	NR	NR	NR	-	-
Evan Cov Ch	18	1,438	1,704	1,871	0.1	0.1
Evan Free Ch	89	19,945	NR	19,945	0.7	1.2
FRND–Consrv Yr Mtgs	9	NR	441	545	0.0	0.0
FRND–Fr Gen Cf	1	NR	11	13	0.0	0.0
FRND–Fr Un Mtg	37	NR	3,120	3,807	0.1	0.2
FRND–Unaffl Mtgs	1	NR	NR	NR	-	-
Grace Gosp Fel	1	NR	NR	NR	-	-
HINDU–I/A Temples	2	NR	NR	488	0.0	0.0
HINDU–Post Ren	8	NR	NR	346	0.0	0.0
HINDU–Trad Temples	3	NR	NR	1,225	0.0	0.1
Ind Fund Churches	14	NR	NR	NR	-	-
Int Cou Comm Ch	1	NR	NR	NR	-	-
Jehovah's Witness	69	NR	NR	NR	-	-
JUD–Conserv	3	353	396	1,069	0.0	0.1
JUD–Orth	4	367	225	510	0.0	0.0
JUD–Reform	6	527	928	2,506	0.1	0.2
LDS–Comm of Christ	49	NR	7,669	7,669	0.3	0.5
LDS–L-D Saints	69	NR	NR	24,614	0.8	1.5
LUTH–Assoc Free Luth	7	NR	NR	NR	-	-
LUTH–Ch of Luth Br	3	295	249	479	0.0	0.0
LUTH–E.L.C.A.	439	61,195	173,837	229,557	7.5	14.0
LUTH–Evan Luth Syn	19	572	1,069	1,292	0.0	0.1
LUTH–Luth Ch-Am Asc	10	NR	NR	NR	-	-
LUTH–Luth Cong Msn Chr	48	7,987	23,705	29,089	1.0	1.8
LUTH–Luth-MO Synod	294	33,416	83,258	105,148	3.5	6.4
LUTH–Nor Amer Luth C	28	NR	NR	NR	-	-
LUTH–Wisc Ev Luth Syn	11	633	1,018	1,338	0.0	0.1
MENN–Amish Undif	52	NR	2,769	7,179	0.2	0.4
MENN–Beachy Amish-Menn	2	370	224	370	0.0	0.0
MENN–Ber Amish-Menn	1	110	60	110	0.0	0.0
MENN–CG in Cr (Menn)	4	NR	347	432	0.0	0.0
MENN–Cons Menn Conf	5	515	449	555	0.0	0.0
MENN–Mennonite USA	22	2,208	3,147	3,851	0.1	0.2
MENN–Tamp Amish-Menn	1	103	61	103	0.0	0.0
METH–AME	12	745	1,784	2,198	0.1	0.1
METH–AME Zion	1	80	110	138	0.0	0.0
METH–C.M.E.	1	0	100	126	0.0	0.0
METH–Evan Meth Ch	2	NR	NR	NR	-	-
METH–Free Methodist	17	567	524	641	0.0	0.0
METH–Un Methodist	810	56,669	179,460	235,190	7.7	14.3
METH–Wesleyan	21	2,146	1,646	2,789	0.1	0.2
Metro Comm Ch	2	95	145	180	0.0	0.0
Missionary Ch	5	342	204	342	0.0	0.0
Muslim Est	18	2,494	NR	6,528	0.2	0.4
Nat Spirit Asso	4	NR	NR	NR	-	-
New Apost Ch	2	NR	NR	NR	-	-
Non-denom Chr Chs	339	53,311	66,780	74,985	2.5	4.6
ORTHE–Ant Orth of NA	3	315	NR	700	0.0	0.0
ORTHE–Greek Orthodox	6	305	NR	1,180	0.0	0.1
ORTHE–Orth Ch in Amer	2	46	NR	61	0.0	0.0
ORTHE–Serb Orth USA	1	35	NR	140	0.0	0.0
ORTHO–Coptic Orth Ch	2	90	NR	130	0.0	0.0
ORTHO–Malan Dioc Am	1	7	NR	21	0.0	0.0
PENT–Assemb of God	129	16,631	7,795	27,755	0.9	1.7
PENT–Ch God (Cleve)	19	791	1,107	1,363	0.0	0.1
PENT–Ch of God Proph	9	NR	358	442	0.0	0.0
PENT–COGIC	9	110	952	1,183	0.0	0.1
PENT–Full Gosp Bapt	2	NR	NR	NR	-	-
PENT–Int Foursq Gos	26	1,890	2,541	3,105	0.1	0.2
PENT–Intl Pent Holiness	4	321	191	239	0.0	0.0
PENT–Open Bible Std	41	3,765	NR	3,765	0.1	0.2
PENT–Pent Ch of God	3	210	NR	327	0.0	0.0
PENT–Un Pent Ch Intl	46	NR	NR	NR	-	-
PENT–United Holy Ch	1	NR	NR	NR	-	-
PENT–Vineyard	16	3,545	5,033	6,111	0.2	0.4
PRES–Cov Ref Pres	1	NR	NR	NR	-	-
PRES–Cumber Presb	1	NR	27	27	0.0	0.0
PRES–Evan Presby Ch	1	NR	145	178	0.0	0.0
PRES–Orth Pres Ch	4	95	104	153	0.0	0.0
PRES–Pres Ref	1	NR	NR	NR	-	-
PRES–Presb Ch (USA)	283	17,150	41,981	51,382	1.7	3.1
PRES–Presb Ch Amer	11	864	1,114	1,419	0.0	0.1
PRES–Ref Pres Han	1	NR	NR	NR	-	-
PRES–Ref Pres of NA	3	101	129	166	0.0	0.0
REF–Christian Ref	59	12,978	16,422	20,457	0.7	1.2
REF–Comm Ref Evan	1	NR	NR	NR	-	-
REF–Heritage Ref	1	NR	75	95	0.0	0.0
REF–Prot Ref Chs	3	724	452	838	0.0	0.1
REF–Ref Ch in Am	80	22,842	35,504	40,714	1.3	2.5
REF–Ref Ch in U.S.	1	NR	109	127	0.0	0.0
REF–Un Ref Chs N.A.	8	NR	NR	NR	-	-
Salvation Army	18	700	1,187	5,536	0.2	0.3
Sev Day Adv	46	2,299	3,995	4,598	0.2	0.3
Sikh	2	NR	NR	NR	-	-
Swedenborgian	1	NR	NR	NR	-	-
Un Breth in Cr	2	19	32	17	0.0	0.0
Un C of Christ	178	10,503	31,842	38,998	1.3	2.4
Unit Univ	12	953	1,723	2,349	0.1	0.1
Unity Ch	5	NR	NR	NR	-	-
Zoroastrian	0	NR	NR	1	0.0	0.0
KANSAS	**4,782**	**381,103**	**729,417**	**1,444,455**	**50.6**	**100.0**
ANG/EPIS–Anglican NA	2	NR	NR	NR	-	-
ANG/EPIS–Episcopal	75	4,778	11,363	13,629	0.5	0.9

NR–Not Reported   - Represents no adherents reported.   Percentages may not total 100 due to rounding.

Table 2: Religious Congregations by State and Group: 2010

Religious Group	Number of Congrega-tions	Number of Attendees	Number of Communicant, Confirmed, or Full Members	Adherents: Number of Adherents	Adherents: % of Total Pop.	Adherents: % of Total Adh.
Ap Chr Ch-Amer	6	902	497	902	0.0	0.1
Bahá'í	6	NR	1,324	1,324	0.0	0.1
BAPT–Amer Bapt Assn	11	NR	1,090	1,364	0.0	0.1
BAPT–Amer Bapt USA	214	17,617	38,986	48,497	1.7	3.4
BAPT–Asc Ref Bap Ch Am	1	NR	NR	NR	-	-
BAPT–Consrv Bapt	1	NR	NR	NR	-	-
BAPT–Converge/BGC	2	150	NR	180	0.0	0.0
BAPT–Free Will Bapt	13	NR	567	713	0.0	0.0
BAPT–Fund Bapt Flwsp	1	NR	NR	NR	-	-
BAPT–Ind Bapt Flwsp Intl	14	NR	NR	NR	-	-
BAPT–N Am Bapt Conf	8	NR	995	1,211	0.0	0.1
BAPT–Natl Mis Bapt Conv	11	620	2,450	3,068	0.1	0.2
BAPT–NBC Amer	7	1,050	1,485	1,905	0.1	0.1
BAPT–NBC USA	33	4,954	15,282	19,492	0.7	1.3
BAPT–Ref Bapt Ch	4	NR	NR	NR	-	-
BAPT–Reg Bapt Gen As	23	NR	NR	NR	-	-
BAPT–S-D Baptist Gen Con	1	22	88	108	0.0	0.0
BAPT–So Bapt Conv	317	37,401	79,152	99,329	3.5	6.9
BRETH–Breth in Chr	7	NR	NR	NR	-	-
BRETH–Brethren (Ash)	3	NR	240	303	0.0	0.0
BRETH–Ch of Brethren	27	1,087	2,237	2,759	0.1	0.2
BRETH–Grace Breth	2	NR	NR	NR	-	-
BRETH–Old Ord Rvr Br	1	NR	4	6	0.0	0.0
BUDD–Mahayana	14	NR	NR	6,122	0.2	0.4
BUDD–Theravada	9	NR	NR	1,443	0.1	0.1
BUDD–Vajrayana	4	NR	NR	638	0.0	0.0
Calv Chpl	12	NR	NR	NR	-	-
Catholic	343	NR	NR	426,611	15.0	29.5
CGOD–Ch God (Ander)	49	7,182	NR	7,182	0.3	0.5
CGOD–Ches God-Gen Con	3	96	138	168	0.0	0.0
Ch Cr, Scientst	9	NR	NR	NR	-	-
Ch God (7th Day)	2	NR	NR	NR	-	-
Ch of Chr (Hol)	1	NR	NR	NR	-	-
Ch of Nazarene	134	18,256	24,782	32,538	1.1	2.3
Chr & Miss Al	5	764	1,159	1,374	0.0	0.1
CHR–Chr Ch (Disc)	123	9,935	31,314	38,890	1.4	2.7
CHR–Chr Chs & Chs Cr	207	NR	49,279	61,549	2.2	4.3
CHR–Chs of Christ	166	13,452	13,408	17,933	0.6	1.2
CHR–Int Chs of Christ	3	NR	514	654	0.0	0.0
Christian Brethren	4	NR	NR	NR	-	-
CONG–Cong Chr, NA	6	NR	969	1,207	0.0	0.1
CONG–Consrv Cong Chr	3	195	418	516	0.0	0.0
Evan Cov Ch	26	5,503	4,424	7,154	0.3	0.5
Evan Free Ch	32	6,615	NR	6,615	0.2	0.5
FRND–Evan Fr Ch Intl	40	2,537	3,474	4,325	0.2	0.3
FRND–Fr Gen Cf	3	NR	42	51	0.0	0.0
FRND–Fr Gen Cf & Un Mtg	1	NR	32	41	0.0	0.0
FRND–Fr Un Mtg	1	NR	437	556	0.0	0.0
FRND–Unaffl Mtgs	1	NR	NR	NR	-	-
HINDU–I/A Temples	2	NR	NR	600	0.0	0.0
HINDU–Post Ren	6	NR	NR	220	0.0	0.0
HINDU–Trad Temples	3	NR	NR	1,570	0.1	0.1
Ind Fund Churches	19	NR	NR	NR	-	-
Intl Fell Bible Ch	1	NR	NR	NR	-	-
Jain	1	NR	NR	NR	-	-
Jehovah's Witness	70	NR	NR	NR	-	-
JUD–Conserv	2	777	872	2,354	0.1	0.2
JUD–Orth	1	360	170	500	0.0	0.0
JUD–Reform	3	1,026	1,808	4,882	0.2	0.3
LDS–Comm of Christ	34	NR	6,061	6,061	0.2	0.4
LDS–L-D Saints	74	NR	NR	34,190	1.2	2.4
LUTH–Assoc Free Luth	2	NR	NR	NR	-	-
LUTH–E.L.C.A.	121	10,987	27,200	34,368	1.2	2.4
LUTH–Luth Ch-Am Asc	1	NR	NR	NR	-	-
LUTH–Luth Cong Msn Chr	10	497	1,491	1,814	0.1	0.1
LUTH–Luth-MO Synod	164	20,119	45,644	59,381	2.1	4.1
LUTH–Nor Amer Luth C	2	NR	NR	NR	-	-
LUTH–Wisc Ev Luth Syn	10	590	797	1,017	0.0	0.1
MENN–Amish Undif	10	NR	444	940	0.0	0.1
MENN–Beachy Amish-Menn	4	652	437	652	0.0	0.0
MENN–CG in Cr (Menn)	26	NR	3,535	4,427	0.2	0.3
MENN–Cons Menn Conf	2	310	228	280	0.0	0.0
MENN–Fel Evg Bib Ch	2	195	160	195	0.0	0.0
MENN–Fel Evg Ch	2	953	617	764	0.0	0.1

Religious Group	Number of Congrega-tions	Number of Attendees	Number of Communicant, Confirmed, or Full Members	Adherents: Number of Adherents	Adherents: % of Total Pop.	Adherents: % of Total Adh.
MENN–Mara Amish-Menn	2	188	101	188	0.0	0.0
MENN–Menn Br US Conf	18	NR	4,327	5,372	0.2	0.4
MENN–Mennonite USA	47	5,827	10,256	12,647	0.4	0.9
METH–AME	41	1,282	5,008	6,285	0.2	0.4
METH–AME Zion	3	0	350	451	0.0	0.0
METH–C.M.E.	8	275	1,340	1,687	0.1	0.1
METH–Free Methodist	19	1,739	1,044	1,789	0.1	0.1
METH–Un Methodist	690	61,584	151,286	202,989	7.1	14.1
METH–Wesleyan	40	4,394	2,719	5,718	0.2	0.4
Metro Comm Ch	2	189	192	242	0.0	0.0
Missionary Ch	5	354	274	407	0.0	0.0
MJEW–Union Mes Cong	1	NR	NR	NR	-	-
Muslim Est	21	2,732	NR	7,744	0.3	0.5
New Apost Ch	1	NR	NR	NR	-	-
Non-denom Chr Chs	609	80,900	101,321	114,013	4.0	7.9
ORTHE–Ant Orth of NA	9	618	NR	1,591	0.1	0.1
ORTHE–Greek Orthodox	2	170	NR	345	0.0	0.0
ORTHE–Orth Ch in Amer	2	171	NR	366	0.0	0.0
ORTHE–Rus Orth Abroad	1	4	NR	15	0.0	0.0
ORTHE–Serb Orth USA	2	275	NR	530	0.0	0.0
ORTHO–Coptic Orth Ch	1	276	NR	535	0.0	0.0
ORTHO–Ethiopian Orth	1	NR	NR	NR	-	-
ORTHO–Malan Dioc Am	1	5	NR	15	0.0	0.0
PENT–Assemb of God	151	19,000	9,839	29,767	1.0	2.1
PENT–Ch God (Cleve)	31	913	1,669	2,080	0.1	0.1
PENT–Ch God Apos Fth	4	NR	NR	NR	-	-
PENT–Ch Lord Jesus Apos	1	NR	NR	NR	-	-
PENT–Ch of God Proph	10	NR	423	536	0.0	0.0
PENT–COGIC	52	2,729	6,938	8,778	0.3	0.6
PENT–Full Gosp Bapt	3	NR	NR	NR	-	-
PENT–Int Foursq Gos	21	1,896	2,830	3,507	0.1	0.2
PENT–Intl Pent Holiness	22	1,303	1,474	1,881	0.1	0.1
PENT–Pent Ch of God	7	490	NR	762	0.0	0.1
PENT–Un Pent Ch Intl	17	NR	NR	NR	-	-
PENT–Vineyard	4	1,442	1,761	2,203	0.1	0.2
PRES–Evan Presby Ch	8	NR	1,598	1,972	0.1	0.1
PRES–Korean Amer Pres	1	NR	NR	NR	-	-
PRES–Korean Pres Amer	1	NR	NR	NR	-	-
PRES–Orth Pres Ch	2	74	102	140	0.0	0.0
PRES–Presb Ch (USA)	175	11,813	29,822	37,211	1.3	2.6
PRES–Presb Ch Amer	7	1,389	1,148	1,569	0.1	0.1
PRES–Ref Pres of NA	10	532	534	688	0.0	0.0
REF–Christian Ref	3	229	351	427	0.0	0.0
REF–Comm Ref Evan	1	NR	NR	NR	-	-
REF–Ref Ch in Am	3	267	397	569	0.0	0.0
Salvation Army	16	731	1,228	6,287	0.2	0.4
Sev Day Adv	66	4,181	7,274	8,368	0.3	0.6
Sikh	1	NR	NR	NR	-	-
Swedenborgian	2	NR	NR	NR	-	-
Un Breth in Cr	5	168	187	144	0.0	0.0
Un C of Christ	55	2,763	7,109	8,730	0.3	0.6
Unit Univ	6	618	901	1,319	0.0	0.1
Unity Ch	7	NR	NR	NR	-	-
Zoroastrian	1	NR	NR	16	0.0	0.0
KENTUCKY	**7,745**	**569,674**	**1,470,009**	**2,237,512**	**51.6**	**100.0**
ANG/EPIS–Anglican NA	17	NR	NR	NR	-	-
ANG/EPIS–Episcopal	71	6,326	14,475	17,278	0.4	0.8
Ap Chr Ch-Amer	1	12	11	12	0.0	0.0
Bahá'í	2	NR	715	715	0.0	0.0
BAPT–Alliance Bapt	3	NR	NR	NR	-	-
BAPT–Amer Bapt Assn	19	NR	3,060	3,714	0.1	0.2
BAPT–Amer Bapt USA	6	823	2,469	2,989	0.1	0.1
BAPT–Asc Ref Bap Ch Am	2	NR	NR	NR	-	-
BAPT–Consrv Bapt	1	NR	NR	NR	-	-
BAPT–Converge/BGC	1	75	NR	90	0.0	0.0
BAPT–Enterprise Bapt Assoc	31	NR	NR	NR	-	-
BAPT–Free Will Bapt	135	NR	12,627	15,275	0.4	0.7
BAPT–Ind Bapt Flwsp Intl	5	NR	NR	NR	-	-
BAPT–Natl Mis Bapt Conv	22	100	2,715	3,282	0.1	0.1
BAPT–NBC Amer	11	1,470	2,860	3,494	0.1	0.2
BAPT–NBC USA	45	6,451	18,208	22,336	0.5	1.0
BAPT–Prim Bapt E Dst	7	175	623	752	0.0	0.0
BAPT–Prog NBC	15	10,950	16,565	20,160	0.5	0.9

NR–Not Reported - Represents no adherents reported. Percentages may not total 100 due to rounding.

Table 2: Religious Congregations by State and Group: 2010

Religious Group	Number of Congrega-tions	Number of Attendees	Number of Communicant, Confirmed, or Full Members	Adherents: Number of Adherents	Adherents: % of Total Pop.	Adherents: % of Total Adh.
BAPT–Ref Bapt Ch	6	NR	NR	NR	-	-
BAPT–Reg Bapt Gen As	2	NR	NR	NR	-	-
BAPT–So Bapt Conv	2,520	273,621	821,201	1,004,205	23.1	44.9
BRETH–Breth in Chr	4	NR	NR	NR	-	-
BRETH–Brethren (Ash)	2	NR	160	192	0.0	0.0
BRETH–Ch of Brethren	4	81	251	306	0.0	0.0
BRETH–Grace Breth	3	NR	NR	NR	-	-
BUDD–Mahayana	11	NR	NR	2,674	0.1	0.1
BUDD–Vajrayana	2	NR	NR	105	0.0	0.0
Calv Chpl	4	NR	NR	NR	-	-
Catholic	308	NR	NR	359,783	8.3	16.1
CGOD–Ch God (Ander)	126	10,152	NR	10,152	0.2	0.5
Ch Christ Chr Union	4	NR	NR	NR	-	-
Ch Cr, Scientst	5	NR	NR	NR	-	-
Ch of Chr (Hol)	1	NR	NR	NR	-	-
Ch of Nazarene	131	8,974	13,108	17,672	0.4	0.8
Chr & Miss Al	22	4,890	854	6,517	0.2	0.3
CHR–Chr Ch (Disc)	227	14,125	44,845	55,034	1.3	2.5
CHR–Chr Chs & Chs Cr	382	NR	112,215	137,241	3.2	6.1
CHR–Chs of Christ	607	45,878	44,793	57,388	1.3	2.6
CHR–Int Chs of Christ	2	NR	200	243	0.0	0.0
Christian Brethren	1	NR	NR	NR	-	-
Evan Assoc RCC	2	NR	NR	NR	-	-
Evan Ch	1	NR	NR	NR	-	-
Evan Cong Ch	1	NR	41	48	0.0	0.0
Evan Cov Ch	1	383	450	498	0.0	0.0
Evan Free Ch	11	2,488	NR	2,488	0.1	0.1
FRND–Fr Gen Cf	4	NR	193	234	0.0	0.0
Grace Gosp Fel	1	NR	NR	NR	-	-
HINDU–Post Ren	7	NR	NR	194	0.0	0.0
HINDU–Trad Temples	2	NR	NR	410	0.0	0.0
Ind Fund Churches	3	NR	NR	NR	-	-
Intl Fell Bible Ch	1	NR	NR	NR	-	-
Jain	1	NR	NR	NR	-	-
Jehovah's Witness	92	NR	NR	NR	-	-
JUD–Conserv	4	848	952	2,571	0.1	0.1
JUD–Orth	1	324	120	450	0.0	0.0
JUD–Reform	6	795	1,404	3,791	0.1	0.2
LDS–Comm of Christ	5	NR	568	568	0.0	0.0
LDS–L-D Saints	74	NR	NR	31,991	0.7	1.4
LUTH–E.L.C.A.	32	2,600	5,177	6,441	0.1	0.3
LUTH–Luth Ch-Am Asc	1	NR	NR	NR	-	-
LUTH–Luth Cong Msn Chr	3	671	1,802	2,316	0.1	0.1
LUTH–Luth–MO Synod	29	2,432	4,474	5,750	0.1	0.3
LUTH–Nor Amer Luth C	1	NR	NR	NR	-	-
LUTH–Wisc Ev Luth Syn	4	281	348	494	0.0	0.0
MENN–Amb Amish-Menn	4	414	202	414	0.0	0.0
MENN–Amish Undif	62	NR	3,088	8,172	0.2	0.4
MENN–Beachy Amish-Menn	3	337	209	337	0.0	0.0
MENN–Ber Amish-Menn	1	109	67	109	0.0	0.0
MENN–CG in Cr (Menn)	4	NR	385	472	0.0	0.0
MENN–Cons Menn Conf	6	228	219	263	0.0	0.0
MENN–Menn Chr Fell	2	243	98	243	0.0	0.0
MENN–Mennonite USA	2	72	47	56	0.0	0.0
MENN–Midw Bchy Am-Menn	3	356	178	356	0.0	0.0
MENN–Unaffil Amish-Menn	2	243	125	243	0.0	0.0
METH–A.W.M.C.	1	46	10	28	0.0	0.0
METH–AME	56	1,370	7,162	8,730	0.2	0.4
METH–AME Zion	24	604	2,662	3,257	0.1	0.1
METH–C.M.E.	20	529	2,350	2,882	0.1	0.1
METH–Evan Meth Ch	2	NR	NR	NR	-	-
METH–Free Methodist	10	995	661	999	0.0	0.0
METH–Un Methodist	914	61,790	165,093	189,596	4.4	8.5
METH–Wesleyan	43	1,596	1,266	2,080	0.0	0.1
Metro Comm Ch	3	145	176	216	0.0	0.0
Missionary Ch	2	125	52	125	0.0	0.0
MJEW–Assoc Mes Cong	1	NR	NR	NR	-	-
Muslim Est	27	3,460	NR	11,123	0.3	0.5
New Apost Ch	2	NR	NR	NR	-	-
Non-denom Chr Chs	354	44,357	59,782	68,184	1.6	3.0
ORTHE–Ant Orth of NA	3	902	NR	1,255	0.0	0.1
ORTHE–Bulgar Orth USA	1	1	NR	3	0.0	0.0
ORTHE–Greek Orthodox	2	210	NR	720	0.0	0.0
ORTHE–Orth Ch in Amer	1	90	NR	120	0.0	0.0
ORTHO–Coptic Orth Ch	1	35	NR	35	0.0	0.0
ORTHO–Ethiopian Orth	1	NR	NR	NR	-	-
PENT–Assemb of God	167	15,624	11,193	22,578	0.5	1.0
PENT–Ch God (Cleve)	245	17,064	33,861	41,216	0.9	1.8
PENT–Ch God Mtn Asm	28	NR	NR	NR	-	-
PENT–Ch Lord Jesus Apos	2	NR	NR	NR	-	-
PENT–Ch of God Proph	73	NR	3,660	4,490	0.1	0.2
PENT–COGIC	11	320	667	817	0.0	0.0
PENT–Cong Hol Ch	1	39	35	42	0.0	0.0
PENT–Fire Bapt Hol Ch	1	NR	NR	NR	-	-
PENT–Full Gosp Bapt	16	NR	NR	NR	-	-
PENT–Int Foursq Gos	8	371	425	523	0.0	0.0
PENT–Int Pent C Chr	8	410	195	640	0.0	0.0
PENT–Intl Pent Holiness	7	269	394	484	0.0	0.0
PENT–Open Bible Std	2	40	NR	40	0.0	0.0
PENT–Pent Ch of God	21	1,470	NR	2,284	0.1	0.1
PENT–Un Pent Ch Intl	92	NR	NR	NR	-	-
PENT–United Holy Ch	1	NR	NR	NR	-	-
PENT–Vineyard	11	2,884	3,765	4,689	0.1	0.2
PRES–As Ref Pres Ch	2	NR	69	84	0.0	0.0
PRES–Cum Pres Am	7	NR	NR	NR	-	-
PRES–Cumber Presb	100	NR	5,247	9,566	0.2	0.4
PRES–Evan Presby Ch	2	NR	164	198	0.0	0.0
PRES–Korean Pres Amer	1	NR	NR	NR	-	-
PRES–Orth Pres Ch	2	84	57	83	0.0	0.0
PRES–Presb Ch (USA)	190	8,962	23,148	28,224	0.7	1.3
PRES–Presb Ch Amer	13	1,406	1,371	1,752	0.0	0.1
REF–Ref Ch in Am	3	160	149	215	0.0	0.0
Salvation Army	18	882	1,773	4,856	0.1	0.2
Sev Day Adv	61	3,870	6,731	7,739	0.2	0.3
Un Breth in Cr	2	54	61	47	0.0	0.0
Un C of Christ	27	1,889	4,697	5,728	0.1	0.3
Unit Univ	8	694	1,031	1,332	0.0	0.1
Unity Ch	3	NR	NR	NR	-	-
Zoroastrian	0	NR	NR	14	0.0	0.0
LOUISIANA	**5,841**	**515,212**	**1,203,923**	**2,746,897**	**60.6**	**100.0**
ANG/EPIS–Anglican NA	7	NR	NR	NR	-	-
ANG/EPIS–Episcopal	95	8,562	21,273	28,214	0.6	1.0
Bahá'í	5	NR	1,319	1,319	0.0	0.0
BAPT–Alliance Bapt	2	NR	NR	NR	-	-
BAPT–Amer Bapt Assn	51	NR	8,669	10,724	0.2	0.4
BAPT–Amer Bapt USA	5	1,780	4,407	5,379	0.1	0.2
BAPT–Asc Ref Bap Ch Am	3	NR	NR	NR	-	-
BAPT–Converge/BGC	2	150	NR	180	0.0	0.0
BAPT–Free Will Bapt	4	NR	368	459	0.0	0.0
BAPT–Ind Bapt Flwsp Intl	18	NR	NR	NR	-	-
BAPT–N Am Bapt Conf	1	NR	105	133	0.0	0.0
BAPT–Natl Mis Bapt Conv	71	1,005	11,651	14,299	0.3	0.5
BAPT–NBC Amer	53	10,376	22,003	27,093	0.6	1.0
BAPT–NBC USA	187	27,260	92,015	113,433	2.5	4.1
BAPT–Prog NBC	5	605	2,675	3,232	0.1	0.1
BAPT–Ref Bapt Ch	7	NR	NR	NR	-	-
BAPT–Reg Bapt Gen As	1	NR	NR	NR	-	-
BAPT–So Bapt Conv	1,607	183,718	572,587	709,650	15.7	25.8
BRETH–Ch of Brethren	1	0	91	114	0.0	0.0
BUDD–Mahayana	12	NR	NR	4,489	0.1	0.2
BUDD–Theravada	2	NR	NR	314	0.0	0.0
BUDD–Vajrayana	2	NR	NR	131	0.0	0.0
Calv Chpl	8	NR	NR	NR	-	-
Catholic	564	NR	NR	1,200,900	26.5	43.7
CGOD–Ch God (Ander)	55	3,615	NR	3,615	0.1	0.1
CGOD–Ches God-Gen Con	1	10	10	12	0.0	0.0
Ch Cr, Scientst	11	NR	NR	NR	-	-
Ch of Chr (Hol)	19	NR	NR	NR	-	-
Ch of God Gen Conf	3	NR	160	203	0.0	0.0
Ch of Nazarene	47	2,009	3,152	4,317	0.1	0.2
Chr & Miss Al	6	129	187	197	0.0	0.0
CHR–Chr Ch (Disc)	20	969	2,822	3,490	0.1	0.1
CHR–Chr Chs & Chs Cr	22	NR	2,286	2,846	0.1	0.1
CHR–Chs of Christ	228	17,975	18,899	24,594	0.5	0.9
CHR–Int Chs of Christ	1	NR	106	127	0.0	0.0
Christian Brethren	2	NR	NR	NR	-	-
Evan Free Ch	2	370	NR	370	0.0	0.0

NR–Not Reported   - Represents no adherents reported.   Percentages may not total 100 due to rounding.

Table 2: Religious Congregations by State and Group: 2010

Religious Group	Number of Congrega-tions	Number of Attendees	Number of Communicant, Confirmed, or Full Members	Adherents		
				Number of Adherents	% of Total Pop.	% of Total Adh.
FRND–Fr Gen Cf	4	NR	56	68	0.0	0.0
HINDU–I/A Temples	3	NR	NR	3,062	0.1	0.1
HINDU–Post Ren	5	NR	NR	150	0.0	0.0
HINDU–Trad Temples	3	NR	NR	920	0.0	0.0
Ind Fund Churches	9	NR	NR	NR	-	-
Intl Fell Bible Ch	1	NR	NR	NR	-	-
Jain	1	NR	NR	NR	-	-
Jehovah's Witness	98	NR	NR	NR	-	-
JUD–Conserv	2	239	268	723	0.0	0.0
JUD–Orth	4	605	300	840	0.0	0.0
JUD–Reform	12	1,525	2,691	7,267	0.2	0.3
LDS–Comm of Christ	5	NR	540	540	0.0	0.0
LDS–L-D Saints	51	NR	NR	28,567	0.6	1.0
LUTH–E.L.C.A.	18	1,544	3,570	4,625	0.1	0.2
LUTH–Luth–MO Synod	58	4,489	8,607	10,872	0.2	0.4
LUTH–Wisc Ev Luth Syn	4	174	310	365	0.0	0.0
MENN–Beachy Amish-Menn	1	19	6	19	0.0	0.0
MENN–CG in Cr (Menn)	3	NR	350	437	0.0	0.0
MENN–Mennonite USA	3	162	143	176	0.0	0.0
METH–A.W.M.C.	1	23	0	23	0.0	0.0
METH–AME	106	2,032	14,512	17,863	0.4	0.7
METH–AME Zion	16	155	1,860	2,300	0.1	0.1
METH–C.M.E.	107	1,361	14,000	17,210	0.4	0.6
METH–Cong Meth	10	NR	352	443	0.0	0.0
METH–Evan Meth Ch	2	NR	NR	NR	-	-
METH–Free Methodist	10	303	377	410	0.0	0.0
METH–So Methodist	10	NR	NR	NR	-	-
METH–Un Methodist	501	40,883	120,466	146,848	3.2	5.3
METH–Wesleyan	4	302	268	392	0.0	0.0
Metro Comm Ch	2	127	145	176	0.0	0.0
MJEW–Union Mes Cong	1	NR	NR	NR	-	-
Muslim Est	27	4,010	NR	9,806	0.2	0.4
New Apost Ch	2	NR	NR	NR	-	-
Non-denom Chr Chs	505	139,786	181,027	195,903	4.3	7.1
ORTHE–Ant Orth of NA	4	202	NR	563	0.0	0.0
ORTHE–Greek Orthodox	4	317	NR	1,347	0.0	0.0
ORTHE–Orth Ch in Amer	2	75	NR	160	0.0	0.0
ORTHO–Armen Ap Etchm	1	50	NR	200	0.0	0.0
ORTHO–Coptic Orth Ch	3	143	NR	178	0.0	0.0
ORTHO–Malan Dioc Am	1	10	NR	30	0.0	0.0
PENT–Assemb of God	221	28,556	24,926	54,478	1.2	2.0
PENT–Ch God (Cleve)	64	4,096	7,621	9,444	0.2	0.3
PENT–Ch God Mtn Asm	1	NR	NR	NR	-	-
PENT–Ch Lord Jesus Apos	6	NR	NR	NR	-	-
PENT–Ch of God Proph	21	NR	677	835	0.0	0.0
PENT–COGIC	132	5,075	17,566	21,746	0.5	0.8
PENT–Fire Bapt Hol Ch	1	NR	NR	NR	-	-
PENT–Full Gosp Bapt	58	NR	NR	NR	-	-
PENT–Int Foursq Gos	14	846	753	938	0.0	0.0
PENT–Intl Pent Holiness	27	4,174	6,510	7,947	0.2	0.3
PENT–Pent Ch of God	5	350	NR	544	0.0	0.0
PENT–Un Pent Ch Intl	310	NR	NR	NR	-	-
PENT–Vineyard	7	2,356	3,060	3,737	0.1	0.1
PRES–As Ref Pres Ch	2	NR	111	141	0.0	0.0
PRES–Cumber Presb	4	NR	43	90	0.0	0.0
PRES–Evan Presby Ch	9	NR	2,576	3,176	0.1	0.1
PRES–Korean Pres Amer	1	NR	NR	NR	-	-
PRES–Orth Pres Ch	2	67	65	77	0.0	0.0
PRES–Presb Ch (USA)	102	3,354	9,856	12,115	0.3	0.4
PRES–Presb Ch Amer	19	1,535	1,962	2,328	0.1	0.1
REF–Comm Ref Evan	3	NR	NR	NR	-	-
Salvation Army	7	764	815	2,080	0.0	0.1
Sev Day Adv	59	6,046	10,512	12,090	0.3	0.4
Sikh	1	NR	NR	NR	-	-
Tao	1	NR	NR	NR	-	-
Un C of Christ	17	407	1,501	1,836	0.0	0.1
Unit Univ	7	517	736	968	0.0	0.0
Unity Ch	5	NR	NR	NR	-	-
Zoroastrian	1	NR	NR	10	0.0	0.0
MAINE	**1,574**	**75,336**	**122,943**	**367,043**	**27.6**	**100.0**
ANG/EPIS–Anglican NA	1	NR	NR	NR	-	-
ANG/EPIS–Episcopal	65	4,662	10,687	12,542	0.9	3.4
Bahá'í	6	NR	898	898	0.1	0.2
BAPT–Alliance Bapt	1	NR	NR	NR	-	-
BAPT–Amer Bapt Assn	3	NR	255	299	0.0	0.1
BAPT–Amer Bapt USA	152	8,851	17,341	20,510	1.5	5.6
BAPT–Asc Ref Bap Ch Am	2	NR	NR	NR	-	-
BAPT–Consrv Bapt	37	NR	NR	NR	-	-
BAPT–Converge/BGC	3	550	NR	660	0.0	0.2
BAPT–Free Will Bapt	2	NR	136	160	0.0	0.0
BAPT–Ref Bapt Ch	2	NR	NR	NR	-	-
BAPT–Reg Bapt Gen As	6	NR	NR	NR	-	-
BAPT–So Bapt Conv	21	1,744	2,263	2,681	0.2	0.7
BRETH–Ch of Brethren	4	167	126	151	0.0	0.0
BUDD–Mahayana	19	NR	NR	1,048	0.1	0.3
BUDD–Theravada	1	NR	NR	395	0.0	0.1
BUDD–Vajrayana	3	NR	NR	123	0.0	0.0
Calv Chpl	6	NR	NR	NR	-	-
Catholic	148	NR	NR	190,106	14.3	51.8
Ch Cr, Scientst	16	NR	NR	NR	-	-
Ch of Nazarene	53	2,356	3,164	4,438	0.3	1.2
Chr & Miss Al	9	625	367	859	0.1	0.2
CHR–Chr Ch (Disc)	1	42	138	162	0.0	0.0
CHR–Chr Chs & Chs Cr	3	NR	36	43	0.0	0.0
CHR–Chs of Christ	22	828	777	1,032	0.1	0.3
Christian Brethren	1	NR	NR	NR	-	-
CONG–Cong Chr Add'l	10	NR	666	788	0.1	0.2
CONG–Cong Chr, NA	38	NR	2,837	3,354	0.3	0.9
CONG–Consrv Cong Chr	10	397	335	394	0.0	0.1
Evan Cov Ch	4	176	173	228	0.0	0.1
Evan Free Ch	7	1,238	NR	1,238	0.1	0.3
FRND–Fr Gen Cf & Un Mtg	24	NR	703	834	0.1	0.2
FRND–Unaffl Mtgs	2	NR	NR	NR	-	-
HINDU–Post Ren	4	NR	NR	116	0.0	0.0
HINDU–Renaiss	1	NR	NR	42	0.0	0.0
Int Cou Comm Ch	3	NR	NR	NR	-	-
Jehovah's Witness	44	NR	NR	NR	-	-
JUD–Conserv	2	377	423	1,142	0.1	0.3
JUD–Orth	4	183	150	255	0.0	0.1
JUD–Reform	3	364	641	1,731	0.1	0.5
LDS–Comm of Christ	10	NR	1,020	1,020	0.1	0.3
LDS–L-D Saints	28	NR	NR	10,684	0.8	2.9
LUTH–E.L.C.A.	17	1,215	3,024	3,791	0.3	1.0
LUTH–Luth–MO Synod	3	87	332	476	0.0	0.1
LUTH–Wisc Ev Luth Syn	1	7	23	31	0.0	0.0
MENN–Amish Undif	3	NR	72	203	0.0	0.1
MENN–CG in Cr (Menn)	1	NR	38	45	0.0	0.0
MENN–Fel Evg Ch	2	185	80	95	0.0	0.0
METH–A.W.M.C.	1	20	0	32	0.0	0.0
METH–AME Zion	2	0	250	297	0.0	0.1
METH–Free Methodist	1	36	29	36	0.0	0.0
METH–Un Methodist	165	8,036	20,411	28,329	2.1	7.7
METH–Wesleyan	11	1,305	763	1,697	0.1	0.5
Muslim Est	5	487	NR	1,332	0.1	0.4
Nat Spirit Asso	5	NR	NR	NR	-	-
New Apost Ch	1	NR	NR	NR	-	-
Non-denom Chr Chs	178	19,387	20,480	25,689	1.9	7.0
ORTHE–Greek Orthodox	4	390	NR	1,325	0.1	0.4
ORTHE–Holy Orth in NA	1	8	NR	10	0.0	0.0
ORTHE–Rus Orth Abroad	2	55	NR	98	0.0	0.0
ORTHE–Serb Orth USA	1	47	NR	315	0.0	0.1
PENT–Assemb of God	47	4,130	2,117	5,747	0.4	1.6
PENT–Ch God (Cleve)	27	1,406	1,806	2,134	0.2	0.6
PENT–Ch of God Proph	1	NR	54	64	0.0	0.0
PENT–COGIC	2	60	240	289	0.0	0.1
PENT–Elim	1	NR	NR	NR	-	-
PENT–I F Chr Assmbl	1	NR	NR	NR	-	-
PENT–Int Foursq Gos	7	239	484	574	0.0	0.2
PENT–Intl Pent Holiness	5	124	148	174	0.0	0.0
PENT–Un Pent Ch Intl	41	NR	NR	NR	-	-
PENT–Vineyard	5	1,728	2,402	2,895	0.2	0.8
PRES–Orth Pres Ch	7	414	445	586	0.0	0.2
PRES–Presb Ch (USA)	10	269	437	523	0.0	0.1
PRES–Presb Ch Amer	2	122	129	160	0.0	0.0
REF–Christian Ref	3	190	118	139	0.0	0.0
REF–Comm Ref Evan	1	NR	NR	NR	-	-
Salvation Army	11	461	1,073	2,479	0.2	0.7

NR–Not Reported - Represents no adherents reported. Percentages may not total 100 due to rounding.

Table 2: Religious Congregations by State and Group: 2010

Religious Group	Number of Congrega-tions	Number of Attendees	Number of Communicant, Confirmed, or Full Members	Adherents: Number of Adherents	Adherents: % of Total Pop.	Adherents: % of Total Adh.
Sev Day Adv	34	1,806	3,139	3,613	0.3	1.0
Swedenborgian	2	NR	NR	NR	-	-
Un C of Christ	153	8,753	19,234	22,747	1.7	6.2
Unit Univ	28	1,809	2,479	3,183	0.2	0.9
Unity Ch	1	NR	NR	NR	-	-
Zoroastrian	0	NR	NR	2	0.0	0.0
MARYLAND	**5,336**	**693,181**	**1,130,888**	**2,415,376**	**41.8**	**100.0**
ANG/EPIS–Anglican NA	27	NR	NR	NR	-	-
ANG/EPIS–Episcopal	207	21,232	52,857	70,836	1.2	2.9
Ap Chr Ch-Amer	1	18	8	18	0.0	0.0
Bahá'í	29	NR	3,109	3,109	0.1	0.1
BAPT–Alliance Bapt	12	NR	NR	NR	-	-
BAPT–Amer Bapt Assn	6	NR	1,636	2,002	0.0	0.1
BAPT–Amer Bapt USA	105	29,827	43,088	52,586	0.9	2.2
BAPT–Consrv Bapt	3	NR	NR	NR	-	-
BAPT–Converge/BGC	19	14,350	NR	17,220	0.3	0.7
BAPT–Free Will Bapt	1	NR	45	55	0.0	0.0
BAPT–Ind Bapt Flwsp Intl	1	NR	NR	NR	-	-
BAPT–Natl Mis Bapt Conv	7	200	1,400	1,709	0.0	0.1
BAPT–NBC Amer	9	5,140	8,670	10,509	0.2	0.4
BAPT–NBC USA	49	9,256	24,265	29,294	0.5	1.2
BAPT–Prog NBC	21	4,250	9,914	12,043	0.2	0.5
BAPT–Ref Bapt Ch	3	NR	NR	NR	-	-
BAPT–Reg Bapt Gen As	10	NR	NR	NR	-	-
BAPT–S-D Baptist Gen Con	2	34	45	55	0.0	0.0
BAPT–So Bapt Conv	541	60,970	123,251	150,345	2.6	6.2
BRETH–Breth in Chr	5	NR	NR	NR	-	-
BRETH–Brethren (Ash)	3	NR	240	292	0.0	0.0
BRETH–Ch of Brethren	62	3,927	8,339	10,144	0.2	0.4
BRETH–Grace Breth	14	NR	NR	NR	-	-
BUDD–Mahayana	25	NR	NR	6,732	0.1	0.3
BUDD–Theravada	9	NR	NR	6,028	0.1	0.2
BUDD–Vajrayana	12	NR	NR	891	0.0	0.0
Calv Chpl	8	NR	NR	NR	-	-
Catholic	300	NR	NR	837,338	14.5	34.7
CGOD–Ch God (Ander)	24	3,308	NR	3,308	0.1	0.1
CGOD–Ches God-Gen Con	18	973	971	1,185	0.0	0.0
Ch Christ Chr Union	3	NR	NR	NR	-	-
Ch Cr, Scientst	18	NR	NR	NR	-	-
Ch God (7th Day)	2	NR	NR	NR	-	-
Ch of Nazarene	68	6,171	6,099	11,027	0.2	0.5
Chr & Miss Al	23	1,964	1,228	2,697	0.0	0.1
CHR–Chr Ch (Disc)	35	1,419	5,237	6,378	0.1	0.3
CHR–Chr Chs & Chs Cr	35	NR	7,178	8,754	0.2	0.4
CHR–Chs of Christ	50	6,317	6,926	8,651	0.1	0.4
CHR–Int Chs of Christ	3	NR	735	907	0.0	0.0
Christian Brethren	4	NR	NR	NR	-	-
CONG–Cong Chr, NA	1	NR	100	116	0.0	0.0
Evan Assoc RCC	2	NR	NR	NR	-	-
Evan Cong Ch	1	NR	0	0	0.0	0.0
Evan Cov Ch	1	43	85	56	0.0	0.0
Evan Free Ch	9	2,378	NR	2,378	0.0	0.1
FRND–Consrv Yr Mtgs	1	NR	0	0	0.0	0.0
FRND–Evan Fr Ch Intl	1	125	80	96	0.0	0.0
FRND–Fr Gen Cf	3	NR	206	243	0.0	0.0
FRND–Fr Gen Cf & Un Mtg	17	NR	2,378	2,900	0.1	0.1
FRND–Unaffl Mtgs	2	NR	NR	NR	-	-
HINDU–I/A Temples	8	NR	NR	5,795	0.1	0.2
HINDU–Post Ren	18	NR	NR	470	0.0	0.0
HINDU–Renaiss	4	NR	NR	484	0.0	0.0
HINDU–Trad Temples	7	NR	NR	7,666	0.1	0.3
Ind Fund Churches	9	NR	NR	NR	-	-
Int Cou Comm Ch	5	NR	NR	NR	-	-
Jain	1	NR	NR	NR	-	-
Jehovah's Witness	72	NR	NR	NR	-	-
JUD–Conserv	21	9,548	10,716	28,933	0.5	1.2
JUD–Orth	53	23,644	9,100	32,840	0.6	1.4
JUD–Reconst	7	1,066	1,361	3,675	0.1	0.2
JUD–Reform	20	3,746	6,606	17,836	0.3	0.7
LDS–Comm of Christ	5	NR	685	685	0.0	0.0
LDS–L-D Saints	79	NR	NR	42,614	0.7	1.8
LUTH–Assoc Free Luth	2	NR	NR	NR	-	-
LUTH–E.L.C.A.	207	20,700	58,451	79,375	1.4	3.3

Religious Group	Number of Congrega-tions	Number of Attendees	Number of Communicant, Confirmed, or Full Members	Adherents: Number of Adherents	Adherents: % of Total Pop.	Adherents: % of Total Adh.
LUTH–Luth Ch-Am Asc	1	NR	NR	NR	-	-
LUTH–Luth Cong Msn Chr	7	1,740	3,915	4,810	0.1	0.2
LUTH–Luth-MO Synod	68	7,470	16,268	21,080	0.4	0.9
LUTH–Nor Amer Luth C	4	NR	NR	NR	-	-
LUTH–Wisc Ev Luth Syn	4	281	457	617	0.0	0.0
MENN–Amish Undif	10	NR	708	1,512	0.0	0.1
MENN–Beachy Amish-Menn	1	82	42	82	0.0	0.0
MENN–Cons Menn Conf	1	375	368	439	0.0	0.0
MENN–Menn Chr Fell	1	100	52	100	0.0	0.0
MENN–Mennonite USA	21	1,707	1,611	1,933	0.0	0.1
METH–A.W.M.C.	1	37	10	47	0.0	0.0
METH–AME	134	33,199	64,613	78,364	1.4	3.2
METH–AME Zion	36	10,530	18,035	21,713	0.4	0.9
METH–C.M.E.	3	250	700	848	0.0	0.0
METH–Evan Meth Ch	1	NR	NR	NR	-	-
METH–Free Methodist	14	895	759	979	0.0	0.0
METH–So Methodist	1	NR	NR	NR	-	-
METH–Un Methodist	876	75,929	205,764	238,774	4.1	9.9
METH–Wesleyan	40	6,670	3,512	8,675	0.2	0.4
Metro Comm Ch	6	227	310	377	0.0	0.0
Missionary Ch	2	67	72	80	0.0	0.0
MJEW–Assoc Mes Cong	1	NR	NR	NR	-	-
MJEW–Union Mes Cong	4	NR	NR	NR	-	-
MORAV–Morav Ch-North	3	295	596	755	0.0	0.0
Muslim Est	54	11,812	NR	36,484	0.6	1.5
New Apost Ch	2	NR	NR	NR	-	-
Non-denom Chr Chs	725	207,696	274,007	298,921	5.2	12.4
OCATH–Pol Natl Cath	1	NR	NR	NR	-	-
ORTHE–Ant Orth of NA	5	604	NR	1,558	0.0	0.1
ORTHE–Carp Rus Orth	2	120	NR	241	0.0	0.0
ORTHE–Georgian Orth	1	40	NR	60	0.0	0.0
ORTHE–Greek Orthodox	9	3,295	NR	14,150	0.2	0.6
ORTHE–Holy Orth in NA	1	77	NR	100	0.0	0.0
ORTHE–Orth Ch in Amer	7	552	NR	1,206	0.0	0.0
ORTHE–Rus Orth Abroad	2	65	NR	110	0.0	0.0
ORTHE–Rus Orth Moscow	1	80	NR	225	0.0	0.0
ORTHE–Serb Orth USA	1	100	NR	2,000	0.0	0.1
ORTHE–Ukrainian Orth	4	270	NR	685	0.0	0.0
ORTHO–Armen Ap Cilic	1	150	NR	2,000	0.0	0.1
ORTHO–Coptic Orth Ch	2	345	NR	750	0.0	0.0
ORTHO–Eritrean Orth	1	225	NR	450	0.0	0.0
ORTHO–Ethiopian Orth	2	NR	NR	NR	-	-
ORTHO–Malan Dioc Am	4	705	NR	1,030	0.0	0.0
ORTHO–Malan Syr Orth	2	120	NR	234	0.0	0.0
PENT–Assemb of God	119	18,716	12,002	29,066	0.5	1.2
PENT–Ch God (Cleve)	126	17,901	25,778	31,273	0.5	1.3
PENT–Ch Lord Jesus Apos	9	NR	NR	NR	-	-
PENT–Ch of God by Faith	1	NR	NR	NR	-	-
PENT–Ch of God Proph	21	NR	993	1,208	0.0	0.1
PENT–COGIC	22	1,529	2,793	3,374	0.1	0.1
PENT–Elim	3	NR	NR	NR	-	-
PENT–Fire Bapt Hol Ch	4	NR	NR	NR	-	-
PENT–Full Gosp Bapt	21	NR	NR	NR	-	-
PENT–I F Chr Assmbl	1	NR	NR	NR	-	-
PENT–Int Foursq Gos	16	2,000	1,712	2,103	0.0	0.1
PENT–Int Pent C Chr	2	48	51	142	0.0	0.0
PENT–Intl Pent Holiness	18	2,335	2,942	3,569	0.1	0.1
PENT–Open Bible Std	1	26	NR	26	0.0	0.0
PENT–Pent Ch of God	7	490	NR	762	0.0	0.0
PENT–Un Pent Ch Intl	48	NR	NR	NR	-	-
PENT–United Holy Ch	6	NR	NR	NR	-	-
PENT–Vineyard	5	465	740	904	0.0	0.0
PRES–AmPres	1	NR	NR	NR	-	-
PRES–As Ref Pres Ch	7	NR	722	886	0.0	0.0
PRES–Cumber Presb	1	NR	14	14	0.0	0.0
PRES–Evan Presby Ch	2	NR	3,048	3,733	0.1	0.2
PRES–Free Ch Scot	1	NR	NR	NR	-	-
PRES–Kor Pres Abroad	2	NR	NR	NR	-	-
PRES–Korean Amer Pres	5	NR	NR	NR	-	-
PRES–Korean Pres Amer	12	NR	NR	NR	-	-
PRES–Orth Pres Ch	7	994	900	1,305	0.0	0.1
PRES–Presb Ch (USA)	140	14,574	27,909	33,966	0.6	1.4
PRES–Presb Ch Amer	57	8,562	10,676	13,852	0.2	0.6
PRES–Ref Pres Han	2	NR	NR	NR	-	-

NR–Not Reported   - Represents no adherents reported.   Percentages may not total 100 due to rounding.

Table 2: Religious Congregations by State and Group: 2010

Religious Group	Number of Congrega-tions	Number of Attendees	Number of Communicant, Confirmed, or Full Members	Adherents		
				Number of Adherents	% of Total Pop.	% of Total Adh.
PRES–Ref Pres of NA	1	114	89	131	0.0	0.0
REF–Christian Ref	2	120	173	212	0.0	0.0
REF–Comm Ref Evan	1	NR	NR	NR	-	-
REF–Ref Ch in Am	1	302	299	299	0.0	0.0
Salvation Army	12	633	1,270	5,106	0.1	0.2
Sev Day Adv	144	20,554	35,739	41,105	0.7	1.7
Sikh	4	NR	NR	NR	-	-
Un Breth in Cr	5	149	161	128	0.0	0.0
Un C of Christ	69	3,879	11,083	13,507	0.2	0.6
Unit Univ	24	3,074	4,986	6,634	0.1	0.3
Unity Ch	9	NR	NR	NR	-	-
Zoroastrian	0	NR	NR	407	0.0	0.0
MASSACHUSETTS	**4,200**	**321,917**	**469,787**	**3,748,058**	**57.2**	**100.0**
ANG/EPIS–Anglican NA	24	NR	NR	NR	-	-
ANG/EPIS–Episcopal	238	23,111	61,712	81,999	1.3	2.2
Bahá'í	25	NR	2,757	2,757	0.0	0.1
BAPT–Alliance Bapt	5	NR	NR	NR	-	-
BAPT–Amer Bapt USA	277	23,613	41,620	49,669	0.8	1.3
BAPT–Asc Ref Bap Ch Am	3	NR	NR	NR	-	-
BAPT–Consrv Bapt	45	NR	NR	NR	-	-
BAPT–Converge/BGC	37	4,075	NR	4,890	0.1	0.1
BAPT–Natl Mis Bapt Conv	3	0	450	530	0.0	0.0
BAPT–NBC USA	7	560	1,315	1,585	0.0	0.0
BAPT–Ref Bapt Ch	9	NR	NR	NR	-	-
BAPT–Reg Bapt Gen As	6	NR	NR	NR	-	-
BAPT–So Bapt Conv	147	12,673	12,915	15,326	0.2	0.4
BRETH–Grace Breth	1	NR	NR	NR	-	-
BUDD–Mahayana	56	NR	NR	15,340	0.2	0.4
BUDD–Theravada	17	NR	NR	11,467	0.2	0.3
BUDD–Vajrayana	18	NR	NR	1,697	0.0	0.0
Calv Chpl	9	NR	NR	NR	-	-
Catholic	641	NR	NR	2,940,199	44.9	78.4
CGOD–Ch God (Ander)	4	6,890	NR	6,890	0.1	0.2
CGOD–Ches God-Gen Con	3	246	125	149	0.0	0.0
Ch Christ Chr Union	2	NR	NR	NR	-	-
Ch Cr, Scientst	49	NR	NR	NR	-	-
Ch God (7th Day)	2	NR	NR	NR	-	-
Ch of Nazarene	66	4,975	7,113	8,908	0.1	0.2
Chr & Miss Al	28	2,727	1,791	4,038	0.1	0.1
CHR–Chr Ch (Disc)	5	0	0	0	0.0	0.0
CHR–Chr Chs & Chs Cr	8	NR	150	181	0.0	0.0
CHR–Chs of Christ	28	1,824	1,656	2,260	0.0	0.1
CHR–Int Chs of Christ	3	NR	2,420	2,851	0.0	0.1
Christian Brethren	7	NR	NR	NR	-	-
CONG–Cong Chr Add'l	7	NR	1,331	1,584	0.0	0.0
CONG–Cong Chr, NA	36	NR	4,350	5,206	0.1	0.1
CONG–Consrv Cong Chr	49	6,968	6,544	7,828	0.1	0.2
Evan Cov Ch	21	3,180	2,793	4,135	0.1	0.1
Evan Free Ch	15	1,879	NR	1,879	0.0	0.1
FRND–Fr Gen Cf & Un Mtg	33	NR	1,777	2,111	0.0	0.1
HINDU–I/A Temples	12	NR	NR	8,594	0.1	0.2
HINDU–Post Ren	20	NR	NR	820	0.0	0.0
HINDU–Renaiss	7	NR	NR	579	0.0	0.0
HINDU–Trad Temples	4	NR	NR	1,648	0.0	0.0
Int Cou Comm Ch	5	NR	NR	NR	-	-
Jain	2	NR	NR	NR	-	-
Jehovah's Witness	83	NR	NR	NR	-	-
JUD–Conserv	34	8,651	9,709	26,215	0.4	0.7
JUD–Orth	49	9,115	3,690	12,660	0.2	0.3
JUD–Reconst	8	761	973	2,628	0.0	0.1
JUD–Reform	41	8,188	14,444	38,999	0.6	1.0
LDS–Comm of Christ	6	NR	612	612	0.0	0.0
LDS–L-D Saints	51	NR	NR	24,965	0.4	0.7
LUTH–Apostolic Luth	2	NR	NR	NR	-	-
LUTH–E.L.C.A.	66	6,440	18,394	24,228	0.4	0.6
LUTH–Evan Luth Syn	2	104	169	230	0.0	0.0
LUTH–Luth Cong Msn Chr	2	57	252	305	0.0	0.0
LUTH–Luth-MO Synod	20	2,291	4,356	5,474	0.1	0.1
LUTH–Wisc Ev Luth Syn	2	88	178	232	0.0	0.0
MENN–Mennonite USA	1	40	49	59	0.0	0.0
METH–AME	17	1,523	4,565	5,405	0.1	0.1
METH–AME Zion	10	100	1,155	1,361	0.0	0.0
METH–C.M.E.	2	40	230	279	0.0	0.0

Religious Group	Number of Congrega-tions	Number of Attendees	Number of Communicant, Confirmed, or Full Members	Adherents		
				Number of Adherents	% of Total Pop.	% of Total Adh.
METH–Free Methodist	14	1,009	999	1,169	0.0	0.0
METH–Prim Meth Ch	7	NR	NR	NR	-	-
METH–Un Methodist	208	12,979	38,984	52,339	0.8	1.4
METH–Wesleyan	3	143	102	186	0.0	0.0
Metro Comm Ch	1	19	20	23	0.0	0.0
Missionary Ch	8	560	381	564	0.0	0.0
MJEW–Union Mes Cong	2	NR	NR	NR	-	-
Muslim Est	39	6,520	NR	21,768	0.3	0.6
Nat Spirit Asso	4	NR	NR	NR	-	-
New Apost Ch	4	NR	NR	NR	-	-
Non-denom Chr Chs	323	55,414	69,835	79,443	1.2	2.1
OCATH–Pol Natl Cath	8	NR	NR	NR	-	-
ORTHE–Alban Orth Dio	1	35	NR	350	0.0	0.0
ORTHE–Ant Orth of NA	11	1,939	NR	6,024	0.1	0.2
ORTHE–Bulgar Orth USA	2	100	NR	236	0.0	0.0
ORTHE–Greek Orthodox	39	8,290	NR	33,755	0.5	0.9
ORTHE–Holy Orth in NA	7	832	NR	1,080	0.0	0.0
ORTHE–Orth Ch in Amer	13	1,021	NR	3,663	0.1	0.1
ORTHE–Romania Orth Ar	3	325	NR	1,070	0.0	0.0
ORTHE–Rus Orth Abroad	5	322	NR	2,339	0.0	0.1
ORTHE–Serb Orth USA	1	100	NR	1,000	0.0	0.0
ORTHE–Ukrainian Orth	1	100	NR	200	0.0	0.0
ORTHO–Armen Ap Cilic	5	4,280	NR	2,300	0.0	0.1
ORTHO–Armen Ap Etchm	8	867	NR	4,050	0.1	0.1
ORTHO–Coptic Orth Ch	1	300	NR	4,000	0.1	0.1
ORTHO–Eritrean Orth	1	325	NR	485	0.0	0.0
ORTHO–Ethiopian Orth	2	NR	NR	NR	-	-
ORTHO–Malan Dioc Am	1	140	NR	220	0.0	0.0
ORTHO–Malan Syr Orth	1	40	NR	72	0.0	0.0
ORTHO–Syrian Orth Ch	2	310	NR	700	0.0	0.0
PENT–Assemb of God	146	22,888	14,132	33,220	0.5	0.9
PENT–Ch God (Cleve)	64	4,662	4,898	5,840	0.1	0.2
PENT–Ch Lord Jesus Apos	7	NR	NR	NR	-	-
PENT–Ch of God Proph	14	NR	688	820	0.0	0.0
PENT–COGIC	17	401	1,720	2,040	0.0	0.1
PENT–Elim	2	NR	NR	NR	-	-
PENT–Fire Bapt Hol Ch	2	NR	NR	NR	-	-
PENT–I F Chr Assmbl	14	NR	NR	NR	-	-
PENT–Int Foursq Gos	31	2,443	2,462	2,966	0.0	0.1
PENT–Intl Pent Holiness	1	350	350	423	0.0	0.0
PENT–Un Pent Asbl God	5	NR	NR	NR	-	-
PENT–Un Pent Ch Intl	20	NR	NR	NR	-	-
PENT–United Holy Ch	6	NR	NR	NR	-	-
PENT–Vineyard	9	1,735	2,259	2,720	0.0	0.1
PRES–Cumber Presb	1	NR	35	35	0.0	0.0
PRES–Evan Presby Ch	2	NR	55	67	0.0	0.0
PRES–Korean Amer Pres	3	NR	NR	NR	-	-
PRES–Korean Pres Amer	7	NR	NR	NR	-	-
PRES–Orth Pres Ch	7	711	621	790	0.0	0.0
PRES–Presb Ch (USA)	34	2,299	3,658	4,382	0.1	0.1
PRES–Presb Ch Amer	9	1,438	941	1,142	0.0	0.0
PRES–Ref Pres of NA	1	80	68	87	0.0	0.0
REF–Christian Ref	5	1,930	1,456	1,766	0.0	0.0
REF–Ref Ch in Am	1	66	101	106	0.0	0.0
Salvation Army	34	1,765	3,045	6,880	0.1	0.2
Sev Day Adv	117	10,465	18,202	20,930	0.3	0.6
Sikh	6	NR	NR	NR	-	-
Swedenborgian	5	NR	NR	NR	-	-
Tao	2	NR	NR	NR	-	-
Un Breth in Cr	1	50	65	43	0.0	0.0
Un C of Christ	374	32,063	72,292	86,639	1.3	2.3
Unit Univ	140	12,482	22,823	31,143	0.5	0.8
Unity Ch	7	NR	NR	NR	-	-
Zoroastrian	1	NR	NR	211	0.0	0.0
MICHIGAN	**9,521**	**1,096,974**	**1,632,731**	**4,165,343**	**42.1**	**100.0**
ANG/EPIS–Anglican NA	13	NR	NR	NR	-	-
ANG/EPIS–Episcopal	216	14,620	32,580	40,383	0.4	1.0
Ap Chr Ch-Amer	3	679	347	679	0.0	0.0
Bahá'í	22	NR	2,979	2,979	0.0	0.1
BAPT–Alliance Bapt	1	NR	NR	NR	-	-
BAPT–Amer Bapt Assn	18	NR	1,234	1,513	0.0	0.0
BAPT–Amer Bapt USA	146	24,371	43,830	53,649	0.5	1.3
BAPT–Consrv Bapt	16	NR	NR	NR	-	-

NR–Not Reported - Represents no adherents reported. Percentages may not total 100 due to rounding.

Table 2: Religious Congregations by State and Group: 2010

Religious Group	Number of Congregations	Number of Attendees	Number of Communicant, Confirmed, or Full Members	Adherents		
				Number of Adherents	% of Total Pop.	% of Total Adh.
BAPT–Converge/BGC	66	8,275	NR	9,930	0.1	0.2
BAPT–Free Will Bapt	43	NR	4,343	5,299	0.1	0.1
BAPT–Fund Bapt Flwsp	1	NR	NR	NR	-	-
BAPT–Ind Bapt Flwsp Intl	23	NR	NR	NR	-	-
BAPT–N Am Bapt Conf	19	NR	3,671	4,452	0.0	0.1
BAPT–Natl Mis Bapt Conv	33	4,765	13,945	17,065	0.2	0.4
BAPT–NBC Amer	14	4,433	10,453	12,962	0.1	0.3
BAPT–NBC USA	183	42,202	93,571	115,165	1.2	2.8
BAPT–NT Ind Bapt	1	NR	NR	NR	-	-
BAPT–Prog NBC	18	2,317	4,410	5,439	0.1	0.1
BAPT–Ref Bapt Ch	6	NR	NR	NR	-	-
BAPT–Reg Bapt Gen As	179	NR	NR	NR	-	-
BAPT–S-D Baptist Gen Con	3	131	165	203	0.0	0.0
BAPT–So Bapt Conv	300	22,516	44,800	54,533	0.6	1.3
BRETH–Breth in Chr	6	NR	NR	NR	-	-
BRETH–Brethren (Ash)	1	NR	80	97	0.0	0.0
BRETH–Ch of Brethren	23	817	1,359	1,634	0.0	0.0
BRETH–Grace Breth	1	NR	NR	NR	-	-
BUDD–Mahayana	27	NR	NR	6,849	0.1	0.2
BUDD–Theravada	11	NR	NR	4,330	0.0	0.1
BUDD–Vajrayana	5	NR	NR	389	0.0	0.0
Calv Chpl	17	NR	NR	NR	-	-
Catholic	839	NR	NR	1,717,296	17.4	41.2
CGOD–Ch God (Ander)	107	11,722	NR	11,722	0.1	0.3
CGOD–Ches God-Gen Con	6	316	216	259	0.0	0.0
Ch Christ Chr Union	4	NR	NR	NR	-	-
Ch Cr, Scientst	41	NR	NR	NR	-	-
Ch God (7th Day)	8	NR	NR	NR	-	-
Ch of Chr (Hol)	4	NR	NR	NR	-	-
Ch of God Gen Conf	5	NR	227	280	0.0	0.0
Ch of Nazarene	185	23,557	24,471	40,375	0.4	1.0
Chr & Miss Al	34	3,716	2,914	5,036	0.1	0.1
CHR–Chr Ch (Disc)	42	2,323	4,918	6,016	0.1	0.1
CHR–Chr Chs & Chs Cr	110	NR	17,233	20,971	0.2	0.5
CHR–Chs of Christ	193	20,645	21,916	28,472	0.3	0.7
CHR–Int Chs of Christ	3	NR	306	377	0.0	0.0
Christian Brethren	11	NR	NR	NR	-	-
CONG–Cong Chr Add'l	3	NR	787	944	0.0	0.0
CONG–Cong Chr, NA	57	NR	9,305	11,315	0.1	0.3
CONG–Consrv Cong Chr	16	1,050	1,289	1,566	0.0	0.0
Evan Assoc RCC	1	NR	NR	NR	-	-
Evan Ch	2	NR	NR	NR	-	-
Evan Cov Ch	52	8,681	7,721	11,285	0.1	0.3
Evan Free Ch	32	7,588	NR	7,588	0.1	0.2
FRND–Consrv Yr Mtgs	2	NR	12	15	0.0	0.0
FRND–Evan Fr Ch Intl	7	768	411	497	0.0	0.0
FRND–Fr Gen Cf	16	NR	325	391	0.0	0.0
FRND–Fr Un Mtg	3	NR	149	180	0.0	0.0
FRND–Unaffl Mtgs	1	NR	NR	NR	-	-
Grace Gosp Fel	20	NR	NR	NR	-	-
HINDU–I/A Temples	11	NR	NR	4,894	0.0	0.1
HINDU–Post Ren	18	NR	NR	606	0.0	0.0
HINDU–Renaiss	3	NR	NR	36	0.0	0.0
HINDU–Trad Temples	10	NR	NR	8,477	0.1	0.2
Ind Fund Churches	110	NR	NR	NR	-	-
Int Cou Comm Ch	13	NR	NR	NR	-	-
Jain	2	NR	NR	NR	-	-
Jehovah's Witness	216	NR	NR	NR	-	-
JUD–Conserv	8	2,737	3,073	8,297	0.1	0.2
JUD–Orth	21	8,935	2,800	12,410	0.1	0.3
JUD–Reconst	4	192	245	662	0.0	0.0
JUD–Reform	22	4,832	8,523	23,013	0.2	0.6
LDS–Comm of Christ	89	NR	14,863	14,863	0.2	0.4
LDS–L-D Saints	105	NR	NR	42,319	0.4	1.0
LUTH–Apostolic Luth	16	NR	NR	NR	-	-
LUTH–Assoc Free Luth	9	NR	NR	NR	-	-
LUTH–Ch Luth Conf	8	NR	NR	NR	-	-
LUTH–E.L.C.A.	320	34,459	91,100	120,598	1.2	2.9
LUTH–Evan Luth Syn	9	580	1,242	1,551	0.0	0.0
LUTH–Luth Ch-Am Asc	1	NR	NR	NR	-	-
LUTH–Luth Cong Msn Chr	18	2,669	7,521	9,075	0.1	0.2
LUTH–Luth–MO Synod	413	77,114	167,409	219,618	2.2	5.3
LUTH–Nor Amer Luth C	10	NR	NR	NR	-	-
LUTH–Wisc Ev Luth Syn	136	14,817	29,810	37,365	0.4	0.9
MENN–Amish Undif	85	NR	4,003	10,218	0.1	0.2
MENN–Beachy Amish-Menn	1	111	67	111	0.0	0.0
MENN–CG in Cr (Menn)	3	NR	378	455	0.0	0.0
MENN–Cons Menn Conf	11	801	727	866	0.0	0.0
MENN–Fel Evg Bib Ch	1	15	15	15	0.0	0.0
MENN–Fel Evg Ch	3	325	178	219	0.0	0.0
MENN–Mennonite USA	28	1,341	1,870	2,278	0.0	0.1
MENN–Ref Mennonite	1	NR	27	30	0.0	0.0
METH–A.W.M.C.	1	32	0	35	0.0	0.0
METH–AME	67	7,124	17,328	21,253	0.2	0.5
METH–AME Zion	16	555	2,760	3,402	0.0	0.1
METH–C.M.E.	25	943	4,382	5,391	0.1	0.1
METH–Free Methodist	128	15,891	10,495	16,273	0.2	0.4
METH–Un Methodist	852	79,939	155,443	228,521	2.3	5.5
METH–Wesleyan	154	30,869	12,717	40,144	0.4	1.0
Metro Comm Ch	6	259	274	333	0.0	0.0
Missionary Ch	72	8,520	4,477	8,603	0.1	0.2
MJEW–Assoc Mes Cong	1	NR	NR	NR	-	-
MJEW–Union Mes Cong	1	NR	NR	NR	-	-
MORAV–Morav Ch-North	3	164	349	423	0.0	0.0
Muslim Est	77	31,647	NR	120,351	1.2	2.9
Nat Spirit Asso	4	NR	NR	NR	-	-
New Apost Ch	26	NR	NR	NR	-	-
Non-denom Chr Chs	924	302,472	360,773	422,916	4.3	10.2
OCATH–Pol Natl Cath	4	NR	NR	NR	-	-
ORTHE–Ant Orth of NA	12	1,436	NR	5,928	0.1	0.1
ORTHE–Bulgar Orth USA	3	205	NR	670	0.0	0.0
ORTHE–Greek Orthodox	21	3,845	NR	13,744	0.1	0.3
ORTHE–Macedonian Orth	2	370	NR	3,275	0.0	0.1
ORTHE–Orth Ch in Amer	18	1,914	NR	4,587	0.0	0.1
ORTHE–Romania Orth Ar	2	180	NR	700	0.0	0.0
ORTHE–Rus Orth Abroad	5	196	NR	575	0.0	0.0
ORTHE–Rus Orth Moscow	5	315	NR	535	0.0	0.0
ORTHE–Serb Orth USA	5	1,602	NR	7,765	0.1	0.2
ORTHE–Ukrainian Orth	2	195	NR	540	0.0	0.0
ORTHO–Armen Ap Cilic	1	200	NR	3,000	0.0	0.1
ORTHO–Armen Ap Etchm	4	345	NR	2,625	0.0	0.1
ORTHO–Coptic Orth Ch	3	730	NR	1,840	0.0	0.0
ORTHO–Eritrean Orth	1	30	NR	50	0.0	0.0
ORTHO–Ethiopian Orth	3	NR	NR	NR	-	-
ORTHO–Malan Dioc Am	3	185	NR	555	0.0	0.0
ORTHO–Malan Syr Orth	1	75	NR	144	0.0	0.0
ORTHO–Syrian Orth Ch	1	375	NR	1,000	0.0	0.0
PENT–Assemb of God	291	44,397	24,732	78,068	0.8	1.9
PENT–Assm God Intl F	1	NR	NR	NR	-	-
PENT–Ch God (Cleve)	115	8,813	19,275	23,514	0.2	0.6
PENT–Ch God Mtn Asm	6	NR	NR	NR	-	-
PENT–Ch Lord Jesus Apos	16	NR	NR	NR	-	-
PENT–Ch of God by Faith	1	NR	NR	NR	-	-
PENT–Ch of God Proph	21	NR	1,100	1,350	0.0	0.0
PENT–COGIC	145	12,893	27,284	33,437	0.3	0.8
PENT–Elim	6	NR	NR	NR	-	-
PENT–Fire Bapt Hol Ch	2	NR	NR	NR	-	-
PENT–Full Gosp Bapt	26	NR	NR	NR	-	-
PENT–I F Chr Assmbl	5	NR	NR	NR	-	-
PENT–Int Foursq Gos	20	1,532	1,000	1,224	0.0	0.0
PENT–Int Pent C Chr	3	180	122	324	0.0	0.0
PENT–Intl Pent Holiness	13	704	842	1,028	0.0	0.0
PENT–Open Bible Std	4	508	NR	508	0.0	0.0
PENT–Pent Ch of God	62	4,340	NR	6,741	0.1	0.2
PENT–Un Pent Asbl God	1	NR	NR	NR	-	-
PENT–Un Pent Ch Intl	109	NR	NR	NR	-	-
PENT–United Holy Ch	1	NR	NR	NR	-	-
PENT–Vineyard	18	3,023	4,087	4,974	0.1	0.1
PRES–Cum Pres Am	1	NR	NR	NR	-	-
PRES–Cumber Presb	2	NR	18	47	0.0	0.0
PRES–Evan Presby Ch	21	NR	9,031	11,053	0.1	0.3
PRES–Free Ch Scot	1	NR	NR	NR	-	-
PRES–Kor Pres Abroad	1	NR	NR	NR	-	-
PRES–Korean Amer Pres	1	NR	NR	NR	-	-
PRES–Korean Pres Amer	4	NR	NR	NR	-	-
PRES–Orth Pres Ch	19	2,147	1,627	2,462	0.0	0.1
PRES–Presb Ch (USA)	258	27,293	62,949	76,644	0.8	1.8
PRES–Presb Ch Amer	10	1,155	1,318	1,615	0.0	0.0

NR–Not Reported   - Represents no adherents reported.   Percentages may not total 100 due to rounding.

Table 2: Religious Congregations by State and Group: 2010

Religious Group	Number of Congrega-tions	Number of Attendees	Number of Communicant, Confirmed, or Full Members	Adherents: Number of Adherents	Adherents: % of Total Pop.	Adherents: % of Total Adh.
PRES–Ref Pres of NA	3	112	89	132	0.0	0.0
REF–Can Amer Ref	1	NR	NR	NR	-	-
REF–Christian Ref	230	57,253	78,367	97,659	1.0	2.3
REF–Comm Ref Evan	4	NR	NR	NR	-	-
REF–Free Ref NA	1	NR	NR	NR	-	-
REF–Heritage Ref	1	NR	447	561	0.0	0.0
REF–Hung Ref Add'l	1	NR	NR	NR	-	-
REF–Prot Ref Chs	14	4,160	2,776	4,639	0.0	0.1
REF–Ref Ch in Am	154	40,558	66,649	75,944	0.8	1.8
REF–Un Ref Chs N.A.	12	NR	NR	NR	-	-
Salvation Army	53	2,922	4,319	19,503	0.2	0.5
Sev Day Adv	225	20,250	35,211	40,503	0.4	1.0
Sikh	10	NR	NR	NR	-	-
Swedenborgian	2	NR	NR	NR	-	-
Un Breth in Cr	36	5,493	3,548	4,684	0.0	0.1
Un C of Christ	151	11,839	31,641	38,557	0.4	0.9
Unit Univ	25	2,369	3,483	4,705	0.0	0.1
Unity Ch	36	NR	NR	NR	-	-
Zoroastrian	1	NR	NR	178	0.0	0.0
MINNESOTA	**5,953**	**676,373**	**1,218,768**	**2,986,450**	**56.3**	**100.0**
ANG/EPIS–Anglican NA	4	NR	NR	NR	-	-
ANG/EPIS–Episcopal	107	7,341	19,916	23,715	0.4	0.8
Ap Chr Ch-Amer	4	1,005	474	1,005	0.0	0.0
Bahá'í	16	NR	1,896	1,896	0.0	0.1
BAPT–Alliance Bapt	2	NR	NR	NR	-	-
BAPT–Amer Bapt Assn	2	NR	100	128	0.0	0.0
BAPT–Amer Bapt USA	38	3,855	8,417	10,218	0.2	0.3
BAPT–Consrv Bapt	37	NR	NR	NR	-	-
BAPT–Converge/BGC	186	52,075	NR	62,490	1.2	2.1
BAPT–N Am Bapt Conf	10	NR	1,502	1,857	0.0	0.1
BAPT–Natl Mis Bapt Conv	2	400	510	620	0.0	0.0
BAPT–NBC Amer	4	1,850	5,850	7,113	0.1	0.2
BAPT–NBC USA	5	1,175	3,300	4,020	0.1	0.1
BAPT–NT Ind Bapt	43	NR	NR	NR	-	-
BAPT–Ref Bapt Ch	2	NR	NR	NR	-	-
BAPT–Reg Bapt Gen As	25	NR	NR	NR	-	-
BAPT–S-D Baptist Gen Con	1	48	90	116	0.0	0.0
BAPT–So Bapt Conv	61	3,493	4,408	5,412	0.1	0.2
BRETH–Ch of Brethren	5	75	280	342	0.0	0.0
BRETH–Grace Breth	1	NR	NR	NR	-	-
BUDD–Mahayana	13	NR	NR	4,617	0.1	0.2
BUDD–Theravada	14	NR	NR	2,636	0.0	0.1
BUDD–Vajrayana	9	NR	NR	502	0.0	0.0
Calv Chpl	9	NR	NR	NR	-	-
Catholic	739	NR	NR	1,150,367	21.7	38.5
CGOD–Ch God (Ander)	5	497	NR	497	0.0	0.0
Ch Cr, Scientst	12	NR	NR	NR	-	-
Ch God (7th Day)	1	NR	NR	NR	-	-
Ch of God Gen Conf	7	NR	206	253	0.0	0.0
Ch of Nazarene	38	2,465	2,747	3,973	0.1	0.1
Chr & Miss Al	99	16,313	13,255	28,669	0.5	1.0
CHR–Chr Ch (Disc)	11	395	3,167	3,752	0.1	0.1
CHR–Chr Chs & Chs Cr	54	NR	5,595	6,912	0.1	0.2
CHR–Chs of Christ	40	2,086	1,891	2,513	0.0	0.1
CHR–Int Chs of Christ	1	NR	205	249	0.0	0.0
Christian Brethren	3	NR	NR	NR	-	-
CONG–Cong Chr, NA	9	NR	4,688	5,706	0.1	0.2
CONG–Consrv Cong Chr	19	6,753	5,993	7,304	0.1	0.2
Evan Ch	7	NR	NR	NR	-	-
Evan Cov Ch	114	20,568	15,909	26,739	0.5	0.9
Evan Free Ch	147	36,727	NR	36,727	0.7	1.2
FRND–Fr Gen Cf	12	NR	377	458	0.0	0.0
FRND–Unaffl Mtgs	2	NR	NR	NR	-	-
Grace Gosp Fel	1	NR	NR	NR	-	-
HINDU–I/A Temples	4	NR	NR	2,252	0.0	0.1
HINDU–Post Ren	7	NR	NR	188	0.0	0.0
HINDU–Renaiss	2	NR	NR	24	0.0	0.0
HINDU–Trad Temples	5	NR	NR	1,575	0.0	0.1
Ind Fund Churches	3	NR	NR	NR	-	-
Int Cou Comm Ch	3	NR	NR	NR	-	-
Jain	1	NR	NR	NR	-	-
Jehovah's Witness	101	NR	NR	NR	-	-
JUD–Conserv	6	3,519	3,950	10,665	0.2	0.4

Religious Group	Number of Congrega-tions	Number of Attendees	Number of Communicant, Confirmed, or Full Members	Adherents: Number of Adherents	Adherents: % of Total Pop.	Adherents: % of Total Adh.
JUD–Orth	8	1,310	675	1,820	0.0	0.1
JUD–Reconst	1	113	144	389	0.0	0.0
JUD–Reform	5	2,324	4,098	11,066	0.2	0.4
LDS–Comm of Christ	7	NR	966	966	0.0	0.0
LDS–L-D Saints	80	NR	NR	30,603	0.6	1.0
LUTH–Apostolic Luth	12	NR	NR	NR	-	-
LUTH–Assoc Free Luth	85	NR	NR	NR	-	-
LUTH–Ch Luth Conf	14	NR	NR	NR	-	-
LUTH–Ch of Luth Br	26	3,408	2,627	9,252	0.2	0.3
LUTH–E.L.C.A.	1,090	179,801	550,438	737,537	13.9	24.7
LUTH–Evan Luth Syn	30	2,561	4,619	6,054	0.1	0.2
LUTH–Luth Ch-Am Asc	8	NR	NR	NR	-	-
LUTH–Luth Cong Msn Chr	97	20,231	47,292	58,774	1.1	2.0
LUTH–Luth-MO Synod	443	57,679	142,321	182,439	3.4	6.1
LUTH–Nor Amer Luth C	12	NR	NR	NR	-	-
LUTH–Wisc Ev Luth Syn	146	20,063	40,711	49,966	0.9	1.7
MENN–Amish Undif	23	NR	1,046	2,765	0.1	0.1
MENN–Beachy Amish-Menn	1	108	64	108	0.0	0.0
MENN–CG in Cr (Menn)	2	NR	77	92	0.0	0.0
MENN–Cons Menn Conf	1	42	37	44	0.0	0.0
MENN–Fel Evg Bib Ch	3	198	162	198	0.0	0.0
MENN–Fel Evg Ch	3	158	162	202	0.0	0.0
MENN–Hutt Breth	10	NR	NR	NR	-	-
MENN–Menn Br US Conf	3	NR	991	1,271	0.0	0.0
MENN–Mennonite USA	11	512	766	938	0.0	0.0
METH–AME	7	350	1,750	2,127	0.0	0.1
METH–C.M.E.	1	20	31	38	0.0	0.0
METH–Free Methodist	11	765	456	772	0.0	0.0
METH–Un Methodist	375	34,242	72,230	101,856	1.9	3.4
METH–Wesleyan	14	1,149	579	1,494	0.0	0.1
Metro Comm Ch	2	258	356	434	0.0	0.0
MORAV–Morav Ch-North	7	430	911	1,119	0.0	0.0
Muslim Est	45	8,146	NR	16,796	0.3	0.6
Nat Spirit Asso	3	NR	NR	NR	-	-
New Apost Ch	2	NR	NR	NR	-	-
Non-denom Chr Chs	390	91,171	116,179	130,263	2.5	4.4
OCATH–Pol Natl Cath	2	NR	NR	NR	-	-
ORTHE–Ant Orth of NA	1	115	NR	333	0.0	0.0
ORTHE–Greek Orthodox	4	700	NR	2,370	0.0	0.1
ORTHE–Holy Orth in NA	1	35	NR	45	0.0	0.0
ORTHE–Orth Ch in Amer	12	754	NR	1,937	0.0	0.1
ORTHE–Romania Orth Ar	1	60	NR	200	0.0	0.0
ORTHE–Rus Orth Abroad	2	120	NR	160	0.0	0.0
ORTHE–Serb Orth USA	6	536	NR	1,137	0.0	0.0
ORTHE–Ukrainian Orth	2	200	NR	750	0.0	0.0
ORTHO–Armen Ap Etchm	1	25	NR	75	0.0	0.0
ORTHO–Coptic Orth Ch	1	300	NR	550	0.0	0.0
ORTHO–Eritrean Orth	1	50	NR	500	0.0	0.0
ORTHO–Ethiopian Orth	2	NR	NR	NR	-	-
PENT–Apos Faith Msn	1	NR	35	43	0.0	0.0
PENT–Assemb of God	234	37,411	15,730	75,302	1.4	2.5
PENT–Ch God (Cleve)	17	1,462	2,151	2,613	0.0	0.1
PENT–Ch Lord Jesus Apos	1	NR	NR	NR	-	-
PENT–Ch of God Proph	6	NR	197	245	0.0	0.0
PENT–COGIC	18	1,160	2,030	2,478	0.0	0.1
PENT–Int Foursq Gos	8	420	455	554	0.0	0.0
PENT–Intl Pent Holiness	8	845	434	539	0.0	0.0
PENT–Open Bible Std	3	128	NR	128	0.0	0.0
PENT–Pent Ch of God	7	490	NR	762	0.0	0.0
PENT–Un Pent Ch Intl	41	NR	NR	NR	-	-
PENT–Vineyard	15	4,083	6,202	7,461	0.1	0.2
PRES–Evan Presby Ch	3	NR	251	311	0.0	0.0
PRES–Kor Pres Abroad	1	NR	NR	NR	-	-
PRES–Orth Pres Ch	2	88	52	83	0.0	0.0
PRES–Presb Ch (USA)	177	13,154	38,001	46,390	0.9	1.6
PRES–Presb Ch Amer	8	492	541	681	0.0	0.0
REF–Christian Ref	30	5,003	6,670	8,221	0.2	0.3
REF–Comm Ref Evan	1	NR	NR	NR	-	-
REF–Prot Ref Chs	1	75	49	84	0.0	0.0
REF–Ref Ch in Am	20	3,626	6,174	6,777	0.1	0.2
REF–Ref Ch in U.S.	2	NR	322	423	0.0	0.0
REF–Un Ref Chs N.A.	2	NR	NR	NR	-	-
Salvation Army	21	1,163	1,693	7,182	0.1	0.2
Sev Day Adv	89	5,227	9,092	10,460	0.2	0.4

NR–Not Reported   - Represents no adherents reported.   Percentages may not total 100 due to rounding.

Table 2: Religious Congregations by State and Group: 2010

Religious Group	Number of Congrega-tions	Number of Attendees	Number of Communicant, Confirmed, or Full Members	Adherents		
				Number of Adherents	% of Total Pop.	% of Total Adh.
Sikh	1	NR	NR	NR	-	-
Swedenborgian	1	NR	NR	NR	-	-
Un C of Christ	136	9,664	29,638	36,194	0.7	1.2
Unit Univ	24	3,308	4,637	6,553	0.1	0.2
Unity Ch	7	NR	NR	NR	-	-
Zoroastrian	1	NR	NR	16	0.0	0.0
MISSISSIPPI	**6,765**	**525,212**	**1,303,304**	**1,742,916**	**58.7**	**100.0**
ANG/EPIS–Anglican NA	5	NR	NR	NR	-	-
ANG/EPIS–Episcopal	81	6,426	16,591	19,239	0.6	1.1
Bahá'í	3	NR	816	816	0.0	0.0
BAPT–Alliance Bapt	3	NR	NR	NR	-	-
BAPT–Amer Bapt Assn	31	NR	3,161	3,900	0.1	0.2
BAPT–Amer Bapt USA	1	100	150	187	0.0	0.0
BAPT–Asc Ref Bap Ch Am	1	NR	NR	NR	-	-
BAPT–Free Will Bapt	51	NR	2,954	3,639	0.1	0.2
BAPT–Ind Bapt Flwsp Intl	2	NR	NR	NR	-	-
BAPT–Natl Mis Bapt Conv	84	1,070	12,020	15,018	0.5	0.9
BAPT–NBC Amer	25	1,772	4,060	5,051	0.2	0.3
BAPT–NBC USA	205	19,014	65,051	81,318	2.7	4.7
BAPT–Prog NBC	7	420	1,075	1,346	0.0	0.1
BAPT–Ref Bapt Ch	7	NR	NR	NR	-	-
BAPT–S-D Baptist Gen Con	1	10	NR	NR	-	-
BAPT–So Bapt Conv	2,149	252,442	728,208	907,384	30.6	52.1
BUDD–Mahayana	3	NR	NR	229	0.0	0.0
BUDD–Theravada	1	NR	NR	14	0.0	0.0
Calv Chpl	5	NR	NR	NR	-	-
Catholic	154	NR	NR	112,488	3.8	6.5
CGOD–Ch God (Ander)	54	3,214	NR	3,214	0.1	0.2
CGOD–Ches God-Gen Con	2	49	0	0	0.0	0.0
Ch Cr, Scientst	4	NR	NR	NR	-	-
Ch of Chr (Hol)	51	NR	NR	NR	-	-
Ch of Nazarene	51	2,673	4,175	4,937	0.2	0.3
Chr & Miss Al	2	NR	NR	NR	-	-
CHR–Chr Ch (Disc)	44	1,140	4,497	5,616	0.2	0.3
CHR–Chr Chs & Chs Cr	28	NR	2,240	2,790	0.1	0.2
CHR–Chs of Christ	369	30,465	32,459	42,166	1.4	2.4
CHR–Int Chs of Christ	1	NR	7	9	0.0	0.0
Evan Cov Ch	2	116	132	151	0.0	0.0
FRND–Fr Gen Cf	1	NR	10	12	0.0	0.0
HINDU–I/A Temples	2	NR	NR	3,304	0.1	0.2
HINDU–Post Ren	2	NR	NR	35	0.0	0.0
HINDU–Trad Temples	3	NR	NR	1,050	0.0	0.1
Jehovah's Witness	86	NR	NR	NR	-	-
JUD–Conserv	1	41	46	124	0.0	0.0
JUD–Reform	9	245	431	1,163	0.0	0.1
LDS–Comm of Christ	6	NR	1,091	1,091	0.0	0.1
LDS–L-D Saints	43	NR	NR	21,217	0.7	1.2
LUTH–E.L.C.A.	13	586	1,402	1,660	0.1	0.1
LUTH–Luth Cong Msn Chr	1	NR	NR	NR	-	-
LUTH–Luth–MO Synod	28	1,394	2,667	3,145	0.1	0.2
LUTH–Wisc Ev Luth Syn	1	9	10	10	0.0	0.0
MENN–Amish Undif	1	NR	65	175	0.0	0.0
MENN–CG in Cr (Menn)	8	NR	973	1,230	0.0	0.1
MENN–Mennonite USA	7	415	442	552	0.0	0.0
METH–AME	130	3,187	18,663	23,243	0.8	1.3
METH–AME Zion	42	190	5,053	6,351	0.2	0.4
METH–C.M.E.	199	1,235	24,517	30,425	1.0	1.7
METH–Cong Meth	37	NR	2,089	2,616	0.1	0.2
METH–Free Methodist	1	13	9	13	0.0	0.0
METH–So Methodist	8	NR	NR	NR	-	-
METH–Un Methodist	1,107	72,463	181,684	204,165	6.9	11.7
METH–Wesleyan	1	62	76	81	0.0	0.0
Muslim Est	16	2,101	NR	5,012	0.2	0.3
New Apost Ch	1	NR	NR	NR	-	-
Non-denom Chr Chs	431	71,586	97,920	104,761	3.5	6.0
ORTHE–Ant Orth of NA	2	170	NR	320	0.0	0.0
ORTHE–Greek Orthodox	2	120	NR	455	0.0	0.0
ORTHE–Orth Ch in Amer	2	100	NR	200	0.0	0.0
PENT–Assemb of God	174	15,254	9,536	21,355	0.7	1.2
PENT–Ch God (Cleve)	176	10,367	19,041	23,720	0.8	1.4
PENT–Ch Lord Jesus Apos	7	NR	NR	NR	-	-
PENT–Ch of God by Faith	2	NR	NR	NR	-	-
PENT–Ch of God Proph	60	NR	1,830	2,268	0.1	0.1
PENT–COGIC	121	3,614	15,866	19,804	0.7	1.1
PENT–Full Gosp Bapt	43	NR	NR	NR	-	-
PENT–Int Foursq Gos	3	87	109	135	0.0	0.0
PENT–Intl Pent Holiness	26	1,202	1,541	1,918	0.1	0.1
PENT–Pent Ch of God	13	910	NR	1,414	0.0	0.1
PENT–Un Pent Ch Intl	168	NR	NR	NR	-	-
PENT–Vineyard	2	115	130	162	0.0	0.0
PRES–As Ref Pres Ch	11	NR	621	776	0.0	0.0
PRES–Cumber Presb	16	NR	1,136	1,695	0.1	0.1
PRES–Evan Presby Ch	10	NR	2,615	3,266	0.1	0.2
PRES–Presb Ch (USA)	108	4,925	10,360	12,822	0.4	0.7
PRES–Presb Ch Amer	121	10,216	15,341	18,439	0.6	1.1
REF–Comm Ref Evan	1	NR	NR	NR	-	-
Salvation Army	12	645	1,344	2,732	0.1	0.2
Sev Day Adv	63	4,896	8,520	9,797	0.3	0.6
Sikh	1	NR	NR	NR	-	-
Un C of Christ	2	0	337	420	0.0	0.0
Unit Univ	6	153	233	269	0.0	0.0
Unity Ch	1	NR	NR	NR	-	-
Zoroastrian	0	NR	NR	2	0.0	0.0
MISSOURI	**9,001**	**799,394**	**1,627,977**	**2,950,894**	**49.3**	**100.0**
ANG/EPIS–Anglican NA	9	NR	NR	NR	-	-
ANG/EPIS–Episcopal	95	7,919	20,298	23,609	0.4	0.8
Ap Chr Ch-Amer	4	446	239	446	0.0	0.0
Bahá'í	17	NR	1,883	1,883	0.0	0.1
BAPT–Alliance Bapt	5	NR	NR	NR	-	-
BAPT–Amer Bapt Assn	23	NR	2,195	2,701	0.0	0.1
BAPT–Amer Bapt USA	27	11,606	16,532	19,991	0.3	0.7
BAPT–Converge/BGC	8	1,250	NR	1,500	0.0	0.1
BAPT–Free Will Bapt	167	NR	10,550	12,932	0.2	0.4
BAPT–Ind Bapt Flwsp Intl	9	NR	NR	NR	-	-
BAPT–N Am Bapt Conf	2	NR	124	153	0.0	0.0
BAPT–Natl Mis Bapt Conv	38	455	5,045	6,142	0.1	0.2
BAPT–NBC Amer	13	3,170	5,731	7,065	0.1	0.2
BAPT–NBC USA	73	18,465	30,090	36,435	0.6	1.2
BAPT–Prog NBC	18	1,295	5,375	6,562	0.1	0.2
BAPT–Ref Bapt Ch	4	NR	NR	NR	-	-
BAPT–Reg Bapt Gen As	12	NR	NR	NR	-	-
BAPT–S-D Baptist Gen Con	2	22	20	24	0.0	0.0
BAPT–So Bapt Conv	2,006	201,188	611,047	749,685	12.5	25.4
BRETH–Ch of Brethren	13	289	478	581	0.0	0.0
BUDD–Mahayana	17	NR	NR	5,130	0.1	0.2
BUDD–Theravada	15	NR	NR	1,853	0.0	0.1
BUDD–Vajrayana	2	NR	NR	87	0.0	0.0
Calv Chpl	16	NR	NR	NR	-	-
Catholic	504	NR	NR	724,315	12.1	24.5
CGOD–Ch God (Ander)	79	5,132	NR	5,132	0.1	0.2
CGOD–Ches God-Gen Con	11	377	588	713	0.0	0.0
Ch Cr, Scientst	25	NR	NR	NR	-	-
Ch God (7th Day)	6	NR	NR	NR	-	-
Ch of Chr (Hol)	6	NR	NR	NR	-	-
Ch of God Gen Conf	9	NR	199	244	0.0	0.0
Ch of Nazarene	177	14,053	19,271	26,451	0.4	0.9
Chr & Miss Al	5	261	267	452	0.0	0.0
CHR–Chr Ch (Disc)	324	18,303	66,555	81,509	1.4	2.8
CHR–Chr Chs & Chs Cr	317	NR	59,163	72,756	1.2	2.5
CHR–Chs of Christ	443	35,038	33,951	42,805	0.7	1.5
CHR–Int Chs of Christ	3	NR	430	521	0.0	0.0
Christian Brethren	7	NR	NR	NR	-	-
Christian Un	19	NR	NR	NR	-	-
CONG–Cong Chr, NA	4	NR	314	391	0.0	0.0
Evan Assoc RCC	3	NR	NR	NR	-	-
Evan Ch	2	NR	NR	NR	-	-
Evan Cov Ch	10	1,395	977	1,815	0.0	0.1
Evan Free Ch	41	9,626	NR	9,626	0.2	0.3
FRND–Consrv Yr Mtgs	1	NR	70	87	0.0	0.0
FRND–Evan Fr Ch Intl	2	114	206	257	0.0	0.0
FRND–Fr Gen Cf	4	NR	152	182	0.0	0.0
Grace Gosp Fel	3	NR	NR	NR	-	-
HINDU–I/A Temples	7	NR	NR	6,271	0.1	0.2
HINDU–Post Ren	9	NR	NR	282	0.0	0.0
HINDU–Renaiss	4	NR	NR	193	0.0	0.0
HINDU–Trad Temples	1	NR	NR	500	0.0	0.0

NR–Not Reported - Represents no adherents reported. Percentages may not total 100 due to rounding.

Table 2: Religious Congregations by State and Group: 2010

Religious Group	Number of Congrega-tions	Number of Attendees	Number of Communicant, Confirmed, or Full Members	Adherents		
				Number of Adherents	% of Total Pop.	% of Total Adh.
Ind Fund Churches	19	NR	NR	NR	-	-
Int Cou Comm Ch	3	NR	NR	NR	-	-
Jain	1	NR	NR	NR	-	-
Jehovah's Witness	152	NR	NR	NR	-	-
JUD–Conserv	3	1,207	1,355	3,659	0.1	0.1
JUD–Orth	10	1,778	800	2,470	0.0	0.1
JUD–Reconst	1	9	12	32	0.0	0.0
JUD–Reform	14	3,362	5,932	16,016	0.3	0.5
LDS–Comm of Christ	108	NR	26,177	26,177	0.4	0.9
LDS–L-D Saints	145	NR	NR	66,071	1.1	2.2
LUTH–Assoc Free Luth	3	NR	NR	NR	-	-
LUTH–Ch Luth Conf	2	NR	NR	NR	-	-
LUTH–E.L.C.A.	72	7,992	17,440	22,260	0.4	0.8
LUTH–Evan Luth Syn	4	121	248	304	0.0	0.0
LUTH–Luth Ch-Am Asc	1	NR	NR	NR	-	-
LUTH–Luth Cong Msn Chr	6	455	1,086	1,302	0.0	0.0
LUTH–Luth-MO Synod	305	52,313	109,219	142,685	2.4	4.8
LUTH–Nor Amer Luth C	4	NR	NR	NR	-	-
LUTH–Wisc Ev Luth Syn	10	611	950	1,261	0.0	0.0
MENN–Amb Amish-Menn	1	136	70	136	0.0	0.0
MENN–Amish Undif	78	NR	3,694	9,833	0.2	0.3
MENN–Beachy Amish-Menn	1	16	13	16	0.0	0.0
MENN–Ber Amish-Menn	2	159	86	159	0.0	0.0
MENN–CG in Cr (Menn)	7	NR	718	881	0.0	0.0
MENN–Fel Evg Ch	4	578	583	728	0.0	0.0
MENN–Mara Amish-Menn	1	79	30	79	0.0	0.0
MENN–Menn Br US Conf	1	NR	10	12	0.0	0.0
MENN–Menn Chr Fell	6	670	312	670	0.0	0.0
MENN–Mennonite USA	5	135	198	239	0.0	0.0
MENN–Tamp Amish-Menn	5	1,701	924	1,701	0.0	0.1
MENN–Unaffil Amish-Menn	2	195	122	195	0.0	0.0
METH–AME	86	3,195	14,124	17,203	0.3	0.6
METH–AME Zion	9	320	1,242	1,514	0.0	0.1
METH–C.M.E.	18	1,530	4,280	5,192	0.1	0.2
METH–Cong Meth	6	NR	279	339	0.0	0.0
METH–Evan Meth Ch	1	NR	NR	NR	-	-
METH–Free Methodist	16	476	425	575	0.0	0.0
METH–Un Methodist	853	79,592	165,525	226,409	3.8	7.7
METH–Wesleyan	16	801	406	1,043	0.0	0.0
Metro Comm Ch	3	429	576	697	0.0	0.0
Missionary Ch	1	13	8	13	0.0	0.0
Muslim Est	39	5,388	NR	11,708	0.2	0.4
Nat Spirit Asso	1	NR	NR	NR	-	-
New Apost Ch	8	NR	NR	NR	-	-
Non-denom Chr Chs	721	164,875	211,993	236,235	3.9	8.0
OCATH–Pol Natl Cath	1	NR	NR	NR	-	-
ORTHE–Ant Orth of NA	2	79	NR	127	0.0	0.0
ORTHE–Greek Orthodox	4	765	NR	4,700	0.1	0.2
ORTHE–Holy Orth in NA	1	15	NR	20	0.0	0.0
ORTHE–Orth Ch in Amer	7	176	NR	292	0.0	0.0
ORTHE–Rus Orth Abroad	3	163	NR	396	0.0	0.0
ORTHE–Serb Orth USA	4	259	NR	785	0.0	0.0
ORTHO–Armen Ap Etchm	1	30	NR	85	0.0	0.0
ORTHO–Coptic Orth Ch	1	150	NR	250	0.0	0.0
ORTHO–Ethiopian Orth	1	NR	NR	NR	-	-
ORTHO–Malan Dioc Am	1	30	NR	90	0.0	0.0
PENT–Apos Faith Msn	1	NR	35	42	0.0	0.0
PENT–Assemb of God	469	70,471	35,481	117,904	2.0	4.0
PENT–Ch God (Cleve)	71	6,811	11,138	13,597	0.2	0.5
PENT–Ch God Apos Fth	7	NR	NR	NR	-	-
PENT–Ch Lord Jesus Apos	5	NR	NR	NR	-	-
PENT–Ch of God Proph	27	NR	753	923	0.0	0.0
PENT–COGIC	65	5,955	11,252	13,787	0.2	0.5
PENT–Full Gosp Bapt	9	NR	NR	NR	-	-
PENT–Int Foursq Gos	25	1,586	1,559	1,902	0.0	0.1
PENT–Intl Pent Holiness	22	1,557	1,776	2,178	0.0	0.1
PENT–Open Bible Std	4	309	NR	309	0.0	0.0
PENT–Pent Ch of God	64	5,610	NR	8,720	0.1	0.3
PENT–Un Pent Ch Intl	169	NR	NR	NR	-	-
PENT–United Holy Ch	3	NR	NR	NR	-	-
PENT–Vineyard	7	3,399	4,941	6,159	0.1	0.2
PRES–As Ref Pres Ch	3	NR	25	32	0.0	0.0
PRES–Cumber Presb	24	NR	731	1,207	0.0	0.0
PRES–Evan Presby Ch	12	NR	5,977	7,299	0.1	0.2
PRES–Free Ch Scot	1	NR	NR	NR	-	-
PRES–Free Pres NA	1	NR	NR	NR	-	-
PRES–Korean Amer Pres	1	NR	NR	NR	-	-
PRES–Korean Pres Amer	2	NR	NR	NR	-	-
PRES–Orth Pres Ch	3	122	103	134	0.0	0.0
PRES–Presb Ch (USA)	264	15,719	37,712	46,060	0.8	1.6
PRES–Presb Ch Amer	34	6,174	6,138	7,815	0.1	0.3
PRES–Ref Pres GA	1	NR	NR	NR	-	-
REF–Christian Ref	2	75	77	93	0.0	0.0
REF–Comm Ref Evan	1	NR	NR	NR	-	-
REF–Ref Ch in Am	1	173	281	336	0.0	0.0
REF–Ref Ch in U.S.	1	NR	56	80	0.0	0.0
REF–Un Ref Chs N.A.	1	NR	NR	NR	-	-
Salvation Army	25	1,534	2,190	9,282	0.2	0.3
Sev Day Adv	85	6,924	12,033	13,841	0.2	0.5
Sikh	5	NR	NR	NR	-	-
Swedenborgian	1	NR	NR	NR	-	-
Un Breth in Cr	1	50	0	43	0.0	0.0
Un C of Christ	151	11,482	33,336	40,802	0.7	1.4
Unit Univ	9	1,236	1,796	2,489	0.0	0.1
Unity Ch	22	NR	NR	NR	-	-
Zoroastrian	1	NR	NR	20	0.0	0.0
MONTANA	**1,778**	**95,105**	**143,149**	**376,976**	**38.1**	**100.0**
ANG/EPIS–Anglican NA	1	NR	NR	NR	-	-
ANG/EPIS–Episcopal	41	1,640	4,371	5,297	0.5	1.4
Bahá'í	6	NR	663	663	0.1	0.2
BAPT–Amer Bapt Assn	9	NR	534	644	0.1	0.2
BAPT–Amer Bapt USA	26	1,639	2,092	2,562	0.3	0.7
BAPT–Consrv Bapt	5	NR	NR	NR	-	-
BAPT–Converge/BGC	3	225	NR	270	0.0	0.1
BAPT–N Am Bapt Conf	3	NR	211	254	0.0	0.1
BAPT–Natl Mis Bapt Conv	1	25	12	15	0.0	0.0
BAPT–NT Ind Bapt	6	NR	NR	NR	-	-
BAPT–Ref Bapt Ch	1	NR	NR	NR	-	-
BAPT–Reg Bapt Gen As	12	NR	NR	NR	-	-
BAPT–So Bapt Conv	131	7,616	11,161	13,537	1.4	3.6
BRETH–Ch of Brethren	1	23	15	20	0.0	0.0
BUDD–Mahayana	8	NR	NR	341	0.0	0.1
BUDD–Theravada	1	NR	NR	267	0.0	0.1
BUDD–Vajrayana	2	NR	NR	250	0.0	0.1
Calv Chpl	10	NR	NR	NR	-	-
Catholic	204	NR	NR	127,612	12.9	33.9
CGOD–Ch God (Ander)	10	442	NR	442	0.0	0.1
Ch Cr, Scientist	9	NR	NR	NR	-	-
Ch of Nazarene	21	1,250	1,661	2,300	0.2	0.6
Chr & Miss Al	37	4,286	2,274	6,398	0.6	1.7
CHR–Chr Ch (Disc)	14	621	1,588	1,924	0.2	0.5
CHR–Chr Chs & Chs Cr	22	NR	2,847	3,468	0.4	0.9
CHR–Chs of Christ	40	2,313	2,108	2,730	0.3	0.7
CHR–Int Chs of Christ	3	NR	89	106	0.0	0.0
Christian Brethren	1	NR	NR	NR	-	-
CONG–Consrv Cong Chr	3	189	381	482	0.0	0.1
Evan Ch	21	NR	NR	NR	-	-
Evan Cov Ch	2	419	188	544	0.1	0.1
Evan Free Ch	13	1,778	NR	1,778	0.2	0.5
FRND–Indep Yr Mtgs	9	NR	65	78	0.0	0.0
HINDU–Post Ren	2	NR	NR	41	0.0	0.0
Jehovah's Witness	47	NR	NR	NR	-	-
JUD–Orth	1	43	50	60	0.0	0.0
JUD–Reform	6	165	291	786	0.1	0.2
LDS–Comm of Christ	7	NR	896	896	0.1	0.2
LDS–L-D Saints	120	NR	NR	46,484	4.7	12.3
LUTH–Assoc Free Luth	5	NR	NR	NR	-	-
LUTH–Ch of Luth Br	4	302	230	724	0.1	0.2
LUTH–E.L.C.A.	126	9,459	29,163	38,665	3.9	10.3
LUTH–Luth Ch-Am Asc	3	NR	NR	NR	-	-
LUTH–Luth Cong Msn Chr	32	1,707	6,335	7,629	0.8	2.0
LUTH–Luth-MO Synod	64	4,803	10,917	14,087	1.4	3.7
LUTH–Wisc Ev Luth Syn	11	499	755	925	0.1	0.2
MENN–Amish Undif	4	NR	163	363	0.0	0.1
MENN–CG in Cr (Menn)	2	NR	135	175	0.0	0.0
MENN–Fel Evg Bib Ch	2	115	43	115	0.0	0.0
MENN–Hutt Breth	52	NR	NR	NR	-	-

NR–Not Reported - Represents no adherents reported. Percentages may not total 100 due to rounding.

Table 2: Religious Congregations by State and Group: 2010

Religious Group	Number of Congrega-tions	Number of Attendees	Number of Communicant, Confirmed, or Full Members	Adherents		
				Number of Adherents	% of Total Pop.	% of Total Adh.
MENN–Menn Br US Conf	2	NR	126	159	0.0	0.0
MENN–Menn Chr Fell	1	81	35	81	0.0	0.0
MENN–Mennonite USA	8	190	362	450	0.0	0.1
METH–A.W.M.C.	2	72	69	88	0.0	0.0
METH–AME	3	40	260	316	0.0	0.1
METH–Free Methodist	1	29	23	29	0.0	0.0
METH–Un Methodist	107	5,755	11,456	16,244	1.6	4.3
METH–Wesleyan	11	541	278	702	0.1	0.2
Metro Comm Ch	1	36	58	70	0.0	0.0
MJEW–Union Mes Cong	1	NR	NR	NR	-	-
Muslim Est	2	139	NR	333	0.0	0.1
New Apost Ch	5	NR	NR	NR	-	-
Non-denom Chr Chs	131	20,593	22,137	27,370	2.8	7.3
ORTHE–Greek Orthodox	2	65	NR	200	0.0	0.1
ORTHE–Orth Ch in Amer	3	132	NR	165	0.0	0.0
ORTHE–Serb Orth USA	1	45	NR	200	0.0	0.1
PENT–Assemb of God	86	10,219	5,100	16,577	1.7	4.4
PENT–Ch God (Cleve)	7	652	651	774	0.1	0.2
PENT–Ch of God Proph	3	NR	58	71	0.0	0.0
PENT–Int Foursq Gos	32	6,681	5,701	6,979	0.7	1.9
PENT–Intl Pent Holiness	4	158	135	163	0.0	0.0
PENT–Open Bible Std	3	215	NR	215	0.0	0.1
PENT–Pent Ch of God	10	700	NR	1,088	0.1	0.3
PENT–Un Pent Ch Intl	17	NR	NR	NR	-	-
PENT–Vineyard	8	675	849	1,013	0.1	0.3
PRES–Bible Pres	1	NR	NR	NR	-	-
PRES–Evan Presby Ch	1	NR	220	264	0.0	0.1
PRES–Kor Pres Abroad	1	NR	NR	NR	-	-
PRES–Korean Pres Amer	1	NR	NR	NR	-	-
PRES–Presb Ch (USA)	51	2,478	5,424	6,609	0.7	1.8
PRES–Presb Ch Amer	5	518	491	631	0.1	0.2
REF–Christian Ref	7	1,132	1,444	1,737	0.2	0.5
REF–Comm Ref Evan	3	NR	NR	NR	-	-
REF–Ref Ch in Am	1	32	45	52	0.0	0.0
REF–Un Ref Chs N.A.	1	NR	NR	NR	-	-
Salvation Army	6	193	297	1,119	0.1	0.3
Sev Day Adv	44	2,285	3,969	4,563	0.5	1.2
Sikh	1	NR	NR	NR	-	-
Un C of Christ	31	1,618	4,437	5,368	0.5	1.4
Unit Univ	5	272	286	414	0.0	0.1
Unity Ch	4	NR	NR	NR	-	-
NEBRASKA	**2,860**	**224,555**	**433,726**	**1,016,529**	**55.7**	**100.0**
ANG/EPIS–Anglican NA	1	NR	NR	NR	-	-
ANG/EPIS–Episcopal	56	2,856	6,714	7,981	0.4	0.8
Bahá'í	5	NR	684	684	0.0	0.1
BAPT–Amer Bapt Assn	2	NR	235	288	0.0	0.0
BAPT–Amer Bapt USA	54	4,296	8,639	10,679	0.6	1.1
BAPT–Asc Ref Bap Ch Am	1	NR	NR	NR	-	-
BAPT–Consrv Bapt	2	NR	NR	NR	-	-
BAPT–Converge/BGC	31	2,975	NR	3,570	0.2	0.4
BAPT–Ind Bapt Flwsp Intl	7	NR	NR	NR	-	-
BAPT–N Am Bapt Conf	3	NR	129	161	0.0	0.0
BAPT–Natl Mis Bapt Conv	1	0	150	189	0.0	0.0
BAPT–NBC Amer	2	150	250	315	0.0	0.0
BAPT–NBC USA	13	1,600	7,175	9,036	0.5	0.9
BAPT–Ref Bapt Ch	1	NR	NR	NR	-	-
BAPT–Reg Bapt Gen As	17	NR	NR	NR	-	-
BAPT–S-D Baptist Gen Con	2	20	153	185	0.0	0.0
BAPT–So Bapt Conv	80	7,168	13,033	16,418	0.9	1.6
BRETH–Brethren (Ash)	1	NR	80	95	0.0	0.0
BRETH–Ch of Brethren	4	94	243	295	0.0	0.0
BUDD–Mahayana	11	NR	NR	4,101	0.2	0.4
BUDD–Theravada	1	NR	NR	15	0.0	0.0
BUDD–Vajrayana	1	NR	NR	107	0.0	0.0
Calv Chpl	4	NR	NR	NR	-	-
Catholic	350	NR	NR	372,838	20.4	36.7
CGOD–Ch God (Ander)	15	559	NR	559	0.0	0.1
Ch Cr, Scientst	8	NR	NR	NR	-	-
Ch God (7th Day)	2	NR	NR	NR	-	-
Ch of Chr (Hol)	1	NR	NR	NR	-	-
Ch of God Gen Conf	1	NR	90	113	0.0	0.0
Ch of Nazarene	31	2,509	2,787	4,281	0.2	0.4
Chr & Miss Al	21	5,789	3,696	13,500	0.7	1.3
CHR–Chr Ch (Disc)	51	1,880	7,165	8,804	0.5	0.9
CHR–Chr Chs & Chs Cr	75	NR	13,227	16,427	0.9	1.6
CHR–Chs of Christ	49	3,573	3,309	4,308	0.2	0.4
CHR–Int Chs of Christ	1	NR	88	111	0.0	0.0
Christian Brethren	1	NR	NR	NR	-	-
CONG–Cong Chr, NA	6	NR	413	498	0.0	0.0
CONG–Consrv Cong Chr	8	685	1,577	1,952	0.1	0.2
Evan Ch	1	NR	NR	NR	-	-
Evan Cov Ch	19	1,723	2,407	2,238	0.1	0.2
Evan Free Ch	73	14,234	NR	14,234	0.8	1.4
FRND–Consrv Yr Mtgs	2	NR	36	44	0.0	0.0
FRND–Evan Fr Ch Intl	1	15	37	45	0.0	0.0
FRND–Fr Gen Cf & Un Mtg	1	NR	54	66	0.0	0.0
FRND–Fr Un Mtg	1	NR	0	0	0.0	0.0
HINDU–Post Ren	5	NR	NR	228	0.0	0.0
HINDU–Trad Temples	1	NR	NR	500	0.0	0.0
Ind Fund Churches	1	NR	NR	NR	-	-
Jehovah's Witness	46	NR	NR	NR	-	-
JUD–Conserv	2	547	614	1,658	0.1	0.2
JUD–Orth	2	310	150	430	0.0	0.0
JUD–Reform	2	469	828	2,236	0.1	0.2
LDS–Comm of Christ	13	NR	2,213	2,213	0.1	0.2
LDS–L-D Saints	62	NR	NR	23,398	1.3	2.3
LUTH–Assoc Free Luth	6	NR	NR	NR	-	-
LUTH–Ch Luth Conf	1	NR	NR	NR	-	-
LUTH–E.L.C.A.	250	32,014	85,175	110,110	6.0	10.8
LUTH–Luth Ch-Am Asc	1	NR	NR	NR	-	-
LUTH–Luth Cong Msn Chr	30	4,597	12,643	15,692	0.9	1.5
LUTH–Luth–MO Synod	269	37,533	87,006	112,585	6.2	11.1
LUTH–Nor Amer Luth C	3	NR	NR	NR	-	-
LUTH–Wisc Ev Luth Syn	34	2,764	4,487	5,744	0.3	0.6
MENN–Amish Undif	3	NR	95	275	0.0	0.0
MENN–CG in Cr (Menn)	3	NR	289	356	0.0	0.0
MENN–Fel Evg Bib Ch	6	887	736	887	0.0	0.1
MENN–Menn Br US Conf	8	NR	621	776	0.0	0.1
MENN–Mennonite USA	11	1,284	2,506	3,040	0.2	0.3
METH–AME	5	100	650	816	0.0	0.1
METH–AME Zion	2	0	200	252	0.0	0.0
METH–C.M.E.	1	0	100	126	0.0	0.0
METH–Free Methodist	6	239	211	259	0.0	0.0
METH–Un Methodist	383	30,119	76,969	109,283	6.0	10.8
METH–Wesleyan	15	1,327	728	1,726	0.1	0.2
Metro Comm Ch	1	145	125	158	0.0	0.0
Missionary Ch	5	346	176	346	0.0	0.0
Muslim Est	8	1,438	NR	6,156	0.3	0.6
Nat Spirit Asso	1	NR	NR	NR	-	-
New Apost Ch	3	NR	NR	NR	-	-
Non-denom Chr Chs	146	22,172	23,754	29,325	1.6	2.9
ORTHE–Ant Orth of NA	3	226	NR	475	0.0	0.0
ORTHE–Greek Orthodox	5	334	NR	725	0.0	0.1
ORTHE–Orth Ch in Amer	2	45	NR	70	0.0	0.0
ORTHE–Serb Orth USA	1	122	NR	223	0.0	0.0
PENT–Assemb of God	98	11,405	4,873	20,118	1.1	2.0
PENT–Ch God (Cleve)	14	789	1,037	1,311	0.1	0.1
PENT–Ch of God Proph	4	NR	154	195	0.0	0.0
PENT–COGIC	17	470	1,885	2,372	0.1	0.2
PENT–Full Gosp Bapt	2	NR	NR	NR	-	-
PENT–Int Foursq Gos	11	693	766	954	0.1	0.1
PENT–Intl Pent Holiness	4	304	171	217	0.0	0.0
PENT–Open Bible Std	5	256	NR	256	0.0	0.0
PENT–Un Pent Ch Intl	17	NR	NR	NR	-	-
PENT–Vineyard	2	210	290	359	0.0	0.0
PRES–Evan Presby Ch	1	NR	850	1,071	0.1	0.1
PRES–Orth Pres Ch	1	55	69	82	0.0	0.0
PRES–Presb Ch (USA)	132	10,151	22,800	28,329	1.6	2.8
PRES–Presb Ch Amer	9	1,042	928	1,128	0.1	0.1
REF–Christian Ref	3	285	245	302	0.0	0.0
REF–Ref Ch in Am	6	1,115	1,844	2,127	0.1	0.2
REF–Ref Ch in U.S.	3	NR	402	509	0.0	0.1
Salvation Army	11	591	940	4,192	0.2	0.4
Sev Day Adv	55	4,220	7,336	8,436	0.5	0.8
Sikh	1	NR	NR	NR	-	-
Tao	1	NR	NR	NR	-	-
Un C of Christ	91	5,479	15,828	19,487	1.1	1.9

NR–Not Reported   - Represents no adherents reported.   Percentages may not total 100 due to rounding.

Table 2: Religious Congregations by State and Group: 2010

Religious Group	Number of Congrega-tions	Number of Attendees	Number of Communicant, Confirmed, or Full Members	Adherents: Number of Adherents	Adherents: % of Total Pop.	Adherents: % of Total Adh.
Unit Univ	4	346	661	868	0.0	0.1
Unity Ch	4	NR	NR	NR	-	-
Zoroastrian	0	NR	NR	11	0.0	0.0
NEVADA	**1,392**	**138,199**	**209,396**	**929,055**	**34.4**	**100.0**
ANG/EPIS–Anglican NA	4	NR	NR	NR	-	-
ANG/EPIS–Episcopal	30	2,169	4,941	5,235	0.2	0.6
Bahá'í	14	NR	1,723	1,723	0.1	0.2
BAPT–Amer Bapt Assn	3	NR	305	379	0.0	0.0
BAPT–Amer Bapt USA	17	2,187	4,484	5,564	0.2	0.6
BAPT–Consrv Bapt	6	NR	NR	NR	-	-
BAPT–Ind Bapt Flwsp Intl	3	NR	NR	NR	-	-
BAPT–Natl Mis Bapt Conv	4	20	490	609	0.0	0.1
BAPT–NBC Amer	1	0	150	186	0.0	0.0
BAPT–NBC USA	4	680	1,145	1,416	0.1	0.2
BAPT–Prog NBC	1	0	0	0	0.0	0.0
BAPT–Ref Bapt Ch	2	NR	NR	NR	-	-
BAPT–Reg Bapt Gen As	3	NR	NR	NR	-	-
BAPT–So Bapt Conv	186	18,820	36,778	45,535	1.7	4.9
BUDD–Mahayana	18	NR	NR	10,504	0.4	1.1
BUDD–Theravada	6	NR	NR	4,016	0.1	0.4
BUDD–Vajrayana	5	NR	NR	207	0.0	0.0
Calv Chpl	22	NR	NR	NR	-	-
Catholic	74	NR	NR	452,170	16.7	48.7
CGOD–Ch God (Ander)	4	225	NR	225	0.0	0.0
Ch Cr, Scientst	4	NR	NR	NR	-	-
Ch God (7th Day)	2	NR	NR	NR	-	-
Ch of Chr (Hol)	2	NR	NR	NR	-	-
Ch of Nazarene	17	1,783	1,510	2,991	0.1	0.3
Chr & Miss Al	5	1,245	665	2,424	0.1	0.3
CHR–Chr Ch (Disc)	7	263	678	841	0.0	0.1
CHR–Chr Chs & Chs Cr	7	NR	14,279	17,727	0.7	1.9
CHR–Chs of Christ	30	2,144	1,982	2,829	0.1	0.3
CHR–Int Chs of Christ	2	NR	253	314	0.0	0.0
Evan Cov Ch	1	55	50	72	0.0	0.0
Evan Free Ch	4	828	NR	828	0.0	0.1
FRND–Evan Fr Ch Intl	1	250	90	112	0.0	0.0
FRND–Indep Yr Mtgs	2	NR	20	24	0.0	0.0
HINDU–Post Ren	6	NR	NR	136	0.0	0.0
HINDU–Renaiss	1	NR	NR	12	0.0	0.0
HINDU–Trad Temples	1	NR	NR	2,000	0.1	0.2
Ind Fund Churches	5	NR	NR	NR	-	-
Jain	1	NR	NR	NR	-	-
Jehovah's Witness	27	NR	NR	NR	-	-
JUD–Conserv	3	614	689	1,861	0.1	0.2
JUD–Orth	8	1,267	650	1,760	0.1	0.2
JUD–Reconst	1	53	68	184	0.0	0.0
JUD–Reform	4	648	1,143	3,085	0.1	0.3
LDS–Comm of Christ	2	NR	317	317	0.0	0.0
LDS–L-D Saints	323	NR	NR	175,149	6.5	18.9
LUTH–E.L.C.A.	21	4,099	7,747	10,576	0.4	1.1
LUTH–Luth Ch-Am Asc	1	NR	NR	NR	-	-
LUTH–Luth Cong Msn Chr	1	30	49	61	0.0	0.0
LUTH–Luth-MO Synod	23	3,771	5,440	7,739	0.3	0.8
LUTH–Wisc Ev Luth Syn	9	1,046	1,451	1,991	0.1	0.2
METH–AME	4	395	1,050	1,301	0.0	0.1
METH–C.M.E.	1	25	35	43	0.0	0.0
METH–Free Methodist	1	23	22	23	0.0	0.0
METH–Un Methodist	37	4,680	7,366	13,148	0.5	1.4
METH–Wesleyan	1	199	126	259	0.0	0.0
Metro Comm Ch	1	155	90	112	0.0	0.0
MJEW–Assoc Mes Cong	1	NR	NR	NR	-	-
MJEW–Union Mes Cong	2	NR	NR	NR	-	-
Muslim Est	7	914	NR	1,700	0.1	0.2
Nat Spirit Asso	2	NR	NR	NR	-	-
New Apost Ch	1	NR	NR	NR	-	-
Non-denom Chr Chs	140	57,080	74,311	82,611	3.1	8.9
ORTHE–Ant Orth of NA	1	79	NR	217	0.0	0.0
ORTHE–Greek Orthodox	2	625	NR	5,375	0.2	0.6
ORTHE–Orth Ch in Amer	2	225	NR	800	0.0	0.1
ORTHE–Romania Orth Ar	1	50	NR	200	0.0	0.0
ORTHE–Rus Orth Abroad	1	30	NR	60	0.0	0.0
ORTHE–Serb Orth USA	2	135	NR	1,355	0.1	0.1
ORTHO–Armen Ap Cilic	1	65	NR	260	0.0	0.0
ORTHO–Armen Ap Etchm	1	50	NR	600	0.0	0.1
ORTHO–Eritrean Orth	1	250	NR	150	0.0	0.0
ORTHO–Ethiopian Orth	1	NR	NR	NR	-	-
ORTHO–Malan Dioc Am	1	8	NR	24	0.0	0.0
ORTHO–Syrian Orth Ch	1	55	NR	240	0.0	0.0
PENT–Assemb of God	61	15,484	16,186	30,545	1.1	3.3
PENT–Ch God (Cleve)	10	665	819	1,017	0.0	0.1
PENT–Ch of God Proph	5	NR	110	136	0.0	0.0
PENT–COGIC	24	2,038	5,001	6,196	0.2	0.7
PENT–Full Gosp Bapt	7	NR	NR	NR	-	-
PENT–Int Foursq Gos	36	3,752	4,047	5,003	0.2	0.5
PENT–Intl Pent Holiness	2	178	154	186	0.0	0.0
PENT–Open Bible Std	1	56	NR	56	0.0	0.0
PENT–Pent Ch of God	3	210	NR	327	0.0	0.0
PENT–Un Pent Ch Intl	8	NR	NR	NR	-	-
PENT–United Holy Ch	1	NR	NR	NR	-	-
PENT–Vineyard	3	453	630	769	0.0	0.1
PRES–Kor Pres Abroad	4	NR	NR	NR	-	-
PRES–Korean Pres Amer	3	NR	NR	NR	-	-
PRES–Orth Pres Ch	2	69	85	125	0.0	0.0
PRES–Presb Ch (USA)	21	2,512	4,142	5,121	0.2	0.6
PRES–Presb Ch Amer	3	261	230	267	0.0	0.0
REF–Christian Ref	5	503	351	436	0.0	0.0
REF–Comm Ref Evan	1	NR	NR	NR	-	-
REF–Hung Ref Add'l	1	NR	NR	NR	-	-
Salvation Army	7	856	702	1,586	0.1	0.2
Sev Day Adv	26	3,308	5,754	6,615	0.2	0.7
Sikh	3	NR	NR	NR	-	-
Un C of Christ	8	408	758	937	0.0	0.1
Unit Univ	2	206	330	445	0.0	0.0
Unity Ch	4	NR	NR	NR	-	-
Zoroastrian	0	NR	NR	8	0.0	0.0
NEW HAMPSHIRE	**1,025**	**61,434**	**101,108**	**462,772**	**35.2**	**100.0**
ANG/EPIS–Anglican NA	5	NR	NR	NR	-	-
ANG/EPIS–Episcopal	47	4,164	11,114	14,563	1.1	3.1
Bahá'í	7	NR	701	701	0.1	0.2
BAPT–Amer Bapt Assn	1	NR	150	174	0.0	0.0
BAPT–Amer Bapt USA	88	5,360	12,099	14,396	1.1	3.1
BAPT–Consrv Bapt	27	NR	NR	NR	-	-
BAPT–Converge/BGC	1	75	NR	90	0.0	0.0
BAPT–Free Will Bapt	1	NR	101	120	0.0	0.0
BAPT–Ref Bapt Ch	5	NR	NR	NR	-	-
BAPT–Reg Bapt Gen As	1	NR	NR	NR	-	-
BAPT–So Bapt Conv	29	1,799	1,907	2,288	0.2	0.5
BUDD–Mahayana	9	NR	NR	229	0.0	0.0
BUDD–Vajrayana	3	NR	NR	88	0.0	0.0
Calv Chpl	4	NR	NR	NR	-	-
Catholic	118	NR	NR	311,028	23.6	67.2
CGOD–Ch God (Ander)	1	0	NR	0	0.0	0.0
Ch Cr, Scientst	15	NR	NR	NR	-	-
Ch of Nazarene	12	971	859	1,444	0.1	0.3
Chr & Miss Al	6	485	334	642	0.0	0.1
CHR–Chr Chs & Chs Cr	10	NR	2,552	3,096	0.2	0.7
CHR–Chs of Christ	13	809	742	1,075	0.1	0.2
CHR–Int Chs of Christ	1	NR	190	231	0.0	0.0
Christian Brethren	2	NR	NR	NR	-	-
CONG–Cong Chr Add'l	3	NR	142	170	0.0	0.0
CONG–Cong Chr, NA	12	NR	969	1,153	0.1	0.2
CONG–Consrv Cong Chr	12	960	919	1,095	0.1	0.2
Evan Cov Ch	6	916	795	1,191	0.1	0.3
Evan Free Ch	7	1,393	NR	1,393	0.1	0.3
FRND–Fr Gen Cf & Un Mtg	13	NR	479	561	0.0	0.1
HINDU–I/A Temples	1	NR	NR	25	0.0	0.0
HINDU–Post Ren	3	NR	NR	118	0.0	0.0
HINDU–Trad Temples	1	NR	NR	40	0.0	0.0
Jehovah's Witness	25	NR	NR	NR	-	-
JUD–Conserv	3	564	632	1,706	0.1	0.4
JUD–Orth	1	43	50	60	0.0	0.0
JUD–Reconst	1	80	102	275	0.0	0.1
JUD–Reform	6	457	808	2,181	0.2	0.5
LDS–L-D Saints	21	NR	NR	8,231	0.6	1.8
LUTH–Apostolic Luth	1	NR	NR	NR	-	-
LUTH–E.L.C.A.	14	1,205	2,785	3,765	0.3	0.8

NR–Not Reported - Represents no adherents reported. Percentages may not total 100 due to rounding.

Table 2: Religious Congregations by State and Group: 2010

Religious Group	Number of Congregations	Number of Attendees	Number of Communicant, Confirmed, or Full Members	Adherents: Number of Adherents	Adherents: % of Total Pop.	Adherents: % of Total Adh.
LUTH–Luth–MO Synod	7	720	1,515	1,912	0.1	0.4
LUTH–Wisc Ev Luth Syn	1	66	103	142	0.0	0.0
METH–Un Methodist	88	4,828	12,715	18,029	1.4	3.9
Muslim Est	3	518	NR	1,616	0.1	0.3
New Apost Ch	2	NR	NR	NR	-	-
Non-denom Chr Chs	83	14,799	14,694	18,741	1.4	4.0
OCATH–Pol Natl Cath	1	NR	NR	NR	-	-
ORTHE–Greek Orthodox	11	1,194	NR	3,985	0.3	0.9
ORTHE–Holy Orth in NA	1	39	NR	50	0.0	0.0
ORTHE–Orth Ch in Amer	3	78	NR	161	0.0	0.0
ORTHE–Rus Orth Moscow	1	50	NR	120	0.0	0.0
ORTHO–Coptic Orth Ch	1	310	NR	610	0.0	0.1
PENT–Assemb of God	39	3,353	1,718	4,740	0.4	1.0
PENT–Ch God (Cleve)	7	251	324	388	0.0	0.1
PENT–Ch of God Proph	1	NR	19	23	0.0	0.0
PENT–Int Foursq Gos	16	2,099	1,730	2,067	0.2	0.4
PENT–Intl Pent Holiness	1	13	18	21	0.0	0.0
PENT–Un Pent Ch Intl	4	NR	NR	NR	-	-
PENT–United Holy Ch	1	NR	NR	NR	-	-
PENT–Vineyard	3	477	478	575	0.0	0.1
PRES–Evan Presby Ch	1	NR	285	343	0.0	0.1
PRES–Free Pres NA	1	NR	NR	NR	-	-
PRES–Korean Pres Amer	2	NR	NR	NR	-	-
PRES–Orth Pres Ch	3	159	155	228	0.0	0.0
PRES–Presb Ch (USA)	10	839	1,783	2,153	0.2	0.5
PRES–Presb Ch Amer	7	359	330	436	0.0	0.1
REF–Christian Ref	2	100	91	108	0.0	0.0
REF–Comm Ref Evan	1	NR	NR	NR	-	-
Salvation Army	10	317	793	2,998	0.2	0.6
Sev Day Adv	18	783	1,360	1,567	0.1	0.3
Un C of Christ	136	9,311	22,107	26,321	2.0	5.7
Unit Univ	23	1,490	2,460	3,301	0.3	0.7
Unity Ch	1	NR	NR	NR	-	-
Zoroastrian	0	NR	NR	8	0.0	0.0
NEW JERSEY	**6,114**	**640,935**	**841,292**	**4,809,520**	**54.7**	**100.0**
ANG/EPIS–Anglican NA	9	NR	NR	NR	-	-
ANG/EPIS–Episcopal	262	23,328	56,204	75,390	0.9	1.6
Bahá'í	12	NR	1,698	1,698	0.0	0.0
BAPT–Alliance Bapt	1	NR	NR	NR	-	-
BAPT–Amer Bapt Assn	2	NR	45	55	0.0	0.0
BAPT–Amer Bapt USA	282	33,132	70,460	86,120	1.0	1.8
BAPT–Asc Ref Bap Ch Am	1	NR	NR	NR	-	-
BAPT–Consrv Bapt	50	NR	NR	NR	-	-
BAPT–Converge/BGC	2	150	NR	180	0.0	0.0
BAPT–Free Will Bapt	3	NR	115	140	0.0	0.0
BAPT–N Am Bapt Conf	2	NR	117	141	0.0	0.0
BAPT–Natl Mis Bapt Conv	7	350	1,600	1,970	0.0	0.0
BAPT–NBC Amer	6	460	1,080	1,330	0.0	0.0
BAPT–NBC USA	115	31,000	60,757	74,106	0.8	1.5
BAPT–NT Ind Bapt	1	NR	NR	NR	-	-
BAPT–Prog NBC	8	1,520	2,450	3,013	0.0	0.1
BAPT–Ref Bapt Ch	10	NR	NR	NR	-	-
BAPT–Reg Bapt Gen As	26	NR	NR	NR	-	-
BAPT–S-D Baptist Gen Con	4	183	459	565	0.0	0.0
BAPT–So Bapt Conv	114	18,229	23,362	28,546	0.3	0.6
BRETH–Breth in Chr	2	NR	NR	NR	-	-
BRETH–Ch of Brethren	1	0	124	150	0.0	0.0
BRETH–Grace Breth	1	NR	NR	NR	-	-
BUDD–Mahayana	49	NR	NR	20,957	0.2	0.4
BUDD–Theravada	3	NR	NR	855	0.0	0.0
BUDD–Vajrayana	9	NR	NR	1,248	0.0	0.0
Calv Chpl	24	NR	NR	NR	-	-
Catholic	729	NR	NR	3,235,290	36.8	67.3
CGOD–Ch God (Ander)	14	643	NR	643	0.0	0.0
CGOD–Ches God-Gen Con	1	0	0	0	0.0	0.0
Ch Cr, Scientst	21	NR	NR	NR	-	-
Ch God (7th Day)	2	NR	NR	NR	-	-
Ch of Nazarene	45	4,324	4,766	6,732	0.1	0.1
Chr & Miss Al	85	14,308	10,193	22,879	0.3	0.5
CHR–Chr Ch (Disc)	23	75	2,165	2,633	0.0	0.1
CHR–Chr Chs & Chs Cr	12	NR	1,058	1,289	0.0	0.0
CHR–Chs of Christ	39	3,469	3,483	4,389	0.0	0.1
CHR–Int Chs of Christ	1	NR	469	572	0.0	0.0
Christian Brethren	16	NR	NR	NR	-	-
CONG–Cong Chr, NA	5	NR	548	670	0.0	0.0
Evan Cong Ch	1	NR	147	180	0.0	0.0
Evan Cov Ch	6	592	531	770	0.0	0.0
Evan Free Ch	28	5,023	NR	5,023	0.1	0.1
FRND–Fr Gen Cf	28	NR	2,040	2,476	0.0	0.1
FRND–Fr Gen Cf & Un Mtg	8	NR	594	725	0.0	0.0
Grace Gosp Fel	3	NR	NR	NR	-	-
HINDU–I/A Temples	36	NR	NR	31,447	0.4	0.7
HINDU–Post Ren	34	NR	NR	918	0.0	0.0
HINDU–Renaiss	3	NR	NR	36	0.0	0.0
HINDU–Trad Temples	21	NR	NR	15,916	0.2	0.3
Ind Fund Churches	23	NR	NR	NR	-	-
Int Cou Comm Ch	7	NR	NR	NR	-	-
Jain	4	NR	NR	NR	-	-
Jehovah's Witness	121	NR	NR	NR	-	-
JUD–Conserv	65	18,765	21,062	56,868	0.6	1.2
JUD–Orth	238	76,981	28,125	106,920	1.2	2.2
JUD–Reconst	7	634	810	2,186	0.0	0.0
JUD–Reform	46	10,653	18,790	50,732	0.6	1.1
LDS–Comm of Christ	3	NR	483	483	0.0	0.0
LDS–L-D Saints	59	NR	NR	31,673	0.4	0.7
LUTH–Ch of Luth Br	5	532	361	1,437	0.0	0.0
LUTH–E.L.C.A.	189	16,304	44,186	62,644	0.7	1.3
LUTH–Luth Cong Msn Chr	1	40	56	69	0.0	0.0
LUTH–Luth–MO Synod	65	5,628	13,032	16,422	0.2	0.3
LUTH–Nor Amer Luth C	1	NR	NR	NR	-	-
LUTH–Wisc Ev Luth Syn	2	92	180	237	0.0	0.0
MENN–Bible Flwshp	9	544	NR	734	0.0	0.0
MENN–Mara Amish-Menn	1	55	21	55	0.0	0.0
MENN–Mennonite USA	9	354	302	368	0.0	0.0
METH–AME	117	9,205	26,976	33,050	0.4	0.7
METH–AME Zion	46	1,408	6,260	7,630	0.1	0.2
METH–C.M.E.	3	385	767	941	0.0	0.0
METH–Free Methodist	10	1,406	1,608	1,700	0.0	0.0
METH–Prim Meth Ch	1	NR	NR	NR	-	-
METH–Un Methodist	557	47,755	91,210	138,052	1.6	2.9
METH–Wesleyan	24	1,572	907	2,047	0.0	0.0
Metro Comm Ch	1	30	31	38	0.0	0.0
Missionary Ch	4	295	246	295	0.0	0.0
MJEW–Assoc Mes Cong	1	NR	NR	NR	-	-
MORAV–Morav Ch-North	4	235	624	814	0.0	0.0
Muslim Est	109	45,780	NR	160,666	1.8	3.3
Nat Spirit Asso	1	NR	NR	NR	-	-
New Apost Ch	16	NR	NR	NR	-	-
Non-denom Chr Chs	554	120,957	144,397	167,015	1.9	3.5
OCATH–Pol Natl Cath	11	NR	NR	NR	-	-
ORTHE–Ant Orth of NA	3	570	NR	2,150	0.0	0.0
ORTHE–Carp Rus Orth	7	488	NR	974	0.0	0.0
ORTHE–Georgian Orth	1	80	NR	150	0.0	0.0
ORTHE–Greek Orthodox	24	6,135	NR	32,370	0.4	0.7
ORTHE–Macedonian Orth	2	200	NR	2,300	0.0	0.0
ORTHE–Orth Ch in Amer	23	1,528	NR	3,854	0.0	0.1
ORTHE–Rus Orth Abroad	12	640	NR	1,145	0.0	0.0
ORTHE–Rus Orth Moscow	6	495	NR	2,150	0.0	0.0
ORTHE–Serb Orth USA	3	175	NR	1,100	0.0	0.0
ORTHE–Ukrainian Orth	11	742	NR	2,485	0.0	0.1
ORTHO–Armen Ap Cilic	1	200	NR	3,000	0.0	0.1
ORTHO–Armen Ap Etchm	5	620	NR	2,490	0.0	0.1
ORTHO–Coptic Orth Ch	16	6,295	NR	14,025	0.2	0.3
ORTHO–Ethiopian Orth	2	NR	NR	NR	-	-
ORTHO–Malan Dioc Am	6	705	NR	1,060	0.0	0.0
ORTHO–Malan Syr Orth	3	245	NR	468	0.0	0.0
ORTHO–Syrian Orth Ch	5	890	NR	2,710	0.0	0.1
PENT–Apos Faith Msn	1	NR	35	43	0.0	0.0
PENT–Assemb of God	307	42,961	30,236	60,430	0.7	1.3
PENT–Ch God (Cleve)	80	7,057	6,714	8,223	0.1	0.2
PENT–Ch Lord Jesus Apos	25	NR	NR	NR	-	-
PENT–Ch of God by Faith	1	NR	NR	NR	-	-
PENT–Ch of God Proph	24	NR	1,532	1,869	0.0	0.0
PENT–COGIC	46	2,155	6,437	7,895	0.1	0.2
PENT–Elim	6	NR	NR	NR	-	-
PENT–Fire Bapt Hol Ch	13	NR	NR	NR	-	-
PENT–Full Gosp Bapt	12	NR	NR	NR	-	-

NR–Not Reported - Represents no adherents reported. Percentages may not total 100 due to rounding.

Table 2: Religious Congregations by State and Group: 2010

Religious Group	Number of Congrega-tions	Number of Attendees	Number of Communicant, Confirmed, or Full Members	Adherents		
				Number of Adherents	% of Total Pop.	% of Total Adh.
PENT–I F Chr Assmbl	3	NR	NR	NR	-	-
PENT–Int Foursq Gos	11	1,087	1,250	1,533	0.0	0.0
PENT–Int Pent C Chr	1	14	69	69	0.0	0.0
PENT–Intl Pent Holiness	5	750	605	742	0.0	0.0
PENT–Pent Ch of God	2	140	NR	218	0.0	0.0
PENT–Un Pent Ch Intl	24	NR	NR	NR	-	-
PENT–United Holy Ch	37	NR	NR	NR	-	-
PENT–Vineyard	5	880	1,145	1,386	0.0	0.0
Pillar of Fire	1	NR	1,500	1,500	0.0	0.0
PRES–AmPres	1	NR	NR	NR	-	-
PRES–As Ref Pres Ch	1	NR	52	63	0.0	0.0
PRES–Cumber Presb	1	NR	36	40	0.0	0.0
PRES–Evan Presby Ch	3	NR	263	322	0.0	0.0
PRES–Kor Pres Abroad	24	NR	NR	NR	-	-
PRES–Korean Amer Pres	12	NR	NR	NR	-	-
PRES–Korean Pres Amer	26	NR	NR	NR	-	-
PRES–Orth Pres Ch	23	1,553	1,534	2,009	0.0	0.0
PRES–Presb Ch (USA)	364	33,120	80,264	97,885	1.1	2.0
PRES–Presb Ch Amer	33	2,470	2,239	2,970	0.0	0.1
PRES–Ref Pres Han	1	NR	NR	NR	-	-
PRES–Ref Pres of NA	1	27	30	34	0.0	0.0
REF–Christian Ref	24	2,767	3,745	4,566	0.1	0.1
REF–Free Ref NA	1	NR	NR	NR	-	-
REF–Heritage Ref	1	NR	94	115	0.0	0.0
REF–Hung Ref Add'l	5	NR	NR	NR	-	-
REF–Ref Ch in Am	129	9,500	20,850	24,366	0.3	0.5
REF–Un Ref Chs N.A.	3	NR	NR	NR	-	-
Salvation Army	28	1,864	2,780	6,244	0.1	0.1
Sev Day Adv	129	12,661	22,018	25,323	0.3	0.5
Sikh	8	NR	NR	NR	-	-
Un Breth in Cr	1	17	22	15	0.0	0.0
Un C of Christ	51	3,065	8,981	10,984	0.1	0.2
Unit Univ	21	2,443	3,962	5,595	0.1	0.1
Unity Ch	7	NR	NR	NR	-	-
Zoroastrian	1	NR	NR	522	0.0	0.0
NEW MEXICO	**2,447**	**171,458**	**272,647**	**1,031,198**	**50.1**	**100.0**
ANG/EPIS–Anglican NA	15	NR	NR	NR	-	-
ANG/EPIS–Episcopal	47	3,695	8,957	10,646	0.5	1.0
Bahá'í	18	NR	2,884	2,884	0.1	0.3
BAPT–Amer Bapt Assn	9	NR	625	808	0.0	0.1
BAPT–Amer Bapt USA	4	341	614	754	0.0	0.1
BAPT–Consrv Bapt	4	NR	NR	NR	-	-
BAPT–Free Will Bapt	3	NR	18	23	0.0	0.0
BAPT–Ind Bapt Flwsp Intl	9	NR	NR	NR	-	-
BAPT–Natl Mis Bapt Conv	2	55	235	294	0.0	0.0
BAPT–NBC Amer	2	125	400	492	0.0	0.0
BAPT–NBC USA	7	265	630	793	0.0	0.1
BAPT–NT Ind Bapt	2	NR	NR	NR	-	-
BAPT–Ref Bapt Ch	4	NR	NR	NR	-	-
BAPT–Reg Bapt Gen As	4	NR	NR	NR	-	-
BAPT–S-D Baptist Gen Con	1	6	8	10	0.0	0.0
BAPT–So Bapt Conv	337	37,003	90,462	113,452	5.5	11.0
BRETH–Breth in Chr	3	NR	NR	NR	-	-
BRETH–Ch of Brethren	2	12	97	124	0.0	0.0
BRETH–Grace Breth	2	NR	NR	NR	-	-
BUDD–Mahayana	24	NR	NR	3,880	0.2	0.4
BUDD–Theravada	3	NR	NR	3,029	0.1	0.3
BUDD–Vajrayana	18	NR	NR	1,271	0.1	0.1
Calv Chpl	23	NR	NR	NR	-	-
Catholic	443	NR	NR	584,941	28.4	56.7
CGOD–Ch God (Ander)	4	790	NR	790	0.0	0.1
CGOD–Ches God-Gen Con	2	54	0	0	0.0	0.0
Ch Cr, Scientst	9	NR	NR	NR	-	-
Ch God (7th Day)	3	NR	NR	NR	-	-
Ch of Nazarene	45	4,469	5,784	8,245	0.4	0.8
Chr & Miss Al	2	415	206	599	0.0	0.1
CHR–Chr Ch (Disc)	16	1,054	2,550	3,129	0.2	0.3
CHR–Chr Chs & Chs Cr	33	NR	3,755	4,696	0.2	0.5
CHR–Chs of Christ	148	11,734	12,452	15,928	0.8	1.5
CHR–Int Chs of Christ	1	NR	110	135	0.0	0.0
Christian Brethren	2	NR	NR	NR	-	-
Evan Free Ch	4	980	NR	980	0.0	0.1
FRND–Fr Gen Cf	12	NR	285	346	0.0	0.0
HINDU–I/A Temples	1	NR	NR	250	0.0	0.0
HINDU–Post Ren	14	NR	NR	750	0.0	0.1
HINDU–Renaiss	4	NR	NR	77	0.0	0.0
HINDU–Trad Temples	2	NR	NR	800	0.0	0.1
Ind Fund Churches	2	NR	NR	NR	-	-
Jehovah's Witness	56	NR	NR	NR	-	-
JUD–Conserv	1	223	250	675	0.0	0.1
JUD–Orth	5	215	250	300	0.0	0.0
JUD–Reform	3	683	1,206	3,257	0.2	0.3
LDS–Comm of Christ	8	NR	555	555	0.0	0.1
LDS–L-D Saints	135	NR	NR	67,637	3.3	6.6
LUTH–Ch Luth Conf	1	NR	NR	NR	-	-
LUTH–E.L.C.A.	22	2,312	4,915	5,991	0.3	0.6
LUTH–Luth Ch-Am Asc	2	NR	NR	NR	-	-
LUTH–Luth Cong Msn Chr	2	1,137	2,193	2,700	0.1	0.3
LUTH–Luth–MO Synod	36	2,322	3,806	4,762	0.2	0.5
LUTH–Wisc Ev Luth Syn	5	368	552	747	0.0	0.1
MENN–Bible Flwshp	1	24	NR	32	0.0	0.0
MENN–CG in Cr (Menn)	3	NR	86	104	0.0	0.0
MENN–Cons Menn Conf	2	115	82	102	0.0	0.0
MENN–Mennonite USA	3	170	135	169	0.0	0.0
METH–A.W.M.C.	2	7	5	7	0.0	0.0
METH–AME	4	95	575	724	0.0	0.1
METH–C.M.E.	6	25	600	756	0.0	0.1
METH–Cong Meth	1	NR	16	21	0.0	0.0
METH–Un Methodist	109	11,641	28,893	36,424	1.8	3.5
METH–Wesleyan	3	99	86	128	0.0	0.0
Metro Comm Ch	2	124	176	218	0.0	0.0
MJEW–Union Mes Cong	1	NR	NR	NR	-	-
Muslim Est	10	1,653	NR	4,116	0.2	0.4
New Apost Ch	3	NR	NR	NR	-	-
Non-denom Chr Chs	197	49,552	56,462	67,353	3.3	6.5
ORTHE–Ant Orth of NA	1	80	NR	112	0.0	0.0
ORTHE–Greek Orthodox	2	345	NR	1,595	0.1	0.2
ORTHE–Orth Ch in Amer	3	111	NR	159	0.0	0.0
ORTHE–Rus Orth Abroad	1	32	NR	75	0.0	0.0
ORTHE–Ukrainian Orth	1	25	NR	30	0.0	0.0
ORTHO–Coptic Orth Ch	1	15	NR	24	0.0	0.0
PENT–Assemb of God	149	20,060	10,965	30,432	1.5	3.0
PENT–Ch God (Cleve)	56	1,786	2,765	3,523	0.2	0.3
PENT–Ch God Apos Fth	1	NR	NR	NR	-	-
PENT–Ch of God Proph	12	NR	369	463	0.0	0.0
PENT–COGIC	11	175	1,005	1,262	0.1	0.1
PENT–Full Gosp Bapt	8	NR	NR	NR	-	-
PENT–Int Foursq Gos	22	1,415	1,228	1,513	0.1	0.1
PENT–Intl Pent Holiness	10	676	618	770	0.0	0.1
PENT–Pent Ch of God	22	1,540	NR	2,393	0.1	0.2
PENT–Un Pent Ch Intl	35	NR	NR	NR	-	-
PENT–Vineyard	6	547	544	661	0.0	0.1
PRES–Cumber Presb	2	NR	1,115	2,573	0.1	0.2
PRES–Orth Pres Ch	2	91	68	84	0.0	0.0
PRES–Presb Ch (USA)	65	4,400	8,617	10,663	0.5	1.0
PRES–Presb Ch Amer	8	501	688	802	0.0	0.1
REF–Christian Ref	16	1,211	1,724	2,237	0.1	0.2
REF–Comm Ref Evan	1	NR	NR	NR	-	-
REF–Ref Ch in Am	3	192	398	448	0.0	0.0
Salvation Army	9	256	407	1,264	0.1	0.1
Sev Day Adv	59	4,348	7,560	8,696	0.4	0.8
Sikh	3	NR	NR	NR	-	-
Swedenborgian	1	NR	NR	NR	-	-
Un C of Christ	9	840	2,053	2,499	0.1	0.2
Unit Univ	9	1,049	1,608	2,007	0.1	0.2
Unity Ch	6	NR	NR	NR	-	-
Zoroastrian	0	NR	NR	9	0.0	0.0
NEW YORK	**14,110**	**1,567,789**	**1,872,223**	**9,923,512**	**51.2**	**100.0**
ANG/EPIS–Anglican NA	19	NR	NR	NR	-	-
ANG/EPIS–Episcopal	653	52,582	121,522	163,730	0.8	1.6
Ap Chr Ch-Amer	1	120	39	120	0.0	0.0
Bahá'í	30	NR	5,118	5,118	0.0	0.1
BAPT–Alliance Bapt	4	NR	NR	NR	-	-
BAPT–Amer Bapt Assn	3	NR	170	203	0.0	0.0
BAPT–Amer Bapt USA	536	89,753	144,518	173,405	0.9	1.7
BAPT–Asc Ref Bap Ch Am	3	NR	NR	NR	-	-

NR–Not Reported   - Represents no adherents reported.   Percentages may not total 100 due to rounding.

Table 2: Religious Congregations by State and Group: 2010

Religious Group	Number of Congregations	Number of Attendees	Number of Communicant, Confirmed, or Full Members	Adherents: Number of Adherents	Adherents: % of Total Pop.	Adherents: % of Total Adh.
BAPT–Consrv Bapt	111	NR	NR	NR	-	-
BAPT–Converge/BGC	23	3,825	NR	4,590	0.0	0.0
BAPT–Fund Bapt Flwsp	1	NR	NR	NR	-	-
BAPT–Ind Bapt Flwsp Intl	4	NR	NR	NR	-	-
BAPT–N Am Bapt Conf	9	NR	1,254	1,504	0.0	0.0
BAPT–Natl Mis Bapt Conv	19	46	2,455	2,962	0.0	0.0
BAPT–NBC Amer	11	1,405	2,750	3,350	0.0	0.0
BAPT–NBC USA	176	26,893	59,320	71,688	0.4	0.7
BAPT–NT Ind Bapt	1	NR	NR	NR	-	-
BAPT–Prog NBC	25	8,205	19,670	23,754	0.1	0.2
BAPT–Ref Bapt Ch	20	NR	NR	NR	-	-
BAPT–Reg Bapt Gen As	136	NR	NR	NR	-	-
BAPT–S-D Baptist Gen Con	11	512	665	798	0.0	0.0
BAPT–So Bapt Conv	327	25,332	26,809	32,271	0.2	0.3
BRETH–Breth in Chr	1	NR	NR	NR	-	-
BRETH–Ch of Brethren	3	39	238	292	0.0	0.0
BRETH–Grace Breth	1	NR	NR	NR	-	-
BUDD–Mahayana	142	NR	NR	53,368	0.3	0.5
BUDD–Theravada	13	NR	NR	8,020	0.0	0.1
BUDD–Vajrayana	64	NR	NR	6,877	0.0	0.1
Calv Chpl	28	NR	NR	NR	-	-
Catholic	1,630	NR	NR	6,286,916	32.4	63.4
CGOD–Ch God (Ander)	33	2,379	NR	2,379	0.0	0.0
CGOD–Ches God-Gen Con	2	157	108	131	0.0	0.0
Ch Christ Chr Union	10	NR	NR	NR	-	-
Ch Cr, Scientst	53	NR	NR	NR	-	-
Ch God (7th Day)	6	NR	NR	NR	-	-
Ch of Chr (Hol)	1	NR	NR	NR	-	-
Ch of Nazarene	142	12,292	13,988	18,302	0.1	0.2
Chr & Miss Al	171	18,737	12,470	25,786	0.1	0.3
CHR–Chr Ch (Disc)	77	1,803	5,149	6,213	0.0	0.1
CHR–Chr Chs & Chs Cr	63	NR	5,607	6,767	0.0	0.1
CHR–Chs of Christ	107	8,521	8,519	10,697	0.1	0.1
CHR–Int Chs of Christ	3	NR	2,640	3,184	0.0	0.0
Christian Brethren	10	NR	NR	NR	-	-
CONG–Cong Chr Add'l	4	NR	564	683	0.0	0.0
CONG–Cong Chr, NA	14	NR	1,423	1,714	0.0	0.0
CONG–Consrv Cong Chr	26	1,811	1,995	2,402	0.0	0.0
Evan Cov Ch	19	2,047	2,323	2,663	0.0	0.0
Evan Free Ch	34	3,710	NR	3,710	0.0	0.0
FRND–Evan Fr Ch Intl	3	200	158	192	0.0	0.0
FRND–Fr Gen Cf & Un Mtg	68	NR	2,722	3,256	0.0	0.0
FRND–Unaffl Mtgs	1	NR	NR	NR	-	-
Grace Gosp Fel	1	NR	NR	NR	-	-
HINDU–I/A Temples	31	NR	NR	16,160	0.1	0.2
HINDU–Post Ren	80	NR	NR	5,914	0.0	0.1
HINDU–Renaiss	15	NR	NR	747	0.0	0.0
HINDU–Trad Temples	39	NR	NR	28,819	0.1	0.3
Ind Fund Churches	9	NR	NR	NR	-	-
Int Cou Comm Ch	17	NR	NR	NR	-	-
Intl Fell Bible Ch	6	NR	NR	NR	-	-
Jain	8	NR	NR	NR	-	-
Jehovah's Witness	287	NR	NR	NR	-	-
JUD–Conserv	126	27,327	31,538	82,809	0.4	0.8
JUD–Orth	788	423,719	145,900	588,500	3.0	5.9
JUD–Reconst	11	1,736	2,286	5,991	0.0	0.1
JUD–Reform	104	22,429	40,167	106,806	0.6	1.1
LDS–Comm of Christ	5	NR	793	793	0.0	0.0
LDS–L-D Saints	151	NR	NR	78,031	0.4	0.8
LUTH–Ch of Luth Br	6	655	435	1,394	0.0	0.0
LUTH–E.L.C.A.	386	31,390	97,021	134,407	0.7	1.4
LUTH–Luth Ch-Am Asc	1	NR	NR	NR	-	-
LUTH–Luth Cong Msn Chr	18	1,135	2,667	3,209	0.0	0.0
LUTH–Luth-MO Synod	189	20,190	49,563	67,408	0.3	0.7
LUTH–Nor Amer Luth C	4	NR	NR	NR	-	-
LUTH–Wisc Ev Luth Syn	7	372	524	707	0.0	0.0
MENN–Amish Undif	86	NR	4,352	10,787	0.1	0.1
MENN–Beachy Amish-Menn	3	244	146	244	0.0	0.0
MENN–Bible Flwshp	4	146	NR	197	0.0	0.0
MENN–Bruderhof Comm	9	1,650	731	1,340	0.0	0.0
MENN–CG in Cr (Menn)	2	NR	45	54	0.0	0.0
MENN–Cons Menn Conf	6	945	817	1,005	0.0	0.0
MENN–Menn Br US Conf	1	NR	0	0	0.0	0.0
MENN–Menn Chr Fell	1	125	85	125	0.0	0.0
MENN–Mennonite USA	31	1,937	2,057	2,505	0.0	0.0
METH–A.W.M.C.	2	60	20	68	0.0	0.0
METH–AME	87	22,373	41,573	49,598	0.3	0.5
METH–AME Zion	89	6,550	19,538	23,650	0.1	0.2
METH–C.M.E.	13	1,325	4,003	4,809	0.0	0.0
METH–Evan Meth Ch	1	NR	NR	NR	-	-
METH–Free Methodist	78	11,725	8,730	12,662	0.1	0.1
METH–Prim Meth Ch	1	NR	NR	NR	-	-
METH–Un Methodist	1,323	78,133	260,984	328,315	1.7	3.3
METH–Wesleyan	121	17,848	7,777	23,212	0.1	0.2
Metro Comm Ch	2	451	604	689	0.0	0.0
Missionary Ch	13	792	852	971	0.0	0.0
MJEW–Union Mes Cong	7	NR	NR	NR	-	-
MORAV–Morav Ch-North	10	981	1,778	2,506	0.0	0.0
Muslim Est	257	104,856	NR	392,953	2.0	4.0
Nat Spirit Asso	8	NR	NR	NR	-	-
New Apost Ch	40	NR	NR	NR	-	-
Non-denom Chr Chs	1,276	262,465	320,403	374,521	1.9	3.8
OCATH–Pol Natl Cath	16	NR	NR	NR	-	-
OCATH–Un Cath Ch	1	NR	NR	702	0.0	0.0
ORTHE–Ant Orth of NA	13	1,155	NR	3,721	0.0	0.0
ORTHE–Bulgar Orth USA	2	95	NR	170	0.0	0.0
ORTHE–Carp Rus Orth	8	625	NR	1,524	0.0	0.0
ORTHE–Greek Orthodox	61	15,446	NR	76,985	0.4	0.8
ORTHE–Holy Orth in NA	4	70	NR	90	0.0	0.0
ORTHE–Macedonian Orth	4	230	NR	1,838	0.0	0.0
ORTHE–Orth Ch in Amer	41	2,180	NR	4,843	0.0	0.0
ORTHE–Romania Orth Ar	6	388	NR	3,473	0.0	0.0
ORTHE–Rus Orth Abroad	19	1,360	NR	3,470	0.0	0.0
ORTHE–Rus Orth Moscow	5	293	NR	6,277	0.0	0.1
ORTHE–Serb Orth USA	2	320	NR	3,530	0.0	0.0
ORTHE–Ukrainian Orth	18	1,379	NR	5,770	0.0	0.1
ORTHO–Armen Ap Cilic	5	400	NR	5,450	0.0	0.1
ORTHO–Armen Ap Etchm	10	665	NR	2,875	0.0	0.0
ORTHO–Coptic Orth Ch	14	4,537	NR	11,397	0.1	0.1
ORTHO–Eritrean Orth	4	820	NR	455	0.0	0.0
ORTHO–Ethiopian Orth	3	NR	NR	NR	-	-
ORTHO–Malan Dioc Am	29	4,185	NR	6,595	0.0	0.1
ORTHO–Malan Syr Orth	9	785	NR	1,494	0.0	0.0
ORTHO–Syrian Orth Ch	2	100	NR	340	0.0	0.0
PENT–Apos Faith Msn	6	NR	210	259	0.0	0.0
PENT–Assemb of God	522	66,949	50,278	92,987	0.5	0.9
PENT–Ch God (Cleve)	216	20,315	25,350	30,989	0.2	0.3
PENT–Ch Lord Jesus Apos	50	NR	NR	NR	-	-
PENT–Ch of God by Faith	9	NR	NR	NR	-	-
PENT–Ch of God Proph	51	NR	4,627	5,635	0.0	0.1
PENT–COGIC	128	6,295	18,559	22,406	0.1	0.2
PENT–Elim	52	NR	NR	NR	-	-
PENT–Fire Bapt Hol Ch	16	NR	NR	NR	-	-
PENT–Full Gosp Bapt	32	NR	NR	NR	-	-
PENT–I F Chr Assmbl	24	NR	NR	NR	-	-
PENT–Int Foursq Gos	13	621	661	778	0.0	0.0
PENT–Intl Pent Holiness	13	2,092	3,089	3,776	0.0	0.0
PENT–Open Bible Std	3	250	NR	250	0.0	0.0
PENT–Pent Ch of God	8	560	NR	871	0.0	0.0
PENT–Un Pent Asbl God	2	NR	NR	NR	-	-
PENT–Un Pent Ch Intl	52	NR	NR	NR	-	-
PENT–United Holy Ch	14	NR	NR	NR	-	-
PENT–Vineyard	19	3,163	4,034	4,840	0.0	0.0
PRES–As Ref Pres Ch	16	NR	1,368	1,631	0.0	0.0
PRES–Bible Pres	2	NR	NR	NR	-	-
PRES–Cumber Presb	2	NR	137	167	0.0	0.0
PRES–Evan Presby Ch	8	NR	1,980	2,421	0.0	0.0
PRES–Free Pres NA	1	NR	NR	NR	-	-
PRES–Kor Pres Abroad	35	NR	NR	NR	-	-
PRES–Korean Amer Pres	32	NR	NR	NR	-	-
PRES–Korean Pres Amer	58	NR	NR	NR	-	-
PRES–Orth Pres Ch	12	725	735	963	0.0	0.0
PRES–Presb Ch (USA)	679	40,632	97,609	116,960	0.6	1.2
PRES–Presb Ch Amer	39	5,085	4,927	5,905	0.0	0.1
PRES–Ref Pres of NA	12	675	597	799	0.0	0.0
REF–Christian Ref	14	1,265	1,573	1,904	0.0	0.0
REF–Comm Ref Evan	2	NR	NR	NR	-	-
REF–Fed Ref Ch	2	NR	NR	NR	-	-

NR–Not Reported   - Represents no adherents reported.   Percentages may not total 100 due to rounding.

Table 2: Religious Congregations by State and Group: 2010

Religious Group	Number of Congregations	Number of Attendees	Number of Communicant, Confirmed, or Full Members	Adherents		
				Number of Adherents	% of Total Pop.	% of Total Adh.
REF–Hung Ref Add'l	4	NR	NR	NR	-	-
REF–Ref Ch in Am	234	17,984	43,050	51,379	0.3	0.5
REF–Un Ref Chs N.A.	3	NR	NR	NR	-	-
Salvation Army	85	5,063	9,665	21,374	0.1	0.2
Sev Day Adv	364	39,635	68,925	79,268	0.4	0.8
Shinto	1	NR	NR	NR	-	-
Sikh	22	NR	NR	NR	-	-
Swedenborgian	3	NR	NR	NR	-	-
Tao	5	NR	NR	NR	-	-
Un Breth in Cr	3	127	191	109	0.0	0.0
Un C of Christ	263	14,023	36,925	44,146	0.2	0.4
Unit Univ	63	5,369	10,150	13,258	0.1	0.1
Unity Ch	26	NR	NR	NR	-	-
Zoroastrian	2	NR	NR	487	0.0	0.0
NORTH CAROLINA	**15,737**	**1,609,384**	**3,250,513**	**4,530,365**	**47.5**	**100.0**
ANG/EPIS–Anglican NA	45	NR	NR	NR	-	-
ANG/EPIS–Episcopal	257	28,310	70,861	83,234	0.9	1.8
Bahá'í	25	NR	5,843	5,843	0.1	0.1
BAPT–Alliance Bapt	21	NR	NR	NR	-	-
BAPT–Amer Bapt Assn	1	NR	60	71	0.0	0.0
BAPT–Amer Bapt USA	44	21,078	39,039	48,513	0.5	1.1
BAPT–Converge/BGC	5	2,300	NR	2,760	0.0	0.1
BAPT–Free Will Bapt	195	NR	21,447	26,165	0.3	0.6
BAPT–Ind Bapt Flwsp Intl	1	NR	NR	NR	-	-
BAPT–N Am Bapt Conf	1	NR	70	88	0.0	0.0
BAPT–Natl Mis Bapt Conv	85	2,320	12,718	15,549	0.2	0.3
BAPT–NBC Amer	5	1,445	2,520	3,085	0.0	0.1
BAPT–NBC USA	105	19,175	39,063	48,281	0.5	1.1
BAPT–Orig Free Will Bapt	238	21,420	29,262	35,921	0.4	0.8
BAPT–Prog NBC	16	1,915	3,907	4,801	0.1	0.1
BAPT–Ref Bapt Ch	15	NR	NR	NR	-	-
BAPT–S-D Baptist Gen Con	1	12	13	15	0.0	0.0
BAPT–So Bapt Conv	4,241	510,890	1,238,976	1,513,059	15.9	33.4
BRETH–Breth in Chr	2	NR	NR	NR	-	-
BRETH–Ch of Brethren	19	681	1,797	2,154	0.0	0.0
BRETH–Grace Breth	1	NR	NR	NR	-	-
BUDD–Mahayana	29	NR	NR	9,883	0.1	0.2
BUDD–Theravada	7	NR	NR	2,442	0.0	0.1
BUDD–Vajrayana	11	NR	NR	1,111	0.0	0.0
Calv Chpl	20	NR	NR	NR	-	-
Catholic	189	NR	NR	392,912	4.1	8.7
CGOD–Ch God (Ander)	49	3,285	NR	3,285	0.0	0.1
Ch Christ Chr Union	4	NR	NR	NR	-	-
Ch Cr, Scientst	21	NR	NR	NR	-	-
Ch God (7th Day)	4	NR	NR	NR	-	-
Ch of God Gen Conf	2	NR	92	110	0.0	0.0
Ch of Nazarene	69	5,608	7,307	8,816	0.1	0.2
Chr & Miss Al	52	6,357	5,121	9,337	0.1	0.2
CHR–Chr Ch (Disc)	305	5,761	21,889	26,932	0.3	0.6
CHR–Chr Chs & Chs Cr	155	NR	25,756	31,344	0.3	0.7
CHR–Chs of Christ	197	17,928	18,198	24,248	0.3	0.5
CHR–Int Chs of Christ	4	NR	509	618	0.0	0.0
Christian Brethren	10	NR	NR	NR	-	-
CONG–Cong Chr Add'l	2	NR	545	669	0.0	0.0
CONG–Cong Chr, NA	3	NR	452	573	0.0	0.0
CONG–Consrv Cong Chr	3	317	681	833	0.0	0.0
Evan Assoc RCC	11	NR	NR	NR	-	-
Evan Cov Ch	6	1,293	1,060	1,682	0.0	0.0
Evan Free Ch	7	3,360	NR	3,360	0.0	0.1
FRND–Consrv Yr Mtgs	8	NR	416	505	0.0	0.0
FRND–Evan Fr Ch Intl	9	535	326	396	0.0	0.0
FRND–Fr Gen Cf	18	NR	515	626	0.0	0.0
FRND–Fr Gen Cf & Un Mtg	4	NR	179	219	0.0	0.0
FRND–Fr Un Mtg	68	NR	6,913	8,471	0.1	0.2
FRND–Unaffl Mtgs	2	NR	NR	NR	-	-
HINDU–I/A Temples	6	NR	NR	4,271	0.0	0.1
HINDU–Post Ren	18	NR	NR	1,616	0.0	0.0
HINDU–Trad Temples	4	NR	NR	4,383	0.0	0.1
Int Cou Comm Ch	1	NR	NR	NR	-	-
Jain	3	NR	NR	NR	-	-
Jehovah's Witness	174	NR	NR	NR	-	-
JUD–Conserv	6	1,754	1,969	5,317	0.1	0.1
JUD–Orth	9	521	443	725	0.0	0.0

Religious Group	Number of Congregations	Number of Attendees	Number of Communicant, Confirmed, or Full Members	Adherents		
				Number of Adherents	% of Total Pop.	% of Total Adh.
JUD–Reconst	2	170	218	589	0.0	0.0
JUD–Reform	18	2,423	4,271	11,530	0.1	0.3
LDS–Comm of Christ	7	NR	845	845	0.0	0.0
LDS–L-D Saints	153	NR	NR	76,782	0.8	1.7
LUTH–Apostolic Luth	1	NR	NR	NR	-	-
LUTH–E.L.C.A.	215	26,775	54,619	69,163	0.7	1.5
LUTH–Luth Ch-Am Asc	2	NR	NR	NR	-	-
LUTH–Luth Cong Msn Chr	15	2,278	5,519	6,830	0.1	0.2
LUTH–Luth-MO Synod	62	9,417	17,159	22,160	0.2	0.5
LUTH–Nor Amer Luth C	32	NR	NR	NR	-	-
LUTH–Wisc Ev Luth Syn	8	563	807	1,070	0.0	0.0
MENN–Amish Undif	1	NR	67	127	0.0	0.0
MENN–Beachy Amish-Menn	1	45	32	45	0.0	0.0
MENN–CG in Cr (Menn)	2	NR	151	183	0.0	0.0
MENN–Menn Br US Conf	6	NR	240	285	0.0	0.0
MENN–Mennonite USA	9	551	572	700	0.0	0.0
METH–AME	189	4,982	29,710	36,281	0.4	0.8
METH–AME Zion	613	15,523	88,511	109,087	1.1	2.4
METH–C.M.E.	33	2,510	6,780	8,324	0.1	0.2
METH–Evan Meth Ch	20	NR	NR	NR	-	-
METH–Free Methodist	3	69	71	79	0.0	0.0
METH–Un Methodist	1,923	202,070	523,213	659,064	6.9	14.5
METH–Wesleyan	170	18,227	17,366	23,708	0.2	0.5
Metro Comm Ch	7	481	564	694	0.0	0.0
Missionary Ch	5	1,052	2,225	2,452	0.0	0.1
MJEW–Assoc Mes Cong	1	NR	NR	NR	-	-
MJEW–Union Mes Cong	1	NR	NR	NR	-	-
MORAV–Morav Ch-South	47	5,869	12,129	14,422	0.2	0.3
Muslim Est	50	11,026	NR	26,045	0.3	0.6
New Apost Ch	6	NR	NR	NR	-	-
Non-denom Chr Chs	1,948	398,815	511,119	565,051	5.9	12.5
ORTHE–Ant Orth of NA	2	198	NR	524	0.0	0.0
ORTHE–Carp Rus Orth	3	58	NR	124	0.0	0.0
ORTHE–Greek Orthodox	15	2,640	NR	11,996	0.1	0.3
ORTHE–Orth Ch in Amer	8	419	NR	662	0.0	0.0
ORTHE–Rus Orth Abroad	3	73	NR	179	0.0	0.0
ORTHE–Serb Orth USA	2	212	NR	600	0.0	0.0
ORTHO–Armen Ap Etchm	1	65	NR	300	0.0	0.0
ORTHO–Coptic Orth Ch	2	475	NR	775	0.0	0.0
ORTHO–Eritrean Orth	2	55	NR	200	0.0	0.0
ORTHO–Ethiopian Orth	3	NR	NR	NR	-	-
ORTHO–Malan Dioc Am	1	25	NR	75	0.0	0.0
ORTHO–Malan Syr Orth	1	30	NR	54	0.0	0.0
PENT–Apos Faith Msn	1	NR	35	43	0.0	0.0
PENT–Assemb of God	277	34,622	21,929	56,086	0.6	1.2
PENT–Assm God Intl F	1	NR	NR	NR	-	-
PENT–Ch God (Cleve)	517	47,653	72,437	89,359	0.9	2.0
PENT–Ch God Mtn Asm	1	NR	NR	NR	-	-
PENT–Ch Lord Jesus Apos	37	NR	NR	NR	-	-
PENT–Ch of God Proph	146	NR	7,046	8,701	0.1	0.2
PENT–COGIC	75	9,360	18,550	22,849	0.2	0.5
PENT–Cong Hol Ch	18	696	564	688	0.0	0.0
PENT–Elim	1	NR	NR	NR	-	-
PENT–Fire Bapt Hol Ch	42	NR	NR	NR	-	-
PENT–Full Gosp Bapt	42	NR	NR	NR	-	-
PENT–Int Foursq Gos	47	7,000	7,665	9,536	0.1	0.2
PENT–Int Pent C Chr	5	171	53	265	0.0	0.0
PENT–Intl Pent Holiness	380	33,687	46,473	57,414	0.6	1.3
PENT–Pent Ch of God	5	350	NR	544	0.0	0.0
PENT–Pent FW Bapt	131	NR	NR	NR	-	-
PENT–Un Pent Ch Intl	68	NR	NR	NR	-	-
PENT–United Holy Ch	158	NR	NR	NR	-	-
PENT–Vineyard	13	1,057	1,289	1,594	0.0	0.0
PRES–As Ref Pres Ch	79	NR	6,865	8,460	0.1	0.2
PRES–Bible Pres	2	NR	NR	NR	-	-
PRES–Evan Presby Ch	28	NR	5,817	7,114	0.1	0.2
PRES–Free Pres NA	1	NR	NR	NR	-	-
PRES–Korean Amer Pres	1	NR	NR	NR	-	-
PRES–Korean Pres Amer	3	NR	NR	NR	-	-
PRES–Orth Pres Ch	12	811	704	981	0.0	0.0
PRES–Pres Ref	1	NR	NR	NR	-	-
PRES–Presb Ch (USA)	710	66,342	150,560	185,669	1.9	4.1
PRES–Presb Ch Amer	109	14,438	15,884	20,084	0.2	0.4
PRES–Ref Pres Han	1	NR	NR	NR	-	-

NR–Not Reported   - Represents no adherents reported.   Percentages may not total 100 due to rounding.

Table 2: Religious Congregations by State and Group: 2010

Religious Group	Number of Congregations	Number of Attendees	Number of Communicant, Confirmed, or Full Members	Adherents		
				Number of Adherents	% of Total Pop.	% of Total Adh.
PRES–Ref Pres of NA	1	53	49	85	0.0	0.0
PRES–Ref Pres US	1	NR	NR	NR	-	-
REF–Christian Ref	1	100	120	145	0.0	0.0
REF–Comm Ref Evan	2	NR	NR	NR	-	-
REF–Ref Ch in Am	1	104	175	197	0.0	0.0
REF–Un Ref Chs N.A.	1	NR	NR	NR	-	-
Salvation Army	42	2,343	3,789	7,560	0.1	0.2
Sev Day Adv	166	14,712	25,578	29,414	0.3	0.6
Sikh	4	NR	NR	NR	-	-
Un C of Christ	161	9,392	26,001	31,795	0.3	0.7
Unit Univ	27	3,132	4,795	6,514	0.1	0.1
Unity Ch	12	NR	NR	NR	-	-
Zoroastrian	0	NR	NR	40	0.0	0.0
NORTH DAKOTA	**1,498**	**82,047**	**199,790**	**451,456**	**67.1**	**100.0**
ANG/EPIS–Anglican NA	1	NR	NR	NR	-	-
ANG/EPIS–Episcopal	19	687	1,686	2,279	0.3	0.5
Bahá'í	1	NR	330	330	0.0	0.1
BAPT–Amer Bapt USA	14	647	1,207	1,462	0.2	0.3
BAPT–Asc Ref Bap Ch Am	1	NR	NR	NR	-	-
BAPT–Consrv Bapt	1	NR	NR	NR	-	-
BAPT–Converge/BGC	3	225	NR	270	0.0	0.1
BAPT–N Am Bapt Conf	30	NR	4,380	5,220	0.8	1.2
BAPT–Ref Bapt Ch	1	NR	NR	NR	-	-
BAPT–So Bapt Conv	37	1,144	1,751	2,151	0.3	0.5
BUDD–Theravada	1	NR	NR	15	0.0	0.0
Calv Chpl	4	NR	NR	NR	-	-
Catholic	235	NR	NR	167,349	24.9	37.1
CGOD–Ch God (Ander)	2	105	NR	105	0.0	0.0
Ch Cr, Scientst	1	NR	NR	NR	-	-
Ch God (7th Day)	3	NR	NR	NR	-	-
Ch of Nazarene	23	2,118	1,935	3,896	0.6	0.9
Chr & Miss Al	3	140	47	171	0.0	0.0
CHR–Chs of Christ	7	395	356	538	0.1	0.1
Christian Brethren	1	NR	NR	NR	-	-
CONG–Cong Chr Add'l	1	NR	22	27	0.0	0.0
CONG–Consrv Cong Chr	8	697	687	814	0.1	0.2
Evan Ch	4	NR	NR	NR	-	-
Evan Cov Ch	3	961	301	1,249	0.2	0.3
Evan Free Ch	28	5,336	NR	5,336	0.8	1.2
FRND–Fr Gen Cf	1	NR	6	7	0.0	0.0
Jehovah's Witness	18	NR	NR	NR	-	-
JUD–Reform	2	37	65	176	0.0	0.0
LDS–Comm of Christ	2	NR	276	276	0.0	0.1
LDS–L-D Saints	16	NR	NR	6,930	1.0	1.5
LUTH–Apostolic Luth	1	NR	NR	NR	-	-
LUTH–Assoc Free Luth	43	NR	NR	NR	-	-
LUTH–Ch Luth Conf	3	NR	NR	NR	-	-
LUTH–Ch of Luth Br	14	1,817	1,246	4,138	0.6	0.9
LUTH–E.L.C.A.	412	35,244	125,426	163,209	24.3	36.2
LUTH–Luth Ch-Am Asc	7	NR	NR	NR	-	-
LUTH–Luth Cong Msn Chr	19	2,682	7,742	9,258	1.4	2.1
LUTH–Luth–MO Synod	85	5,967	17,430	22,003	3.3	4.9
LUTH–Nor Amer Luth C	2	NR	NR	NR	-	-
LUTH–Wisc Ev Luth Syn	12	512	1,042	1,283	0.2	0.3
MENN–CG in Cr (Menn)	1	NR	104	125	0.0	0.0
MENN–Hutt Breth	7	NR	NR	NR	-	-
MENN–Menn Br US Conf	2	NR	184	218	0.0	0.0
MENN–Mennonite USA	2	65	79	93	0.0	0.0
METH–Free Methodist	2	33	17	33	0.0	0.0
METH–Un Methodist	111	6,016	12,473	17,336	2.6	3.8
METH–Wesleyan	4	729	271	948	0.1	0.2
MORAV–Morav Ch-North	4	159	407	502	0.1	0.1
Muslim Est	3	283	NR	636	0.1	0.1
Non-denom Chr Chs	33	2,899	3,226	4,091	0.6	0.9
ORTHE–Orth Ch in Amer	2	60	NR	110	0.0	0.0
ORTHE–Ukrainian Orth	1	10	NR	10	0.0	0.0
PENT–Assemb of God	65	6,618	3,101	10,838	1.6	2.4
PENT–Assm God Intl F	1	NR	NR	NR	-	-
PENT–Ch God (Cleve)	16	715	784	953	0.1	0.2
PENT–Ch of God Proph	2	NR	54	66	0.0	0.0
PENT–Int Foursq Gos	2	398	437	529	0.1	0.1
PENT–Open Bible Std	1	81	NR	81	0.0	0.0
PENT–Pent Ch of God	2	140	NR	217	0.0	0.0

Religious Group	Number of Congregations	Number of Attendees	Number of Communicant, Confirmed, or Full Members	Adherents		
				Number of Adherents	% of Total Pop.	% of Total Adh.
PENT–Un Pent Ch Intl	15	NR	NR	NR	-	-
PRES–Orth Pres Ch	2	48	42	49	0.0	0.0
PRES–Presb Ch (USA)	54	1,832	4,569	5,529	0.8	1.2
REF–Christian Ref	1	47	75	88	0.0	0.0
REF–Ref Ch in Am	6	386	803	953	0.1	0.2
REF–Ref Ch in U.S.	3	NR	82	93	0.0	0.0
Salvation Army	6	227	303	1,331	0.2	0.3
Sev Day Adv	29	1,210	2,104	2,422	0.4	0.5
Un C of Christ	50	1,273	4,605	5,535	0.8	1.2
Unit Univ	2	104	135	177	0.0	0.0
Zoroastrian	0	NR	NR	1	0.0	0.0
OHIO	**13,606**	**1,265,197**	**2,160,933**	**5,071,684**	**44.0**	**100.0**
ANG/EPIS–Anglican NA	25	NR	NR	NR	-	-
ANG/EPIS–Episcopal	171	15,816	38,152	45,904	0.4	0.9
Ap Chr Ch-Amer	9	3,028	1,471	3,028	0.0	0.1
Bahá'í	18	NR	2,159	2,159	0.0	0.0
BAPT–Alliance Bapt	4	NR	NR	NR	-	-
BAPT–Amer Bapt Assn	10	NR	910	1,119	0.0	0.0
BAPT–Amer Bapt USA	286	40,208	80,599	98,102	0.9	1.9
BAPT–Asc Ref Bap Ch Am	2	NR	NR	NR	-	-
BAPT–Consrv Bapt	7	NR	NR	NR	-	-
BAPT–Converge/BGC	24	10,550	NR	12,660	0.1	0.2
BAPT–Enterprise Bapt Assoc	24	NR	NR	NR	-	-
BAPT–Free Will Bapt	149	NR	10,041	12,272	0.1	0.2
BAPT–Fund Bapt Flwsp	1	NR	NR	NR	-	-
BAPT–Ind Bapt Flwsp Intl	73	NR	NR	NR	-	-
BAPT–N Am Bapt Conf	6	NR	2,179	2,645	0.0	0.1
BAPT–Natl Mis Bapt Conv	54	1,705	7,870	9,574	0.1	0.2
BAPT–NBC Amer	12	1,780	5,800	7,102	0.1	0.1
BAPT–NBC USA	176	27,570	75,151	91,223	0.8	1.8
BAPT–Prim Bapt E Dst	4	100	356	431	0.0	0.0
BAPT–Prog NBC	11	1,900	3,830	4,626	0.0	0.1
BAPT–Ref Bapt Ch	7	NR	NR	NR	-	-
BAPT–Reg Bapt Gen As	152	NR	NR	NR	-	-
BAPT–S-D Baptist Gen Con	1	37	53	65	0.0	0.0
BAPT–So Bapt Conv	668	65,926	140,149	171,951	1.5	3.4
BRETH–Breth in Chr	13	NR	NR	NR	-	-
BRETH–Brethren (Ash)	24	NR	2,290	2,807	0.0	0.1
BRETH–Ch of Brethren	99	6,256	12,838	15,723	0.1	0.3
BRETH–Grace Breth	65	NR	NR	NR	-	-
BUDD–Mahayana	25	NR	NR	9,329	0.1	0.2
BUDD–Theravada	8	NR	NR	1,831	0.0	0.0
BUDD–Vajrayana	9	NR	NR	509	0.0	0.0
Calv Chpl	12	NR	NR	NR	-	-
Catholic	881	NR	NR	1,992,567	17.3	39.3
CGOD–Ch God (Ander)	223	28,224	NR	28,224	0.2	0.6
CGOD–Ches God-Gen Con	32	3,057	3,664	4,510	0.0	0.1
Ch Christ Chr Union	139	NR	NR	NR	-	-
Ch Cr, Scientst	42	NR	NR	NR	-	-
Ch God (7th Day)	2	NR	NR	NR	-	-
Ch of Chr (Hol)	3	NR	NR	NR	-	-
Ch of God Gen Conf	8	NR	382	467	0.0	0.0
Ch of Nazarene	366	49,419	59,752	85,226	0.7	1.7
Chr & Miss Al	120	25,828	14,711	41,258	0.4	0.8
CHR–Chr Ch (Disc)	182	12,908	42,331	51,486	0.4	1.0
CHR–Chr Chs & Chs Cr	466	NR	115,285	141,311	1.2	2.8
CHR–Chs of Christ	402	34,146	33,727	44,859	0.4	0.9
CHR–Int Chs of Christ	5	NR	755	921	0.0	0.0
Christian Brethren	3	NR	NR	NR	-	-
Christian Un	57	NR	NR	NR	-	-
CONG–Cong Chr, NA	25	NR	4,379	5,310	0.0	0.1
CONG–Consrv Cong Chr	23	1,960	3,365	4,088	0.0	0.1
CONG–Midw Cong Chr Fel	11	363	405	505	0.0	0.0
Evan Assoc RCC	8	NR	NR	NR	-	-
Evan Ch	3	NR	NR	NR	-	-
Evan Cong Ch	5	NR	454	546	0.0	0.0
Evan Cov Ch	16	1,870	2,299	2,431	0.0	0.0
Evan Free Ch	24	6,687	NR	6,687	0.1	0.1
FRND–Central Yr Mtg	1	25	0	0	0.0	0.0
FRND–Consrv Yr Mtgs	8	NR	455	540	0.0	0.0
FRND–Evan Fr Ch Intl	49	10,536	5,940	7,188	0.1	0.1
FRND–Fr Gen Cf	22	NR	631	768	0.0	0.0
FRND–Fr Gen Cf & Un Mtg	2	NR	73	89	0.0	0.0

NR–Not Reported   - Represents no adherents reported.   Percentages may not total 100 due to rounding.

Table 2: Religious Congregations by State and Group: 2010

Religious Group	Number of Congregations	Number of Attendees	Number of Communicant, Confirmed, or Full Members	Adherents: Number of Adherents	Adherents: % of Total Pop.	Adherents: % of Total Adh.
FRND–Fr Un Mtg	29	NR	1,353	1,663	0.0	0.0
Grace Gosp Fel	9	NR	NR	NR	-	-
HINDU–I/A Temples	14	NR	NR	13,173	0.1	0.3
HINDU–Post Ren	21	NR	NR	597	0.0	0.0
HINDU–Trad Temples	10	NR	NR	14,982	0.1	0.3
Ind Fund Churches	5	NR	NR	NR	-	-
Int Cou Comm Ch	12	NR	NR	NR	-	-
Jain	4	NR	NR	NR	-	-
Jehovah's Witness	230	NR	NR	NR	-	-
JUD–Conserv	14	5,533	6,210	16,767	0.1	0.3
JUD–Orth	40	13,006	4,870	18,065	0.2	0.4
JUD–Reconst	4	176	224	605	0.0	0.0
JUD–Reform	35	6,099	10,756	29,042	0.3	0.6
LDS–Comm of Christ	34	NR	4,452	4,452	0.0	0.1
LDS–L-D Saints	129	NR	NR	58,605	0.5	1.2
LUTH–Assoc Free Luth	4	NR	NR	NR	-	-
LUTH–Ch of Luth Br	1	355	227	602	0.0	0.0
LUTH–E.L.C.A.	566	63,585	170,924	223,253	1.9	4.4
LUTH–Evan Luth Syn	3	251	541	748	0.0	0.0
LUTH–Luth Ch-Am Asc	3	NR	NR	NR	-	-
LUTH–Luth Cong Msn Chr	29	4,898	13,159	16,116	0.1	0.3
LUTH–Luth-MO Synod	184	24,163	52,876	68,642	0.6	1.4
LUTH–Nor Amer Luth C	47	NR	NR	NR	-	-
LUTH–Wisc Ev Luth Syn	20	1,954	3,268	4,143	0.0	0.1
MENN–Amish Undif	432	NR	26,430	59,103	0.5	1.2
MENN–Beachy Amish-Menn	22	2,731	1,617	2,731	0.0	0.1
MENN–Ber Amish-Menn	2	160	92	160	0.0	0.0
MENN–CG in Cr (Menn)	4	NR	411	504	0.0	0.0
MENN–Cons Menn Conf	24	4,296	3,254	4,116	0.0	0.1
MENN–Fel Evg Ch	9	2,108	1,392	1,721	0.0	0.0
MENN–Menn Chr Fell	2	141	66	141	0.0	0.0
MENN–Mennonite USA	80	9,445	12,011	14,978	0.1	0.3
MENN–Ref Mennonite	3	NR	63	70	0.0	0.0
MENN–Unaffil Amish-Menn	2	162	110	162	0.0	0.0
METH–A.W.M.C.	18	734	310	866	0.0	0.0
METH–AME	113	5,341	20,633	25,097	0.2	0.5
METH–AME Zion	23	1,015	3,691	4,478	0.0	0.1
METH–C.M.E.	25	2,160	6,085	7,388	0.1	0.1
METH–Evan Meth Ch	1	NR	NR	NR	-	-
METH–Free Methodist	39	7,732	4,073	7,876	0.1	0.2
METH–Prim Meth Ch	2	NR	NR	NR	-	-
METH–Un Methodist	1,893	176,511	364,909	496,232	4.3	9.8
METH–Wesleyan	85	8,674	5,502	11,280	0.1	0.2
Metro Comm Ch	3	107	122	149	0.0	0.0
Missionary Ch	37	3,539	2,125	3,573	0.0	0.1
MJEW–Union Mes Cong	2	NR	NR	NR	-	-
MORAV–Morav Ch-North	8	692	1,406	1,672	0.0	0.0
Muslim Est	60	11,246	NR	33,408	0.3	0.7
Nat Spirit Asso	4	NR	NR	NR	-	-
New Apost Ch	16	NR	NR	NR	-	-
Non-denom Chr Chs	1,420	340,269	404,814	468,412	4.1	9.2
OCATH–Pol Natl Cath	4	NR	NR	NR	-	-
ORTHE–Ant Orth of NA	10	1,158	NR	3,661	0.0	0.1
ORTHE–Bulgar Orth USA	2	110	NR	205	0.0	0.0
ORTHE–Carp Rus Orth	6	292	NR	602	0.0	0.0
ORTHE–Greek Orthodox	26	5,843	NR	27,806	0.2	0.5
ORTHE–Macedonian Orth	4	320	NR	1,540	0.0	0.0
ORTHE–Orth Ch in Amer	35	2,940	NR	6,297	0.1	0.1
ORTHE–Romania Orth Ar	1	140	NR	650	0.0	0.0
ORTHE–Rus Orth Abroad	5	217	NR	645	0.0	0.0
ORTHE–Rus Orth Moscow	1	45	NR	80	0.0	0.0
ORTHE–Serb Orth USA	15	1,086	NR	4,749	0.0	0.1
ORTHE–Ukrainian Orth	7	507	NR	2,107	0.0	0.0
ORTHO–Armen Ap Cilic	1	40	NR	100	0.0	0.0
ORTHO–Armen Ap Etchm	2	55	NR	140	0.0	0.0
ORTHO–Coptic Orth Ch	4	1,726	NR	2,715	0.0	0.1
ORTHO–Eritrean Orth	3	335	NR	820	0.0	0.0
ORTHO–Ethiopian Orth	1	NR	NR	NR	-	-
ORTHO–Malan Dioc Am	1	15	NR	45	0.0	0.0
ORTHO–Malan Syr Orth	1	30	NR	54	0.0	0.0
PENT–Assemb of God	285	41,432	23,711	62,230	0.5	1.2
PENT–Assm God Intl F	1	NR	NR	NR	-	-
PENT–Ch God (Cleve)	224	22,736	43,687	53,489	0.5	1.1
PENT–Ch God Mtn Asm	26	NR	NR	NR	-	-

Religious Group	Number of Congregations	Number of Attendees	Number of Communicant, Confirmed, or Full Members	Adherents: Number of Adherents	Adherents: % of Total Pop.	Adherents: % of Total Adh.
PENT–Ch Lord Jesus Apos	17	NR	NR	NR	-	-
PENT–Ch of God Proph	42	NR	1,829	2,234	0.0	0.0
PENT–COGIC	117	6,445	17,214	20,900	0.2	0.4
PENT–Elim	1	NR	NR	NR	-	-
PENT–Fire Bapt Hol Ch	8	NR	NR	NR	-	-
PENT–Full Gosp Bapt	32	NR	NR	NR	-	-
PENT–I F Chr Assmbl	5	NR	NR	NR	-	-
PENT–Int Foursq Gos	42	3,492	3,958	4,837	0.0	0.1
PENT–Int Pent C Chr	24	537	362	1,298	0.0	0.0
PENT–Intl Pent Holiness	24	835	1,571	1,913	0.0	0.0
PENT–Open Bible Std	23	1,525	NR	1,525	0.0	0.0
PENT–Pent Ch of God	34	2,380	NR	3,700	0.0	0.1
PENT–Un Pent Ch Intl	124	NR	NR	NR	-	-
PENT–United Holy Ch	19	NR	NR	NR	-	-
PENT–Vineyard	57	27,172	35,738	44,027	0.4	0.9
Pillar of Fire	1	NR	125	125	0.0	0.0
PRES–Bible Pres	1	NR	NR	NR	-	-
PRES–Cum Pres Am	2	NR	NR	NR	-	-
PRES–Evan Presby Ch	12	NR	3,909	4,727	0.0	0.1
PRES–Kor Pres Abroad	2	NR	NR	NR	-	-
PRES–Korean Amer Pres	2	NR	NR	NR	-	-
PRES–Orth Pres Ch	7	629	686	934	0.0	0.0
PRES–Presb Ch (USA)	560	39,201	89,490	109,232	0.9	2.2
PRES–Presb Ch Amer	20	2,250	2,465	3,105	0.0	0.1
PRES–Ref Pres of NA	2	65	50	68	0.0	0.0
REF–Christian Ref	6	629	692	848	0.0	0.0
REF–Fed Ref Ch	1	NR	NR	NR	-	-
REF–Hung Ref Add'l	1	NR	NR	NR	-	-
REF–Ref Ch in Am	8	1,283	2,191	2,818	0.0	0.1
REF–Ref Ch in U.S.	1	NR	73	92	0.0	0.0
Salvation Army	67	3,093	6,688	21,376	0.2	0.4
Sev Day Adv	139	12,328	21,433	24,655	0.2	0.5
Sikh	13	NR	NR	NR	-	-
Swedenborgian	3	NR	NR	NR	-	-
Un Breth in Cr	44	3,803	3,047	3,256	0.0	0.1
Un C of Christ	366	30,242	96,646	117,783	1.0	2.3
Unit Univ	38	3,279	4,936	6,588	0.1	0.1
Unity Ch	21	NR	NR	NR	-	-
Zoroastrian	2	NR	NR	95	0.0	0.0
OKLAHOMA	**7,057**	**690,853**	**1,550,418**	**2,226,379**	**59.3**	**100.0**
ANG/EPIS–Anglican NA	6	NR	NR	NR	-	-
ANG/EPIS–Episcopal	69	5,585	13,356	15,955	0.4	0.7
Bahá'í	9	NR	1,840	1,840	0.0	0.1
BAPT–Amer Bapt Assn	84	NR	9,152	11,345	0.3	0.5
BAPT–Amer Bapt USA	15	2,104	4,518	5,640	0.2	0.3
BAPT–Asc Ref Bap Ch Am	1	NR	NR	NR	-	-
BAPT–Free Will Bapt	218	NR	20,707	25,619	0.7	1.2
BAPT–Ind Bapt Flwsp Intl	23	NR	NR	NR	-	-
BAPT–N Am Bapt Conf	5	NR	319	394	0.0	0.0
BAPT–Natl Mis Bapt Conv	15	0	2,010	2,485	0.1	0.1
BAPT–NBC Amer	9	1,185	2,335	2,917	0.1	0.1
BAPT–NBC USA	42	6,439	15,827	19,748	0.5	0.9
BAPT–Prog NBC	10	1,855	5,225	6,539	0.2	0.3
BAPT–Ref Bapt Ch	10	NR	NR	NR	-	-
BAPT–Reg Bapt Gen As	1	NR	NR	NR	-	-
BAPT–S-D Baptist Gen Con	2	NR	NR	NR	-	-
BAPT–So Bapt Conv	1,829	202,028	715,396	886,394	23.6	39.8
BRETH–Breth in Chr	2	NR	NR	NR	-	-
BRETH–Ch of Brethren	4	108	351	427	0.0	0.0
BUDD–Mahayana	16	NR	NR	7,490	0.2	0.3
BUDD–Theravada	6	NR	NR	2,083	0.1	0.1
BUDD–Vajrayana	2	NR	NR	46	0.0	0.0
Calv Chpl	5	NR	NR	NR	-	-
Catholic	190	NR	NR	178,430	4.8	8.0
CGOD–Ch God (Ander)	32	7,079	NR	7,079	0.2	0.3
CGOD–Ches God-Gen Con	9	371	632	783	0.0	0.0
Ch Cr, Scientst	12	NR	NR	NR	-	-
Ch God (7th Day)	9	NR	NR	NR	-	-
Ch of Nazarene	187	18,736	30,802	37,278	1.0	1.7
Chr & Miss Al	9	721	921	1,133	0.0	0.1
CHR–Chr Ch (Disc)	175	13,048	35,454	43,928	1.2	2.0
CHR–Chr Chs & Chs Cr	197	NR	28,964	35,809	1.0	1.6
CHR–Chs of Christ	583	59,195	59,809	77,495	2.1	3.5

NR–Not Reported   - Represents no adherents reported.   Percentages may not total 100 due to rounding.

Table 2: Religious Congregations by State and Group: 2010

Religious Group	Number of Congregations	Number of Attendees	Number of Communicant, Confirmed, or Full Members	Adherents		
				Number of Adherents	% of Total Pop.	% of Total Adh.
CHR–Int Chs of Christ	2	NR	105	132	0.0	0.0
Christian Brethren	2	NR	NR	NR	-	-
Christian Un	8	NR	NR	NR	-	-
CONG–Cong Chr, NA	1	NR	30	38	0.0	0.0
Evan Assoc RCC	1	NR	NR	NR	-	-
Evan Cov Ch	6	33,775	10,290	43,907	1.2	2.0
Evan Free Ch	9	502	NR	502	0.0	0.0
FRND–Evan Fr Ch Intl	11	430	509	620	0.0	0.0
FRND–Fr Gen Cf	5	NR	88	107	0.0	0.0
FRND–Fr Un Mtg	2	NR	84	104	0.0	0.0
Grace Gosp Fel	2	NR	NR	NR	-	-
HINDU–I/A Temples	3	NR	NR	916	0.0	0.0
HINDU–Post Ren	7	NR	NR	250	0.0	0.0
HINDU–Trad Temples	2	NR	NR	4,360	0.1	0.2
Ind Fund Churches	6	NR	NR	NR	-	-
Int Cou Comm Ch	1	NR	NR	NR	-	-
Intl Fell Bible Ch	2	NR	NR	NR	-	-
Jain	1	NR	NR	NR	-	-
Jehovah's Witness	97	NR	NR	NR	-	-
JUD–Conserv	2	580	651	1,757	0.0	0.1
JUD–Reform	5	424	747	2,016	0.1	0.1
LDS–Comm of Christ	24	NR	3,660	3,660	0.1	0.2
LDS–L-D Saints	83	NR	NR	43,033	1.1	1.9
LUTH–Assoc Free Luth	2	NR	NR	NR	-	-
LUTH–E.L.C.A.	34	2,465	5,363	6,426	0.2	0.3
LUTH–Luth Cong Msn Chr	2	NR	NR	NR	-	-
LUTH–Luth–MO Synod	82	7,586	16,241	21,622	0.6	1.0
LUTH–Nor Amer Luth C	1	NR	NR	NR	-	-
LUTH–Wisc Ev Luth Syn	4	275	424	554	0.0	0.0
MENN–Amish Undif	6	NR	273	523	0.0	0.0
MENN–Beachy Amish-Menn	1	58	27	58	0.0	0.0
MENN–CG in Cr (Menn)	6	NR	527	643	0.0	0.0
MENN–Cons Menn Conf	2	175	162	201	0.0	0.0
MENN–Fel Evg Bib Ch	3	159	135	159	0.0	0.0
MENN–Menn Br US Conf	14	NR	2,810	3,482	0.1	0.2
MENN–Mennonite USA	13	726	954	1,188	0.0	0.1
METH–AME	42	452	6,933	8,633	0.2	0.4
METH–AME Zion	5	0	600	748	0.0	0.0
METH–C.M.E.	29	230	3,560	4,445	0.1	0.2
METH–Cong Meth	1	NR	17	21	0.0	0.0
METH–Evan Meth Ch	2	NR	NR	NR	-	-
METH–Free Methodist	51	2,967	1,256	3,467	0.1	0.2
METH–Un Methodist	598	58,182	241,977	282,347	7.5	12.7
METH–Wesleyan	16	1,764	1,284	2,295	0.1	0.1
Metro Comm Ch	1	21	35	44	0.0	0.0
Muslim Est	18	3,591	NR	7,392	0.2	0.3
Nat Spirit Asso	1	NR	NR	NR	-	-
New Apost Ch	2	NR	NR	NR	-	-
Non-denom Chr Chs	704	157,913	197,618	220,387	5.9	9.9
ORTHE–Ant Orth of NA	5	604	NR	1,364	0.0	0.1
ORTHE–Greek Orthodox	2	220	NR	515	0.0	0.0
ORTHE–Orth Ch in Amer	2	77	NR	112	0.0	0.0
ORTHE–Rus Orth Abroad	1	48	NR	94	0.0	0.0
ORTHE–Ukrainian Orth	1	35	NR	75	0.0	0.0
ORTHO–Armen Ap Etchm	2	80	NR	160	0.0	0.0
ORTHO–Coptic Orth Ch	2	74	NR	115	0.0	0.0
ORTHO–Ethiopian Orth	1	NR	NR	NR	-	-
ORTHO–Malan Dioc Am	1	40	NR	120	0.0	0.0
ORTHO–Malan Syr Orth	1	75	NR	144	0.0	0.0
PENT–Assemb of God	497	58,119	34,692	85,926	2.3	3.9
PENT–Ch God (Cleve)	76	4,177	5,901	7,309	0.2	0.3
PENT–Ch God Apos Fth	10	NR	NR	NR	-	-
PENT–Ch of God Proph	29	NR	1,513	1,891	0.1	0.1
PENT–COGIC	40	880	4,897	6,106	0.2	0.3
PENT–Full Gosp Bapt	7	NR	NR	NR	-	-
PENT–Int Foursq Gos	20	1,380	1,474	1,828	0.0	0.1
PENT–Intl Pent Holiness	142	10,792	16,211	20,163	0.5	0.9
PENT–Pent Ch of God	84	5,880	NR	9,134	0.2	0.4
PENT–Un Pent Ch Intl	116	NR	NR	NR	-	-
PENT–Vineyard	3	233	225	278	0.0	0.0
PRES–Cum Pres Am	1	NR	NR	NR	-	-
PRES–Cumber Presb	16	NR	600	856	0.0	0.0
PRES–Evan Presby Ch	1	NR	2,125	2,660	0.1	0.1
PRES–Korean Amer Pres	2	NR	NR	NR	-	-

Religious Group	Number of Congregations	Number of Attendees	Number of Communicant, Confirmed, or Full Members	Adherents		
				Number of Adherents	% of Total Pop.	% of Total Adh.
PRES–Korean Pres Amer	1	NR	NR	NR	-	-
PRES–Orth Pres Ch	3	71	92	108	0.0	0.0
PRES–Presb Ch (USA)	134	6,859	20,341	25,267	0.7	1.1
PRES–Presb Ch Amer	10	1,028	1,144	1,361	0.0	0.1
PRES–Ref Pres of NA	2	84	60	98	0.0	0.0
REF–Ref Ch in Am	3	371	693	814	0.0	0.0
Salvation Army	19	1,145	1,755	5,350	0.1	0.2
Sev Day Adv	83	5,450	9,479	10,902	0.3	0.5
Sikh	1	NR	NR	NR	-	-
Un C of Christ	16	1,027	2,497	3,116	0.1	0.1
Unit Univ	10	1,375	2,741	3,603	0.1	0.2
Unity Ch	5	NR	NR	NR	-	-
Zoroastrian	0	NR	NR	16	0.0	0.0
OREGON	**4,026**	**324,981**	**455,240**	**1,194,793**	**31.2**	**100.0**
ANG/EPIS–Anglican NA	4	NR	NR	NR	-	-
ANG/EPIS–Episcopal	96	7,652	16,187	20,348	0.5	1.7
Ap Chr Ch-Amer	2	441	202	441	0.0	0.0
Bahá'í	45	NR	5,281	5,281	0.1	0.4
BAPT–Amer Bapt Assn	20	NR	1,575	1,899	0.0	0.2
BAPT–Amer Bapt USA	42	5,770	9,385	11,329	0.3	0.9
BAPT–Asc Ref Bap Ch Am	2	NR	NR	NR	-	-
BAPT–Consrv Bapt	166	NR	NR	NR	-	-
BAPT–Converge/BGC	16	1,200	NR	1,440	0.0	0.1
BAPT–Free Will Bapt	3	NR	123	150	0.0	0.0
BAPT–Ind Bapt Flwsp Intl	3	NR	NR	NR	-	-
BAPT–N Am Bapt Conf	11	NR	1,557	1,911	0.0	0.2
BAPT–Natl Mis Bapt Conv	3	0	450	543	0.0	0.0
BAPT–NBC Amer	2	225	400	478	0.0	0.0
BAPT–Ref Bapt Ch	8	NR	NR	NR	-	-
BAPT–Reg Bapt Gen As	12	NR	NR	NR	-	-
BAPT–S-D Baptist Gen Con	1	30	28	33	0.0	0.0
BAPT–So Bapt Conv	147	11,328	22,245	26,925	0.7	2.3
BRETH–Breth in Chr	2	NR	NR	NR	-	-
BRETH–Ch of Brethren	4	51	212	261	0.0	0.0
BRETH–Grace Breth	1	NR	NR	NR	-	-
BUDD–Mahayana	41	NR	NR	11,992	0.3	1.0
BUDD–Theravada	4	NR	NR	1,255	0.0	0.1
BUDD–Vajrayana	26	NR	NR	1,538	0.0	0.1
Calv Chpl	57	NR	NR	NR	-	-
Catholic	208	NR	NR	398,738	10.4	33.4
CGOD–Ch God (Ander)	46	4,517	NR	4,517	0.1	0.4
Ch Cr, Scientst	31	NR	NR	NR	-	-
Ch God (7th Day)	5	NR	NR	NR	-	-
Ch of Nazarene	99	12,973	15,259	21,444	0.6	1.8
Chr & Miss Al	23	5,823	3,610	12,254	0.3	1.0
CHR–Chr Ch (Disc)	38	3,502	8,897	10,866	0.3	0.9
CHR–Chr Chs & Chs Cr	151	NR	29,437	35,623	0.9	3.0
CHR–Chs of Christ	116	8,959	8,200	10,955	0.3	0.9
CONG–Cong Chr, NA	2	NR	199	252	0.0	0.0
Evan Ch	41	NR	NR	NR	-	-
Evan Cov Ch	19	3,317	2,398	4,313	0.1	0.4
Evan Free Ch	14	1,898	NR	1,898	0.0	0.2
FRND–Evan Fr Ch Intl	37	2,638	3,704	4,547	0.1	0.4
FRND–Indep Yr Mtgs	11	NR	360	429	0.0	0.0
FRND–Unaffl Mtgs	1	NR	NR	NR	-	-
Grace Gosp Fel	2	NR	NR	NR	-	-
HINDU–I/A Temples	6	NR	NR	5,604	0.1	0.5
HINDU–Post Ren	21	NR	NR	859	0.0	0.1
HINDU–Renaiss	7	NR	NR	186	0.0	0.0
HINDU–Trad Temples	1	NR	NR	2,000	0.1	0.2
Ind Fund Churches	16	NR	NR	NR	-	-
Int Cou Comm Ch	1	NR	NR	NR	-	-
Intl Fell Bible Ch	1	NR	NR	NR	-	-
Jain	2	NR	NR	NR	-	-
Jehovah's Witness	121	NR	NR	NR	-	-
JUD–Conserv	1	864	970	2,619	0.1	0.2
JUD–Orth	8	709	400	985	0.0	0.1
JUD–Reconst	3	643	821	2,217	0.1	0.2
JUD–Reform	4	645	1,137	3,070	0.1	0.3
LDS–Comm of Christ	13	NR	2,132	2,132	0.1	0.2
LDS–L-D Saints	304	NR	NR	147,965	3.9	12.4
LUTH–Apostolic Luth	3	NR	NR	NR	-	-
LUTH–Assoc Free Luth	3	NR	NR	NR	-	-

NR–Not Reported   - Represents no adherents reported.   Percentages may not total 100 due to rounding.

Table 2: Religious Congregations by State and Group: 2010

Religious Group	Number of Congrega-tions	Number of Attendees	Number of Communicant, Confirmed, or Full Members	Adherents: Number of Adherents	Adherents: % of Total Pop.	Adherents: % of Total Adh.
LUTH–Ch of Luth Br	3	193	109	303	0.0	0.0
LUTH–E.L.C.A.	117	11,913	27,331	35,764	0.9	3.0
LUTH–Evan Luth Syn	10	297	514	657	0.0	0.1
LUTH–Luth Cong Msn Chr	7	485	725	899	0.0	0.1
LUTH–Luth–MO Synod	87	8,162	14,135	18,092	0.5	1.5
LUTH–Nor Amer Luth C	2	NR	NR	NR	-	-
LUTH–Wisc Ev Luth Syn	11	516	953	1,190	0.0	0.1
MENN–CG in Cr (Menn)	2	NR	142	174	0.0	0.0
MENN–Cons Menn Conf	1	200	196	241	0.0	0.0
MENN–Fel Evg Bib Ch	1	504	504	504	0.0	0.0
MENN–Hutt Breth	1	NR	NR	NR	-	-
MENN–Menn Br US Conf	10	NR	3,477	4,222	0.1	0.4
MENN–Mennonite USA	24	1,955	2,016	2,472	0.1	0.2
METH–AME	2	275	400	478	0.0	0.0
METH–AME Zion	2	0	250	308	0.0	0.0
METH–C.M.E.	3	100	350	417	0.0	0.0
METH–Evan Meth Ch	3	NR	NR	NR	-	-
METH–Free Methodist	29	3,383	2,336	3,560	0.1	0.3
METH–Un Methodist	166	10,003	20,298	29,406	0.8	2.5
METH–Wesleyan	12	827	483	1,077	0.0	0.1
Metro Comm Ch	1	203	251	300	0.0	0.0
Missionary Ch	5	326	238	337	0.0	0.0
MJEW–Union Mes Cong	1	NR	NR	NR	-	-
Muslim Est	12	1,974	NR	3,988	0.1	0.3
New Apost Ch	3	NR	NR	NR	-	-
Non-denom Chr Chs	443	99,987	118,968	137,748	3.6	11.5
OCATH–Un Cath Ch	1	NR	NR	702	0.0	0.1
ORTHE–Ant Orth of NA	1	175	NR	500	0.0	0.0
ORTHE–Greek Orthodox	3	615	NR	2,750	0.1	0.2
ORTHE–Holy Orth in NA	1	77	NR	100	0.0	0.0
ORTHE–Orth Ch in Amer	7	649	NR	1,211	0.0	0.1
ORTHE–Rus Orth Abroad	3	144	NR	560	0.0	0.0
ORTHE–Serb Orth USA	3	160	NR	690	0.0	0.1
ORTHE–Ukrainian Orth	1	65	NR	120	0.0	0.0
ORTHO–Armen Ap Etchm	1	75	NR	800	0.0	0.1
ORTHO–Coptic Orth Ch	1	50	NR	100	0.0	0.0
ORTHO–Eritrean Orth	2	325	NR	205	0.0	0.0
ORTHO–Ethiopian Orth	1	NR	NR	NR	-	-
ORTHO–Syrian Orth Ch	1	85	NR	280	0.0	0.0
PENT–Apos Faith Msn	5	NR	955	1,141	0.0	0.1
PENT–Assemb of God	223	27,925	16,068	45,492	1.2	3.8
PENT–Ch God (Cleve)	37	2,686	3,483	4,195	0.1	0.4
PENT–Ch God Apos Fth	1	NR	NR	NR	-	-
PENT–Ch of God Proph	21	NR	596	731	0.0	0.1
PENT–COGIC	12	835	1,880	2,247	0.1	0.2
PENT–Cong Hol Ch	1	39	35	44	0.0	0.0
PENT–Full Gosp Bapt	4	NR	NR	NR	-	-
PENT–Int Foursq Gos	115	28,292	31,202	37,670	1.0	3.2
PENT–Intl Pent Holiness	10	652	372	454	0.0	0.0
PENT–Open Bible Std	24	2,452	NR	2,452	0.1	0.2
PENT–Pent Ch of God	32	2,240	NR	3,482	0.1	0.3
PENT–Un Pent Ch Intl	47	NR	NR	NR	-	-
PENT–Vineyard	12	1,772	2,317	2,821	0.1	0.2
PRES–Bible Pres	1	NR	NR	NR	-	-
PRES–Evan Presby Ch	4	NR	1,904	2,358	0.1	0.2
PRES–Kor Pres Abroad	1	NR	NR	NR	-	-
PRES–Korean Amer Pres	2	NR	NR	NR	-	-
PRES–Korean Pres Amer	3	NR	NR	NR	-	-
PRES–Orth Pres Ch	7	604	566	718	0.0	0.1
PRES–Presb Ch (USA)	127	11,953	20,107	24,307	0.6	2.0
PRES–Presb Ch Amer	7	603	594	672	0.0	0.1
REF–Christian Ref	8	640	824	1,016	0.0	0.1
REF–Comm Ref Evan	3	NR	NR	NR	-	-
REF–Un Ref Chs N.A.	2	NR	NR	NR	-	-
Salvation Army	17	913	1,285	3,475	0.1	0.3
Sev Day Adv	159	20,081	34,920	40,162	1.0	3.4
Sikh	5	NR	NR	NR	-	-
Tao	1	NR	NR	NR	-	-
Un Breth in Cr	1	45	48	39	0.0	0.0
Un C of Christ	36	3,615	5,997	7,247	0.2	0.6
Unit Univ	21	2,726	3,242	4,596	0.1	0.4
Unity Ch	16	NR	NR	NR	-	-
Zoroastrian	0	NR	NR	22	0.0	0.0

Religious Group	Number of Congrega-tions	Number of Attendees	Number of Communicant, Confirmed, or Full Members	Adherents: Number of Adherents	Adherents: % of Total Pop.	Adherents: % of Total Adh.
PENNSYLVANIA	**15,359**	**1,280,678**	**2,268,785**	**6,838,440**	**53.8**	**100.0**
ANG/EPIS–Anglican NA	72	NR	NR	NR	-	-
ANG/EPIS–Episcopal	331	27,352	68,093	84,482	0.7	1.2
Ap Chr Ch-Amer	1	76	37	76	0.0	0.0
Bahá'í	12	NR	1,884	1,884	0.0	0.0
BAPT–Alliance Bapt	1	NR	NR	NR	-	-
BAPT–Amer Bapt Assn	5	NR	300	362	0.0	0.0
BAPT–Amer Bapt USA	416	72,190	115,214	138,255	1.1	2.0
BAPT–Asc Ref Bap Ch Am	6	NR	NR	NR	-	-
BAPT–Consrv Bapt	54	NR	NR	NR	-	-
BAPT–Converge/BGC	18	3,125	NR	3,750	0.0	0.1
BAPT–Free Will Bapt	3	NR	179	214	0.0	0.0
BAPT–Fund Bapt Flwsp	2	NR	NR	NR	-	-
BAPT–Ind Bapt Flwsp Intl	7	NR	NR	NR	-	-
BAPT–N Am Bapt Conf	11	NR	2,290	2,752	0.0	0.0
BAPT–Natl Mis Bapt Conv	5	100	500	605	0.0	0.0
BAPT–NBC Amer	8	985	1,610	1,964	0.0	0.0
BAPT–NBC USA	100	19,255	38,578	46,489	0.4	0.7
BAPT–Prog NBC	21	1,970	4,990	6,028	0.0	0.1
BAPT–Ref Bapt Ch	24	NR	NR	NR	-	-
BAPT–Reg Bapt Gen As	59	NR	NR	NR	-	-
BAPT–S-D Baptist Gen Con	3	111	145	174	0.0	0.0
BAPT–So Bapt Conv	381	41,164	49,885	60,116	0.5	0.9
BRETH–Breth in Chr	112	NR	NR	NR	-	-
BRETH–Brethren (Ash)	17	NR	1,360	1,605	0.0	0.0
BRETH–Ch of Brethren	241	19,639	37,750	45,418	0.4	0.7
BRETH–Grace Breth	57	NR	NR	NR	-	-
BRETH–Old Ord Rvr Br	4	NR	306	537	0.0	0.0
BRETH–United Zion Ch	12	NR	585	721	0.0	0.0
BUDD–Mahayana	41	NR	NR	14,285	0.1	0.2
BUDD–Theravada	7	NR	NR	3,547	0.0	0.1
BUDD–Vajrayana	15	NR	NR	1,530	0.0	0.0
Calv Chpl	22	NR	NR	NR	-	-
Catholic	1,365	NR	NR	3,503,028	27.6	51.2
CGOD–Ch God (Ander)	89	12,392	NR	12,392	0.1	0.2
CGOD–Ches God-Gen Con	158	14,507	17,530	21,059	0.2	0.3
Ch Christ Chr Union	5	NR	NR	NR	-	-
Ch Cr, Scientst	31	NR	NR	NR	-	-
Ch God (7th Day)	2	NR	NR	NR	-	-
Ch of Nazarene	159	14,121	16,417	25,986	0.2	0.4
Chr & Miss Al	245	32,620	20,650	50,899	0.4	0.7
CHR–Chr Ch (Disc)	63	2,081	10,949	12,968	0.1	0.2
CHR–Chr Chs & Chs Cr	121	NR	19,183	22,658	0.2	0.3
CHR–Chs of Christ	138	8,191	7,894	10,595	0.1	0.2
CHR–Int Chs of Christ	6	NR	962	1,155	0.0	0.0
Christian Brethren	19	NR	NR	NR	-	-
CONG–Cong Chr Add'l	4	NR	310	374	0.0	0.0
CONG–Cong Chr, NA	6	NR	307	364	0.0	0.0
CONG–Consrv Cong Chr	21	1,487	2,556	3,063	0.0	0.0
Evan Assoc RCC	22	NR	NR	NR	-	-
Evan Ch	9	NR	NR	NR	-	-
Evan Cong Ch	114	NR	15,800	19,146	0.2	0.3
Evan Cov Ch	18	1,410	2,166	1,834	0.0	0.0
Evan Free Ch	63	19,091	NR	19,091	0.2	0.3
FRND–Consrv Yr Mtgs	1	NR	10	12	0.0	0.0
FRND–Evan Fr Ch Intl	3	443	241	290	0.0	0.0
FRND–Fr Gen Cf	88	NR	8,526	10,354	0.1	0.2
FRND–Fr Gen Cf & Un Mtg	11	NR	706	835	0.0	0.0
Grace Gosp Fel	4	NR	NR	NR	-	-
HINDU–I/A Temples	16	NR	NR	25,212	0.2	0.4
HINDU–Post Ren	22	NR	NR	4,556	0.0	0.1
HINDU–Renaiss	3	NR	NR	36	0.0	0.0
HINDU–Trad Temples	10	NR	NR	13,948	0.1	0.2
Ind Fund Churches	37	NR	NR	NR	-	-
Int Cou Comm Ch	4	NR	NR	NR	-	-
Intl Fell Bible Ch	3	NR	NR	NR	-	-
Jain	6	NR	NR	NR	-	-
Jehovah's Witness	245	NR	NR	NR	-	-
JUD–Conserv	41	11,685	13,115	35,412	0.3	0.5
JUD–Orth	59	16,036	6,375	22,275	0.2	0.3
JUD–Reconst	13	1,660	2,121	5,726	0.0	0.1
JUD–Reform	46	8,168	14,407	38,899	0.3	0.6
LDS–Comm of Christ	14	NR	2,227	2,227	0.0	0.0
LDS–L-D Saints	108	NR	NR	49,794	0.4	0.7

NR–Not Reported   - Represents no adherents reported.   Percentages may not total 100 due to rounding.

Table 2: Religious Congregations by State and Group: 2010

Religious Group	Number of Congrega-tions	Number of Attendees	Number of Communicant, Confirmed, or Full Members	Adherents		
				Number of Adherents	% of Total Pop.	% of Total Adh.
LUTH–Assoc Free Luth	10	NR	NR	NR	-	-
LUTH–Ch of Luth Br	3	363	330	965	0.0	0.0
LUTH–E.L.C.A.	1,242	113,935	379,301	501,974	4.0	7.3
LUTH–Evan Luth Syn	1	21	14	22	0.0	0.0
LUTH–Luth Ch-Am Asc	2	NR	NR	NR	-	-
LUTH–Luth Cong Msn Chr	12	1,436	5,934	7,162	0.1	0.1
LUTH–Luth–MO Synod	84	6,337	13,928	17,861	0.1	0.3
LUTH–Nor Amer Luth C	32	NR	NR	NR	-	-
LUTH–Wisc Ev Luth Syn	4	193	334	402	0.0	0.0
MENN–Amish Undif	397	NR	24,721	58,009	0.5	0.8
MENN–Beachy Amish-Menn	14	2,523	1,575	2,523	0.0	0.0
MENN–Bible Flwshp	44	8,807	NR	11,892	0.1	0.2
MENN–Bruderhof Comm	2	534	255	434	0.0	0.0
MENN–CG in Cr (Menn)	5	NR	512	615	0.0	0.0
MENN–Cons Menn Conf	12	1,594	1,595	1,922	0.0	0.0
MENN–Mara Amish-Menn	2	409	235	409	0.0	0.0
MENN–Menn Chr Fell	5	676	339	676	0.0	0.0
MENN–Mennonite USA	248	24,914	28,160	34,344	0.3	0.5
MENN–Ref Mennonite	3	NR	115	125	0.0	0.0
MENN–Unaffil Amish-Menn	5	676	401	676	0.0	0.0
METH–A.W.M.C.	49	1,614	741	2,126	0.0	0.0
METH–AME	150	7,723	26,001	31,195	0.2	0.5
METH–AME Zion	51	1,224	5,719	6,846	0.1	0.1
METH–C.M.E.	13	145	2,156	2,603	0.0	0.0
METH–Evan Meth Ch	3	NR	NR	NR	-	-
METH–Free Methodist	96	5,962	4,430	6,288	0.0	0.1
METH–Prim Meth Ch	36	NR	NR	NR	-	-
METH–Un Methodist	2,241	170,428	455,172	591,734	4.7	8.7
METH–Wesleyan	78	9,165	6,449	11,919	0.1	0.2
Metro Comm Ch	6	333	382	558	0.0	0.0
Missionary Ch	14	1,185	816	1,234	0.0	0.0
MJEW–Assoc Mes Cong	1	NR	NR	NR	-	-
MJEW–Union Mes Cong	2	NR	NR	NR	-	-
MORAV–Morav Ch-North	23	2,588	6,188	7,610	0.1	0.1
Muslim Est	99	25,839	NR	80,487	0.6	1.2
Nat Spirit Asso	3	NR	NR	NR	-	-
New Apost Ch	14	NR	NR	NR	-	-
Non-denom Chr Chs	1,532	278,826	316,441	384,912	3.0	5.6
OCATH–Pol Natl Cath	31	NR	NR	NR	-	-
ORTHE–Ant Orth of NA	20	2,365	NR	6,688	0.1	0.1
ORTHE–Bulgar Orth USA	1	15	NR	80	0.0	0.0
ORTHE–Carp Rus Orth	34	2,341	NR	4,513	0.0	0.1
ORTHE–Georgian Orth	2	75	NR	310	0.0	0.0
ORTHE–Greek Orthodox	37	6,015	NR	18,685	0.1	0.3
ORTHE–Holy Orth in NA	2	97	NR	127	0.0	0.0
ORTHE–Macedonian Orth	1	6	NR	50	0.0	0.0
ORTHE–Orth Ch in Amer	83	4,889	NR	9,430	0.1	0.1
ORTHE–Romania Orth Ar	2	100	NR	600	0.0	0.0
ORTHE–Rus Orth Abroad	9	893	NR	1,162	0.0	0.0
ORTHE–Rus Orth Moscow	8	519	NR	1,910	0.0	0.0
ORTHE–Serb Orth USA	13	741	NR	4,359	0.0	0.1
ORTHE–Ukrainian Orth	24	1,688	NR	4,620	0.0	0.1
ORTHO–Armen Ap Cilic	1	200	NR	3,000	0.0	0.0
ORTHO–Armen Ap Etchm	3	325	NR	1,050	0.0	0.0
ORTHO–Coptic Orth Ch	8	895	NR	1,540	0.0	0.0
ORTHO–Eritrean Orth	1	25	NR	260	0.0	0.0
ORTHO–Ethiopian Orth	1	NR	NR	NR	-	-
ORTHO–Malan Dioc Am	6	1,295	NR	2,100	0.0	0.0
ORTHO–Malan Syr Orth	2	295	NR	558	0.0	0.0
PENT–Apos Faith Msn	1	NR	35	42	0.0	0.0
PENT–Assemb of God	381	63,869	38,626	106,689	0.8	1.6
PENT–Assm God Intl F	1	NR	NR	NR	-	-
PENT–Ch God (Cleve)	120	11,376	15,584	18,752	0.1	0.3
PENT–Ch Lord Jesus Apos	14	NR	NR	NR	-	-
PENT–Ch of God by Faith	3	NR	NR	NR	-	-
PENT–Ch of God Proph	30	NR	1,472	1,766	0.0	0.0
PENT–COGIC	86	6,230	15,467	18,607	0.1	0.3
PENT–Cong Hol Ch	2	78	70	84	0.0	0.0
PENT–Elim	16	NR	NR	NR	-	-
PENT–Fire Bapt Hol Ch	11	NR	NR	NR	-	-
PENT–Full Gosp Bapt	28	NR	NR	NR	-	-
PENT–I F Chr Assmbl	16	NR	NR	NR	-	-
PENT–Int Foursq Gos	22	1,230	1,206	1,448	0.0	0.0
PENT–Intl Pent Holiness	22	1,525	1,899	2,271	0.0	0.0

Religious Group	Number of Congrega-tions	Number of Attendees	Number of Communicant, Confirmed, or Full Members	Adherents		
				Number of Adherents	% of Total Pop.	% of Total Adh.
PENT–Open Bible Std	6	301	NR	301	0.0	0.0
PENT–Pent Ch of God	3	210	NR	327	0.0	0.0
PENT–Pent FW Bapt	1	NR	NR	NR	-	-
PENT–Un Pent Ch Intl	49	NR	NR	NR	-	-
PENT–United Holy Ch	22	NR	NR	NR	-	-
PENT–Vineyard	10	1,695	2,256	2,736	0.0	0.0
PRES–AmPres	1	NR	NR	NR	-	-
PRES–As Ref Pres Ch	4	NR	189	223	0.0	0.0
PRES–Bible Pres	1	NR	NR	NR	-	-
PRES–Cumber Presb	1	NR	100	96	0.0	0.0
PRES–Evan Presby Ch	18	NR	5,740	6,817	0.1	0.1
PRES–Free Pres NA	2	NR	NR	NR	-	-
PRES–Kor Pres Abroad	4	NR	NR	NR	-	-
PRES–Korean Amer Pres	8	NR	NR	NR	-	-
PRES–Korean Pres Amer	26	NR	NR	NR	-	-
PRES–Orth Pres Ch	34	2,443	2,328	3,056	0.0	0.0
PRES–Presb Ch (USA)	1,011	83,604	202,369	241,659	1.9	3.5
PRES–Presb Ch Amer	112	16,061	18,503	23,331	0.2	0.3
PRES–Ref Pres of NA	16	1,327	1,156	1,532	0.0	0.0
REF–Can Amer Ref	1	NR	NR	NR	-	-
REF–Christian Ref	11	473	404	490	0.0	0.0
REF–Comm Ref Evan	1	NR	NR	NR	-	-
REF–Hung Ref Add'l	4	NR	NR	NR	-	-
REF–Ref Ch in Am	11	1,089	1,753	2,076	0.0	0.0
REF–Ref Ch in U.S.	1	NR	20	27	0.0	0.0
REF–Un Ref Chs N.A.	2	NR	NR	NR	-	-
Salvation Army	89	4,341	9,071	31,161	0.2	0.5
Schwenkfelder	4	NR	2,227	2,695	0.0	0.0
Sev Day Adv	152	10,692	18,596	21,391	0.2	0.3
Sikh	6	NR	NR	NR	-	-
Swedenborgian	1	NR	NR	NR	-	-
Tao	1	NR	NR	NR	-	-
Un Breth in Cr	31	5,658	5,821	4,821	0.0	0.1
Un C of Christ	627	44,760	149,448	180,248	1.4	2.6
Unit Univ	38	3,628	6,043	7,936	0.1	0.1
Unity Ch	9	NR	NR	NR	-	-
Zoroastrian	1	NR	NR	311	0.0	0.0
RHODE ISLAND	**677**	**42,181**	**69,563**	**576,919**	**54.8**	**100.0**
ANG/EPIS–Episcopal	54	5,523	14,480	19,377	1.8	3.4
Bahá'í	2	NR	273	273	0.0	0.0
BAPT–Alliance Bapt	1	NR	NR	NR	-	-
BAPT–Amer Bapt USA	75	5,337	12,778	15,220	1.4	2.6
BAPT–Consrv Bapt	8	NR	NR	NR	-	-
BAPT–Converge/BGC	1	75	NR	90	0.0	0.0
BAPT–Free Will Bapt	1	NR	101	118	0.0	0.0
BAPT–Ref Bapt Ch	1	NR	NR	NR	-	-
BAPT–Reg Bapt Gen As	1	NR	NR	NR	-	-
BAPT–S-D Baptist Gen Con	4	87	246	289	0.0	0.1
BAPT–So Bapt Conv	15	692	907	1,071	0.1	0.2
BUDD–Mahayana	9	NR	NR	713	0.1	0.1
BUDD–Theravada	4	NR	NR	1,487	0.1	0.3
BUDD–Vajrayana	3	NR	NR	116	0.0	0.0
Calv Chpl	1	NR	NR	NR	-	-
Catholic	159	NR	NR	466,598	44.3	80.9
CGOD–Ch God (Ander)	2	165	NR	165	0.0	0.0
Ch Cr, Scientist	4	NR	NR	NR	-	-
Ch of Nazarene	7	525	602	693	0.1	0.1
Chr & Miss Al	3	392	385	551	0.1	0.1
CHR–Chr Chs & Chs Cr	3	NR	0	0	0.0	0.0
CHR–Chs of Christ	7	455	451	644	0.1	0.1
CONG–Cong Chr Add'l	2	NR	863	1,013	0.1	0.2
CONG–Cong Chr, NA	1	NR	25	30	0.0	0.0
CONG–Consrv Cong Chr	2	290	468	556	0.1	0.1
Evan Cov Ch	4	853	587	1,108	0.1	0.2
Evan Free Ch	1	20	NR	20	0.0	0.0
FRND–Evan Fr Ch Intl	2	361	145	170	0.0	0.0
FRND–Fr Gen Cf & Un Mtg	5	NR	328	392	0.0	0.1
HINDU–Post Ren	1	NR	NR	25	0.0	0.0
HINDU–Renaiss	1	NR	NR	84	0.0	0.0
Jehovah's Witness	14	NR	NR	NR	-	-
JUD–Conserv	4	1,134	1,272	3,434	0.3	0.6
JUD–Orth	8	1,137	590	1,580	0.2	0.3
JUD–Reform	4	804	1,419	3,831	0.4	0.7

NR–Not Reported - Represents no adherents reported. Percentages may not total 100 due to rounding.

Table 2: Religious Congregations by State and Group: 2010

Religious Group	Number of Congrega-tions	Number of Attendees	Number of Communicant, Confirmed, or Full Members	Adherents		
				Number of Adherents	% of Total Pop.	% of Total Adh.
LDS–Comm of Christ	2	NR	204	204	0.0	0.0
LDS–L-D Saints	7	NR	NR	3,833	0.4	0.7
LUTH–Ch of Luth Br	1	47	30	82	0.0	0.0
LUTH–E.L.C.A.	13	1,490	3,836	5,261	0.5	0.9
LUTH–Luth–MO Synod	3	431	824	1,015	0.1	0.2
METH–AME	3	75	425	507	0.0	0.1
METH–AME Zion	2	0	250	300	0.0	0.1
METH–Free Methodist	1	348	159	348	0.0	0.1
METH–Prim Meth Ch	4	NR	NR	NR	-	-
METH–Un Methodist	23	1,814	5,513	6,901	0.7	1.2
Missionary Ch	1	15	14	15	0.0	0.0
Muslim Est	6	588	NR	1,444	0.1	0.3
New Apost Ch	1	NR	NR	NR	-	-
Non-denom Chr Chs	37	7,466	7,823	9,604	0.9	1.7
OCATH–Pol Natl Cath	2	NR	NR	NR	-	-
ORTHE–Ant Orth of NA	1	105	NR	450	0.0	0.1
ORTHE–Greek Orthodox	3	620	NR	2,625	0.2	0.5
ORTHE–Orth Ch in Amer	2	95	NR	525	0.0	0.1
ORTHE–Ukrainian Orth	1	80	NR	175	0.0	0.0
ORTHO–Armen Ap Cilic	1	200	NR	2,500	0.2	0.4
ORTHO–Armen Ap Etchm	1	175	NR	500	0.0	0.1
ORTHO–Coptic Orth Ch	1	275	NR	450	0.0	0.1
ORTHO–Syrian Orth Ch	1	80	NR	400	0.0	0.1
PENT–Assemb of God	31	3,417	2,045	4,666	0.4	0.8
PENT–Ch God (Cleve)	25	1,436	1,550	1,858	0.2	0.3
PENT–Ch Lord Jesus Apos	1	NR	NR	NR	-	-
PENT–Ch of God Proph	4	NR	121	145	0.0	0.0
PENT–COGIC	1	15	18	22	0.0	0.0
PENT–Full Gosp Bapt	2	NR	NR	NR	-	-
PENT–Int Foursq Gos	1	107	52	62	0.0	0.0
PENT–Un Pent Ch Intl	9	NR	NR	NR	-	-
PENT–United Holy Ch	1	NR	NR	NR	-	-
PRES–Pres Ref	1	NR	NR	NR	-	-
PRES–Presb Ch (USA)	9	919	1,784	2,109	0.2	0.4
PRES–Presb Ch Amer	2	210	203	265	0.0	0.0
PRES–Ref Pres of NA	1	40	30	50	0.0	0.0
REF–Christian Ref	1	NR	0	0	0.0	0.0
Salvation Army	4	175	400	840	0.1	0.1
Sev Day Adv	17	908	1,580	1,817	0.2	0.3
Un C of Christ	28	2,522	5,711	6,800	0.6	1.2
Unit Univ	8	678	1,071	1,486	0.1	0.3
Zoroastrian	0	NR	NR	12	0.0	0.0
SOUTH CAROLINA	**8,051**	**867,878**	**1,782,676**	**2,413,443**	**52.2**	**100.0**
ANG/EPIS–Anglican NA	54	NR	NR	NR	-	-
ANG/EPIS–Episcopal	130	20,118	47,215	54,615	1.2	2.3
Bahá'í	22	NR	17,559	17,559	0.4	0.7
BAPT–Alliance Bapt	4	NR	NR	NR	-	-
BAPT–Amer Bapt Assn	6	NR	475	584	0.0	0.0
BAPT–Amer Bapt USA	2	535	770	934	0.0	0.0
BAPT–Asc Ref Bap Ch Am	1	NR	NR	NR	-	-
BAPT–Consrv Bapt	1	NR	NR	NR	-	-
BAPT–Free Will Bapt	118	NR	4,712	5,770	0.1	0.2
BAPT–Fund Bapt Flwsp	2	NR	NR	NR	-	-
BAPT–Ind Bapt Flwsp Intl	4	NR	NR	NR	-	-
BAPT–Natl Mis Bapt Conv	27	531	4,005	4,845	0.1	0.2
BAPT–NBC Amer	12	1,515	4,110	4,976	0.1	0.2
BAPT–NBC USA	185	20,862	53,212	64,925	1.4	2.7
BAPT–NT Ind Bapt	1	NR	NR	NR	-	-
BAPT–Orig Free Will Bapt	2	180	246	292	0.0	0.0
BAPT–Prog NBC	44	11,423	19,605	23,963	0.5	1.0
BAPT–Ref Bapt Ch	6	NR	NR	NR	-	-
BAPT–Reg Bapt Gen As	1	NR	NR	NR	-	-
BAPT–S-D Baptist Gen Con	3	NR	NR	NR	-	-
BAPT–So Bapt Conv	2,110	312,726	747,718	913,763	19.8	37.9
BRETH–Ch of Brethren	1	42	60	74	0.0	0.0
BRETH–Grace Breth	2	NR	NR	NR	-	-
BUDD–Mahayana	5	NR	NR	2,148	0.0	0.1
BUDD–Theravada	2	NR	NR	695	0.0	0.0
BUDD–Vajrayana	4	NR	NR	521	0.0	0.0
Calv Chpl	14	NR	NR	NR	-	-
Catholic	119	NR	NR	181,743	3.9	7.5
CGOD–Ch God (Ander)	39	2,415	NR	2,415	0.1	0.1
CGOD–Ches God-Gen Con	2	0	0	0	0.0	0.0
Ch Cr, Scientst	11	NR	NR	NR	-	-
Ch of God Gen Conf	4	NR	323	399	0.0	0.0
Ch of Nazarene	66	6,528	9,999	11,886	0.3	0.5
Chr & Miss Al	13	2,044	1,201	2,615	0.1	0.1
CHR–Chr Ch (Disc)	43	2,527	5,359	6,591	0.1	0.3
CHR–Chr Chs & Chs Cr	35	NR	4,027	4,919	0.1	0.2
CHR–Chs of Christ	127	10,958	10,655	13,816	0.3	0.6
CHR–Int Chs of Christ	3	NR	458	562	0.0	0.0
Christian Brethren	2	NR	NR	NR	-	-
Evan Cov Ch	1	43	6	56	0.0	0.0
Evan Free Ch	3	290	NR	290	0.0	0.0
FRND–Consrv Yr Mtgs	2	NR	0	0	0.0	0.0
FRND–Fr Gen Cf	8	NR	30	36	0.0	0.0
HINDU–Post Ren	6	NR	NR	169	0.0	0.0
HINDU–Trad Temples	4	NR	NR	3,816	0.1	0.2
Ind Fund Churches	2	NR	NR	NR	-	-
Int Cou Comm Ch	1	NR	NR	NR	-	-
Intl Fell Bible Ch	1	NR	NR	NR	-	-
Jehovah's Witness	93	NR	NR	NR	-	-
JUD–Conserv	4	693	778	2,100	0.0	0.1
JUD–Orth	6	424	280	590	0.0	0.0
JUD–Reform	9	801	1,415	3,820	0.1	0.2
LDS–Comm of Christ	4	NR	472	472	0.0	0.0
LDS–L-D Saints	64	NR	NR	37,391	0.8	1.5
LUTH–Apostolic Luth	2	NR	NR	NR	-	-
LUTH–Ch Luth Conf	1	NR	NR	NR	-	-
LUTH–E.L.C.A.	163	19,402	40,703	53,916	1.2	2.2
LUTH–Luth Cong Msn Chr	8	711	1,223	1,488	0.0	0.1
LUTH–Luth–MO Synod	17	1,784	2,511	3,039	0.1	0.1
LUTH–Nor Amer Luth C	4	NR	NR	NR	-	-
LUTH–Wisc Ev Luth Syn	4	497	556	812	0.0	0.0
MENN–Beachy Amish-Menn	3	363	218	363	0.0	0.0
MENN–Cons Menn Conf	1	34	19	23	0.0	0.0
METH–AME	564	21,741	99,489	120,854	2.6	5.0
METH–AME Zion	138	1,625	17,890	21,956	0.5	0.9
METH–C.M.E.	42	1,420	6,479	7,937	0.2	0.3
METH–Free Methodist	2	102	50	102	0.0	0.0
METH–So Methodist	54	NR	NR	NR	-	-
METH–Un Methodist	1,016	93,718	235,850	274,111	5.9	11.4
METH–Wesleyan	62	4,197	4,113	5,463	0.1	0.2
Metro Comm Ch	2	112	119	144	0.0	0.0
Missionary Ch	5	315	230	340	0.0	0.0
MJEW–Union Mes Cong	1	NR	NR	NR	-	-
Muslim Est	21	2,531	NR	5,792	0.1	0.2
New Apost Ch	3	NR	NR	NR	-	-
Non-denom Chr Chs	826	178,320	201,662	241,583	5.2	10.0
ORTHE–Ant Orth of NA	4	138	NR	220	0.0	0.0
ORTHE–Greek Orthodox	8	1,305	NR	4,333	0.1	0.2
ORTHE–Orth Ch in Amer	6	366	NR	499	0.0	0.0
ORTHE–Rus Orth Abroad	2	80	NR	175	0.0	0.0
ORTHO–Coptic Orth Ch	2	175	NR	330	0.0	0.0
PENT–Apos Faith Msn	4	NR	140	171	0.0	0.0
PENT–Assemb of God	118	14,483	9,953	21,606	0.5	0.9
PENT–Ch God (Cleve)	293	30,407	50,691	62,068	1.3	2.6
PENT–Ch Lord Jesus Apos	38	NR	NR	NR	-	-
PENT–Ch of God by Faith	10	NR	NR	NR	-	-
PENT–Ch of God Proph	117	NR	4,721	5,790	0.1	0.2
PENT–COGIC	36	2,395	5,514	6,722	0.1	0.3
PENT–Cong Hol Ch	18	1,247	1,257	1,539	0.0	0.1
PENT–Elim	1	NR	NR	NR	-	-
PENT–Fire Bapt Hol Ch	53	NR	NR	NR	-	-
PENT–Full Gosp Bapt	8	NR	NR	NR	-	-
PENT–Int Foursq Gos	9	522	658	817	0.0	0.0
PENT–Intl Pent Holiness	259	36,373	45,833	56,230	1.2	2.3
PENT–Pent FW Bapt	2	NR	NR	NR	-	-
PENT–Un Pent Asbl God	8	NR	NR	NR	-	-
PENT–Un Pent Ch Intl	46	NR	NR	NR	-	-
PENT–United Holy Ch	4	NR	NR	NR	-	-
PENT–Vineyard	5	721	833	1,000	0.0	0.0
PRES–As Ref Pres Ch	65	NR	8,609	10,567	0.2	0.4
PRES–Bible Pres	1	NR	NR	NR	-	-
PRES–Evan Presby Ch	7	NR	889	1,086	0.0	0.0
PRES–Free Ch Scot	1	NR	NR	NR	-	-
PRES–Free Pres NA	3	NR	NR	NR	-	-

NR–Not Reported - Represents no adherents reported. Percentages may not total 100 due to rounding.

Table 2: Religious Congregations by State and Group: 2010

Religious Group	Number of Congrega-tions	Number of Attendees	Number of Communicant, Confirmed, or Full Members	Adherents		
				Number of Adherents	% of Total Pop.	% of Total Adh.
PRES–Kor Pres Abroad	2	NR	NR	NR	-	-
PRES–Orth Pres Ch	2	112	89	125	0.0	0.0
PRES–Presb Ch (USA)	318	34,889	74,690	91,064	2.0	3.8
PRES–Presb Ch Amer	110	15,308	20,042	25,461	0.6	1.1
PRES–Ref Pres GA	1	NR	NR	NR	-	-
REF–Christian Ref	1	30	25	30	0.0	0.0
REF–Comm Ref Evan	2	NR	NR	NR	-	-
Salvation Army	18	971	1,298	2,634	0.1	0.1
Sev Day Adv	75	5,603	9,746	11,210	0.2	0.5
Sikh	1	NR	NR	NR	-	-
Un C of Christ	3	332	576	692	0.0	0.0
Unit Univ	10	894	1,310	1,785	0.0	0.1
Unity Ch	6	NR	NR	NR	-	-
Zoroastrian	0	NR	NR	16	0.0	0.0
SOUTH DAKOTA	**1,819**	**118,799**	**221,469**	**476,832**	**58.6**	**100.0**
ANG/EPIS–Episcopal	74	2,089	5,075	9,359	1.1	2.0
Bahá'í	3	NR	1,017	1,017	0.1	0.2
BAPT–Amer Bapt Assn	1	NR	85	106	0.0	0.0
BAPT–Amer Bapt USA	34	2,985	5,146	6,338	0.8	1.3
BAPT–Converge/BGC	16	2,250	NR	2,700	0.3	0.6
BAPT–Ind Bapt Flwsp Intl	1	NR	NR	NR	-	-
BAPT–N Am Bapt Conf	21	NR	3,247	4,001	0.5	0.8
BAPT–NT Ind Bapt	4	NR	NR	NR	-	-
BAPT–Ref Bapt Ch	1	NR	NR	NR	-	-
BAPT–Reg Bapt Gen As	1	NR	NR	NR	-	-
BAPT–S-D Baptist Gen Con	1	NR	NR	NR	-	-
BAPT–So Bapt Conv	63	2,188	4,896	6,069	0.7	1.3
BUDD–Mahayana	2	NR	NR	205	0.0	0.0
BUDD–Theravada	1	NR	NR	14	0.0	0.0
Calv Chpl	3	NR	NR	NR	-	-
Catholic	243	NR	NR	148,883	18.3	31.2
CGOD–Ch God (Ander)	6	608	NR	608	0.1	0.1
Ch Cr, Scientst	2	NR	NR	NR	-	-
Ch God (7th Day)	3	NR	NR	NR	-	-
Ch of Nazarene	17	752	840	1,386	0.2	0.3
Chr & Miss Al	15	902	532	1,396	0.2	0.3
CHR–Chr Ch (Disc)	3	106	349	431	0.1	0.1
CHR–Chr Chs & Chs Cr	12	NR	1,367	1,666	0.2	0.3
CHR–Chs of Christ	23	940	870	1,143	0.1	0.2
Christian Brethren	1	NR	NR	NR	-	-
CONG–Cong Chr Add'l	1	NR	28	41	0.0	0.0
CONG–Consrv Cong Chr	2	250	376	454	0.1	0.1
Evan Assoc RCC	1	NR	NR	NR	-	-
Evan Cov Ch	8	648	713	841	0.1	0.2
Evan Free Ch	18	3,121	NR	3,121	0.4	0.7
FRND–Consrv Yr Mtgs	1	NR	0	0	0.0	0.0
FRND–Fr Gen Cf	2	NR	0	0	0.0	0.0
Grace Gosp Fel	2	NR	NR	NR	-	-
HINDU–Post Ren	2	NR	NR	32	0.0	0.0
Jehovah's Witness	18	NR	NR	NR	-	-
JUD–Conserv	1	8	9	24	0.0	0.0
JUD–Reform	2	55	96	260	0.0	0.1
LDS–Comm of Christ	1	NR	189	189	0.0	0.0
LDS–L-D Saints	33	NR	NR	9,812	1.2	2.1
LUTH–Apostolic Luth	3	NR	NR	NR	-	-
LUTH–Assoc Free Luth	25	NR	NR	NR	-	-
LUTH–Ch Luth Conf	11	NR	NR	NR	-	-
LUTH–Ch of Luth Br	3	101	76	162	0.0	0.0
LUTH–E.L.C.A.	223	29,565	82,851	112,649	13.8	23.6
LUTH–Luth Ch-Am Asc	2	NR	NR	NR	-	-
LUTH–Luth Cong Msn Chr	34	2,327	5,977	7,313	0.9	1.5
LUTH–Luth-MO Synod	114	9,717	23,970	30,487	3.7	6.4
LUTH–Nor Amer Luth C	14	NR	NR	NR	-	-
LUTH–Wisc Ev Luth Syn	50	3,557	6,891	8,709	1.1	1.8
MENN–Amish Undif	1	NR	13	31	0.0	0.0
MENN–CG in Cr (Menn)	2	NR	217	263	0.0	0.1
MENN–Fel Evg Bib Ch	1	48	30	48	0.0	0.0
MENN–Hutt Breth	60	NR	NR	NR	-	-
MENN–Menn Br US Conf	10	NR	911	1,123	0.1	0.2
MENN–Mennonite USA	8	990	1,492	1,816	0.2	0.4
METH–Free Methodist	3	73	58	81	0.0	0.0
METH–Un Methodist	149	13,300	24,967	36,020	4.4	7.6
METH–Wesleyan	31	9,010	2,883	11,712	1.4	2.5
Missionary Ch	2	59	63	63	0.0	0.0
Muslim Est	5	566	NR	1,332	0.2	0.3
Non-denom Chr Chs	76	7,057	8,009	9,878	1.2	2.1
ORTHE–Ant Orth of NA	1	27	NR	60	0.0	0.0
ORTHE–Greek Orthodox	1	60	NR	250	0.0	0.1
ORTHE–Holy Orth in NA	1	8	NR	10	0.0	0.0
PENT–Assemb of God	45	5,019	2,713	7,541	0.9	1.6
PENT–Ch God (Cleve)	12	534	408	498	0.1	0.1
PENT–Ch of God Proph	2	NR	53	66	0.0	0.0
PENT–COGIC	2	250	350	435	0.1	0.1
PENT–Int Foursq Gos	4	708	784	973	0.1	0.2
PENT–Open Bible Std	9	1,219	NR	1,219	0.1	0.3
PENT–Pent Ch of God	1	70	NR	109	0.0	0.0
PENT–Un Pent Ch Intl	8	NR	NR	NR	-	-
PENT–Vineyard	1	5	6	7	0.0	0.0
PRES–Orth Pres Ch	6	182	268	349	0.0	0.1
PRES–Presb Ch (USA)	82	4,347	8,190	10,169	1.2	2.1
PRES–Presb Ch Amer	9	615	1,053	1,199	0.1	0.3
REF–Christian Ref	14	2,385	3,705	4,588	0.6	1.0
REF–Prot Ref Chs	1	48	32	53	0.0	0.0
REF–Ref Ch in Am	26	4,457	6,842	8,236	1.0	1.7
REF–Ref Ch in U.S.	11	NR	840	1,066	0.1	0.2
REF–Un Ref Chs N.A.	1	NR	NR	NR	-	-
Salvation Army	7	210	391	2,879	0.4	0.6
Sev Day Adv	21	1,203	2,091	2,406	0.3	0.5
Un Breth in Cr	1	13	0	12	0.0	0.0
Un C of Christ	79	4,055	10,378	12,758	1.6	2.7
Unit Univ	3	112	122	166	0.0	0.0
Unity Ch	1	NR	NR	NR	-	-
TENNESSEE	**11,542**	**1,240,173**	**2,620,536**	**3,522,345**	**55.5**	**100.0**
ANG/EPIS–Anglican NA	20	NR	NR	NR	-	-
ANG/EPIS–Episcopal	126	14,249	33,746	40,053	0.6	1.1
Ap Chr Ch-Amer	1	24	12	24	0.0	0.0
Bahá'í	15	NR	2,050	2,050	0.0	0.1
BAPT–Alliance Bapt	3	NR	NR	NR	-	-
BAPT–Amer Bapt Assn	9	NR	585	727	0.0	0.0
BAPT–Amer Bapt USA	10	1,195	3,368	4,158	0.1	0.1
BAPT–Asc Ref Bap Ch Am	2	NR	NR	NR	-	-
BAPT–Free Will Bapt	214	NR	20,183	24,351	0.4	0.7
BAPT–Ind Bapt Flwsp Intl	6	NR	NR	NR	-	-
BAPT–Natl Mis Bapt Conv	77	2,025	11,565	14,146	0.2	0.4
BAPT–NBC Amer	23	4,270	8,026	9,935	0.2	0.3
BAPT–NBC USA	211	46,885	101,657	125,748	2.0	3.6
BAPT–NT Ind Bapt	1	NR	NR	NR	-	-
BAPT–Prim Bapt E Dst	25	625	2,222	2,662	0.0	0.1
BAPT–Prog NBC	12	5,149	10,910	13,631	0.2	0.4
BAPT–Ref Bapt Ch	9	NR	NR	NR	-	-
BAPT–Reg Bapt Gen As	3	NR	NR	NR	-	-
BAPT–S-D Baptist Gen Con	2	38	27	33	0.0	0.0
BAPT–So Bapt Conv	3,189	429,953	1,217,885	1,483,356	23.4	42.1
BRETH–Breth in Chr	4	NR	NR	NR	-	-
BRETH–Ch of Brethren	16	367	1,048	1,245	0.0	0.0
BRETH–Grace Breth	1	NR	NR	NR	-	-
BUDD–Mahayana	12	NR	NR	1,594	0.0	0.0
BUDD–Theravada	7	NR	NR	1,796	0.0	0.1
BUDD–Vajrayana	3	NR	NR	130	0.0	0.0
Calv Chpl	22	NR	NR	NR	-	-
Catholic	151	NR	NR	222,343	3.5	6.3
CGOD–Ch God (Ander)	71	4,742	NR	4,742	0.1	0.1
Ch Christ Chr Union	2	NR	NR	NR	-	-
Ch Cr, Scientst	10	NR	NR	NR	-	-
Ch God (7th Day)	4	NR	NR	NR	-	-
Ch of Chr (Hol)	4	NR	NR	NR	-	-
Ch of God Gen Conf	1	NR	5	6	0.0	0.0
Ch of Nazarene	172	17,289	23,198	27,874	0.4	0.8
Chr & Miss Al	8	686	493	1,028	0.0	0.0
CHR–Chr Ch (Disc)	61	5,125	32,391	40,314	0.6	1.1
CHR–Chr Chs & Chs Cr	173	NR	29,799	35,847	0.6	1.0
CHR–Chs of Christ	1,432	170,861	167,265	214,118	3.4	6.1
CHR–Int Chs of Christ	4	NR	629	764	0.0	0.0
Christian Brethren	2	NR	NR	NR	-	-
CONG–Cong Chr, NA	1	NR	67	78	0.0	0.0
Evan Cov Ch	2	71	41	93	0.0	0.0

NR–Not Reported - Represents no adherents reported. Percentages may not total 100 due to rounding.

Table 2: Religious Congregations by State and Group: 2010

Religious Group	Number of Congregations	Number of Attendees	Number of Communicant, Confirmed, or Full Members	Adherents		
				Number of Adherents	% of Total Pop.	% of Total Adh.
Evan Free Ch	10	5,400	NR	5,400	0.1	0.2
FRND–Fr Gen Cf	12	NR	196	237	0.0	0.0
FRND–Fr Un Mtg	7	NR	230	277	0.0	0.0
HINDU–I/A Temples	6	NR	NR	5,584	0.1	0.2
HINDU–Post Ren	8	NR	NR	329	0.0	0.0
HINDU–Renaiss	1	NR	NR	12	0.0	0.0
HINDU–Trad Temples	4	NR	NR	4,483	0.1	0.1
Ind Fund Churches	6	NR	NR	NR	-	-
Int Cou Comm Ch	4	NR	NR	NR	-	-
Jain	2	NR	NR	NR	-	-
Jehovah's Witness	126	NR	NR	NR	-	-
JUD–Conserv	4	889	998	2,694	0.0	0.1
JUD–Orth	7	3,175	1,260	4,410	0.1	0.1
JUD–Reform	8	1,781	3,143	8,486	0.1	0.2
LDS–Comm of Christ	11	NR	1,716	1,716	0.0	0.0
LDS–L-D Saints	99	NR	NR	45,675	0.7	1.3
LUTH–Assoc Free Luth	1	NR	NR	NR	-	-
LUTH–E.L.C.A.	47	4,797	9,514	11,840	0.2	0.3
LUTH–Luth Cong Msn Chr	1	45	60	75	0.0	0.0
LUTH–Luth–MO Synod	58	7,079	11,938	14,681	0.2	0.4
LUTH–Nor Amer Luth C	3	NR	NR	NR	-	-
LUTH–Wisc Ev Luth Syn	10	1,012	1,428	1,914	0.0	0.1
MENN–Amish Undif	15	NR	715	1,948	0.0	0.1
MENN–Beachy Amish-Menn	3	285	178	285	0.0	0.0
MENN–CG in Cr (Menn)	2	NR	191	230	0.0	0.0
MENN–Mara Amish-Menn	5	742	373	742	0.0	0.0
MENN–Menn Chr Fell	3	441	209	441	0.0	0.0
MENN–Mennonite USA	3	70	72	87	0.0	0.0
MENN–Ref Mennonite	1	NR	6	8	0.0	0.0
MENN–Unaffil Amish-Menn	1	116	50	116	0.0	0.0
METH–A.W.M.C.	2	34	9	38	0.0	0.0
METH–AME	129	2,302	17,922	22,016	0.3	0.6
METH–AME Zion	64	1,027	7,946	9,606	0.2	0.3
METH–C.M.E.	133	2,043	18,695	23,068	0.4	0.7
METH–Cong Meth	9	NR	321	389	0.0	0.0
METH–Evan Meth Ch	1	NR	NR	NR	-	-
METH–Free Methodist	10	471	436	518	0.0	0.0
METH–So Methodist	6	NR	NR	NR	-	-
METH–Un Methodist	1,508	126,611	317,223	375,693	5.9	10.7
METH–Wesleyan	25	1,407	1,131	1,833	0.0	0.1
Metro Comm Ch	2	142	170	204	0.0	0.0
Missionary Ch	5	285	30	285	0.0	0.0
MJEW–Union Mes Cong	2	NR	NR	NR	-	-
Muslim Est	38	6,304	NR	15,384	0.2	0.4
New Apost Ch	3	NR	NR	NR	-	-
Non-denom Chr Chs	917	208,518	259,941	292,248	4.6	8.3
OCATH–Un Cath Ch	1	NR	NR	702	0.0	0.0
ORTHE–Ant Orth of NA	4	437	NR	909	0.0	0.0
ORTHE–Greek Orthodox	6	710	NR	2,320	0.0	0.1
ORTHE–Orth Ch in Amer	5	265	NR	582	0.0	0.0
ORTHE–Romania Orth Ar	1	25	NR	100	0.0	0.0
ORTHE–Serb Orth USA	1	50	NR	70	0.0	0.0
ORTHO–Armen Ap Etchm	2	90	NR	225	0.0	0.0
ORTHO–Coptic Orth Ch	7	2,022	NR	6,195	0.1	0.2
ORTHO–Ethiopian Orth	1	NR	NR	NR	-	-
ORTHO–Malan Dioc Am	1	7	NR	21	0.0	0.0
PENT–Assemb of God	225	32,043	30,940	49,330	0.8	1.4
PENT–Assm God Intl F	1	NR	NR	NR	-	-
PENT–Ch God (Cleve)	379	38,808	64,984	78,597	1.2	2.2
PENT–Ch God Mtn Asm	14	NR	NR	NR	-	-
PENT–Ch Lord Jesus Apos	5	NR	NR	NR	-	-
PENT–Ch of God by Faith	2	NR	NR	NR	-	-
PENT–Ch of God Proph	124	NR	6,932	8,448	0.1	0.2
PENT–COGIC	141	21,209	44,821	55,739	0.9	1.6
PENT–Cong Hol Ch	3	155	120	142	0.0	0.0
PENT–Fire Bapt Hol Ch	9	NR	NR	NR	-	-
PENT–Full Gosp Bapt	23	NR	NR	NR	-	-
PENT–Int Foursq Gos	8	1,123	1,564	1,966	0.0	0.1
PENT–Intl Pent Holiness	36	2,184	3,080	3,719	0.1	0.1
PENT–Open Bible Std	1	40	NR	40	0.0	0.0
PENT–Orig Ch of God	4	NR	NR	NR	-	-
PENT–Pent Ch of God	13	910	NR	1,415	0.0	0.0
PENT–Un Pent Ch Intl	160	NR	NR	NR	-	-
PENT–Vineyard	10	1,420	1,791	2,207	0.0	0.1
PRES–As Ref Pres Ch	11	NR	862	1,068	0.0	0.0
PRES–Bible Pres	1	NR	NR	NR	-	-
PRES–Cum Pres Am	25	NR	NR	NR	-	-
PRES–Cumber Presb	268	NR	17,688	29,453	0.5	0.8
PRES–Evan Presby Ch	20	NR	17,614	21,754	0.3	0.6
PRES–Korean Pres Amer	5	NR	NR	NR	-	-
PRES–Orth Pres Ch	4	184	136	187	0.0	0.0
PRES–Presb Ch (USA)	280	19,817	47,142	57,490	0.9	1.6
PRES–Presb Ch Amer	73	16,927	20,074	26,036	0.4	0.7
PRES–Ref Pres GA	1	NR	NR	NR	-	-
PRES–Ref Pres US	1	NR	NR	NR	-	-
REF–Christian Ref	1	71	130	158	0.0	0.0
REF–Comm Ref Evan	2	NR	NR	NR	-	-
Salvation Army	17	1,012	1,330	3,372	0.1	0.1
Sev Day Adv	159	19,192	33,370	38,381	0.6	1.1
Sikh	3	NR	NR	NR	-	-
Un C of Christ	15	1,453	2,310	2,801	0.0	0.1
Unit Univ	14	1,489	2,375	3,104	0.0	0.1
Unity Ch	12	NR	NR	NR	-	-
Zoroastrian	0	NR	NR	16	0.0	0.0
TEXAS	**27,848**	**3,509,943**	**6,708,243**	**14,083,008**	**56.0**	**100.0**
ANG/EPIS–Anglican NA	111	NR	NR	NR	-	-
ANG/EPIS–Episcopal	377	51,182	123,872	148,439	0.6	1.1
Ap Chr Ch-Amer	2	46	25	46	0.0	0.0
Bahá'í	68	NR	13,235	13,235	0.1	0.1
BAPT–Alliance Bapt	9	NR	NR	NR	-	-
BAPT–Amer Bapt Assn	264	NR	31,568	39,354	0.2	0.3
BAPT–Amer Bapt USA	15	1,558	5,634	7,172	0.0	0.1
BAPT–Asc Ref Bap Ch Am	3	NR	NR	NR	-	-
BAPT–Consrv Bapt	1	NR	NR	NR	-	-
BAPT–Converge/BGC	6	1,100	NR	1,320	0.0	0.0
BAPT–Free Will Bapt	48	NR	2,496	3,111	0.0	0.0
BAPT–Ind Bapt Flwsp Intl	258	NR	NR	NR	-	-
BAPT–N Am Bapt Conf	13	NR	915	1,157	0.0	0.0
BAPT–Natl Mis Bapt Conv	170	5,254	26,917	34,039	0.1	0.2
BAPT–NBC Amer	140	27,860	70,341	89,050	0.4	0.6
BAPT–NBC USA	133	20,571	47,447	59,529	0.2	0.4
BAPT–Prog NBC	8	800	2,105	2,683	0.0	0.0
BAPT–Ref Bapt Ch	27	NR	NR	NR	-	-
BAPT–Reg Bapt Gen As	6	NR	NR	NR	-	-
BAPT–S-D Baptist Gen Con	3	33	52	67	0.0	0.0
BAPT–So Bapt Conv	8,133	1,096,785	2,949,823	3,722,194	14.8	26.4
BRETH–Breth in Chr	1	NR	NR	NR	-	-
BRETH–Ch of Brethren	1	0	96	118	0.0	0.0
BRETH–Grace Breth	3	NR	NR	NR	-	-
BUDD–Mahayana	95	NR	NR	49,874	0.2	0.4
BUDD–Theravada	30	NR	NR	13,461	0.1	0.1
BUDD–Vajrayana	23	NR	NR	2,781	0.0	0.0
Calv Chpl	57	NR	NR	NR	-	-
Catholic	1,348	NR	NR	4,673,500	18.6	33.2
CGOD–Ch God (Ander)	86	3,990	NR	3,990	0.0	0.0
Ch Christ Chr Union	2	NR	NR	NR	-	-
Ch Cr, Scientst	64	NR	NR	NR	-	-
Ch God (7th Day)	70	NR	NR	NR	-	-
Ch of Chr (Hol)	4	NR	NR	NR	-	-
Ch of God Gen Conf	1	NR	50	65	0.0	0.0
Ch of Nazarene	301	22,227	34,688	44,836	0.2	0.3
Chr & Miss Al	48	3,974	2,943	5,465	0.0	0.0
CHR–Chr Ch (Disc)	383	21,697	59,302	74,817	0.3	0.5
CHR–Chr Chs & Chs Cr	136	NR	31,474	40,078	0.2	0.3
CHR–Chs of Christ	2,042	250,602	272,216	351,129	1.4	2.5
CHR–Int Chs of Christ	9	NR	2,236	2,857	0.0	0.0
Christian Brethren	4	NR	NR	NR	-	-
CONG–Consrv Cong Chr	1	30	23	29	0.0	0.0
Evan Assoc RCC	5	NR	NR	NR	-	-
Evan Cov Ch	13	1,073	1,030	1,393	0.0	0.0
Evan Free Ch	64	13,486	NR	13,486	0.1	0.1
FRND–Evan Fr Ch Intl	11	688	1,474	1,845	0.0	0.0
FRND–Fr Gen Cf	16	NR	734	929	0.0	0.0
FRND–Unaffl Mtgs	2	NR	NR	NR	-	-
Grace Gosp Fel	4	NR	NR	NR	-	-
HINDU–I/A Temples	42	NR	NR	36,550	0.1	0.3
HINDU–Post Ren	31	NR	NR	968	0.0	0.0

NR–Not Reported - Represents no adherents reported. Percentages may not total 100 due to rounding.

Table 2: Religious Congregations by State and Group: 2010

Religious Group	Number of Congrega-tions	Number of Attendees	Number of Communicant, Confirmed, or Full Members	Adherents: Number of Adherents	Adherents: % of Total Pop.	Adherents: % of Total Adh.
HINDU–Renaiss	5	NR	NR	98	0.0	0.0
HINDU–Trad Temples	20	NR	NR	23,109	0.1	0.2
Ind Fund Churches	1	NR	NR	NR	-	-
Jain	6	NR	NR	NR	-	-
Jehovah's Witness	426	NR	NR	NR	-	-
JUD–Conserv	13	5,904	6,626	17,889	0.1	0.1
JUD–Orth	30	6,054	2,800	8,410	0.0	0.1
JUD–Reconst	3	104	132	356	0.0	0.0
JUD–Reform	36	7,139	12,589	33,990	0.1	0.2
LDS–Comm of Christ	42	NR	4,450	4,450	0.0	0.0
LDS–L-D Saints	577	NR	NR	296,141	1.2	2.1
LUTH–Assoc Free Luth	8	NR	NR	NR	-	-
LUTH–Ch Luth Conf	4	NR	NR	NR	-	-
LUTH–Ch of Luth Br	1	58	37	72	0.0	0.0
LUTH–E.L.C.A.	362	38,788	88,108	111,647	0.4	0.8
LUTH–Evan Luth Syn	1	43	44	75	0.0	0.0
LUTH–Luth Cong Msn Chr	47	5,352	16,822	20,936	0.1	0.1
LUTH–Luth-MO Synod	345	55,171	103,430	132,508	0.5	0.9
LUTH–Nor Amer Luth C	26	NR	NR	NR	-	-
LUTH–Wisc Ev Luth Syn	38	3,342	5,025	6,828	0.0	0.0
MENN–Amish Undif	1	NR	20	52	0.0	0.0
MENN–Beachy Amish-Menn	2	265	131	265	0.0	0.0
MENN–CG in Cr (Menn)	11	NR	838	1,068	0.0	0.0
MENN–Cons Menn Conf	3	50	83	106	0.0	0.0
MENN–Menn Br US Conf	8	NR	296	403	0.0	0.0
MENN–Mennonite USA	23	697	952	1,233	0.0	0.0
MENN–Unaffil Amish-Menn	4	309	148	309	0.0	0.0
METH–AME	247	6,570	34,901	43,839	0.2	0.3
METH–AME Zion	11	318	1,040	1,327	0.0	0.0
METH–C.M.E.	157	6,673	30,277	37,986	0.2	0.3
METH–Cong Meth	41	NR	1,879	2,396	0.0	0.0
METH–Evan Meth Ch	11	NR	NR	NR	-	-
METH–Free Methodist	21	1,673	1,217	1,864	0.0	0.0
METH–So Methodist	2	NR	NR	NR	-	-
METH–Un Methodist	1,967	284,502	804,098	1,122,736	4.5	8.0
METH–Wesleyan	13	1,668	620	2,169	0.0	0.0
Metro Comm Ch	16	1,642	2,185	2,765	0.0	0.0
Missionary Ch	24	3,028	1,614	3,119	0.0	0.0
MJEW–Assoc Mes Cong	1	NR	NR	NR	-	-
MJEW–Union Mes Cong	5	NR	NR	NR	-	-
MORAV–Unity Of Breth	26	NR	NR	NR	-	-
Muslim Est	166	103,584	NR	421,972	1.7	3.0
Nat Spirit Asso	4	NR	NR	NR	-	-
New Apost Ch	13	NR	NR	NR	-	-
Non-denom Chr Chs	3,685	1,077,353	1,402,964	1,546,542	6.2	11.0
OCATH–Pol Natl Cath	3	NR	NR	NR	-	-
ORTHE–Ant Orth of NA	21	2,178	NR	5,348	0.0	0.0
ORTHE–Greek Orthodox	19	2,656	NR	12,167	0.0	0.1
ORTHE–Orth Ch in Amer	17	1,004	NR	2,657	0.0	0.0
ORTHE–Romania Orth Ar	3	105	NR	600	0.0	0.0
ORTHE–Rus Orth Abroad	7	290	NR	1,022	0.0	0.0
ORTHE–Serb Orth USA	4	493	NR	1,375	0.0	0.0
ORTHO–Armen Ap Etchm	5	225	NR	515	0.0	0.0
ORTHO–Coptic Orth Ch	12	1,789	NR	3,866	0.0	0.0
ORTHO–Eritrean Orth	2	100	NR	1,000	0.0	0.0
ORTHO–Ethiopian Orth	4	NR	NR	NR	-	-
ORTHO–Malan Dioc Am	12	811	NR	2,433	0.0	0.0
ORTHO–Malan Syr Orth	5	670	NR	1,260	0.0	0.0
ORTHO–Syrian Orth Ch	2	83	NR	210	0.0	0.0
PENT–Apos Faith Msn	3	NR	105	135	0.0	0.0
PENT–Assemb of God	1,322	181,298	137,421	275,565	1.1	2.0
PENT–Assm God Intl F	3	NR	NR	NR	-	-
PENT–Ch God (Cleve)	269	24,102	37,900	47,709	0.2	0.3
PENT–Ch God Apos Fth	18	NR	NR	NR	-	-
PENT–Ch Lord Jesus Apos	22	NR	NR	NR	-	-
PENT–Ch of God Proph	87	NR	2,852	3,610	0.0	0.0
PENT–COGIC	393	17,324	61,386	77,545	0.3	0.6
PENT–Cong Hol Ch	28	1,092	980	1,280	0.0	0.0
PENT–Full Gosp Bapt	52	NR	NR	NR	-	-
PENT–Int Foursq Gos	85	6,736	8,722	11,047	0.0	0.1
PENT–Intl Pent Holiness	147	12,278	12,109	15,576	0.1	0.1
PENT–Open Bible Std	6	148	NR	148	0.0	0.0
PENT–Pent Ch of God	124	8,680	NR	13,486	0.1	0.1
PENT–Un Pent Ch Intl	656	NR	NR	NR	-	-

Religious Group	Number of Congrega-tions	Number of Attendees	Number of Communicant, Confirmed, or Full Members	Adherents: Number of Adherents	Adherents: % of Total Pop.	Adherents: % of Total Adh.
PENT–Vineyard	33	4,547	6,697	8,527	0.0	0.1
PRES–As Ref Pres Ch	5	NR	175	223	0.0	0.0
PRES–Cum Pres Am	19	NR	NR	NR	-	-
PRES–Cumber Presb	41	NR	4,000	6,355	0.0	0.0
PRES–Evan Presby Ch	13	NR	2,256	2,883	0.0	0.0
PRES–Kor Pres Abroad	2	NR	NR	NR	-	-
PRES–Korean Amer Pres	4	NR	NR	NR	-	-
PRES–Korean Pres Amer	8	NR	NR	NR	-	-
PRES–Orth Pres Ch	13	703	609	824	0.0	0.0
PRES–Presb Ch (USA)	507	46,564	122,473	155,046	0.6	1.1
PRES–Presb Ch Amer	90	10,342	13,711	17,959	0.1	0.1
PRES–Ref Pres GA	1	NR	NR	NR	-	-
PRES–Ref Pres Han	1	NR	NR	NR	-	-
PRES–Ref Pres US	1	NR	NR	NR	-	-
REF–Christian Ref	13	1,623	1,110	1,416	0.0	0.0
REF–Comm Ref Evan	5	NR	NR	NR	-	-
REF–Hung Ref Add'l	2	NR	NR	NR	-	-
REF–Ref Ch in Am	1	160	504	512	0.0	0.0
Salvation Army	64	4,795	6,967	23,761	0.1	0.2
Sev Day Adv	367	37,028	64,388	74,055	0.3	0.5
Sikh	24	NR	NR	NR	-	-
Tao	1	NR	NR	NR	-	-
Un C of Christ	62	4,964	13,803	17,464	0.1	0.1
Unit Univ	49	3,912	6,053	8,107	0.0	0.1
Unity Ch	43	NR	NR	NR	-	-
Zoroastrian	3	NR	NR	1,095	0.0	0.0
UTAH	**5,557**	**50,875**	**62,560**	**2,186,403**	**79.1**	**100.0**
ANG/EPIS–Anglican NA	1	NR	NR	NR	-	-
ANG/EPIS–Episcopal	27	1,786	4,737	5,407	0.2	0.2
Bahá'í	14	NR	1,129	1,129	0.0	0.1
BAPT–Amer Bapt Assn	2	NR	170	228	0.0	0.0
BAPT–Amer Bapt USA	8	1,158	1,591	2,082	0.1	0.1
BAPT–Consrv Bapt	11	NR	NR	NR	-	-
BAPT–Converge/BGC	2	150	NR	180	0.0	0.0
BAPT–Free Will Bapt	2	NR	84	110	0.0	0.0
BAPT–Ind Bapt Flwsp Intl	3	NR	NR	NR	-	-
BAPT–NBC USA	3	710	770	1,017	0.0	0.0
BAPT–Ref Bapt Ch	1	NR	NR	NR	-	-
BAPT–Reg Bapt Gen As	5	NR	NR	NR	-	-
BAPT–So Bapt Conv	79	5,325	9,497	12,593	0.5	0.6
BUDD–Mahayana	13	NR	NR	6,496	0.2	0.3
BUDD–Theravada	3	NR	NR	2,061	0.1	0.1
BUDD–Vajrayana	1	NR	NR	45	0.0	0.0
Calv Chpl	7	NR	NR	NR	-	-
Catholic	68	NR	NR	160,125	5.8	7.3
Ch Cr, Scientst	5	NR	NR	NR	-	-
Ch God (7th Day)	1	NR	NR	NR	-	-
Ch of Nazarene	5	214	242	412	0.0	0.0
Chr & Miss Al	9	491	310	701	0.0	0.0
CHR–Chr Ch (Disc)	3	230	503	652	0.0	0.0
CHR–Chr Chs & Chs Cr	5	NR	761	1,005	0.0	0.0
CHR–Chs of Christ	19	977	889	1,135	0.0	0.1
CHR–Int Chs of Christ	1	NR	30	39	0.0	0.0
CONG–Armen Evang Add'l	1	NR	NR	NR	-	-
CONG–Cong Chr, NA	1	NR	219	285	0.0	0.0
Evan Free Ch	12	2,460	NR	2,460	0.1	0.1
FRND–Fr Gen Cf	3	NR	56	74	0.0	0.0
HINDU–I/A Temples	2	NR	NR	1,812	0.1	0.1
HINDU–Post Ren	7	NR	NR	231	0.0	0.0
HINDU–Trad Temples	1	NR	NR	50	0.0	0.0
Ind Fund Churches	2	NR	NR	NR	-	-
Jehovah's Witness	28	NR	NR	NR	-	-
JUD–Conserv	0	105	118	317	0.0	0.0
JUD–Orth	2	72	75	100	0.0	0.0
JUD–Reconst	1	23	30	81	0.0	0.0
JUD–Reform	2	240	424	1,143	0.0	0.1
LDS–Comm of Christ	4	NR	543	543	0.0	0.0
LDS–L-D Saints	4,835	NR	NR	1,910,504	69.1	87.4
LUTH–E.L.C.A.	12	1,151	2,450	3,186	0.1	0.1
LUTH–Evan Luth Syn	1	46	88	147	0.0	0.0
LUTH–Luth Cong Msn Chr	4	759	2,078	2,731	0.1	0.1
LUTH–Luth–MO Synod	19	1,406	3,081	4,070	0.1	0.2
LUTH–Wisc Ev Luth Syn	2	235	348	484	0.0	0.0

NR–Not Reported - Represents no adherents reported. Percentages may not total 100 due to rounding.

Table 2: Religious Congregations by State and Group: 2010

Religious Group	Number of Congrega-tions	Number of Attendees	Number of Communicant, Confirmed, or Full Members	Adherents		
				Number of Adherents	% of Total Pop.	% of Total Adh.
MENN–Menn Br US Conf	4	NR	500	651	0.0	0.0
METH–AME	2	0	300	392	0.0	0.0
METH–Un Methodist	19	2,287	4,331	6,156	0.2	0.3
METH–Wesleyan	1	25	2	33	0.0	0.0
Muslim Est	9	1,534	NR	4,998	0.2	0.2
New Apost Ch	1	NR	NR	NR	-	-
Non-denom Chr Chs	89	11,921	11,758	15,580	0.6	0.7
ORTHE–Ant Orth of NA	1	92	NR	255	0.0	0.0
ORTHE–Greek Orthodox	4	985	NR	5,130	0.2	0.2
ORTHE–Holy Orth in NA	1	27	NR	35	0.0	0.0
ORTHE–Rus Orth Abroad	1	75	NR	250	0.0	0.0
ORTHE–Serb Orth USA	1	70	NR	300	0.0	0.0
ORTHO–Coptic Orth Ch	1	6	NR	12	0.0	0.0
PENT–Assemb of God	42	7,516	2,729	11,944	0.4	0.5
PENT–Ch God (Cleve)	14	1,404	1,292	1,714	0.1	0.1
PENT–Ch of God Proph	9	NR	295	384	0.0	0.0
PENT–COGIC	9	0	1,400	1,849	0.1	0.1
PENT–Int Foursq Gos	13	1,429	789	1,037	0.0	0.0
PENT–Intl Pent Holiness	2	145	80	106	0.0	0.0
PENT–Open Bible Std	1	25	NR	25	0.0	0.0
PENT–Pent Ch of God	5	350	NR	544	0.0	0.0
PENT–Un Pent Ch Intl	7	NR	NR	NR	-	-
PENT–Vineyard	5	409	440	570	0.0	0.0
PRES–Kor Pres Abroad	1	NR	NR	NR	-	-
PRES–Orth Pres Ch	2	82	57	80	0.0	0.0
PRES–Presb Ch (USA)	23	1,989	3,508	4,624	0.2	0.2
PRES–Presb Ch Amer	7	323	278	348	0.0	0.0
REF–Christian Ref	4	192	214	279	0.0	0.0
Salvation Army	3	125	225	384	0.0	0.0
Sev Day Adv	19	1,535	2,667	3,066	0.1	0.1
Sikh	3	NR	NR	NR	-	-
Un C of Christ	10	576	817	1,080	0.0	0.0
Unit Univ	4	215	655	940	0.0	0.0
Unity Ch	3	NR	NR	NR	-	-
Zoroastrian	0	NR	NR	2	0.0	0.0
VERMONT	**854**	**33,702**	**56,004**	**210,391**	**33.6**	**100.0**
ANG/EPIS–Anglican NA	3	NR	NR	NR	-	-
ANG/EPIS–Episcopal	47	2,387	5,498	6,999	1.1	3.3
Ap Chr Ch-Amer	1	30	10	30	0.0	0.0
Bahá'í	2	NR	345	345	0.1	0.2
BAPT–Amer Bapt Assn	1	NR	85	99	0.0	0.0
BAPT–Amer Bapt USA	57	2,623	6,081	7,178	1.1	3.4
BAPT–Consrv Bapt	4	NR	NR	NR	-	-
BAPT–Converge/BGC	2	475	NR	570	0.1	0.3
BAPT–N Am Bapt Conf	1	NR	37	43	0.0	0.0
BAPT–Ref Bapt Ch	1	NR	NR	NR	-	-
BAPT–So Bapt Conv	38	1,950	1,583	1,870	0.3	0.9
BRETH–Grace Breth	1	NR	NR	NR	-	-
BUDD–Mahayana	11	NR	NR	213	0.0	0.1
BUDD–Vajrayana	13	NR	NR	713	0.1	0.3
Calv Chpl	2	NR	NR	NR	-	-
Catholic	129	NR	NR	128,293	20.5	61.0
Ch Cr, Scientst	10	NR	NR	NR	-	-
Ch of Nazarene	10	476	501	1,033	0.2	0.5
Chr & Miss Al	10	2,355	1,018	4,704	0.8	2.2
CHR–Chr Chs & Chs Cr	3	NR	110	129	0.0	0.1
CHR–Chs of Christ	10	524	469	651	0.1	0.3
CHR–Int Chs of Christ	1	NR	21	25	0.0	0.0
CONG–Cong Chr Add'l	9	NR	292	347	0.1	0.2
CONG–Cong Chr, NA	3	NR	304	361	0.1	0.2
CONG–Consrv Cong Chr	8	482	588	699	0.1	0.3
Evan Cov Ch	1	76	94	99	0.0	0.0
Evan Free Ch	7	608	NR	608	0.1	0.3
FRND–Fr Gen Cf & Un Mtg	13	NR	293	346	0.1	0.2
HINDU–Post Ren	4	NR	NR	172	0.0	0.1
Ind Fund Churches	2	NR	NR	NR	-	-
Jehovah's Witness	15	NR	NR	NR	-	-
JUD–Conserv	2	332	373	1,007	0.2	0.5
JUD–Orth	1	43	50	60	0.0	0.0
JUD–Reconst	1	85	108	292	0.0	0.1
JUD–Reform	3	227	400	1,080	0.2	0.5
LDS–L-D Saints	12	NR	NR	4,384	0.7	2.1
LUTH–E.L.C.A.	7	343	877	971	0.2	0.5

Religious Group	Number of Congrega-tions	Number of Attendees	Number of Communicant, Confirmed, or Full Members	Adherents		
				Number of Adherents	% of Total Pop.	% of Total Adh.
LUTH–Luth–MO Synod	3	214	425	497	0.1	0.2
LUTH–Wisc Ev Luth Syn	1	39	56	69	0.0	0.0
MENN–Mennonite USA	2	95	98	115	0.0	0.1
METH–Free Methodist	1	0	0	0	0.0	0.0
METH–Un Methodist	117	3,940	11,630	14,710	2.4	7.0
METH–Wesleyan	3	110	51	144	0.0	0.1
Muslim Est	1	100	NR	300	0.0	0.1
New Apost Ch	1	NR	NR	NR	-	-
Non-denom Chr Chs	50	5,038	5,543	6,989	1.1	3.3
ORTHE–Greek Orthodox	2	55	NR	185	0.0	0.1
ORTHE–Orth Ch in Amer	2	55	NR	105	0.0	0.0
PENT–Assemb of God	23	1,748	1,126	2,330	0.4	1.1
PENT–Ch God (Cleve)	2	144	65	77	0.0	0.0
PENT–Ch of God Proph	2	NR	48	57	0.0	0.0
PENT–COGIC	1	30	30	36	0.0	0.0
PENT–I F Chr Assmbl	1	NR	NR	NR	-	-
PENT–Int Foursq Gos	1	86	84	99	0.0	0.0
PENT–Un Pent Ch Intl	7	NR	NR	NR	-	-
PENT–Vineyard	1	17	23	27	0.0	0.0
PRES–Orth Pres Ch	1	71	70	95	0.0	0.0
PRES–Presb Ch (USA)	9	314	611	725	0.1	0.3
PRES–Presb Ch Amer	1	48	48	66	0.0	0.0
REF–Christian Ref	1	90	143	168	0.0	0.1
REF–Un Ref Chs N.A.	1	NR	NR	NR	-	-
Salvation Army	3	109	196	441	0.1	0.2
Sev Day Adv	14	450	777	896	0.1	0.4
Tao	1	NR	NR	NR	-	-
Un C of Christ	135	6,615	13,905	16,392	2.6	7.8
Unit Univ	21	1,318	1,938	2,547	0.4	1.2
Unity Ch	1	NR	NR	NR	-	-
VIRGINIA	**10,088**	**1,094,227**	**2,067,179**	**3,586,592**	**44.8**	**100.0**
ANG/EPIS–Anglican NA	54	NR	NR	NR	-	-
ANG/EPIS–Episcopal	349	38,772	97,452	120,579	1.5	3.4
Bahá'í	37	NR	4,728	4,728	0.1	0.1
BAPT–Alliance Bapt	17	NR	NR	NR	-	-
BAPT–Amer Bapt Assn	4	NR	315	390	0.0	0.0
BAPT–Amer Bapt USA	107	27,693	54,887	65,881	0.8	1.8
BAPT–Asc Ref Bap Ch Am	3	NR	NR	NR	-	-
BAPT–Consrv Bapt	1	NR	NR	NR	-	-
BAPT–Converge/BGC	5	375	NR	450	0.0	0.0
BAPT–Free Will Bapt	80	NR	4,292	5,141	0.1	0.1
BAPT–Fund Bapt Flwsp	3	NR	NR	NR	-	-
BAPT–Ind Bapt Flwsp Intl	5	NR	NR	NR	-	-
BAPT–Natl Mis Bapt Conv	10	115	1,450	1,732	0.0	0.0
BAPT–NBC Amer	8	1,695	2,570	3,125	0.0	0.1
BAPT–NBC USA	74	27,561	47,051	56,554	0.7	1.6
BAPT–Prim Bapt E Dst	21	525	1,864	2,201	0.0	0.1
BAPT–Prog NBC	17	2,275	4,646	5,591	0.1	0.2
BAPT–Ref Bapt Ch	13	NR	NR	NR	-	-
BAPT–Reg Bapt Gen As	7	NR	NR	NR	-	-
BAPT–S-D Baptist Gen Con	1	90	70	80	0.0	0.0
BAPT–So Bapt Conv	1,914	259,397	632,828	763,655	9.5	21.3
BRETH–Breth in Chr	6	NR	NR	NR	-	-
BRETH–Brethren (Ash)	9	NR	1,460	1,766	0.0	0.0
BRETH–Ch of Brethren	185	11,177	24,754	29,841	0.4	0.8
BRETH–Grace Breth	16	NR	NR	NR	-	-
BUDD–Mahayana	39	NR	NR	17,210	0.2	0.5
BUDD–Theravada	8	NR	NR	3,796	0.0	0.1
BUDD–Vajrayana	15	NR	NR	1,989	0.0	0.1
Calv Chpl	28	NR	NR	NR	-	-
Catholic	230	NR	NR	673,853	8.4	18.8
CGOD–Ch God (Ander)	55	4,634	NR	4,634	0.1	0.1
CGOD–Ches God-Gen Con	1	62	56	72	0.0	0.0
Ch Christ Chr Union	1	NR	NR	NR	-	-
Ch Cr, Scientst	24	NR	NR	NR	-	-
Ch God (7th Day)	4	NR	NR	NR	-	-
Ch of Chr (Hol)	8	NR	NR	NR	-	-
Ch of God Gen Conf	4	NR	122	149	0.0	0.0
Ch of Nazarene	93	11,644	12,859	30,852	0.4	0.9
Chr & Miss Al	29	2,148	1,859	2,923	0.0	0.1
CHR–Chr Ch (Disc)	179	6,676	23,538	28,209	0.4	0.8
CHR–Chr Chs & Chs Cr	218	NR	38,969	47,041	0.6	1.3
CHR–Chs of Christ	165	13,267	12,485	16,591	0.2	0.5

NR–Not Reported - Represents no adherents reported. Percentages may not total 100 due to rounding.

Table 2: Religious Congregations by State and Group: 2010

Religious Group	Number of Congrega-tions	Number of Attendees	Number of Communicant, Confirmed, or Full Members	Adherents		
				Number of Adherents	% of Total Pop.	% of Total Adh.
CHR–Int Chs of Christ	6	NR	1,488	1,813	0.0	0.1
Christian Brethren	2	NR	NR	NR	-	-
CONG–Cong Chr Add'l	3	NR	195	225	0.0	0.0
CONG–Cong Chr, NA	1	NR	44	53	0.0	0.0
CONG–Consrv Cong Chr	5	350	878	1,082	0.0	0.0
Evan Assoc RCC	3	NR	NR	NR	-	-
Evan Cov Ch	2	72	133	93	0.0	0.0
Evan Free Ch	10	2,395	NR	2,395	0.0	0.1
FRND–Consrv Yr Mtgs	2	NR	178	218	0.0	0.0
FRND–Evan Fr Ch Intl	16	1,044	696	841	0.0	0.0
FRND–Fr Gen Cf & Un Mtg	23	NR	1,333	1,627	0.0	0.0
FRND–Fr Un Mtg	5	NR	213	256	0.0	0.0
FRND–Unaffl Mtgs	2	NR	NR	NR	-	-
Grace Gosp Fel	1	NR	NR	NR	-	-
HINDU–I/A Temples	8	NR	NR	4,989	0.1	0.1
HINDU–Post Ren	25	NR	NR	562	0.0	0.0
HINDU–Renaiss	5	NR	NR	348	0.0	0.0
HINDU–Trad Temples	6	NR	NR	6,150	0.1	0.2
Ind Fund Churches	5	NR	NR	NR	-	-
Int Cou Comm Ch	3	NR	NR	NR	-	-
Jain	1	NR	NR	NR	-	-
Jehovah's Witness	131	NR	NR	NR	-	-
JUD–Conserv	13	3,364	3,774	10,190	0.1	0.3
JUD–Orth	10	1,051	620	1,460	0.0	0.0
JUD–Reconst	1	29	37	100	0.0	0.0
JUD–Reform	21	3,574	6,305	17,025	0.2	0.5
LDS–Comm of Christ	4	NR	548	548	0.0	0.0
LDS–L-D Saints	196	NR	NR	89,800	1.1	2.5
LUTH–Ch Luth Conf	1	NR	NR	NR	-	-
LUTH–E.L.C.A.	191	19,331	44,461	56,754	0.7	1.6
LUTH–Luth Ch-Am Asc	1	NR	NR	NR	-	-
LUTH–Luth Cong Msn Chr	4	850	1,651	1,988	0.0	0.1
LUTH–Luth–MO Synod	50	7,589	13,215	17,337	0.2	0.5
LUTH–Nor Amer Luth C	4	NR	NR	NR	-	-
LUTH–Wisc Ev Luth Syn	9	955	1,407	1,858	0.0	0.1
MENN–Amish Undif	4	NR	195	547	0.0	0.0
MENN–Beachy Amish-Menn	9	1,017	605	1,017	0.0	0.0
MENN–Ber Amish-Menn	1	17	9	17	0.0	0.0
MENN–CG in Cr (Menn)	1	NR	21	26	0.0	0.0
MENN–Cons Menn Conf	3	243	128	154	0.0	0.0
MENN–Mara Amish-Menn	1	75	29	75	0.0	0.0
MENN–Mennonite USA	54	5,849	7,561	9,046	0.1	0.3
MENN–Unaffil Amish-Menn	1	38	31	38	0.0	0.0
METH–A.W.M.C.	4	52	18	69	0.0	0.0
METH–AME	78	2,617	12,840	15,583	0.2	0.4
METH–AME Zion	66	1,511	8,449	10,148	0.1	0.3
METH–C.M.E.	13	650	2,382	2,842	0.0	0.1
METH–Evan Meth Ch	4	NR	NR	NR	-	-
METH–Free Methodist	6	572	408	575	0.0	0.0
METH–So Methodist	1	NR	NR	NR	-	-
METH–Un Methodist	1,540	126,973	372,251	467,417	5.8	13.0
METH–Wesleyan	55	4,809	4,713	6,251	0.1	0.2
Metro Comm Ch	5	319	449	538	0.0	0.0
MJEW–Assoc Mes Cong	1	NR	NR	NR	-	-
MJEW–Union Mes Cong	4	NR	NR	NR	-	-
MORAV–Morav Ch-South	3	181	177	219	0.0	0.0
Muslim Est	62	49,104	NR	213,032	2.7	5.9
Nat Spirit Asso	2	NR	NR	NR	-	-
New Apost Ch	6	NR	NR	NR	-	-
Non-denom Chr Chs	1,237	272,025	342,054	378,934	4.7	10.6
OCATH–Un Cath Ch	1	NR	NR	702	0.0	0.0
ORTHE–Ant Orth of NA	4	205	NR	380	0.0	0.0
ORTHE–Bulgar Orth USA	2	23	NR	33	0.0	0.0
ORTHE–Carp Rus Orth	2	87	NR	185	0.0	0.0
ORTHE–Greek Orthodox	12	2,405	NR	10,772	0.1	0.3
ORTHE–Holy Orth in NA	3	62	NR	80	0.0	0.0
ORTHE–Orth Ch in Amer	10	526	NR	1,542	0.0	0.0
ORTHE–Romania Orth Ar	1	50	NR	150	0.0	0.0
ORTHE–Rus Orth Abroad	3	83	NR	142	0.0	0.0
ORTHE–Ukrainian Orth	1	40	NR	120	0.0	0.0
ORTHO–Armen Ap Etchm	2	90	NR	210	0.0	0.0
ORTHO–Coptic Orth Ch	6	1,600	NR	4,150	0.1	0.1
ORTHO–Ethiopian Orth	1	NR	NR	NR	-	-
ORTHO–Malan Dioc Am	1	60	NR	100	0.0	0.0

Religious Group	Number of Congrega-tions	Number of Attendees	Number of Communicant, Confirmed, or Full Members	Adherents		
				Number of Adherents	% of Total Pop.	% of Total Adh.
ORTHO–Malan Syr Orth	1	30	NR	54	0.0	0.0
ORTHO–Syrian Orth Ch	2	125	NR	335	0.0	0.0
PENT–Apos Faith Msn	1	NR	35	41	0.0	0.0
PENT–Assemb of God	224	37,372	23,773	56,241	0.7	1.6
PENT–Assm God Intl F	1	NR	NR	NR	-	-
PENT–Ch God (Cleve)	200	22,692	35,181	42,530	0.5	1.2
PENT–Ch God Mtn Asm	3	NR	NR	NR	-	-
PENT–Ch Lord Jesus Apos	45	NR	NR	NR	-	-
PENT–Ch of God by Faith	1	NR	NR	NR	-	-
PENT–Ch of God Proph	102	NR	4,923	5,911	0.1	0.2
PENT–COGIC	71	4,998	12,920	15,453	0.2	0.4
PENT–Cong Hol Ch	14	522	357	422	0.0	0.0
PENT–Elim	3	NR	NR	NR	-	-
PENT–Fire Bapt Hol Ch	2	NR	NR	NR	-	-
PENT–Full Gosp Bapt	21	NR	NR	NR	-	-
PENT–Int Foursq Gos	21	3,073	2,591	3,085	0.0	0.1
PENT–Int Pent C Chr	5	156	92	295	0.0	0.0
PENT–Intl Pent Holiness	207	19,080	25,576	30,327	0.4	0.8
PENT–Open Bible Std	2	85	NR	85	0.0	0.0
PENT–Orig Ch of God	2	NR	NR	NR	-	-
PENT–Pent Ch of God	8	560	NR	872	0.0	0.0
PENT–Pent FW Bapt	7	NR	NR	NR	-	-
PENT–Un Pent Ch Intl	53	NR	NR	NR	-	-
PENT–United Holy Ch	43	NR	NR	NR	-	-
PENT–Vineyard	12	1,874	2,403	2,958	0.0	0.1
PRES–As Ref Pres Ch	12	NR	932	1,085	0.0	0.0
PRES–Bible Pres	2	NR	NR	NR	-	-
PRES–Evan Presby Ch	16	NR	3,645	4,424	0.1	0.1
PRES–Kor Pres Abroad	4	NR	NR	NR	-	-
PRES–Korean Amer Pres	18	NR	NR	NR	-	-
PRES–Korean Pres Amer	23	NR	NR	NR	-	-
PRES–Orth Pres Ch	11	875	817	1,144	0.0	0.0
PRES–Presb Ch (USA)	498	44,149	96,116	115,955	1.4	3.2
PRES–Presb Ch Amer	92	16,556	17,883	22,532	0.3	0.6
PRES–Ref Pres GA	1	NR	NR	NR	-	-
PRES–Ref Pres Han	1	NR	NR	NR	-	-
PRES–Ref Pres US	2	NR	NR	NR	-	-
REF–Christian Ref	2	135	204	250	0.0	0.0
REF–Comm Ref Evan	4	NR	NR	NR	-	-
REF–Fed Ref Ch	2	NR	NR	NR	-	-
Salvation Army	29	1,562	3,685	4,480	0.1	0.1
Sev Day Adv	148	12,193	21,206	24,388	0.3	0.7
Sikh	11	NR	NR	NR	-	-
Un Breth in Cr	6	587	628	501	0.0	0.0
Un C of Christ	86	4,012	10,799	13,129	0.2	0.4
Unit Univ	24	3,598	5,662	8,001	0.1	0.2
Unity Ch	17	NR	NR	NR	-	-
Zoroastrian	1	NR	NR	255	0.0	0.0
WASHINGTON	**6,114**	**650,432**	**835,492**	**2,328,005**	**34.6**	**100.0**
ANG/EPIS–Anglican NA	24	NR	NR	NR	-	-
ANG/EPIS–Episcopal	127	11,285	27,113	33,410	0.5	1.4
Bahá'í	82	NR	7,087	7,087	0.1	0.3
BAPT–Amer Bapt Assn	13	NR	1,085	1,317	0.0	0.1
BAPT–Amer Bapt USA	119	13,218	21,973	26,638	0.4	1.1
BAPT–Asc Ref Bap Ch Am	2	NR	NR	NR	-	-
BAPT–Consrv Bapt	64	NR	NR	NR	-	-
BAPT–Converge/BGC	62	11,825	NR	14,190	0.2	0.6
BAPT–Free Will Bapt	2	NR	82	101	0.0	0.0
BAPT–Ind Bapt Flwsp Intl	8	NR	NR	NR	-	-
BAPT–N Am Bapt Conf	18	NR	1,746	2,132	0.0	0.1
BAPT–Natl Mis Bapt Conv	4	180	590	713	0.0	0.0
BAPT–NBC Amer	1	112	140	173	0.0	0.0
BAPT–NBC USA	5	510	1,750	2,151	0.0	0.1
BAPT–Ref Bapt Ch	10	NR	NR	NR	-	-
BAPT–Reg Bapt Gen As	54	NR	NR	NR	-	-
BAPT–S-D Baptist Gen Con	2	73	83	103	0.0	0.0
BAPT–So Bapt Conv	280	24,918	42,106	51,665	0.8	2.2
BRETH–Ch of Brethren	12	299	700	854	0.0	0.0
BRETH–Grace Breth	11	NR	NR	NR	-	-
BUDD–Mahayana	70	NR	NR	31,254	0.5	1.3
BUDD–Theravada	18	NR	NR	14,711	0.2	0.6
BUDD–Vajrayana	30	NR	NR	3,100	0.0	0.1
Calv Chpl	57	NR	NR	NR	-	-

NR–Not Reported   - Represents no adherents reported.   Percentages may not total 100 due to rounding.

Table 2: Religious Congregations by State and Group: 2010

Religious Group	Number of Congrega-tions	Number of Attendees	Number of Communicant, Confirmed, or Full Members	Adherents		
				Number of Adherents	% of Total Pop.	% of Total Adh.
Catholic	312	NR	NR	784,332	11.7	33.7
CGOD–Ch God (Ander)	47	7,228	NR	7,228	0.1	0.3
Ch Cr, Scientist	44	NR	NR	NR	-	-
Ch God (7th Day)	3	NR	NR	NR	-	-
Ch of God Gen Conf	2	NR	80	101	0.0	0.0
Ch of Nazarene	154	19,876	24,663	36,477	0.5	1.6
Chr & Miss Al	85	11,819	7,936	18,843	0.3	0.8
CHR–Chr Ch (Disc)	53	2,490	6,265	7,697	0.1	0.3
CHR–Chr Chs & Chs Cr	62	NR	17,270	21,011	0.3	0.9
CHR–Chs of Christ	133	10,560	10,071	13,233	0.2	0.6
CHR–Int Chs of Christ	4	NR	825	998	0.0	0.0
Christian Brethren	3	NR	NR	NR	-	-
CONG–Cong Chr, NA	5	NR	427	537	0.0	0.0
CONG–Consrv Cong Chr	4	115	127	151	0.0	0.0
Evan Ch	14	NR	NR	NR	-	-
Evan Cov Ch	50	9,248	6,988	12,023	0.2	0.5
Evan Free Ch	41	5,342	NR	5,342	0.1	0.2
FRND–Evan Fr Ch Intl	18	976	1,091	1,348	0.0	0.1
FRND–Fr Gen Cf	1	NR	61	74	0.0	0.0
FRND–Indep Yr Mtgs	23	NR	468	560	0.0	0.0
Grace Gosp Fel	5	NR	NR	NR	-	-
HINDU–I/A Temples	8	NR	NR	3,263	0.0	0.1
HINDU–Post Ren	25	NR	NR	903	0.0	0.0
HINDU–Renaiss	7	NR	NR	520	0.0	0.0
HINDU–Trad Temples	2	NR	NR	5,150	0.1	0.2
Ind Fund Churches	38	NR	NR	NR	-	-
Int Cou Comm Ch	1	NR	NR	NR	-	-
Intl Fell Bible Ch	1	NR	NR	NR	-	-
Jehovah's Witness	166	NR	NR	NR	-	-
JUD–Conserv	5	1,273	1,428	3,856	0.1	0.2
JUD–Orth	14	2,130	1,100	2,960	0.0	0.1
JUD–Reconst	2	199	254	685	0.0	0.0
JUD–Reform	17	2,511	4,426	11,950	0.2	0.5
LDS–Comm of Christ	26	NR	4,147	4,147	0.1	0.2
LDS–L-D Saints	520	NR	NR	267,267	4.0	11.5
LUTH–Apostolic Luth	7	NR	NR	NR	-	-
LUTH–Assoc Free Luth	7	NR	NR	NR	-	-
LUTH–Ch Luth Conf	5	NR	NR	NR	-	-
LUTH–Ch of Luth Br	12	1,136	813	1,858	0.0	0.1
LUTH–Cons Luth Assn	1	NR	NR	NR	-	-
LUTH–E.L.C.A.	259	31,599	71,264	96,555	1.4	4.1
LUTH–Evan Luth Syn	5	542	962	1,347	0.0	0.1
LUTH–Luth Ch-Am Asc	2	NR	NR	NR	-	-
LUTH–Luth Cong Msn Chr	22	2,704	7,240	8,790	0.1	0.4
LUTH–Luth–MO Synod	117	13,047	24,497	32,807	0.5	1.4
LUTH–Nor Amer Luth C	2	NR	NR	NR	-	-
LUTH–Wisc Ev Luth Syn	25	1,933	3,106	3,887	0.1	0.2
MENN–CG in Cr (Menn)	2	NR	178	236	0.0	0.0
MENN–Hutt Breth	5	NR	NR	NR	-	-
MENN–Menn Br US Conf	22	NR	7,161	8,819	0.1	0.4
MENN–Mennonite USA	6	297	432	550	0.0	0.0
METH–AME	9	960	2,450	2,969	0.0	0.1
METH–AME Zion	4	0	410	501	0.0	0.0
METH–C.M.E.	6	30	750	944	0.0	0.0
METH–Evan Meth Ch	4	NR	NR	NR	-	-
METH–Free Methodist	49	9,723	6,134	10,057	0.1	0.4
METH–Un Methodist	244	20,441	48,102	66,616	1.0	2.9
METH–Wesleyan	6	362	259	470	0.0	0.0
Metro Comm Ch	6	199	188	233	0.0	0.0
Missionary Ch	8	243	176	268	0.0	0.0
MJEW–Union Mes Cong	2	NR	NR	NR	-	-
Muslim Est	36	5,289	NR	19,092	0.3	0.8
Nat Spirit Asso	3	NR	NR	NR	-	-
New Apost Ch	5	NR	NR	NR	-	-
Non-denom Chr Chs	743	226,196	265,485	309,440	4.6	13.3
OCATH–Pol Natl Cath	1	NR	NR	NR	-	-
ORTHE–Ant Orth of NA	8	777	NR	1,232	0.0	0.1
ORTHE–Greek Orthodox	8	910	NR	6,017	0.1	0.3
ORTHE–Holy Orth in NA	3	123	NR	160	0.0	0.0
ORTHE–Orth Ch in Amer	9	624	NR	1,496	0.0	0.1
ORTHE–Pal/Jor Orth	1	30	NR	125	0.0	0.0
ORTHE–Rus Orth Abroad	3	250	NR	525	0.0	0.0
ORTHE–Serb Orth USA	1	70	NR	1,500	0.0	0.1
ORTHE–Ukrainian Orth	1	45	NR	150	0.0	0.0
ORTHO–Armen Ap Etchm	1	125	NR	2,500	0.0	0.1
ORTHO–Coptic Orth Ch	3	485	NR	1,735	0.0	0.1
ORTHO–Eritrean Orth	3	700	NR	1,400	0.0	0.1
ORTHO–Ethiopian Orth	2	NR	NR	NR	-	-
ORTHO–Malan Dioc Am	1	25	NR	75	0.0	0.0
ORTHO–Malan Syr Orth	1	40	NR	72	0.0	0.0
PENT–Apos Faith Msn	6	NR	210	254	0.0	0.0
PENT–Assemb of God	342	63,932	29,810	125,005	1.9	5.4
PENT–Ch God (Cleve)	38	2,624	3,846	4,859	0.1	0.2
PENT–Ch of God by Faith	4	NR	NR	NR	-	-
PENT–Ch of God Proph	21	NR	895	1,121	0.0	0.0
PENT–COGIC	30	2,629	5,617	6,838	0.1	0.3
PENT–Int Foursq Gos	160	35,793	31,642	38,874	0.6	1.7
PENT–Intl Pent Holiness	20	1,435	895	1,183	0.0	0.1
PENT–Open Bible Std	23	3,118	NR	3,118	0.0	0.1
PENT–Pent Ch of God	18	1,260	NR	1,959	0.0	0.1
PENT–Un Pent Ch Intl	55	NR	NR	NR	-	-
PENT–Vineyard	14	1,651	2,194	2,696	0.0	0.1
PRES–Bible Pres	3	NR	NR	NR	-	-
PRES–Evan Presby Ch	4	NR	1,480	1,767	0.0	0.1
PRES–Kor Pres Abroad	10	NR	NR	NR	-	-
PRES–Korean Amer Pres	9	NR	NR	NR	-	-
PRES–Korean Pres Amer	19	NR	NR	NR	-	-
PRES–Orth Pres Ch	10	764	629	933	0.0	0.0
PRES–Presb Ch (USA)	217	34,783	50,418	61,502	0.9	2.6
PRES–Presb Ch Amer	24	2,577	2,579	3,149	0.0	0.1
PRES–Ref Pres Han	1	NR	NR	NR	-	-
PRES–Ref Pres of NA	1	65	71	83	0.0	0.0
REF–Can Amer Ref	1	NR	NR	NR	-	-
REF–Christian Ref	52	6,187	7,784	9,497	0.1	0.4
REF–Comm Ref Evan	6	NR	NR	NR	-	-
REF–Prot Ref Chs	2	102	65	117	0.0	0.0
REF–Ref Ch in Am	9	1,598	2,332	2,735	0.0	0.1
REF–Un Ref Chs N.A.	5	NR	NR	NR	-	-
Salvation Army	24	1,364	2,158	7,390	0.1	0.3
Sev Day Adv	206	26,471	46,036	52,944	0.8	2.3
Shinto	1	NR	NR	NR	-	-
Sikh	6	NR	NR	NR	-	-
Swedenborgian	1	NR	NR	NR	-	-
Tao	2	NR	NR	NR	-	-
Un Breth in Cr	1	56	24	48	0.0	0.0
Un C of Christ	77	5,038	9,730	11,735	0.2	0.5
Unit Univ	28	3,893	5,388	7,488	0.1	0.3
Unity Ch	23	NR	NR	NR	-	-
Zoroastrian	1	NR	NR	29	0.0	0.0
WEST VIRGINIA	**4,413**	**240,457**	**428,729**	**658,313**	**35.5**	**100.0**
ANG/EPIS–Anglican NA	2	NR	NR	NR	-	-
ANG/EPIS–Episcopal	67	3,015	7,434	8,529	0.5	1.3
Ap Chr Ch-Amer	1	0	0	0	0.0	0.0
Bahá'í	3	NR	520	520	0.0	0.1
BAPT–Amer Bapt Assn	5	NR	940	1,160	0.1	0.2
BAPT–Amer Bapt USA	381	31,948	74,045	88,193	4.8	13.4
BAPT–Consrv Bapt	1	NR	NR	NR	-	-
BAPT–Free Will Bapt	174	NR	7,665	9,161	0.5	1.4
BAPT–Fund Bapt Flwsp	1	NR	NR	NR	-	-
BAPT–Ind Bapt Flwsp Intl	1	NR	NR	NR	-	-
BAPT–Natl Mis Bapt Conv	11	200	1,405	1,701	0.1	0.3
BAPT–NBC USA	22	1,685	4,498	5,341	0.3	0.8
BAPT–Prog NBC	2	180	500	613	0.0	0.1
BAPT–Ref Bapt Ch	2	NR	NR	NR	-	-
BAPT–Reg Bapt Gen As	18	NR	NR	NR	-	-
BAPT–S-D Baptist Gen Con	3	118	238	285	0.0	0.0
BAPT–So Bapt Conv	232	16,878	35,804	42,834	2.3	6.5
BRETH–Breth in Chr	1	NR	NR	NR	-	-
BRETH–Brethren (Ash)	4	NR	320	380	0.0	0.1
BRETH–Ch of Brethren	77	2,713	6,468	7,727	0.4	1.2
BRETH–Grace Breth	4	NR	NR	NR	-	-
BUDD–Mahayana	1	NR	NR	11	0.0	0.0
BUDD–Theravada	1	NR	NR	300	0.0	0.0
Calv Chpl	3	NR	NR	NR	-	-
Catholic	139	NR	NR	95,849	5.2	14.6
CGOD–Ch God (Ander)	79	4,689	NR	4,689	0.3	0.7
CGOD–Ches God-Gen Con	6	252	273	323	0.0	0.0

NR–Not Reported - Represents no adherents reported. Percentages may not total 100 due to rounding.

Table 2: Religious Congregations by State and Group: 2010

Religious Group	Number of Congrega-tions	Number of Attendees	Number of Communicant, Confirmed, or Full Members	Adherents		
				Number of Adherents	% of Total Pop.	% of Total Adh.
Ch Cr, Scientst	6	NR	NR	NR	-	-
Ch God (7th Day)	2	NR	NR	NR	-	-
Ch of Nazarene	125	9,009	13,921	18,305	1.0	2.8
Chr & Miss Al	19	1,530	810	2,212	0.1	0.3
CHR–Chr Ch (Disc)	41	1,877	6,715	7,955	0.4	1.2
CHR–Chr Chs & Chs Cr	88	NR	9,190	10,927	0.6	1.7
CHR–Chs of Christ	287	18,002	17,853	22,167	1.2	3.4
CONG–Cong Chr, NA	1	NR	25	30	0.0	0.0
Evan Assoc RCC	1	NR	NR	NR	-	-
Evan Free Ch	1	35	NR	35	0.0	0.0
FRND–Fr Gen Cf	3	NR	20	23	0.0	0.0
FRND–Fr Gen Cf & Un Mtg	1	NR	0	0	0.0	0.0
Grace Gosp Fel	1	NR	NR	NR	-	-
HINDU–I/A Temples	2	NR	NR	1,691	0.1	0.3
HINDU–Post Ren	3	NR	NR	42	0.0	0.0
Ind Fund Churches	1	NR	NR	NR	-	-
Jain	1	NR	NR	NR	-	-
Jehovah's Witness	51	NR	NR	NR	-	-
JUD–Conserv	0	51	57	154	0.0	0.0
JUD–Orth	1	43	50	60	0.0	0.0
JUD–Reform	6	243	431	1,164	0.1	0.2
LDS–Comm of Christ	7	NR	845	845	0.0	0.1
LDS–L-D Saints	38	NR	NR	16,710	0.9	2.5
LUTH–E.L.C.A.	52	2,644	9,140	12,809	0.7	1.9
LUTH–Luth-MO Synod	3	196	289	370	0.0	0.1
LUTH–Nor Amer Luth C	2	NR	NR	NR	-	-
MENN–Amish Undif	3	NR	73	217	0.0	0.0
MENN–Beachy Amish-Menn	1	79	36	79	0.0	0.0
MENN–Bruderhof Comm	1	32	6	17	0.0	0.0
MENN–Menn Chr Fell	1	60	37	60	0.0	0.0
MENN–Mennonite USA	5	125	176	205	0.0	0.0
MENN–Unaffil Amish-Menn	1	13	10	13	0.0	0.0
METH–A.W.M.C.	10	321	79	373	0.0	0.1
METH–AME	23	195	2,311	2,748	0.1	0.4
METH–AME Zion	1	40	80	95	0.0	0.0
METH–C.M.E.	1	0	100	115	0.0	0.0
METH–Evan Meth Ch	7	NR	NR	NR	-	-
METH–Free Methodist	18	840	770	963	0.1	0.1
METH–Un Methodist	1,197	49,033	109,996	136,929	7.4	20.8
METH–Wesleyan	26	1,034	668	1,348	0.1	0.2
Metro Comm Ch	1	16	23	27	0.0	0.0
Muslim Est	7	844	NR	1,908	0.1	0.3
New Apost Ch	1	NR	NR	NR	-	-
Non-denom Chr Chs	312	53,004	60,473	71,205	3.8	10.8
ORTHE–Ant Orth of NA	3	510	NR	1,235	0.1	0.2
ORTHE–Carp Rus Orth	2	93	NR	146	0.0	0.0
ORTHE–Greek Orthodox	6	380	NR	1,170	0.1	0.2
ORTHE–Orth Ch in Amer	2	53	NR	85	0.0	0.0
ORTHE–Rus Orth Abroad	3	100	NR	115	0.0	0.0
ORTHE–Serb Orth USA	1	10	NR	25	0.0	0.0
PENT–Assemb of God	118	9,511	6,737	15,473	0.8	2.4
PENT–Assm God Intl F	2	NR	NR	NR	-	-
PENT–Ch God (Cleve)	178	11,826	18,242	21,740	1.2	3.3
PENT–Ch God Mtn Asm	1	NR	NR	NR	-	-
PENT–Ch Lord Jesus Apos	5	NR	NR	NR	-	-
PENT–Ch of God Proph	27	NR	577	685	0.0	0.1
PENT–COGIC	6	100	750	892	0.0	0.1
PENT–I F Chr Assmbl	4	NR	NR	NR	-	-
PENT–Int Foursq Gos	7	432	469	563	0.0	0.1
PENT–Int Pent C Chr	7	180	102	273	0.0	0.0
PENT–Intl Pent Holiness	53	2,198	3,602	4,277	0.2	0.6
PENT–Open Bible Std	2	135	NR	135	0.0	0.0
PENT–Orig Ch of God	1	NR	NR	NR	-	-
PENT–Pent Ch of God	22	1,540	NR	2,394	0.1	0.4
PENT–Un Pent Ch Intl	59	NR	NR	NR	-	-
PENT–United Holy Ch	14	NR	NR	NR	-	-
PENT–Vineyard	2	773	1,175	1,380	0.1	0.2
PRES–As Ref Pres Ch	3	NR	66	78	0.0	0.0
PRES–Evan Presby Ch	2	NR	482	573	0.0	0.1
PRES–Orth Pres Ch	2	72	63	78	0.0	0.0
PRES–Presb Ch (USA)	196	7,847	16,549	19,689	1.1	3.0
PRES–Presb Ch Amer	12	701	678	817	0.0	0.1
REF–Comm Ref Evan	1	NR	NR	NR	-	-
Salvation Army	16	707	1,094	2,561	0.1	0.4
Sev Day Adv	43	1,692	2,954	3,396	0.2	0.5
Un Breth in Cr	2	327	240	278	0.0	0.0
Un C of Christ	5	169	482	582	0.0	0.1
Unit Univ	4	157	173	245	0.0	0.0
Unity Ch	2	NR	NR	NR	-	-
Zoroastrian	0	NR	NR	11	0.0	0.0
WISCONSIN	**6,078**	**611,541**	**1,126,174**	**3,047,442**	**53.6**	**100.0**
ANG/EPIS–Anglican NA	6	NR	NR	NR	-	-
ANG/EPIS–Episcopal	114	7,016	15,530	18,314	0.3	0.6
Bahá'í	18	NR	2,149	2,149	0.0	0.1
BAPT–Alliance Bapt	1	NR	NR	NR	-	-
BAPT–Amer Bapt Assn	2	NR	150	185	0.0	0.0
BAPT–Amer Bapt USA	61	7,213	13,688	16,820	0.3	0.6
BAPT–Consrv Bapt	9	NR	NR	NR	-	-
BAPT–Converge/BGC	93	13,675	NR	16,410	0.3	0.5
BAPT–Free Will Bapt	2	NR	124	153	0.0	0.0
BAPT–Fund Bapt Flwsp	1	NR	NR	NR	-	-
BAPT–Ind Bapt Flwsp Intl	1	NR	NR	NR	-	-
BAPT–N Am Bapt Conf	10	NR	2,621	3,236	0.1	0.1
BAPT–Natl Mis Bapt Conv	11	200	2,100	2,606	0.0	0.1
BAPT–NBC Amer	1	300	600	745	0.0	0.0
BAPT–NBC USA	32	6,337	16,577	20,560	0.4	0.7
BAPT–NT Ind Bapt	18	NR	NR	NR	-	-
BAPT–Prog NBC	2	0	300	371	0.0	0.0
BAPT–Ref Bapt Ch	5	NR	NR	NR	-	-
BAPT–Reg Bapt Gen As	36	NR	NR	NR	-	-
BAPT–S-D Baptist Gen Con	6	322	305	374	0.0	0.0
BAPT–So Bapt Conv	95	8,798	14,367	17,767	0.3	0.6
BRETH–Breth in Chr	2	NR	NR	NR	-	-
BRETH–Ch of Brethren	1	0	21	26	0.0	0.0
BUDD–Mahayana	20	NR	NR	2,378	0.0	0.1
BUDD–Theravada	6	NR	NR	1,400	0.0	0.0
BUDD–Vajrayana	17	NR	NR	977	0.0	0.0
Calv Chpl	13	NR	NR	NR	-	-
Catholic	764	NR	NR	1,425,523	25.1	46.8
CGOD–Ch God (Ander)	10	585	NR	585	0.0	0.0
Ch Cr, Scientst	32	NR	NR	NR	-	-
Ch of God Gen Conf	1	NR	17	21	0.0	0.0
Ch of Nazarene	41	1,612	2,360	3,054	0.1	0.1
Chr & Miss Al	55	13,055	10,051	21,247	0.4	0.7
CHR–Chr Ch (Disc)	2	137	158	196	0.0	0.0
CHR–Chr Chs & Chs Cr	34	NR	5,232	6,409	0.1	0.2
CHR–Chs of Christ	69	4,252	4,351	5,941	0.1	0.2
CHR–Int Chs of Christ	4	NR	409	502	0.0	0.0
CONG–Cong Chr, NA	33	NR	4,788	5,872	0.1	0.2
CONG–Consrv Cong Chr	15	1,222	1,665	2,038	0.0	0.1
Evan Ch	1	NR	NR	NR	-	-
Evan Cov Ch	28	2,861	2,635	3,720	0.1	0.1
Evan Free Ch	100	29,881	NR	29,881	0.5	1.0
FRND–Consrv Yr Mtgs	1	NR	8	10	0.0	0.0
FRND–Fr Gen Cf	21	NR	562	683	0.0	0.0
FRND–Fr Un Mtg	2	NR	77	93	0.0	0.0
Grace Gosp Fel	12	NR	NR	NR	-	-
HINDU–I/A Temples	1	NR	NR	16	0.0	0.0
HINDU–Post Ren	7	NR	NR	283	0.0	0.0
HINDU–Trad Temples	3	NR	NR	6,475	0.1	0.2
Ind Fund Churches	38	NR	NR	NR	-	-
Int Cou Comm Ch	1	NR	NR	NR	-	-
Jain	1	NR	NR	NR	-	-
Jehovah's Witness	131	NR	NR	NR	-	-
JUD–Conserv	6	761	854	2,306	0.0	0.1
JUD–Orth	10	1,278	650	1,775	0.0	0.1
JUD–Reconst	2	147	188	508	0.0	0.0
JUD–Reform	9	1,703	3,003	8,108	0.1	0.3
LDS–Comm of Christ	9	NR	1,242	1,242	0.0	0.0
LDS–L-D Saints	69	NR	NR	24,496	0.4	0.8
LUTH–Assoc Free Luth	15	NR	NR	NR	-	-
LUTH–Ch Luth Conf	9	NR	NR	NR	-	-
LUTH–Ch of Luth Br	5	935	513	1,810	0.0	0.1
LUTH–E.L.C.A.	695	100,161	310,421	414,326	7.3	13.6
LUTH–Evan Luth Syn	22	2,090	3,870	4,633	0.1	0.2
LUTH–Luth Ch-Am Asc	4	NR	NR	NR	-	-
LUTH–Luth Cong Msn Chr	49	6,141	18,498	22,401	0.4	0.7

NR–Not Reported   - Represents no adherents reported.   Percentages may not total 100 due to rounding.

Table 2: Religious Congregations by State and Group: 2010

Religious Group	Number of Congrega-tions	Number of Attendees	Number of Communicant, Confirmed, or Full Members	Adherents: Number of Adherents	Adherents: % of Total Pop.	Adherents: % of Total Adh.
LUTH–Luth–MO Synod	431	72,412	173,187	223,279	3.9	7.3
LUTH–Nor Amer Luth C	15	NR	NR	NR	-	-
LUTH–Wisc Ev Luth Syn	419	81,120	159,003	198,667	3.5	6.5
MENN–Amish Undif	115	NR	5,536	14,957	0.3	0.5
MENN–CG in Cr (Menn)	4	NR	399	481	0.0	0.0
MENN–Mennonite USA	7	251	292	352	0.0	0.0
MENN–Tamp Amish-Menn	2	207	127	207	0.0	0.0
METH–AME	13	1,230	2,630	3,250	0.1	0.1
METH–AME Zion	1	0	100	124	0.0	0.0
METH–C.M.E.	10	512	2,468	3,063	0.1	0.1
METH–Free Methodist	10	866	611	908	0.0	0.0
METH–Prim Meth Ch	11	NR	NR	NR	-	-
METH–Un Methodist	473	37,722	79,325	114,938	2.0	3.8
METH–Wesleyan	30	3,691	2,186	4,800	0.1	0.2
Metro Comm Ch	2	56	51	63	0.0	0.0
Missionary Ch	2	69	25	69	0.0	0.0
MJEW–Union Mes Cong	1	NR	NR	NR	-	-
MORAV–Morav Ch-North	17	1,182	3,069	3,640	0.1	0.1
Muslim Est	23	4,617	NR	14,744	0.3	0.5
New Apost Ch	7	NR	NR	NR	-	-
Non-denom Chr Chs	568	103,654	112,369	138,672	2.4	4.6
OCATH–Pol Natl Cath	6	NR	NR	NR	-	-
ORTHE–Ant Orth of NA	3	280	NR	515	0.0	0.0
ORTHE–Greek Orthodox	8	1,480	NR	5,020	0.1	0.2
ORTHE–Orth Ch in Amer	8	342	NR	579	0.0	0.0
ORTHE–Rus Orth Abroad	4	182	NR	779	0.0	0.0
ORTHE–Serb Orth USA	5	1,789	NR	5,060	0.1	0.2
ORTHE–Ukrainian Orth	1	35	NR	100	0.0	0.0
ORTHO–Armen Ap Cilic	1	60	NR	400	0.0	0.0
ORTHO–Armen Ap Etchm	2	180	NR	535	0.0	0.0
ORTHO–Coptic Orth Ch	2	218	NR	235	0.0	0.0
PENT–Apos Faith Msn	2	NR	70	85	0.0	0.0
PENT–Assemb of God	182	27,106	14,722	45,895	0.8	1.5
PENT–Assm God Intl F	2	NR	NR	NR	-	-
PENT–Ch God (Cleve)	17	914	1,252	1,519	0.0	0.0
PENT–Ch Lord Jesus Apos	1	NR	NR	NR	-	-
PENT–Ch of God Proph	5	NR	140	171	0.0	0.0
PENT–COGIC	35	5,531	10,870	13,484	0.2	0.4
PENT–Full Gosp Bapt	12	NR	NR	NR	-	-
PENT–Int Foursq Gos	16	904	1,227	1,463	0.0	0.0
PENT–Intl Pent Holiness	3	69	103	126	0.0	0.0
PENT–Open Bible Std	2	85	NR	85	0.0	0.0
PENT–Pent Ch of God	5	350	NR	545	0.0	0.0
PENT–Un Pent Ch Intl	74	NR	NR	NR	-	-
PENT–United Holy Ch	6	NR	NR	NR	-	-
PENT–Vineyard	10	1,011	1,576	1,901	0.0	0.1
PRES–Cov Ref Pres	1	NR	NR	NR	-	-
PRES–Evan Presby Ch	2	NR	250	305	0.0	0.0
PRES–Korean Pres Amer	1	NR	NR	NR	-	-
PRES–Orth Pres Ch	14	1,311	1,475	2,042	0.0	0.1
PRES–Presb Ch (USA)	154	11,741	26,067	31,692	0.6	1.0
PRES–Presb Ch Amer	10	740	766	946	0.0	0.0
PRES–Ref Pres GA	1	NR	NR	NR	-	-
REF–Christian Ref	23	3,817	5,334	6,494	0.1	0.2
REF–Heritage Ref	1	NR	9	11	0.0	0.0
REF–Prot Ref Chs	1	189	122	214	0.0	0.0
REF–Ref Ch in Am	27	5,650	10,763	11,601	0.2	0.4
REF–Ref Ch in U.S.	1	NR	196	222	0.0	0.0
REF–Un Ref Chs N.A.	1	NR	NR	NR	-	-
Salvation Army	23	1,247	1,444	11,175	0.2	0.4
Sev Day Adv	82	5,018	8,724	10,034	0.2	0.3
Sikh	3	NR	NR	NR	-	-
Un C of Christ	229	20,658	54,005	65,797	1.2	2.2
Unit Univ	28	2,363	5,597	7,553	0.1	0.2
Unity Ch	9	NR	NR	NR	-	-
Zoroastrian	0	NR	NR	20	0.0	0.0
WYOMING	**948**	**43,712**	**69,169**	**223,074**	**39.6**	**100.0**
ANG/EPIS–Anglican NA	5	NR	NR	NR	-	-
ANG/EPIS–Episcopal	46	1,972	5,883	7,279	1.3	3.3
Bahá'í	3	NR	290	290	0.1	0.1
BAPT–Amer Bapt Assn	3	NR	320	394	0.1	0.2
BAPT–Amer Bapt USA	16	1,390	2,190	2,670	0.5	1.2
BAPT–Consrv Bapt	13	NR	NR	NR	-	-
BAPT–Converge/BGC	6	1,175	NR	1,410	0.3	0.6
BAPT–Free Will Bapt	1	NR	10	12	0.0	0.0
BAPT–Ind Bapt Flwsp Intl	1	NR	NR	NR	-	-
BAPT–Natl Mis Bapt Conv	1	10	12	15	0.0	0.0
BAPT–NBC USA	1	0	0	0	0.0	0.0
BAPT–NT Ind Bapt	2	NR	NR	NR	-	-
BAPT–Ref Bapt Ch	2	NR	NR	NR	-	-
BAPT–So Bapt Conv	100	5,461	12,720	15,812	2.8	7.1
BRETH–Brethren (Ash)	1	NR	80	99	0.0	0.0
BUDD–Mahayana	2	NR	NR	22	0.0	0.0
BUDD–Vajrayana	2	NR	NR	105	0.0	0.0
Calv Chpl	6	NR	NR	NR	-	-
Catholic	70	NR	NR	61,222	10.9	27.4
CGOD–Ch God (Ander)	6	2,030	NR	2,030	0.4	0.9
Ch Cr, Scientist	4	NR	NR	NR	-	-
Ch of Nazarene	16	811	972	1,327	0.2	0.6
Chr & Miss Al	14	1,453	770	2,464	0.4	1.1
CHR–Chr Ch (Disc)	4	504	1,435	1,738	0.3	0.8
CHR–Chr Chs & Chs Cr	17	NR	1,372	1,681	0.3	0.8
CHR–Chs of Christ	33	1,694	1,486	1,957	0.3	0.9
CONG–Cong Chr, NA	1	NR	20	25	0.0	0.0
Evan Ch	3	NR	NR	NR	-	-
Evan Free Ch	10	1,518	NR	1,518	0.3	0.7
FRND–Fr Gen Cf	5	NR	25	30	0.0	0.0
FRND–Indep Yr Mtgs	1	NR	4	5	0.0	0.0
Grace Gosp Fel	1	NR	NR	NR	-	-
HINDU–Post Ren	1	NR	NR	76	0.0	0.0
Jehovah's Witness	22	NR	NR	NR	-	-
JUD–Reform	1	27	47	127	0.0	0.1
LDS–Comm of Christ	4	NR	512	512	0.1	0.2
LDS–L-D Saints	153	NR	NR	62,804	11.1	28.2
LUTH–Ch Luth Conf	1	NR	NR	NR	-	-
LUTH–E.L.C.A.	22	1,927	5,863	7,541	1.3	3.4
LUTH–Luth Ch-Am Asc	1	NR	NR	NR	-	-
LUTH–Luth Cong Msn Chr	1	NR	NR	NR	-	-
LUTH–Luth–MO Synod	41	3,002	7,153	9,344	1.7	4.2
LUTH–Nor Amer Luth C	2	NR	NR	NR	-	-
LUTH–Wisc Ev Luth Syn	4	219	333	429	0.1	0.2
MENN–CG in Cr (Menn)	1	NR	8	10	0.0	0.0
METH–A.W.M.C.	1	14	0	18	0.0	0.0
METH–AME	2	45	175	216	0.0	0.1
METH–Un Methodist	40	3,119	7,513	10,768	1.9	4.8
METH–Wesleyan	3	972	362	1,264	0.2	0.6
Muslim Est	3	303	NR	716	0.1	0.3
Non-denom Chr Chs	85	7,936	9,262	10,735	1.9	4.8
ORTHE–Ant Orth of NA	1	18	NR	40	0.0	0.0
ORTHE–Greek Orthodox	3	200	NR	745	0.1	0.3
PENT–Assemb of God	43	2,987	1,570	4,419	0.8	2.0
PENT–Ch God (Cleve)	2	39	39	50	0.0	0.0
PENT–Ch of God Proph	6	NR	315	384	0.1	0.2
PENT–COGIC	2	30	40	50	0.0	0.0
PENT–Cong Hol Ch	2	78	70	88	0.0	0.0
PENT–Int Foursq Gos	9	791	714	878	0.2	0.4
PENT–Open Bible Std	1	25	NR	25	0.0	0.0
PENT–Pent Ch of God	1	70	NR	109	0.0	0.0
PENT–Un Pent Ch Intl	17	NR	NR	NR	-	-
PENT–Vineyard	3	190	300	376	0.1	0.2
PRES–Presb Ch (USA)	31	2,086	4,397	5,348	0.9	2.4
PRES–Presb Ch Amer	3	267	223	273	0.0	0.1
PRES–Ref Pres of NA	1	25	12	20	0.0	0.0
REF–Ref Ch in U.S.	1	NR	38	53	0.0	0.0
Salvation Army	3	92	285	731	0.1	0.3
Sev Day Adv	22	668	1,161	1,337	0.2	0.6
Un C of Christ	9	366	920	1,135	0.2	0.5
Unit Univ	4	198	268	344	0.1	0.2
Zoroastrian	0	NR	NR	4	0.0	0.0

NR–Not Reported - Represents no adherents reported. Percentages may not total 100 due to rounding.

This page intentionally left blank.

Table 3: Religious Congregations by County and Group: 2010

Religious Group	Number of Congregations	Number of Attendees	Number of Communicant, Confirmed, or Full Members	Adherents		
				Number of Adherents	% of Total Pop.	% of Total Adh.
ALABAMA	**10,514**	**1,003,980**	**2,251,695**	**3,007,553**	**62.9**	**100.0**
AUTAUGA	**106**	**11,111**	**27,062**	**36,938**	**67.7**	**100.0**
ANG/EPIS–Anglican NA	1	NR	NR	NR	-	-
ANG/EPIS–Episcopal	1	150	300	415	0.8	1.1
Bahá'í	0	NR	33	33	0.1	0.1
BAPT–Amer Bapt Assn	1	NR	150	188	0.3	0.5
BAPT–Free Will Bapt	1	NR	104	130	0.2	0.4
BAPT–NBC USA	3	350	725	908	1.7	2.5
BAPT–So Bapt Conv	37	4,585	13,711	17,171	31.5	46.5
Catholic	1	NR	NR	1,766	3.2	4.8
CGOD–Ch God (Ander)	1	40	NR	40	0.1	0.1
Chr & Miss Al	1	130	75	186	0.3	0.5
CHR–Chr Chs & Chs Cr	1	NR	55	69	0.1	0.2
CHR–Chs of Christ	6	952	813	1,137	2.1	3.1
Grace Gosp Fel	1	NR	NR	NR	-	-
LDS–L-D Saints	1	NR	NR	820	1.5	2.2
LUTH–E.L.C.A.	1	38	83	161	0.3	0.4
LUTH–Luth Cong Msn Chr	1	25	30	38	0.1	0.1
LUTH–Luth–MO Synod	1	21	35	46	0.1	0.1
METH–AME	6	0	700	877	1.6	2.4
METH–AME Zion	2	20	134	168	0.3	0.5
METH–C.M.E.	1	20	120	150	0.3	0.4
METH–Un Methodist	10	1,034	2,986	3,946	7.2	10.7
METH–Wesleyan	1	112	151	146	0.3	0.4
Non-denom Chr Chs	10	1,520	1,615	1,945	3.6	5.3
PENT–Assemb of God	4	242	168	275	0.5	0.7
PENT–Ch God (Cleve)	5	367	763	956	1.8	2.6
PENT–COGIC	1	0	150	188	0.3	0.5
PENT–Intl Pent Holiness	1	1,304	3,800	4,759	8.7	12.9
PENT–Un Pent Ch Intl	2	NR	NR	NR	-	-
PRES–As Ref Pres Ch	1	NR	0	0	0.0	0.0
PRES–Evan Presby Ch	1	NR	13	16	0.0	0.0
PRES–Presb Ch Amer	1	155	267	308	0.6	0.8
Sev Day Adv	1	46	81	93	0.2	0.3
Zoroastrian	0	NR	NR	3	0.0	0.0
BALDWIN	**271**	**34,068**	**65,965**	**96,918**	**53.2**	**100.0**
ANG/EPIS–Anglican NA	1	NR	NR	NR	-	-
ANG/EPIS–Episcopal	9	1,323	3,090	3,399	1.9	3.5
Bahá'í	1	NR	37	37	0.0	0.0
BAPT–Amer Bapt Assn	1	NR	150	182	0.1	0.2
BAPT–Free Will Bapt	1	NR	104	126	0.1	0.1
BAPT–Natl Mis Bapt Conv	3	0	450	547	0.3	0.6
BAPT–So Bapt Conv	67	10,875	30,302	36,823	20.2	38.0
Calv Chpl	2	NR	NR	NR	-	-
Catholic	13	NR	NR	14,009	7.7	14.5
CGOD–Ch God (Ander)	2	102	NR	102	0.1	0.1
Ch Cr, Scientst	2	NR	NR	NR	-	-
Ch of Nazarene	1	34	39	39	0.0	0.0
Chr & Miss Al	1	310	176	376	0.2	0.4
CHR–Chr Ch (Disc)	3	158	443	538	0.3	0.6
CHR–Chr Chs & Chs Cr	2	NR	441	536	0.3	0.6
CHR–Chs of Christ	12	1,457	1,167	1,515	0.8	1.6
Evan Cov Ch	3	139	243	180	0.1	0.2
FRND–Fr Gen Cf	1	NR	20	24	0.0	0.0
Grace Gosp Fel	1	NR	NR	NR	-	-
Jehovah's Witness	4	NR	NR	NR	-	-
LDS–Comm of Christ	2	NR	323	323	0.2	0.3
LDS–L-D Saints	2	NR	NR	1,022	0.6	1.1
LUTH–Assoc Free Luth	1	NR	NR	NR	-	-
LUTH–E.L.C.A.	2	183	233	264	0.1	0.3
LUTH–Luth Cong Msn Chr	1	39	43	52	0.0	0.1
LUTH–Luth–MO Synod	8	806	1,278	1,544	0.8	1.6
METH–AME	7	75	850	1,033	0.6	1.1
METH–AME Zion	2	70	300	365	0.2	0.4
METH–C.M.E.	1	0	150	182	0.1	0.2
METH–Un Methodist	24	4,926	10,650	13,540	7.4	14.0
METH–Wesleyan	1	101	87	131	0.1	0.1
New Apost Ch	1	NR	NR	NR	-	-
Non-denom Chr Chs	26	4,508	5,361	6,065	3.3	6.3
ORTHE–Greek Orthodox	1	45	NR	190	0.1	0.2
PENT–Assemb of God	17	2,465	1,530	3,410	1.9	3.5
PENT–Ch God (Cleve)	11	3,902	3,640	4,423	2.4	4.6
PENT–Ch of God Proph	1	NR	50	61	0.0	0.1
PENT–COGIC	4	100	825	1,003	0.6	1.0
PENT–Intl Pent Holiness	6	579	924	1,123	0.6	1.2
PENT–Un Pent Ch Intl	4	NR	NR	NR	-	-
PRES–Presb Ch (USA)	9	1,056	1,901	2,310	1.3	2.4
PRES–Presb Ch Amer	5	530	665	890	0.5	0.9
Sev Day Adv	3	204	354	408	0.2	0.4
Unit Univ	1	81	139	146	0.1	0.2
Unity Ch	1	NR	NR	NR	-	-
BARBOUR	**89**	**4,621**	**11,656**	**15,101**	**55.0**	**100.0**
ANG/EPIS–Episcopal	1	87	338	338	1.2	2.2
BAPT–Free Will Bapt	1	NR	104	125	0.5	0.8
BAPT–NBC USA	5	100	700	841	3.1	5.6
BAPT–So Bapt Conv	25	1,905	5,526	6,639	24.2	44.0
Catholic	1	NR	NR	575	2.1	3.8
CGOD–Ch God (Ander)	1	0	NR	0	0.0	0.0
CHR–Chs of Christ	2	120	107	147	0.5	1.0
Jehovah's Witness	1	NR	NR	NR	-	-
LDS–L-D Saints	1	NR	NR	265	1.0	1.8
METH–AME	13	260	1,900	2,283	8.3	15.1
METH–Un Methodist	11	538	1,206	1,473	5.4	9.8
Non-denom Chr Chs	7	733	730	918	3.3	6.1
PENT–Assemb of God	8	460	345	663	2.4	4.4
PENT–Ch God (Cleve)	1	72	84	101	0.4	0.7
PENT–COGIC	3	120	170	204	0.7	1.4
PENT–Un Pent Ch Intl	1	NR	NR	NR	-	-
PRES–Presb Ch (USA)	1	70	223	268	1.0	1.8
PRES–Presb Ch Amer	4	106	146	170	0.6	1.1
Sev Day Adv	1	15	26	30	0.1	0.2
Un C of Christ	1	35	51	61	0.2	0.4
BIBB	**81**	**3,896**	**9,480**	**11,430**	**49.9**	**100.0**
Bahá'í	0	NR	3	3	0.0	0.0
BAPT–Free Will Bapt	1	NR	104	126	0.5	1.1
BAPT–NBC USA	1	0	150	181	0.8	1.6
BAPT–So Bapt Conv	42	2,928	7,125	8,609	37.6	75.3
Ch of Nazarene	2	123	170	170	0.7	1.5
CHR–Chs of Christ	3	120	100	134	0.6	1.2
Jehovah's Witness	1	NR	NR	NR	-	-
METH–AME	3	0	350	423	1.8	3.7
METH–AME Zion	3	0	300	362	1.6	3.2
METH–Un Methodist	8	140	246	279	1.2	2.4
Non-denom Chr Chs	2	210	270	288	1.3	2.5
PENT–Assemb of God	2	130	111	203	0.9	1.8
PENT–Ch God (Cleve)	2	147	252	304	1.3	2.7
PENT–Ch Lord Jesus Apos	1	NR	NR	NR	-	-
PENT–Ch of God Proph	3	NR	150	181	0.8	1.6
PENT–Un Pent Ch Intl	3	NR	NR	NR	-	-
PRES–Presb Ch (USA)	1	18	19	23	0.1	0.2
PRES–Presb Ch Amer	2	60	95	104	0.5	0.9
Sev Day Adv	1	20	35	40	0.2	0.3
BLOUNT	**156**	**10,849**	**26,537**	**37,352**	**65.2**	**100.0**
ANG/EPIS–Episcopal	1	20	39	44	0.1	0.1
Bahá'í	0	NR	1	1	0.0	0.0
BAPT–Free Will Bapt	1	NR	104	128	0.2	0.3
BAPT–Natl Mis Bapt Conv	1	12	17	21	0.0	0.1
BAPT–NBC USA	1	30	30	37	0.1	0.1
BAPT–So Bapt Conv	79	7,057	19,916	24,529	42.8	65.7
BRETH–Ch of Brethren	1	0	43	53	0.1	0.1
Catholic	1	NR	NR	4,744	8.3	12.7
Ch of Nazarene	5	254	356	623	1.1	1.7
Chr & Miss Al	1	21	10	30	0.1	0.1
CHR–Chs of Christ	8	368	427	517	0.9	1.4
FRND–Fr Gen Cf	1	NR	0	0	0.0	0.0
Jehovah's Witness	1	NR	NR	NR	-	-
LDS–L-D Saints	1	NR	NR	291	0.5	0.8
METH–Un Methodist	27	1,329	2,766	2,991	5.2	8.0
Non-denom Chr Chs	8	680	1,020	1,020	1.8	2.7
PENT–Assemb of God	3	118	105	227	0.4	0.6
PENT–Ch God (Cleve)	10	824	1,354	1,668	2.9	4.5

NR–Not Reported - Represents no adherents reported. Percentages may not total 100 due to rounding.

Table 3: Religious Congregations by County and Group: 2010

Religious Group	Number of Congregations	Number of Attendees	Number of Communicant, Confirmed, or Full Members	Adherents: Number of Adherents	Adherents: % of Total Pop.	Adherents: % of Total Adh.
PENT–Intl Pent Holiness	1	130	296	365	0.6	1.0
PRES–Cumber Presb	3	NR	42	50	0.1	0.1
PRES–Presb Ch Amer	1	0	0	0	0.0	0.0
Sev Day Adv	1	6	11	13	0.0	0.0
BULLOCK	**47**	**1,044**	**5,151**	**6,300**	**57.7**	**100.0**
Bahá'í	0	NR	53	53	0.5	0.8
BAPT–Natl Mis Bapt Conv	1	0	150	181	1.7	2.9
BAPT–NBC USA	3	85	725	875	8.0	13.9
BAPT–So Bapt Conv	8	446	1,487	1,794	16.4	28.5
Catholic	1	NR	NR	49	0.4	0.8
Ch of Chr (Hol)	1	NR	NR	NR	-	-
CHR–Chs of Christ	1	38	30	60	0.5	1.0
Jehovah's Witness	1	NR	NR	NR	-	-
METH–AME	11	35	1,280	1,544	14.1	24.5
METH–AME Zion	4	0	450	543	5.0	8.6
METH–C.M.E.	2	0	250	302	2.8	4.8
METH–Un Methodist	8	211	408	562	5.1	8.9
Non-denom Chr Chs	2	138	200	200	1.8	3.2
PENT–Cong Hol Ch	1	39	35	42	0.4	0.7
PRES–Presb Ch (USA)	1	15	32	39	0.4	0.6
PRES–Presb Ch Amer	1	17	17	17	0.2	0.3
Sev Day Adv	1	20	34	39	0.4	0.6
BUTLER	**92**	**4,299**	**10,167**	**12,278**	**58.6**	**100.0**
ANG/EPIS–Episcopal	1	64	231	235	1.1	1.9
BAPT–NBC Amer	1	0	150	184	0.9	1.5
BAPT–NBC USA	2	0	500	614	2.9	5.0
BAPT–So Bapt Conv	35	2,101	5,440	6,675	31.9	54.4
Catholic	1	NR	NR	77	0.4	0.6
CHR–Chr Ch (Disc)	3	194	458	562	2.7	4.6
CHR–Chr Chs & Chs Cr	1	NR	50	61	0.3	0.5
CHR–Chs of Christ	11	613	647	786	3.8	6.4
Jehovah's Witness	1	NR	NR	NR	-	-
LDS–Comm of Christ	1	NR	136	136	0.6	1.1
LDS–L-D Saints	1	NR	NR	102	0.5	0.8
METH–AME Zion	4	0	550	675	3.2	5.5
METH–Un Methodist	13	370	801	856	4.1	7.0
Non-denom Chr Chs	5	500	675	700	3.3	5.7
PENT–Assemb of God	1	95	80	95	0.5	0.8
PENT–Ch God (Cleve)	3	165	41	50	0.2	0.4
PENT–COGIC	1	0	150	184	0.9	1.5
PENT–Intl Pent Holiness	4	91	80	98	0.5	0.8
PENT–Un Pent Ch Intl	1	NR	NR	NR	-	-
PRES–Presb Ch Amer	1	90	149	155	0.7	1.3
Sev Day Adv	1	16	29	33	0.2	0.3
CALHOUN	**281**	**28,966**	**65,163**	**84,615**	**71.4**	**100.0**
ANG/EPIS–Episcopal	3	322	664	744	0.6	0.9
Bahá'í	0	NR	20	20	0.0	0.0
BAPT–Natl Mis Bapt Conv	1	0	150	182	0.2	0.2
BAPT–NBC USA	6	515	2,500	3,038	2.6	3.6
BAPT–So Bapt Conv	91	12,320	38,120	46,326	39.1	54.7
Catholic	4	NR	NR	3,192	2.7	3.8
CGOD–Ch God (Ander)	1	34	NR	34	0.0	0.0
Ch of Nazarene	2	109	191	193	0.2	0.2
CHR–Chr Ch (Disc)	2	39	155	188	0.2	0.2
CHR–Chr Chs & Chs Cr	2	NR	185	225	0.2	0.3
CHR–Chs of Christ	16	2,035	2,009	2,569	2.2	3.0
Jehovah's Witness	2	NR	NR	NR	-	-
JUD–Reform	1	24	42	113	0.1	0.1
LDS–L-D Saints	2	NR	NR	1,149	1.0	1.4
LUTH–E.L.C.A.	2	75	129	218	0.2	0.3
METH–AME	1	0	100	122	0.1	0.1
METH–AME Zion	1	0	100	122	0.1	0.1
METH–C.M.E.	11	260	1,078	1,310	1.1	1.5
METH–Cong Meth	8	NR	733	891	0.8	1.1
METH–Un Methodist	27	2,091	4,119	5,160	4.4	6.1
METH–Wesleyan	1	30	32	39	0.0	0.0
Muslim Est	1	134	NR	308	0.3	0.4
Non-denom Chr Chs	30	7,355	7,950	9,712	8.2	11.5
ORTHE–Orth Ch in Amer	1	30	NR	40	0.0	0.0
PENT–Apos Faith Msn	1	NR	35	43	0.0	0.1
PENT–Assemb of God	6	331	239	511	0.4	0.6
PENT–Ch God (Cleve)	13	1,531	3,537	4,298	3.6	5.1
PENT–Ch Lord Jesus Apos	1	NR	NR	NR	-	-
PENT–Ch of God by Faith	1	NR	NR	NR	-	-
PENT–Ch of God Proph	1	NR	66	80	0.1	0.1
PENT–COGIC	3	15	320	389	0.3	0.5
PENT–Cong Hol Ch	16	717	640	778	0.7	0.9
PENT–Fire Bapt Hol Ch	2	NR	NR	NR	-	-
PENT–Int Foursq Gos	1	163	485	589	0.5	0.7
PENT–Intl Pent Holiness	2	249	258	314	0.3	0.4
PENT–Un Pent Ch Intl	2	NR	NR	NR	-	-
PRES–Cumber Presb	1	NR	61	90	0.1	0.1
PRES–Presb Ch (USA)	8	186	622	756	0.6	0.9
PRES–Presb Ch Amer	2	140	176	228	0.2	0.3
Salvation Army	1	71	116	264	0.2	0.3
Sev Day Adv	4	190	331	380	0.3	0.4
CHAMBERS	**119**	**6,516**	**17,966**	**22,251**	**65.0**	**100.0**
Bahá'í	0	NR	2	2	0.0	0.0
BAPT–NBC Amer	2	80	106	127	0.4	0.6
BAPT–NBC USA	9	1,175	3,660	4,402	12.9	19.8
BAPT–So Bapt Conv	36	2,422	8,504	10,229	29.9	46.0
Catholic	1	NR	NR	249	0.7	1.1
CGOD–Ch God (Ander)	2	84	NR	84	0.2	0.4
Ch of Nazarene	4	300	520	584	1.7	2.6
CHR–Chr Ch (Disc)	2	0	75	90	0.3	0.4
CHR–Chr Chs & Chs Cr	2	NR	400	481	1.4	2.2
CHR–Chs of Christ	4	241	223	282	0.8	1.3
CONG–Cong Chr, NA	2	NR	75	90	0.3	0.4
Jehovah's Witness	1	NR	NR	NR	-	-
LDS–L-D Saints	1	NR	NR	237	0.7	1.1
METH–AME	4	68	400	481	1.4	2.2
METH–C.M.E.	6	0	640	770	2.3	3.5
METH–Un Methodist	26	1,345	2,338	2,792	8.2	12.5
Non-denom Chr Chs	4	390	505	513	1.5	2.3
PENT–Assemb of God	4	233	190	335	1.0	1.5
PENT–Ch God (Cleve)	1	37	173	208	0.6	0.9
PENT–Cong Hol Ch	1	31	28	34	0.1	0.2
PENT–Pent Ch of God	1	70	NR	109	0.3	0.5
PENT–Un Pent Ch Intl	1	NR	NR	NR	-	-
PENT–Vineyard	1	16	20	24	0.1	0.1
PRES–Presb Ch (USA)	1	0	11	13	0.0	0.1
Sev Day Adv	1	10	17	20	0.1	0.1
Un C of Christ	2	14	79	95	0.3	0.4
CHEROKEE	**79**	**4,463**	**10,463**	**12,455**	**47.9**	**100.0**
BAPT–So Bapt Conv	49	3,066	8,394	10,013	38.5	80.4
CHR–Chs of Christ	3	120	120	149	0.6	1.2
Jehovah's Witness	1	NR	NR	NR	-	-
METH–Cong Meth	1	NR	39	47	0.2	0.4
METH–Un Methodist	16	894	1,329	1,590	6.1	12.8
Non-denom Chr Chs	2	135	195	195	0.8	1.6
PENT–Ch God (Cleve)	2	131	203	242	0.9	1.9
PENT–Ch of God Proph	1	NR	61	73	0.3	0.6
PENT–Cong Hol Ch	3	117	122	146	0.6	1.2
PENT–Un Pent Ch Intl	1	NR	NR	NR	-	-
CHILTON	**122**	**9,993**	**24,157**	**30,488**	**69.9**	**100.0**
ANG/EPIS–Episcopal	1	38	65	66	0.2	0.2
Bahá'í	0	NR	3	3	0.0	0.0
BAPT–Amer Bapt Assn	2	NR	145	180	0.4	0.6
BAPT–Natl Mis Bapt Conv	2	0	300	372	0.9	1.2
BAPT–NBC USA	2	0	300	372	0.9	1.2
BAPT–So Bapt Conv	59	5,965	17,026	21,118	48.4	69.3
Catholic	1	NR	NR	709	1.6	2.3
CGOD–Ch God (Ander)	1	60	NR	60	0.1	0.2
Ch of Nazarene	1	41	20	41	0.1	0.1
CHR–Chs of Christ	5	203	318	304	0.7	1.0
CONG–Cong Chr, NA	1	NR	105	130	0.3	0.4
Jehovah's Witness	1	NR	NR	NR	-	-
LDS–L-D Saints	1	NR	NR	247	0.6	0.8
METH–AME	2	0	300	372	0.9	1.2
METH–Un Methodist	12	895	1,423	1,609	3.7	5.3

NR–Not Reported - Represents no adherents reported. Percentages may not total 100 due to rounding.

Table 3: Religious Congregations by County and Group: 2010

Religious Group	Number of Congregations	Number of Attendees	Number of Communicant, Confirmed, or Full Members	Adherents: Number of Adherents	Adherents: % of Total Pop.	Adherents: % of Total Adh.
Non-denom Chr Chs	10	1,235	1,895	1,943	4.5	6.4
PENT–Assemb of God	8	784	853	1,232	2.8	4.0
PENT–Ch God (Cleve)	9	654	1,244	1,543	3.5	5.1
PENT–Ch of God Proph	1	NR	9	11	0.0	0.0
PENT–Full Gosp Bapt	1	NR	NR	NR	-	-
PRES–Presb Ch Amer	1	60	50	60	0.1	0.2
Sev Day Adv	1	58	101	116	0.3	0.4
CHOCTAW	**83**	**3,400**	**7,527**	**9,721**	**70.1**	**100.0**
BAPT–NBC USA	3	200	500	602	4.3	6.2
BAPT–So Bapt Conv	29	1,395	3,418	4,115	29.7	42.3
Catholic	1	NR	NR	60	0.4	0.6
CGOD–Ch God (Ander)	1	0	NR	0	0.0	0.0
CHR–Chs of Christ	2	100	97	145	1.0	1.5
Christian Brethren	1	NR	NR	NR	-	-
LDS–L-D Saints	1	NR	NR	157	1.1	1.6
METH–AME	1	0	100	120	0.9	1.2
METH–AME Zion	5	150	855	1,029	7.4	10.6
METH–C.M.E.	5	0	550	662	4.8	6.8
METH–Cong Meth	1	NR	65	78	0.6	0.8
METH–Un Methodist	12	290	692	778	5.6	8.0
Non-denom Chr Chs	3	265	350	381	2.7	3.9
PENT–Assemb of God	9	747	361	947	6.8	9.7
PENT–Ch God (Cleve)	3	184	279	336	2.4	3.5
PENT–COGIC	2	20	184	222	1.6	2.3
PENT–Intl Pent Holiness	1	15	20	24	0.2	0.2
PENT–Un Pent Ch Intl	1	NR	NR	NR	-	-
PRES–Presb Ch (USA)	1	7	9	11	0.1	0.1
Sev Day Adv	1	27	47	54	0.4	0.6
CLARKE	**122**	**5,800**	**16,594**	**20,470**	**79.2**	**100.0**
ANG/EPIS–Episcopal	1	25	38	38	0.1	0.2
BAPT–Ind Bapt Flwsp Intl	2	NR	NR	NR	-	-
BAPT–NBC USA	4	425	1,450	1,774	6.9	8.7
BAPT–So Bapt Conv	49	3,162	9,649	11,803	45.7	57.7
Catholic	3	NR	NR	11	0.0	0.1
CGOD–Ch God (Ander)	1	0	NR	0	0.0	0.0
Ch of Nazarene	1	8	21	31	0.1	0.2
CHR–Chs of Christ	5	210	218	282	1.1	1.4
Jehovah's Witness	2	NR	NR	NR	-	-
LDS–L-D Saints	1	NR	NR	95	0.4	0.5
LUTH–Luth–MO Synod	1	25	23	23	0.1	0.1
METH–AME	9	190	1,160	1,419	5.5	6.9
METH–AME Zion	4	20	507	620	2.4	3.0
METH–C.M.E.	5	0	550	673	2.6	3.3
METH–Un Methodist	14	336	1,400	1,551	6.0	7.6
Non-denom Chr Chs	5	473	616	666	2.6	3.3
PENT–Apos Faith Msn	1	NR	35	43	0.2	0.2
PENT–Assemb of God	5	283	83	417	1.6	2.0
PENT–Ch God (Cleve)	2	94	179	219	0.8	1.1
PENT–Ch of God Proph	1	NR	10	12	0.0	0.1
PENT–COGIC	1	455	500	612	2.4	3.0
PENT–Un Pent Ch Intl	2	NR	NR	NR	-	-
PRES–Presb Ch (USA)	1	25	35	43	0.2	0.2
Sev Day Adv	2	69	120	138	0.5	0.7
CLAY	**69**	**3,442**	**8,357**	**10,305**	**74.0**	**100.0**
Bahá'í	0	NR	1	1	0.0	0.0
BAPT–NBC USA	1	0	150	181	1.3	1.8
BAPT–So Bapt Conv	39	2,139	6,502	7,848	56.3	76.2
Catholic	1	NR	NR	186	1.3	1.8
CHR–Chs of Christ	6	306	316	381	2.7	3.7
Jehovah's Witness	1	NR	NR	NR	-	-
METH–Cong Meth	1	NR	17	21	0.2	0.2
METH–Un Methodist	12	439	823	1,038	7.5	10.1
Non-denom Chr Chs	2	180	175	225	1.6	2.2
PENT–Assemb of God	1	236	232	256	1.8	2.5
PENT–Ch God (Cleve)	2	107	92	111	0.8	1.1
PENT–Ch Lord Jesus Apos	1	NR	NR	NR	-	-
PENT–Intl Pent Holiness	1	15	15	18	0.1	0.2
Sev Day Adv	1	20	34	39	0.3	0.4

Religious Group	Number of Congregations	Number of Attendees	Number of Communicant, Confirmed, or Full Members	Adherents: Number of Adherents	Adherents: % of Total Pop.	Adherents: % of Total Adh.
CLEBURNE	**66**	**3,900**	**9,452**	**11,463**	**76.6**	**100.0**
ANG/EPIS–Episcopal	1	35	91	104	0.7	0.9
Bahá'í	0	NR	1	1	0.0	0.0
BAPT–Natl Mis Bapt Conv	1	0	150	183	1.2	1.6
BAPT–So Bapt Conv	38	2,914	7,628	9,308	62.2	81.2
CHR–Chs of Christ	3	113	157	186	1.2	1.6
METH–Cong Meth	1	NR	225	275	1.8	2.4
METH–Un Methodist	16	427	637	740	4.9	6.5
Non-denom Chr Chs	1	100	150	150	1.0	1.3
PENT–Assemb of God	1	85	60	85	0.6	0.7
PENT–Ch God (Cleve)	4	226	353	431	2.9	3.8
COFFEE	**120**	**10,431**	**24,391**	**33,021**	**66.1**	**100.0**
ANG/EPIS–Episcopal	1	40	80	110	0.2	0.3
BAPT–Free Will Bapt	2	NR	208	255	0.5	0.8
BAPT–NBC USA	1	200	300	368	0.7	1.1
BAPT–So Bapt Conv	54	6,581	17,791	21,848	43.7	66.2
Calv Chpl	1	NR	NR	NR	-	-
Catholic	1	NR	NR	1,550	3.1	4.7
Ch Cr, Scientst	1	NR	NR	NR	-	-
CHR–Chs of Christ	7	697	668	882	1.8	2.7
Jehovah's Witness	2	NR	NR	NR	-	-
LDS–L-D Saints	1	NR	NR	805	1.6	2.4
LUTH–Luth–MO Synod	1	55	115	129	0.3	0.4
METH–AME	4	0	450	553	1.1	1.7
METH–Un Methodist	11	1,174	2,680	3,236	6.5	9.8
Non-denom Chr Chs	3	280	425	425	0.9	1.3
PENT–Assemb of God	15	938	468	1,371	2.7	4.2
PENT–Ch God (Cleve)	3	249	614	754	1.5	2.3
PENT–Ch of God by Faith	1	NR	NR	NR	-	-
PENT–Ch of God Proph	1	NR	33	41	0.1	0.1
PENT–COGIC	3	20	325	399	0.8	1.2
PENT–Full Gosp Bapt	3	NR	NR	NR	-	-
PENT–Intl Pent Holiness	1	49	45	55	0.1	0.2
PENT–Un Pent Ch Intl	1	NR	NR	NR	-	-
PRES–Presb Ch (USA)	1	70	90	111	0.2	0.3
PRES–Presb Ch Amer	1	78	99	129	0.3	0.4
COLBERT	**140**	**14,166**	**30,230**	**37,805**	**69.5**	**100.0**
ANG/EPIS–Episcopal	1	92	250	278	0.5	0.7
Bahá'í	0	NR	7	7	0.0	0.0
BAPT–Amer Bapt Assn	2	NR	186	224	0.4	0.6
BAPT–Free Will Bapt	1	NR	104	125	0.2	0.3
BAPT–Natl Mis Bapt Conv	2	0	300	360	0.7	1.0
BAPT–NBC USA	6	765	1,525	1,833	3.4	4.8
BAPT–So Bapt Conv	40	6,164	17,972	21,596	39.7	57.1
Catholic	1	NR	NR	1,415	2.6	3.7
Ch of Nazarene	3	266	274	305	0.6	0.8
CHR–Chs of Christ	33	4,093	3,909	4,821	8.9	12.8
Jehovah's Witness	1	NR	NR	NR	-	-
LUTH–Luth–MO Synod	1	55	66	94	0.2	0.2
METH–AME	4	0	450	541	1.0	1.4
METH–C.M.E.	4	55	285	342	0.6	0.9
METH–Un Methodist	14	1,152	2,429	2,945	5.4	7.8
Non-denom Chr Chs	8	907	1,212	1,298	2.4	3.4
PENT–Assemb of God	1	94	69	180	0.3	0.5
PENT–Ch God (Cleve)	3	199	347	417	0.8	1.1
PENT–Ch of God Proph	1	NR	120	144	0.3	0.4
PENT–COGIC	1	0	150	180	0.3	0.5
PENT–Un Pent Ch Intl	2	NR	NR	NR	-	-
PRES–Cum Pres Am	1	NR	NR	NR	-	-
PRES–Cumber Presb	6	NR	137	184	0.3	0.5
PRES–Presb Ch (USA)	2	80	121	145	0.3	0.4
PRES–Presb Ch Amer	1	220	276	324	0.6	0.9
Sev Day Adv	1	24	41	47	0.1	0.1
CONECUH	**62**	**1,907**	**6,392**	**7,550**	**57.1**	**100.0**
BAPT–Free Will Bapt	3	NR	312	376	2.8	5.0
BAPT–Ind Bapt Flwsp Intl	1	NR	NR	NR	-	-
BAPT–NBC USA	1	0	754	909	6.9	12.0
BAPT–Prog NBC	2	0	500	603	4.6	8.0
BAPT–So Bapt Conv	18	878	2,575	3,105	23.5	41.1

NR–Not Reported - Represents no adherents reported. Percentages may not total 100 due to rounding.

Table 3: Religious Congregations by County and Group: 2010

Religious Group	Number of Congrega-tions	Number of Attendees	Number of Communicant, Confirmed, or Full Members	Adherents		
				Number of Adherents	% of Total Pop.	% of Total Adh.
CHR–Chs of Christ	4	260	274	348	2.6	4.6
Jehovah's Witness	1	NR	NR	NR	-	-
LDS–Comm of Christ	2	NR	272	272	2.1	3.6
METH–AME Zion	4	75	405	488	3.7	6.5
METH–Un Methodist	17	482	914	965	7.3	12.8
PENT–Assemb of God	4	119	96	134	1.0	1.8
PENT–Ch God (Cleve)	1	45	68	82	0.6	1.1
PENT–Intl Pent Holiness	2	48	209	252	1.9	3.3
PRES–Presb Ch (USA)	1	0	13	16	0.1	0.2
Sev Day Adv	1	0	0	0	0.0	0.0
COOSA	**49**	**1,767**	**5,311**	**6,148**	**53.3**	**100.0**
Bahá'í	0	NR	3	3	0.0	0.0
BAPT–Ind Bapt Flwsp Intl	1	NR	NR	NR	-	-
BAPT–Natl Mis Bapt Conv	2	0	300	353	3.1	5.7
BAPT–NBC USA	3	0	330	388	3.4	6.3
BAPT–So Bapt Conv	19	923	2,837	3,336	28.9	54.3
CHR–Chs of Christ	2	60	60	73	0.6	1.2
METH–AME	4	0	450	529	4.6	8.6
METH–C.M.E.	1	0	100	118	1.0	1.9
METH–Un Methodist	8	200	465	499	4.3	8.1
Non-denom Chr Chs	3	465	560	606	5.3	9.9
PENT–Ch God (Cleve)	2	61	111	131	1.1	2.1
PENT–Ch of God by Faith	1	NR	NR	NR	-	-
PENT–Ch of God Proph	1	NR	29	34	0.3	0.6
PRES–Presb Ch (USA)	2	58	66	78	0.7	1.3
COVINGTON	**126**	**7,581**	**18,765**	**23,386**	**61.9**	**100.0**
ANG/EPIS–Episcopal	1	47	59	85	0.2	0.4
Bahá'í	0	NR	4	4	0.0	0.0
BAPT–NBC USA	2	0	150	181	0.5	0.8
BAPT–So Bapt Conv	53	4,279	13,261	16,036	42.5	68.6
Catholic	1	NR	NR	291	0.8	1.2
Ch of Nazarene	1	21	42	44	0.1	0.2
CHR–Chs of Christ	12	772	871	1,128	3.0	4.8
Jehovah's Witness	2	NR	NR	NR	-	-
LDS–L-D Saints	1	NR	NR	269	0.7	1.2
LUTH–Luth–MO Synod	2	55	67	80	0.2	0.3
METH–AME	3	0	350	423	1.1	1.8
METH–Cong Meth	1	NR	24	29	0.1	0.1
METH–Un Methodist	11	652	1,657	1,792	4.7	7.7
Non-denom Chr Chs	8	845	1,212	1,225	3.2	5.2
PENT–Assemb of God	14	588	372	962	2.5	4.1
PENT–Ch God (Cleve)	5	175	300	363	1.0	1.6
PENT–Ch of God by Faith	1	NR	NR	NR	-	-
PENT–COGIC	1	0	60	73	0.2	0.3
PENT–Intl Pent Holiness	1	20	20	24	0.1	0.1
PENT–Un Pent Ch Intl	2	NR	NR	NR	-	-
PRES–As Ref Pres Ch	1	NR	68	82	0.2	0.4
PRES–Presb Ch (USA)	1	65	179	216	0.6	0.9
PRES–Presb Ch Amer	1	40	31	35	0.1	0.1
Sev Day Adv	1	22	38	44	0.1	0.2
CRENSHAW	**68**	**3,379**	**7,001**	**8,784**	**63.2**	**100.0**
Bahá'í	0	NR	2	2	0.0	0.0
BAPT–So Bapt Conv	28	1,779	4,759	5,807	41.8	66.1
CHR–Chs of Christ	11	546	499	645	4.6	7.3
LDS–L-D Saints	1	NR	NR	221	1.6	2.5
METH–AME	1	0	100	122	0.9	1.4
METH–AME Zion	1	0	100	122	0.9	1.4
METH–Un Methodist	12	403	718	869	6.2	9.9
Non-denom Chr Chs	2	200	300	300	2.2	3.4
PENT–Assemb of God	8	247	214	319	2.3	3.6
PENT–Ch God (Cleve)	3	204	304	371	2.7	4.2
Un C of Christ	1	0	5	6	0.0	0.1
CULLMAN	**227**	**22,486**	**46,669**	**62,799**	**78.1**	**100.0**
ANG/EPIS–Episcopal	1	141	257	275	0.3	0.4
Bahá'í	0	NR	5	5	0.0	0.0
BAPT–Free Will Bapt	2	NR	208	253	0.3	0.4
BAPT–So Bapt Conv	118	11,095	30,939	37,629	46.8	59.9
Catholic	2	NR	NR	4,614	5.7	7.3
CGOD–Ch God (Ander)	1	150	NR	150	0.2	0.2
Ch of Nazarene	5	401	479	793	1.0	1.3
CHR–Chr Ch (Disc)	1	0	0	0	0.0	0.0
CHR–Chr Chs & Chs Cr	1	NR	30	36	0.0	0.1
CHR–Chs of Christ	29	2,146	2,072	2,684	3.3	4.3
Evan Assoc RCC	1	NR	NR	NR	-	-
Jehovah's Witness	1	NR	NR	NR	-	-
LDS–L-D Saints	1	NR	NR	619	0.8	1.0
LUTH–E.L.C.A.	1	45	81	89	0.1	0.1
LUTH–Luth–MO Synod	2	342	926	1,192	1.5	1.9
METH–Cong Meth	1	NR	90	109	0.1	0.2
METH–Un Methodist	20	1,450	2,644	3,242	4.0	5.2
Non-denom Chr Chs	14	3,796	3,915	4,823	6.0	7.7
PENT–Assemb of God	3	125	114	153	0.2	0.2
PENT–Ch God (Cleve)	11	2,439	3,852	4,685	5.8	7.5
PENT–Intl Pent Holiness	1	30	30	36	0.0	0.1
PENT–Un Pent Ch Intl	1	NR	NR	NR	-	-
PRES–Cumber Presb	7	NR	503	769	1.0	1.2
PRES–Presb Ch (USA)	1	45	76	92	0.1	0.1
PRES–Presb Ch Amer	1	225	351	439	0.5	0.7
Sev Day Adv	1	56	97	112	0.1	0.2
DALE	**109**	**6,910**	**18,173**	**24,732**	**49.2**	**100.0**
ANG/EPIS–Episcopal	1	27	58	87	0.2	0.4
Bahá'í	0	NR	9	9	0.0	0.0
BAPT–Free Will Bapt	6	NR	624	777	1.5	3.1
BAPT–NBC USA	1	175	418	521	1.0	2.1
BAPT–So Bapt Conv	27	2,649	10,360	12,904	25.7	52.2
Catholic	1	NR	NR	278	0.6	1.1
Ch of Nazarene	1	28	48	48	0.1	0.2
CHR–Chs of Christ	5	460	475	576	1.1	2.3
Jehovah's Witness	2	NR	NR	NR	-	-
LDS–L-D Saints	2	NR	NR	863	1.7	3.5
LUTH–Luth–MO Synod	1	69	99	124	0.2	0.5
METH–AME	5	0	500	623	1.2	2.5
METH–AME Zion	2	0	250	311	0.6	1.3
METH–Cong Meth	1	NR	19	24	0.0	0.1
METH–Un Methodist	25	1,443	3,121	3,615	7.2	14.6
Non-denom Chr Chs	8	955	1,140	1,313	2.6	5.3
PENT–Assemb of God	12	885	406	1,869	3.7	7.6
PENT–Ch God (Cleve)	4	149	174	217	0.4	0.9
PENT–Ch of God by Faith	1	NR	NR	NR	-	-
PENT–COGIC	1	0	350	436	0.9	1.8
PRES–Presb Ch (USA)	1	0	8	10	0.0	0.0
PRES–Presb Ch Amer	1	44	70	76	0.2	0.3
Sev Day Adv	1	26	44	51	0.1	0.2
DALLAS	**140**	**7,306**	**21,163**	**26,546**	**60.6**	**100.0**
ANG/EPIS–Episcopal	2	145	426	439	1.0	1.7
Bahá'í	0	NR	32	32	0.1	0.1
BAPT–Natl Mis Bapt Conv	3	0	650	816	1.9	3.1
BAPT–NBC USA	10	250	2,450	3,075	7.0	11.6
BAPT–So Bapt Conv	30	2,685	8,702	10,923	24.9	41.1
Catholic	2	NR	NR	536	1.2	2.0
CGOD–Ch God (Ander)	1	45	NR	45	0.1	0.2
Ch of Chr (Hol)	1	NR	NR	NR	-	-
Ch of Nazarene	2	170	202	256	0.6	1.0
CHR–Chr Ch (Disc)	1	0	60	75	0.2	0.3
CHR–Chr Chs & Chs Cr	2	NR	90	113	0.3	0.4
CHR–Chs of Christ	8	434	489	639	1.5	2.4
Int Cou Comm Ch	1	NR	NR	NR	-	-
Jehovah's Witness	2	NR	NR	NR	-	-
JUD–Reform	1	4	7	19	0.0	0.1
LDS–L-D Saints	1	NR	NR	329	0.8	1.2
LUTH–Luth–MO Synod	2	126	213	263	0.6	1.0
MENN–Unaffil Amish-Menn	1	54	33	54	0.1	0.2
METH–AME	9	75	1,097	1,377	3.1	5.2
METH–AME Zion	4	0	450	565	1.3	2.1
METH–C.M.E.	3	0	300	377	0.9	1.4
METH–Un Methodist	15	585	1,132	1,225	2.8	4.6
Muslim Est	1	30	NR	30	0.1	0.1
Non-denom Chr Chs	13	1,980	3,108	3,234	7.4	12.2
PENT–Assemb of God	1	70	43	100	0.2	0.4

NR–Not Reported   - Represents no adherents reported.   Percentages may not total 100 due to rounding.

Table 3: Religious Congregations by County and Group: 2010

Religious Group	Number of Congrega-tions	Number of Attendees	Number of Communicant, Confirmed, or Full Members	Adherents		
				Number of Adherents	% of Total Pop.	% of Total Adh.
PENT–Ch God (Cleve)	4	136	357	448	1.0	1.7
PENT–COGIC	1	0	150	188	0.4	0.7
PENT–Un Pent Ch Intl	1	NR	NR	NR	-	-
PRES–As Ref Pres Ch	1	NR	5	6	0.0	0.0
PRES–Cum Pres Am	4	NR	NR	NR	-	-
PRES–Presb Ch (USA)	7	152	557	699	1.6	2.6
PRES–Presb Ch Amer	2	110	206	227	0.5	0.9
PRES–Ref Pres of NA	1	37	37	47	0.1	0.2
Salvation Army	1	56	84	84	0.2	0.3
Sev Day Adv	2	162	283	325	0.7	1.2
DEKALB	**184**	**13,220**	**29,525**	**39,370**	**55.4**	**100.0**
ANG/EPIS–Episcopal	2	95	148	184	0.3	0.5
Bahá'í	0	NR	1	1	0.0	0.0
BAPT–So Bapt Conv	84	7,546	20,477	25,620	36.0	65.1
Catholic	1	NR	NR	2,657	3.7	6.7
Ch God (7th Day)	1	NR	NR	NR	-	-
Ch of Nazarene	4	190	279	431	0.6	1.1
CHR–Chr Chs & Chs Cr	1	NR	70	88	0.1	0.2
CHR–Chs of Christ	10	578	519	695	1.0	1.8
Jehovah's Witness	1	NR	NR	NR	-	-
LDS–L-D Saints	1	NR	NR	251	0.4	0.6
LUTH–Luth-MO Synod	1	20	25	27	0.0	0.1
METH–Un Methodist	31	1,423	3,171	3,596	5.1	9.1
METH–Wesleyan	2	197	154	256	0.4	0.7
Non-denom Chr Chs	10	1,150	1,580	1,704	2.4	4.3
PENT–Assemb of God	1	35	16	41	0.1	0.1
PENT–Ch God (Cleve)	17	1,564	2,117	2,649	3.7	6.7
PENT–Ch Lord Jesus Apos	1	NR	NR	NR	-	-
PENT–Ch of God Proph	5	NR	263	329	0.5	0.8
PENT–Cong Hol Ch	1	35	16	20	0.0	0.1
PENT–Un Pent Ch Intl	1	NR	NR	NR	-	-
PRES–Presb Ch (USA)	3	25	116	145	0.2	0.4
PRES–Presb Ch Amer	2	95	109	142	0.2	0.4
Sev Day Adv	4	267	464	534	0.8	1.4
ELMORE	**141**	**14,074**	**28,708**	**37,247**	**47.0**	**100.0**
ANG/EPIS–Episcopal	3	213	426	487	0.6	1.3
Bahá'í	0	NR	13	13	0.0	0.0
BAPT–Amer Bapt Assn	1	NR	920	1,122	1.4	3.0
BAPT–NBC USA	3	150	550	671	0.8	1.8
BAPT–So Bapt Conv	45	6,303	16,287	19,858	25.0	53.3
Catholic	2	NR	NR	677	0.9	1.8
CGOD–Ch God (Ander)	1	0	NR	0	0.0	0.0
Ch of Nazarene	1	110	109	110	0.1	0.3
CHR–Chr Ch (Disc)	1	72	174	212	0.3	0.6
CHR–Chs of Christ	14	1,070	951	1,241	1.6	3.3
Christian Brethren	1	NR	NR	NR	-	-
CONG–Cong Chr, NA	1	NR	50	61	0.1	0.2
Jehovah's Witness	3	NR	NR	NR	-	-
LDS–L-D Saints	1	NR	NR	518	0.7	1.4
METH–AME Zion	9	50	960	1,171	1.5	3.1
METH–Un Methodist	24	2,085	4,176	4,942	6.2	13.3
Non-denom Chr Chs	11	2,340	1,660	3,014	3.8	8.1
PENT–Assemb of God	6	680	469	806	1.0	2.2
PENT–Ch God (Cleve)	5	602	1,128	1,375	1.7	3.7
PENT–COGIC	1	20	49	60	0.1	0.2
PENT–Cong Hol Ch	2	51	41	50	0.1	0.1
PENT–Intl Pent Holiness	1	55	51	62	0.1	0.2
PRES–Cumber Presb	1	NR	169	169	0.2	0.5
PRES–Evan Presby Ch	1	NR	36	44	0.1	0.1
PRES–Presb Ch (USA)	1	101	164	200	0.3	0.5
PRES–Presb Ch Amer	1	144	277	329	0.4	0.9
Sev Day Adv	1	28	48	55	0.1	0.1
ESCAMBIA	**124**	**7,202**	**18,317**	**23,014**	**60.1**	**100.0**
ANG/EPIS–Episcopal	3	94	287	340	0.9	1.5
Bahá'í	0	NR	10	10	0.0	0.0
BAPT–Amer Bapt Assn	1	NR	85	103	0.3	0.4
BAPT–Free Will Bapt	1	NR	104	126	0.3	0.5
BAPT–Ind Bapt Flwsp Intl	1	NR	NR	NR	-	-
BAPT–Natl Mis Bapt Conv	2	50	225	273	0.7	1.2
BAPT–NBC USA	2	150	871	1,055	2.8	4.6
BAPT–So Bapt Conv	43	3,140	10,964	13,280	34.7	57.7
Catholic	2	NR	NR	530	1.4	2.3
Ch of Nazarene	2	117	154	180	0.5	0.8
CHR–Chs of Christ	7	405	390	507	1.3	2.2
Jehovah's Witness	2	NR	NR	NR	-	-
LDS–Comm of Christ	4	NR	544	544	1.4	2.4
LUTH–Luth-MO Synod	1	20	28	30	0.1	0.1
MENN–Mennonite USA	1	58	45	55	0.1	0.2
METH–AME	5	120	540	654	1.7	2.8
METH–Un Methodist	15	558	1,423	1,509	3.9	6.6
Non-denom Chr Chs	6	895	1,104	1,168	3.0	5.1
PENT–Assemb of God	7	917	401	1,310	3.4	5.7
PENT–Ch God (Cleve)	4	126	136	165	0.4	0.7
PENT–Ch of God Proph	1	NR	7	8	0.0	0.0
PENT–COGIC	1	0	150	182	0.5	0.8
PENT–Intl Pent Holiness	8	330	542	656	1.7	2.9
PENT–Un Pent Ch Intl	2	NR	NR	NR	-	-
PRES–Presb Ch Amer	2	186	244	257	0.7	1.1
Sev Day Adv	1	36	63	72	0.2	0.3
ETOWAH	**256**	**24,281**	**62,151**	**84,006**	**80.4**	**100.0**
ANG/EPIS–Episcopal	2	194	579	669	0.6	0.8
Bahá'í	0	NR	7	7	0.0	0.0
BAPT–Natl Mis Bapt Conv	2	0	300	363	0.3	0.4
BAPT–NBC USA	12	965	3,039	3,681	3.5	4.4
BAPT–Ref Bapt Ch	1	NR	NR	NR	-	-
BAPT–So Bapt Conv	104	12,786	41,818	50,648	48.5	60.3
Catholic	1	NR	NR	7,624	7.3	9.1
CGOD–Ch God (Ander)	1	21	NR	21	0.0	0.0
Ch Cr, Scientst	1	NR	NR	NR	-	-
Ch of Nazarene	2	172	355	355	0.3	0.4
Chr & Miss Al	1	48	39	64	0.1	0.1
CHR–Chs of Christ	14	1,367	1,431	1,760	1.7	2.1
Jehovah's Witness	2	NR	NR	NR	-	-
LDS–L-D Saints	1	NR	NR	814	0.8	1.0
LUTH–Luth-MO Synod	3	138	191	235	0.2	0.3
METH–AME	2	40	225	273	0.3	0.3
METH–C.M.E.	3	40	310	375	0.4	0.4
METH–Un Methodist	32	2,318	4,673	5,119	4.9	6.1
Muslim Est	2	268	NR	616	0.6	0.7
Non-denom Chr Chs	23	2,875	3,660	3,962	3.8	4.7
PENT–Assemb of God	7	582	538	1,086	1.0	1.3
PENT–Ch God (Cleve)	17	1,326	2,823	3,419	3.3	4.1
PENT–Ch Lord Jesus Apos	1	NR	NR	NR	-	-
PENT–Ch of God Proph	2	NR	70	85	0.1	0.1
PENT–COGIC	1	75	100	121	0.1	0.1
PENT–Cong Hol Ch	5	134	116	140	0.1	0.2
PENT–Fire Bapt Hol Ch	1	NR	NR	NR	-	-
PENT–Intl Pent Holiness	1	260	620	751	0.7	0.9
PENT–Un Pent Ch Intl	2	NR	NR	NR	-	-
PENT–Vineyard	1	110	140	170	0.2	0.2
PRES–Cumber Presb	3	NR	247	512	0.5	0.6
PRES–Presb Ch (USA)	1	15	23	28	0.0	0.0
PRES–Presb Ch Amer	2	334	458	543	0.5	0.6
Salvation Army	1	24	60	187	0.2	0.2
Sev Day Adv	2	189	329	378	0.4	0.4
FAYETTE	**94**	**4,643**	**8,891**	**11,039**	**64.0**	**100.0**
ANG/EPIS–Episcopal	1	35	69	74	0.4	0.7
BAPT–Free Will Bapt	3	NR	312	375	2.2	3.4
BAPT–So Bapt Conv	36	2,149	5,310	6,385	37.0	57.8
Catholic	1	NR	NR	90	0.5	0.8
Ch of Nazarene	4	165	151	193	1.1	1.7
CHR–Chs of Christ	21	1,330	1,238	1,591	9.2	14.4
Jehovah's Witness	1	NR	NR	NR	-	-
LDS–L-D Saints	1	NR	NR	123	0.7	1.1
METH–AME Zion	3	0	350	421	2.4	3.8
METH–C.M.E.	1	0	100	120	0.7	1.1
METH–Un Methodist	10	409	616	721	4.2	6.5
Non-denom Chr Chs	2	105	120	132	0.8	1.2
PENT–Assemb of God	2	190	110	195	1.1	1.8
PENT–Ch God (Cleve)	5	260	447	537	3.1	4.9
PENT–Ch of God Proph	1	NR	68	82	0.5	0.7

NR–Not Reported   - Represents no adherents reported.   Percentages may not total 100 due to rounding.

Table 3: Religious Congregations by County and Group: 2010

Religious Group	Number of Congregations	Number of Attendees	Number of Communicant, Confirmed, or Full Members	Adherents		
				Number of Adherents	% of Total Pop.	% of Total Adh.
PENT–Orig Ch of God	1	NR	NR	NR	-	-
PENT–Un Pent Ch Intl	1	NR	NR	NR	-	-
FRANKLIN	**102**	**6,786**	**14,840**	**20,416**	**64.4**	**100.0**
BAPT–Amer Bapt Assn	6	NR	740	916	2.9	4.5
BAPT–Free Will Bapt	3	NR	312	386	1.2	1.9
BAPT–So Bapt Conv	36	3,271	8,920	11,041	34.8	54.1
Catholic	1	NR	NR	1,487	4.7	7.3
Ch of Nazarene	2	67	120	246	0.8	1.2
CHR–Chs of Christ	25	1,809	1,699	2,173	6.9	10.6
Jehovah's Witness	1	NR	NR	NR	-	-
LDS–L-D Saints	1	NR	NR	475	1.5	2.3
METH–C.M.E.	3	0	350	433	1.4	2.1
METH–Un Methodist	5	420	1,046	1,189	3.8	5.8
Non-denom Chr Chs	6	630	775	862	2.7	4.2
PENT–Assemb of God	1	125	145	197	0.6	1.0
PENT–Ch God (Cleve)	3	305	528	654	2.1	3.2
PENT–Ch of God Proph	3	NR	94	116	0.4	0.6
PENT–COGIC	1	60	75	93	0.3	0.5
PENT–Pent Ch of God	1	70	NR	109	0.3	0.5
PENT–Un Pent Ch Intl	1	NR	NR	NR	-	-
PRES–Presb Ch (USA)	1	6	5	6	0.0	0.0
PRES–Presb Ch Amer	1	15	18	18	0.1	0.1
Sev Day Adv	1	8	13	15	0.0	0.1
GENEVA	**102**	**5,424**	**13,037**	**16,488**	**61.5**	**100.0**
Bahá'í	0	NR	4	4	0.0	0.0
BAPT–Free Will Bapt	3	NR	312	376	1.4	2.3
BAPT–Natl Mis Bapt Conv	2	0	300	361	1.3	2.2
BAPT–So Bapt Conv	36	3,022	8,932	10,760	40.2	65.3
Catholic	1	NR	NR	50	0.2	0.3
CHR–Chs of Christ	7	340	308	404	1.5	2.5
Jehovah's Witness	1	NR	NR	NR	-	-
LDS–L-D Saints	1	NR	NR	203	0.8	1.2
METH–AME	4	0	450	542	2.0	3.3
METH–Un Methodist	19	830	1,791	1,944	7.3	11.8
Muslim Est	1	134	NR	308	1.1	1.9
Non-denom Chr Chs	2	210	260	288	1.1	1.7
PENT–Assemb of God	16	675	414	928	3.5	5.6
PENT–Ch God (Cleve)	2	44	31	37	0.1	0.2
PENT–Ch God Mtn Asm	1	NR	NR	NR	-	-
PENT–COGIC	3	130	210	253	0.9	1.5
PENT–Cong Hol Ch	1	24	12	14	0.1	0.1
PENT–Un Pent Ch Intl	1	NR	NR	NR	-	-
PRES–Presb Ch (USA)	1	15	13	16	0.1	0.1
GREENE	**28**	**582**	**2,067**	**2,425**	**26.8**	**100.0**
ANG/EPIS–Episcopal	3	48	108	109	1.2	4.5
Bahá'í	0	NR	22	22	0.2	0.9
BAPT–NBC USA	1	0	150	184	2.0	7.6
BAPT–So Bapt Conv	4	93	504	617	6.8	25.4
Catholic	1	NR	NR	37	0.4	1.5
CHR–Chr Ch (Disc)	1	0	25	31	0.3	1.3
CHR–Chs of Christ	2	36	39	41	0.5	1.7
METH–AME Zion	1	0	100	122	1.3	5.0
METH–C.M.E.	3	0	450	551	6.1	22.7
METH–Un Methodist	4	131	230	235	2.6	9.7
Non-denom Chr Chs	1	200	300	300	3.3	12.4
PRES–Cum Pres Am	2	NR	NR	NR	-	-
PRES–Cumber Presb	1	NR	15	37	0.4	1.5
PRES–Presb Ch Amer	3	59	98	109	1.2	4.5
Sev Day Adv	1	15	26	30	0.3	1.2
HALE	**69**	**2,254**	**7,727**	**9,531**	**60.5**	**100.0**
ANG/EPIS–Episcopal	1	37	92	100	0.6	1.0
Bahá'í	0	NR	6	6	0.0	0.1
BAPT–Natl Mis Bapt Conv	2	0	300	368	2.3	3.9
BAPT–NBC USA	1	100	175	214	1.4	2.2
BAPT–So Bapt Conv	15	972	2,932	3,593	22.8	37.7
Catholic	1	NR	NR	25	0.2	0.3
CGOD–Ch God (Ander)	1	50	NR	50	0.3	0.5
Ch of Nazarene	2	63	126	126	0.8	1.3
CHR–Chs of Christ	2	105	87	106	0.7	1.1
Jehovah's Witness	1	NR	NR	NR	-	-
LDS–L-D Saints	1	NR	NR	159	1.0	1.7
METH–AME	10	0	1,050	1,287	8.2	13.5
METH–AME Zion	2	0	300	368	2.3	3.9
METH–C.M.E.	9	85	1,025	1,256	8.0	13.2
METH–Un Methodist	14	512	1,143	1,277	8.1	13.4
Non-denom Chr Chs	3	235	395	395	2.5	4.1
ORTHE–Orth Ch in Amer	1	35	NR	100	0.6	1.0
PRES–Presb Ch (USA)	1	0	7	9	0.1	0.1
PRES–Presb Ch Amer	2	60	89	92	0.6	1.0
HENRY	**43**	**2,216**	**6,888**	**8,195**	**47.4**	**100.0**
BAPT–Free Will Bapt	6	NR	624	752	4.3	9.2
BAPT–NBC USA	2	100	300	362	2.1	4.4
BAPT–So Bapt Conv	18	1,491	4,083	4,922	28.4	60.1
CHR–Chs of Christ	2	75	70	88	0.5	1.1
METH–AME	5	0	600	723	4.2	8.8
METH–Un Methodist	5	379	849	904	5.2	11.0
Non-denom Chr Chs	2	120	190	190	1.1	2.3
PENT–Assemb of God	1	25	0	46	0.3	0.6
PENT–COGIC	1	0	150	181	1.0	2.2
PENT–Intl Pent Holiness	1	26	22	27	0.2	0.3
HOUSTON	**210**	**27,946**	**61,733**	**81,059**	**79.8**	**100.0**
ANG/EPIS–Anglican NA	1	NR	NR	NR	-	-
ANG/EPIS–Episcopal	1	152	435	514	0.5	0.6
Bahá'í	0	NR	4	4	0.0	0.0
BAPT–Amer Bapt Assn	1	NR	85	105	0.1	0.1
BAPT–Free Will Bapt	9	NR	936	1,156	1.1	1.4
BAPT–Fund Bapt Flwsp	1	NR	NR	NR	-	-
BAPT–Natl Mis Bapt Conv	3	0	450	556	0.5	0.7
BAPT–NBC USA	4	720	1,620	2,002	2.0	2.5
BAPT–Ref Bapt Ch	1	NR	NR	NR	-	-
BAPT–So Bapt Conv	71	12,955	37,159	45,912	45.2	56.6
Calv Chpl	1	NR	NR	NR	-	-
Catholic	1	NR	NR	2,551	2.5	3.1
Ch of Nazarene	2	164	274	277	0.3	0.3
CHR–Chr Ch (Disc)	1	45	131	162	0.2	0.2
CHR–Chs of Christ	9	1,066	1,196	1,513	1.5	1.9
Ind Fund Churches	1	NR	NR	NR	-	-
Jehovah's Witness	1	NR	NR	NR	-	-
JUD–Reform	1	30	53	143	0.1	0.2
LDS–L-D Saints	2	NR	NR	1,119	1.1	1.4
LUTH–E.L.C.A.	1	51	89	112	0.1	0.1
LUTH–Luth-MO Synod	1	103	219	254	0.3	0.3
METH–AME	6	200	900	1,112	1.1	1.4
METH–Un Methodist	26	4,707	8,415	11,049	10.9	13.6
Muslim Est	2	268	NR	616	0.6	0.8
Non-denom Chr Chs	23	4,940	6,806	7,135	7.0	8.8
ORTHE–Ant Orth of NA	1	25	NR	40	0.0	0.0
PENT–Assemb of God	16	1,451	1,175	2,510	2.5	3.1
PENT–Ch God (Cleve)	1	35	115	142	0.1	0.2
PENT–Ch Lord Jesus Apos	3	NR	NR	NR	-	-
PENT–Ch of God by Faith	3	NR	NR	NR	-	-
PENT–Ch of God Proph	1	NR	21	26	0.0	0.0
PENT–COGIC	2	50	150	185	0.2	0.2
PENT–Cong Hol Ch	2	107	65	80	0.1	0.1
PENT–Intl Pent Holiness	1	6	6	7	0.0	0.0
PENT–Un Pent Ch Intl	1	NR	NR	NR	-	-
PENT–Vineyard	1	130	200	247	0.2	0.3
PRES–Presb Ch (USA)	2	143	330	408	0.4	0.5
PRES–Presb Ch Amer	2	445	600	740	0.7	0.9
Salvation Army	1	25	77	127	0.1	0.2
Sev Day Adv	2	128	222	255	0.3	0.3
Unity Ch	1	NR	NR	NR	-	-
JACKSON	**145**	**9,708**	**22,315**	**28,922**	**54.3**	**100.0**
ANG/EPIS–Episcopal	1	72	227	246	0.5	0.9
Bahá'í	0	NR	7	7	0.0	0.0
BAPT–Natl Mis Bapt Conv	2	0	300	362	0.7	1.3
BAPT–NBC USA	1	0	150	181	0.3	0.6
BAPT–S-D Baptist Gen Con	1	41	60	72	0.1	0.2

NR–Not Reported   - Represents no adherents reported.   Percentages may not total 100 due to rounding.

Table 3: Religious Congregations by County and Group: 2010

Religious Group	Number of Congrega-tions	Number of Attendees	Number of Communicant, Confirmed, or Full Members	Adherents		
				Number of Adherents	% of Total Pop.	% of Total Adh.
BAPT–So Bapt Conv	63	5,218	15,384	18,570	34.9	64.2
Catholic	1	NR	NR	1,515	2.8	5.2
Ch of Nazarene	2	60	63	167	0.3	0.6
CHR–Chs of Christ	19	1,197	1,235	1,544	2.9	5.3
Jehovah's Witness	1	NR	NR	NR	-	-
LDS–L-D Saints	1	NR	NR	323	0.6	1.1
LUTH–Luth-MO Synod	1	20	32	32	0.1	0.1
METH–AME	2	80	250	302	0.6	1.0
METH–Un Methodist	17	1,139	1,666	1,870	3.5	6.5
Non-denom Chr Chs	3	350	475	513	1.0	1.8
PENT–Assemb of God	1	29	9	29	0.1	0.1
PENT–Ch God (Cleve)	17	1,284	1,737	2,097	3.9	7.3
PENT–Un Pent Ch Intl	2	NR	NR	NR	-	-
PRES–Cum Pres Am	1	NR	NR	NR	-	-
PRES–Cumber Presb	5	NR	342	657	1.2	2.3
Sev Day Adv	4	218	378	435	0.8	1.5
JEFFERSON	**1,198**	**182,387**	**405,223**	**552,254**	**83.9**	**100.0**
ANG/EPIS–Anglican NA	6	NR	NR	NR	-	-
ANG/EPIS–Episcopal	17	3,818	12,373	14,025	2.1	2.5
Bahá'í	2	NR	280	280	0.0	0.1
BAPT–Alliance Bapt	2	NR	NR	NR	-	-
BAPT–Amer Bapt Assn	1	NR	85	104	0.0	0.0
BAPT–Free Will Bapt	8	NR	832	1,017	0.2	0.2
BAPT–Natl Mis Bapt Conv	8	0	1,110	1,357	0.2	0.2
BAPT–NBC Amer	10	1,975	4,430	5,414	0.8	1.0
BAPT–NBC USA	117	21,625	55,075	67,313	10.2	12.2
BAPT–Prog NBC	3	1,030	2,716	3,320	0.5	0.6
BAPT–Ref Bapt Ch	1	NR	NR	NR	-	-
BAPT–So Bapt Conv	272	49,857	151,897	185,650	28.2	33.6
BUDD–Mahayana	1	NR	NR	11	0.0	0.0
BUDD–Vajrayana	1	NR	NR	53	0.0	0.0
Catholic	32	NR	NR	55,083	8.4	10.0
CGOD–Ch God (Ander)	15	917	NR	917	0.1	0.2
Ch Cr, Scientst	1	NR	NR	NR	-	-
Ch of Chr (Hol)	1	NR	NR	NR	-	-
Ch of Nazarene	9	585	1,227	1,356	0.2	0.2
Chr & Miss Al	9	340	282	459	0.1	0.1
CHR–Chr Ch (Disc)	5	89	493	603	0.1	0.1
CHR–Chr Chs & Chs Cr	1	NR	165	202	0.0	0.0
CHR–Chs of Christ	69	8,862	8,976	11,267	1.7	2.0
CHR–Int Chs of Christ	1	NR	64	78	0.0	0.0
Christian Brethren	1	NR	NR	NR	-	-
Christian Un	2	NR	NR	NR	-	-
Evan Cov Ch	1	25	125	32	0.0	0.0
Evan Free Ch	1	300	NR	300	0.0	0.1
FRND–Fr Gen Cf	1	NR	19	23	0.0	0.0
HINDU–I/A Temples	2	NR	NR	129	0.0	0.0
HINDU–Post Ren	1	NR	NR	77	0.0	0.0
Ind Fund Churches	1	NR	NR	NR	-	-
Int Cou Comm Ch	6	NR	NR	NR	-	-
Jehovah's Witness	15	NR	NR	NR	-	-
JUD–Conserv	1	585	657	1,774	0.3	0.3
JUD–Orth	2	266	135	375	0.1	0.1
JUD–Reform	1	414	730	1,971	0.3	0.4
LDS–L-D Saints	8	NR	NR	4,753	0.7	0.9
LUTH–E.L.C.A.	3	276	487	594	0.1	0.1
LUTH–Luth Cong Msn Chr	1	275	642	785	0.1	0.1
LUTH–Luth-MO Synod	11	542	1,217	1,645	0.2	0.3
LUTH–Wisc Ev Luth Syn	1	51	51	79	0.0	0.0
METH–AME	42	1,920	7,750	9,472	1.4	1.7
METH–AME Zion	21	265	2,586	3,161	0.5	0.6
METH–C.M.E.	29	995	4,455	5,445	0.8	1.0
METH–Free Methodist	2	57	53	62	0.0	0.0
METH–So Methodist	1	NR	NR	NR	-	-
METH–Un Methodist	86	14,928	37,051	43,422	6.6	7.9
METH–Wesleyan	1	97	92	126	0.0	0.0
Metro Comm Ch	1	7	5	6	0.0	0.0
Muslim Est	7	1,254	NR	3,348	0.5	0.6
Non-denom Chr Chs	170	49,935	65,377	69,878	10.6	12.7
ORTHE–Greek Orthodox	1	340	NR	1,100	0.2	0.2
ORTHE–Orth Ch in Amer	1	120	NR	200	0.0	0.0
ORTHE–Rus Orth Moscow	1	30	NR	70	0.0	0.0
ORTHO–Coptic Orth Ch	1	15	NR	54	0.0	0.0

Religious Group	Number of Congrega-tions	Number of Attendees	Number of Communicant, Confirmed, or Full Members	Adherents		
				Number of Adherents	% of Total Pop.	% of Total Adh.
PENT–Apos Faith Msn	1	NR	35	43	0.0	0.0
PENT–Assemb of God	18	2,755	2,157	3,411	0.5	0.6
PENT–Ch God (Cleve)	45	6,026	13,008	15,899	2.4	2.9
PENT–Ch Lord Jesus Apos	3	NR	NR	NR	-	-
PENT–Ch of God by Faith	1	NR	NR	NR	-	-
PENT–Ch of God Proph	8	NR	620	758	0.1	0.1
PENT–COGIC	16	1,575	9,140	11,171	1.7	2.0
PENT–Cong Hol Ch	1	29	23	28	0.0	0.0
PENT–Full Gosp Bapt	3	NR	NR	NR	-	-
PENT–Intl Pent Holiness	5	292	496	606	0.1	0.1
PENT–Pent Ch of God	1	70	NR	109	0.0	0.0
PENT–Un Pent Ch Intl	5	NR	NR	NR	-	-
PRES–As Ref Pres Ch	1	NR	25	31	0.0	0.0
PRES–Cum Pres Am	5	NR	NR	NR	-	-
PRES–Cumber Presb	7	NR	314	684	0.1	0.1
PRES–Orth Pres Ch	1	50	26	46	0.0	0.0
PRES–Presb Ch (USA)	26	2,483	6,523	7,972	1.2	1.4
PRES–Presb Ch Amer	13	4,771	7,242	9,173	1.4	1.7
REF–Comm Ref Evan	1	NR	NR	NR	-	-
Salvation Army	2	267	164	232	0.0	0.0
Sev Day Adv	14	2,004	3,483	4,007	0.6	0.7
Sikh	1	NR	NR	NR	-	-
Un C of Christ	3	135	321	392	0.1	0.1
Unit Univ	1	135	209	300	0.0	0.1
Unity Ch	1	NR	NR	NR	-	-
Zoroastrian	0	NR	NR	2	0.0	0.0
LAMAR	**90**	**4,008**	**9,097**	**11,042**	**75.8**	**100.0**
BAPT–Free Will Bapt	15	NR	1,560	1,881	12.9	17.0
BAPT–Natl Mis Bapt Conv	1	0	150	181	1.2	1.6
BAPT–So Bapt Conv	24	1,416	3,587	4,326	29.7	39.2
Ch of Nazarene	1	9	8	13	0.1	0.1
CHR–Chs of Christ	13	879	858	1,115	7.7	10.1
METH–C.M.E.	6	0	750	904	6.2	8.2
METH–Un Methodist	15	603	942	1,055	7.2	9.6
Non-denom Chr Chs	2	600	600	775	5.3	7.0
PENT–Assemb of God	2	170	150	199	1.4	1.8
PENT–Ch God (Cleve)	9	331	492	593	4.1	5.4
PENT–Un Pent Ch Intl	2	NR	NR	NR	-	-
LAUDERDALE	**206**	**25,046**	**42,759**	**54,063**	**58.3**	**100.0**
ANG/EPIS–Episcopal	2	230	740	747	0.8	1.4
Bahá'í	0	NR	16	16	0.0	0.0
BAPT–Amer Bapt Assn	1	NR	85	102	0.1	0.2
BAPT–Free Will Bapt	3	NR	312	373	0.4	0.7
BAPT–Natl Mis Bapt Conv	2	0	150	179	0.2	0.3
BAPT–NBC USA	2	70	250	299	0.3	0.6
BAPT–Prog NBC	1	155	275	329	0.4	0.6
BAPT–Ref Bapt Ch	1	NR	NR	NR	-	-
BAPT–So Bapt Conv	38	6,043	16,744	20,028	21.6	37.0
Catholic	2	NR	NR	1,948	2.1	3.6
CGOD–Ch God (Ander)	2	105	NR	105	0.1	0.2
Ch of Nazarene	3	156	179	192	0.2	0.4
CHR–Chr Ch (Disc)	1	156	265	317	0.3	0.6
CHR–Chr Chs & Chs Cr	1	NR	0	0	0.0	0.0
CHR–Chs of Christ	62	11,030	10,301	13,366	14.4	24.7
Int Cou Comm Ch	1	NR	NR	NR	-	-
Jehovah's Witness	1	NR	NR	NR	-	-
LDS–L-D Saints	1	NR	NR	679	0.7	1.3
LUTH–Luth Cong Msn Chr	1	41	101	121	0.1	0.2
LUTH–Luth-MO Synod	1	70	145	162	0.2	0.3
METH–AME	7	180	1,037	1,240	1.3	2.3
METH–C.M.E.	1	0	100	120	0.1	0.2
METH–Un Methodist	31	2,702	5,615	6,527	7.0	12.1
Non-denom Chr Chs	15	3,280	4,475	4,606	5.0	8.5
PENT–Assemb of God	1	280	280	311	0.3	0.6
PENT–Ch God (Cleve)	3	113	261	312	0.3	0.6
PENT–COGIC	2	0	150	179	0.2	0.3
PENT–Un Pent Ch Intl	2	NR	NR	NR	-	-
PRES–Cum Pres Am	4	NR	NR	NR	-	-
PRES–Cumber Presb	6	NR	449	773	0.8	1.4
PRES–Presb Ch (USA)	3	178	408	488	0.5	0.9
PRES–Presb Ch Amer	1	67	76	95	0.1	0.2

NR–Not Reported - Represents no adherents reported. Percentages may not total 100 due to rounding.

Table 3: Religious Congregations by County and Group: 2010

Religious Group	Number of Congrega-tions	Number of Attendees	Number of Communicant, Confirmed, or Full Members	Adherents		
				Number of Adherents	% of Total Pop.	% of Total Adh.
Salvation Army	1	55	127	198	0.2	0.4
Sev Day Adv	2	110	191	219	0.2	0.4
Unit Univ	1	25	27	31	0.0	0.1
Zoroastrian	0	NR	NR	1	0.0	0.0
LAWRENCE	**81**	**6,375**	**14,614**	**17,919**	**52.2**	**100.0**
Bahá'í	0	NR	2	2	0.0	0.0
BAPT–Free Will Bapt	1	NR	104	126	0.4	0.7
BAPT–NBC USA	1	150	400	484	1.4	2.7
BAPT–So Bapt Conv	31	3,533	10,621	12,863	37.5	71.8
Catholic	1	NR	NR	87	0.3	0.5
CHR–Chs of Christ	17	1,418	1,317	1,716	5.0	9.6
METH–C.M.E.	2	0	300	363	1.1	2.0
METH–Un Methodist	11	513	941	1,117	3.3	6.2
Non-denom Chr Chs	1	400	450	500	1.5	2.8
PENT–Assemb of God	2	119	40	130	0.4	0.7
PENT–Ch God (Cleve)	1	89	168	203	0.6	1.1
PENT–Ch of God Proph	2	NR	61	74	0.2	0.4
PENT–COGIC	1	75	80	97	0.3	0.5
PENT–Un Pent Ch Intl	3	NR	NR	NR	-	-
PRES–Cum Pres Am	3	NR	NR	NR	-	-
PRES–Cumber Presb	1	NR	25	37	0.1	0.2
PRES–Presb Ch (USA)	1	40	48	58	0.2	0.3
PRES–Presb Ch Amer	1	20	26	26	0.1	0.1
Sev Day Adv	1	18	31	36	0.1	0.2
LEE	**175**	**19,585**	**41,274**	**56,996**	**40.6**	**100.0**
ANG/EPIS–Episcopal	4	424	940	1,289	0.9	2.3
Bahá'í	0	NR	28	28	0.0	0.0
BAPT–Free Will Bapt	1	NR	104	126	0.1	0.2
BAPT–NBC USA	10	380	2,460	2,976	2.1	5.2
BAPT–Ref Bapt Ch	1	NR	NR	NR	-	-
BAPT–So Bapt Conv	35	7,837	17,659	21,366	15.2	37.5
Catholic	2	NR	NR	2,872	2.0	5.0
CGOD–Ch God (Ander)	1	26	NR	26	0.0	0.0
Ch of Nazarene	3	212	434	498	0.4	0.9
CHR–Chr Ch (Disc)	2	58	173	209	0.1	0.4
CHR–Chs of Christ	9	1,108	1,052	1,468	1.0	2.6
CHR–Int Chs of Christ	1	NR	20	24	0.0	0.0
FRND–Fr Gen Cf	1	NR	0	0	0.0	0.0
Jehovah's Witness	4	NR	NR	NR	-	-
JUD–Reform	1	26	46	124	0.1	0.2
LDS–L-D Saints	2	NR	NR	830	0.6	1.5
LUTH–Luth-MO Synod	1	154	180	243	0.2	0.4
METH–AME	10	125	1,200	1,452	1.0	2.5
METH–AME Zion	11	0	1,250	1,512	1.1	2.7
METH–C.M.E.	10	315	1,180	1,428	1.0	2.5
METH–Un Methodist	21	4,202	9,181	12,794	9.1	22.4
Missionary Ch	1	24	0	24	0.0	0.0
Muslim Est	1	134	NR	308	0.2	0.5
Non-denom Chr Chs	18	1,811	2,370	2,508	1.8	4.4
PENT–Assemb of God	8	1,449	982	2,423	1.7	4.3
PENT–Ch God (Cleve)	1	57	148	179	0.1	0.3
PENT–Ch of God by Faith	1	NR	NR	NR	-	-
PENT–Cong Hol Ch	3	90	65	79	0.1	0.1
PENT–Un Pent Ch Intl	1	NR	NR	NR	-	-
PRES–Evan Presby Ch	1	NR	155	188	0.1	0.3
PRES–Presb Ch (USA)	2	275	792	958	0.7	1.7
PRES–Presb Ch Amer	4	687	557	706	0.5	1.2
Sev Day Adv	3	116	202	232	0.2	0.4
Unit Univ	1	75	96	126	0.1	0.2
LIMESTONE	**166**	**19,051**	**32,228**	**43,018**	**52.0**	**100.0**
ANG/EPIS–Episcopal	1	48	91	91	0.1	0.2
Ap Chr Ch-Amer	1	55	33	55	0.1	0.1
Bahá'í	0	NR	2	2	0.0	0.0
BAPT–Natl Mis Bapt Conv	3	185	350	430	0.5	1.0
BAPT–So Bapt Conv	42	7,863	18,820	23,120	27.9	53.7
Catholic	1	NR	NR	2,462	3.0	5.7
CGOD–Ch God (Ander)	1	50	NR	50	0.1	0.1
Ch of Nazarene	1	60	63	160	0.2	0.4
CHR–Chr Ch (Disc)	1	69	188	231	0.3	0.5
CHR–Chs of Christ	51	5,991	5,565	6,901	8.3	16.0

Religious Group	Number of Congrega-tions	Number of Attendees	Number of Communicant, Confirmed, or Full Members	Adherents		
				Number of Adherents	% of Total Pop.	% of Total Adh.
HINDU–Post Ren	1	NR	NR	16	0.0	0.0
HINDU–Trad Temples	1	NR	NR	600	0.7	1.4
Jehovah's Witness	1	NR	NR	NR	-	-
LDS–L-D Saints	1	NR	NR	591	0.7	1.4
LUTH–Wisc Ev Luth Syn	1	80	115	147	0.2	0.3
METH–C.M.E.	3	35	355	436	0.5	1.0
METH–Un Methodist	19	2,358	3,641	4,118	5.0	9.6
Non-denom Chr Chs	13	1,680	2,084	2,219	2.7	5.2
PENT–Assemb of God	1	177	108	397	0.5	0.9
PENT–Ch of God Proph	2	NR	95	117	0.1	0.3
PENT–Full Gosp Bapt	3	NR	NR	NR	-	-
PENT–Intl Pent Holiness	1	75	30	37	0.0	0.1
PENT–Un Pent Ch Intl	3	NR	NR	NR	-	-
PRES–Cum Pres Am	5	NR	NR	NR	-	-
PRES–Cumber Presb	1	NR	76	106	0.1	0.2
PRES–Presb Ch (USA)	3	159	339	416	0.5	1.0
Sev Day Adv	4	136	238	273	0.3	0.6
Un C of Christ	1	30	35	43	0.1	0.1
LOWNDES	**50**	**2,364**	**5,108**	**6,217**	**55.0**	**100.0**
ANG/EPIS–Episcopal	1	45	57	57	0.5	0.9
Bahá'í	0	NR	1	1	0.0	0.0
BAPT–Natl Mis Bapt Conv	2	0	300	367	3.2	5.9
BAPT–NBC USA	4	100	800	979	8.7	15.7
BAPT–So Bapt Conv	9	1,218	1,440	1,763	15.6	28.4
CHR–Chr Ch (Disc)	11	398	1,072	1,312	11.6	21.1
CHR–Chs of Christ	6	296	313	400	3.5	6.4
Jehovah's Witness	1	NR	NR	NR	-	-
METH–AME Zion	3	0	400	490	4.3	7.9
METH–C.M.E.	3	0	350	429	3.8	6.9
METH–Un Methodist	4	77	133	143	1.3	2.3
Non-denom Chr Chs	1	100	150	150	1.3	2.4
PENT–Assemb of God	1	20	0	20	0.2	0.3
PRES–Presb Ch Amer	4	110	92	106	0.9	1.7
MACON	**67**	**3,046**	**7,412**	**9,583**	**44.7**	**100.0**
ANG/EPIS–Episcopal	1	49	68	70	0.3	0.7
Bahá'í	0	NR	78	78	0.4	0.8
BAPT–NBC Amer	1	0	150	177	0.8	1.8
BAPT–NBC USA	6	630	1,421	1,672	7.8	17.4
BAPT–So Bapt Conv	8	293	918	1,080	5.0	11.3
Catholic	1	NR	NR	100	0.5	1.0
CHR–Chr Ch (Disc)	2	129	220	259	1.2	2.7
CHR–Chs of Christ	3	188	213	264	1.2	2.8
Jehovah's Witness	1	NR	NR	NR	-	-
LDS–L-D Saints	1	NR	NR	233	1.1	2.4
LUTH–E.L.C.A.	1	55	0	12	0.1	0.1
METH–AME	6	125	750	883	4.1	9.2
METH–AME Zion	14	110	1,730	2,036	9.5	21.2
METH–Un Methodist	9	273	577	723	3.4	7.5
Muslim Est	2	194	NR	368	1.7	3.8
Non-denom Chr Chs	5	815	815	1,062	5.0	11.1
PENT–Assemb of God	1	30	15	34	0.2	0.4
PENT–COGIC	1	0	150	177	0.8	1.8
PRES–Presb Ch (USA)	3	27	85	100	0.5	1.0
Sev Day Adv	1	128	222	255	1.2	2.7
MADISON	**432**	**60,679**	**120,937**	**168,830**	**50.4**	**100.0**
ANG/EPIS–Anglican NA	1	NR	NR	NR	-	-
ANG/EPIS–Episcopal	6	1,171	2,746	3,325	1.0	2.0
Bahá'í	2	NR	145	145	0.0	0.1
BAPT–Amer Bapt Assn	1	NR	70	85	0.0	0.1
BAPT–Amer Bapt USA	1	1,124	1,672	2,040	0.6	1.2
BAPT–Free Will Bapt	3	NR	312	381	0.1	0.2
BAPT–Natl Mis Bapt Conv	4	0	1,150	1,403	0.4	0.8
BAPT–NBC USA	1	85	155	189	0.1	0.1
BAPT–Prog NBC	2	900	1,800	2,196	0.7	1.3
BAPT–Ref Bapt Ch	2	NR	NR	NR	-	-
BAPT–S-D Baptist Gen Con	1	NR	11	13	0.0	0.0
BAPT–So Bapt Conv	94	19,892	54,606	66,627	19.9	39.5
BUDD–Mahayana	3	NR	NR	364	0.1	0.2
Calv Chpl	1	NR	NR	NR	-	-
Catholic	6	NR	NR	14,157	4.2	8.4

NR–Not Reported - Represents no adherents reported. Percentages may not total 100 due to rounding.

Table 3: Religious Congregations by County and Group: 2010

Religious Group	Number of Congregations	Number of Attendees	Number of Communicant, Confirmed, or Full Members	Adherents: Number of Adherents	Adherents: % of Total Pop.	Adherents: % of Total Adh.
CGOD–Ch God (Ander)	1	102	NR	102	0.0	0.1
Ch Cr, Scientst	1	NR	NR	NR	-	-
Ch of Nazarene	7	619	944	1,118	0.3	0.7
Chr & Miss Al	1	48	33	69	0.0	0.0
CHR–Chr Ch (Disc)	3	369	735	897	0.3	0.5
CHR–Chr Chs & Chs Cr	2	NR	225	275	0.1	0.2
CHR–Chs of Christ	39	8,282	8,154	10,538	3.1	6.2
Evan Free Ch	1	200	NR	200	0.1	0.1
FRND–Fr Gen Cf	1	NR	4	5	0.0	0.0
HINDU–Post Ren	2	NR	NR	41	0.0	0.0
Jehovah's Witness	3	NR	NR	NR	-	-
JUD–Conserv	1	57	64	173	0.1	0.1
JUD–Reform	1	99	175	473	0.1	0.3
LDS–Comm of Christ	1	NR	156	156	0.0	0.1
LDS–L-D Saints	7	NR	NR	4,137	1.2	2.5
LUTH–E.L.C.A.	4	689	1,214	1,670	0.5	1.0
LUTH–Luth–MO Synod	5	485	952	1,160	0.3	0.7
METH–AME	3	150	500	610	0.2	0.4
METH–AME Zion	2	0	200	244	0.1	0.1
METH–C.M.E.	8	270	995	1,214	0.4	0.7
METH–So Methodist	1	NR	NR	NR	-	-
METH–Un Methodist	47	10,033	19,482	24,591	7.3	14.6
Muslim Est	3	402	NR	924	0.3	0.5
New Apost Ch	1	NR	NR	NR	-	-
Non-denom Chr Chs	60	7,838	10,050	11,137	3.3	6.6
ORTHE–Greek Orthodox	1	65	NR	280	0.1	0.2
ORTHE–Serb Orth USA	1	45	NR	60	0.0	0.0
PENT–Assemb of God	7	462	277	547	0.2	0.3
PENT–Ch God (Cleve)	7	857	1,865	2,276	0.7	1.3
PENT–Ch Lord Jesus Apos	1	NR	NR	NR	-	-
PENT–Ch of God Proph	4	NR	154	188	0.1	0.1
PENT–COGIC	4	40	700	854	0.3	0.5
PENT–Full Gosp Bapt	2	NR	NR	NR	-	-
PENT–Int Foursq Gos	2	245	232	283	0.1	0.2
PENT–Intl Pent Holiness	3	194	257	314	0.1	0.2
PENT–Un Pent Ch Intl	6	NR	NR	NR	-	-
PENT–Vineyard	1	85	85	104	0.0	0.1
PRES–As Ref Pres Ch	3	NR	61	74	0.0	0.0
PRES–Cum Pres Am	14	NR	NR	NR	-	-
PRES–Cumber Presb	8	NR	326	569	0.2	0.3
PRES–Evan Presby Ch	1	NR	292	356	0.1	0.2
PRES–Korean Pres Amer	1	NR	NR	NR	-	-
PRES–Orth Pres Ch	1	35	28	38	0.0	0.0
PRES–Presb Ch (USA)	9	794	2,275	2,776	0.8	1.6
PRES–Presb Ch Amer	6	1,604	1,938	2,507	0.7	1.5
REF–Fed Ref Ch	2	NR	NR	NR	-	-
Salvation Army	1	108	115	241	0.1	0.1
Sev Day Adv	11	3,150	5,478	6,301	1.9	3.7
Un C of Christ	1	97	188	229	0.1	0.1
Unit Univ	1	83	116	166	0.0	0.1
Unity Ch	1	NR	NR	NR	-	-
Zoroastrian	0	NR	NR	8	0.0	0.0
MARENGO	**88**	**4,245**	**13,006**	**16,244**	**77.3**	**100.0**
ANG/EPIS–Episcopal	2	97	208	231	1.1	1.4
Bahá'í	0	NR	6	6	0.0	0.0
BAPT–Natl Mis Bapt Conv	1	0	150	183	0.9	1.1
BAPT–NBC USA	3	140	1,300	1,590	7.6	9.8
BAPT–So Bapt Conv	31	2,331	7,350	8,990	42.8	55.3
Catholic	1	NR	NR	386	1.8	2.4
Ch of Nazarene	1	20	36	36	0.2	0.2
CHR–Chr Chs & Chs Cr	1	NR	60	73	0.3	0.4
CHR–Chs of Christ	3	154	154	200	1.0	1.2
Jehovah's Witness	1	NR	NR	NR	-	-
LDS–L-D Saints	2	NR	NR	218	1.0	1.3
MENN–CG in Cr (Menn)	1	NR	146	179	0.9	1.1
METH–AME	4	0	450	550	2.6	3.4
METH–AME Zion	5	0	500	612	2.9	3.8
METH–C.M.E.	1	0	100	122	0.6	0.8
METH–Un Methodist	18	680	1,461	1,675	8.0	10.3
Non-denom Chr Chs	7	595	770	810	3.9	5.0
PENT–Assemb of God	1	45	30	47	0.2	0.3
PENT–Ch God (Cleve)	1	6	25	31	0.1	0.2
PRES–Presb Ch Amer	3	165	240	282	1.3	1.7

Religious Group	Number of Congregations	Number of Attendees	Number of Communicant, Confirmed, or Full Members	Adherents: Number of Adherents	Adherents: % of Total Pop.	Adherents: % of Total Adh.
Sev Day Adv	1	12	20	23	0.1	0.1
MARION	**112**	**6,958**	**15,005**	**18,828**	**61.2**	**100.0**
BAPT–Amer Bapt Assn	3	NR	370	443	1.4	2.4
BAPT–Free Will Bapt	18	NR	1,872	2,243	7.3	11.9
BAPT–Natl Mis Bapt Conv	1	0	150	180	0.6	1.0
BAPT–So Bapt Conv	29	3,172	7,379	8,842	28.7	47.0
Catholic	1	NR	NR	474	1.5	2.5
Chr & Miss Al	1	19	26	32	0.1	0.2
CHR–Chs of Christ	24	1,740	1,682	2,145	7.0	11.4
LDS–L-D Saints	1	NR	NR	220	0.7	1.2
METH–C.M.E.	2	30	155	186	0.6	1.0
METH–Un Methodist	12	631	1,174	1,460	4.7	7.8
Non-denom Chr Chs	5	795	940	1,044	3.4	5.5
PENT–Assemb of God	2	259	335	346	1.1	1.8
PENT–Ch God (Cleve)	7	242	597	715	2.3	3.8
PENT–Ch of God Proph	3	NR	325	389	1.3	2.1
PENT–Pent Ch of God	1	70	NR	109	0.4	0.6
PENT–Un Pent Ch Intl	2	NR	NR	NR	-	-
MARSHALL	**216**	**20,009**	**42,100**	**60,942**	**65.5**	**100.0**
ANG/EPIS–Episcopal	2	231	502	669	0.7	1.1
Bahá'í	0	NR	4	4	0.0	0.0
BAPT–Natl Mis Bapt Conv	1	35	50	62	0.1	0.1
BAPT–So Bapt Conv	103	11,018	28,694	35,556	38.2	58.3
Catholic	2	NR	NR	8,382	9.0	13.8
CGOD–Ch God (Ander)	3	95	NR	95	0.1	0.2
Ch of Nazarene	4	335	244	386	0.4	0.6
CHR–Chs of Christ	22	2,153	2,107	2,495	2.7	4.1
Jehovah's Witness	2	NR	NR	NR	-	-
LDS–L-D Saints	1	NR	NR	609	0.7	1.0
LUTH–Luth–MO Synod	1	55	91	98	0.1	0.2
MENN–CG in Cr (Menn)	1	NR	59	73	0.1	0.1
METH–AME	2	0	250	310	0.3	0.5
METH–Cong Meth	1	NR	387	480	0.5	0.8
METH–Un Methodist	34	3,020	5,906	6,908	7.4	11.3
Non-denom Chr Chs	4	350	460	487	0.5	0.8
PENT–Assemb of God	5	603	405	692	0.7	1.1
PENT–Ch God (Cleve)	15	1,719	2,268	2,810	3.0	4.6
PENT–Ch Lord Jesus Apos	1	NR	NR	NR	-	-
PENT–Ch of God Proph	3	NR	93	115	0.1	0.2
PENT–Un Pent Ch Intl	2	NR	NR	NR	-	-
PENT–Vineyard	1	75	100	124	0.1	0.2
PRES–Presb Ch (USA)	2	140	235	291	0.3	0.5
PRES–Presb Ch Amer	1	102	110	141	0.2	0.2
Sev Day Adv	3	78	135	155	0.2	0.3
MOBILE	**599**	**72,610**	**175,670**	**253,133**	**61.3**	**100.0**
ANG/EPIS–Anglican NA	2	NR	NR	NR	-	-
ANG/EPIS–Episcopal	15	1,539	4,345	5,794	1.4	2.3
Bahá'í	1	NR	82	82	0.0	0.0
BAPT–Amer Bapt Assn	5	NR	835	1,033	0.3	0.4
BAPT–Amer Bapt USA	1	425	850	1,052	0.3	0.4
BAPT–Ind Bapt Flwsp Intl	1	NR	NR	NR	-	-
BAPT–Natl Mis Bapt Conv	1	12	15	19	0.0	0.0
BAPT–NBC Amer	2	0	575	712	0.2	0.3
BAPT–NBC USA	46	7,605	19,942	24,679	6.0	9.7
BAPT–So Bapt Conv	116	18,164	73,193	90,579	21.9	35.8
BRETH–Ch of Brethren	1	40	83	103	0.0	0.0
BUDD–Mahayana	1	NR	NR	506	0.1	0.2
BUDD–Theravada	1	NR	NR	395	0.1	0.2
Calv Chpl	1	NR	NR	NR	-	-
Catholic	35	NR	NR	32,003	7.7	12.6
CGOD–Ch God (Ander)	4	100	NR	100	0.0	0.0
Ch Cr, Scientst	1	NR	NR	NR	-	-
Ch of Nazarene	5	295	406	460	0.1	0.2
CHR–Chr Ch (Disc)	2	113	301	372	0.1	0.1
CHR–Chr Chs & Chs Cr	4	NR	410	507	0.1	0.2
CHR–Chs of Christ	20	2,466	2,286	2,941	0.7	1.2
Grace Gosp Fel	4	NR	NR	NR	-	-
HINDU–Post Ren	1	NR	NR	16	0.0	0.0
Jehovah's Witness	9	NR	NR	NR	-	-
JUD–Conserv	1	119	133	359	0.1	0.1

NR–Not Reported - Represents no adherents reported. Percentages may not total 100 due to rounding.

Table 3: Religious Congregations by County and Group: 2010

Religious Group	Number of Congrega-tions	Number of Attendees	Number of Communicant, Confirmed, or Full Members	Adherents		
				Number of Adherents	% of Total Pop.	% of Total Adh.
JUD–Reform	1	126	223	602	0.1	0.2
LDS–Comm of Christ	4	NR	748	748	0.2	0.3
LDS–L-D Saints	3	NR	NR	2,366	0.6	0.9
LUTH–E.L.C.A.	2	142	241	354	0.1	0.1
LUTH–Luth–MO Synod	6	683	1,106	1,342	0.3	0.5
LUTH–Wisc Ev Luth Syn	1	77	76	117	0.0	0.0
METH–AME	17	370	2,240	2,772	0.7	1.1
METH–AME Zion	17	445	2,460	3,044	0.7	1.2
METH–C.M.E.	2	0	200	248	0.1	0.1
METH–Cong Meth	1	NR	NR	NR	-	-
METH–Evan Meth Ch	1	NR	NR	NR	-	-
METH–So Methodist	1	NR	NR	NR	-	-
METH–Un Methodist	45	6,353	16,228	19,897	4.8	7.9
METH–Wesleyan	1	138	121	179	0.0	0.1
Metro Comm Ch	1	64	114	141	0.0	0.1
Muslim Est	5	670	NR	1,540	0.4	0.6
Non-denom Chr Chs	96	17,738	26,557	27,284	6.6	10.8
ORTHE–Greek Orthodox	1	185	NR	700	0.2	0.3
ORTHO–Coptic Orth Ch	1	20	NR	24	0.0	0.0
PENT–Apos Faith Msn	1	NR	35	43	0.0	0.0
PENT–Assemb of God	36	6,377	5,546	9,878	2.4	3.9
PENT–Ch God (Cleve)	24	4,589	9,170	11,348	2.7	4.5
PENT–Ch Lord Jesus Apos	2	NR	NR	NR	-	-
PENT–Ch of God Proph	4	NR	56	69	0.0	0.0
PENT–COGIC	12	1,050	2,141	2,650	0.6	1.0
PENT–Intl Pent Holiness	2	29	52	64	0.0	0.0
PENT–Un Pent Ch Intl	7	NR	NR	NR	-	-
PRES–Orth Pres Ch	1	48	22	26	0.0	0.0
PRES–Presb Ch (USA)	13	927	2,183	2,702	0.7	1.1
PRES–Presb Ch Amer	2	261	236	323	0.1	0.1
Salvation Army	2	117	173	324	0.1	0.1
Sev Day Adv	5	1,283	2,231	2,566	0.6	1.0
Unit Univ	1	40	55	70	0.0	0.0
Unity Ch	1	NR	NR	NR	-	-
MONROE	**88**	**4,349**	**11,818**	**14,959**	**64.8**	**100.0**
ANG/EPIS–Episcopal	1	52	107	148	0.6	1.0
Bahá'í	0	NR	2	2	0.0	0.0
BAPT–Free Will Bapt	1	NR	104	128	0.6	0.9
BAPT–Natl Mis Bapt Conv	2	0	300	369	1.6	2.5
BAPT–NBC USA	8	675	2,369	2,916	12.6	19.5
BAPT–So Bapt Conv	31	1,958	5,518	6,792	29.4	45.4
Catholic	1	NR	NR	100	0.4	0.7
Ch of Nazarene	2	113	207	242	1.0	1.6
CHR–Chs of Christ	2	115	174	218	0.9	1.5
Jehovah's Witness	1	NR	NR	NR	-	-
LDS–L-D Saints	1	NR	NR	305	1.3	2.0
LUTH–Luth–MO Synod	1	18	35	40	0.2	0.3
METH–AME	5	0	550	677	2.9	4.5
METH–AME Zion	1	0	150	185	0.8	1.2
METH–C.M.E.	2	30	200	246	1.1	1.6
METH–Un Methodist	14	554	1,094	1,229	5.3	8.2
Non-denom Chr Chs	3	190	270	275	1.2	1.8
PENT–Assemb of God	7	505	352	610	2.6	4.1
PENT–Ch God (Cleve)	1	41	96	118	0.5	0.8
PENT–COGIC	1	0	150	185	0.8	1.2
PENT–Intl Pent Holiness	1	41	14	17	0.1	0.1
PENT–Un Pent Ch Intl	1	NR	NR	NR	-	-
PRES–Presb Ch Amer	1	57	126	157	0.7	1.0
MONTGOMERY	**354**	**53,950**	**119,506**	**159,955**	**69.7**	**100.0**
ANG/EPIS–Anglican NA	2	NR	NR	NR	-	-
ANG/EPIS–Episcopal	6	880	2,541	2,782	1.2	1.7
Bahá'í	1	NR	287	287	0.1	0.2
BAPT–Amer Bapt Assn	1	NR	85	105	0.0	0.1
BAPT–Amer Bapt USA	2	1,500	4,100	5,065	2.2	3.2
BAPT–Free Will Bapt	1	NR	104	128	0.1	0.1
BAPT–Natl Mis Bapt Conv	1	0	150	185	0.1	0.1
BAPT–NBC Amer	2	1,945	4,700	5,806	2.5	3.6
BAPT–NBC USA	39	6,335	17,315	21,390	9.3	13.4
BAPT–Prog NBC	1	150	395	488	0.2	0.3
BAPT–So Bapt Conv	54	10,397	34,827	43,024	18.8	26.9
BUDD–Theravada	1	NR	NR	15	0.0	0.0

Religious Group	Number of Congrega-tions	Number of Attendees	Number of Communicant, Confirmed, or Full Members	Adherents		
				Number of Adherents	% of Total Pop.	% of Total Adh.
Catholic	9	NR	NR	9,480	4.1	5.9
CGOD–Ch God (Ander)	2	220	NR	220	0.1	0.1
Ch Cr, Scientst	1	NR	NR	NR	-	-
Ch of Chr (Hol)	1	NR	NR	NR	-	-
Ch of Nazarene	2	78	115	148	0.1	0.1
CHR–Chr Ch (Disc)	3	124	334	413	0.2	0.3
CHR–Chr Chs & Chs Cr	1	NR	100	124	0.1	0.1
CHR–Chs of Christ	38	6,151	6,332	8,411	3.7	5.3
Jehovah's Witness	6	NR	NR	NR	-	-
JUD–Conserv	1	177	199	537	0.2	0.3
JUD–Reform	1	96	170	459	0.2	0.3
LDS–Comm of Christ	1	NR	136	136	0.1	0.1
LDS–L-D Saints	2	NR	NR	1,893	0.8	1.2
LUTH–E.L.C.A.	1	112	234	291	0.1	0.2
LUTH–Luth–MO Synod	2	187	304	377	0.2	0.2
METH–AME	7	400	1,863	2,301	1.0	1.4
METH–AME Zion	25	758	3,926	4,850	2.1	3.0
METH–C.M.E.	3	110	281	347	0.2	0.2
METH–Un Methodist	32	7,915	17,535	21,940	9.6	13.7
Metro Comm Ch	1	31	46	57	0.0	0.0
Muslim Est	3	574	NR	968	0.4	0.6
Non-denom Chr Chs	48	7,289	9,050	9,817	4.3	6.1
ORTHE–Greek Orthodox	1	40	NR	85	0.0	0.1
PENT–Assemb of God	6	1,089	1,158	1,471	0.6	0.9
PENT–Ch God (Cleve)	3	370	628	776	0.3	0.5
PENT–Ch of God Proph	1	NR	15	19	0.0	0.0
PENT–COGIC	8	3,550	7,060	8,722	3.8	5.5
PENT–Full Gosp Bapt	3	NR	NR	NR	-	-
PENT–Intl Pent Holiness	2	92	65	80	0.0	0.1
PENT–Un Pent Ch Intl	4	NR	NR	NR	-	-
PRES–Evan Presby Ch	1	NR	81	100	0.0	0.1
PRES–Presb Ch (USA)	6	370	785	970	0.4	0.6
PRES–Presb Ch Amer	7	1,546	2,197	2,717	1.2	1.7
Salvation Army	1	102	85	292	0.1	0.2
Sev Day Adv	5	1,042	1,813	2,085	0.9	1.3
Un C of Christ	3	250	376	465	0.2	0.3
Unit Univ	1	70	114	129	0.1	0.1
Unity Ch	1	NR	NR	NR	-	-
MORGAN	**250**	**28,765**	**58,247**	**83,260**	**69.7**	**100.0**
ANG/EPIS–Episcopal	3	295	785	833	0.7	1.0
Bahá'í	0	NR	26	26	0.0	0.0
BAPT–Free Will Bapt	3	NR	312	382	0.3	0.5
BAPT–Ind Bapt Flwsp Intl	2	NR	NR	NR	-	-
BAPT–Natl Mis Bapt Conv	6	80	950	1,164	1.0	1.4
BAPT–So Bapt Conv	78	11,450	33,007	40,438	33.8	48.6
Catholic	1	NR	NR	8,380	7.0	10.1
CGOD–Ch God (Ander)	7	867	NR	867	0.7	1.0
Ch Cr, Scientst	1	NR	NR	NR	-	-
Ch of Nazarene	4	204	400	521	0.4	0.6
CHR–Chr Ch (Disc)	4	204	518	635	0.5	0.8
CHR–Chr Chs & Chs Cr	3	NR	295	361	0.3	0.4
CHR–Chs of Christ	23	3,730	3,613	4,570	3.8	5.5
Jehovah's Witness	2	NR	NR	NR	-	-
LDS–Comm of Christ	1	NR	156	156	0.1	0.2
LDS–L-D Saints	1	NR	NR	759	0.6	0.9
LUTH–Luth–MO Synod	2	441	586	707	0.6	0.8
MENN–Beachy Amish-Menn	2	139	78	139	0.1	0.2
METH–AME	1	0	100	123	0.1	0.1
METH–AME Zion	2	0	300	368	0.3	0.4
METH–C.M.E.	5	70	625	766	0.6	0.9
METH–Un Methodist	35	3,443	7,431	9,481	7.9	11.4
Non-denom Chr Chs	28	4,403	5,155	5,970	5.0	7.2
PENT–Assemb of God	4	2,085	1,066	3,075	2.6	3.7
PENT–Ch God (Cleve)	8	562	1,089	1,334	1.1	1.6
PENT–Ch of God Proph	3	NR	78	96	0.1	0.1
PENT–COGIC	1	0	150	184	0.2	0.2
PENT–Intl Pent Holiness	1	114	169	207	0.2	0.2
PENT–Un Pent Ch Intl	3	NR	NR	NR	-	-
PRES–Cum Pres Am	4	NR	NR	NR	-	-
PRES–Free Pres NA	1	NR	NR	NR	-	-
PRES–Presb Ch (USA)	4	253	602	738	0.6	0.9
PRES–Presb Ch Amer	2	197	290	360	0.3	0.4
Salvation Army	1	32	127	229	0.2	0.3

NR–Not Reported   - Represents no adherents reported.   Percentages may not total 100 due to rounding.

Table 3: Religious Congregations by County and Group: 2010

Religious Group	Number of Congrega-tions	Number of Attendees	Number of Communicant, Confirmed, or Full Members	Adherents		
				Number of Adherents	% of Total Pop.	% of Total Adh.
Sev Day Adv	4	196	339	391	0.3	0.5
PERRY	**44**	**1,778**	**4,775**	**5,710**	**53.9**	**100.0**
ANG/EPIS–Episcopal	1	40	80	92	0.9	1.6
Bahá'í	0	NR	5	5	0.0	0.1
BAPT–Free Will Bapt	1	NR	104	127	1.2	2.2
BAPT–NBC USA	2	475	575	703	6.6	12.3
BAPT–So Bapt Conv	11	539	1,937	2,369	22.4	41.5
CHR–Chs of Christ	1	40	60	80	0.8	1.4
METH–AME	3	40	350	428	4.0	7.5
METH–AME Zion	4	0	450	550	5.2	9.6
METH–Un Methodist	10	408	742	822	7.8	14.4
Non-denom Chr Chs	2	110	160	162	1.5	2.8
PENT–Assemb of God	1	8	4	8	0.1	0.1
PENT–Ch God (Cleve)	2	62	61	75	0.7	1.3
PENT–Ch Lord Jesus Apos	1	NR	NR	NR	-	-
PENT–COGIC	1	0	150	183	1.7	3.2
PENT–Un Pent Ch Intl	1	NR	NR	NR	-	-
PRES–Presb Ch Amer	2	45	79	84	0.8	1.5
Un C of Christ	1	11	18	22	0.2	0.4
PICKENS	**98**	**4,077**	**10,714**	**13,500**	**68.4**	**100.0**
ANG/EPIS–Episcopal	1	5	0	4	0.0	0.0
Bahá'í	0	NR	4	4	0.0	0.0
BAPT–Free Will Bapt	6	NR	624	759	3.8	5.6
BAPT–NBC USA	1	0	150	183	0.9	1.4
BAPT–So Bapt Conv	39	2,683	6,558	7,979	40.4	59.1
Catholic	1	NR	NR	74	0.4	0.5
CHR–Chs of Christ	4	167	168	219	1.1	1.6
METH–C.M.E.	9	0	1,200	1,460	7.4	10.8
METH–Un Methodist	17	735	1,392	1,558	7.9	11.5
Muslim Est	1	134	NR	308	1.6	2.3
PENT–Assemb of God	2	48	42	74	0.4	0.5
PENT–Ch God (Cleve)	3	80	137	167	0.8	1.2
PENT–Ch of God Proph	3	NR	82	100	0.5	0.7
PENT–COGIC	1	0	60	73	0.4	0.5
PENT–Pent Ch of God	2	140	NR	217	1.1	1.6
PENT–Un Pent Ch Intl	1	NR	NR	NR	-	-
PRES–Cum Pres Am	4	NR	NR	NR	-	-
PRES–Cumber Presb	1	NR	33	40	0.2	0.3
PRES–Presb Ch (USA)	1	0	34	41	0.2	0.3
PRES–Presb Ch Amer	1	85	230	240	1.2	1.8
PIKE	**89**	**5,128**	**13,498**	**16,755**	**50.9**	**100.0**
ANG/EPIS–Episcopal	1	60	158	171	0.5	1.0
Bahá'í	0	NR	2	2	0.0	0.0
BAPT–Natl Mis Bapt Conv	4	0	600	711	2.2	4.2
BAPT–NBC USA	3	525	900	1,067	3.2	6.4
BAPT–So Bapt Conv	32	2,555	7,062	8,370	25.4	50.0
Catholic	1	NR	NR	215	0.7	1.3
CHR–Chs of Christ	7	610	544	740	2.2	4.4
Jehovah's Witness	2	NR	NR	NR	-	-
LDS–L-D Saints	1	NR	NR	323	1.0	1.9
METH–AME	9	0	1,250	1,482	4.5	8.8
METH–C.M.E.	3	0	350	415	1.3	2.5
METH–Un Methodist	12	757	1,932	2,256	6.9	13.5
Non-denom Chr Chs	1	100	150	150	0.5	0.9
PENT–Assemb of God	6	345	193	441	1.3	2.6
PENT–Ch God (Cleve)	3	50	102	121	0.4	0.7
PRES–Presb Ch (USA)	1	0	13	15	0.0	0.1
PRES–Presb Ch Amer	1	77	156	178	0.5	1.1
Sev Day Adv	2	49	86	98	0.3	0.6
RANDOLPH	**106**	**5,003**	**10,931**	**13,134**	**57.3**	**100.0**
ANG/EPIS–Episcopal	1	30	65	65	0.3	0.5
Bahá'í	0	NR	1	1	0.0	0.0
BAPT–Natl Mis Bapt Conv	1	0	150	183	0.8	1.4
BAPT–NBC USA	6	250	1,250	1,526	6.7	11.6
BAPT–So Bapt Conv	35	2,123	5,097	6,224	27.2	47.4
Catholic	1	NR	NR	149	0.7	1.1
CGOD–Ch God (Ander)	1	0	NR	0	0.0	0.0
Ch of Nazarene	2	143	170	240	1.0	1.8

Religious Group	Number of Congrega-tions	Number of Attendees	Number of Communicant, Confirmed, or Full Members	Adherents		
				Number of Adherents	% of Total Pop.	% of Total Adh.
CHR–Chr Chs & Chs Cr	1	NR	106	129	0.6	1.0
CHR–Chs of Christ	11	594	529	682	3.0	5.2
CONG–Cong Chr, NA	1	NR	50	61	0.3	0.5
Jehovah's Witness	1	NR	NR	NR	-	-
METH–AME	1	0	100	122	0.5	0.9
METH–C.M.E.	1	0	100	122	0.5	0.9
METH–Cong Meth	5	NR	238	291	1.3	2.2
METH–Un Methodist	24	1,029	1,725	1,852	8.1	14.1
Non-denom Chr Chs	4	520	725	725	3.2	5.5
PENT–Assemb of God	1	0	0	0	0.0	0.0
PENT–Ch God (Cleve)	7	306	611	746	3.3	5.7
Sev Day Adv	2	8	14	16	0.1	0.1
RUSSELL	**133**	**10,348**	**27,632**	**36,790**	**69.5**	**100.0**
ANG/EPIS–Episcopal	1	17	22	22	0.0	0.1
Bahá'í	0	NR	20	20	0.0	0.1
BAPT–Free Will Bapt	3	NR	219	272	0.5	0.7
BAPT–Natl Mis Bapt Conv	1	0	150	187	0.4	0.5
BAPT–NBC USA	6	910	2,375	2,954	5.6	8.0
BAPT–So Bapt Conv	32	4,212	13,827	17,198	32.5	46.7
BUDD–Mahayana	1	NR	NR	20	0.0	0.1
Catholic	4	NR	NR	1,595	3.0	4.3
CGOD–Ch God (Ander)	1	0	NR	0	0.0	0.0
CHR–Chr Ch (Disc)	1	0	52	65	0.1	0.2
CHR–Chs of Christ	5	346	465	603	1.1	1.6
Jehovah's Witness	1	NR	NR	NR	-	-
LDS–L-D Saints	1	NR	NR	758	1.4	2.1
METH–AME	21	150	2,950	3,669	6.9	10.0
METH–AME Zion	4	20	500	622	1.2	1.7
METH–C.M.E.	4	110	550	684	1.3	1.9
METH–Un Methodist	11	781	1,883	2,330	4.4	6.3
Non-denom Chr Chs	18	2,095	2,900	3,035	5.7	8.2
PENT–Assemb of God	8	1,327	944	1,715	3.2	4.7
PENT–Ch God (Cleve)	2	78	259	322	0.6	0.9
PENT–COGIC	1	0	150	187	0.4	0.5
PENT–Full Gosp Bapt	1	NR	NR	NR	-	-
PENT–Pent Ch of God	1	70	NR	109	0.2	0.3
PENT–Un Pent Ch Intl	1	NR	NR	NR	-	-
PRES–Presb Ch (USA)	1	34	22	27	0.1	0.1
Sev Day Adv	3	198	344	396	0.7	1.1
ST. CLAIR	**154**	**12,218**	**31,749**	**39,768**	**47.6**	**100.0**
ANG/EPIS–Episcopal	1	100	221	280	0.3	0.7
Bahá'í	0	NR	12	12	0.0	0.0
BAPT–Amer Bapt Assn	1	NR	85	104	0.1	0.3
BAPT–Free Will Bapt	5	NR	520	637	0.8	1.6
BAPT–Natl Mis Bapt Conv	2	0	300	368	0.4	0.9
BAPT–NBC USA	1	250	500	613	0.7	1.5
BAPT–So Bapt Conv	67	7,239	22,397	27,457	32.8	69.0
Catholic	1	NR	NR	1,056	1.3	2.7
Ch of Nazarene	1	24	46	50	0.1	0.1
CHR–Chs of Christ	8	336	305	393	0.5	1.0
Jehovah's Witness	2	NR	NR	NR	-	-
METH–C.M.E.	2	0	200	245	0.3	0.6
METH–Un Methodist	15	1,184	2,207	2,482	3.0	6.2
Non-denom Chr Chs	14	1,575	1,910	2,164	2.6	5.4
PENT–Assemb of God	6	483	527	823	1.0	2.1
PENT–Ch God (Cleve)	8	870	1,165	1,428	1.7	3.6
PENT–Ch Lord Jesus Apos	4	NR	NR	NR	-	-
PENT–Ch of God Proph	2	NR	147	180	0.2	0.5
PENT–COGIC	3	0	450	552	0.7	1.4
PENT–Un Pent Ch Intl	2	NR	NR	NR	-	-
PRES–Cumber Presb	2	NR	143	163	0.2	0.4
PRES–Presb Ch (USA)	2	35	77	94	0.1	0.2
PRES–Presb Ch Amer	2	49	410	521	0.6	1.3
REF–Comm Ref Evan	1	NR	NR	NR	-	-
Sev Day Adv	2	73	127	146	0.2	0.4
SHELBY	**230**	**34,104**	**61,747**	**85,708**	**43.9**	**100.0**
ANG/EPIS–Anglican NA	3	NR	NR	NR	-	-
ANG/EPIS–Episcopal	5	393	963	1,073	0.6	1.3
Bahá'í	0	NR	20	20	0.0	0.0
BAPT–Alliance Bapt	2	NR	NR	NR	-	-

NR–Not Reported   - Represents no adherents reported.   Percentages may not total 100 due to rounding.

Table 3: Religious Congregations by County and Group: 2010

Religious Group	Number of Congregations	Number of Attendees	Number of Communicant, Confirmed, or Full Members	Adherents: Number of Adherents	Adherents: % of Total Pop.	Adherents: % of Total Adh.
BAPT–Amer Bapt Assn	1	NR	85	106	0.1	0.1
BAPT–Free Will Bapt	3	NR	312	390	0.2	0.5
BAPT–Natl Mis Bapt Conv	1	0	150	187	0.1	0.2
BAPT–NBC USA	4	600	1,050	1,311	0.7	1.5
BAPT–So Bapt Conv	81	16,579	35,174	43,917	22.5	51.2
Catholic	1	NR	NR	2,883	1.5	3.4
CGOD–Ch God (Ander)	3	32	NR	32	0.0	0.0
Ch of Nazarene	2	161	322	342	0.2	0.4
Chr & Miss Al	1	42	20	42	0.0	0.0
CHR–Chr Ch (Disc)	2	262	696	869	0.4	1.0
CHR–Chs of Christ	16	1,222	1,139	1,442	0.7	1.7
HINDU–Trad Temples	1	NR	NR	500	0.3	0.6
Ind Fund Churches	1	NR	NR	NR	-	-
Jehovah's Witness	1	NR	NR	NR	-	-
LDS–L-D Saints	3	NR	NR	1,508	0.8	1.8
LUTH–E.L.C.A.	1	130	266	301	0.2	0.4
METH–AME	6	75	639	798	0.4	0.9
METH–AME Zion	1	0	100	125	0.1	0.1
METH–Un Methodist	26	6,178	10,415	13,711	7.0	16.0
METH–Wesleyan	1	89	8	116	0.1	0.1
Muslim Est	1	134	NR	308	0.2	0.4
Non-denom Chr Chs	19	2,310	3,070	3,210	1.6	3.7
ORTHE–Ant Orth of NA	1	21	NR	58	0.0	0.1
PENT–Assemb of God	11	2,276	1,051	4,272	2.2	5.0
PENT–Ch God (Cleve)	9	861	1,383	1,727	0.9	2.0
PENT–Ch of God Proph	4	NR	182	227	0.1	0.3
PENT–Intl Pent Holiness	1	347	446	557	0.3	0.6
PENT–Un Pent Ch Intl	3	NR	NR	NR	-	-
PENT–Vineyard	1	286	533	665	0.3	0.8
PRES–Cumber Presb	4	NR	616	843	0.4	1.0
PRES–Presb Ch (USA)	2	33	98	122	0.1	0.1
PRES–Presb Ch Amer	5	1,997	2,921	3,950	2.0	4.6
Salvation Army	1	48	40	40	0.0	0.0
Sev Day Adv	2	28	48	55	0.0	0.1
Zoroastrian	0	NR	NR	1	0.0	0.0
SUMTER	**52**	**1,136**	**4,179**	**4,970**	**36.1**	**100.0**
ANG/EPIS–Episcopal	2	29	31	38	0.3	0.8
Bahá'í	0	NR	1	1	0.0	0.0
BAPT–Free Will Bapt	2	NR	208	248	1.8	5.0
BAPT–NBC USA	4	0	450	536	3.9	10.8
BAPT–So Bapt Conv	12	598	1,549	1,845	13.4	37.1
Catholic	1	NR	NR	37	0.3	0.7
CHR–Chs of Christ	1	75	75	85	0.6	1.7
Jehovah's Witness	1	NR	NR	NR	-	-
MENN–CG in Cr (Menn)	1	NR	156	186	1.4	3.7
METH–AME Zion	2	0	300	357	2.6	7.2
METH–C.M.E.	5	63	509	606	4.4	12.2
METH–Cong Meth	1	NR	46	55	0.4	1.1
METH–Un Methodist	8	186	475	561	4.1	11.3
Non-denom Chr Chs	1	100	150	150	1.1	3.0
PENT–Ch God (Cleve)	1	19	25	30	0.2	0.6
PENT–Un Pent Ch Intl	2	NR	NR	NR	-	-
PRES–Presb Ch (USA)	3	0	143	170	1.2	3.4
PRES–Presb Ch Amer	5	66	61	65	0.5	1.3
TALLADEGA	**209**	**13,927**	**34,397**	**44,005**	**53.5**	**100.0**
ANG/EPIS–Episcopal	4	160	285	324	0.4	0.7
Bahá'í	0	NR	9	9	0.0	0.0
BAPT–Free Will Bapt	3	NR	312	380	0.5	0.9
BAPT–NBC USA	7	1,075	1,550	1,886	2.3	4.3
BAPT–So Bapt Conv	69	6,306	20,584	25,051	30.4	56.9
Catholic	4	NR	NR	1,769	2.1	4.0
CGOD–Ch God (Ander)	2	38	NR	38	0.0	0.1
Ch of Nazarene	2	73	126	152	0.2	0.3
CHR–Chs of Christ	11	1,072	1,017	1,326	1.6	3.0
Jehovah's Witness	2	NR	NR	NR	-	-
LDS–L-D Saints	2	NR	NR	545	0.7	1.2
METH–AME	1	0	150	183	0.2	0.4
METH–AME Zion	2	75	195	237	0.3	0.5
METH–C.M.E.	8	50	925	1,126	1.4	2.6
METH–Un Methodist	28	1,490	3,235	3,817	4.6	8.7
Non-denom Chr Chs	18	1,750	2,330	2,553	3.1	5.8
PENT–Assemb of God	7	423	272	490	0.6	1.1
PENT–Ch God (Cleve)	9	767	2,143	2,608	3.2	5.9
PENT–Ch Lord Jesus Apos	5	NR	NR	NR	-	-
PENT–Ch of God Proph	3	NR	51	62	0.1	0.1
PENT–COGIC	2	30	175	213	0.3	0.5
PENT–Cong Hol Ch	5	174	149	181	0.2	0.4
PENT–Fire Bapt Hol Ch	1	NR	NR	NR	-	-
PENT–Intl Pent Holiness	1	75	152	185	0.2	0.4
PENT–Un Pent Ch Intl	3	NR	NR	NR	-	-
PRES–Presb Ch (USA)	3	118	270	329	0.4	0.7
PRES–Presb Ch Amer	2	75	131	151	0.2	0.3
Sev Day Adv	3	161	280	322	0.4	0.7
Un C of Christ	2	15	56	68	0.1	0.2
TALLAPOOSA	**142**	**9,593**	**23,619**	**28,905**	**69.5**	**100.0**
ANG/EPIS–Episcopal	1	98	247	248	0.6	0.9
Bahá'í	0	NR	1	1	0.0	0.0
BAPT–Natl Mis Bapt Conv	2	30	210	252	0.6	0.9
BAPT–NBC USA	7	425	2,170	2,602	6.3	9.0
BAPT–So Bapt Conv	58	5,235	14,310	17,160	41.2	59.4
BUDD–Mahayana	1	NR	NR	20	0.0	0.1
Catholic	1	NR	NR	894	2.1	3.1
CGOD–Ch God (Ander)	1	22	NR	22	0.1	0.1
Ch of Nazarene	1	52	67	67	0.2	0.2
CHR–Chr Ch (Disc)	1	10	15	18	0.0	0.1
CHR–Chs of Christ	8	580	636	764	1.8	2.6
Jehovah's Witness	3	NR	NR	NR	-	-
LDS–L-D Saints	1	NR	NR	158	0.4	0.5
METH–AME Zion	3	0	260	312	0.7	1.1
METH–C.M.E.	3	0	300	360	0.9	1.2
METH–Un Methodist	27	1,903	3,698	4,015	9.6	13.9
Non-denom Chr Chs	6	570	945	990	2.4	3.4
PENT–Assemb of God	4	209	88	219	0.5	0.8
PENT–Ch God (Cleve)	2	132	183	219	0.5	0.8
PENT–Ch Lord Jesus Apos	1	NR	NR	NR	-	-
PENT–Ch of God Proph	1	NR	54	65	0.2	0.2
PENT–Cong Hol Ch	2	48	46	55	0.1	0.2
PENT–Intl Pent Holiness	1	154	128	153	0.4	0.5
PENT–Un Pent Ch Intl	2	NR	NR	NR	-	-
PRES–Presb Ch (USA)	4	125	249	299	0.7	1.0
Unit Univ	1	0	12	12	0.0	0.0
TUSCALOOSA	**311**	**36,771**	**83,961**	**104,315**	**53.6**	**100.0**
ANG/EPIS–Episcopal	3	521	1,812	1,825	0.9	1.7
Bahá'í	1	NR	109	109	0.1	0.1
BAPT–Amer Bapt Assn	1	NR	120	144	0.1	0.1
BAPT–Free Will Bapt	10	NR	1,040	1,248	0.6	1.2
BAPT–Natl Mis Bapt Conv	2	0	300	360	0.2	0.3
BAPT–NBC Amer	1	800	1,100	1,320	0.7	1.3
BAPT–NBC USA	12	2,395	6,268	7,519	3.9	7.2
BAPT–So Bapt Conv	107	16,021	43,682	52,402	26.9	50.2
Catholic	2	NR	NR	3,729	1.9	3.6
CGOD–Ch God (Ander)	4	85	NR	85	0.0	0.1
Ch of Nazarene	7	364	669	686	0.4	0.7
CHR–Chr Ch (Disc)	2	90	189	227	0.1	0.2
CHR–Chs of Christ	9	1,856	1,933	2,479	1.3	2.4
Jehovah's Witness	2	NR	NR	NR	-	-
JUD–Reform	1	37	66	178	0.1	0.2
LDS–L-D Saints	2	NR	NR	1,246	0.6	1.2
LUTH–Luth-MO Synod	3	101	171	181	0.1	0.2
METH–AME	5	0	700	840	0.4	0.8
METH–AME Zion	14	150	1,850	2,219	1.1	2.1
METH–C.M.E.	6	220	1,509	1,810	0.9	1.7
METH–So Methodist	1	NR	NR	NR	-	-
METH–Un Methodist	36	3,557	7,489	8,417	4.3	8.1
METH–Wesleyan	3	621	890	808	0.4	0.8
Muslim Est	1	134	NR	308	0.2	0.3
Non-denom Chr Chs	33	6,616	8,564	9,293	4.8	8.9
PENT–Assemb of God	5	368	376	505	0.3	0.5
PENT–Ch God (Cleve)	10	1,005	1,616	1,939	1.0	1.9
PENT–Ch Lord Jesus Apos	1	NR	NR	NR	-	-
PENT–Ch of God by Faith	1	NR	NR	NR	-	-
PENT–Ch of God Proph	2	NR	130	156	0.1	0.1

NR–Not Reported - Represents no adherents reported. Percentages may not total 100 due to rounding.

Table 3: Religious Congregations by County and Group: 2010

Religious Group	Number of Congregations	Number of Attendees	Number of Communicant, Confirmed, or Full Members	Adherents		
				Number of Adherents	% of Total Pop.	% of Total Adh.
PENT–COGIC	2	0	300	360	0.2	0.3
PENT–Full Gosp Bapt	1	NR	NR	NR	-	-
PENT–Un Pent Ch Intl	2	NR	NR	NR	-	-
PENT–Vineyard	1	270	325	390	0.2	0.4
PRES–Cum Pres Am	1	NR	NR	NR	-	-
PRES–Cumber Presb	2	NR	102	191	0.1	0.2
PRES–Presb Ch (USA)	6	698	1,622	1,946	1.0	1.9
PRES–Presb Ch Amer	2	555	533	638	0.3	0.6
Salvation Army	1	57	79	263	0.1	0.3
Sev Day Adv	4	198	343	395	0.2	0.4
Unit Univ	1	52	74	99	0.1	0.1
Unity Ch	1	NR	NR	NR	-	-
WALKER	**217**	**15,254**	**34,911**	**43,800**	**65.4**	**100.0**
ANG/EPIS–Episcopal	1	51	114	114	0.2	0.3
Bahá'í	0	NR	8	8	0.0	0.0
BAPT–Amer Bapt Assn	1	NR	85	103	0.2	0.2
BAPT–Free Will Bapt	9	NR	936	1,130	1.7	2.6
BAPT–So Bapt Conv	73	6,664	20,422	24,658	36.8	56.3
Catholic	1	NR	NR	523	0.8	1.2
CGOD–Ch God (Ander)	2	110	NR	110	0.2	0.3
Ch of Nazarene	7	609	884	1,034	1.5	2.4
Chr & Miss Al	1	6	4	7	0.0	0.0
CHR–Chr Ch (Disc)	1	30	70	85	0.1	0.2
CHR–Chs of Christ	41	3,011	2,914	3,950	5.9	9.0
Jehovah's Witness	2	NR	NR	NR	-	-
LDS–L-D Saints	1	NR	NR	512	0.8	1.2
METH–AME	2	0	250	302	0.5	0.7
METH–AME Zion	1	0	100	121	0.2	0.3
METH–C.M.E.	4	25	450	543	0.8	1.2
METH–Un Methodist	22	1,019	1,875	2,265	3.4	5.2
Non-denom Chr Chs	8	1,024	1,205	1,411	2.1	3.2
PENT–Assemb of God	9	569	466	735	1.1	1.7
PENT–Ch God (Cleve)	20	1,894	4,545	5,488	8.2	12.5
PENT–Ch of God Proph	6	NR	288	348	0.5	0.8
PENT–COGIC	1	95	100	121	0.2	0.3
PENT–Un Pent Ch Intl	1	NR	NR	NR	-	-
PRES–Presb Ch (USA)	1	50	73	88	0.1	0.2
PRES–Presb Ch Amer	1	75	84	100	0.1	0.2
Sev Day Adv	1	22	38	44	0.1	0.1
WASHINGTON	**88**	**3,686**	**8,098**	**10,284**	**58.5**	**100.0**
BAPT–Natl Mis Bapt Conv	1	0	150	185	1.1	1.8
BAPT–NBC USA	2	60	275	339	1.9	3.3
BAPT–So Bapt Conv	34	2,133	4,872	6,009	34.2	58.4
BRETH–Ch of Brethren	1	0	60	74	0.4	0.7
Catholic	2	NR	NR	30	0.2	0.3
Ch of Nazarene	2	52	51	70	0.4	0.7
FRND–Fr Un Mtg	1	NR	0	0	0.0	0.0
METH–AME	2	50	200	247	1.4	2.4
METH–AME Zion	5	0	550	678	3.9	6.6
METH–C.M.E.	1	0	100	123	0.7	1.2
METH–Un Methodist	18	462	1,145	1,242	7.1	12.1
Non-denom Chr Chs	3	230	218	288	1.6	2.8
PENT–Assemb of God	10	609	284	761	4.3	7.4
PENT–Ch God (Cleve)	3	60	153	189	1.1	1.8
PENT–COGIC	1	30	40	49	0.3	0.5
PENT–Un Pent Ch Intl	2	NR	NR	NR	-	-
WILCOX	**72**	**1,694**	**5,633**	**7,124**	**61.0**	**100.0**
BAPT–So Bapt Conv	16	755	1,738	2,177	18.7	30.6
Catholic	3	NR	NR	12	0.1	0.2
CHR–Chs of Christ	5	170	163	206	1.8	2.9
Jehovah's Witness	1	NR	NR	NR	-	-
LDS–L-D Saints	1	NR	NR	95	0.8	1.3
LUTH–Luth–MO Synod	3	122	178	262	2.2	3.7
METH–AME	19	0	1,950	2,443	20.9	34.3
METH–AME Zion	1	0	100	125	1.1	1.8
METH–C.M.E.	2	0	200	251	2.2	3.5
METH–Un Methodist	6	179	412	463	4.0	6.5
Non-denom Chr Chs	4	365	395	477	4.1	6.7
PENT–Ch God (Cleve)	2	61	106	133	1.1	1.9
PENT–COGIC	1	0	150	188	1.6	2.6

Religious Group	Number of Congregations	Number of Attendees	Number of Communicant, Confirmed, or Full Members	Adherents		
				Number of Adherents	% of Total Pop.	% of Total Adh.
PRES–As Ref Pres Ch	2	NR	72	90	0.8	1.3
PRES–Cum Pres Am	2	NR	NR	NR	-	-
PRES–Presb Ch (USA)	2	0	84	105	0.9	1.5
PRES–Presb Ch Amer	2	42	85	97	0.8	1.4
WINSTON	**75**	**5,199**	**11,856**	**14,974**	**61.2**	**100.0**
BAPT–Amer Bapt Assn	1	NR	85	102	0.4	0.7
BAPT–So Bapt Conv	38	3,187	9,286	11,113	45.4	74.2
Catholic	1	NR	NR	223	0.9	1.5
Ch of Nazarene	1	17	23	23	0.1	0.2
CHR–Chs of Christ	9	843	768	978	4.0	6.5
Intl Fell Bible Ch	1	NR	NR	NR	-	-
Jehovah's Witness	1	NR	NR	NR	-	-
LDS–L-D Saints	1	NR	NR	135	0.6	0.9
METH–Un Methodist	10	460	840	1,117	4.6	7.5
PENT–Assemb of God	2	230	120	295	1.2	2.0
PENT–Ch God (Cleve)	6	392	655	784	3.2	5.2
PENT–Ch of God Proph	2	NR	79	95	0.4	0.6
PENT–Pent Ch of God	1	70	NR	109	0.4	0.7
PENT–Un Pent Ch Intl	1	NR	NR	NR	-	-
ALASKA	**1,246**	**71,303**	**97,674**	**240,833**	**33.9**	**100.0**
ALEUTIANS EAST	**8**	**244**	**48**	**741**	**23.6**	**100.0**
Bahá'í	0	NR	8	8	0.3	1.1
BAPT–Converge/BGC	1	75	NR	90	2.9	12.1
BAPT–Ind Bapt Flwsp Intl	1	NR	NR	NR	-	-
BAPT–So Bapt Conv	2	40	40	44	1.4	5.9
ORTHE–Orth Ch in Amer	4	129	NR	599	19.1	80.8
ALEUTIANS WEST	**12**	**319**	**185**	**1,365**	**24.5**	**100.0**
Bahá'í	0	NR	6	6	0.1	0.4
Catholic	1	NR	NR	185	3.3	13.6
Ind Fund Churches	1	NR	NR	NR	-	-
LDS–L-D Saints	1	NR	NR	106	1.9	7.8
METH–Un Methodist	1	28	29	82	1.5	6.0
Non-denom Chr Chs	1	180	150	225	4.0	16.5
ORTHE–Orth Ch in Amer	6	107	NR	754	13.6	55.2
PENT–Assemb of God	1	4	0	7	0.1	0.5
ANCHORAGE	**326**	**30,423**	**41,624**	**102,804**	**35.2**	**100.0**
ANG/EPIS–Episcopal	5	426	1,388	1,635	0.6	1.6
Bahá'í	1	NR	382	382	0.1	0.4
BAPT–Amer Bapt USA	4	510	1,186	1,486	0.5	1.4
BAPT–Converge/BGC	3	225	NR	270	0.1	0.3
BAPT–Natl Mis Bapt Conv	3	0	450	564	0.2	0.5
BAPT–NBC USA	1	0	0	0	0.0	0.0
BAPT–Reg Bapt Gen As	2	NR	NR	NR	-	-
BAPT–S-D Baptist Gen Con	1	NR	NR	NR	-	-
BAPT–So Bapt Conv	33	3,563	7,225	9,056	3.1	8.8
BRETH–Grace Breth	2	NR	NR	NR	-	-
BUDD–Mahayana	3	NR	NR	618	0.2	0.6
BUDD–Theravada	4	NR	NR	3,405	1.2	3.3
BUDD–Vajrayana	1	NR	NR	20	0.0	0.0
Calv Chpl	1	NR	NR	NR	-	-
Catholic	12	NR	NR	22,969	7.9	22.3
CGOD–Ch God (Ander)	2	380	NR	380	0.1	0.4
Ch Cr, Scientst	1	NR	NR	NR	-	-
Ch of Nazarene	8	494	641	865	0.3	0.8
Chr & Miss Al	4	610	528	853	0.3	0.8
CHR–Chr Ch (Disc)	1	0	155	194	0.1	0.2
CHR–Chr Chs & Chs Cr	4	NR	1,935	2,425	0.8	2.4
CHR–Chs of Christ	5	650	672	1,043	0.4	1.0
CHR–Int Chs of Christ	1	NR	105	132	0.0	0.1
Christian Brethren	1	NR	NR	NR	-	-
CONG–Cong Chr, NA	3	NR	252	316	0.1	0.3
Evan Cov Ch	4	973	564	1,266	0.4	1.2
Evan Free Ch	1	30	NR	30	0.0	0.0
FRND–Evan Fr Ch Intl	1	60	90	113	0.0	0.1
FRND–Fr Gen Cf	1	NR	60	75	0.0	0.1
HINDU–Post Ren	2	NR	NR	35	0.0	0.0

NR–Not Reported - Represents no adherents reported. Percentages may not total 100 due to rounding.

Table 3: Religious Congregations by County and Group: 2010

Religious Group	Number of Congrega-tions	Number of Attendees	Number of Communicant, Confirmed, or Full Members	Adherents		
				Number of Adherents	% of Total Pop.	% of Total Adh.
HINDU–Renaiss	1	NR	NR	12	0.0	0.0
HINDU–Trad Temples	1	NR	NR	160	0.1	0.2
Jehovah's Witness	5	NR	NR	NR	-	-
JUD–Orth	1	43	50	60	0.0	0.1
JUD–Reform	1	87	154	416	0.1	0.4
LDS–Comm of Christ	1	NR	167	167	0.1	0.2
LDS–L-D Saints	28	NR	NR	13,867	4.8	13.5
LUTH–Ch Luth Conf	1	NR	NR	NR	-	-
LUTH–E.L.C.A.	9	1,004	2,721	3,334	1.1	3.2
LUTH–Luth Cong Msn Chr	1	16	13	16	0.0	0.0
LUTH–Luth–MO Synod	4	462	826	1,141	0.4	1.1
LUTH–Wisc Ev Luth Syn	3	266	432	547	0.2	0.5
MENN–Mennonite USA	1	40	40	50	0.0	0.0
METH–AME Zion	1	65	100	125	0.0	0.1
METH–C.M.E.	3	0	350	439	0.2	0.4
METH–Free Methodist	2	120	91	120	0.0	0.1
METH–Un Methodist	10	1,146	1,872	2,836	1.0	2.8
METH–Wesleyan	1	59	5	77	0.0	0.1
Metro Comm Ch	1	7	14	18	0.0	0.0
MORAV–Morav Ch-AK	1	NR	85	107	0.0	0.1
Muslim Est	3	402	NR	924	0.3	0.9
Non-denom Chr Chs	51	12,474	12,761	17,405	6.0	16.9
ORTHE–Ant Orth of NA	1	225	NR	350	0.1	0.3
ORTHE–Greek Orthodox	1	86	NR	234	0.1	0.2
ORTHE–Orth Ch in Amer	5	306	NR	1,591	0.5	1.5
ORTHE–Serb Orth USA	1	30	NR	40	0.0	0.0
PENT–Assemb of God	24	2,695	1,533	4,632	1.6	4.5
PENT–Ch God (Cleve)	6	360	903	1,132	0.4	1.1
PENT–Ch of God Proph	2	NR	79	99	0.0	0.1
PENT–Int Foursq Gos	1	127	187	234	0.1	0.2
PENT–Intl Pent Holiness	3	174	155	194	0.1	0.2
PENT–Un Pent Ch Intl	6	NR	NR	NR	-	-
PRES–Kor Pres Abroad	1	NR	NR	NR	-	-
PRES–Korean Pres Amer	1	NR	NR	NR	-	-
PRES–Presb Ch (USA)	7	696	1,077	1,350	0.5	1.3
PRES–Presb Ch Amer	1	90	51	72	0.0	0.1
REF–Christian Ref	3	259	211	264	0.1	0.3
REF–Comm Ref Evan	1	NR	NR	NR	-	-
Salvation Army	2	136	312	477	0.2	0.5
Sev Day Adv	9	892	1,552	1,785	0.6	1.7
Sikh	2	NR	NR	NR	-	-
Un C of Christ	2	80	61	76	0.0	0.1
Unit Univ	1	155	189	321	0.1	0.3
Unity Ch	1	NR	NR	NR	-	-
BETHEL	**55**	**950**	**1,961**	**9,011**	**53.0**	**100.0**
Bahá'í	0	NR	26	26	0.2	0.3
Catholic	8	NR	NR	3,244	19.1	36.0
Evan Cov Ch	3	108	113	141	0.8	1.6
LDS–L-D Saints	1	NR	NR	172	1.0	1.9
LUTH–E.L.C.A.	1	28	0	37	0.2	0.4
MORAV–Morav Ch-AK	17	NR	1,547	2,179	12.8	24.2
Non-denom Chr Chs	1	100	150	150	0.9	1.7
ORTHE–Orth Ch in Amer	17	569	NR	2,852	16.8	31.7
PENT–Assemb of God	2	50	23	70	0.4	0.8
PENT–Intl Pent Holiness	2	85	85	120	0.7	1.3
PENT–Un Pent Ch Intl	2	NR	NR	NR	-	-
Sev Day Adv	1	10	17	20	0.1	0.2
BRISTOL BAY	**6**	**66**	**6**	**293**	**29.4**	**100.0**
Bahá'í	0	NR	1	1	0.1	0.3
BAPT–So Bapt Conv	1	11	5	6	0.6	2.0
Catholic	1	NR	NR	60	6.0	20.5
ORTHE–Orth Ch in Amer	3	55	NR	226	22.7	77.1
PENT–Un Pent Ch Intl	1	NR	NR	NR	-	-
DENALI	**8**	**233**	**263**	**509**	**27.9**	**100.0**
Bahá'í	0	NR	5	5	0.3	1.0
BAPT–So Bapt Conv	2	99	78	95	5.2	18.7
Catholic	1	NR	NR	112	6.1	22.0
LDS–L-D Saints	1	NR	NR	82	4.5	16.1
Non-denom Chr Chs	2	105	162	181	9.9	35.6
PENT–Assemb of God	2	29	18	34	1.9	6.7
DILLINGHAM	**25**	**471**	**641**	**2,502**	**51.6**	**100.0**
Bahá'í	0	NR	14	14	0.3	0.6
BAPT–So Bapt Conv	3	90	61	82	1.7	3.3
Catholic	2	NR	NR	578	11.9	23.1
CHR–Chs of Christ	1	10	10	10	0.2	0.4
LDS–L-D Saints	1	NR	NR	44	0.9	1.8
LUTH–E.L.C.A.	1	26	50	73	1.5	2.9
MORAV–Morav Ch-AK	5	NR	272	363	7.5	14.5
ORTHE–Orth Ch in Amer	7	160	NR	988	20.4	39.5
PENT–Assemb of God	3	63	22	106	2.2	4.2
Sev Day Adv	2	122	212	244	5.0	9.8
FAIRBANKS NORTH STAR	**123**	**9,721**	**14,925**	**28,104**	**28.8**	**100.0**
ANG/EPIS–Episcopal	2	326	1,297	1,305	1.3	4.6
Bahá'í	3	NR	98	98	0.1	0.3
BAPT–Amer Bapt USA	4	208	273	343	0.4	1.2
BAPT–Consrv Bapt	3	NR	NR	NR	-	-
BAPT–Free Will Bapt	1	NR	73	92	0.1	0.3
BAPT–Fund Bapt Flwsp	1	NR	NR	NR	-	-
BAPT–Ind Bapt Flwsp Intl	1	NR	NR	NR	-	-
BAPT–So Bapt Conv	14	912	2,902	3,646	3.7	13.0
BUDD–Mahayana	2	NR	NR	265	0.3	0.9
Catholic	5	NR	NR	4,195	4.3	14.9
CGOD–Ch God (Ander)	1	200	NR	200	0.2	0.7
Ch Cr, Scientst	1	NR	NR	NR	-	-
Ch of Nazarene	3	118	129	296	0.3	1.1
CHR–Chr Chs & Chs Cr	1	NR	160	201	0.2	0.7
CHR–Chs of Christ	3	255	233	275	0.3	1.0
Christian Brethren	2	NR	NR	NR	-	-
Evan Cov Ch	1	135	47	176	0.2	0.6
FRND–Evan Fr Ch Intl	1	10	15	19	0.0	0.1
FRND–Fr Gen Cf	1	NR	50	63	0.1	0.2
HINDU–Post Ren	1	NR	NR	25	0.0	0.1
Jehovah's Witness	3	NR	NR	NR	-	-
JUD–Reform	1	32	56	151	0.2	0.5
LDS–Comm of Christ	1	NR	167	167	0.2	0.6
LDS–L-D Saints	10	NR	NR	4,525	4.6	16.1
LUTH–Ch Luth Conf	1	NR	NR	NR	-	-
LUTH–E.L.C.A.	3	296	868	1,013	1.0	3.6
LUTH–Luth–MO Synod	1	374	652	825	0.8	2.9
LUTH–Wisc Ev Luth Syn	1	46	53	64	0.1	0.2
METH–AME	1	15	20	25	0.0	0.1
METH–AME Zion	2	50	150	188	0.2	0.7
METH–Un Methodist	2	279	393	587	0.6	2.1
Non-denom Chr Chs	18	4,700	5,468	6,339	6.5	22.6
ORTHE–Orth Ch in Amer	1	35	NR	135	0.1	0.5
PENT–Assemb of God	6	673	366	1,080	1.1	3.8
PENT–Ch God (Cleve)	3	82	117	147	0.2	0.5
PENT–Ch of God Proph	1	NR	22	28	0.0	0.1
PENT–COGIC	3	215	205	258	0.3	0.9
PENT–Int Foursq Gos	1	0	0	0	0.0	0.0
PENT–Intl Pent Holiness	2	63	35	44	0.0	0.2
PENT–Un Pent Ch Intl	2	NR	NR	NR	-	-
PRES–Presb Ch (USA)	5	372	524	658	0.7	2.3
Salvation Army	1	30	39	75	0.1	0.3
Sev Day Adv	2	240	418	480	0.5	1.7
Unit Univ	1	55	95	116	0.1	0.4
HAINES	**16**	**297**	**309**	**877**	**35.0**	**100.0**
ANG/EPIS–Episcopal	1	18	35	74	3.0	8.4
Bahá'í	1	NR	15	15	0.6	1.7
BAPT–So Bapt Conv	2	63	70	82	3.3	9.4
BUDD–Mahayana	1	NR	NR	103	4.1	11.7
Catholic	3	NR	NR	185	7.4	21.1
LDS–L-D Saints	1	NR	NR	81	3.2	9.2
Non-denom Chr Chs	1	60	70	75	3.0	8.6
PENT–Assemb of God	2	49	5	62	2.5	7.1
PENT–Int Foursq Gos	1	0	0	0	0.0	0.0
PENT–Un Pent Ch Intl	1	NR	NR	NR	-	-
PRES–Presb Ch (USA)	1	90	64	75	3.0	8.6
Salvation Army	1	17	50	125	5.0	14.3

NR–Not Reported   - Represents no adherents reported.   Percentages may not total 100 due to rounding.

Table 3: Religious Congregations by County and Group: 2010

Religious Group	Number of Congregations	Number of Attendees	Number of Communicant, Confirmed, or Full Members	Adherents: Number of Adherents	Adherents: % of Total Pop.	Adherents: % of Total Adh.
HOONAH-ANGOON	**15**	**164**	**105**	**633**	**29.4**	**100.0**
Bahá'í	0	NR	11	11	0.5	1.7
Catholic	6	NR	NR	125	5.8	19.7
LDS–L-D Saints	1	NR	NR	78	3.6	12.3
ORTHE–Orth Ch in Amer	2	45	NR	200	9.3	31.6
PENT–Assemb of God	3	94	40	114	5.3	18.0
PENT–Un Pent Ch Intl	1	NR	NR	NR	-	-
PRES–Presb Ch (USA)	1	0	21	21	1.0	3.3
Salvation Army	1	25	33	84	3.9	13.3
JUNEAU	**47**	**2,185**	**3,657**	**8,969**	**28.7**	**100.0**
ANG/EPIS–Episcopal	2	135	257	292	0.9	3.3
Bahá'í	1	NR	162	162	0.5	1.8
BAPT–So Bapt Conv	4	208	634	771	2.5	8.6
BUDD–Vajrayana	1	NR	NR	53	0.2	0.6
Calv Chpl	1	NR	NR	NR	-	-
Catholic	2	NR	NR	1,900	6.1	21.2
CGOD–Ch God (Ander)	1	65	NR	65	0.2	0.7
Ch of Nazarene	1	110	131	160	0.5	1.8
Chr & Miss Al	1	55	0	81	0.3	0.9
CHR–Chs of Christ	1	95	84	110	0.4	1.2
FRND–Fr Gen Cf	1	NR	25	30	0.1	0.3
HINDU–Post Ren	1	NR	NR	16	0.1	0.2
Jehovah's Witness	1	NR	NR	NR	-	-
JUD–Reform	1	27	48	130	0.4	1.4
LDS–L-D Saints	4	NR	NR	1,711	5.5	19.1
LUTH–E.L.C.A.	2	125	368	464	1.5	5.2
LUTH–Luth–MO Synod	1	30	56	63	0.2	0.7
LUTH–Wisc Ev Luth Syn	1	68	85	117	0.4	1.3
METH–Un Methodist	3	131	280	446	1.4	5.0
New Apost Ch	1	NR	NR	NR	-	-
Non-denom Chr Chs	4	520	570	675	2.2	7.5
ORTHE–Orth Ch in Amer	1	25	NR	150	0.5	1.7
PENT–Assemb of God	1	350	0	350	1.1	3.9
PENT–Ch God (Cleve)	1	120	176	214	0.7	2.4
PENT–Int Foursq Gos	1	14	4	5	0.0	0.1
PENT–Un Pent Ch Intl	2	NR	NR	NR	-	-
PRES–Presb Ch (USA)	2	0	576	701	2.2	7.8
Salvation Army	1	26	62	139	0.4	1.5
Sev Day Adv	1	58	102	117	0.4	1.3
Unit Univ	1	23	37	47	0.2	0.5
Unity Ch	1	NR	NR	NR	-	-
KENAI PENINSULA	**123**	**6,647**	**8,111**	**17,843**	**32.2**	**100.0**
ANG/EPIS–Episcopal	3	61	88	91	0.2	0.5
Bahá'í	2	NR	93	93	0.2	0.5
BAPT–Consrv Bapt	1	NR	NR	NR	-	-
BAPT–Ind Bapt Flwsp Intl	3	NR	NR	NR	-	-
BAPT–Reg Bapt Gen As	1	NR	NR	NR	-	-
BAPT–So Bapt Conv	8	559	1,276	1,553	2.8	8.7
BRETH–Grace Breth	2	NR	NR	NR	-	-
Catholic	6	NR	NR	2,810	5.1	15.7
Ch Cr, Scientst	1	NR	NR	NR	-	-
Ch of Nazarene	5	327	384	481	0.9	2.7
CHR–Chr Chs & Chs Cr	4	NR	525	639	1.2	3.6
CHR–Chs of Christ	8	417	369	515	0.9	2.9
Evan Cov Ch	1	70	0	91	0.2	0.5
FRND–Fr Gen Cf	1	NR	25	30	0.1	0.2
Ind Fund Churches	1	NR	NR	NR	-	-
Jehovah's Witness	3	NR	NR	NR	-	-
JUD–Reform	1	12	21	57	0.1	0.3
LDS–L-D Saints	5	NR	NR	2,929	5.3	16.4
LUTH–E.L.C.A.	2	168	327	387	0.7	2.2
LUTH–Luth–MO Synod	4	229	329	391	0.7	2.2
LUTH–Wisc Ev Luth Syn	1	92	90	124	0.2	0.7
MENN–CG in Cr (Menn)	1	NR	4	5	0.0	0.0
METH–Un Methodist	7	328	593	899	1.6	5.0
METH–Wesleyan	1	89	21	116	0.2	0.7
Non-denom Chr Chs	20	2,770	3,121	3,881	7.0	21.8
ORTHE–Ant Orth of NA	1	47	NR	60	0.1	0.3
ORTHE–Orth Ch in Amer	7	165	NR	799	1.4	4.5
PENT–Assemb of God	9	724	293	1,074	1.9	6.0
PENT–Ch God (Cleve)	2	229	176	214	0.4	1.2
PENT–Int Foursq Gos	1	60	57	69	0.1	0.4
PENT–Intl Pent Holiness	1	55	55	67	0.1	0.4
PENT–Pent Ch of God	1	70	NR	109	0.2	0.6
PENT–Un Pent Ch Intl	4	NR	NR	NR	-	-
Salvation Army	2	49	43	115	0.2	0.6
Sev Day Adv	2	122	212	244	0.4	1.4
Unit Univ	1	4	9	NR	-	-
KETCHIKAN GATEWAY	**31**	**1,516**	**1,521**	**4,246**	**31.5**	**100.0**
ANG/EPIS–Episcopal	1	48	114	142	1.1	3.3
Bahá'í	2	NR	35	35	0.3	0.8
BAPT–So Bapt Conv	3	118	167	204	1.5	4.8
Catholic	2	NR	NR	920	6.8	21.7
Ch of Nazarene	1	56	38	125	0.9	2.9
Chr & Miss Al	5	479	180	484	3.6	11.4
CHR–Chs of Christ	1	75	70	105	0.8	2.5
Jehovah's Witness	1	NR	NR	NR	-	-
LDS–L-D Saints	1	NR	NR	731	5.4	17.2
LUTH–Ch Luth Conf	1	NR	NR	NR	-	-
LUTH–E.L.C.A.	1	107	233	365	2.7	8.6
METH–Un Methodist	1	47	68	85	0.6	2.0
Non-denom Chr Chs	2	110	100	137	1.0	3.2
PENT–Assemb of God	1	170	60	242	1.8	5.7
PENT–Ch God (Cleve)	1	105	240	293	2.2	6.9
PENT–Int Foursq Gos	2	18	11	13	0.1	0.3
PENT–Pent Ch of God	1	70	NR	109	0.8	2.6
PENT–Un Pent Ch Intl	1	NR	NR	NR	-	-
PRES–Presb Ch (USA)	1	30	42	51	0.4	1.2
Salvation Army	1	46	99	131	1.0	3.1
Sev Day Adv	1	37	64	74	0.5	1.7
KODIAK ISLAND	**34**	**1,545**	**1,011**	**3,818**	**28.1**	**100.0**
ANG/EPIS–Episcopal	1	36	53	87	0.6	2.3
Bahá'í	0	NR	8	8	0.1	0.2
BAPT–Amer Bapt USA	2	174	101	130	1.0	3.4
BAPT–Reg Bapt Gen As	1	NR	NR	NR	-	-
BAPT–So Bapt Conv	1	47	75	97	0.7	2.5
Catholic	1	NR	NR	500	3.7	13.1
Ch Cr, Scientst	1	NR	NR	NR	-	-
Ch of Nazarene	1	70	71	108	0.8	2.8
Chr & Miss Al	1	232	123	123	0.9	3.2
CHR–Chs of Christ	1	40	35	45	0.3	1.2
Jehovah's Witness	1	NR	NR	NR	-	-
JUD–Orth	0	40	0	0	0.0	0.0
LDS–L-D Saints	1	NR	NR	439	3.2	11.5
LUTH–Luth Cong Msn Chr	1	77	257	331	2.4	8.7
LUTH–Wisc Ev Luth Syn	1	10	6	12	0.1	0.3
Non-denom Chr Chs	3	165	166	206	1.5	5.4
ORTHE–Bulgar Orth USA	1	25	NR	25	0.2	0.7
ORTHE–Orth Ch in Amer	7	348	NR	1,367	10.1	35.8
ORTHE–Serb Orth USA	2	7	NR	7	0.1	0.2
PENT–Assemb of God	1	200	0	200	1.5	5.2
PENT–Ch of God Proph	1	NR	3	4	0.0	0.1
PENT–Un Pent Ch Intl	1	NR	NR	NR	-	-
PRES–Korean Pres Amer	1	NR	NR	NR	-	-
Salvation Army	1	19	27	32	0.2	0.8
Sev Day Adv	1	40	70	81	0.6	2.1
Unit Univ	1	15	16	16	0.1	0.4
LAKE AND PENINSULA	**10**	**232**	**5**	**1,148**	**70.4**	**100.0**
Bahá'í	0	NR	5	5	0.3	0.4
ORTHE–Orth Ch in Amer	10	232	NR	1,143	70.1	99.6
MATANUSKA-SUSITNA	**116**	**8,923**	**12,209**	**26,656**	**30.0**	**100.0**
ANG/EPIS–Episcopal	4	97	135	162	0.2	0.6
Bahá'í	3	NR	105	105	0.1	0.4
BAPT–Amer Bapt USA	2	54	94	121	0.1	0.5
BAPT–Ind Bapt Flwsp Intl	1	NR	NR	NR	-	-
BAPT–Natl Mis Bapt Conv	1	0	150	193	0.2	0.7
BAPT–Reg Bapt Gen As	1	NR	NR	NR	-	-
BAPT–So Bapt Conv	12	933	2,416	3,103	3.5	11.6
Catholic	4	NR	NR	3,354	3.8	12.6

NR–Not Reported - Represents no adherents reported. Percentages may not total 100 due to rounding.

Table 3: Religious Congregations by County and Group: 2010

Religious Group	Number of Congrega-tions	Number of Attendees	Number of Communicant, Confirmed, or Full Members	Adherents: Number of Adherents	Adherents: % of Total Pop.	Adherents: % of Total Adh.
CGOD–Ch God (Ander)	2	225	NR	225	0.3	0.8
Ch Cr, Scientst	1	NR	NR	NR	-	-
Ch of Nazarene	3	290	382	716	0.8	2.7
Chr & Miss Al	2	36	17	46	0.1	0.2
CHR–Chr Chs & Chs Cr	2	NR	250	321	0.4	1.2
CHR–Chs of Christ	2	225	224	306	0.3	1.1
Evan Cov Ch	1	88	65	114	0.1	0.4
FRND–Fr Gen Cf	2	NR	25	32	0.0	0.1
Jehovah's Witness	3	NR	NR	NR	-	-
LDS–Comm of Christ	1	NR	167	167	0.2	0.6
LDS–L-D Saints	11	NR	NR	5,378	6.0	20.2
LUTH–E.L.C.A.	5	210	702	1,087	1.2	4.1
LUTH–Luth–MO Synod	2	191	764	1,075	1.2	4.0
LUTH–Wisc Ev Luth Syn	1	73	102	137	0.2	0.5
METH–Un Methodist	2	145	238	387	0.4	1.5
METH–Wesleyan	1	28	2	36	0.0	0.1
Non-denom Chr Chs	28	5,218	4,820	7,009	7.9	26.3
ORTHE–Ant Orth of NA	1	41	NR	112	0.1	0.4
PENT–Assemb of God	4	224	107	304	0.3	1.1
PENT–Ch God (Cleve)	3	126	353	453	0.5	1.7
PENT–Open Bible Std	1	47	NR	47	0.1	0.2
PENT–Pent Ch of God	1	70	NR	109	0.1	0.4
PENT–Un Pent Ch Intl	2	NR	NR	NR	-	-
PRES–Orth Pres Ch	1	70	61	79	0.1	0.3
PRES–Presb Ch (USA)	2	134	375	482	0.5	1.8
Salvation Army	1	48	46	296	0.3	1.1
Sev Day Adv	3	350	609	700	0.8	2.6
NOME	**35**	**931**	**1,794**	**4,463**	**47.0**	**100.0**
Bahá'í	0	NR	39	39	0.4	0.9
BAPT–So Bapt Conv	1	20	25	34	0.4	0.8
Catholic	5	NR	NR	880	9.3	19.7
Ch of Nazarene	1	30	49	81	0.9	1.8
Evan Cov Ch	7	381	288	496	5.2	11.1
LDS–L-D Saints	1	NR	NR	119	1.3	2.7
LUTH–E.L.C.A.	5	205	891	1,889	19.9	42.3
METH–Un Methodist	1	25	48	126	1.3	2.8
Non-denom Chr Chs	1	45	50	56	0.6	1.3
ORTHE–Orth Ch in Amer	2	20	NR	100	1.1	2.2
PENT–Assemb of God	5	92	105	270	2.8	6.0
PRES–Presb Ch (USA)	3	18	133	183	1.9	4.1
Sev Day Adv	3	95	166	190	2.0	4.3
NORTH SLOPE	**17**	**475**	**840**	**1,539**	**16.3**	**100.0**
ANG/EPIS–Episcopal	2	24	283	309	3.3	20.1
Bahá'í	0	NR	13	13	0.1	0.8
Catholic	2	NR	NR	165	1.7	10.7
LDS–L-D Saints	1	NR	NR	111	1.2	7.2
Non-denom Chr Chs	2	30	21	37	0.4	2.4
PENT–Assemb of God	4	170	63	336	3.6	21.8
PENT–Ch God (Cleve)	1	91	65	80	0.8	5.2
PRES–Presb Ch (USA)	5	160	395	488	5.2	31.7
NORTHWEST ARCTIC	**25**	**849**	**1,269**	**2,385**	**31.7**	**100.0**
ANG/EPIS–Episcopal	3	51	100	408	5.4	17.1
Bahá'í	0	NR	29	29	0.4	1.2
BAPT–So Bapt Conv	5	118	92	129	1.7	5.4
Catholic	1	NR	NR	240	3.2	10.1
CHR–Chs of Christ	1	6	6	8	0.1	0.3
FRND–Evan Fr Ch Intl	10	591	895	1,255	16.7	52.6
LDS–L-D Saints	1	NR	NR	64	0.9	2.7
Non-denom Chr Chs	1	20	25	25	0.3	1.0
PENT–Assemb of God	2	19	3	60	0.8	2.5
PENT–Ch God (Cleve)	1	44	119	167	2.2	7.0
PETERSBURG	**14**	**364**	**650**	**1,184**	**31.0**	**100.0**
ANG/EPIS–Episcopal	1	10	17	22	0.6	1.9
Bahá'í	0	NR	32	32	0.8	2.7
BAPT–So Bapt Conv	1	30	29	35	0.9	3.0
Catholic	1	NR	NR	90	2.4	7.6
LDS–L-D Saints	1	NR	NR	110	2.9	9.3
LUTH–E.L.C.A.	1	105	274	420	11.0	35.5
ORTHE–Orth Ch in Amer	1	14	NR	15	0.4	1.3
PENT–Assemb of God	2	105	69	150	3.9	12.7
PENT–Un Pent Ch Intl	1	NR	NR	NR	-	-
PRES–Presb Ch (USA)	2	37	52	63	1.7	5.3
Salvation Army	2	45	147	212	5.6	17.9
Sev Day Adv	1	18	30	35	0.9	3.0
PRINCE OF WALES-HYDER	**30**	**623**	**828**	**1,759**	**31.6**	**100.0**
Bahá'í	0	NR	25	25	0.4	1.4
BAPT–So Bapt Conv	3	100	113	141	2.5	8.0
Catholic	9	NR	NR	450	8.1	25.6
Chr & Miss Al	3	80	64	104	1.9	5.9
Jehovah's Witness	2	NR	NR	NR	-	-
LDS–L-D Saints	1	NR	NR	174	3.1	9.9
Non-denom Chr Chs	3	150	198	213	3.8	12.1
PENT–Assemb of God	2	78	60	112	2.0	6.4
PENT–Ch God (Cleve)	2	65	143	178	3.2	10.1
PRES–Presb Ch (USA)	3	70	116	145	2.6	8.2
Salvation Army	1	40	40	138	2.5	7.8
Sev Day Adv	1	40	69	79	1.4	4.5
SITKA	**21**	**666**	**1,195**	**2,895**	**32.6**	**100.0**
ANG/EPIS–Episcopal	1	90	202	202	2.3	7.0
Bahá'í	1	NR	34	34	0.4	1.2
BAPT–Consrv Bapt	1	NR	NR	NR	-	-
BAPT–So Bapt Conv	1	29	133	163	1.8	5.6
Catholic	1	NR	NR	460	5.2	15.9
Ch of Nazarene	1	62	70	167	1.9	5.8
CHR–Chs of Christ	1	8	8	9	0.1	0.3
FRND–Fr Gen Cf	1	NR	0	0	0.0	0.0
Jehovah's Witness	1	NR	NR	NR	-	-
LDS–L-D Saints	1	NR	NR	344	3.9	11.9
LUTH–E.L.C.A.	1	50	247	374	4.2	12.9
LUTH–Wisc Ev Luth Syn	1	9	11	11	0.1	0.4
METH–Un Methodist	1	48	77	137	1.5	4.7
Non-denom Chr Chs	1	75	125	125	1.4	4.3
ORTHE–Orth Ch in Amer	1	40	NR	300	3.4	10.4
PENT–Assemb of God	1	175	60	280	3.2	9.7
PENT–Un Pent Ch Intl	1	NR	NR	NR	-	-
PRES–Presb Ch (USA)	1	0	73	89	1.0	3.1
Salvation Army	1	39	65	91	1.0	3.1
Sev Day Adv	1	41	71	82	0.9	2.8
Unit Univ	1	0	19	27	0.3	0.9
SKAGWAY	**7**	**65**	**60**	**270**	**27.9**	**100.0**
ANG/EPIS–Episcopal	1	3	2	3	0.3	1.1
Bahá'í	0	NR	1	1	0.1	0.4
BAPT–So Bapt Conv	1	3	2	2	0.2	0.7
Catholic	1	NR	NR	125	12.9	46.3
LDS–L-D Saints	1	NR	NR	77	8.0	28.5
PRES–Presb Ch (USA)	3	59	55	62	6.4	23.0
SOUTHEAST FAIRBANKS	**26**	**703**	**844**	**1,996**	**28.4**	**100.0**
ANG/EPIS–Episcopal	2	25	120	120	1.7	6.0
Bahá'í	0	NR	30	30	0.4	1.5
BAPT–Ind Bapt Flwsp Intl	1	NR	NR	NR	-	-
BAPT–S-D Baptist Gen Con	1	13	NR	NR	-	-
BAPT–So Bapt Conv	3	225	340	427	6.1	21.4
Catholic	2	NR	NR	366	5.2	18.3
LDS–L-D Saints	2	NR	NR	404	5.7	20.2
LUTH–E.L.C.A.	1	17	30	31	0.4	1.6
Non-denom Chr Chs	5	195	134	248	3.5	12.4
PENT–Assemb of God	2	50	12	50	0.7	2.5
PENT–Ch God (Cleve)	2	22	34	43	0.6	2.2
PENT–Pent Ch of God	1	70	NR	109	1.6	5.5
PENT–Un Pent Ch Intl	1	NR	NR	NR	-	-
PRES–Presb Ch (USA)	1	18	25	31	0.4	1.6
Sev Day Adv	2	68	119	137	1.9	6.9
VALDEZ-CORDOVA	**39**	**1,432**	**1,555**	**3,329**	**34.5**	**100.0**
ANG/EPIS–Episcopal	2	50	146	166	1.7	5.0
Bahá'í	0	NR	15	15	0.2	0.5

NR–Not Reported   - Represents no adherents reported.   Percentages may not total 100 due to rounding.

Table 3: Religious Congregations by County and Group: 2010

Religious Group	Number of Congrega-tions	Number of Attendees	Number of Communicant, Confirmed, or Full Members	Adherents: Number of Adherents	Adherents: % of Total Pop.	Adherents: % of Total Adh.
BAPT–Amer Bapt USA	1	55	54	66	0.7	2.0
BAPT–So Bapt Conv	2	101	180	221	2.3	6.6
Catholic	3	NR	NR	437	4.5	13.1
Ch of Nazarene	2	107	91	176	1.8	5.3
CHR–Chs of Christ	1	10	10	15	0.2	0.5
FRND–Fr Gen Cf	1	NR	0	0	0.0	0.0
Jehovah's Witness	2	NR	NR	NR	-	-
LDS–L-D Saints	3	NR	NR	457	4.7	13.7
LUTH–E.L.C.A.	1	30	75	113	1.2	3.4
LUTH–Luth–MO Synod	2	303	120	170	1.8	5.1
Non-denom Chr Chs	9	626	655	813	8.4	24.4
ORTHE–Orth Ch in Amer	4	70	NR	328	3.4	9.9
PENT–Assemb of God	2	56	24	75	0.8	2.3
PENT–COGIC	1	0	150	184	1.9	5.5
Salvation Army	1	4	1	53	0.6	1.6
Sev Day Adv	2	20	34	40	0.4	1.2
WADE HAMPTON	**26**	**497**	**368**	**6,478**	**86.8**	**100.0**
Bahá'í	0	NR	31	31	0.4	0.5
Catholic	12	NR	NR	4,713	63.2	72.8
Evan Cov Ch	3	158	167	205	2.7	3.2
Non-denom Chr Chs	2	115	170	170	2.3	2.6
ORTHE–Orth Ch in Amer	5	155	NR	1,020	13.7	15.7
PENT–Assemb of God	4	69	0	339	4.5	5.2
WRANGELL	**12**	**227**	**321**	**916**	**38.7**	**100.0**
ANG/EPIS–Episcopal	1	23	55	68	2.9	7.4
Bahá'í	1	NR	40	40	1.7	4.4
Catholic	2	NR	NR	300	12.7	32.8
CGOD–Ch God (Ander)	1	22	NR	22	0.9	2.4
LDS–L-D Saints	1	NR	NR	110	4.6	12.0
LUTH–E.L.C.A.	2	16	33	55	2.3	6.0
PENT–Assemb of God	1	100	66	207	8.7	22.6
PRES–Presb Ch (USA)	1	24	51	61	2.6	6.7
Salvation Army	1	16	30	0	0.0	0.0
Sev Day Adv	1	26	46	53	2.2	5.8
YAKUTAT	**3**	**40**	**25**	**163**	**24.6**	**100.0**
Bahá'í	0	NR	3	3	0.5	1.8
Catholic	1	NR	NR	50	7.6	30.7
LDS–L-D Saints	1	NR	NR	57	8.6	35.0
PENT–Assemb of God	1	40	22	53	8.0	32.5
YUKON-KOYUKUK	**36**	**495**	**1,344**	**3,937**	**70.5**	**100.0**
ANG/EPIS–Episcopal	18	354	1,184	2,148	38.4	54.6
Bahá'í	0	NR	87	87	1.6	2.2
Catholic	10	NR	NR	1,453	26.0	36.9
CHR–Chs of Christ	1	8	5	10	0.2	0.3
Non-denom Chr Chs	2	80	58	100	1.8	2.5
ORTHE–Orth Ch in Amer	3	23	NR	85	1.5	2.2
PENT–Assemb of God	2	30	10	54	1.0	1.4
ARIZONA	**4,673**	**506,056**	**708,851**	**2,379,928**	**37.2**	**100.0**
APACHE	**132**	**2,633**	**3,470**	**34,926**	**48.8**	**100.0**
ANG/EPIS–Episcopal	3	75	213	259	0.4	0.7
Bahá'í	2	NR	324	324	0.5	0.9
BAPT–Amer Bapt Assn	1	NR	85	112	0.2	0.3
BAPT–Amer Bapt USA	1	17	17	22	0.0	0.1
BAPT–Asc Ref Bap Ch Am	1	NR	NR	NR	-	-
BAPT–Ind Bapt Flwsp Intl	3	NR	NR	NR	-	-
BAPT–So Bapt Conv	14	462	710	933	1.3	2.7
BUDD–Mahayana	1	NR	NR	103	0.1	0.3
Calv Chpl	1	NR	NR	NR	-	-
Catholic	13	NR	NR	15,000	21.0	42.9
CGOD–Ch God (Ander)	1	92	NR	92	0.1	0.3
CGOD–Ches God-Gen Con	1	60	0	0	0.0	0.0
Ch of Nazarene	3	103	116	139	0.2	0.4
CHR–Chs of Christ	5	100	102	158	0.2	0.5
FRND–Evan Fr Ch Intl	4	NR	0	0	0.0	0.0
Ind Fund Churches	1	NR	NR	NR	-	-
Jehovah's Witness	5	NR	NR	NR	-	-
LDS–L-D Saints	27	NR	NR	14,950	20.9	42.8
LUTH–E.L.C.A.	1	22	37	37	0.1	0.1
LUTH–Wisc Ev Luth Syn	2	56	63	85	0.1	0.2
MENN–CG in Cr (Menn)	1	NR	9	12	0.0	0.0
METH–Un Methodist	1	43	62	62	0.1	0.2
Non-denom Chr Chs	5	315	365	423	0.6	1.2
PENT–Assemb of God	9	458	258	683	1.0	2.0
PENT–Ch God (Cleve)	12	346	419	550	0.8	1.6
PENT–Intl Pent Holiness	1	35	30	39	0.1	0.1
PENT–Pent Ch of God	1	70	NR	109	0.2	0.3
PRES–Presb Ch (USA)	5	149	255	335	0.5	1.0
REF–Christian Ref	3	120	212	278	0.4	0.8
Sev Day Adv	4	110	193	221	0.3	0.6
COCHISE	**207**	**8,806**	**13,938**	**53,070**	**40.4**	**100.0**
ANG/EPIS–Anglican NA	1	NR	NR	NR	-	-
ANG/EPIS–Episcopal	5	194	378	451	0.3	0.8
Bahá'í	1	NR	159	159	0.1	0.3
BAPT–Consrv Bapt	6	NR	NR	NR	-	-
BAPT–Free Will Bapt	1	NR	26	32	0.0	0.1
BAPT–NBC USA	1	105	500	607	0.5	1.1
BAPT–So Bapt Conv	26	1,847	4,410	5,357	4.1	10.1
BUDD–Mahayana	1	NR	NR	102	0.1	0.2
BUDD–Vajrayana	1	NR	NR	20	0.0	0.0
Calv Chpl	1	NR	NR	NR	-	-
Catholic	16	NR	NR	26,615	20.3	50.2
CGOD–Ch God (Ander)	1	55	NR	55	0.0	0.1
Ch Christ Chr Union	1	NR	NR	NR	-	-
Ch Cr, Scientst	1	NR	NR	NR	-	-
Ch God (7th Day)	1	NR	NR	NR	-	-
Ch of Nazarene	7	198	186	225	0.2	0.4
CHR–Chr Chs & Chs Cr	3	NR	690	838	0.6	1.6
CHR–Chs of Christ	9	485	438	586	0.4	1.1
CONG–Cong Chr, NA	1	NR	47	57	0.0	0.1
Evan Free Ch	2	135	NR	135	0.1	0.3
FRND–Fr Gen Cf	2	NR	0	0	0.0	0.0
Jehovah's Witness	6	NR	NR	NR	-	-
JUD–Reform	1	16	28	76	0.1	0.1
LDS–L-D Saints	17	NR	NR	7,933	6.0	14.9
LUTH–E.L.C.A.	3	294	453	516	0.4	1.0
LUTH–Luth–MO Synod	3	186	371	421	0.3	0.8
LUTH–Wisc Ev Luth Syn	4	129	189	231	0.2	0.4
MENN–CG in Cr (Menn)	1	NR	63	77	0.1	0.1
METH–Un Methodist	9	572	947	1,558	1.2	2.9
Non-denom Chr Chs	29	2,381	2,745	3,219	2.5	6.1
ORTHE–Serb Orth USA	1	30	NR	50	0.0	0.1
PENT–Assemb of God	15	1,074	632	1,597	1.2	3.0
PENT–Ch God (Cleve)	3	189	248	301	0.2	0.6
PENT–COGIC	2	0	210	255	0.2	0.5
PENT–Int Foursq Gos	2	85	76	92	0.1	0.2
PENT–Pent Ch of God	1	70	NR	109	0.1	0.2
PENT–Un Pent Ch Intl	5	NR	NR	NR	-	-
PRES–Korean Amer Pres	1	NR	NR	NR	-	-
PRES–Presb Ch (USA)	4	278	491	596	0.5	1.1
PRES–Presb Ch Amer	2	67	58	58	0.0	0.1
Salvation Army	1	28	39	104	0.1	0.2
Sev Day Adv	5	168	292	336	0.3	0.6
Un C of Christ	2	150	171	208	0.2	0.4
Unit Univ	1	70	91	94	0.1	0.2
Unity Ch	1	NR	NR	NR	-	-
COCONINO	**182**	**8,111**	**11,075**	**39,909**	**29.7**	**100.0**
ANG/EPIS–Anglican NA	1	NR	NR	NR	-	-
ANG/EPIS–Episcopal	3	216	616	692	0.5	1.7
Bahá'í	2	NR	283	283	0.2	0.7
BAPT–Amer Bapt USA	1	20	0	0	0.0	0.0
BAPT–Consrv Bapt	10	NR	NR	NR	-	-
BAPT–Converge/BGC	1	75	NR	90	0.1	0.2
BAPT–Ind Bapt Flwsp Intl	2	NR	NR	NR	-	-
BAPT–So Bapt Conv	12	650	1,003	1,227	0.9	3.1
BUDD–Mahayana	3	NR	NR	649	0.5	1.6

NR–Not Reported   - Represents no adherents reported.   Percentages may not total 100 due to rounding.

Table 3: Religious Congregations by County and Group: 2010

Religious Group	Number of Congregations	Number of Attendees	Number of Communicant, Confirmed, or Full Members	Adherents: Number of Adherents	Adherents: % of Total Pop.	Adherents: % of Total Adh.
BUDD–Vajrayana	3	NR	NR	146	0.1	0.4
Calv Chpl	2	NR	NR	NR	-	-
Catholic	9	NR	NR	6,750	5.0	16.9
Ch Cr, Scientst	2	NR	NR	NR	-	-
Ch of Nazarene	10	609	713	963	0.7	2.4
Chr & Miss Al	2	40	36	56	0.0	0.1
CHR–Chr Chs & Chs Cr	1	NR	1,400	1,713	1.3	4.3
CHR–Chs of Christ	5	158	155	198	0.1	0.5
Evan Free Ch	1	400	NR	400	0.3	1.0
FRND–Fr Gen Cf	1	NR	24	29	0.0	0.1
HINDU–Post Ren	2	NR	NR	41	0.0	0.1
Ind Fund Churches	2	NR	NR	NR	-	-
Int Cou Comm Ch	1	NR	NR	NR	-	-
Jehovah's Witness	3	NR	NR	NR	-	-
JUD–Orth	1	43	50	60	0.0	0.2
JUD–Reform	1	24	42	113	0.1	0.3
LDS–L-D Saints	32	NR	NR	16,633	12.4	41.7
LUTH–E.L.C.A.	2	216	362	457	0.3	1.1
LUTH–Luth–MO Synod	2	25	208	257	0.2	0.6
LUTH–Wisc Ev Luth Syn	1	106	119	163	0.1	0.4
METH–AME	1	0	100	122	0.1	0.3
METH–Un Methodist	5	728	1,048	1,534	1.1	3.8
METH–Wesleyan	2	137	87	178	0.1	0.4
Muslim Est	1	60	NR	150	0.1	0.4
Non-denom Chr Chs	21	2,495	2,930	3,415	2.5	8.6
ORTHE–Greek Orthodox	1	60	NR	150	0.1	0.4
PENT–Assemb of God	9	718	228	930	0.7	2.3
PENT–Ch God (Cleve)	1	70	51	62	0.0	0.2
PENT–COGIC	1	25	40	49	0.0	0.1
PENT–Int Foursq Gos	2	156	229	280	0.2	0.7
PENT–Pent Ch of God	4	280	NR	435	0.3	1.1
PENT–Un Pent Ch Intl	2	NR	NR	NR	-	-
PRES–Presb Ch (USA)	3	132	188	230	0.2	0.6
PRES–Presb Ch Amer	1	81	67	67	0.0	0.2
REF–Christian Ref	1	58	58	71	0.1	0.2
Salvation Army	1	43	95	178	0.1	0.4
Sev Day Adv	2	51	89	102	0.1	0.3
Sikh	1	NR	NR	NR	-	-
Un C of Christ	2	317	665	814	0.6	2.0
Unit Univ	2	118	189	219	0.2	0.5
Unity Ch	1	NR	NR	NR	-	-
Zoroastrian	0	NR	NR	3	0.0	0.0
GILA	**92**	**4,120**	**4,625**	**20,145**	**37.6**	**100.0**
ANG/EPIS–Episcopal	2	155	303	345	0.6	1.7
Bahá'í	0	NR	35	35	0.1	0.2
BAPT–Consrv Bapt	3	NR	NR	NR	-	-
BAPT–So Bapt Conv	12	523	854	1,018	1.9	5.1
Calv Chpl	1	NR	NR	NR	-	-
Catholic	10	NR	NR	8,519	15.9	42.3
Ch Cr, Scientst	1	NR	NR	NR	-	-
Ch of Nazarene	2	174	206	217	0.4	1.1
CHR–Chr Ch (Disc)	1	80	102	122	0.2	0.6
CHR–Chr Chs & Chs Cr	1	NR	25	30	0.1	0.1
CHR–Chs of Christ	3	192	200	245	0.5	1.2
Evan Free Ch	1	500	NR	500	0.9	2.5
Ind Fund Churches	1	NR	NR	NR	-	-
Jehovah's Witness	3	NR	NR	NR	-	-
LDS–L-D Saints	12	NR	NR	4,719	8.8	23.4
LUTH–E.L.C.A.	2	234	343	362	0.7	1.8
LUTH–Luth–MO Synod	1	99	114	122	0.2	0.6
LUTH–Wisc Ev Luth Syn	5	396	594	1,212	2.3	6.0
METH–Un Methodist	3	150	334	402	0.8	2.0
Non-denom Chr Chs	9	829	902	1,098	2.0	5.5
PENT–Assemb of God	7	409	240	534	1.0	2.7
PENT–Ch God (Cleve)	1	9	11	13	0.0	0.1
PENT–Int Foursq Gos	1	52	8	10	0.0	0.0
PENT–Pent Ch of God	1	70	NR	109	0.2	0.5
PENT–Un Pent Ch Intl	2	NR	NR	NR	-	-
PRES–Presb Ch (USA)	3	143	187	223	0.4	1.1
Salvation Army	1	29	34	155	0.3	0.8
Sev Day Adv	2	76	133	153	0.3	0.8
Unity Ch	1	NR	NR	NR	-	-
Zoroastrian	0	NR	NR	2	0.0	0.0

Religious Group	Number of Congregations	Number of Attendees	Number of Communicant, Confirmed, or Full Members	Adherents: Number of Adherents	Adherents: % of Total Pop.	Adherents: % of Total Adh.
GRAHAM	**65**	**1,333**	**1,748**	**20,563**	**55.2**	**100.0**
ANG/EPIS–Episcopal	1	18	37	37	0.1	0.2
Bahá'í	0	NR	27	27	0.1	0.1
BAPT–Consrv Bapt	1	NR	NR	NR	-	-
BAPT–So Bapt Conv	3	57	212	274	0.7	1.3
Calv Chpl	1	NR	NR	NR	-	-
Catholic	6	NR	NR	6,194	16.6	30.1
Ch of Nazarene	1	55	61	102	0.3	0.5
CHR–Chr Chs & Chs Cr	1	NR	40	52	0.1	0.3
CHR–Chs of Christ	2	105	107	165	0.4	0.8
Jehovah's Witness	1	NR	NR	NR	-	-
LDS–L-D Saints	29	NR	NR	11,766	31.6	57.2
LUTH–E.L.C.A.	1	20	60	66	0.2	0.3
LUTH–Luth–MO Synod	1	15	9	15	0.0	0.1
LUTH–Wisc Ev Luth Syn	2	107	267	370	1.0	1.8
METH–Un Methodist	1	140	256	378	1.0	1.8
Non-denom Chr Chs	5	530	470	668	1.8	3.2
ORTHE–Serb Orth USA	1	40	NR	30	0.1	0.1
PENT–Assemb of God	3	130	33	214	0.6	1.0
PENT–Ch God (Cleve)	1	15	11	14	0.0	0.1
PENT–Un Pent Ch Intl	1	NR	NR	NR	-	-
PRES–Presb Ch (USA)	1	45	62	80	0.2	0.4
Sev Day Adv	2	56	96	111	0.3	0.5
GREENLEE	**19**	**380**	**428**	**4,442**	**52.6**	**100.0**
ANG/EPIS–Episcopal	1	7	10	10	0.1	0.2
Bahá'í	0	NR	8	8	0.1	0.2
BAPT–Consrv Bapt	2	NR	NR	NR	-	-
BAPT–So Bapt Conv	2	70	87	112	1.3	2.5
Catholic	3	NR	NR	2,608	30.9	58.7
CHR–Chs of Christ	2	130	117	158	1.9	3.6
Jehovah's Witness	1	NR	NR	NR	-	-
LDS–L-D Saints	3	NR	NR	1,221	14.5	27.5
LUTH–Luth–MO Synod	1	4	4	4	0.0	0.1
METH–Un Methodist	1	12	16	24	0.3	0.5
Non-denom Chr Chs	2	75	150	150	1.8	3.4
PENT–Assemb of God	1	82	36	147	1.7	3.3
LA PAZ	**39**	**1,312**	**1,533**	**4,909**	**24.0**	**100.0**
Bahá'í	0	NR	19	19	0.1	0.4
BAPT–Amer Bapt USA	1	35	50	58	0.3	1.2
BAPT–Consrv Bapt	3	NR	NR	NR	-	-
BAPT–So Bapt Conv	3	187	543	630	3.1	12.8
Calv Chpl	1	NR	NR	NR	-	-
Catholic	4	NR	NR	1,109	5.4	22.6
Ch of Nazarene	2	47	29	135	0.7	2.8
Chr & Miss Al	1	204	97	574	2.8	11.7
CHR–Chr Chs & Chs Cr	1	NR	0	0	0.0	0.0
CHR–Chs of Christ	3	130	55	60	0.3	1.2
Ind Fund Churches	2	NR	NR	NR	-	-
Jehovah's Witness	1	NR	NR	NR	-	-
LDS–L-D Saints	3	NR	NR	991	4.8	20.2
LUTH–E.L.C.A.	1	0	0	0	0.0	0.0
LUTH–Luth–MO Synod	1	96	83	96	0.5	2.0
LUTH–Wisc Ev Luth Syn	1	100	122	152	0.7	3.1
METH–Un Methodist	1	52	88	244	1.2	5.0
Non-denom Chr Chs	2	135	142	169	0.8	3.4
PENT–Assemb of God	4	238	124	353	1.7	7.2
PENT–COGIC	1	0	150	174	0.8	3.5
PENT–Pent Ch of God	1	70	NR	109	0.5	2.2
PENT–Un Pent Ch Intl	1	NR	NR	NR	-	-
Sev Day Adv	1	18	31	36	0.2	0.7
MARICOPA	**2,299**	**341,031**	**482,806**	**1,491,480**	**39.1**	**100.0**
ANG/EPIS–Anglican NA	7	NR	NR	NR	-	-
ANG/EPIS–Episcopal	29	5,166	9,865	13,203	0.3	0.9
Ap Chr Ch-Amer	1	260	145	260	0.0	0.0
Bahá'í	12	NR	4,766	4,766	0.1	0.3
BAPT–Amer Bapt Assn	5	NR	455	573	0.0	0.0
BAPT–Amer Bapt USA	14	2,762	5,177	6,524	0.2	0.4
BAPT–Asc Ref Bap Ch Am	2	NR	NR	NR	-	-
BAPT–Consrv Bapt	36	NR	NR	NR	-	-

NR–Not Reported - Represents no adherents reported. Percentages may not total 100 due to rounding.

Table 3: Religious Congregations by County and Group: 2010

Religious Group	Number of Congregations	Number of Attendees	Number of Communicant, Confirmed, or Full Members	Adherents: Number of Adherents	Adherents: % of Total Pop.	Adherents: % of Total Adh.
BAPT–Converge/BGC	18	5,775	NR	6,930	0.2	0.5
BAPT–Free Will Bapt	5	NR	265	334	0.0	0.0
BAPT–Fund Bapt Flwsp	1	NR	NR	NR	-	-
BAPT–Ind Bapt Flwsp Intl	5	NR	NR	NR	-	-
BAPT–Natl Mis Bapt Conv	1	0	150	189	0.0	0.0
BAPT–NBC Amer	3	120	650	819	0.0	0.1
BAPT–NBC USA	4	320	520	655	0.0	0.0
BAPT–NT Ind Bapt	2	NR	NR	NR	-	-
BAPT–Ref Bapt Ch	5	NR	NR	NR	-	-
BAPT–Reg Bapt Gen As	6	NR	NR	NR	-	-
BAPT–So Bapt Conv	149	24,094	58,093	73,207	1.9	4.9
BRETH–Brethren (Ash)	1	NR	80	101	0.0	0.0
BRETH–Ch of Brethren	2	127	148	187	0.0	0.0
BRETH–Grace Breth	1	NR	NR	NR	-	-
BUDD–Mahayana	21	NR	NR	10,159	0.3	0.7
BUDD–Theravada	3	NR	NR	2,060	0.1	0.1
BUDD–Vajrayana	2	NR	NR	623	0.0	0.0
Calv Chpl	17	NR	NR	NR	-	-
Catholic	99	NR	NR	519,950	13.6	34.9
CGOD–Ch God (Ander)	16	3,435	NR	3,435	0.1	0.2
Ch Cr, Scientst	10	NR	NR	NR	-	-
Ch God (7th Day)	4	NR	NR	NR	-	-
Ch of God Gen Conf	1	NR	62	78	0.0	0.0
Ch of Nazarene	38	5,365	6,703	8,973	0.2	0.6
Chr & Miss Al	10	977	448	1,158	0.0	0.1
CHR–Chr Ch (Disc)	20	1,559	2,581	3,252	0.1	0.2
CHR–Chr Chs & Chs Cr	29	NR	28,412	35,804	0.9	2.4
CHR–Chs of Christ	49	5,812	6,063	7,719	0.2	0.5
CHR–Int Chs of Christ	1	NR	556	701	0.0	0.0
Christian Brethren	1	NR	NR	NR	-	-
CONG–Cong Chr, NA	2	NR	502	633	0.0	0.0
CONG–Consrv Cong Chr	1	0	0	0	0.0	0.0
Evan Cov Ch	8	1,396	808	1,814	0.0	0.1
Evan Free Ch	14	4,774	NR	4,774	0.1	0.3
FRND–Evan Fr Ch Intl	4	181	85	107	0.0	0.0
FRND–Fr Gen Cf	2	NR	87	110	0.0	0.0
Grace Gosp Fel	3	NR	NR	NR	-	-
HINDU–I/A Temples	7	NR	NR	4,471	0.1	0.3
HINDU–Post Ren	7	NR	NR	255	0.0	0.0
HINDU–Renaiss	2	NR	NR	13,000	0.3	0.9
HINDU–Trad Temples	4	NR	NR	11,500	0.3	0.8
Ind Fund Churches	1	NR	NR	NR	-	-
Int Cou Comm Ch	3	NR	NR	NR	-	-
Jain	1	NR	NR	NR	-	-
Jehovah's Witness	40	NR	NR	NR	-	-
JUD–Conserv	4	789	885	2,390	0.1	0.2
JUD–Orth	12	1,598	600	2,250	0.1	0.2
JUD–Reform	7	1,935	3,412	9,212	0.2	0.6
LDS–Comm of Christ	4	NR	856	856	0.0	0.1
LDS–L-D Saints	503	NR	NR	242,732	6.4	16.3
LUTH–Apostolic Luth	1	NR	NR	NR	-	-
LUTH–Assoc Free Luth	2	NR	NR	NR	-	-
LUTH–Ch Luth Conf	1	NR	NR	NR	-	-
LUTH–Ch of Luth Br	3	191	102	271	0.0	0.0
LUTH–E.L.C.A.	47	14,397	23,508	30,014	0.8	2.0
LUTH–Evan Luth Syn	1	47	69	81	0.0	0.0
LUTH–Luth Ch-Am Asc	1	NR	NR	NR	-	-
LUTH–Luth Cong Msn Chr	12	3,950	9,709	12,235	0.3	0.8
LUTH–Luth-MO Synod	34	10,050	14,658	18,408	0.5	1.2
LUTH–Nor Amer Luth C	1	NR	NR	NR	-	-
LUTH–Wisc Ev Luth Syn	20	3,267	4,376	5,842	0.2	0.4
MENN–CG in Cr (Menn)	1	NR	100	126	0.0	0.0
MENN–Cons Menn Conf	4	210	133	168	0.0	0.0
MENN–Menn Br US Conf	4	NR	24	30	0.0	0.0
MENN–Mennonite USA	6	621	678	854	0.0	0.1
METH–AME	5	630	1,580	1,991	0.1	0.1
METH–AME Zion	1	60	100	126	0.0	0.0
METH–C.M.E.	2	80	310	391	0.0	0.0
METH–Evan Meth Ch	2	NR	NR	NR	-	-
METH–Free Methodist	9	967	719	1,015	0.0	0.1
METH–Un Methodist	55	12,044	19,368	28,634	0.8	1.9
METH–Wesleyan	7	471	300	614	0.0	0.0
Metro Comm Ch	1	56	67	84	0.0	0.0
Missionary Ch	3	83	15	83	0.0	0.0

Religious Group	Number of Congregations	Number of Attendees	Number of Communicant, Confirmed, or Full Members	Adherents: Number of Adherents	Adherents: % of Total Pop.	Adherents: % of Total Adh.
Muslim Est	22	3,091	NR	6,817	0.2	0.5
Nat Spirit Asso	1	NR	NR	NR	-	-
New Apost Ch	2	NR	NR	NR	-	-
Non-denom Chr Chs	309	153,106	191,707	213,640	5.6	14.3
OCATH–Un Cath Ch	1	NR	NR	701	0.0	0.0
ORTHE–Ant Orth of NA	2	430	NR	1,120	0.0	0.1
ORTHE–Bulgar Orth USA	1	25	NR	150	0.0	0.0
ORTHE–Greek Orthodox	4	1,155	NR	5,650	0.1	0.4
ORTHE–Macedonian Orth	1	50	NR	150	0.0	0.0
ORTHE–Orth Ch in Amer	5	355	NR	700	0.0	0.0
ORTHE–Rus Orth Abroad	1	30	NR	80	0.0	0.0
ORTHE–Serb Orth USA	1	80	NR	700	0.0	0.0
ORTHE–Ukrainian Orth	1	20	NR	40	0.0	0.0
ORTHO–Armen Ap Etchm	1	125	NR	3,600	0.1	0.2
ORTHO–Coptic Orth Ch	2	287	NR	559	0.0	0.0
ORTHO–Eritrean Orth	1	325	NR	150	0.0	0.0
ORTHO–Ethiopian Orth	1	NR	NR	NR	-	-
ORTHO–Malan Dioc Am	1	20	NR	60	0.0	0.0
ORTHO–Malan Syr Orth	1	95	NR	180	0.0	0.0
ORTHO–Syrian Orth Ch	1	125	NR	240	0.0	0.0
PENT–Assemb of God	120	35,500	31,347	93,252	2.4	6.3
PENT–Ch God (Cleve)	34	2,358	3,125	3,938	0.1	0.3
PENT–Ch Lord Jesus Apos	1	NR	NR	NR	-	-
PENT–Ch of God Proph	19	NR	953	1,201	0.0	0.1
PENT–COGIC	16	702	1,672	2,107	0.1	0.1
PENT–Cong Hol Ch	1	39	35	44	0.0	0.0
PENT–Full Gosp Bapt	15	NR	NR	NR	-	-
PENT–Int Foursq Gos	13	1,859	1,734	2,185	0.1	0.1
PENT–Int Pent C Chr	1	0	NR	35	0.0	0.0
PENT–Intl Pent Holiness	14	1,086	986	1,243	0.0	0.1
PENT–Open Bible Std	1	263	NR	263	0.0	0.0
PENT–Pent Ch of God	21	1,470	NR	2,284	0.1	0.2
PENT–Un Pent Ch Intl	16	NR	NR	NR	-	-
PENT–Vineyard	13	5,381	9,895	12,469	0.3	0.8
PRES–Evan Presby Ch	2	NR	236	297	0.0	0.0
PRES–Free Pres NA	1	NR	NR	NR	-	-
PRES–Kor Pres Abroad	6	NR	NR	NR	-	-
PRES–Korean Amer Pres	1	NR	NR	NR	-	-
PRES–Korean Pres Amer	2	NR	NR	NR	-	-
PRES–Orth Pres Ch	2	130	138	200	0.0	0.0
PRES–Presb Ch (USA)	42	6,394	11,904	15,001	0.4	1.0
PRES–Presb Ch Amer	9	899	780	922	0.0	0.1
PRES–Ref Pres of NA	1	48	23	40	0.0	0.0
REF–Christian Ref	4	350	477	601	0.0	0.0
REF–Comm Ref Evan	1	NR	NR	NR	-	-
REF–Hung Ref Add'l	1	NR	NR	NR	-	-
REF–Ref Ch in Am	5	962	820	1,101	0.0	0.1
REF–Un Ref Chs N.A.	1	NR	NR	NR	-	-
Salvation Army	12	1,003	1,459	2,393	0.1	0.2
Sev Day Adv	47	6,782	11,792	13,564	0.4	0.9
Sikh	4	NR	NR	NR	-	-
Tao	1	NR	NR	NR	-	-
Un Breth in Cr	1	0	0	0	0.0	0.0
Un C of Christ	19	2,225	4,435	5,589	0.1	0.4
Unit Univ	4	692	1,098	1,390	0.0	0.1
Unity Ch	7	NR	NR	NR	-	-
Zoroastrian	0	NR	NR	93	0.0	0.0
MOHAVE	**139**	**10,828**	**12,556**	**44,735**	**22.3**	**100.0**
ANG/EPIS–Episcopal	3	176	202	400	0.2	0.9
Bahá'í	0	NR	64	64	0.0	0.1
BAPT–Consrv Bapt	3	NR	NR	NR	-	-
BAPT–Converge/BGC	1	75	NR	90	0.0	0.2
BAPT–Reg Bapt Gen As	1	NR	NR	NR	-	-
BAPT–So Bapt Conv	17	2,317	3,518	4,178	2.1	9.3
Calv Chpl	4	NR	NR	NR	-	-
Catholic	5	NR	NR	18,500	9.2	41.4
Ch Cr, Scientst	1	NR	NR	NR	-	-
Ch of Nazarene	3	290	308	479	0.2	1.1
Chr & Miss Al	2	122	21	165	0.1	0.4
CHR–Chr Chs & Chs Cr	4	NR	485	576	0.3	1.3
CHR–Chs of Christ	6	372	356	490	0.2	1.1
Evan Free Ch	2	650	NR	650	0.3	1.5
Ind Fund Churches	1	NR	NR	NR	-	-

NR–Not Reported   - Represents no adherents reported.   Percentages may not total 100 due to rounding.

Table 3: Religious Congregations by County and Group: 2010

Religious Group	Number of Congregations	Number of Attendees	Number of Communicant, Confirmed, or Full Members	Adherents: Number of Adherents	Adherents: % of Total Pop.	Adherents: % of Total Adh.
Jehovah's Witness	3	NR	NR	NR	-	-
JUD–Reform	2	22	38	103	0.1	0.2
LDS–L-D Saints	12	NR	NR	8,147	4.1	18.2
LUTH–E.L.C.A.	3	874	1,251	1,479	0.7	3.3
LUTH–Evan Luth Syn	2	166	207	268	0.1	0.6
LUTH–Luth Cong Msn Chr	1	35	NR	NR	-	-
LUTH–Luth-MO Synod	3	402	530	615	0.3	1.4
LUTH–Wisc Ev Luth Syn	1	108	158	180	0.1	0.4
METH–Un Methodist	4	867	1,167	1,703	0.9	3.8
Muslim Est	2	268	NR	616	0.3	1.4
Non-denom Chr Chs	21	1,966	2,500	2,732	1.4	6.1
ORTHE–Orth Ch in Amer	1	28	NR	50	0.0	0.1
ORTHO–Coptic Orth Ch	1	10	NR	14	0.0	0.0
PENT–Assemb of God	10	1,043	494	1,519	0.8	3.4
PENT–Ch God (Cleve)	2	35	36	43	0.0	0.1
PENT–Full Gosp Bapt	1	NR	NR	NR	-	-
PENT–Int Foursq Gos	3	342	326	387	0.2	0.9
PENT–Pent Ch of God	1	70	NR	109	0.1	0.2
PENT–Un Pent Ch Intl	3	NR	NR	NR	-	-
PRES–Presb Ch (USA)	2	296	403	479	0.2	1.1
Salvation Army	3	58	81	227	0.1	0.5
Sev Day Adv	3	236	411	472	0.2	1.1
Unity Ch	2	NR	NR	NR	-	-
NAVAJO	**194**	**6,336**	**8,150**	**46,910**	**43.7**	**100.0**
ANG/EPIS–Episcopal	3	102	166	187	0.2	0.4
Bahá'í	2	NR	212	212	0.2	0.5
BAPT–Amer Bapt USA	5	139	128	166	0.2	0.4
BAPT–Consrv Bapt	1	NR	NR	NR	-	-
BAPT–Reg Bapt Gen As	3	NR	NR	NR	-	-
BAPT–So Bapt Conv	15	1,253	2,070	2,680	2.5	5.7
Calv Chpl	3	NR	NR	NR	-	-
Catholic	14	NR	NR	6,600	6.1	14.1
Ch Cr, Scientst	1	NR	NR	NR	-	-
Ch of Nazarene	10	323	416	533	0.5	1.1
Chr & Miss Al	1	15	15	23	0.0	0.0
CHR–Chr Chs & Chs Cr	3	NR	93	120	0.1	0.3
CHR–Chs of Christ	6	214	178	246	0.2	0.5
Jehovah's Witness	4	NR	NR	NR	-	-
LDS–Comm of Christ	1	NR	214	214	0.2	0.5
LDS–L-D Saints	53	NR	NR	24,301	22.6	51.8
LUTH–E.L.C.A.	1	12	22	24	0.0	0.1
LUTH–Luth Ch-Am Asc	1	NR	NR	NR	-	-
LUTH–Luth Cong Msn Chr	1	10	15	19	0.0	0.0
LUTH–Luth-MO Synod	2	120	108	203	0.2	0.4
LUTH–Wisc Ev Luth Syn	6	586	969	1,955	1.8	4.2
METH–AME	1	0	100	129	0.1	0.3
METH–Un Methodist	5	253	406	792	0.7	1.7
METH–Wesleyan	2	48	82	62	0.1	0.1
Non-denom Chr Chs	13	1,026	1,502	1,573	1.5	3.4
PENT–Assemb of God	17	1,429	660	5,383	5.0	11.5
PENT–Ch God (Cleve)	2	25	32	41	0.0	0.1
PENT–COGIC	1	0	60	78	0.1	0.2
PENT–Int Foursq Gos	1	0	0	0	0.0	0.0
PENT–Pent Ch of God	5	350	NR	544	0.5	1.2
PENT–Un Pent Ch Intl	2	NR	NR	NR	-	-
PRES–Presb Ch (USA)	4	154	186	241	0.2	0.5
Salvation Army	1	17	63	63	0.1	0.1
Sev Day Adv	3	260	453	521	0.5	1.1
Unity Ch	1	NR	NR	NR	-	-
PIMA	**636**	**77,146**	**111,121**	**390,546**	**39.8**	**100.0**
ANG/EPIS–Anglican NA	1	NR	NR	NR	-	-
ANG/EPIS–Episcopal	9	1,975	6,658	7,601	0.8	1.9
Ap Chr Ch-Amer	1	39	22	39	0.0	0.0
Bahá'í	7	NR	948	948	0.1	0.2
BAPT–Amer Bapt Assn	1	NR	150	182	0.0	0.0
BAPT–Amer Bapt USA	2	345	316	384	0.0	0.1
BAPT–Consrv Bapt	14	NR	NR	NR	-	-
BAPT–Free Will Bapt	1	NR	26	32	0.0	0.0
BAPT–Fund Bapt Flwsp	1	NR	NR	NR	-	-
BAPT–Ind Bapt Flwsp Intl	1	NR	NR	NR	-	-
BAPT–NBC Amer	1	800	850	1,034	0.1	0.3
BAPT–NBC USA	4	920	1,510	1,836	0.2	0.5
BAPT–Reg Bapt Gen As	2	NR	NR	NR	-	-
BAPT–So Bapt Conv	66	8,694	18,328	22,286	2.3	5.7
BRETH–Brethren (Ash)	2	NR	160	195	0.0	0.0
BRETH–Ch of Brethren	1	27	26	32	0.0	0.0
BUDD–Mahayana	13	NR	NR	2,776	0.3	0.7
BUDD–Theravada	1	NR	NR	1,364	0.1	0.3
BUDD–Vajrayana	8	NR	NR	642	0.1	0.2
Calv Chpl	5	NR	NR	NR	-	-
Catholic	50	NR	NR	203,770	20.8	52.2
CGOD–Ch God (Ander)	5	113	NR	113	0.0	0.0
Ch Christ Chr Union	2	NR	NR	NR	-	-
Ch Cr, Scientst	4	NR	NR	NR	-	-
Ch of Nazarene	15	1,890	1,768	2,596	0.3	0.7
Chr & Miss Al	4	268	206	337	0.0	0.1
CHR–Chr Ch (Disc)	8	637	970	1,179	0.1	0.3
CHR–Chr Chs & Chs Cr	8	NR	3,085	3,751	0.4	1.0
CHR–Chs of Christ	16	1,555	1,603	2,047	0.2	0.5
Evan Cov Ch	2	398	326	518	0.1	0.1
Evan Free Ch	8	1,839	NR	1,839	0.2	0.5
FRND–Evan Fr Ch Intl	1	66	72	88	0.0	0.0
FRND–Fr Gen Cf	1	NR	88	107	0.0	0.0
HINDU–I/A Temples	2	NR	NR	3,304	0.3	0.8
HINDU–Post Ren	5	NR	NR	153	0.0	0.0
Ind Fund Churches	1	NR	NR	NR	-	-
Jehovah's Witness	14	NR	NR	NR	-	-
JUD–Conserv	2	722	810	2,187	0.2	0.6
JUD–Orth	3	284	150	400	0.0	0.1
JUD–Reform	3	656	1,157	3,124	0.3	0.8
LDS–Comm of Christ	2	NR	428	428	0.0	0.1
LDS–L-D Saints	53	NR	NR	28,659	2.9	7.3
LUTH–Assoc Free Luth	1	NR	NR	NR	-	-
LUTH–E.L.C.A.	16	3,961	6,343	8,620	0.9	2.2
LUTH–Luth Cong Msn Chr	4	552	775	942	0.1	0.2
LUTH–Luth-MO Synod	9	1,495	3,072	3,600	0.4	0.9
LUTH–Wisc Ev Luth Syn	6	995	1,446	1,775	0.2	0.5
MENN–Mennonite USA	1	55	65	79	0.0	0.0
METH–AME	2	200	470	572	0.1	0.1
METH–C.M.E.	2	8	165	201	0.0	0.1
METH–Free Methodist	2	120	93	122	0.0	0.0
METH–Un Methodist	17	4,375	6,786	10,445	1.1	2.7
METH–Wesleyan	7	764	390	994	0.1	0.3
Metro Comm Ch	1	80	97	118	0.0	0.0
Missionary Ch	1	52	45	52	0.0	0.0
MJEW–Assoc Mes Cong	1	NR	NR	NR	-	-
Muslim Est	1	134	NR	308	0.0	0.1
New Apost Ch	1	NR	NR	NR	-	-
Non-denom Chr Chs	89	22,539	33,965	37,035	3.8	9.5
ORTHE–Ant Orth of NA	1	150	NR	200	0.0	0.1
ORTHE–Greek Orthodox	1	300	NR	2,000	0.2	0.5
ORTHE–Holy Orth in NA	1	15	NR	20	0.0	0.0
ORTHE–Rus Orth Abroad	1	5	NR	5	0.0	0.0
ORTHO–Coptic Orth Ch	1	22	NR	35	0.0	0.0
PENT–Assemb of God	32	8,628	1,948	10,261	1.0	2.6
PENT–Ch God (Cleve)	9	1,964	1,348	1,639	0.2	0.4
PENT–Ch of God Proph	2	NR	81	98	0.0	0.0
PENT–COGIC	5	190	450	547	0.1	0.1
PENT–Cong Hol Ch	1	39	35	43	0.0	0.0
PENT–Int Foursq Gos	4	1,238	1,269	1,543	0.2	0.4
PENT–Intl Pent Holiness	1	500	420	511	0.1	0.1
PENT–Pent Ch of God	3	210	NR	326	0.0	0.1
PENT–Un Pent Ch Intl	4	NR	NR	NR	-	-
PENT–Vineyard	3	244	357	434	0.0	0.1
PRES–Cumber Presb	1	NR	24	24	0.0	0.0
PRES–Kor Pres Abroad	1	NR	NR	NR	-	-
PRES–Orth Pres Ch	1	35	18	20	0.0	0.0
PRES–Presb Ch (USA)	15	2,680	5,564	6,766	0.7	1.7
PRES–Presb Ch Amer	4	1,382	1,507	1,554	0.2	0.4
REF–Christian Ref	1	0	0	0	0.0	0.0
REF–Ref Ch in Am	2	151	218	299	0.0	0.1
Salvation Army	5	341	218	346	0.0	0.1
Sev Day Adv	12	1,412	2,457	2,825	0.3	0.7
Sikh	1	NR	NR	NR	-	-
Un C of Christ	6	728	1,248	1,518	0.2	0.4

NR–Not Reported   - Represents no adherents reported.   Percentages may not total 100 due to rounding.

Table 3: Religious Congregations by County and Group: 2010

Religious Group	Number of Congregations	Number of Attendees	Number of Communicant, Confirmed, or Full Members	Adherents: Number of Adherents	Adherents: % of Total Pop.	Adherents: % of Total Adh.
Unit Univ	3	354	590	687	0.1	0.2
Unity Ch	3	NR	NR	NR	-	-
Zoroastrian	1	NR	NR	31	0.0	0.0
PINAL	**245**	**13,618**	**18,091**	**81,614**	**21.7**	**100.0**
ANG/EPIS–Episcopal	2	111	241	249	0.1	0.3
Bahá'í	3	NR	358	358	0.1	0.4
BAPT–Amer Bapt USA	1	30	25	32	0.0	0.0
BAPT–Consrv Bapt	6	NR	NR	NR	-	-
BAPT–Converge/BGC	1	75	NR	90	0.0	0.1
BAPT–Free Will Bapt	1	NR	26	33	0.0	0.0
BAPT–Ind Bapt Flwsp Intl	1	NR	NR	NR	-	-
BAPT–NT Ind Bapt	1	NR	NR	NR	-	-
BAPT–So Bapt Conv	39	2,330	5,377	6,846	1.8	8.4
BUDD–Mahayana	1	NR	NR	300	0.1	0.4
BUDD–Theravada	1	NR	NR	291	0.1	0.4
Calv Chpl	4	NR	NR	NR	-	-
Catholic	20	NR	NR	39,268	10.5	48.1
CGOD–Ch God (Ander)	1	0	NR	0	0.0	0.0
Ch Cr, Scientst	1	NR	NR	NR	-	-
Ch of Nazarene	5	833	756	1,215	0.3	1.5
Chr & Miss Al	1	195	0	440	0.1	0.5
CHR–Chr Chs & Chs Cr	3	NR	1,470	1,872	0.5	2.3
CHR–Chs of Christ	12	687	638	816	0.2	1.0
Evan Free Ch	1	95	NR	95	0.0	0.1
Ind Fund Churches	1	NR	NR	NR	-	-
Jehovah's Witness	6	NR	NR	NR	-	-
LDS–L-D Saints	31	NR	NR	14,082	3.7	17.3
LUTH–E.L.C.A.	2	190	239	262	0.1	0.3
LUTH–Luth Ch-Am Asc	1	NR	NR	NR	-	-
LUTH–Luth–MO Synod	3	762	598	734	0.2	0.9
LUTH–Wisc Ev Luth Syn	1	82	121	161	0.0	0.2
METH–Evan Meth Ch	5	NR	NR	NR	-	-
METH–Un Methodist	7	1,738	1,411	4,297	1.1	5.3
METH–Wesleyan	1	39	37	51	0.0	0.1
Muslim Est	2	144	NR	358	0.1	0.4
Non-denom Chr Chs	21	2,891	3,646	3,949	1.1	4.8
ORTHE–Greek Orthodox	1	150	NR	200	0.1	0.2
PENT–Assemb of God	26	1,873	1,000	2,811	0.7	3.4
PENT–Ch God (Cleve)	5	192	229	292	0.1	0.4
PENT–Ch of God Proph	1	NR	150	191	0.1	0.2
PENT–COGIC	2	55	290	369	0.1	0.5
PENT–Int Foursq Gos	1	9	10	13	0.0	0.0
PENT–Intl Pent Holiness	1	50	50	64	0.0	0.1
PENT–Pent Ch of God	1	70	NR	109	0.0	0.1
PENT–Un Pent Ch Intl	3	NR	NR	NR	-	-
PENT–United Holy Ch	1	NR	NR	NR	-	-
PRES–As Ref Pres Ch	1	NR	25	32	0.0	0.0
PRES–Presb Ch (USA)	9	690	808	1,029	0.3	1.3
Salvation Army	1	15	44	76	0.0	0.1
Sev Day Adv	6	312	542	624	0.2	0.8
Zoroastrian	0	NR	NR	5	0.0	0.0
SANTA CRUZ	**43**	**1,595**	**1,830**	**18,651**	**39.3**	**100.0**
ANG/EPIS–Episcopal	1	70	172	248	0.5	1.3
Bahá'í	1	NR	70	70	0.1	0.4
BAPT–Consrv Bapt	3	NR	NR	NR	-	-
BAPT–Fund Bapt Flwsp	1	NR	NR	NR	-	-
BAPT–So Bapt Conv	4	221	141	183	0.4	1.0
Catholic	7	NR	NR	15,217	32.1	81.6
Ch of Nazarene	1	30	20	42	0.1	0.2
CHR–Chs of Christ	1	28	26	34	0.1	0.2
Evan Free Ch	2	70	NR	70	0.1	0.4
HINDU–Post Ren	1	NR	NR	20	0.0	0.1
LDS–L-D Saints	1	NR	NR	876	1.8	4.7
LUTH–Assoc Free Luth	1	NR	NR	NR	-	-
LUTH–Luth–MO Synod	1	26	34	35	0.1	0.2
METH–Un Methodist	2	94	110	164	0.3	0.9
Non-denom Chr Chs	3	200	250	276	0.6	1.5
PENT–Assemb of God	4	670	663	985	2.1	5.3
PENT–Ch God (Cleve)	1	48	91	118	0.2	0.6
PENT–Ch of God Proph	1	NR	54	70	0.1	0.4
PENT–Int Foursq Gos	1	53	52	68	0.1	0.4
PENT–Open Bible Std	1	0	NR	0	0.0	0.0
PRES–Korean Pres Amer	1	NR	NR	NR	-	-
Sev Day Adv	3	64	111	128	0.3	0.7
Un C of Christ	1	21	36	47	0.1	0.3
YAVAPAI	**240**	**17,392**	**21,705**	**54,822**	**26.0**	**100.0**
ANG/EPIS–Anglican NA	2	NR	NR	NR	-	-
ANG/EPIS–Episcopal	3	408	928	981	0.5	1.8
Ap Chr Ch-Amer	1	39	22	39	0.0	0.1
Bahá'í	3	NR	209	209	0.1	0.4
BAPT–Amer Bapt Assn	2	NR	235	275	0.1	0.5
BAPT–Amer Bapt USA	1	42	15	18	0.0	0.0
BAPT–Asc Ref Bap Ch Am	1	NR	NR	NR	-	-
BAPT–Consrv Bapt	5	NR	NR	NR	-	-
BAPT–Free Will Bapt	1	NR	26	30	0.0	0.1
BAPT–Ind Bapt Flwsp Intl	1	NR	NR	NR	-	-
BAPT–Ref Bapt Ch	1	NR	NR	NR	-	-
BAPT–Reg Bapt Gen As	1	NR	NR	NR	-	-
BAPT–So Bapt Conv	27	1,911	3,539	4,141	2.0	7.6
BUDD–Vajrayana	1	NR	NR	26	0.0	0.0
Calv Chpl	6	NR	NR	NR	-	-
Catholic	14	NR	NR	16,500	7.8	30.1
CGOD–Ch God (Ander)	2	150	NR	150	0.1	0.3
Ch Cr, Scientst	2	NR	NR	NR	-	-
Ch of Nazarene	4	662	833	872	0.4	1.6
Chr & Miss Al	1	110	74	107	0.1	0.2
CHR–Chr Ch (Disc)	1	28	32	37	0.0	0.1
CHR–Chr Chs & Chs Cr	6	NR	1,121	1,312	0.6	2.4
CHR–Chs of Christ	11	601	601	669	0.3	1.2
Evan Free Ch	2	145	NR	145	0.1	0.3
HINDU–Post Ren	3	NR	NR	71	0.0	0.1
HINDU–Renaiss	1	NR	NR	12	0.0	0.0
Int Cou Comm Ch	1	NR	NR	NR	-	-
Jehovah's Witness	7	NR	NR	NR	-	-
JUD–Reform	1	84	148	400	0.2	0.7
LDS–Comm of Christ	1	NR	214	214	0.1	0.4
LDS–L-D Saints	22	NR	NR	9,608	4.6	17.5
LUTH–E.L.C.A.	3	457	640	689	0.3	1.3
LUTH–Luth Cong Msn Chr	1	725	986	1,154	0.5	2.1
LUTH–Luth–MO Synod	8	640	731	914	0.4	1.7
LUTH–Wisc Ev Luth Syn	4	327	511	563	0.3	1.0
MENN–CG in Cr (Menn)	1	NR	6	7	0.0	0.0
METH–A.W.M.C.	1	18	0	20	0.0	0.0
METH–Free Methodist	1	40	26	40	0.0	0.1
METH–Un Methodist	6	953	1,503	1,710	0.8	3.1
METH–Wesleyan	1	18	2	23	0.0	0.0
Missionary Ch	1	0	0	0	0.0	0.0
New Apost Ch	1	NR	NR	NR	-	-
Non-denom Chr Chs	28	6,173	6,229	7,886	3.7	14.4
ORTHE–Greek Orthodox	1	80	NR	100	0.0	0.2
PENT–Assemb of God	15	2,000	835	2,810	1.3	5.1
PENT–Ch God (Cleve)	1	32	36	42	0.0	0.1
PENT–Ch of God Proph	1	NR	15	18	0.0	0.0
PENT–Int Foursq Gos	3	117	90	105	0.0	0.2
PENT–Pent Ch of God	2	140	NR	217	0.1	0.4
PENT–Un Pent Ch Intl	3	NR	NR	NR	-	-
PENT–Vineyard	2	139	180	211	0.1	0.4
PRES–Orth Pres Ch	2	60	68	82	0.0	0.1
PRES–Presb Ch (USA)	4	463	593	694	0.3	1.3
REF–Ref Ch in Am	1	125	170	218	0.1	0.4
Salvation Army	1	52	51	294	0.1	0.5
Sev Day Adv	6	416	723	831	0.4	1.5
Un C of Christ	2	105	152	178	0.1	0.3
Unit Univ	2	132	161	200	0.1	0.4
Unity Ch	3	NR	NR	NR	-	-
YUMA	**141**	**11,415**	**15,775**	**73,206**	**37.4**	**100.0**
ANG/EPIS–Anglican NA	1	NR	NR	NR	-	-
ANG/EPIS–Episcopal	1	134	190	190	0.1	0.3
Bahá'í	1	NR	177	177	0.1	0.2
BAPT–Amer Bapt Assn	2	NR	140	178	0.1	0.2
BAPT–Consrv Bapt	5	NR	NR	NR	-	-
BAPT–Converge/BGC	1	75	NR	90	0.0	0.1

NR–Not Reported   - Represents no adherents reported.   Percentages may not total 100 due to rounding.

Table 3: Religious Congregations by County and Group: 2010

Religious Group	Number of Congregations	Number of Attendees	Number of Communicant, Confirmed, or Full Members	Adherents: Number of Adherents	Adherents: % of Total Pop.	Adherents: % of Total Adh.
BAPT–Ind Bapt Flwsp Intl	2	NR	NR	NR	-	-
BAPT–Natl Mis Bapt Conv	1	0	0	0	0.0	0.0
BAPT–So Bapt Conv	15	2,722	2,950	3,758	1.9	5.1
Calv Chpl	1	NR	NR	NR	-	-
Catholic	7	NR	NR	43,401	22.2	59.3
Ch Cr, Scientst	1	NR	NR	NR	-	-
Ch of Nazarene	5	285	395	500	0.3	0.7
CHR–Chr Chs & Chs Cr	2	NR	1,820	2,318	1.2	3.2
CHR–Chs of Christ	7	425	430	560	0.3	0.8
Evan Free Ch	1	130	NR	130	0.1	0.2
HINDU–Renaiss	1	NR	NR	60	0.0	0.1
Jehovah's Witness	4	NR	NR	NR	-	-
JUD–Reform	1	19	33	89	0.0	0.1
LDS–Comm of Christ	1	NR	214	214	0.1	0.3
LDS–L-D Saints	13	NR	NR	6,300	3.2	8.6
LUTH–Ch of Luth Br	1	155	48	320	0.2	0.4
LUTH–E.L.C.A.	2	383	370	418	0.2	0.6
LUTH–Luth–MO Synod	3	183	698	898	0.5	1.2
LUTH–Wisc Ev Luth Syn	1	54	64	71	0.0	0.1
MENN–CG in Cr (Menn)	1	NR	42	53	0.0	0.1
METH–Un Methodist	5	752	764	3,030	1.5	4.1
Muslim Est	1	134	NR	308	0.2	0.4
Non-denom Chr Chs	17	3,075	4,594	4,872	2.5	6.7
PENT–Assemb of God	13	1,712	990	2,234	1.1	3.1
PENT–Ch God (Cleve)	1	108	137	175	0.1	0.2
PENT–Ch of God Proph	2	NR	74	94	0.0	0.1
PENT–COGIC	2	30	174	222	0.1	0.3
PENT–Int Foursq Gos	1	33	38	48	0.0	0.1
PENT–Intl Pent Holiness	1	115	123	157	0.1	0.2
PENT–Pent Ch of God	1	70	NR	109	0.1	0.1
PRES–Korean Pres Amer	2	NR	NR	NR	-	-
PRES–Presb Ch (USA)	5	153	317	404	0.2	0.6
Salvation Army	2	130	80	776	0.4	1.1
Sev Day Adv	4	500	869	1,000	0.5	1.4
Un C of Christ	1	20	28	36	0.0	0.0
Unit Univ	1	18	16	16	0.0	0.0
Unity Ch	1	NR	NR	NR	-	-
ARKANSAS	**6,697**	**515,358**	**1,155,819**	**1,614,357**	**55.4**	**100.0**
ARKANSAS	**66**	**3,339**	**10,894**	**13,578**	**71.4**	**100.0**
ANG/EPIS–Episcopal	1	40	91	91	0.5	0.7
Bahá'í	0	NR	37	37	0.2	0.3
BAPT–Amer Bapt Assn	7	NR	1,161	1,410	7.4	10.4
BAPT–Natl Mis Bapt Conv	1	0	150	182	1.0	1.3
BAPT–So Bapt Conv	16	1,297	5,213	6,332	33.3	46.6
Catholic	1	NR	NR	300	1.6	2.2
Ch of Nazarene	1	22	27	42	0.2	0.3
CHR–Chr Ch (Disc)	1	70	230	279	1.5	2.1
CHR–Chr Chs & Chs Cr	1	NR	15	18	0.1	0.1
CHR–Chs of Christ	4	130	112	140	0.7	1.0
FRND–Central Yr Mtg	1	11	8	10	0.1	0.1
Jehovah's Witness	1	NR	NR	NR	-	-
LUTH–E.L.C.A.	1	42	91	115	0.6	0.8
LUTH–Luth–MO Synod	3	317	788	944	5.0	7.0
METH–AME	5	0	550	668	3.5	4.9
METH–Un Methodist	12	805	1,727	1,976	10.4	14.6
Non-denom Chr Chs	2	325	350	407	2.1	3.0
PENT–Assemb of God	4	197	162	297	1.6	2.2
PENT–COGIC	1	0	150	182	1.0	1.3
PENT–Pent Ch of God	1	70	NR	109	0.6	0.8
PENT–Un Pent Ch Intl	1	NR	NR	NR	-	-
PRES–Presb Ch (USA)	1	13	32	39	0.2	0.3
ASHLEY	**100**	**4,263**	**15,118**	**19,524**	**89.3**	**100.0**
ANG/EPIS–Episcopal	1	19	40	45	0.2	0.2
Bahá'í	0	NR	6	6	0.0	0.0
BAPT–Amer Bapt Assn	9	NR	1,540	1,891	8.7	9.7
BAPT–Free Will Bapt	6	NR	552	678	3.1	3.5
BAPT–Natl Mis Bapt Conv	1	0	150	184	0.8	0.9
BAPT–NBC USA	2	0	650	798	3.7	4.1
BAPT–So Bapt Conv	28	2,322	8,135	9,991	45.7	51.2
Catholic	2	NR	NR	694	3.2	3.6
CGOD–Ch God (Ander)	1	84	NR	84	0.4	0.4
Ch of Chr (Hol)	1	NR	NR	NR	-	-
CHR–Chs of Christ	6	290	422	496	2.3	2.5
Jehovah's Witness	1	NR	NR	NR	-	-
LDS–Comm of Christ	1	NR	81	81	0.4	0.4
LUTH–Luth–MO Synod	1	9	19	23	0.1	0.1
METH–AME	9	150	1,075	1,320	6.0	6.8
METH–AME Zion	3	0	300	368	1.7	1.9
METH–C.M.E.	2	0	200	246	1.1	1.3
METH–Un Methodist	10	419	907	914	4.2	4.7
Non-denom Chr Chs	4	275	350	382	1.7	2.0
PENT–Assemb of God	4	315	200	394	1.8	2.0
PENT–COGIC	2	150	450	553	2.5	2.8
PENT–Pent Ch of God	3	210	NR	326	1.5	1.7
PENT–Un Pent Ch Intl	2	NR	NR	NR	-	-
PRES–Presb Ch (USA)	1	20	41	50	0.2	0.3
BAXTER	**92**	**8,265**	**15,184**	**21,158**	**51.0**	**100.0**
ANG/EPIS–Anglican NA	1	NR	NR	NR	-	-
ANG/EPIS–Episcopal	1	85	124	124	0.3	0.6
Bahá'í	0	NR	13	13	0.0	0.1
BAPT–Amer Bapt Assn	2	NR	124	144	0.3	0.7
BAPT–Free Will Bapt	2	NR	184	214	0.5	1.0
BAPT–Natl Mis Bapt Conv	1	0	150	174	0.4	0.8
BAPT–NT Ind Bapt	1	NR	NR	NR	-	-
BAPT–So Bapt Conv	24	2,681	7,215	8,376	20.2	39.6
Calv Chpl	1	NR	NR	NR	-	-
Catholic	1	NR	NR	2,359	5.7	11.1
Ch Cr, Scientst	1	NR	NR	NR	-	-
Ch of Nazarene	2	107	148	217	0.5	1.0
CHR–Chr Ch (Disc)	1	150	258	300	0.7	1.4
CHR–Chr Chs & Chs Cr	1	NR	200	232	0.6	1.1
CHR–Chs of Christ	15	1,429	1,299	1,545	3.7	7.3
Ind Fund Churches	1	NR	NR	NR	-	-
Jehovah's Witness	1	NR	NR	NR	-	-
LDS–Comm of Christ	1	NR	135	135	0.3	0.6
LDS–L-D Saints	1	NR	NR	730	1.8	3.5
LUTH–E.L.C.A.	1	111	332	400	1.0	1.9
LUTH–Luth–MO Synod	1	350	550	607	1.5	2.9
LUTH–Wisc Ev Luth Syn	1	72	99	120	0.3	0.6
METH–Un Methodist	4	782	1,294	1,479	3.6	7.0
Non-denom Chr Chs	10	1,230	1,707	1,939	4.7	9.2
PENT–Assemb of God	4	573	427	799	1.9	3.8
PENT–Ch God (Cleve)	2	49	60	70	0.2	0.3
PENT–COGIC	1	280	280	325	0.8	1.5
PENT–Pent Ch of God	1	70	NR	109	0.3	0.5
PENT–Un Pent Ch Intl	1	NR	NR	NR	-	-
PRES–Cumber Presb	2	NR	121	196	0.5	0.9
PRES–Presb Ch (USA)	2	128	194	225	0.5	1.1
Salvation Army	1	75	119	154	0.4	0.7
Sev Day Adv	1	81	141	162	0.4	0.8
Unit Univ	1	12	10	10	0.0	0.0
Unity Ch	1	NR	NR	NR	-	-
BENTON	**295**	**38,402**	**68,244**	**109,019**	**49.3**	**100.0**
ANG/EPIS–Episcopal	4	454	858	905	0.4	0.8
Bahá'í	1	NR	89	89	0.0	0.1
BAPT–Amer Bapt Assn	5	NR	830	1,069	0.5	1.0
BAPT–Amer Bapt USA	1	43	88	113	0.1	0.1
BAPT–Free Will Bapt	7	NR	644	829	0.4	0.8
BAPT–Ref Bapt Ch	1	NR	NR	NR	-	-
BAPT–Reg Bapt Gen As	2	NR	NR	NR	-	-
BAPT–So Bapt Conv	61	10,753	28,597	36,819	16.6	33.8
BRETH–Ch of Brethren	0	0	13	17	0.0	0.0
Calv Chpl	1	NR	NR	NR	-	-
Catholic	4	NR	NR	16,757	7.6	15.4
Ch Cr, Scientst	1	NR	NR	NR	-	-
Ch of Nazarene	10	936	1,123	1,509	0.7	1.4
Chr & Miss Al	2	85	78	113	0.1	0.1
CHR–Chr Ch (Disc)	5	414	924	1,190	0.5	1.1
CHR–Chr Chs & Chs Cr	8	NR	1,906	2,454	1.1	2.3
CHR–Chs of Christ	19	3,075	3,050	3,992	1.8	3.7

NR–Not Reported - Represents no adherents reported. Percentages may not total 100 due to rounding.

Table 3: Religious Congregations by County and Group: 2010

Religious Group	Number of Congregations	Number of Attendees	Number of Communicant, Confirmed, or Full Members	Adherents		
				Number of Adherents	% of Total Pop.	% of Total Adh.
Evan Free Ch	3	390	NR	390	0.2	0.4
HINDU–I/A Temples	1	NR	NR	250	0.1	0.2
Ind Fund Churches	2	NR	NR	NR	-	-
Int Cou Comm Ch	1	NR	NR	NR	-	-
Jehovah's Witness	5	NR	NR	NR	-	-
LDS–L-D Saints	10	NR	NR	4,210	1.9	3.9
LUTH–E.L.C.A.	4	602	1,015	1,198	0.5	1.1
LUTH–Luth Cong Msn Chr	1	44	56	72	0.0	0.1
LUTH–Luth–MO Synod	5	696	960	1,126	0.5	1.0
LUTH–Wisc Ev Luth Syn	2	184	238	362	0.2	0.3
MENN–CG in Cr (Menn)	1	NR	145	187	0.1	0.2
METH–Free Methodist	1	48	10	48	0.0	0.0
METH–Un Methodist	20	3,050	6,861	9,280	4.2	8.5
METH–Wesleyan	2	54	59	70	0.0	0.1
Muslim Est	1	134	NR	308	0.1	0.3
Non-denom Chr Chs	37	11,286	14,291	15,423	7.0	14.1
PENT–Assemb of God	23	2,981	1,772	3,888	1.8	3.6
PENT–Ch God (Cleve)	3	236	254	327	0.1	0.3
PENT–Ch God Apos Fth	1	NR	NR	NR	-	-
PENT–Ch of God Proph	1	NR	54	70	0.0	0.1
PENT–Intl Pent Holiness	4	381	393	506	0.2	0.5
PENT–Open Bible Std	2	192	NR	192	0.1	0.2
PENT–Pent Ch of God	4	280	NR	435	0.2	0.4
PENT–Un Pent Ch Intl	6	NR	NR	NR	-	-
PRES–Presb Ch (USA)	8	700	1,672	2,153	1.0	2.0
PRES–Presb Ch Amer	1	174	143	229	0.1	0.2
REF–Ref Ch in U.S.	1	NR	18	20	0.0	0.0
Sev Day Adv	12	1,210	2,103	2,419	1.1	2.2
Unity Ch	1	NR	NR	NR	-	-
BOONE	**98**	**12,926**	**20,685**	**27,467**	**74.4**	**100.0**
ANG/EPIS–Episcopal	1	53	100	181	0.5	0.7
Bahá'í	0	NR	2	2	0.0	0.0
BAPT–Amer Bapt Assn	4	NR	405	493	1.3	1.8
BAPT–Free Will Bapt	1	NR	92	112	0.3	0.4
BAPT–So Bapt Conv	27	4,278	8,998	10,943	29.7	39.8
Catholic	1	NR	NR	970	2.6	3.5
CGOD–Ch God (Ander)	1	901	NR	901	2.4	3.3
Ch of Nazarene	1	54	72	90	0.2	0.3
CHR–Chr Ch (Disc)	1	235	606	737	2.0	2.7
CHR–Chr Chs & Chs Cr	1	NR	85	103	0.3	0.4
CHR–Chs of Christ	13	1,186	1,057	1,243	3.4	4.5
Jehovah's Witness	1	NR	NR	NR	-	-
LDS–L-D Saints	1	NR	NR	573	1.6	2.1
LUTH–E.L.C.A.	1	26	43	43	0.1	0.2
LUTH–Luth–MO Synod	1	70	168	223	0.6	0.8
MENN–Beachy Amish-Menn	2	182	90	182	0.5	0.7
METH–Un Methodist	9	451	935	1,082	2.9	3.9
METH–Wesleyan	1	17	28	22	0.1	0.1
Non-denom Chr Chs	10	3,785	5,920	6,068	16.4	22.1
PENT–Assemb of God	10	1,313	1,295	2,444	6.6	8.9
PENT–Ch God (Cleve)	1	58	234	285	0.8	1.0
PENT–Ch God Apos Fth	3	NR	NR	NR	-	-
PENT–Pent Ch of God	1	70	NR	109	0.3	0.4
PENT–Un Pent Ch Intl	3	NR	NR	NR	-	-
PRES–Presb Ch (USA)	1	125	324	394	1.1	1.4
REF–Heritage Ref	1	NR	18	22	0.1	0.1
Sev Day Adv	1	122	213	245	0.7	0.9
BRADLEY	**58**	**1,704**	**7,395**	**9,409**	**81.8**	**100.0**
BAPT–Amer Bapt Assn	1	NR	160	196	1.7	2.1
BAPT–Free Will Bapt	7	NR	644	788	6.8	8.4
BAPT–So Bapt Conv	12	901	3,392	4,151	36.1	44.1
Catholic	1	NR	NR	389	3.4	4.1
CHR–Chs of Christ	3	100	95	121	1.1	1.3
Jehovah's Witness	1	NR	NR	NR	-	-
MENN–CG in Cr (Menn)	1	NR	72	88	0.8	0.9
METH–AME	10	0	1,200	1,468	12.8	15.6
METH–AME Zion	1	0	100	122	1.1	1.3
METH–Un Methodist	9	350	823	839	7.3	8.9
Non-denom Chr Chs	1	60	100	100	0.9	1.1
PENT–Assemb of God	1	99	69	133	1.2	1.4
PENT–Ch God (Cleve)	1	17	76	93	0.8	1.0
PENT–COGIC	4	75	550	673	5.8	7.2
PENT–Pent Ch of God	1	70	NR	109	0.9	1.2
PENT–Un Pent Ch Intl	1	NR	NR	NR	-	-
PRES–As Ref Pres Ch	1	NR	5	6	0.1	0.1
PRES–Presb Ch (USA)	2	32	109	133	1.2	1.4
CALHOUN	**22**	**861**	**1,928**	**2,405**	**44.8**	**100.0**
BAPT–Amer Bapt Assn	2	NR	85	100	1.9	4.2
BAPT–So Bapt Conv	6	337	1,057	1,244	23.2	51.7
Ch of Nazarene	1	53	41	84	1.6	3.5
CHR–Chs of Christ	3	191	177	231	4.3	9.6
METH–AME	1	0	150	177	3.3	7.4
METH–Un Methodist	4	108	203	236	4.4	9.8
PENT–Assemb of God	4	172	162	203	3.8	8.4
PRES–Cumber Presb	1	NR	53	130	2.4	5.4
CARROLL	**73**	**3,977**	**7,266**	**10,843**	**39.5**	**100.0**
ANG/EPIS–Episcopal	1	58	142	142	0.5	1.3
Bahá'í	0	NR	6	6	0.0	0.1
BAPT–Amer Bapt Assn	2	NR	125	151	0.6	1.4
BAPT–Free Will Bapt	5	NR	460	557	2.0	5.1
BAPT–Ind Bapt Flwsp Intl	1	NR	NR	NR	-	-
BAPT–So Bapt Conv	16	1,317	3,408	4,129	15.0	38.1
Calv Chpl	1	NR	NR	NR	-	-
Catholic	2	NR	NR	950	3.5	8.8
Ch Cr, Scientst	1	NR	NR	NR	-	-
Ch of Nazarene	1	27	25	68	0.2	0.6
CHR–Chr Ch (Disc)	1	52	155	188	0.7	1.7
CHR–Chr Chs & Chs Cr	1	NR	85	103	0.4	0.9
CHR–Chs of Christ	4	188	166	201	0.7	1.9
Jehovah's Witness	1	NR	NR	NR	-	-
LDS–Comm of Christ	1	NR	135	135	0.5	1.2
LDS–L-D Saints	1	NR	NR	280	1.0	2.6
LUTH–Luth–MO Synod	2	57	67	73	0.3	0.7
MENN–Tamp Amish-Menn	1	233	139	233	0.8	2.1
METH–Un Methodist	4	316	803	1,033	3.8	9.5
New Apost Ch	1	NR	NR	NR	-	-
Non-denom Chr Chs	6	673	978	1,047	3.8	9.7
PENT–Assemb of God	5	917	324	1,261	4.6	11.6
PENT–Ch God (Cleve)	1	11	14	17	0.1	0.2
PENT–Ch God Apos Fth	6	NR	NR	NR	-	-
PENT–Un Pent Ch Intl	2	NR	NR	NR	-	-
PRES–Presb Ch (USA)	2	38	96	116	0.4	1.1
Sev Day Adv	2	43	74	86	0.3	0.8
Tao	1	NR	NR	NR	-	-
Unit Univ	1	47	64	67	0.2	0.6
CHICOT	**39**	**1,085**	**4,673**	**6,282**	**53.2**	**100.0**
ANG/EPIS–Episcopal	1	11	38	39	0.3	0.6
Bahá'í	0	NR	1	1	0.0	0.0
BAPT–Amer Bapt Assn	2	NR	184	224	1.9	3.6
BAPT–Free Will Bapt	1	NR	92	112	0.9	1.8
BAPT–Natl Mis Bapt Conv	1	0	150	183	1.6	2.9
BAPT–NBC USA	1	0	150	183	1.6	2.9
BAPT–So Bapt Conv	13	764	3,044	3,708	31.4	59.0
Catholic	1	NR	NR	525	4.4	8.4
CHR–Chs of Christ	3	93	88	115	1.0	1.8
Jehovah's Witness	1	NR	NR	NR	-	-
JUD–Reform	1	4	7	19	0.2	0.3
METH–AME	3	0	400	487	4.1	7.8
METH–AME Zion	1	0	100	122	1.0	1.9
METH–Un Methodist	3	119	277	355	3.0	5.7
PENT–Assemb of God	3	74	37	81	0.7	1.3
PENT–COGIC	1	20	20	24	0.2	0.4
PENT–Un Pent Ch Intl	1	NR	NR	NR	-	-
PRES–Presb Ch (USA)	2	0	85	104	0.9	1.7
CLARK	**84**	**5,569**	**12,717**	**15,623**	**67.9**	**100.0**
Bahá'í	0	NR	15	15	0.1	0.1
BAPT–Amer Bapt Assn	4	NR	1,025	1,204	5.2	7.7
BAPT–Free Will Bapt	1	NR	92	108	0.5	0.7
BAPT–NBC USA	1	0	200	235	1.0	1.5

NR–Not Reported - Represents no adherents reported. Percentages may not total 100 due to rounding.

Table 3: Religious Congregations by County and Group: 2010

Religious Group	Number of Congrega-tions	Number of Attendees	Number of Communicant, Confirmed, or Full Members	Adherents: Number of Adherents	Adherents: % of Total Pop.	Adherents: % of Total Adh.
BAPT–So Bapt Conv	32	3,905	8,274	9,716	42.3	62.2
Catholic	1	NR	NR	80	0.3	0.5
CGOD–Ch God (Ander)	2	70	NR	70	0.3	0.4
Ch of Chr (Hol)	1	NR	NR	NR	-	-
Ch of Nazarene	1	35	50	70	0.3	0.4
CHR–Chr Ch (Disc)	1	7	14	16	0.1	0.1
CHR–Chs of Christ	4	195	184	246	1.1	1.6
LDS–L-D Saints	1	NR	NR	243	1.1	1.6
METH–AME	7	0	800	939	4.1	6.0
METH–C.M.E.	1	0	100	117	0.5	0.7
METH–Un Methodist	10	583	1,303	1,469	6.4	9.4
Non-denom Chr Chs	2	190	190	238	1.0	1.5
PENT–Assemb of God	5	327	152	378	1.6	2.4
PENT–Pent Ch of God	1	70	NR	109	0.5	0.7
PENT–Un Pent Ch Intl	3	NR	NR	NR	-	-
PRES–Presb Ch (USA)	4	127	213	250	1.1	1.6
Sev Day Adv	2	60	105	120	0.5	0.8
CLAY	**57**	**2,478**	**5,662**	**7,159**	**44.5**	**100.0**
BAPT–Amer Bapt Assn	4	NR	305	367	2.3	5.1
BAPT–Free Will Bapt	1	NR	92	111	0.7	1.6
BAPT–So Bapt Conv	16	1,153	3,516	4,229	26.3	59.1
Catholic	1	NR	NR	30	0.2	0.4
CGOD–Ch God (Ander)	1	30	NR	30	0.2	0.4
Ch of Nazarene	1	12	12	42	0.3	0.6
CHR–Chr Chs & Chs Cr	2	NR	120	144	0.9	2.0
CHR–Chs of Christ	14	904	846	1,115	6.9	15.6
Jehovah's Witness	2	NR	NR	NR	-	-
LUTH–Luth-MO Synod	1	38	85	104	0.6	1.5
MENN–Amish Undif	1	NR	24	65	0.4	0.9
METH–Un Methodist	5	238	649	758	4.7	10.6
PENT–Assemb of God	2	33	0	39	0.2	0.5
PENT–Pent Ch of God	1	70	NR	109	0.7	1.5
PENT–Un Pent Ch Intl	4	NR	NR	NR	-	-
PRES–Presb Ch (USA)	1	0	13	16	0.1	0.2
CLEBURNE	**62**	**5,150**	**9,566**	**12,988**	**50.0**	**100.0**
ANG/EPIS–Episcopal	1	53	97	97	0.4	0.7
Bahá'í	0	NR	4	4	0.0	0.0
BAPT–Amer Bapt Assn	3	NR	255	301	1.2	2.3
BAPT–Free Will Bapt	1	NR	92	109	0.4	0.8
BAPT–So Bapt Conv	22	2,556	5,619	6,630	25.5	51.0
Catholic	1	NR	NR	405	1.6	3.1
Ch of Nazarene	1	76	64	151	0.6	1.2
CHR–Chr Chs & Chs Cr	1	NR	60	71	0.3	0.5
CHR–Chs of Christ	6	389	402	474	1.8	3.6
Jehovah's Witness	1	NR	NR	NR	-	-
LDS–L-D Saints	1	NR	NR	591	2.3	4.6
LUTH–E.L.C.A.	2	126	247	251	1.0	1.9
LUTH–Luth-MO Synod	1	0	26	26	0.1	0.2
METH–Un Methodist	4	737	1,675	1,954	7.5	15.0
Non-denom Chr Chs	5	680	515	849	3.3	6.5
PENT–Assemb of God	2	305	237	645	2.5	5.0
PENT–Ch God (Cleve)	3	90	140	165	0.6	1.3
PENT–Pent Ch of God	1	70	NR	109	0.4	0.8
PENT–Un Pent Ch Intl	3	NR	NR	NR	-	-
PRES–As Ref Pres Ch	1	NR	29	34	0.1	0.3
PRES–Presb Ch (USA)	1	60	90	106	0.4	0.8
Sev Day Adv	1	8	14	16	0.1	0.1
CLEVELAND	**36**	**817**	**3,417**	**4,269**	**49.1**	**100.0**
BAPT–Amer Bapt Assn	11	NR	1,500	1,861	21.4	43.6
BAPT–Free Will Bapt	2	NR	184	228	2.6	5.3
BAPT–So Bapt Conv	5	343	791	982	11.3	23.0
CGOD–Ch God (Ander)	1	50	NR	50	0.6	1.2
CHR–Chs of Christ	1	70	80	90	1.0	2.1
METH–AME	2	0	250	310	3.6	7.3
METH–Un Methodist	10	240	519	546	6.3	12.8
PENT–Assemb of God	2	95	32	126	1.5	3.0
PENT–Ch God (Cleve)	1	19	44	55	0.6	1.3
PENT–COGIC	1	0	17	21	0.2	0.5

Religious Group	Number of Congrega-tions	Number of Attendees	Number of Communicant, Confirmed, or Full Members	Adherents: Number of Adherents	Adherents: % of Total Pop.	Adherents: % of Total Adh.
COLUMBIA	**73**	**3,061**	**10,699**	**12,995**	**52.9**	**100.0**
ANG/EPIS–Episcopal	1	14	46	46	0.2	0.4
Bahá'í	0	NR	1	1	0.0	0.0
BAPT–Amer Bapt Assn	8	NR	960	1,160	4.7	8.9
BAPT–NBC USA	2	100	410	496	2.0	3.8
BAPT–So Bapt Conv	8	694	3,836	4,637	18.9	35.7
Catholic	1	NR	NR	220	0.9	1.7
CHR–Chs of Christ	7	551	655	762	3.1	5.9
Jehovah's Witness	1	NR	NR	NR	-	-
LDS–L-D Saints	1	NR	NR	233	0.9	1.8
LUTH–Luth-MO Synod	1	12	15	20	0.1	0.2
METH–AME	10	55	1,050	1,269	5.2	9.8
METH–C.M.E.	6	0	700	846	3.4	6.5
METH–Un Methodist	14	638	1,687	1,779	7.2	13.7
Non-denom Chr Chs	4	590	735	800	3.3	6.2
PENT–Assemb of God	2	32	24	32	0.1	0.2
PENT–COGIC	3	270	390	471	1.9	3.6
PENT–Un Pent Ch Intl	1	NR	NR	NR	-	-
PRES–Cumber Presb	1	NR	15	15	0.1	0.1
PRES–Presb Ch (USA)	1	75	122	147	0.6	1.1
Sev Day Adv	1	30	53	61	0.2	0.5
CONWAY	**66**	**3,053**	**6,148**	**10,387**	**48.8**	**100.0**
Bahá'í	0	NR	3	3	0.0	0.0
BAPT–Amer Bapt Assn	9	NR	800	983	4.6	9.5
BAPT–Free Will Bapt	3	NR	276	339	1.6	3.3
BAPT–So Bapt Conv	9	865	2,141	2,630	12.4	25.3
Catholic	4	NR	NR	1,791	8.4	17.2
Ch of God Gen Conf	1	NR	7	9	0.0	0.1
Ch of Nazarene	1	58	100	100	0.5	1.0
CHR–Chs of Christ	15	918	869	1,300	6.1	12.5
Jehovah's Witness	1	NR	NR	NR	-	-
LDS–L-D Saints	1	NR	NR	342	1.6	3.3
METH–AME	1	0	150	184	0.9	1.8
METH–AME Zion	2	85	260	319	1.5	3.1
METH–C.M.E.	3	0	300	369	1.7	3.6
METH–Un Methodist	6	215	546	590	2.8	5.7
Non-denom Chr Chs	1	160	200	200	0.9	1.9
PENT–Assemb of God	4	593	279	798	3.8	7.7
PENT–Pent Ch of God	1	70	NR	109	0.5	1.0
PENT–Un Pent Ch Intl	1	NR	NR	NR	-	-
PRES–Cumber Presb	1	NR	9	65	0.3	0.6
PRES–Presb Ch (USA)	2	89	208	256	1.2	2.5
CRAIGHEAD	**170**	**20,025**	**40,508**	**54,194**	**56.2**	**100.0**
ANG/EPIS–Anglican NA	1	NR	NR	NR	-	-
ANG/EPIS–Episcopal	1	106	193	277	0.3	0.5
Bahá'í	0	NR	5	5	0.0	0.0
BAPT–Amer Bapt Assn	3	NR	485	605	0.6	1.1
BAPT–Free Will Bapt	3	NR	276	344	0.4	0.6
BAPT–So Bapt Conv	51	8,987	24,599	30,671	31.8	56.6
Calv Chpl	1	NR	NR	NR	-	-
Catholic	2	NR	NR	2,470	2.6	4.6
Ch God (7th Day)	1	NR	NR	NR	-	-
Ch of Nazarene	2	272	368	637	0.7	1.2
CHR–Chr Ch (Disc)	2	104	191	238	0.2	0.4
CHR–Chr Chs & Chs Cr	4	NR	480	598	0.6	1.1
CHR–Chs of Christ	21	3,917	4,213	5,276	5.5	9.7
Jehovah's Witness	3	NR	NR	NR	-	-
JUD–Reform	1	18	32	86	0.1	0.2
LDS–Comm of Christ	3	NR	405	405	0.4	0.7
LDS–L-D Saints	1	NR	NR	653	0.7	1.2
LUTH–E.L.C.A.	1	18	65	76	0.1	0.1
LUTH–Luth-MO Synod	1	62	123	158	0.2	0.3
METH–AME	2	0	250	312	0.3	0.6
METH–C.M.E.	1	0	100	125	0.1	0.2
METH–Un Methodist	19	2,150	4,052	4,578	4.7	8.4
Muslim Est	1	134	NR	308	0.3	0.6
Non-denom Chr Chs	16	2,455	3,100	3,357	3.5	6.2
PENT–Assemb of God	11	634	522	1,350	1.4	2.5
PENT–Ch God (Cleve)	2	553	469	585	0.6	1.1
PENT–Ch of God Proph	1	NR	37	46	0.0	0.1
PENT–COGIC	2	190	175	218	0.2	0.4

NR–Not Reported   - Represents no adherents reported.   Percentages may not total 100 due to rounding.

Table 3: Religious Congregations by County and Group: 2010

Religious Group	Number of Congrega-tions	Number of Attendees	Number of Communicant, Confirmed, or Full Members	Adherents: Number of Adherents	Adherents: % of Total Pop.	Adherents: % of Total Adh.
PENT–Pent Ch of God	3	210	NR	326	0.3	0.6
PENT–Un Pent Ch Intl	6	NR	NR	NR	-	-
PRES–Presb Ch (USA)	1	113	192	239	0.2	0.4
Salvation Army	1	33	68	124	0.1	0.2
Sev Day Adv	1	54	93	107	0.1	0.2
Unit Univ	1	15	15	20	0.0	0.0
CRAWFORD	**128**	**10,964**	**21,330**	**31,172**	**50.3**	**100.0**
ANG/EPIS–Episcopal	1	70	146	146	0.2	0.5
Bahá'í	0	NR	6	6	0.0	0.0
BAPT–Amer Bapt Assn	9	NR	870	1,093	1.8	3.5
BAPT–Free Will Bapt	13	NR	1,196	1,503	2.4	4.8
BAPT–So Bapt Conv	25	3,871	11,033	13,862	22.4	44.5
Catholic	2	NR	NR	1,263	2.0	4.1
CGOD–Ch God (Ander)	1	97	NR	97	0.2	0.3
CGOD–Ches God-Gen Con	1	15	14	18	0.0	0.1
Ch of Nazarene	3	117	280	315	0.5	1.0
Chr & Miss Al	1	38	17	37	0.1	0.1
CHR–Chr Ch (Disc)	1	0	72	90	0.1	0.3
CHR–Chs of Christ	10	756	742	956	1.5	3.1
Intl Fell Bible Ch	1	NR	NR	NR	-	-
Jehovah's Witness	2	NR	NR	NR	-	-
LDS–L-D Saints	1	NR	NR	610	1.0	2.0
LUTH–Luth-MO Synod	1	19	41	49	0.1	0.2
METH–Un Methodist	11	1,168	2,143	3,079	5.0	9.9
Non-denom Chr Chs	11	1,339	1,660	1,824	2.9	5.9
PENT–Apos Faith Msn	1	NR	35	44	0.1	0.1
PENT–Assemb of God	16	2,641	2,585	4,600	7.4	14.8
PENT–Pent Ch of God	9	630	NR	979	1.6	3.1
PENT–Un Pent Ch Intl	2	NR	NR	NR	-	-
PRES–Presb Ch (USA)	3	129	360	452	0.7	1.5
Sev Day Adv	3	74	130	149	0.2	0.5
CRITTENDEN	**79**	**6,746**	**18,716**	**24,856**	**48.8**	**100.0**
ANG/EPIS–Anglican NA	1	NR	NR	NR	-	-
ANG/EPIS–Episcopal	1	45	72	82	0.2	0.3
Bahá'í	0	NR	6	6	0.0	0.0
BAPT–Amer Bapt Assn	3	NR	535	688	1.4	2.8
BAPT–Natl Mis Bapt Conv	4	0	600	772	1.5	3.1
BAPT–NBC Amer	1	200	350	450	0.9	1.8
BAPT–NBC USA	2	925	1,400	1,801	3.5	7.2
BAPT–So Bapt Conv	15	1,952	9,122	11,737	23.1	47.2
Catholic	3	NR	NR	525	1.0	2.1
Ch of Chr (Hol)	1	NR	NR	NR	-	-
Ch of Nazarene	1	29	69	84	0.2	0.3
CHR–Chr Ch (Disc)	1	45	111	143	0.3	0.6
CHR–Chs of Christ	7	836	857	1,061	2.1	4.3
Jehovah's Witness	1	NR	NR	NR	-	-
LDS–L-D Saints	1	NR	NR	405	0.8	1.6
LUTH–Luth-MO Synod	1	22	26	27	0.1	0.1
METH–AME	2	50	248	319	0.6	1.3
METH–C.M.E.	3	0	350	450	0.9	1.8
METH–Un Methodist	5	672	2,077	2,368	4.7	9.5
New Apost Ch	1	NR	NR	NR	-	-
Non-denom Chr Chs	8	830	1,155	1,162	2.3	4.7
PENT–Assemb of God	3	480	575	972	1.9	3.9
PENT–Ch God (Cleve)	2	196	322	414	0.8	1.7
PENT–Ch of God Proph	1	NR	24	31	0.1	0.1
PENT–COGIC	5	70	524	674	1.3	2.7
PENT–Pent Ch of God	3	210	NR	326	0.6	1.3
PENT–Un Pent Ch Intl	1	NR	NR	NR	-	-
PRES–Presb Ch (USA)	1	110	165	212	0.4	0.9
Sev Day Adv	1	74	128	147	0.3	0.6
CROSS	**59**	**3,949**	**9,483**	**12,130**	**67.9**	**100.0**
ANG/EPIS–Episcopal	1	5	4	4	0.0	0.0
BAPT–Amer Bapt Assn	2	NR	170	209	1.2	1.7
BAPT–Natl Mis Bapt Conv	1	0	150	184	1.0	1.5
BAPT–NBC USA	1	200	500	614	3.4	5.1
BAPT–So Bapt Conv	17	1,808	5,225	6,415	35.9	52.9
BRETH–Ch of Brethren	1	10	16	20	0.1	0.2
Catholic	1	NR	NR	350	2.0	2.9
CHR–Chs of Christ	3	430	370	475	2.7	3.9

Religious Group	Number of Congrega-tions	Number of Attendees	Number of Communicant, Confirmed, or Full Members	Adherents: Number of Adherents	Adherents: % of Total Pop.	Adherents: % of Total Adh.
METH–AME	1	0	100	123	0.7	1.0
METH–C.M.E.	3	0	300	368	2.1	3.0
METH–Un Methodist	8	404	1,234	1,358	7.6	11.2
Non-denom Chr Chs	4	350	500	500	2.8	4.1
PENT–Assemb of God	8	469	519	916	5.1	7.6
PENT–Ch God (Cleve)	4	143	280	344	1.9	2.8
PENT–Orig Ch of God	1	NR	NR	NR	-	-
PENT–Pent Ch of God	1	70	NR	109	0.6	0.9
PENT–Un Pent Ch Intl	1	NR	NR	NR	-	-
PRES–Presb Ch (USA)	1	60	115	141	0.8	1.2
DALLAS	**40**	**1,162**	**3,769**	**4,735**	**58.3**	**100.0**
BAPT–Amer Bapt Assn	2	NR	652	795	9.8	16.8
BAPT–NBC USA	1	0	150	183	2.3	3.9
BAPT–So Bapt Conv	6	427	1,035	1,262	15.5	26.7
Catholic	1	NR	NR	36	0.4	0.8
CHR–Chs of Christ	3	70	68	82	1.0	1.7
Jehovah's Witness	2	NR	NR	NR	-	-
LDS–L-D Saints	1	NR	NR	64	0.8	1.4
METH–AME	5	0	550	671	8.3	14.2
METH–Un Methodist	7	184	506	552	6.8	11.7
Non-denom Chr Chs	2	225	350	350	4.3	7.4
PENT–Assemb of God	4	216	126	335	4.1	7.1
PENT–COGIC	2	40	300	366	4.5	7.7
PENT–Un Pent Ch Intl	1	NR	NR	NR	-	-
PRES–Presb Ch (USA)	3	0	32	39	0.5	0.8
DESHA	**52**	**1,933**	**6,616**	**8,525**	**65.5**	**100.0**
ANG/EPIS–Episcopal	1	6	7	7	0.1	0.1
Bahá'í	0	NR	34	34	0.3	0.4
BAPT–Amer Bapt Assn	2	NR	170	214	1.6	2.5
BAPT–Natl Mis Bapt Conv	1	0	150	188	1.4	2.2
BAPT–NBC USA	4	0	400	502	3.9	5.9
BAPT–So Bapt Conv	13	887	3,492	4,386	33.7	51.4
Catholic	2	NR	NR	82	0.6	1.0
Ch of Nazarene	1	17	137	137	1.1	1.6
CHR–Chr Chs & Chs Cr	1	NR	115	144	1.1	1.7
CHR–Chs of Christ	3	158	172	202	1.6	2.4
Jehovah's Witness	1	NR	NR	NR	-	-
MENN–CG in Cr (Menn)	1	NR	129	162	1.2	1.9
METH–AME	4	20	400	502	3.9	5.9
METH–Un Methodist	5	226	710	749	5.8	8.8
Non-denom Chr Chs	2	200	300	300	2.3	3.5
PENT–Assemb of God	5	243	139	372	2.9	4.4
PENT–Ch of God Proph	1	NR	31	39	0.3	0.5
PENT–COGIC	1	0	150	188	1.4	2.2
PENT–Pent Ch of God	2	140	NR	217	1.7	2.5
PENT–Un Pent Ch Intl	1	NR	NR	NR	-	-
PRES–Presb Ch (USA)	1	36	80	100	0.8	1.2
DREW	**68**	**3,445**	**10,425**	**13,284**	**71.8**	**100.0**
ANG/EPIS–Episcopal	1	12	14	16	0.1	0.1
Bahá'í	0	NR	2	2	0.0	0.0
BAPT–Amer Bapt Assn	4	NR	1,055	1,288	7.0	9.7
BAPT–Free Will Bapt	2	NR	184	225	1.2	1.7
BAPT–Natl Mis Bapt Conv	1	35	45	55	0.3	0.4
BAPT–NBC USA	1	200	250	305	1.6	2.3
BAPT–So Bapt Conv	17	1,376	4,696	5,734	31.0	43.2
Catholic	1	NR	NR	242	1.3	1.8
CHR–Chr Chs & Chs Cr	1	NR	20	24	0.1	0.2
CHR–Chs of Christ	2	230	200	270	1.5	2.0
Jehovah's Witness	1	NR	NR	NR	-	-
LDS–Comm of Christ	1	NR	81	81	0.4	0.6
LDS–L-D Saints	1	NR	NR	219	1.2	1.6
METH–AME	9	60	1,050	1,282	6.9	9.7
METH–AME Zion	1	0	100	122	0.7	0.9
METH–Un Methodist	9	377	1,105	1,245	6.7	9.4
Non-denom Chr Chs	4	240	313	353	1.9	2.7
PENT–Assemb of God	3	426	487	722	3.9	5.4
PENT–Ch God (Cleve)	1	28	38	46	0.2	0.3
PENT–COGIC	1	225	250	305	1.6	2.3
PENT–Pent Ch of God	1	70	NR	109	0.6	0.8
PENT–Un Pent Ch Intl	1	NR	NR	NR	-	-

NR–Not Reported   - Represents no adherents reported.   Percentages may not total 100 due to rounding.

Table 3: Religious Congregations by County and Group: 2010

Religious Group	Number of Congrega-tions	Number of Attendees	Number of Communicant, Confirmed, or Full Members	Adherents		
				Number of Adherents	% of Total Pop.	% of Total Adh.
PRES–As Ref Pres Ch	1	NR	32	39	0.2	0.3
PRES–Cumber Presb	1	NR	53	54	0.3	0.4
PRES–Presb Ch (USA)	2	140	404	493	2.7	3.7
Sev Day Adv	1	26	46	53	0.3	0.4
FAULKNER	**144**	**21,422**	**38,435**	**53,936**	**47.6**	**100.0**
ANG/EPIS–Episcopal	1	139	298	358	0.3	0.7
Bahá'í	0	NR	20	20	0.0	0.0
BAPT–Amer Bapt Assn	3	NR	670	829	0.7	1.5
BAPT–Free Will Bapt	6	NR	552	683	0.6	1.3
BAPT–Natl Mis Bapt Conv	1	0	150	186	0.2	0.3
BAPT–Ref Bapt Ch	1	NR	NR	NR	-	-
BAPT–So Bapt Conv	36	6,063	16,158	20,003	17.7	37.1
Catholic	1	NR	NR	5,089	4.5	9.4
Ch of Chr (Hol)	1	NR	NR	NR	-	-
Ch of God Gen Conf	1	NR	70	87	0.1	0.2
Ch of Nazarene	7	886	1,365	1,597	1.4	3.0
CHR–Chr Ch (Disc)	1	45	70	87	0.1	0.2
CHR–Chs of Christ	20	2,252	2,114	2,773	2.4	5.1
Jehovah's Witness	1	NR	NR	NR	-	-
LDS–L-D Saints	3	NR	NR	1,457	1.3	2.7
LUTH–E.L.C.A.	1	45	98	100	0.1	0.2
LUTH–Luth–MO Synod	3	200	288	385	0.3	0.7
METH–AME	1	0	100	124	0.1	0.2
METH–AME Zion	1	0	100	124	0.1	0.2
METH–C.M.E.	1	0	100	124	0.1	0.2
METH–Un Methodist	17	1,571	4,377	5,578	4.9	10.3
METH–Wesleyan	1	65	100	85	0.1	0.2
Muslim Est	1	35	NR	50	0.0	0.1
Non-denom Chr Chs	14	8,305	10,390	10,731	9.5	19.9
PENT–Assemb of God	7	1,205	535	2,056	1.8	3.8
PENT–Ch God (Cleve)	1	77	121	150	0.1	0.3
PENT–COGIC	1	0	150	186	0.2	0.3
PENT–Pent Ch of God	3	210	NR	326	0.3	0.6
PENT–Un Pent Ch Intl	5	NR	NR	NR	-	-
PRES–Presb Ch (USA)	1	197	489	605	0.5	1.1
PRES–Presb Ch Amer	1	25	0	0	0.0	0.0
Salvation Army	1	45	21	29	0.0	0.1
Sev Day Adv	1	57	99	114	0.1	0.2
FRANKLIN	**46**	**1,783**	**5,450**	**7,578**	**41.8**	**100.0**
Bahá'í	0	NR	3	3	0.0	0.0
BAPT–Amer Bapt Assn	5	NR	1,032	1,271	7.0	16.8
BAPT–Free Will Bapt	6	NR	552	680	3.8	9.0
BAPT–So Bapt Conv	6	525	2,278	2,805	15.5	37.0
Catholic	2	NR	NR	710	3.9	9.4
Ch of Nazarene	2	60	116	136	0.8	1.8
CHR–Chr Ch (Disc)	1	40	64	79	0.4	1.0
CHR–Chs of Christ	5	248	220	293	1.6	3.9
Jehovah's Witness	1	NR	NR	NR	-	-
METH–Un Methodist	7	508	936	1,034	5.7	13.6
PENT–Assemb of God	6	276	115	308	1.7	4.1
PENT–Pent Ch of God	1	70	NR	109	0.6	1.4
PENT–Un Pent Ch Intl	1	NR	NR	NR	-	-
PRES–Cumber Presb	1	NR	50	50	0.3	0.7
PRES–Presb Ch (USA)	1	32	43	53	0.3	0.7
Sev Day Adv	1	24	41	47	0.3	0.6
FULTON	**49**	**2,875**	**4,068**	**5,397**	**44.1**	**100.0**
Bahá'í	0	NR	2	2	0.0	0.0
BAPT–Amer Bapt Assn	1	NR	25	30	0.2	0.6
BAPT–Free Will Bapt	1	NR	63	75	0.6	1.4
BAPT–Reg Bapt Gen As	1	NR	NR	NR	-	-
BAPT–So Bapt Conv	10	1,146	2,482	2,951	24.1	54.7
CHR–Chr Ch (Disc)	1	45	60	71	0.6	1.3
CHR–Chs of Christ	17	973	828	1,055	8.6	19.5
Jehovah's Witness	2	NR	NR	NR	-	-
MENN–Amish Undif	1	NR	24	65	0.5	1.2
MENN–Tamp Amish-Menn	1	175	80	175	1.4	3.2
METH–Un Methodist	5	159	270	331	2.7	6.1
PENT–Assemb of God	3	275	144	431	3.5	8.0
PENT–Pent Ch of God	1	70	NR	109	0.9	2.0
PENT–Un Pent Ch Intl	1	NR	NR	NR	-	-

Religious Group	Number of Congrega-tions	Number of Attendees	Number of Communicant, Confirmed, or Full Members	Adherents		
				Number of Adherents	% of Total Pop.	% of Total Adh.
PRES–Cumber Presb	3	NR	34	38	0.3	0.7
Sev Day Adv	1	32	56	64	0.5	1.2
GARLAND	**193**	**18,527**	**37,276**	**51,057**	**53.2**	**100.0**
ANG/EPIS–Anglican NA	2	NR	NR	NR	-	-
ANG/EPIS–Episcopal	2	304	626	921	1.0	1.8
Bahá'í	0	NR	33	33	0.0	0.1
BAPT–Amer Bapt Assn	21	NR	2,635	3,136	3.3	6.1
BAPT–Free Will Bapt	3	NR	276	329	0.3	0.6
BAPT–Natl Mis Bapt Conv	1	0	150	179	0.2	0.4
BAPT–NBC USA	4	205	765	911	0.9	1.8
BAPT–Reg Bapt Gen As	1	NR	NR	NR	-	-
BAPT–So Bapt Conv	44	4,742	12,903	15,358	16.0	30.1
Catholic	3	NR	NR	4,501	4.7	8.8
CGOD–Ch God (Ander)	2	205	NR	205	0.2	0.4
Ch Cr, Scientst	1	NR	NR	NR	-	-
Ch of Nazarene	4	530	837	897	0.9	1.8
CHR–Chr Ch (Disc)	2	90	286	340	0.4	0.7
CHR–Chr Chs & Chs Cr	2	NR	133	158	0.2	0.3
CHR–Chs of Christ	9	983	1,002	1,216	1.3	2.4
Evan Free Ch	1	519	NR	519	0.5	1.0
HINDU–Post Ren	1	NR	NR	77	0.1	0.2
Jehovah's Witness	2	NR	NR	NR	-	-
JUD–Reform	1	31	55	148	0.2	0.3
LDS–Comm of Christ	1	NR	135	135	0.1	0.3
LDS–L-D Saints	1	NR	NR	1,082	1.1	2.1
LUTH–E.L.C.A.	3	325	504	512	0.5	1.0
LUTH–Luth–MO Synod	3	486	653	739	0.8	1.4
LUTH–Wisc Ev Luth Syn	1	31	36	36	0.0	0.1
METH–AME	2	250	600	714	0.7	1.4
METH–AME Zion	1	0	100	119	0.1	0.2
METH–C.M.E.	1	0	100	119	0.1	0.2
METH–Un Methodist	17	2,671	6,613	7,333	7.6	14.4
Non-denom Chr Chs	21	4,469	5,089	5,848	6.1	11.5
ORTHE–Ant Orth of NA	1	25	NR	40	0.0	0.1
ORTHE–Greek Orthodox	1	15	NR	30	0.0	0.1
ORTHE–Serb Orth USA	2	55	NR	321	0.3	0.6
PENT–Assemb of God	6	1,040	731	1,412	1.5	2.8
PENT–Ch God (Cleve)	1	162	163	194	0.2	0.4
PENT–Ch of God Proph	1	NR	37	44	0.0	0.1
PENT–COGIC	4	95	450	536	0.6	1.0
PENT–Intl Pent Holiness	1	55	117	139	0.1	0.3
PENT–Pent Ch of God	1	70	NR	109	0.1	0.2
PENT–Un Pent Ch Intl	3	NR	NR	NR	-	-
PRES–Cumber Presb	1	NR	74	91	0.1	0.2
PRES–Presb Ch (USA)	5	658	1,376	1,638	1.7	3.2
PRES–Presb Ch Amer	1	50	0	0	0.0	0.0
Salvation Army	1	31	96	147	0.2	0.3
Sev Day Adv	4	338	589	677	0.7	1.3
Unit Univ	2	92	112	114	0.1	0.2
Unity Ch	1	NR	NR	NR	-	-
GRANT	**50**	**1,688**	**6,739**	**8,562**	**48.0**	**100.0**
BAPT–Amer Bapt Assn	20	NR	3,283	4,026	22.6	47.0
BAPT–So Bapt Conv	7	652	1,866	2,288	12.8	26.7
Catholic	1	NR	NR	68	0.4	0.8
CHR–Chr Ch (Disc)	1	0	25	31	0.2	0.4
CHR–Chs of Christ	2	158	166	204	1.1	2.4
Grace Gosp Fel	1	NR	NR	NR	-	-
Jehovah's Witness	1	NR	NR	NR	-	-
METH–AME	2	0	250	307	1.7	3.6
METH–Un Methodist	7	396	773	873	4.9	10.2
Non-denom Chr Chs	1	100	150	150	0.8	1.8
PENT–Assemb of God	4	312	201	471	2.6	5.5
PENT–Pent Ch of God	1	70	NR	109	0.6	1.3
PENT–Un Pent Ch Intl	1	NR	NR	NR	-	-
PRES–Cumber Presb	1	NR	25	35	0.2	0.4
GREENE	**100**	**8,863**	**17,784**	**23,179**	**55.1**	**100.0**
ANG/EPIS–Episcopal	1	29	38	38	0.1	0.2
Bahá'í	0	NR	1	1	0.0	0.0
BAPT–Amer Bapt Assn	4	NR	405	503	1.2	2.2
BAPT–Free Will Bapt	2	NR	184	228	0.5	1.0

NR–Not Reported   - Represents no adherents reported.   Percentages may not total 100 due to rounding.

Table 3: Religious Congregations by County and Group: 2010

Religious Group	Number of Congrega-tions	Number of Attendees	Number of Communicant, Confirmed, or Full Members	Adherents: Number of Adherents	Adherents: % of Total Pop.	Adherents: % of Total Adh.
BAPT–So Bapt Conv	36	4,272	11,421	14,182	33.7	61.2
Catholic	1	NR	NR	410	1.0	1.8
CGOD–Ch God (Ander)	1	230	NR	230	0.5	1.0
Ch of Nazarene	3	70	123	155	0.4	0.7
CHR–Chr Chs & Chs Cr	1	NR	90	112	0.3	0.5
CHR–Chs of Christ	19	2,572	2,318	3,162	7.5	13.6
Jehovah's Witness	1	NR	NR	NR	-	-
LDS–L-D Saints	1	NR	NR	222	0.5	1.0
LUTH–Luth–MO Synod	2	185	354	470	1.1	2.0
METH–Un Methodist	14	941	2,193	2,503	5.9	10.8
Non-denom Chr Chs	2	310	310	387	0.9	1.7
PENT–Assemb of God	2	86	56	106	0.3	0.5
PENT–Ch God (Cleve)	2	98	258	320	0.8	1.4
PENT–Ch God Apos Fth	1	NR	NR	NR	-	-
PENT–Pent Ch of God	1	70	NR	109	0.3	0.5
PENT–Un Pent Ch Intl	5	NR	NR	NR	-	-
PRES–Presb Ch (USA)	1	0	33	41	0.1	0.2
HEMPSTEAD	**67**	**2,766**	**8,679**	**11,496**	**50.8**	**100.0**
ANG/EPIS–Episcopal	1	22	28	28	0.1	0.2
Bahá'í	0	NR	1	1	0.0	0.0
BAPT–Amer Bapt Assn	2	NR	170	214	0.9	1.9
BAPT–Ind Bapt Flwsp Intl	1	NR	NR	NR	-	-
BAPT–NBC USA	1	150	500	630	2.8	5.5
BAPT–So Bapt Conv	14	1,064	4,444	5,600	24.8	48.7
Catholic	1	NR	NR	386	1.7	3.4
CGOD–Ch God (Ander)	1	85	NR	85	0.4	0.7
Ch of Nazarene	3	79	122	132	0.6	1.1
CHR–Chr Ch (Disc)	1	0	0	0	0.0	0.0
CHR–Chr Chs & Chs Cr	1	NR	0	0	0.0	0.0
CHR–Chs of Christ	9	613	621	770	3.4	6.7
Jehovah's Witness	1	NR	NR	NR	-	-
LDS–L-D Saints	1	NR	NR	224	1.0	1.9
METH–AME	3	0	300	378	1.7	3.3
METH–C.M.E.	7	0	850	1,071	4.7	9.3
METH–Un Methodist	11	446	1,040	1,156	5.1	10.1
Non-denom Chr Chs	2	100	251	251	1.1	2.2
PENT–Assemb of God	2	137	95	137	0.6	1.2
PENT–Ch of God Proph	1	NR	33	42	0.2	0.4
PENT–COGIC	1	0	150	189	0.8	1.6
PENT–Pent Ch of God	1	70	NR	109	0.5	0.9
PENT–Un Pent Ch Intl	1	NR	NR	NR	-	-
PRES–Presb Ch (USA)	1	0	74	93	0.4	0.8
HOT SPRING	**94**	**3,911**	**12,865**	**15,885**	**48.2**	**100.0**
Bahá'í	0	NR	2	2	0.0	0.0
BAPT–Amer Bapt Assn	30	NR	4,833	5,860	17.8	36.9
BAPT–Free Will Bapt	1	NR	92	112	0.3	0.7
BAPT–Natl Mis Bapt Conv	1	90	160	194	0.6	1.2
BAPT–NBC Amer	1	40	120	146	0.4	0.9
BAPT–NBC USA	3	400	700	849	2.6	5.3
BAPT–So Bapt Conv	13	1,028	3,412	4,137	12.6	26.0
Catholic	1	NR	NR	90	0.3	0.6
Ch of God Gen Conf	1	NR	15	18	0.1	0.1
Ch of Nazarene	1	8	24	24	0.1	0.2
CHR–Chs of Christ	5	235	223	268	0.8	1.7
Jehovah's Witness	1	NR	NR	NR	-	-
LUTH–Luth–MO Synod	1	15	26	27	0.1	0.2
METH–AME	1	100	200	243	0.7	1.5
METH–Un Methodist	12	535	1,259	1,428	4.3	9.0
Non-denom Chr Chs	4	525	800	819	2.5	5.2
PENT–Assemb of God	11	685	487	1,064	3.2	6.7
PENT–Ch God (Cleve)	1	33	79	96	0.3	0.6
PENT–COGIC	1	0	60	73	0.2	0.5
PENT–Un Pent Ch Intl	2	NR	NR	NR	-	-
PRES–Presb Ch (USA)	1	61	102	124	0.4	0.8
Sev Day Adv	2	156	271	311	0.9	2.0
HOWARD	**59**	**3,125**	**6,400**	**8,135**	**59.0**	**100.0**
BAPT–Amer Bapt Assn	2	NR	310	389	2.8	4.8
BAPT–So Bapt Conv	9	773	2,072	2,603	18.9	32.0
Catholic	1	NR	NR	150	1.1	1.8
CGOD–Ch God (Ander)	3	82	NR	82	0.6	1.0

Religious Group	Number of Congrega-tions	Number of Attendees	Number of Communicant, Confirmed, or Full Members	Adherents: Number of Adherents	Adherents: % of Total Pop.	Adherents: % of Total Adh.
CHR–Chr Chs & Chs Cr	1	NR	65	82	0.6	1.0
CHR–Chs of Christ	12	1,003	1,196	1,428	10.4	17.6
Jehovah's Witness	2	NR	NR	NR	-	-
LDS–Comm of Christ	1	NR	81	81	0.6	1.0
MENN–Tamp Amish-Menn	1	189	113	189	1.4	2.3
METH–AME	1	0	150	188	1.4	2.3
METH–C.M.E.	8	75	900	1,131	8.2	13.9
METH–Un Methodist	8	288	717	794	5.8	9.8
Non-denom Chr Chs	3	270	370	388	2.8	4.8
PENT–Assemb of God	2	151	121	249	1.8	3.1
PENT–COGIC	2	215	215	270	2.0	3.3
PENT–Intl Pent Holiness	1	65	65	82	0.6	1.0
PENT–Un Pent Ch Intl	1	NR	NR	NR	-	-
Sev Day Adv	1	14	25	29	0.2	0.4
INDEPENDENCE	**107**	**6,939**	**16,323**	**21,239**	**58.0**	**100.0**
ANG/EPIS–Episcopal	1	126	218	239	0.7	1.1
Bahá'í	0	NR	6	6	0.0	0.0
BAPT–Amer Bapt Assn	14	NR	1,488	1,832	5.0	8.6
BAPT–Free Will Bapt	8	NR	736	906	2.5	4.3
BAPT–Natl Mis Bapt Conv	1	0	150	185	0.5	0.9
BAPT–So Bapt Conv	25	2,656	7,623	9,386	25.6	44.2
Catholic	1	NR	NR	350	1.0	1.6
Ch Cr, Scientst	1	NR	NR	NR	-	-
Ch of Nazarene	1	82	219	219	0.6	1.0
CHR–Chs of Christ	14	1,323	1,340	1,698	4.6	8.0
Jehovah's Witness	1	NR	NR	NR	-	-
LDS–L-D Saints	1	NR	NR	360	1.0	1.7
LUTH–Luth–MO Synod	1	51	93	124	0.3	0.6
METH–AME	1	0	100	123	0.3	0.6
METH–Un Methodist	14	719	2,290	2,504	6.8	11.8
Non-denom Chr Chs	6	970	1,280	1,362	3.7	6.4
PENT–Assemb of God	7	682	287	1,091	3.0	5.1
PENT–Ch God (Cleve)	1	78	57	70	0.2	0.3
PENT–Ch of God Proph	1	NR	16	20	0.1	0.1
PENT–Pent Ch of God	2	140	NR	217	0.6	1.0
PENT–Un Pent Ch Intl	2	NR	NR	NR	-	-
PRES–Cumber Presb	2	NR	113	178	0.5	0.8
PRES–Presb Ch (USA)	1	50	199	245	0.7	1.2
Sev Day Adv	1	62	108	124	0.3	0.6
IZARD	**61**	**2,129**	**5,396**	**6,748**	**49.3**	**100.0**
ANG/EPIS–Episcopal	1	12	14	15	0.1	0.2
Bahá'í	0	NR	11	11	0.1	0.2
BAPT–Amer Bapt Assn	7	NR	550	643	4.7	9.5
BAPT–Free Will Bapt	2	NR	184	215	1.6	3.2
BAPT–Natl Mis Bapt Conv	1	35	150	175	1.3	2.6
BAPT–So Bapt Conv	14	1,091	3,063	3,580	26.1	53.1
Catholic	1	NR	NR	125	0.9	1.9
Ch of Nazarene	1	15	35	35	0.3	0.5
CHR–Chs of Christ	9	313	235	346	2.5	5.1
Jehovah's Witness	1	NR	NR	NR	-	-
LUTH–Luth–MO Synod	1	77	95	102	0.7	1.5
MENN–Mennonite USA	1	28	40	47	0.3	0.7
METH–Un Methodist	8	289	528	684	5.0	10.1
PENT–Assemb of God	5	172	62	256	1.9	3.8
PENT–Ch God (Cleve)	1	30	37	43	0.3	0.6
PENT–Un Pent Ch Intl	1	NR	NR	NR	-	-
PRES–Cumber Presb	6	NR	319	386	2.8	5.7
PRES–Presb Ch (USA)	1	67	73	85	0.6	1.3
JACKSON	**73**	**3,449**	**8,134**	**10,150**	**56.4**	**100.0**
ANG/EPIS–Episcopal	1	53	125	125	0.7	1.2
BAPT–Amer Bapt Assn	5	NR	600	714	4.0	7.0
BAPT–Free Will Bapt	4	NR	368	438	2.4	4.3
BAPT–So Bapt Conv	15	962	3,828	4,556	25.3	44.9
Catholic	1	NR	NR	50	0.3	0.5
Ch of Nazarene	1	5	15	16	0.1	0.2
CHR–Chr Ch (Disc)	1	0	72	86	0.5	0.8
CHR–Chs of Christ	22	1,652	1,685	2,069	11.5	20.4
Jehovah's Witness	1	NR	NR	NR	-	-
METH–AME	3	0	300	357	2.0	3.5
METH–Un Methodist	7	237	642	662	3.7	6.5

NR–Not Reported - Represents no adherents reported. Percentages may not total 100 due to rounding.

Table 3: Religious Congregations by County and Group: 2010

Religious Group	Number of Congrega-tions	Number of Attendees	Number of Communicant, Confirmed, or Full Members	Adherents: Number of Adherents	Adherents: % of Total Pop.	Adherents: % of Total Adh.
PENT–Assemb of God	5	250	143	327	1.8	3.2
PENT–Ch God (Cleve)	1	20	95	113	0.6	1.1
PENT–COGIC	1	0	150	179	1.0	1.8
PENT–Pent Ch of God	3	210	NR	326	1.8	3.2
PENT–Un Pent Ch Intl	1	NR	NR	NR	-	-
PRES–Presb Ch (USA)	1	60	111	132	0.7	1.3
JEFFERSON	**188**	**12,605**	**35,489**	**46,297**	**59.8**	**100.0**
ANG/EPIS–Episcopal	2	158	511	511	0.7	1.1
Bahá'í	0	NR	26	26	0.0	0.1
BAPT–Amer Bapt Assn	18	NR	3,470	4,246	5.5	9.2
BAPT–Free Will Bapt	1	NR	92	113	0.1	0.2
BAPT–Ind Bapt Flwsp Intl	1	NR	NR	NR	-	-
BAPT–Natl Mis Bapt Conv	8	70	1,043	1,276	1.6	2.8
BAPT–NBC USA	22	2,455	5,170	6,327	8.2	13.7
BAPT–So Bapt Conv	29	3,652	12,849	15,724	20.3	34.0
Catholic	3	NR	NR	1,121	1.4	2.4
CGOD–Ch God (Ander)	1	0	NR	0	0.0	0.0
Ch Cr, Scientst	1	NR	NR	NR	-	-
Ch of Chr (Hol)	1	NR	NR	NR	-	-
Ch of Nazarene	1	15	96	96	0.1	0.2
CHR–Chr Ch (Disc)	2	67	139	170	0.2	0.4
CHR–Chr Chs & Chs Cr	1	NR	50	61	0.1	0.1
CHR–Chs of Christ	9	671	741	922	1.2	2.0
Jehovah's Witness	1	NR	NR	NR	-	-
JUD–Reform	1	10	17	46	0.1	0.1
LDS–L-D Saints	1	NR	NR	595	0.8	1.3
LUTH–Luth–MO Synod	1	83	161	195	0.3	0.4
MENN–CG in Cr (Menn)	1	NR	51	62	0.1	0.1
METH–AME	13	250	1,825	2,233	2.9	4.8
METH–AME Zion	1	0	100	122	0.2	0.3
METH–C.M.E.	2	0	250	306	0.4	0.7
METH–Un Methodist	15	1,240	3,315	4,352	5.6	9.4
Muslim Est	1	134	NR	308	0.4	0.7
Non-denom Chr Chs	17	1,665	2,650	2,710	3.5	5.9
PENT–Assemb of God	6	797	659	1,233	1.6	2.7
PENT–Ch God (Cleve)	3	137	328	401	0.5	0.9
PENT–COGIC	7	300	875	1,071	1.4	2.3
PENT–Pent Ch of God	5	350	NR	544	0.7	1.2
PENT–Un Pent Ch Intl	4	NR	NR	NR	-	-
PRES–Cumber Presb	2	NR	27	141	0.2	0.3
PRES–Presb Ch (USA)	3	272	693	848	1.1	1.8
Salvation Army	1	117	70	214	0.3	0.5
Sev Day Adv	3	162	281	323	0.4	0.7
JOHNSON	**60**	**3,869**	**8,700**	**12,182**	**47.7**	**100.0**
Bahá'í	0	NR	4	4	0.0	0.0
BAPT–Amer Bapt Assn	2	NR	460	570	2.2	4.7
BAPT–Free Will Bapt	2	NR	184	228	0.9	1.9
BAPT–So Bapt Conv	17	1,588	5,191	6,430	25.2	52.8
Catholic	1	NR	NR	618	2.4	5.1
Ch of Nazarene	1	55	118	123	0.5	1.0
CHR–Chs of Christ	7	511	612	722	2.8	5.9
Jehovah's Witness	1	NR	NR	NR	-	-
LDS–L-D Saints	1	NR	NR	573	2.2	4.7
LUTH–Luth–MO Synod	1	73	160	192	0.8	1.6
MENN–Tamp Amish-Menn	1	124	70	124	0.5	1.0
METH–Un Methodist	5	352	694	706	2.8	5.8
METH–Wesleyan	1	50	146	65	0.3	0.5
Muslim Est	1	134	NR	308	1.2	2.5
Non-denom Chr Chs	2	200	300	300	1.2	2.5
PENT–Assemb of God	9	540	463	752	2.9	6.2
PENT–Int Foursq Gos	1	15	17	21	0.1	0.2
PENT–Pent Ch of God	1	70	NR	109	0.4	0.9
PENT–Un Pent Ch Intl	2	NR	NR	NR	-	-
PRES–Presb Ch (USA)	2	93	169	209	0.8	1.7
Sev Day Adv	2	64	112	128	0.5	1.1
LAFAYETTE	**23**	**860**	**2,678**	**3,367**	**44.0**	**100.0**
Bahá'í	0	NR	2	2	0.0	0.1
BAPT–Amer Bapt Assn	1	NR	85	103	1.3	3.1
BAPT–NBC USA	1	5	10	12	0.2	0.4
BAPT–So Bapt Conv	6	389	1,587	1,924	25.2	57.1
Ch of Nazarene	1	0	0	0	0.0	0.0
CHR–Chs of Christ	5	224	225	327	4.3	9.7
METH–AME	1	0	100	121	1.6	3.6
METH–C.M.E.	1	0	150	182	2.4	5.4
METH–Un Methodist	4	161	328	373	4.9	11.1
PENT–Assemb of God	2	81	41	141	1.8	4.2
PENT–COGIC	1	0	150	182	2.4	5.4
LAWRENCE	**72**	**3,092**	**7,047**	**9,202**	**52.8**	**100.0**
Bahá'í	0	NR	1	1	0.0	0.0
BAPT–Amer Bapt Assn	7	NR	848	1,027	5.9	11.2
BAPT–Free Will Bapt	7	NR	644	780	4.5	8.5
BAPT–So Bapt Conv	19	945	3,391	4,107	23.6	44.6
Catholic	1	NR	NR	85	0.5	0.9
CHR–Chs of Christ	13	1,305	976	1,383	7.9	15.0
Jehovah's Witness	1	NR	NR	NR	-	-
METH–Un Methodist	11	360	817	930	5.3	10.1
Non-denom Chr Chs	1	150	150	188	1.1	2.0
PENT–Assemb of God	5	217	131	484	2.8	5.3
PENT–Pent Ch of God	1	70	NR	109	0.6	1.2
PENT–Un Pent Ch Intl	4	NR	NR	NR	-	-
PRES–Presb Ch (USA)	1	45	89	108	0.6	1.2
REF–Comm Ref Evan	1	NR	NR	NR	-	-
LEE	**34**	**840**	**2,941**	**3,719**	**35.7**	**100.0**
ANG/EPIS–Episcopal	1	22	40	51	0.5	1.4
Bahá'í	0	NR	1	1	0.0	0.0
BAPT–Amer Bapt Assn	5	NR	390	462	4.4	12.4
BAPT–So Bapt Conv	3	194	949	1,125	10.8	30.3
Catholic	1	NR	NR	54	0.5	1.5
CHR–Chr Chs & Chs Cr	1	NR	50	59	0.6	1.6
CHR–Chs of Christ	5	209	192	255	2.4	6.9
Jehovah's Witness	1	NR	NR	NR	-	-
METH–AME	2	0	250	296	2.8	8.0
METH–Un Methodist	4	87	314	315	3.0	8.5
Non-denom Chr Chs	2	220	270	300	2.9	8.1
PENT–Assemb of God	1	75	50	285	2.7	7.7
PENT–Ch God (Cleve)	2	18	57	68	0.7	1.8
PENT–Ch of God Proph	1	NR	54	64	0.6	1.7
PENT–COGIC	2	0	300	356	3.4	9.6
PENT–Un Pent Ch Intl	2	NR	NR	NR	-	-
PRES–Presb Ch (USA)	1	15	24	28	0.3	0.8
LINCOLN	**40**	**1,065**	**4,261**	**5,145**	**36.4**	**100.0**
Bahá'í	0	NR	5	5	0.0	0.1
BAPT–Amer Bapt Assn	8	NR	745	875	6.2	17.0
BAPT–Free Will Bapt	3	NR	276	324	2.3	6.3
BAPT–Natl Mis Bapt Conv	2	0	300	352	2.5	6.8
BAPT–NBC USA	1	0	150	176	1.2	3.4
BAPT–So Bapt Conv	7	313	1,518	1,782	12.6	34.6
Catholic	2	NR	NR	105	0.7	2.0
CHR–Chr Chs & Chs Cr	1	NR	79	93	0.7	1.8
CHR–Chs of Christ	3	135	126	164	1.2	3.2
METH–AME	1	0	100	117	0.8	2.3
METH–Un Methodist	4	205	397	451	3.2	8.8
Non-denom Chr Chs	2	225	275	306	2.2	5.9
PENT–Assemb of God	3	187	134	212	1.5	4.1
PENT–COGIC	1	0	150	176	1.2	3.4
PENT–Un Pent Ch Intl	1	NR	NR	NR	-	-
PRES–Cumber Presb	1	NR	6	7	0.0	0.1
LITTLE RIVER	**51**	**2,785**	**6,420**	**7,838**	**59.5**	**100.0**
ANG/EPIS–Episcopal	1	15	43	43	0.3	0.5
Bahá'í	0	NR	2	2	0.0	0.0
BAPT–Amer Bapt Assn	2	NR	105	128	1.0	1.6
BAPT–NBC USA	1	80	120	146	1.1	1.9
BAPT–So Bapt Conv	12	1,006	3,371	4,113	31.2	52.5
Catholic	2	NR	NR	86	0.7	1.1
Ch of Nazarene	1	53	126	146	1.1	1.9
CHR–Chs of Christ	4	331	344	449	3.4	5.7
Jehovah's Witness	2	NR	NR	NR	-	-
LDS–Comm of Christ	1	NR	81	81	0.6	1.0

NR–Not Reported   - Represents no adherents reported.   Percentages may not total 100 due to rounding.

Table 3: Religious Congregations by County and Group: 2010

Religious Group	Number of Congrega-tions	Number of Attendees	Number of Communicant, Confirmed, or Full Members	Adherents: Number of Adherents	Adherents: % of Total Pop.	Adherents: % of Total Adh.
METH–AME	2	0	250	305	2.3	3.9
METH–C.M.E.	2	35	135	165	1.3	2.1
METH–Un Methodist	6	285	632	685	5.2	8.7
Non-denom Chr Chs	8	745	1,080	1,088	8.3	13.9
PENT–Assemb of God	2	165	106	238	1.8	3.0
PENT–COGIC	1	0	0	0	0.0	0.0
PENT–Full Gosp Bapt	1	NR	NR	NR	-	-
PENT–Pent Ch of God	1	70	NR	109	0.8	1.4
PRES–Cumber Presb	2	NR	25	54	0.4	0.7
LOGAN	**95**	**4,401**	**12,152**	**17,807**	**79.7**	**100.0**
Bahá'í	0	NR	6	6	0.0	0.0
BAPT–Amer Bapt Assn	4	NR	310	380	1.7	2.1
BAPT–Free Will Bapt	4	NR	368	451	2.0	2.5
BAPT–So Bapt Conv	25	1,989	8,286	10,144	45.4	57.0
Catholic	8	NR	NR	1,507	6.7	8.5
CGOD–Ches God-Gen Con	1	9	0	0	0.0	0.0
Ch of God Gen Conf	1	NR	10	12	0.1	0.1
Chr & Miss Al	1	60	74	74	0.3	0.4
CHR–Chr Ch (Disc)	1	56	112	137	0.6	0.8
CHR–Chs of Christ	5	287	295	368	1.6	2.1
Jehovah's Witness	3	NR	NR	NR	-	-
LUTH–E.L.C.A.	1	41	37	114	0.5	0.6
METH–Un Methodist	6	262	971	1,084	4.8	6.1
Non-denom Chr Chs	4	332	432	465	2.1	2.6
PENT–Assemb of God	12	951	481	1,424	6.4	8.0
PENT–Ch God (Cleve)	1	15	92	113	0.5	0.6
PENT–COGIC	2	0	300	367	1.6	2.1
PENT–Intl Pent Holiness	1	33	19	23	0.1	0.1
PENT–Pent Ch of God	5	350	NR	544	2.4	3.1
PENT–Un Pent Ch Intl	2	NR	NR	NR	-	-
PRES–Cumber Presb	7	NR	332	563	2.5	3.2
Sev Day Adv	1	16	27	31	0.1	0.2
LONOKE	**114**	**9,526**	**22,543**	**30,607**	**44.8**	**100.0**
Bahá'í	0	NR	62	62	0.1	0.2
BAPT–Amer Bapt Assn	12	NR	1,465	1,863	2.7	6.1
BAPT–Free Will Bapt	1	NR	92	117	0.2	0.4
BAPT–NBC Amer	1	25	25	32	0.0	0.1
BAPT–NBC USA	1	0	150	191	0.3	0.6
BAPT–Ref Bapt Ch	1	NR	NR	NR	-	-
BAPT–So Bapt Conv	34	4,288	13,103	16,665	24.4	54.4
Calv Chpl	1	NR	NR	NR	-	-
Catholic	2	NR	NR	155	0.2	0.5
Ch of Nazarene	1	49	90	159	0.2	0.5
CHR–Chs of Christ	10	954	1,084	1,510	2.2	4.9
Jehovah's Witness	1	NR	NR	NR	-	-
LDS–L-D Saints	2	NR	NR	924	1.4	3.0
LUTH–Luth–MO Synod	1	188	336	459	0.7	1.5
METH–AME	1	0	100	127	0.2	0.4
METH–Un Methodist	16	1,287	3,370	3,883	5.7	12.7
Muslim Est	1	134	NR	308	0.5	1.0
Non-denom Chr Chs	12	1,692	2,020	2,247	3.3	7.3
PENT–Assemb of God	4	456	234	729	1.1	2.4
PENT–Ch of God Proph	1	NR	69	88	0.1	0.3
PENT–COGIC	1	0	150	191	0.3	0.6
PENT–Pent Ch of God	6	420	NR	652	1.0	2.1
PENT–Un Pent Ch Intl	2	NR	NR	NR	-	-
PRES–Evan Presby Ch	1	NR	70	89	0.1	0.3
PRES–Presb Ch (USA)	1	33	123	156	0.2	0.5
MADISON	**41**	**2,104**	**4,096**	**5,874**	**37.4**	**100.0**
Bahá'í	0	NR	6	6	0.0	0.1
BAPT–Amer Bapt Assn	1	NR	60	73	0.5	1.2
BAPT–Free Will Bapt	3	NR	276	338	2.2	5.8
BAPT–So Bapt Conv	6	652	2,199	2,690	17.1	45.8
Catholic	1	NR	NR	150	1.0	2.6
CHR–Chs of Christ	13	664	669	875	5.6	14.9
Christian Un	1	NR	NR	NR	-	-
Jehovah's Witness	1	NR	NR	NR	-	-
LDS–L-D Saints	1	NR	NR	252	1.6	4.3
MENN–Beachy Amish-Menn	1	105	61	105	0.7	1.8
METH–Un Methodist	3	132	256	343	2.2	5.8
Non-denom Chr Chs	3	215	265	307	2.0	5.2
PENT–Assemb of God	4	260	116	509	3.2	8.7
PENT–Un Pent Ch Intl	1	NR	NR	NR	-	-
PRES–Presb Ch (USA)	1	46	135	165	1.0	2.8
Sev Day Adv	1	30	53	61	0.4	1.0
MARION	**40**	**2,449**	**5,060**	**6,353**	**38.1**	**100.0**
Bahá'í	0	NR	3	3	0.0	0.0
BAPT–Amer Bapt Assn	1	NR	85	98	0.6	1.5
BAPT–So Bapt Conv	10	1,035	2,857	3,293	19.8	51.8
Catholic	1	NR	NR	340	2.0	5.4
CHR–Chr Chs & Chs Cr	2	NR	340	392	2.4	6.2
CHR–Chs of Christ	7	337	327	389	2.3	6.1
Jehovah's Witness	1	NR	NR	NR	-	-
LUTH–E.L.C.A.	1	97	192	207	1.2	3.3
METH–Un Methodist	5	206	506	535	3.2	8.4
Non-denom Chr Chs	3	420	420	550	3.3	8.7
PENT–Assemb of God	2	97	63	129	0.8	2.0
PENT–Ch God (Cleve)	1	48	84	97	0.6	1.5
PENT–Ch God Apos Fth	1	NR	NR	NR	-	-
PENT–Pent Ch of God	1	70	NR	109	0.7	1.7
PENT–Un Pent Ch Intl	1	NR	NR	NR	-	-
PRES–Presb Ch (USA)	2	121	152	175	1.1	2.8
Sev Day Adv	1	18	31	36	0.2	0.6
MILLER	**94**	**7,459**	**20,200**	**26,253**	**60.4**	**100.0**
Bahá'í	0	NR	2	2	0.0	0.0
BAPT–Amer Bapt Assn	3	NR	830	1,025	2.4	3.9
BAPT–NBC USA	3	510	1,000	1,235	2.8	4.7
BAPT–Ref Bapt Ch	1	NR	NR	NR	-	-
BAPT–S-D Baptist Gen Con	1	NR	88	109	0.3	0.4
BAPT–So Bapt Conv	26	3,118	11,905	14,706	33.8	56.0
Catholic	1	NR	NR	1,404	3.2	5.3
CGOD–Ch God (Ander)	2	27	NR	27	0.1	0.1
Ch of Nazarene	1	71	249	249	0.6	0.9
CHR–Chs of Christ	10	713	766	855	2.0	3.3
Jehovah's Witness	1	NR	NR	NR	-	-
METH–AME	1	0	100	124	0.3	0.5
METH–C.M.E.	4	0	400	494	1.1	1.9
METH–Cong Meth	1	NR	12	15	0.0	0.1
METH–Un Methodist	10	823	2,273	2,558	5.9	9.7
Non-denom Chr Chs	12	1,250	1,850	1,888	4.3	7.2
PENT–Assemb of God	6	558	315	621	1.4	2.4
PENT–COGIC	1	0	150	185	0.4	0.7
PENT–Full Gosp Bapt	2	NR	NR	NR	-	-
PENT–Pent Ch of God	4	280	NR	435	1.0	1.7
PENT–Un Pent Ch Intl	2	NR	NR	NR	-	-
PRES–Presb Ch (USA)	1	109	260	321	0.7	1.2
REF–Comm Ref Evan	1	NR	NR	NR	-	-
MISSISSIPPI	**131**	**7,795**	**22,487**	**31,145**	**67.0**	**100.0**
ANG/EPIS–Episcopal	2	38	73	73	0.2	0.2
Bahá'í	0	NR	8	8	0.0	0.0
BAPT–Natl Mis Bapt Conv	2	185	350	448	1.0	1.4
BAPT–NBC USA	4	375	800	1,024	2.2	3.3
BAPT–So Bapt Conv	40	2,885	14,632	18,722	40.3	60.1
Catholic	2	NR	NR	500	1.1	1.6
Ch of Nazarene	2	31	89	89	0.2	0.3
CHR–Chr Ch (Disc)	2	75	296	379	0.8	1.2
CHR–Chr Chs & Chs Cr	1	NR	150	192	0.4	0.6
CHR–Chs of Christ	16	938	959	1,131	2.4	3.6
Jehovah's Witness	1	NR	NR	NR	-	-
LDS–L-D Saints	1	NR	NR	384	0.8	1.2
LUTH–Luth–MO Synod	1	40	75	90	0.2	0.3
METH–AME	3	0	300	384	0.8	1.2
METH–C.M.E.	2	0	165	211	0.5	0.7
METH–Un Methodist	10	511	1,284	1,402	3.0	4.5
Muslim Est	1	134	NR	308	0.7	1.0
Non-denom Chr Chs	9	685	985	1,018	2.2	3.3
PENT–Assemb of God	7	515	389	1,767	3.8	5.7
PENT–Ch God (Cleve)	6	559	943	1,207	2.6	3.9
PENT–Ch of God Proph	1	NR	10	13	0.0	0.0
PENT–COGIC	5	330	750	960	2.1	3.1

NR–Not Reported - Represents no adherents reported. Percentages may not total 100 due to rounding.

Table 3: Religious Congregations by County and Group: 2010

Religious Group	Number of Congregations	Number of Attendees	Number of Communicant, Confirmed, or Full Members	Adherents: Number of Adherents	Adherents: % of Total Pop.	Adherents: % of Total Adh.
PENT–Intl Pent Holiness	1	48	40	51	0.1	0.2
PENT–Pent Ch of God	5	350	NR	544	1.2	1.7
PENT–Un Pent Ch Intl	5	NR	NR	NR	-	-
PRES–Presb Ch (USA)	1	80	171	219	0.5	0.7
PRES–Presb Ch Amer	1	16	18	21	0.0	0.1
MONROE	**38**	**1,321**	**4,678**	**5,668**	**69.6**	**100.0**
BAPT–Amer Bapt Assn	5	NR	565	676	8.3	11.9
BAPT–So Bapt Conv	6	449	2,015	2,412	29.6	42.6
Catholic	1	NR	NR	65	0.8	1.1
CHR–Chs of Christ	4	205	241	339	4.2	6.0
LUTH–Luth–MO Synod	1	20	72	86	1.1	1.5
METH–AME	4	0	450	539	6.6	9.5
METH–C.M.E.	2	0	250	299	3.7	5.3
METH–Un Methodist	6	239	617	658	8.1	11.6
Non-denom Chr Chs	1	150	225	225	2.8	4.0
PENT–Assemb of God	2	138	97	200	2.5	3.5
PENT–Ch of God Proph	1	NR	20	24	0.3	0.4
PENT–COGIC	1	45	0	0	0.0	0.0
PRES–Presb Ch (USA)	2	32	62	74	0.9	1.3
PRES–Presb Ch Amer	1	35	49	54	0.7	1.0
Sev Day Adv	1	8	15	17	0.2	0.3
MONTGOMERY	**31**	**1,530**	**3,416**	**4,163**	**43.9**	**100.0**
BAPT–Amer Bapt Assn	2	NR	170	202	2.1	4.9
BAPT–Natl Mis Bapt Conv	1	0	150	178	1.9	4.3
BAPT–So Bapt Conv	14	669	2,013	2,392	25.2	57.5
Catholic	1	NR	NR	100	1.1	2.4
Ch of Nazarene	1	118	226	240	2.5	5.8
CHR–Chs of Christ	3	150	120	160	1.7	3.8
METH–Un Methodist	3	162	312	321	3.4	7.7
Non-denom Chr Chs	1	300	350	375	4.0	9.0
PENT–Assemb of God	2	87	14	124	1.3	3.0
PENT–Un Pent Ch Intl	1	NR	NR	NR	-	-
PRES–Presb Ch (USA)	1	24	27	32	0.3	0.8
Sev Day Adv	1	20	34	39	0.4	0.9
NEVADA	**35**	**1,019**	**3,276**	**4,045**	**45.0**	**100.0**
BAPT–Amer Bapt Assn	2	NR	170	208	2.3	5.1
BAPT–So Bapt Conv	3	140	760	931	10.3	23.0
CGOD–Ch God (Ander)	1	25	NR	25	0.3	0.6
Ch of Nazarene	2	95	105	123	1.4	3.0
CHR–Chs of Christ	6	316	349	424	4.7	10.5
METH–AME	10	0	1,100	1,347	15.0	33.3
METH–C.M.E.	1	0	100	122	1.4	3.0
METH–Un Methodist	5	246	478	558	6.2	13.8
Non-denom Chr Chs	1	100	150	150	1.7	3.7
PENT–Assemb of God	1	82	46	135	1.5	3.3
PENT–Un Pent Ch Intl	2	NR	NR	NR	-	-
PRES–Presb Ch (USA)	1	15	18	22	0.2	0.5
NEWTON	**29**	**1,021**	**1,659**	**2,244**	**26.9**	**100.0**
Bahá'í	0	NR	2	2	0.0	0.1
BAPT–Amer Bapt Assn	1	NR	150	179	2.1	8.0
BAPT–Free Will Bapt	1	NR	92	109	1.3	4.9
BAPT–So Bapt Conv	9	481	1,000	1,190	14.3	53.0
Ch God (7th Day)	1	NR	NR	NR	-	-
CHR–Chs of Christ	6	203	193	241	2.9	10.7
Christian Un	1	NR	NR	NR	-	-
HINDU–Post Ren	1	NR	NR	25	0.3	1.1
Jehovah's Witness	2	NR	NR	NR	-	-
METH–Un Methodist	1	32	80	80	1.0	3.6
Non-denom Chr Chs	1	25	30	31	0.4	1.4
PENT–Assemb of God	4	280	112	387	4.6	17.2
PENT–Un Pent Ch Intl	1	NR	NR	NR	-	-
OUACHITA	**131**	**6,450**	**19,212**	**23,963**	**91.7**	**100.0**
ANG/EPIS–Episcopal	1	19	33	33	0.1	0.1
Bahá'í	0	NR	2	2	0.0	0.0
BAPT–Amer Bapt Assn	7	NR	740	903	3.5	3.8
BAPT–Natl Mis Bapt Conv	3	0	300	366	1.4	1.5
BAPT–NBC USA	9	554	1,839	2,245	8.6	9.4

Religious Group	Number of Congregations	Number of Attendees	Number of Communicant, Confirmed, or Full Members	Adherents: Number of Adherents	Adherents: % of Total Pop.	Adherents: % of Total Adh.
BAPT–So Bapt Conv	23	2,113	7,363	8,989	34.4	37.5
Catholic	1	NR	NR	100	0.4	0.4
CGOD–Ch God (Ander)	1	0	NR	0	0.0	0.0
Ch of Nazarene	1	26	60	60	0.2	0.3
CHR–Chr Ch (Disc)	1	0	26	32	0.1	0.1
CHR–Chs of Christ	8	542	582	750	2.9	3.1
Jehovah's Witness	1	NR	NR	NR	-	-
LDS–L-D Saints	1	NR	NR	171	0.7	0.7
METH–AME	22	0	2,800	3,418	13.1	14.3
METH–C.M.E.	1	0	150	183	0.7	0.8
METH–Un Methodist	17	734	1,643	1,873	7.2	7.8
Non-denom Chr Chs	10	980	1,425	1,444	5.5	6.0
PENT–Assemb of God	8	864	331	989	3.8	4.1
PENT–COGIC	7	520	1,600	1,953	7.5	8.2
PENT–Un Pent Ch Intl	2	NR	NR	NR	-	-
PRES–Cumber Presb	4	NR	143	240	0.9	1.0
PRES–Presb Ch (USA)	2	80	144	176	0.7	0.7
Sev Day Adv	1	18	31	36	0.1	0.2
PERRY	**24**	**1,086**	**2,756**	**3,744**	**35.8**	**100.0**
BAPT–Free Will Bapt	2	NR	184	221	2.1	5.9
BAPT–So Bapt Conv	8	586	2,022	2,431	23.3	64.9
Catholic	1	NR	NR	250	2.4	6.7
Ch of Nazarene	1	22	43	43	0.4	1.1
CHR–Chs of Christ	4	170	165	216	2.1	5.8
Jehovah's Witness	1	NR	NR	NR	-	-
METH–AME	1	0	100	120	1.1	3.2
METH–Un Methodist	1	19	27	50	0.5	1.3
PENT–Assemb of God	4	289	215	413	4.0	11.0
PENT–Un Pent Ch Intl	1	NR	NR	NR	-	-
PHILLIPS	**59**	**1,955**	**8,528**	**11,039**	**50.7**	**100.0**
ANG/EPIS–Episcopal	1	53	298	298	1.4	2.7
Bahá'í	0	NR	1	1	0.0	0.0
BAPT–Amer Bapt Assn	1	NR	85	108	0.5	1.0
BAPT–Natl Mis Bapt Conv	4	50	558	708	3.3	6.4
BAPT–NBC USA	3	0	800	1,015	4.7	9.2
BAPT–So Bapt Conv	12	818	3,778	4,792	22.0	43.4
Catholic	1	NR	NR	216	1.0	2.0
Ch of Nazarene	1	16	9	19	0.1	0.2
CHR–Chr Chs & Chs Cr	1	NR	59	75	0.3	0.7
CHR–Chs of Christ	5	431	455	640	2.9	5.8
Jehovah's Witness	1	NR	NR	NR	-	-
LDS–L-D Saints	1	NR	NR	166	0.8	1.5
METH–AME	5	0	550	698	3.2	6.3
METH–C.M.E.	2	0	250	317	1.5	2.9
METH–Un Methodist	5	229	605	647	3.0	5.9
Non-denom Chr Chs	2	200	250	275	1.3	2.5
PENT–Assemb of God	2	32	18	37	0.2	0.3
PENT–Ch God (Cleve)	1	9	91	115	0.5	1.0
PENT–Ch of God Proph	2	NR	68	86	0.4	0.8
PENT–COGIC	4	75	549	696	3.2	6.3
PENT–Un Pent Ch Intl	2	NR	NR	NR	-	-
PRES–Presb Ch (USA)	2	30	84	107	0.5	1.0
Sev Day Adv	1	12	20	23	0.1	0.2
PIKE	**57**	**1,978**	**4,863**	**6,601**	**58.5**	**100.0**
BAPT–Amer Bapt Assn	11	NR	1,115	1,367	12.1	20.7
BAPT–Free Will Bapt	4	NR	368	451	4.0	6.8
BAPT–So Bapt Conv	7	408	1,193	1,462	12.9	22.1
Catholic	1	NR	NR	250	2.2	3.8
Ch of Nazarene	1	65	45	65	0.6	1.0
CHR–Chr Chs & Chs Cr	1	NR	300	368	3.3	5.6
CHR–Chs of Christ	12	780	788	1,039	9.2	15.7
Jehovah's Witness	1	NR	NR	NR	-	-
LDS–L-D Saints	1	NR	NR	171	1.5	2.6
METH–Un Methodist	8	216	443	456	4.0	6.9
PENT–Assemb of God	5	330	324	408	3.6	6.2
PENT–Ch God (Cleve)	1	0	69	85	0.8	1.3
PENT–COGIC	1	0	150	184	1.6	2.8
PENT–Pent Ch of God	2	140	NR	217	1.9	3.3
Sev Day Adv	1	39	68	78	0.7	1.2

NR–Not Reported   - Represents no adherents reported.   Percentages may not total 100 due to rounding.

Table 3: Religious Congregations by County and Group: 2010

Religious Group	Number of Congrega-tions	Number of Attendees	Number of Communicant, Confirmed, or Full Members	Adherents: Number of Adherents	Adherents: % of Total Pop.	Adherents: % of Total Adh.
POINSETT	**89**	**4,521**	**13,174**	**16,482**	**67.0**	**100.0**
BAPT–Amer Bapt Assn	1	NR	60	74	0.3	0.4
BAPT–So Bapt Conv	34	2,100	9,066	11,142	45.3	67.6
Catholic	2	NR	NR	209	0.9	1.3
CHR–Chr Ch (Disc)	2	20	142	175	0.7	1.1
CHR–Chr Chs & Chs Cr	1	NR	200	246	1.0	1.5
CHR–Chs of Christ	11	656	759	915	3.7	5.6
Jehovah's Witness	1	NR	NR	NR	-	-
LDS–Comm of Christ	1	NR	135	135	0.5	0.8
LUTH–Luth–MO Synod	1	61	130	177	0.7	1.1
METH–AME	2	0	160	197	0.8	1.2
METH–Un Methodist	9	321	1,090	1,103	4.5	6.7
Non-denom Chr Chs	6	560	770	800	3.3	4.9
PENT–Assemb of God	5	452	282	625	2.5	3.8
PENT–Ch God (Cleve)	5	211	315	387	1.6	2.3
PENT–Ch of God Proph	4	NR	65	80	0.3	0.5
PENT–Pent Ch of God	2	140	NR	217	0.9	1.3
PENT–Un Pent Ch Intl	2	NR	NR	NR	-	-
POLK	**70**	**4,127**	**7,892**	**11,099**	**53.7**	**100.0**
ANG/EPIS–Anglican NA	1	NR	NR	NR	-	-
ANG/EPIS–Episcopal	1	25	37	39	0.2	0.4
Bahá'í	0	NR	5	5	0.0	0.0
BAPT–Amer Bapt Assn	1	NR	85	104	0.5	0.9
BAPT–Free Will Bapt	1	NR	92	113	0.5	1.0
BAPT–So Bapt Conv	18	1,446	3,830	4,695	22.7	42.3
Catholic	1	NR	NR	570	2.8	5.1
Ch of Nazarene	3	177	417	428	2.1	3.9
CHR–Chr Chs & Chs Cr	5	NR	440	539	2.6	4.9
CHR–Chs of Christ	8	295	304	362	1.8	3.3
Jehovah's Witness	1	NR	NR	NR	-	-
LDS–L-D Saints	1	NR	NR	527	2.6	4.7
LUTH–Luth–MO Synod	1	24	54	57	0.3	0.5
MENN–Tamp Amish-Menn	1	34	21	34	0.2	0.3
METH–Un Methodist	5	341	915	1,081	5.2	9.7
Non-denom Chr Chs	8	745	1,010	1,069	5.2	9.6
PENT–Assemb of God	3	313	146	502	2.4	4.5
PENT–Ch God (Cleve)	2	162	256	314	1.5	2.8
PENT–Ch of God Proph	1	NR	19	23	0.1	0.2
PENT–Int Foursq Gos	1	240	81	99	0.5	0.9
PENT–Pent Ch of God	3	210	NR	326	1.6	2.9
PENT–Un Pent Ch Intl	2	NR	NR	NR	-	-
PRES–Presb Ch (USA)	1	53	73	89	0.4	0.8
Sev Day Adv	1	62	107	123	0.6	1.1
POPE	**151**	**10,798**	**18,524**	**28,676**	**46.4**	**100.0**
ANG/EPIS–Episcopal	1	137	317	406	0.7	1.4
Bahá'í	0	NR	16	16	0.0	0.1
BAPT–Amer Bapt Assn	6	NR	1,000	1,217	2.0	4.2
BAPT–Free Will Bapt	16	NR	1,472	1,791	2.9	6.2
BAPT–So Bapt Conv	21	2,740	6,571	7,995	12.9	27.9
Catholic	3	NR	NR	1,527	2.5	5.3
Ch of Nazarene	1	31	45	53	0.1	0.2
Chr & Miss Al	1	55	41	91	0.1	0.3
CHR–Chr Ch (Disc)	2	37	67	82	0.1	0.3
CHR–Chr Chs & Chs Cr	2	NR	65	79	0.1	0.3
CHR–Chs of Christ	13	1,049	1,087	1,424	2.3	5.0
Jehovah's Witness	1	NR	NR	NR	-	-
LDS–L-D Saints	1	NR	NR	782	1.3	2.7
LUTH–Luth–MO Synod	2	184	420	534	0.9	1.9
LUTH–Wisc Ev Luth Syn	1	19	27	28	0.0	0.1
METH–AME	1	0	100	122	0.2	0.4
METH–C.M.E.	2	0	200	243	0.4	0.8
METH–Un Methodist	8	940	2,367	3,211	5.2	11.2
METH–Wesleyan	3	103	55	134	0.2	0.5
Muslim Est	1	134	NR	308	0.5	1.1
Non-denom Chr Chs	11	1,570	1,765	2,036	3.3	7.1
PENT–Assemb of God	26	2,956	1,689	4,530	7.3	15.8
PENT–Ch God (Cleve)	3	119	214	260	0.4	0.9
PENT–Ch of God Proph	1	NR	41	50	0.1	0.2
PENT–Int Foursq Gos	1	0	0	0	0.0	0.0
PENT–Intl Pent Holiness	3	182	102	124	0.2	0.4
PENT–Pent Ch of God	4	280	NR	435	0.7	1.5
PENT–Un Pent Ch Intl	4	NR	NR	NR	-	-
PRES–As Ref Pres Ch	1	NR	45	55	0.1	0.2
PRES–Cumber Presb	6	NR	269	446	0.7	1.6
PRES–Presb Ch (USA)	2	145	381	464	0.8	1.6
PRES–Presb Ch Amer	1	40	25	35	0.1	0.1
Salvation Army	1	13	32	70	0.1	0.2
Sev Day Adv	1	64	111	128	0.2	0.4
PRAIRIE	**29**	**1,030**	**3,416**	**4,362**	**50.1**	**100.0**
ANG/EPIS–Episcopal	1	29	142	180	2.1	4.1
BAPT–Amer Bapt Assn	7	NR	950	1,128	12.9	25.9
BAPT–Natl Mis Bapt Conv	1	0	150	178	2.0	4.1
BAPT–So Bapt Conv	4	418	1,345	1,597	18.3	36.6
Catholic	1	NR	NR	176	2.0	4.0
Ch of Nazarene	1	27	23	32	0.4	0.7
CHR–Chs of Christ	3	108	100	125	1.4	2.9
LUTH–Luth–MO Synod	1	57	119	128	1.5	2.9
METH–Un Methodist	4	240	503	580	6.7	13.3
PENT–Assemb of God	2	81	57	97	1.1	2.2
PENT–Ch of God Proph	1	NR	27	32	0.4	0.7
PENT–Orig Ch of God	1	NR	NR	NR	-	-
PENT–Pent Ch of God	1	70	NR	109	1.3	2.5
PENT–Un Pent Ch Intl	1	NR	NR	NR	-	-
PULASKI	**557**	**74,512**	**154,383**	**222,466**	**58.1**	**100.0**
ANG/EPIS–Anglican NA	2	NR	NR	NR	-	-
ANG/EPIS–Episcopal	9	1,378	3,874	4,194	1.1	1.9
Bahá'í	2	NR	545	545	0.1	0.2
BAPT–Alliance Bapt	1	NR	NR	NR	-	-
BAPT–Amer Bapt Assn	22	NR	5,285	6,520	1.7	2.9
BAPT–Free Will Bapt	5	NR	460	567	0.1	0.3
BAPT–Ind Bapt Flwsp Intl	1	NR	NR	NR	-	-
BAPT–Natl Mis Bapt Conv	3	0	450	555	0.1	0.2
BAPT–NBC Amer	6	330	755	931	0.2	0.4
BAPT–NBC USA	22	3,855	9,808	12,100	3.2	5.4
BAPT–Prog NBC	1	0	150	185	0.0	0.1
BAPT–S-D Baptist Gen Con	1	24	43	53	0.0	0.0
BAPT–So Bapt Conv	117	18,579	55,107	67,984	17.8	30.6
BUDD–Mahayana	5	NR	NR	433	0.1	0.2
BUDD–Theravada	1	NR	NR	15	0.0	0.0
Catholic	15	NR	NR	23,960	6.3	10.8
CGOD–Ch God (Ander)	2	93	NR	93	0.0	0.0
Ch Cr, Scientist	2	NR	NR	NR	-	-
Ch of Chr (Hol)	1	NR	NR	NR	-	-
Ch of God Gen Conf	1	NR	7	9	0.0	0.0
Ch of Nazarene	12	1,767	2,808	3,872	1.0	1.7
Chr & Miss Al	1	35	33	49	0.0	0.0
CHR–Chr Ch (Disc)	10	599	1,347	1,662	0.4	0.7
CHR–Chr Chs & Chs Cr	3	NR	125	154	0.0	0.1
CHR–Chs of Christ	32	6,392	6,743	8,542	2.2	3.8
CHR–Int Chs of Christ	1	NR	33	41	0.0	0.0
FRND–Fr Gen Cf	1	NR	47	58	0.0	0.0
HINDU–I/A Temples	1	NR	NR	1,742	0.5	0.8
HINDU–Post Ren	1	NR	NR	16	0.0	0.0
HINDU–Trad Temples	1	NR	NR	400	0.1	0.2
Ind Fund Churches	1	NR	NR	NR	-	-
Jehovah's Witness	4	NR	NR	NR	-	-
JUD–Orth	1	43	50	60	0.0	0.0
JUD–Reform	1	197	347	937	0.2	0.4
LDS–Comm of Christ	1	NR	135	135	0.0	0.1
LDS–L-D Saints	6	NR	NR	3,965	1.0	1.8
LUTH–E.L.C.A.	2	94	220	247	0.1	0.1
LUTH–Luth–MO Synod	7	901	1,502	1,829	0.5	0.8
LUTH–Wisc Ev Luth Syn	1	27	35	41	0.0	0.0
METH–AME	14	535	2,516	3,104	0.8	1.4
METH–AME Zion	3	30	299	369	0.1	0.2
METH–C.M.E.	10	450	1,235	1,524	0.4	0.7
METH–Un Methodist	47	7,873	24,002	28,299	7.4	12.7
Muslim Est	2	268	NR	616	0.2	0.3
Non-denom Chr Chs	75	20,182	23,631	26,955	7.0	12.1
ORTHE–Ant Orth of NA	1	45	NR	80	0.0	0.0
ORTHE–Greek Orthodox	1	150	NR	300	0.1	0.1
ORTHO–Coptic Orth Ch	1	14	NR	18	0.0	0.0

NR–Not Reported - Represents no adherents reported. Percentages may not total 100 due to rounding.

Table 3: Religious Congregations by County and Group: 2010

Religious Group	Number of Congrega-tions	Number of Attendees	Number of Communicant, Confirmed, or Full Members	Adherents: Number of Adherents	Adherents: % of Total Pop.	Adherents: % of Total Adh.
PENT–Assemb of God	24	6,673	4,466	8,121	2.1	3.7
PENT–Ch God (Cleve)	2	112	325	401	0.1	0.2
PENT–Ch of God Proph	2	NR	108	133	0.0	0.1
PENT–COGIC	16	750	2,275	2,807	0.7	1.3
PENT–Int Foursq Gos	1	63	94	116	0.0	0.1
PENT–Orig Ch of God	1	NR	NR	NR	-	-
PENT–Pent Ch of God	7	490	NR	761	0.2	0.3
PENT–Un Pent Ch Intl	16	NR	NR	NR	-	-
PRES–Cumber Presb	2	NR	96	272	0.1	0.1
PRES–Korean Pres Amer	1	NR	NR	NR	-	-
PRES–Presb Ch (USA)	11	1,289	3,434	4,236	1.1	1.9
PRES–Presb Ch Amer	2	272	311	381	0.1	0.2
Salvation Army	3	165	162	310	0.1	0.1
Sev Day Adv	5	744	1,294	1,488	0.4	0.7
Un C of Christ	1	13	27	33	0.0	0.0
Unit Univ	1	80	199	248	0.1	0.1
Unity Ch	2	NR	NR	NR	-	-
RANDOLPH	**54**	**2,649**	**6,893**	**10,577**	**58.9**	**100.0**
BAPT–Amer Bapt Assn	1	NR	85	103	0.6	1.0
BAPT–Free Will Bapt	7	NR	644	781	4.3	7.4
BAPT–So Bapt Conv	12	753	4,429	5,371	29.9	50.8
Catholic	2	NR	NR	1,300	7.2	12.3
Ch God (7th Day)	1	NR	NR	NR	-	-
CHR–Chs of Christ	18	1,253	1,080	1,380	7.7	13.0
LDS–L-D Saints	1	NR	NR	300	1.7	2.8
LUTH–Luth–MO Synod	1	15	31	36	0.2	0.3
MENN–Tamp Amish-Menn	1	128	74	128	0.7	1.2
METH–Un Methodist	1	106	231	270	1.5	2.6
Non-denom Chr Chs	2	185	235	241	1.3	2.3
PENT–Assemb of God	2	97	0	460	2.6	4.3
PENT–Ch of God Proph	1	NR	13	16	0.1	0.2
PENT–Pent Ch of God	1	70	NR	109	0.6	1.0
PENT–Un Pent Ch Intl	1	NR	NR	NR	-	-
PRES–Presb Ch (USA)	1	10	15	18	0.1	0.2
Sev Day Adv	1	32	56	64	0.4	0.6
ST. FRANCIS	**77**	**3,247**	**12,012**	**14,687**	**52.0**	**100.0**
ANG/EPIS–Episcopal	2	56	87	103	0.4	0.7
BAPT–Amer Bapt Assn	3	NR	235	288	1.0	2.0
BAPT–Natl Mis Bapt Conv	4	0	600	734	2.6	5.0
BAPT–NBC USA	5	170	1,150	1,408	5.0	9.6
BAPT–So Bapt Conv	19	1,390	5,878	7,195	25.5	49.0
Catholic	1	NR	NR	92	0.3	0.6
Ch of Nazarene	1	20	22	34	0.1	0.2
CHR–Chs of Christ	6	260	324	414	1.5	2.8
Jehovah's Witness	2	NR	NR	NR	-	-
LUTH–Luth–MO Synod	1	13	32	46	0.2	0.3
METH–AME	2	0	200	245	0.9	1.7
METH–C.M.E.	4	150	600	734	2.6	5.0
METH–Un Methodist	8	299	874	1,012	3.6	6.9
Non-denom Chr Chs	5	420	620	625	2.2	4.3
PENT–Assemb of God	2	86	73	126	0.4	0.9
PENT–Ch God (Cleve)	3	271	593	726	2.6	4.9
PENT–COGIC	4	100	500	612	2.2	4.2
PENT–Orig Ch of God	1	NR	NR	NR	-	-
PENT–Un Pent Ch Intl	1	NR	NR	NR	-	-
PRES–Cumber Presb	1	NR	79	117	0.4	0.8
PRES–Presb Ch (USA)	1	0	123	151	0.5	1.0
Sev Day Adv	1	12	22	25	0.1	0.2
SALINE	**146**	**13,044**	**32,756**	**43,486**	**40.6**	**100.0**
ANG/EPIS–Episcopal	1	48	82	123	0.1	0.3
Bahá'í	0	NR	3	3	0.0	0.0
BAPT–Amer Bapt Assn	33	NR	7,133	8,814	8.2	20.3
BAPT–Free Will Bapt	2	NR	184	227	0.2	0.5
BAPT–Ind Bapt Flwsp Intl	1	NR	NR	NR	-	-
BAPT–Natl Mis Bapt Conv	1	0	150	185	0.2	0.4
BAPT–NBC USA	1	100	150	185	0.2	0.4
BAPT–So Bapt Conv	32	5,461	13,176	16,282	15.2	37.4
Calv Chpl	1	NR	NR	NR	-	-
Catholic	1	NR	NR	2,113	2.0	4.9
CGOD–Ch God (Ander)	4	273	NR	273	0.3	0.6

Religious Group	Number of Congrega-tions	Number of Attendees	Number of Communicant, Confirmed, or Full Members	Adherents: Number of Adherents	Adherents: % of Total Pop.	Adherents: % of Total Adh.
Ch of Nazarene	4	361	720	1,114	1.0	2.6
CHR–Chr Ch (Disc)	2	40	151	187	0.2	0.4
CHR–Chs of Christ	12	1,307	1,285	1,713	1.6	3.9
Grace Gosp Fel	1	NR	NR	NR	-	-
Jehovah's Witness	1	NR	NR	NR	-	-
LUTH–Luth–MO Synod	4	359	614	747	0.7	1.7
METH–AME	2	0	250	309	0.3	0.7
METH–Un Methodist	13	1,955	5,056	6,182	5.8	14.2
Non-denom Chr Chs	12	1,779	2,300	2,399	2.2	5.5
PENT–Assemb of God	7	869	454	1,131	1.1	2.6
PENT–Ch God (Cleve)	1	12	74	91	0.1	0.2
PENT–COGIC	2	100	325	402	0.4	0.9
PENT–Int Foursq Gos	1	76	342	423	0.4	1.0
PENT–Pent Ch of God	2	140	NR	217	0.2	0.5
PENT–Un Pent Ch Intl	3	NR	NR	NR	-	-
PRES–Presb Ch (USA)	1	75	152	188	0.2	0.4
Sev Day Adv	1	89	155	178	0.2	0.4
SCOTT	**56**	**2,365**	**4,025**	**6,417**	**57.1**	**100.0**
Bahá'í	0	NR	6	6	0.1	0.1
BAPT–Amer Bapt Assn	2	NR	170	211	1.9	3.3
BAPT–Free Will Bapt	4	NR	368	457	4.1	7.1
BAPT–So Bapt Conv	16	862	2,255	2,803	25.0	43.7
BUDD–Theravada	1	NR	NR	300	2.7	4.7
Catholic	1	NR	NR	429	3.8	6.7
Ch of Nazarene	2	189	203	231	2.1	3.6
CHR–Chs of Christ	4	203	176	247	2.2	3.8
Jehovah's Witness	2	NR	NR	NR	-	-
METH–Un Methodist	5	91	248	248	2.2	3.9
Non-denom Chr Chs	5	375	455	531	4.7	8.3
PENT–Assemb of God	6	225	136	288	2.6	4.5
PENT–Pent Ch of God	6	420	NR	652	5.8	10.2
PENT–Un Pent Ch Intl	1	NR	NR	NR	-	-
PRES–Cumber Presb	1	NR	8	14	0.1	0.2
SEARCY	**36**	**1,374**	**3,074**	**3,744**	**45.7**	**100.0**
BAPT–Amer Bapt Assn	2	NR	185	219	2.7	5.8
BAPT–Free Will Bapt	1	NR	92	109	1.3	2.9
BAPT–So Bapt Conv	10	496	1,557	1,847	22.5	49.3
Ch of Nazarene	1	7	27	27	0.3	0.7
CHR–Chr Chs & Chs Cr	1	NR	86	102	1.2	2.7
CHR–Chs of Christ	5	193	185	234	2.9	6.3
Jehovah's Witness	1	NR	NR	NR	-	-
MENN–Menn Br US Conf	1	NR	53	63	0.8	1.7
METH–Un Methodist	2	78	211	216	2.6	5.8
Non-denom Chr Chs	2	200	300	300	3.7	8.0
PENT–Assemb of God	5	356	167	379	4.6	10.1
PENT–Ch God (Cleve)	1	20	18	21	0.3	0.6
PENT–COGIC	1	0	150	178	2.2	4.8
PENT–Un Pent Ch Intl	2	NR	NR	NR	-	-
Sev Day Adv	1	24	43	49	0.6	1.3
SEBASTIAN	**215**	**24,389**	**54,858**	**86,374**	**68.7**	**100.0**
ANG/EPIS–Episcopal	3	244	559	849	0.7	1.0
Bahá'í	0	NR	30	30	0.0	0.0
BAPT–Amer Bapt Assn	6	NR	1,295	1,616	1.3	1.9
BAPT–Free Will Bapt	9	NR	828	1,033	0.8	1.2
BAPT–So Bapt Conv	51	8,316	27,804	34,690	27.6	40.2
BUDD–Theravada	2	NR	NR	675	0.5	0.8
Calv Chpl	1	NR	NR	NR	-	-
Catholic	6	NR	NR	12,251	9.7	14.2
CGOD–Ch God (Ander)	1	32	NR	32	0.0	0.0
Ch God (7th Day)	1	NR	NR	NR	-	-
Ch of Nazarene	5	333	692	754	0.6	0.9
CHR–Chr Ch (Disc)	1	195	410	512	0.4	0.6
CHR–Chr Chs & Chs Cr	2	NR	692	863	0.7	1.0
CHR–Chs of Christ	20	1,957	2,447	2,986	2.4	3.5
Int Cou Comm Ch	1	NR	NR	NR	-	-
Jehovah's Witness	3	NR	NR	NR	-	-
JUD–Reform	1	14	24	65	0.1	0.1
LDS–Comm of Christ	1	NR	156	156	0.1	0.2
LDS–L-D Saints	2	NR	NR	1,699	1.4	2.0
LUTH–E.L.C.A.	1	130	311	380	0.3	0.4

NR–Not Reported - Represents no adherents reported. Percentages may not total 100 due to rounding.

Table 3: Religious Congregations by County and Group: 2010

Religious Group	Number of Congrega-tions	Number of Attendees	Number of Communicant, Confirmed, or Full Members	Adherents: Number of Adherents	% of Total Pop.	% of Total Adh.
LUTH–Luth-MO Synod	4	370	721	868	0.7	1.0
METH–AME	1	60	100	125	0.1	0.1
METH–C.M.E.	1	0	150	187	0.1	0.2
METH–Un Methodist	25	3,093	8,285	9,105	7.2	10.5
Muslim Est	2	268	NR	616	0.5	0.7
New Apost Ch	1	NR	NR	NR	-	-
Non-denom Chr Chs	20	5,745	6,980	7,950	6.3	9.2
ORTHE–Orth Ch in Amer	1	30	NR	60	0.0	0.1
PENT–Assemb of God	18	2,063	933	4,498	3.6	5.2
PENT–COGIC	2	35	195	243	0.2	0.3
PENT–Int Foursq Gos	1	57	66	82	0.1	0.1
PENT–Intl Pent Holiness	1	50	50	62	0.0	0.1
PENT–Pent Ch of God	8	560	NR	870	0.7	1.0
PENT–Un Pent Ch Intl	3	NR	NR	NR	-	-
PENT–Vineyard	1	140	165	206	0.2	0.2
PRES–Cumber Presb	1	NR	25	170	0.1	0.2
PRES–Presb Ch (USA)	3	304	1,264	1,577	1.3	1.8
Salvation Army	1	85	140	548	0.4	0.6
Sev Day Adv	3	308	536	616	0.5	0.7
Unity Ch	1	NR	NR	NR	-	-
SEVIER	**50**	**2,436**	**5,860**	**9,174**	**53.8**	**100.0**
Bahá'í	0	NR	1	1	0.0	0.0
BAPT–Amer Bapt Assn	5	NR	778	1,014	5.9	11.1
BAPT–Natl Mis Bapt Conv	1	0	150	196	1.1	2.1
BAPT–So Bapt Conv	12	939	3,136	4,088	24.0	44.6
Catholic	1	NR	NR	1,200	7.0	13.1
Ch of Nazarene	1	12	16	51	0.3	0.6
CHR–Chr Chs & Chs Cr	1	NR	50	65	0.4	0.7
CHR–Chs of Christ	5	460	475	556	3.3	6.1
Jehovah's Witness	1	NR	NR	NR	-	-
METH–Un Methodist	8	284	550	651	3.8	7.1
Non-denom Chr Chs	1	55	50	69	0.4	0.8
ORTHE–Rus Orth Abroad	1	14	NR	51	0.3	0.6
PENT–Assemb of God	3	424	264	636	3.7	6.9
PENT–Pent Ch of God	1	70	NR	109	0.6	1.2
PENT–Un Pent Ch Intl	1	NR	NR	NR	-	-
PRES–Cumber Presb	5	NR	86	136	0.8	1.5
PRES–Presb Ch (USA)	1	9	10	13	0.1	0.1
Sev Day Adv	2	169	294	338	2.0	3.7
SHARP	**78**	**3,758**	**8,917**	**11,580**	**67.1**	**100.0**
ANG/EPIS–Episcopal	1	13	18	18	0.1	0.2
Bahá'í	0	NR	1	1	0.0	0.0
BAPT–Amer Bapt Assn	10	NR	1,528	1,821	10.5	15.7
BAPT–Free Will Bapt	2	NR	184	219	1.3	1.9
BAPT–Reg Bapt Gen As	1	NR	NR	NR	-	-
BAPT–So Bapt Conv	15	1,217	3,873	4,614	26.7	39.8
Catholic	1	NR	NR	471	2.7	4.1
Ch Cr, Scientst	1	NR	NR	NR	-	-
CHR–Chr Ch (Disc)	1	12	16	19	0.1	0.2
CHR–Chr Chs & Chs Cr	1	NR	20	24	0.1	0.2
CHR–Chs of Christ	12	843	845	1,067	6.2	9.2
Evan Free Ch	1	35	NR	35	0.2	0.3
Jehovah's Witness	1	NR	NR	NR	-	-
LDS–Comm of Christ	1	NR	135	135	0.8	1.2
LDS–L-D Saints	1	NR	NR	250	1.4	2.2
LUTH–E.L.C.A.	1	65	90	90	0.5	0.8
LUTH–Luth-MO Synod	1	99	203	218	1.3	1.9
METH–Un Methodist	10	560	1,080	1,201	7.0	10.4
Non-denom Chr Chs	2	280	420	425	2.5	3.7
PENT–Assemb of God	5	384	196	487	2.8	4.2
PENT–Ch God (Cleve)	3	123	224	267	1.5	2.3
PENT–Pent Ch of God	1	70	NR	109	0.6	0.9
PENT–Un Pent Ch Intl	2	NR	NR	NR	-	-
PRES–Cumber Presb	2	NR	15	28	0.2	0.2
PRES–Presb Ch (USA)	1	45	47	56	0.3	0.5
Sev Day Adv	1	12	22	25	0.1	0.2
STONE	**41**	**2,172**	**4,367**	**5,975**	**48.2**	**100.0**
Bahá'í	0	NR	4	4	0.0	0.1
BAPT–Amer Bapt Assn	6	NR	966	1,149	9.3	19.2
BAPT–So Bapt Conv	9	687	1,848	2,198	17.7	36.8

Religious Group	Number of Congrega-tions	Number of Attendees	Number of Communicant, Confirmed, or Full Members	Adherents: Number of Adherents	% of Total Pop.	% of Total Adh.
Catholic	1	NR	NR	138	1.1	2.3
CHR–Chr Chs & Chs Cr	1	NR	35	42	0.3	0.7
CHR–Chs of Christ	6	465	445	551	4.4	9.2
Jehovah's Witness	1	NR	NR	NR	-	-
LDS–L-D Saints	1	NR	NR	206	1.7	3.4
LUTH–Luth-MO Synod	1	20	19	19	0.2	0.3
MENN–Beachy Amish-Menn	1	144	62	144	1.2	2.4
MENN–Cons Menn Conf	1	18	25	30	0.2	0.5
METH–Un Methodist	2	217	389	568	4.6	9.5
Non-denom Chr Chs	3	210	304	363	2.9	6.1
PENT–Assemb of God	3	342	128	397	3.2	6.6
PENT–Ch God (Cleve)	1	23	57	68	0.5	1.1
PENT–Ch of God Proph	1	NR	6	7	0.1	0.1
PENT–Un Pent Ch Intl	2	NR	NR	NR	-	-
Sev Day Adv	1	46	79	91	0.7	1.5
UNION	**158**	**9,305**	**27,594**	**34,674**	**83.3**	**100.0**
ANG/EPIS–Episcopal	1	95	281	302	0.7	0.9
Bahá'í	0	NR	1	1	0.0	0.0
BAPT–Amer Bapt Assn	8	NR	760	933	2.2	2.7
BAPT–Ind Bapt Flwsp Intl	1	NR	NR	NR	-	-
BAPT–Natl Mis Bapt Conv	3	0	450	552	1.3	1.6
BAPT–NBC USA	7	1,120	3,405	4,178	10.0	12.0
BAPT–So Bapt Conv	39	3,751	13,106	16,082	38.6	46.4
Catholic	1	NR	NR	671	1.6	1.9
CGOD–Ch God (Ander)	2	63	NR	63	0.2	0.2
Ch of Nazarene	1	16	33	33	0.1	0.1
CHR–Chr Ch (Disc)	1	0	50	61	0.1	0.2
CHR–Chs of Christ	13	919	937	1,262	3.0	3.6
Jehovah's Witness	1	NR	NR	NR	-	-
LDS–Comm of Christ	1	NR	81	81	0.2	0.2
LDS–L-D Saints	1	NR	NR	297	0.7	0.9
LUTH–Luth-MO Synod	1	60	84	105	0.3	0.3
MENN–Cons Menn Conf	1	26	40	49	0.1	0.1
MENN–Mennonite USA	1	16	20	25	0.1	0.1
METH–AME	11	0	1,300	1,595	3.8	4.6
METH–C.M.E.	5	0	600	736	1.8	2.1
METH–So Methodist	1	NR	NR	NR	-	-
METH–Un Methodist	15	741	2,133	2,242	5.4	6.5
Non-denom Chr Chs	14	1,521	2,515	2,561	6.2	7.4
PENT–Assemb of God	11	736	552	1,102	2.6	3.2
PENT–Ch God (Cleve)	1	18	80	98	0.2	0.3
PENT–COGIC	7	61	709	870	2.1	2.5
PENT–Pent Ch of God	2	140	NR	217	0.5	0.6
PENT–Un Pent Ch Intl	3	NR	NR	NR	-	-
PRES–Cumber Presb	1	NR	8	10	0.0	0.0
PRES–Evan Presby Ch	1	NR	37	45	0.1	0.1
PRES–Presb Ch (USA)	2	0	374	459	1.1	1.3
Sev Day Adv	1	22	38	44	0.1	0.1
VAN BUREN	**49**	**2,707**	**5,529**	**7,057**	**40.8**	**100.0**
Bahá'í	0	NR	1	1	0.0	0.0
BAPT–Amer Bapt Assn	2	NR	170	201	1.2	2.8
BAPT–So Bapt Conv	18	1,283	3,392	4,017	23.2	56.9
Catholic	2	NR	NR	354	2.0	5.0
Ch of Nazarene	1	24	53	63	0.4	0.9
CHR–Chs of Christ	10	558	529	657	3.8	9.3
Evan Ch	1	NR	NR	NR	-	-
Jehovah's Witness	1	NR	NR	NR	-	-
LUTH–Luth-MO Synod	1	64	84	84	0.5	1.2
METH–Un Methodist	3	248	708	831	4.8	11.8
Non-denom Chr Chs	3	33	60	65	0.4	0.9
PENT–Assemb of God	3	241	131	311	1.8	4.4
PENT–Int Foursq Gos	2	122	157	186	1.1	2.6
PRES–Presb Ch (USA)	1	100	186	220	1.3	3.1
Sev Day Adv	1	34	58	67	0.4	0.9
WASHINGTON	**275**	**33,446**	**68,676**	**115,249**	**56.8**	**100.0**
ANG/EPIS–Anglican NA	1	NR	NR	NR	-	-
ANG/EPIS–Episcopal	2	550	1,742	2,198	1.1	1.9
Bahá'í	2	NR	158	158	0.1	0.1
BAPT–Amer Bapt Assn	7	NR	645	808	0.4	0.7
BAPT–Free Will Bapt	13	NR	1,196	1,499	0.7	1.3

NR–Not Reported - Represents no adherents reported. Percentages may not total 100 due to rounding.

Table 3: Religious Congregations by County and Group: 2010

Religious Group	Number of Congrega-tions	Number of Attendees	Number of Communicant, Confirmed, or Full Members	Adherents: Number of Adherents	Adherents: % of Total Pop.	Adherents: % of Total Adh.
BAPT–NBC USA	1	500	500	626	0.3	0.5
BAPT–Reg Bapt Gen As	2	NR	NR	NR	-	-
BAPT–So Bapt Conv	49	11,864	34,847	43,661	21.5	37.9
BUDD–Mahayana	2	NR	NR	219	0.1	0.2
BUDD–Theravada	2	NR	NR	314	0.2	0.3
Calv Chpl	1	NR	NR	NR	-	-
Catholic	4	NR	NR	25,134	12.4	21.8
CGOD–Ch God (Ander)	1	50	NR	50	0.0	0.0
Ch Cr, Scientst	2	NR	NR	NR	-	-
Ch of Nazarene	5	276	396	475	0.2	0.4
CHR–Chr Ch (Disc)	1	187	299	375	0.2	0.3
CHR–Chr Chs & Chs Cr	4	NR	980	1,228	0.6	1.1
CHR–Chs of Christ	25	2,983	2,783	3,709	1.8	3.2
Christian Un	2	NR	NR	NR	-	-
FRND–Fr Gen Cf	1	NR	39	49	0.0	0.0
HINDU–Post Ren	1	NR	NR	10	0.0	0.0
Jehovah's Witness	2	NR	NR	NR	-	-
JUD–Reform	1	39	69	186	0.1	0.2
LDS–Comm of Christ	1	NR	135	135	0.1	0.1
LDS–L-D Saints	8	NR	NR	2,962	1.5	2.6
LUTH–E.L.C.A.	1	225	592	717	0.4	0.6
LUTH–Luth–MO Synod	4	341	543	664	0.3	0.6
METH–Un Methodist	21	3,724	9,687	11,458	5.6	9.9
Missionary Ch	1	15	15	15	0.0	0.0
Muslim Est	1	134	NR	308	0.2	0.3
Non-denom Chr Chs	36	7,571	9,123	10,116	5.0	8.8
ORTHE–Ant Orth of NA	1	50	NR	300	0.1	0.3
PENT–Assemb of God	14	1,907	1,236	2,325	1.1	2.0
PENT–Ch God (Cleve)	12	654	815	1,021	0.5	0.9
PENT–Intl Pent Holiness	3	119	127	159	0.1	0.1
PENT–Pent Ch of God	8	560	NR	870	0.4	0.8
PENT–Un Pent Ch Intl	8	NR	NR	NR	-	-
PRES–Cumber Presb	2	NR	67	70	0.0	0.1
PRES–Presb Ch (USA)	9	496	1,140	1,428	0.7	1.2
PRES–Presb Ch Amer	1	145	140	208	0.1	0.2
Salvation Army	4	496	347	493	0.2	0.4
Sev Day Adv	5	424	736	847	0.4	0.7
Un C of Christ	2	0	162	203	0.1	0.2
Unit Univ	1	136	157	251	0.1	0.2
Unity Ch	1	NR	NR	NR	-	-
WHITE	**206**	**19,300**	**33,808**	**45,037**	**58.4**	**100.0**
ANG/EPIS–Episcopal	1	60	122	122	0.2	0.3
Bahá'í	0	NR	14	14	0.0	0.0
BAPT–Amer Bapt Assn	30	NR	2,928	3,596	4.7	8.0
BAPT–Free Will Bapt	5	NR	460	565	0.7	1.3
BAPT–NBC USA	1	0	150	184	0.2	0.4
BAPT–So Bapt Conv	34	4,731	14,609	17,940	23.3	39.8
Catholic	2	NR	NR	749	1.0	1.7
Ch of Chr (Hol)	1	NR	NR	NR	-	-
Ch of Nazarene	3	253	378	717	0.9	1.6
CHR–Chr Ch (Disc)	2	61	147	181	0.2	0.4
CHR–Chr Chs & Chs Cr	2	NR	121	149	0.2	0.3
CHR–Chs of Christ	38	7,018	6,862	8,395	10.9	18.6
Jehovah's Witness	2	NR	NR	NR	-	-
LDS–Comm of Christ	1	NR	135	135	0.2	0.3
LDS–L-D Saints	1	NR	NR	645	0.8	1.4
LUTH–Luth–MO Synod	1	52	82	82	0.1	0.2
METH–C.M.E.	2	0	227	279	0.4	0.6
METH–Un Methodist	25	1,464	2,949	3,313	4.3	7.4
METH–Wesleyan	1	56	20	73	0.1	0.2
Non-denom Chr Chs	17	2,980	2,885	3,881	5.0	8.6
PENT–Assemb of God	11	1,777	603	2,197	2.9	4.9
PENT–Ch God (Cleve)	7	444	643	790	1.0	1.8
PENT–Ch of God Proph	2	NR	22	27	0.0	0.1
PENT–COGIC	1	0	150	184	0.2	0.4
PENT–Pent Ch of God	4	280	NR	435	0.6	1.0
PENT–Un Pent Ch Intl	5	NR	NR	NR	-	-
PRES–Cumber Presb	3	NR	40	70	0.1	0.2
PRES–Presb Ch (USA)	2	78	181	222	0.3	0.5
REF–Comm Ref Evan	1	NR	NR	NR	-	-
Sev Day Adv	1	46	80	92	0.1	0.2

Religious Group	Number of Congrega-tions	Number of Attendees	Number of Communicant, Confirmed, or Full Members	Adherents: Number of Adherents	Adherents: % of Total Pop.	Adherents: % of Total Adh.
WOODRUFF	**28**	**1,100**	**2,725**	**3,317**	**45.7**	**100.0**
Bahá'í	0	NR	38	38	0.5	1.1
BAPT–Amer Bapt Assn	1	NR	85	103	1.4	3.1
BAPT–So Bapt Conv	8	408	1,341	1,625	22.4	49.0
Catholic	1	NR	NR	45	0.6	1.4
Ch of Nazarene	1	59	122	185	2.5	5.6
CHR–Chs of Christ	4	275	265	330	4.5	9.9
METH–Un Methodist	6	177	472	491	6.8	14.8
PENT–Assemb of God	1	39	22	39	0.5	1.2
PENT–Ch God (Cleve)	2	42	65	79	1.1	2.4
PENT–Ch of God Proph	1	NR	65	79	1.1	2.4
PENT–COGIC	2	100	250	303	4.2	9.1
PENT–Orig Ch of God	1	NR	NR	NR	-	-
YELL	**85**	**3,217**	**6,882**	**11,304**	**51.0**	**100.0**
Bahá'í	0	NR	1	1	0.0	0.0
BAPT–Amer Bapt Assn	5	NR	405	509	2.3	4.5
BAPT–Free Will Bapt	12	NR	1,104	1,387	6.3	12.3
BAPT–So Bapt Conv	13	907	2,784	3,499	15.8	31.0
Catholic	2	NR	NR	1,800	8.1	15.9
CGOD–Ch God (Ander)	1	0	NR	0	0.0	0.0
Ch of Nazarene	1	30	53	53	0.2	0.5
Chr & Miss Al	1	39	32	58	0.3	0.5
CHR–Chs of Christ	12	737	692	932	4.2	8.2
Jehovah's Witness	1	NR	NR	NR	-	-
LDS–L-D Saints	1	NR	NR	192	0.9	1.7
MENN–Ber Amish-Menn	1	107	63	107	0.5	0.9
METH–C.M.E.	2	0	200	251	1.1	2.2
METH–Un Methodist	14	476	947	1,153	5.2	10.2
Non-denom Chr Chs	2	120	130	150	0.7	1.3
PENT–Assemb of God	9	580	295	785	3.5	6.9
PENT–Pent Ch of God	2	140	NR	217	1.0	1.9
PENT–Un Pent Ch Intl	2	NR	NR	NR	-	-
PRES–As Ref Pres Ch	1	NR	14	18	0.1	0.2
PRES–Cumber Presb	1	NR	16	16	0.1	0.1
PRES–Presb Ch (USA)	1	40	75	94	0.4	0.8
Sev Day Adv	1	41	71	82	0.4	0.7
CALIFORNIA	**23,558**	**2,840,602**	**3,642,008**	**16,765,751**	**45.0**	**100.0**
ALAMEDA	**1,091**	**114,283**	**150,811**	**509,573**	**33.7**	**100.0**
ANG/EPIS–Episcopal	18	1,878	4,440	5,174	0.3	1.0
Bahá'í	12	NR	982	982	0.1	0.2
BAPT–Alliance Bapt	3	NR	NR	NR	-	-
BAPT–Amer Bapt Assn	2	NR	135	164	0.0	0.0
BAPT–Amer Bapt USA	27	5,142	6,612	8,017	0.5	1.6
BAPT–Consrv Bapt	8	NR	NR	NR	-	-
BAPT–Converge/BGC	5	1,100	NR	1,320	0.1	0.3
BAPT–Free Will Bapt	1	NR	46	56	0.0	0.0
BAPT–N Am Bapt Conf	1	NR	85	103	0.0	0.0
BAPT–Natl Mis Bapt Conv	16	1,010	3,625	4,395	0.3	0.9
BAPT–NBC Amer	5	500	1,500	1,819	0.1	0.4
BAPT–NBC USA	2	0	750	909	0.1	0.2
BAPT–NT Ind Bapt	1	NR	NR	NR	-	-
BAPT–Prog NBC	2	0	300	364	0.0	0.1
BAPT–Ref Bapt Ch	1	NR	NR	NR	-	-
BAPT–Reg Bapt Gen As	3	NR	NR	NR	-	-
BAPT–So Bapt Conv	119	10,993	18,103	21,951	1.5	4.3
BUDD–Mahayana	32	NR	NR	9,391	0.6	1.8
BUDD–Theravada	6	NR	NR	4,105	0.3	0.8
BUDD–Vajrayana	11	NR	NR	883	0.1	0.2
Calv Chpl	4	NR	NR	NR	-	-
Catholic	53	NR	NR	231,500	15.3	45.4
CGOD–Ch God (Ander)	4	233	NR	233	0.0	0.0
Ch Cr, Scientst	8	NR	NR	NR	-	-
Ch God (7th Day)	1	NR	NR	NR	-	-
Ch of Chr (Hol)	4	NR	NR	NR	-	-
Ch of Nazarene	13	1,126	1,225	1,420	0.1	0.3
Chr & Miss Al	12	1,174	3,466	3,812	0.3	0.7
CHR–Chr Ch (Disc)	15	417	737	894	0.1	0.2
CHR–Chr Chs & Chs Cr	6	NR	485	588	0.0	0.1
CHR–Chs of Christ	19	1,604	1,797	2,429	0.2	0.5

NR–Not Reported   - Represents no adherents reported.   Percentages may not total 100 due to rounding.

Table 3: Religious Congregations by County and Group: 2010

Religious Group	Number of Congregations	Number of Attendees	Number of Communicant, Confirmed, or Full Members	Adherents		
				Number of Adherents	% of Total Pop.	% of Total Adh.
Christian Brethren	3	NR	NR	NR	-	-
CONG–Cong Chr, NA	1	NR	40	49	0.0	0.0
Evan Cov Ch	9	2,037	1,982	2,649	0.2	0.5
Evan Free Ch	9	1,920	NR	1,920	0.1	0.4
FRND–Fr Un Mtg	1	NR	28	34	0.0	0.0
FRND–Indep Yr Mtgs	3	NR	202	245	0.0	0.0
HINDU–I/A Temples	6	NR	NR	4,573	0.3	0.9
HINDU–Post Ren	14	NR	NR	622	0.0	0.1
HINDU–Renaiss	6	NR	NR	144	0.0	0.0
HINDU–Trad Temples	1	NR	NR	1,000	0.1	0.2
Ind Fund Churches	1	NR	NR	NR	-	-
Int Cou Comm Ch	3	NR	NR	NR	-	-
Jain	1	NR	NR	NR	-	-
Jehovah's Witness	20	NR	NR	NR	-	-
JUD–Conserv	2	693	778	2,101	0.1	0.4
JUD–Orth	6	1,047	500	1,475	0.1	0.3
JUD–Reconst	1	20	25	68	0.0	0.0
JUD–Reform	6	1,170	2,063	5,570	0.4	1.1
LDS–Comm of Christ	1	NR	158	158	0.0	0.0
LDS–L-D Saints	46	NR	NR	24,929	1.7	4.9
LUTH–Apostolic Luth	1	NR	NR	NR	-	-
LUTH–Ch Luth Conf	1	NR	NR	NR	-	-
LUTH–E.L.C.A.	25	1,854	3,777	4,776	0.3	0.9
LUTH–Luth-MO Synod	17	1,794	3,075	3,869	0.3	0.8
LUTH–Wisc Ev Luth Syn	1	45	90	118	0.0	0.0
METH–AME	7	1,440	5,850	7,093	0.5	1.4
METH–AME Zion	3	175	560	679	0.0	0.1
METH–C.M.E.	5	430	1,100	1,334	0.1	0.3
METH–Free Methodist	3	205	252	252	0.0	0.0
METH–Un Methodist	30	3,311	6,635	9,345	0.6	1.8
METH–Wesleyan	3	88	81	115	0.0	0.0
Metro Comm Ch	1	68	114	138	0.0	0.0
Muslim Est	27	9,318	NR	29,941	2.0	5.9
Nat Spirit Asso	1	NR	NR	NR	-	-
New Apost Ch	2	NR	NR	NR	-	-
Non-denom Chr Chs	147	41,124	53,716	61,109	4.0	12.0
ORTHE–Greek Orthodox	2	925	NR	1,600	0.1	0.3
ORTHE–Orth Ch in Amer	5	237	NR	630	0.0	0.1
ORTHE–Romania Orth Ar	1	50	NR	350	0.0	0.1
ORTHO–Armen Ap Etchm	1	125	NR	1,500	0.1	0.3
ORTHO–Coptic Orth Ch	2	550	NR	1,210	0.1	0.2
ORTHO–Eritrean Orth	2	375	NR	1,050	0.1	0.2
ORTHO–Ethiopian Orth	2	NR	NR	NR	-	-
ORTHO–Malan Dioc Am	1	100	NR	300	0.0	0.1
PENT–Assemb of God	59	7,213	4,933	11,268	0.7	2.2
PENT–Ch God (Cleve)	9	772	729	884	0.1	0.2
PENT–Ch Lord Jesus Apos	3	NR	NR	NR	-	-
PENT–Ch of God Proph	1	NR	15	18	0.0	0.0
PENT–COGIC	26	1,120	3,400	4,123	0.3	0.8
PENT–Full Gosp Bapt	7	NR	NR	NR	-	-
PENT–Int Foursq Gos	11	1,707	1,131	1,371	0.1	0.3
PENT–Intl Pent Holiness	4	385	371	450	0.0	0.1
PENT–Open Bible Std	1	77	NR	77	0.0	0.0
PENT–Pent Ch of God	2	140	NR	217	0.0	0.0
PENT–Un Pent Ch Intl	9	NR	NR	NR	-	-
PENT–Vineyard	1	110	135	164	0.0	0.0
PRES–Kor Pres Abroad	2	NR	NR	NR	-	-
PRES–Korean Amer Pres	4	NR	NR	NR	-	-
PRES–Korean Pres Amer	7	NR	NR	NR	-	-
PRES–Orth Pres Ch	1	53	49	58	0.0	0.0
PRES–Presb Ch (USA)	30	3,749	6,613	8,019	0.5	1.6
PRES–Presb Ch Amer	5	60	24	48	0.0	0.0
REF–Christian Ref	4	402	427	518	0.0	0.1
REF–Ref Ch in Am	2	138	215	310	0.0	0.1
Salvation Army	4	276	395	2,075	0.1	0.4
Sev Day Adv	15	2,083	3,622	4,166	0.3	0.8
Sikh	4	NR	NR	NR	-	-
Tao	3	NR	NR	NR	-	-
Un C of Christ	22	1,115	2,626	3,184	0.2	0.6
Unit Univ	5	605	812	1,025	0.1	0.2
Unity Ch	6	NR	NR	NR	-	-
Zoroastrian	0	NR	NR	143	0.0	0.0

Religious Group	Number of Congregations	Number of Attendees	Number of Communicant, Confirmed, or Full Members	Adherents		
				Number of Adherents	% of Total Pop.	% of Total Adh.
ALPINE	**1**	**NR**	**NR**	**50**	**4.3**	**100.0**
Non-denom Chr Chs	1	NR	NR	50	4.3	100.0
AMADOR	**47**	**2,316**	**2,590**	**9,307**	**24.4**	**100.0**
ANG/EPIS–Episcopal	1	89	129	152	0.4	1.6
Bahá'í	0	NR	4	4	0.0	0.0
BAPT–Amer Bapt Assn	1	NR	85	97	0.3	1.0
BAPT–Consrv Bapt	2	NR	NR	NR	-	-
BAPT–Free Will Bapt	1	NR	46	52	0.1	0.6
BAPT–So Bapt Conv	6	243	440	500	1.3	5.4
Calv Chpl	2	NR	NR	NR	-	-
Catholic	6	NR	NR	3,887	10.2	41.8
Ch Cr, Scientst	1	NR	NR	NR	-	-
Ch of Nazarene	1	466	326	866	2.3	9.3
CHR–Chs of Christ	3	80	61	81	0.2	0.9
Evan Free Ch	1	65	NR	65	0.2	0.7
FRND–Indep Yr Mtgs	1	NR	0	0	0.0	0.0
HINDU–Post Ren	1	NR	NR	16	0.0	0.2
Jehovah's Witness	2	NR	NR	NR	-	-
LDS–L-D Saints	2	NR	NR	1,196	3.1	12.9
LUTH–E.L.C.A.	1	60	211	283	0.7	3.0
METH–Un Methodist	3	126	302	331	0.9	3.6
Non-denom Chr Chs	2	560	400	700	1.8	7.5
ORTHE–Serb Orth USA	1	45	NR	150	0.4	1.6
PENT–Assemb of God	4	201	166	339	0.9	3.6
PENT–Int Foursq Gos	2	204	219	249	0.7	2.7
PENT–Intl Pent Holiness	1	15	40	45	0.1	0.5
PENT–Pent Ch of God	1	70	NR	109	0.3	1.2
Sev Day Adv	1	92	161	185	0.5	2.0
BUTTE	**202**	**16,872**	**21,131**	**74,981**	**34.1**	**100.0**
ANG/EPIS–Episcopal	4	277	650	661	0.3	0.9
Bahá'í	2	NR	218	218	0.1	0.3
BAPT–Amer Bapt Assn	1	NR	0	0	0.0	0.0
BAPT–Amer Bapt USA	2	123	215	256	0.1	0.3
BAPT–Consrv Bapt	4	NR	NR	NR	-	-
BAPT–Converge/BGC	1	75	NR	90	0.0	0.1
BAPT–NBC USA	1	0	0	0	0.0	0.0
BAPT–Reg Bapt Gen As	3	NR	NR	NR	-	-
BAPT–So Bapt Conv	16	1,102	1,931	2,296	1.0	3.1
BRETH–Ch of Brethren	1	0	43	51	0.0	0.1
BRETH–Grace Breth	1	NR	NR	NR	-	-
BUDD–Mahayana	3	NR	NR	216	0.1	0.3
BUDD–Vajrayana	1	NR	NR	20	0.0	0.0
Calv Chpl	4	NR	NR	NR	-	-
Catholic	7	NR	NR	34,101	15.5	45.5
CGOD–Ch God (Ander)	2	100	NR	100	0.0	0.1
Ch Cr, Scientst	3	NR	NR	NR	-	-
Ch of Nazarene	4	866	626	1,840	0.8	2.5
Chr & Miss Al	6	2,229	2,335	4,073	1.9	5.4
CHR–Chr Ch (Disc)	2	161	298	354	0.2	0.5
CHR–Chr Chs & Chs Cr	4	NR	380	452	0.2	0.6
CHR–Chs of Christ	7	382	430	515	0.2	0.7
Christian Brethren	1	NR	NR	NR	-	-
CONG–Cong Chr, NA	1	NR	155	184	0.1	0.2
Evan Free Ch	5	1,085	NR	1,085	0.5	1.4
FRND–Indep Yr Mtgs	1	NR	18	21	0.0	0.0
Jehovah's Witness	7	NR	NR	NR	-	-
JUD–Reconst	1	9	12	32	0.0	0.0
LDS–L-D Saints	16	NR	NR	9,357	4.3	12.5
LUTH–E.L.C.A.	2	243	859	1,088	0.5	1.5
LUTH–Luth-MO Synod	4	342	703	805	0.4	1.1
MENN–CG in Cr (Menn)	1	NR	27	32	0.0	0.0
MENN–Menn Chr Fell	1	41	21	41	0.0	0.1
METH–AME	1	0	150	178	0.1	0.2
METH–C.M.E.	1	0	100	119	0.1	0.2
METH–Free Methodist	1	345	210	345	0.2	0.5
METH–Un Methodist	7	657	1,234	1,607	0.7	2.1
Muslim Est	1	346	NR	1,109	0.5	1.5
Non-denom Chr Chs	21	3,345	3,916	4,392	2.0	5.9
ORTHE–Orth Ch in Amer	1	40	NR	40	0.0	0.1
ORTHO–Syrian Orth Ch	1	90	NR	240	0.1	0.3
PENT–Assemb of God	11	750	386	946	0.4	1.3

NR–Not Reported - Represents no adherents reported. Percentages may not total 100 due to rounding.

Table 3: Religious Congregations by County and Group: 2010

Religious Group	Number of Congregations	Number of Attendees	Number of Communicant, Confirmed, or Full Members	Adherents		
				Number of Adherents	% of Total Pop.	% of Total Adh.
PENT–Ch God (Cleve)	3	458	314	373	0.2	0.5
PENT–Ch God Apos Fth	1	NR	NR	NR	-	-
PENT–Ch of God Proph	1	NR	30	36	0.0	0.0
PENT–COGIC	1	0	150	178	0.1	0.2
PENT–Int Foursq Gos	3	190	290	345	0.2	0.5
PENT–Pent Ch of God	7	490	NR	761	0.3	1.0
PENT–Un Pent Ch Intl	3	NR	NR	NR	-	-
PENT–Vineyard	1	125	225	268	0.1	0.4
PRES–Evan Presby Ch	1	NR	52	62	0.0	0.1
PRES–Presb Ch (USA)	2	890	1,634	1,943	0.9	2.6
PRES–Presb Ch Amer	1	144	152	182	0.1	0.2
REF–Ref Ch in U.S.	1	NR	22	29	0.0	0.0
Salvation Army	2	175	280	398	0.2	0.5
Sev Day Adv	7	1,652	2,874	3,305	1.5	4.4
Un C of Christ	2	98	133	158	0.1	0.2
Unit Univ	1	42	58	79	0.0	0.1
Unity Ch	1	NR	NR	NR	-	-
CALAVERAS	**61**	**3,038**	**3,710**	**31,428**	**69.0**	**100.0**
ANG/EPIS–Anglican NA	1	NR	NR	NR	-	-
ANG/EPIS–Episcopal	2	56	90	112	0.2	0.4
Bahá'í	0	NR	17	17	0.0	0.1
BAPT–Amer Bapt Assn	1	NR	85	99	0.2	0.3
BAPT–Amer Bapt USA	1	30	45	52	0.1	0.2
BAPT–So Bapt Conv	6	335	396	461	1.0	1.5
BUDD–Mahayana	1	NR	NR	28	0.1	0.1
Calv Chpl	1	NR	NR	NR	-	-
Catholic	5	NR	NR	25,052	55.0	79.7
Ch of Nazarene	1	43	43	43	0.1	0.1
CHR–Chs of Christ	4	100	97	113	0.2	0.4
Evan Cov Ch	5	869	854	1,129	2.5	3.6
Evan Free Ch	1	18	NR	18	0.0	0.1
Jehovah's Witness	2	NR	NR	NR	-	-
LDS–L-D Saints	3	NR	NR	1,597	3.5	5.1
LUTH–E.L.C.A.	2	67	78	138	0.3	0.4
LUTH–Luth Cong Msn Chr	1	NR	NR	NR	-	-
LUTH–Luth-MO Synod	1	26	37	43	0.1	0.1
METH–Un Methodist	1	80	114	160	0.4	0.5
Non-denom Chr Chs	10	970	1,185	1,331	2.9	4.2
ORTHE–Ant Orth of NA	1	30	NR	35	0.1	0.1
ORTHE–Serb Orth USA	1	6	NR	10	0.0	0.0
PENT–Assemb of God	4	117	63	167	0.4	0.5
PENT–Open Bible Std	1	11	NR	11	0.0	0.0
PENT–Pent Ch of God	1	70	NR	109	0.2	0.3
Sev Day Adv	2	96	168	193	0.4	0.6
Un C of Christ	2	114	438	510	1.1	1.6
COLUSA	**29**	**1,070**	**1,209**	**11,399**	**53.2**	**100.0**
ANG/EPIS–Episcopal	1	21	34	54	0.3	0.5
Bahá'í	0	NR	7	7	0.0	0.1
BAPT–Amer Bapt USA	1	25	25	32	0.1	0.3
BAPT–Reg Bapt Gen As	1	NR	NR	NR	-	-
BAPT–So Bapt Conv	2	28	78	101	0.5	0.9
Catholic	6	NR	NR	9,170	42.8	80.4
Chr & Miss Al	1	33	0	53	0.2	0.5
CHR–Chr Ch (Disc)	1	8	25	32	0.1	0.3
Jehovah's Witness	1	NR	NR	NR	-	-
LDS–L-D Saints	1	NR	NR	372	1.7	3.3
LUTH–Luth-MO Synod	1	25	51	57	0.3	0.5
METH–Un Methodist	4	139	312	423	2.0	3.7
Non-denom Chr Chs	3	360	360	450	2.1	3.9
PENT–Assemb of God	5	316	161	445	2.1	3.9
PRES–Presb Ch (USA)	1	115	156	203	0.9	1.8
CONTRA COSTA	**652**	**72,283**	**90,143**	**403,596**	**38.5**	**100.0**
ANG/EPIS–Anglican NA	2	NR	NR	NR	-	-
ANG/EPIS–Episcopal	15	1,671	4,103	5,303	0.5	1.3
Bahá'í	16	NR	897	897	0.1	0.2
BAPT–Alliance Bapt	1	NR	NR	NR	-	-
BAPT–Amer Bapt Assn	5	NR	464	572	0.1	0.1
BAPT–Amer Bapt USA	17	1,820	2,138	2,637	0.3	0.7
BAPT–Consrv Bapt	7	NR	NR	NR	-	-
BAPT–Converge/BGC	8	2,525	NR	3,030	0.3	0.8

Religious Group	Number of Congregations	Number of Attendees	Number of Communicant, Confirmed, or Full Members	Adherents		
				Number of Adherents	% of Total Pop.	% of Total Adh.
BAPT–Free Will Bapt	4	NR	184	227	0.0	0.1
BAPT–Natl Mis Bapt Conv	5	25	635	783	0.1	0.2
BAPT–NBC Amer	2	250	1,300	1,603	0.2	0.4
BAPT–NBC USA	6	500	3,850	4,749	0.5	1.2
BAPT–Reg Bapt Gen As	8	NR	NR	NR	-	-
BAPT–S-D Baptist Gen Con	1	24	59	73	0.0	0.0
BAPT–So Bapt Conv	65	7,372	10,650	13,136	1.3	3.3
BUDD–Mahayana	7	NR	NR	9,031	0.9	2.2
BUDD–Theravada	3	NR	NR	641	0.1	0.2
BUDD–Vajrayana	3	NR	NR	150	0.0	0.0
Calv Chpl	5	NR	NR	NR	-	-
Catholic	34	NR	NR	228,400	21.8	56.6
CGOD–Ch God (Ander)	2	0	NR	0	0.0	0.0
Ch Cr, Scientst	5	NR	NR	NR	-	-
Ch of Nazarene	4	690	1,154	1,326	0.1	0.3
Chr & Miss Al	4	848	646	1,413	0.1	0.4
CHR–Chr Ch (Disc)	5	257	480	592	0.1	0.1
CHR–Chr Chs & Chs Cr	4	NR	580	715	0.1	0.2
CHR–Chs of Christ	20	1,789	1,988	2,489	0.2	0.6
CONG–Cong Chr, NA	1	NR	54	67	0.0	0.0
Evan Cov Ch	11	1,946	1,663	2,531	0.2	0.6
Evan Free Ch	4	1,990	NR	1,990	0.2	0.5
FRND–Evan Fr Ch Intl	1	76	36	44	0.0	0.0
HINDU–Post Ren	5	NR	NR	218	0.0	0.1
HINDU–Trad Temples	1	NR	NR	50	0.0	0.0
Jehovah's Witness	13	NR	NR	NR	-	-
JUD–Conserv	1	277	311	840	0.1	0.2
JUD–Orth	2	85	100	120	0.0	0.0
JUD–Reform	4	767	1,352	3,650	0.3	0.9
LDS–Comm of Christ	1	NR	158	158	0.0	0.0
LDS–L-D Saints	42	NR	NR	21,505	2.0	5.3
LUTH–E.L.C.A.	13	1,928	3,431	5,013	0.5	1.2
LUTH–Luth Cong Msn Chr	1	1,009	133	164	0.0	0.0
LUTH–Luth-MO Synod	13	903	1,396	1,753	0.2	0.4
LUTH–Wisc Ev Luth Syn	1	23	34	38	0.0	0.0
METH–AME	4	50	450	555	0.1	0.1
METH–C.M.E.	3	205	703	867	0.1	0.2
METH–Free Methodist	4	245	184	250	0.0	0.1
METH–Un Methodist	23	2,373	4,849	7,676	0.7	1.9
METH–Wesleyan	3	186	94	242	0.0	0.1
Muslim Est	9	3,106	NR	9,980	1.0	2.5
New Apost Ch	2	NR	NR	NR	-	-
Non-denom Chr Chs	72	17,650	23,148	26,080	2.5	6.5
ORTHE–Ant Orth of NA	1	110	NR	350	0.0	0.1
ORTHE–Greek Orthodox	1	100	NR	600	0.1	0.1
ORTHE–Orth Ch in Amer	2	49	NR	125	0.0	0.0
ORTHE–Rus Orth Abroad	1	40	NR	175	0.0	0.0
ORTHE–Serb Orth USA	2	75	NR	650	0.1	0.2
ORTHO–Coptic Orth Ch	1	276	NR	535	0.1	0.1
PENT–Apos Faith Msn	1	NR	35	43	0.0	0.0
PENT–Assemb of God	22	6,796	2,905	10,764	1.0	2.7
PENT–Ch God (Cleve)	10	516	715	882	0.1	0.2
PENT–Ch of God Proph	3	NR	133	164	0.0	0.0
PENT–COGIC	13	275	1,490	1,838	0.2	0.5
PENT–Full Gosp Bapt	1	NR	NR	NR	-	-
PENT–Int Foursq Gos	14	1,341	2,333	2,878	0.3	0.7
PENT–Intl Pent Holiness	4	522	296	365	0.0	0.1
PENT–Open Bible Std	5	936	NR	936	0.1	0.2
PENT–Pent Ch of God	10	1,830	NR	2,843	0.3	0.7
PENT–Un Pent Ch Intl	6	NR	NR	NR	-	-
PENT–Vineyard	2	228	312	385	0.0	0.1
PRES–Evan Presby Ch	2	NR	521	643	0.1	0.2
PRES–Kor Pres Abroad	2	NR	NR	NR	-	-
PRES–Korean Pres Amer	1	NR	NR	NR	-	-
PRES–Orth Pres Ch	1	79	89	107	0.0	0.0
PRES–Presb Ch (USA)	15	4,319	7,617	9,395	0.9	2.3
PRES–Presb Ch Amer	4	712	783	1,040	0.1	0.3
REF–Christian Ref	2	185	204	252	0.0	0.1
REF–Ref Ch in Am	1	140	68	178	0.0	0.0
REF–Un Ref Chs N.A.	1	NR	NR	NR	-	-
Salvation Army	3	179	286	556	0.1	0.1
Sev Day Adv	10	1,594	2,774	3,189	0.3	0.8
Sikh	3	NR	NR	NR	-	-
Swedenborgian	1	NR	NR	NR	-	-

NR–Not Reported - Represents no adherents reported. Percentages may not total 100 due to rounding.

Table 3: Religious Congregations by County and Group: 2010

Religious Group	Number of Congrega-tions	Number of Attendees	Number of Communicant, Confirmed, or Full Members	Adherents		
				Number of Adherents	% of Total Pop.	% of Total Adh.
Un C of Christ	10	706	1,485	1,832	0.2	0.5
Unit Univ	2	685	873	1,180	0.1	0.3
Unity Ch	3	NR	NR	NR	-	-
Zoroastrian	0	NR	NR	133	0.0	0.0
DEL NORTE	**32**	**1,859**	**1,983**	**5,962**	**20.8**	**100.0**
ANG/EPIS–Episcopal	1	19	50	68	0.2	1.1
Bahá'í	1	NR	36	36	0.1	0.6
BAPT–Reg Bapt Gen As	1	NR	NR	NR	-	-
BAPT–So Bapt Conv	3	147	145	173	0.6	2.9
BUDD–Mahayana	1	NR	NR	10	0.0	0.2
Calv Chpl	1	NR	NR	NR	-	-
Catholic	1	NR	NR	1,585	5.5	26.6
Ch of Nazarene	1	29	49	49	0.2	0.8
Chr & Miss Al	1	30	47	47	0.2	0.8
CHR–Chr Chs & Chs Cr	1	NR	85	102	0.4	1.7
Evan Free Ch	1	130	NR	130	0.5	2.2
Ind Fund Churches	1	NR	NR	NR	-	-
Jehovah's Witness	1	NR	NR	NR	-	-
LDS–L-D Saints	2	NR	NR	1,213	4.2	20.3
LUTH–Luth–MO Synod	1	128	382	503	1.8	8.4
METH–Un Methodist	3	147	266	368	1.3	6.2
Non-denom Chr Chs	3	370	200	462	1.6	7.7
PENT–Assemb of God	2	216	99	374	1.3	6.3
PENT–Ch of God Proph	1	NR	54	65	0.2	1.1
PENT–Int Foursq Gos	2	408	283	338	1.2	5.7
PENT–Pent Ch of God	1	70	NR	109	0.4	1.8
PENT–Un Pent Ch Intl	1	NR	NR	NR	-	-
Sev Day Adv	1	165	287	330	1.2	5.5
EL DORADO	**118**	**14,223**	**13,873**	**52,016**	**28.7**	**100.0**
ANG/EPIS–Episcopal	2	393	649	724	0.4	1.4
Bahá'í	2	NR	142	142	0.1	0.3
BAPT–Amer Bapt Assn	1	NR	85	102	0.1	0.2
BAPT–Amer Bapt USA	1	398	239	287	0.2	0.6
BAPT–Asc Ref Bap Ch Am	1	NR	NR	NR	-	-
BAPT–Consrv Bapt	5	NR	NR	NR	-	-
BAPT–N Am Bapt Conf	1	NR	163	196	0.1	0.4
BAPT–Ref Bapt Ch	1	NR	NR	NR	-	-
BAPT–So Bapt Conv	6	431	400	481	0.3	0.9
Calv Chpl	4	NR	NR	NR	-	-
Catholic	6	NR	NR	23,298	12.9	44.8
Ch Cr, Scientst	2	NR	NR	NR	-	-
Ch of Nazarene	1	128	132	190	0.1	0.4
Chr & Miss Al	1	757	526	1,472	0.8	2.8
CHR–Chr Chs & Chs Cr	1	NR	85	102	0.1	0.2
CHR–Chs of Christ	5	260	243	296	0.2	0.6
CONG–Cong Chr, NA	1	NR	50	60	0.0	0.1
Evan Cov Ch	3	741	344	963	0.5	1.9
Evan Free Ch	3	530	NR	530	0.3	1.0
HINDU–Post Ren	2	NR	NR	516	0.3	1.0
Jehovah's Witness	6	NR	NR	NR	-	-
JUD–Reform	1	27	48	130	0.1	0.2
LDS–L-D Saints	15	NR	NR	7,030	3.9	13.5
LUTH–E.L.C.A.	2	160	340	476	0.3	0.9
LUTH–Luth–MO Synod	3	401	687	887	0.5	1.7
METH–Un Methodist	3	580	638	841	0.5	1.6
Muslim Est	1	345	NR	1,109	0.6	2.1
Non-denom Chr Chs	19	7,375	7,100	9,350	5.2	18.0
ORTHE–Pal/Jor Orth	1	40	NR	250	0.1	0.5
ORTHE–Rus Orth Abroad	1	40	NR	65	0.0	0.1
PENT–Assemb of God	3	210	156	255	0.1	0.5
PENT–Int Foursq Gos	2	191	133	160	0.1	0.3
PENT–Pent Ch of God	1	70	NR	109	0.1	0.2
PENT–Un Pent Ch Intl	2	NR	NR	NR	-	-
PRES–Presb Ch (USA)	2	424	456	549	0.3	1.1
Sev Day Adv	6	722	1,257	1,445	0.8	2.8
Unity Ch	1	NR	NR	NR	-	-
Zoroastrian	0	NR	NR	1	0.0	0.0
FRESNO	**701**	**80,389**	**100,163**	**481,076**	**51.7**	**100.0**
ANG/EPIS–Anglican NA	7	NR	NR	NR	-	-
ANG/EPIS–Episcopal	1	133	250	285	0.0	0.1

Religious Group	Number of Congrega-tions	Number of Attendees	Number of Communicant, Confirmed, or Full Members	Adherents		
				Number of Adherents	% of Total Pop.	% of Total Adh.
Bahá'í	2	NR	474	474	0.1	0.1
BAPT–Amer Bapt Assn	3	NR	450	585	0.1	0.1
BAPT–Amer Bapt USA	17	3,228	4,216	5,476	0.6	1.1
BAPT–Consrv Bapt	3	NR	NR	NR	-	-
BAPT–Converge/BGC	9	3,175	NR	3,810	0.4	0.8
BAPT–Free Will Bapt	5	NR	230	299	0.0	0.1
BAPT–Natl Mis Bapt Conv	3	30	400	520	0.1	0.1
BAPT–Ref Bapt Ch	1	NR	NR	NR	-	-
BAPT–Reg Bapt Gen As	4	NR	NR	NR	-	-
BAPT–So Bapt Conv	57	7,802	11,739	15,248	1.6	3.2
BRETH–Ch of Brethren	2	96	108	140	0.0	0.0
BUDD–Mahayana	11	NR	NR	6,672	0.7	1.4
BUDD–Theravada	5	NR	NR	2,755	0.3	0.6
Calv Chpl	2	NR	NR	NR	-	-
Catholic	43	NR	NR	288,324	31.0	59.9
CGOD–Ch God (Ander)	9	860	NR	860	0.1	0.2
Ch Cr, Scientst	1	NR	NR	NR	-	-
Ch of Chr (Hol)	2	NR	NR	NR	-	-
Ch of Nazarene	23	1,324	1,592	2,384	0.3	0.5
Chr & Miss Al	5	1,018	2,198	2,206	0.2	0.5
CHR–Chr Ch (Disc)	3	134	270	351	0.0	0.1
CHR–Chr Chs & Chs Cr	5	NR	2,430	3,156	0.3	0.7
CHR–Chs of Christ	27	2,971	2,685	3,398	0.4	0.7
CHR–Int Chs of Christ	1	NR	71	92	0.0	0.0
CONG–Armen Evang Add'l	1	NR	NR	NR	-	-
CONG–Consrv Cong Chr	1	85	170	221	0.0	0.0
Evan Cov Ch	7	691	669	897	0.1	0.2
Evan Free Ch	6	2,660	NR	2,660	0.3	0.6
FRND–Evan Fr Ch Intl	1	72	70	91	0.0	0.0
FRND–Indep Yr Mtgs	1	NR	8	10	0.0	0.0
HINDU–I/A Temples	2	NR	NR	1,992	0.2	0.4
HINDU–Post Ren	3	NR	NR	85	0.0	0.0
Jehovah's Witness	18	NR	NR	NR	-	-
JUD–Conserv	1	29	32	86	0.0	0.0
JUD–Orth	1	43	50	60	0.0	0.0
JUD–Reform	1	200	352	950	0.1	0.2
LDS–Comm of Christ	1	NR	158	158	0.0	0.0
LDS–L-D Saints	36	NR	NR	21,404	2.3	4.4
LUTH–E.L.C.A.	14	1,753	3,304	4,331	0.5	0.9
LUTH–Luth Cong Msn Chr	2	243	545	708	0.1	0.1
LUTH–Luth–MO Synod	5	571	720	961	0.1	0.2
LUTH–Nor Amer Luth C	1	NR	NR	NR	-	-
LUTH–Wisc Ev Luth Syn	1	113	129	162	0.0	0.0
MENN–Menn Br US Conf	23	NR	3,821	4,963	0.5	1.0
MENN–Mennonite USA	4	250	417	542	0.1	0.1
MENN–Unaffil Amish-Menn	1	114	53	114	0.0	0.0
METH–AME	3	25	250	325	0.0	0.1
METH–AME Zion	1	0	150	195	0.0	0.0
METH–C.M.E.	1	0	150	195	0.0	0.0
METH–Free Methodist	1	101	78	101	0.0	0.0
METH–Un Methodist	20	1,329	2,907	3,511	0.4	0.7
Muslim Est	4	1,875	NR	2,868	0.3	0.6
New Apost Ch	1	NR	NR	NR	-	-
Non-denom Chr Chs	102	25,232	33,833	36,092	3.9	7.5
ORTHE–Greek Orthodox	2	320	NR	1,788	0.2	0.4
ORTHE–Serb Orth USA	1	125	NR	400	0.0	0.1
ORTHO–Armen Ap Cilic	1	115	NR	460	0.0	0.1
ORTHO–Armen Ap Etchm	3	415	NR	5,000	0.5	1.0
ORTHO–Coptic Orth Ch	1	75	NR	120	0.0	0.0
ORTHO–Ethiopian Orth	1	NR	NR	NR	-	-
PENT–Assemb of God	50	12,583	6,454	27,227	2.9	5.7
PENT–Ch God (Cleve)	8	661	992	1,289	0.1	0.3
PENT–Ch of God Proph	9	NR	345	448	0.0	0.1
PENT–COGIC	10	632	2,252	2,925	0.3	0.6
PENT–Full Gosp Bapt	3	NR	NR	NR	-	-
PENT–Int Foursq Gos	14	1,838	3,441	4,470	0.5	0.9
PENT–Intl Pent Holiness	6	404	371	482	0.1	0.1
PENT–Pent Ch of God	16	1,120	NR	1,740	0.2	0.4
PENT–Un Pent Ch Intl	5	NR	NR	NR	-	-
PENT–Vineyard	1	283	432	561	0.1	0.1
PRES–Evan Presby Ch	5	NR	1,684	2,187	0.2	0.5
PRES–Presb Ch (USA)	10	801	1,279	1,661	0.2	0.3
PRES–Presb Ch Amer	1	100	90	115	0.0	0.0
PRES–Ref Pres of NA	1	93	76	93	0.0	0.0

NR–Not Reported   - Represents no adherents reported.   Percentages may not total 100 due to rounding.

Table 3: Religious Congregations by County and Group: 2010

Religious Group	Number of Congrega-tions	Number of Attendees	Number of Communicant, Confirmed, or Full Members	Adherents		
				Number of Adherents	% of Total Pop.	% of Total Adh.
REF–Christian Ref	4	230	272	353	0.0	0.1
REF–Ref Ch in Am	1	130	140	175	0.0	0.0
REF–Un Ref Chs N.A.	1	NR	NR	NR	-	-
Salvation Army	3	230	201	431	0.0	0.1
Sev Day Adv	18	3,459	6,014	6,918	0.7	1.4
Sikh	6	NR	NR	NR	-	-
Un C of Christ	3	358	803	1,043	0.1	0.2
Unit Univ	1	260	338	468	0.1	0.1
Unity Ch	1	NR	NR	NR	-	-
Zoroastrian	0	NR	NR	5	0.0	0.0
GLENN	**49**	**1,735**	**2,419**	**11,126**	**39.6**	**100.0**
ANG/EPIS–Episcopal	2	24	36	88	0.3	0.8
Bahá'í	0	NR	12	12	0.0	0.1
BAPT–Amer Bapt USA	3	152	200	255	0.9	2.3
BAPT–So Bapt Conv	2	53	95	121	0.4	1.1
Calv Chpl	1	NR	NR	NR	-	-
Catholic	3	NR	NR	6,112	21.7	54.9
CGOD–Ch God (Ander)	1	0	NR	0	0.0	0.0
Ch of Nazarene	1	23	21	37	0.1	0.3
CHR–Chr Chs & Chs Cr	2	NR	181	231	0.8	2.1
CHR–Chs of Christ	2	26	29	34	0.1	0.3
Evan Free Ch	2	419	NR	419	1.5	3.8
Jehovah's Witness	2	NR	NR	NR	-	-
LDS–L-D Saints	3	NR	NR	820	2.9	7.4
LUTH–E.L.C.A.	1	51	163	287	1.0	2.6
LUTH–Luth-MO Synod	2	57	179	220	0.8	2.0
MENN–CG in Cr (Menn)	2	NR	238	303	1.1	2.7
MENN–Menn Br US Conf	1	NR	54	69	0.2	0.6
METH–Un Methodist	2	156	280	614	2.2	5.5
Non-denom Chr Chs	6	500	545	660	2.3	5.9
PENT–Assemb of God	3	170	63	328	1.2	2.9
PENT–COGIC	1	0	150	191	0.7	1.7
PENT–Int Foursq Gos	1	0	0	0	0.0	0.0
PENT–Pent Ch of God	1	70	NR	109	0.4	1.0
PENT–Un Pent Ch Intl	1	NR	NR	NR	-	-
PRES–Presb Ch (USA)	1	0	78	99	0.4	0.9
REF–Ref Ch in U.S.	1	NR	35	48	0.2	0.4
Sev Day Adv	2	34	60	69	0.2	0.6
HUMBOLDT	**177**	**7,996**	**9,801**	**28,959**	**21.5**	**100.0**
ANG/EPIS–Episcopal	4	230	438	627	0.5	2.2
Bahá'í	1	NR	127	127	0.1	0.4
BAPT–Amer Bapt Assn	4	NR	340	402	0.3	1.4
BAPT–Amer Bapt USA	2	661	434	514	0.4	1.8
BAPT–Consrv Bapt	2	NR	NR	NR	-	-
BAPT–Reg Bapt Gen As	3	NR	NR	NR	-	-
BAPT–So Bapt Conv	15	782	1,541	1,824	1.4	6.3
BUDD–Mahayana	7	NR	NR	389	0.3	1.3
BUDD–Vajrayana	3	NR	NR	150	0.1	0.5
Calv Chpl	3	NR	NR	NR	-	-
Catholic	13	NR	NR	9,901	7.4	34.2
Ch Cr, Scientst	3	NR	NR	NR	-	-
Ch of Nazarene	4	362	674	868	0.6	3.0
CHR–Chr Ch (Disc)	1	23	30	36	0.0	0.1
CHR–Chr Chs & Chs Cr	2	NR	80	95	0.1	0.3
CHR–Chs of Christ	5	142	163	215	0.2	0.7
Christian Brethren	1	NR	NR	NR	-	-
Evan Cov Ch	1	142	146	185	0.1	0.6
Evan Free Ch	2	610	NR	610	0.5	2.1
FRND–Indep Yr Mtgs	2	NR	17	20	0.0	0.1
HINDU–Post Ren	1	NR	NR	77	0.1	0.3
HINDU–Renaiss	2	NR	NR	387	0.3	1.3
Ind Fund Churches	1	NR	NR	NR	-	-
Jehovah's Witness	5	NR	NR	NR	-	-
JUD–Reform	1	71	126	340	0.3	1.2
LDS–Comm of Christ	1	NR	158	158	0.1	0.5
LDS–L-D Saints	7	NR	NR	3,557	2.6	12.3
LUTH–E.L.C.A.	6	254	396	591	0.4	2.0
LUTH–Luth Cong Msn Chr	1	19	32	38	0.0	0.1
LUTH–Luth-MO Synod	3	158	221	286	0.2	1.0
METH–Un Methodist	4	420	649	1,395	1.0	4.8
METH–Wesleyan	1	58	65	75	0.1	0.3

Religious Group	Number of Congrega-tions	Number of Attendees	Number of Communicant, Confirmed, or Full Members	Adherents		
				Number of Adherents	% of Total Pop.	% of Total Adh.
Non-denom Chr Chs	11	585	765	872	0.6	3.0
ORTHE–Orth Ch in Amer	1	35	NR	65	0.0	0.2
PENT–Apos Faith Msn	1	NR	35	41	0.0	0.1
PENT–Assemb of God	16	925	416	1,228	0.9	4.2
PENT–Ch God (Cleve)	3	73	82	97	0.1	0.3
PENT–Int Foursq Gos	4	1,041	509	602	0.4	2.1
PENT–Pent Ch of God	4	280	NR	435	0.3	1.5
PENT–Un Pent Ch Intl	2	NR	NR	NR	-	-
PENT–Vineyard	2	80	125	148	0.1	0.5
PRES–Presb Ch (USA)	13	304	900	1,065	0.8	3.7
Salvation Army	1	47	163	163	0.1	0.6
Sev Day Adv	5	536	931	1,072	0.8	3.7
Un C of Christ	1	60	98	116	0.1	0.4
Unit Univ	1	98	140	188	0.1	0.6
Unity Ch	1	NR	NR	NR	-	-
IMPERIAL	**123**	**6,499**	**9,893**	**67,372**	**38.6**	**100.0**
ANG/EPIS–Episcopal	3	127	196	211	0.1	0.3
Bahá'í	0	NR	119	119	0.1	0.2
BAPT–Amer Bapt USA	3	368	265	341	0.2	0.5
BAPT–N Am Bapt Conf	1	NR	120	155	0.1	0.2
BAPT–Natl Mis Bapt Conv	2	0	210	270	0.2	0.4
BAPT–NBC USA	1	50	100	129	0.1	0.2
BAPT–Reg Bapt Gen As	2	NR	NR	NR	-	-
BAPT–So Bapt Conv	11	765	2,450	3,155	1.8	4.7
BUDD–Vajrayana	1	NR	NR	166	0.1	0.2
Calv Chpl	3	NR	NR	NR	-	-
Catholic	12	NR	NR	49,226	28.2	73.1
Ch Cr, Scientst	1	NR	NR	NR	-	-
Ch of Nazarene	5	201	239	309	0.2	0.5
CHR–Chr Chs & Chs Cr	3	NR	601	774	0.4	1.1
CHR–Chs of Christ	7	248	210	276	0.2	0.4
FRND–Evan Fr Ch Intl	2	34	25	32	0.0	0.0
Ind Fund Churches	1	NR	NR	NR	-	-
Jehovah's Witness	5	NR	NR	NR	-	-
JUD–Reform	1	10	18	49	0.0	0.1
LDS–L-D Saints	5	NR	NR	3,149	1.8	4.7
LUTH–Luth-MO Synod	4	169	336	389	0.2	0.6
METH–AME	1	0	150	193	0.1	0.3
METH–C.M.E.	1	0	60	77	0.0	0.1
METH–Un Methodist	4	116	341	419	0.2	0.6
Muslim Est	1	30	NR	150	0.1	0.2
Non-denom Chr Chs	10	1,335	2,010	2,137	1.2	3.2
PENT–Assemb of God	16	2,137	900	3,735	2.1	5.5
PENT–Ch God (Cleve)	1	12	7	9	0.0	0.0
PENT–Ch of God Proph	3	NR	123	158	0.1	0.2
PENT–Int Foursq Gos	1	78	79	102	0.1	0.2
PENT–Intl Pent Holiness	1	20	20	26	0.0	0.0
PRES–Kor Pres Abroad	1	NR	NR	NR	-	-
PRES–Korean Pres Amer	1	NR	NR	NR	-	-
PRES–Presb Ch (USA)	2	98	129	166	0.1	0.2
PRES–Presb Ch Amer	1	0	0	0	0.0	0.0
Salvation Army	1	100	139	248	0.1	0.4
Sev Day Adv	5	601	1,046	1,202	0.7	1.8
INYO	**38**	**1,284**	**1,867**	**7,973**	**43.0**	**100.0**
ANG/EPIS–Anglican NA	2	NR	NR	NR	-	-
Bahá'í	0	NR	8	8	0.0	0.1
BAPT–Consrv Bapt	2	NR	NR	NR	-	-
BAPT–So Bapt Conv	3	107	101	120	0.6	1.5
Calv Chpl	1	NR	NR	NR	-	-
Catholic	5	NR	NR	4,827	26.0	60.5
Ch Cr, Scientst	1	NR	NR	NR	-	-
Ch of Nazarene	2	90	98	138	0.7	1.7
CHR–Chs of Christ	1	15	15	20	0.1	0.3
Evan Free Ch	1	50	NR	50	0.3	0.6
Jehovah's Witness	1	NR	NR	NR	-	-
LDS–L-D Saints	2	NR	NR	621	3.3	7.8
LUTH–Evan Luth Syn	1	13	22	27	0.1	0.3
LUTH–Luth-MO Synod	1	100	190	204	1.1	2.6
METH–Un Methodist	3	188	313	682	3.7	8.6
Non-denom Chr Chs	3	331	565	565	3.0	7.1
PENT–Assemb of God	2	120	78	150	0.8	1.9

NR–Not Reported - Represents no adherents reported. Percentages may not total 100 due to rounding.

Table 3: Religious Congregations by County and Group: 2010

Religious Group	Number of Congrega-tions	Number of Attendees	Number of Communicant, Confirmed, or Full Members	Adherents: Number of Adherents	Adherents: % of Total Pop.	Adherents: % of Total Adh.
PENT–COGIC	1	0	150	178	1.0	2.2
PENT–Int Foursq Gos	1	73	84	100	0.5	1.3
PRES–Presb Ch (USA)	2	100	137	163	0.9	2.0
Salvation Army	1	43	12	12	0.1	0.2
Sev Day Adv	2	54	94	108	0.6	1.4
KERN	**615**	**71,743**	**97,856**	**403,182**	**48.0**	**100.0**
ANG/EPIS–Anglican NA	7	NR	NR	NR	-	-
ANG/EPIS–Episcopal	4	121	201	220	0.0	0.1
Bahá'í	1	NR	167	167	0.0	0.0
BAPT–Amer Bapt Assn	9	NR	674	880	0.1	0.2
BAPT–Amer Bapt USA	8	1,044	1,614	2,106	0.3	0.5
BAPT–Consrv Bapt	2	NR	NR	NR	-	-
BAPT–Converge/BGC	3	225	NR	270	0.0	0.1
BAPT–Free Will Bapt	9	NR	414	540	0.1	0.1
BAPT–NBC Amer	1	150	260	339	0.0	0.1
BAPT–Ref Bapt Ch	1	NR	NR	NR	-	-
BAPT–So Bapt Conv	74	9,483	20,747	27,075	3.2	6.7
BRETH–Ch of Brethren	2	52	160	209	0.0	0.1
BUDD–Mahayana	3	NR	NR	1,578	0.2	0.4
BUDD–Theravada	1	NR	NR	1,365	0.2	0.3
Calv Chpl	6	NR	NR	NR	-	-
Catholic	30	NR	NR	245,836	29.3	61.0
CGOD–Ch God (Ander)	1	160	NR	160	0.0	0.0
Ch Cr, Scientst	4	NR	NR	NR	-	-
Ch of Nazarene	15	2,491	2,682	3,335	0.4	0.8
Chr & Miss Al	3	1,025	742	1,769	0.2	0.4
CHR–Chr Ch (Disc)	2	21	325	424	0.1	0.1
CHR–Chr Chs & Chs Cr	6	NR	690	900	0.1	0.2
CHR–Chs of Christ	32	2,936	3,111	4,069	0.5	1.0
CHR–Int Chs of Christ	1	NR	42	55	0.0	0.0
Evan Free Ch	4	275	NR	275	0.0	0.1
FRND–Fr Un Mtg	1	NR	10	13	0.0	0.0
HINDU–I/A Temples	2	NR	NR	379	0.0	0.1
HINDU–Post Ren	1	NR	NR	10	0.0	0.0
HINDU–Trad Temples	1	NR	NR	900	0.1	0.2
Ind Fund Churches	3	NR	NR	NR	-	-
Jehovah's Witness	18	NR	NR	NR	-	-
JUD–Orth	1	43	50	60	0.0	0.0
JUD–Reform	2	109	192	518	0.1	0.1
LDS–Comm of Christ	2	NR	317	317	0.0	0.1
LDS–L-D Saints	39	NR	NR	21,095	2.5	5.2
LUTH–Assoc Free Luth	1	NR	NR	NR	-	-
LUTH–E.L.C.A.	2	145	284	375	0.0	0.1
LUTH–Luth Ch-Am Asc	1	NR	NR	NR	-	-
LUTH–Luth Cong Msn Chr	1	225	1,403	1,831	0.2	0.5
LUTH–Luth-MO Synod	12	1,210	2,454	3,187	0.4	0.8
LUTH–Wisc Ev Luth Syn	1	15	15	16	0.0	0.0
MENN–Menn Br US Conf	7	NR	1,787	2,332	0.3	0.6
METH–AME	3	225	875	1,142	0.1	0.3
METH–C.M.E.	1	0	150	196	0.0	0.0
METH–Un Methodist	13	1,115	1,956	2,952	0.4	0.7
METH–Wesleyan	5	225	299	294	0.0	0.1
Muslim Est	4	1,340	NR	4,218	0.5	1.0
Non-denom Chr Chs	81	28,549	36,385	38,689	4.6	9.6
ORTHE–Greek Orthodox	1	100	NR	200	0.0	0.0
ORTHE–Holy Orth in NA	1	15	NR	20	0.0	0.0
ORTHO–Coptic Orth Ch	1	200	NR	230	0.0	0.1
PENT–Apos Faith Msn	1	NR	35	46	0.0	0.0
PENT–Assemb of God	45	9,415	5,688	13,060	1.6	3.2
PENT–Ch God (Cleve)	9	470	963	1,257	0.1	0.3
PENT–Ch of God Proph	7	NR	203	265	0.0	0.1
PENT–COGIC	15	830	1,800	2,349	0.3	0.6
PENT–Full Gosp Bapt	4	NR	NR	NR	-	-
PENT–Int Foursq Gos	18	3,581	2,969	3,874	0.5	1.0
PENT–Intl Pent Holiness	10	1,200	1,008	1,315	0.2	0.3
PENT–Pent Ch of God	17	1,190	NR	1,849	0.2	0.5
PENT–Un Pent Ch Intl	14	NR	NR	NR	-	-
PENT–United Holy Ch	1	NR	NR	NR	-	-
PENT–Vineyard	2	210	75	98	0.0	0.0
PRES–Evan Presby Ch	1	NR	934	1,219	0.1	0.3
PRES–Presb Ch (USA)	4	111	550	718	0.1	0.2
PRES–Presb Ch Amer	1	41	30	37	0.0	0.0
REF–Christian Ref	2	55	41	54	0.0	0.0

Religious Group	Number of Congrega-tions	Number of Attendees	Number of Communicant, Confirmed, or Full Members	Adherents: Number of Adherents	Adherents: % of Total Pop.	Adherents: % of Total Adh.
REF–Ref Ch in U.S.	2	NR	236	311	0.0	0.1
Salvation Army	2	123	121	121	0.0	0.0
Sev Day Adv	18	2,666	4,638	5,332	0.6	1.3
Sikh	2	NR	NR	NR	-	-
Un C of Christ	4	304	499	651	0.1	0.2
Unit Univ	1	48	60	75	0.0	0.0
Unity Ch	1	NR	NR	NR	-	-
Zoroastrian	0	NR	NR	5	0.0	0.0
KINGS	**112**	**9,080**	**9,419**	**84,795**	**55.4**	**100.0**
ANG/EPIS–Anglican NA	2	NR	NR	NR	-	-
ANG/EPIS–Episcopal	1	48	86	93	0.1	0.1
Bahá'í	0	NR	22	22	0.0	0.0
BAPT–Amer Bapt Assn	2	NR	185	237	0.2	0.3
BAPT–Amer Bapt USA	3	1,659	1,408	1,803	1.2	2.1
BAPT–Consrv Bapt	1	NR	NR	NR	-	-
BAPT–Free Will Bapt	3	NR	138	177	0.1	0.2
BAPT–So Bapt Conv	5	250	271	347	0.2	0.4
BUDD–Mahayana	1	NR	NR	1,250	0.8	1.5
Calv Chpl	1	NR	NR	NR	-	-
Catholic	8	NR	NR	66,133	43.2	78.0
CGOD–Ch God (Ander)	2	93	NR	93	0.1	0.1
Ch of Nazarene	4	382	300	525	0.3	0.6
CHR–Chr Ch (Disc)	1	75	144	184	0.1	0.2
CHR–Chs of Christ	6	530	520	716	0.5	0.8
Ind Fund Churches	1	NR	NR	NR	-	-
Jehovah's Witness	4	NR	NR	NR	-	-
LDS–L-D Saints	5	NR	NR	2,362	1.5	2.8
LUTH–E.L.C.A.	1	65	165	278	0.2	0.3
LUTH–Luth-MO Synod	1	50	123	150	0.1	0.2
MENN–Menn Br US Conf	1	NR	40	51	0.0	0.1
METH–AME Zion	1	0	100	128	0.1	0.2
METH–Un Methodist	4	237	366	764	0.5	0.9
Muslim Est	1	345	NR	1,108	0.7	1.3
Non-denom Chr Chs	11	1,975	2,293	2,651	1.7	3.1
PENT–Assemb of God	13	1,235	686	1,489	1.0	1.8
PENT–COGIC	1	0	150	192	0.1	0.2
PENT–Int Foursq Gos	3	309	136	174	0.1	0.2
PENT–Intl Pent Holiness	2	57	77	99	0.1	0.1
PENT–Pent Ch of God	9	630	NR	979	0.6	1.2
PENT–Un Pent Ch Intl	1	NR	NR	NR	-	-
PRES–Orth Pres Ch	1	65	58	91	0.1	0.1
PRES–Presb Ch (USA)	3	60	362	464	0.3	0.5
REF–Christian Ref	1	235	488	625	0.4	0.7
REF–Un Ref Chs N.A.	1	NR	NR	NR	-	-
Salvation Army	1	54	40	159	0.1	0.2
Sev Day Adv	6	726	1,261	1,451	0.9	1.7
LAKE	**81**	**4,170**	**4,630**	**16,501**	**25.5**	**100.0**
ANG/EPIS–Episcopal	1	22	53	70	0.1	0.4
Bahá'í	0	NR	49	49	0.1	0.3
BAPT–Amer Bapt USA	1	30	46	55	0.1	0.3
BAPT–Consrv Bapt	1	NR	NR	NR	-	-
BAPT–Reg Bapt Gen As	1	NR	NR	NR	-	-
BAPT–So Bapt Conv	9	961	1,030	1,224	1.9	7.4
BUDD–Mahayana	2	NR	NR	57	0.1	0.3
Calv Chpl	1	NR	NR	NR	-	-
Catholic	6	NR	NR	6,857	10.6	41.6
Ch Cr, Scientst	1	NR	NR	NR	-	-
Ch of Nazarene	2	95	64	146	0.2	0.9
CHR–Chr Ch (Disc)	1	120	73	87	0.1	0.5
CHR–Chr Chs & Chs Cr	1	NR	25	30	0.0	0.2
CHR–Chs of Christ	4	140	144	190	0.3	1.2
Evan Free Ch	1	300	NR	300	0.5	1.8
FRND–Indep Yr Mtgs	1	NR	0	0	0.0	0.0
HINDU–Post Ren	1	NR	NR	77	0.1	0.5
HINDU–Renaiss	1	NR	NR	375	0.6	2.3
Jehovah's Witness	3	NR	NR	NR	-	-
LDS–Comm of Christ	1	NR	158	158	0.2	1.0
LDS–L-D Saints	5	NR	NR	2,294	3.5	13.9
LUTH–E.L.C.A.	1	44	83	90	0.1	0.5
LUTH–Luth-MO Synod	2	98	134	145	0.2	0.9
METH–Un Methodist	7	347	482	654	1.0	4.0

NR–Not Reported - Represents no adherents reported. Percentages may not total 100 due to rounding.

Table 3: Religious Congregations by County and Group: 2010

Religious Group	Number of Congrega-tions	Number of Attendees	Number of Communicant, Confirmed, or Full Members	Adherents: Number of Adherents	Adherents: % of Total Pop.	Adherents: % of Total Adh.
Non-denom Chr Chs	10	890	1,115	1,219	1.9	7.4
ORTHE–Holy Orth in NA	1	39	NR	50	0.1	0.3
PENT–Assemb of God	4	523	296	1,233	1.9	7.5
PENT–Ch God (Cleve)	1	10	24	29	0.0	0.2
PENT–Int Foursq Gos	1	34	24	29	0.0	0.2
PENT–Intl Pent Holiness	1	45	55	65	0.1	0.4
PENT–Pent Ch of God	1	70	NR	109	0.2	0.7
PRES–Presb Ch (USA)	2	30	156	185	0.3	1.1
Sev Day Adv	4	327	569	654	1.0	4.0
Unit Univ	1	45	50	70	0.1	0.4
Unity Ch	1	NR	NR	NR	-	-
LASSEN	**41**	**2,121**	**1,841**	**8,154**	**23.4**	**100.0**
ANG/EPIS–Episcopal	1	15	23	31	0.1	0.4
Bahá'í	0	NR	19	19	0.1	0.2
BAPT–So Bapt Conv	6	161	375	433	1.2	5.3
Calv Chpl	3	NR	NR	NR	-	-
Catholic	3	NR	NR	3,389	9.7	41.6
Ch of Nazarene	1	158	92	187	0.5	2.3
CHR–Chr Chs & Chs Cr	1	NR	30	35	0.1	0.4
CHR–Chs of Christ	1	60	45	50	0.1	0.6
Evan Free Ch	1	450	NR	450	1.3	5.5
Ind Fund Churches	1	NR	NR	NR	-	-
Jehovah's Witness	3	NR	NR	NR	-	-
LDS–L-D Saints	3	NR	NR	1,341	3.8	16.4
LUTH–Luth-MO Synod	1	39	153	192	0.6	2.4
MENN–Menn Chr Fell	1	51	23	51	0.1	0.6
METH–Un Methodist	1	65	161	292	0.8	3.6
Non-denom Chr Chs	5	521	501	651	1.9	8.0
PENT–Assemb of God	4	251	145	500	1.4	6.1
PENT–Int Foursq Gos	1	69	29	34	0.1	0.4
PENT–Pent Ch of God	2	140	NR	217	0.6	2.7
Sev Day Adv	2	141	245	282	0.8	3.5
LOS ANGELES	**5,773**	**743,177**	**963,619**	**5,214,110**	**53.1**	**100.0**
ANG/EPIS–Anglican NA	8	NR	NR	NR	-	-
ANG/EPIS–Episcopal	83	11,400	27,150	38,108	0.4	0.7
Ap Chr Ch-Amer	1	78	49	78	0.0	0.0
Bahá'í	39	NR	8,061	8,061	0.1	0.2
BAPT–Amer Bapt Assn	11	NR	1,065	1,307	0.0	0.0
BAPT–Amer Bapt USA	180	39,912	40,359	49,515	0.5	0.9
BAPT–Asc Ref Bap Ch Am	4	NR	NR	NR	-	-
BAPT–Consrv Bapt	52	NR	NR	NR	-	-
BAPT–Converge/BGC	27	5,325	NR	6,390	0.1	0.1
BAPT–Free Will Bapt	5	NR	230	282	0.0	0.0
BAPT–N Am Bapt Conf	3	NR	85	104	0.0	0.0
BAPT–Natl Mis Bapt Conv	25	500	2,708	3,322	0.0	0.1
BAPT–NBC Amer	16	5,006	8,237	10,106	0.1	0.2
BAPT–NBC USA	52	5,417	19,284	23,659	0.2	0.5
BAPT–Prog NBC	12	535	2,007	2,462	0.0	0.0
BAPT–Ref Bapt Ch	5	NR	NR	NR	-	-
BAPT–Reg Bapt Gen As	18	NR	NR	NR	-	-
BAPT–S-D Baptist Gen Con	3	39	55	67	0.0	0.0
BAPT–So Bapt Conv	517	55,784	81,777	100,329	1.0	1.9
BRETH–Breth in Chr	3	NR	NR	NR	-	-
BRETH–Brethren (Ash)	2	NR	160	196	0.0	0.0
BRETH–Ch of Brethren	11	510	991	1,216	0.0	0.0
BRETH–Grace Breth	13	NR	NR	NR	-	-
BUDD–Mahayana	126	NR	NR	70,397	0.7	1.4
BUDD–Theravada	29	NR	NR	19,132	0.2	0.4
BUDD–Vajrayana	27	NR	NR	2,168	0.0	0.0
Calv Chpl	49	NR	NR	NR	-	-
Catholic	274	NR	NR	3,542,994	36.1	68.0
CGOD–Ch God (Ander)	30	4,941	NR	4,941	0.1	0.1
Ch Cr, Scientst	41	NR	NR	NR	-	-
Ch God (7th Day)	10	NR	NR	NR	-	-
Ch of Chr (Hol)	20	NR	NR	NR	-	-
Ch of God Gen Conf	1	NR	30	37	0.0	0.0
Ch of Nazarene	105	12,102	15,134	21,870	0.2	0.4
Chr & Miss Al	48	5,052	5,041	6,729	0.1	0.1
CHR–Chr Ch (Disc)	79	2,735	6,757	8,290	0.1	0.2
CHR–Chr Chs & Chs Cr	56	NR	22,468	27,565	0.3	0.5
CHR–Chs of Christ	99	11,403	13,071	16,763	0.2	0.3

Religious Group	Number of Congrega-tions	Number of Attendees	Number of Communicant, Confirmed, or Full Members	Adherents: Number of Adherents	Adherents: % of Total Pop.	Adherents: % of Total Adh.
CHR–Int Chs of Christ	2	NR	5,028	6,169	0.1	0.1
Christian Brethren	2	NR	NR	NR	-	-
CONG–Armen Evang Add'l	6	NR	NR	NR	-	-
CONG–Cong Chr, NA	8	NR	1,984	2,434	0.0	0.0
CONG–Consrv Cong Chr	6	3,685	3,984	4,888	0.0	0.1
Evan Cov Ch	30	6,152	4,636	7,999	0.1	0.2
Evan Free Ch	33	7,305	NR	7,305	0.1	0.1
FRND–Evan Fr Ch Intl	16	1,867	1,340	1,644	0.0	0.0
FRND–Fr Un Mtg	1	NR	340	417	0.0	0.0
FRND–Indep Yr Mtgs	5	NR	197	242	0.0	0.0
Grace Gosp Fel	1	NR	NR	NR	-	-
HINDU–I/A Temples	16	NR	NR	9,759	0.1	0.2
HINDU–Post Ren	34	NR	NR	946	0.0	0.0
HINDU–Renaiss	15	NR	NR	572	0.0	0.0
HINDU–Trad Temples	13	NR	NR	8,336	0.1	0.2
Ind Fund Churches	13	NR	NR	NR	-	-
Int Cou Comm Ch	5	NR	NR	NR	-	-
Jehovah's Witness	133	NR	NR	NR	-	-
JUD–Conserv	23	8,803	9,880	26,676	0.3	0.5
JUD–Orth	150	31,524	12,000	44,400	0.5	0.9
JUD–Reconst	3	1,091	1,393	3,761	0.0	0.1
JUD–Reform	26	7,063	12,456	33,631	0.3	0.6
LDS–Comm of Christ	5	NR	820	820	0.0	0.0
LDS–L-D Saints	226	NR	NR	150,569	1.5	2.9
LUTH–Apostolic Luth	1	NR	NR	NR	-	-
LUTH–Ch Luth Conf	1	NR	NR	NR	-	-
LUTH–Ch of Luth Br	1	35	39	70	0.0	0.0
LUTH–Cons Luth Assn	1	NR	NR	NR	-	-
LUTH–E.L.C.A.	109	9,725	17,549	23,713	0.2	0.5
LUTH–Evan Luth Syn	1	22	29	49	0.0	0.0
LUTH–Luth Ch-Am Asc	1	NR	NR	NR	-	-
LUTH–Luth Cong Msn Chr	10	1,528	3,523	4,322	0.0	0.1
LUTH–Luth-MO Synod	90	8,308	14,969	18,317	0.2	0.4
LUTH–Wisc Ev Luth Syn	8	517	920	1,173	0.0	0.0
MENN–Cons Menn Conf	1	0	65	80	0.0	0.0
MENN–Menn Br US Conf	11	NR	887	1,088	0.0	0.0
MENN–Mennonite USA	24	1,466	1,725	2,116	0.0	0.0
METH–AME	34	20,455	33,843	41,521	0.4	0.8
METH–AME Zion	11	343	1,325	1,626	0.0	0.0
METH–C.M.E.	14	1,075	3,034	3,722	0.0	0.1
METH–Evan Meth Ch	2	NR	NR	NR	-	-
METH–Free Methodist	31	3,793	2,536	3,972	0.0	0.1
METH–Un Methodist	154	20,095	35,076	49,927	0.5	1.0
METH–Wesleyan	29	3,220	3,504	4,190	0.0	0.1
Metro Comm Ch	4	362	460	564	0.0	0.0
Missionary Ch	18	3,944	3,992	4,611	0.0	0.1
MJEW–Union Mes Cong	2	NR	NR	NR	-	-
MORAV–Morav Ch-North	1	52	159	216	0.0	0.0
Muslim Est	59	18,839	NR	69,080	0.7	1.3
Nat Spirit Asso	1	NR	NR	NR	-	-
New Apost Ch	5	NR	NR	NR	-	-
Non-denom Chr Chs	720	224,955	319,864	345,848	3.5	6.6
OCATH–Pol Natl Cath	1	NR	NR	NR	-	-
ORTHE–Ant Orth of NA	6	922	NR	3,565	0.0	0.1
ORTHE–Bulgar Orth USA	1	0	NR	0	0.0	0.0
ORTHE–Georgian Orth	1	40	NR	150	0.0	0.0
ORTHE–Greek Orthodox	8	2,125	NR	9,155	0.1	0.2
ORTHE–Holy Orth in NA	1	92	NR	120	0.0	0.0
ORTHE–Macedonian Orth	1	45	NR	300	0.0	0.0
ORTHE–Orth Ch in Amer	8	387	NR	1,101	0.0	0.0
ORTHE–Pal/Jor Orth	1	50	NR	250	0.0	0.0
ORTHE–Romania Orth Ar	2	100	NR	250	0.0	0.0
ORTHE–Rus Orth Abroad	3	740	NR	4,100	0.0	0.1
ORTHE–Serb Orth USA	3	540	NR	5,240	0.1	0.1
ORTHE–Ukrainian Orth	2	125	NR	400	0.0	0.0
ORTHO–Armen Ap Cilic	7	1,025	NR	4,100	0.0	0.1
ORTHO–Armen Ap Etchm	10	2,075	NR	17,050	0.2	0.3
ORTHO–Coptic Orth Ch	12	8,680	NR	11,650	0.1	0.2
ORTHO–Eritrean Orth	1	75	NR	650	0.0	0.0
ORTHO–Ethiopian Orth	3	NR	NR	NR	-	-
ORTHO–Malan Dioc Am	3	140	NR	420	0.0	0.0
ORTHO–Malan Syr Orth	1	115	NR	216	0.0	0.0
ORTHO–Syrian Orth Ch	2	700	NR	4,800	0.0	0.1
PENT–Apos Faith Msn	1	NR	35	43	0.0	0.0

NR–Not Reported - Represents no adherents reported. Percentages may not total 100 due to rounding.

Table 3: Religious Congregations by County and Group: 2010

Religious Group	Number of Congrega-tions	Number of Attendees	Number of Communicant, Confirmed, or Full Members	Adherents		
				Number of Adherents	% of Total Pop.	% of Total Adh.
PENT–Assemb of God	269	49,713	31,006	69,317	0.7	1.3
PENT–Assm God Intl F	1	NR	NR	NR	-	-
PENT–Ch God (Cleve)	44	3,496	3,886	4,768	0.0	0.1
PENT–Ch Lord Jesus Apos	3	NR	NR	NR	-	-
PENT–Ch of God Proph	23	NR	957	1,174	0.0	0.0
PENT–COGIC	97	7,551	21,127	25,920	0.3	0.5
PENT–Fire Bapt Hol Ch	1	NR	NR	NR	-	-
PENT–Full Gosp Bapt	23	NR	NR	NR	-	-
PENT–Int Foursq Gos	234	39,024	44,541	54,646	0.6	1.0
PENT–Intl Pent Holiness	20	5,549	3,818	4,684	0.0	0.1
PENT–Open Bible Std	11	510	NR	510	0.0	0.0
PENT–Pent Ch of God	14	2,110	NR	3,278	0.0	0.1
PENT–Pent FW Bapt	2	NR	NR	NR	-	-
PENT–Un Pent Ch Intl	33	NR	NR	NR	-	-
PENT–United Holy Ch	3	NR	NR	NR	-	-
PENT–Vineyard	17	6,758	8,482	10,406	0.1	0.2
Pillar of Fire	1	NR	50	50	0.0	0.0
PRES–As Ref Pres Ch	14	NR	344	422	0.0	0.0
PRES–Evan Presby Ch	1	NR	28	34	0.0	0.0
PRES–Kor Pres Abroad	39	NR	NR	NR	-	-
PRES–Korean Amer Pres	48	NR	NR	NR	-	-
PRES–Korean Pres Amer	70	NR	NR	NR	-	-
PRES–Orth Pres Ch	4	505	489	632	0.0	0.0
PRES–Presb Ch (USA)	150	20,185	31,361	38,476	0.4	0.7
PRES–Presb Ch Amer	35	728	859	1,027	0.0	0.0
PRES–Ref Pres of NA	1	60	45	63	0.0	0.0
REF–Christian Ref	52	9,296	8,063	9,892	0.1	0.2
REF–Comm Ref Evan	1	NR	NR	NR	-	-
REF–Hung Ref Add'l	1	NR	NR	NR	-	-
REF–Ref Ch in Am	13	3,101	3,162	6,293	0.1	0.1
REF–Ref Ch in U.S.	1	NR	30	44	0.0	0.0
REF–Un Ref Chs N.A.	2	NR	NR	NR	-	-
Salvation Army	23	2,138	3,350	7,529	0.1	0.1
Sev Day Adv	140	22,188	38,582	44,377	0.5	0.9
Sikh	14	NR	NR	NR	-	-
Swedenborgian	1	NR	NR	NR	-	-
Tao	5	NR	NR	NR	-	-
Un C of Christ	54	3,795	8,853	10,861	0.1	0.2
Unit Univ	14	1,531	2,275	2,869	0.0	0.1
Unity Ch	14	NR	NR	NR	-	-
Zoroastrian	2	NR	NR	417	0.0	0.0
MADERA	**126**	**11,539**	**14,116**	**79,953**	**53.0**	**100.0**
ANG/EPIS–Anglican NA	1	NR	NR	NR	-	-
ANG/EPIS–Episcopal	2	31	44	45	0.0	0.1
Bahá'í	1	NR	58	58	0.0	0.1
BAPT–Amer Bapt Assn	1	NR	75	96	0.1	0.1
BAPT–Amer Bapt USA	3	385	294	377	0.2	0.5
BAPT–Converge/BGC	2	150	NR	180	0.1	0.2
BAPT–Free Will Bapt	1	NR	46	59	0.0	0.1
BAPT–NBC Amer	1	200	250	320	0.2	0.4
BAPT–Reg Bapt Gen As	1	NR	NR	NR	-	-
BAPT–So Bapt Conv	13	1,231	1,512	1,937	1.3	2.4
BUDD–Mahayana	1	NR	NR	27	0.0	0.0
BUDD–Theravada	1	NR	NR	267	0.2	0.3
Calv Chpl	2	NR	NR	NR	-	-
Catholic	3	NR	NR	56,566	37.5	70.7
CGOD–Ch God (Ander)	3	745	NR	745	0.5	0.9
Ch Cr, Scientst	1	NR	NR	NR	-	-
Ch God (7th Day)	1	NR	NR	NR	-	-
Ch of Nazarene	3	112	156	173	0.1	0.2
CHR–Chr Chs & Chs Cr	1	NR	155	199	0.1	0.2
CHR–Chs of Christ	5	425	360	516	0.3	0.6
Evan Free Ch	2	325	NR	325	0.2	0.4
Jehovah's Witness	5	NR	NR	NR	-	-
LDS–L-D Saints	5	NR	NR	3,355	2.2	4.2
LUTH–E.L.C.A.	2	149	364	515	0.3	0.6
LUTH–Luth Cong Msn Chr	3	217	812	1,040	0.7	1.3
LUTH–Luth–MO Synod	1	42	53	59	0.0	0.1
MENN–Menn Br US Conf	2	NR	134	172	0.1	0.2
METH–AME Zion	1	0	100	128	0.1	0.2
METH–Un Methodist	3	302	478	602	0.4	0.8
Muslim Est	1	345	NR	1,109	0.7	1.4
Non-denom Chr Chs	21	3,838	5,986	6,190	4.1	7.7

Religious Group	Number of Congrega-tions	Number of Attendees	Number of Communicant, Confirmed, or Full Members	Adherents		
				Number of Adherents	% of Total Pop.	% of Total Adh.
PENT–Assemb of God	10	978	627	1,335	0.9	1.7
PENT–Ch God (Cleve)	3	165	125	160	0.1	0.2
PENT–Ch of God Proph	1	NR	37	47	0.0	0.1
PENT–COGIC	3	20	185	237	0.2	0.3
PENT–Int Foursq Gos	2	41	42	54	0.0	0.1
PENT–Pent Ch of God	3	210	NR	326	0.2	0.4
PENT–Un Pent Ch Intl	1	NR	NR	NR	-	-
PENT–Vineyard	1	75	120	154	0.1	0.2
PRES–Presb Ch (USA)	2	466	536	687	0.5	0.9
REF–Ref Ch in Am	1	402	376	517	0.3	0.6
Sev Day Adv	5	655	1,140	1,310	0.9	1.6
Un C of Christ	1	30	51	65	0.0	0.1
Zoroastrian	0	NR	NR	1	0.0	0.0
MARIN	**204**	**12,120**	**17,396**	**109,808**	**43.5**	**100.0**
ANG/EPIS–Anglican NA	1	NR	NR	NR	-	-
ANG/EPIS–Episcopal	12	1,056	3,101	3,501	1.4	3.2
Bahá'í	4	NR	243	243	0.1	0.2
BAPT–Amer Bapt USA	6	1,075	806	961	0.4	0.9
BAPT–Consrv Bapt	1	NR	NR	NR	-	-
BAPT–Natl Mis Bapt Conv	1	80	500	596	0.2	0.5
BAPT–So Bapt Conv	30	2,324	2,832	3,378	1.3	3.1
BUDD–Mahayana	10	NR	NR	1,506	0.6	1.4
BUDD–Theravada	2	NR	NR	800	0.3	0.7
BUDD–Vajrayana	7	NR	NR	331	0.1	0.3
Calv Chpl	1	NR	NR	NR	-	-
Catholic	30	NR	NR	77,114	30.6	70.2
CGOD–Ch God (Ander)	1	70	NR	70	0.0	0.1
Ch Cr, Scientst	4	NR	NR	NR	-	-
Ch of Nazarene	2	45	157	157	0.1	0.1
CHR–Chr Chs & Chs Cr	1	NR	100	119	0.0	0.1
CHR–Chs of Christ	1	15	12	16	0.0	0.0
Evan Cov Ch	1	503	232	654	0.3	0.6
FRND–Indep Yr Mtgs	1	NR	15	18	0.0	0.0
HINDU–Post Ren	6	NR	NR	329	0.1	0.3
HINDU–Renaiss	1	NR	NR	375	0.1	0.3
Jehovah's Witness	4	NR	NR	NR	-	-
JUD–Conserv	1	417	468	1,264	0.5	1.2
JUD–Orth	2	86	100	120	0.0	0.1
JUD–Reform	1	663	1,170	3,159	1.3	2.9
LDS–Comm of Christ	1	NR	158	158	0.1	0.1
LDS–L-D Saints	4	NR	NR	2,468	1.0	2.2
LUTH–E.L.C.A.	5	420	779	1,020	0.4	0.9
LUTH–Luth–MO Synod	3	240	426	532	0.2	0.5
METH–Un Methodist	4	276	541	915	0.4	0.8
Muslim Est	1	346	NR	1,109	0.4	1.0
Non-denom Chr Chs	16	1,590	2,023	2,237	0.9	2.0
ORTHE–Greek Orthodox	1	190	NR	1,200	0.5	1.1
ORTHE–Orth Ch in Amer	1	90	NR	200	0.1	0.2
ORTHE–Pal/Jor Orth	1	40	NR	125	0.0	0.1
PENT–Assemb of God	4	414	357	920	0.4	0.8
PENT–Ch God (Cleve)	1	60	106	126	0.0	0.1
PENT–COGIC	1	100	150	179	0.1	0.2
PENT–Un Pent Ch Intl	1	NR	NR	NR	-	-
PRES–Korean Amer Pres	1	NR	NR	NR	-	-
PRES–Orth Pres Ch	1	36	31	37	0.0	0.0
PRES–Presb Ch (USA)	16	1,330	2,193	2,616	1.0	2.4
PRES–Presb Ch Amer	1	106	71	87	0.0	0.1
Salvation Army	1	66	10	144	0.1	0.1
Sev Day Adv	3	170	295	340	0.1	0.3
Un C of Christ	4	217	358	427	0.2	0.4
Unit Univ	1	95	162	232	0.1	0.2
Unity Ch	1	NR	NR	NR	-	-
Zoroastrian	0	NR	NR	25	0.0	0.0
MARIPOSA	**31**	**1,663**	**2,009**	**7,728**	**42.3**	**100.0**
ANG/EPIS–Anglican NA	1	NR	NR	NR	-	-
Bahá'í	1	NR	39	39	0.2	0.5
BAPT–Consrv Bapt	1	NR	NR	NR	-	-
BAPT–So Bapt Conv	1	35	26	30	0.2	0.4
Catholic	3	NR	NR	4,671	25.6	60.4
CGOD–Ch God (Ander)	1	205	NR	205	1.1	2.7
Ch Cr, Scientst	1	NR	NR	NR	-	-

NR–Not Reported   - Represents no adherents reported.   Percentages may not total 100 due to rounding.

Table 3: Religious Congregations by County and Group: 2010

Religious Group	Number of Congrega-tions	Number of Attendees	Number of Communicant, Confirmed, or Full Members	Adherents		
				Number of Adherents	% of Total Pop.	% of Total Adh.
CHR–Chs of Christ	2	55	64	74	0.4	1.0
Jehovah's Witness	2	NR	NR	NR	-	-
LDS–L-D Saints	1	NR	NR	392	2.1	5.1
LUTH–E.L.C.A.	1	82	118	172	0.9	2.2
METH–Un Methodist	2	112	253	406	2.2	5.3
Non-denom Chr Chs	10	1,020	1,341	1,501	8.2	19.4
PENT–Assemb of God	1	45	0	45	0.2	0.6
PENT–Int Foursq Gos	1	37	43	49	0.3	0.6
Sev Day Adv	2	72	125	144	0.8	1.9
MENDOCINO	**119**	**3,952**	**5,722**	**28,737**	**32.7**	**100.0**
ANG/EPIS–Episcopal	4	137	242	287	0.3	1.0
Bahá'í	0	NR	84	84	0.1	0.3
BAPT–Amer Bapt USA	2	294	360	434	0.5	1.5
BAPT–Consrv Bapt	2	NR	NR	NR	-	-
BAPT–Reg Bapt Gen As	1	NR	NR	NR	-	-
BAPT–So Bapt Conv	9	395	1,059	1,276	1.5	4.4
BUDD–Mahayana	6	NR	NR	1,185	1.3	4.1
BUDD–Theravada	2	NR	NR	1,664	1.9	5.8
BUDD–Vajrayana	4	NR	NR	239	0.3	0.8
Calv Chpl	2	NR	NR	NR	-	-
Catholic	11	NR	NR	15,081	17.2	52.5
Ch Cr, Scientst	2	NR	NR	NR	-	-
Ch of Nazarene	2	30	85	98	0.1	0.3
CHR–Chr Ch (Disc)	1	15	18	22	0.0	0.1
CHR–Chs of Christ	3	144	127	158	0.2	0.5
Evan Free Ch	1	150	NR	150	0.2	0.5
FRND–Indep Yr Mtgs	2	NR	12	14	0.0	0.0
HINDU–I/A Temples	2	NR	NR	500	0.6	1.7
Ind Fund Churches	2	NR	NR	NR	-	-
Jehovah's Witness	7	NR	NR	NR	-	-
LDS–L-D Saints	4	NR	NR	2,335	2.7	8.1
LUTH–E.L.C.A.	3	161	278	383	0.4	1.3
LUTH–Evan Luth Syn	1	30	28	35	0.0	0.1
LUTH–Luth–MO Synod	3	88	229	253	0.3	0.9
METH–Un Methodist	8	299	615	889	1.0	3.1
Non-denom Chr Chs	8	864	765	1,080	1.2	3.8
PENT–Assemb of God	8	283	199	451	0.5	1.6
PENT–Ch of God Proph	1	NR	54	65	0.1	0.2
PENT–Int Foursq Gos	2	89	93	112	0.1	0.4
PENT–Pent Ch of God	2	140	NR	217	0.2	0.8
PENT–Un Pent Ch Intl	3	NR	NR	NR	-	-
PRES–Presb Ch (USA)	5	311	582	701	0.8	2.4
Sev Day Adv	4	508	885	1,017	1.2	3.5
Unit Univ	1	14	7	7	0.0	0.0
Unity Ch	1	NR	NR	NR	-	-
MERCED	**192**	**14,592**	**22,568**	**139,353**	**54.5**	**100.0**
ANG/EPIS–Anglican NA	3	NR	NR	NR	-	-
ANG/EPIS–Episcopal	1	9	12	17	0.0	0.0
Bahá'í	1	NR	251	251	0.1	0.2
BAPT–Amer Bapt Assn	1	NR	150	198	0.1	0.1
BAPT–Amer Bapt USA	2	119	292	385	0.2	0.3
BAPT–Consrv Bapt	2	NR	NR	NR	-	-
BAPT–Natl Mis Bapt Conv	1	0	150	198	0.1	0.1
BAPT–So Bapt Conv	24	1,301	3,526	4,649	1.8	3.3
BUDD–Mahayana	1	NR	NR	11	0.0	0.0
Calv Chpl	2	NR	NR	NR	-	-
Catholic	18	NR	NR	102,005	39.9	73.2
CGOD–Ch God (Ander)	2	190	NR	190	0.1	0.1
Ch Cr, Scientst	1	NR	NR	NR	-	-
Ch of Chr (Hol)	2	NR	NR	NR	-	-
Ch of Nazarene	6	339	505	695	0.3	0.5
Chr & Miss Al	1	260	503	503	0.2	0.4
CHR–Chr Ch (Disc)	2	36	61	80	0.0	0.1
CHR–Chr Chs & Chs Cr	1	NR	120	158	0.1	0.1
CHR–Chs of Christ	8	490	467	605	0.2	0.4
Evan Cov Ch	1	151	410	196	0.1	0.1
Evan Free Ch	2	200	NR	200	0.1	0.1
Ind Fund Churches	1	NR	NR	NR	-	-
Jehovah's Witness	5	NR	NR	NR	-	-
JUD–Reform	1	14	24	65	0.0	0.0
LDS–L-D Saints	10	NR	NR	4,448	1.7	3.2
LUTH–E.L.C.A.	3	165	248	356	0.1	0.3
LUTH–Luth Cong Msn Chr	1	49	146	193	0.1	0.1
LUTH–Luth–MO Synod	2	172	346	755	0.3	0.5
MENN–CG in Cr (Menn)	3	NR	563	742	0.3	0.5
METH–AME Zion	1	0	100	132	0.1	0.1
METH–C.M.E.	1	0	100	132	0.1	0.1
METH–Un Methodist	6	471	1,146	1,832	0.7	1.3
Muslim Est	1	345	NR	1,109	0.4	0.8
Non-denom Chr Chs	18	5,898	8,998	11,412	4.5	8.2
ORTHE–Orth Ch in Amer	1	35	NR	64	0.0	0.0
PENT–Assemb of God	16	1,930	846	2,442	1.0	1.8
PENT–Ch God (Cleve)	1	75	32	42	0.0	0.0
PENT–Ch of God Proph	1	NR	14	18	0.0	0.0
PENT–COGIC	5	10	474	625	0.2	0.4
PENT–Int Foursq Gos	4	312	344	454	0.2	0.3
PENT–Pent Ch of God	8	560	NR	870	0.3	0.6
PENT–Un Pent Ch Intl	6	NR	NR	NR	-	-
PRES–Presb Ch (USA)	4	568	761	1,003	0.4	0.7
REF–Christian Ref	2	351	379	500	0.2	0.4
Salvation Army	2	43	732	820	0.3	0.6
Sev Day Adv	4	499	868	998	0.4	0.7
Sikh	2	NR	NR	NR	-	-
Unity Ch	1	NR	NR	NR	-	-
MODOC	**16**	**226**	**440**	**1,465**	**15.1**	**100.0**
ANG/EPIS–Episcopal	1	18	36	36	0.4	2.5
Bahá'í	0	NR	19	19	0.2	1.3
BAPT–Consrv Bapt	1	NR	NR	NR	-	-
BAPT–So Bapt Conv	2	87	151	180	1.9	12.3
Catholic	2	NR	NR	606	6.3	41.4
CHR–Chs of Christ	2	48	46	48	0.5	3.3
Jehovah's Witness	1	NR	NR	NR	-	-
LDS–L-D Saints	2	NR	NR	344	3.6	23.5
PENT–Assemb of God	1	31	24	39	0.4	2.7
Sev Day Adv	2	42	72	83	0.9	5.7
Un C of Christ	2	0	92	110	1.1	7.5
MONO	**16**	**400**	**279**	**13,645**	**96.1**	**100.0**
Bahá'í	0	NR	3	3	0.0	0.0
BAPT–So Bapt Conv	3	111	91	109	0.8	0.8
Calv Chpl	2	NR	NR	NR	-	-
Catholic	3	NR	NR	12,852	90.5	94.2
Evan Free Ch	1	100	NR	100	0.7	0.7
Jehovah's Witness	1	NR	NR	NR	-	-
LDS–L-D Saints	2	NR	NR	337	2.4	2.5
LUTH–Luth–MO Synod	1	45	49	61	0.4	0.4
METH–Un Methodist	1	33	45	45	0.3	0.3
Non-denom Chr Chs	1	100	80	125	0.9	0.9
PRES–Presb Ch (USA)	1	11	11	13	0.1	0.1
MONTEREY	**287**	**19,467**	**31,298**	**205,066**	**49.4**	**100.0**
ANG/EPIS–Anglican NA	1	NR	NR	NR	-	-
ANG/EPIS–Episcopal	14	1,080	2,371	3,120	0.8	1.5
Bahá'í	1	NR	1,480	1,480	0.4	0.7
BAPT–Amer Bapt Assn	1	NR	85	107	0.0	0.1
BAPT–Amer Bapt USA	4	360	378	477	0.1	0.2
BAPT–Consrv Bapt	7	NR	NR	NR	-	-
BAPT–Free Will Bapt	2	NR	92	116	0.0	0.1
BAPT–Fund Bapt Flwsp	1	NR	NR	NR	-	-
BAPT–NBC Amer	1	150	300	379	0.1	0.2
BAPT–NBC USA	2	160	270	341	0.1	0.2
BAPT–Ref Bapt Ch	1	NR	NR	NR	-	-
BAPT–So Bapt Conv	23	1,263	3,063	3,866	0.9	1.9
BUDD–Mahayana	11	NR	NR	5,351	1.3	2.6
BUDD–Theravada	1	NR	NR	1,365	0.3	0.7
BUDD–Vajrayana	1	NR	NR	53	0.0	0.0
Calv Chpl	3	NR	NR	NR	-	-
Catholic	26	NR	NR	150,050	36.2	73.2
CGOD–Ch God (Ander)	1	45	NR	45	0.0	0.0
Ch Cr, Scientst	3	NR	NR	NR	-	-
Ch of Nazarene	4	414	570	733	0.2	0.4
Chr & Miss Al	2	93	85	106	0.0	0.1
CHR–Chr Ch (Disc)	1	55	100	126	0.0	0.1

NR–Not Reported - Represents no adherents reported. Percentages may not total 100 due to rounding.

Table 3: Religious Congregations by County and Group: 2010

Religious Group	Number of Congregations	Number of Attendees	Number of Communicant, Confirmed, or Full Members	Adherents: Number of Adherents	Adherents: % of Total Pop.	Adherents: % of Total Adh.
CHR–Chr Chs & Chs Cr	1	NR	147	186	0.0	0.1
CHR–Chs of Christ	9	518	477	605	0.1	0.3
CONG–Cong Chr, NA	1	NR	51	64	0.0	0.0
Evan Cov Ch	1	10	9	13	0.0	0.0
FRND–Indep Yr Mtgs	2	NR	24	30	0.0	0.0
Grace Gosp Fel	1	NR	NR	NR	-	-
HINDU–Post Ren	2	NR	NR	102	0.0	0.0
Jehovah's Witness	7	NR	NR	NR	-	-
JUD–Conserv	1	9	10	27	0.0	0.0
JUD–Orth	1	43	50	60	0.0	0.0
JUD–Reform	2	210	371	1,002	0.2	0.5
LDS–Comm of Christ	1	NR	158	158	0.0	0.1
LDS–L-D Saints	10	NR	NR	5,906	1.4	2.9
LUTH–Assoc Free Luth	1	NR	NR	NR	-	-
LUTH–E.L.C.A.	6	460	1,082	1,408	0.3	0.7
LUTH–Luth–MO Synod	3	282	386	442	0.1	0.2
METH–C.M.E.	2	40	180	227	0.1	0.1
METH–Un Methodist	10	698	1,137	1,548	0.4	0.8
MJEW–Union Mes Cong	1	NR	NR	NR	-	-
Muslim Est	3	790	NR	2,518	0.6	1.2
Non-denom Chr Chs	31	6,460	11,820	12,026	2.9	5.9
ORTHE–Greek Orthodox	1	55	NR	140	0.0	0.1
ORTHE–Rus Orth Abroad	1	40	NR	250	0.1	0.1
ORTHO–Coptic Orth Ch	1	45	NR	250	0.1	0.1
PENT–Assemb of God	18	1,329	853	1,880	0.5	0.9
PENT–Assm God Intl F	1	NR	NR	NR	-	-
PENT–Ch God (Cleve)	5	164	138	174	0.0	0.1
PENT–Ch of God Proph	1	NR	23	29	0.0	0.0
PENT–COGIC	3	50	200	252	0.1	0.1
PENT–Int Foursq Gos	2	139	139	175	0.0	0.1
PENT–Intl Pent Holiness	1	12	10	13	0.0	0.0
PENT–Pent Ch of God	11	770	NR	1,196	0.3	0.6
PENT–Un Pent Ch Intl	3	NR	NR	NR	-	-
PENT–Vineyard	1	50	75	95	0.0	0.0
PRES–Korean Amer Pres	3	NR	NR	NR	-	-
PRES–Korean Pres Amer	4	NR	NR	NR	-	-
PRES–Orth Pres Ch	1	93	89	116	0.0	0.1
PRES–Presb Ch (USA)	9	2,661	3,481	4,394	1.1	2.1
PRES–Presb Ch Amer	1	45	42	50	0.0	0.0
Salvation Army	2	82	83	309	0.1	0.2
Sev Day Adv	7	671	1,167	1,342	0.3	0.7
Sikh	1	NR	NR	NR	-	-
Un C of Christ	1	0	61	77	0.0	0.0
Unit Univ	1	121	241	286	0.1	0.1
Unity Ch	1	NR	NR	NR	-	-
Zoroastrian	0	NR	NR	1	0.0	0.0
NAPA	**101**	**9,290**	**13,127**	**71,383**	**52.3**	**100.0**
ANG/EPIS–Episcopal	3	395	528	765	0.6	1.1
Bahá'í	1	NR	56	56	0.0	0.1
BAPT–Amer Bapt USA	2	317	267	324	0.2	0.5
BAPT–Converge/BGC	1	75	NR	90	0.1	0.1
BAPT–Ind Bapt Flwsp Intl	1	NR	NR	NR	-	-
BAPT–So Bapt Conv	7	486	946	1,147	0.8	1.6
BUDD–Mahayana	2	NR	NR	516	0.4	0.7
BUDD–Vajrayana	1	NR	NR	20	0.0	0.0
Calv Chpl	1	NR	NR	NR	-	-
Catholic	8	NR	NR	47,968	35.1	67.2
Ch Cr, Scientst	1	NR	NR	NR	-	-
Ch of Nazarene	1	50	78	95	0.1	0.1
Chr & Miss Al	3	211	184	243	0.2	0.3
CHR–Chr Chs & Chs Cr	2	NR	800	970	0.7	1.4
CHR–Chs of Christ	2	70	65	84	0.1	0.1
Evan Free Ch	1	110	NR	110	0.1	0.2
FRND–Indep Yr Mtgs	1	NR	8	10	0.0	0.0
HINDU–Post Ren	1	NR	NR	100	0.1	0.1
Jehovah's Witness	2	NR	NR	NR	-	-
JUD–Reform	1	87	153	413	0.3	0.6
LDS–L-D Saints	6	NR	NR	2,209	1.6	3.1
LUTH–E.L.C.A.	2	99	248	281	0.2	0.4
LUTH–Luth–MO Synod	1	298	636	835	0.6	1.2
METH–Un Methodist	2	201	503	641	0.5	0.9
Muslim Est	3	1,035	NR	3,327	2.4	4.7
Non-denom Chr Chs	11	2,050	2,525	2,687	2.0	3.8

Religious Group	Number of Congregations	Number of Attendees	Number of Communicant, Confirmed, or Full Members	Adherents: Number of Adherents	Adherents: % of Total Pop.	Adherents: % of Total Adh.
ORTHE–Orth Ch in Amer	1	15	NR	50	0.0	0.1
ORTHE–Rus Orth Abroad	1	15	NR	30	0.0	0.0
PENT–Assemb of God	5	552	361	1,407	1.0	2.0
PENT–COGIC	2	0	300	364	0.3	0.5
PENT–Int Foursq Gos	1	46	90	109	0.1	0.2
PENT–Pent Ch of God	2	140	NR	217	0.2	0.3
PENT–Un Pent Ch Intl	3	NR	NR	NR	-	-
PRES–Presb Ch (USA)	4	330	744	902	0.7	1.3
REF–Christian Ref	1	20	3	4	0.0	0.0
Salvation Army	1	40	57	150	0.1	0.2
Sev Day Adv	11	2,588	4,499	5,175	3.8	7.2
Unit Univ	1	60	76	84	0.1	0.1
Unity Ch	1	NR	NR	NR	-	-
NEVADA	**87**	**13,073**	**18,352**	**31,053**	**31.4**	**100.0**
ANG/EPIS–Episcopal	2	323	615	669	0.7	2.2
Bahá'í	2	NR	124	124	0.1	0.4
BAPT–Amer Bapt USA	1	46	51	59	0.1	0.2
BAPT–Consrv Bapt	1	NR	NR	NR	-	-
BAPT–Reg Bapt Gen As	1	NR	NR	NR	-	-
BAPT–So Bapt Conv	5	2,058	1,634	1,901	1.9	6.1
BUDD–Mahayana	4	NR	NR	108	0.1	0.3
BUDD–Vajrayana	3	NR	NR	112	0.1	0.4
Calv Chpl	3	NR	NR	NR	-	-
Catholic	4	NR	NR	7,999	8.1	25.8
CGOD–Ch God (Ander)	2	0	NR	0	0.0	0.0
Ch Cr, Scientst	2	NR	NR	NR	-	-
Ch of Nazarene	2	217	192	390	0.4	1.3
Chr & Miss Al	1	280	135	350	0.4	1.1
CHR–Chs of Christ	4	150	166	234	0.2	0.8
FRND–Indep Yr Mtgs	1	NR	51	59	0.1	0.2
HINDU–Post Ren	5	NR	NR	310	0.3	1.0
HINDU–Renaiss	1	NR	NR	12	0.0	0.0
Jehovah's Witness	3	NR	NR	NR	-	-
JUD–Reform	1	52	91	246	0.2	0.8
LDS–L-D Saints	3	NR	NR	1,683	1.7	5.4
LUTH–E.L.C.A.	2	258	527	614	0.6	2.0
LUTH–Luth–MO Synod	1	105	159	175	0.2	0.6
METH–Un Methodist	5	531	875	1,332	1.3	4.3
Non-denom Chr Chs	13	8,156	12,011	12,578	12.7	40.5
PENT–Assemb of God	2	190	182	297	0.3	1.0
PENT–Ch God (Cleve)	1	20	22	26	0.0	0.1
PENT–Int Foursq Gos	2	136	129	150	0.2	0.5
PENT–Un Pent Ch Intl	1	NR	NR	NR	-	-
PRES–Evan Presby Ch	1	NR	441	513	0.5	1.7
PRES–Presb Ch (USA)	1	33	53	62	0.1	0.2
REF–Ref Ch in U.S.	1	NR	40	54	0.1	0.2
Salvation Army	1	34	48	55	0.1	0.2
Sev Day Adv	3	402	699	804	0.8	2.6
Unit Univ	1	82	107	136	0.1	0.4
Unity Ch	1	NR	NR	NR	-	-
Zoroastrian	0	NR	NR	1	0.0	0.0
ORANGE	**1,519**	**266,839**	**344,038**	**1,377,585**	**45.8**	**100.0**
ANG/EPIS–Anglican NA	7	NR	NR	NR	-	-
ANG/EPIS–Episcopal	22	3,963	8,426	11,531	0.4	0.8
Bahá'í	24	NR	2,729	2,729	0.1	0.2
BAPT–Amer Bapt Assn	2	NR	85	104	0.0	0.0
BAPT–Amer Bapt USA	26	3,972	5,180	6,357	0.2	0.5
BAPT–Consrv Bapt	11	NR	NR	NR	-	-
BAPT–Converge/BGC	6	1,500	NR	1,800	0.1	0.1
BAPT–Free Will Bapt	1	NR	46	56	0.0	0.0
BAPT–N Am Bapt Conf	8	NR	1,413	1,734	0.1	0.1
BAPT–NBC USA	1	0	150	184	0.0	0.0
BAPT–Ref Bapt Ch	1	NR	NR	NR	-	-
BAPT–Reg Bapt Gen As	3	NR	NR	NR	-	-
BAPT–So Bapt Conv	133	31,557	56,400	69,216	2.3	5.0
BRETH–Ch of Brethren	1	90	127	156	0.0	0.0
BRETH–Grace Breth	3	NR	NR	NR	-	-
BUDD–Mahayana	56	NR	NR	24,964	0.8	1.8
BUDD–Theravada	3	NR	NR	996	0.0	0.1
BUDD–Vajrayana	2	NR	NR	71	0.0	0.0
Calv Chpl	48	NR	NR	NR	-	-

NR–Not Reported - Represents no adherents reported. Percentages may not total 100 due to rounding.

Table 3: Religious Congregations by County and Group: 2010

Religious Group	Number of Congregations	Number of Attendees	Number of Communicant, Confirmed, or Full Members	Adherents: Number of Adherents	Adherents: % of Total Pop.	Adherents: % of Total Adh.
Catholic	67	NR	NR	797,473	26.5	57.9
CGOD–Ch God (Ander)	6	252	NR	252	0.0	0.0
Ch Cr, Scientst	12	NR	NR	NR	-	-
Ch God (7th Day)	1	NR	NR	NR	-	-
Ch of Nazarene	26	1,993	3,002	3,867	0.1	0.3
Chr & Miss Al	22	8,451	3,121	9,387	0.3	0.7
CHR–Chr Ch (Disc)	14	774	1,849	2,269	0.1	0.2
CHR–Chr Chs & Chs Cr	20	NR	12,767	15,668	0.5	1.1
CHR–Chs of Christ	31	3,157	2,941	3,801	0.1	0.3
CHR–Int Chs of Christ	0	NR	319	391	0.0	0.0
CONG–Cong Chr, NA	3	NR	275	337	0.0	0.0
Evan Cov Ch	6	2,678	1,185	3,482	0.1	0.3
Evan Free Ch	15	9,100	NR	9,100	0.3	0.7
FRND–Evan Fr Ch Intl	9	7,817	2,660	3,264	0.1	0.2
FRND–Indep Yr Mtgs	1	NR	41	50	0.0	0.0
Grace Gosp Fel	1	NR	NR	NR	-	-
HINDU–I/A Temples	5	NR	NR	4,204	0.1	0.3
HINDU–Post Ren	7	NR	NR	303	0.0	0.0
HINDU–Renaiss	1	NR	NR	12	0.0	0.0
HINDU–Trad Temples	2	NR	NR	900	0.0	0.1
Ind Fund Churches	9	NR	NR	NR	-	-
Jain	1	NR	NR	NR	-	-
Jehovah's Witness	29	NR	NR	NR	-	-
JUD–Conserv	4	1,083	1,215	3,280	0.1	0.2
JUD–Orth	13	959	700	1,350	0.0	0.1
JUD–Reconst	1	485	619	1,671	0.1	0.1
JUD–Reform	6	1,729	3,049	8,232	0.3	0.6
LDS–Comm of Christ	3	NR	492	492	0.0	0.0
LDS–L-D Saints	121	NR	NR	66,772	2.2	4.8
LUTH–Assoc Free Luth	1	NR	NR	NR	-	-
LUTH–Ch of Luth Br	1	115	59	180	0.0	0.0
LUTH–Cons Luth Assn	2	NR	NR	NR	-	-
LUTH–E.L.C.A.	35	4,519	8,401	10,846	0.4	0.8
LUTH–Evan Luth Syn	2	98	128	107	0.0	0.0
LUTH–Luth Cong Msn Chr	7	2,364	7,305	8,965	0.3	0.7
LUTH–Luth-MO Synod	30	7,509	13,163	17,377	0.6	1.3
LUTH–Nor Amer Luth C	2	NR	NR	NR	-	-
LUTH–Wisc Ev Luth Syn	5	406	579	745	0.0	0.1
MENN–CG in Cr (Menn)	1	NR	1	1	0.0	0.0
MENN–Menn Br US Conf	1	NR	350	430	0.0	0.0
MENN–Mennonite USA	1	33	42	52	0.0	0.0
METH–AME	2	600	1,350	1,657	0.1	0.1
METH–C.M.E.	1	0	100	123	0.0	0.0
METH–Free Methodist	8	1,075	762	1,105	0.0	0.1
METH–Un Methodist	42	5,591	8,964	12,194	0.4	0.9
METH–Wesleyan	7	157	115	204	0.0	0.0
Metro Comm Ch	2	50	65	79	0.0	0.0
Missionary Ch	1	45	60	60	0.0	0.0
MJEW–Assoc Mes Cong	1	NR	NR	NR	-	-
MJEW–Union Mes Cong	1	NR	NR	NR	-	-
Muslim Est	20	8,307	NR	24,674	0.8	1.8
New Apost Ch	1	NR	NR	NR	-	-
Non-denom Chr Chs	193	84,866	112,111	122,205	4.1	8.9
ORTHE–Ant Orth of NA	5	771	NR	1,831	0.1	0.1
ORTHE–Greek Orthodox	3	805	NR	2,575	0.1	0.2
ORTHE–Orth Ch in Amer	1	150	NR	1,000	0.0	0.1
ORTHE–Rus Orth Abroad	1	5	NR	10	0.0	0.0
ORTHE–Serb Orth USA	1	60	NR	250	0.0	0.0
ORTHO–Armen Ap Cilic	1	90	NR	360	0.0	0.0
ORTHO–Armen Ap Etchm	1	100	NR	1,200	0.0	0.1
ORTHO–Coptic Orth Ch	4	3,650	NR	5,050	0.2	0.4
ORTHO–Eritrean Orth	1	50	NR	50	0.0	0.0
ORTHO–Syrian Orth Ch	1	215	NR	1,080	0.0	0.1
PENT–Assemb of God	68	20,851	22,371	29,899	1.0	2.2
PENT–Ch God (Cleve)	15	4,006	4,390	5,388	0.2	0.4
PENT–Ch of God Proph	6	NR	540	663	0.0	0.0
PENT–COGIC	2	305	375	460	0.0	0.0
PENT–Full Gosp Bapt	1	NR	NR	NR	-	-
PENT–Int Foursq Gos	34	7,213	4,806	5,898	0.2	0.4
PENT–Intl Pent Holiness	1	97	115	141	0.0	0.0
PENT–Pent Ch of God	3	210	NR	326	0.0	0.0
PENT–Un Pent Ch Intl	9	NR	NR	NR	-	-
PENT–United Holy Ch	1	NR	NR	NR	-	-
PENT–Vineyard	11	3,355	5,981	7,340	0.2	0.5
PRES–As Ref Pres Ch	1	NR	30	37	0.0	0.0
PRES–Kor Pres Abroad	16	NR	NR	NR	-	-
PRES–Korean Amer Pres	17	NR	NR	NR	-	-
PRES–Korean Pres Amer	15	NR	NR	NR	-	-
PRES–Orth Pres Ch	6	296	280	340	0.0	0.0
PRES–Presb Ch (USA)	37	11,418	17,649	21,660	0.7	1.6
PRES–Presb Ch Amer	13	3,453	3,580	3,914	0.1	0.3
REF–Christian Ref	23	2,697	2,456	3,014	0.1	0.2
REF–Ref Ch in Am	3	3,955	6,200	9,273	0.3	0.7
REF–Ref Ch in U.S.	1	NR	29	49	0.0	0.0
REF–Un Ref Chs N.A.	2	NR	NR	NR	-	-
Salvation Army	4	908	1,160	4,281	0.1	0.3
Sev Day Adv	20	5,447	9,473	10,894	0.4	0.8
Sikh	5	NR	NR	NR	-	-
Un C of Christ	14	1,005	1,612	1,978	0.1	0.1
Unit Univ	5	432	645	830	0.0	0.1
Unity Ch	4	NR	NR	NR	-	-
Zoroastrian	2	NR	NR	335	0.0	0.0
PLACER	**253**	**40,058**	**46,172**	**133,715**	**38.4**	**100.0**
ANG/EPIS–Anglican NA	2	NR	NR	NR	-	-
ANG/EPIS–Episcopal	5	423	1,050	1,062	0.3	0.8
Bahá'í	4	NR	233	233	0.1	0.2
BAPT–Consrv Bapt	3	NR	NR	NR	-	-
BAPT–Converge/BGC	1	75	NR	90	0.0	0.1
BAPT–N Am Bapt Conf	6	NR	1,039	1,275	0.4	1.0
BAPT–Reg Bapt Gen As	1	NR	NR	NR	-	-
BAPT–So Bapt Conv	16	1,284	1,349	1,655	0.5	1.2
BRETH–Grace Breth	1	NR	NR	NR	-	-
BUDD–Mahayana	1	NR	NR	1,250	0.4	0.9
Calv Chpl	6	NR	NR	NR	-	-
Catholic	12	NR	NR	51,342	14.7	38.4
CGOD–Ch God (Ander)	2	0	NR	0	0.0	0.0
Ch Cr, Scientst	2	NR	NR	NR	-	-
Ch God (7th Day)	1	NR	NR	NR	-	-
Ch of Nazarene	3	690	665	741	0.2	0.6
Chr & Miss Al	3	191	89	364	0.1	0.3
CHR–Chr Ch (Disc)	2	41	76	93	0.0	0.1
CHR–Chr Chs & Chs Cr	3	NR	5,000	6,134	1.8	4.6
CHR–Chs of Christ	6	510	451	585	0.2	0.4
Evan Cov Ch	7	10,500	4,754	13,649	3.9	10.2
Evan Free Ch	2	460	NR	460	0.1	0.3
HINDU–I/A Temples	1	NR	NR	250	0.1	0.2
Ind Fund Churches	1	NR	NR	NR	-	-
Jehovah's Witness	9	NR	NR	NR	-	-
JUD–Orth	1	43	50	60	0.0	0.0
JUD–Reform	1	72	127	343	0.1	0.3
LDS–L-D Saints	33	NR	NR	15,179	4.4	11.4
LUTH–E.L.C.A.	6	895	1,795	2,176	0.6	1.6
LUTH–Luth-MO Synod	3	582	769	927	0.3	0.7
LUTH–Wisc Ev Luth Syn	1	133	178	228	0.1	0.2
METH–Free Methodist	2	30	24	32	0.0	0.0
METH–Un Methodist	10	767	1,540	1,835	0.5	1.4
METH–Wesleyan	4	405	251	527	0.2	0.4
Nat Spirit Asso	2	NR	NR	NR	-	-
Non-denom Chr Chs	35	14,701	18,509	19,781	5.7	14.8
ORTHE–Greek Orthodox	1	210	NR	400	0.1	0.3
PENT–Assemb of God	13	4,023	2,013	5,256	1.5	3.9
PENT–Ch God (Cleve)	1	11	37	45	0.0	0.0
PENT–Ch of God Proph	1	NR	23	28	0.0	0.0
PENT–Int Foursq Gos	6	577	387	475	0.1	0.4
PENT–Open Bible Std	1	34	NR	34	0.0	0.0
PENT–Pent Ch of God	2	140	NR	217	0.1	0.2
PENT–Un Pent Ch Intl	4	NR	NR	NR	-	-
PENT–Vineyard	2	195	240	294	0.1	0.2
PRES–Evan Presby Ch	1	NR	1,181	1,449	0.4	1.1
PRES–Orth Pres Ch	1	159	126	181	0.1	0.1
PRES–Presb Ch (USA)	2	339	505	619	0.2	0.5
PRES–Presb Ch Amer	1	534	494	665	0.2	0.5
REF–Christian Ref	1	337	200	245	0.1	0.2
Salvation Army	2	98	231	274	0.1	0.2
Sev Day Adv	9	1,262	2,195	2,524	0.7	1.9
Un C of Christ	4	253	482	591	0.2	0.4
Unit Univ	1	84	109	143	0.0	0.1

NR–Not Reported - Represents no adherents reported. Percentages may not total 100 due to rounding.

Table 3: Religious Congregations by County and Group: 2010

Religious Group	Number of Congregations	Number of Attendees	Number of Communicant, Confirmed, or Full Members	Adherents: Number of Adherents	Adherents: % of Total Pop.	Adherents: % of Total Adh.
Unity Ch	2	NR	NR	NR	-	-
Zoroastrian	0	NR	NR	4	0.0	0.0
PLUMAS	**41**	**1,327**	**1,706**	**4,493**	**22.5**	**100.0**
ANG/EPIS–Anglican NA	2	NR	NR	NR	-	-
ANG/EPIS–Episcopal	2	24	45	53	0.3	1.2
Bahá'í	0	NR	9	9	0.0	0.2
BAPT–Reg Bapt Gen As	1	NR	NR	NR	-	-
BAPT–So Bapt Conv	4	306	400	461	2.3	10.3
Catholic	4	NR	NR	1,216	6.1	27.1
CHR–Chs of Christ	2	62	47	70	0.3	1.6
Jehovah's Witness	3	NR	NR	NR	-	-
LDS–L-D Saints	3	NR	NR	755	3.8	16.8
LUTH–E.L.C.A.	1	35	121	143	0.7	3.2
LUTH–Luth-MO Synod	3	44	71	76	0.4	1.7
METH–Un Methodist	5	179	405	650	3.2	14.5
METH–Wesleyan	1	26	26	34	0.2	0.8
Non-denom Chr Chs	3	385	305	494	2.5	11.0
PENT–Assemb of God	4	133	51	272	1.4	6.1
PENT–Vineyard	1	75	125	144	0.7	3.2
Sev Day Adv	2	58	101	116	0.6	2.6
RIVERSIDE	**1,140**	**186,542**	**231,349**	**973,004**	**44.4**	**100.0**
ANG/EPIS–Anglican NA	1	NR	NR	NR	-	-
ANG/EPIS–Episcopal	16	2,048	4,450	4,793	0.2	0.5
Bahá'í	10	NR	834	834	0.0	0.1
BAPT–Amer Bapt Assn	2	NR	170	217	0.0	0.0
BAPT–Amer Bapt USA	8	417	820	1,044	0.0	0.1
BAPT–Consrv Bapt	12	NR	NR	NR	-	-
BAPT–Converge/BGC	12	900	NR	1,080	0.0	0.1
BAPT–N Am Bapt Conf	1	NR	182	232	0.0	0.0
BAPT–Natl Mis Bapt Conv	5	200	475	605	0.0	0.1
BAPT–NBC USA	3	60	1,600	2,038	0.1	0.2
BAPT–Ref Bapt Ch	1	NR	NR	NR	-	-
BAPT–Reg Bapt Gen As	3	NR	NR	NR	-	-
BAPT–S-D Baptist Gen Con	2	93	248	316	0.0	0.0
BAPT–So Bapt Conv	128	16,172	21,161	26,952	1.2	2.8
BRETH–Breth in Chr	6	NR	NR	NR	-	-
BRETH–Grace Breth	2	NR	NR	NR	-	-
BUDD–Mahayana	9	NR	NR	7,293	0.3	0.7
BUDD–Theravada	3	NR	NR	3,028	0.1	0.3
BUDD–Vajrayana	1	NR	NR	36	0.0	0.0
Calv Chpl	33	NR	NR	NR	-	-
Catholic	51	NR	NR	602,765	27.5	61.9
CGOD–Ch God (Ander)	4	663	NR	663	0.0	0.1
CGOD–Ches God-Gen Con	1	45	62	79	0.0	0.0
Ch Cr, Scientst	7	NR	NR	NR	-	-
Ch God (7th Day)	1	NR	NR	NR	-	-
Ch of Nazarene	17	1,900	2,778	3,252	0.1	0.3
Chr & Miss Al	15	4,340	2,352	6,035	0.3	0.6
CHR–Chr Ch (Disc)	6	242	441	562	0.0	0.1
CHR–Chr Chs & Chs Cr	9	NR	2,555	3,254	0.1	0.3
CHR–Chs of Christ	29	3,377	3,530	4,344	0.2	0.4
CHR–Int Chs of Christ	1	NR	417	531	0.0	0.1
Evan Cov Ch	1	84	82	109	0.0	0.0
Evan Free Ch	7	6,018	NR	6,018	0.3	0.6
FRND–Evan Fr Ch Intl	3	372	107	136	0.0	0.0
FRND–Indep Yr Mtgs	1	NR	23	29	0.0	0.0
Grace Gosp Fel	3	NR	NR	NR	-	-
HINDU–I/A Temples	1	NR	NR	348	0.0	0.0
HINDU–Post Ren	4	NR	NR	70	0.0	0.0
HINDU–Trad Temples	1	NR	NR	200	0.0	0.0
Ind Fund Churches	9	NR	NR	NR	-	-
Jehovah's Witness	34	NR	NR	NR	-	-
JUD–Conserv	3	227	255	688	0.0	0.1
JUD–Orth	3	129	150	180	0.0	0.0
JUD–Reform	3	236	416	1,123	0.1	0.1
LDS–Comm of Christ	1	NR	159	159	0.0	0.0
LDS–L-D Saints	96	NR	NR	51,957	2.4	5.3
LUTH–E.L.C.A.	17	2,290	4,387	5,666	0.3	0.6
LUTH–Luth-MO Synod	21	3,260	4,585	5,663	0.3	0.6
LUTH–Wisc Ev Luth Syn	5	463	589	723	0.0	0.1
MENN–Menn Br US Conf	1	NR	0	0	0.0	0.0
METH–AME	10	264	1,294	1,648	0.1	0.2
METH–C.M.E.	3	170	500	637	0.0	0.1
METH–Evan Meth Ch	1	NR	NR	NR	-	-
METH–Free Methodist	6	2,104	742	2,126	0.1	0.2
METH–Un Methodist	20	2,477	3,673	5,134	0.2	0.5
METH–Wesleyan	2	173	103	225	0.0	0.0
Metro Comm Ch	1	94	123	157	0.0	0.0
Missionary Ch	7	824	727	894	0.0	0.1
MORAV–Morav Ch-North	1	42	87	125	0.0	0.0
Muslim Est	8	3,656	NR	11,376	0.5	1.2
Non-denom Chr Chs	192	88,629	116,340	127,724	5.8	13.1
ORTHE–Ant Orth of NA	2	286	NR	542	0.0	0.1
ORTHE–Greek Orthodox	2	200	NR	650	0.0	0.1
ORTHE–Orth Ch in Amer	1	20	NR	45	0.0	0.0
ORTHO–Armen Ap Cilic	1	45	NR	180	0.0	0.0
ORTHO–Armen Ap Etchm	1	40	NR	1,200	0.1	0.1
ORTHO–Coptic Orth Ch	4	690	NR	1,030	0.0	0.1
PENT–Assemb of God	65	12,598	11,074	19,205	0.9	2.0
PENT–Ch God (Cleve)	13	946	940	1,197	0.1	0.1
PENT–Ch of God Proph	7	NR	260	331	0.0	0.0
PENT–COGIC	12	4,704	11,182	14,242	0.7	1.5
PENT–Full Gosp Bapt	7	NR	NR	NR	-	-
PENT–Int Foursq Gos	24	3,154	2,709	3,450	0.2	0.4
PENT–Intl Pent Holiness	11	830	793	1,010	0.0	0.1
PENT–Open Bible Std	2	266	NR	266	0.0	0.0
PENT–Pent Ch of God	6	420	NR	652	0.0	0.1
PENT–Un Pent Ch Intl	15	NR	NR	NR	-	-
PENT–Vineyard	5	751	1,038	1,322	0.1	0.1
PRES–Evan Presby Ch	1	NR	57	73	0.0	0.0
PRES–Kor Pres Abroad	1	NR	NR	NR	-	-
PRES–Korean Amer Pres	1	NR	NR	NR	-	-
PRES–Korean Pres Amer	1	NR	NR	NR	-	-
PRES–Orth Pres Ch	1	130	128	153	0.0	0.0
PRES–Presb Ch (USA)	15	2,704	3,449	4,393	0.2	0.5
PRES–Presb Ch Amer	2	149	105	154	0.0	0.0
REF–Christian Ref	6	523	560	713	0.0	0.1
REF–Ref Ch in Am	8	4,699	2,784	6,199	0.3	0.6
Salvation Army	5	280	561	561	0.0	0.1
Sev Day Adv	39	10,323	17,951	20,646	0.9	2.1
Sikh	3	NR	NR	NR	-	-
Un C of Christ	8	632	1,125	1,433	0.1	0.1
Unit Univ	3	183	216	263	0.0	0.0
Unity Ch	3	NR	NR	NR	-	-
Zoroastrian	1	NR	NR	26	0.0	0.0
SACRAMENTO	**876**	**110,848**	**153,573**	**525,985**	**37.1**	**100.0**
ANG/EPIS–Anglican NA	2	NR	NR	NR	-	-
ANG/EPIS–Episcopal	12	1,410	3,295	3,752	0.3	0.7
Bahá'í	8	NR	1,562	1,562	0.1	0.3
BAPT–Amer Bapt Assn	3	NR	420	523	0.0	0.1
BAPT–Amer Bapt USA	15	2,739	5,066	6,303	0.4	1.2
BAPT–Consrv Bapt	7	NR	NR	NR	-	-
BAPT–Converge/BGC	5	375	NR	450	0.0	0.1
BAPT–Free Will Bapt	1	NR	46	57	0.0	0.0
BAPT–N Am Bapt Conf	19	NR	7,111	8,848	0.6	1.7
BAPT–Natl Mis Bapt Conv	3	45	345	429	0.0	0.1
BAPT–NBC Amer	2	175	500	622	0.0	0.1
BAPT–NBC USA	5	2,561	3,950	4,915	0.3	0.9
BAPT–Ref Bapt Ch	1	NR	NR	NR	-	-
BAPT–Reg Bapt Gen As	2	NR	NR	NR	-	-
BAPT–So Bapt Conv	75	8,404	19,732	24,551	1.7	4.7
BRETH–Ch of Brethren	1	22	57	71	0.0	0.0
BUDD–Mahayana	25	NR	NR	12,955	0.9	2.5
BUDD–Theravada	2	NR	NR	600	0.0	0.1
BUDD–Vajrayana	1	NR	NR	63	0.0	0.0
Calv Chpl	8	NR	NR	NR	-	-
Catholic	45	NR	NR	229,725	16.2	43.7
CGOD–Ch God (Ander)	7	580	NR	580	0.0	0.1
Ch Cr, Scientst	4	NR	NR	NR	-	-
Ch God (7th Day)	5	NR	NR	NR	-	-
Ch of Chr (Hol)	2	NR	NR	NR	-	-
Ch of Nazarene	11	1,675	2,164	2,844	0.2	0.5
Chr & Miss Al	14	2,370	3,250	4,498	0.3	0.9
CHR–Chr Ch (Disc)	6	337	658	819	0.1	0.2

NR–Not Reported   - Represents no adherents reported.   Percentages may not total 100 due to rounding.

Table 3: Religious Congregations by County and Group: 2010

Religious Group	Number of Congrega-tions	Number of Attendees	Number of Communicant, Confirmed, or Full Members	Adherents		
				Number of Adherents	% of Total Pop.	% of Total Adh.
CHR–Chr Chs & Chs Cr	3	NR	730	908	0.1	0.2
CHR–Chs of Christ	21	2,802	2,513	3,317	0.2	0.6
CHR–Int Chs of Christ	1	NR	105	131	0.0	0.0
CONG–Armen Evang Add'l	1	NR	NR	NR	-	-
CONG–Cong Chr, NA	1	NR	28	35	0.0	0.0
Evan Cov Ch	11	4,863	2,750	6,322	0.4	1.2
Evan Free Ch	4	620	NR	620	0.0	0.1
FRND–Evan Fr Ch Intl	3	209	153	190	0.0	0.0
FRND–Fr Gen Cf	1	NR	45	56	0.0	0.0
FRND–Indep Yr Mtgs	1	NR	45	56	0.0	0.0
HINDU–I/A Temples	4	NR	NR	1,443	0.1	0.3
HINDU–Post Ren	6	NR	NR	202	0.0	0.0
HINDU–Renaiss	1	NR	NR	85	0.0	0.0
HINDU–Trad Temples	2	NR	NR	7,000	0.5	1.3
Ind Fund Churches	5	NR	NR	NR	-	-
Jain	1	NR	NR	NR	-	-
Jehovah's Witness	24	NR	NR	NR	-	-
JUD–Conserv	1	433	486	1,312	0.1	0.2
JUD–Orth	3	355	200	500	0.0	0.1
JUD–Reform	3	580	1,023	2,762	0.2	0.5
LDS–Comm of Christ	1	NR	158	158	0.0	0.0
LDS–L-D Saints	77	NR	NR	44,951	3.2	8.5
LUTH–E.L.C.A.	16	2,389	4,540	6,743	0.5	1.3
LUTH–Luth Ch-Am Asc	2	NR	NR	NR	-	-
LUTH–Luth–MO Synod	10	1,350	2,244	2,778	0.2	0.5
LUTH–Wisc Ev Luth Syn	2	430	643	806	0.1	0.2
MENN–Menn Br US Conf	6	NR	1,131	1,407	0.1	0.3
METH–A.W.M.C.	1	96	18	151	0.0	0.0
METH–AME	4	320	781	972	0.1	0.2
METH–AME Zion	2	155	389	484	0.0	0.1
METH–C.M.E.	2	0	300	373	0.0	0.1
METH–Free Methodist	3	171	234	234	0.0	0.0
METH–Un Methodist	27	2,664	5,263	7,534	0.5	1.4
METH–Wesleyan	7	1,238	663	1,610	0.1	0.3
Metro Comm Ch	1	40	39	49	0.0	0.0
Missionary Ch	2	220	230	230	0.0	0.0
MJEW–Union Mes Cong	1	NR	NR	NR	-	-
Muslim Est	11	3,797	NR	12,198	0.9	2.3
Nat Spirit Asso	1	NR	NR	NR	-	-
New Apost Ch	1	NR	NR	NR	-	-
Non-denom Chr Chs	110	36,805	46,805	54,060	3.8	10.3
ORTHE–Ant Orth of NA	1	75	NR	130	0.0	0.0
ORTHE–Greek Orthodox	2	500	NR	2,750	0.2	0.5
ORTHE–Orth Ch in Amer	2	195	NR	450	0.0	0.1
ORTHE–Romania Orth Ar	1	40	NR	150	0.0	0.0
ORTHE–Rus Orth Abroad	1	115	NR	250	0.0	0.0
ORTHE–Serb Orth USA	1	160	NR	400	0.0	0.1
ORTHO–Armen Ap Etchm	1	90	NR	1,200	0.1	0.2
ORTHO–Coptic Orth Ch	1	75	NR	300	0.0	0.1
ORTHO–Ethiopian Orth	1	NR	NR	NR	-	-
ORTHO–Malan Dioc Am	1	15	NR	45	0.0	0.0
PENT–Apos Faith Msn	1	NR	35	44	0.0	0.0
PENT–Assemb of God	56	15,541	9,673	25,208	1.8	4.8
PENT–Ch God (Cleve)	7	743	1,022	1,272	0.1	0.2
PENT–Ch Lord Jesus Apos	1	NR	NR	NR	-	-
PENT–Ch of God Proph	4	NR	127	158	0.0	0.0
PENT–COGIC	18	1,265	3,850	4,790	0.3	0.9
PENT–Full Gosp Bapt	1	NR	NR	NR	-	-
PENT–Int Foursq Gos	9	1,562	1,565	1,947	0.1	0.4
PENT–Intl Pent Holiness	4	234	305	379	0.0	0.1
PENT–Open Bible Std	1	147	NR	147	0.0	0.0
PENT–Pent Ch of God	6	420	NR	652	0.0	0.1
PENT–Un Pent Ch Intl	10	NR	NR	NR	-	-
PENT–Vineyard	2	140	205	255	0.0	0.0
PRES–Evan Presby Ch	1	NR	1,726	2,147	0.2	0.4
PRES–Kor Pres Abroad	2	NR	NR	NR	-	-
PRES–Korean Pres Amer	1	NR	NR	NR	-	-
PRES–Presb Ch (USA)	17	2,476	4,703	5,851	0.4	1.1
PRES–Presb Ch Amer	5	285	328	364	0.0	0.1
REF–Christian Ref	7	389	310	386	0.0	0.1
REF–Comm Ref Evan	1	NR	NR	NR	-	-
REF–Ref Ch in Am	3	1,317	1,500	2,057	0.1	0.4
REF–Ref Ch in U.S.	1	NR	156	211	0.0	0.0
Salvation Army	2	283	446	1,325	0.1	0.3

Religious Group	Number of Congrega-tions	Number of Attendees	Number of Communicant, Confirmed, or Full Members	Adherents		
				Number of Adherents	% of Total Pop.	% of Total Adh.
Sev Day Adv	18	3,970	6,903	7,940	0.6	1.5
Sikh	1	NR	NR	NR	-	-
Un C of Christ	5	265	590	734	0.1	0.1
Unit Univ	2	316	457	567	0.0	0.1
Unity Ch	3	NR	NR	NR	-	-
Zoroastrian	0	NR	NR	32	0.0	0.0
SAN BENITO	**32**	**2,177**	**2,367**	**35,690**	**64.6**	**100.0**
ANG/EPIS–Episcopal	1	56	79	79	0.1	0.2
Bahá'í	1	NR	49	49	0.1	0.1
BAPT–Converge/BGC	1	400	NR	480	0.9	1.3
BAPT–So Bapt Conv	1	25	25	32	0.1	0.1
Catholic	3	NR	NR	31,105	56.3	87.2
CHR–Chs of Christ	2	38	35	40	0.1	0.1
Jehovah's Witness	1	NR	NR	NR	-	-
LDS–L-D Saints	3	NR	NR	1,151	2.1	3.2
MENN–Menn Br US Conf	1	NR	40	51	0.1	0.1
METH–Un Methodist	1	87	235	298	0.5	0.8
Non-denom Chr Chs	7	740	1,080	1,090	2.0	3.1
PENT–Assemb of God	2	248	137	331	0.6	0.9
PENT–Ch God (Cleve)	1	30	32	41	0.1	0.1
PENT–Ch of God Proph	1	NR	53	68	0.1	0.2
PENT–Int Foursq Gos	1	154	78	100	0.2	0.3
PENT–Pent Ch of God	1	70	NR	109	0.2	0.3
PENT–Un Pent Ch Intl	1	NR	NR	NR	-	-
PRES–Presb Ch (USA)	1	144	242	310	0.6	0.9
Salvation Army	1	47	43	77	0.1	0.2
Sev Day Adv	1	138	239	275	0.5	0.8
Zoroastrian	0	NR	NR	4	0.0	0.0
SAN BERNARDINO	**1,274**	**162,002**	**228,791**	**813,804**	**40.0**	**100.0**
ANG/EPIS–Anglican NA	2	NR	NR	NR	-	-
ANG/EPIS–Episcopal	17	1,081	2,202	2,984	0.1	0.4
Bahá'í	6	NR	667	667	0.0	0.1
BAPT–Amer Bapt Assn	5	NR	262	336	0.0	0.0
BAPT–Amer Bapt USA	20	4,129	4,017	5,157	0.3	0.6
BAPT–Asc Ref Bap Ch Am	1	NR	NR	NR	-	-
BAPT–Consrv Bapt	12	NR	NR	NR	-	-
BAPT–Converge/BGC	5	1,825	NR	2,190	0.1	0.3
BAPT–Free Will Bapt	1	NR	46	59	0.0	0.0
BAPT–N Am Bapt Conf	4	NR	466	598	0.0	0.1
BAPT–Natl Mis Bapt Conv	3	65	350	449	0.0	0.1
BAPT–NBC USA	2	1,200	5,350	6,868	0.3	0.8
BAPT–Ref Bapt Ch	2	NR	NR	NR	-	-
BAPT–Reg Bapt Gen As	2	NR	NR	NR	-	-
BAPT–S-D Baptist Gen Con	1	25	NR	NR	-	-
BAPT–So Bapt Conv	122	15,920	35,104	45,066	2.2	5.5
BRETH–Breth in Chr	8	NR	NR	NR	-	-
BRETH–Grace Breth	3	NR	NR	NR	-	-
BUDD–Mahayana	3	NR	NR	1,022	0.1	0.1
BUDD–Theravada	10	NR	NR	7,587	0.4	0.9
Calv Chpl	30	NR	NR	NR	-	-
Catholic	55	NR	NR	445,334	21.9	54.7
CGOD–Ch God (Ander)	6	372	NR	372	0.0	0.0
Ch Cr, Scientst	8	NR	NR	NR	-	-
Ch God (7th Day)	2	NR	NR	NR	-	-
Ch of Chr (Hol)	2	NR	NR	NR	-	-
Ch of Nazarene	33	4,404	4,813	6,811	0.3	0.8
Chr & Miss Al	13	1,492	1,043	1,750	0.1	0.2
CHR–Chr Ch (Disc)	13	374	848	1,089	0.1	0.1
CHR–Chr Chs & Chs Cr	15	NR	3,325	4,269	0.2	0.5
CHR–Chs of Christ	36	2,654	2,684	3,456	0.2	0.4
CONG–Cong Chr, NA	3	NR	1,960	2,516	0.1	0.3
Evan Cov Ch	2	165	108	214	0.0	0.0
Evan Free Ch	10	4,063	NR	4,063	0.2	0.5
FRND–Evan Fr Ch Intl	1	91	34	44	0.0	0.0
HINDU–I/A Temples	3	NR	NR	3,984	0.2	0.5
HINDU–Post Ren	5	NR	NR	272	0.0	0.0
Ind Fund Churches	8	NR	NR	NR	-	-
Int Cou Comm Ch	1	NR	NR	NR	-	-
Jehovah's Witness	36	NR	NR	NR	-	-
JUD–Conserv	2	89	100	270	0.0	0.0
JUD–Orth	1	43	50	60	0.0	0.0

NR–Not Reported - Represents no adherents reported. Percentages may not total 100 due to rounding.

Table 3: Religious Congregations by County and Group: 2010

Religious Group	Number of Congrega-tions	Number of Attendees	Number of Communicant, Confirmed, or Full Members	Adherents		
				Number of Adherents	% of Total Pop.	% of Total Adh.
JUD–Reform	3	180	317	856	0.0	0.1
LDS–Comm of Christ	3	NR	487	487	0.0	0.1
LDS–L-D Saints	103	NR	NR	52,314	2.6	6.4
LUTH–Ch of Luth Br	1	113	83	420	0.0	0.1
LUTH–E.L.C.A.	19	1,285	2,445	3,205	0.2	0.4
LUTH–Luth Cong Msn Chr	2	139	194	249	0.0	0.0
LUTH–Luth–MO Synod	22	2,467	4,826	5,781	0.3	0.7
LUTH–Wisc Ev Luth Syn	3	148	182	214	0.0	0.0
MENN–Menn Br US Conf	1	NR	20	26	0.0	0.0
MENN–Mennonite USA	3	66	174	223	0.0	0.0
METH–AME	7	665	1,681	2,158	0.1	0.3
METH–AME Zion	1	30	40	51	0.0	0.0
METH–C.M.E.	4	900	1,900	2,439	0.1	0.3
METH–Free Methodist	11	1,535	1,314	1,818	0.1	0.2
METH–Un Methodist	25	2,012	3,262	4,043	0.2	0.5
METH–Wesleyan	3	383	270	498	0.0	0.1
Missionary Ch	1	120	150	150	0.0	0.0
MJEW–Union Mes Cong	1	NR	NR	NR	-	-
Muslim Est	14	5,131	NR	12,321	0.6	1.5
New Apost Ch	3	NR	NR	NR	-	-
Non-denom Chr Chs	208	70,664	98,290	105,314	5.2	12.9
ORTHE–Ant Orth of NA	1	104	NR	288	0.0	0.0
ORTHE–Greek Orthodox	2	155	NR	500	0.0	0.1
ORTHE–Orth Ch in Amer	1	30	NR	60	0.0	0.0
ORTHE–Romania Orth Ar	1	70	NR	800	0.0	0.1
ORTHO–Coptic Orth Ch	4	1,450	NR	1,940	0.1	0.2
ORTHO–Syrian Orth Ch	1	85	NR	280	0.0	0.0
PENT–Assemb of God	69	8,437	4,575	13,916	0.7	1.7
PENT–Ch God (Cleve)	14	854	675	867	0.0	0.1
PENT–Ch of God Proph	8	NR	565	725	0.0	0.1
PENT–COGIC	16	615	2,340	3,004	0.1	0.4
PENT–Full Gosp Bapt	4	NR	NR	NR	-	-
PENT–Int Foursq Gos	45	3,597	3,900	5,007	0.2	0.6
PENT–Intl Pent Holiness	4	363	426	547	0.0	0.1
PENT–Open Bible Std	1	89	NR	89	0.0	0.0
PENT–Pent Ch of God	7	490	NR	761	0.0	0.1
PENT–Un Pent Ch Intl	13	NR	NR	NR	-	-
PENT–Vineyard	4	298	323	415	0.0	0.1
PRES–Cumber Presb	1	NR	14	36	0.0	0.0
PRES–Kor Pres Abroad	2	NR	NR	NR	-	-
PRES–Korean Amer Pres	4	NR	NR	NR	-	-
PRES–Korean Pres Amer	8	NR	NR	NR	-	-
PRES–Orth Pres Ch	2	85	53	72	0.0	0.0
PRES–Presb Ch (USA)	18	1,734	3,811	4,893	0.2	0.6
REF–Christian Ref	6	1,331	2,175	2,792	0.1	0.3
REF–Hung Ref Add'l	1	NR	NR	NR	-	-
REF–Prot Ref Chs	1	221	155	239	0.0	0.0
REF–Ref Ch in Am	3	778	585	931	0.0	0.1
REF–Un Ref Chs N.A.	3	NR	NR	NR	-	-
Salvation Army	4	373	482	1,306	0.1	0.2
Sev Day Adv	58	16,416	28,552	32,831	1.6	4.0
Sikh	1	NR	NR	NR	-	-
Un C of Christ	12	507	969	1,244	0.1	0.2
Unit Univ	1	90	127	167	0.0	0.0
Unity Ch	1	NR	NR	NR	-	-
Zoroastrian	1	NR	NR	40	0.0	0.0
SAN DIEGO	**1,720**	**252,258**	**305,688**	**1,359,377**	**43.9**	**100.0**
ANG/EPIS–Anglican NA	8	NR	NR	NR	-	-
ANG/EPIS–Episcopal	35	5,015	10,915	12,532	0.4	0.9
Ap Chr Ch-Amer	1	60	40	60	0.0	0.0
Bahá'í	19	NR	3,238	3,238	0.1	0.2
BAPT–Amer Bapt Assn	1	NR	15	18	0.0	0.0
BAPT–Amer Bapt USA	25	2,363	2,573	3,135	0.1	0.2
BAPT–Asc Ref Bap Ch Am	1	NR	NR	NR	-	-
BAPT–Consrv Bapt	11	NR	NR	NR	-	-
BAPT–Converge/BGC	20	5,125	NR	6,150	0.2	0.5
BAPT–Free Will Bapt	1	NR	46	56	0.0	0.0
BAPT–Ind Bapt Flwsp Intl	2	NR	NR	NR	-	-
BAPT–Natl Mis Bapt Conv	5	82	380	463	0.0	0.0
BAPT–NBC Amer	4	816	1,250	1,523	0.0	0.1
BAPT–NBC USA	7	575	1,650	2,010	0.1	0.1
BAPT–Prog NBC	1	600	650	792	0.0	0.1
BAPT–Ref Bapt Ch	3	NR	NR	NR	-	-
BAPT–Reg Bapt Gen As	7	NR	NR	NR	-	-
BAPT–So Bapt Conv	206	24,645	27,482	33,486	1.1	2.5
BRETH–Ch of Brethren	1	24	47	57	0.0	0.0
BRETH–Grace Breth	1	NR	NR	NR	-	-
BUDD–Mahayana	40	NR	NR	33,289	1.1	2.4
BUDD–Theravada	9	NR	NR	4,201	0.1	0.3
BUDD–Vajrayana	10	NR	NR	809	0.0	0.1
Calv Chpl	35	NR	NR	NR	-	-
Catholic	115	NR	NR	801,850	25.9	59.0
CGOD–Ch God (Ander)	9	1,604	NR	1,604	0.1	0.1
CGOD–Ches God-Gen Con	3	104	150	183	0.0	0.0
Ch Cr, Scientst	15	NR	NR	NR	-	-
Ch God (7th Day)	2	NR	NR	NR	-	-
Ch of Chr (Hol)	2	NR	NR	NR	-	-
Ch of Nazarene	29	3,053	4,311	5,267	0.2	0.4
Chr & Miss Al	18	1,292	1,537	1,978	0.1	0.1
CHR–Chr Ch (Disc)	11	1,355	2,691	3,279	0.1	0.2
CHR–Chr Chs & Chs Cr	13	NR	2,625	3,198	0.1	0.2
CHR–Chs of Christ	47	5,113	4,911	6,668	0.2	0.5
CHR–Int Chs of Christ	1	NR	981	1,195	0.0	0.1
Christian Brethren	2	NR	NR	NR	-	-
CONG–Armen Evang Add'l	1	NR	NR	NR	-	-
CONG–Cong Chr, NA	6	NR	487	593	0.0	0.0
CONG–Consrv Cong Chr	1	370	431	525	0.0	0.0
Evan Cov Ch	9	1,441	1,564	1,873	0.1	0.1
Evan Free Ch	13	10,395	NR	10,395	0.3	0.8
FRND–Evan Fr Ch Intl	3	125	102	124	0.0	0.0
FRND–Indep Yr Mtgs	2	NR	91	111	0.0	0.0
HINDU–I/A Temples	3	NR	NR	3,374	0.1	0.2
HINDU–Post Ren	10	NR	NR	247	0.0	0.0
HINDU–Renaiss	4	NR	NR	48	0.0	0.0
HINDU–Trad Temples	2	NR	NR	3,200	0.1	0.2
Ind Fund Churches	3	NR	NR	NR	-	-
Jain	1	NR	NR	NR	-	-
Jehovah's Witness	43	NR	NR	NR	-	-
JUD–Conserv	8	1,760	1,975	5,332	0.2	0.4
JUD–Orth	16	1,704	650	2,400	0.1	0.2
JUD–Reconst	1	135	172	464	0.0	0.0
JUD–Reform	5	1,805	3,184	8,597	0.3	0.6
LDS–Comm of Christ	5	NR	850	850	0.0	0.1
LDS–L-D Saints	120	NR	NR	71,495	2.3	5.3
LUTH–Assoc Free Luth	2	NR	NR	NR	-	-
LUTH–E.L.C.A.	34	4,744	9,609	11,563	0.4	0.9
LUTH–Luth Ch-Am Asc	1	NR	NR	NR	-	-
LUTH–Luth Cong Msn Chr	5	1,586	3,739	4,556	0.1	0.3
LUTH–Luth–MO Synod	37	5,593	9,001	12,060	0.4	0.9
LUTH–Wisc Ev Luth Syn	7	714	1,033	1,247	0.0	0.1
MENN–Menn Br US Conf	1	NR	17	21	0.0	0.0
MENN–Mennonite USA	1	6	7	9	0.0	0.0
METH–AME	5	150	700	853	0.0	0.1
METH–AME Zion	4	50	430	524	0.0	0.0
METH–C.M.E.	1	100	275	335	0.0	0.0
METH–Evan Meth Ch	2	NR	NR	NR	-	-
METH–Free Methodist	3	378	288	385	0.0	0.0
METH–Un Methodist	43	8,417	14,758	20,797	0.7	1.5
METH–Wesleyan	15	4,055	4,126	5,272	0.2	0.4
Metro Comm Ch	1	308	304	370	0.0	0.0
Missionary Ch	2	215	250	290	0.0	0.0
MJEW–Union Mes Cong	1	NR	NR	NR	-	-
Muslim Est	19	6,737	NR	21,994	0.7	1.6
New Apost Ch	3	NR	NR	NR	-	-
Non-denom Chr Chs	212	103,623	134,283	148,930	4.8	11.0
ORTHE–Ant Orth of NA	2	244	NR	543	0.0	0.0
ORTHE–Greek Orthodox	3	645	NR	3,000	0.1	0.2
ORTHE–Orth Ch in Amer	3	150	NR	375	0.0	0.0
ORTHE–Rus Orth Abroad	1	40	NR	200	0.0	0.0
ORTHE–Rus Orth Moscow	1	35	NR	90	0.0	0.0
ORTHE–Serb Orth USA	3	180	NR	860	0.0	0.1
ORTHE–Ukrainian Orth	1	20	NR	60	0.0	0.0
ORTHO–Armen Ap Etchm	1	80	NR	1,150	0.0	0.1
ORTHO–Coptic Orth Ch	1	350	NR	500	0.0	0.0
ORTHO–Eritrean Orth	1	125	NR	450	0.0	0.0
ORTHO–Ethiopian Orth	1	NR	NR	NR	-	-
ORTHO–Syrian Orth Ch	1	155	NR	600	0.0	0.0

NR–Not Reported   - Represents no adherents reported.   Percentages may not total 100 due to rounding.

Table 3: Religious Congregations by County and Group: 2010

Religious Group	Number of Congrega-tions	Number of Attendees	Number of Communicant, Confirmed, or Full Members	Adherents		
				Number of Adherents	% of Total Pop.	% of Total Adh.
PENT–Assemb of God	66	15,984	8,069	23,905	0.8	1.8
PENT–Assm God Intl F	1	NR	NR	NR	-	-
PENT–Ch God (Cleve)	5	222	170	207	0.0	0.0
PENT–Ch Lord Jesus Apos	4	NR	NR	NR	-	-
PENT–Ch of God Proph	5	NR	264	322	0.0	0.0
PENT–COGIC	21	1,617	3,576	4,357	0.1	0.3
PENT–Int Foursq Gos	22	1,620	1,418	1,728	0.1	0.1
PENT–Intl Pent Holiness	6	278	308	375	0.0	0.0
PENT–Open Bible Std	1	100	NR	100	0.0	0.0
PENT–Pent Ch of God	4	280	NR	435	0.0	0.0
PENT–Un Pent Ch Intl	29	NR	NR	NR	-	-
PENT–Vineyard	5	606	755	920	0.0	0.1
PRES–As Ref Pres Ch	2	NR	54	66	0.0	0.0
PRES–Evan Presby Ch	2	NR	517	630	0.0	0.0
PRES–Kor Pres Abroad	1	NR	NR	NR	-	-
PRES–Korean Amer Pres	4	NR	NR	NR	-	-
PRES–Korean Pres Amer	3	NR	NR	NR	-	-
PRES–Orth Pres Ch	4	374	359	466	0.0	0.0
PRES–Presb Ch (USA)	29	8,211	13,959	17,009	0.5	1.3
PRES–Presb Ch Amer	20	2,726	1,839	2,285	0.1	0.2
PRES–Ref Pres of NA	1	30	27	44	0.0	0.0
REF–Christian Ref	7	602	800	975	0.0	0.1
REF–Hung Ref Add'l	1	NR	NR	NR	-	-
REF–Ref Ch in Am	1	150	210	360	0.0	0.0
REF–Ref Ch in U.S.	1	NR	16	20	0.0	0.0
REF–Un Ref Chs N.A.	3	NR	NR	NR	-	-
Salvation Army	7	620	666	9,133	0.3	0.7
Sev Day Adv	34	7,551	13,132	15,102	0.5	1.1
Sikh	2	NR	NR	NR	-	-
Swedenborgian	1	NR	NR	NR	-	-
Tao	1	NR	NR	NR	-	-
Un C of Christ	22	1,969	4,303	5,243	0.2	0.4
Unit Univ	5	1,057	1,428	1,851	0.1	0.1
Unity Ch	6	NR	NR	NR	-	-
Zoroastrian	0	NR	NR	141	0.0	0.0
SAN FRANCISCO	**521**	**44,759**	**72,673**	**284,310**	**35.3**	**100.0**
ANG/EPIS–Episcopal	18	2,131	5,225	6,145	0.8	2.2
Bahá'í	1	NR	790	790	0.1	0.3
BAPT–Alliance Bapt	1	NR	NR	NR	-	-
BAPT–Amer Bapt USA	13	2,498	4,412	4,930	0.6	1.7
BAPT–Consrv Bapt	1	NR	NR	NR	-	-
BAPT–Converge/BGC	3	225	NR	270	0.0	0.1
BAPT–Fund Bapt Flwsp	1	NR	NR	NR	-	-
BAPT–N Am Bapt Conf	2	NR	361	403	0.1	0.1
BAPT–Natl Mis Bapt Conv	4	250	800	894	0.1	0.3
BAPT–NBC Amer	9	710	1,275	1,425	0.2	0.5
BAPT–NBC USA	16	4,355	7,451	8,326	1.0	2.9
BAPT–So Bapt Conv	44	3,330	4,800	5,364	0.7	1.9
BRETH–Grace Breth	1	NR	NR	NR	-	-
BUDD–Mahayana	28	NR	NR	14,020	1.7	4.9
BUDD–Theravada	2	NR	NR	2,729	0.3	1.0
BUDD–Vajrayana	10	NR	NR	991	0.1	0.3
Calv Chpl	2	NR	NR	NR	-	-
Catholic	50	NR	NR	120,988	15.0	42.6
CGOD–Ch God (Ander)	1	65	NR	65	0.0	0.0
Ch Cr, Scientist	4	NR	NR	NR	-	-
Ch of Chr (Hol)	2	NR	NR	NR	-	-
Ch of Nazarene	9	372	470	582	0.1	0.2
Chr & Miss Al	2	546	604	681	0.1	0.2
CHR–Chr Ch (Disc)	2	34	73	82	0.0	0.0
CHR–Chr Chs & Chs Cr	1	NR	30	34	0.0	0.0
CHR–Chs of Christ	7	422	487	827	0.1	0.3
CONG–Armen Evang Add'l	1	NR	NR	NR	-	-
Evan Cov Ch	5	367	301	477	0.1	0.2
Evan Free Ch	3	550	NR	550	0.1	0.2
FRND–Indep Yr Mtgs	1	NR	91	102	0.0	0.0
HINDU–I/A Temples	1	NR	NR	1,742	0.2	0.6
HINDU–Post Ren	8	NR	NR	268	0.0	0.1
HINDU–Renaiss	5	NR	NR	1,048	0.1	0.4
Int Cou Comm Ch	2	NR	NR	NR	-	-
Jehovah's Witness	12	NR	NR	NR	-	-
JUD–Conserv	3	556	624	1,685	0.2	0.6
JUD–Orth	8	1,065	700	1,500	0.2	0.5
JUD–Reconst	1	78	100	270	0.0	0.1
JUD–Reform	4	1,984	3,499	9,447	1.2	3.3
LDS–Comm of Christ	1	NR	158	158	0.0	0.1
LDS–L-D Saints	5	NR	NR	5,923	0.7	2.1
LUTH–E.L.C.A.	9	594	1,189	1,590	0.2	0.6
LUTH–Luth Cong Msn Chr	1	110	199	222	0.0	0.1
LUTH–Luth–MO Synod	8	905	1,367	1,812	0.2	0.6
MENN–Mennonite USA	2	141	106	118	0.0	0.0
METH–AME	3	350	650	726	0.1	0.3
METH–AME Zion	1	0	100	112	0.0	0.0
METH–C.M.E.	2	125	460	514	0.1	0.2
METH–Free Methodist	2	70	90	90	0.0	0.0
METH–Un Methodist	12	4,017	14,731	39,312	4.9	13.8
Metro Comm Ch	1	231	270	302	0.0	0.1
Muslim Est	6	2,071	NR	6,654	0.8	2.3
Nat Spirit Asso	3	NR	NR	NR	-	-
New Apost Ch	1	NR	NR	NR	-	-
Non-denom Chr Chs	39	6,077	8,251	9,020	1.1	3.2
ORTHE–Ant Orth of NA	1	220	NR	1,000	0.1	0.4
ORTHE–Greek Orthodox	2	550	NR	3,600	0.4	1.3
ORTHE–Orth Ch in Amer	2	155	NR	200	0.0	0.1
ORTHE–Pal/Jor Orth	1	300	NR	3,750	0.5	1.3
ORTHE–Rus Orth Abroad	5	355	NR	810	0.1	0.3
ORTHE–Rus Orth Moscow	1	50	NR	800	0.1	0.3
ORTHE–Serb Orth USA	1	60	NR	250	0.0	0.1
ORTHE–Ukrainian Orth	1	45	NR	100	0.0	0.0
ORTHO–Armen Ap Cilic	1	90	NR	360	0.0	0.1
ORTHO–Armen Ap Etchm	1	120	NR	1,800	0.2	0.6
PENT–Assemb of God	19	3,076	2,188	4,193	0.5	1.5
PENT–Ch God (Cleve)	5	410	439	491	0.1	0.2
PENT–Ch Lord Jesus Apos	2	NR	NR	NR	-	-
PENT–Ch of God Proph	2	NR	159	178	0.0	0.1
PENT–COGIC	12	280	1,055	1,179	0.1	0.4
PENT–Full Gosp Bapt	2	NR	NR	NR	-	-
PENT–Int Foursq Gos	3	116	171	191	0.0	0.1
PENT–Intl Pent Holiness	1	43	25	28	0.0	0.0
PENT–Open Bible Std	2	35	NR	35	0.0	0.0
PENT–Un Pent Ch Intl	4	NR	NR	NR	-	-
PRES–Cumber Presb	3	NR	881	901	0.1	0.3
PRES–Korean Amer Pres	2	NR	NR	NR	-	-
PRES–Korean Pres Amer	3	NR	NR	NR	-	-
PRES–Orth Pres Ch	1	53	50	58	0.0	0.0
PRES–Presb Ch (USA)	23	1,105	3,265	3,648	0.5	1.3
REF–Christian Ref	1	410	311	348	0.0	0.1
REF–Ref Ch in Am	1	802	634	1,924	0.2	0.7
Salvation Army	7	615	702	1,656	0.2	0.6
Sev Day Adv	10	877	1,525	1,754	0.2	0.6
Sikh	1	NR	NR	NR	-	-
Swedenborgian	1	NR	NR	NR	-	-
Tao	6	NR	NR	NR	-	-
Un C of Christ	7	558	1,139	1,273	0.2	0.4
Unit Univ	1	205	465	543	0.1	0.2
Unity Ch	2	NR	NR	NR	-	-
Zoroastrian	0	NR	NR	52	0.0	0.0
SAN JOAQUIN	**452**	**49,102**	**63,099**	**302,267**	**44.1**	**100.0**
ANG/EPIS–Anglican NA	2	NR	NR	NR	-	-
ANG/EPIS–Episcopal	3	278	500	657	0.1	0.2
Bahá'í	1	NR	425	425	0.1	0.1
BAPT–Amer Bapt Assn	4	NR	200	258	0.0	0.1
BAPT–Amer Bapt USA	5	1,655	1,436	1,851	0.3	0.6
BAPT–Consrv Bapt	6	NR	NR	NR	-	-
BAPT–Converge/BGC	3	225	NR	270	0.0	0.1
BAPT–Free Will Bapt	2	NR	92	119	0.0	0.0
BAPT–N Am Bapt Conf	6	NR	3,135	4,042	0.6	1.3
BAPT–Natl Mis Bapt Conv	2	0	300	387	0.1	0.1
BAPT–NBC Amer	4	575	1,050	1,354	0.2	0.4
BAPT–NBC USA	1	0	150	193	0.0	0.1
BAPT–Reg Bapt Gen As	4	NR	NR	NR	-	-
BAPT–So Bapt Conv	46	4,584	5,925	7,639	1.1	2.5
BRETH–Brethren (Ash)	3	NR	240	309	0.0	0.1
BRETH–Grace Breth	4	NR	NR	NR	-	-
BUDD–Mahayana	5	NR	NR	3,570	0.5	1.2
BUDD–Theravada	6	NR	NR	3,152	0.5	1.0

NR–Not Reported   - Represents no adherents reported.   Percentages may not total 100 due to rounding.

Table 3: Religious Congregations by County and Group: 2010

Religious Group	Number of Congregations	Number of Attendees	Number of Communicant, Confirmed, or Full Members	Adherents: Number of Adherents	Adherents: % of Total Pop.	Adherents: % of Total Adh.
Calv Chpl	4	NR	NR	NR	-	-
Catholic	18	NR	NR	183,692	26.8	60.8
CGOD–Ch God (Ander)	2	12	NR	12	0.0	0.0
CGOD–Ches God-Gen Con	1	27	28	36	0.0	0.0
Ch Cr, Scientst	2	NR	NR	NR	-	-
Ch God (7th Day)	2	NR	NR	NR	-	-
Ch of Nazarene	7	1,108	711	1,626	0.2	0.5
Chr & Miss Al	8	1,000	1,314	1,523	0.2	0.5
CHR–Chr Ch (Disc)	2	109	187	241	0.0	0.1
CHR–Chr Chs & Chs Cr	3	NR	150	193	0.0	0.1
CHR–Chs of Christ	20	1,673	1,510	2,023	0.3	0.7
Christian Brethren	1	NR	NR	NR	-	-
Evan Cov Ch	4	444	399	577	0.1	0.2
Evan Free Ch	4	220	NR	220	0.0	0.1
FRND–Indep Yr Mtgs	1	NR	12	15	0.0	0.0
HINDU–Post Ren	2	NR	NR	50	0.0	0.0
Ind Fund Churches	2	NR	NR	NR	-	-
Jehovah's Witness	10	NR	NR	NR	-	-
JUD–Orth	1	43	50	60	0.0	0.0
JUD–Reform	1	142	250	675	0.1	0.2
LDS–Comm of Christ	1	NR	158	158	0.0	0.1
LDS–L-D Saints	24	NR	NR	15,653	2.3	5.2
LUTH–Assoc Free Luth	1	NR	NR	NR	-	-
LUTH–E.L.C.A.	3	560	1,186	1,380	0.2	0.5
LUTH–Luth Cong Msn Chr	1	211	458	590	0.1	0.2
LUTH–Luth–MO Synod	5	1,065	1,983	2,795	0.4	0.9
LUTH–Wisc Ev Luth Syn	1	57	90	111	0.0	0.0
MENN–Menn Br US Conf	2	NR	292	376	0.1	0.1
METH–AME	1	80	200	258	0.0	0.1
METH–AME Zion	1	70	150	193	0.0	0.1
METH–C.M.E.	1	0	150	193	0.0	0.1
METH–Free Methodist	2	157	82	157	0.0	0.1
METH–Un Methodist	12	1,361	3,153	4,542	0.7	1.5
METH–Wesleyan	1	76	53	99	0.0	0.0
Metro Comm Ch	1	82	53	68	0.0	0.0
Muslim Est	9	3,107	NR	9,980	1.5	3.3
Nat Spirit Asso	1	NR	NR	NR	-	-
New Apost Ch	1	NR	NR	NR	-	-
Non-denom Chr Chs	57	15,069	23,356	25,366	3.7	8.4
ORTHE–Greek Orthodox	1	250	NR	1,250	0.2	0.4
ORTHO–Coptic Orth Ch	1	95	NR	118	0.0	0.0
PENT–Assemb of God	24	6,545	2,350	7,739	1.1	2.6
PENT–Ch God (Cleve)	5	427	438	565	0.1	0.2
PENT–COGIC	7	105	522	673	0.1	0.2
PENT–Int Foursq Gos	10	453	629	811	0.1	0.3
PENT–Intl Pent Holiness	2	77	177	228	0.0	0.1
PENT–Open Bible Std	2	465	NR	465	0.1	0.2
PENT–Pent Ch of God	13	910	NR	1,414	0.2	0.5
PENT–Un Pent Ch Intl	17	NR	NR	NR	-	-
PRES–Korean Pres Amer	1	NR	NR	NR	-	-
PRES–Presb Ch (USA)	8	657	1,351	1,742	0.3	0.6
PRES–Presb Ch Amer	1	110	136	146	0.0	0.0
REF–Christian Ref	6	1,805	2,205	2,843	0.4	0.9
REF–Ref Ch in Am	2	557	1,169	1,218	0.2	0.4
REF–Ref Ch in U.S.	2	NR	50	64	0.0	0.0
REF–Un Ref Chs N.A.	1	NR	NR	NR	-	-
Salvation Army	2	201	285	809	0.1	0.3
Sev Day Adv	14	2,258	3,925	4,515	0.7	1.5
Sikh	2	NR	NR	NR	-	-
Un C of Christ	2	123	274	353	0.1	0.1
Unit Univ	1	74	160	195	0.0	0.1
Unity Ch	1	NR	NR	NR	-	-
Zoroastrian	0	NR	NR	31	0.0	0.0
SAN LUIS OBISPO	**263**	**28,195**	**32,787**	**145,470**	**54.0**	**100.0**
ANG/EPIS–Anglican NA	3	NR	NR	NR	-	-
ANG/EPIS–Episcopal	7	479	931	1,158	0.4	0.8
Bahá'í	3	NR	237	237	0.1	0.2
BAPT–Amer Bapt Assn	2	NR	110	128	0.0	0.1
BAPT–Amer Bapt USA	2	760	475	554	0.2	0.4
BAPT–Consrv Bapt	1	NR	NR	NR	-	-
BAPT–Converge/BGC	4	625	NR	750	0.3	0.5
BAPT–NBC USA	3	167	925	1,078	0.4	0.7
BAPT–Reg Bapt Gen As	3	NR	NR	NR	-	-

Religious Group	Number of Congregations	Number of Attendees	Number of Communicant, Confirmed, or Full Members	Adherents: Number of Adherents	Adherents: % of Total Pop.	Adherents: % of Total Adh.
BAPT–So Bapt Conv	11	587	840	979	0.4	0.7
BUDD–Mahayana	2	NR	NR	1,275	0.5	0.9
BUDD–Vajrayana	2	NR	NR	221	0.1	0.2
Calv Chpl	7	NR	NR	NR	-	-
Catholic	17	NR	NR	89,075	33.0	61.2
CGOD–Ch God (Ander)	1	0	NR	0	0.0	0.0
Ch Cr, Scientst	5	NR	NR	NR	-	-
Ch of Nazarene	6	3,325	1,856	4,489	1.7	3.1
Chr & Miss Al	1	140	478	478	0.2	0.3
CHR–Chr Ch (Disc)	1	0	0	0	0.0	0.0
CHR–Chr Chs & Chs Cr	4	NR	393	458	0.2	0.3
CHR–Chs of Christ	9	523	479	622	0.2	0.4
Evan Free Ch	5	1,470	NR	1,470	0.5	1.0
FRND–Indep Yr Mtgs	1	NR	20	23	0.0	0.0
HINDU–Post Ren	2	NR	NR	41	0.0	0.0
Jehovah's Witness	10	NR	NR	NR	-	-
JUD–Conserv	1	36	40	108	0.0	0.1
JUD–Reform	2	172	303	818	0.3	0.6
LDS–Comm of Christ	1	NR	158	158	0.1	0.1
LDS–L-D Saints	12	NR	NR	6,216	2.3	4.3
LUTH–E.L.C.A.	28	4,885	7,871	10,062	3.7	6.9
LUTH–Luth Cong Msn Chr	1	220	485	565	0.2	0.4
LUTH–Luth–MO Synod	4	405	685	769	0.3	0.5
LUTH–Nor Amer Luth C	1	NR	NR	NR	-	-
MENN–Mennonite USA	1	45	60	70	0.0	0.0
METH–Un Methodist	7	754	1,295	1,807	0.7	1.2
Muslim Est	2	690	NR	2,218	0.8	1.5
New Apost Ch	1	NR	NR	NR	-	-
Non-denom Chr Chs	37	6,765	7,624	9,600	3.6	6.6
ORTHE–Greek Orthodox	1	60	NR	180	0.1	0.1
ORTHE–Pal/Jor Orth	1	5	NR	25	0.0	0.0
PENT–Assemb of God	12	1,077	534	1,479	0.5	1.0
PENT–Ch God (Cleve)	1	24	7	8	0.0	0.0
PENT–Ch of God Proph	2	NR	68	79	0.0	0.1
PENT–Int Foursq Gos	5	529	198	231	0.1	0.2
PENT–Pent Ch of God	2	140	NR	217	0.1	0.1
PENT–Un Pent Ch Intl	2	NR	NR	NR	-	-
PENT–Vineyard	5	2,074	2,720	3,171	1.2	2.2
PRES–Korean Pres Amer	1	NR	NR	NR	-	-
PRES–Presb Ch (USA)	7	896	1,407	1,640	0.6	1.1
PRES–Presb Ch Amer	2	186	251	285	0.1	0.2
Sev Day Adv	5	818	1,421	1,635	0.6	1.1
Un C of Christ	3	228	733	855	0.3	0.6
Unit Univ	1	110	183	225	0.1	0.2
Unity Ch	3	NR	NR	NR	-	-
Zoroastrian	0	NR	NR	13	0.0	0.0
SAN MATEO	**357**	**32,482**	**43,842**	**331,338**	**46.1**	**100.0**
ANG/EPIS–Episcopal	16	1,444	4,150	5,149	0.7	1.6
Bahá'í	7	NR	603	603	0.1	0.2
BAPT–Amer Bapt USA	10	1,542	2,021	2,447	0.3	0.7
BAPT–Consrv Bapt	8	NR	NR	NR	-	-
BAPT–Converge/BGC	3	225	NR	270	0.0	0.1
BAPT–NBC USA	3	410	800	969	0.1	0.3
BAPT–So Bapt Conv	29	2,471	2,848	3,448	0.5	1.0
BUDD–Mahayana	12	NR	NR	4,067	0.6	1.2
BUDD–Theravada	3	NR	NR	1,947	0.3	0.6
BUDD–Vajrayana	2	NR	NR	237	0.0	0.1
Calv Chpl	2	NR	NR	NR	-	-
Catholic	22	NR	NR	243,634	33.9	73.5
CGOD–Ch God (Ander)	2	75	NR	75	0.0	0.0
Ch Cr, Scientst	3	NR	NR	NR	-	-
Ch of Nazarene	3	175	243	246	0.0	0.1
Chr & Miss Al	5	324	374	488	0.1	0.1
CHR–Chr Ch (Disc)	1	13	35	42	0.0	0.0
CHR–Chr Chs & Chs Cr	2	NR	220	266	0.0	0.1
CHR–Chs of Christ	7	548	570	746	0.1	0.2
Evan Cov Ch	3	1,093	665	1,421	0.2	0.4
Evan Free Ch	3	104	NR	104	0.0	0.0
HINDU–I/A Temples	1	NR	NR	238	0.0	0.1
HINDU–Post Ren	3	NR	NR	60	0.0	0.0
HINDU–Renaiss	1	NR	NR	12	0.0	0.0
HINDU–Trad Temples	2	NR	NR	150	0.0	0.0
Ind Fund Churches	1	NR	NR	NR	-	-

NR–Not Reported - Represents no adherents reported. Percentages may not total 100 due to rounding.

Table 3: Religious Congregations by County and Group: 2010

Religious Group	Number of Congregations	Number of Attendees	Number of Communicant, Confirmed, or Full Members	Adherents: Number of Adherents	Adherents: % of Total Pop.	Adherents: % of Total Adh.
Jehovah's Witness	10	NR	NR	NR	-	-
JUD–Conserv	2	549	616	1,663	0.2	0.5
JUD–Orth	1	43	50	60	0.0	0.0
JUD–Reform	2	866	1,527	4,123	0.6	1.2
LDS–Comm of Christ	1	NR	158	158	0.0	0.0
LDS–L-D Saints	21	NR	NR	13,240	1.8	4.0
LUTH–E.L.C.A.	10	673	1,561	1,798	0.3	0.5
LUTH–Luth–MO Synod	7	720	1,282	1,600	0.2	0.5
LUTH–Wisc Ev Luth Syn	1	64	101	135	0.0	0.0
METH–AME Zion	2	17	230	278	0.0	0.1
METH–C.M.E.	2	0	200	242	0.0	0.1
METH–Free Methodist	6	441	399	510	0.1	0.2
METH–Un Methodist	12	1,447	2,628	3,579	0.5	1.1
Metro Comm Ch	1	45	53	64	0.0	0.0
Muslim Est	4	1,381	NR	4,436	0.6	1.3
Non-denom Chr Chs	29	6,071	7,794	8,802	1.2	2.7
ORTHE–Georgian Orth	1	35	NR	100	0.0	0.0
ORTHE–Greek Orthodox	1	400	NR	3,750	0.5	1.1
ORTHE–Orth Ch in Amer	1	85	NR	500	0.1	0.2
ORTHE–Rus Orth Abroad	1	90	NR	800	0.1	0.2
ORTHO–Coptic Orth Ch	1	100	NR	200	0.0	0.1
PENT–Assemb of God	25	2,695	2,092	3,299	0.5	1.0
PENT–Ch God (Cleve)	5	1,109	617	747	0.1	0.2
PENT–COGIC	5	50	460	557	0.1	0.2
PENT–Int Foursq Gos	5	504	447	541	0.1	0.2
PENT–Intl Pent Holiness	1	20	35	42	0.0	0.0
PENT–Un Pent Ch Intl	2	NR	NR	NR	-	-
PENT–Vineyard	2	251	350	424	0.1	0.1
Pillar of Fire	1	NR	225	225	0.0	0.1
PRES–Korean Pres Amer	1	NR	NR	NR	-	-
PRES–Orth Pres Ch	1	40	40	48	0.0	0.0
PRES–Presb Ch (USA)	9	4,286	6,927	8,387	1.2	2.5
PRES–Presb Ch Amer	1	0	0	0	0.0	0.0
REF–Christian Ref	1	20	25	30	0.0	0.0
REF–Hung Ref Add'l	1	NR	NR	NR	-	-
Salvation Army	1	73	65	65	0.0	0.0
Sev Day Adv	9	620	1,077	1,239	0.2	0.4
Un C of Christ	14	1,040	1,961	2,374	0.3	0.7
Unit Univ	2	323	393	602	0.1	0.2
Zoroastrian	1	NR	NR	101	0.0	0.0
SANTA BARBARA	**299**	**23,449**	**28,505**	**201,791**	**47.6**	**100.0**
ANG/EPIS–Episcopal	7	1,082	2,928	3,136	0.7	1.6
Bahá'í	3	NR	309	309	0.1	0.2
BAPT–Amer Bapt Assn	2	NR	40	49	0.0	0.0
BAPT–Amer Bapt USA	6	269	355	431	0.1	0.2
BAPT–Consrv Bapt	3	NR	NR	NR	-	-
BAPT–Converge/BGC	6	2,150	NR	2,580	0.6	1.3
BAPT–NBC USA	5	120	770	935	0.2	0.5
BAPT–Ref Bapt Ch	1	NR	NR	NR	-	-
BAPT–Reg Bapt Gen As	2	NR	NR	NR	-	-
BAPT–So Bapt Conv	19	1,069	1,455	1,766	0.4	0.9
BUDD–Mahayana	6	NR	NR	3,281	0.8	1.6
BUDD–Vajrayana	4	NR	NR	573	0.1	0.3
Calv Chpl	6	NR	NR	NR	-	-
Catholic	17	NR	NR	146,940	34.7	72.8
CGOD–Ch God (Ander)	1	84	NR	84	0.0	0.0
Ch Cr, Scientst	4	NR	NR	NR	-	-
Ch of Nazarene	4	678	717	810	0.2	0.4
Chr & Miss Al	1	120	161	165	0.0	0.1
CHR–Chr Ch (Disc)	2	81	155	188	0.0	0.1
CHR–Chr Chs & Chs Cr	1	NR	45	55	0.0	0.0
CHR–Chs of Christ	9	548	542	714	0.2	0.4
CONG–Consrv Cong Chr	1	125	100	121	0.0	0.1
Evan Cov Ch	4	1,078	717	1,402	0.3	0.7
Evan Free Ch	4	570	NR	570	0.1	0.3
FRND–Indep Yr Mtgs	1	NR	39	47	0.0	0.0
HINDU–Post Ren	5	NR	NR	153	0.0	0.1
HINDU–Renaiss	1	NR	NR	12	0.0	0.0
Jehovah's Witness	8	NR	NR	NR	-	-
JUD–Orth	1	43	50	60	0.0	0.0
JUD–Reform	3	452	797	2,152	0.5	1.1
LDS–Comm of Christ	1	NR	164	164	0.0	0.1
LDS–L-D Saints	14	NR	NR	7,241	1.7	3.6

Religious Group	Number of Congregations	Number of Attendees	Number of Communicant, Confirmed, or Full Members	Adherents: Number of Adherents	Adherents: % of Total Pop.	Adherents: % of Total Adh.
LUTH–E.L.C.A.	6	573	1,543	1,688	0.4	0.8
LUTH–Luth Cong Msn Chr	1	96	201	244	0.1	0.1
LUTH–Luth–MO Synod	8	846	1,282	1,808	0.4	0.9
LUTH–Nor Amer Luth C	1	NR	NR	NR	-	-
LUTH–Wisc Ev Luth Syn	2	131	206	234	0.1	0.1
METH–AME	3	40	260	316	0.1	0.2
METH–C.M.E.	1	0	100	121	0.0	0.1
METH–Free Methodist	2	503	484	520	0.1	0.3
METH–Un Methodist	8	877	1,484	2,049	0.5	1.0
Missionary Ch	2	182	173	182	0.0	0.1
Muslim Est	2	130	NR	1,259	0.3	0.6
Nat Spirit Asso	1	NR	NR	NR	-	-
Non-denom Chr Chs	23	2,662	3,457	3,682	0.9	1.8
ORTHE–Ant Orth of NA	2	225	NR	350	0.1	0.2
ORTHE–Greek Orthodox	1	125	NR	650	0.2	0.3
ORTHE–Orth Ch in Amer	2	66	NR	66	0.0	0.0
ORTHE–Rus Orth Abroad	1	12	NR	70	0.0	0.0
ORTHO–Armen Ap Etchm	1	40	NR	400	0.1	0.2
PENT–Assemb of God	12	2,635	1,407	3,176	0.7	1.6
PENT–Ch God (Cleve)	2	146	146	177	0.0	0.1
PENT–Ch of God Proph	7	NR	313	380	0.1	0.2
PENT–COGIC	4	100	500	607	0.1	0.3
PENT–Int Foursq Gos	12	1,849	2,532	3,073	0.7	1.5
PENT–Open Bible Std	1	200	NR	200	0.0	0.1
PENT–Pent Ch of God	1	70	NR	109	0.0	0.1
PENT–Un Pent Ch Intl	3	NR	NR	NR	-	-
PENT–Vineyard	4	474	577	700	0.2	0.3
PRES–Evan Presby Ch	1	NR	75	91	0.0	0.0
PRES–Korean Pres Amer	3	NR	NR	NR	-	-
PRES–Orth Pres Ch	2	113	109	153	0.0	0.1
PRES–Presb Ch (USA)	11	1,519	2,370	2,877	0.7	1.4
PRES–Presb Ch Amer	1	108	86	105	0.0	0.1
REF–Christian Ref	2	148	90	109	0.0	0.1
Salvation Army	2	81	88	467	0.1	0.2
Sev Day Adv	5	524	912	1,049	0.2	0.5
Un C of Christ	2	110	160	194	0.0	0.1
Unit Univ	2	395	606	737	0.2	0.4
Unity Ch	3	NR	NR	NR	-	-
Zoroastrian	0	NR	NR	10	0.0	0.0
SANTA CLARA	**927**	**133,049**	**151,806**	**776,028**	**43.6**	**100.0**
ANG/EPIS–Anglican NA	3	NR	NR	NR	-	-
ANG/EPIS–Episcopal	21	2,594	6,636	8,025	0.5	1.0
Bahá'í	14	NR	1,397	1,397	0.1	0.2
BAPT–Amer Bapt Assn	1	NR	70	86	0.0	0.0
BAPT–Amer Bapt USA	10	1,432	1,521	1,876	0.1	0.2
BAPT–Consrv Bapt	16	NR	NR	NR	-	-
BAPT–Converge/BGC	7	1,175	NR	1,410	0.1	0.2
BAPT–N Am Bapt Conf	1	NR	42	52	0.0	0.0
BAPT–Natl Mis Bapt Conv	1	50	100	123	0.0	0.0
BAPT–NBC USA	2	270	360	444	0.0	0.1
BAPT–Ref Bapt Ch	2	NR	NR	NR	-	-
BAPT–Reg Bapt Gen As	4	NR	NR	NR	-	-
BAPT–So Bapt Conv	71	10,441	13,446	16,587	0.9	2.1
BUDD–Mahayana	43	NR	NR	19,243	1.1	2.5
BUDD–Theravada	8	NR	NR	3,128	0.2	0.4
BUDD–Vajrayana	8	NR	NR	543	0.0	0.1
Calv Chpl	2	NR	NR	NR	-	-
Catholic	56	NR	NR	447,369	25.1	57.6
CGOD–Ch God (Ander)	4	4,887	NR	4,887	0.3	0.6
Ch Cr, Scientst	8	NR	NR	NR	-	-
Ch God (7th Day)	3	NR	NR	NR	-	-
Ch of Nazarene	10	1,216	1,552	2,315	0.1	0.3
Chr & Miss Al	15	2,197	2,217	2,921	0.2	0.4
CHR–Chr Ch (Disc)	8	243	496	612	0.0	0.1
CHR–Chr Chs & Chs Cr	10	NR	1,475	1,820	0.1	0.2
CHR–Chs of Christ	14	1,534	1,450	1,963	0.1	0.3
Christian Brethren	3	NR	NR	NR	-	-
Evan Assoc RCC	1	NR	NR	NR	-	-
Evan Cov Ch	9	658	501	857	0.0	0.1
Evan Free Ch	3	850	NR	850	0.0	0.1
FRND–Indep Yr Mtgs	2	NR	147	181	0.0	0.0
HINDU–I/A Temples	12	NR	NR	10,096	0.6	1.3
HINDU–Post Ren	11	NR	NR	314	0.0	0.0

NR–Not Reported - Represents no adherents reported. Percentages may not total 100 due to rounding.

Table 3: Religious Congregations by County and Group: 2010

Religious Group	Number of Congregations	Number of Attendees	Number of Communicant, Confirmed, or Full Members	Adherents: Number of Adherents	Adherents: % of Total Pop.	Adherents: % of Total Adh.
HINDU–Renaiss	3	NR	NR	2,024	0.1	0.3
HINDU–Trad Temples	5	NR	NR	31,340	1.8	4.0
Ind Fund Churches	1	NR	NR	NR	-	-
Jain	1	NR	NR	NR	-	-
Jehovah's Witness	14	NR	NR	NR	-	-
JUD–Conserv	3	1,191	1,337	3,610	0.2	0.5
JUD–Orth	8	1,065	700	1,500	0.1	0.2
JUD–Reconst	1	88	113	305	0.0	0.0
JUD–Reform	4	1,402	2,473	6,677	0.4	0.9
LDS–Comm of Christ	1	NR	158	158	0.0	0.0
LDS–L-D Saints	45	NR	NR	24,739	1.4	3.2
LUTH–Ch Luth Conf	1	NR	NR	NR	-	-
LUTH–E.L.C.A.	21	2,203	3,768	5,439	0.3	0.7
LUTH–Luth Cong Msn Chr	1	120	281	347	0.0	0.0
LUTH–Luth–MO Synod	13	1,468	2,996	3,755	0.2	0.5
LUTH–Nor Amer Luth C	1	NR	NR	NR	-	-
LUTH–Wisc Ev Luth Syn	2	418	741	903	0.1	0.1
MENN–Menn Br US Conf	4	NR	1,329	1,639	0.1	0.2
METH–AME	2	0	250	308	0.0	0.0
METH–AME Zion	4	0	360	444	0.0	0.1
METH–C.M.E.	2	0	250	308	0.0	0.0
METH–Free Methodist	1	61	104	104	0.0	0.0
METH–Un Methodist	32	4,654	9,924	16,731	0.9	2.2
Metro Comm Ch	1	27	29	36	0.0	0.0
MJEW–Union Mes Cong	1	NR	NR	NR	-	-
Muslim Est	17	5,867	NR	18,851	1.1	2.4
Nat Spirit Asso	1	NR	NR	NR	-	-
New Apost Ch	2	NR	NR	NR	-	-
Non-denom Chr Chs	125	57,425	66,705	76,984	4.3	9.9
ORTHE–Ant Orth of NA	2	310	NR	704	0.0	0.1
ORTHE–Greek Orthodox	2	950	NR	2,700	0.2	0.3
ORTHE–Orth Ch in Amer	2	100	NR	232	0.0	0.0
ORTHE–Pal/Jor Orth	1	100	NR	750	0.0	0.1
ORTHE–Rus Orth Abroad	2	265	NR	300	0.0	0.0
ORTHE–Serb Orth USA	1	95	NR	350	0.0	0.0
ORTHO–Armen Ap Etchm	1	100	NR	1,600	0.1	0.2
ORTHO–Coptic Orth Ch	1	250	NR	350	0.0	0.0
ORTHO–Eritrean Orth	1	75	NR	350	0.0	0.0
ORTHO–Ethiopian Orth	2	NR	NR	NR	-	-
ORTHO–Malan Syr Orth	1	75	NR	144	0.0	0.0
ORTHO–Syrian Orth Ch	1	100	NR	240	0.0	0.0
PENT–Assemb of God	45	11,019	6,776	15,643	0.9	2.0
PENT–Ch God (Cleve)	7	435	522	644	0.0	0.1
PENT–Ch of God Proph	3	NR	71	88	0.0	0.0
PENT–COGIC	9	132	750	925	0.1	0.1
PENT–Int Foursq Gos	10	1,106	1,019	1,257	0.1	0.2
PENT–Intl Pent Holiness	10	2,250	1,333	1,644	0.1	0.2
PENT–Open Bible Std	2	111	NR	111	0.0	0.0
PENT–Pent Ch of God	7	490	NR	761	0.0	0.1
PENT–Un Pent Ch Intl	12	NR	NR	NR	-	-
PENT–Vineyard	1	255	240	296	0.0	0.0
PRES–Kor Pres Abroad	3	NR	NR	NR	-	-
PRES–Korean Amer Pres	3	NR	NR	NR	-	-
PRES–Korean Pres Amer	8	NR	NR	NR	-	-
PRES–Orth Pres Ch	2	270	235	312	0.0	0.0
PRES–Presb Ch (USA)	25	3,757	6,596	8,137	0.5	1.0
PRES–Presb Ch Amer	7	561	466	566	0.0	0.1
REF–Christian Ref	5	489	481	593	0.0	0.1
REF–Ref Ch in Am	2	578	385	993	0.1	0.1
Salvation Army	4	326	345	1,374	0.1	0.2
Sev Day Adv	24	3,915	6,806	7,830	0.4	1.0
Sikh	3	NR	NR	NR	-	-
Un C of Christ	10	919	2,102	2,593	0.1	0.3
Unit Univ	4	480	751	987	0.1	0.1
Unity Ch	3	NR	NR	NR	-	-
Zoroastrian	1	NR	NR	253	0.0	0.0
SANTA CRUZ	**184**	**12,340**	**13,902**	**81,322**	**31.0**	**100.0**
ANG/EPIS–Anglican NA	1	NR	NR	NR	-	-
ANG/EPIS–Episcopal	6	510	1,101	1,626	0.6	2.0
Bahá'í	6	NR	706	706	0.3	0.9
BAPT–Amer Bapt Assn	2	NR	60	72	0.0	0.1
BAPT–Amer Bapt USA	1	40	75	89	0.0	0.1
BAPT–Consrv Bapt	5	NR	NR	NR	-	-

Religious Group	Number of Congregations	Number of Attendees	Number of Communicant, Confirmed, or Full Members	Adherents: Number of Adherents	Adherents: % of Total Pop.	Adherents: % of Total Adh.
BAPT–Converge/BGC	1	75	NR	90	0.0	0.1
BAPT–Prog NBC	1	0	0	0	0.0	0.0
BAPT–So Bapt Conv	7	295	409	488	0.2	0.6
BUDD–Mahayana	8	NR	NR	2,132	0.8	2.6
BUDD–Theravada	1	NR	NR	292	0.1	0.4
BUDD–Vajrayana	7	NR	NR	730	0.3	0.9
Calv Chpl	3	NR	NR	NR	-	-
Catholic	13	NR	NR	50,500	19.2	62.1
Ch Cr, Scientst	2	NR	NR	NR	-	-
Ch of Nazarene	2	300	436	517	0.2	0.6
Chr & Miss Al	1	15	0	15	0.0	0.0
CHR–Chr Ch (Disc)	2	62	115	137	0.1	0.2
CHR–Chs of Christ	2	130	130	165	0.1	0.2
CONG–Cong Chr, NA	1	NR	224	267	0.1	0.3
Evan Cov Ch	1	141	183	183	0.1	0.2
Evan Free Ch	2	200	NR	200	0.1	0.2
FRND–Indep Yr Mtgs	1	NR	78	93	0.0	0.1
HINDU–I/A Temples	1	NR	NR	110	0.0	0.1
HINDU–Post Ren	6	NR	NR	258	0.1	0.3
HINDU–Renaiss	2	NR	NR	24	0.0	0.0
Jehovah's Witness	7	NR	NR	NR	-	-
JUD–Conserv	1	41	46	124	0.0	0.2
JUD–Reform	1	262	462	1,247	0.5	1.5
LDS–L-D Saints	6	NR	NR	3,709	1.4	4.6
LUTH–E.L.C.A.	3	180	531	695	0.3	0.9
LUTH–Luth–MO Synod	3	134	301	345	0.1	0.4
MENN–Menn Br US Conf	2	NR	33	39	0.0	0.0
METH–Free Methodist	1	179	135	179	0.1	0.2
METH–Un Methodist	4	312	502	713	0.3	0.9
Missionary Ch	1	116	0	116	0.0	0.1
Muslim Est	1	345	NR	1,109	0.4	1.4
Non-denom Chr Chs	18	5,050	3,880	6,713	2.6	8.3
ORTHE–Ant Orth of NA	1	100	NR	200	0.1	0.2
ORTHE–Greek Orthodox	1	35	NR	150	0.1	0.2
ORTHE–Pal/Jor Orth	1	150	NR	750	0.3	0.9
ORTHE–Rus Orth Abroad	1	4	NR	4	0.0	0.0
PENT–Assemb of God	8	791	517	1,201	0.5	1.5
PENT–Ch God (Cleve)	3	147	203	242	0.1	0.3
PENT–COGIC	2	35	200	238	0.1	0.3
PENT–Int Foursq Gos	4	543	493	588	0.2	0.7
PENT–Intl Pent Holiness	2	94	127	151	0.1	0.2
PENT–Pent Ch of God	2	140	NR	217	0.1	0.3
PENT–Un Pent Ch Intl	2	NR	NR	NR	-	-
PENT–Vineyard	2	225	335	399	0.2	0.5
PRES–Korean Pres Amer	1	NR	NR	NR	-	-
PRES–Presb Ch (USA)	7	478	675	805	0.3	1.0
REF–Comm Ref Evan	1	NR	NR	NR	-	-
Salvation Army	2	204	173	625	0.2	0.8
Sev Day Adv	5	646	1,124	1,293	0.5	1.6
Tao	1	NR	NR	NR	-	-
Un C of Christ	3	291	523	624	0.2	0.8
Unit Univ	1	70	125	145	0.1	0.2
Unity Ch	1	NR	NR	NR	-	-
Zoroastrian	0	NR	NR	7	0.0	0.0
SHASTA	**164**	**21,106**	**22,299**	**47,852**	**27.0**	**100.0**
ANG/EPIS–Episcopal	2	180	523	527	0.3	1.1
Bahá'í	1	NR	84	84	0.0	0.2
BAPT–Amer Bapt Assn	2	NR	175	210	0.1	0.4
BAPT–Consrv Bapt	6	NR	NR	NR	-	-
BAPT–Free Will Bapt	1	NR	46	55	0.0	0.1
BAPT–Reg Bapt Gen As	2	NR	NR	NR	-	-
BAPT–So Bapt Conv	12	648	764	918	0.5	1.9
BUDD–Mahayana	1	NR	NR	11	0.0	0.0
Calv Chpl	4	NR	NR	NR	-	-
Catholic	8	NR	NR	8,629	4.9	18.0
CGOD–Ch God (Ander)	1	40	NR	40	0.0	0.1
Ch Cr, Scientst	1	NR	NR	NR	-	-
Ch of Nazarene	3	551	625	913	0.5	1.9
Chr & Miss Al	4	3,307	1,218	5,005	2.8	10.5
CHR–Chr Ch (Disc)	1	144	184	221	0.1	0.5
CHR–Chs of Christ	6	563	640	708	0.4	1.5
Evan Free Ch	2	326	NR	326	0.2	0.7
FRND–Indep Yr Mtgs	1	NR	9	11	0.0	0.0

NR–Not Reported - Represents no adherents reported. Percentages may not total 100 due to rounding.

Table 3: Religious Congregations by County and Group: 2010

Religious Group	Number of Congregations	Number of Attendees	Number of Communicant, Confirmed, or Full Members	Adherents: Number of Adherents	Adherents: % of Total Pop.	Adherents: % of Total Adh.
Ind Fund Churches	1	NR	NR	NR	-	-
Jehovah's Witness	9	NR	NR	NR	-	-
JUD–Reform	1	28	49	132	0.1	0.3
LDS–Comm of Christ	1	NR	158	158	0.1	0.3
LDS–L-D Saints	11	NR	NR	6,843	3.9	14.3
LUTH–E.L.C.A.	1	222	376	479	0.3	1.0
LUTH–Luth-MO Synod	2	235	461	504	0.3	1.1
LUTH–Wisc Ev Luth Syn	2	225	373	490	0.3	1.0
METH–C.M.E.	1	0	100	120	0.1	0.3
METH–Un Methodist	4	434	766	1,072	0.6	2.2
Muslim Est	1	14	NR	35	0.0	0.1
Non-denom Chr Chs	27	11,395	12,663	15,194	8.6	31.8
ORTHE–Greek Orthodox	1	30	NR	75	0.0	0.2
ORTHE–Orth Ch in Amer	1	20	NR	30	0.0	0.1
ORTHE–Serb Orth USA	3	56	NR	86	0.0	0.2
PENT–Assemb of God	6	494	304	879	0.5	1.8
PENT–Ch God (Cleve)	2	120	112	135	0.1	0.3
PENT–Ch of God Proph	1	NR	10	12	0.0	0.0
PENT–Int Foursq Gos	7	554	471	566	0.3	1.2
PENT–Pent Ch of God	5	350	NR	544	0.3	1.1
PENT–Un Pent Ch Intl	2	NR	NR	NR	-	-
PENT–Vineyard	1	105	125	150	0.1	0.3
PRES–Orth Pres Ch	1	27	19	25	0.0	0.1
PRES–Presb Ch (USA)	2	50	216	260	0.1	0.5
REF–Ref Ch in U.S.	1	NR	24	29	0.0	0.1
Salvation Army	1	44	82	382	0.2	0.8
Sev Day Adv	7	860	1,496	1,720	1.0	3.6
Sikh	1	NR	NR	NR	-	-
Un C of Christ	1	72	216	260	0.1	0.5
Unit Univ	1	12	10	10	0.0	0.0
Unity Ch	1	NR	NR	NR	-	-
Zoroastrian	0	NR	NR	4	0.0	0.0
SIERRA	**9**	**177**	**161**	**489**	**15.1**	**100.0**
Bahá'í	0	NR	3	3	0.1	0.6
Catholic	2	NR	NR	122	3.8	24.9
Ind Fund Churches	1	NR	NR	NR	-	-
LDS–L-D Saints	1	NR	NR	101	3.1	20.7
METH–Un Methodist	2	19	41	64	2.0	13.1
Non-denom Chr Chs	1	30	30	38	1.2	7.8
PENT–Assemb of God	2	128	87	161	5.0	32.9
SISKIYOU	**92**	**3,687**	**5,008**	**12,853**	**28.6**	**100.0**
ANG/EPIS–Anglican NA	1	NR	NR	NR	-	-
ANG/EPIS–Episcopal	2	61	71	71	0.2	0.6
Bahá'í	0	NR	37	37	0.1	0.3
BAPT–Amer Bapt USA	3	114	113	134	0.3	1.0
BAPT–So Bapt Conv	7	533	1,382	1,640	3.7	12.8
BUDD–Mahayana	1	NR	NR	250	0.6	1.9
Calv Chpl	3	NR	NR	NR	-	-
Catholic	12	NR	NR	4,089	9.1	31.8
Ch Cr, Scientst	1	NR	NR	NR	-	-
Ch of Nazarene	3	244	184	274	0.6	2.1
Chr & Miss Al	1	170	81	170	0.4	1.3
CHR–Chr Chs & Chs Cr	2	NR	95	113	0.3	0.9
CHR–Chs of Christ	2	48	51	60	0.1	0.5
Evan Free Ch	2	265	NR	265	0.6	2.1
HINDU–Post Ren	1	NR	NR	77	0.2	0.6
Ind Fund Churches	1	NR	NR	NR	-	-
Jehovah's Witness	4	NR	NR	NR	-	-
LDS–L-D Saints	5	NR	NR	1,629	3.6	12.7
LUTH–E.L.C.A.	2	75	179	237	0.5	1.8
LUTH–Luth-MO Synod	1	42	76	80	0.2	0.6
METH–Evan Meth Ch	1	NR	NR	NR	-	-
METH–Un Methodist	6	328	570	851	1.9	6.6
Non-denom Chr Chs	13	940	1,253	1,360	3.0	10.6
PENT–Assemb of God	8	327	134	494	1.1	3.8
PENT–COGIC	1	0	150	178	0.4	1.4
PENT–Int Foursq Gos	1	145	83	98	0.2	0.8
PENT–Pent Ch of God	1	70	NR	109	0.2	0.8
PRES–Presb Ch (USA)	3	63	127	151	0.3	1.2
REF–Christian Ref	1	35	27	32	0.1	0.2
Sev Day Adv	3	227	395	454	1.0	3.5

Religious Group	Number of Congregations	Number of Attendees	Number of Communicant, Confirmed, or Full Members	Adherents: Number of Adherents	Adherents: % of Total Pop.	Adherents: % of Total Adh.
SOLANO	**294**	**33,694**	**46,440**	**155,307**	**37.6**	**100.0**
ANG/EPIS–Anglican NA	1	NR	NR	NR	-	-
ANG/EPIS–Episcopal	4	349	1,007	1,130	0.3	0.7
Bahá'í	4	NR	205	205	0.0	0.1
BAPT–Amer Bapt USA	12	1,525	1,985	2,439	0.6	1.6
BAPT–Consrv Bapt	4	NR	NR	NR	-	-
BAPT–Converge/BGC	4	625	NR	750	0.2	0.5
BAPT–Free Will Bapt	1	NR	46	57	0.0	0.0
BAPT–Natl Mis Bapt Conv	1	0	150	184	0.0	0.1
BAPT–NBC USA	1	115	180	221	0.1	0.1
BAPT–Reg Bapt Gen As	3	NR	NR	NR	-	-
BAPT–So Bapt Conv	35	6,912	11,268	13,845	3.3	8.9
BUDD–Mahayana	3	NR	NR	544	0.1	0.4
Calv Chpl	5	NR	NR	NR	-	-
Catholic	10	NR	NR	81,158	19.6	52.3
CGOD–Ches God-Gen Con	1	15	8	10	0.0	0.0
Ch Cr, Scientst	1	NR	NR	NR	-	-
Ch of Chr (Hol)	2	NR	NR	NR	-	-
Ch of Nazarene	6	1,027	1,230	1,729	0.4	1.1
Chr & Miss Al	2	140	193	228	0.1	0.1
CHR–Chr Ch (Disc)	2	99	172	211	0.1	0.1
CHR–Chr Chs & Chs Cr	4	NR	1,355	1,665	0.4	1.1
CHR–Chs of Christ	13	1,045	911	1,183	0.3	0.8
CONG–Cong Chr, NA	1	NR	80	98	0.0	0.1
Evan Free Ch	2	1,040	NR	1,040	0.3	0.7
HINDU–I/A Temples	2	NR	NR	500	0.1	0.3
Ind Fund Churches	1	NR	NR	NR	-	-
Jehovah's Witness	7	NR	NR	NR	-	-
JUD–Conserv	1	12	13	35	0.0	0.0
LDS–Comm of Christ	1	NR	158	158	0.0	0.1
LDS–L-D Saints	21	NR	NR	10,313	2.5	6.6
LUTH–E.L.C.A.	4	409	946	1,221	0.3	0.8
LUTH–Luth-MO Synod	3	434	1,027	1,328	0.3	0.9
LUTH–Wisc Ev Luth Syn	2	109	160	227	0.1	0.1
METH–AME	3	0	400	491	0.1	0.3
METH–AME Zion	1	0	100	123	0.0	0.1
METH–C.M.E.	3	160	500	614	0.1	0.4
METH–Un Methodist	6	683	1,291	1,724	0.4	1.1
Muslim Est	3	1,035	NR	3,327	0.8	2.1
Non-denom Chr Chs	43	12,329	16,854	18,923	4.6	12.2
ORTHE–Ant Orth of NA	1	95	NR	166	0.0	0.1
ORTHE–Greek Orthodox	1	65	NR	400	0.1	0.3
PENT–Assemb of God	18	2,586	1,611	3,275	0.8	2.1
PENT–Ch God (Cleve)	3	216	287	353	0.1	0.2
PENT–Ch of God Proph	3	NR	119	146	0.0	0.1
PENT–COGIC	6	360	760	934	0.2	0.6
PENT–Full Gosp Bapt	1	NR	NR	NR	-	-
PENT–Int Foursq Gos	6	302	292	359	0.1	0.2
PENT–Intl Pent Holiness	2	58	79	97	0.0	0.1
PENT–Open Bible Std	1	49	NR	49	0.0	0.0
PENT–Pent Ch of God	2	140	NR	217	0.1	0.1
PENT–Un Pent Ch Intl	5	NR	NR	NR	-	-
PRES–Korean Pres Amer	1	NR	NR	NR	-	-
PRES–Presb Ch (USA)	8	873	1,368	1,681	0.4	1.1
REF–Christian Ref	1	100	94	115	0.0	0.1
Salvation Army	1	14	145	145	0.0	0.1
Sev Day Adv	6	670	1,165	1,340	0.3	0.9
Sikh	1	NR	NR	NR	-	-
Un C of Christ	3	103	281	345	0.1	0.2
Unity Ch	1	NR	NR	NR	-	-
Zoroastrian	0	NR	NR	4	0.0	0.0
SONOMA	**315**	**22,750**	**29,314**	**169,992**	**35.1**	**100.0**
ANG/EPIS–Anglican NA	1	NR	NR	NR	-	-
ANG/EPIS–Episcopal	8	697	1,532	1,756	0.4	1.0
Bahá'í	2	NR	318	318	0.1	0.2
BAPT–Amer Bapt Assn	1	NR	30	36	0.0	0.0
BAPT–Amer Bapt USA	1	730	127	153	0.0	0.1
BAPT–Consrv Bapt	3	NR	NR	NR	-	-
BAPT–Converge/BGC	1	75	NR	90	0.0	0.1
BAPT–Free Will Bapt	1	NR	46	55	0.0	0.0
BAPT–Reg Bapt Gen As	4	NR	NR	NR	-	-
BAPT–So Bapt Conv	19	1,945	3,934	4,727	1.0	2.8

NR–Not Reported - Represents no adherents reported. Percentages may not total 100 due to rounding.

Table 3: Religious Congregations by County and Group: 2010

Religious Group	Number of Congregations	Number of Attendees	Number of Communicant, Confirmed, or Full Members	Adherents: Number of Adherents	Adherents: % of Total Pop.	Adherents: % of Total Adh.
BUDD–Mahayana	8	NR	NR	5,503	1.1	3.2
BUDD–Theravada	7	NR	NR	2,344	0.5	1.4
BUDD–Vajrayana	11	NR	NR	1,298	0.3	0.8
Calv Chpl	5	NR	NR	NR	-	-
Catholic	23	NR	NR	107,737	22.3	63.4
CGOD–Ch God (Ander)	2	30	NR	30	0.0	0.0
Ch Cr, Scientst	5	NR	NR	NR	-	-
Ch of Nazarene	3	459	613	1,019	0.2	0.6
Chr & Miss Al	4	376	284	512	0.1	0.3
CHR–Chr Ch (Disc)	1	12	25	30	0.0	0.0
CHR–Chr Chs & Chs Cr	3	NR	645	775	0.2	0.5
CHR–Chs of Christ	11	636	671	842	0.2	0.5
Evan Cov Ch	2	1,178	415	1,531	0.3	0.9
Evan Free Ch	2	115	NR	115	0.0	0.1
FRND–Indep Yr Mtgs	3	NR	92	111	0.0	0.1
HINDU–Post Ren	1	NR	NR	25	0.0	0.0
HINDU–Renaiss	1	NR	NR	12	0.0	0.0
Ind Fund Churches	1	NR	NR	NR	-	-
Jehovah's Witness	13	NR	NR	NR	-	-
JUD–Conserv	1	171	192	518	0.1	0.3
JUD–Orth	1	43	50	60	0.0	0.0
JUD–Reconst	1	58	74	200	0.0	0.1
JUD–Reform	2	252	445	1,202	0.2	0.7
LDS–Comm of Christ	1	NR	158	158	0.0	0.1
LDS–L-D Saints	17	NR	NR	9,069	1.9	5.3
LUTH–E.L.C.A.	5	787	1,745	2,382	0.5	1.4
LUTH–Evan Luth Syn	1	26	35	35	0.0	0.0
LUTH–Luth–MO Synod	8	897	1,584	2,269	0.5	1.3
LUTH–Wisc Ev Luth Syn	1	33	47	49	0.0	0.0
METH–Free Methodist	1	47	52	52	0.0	0.0
METH–Un Methodist	9	1,296	1,707	2,923	0.6	1.7
Metro Comm Ch	2	43	54	65	0.0	0.0
Muslim Est	2	690	NR	2,217	0.5	1.3
Non-denom Chr Chs	35	5,355	6,496	7,441	1.5	4.4
ORTHE–Ant Orth of NA	1	14	NR	37	0.0	0.0
ORTHE–Bulgar Orth USA	1	65	NR	110	0.0	0.1
ORTHE–Orth Ch in Amer	2	182	NR	272	0.1	0.2
ORTHE–Pal/Jor Orth	1	100	NR	750	0.2	0.4
ORTHE–Rus Orth Abroad	2	110	NR	220	0.0	0.1
PENT–Assemb of God	17	1,360	839	1,634	0.3	1.0
PENT–Ch God (Cleve)	2	257	251	302	0.1	0.2
PENT–Ch of God Proph	1	NR	150	180	0.0	0.1
PENT–COGIC	1	80	85	102	0.0	0.1
PENT–Int Foursq Gos	5	472	569	684	0.1	0.4
PENT–Open Bible Std	1	29	NR	29	0.0	0.0
PENT–Pent Ch of God	4	280	NR	435	0.1	0.3
PENT–Un Pent Ch Intl	5	NR	NR	NR	-	-
PRES–Cumber Presb	1	NR	15	15	0.0	0.0
PRES–Presb Ch (USA)	11	1,406	2,028	2,437	0.5	1.4
PRES–Presb Ch Amer	2	240	173	224	0.0	0.1
REF–Ref Ch in Am	1	40	41	97	0.0	0.1
Salvation Army	2	92	107	477	0.1	0.3
Sev Day Adv	10	1,131	1,968	2,262	0.5	1.3
Un C of Christ	8	651	1,325	1,592	0.3	0.9
Unit Univ	2	290	392	460	0.1	0.3
Unity Ch	1	NR	NR	NR	-	-
Zoroastrian	0	NR	NR	14	0.0	0.0
STANISLAUS	**389**	**39,503**	**50,976**	**202,370**	**39.3**	**100.0**
ANG/EPIS–Anglican NA	4	NR	NR	NR	-	-
ANG/EPIS–Episcopal	3	167	330	480	0.1	0.2
Bahá'í	2	NR	280	280	0.1	0.1
BAPT–Amer Bapt Assn	7	NR	645	826	0.2	0.4
BAPT–Amer Bapt USA	5	726	779	997	0.2	0.5
BAPT–Asc Ref Bap Ch Am	1	NR	NR	NR	-	-
BAPT–Consrv Bapt	6	NR	NR	NR	-	-
BAPT–Converge/BGC	1	400	NR	480	0.1	0.2
BAPT–Free Will Bapt	4	NR	184	235	0.0	0.1
BAPT–N Am Bapt Conf	1	NR	30	38	0.0	0.0
BAPT–Natl Mis Bapt Conv	1	75	100	128	0.0	0.1
BAPT–Prog NBC	1	0	350	448	0.1	0.2
BAPT–Ref Bapt Ch	1	NR	NR	NR	-	-
BAPT–Reg Bapt Gen As	2	NR	NR	NR	-	-
BAPT–So Bapt Conv	35	2,592	6,082	7,784	1.5	3.8
BRETH–Ch of Brethren	3	211	353	452	0.1	0.2
BRETH–Grace Breth	1	NR	NR	NR	-	-
BUDD–Mahayana	3	NR	NR	573	0.1	0.3
BUDD–Theravada	2	NR	NR	695	0.1	0.3
Calv Chpl	3	NR	NR	NR	-	-
Catholic	18	NR	NR	107,529	20.9	53.1
CGOD–Ch God (Ander)	1	255	NR	255	0.0	0.1
Ch Cr, Scientst	1	NR	NR	NR	-	-
Ch of Nazarene	13	1,225	1,484	2,339	0.5	1.2
Chr & Miss Al	2	116	168	168	0.0	0.1
CHR–Chr Ch (Disc)	4	203	405	518	0.1	0.3
CHR–Chr Chs & Chs Cr	3	NR	1,332	1,705	0.3	0.8
CHR–Chs of Christ	19	1,462	1,481	1,899	0.4	0.9
CONG–Cong Chr, NA	1	NR	74	95	0.0	0.0
Evan Cov Ch	7	1,511	1,147	1,965	0.4	1.0
Evan Free Ch	4	827	NR	827	0.2	0.4
FRND–Evan Fr Ch Intl	1	62	61	78	0.0	0.0
HINDU–Trad Temples	1	NR	NR	2,000	0.4	1.0
Ind Fund Churches	1	NR	NR	NR	-	-
Jehovah's Witness	12	NR	NR	NR	-	-
JUD–Conserv	1	120	135	364	0.1	0.2
LDS–Comm of Christ	1	NR	158	158	0.0	0.1
LDS–L-D Saints	31	NR	NR	13,859	2.7	6.8
LUTH–Ch Luth Conf	1	NR	NR	NR	-	-
LUTH–E.L.C.A.	2	153	408	545	0.1	0.3
LUTH–Luth Ch-Am Asc	1	NR	NR	NR	-	-
LUTH–Luth Cong Msn Chr	1	102	331	424	0.1	0.2
LUTH–Luth–MO Synod	5	563	1,094	1,321	0.3	0.7
LUTH–Wisc Ev Luth Syn	1	134	237	281	0.1	0.1
METH–AME	1	0	100	128	0.0	0.1
METH–AME Zion	1	0	100	128	0.0	0.1
METH–C.M.E.	1	0	50	64	0.0	0.0
METH–Free Methodist	3	318	300	343	0.1	0.2
METH–Un Methodist	7	1,060	2,229	2,931	0.6	1.4
Missionary Ch	1	80	80	80	0.0	0.0
Muslim Est	1	346	NR	1,109	0.2	0.5
Non-denom Chr Chs	42	11,910	17,393	18,265	3.6	9.0
ORTHE–Ant Orth of NA	1	50	NR	75	0.0	0.0
ORTHE–Greek Orthodox	1	315	NR	550	0.1	0.3
PENT–Assemb of God	34	8,427	4,186	15,432	3.0	7.6
PENT–Ch God (Cleve)	4	155	297	380	0.1	0.2
PENT–Ch of God Proph	1	NR	39	50	0.0	0.0
PENT–COGIC	3	165	325	416	0.1	0.2
PENT–Int Foursq Gos	9	781	1,455	1,862	0.4	0.9
PENT–Intl Pent Holiness	3	525	405	518	0.1	0.3
PENT–Pent Ch of God	13	910	NR	1,414	0.3	0.7
PENT–Un Pent Ch Intl	12	NR	NR	NR	-	-
PENT–Vineyard	1	30	50	64	0.0	0.0
PRES–Orth Pres Ch	2	153	115	165	0.0	0.1
PRES–Presb Ch (USA)	8	435	1,299	1,663	0.3	0.8
REF–Christian Ref	2	425	815	1,043	0.2	0.5
REF–Ref Ch in Am	2	158	200	232	0.0	0.1
REF–Ref Ch in U.S.	1	NR	62	77	0.0	0.0
Salvation Army	3	175	129	1,336	0.3	0.7
Sev Day Adv	9	1,935	3,364	3,870	0.8	1.9
Sikh	2	NR	NR	NR	-	-
Un C of Christ	1	150	210	269	0.1	0.1
Unit Univ	1	96	125	145	0.0	0.1
Unity Ch	1	NR	NR	NR	-	-
Zoroastrian	0	NR	NR	15	0.0	0.0
SUTTER	**70**	**11,666**	**8,015**	**29,782**	**31.4**	**100.0**
ANG/EPIS–Anglican NA	1	NR	NR	NR	-	-
ANG/EPIS–Episcopal	1	23	40	40	0.0	0.1
Bahá'í	0	NR	9	9	0.0	0.0
BAPT–Amer Bapt Assn	1	NR	85	108	0.1	0.4
BAPT–Consrv Bapt	1	NR	NR	NR	-	-
BAPT–Reg Bapt Gen As	1	NR	NR	NR	-	-
BAPT–So Bapt Conv	6	437	695	882	0.9	3.0
BRETH–Ch of Brethren	1	40	85	108	0.1	0.4
Calv Chpl	1	NR	NR	NR	-	-
Catholic	3	NR	NR	9,181	9.7	30.8
CGOD–Ch God (Ander)	2	2,956	NR	2,956	3.1	9.9
Ch Cr, Scientst	1	NR	NR	NR	-	-

NR–Not Reported - Represents no adherents reported. Percentages may not total 100 due to rounding.

Table 3: Religious Congregations by County and Group: 2010

Religious Group	Number of Congregations	Number of Attendees	Number of Communicant, Confirmed, or Full Members	Adherents: Number of Adherents	Adherents: % of Total Pop.	Adherents: % of Total Adh.
Ch of Nazarene	2	2,061	1,049	2,777	2.9	9.3
Chr & Miss Al	2	405	712	762	0.8	2.6
CHR–Chr Chs & Chs Cr	2	NR	135	171	0.2	0.6
CHR–Chs of Christ	4	375	376	458	0.5	1.5
Evan Free Ch	1	450	NR	450	0.5	1.5
HINDU–Trad Temples	1	NR	NR	300	0.3	1.0
Jehovah's Witness	1	NR	NR	NR	-	-
JUD–Reform	1	11	20	54	0.1	0.2
LDS–Comm of Christ	1	NR	158	158	0.2	0.5
LDS–L-D Saints	7	NR	NR	3,135	3.3	10.5
LUTH–Luth Ch-Am Asc	1	NR	NR	NR	-	-
LUTH–Luth–MO Synod	1	130	140	241	0.3	0.8
METH–Un Methodist	5	207	427	839	0.9	2.8
Muslim Est	1	345	NR	1,109	1.2	3.7
Non-denom Chr Chs	4	1,880	2,450	2,525	2.7	8.5
PENT–Assemb of God	5	1,440	478	1,883	2.0	6.3
PENT–Int Foursq Gos	1	162	119	151	0.2	0.5
PENT–Pent Ch of God	2	140	NR	217	0.2	0.7
PENT–Un Pent Ch Intl	1	NR	NR	NR	-	-
PRES–Presb Ch (USA)	1	375	587	745	0.8	2.5
REF–Ref Ch in U.S.	1	NR	52	65	0.1	0.2
Sev Day Adv	2	229	398	458	0.5	1.5
Sikh	4	NR	NR	NR	-	-
TEHAMA	**60**	**3,222**	**3,651**	**18,773**	**29.6**	**100.0**
ANG/EPIS–Episcopal	2	54	117	124	0.2	0.7
Bahá'í	1	NR	52	52	0.1	0.3
BAPT–Amer Bapt USA	1	78	239	296	0.5	1.6
BAPT–Consrv Bapt	2	NR	NR	NR	-	-
BAPT–Reg Bapt Gen As	1	NR	NR	NR	-	-
BAPT–So Bapt Conv	5	240	339	420	0.7	2.2
Calv Chpl	1	NR	NR	NR	-	-
Catholic	3	NR	NR	11,243	17.7	59.9
CGOD–Ch God (Ander)	3	339	NR	339	0.5	1.8
Ch of Nazarene	1	81	53	81	0.1	0.4
CHR–Chr Ch (Disc)	1	22	30	37	0.1	0.2
CHR–Chs of Christ	2	158	175	180	0.3	1.0
Jehovah's Witness	2	NR	NR	NR	-	-
LDS–L-D Saints	3	NR	NR	2,078	3.3	11.1
LUTH–Luth–MO Synod	2	126	208	252	0.4	1.3
METH–Un Methodist	5	139	361	479	0.8	2.6
Non-denom Chr Chs	5	340	398	451	0.7	2.4
ORTHE–Orth Ch in Amer	1	20	NR	20	0.0	0.1
PENT–Assemb of God	4	444	283	495	0.8	2.6
PENT–Ch God (Cleve)	2	103	88	109	0.2	0.6
PENT–Int Foursq Gos	2	0	0	0	0.0	0.0
PENT–Intl Pent Holiness	1	19	27	33	0.1	0.2
PENT–Pent Ch of God	4	280	NR	435	0.7	2.3
PENT–Vineyard	1	375	600	743	1.2	4.0
PRES–Presb Ch (USA)	2	157	278	344	0.5	1.8
Salvation Army	1	33	32	135	0.2	0.7
Sev Day Adv	2	214	371	427	0.7	2.3
TRINITY	**26**	**716**	**753**	**1,808**	**13.1**	**100.0**
Bahá'í	0	NR	7	7	0.1	0.4
BAPT–Consrv Bapt	1	NR	NR	NR	-	-
BAPT–Reg Bapt Gen As	1	NR	NR	NR	-	-
BUDD–Vajrayana	1	NR	NR	20	0.1	1.1
Catholic	3	NR	NR	269	2.0	14.9
Ch Cr, Scientst	1	NR	NR	NR	-	-
Ch of Nazarene	1	115	151	151	1.1	8.4
CHR–Chs of Christ	2	60	60	76	0.6	4.2
Jehovah's Witness	2	NR	NR	NR	-	-
LDS–L-D Saints	2	NR	NR	385	2.8	21.3
LUTH–E.L.C.A.	1	30	63	74	0.5	4.1
New Apost Ch	1	NR	NR	NR	-	-
Non-denom Chr Chs	4	185	136	236	1.7	13.1
PENT–Assemb of God	3	202	127	350	2.5	19.4
Sev Day Adv	2	74	129	148	1.1	8.2
Un C of Christ	1	50	80	92	0.7	5.1
TULARE	**407**	**35,933**	**40,587**	**180,137**	**40.7**	**100.0**
ANG/EPIS–Anglican NA	4	NR	NR	NR	-	-
ANG/EPIS–Episcopal	2	87	143	203	0.0	0.1
Bahá'í	1	NR	274	274	0.1	0.2
BAPT–Amer Bapt Assn	4	NR	410	549	0.1	0.3
BAPT–Amer Bapt USA	5	1,067	1,222	1,637	0.4	0.9
BAPT–Converge/BGC	4	300	NR	360	0.1	0.2
BAPT–Free Will Bapt	5	NR	230	308	0.1	0.2
BAPT–Prog NBC	1	0	150	201	0.0	0.1
BAPT–Reg Bapt Gen As	4	NR	NR	NR	-	-
BAPT–So Bapt Conv	31	1,624	3,415	4,575	1.0	2.5
BRETH–Breth in Chr	1	NR	NR	NR	-	-
BRETH–Ch of Brethren	1	60	55	74	0.0	0.0
BUDD–Mahayana	3	NR	NR	2,511	0.6	1.4
BUDD–Theravada	2	NR	NR	1,664	0.4	0.9
Calv Chpl	3	NR	NR	NR	-	-
Catholic	26	NR	NR	102,772	23.2	57.1
CGOD–Ch God (Ander)	5	698	NR	698	0.2	0.4
CGOD–Ches God-Gen Con	1	35	50	67	0.0	0.0
Ch Cr, Scientst	1	NR	NR	NR	-	-
Ch God (7th Day)	1	NR	NR	NR	-	-
Ch of Nazarene	25	3,614	4,322	4,927	1.1	2.7
Chr & Miss Al	3	567	513	1,114	0.3	0.6
CHR–Chr Ch (Disc)	3	81	135	181	0.0	0.1
CHR–Chr Chs & Chs Cr	5	NR	1,391	1,864	0.4	1.0
CHR–Chs of Christ	23	1,597	1,598	2,124	0.5	1.2
Evan Cov Ch	2	141	98	183	0.0	0.1
Evan Free Ch	3	580	NR	580	0.1	0.3
FRND–Indep Yr Mtgs	1	NR	36	48	0.0	0.0
Jehovah's Witness	9	NR	NR	NR	-	-
JUD–Reform	1	44	78	211	0.0	0.1
LDS–Comm of Christ	1	NR	158	158	0.0	0.1
LDS–L-D Saints	15	NR	NR	7,740	1.8	4.3
LUTH–E.L.C.A.	2	498	721	868	0.2	0.5
LUTH–Luth–MO Synod	5	442	1,084	1,460	0.3	0.8
LUTH–Nor Amer Luth C	1	NR	NR	NR	-	-
MENN–Menn Br US Conf	5	NR	1,122	1,503	0.3	0.8
METH–AME	2	0	250	335	0.1	0.2
METH–Un Methodist	9	961	1,665	2,811	0.6	1.6
Muslim Est	2	495	NR	1,359	0.3	0.8
Non-denom Chr Chs	45	8,690	9,460	11,423	2.6	6.3
ORTHO–Armen Ap Etchm	1	50	NR	500	0.1	0.3
ORTHO–Coptic Orth Ch	1	120	NR	150	0.0	0.1
PENT–Apos Faith Msn	1	NR	35	47	0.0	0.0
PENT–Assemb of God	34	6,282	2,334	10,611	2.4	5.9
PENT–Ch God (Cleve)	15	802	814	1,091	0.2	0.6
PENT–Ch of God Proph	6	NR	338	453	0.1	0.3
PENT–COGIC	2	10	165	221	0.0	0.1
PENT–Int Foursq Gos	9	813	700	938	0.2	0.5
PENT–Intl Pent Holiness	4	210	213	285	0.1	0.2
PENT–Pent Ch of God	20	1,400	NR	2,175	0.5	1.2
PENT–Un Pent Ch Intl	9	NR	NR	NR	-	-
PENT–Vineyard	1	125	170	228	0.1	0.1
PRES–Presb Ch (USA)	10	585	1,036	1,388	0.3	0.8
REF–Christian Ref	1	800	994	1,332	0.3	0.7
REF–Ref Ch in Am	3	827	1,035	1,183	0.3	0.7
REF–Un Ref Chs N.A.	1	NR	NR	NR	-	-
Salvation Army	2	254	517	517	0.1	0.3
Sev Day Adv	15	1,890	3,286	3,780	0.9	2.1
Un Breth in Cr	1	22	30	19	0.0	0.0
Un C of Christ	2	114	277	371	0.1	0.2
Unit Univ	2	48	63	66	0.0	0.0
TUOLUMNE	**66**	**5,517**	**6,228**	**24,907**	**45.0**	**100.0**
ANG/EPIS–Anglican NA	2	NR	NR	NR	-	-
ANG/EPIS–Episcopal	1	13	22	22	0.0	0.1
Bahá'í	1	NR	39	39	0.1	0.2
BAPT–Amer Bapt USA	1	86	94	108	0.2	0.4
BAPT–So Bapt Conv	4	335	429	492	0.9	2.0
BUDD–Vajrayana	1	NR	NR	53	0.1	0.2
Calv Chpl	1	NR	NR	NR	-	-
Catholic	5	NR	NR	14,728	26.6	59.1
Ch Cr, Scientst	1	NR	NR	NR	-	-
Ch of Nazarene	1	40	35	40	0.1	0.2
CHR–Chr Chs & Chs Cr	1	NR	50	57	0.1	0.2
CHR–Chs of Christ	4	176	176	212	0.4	0.9

NR–Not Reported - Represents no adherents reported. Percentages may not total 100 due to rounding.

Table 3: Religious Congregations by County and Group: 2010

Religious Group	Number of Congregations	Number of Attendees	Number of Communicant, Confirmed, or Full Members	Adherents: Number of Adherents	Adherents: % of Total Pop.	Adherents: % of Total Adh.
Evan Free Ch	2	310	NR	310	0.6	1.2
Jehovah's Witness	2	NR	NR	NR	-	-
LDS–L-D Saints	3	NR	NR	1,425	2.6	5.7
LUTH–E.L.C.A.	2	108	182	210	0.4	0.8
LUTH–Luth–MO Synod	1	179	288	289	0.5	1.2
METH–Un Methodist	4	150	247	326	0.6	1.3
Non-denom Chr Chs	12	2,255	3,215	3,491	6.3	14.0
ORTHE–Orth Ch in Amer	1	25	NR	59	0.1	0.2
PENT–Assemb of God	5	997	212	1,522	2.7	6.1
PENT–Int Foursq Gos	2	58	82	94	0.2	0.4
PENT–Pent Ch of God	1	70	NR	109	0.2	0.4
PENT–Un Pent Ch Intl	1	NR	NR	NR	-	-
PRES–Orth Pres Ch	1	52	43	52	0.1	0.2
PRES–Presb Ch (USA)	1	83	113	130	0.2	0.5
Sev Day Adv	3	530	921	1,059	1.9	4.3
Unit Univ	1	50	80	80	0.1	0.3
Unity Ch	1	NR	NR	NR	-	-
VENTURA	**482**	**59,797**	**78,493**	**368,982**	**44.8**	**100.0**
ANG/EPIS–Episcopal	9	949	2,299	2,449	0.3	0.7
Bahá'í	8	NR	552	552	0.1	0.1
BAPT–Amer Bapt Assn	3	NR	235	292	0.0	0.1
BAPT–Amer Bapt USA	2	319	334	415	0.1	0.1
BAPT–Consrv Bapt	2	NR	NR	NR	-	-
BAPT–Converge/BGC	7	1,575	NR	1,890	0.2	0.5
BAPT–Free Will Bapt	2	NR	92	114	0.0	0.0
BAPT–Natl Mis Bapt Conv	1	0	0	0	0.0	0.0
BAPT–Prog NBC	1	500	1,200	1,490	0.2	0.4
BAPT–Ref Bapt Ch	1	NR	NR	NR	-	-
BAPT–Reg Bapt Gen As	2	NR	NR	NR	-	-
BAPT–So Bapt Conv	24	1,815	4,307	5,347	0.6	1.4
BRETH–Grace Breth	1	NR	NR	NR	-	-
BUDD–Mahayana	9	NR	NR	4,017	0.5	1.1
BUDD–Vajrayana	2	NR	NR	528	0.1	0.1
Calv Chpl	9	NR	NR	NR	-	-
Catholic	20	NR	NR	232,571	28.2	63.0
Ch Cr, Scientst	5	NR	NR	NR	-	-
Ch God (7th Day)	1	NR	NR	NR	-	-
Ch of God Gen Conf	1	NR	8	10	0.0	0.0
Ch of Nazarene	6	474	642	796	0.1	0.2
Chr & Miss Al	3	54	68	74	0.0	0.0
CHR–Chr Ch (Disc)	4	106	296	367	0.0	0.1
CHR–Chr Chs & Chs Cr	9	NR	2,920	3,625	0.4	1.0
CHR–Chs of Christ	16	1,423	1,391	1,755	0.2	0.5
CHR–Int Chs of Christ	0	NR	319	396	0.0	0.1
Evan Cov Ch	2	391	452	508	0.1	0.1
Evan Free Ch	6	2,382	NR	2,382	0.3	0.6
FRND–Indep Yr Mtgs	2	NR	0	0	0.0	0.0
HINDU–I/A Temples	1	NR	NR	1,742	0.2	0.5
HINDU–Post Ren	8	NR	NR	305	0.0	0.1
HINDU–Trad Temples	2	NR	NR	250	0.0	0.1
Ind Fund Churches	1	NR	NR	NR	-	-
Jehovah's Witness	14	NR	NR	NR	-	-
JUD–Conserv	2	579	650	1,755	0.2	0.5
JUD–Orth	9	383	450	540	0.1	0.1
JUD–Reform	3	662	1,168	3,154	0.4	0.9
LDS–Comm of Christ	2	NR	328	328	0.0	0.1
LDS–L-D Saints	44	NR	NR	20,123	2.4	5.5
LUTH–Assoc Free Luth	1	NR	NR	NR	-	-
LUTH–E.L.C.A.	11	2,211	5,554	7,765	0.9	2.1
LUTH–Luth Cong Msn Chr	1	35	54	67	0.0	0.0
LUTH–Luth–MO Synod	12	1,381	2,955	4,296	0.5	1.2
LUTH–Wisc Ev Luth Syn	1	51	77	96	0.0	0.0
METH–AME	1	200	350	434	0.1	0.1
METH–Un Methodist	18	2,118	3,774	5,325	0.6	1.4
METH–Wesleyan	1	40	31	52	0.0	0.0
Missionary Ch	6	3,038	1,175	3,049	0.4	0.8
Muslim Est	3	940	NR	3,417	0.4	0.9
New Apost Ch	1	NR	NR	NR	-	-
Non-denom Chr Chs	58	23,730	31,264	34,105	4.1	9.2
ORTHE–Greek Orthodox	1	150	NR	600	0.1	0.2
ORTHE–Orth Ch in Amer	2	107	NR	135	0.0	0.0
ORTHE–Rus Orth Abroad	1	30	NR	70	0.0	0.0
ORTHO–Armen Ap Etchm	1	50	NR	300	0.0	0.1
ORTHO–Coptic Orth Ch	2	420	NR	575	0.1	0.2
PENT–Assemb of God	24	2,404	1,638	3,268	0.4	0.9
PENT–Ch God (Cleve)	9	968	775	962	0.1	0.3
PENT–Ch of God Proph	3	NR	93	115	0.0	0.0
PENT–COGIC	1	100	50	62	0.0	0.0
PENT–Int Foursq Gos	25	3,967	3,532	4,384	0.5	1.2
PENT–Intl Pent Holiness	2	150	227	282	0.0	0.1
PENT–Pent Ch of God	3	210	NR	326	0.0	0.1
PENT–Un Pent Ch Intl	4	NR	NR	NR	-	-
PENT–Vineyard	5	785	1,034	1,284	0.2	0.3
PRES–Korean Amer Pres	1	NR	NR	NR	-	-
PRES–Korean Pres Amer	1	NR	NR	NR	-	-
PRES–Orth Pres Ch	1	38	33	42	0.0	0.0
PRES–Presb Ch (USA)	14	2,776	4,032	5,005	0.6	1.4
PRES–Presb Ch Amer	1	49	51	58	0.0	0.0
REF–Christian Ref	2	130	124	154	0.0	0.0
Salvation Army	2	57	100	352	0.0	0.1
Sev Day Adv	10	1,630	2,834	3,260	0.4	0.9
Un C of Christ	4	45	548	680	0.1	0.2
Unit Univ	3	375	477	673	0.1	0.2
Unity Ch	2	NR	NR	NR	-	-
Zoroastrian	0	NR	NR	14	0.0	0.0
YOLO	**138**	**12,829**	**12,964**	**72,964**	**36.3**	**100.0**
ANG/EPIS–Episcopal	2	264	573	680	0.3	0.9
Bahá'í	3	NR	213	213	0.1	0.3
BAPT–Amer Bapt USA	1	78	67	81	0.0	0.1
BAPT–Consrv Bapt	1	NR	NR	NR	-	-
BAPT–Converge/BGC	1	75	NR	90	0.0	0.1
BAPT–Free Will Bapt	1	NR	46	56	0.0	0.1
BAPT–N Am Bapt Conf	1	NR	NR	NR	-	-
BAPT–Reg Bapt Gen As	1	NR	NR	NR	-	-
BAPT–So Bapt Conv	11	3,205	3,001	3,631	1.8	5.0
BUDD–Mahayana	2	NR	NR	202	0.1	0.3
BUDD–Theravada	1	NR	NR	1,006	0.5	1.4
BUDD–Vajrayana	2	NR	NR	67	0.0	0.1
Calv Chpl	2	NR	NR	NR	-	-
Catholic	11	NR	NR	42,656	21.2	58.5
CGOD–Ch God (Ander)	2	80	NR	80	0.0	0.1
Ch Cr, Scientst	1	NR	NR	NR	-	-
Ch of Nazarene	2	160	223	272	0.1	0.4
Chr & Miss Al	2	113	44	198	0.1	0.3
CHR–Chr Ch (Disc)	1	74	390	472	0.2	0.6
CHR–Chs of Christ	7	290	295	415	0.2	0.6
Christian Brethren	1	NR	NR	NR	-	-
Evan Cov Ch	3	1,306	746	1,698	0.8	2.3
FRND–Evan Fr Ch Intl	1	45	32	39	0.0	0.1
FRND–Fr Gen Cf	1	NR	47	57	0.0	0.1
FRND–Indep Yr Mtgs	1	NR	47	57	0.0	0.1
HINDU–Post Ren	1	NR	NR	77	0.0	0.1
Jehovah's Witness	3	NR	NR	NR	-	-
JUD–Reform	1	156	275	742	0.4	1.0
LDS–L-D Saints	9	NR	NR	4,839	2.4	6.6
LUTH–E.L.C.A.	4	326	648	808	0.4	1.1
LUTH–Luth–MO Synod	2	95	336	418	0.2	0.6
MENN–Menn Br US Conf	1	NR	0	0	0.0	0.0
METH–Un Methodist	4	416	788	1,200	0.6	1.6
Muslim Est	4	1,381	NR	4,436	2.2	6.1
Non-denom Chr Chs	12	2,220	2,385	2,797	1.4	3.8
OCATH–Un Cath Ch	1	NR	NR	702	0.3	1.0
ORTHE–Ant Orth of NA	1	50	NR	250	0.1	0.3
ORTHE–Orth Ch in Amer	1	60	NR	100	0.0	0.1
PENT–Assemb of God	8	958	561	1,666	0.8	2.3
PENT–Ch God (Cleve)	1	73	111	134	0.1	0.2
PENT–Ch of God Proph	1	NR	16	19	0.0	0.0
PENT–Int Foursq Gos	3	92	147	178	0.1	0.2
PENT–Pent Ch of God	2	140	NR	217	0.1	0.3
PENT–Un Pent Ch Intl	3	NR	NR	NR	-	-
PRES–Evan Presby Ch	1	NR	50	60	0.0	0.1
PRES–Presb Ch (USA)	4	576	1,052	1,273	0.6	1.7
REF–Christian Ref	1	NR	0	0	0.0	0.0
Sev Day Adv	3	218	380	437	0.2	0.6
Sikh	1	NR	NR	NR	-	-
Un C of Christ	2	178	219	265	0.1	0.4

NR–Not Reported   - Represents no adherents reported.   Percentages may not total 100 due to rounding.

Table 3: Religious Congregations by County and Group: 2010

Religious Group	Number of Congrega-tions	Number of Attendees	Number of Communicant, Confirmed, or Full Members	Adherents		
				Number of Adherents	% of Total Pop.	% of Total Adh.
Unit Univ	1	200	272	372	0.2	0.5
Unity Ch	1	NR	NR	NR	-	-
Zoroastrian	0	NR	NR	4	0.0	0.0
YUBA	**66**	**4,118**	**4,556**	**23,605**	**32.7**	**100.0**
ANG/EPIS–Episcopal	2	59	104	124	0.2	0.5
Bahá'í	0	NR	59	59	0.1	0.2
BAPT–So Bapt Conv	7	389	427	554	0.8	2.3
BUDD–Mahayana	1	NR	NR	1,250	1.7	5.3
Calv Chpl	1	NR	NR	NR	-	-
Catholic	3	NR	NR	12,138	16.8	51.4
CGOD–Ches God-Gen Con	1	100	116	150	0.2	0.6
Ch of Nazarene	2	118	153	156	0.2	0.7
Chr & Miss Al	1	85	166	166	0.2	0.7
CHR–Chr Ch (Disc)	1	49	43	56	0.1	0.2
CHR–Chr Chs & Chs Cr	1	NR	85	110	0.2	0.5
CHR–Chs of Christ	3	138	133	158	0.2	0.7
Evan Cov Ch	1	244	0	317	0.4	1.3
Int Cou Comm Ch	1	NR	NR	NR	-	-
Jehovah's Witness	2	NR	NR	NR	-	-
LDS–L-D Saints	5	NR	NR	3,096	4.3	13.1
LUTH–E.L.C.A.	1	49	112	137	0.2	0.6
METH–AME	1	135	205	266	0.4	1.1
METH–Un Methodist	1	160	312	465	0.6	2.0
METH–Wesleyan	1	71	36	92	0.1	0.4
Non-denom Chr Chs	9	1,315	1,555	1,750	2.4	7.4
PENT–Assemb of God	7	531	339	714	1.0	3.0
PENT–Ch God (Cleve)	1	33	57	74	0.1	0.3
PENT–Ch of God Proph	2	NR	16	21	0.0	0.1
PENT–Intl Pent Holiness	2	225	207	268	0.4	1.1
PENT–Pent Ch of God	2	140	NR	217	0.3	0.9
PENT–Un Pent Ch Intl	1	NR	NR	NR	-	-
PRES–Presb Ch (USA)	1	67	84	109	0.2	0.5
Salvation Army	1	67	98	871	1.2	3.7
Sev Day Adv	3	143	249	286	0.4	1.2
Sikh	1	NR	NR	NR	-	-
Zoroastrian	0	NR	NR	1	0.0	0.0
COLORADO	**4,188**	**472,288**	**654,157**	**1,902,282**	**37.8**	**100.0**
ADAMS	**244**	**23,290**	**28,303**	**129,651**	**29.4**	**100.0**
ANG/EPIS–Episcopal	3	177	384	409	0.1	0.3
Bahá'í	4	NR	315	315	0.1	0.2
BAPT–Amer Bapt Assn	2	NR	170	221	0.1	0.2
BAPT–Amer Bapt USA	1	50	75	97	0.0	0.1
BAPT–Consrv Bapt	2	NR	NR	NR	-	-
BAPT–Converge/BGC	4	625	NR	750	0.2	0.6
BAPT–Free Will Bapt	1	NR	10	13	0.0	0.0
BAPT–N Am Bapt Conf	1	NR	52	67	0.0	0.1
BAPT–NT Ind Bapt	3	NR	NR	NR	-	-
BAPT–Reg Bapt Gen As	4	NR	NR	NR	-	-
BAPT–S-D Baptist Gen Con	1	50	60	78	0.0	0.1
BAPT–So Bapt Conv	19	1,252	2,268	2,944	0.7	2.3
BUDD–Theravada	2	NR	NR	2,729	0.6	2.1
Calv Chpl	2	NR	NR	NR	-	-
Catholic	11	NR	NR	70,598	16.0	54.5
CGOD–Ch God (Ander)	1	19	NR	19	0.0	0.0
Ch Cr, Scientst	1	NR	NR	NR	-	-
Ch God (7th Day)	2	NR	NR	NR	-	-
Ch of Nazarene	7	2,180	1,539	3,204	0.7	2.5
Chr & Miss Al	3	556	762	888	0.2	0.7
CHR–Chr Ch (Disc)	2	15	31	40	0.0	0.0
CHR–Chr Chs & Chs Cr	3	NR	915	1,188	0.3	0.9
CHR–Chs of Christ	4	327	320	396	0.1	0.3
CONG–Consrv Cong Chr	1	80	130	169	0.0	0.1
Evan Cov Ch	1	212	96	276	0.1	0.2
Evan Free Ch	2	140	NR	140	0.0	0.1
FRND–Consrv Yr Mtgs	1	NR	0	0	0.0	0.0
Grace Gosp Fel	2	NR	NR	NR	-	-
HINDU–I/A Temples	1	NR	NR	1,562	0.4	1.2
Jehovah's Witness	5	NR	NR	NR	-	-
JUD–Reform	1	32	56	151	0.0	0.1

Religious Group	Number of Congrega-tions	Number of Attendees	Number of Communicant, Confirmed, or Full Members	Adherents		
				Number of Adherents	% of Total Pop.	% of Total Adh.
LDS–Comm of Christ	3	NR	384	384	0.1	0.3
LDS–L-D Saints	18	NR	NR	11,400	2.6	8.8
LUTH–E.L.C.A.	6	655	1,391	1,683	0.4	1.3
LUTH–Luth Ch-Am Asc	1	NR	NR	NR	-	-
LUTH–Luth–MO Synod	8	1,084	2,449	3,169	0.7	2.4
LUTH–Wisc Ev Luth Syn	2	254	387	535	0.1	0.4
MENN–Mennonite USA	1	0	45	58	0.0	0.0
METH–Free Methodist	3	230	201	241	0.1	0.2
METH–Un Methodist	9	893	1,941	2,868	0.6	2.2
Muslim Est	2	268	NR	616	0.1	0.5
New Apost Ch	1	NR	NR	NR	-	-
Non-denom Chr Chs	24	6,705	6,985	8,558	1.9	6.6
ORTHO–Ethiopian Orth	1	NR	NR	NR	-	-
PENT–Assemb of God	11	3,007	1,246	6,203	1.4	4.8
PENT–Ch God (Cleve)	2	150	247	321	0.1	0.2
PENT–Ch of God Proph	2	NR	91	118	0.0	0.1
PENT–COGIC	2	0	150	195	0.0	0.2
PENT–Int Foursq Gos	14	1,261	1,245	1,616	0.4	1.2
PENT–Intl Pent Holiness	5	922	813	1,055	0.2	0.8
PENT–Un Pent Ch Intl	6	NR	NR	NR	-	-
PENT–Vineyard	1	50	70	91	0.0	0.1
Pillar of Fire	1	NR	125	125	0.0	0.1
PRES–Presb Ch (USA)	9	797	1,367	1,774	0.4	1.4
PRES–Presb Ch Amer	1	157	147	205	0.0	0.2
PRES–Ref Pres of NA	1	70	60	99	0.0	0.1
REF–Christian Ref	1	50	65	84	0.0	0.1
Salvation Army	1	48	63	73	0.0	0.1
Sev Day Adv	8	832	1,446	1,664	0.4	1.3
Un C of Christ	3	142	202	262	0.1	0.2
ALAMOSA	**31**	**1,239**	**2,052**	**11,445**	**74.1**	**100.0**
ANG/EPIS–Episcopal	1	18	45	45	0.3	0.4
Bahá'í	0	NR	20	20	0.1	0.2
BAPT–Converge/BGC	1	75	NR	90	0.6	0.8
BAPT–So Bapt Conv	5	153	687	854	5.5	7.5
Calv Chpl	1	NR	NR	NR	-	-
Catholic	1	NR	NR	6,996	45.3	61.1
Ch Cr, Scientst	1	NR	NR	NR	-	-
Ch of Nazarene	1	0	0	0	0.0	0.0
CHR–Chr Ch (Disc)	1	53	84	104	0.7	0.9
CHR–Chr Chs & Chs Cr	1	NR	100	124	0.8	1.1
CHR–Chs of Christ	1	65	56	82	0.5	0.7
Jehovah's Witness	1	NR	NR	NR	-	-
LDS–L-D Saints	5	NR	NR	1,547	10.0	13.5
LUTH–Luth–MO Synod	1	64	131	168	1.1	1.5
METH–Un Methodist	2	101	262	415	2.7	3.6
Non-denom Chr Chs	1	50	59	62	0.4	0.5
PENT–Assemb of God	1	250	69	280	1.8	2.4
PENT–Ch God (Cleve)	1	200	86	107	0.7	0.9
PENT–Un Pent Ch Intl	1	NR	NR	NR	-	-
PENT–Vineyard	1	30	52	65	0.4	0.6
PRES–Presb Ch (USA)	1	0	102	127	0.8	1.1
REF–Christian Ref	1	100	160	199	1.3	1.7
Sev Day Adv	1	80	139	160	1.0	1.4
ARAPAHOE	**302**	**50,681**	**70,470**	**190,837**	**33.4**	**100.0**
ANG/EPIS–Anglican NA	3	NR	NR	NR	-	-
ANG/EPIS–Episcopal	5	881	2,120	2,364	0.4	1.2
Ap Chr Ch-Amer	1	81	44	81	0.0	0.0
Bahá'í	3	NR	140	140	0.0	0.1
BAPT–Amer Bapt Assn	1	NR	85	106	0.0	0.1
BAPT–Amer Bapt USA	5	453	684	854	0.1	0.4
BAPT–Consrv Bapt	3	NR	NR	NR	-	-
BAPT–Converge/BGC	3	2,875	NR	3,450	0.6	1.8
BAPT–Fund Bapt Flwsp	1	NR	NR	NR	-	-
BAPT–Ind Bapt Flwsp Intl	1	NR	NR	NR	-	-
BAPT–N Am Bapt Conf	1	NR	88	110	0.0	0.1
BAPT–Natl Mis Bapt Conv	1	0	150	187	0.0	0.1
BAPT–Reg Bapt Gen As	1	NR	NR	NR	-	-
BAPT–So Bapt Conv	30	2,896	7,126	8,901	1.6	4.7
BRETH–Ch of Brethren	1	41	141	176	0.0	0.1
BUDD–Mahayana	2	NR	NR	520	0.1	0.3
BUDD–Vajrayana	3	NR	NR	76	0.0	0.0

NR–Not Reported - Represents no adherents reported. Percentages may not total 100 due to rounding.

Table 3: Religious Congregations by County and Group: 2010

Religious Group	Number of Congregations	Number of Attendees	Number of Communicant, Confirmed, or Full Members	Adherents		
				Number of Adherents	% of Total Pop.	% of Total Adh.
Calv Chpl	1	NR	NR	NR	-	-
Catholic	13	NR	NR	69,031	12.1	36.2
Ch Cr, Scientst	3	NR	NR	NR	-	-
Ch of Nazarene	1	256	388	388	0.1	0.2
Chr & Miss Al	2	178	117	273	0.0	0.1
CHR–Chr Ch (Disc)	3	991	1,875	2,342	0.4	1.2
CHR–Chr Chs & Chs Cr	2	NR	325	406	0.1	0.2
CHR–Chs of Christ	9	1,651	1,372	1,960	0.3	1.0
CHR–Int Chs of Christ	0	NR	160	200	0.0	0.1
Christian Brethren	1	NR	NR	NR	-	-
Evan Cov Ch	1	277	251	360	0.1	0.2
Evan Free Ch	7	1,818	NR	1,818	0.3	1.0
HINDU–Post Ren	3	NR	NR	112	0.0	0.1
Ind Fund Churches	2	NR	NR	NR	-	-
Jehovah's Witness	5	NR	NR	NR	-	-
JUD–Orth	1	131	50	185	0.0	0.1
LDS–Comm of Christ	1	NR	128	128	0.0	0.1
LDS–L-D Saints	27	NR	NR	14,505	2.5	7.6
LUTH–Ch of Luth Br	1	0	20	50	0.0	0.0
LUTH–E.L.C.A.	13	2,900	8,238	11,536	2.0	6.0
LUTH–Luth–MO Synod	8	2,292	4,244	5,552	1.0	2.9
LUTH–Wisc Ev Luth Syn	1	223	304	379	0.1	0.2
MENN–Menn Br US Conf	2	NR	470	587	0.1	0.3
MENN–Mennonite USA	2	81	106	132	0.0	0.1
METH–Free Methodist	1	73	5	73	0.0	0.0
METH–Un Methodist	10	1,746	4,332	5,692	1.0	3.0
METH–Wesleyan	2	132	80	172	0.0	0.1
Muslim Est	3	2,268	NR	10,616	1.9	5.6
Non-denom Chr Chs	35	17,477	22,045	25,169	4.4	13.2
ORTHE–Greek Orthodox	1	350	NR	1,100	0.2	0.6
ORTHE–Orth Ch in Amer	1	85	NR	100	0.0	0.1
ORTHO–Armen Ap Cilic	1	45	NR	180	0.0	0.1
ORTHO–Coptic Orth Ch	1	150	NR	400	0.1	0.2
PENT–Assemb of God	11	2,671	1,839	3,602	0.6	1.9
PENT–Ch God (Cleve)	6	304	683	853	0.1	0.4
PENT–COGIC	1	400	700	874	0.2	0.5
PENT–Full Gosp Bapt	2	NR	NR	NR	-	-
PENT–Int Foursq Gos	2	124	53	66	0.0	0.0
PENT–Intl Pent Holiness	7	475	408	510	0.1	0.3
PENT–Un Pent Ch Intl	2	NR	NR	NR	-	-
PENT–Vineyard	1	1,232	2,200	2,748	0.5	1.4
PRES–As Ref Pres Ch	1	NR	0	0	0.0	0.0
PRES–Evan Presby Ch	8	NR	2,849	3,559	0.6	1.9
PRES–Kor Pres Abroad	1	NR	NR	NR	-	-
PRES–Korean Pres Amer	1	NR	NR	NR	-	-
PRES–Presb Ch (USA)	8	1,391	2,633	3,289	0.6	1.7
PRES–Presb Ch Amer	2	135	122	145	0.0	0.1
REF–Christian Ref	1	2,000	656	819	0.1	0.4
REF–Ref Ch in Am	1	123	204	252	0.0	0.1
REF–Un Ref Chs N.A.	1	NR	NR	NR	-	-
Salvation Army	2	89	122	157	0.0	0.1
Sev Day Adv	8	701	1,219	1,402	0.2	0.7
Un C of Christ	5	593	1,551	1,937	0.3	1.0
Unit Univ	1	92	143	212	0.0	0.1
Unity Ch	1	NR	NR	NR	-	-
Zoroastrian	0	NR	NR	1	0.0	0.0
ARCHULETA	**25**	**1,465**	**1,404**	**9,403**	**77.8**	**100.0**
ANG/EPIS–Anglican NA	1	NR	NR	NR	-	-
ANG/EPIS–Episcopal	1	85	165	165	1.4	1.8
Bahá'í	0	NR	15	15	0.1	0.2
BAPT–So Bapt Conv	3	348	468	550	4.6	5.8
BUDD–Vajrayana	1	NR	NR	1,235	10.2	13.1
Calv Chpl	1	NR	NR	NR	-	-
Catholic	6	NR	NR	5,643	46.7	60.0
CHR–Chs of Christ	2	54	39	56	0.5	0.6
Evan Free Ch	1	300	NR	300	2.5	3.2
Jehovah's Witness	1	NR	NR	NR	-	-
LDS–L-D Saints	1	NR	NR	382	3.2	4.1
LUTH–Luth–MO Synod	1	60	121	154	1.3	1.6
METH–Un Methodist	1	153	170	170	1.4	1.8
Non-denom Chr Chs	2	330	330	413	3.4	4.4
PENT–Assemb of God	1	65	0	200	1.7	2.1
Sev Day Adv	1	35	61	70	0.6	0.7
Unit Univ	1	35	35	50	0.4	0.5
BACA	**21**	**557**	**544**	**1,119**	**29.5**	**100.0**
Bahá'í	0	NR	3	3	0.1	0.3
BAPT–So Bapt Conv	2	41	42	50	1.3	4.5
Catholic	2	NR	NR	200	5.3	17.9
CGOD–Ch God (Ander)	2	74	NR	74	2.0	6.6
CHR–Chs of Christ	4	101	101	137	3.6	12.2
FRND–Evan Fr Ch Intl	3	18	31	37	1.0	3.3
METH–Un Methodist	3	107	239	342	9.0	30.6
METH–Wesleyan	2	74	36	96	2.5	8.6
PENT–Assemb of God	1	70	24	100	2.6	8.9
PENT–Intl Pent Holiness	1	68	60	71	1.9	6.3
Sev Day Adv	1	4	8	9	0.2	0.8
BENT	**13**	**371**	**537**	**2,099**	**32.3**	**100.0**
Bahá'í	0	NR	7	7	0.1	0.3
BAPT–Consrv Bapt	1	NR	NR	NR	-	-
BAPT–So Bapt Conv	2	66	58	67	1.0	3.2
Catholic	1	NR	NR	1,469	22.6	70.0
Ch of Nazarene	1	24	18	24	0.4	1.1
CHR–Chs of Christ	2	42	34	52	0.8	2.5
FRND–Evan Fr Ch Intl	2	51	83	95	1.5	4.5
LUTH–Wisc Ev Luth Syn	1	27	36	47	0.7	2.2
METH–Un Methodist	2	91	214	238	3.7	11.3
PRES–Presb Ch (USA)	1	70	87	100	1.5	4.8
BOULDER	**233**	**27,303**	**36,882**	**122,268**	**41.5**	**100.0**
ANG/EPIS–Anglican NA	2	NR	NR	NR	-	-
ANG/EPIS–Episcopal	5	874	2,699	3,097	1.1	2.5
Bahá'í	5	NR	222	222	0.1	0.2
BAPT–Amer Bapt USA	2	138	257	308	0.1	0.3
BAPT–Asc Ref Bap Ch Am	1	NR	NR	NR	-	-
BAPT–Consrv Bapt	2	NR	NR	NR	-	-
BAPT–Converge/BGC	2	875	NR	1,050	0.4	0.9
BAPT–Fund Bapt Flwsp	1	NR	NR	NR	-	-
BAPT–Ref Bapt Ch	1	NR	NR	NR	-	-
BAPT–Reg Bapt Gen As	1	NR	NR	NR	-	-
BAPT–S-D Baptist Gen Con	1	65	49	59	0.0	0.0
BAPT–So Bapt Conv	8	1,246	941	1,128	0.4	0.9
BRETH–Ch of Brethren	1	69	91	109	0.0	0.1
BUDD–Mahayana	7	NR	NR	264	0.1	0.2
BUDD–Theravada	2	NR	NR	662	0.2	0.5
BUDD–Vajrayana	9	NR	NR	492	0.2	0.4
Calv Chpl	2	NR	NR	NR	-	-
Catholic	10	NR	NR	59,240	20.1	48.5
Ch Cr, Scientst	2	NR	NR	NR	-	-
Ch of Nazarene	2	164	154	263	0.1	0.2
CHR–Chr Ch (Disc)	1	63	190	228	0.1	0.2
CHR–Chr Chs & Chs Cr	3	NR	2,800	3,356	1.1	2.7
CHR–Chs of Christ	5	642	573	673	0.2	0.6
CHR–Int Chs of Christ	0	NR	160	192	0.1	0.2
CONG–Cong Chr Add'l	1	NR	0	0	0.0	0.0
CONG–Cong Chr, NA	1	NR	31	37	0.0	0.0
CONG–Consrv Cong Chr	1	20	48	58	0.0	0.0
Evan Cov Ch	3	112	104	145	0.0	0.1
Evan Free Ch	3	1,730	NR	1,730	0.6	1.4
FRND–Fr Gen Cf	1	NR	148	177	0.1	0.1
HINDU–Post Ren	14	NR	NR	552	0.2	0.5
HINDU–Renaiss	1	NR	NR	12	0.0	0.0
Jehovah's Witness	4	NR	NR	NR	-	-
JUD–Conserv	1	182	204	551	0.2	0.5
JUD–Orth	2	178	100	250	0.1	0.2
JUD–Reform	1	323	569	1,536	0.5	1.3
LDS–Comm of Christ	1	NR	128	128	0.0	0.1
LDS–L-D Saints	17	NR	NR	8,620	2.9	7.1
LUTH–E.L.C.A.	9	2,228	4,677	6,350	2.2	5.2
LUTH–Luth Cong Msn Chr	1	577	1,074	1,287	0.4	1.1
LUTH–Luth–MO Synod	5	517	1,018	1,271	0.4	1.0
LUTH–Wisc Ev Luth Syn	2	120	168	213	0.1	0.2
MENN–Mennonite USA	1	78	115	138	0.0	0.1
METH–Un Methodist	11	1,326	2,676	3,424	1.2	2.8
Missionary Ch	1	0	0	0	0.0	0.0

NR–Not Reported   - Represents no adherents reported.   Percentages may not total 100 due to rounding.

Table 3: Religious Congregations by County and Group: 2010

Religious Group	Number of Congrega-tions	Number of Attendees	Number of Communicant, Confirmed, or Full Members	Adherents		
				Number of Adherents	% of Total Pop.	% of Total Adh.
Muslim Est	1	200	NR	400	0.1	0.3
Non-denom Chr Chs	25	10,652	10,526	13,992	4.8	11.4
OCATH–Pol Natl Cath	1	NR	NR	NR	-	-
ORTHE–Ant Orth of NA	3	184	NR	468	0.2	0.4
ORTHE–Greek Orthodox	1	150	NR	250	0.1	0.2
PENT–Assemb of God	8	606	369	1,110	0.4	0.9
PENT–Int Foursq Gos	3	148	145	174	0.1	0.1
PENT–Intl Pent Holiness	2	102	90	108	0.0	0.1
PENT–Un Pent Ch Intl	6	NR	NR	NR	-	-
PRES–Korean Pres Amer	1	NR	NR	NR	-	-
PRES–Presb Ch (USA)	9	1,820	3,197	3,832	1.3	3.1
PRES–Ref Pres of NA	1	48	45	63	0.0	0.1
REF–Christian Ref	2	250	307	368	0.1	0.3
Sev Day Adv	4	669	1,164	1,338	0.5	1.1
Sikh	2	NR	NR	NR	-	-
Un C of Christ	3	628	1,396	1,673	0.6	1.4
Unit Univ	2	319	447	670	0.2	0.5
Unity Ch	3	NR	NR	NR	-	-
BROOMFIELD	**37**	**6,557**	**9,920**	**17,012**	**30.4**	**100.0**
ANG/EPIS–Anglican NA	2	NR	NR	NR	-	-
ANG/EPIS–Episcopal	1	142	147	262	0.5	1.5
Bahá'í	1	NR	32	32	0.1	0.2
BAPT–Consrv Bapt	1	NR	NR	NR	-	-
BAPT–So Bapt Conv	2	120	922	1,162	2.1	6.8
BUDD–Vajrayana	1	NR	NR	32	0.1	0.2
Calv Chpl	1	NR	NR	NR	-	-
Catholic	1	NR	NR	4,000	7.2	23.5
CHR–Chr Chs & Chs Cr	1	NR	250	315	0.6	1.9
CHR–Chs of Christ	2	360	310	410	0.7	2.4
Evan Free Ch	1	350	NR	350	0.6	2.1
Jehovah's Witness	1	NR	NR	NR	-	-
LUTH–E.L.C.A.	2	665	1,527	2,373	4.2	13.9
LUTH–Luth Cong Msn Chr	1	35	35	44	0.1	0.3
LUTH–Luth–MO Synod	2	635	972	1,284	2.3	7.5
METH–Un Methodist	1	805	1,621	2,029	3.6	11.9
Non-denom Chr Chs	8	2,380	3,000	3,206	5.7	18.8
PENT–Assemb of God	1	95	48	142	0.3	0.8
PENT–Intl Pent Holiness	1	100	92	116	0.2	0.7
PENT–Un Pent Ch Intl	1	NR	NR	NR	-	-
PRES–Orth Pres Ch	1	135	81	131	0.2	0.8
REF–Christian Ref	1	567	571	720	1.3	4.2
Salvation Army	1	22	69	109	0.2	0.6
Sev Day Adv	1	58	101	116	0.2	0.7
Un C of Christ	1	88	142	179	0.3	1.1
CHAFFEE	**36**	**2,312**	**4,297**	**7,784**	**43.7**	**100.0**
ANG/EPIS–Anglican NA	1	NR	NR	NR	-	-
ANG/EPIS–Episcopal	2	120	290	290	1.6	3.7
Bahá'í	0	NR	11	11	0.1	0.1
BAPT–Consrv Bapt	1	NR	NR	NR	-	-
BAPT–So Bapt Conv	3	205	1,874	2,143	12.0	27.5
Catholic	2	NR	NR	2,024	11.4	26.0
Ch Cr, Scientst	1	NR	NR	NR	-	-
Ch of Nazarene	1	55	54	55	0.3	0.7
CHR–Chr Ch (Disc)	2	39	112	128	0.7	1.6
CHR–Chs of Christ	3	185	165	240	1.3	3.1
Evan Free Ch	1	65	NR	65	0.4	0.8
FRND–Fr Gen Cf	1	NR	0	0	0.0	0.0
Jehovah's Witness	2	NR	NR	NR	-	-
LDS–L-D Saints	2	NR	NR	435	2.4	5.6
LUTH–Luth–MO Synod	2	136	238	271	1.5	3.5
METH–Un Methodist	1	62	140	173	1.0	2.2
Non-denom Chr Chs	3	555	535	693	3.9	8.9
PENT–Assemb of God	2	285	151	424	2.4	5.4
PENT–Ch God (Cleve)	1	71	34	39	0.2	0.5
PENT–Un Pent Ch Intl	1	NR	NR	NR	-	-
PENT–Vineyard	1	205	300	343	1.9	4.4
PRES–Presb Ch (USA)	1	217	206	236	1.3	3.0
Sev Day Adv	1	8	15	17	0.1	0.2
Un C of Christ	1	104	172	197	1.1	2.5

Religious Group	Number of Congrega-tions	Number of Attendees	Number of Communicant, Confirmed, or Full Members	Adherents		
				Number of Adherents	% of Total Pop.	% of Total Adh.
CHEYENNE	**11**	**289**	**562**	**960**	**52.3**	**100.0**
BAPT–So Bapt Conv	1	8	8	10	0.5	1.0
Catholic	1	NR	NR	280	15.3	29.2
CHR–Chr Chs & Chs Cr	1	NR	120	147	8.0	15.3
CHR–Chs of Christ	1	18	17	22	1.2	2.3
LUTH–E.L.C.A.	1	7	6	6	0.3	0.6
LUTH–Luth–MO Synod	2	53	112	134	7.3	14.0
METH–Un Methodist	2	58	104	166	9.0	17.3
Non-denom Chr Chs	2	145	195	195	10.6	20.3
CLEAR CREEK	**12**	**217**	**314**	**1,411**	**15.5**	**100.0**
ANG/EPIS–Episcopal	1	14	18	18	0.2	1.3
Bahá'í	0	NR	5	5	0.1	0.4
BAPT–Converge/BGC	1	75	NR	90	1.0	6.4
BAPT–So Bapt Conv	1	12	20	23	0.3	1.6
Catholic	3	NR	NR	708	7.8	50.2
Jehovah's Witness	1	NR	NR	NR	-	-
LDS–L-D Saints	1	NR	NR	232	2.6	16.4
LUTH–E.L.C.A.	1	25	74	86	0.9	6.1
METH–Un Methodist	1	30	73	106	1.2	7.5
PRES–Presb Ch (USA)	2	61	124	143	1.6	10.1
CONEJOS	**25**	**98**	**123**	**6,141**	**74.4**	**100.0**
Bahá'í	0	NR	15	15	0.2	0.2
Catholic	11	NR	NR	3,510	42.5	57.2
LDS–L-D Saints	8	NR	NR	2,343	28.4	38.2
MENN–Amish Undif	1	NR	44	119	1.4	1.9
MENN–Mennonite USA	1	0	7	9	0.1	0.1
PENT–Assemb of God	2	69	22	100	1.2	1.6
PRES–Presb Ch (USA)	2	29	35	45	0.5	0.7
COSTILLA	**11**	**13**	**41**	**3,466**	**98.4**	**100.0**
Bahá'í	0	NR	21	21	0.6	0.6
Catholic	9	NR	NR	3,260	92.5	94.1
LDS–L-D Saints	1	NR	NR	161	4.6	4.6
PRES–Presb Ch (USA)	1	13	20	24	0.7	0.7
CROWLEY	**10**	**415**	**589**	**1,784**	**30.6**	**100.0**
Bahá'í	0	NR	2	2	0.0	0.1
BAPT–So Bapt Conv	1	25	25	28	0.5	1.6
Catholic	1	NR	NR	1,092	18.8	61.2
CHR–Chr Ch (Disc)	1	30	75	84	1.4	4.7
LUTH–E.L.C.A.	1	14	13	16	0.3	0.9
LUTH–Luth–MO Synod	1	7	8	8	0.1	0.4
METH–Un Methodist	2	69	156	212	3.6	11.9
Non-denom Chr Chs	2	250	310	312	5.4	17.5
PENT–Assemb of God	1	20	0	30	0.5	1.7
CUSTER	**11**	**452**	**737**	**1,629**	**38.3**	**100.0**
ANG/EPIS–Episcopal	1	25	52	52	1.2	3.2
Bahá'í	0	NR	2	2	0.0	0.1
BAPT–So Bapt Conv	1	205	185	211	5.0	13.0
Catholic	1	NR	NR	543	12.8	33.3
CHR–Chs of Christ	1	25	31	34	0.8	2.1
LDS–L-D Saints	1	NR	NR	117	2.7	7.2
LUTH–Luth–MO Synod	1	0	221	255	6.0	15.7
MENN–Amish Undif	1	NR	24	65	1.5	4.0
METH–Un Methodist	1	87	122	212	5.0	13.0
Non-denom Chr Chs	2	110	100	138	3.2	8.5
Tao	1	NR	NR	NR	-	-
DELTA	**61**	**3,248**	**4,186**	**11,255**	**36.4**	**100.0**
ANG/EPIS–Episcopal	1	54	81	81	0.3	0.7
Bahá'í	0	NR	13	13	0.0	0.1
BAPT–Amer Bapt Assn	1	NR	85	102	0.3	0.9
BAPT–Amer Bapt USA	2	215	251	301	1.0	2.7
BAPT–NT Ind Bapt	1	NR	NR	NR	-	-
BAPT–So Bapt Conv	2	131	361	433	1.4	3.8
Catholic	4	NR	NR	3,630	11.7	32.3
CGOD–Ch God (Ander)	2	49	NR	49	0.2	0.4
Ch Cr, Scientst	1	NR	NR	NR	-	-

NR–Not Reported - Represents no adherents reported. Percentages may not total 100 due to rounding.

Table 3: Religious Congregations by County and Group: 2010

Religious Group	Number of Congrega-tions	Number of Attendees	Number of Communicant, Confirmed, or Full Members	Adherents: Number of Adherents	Adherents: % of Total Pop.	Adherents: % of Total Adh.
Ch of Nazarene	3	82	111	148	0.5	1.3
CHR–Chr Chs & Chs Cr	3	NR	404	485	1.6	4.3
CHR–Chs of Christ	4	203	188	240	0.8	2.1
Evan Free Ch	1	100	NR	100	0.3	0.9
FRND–Evan Fr Ch Intl	2	173	341	409	1.3	3.6
Ind Fund Churches	2	NR	NR	NR	-	-
Jehovah's Witness	4	NR	NR	NR	-	-
LDS–Comm of Christ	1	NR	128	128	0.4	1.1
LDS–L-D Saints	3	NR	NR	1,535	5.0	13.6
LUTH–E.L.C.A.	1	47	85	106	0.3	0.9
LUTH–Luth–MO Synod	2	135	333	388	1.3	3.4
MENN–Tamp Amish-Menn	1	70	38	70	0.2	0.6
METH–Un Methodist	5	383	686	903	2.9	8.0
Non-denom Chr Chs	3	431	405	538	1.7	4.8
ORTHE–Orth Ch in Amer	1	80	NR	96	0.3	0.9
PENT–Assemb of God	4	730	245	886	2.9	7.9
PENT–Pent Ch of God	1	70	NR	109	0.4	1.0
PENT–Vineyard	1	22	20	24	0.1	0.2
PRES–Presb Ch (USA)	2	145	187	224	0.7	2.0
Sev Day Adv	3	128	224	257	0.8	2.3
DENVER	**439**	**56,912**	**82,542**	**304,759**	**50.8**	**100.0**
ANG/EPIS–Anglican NA	2	NR	NR	NR	-	-
ANG/EPIS–Episcopal	14	2,426	4,977	6,399	1.1	2.1
Bahá'í	1	NR	456	456	0.1	0.1
BAPT–Amer Bapt USA	19	5,507	10,257	12,445	2.1	4.1
BAPT–Consrv Bapt	5	NR	NR	NR	-	-
BAPT–Converge/BGC	3	225	NR	270	0.0	0.1
BAPT–Natl Mis Bapt Conv	3	150	450	546	0.1	0.2
BAPT–NBC Amer	1	0	200	243	0.0	0.1
BAPT–NBC USA	4	1,800	3,400	4,125	0.7	1.4
BAPT–NT Ind Bapt	3	NR	NR	NR	-	-
BAPT–Ref Bapt Ch	1	NR	NR	NR	-	-
BAPT–So Bapt Conv	30	3,209	4,512	5,474	0.9	1.8
BRETH–Ch of Brethren	1	0	0	0	0.0	0.0
BUDD–Mahayana	11	NR	NR	10,517	1.8	3.5
BUDD–Theravada	1	NR	NR	396	0.1	0.1
BUDD–Vajrayana	3	NR	NR	541	0.1	0.2
Calv Chpl	1	NR	NR	NR	-	-
Catholic	38	NR	NR	159,489	26.6	52.3
CGOD–Ch God (Ander)	2	145	NR	145	0.0	0.0
Ch Cr, Scientst	4	NR	NR	NR	-	-
Ch of Nazarene	5	1,711	2,410	2,642	0.4	0.9
CHR–Chr Ch (Disc)	6	754	1,461	1,773	0.3	0.6
CHR–Chr Chs & Chs Cr	4	NR	695	843	0.1	0.3
CHR–Chs of Christ	7	1,165	1,321	1,692	0.3	0.6
Evan Cov Ch	1	44	0	57	0.0	0.0
Evan Free Ch	7	1,420	NR	1,420	0.2	0.5
FRND–Evan Fr Ch Intl	1	192	361	438	0.1	0.1
FRND–Fr Gen Cf	1	NR	173	210	0.0	0.1
Grace Gosp Fel	3	NR	NR	NR	-	-
HINDU–Post Ren	3	NR	NR	95	0.0	0.0
HINDU–Renaiss	1	NR	NR	12	0.0	0.0
Ind Fund Churches	1	NR	NR	NR	-	-
Jehovah's Witness	4	NR	NR	NR	-	-
JUD–Conserv	2	1,069	1,200	3,240	0.5	1.1
JUD–Orth	7	1,065	650	1,500	0.2	0.5
JUD–Reconst	1	244	311	840	0.1	0.3
JUD–Reform	3	1,836	3,238	8,743	1.5	2.9
LDS–Comm of Christ	1	NR	128	128	0.0	0.0
LDS–L-D Saints	13	NR	NR	10,092	1.7	3.3
LUTH–E.L.C.A.	12	826	1,653	2,155	0.4	0.7
LUTH–Luth–MO Synod	10	1,055	1,651	1,938	0.3	0.6
LUTH–Nor Amer Luth C	1	NR	NR	NR	-	-
LUTH–Wisc Ev Luth Syn	2	275	481	621	0.1	0.2
MENN–Menn Br US Conf	1	NR	38	46	0.0	0.0
MENN–Mennonite USA	1	215	325	394	0.1	0.1
METH–AME	4	870	1,366	1,657	0.3	0.5
METH–AME Zion	2	0	200	243	0.0	0.1
METH–C.M.E.	2	260	760	922	0.2	0.3
METH–Un Methodist	20	2,561	5,735	7,357	1.2	2.4
METH–Wesleyan	1	53	53	69	0.0	0.0
Metro Comm Ch	1	244	293	355	0.1	0.1
Muslim Est	4	1,452	NR	2,924	0.5	1.0
Non-denom Chr Chs	50	15,947	19,453	20,807	3.5	6.8
OCATH–Pol Natl Cath	1	NR	NR	NR	-	-
ORTHE–Ant Orth of NA	2	170	NR	290	0.0	0.1
ORTHE–Greek Orthodox	2	600	NR	4,000	0.7	1.3
ORTHE–Orth Ch in Amer	2	300	NR	350	0.1	0.1
ORTHE–Rus Orth Abroad	1	130	NR	600	0.1	0.2
ORTHO–Eritrean Orth	1	75	NR	500	0.1	0.2
ORTHO–Ethiopian Orth	3	NR	NR	NR	-	-
ORTHO–Malan Syr Orth	1	50	NR	90	0.0	0.0
PENT–Assemb of God	9	1,187	681	1,656	0.3	0.5
PENT–Ch God (Cleve)	1	20	10	12	0.0	0.0
PENT–Ch of God Proph	1	NR	20	24	0.0	0.0
PENT–COGIC	7	100	595	722	0.1	0.2
PENT–Int Foursq Gos	2	88	88	107	0.0	0.0
PENT–Intl Pent Holiness	6	463	477	579	0.1	0.2
PENT–Pent Ch of God	2	140	NR	217	0.0	0.1
PENT–Un Pent Ch Intl	5	NR	NR	NR	-	-
PENT–Vineyard	1	16	20	24	0.0	0.0
Pillar of Fire	1	NR	75	75	0.0	0.0
PRES–Evan Presby Ch	1	NR	84	102	0.0	0.0
PRES–Orth Pres Ch	2	100	93	132	0.0	0.0
PRES–Presb Ch (USA)	14	1,975	4,522	5,487	0.9	1.8
PRES–Presb Ch Amer	3	0	0	0	0.0	0.0
REF–Christian Ref	5	782	981	1,190	0.2	0.4
REF–Hung Ref Add'l	1	NR	NR	NR	-	-
REF–Ref Ch in Am	4	289	463	505	0.1	0.2
Salvation Army	3	221	313	6,817	1.1	2.2
Sev Day Adv	13	2,244	3,901	4,487	0.7	1.5
Tao	1	NR	NR	NR	-	-
Un C of Christ	9	521	1,102	1,337	0.2	0.4
Unit Univ	2	721	909	1,197	0.2	0.4
Unity Ch	3	NR	NR	NR	-	-
Zoroastrian	1	NR	NR	NR	-	-
DOLORES	**7**	**101**	**217**	**341**	**16.5**	**100.0**
Bahá'í	0	NR	1	1	0.0	0.3
BAPT–So Bapt Conv	2	65	131	158	7.7	46.3
BUDD–Vajrayana	1	NR	NR	20	1.0	5.9
Catholic	2	NR	NR	73	3.5	21.4
METH–Un Methodist	1	20	57	57	2.8	16.7
Sev Day Adv	1	16	28	32	1.6	9.4
DOUGLAS	**136**	**29,301**	**45,702**	**100,018**	**35.0**	**100.0**
ANG/EPIS–Anglican NA	1	NR	NR	NR	-	-
ANG/EPIS–Episcopal	3	369	987	1,045	0.4	1.0
Bahá'í	4	NR	170	170	0.1	0.2
BAPT–Consrv Bapt	1	NR	NR	NR	-	-
BAPT–Converge/BGC	1	75	NR	90	0.0	0.1
BAPT–Ref Bapt Ch	1	NR	NR	NR	-	-
BAPT–So Bapt Conv	14	910	1,542	2,031	0.7	2.0
BUDD–Mahayana	1	NR	NR	300	0.1	0.3
Calv Chpl	3	NR	NR	NR	-	-
Catholic	4	NR	NR	22,360	7.8	22.4
Ch of Nazarene	3	166	64	350	0.1	0.3
CHR–Chr Chs & Chs Cr	4	NR	5,450	7,178	2.5	7.2
CHR–Chs of Christ	3	370	373	428	0.1	0.4
Evan Cov Ch	1	151	96	196	0.1	0.2
Evan Free Ch	2	540	NR	540	0.2	0.5
JUD–Orth	1	43	50	60	0.0	0.1
LDS–L-D Saints	28	NR	NR	13,111	4.6	13.1
LUTH–Ch of Luth Br	1	125	65	105	0.0	0.1
LUTH–E.L.C.A.	2	838	1,607	2,312	0.8	2.3
LUTH–Luth Cong Msn Chr	2	273	729	960	0.3	1.0
LUTH–Luth–MO Synod	5	811	1,155	1,508	0.5	1.5
LUTH–Wisc Ev Luth Syn	1	141	187	249	0.1	0.2
MENN–Menn Br US Conf	1	NR	45	59	0.0	0.1
METH–Free Methodist	1	593	595	595	0.2	0.6
METH–Un Methodist	4	2,606	4,865	8,499	3.0	8.5
Non-denom Chr Chs	23	18,148	18,145	24,002	8.4	24.0
PENT–Assemb of God	5	1,279	191	1,588	0.6	1.6
PENT–Int Foursq Gos	2	542	626	824	0.3	0.8
PENT–Un Pent Ch Intl	1	NR	NR	NR	-	-
PRES–Evan Presby Ch	3	NR	6,761	8,904	3.1	8.9

NR–Not Reported - Represents no adherents reported. Percentages may not total 100 due to rounding.

Table 3: Religious Congregations by County and Group: 2010

Religious Group	Number of Congrega-tions	Number of Attendees	Number of Communicant, Confirmed, or Full Members	Adherents		
				Number of Adherents	% of Total Pop.	% of Total Adh.
PRES–Orth Pres Ch	1	285	224	269	0.1	0.3
PRES–Presb Ch (USA)	2	590	928	1,222	0.4	1.2
PRES–Presb Ch Amer	2	75	50	66	0.0	0.1
REF–Christian Ref	2	100	353	465	0.2	0.5
Sev Day Adv	2	210	365	420	0.1	0.4
Un C of Christ	1	61	79	104	0.0	0.1
Zoroastrian	0	NR	NR	8	0.0	0.0
EAGLE	**36**	**1,943**	**2,368**	**16,081**	**30.8**	**100.0**
ANG/EPIS–Anglican NA	1	NR	NR	NR	-	-
ANG/EPIS–Episcopal	1	185	250	322	0.6	2.0
Bahá'í	0	NR	4	4	0.0	0.0
BAPT–So Bapt Conv	4	195	302	377	0.7	2.3
Calv Chpl	2	NR	NR	NR	-	-
Catholic	6	NR	NR	11,373	21.8	70.7
Chr & Miss Al	1	22	0	46	0.1	0.3
Jehovah's Witness	2	NR	NR	NR	-	-
JUD–Orth	1	43	50	60	0.1	0.4
LDS–L-D Saints	2	NR	NR	818	1.6	5.1
LUTH–E.L.C.A.	2	163	119	614	1.2	3.8
LUTH–Luth–MO Synod	1	130	310	386	0.7	2.4
LUTH–Wisc Ev Luth Syn	1	67	116	158	0.3	1.0
METH–Un Methodist	2	152	243	499	1.0	3.1
Non-denom Chr Chs	4	655	725	831	1.6	5.2
PENT–Assemb of God	2	204	12	300	0.6	1.9
PRES–Evan Presby Ch	1	NR	61	76	0.1	0.5
PRES–Presb Ch (USA)	1	115	154	192	0.4	1.2
Sev Day Adv	1	12	22	25	0.0	0.2
Unity Ch	1	NR	NR	NR	-	-
ELBERT	**23**	**999**	**1,493**	**3,467**	**15.0**	**100.0**
ANG/EPIS–Episcopal	1	7	8	8	0.0	0.2
Bahá'í	0	NR	6	6	0.0	0.2
BAPT–Amer Bapt USA	1	12	18	22	0.1	0.6
BAPT–Consrv Bapt	1	NR	NR	NR	-	-
BAPT–So Bapt Conv	3	202	229	280	1.2	8.1
Calv Chpl	1	NR	NR	NR	-	-
Catholic	1	NR	NR	1,022	4.4	29.5
Ch of Nazarene	1	9	14	14	0.1	0.4
Chr & Miss Al	1	240	240	310	1.3	8.9
CHR–Chr Chs & Chs Cr	1	NR	23	28	0.1	0.8
CONG–Consrv Cong Chr	1	14	12	15	0.1	0.4
LDS–L-D Saints	2	NR	NR	738	3.2	21.3
LUTH–E.L.C.A.	1	47	58	64	0.3	1.8
LUTH–Luth–MO Synod	1	45	46	70	0.3	2.0
METH–Un Methodist	1	16	22	25	0.1	0.7
Non-denom Chr Chs	3	380	600	600	2.6	17.3
PRES–Presb Ch (USA)	3	27	217	265	1.1	7.6
EL PASO	**426**	**72,417**	**104,996**	**207,699**	**33.4**	**100.0**
ANG/EPIS–Anglican NA	4	NR	NR	NR	-	-
ANG/EPIS–Episcopal	7	989	1,933	2,536	0.4	1.2
Bahá'í	2	NR	359	359	0.1	0.2
BAPT–Amer Bapt Assn	2	NR	170	213	0.0	0.1
BAPT–Amer Bapt USA	5	1,106	1,561	1,959	0.3	0.9
BAPT–Consrv Bapt	1	NR	NR	NR	-	-
BAPT–Converge/BGC	2	150	NR	180	0.0	0.1
BAPT–Free Will Bapt	1	NR	10	13	0.0	0.0
BAPT–NBC Amer	1	200	275	345	0.1	0.2
BAPT–NBC USA	3	550	985	1,236	0.2	0.6
BAPT–Reg Bapt Gen As	1	NR	NR	NR	-	-
BAPT–S-D Baptist Gen Con	1	30	45	56	0.0	0.0
BAPT–So Bapt Conv	48	6,934	12,918	16,213	2.6	7.8
BRETH–Breth in Chr	1	NR	NR	NR	-	-
BRETH–Grace Breth	1	NR	NR	NR	-	-
BUDD–Mahayana	3	NR	NR	1,859	0.3	0.9
Calv Chpl	4	NR	NR	NR	-	-
Catholic	23	NR	NR	52,310	8.4	25.2
CGOD–Ch God (Ander)	1	148	NR	148	0.0	0.1
Ch Cr, Scientst	1	NR	NR	NR	-	-
Ch God (7th Day)	1	NR	NR	NR	-	-
Ch of Chr (Hol)	1	NR	NR	NR	-	-
Ch of Nazarene	16	1,970	2,238	2,751	0.4	1.3
Chr & Miss Al	5	930	618	1,365	0.2	0.7
CHR–Chr Ch (Disc)	2	251	369	463	0.1	0.2
CHR–Chr Chs & Chs Cr	8	NR	3,030	3,803	0.6	1.8
CHR–Chs of Christ	12	1,895	1,852	2,223	0.4	1.1
CHR–Int Chs of Christ	1	NR	124	156	0.0	0.1
Christian Brethren	1	NR	NR	NR	-	-
Evan Cov Ch	4	476	557	618	0.1	0.3
Evan Free Ch	6	1,439	NR	1,439	0.2	0.7
FRND–Evan Fr Ch Intl	1	88	104	131	0.0	0.1
FRND–Fr Gen Cf	1	NR	24	30	0.0	0.0
HINDU–Post Ren	2	NR	NR	102	0.0	0.0
Ind Fund Churches	5	NR	NR	NR	-	-
Jehovah's Witness	10	NR	NR	NR	-	-
JUD–Conserv	0	106	119	321	0.1	0.2
JUD–Reform	2	124	219	591	0.1	0.3
LDS–Comm of Christ	1	NR	128	128	0.0	0.1
LDS–L-D Saints	36	NR	NR	18,602	3.0	9.0
LUTH–E.L.C.A.	10	2,029	4,700	6,040	1.0	2.9
LUTH–Luth Cong Msn Chr	2	567	1,250	1,569	0.3	0.8
LUTH–Luth–MO Synod	8	1,663	3,082	4,058	0.7	2.0
LUTH–Nor Amer Luth C	2	NR	NR	NR	-	-
LUTH–Wisc Ev Luth Syn	2	233	418	564	0.1	0.3
MENN–CG in Cr (Menn)	1	NR	10	13	0.0	0.0
MENN–Mennonite USA	3	278	344	432	0.1	0.2
METH–AME	1	300	375	471	0.1	0.2
METH–Free Methodist	1	95	90	95	0.0	0.0
METH–Un Methodist	18	4,178	8,085	12,181	2.0	5.9
METH–Wesleyan	4	443	322	575	0.1	0.3
Metro Comm Ch	1	72	103	129	0.0	0.1
Muslim Est	1	100	NR	300	0.0	0.1
New Apost Ch	1	NR	NR	NR	-	-
Non-denom Chr Chs	57	34,245	43,250	46,932	7.5	22.6
ORTHE–Greek Orthodox	1	60	NR	500	0.1	0.2
ORTHE–Orth Ch in Amer	2	215	NR	322	0.1	0.2
ORTHE–Serb Orth USA	1	30	NR	125	0.0	0.1
PENT–Assemb of God	17	3,543	1,588	4,927	0.8	2.4
PENT–Ch God (Cleve)	7	194	192	241	0.0	0.1
PENT–Ch of God Proph	1	NR	27	34	0.0	0.0
PENT–COGIC	6	428	505	634	0.1	0.3
PENT–Int Foursq Gos	3	454	411	516	0.1	0.2
PENT–Intl Pent Holiness	3	137	125	157	0.0	0.1
PENT–Open Bible Std	2	10	NR	10	0.0	0.0
PENT–Pent Ch of God	2	140	NR	217	0.0	0.1
PENT–Un Pent Ch Intl	4	NR	NR	NR	-	-
PENT–Vineyard	1	156	140	176	0.0	0.1
PRES–Korean Amer Pres	1	NR	NR	NR	-	-
PRES–Korean Pres Amer	1	NR	NR	NR	-	-
PRES–Orth Pres Ch	1	28	29	35	0.0	0.0
PRES–Presb Ch (USA)	7	803	5,138	6,448	1.0	3.1
PRES–Presb Ch Amer	5	1,818	1,966	2,589	0.4	1.2
PRES–Ref Pres of NA	1	145	111	167	0.0	0.1
REF–Christian Ref	1	140	222	279	0.0	0.1
REF–Ref Ch in Am	2	507	691	937	0.2	0.5
REF–Ref Ch in U.S.	1	NR	45	68	0.0	0.0
Salvation Army	2	203	362	1,133	0.2	0.5
Sev Day Adv	5	594	1,033	1,188	0.2	0.6
Un C of Christ	7	954	2,370	2,974	0.5	1.4
Unit Univ	2	269	374	509	0.1	0.2
Unity Ch	1	NR	NR	NR	-	-
Zoroastrian	0	NR	NR	4	0.0	0.0
FREMONT	**53**	**4,607**	**6,456**	**19,097**	**40.8**	**100.0**
ANG/EPIS–Episcopal	1	76	148	275	0.6	1.4
Bahá'í	0	NR	31	31	0.1	0.2
BAPT–Amer Bapt USA	2	84	329	379	0.8	2.0
BAPT–So Bapt Conv	7	369	1,297	1,494	3.2	7.8
Calv Chpl	1	NR	NR	NR	-	-
Catholic	3	NR	NR	9,031	19.3	47.3
Ch Cr, Scientst	1	NR	NR	NR	-	-
Ch of Nazarene	3	128	196	223	0.5	1.2
CHR–Chr Ch (Disc)	1	147	386	445	1.0	2.3
CHR–Chr Chs & Chs Cr	2	NR	260	299	0.6	1.6
CHR–Chs of Christ	3	120	136	160	0.3	0.8
Evan Free Ch	1	542	NR	542	1.2	2.8

NR–Not Reported - Represents no adherents reported. Percentages may not total 100 due to rounding.

Table 3: Religious Congregations by County and Group: 2010

Religious Group	Number of Congrega-tions	Number of Attendees	Number of Communicant, Confirmed, or Full Members	Adherents		
				Number of Adherents	% of Total Pop.	% of Total Adh.
FRND–Evan Fr Ch Intl	1	100	38	44	0.1	0.2
HINDU–Post Ren	1	NR	NR	77	0.2	0.4
Jehovah's Witness	1	NR	NR	NR	-	-
LDS–L-D Saints	2	NR	NR	1,434	3.1	7.5
LUTH–E.L.C.A.	1	157	238	361	0.8	1.9
LUTH–Luth–MO Synod	1	78	107	120	0.3	0.6
METH–Free Methodist	1	43	36	43	0.1	0.2
METH–Un Methodist	2	275	388	417	0.9	2.2
METH–Wesleyan	1	104	74	135	0.3	0.7
Non-denom Chr Chs	7	640	540	806	1.7	4.2
PENT–Assemb of God	2	136	79	278	0.6	1.5
PENT–Int Foursq Gos	1	51	43	50	0.1	0.3
PENT–Intl Pent Holiness	1	37	33	38	0.1	0.2
PENT–Un Pent Ch Intl	1	NR	NR	NR	-	-
PENT–Vineyard	1	1,166	1,600	1,843	3.9	9.7
PRES–Presb Ch (USA)	2	197	224	258	0.6	1.4
Sev Day Adv	2	157	273	314	0.7	1.6
GARFIELD	**70**	**4,147**	**4,865**	**15,502**	**27.5**	**100.0**
ANG/EPIS–Episcopal	3	95	238	255	0.5	1.6
Bahá'í	0	NR	31	31	0.1	0.2
BAPT–Amer Bapt USA	1	250	175	223	0.4	1.4
BAPT–Converge/BGC	2	475	NR	570	1.0	3.7
BAPT–NT Ind Bapt	2	NR	NR	NR	-	-
BAPT–So Bapt Conv	6	436	516	657	1.2	4.2
Calv Chpl	1	NR	NR	NR	-	-
Catholic	6	NR	NR	6,368	11.3	41.1
Ch Cr, Scientst	1	NR	NR	NR	-	-
CHR–Chr Chs & Chs Cr	2	NR	250	319	0.6	2.1
CHR–Chs of Christ	3	270	235	355	0.6	2.3
FRND–Fr Gen Cf	1	NR	0	0	0.0	0.0
HINDU–Renaiss	1	NR	NR	12	0.0	0.1
Ind Fund Churches	1	NR	NR	NR	-	-
Jehovah's Witness	3	NR	NR	NR	-	-
LDS–Comm of Christ	1	NR	128	128	0.2	0.8
LDS–L-D Saints	5	NR	NR	2,085	3.7	13.4
LUTH–E.L.C.A.	1	96	293	410	0.7	2.6
LUTH–Luth–MO Synod	2	158	345	429	0.8	2.8
LUTH–Wisc Ev Luth Syn	1	33	27	41	0.1	0.3
MENN–Mennonite USA	1	36	30	38	0.1	0.2
METH–Un Methodist	4	256	422	669	1.2	4.3
Non-denom Chr Chs	7	1,185	1,275	1,480	2.6	9.5
PENT–Assemb of God	7	492	209	600	1.1	3.9
PENT–Ch of God Proph	1	NR	15	19	0.0	0.1
PENT–Int Foursq Gos	1	85	145	185	0.3	1.2
PRES–Presb Ch (USA)	1	42	113	144	0.3	0.9
Sev Day Adv	3	208	361	415	0.7	2.7
Un C of Christ	1	0	25	32	0.1	0.2
Unit Univ	1	30	32	37	0.1	0.2
GILPIN	**3**	**65**	**119**	**285**	**5.2**	**100.0**
ANG/EPIS–Episcopal	1	14	14	14	0.3	4.9
Bahá'í	0	NR	2	2	0.0	0.7
Catholic	1	NR	NR	126	2.3	44.2
METH–Un Methodist	1	51	103	143	2.6	50.2
GRAND	**24**	**1,062**	**1,660**	**3,717**	**25.0**	**100.0**
ANG/EPIS–Episcopal	2	69	154	158	1.1	4.3
Bahá'í	0	NR	4	4	0.0	0.1
BAPT–So Bapt Conv	5	289	582	693	4.7	18.6
Catholic	5	NR	NR	1,544	10.4	41.5
Ch of Nazarene	1	17	20	20	0.1	0.5
CHR–Chs of Christ	2	47	33	43	0.3	1.2
Jehovah's Witness	1	NR	NR	NR	-	-
LDS–L-D Saints	1	NR	NR	253	1.7	6.8
LUTH–E.L.C.A.	1	96	224	224	1.5	6.0
Non-denom Chr Chs	3	215	255	274	1.8	7.4
PENT–Assemb of God	1	67	21	67	0.5	1.8
PRES–Presb Ch (USA)	2	262	367	437	2.9	11.8
GUNNISON	**21**	**931**	**1,306**	**6,095**	**39.8**	**100.0**
ANG/EPIS–Episcopal	2	54	145	162	1.1	2.7
Bahá'í	0	NR	7	7	0.0	0.1
BAPT–Converge/BGC	1	75	NR	90	0.6	1.5
BAPT–NT Ind Bapt	1	NR	NR	NR	-	-
BAPT–So Bapt Conv	3	337	543	634	4.1	10.4
BUDD–Mahayana	1	NR	NR	11	0.1	0.2
Calv Chpl	1	NR	NR	NR	-	-
Catholic	2	NR	NR	4,157	27.1	68.2
CHR–Chs of Christ	1	100	75	95	0.6	1.6
Jehovah's Witness	1	NR	NR	NR	-	-
LDS–L-D Saints	1	NR	NR	308	2.0	5.1
LUTH–Luth–MO Synod	1	44	66	76	0.5	1.2
Non-denom Chr Chs	2	120	130	155	1.0	2.5
PENT–Assemb of God	1	30	23	31	0.2	0.5
Sev Day Adv	1	20	35	40	0.3	0.7
Un C of Christ	2	151	282	329	2.1	5.4
HINSDALE	**4**	**172**	**188**	**280**	**33.2**	**100.0**
ANG/EPIS–Episcopal	1	42	57	65	7.7	23.2
BAPT–So Bapt Conv	1	60	68	82	9.7	29.3
Catholic	1	NR	NR	57	6.8	20.4
PRES–Presb Ch (USA)	1	70	63	76	9.0	27.1
HUERFANO	**16**	**410**	**721**	**4,499**	**67.0**	**100.0**
ANG/EPIS–Episcopal	1	26	75	75	1.1	1.7
Bahá'í	0	NR	9	9	0.1	0.2
BAPT–Amer Bapt USA	1	57	18	21	0.3	0.5
BAPT–So Bapt Conv	2	57	258	296	4.4	6.6
BUDD–Vajrayana	1	NR	NR	52	0.8	1.2
Catholic	4	NR	NR	3,508	52.3	78.0
CHR–Chs of Christ	1	40	33	46	0.7	1.0
Jehovah's Witness	1	NR	NR	NR	-	-
LUTH–Luth–MO Synod	1	12	19	29	0.4	0.6
METH–Un Methodist	2	83	147	278	4.1	6.2
Non-denom Chr Chs	1	100	150	150	2.2	3.3
PENT–Assemb of God	1	35	12	35	0.5	0.8
JACKSON	**7**	**122**	**235**	**346**	**24.8**	**100.0**
BAPT–NT Ind Bapt	1	NR	NR	NR	-	-
BAPT–So Bapt Conv	1	30	40	47	3.4	13.6
Catholic	1	NR	NR	85	6.1	24.6
CHR–Chs of Christ	1	25	20	28	2.0	8.1
METH–Un Methodist	1	20	123	124	8.9	35.8
Non-denom Chr Chs	2	47	52	62	4.4	17.9
JEFFERSON	**335**	**53,456**	**74,307**	**190,765**	**35.7**	**100.0**
ANG/EPIS–Anglican NA	2	NR	NR	NR	-	-
ANG/EPIS–Episcopal	9	1,158	2,451	2,749	0.5	1.4
Bahá'í	3	NR	181	181	0.0	0.1
BAPT–Amer Bapt Assn	1	NR	26	31	0.0	0.0
BAPT–Amer Bapt USA	2	65	76	91	0.0	0.0
BAPT–Consrv Bapt	9	NR	NR	NR	-	-
BAPT–Converge/BGC	9	1,400	NR	1,680	0.3	0.9
BAPT–NT Ind Bapt	3	NR	NR	NR	-	-
BAPT–Ref Bapt Ch	1	NR	NR	NR	-	-
BAPT–Reg Bapt Gen As	1	NR	NR	NR	-	-
BAPT–So Bapt Conv	25	5,512	5,460	6,571	1.2	3.4
BRETH–Ch of Brethren	1	0	14	17	0.0	0.0
BUDD–Mahayana	6	NR	NR	1,636	0.3	0.9
BUDD–Theravada	1	NR	NR	300	0.1	0.2
Calv Chpl	2	NR	NR	NR	-	-
Catholic	17	NR	NR	80,219	15.0	42.1
CGOD–Ch God (Ander)	2	130	NR	130	0.0	0.1
Ch Cr, Scientst	3	NR	NR	NR	-	-
Ch of Nazarene	5	519	859	944	0.2	0.5
Chr & Miss Al	1	108	24	150	0.0	0.1
CHR–Chr Ch (Disc)	4	151	438	527	0.1	0.3
CHR–Chr Chs & Chs Cr	5	NR	552	664	0.1	0.3
CHR–Chs of Christ	9	1,168	1,072	1,522	0.3	0.8
CHR–Int Chs of Christ	1	NR	322	388	0.1	0.2
Evan Cov Ch	5	2,072	1,679	2,693	0.5	1.4
Evan Free Ch	6	1,180	NR	1,180	0.2	0.6
FRND–Evan Fr Ch Intl	1	129	158	190	0.0	0.1

NR–Not Reported - Represents no adherents reported. Percentages may not total 100 due to rounding.

Table 3: Religious Congregations by County and Group: 2010

Religious Group	Number of Congrega-tions	Number of Attendees	Number of Communicant, Confirmed, or Full Members	Adherents		
				Number of Adherents	% of Total Pop.	% of Total Adh.
Grace Gosp Fel	3	NR	NR	NR	-	-
HINDU–Post Ren	1	NR	NR	77	0.0	0.0
HINDU–Trad Temples	1	NR	NR	2,000	0.4	1.0
Ind Fund Churches	2	NR	NR	NR	-	-
Jain	1	NR	NR	NR	-	-
Jehovah's Witness	9	NR	NR	NR	-	-
JUD–Orth	1	43	50	60	0.0	0.0
JUD–Reconst	1	122	156	421	0.1	0.2
JUD–Reform	1	69	121	327	0.1	0.2
LDS–Comm of Christ	1	NR	128	128	0.0	0.1
LDS–L-D Saints	22	NR	NR	11,175	2.1	5.9
LUTH–Ch Luth Conf	1	NR	NR	NR	-	-
LUTH–Ch of Luth Br	1	52	47	98	0.0	0.1
LUTH–E.L.C.A.	14	3,212	7,242	9,048	1.7	4.7
LUTH–Luth Cong Msn Chr	2	141	643	774	0.1	0.4
LUTH–Luth–MO Synod	11	2,538	4,475	6,076	1.1	3.2
LUTH–Wisc Ev Luth Syn	2	268	397	562	0.1	0.3
MENN–Menn Br US Conf	1	NR	152	183	0.0	0.1
MENN–Mennonite USA	2	90	115	138	0.0	0.1
METH–Free Methodist	1	315	130	315	0.1	0.2
METH–Un Methodist	12	1,853	4,153	5,756	1.1	3.0
Muslim Est	2	194	NR	558	0.1	0.3
Nat Spirit Asso	1	NR	NR	NR	-	-
New Apost Ch	2	NR	NR	NR	-	-
Non-denom Chr Chs	44	22,608	32,841	34,140	6.4	17.9
ORTHE–Ant Orth of NA	1	275	NR	400	0.1	0.2
ORTHE–Serb Orth USA	1	30	NR	640	0.1	0.3
ORTHO–Malan Dioc Am	1	10	NR	30	0.0	0.0
PENT–Assemb of God	9	2,993	987	4,501	0.8	2.4
PENT–Ch God (Cleve)	3	196	792	953	0.2	0.5
PENT–Ch of God Proph	1	NR	55	66	0.0	0.0
PENT–Int Foursq Gos	5	305	257	309	0.1	0.2
PENT–Un Pent Ch Intl	3	NR	NR	NR	-	-
PENT–Vineyard	2	725	760	915	0.2	0.5
PRES–Evan Presby Ch	2	NR	719	865	0.2	0.5
PRES–Korean Pres Amer	2	NR	NR	NR	-	-
PRES–Presb Ch (USA)	8	1,130	2,067	2,488	0.5	1.3
PRES–Presb Ch Amer	2	413	318	516	0.1	0.3
REF–Can Amer Ref	1	NR	NR	NR	-	-
REF–Ref Ch in Am	3	331	399	573	0.1	0.3
Sev Day Adv	7	1,112	1,933	2,223	0.4	1.2
Sikh	1	NR	NR	NR	-	-
Tao	1	NR	NR	NR	-	-
Un C of Christ	5	292	1,233	1,484	0.3	0.8
Unit Univ	2	547	825	1,103	0.2	0.6
Unity Ch	2	NR	NR	NR	-	-
KIOWA	**8**	**1,046**	**1,144**	**1,612**	**115.3**	**100.0**
Bahá'í	0	NR	1	1	0.1	0.1
BAPT–So Bapt Conv	1	57	106	127	9.1	7.9
CHR–Chr Chs & Chs Cr	1	NR	60	72	5.2	4.5
FRND–Evan Fr Ch Intl	1	18	18	21	1.5	1.3
METH–Un Methodist	3	66	137	255	18.2	15.8
Non-denom Chr Chs	1	880	800	1,100	78.7	68.2
PENT–Assemb of God	1	25	22	36	2.6	2.2
KIT CARSON	**29**	**1,291**	**2,375**	**4,493**	**54.3**	**100.0**
BAPT–Amer Bapt USA	1	67	198	238	2.9	5.3
BAPT–Consrv Bapt	1	NR	NR	NR	-	-
BAPT–So Bapt Conv	2	88	280	337	4.1	7.5
Catholic	3	NR	NR	1,031	12.5	22.9
CGOD–Ch God (Ander)	1	83	NR	83	1.0	1.8
CHR–Chr Ch (Disc)	1	65	220	265	3.2	5.9
CHR–Chr Chs & Chs Cr	2	NR	50	60	0.7	1.3
CHR–Chs of Christ	2	140	126	166	2.0	3.7
CONG–Consrv Cong Chr	2	122	187	225	2.7	5.0
Evan Free Ch	2	180	NR	180	2.2	4.0
LDS–Comm of Christ	1	NR	128	128	1.5	2.8
LDS–L-D Saints	1	NR	NR	226	2.7	5.0
LUTH–E.L.C.A.	2	134	306	436	5.3	9.7
LUTH–Luth–MO Synod	2	101	373	492	5.9	11.0
METH–Un Methodist	2	85	267	290	3.5	6.5
Non-denom Chr Chs	2	150	200	212	2.6	4.7

Religious Group	Number of Congrega-tions	Number of Attendees	Number of Communicant, Confirmed, or Full Members	Adherents		
				Number of Adherents	% of Total Pop.	% of Total Adh.
PENT–Assemb of God	1	70	30	112	1.4	2.5
Sev Day Adv	1	6	10	12	0.1	0.3
LAKE	**10**	**271**	**233**	**1,184**	**16.2**	**100.0**
ANG/EPIS–Episcopal	1	23	41	52	0.7	4.4
Bahá'í	0	NR	6	6	0.1	0.5
BAPT–NT Ind Bapt	1	NR	NR	NR	-	-
BAPT–So Bapt Conv	1	20	29	36	0.5	3.0
Catholic	1	NR	NR	683	9.3	57.7
Evan Free Ch	1	110	NR	110	1.5	9.3
Jehovah's Witness	1	NR	NR	NR	-	-
LUTH–Luth–MO Synod	1	24	46	63	0.9	5.3
PENT–Assemb of God	1	25	0	100	1.4	8.4
PRES–Presb Ch (USA)	1	39	59	74	1.0	6.3
Sev Day Adv	1	30	52	60	0.8	5.1
LA PLATA	**63**	**3,640**	**5,572**	**20,185**	**39.3**	**100.0**
ANG/EPIS–Anglican NA	1	NR	NR	NR	-	-
ANG/EPIS–Episcopal	1	143	354	354	0.7	1.8
Bahá'í	2	NR	81	81	0.2	0.4
BAPT–Consrv Bapt	1	NR	NR	NR	-	-
BAPT–So Bapt Conv	10	426	599	711	1.4	3.5
Catholic	5	NR	NR	11,484	22.4	56.9
Ch Cr, Scientst	1	NR	NR	NR	-	-
Ch of Nazarene	1	129	167	222	0.4	1.1
CHR–Chr Chs & Chs Cr	2	NR	136	162	0.3	0.8
CHR–Chs of Christ	7	348	266	331	0.6	1.6
Evan Free Ch	1	50	NR	50	0.1	0.2
FRND–Fr Gen Cf	1	NR	34	40	0.1	0.2
Jehovah's Witness	3	NR	NR	NR	-	-
JUD–Reform	1	39	68	184	0.4	0.9
LDS–Comm of Christ	1	NR	128	128	0.2	0.6
LDS–L-D Saints	4	NR	NR	2,126	4.1	10.5
LUTH–E.L.C.A.	1	190	446	507	1.0	2.5
LUTH–Luth–MO Synod	1	0	108	118	0.2	0.6
METH–Un Methodist	2	446	717	756	1.5	3.7
Non-denom Chr Chs	4	535	750	806	1.6	4.0
PENT–Assemb of God	3	140	90	190	0.4	0.9
PENT–Int Foursq Gos	2	729	912	1,083	2.1	5.4
PENT–Un Pent Ch Intl	1	NR	NR	NR	-	-
PRES–Presb Ch (USA)	4	287	436	518	1.0	2.6
PRES–Presb Ch Amer	1	0	0	0	0.0	0.0
Sev Day Adv	1	99	172	198	0.4	1.0
Unit Univ	1	79	108	136	0.3	0.7
LARIMER	**231**	**42,966**	**50,358**	**121,885**	**40.7**	**100.0**
ANG/EPIS–Anglican NA	2	NR	NR	NR	-	-
ANG/EPIS–Episcopal	4	600	1,516	1,656	0.6	1.4
Bahá'í	3	NR	243	243	0.1	0.2
BAPT–Amer Bapt Assn	2	NR	142	170	0.1	0.1
BAPT–Amer Bapt USA	2	170	320	383	0.1	0.3
BAPT–Consrv Bapt	2	NR	NR	NR	-	-
BAPT–Converge/BGC	2	475	NR	570	0.2	0.5
BAPT–Free Will Bapt	1	NR	10	12	0.0	0.0
BAPT–So Bapt Conv	16	994	1,738	2,082	0.7	1.7
BUDD–Mahayana	2	NR	NR	770	0.3	0.6
BUDD–Vajrayana	3	NR	NR	562	0.2	0.5
Calv Chpl	2	NR	NR	NR	-	-
Catholic	7	NR	NR	35,495	11.8	29.1
CGOD–Ch God (Ander)	1	125	NR	125	0.0	0.1
Ch Cr, Scientst	2	NR	NR	NR	-	-
Ch of Nazarene	3	349	336	688	0.2	0.6
CHR–Chr Ch (Disc)	3	459	1,274	1,526	0.5	1.3
CHR–Chr Chs & Chs Cr	4	NR	855	1,024	0.3	0.8
CHR–Chs of Christ	6	691	671	767	0.3	0.6
CHR–Int Chs of Christ	1	NR	63	75	0.0	0.1
Evan Cov Ch	5	4,343	1,464	5,645	1.9	4.6
Evan Free Ch	6	2,490	NR	2,490	0.8	2.0
FRND–Fr Gen Cf	1	NR	51	61	0.0	0.1
HINDU–Post Ren	1	NR	NR	25	0.0	0.0
Jehovah's Witness	7	NR	NR	NR	-	-
JUD–Reform	1	26	45	122	0.0	0.1
LDS–Comm of Christ	2	NR	256	256	0.1	0.2

NR–Not Reported   - Represents no adherents reported.   Percentages may not total 100 due to rounding.

Table 3: Religious Congregations by County and Group: 2010

Religious Group	Number of Congrega-tions	Number of Attendees	Number of Communicant, Confirmed, or Full Members	Adherents		
				Number of Adherents	% of Total Pop.	% of Total Adh.
LDS–L-D Saints	20	NR	NR	8,622	2.9	7.1
LUTH–Assoc Free Luth	1	NR	NR	NR	-	-
LUTH–Ch Luth Conf	1	NR	NR	NR	-	-
LUTH–Ch of Luth Br	1	45	37	138	0.0	0.1
LUTH–E.L.C.A.	8	1,741	3,227	4,698	1.6	3.9
LUTH–Luth Cong Msn Chr	1	NR	NR	NR	-	-
LUTH–Luth–MO Synod	6	2,200	3,538	5,093	1.7	4.2
LUTH–Wisc Ev Luth Syn	2	263	344	433	0.1	0.4
MENN–Mennonite USA	1	50	57	68	0.0	0.1
METH–Un Methodist	7	1,697	3,783	4,933	1.6	4.0
METH–Wesleyan	1	95	46	124	0.0	0.1
Metro Comm Ch	1	30	25	30	0.0	0.0
Missionary Ch	2	645	500	645	0.2	0.5
Muslim Est	1	200	NR	400	0.1	0.3
Non-denom Chr Chs	35	13,116	17,630	19,081	6.4	15.7
ORTHE–Ant Orth of NA	1	75	NR	120	0.0	0.1
ORTHE–Greek Orthodox	1	140	NR	250	0.1	0.2
PENT–Assemb of God	7	5,905	2,361	10,394	3.5	8.5
PENT–Int Foursq Gos	6	326	226	271	0.1	0.2
PENT–Un Pent Ch Intl	4	NR	NR	NR	-	-
PENT–Vineyard	2	1,870	2,900	3,474	1.2	2.9
PRES–Evan Presby Ch	2	NR	588	704	0.2	0.6
PRES–Orth Pres Ch	1	50	43	58	0.0	0.0
PRES–Presb Ch (USA)	10	1,775	2,832	3,392	1.1	2.8
PRES–Presb Ch Amer	3	177	64	85	0.0	0.1
REF–Christian Ref	1	215	184	220	0.1	0.2
REF–Prot Ref Chs	1	243	160	273	0.1	0.2
REF–Un Ref Chs N.A.	1	NR	NR	NR	-	-
Salvation Army	1	31	56	216	0.1	0.2
Sev Day Adv	5	732	1,275	1,465	0.5	1.2
Un C of Christ	2	363	870	1,042	0.3	0.9
Unit Univ	2	260	628	909	0.3	0.7
Unity Ch	2	NR	NR	NR	-	-
LAS ANIMAS	**22**	**771**	**1,339**	**13,829**	**89.2**	**100.0**
Bahá'í	0	NR	8	8	0.1	0.1
BAPT–So Bapt Conv	2	137	496	589	3.8	4.3
Catholic	4	NR	NR	12,196	78.6	88.2
Ch of Nazarene	1	20	43	56	0.4	0.4
CHR–Chs of Christ	2	65	58	90	0.6	0.7
Ind Fund Churches	1	NR	NR	NR	-	-
Jehovah's Witness	1	NR	NR	NR	-	-
JUD–Reform	1	5	9	24	0.2	0.2
LUTH–E.L.C.A.	1	23	86	99	0.6	0.7
METH–Un Methodist	1	43	100	119	0.8	0.9
Non-denom Chr Chs	4	353	455	479	3.1	3.5
PENT–Assemb of God	2	75	4	76	0.5	0.5
PRES–Presb Ch (USA)	1	24	34	40	0.3	0.3
Sev Day Adv	1	26	46	53	0.3	0.4
LINCOLN	**25**	**821**	**1,281**	**2,298**	**42.0**	**100.0**
ANG/EPIS–Episcopal	1	14	21	21	0.4	0.9
BAPT–So Bapt Conv	3	170	182	214	3.9	9.3
BRETH–Ch of Brethren	1	21	25	29	0.5	1.3
Catholic	2	NR	NR	444	8.1	19.3
Ch of Nazarene	1	20	21	21	0.4	0.9
CHR–Chs of Christ	1	70	50	75	1.4	3.3
CONG–Consrv Cong Chr	1	15	20	24	0.4	1.0
Evan Free Ch	1	40	NR	40	0.7	1.7
Jehovah's Witness	1	NR	NR	NR	-	-
LDS–Comm of Christ	1	NR	128	128	2.3	5.6
LDS–L-D Saints	1	NR	NR	82	1.5	3.6
LUTH–E.L.C.A.	1	50	110	118	2.2	5.1
LUTH–Luth–MO Synod	3	58	68	81	1.5	3.5
METH–Un Methodist	4	238	464	801	14.7	34.9
Non-denom Chr Chs	2	125	150	156	2.9	6.8
REF–Ref Ch in U.S.	1	NR	42	64	1.2	2.8
LOGAN	**35**	**2,533**	**3,724**	**8,437**	**37.2**	**100.0**
ANG/EPIS–Episcopal	1	23	66	66	0.3	0.8
Bahá'í	0	NR	1	1	0.0	0.0
BAPT–Amer Bapt USA	1	175	428	505	2.2	6.0
BAPT–So Bapt Conv	2	317	322	380	1.7	4.5

Religious Group	Number of Congrega-tions	Number of Attendees	Number of Communicant, Confirmed, or Full Members	Adherents		
				Number of Adherents	% of Total Pop.	% of Total Adh.
Catholic	3	NR	NR	3,136	13.8	37.2
CGOD–Ch God (Ander)	1	32	NR	32	0.1	0.4
Ch of Nazarene	1	243	287	287	1.3	3.4
CHR–Chr Ch (Disc)	1	80	243	287	1.3	3.4
CHR–Chs of Christ	1	45	40	50	0.2	0.6
Evan Free Ch	1	85	NR	85	0.4	1.0
LDS–L-D Saints	1	NR	NR	554	2.4	6.6
LUTH–E.L.C.A.	1	50	101	125	0.6	1.5
LUTH–Luth–MO Synod	3	279	406	598	2.6	7.1
METH–Un Methodist	7	293	775	1,084	4.8	12.8
Non-denom Chr Chs	3	370	500	500	2.2	5.9
PENT–Assemb of God	3	136	68	174	0.8	2.1
PENT–Int Foursq Gos	1	213	25	29	0.1	0.3
PENT–Un Pent Ch Intl	1	NR	NR	NR	-	-
PRES–Presb Ch (USA)	1	131	301	355	1.6	4.2
Sev Day Adv	1	26	44	51	0.2	0.6
Un C of Christ	1	35	117	138	0.6	1.6
MESA	**148**	**17,721**	**23,526**	**50,728**	**34.6**	**100.0**
ANG/EPIS–Anglican NA	1	NR	NR	NR	-	-
ANG/EPIS–Episcopal	2	302	566	569	0.4	1.1
Bahá'í	2	NR	115	115	0.1	0.2
BAPT–Amer Bapt USA	4	193	411	503	0.3	1.0
BAPT–Consrv Bapt	1	NR	NR	NR	-	-
BAPT–Converge/BGC	1	75	NR	90	0.1	0.2
BAPT–Free Will Bapt	1	NR	10	12	0.0	0.0
BAPT–NT Ind Bapt	1	NR	NR	NR	-	-
BAPT–So Bapt Conv	15	992	1,154	1,412	1.0	2.8
BRETH–Ch of Brethren	1	33	116	142	0.1	0.3
Calv Chpl	1	NR	NR	NR	-	-
Catholic	5	NR	NR	7,939	5.4	15.7
CGOD–Ch God (Ander)	1	32	NR	32	0.0	0.1
Ch Cr, Scientst	1	NR	NR	NR	-	-
Ch of Nazarene	2	283	310	410	0.3	0.8
Chr & Miss Al	1	300	118	475	0.3	0.9
CHR–Chr Ch (Disc)	1	128	253	310	0.2	0.6
CHR–Chr Chs & Chs Cr	6	NR	1,355	1,658	1.1	3.3
CHR–Chs of Christ	4	334	439	512	0.3	1.0
Evan Free Ch	2	215	NR	215	0.1	0.4
FRND–Fr Gen Cf	1	NR	0	0	0.0	0.0
Ind Fund Churches	3	NR	NR	NR	-	-
Jehovah's Witness	4	NR	NR	NR	-	-
JUD–Reform	1	39	69	186	0.1	0.4
LDS–Comm of Christ	1	NR	128	128	0.1	0.3
LDS–L-D Saints	18	NR	NR	10,060	6.9	19.8
LUTH–E.L.C.A.	2	282	649	781	0.5	1.5
LUTH–Luth–MO Synod	1	352	913	1,177	0.8	2.3
LUTH–Wisc Ev Luth Syn	1	60	90	110	0.1	0.2
METH–Un Methodist	6	859	1,900	3,663	2.5	7.2
Non-denom Chr Chs	22	6,610	8,010	9,099	6.2	17.9
ORTHE–Greek Orthodox	1	55	NR	80	0.1	0.2
PENT–Assemb of God	9	1,977	953	3,341	2.3	6.6
PENT–Ch God (Cleve)	1	100	46	56	0.0	0.1
PENT–Ch of God Proph	1	NR	4	5	0.0	0.0
PENT–Int Foursq Gos	3	339	525	642	0.4	1.3
PENT–Intl Pent Holiness	2	124	110	135	0.1	0.3
PENT–Pent Ch of God	1	70	NR	109	0.1	0.2
PENT–Un Pent Ch Intl	1	NR	NR	NR	-	-
PENT–Vineyard	2	2,550	3,450	4,222	2.9	8.3
PRES–Presb Ch (USA)	3	669	757	926	0.6	1.8
REF–Christian Ref	1	145	107	131	0.1	0.3
REF–Comm Ref Evan	1	NR	NR	NR	-	-
Salvation Army	1	44	78	430	0.3	0.8
Sev Day Adv	3	320	555	639	0.4	1.3
Sikh	1	NR	NR	NR	-	-
Un C of Christ	2	168	253	310	0.2	0.6
Unit Univ	1	71	82	104	0.1	0.2
Unity Ch	1	NR	NR	NR	-	-
MINERAL	**5**	**116**	**465**	**567**	**79.6**	**100.0**
ANG/EPIS–Episcopal	1	10	9	9	1.3	1.6
BAPT–So Bapt Conv	1	26	350	390	54.8	68.8
Catholic	1	NR	NR	40	5.6	7.1

NR–Not Reported — - Represents no adherents reported. — Percentages may not total 100 due to rounding.

Table 3: Religious Congregations by County and Group: 2010

Religious Group	Number of Congrega-tions	Number of Attendees	Number of Communicant, Confirmed, or Full Members	Adherents: Number of Adherents	Adherents: % of Total Pop.	Adherents: % of Total Adh.
CHR–Chs of Christ	1	35	19	31	4.4	5.5
Un C of Christ	1	45	87	97	13.6	17.1
MOFFAT	**23**	**668**	**1,300**	**4,428**	**32.1**	**100.0**
ANG/EPIS–Episcopal	1	13	14	17	0.1	0.4
BAPT–Converge/BGC	1	75	NR	90	0.7	2.0
BAPT–So Bapt Conv	2	122	424	541	3.9	12.2
Catholic	1	NR	NR	1,138	8.2	25.7
CHR–Chr Chs & Chs Cr	1	NR	250	319	2.3	7.2
CHR–Chs of Christ	1	80	86	123	0.9	2.8
Jehovah's Witness	1	NR	NR	NR	-	-
LDS–L-D Saints	3	NR	NR	1,339	9.7	30.2
LUTH–E.L.C.A.	1	8	33	33	0.2	0.7
LUTH–Luth–MO Synod	1	48	94	110	0.8	2.5
METH–Un Methodist	1	21	40	67	0.5	1.5
Non-denom Chr Chs	2	170	150	213	1.5	4.8
ORTHE–Greek Orthodox	1	30	NR	150	1.1	3.4
PENT–Assemb of God	1	27	13	42	0.3	0.9
PENT–Ch God (Cleve)	1	30	129	164	1.2	3.7
PENT–Un Pent Ch Intl	1	NR	NR	NR	-	-
Sev Day Adv	1	18	32	37	0.3	0.8
Un C of Christ	2	26	35	45	0.3	1.0
MONTEZUMA	**47**	**2,749**	**3,373**	**8,018**	**31.4**	**100.0**
ANG/EPIS–Anglican NA	1	NR	NR	NR	-	-
ANG/EPIS–Episcopal	2	44	154	187	0.7	2.3
Bahá'í	0	NR	26	26	0.1	0.3
BAPT–Amer Bapt USA	1	52	41	50	0.2	0.6
BAPT–Consrv Bapt	1	NR	NR	NR	-	-
BAPT–Ind Bapt Flwsp Intl	1	NR	NR	NR	-	-
BAPT–So Bapt Conv	6	490	684	835	3.3	10.4
BUDD–Mahayana	1	NR	NR	28	0.1	0.3
Calv Chpl	1	NR	NR	NR	-	-
Catholic	3	NR	NR	1,288	5.0	16.1
Ch of Nazarene	1	84	100	107	0.4	1.3
CHR–Chr Chs & Chs Cr	1	NR	40	49	0.2	0.6
CHR–Chs of Christ	3	160	168	200	0.8	2.5
Evan Free Ch	1	100	NR	100	0.4	1.2
FRND–Fr Gen Cf	1	NR	0	0	0.0	0.0
Jehovah's Witness	2	NR	NR	NR	-	-
LDS–L-D Saints	5	NR	NR	2,277	8.9	28.4
LUTH–Luth–MO Synod	1	100	156	173	0.7	2.2
METH–Un Methodist	3	224	525	708	2.8	8.8
Non-denom Chr Chs	5	805	855	1,006	3.9	12.5
PENT–Assemb of God	2	415	145	415	1.6	5.2
PENT–Int Foursq Gos	2	86	160	195	0.8	2.4
PENT–Un Pent Ch Intl	1	NR	NR	NR	-	-
PRES–Presb Ch (USA)	1	62	98	120	0.5	1.5
Sev Day Adv	1	127	221	254	1.0	3.2
MONTROSE	**59**	**3,672**	**3,871**	**11,248**	**27.3**	**100.0**
ANG/EPIS–Anglican NA	2	NR	NR	NR	-	-
ANG/EPIS–Episcopal	1	21	31	32	0.1	0.3
Bahá'í	0	NR	26	26	0.1	0.2
BAPT–Amer Bapt USA	2	77	96	119	0.3	1.1
BAPT–Consrv Bapt	1	NR	NR	NR	-	-
BAPT–So Bapt Conv	7	240	307	379	0.9	3.4
Calv Chpl	1	NR	NR	NR	-	-
Catholic	3	NR	NR	2,916	7.1	25.9
Ch Cr, Scientst	1	NR	NR	NR	-	-
Ch of Nazarene	1	77	92	127	0.3	1.1
CHR–Chr Chs & Chs Cr	3	NR	717	885	2.1	7.9
CHR–Chs of Christ	1	110	94	131	0.3	1.2
Evan Free Ch	1	210	NR	210	0.5	1.9
Jehovah's Witness	1	NR	NR	NR	-	-
LDS–L-D Saints	6	NR	NR	2,800	6.8	24.9
LUTH–E.L.C.A.	1	105	346	437	1.1	3.9
LUTH–Luth–MO Synod	1	56	97	124	0.3	1.1
LUTH–Wisc Ev Luth Syn	1	53	66	84	0.2	0.7
MENN–CG in Cr (Menn)	1	NR	69	85	0.2	0.8
METH–Un Methodist	2	364	537	777	1.9	6.9
Non-denom Chr Chs	1	100	150	150	0.4	1.3
PENT–Assemb of God	4	417	199	498	1.2	4.4

Religious Group	Number of Congrega-tions	Number of Attendees	Number of Communicant, Confirmed, or Full Members	Adherents: Number of Adherents	Adherents: % of Total Pop.	Adherents: % of Total Adh.
PENT–Ch God (Cleve)	1	56	85	105	0.3	0.9
PENT–Ch of God Proph	1	NR	6	7	0.0	0.1
PENT–Int Foursq Gos	4	1,117	129	159	0.4	1.4
PENT–Pent Ch of God	2	140	NR	217	0.5	1.9
PENT–Un Pent Ch Intl	1	NR	NR	NR	-	-
PRES–Presb Ch (USA)	1	167	197	243	0.6	2.2
PRES–Presb Ch Amer	1	90	109	129	0.3	1.1
Sev Day Adv	4	216	375	431	1.0	3.8
Un C of Christ	2	56	143	177	0.4	1.6
MORGAN	**45**	**2,682**	**4,913**	**14,188**	**50.4**	**100.0**
ANG/EPIS–Episcopal	1	42	84	126	0.4	0.9
Bahá'í	0	NR	19	19	0.1	0.1
BAPT–Amer Bapt USA	1	55	137	175	0.6	1.2
BAPT–Consrv Bapt	1	NR	NR	NR	-	-
BAPT–So Bapt Conv	3	184	440	562	2.0	4.0
Catholic	4	NR	NR	6,871	24.4	48.4
Ch of Nazarene	2	151	216	310	1.1	2.2
CHR–Chr Ch (Disc)	1	77	273	349	1.2	2.5
CHR–Chs of Christ	2	85	65	94	0.3	0.7
CONG–Consrv Cong Chr	3	145	440	562	2.0	4.0
Jehovah's Witness	1	NR	NR	NR	-	-
LDS–Comm of Christ	1	NR	128	128	0.5	0.9
LDS–L-D Saints	1	NR	NR	616	2.2	4.3
LUTH–E.L.C.A.	3	184	510	671	2.4	4.7
LUTH–Luth–MO Synod	1	160	474	634	2.3	4.5
LUTH–Wisc Ev Luth Syn	1	45	74	89	0.3	0.6
METH–Un Methodist	2	219	577	651	2.3	4.6
Non-denom Chr Chs	3	340	335	450	1.6	3.2
PENT–Assemb of God	4	307	204	696	2.5	4.9
PENT–Ch of God Proph	1	NR	18	23	0.1	0.2
PENT–Int Foursq Gos	3	346	190	243	0.9	1.7
PENT–Un Pent Ch Intl	1	NR	NR	NR	-	-
PRES–Presb Ch (USA)	3	182	344	439	1.6	3.1
Sev Day Adv	1	50	88	101	0.4	0.7
Un C of Christ	1	110	297	379	1.3	2.7
OTERO	**53**	**1,952**	**3,001**	**14,989**	**79.6**	**100.0**
ANG/EPIS–Anglican NA	1	NR	NR	NR	-	-
ANG/EPIS–Episcopal	1	27	48	48	0.3	0.3
Bahá'í	0	NR	10	10	0.1	0.1
BAPT–Amer Bapt USA	1	35	69	85	0.5	0.6
BAPT–Consrv Bapt	2	NR	NR	NR	-	-
BAPT–NBC USA	1	3	3	4	0.0	0.0
BAPT–Reg Bapt Gen As	2	NR	NR	NR	-	-
BAPT–So Bapt Conv	6	306	412	508	2.7	3.4
Catholic	3	NR	NR	10,415	55.3	69.5
CGOD–Ch God (Ander)	2	85	NR	85	0.5	0.6
Ch of Nazarene	3	176	166	191	1.0	1.3
CHR–Chr Ch (Disc)	2	70	249	307	1.6	2.0
CHR–Chr Chs & Chs Cr	1	NR	60	74	0.4	0.5
CHR–Chs of Christ	3	166	154	196	1.0	1.3
Jehovah's Witness	2	NR	NR	NR	-	-
LDS–L-D Saints	1	NR	NR	582	3.1	3.9
LUTH–E.L.C.A.	2	65	185	199	1.1	1.3
LUTH–Luth–MO Synod	2	72	109	140	0.7	0.9
MENN–Mennonite USA	3	171	300	370	2.0	2.5
METH–Un Methodist	6	274	704	984	5.2	6.6
Non-denom Chr Chs	2	125	148	158	0.8	1.1
PENT–Assemb of God	3	133	55	200	1.1	1.3
PENT–Open Bible Std	1	33	NR	33	0.2	0.2
PRES–Presb Ch (USA)	2	170	258	318	1.7	2.1
Sev Day Adv	1	41	71	82	0.4	0.5
OURAY	**9**	**261**	**376**	**926**	**20.9**	**100.0**
ANG/EPIS–Episcopal	1	28	85	94	2.1	10.2
Bahá'í	0	NR	1	1	0.0	0.1
BAPT–So Bapt Conv	1	80	26	30	0.7	3.2
Catholic	1	NR	NR	499	11.2	53.9
CHR–Chs of Christ	1	9	9	9	0.2	1.0
LUTH–E.L.C.A.	1	0	0	0	0.0	0.0
Non-denom Chr Chs	1	120	175	175	3.9	18.9
PENT–Assemb of God	1	24	0	26	0.6	2.8

NR–Not Reported - Represents no adherents reported. Percentages may not total 100 due to rounding.

Table 3: Religious Congregations by County and Group: 2010

Religious Group	Number of Congregations	Number of Attendees	Number of Communicant, Confirmed, or Full Members	Adherents: Number of Adherents	Adherents: % of Total Pop.	Adherents: % of Total Adh.
PRES–Presb Ch (USA)	2	0	80	92	2.1	9.9
PARK	**19**	**801**	**976**	**2,074**	**12.8**	**100.0**
Bahá'í	0	NR	14	14	0.1	0.7
BAPT–Converge/BGC	1	75	NR	90	0.6	4.3
BAPT–So Bapt Conv	3	80	114	133	0.8	6.4
Catholic	2	NR	NR	700	4.3	33.8
CHR–Chr Chs & Chs Cr	1	NR	60	70	0.4	3.4
CHR–Chs of Christ	1	25	25	25	0.2	1.2
HINDU–Post Ren	1	NR	NR	77	0.5	3.7
Jehovah's Witness	1	NR	NR	NR	-	-
LUTH–Luth–MO Synod	1	70	119	182	1.1	8.8
LUTH–Wisc Ev Luth Syn	1	6	8	12	0.1	0.6
METH–Un Methodist	1	44	77	111	0.7	5.4
Non-denom Chr Chs	3	443	475	560	3.5	27.0
ORTHE–Orth Ch in Amer	1	2	NR	2	0.0	0.1
PRES–Presb Ch (USA)	1	45	65	76	0.5	3.7
Sev Day Adv	1	11	19	22	0.1	1.1
PHILLIPS	**18**	**681**	**1,526**	**2,583**	**58.1**	**100.0**
BAPT–Consrv Bapt	2	NR	NR	NR	-	-
BAPT–So Bapt Conv	1	25	13	16	0.4	0.6
BRETH–Ch of Brethren	1	0	74	92	2.1	3.6
Catholic	3	NR	NR	613	13.8	23.7
CHR–Chr Chs & Chs Cr	1	NR	150	186	4.2	7.2
CHR–Chs of Christ	2	81	72	99	2.2	3.8
Evan Cov Ch	1	19	26	25	0.6	1.0
LUTH–Luth–MO Synod	3	250	579	761	17.1	29.5
METH–Un Methodist	2	164	436	569	12.8	22.0
Non-denom Chr Chs	1	100	150	150	3.4	5.8
PENT–Assemb of God	1	42	26	72	1.6	2.8
PITKIN	**16**	**663**	**1,052**	**3,123**	**18.2**	**100.0**
ANG/EPIS–Episcopal	2	181	394	420	2.4	13.4
Bahá'í	0	NR	9	9	0.1	0.3
BAPT–Consrv Bapt	1	NR	NR	NR	-	-
BUDD–Vajrayana	1	NR	NR	25	0.1	0.8
Catholic	2	NR	NR	1,234	7.2	39.5
Ch Cr, Scientst	1	NR	NR	NR	-	-
Jehovah's Witness	1	NR	NR	NR	-	-
JUD–Orth	1	43	50	60	0.3	1.9
JUD–Reform	1	114	201	543	3.2	17.4
LDS–L-D Saints	1	NR	NR	268	1.6	8.6
LUTH–Luth–MO Synod	1	42	51	67	0.4	2.1
METH–Un Methodist	2	33	121	155	0.9	5.0
Non-denom Chr Chs	1	250	200	312	1.8	10.0
PENT–Ch of God Proph	1	NR	26	30	0.2	1.0
PROWERS	**39**	**1,033**	**2,256**	**6,938**	**55.3**	**100.0**
ANG/EPIS–Episcopal	1	18	34	34	0.3	0.5
Bahá'í	0	NR	6	6	0.0	0.1
BAPT–Amer Bapt USA	1	94	183	232	1.8	3.3
BAPT–So Bapt Conv	2	36	64	81	0.6	1.2
BRETH–Ch of Brethren	1	0	78	99	0.8	1.4
Catholic	3	NR	NR	3,617	28.8	52.1
CGOD–Ch God (Ander)	1	23	NR	23	0.2	0.3
Ch Cr, Scientst	1	NR	NR	NR	-	-
Ch of Nazarene	3	76	65	127	1.0	1.8
CHR–Chr Chs & Chs Cr	2	NR	550	698	5.6	10.1
CHR–Chs of Christ	5	133	128	195	1.6	2.8
Evan Free Ch	1	40	NR	40	0.3	0.6
FRND–Evan Fr Ch Intl	1	9	20	25	0.2	0.4
Jehovah's Witness	1	NR	NR	NR	-	-
LDS–L-D Saints	2	NR	NR	439	3.5	6.3
LUTH–Ch Luth Conf	1	NR	NR	NR	-	-
LUTH–Luth–MO Synod	1	40	61	84	0.7	1.2
METH–Un Methodist	5	203	572	681	5.4	9.8
Non-denom Chr Chs	2	200	300	300	2.4	4.3
PENT–Assemb of God	1	15	0	15	0.1	0.2
PENT–Int Foursq Gos	1	62	71	90	0.7	1.3
PRES–Presb Ch (USA)	2	55	74	94	0.7	1.4
Sev Day Adv	1	29	50	58	0.5	0.8
PUEBLO	**157**	**12,572**	**16,187**	**99,012**	**62.2**	**100.0**
ANG/EPIS–Anglican NA	1	NR	NR	NR	-	-
ANG/EPIS–Episcopal	2	226	500	571	0.4	0.6
Bahá'í	1	NR	85	85	0.1	0.1
BAPT–Amer Bapt USA	4	328	584	720	0.5	0.7
BAPT–Free Will Bapt	1	NR	10	12	0.0	0.0
BAPT–NBC USA	2	100	349	430	0.3	0.4
BAPT–Reg Bapt Gen As	2	NR	NR	NR	-	-
BAPT–So Bapt Conv	14	1,901	2,345	2,890	1.8	2.9
Calv Chpl	1	NR	NR	NR	-	-
Catholic	18	NR	NR	72,405	45.5	73.1
CGOD–Ch God (Ander)	1	70	NR	70	0.0	0.1
Ch Cr, Scientst	1	NR	NR	NR	-	-
Ch of God Gen Conf	1	NR	5	6	0.0	0.0
Ch of Nazarene	2	279	347	410	0.3	0.4
CHR–Chr Ch (Disc)	3	380	1,190	1,467	0.9	1.5
CHR–Chr Chs & Chs Cr	3	NR	280	345	0.2	0.3
CHR–Chs of Christ	5	547	614	844	0.5	0.9
Evan Free Ch	3	220	NR	220	0.1	0.2
Ind Fund Churches	1	NR	NR	NR	-	-
Jehovah's Witness	5	NR	NR	NR	-	-
JUD–Reform	1	17	30	81	0.1	0.1
LDS–Comm of Christ	1	NR	128	128	0.1	0.1
LDS–L-D Saints	8	NR	NR	4,287	2.7	4.3
LUTH–E.L.C.A.	2	257	603	723	0.5	0.7
LUTH–Luth–MO Synod	3	132	628	838	0.5	0.8
LUTH–Wisc Ev Luth Syn	1	120	172	218	0.1	0.2
MENN–Mennonite USA	1	30	50	62	0.0	0.1
METH–AME	1	0	150	185	0.1	0.2
METH–Free Methodist	1	55	26	55	0.0	0.1
METH–Un Methodist	8	825	1,609	1,823	1.1	1.8
Metro Comm Ch	1	10	12	15	0.0	0.0
MJEW–Union Mes Cong	1	NR	NR	NR	-	-
Muslim Est	1	134	NR	308	0.2	0.3
Non-denom Chr Chs	24	2,807	3,450	3,822	2.4	3.9
ORTHE–Greek Orthodox	1	24	NR	65	0.0	0.1
ORTHE–Orth Ch in Amer	1	70	NR	70	0.0	0.1
PENT–Assemb of God	9	1,749	850	3,203	2.0	3.2
PENT–Ch God (Cleve)	3	1,306	428	527	0.3	0.5
PENT–Ch of God Proph	1	NR	38	47	0.0	0.0
PENT–Int Foursq Gos	2	18	10	12	0.0	0.0
PENT–Intl Pent Holiness	1	6	5	6	0.0	0.0
PENT–Un Pent Ch Intl	1	NR	NR	NR	-	-
PENT–Vineyard	1	45	60	74	0.0	0.1
PRES–Presb Ch (USA)	4	470	879	1,083	0.7	1.1
PRES–Presb Ch Amer	1	60	46	59	0.0	0.1
Salvation Army	1	38	84	120	0.1	0.1
Sev Day Adv	3	250	434	499	0.3	0.5
Un C of Christ	2	59	138	170	0.1	0.2
Unit Univ	1	39	48	57	0.0	0.1
RIO BLANCO	**25**	**645**	**949**	**2,995**	**44.9**	**100.0**
ANG/EPIS–Episcopal	2	40	100	100	1.5	3.3
Bahá'í	0	NR	3	3	0.0	0.1
BAPT–Amer Bapt USA	1	70	30	37	0.6	1.2
BAPT–So Bapt Conv	5	283	374	463	6.9	15.5
Catholic	2	NR	NR	604	9.1	20.2
CHR–Chr Chs & Chs Cr	2	NR	180	223	3.3	7.4
CHR–Chs of Christ	2	38	27	35	0.5	1.2
Ind Fund Churches	1	NR	NR	NR	-	-
Jehovah's Witness	1	NR	NR	NR	-	-
LDS–L-D Saints	3	NR	NR	1,055	15.8	35.2
LUTH–Luth–MO Synod	1	17	18	25	0.4	0.8
METH–Un Methodist	1	90	126	297	4.5	9.9
Non-denom Chr Chs	1	56	70	70	1.1	2.3
PENT–Assemb of God	2	51	21	83	1.2	2.8
REF–Comm Ref Evan	1	NR	NR	NR	-	-
RIO GRANDE	**37**	**1,586**	**2,008**	**8,001**	**66.8**	**100.0**
ANG/EPIS–Episcopal	2	21	42	42	0.4	0.5
Bahá'í	0	NR	1	1	0.0	0.0
BAPT–So Bapt Conv	5	342	514	639	5.3	8.0
Catholic	4	NR	NR	4,474	37.3	55.9

NR–Not Reported - Represents no adherents reported. Percentages may not total 100 due to rounding.

Table 3: Religious Congregations by County and Group: 2010

Religious Group	Number of Congrega-tions	Number of Attendees	Number of Communicant, Confirmed, or Full Members	Adherents: Number of Adherents	Adherents: % of Total Pop.	Adherents: % of Total Adh.
Ch of Nazarene	1	152	167	246	2.1	3.1
CHR–Chr Ch (Disc)	1	21	44	55	0.5	0.7
CHR–Chs of Christ	2	155	120	140	1.2	1.7
Jehovah's Witness	2	NR	NR	NR	-	-
LDS–L-D Saints	2	NR	NR	579	4.8	7.2
LUTH–Luth–MO Synod	1	58	137	174	1.5	2.2
LUTH–Wisc Ev Luth Syn	1	11	13	15	0.1	0.2
MENN–Amish Undif	2	NR	50	146	1.2	1.8
METH–Un Methodist	3	88	214	307	2.6	3.8
Non-denom Chr Chs	4	360	372	500	4.2	6.2
PENT–Assemb of God	4	272	144	451	3.8	5.6
PRES–Presb Ch (USA)	2	83	150	186	1.6	2.3
Sev Day Adv	1	23	40	46	0.4	0.6
ROUTT	**24**	**1,558**	**2,035**	**6,665**	**28.4**	**100.0**
ANG/EPIS–Episcopal	1	115	476	476	2.0	7.1
Bahá'í	0	NR	10	10	0.0	0.2
BAPT–NT Ind Bapt	1	NR	NR	NR	-	-
BAPT–So Bapt Conv	3	243	173	206	0.9	3.1
Catholic	2	NR	NR	3,380	14.4	50.7
Ch Cr, Scientst	1	NR	NR	NR	-	-
CHR–Chs of Christ	1	28	28	39	0.2	0.6
Evan Free Ch	1	85	NR	85	0.4	1.3
HINDU–Post Ren	1	NR	NR	10	0.0	0.2
Ind Fund Churches	1	NR	NR	NR	-	-
LDS–L-D Saints	1	NR	NR	356	1.5	5.3
LUTH–Luth–MO Synod	1	0	310	310	1.3	4.7
LUTH–Wisc Ev Luth Syn	1	11	10	12	0.1	0.2
METH–Un Methodist	1	185	394	741	3.2	11.1
Non-denom Chr Chs	3	320	360	400	1.7	6.0
PENT–Assemb of God	1	500	156	500	2.1	7.5
REF–Comm Ref Evan	1	NR	NR	NR	-	-
Sev Day Adv	2	8	15	17	0.1	0.3
Un C of Christ	1	63	103	123	0.5	1.8
SAGUACHE	**23**	**231**	**571**	**4,004**	**65.6**	**100.0**
Bahá'í	0	NR	11	11	0.2	0.3
BAPT–Amer Bapt USA	1	17	32	39	0.6	1.0
BAPT–So Bapt Conv	5	122	218	267	4.4	6.7
BUDD–Mahayana	1	NR	NR	25	0.4	0.6
BUDD–Vajrayana	4	NR	NR	568	9.3	14.2
Catholic	1	NR	NR	2,244	36.7	56.0
CHR–Chs of Christ	2	28	28	33	0.5	0.8
HINDU–I/A Temples	1	NR	NR	250	4.1	6.2
HINDU–Post Ren	2	NR	NR	50	0.8	1.2
HINDU–Renaiss	1	NR	NR	12	0.2	0.3
LDS–L-D Saints	1	NR	NR	196	3.2	4.9
MENN–CG in Cr (Menn)	1	NR	113	138	2.3	3.4
METH–Un Methodist	2	54	159	159	2.6	4.0
Non-denom Chr Chs	1	10	10	12	0.2	0.3
SAN JUAN	**7**	**92**	**131**	**354**	**50.6**	**100.0**
Bahá'í	0	NR	2	2	0.3	0.6
BAPT–So Bapt Conv	1	50	25	29	4.1	8.2
Catholic	2	NR	NR	167	23.9	47.2
CHR–Chs of Christ	1	25	5	5	0.7	1.4
LDS–L-D Saints	1	NR	NR	35	5.0	9.9
Un C of Christ	2	17	99	116	16.6	32.8
SAN MIGUEL	**8**	**311**	**425**	**2,171**	**29.5**	**100.0**
Bahá'í	0	NR	2	2	0.0	0.1
BAPT–So Bapt Conv	2	137	209	248	3.4	11.4
Catholic	1	NR	NR	1,651	22.4	76.0
CHR–Chr Chs & Chs Cr	1	NR	50	59	0.8	2.7
Jehovah's Witness	1	NR	NR	NR	-	-
Non-denom Chr Chs	1	60	50	75	1.0	3.5
PENT–Intl Pent Holiness	1	29	26	31	0.4	1.4
PRES–Presb Ch (USA)	1	85	88	105	1.4	4.8
SEDGWICK	**12**	**392**	**826**	**1,302**	**54.7**	**100.0**
BAPT–Consrv Bapt	1	NR	NR	NR	-	-
BAPT–So Bapt Conv	1	35	36	42	1.8	3.2
Catholic	2	NR	NR	317	13.3	24.3
CHR–Chr Chs & Chs Cr	1	NR	150	176	7.4	13.5
LUTH–Luth–MO Synod	1	75	198	208	8.7	16.0
MENN–Mennonite USA	1	41	54	64	2.7	4.9
METH–Un Methodist	2	71	158	241	10.1	18.5
Non-denom Chr Chs	2	150	205	225	9.5	17.3
PRES–Presb Ch (USA)	1	20	25	29	1.2	2.2
SUMMIT	**27**	**1,929**	**1,767**	**5,879**	**21.0**	**100.0**
ANG/EPIS–Episcopal	1	106	199	199	0.7	3.4
Bahá'í	0	NR	5	5	0.0	0.1
BAPT–So Bapt Conv	6	366	305	354	1.3	6.0
Calv Chpl	1	NR	NR	NR	-	-
Catholic	4	NR	NR	2,563	9.2	43.6
CHR–Chs of Christ	1	65	45	65	0.2	1.1
Ind Fund Churches	1	NR	NR	NR	-	-
Jehovah's Witness	1	NR	NR	NR	-	-
LDS–L-D Saints	1	NR	NR	557	2.0	9.5
LUTH–E.L.C.A.	1	170	368	483	1.7	8.2
LUTH–Luth–MO Synod	1	45	45	57	0.2	1.0
METH–Free Methodist	1	44	42	44	0.2	0.7
METH–Un Methodist	1	212	214	326	1.2	5.5
Non-denom Chr Chs	3	835	485	1,044	3.7	17.8
PENT–Assemb of God	2	49	0	118	0.4	2.0
Sev Day Adv	1	12	21	24	0.1	0.4
Unit Univ	1	25	38	40	0.1	0.7
TELLER	**24**	**1,773**	**3,204**	**7,029**	**30.1**	**100.0**
ANG/EPIS–Episcopal	2	54	116	136	0.6	1.9
Bahá'í	0	NR	17	17	0.1	0.2
BAPT–Amer Bapt USA	1	0	78	92	0.4	1.3
BAPT–So Bapt Conv	3	215	363	427	1.8	6.1
BUDD–Mahayana	1	NR	NR	300	1.3	4.3
Catholic	3	NR	NR	1,785	7.6	25.4
Ch of Nazarene	1	140	70	210	0.9	3.0
CHR–Chr Chs & Chs Cr	1	NR	450	529	2.3	7.5
CHR–Chs of Christ	1	50	45	70	0.3	1.0
Evan Free Ch	1	0	NR	0	0.0	0.0
Jehovah's Witness	1	NR	NR	NR	-	-
LDS–L-D Saints	1	NR	NR	713	3.1	10.1
LUTH–Luth–MO Synod	1	148	510	510	2.2	7.3
METH–Un Methodist	1	248	492	798	3.4	11.4
Muslim Est	1	134	NR	308	1.3	4.4
Non-denom Chr Chs	4	745	995	1,056	4.5	15.0
Sev Day Adv	1	39	68	78	0.3	1.1
WASHINGTON	**20**	**527**	**914**	**1,795**	**37.3**	**100.0**
BAPT–NT Ind Bapt	1	NR	NR	NR	-	-
BAPT–So Bapt Conv	3	37	97	117	2.4	6.5
Catholic	1	NR	NR	639	13.3	35.6
CHR–Chs of Christ	2	16	15	20	0.4	1.1
Grace Gosp Fel	2	NR	NR	NR	-	-
LUTH–E.L.C.A.	2	35	71	93	1.9	5.2
LUTH–Luth Ch-Am Asc	1	NR	NR	NR	-	-
LUTH–Luth–MO Synod	1	27	54	64	1.3	3.6
METH–Un Methodist	2	72	226	314	6.5	17.5
PENT–Assemb of God	1	15	9	15	0.3	0.8
PENT–Int Foursq Gos	1	212	249	301	6.3	16.8
PRES–Presb Ch (USA)	2	105	178	215	4.5	12.0
Sev Day Adv	1	8	15	17	0.4	0.9
WELD	**205**	**17,661**	**21,411**	**72,815**	**28.8**	**100.0**
ANG/EPIS–Episcopal	4	369	615	628	0.2	0.9
Bahá'í	1	NR	70	70	0.0	0.1
BAPT–Amer Bapt Assn	1	NR	50	64	0.0	0.1
BAPT–Amer Bapt USA	2	81	118	152	0.1	0.2
BAPT–Consrv Bapt	4	NR	NR	NR	-	-
BAPT–Converge/BGC	1	75	NR	90	0.0	0.1
BAPT–Free Will Bapt	1	NR	10	13	0.0	0.0
BAPT–Ind Bapt Flwsp Intl	1	NR	NR	NR	-	-
BAPT–N Am Bapt Conf	2	NR	211	271	0.1	0.4
BAPT–NT Ind Bapt	2	NR	NR	NR	-	-

NR–Not Reported   - Represents no adherents reported.   Percentages may not total 100 due to rounding.

Table 3: Religious Congregations by County and Group: 2010

Religious Group	Number of Congrega-tions	Number of Attendees	Number of Communicant, Confirmed, or Full Members	Adherents: Number of Adherents	Adherents: % of Total Pop.	Adherents: % of Total Adh.
BAPT–Reg Bapt Gen As	2	NR	NR	NR	-	-
BAPT–So Bapt Conv	16	1,042	1,852	2,378	0.9	3.3
BRETH–Ch of Brethren	1	0	41	53	0.0	0.1
Calv Chpl	2	NR	NR	NR	-	-
Catholic	14	NR	NR	34,138	13.5	46.9
CGOD–Ch God (Ander)	1	30	NR	30	0.0	0.0
Ch Cr, Scientst	1	NR	NR	NR	-	-
Ch of Nazarene	3	318	384	438	0.2	0.6
Chr & Miss Al	1	40	29	64	0.0	0.1
CHR–Chr Ch (Disc)	3	201	460	591	0.2	0.8
CHR–Chr Chs & Chs Cr	4	NR	475	610	0.2	0.8
CHR–Chs of Christ	4	365	362	450	0.2	0.6
CONG–Consrv Cong Chr	2	205	475	610	0.2	0.8
Evan Cov Ch	1	115	0	150	0.1	0.2
Evan Free Ch	5	3,188	NR	3,188	1.3	4.4
Ind Fund Churches	1	NR	NR	NR	-	-
Jehovah's Witness	5	NR	NR	NR	-	-
LDS–Comm of Christ	1	NR	128	128	0.1	0.2
LDS–L-D Saints	11	NR	NR	4,811	1.9	6.6
LUTH–E.L.C.A.	7	842	2,340	2,786	1.1	3.8
LUTH–Luth–MO Synod	7	755	1,635	2,092	0.8	2.9
LUTH–Nor Amer Luth C	1	NR	NR	NR	-	-
LUTH–Wisc Ev Luth Syn	2	119	161	216	0.1	0.3
MENN–Mennonite USA	1	60	57	73	0.0	0.1
METH–Un Methodist	12	1,053	2,371	3,394	1.3	4.7
METH–Wesleyan	1	1,431	474	1,860	0.7	2.6
Missionary Ch	2	235	0	235	0.1	0.3
Muslim Est	1	134	NR	308	0.1	0.4
Non-denom Chr Chs	26	2,942	3,250	3,892	1.5	5.3
ORTHE–Orth Ch in Amer	1	30	NR	35	0.0	0.0
PENT–Assemb of God	14	1,955	933	2,713	1.1	3.7
PENT–Ch God (Cleve)	1	100	100	128	0.1	0.2
PENT–Ch of God Proph	1	NR	54	69	0.0	0.1
PENT–Int Foursq Gos	5	239	941	1,208	0.5	1.7
PENT–Intl Pent Holiness	2	69	60	77	0.0	0.1
PENT–Pent Ch of God	1	70	NR	109	0.0	0.1
PENT–Un Pent Ch Intl	2	NR	NR	NR	-	-
PENT–Vineyard	1	120	299	384	0.2	0.5
PRES–Evan Presby Ch	1	NR	407	523	0.2	0.7
PRES–Presb Ch (USA)	4	183	414	532	0.2	0.7
PRES–Presb Ch Amer	1	118	80	105	0.0	0.1
REF–Christian Ref	1	135	101	130	0.1	0.2
REF–Ref Ch in U.S.	1	NR	57	78	0.0	0.1
Salvation Army	1	8	73	84	0.0	0.1
Sev Day Adv	6	541	941	1,082	0.4	1.5
Un C of Christ	4	463	1,345	1,727	0.7	2.4
Unit Univ	1	30	38	48	0.0	0.1
YUMA	**32**	**1,521**	**2,932**	**5,312**	**52.9**	**100.0**
BAPT–NT Ind Bapt	1	NR	NR	NR	-	-
BAPT–So Bapt Conv	3	153	185	232	2.3	4.4
Catholic	2	NR	NR	1,578	15.7	29.7
Ch of Nazarene	3	155	206	220	2.2	4.1
CHR–Chr Chs & Chs Cr	1	NR	85	107	1.1	2.0
CHR–Chs of Christ	2	54	51	71	0.7	1.3
Grace Gosp Fel	1	NR	NR	NR	-	-
Jehovah's Witness	1	NR	NR	NR	-	-
LDS–Comm of Christ	1	NR	128	128	1.3	2.4
LUTH–Luth–MO Synod	2	193	635	834	8.3	15.7
METH–Un Methodist	4	202	769	922	9.2	17.4
Non-denom Chr Chs	3	365	375	463	4.6	8.7
PENT–Assemb of God	2	70	60	103	1.0	1.9
PENT–Intl Pent Holiness	1	68	60	75	0.7	1.4
PENT–Pent Ch of God	1	70	NR	109	1.1	2.1
PRES–Presb Ch (USA)	2	125	246	309	3.1	5.8
Sev Day Adv	1	26	46	53	0.5	1.0
Un C of Christ	1	40	86	108	1.1	2.0
CONNECTICUT	**2,597**	**214,657**	**383,701**	**1,830,862**	**51.2**	**100.0**
FAIRFIELD	**654**	**66,033**	**112,138**	**579,693**	**63.2**	**100.0**
ANG/EPIS–Anglican NA	2	NR	NR	NR	-	-

Religious Group	Number of Congrega-tions	Number of Attendees	Number of Communicant, Confirmed, or Full Members	Adherents: Number of Adherents	Adherents: % of Total Pop.	Adherents: % of Total Adh.
ANG/EPIS–Episcopal	43	5,717	18,239	22,774	2.5	3.9
Bahá'í	1	NR	230	230	0.0	0.0
BAPT–Amer Bapt USA	25	5,114	10,281	12,673	1.4	2.2
BAPT–Consrv Bapt	3	NR	NR	NR	-	-
BAPT–Converge/BGC	1	400	NR	480	0.1	0.1
BAPT–Natl Mis Bapt Conv	1	0	150	185	0.0	0.0
BAPT–NBC USA	1	200	400	493	0.1	0.1
BAPT–So Bapt Conv	17	1,873	2,582	3,183	0.3	0.5
BUDD–Mahayana	4	NR	NR	555	0.1	0.1
BUDD–Theravada	2	NR	NR	696	0.1	0.1
Catholic	93	NR	NR	404,341	44.1	69.8
Ch Cr, Scientst	8	NR	NR	NR	-	-
Ch God (7th Day)	1	NR	NR	NR	-	-
Ch of Nazarene	10	599	589	786	0.1	0.1
Chr & Miss Al	6	439	420	626	0.1	0.1
CHR–Chr Ch (Disc)	4	37	136	168	0.0	0.0
CHR–Chr Chs & Chs Cr	1	NR	56	69	0.0	0.0
CHR–Chs of Christ	5	435	410	549	0.1	0.1
CHR–Int Chs of Christ	1	NR	116	143	0.0	0.0
Christian Brethren	2	NR	NR	NR	-	-
CONG–Cong Chr, NA	1	NR	34	42	0.0	0.0
CONG–Consrv Cong Chr	1	100	171	211	0.0	0.0
Evan Cov Ch	2	242	306	315	0.0	0.1
Evan Free Ch	8	1,463	NR	1,463	0.2	0.3
FRND–Fr Gen Cf & Un Mtg	2	NR	109	134	0.0	0.0
HINDU–I/A Temples	2	NR	NR	320	0.0	0.1
HINDU–Post Ren	7	NR	NR	226	0.0	0.0
HINDU–Trad Temples	1	NR	NR	1,033	0.1	0.2
Jain	1	NR	NR	NR	-	-
Jehovah's Witness	10	NR	NR	NR	-	-
JUD–Conserv	8	1,763	1,979	5,343	0.6	0.9
JUD–Orth	11	2,952	1,200	4,100	0.4	0.7
JUD–Reform	8	1,865	3,289	8,880	1.0	1.5
LDS–Comm of Christ	1	NR	161	161	0.0	0.0
LDS–L-D Saints	10	NR	NR	4,531	0.5	0.8
LUTH–E.L.C.A.	16	1,274	3,576	4,865	0.5	0.8
LUTH–Luth Cong Msn Chr	1	NR	NR	NR	-	-
LUTH–Luth–MO Synod	10	1,004	2,154	2,780	0.3	0.5
LUTH–Wisc Ev Luth Syn	1	57	85	100	0.0	0.0
METH–AME	6	645	1,390	1,713	0.2	0.3
METH–AME Zion	2	0	250	308	0.0	0.1
METH–C.M.E.	2	100	300	370	0.0	0.1
METH–Free Methodist	6	930	898	974	0.1	0.2
METH–Un Methodist	32	3,072	11,204	14,712	1.6	2.5
METH–Wesleyan	2	32	13	41	0.0	0.0
Muslim Est	13	1,686	NR	5,172	0.6	0.9
Nat Spirit Asso	1	NR	NR	NR	-	-
Non-denom Chr Chs	70	15,010	18,319	21,565	2.4	3.7
OCATH–Pol Natl Cath	1	NR	NR	NR	-	-
ORTHE–Ant Orth of NA	2	335	NR	1,061	0.1	0.2
ORTHE–Carp Rus Orth	4	317	NR	1,003	0.1	0.2
ORTHE–Greek Orthodox	5	1,225	NR	4,901	0.5	0.8
ORTHE–Orth Ch in Amer	5	430	NR	1,335	0.1	0.2
ORTHE–Rus Orth Abroad	2	75	NR	165	0.0	0.0
ORTHE–Ukrainian Orth	2	47	NR	150	0.0	0.0
ORTHO–Armen Ap Etchm	1	70	NR	600	0.1	0.1
PENT–Assemb of God	23	3,886	2,512	5,057	0.6	0.9
PENT–Ch God (Cleve)	22	2,542	3,151	3,884	0.4	0.7
PENT–Ch Lord Jesus Apos	5	NR	NR	NR	-	-
PENT–Ch of God Proph	4	NR	216	266	0.0	0.0
PENT–COGIC	7	415	872	1,075	0.1	0.2
PENT–Fire Bapt Hol Ch	2	NR	NR	NR	-	-
PENT–Full Gosp Bapt	1	NR	NR	NR	-	-
PENT–I F Chr Assmbl	1	NR	NR	NR	-	-
PENT–Int Foursq Gos	2	48	54	67	0.0	0.0
PENT–Int Pent C Chr	1	0	NR	75	0.0	0.0
PENT–Intl Pent Holiness	1	111	123	152	0.0	0.0
PENT–Pent Ch of God	1	70	NR	109	0.0	0.0
PENT–Un Pent Asbl God	1	NR	NR	NR	-	-
PENT–Un Pent Ch Intl	5	NR	NR	NR	-	-
PENT–United Holy Ch	2	NR	NR	NR	-	-
PRES–Korean Pres Amer	1	NR	NR	NR	-	-
PRES–Orth Pres Ch	1	59	41	72	0.0	0.0
PRES–Presb Ch (USA)	9	1,483	4,389	5,410	0.6	0.9

NR–Not Reported - Represents no adherents reported. Percentages may not total 100 due to rounding.

Table 3: Religious Congregations by County and Group: 2010

Religious Group	Number of Congrega-tions	Number of Attendees	Number of Communicant, Confirmed, or Full Members	Adherents: Number of Adherents	Adherents: % of Total Pop.	Adherents: % of Total Adh.
PRES–Presb Ch Amer	5	314	224	359	0.0	0.1
Salvation Army	5	211	457	689	0.1	0.1
Sev Day Adv	17	1,436	2,499	2,873	0.3	0.5
Sikh	1	NR	NR	NR	-	-
Un C of Christ	43	5,316	17,706	21,826	2.4	3.8
Unit Univ	4	634	847	1,192	0.1	0.2
Unity Ch	2	NR	NR	NR	-	-
Zoroastrian	0	NR	NR	62	0.0	0.0
HARTFORD	**630**	**58,738**	**110,698**	**442,638**	**49.5**	**100.0**
ANG/EPIS–Anglican NA	1	NR	NR	NR	-	-
ANG/EPIS–Episcopal	35	3,641	9,816	11,593	1.3	2.6
Bahá'í	5	NR	324	324	0.0	0.1
BAPT–Amer Bapt USA	33	3,101	10,006	12,085	1.4	2.7
BAPT–Consrv Bapt	1	NR	NR	NR	-	-
BAPT–Converge/BGC	9	2,925	NR	3,510	0.4	0.8
BAPT–Natl Mis Bapt Conv	1	0	150	181	0.0	0.0
BAPT–NBC Amer	2	1,000	1,600	1,932	0.2	0.4
BAPT–NBC USA	1	250	257	310	0.0	0.1
BAPT–Ref Bapt Ch	1	NR	NR	NR	-	-
BAPT–Reg Bapt Gen As	2	NR	NR	NR	-	-
BAPT–S-D Baptist Gen Con	1	27	9	11	0.0	0.0
BAPT–So Bapt Conv	10	800	1,155	1,395	0.2	0.3
BRETH–Grace Breth	1	NR	NR	NR	-	-
BUDD–Mahayana	8	NR	NR	1,322	0.1	0.3
BUDD–Vajrayana	5	NR	NR	689	0.1	0.2
Catholic	95	NR	NR	278,203	31.1	62.9
CGOD–Ch God (Ander)	1	0	NR	0	0.0	0.0
Ch Cr, Scientst	4	NR	NR	NR	-	-
Ch of Nazarene	4	342	431	659	0.1	0.1
Chr & Miss Al	4	222	286	521	0.1	0.1
CHR–Chr Ch (Disc)	3	0	0	0	0.0	0.0
CHR–Chr Chs & Chs Cr	2	NR	300	362	0.0	0.1
CHR–Chs of Christ	6	656	551	758	0.1	0.2
CHR–Int Chs of Christ	1	NR	282	341	0.0	0.1
CONG–Cong Chr Add'l	1	NR	84	101	0.0	0.0
CONG–Cong Chr, NA	3	NR	479	579	0.1	0.1
CONG–Consrv Cong Chr	1	80	91	110	0.0	0.0
Evan Cov Ch	5	1,194	1,179	1,553	0.2	0.4
Evan Free Ch	4	738	NR	738	0.1	0.2
FRND–Fr Gen Cf & Un Mtg	1	NR	187	226	0.0	0.1
HINDU–I/A Temples	4	NR	NR	3,570	0.4	0.8
HINDU–Post Ren	5	NR	NR	92	0.0	0.0
Int Cou Comm Ch	1	NR	NR	NR	-	-
Jehovah's Witness	13	NR	NR	NR	-	-
JUD–Conserv	7	2,078	2,332	6,296	0.7	1.4
JUD–Orth	7	1,368	600	1,900	0.2	0.4
JUD–Reform	6	1,246	2,198	5,935	0.7	1.3
LDS–Comm of Christ	1	NR	102	102	0.0	0.0
LDS–L-D Saints	8	NR	NR	3,450	0.4	0.8
LUTH–Ch of Luth Br	1	180	109	204	0.0	0.0
LUTH–E.L.C.A.	20	2,214	7,030	8,990	1.0	2.0
LUTH–Luth–MO Synod	8	1,002	2,101	2,995	0.3	0.7
LUTH–Wisc Ev Luth Syn	1	84	115	143	0.0	0.0
MENN–CG in Cr (Menn)	1	NR	0	0	0.0	0.0
METH–AME	3	350	1,244	1,502	0.2	0.3
METH–AME Zion	7	570	1,773	2,141	0.2	0.5
METH–C.M.E.	3	700	1,100	1,329	0.1	0.3
METH–Un Methodist	28	2,733	9,204	12,141	1.4	2.7
METH–Wesleyan	1	33	39	43	0.0	0.0
Metro Comm Ch	1	32	51	62	0.0	0.0
MJEW–Union Mes Cong	1	NR	NR	NR	-	-
Muslim Est	10	1,348	NR	3,056	0.3	0.7
Nat Spirit Asso	1	NR	NR	NR	-	-
Non-denom Chr Chs	69	12,976	21,186	22,427	2.5	5.1
OCATH–Pol Natl Cath	5	NR	NR	NR	-	-
ORTHE–Greek Orthodox	4	465	NR	1,780	0.2	0.4
ORTHE–Orth Ch in Amer	3	205	NR	525	0.1	0.1
ORTHE–Rus Orth Abroad	1	50	NR	125	0.0	0.0
ORTHE–Ukrainian Orth	2	155	NR	335	0.0	0.1
ORTHO–Armen Ap Cilic	1	60	NR	500	0.1	0.1
ORTHO–Armen Ap Etchm	2	135	NR	400	0.0	0.1
PENT–Assemb of God	16	3,255	2,026	5,654	0.6	1.3
PENT–Ch God (Cleve)	17	1,694	2,532	3,058	0.3	0.7
PENT–Ch Lord Jesus Apos	1	NR	NR	NR	-	-
PENT–Ch of God Proph	1	NR	580	700	0.1	0.2
PENT–COGIC	6	240	870	1,051	0.1	0.2
PENT–Elim	2	NR	NR	NR	-	-
PENT–Fire Bapt Hol Ch	1	NR	NR	NR	-	-
PENT–Full Gosp Bapt	1	NR	NR	NR	-	-
PENT–I F Chr Assmbl	1	NR	NR	NR	-	-
PENT–Pent Ch of God	1	70	NR	109	0.0	0.0
PENT–Un Pent Ch Intl	13	NR	NR	NR	-	-
PENT–United Holy Ch	1	NR	NR	NR	-	-
PRES–Evan Presby Ch	1	NR	152	184	0.0	0.0
PRES–Korean Pres Amer	1	NR	NR	NR	-	-
PRES–Presb Ch (USA)	4	426	688	831	0.1	0.2
PRES–Presb Ch Amer	4	265	219	274	0.0	0.1
REF–Christian Ref	1	146	203	245	0.0	0.1
Salvation Army	7	399	894	1,393	0.2	0.3
Sev Day Adv	14	1,616	2,808	3,232	0.4	0.7
Sikh	1	NR	NR	NR	-	-
Tao	1	NR	NR	NR	-	-
Un C of Christ	52	6,989	22,284	26,914	3.0	6.1
Unit Univ	5	678	1,071	1,434	0.2	0.3
Unity Ch	2	NR	NR	NR	-	-
Zoroastrian	0	NR	NR	13	0.0	0.0
LITCHFIELD	**176**	**8,273**	**20,788**	**80,273**	**42.3**	**100.0**
ANG/EPIS–Anglican NA	1	NR	NR	NR	-	-
ANG/EPIS–Episcopal	20	1,331	3,188	4,324	2.3	5.4
Bahá'í	0	NR	43	43	0.0	0.1
BAPT–Amer Bapt USA	6	346	626	744	0.4	0.9
BAPT–Converge/BGC	1	75	NR	90	0.0	0.1
BAPT–Reg Bapt Gen As	1	NR	NR	NR	-	-
BAPT–So Bapt Conv	5	318	428	509	0.3	0.6
BUDD–Mahayana	1	NR	NR	2,906	1.5	3.6
BUDD–Theravada	1	NR	NR	300	0.2	0.4
BUDD–Vajrayana	1	NR	NR	71	0.0	0.1
Catholic	28	NR	NR	49,652	26.1	61.9
Chr & Miss Al	1	110	71	175	0.1	0.2
CHR–Chs of Christ	2	80	92	125	0.1	0.2
CONG–Cong Chr, NA	5	NR	414	492	0.3	0.6
Evan Cov Ch	2	222	521	288	0.2	0.4
FRND–Fr Gen Cf & Un Mtg	3	NR	36	43	0.0	0.1
FRND–Unaffl Mtgs	1	NR	NR	NR	-	-
HINDU–Post Ren	1	NR	NR	65	0.0	0.1
Jehovah's Witness	5	NR	NR	NR	-	-
JUD–Conserv	1	89	100	270	0.1	0.3
JUD–Reform	1	56	99	267	0.1	0.3
LDS–L-D Saints	1	NR	NR	377	0.2	0.5
LUTH–Ch of Luth Br	1	150	125	395	0.2	0.5
LUTH–E.L.C.A.	6	488	1,212	1,495	0.8	1.9
LUTH–Luth Cong Msn Chr	1	50	110	131	0.1	0.2
LUTH–Luth–MO Synod	4	349	657	705	0.4	0.9
METH–AME Zion	2	12	135	160	0.1	0.2
METH–Un Methodist	15	844	4,252	5,071	2.7	6.3
New Apost Ch	1	NR	NR	NR	-	-
Non-denom Chr Chs	11	985	1,000	1,283	0.7	1.6
OCATH–Pol Natl Cath	1	NR	NR	NR	-	-
OCATH–Un Cath Ch	1	NR	NR	702	0.4	0.9
ORTHE–Orth Ch in Amer	2	90	NR	175	0.1	0.2
PENT–Assemb of God	2	190	248	559	0.3	0.7
PENT–Ch God (Cleve)	1	4	29	34	0.0	0.0
PENT–Int Foursq Gos	1	33	38	45	0.0	0.1
PENT–Open Bible Std	1	29	NR	29	0.0	0.0
PENT–Un Pent Ch Intl	1	NR	NR	NR	-	-
Salvation Army	1	48	44	51	0.0	0.1
Sev Day Adv	2	32	55	64	0.0	0.1
Un C of Christ	31	2,294	7,163	8,512	4.5	10.6
Unit Univ	2	48	102	120	0.1	0.1
Unity Ch	1	NR	NR	NR	-	-
Zoroastrian	0	NR	NR	1	0.0	0.0
MIDDLESEX	**120**	**7,509**	**15,848**	**69,773**	**42.1**	**100.0**
ANG/EPIS–Episcopal	12	920	1,873	2,748	1.7	3.9
Bahá'í	0	NR	44	44	0.0	0.1

NR–Not Reported - Represents no adherents reported. Percentages may not total 100 due to rounding.

Table 3: Religious Congregations by County and Group: 2010

Religious Group	Number of Congrega-tions	Number of Attendees	Number of Communicant, Confirmed, or Full Members	Adherents		
				Number of Adherents	% of Total Pop.	% of Total Adh.
BAPT–Amer Bapt USA	6	139	766	911	0.5	1.3
BAPT–NBC USA	1	140	170	202	0.1	0.3
BAPT–S-D Baptist Gen Con	1	18	26	31	0.0	0.0
BAPT–So Bapt Conv	1	25	10	12	0.0	0.0
BUDD–Mahayana	2	NR	NR	123	0.1	0.2
Catholic	18	NR	NR	46,800	28.2	67.1
Ch Cr, Scientst	1	NR	NR	NR	-	-
CONG–Cong Chr Add'l	1	NR	402	478	0.3	0.7
CONG–Cong Chr, NA	1	NR	120	143	0.1	0.2
Evan Cov Ch	2	105	235	137	0.1	0.2
Evan Free Ch	1	252	NR	252	0.2	0.4
FRND–Fr Gen Cf & Un Mtg	1	NR	19	23	0.0	0.0
HINDU–Post Ren	1	NR	NR	77	0.0	0.1
HINDU–Trad Temples	1	NR	NR	850	0.5	1.2
Jehovah's Witness	2	NR	NR	NR	-	-
JUD–Conserv	1	160	180	486	0.3	0.7
JUD–Reform	1	121	214	578	0.3	0.8
LDS–L-D Saints	1	NR	NR	663	0.4	1.0
LUTH–E.L.C.A.	7	684	1,905	2,473	1.5	3.5
LUTH–Luth–MO Synod	1	97	305	401	0.2	0.6
METH–AME	1	0	150	178	0.1	0.3
METH–AME Zion	1	0	500	594	0.4	0.9
METH–Un Methodist	9	505	1,258	1,927	1.2	2.8
Muslim Est	1	40	NR	100	0.1	0.1
Non-denom Chr Chs	15	1,810	2,103	2,506	1.5	3.6
ORTHE–Orth Ch in Amer	1	40	NR	85	0.1	0.1
PENT–Assemb of God	3	298	167	362	0.2	0.5
PENT–Ch God (Cleve)	1	15	9	11	0.0	0.0
PENT–COGIC	1	15	0	0	0.0	0.0
PENT–Elim	1	NR	NR	NR	-	-
PENT–Full Gosp Bapt	1	NR	NR	NR	-	-
PENT–Un Pent Ch Intl	1	NR	NR	NR	-	-
Salvation Army	1	15	49	228	0.1	0.3
Sev Day Adv	1	19	33	38	0.0	0.1
Un C of Christ	19	2,091	5,310	6,312	3.8	9.0
NEW HAVEN	**586**	**47,665**	**77,355**	**421,157**	**48.8**	**100.0**
ANG/EPIS–Anglican NA	2	NR	NR	NR	-	-
ANG/EPIS–Episcopal	39	3,970	9,681	12,239	1.4	2.9
Bahá'í	1	NR	194	194	0.0	0.0
BAPT–Amer Bapt USA	19	2,186	6,569	7,900	0.9	1.9
BAPT–Asc Ref Bap Ch Am	1	NR	NR	NR	-	-
BAPT–Consrv Bapt	1	NR	NR	NR	-	-
BAPT–Converge/BGC	5	700	NR	840	0.1	0.2
BAPT–N Am Bapt Conf	1	NR	NR	NR	-	-
BAPT–Natl Mis Bapt Conv	2	55	300	361	0.0	0.1
BAPT–NBC Amer	1	300	700	842	0.1	0.2
BAPT–NBC USA	1	0	150	180	0.0	0.0
BAPT–Prog NBC	1	125	200	241	0.0	0.1
BAPT–Ref Bapt Ch	1	NR	NR	NR	-	-
BAPT–So Bapt Conv	9	915	855	1,028	0.1	0.2
BUDD–Mahayana	4	NR	NR	330	0.0	0.1
BUDD–Vajrayana	4	NR	NR	157	0.0	0.0
Calv Chpl	1	NR	NR	NR	-	-
Catholic	101	NR	NR	303,975	35.2	72.2
CGOD–Ch God (Ander)	1	100	NR	100	0.0	0.0
Ch Cr, Scientst	3	NR	NR	NR	-	-
Ch God (7th Day)	1	NR	NR	NR	-	-
Ch of Nazarene	2	45	49	129	0.0	0.0
Chr & Miss Al	4	418	314	530	0.1	0.1
CHR–Chr Ch (Disc)	1	0	0	0	0.0	0.0
CHR–Chr Chs & Chs Cr	3	NR	223	268	0.0	0.1
CHR–Chs of Christ	6	560	565	892	0.1	0.2
Christian Brethren	2	NR	NR	NR	-	-
CONG–Cong Chr, NA	2	NR	205	247	0.0	0.1
Evan Cov Ch	2	59	156	77	0.0	0.0
Evan Free Ch	7	980	NR	980	0.1	0.2
FRND–Fr Gen Cf & Un Mtg	1	NR	74	89	0.0	0.0
HINDU–Post Ren	4	NR	NR	169	0.0	0.0
Int Cou Comm Ch	1	NR	NR	NR	-	-
Jehovah's Witness	14	NR	NR	NR	-	-
JUD–Conserv	7	1,680	1,885	5,090	0.6	1.2
JUD–Orth	13	1,224	450	1,700	0.2	0.4
JUD–Reform	5	844	1,489	4,020	0.5	1.0
LDS–L-D Saints	6	NR	NR	3,010	0.3	0.7
LUTH–E.L.C.A.	16	1,211	3,310	4,196	0.5	1.0
LUTH–Luth–MO Synod	7	685	1,365	1,635	0.2	0.4
METH–AME	2	400	700	842	0.1	0.2
METH–AME Zion	7	440	1,550	1,864	0.2	0.4
METH–C.M.E.	2	200	400	481	0.1	0.1
METH–Un Methodist	19	1,621	6,583	8,912	1.0	2.1
Metro Comm Ch	1	41	54	65	0.0	0.0
MJEW–Union Mes Cong	1	NR	NR	NR	-	-
Muslim Est	10	1,756	NR	4,432	0.5	1.1
New Apost Ch	2	NR	NR	NR	-	-
Non-denom Chr Chs	67	12,688	15,529	17,153	2.0	4.1
OCATH–Pol Natl Cath	2	NR	NR	NR	-	-
OCATH–Un Cath Ch	1	NR	NR	702	0.1	0.2
ORTHE–Greek Orthodox	4	570	NR	2,446	0.3	0.6
ORTHE–Orth Ch in Amer	5	355	NR	855	0.1	0.2
ORTHE–Ukrainian Orth	1	25	NR	40	0.0	0.0
ORTHO–Coptic Orth Ch	1	275	NR	390	0.0	0.1
PENT–Assemb of God	30	3,996	1,669	4,535	0.5	1.1
PENT–Ch God (Cleve)	19	1,487	1,361	1,637	0.2	0.4
PENT–Ch Lord Jesus Apos	4	NR	NR	NR	-	-
PENT–Ch of God Proph	3	NR	152	183	0.0	0.0
PENT–COGIC	12	425	1,380	1,660	0.2	0.4
PENT–Elim	1	NR	NR	NR	-	-
PENT–Fire Bapt Hol Ch	1	NR	NR	NR	-	-
PENT–I F Chr Assmbl	1	NR	NR	NR	-	-
PENT–Int Foursq Gos	1	62	68	82	0.0	0.0
PENT–Pent Ch of God	1	70	NR	109	0.0	0.0
PENT–Un Pent Ch Intl	4	NR	NR	NR	-	-
PENT–United Holy Ch	3	NR	NR	NR	-	-
PENT–Vineyard	3	251	392	471	0.1	0.1
PRES–Korean Pres Amer	2	NR	NR	NR	-	-
PRES–Orth Pres Ch	1	50	41	60	0.0	0.0
PRES–Presb Ch (USA)	4	263	638	767	0.1	0.2
PRES–Presb Ch Amer	1	200	132	179	0.0	0.0
Salvation Army	5	204	438	765	0.1	0.2
Sev Day Adv	12	916	1,591	1,831	0.2	0.4
Tao	1	NR	NR	NR	-	-
Un C of Christ	46	4,896	15,329	18,436	2.1	4.4
Unit Univ	4	417	614	829	0.1	0.2
Zoroastrian	0	NR	NR	12	0.0	0.0
NEW LONDON	**234**	**14,039**	**25,663**	**123,150**	**44.9**	**100.0**
ANG/EPIS–Anglican NA	1	NR	NR	NR	-	-
ANG/EPIS–Episcopal	10	1,259	2,550	3,620	1.3	2.9
Bahá'í	1	NR	83	83	0.0	0.1
BAPT–Alliance Bapt	1	NR	NR	NR	-	-
BAPT–Amer Bapt USA	21	1,714	4,173	4,988	1.8	4.1
BAPT–Consrv Bapt	5	NR	NR	NR	-	-
BAPT–Converge/BGC	1	75	NR	90	0.0	0.1
BAPT–NBC USA	1	700	1,400	1,673	0.6	1.4
BAPT–S-D Baptist Gen Con	1	4	13	16	0.0	0.0
BAPT–So Bapt Conv	6	271	375	448	0.2	0.4
BUDD–Mahayana	2	NR	NR	22	0.0	0.0
Calv Chpl	1	NR	NR	NR	-	-
Catholic	32	NR	NR	84,765	30.9	68.8
Ch Cr, Scientst	1	NR	NR	NR	-	-
Ch of Nazarene	1	33	35	38	0.0	0.0
Chr & Miss Al	2	203	229	449	0.2	0.4
CHR–Chs of Christ	1	83	100	125	0.0	0.1
CHR–Int Chs of Christ	1	NR	115	137	0.0	0.1
Christian Brethren	1	NR	NR	NR	-	-
CONG–Cong Chr Add'l	1	NR	41	49	0.0	0.0
CONG–Cong Chr, NA	12	NR	1,493	1,784	0.7	1.4
Evan Free Ch	2	188	NR	188	0.1	0.2
FRND–Fr Gen Cf & Un Mtg	1	NR	33	39	0.0	0.0
HINDU–Post Ren	3	NR	NR	57	0.0	0.0
Jehovah's Witness	5	NR	NR	NR	-	-
JUD–Conserv	2	360	404	1,091	0.4	0.9
JUD–Orth	3	310	150	430	0.2	0.3
JUD–Reform	1	144	254	686	0.3	0.6
LDS–Comm of Christ	1	NR	102	102	0.0	0.1
LDS–L-D Saints	4	NR	NR	1,888	0.7	1.5
LUTH–E.L.C.A.	2	342	808	1,018	0.4	0.8

NR–Not Reported   - Represents no adherents reported.   Percentages may not total 100 due to rounding.

Table 3: Religious Congregations by County and Group: 2010

Religious Group	Number of Congregations	Number of Attendees	Number of Communicant, Confirmed, or Full Members	Adherents: Number of Adherents	Adherents: % of Total Pop.	Adherents: % of Total Adh.
LUTH–Luth–MO Synod	4	282	625	793	0.3	0.6
METH–AME	2	0	200	239	0.1	0.2
METH–AME Zion	4	100	500	598	0.2	0.5
METH–Un Methodist	11	546	1,729	2,086	0.8	1.7
Muslim Est	1	120	NR	350	0.1	0.3
Nat Spirit Asso	3	NR	NR	NR	-	-
New Apost Ch	1	NR	NR	NR	-	-
Non-denom Chr Chs	25	3,245	3,930	4,374	1.6	3.6
OCATH–Pol Natl Cath	2	NR	NR	NR	-	-
ORTHE–Greek Orthodox	2	500	NR	2,350	0.9	1.9
ORTHE–Orth Ch in Amer	1	35	NR	56	0.0	0.0
ORTHE–Rus Orth Abroad	1	25	NR	50	0.0	0.0
PENT–Assemb of God	9	836	495	1,133	0.4	0.9
PENT–Ch God (Cleve)	2	110	354	423	0.2	0.3
PENT–Ch Lord Jesus Apos	2	NR	NR	NR	-	-
PENT–COGIC	1	25	70	84	0.0	0.1
PENT–Fire Bapt Hol Ch	1	NR	NR	NR	-	-
PENT–Int Foursq Gos	2	46	82	98	0.0	0.1
PENT–Un Pent Ch Intl	1	NR	NR	NR	-	-
PRES–Presb Ch (USA)	2	232	311	372	0.1	0.3
PRES–Presb Ch Amer	1	55	26	42	0.0	0.0
Salvation Army	2	62	193	566	0.2	0.5
Sev Day Adv	5	200	348	400	0.1	0.3
Un C of Christ	18	1,738	4,214	5,037	1.8	4.1
Unit Univ	2	196	228	313	0.1	0.3
Unity Ch	2	NR	NR	NR	-	-
TOLLAND	**88**	**6,457**	**12,203**	**60,149**	**39.4**	**100.0**
ANG/EPIS–Episcopal	5	407	876	1,004	0.7	1.7
Ap Chr Ch-Amer	1	575	360	575	0.4	1.0
Bahá'í	0	NR	60	60	0.0	0.1
BAPT–Amer Bapt USA	3	166	357	420	0.3	0.7
BAPT–Consrv Bapt	3	NR	NR	NR	-	-
BAPT–So Bapt Conv	3	401	565	665	0.4	1.1
BUDD–Mahayana	1	NR	NR	28	0.0	0.0
BUDD–Theravada	1	NR	NR	300	0.2	0.5
Catholic	14	NR	NR	43,500	28.5	72.3
Ch of Nazarene	1	175	129	235	0.2	0.4
Chr & Miss Al	1	100	140	160	0.1	0.3
CHR–Chs of Christ	2	98	91	114	0.1	0.2
CONG–Cong Chr, NA	1	NR	106	125	0.1	0.2
CONG–Consrv Cong Chr	2	95	92	108	0.1	0.2
FRND–Fr Gen Cf & Un Mtg	1	NR	63	74	0.0	0.1
Int Cou Comm Ch	1	NR	NR	NR	-	-
Jain	1	NR	NR	NR	-	-
Jehovah's Witness	1	NR	NR	NR	-	-
JUD–Orth	1	22	25	30	0.0	0.0
LDS–L-D Saints	1	NR	NR	549	0.4	0.9
LUTH–E.L.C.A.	3	423	699	927	0.6	1.5
LUTH–Luth–MO Synod	3	203	352	476	0.3	0.8
METH–Un Methodist	6	400	1,122	1,515	1.0	2.5
METH–Wesleyan	1	73	49	95	0.1	0.2
Muslim Est	1	134	NR	308	0.2	0.5
Non-denom Chr Chs	6	820	715	1,086	0.7	1.8
ORTHE–Greek Orthodox	1	30	NR	100	0.1	0.2
PENT–Assemb of God	2	129	48	189	0.1	0.3
PRES–Presb Ch Amer	1	207	192	251	0.2	0.4
Sev Day Adv	1	58	100	115	0.1	0.2
Un C of Christ	18	1,922	6,039	7,113	4.7	11.8
Unit Univ	1	19	23	27	0.0	0.0
WINDHAM	**109**	**5,943**	**9,008**	**54,029**	**45.6**	**100.0**
ANG/EPIS–Episcopal	7	522	878	959	0.8	1.8
Bahá'í	0	NR	36	36	0.0	0.1
BAPT–Amer Bapt USA	9	577	792	951	0.8	1.8
BAPT–Consrv Bapt	1	NR	NR	NR	-	-
BAPT–So Bapt Conv	1	75	26	31	0.0	0.1
BUDD–Mahayana	1	NR	NR	11	0.0	0.0
Catholic	18	NR	NR	41,700	35.2	77.2
Ch Cr, Scientst	1	NR	NR	NR	-	-
Ch of Nazarene	2	116	146	160	0.1	0.3
Chr & Miss Al	1	125	70	140	0.1	0.3
CHR–Chs of Christ	1	40	41	55	0.0	0.1

Religious Group	Number of Congregations	Number of Attendees	Number of Communicant, Confirmed, or Full Members	Adherents: Number of Adherents	Adherents: % of Total Pop.	Adherents: % of Total Adh.
CONG–Cong Chr Add'l	1	NR	24	29	0.0	0.1
CONG–Consrv Cong Chr	4	148	120	144	0.1	0.3
Evan Cov Ch	1	211	195	274	0.2	0.5
Evan Free Ch	1	45	NR	45	0.0	0.1
Jehovah's Witness	5	NR	NR	NR	-	-
JUD–Conserv	1	35	39	105	0.1	0.2
JUD–Reconst	1	125	160	432	0.4	0.8
LDS–L-D Saints	1	NR	NR	522	0.4	1.0
LUTH–E.L.C.A.	3	109	699	772	0.7	1.4
MENN–Bible Flwshp	1	32	NR	43	0.0	0.1
METH–AME Zion	1	0	150	180	0.2	0.3
METH–Un Methodist	4	200	841	1,263	1.1	2.3
Nat Spirit Asso	1	NR	NR	NR	-	-
Non-denom Chr Chs	13	1,960	2,102	2,469	2.1	4.6
ORTHE–Greek Orthodox	1	50	NR	150	0.1	0.3
ORTHE–Orth Ch in Amer	1	30	NR	55	0.0	0.1
PENT–Assemb of God	4	343	229	458	0.4	0.8
PENT–Ch God (Cleve)	1	261	277	332	0.3	0.6
PENT–Un Pent Ch Intl	2	NR	NR	NR	-	-
Salvation Army	1	42	37	148	0.1	0.3
Sev Day Adv	3	98	170	196	0.2	0.4
Un C of Christ	15	787	1,963	2,356	2.0	4.4
Unit Univ	1	12	13	13	0.0	0.0
DELAWARE	**831**	**75,229**	**129,616**	**374,917**	**41.8**	**100.0**
KENT	**158**	**13,513**	**23,010**	**52,665**	**32.4**	**100.0**
ANG/EPIS–Anglican NA	1	NR	NR	NR	-	-
ANG/EPIS–Episcopal	5	378	980	1,115	0.7	2.1
Bahá'í	2	NR	73	73	0.0	0.1
BAPT–Amer Bapt Assn	1	NR	85	105	0.1	0.2
BAPT–Amer Bapt USA	3	233	632	784	0.5	1.5
BAPT–NBC USA	1	0	150	186	0.1	0.4
BAPT–Reg Bapt Gen As	1	NR	NR	NR	-	-
BAPT–So Bapt Conv	8	751	1,123	1,392	0.9	2.6
BRETH–Ch of Brethren	1	0	100	124	0.1	0.2
BUDD–Mahayana	1	NR	NR	100	0.1	0.2
Catholic	5	NR	NR	16,679	10.3	31.7
CGOD–Ch God (Ander)	2	130	NR	130	0.1	0.2
Ch of Nazarene	6	521	626	844	0.5	1.6
Chr & Miss Al	1	42	36	65	0.0	0.1
CHR–Chr Chs & Chs Cr	2	NR	200	248	0.2	0.5
CHR–Chs of Christ	2	80	90	120	0.1	0.2
FRND–Fr Gen Cf	1	NR	49	61	0.0	0.1
Jehovah's Witness	3	NR	NR	NR	-	-
JUD–Conserv	1	58	65	176	0.1	0.3
LDS–Comm of Christ	1	NR	161	161	0.1	0.3
LDS–L-D Saints	4	NR	NR	1,839	1.1	3.5
LUTH–E.L.C.A.	1	150	440	595	0.4	1.1
LUTH–Luth–MO Synod	2	210	528	744	0.5	1.4
MENN–Amish Undif	9	NR	610	1,424	0.9	2.7
MENN–Bible Flwshp	1	30	NR	41	0.0	0.1
MENN–Cons Menn Conf	1	110	52	64	0.0	0.1
METH–AME	14	370	2,097	2,600	1.6	4.9
METH–Un Methodist	28	3,194	7,824	11,655	7.2	22.1
METH–Wesleyan	5	992	553	1,290	0.8	2.4
Muslim Est	1	134	NR	308	0.2	0.6
Non-denom Chr Chs	21	3,155	3,737	4,216	2.6	8.0
ORTHE–Ukrainian Orth	1	45	NR	100	0.1	0.2
PENT–Assemb of God	1	1,408	567	2,467	1.5	4.7
PENT–Ch God (Cleve)	3	177	195	242	0.1	0.5
PENT–Ch of God Proph	1	NR	11	14	0.0	0.0
PENT–COGIC	2	225	370	459	0.3	0.9
PENT–Fire Bapt Hol Ch	1	NR	NR	NR	-	-
PENT–Pent Ch of God	1	70	NR	109	0.1	0.2
PENT–United Holy Ch	1	NR	NR	NR	-	-
PRES–Presb Ch (USA)	2	149	361	448	0.3	0.9
PRES–Presb Ch Amer	1	346	290	432	0.3	0.8
Salvation Army	1	16	50	135	0.1	0.3
Sev Day Adv	6	393	684	786	0.5	1.5
Un C of Christ	1	103	220	273	0.2	0.5
Unit Univ	1	43	51	61	0.0	0.1

NR–Not Reported - Represents no adherents reported. Percentages may not total 100 due to rounding.

Table 3: Religious Congregations by County and Group: 2010

Religious Group	Number of Congrega-tions	Number of Attendees	Number of Communicant, Confirmed, or Full Members	Adherents		
				Number of Adherents	% of Total Pop.	% of Total Adh.
NEW CASTLE	**413**	**42,245**	**70,412**	**250,339**	**46.5**	**100.0**
ANG/EPIS–Episcopal	19	2,312	5,809	7,374	1.4	2.9
Bahá'í	3	NR	136	136	0.0	0.1
BAPT–Amer Bapt USA	13	1,816	3,222	3,915	0.7	1.6
BAPT–Consrv Bapt	1	NR	NR	NR	-	-
BAPT–Converge/BGC	2	875	NR	1,050	0.2	0.4
BAPT–Free Will Bapt	2	NR	90	109	0.0	0.0
BAPT–Natl Mis Bapt Conv	1	0	150	182	0.0	0.1
BAPT–NBC Amer	1	0	0	0	0.0	0.0
BAPT–NBC USA	9	605	1,534	1,864	0.3	0.7
BAPT–Reg Bapt Gen As	1	NR	NR	NR	-	-
BAPT–So Bapt Conv	17	1,991	3,859	4,689	0.9	1.9
BRETH–Breth in Chr	1	NR	NR	NR	-	-
BRETH–Ch of Brethren	1	58	119	145	0.0	0.1
BUDD–Mahayana	3	NR	NR	321	0.1	0.1
BUDD–Vajrayana	1	NR	NR	13	0.0	0.0
Calv Chpl	1	NR	NR	NR	-	-
Catholic	33	NR	NR	138,172	25.7	55.2
CGOD–Ch God (Ander)	3	185	NR	185	0.0	0.1
Ch Cr, Scientst	2	NR	NR	NR	-	-
Ch of Chr (Hol)	1	NR	NR	NR	-	-
Ch of Nazarene	4	247	217	279	0.1	0.1
Chr & Miss Al	4	147	152	297	0.1	0.1
CHR–Chr Chs & Chs Cr	1	NR	0	0	0.0	0.0
CHR–Chs of Christ	6	582	733	908	0.2	0.4
CHR–Int Chs of Christ	1	NR	52	63	0.0	0.0
Christian Brethren	1	NR	NR	NR	-	-
Evan Free Ch	4	695	NR	695	0.1	0.3
FRND–Fr Gen Cf	6	NR	445	541	0.1	0.2
HINDU–I/A Temples	1	NR	NR	1,742	0.3	0.7
HINDU–Post Ren	3	NR	NR	51	0.0	0.0
HINDU–Renaiss	1	NR	NR	12	0.0	0.0
HINDU–Trad Temples	1	NR	NR	6,000	1.1	2.4
Jehovah's Witness	8	NR	NR	NR	-	-
JUD–Conserv	1	356	399	1,077	0.2	0.4
JUD–Orth	1	43	50	60	0.0	0.0
JUD–Reconst	1	217	277	748	0.1	0.3
JUD–Reform	1	380	671	1,812	0.3	0.7
LDS–Comm of Christ	1	NR	161	161	0.0	0.1
LDS–L-D Saints	7	NR	NR	2,541	0.5	1.0
LUTH–E.L.C.A.	10	1,363	3,095	4,991	0.9	2.0
LUTH–Luth–MO Synod	3	294	632	829	0.2	0.3
LUTH–Wisc Ev Luth Syn	1	92	151	187	0.0	0.1
MENN–Bible Flwshp	1	475	NR	641	0.1	0.3
MENN–Mennonite USA	4	153	99	120	0.0	0.0
METH–AME	10	1,415	3,882	4,717	0.9	1.9
METH–AME Zion	3	0	350	425	0.1	0.2
METH–Un Methodist	51	6,875	18,085	22,761	4.2	9.1
METH–Wesleyan	2	129	155	168	0.0	0.1
Muslim Est	4	1,268	NR	6,816	1.3	2.7
Non-denom Chr Chs	59	10,221	11,802	13,920	2.6	5.6
ORTHE–Ant Orth of NA	1	12	NR	31	0.0	0.0
ORTHE–Greek Orthodox	1	280	NR	550	0.1	0.2
ORTHE–Orth Ch in Amer	1	110	NR	200	0.0	0.1
ORTHE–Ukrainian Orth	1	100	NR	175	0.0	0.1
ORTHO–Coptic Orth Ch	1	95	NR	210	0.0	0.1
PENT–Assemb of God	11	1,806	1,137	2,721	0.5	1.1
PENT–Ch God (Cleve)	3	258	269	327	0.1	0.1
PENT–Ch Lord Jesus Apos	3	NR	NR	NR	-	-
PENT–Ch of God Proph	4	NR	271	329	0.1	0.1
PENT–COGIC	1	20	20	24	0.0	0.0
PENT–Full Gosp Bapt	5	NR	NR	NR	-	-
PENT–Intl Pent Holiness	2	144	199	242	0.0	0.1
PENT–Un Pent Ch Intl	5	NR	NR	NR	-	-
PENT–United Holy Ch	3	NR	NR	NR	-	-
PRES–Kor Pres Abroad	1	NR	NR	NR	-	-
PRES–Orth Pres Ch	2	187	218	268	0.0	0.1
PRES–Presb Ch (USA)	25	2,568	6,838	8,308	1.5	3.3
PRES–Presb Ch Amer	9	2,246	2,059	2,452	0.5	1.0
Salvation Army	2	114	372	385	0.1	0.2
Sev Day Adv	9	992	1,724	1,984	0.4	0.8
Sikh	1	NR	NR	NR	-	-
Swedenborgian	1	NR	NR	NR	-	-
Un C of Christ	1	60	193	234	0.0	0.1

Religious Group	Number of Congrega-tions	Number of Attendees	Number of Communicant, Confirmed, or Full Members	Adherents		
				Number of Adherents	% of Total Pop.	% of Total Adh.
Unit Univ	3	459	785	1,139	0.2	0.5
Unity Ch	1	NR	NR	NR	-	-
Zoroastrian	0	NR	NR	43	0.0	0.0
SUSSEX	**260**	**19,471**	**36,194**	**71,913**	**36.5**	**100.0**
ANG/EPIS–Episcopal	11	996	2,030	2,319	1.2	3.2
Bahá'í	1	NR	70	70	0.0	0.1
BAPT–Asc Ref Bap Ch Am	1	NR	NR	NR	-	-
BAPT–Reg Bapt Gen As	3	NR	NR	NR	-	-
BAPT–So Bapt Conv	8	852	1,100	1,306	0.7	1.8
BRETH–Brethren (Ash)	1	NR	80	95	0.0	0.1
Catholic	7	NR	NR	27,681	14.0	38.5
CGOD–Ches God-Gen Con	1	0	0	0	0.0	0.0
Ch Cr, Scientst	2	NR	NR	NR	-	-
Ch of Nazarene	5	562	472	580	0.3	0.8
Chr & Miss Al	3	394	269	625	0.3	0.9
CHR–Chr Ch (Disc)	2	47	90	107	0.1	0.1
CHR–Chr Chs & Chs Cr	6	NR	870	1,033	0.5	1.4
CHR–Chs of Christ	4	220	221	278	0.1	0.4
Evan Free Ch	1	140	NR	140	0.1	0.2
FRND–Fr Gen Cf	1	NR	0	0	0.0	0.0
Ind Fund Churches	1	NR	NR	NR	-	-
Jehovah's Witness	3	NR	NR	NR	-	-
LDS–L-D Saints	1	NR	NR	452	0.2	0.6
LUTH–E.L.C.A.	3	285	764	926	0.5	1.3
LUTH–Luth–MO Synod	2	377	531	560	0.3	0.8
MENN–Bible Flwshp	1	54	NR	73	0.0	0.1
MENN–Cons Menn Conf	2	361	376	446	0.2	0.6
MENN–Mennonite USA	2	115	145	172	0.1	0.2
METH–AME	15	220	1,724	2,047	1.0	2.8
METH–AME Zion	4	120	380	451	0.2	0.6
METH–Un Methodist	79	6,802	16,443	19,240	9.8	26.8
METH–Wesleyan	9	1,088	765	1,414	0.7	2.0
Metro Comm Ch	1	28	35	42	0.0	0.1
Non-denom Chr Chs	26	3,601	4,224	4,837	2.5	6.7
ORTHE–Ant Orth of NA	1	50	NR	100	0.1	0.1
ORTHE–Orth Ch in Amer	1	40	NR	120	0.1	0.2
PENT–Assemb of God	4	384	291	532	0.3	0.7
PENT–Ch God (Cleve)	14	1,390	2,935	3,485	1.8	4.8
PENT–Ch of God Proph	3	NR	183	217	0.1	0.3
PENT–COGIC	2	140	350	416	0.2	0.6
PENT–Elim	2	NR	NR	NR	-	-
PENT–Fire Bapt Hol Ch	2	NR	NR	NR	-	-
PENT–Un Pent Ch Intl	4	NR	NR	NR	-	-
PRES–Presb Ch (USA)	9	555	969	1,151	0.6	1.6
PRES–Presb Ch Amer	2	260	240	275	0.1	0.4
Salvation Army	1	42	50	51	0.0	0.1
Sev Day Adv	7	260	453	521	0.3	0.7
Un C of Christ	1	15	15	18	0.0	0.0
Unit Univ	1	73	119	131	0.1	0.2
Zoroastrian	0	NR	NR	2	0.0	0.0
DISTRICT OF COLUMBIA	**609**	**92,261**	**188,990**	**332,342**	**55.2**	**100.0**
DISTRICT OF COLUMBIA	**609**	**92,261**	**188,990**	**332,342**	**55.2**	**100.0**
ANG/EPIS–Anglican NA	4	NR	NR	NR	-	-
ANG/EPIS–Episcopal	32	7,313	15,029	18,551	3.1	5.6
Bahá'í	1	NR	521	521	0.1	0.2
BAPT–Alliance Bapt	3	NR	NR	NR	-	-
BAPT–Amer Bapt USA	63	15,077	32,493	37,379	6.2	11.2
BAPT–Consrv Bapt	1	NR	NR	NR	-	-
BAPT–Natl Mis Bapt Conv	4	140	350	403	0.1	0.1
BAPT–NBC USA	30	3,625	19,645	22,599	3.8	6.8
BAPT–Prog NBC	22	6,107	13,090	15,059	2.5	4.5
BAPT–S-D Baptist Gen Con	1	49	51	59	0.0	0.0
BAPT–So Bapt Conv	63	8,825	23,123	26,600	4.4	8.0
BRETH–Brethren (Ash)	1	NR	80	92	0.0	0.0
BRETH–Ch of Brethren	1	15	135	155	0.0	0.0
BRETH–Grace Breth	2	NR	NR	NR	-	-
BUDD–Mahayana	10	NR	NR	4,391	0.7	1.3
BUDD–Theravada	1	NR	NR	1,007	0.2	0.3
BUDD–Vajrayana	3	NR	NR	523	0.1	0.2

NR–Not Reported - Represents no adherents reported. Percentages may not total 100 due to rounding.

Table 3: Religious Congregations by County and Group: 2010

Religious Group	Number of Congrega-tions	Number of Attendees	Number of Communicant, Confirmed, or Full Members	Adherents		
				Number of Adherents	% of Total Pop.	% of Total Adh.
Catholic	45	NR	NR	75,948	12.6	22.9
CGOD–Ch God (Ander)	6	446	NR	446	0.1	0.1
Ch Cr, Scientist	6	NR	NR	NR	-	-
Ch of Chr (Hol)	1	NR	NR	NR	-	-
Ch of Nazarene	5	282	602	669	0.1	0.2
Chr & Miss Al	2	240	190	375	0.1	0.1
CHR–Chr Ch (Disc)	4	490	1,395	1,605	0.3	0.5
CHR–Chs of Christ	4	492	543	620	0.1	0.2
CONG–Armen Evang Add'l	1	NR	NR	NR	-	-
Evan Cov Ch	1	29	0	38	0.0	0.0
Evan Free Ch	1	20	NR	20	0.0	0.0
FRND–Fr Gen Cf & Un Mtg	3	NR	432	497	0.1	0.1
FRND–Unaffl Mtgs	1	NR	NR	NR	-	-
HINDU–I/A Temples	5	NR	NR	3,853	0.6	1.2
HINDU–Post Ren	4	NR	NR	60	0.0	0.0
Int Cou Comm Ch	3	NR	NR	NR	-	-
Jehovah's Witness	4	NR	NR	NR	-	-
JUD–Conserv	2	1,553	1,743	4,706	0.8	1.4
JUD–Orth	3	864	600	1,200	0.2	0.4
JUD–Reform	3	2,469	4,355	11,758	2.0	3.5
LDS–Comm of Christ	1	NR	137	137	0.0	0.0
LDS–L-D Saints	1	NR	NR	420	0.1	0.1
LUTH–E.L.C.A.	13	1,322	2,002	3,305	0.5	1.0
LUTH–Luth–MO Synod	2	223	373	821	0.1	0.2
LUTH–Nor Amer Luth C	1	NR	NR	NR	-	-
MENN–Mennonite USA	3	205	110	127	0.0	0.0
MENN–Unaffil Amish-Menn	1	10	5	10	0.0	0.0
METH–AME	13	1,762	4,751	5,465	0.9	1.6
METH–AME Zion	14	1,132	2,741	3,153	0.5	0.9
METH–C.M.E.	5	950	2,110	2,427	0.4	0.7
METH–Free Methodist	1	25	56	56	0.0	0.0
METH–Un Methodist	29	3,683	8,960	10,664	1.8	3.2
METH–Wesleyan	1	54	107	70	0.0	0.0
Metro Comm Ch	1	242	358	412	0.1	0.1
MJEW–Union Mes Cong	1	NR	NR	NR	-	-
MORAV–Morav Ch-North	1	91	108	143	0.0	0.0
Muslim Est	7	1,586	NR	4,032	0.7	1.2
Nat Spirit Asso	1	NR	NR	NR	-	-
Non-denom Chr Chs	61	18,224	33,785	34,292	5.7	10.3
ORTHE–Ant Orth of NA	2	65	NR	100	0.0	0.0
ORTHE–Greek Orthodox	2	1,500	NR	9,500	1.6	2.9
ORTHE–Orth Ch in Amer	1	300	NR	1,500	0.2	0.5
ORTHE–Rus Orth Abroad	1	350	NR	800	0.1	0.2
ORTHO–Armen Ap Etchm	1	150	NR	1,000	0.2	0.3
ORTHO–Eritrean Orth	2	400	NR	1,150	0.2	0.3
ORTHO–Ethiopian Orth	3	NR	NR	NR	-	-
PENT–Apos Faith Msn	1	NR	35	40	0.0	0.0
PENT–Assemb of God	7	3,619	2,170	4,033	0.7	1.2
PENT–Ch God (Cleve)	3	87	168	193	0.0	0.1
PENT–Ch Lord Jesus Apos	4	NR	NR	NR	-	-
PENT–Ch of God Proph	4	NR	303	349	0.1	0.1
PENT–COGIC	9	650	1,300	1,496	0.2	0.5
PENT–Fire Bapt Hol Ch	3	NR	NR	NR	-	-
PENT–Full Gosp Bapt	4	NR	NR	NR	-	-
PENT–Int Foursq Gos	1	11	13	15	0.0	0.0
PENT–Un Pent Ch Intl	2	NR	NR	NR	-	-
PENT–United Holy Ch	4	NR	NR	NR	-	-
PRES–Presb Ch (USA)	16	2,436	5,594	6,435	1.1	1.9
PRES–Presb Ch Amer	1	495	433	494	0.1	0.1
REF–Christian Ref	1	100	136	156	0.0	0.0
REF–Hung Ref Add'l	1	NR	NR	NR	-	-
REF–Un Ref Chs N.A.	1	NR	NR	NR	-	-
Salvation Army	3	168	288	357	0.1	0.1
Sev Day Adv	11	2,610	4,537	5,219	0.9	1.6
Sikh	1	NR	NR	NR	-	-
Swedenborgian	1	NR	NR	NR	-	-
Tao	1	NR	NR	NR	-	-
Un C of Christ	9	992	2,953	3,397	0.6	1.0
Unit Univ	3	783	1,080	1,426	0.2	0.4
Unity Ch	2	NR	NR	NR	-	-
Zoroastrian	1	NR	NR	14	0.0	0.0
FLORIDA	**15,611**	**2,142,198**	**3,457,120**	**7,357,588**	**39.1**	**100.0**

Religious Group	Number of Congrega-tions	Number of Attendees	Number of Communicant, Confirmed, or Full Members	Adherents		
				Number of Adherents	% of Total Pop.	% of Total Adh.
ALACHUA	**302**	**32,428**	**55,618**	**102,841**	**41.6**	**100.0**
ANG/EPIS–Anglican NA	2	NR	NR	NR	-	-
ANG/EPIS–Episcopal	7	609	1,394	1,668	0.7	1.6
Bahá'í	2	NR	316	316	0.1	0.3
BAPT–Amer Bapt Assn	2	NR	185	215	0.1	0.2
BAPT–Natl Mis Bapt Conv	5	100	600	696	0.3	0.7
BAPT–NBC USA	6	375	1,125	1,305	0.5	1.3
BAPT–Ref Bapt Ch	3	NR	NR	NR	-	-
BAPT–So Bapt Conv	62	7,859	19,191	22,268	9.0	21.7
BUDD–Mahayana	5	NR	NR	297	0.1	0.3
BUDD–Vajrayana	3	NR	NR	150	0.1	0.1
Calv Chpl	1	NR	NR	NR	-	-
Catholic	6	NR	NR	20,004	8.1	19.5
CGOD–Ch God (Ander)	1	92	NR	92	0.0	0.1
Ch Cr, Scientist	1	NR	NR	NR	-	-
Ch of Nazarene	3	192	442	450	0.2	0.4
Chr & Miss Al	1	23	0	42	0.0	0.0
CHR–Chr Ch (Disc)	1	62	95	110	0.0	0.1
CHR–Chr Chs & Chs Cr	1	NR	100	116	0.0	0.1
CHR–Chs of Christ	12	1,575	1,508	1,845	0.7	1.8
CHR–Int Chs of Christ	1	NR	270	313	0.1	0.3
Evan Free Ch	1	400	NR	400	0.2	0.4
FRND–Fr Gen Cf	1	NR	60	70	0.0	0.1
HINDU–I/A Temples	2	NR	NR	3,124	1.3	3.0
HINDU–Post Ren	2	NR	NR	93	0.0	0.1
Jehovah's Witness	5	NR	NR	NR	-	-
JUD–Conserv	1	267	300	810	0.3	0.8
JUD–Reform	1	74	131	354	0.1	0.3
LDS–Comm of Christ	1	NR	121	121	0.0	0.1
LDS–L-D Saints	6	NR	NR	2,601	1.1	2.5
LUTH–E.L.C.A.	2	151	255	388	0.2	0.4
LUTH–Luth–MO Synod	2	425	748	905	0.4	0.9
LUTH–Wisc Ev Luth Syn	1	65	92	106	0.0	0.1
MENN–Mennonite USA	1	35	45	52	0.0	0.1
METH–AME	12	450	2,100	2,437	1.0	2.4
METH–C.M.E.	1	0	100	116	0.0	0.1
METH–Un Methodist	35	4,381	8,881	13,617	5.5	13.2
Metro Comm Ch	1	61	73	85	0.0	0.1
Muslim Est	2	812	NR	2,794	1.1	2.7
New Apost Ch	1	NR	NR	NR	-	-
Non-denom Chr Chs	34	7,788	9,470	11,267	4.6	11.0
ORTHE–Greek Orthodox	1	50	NR	200	0.1	0.2
ORTHO–Coptic Orth Ch	1	23	NR	33	0.0	0.0
PENT–Assemb of God	13	2,672	1,314	5,667	2.3	5.5
PENT–Ch God (Cleve)	6	843	1,407	1,633	0.7	1.6
PENT–Ch of God by Faith	9	NR	NR	NR	-	-
PENT–Ch of God Proph	2	NR	79	92	0.0	0.1
PENT–COGIC	5	135	750	870	0.4	0.8
PENT–Full Gosp Bapt	1	NR	NR	NR	-	-
PENT–Intl Pent Holiness	3	135	130	151	0.1	0.1
PENT–Un Pent Ch Intl	2	NR	NR	NR	-	-
PENT–Vineyard	1	260	325	377	0.2	0.4
PRES–Orth Pres Ch	1	47	27	40	0.0	0.0
PRES–Presb Ch (USA)	9	740	1,407	1,633	0.7	1.6
PRES–Presb Ch Amer	2	452	416	416	0.2	0.4
Salvation Army	1	52	60	78	0.0	0.1
Sev Day Adv	5	660	1,148	1,320	0.5	1.3
Un C of Christ	1	375	681	790	0.3	0.8
Unit Univ	1	188	272	312	0.1	0.3
Unity Ch	1	NR	NR	NR	-	-
Zoroastrian	0	NR	NR	2	0.0	0.0
BAKER	**36**	**3,136**	**4,621**	**6,865**	**25.3**	**100.0**
ANG/EPIS–Anglican NA	1	NR	NR	NR	-	-
Bahá'í	0	NR	1	1	0.0	0.0
BAPT–NBC USA	1	0	150	188	0.7	2.7
BAPT–So Bapt Conv	7	964	2,128	2,670	9.8	38.9
Catholic	1	NR	NR	383	1.4	5.6
CHR–Chr Chs & Chs Cr	1	NR	0	0	0.0	0.0
CHR–Chs of Christ	2	145	115	201	0.7	2.9
Jehovah's Witness	1	NR	NR	NR	-	-
LDS–L-D Saints	1	NR	NR	612	2.3	8.9
METH–AME	1	0	100	125	0.5	1.8

NR–Not Reported   - Represents no adherents reported.   Percentages may not total 100 due to rounding.

Table 3: Religious Congregations by County and Group: 2010

Religious Group	Number of Congrega-tions	Number of Attendees	Number of Communicant, Confirmed, or Full Members	Adherents		
				Number of Adherents	% of Total Pop.	% of Total Adh.
METH–Cong Meth	1	NR	18	23	0.1	0.3
METH–Un Methodist	1	150	267	339	1.3	4.9
Non-denom Chr Chs	8	1,190	1,215	1,488	5.5	21.7
PENT–Assemb of God	2	150	83	152	0.6	2.2
PENT–Ch God (Cleve)	3	377	387	486	1.8	7.1
PENT–Ch Lord Jesus Apos	1	NR	NR	NR	-	-
PENT–Ch of God by Faith	1	NR	NR	NR	-	-
PENT–COGIC	1	15	25	31	0.1	0.5
PENT–Cong Hol Ch	2	145	132	166	0.6	2.4
BAY	**205**	**24,230**	**44,995**	**69,639**	**41.2**	**100.0**
ANG/EPIS–Anglican NA	1	NR	NR	NR	-	-
ANG/EPIS–Episcopal	5	449	1,084	1,232	0.7	1.8
Bahá'í	0	NR	38	38	0.0	0.1
BAPT–Amer Bapt Assn	1	NR	0	0	0.0	0.0
BAPT–Free Will Bapt	1	NR	89	107	0.1	0.2
BAPT–Natl Mis Bapt Conv	2	0	300	361	0.2	0.5
BAPT–NBC Amer	2	600	1,150	1,385	0.8	2.0
BAPT–So Bapt Conv	35	7,553	22,118	26,635	15.8	38.2
BUDD–Mahayana	1	NR	NR	102	0.1	0.1
Calv Chpl	1	NR	NR	NR	-	-
Catholic	7	NR	NR	7,744	4.6	11.1
CGOD–Ch God (Ander)	1	35	NR	35	0.0	0.1
Ch Cr, Scientst	1	NR	NR	NR	-	-
Ch of Nazarene	1	78	129	183	0.1	0.3
Chr & Miss Al	3	165	134	177	0.1	0.3
CHR–Chr Chs & Chs Cr	3	NR	180	217	0.1	0.3
CHR–Chs of Christ	8	981	1,025	1,215	0.7	1.7
Jehovah's Witness	6	NR	NR	NR	-	-
JUD–Reform	1	27	47	127	0.1	0.2
LDS–Comm of Christ	1	NR	136	136	0.1	0.2
LDS–L-D Saints	4	NR	NR	2,215	1.3	3.2
LUTH–E.L.C.A.	1	99	254	315	0.2	0.5
LUTH–Luth-MO Synod	4	382	727	837	0.5	1.2
LUTH–Wisc Ev Luth Syn	1	70	96	119	0.1	0.2
METH–AME	6	119	700	843	0.5	1.2
METH–Un Methodist	20	3,520	6,460	8,630	5.1	12.4
Muslim Est	1	406	NR	1,397	0.8	2.0
New Apost Ch	1	NR	NR	NR	-	-
Non-denom Chr Chs	37	5,255	6,031	6,958	4.1	10.0
ORTHE–Greek Orthodox	1	60	NR	70	0.0	0.1
PENT–Assemb of God	19	2,018	942	4,544	2.7	6.5
PENT–Ch God (Cleve)	4	113	131	158	0.1	0.2
PENT–Ch of God Proph	2	NR	45	54	0.0	0.1
PENT–COGIC	1	50	80	96	0.1	0.1
PENT–Intl Pent Holiness	3	513	648	780	0.5	1.1
PENT–Pent Ch of God	1	70	NR	109	0.1	0.2
PENT–Un Pent Ch Intl	2	NR	NR	NR	-	-
PENT–Vineyard	1	127	140	169	0.1	0.2
PRES–Presb Ch (USA)	5	601	866	1,043	0.6	1.5
PRES–Presb Ch Amer	3	445	616	678	0.4	1.0
Salvation Army	1	89	136	136	0.1	0.2
Sev Day Adv	4	370	644	741	0.4	1.1
Unit Univ	1	35	49	53	0.0	0.1
Unity Ch	1	NR	NR	NR	-	-
BRADFORD	**55**	**3,695**	**10,256**	**13,176**	**46.2**	**100.0**
ANG/EPIS–Episcopal	1	46	101	110	0.4	0.8
Bahá'í	0	NR	2	2	0.0	0.0
BAPT–Ind Bapt Flwsp Intl	1	NR	NR	NR	-	-
BAPT–NBC USA	2	0	0	0	0.0	0.0
BAPT–So Bapt Conv	16	1,792	6,635	7,867	27.6	59.7
Catholic	1	NR	NR	142	0.5	1.1
Ch of Nazarene	1	32	26	42	0.1	0.3
CHR–Chr Chs & Chs Cr	2	NR	130	154	0.5	1.2
CHR–Chs of Christ	4	149	133	167	0.6	1.3
Jehovah's Witness	1	NR	NR	NR	-	-
LDS–L-D Saints	1	NR	NR	565	2.0	4.3
LUTH–Luth-MO Synod	1	40	0	35	0.1	0.3
METH–AME	3	90	368	436	1.5	3.3
METH–Cong Meth	1	NR	0	0	0.0	0.0
METH–Un Methodist	4	587	1,373	1,960	6.9	14.9
Non-denom Chr Chs	5	470	615	663	2.3	5.0
PENT–Ch God (Cleve)	3	329	598	709	2.5	5.4
PENT–Ch of God by Faith	1	NR	NR	NR	-	-
PENT–Ch of God Proph	1	NR	30	36	0.1	0.3
PENT–Cong Hol Ch	2	36	33	39	0.1	0.3
PENT–Un Pent Ch Intl	1	NR	NR	NR	-	-
PRES–Presb Ch (USA)	2	100	169	200	0.7	1.5
Sev Day Adv	1	24	43	49	0.2	0.4
BREVARD	**414**	**58,131**	**95,955**	**189,430**	**34.9**	**100.0**
ANG/EPIS–Anglican NA	3	NR	NR	NR	-	-
ANG/EPIS–Episcopal	11	1,566	2,804	3,239	0.6	1.7
Bahá'í	3	NR	185	185	0.0	0.1
BAPT–Amer Bapt Assn	2	NR	20	23	0.0	0.0
BAPT–Amer Bapt USA	1	37	24	28	0.0	0.0
BAPT–Converge/BGC	2	150	NR	180	0.0	0.1
BAPT–Free Will Bapt	5	NR	445	522	0.1	0.3
BAPT–Ind Bapt Flwsp Intl	1	NR	NR	NR	-	-
BAPT–Natl Mis Bapt Conv	1	0	150	176	0.0	0.1
BAPT–NBC Amer	1	350	500	587	0.1	0.3
BAPT–NBC USA	5	1,050	1,576	1,849	0.3	1.0
BAPT–Ref Bapt Ch	2	NR	NR	NR	-	-
BAPT–So Bapt Conv	57	10,141	22,652	26,576	4.9	14.0
BRETH–Grace Breth	1	NR	NR	NR	-	-
BUDD–Mahayana	3	NR	NR	132	0.0	0.1
BUDD–Theravada	1	NR	NR	375	0.1	0.2
Calv Chpl	4	NR	NR	NR	-	-
Catholic	14	NR	NR	64,831	11.9	34.2
CGOD–Ch God (Ander)	2	55	NR	55	0.0	0.0
Ch Cr, Scientst	2	NR	NR	NR	-	-
Ch of Nazarene	9	737	1,264	1,445	0.3	0.8
Chr & Miss Al	3	127	88	149	0.0	0.1
CHR–Chr Ch (Disc)	2	269	451	529	0.1	0.3
CHR–Chr Chs & Chs Cr	9	NR	2,044	2,398	0.4	1.3
CHR–Chs of Christ	12	1,740	1,871	2,192	0.4	1.2
CHR–Int Chs of Christ	0	NR	112	131	0.0	0.1
Evan Free Ch	1	800	NR	800	0.1	0.4
FRND–Fr Gen Cf	1	NR	14	16	0.0	0.0
Grace Gosp Fel	1	NR	NR	NR	-	-
HINDU–Post Ren	3	NR	NR	200	0.0	0.1
HINDU–Renaiss	1	NR	NR	12	0.0	0.0
HINDU–Trad Temples	1	NR	NR	100	0.0	0.1
Jehovah's Witness	8	NR	NR	NR	-	-
JUD–Orth	1	0	50	0	0.0	0.0
JUD–Reform	1	109	192	518	0.1	0.3
LDS–Comm of Christ	1	NR	121	121	0.0	0.1
LDS–L-D Saints	7	NR	NR	5,136	0.9	2.7
LUTH–E.L.C.A.	10	1,339	2,637	3,027	0.6	1.6
LUTH–Luth Cong Msn Chr	2	270	547	642	0.1	0.3
LUTH–Luth-MO Synod	10	1,460	2,178	2,513	0.5	1.3
LUTH–Wisc Ev Luth Syn	2	175	264	304	0.1	0.2
METH–AME	7	660	1,743	2,045	0.4	1.1
METH–AME Zion	1	0	100	117	0.0	0.1
METH–Free Methodist	1	8	4	8	0.0	0.0
METH–Un Methodist	22	6,257	13,859	18,514	3.4	9.8
METH–Wesleyan	1	26	23	34	0.0	0.0
Muslim Est	3	1,218	NR	4,191	0.8	2.2
Non-denom Chr Chs	75	20,566	27,706	29,047	5.3	15.3
ORTHE–Ant Orth of NA	1	46	NR	65	0.0	0.0
ORTHE–Greek Orthodox	1	150	NR	1,000	0.2	0.5
ORTHE–Orth Ch in Amer	1	15	NR	30	0.0	0.0
ORTHO–Coptic Orth Ch	2	152	NR	172	0.0	0.1
PENT–Assemb of God	13	1,483	1,062	1,891	0.3	1.0
PENT–Ch God (Cleve)	17	1,546	2,287	2,683	0.5	1.4
PENT–Ch God Mtn Asm	1	NR	NR	NR	-	-
PENT–Ch Lord Jesus Apos	2	NR	NR	NR	-	-
PENT–Ch of God by Faith	2	NR	NR	NR	-	-
PENT–Ch of God Proph	2	NR	41	48	0.0	0.0
PENT–COGIC	6	230	575	675	0.1	0.4
PENT–Full Gosp Bapt	2	NR	NR	NR	-	-
PENT–Intl Pent Holiness	1	118	146	171	0.0	0.1
PENT–Un Pent Ch Intl	4	NR	NR	NR	-	-
PENT–Vineyard	2	65	105	123	0.0	0.1
PRES–As Ref Pres Ch	2	NR	323	379	0.1	0.2
PRES–Bible Pres	1	NR	NR	NR	-	-

NR–Not Reported - Represents no adherents reported. Percentages may not total 100 due to rounding.

Table 3: Religious Congregations by County and Group: 2010

Religious Group	Number of Congrega-tions	Number of Attendees	Number of Communicant, Confirmed, or Full Members	Adherents		
				Number of Adherents	% of Total Pop.	% of Total Adh.
PRES–Cov Ref Pres	1	NR	NR	NR	-	-
PRES–Presb Ch (USA)	12	2,478	4,029	4,727	0.9	2.5
PRES–Presb Ch Amer	5	1,001	1,033	1,298	0.2	0.7
REF–Christian Ref	1	30	13	15	0.0	0.0
Salvation Army	2	115	224	328	0.1	0.2
Sev Day Adv	7	969	1,685	1,938	0.4	1.0
Un C of Christ	4	491	679	797	0.1	0.4
Unit Univ	3	132	129	143	0.0	0.1
Unity Ch	3	NR	NR	NR	-	-
BROWARD	**1,040**	**174,697**	**247,936**	**641,572**	**36.7**	**100.0**
ANG/EPIS–Anglican NA	3	NR	NR	NR	-	-
ANG/EPIS–Episcopal	17	2,684	5,803	6,803	0.4	1.1
Ap Chr Ch-Amer	1	35	18	35	0.0	0.0
Bahá'í	15	NR	1,297	1,297	0.1	0.2
BAPT–Amer Bapt Assn	3	NR	320	385	0.0	0.1
BAPT–Amer Bapt USA	2	3,400	10,818	13,028	0.7	2.0
BAPT–Consrv Bapt	1	NR	NR	NR	-	-
BAPT–Converge/BGC	6	775	NR	930	0.1	0.1
BAPT–Free Will Bapt	1	NR	89	107	0.0	0.0
BAPT–Ind Bapt Flwsp Intl	1	NR	NR	NR	-	-
BAPT–Natl Mis Bapt Conv	4	325	750	903	0.1	0.1
BAPT–NBC Amer	1	200	1,000	1,204	0.1	0.2
BAPT–NBC USA	16	3,568	7,860	9,466	0.5	1.5
BAPT–NT Ind Bapt	1	NR	NR	NR	-	-
BAPT–Ref Bapt Ch	2	NR	NR	NR	-	-
BAPT–Reg Bapt Gen As	2	NR	NR	NR	-	-
BAPT–S-D Baptist Gen Con	1	66	55	66	0.0	0.0
BAPT–So Bapt Conv	181	43,266	60,783	73,203	4.2	11.4
BRETH–Breth in Chr	6	NR	NR	NR	-	-
BRETH–Grace Breth	1	NR	NR	NR	-	-
BUDD–Mahayana	8	NR	NR	11,728	0.7	1.8
BUDD–Vajrayana	3	NR	NR	700	0.0	0.1
Calv Chpl	6	NR	NR	NR	-	-
Catholic	46	NR	NR	280,324	16.0	43.7
CGOD–Ch God (Ander)	10	1,629	NR	1,629	0.1	0.3
Ch Cr, Scientst	3	NR	NR	NR	-	-
Ch of Nazarene	12	1,012	1,643	1,930	0.1	0.3
Chr & Miss Al	18	1,431	910	1,697	0.1	0.3
CHR–Chr Ch (Disc)	9	409	1,531	1,844	0.1	0.3
CHR–Chr Chs & Chs Cr	9	NR	405	488	0.0	0.1
CHR–Chs of Christ	19	3,515	5,242	6,372	0.4	1.0
CHR–Int Chs of Christ	0	NR	252	303	0.0	0.0
Christian Brethren	1	NR	NR	NR	-	-
Evan Cov Ch	1	44	93	57	0.0	0.0
Evan Free Ch	3	200	NR	200	0.0	0.0
FRND–Fr Gen Cf	1	NR	7	8	0.0	0.0
HINDU–Post Ren	4	NR	NR	153	0.0	0.0
HINDU–Renaiss	2	NR	NR	24	0.0	0.0
HINDU–Trad Temples	3	NR	NR	600	0.0	0.1
Ind Fund Churches	2	NR	NR	NR	-	-
Int Cou Comm Ch	1	NR	NR	NR	-	-
Jehovah's Witness	20	NR	NR	NR	-	-
JUD–Conserv	8	2,151	2,414	6,518	0.4	1.0
JUD–Orth	30	3,960	2,500	5,500	0.3	0.9
JUD–Reform	8	2,050	3,615	9,760	0.6	1.5
LDS–Comm of Christ	1	NR	121	121	0.0	0.0
LDS–L-D Saints	13	NR	NR	8,206	0.5	1.3
LUTH–E.L.C.A.	16	1,440	2,754	3,485	0.2	0.5
LUTH–Luth-MO Synod	13	1,292	2,464	3,173	0.2	0.5
LUTH–Wisc Ev Luth Syn	1	53	77	102	0.0	0.0
MENN–Mennonite USA	1	0	18	22	0.0	0.0
METH–AME	10	1,450	3,425	4,125	0.2	0.6
METH–AME Zion	1	0	100	120	0.0	0.0
METH–C.M.E.	3	0	400	482	0.0	0.1
METH–Free Methodist	1	75	112	112	0.0	0.0
METH–Un Methodist	21	5,468	12,293	22,462	1.3	3.5
METH–Wesleyan	4	206	123	268	0.0	0.0
Metro Comm Ch	1	579	524	631	0.0	0.1
Missionary Ch	1	15	0	15	0.0	0.0
MJEW–Union Mes Cong	1	NR	NR	NR	-	-
Muslim Est	13	6,048	NR	18,176	1.0	2.8
New Apost Ch	1	NR	NR	NR	-	-
Non-denom Chr Chs	173	54,377	78,803	81,534	4.7	12.7
OCATH–Pol Natl Cath	1	NR	NR	NR	-	-
ORTHE–Ant Orth of NA	1	250	NR	650	0.0	0.1
ORTHE–Carp Rus Orth	1	20	NR	50	0.0	0.0
ORTHE–Greek Orthodox	2	500	NR	2,385	0.1	0.4
ORTHE–Macedonian Orth	1	85	NR	660	0.0	0.1
ORTHE–Orth Ch in Amer	3	295	NR	1,100	0.1	0.2
ORTHE–Rus Orth Abroad	1	25	NR	25	0.0	0.0
ORTHE–Ukrainian Orth	1	40	NR	80	0.0	0.0
ORTHO–Armen Ap Cilic	1	80	NR	80	0.0	0.0
ORTHO–Coptic Orth Ch	1	300	NR	330	0.0	0.1
ORTHO–Malan Dioc Am	3	60	NR	180	0.0	0.0
ORTHO–Malan Syr Orth	1	55	NR	108	0.0	0.0
PENT–Assemb of God	54	8,730	4,893	13,900	0.8	2.2
PENT–Ch God (Cleve)	58	6,052	8,595	10,351	0.6	1.6
PENT–Ch God Mtn Asm	1	NR	NR	NR	-	-
PENT–Ch Lord Jesus Apos	3	NR	NR	NR	-	-
PENT–Ch of God by Faith	3	NR	NR	NR	-	-
PENT–Ch of God Proph	13	NR	775	933	0.1	0.1
PENT–COGIC	7	450	1,300	1,566	0.1	0.2
PENT–Fire Bapt Hol Ch	3	NR	NR	NR	-	-
PENT–Int Foursq Gos	2	0	0	0	0.0	0.0
PENT–Int Pent C Chr	1	0	NR	40	0.0	0.0
PENT–Intl Pent Holiness	8	1,739	1,630	1,963	0.1	0.3
PENT–Open Bible Std	3	958	NR	958	0.1	0.1
PENT–Un Pent Ch Intl	9	NR	NR	NR	-	-
PRES–As Ref Pres Ch	1	NR	280	337	0.0	0.1
PRES–Evan Presby Ch	1	NR	385	464	0.0	0.1
PRES–Orth Pres Ch	1	60	41	43	0.0	0.0
PRES–Presb Ch (USA)	12	1,938	3,697	4,452	0.3	0.7
PRES–Presb Ch Amer	9	2,691	3,174	3,830	0.2	0.6
REF–Christian Ref	1	160	136	164	0.0	0.0
REF–Ref Ch in Am	3	276	249	359	0.0	0.1
Salvation Army	1	171	376	376	0.0	0.1
Sev Day Adv	48	7,636	13,278	15,271	0.9	2.4
Sikh	2	NR	NR	NR	-	-
Tao	1	NR	NR	NR	-	-
Un C of Christ	4	262	282	340	0.0	0.1
Unit Univ	3	141	226	258	0.0	0.0
Unity Ch	4	NR	NR	NR	-	-
Zoroastrian	0	NR	NR	23	0.0	0.0
CALHOUN	**37**	**2,268**	**3,675**	**5,966**	**40.8**	**100.0**
BAPT–Amer Bapt Assn	1	NR	85	102	0.7	1.7
BAPT–Free Will Bapt	2	NR	178	214	1.5	3.6
BAPT–So Bapt Conv	7	456	1,511	1,815	12.4	30.4
Catholic	1	NR	NR	53	0.4	0.9
Ch of Nazarene	1	16	30	39	0.3	0.7
Jehovah's Witness	1	NR	NR	NR	-	-
METH–AME	1	75	126	151	1.0	2.5
METH–Un Methodist	3	129	402	416	2.8	7.0
Muslim Est	1	406	NR	1,397	9.6	23.4
Non-denom Chr Chs	3	595	555	745	5.1	12.5
PENT–Assemb of God	5	189	104	213	1.5	3.6
PENT–Ch God (Cleve)	3	166	203	244	1.7	4.1
PENT–COGIC	2	15	175	210	1.4	3.5
PENT–Intl Pent Holiness	4	211	294	353	2.4	5.9
PENT–Un Pent Ch Intl	1	NR	NR	NR	-	-
PRES–Presb Ch (USA)	1	10	12	14	0.1	0.2
CHARLOTTE	**111**	**15,393**	**19,197**	**64,078**	**40.1**	**100.0**
ANG/EPIS–Episcopal	2	383	998	1,050	0.7	1.6
Bahá'í	0	NR	15	15	0.0	0.0
BAPT–Converge/BGC	1	75	NR	90	0.1	0.1
BAPT–Reg Bapt Gen As	1	NR	NR	NR	-	-
BAPT–So Bapt Conv	15	2,523	3,570	3,991	2.5	6.2
Catholic	5	NR	NR	35,400	22.1	55.2
CGOD–Ch God (Ander)	1	0	NR	0	0.0	0.0
Ch Cr, Scientst	1	NR	NR	NR	-	-
Ch of Nazarene	2	105	140	428	0.3	0.7
Chr & Miss Al	4	1,067	449	1,607	1.0	2.5
CHR–Chr Chs & Chs Cr	3	NR	850	950	0.6	1.5
CHR–Chs of Christ	4	234	179	246	0.2	0.4
Jehovah's Witness	3	NR	NR	NR	-	-

NR–Not Reported - Represents no adherents reported. Percentages may not total 100 due to rounding.

Table 3: Religious Congregations by County and Group: 2010

Religious Group	Number of Congregations	Number of Attendees	Number of Communicant, Confirmed, or Full Members	Adherents: Number of Adherents	Adherents: % of Total Pop.	Adherents: % of Total Adh.
JUD–Orth	1	43	50	60	0.0	0.1
JUD–Reconst	1	7	9	24	0.0	0.0
JUD–Reform	1	57	101	273	0.2	0.4
LDS–L-D Saints	1	NR	NR	845	0.5	1.3
LUTH–E.L.C.A.	3	650	967	1,068	0.7	1.7
LUTH–Luth–MO Synod	3	516	666	754	0.5	1.2
LUTH–Wisc Ev Luth Syn	1	78	69	80	0.1	0.1
METH–AME	1	0	150	168	0.1	0.3
METH–Free Methodist	1	29	30	30	0.0	0.0
METH–Un Methodist	7	2,509	3,270	5,692	3.6	8.9
METH–Wesleyan	1	51	17	66	0.0	0.1
Muslim Est	1	407	NR	1,397	0.9	2.2
Non-denom Chr Chs	15	2,645	3,305	3,646	2.3	5.7
ORTHE–Greek Orthodox	1	65	NR	384	0.2	0.6
ORTHE–Orth Ch in Amer	1	25	NR	50	0.0	0.1
PENT–Assemb of God	5	783	219	888	0.6	1.4
PENT–Ch God (Cleve)	5	330	490	548	0.3	0.9
PENT–Ch of God Proph	1	NR	107	120	0.1	0.2
PENT–Int Foursq Gos	1	33	47	53	0.0	0.1
PENT–Intl Pent Holiness	1	150	150	168	0.1	0.3
PENT–Open Bible Std	1	58	NR	58	0.0	0.1
PRES–Presb Ch (USA)	4	1,130	1,258	1,406	0.9	2.2
Salvation Army	1	117	105	275	0.2	0.4
Sev Day Adv	7	663	1,152	1,326	0.8	2.1
Un C of Christ	2	596	745	833	0.5	1.3
Unit Univ	1	64	89	89	0.1	0.1
Unity Ch	1	NR	NR	NR	-	-
CITRUS	**137**	**15,122**	**22,540**	**43,216**	**30.6**	**100.0**
ANG/EPIS–Anglican NA	3	NR	NR	NR	-	-
ANG/EPIS–Episcopal	3	481	896	957	0.7	2.2
Bahá'í	1	NR	44	44	0.0	0.1
BAPT–Amer Bapt Assn	1	NR	85	96	0.1	0.2
BAPT–Converge/BGC	1	75	NR	90	0.1	0.2
BAPT–Natl Mis Bapt Conv	2	50	190	215	0.2	0.5
BAPT–Ref Bapt Ch	1	NR	NR	NR	-	-
BAPT–Reg Bapt Gen As	1	NR	NR	NR	-	-
BAPT–So Bapt Conv	21	4,230	7,118	8,055	5.7	18.6
Catholic	6	NR	NR	13,612	9.6	31.5
CGOD–Ch God (Ander)	2	237	NR	237	0.2	0.5
Ch Cr, Scientst	1	NR	NR	NR	-	-
Ch of Nazarene	1	272	315	344	0.2	0.8
CHR–Chr Chs & Chs Cr	6	NR	397	449	0.3	1.0
CHR–Chs of Christ	9	595	515	707	0.5	1.6
CONG–Cong Chr, NA	1	NR	121	137	0.1	0.3
HINDU–I/A Temples	1	NR	NR	1,000	0.7	2.3
Jehovah's Witness	4	NR	NR	NR	-	-
LDS–L-D Saints	1	NR	NR	770	0.5	1.8
LUTH–E.L.C.A.	2	455	384	1,026	0.7	2.4
LUTH–Luth–MO Synod	2	323	574	640	0.5	1.5
LUTH–Wisc Ev Luth Syn	1	140	141	194	0.1	0.4
METH–AME	2	0	200	226	0.2	0.5
METH–Un Methodist	7	1,600	2,895	3,431	2.4	7.9
Non-denom Chr Chs	21	2,451	3,014	3,507	2.5	8.1
ORTHE–Greek Orthodox	1	60	NR	150	0.1	0.3
ORTHE–Orth Ch in Amer	1	41	NR	96	0.1	0.2
PENT–Assemb of God	7	870	852	1,624	1.1	3.8
PENT–Ch God (Cleve)	7	1,032	1,838	2,080	1.5	4.8
PENT–Ch God Mtn Asm	1	NR	NR	NR	-	-
PENT–Ch of God by Faith	1	NR	NR	NR	-	-
PENT–Int Foursq Gos	1	22	35	40	0.0	0.1
PENT–Un Pent Ch Intl	3	NR	NR	NR	-	-
PENT–Vineyard	1	50	50	57	0.0	0.1
PRES–Presb Ch (USA)	2	513	900	1,018	0.7	2.4
PRES–Presb Ch Amer	4	1,345	1,534	1,918	1.4	4.4
Salvation Army	1	42	54	61	0.0	0.1
Sev Day Adv	4	183	319	366	0.3	0.8
Unit Univ	1	55	69	69	0.0	0.2
Unity Ch	1	NR	NR	NR	-	-

Religious Group	Number of Congregations	Number of Attendees	Number of Communicant, Confirmed, or Full Members	Adherents: Number of Adherents	Adherents: % of Total Pop.	Adherents: % of Total Adh.
CLAY	**152**	**24,839**	**46,199**	**82,790**	**43.4**	**100.0**
ANG/EPIS–Anglican NA	3	NR	NR	NR	-	-
ANG/EPIS–Episcopal	3	304	710	712	0.4	0.9
Bahá'í	1	NR	54	54	0.0	0.1
BAPT–Free Will Bapt	1	NR	89	111	0.1	0.1
BAPT–Natl Mis Bapt Conv	1	0	150	187	0.1	0.2
BAPT–So Bapt Conv	45	9,792	25,074	31,203	16.3	37.7
BRETH–Ch of Brethren	1	0	73	91	0.0	0.1
Calv Chpl	1	NR	NR	NR	-	-
Catholic	4	NR	NR	22,260	11.7	26.9
CGOD–Ch God (Ander)	1	40	NR	40	0.0	0.0
Ch of Nazarene	1	111	118	175	0.1	0.2
Chr & Miss Al	2	144	136	235	0.1	0.3
CHR–Chr Ch (Disc)	1	44	49	61	0.0	0.1
CHR–Chr Chs & Chs Cr	2	NR	255	317	0.2	0.4
CHR–Chs of Christ	8	865	870	1,061	0.6	1.3
Christian Brethren	1	NR	NR	NR	-	-
Evan Free Ch	1	79	NR	79	0.0	0.1
Jehovah's Witness	2	NR	NR	NR	-	-
LDS–Comm of Christ	1	NR	121	121	0.1	0.1
LDS–L-D Saints	5	NR	NR	2,888	1.5	3.5
LUTH–E.L.C.A.	2	553	1,178	1,333	0.7	1.6
LUTH–Luth–MO Synod	1	160	255	325	0.2	0.4
LUTH–Wisc Ev Luth Syn	1	25	42	52	0.0	0.1
METH–AME	2	0	200	249	0.1	0.3
METH–Un Methodist	6	1,324	3,393	4,151	2.2	5.0
METH–Wesleyan	1	37	41	48	0.0	0.1
Muslim Est	1	406	NR	1,397	0.7	1.7
Non-denom Chr Chs	25	8,351	9,920	10,926	5.7	13.2
PENT–Assemb of God	7	642	435	780	0.4	0.9
PENT–Ch God (Cleve)	5	228	449	559	0.3	0.7
PENT–Ch Lord Jesus Apos	2	NR	NR	NR	-	-
PENT–Cong Hol Ch	1	70	64	80	0.0	0.1
PENT–Intl Pent Holiness	3	186	301	375	0.2	0.5
PENT–Un Pent Ch Intl	2	NR	NR	NR	-	-
PRES–Presb Ch (USA)	4	594	1,154	1,436	0.8	1.7
PRES–Presb Ch Amer	1	641	744	1,071	0.6	1.3
Salvation Army	1	90	97	118	0.1	0.1
Sev Day Adv	1	66	116	133	0.1	0.2
Unit Univ	1	87	111	162	0.1	0.2
COLLIER	**210**	**30,215**	**46,404**	**111,034**	**34.5**	**100.0**
ANG/EPIS–Anglican NA	1	NR	NR	NR	-	-
ANG/EPIS–Episcopal	5	1,251	2,907	3,103	1.0	2.8
Bahá'í	1	NR	150	150	0.0	0.1
BAPT–Natl Mis Bapt Conv	2	300	650	764	0.2	0.7
BAPT–Ref Bapt Ch	1	NR	NR	NR	-	-
BAPT–So Bapt Conv	36	7,205	13,454	15,818	4.9	14.2
BRETH–Ch of Brethren	1	0	0	0	0.0	0.0
BUDD–Mahayana	3	NR	NR	124	0.0	0.1
BUDD–Vajrayana	1	NR	NR	39	0.0	0.0
Catholic	10	NR	NR	47,000	14.6	42.3
Ch Cr, Scientst	1	NR	NR	NR	-	-
Ch of Nazarene	6	828	1,194	1,323	0.4	1.2
Chr & Miss Al	4	187	105	263	0.1	0.2
CHR–Chr Ch (Disc)	2	124	144	169	0.1	0.2
CHR–Chr Chs & Chs Cr	3	NR	525	617	0.2	0.6
CHR–Chs of Christ	2	285	233	317	0.1	0.3
CONG–Cong Chr, NA	2	NR	517	608	0.2	0.5
Evan Free Ch	1	52	NR	52	0.0	0.0
Grace Gosp Fel	1	NR	NR	NR	-	-
HINDU–Post Ren	1	NR	NR	50	0.0	0.0
Jehovah's Witness	6	NR	NR	NR	-	-
JUD–Conserv	1	67	75	202	0.1	0.2
JUD–Orth	1	43	50	60	0.0	0.1
JUD–Reform	1	333	587	1,585	0.5	1.4
LDS–L-D Saints	5	NR	NR	1,793	0.6	1.6
LUTH–E.L.C.A.	3	988	1,187	1,605	0.5	1.4
LUTH–Evan Luth Syn	1	153	160	195	0.1	0.2
LUTH–Luth–MO Synod	5	889	1,528	1,749	0.5	1.6
MENN–Mennonite USA	1	NR	NR	NR	-	-
METH–AME	2	0	300	353	0.1	0.3
METH–Free Methodist	2	496	444	523	0.2	0.5

NR–Not Reported - Represents no adherents reported. Percentages may not total 100 due to rounding.

Table 3: Religious Congregations by County and Group: 2010

Religious Group	Number of Congrega-tions	Number of Attendees	Number of Communicant, Confirmed, or Full Members	Adherents		
				Number of Adherents	% of Total Pop.	% of Total Adh.
METH–Un Methodist	6	2,764	4,550	7,886	2.5	7.1
METH–Wesleyan	1	68	16	88	0.0	0.1
Metro Comm Ch	1	34	35	41	0.0	0.0
Missionary Ch	1	25	25	25	0.0	0.0
Muslim Est	1	406	NR	1,397	0.4	1.3
Non-denom Chr Chs	36	6,145	7,990	8,817	2.7	7.9
OCATH–Un Cath Ch	1	NR	NR	702	0.2	0.6
ORTHE–Ant Orth of NA	1	120	NR	250	0.1	0.2
ORTHE–Greek Orthodox	1	330	NR	1,000	0.3	0.9
ORTHE–Orth Ch in Amer	2	130	NR	400	0.1	0.4
ORTHO–Armen Ap Etchm	1	35	NR	80	0.0	0.1
PENT–Assemb of God	9	1,868	1,154	2,183	0.7	2.0
PENT–Ch God (Cleve)	8	768	1,332	1,566	0.5	1.4
PENT–Int Foursq Gos	1	14	25	29	0.0	0.0
PENT–Intl Pent Holiness	1	35	70	82	0.0	0.1
PENT–Un Pent Ch Intl	2	NR	NR	NR	-	-
PENT–Vineyard	1	40	55	65	0.0	0.1
PRES–Presb Ch (USA)	4	1,187	2,811	3,305	1.0	3.0
PRES–Presb Ch Amer	5	955	678	704	0.2	0.6
Salvation Army	2	165	255	255	0.1	0.2
Sev Day Adv	8	752	1,309	1,505	0.5	1.4
Un C of Christ	3	1,036	1,601	1,882	0.6	1.7
Unit Univ	1	137	288	310	0.1	0.3
Unity Ch	1	NR	NR	NR	-	-
COLUMBIA	**120**	**10,249**	**20,178**	**27,171**	**40.2**	**100.0**
ANG/EPIS–Anglican NA	1	NR	NR	NR	-	-
ANG/EPIS–Episcopal	1	109	196	201	0.3	0.7
Bahá'í	0	NR	5	5	0.0	0.0
BAPT–Ind Bapt Flwsp Intl	1	NR	NR	NR	-	-
BAPT–Natl Mis Bapt Conv	1	0	150	182	0.3	0.7
BAPT–NBC USA	2	215	600	727	1.1	2.7
BAPT–Reg Bapt Gen As	1	NR	NR	NR	-	-
BAPT–So Bapt Conv	31	4,050	9,952	12,056	17.9	44.4
BRETH–Breth in Chr	1	NR	NR	NR	-	-
BUDD–Mahayana	1	NR	NR	103	0.2	0.4
Catholic	1	NR	NR	1,652	2.4	6.1
Ch Cr, Scientst	1	NR	NR	NR	-	-
Ch of Nazarene	1	86	200	200	0.3	0.7
CHR–Chr Chs & Chs Cr	2	NR	118	143	0.2	0.5
CHR–Chs of Christ	6	335	344	449	0.7	1.7
Jehovah's Witness	1	NR	NR	NR	-	-
LDS–L-D Saints	3	NR	NR	1,002	1.5	3.7
LUTH–E.L.C.A.	2	84	167	214	0.3	0.8
LUTH–Luth–MO Synod	1	98	188	210	0.3	0.8
METH–AME	8	290	1,180	1,429	2.1	5.3
METH–Cong Meth	1	NR	148	179	0.3	0.7
METH–So Methodist	1	NR	NR	NR	-	-
METH–Un Methodist	11	924	1,792	2,260	3.3	8.3
Non-denom Chr Chs	19	3,125	3,755	4,265	6.3	15.7
PENT–Assemb of God	4	171	158	319	0.5	1.2
PENT–Ch God (Cleve)	4	251	469	568	0.8	2.1
PENT–Ch Lord Jesus Apos	2	NR	NR	NR	-	-
PENT–Ch of God by Faith	1	NR	NR	NR	-	-
PENT–COGIC	1	0	0	0	0.0	0.0
PENT–Cong Hol Ch	2	23	21	25	0.0	0.1
PENT–Full Gosp Bapt	1	NR	NR	NR	-	-
PENT–Intl Pent Holiness	1	21	35	42	0.1	0.2
PENT–Pent Ch of God	1	70	NR	109	0.2	0.4
PRES–Presb Ch (USA)	2	245	435	527	0.8	1.9
Sev Day Adv	3	152	265	304	0.5	1.1
DESOTO	**57**	**3,102**	**8,186**	**14,282**	**41.0**	**100.0**
ANG/EPIS–Episcopal	1	48	57	66	0.2	0.5
Bahá'í	0	NR	9	9	0.0	0.1
BAPT–Amer Bapt Assn	1	NR	80	97	0.3	0.7
BAPT–Ind Bapt Flwsp Intl	1	NR	NR	NR	-	-
BAPT–NBC Amer	4	25	375	453	1.3	3.2
BAPT–So Bapt Conv	12	1,112	3,836	4,636	13.3	32.5
BRETH–Ch of Brethren	1	0	27	33	0.1	0.2
Catholic	2	NR	NR	4,300	12.3	30.1
Ch of Nazarene	1	55	116	137	0.4	1.0
CHR–Chr Chs & Chs Cr	2	NR	195	236	0.7	1.7

Religious Group	Number of Congrega-tions	Number of Attendees	Number of Communicant, Confirmed, or Full Members	Adherents		
				Number of Adherents	% of Total Pop.	% of Total Adh.
CHR–Chs of Christ	3	155	152	191	0.5	1.3
LDS–L-D Saints	1	NR	NR	213	0.6	1.5
LUTH–Luth–MO Synod	1	60	75	85	0.2	0.6
MENN–CG in Cr (Menn)	1	NR	21	25	0.1	0.2
MENN–Mennonite USA	1	73	51	62	0.2	0.4
METH–AME	3	52	400	483	1.4	3.4
METH–C.M.E.	2	0	250	302	0.9	2.1
METH–Un Methodist	5	579	1,166	1,413	4.1	9.9
Non-denom Chr Chs	4	360	510	550	1.6	3.9
PENT–Assemb of God	2	130	180	180	0.5	1.3
PENT–Ch God (Cleve)	4	240	312	377	1.1	2.6
PENT–Ch of God Proph	1	NR	45	54	0.2	0.4
PENT–Un Pent Ch Intl	1	NR	NR	NR	-	-
PRES–Presb Ch (USA)	1	118	213	257	0.7	1.8
PRES–Presb Ch Amer	1	67	67	67	0.2	0.5
Sev Day Adv	1	28	49	56	0.2	0.4
DIXIE	**28**	**1,624**	**3,704**	**4,741**	**28.9**	**100.0**
Bahá'í	0	NR	3	3	0.0	0.1
BAPT–So Bapt Conv	10	852	2,581	3,031	18.5	63.9
Catholic	1	NR	NR	164	1.0	3.5
CHR–Chs of Christ	2	80	87	111	0.7	2.3
Jehovah's Witness	1	NR	NR	NR	-	-
LDS–L-D Saints	1	NR	NR	185	1.1	3.9
METH–Un Methodist	3	141	369	442	2.7	9.3
Non-denom Chr Chs	1	50	100	100	0.6	2.1
PENT–Assemb of God	2	93	62	118	0.7	2.5
PENT–Ch God (Cleve)	2	190	260	305	1.9	6.4
PENT–Intl Pent Holiness	4	176	168	197	1.2	4.2
Sev Day Adv	1	42	74	85	0.5	1.8
DUVAL	**885**	**157,878**	**311,115**	**480,455**	**55.6**	**100.0**
ANG/EPIS–Anglican NA	7	NR	NR	NR	-	-
ANG/EPIS–Episcopal	20	3,236	7,409	10,064	1.2	2.1
Bahá'í	1	NR	480	480	0.1	0.1
BAPT–Alliance Bapt	1	NR	NR	NR	-	-
BAPT–Amer Bapt Assn	3	NR	95	116	0.0	0.0
BAPT–Amer Bapt USA	2	170	414	507	0.1	0.1
BAPT–Converge/BGC	2	150	NR	180	0.0	0.0
BAPT–Free Will Bapt	2	NR	178	218	0.0	0.0
BAPT–Ind Bapt Flwsp Intl	2	NR	NR	NR	-	-
BAPT–Natl Mis Bapt Conv	8	3,550	4,950	6,066	0.7	1.3
BAPT–NBC Amer	6	1,725	2,745	3,364	0.4	0.7
BAPT–NBC USA	20	13,000	14,160	17,352	2.0	3.6
BAPT–Prog NBC	1	0	150	184	0.0	0.0
BAPT–Reg Bapt Gen As	2	NR	NR	NR	-	-
BAPT–So Bapt Conv	197	35,184	111,399	136,508	15.8	28.4
BRETH–Ch of Brethren	1	30	29	36	0.0	0.0
BUDD–Mahayana	4	NR	NR	1,607	0.2	0.3
BUDD–Theravada	3	NR	NR	1,091	0.1	0.2
BUDD–Vajrayana	2	NR	NR	528	0.1	0.1
Calv Chpl	1	NR	NR	NR	-	-
Catholic	25	NR	NR	78,167	9.0	16.3
CGOD–Ch God (Ander)	10	737	NR	737	0.1	0.2
Ch Christ Chr Union	1	NR	NR	NR	-	-
Ch Cr, Scientst	3	NR	NR	NR	-	-
Ch God (7th Day)	1	NR	NR	NR	-	-
Ch of Nazarene	9	657	1,021	1,040	0.1	0.2
Chr & Miss Al	5	701	868	934	0.1	0.2
CHR–Chr Ch (Disc)	9	780	1,913	2,344	0.3	0.5
CHR–Chr Chs & Chs Cr	9	NR	5,565	6,819	0.8	1.4
CHR–Chs of Christ	26	4,710	5,808	6,981	0.8	1.5
CHR–Int Chs of Christ	1	NR	255	312	0.0	0.1
Evan Free Ch	3	450	NR	450	0.1	0.1
FRND–Fr Gen Cf	1	NR	8	10	0.0	0.0
Grace Gosp Fel	1	NR	NR	NR	-	-
HINDU–I/A Temples	1	NR	NR	1,742	0.2	0.4
HINDU–Post Ren	2	NR	NR	41	0.0	0.0
HINDU–Trad Temples	1	NR	NR	1,000	0.1	0.2
Int Cou Comm Ch	1	NR	NR	NR	-	-
Jain	1	NR	NR	NR	-	-
Jehovah's Witness	13	NR	NR	NR	-	-
JUD–Conserv	2	825	926	2,500	0.3	0.5

NR–Not Reported   - Represents no adherents reported.   Percentages may not total 100 due to rounding.

Table 3: Religious Congregations by County and Group: 2010

Religious Group	Number of Congrega-tions	Number of Attendees	Number of Communicant, Confirmed, or Full Members	Adherents		
				Number of Adherents	% of Total Pop.	% of Total Adh.
JUD–Orth	2	522	230	725	0.1	0.2
JUD–Reconst	1	20	25	68	0.0	0.0
JUD–Reform	1	376	663	1,790	0.2	0.4
LDS–Comm of Christ	1	NR	121	121	0.0	0.0
LDS–L-D Saints	13	NR	NR	9,220	1.1	1.9
LUTH–E.L.C.A.	8	866	1,592	2,445	0.3	0.5
LUTH–Luth Cong Msn Chr	1	360	760	931	0.1	0.2
LUTH–Luth–MO Synod	6	865	1,887	2,236	0.3	0.5
LUTH–Wisc Ev Luth Syn	2	206	294	378	0.0	0.1
METH–AME	30	3,822	20,296	24,871	2.9	5.2
METH–AME Zion	1	35	100	123	0.0	0.0
METH–C.M.E.	4	0	400	490	0.1	0.1
METH–Un Methodist	40	8,463	18,576	23,519	2.7	4.9
Metro Comm Ch	1	18	0	22	0.0	0.0
Muslim Est	5	1,704	NR	5,787	0.7	1.2
New Apost Ch	1	NR	NR	NR	-	-
Non-denom Chr Chs	183	57,333	79,739	85,110	9.8	17.7
ORTHE–Ant Orth of NA	1	275	NR	800	0.1	0.2
ORTHE–Greek Orthodox	1	200	NR	750	0.1	0.2
ORTHE–Orth Ch in Amer	3	255	NR	570	0.1	0.1
ORTHE–Serb Orth USA	1	60	NR	400	0.0	0.1
ORTHO–Armen Ap Etchm	1	60	NR	100	0.0	0.0
ORTHO–Coptic Orth Ch	2	250	NR	370	0.0	0.1
ORTHO–Ethiopian Orth	1	NR	NR	NR	-	-
ORTHO–Malan Dioc Am	1	8	NR	24	0.0	0.0
ORTHO–Syrian Orth Ch	1	75	NR	400	0.0	0.1
PENT–Assemb of God	28	5,221	7,509	12,828	1.5	2.7
PENT–Ch God (Cleve)	27	2,312	2,792	3,421	0.4	0.7
PENT–Ch Lord Jesus Apos	3	NR	NR	NR	-	-
PENT–Ch of God by Faith	3	NR	NR	NR	-	-
PENT–Ch of God Proph	10	NR	508	623	0.1	0.1
PENT–COGIC	8	235	863	1,058	0.1	0.2
PENT–Cong Hol Ch	3	126	114	140	0.0	0.0
PENT–Fire Bapt Hol Ch	1	NR	NR	NR	-	-
PENT–Full Gosp Bapt	5	NR	NR	NR	-	-
PENT–Int Foursq Gos	2	70	67	82	0.0	0.0
PENT–Intl Pent Holiness	5	260	622	762	0.1	0.2
PENT–Open Bible Std	1	18	NR	18	0.0	0.0
PENT–Un Pent Ch Intl	6	NR	NR	NR	-	-
PENT–Vineyard	2	785	1,025	1,256	0.1	0.3
PRES–As Ref Pres Ch	1	NR	24	29	0.0	0.0
PRES–Kor Pres Abroad	1	NR	NR	NR	-	-
PRES–Presb Ch (USA)	25	4,626	10,374	12,712	1.5	2.6
PRES–Presb Ch Amer	8	687	692	925	0.1	0.2
REF–Christian Ref	1	65	55	67	0.0	0.0
Salvation Army	1	99	249	249	0.0	0.1
Sev Day Adv	12	1,485	2,583	2,970	0.3	0.6
Sikh	1	NR	NR	NR	-	-
Un C of Christ	3	211	339	415	0.0	0.1
Unit Univ	1	0	243	268	0.0	0.1
Unity Ch	4	NR	NR	NR	-	-
Zoroastrian	1	NR	NR	4	0.0	0.0
ESCAMBIA	**365**	**56,927**	**110,539**	**158,284**	**53.2**	**100.0**
ANG/EPIS–Anglican NA	1	NR	NR	NR	-	-
ANG/EPIS–Episcopal	7	1,067	2,653	4,166	1.4	2.6
Bahá'í	1	NR	75	75	0.0	0.0
BAPT–Amer Bapt Assn	6	NR	603	724	0.2	0.5
BAPT–Free Will Bapt	3	NR	267	320	0.1	0.2
BAPT–Ind Bapt Flwsp Intl	5	NR	NR	NR	-	-
BAPT–Natl Mis Bapt Conv	4	325	775	930	0.3	0.6
BAPT–NBC Amer	2	300	850	1,020	0.3	0.6
BAPT–NBC USA	13	1,495	4,775	5,730	1.9	3.6
BAPT–Ref Bapt Ch	1	NR	NR	NR	-	-
BAPT–So Bapt Conv	70	12,648	37,668	45,204	15.2	28.6
BUDD–Mahayana	1	NR	NR	505	0.2	0.3
Calv Chpl	1	NR	NR	NR	-	-
Catholic	18	NR	NR	18,231	6.1	11.5
Ch Cr, Scientst	1	NR	NR	NR	-	-
Ch of Nazarene	2	311	396	417	0.1	0.3
Chr & Miss Al	2	65	56	116	0.0	0.1
CHR–Chr Ch (Disc)	3	240	583	700	0.2	0.4
CHR–Chr Chs & Chs Cr	2	NR	185	222	0.1	0.1
CHR–Chs of Christ	17	2,041	2,014	2,474	0.8	1.6

Religious Group	Number of Congrega-tions	Number of Attendees	Number of Communicant, Confirmed, or Full Members	Adherents		
				Number of Adherents	% of Total Pop.	% of Total Adh.
Evan Free Ch	1	225	NR	225	0.1	0.1
HINDU–Post Ren	1	NR	NR	25	0.0	0.0
Jehovah's Witness	5	NR	NR	NR	-	-
JUD–Conserv	1	62	70	189	0.1	0.1
JUD–Reform	1	83	147	397	0.1	0.3
LDS–Comm of Christ	4	NR	544	544	0.2	0.3
LDS–L-D Saints	6	NR	NR	3,057	1.0	1.9
LUTH–E.L.C.A.	1	155	435	550	0.2	0.3
LUTH–Luth–MO Synod	7	881	1,610	2,062	0.7	1.3
MENN–CG in Cr (Menn)	2	NR	178	214	0.1	0.1
METH–AME	6	555	1,395	1,674	0.6	1.1
METH–AME Zion	9	150	1,250	1,500	0.5	0.9
METH–C.M.E.	3	0	350	420	0.1	0.3
METH–Un Methodist	25	4,400	12,352	16,020	5.4	10.1
METH–Wesleyan	1	18	14	23	0.0	0.0
Metro Comm Ch	1	188	198	238	0.1	0.2
Muslim Est	2	812	NR	2,794	0.9	1.8
New Apost Ch	1	NR	NR	NR	-	-
Non-denom Chr Chs	59	24,964	32,226	35,536	11.9	22.5
ORTHE–Ant Orth of NA	1	80	NR	145	0.0	0.1
ORTHE–Greek Orthodox	1	130	NR	500	0.2	0.3
ORTHO–Coptic Orth Ch	1	25	NR	29	0.0	0.0
PENT–Apos Faith Msn	2	NR	70	84	0.0	0.1
PENT–Assemb of God	21	2,500	2,761	3,946	1.3	2.5
PENT–Ch God (Cleve)	5	198	508	610	0.2	0.4
PENT–COGIC	7	200	725	870	0.3	0.5
PENT–Intl Pent Holiness	5	758	909	1,091	0.4	0.7
PENT–Open Bible Std	1	30	NR	30	0.0	0.0
PENT–Un Pent Ch Intl	4	NR	NR	NR	-	-
PRES–Orth Pres Ch	1	75	71	79	0.0	0.0
PRES–Presb Ch (USA)	5	670	1,815	2,178	0.7	1.4
PRES–Presb Ch Amer	6	522	762	898	0.3	0.6
REF–Comm Ref Evan	1	NR	NR	NR	-	-
Salvation Army	1	50	110	175	0.1	0.1
Sev Day Adv	4	484	842	968	0.3	0.6
Un C of Christ	1	115	192	230	0.1	0.1
Unit Univ	1	105	105	147	0.0	0.1
Unity Ch	1	NR	NR	NR	-	-
Zoroastrian	0	NR	NR	2	0.0	0.0
FLAGLER	**70**	**7,992**	**11,181**	**31,746**	**33.2**	**100.0**
ANG/EPIS–Episcopal	1	323	648	805	0.8	2.5
Bahá'í	0	NR	5	5	0.0	0.0
BAPT–So Bapt Conv	16	2,235	3,478	4,092	4.3	12.9
Calv Chpl	1	NR	NR	NR	-	-
Catholic	4	NR	NR	18,033	18.8	56.8
Ch Cr, Scientst	1	NR	NR	NR	-	-
Ch of Nazarene	1	0	0	0	0.0	0.0
Chr & Miss Al	1	273	215	540	0.6	1.7
CHR–Chr Ch (Disc)	1	0	0	0	0.0	0.0
CHR–Chr Chs & Chs Cr	1	NR	90	106	0.1	0.3
CHR–Chs of Christ	1	80	82	90	0.1	0.3
Jehovah's Witness	2	NR	NR	NR	-	-
JUD–Conserv	1	45	50	135	0.1	0.4
LUTH–E.L.C.A.	1	124	240	240	0.3	0.8
LUTH–Luth Cong Msn Chr	1	168	220	259	0.3	0.8
LUTH–Luth–MO Synod	1	257	386	452	0.5	1.4
LUTH–Wisc Ev Luth Syn	1	86	63	93	0.1	0.3
METH–AME	1	300	100	118	0.1	0.4
METH–Un Methodist	3	804	1,469	2,254	2.4	7.1
Non-denom Chr Chs	17	2,640	3,405	3,535	3.7	11.1
ORTHE–Holy Orth in NA	1	15	NR	20	0.0	0.1
ORTHE–Orth Ch in Amer	1	20	NR	40	0.0	0.1
ORTHE–Rus Orth Abroad	1	40	NR	80	0.1	0.3
PENT–Assemb of God	2	130	112	130	0.1	0.4
PENT–Ch God (Cleve)	2	101	72	85	0.1	0.3
PENT–Intl Pent Holiness	1	25	20	24	0.0	0.1
PENT–Un Pent Ch Intl	2	NR	NR	NR	-	-
PRES–Presb Ch Amer	1	44	37	45	0.0	0.1
Sev Day Adv	3	282	489	563	0.6	1.8
Zoroastrian	0	NR	NR	2	0.0	0.0

NR–Not Reported   - Represents no adherents reported.   Percentages may not total 100 due to rounding.

Table 3: Religious Congregations by County and Group: 2010

Religious Group	Number of Congrega-tions	Number of Attendees	Number of Communicant, Confirmed, or Full Members	Adherents		
				Number of Adherents	% of Total Pop.	% of Total Adh.
FRANKLIN	**33**	**1,870**	**3,047**	**4,723**	**40.9**	**100.0**
ANG/EPIS–Episcopal	2	97	161	186	1.6	3.9
BAPT–So Bapt Conv	7	332	950	1,099	9.5	23.3
Catholic	2	NR	NR	800	6.9	16.9
CHR–Chs of Christ	1	16	14	14	0.1	0.3
Jehovah's Witness	1	NR	NR	NR	-	-
LDS–L-D Saints	1	NR	NR	133	1.2	2.8
METH–AME	2	0	250	289	2.5	6.1
METH–Un Methodist	4	245	436	597	5.2	12.6
Non-denom Chr Chs	4	370	500	508	4.4	10.8
PENT–Assemb of God	4	146	93	354	3.1	7.5
PENT–Ch God (Cleve)	2	375	371	429	3.7	9.1
PENT–Cong Hol Ch	1	39	35	40	0.3	0.8
PENT–Full Gosp Bapt	1	NR	NR	NR	-	-
PENT–Intl Pent Holiness	1	250	237	274	2.4	5.8
GADSDEN	**116**	**4,959**	**15,908**	**20,843**	**44.9**	**100.0**
ANG/EPIS–Episcopal	1	64	78	78	0.2	0.4
Bahá'í	0	NR	134	134	0.3	0.6
BAPT–Free Will Bapt	1	NR	73	90	0.2	0.4
BAPT–Natl Mis Bapt Conv	2	0	300	370	0.8	1.8
BAPT–NBC USA	1	0	350	431	0.9	2.1
BAPT–So Bapt Conv	18	1,130	4,588	5,651	12.2	27.1
Catholic	2	NR	NR	1,535	3.3	7.4
CHR–Chs of Christ	2	150	138	171	0.4	0.8
Jehovah's Witness	3	NR	NR	NR	-	-
LDS–L-D Saints	1	NR	NR	215	0.5	1.0
METH–AME	31	800	4,600	5,666	12.2	27.2
METH–C.M.E.	3	0	400	493	1.1	2.4
METH–Un Methodist	8	585	1,321	1,470	3.2	7.1
Non-denom Chr Chs	15	1,370	2,054	2,072	4.5	9.9
PENT–Assemb of God	7	273	134	321	0.7	1.5
PENT–Ch of God Proph	3	NR	70	86	0.2	0.4
PENT–COGIC	5	180	750	924	2.0	4.4
PENT–Full Gosp Bapt	2	NR	NR	NR	-	-
PENT–Intl Pent Holiness	2	95	190	234	0.5	1.1
PENT–Un Pent Ch Intl	2	NR	NR	NR	-	-
PRES–Presb Ch (USA)	4	218	594	732	1.6	3.5
PRES–Presb Ch Amer	2	68	88	117	0.3	0.6
Sev Day Adv	1	26	46	53	0.1	0.3
GILCHRIST	**32**	**2,034**	**5,358**	**6,493**	**38.3**	**100.0**
Bahá'í	0	NR	4	4	0.0	0.1
BAPT–NBC USA	1	0	150	179	1.1	2.8
BAPT–So Bapt Conv	12	1,041	4,066	4,845	28.6	74.6
Ch Christ Chr Union	1	NR	NR	NR	-	-
Ch of Nazarene	1	51	60	60	0.4	0.9
CHR–Chs of Christ	6	495	460	531	3.1	8.2
Intl Fell Bible Ch	1	NR	NR	NR	-	-
METH–AME	1	0	100	119	0.7	1.8
METH–Un Methodist	1	53	89	93	0.5	1.4
Non-denom Chr Chs	3	148	190	205	1.2	3.2
PENT–Assemb of God	2	86	0	175	1.0	2.7
PENT–Ch God (Cleve)	2	132	190	226	1.3	3.5
Sev Day Adv	1	28	49	56	0.3	0.9
GLADES	**13**	**798**	**1,958**	**3,140**	**24.4**	**100.0**
Bahá'í	0	NR	50	50	0.4	1.6
BAPT–Natl Mis Bapt Conv	1	0	150	176	1.4	5.6
BAPT–So Bapt Conv	4	336	1,174	1,376	10.7	43.8
Catholic	1	NR	NR	700	5.4	22.3
CHR–Chr Chs & Chs Cr	1	NR	60	70	0.5	2.2
METH–AME	1	0	100	117	0.9	3.7
METH–Un Methodist	1	65	102	114	0.9	3.6
Non-denom Chr Chs	2	285	240	356	2.8	11.3
PENT–Ch God (Cleve)	1	27	82	96	0.7	3.1
PENT–Open Bible Std	1	85	NR	85	0.7	2.7
GULF	**42**	**2,366**	**5,207**	**6,830**	**43.1**	**100.0**
ANG/EPIS–Episcopal	2	82	166	169	1.1	2.5
Bahá'í	0	NR	2	2	0.0	0.0
BAPT–Amer Bapt Assn	1	NR	85	97	0.6	1.4
BAPT–Natl Mis Bapt Conv	1	0	150	171	1.1	2.5
BAPT–So Bapt Conv	9	994	2,661	3,035	19.1	44.4
Catholic	3	NR	NR	330	2.1	4.8
Ch of Nazarene	1	28	11	30	0.2	0.4
CHR–Chs of Christ	2	35	26	42	0.3	0.6
Jehovah's Witness	1	NR	NR	NR	-	-
LDS–L-D Saints	1	NR	NR	251	1.6	3.7
METH–AME	3	0	400	456	2.9	6.7
METH–Un Methodist	3	333	844	940	5.9	13.8
Non-denom Chr Chs	4	305	440	440	2.8	6.4
PENT–Assemb of God	4	439	258	681	4.3	10.0
PENT–Ch God (Cleve)	1	19	46	52	0.3	0.8
PENT–Intl Pent Holiness	3	100	72	82	0.5	1.2
PENT–Un Pent Ch Intl	1	NR	NR	NR	-	-
PRES–Presb Ch (USA)	2	31	46	52	0.3	0.8
HAMILTON	**40**	**1,432**	**4,500**	**5,756**	**38.9**	**100.0**
Bahá'í	0	NR	1	1	0.0	0.0
BAPT–NBC USA	1	0	125	147	1.0	2.6
BAPT–So Bapt Conv	9	630	2,406	2,829	19.1	49.1
Catholic	1	NR	NR	53	0.4	0.9
Ch of Nazarene	1	25	26	36	0.2	0.6
CHR–Chr Chs & Chs Cr	1	NR	175	206	1.4	3.6
CHR–Chs of Christ	2	103	83	117	0.8	2.0
Int Cou Comm Ch	1	NR	NR	NR	-	-
LDS–L-D Saints	1	NR	NR	440	3.0	7.6
METH–AME	3	0	350	411	2.8	7.1
METH–C.M.E.	1	0	100	118	0.8	2.1
METH–Cong Meth	2	NR	61	72	0.5	1.3
METH–Un Methodist	3	85	274	299	2.0	5.2
Non-denom Chr Chs	3	325	430	440	3.0	7.6
PENT–Assemb of God	2	60	52	98	0.7	1.7
PENT–Ch God (Cleve)	4	120	288	339	2.3	5.9
PENT–Ch Lord Jesus Apos	1	NR	NR	NR	-	-
PENT–Cong Hol Ch	1	13	12	14	0.1	0.2
PRES–Presb Ch (USA)	2	45	71	83	0.6	1.4
Sev Day Adv	1	26	46	53	0.4	0.9
HARDEE	**58**	**3,414**	**9,705**	**14,114**	**50.9**	**100.0**
ANG/EPIS–Episcopal	1	13	32	32	0.1	0.2
Bahá'í	0	NR	33	33	0.1	0.2
BAPT–Amer Bapt Assn	1	NR	200	256	0.9	1.8
BAPT–Natl Mis Bapt Conv	1	0	150	192	0.7	1.4
BAPT–NBC Amer	1	75	100	128	0.5	0.9
BAPT–So Bapt Conv	19	1,633	5,972	7,642	27.6	54.1
Catholic	4	NR	NR	1,700	6.1	12.0
Ch of Nazarene	1	0	11	11	0.0	0.1
CHR–Chr Chs & Chs Cr	2	NR	350	448	1.6	3.2
CHR–Chs of Christ	2	85	111	141	0.5	1.0
Jehovah's Witness	1	NR	NR	NR	-	-
LDS–L-D Saints	1	NR	NR	110	0.4	0.8
LUTH–Luth-MO Synod	1	36	38	38	0.1	0.3
METH–AME	2	0	250	320	1.2	2.3
METH–Prim Meth Ch	1	NR	NR	NR	-	-
METH–Un Methodist	4	267	566	630	2.3	4.5
Non-denom Chr Chs	5	482	850	916	3.3	6.5
PENT–Assemb of God	2	434	275	551	2.0	3.9
PENT–Ch God (Cleve)	5	304	629	805	2.9	5.7
PENT–Un Pent Ch Intl	1	NR	NR	NR	-	-
PRES–Presb Ch Amer	1	40	60	71	0.3	0.5
Sev Day Adv	2	45	78	90	0.3	0.6
HENDRY	**59**	**4,300**	**6,153**	**11,165**	**28.5**	**100.0**
ANG/EPIS–Episcopal	2	73	139	168	0.4	1.5
Bahá'í	0	NR	123	123	0.3	1.1
BAPT–NBC Amer	1	130	300	383	1.0	3.4
BAPT–Reg Bapt Gen As	1	NR	NR	NR	-	-
BAPT–So Bapt Conv	11	799	1,773	2,261	5.8	20.3
Catholic	3	NR	NR	2,600	6.6	23.3
CGOD–Ch God (Ander)	1	20	NR	20	0.1	0.2
Ch God (7th Day)	1	NR	NR	NR	-	-
CHR–Chr Ch (Disc)	1	90	178	227	0.6	2.0
CHR–Chr Chs & Chs Cr	1	NR	55	70	0.2	0.6

NR–Not Reported   - Represents no adherents reported.   Percentages may not total 100 due to rounding.

Table 3: Religious Congregations by County and Group: 2010

Religious Group	Number of Congregations	Number of Attendees	Number of Communicant, Confirmed, or Full Members	Adherents: Number of Adherents	Adherents: % of Total Pop.	Adherents: % of Total Adh.
CHR–Chs of Christ	3	110	85	125	0.3	1.1
Jehovah's Witness	2	NR	NR	NR	-	-
LUTH–Luth-MO Synod	2	71	73	83	0.2	0.7
METH–AME	1	0	150	191	0.5	1.7
METH–Un Methodist	2	306	641	930	2.4	8.3
Non-denom Chr Chs	11	1,550	1,650	2,062	5.3	18.5
PENT–Assemb of God	4	730	282	926	2.4	8.3
PENT–Ch God (Cleve)	4	232	509	649	1.7	5.8
PENT–Ch of God Proph	2	NR	35	45	0.1	0.4
PENT–Intl Pent Holiness	1	25	20	26	0.1	0.2
PENT–Pent Ch of God	1	70	NR	109	0.3	1.0
PENT–Un Pent Ch Intl	2	NR	NR	NR	-	-
PRES–Presb Ch (USA)	1	40	46	59	0.2	0.5
Sev Day Adv	1	54	94	108	0.3	1.0
HERNANDO	**120**	**14,243**	**18,876**	**47,057**	**27.2**	**100.0**
ANG/EPIS–Episcopal	2	315	575	711	0.4	1.5
Bahá'í	1	NR	57	57	0.0	0.1
BAPT–Reg Bapt Gen As	1	NR	NR	NR	-	-
BAPT–So Bapt Conv	18	2,557	5,256	6,176	3.6	13.1
BRETH–Breth in Chr	1	NR	NR	NR	-	-
BRETH–Grace Breth	1	NR	NR	NR	-	-
Calv Chpl	1	NR	NR	NR	-	-
Catholic	7	NR	NR	17,068	9.9	36.3
CGOD–Ch God (Ander)	1	0	NR	0	0.0	0.0
Ch of Nazarene	3	316	431	608	0.4	1.3
Chr & Miss Al	1	197	159	304	0.2	0.6
CHR–Chr Ch (Disc)	1	27	39	46	0.0	0.1
CHR–Chr Chs & Chs Cr	3	NR	992	1,166	0.7	2.5
CHR–Chs of Christ	5	365	313	389	0.2	0.8
Christian Brethren	1	NR	NR	NR	-	-
Evan Free Ch	1	150	NR	150	0.1	0.3
Int Cou Comm Ch	1	NR	NR	NR	-	-
Jehovah's Witness	3	NR	NR	NR	-	-
JUD–Reform	1	66	117	316	0.2	0.7
LDS–L-D Saints	1	NR	NR	982	0.6	2.1
LUTH–E.L.C.A.	3	579	946	1,166	0.7	2.5
LUTH–Luth-MO Synod	3	514	701	852	0.5	1.8
LUTH–Wisc Ev Luth Syn	1	104	112	139	0.1	0.3
METH–AME	2	40	249	293	0.2	0.6
METH–Un Methodist	7	1,908	2,756	3,376	2.0	7.2
METH–Wesleyan	3	582	404	757	0.4	1.6
Muslim Est	1	406	NR	1,397	0.8	3.0
New Apost Ch	1	NR	NR	NR	-	-
Non-denom Chr Chs	19	2,746	2,717	3,567	2.1	7.6
ORTHE–Carp Rus Orth	1	35	NR	60	0.0	0.1
ORTHE–Greek Orthodox	1	50	NR	125	0.1	0.3
ORTHE–Orth Ch in Amer	1	20	NR	50	0.0	0.1
PENT–Assemb of God	4	1,997	764	4,527	2.6	9.6
PENT–Ch God (Cleve)	3	183	322	378	0.2	0.8
PENT–Ch of God by Faith	1	NR	NR	NR	-	-
PENT–Ch of God Proph	1	NR	105	123	0.1	0.3
PENT–Full Gosp Bapt	1	NR	NR	NR	-	-
PENT–Pent Ch of God	1	70	NR	109	0.1	0.2
PENT–Un Pent Ch Intl	1	NR	NR	NR	-	-
PRES–Evan Presby Ch	1	NR	360	423	0.2	0.9
PRES–Presb Ch (USA)	2	463	750	881	0.5	1.9
PRES–Presb Ch Amer	1	61	52	65	0.0	0.1
Salvation Army	1	68	82	82	0.0	0.2
Sev Day Adv	3	195	340	390	0.2	0.8
Un C of Christ	2	207	257	302	0.2	0.6
Unit Univ	1	22	20	22	0.0	0.0
HIGHLANDS	**138**	**12,399**	**22,023**	**34,002**	**34.4**	**100.0**
ANG/EPIS–Episcopal	3	303	481	664	0.7	2.0
Bahá'í	0	NR	20	20	0.0	0.1
BAPT–Free Will Bapt	1	NR	89	103	0.1	0.3
BAPT–Natl Mis Bapt Conv	3	0	375	436	0.4	1.3
BAPT–Ref Bapt Ch	1	NR	NR	NR	-	-
BAPT–Reg Bapt Gen As	4	NR	NR	NR	-	-
BAPT–So Bapt Conv	23	2,933	6,713	7,804	7.9	23.0
BRETH–Ch of Brethren	2	0	185	215	0.2	0.6
BRETH–Grace Breth	1	NR	NR	NR	-	-
Catholic	3	NR	NR	4,000	4.0	11.8
CGOD–Ch God (Ander)	2	147	NR	147	0.1	0.4
Ch Christ Chr Union	1	NR	NR	NR	-	-
Ch Cr, Scientst	1	NR	NR	NR	-	-
Ch of Nazarene	3	295	368	485	0.5	1.4
Chr & Miss Al	1	31	0	52	0.1	0.2
CHR–Chr Ch (Disc)	2	170	202	235	0.2	0.7
CHR–Chr Chs & Chs Cr	4	NR	709	824	0.8	2.4
CHR–Chs of Christ	5	420	397	506	0.5	1.5
Jehovah's Witness	2	NR	NR	NR	-	-
JUD–Reform	1	26	46	124	0.1	0.4
LDS–L-D Saints	1	NR	NR	492	0.5	1.4
LUTH–E.L.C.A.	2	159	215	221	0.2	0.6
LUTH–Evan Luth Syn	1	50	43	45	0.0	0.1
LUTH–Luth Ch-Am Asc	1	NR	NR	NR	-	-
LUTH–Luth-MO Synod	3	330	363	403	0.4	1.2
METH–AME	4	0	550	639	0.6	1.9
METH–C.M.E.	1	0	100	116	0.1	0.3
METH–Un Methodist	6	1,422	2,504	3,914	4.0	11.5
Missionary Ch	1	100	65	100	0.1	0.3
Muslim Est	1	407	NR	1,397	1.4	4.1
Non-denom Chr Chs	17	3,145	2,935	4,203	4.3	12.4
PENT–Assemb of God	5	600	423	741	0.8	2.2
PENT–Ch God (Cleve)	5	470	789	917	0.9	2.7
PENT–Ch Lord Jesus Apos	1	NR	NR	NR	-	-
PENT–Ch of God by Faith	3	NR	NR	NR	-	-
PENT–Ch of God Proph	1	NR	31	36	0.0	0.1
PENT–COGIC	3	20	340	395	0.4	1.2
PENT–Intl Pent Holiness	1	50	150	174	0.2	0.5
PENT–Un Pent Ch Intl	1	NR	NR	NR	-	-
PENT–Vineyard	1	22	25	29	0.0	0.1
PRES–As Ref Pres Ch	3	NR	973	1,131	1.1	3.3
PRES–Presb Ch (USA)	1	90	90	105	0.1	0.3
PRES–Presb Ch Amer	1	0	0	0	0.0	0.0
Salvation Army	1	40	31	84	0.1	0.2
Sev Day Adv	7	1,068	1,856	2,135	2.2	6.3
Un C of Christ	2	101	955	1,110	1.1	3.3
Unity Ch	1	NR	NR	NR	-	-
HILLSBOROUGH	**1,005**	**156,885**	**246,577**	**488,899**	**39.8**	**100.0**
ANG/EPIS–Anglican NA	3	NR	NR	NR	-	-
ANG/EPIS–Episcopal	14	2,524	5,693	6,738	0.5	1.4
Bahá'í	3	NR	378	378	0.0	0.1
BAPT–Amer Bapt Assn	5	NR	490	601	0.0	0.1
BAPT–Amer Bapt USA	2	208	168	206	0.0	0.0
BAPT–Converge/BGC	7	850	NR	1,020	0.1	0.2
BAPT–Free Will Bapt	3	NR	267	327	0.0	0.1
BAPT–Ind Bapt Flwsp Intl	1	NR	NR	NR	-	-
BAPT–Natl Mis Bapt Conv	5	0	660	809	0.1	0.2
BAPT–NBC Amer	8	1,726	6,550	8,029	0.7	1.6
BAPT–NBC USA	3	570	2,150	2,635	0.2	0.5
BAPT–Prog NBC	2	250	775	950	0.1	0.2
BAPT–Ref Bapt Ch	2	NR	NR	NR	-	-
BAPT–So Bapt Conv	195	42,863	83,361	102,178	8.3	20.9
BRETH–Breth in Chr	1	NR	NR	NR	-	-
BRETH–Grace Breth	2	NR	NR	NR	-	-
BUDD–Mahayana	8	NR	NR	840	0.1	0.2
BUDD–Theravada	3	NR	NR	2,663	0.2	0.5
BUDD–Vajrayana	3	NR	NR	138	0.0	0.0
Calv Chpl	3	NR	NR	NR	-	-
Catholic	28	NR	NR	130,973	10.7	26.8
CGOD–Ch God (Ander)	9	1,219	NR	1,219	0.1	0.2
Ch Cr, Scientst	4	NR	NR	NR	-	-
Ch God (7th Day)	1	NR	NR	NR	-	-
Ch of Nazarene	17	1,498	2,222	2,471	0.2	0.5
Chr & Miss Al	7	576	194	587	0.0	0.1
CHR–Chr Ch (Disc)	6	468	602	738	0.1	0.2
CHR–Chr Chs & Chs Cr	8	NR	1,390	1,704	0.1	0.3
CHR–Chs of Christ	44	5,915	5,659	7,164	0.6	1.5
CHR–Int Chs of Christ	1	NR	282	346	0.0	0.1
Christian Brethren	1	NR	NR	NR	-	-
Evan Free Ch	1	245	NR	245	0.0	0.1
FRND–Fr Gen Cf	1	NR	23	28	0.0	0.0
HINDU–I/A Temples	4	NR	NR	2,262	0.2	0.5

NR–Not Reported - Represents no adherents reported. Percentages may not total 100 due to rounding.

Table 3: Religious Congregations by County and Group: 2010

Religious Group	Number of Congrega-tions	Number of Attendees	Number of Communicant, Confirmed, or Full Members	Adherents		
				Number of Adherents	% of Total Pop.	% of Total Adh.
HINDU–Post Ren	5	NR	NR	189	0.0	0.0
HINDU–Trad Temples	4	NR	NR	7,283	0.6	1.5
Ind Fund Churches	1	NR	NR	NR	-	-
Int Cou Comm Ch	2	NR	NR	NR	-	-
Jehovah's Witness	22	NR	NR	NR	-	-
JUD–Conserv	2	785	881	2,379	0.2	0.5
JUD–Orth	4	396	250	550	0.0	0.1
JUD–Reform	4	818	1,442	3,893	0.3	0.8
LDS–Comm of Christ	1	NR	121	121	0.0	0.0
LDS–L-D Saints	16	NR	NR	8,990	0.7	1.8
LUTH–E.L.C.A.	12	2,184	4,802	6,061	0.5	1.2
LUTH–Luth–MO Synod	11	1,930	3,224	4,039	0.3	0.8
LUTH–Wisc Ev Luth Syn	2	162	235	311	0.0	0.1
MENN–Mennonite USA	1	25	25	31	0.0	0.0
METH–AME	21	900	3,263	4,000	0.3	0.8
METH–AME Zion	5	10	430	527	0.0	0.1
METH–C.M.E.	3	75	400	490	0.0	0.1
METH–Free Methodist	3	429	377	433	0.0	0.1
METH–So Methodist	1	NR	NR	NR	-	-
METH–Un Methodist	42	12,444	23,611	35,452	2.9	7.3
METH–Wesleyan	1	84	NR	109	0.0	0.0
Metro Comm Ch	1	176	128	157	0.0	0.0
Missionary Ch	1	10	0	10	0.0	0.0
Muslim Est	11	5,261	NR	20,970	1.7	4.3
New Apost Ch	1	NR	NR	NR	-	-
Non-denom Chr Chs	173	44,724	61,735	67,239	5.5	13.8
ORTHE–Greek Orthodox	1	350	NR	1,200	0.1	0.2
ORTHE–Orth Ch in Amer	1	35	NR	35	0.0	0.0
ORTHE–Rus Orth Moscow	1	25	NR	80	0.0	0.0
ORTHE–Ukrainian Orth	1	80	NR	175	0.0	0.0
ORTHO–Coptic Orth Ch	2	320	NR	673	0.1	0.1
ORTHO–Ethiopian Orth	1	NR	NR	NR	-	-
ORTHO–Malan Dioc Am	1	40	NR	120	0.0	0.0
ORTHO–Malan Syr Orth	1	95	NR	180	0.0	0.0
PENT–Assemb of God	53	8,571	5,048	10,708	0.9	2.2
PENT–Ch God (Cleve)	46	5,913	9,156	11,223	0.9	2.3
PENT–Ch Lord Jesus Apos	4	NR	NR	NR	-	-
PENT–Ch of God by Faith	2	NR	NR	NR	-	-
PENT–Ch of God Proph	7	NR	278	341	0.0	0.1
PENT–COGIC	10	700	3,035	3,720	0.3	0.8
PENT–Fire Bapt Hol Ch	1	NR	NR	NR	-	-
PENT–Full Gosp Bapt	1	NR	NR	NR	-	-
PENT–I F Chr Assmbl	1	NR	NR	NR	-	-
PENT–Int Foursq Gos	6	377	450	552	0.0	0.1
PENT–Intl Pent Holiness	6	664	689	845	0.1	0.2
PENT–Open Bible Std	2	78	NR	78	0.0	0.0
PENT–Pent Ch of God	8	560	NR	870	0.1	0.2
PENT–Pent FW Bapt	1	NR	NR	NR	-	-
PENT–Un Pent Asbl God	1	NR	NR	NR	-	-
PENT–Un Pent Ch Intl	15	NR	NR	NR	-	-
PENT–Vineyard	1	84	84	103	0.0	0.0
PRES–As Ref Pres Ch	4	NR	281	344	0.0	0.1
PRES–Cumber Presb	4	NR	354	381	0.0	0.1
PRES–Evan Presby Ch	1	NR	344	422	0.0	0.1
PRES–Kor Pres Abroad	2	NR	NR	NR	-	-
PRES–Presb Ch (USA)	20	4,461	7,100	8,703	0.7	1.8
PRES–Presb Ch Amer	7	1,233	1,067	1,403	0.1	0.3
REF–Ref Ch in Am	1	135	187	262	0.0	0.1
Salvation Army	2	300	597	874	0.1	0.2
Sev Day Adv	22	2,938	5,109	5,876	0.5	1.2
Sikh	1	NR	NR	NR	-	-
Un C of Christ	3	467	818	1,003	0.1	0.2
Unit Univ	3	134	194	225	0.0	0.0
Unity Ch	5	NR	NR	NR	-	-
Zoroastrian	1	NR	NR	20	0.0	0.0
HOLMES	**69**	**3,358**	**6,766**	**9,877**	**49.6**	**100.0**
Bahá'í	0	NR	3	3	0.0	0.0
BAPT–Free Will Bapt	1	NR	89	106	0.5	1.1
BAPT–Natl Mis Bapt Conv	1	0	150	179	0.9	1.8
BAPT–So Bapt Conv	20	1,419	4,644	5,532	27.8	56.0
Catholic	1	NR	NR	102	0.5	1.0
CHR–Chs of Christ	3	122	121	140	0.7	1.4
Jehovah's Witness	1	NR	NR	NR	-	-

Religious Group	Number of Congrega-tions	Number of Attendees	Number of Communicant, Confirmed, or Full Members	Adherents		
				Number of Adherents	% of Total Pop.	% of Total Adh.
LDS–L-D Saints	2	NR	NR	714	3.6	7.2
LUTH–Luth–MO Synod	1	17	15	15	0.1	0.2
METH–AME	2	0	200	238	1.2	2.4
METH–Cong Meth	2	NR	37	44	0.2	0.4
METH–Un Methodist	8	292	478	561	2.8	5.7
Non-denom Chr Chs	1	100	150	150	0.8	1.5
PENT–Assemb of God	18	1,317	688	1,867	9.4	18.9
PENT–Ch God (Cleve)	1	24	29	35	0.2	0.4
PENT–Ch of God Proph	2	NR	55	66	0.3	0.7
PENT–COGIC	1	25	35	42	0.2	0.4
PENT–Un Pent Ch Intl	2	NR	NR	NR	-	-
PRES–Presb Ch (USA)	1	4	7	8	0.0	0.1
Sev Day Adv	1	38	65	75	0.4	0.8
INDIAN RIVER	**123**	**14,018**	**20,100**	**65,226**	**47.3**	**100.0**
ANG/EPIS–Anglican NA	2	NR	NR	NR	-	-
ANG/EPIS–Episcopal	3	696	1,139	1,252	0.9	1.9
Bahá'í	1	NR	72	72	0.1	0.1
BAPT–Consrv Bapt	1	NR	NR	NR	-	-
BAPT–Free Will Bapt	2	NR	178	207	0.1	0.3
BAPT–Reg Bapt Gen As	1	NR	NR	NR	-	-
BAPT–So Bapt Conv	18	2,168	3,751	4,367	3.2	6.7
BRETH–Breth in Chr	1	NR	NR	NR	-	-
Calv Chpl	1	NR	NR	NR	-	-
Catholic	5	NR	NR	36,514	26.5	56.0
CGOD–Ch God (Ander)	2	1,473	NR	1,473	1.1	2.3
Ch Cr, Scientst	1	NR	NR	NR	-	-
Ch of Nazarene	2	305	492	867	0.6	1.3
Chr & Miss Al	1	118	71	224	0.2	0.3
CHR–Chr Ch (Disc)	1	73	88	102	0.1	0.2
CHR–Chr Chs & Chs Cr	3	NR	470	547	0.4	0.8
CHR–Chs of Christ	3	328	277	392	0.3	0.6
Evan Cov Ch	1	96	80	125	0.1	0.2
HINDU–Post Ren	1	NR	NR	84	0.1	0.1
Jehovah's Witness	2	NR	NR	NR	-	-
JUD–Reform	1	101	179	483	0.3	0.7
LDS–L-D Saints	1	NR	NR	780	0.6	1.2
LUTH–E.L.C.A.	3	576	1,002	1,252	0.9	1.9
LUTH–Evan Luth Syn	2	189	292	339	0.2	0.5
LUTH–Luth–MO Synod	1	118	181	219	0.2	0.3
METH–AME	5	0	700	815	0.6	1.2
METH–AME Zion	1	0	100	116	0.1	0.2
METH–Un Methodist	5	1,265	2,691	3,546	2.6	5.4
METH–Wesleyan	1	5	3	7	0.0	0.0
Muslim Est	1	406	NR	1,397	1.0	2.1
Non-denom Chr Chs	11	1,480	1,630	1,980	1.4	3.0
PENT–Assemb of God	5	1,050	1,097	1,509	1.1	2.3
PENT–Ch God (Cleve)	8	603	978	1,139	0.8	1.7
PENT–Ch Lord Jesus Apos	4	NR	NR	NR	-	-
PENT–Ch of God by Faith	2	NR	NR	NR	-	-
PENT–Ch of God Proph	1	NR	35	41	0.0	0.1
PENT–COGIC	5	20	535	623	0.5	1.0
PENT–Un Pent Ch Intl	1	NR	NR	NR	-	-
PENT–Vineyard	1	100	130	151	0.1	0.2
PRES–As Ref Pres Ch	1	NR	99	115	0.1	0.2
PRES–Presb Ch (USA)	3	667	1,052	1,225	0.9	1.9
PRES–Presb Ch Amer	1	55	48	53	0.0	0.1
Salvation Army	1	69	89	150	0.1	0.2
Sev Day Adv	2	128	222	256	0.2	0.4
Un C of Christ	2	1,768	2,231	2,598	1.9	4.0
Unit Univ	1	161	188	206	0.1	0.3
Unity Ch	1	NR	NR	NR	-	-
JACKSON	**145**	**7,542**	**18,531**	**23,692**	**47.6**	**100.0**
ANG/EPIS–Episcopal	1	80	142	142	0.3	0.6
Bahá'í	0	NR	3	3	0.0	0.0
BAPT–Free Will Bapt	7	NR	623	735	1.5	3.1
BAPT–Ind Bapt Flwsp Intl	1	NR	NR	NR	-	-
BAPT–Natl Mis Bapt Conv	4	0	600	708	1.4	3.0
BAPT–So Bapt Conv	45	3,395	9,237	10,894	21.9	46.0
Catholic	1	NR	NR	371	0.7	1.6
Ch of Nazarene	1	30	33	37	0.1	0.2
CHR–Chs of Christ	2	127	121	148	0.3	0.6

NR–Not Reported   - Represents no adherents reported.   Percentages may not total 100 due to rounding.

Table 3: Religious Congregations by County and Group: 2010

Religious Group	Number of Congregations	Number of Attendees	Number of Communicant, Confirmed, or Full Members	Adherents		
				Number of Adherents	% of Total Pop.	% of Total Adh.
Jehovah's Witness	1	NR	NR	NR	-	-
LDS–L-D Saints	1	NR	NR	672	1.4	2.8
LUTH–Luth–MO Synod	1	33	62	67	0.1	0.3
METH–AME	20	135	2,578	3,040	6.1	12.8
METH–C.M.E.	2	30	150	177	0.4	0.7
METH–Un Methodist	18	748	1,705	2,155	4.3	9.1
METH–Wesleyan	1	47	60	61	0.1	0.3
Non-denom Chr Chs	9	710	894	961	1.9	4.1
PENT–Assemb of God	16	1,612	1,380	2,304	4.6	9.7
PENT–Ch God (Cleve)	3	80	211	249	0.5	1.1
PENT–Ch of God by Faith	1	NR	NR	NR	-	-
PENT–Ch of God Proph	1	NR	3	4	0.0	0.0
PENT–Intl Pent Holiness	4	245	308	363	0.7	1.5
PENT–Pent Ch of God	1	70	NR	109	0.2	0.5
PENT–Un Pent Ch Intl	1	NR	NR	NR	-	-
PRES–Presb Ch (USA)	1	88	227	268	0.5	1.1
Sev Day Adv	2	112	194	224	0.5	0.9
JEFFERSON	**51**	**1,940**	**7,236**	**9,009**	**61.0**	**100.0**
ANG/EPIS–Episcopal	1	63	151	180	1.2	2.0
Bahá'í	0	NR	35	35	0.2	0.4
BAPT–Natl Mis Bapt Conv	1	0	150	176	1.2	2.0
BAPT–So Bapt Conv	10	766	2,675	3,131	21.2	34.8
Catholic	1	NR	NR	273	1.8	3.0
Ch of Nazarene	1	76	109	109	0.7	1.2
CHR–Chs of Christ	2	87	66	92	0.6	1.0
Jehovah's Witness	1	NR	NR	NR	-	-
METH–AME	16	23	2,049	2,399	16.3	26.6
METH–Un Methodist	6	400	819	1,250	8.5	13.9
Non-denom Chr Chs	2	200	300	300	2.0	3.3
PENT–Assemb of God	1	62	26	62	0.4	0.7
PENT–Ch God (Cleve)	1	56	64	75	0.5	0.8
PENT–Ch Lord Jesus Apos	1	NR	NR	NR	-	-
PENT–Ch of God Proph	2	NR	132	155	1.1	1.7
PENT–COGIC	2	0	300	351	2.4	3.9
PENT–Intl Pent Holiness	2	207	295	345	2.3	3.8
PRES–Presb Ch (USA)	1	0	65	76	0.5	0.8
LAFAYETTE	**20**	**1,385**	**2,808**	**3,754**	**42.3**	**100.0**
ANG/EPIS–Episcopal	1	7	7	7	0.1	0.2
BAPT–So Bapt Conv	9	850	1,888	2,245	25.3	59.8
Catholic	1	NR	NR	460	5.2	12.3
CHR–Chs of Christ	2	65	50	71	0.8	1.9
METH–Un Methodist	2	60	143	156	1.8	4.2
Non-denom Chr Chs	2	210	300	300	3.4	8.0
PENT–Assemb of God	1	80	54	80	0.9	2.1
PENT–Ch God (Cleve)	1	113	216	257	2.9	6.8
PENT–COGIC	1	0	150	178	2.0	4.7
LAKE	**323**	**41,249**	**63,635**	**114,251**	**38.5**	**100.0**
ANG/EPIS–Anglican NA	1	NR	NR	NR	-	-
ANG/EPIS–Episcopal	7	1,238	2,176	2,509	0.8	2.2
Bahá'í	0	NR	73	73	0.0	0.1
BAPT–Amer Bapt Assn	6	NR	774	921	0.3	0.8
BAPT–Converge/BGC	1	75	NR	90	0.0	0.1
BAPT–Ind Bapt Flwsp Intl	3	NR	NR	NR	-	-
BAPT–Natl Mis Bapt Conv	1	0	150	178	0.1	0.2
BAPT–NBC USA	6	465	1,265	1,505	0.5	1.3
BAPT–Prog NBC	1	0	150	178	0.1	0.2
BAPT–Ref Bapt Ch	1	NR	NR	NR	-	-
BAPT–Reg Bapt Gen As	2	NR	NR	NR	-	-
BAPT–So Bapt Conv	49	7,890	15,092	17,955	6.0	15.7
Calv Chpl	2	NR	NR	NR	-	-
Catholic	7	NR	NR	26,872	9.0	23.5
CGOD–Ch God (Ander)	3	335	NR	335	0.1	0.3
Ch Cr, Scientst	3	NR	NR	NR	-	-
Ch of Nazarene	4	349	257	419	0.1	0.4
Chr & Miss Al	4	262	223	313	0.1	0.3
CHR–Chr Ch (Disc)	1	58	130	155	0.1	0.1
CHR–Chr Chs & Chs Cr	7	NR	2,799	3,330	1.1	2.9
CHR–Chs of Christ	12	1,230	1,163	1,492	0.5	1.3
CHR–Int Chs of Christ	0	NR	112	133	0.0	0.1
CONG–Cong Chr, NA	2	NR	148	176	0.1	0.2

Religious Group	Number of Congregations	Number of Attendees	Number of Communicant, Confirmed, or Full Members	Adherents		
				Number of Adherents	% of Total Pop.	% of Total Adh.
Evan Cov Ch	1	87	57	113	0.0	0.1
Evan Free Ch	3	580	NR	580	0.2	0.5
Int Cou Comm Ch	1	NR	NR	NR	-	-
Jehovah's Witness	6	NR	NR	NR	-	-
LDS–Comm of Christ	2	NR	242	242	0.1	0.2
LDS–L-D Saints	4	NR	NR	2,463	0.8	2.2
LUTH–E.L.C.A.	4	558	1,160	1,292	0.4	1.1
LUTH–Luth–MO Synod	3	900	1,539	1,876	0.6	1.6
LUTH–Wisc Ev Luth Syn	1	116	113	116	0.0	0.1
MENN–Cons Menn Conf	1	54	25	30	0.0	0.0
METH–A.W.M.C.	1	13	0	16	0.0	0.0
METH–AME	10	115	1,412	1,680	0.6	1.5
METH–C.M.E.	1	60	70	83	0.0	0.1
METH–Un Methodist	12	3,976	7,555	11,224	3.8	9.8
METH–Wesleyan	2	93	77	121	0.0	0.1
Muslim Est	3	1,218	NR	4,191	1.4	3.7
Non-denom Chr Chs	60	12,585	14,319	16,890	5.7	14.8
ORTHE–Ant Orth of NA	1	47	NR	130	0.0	0.1
ORTHE–Serb Orth USA	1	115	NR	1,000	0.3	0.9
PENT–Assemb of God	9	1,063	720	1,505	0.5	1.3
PENT–Ch God (Cleve)	21	2,578	3,945	4,693	1.6	4.1
PENT–Ch Lord Jesus Apos	2	NR	NR	NR	-	-
PENT–Ch of God by Faith	5	NR	NR	NR	-	-
PENT–Ch of God Proph	3	NR	67	80	0.0	0.1
PENT–COGIC	5	20	620	738	0.2	0.6
PENT–Int Foursq Gos	2	96	47	56	0.0	0.0
PENT–Intl Pent Holiness	3	155	220	262	0.1	0.2
PENT–Un Pent Ch Intl	2	NR	NR	NR	-	-
PENT–Vineyard	1	300	345	410	0.1	0.4
PRES–Presb Ch (USA)	9	3,276	4,502	5,356	1.8	4.7
PRES–Presb Ch Amer	2	155	180	222	0.1	0.2
Salvation Army	1	54	51	105	0.0	0.1
Sev Day Adv	12	906	1,575	1,812	0.6	1.6
Un C of Christ	2	177	229	272	0.1	0.2
Unit Univ	1	50	53	53	0.0	0.0
Unity Ch	3	NR	NR	NR	-	-
Zoroastrian	0	NR	NR	6	0.0	0.0
LEE	**430**	**68,452**	**84,066**	**233,165**	**37.7**	**100.0**
ANG/EPIS–Anglican NA	1	NR	NR	NR	-	-
ANG/EPIS–Episcopal	12	1,852	3,360	3,482	0.6	1.5
Ap Chr Ch-Amer	1	33	17	33	0.0	0.0
Bahá'í	3	NR	140	140	0.0	0.1
BAPT–Amer Bapt Assn	1	NR	85	100	0.0	0.0
BAPT–Consrv Bapt	1	NR	NR	NR	-	-
BAPT–Converge/BGC	3	225	NR	270	0.0	0.1
BAPT–Ind Bapt Flwsp Intl	1	NR	NR	NR	-	-
BAPT–Natl Mis Bapt Conv	1	0	150	177	0.0	0.1
BAPT–NBC Amer	1	0	300	353	0.1	0.2
BAPT–Ref Bapt Ch	1	NR	NR	NR	-	-
BAPT–Reg Bapt Gen As	2	NR	NR	NR	-	-
BAPT–So Bapt Conv	68	12,741	20,802	24,505	4.0	10.5
BRETH–Ch of Brethren	2	33	51	60	0.0	0.0
BRETH–Grace Breth	2	NR	NR	NR	-	-
BUDD–Theravada	1	NR	NR	1,365	0.2	0.6
BUDD–Vajrayana	1	NR	NR	457	0.1	0.2
Calv Chpl	2	NR	NR	NR	-	-
Catholic	20	NR	NR	100,300	16.2	43.0
CGOD–Ch God (Ander)	3	120	NR	120	0.0	0.1
Ch Cr, Scientst	4	NR	NR	NR	-	-
Ch God (7th Day)	2	NR	NR	NR	-	-
Ch of Nazarene	5	554	778	832	0.1	0.4
Chr & Miss Al	7	1,228	965	1,924	0.3	0.8
CHR–Chr Ch (Disc)	3	220	542	638	0.1	0.3
CHR–Chr Chs & Chs Cr	10	NR	2,915	3,434	0.6	1.5
CHR–Chs of Christ	7	1,047	951	1,396	0.2	0.6
CHR–Int Chs of Christ	1	NR	45	53	0.0	0.0
CONG–Cong Chr, NA	2	NR	134	158	0.0	0.1
Evan Free Ch	1	125	NR	125	0.0	0.1
FRND–Fr Gen Cf	1	NR	26	31	0.0	0.0
HINDU–Post Ren	1	NR	NR	16	0.0	0.0
HINDU–Trad Temples	1	NR	NR	300	0.0	0.1
Ind Fund Churches	1	NR	NR	NR	-	-
Int Cou Comm Ch	1	NR	NR	NR	-	-

NR–Not Reported   - Represents no adherents reported.   Percentages may not total 100 due to rounding.

Table 3: Religious Congregations by County and Group: 2010

Religious Group	Number of Congrega-tions	Number of Attendees	Number of Communicant, Confirmed, or Full Members	Adherents		
				Number of Adherents	% of Total Pop.	% of Total Adh.
Jain	1	NR	NR	NR	-	-
Jehovah's Witness	10	NR	NR	NR	-	-
JUD–Conserv	1	96	108	292	0.0	0.1
JUD–Orth	1	43	50	60	0.0	0.0
JUD–Reform	2	235	414	1,118	0.2	0.5
LDS–Comm of Christ	1	NR	121	121	0.0	0.1
LDS–L-D Saints	6	NR	NR	2,998	0.5	1.3
LUTH–Ch of Luth Br	1	137	95	205	0.0	0.1
LUTH–E.L.C.A.	8	1,781	2,344	3,219	0.5	1.4
LUTH–Luth–MO Synod	7	1,913	2,810	3,421	0.6	1.5
LUTH–Wisc Ev Luth Syn	3	335	417	525	0.1	0.2
MENN–Mennonite USA	3	1,325	740	872	0.1	0.4
METH–AME	4	500	800	942	0.2	0.4
METH–C.M.E.	3	0	300	353	0.1	0.2
METH–Free Methodist	1	275	230	275	0.0	0.1
METH–Un Methodist	20	7,140	8,091	14,133	2.3	6.1
METH–Wesleyan	4	241	109	313	0.1	0.1
Metro Comm Ch	1	122	166	196	0.0	0.1
MJEW–Union Mes Cong	1	NR	NR	NR	-	-
Muslim Est	4	1,624	NR	5,587	0.9	2.4
New Apost Ch	2	NR	NR	NR	-	-
Non-denom Chr Chs	62	12,830	16,444	18,668	3.0	8.0
ORTHE–Ant Orth of NA	1	30	NR	50	0.0	0.0
ORTHE–Greek Orthodox	1	145	NR	640	0.1	0.3
ORTHE–Orth Ch in Amer	1	36	NR	60	0.0	0.0
ORTHO–Coptic Orth Ch	1	170	NR	220	0.0	0.1
PENT–Assemb of God	21	11,257	4,180	20,401	3.3	8.7
PENT–Ch God (Cleve)	15	989	2,458	2,896	0.5	1.2
PENT–Ch God Mtn Asm	2	NR	NR	NR	-	-
PENT–Ch of God by Faith	1	NR	NR	NR	-	-
PENT–Ch of God Proph	8	NR	342	403	0.1	0.2
PENT–COGIC	2	65	80	94	0.0	0.0
PENT–Int Foursq Gos	2	27	57	67	0.0	0.0
PENT–Intl Pent Holiness	13	1,720	1,805	2,126	0.3	0.9
PENT–Open Bible Std	2	50	NR	50	0.0	0.0
PENT–Un Pent Ch Intl	4	NR	NR	NR	-	-
PENT–Vineyard	2	683	780	919	0.1	0.4
PRES–Evan Presby Ch	1	NR	1,114	1,312	0.2	0.6
PRES–Presb Ch (USA)	10	4,101	4,843	5,705	0.9	2.4
PRES–Presb Ch Amer	4	511	563	627	0.1	0.3
REF–Un Ref Chs N.A.	1	NR	NR	NR	-	-
Salvation Army	1	233	195	386	0.1	0.2
Sev Day Adv	10	1,184	2,059	2,369	0.4	1.0
Swedenborgian	1	NR	NR	NR	-	-
Un C of Christ	2	476	885	1,043	0.2	0.4
Unit Univ	2	0	205	230	0.0	0.1
Unity Ch	2	NR	NR	NR	-	-
LEON	**274**	**47,022**	**89,398**	**130,227**	**47.3**	**100.0**
ANG/EPIS–Anglican NA	4	NR	NR	NR	-	-
ANG/EPIS–Episcopal	7	885	2,165	2,226	0.8	1.7
Bahá'í	2	NR	133	133	0.0	0.1
BAPT–Amer Bapt Assn	2	NR	170	201	0.1	0.2
BAPT–Ind Bapt Flwsp Intl	1	NR	NR	NR	-	-
BAPT–Natl Mis Bapt Conv	4	0	750	885	0.3	0.7
BAPT–NBC USA	4	5,800	10,950	12,920	4.7	9.9
BAPT–Reg Bapt Gen As	1	NR	NR	NR	-	-
BAPT–So Bapt Conv	45	9,442	25,418	29,991	10.9	23.0
BUDD–Mahayana	2	NR	NR	112	0.0	0.1
BUDD–Vajrayana	3	NR	NR	118	0.0	0.1
Calv Chpl	1	NR	NR	NR	-	-
Catholic	1	NR	NR	15,677	5.7	12.0
CGOD–Ch God (Ander)	1	30	NR	30	0.0	0.0
Ch Cr, Scientst	1	NR	NR	NR	-	-
Ch of Nazarene	2	159	251	256	0.1	0.2
Chr & Miss Al	1	174	123	301	0.1	0.2
CHR–Chr Ch (Disc)	1	0	0	0	0.0	0.0
CHR–Chr Chs & Chs Cr	3	NR	455	537	0.2	0.4
CHR–Chs of Christ	6	1,075	1,125	1,421	0.5	1.1
CHR–Int Chs of Christ	2	NR	297	350	0.1	0.3
Evan Free Ch	1	1,000	NR	1,000	0.4	0.8
FRND–Fr Gen Cf	1	NR	54	64	0.0	0.0
HINDU–I/A Temples	1	NR	NR	1,562	0.6	1.2
HINDU–Post Ren	2	NR	NR	102	0.0	0.1

Religious Group	Number of Congrega-tions	Number of Attendees	Number of Communicant, Confirmed, or Full Members	Adherents		
				Number of Adherents	% of Total Pop.	% of Total Adh.
Jehovah's Witness	4	NR	NR	NR	-	-
JUD–Conserv	1	106	119	321	0.1	0.2
JUD–Orth	1	43	50	60	0.0	0.0
JUD–Reform	1	200	352	950	0.3	0.7
LDS–Comm of Christ	1	NR	121	121	0.0	0.1
LDS–L-D Saints	5	NR	NR	3,048	1.1	2.3
LUTH–E.L.C.A.	2	358	732	939	0.3	0.7
LUTH–Luth–MO Synod	2	395	518	665	0.2	0.5
LUTH–Wisc Ev Luth Syn	1	95	114	150	0.1	0.1
METH–AME	18	2,800	5,940	7,009	2.5	5.4
METH–AME Zion	1	0	150	177	0.1	0.1
METH–C.M.E.	4	0	450	531	0.2	0.4
METH–Un Methodist	15	3,400	9,913	12,553	4.6	9.6
Metro Comm Ch	1	39	46	54	0.0	0.0
Muslim Est	3	1,023	NR	3,294	1.2	2.5
Non-denom Chr Chs	53	13,525	20,670	21,154	7.7	16.2
ORTHE–Greek Orthodox	1	65	NR	280	0.1	0.2
ORTHO–Coptic Orth Ch	1	200	NR	325	0.1	0.2
PENT–Assemb of God	7	1,362	842	1,563	0.6	1.2
PENT–Ch God (Cleve)	3	486	475	560	0.2	0.4
PENT–Ch of God by Faith	1	NR	NR	NR	-	-
PENT–Ch of God Proph	3	NR	239	282	0.1	0.2
PENT–COGIC	6	455	585	690	0.3	0.5
PENT–Cong Hol Ch	1	7	6	7	0.0	0.0
PENT–Full Gosp Bapt	1	NR	NR	NR	-	-
PENT–Int Foursq Gos	1	25	58	68	0.0	0.1
PENT–Intl Pent Holiness	9	952	1,152	1,359	0.5	1.0
PENT–Open Bible Std	1	40	NR	40	0.0	0.0
PENT–Un Pent Ch Intl	2	NR	NR	NR	-	-
PRES–Evan Presby Ch	2	NR	37	44	0.0	0.0
PRES–Orth Pres Ch	1	188	129	159	0.1	0.1
PRES–Presb Ch (USA)	8	970	2,312	2,728	1.0	2.1
PRES–Presb Ch Amer	5	1,026	1,332	1,795	0.7	1.4
Salvation Army	1	36	92	150	0.1	0.1
Sev Day Adv	4	435	757	870	0.3	0.7
Un C of Christ	1	93	129	152	0.1	0.1
Unit Univ	1	133	187	243	0.1	0.2
Unity Ch	2	NR	NR	NR	-	-
LEVY	**80**	**5,381**	**13,706**	**19,438**	**47.6**	**100.0**
ANG/EPIS–Episcopal	3	157	220	222	0.5	1.1
Bahá'í	0	NR	18	18	0.0	0.1
BAPT–Natl Mis Bapt Conv	1	0	150	179	0.4	0.9
BAPT–NBC USA	2	0	150	179	0.4	0.9
BAPT–So Bapt Conv	20	2,952	9,790	11,657	28.6	60.0
Catholic	3	NR	NR	1,695	4.2	8.7
CHR–Chr Chs & Chs Cr	1	NR	38	45	0.1	0.2
CHR–Chs of Christ	9	444	422	577	1.4	3.0
Evan Free Ch	1	65	NR	65	0.2	0.3
Jehovah's Witness	3	NR	NR	NR	-	-
LDS–L-D Saints	2	NR	NR	873	2.1	4.5
LUTH–Luth–MO Synod	1	49	58	76	0.2	0.4
METH–AME	6	40	698	831	2.0	4.3
METH–Un Methodist	7	428	923	1,404	3.4	7.2
Non-denom Chr Chs	4	425	490	556	1.4	2.9
ORTHE–Greek Orthodox	1	20	NR	30	0.1	0.2
PENT–Assemb of God	2	105	0	140	0.3	0.7
PENT–Ch God (Cleve)	5	594	579	689	1.7	3.5
PENT–Ch of God by Faith	3	NR	NR	NR	-	-
PENT–COGIC	1	0	50	60	0.1	0.3
PENT–Un Pent Ch Intl	2	NR	NR	NR	-	-
PENT–Vineyard	1	45	55	65	0.2	0.3
PRES–Presb Ch (USA)	2	57	65	77	0.2	0.4
LIBERTY	**21**	**802**	**2,241**	**3,565**	**42.6**	**100.0**
BAPT–So Bapt Conv	4	333	1,322	1,585	18.9	44.5
CHR–Chr Chs & Chs Cr	1	NR	90	108	1.3	3.0
LDS–L-D Saints	2	NR	NR	869	10.4	24.4
METH–AME	2	0	200	240	2.9	6.7
METH–Un Methodist	2	82	134	134	1.6	3.8
Non-denom Chr Chs	1	100	150	150	1.8	4.2
PENT–Assemb of God	5	170	97	181	2.2	5.1
PENT–Ch God (Cleve)	1	64	130	156	1.9	4.4

NR–Not Reported   - Represents no adherents reported.   Percentages may not total 100 due to rounding.

Table 3: Religious Congregations by County and Group: 2010

Religious Group	Number of Congrega-tions	Number of Attendees	Number of Communicant, Confirmed, or Full Members	Adherents: Number of Adherents	Adherents: % of Total Pop.	Adherents: % of Total Adh.
PENT–Ch of God Proph	1	NR	54	65	0.8	1.8
PENT–Intl Pent Holiness	1	53	64	77	0.9	2.2
PENT–Un Pent Ch Intl	1	NR	NR	NR	-	-
MADISON	**55**	**2,469**	**7,624**	**9,381**	**48.8**	**100.0**
ANG/EPIS–Episcopal	1	30	87	87	0.5	0.9
Bahá'í	0	NR	1	1	0.0	0.0
BAPT–Amer Bapt Assn	1	NR	85	102	0.5	1.1
BAPT–Natl Mis Bapt Conv	2	0	210	252	1.3	2.7
BAPT–NBC USA	2	80	325	390	2.0	4.2
BAPT–So Bapt Conv	20	1,467	4,174	5,007	26.0	53.4
Catholic	1	NR	NR	216	1.1	2.3
Ch of Nazarene	1	8	14	19	0.1	0.2
CHR–Chs of Christ	2	62	45	66	0.3	0.7
Jehovah's Witness	1	NR	NR	NR	-	-
LDS–L-D Saints	1	NR	NR	186	1.0	2.0
METH–AME	9	60	1,060	1,272	6.6	13.6
METH–Un Methodist	8	589	1,301	1,400	7.3	14.9
PENT–Ch God (Cleve)	2	120	186	223	1.2	2.4
PENT–Ch Lord Jesus Apos	2	NR	NR	NR	-	-
PRES–Presb Ch Amer	1	40	113	134	0.7	1.4
Sev Day Adv	1	13	23	26	0.1	0.3
MANATEE	**244**	**33,780**	**52,946**	**121,961**	**37.8**	**100.0**
ANG/EPIS–Episcopal	5	926	1,670	1,949	0.6	1.6
Bahá'í	1	NR	98	98	0.0	0.1
BAPT–Converge/BGC	2	475	NR	570	0.2	0.5
BAPT–Natl Mis Bapt Conv	3	45	360	428	0.1	0.4
BAPT–NBC Amer	2	0	300	356	0.1	0.3
BAPT–Reg Bapt Gen As	1	NR	NR	NR	-	-
BAPT–S-D Baptist Gen Con	1	12	22	26	0.0	0.0
BAPT–So Bapt Conv	39	7,167	15,026	17,856	5.5	14.6
BRETH–Brethren (Ash)	2	NR	160	190	0.1	0.2
BRETH–Ch of Brethren	1	0	342	406	0.1	0.3
BUDD–Mahayana	2	NR	NR	205	0.1	0.2
BUDD–Vajrayana	1	NR	NR	55	0.0	0.0
Calv Chpl	1	NR	NR	NR	-	-
Catholic	9	NR	NR	50,700	15.7	41.6
CGOD–Ch God (Ander)	1	430	NR	430	0.1	0.4
Ch Cr, Scientst	1	NR	NR	NR	-	-
Ch of Nazarene	4	812	1,106	1,687	0.5	1.4
Chr & Miss Al	4	247	102	302	0.1	0.2
CHR–Chr Ch (Disc)	1	0	110	131	0.0	0.1
CHR–Chr Chs & Chs Cr	4	NR	585	695	0.2	0.6
CHR–Chs of Christ	12	980	992	1,246	0.4	1.0
Evan Cov Ch	3	223	436	290	0.1	0.2
Evan Free Ch	1	85	NR	85	0.0	0.1
Grace Gosp Fel	1	NR	NR	NR	-	-
Int Cou Comm Ch	4	NR	NR	NR	-	-
Jehovah's Witness	4	NR	NR	NR	-	-
JUD–Orth	1	43	50	60	0.0	0.0
LDS–Comm of Christ	1	NR	121	121	0.0	0.1
LDS–L-D Saints	3	NR	NR	1,686	0.5	1.4
LUTH–E.L.C.A.	4	809	1,219	1,381	0.4	1.1
LUTH–Luth–MO Synod	3	827	1,155	1,293	0.4	1.1
LUTH–Wisc Ev Luth Syn	2	204	194	242	0.1	0.2
METH–AME	6	0	700	832	0.3	0.7
METH–C.M.E.	3	0	350	416	0.1	0.3
METH–Free Methodist	1	88	74	88	0.0	0.1
METH–Un Methodist	16	3,263	5,916	10,994	3.4	9.0
METH–Wesleyan	1	35	28	46	0.0	0.0
New Apost Ch	1	NR	NR	NR	-	-
Non-denom Chr Chs	44	12,196	15,380	17,481	5.4	14.3
ORTHE–Greek Orthodox	1	195	NR	870	0.3	0.7
ORTHE–Orth Ch in Amer	1	65	NR	90	0.0	0.1
PENT–Assemb of God	4	570	207	962	0.3	0.8
PENT–Ch God (Cleve)	8	977	901	1,071	0.3	0.9
PENT–Ch of God Proph	1	NR	54	64	0.0	0.1
PENT–COGIC	3	150	410	487	0.2	0.4
PENT–Full Gosp Bapt	1	NR	NR	NR	-	-
PENT–Intl Pent Holiness	1	150	150	178	0.1	0.1
PENT–Pent Ch of God	1	70	NR	109	0.0	0.1
PENT–Un Pent Ch Intl	1	NR	NR	NR	-	-

Religious Group	Number of Congrega-tions	Number of Attendees	Number of Communicant, Confirmed, or Full Members	Adherents: Number of Adherents	Adherents: % of Total Pop.	Adherents: % of Total Adh.
PRES–As Ref Pres Ch	1	NR	200	238	0.1	0.2
PRES–Orth Pres Ch	1	85	52	73	0.0	0.1
PRES–Presb Ch (USA)	7	1,051	1,829	2,173	0.7	1.8
PRES–Presb Ch Amer	2	409	415	511	0.2	0.4
REF–Christian Ref	2	24	612	727	0.2	0.6
REF–Ref Ch in Am	1	98	77	119	0.0	0.1
Salvation Army	2	133	150	289	0.1	0.2
Sev Day Adv	5	503	874	1,006	0.3	0.8
Un Breth in Cr	1	110	52	94	0.0	0.1
Un C of Christ	2	243	364	433	0.1	0.4
Unit Univ	1	80	103	116	0.0	0.1
Unity Ch	1	NR	NR	NR	-	-
Zoroastrian	0	NR	NR	6	0.0	0.0
MARION	**364**	**46,345**	**66,715**	**115,580**	**34.9**	**100.0**
ANG/EPIS–Anglican NA	1	NR	NR	NR	-	-
ANG/EPIS–Episcopal	7	638	1,079	1,269	0.4	1.1
Bahá'í	2	NR	87	87	0.0	0.1
BAPT–Amer Bapt Assn	2	NR	230	270	0.1	0.2
BAPT–Converge/BGC	2	150	NR	180	0.1	0.2
BAPT–Free Will Bapt	1	NR	89	104	0.0	0.1
BAPT–Natl Mis Bapt Conv	1	0	150	176	0.1	0.2
BAPT–NBC USA	5	435	675	792	0.2	0.7
BAPT–Prog NBC	1	0	0	0	0.0	0.0
BAPT–Reg Bapt Gen As	2	NR	NR	NR	-	-
BAPT–So Bapt Conv	70	11,751	17,078	20,032	6.0	17.3
BRETH–Breth in Chr	1	NR	NR	NR	-	-
BRETH–Grace Breth	1	NR	NR	NR	-	-
Catholic	10	NR	NR	31,957	9.6	27.6
CGOD–Ch God (Ander)	2	2,270	NR	2,270	0.7	2.0
Ch Cr, Scientst	1	NR	NR	NR	-	-
Ch of Nazarene	4	259	262	287	0.1	0.2
Chr & Miss Al	2	206	131	345	0.1	0.3
CHR–Chr Ch (Disc)	4	234	528	619	0.2	0.5
CHR–Chr Chs & Chs Cr	7	NR	1,150	1,349	0.4	1.2
CHR–Chs of Christ	13	1,257	1,203	1,486	0.4	1.3
Evan Free Ch	1	80	NR	80	0.0	0.1
FRND–Fr Gen Cf	1	NR	0	0	0.0	0.0
HINDU–Post Ren	2	NR	NR	177	0.1	0.2
Jehovah's Witness	9	NR	NR	NR	-	-
JUD–Orth	1	43	50	60	0.0	0.1
JUD–Reform	1	67	119	321	0.1	0.3
LDS–Comm of Christ	1	NR	121	121	0.0	0.1
LDS–L-D Saints	4	NR	NR	2,176	0.7	1.9
LUTH–E.L.C.A.	7	1,040	1,415	1,725	0.5	1.5
LUTH–Luth–MO Synod	6	1,306	1,643	1,766	0.5	1.5
LUTH–Wisc Ev Luth Syn	1	62	76	80	0.0	0.1
METH–AME	15	230	1,791	2,101	0.6	1.8
METH–AME Zion	1	100	150	176	0.1	0.2
METH–C.M.E.	2	350	190	223	0.1	0.2
METH–Free Methodist	1	65	58	65	0.0	0.1
METH–Prim Meth Ch	1	NR	NR	NR	-	-
METH–Un Methodist	26	3,554	7,720	9,267	2.8	8.0
METH–Wesleyan	1	47	31	61	0.0	0.1
Metro Comm Ch	1	20	17	20	0.0	0.0
MJEW–Union Mes Cong	1	NR	NR	NR	-	-
Muslim Est	1	406	NR	1,397	0.4	1.2
New Apost Ch	1	NR	NR	NR	-	-
Non-denom Chr Chs	56	13,725	19,540	20,476	6.2	17.7
OCATH–Pol Natl Cath	1	NR	NR	NR	-	-
ORTHE–Ant Orth of NA	1	14	NR	39	0.0	0.0
ORTHE–Greek Orthodox	1	3	NR	3	0.0	0.0
ORTHO–Armen Ap Etchm	1	10	NR	40	0.0	0.0
PENT–Assemb of God	13	2,159	1,373	2,598	0.8	2.2
PENT–Ch God (Cleve)	16	2,199	3,648	4,279	1.3	3.7
PENT–Ch of God by Faith	2	NR	NR	NR	-	-
PENT–Ch of God Proph	4	NR	119	140	0.0	0.1
PENT–COGIC	3	0	450	528	0.2	0.5
PENT–Int Foursq Gos	1	100	52	61	0.0	0.1
PENT–Intl Pent Holiness	6	251	318	373	0.1	0.3
PENT–Un Pent Ch Intl	3	NR	NR	NR	-	-
PRES–Orth Pres Ch	1	27	23	29	0.0	0.0
PRES–Presb Ch (USA)	10	1,226	2,453	2,877	0.9	2.5
PRES–Presb Ch Amer	5	755	598	725	0.2	0.6

NR–Not Reported - Represents no adherents reported. Percentages may not total 100 due to rounding.

Table 3: Religious Congregations by County and Group: 2010

Religious Group	Number of Congrega-tions	Number of Attendees	Number of Communicant, Confirmed, or Full Members	Adherents: Number of Adherents	Adherents: % of Total Pop.	Adherents: % of Total Adh.
PRES–Ref Pres GA	2	NR	NR	NR	-	-
Salvation Army	1	134	186	186	0.1	0.2
Sev Day Adv	8	908	1,578	1,815	0.5	1.6
Un C of Christ	2	164	217	255	0.1	0.2
Unit Univ	1	100	117	117	0.0	0.1
Unity Ch	2	NR	NR	NR	-	-
MARTIN	**117**	**13,836**	**22,201**	**61,237**	**41.9**	**100.0**
ANG/EPIS–Anglican NA	1	NR	NR	NR	-	-
ANG/EPIS–Episcopal	6	1,021	2,196	2,490	1.7	4.1
Bahá'í	1	NR	55	55	0.0	0.1
BAPT–Amer Bapt Assn	2	NR	170	196	0.1	0.3
BAPT–Ind Bapt Flwsp Intl	1	NR	NR	NR	-	-
BAPT–Natl Mis Bapt Conv	1	0	150	173	0.1	0.3
BAPT–NBC USA	2	50	250	288	0.2	0.5
BAPT–So Bapt Conv	18	3,110	4,186	4,820	3.3	7.9
BRETH–Breth in Chr	1	NR	NR	NR	-	-
BUDD–Mahayana	1	NR	NR	102	0.1	0.2
BUDD–Vajrayana	1	NR	NR	167	0.1	0.3
Calv Chpl	2	NR	NR	NR	-	-
Catholic	6	NR	NR	31,282	21.4	51.1
Ch Cr, Scientst	1	NR	NR	NR	-	-
Ch of Nazarene	2	624	814	814	0.6	1.3
Chr & Miss Al	1	57	28	72	0.0	0.1
CHR–Chr Chs & Chs Cr	2	NR	130	150	0.1	0.2
CHR–Chs of Christ	3	295	352	409	0.3	0.7
CONG–Cong Chr, NA	1	NR	356	410	0.3	0.7
Jehovah's Witness	4	NR	NR	NR	-	-
JUD–Orth	1	43	50	60	0.0	0.1
JUD–Reform	1	138	243	656	0.4	1.1
LDS–L-D Saints	1	NR	NR	947	0.6	1.5
LUTH–E.L.C.A.	2	530	1,245	1,427	1.0	2.3
LUTH–Luth-MO Synod	2	424	733	867	0.6	1.4
METH–AME	3	100	440	507	0.3	0.8
METH–C.M.E.	2	0	200	230	0.2	0.4
METH–So Methodist	1	NR	NR	NR	-	-
METH–Un Methodist	4	1,278	3,656	5,425	3.7	8.9
Muslim Est	1	406	NR	1,397	1.0	2.3
Non-denom Chr Chs	13	3,485	4,075	4,532	3.1	7.4
ORTHE–Greek Orthodox	1	90	NR	200	0.1	0.3
PENT–Assemb of God	2	171	198	344	0.2	0.6
PENT–Ch God (Cleve)	9	692	741	853	0.6	1.4
PENT–Ch of God by Faith	1	NR	NR	NR	-	-
PENT–Ch of God Proph	2	NR	62	71	0.0	0.1
PENT–Un Pent Ch Intl	1	NR	NR	NR	-	-
PRES–Presb Ch (USA)	4	823	1,286	1,481	1.0	2.4
PRES–Presb Ch Amer	2	150	152	179	0.1	0.3
Salvation Army	1	36	52	200	0.1	0.3
Sev Day Adv	1	64	112	129	0.1	0.2
Un C of Christ	2	200	203	234	0.2	0.4
Unit Univ	1	49	66	70	0.0	0.1
Unity Ch	2	NR	NR	NR	-	-
MIAMI-DADE	**1,437**	**211,320**	**307,548**	**992,522**	**39.8**	**100.0**
ANG/EPIS–Anglican NA	1	NR	NR	NR	-	-
ANG/EPIS–Episcopal	30	4,746	9,661	12,569	0.5	1.3
Bahá'í	6	NR	794	794	0.0	0.1
BAPT–Amer Bapt Assn	1	NR	85	102	0.0	0.0
BAPT–Amer Bapt USA	3	695	559	671	0.0	0.1
BAPT–Consrv Bapt	1	NR	NR	NR	-	-
BAPT–Converge/BGC	6	450	NR	540	0.0	0.1
BAPT–Free Will Bapt	5	NR	445	534	0.0	0.1
BAPT–Natl Mis Bapt Conv	9	300	2,297	2,757	0.1	0.3
BAPT–NBC USA	44	14,015	39,921	47,921	1.9	4.8
BAPT–Ref Bapt Ch	3	NR	NR	NR	-	-
BAPT–Reg Bapt Gen As	1	NR	NR	NR	-	-
BAPT–S-D Baptist Gen Con	1	56	80	96	0.0	0.0
BAPT–So Bapt Conv	313	44,398	66,747	80,123	3.2	8.1
BRETH–Breth in Chr	35	NR	NR	NR	-	-
BRETH–Ch of Brethren	3	210	338	406	0.0	0.0
BRETH–Grace Breth	1	NR	NR	NR	-	-
BUDD–Mahayana	13	NR	NR	915	0.0	0.1
BUDD–Vajrayana	9	NR	NR	427	0.0	0.0

Religious Group	Number of Congrega-tions	Number of Attendees	Number of Communicant, Confirmed, or Full Members	Adherents: Number of Adherents	Adherents: % of Total Pop.	Adherents: % of Total Adh.
Calv Chpl	6	NR	NR	NR	-	-
Catholic	65	NR	NR	544,449	21.8	54.9
CGOD–Ch God (Ander)	7	665	NR	665	0.0	0.1
CGOD–Ches God-Gen Con	1	48	0	0	0.0	0.0
Ch Cr, Scientst	5	NR	NR	NR	-	-
Ch God (7th Day)	3	NR	NR	NR	-	-
Ch of Nazarene	26	4,750	6,559	6,796	0.3	0.7
Chr & Miss Al	11	916	589	1,257	0.1	0.1
CHR–Chr Ch (Disc)	24	264	486	583	0.0	0.1
CHR–Chr Chs & Chs Cr	5	NR	265	318	0.0	0.0
CHR–Chs of Christ	24	2,710	3,026	4,046	0.2	0.4
CHR–Int Chs of Christ	1	NR	758	910	0.0	0.1
Christian Brethren	1	NR	NR	NR	-	-
Evan Cov Ch	5	423	640	549	0.0	0.1
Evan Free Ch	1	40	NR	40	0.0	0.0
FRND–Evan Fr Ch Intl	1	280	0	0	0.0	0.0
FRND–Fr Gen Cf	1	NR	64	77	0.0	0.0
FRND–Fr Un Mtg	1	NR	0	0	0.0	0.0
HINDU–I/A Temples	6	NR	NR	2,716	0.1	0.3
HINDU–Post Ren	7	NR	NR	177	0.0	0.0
HINDU–Renaiss	5	NR	NR	86	0.0	0.0
HINDU–Trad Temples	2	NR	NR	90	0.0	0.0
Ind Fund Churches	2	NR	NR	NR	-	-
Jain	1	NR	NR	NR	-	-
Jehovah's Witness	32	NR	NR	NR	-	-
JUD–Conserv	8	2,102	2,359	6,369	0.3	0.6
JUD–Orth	53	7,380	3,650	10,250	0.4	1.0
JUD–Reconst	1	110	141	381	0.0	0.0
JUD–Reform	6	2,343	4,132	11,156	0.4	1.1
LDS–Comm of Christ	2	NR	242	242	0.0	0.0
LDS–L-D Saints	18	NR	NR	14,628	0.6	1.5
LUTH–E.L.C.A.	18	1,671	3,997	5,571	0.2	0.6
LUTH–Luth Cong Msn Chr	2	300	500	600	0.0	0.1
LUTH–Luth-MO Synod	12	690	1,295	1,888	0.1	0.2
LUTH–Nor Amer Luth C	1	NR	NR	NR	-	-
LUTH–Wisc Ev Luth Syn	1	214	151	225	0.0	0.0
MENN–Cons Menn Conf	1	31	14	17	0.0	0.0
MENN–Mennonite USA	6	294	278	334	0.0	0.0
METH–AME	22	2,540	5,442	6,533	0.3	0.7
METH–AME Zion	1	0	150	180	0.0	0.0
METH–C.M.E.	1	150	400	480	0.0	0.0
METH–Free Methodist	6	532	696	708	0.0	0.1
METH–Un Methodist	32	3,716	9,488	11,880	0.5	1.2
METH–Wesleyan	2	122	46	159	0.0	0.0
Metro Comm Ch	1	16	15	18	0.0	0.0
MJEW–Union Mes Cong	1	NR	NR	NR	-	-
MORAV–Morav Ch-South	3	408	549	794	0.0	0.1
Muslim Est	15	6,307	NR	23,064	0.9	2.3
New Apost Ch	2	NR	NR	NR	-	-
Non-denom Chr Chs	197	67,301	87,452	96,749	3.9	9.7
ORTHE–Ant Orth of NA	2	195	NR	1,100	0.0	0.1
ORTHE–Greek Orthodox	3	340	NR	1,620	0.1	0.2
ORTHE–Orth Ch in Amer	2	85	NR	220	0.0	0.0
ORTHE–Rus Orth Abroad	1	40	NR	300	0.0	0.0
ORTHE–Serb Orth USA	1	200	NR	1,000	0.0	0.1
ORTHO–Syrian Orth Ch	1	40	NR	200	0.0	0.0
PENT–Assemb of God	45	9,748	5,905	25,244	1.0	2.5
PENT–Ch God (Cleve)	37	3,895	4,617	5,542	0.2	0.6
PENT–Ch God Mtn Asm	1	NR	NR	NR	-	-
PENT–Ch Lord Jesus Apos	4	NR	NR	NR	-	-
PENT–Ch of God by Faith	3	NR	NR	NR	-	-
PENT–Ch of God Proph	14	NR	929	1,115	0.0	0.1
PENT–COGIC	11	750	1,835	2,203	0.1	0.2
PENT–Elim	2	NR	NR	NR	-	-
PENT–Fire Bapt Hol Ch	1	NR	NR	NR	-	-
PENT–Full Gosp Bapt	2	NR	NR	NR	-	-
PENT–I F Chr Assmbl	1	NR	NR	NR	-	-
PENT–Int Foursq Gos	5	280	319	383	0.0	0.0
PENT–Intl Pent Holiness	18	1,199	1,321	1,586	0.1	0.2
PENT–Open Bible Std	7	789	NR	789	0.0	0.1
PENT–Pent FW Bapt	1	NR	NR	NR	-	-
PENT–Un Pent Ch Intl	4	NR	NR	NR	-	-
PENT–Vineyard	2	2,290	3,435	4,123	0.2	0.4
PRES–Cumber Presb	1	NR	45	78	0.0	0.0

NR–Not Reported   - Represents no adherents reported.   Percentages may not total 100 due to rounding.

Table 3: Religious Congregations by County and Group: 2010

Religious Group	Number of Congrega-tions	Number of Attendees	Number of Communicant, Confirmed, or Full Members	Adherents: Number of Adherents	Adherents: % of Total Pop.	Adherents: % of Total Adh.
PRES–Evan Presby Ch	1	NR	86	103	0.0	0.0
PRES–Kor Pres Abroad	1	NR	NR	NR	-	-
PRES–Orth Pres Ch	1	15	14	23	0.0	0.0
PRES–Presb Ch (USA)	17	1,775	2,708	3,251	0.1	0.3
PRES–Presb Ch Amer	14	1,779	2,432	2,909	0.1	0.3
REF–Christian Ref	5	427	435	522	0.0	0.1
REF–Hung Ref Add'l	1	NR	NR	NR	-	-
REF–Ref Ch in Am	2	115	91	151	0.0	0.0
Salvation Army	4	532	748	4,434	0.2	0.4
Sev Day Adv	62	13,950	24,260	27,901	1.1	2.8
Un C of Christ	12	1,603	3,934	4,722	0.2	0.5
Unit Univ	1	80	123	143	0.0	0.0
Unity Ch	6	NR	NR	NR	-	-
Zoroastrian	1	NR	NR	20	0.0	0.0
MONROE	**81**	**4,728**	**7,270**	**24,391**	**33.4**	**100.0**
ANG/EPIS–Episcopal	5	359	762	967	1.3	4.0
Bahá'í	1	NR	103	103	0.1	0.4
BAPT–Converge/BGC	1	75	NR	90	0.1	0.4
BAPT–NBC Amer	1	0	150	169	0.2	0.7
BAPT–So Bapt Conv	12	793	2,205	2,490	3.4	10.2
BUDD–Mahayana	1	NR	NR	11	0.0	0.0
BUDD–Vajrayana	1	NR	NR	36	0.0	0.1
Catholic	5	NR	NR	13,346	18.3	54.7
Ch Cr, Scientist	1	NR	NR	NR	-	-
Ch of Nazarene	2	15	29	29	0.0	0.1
CHR–Chs of Christ	3	118	67	103	0.1	0.4
Evan Cov Ch	1	31	36	40	0.1	0.2
FRND–Fr Gen Cf	1	NR	0	0	0.0	0.0
Jehovah's Witness	2	NR	NR	NR	-	-
JUD–Orth	1	43	50	60	0.1	0.2
LDS–L-D Saints	2	NR	NR	598	0.8	2.5
LUTH–E.L.C.A.	1	49	52	64	0.1	0.3
LUTH–Luth–MO Synod	3	90	269	331	0.5	1.4
METH–AME	3	0	400	452	0.6	1.9
METH–AME Zion	1	60	120	136	0.2	0.6
METH–Un Methodist	6	737	905	1,355	1.9	5.6
Metro Comm Ch	1	53	67	76	0.1	0.3
Muslim Est	1	407	NR	1,397	1.9	5.7
Non-denom Chr Chs	3	419	470	524	0.7	2.1
ORTHO–Coptic Orth Ch	1	16	NR	20	0.0	0.1
PENT–Assemb of God	3	284	115	307	0.4	1.3
PENT–Ch God (Cleve)	3	123	218	246	0.3	1.0
PENT–Ch of God Proph	1	NR	12	14	0.0	0.1
PENT–Un Pent Ch Intl	1	NR	NR	NR	-	-
PENT–Vineyard	1	500	700	790	1.1	3.2
PRES–Orth Pres Ch	1	25	15	22	0.0	0.1
PRES–Presb Ch (USA)	3	278	233	263	0.4	1.1
Salvation Army	1	55	39	61	0.1	0.3
Sev Day Adv	3	54	94	109	0.1	0.4
Un C of Christ	2	89	109	123	0.2	0.5
Unit Univ	1	55	50	59	0.1	0.2
Unity Ch	1	NR	NR	NR	-	-
NASSAU	**101**	**11,440**	**22,042**	**34,276**	**46.8**	**100.0**
ANG/EPIS–Anglican NA	1	NR	NR	NR	-	-
ANG/EPIS–Episcopal	2	292	812	812	1.1	2.4
Bahá'í	1	NR	14	14	0.0	0.0
BAPT–Ind Bapt Flwsp Intl	2	NR	NR	NR	-	-
BAPT–Natl Mis Bapt Conv	1	0	150	180	0.2	0.5
BAPT–NBC USA	3	275	535	641	0.9	1.9
BAPT–Ref Bapt Ch	1	NR	NR	NR	-	-
BAPT–So Bapt Conv	28	4,955	13,023	15,610	21.3	45.5
Catholic	2	NR	NR	5,192	7.1	15.1
CGOD–Ch God (Ander)	1	0	NR	0	0.0	0.0
Ch of Nazarene	1	89	204	204	0.3	0.6
Chr & Miss Al	2	66	50	144	0.2	0.4
CHR–Chs of Christ	3	243	231	288	0.4	0.8
Jehovah's Witness	2	NR	NR	NR	-	-
LDS–L-D Saints	2	NR	NR	878	1.2	2.6
LUTH–E.L.C.A.	1	122	252	280	0.4	0.8
METH–AME	3	38	300	360	0.5	1.1
METH–Free Methodist	1	20	38	38	0.1	0.1
METH–Un Methodist	5	734	1,677	2,483	3.4	7.2
Non-denom Chr Chs	16	2,840	2,148	3,700	5.0	10.8
PENT–Assemb of God	5	581	390	776	1.1	2.3
PENT–Ch God (Cleve)	8	563	1,013	1,214	1.7	3.5
PENT–Ch of God by Faith	3	NR	NR	NR	-	-
PENT–Ch of God Proph	1	NR	39	47	0.1	0.1
PENT–Int Foursq Gos	1	41	39	47	0.1	0.1
PENT–Intl Pent Holiness	1	100	125	150	0.2	0.4
PENT–Un Pent Ch Intl	1	NR	NR	NR	-	-
PRES–Presb Ch (USA)	1	380	909	1,090	1.5	3.2
PRES–Presb Ch Amer	1	78	63	92	0.1	0.3
Un C of Christ	1	23	30	36	0.0	0.1
OKALOOSA	**222**	**26,413**	**53,886**	**86,390**	**47.8**	**100.0**
ANG/EPIS–Anglican NA	2	NR	NR	NR	-	-
ANG/EPIS–Episcopal	4	505	889	1,057	0.6	1.2
Bahá'í	1	NR	36	36	0.0	0.0
BAPT–Amer Bapt Assn	1	NR	85	103	0.1	0.1
BAPT–Natl Mis Bapt Conv	1	45	200	241	0.1	0.3
BAPT–So Bapt Conv	59	8,214	25,844	31,192	17.3	36.1
BUDD–Mahayana	2	NR	NR	921	0.5	1.1
BUDD–Theravada	1	NR	NR	1,364	0.8	1.6
Catholic	6	NR	NR	9,085	5.0	10.5
Ch Cr, Scientst	1	NR	NR	NR	-	-
Ch of Nazarene	2	89	135	145	0.1	0.2
CHR–Chr Ch (Disc)	2	116	220	266	0.1	0.3
CHR–Chr Chs & Chs Cr	2	NR	70	84	0.0	0.1
CHR–Chs of Christ	12	1,265	1,176	1,453	0.8	1.7
HINDU–Post Ren	1	NR	NR	25	0.0	0.0
Jehovah's Witness	3	NR	NR	NR	-	-
JUD–Reform	1	43	75	202	0.1	0.2
LDS–Comm of Christ	2	NR	272	272	0.2	0.3
LDS–L-D Saints	7	NR	NR	3,298	1.8	3.8
LUTH–E.L.C.A.	2	559	1,269	1,731	1.0	2.0
LUTH–Luth–MO Synod	3	627	1,086	1,500	0.8	1.7
METH–AME	3	175	502	606	0.3	0.7
METH–AME Zion	1	75	227	274	0.2	0.3
METH–Un Methodist	12	5,482	11,883	16,699	9.2	19.3
Muslim Est	1	406	NR	1,397	0.8	1.6
Non-denom Chr Chs	34	4,224	5,464	5,938	3.3	6.9
ORTHE–Greek Orthodox	1	70	NR	310	0.2	0.4
ORTHO–Coptic Orth Ch	1	24	NR	27	0.0	0.0
PENT–Assemb of God	19	2,928	1,850	5,057	2.8	5.9
PENT–Ch God (Cleve)	4	230	502	606	0.3	0.7
PENT–Ch of God by Faith	1	NR	NR	NR	-	-
PENT–Ch of God Proph	1	NR	18	22	0.0	0.0
PENT–COGIC	4	130	440	531	0.3	0.6
PENT–Full Gosp Bapt	1	NR	NR	NR	-	-
PENT–Un Pent Ch Intl	3	NR	NR	NR	-	-
PRES–Korean Pres Amer	1	NR	NR	NR	-	-
PRES–Orth Pres Ch	1	20	16	17	0.0	0.0
PRES–Presb Ch (USA)	6	317	548	661	0.4	0.8
PRES–Presb Ch Amer	6	538	556	665	0.4	0.8
REF–Comm Ref Evan	1	NR	NR	NR	-	-
Salvation Army	1	51	69	71	0.0	0.1
Sev Day Adv	3	192	333	383	0.2	0.4
Unit Univ	1	88	121	151	0.1	0.2
Unity Ch	1	NR	NR	NR	-	-
OKEECHOBEE	**53**	**4,380**	**9,612**	**14,331**	**35.8**	**100.0**
ANG/EPIS–Episcopal	1	126	180	253	0.6	1.8
Bahá'í	0	NR	10	10	0.0	0.1
BAPT–Amer Bapt Assn	1	NR	200	244	0.6	1.7
BAPT–Free Will Bapt	1	NR	89	109	0.3	0.8
BAPT–Natl Mis Bapt Conv	3	100	675	825	2.1	5.8
BAPT–So Bapt Conv	8	1,307	3,535	4,321	10.8	30.2
BRETH–Grace Breth	1	NR	NR	NR	-	-
Calv Chpl	1	NR	NR	NR	-	-
Catholic	3	NR	NR	2,534	6.3	17.7
Ch of Nazarene	1	61	50	62	0.2	0.4
CHR–Chr Chs & Chs Cr	3	NR	477	583	1.5	4.1
CHR–Chs of Christ	3	100	93	115	0.3	0.8
Jehovah's Witness	1	NR	NR	NR	-	-

NR–Not Reported - Represents no adherents reported. Percentages may not total 100 due to rounding.

Table 3: Religious Congregations by County and Group: 2010

Religious Group	Number of Congregations	Number of Attendees	Number of Communicant, Confirmed, or Full Members	Adherents: Number of Adherents	Adherents: % of Total Pop.	Adherents: % of Total Adh.
LDS–L-D Saints	1	NR	NR	304	0.8	2.1
LUTH–Luth-MO Synod	1	176	452	544	1.4	3.8
METH–AME	1	0	100	122	0.3	0.9
METH–Un Methodist	1	256	552	733	1.8	5.1
Non-denom Chr Chs	11	1,590	2,350	2,444	6.1	17.1
PENT–Assemb of God	2	155	80	195	0.5	1.4
PENT–Ch God (Cleve)	3	346	516	631	1.6	4.4
PENT–Ch of God by Faith	1	NR	NR	NR	-	-
PENT–Ch of God Proph	1	NR	58	71	0.2	0.5
PENT–Cong Hol Ch	1	39	35	43	0.1	0.3
PENT–Un Pent Ch Intl	1	NR	NR	NR	-	-
PRES–Presb Ch (USA)	1	64	56	68	0.2	0.5
Sev Day Adv	1	60	104	120	0.3	0.8
ORANGE	**824**	**141,643**	**227,045**	**482,253**	**42.1**	**100.0**
ANG/EPIS–Anglican NA	2	NR	NR	NR	-	-
ANG/EPIS–Episcopal	16	2,941	6,459	8,366	0.7	1.7
Bahá'í	3	NR	397	397	0.0	0.1
BAPT–Amer Bapt Assn	5	NR	715	874	0.1	0.2
BAPT–Amer Bapt USA	6	1,147	2,599	3,175	0.3	0.7
BAPT–Converge/BGC	9	1,725	NR	2,070	0.2	0.4
BAPT–Free Will Bapt	3	NR	267	326	0.0	0.1
BAPT–Ind Bapt Flwsp Intl	2	NR	NR	NR	-	-
BAPT–Natl Mis Bapt Conv	6	30	750	916	0.1	0.2
BAPT–NBC Amer	5	1,688	5,075	6,200	0.5	1.3
BAPT–NBC USA	2	599	710	867	0.1	0.2
BAPT–Ref Bapt Ch	2	NR	NR	NR	-	-
BAPT–So Bapt Conv	118	21,554	51,173	62,518	5.5	13.0
BRETH–Breth in Chr	2	NR	NR	NR	-	-
BRETH–Ch of Brethren	4	77	291	356	0.0	0.1
BUDD–Mahayana	9	NR	NR	6,834	0.6	1.4
BUDD–Vajrayana	4	NR	NR	706	0.1	0.1
Calv Chpl	2	NR	NR	NR	-	-
Catholic	21	NR	NR	145,082	12.7	30.1
CGOD–Ch God (Ander)	5	632	NR	632	0.1	0.1
CGOD–Ches God-Gen Con	1	0	53	65	0.0	0.0
Ch Cr, Scientst	3	NR	NR	NR	-	-
Ch of Chr (Hol)	1	NR	NR	NR	-	-
Ch of Nazarene	19	3,375	4,754	5,203	0.5	1.1
Chr & Miss Al	11	1,745	1,044	2,300	0.2	0.5
CHR–Chr Ch (Disc)	7	1,012	1,929	2,357	0.2	0.5
CHR–Chr Chs & Chs Cr	12	NR	3,370	4,117	0.4	0.9
CHR–Chs of Christ	20	2,455	2,341	3,052	0.3	0.6
CHR–Int Chs of Christ	1	NR	226	276	0.0	0.1
Christian Brethren	1	NR	NR	NR	-	-
Evan Cov Ch	2	160	290	208	0.0	0.0
Evan Free Ch	1	330	NR	330	0.0	0.1
FRND–Fr Gen Cf	2	NR	64	78	0.0	0.0
Grace Gosp Fel	1	NR	NR	NR	-	-
HINDU–I/A Temples	4	NR	NR	2,467	0.2	0.5
HINDU–Post Ren	3	NR	NR	140	0.0	0.0
HINDU–Trad Temples	7	NR	NR	2,443	0.2	0.5
Int Cou Comm Ch	1	NR	NR	NR	-	-
Intl Fell Bible Ch	1	NR	NR	NR	-	-
Jain	1	NR	NR	NR	-	-
Jehovah's Witness	12	NR	NR	NR	-	-
JUD–Conserv	2	746	837	2,260	0.2	0.5
JUD–Orth	2	86	100	120	0.0	0.0
JUD–Reform	1	401	707	1,909	0.2	0.4
LDS–Comm of Christ	1	NR	121	121	0.0	0.0
LDS–L-D Saints	17	NR	NR	10,830	0.9	2.2
LUTH–Ch Luth Conf	1	NR	NR	NR	-	-
LUTH–E.L.C.A.	10	1,407	3,009	3,696	0.3	0.8
LUTH–Luth-MO Synod	8	1,374	2,956	3,644	0.3	0.8
LUTH–Wisc Ev Luth Syn	3	378	633	826	0.1	0.2
MENN–Mennonite USA	2	100	75	92	0.0	0.0
METH–AME	16	1,040	3,378	4,127	0.4	0.9
METH–AME Zion	2	0	250	305	0.0	0.1
METH–C.M.E.	3	1,650	3,100	3,787	0.3	0.8
METH–Free Methodist	3	72	86	91	0.0	0.0
METH–Un Methodist	23	7,654	19,086	25,787	2.3	5.3
METH–Wesleyan	3	57	66	75	0.0	0.0
Metro Comm Ch	1	215	279	341	0.0	0.1
Missionary Ch	1	25	30	30	0.0	0.0
Muslim Est	9	3,549	NR	12,572	1.1	2.6
Nat Spirit Asso	2	NR	NR	NR	-	-
New Apost Ch	1	NR	NR	NR	-	-
Non-denom Chr Chs	165	41,763	57,634	60,381	5.3	12.5
ORTHE–Ant Orth of NA	1	75	NR	225	0.0	0.0
ORTHE–Greek Orthodox	1	300	NR	2,500	0.2	0.5
ORTHE–Romania Orth Ar	1	20	NR	100	0.0	0.0
ORTHO–Armen Ap Etchm	2	95	NR	850	0.1	0.2
ORTHO–Coptic Orth Ch	1	240	NR	520	0.0	0.1
ORTHO–Eritrean Orth	1	300	NR	200	0.0	0.0
ORTHO–Malan Dioc Am	1	25	NR	75	0.0	0.0
ORTHO–Syrian Orth Ch	1	85	NR	150	0.0	0.0
PENT–Apos Faith Msn	2	NR	70	86	0.0	0.0
PENT–Assemb of God	28	15,740	11,427	35,280	3.1	7.3
PENT–Ch God (Cleve)	36	2,983	4,574	5,588	0.5	1.2
PENT–Ch God Apos Fth	1	NR	NR	NR	-	-
PENT–Ch Lord Jesus Apos	2	NR	NR	NR	-	-
PENT–Ch of God by Faith	4	NR	NR	NR	-	-
PENT–Ch of God Proph	10	NR	496	606	0.1	0.1
PENT–COGIC	5	275	850	1,038	0.1	0.2
PENT–Fire Bapt Hol Ch	1	NR	NR	NR	-	-
PENT–Int Foursq Gos	11	760	1,030	1,258	0.1	0.3
PENT–Intl Pent Holiness	5	682	966	1,180	0.1	0.2
PENT–Open Bible Std	2	47	NR	47	0.0	0.0
PENT–Pent Ch of God	1	70	NR	109	0.0	0.0
PENT–Un Pent Ch Intl	4	NR	NR	NR	-	-
PENT–Vineyard	1	85	115	140	0.0	0.0
PRES–As Ref Pres Ch	1	NR	41	50	0.0	0.0
PRES–Bible Pres	1	NR	NR	NR	-	-
PRES–Free Pres NA	1	NR	NR	NR	-	-
PRES–Kor Pres Abroad	1	NR	NR	NR	-	-
PRES–Orth Pres Ch	1	102	133	146	0.0	0.0
PRES–Presb Ch (USA)	20	5,394	9,688	11,836	1.0	2.5
PRES–Presb Ch Amer	10	2,467	2,541	3,413	0.3	0.7
PRES–Ref Pres of NA	1	55	81	106	0.0	0.0
REF–Christian Ref	2	190	115	140	0.0	0.0
REF–Ref Ch in Am	2	177	169	242	0.0	0.1
Salvation Army	1	180	276	331	0.0	0.1
Sev Day Adv	39	10,517	18,290	21,034	1.8	4.4
Un C of Christ	5	550	989	1,208	0.1	0.3
Unit Univ	2	242	340	441	0.0	0.1
Unity Ch	2	NR	NR	NR	-	-
Zoroastrian	0	NR	NR	5	0.0	0.0
OSCEOLA	**206**	**27,532**	**33,018**	**98,652**	**36.7**	**100.0**
ANG/EPIS–Anglican NA	2	NR	NR	NR	-	-
ANG/EPIS–Episcopal	2	443	784	893	0.3	0.9
Bahá'í	1	NR	57	57	0.0	0.1
BAPT–Amer Bapt Assn	3	NR	235	293	0.1	0.3
BAPT–Amer Bapt USA	2	21	26	32	0.0	0.0
BAPT–Converge/BGC	7	525	NR	630	0.2	0.6
BAPT–NBC USA	1	100	175	218	0.1	0.2
BAPT–Reg Bapt Gen As	1	NR	NR	NR	-	-
BAPT–S-D Baptist Gen Con	1	17	NR	NR	-	-
BAPT–So Bapt Conv	30	4,967	6,275	7,812	2.9	7.9
BUDD–Mahayana	1	NR	NR	102	0.0	0.1
BUDD–Theravada	1	NR	NR	375	0.1	0.4
Catholic	5	NR	NR	41,710	15.5	42.3
CGOD–Ch God (Ander)	1	350	NR	350	0.1	0.4
Ch Cr, Scientst	1	NR	NR	NR	-	-
Ch of Nazarene	5	442	600	1,034	0.4	1.0
Chr & Miss Al	1	432	231	440	0.2	0.4
CHR–Chr Ch (Disc)	4	670	608	757	0.3	0.8
CHR–Chr Chs & Chs Cr	5	NR	2,300	2,863	1.1	2.9
CHR–Chs of Christ	4	325	282	366	0.1	0.4
Christian Brethren	1	NR	NR	NR	-	-
Ind Fund Churches	1	NR	NR	NR	-	-
Jehovah's Witness	6	NR	NR	NR	-	-
JUD–Reform	1	27	48	130	0.0	0.1
LDS–L-D Saints	6	NR	NR	3,277	1.2	3.3
LUTH–E.L.C.A.	1	330	615	788	0.3	0.8
LUTH–Evan Luth Syn	1	98	102	120	0.0	0.1
LUTH–Luth-MO Synod	1	85	141	225	0.1	0.2
METH–AME	2	25	187	233	0.1	0.2

NR–Not Reported   - Represents no adherents reported.   Percentages may not total 100 due to rounding.

Table 3: Religious Congregations by County and Group: 2010

Religious Group	Number of Congrega-tions	Number of Attendees	Number of Communicant, Confirmed, or Full Members	Adherents		
				Number of Adherents	% of Total Pop.	% of Total Adh.
METH–AME Zion	1	0	100	124	0.0	0.1
METH–Free Methodist	1	101	64	101	0.0	0.1
METH–Un Methodist	3	617	2,657	3,248	1.2	3.3
METH–Wesleyan	1	21	20	27	0.0	0.0
Missionary Ch	2	56	27	56	0.0	0.1
Muslim Est	6	2,436	NR	8,382	3.1	8.5
Non-denom Chr Chs	42	7,995	10,695	11,455	4.3	11.6
OCATH–Un Cath Ch	1	NR	NR	702	0.3	0.7
ORTHE–Rus Orth Abroad	1	20	NR	80	0.0	0.1
ORTHO–Armen Ap Cilic	1	50	NR	150	0.1	0.2
PENT–Assemb of God	13	4,629	2,391	6,273	2.3	6.4
PENT–Ch God (Cleve)	13	1,359	1,899	2,364	0.9	2.4
PENT–Ch of God Proph	2	NR	159	198	0.1	0.2
PENT–COGIC	2	75	300	373	0.1	0.4
PENT–Full Gosp Bapt	1	NR	NR	NR	-	-
PENT–Int Foursq Gos	4	232	220	274	0.1	0.3
PENT–Pent FW Bapt	1	NR	NR	NR	-	-
PENT–Un Pent Ch Intl	2	NR	NR	NR	-	-
PRES–Presb Ch (USA)	3	426	655	815	0.3	0.8
Salvation Army	1	41	91	91	0.0	0.1
Sev Day Adv	6	617	1,074	1,234	0.5	1.3
Sikh	1	NR	NR	NR	-	-
PALM BEACH	**775**	**131,770**	**185,049**	**483,715**	**36.6**	**100.0**
ANG/EPIS–Anglican NA	1	NR	NR	NR	-	-
ANG/EPIS–Episcopal	20	3,970	9,501	10,519	0.8	2.2
Bahá'í	10	NR	1,968	1,968	0.1	0.4
BAPT–Amer Bapt Assn	2	NR	170	201	0.0	0.0
BAPT–Consrv Bapt	1	NR	NR	NR	-	-
BAPT–Converge/BGC	2	150	NR	180	0.0	0.0
BAPT–Free Will Bapt	2	NR	178	211	0.0	0.0
BAPT–Ind Bapt Flwsp Intl	1	NR	NR	NR	-	-
BAPT–N Am Bapt Conf	8	NR	950	1,125	0.1	0.2
BAPT–Natl Mis Bapt Conv	5	100	1,000	1,184	0.1	0.2
BAPT–NBC Amer	2	1,600	2,950	3,492	0.3	0.7
BAPT–NBC USA	8	2,200	6,350	7,517	0.6	1.6
BAPT–Reg Bapt Gen As	3	NR	NR	NR	-	-
BAPT–S-D Baptist Gen Con	1	28	23	27	0.0	0.0
BAPT–So Bapt Conv	127	21,099	29,054	34,395	2.6	7.1
BRETH–Breth in Chr	4	NR	NR	NR	-	-
BRETH–Ch of Brethren	1	0	0	0	0.0	0.0
BUDD–Mahayana	2	NR	NR	623	0.0	0.1
BUDD–Vajrayana	1	NR	NR	39	0.0	0.0
Calv Chpl	7	NR	NR	NR	-	-
Catholic	36	NR	NR	210,006	15.9	43.4
CGOD–Ch God (Ander)	5	398	NR	398	0.0	0.1
Ch Cr, Scientst	6	NR	NR	NR	-	-
Ch God (7th Day)	1	NR	NR	NR	-	-
Ch of Nazarene	15	1,361	2,447	2,764	0.2	0.6
Chr & Miss Al	19	2,015	1,166	2,708	0.2	0.6
CHR–Chr Ch (Disc)	3	415	544	644	0.0	0.1
CHR–Chr Chs & Chs Cr	5	NR	965	1,142	0.1	0.2
CHR–Chs of Christ	12	1,975	2,088	2,696	0.2	0.6
CHR–Int Chs of Christ	0	NR	252	298	0.0	0.1
Christian Brethren	1	NR	NR	NR	-	-
CONG–Cong Chr, NA	1	NR	1,830	2,166	0.2	0.4
Evan Cov Ch	1	120	66	156	0.0	0.0
Evan Free Ch	1	32	NR	32	0.0	0.0
FRND–Fr Gen Cf	1	NR	50	59	0.0	0.0
HINDU–I/A Temples	1	NR	NR	1,742	0.1	0.4
HINDU–Post Ren	7	NR	NR	204	0.0	0.0
HINDU–Renaiss	2	NR	NR	24	0.0	0.0
HINDU–Trad Temples	1	NR	NR	3,000	0.2	0.6
Jain	1	NR	NR	NR	-	-
Jehovah's Witness	16	NR	NR	NR	-	-
JUD–Conserv	12	5,138	5,766	15,568	1.2	3.2
JUD–Orth	28	5,040	3,500	7,000	0.5	1.4
JUD–Reconst	1	24	31	84	0.0	0.0
JUD–Reform	9	3,030	5,344	14,429	1.1	3.0
LDS–Comm of Christ	1	NR	121	121	0.0	0.0
LDS–L-D Saints	7	NR	NR	5,930	0.4	1.2
LUTH–Apostolic Luth	1	NR	NR	NR	-	-
LUTH–E.L.C.A.	11	1,643	2,999	3,765	0.3	0.8
LUTH–Luth Cong Msn Chr	1	180	618	732	0.1	0.2

Religious Group	Number of Congrega-tions	Number of Attendees	Number of Communicant, Confirmed, or Full Members	Adherents		
				Number of Adherents	% of Total Pop.	% of Total Adh.
LUTH–Luth-MO Synod	11	2,007	3,796	5,245	0.4	1.1
LUTH–Nor Amer Luth C	1	NR	NR	NR	-	-
LUTH–Wisc Ev Luth Syn	1	183	241	301	0.0	0.1
METH–AME	18	685	3,383	4,005	0.3	0.8
METH–C.M.E.	1	0	150	178	0.0	0.0
METH–Free Methodist	4	213	86	213	0.0	0.0
METH–So Methodist	1	NR	NR	NR	-	-
METH–Un Methodist	21	5,092	12,737	17,668	1.3	3.7
METH–Wesleyan	1	20	26	26	0.0	0.0
Metro Comm Ch	2	138	155	184	0.0	0.0
MJEW–Union Mes Cong	1	NR	NR	NR	-	-
MORAV–Morav Ch-South	1	34	26	41	0.0	0.0
MORAV–Unity Of Breth	1	NR	NR	NR	-	-
Muslim Est	9	3,299	NR	11,426	0.9	2.4
New Apost Ch	3	NR	NR	NR	-	-
Non-denom Chr Chs	86	37,484	47,833	52,936	4.0	10.9
ORTHE–Ant Orth of NA	1	100	NR	230	0.0	0.0
ORTHE–Greek Orthodox	2	625	NR	3,750	0.3	0.8
ORTHE–Orth Ch in Amer	2	50	NR	110	0.0	0.0
ORTHO–Armen Ap Etchm	1	200	NR	1,000	0.1	0.2
ORTHO–Coptic Orth Ch	2	398	NR	605	0.0	0.1
PENT–Assemb of God	18	9,709	3,732	10,272	0.8	2.1
PENT–Ch God (Cleve)	47	3,947	6,086	7,205	0.5	1.5
PENT–Ch Lord Jesus Apos	2	NR	NR	NR	-	-
PENT–Ch of God by Faith	3	NR	NR	NR	-	-
PENT–Ch of God Proph	16	NR	906	1,073	0.1	0.2
PENT–COGIC	8	240	977	1,157	0.1	0.2
PENT–Full Gosp Bapt	3	NR	NR	NR	-	-
PENT–Intl Pent Holiness	19	5,635	6,328	7,491	0.6	1.5
PENT–Open Bible Std	1	35	NR	35	0.0	0.0
PENT–Un Pent Ch Intl	3	NR	NR	NR	-	-
PENT–Vineyard	1	42	68	81	0.0	0.0
PRES–Orth Pres Ch	1	47	26	39	0.0	0.0
PRES–Presb Ch (USA)	15	2,334	4,445	5,262	0.4	1.1
PRES–Presb Ch Amer	11	2,710	3,610	3,795	0.3	0.8
REF–Christian Ref	2	155	214	253	0.0	0.1
REF–Ref Ch in Am	1	35	40	63	0.0	0.0
Salvation Army	3	235	314	356	0.0	0.1
Sev Day Adv	24	3,676	6,392	7,352	0.6	1.5
Un C of Christ	7	1,809	3,254	3,852	0.3	0.8
Unit Univ	2	115	293	353	0.0	0.1
Unity Ch	4	NR	NR	NR	-	-
Zoroastrian	0	NR	NR	9	0.0	0.0
PASCO	**273**	**29,325**	**39,288**	**101,424**	**21.8**	**100.0**
ANG/EPIS–Episcopal	4	529	853	984	0.2	1.0
Bahá'í	2	NR	108	108	0.0	0.1
BAPT–Amer Bapt Assn	1	NR	85	102	0.0	0.1
BAPT–Ind Bapt Flwsp Intl	1	NR	NR	NR	-	-
BAPT–Ref Bapt Ch	1	NR	NR	NR	-	-
BAPT–Reg Bapt Gen As	3	NR	NR	NR	-	-
BAPT–So Bapt Conv	53	7,095	12,807	15,293	3.3	15.1
BRETH–Grace Breth	1	NR	NR	NR	-	-
BUDD–Vajrayana	2	NR	NR	235	0.1	0.2
Catholic	13	NR	NR	41,497	8.9	40.9
CGOD–Ch God (Ander)	2	30	NR	30	0.0	0.0
Ch Cr, Scientst	2	NR	NR	NR	-	-
Ch of Nazarene	5	430	429	589	0.1	0.6
Chr & Miss Al	2	243	129	318	0.1	0.3
CHR–Chr Ch (Disc)	2	72	148	177	0.0	0.2
CHR–Chr Chs & Chs Cr	4	NR	360	430	0.1	0.4
CHR–Chs of Christ	9	817	760	933	0.2	0.9
CONG–Cong Chr, NA	1	NR	140	167	0.0	0.2
Evan Free Ch	2	180	NR	180	0.0	0.2
Jehovah's Witness	6	NR	NR	NR	-	-
JUD–Orth	2	86	100	120	0.0	0.1
LDS–Comm of Christ	2	NR	242	242	0.1	0.2
LDS–L-D Saints	2	NR	NR	1,874	0.4	1.8
LUTH–Ch of Luth Br	2	150	78	266	0.1	0.3
LUTH–E.L.C.A.	4	815	814	1,027	0.2	1.0
LUTH–Luth Cong Msn Chr	1	110	117	140	0.0	0.1
LUTH–Luth-MO Synod	4	638	947	1,191	0.3	1.2
LUTH–Nor Amer Luth C	1	NR	NR	NR	-	-
LUTH–Wisc Ev Luth Syn	3	169	212	240	0.1	0.2

NR–Not Reported - Represents no adherents reported. Percentages may not total 100 due to rounding.

Table 3: Religious Congregations by County and Group: 2010

Religious Group	Number of Congrega-tions	Number of Attendees	Number of Communicant, Confirmed, or Full Members	Adherents: Number of Adherents	Adherents: % of Total Pop.	Adherents: % of Total Adh.
MENN–Beachy Amish-Menn	1	46	12	46	0.0	0.0
MENN–Mennonite USA	1	64	55	66	0.0	0.1
METH–AME	4	11	372	444	0.1	0.4
METH–Free Methodist	2	103	93	103	0.0	0.1
METH–Prim Meth Ch	1	NR	NR	NR	-	-
METH–Un Methodist	15	3,294	5,212	8,202	1.8	8.1
METH–Wesleyan	2	179	98	233	0.1	0.2
Metro Comm Ch	1	51	65	78	0.0	0.1
Muslim Est	1	190	NR	400	0.1	0.4
New Apost Ch	1	NR	NR	NR	-	-
Non-denom Chr Chs	50	6,070	7,747	8,600	1.9	8.5
ORTHE–Greek Orthodox	1	275	NR	1,225	0.3	1.2
ORTHE–Orth Ch in Amer	1	40	NR	80	0.0	0.1
ORTHO–Malan Dioc Am	1	15	NR	45	0.0	0.0
PENT–Assemb of God	14	3,893	1,633	8,470	1.8	8.4
PENT–Ch God (Cleve)	12	1,380	2,680	3,200	0.7	3.2
PENT–Ch of God by Faith	1	NR	NR	NR	-	-
PENT–Ch of God Proph	1	NR	23	27	0.0	0.0
PENT–COGIC	1	0	150	179	0.0	0.2
PENT–Int Foursq Gos	1	96	60	72	0.0	0.1
PENT–Intl Pent Holiness	2	90	50	60	0.0	0.1
PENT–Pent Ch of God	1	70	NR	109	0.0	0.1
PENT–Un Pent Ch Intl	3	NR	NR	NR	-	-
PRES–Evan Presby Ch	1	NR	54	64	0.0	0.1
PRES–Presb Ch (USA)	6	1,021	1,214	1,450	0.3	1.4
PRES–Presb Ch Amer	1	266	200	285	0.1	0.3
Salvation Army	1	104	109	531	0.1	0.5
Sev Day Adv	5	510	888	1,021	0.2	1.0
Un C of Christ	2	193	244	291	0.1	0.3
Unity Ch	2	NR	NR	NR	-	-
PINELLAS	**618**	**83,984**	**135,032**	**330,099**	**36.0**	**100.0**
ANG/EPIS–Anglican NA	2	NR	NR	NR	-	-
ANG/EPIS–Episcopal	20	3,287	6,496	7,790	0.8	2.4
Bahá'í	4	NR	599	599	0.1	0.2
BAPT–Amer Bapt Assn	3	NR	320	369	0.0	0.1
BAPT–Amer Bapt USA	3	510	844	974	0.1	0.3
BAPT–Converge/BGC	3	550	NR	660	0.1	0.2
BAPT–Free Will Bapt	1	NR	89	103	0.0	0.0
BAPT–Ind Bapt Flwsp Intl	1	NR	NR	NR	-	-
BAPT–Natl Mis Bapt Conv	9	250	1,210	1,397	0.2	0.4
BAPT–NBC Amer	4	100	450	520	0.1	0.2
BAPT–NBC USA	2	1,600	3,450	3,983	0.4	1.2
BAPT–Prog NBC	1	0	150	173	0.0	0.1
BAPT–Reg Bapt Gen As	1	NR	NR	NR	-	-
BAPT–So Bapt Conv	71	11,937	24,699	28,514	3.1	8.6
BRETH–Ch of Brethren	1	0	100	115	0.0	0.0
BRETH–Grace Breth	1	NR	NR	NR	-	-
BUDD–Mahayana	7	NR	NR	2,313	0.3	0.7
BUDD–Theravada	3	NR	NR	996	0.1	0.3
BUDD–Vajrayana	4	NR	NR	703	0.1	0.2
Calv Chpl	2	NR	NR	NR	-	-
Catholic	32	NR	NR	112,948	12.3	34.2
CGOD–Ch God (Ander)	4	1,091	NR	1,091	0.1	0.3
Ch Cr, Scientst	5	NR	NR	NR	-	-
Ch of Nazarene	10	972	1,413	1,688	0.2	0.5
Chr & Miss Al	7	874	789	1,162	0.1	0.4
CHR–Chr Ch (Disc)	3	224	824	951	0.1	0.3
CHR–Chr Chs & Chs Cr	7	NR	4,310	4,976	0.5	1.5
CHR–Chs of Christ	21	2,417	2,624	3,332	0.4	1.0
Christian Brethren	1	NR	NR	NR	-	-
CONG–Cong Chr, NA	1	NR	55	63	0.0	0.0
Evan Cov Ch	4	659	728	855	0.1	0.3
Evan Free Ch	1	100	NR	100	0.0	0.0
FRND–Fr Gen Cf	2	NR	68	79	0.0	0.0
Grace Gosp Fel	1	NR	NR	NR	-	-
HINDU–Post Ren	2	NR	NR	93	0.0	0.0
HINDU–Renaiss	2	NR	NR	97	0.0	0.0
Int Cou Comm Ch	4	NR	NR	NR	-	-
Jain	1	NR	NR	NR	-	-
Jehovah's Witness	17	NR	NR	NR	-	-
JUD–Conserv	2	556	624	1,685	0.2	0.5
JUD–Orth	2	130	150	180	0.0	0.1
JUD–Reform	4	902	1,590	4,293	0.5	1.3

Religious Group	Number of Congrega-tions	Number of Attendees	Number of Communicant, Confirmed, or Full Members	Adherents: Number of Adherents	Adherents: % of Total Pop.	Adherents: % of Total Adh.
LDS–Comm of Christ	3	NR	363	363	0.0	0.1
LDS–L-D Saints	7	NR	NR	5,257	0.6	1.6
LUTH–E.L.C.A.	15	2,573	4,413	6,149	0.7	1.9
LUTH–Luth Cong Msn Chr	1	75	130	150	0.0	0.0
LUTH–Luth–MO Synod	7	2,262	3,998	5,332	0.6	1.6
LUTH–Wisc Ev Luth Syn	3	290	521	640	0.1	0.2
MENN–Bruderhof Comm	1	37	11	22	0.0	0.0
MENN–Mennonite USA	1	40	20	23	0.0	0.0
METH–AME	11	850	2,503	2,890	0.3	0.9
METH–AME Zion	1	0	100	115	0.0	0.0
METH–C.M.E.	2	0	200	231	0.0	0.1
METH–Free Methodist	2	336	476	491	0.1	0.1
METH–Un Methodist	35	10,658	26,134	38,776	4.2	11.7
METH–Wesleyan	3	636	702	827	0.1	0.3
Metro Comm Ch	1	242	226	261	0.0	0.1
Missionary Ch	1	16	11	16	0.0	0.0
MJEW–Union Mes Cong	1	NR	NR	NR	-	-
Muslim Est	10	4,006	NR	13,372	1.5	4.1
New Apost Ch	1	NR	NR	NR	-	-
Non-denom Chr Chs	79	17,563	22,334	25,698	2.8	7.8
OCATH–Pol Natl Cath	1	NR	NR	NR	-	-
ORTHE–Ant Orth of NA	1	80	NR	200	0.0	0.1
ORTHE–Greek Orthodox	4	1,565	NR	11,375	1.2	3.4
ORTHE–Macedonian Orth	1	50	NR	500	0.1	0.2
ORTHE–Orth Ch in Amer	1	45	NR	85	0.0	0.0
ORTHE–Rus Orth Abroad	1	75	NR	2,000	0.2	0.6
ORTHE–Serb Orth USA	2	180	NR	1,625	0.2	0.5
ORTHE–Ukrainian Orth	1	25	NR	60	0.0	0.0
ORTHO–Armen Ap Etchm	1	90	NR	740	0.1	0.2
ORTHO–Coptic Orth Ch	1	600	NR	1,100	0.1	0.3
ORTHO–Syrian Orth Ch	1	225	NR	600	0.1	0.2
PENT–Assemb of God	20	4,371	3,988	7,858	0.9	2.4
PENT–Ch God (Cleve)	16	2,190	3,412	3,939	0.4	1.2
PENT–Ch of God by Faith	2	NR	NR	NR	-	-
PENT–Ch of God Proph	1	NR	73	84	0.0	0.0
PENT–COGIC	6	150	560	646	0.1	0.2
PENT–Fire Bapt Hol Ch	1	NR	NR	NR	-	-
PENT–Full Gosp Bapt	4	NR	NR	NR	-	-
PENT–I F Chr Assmbl	1	NR	NR	NR	-	-
PENT–Int Foursq Gos	4	236	385	444	0.0	0.1
PENT–Intl Pent Holiness	1	60	60	69	0.0	0.0
PENT–Open Bible Std	7	394	NR	394	0.0	0.1
PENT–Un Pent Ch Intl	5	NR	NR	NR	-	-
PENT–Vineyard	2	220	275	317	0.0	0.1
PRES–As Ref Pres Ch	1	NR	90	104	0.0	0.0
PRES–Bible Pres	1	NR	NR	NR	-	-
PRES–Evan Presby Ch	1	NR	107	124	0.0	0.0
PRES–Presb Ch (USA)	28	3,758	6,751	7,794	0.9	2.4
PRES–Presb Ch Amer	5	297	284	357	0.0	0.1
REF–Christian Ref	2	105	50	58	0.0	0.0
Salvation Army	4	602	799	1,007	0.1	0.3
Sev Day Adv	11	1,052	1,827	2,103	0.2	0.6
Un C of Christ	9	1,485	2,156	2,489	0.3	0.8
Unit Univ	4	386	491	610	0.1	0.2
Unity Ch	6	NR	NR	NR	-	-
Zoroastrian	0	NR	NR	2	0.0	0.0
POLK	**676**	**86,055**	**149,327**	**244,720**	**40.6**	**100.0**
ANG/EPIS–Anglican NA	1	NR	NR	NR	-	-
ANG/EPIS–Episcopal	12	1,563	2,727	3,473	0.6	1.4
Bahá'í	2	NR	169	169	0.0	0.1
BAPT–Amer Bapt Assn	9	NR	2,410	2,947	0.5	1.2
BAPT–Amer Bapt USA	1	83	99	121	0.0	0.0
BAPT–Converge/BGC	1	75	NR	90	0.0	0.0
BAPT–Free Will Bapt	9	NR	801	980	0.2	0.4
BAPT–Natl Mis Bapt Conv	6	55	805	984	0.2	0.4
BAPT–NBC Amer	10	1,130	3,704	4,530	0.8	1.9
BAPT–Reg Bapt Gen As	7	NR	NR	NR	-	-
BAPT–So Bapt Conv	152	20,093	54,090	66,149	11.0	27.0
BRETH–Grace Breth	1	NR	NR	NR	-	-
BUDD–Mahayana	1	NR	NR	102	0.0	0.0
Calv Chpl	1	NR	NR	NR	-	-
Catholic	13	NR	NR	45,251	7.5	18.5
CGOD–Ch God (Ander)	10	1,989	NR	1,989	0.3	0.8

NR–Not Reported - Represents no adherents reported. Percentages may not total 100 due to rounding.

Table 3: Religious Congregations by County and Group: 2010

Religious Group	Number of Congrega-tions	Number of Attendees	Number of Communicant, Confirmed, or Full Members	Adherents: Number of Adherents	Adherents: % of Total Pop.	Adherents: % of Total Adh.
Ch Cr, Scientst	3	NR	NR	NR	-	-
Ch God (7th Day)	2	NR	NR	NR	-	-
Ch of Nazarene	14	4,001	4,312	4,819	0.8	2.0
Chr & Miss Al	4	394	338	631	0.1	0.3
CHR–Chr Ch (Disc)	6	317	613	750	0.1	0.3
CHR–Chr Chs & Chs Cr	8	NR	1,484	1,815	0.3	0.7
CHR–Chs of Christ	26	2,746	2,750	3,597	0.6	1.5
Evan Free Ch	1	160	NR	160	0.0	0.1
FRND–Fr Gen Cf	1	NR	0	0	0.0	0.0
HINDU–I/A Temples	1	NR	NR	350	0.1	0.1
Jehovah's Witness	12	NR	NR	NR	-	-
JUD–Conserv	1	89	100	270	0.0	0.1
JUD–Reform	1	35	61	165	0.0	0.1
LDS–Comm of Christ	1	NR	121	121	0.0	0.0
LDS–L-D Saints	9	NR	NR	4,568	0.8	1.9
LUTH–Ch Luth Conf	1	NR	NR	NR	-	-
LUTH–E.L.C.A.	4	643	1,139	1,216	0.2	0.5
LUTH–Evan Luth Syn	3	151	198	239	0.0	0.1
LUTH–Luth Cong Msn Chr	2	186	258	316	0.1	0.1
LUTH–Luth-MO Synod	5	1,732	3,219	3,860	0.6	1.6
LUTH–Nor Amer Luth C	1	NR	NR	NR	-	-
MENN–Mennonite USA	1	45	36	44	0.0	0.0
METH–AME	17	1,120	3,740	4,574	0.8	1.9
METH–AME Zion	1	0	150	183	0.0	0.1
METH–C.M.E.	2	30	160	196	0.0	0.1
METH–Free Methodist	3	316	234	326	0.1	0.1
METH–Prim Meth Ch	1	NR	NR	NR	-	-
METH–Un Methodist	33	6,027	12,155	18,798	3.1	7.7
METH–Wesleyan	1	94	50	122	0.0	0.0
Missionary Ch	3	301	125	301	0.0	0.1
Muslim Est	2	812	NR	2,794	0.5	1.1
Non-denom Chr Chs	95	20,791	26,949	30,343	5.0	12.4
ORTHE–Carp Rus Orth	1	38	NR	67	0.0	0.0
ORTHE–Greek Orthodox	1	100	NR	200	0.0	0.1
ORTHE–Rus Orth Abroad	1	20	NR	40	0.0	0.0
PENT–Assemb of God	45	9,560	7,270	13,492	2.2	5.5
PENT–Ch God (Cleve)	35	4,231	7,318	8,950	1.5	3.7
PENT–Ch Lord Jesus Apos	6	NR	NR	NR	-	-
PENT–Ch of God by Faith	11	NR	NR	NR	-	-
PENT–Ch of God Proph	3	NR	82	100	0.0	0.0
PENT–COGIC	4	40	240	294	0.0	0.1
PENT–Int Foursq Gos	1	21	53	65	0.0	0.0
PENT–Intl Pent Holiness	5	602	595	728	0.1	0.3
PENT–Pent Ch of God	2	140	NR	217	0.0	0.1
PENT–Pent FW Bapt	1	NR	NR	NR	-	-
PENT–Un Pent Asbl God	1	NR	NR	NR	-	-
PENT–Un Pent Ch Intl	4	NR	NR	NR	-	-
PENT–Vineyard	1	128	213	260	0.0	0.1
PRES–As Ref Pres Ch	4	NR	1,227	1,501	0.2	0.6
PRES–Bible Pres	1	NR	NR	NR	-	-
PRES–Presb Ch (USA)	14	3,284	5,563	6,803	1.1	2.8
PRES–Presb Ch Amer	7	1,363	1,216	1,583	0.3	0.6
PRES–Ref Pres GA	1	NR	NR	NR	-	-
REF–Comm Ref Evan	1	NR	NR	NR	-	-
Salvation Army	2	242	326	492	0.1	0.2
Sev Day Adv	18	1,154	2,006	2,308	0.4	0.9
Un C of Christ	2	103	152	186	0.0	0.1
Unit Univ	1	51	69	91	0.0	0.0
Unity Ch	2	NR	NR	NR	-	-
PUTNAM	**136**	**9,095**	**21,429**	**30,972**	**41.6**	**100.0**
ANG/EPIS–Episcopal	7	330	493	645	0.9	2.1
Bahá'í	0	NR	15	15	0.0	0.0
BAPT–NBC Amer	1	175	250	303	0.4	1.0
BAPT–NBC USA	1	0	500	605	0.8	2.0
BAPT–S-D Baptist Gen Con	1	15	9	11	0.0	0.0
BAPT–So Bapt Conv	34	4,061	12,877	15,586	21.0	50.3
BUDD–Theravada	1	NR	NR	300	0.4	1.0
Catholic	3	NR	NR	2,783	3.7	9.0
CGOD–Ch God (Ander)	2	82	NR	82	0.1	0.3
Ch of Nazarene	2	54	68	84	0.1	0.3
Chr & Miss Al	1	45	16	51	0.1	0.2
CHR–Chs of Christ	6	391	394	490	0.7	1.6
CONG–Cong Chr, NA	1	NR	55	67	0.1	0.2

Religious Group	Number of Congrega-tions	Number of Attendees	Number of Communicant, Confirmed, or Full Members	Adherents: Number of Adherents	Adherents: % of Total Pop.	Adherents: % of Total Adh.
Jehovah's Witness	3	NR	NR	NR	-	-
LDS–L-D Saints	4	NR	NR	1,457	2.0	4.7
LUTH–Assoc Free Luth	1	NR	NR	NR	-	-
LUTH–E.L.C.A.	1	60	74	74	0.1	0.2
LUTH–Luth Cong Msn Chr	1	31	67	81	0.1	0.3
METH–AME	8	0	950	1,150	1.5	3.7
METH–Un Methodist	10	747	1,967	2,383	3.2	7.7
Non-denom Chr Chs	13	1,435	1,685	1,911	2.6	6.2
PENT–Assemb of God	3	583	282	820	1.1	2.6
PENT–Ch God (Cleve)	7	236	248	300	0.4	1.0
PENT–Ch God Mtn Asm	1	NR	NR	NR	-	-
PENT–Ch Lord Jesus Apos	1	NR	NR	NR	-	-
PENT–Ch of God by Faith	6	NR	NR	NR	-	-
PENT–Ch of God Proph	2	NR	100	121	0.2	0.4
PENT–COGIC	2	0	210	254	0.3	0.8
PENT–Intl Pent Holiness	3	460	442	535	0.7	1.7
PENT–Pent FW Bapt	1	NR	NR	NR	-	-
PENT–Un Pent Ch Intl	1	NR	NR	NR	-	-
PRES–Presb Ch (USA)	3	197	418	506	0.7	1.6
Sev Day Adv	3	150	261	300	0.4	1.0
Sikh	1	NR	NR	NR	-	-
Un C of Christ	1	43	48	58	0.1	0.2
ST. JOHNS	**134**	**16,677**	**30,149**	**69,667**	**36.7**	**100.0**
ANG/EPIS–Anglican NA	1	NR	NR	NR	-	-
ANG/EPIS–Episcopal	5	2,183	6,772	7,127	3.8	10.2
Bahá'í	1	NR	101	101	0.1	0.1
BAPT–NBC USA	3	0	290	351	0.2	0.5
BAPT–So Bapt Conv	27	6,259	11,909	14,404	7.6	20.7
BUDD–Mahayana	1	NR	NR	102	0.1	0.1
BUDD–Vajrayana	2	NR	NR	202	0.1	0.3
Catholic	11	NR	NR	27,153	14.3	39.0
CGOD–Ch God (Ander)	1	0	NR	0	0.0	0.0
Ch Cr, Scientist	1	NR	NR	NR	-	-
Ch of Nazarene	2	221	179	385	0.2	0.6
Chr & Miss Al	1	NR	NR	NR	-	-
CHR–Chr Chs & Chs Cr	2	NR	700	847	0.4	1.2
CHR–Chs of Christ	3	330	275	315	0.2	0.5
Evan Free Ch	1	120	NR	120	0.1	0.2
HINDU–I/A Temples	2	NR	NR	1,812	1.0	2.6
Jehovah's Witness	2	NR	NR	NR	-	-
JUD–Orth	3	461	200	640	0.3	0.9
JUD–Reform	1	64	113	305	0.2	0.4
LDS–L-D Saints	2	NR	NR	1,288	0.7	1.8
LUTH–E.L.C.A.	2	196	389	659	0.3	0.9
LUTH–Luth-MO Synod	2	183	167	249	0.1	0.4
METH–AME	4	253	690	835	0.4	1.2
METH–AME Zion	1	18	45	54	0.0	0.1
METH–C.M.E.	1	35	50	60	0.0	0.1
METH–Un Methodist	7	701	1,859	2,267	1.2	3.3
Metro Comm Ch	1	71	154	186	0.1	0.3
Muslim Est	1	406	NR	1,397	0.7	2.0
Non-denom Chr Chs	19	2,361	2,783	3,136	1.7	4.5
ORTHE–Greek Orthodox	1	100	NR	320	0.2	0.5
PENT–Assemb of God	3	143	90	223	0.1	0.3
PENT–Ch God (Cleve)	2	101	185	224	0.1	0.3
PENT–Ch of God by Faith	2	NR	NR	NR	-	-
PENT–Ch of God Proph	1	NR	28	34	0.0	0.0
PENT–Cong Hol Ch	1	39	35	42	0.0	0.1
PENT–Intl Pent Holiness	3	230	377	456	0.2	0.7
PENT–Vineyard	1	47	62	75	0.0	0.1
PRES–Orth Pres Ch	1	85	59	71	0.0	0.1
PRES–Presb Ch (USA)	2	521	869	1,051	0.6	1.5
PRES–Presb Ch Amer	2	1,318	1,394	2,717	1.4	3.9
Salvation Army	1	10	30	71	0.0	0.1
Sev Day Adv	2	134	232	267	0.1	0.4
Un C of Christ	1	25	32	39	0.0	0.1
Unit Univ	1	62	80	81	0.0	0.1
Zoroastrian	0	NR	NR	1	0.0	0.0
ST. LUCIE	**213**	**26,544**	**33,864**	**79,604**	**28.7**	**100.0**
ANG/EPIS–Episcopal	4	569	986	1,302	0.5	1.6
Bahá'í	1	NR	56	56	0.0	0.1

NR–Not Reported - Represents no adherents reported. Percentages may not total 100 due to rounding.

Table 3: Religious Congregations by County and Group: 2010

Religious Group	Number of Congrega-tions	Number of Attendees	Number of Communicant, Confirmed, or Full Members	Adherents		
				Number of Adherents	% of Total Pop.	% of Total Adh.
BAPT–Amer Bapt Assn	1	NR	50	60	0.0	0.1
BAPT–Converge/BGC	1	75	NR	90	0.0	0.1
BAPT–N Am Bapt Conf	1	NR	NR	NR	-	-
BAPT–Natl Mis Bapt Conv	1	0	0	0	0.0	0.0
BAPT–NBC USA	4	400	1,650	1,991	0.7	2.5
BAPT–Reg Bapt Gen As	1	NR	NR	NR	-	-
BAPT–So Bapt Conv	40	4,803	7,289	8,796	3.2	11.0
Calv Chpl	1	NR	NR	NR	-	-
Catholic	8	NR	NR	33,797	12.2	42.5
CGOD–Ch God (Ander)	1	40	NR	40	0.0	0.1
Ch God (7th Day)	1	NR	NR	NR	-	-
Ch of Nazarene	6	631	754	910	0.3	1.1
Chr & Miss Al	4	312	159	376	0.1	0.5
CHR–Chr Ch (Disc)	3	30	70	84	0.0	0.1
CHR–Chr Chs & Chs Cr	3	NR	282	340	0.1	0.4
CHR–Chs of Christ	5	500	556	659	0.2	0.8
Evan Free Ch	1	170	NR	170	0.1	0.2
FRND–Evan Fr Ch Intl	3	1,749	680	821	0.3	1.0
FRND–Fr Gen Cf	1	NR	0	0	0.0	0.0
Jehovah's Witness	6	NR	NR	NR	-	-
LDS–L-D Saints	1	NR	NR	906	0.3	1.1
LUTH–E.L.C.A.	4	517	680	855	0.3	1.1
LUTH–Evan Luth Syn	1	68	86	122	0.0	0.2
LUTH–Luth Cong Msn Chr	1	46	105	127	0.0	0.2
LUTH–Luth-MO Synod	2	291	453	578	0.2	0.7
METH–AME	2	150	700	845	0.3	1.1
METH–So Methodist	1	NR	NR	NR	-	-
METH–Un Methodist	8	1,643	2,500	3,990	1.4	5.0
METH–Wesleyan	1	73	0	95	0.0	0.1
Muslim Est	2	556	NR	1,747	0.6	2.2
New Apost Ch	2	NR	NR	NR	-	-
Non-denom Chr Chs	35	6,154	8,055	8,434	3.0	10.6
ORTHE–Greek Orthodox	1	220	NR	1,000	0.4	1.3
ORTHE–Orth Ch in Amer	1	84	NR	105	0.0	0.1
PENT–Assemb of God	7	916	644	1,119	0.4	1.4
PENT–Ch God (Cleve)	10	2,279	2,983	3,600	1.3	4.5
PENT–Ch of God by Faith	1	NR	NR	NR	-	-
PENT–Ch of God Proph	2	NR	84	101	0.0	0.1
PENT–Cong Hol Ch	1	39	35	42	0.0	0.1
PENT–Int Foursq Gos	1	21	21	25	0.0	0.0
PENT–Intl Pent Holiness	2	150	65	78	0.0	0.1
PENT–Open Bible Std	1	45	NR	45	0.0	0.1
PENT–Pent Ch of God	4	280	NR	435	0.2	0.5
PENT–Un Pent Ch Intl	1	NR	NR	NR	-	-
PENT–Vineyard	2	865	990	1,195	0.4	1.5
PRES–Orth Pres Ch	1	61	59	80	0.0	0.1
PRES–Presb Ch (USA)	4	725	1,010	1,219	0.4	1.5
PRES–Presb Ch Amer	1	27	31	31	0.0	0.0
REF–Christian Ref	2	435	354	427	0.2	0.5
Salvation Army	1	77	89	145	0.1	0.2
Sev Day Adv	8	1,168	2,031	2,335	0.8	2.9
Un C of Christ	3	375	357	431	0.2	0.5
Unity Ch	2	NR	NR	NR	-	-
SANTA ROSA	**156**	**20,635**	**45,571**	**67,058**	**44.3**	**100.0**
ANG/EPIS–Anglican NA	1	NR	NR	NR	-	-
ANG/EPIS–Episcopal	3	258	608	711	0.5	1.1
Bahá'í	1	NR	43	43	0.0	0.1
BAPT–Amer Bapt Assn	6	NR	510	623	0.4	0.9
BAPT–Ind Bapt Flwsp Intl	2	NR	NR	NR	-	-
BAPT–So Bapt Conv	40	8,966	26,419	32,263	21.3	48.1
BUDD–Vajrayana	1	NR	NR	41	0.0	0.1
Calv Chpl	1	NR	NR	NR	-	-
Catholic	3	NR	NR	6,667	4.4	9.9
CGOD–Ch God (Ander)	1	10	NR	10	0.0	0.0
Ch of Nazarene	1	31	26	40	0.0	0.1
CHR–Chs of Christ	8	749	759	925	0.6	1.4
Jehovah's Witness	2	NR	NR	NR	-	-
LDS–Comm of Christ	2	NR	272	272	0.2	0.4
LDS–L-D Saints	4	NR	NR	1,451	1.0	2.2
LUTH–Luth-MO Synod	2	171	321	382	0.3	0.6
LUTH–Wisc Ev Luth Syn	1	77	89	155	0.1	0.2
METH–AME	2	0	200	244	0.2	0.4
METH–AME Zion	1	0	150	183	0.1	0.3
METH–Un Methodist	16	4,498	9,212	14,165	9.4	21.1
Non-denom Chr Chs	21	2,842	4,183	4,633	3.1	6.9
PENT–Assemb of God	19	2,435	1,547	2,790	1.8	4.2
PENT–Ch God (Cleve)	1	50	116	142	0.1	0.2
PENT–Ch of God Proph	1	NR	16	20	0.0	0.0
PENT–Intl Pent Holiness	2	56	55	67	0.0	0.1
PENT–Un Pent Ch Intl	5	NR	NR	NR	-	-
PENT–Vineyard	1	40	50	61	0.0	0.1
PRES–Presb Ch (USA)	4	278	700	855	0.6	1.3
PRES–Presb Ch Amer	2	120	201	207	0.1	0.3
Sev Day Adv	1	54	94	108	0.1	0.2
Unity Ch	1	NR	NR	NR	-	-
SARASOTA	**292**	**44,328**	**67,088**	**165,091**	**43.5**	**100.0**
ANG/EPIS–Anglican NA	2	NR	NR	NR	-	-
ANG/EPIS–Episcopal	11	2,641	5,804	6,032	1.6	3.7
Ap Chr Ch-Amer	1	102	73	102	0.0	0.1
Bahá'í	1	NR	133	133	0.0	0.1
BAPT–NBC Amer	3	360	850	963	0.3	0.6
BAPT–Ref Bapt Ch	1	NR	NR	NR	-	-
BAPT–Reg Bapt Gen As	2	NR	NR	NR	-	-
BAPT–So Bapt Conv	24	6,012	13,160	14,915	3.9	9.0
BRETH–Breth in Chr	1	NR	NR	NR	-	-
BRETH–Brethren (Ash)	2	NR	160	181	0.0	0.1
BRETH–Ch of Brethren	1	16	14	16	0.0	0.0
BUDD–Mahayana	2	NR	NR	31	0.0	0.0
BUDD–Vajrayana	2	NR	NR	260	0.1	0.2
Calv Chpl	3	NR	NR	NR	-	-
Catholic	13	NR	NR	76,000	20.0	46.0
CGOD–Ch God (Ander)	4	348	NR	348	0.1	0.2
Ch Cr, Scientst	5	NR	NR	NR	-	-
Ch of Nazarene	7	1,154	1,279	1,570	0.4	1.0
Chr & Miss Al	2	490	145	1,034	0.3	0.6
CHR–Chr Ch (Disc)	4	453	559	634	0.2	0.4
CHR–Chr Chs & Chs Cr	7	NR	1,160	1,315	0.3	0.8
CHR–Chs of Christ	7	521	517	668	0.2	0.4
CONG–Cong Chr, NA	1	NR	72	82	0.0	0.0
Evan Cov Ch	3	326	379	424	0.1	0.3
Evan Free Ch	1	100	NR	100	0.0	0.1
FRND–Fr Gen Cf	1	NR	49	56	0.0	0.0
Grace Gosp Fel	1	NR	NR	NR	-	-
HINDU–Post Ren	3	NR	NR	193	0.1	0.1
Jehovah's Witness	7	NR	NR	NR	-	-
JUD–Conserv	2	605	679	1,833	0.5	1.1
JUD–Orth	2	86	100	120	0.0	0.1
JUD–Reconst	1	70	90	243	0.1	0.1
JUD–Reform	3	691	1,218	3,289	0.9	2.0
LDS–L-D Saints	3	NR	NR	1,682	0.4	1.0
LUTH–Assoc Free Luth	1	NR	NR	NR	-	-
LUTH–E.L.C.A.	8	1,640	2,100	2,679	0.7	1.6
LUTH–Luth-MO Synod	3	754	1,157	1,350	0.4	0.8
LUTH–Wisc Ev Luth Syn	2	170	226	280	0.1	0.2
MENN–Amish Undif	1	NR	111	125	0.0	0.1
MENN–Beachy Amish-Menn	1	125	85	125	0.0	0.1
MENN–CG in Cr (Menn)	1	NR	0	0	0.0	0.0
MENN–Cons Menn Conf	2	864	566	641	0.2	0.4
MENN–Mennonite USA	8	1,183	1,215	1,377	0.4	0.8
METH–AME	2	145	350	397	0.1	0.2
METH–C.M.E.	1	200	327	371	0.1	0.2
METH–Un Methodist	11	4,700	8,972	11,428	3.0	6.9
Metro Comm Ch	2	273	340	386	0.1	0.2
Muslim Est	1	300	NR	800	0.2	0.5
New Apost Ch	2	NR	NR	NR	-	-
Non-denom Chr Chs	54	9,728	11,322	12,910	3.4	7.8
ORTHE–Orth Ch in Amer	1	70	NR	120	0.0	0.1
ORTHE–Serb Orth USA	1	100	NR	500	0.1	0.3
PENT–Assemb of God	7	3,436	1,410	5,029	1.3	3.0
PENT–Ch God (Cleve)	6	516	1,374	1,557	0.4	0.9
PENT–Ch of God Proph	1	NR	54	61	0.0	0.0
PENT–COGIC	1	0	150	170	0.0	0.1
PENT–Int Foursq Gos	1	43	38	43	0.0	0.0
PENT–Intl Pent Holiness	2	89	89	101	0.0	0.1
PENT–Un Pent Ch Intl	3	NR	NR	NR	-	-
PRES–Korean Amer Pres	1	NR	NR	NR	-	-

NR–Not Reported - Represents no adherents reported. Percentages may not total 100 due to rounding.

Table 3: Religious Congregations by County and Group: 2010

Religious Group	Number of Congregations	Number of Attendees	Number of Communicant, Confirmed, or Full Members	Adherents: Number of Adherents	Adherents: % of Total Pop.	Adherents: % of Total Adh.
PRES–Korean Pres Amer	1	NR	NR	NR	-	-
PRES–Presb Ch (USA)	13	3,092	7,135	8,087	2.1	4.9
PRES–Presb Ch Amer	4	1,044	931	978	0.3	0.6
REF–Ref Ch in Am	2	155	79	234	0.1	0.1
Salvation Army	2	346	215	415	0.1	0.3
Sev Day Adv	4	312	543	625	0.2	0.4
Un C of Christ	5	750	1,388	1,573	0.4	1.0
Unit Univ	2	318	470	503	0.1	0.3
Unity Ch	2	NR	NR	NR	-	-
Zoroastrian	0	NR	NR	2	0.0	0.0
SEMINOLE	**283**	**54,353**	**76,858**	**172,072**	**40.7**	**100.0**
ANG/EPIS–Anglican NA	3	NR	NR	NR	-	-
ANG/EPIS–Episcopal	6	1,024	1,994	2,324	0.5	1.4
Bahá'í	2	NR	143	143	0.0	0.1
BAPT–Amer Bapt USA	1	12	16	19	0.0	0.0
BAPT–Consrv Bapt	1	NR	NR	NR	-	-
BAPT–Converge/BGC	3	550	NR	660	0.2	0.4
BAPT–Ind Bapt Flwsp Intl	1	NR	NR	NR	-	-
BAPT–Natl Mis Bapt Conv	4	0	300	362	0.1	0.2
BAPT–NBC USA	3	400	625	753	0.2	0.4
BAPT–Ref Bapt Ch	3	NR	NR	NR	-	-
BAPT–So Bapt Conv	36	8,530	15,977	19,257	4.6	11.2
BUDD–Theravada	1	NR	NR	300	0.1	0.2
BUDD–Vajrayana	1	NR	NR	39	0.0	0.0
Calv Chpl	1	NR	NR	NR	-	-
Catholic	8	NR	NR	67,501	16.0	39.2
CGOD–Ch God (Ander)	1	250	NR	250	0.1	0.1
Ch God (7th Day)	1	NR	NR	NR	-	-
Ch of Nazarene	5	190	227	372	0.1	0.2
Chr & Miss Al	4	372	224	578	0.1	0.3
CHR–Chr Ch (Disc)	1	326	346	417	0.1	0.2
CHR–Chr Chs & Chs Cr	2	NR	350	422	0.1	0.2
CHR–Chs of Christ	10	683	639	788	0.2	0.5
CHR–Int Chs of Christ	0	NR	112	135	0.0	0.1
CONG–Cong Chr, NA	1	NR	44	53	0.0	0.0
Evan Cov Ch	1	6	6	8	0.0	0.0
HINDU–I/A Temples	2	NR	NR	267	0.1	0.2
HINDU–Trad Temples	1	NR	NR	1,000	0.2	0.6
Jain	1	NR	NR	NR	-	-
Jehovah's Witness	4	NR	NR	NR	-	-
JUD–Conserv	1	168	188	508	0.1	0.3
JUD–Orth	1	43	50	60	0.0	0.0
JUD–Reform	2	81	143	386	0.1	0.2
LDS–Comm of Christ	1	NR	121	121	0.0	0.1
LDS–L-D Saints	6	NR	NR	3,495	0.8	2.0
LUTH–E.L.C.A.	3	501	818	928	0.2	0.5
LUTH–Luth–MO Synod	5	2,144	4,676	6,306	1.5	3.7
LUTH–Nor Amer Luth C	1	NR	NR	NR	-	-
METH–AME	9	707	1,413	1,703	0.4	1.0
METH–Un Methodist	12	3,548	7,161	9,737	2.3	5.7
METH–Wesleyan	1	55	36	72	0.0	0.0
MORAV–Morav Ch-South	1	70	91	107	0.0	0.1
Muslim Est	2	812	NR	2,794	0.7	1.6
Non-denom Chr Chs	56	23,423	29,368	32,805	7.8	19.1
ORTHE–Orth Ch in Amer	1	125	NR	300	0.1	0.2
ORTHO–Coptic Orth Ch	1	500	NR	804	0.2	0.5
PENT–Assemb of God	12	3,064	938	3,559	0.8	2.1
PENT–Ch God (Cleve)	8	551	877	1,057	0.3	0.6
PENT–Ch Lord Jesus Apos	2	NR	NR	NR	-	-
PENT–Ch of God by Faith	2	NR	NR	NR	-	-
PENT–Ch of God Proph	5	NR	309	372	0.1	0.2
PENT–COGIC	3	0	350	422	0.1	0.2
PENT–Fire Bapt Hol Ch	1	NR	NR	NR	-	-
PENT–Int Foursq Gos	3	237	222	268	0.1	0.2
PENT–Intl Pent Holiness	3	310	325	392	0.1	0.2
PENT–Un Pent Ch Intl	2	NR	NR	NR	-	-
PRES–As Ref Pres Ch	1	NR	0	0	0.0	0.0
PRES–Orth Pres Ch	1	59	48	71	0.0	0.0
PRES–Presb Ch (USA)	11	1,951	2,939	3,542	0.8	2.1
PRES–Presb Ch Amer	3	893	1,097	1,138	0.3	0.7
REF–Christian Ref	1	45	9	11	0.0	0.0
Salvation Army	1	45	88	165	0.0	0.1
Sev Day Adv	8	2,453	4,267	4,906	1.2	2.9
Sikh	2	NR	NR	NR	-	-
Un C of Christ	2	225	321	387	0.1	0.2
Unity Ch	1	NR	NR	NR	-	-
Zoroastrian	0	NR	NR	8	0.0	0.0
SUMTER	**99**	**9,756**	**14,828**	**22,000**	**23.5**	**100.0**
ANG/EPIS–Episcopal	1	61	93	93	0.1	0.4
Bahá'í	0	NR	14	14	0.0	0.1
BAPT–Amer Bapt Assn	3	NR	320	344	0.4	1.6
BAPT–Free Will Bapt	1	NR	89	96	0.1	0.4
BAPT–Natl Mis Bapt Conv	1	0	150	161	0.2	0.7
BAPT–NBC USA	1	40	40	43	0.0	0.2
BAPT–So Bapt Conv	18	2,108	4,468	4,799	5.1	21.8
Catholic	3	NR	NR	3,815	4.1	17.3
CGOD–Ch God (Ander)	2	67	NR	67	0.1	0.3
Ch of Nazarene	1	0	0	0	0.0	0.0
CHR–Chr Ch (Disc)	1	74	161	173	0.2	0.8
CHR–Chr Chs & Chs Cr	1	NR	465	499	0.5	2.3
CHR–Chs of Christ	5	271	285	351	0.4	1.6
Jehovah's Witness	1	NR	NR	NR	-	-
LDS–L-D Saints	1	NR	NR	223	0.2	1.0
LUTH–E.L.C.A.	2	1,104	1,351	1,356	1.5	6.2
LUTH–Luth Cong Msn Chr	1	22	NR	NR	-	-
LUTH–Luth–MO Synod	1	71	107	114	0.1	0.5
LUTH–Wisc Ev Luth Syn	1	82	79	83	0.1	0.4
METH–AME	5	135	555	596	0.6	2.7
METH–Un Methodist	9	2,070	2,322	3,756	4.0	17.1
Metro Comm Ch	1	67	0	72	0.1	0.3
Non-denom Chr Chs	15	1,935	2,431	2,680	2.9	12.2
PENT–Assemb of God	5	801	537	1,201	1.3	5.5
PENT–Ch God (Cleve)	7	384	634	681	0.7	3.1
PENT–Ch Lord Jesus Apos	1	NR	NR	NR	-	-
PENT–Ch of God by Faith	1	NR	NR	NR	-	-
PENT–COGIC	2	0	150	161	0.2	0.7
PENT–Intl Pent Holiness	1	180	180	193	0.2	0.9
PENT–Un Pent Ch Intl	1	NR	NR	NR	-	-
PRES–As Ref Pres Ch	1	NR	58	62	0.1	0.3
PRES–Presb Ch (USA)	3	160	159	171	0.2	0.8
Sev Day Adv	1	24	42	48	0.1	0.2
Un C of Christ	1	100	138	148	0.2	0.7
SUWANNEE	**101**	**6,241**	**16,308**	**21,885**	**52.7**	**100.0**
ANG/EPIS–Episcopal	1	135	300	312	0.8	1.4
Bahá'í	0	NR	5	5	0.0	0.0
BAPT–Free Will Bapt	1	NR	89	108	0.3	0.5
BAPT–Ind Bapt Flwsp Intl	1	NR	NR	NR	-	-
BAPT–Natl Mis Bapt Conv	1	0	150	182	0.4	0.8
BAPT–NBC USA	2	0	650	788	1.9	3.6
BAPT–So Bapt Conv	36	3,809	10,891	13,211	31.8	60.4
BUDD–Mahayana	1	NR	NR	14	0.0	0.1
Catholic	2	NR	NR	1,070	2.6	4.9
CGOD–Ch God (Ander)	2	23	NR	23	0.1	0.1
Ch Cr, Scientst	1	NR	NR	NR	-	-
Ch of Nazarene	1	127	84	127	0.3	0.6
CHR–Chr Chs & Chs Cr	1	NR	70	85	0.2	0.4
CHR–Chs of Christ	5	416	418	524	1.3	2.4
Jehovah's Witness	2	NR	NR	NR	-	-
LDS–L-D Saints	2	NR	NR	938	2.3	4.3
LUTH–Ch Luth Conf	1	NR	NR	NR	-	-
METH–AME	8	20	1,050	1,274	3.1	5.8
METH–Un Methodist	7	385	803	1,041	2.5	4.8
Non-denom Chr Chs	8	615	870	891	2.1	4.1
PENT–Assemb of God	2	145	72	168	0.4	0.8
PENT–Ch God (Cleve)	6	306	524	636	1.5	2.9
PENT–Ch of God by Faith	1	NR	NR	NR	-	-
PENT–COGIC	1	10	15	18	0.0	0.1
PENT–Fire Bapt Hol Ch	1	NR	NR	NR	-	-
PENT–Pent Ch of God	1	70	NR	109	0.3	0.5
PENT–Un Pent Ch Intl	1	NR	NR	NR	-	-
PRES–Presb Ch (USA)	2	35	72	87	0.2	0.4
PRES–Presb Ch Amer	1	83	138	151	0.4	0.7
Sev Day Adv	2	62	107	123	0.3	0.6

NR–Not Reported   - Represents no adherents reported.   Percentages may not total 100 due to rounding.

Table 3: Religious Congregations by County and Group: 2010

Religious Group	Number of Congregations	Number of Attendees	Number of Communicant, Confirmed, or Full Members	Adherents: Number of Adherents	Adherents: % of Total Pop.	Adherents: % of Total Adh.
TAYLOR	**64**	**3,845**	**8,907**	**11,088**	**49.1**	**100.0**
ANG/EPIS–Episcopal	1	50	84	84	0.4	0.8
Bahá'í	0	NR	3	3	0.0	0.0
BAPT–Ind Bapt Flwsp Intl	1	NR	NR	NR	-	-
BAPT–Natl Mis Bapt Conv	2	0	300	354	1.6	3.2
BAPT–So Bapt Conv	23	2,120	5,925	6,992	31.0	63.1
Catholic	1	NR	NR	278	1.2	2.5
CGOD–Ch God (Ander)	1	100	NR	100	0.4	0.9
CHR–Chs of Christ	4	241	235	299	1.3	2.7
Jehovah's Witness	1	NR	NR	NR	-	-
LDS–L-D Saints	1	NR	NR	167	0.7	1.5
METH–AME	2	75	450	531	2.4	4.8
METH–Un Methodist	5	194	477	560	2.5	5.1
Non-denom Chr Chs	8	615	850	872	3.9	7.9
PENT–Assemb of God	1	137	58	230	1.0	2.1
PENT–Ch God (Cleve)	5	141	172	203	0.9	1.8
PENT–Ch of God Proph	3	NR	73	86	0.4	0.8
PENT–Intl Pent Holiness	2	27	27	32	0.1	0.3
PENT–Un Pent Ch Intl	1	NR	NR	NR	-	-
PRES–Presb Ch (USA)	1	107	187	221	1.0	2.0
Sev Day Adv	1	38	66	76	0.3	0.7
UNION	**22**	**932**	**2,361**	**3,294**	**21.2**	**100.0**
Bahá'í	0	NR	3	3	0.0	0.1
BAPT–Free Will Bapt	1	NR	89	105	0.7	3.2
BAPT–So Bapt Conv	7	472	1,389	1,631	10.5	49.5
CHR–Chr Chs & Chs Cr	1	NR	300	352	2.3	10.7
CHR–Chs of Christ	2	183	136	185	1.2	5.6
LDS–L-D Saints	1	NR	NR	478	3.1	14.5
METH–AME	1	0	100	117	0.8	3.6
METH–Cong Meth	1	NR	28	33	0.2	1.0
METH–Un Methodist	2	36	78	100	0.6	3.0
Non-denom Chr Chs	2	135	135	169	1.1	5.1
PENT–Ch God (Cleve)	2	106	103	121	0.8	3.7
PENT–Ch of God by Faith	2	NR	NR	NR	-	-
VOLUSIA	**425**	**63,346**	**84,174**	**172,437**	**34.9**	**100.0**
ANG/EPIS–Anglican NA	1	NR	NR	NR	-	-
ANG/EPIS–Episcopal	11	1,832	3,206	4,018	0.8	2.3
Bahá'í	0	NR	128	128	0.0	0.1
BAPT–Amer Bapt Assn	1	NR	89	104	0.0	0.1
BAPT–Amer Bapt USA	1	210	160	187	0.0	0.1
BAPT–Free Will Bapt	1	NR	89	104	0.0	0.1
BAPT–Natl Mis Bapt Conv	3	50	400	467	0.1	0.3
BAPT–NBC USA	6	755	900	1,050	0.2	0.6
BAPT–Ref Bapt Ch	1	NR	NR	NR	-	-
BAPT–Reg Bapt Gen As	3	NR	NR	NR	-	-
BAPT–S-D Baptist Gen Con	2	63	124	145	0.0	0.1
BAPT–So Bapt Conv	56	8,422	17,119	19,969	4.0	11.6
BRETH–Grace Breth	1	NR	NR	NR	-	-
BUDD–Theravada	1	NR	NR	291	0.1	0.2
Calv Chpl	2	NR	NR	NR	-	-
Catholic	15	NR	NR	50,934	10.3	29.5
CGOD–Ch God (Ander)	4	888	NR	888	0.2	0.5
Ch Cr, Scientst	5	NR	NR	NR	-	-
Ch of Nazarene	6	551	682	887	0.2	0.5
Chr & Miss Al	9	1,680	1,287	2,504	0.5	1.5
CHR–Chr Ch (Disc)	7	1,263	2,173	2,535	0.5	1.5
CHR–Chr Chs & Chs Cr	13	NR	4,267	4,977	1.0	2.9
CHR–Chs of Christ	14	1,277	1,322	1,634	0.3	0.9
CHR–Int Chs of Christ	1	NR	28	33	0.0	0.0
Evan Cov Ch	1	85	28	110	0.0	0.1
Evan Free Ch	1	500	NR	500	0.1	0.3
FRND–Fr Gen Cf	2	NR	0	0	0.0	0.0
Jain	1	NR	NR	NR	-	-
Jehovah's Witness	13	NR	NR	NR	-	-
JUD–Conserv	1	117	131	354	0.1	0.2
JUD–Orth	1	43	50	60	0.0	0.0
JUD–Reform	1	130	230	621	0.1	0.4
LDS–L-D Saints	6	NR	NR	3,807	0.8	2.2
LUTH–E.L.C.A.	8	1,031	2,510	2,894	0.6	1.7
LUTH–Luth Ch-Am Asc	1	NR	NR	NR	-	-
LUTH–Luth–MO Synod	3	621	830	948	0.2	0.5

Religious Group	Number of Congregations	Number of Attendees	Number of Communicant, Confirmed, or Full Members	Adherents: Number of Adherents	Adherents: % of Total Pop.	Adherents: % of Total Adh.
LUTH–Wisc Ev Luth Syn	2	291	348	481	0.1	0.3
METH–AME	13	805	2,472	2,884	0.6	1.7
METH–C.M.E.	3	0	300	350	0.1	0.2
METH–Un Methodist	25	5,011	9,476	13,869	2.8	8.0
METH–Wesleyan	3	105	83	136	0.0	0.1
Muslim Est	2	640	NR	1,550	0.3	0.9
New Apost Ch	1	NR	NR	NR	-	-
Non-denom Chr Chs	65	17,062	20,950	23,607	4.8	13.7
ORTHE–Ant Orth of NA	1	80	NR	206	0.0	0.1
ORTHE–Greek Orthodox	1	175	NR	500	0.1	0.3
ORTHE–Orth Ch in Amer	1	25	NR	100	0.0	0.1
ORTHE–Rus Orth Abroad	1	20	NR	25	0.0	0.0
ORTHO–Coptic Orth Ch	1	275	NR	375	0.1	0.2
PENT–Assemb of God	14	9,851	3,254	14,139	2.9	8.2
PENT–Ch God (Cleve)	12	1,176	2,196	2,562	0.5	1.5
PENT–Ch Lord Jesus Apos	2	NR	NR	NR	-	-
PENT–Ch of God by Faith	2	NR	NR	NR	-	-
PENT–Ch of God Proph	5	NR	179	209	0.0	0.1
PENT–COGIC	7	220	430	502	0.1	0.3
PENT–Int Foursq Gos	2	93	34	40	0.0	0.0
PENT–Intl Pent Holiness	9	867	1,132	1,320	0.3	0.8
PENT–Open Bible Std	2	152	NR	152	0.0	0.1
PENT–Pent Ch of God	1	70	NR	109	0.0	0.1
PENT–Un Pent Ch Intl	3	NR	NR	NR	-	-
PRES–Presb Ch (USA)	12	4,234	4,023	4,693	0.9	2.7
PRES–Presb Ch Amer	3	421	443	522	0.1	0.3
Salvation Army	2	108	135	250	0.1	0.1
Sev Day Adv	8	874	1,520	1,749	0.4	1.0
Swedenborgian	1	NR	NR	NR	-	-
Un Breth in Cr	2	403	62	344	0.1	0.2
Un C of Christ	10	667	1,157	1,350	0.3	0.8
Unit Univ	4	203	227	259	0.1	0.2
Unity Ch	2	NR	NR	NR	-	-
Zoroastrian	0	NR	NR	5	0.0	0.0
WAKULLA	**44**	**3,219**	**4,941**	**6,972**	**22.7**	**100.0**
ANG/EPIS–Anglican NA	1	NR	NR	NR	-	-
Bahá'í	0	NR	6	6	0.0	0.1
BAPT–Natl Mis Bapt Conv	3	0	450	543	1.8	7.8
BAPT–So Bapt Conv	9	873	1,686	2,036	6.6	29.2
BUDD–Mahayana	1	NR	NR	115	0.4	1.6
Catholic	1	NR	NR	300	1.0	4.3
CHR–Chs of Christ	3	70	65	80	0.3	1.1
Jehovah's Witness	1	NR	NR	NR	-	-
LDS–L-D Saints	1	NR	NR	388	1.3	5.6
LUTH–Luth–MO Synod	1	34	42	56	0.2	0.8
METH–AME	1	0	100	121	0.4	1.7
METH–Un Methodist	4	416	809	985	3.2	14.1
Non-denom Chr Chs	9	1,055	1,105	1,334	4.3	19.1
PENT–Assemb of God	3	497	304	562	1.8	8.1
PENT–Cong Hol Ch	2	28	26	31	0.1	0.4
PENT–Intl Pent Holiness	2	190	250	302	1.0	4.3
PENT–Un Pent Ch Intl	1	NR	NR	NR	-	-
Sev Day Adv	1	56	98	113	0.4	1.6
WALTON	**120**	**7,231**	**14,428**	**22,237**	**40.4**	**100.0**
ANG/EPIS–Episcopal	2	179	327	343	0.6	1.5
Bahá'í	0	NR	6	6	0.0	0.0
BAPT–Free Will Bapt	1	NR	89	106	0.2	0.5
BAPT–So Bapt Conv	43	2,726	7,761	9,248	16.8	41.6
Catholic	4	NR	NR	3,638	6.6	16.4
CHR–Chr Chs & Chs Cr	1	NR	50	60	0.1	0.3
CHR–Chs of Christ	6	268	201	255	0.5	1.1
Jehovah's Witness	3	NR	NR	NR	-	-
LDS–L-D Saints	2	NR	NR	870	1.6	3.9
LUTH–E.L.C.A.	1	20	25	29	0.1	0.1
LUTH–Luth–MO Synod	2	56	39	49	0.1	0.2
METH–AME	8	100	1,027	1,224	2.2	5.5
METH–Un Methodist	12	1,090	1,868	2,566	4.7	11.5
Non-denom Chr Chs	12	2,165	2,340	2,752	5.0	12.4
PENT–Assemb of God	10	378	150	444	0.8	2.0
PENT–Ch God (Cleve)	2	25	51	61	0.1	0.3
PENT–COGIC	1	20	35	42	0.1	0.2

NR–Not Reported   - Represents no adherents reported.   Percentages may not total 100 due to rounding.

Table 3: Religious Congregations by County and Group: 2010

Religious Group	Number of Congregations	Number of Attendees	Number of Communicant, Confirmed, or Full Members	Adherents: Number of Adherents	Adherents: % of Total Pop.	Adherents: % of Total Adh.
PENT–Full Gosp Bapt	1	NR	NR	NR	-	-
PENT–Un Pent Ch Intl	2	NR	NR	NR	-	-
PRES–Evan Presby Ch	1	NR	86	102	0.2	0.5
PRES–Presb Ch (USA)	5	176	324	386	0.7	1.7
Sev Day Adv	1	28	49	56	0.1	0.3
WASHINGTON	**60**	**3,201**	**7,513**	**9,767**	**39.2**	**100.0**
ANG/EPIS–Episcopal	1	41	71	71	0.3	0.7
BAPT–Free Will Bapt	3	NR	267	318	1.3	3.3
BAPT–Natl Mis Bapt Conv	1	0	150	179	0.7	1.8
BAPT–So Bapt Conv	23	1,799	4,803	5,720	23.0	58.6
Catholic	2	NR	NR	325	1.3	3.3
CHR–Chs of Christ	2	155	140	185	0.7	1.9
Jehovah's Witness	1	NR	NR	NR	-	-
METH–AME	6	105	750	893	3.6	9.1
METH–Un Methodist	5	227	489	581	2.3	5.9
Non-denom Chr Chs	3	260	260	325	1.3	3.3
PENT–Assemb of God	6	494	274	801	3.2	8.2
PENT–Ch God (Cleve)	1	44	26	31	0.1	0.3
PENT–Ch of God by Faith	1	NR	NR	NR	-	-
PENT–Ch of God Proph	1	NR	45	54	0.2	0.6
PENT–COGIC	1	0	150	179	0.7	1.8
PENT–Intl Pent Holiness	1	37	36	43	0.2	0.4
PENT–Un Pent Ch Intl	1	NR	NR	NR	-	-
PRES–Presb Ch (USA)	1	39	52	62	0.2	0.6
GEORGIA	**12,292**	**1,569,696**	**3,333,256**	**4,924,398**	**50.8**	**100.0**
APPLING	**63**	**4,107**	**11,502**	**15,075**	**82.7**	**100.0**
ANG/EPIS–Episcopal	1	12	15	17	0.1	0.1
Bahá'í	0	NR	1	1	0.0	0.0
BAPT–Free Will Bapt	5	NR	365	456	2.5	3.0
BAPT–So Bapt Conv	25	2,518	7,239	9,054	49.6	60.1
Catholic	1	NR	NR	742	4.1	4.9
CHR–Chs of Christ	1	5	6	6	0.0	0.0
Jehovah's Witness	1	NR	NR	NR	-	-
METH–AME	2	0	200	250	1.4	1.7
METH–C.M.E.	2	0	250	313	1.7	2.1
METH–Un Methodist	9	465	1,332	1,455	8.0	9.7
Non-denom Chr Chs	3	250	330	342	1.9	2.3
PENT–Assemb of God	2	323	78	335	1.8	2.2
PENT–Ch God (Cleve)	6	507	1,434	1,793	9.8	11.9
PENT–Ch of God Proph	2	NR	55	69	0.4	0.5
PENT–COGIC	1	0	150	188	1.0	1.2
PENT–Un Pent Ch Intl	1	NR	NR	NR	-	-
Sev Day Adv	1	27	47	54	0.3	0.4
ATKINSON	**24**	**735**	**2,199**	**3,436**	**41.0**	**100.0**
BAPT–Free Will Bapt	2	NR	146	189	2.3	5.5
BAPT–So Bapt Conv	6	332	991	1,282	15.3	37.3
Catholic	1	NR	NR	152	1.8	4.4
LDS–L-D Saints	1	NR	NR	464	5.5	13.5
METH–AME	4	0	550	712	8.5	20.7
METH–Un Methodist	5	146	296	298	3.6	8.7
PENT–Assemb of God	2	52	32	101	1.2	2.9
PENT–Ch God (Cleve)	2	205	149	193	2.3	5.6
PENT–Ch of God Proph	1	NR	35	45	0.5	1.3
BACON	**35**	**2,654**	**4,732**	**6,424**	**57.9**	**100.0**
BAPT–Free Will Bapt	3	NR	219	275	2.5	4.3
BAPT–Natl Mis Bapt Conv	1	40	40	50	0.5	0.8
BAPT–So Bapt Conv	10	1,149	2,295	2,881	26.0	44.8
Catholic	1	NR	NR	158	1.4	2.5
Ch of Nazarene	1	125	78	231	2.1	3.6
CHR–Chs of Christ	1	24	23	28	0.3	0.4
LDS–L-D Saints	1	NR	NR	236	2.1	3.7
METH–Cong Meth	2	NR	185	232	2.1	3.6
METH–Un Methodist	4	119	344	355	3.2	5.5
METH–Wesleyan	1	22	13	29	0.3	0.5
Non-denom Chr Chs	4	670	650	839	7.6	13.1
PENT–Ch God (Cleve)	4	505	722	906	8.2	14.1

Religious Group	Number of Congregations	Number of Attendees	Number of Communicant, Confirmed, or Full Members	Adherents: Number of Adherents	Adherents: % of Total Pop.	Adherents: % of Total Adh.
PENT–Ch of God Proph	1	NR	13	16	0.1	0.2
PENT–COGIC	1	0	150	188	1.7	2.9
BAKER	**15**	**335**	**1,047**	**1,383**	**40.1**	**100.0**
Bahá'í	0	NR	10	10	0.3	0.7
BAPT–Free Will Bapt	2	NR	146	178	5.2	12.9
BAPT–NBC USA	1	0	100	122	3.5	8.8
BAPT–Orig Free Will Bapt	1	90	123	150	4.3	10.8
BAPT–So Bapt Conv	4	139	362	441	12.8	31.9
CHR–Chs of Christ	1	5	5	6	0.2	0.4
METH–C.M.E.	2	0	250	305	8.8	22.1
METH–Un Methodist	1	6	11	11	0.3	0.8
PENT–Assemb of God	1	25	19	25	0.7	1.8
PENT–Pent Ch of God	1	70	NR	109	3.2	7.9
PRES–Presb Ch (USA)	1	0	21	26	0.8	1.9
BALDWIN	**57**	**4,293**	**10,537**	**14,224**	**31.1**	**100.0**
ANG/EPIS–Episcopal	1	107	285	285	0.6	2.0
Bahá'í	0	NR	58	58	0.1	0.4
BAPT–So Bapt Conv	16	1,625	4,647	5,540	12.1	38.9
Catholic	1	NR	NR	1,100	2.4	7.7
Ch of Nazarene	1	19	15	33	0.1	0.2
CHR–Chr Chs & Chs Cr	3	NR	942	1,123	2.5	7.9
CHR–Chs of Christ	3	97	83	109	0.2	0.8
Jehovah's Witness	2	NR	NR	NR	-	-
LDS–L-D Saints	1	NR	NR	675	1.5	4.7
LUTH–Luth–MO Synod	1	22	36	37	0.1	0.3
METH–AME	3	175	500	596	1.3	4.2
METH–C.M.E.	1	0	150	179	0.4	1.3
METH–Un Methodist	6	583	1,513	1,850	4.0	13.0
Non-denom Chr Chs	8	1,140	1,380	1,525	3.3	10.7
PENT–Assemb of God	1	22	16	22	0.0	0.2
PENT–Ch God (Cleve)	2	144	295	352	0.8	2.5
PENT–COGIC	2	95	195	232	0.5	1.6
PENT–Int Foursq Gos	1	24	35	42	0.1	0.3
PRES–Presb Ch (USA)	1	100	197	235	0.5	1.7
PRES–Presb Ch Amer	1	65	60	81	0.2	0.6
Sev Day Adv	2	75	130	150	0.3	1.1
BANKS	**30**	**2,997**	**8,577**	**10,613**	**57.7**	**100.0**
Bahá'í	0	NR	4	4	0.0	0.0
BAPT–Ref Bapt Ch	1	NR	NR	NR	-	-
BAPT–So Bapt Conv	13	2,278	7,136	8,853	48.1	83.4
Chr & Miss Al	1	11	0	12	0.1	0.1
CHR–Chr Chs & Chs Cr	3	NR	253	314	1.7	3.0
Jehovah's Witness	1	NR	NR	NR	-	-
METH–Un Methodist	4	269	508	639	3.5	6.0
Non-denom Chr Chs	1	150	200	200	1.1	1.9
PENT–Ch God (Cleve)	3	138	303	376	2.0	3.5
PENT–Cong Hol Ch	2	116	103	128	0.7	1.2
PRES–Presb Ch (USA)	1	35	70	87	0.5	0.8
BARROW	**75**	**7,368**	**17,149**	**26,145**	**37.7**	**100.0**
ANG/EPIS–Episcopal	1	46	75	85	0.1	0.3
Bahá'í	0	NR	21	21	0.0	0.1
BAPT–Amer Bapt Assn	1	NR	150	194	0.3	0.7
BAPT–NBC USA	3	100	380	491	0.7	1.9
BAPT–So Bapt Conv	21	3,163	8,344	10,782	15.5	41.2
Calv Chpl	1	NR	NR	NR	-	-
Catholic	1	NR	NR	3,825	5.5	14.6
Chr & Miss Al	2	606	1,173	1,183	1.7	4.5
CHR–Chr Ch (Disc)	3	175	522	675	1.0	2.6
CHR–Chr Chs & Chs Cr	5	NR	795	1,027	1.5	3.9
CHR–Chs of Christ	1	93	67	82	0.1	0.3
Jehovah's Witness	1	NR	NR	NR	-	-
LDS–L-D Saints	2	NR	NR	780	1.1	3.0
LUTH–E.L.C.A.	1	52	83	94	0.1	0.4
LUTH–Luth–MO Synod	1	41	42	60	0.1	0.2
METH–AME Zion	1	0	150	194	0.3	0.7
METH–Un Methodist	10	1,284	3,154	3,850	5.6	14.7
METH–Wesleyan	1	153	113	199	0.3	0.8
Non-denom Chr Chs	7	1,110	1,285	1,451	2.1	5.5

NR–Not Reported - Represents no adherents reported. Percentages may not total 100 due to rounding.

Table 3: Religious Congregations by County and Group: 2010

Religious Group	Number of Congregations	Number of Attendees	Number of Communicant, Confirmed, or Full Members	Adherents		
				Number of Adherents	% of Total Pop.	% of Total Adh.
ORTHO–Malan Syr Orth	1	55	NR	108	0.2	0.4
PENT–Assemb of God	1	68	34	92	0.1	0.4
PENT–Ch God (Cleve)	3	67	243	314	0.5	1.2
PENT–Ch of God Proph	1	NR	54	70	0.1	0.3
PENT–Cong Hol Ch	1	39	35	45	0.1	0.2
PENT–Fire Bapt Hol Ch	1	NR	NR	NR	-	-
PRES–Presb Ch (USA)	2	130	159	205	0.3	0.8
PRES–Presb Ch Amer	1	71	70	88	0.1	0.3
Sev Day Adv	1	115	200	230	0.3	0.9
BARTOW	**121**	**14,749**	**34,634**	**46,779**	**46.7**	**100.0**
ANG/EPIS–Episcopal	1	121	225	225	0.2	0.5
Bahá'í	0	NR	40	40	0.0	0.1
BAPT–Alliance Bapt	1	NR	NR	NR	-	-
BAPT–Free Will Bapt	1	NR	73	92	0.1	0.2
BAPT–Natl Mis Bapt Conv	1	50	70	88	0.1	0.2
BAPT–NBC USA	2	100	700	883	0.9	1.9
BAPT–So Bapt Conv	42	6,338	17,790	22,435	22.4	48.0
Catholic	1	NR	NR	2,401	2.4	5.1
Ch of Nazarene	1	42	67	69	0.1	0.1
CHR–Chr Chs & Chs Cr	2	NR	310	391	0.4	0.8
CHR–Chs of Christ	5	397	348	490	0.5	1.0
Jehovah's Witness	2	NR	NR	NR	-	-
LDS–L-D Saints	3	NR	NR	1,029	1.0	2.2
LUTH–Luth–MO Synod	1	118	281	319	0.3	0.7
METH–AME	3	75	450	567	0.6	1.2
METH–Cong Meth	1	NR	147	185	0.2	0.4
METH–Un Methodist	15	1,634	4,512	5,707	5.7	12.2
METH–Wesleyan	1	26	5	34	0.0	0.1
Muslim Est	1	35	NR	120	0.1	0.3
Non-denom Chr Chs	19	2,395	3,095	3,482	3.5	7.4
PENT–Assemb of God	1	38	20	38	0.0	0.1
PENT–Ch God (Cleve)	4	2,781	5,057	6,377	6.4	13.6
PENT–Ch of God Proph	1	NR	39	49	0.0	0.1
PENT–COGIC	1	0	150	189	0.2	0.4
PENT–Full Gosp Bapt	1	NR	NR	NR	-	-
PENT–Int Foursq Gos	2	93	103	130	0.1	0.3
PRES–Cumber Presb	1	NR	92	148	0.1	0.3
PRES–Presb Ch (USA)	2	280	712	898	0.9	1.9
Salvation Army	1	59	59	59	0.1	0.1
Sev Day Adv	4	167	289	334	0.3	0.7
BEN HILL	**40**	**3,301**	**9,475**	**12,280**	**69.6**	**100.0**
ANG/EPIS–Episcopal	1	14	27	27	0.2	0.2
Bahá'í	0	NR	3	3	0.0	0.0
BAPT–NBC USA	1	0	150	190	1.1	1.5
BAPT–So Bapt Conv	16	1,577	6,159	7,791	44.2	63.4
Catholic	1	NR	NR	555	3.1	4.5
Ch of Nazarene	1	108	198	198	1.1	1.6
CHR–Chs of Christ	2	196	215	266	1.5	2.2
Jehovah's Witness	1	NR	NR	NR	-	-
METH–AME	1	0	100	126	0.7	1.0
METH–C.M.E.	1	0	100	126	0.7	1.0
METH–Un Methodist	3	340	821	970	5.5	7.9
Non-denom Chr Chs	6	720	841	955	5.4	7.8
PENT–Assemb of God	1	15	15	15	0.1	0.1
PENT–Ch God (Cleve)	1	237	696	880	5.0	7.2
PENT–Ch of God by Faith	1	NR	NR	NR	-	-
PENT–Un Pent Ch Intl	1	NR	NR	NR	-	-
PRES–Presb Ch (USA)	1	36	49	62	0.4	0.5
Sev Day Adv	1	58	101	116	0.7	0.9
BERRIEN	**34**	**2,313**	**5,490**	**7,051**	**36.6**	**100.0**
BAPT–So Bapt Conv	10	919	3,298	4,113	21.3	58.3
Catholic	2	NR	NR	285	1.5	4.0
Ch of Nazarene	2	87	72	152	0.8	2.2
CHR–Chs of Christ	1	24	25	30	0.2	0.4
METH–AME	3	0	300	374	1.9	5.3
METH–C.M.E.	1	0	100	125	0.6	1.8
METH–Un Methodist	6	588	803	827	4.3	11.7
Non-denom Chr Chs	4	365	405	506	2.6	7.2
PENT–Assemb of God	1	90	47	90	0.5	1.3
PENT–Ch God (Cleve)	4	240	440	549	2.8	7.8
BIBB	**235**	**34,704**	**70,284**	**93,858**	**60.3**	**100.0**
ANG/EPIS–Episcopal	4	496	1,395	1,541	1.0	1.6
Bahá'í	0	NR	56	56	0.0	0.1
BAPT–Free Will Bapt	1	NR	73	91	0.1	0.1
BAPT–Natl Mis Bapt Conv	2	65	275	343	0.2	0.4
BAPT–NBC USA	22	3,697	9,738	12,163	7.8	13.0
BAPT–So Bapt Conv	46	9,933	22,439	28,028	18.0	29.9
Catholic	3	NR	NR	6,153	4.0	6.6
CGOD–Ch God (Ander)	2	437	NR	437	0.3	0.5
Ch Cr, Scientst	1	NR	NR	NR	-	-
Ch of Nazarene	3	122	169	196	0.1	0.2
CHR–Chr Ch (Disc)	2	45	213	266	0.2	0.3
CHR–Chr Chs & Chs Cr	3	NR	228	285	0.2	0.3
CHR–Chs of Christ	8	900	941	1,241	0.8	1.3
CHR–Int Chs of Christ	1	NR	37	46	0.0	0.0
Jehovah's Witness	3	NR	NR	NR	-	-
JUD–Conserv	1	115	129	348	0.2	0.4
JUD–Reform	1	62	110	297	0.2	0.3
LDS–L-D Saints	1	NR	NR	1,317	0.8	1.4
LUTH–E.L.C.A.	1	101	391	559	0.4	0.6
LUTH–Luth–MO Synod	1	30	46	55	0.0	0.1
METH–AME	19	740	2,490	3,110	2.0	3.3
METH–C.M.E.	4	250	910	1,137	0.7	1.2
METH–Free Methodist	1	20	25	25	0.0	0.0
METH–Un Methodist	24	3,619	11,752	13,564	8.7	14.5
METH–Wesleyan	1	60	57	78	0.1	0.1
Muslim Est	2	320	NR	837	0.5	0.9
Non-denom Chr Chs	36	8,880	12,735	13,228	8.5	14.1
ORTHE–Greek Orthodox	1	40	NR	120	0.1	0.1
ORTHE–Orth Ch in Amer	1	35	NR	80	0.1	0.1
PENT–Assemb of God	5	1,719	1,089	1,937	1.2	2.1
PENT–Ch God (Cleve)	8	1,051	1,730	2,161	1.4	2.3
PENT–Ch of God Proph	2	NR	160	200	0.1	0.2
PENT–COGIC	5	150	365	456	0.3	0.5
PENT–Cong Hol Ch	3	75	62	77	0.0	0.1
PENT–Fire Bapt Hol Ch	1	NR	NR	NR	-	-
PENT–Intl Pent Holiness	2	202	222	277	0.2	0.3
PENT–Un Pent Ch Intl	2	NR	NR	NR	-	-
PRES–Presb Ch (USA)	3	180	404	505	0.3	0.5
PRES–Presb Ch Amer	5	784	1,150	1,441	0.9	1.5
Salvation Army	1	129	144	305	0.2	0.3
Sev Day Adv	2	374	649	747	0.5	0.8
Unit Univ	1	73	100	144	0.1	0.2
Zoroastrian	0	NR	NR	7	0.0	0.0
BLECKLEY	**29**	**1,627**	**4,152**	**5,501**	**42.1**	**100.0**
ANG/EPIS–Episcopal	1	38	55	83	0.6	1.5
Bahá'í	0	NR	14	14	0.1	0.3
BAPT–Free Will Bapt	2	NR	146	175	1.3	3.2
BAPT–Natl Mis Bapt Conv	1	0	150	180	1.4	3.3
BAPT–So Bapt Conv	10	779	2,275	2,731	20.9	49.6
Ch of Nazarene	1	45	89	89	0.7	1.6
CHR–Chs of Christ	1	30	25	35	0.3	0.6
LDS–L-D Saints	1	NR	NR	560	4.3	10.2
METH–AME	2	0	250	300	2.3	5.5
METH–Un Methodist	2	103	333	366	2.8	6.7
Non-denom Chr Chs	2	275	325	369	2.8	6.7
PENT–Assemb of God	2	15	20	35	0.3	0.6
PENT–Ch God (Cleve)	1	181	231	277	2.1	5.0
PENT–Ch of God by Faith	1	NR	NR	NR	-	-
PENT–Ch of God Proph	1	NR	32	38	0.3	0.7
PENT–Intl Pent Holiness	1	161	207	249	1.9	4.5
BRANTLEY	**27**	**1,978**	**5,126**	**6,382**	**34.7**	**100.0**
Bahá'í	0	NR	1	1	0.0	0.0
BAPT–So Bapt Conv	10	1,481	3,932	4,942	26.8	77.4
Ch of Nazarene	1	30	21	39	0.2	0.6
METH–AME	1	0	100	126	0.7	2.0
METH–Un Methodist	4	120	213	239	1.3	3.7
METH–Wesleyan	2	78	101	102	0.6	1.6
Non-denom Chr Chs	1	50	75	75	0.4	1.2
PENT–Ch God (Cleve)	5	219	504	633	3.4	9.9
PENT–Ch of God Proph	3	NR	179	225	1.2	3.5

NR–Not Reported   - Represents no adherents reported.   Percentages may not total 100 due to rounding.

Table 3: Religious Congregations by County and Group: 2010

Religious Group	Number of Congrega-tions	Number of Attendees	Number of Communicant, Confirmed, or Full Members	Adherents		
				Number of Adherents	% of Total Pop.	% of Total Adh.
BROOKS	**51**	**2,193**	**6,200**	**7,412**	**45.6**	**100.0**
ANG/EPIS–Episcopal	1	22	54	54	0.3	0.7
Bahá'í	0	NR	4	4	0.0	0.1
BAPT–So Bapt Conv	16	1,063	3,108	3,792	23.3	51.2
Ch of Nazarene	2	46	68	138	0.8	1.9
CHR–Chr Ch (Disc)	1	0	130	159	1.0	2.1
CHR–Chs of Christ	4	247	299	341	2.1	4.6
Jehovah's Witness	1	NR	NR	NR	-	-
METH–AME	7	125	950	1,159	7.1	15.6
METH–C.M.E.	2	0	250	305	1.9	4.1
METH–Un Methodist	10	287	721	737	4.5	9.9
Non-denom Chr Chs	2	150	250	250	1.5	3.4
PENT–Assemb of God	1	60	35	75	0.5	1.0
PENT–Ch God (Cleve)	2	116	188	229	1.4	3.1
PRES–Presb Ch (USA)	1	25	53	65	0.4	0.9
Sev Day Adv	1	52	90	104	0.6	1.4
BRYAN	**35**	**3,138**	**8,061**	**12,121**	**40.1**	**100.0**
ANG/EPIS–Episcopal	1	81	150	231	0.8	1.9
Bahá'í	0	NR	10	10	0.0	0.1
BAPT–NBC Amer	1	175	275	354	1.2	2.9
BAPT–So Bapt Conv	8	968	3,981	5,124	16.9	42.3
Catholic	2	NR	NR	2,030	6.7	16.7
CHR–Chr Chs & Chs Cr	2	NR	150	193	0.6	1.6
CHR–Chs of Christ	2	138	105	171	0.6	1.4
Jehovah's Witness	1	NR	NR	NR	-	-
LUTH–E.L.C.A.	1	68	90	134	0.4	1.1
METH–AME	2	0	200	257	0.9	2.1
METH–Un Methodist	3	574	1,663	1,938	6.4	16.0
METH–Wesleyan	1	85	36	111	0.4	0.9
Non-denom Chr Chs	6	800	1,050	1,125	3.7	9.3
PENT–Assemb of God	1	25	30	30	0.1	0.2
PENT–Ch God (Cleve)	1	64	80	103	0.3	0.8
PRES–Presb Ch (USA)	1	160	241	310	1.0	2.6
PRES–Presb Ch Amer	1	0	0	0	0.0	0.0
Shinto	1	NR	NR	NR	-	-
BULLOCH	**82**	**8,868**	**18,594**	**25,514**	**36.3**	**100.0**
ANG/EPIS–Episcopal	1	105	167	178	0.3	0.7
Bahá'í	0	NR	21	21	0.0	0.1
BAPT–Free Will Bapt	1	NR	73	87	0.1	0.3
BAPT–Natl Mis Bapt Conv	1	0	150	179	0.3	0.7
BAPT–NBC USA	2	0	300	357	0.5	1.4
BAPT–So Bapt Conv	28	4,219	9,693	11,548	16.4	45.3
BUDD–Mahayana	2	NR	NR	40	0.1	0.2
Catholic	1	NR	NR	1,897	2.7	7.4
CGOD–Ch God (Ander)	4	163	NR	163	0.2	0.6
CHR–Chr Chs & Chs Cr	1	NR	0	0	0.0	0.0
CHR–Chs of Christ	1	69	75	89	0.1	0.3
Jehovah's Witness	2	NR	NR	NR	-	-
LDS–L-D Saints	1	NR	NR	769	1.1	3.0
LUTH–Luth-MO Synod	1	57	66	85	0.1	0.3
METH–AME	4	0	500	596	0.8	2.3
METH–Un Methodist	10	1,462	3,635	4,658	6.6	18.3
Non-denom Chr Chs	9	1,648	1,889	2,112	3.0	8.3
PENT–Assemb of God	2	147	0	276	0.4	1.1
PENT–Ch God (Cleve)	4	465	1,139	1,357	1.9	5.3
PENT–COGIC	1	0	150	179	0.3	0.7
PENT–Intl Pent Holiness	1	60	63	75	0.1	0.3
PENT–Un Pent Ch Intl	1	NR	NR	NR	-	-
PRES–Presb Ch (USA)	1	119	258	307	0.4	1.2
PRES–Presb Ch Amer	1	235	245	328	0.5	1.3
Sev Day Adv	1	64	111	128	0.2	0.5
Unit Univ	1	55	59	85	0.1	0.3
BURKE	**57**	**3,026**	**8,389**	**11,271**	**48.3**	**100.0**
ANG/EPIS–Episcopal	1	48	123	123	0.5	1.1
Bahá'í	0	NR	97	97	0.4	0.9
BAPT–Free Will Bapt	1	NR	73	93	0.4	0.8
BAPT–Natl Mis Bapt Conv	2	60	250	320	1.4	2.8
BAPT–NBC USA	1	0	150	192	0.8	1.7
BAPT–So Bapt Conv	18	1,685	4,437	5,671	24.3	50.3

Religious Group	Number of Congrega-tions	Number of Attendees	Number of Communicant, Confirmed, or Full Members	Adherents		
				Number of Adherents	% of Total Pop.	% of Total Adh.
Catholic	1	NR	NR	350	1.5	3.1
CGOD–Ch God (Ander)	1	25	NR	25	0.1	0.2
CHR–Chs of Christ	1	28	36	64	0.3	0.6
LDS–L-D Saints	1	NR	NR	467	2.0	4.1
METH–AME	5	40	549	702	3.0	6.2
METH–AME Zion	1	0	100	128	0.5	1.1
METH–C.M.E.	2	0	250	320	1.4	2.8
METH–Un Methodist	12	553	1,217	1,449	6.2	12.9
Non-denom Chr Chs	4	380	530	550	2.4	4.9
PENT–Ch God (Cleve)	1	118	282	360	1.5	3.2
PENT–Ch Lord Jesus Apos	1	NR	NR	NR	-	-
PENT–COGIC	1	0	150	192	0.8	1.7
PENT–Un Pent Ch Intl	1	NR	NR	NR	-	-
PRES–Presb Ch (USA)	1	29	41	52	0.2	0.5
PRES–Presb Ch Amer	1	60	104	116	0.5	1.0
BUTTS	**40**	**3,647**	**7,634**	**9,947**	**42.1**	**100.0**
Bahá'í	0	NR	6	6	0.0	0.1
BAPT–Amer Bapt Assn	1	NR	85	103	0.4	1.0
BAPT–NBC USA	1	400	582	705	3.0	7.1
BAPT–Ref Bapt Ch	1	NR	NR	NR	-	-
BAPT–So Bapt Conv	10	1,870	4,490	5,441	23.0	54.7
Catholic	1	NR	NR	657	2.8	6.6
Ch of Nazarene	1	53	95	95	0.4	1.0
CHR–Chr Chs & Chs Cr	1	NR	77	93	0.4	0.9
CHR–Chs of Christ	1	30	25	30	0.1	0.3
Jehovah's Witness	1	NR	NR	NR	-	-
METH–AME	3	0	300	364	1.5	3.7
METH–C.M.E.	2	105	235	285	1.2	2.9
METH–Cong Meth	1	NR	NR	NR	-	-
METH–Un Methodist	6	428	834	1,022	4.3	10.3
Non-denom Chr Chs	4	300	450	475	2.0	4.8
PENT–Assemb of God	1	400	215	400	1.7	4.0
PENT–Int Pent C Chr	1	12	115	115	0.5	1.2
PENT–Un Pent Ch Intl	1	NR	NR	NR	-	-
PRES–Presb Ch (USA)	2	43	114	138	0.6	1.4
Sev Day Adv	1	6	11	13	0.1	0.1
Zoroastrian	0	NR	NR	5	0.0	0.1
CALHOUN	**29**	**716**	**3,435**	**4,042**	**60.4**	**100.0**
Bahá'í	0	NR	26	26	0.4	0.6
BAPT–Alliance Bapt	1	NR	NR	NR	-	-
BAPT–Free Will Bapt	1	NR	73	87	1.3	2.2
BAPT–Natl Mis Bapt Conv	5	100	800	948	14.2	23.5
BAPT–NBC USA	1	0	150	178	2.7	4.4
BAPT–So Bapt Conv	7	424	1,480	1,754	26.2	43.4
CHR–Chs of Christ	1	15	10	18	0.3	0.4
METH–AME	2	0	200	237	3.5	5.9
METH–C.M.E.	2	0	300	356	5.3	8.8
METH–Un Methodist	8	163	385	425	6.3	10.5
PENT–Ch God (Cleve)	1	14	11	13	0.2	0.3
CAMDEN	**73**	**6,114**	**13,922**	**19,500**	**38.6**	**100.0**
ANG/EPIS–Episcopal	4	227	384	425	0.8	2.2
Bahá'í	0	NR	6	6	0.0	0.0
BAPT–Amer Bapt Assn	2	NR	185	234	0.5	1.2
BAPT–Free Will Bapt	1	NR	73	92	0.2	0.5
BAPT–NBC USA	3	800	1,400	1,772	3.5	9.1
BAPT–Ref Bapt Ch	1	NR	NR	NR	-	-
BAPT–So Bapt Conv	14	1,317	5,632	7,128	14.1	36.6
Catholic	1	NR	NR	1,656	3.3	8.5
CHR–Chs of Christ	2	135	128	163	0.3	0.8
Evan Free Ch	1	70	NR	70	0.1	0.4
Jehovah's Witness	1	NR	NR	NR	-	-
LDS–L-D Saints	1	NR	NR	913	1.8	4.7
LUTH–Luth-MO Synod	1	90	104	134	0.3	0.7
METH–AME	3	40	350	443	0.9	2.3
METH–C.M.E.	1	0	100	127	0.3	0.7
METH–Un Methodist	11	910	2,356	2,462	4.9	12.6
Non-denom Chr Chs	10	1,485	1,720	1,931	3.8	9.9
PENT–Assemb of God	1	150	58	150	0.3	0.8
PENT–Ch God (Cleve)	7	652	964	1,220	2.4	6.3
PENT–Ch of God by Faith	3	NR	NR	NR	-	-

NR–Not Reported   - Represents no adherents reported.   Percentages may not total 100 due to rounding.

Table 3: Religious Congregations by County and Group: 2010

Religious Group	Number of Congregations	Number of Attendees	Number of Communicant, Confirmed, or Full Members	Adherents: Number of Adherents	Adherents: % of Total Pop.	Adherents: % of Total Adh.
PENT–Ch of God Proph	1	NR	26	33	0.1	0.2
PENT–COGIC	1	30	50	63	0.1	0.3
PENT–Un Pent Ch Intl	1	NR	NR	NR	-	-
PRES–Presb Ch (USA)	1	158	298	377	0.7	1.9
Sev Day Adv	1	50	88	101	0.2	0.5
CANDLER	**23**	**1,249**	**3,558**	**4,744**	**43.1**	**100.0**
BAPT–Free Will Bapt	1	NR	73	91	0.8	1.9
BAPT–Natl Mis Bapt Conv	1	0	150	188	1.7	4.0
BAPT–NBC USA	1	0	150	188	1.7	4.0
BAPT–So Bapt Conv	9	791	2,245	2,811	25.6	59.3
Catholic	1	NR	NR	319	2.9	6.7
CGOD–Ch God (Ander)	1	0	NR	0	0.0	0.0
CHR–Chs of Christ	2	55	42	65	0.6	1.4
Jehovah's Witness	1	NR	NR	NR	-	-
METH–Un Methodist	3	157	355	402	3.7	8.5
PENT–Ch God (Cleve)	2	225	504	631	5.7	13.3
PRES–Presb Ch (USA)	1	21	39	49	0.4	1.0
CARROLL	**154**	**18,105**	**40,215**	**53,677**	**48.6**	**100.0**
ANG/EPIS–Episcopal	1	157	410	663	0.6	1.2
Bahá'í	0	NR	42	42	0.0	0.1
BAPT–Natl Mis Bapt Conv	2	0	300	374	0.3	0.7
BAPT–NBC USA	1	0	125	156	0.1	0.3
BAPT–So Bapt Conv	47	7,585	20,433	25,480	23.1	47.5
Catholic	1	NR	NR	4,462	4.0	8.3
Ch Cr, Scientst	1	NR	NR	NR	-	-
CHR–Chr Chs & Chs Cr	8	NR	1,915	2,388	2.2	4.4
CHR–Chs of Christ	9	699	672	807	0.7	1.5
Jehovah's Witness	1	NR	NR	NR	-	-
LDS–L-D Saints	1	NR	NR	780	0.7	1.5
LUTH–E.L.C.A.	1	64	142	160	0.1	0.3
METH–AME	2	0	250	312	0.3	0.6
METH–Un Methodist	24	2,347	5,545	6,534	5.9	12.2
Non-denom Chr Chs	24	5,348	7,324	7,636	6.9	14.2
PENT–Assemb of God	2	98	55	104	0.1	0.2
PENT–Ch God (Cleve)	8	836	1,677	2,091	1.9	3.9
PENT–Ch of God Proph	3	NR	108	135	0.1	0.3
PENT–COGIC	1	10	20	25	0.0	0.0
PENT–Cong Hol Ch	6	459	455	567	0.5	1.1
PENT–Intl Pent Holiness	2	73	52	65	0.1	0.1
PENT–Un Pent Ch Intl	2	NR	NR	NR	-	-
PRES–Free Pres NA	1	NR	NR	NR	-	-
PRES–Presb Ch (USA)	2	129	349	435	0.4	0.8
PRES–Presb Ch Amer	2	230	220	318	0.3	0.6
Sev Day Adv	2	70	121	139	0.1	0.3
Zoroastrian	0	NR	NR	4	0.0	0.0
CATOOSA	**62**	**6,605**	**15,458**	**19,480**	**30.5**	**100.0**
ANG/EPIS–Episcopal	1	88	135	135	0.2	0.7
Bahá'í	0	NR	7	7	0.0	0.0
BAPT–So Bapt Conv	32	4,202	10,926	13,507	21.1	69.3
Catholic	1	NR	NR	523	0.8	2.7
Ch of Nazarene	1	208	434	434	0.7	2.2
CHR–Chs of Christ	2	320	286	367	0.6	1.9
Jehovah's Witness	1	NR	NR	NR	-	-
METH–AME Zion	1	0	150	185	0.3	0.9
METH–Un Methodist	8	843	2,097	2,596	4.1	13.3
METH–Wesleyan	1	131	71	170	0.3	0.9
Non-denom Chr Chs	4	350	500	512	0.8	2.6
PENT–Ch God (Cleve)	4	204	471	582	0.9	3.0
PENT–Ch of God Proph	1	NR	14	17	0.0	0.1
PRES–Presb Ch (USA)	2	48	68	84	0.1	0.4
PRES–Presb Ch Amer	1	75	62	88	0.1	0.5
Sev Day Adv	2	136	237	273	0.4	1.4
CHARLTON	**25**	**1,122**	**3,521**	**4,486**	**36.9**	**100.0**
BAPT–Amer Bapt Assn	1	NR	300	359	2.9	8.0
BAPT–Free Will Bapt	1	NR	73	87	0.7	1.9
BAPT–NBC Amer	1	125	650	778	6.4	17.3
BAPT–So Bapt Conv	7	575	1,604	1,920	15.8	42.8
Catholic	1	NR	NR	270	2.2	6.0

Religious Group	Number of Congregations	Number of Attendees	Number of Communicant, Confirmed, or Full Members	Adherents: Number of Adherents	Adherents: % of Total Pop.	Adherents: % of Total Adh.
CHR–Chs of Christ	1	15	17	24	0.2	0.5
METH–AME	1	0	100	120	1.0	2.7
METH–Un Methodist	5	197	476	568	4.7	12.7
PENT–Assemb of God	1	26	40	48	0.4	1.1
PENT–Ch God (Cleve)	4	184	240	287	2.4	6.4
PENT–Ch of God by Faith	1	NR	NR	NR	-	-
PENT–Ch of God Proph	1	NR	21	25	0.2	0.6
CHATHAM	**324**	**48,091**	**101,268**	**150,853**	**56.9**	**100.0**
ANG/EPIS–Anglican NA	2	NR	NR	NR	-	-
ANG/EPIS–Episcopal	12	1,648	3,357	4,592	1.7	3.0
Bahá'í	2	NR	268	268	0.1	0.2
BAPT–Amer Bapt Assn	2	NR	170	207	0.1	0.1
BAPT–Amer Bapt USA	2	465	1,637	1,993	0.8	1.3
BAPT–Free Will Bapt	1	NR	73	89	0.0	0.1
BAPT–Natl Mis Bapt Conv	3	75	950	1,156	0.4	0.8
BAPT–NBC USA	28	3,865	11,092	13,501	5.1	8.9
BAPT–Prog NBC	3	750	1,390	1,692	0.6	1.1
BAPT–So Bapt Conv	52	6,788	20,299	24,708	9.3	16.4
BUDD–Mahayana	1	NR	NR	11	0.0	0.0
Calv Chpl	1	NR	NR	NR	-	-
Catholic	10	NR	NR	22,109	8.3	14.7
CGOD–Ch God (Ander)	3	118	NR	118	0.0	0.1
Ch Cr, Scientst	1	NR	NR	NR	-	-
Ch of Nazarene	4	111	144	178	0.1	0.1
Chr & Miss Al	4	342	240	459	0.2	0.3
CHR–Chr Ch (Disc)	2	0	0	0	0.0	0.0
CHR–Chr Chs & Chs Cr	6	NR	5,633	6,857	2.6	4.5
CHR–Chs of Christ	10	893	1,058	1,395	0.5	0.9
FRND–Fr Gen Cf	1	NR	7	9	0.0	0.0
HINDU–I/A Temples	1	NR	NR	1,742	0.7	1.2
Jehovah's Witness	7	NR	NR	NR	-	-
JUD–Conserv	1	239	268	724	0.3	0.5
JUD–Orth	1	1,001	375	1,390	0.5	0.9
JUD–Reform	1	167	295	796	0.3	0.5
LDS–L-D Saints	3	NR	NR	2,905	1.1	1.9
LUTH–E.L.C.A.	8	794	2,161	2,526	1.0	1.7
LUTH–Luth–MO Synod	1	205	412	503	0.2	0.3
LUTH–Wisc Ev Luth Syn	1	126	141	141	0.1	0.1
METH–AME	13	765	3,225	3,926	1.5	2.6
METH–C.M.E.	5	3,750	5,650	6,877	2.6	4.6
METH–So Methodist	1	NR	NR	NR	-	-
METH–Un Methodist	29	4,398	11,881	14,125	5.3	9.4
Muslim Est	2	275	NR	600	0.2	0.4
Non-denom Chr Chs	47	14,690	20,000	21,761	8.2	14.4
ORTHE–Greek Orthodox	1	180	NR	350	0.1	0.2
ORTHO–Coptic Orth Ch	1	13	NR	15	0.0	0.0
PENT–Assemb of God	9	722	601	1,116	0.4	0.7
PENT–Ch God (Cleve)	8	1,344	2,324	2,829	1.1	1.9
PENT–Ch of God Proph	1	NR	24	29	0.0	0.0
PENT–COGIC	4	425	950	1,156	0.4	0.8
PENT–Fire Bapt Hol Ch	1	NR	NR	NR	-	-
PENT–Full Gosp Bapt	1	NR	NR	NR	-	-
PENT–Intl Pent Holiness	2	850	1,040	1,266	0.5	0.8
PENT–Un Pent Ch Intl	2	NR	NR	NR	-	-
PENT–Vineyard	2	145	195	237	0.1	0.2
PRES–Presb Ch (USA)	8	825	1,931	2,350	0.9	1.6
PRES–Presb Ch Amer	5	446	638	724	0.3	0.5
Salvation Army	1	91	114	263	0.1	0.2
Sev Day Adv	4	1,462	2,542	2,924	1.1	1.9
Un C of Christ	1	27	53	65	0.0	0.0
Unit Univ	1	96	130	171	0.1	0.1
Unity Ch	1	NR	NR	NR	-	-
CHATTAHOOCHEE	**8**	**153**	**797**	**1,023**	**9.1**	**100.0**
Bahá'í	0	NR	3	3	0.0	0.3
BAPT–NBC USA	1	0	150	194	1.7	19.0
BAPT–So Bapt Conv	1	100	263	341	3.0	33.3
CHR–Chs of Christ	1	25	25	32	0.3	3.1
Jehovah's Witness	1	NR	NR	NR	-	-
METH–AME	2	0	200	259	2.3	25.3
METH–C.M.E.	1	0	100	130	1.2	12.7
METH–Un Methodist	1	28	56	64	0.6	6.3

NR–Not Reported   - Represents no adherents reported.   Percentages may not total 100 due to rounding.

Table 3: Religious Congregations by County and Group: 2010

Religious Group	Number of Congrega-tions	Number of Attendees	Number of Communicant, Confirmed, or Full Members	Adherents		
				Number of Adherents	% of Total Pop.	% of Total Adh.
CHATTOOGA	**80**	**4,667**	**10,179**	**12,417**	**47.7**	**100.0**
ANG/EPIS–Episcopal	1	24	41	77	0.3	0.6
BAPT–Ind Bapt Flwsp Intl	1	NR	NR	NR	-	-
BAPT–NBC USA	1	0	150	182	0.7	1.5
BAPT–So Bapt Conv	34	2,849	6,881	8,335	32.0	67.1
Chr & Miss Al	1	65	84	88	0.3	0.7
CHR–Chs of Christ	13	715	794	1,039	4.0	8.4
Jehovah's Witness	1	NR	NR	NR	-	-
METH–AME Zion	4	0	400	485	1.9	3.9
METH–Un Methodist	7	396	794	949	3.6	7.6
Non-denom Chr Chs	2	190	180	238	0.9	1.9
PENT–Ch God (Cleve)	3	182	369	447	1.7	3.6
PENT–Ch of God Proph	2	NR	111	134	0.5	1.1
PENT–Cong Hol Ch	2	92	97	118	0.5	1.0
PENT–Un Pent Ch Intl	1	NR	NR	NR	-	-
PRES–Evan Presby Ch	1	NR	30	36	0.1	0.3
PRES–Presb Ch (USA)	4	91	152	184	0.7	1.5
PRES–Presb Ch Amer	1	33	45	46	0.2	0.4
Sev Day Adv	1	30	51	59	0.2	0.5
CHEROKEE	**154**	**29,688**	**59,343**	**91,450**	**42.7**	**100.0**
ANG/EPIS–Anglican NA	1	NR	NR	NR	-	-
ANG/EPIS–Episcopal	1	158	281	281	0.1	0.3
Bahá'í	2	NR	136	136	0.1	0.1
BAPT–Amer Bapt Assn	1	NR	775	990	0.5	1.1
BAPT–NBC USA	1	0	150	192	0.1	0.2
BAPT–So Bapt Conv	49	14,857	35,137	44,883	20.9	49.1
Catholic	2	NR	NR	9,617	4.5	10.5
Ch Cr, Scientst	1	NR	NR	NR	-	-
Ch of Nazarene	1	87	211	211	0.1	0.2
CHR–Chr Chs & Chs Cr	2	NR	1,000	1,277	0.6	1.4
CHR–Chs of Christ	6	487	521	682	0.3	0.7
FRND–Fr Gen Cf	1	NR	0	0	0.0	0.0
Jehovah's Witness	1	NR	NR	NR	-	-
LDS–L-D Saints	4	NR	NR	1,725	0.8	1.9
LUTH–E.L.C.A.	2	351	764	1,091	0.5	1.2
LUTH–Luth-MO Synod	1	202	377	471	0.2	0.5
METH–AME	3	350	1,750	2,235	1.0	2.4
METH–Un Methodist	19	4,435	9,459	14,873	6.9	16.3
Missionary Ch	2	77	0	77	0.0	0.1
Non-denom Chr Chs	20	5,375	5,275	7,901	3.7	8.6
ORTHE–Carp Rus Orth	1	38	NR	60	0.0	0.1
PENT–Assemb of God	6	574	280	695	0.3	0.8
PENT–Ch God (Cleve)	11	1,686	1,770	2,261	1.1	2.5
PENT–Ch of God Proph	2	NR	77	98	0.0	0.1
PENT–Cong Hol Ch	2	89	106	135	0.1	0.1
PENT–Full Gosp Bapt	1	NR	NR	NR	-	-
PENT–Un Pent Ch Intl	1	NR	NR	NR	-	-
PRES–Presb Ch (USA)	5	474	730	932	0.4	1.0
PRES–Presb Ch Amer	2	294	275	318	0.1	0.3
Sev Day Adv	3	154	269	309	0.1	0.3
CLARKE	**104**	**12,986**	**27,671**	**43,817**	**37.5**	**100.0**
ANG/EPIS–Episcopal	2	567	1,264	1,269	1.1	2.9
Bahá'í	1	NR	73	73	0.1	0.2
BAPT–NBC USA	2	500	550	641	0.5	1.5
BAPT–So Bapt Conv	13	2,367	5,473	6,380	5.5	14.6
BUDD–Mahayana	1	NR	NR	28	0.0	0.1
Catholic	1	NR	NR	8,475	7.3	19.3
Ch Cr, Scientst	1	NR	NR	NR	-	-
Chr & Miss Al	1	90	73	170	0.1	0.4
CHR–Chr Ch (Disc)	2	79	287	335	0.3	0.8
CHR–Chr Chs & Chs Cr	1	NR	0	0	0.0	0.0
CHR–Chs of Christ	3	485	449	645	0.6	1.5
CHR–Int Chs of Christ	1	NR	341	398	0.3	0.9
FRND–Fr Gen Cf	1	NR	11	13	0.0	0.0
HINDU–Post Ren	2	NR	NR	153	0.1	0.3
Jehovah's Witness	3	NR	NR	NR	-	-
JUD–Orth	1	22	25	30	0.0	0.1
JUD–Reform	1	78	138	373	0.3	0.9
LDS–L-D Saints	4	NR	NR	1,550	1.3	3.5
LUTH–E.L.C.A.	1	137	214	255	0.2	0.6
LUTH–Luth-MO Synod	2	216	381	455	0.4	1.0
METH–AME	4	680	2,600	3,031	2.6	6.9
METH–Un Methodist	10	2,383	7,821	9,400	8.1	21.5
Metro Comm Ch	1	36	44	51	0.0	0.1
Muslim Est	1	269	NR	762	0.7	1.7
Non-denom Chr Chs	17	2,065	2,710	2,988	2.6	6.8
PENT–Assemb of God	2	143	100	260	0.2	0.6
PENT–Ch God (Cleve)	2	900	1,453	1,694	1.5	3.9
PENT–Ch Lord Jesus Apos	2	NR	NR	NR	-	-
PENT–COGIC	1	0	150	175	0.1	0.4
PENT–Cong Hol Ch	1	80	90	105	0.1	0.2
PENT–Fire Bapt Hol Ch	1	NR	NR	NR	-	-
PENT–Full Gosp Bapt	1	NR	NR	NR	-	-
PENT–Intl Pent Holiness	1	101	341	398	0.3	0.9
PENT–Un Pent Ch Intl	3	NR	NR	NR	-	-
PENT–Vineyard	1	110	160	187	0.2	0.4
PRES–Presb Ch (USA)	3	754	1,786	2,082	1.8	4.8
PRES–Presb Ch Amer	2	461	378	472	0.4	1.1
Salvation Army	1	48	91	175	0.1	0.4
Sev Day Adv	4	248	432	497	0.4	1.1
Unit Univ	1	167	236	297	0.3	0.7
Unity Ch	1	NR	NR	NR	-	-
CLAY	**15**	**364**	**1,610**	**1,937**	**60.9**	**100.0**
Bahá'í	0	NR	4	4	0.1	0.2
BAPT–Natl Mis Bapt Conv	1	0	150	182	5.7	9.4
BAPT–So Bapt Conv	4	248	681	827	26.0	42.7
METH–AME	6	0	600	728	22.9	37.6
METH–Un Methodist	3	81	135	147	4.6	7.6
PRES–Presb Ch (USA)	1	35	40	49	1.5	2.5
CLAYTON	**189**	**38,631**	**77,426**	**115,088**	**44.4**	**100.0**
ANG/EPIS–Anglican NA	2	NR	NR	NR	-	-
ANG/EPIS–Episcopal	1	101	292	312	0.1	0.3
Bahá'í	0	NR	78	78	0.0	0.1
BAPT–Ind Bapt Flwsp Intl	1	NR	NR	NR	-	-
BAPT–Natl Mis Bapt Conv	2	0	300	388	0.1	0.3
BAPT–NBC USA	2	1,650	3,100	4,011	1.5	3.5
BAPT–So Bapt Conv	44	5,346	20,384	26,374	10.2	22.9
BUDD–Mahayana	1	NR	NR	506	0.2	0.4
BUDD–Theravada	2	NR	NR	600	0.2	0.5
Catholic	3	NR	NR	10,533	4.1	9.2
CGOD–Ch God (Ander)	1	57	NR	57	0.0	0.0
Ch of Chr (Hol)	1	NR	NR	NR	-	-
Ch of Nazarene	3	195	367	473	0.2	0.4
Chr & Miss Al	1	133	147	167	0.1	0.1
CHR–Chr Ch (Disc)	1	0	0	0	0.0	0.0
CHR–Chr Chs & Chs Cr	4	NR	708	916	0.4	0.8
CHR–Chs of Christ	8	695	628	786	0.3	0.7
HINDU–I/A Temples	1	NR	NR	863	0.3	0.7
HINDU–Trad Temples	2	NR	NR	9,000	3.5	7.8
Jehovah's Witness	3	NR	NR	NR	-	-
LDS–L-D Saints	3	NR	NR	1,456	0.6	1.3
LUTH–Luth-MO Synod	1	57	142	160	0.1	0.1
METH–AME	6	475	1,580	2,044	0.8	1.8
METH–Un Methodist	14	1,345	4,868	5,472	2.1	4.8
Muslim Est	1	300	NR	1,000	0.4	0.9
Non-denom Chr Chs	48	25,795	40,530	44,049	17.0	38.3
PENT–Assemb of God	4	476	414	714	0.3	0.6
PENT–Ch God (Cleve)	4	373	901	1,166	0.4	1.0
PENT–Ch of God Proph	2	NR	92	119	0.0	0.1
PENT–COGIC	4	800	1,300	1,682	0.6	1.5
PENT–Fire Bapt Hol Ch	1	NR	NR	NR	-	-
PENT–Pent Ch of God	1	70	NR	109	0.0	0.1
PENT–Un Pent Ch Intl	3	NR	NR	NR	-	-
PENT–United Holy Ch	1	NR	NR	NR	-	-
PRES–Presb Ch (USA)	4	199	704	911	0.4	0.8
Salvation Army	1	88	65	191	0.1	0.2
Sev Day Adv	7	476	826	951	0.4	0.8
Unity Ch	1	NR	NR	NR	-	-
CLINCH	**21**	**873**	**2,126**	**2,744**	**40.4**	**100.0**
BAPT–Free Will Bapt	1	NR	73	92	1.4	3.4
BAPT–So Bapt Conv	5	282	594	752	11.1	27.4

NR–Not Reported - Represents no adherents reported. Percentages may not total 100 due to rounding.

Table 3: Religious Congregations by County and Group: 2010

Religious Group	Number of Congregations	Number of Attendees	Number of Communicant, Confirmed, or Full Members	Adherents: Number of Adherents	Adherents: % of Total Pop.	Adherents: % of Total Adh.
CHR–Chs of Christ	1	22	18	22	0.3	0.8
METH–AME	2	0	200	253	3.7	9.2
METH–Cong Meth	1	NR	84	106	1.6	3.9
METH–Un Methodist	2	97	203	217	3.2	7.9
PENT–Assemb of God	1	60	0	94	1.4	3.4
PENT–Ch God (Cleve)	5	412	828	1,049	15.4	38.2
PENT–Ch of God Proph	2	NR	54	68	1.0	2.5
PRES–Presb Ch (USA)	1	0	72	91	1.3	3.3
COBB	**449**	**104,895**	**229,079**	**374,323**	**54.4**	**100.0**
ANG/EPIS–Anglican NA	5	NR	NR	NR	-	-
ANG/EPIS–Episcopal	8	2,235	4,798	5,870	0.9	1.6
Bahá'í	9	NR	785	785	0.1	0.2
BAPT–Amer Bapt USA	1	165	300	374	0.1	0.1
BAPT–Asc Ref Bap Ch Am	1	NR	NR	NR	-	-
BAPT–Free Will Bapt	1	NR	73	91	0.0	0.0
BAPT–Natl Mis Bapt Conv	1	0	150	187	0.0	0.0
BAPT–NBC USA	6	300	1,250	1,560	0.2	0.4
BAPT–Ref Bapt Ch	1	NR	NR	NR	-	-
BAPT–So Bapt Conv	124	28,376	84,249	105,130	15.3	28.1
BRETH–Grace Breth	1	NR	NR	NR	-	-
Calv Chpl	1	NR	NR	NR	-	-
Catholic	7	NR	NR	76,988	11.2	20.6
CGOD–Ch God (Ander)	2	609	NR	609	0.1	0.2
Ch Cr, Scientst	1	NR	NR	NR	-	-
Ch of Nazarene	5	394	407	473	0.1	0.1
Chr & Miss Al	2	250	134	259	0.0	0.1
CHR–Chr Ch (Disc)	2	155	450	562	0.1	0.2
CHR–Chr Chs & Chs Cr	6	NR	641	800	0.1	0.2
CHR–Chs of Christ	12	2,386	2,347	3,028	0.4	0.8
CHR–Int Chs of Christ	1	NR	527	658	0.1	0.2
HINDU–I/A Temples	1	NR	NR	250	0.0	0.1
HINDU–Post Ren	3	NR	NR	42	0.0	0.0
HINDU–Renaiss	1	NR	NR	12	0.0	0.0
HINDU–Trad Temples	1	NR	NR	200	0.0	0.1
Jehovah's Witness	6	NR	NR	NR	-	-
JUD–Conserv	1	586	658	1,777	0.3	0.5
JUD–Orth	2	86	100	120	0.0	0.0
JUD–Reform	1	297	523	1,412	0.2	0.4
LDS–L-D Saints	14	NR	NR	6,642	1.0	1.8
LUTH–E.L.C.A.	6	1,226	2,656	3,310	0.5	0.9
LUTH–Luth-MO Synod	2	486	786	1,028	0.1	0.3
LUTH–Wisc Ev Luth Syn	1	165	308	384	0.1	0.1
METH–AME	7	4,600	7,950	9,920	1.4	2.7
METH–AME Zion	1	0	150	187	0.0	0.0
METH–Cong Meth	1	NR	NR	NR	-	-
METH–Evan Meth Ch	2	NR	NR	NR	-	-
METH–Un Methodist	37	12,139	39,472	53,622	7.8	14.3
Missionary Ch	1	50	0	50	0.0	0.0
Muslim Est	6	1,253	NR	4,087	0.6	1.1
Non-denom Chr Chs	61	34,136	47,066	50,131	7.3	13.4
ORTHE–Greek Orthodox	1	400	NR	1,700	0.2	0.5
PENT–Assemb of God	13	1,609	1,632	2,472	0.4	0.7
PENT–Ch God (Cleve)	18	5,598	19,049	23,770	3.5	6.4
PENT–Ch God Mtn Asm	1	NR	NR	NR	-	-
PENT–Ch of God Proph	8	NR	582	726	0.1	0.2
PENT–COGIC	3	0	300	374	0.1	0.1
PENT–Int Foursq Gos	4	243	337	421	0.1	0.1
PENT–Un Pent Ch Intl	2	NR	NR	NR	-	-
PENT–Vineyard	3	865	1,025	1,279	0.2	0.3
PRES–As Ref Pres Ch	1	NR	24	30	0.0	0.0
PRES–Kor Pres Abroad	1	NR	NR	NR	-	-
PRES–Orth Pres Ch	1	75	68	94	0.0	0.0
PRES–Presb Ch (USA)	15	2,887	5,555	6,932	1.0	1.9
PRES–Presb Ch Amer	9	1,545	1,661	2,137	0.3	0.6
REF–Comm Ref Evan	1	NR	NR	NR	-	-
Salvation Army	1	45	82	295	0.0	0.1
Sev Day Adv	11	1,490	2,590	2,981	0.4	0.8
Un C of Christ	1	111	279	348	0.1	0.1
Unit Univ	1	133	115	186	0.0	0.0
Unity Ch	2	NR	NR	NR	-	-
Zoroastrian	0	NR	NR	30	0.0	0.0

Religious Group	Number of Congregations	Number of Attendees	Number of Communicant, Confirmed, or Full Members	Adherents: Number of Adherents	Adherents: % of Total Pop.	Adherents: % of Total Adh.
COFFEE	**91**	**6,932**	**14,303**	**20,167**	**47.6**	**100.0**
ANG/EPIS–Episcopal	1	69	151	203	0.5	1.0
Bahá'í	0	NR	2	2	0.0	0.0
BAPT–So Bapt Conv	29	3,336	7,848	9,852	23.3	48.9
Catholic	1	NR	NR	1,208	2.9	6.0
CGOD–Ch God (Ander)	1	7	NR	7	0.0	0.0
CHR–Chs of Christ	2	66	67	87	0.2	0.4
Jehovah's Witness	1	NR	NR	NR	-	-
LDS–L-D Saints	2	NR	NR	1,073	2.5	5.3
METH–AME	4	40	430	540	1.3	2.7
METH–C.M.E.	2	0	250	314	0.7	1.6
METH–Un Methodist	9	421	1,190	1,346	3.2	6.7
Non-denom Chr Chs	13	1,300	1,631	1,763	4.2	8.7
PENT–Assemb of God	2	265	31	275	0.6	1.4
PENT–Ch God (Cleve)	14	1,280	2,368	2,973	7.0	14.7
PENT–Ch of God by Faith	3	NR	NR	NR	-	-
PENT–Ch of God Proph	3	NR	165	207	0.5	1.0
PENT–Pent Ch of God	1	70	NR	109	0.3	0.5
PRES–Presb Ch (USA)	1	50	122	153	0.4	0.8
Sev Day Adv	2	28	48	55	0.1	0.3
COLQUITT	**95**	**8,017**	**19,522**	**26,293**	**57.8**	**100.0**
ANG/EPIS–Episcopal	2	53	93	93	0.2	0.4
Bahá'í	0	NR	20	20	0.0	0.1
BAPT–Amer Bapt Assn	1	NR	85	109	0.2	0.4
BAPT–Free Will Bapt	5	NR	365	466	1.0	1.8
BAPT–NBC USA	1	0	0	0	0.0	0.0
BAPT–So Bapt Conv	47	4,839	13,798	17,631	38.8	67.1
Catholic	1	NR	NR	1,300	2.9	4.9
Ch of Nazarene	1	112	225	274	0.6	1.0
Chr & Miss Al	1	163	90	210	0.5	0.8
CHR–Chs of Christ	1	75	68	75	0.2	0.3
Jehovah's Witness	1	NR	NR	NR	-	-
LDS–L-D Saints	1	NR	NR	506	1.1	1.9
METH–AME	3	0	300	383	0.8	1.5
METH–C.M.E.	1	0	100	128	0.3	0.5
METH–Un Methodist	9	407	1,120	1,178	2.6	4.5
Non-denom Chr Chs	6	1,330	1,820	1,896	4.2	7.2
PENT–Assemb of God	4	529	326	625	1.4	2.4
PENT–Ch God (Cleve)	3	247	274	350	0.8	1.3
PENT–Ch of God Proph	1	NR	24	31	0.1	0.1
PENT–COGIC	2	0	300	383	0.8	1.5
PENT–Un Pent Ch Intl	1	NR	NR	NR	-	-
PRES–Presb Ch (USA)	1	160	338	432	0.9	1.6
Sev Day Adv	2	102	176	203	0.4	0.8
COLUMBIA	**103**	**16,780**	**29,672**	**47,891**	**38.6**	**100.0**
ANG/EPIS–Episcopal	3	295	609	676	0.5	1.4
Bahá'í	1	NR	75	75	0.1	0.2
BAPT–Free Will Bapt	1	NR	73	92	0.1	0.2
BAPT–NBC USA	4	240	829	1,046	0.8	2.2
BAPT–So Bapt Conv	25	6,474	14,569	18,377	14.8	38.4
Catholic	1	NR	NR	4,666	3.8	9.7
Ch Cr, Scientst	1	NR	NR	NR	-	-
CHR–Chr Chs & Chs Cr	2	NR	360	454	0.4	0.9
CHR–Chs of Christ	4	493	480	647	0.5	1.4
Christian Brethren	1	NR	NR	NR	-	-
HINDU–I/A Temples	1	NR	NR	1,742	1.4	3.6
HINDU–Trad Temples	1	NR	NR	1,500	1.2	3.1
Jain	2	NR	NR	NR	-	-
Jehovah's Witness	2	NR	NR	NR	-	-
JUD–Orth	1	43	50	60	0.0	0.1
LDS–L-D Saints	3	NR	NR	2,008	1.6	4.2
LUTH–Nor Amer Luth C	1	NR	NR	NR	-	-
LUTH–Wisc Ev Luth Syn	1	121	183	238	0.2	0.5
METH–C.M.E.	1	21	100	126	0.1	0.3
METH–Un Methodist	13	2,750	6,132	8,483	6.8	17.7
METH–Wesleyan	1	176	89	229	0.2	0.5
Non-denom Chr Chs	11	1,504	1,675	1,931	1.6	4.0
ORTHO–Coptic Orth Ch	1	22	NR	26	0.0	0.1
ORTHO–Malan Dioc Am	1	8	NR	24	0.0	0.1
PENT–Assemb of God	1	72	79	79	0.1	0.2
PENT–Ch God (Cleve)	4	3,166	2,421	3,054	2.5	6.4

NR–Not Reported - Represents no adherents reported. Percentages may not total 100 due to rounding.

Table 3: Religious Congregations by County and Group: 2010

Religious Group	Number of Congrega-tions	Number of Attendees	Number of Communicant, Confirmed, or Full Members	Adherents: Number of Adherents	Adherents: % of Total Pop.	Adherents: % of Total Adh.
PENT–Cong Hol Ch	2	102	63	79	0.1	0.2
PENT–Un Pent Ch Intl	2	NR	NR	NR	-	-
PENT–Vineyard	1	378	552	696	0.6	1.5
PRES–Presb Ch (USA)	1	35	41	52	0.0	0.1
PRES–Presb Ch Amer	5	558	731	886	0.7	1.9
Sev Day Adv	3	322	561	645	0.5	1.3
Sikh	1	NR	NR	NR	-	-
COOK	**39**	**2,582**	**6,938**	**8,878**	**51.6**	**100.0**
Bahá'í	0	NR	3	3	0.0	0.0
BAPT–Asc Ref Bap Ch Am	1	NR	NR	NR	-	-
BAPT–Free Will Bapt	1	NR	73	93	0.5	1.0
BAPT–Ref Bapt Ch	1	NR	NR	NR	-	-
BAPT–So Bapt Conv	13	1,451	4,027	5,112	29.7	57.6
Catholic	1	NR	NR	279	1.6	3.1
CHR–Chs of Christ	2	183	220	266	1.5	3.0
Jehovah's Witness	1	NR	NR	NR	-	-
METH–AME	4	0	500	635	3.7	7.2
METH–Un Methodist	6	339	824	965	5.6	10.9
Non-denom Chr Chs	4	400	550	575	3.3	6.5
PENT–Assemb of God	1	111	130	175	1.0	2.0
PENT–Ch God (Cleve)	2	90	454	576	3.3	6.5
PENT–COGIC	1	0	150	190	1.1	2.1
PRES–Presb Ch (USA)	1	8	7	9	0.1	0.1
COWETA	**158**	**21,706**	**42,592**	**59,535**	**46.8**	**100.0**
ANG/EPIS–Anglican NA	1	NR	NR	NR	-	-
ANG/EPIS–Episcopal	1	222	639	709	0.6	1.2
Bahá'í	0	NR	88	88	0.1	0.1
BAPT–Ind Bapt Flwsp Intl	1	NR	NR	NR	-	-
BAPT–NBC USA	3	0	650	825	0.6	1.4
BAPT–Ref Bapt Ch	1	NR	NR	NR	-	-
BAPT–So Bapt Conv	47	10,807	21,233	26,951	21.2	45.3
Catholic	2	NR	NR	5,383	4.2	9.0
Ch of Nazarene	1	86	78	95	0.1	0.2
CHR–Chr Ch (Disc)	1	0	27	34	0.0	0.1
CHR–Chr Chs & Chs Cr	3	NR	1,075	1,364	1.1	2.3
CHR–Chs of Christ	6	501	507	688	0.5	1.2
Jehovah's Witness	2	NR	NR	NR	-	-
LDS–L-D Saints	4	NR	NR	1,581	1.2	2.7
LUTH–E.L.C.A.	1	120	173	187	0.1	0.3
LUTH–Luth Cong Msn Chr	1	10	45	57	0.0	0.1
LUTH–Luth–MO Synod	1	60	68	86	0.1	0.1
LUTH–Wisc Ev Luth Syn	1	221	242	379	0.3	0.6
METH–AME	7	50	848	1,076	0.8	1.8
METH–C.M.E.	1	0	150	190	0.1	0.3
METH–Free Methodist	1	55	0	55	0.0	0.1
METH–Un Methodist	28	2,644	7,156	8,276	6.5	13.9
Non-denom Chr Chs	20	3,845	5,505	6,045	4.7	10.2
PENT–Assemb of God	4	624	506	828	0.7	1.4
PENT–Ch God (Cleve)	5	1,228	1,518	1,927	1.5	3.2
PENT–Ch of God Proph	2	NR	72	91	0.1	0.2
PENT–COGIC	1	0	0	0	0.0	0.0
PENT–Cong Hol Ch	1	410	469	595	0.5	1.0
PENT–Intl Pent Holiness	1	40	79	100	0.1	0.2
PENT–Pent Ch of God	1	70	NR	109	0.1	0.2
PENT–Un Pent Ch Intl	3	NR	NR	NR	-	-
PENT–Vineyard	1	110	131	166	0.1	0.3
PRES–As Ref Pres Ch	1	NR	226	287	0.2	0.5
PRES–Presb Ch (USA)	1	177	471	598	0.5	1.0
PRES–Presb Ch Amer	1	100	69	111	0.1	0.2
Sev Day Adv	2	326	567	652	0.5	1.1
Zoroastrian	0	NR	NR	2	0.0	0.0
CRAWFORD	**19**	**590**	**2,082**	**2,430**	**19.2**	**100.0**
Bahá'í	0	NR	38	38	0.3	1.6
BAPT–Asc Ref Bap Ch Am	1	NR	NR	NR	-	-
BAPT–NBC USA	1	0	150	181	1.4	7.4
BAPT–Ref Bapt Ch	1	NR	NR	NR	-	-
BAPT–So Bapt Conv	3	268	667	805	6.4	33.1
CHR–Chs of Christ	1	10	10	10	0.1	0.4
METH–AME	2	0	250	302	2.4	12.4
METH–C.M.E.	3	50	490	591	4.7	24.3
METH–Un Methodist	4	162	327	353	2.8	14.5
Non-denom Chr Chs	1	100	150	150	1.2	6.2
PENT–Ch Lord Jesus Apos	1	NR	NR	NR	-	-
PENT–Ch of God by Faith	1	NR	NR	NR	-	-
CRISP	**50**	**2,980**	**8,231**	**10,592**	**45.2**	**100.0**
ANG/EPIS–Episcopal	1	47	76	81	0.3	0.8
Bahá'í	0	NR	26	26	0.1	0.2
BAPT–Free Will Bapt	1	NR	73	91	0.4	0.9
BAPT–So Bapt Conv	25	1,979	5,740	7,173	30.6	67.7
Catholic	1	NR	NR	604	2.6	5.7
CHR–Chs of Christ	3	153	128	168	0.7	1.6
Jehovah's Witness	1	NR	NR	NR	-	-
METH–AME	1	0	100	125	0.5	1.2
METH–Un Methodist	6	421	1,439	1,566	6.7	14.8
Non-denom Chr Chs	2	215	275	294	1.3	2.8
PENT–Assemb of God	1	32	28	32	0.1	0.3
PENT–Ch God (Cleve)	1	83	94	117	0.5	1.1
PENT–Ch of God by Faith	1	NR	NR	NR	-	-
PENT–Ch of God Proph	2	NR	124	155	0.7	1.5
PENT–COGIC	1	50	75	94	0.4	0.9
PENT–Un Pent Ch Intl	1	NR	NR	NR	-	-
PRES–Presb Ch (USA)	2	0	53	66	0.3	0.6
DADE	**32**	**2,767**	**4,954**	**6,092**	**36.6**	**100.0**
Bahá'í	0	NR	2	2	0.0	0.0
BAPT–So Bapt Conv	8	1,041	2,341	2,789	16.8	45.8
Catholic	1	NR	NR	274	1.6	4.5
CHR–Chs of Christ	4	255	273	333	2.0	5.5
Jehovah's Witness	1	NR	NR	NR	-	-
METH–Un Methodist	7	516	1,059	1,254	7.5	20.6
Non-denom Chr Chs	3	530	650	700	4.2	11.5
PENT–Ch God (Cleve)	5	278	374	446	2.7	7.3
Sev Day Adv	3	147	255	294	1.8	4.8
DAWSON	**41**	**4,423**	**7,649**	**10,477**	**46.9**	**100.0**
Bahá'í	0	NR	3	3	0.0	0.0
BAPT–Ref Bapt Ch	1	NR	NR	NR	-	-
BAPT–So Bapt Conv	16	1,773	3,868	4,700	21.0	44.9
Catholic	1	NR	NR	447	2.0	4.3
CHR–Chr Chs & Chs Cr	1	NR	205	249	1.1	2.4
CHR–Chs of Christ	1	30	37	40	0.2	0.4
Jehovah's Witness	1	NR	NR	NR	-	-
LDS–L-D Saints	2	NR	NR	1,032	4.6	9.9
METH–Un Methodist	5	412	812	935	4.2	8.9
Non-denom Chr Chs	8	1,898	2,210	2,460	11.0	23.5
PENT–Ch God (Cleve)	1	160	250	304	1.4	2.9
PENT–Ch of God Proph	1	NR	122	148	0.7	1.4
PRES–Presb Ch Amer	2	100	55	59	0.3	0.6
Sev Day Adv	1	50	87	100	0.4	1.0
DECATUR	**88**	**4,692**	**13,271**	**17,348**	**62.3**	**100.0**
ANG/EPIS–Episcopal	1	45	72	88	0.3	0.5
Bahá'í	0	NR	23	23	0.1	0.1
BAPT–Free Will Bapt	3	NR	219	272	1.0	1.6
BAPT–Natl Mis Bapt Conv	3	0	450	559	2.0	3.2
BAPT–NBC USA	1	0	150	186	0.7	1.1
BAPT–So Bapt Conv	32	2,827	7,417	9,221	33.1	53.2
Catholic	1	NR	NR	699	2.5	4.0
CGOD–Ch God (Ander)	1	38	NR	38	0.1	0.2
Ch of Nazarene	1	80	83	83	0.3	0.5
CHR–Chr Chs & Chs Cr	1	NR	120	149	0.5	0.9
CHR–Chs of Christ	3	188	188	223	0.8	1.3
Jehovah's Witness	1	NR	NR	NR	-	-
JUD–Reform	1	6	11	30	0.1	0.2
LDS–L-D Saints	1	NR	NR	230	0.8	1.3
METH–AME	13	0	1,500	1,865	6.7	10.8
METH–Un Methodist	11	538	1,477	1,709	6.1	9.9
Non-denom Chr Chs	4	420	530	592	2.1	3.4
PENT–Assemb of God	3	175	98	228	0.8	1.3
PENT–Ch God (Cleve)	3	190	530	659	2.4	3.8
PENT–Ch of God Proph	1	NR	19	24	0.1	0.1

NR–Not Reported - Represents no adherents reported. Percentages may not total 100 due to rounding.

Table 3: Religious Congregations by County and Group: 2010

Religious Group	Number of Congregations	Number of Attendees	Number of Communicant, Confirmed, or Full Members	Adherents: Number of Adherents	Adherents: % of Total Pop.	Adherents: % of Total Adh.
PENT–Un Pent Ch Intl	1	NR	NR	NR	-	-
PRES–Presb Ch (USA)	1	140	306	380	1.4	2.2
Sev Day Adv	1	45	78	90	0.3	0.5
DEKALB	**520**	**112,371**	**194,172**	**331,999**	**48.0**	**100.0**
ANG/EPIS–Anglican NA	2	NR	NR	NR	-	-
ANG/EPIS–Episcopal	9	2,081	5,099	7,158	1.0	2.2
Bahá'í	6	NR	998	998	0.1	0.3
BAPT–Alliance Bapt	1	NR	NR	NR	-	-
BAPT–Amer Bapt USA	1	275	610	751	0.1	0.2
BAPT–Natl Mis Bapt Conv	2	0	1,150	1,416	0.2	0.4
BAPT–NBC Amer	1	275	250	308	0.0	0.1
BAPT–NBC USA	11	6,160	9,586	11,807	1.7	3.6
BAPT–S-D Baptist Gen Con	2	NR	NR	NR	-	-
BAPT–So Bapt Conv	85	17,461	44,132	54,355	7.9	16.4
BUDD–Mahayana	9	NR	NR	4,271	0.6	1.3
BUDD–Theravada	4	NR	NR	2,427	0.4	0.7
BUDD–Vajrayana	3	NR	NR	124	0.0	0.0
Catholic	11	NR	NR	62,844	9.1	18.9
CGOD–Ch God (Ander)	1	21	NR	21	0.0	0.0
Ch Cr, Scientst	1	NR	NR	NR	-	-
Ch of Chr (Hol)	2	NR	NR	NR	-	-
Chr & Miss Al	4	318	420	507	0.1	0.2
CHR–Chr Ch (Disc)	5	1,439	8,470	10,432	1.5	3.1
CHR–Chr Chs & Chs Cr	3	NR	1,165	1,435	0.2	0.4
CHR–Chs of Christ	12	4,372	4,797	6,175	0.9	1.9
Evan Cov Ch	1	435	223	566	0.1	0.2
Evan Free Ch	1	75	NR	75	0.0	0.0
FRND–Fr Gen Cf	1	NR	131	161	0.0	0.0
HINDU–Post Ren	2	NR	NR	35	0.0	0.0
Jehovah's Witness	8	NR	NR	NR	-	-
JUD–Conserv	1	436	489	1,320	0.2	0.4
JUD–Orth	7	3,600	1,350	5,000	0.7	1.5
JUD–Reconst	1	157	201	543	0.1	0.2
LDS–L-D Saints	4	NR	NR	2,763	0.4	0.8
LUTH–E.L.C.A.	12	778	1,281	1,659	0.2	0.5
LUTH–Luth–MO Synod	5	449	822	1,022	0.1	0.3
LUTH–Nor Amer Luth C	1	NR	NR	NR	-	-
MENN–Mennonite USA	1	25	21	26	0.0	0.0
METH–AME	15	2,227	6,396	7,878	1.1	2.4
METH–AME Zion	3	150	425	523	0.1	0.2
METH–C.M.E.	1	0	100	123	0.0	0.0
METH–Un Methodist	45	7,784	24,946	30,527	4.4	9.2
METH–Wesleyan	2	117	114	152	0.0	0.0
Metro Comm Ch	2	225	332	409	0.1	0.1
MORAV–Morav Ch-South	1	53	124	154	0.0	0.0
Muslim Est	12	4,688	NR	12,885	1.9	3.9
New Apost Ch	1	NR	NR	NR	-	-
Non-denom Chr Chs	90	36,687	46,640	52,696	7.6	15.9
ORTHE–Greek Orthodox	1	600	NR	3,000	0.4	0.9
ORTHO–Eritrean Orth	2	625	NR	1,050	0.2	0.3
ORTHO–Ethiopian Orth	3	NR	NR	NR	-	-
ORTHO–Malan Dioc Am	1	100	NR	300	0.0	0.1
ORTHO–Malan Syr Orth	1	55	NR	108	0.0	0.0
PENT–Assemb of God	3	1,078	833	3,569	0.5	1.1
PENT–Ch God (Cleve)	12	1,406	2,137	2,632	0.4	0.8
PENT–Ch Lord Jesus Apos	3	NR	NR	NR	-	-
PENT–Ch of God by Faith	1	NR	NR	NR	-	-
PENT–Ch of God Proph	5	NR	411	506	0.1	0.2
PENT–COGIC	13	2,075	4,200	5,173	0.7	1.6
PENT–Full Gosp Bapt	7	NR	NR	NR	-	-
PENT–Int Foursq Gos	1	43	32	39	0.0	0.0
PENT–Int Pent C Chr	1	15	NR	40	0.0	0.0
PENT–Intl Pent Holiness	2	595	710	874	0.1	0.3
PENT–Un Pent Ch Intl	5	NR	NR	NR	-	-
PENT–United Holy Ch	2	NR	NR	NR	-	-
PENT–Vineyard	1	340	600	739	0.1	0.2
PRES–As Ref Pres Ch	1	NR	46	57	0.0	0.0
PRES–Korean Pres Amer	1	NR	NR	NR	-	-
PRES–Orth Pres Ch	1	122	130	163	0.0	0.0
PRES–Presb Ch (USA)	23	4,774	8,654	10,659	1.5	3.2
PRES–Presb Ch Amer	8	2,550	3,135	3,630	0.5	1.1
REF–Christian Ref	1	70	90	111	0.0	0.0
Salvation Army	4	575	725	991	0.1	0.3

Religious Group	Number of Congregations	Number of Attendees	Number of Communicant, Confirmed, or Full Members	Adherents: Number of Adherents	Adherents: % of Total Pop.	Adherents: % of Total Adh.
Sev Day Adv	17	3,212	5,585	6,425	0.9	1.9
Sikh	1	NR	NR	NR	-	-
Un C of Christ	4	3,346	5,890	7,254	1.0	2.2
Unit Univ	2	502	722	1,102	0.2	0.3
Unity Ch	1	NR	NR	NR	-	-
Zoroastrian	0	NR	NR	31	0.0	0.0
DODGE	**77**	**4,265**	**11,117**	**13,725**	**63.0**	**100.0**
Bahá'í	0	NR	9	9	0.0	0.1
BAPT–Free Will Bapt	5	NR	365	440	2.0	3.2
BAPT–So Bapt Conv	43	3,325	9,222	11,124	51.0	81.0
Catholic	1	NR	NR	328	1.5	2.4
Ch of Nazarene	1	80	102	103	0.5	0.8
CHR–Chr Ch (Disc)	2	20	60	72	0.3	0.5
CHR–Chs of Christ	1	48	45	58	0.3	0.4
Jehovah's Witness	1	NR	NR	NR	-	-
METH–AME	2	45	150	181	0.8	1.3
METH–C.M.E.	1	10	20	24	0.1	0.2
METH–Un Methodist	8	271	551	638	2.9	4.6
Non-denom Chr Chs	1	50	50	62	0.3	0.5
PENT–Assemb of God	1	80	75	122	0.6	0.9
PENT–Ch God (Cleve)	5	277	347	419	1.9	3.1
PENT–Cong Hol Ch	2	59	41	49	0.2	0.4
PENT–Un Pent Ch Intl	1	NR	NR	NR	-	-
PRES–Presb Ch (USA)	2	0	80	96	0.4	0.7
DOOLY	**40**	**1,773**	**4,731**	**5,603**	**37.6**	**100.0**
Bahá'í	0	NR	100	100	0.7	1.8
BAPT–Amer Bapt Assn	1	NR	85	102	0.7	1.8
BAPT–Free Will Bapt	2	NR	146	175	1.2	3.1
BAPT–NBC USA	1	0	150	179	1.2	3.2
BAPT–So Bapt Conv	21	1,049	2,968	3,548	23.8	63.3
Jehovah's Witness	1	NR	NR	NR	-	-
METH–C.M.E.	1	20	40	48	0.3	0.9
METH–Un Methodist	10	404	900	1,075	7.2	19.2
Non-denom Chr Chs	2	168	224	235	1.6	4.2
PENT–Ch God (Cleve)	1	132	118	141	0.9	2.5
DOUGHERTY	**134**	**20,843**	**41,404**	**54,726**	**57.9**	**100.0**
ANG/EPIS–Episcopal	3	413	813	995	1.1	1.8
Bahá'í	0	NR	78	78	0.1	0.1
BAPT–Free Will Bapt	3	NR	219	275	0.3	0.5
BAPT–NBC USA	11	1,350	3,125	3,919	4.1	7.2
BAPT–So Bapt Conv	22	4,537	11,700	14,674	15.5	26.8
Catholic	1	NR	NR	3,963	4.2	7.2
Ch of Nazarene	2	107	207	207	0.2	0.4
CHR–Chr Ch (Disc)	1	50	108	135	0.1	0.2
CHR–Chr Chs & Chs Cr	1	NR	150	188	0.2	0.3
CHR–Chs of Christ	7	1,041	1,306	1,418	1.5	2.6
Christian Brethren	1	NR	NR	NR	-	-
Jehovah's Witness	2	NR	NR	NR	-	-
JUD–Reform	1	50	88	238	0.3	0.4
LDS–L-D Saints	1	NR	NR	1,121	1.2	2.0
LUTH–E.L.C.A.	1	44	85	92	0.1	0.2
LUTH–Luth–MO Synod	1	70	96	110	0.1	0.2
METH–AME	1	200	370	464	0.5	0.8
METH–C.M.E.	2	0	250	314	0.3	0.6
METH–So Methodist	1	NR	NR	NR	-	-
METH–Un Methodist	9	1,701	6,297	7,170	7.6	13.1
Muslim Est	2	540	NR	1,524	1.6	2.8
Non-denom Chr Chs	42	9,280	13,631	14,230	15.0	26.0
ORTHE–Holy Orth in NA	1	15	NR	20	0.0	0.0
PENT–Assemb of God	1	360	510	510	0.5	0.9
PENT–Ch God (Cleve)	4	229	454	569	0.6	1.0
PENT–Ch of God Proph	1	NR	6	8	0.0	0.0
PENT–COGIC	3	250	700	878	0.9	1.6
PENT–Un Pent Ch Intl	1	NR	NR	NR	-	-
PRES–Presb Ch (USA)	3	299	641	804	0.9	1.5
PRES–Presb Ch Amer	1	52	54	67	0.1	0.1
Salvation Army	1	52	163	349	0.4	0.6
Sev Day Adv	2	203	353	406	0.4	0.7
Unity Ch	1	NR	NR	NR	-	-

NR–Not Reported   - Represents no adherents reported.   Percentages may not total 100 due to rounding.

Table 3: Religious Congregations by County and Group: 2010

Religious Group	Number of Congregations	Number of Attendees	Number of Communicant, Confirmed, or Full Members	Adherents		
				Number of Adherents	% of Total Pop.	% of Total Adh.
DOUGLAS	**118**	**21,312**	**43,275**	**66,045**	**49.9**	**100.0**
ANG/EPIS–Anglican NA	2	NR	NR	NR	-	-
ANG/EPIS–Episcopal	2	146	225	225	0.2	0.3
Bahá'í	1	NR	87	87	0.1	0.1
BAPT–NBC USA	1	300	300	383	0.3	0.6
BAPT–Ref Bapt Ch	1	NR	NR	NR	-	-
BAPT–So Bapt Conv	28	8,039	22,686	28,984	21.9	43.9
Catholic	2	NR	NR	9,360	7.1	14.2
CGOD–Ch God (Ander)	1	42	NR	42	0.0	0.1
Ch of Nazarene	1	59	104	104	0.1	0.2
CHR–Chr Chs & Chs Cr	3	NR	450	575	0.4	0.9
CHR–Chs of Christ	6	419	398	526	0.4	0.8
Evan Cov Ch	1	49	53	64	0.0	0.1
Jehovah's Witness	2	NR	NR	NR	-	-
LDS–L-D Saints	3	NR	NR	1,169	0.9	1.8
LUTH–E.L.C.A.	1	139	225	333	0.3	0.5
LUTH–Luth–MO Synod	1	105	189	231	0.2	0.3
METH–AME	3	205	285	364	0.3	0.6
METH–Evan Meth Ch	1	NR	NR	NR	-	-
METH–Un Methodist	8	1,810	5,113	6,305	4.8	9.5
Muslim Est	1	269	NR	762	0.6	1.2
Non-denom Chr Chs	28	5,413	6,933	7,357	5.6	11.1
PENT–Assemb of God	4	2,198	1,808	3,555	2.7	5.4
PENT–Ch God (Cleve)	6	873	2,420	3,092	2.3	4.7
PENT–Ch of God Proph	1	NR	92	118	0.1	0.2
PENT–Intl Pent Holiness	1	28	28	36	0.0	0.1
PENT–Un Pent Ch Intl	2	NR	NR	NR	-	-
PENT–Vineyard	1	80	100	128	0.1	0.2
PRES–Presb Ch (USA)	1	437	846	1,081	0.8	1.6
PRES–Presb Ch Amer	2	319	269	399	0.3	0.6
Sev Day Adv	3	382	664	765	0.6	1.2
EARLY	**55**	**1,877**	**6,989**	**8,791**	**79.9**	**100.0**
ANG/EPIS–Episcopal	1	8	14	14	0.1	0.2
Bahá'í	0	NR	7	7	0.1	0.1
BAPT–Free Will Bapt	4	NR	292	364	3.3	4.1
BAPT–Natl Mis Bapt Conv	4	0	600	749	6.8	8.5
BAPT–Orig Free Will Bapt	3	270	369	460	4.2	5.2
BAPT–So Bapt Conv	12	852	2,929	3,655	33.2	41.6
Catholic	1	NR	NR	135	1.2	1.5
CHR–Chs of Christ	3	103	95	126	1.1	1.4
Jehovah's Witness	1	NR	NR	NR	-	-
METH–AME	11	65	1,310	1,635	14.9	18.6
METH–C.M.E.	1	0	150	187	1.7	2.1
METH–Un Methodist	5	290	752	790	7.2	9.0
Non-denom Chr Chs	1	30	50	50	0.5	0.6
PENT–Assemb of God	3	65	95	222	2.0	2.5
PENT–Ch God (Cleve)	1	40	76	95	0.9	1.1
PENT–Un Pent Ch Intl	1	NR	NR	NR	-	-
PRES–Presb Ch (USA)	2	97	151	188	1.7	2.1
Sev Day Adv	1	57	99	114	1.0	1.3
ECHOLS	**6**	**276**	**588**	**776**	**19.2**	**100.0**
BAPT–So Bapt Conv	2	125	347	448	11.1	57.7
CHR–Chs of Christ	1	35	35	40	1.0	5.2
METH–Un Methodist	2	62	116	172	4.3	22.2
PENT–Ch God (Cleve)	1	54	90	116	2.9	14.9
EFFINGHAM	**77**	**7,270**	**15,618**	**20,859**	**39.9**	**100.0**
ANG/EPIS–Episcopal	1	44	80	80	0.2	0.4
Bahá'í	0	NR	2	2	0.0	0.0
BAPT–Asc Ref Bap Ch Am	1	NR	NR	NR	-	-
BAPT–NBC USA	1	0	150	192	0.4	0.9
BAPT–Ref Bapt Ch	1	NR	NR	NR	-	-
BAPT–So Bapt Conv	22	3,497	7,847	10,040	19.2	48.1
Catholic	1	NR	NR	400	0.8	1.9
CGOD–Ch God (Ander)	1	25	NR	25	0.0	0.1
CHR–Chr Ch (Disc)	1	91	169	216	0.4	1.0
CHR–Chr Chs & Chs Cr	3	NR	200	256	0.5	1.2
CHR–Chs of Christ	2	163	127	187	0.4	0.9
Evan Free Ch	1	60	NR	60	0.1	0.3
Jehovah's Witness	1	NR	NR	NR	-	-
LDS–L-D Saints	1	NR	NR	480	0.9	2.3
LUTH–E.L.C.A.	3	227	825	1,124	2.2	5.4
LUTH–Luth Cong Msn Chr	5	410	924	1,182	2.3	5.7
METH–AME	4	40	510	653	1.2	3.1
METH–So Methodist	1	NR	NR	NR	-	-
METH–Un Methodist	11	1,099	2,542	3,108	5.9	14.9
Non-denom Chr Chs	6	905	1,097	1,168	2.2	5.6
ORTHE–Orth Ch in Amer	1	40	NR	75	0.1	0.4
PENT–Assemb of God	2	108	30	185	0.4	0.9
PENT–Ch God (Cleve)	3	486	1,025	1,311	2.5	6.3
PENT–Ch Lord Jesus Apos	1	NR	NR	NR	-	-
PENT–Ch of God Proph	1	NR	18	23	0.0	0.1
PENT–Intl Pent Holiness	1	40	21	27	0.1	0.1
PRES–Presb Ch (USA)	1	35	51	65	0.1	0.3
ELBERT	**66**	**3,276**	**9,328**	**11,434**	**56.7**	**100.0**
ANG/EPIS–Episcopal	1	17	35	35	0.2	0.3
Bahá'í	0	NR	1	1	0.0	0.0
BAPT–NBC USA	2	75	350	426	2.1	3.7
BAPT–So Bapt Conv	20	1,724	4,861	5,913	29.3	51.7
Catholic	1	NR	NR	178	0.9	1.6
CHR–Chr Chs & Chs Cr	1	NR	250	304	1.5	2.7
CHR–Chs of Christ	2	65	65	65	0.3	0.6
CONG–Cong Chr, NA	1	NR	45	55	0.3	0.5
Jehovah's Witness	1	NR	NR	NR	-	-
LDS–L-D Saints	1	NR	NR	192	1.0	1.7
LUTH–E.L.C.A.	1	25	59	59	0.3	0.5
METH–AME	1	0	100	122	0.6	1.1
METH–C.M.E.	4	0	600	730	3.6	6.4
METH–Un Methodist	14	740	1,923	2,074	10.3	18.1
METH–Wesleyan	1	12	16	16	0.1	0.1
Non-denom Chr Chs	1	25	25	31	0.2	0.3
PENT–Assemb of God	1	20	0	20	0.1	0.2
PENT–Ch God (Cleve)	3	206	518	630	3.1	5.5
PENT–Ch of God Proph	1	NR	6	7	0.0	0.1
PENT–Fire Bapt Hol Ch	1	NR	NR	NR	-	-
PENT–Intl Pent Holiness	4	276	310	377	1.9	3.3
PRES–As Ref Pres Ch	1	NR	24	29	0.1	0.3
PRES–Presb Ch (USA)	3	91	140	170	0.8	1.5
EMANUEL	**53**	**2,760**	**7,270**	**9,479**	**41.9**	**100.0**
ANG/EPIS–Episcopal	1	25	41	60	0.3	0.6
BAPT–Free Will Bapt	2	NR	146	182	0.8	1.9
BAPT–Natl Mis Bapt Conv	1	0	150	187	0.8	2.0
BAPT–NBC USA	1	95	196	245	1.1	2.6
BAPT–So Bapt Conv	16	1,395	4,093	5,106	22.6	53.9
Catholic	1	NR	NR	495	2.2	5.2
Ch of Nazarene	1	44	34	56	0.2	0.6
CHR–Chs of Christ	1	20	20	25	0.1	0.3
Jehovah's Witness	1	NR	NR	NR	-	-
LDS–L-D Saints	1	NR	NR	146	0.6	1.5
METH–AME	8	0	800	998	4.4	10.5
METH–Un Methodist	9	597	1,160	1,212	5.4	12.8
Non-denom Chr Chs	1	100	150	150	0.7	1.6
PENT–Assemb of God	1	16	0	18	0.1	0.2
PENT–Ch God (Cleve)	5	416	415	518	2.3	5.5
PENT–Intl Pent Holiness	2	52	57	71	0.3	0.7
PRES–Presb Ch (USA)	1	0	8	10	0.0	0.1
EVANS	**26**	**1,544**	**3,751**	**4,771**	**43.4**	**100.0**
Bahá'í	0	NR	2	2	0.0	0.0
BAPT–So Bapt Conv	10	935	2,305	2,902	26.4	60.8
Catholic	2	NR	NR	250	2.3	5.2
Ch of Nazarene	1	21	59	59	0.5	1.2
CHR–Chs of Christ	1	30	30	36	0.3	0.8
METH–AME	1	40	60	76	0.7	1.6
METH–Un Methodist	7	429	1,110	1,213	11.0	25.4
PENT–Ch God (Cleve)	3	89	135	170	1.5	3.6
PENT–Ch of God Proph	1	NR	50	63	0.6	1.3
FANNIN	**58**	**4,100**	**12,442**	**14,936**	**63.1**	**100.0**
ANG/EPIS–Anglican NA	1	NR	NR	NR	-	-

NR–Not Reported   - Represents no adherents reported.   Percentages may not total 100 due to rounding.

Table 3: Religious Congregations by County and Group: 2010

Religious Group	Number of Congregations	Number of Attendees	Number of Communicant, Confirmed, or Full Members	Adherents: Number of Adherents	Adherents: % of Total Pop.	Adherents: % of Total Adh.
Bahá'í	0	NR	6	6	0.0	0.0
BAPT–So Bapt Conv	34	2,401	8,945	10,493	44.3	70.3
Catholic	1	NR	NR	541	2.3	3.6
Chr & Miss Al	1	50	50	55	0.2	0.4
CHR–Chs of Christ	4	285	291	367	1.5	2.5
Jehovah's Witness	1	NR	NR	NR	-	-
LUTH–E.L.C.A.	1	50	79	85	0.4	0.6
METH–Un Methodist	6	374	651	827	3.5	5.5
Non-denom Chr Chs	5	710	1,980	2,049	8.7	13.7
PENT–Ch God (Cleve)	2	158	288	338	1.4	2.3
PENT–Ch of God Proph	1	NR	26	30	0.1	0.2
Sev Day Adv	1	72	126	145	0.6	1.0
FAYETTE	**117**	**19,451**	**46,519**	**70,334**	**66.0**	**100.0**
ANG/EPIS–Anglican NA	1	NR	NR	NR	-	-
ANG/EPIS–Episcopal	2	194	425	722	0.7	1.0
Bahá'í	0	NR	50	50	0.0	0.1
BAPT–Asc Ref Bap Ch Am	1	NR	NR	NR	-	-
BAPT–Ind Bapt Flwsp Intl	1	NR	NR	NR	-	-
BAPT–NBC USA	1	130	150	184	0.2	0.3
BAPT–Ref Bapt Ch	1	NR	NR	NR	-	-
BAPT–So Bapt Conv	28	8,214	23,103	28,342	26.6	40.3
Catholic	2	NR	NR	10,392	9.8	14.8
Ch Cr, Scientst	1	NR	NR	NR	-	-
Ch of God Gen Conf	1	NR	10	12	0.0	0.0
CHR–Chr Ch (Disc)	1	25	34	42	0.0	0.1
CHR–Chr Chs & Chs Cr	7	NR	3,168	3,886	3.6	5.5
CHR–Chs of Christ	5	851	801	1,098	1.0	1.6
Jehovah's Witness	1	NR	NR	NR	-	-
JUD–Reform	1	57	101	273	0.3	0.4
LDS–Comm of Christ	1	NR	118	118	0.1	0.2
LDS–L-D Saints	3	NR	NR	1,256	1.2	1.8
LUTH–E.L.C.A.	1	404	1,136	1,393	1.3	2.0
LUTH–Luth Cong Msn Chr	1	120	NR	NR	-	-
LUTH–Luth–MO Synod	1	240	319	440	0.4	0.6
LUTH–Nor Amer Luth C	2	NR	NR	NR	-	-
METH–AME	3	0	450	552	0.5	0.8
METH–Free Methodist	1	47	46	47	0.0	0.1
METH–Un Methodist	12	2,988	9,437	12,045	11.3	17.1
Muslim Est	1	150	NR	300	0.3	0.4
Non-denom Chr Chs	18	3,865	4,297	5,336	5.0	7.6
ORTHE–Greek Orthodox	1	85	NR	200	0.2	0.3
PENT–Assemb of God	1	45	25	50	0.0	0.1
PENT–Ch God (Cleve)	3	386	501	615	0.6	0.9
PENT–Ch of God Proph	1	NR	45	55	0.1	0.1
PENT–Cong Hol Ch	2	45	34	42	0.0	0.1
PENT–Full Gosp Bapt	1	NR	NR	NR	-	-
PENT–Un Pent Ch Intl	1	NR	NR	NR	-	-
PENT–Vineyard	1	26	39	48	0.0	0.1
PRES–Presb Ch (USA)	3	713	1,163	1,427	1.3	2.0
PRES–Presb Ch Amer	4	675	735	1,027	1.0	1.5
Sev Day Adv	1	191	332	382	0.4	0.5
FLOYD	**170**	**17,539**	**44,155**	**60,906**	**63.2**	**100.0**
ANG/EPIS–Anglican NA	1	NR	NR	NR	-	-
ANG/EPIS–Episcopal	2	258	586	1,049	1.1	1.7
Bahá'í	0	NR	18	18	0.0	0.0
BAPT–NBC USA	3	225	515	635	0.7	1.0
BAPT–So Bapt Conv	67	10,173	29,590	36,500	37.9	59.9
Catholic	1	NR	NR	5,282	5.5	8.7
Ch Cr, Scientst	1	NR	NR	NR	-	-
Ch of Nazarene	1	32	43	43	0.0	0.1
CHR–Chr Ch (Disc)	1	39	123	152	0.2	0.2
CHR–Chr Chs & Chs Cr	2	NR	146	180	0.2	0.3
CHR–Chs of Christ	6	700	668	813	0.8	1.3
Jehovah's Witness	2	NR	NR	NR	-	-
JUD–Reform	1	22	39	105	0.1	0.2
LDS–L-D Saints	1	NR	NR	742	0.8	1.2
LUTH–Luth–MO Synod	1	96	183	203	0.2	0.3
METH–AME	3	0	300	370	0.4	0.6
METH–AME Zion	1	0	150	185	0.2	0.3
METH–C.M.E.	2	0	200	247	0.3	0.4
METH–Cong Meth	1	NR	21	26	0.0	0.0

Religious Group	Number of Congregations	Number of Attendees	Number of Communicant, Confirmed, or Full Members	Adherents: Number of Adherents	Adherents: % of Total Pop.	Adherents: % of Total Adh.
METH–So Methodist	2	NR	NR	NR	-	-
METH–Un Methodist	31	1,866	4,950	5,622	5.8	9.2
Missionary Ch	1	350	0	350	0.4	0.6
Non-denom Chr Chs	12	2,045	2,335	2,846	3.0	4.7
PENT–Assemb of God	3	223	193	336	0.3	0.6
PENT–Ch God (Cleve)	7	1,052	2,308	2,847	3.0	4.7
PENT–Ch of God Proph	2	NR	58	72	0.1	0.1
PENT–Cong Hol Ch	3	96	86	106	0.1	0.2
PENT–Fire Bapt Hol Ch	1	NR	NR	NR	-	-
PENT–Un Pent Ch Intl	1	NR	NR	NR	-	-
PRES–Evan Presby Ch	1	NR	955	1,178	1.2	1.9
PRES–Korean Pres Amer	1	NR	NR	NR	-	-
PRES–Presb Ch (USA)	2	203	415	512	0.5	0.8
PRES–Presb Ch Amer	1	0	0	0	0.0	0.0
REF–Comm Ref Evan	1	NR	NR	NR	-	-
Salvation Army	1	41	68	251	0.3	0.4
Sev Day Adv	3	118	205	236	0.2	0.4
FORSYTH	**108**	**22,452**	**43,899**	**73,982**	**42.2**	**100.0**
ANG/EPIS–Episcopal	1	144	312	312	0.2	0.4
Bahá'í	1	NR	75	75	0.0	0.1
BAPT–Free Will Bapt	1	NR	73	97	0.1	0.1
BAPT–So Bapt Conv	46	11,589	23,827	31,542	18.0	42.6
Catholic	2	NR	NR	16,643	9.5	22.5
Ch of Nazarene	2	41	43	73	0.0	0.1
CHR–Chr Chs & Chs Cr	2	NR	500	662	0.4	0.9
CHR–Chs of Christ	5	594	475	713	0.4	1.0
Jehovah's Witness	1	NR	NR	NR	-	-
LDS–L-D Saints	2	NR	NR	906	0.5	1.2
LUTH–E.L.C.A.	2	362	682	883	0.5	1.2
LUTH–Luth–MO Synod	1	105	116	168	0.1	0.2
METH–Un Methodist	12	2,401	6,610	9,016	5.1	12.2
Non-denom Chr Chs	13	5,470	9,525	9,719	5.5	13.1
ORTHE–Greek Orthodox	1	100	NR	275	0.2	0.4
ORTHE–Rus Orth Abroad	1	60	NR	225	0.1	0.3
ORTHE–Ukrainian Orth	1	39	NR	200	0.1	0.3
PENT–Assemb of God	2	455	194	470	0.3	0.6
PENT–Ch God (Cleve)	3	286	511	676	0.4	0.9
PENT–Ch of God Proph	1	NR	28	37	0.0	0.1
PENT–Cong Hol Ch	1	39	35	46	0.0	0.1
PENT–Intl Pent Holiness	1	61	34	45	0.0	0.1
PRES–Presb Ch (USA)	2	286	595	788	0.4	1.1
PRES–Presb Ch Amer	3	420	264	411	0.2	0.6
PRES–Ref Pres US	1	NR	NR	NR	-	-
FRANKLIN	**70**	**5,886**	**12,782**	**15,468**	**70.0**	**100.0**
BAPT–So Bapt Conv	20	2,831	7,248	8,753	39.6	56.6
CHR–Chr Chs & Chs Cr	1	NR	200	242	1.1	1.6
CHR–Chs of Christ	2	142	127	167	0.8	1.1
METH–C.M.E.	2	0	300	362	1.6	2.3
METH–Un Methodist	13	776	1,535	1,905	8.6	12.3
Non-denom Chr Chs	5	495	560	656	3.0	4.2
PENT–Ch God (Cleve)	9	723	1,505	1,817	8.2	11.7
PENT–Cong Hol Ch	4	408	436	527	2.4	3.4
PENT–Intl Pent Holiness	8	341	609	735	3.3	4.8
PRES–Presb Ch (USA)	4	48	83	100	0.5	0.6
Sev Day Adv	1	97	169	194	0.9	1.3
Unit Univ	1	25	10	10	0.0	0.1
FULTON	**755**	**177,741**	**392,716**	**605,740**	**65.8**	**100.0**
ANG/EPIS–Anglican NA	2	NR	NR	NR	-	-
ANG/EPIS–Episcopal	16	4,930	16,973	19,551	2.1	3.2
Ap Chr Ch-Amer	1	41	22	41	0.0	0.0
Bahá'í	6	NR	1,086	1,086	0.1	0.2
BAPT–Alliance Bapt	3	NR	NR	NR	-	-
BAPT–Amer Bapt USA	8	1,878	6,207	7,637	0.8	1.3
BAPT–Converge/BGC	1	75	NR	90	0.0	0.0
BAPT–Natl Mis Bapt Conv	6	225	1,000	1,230	0.1	0.2
BAPT–NBC Amer	1	35	60	74	0.0	0.0
BAPT–NBC USA	45	19,235	48,774	60,012	6.5	9.9
BAPT–Prog NBC	10	2,300	3,625	4,460	0.5	0.7
BAPT–Ref Bapt Ch	1	NR	NR	NR	-	-
BAPT–Reg Bapt Gen As	1	NR	NR	NR	-	-

NR–Not Reported - Represents no adherents reported. Percentages may not total 100 due to rounding.

Table 3: Religious Congregations by County and Group: 2010

Religious Group	Number of Congrega-tions	Number of Attendees	Number of Communicant, Confirmed, or Full Members	Adherents		
				Number of Adherents	% of Total Pop.	% of Total Adh.
BAPT–So Bapt Conv	111	23,629	59,433	73,127	7.9	12.1
BUDD–Mahayana	8	NR	NR	5,000	0.5	0.8
BUDD–Theravada	1	NR	NR	396	0.0	0.1
BUDD–Vajrayana	2	NR	NR	478	0.1	0.1
Calv Chpl	1	NR	NR	NR	-	-
Catholic	18	NR	NR	91,391	9.9	15.1
CGOD–Ch God (Ander)	4	437	NR	437	0.0	0.1
Ch Cr, Scientst	3	NR	NR	NR	-	-
Ch of Chr (Hol)	1	NR	NR	NR	-	-
Ch of Nazarene	2	135	219	228	0.0	0.0
Chr & Miss Al	4	228	86	323	0.0	0.1
CHR–Chr Ch (Disc)	5	701	1,573	1,935	0.2	0.3
CHR–Chr Chs & Chs Cr	15	NR	2,688	3,307	0.4	0.5
CHR–Chs of Christ	15	3,139	3,512	4,640	0.5	0.8
CHR–Int Chs of Christ	2	NR	688	847	0.1	0.1
CONG–Cong Chr, NA	1	NR	28	34	0.0	0.0
Evan Cov Ch	2	270	37	351	0.0	0.1
HINDU–I/A Temples	5	NR	NR	3,180	0.3	0.5
HINDU–Post Ren	5	NR	NR	211	0.0	0.0
HINDU–Renaiss	1	NR	NR	12	0.0	0.0
Int Cou Comm Ch	1	NR	NR	NR	-	-
Jehovah's Witness	10	NR	NR	NR	-	-
JUD–Conserv	5	2,089	2,345	6,332	0.7	1.0
JUD–Orth	5	540	250	750	0.1	0.1
JUD–Reform	6	2,641	4,657	12,574	1.4	2.1
LDS–Comm of Christ	1	NR	118	118	0.0	0.0
LDS–L-D Saints	8	NR	NR	6,706	0.7	1.1
LUTH–E.L.C.A.	11	1,836	4,669	5,468	0.6	0.9
LUTH–Luth-MO Synod	5	631	717	817	0.1	0.1
LUTH–Wisc Ev Luth Syn	1	93	129	157	0.0	0.0
MENN–Mennonite USA	2	35	20	25	0.0	0.0
METH–AME	33	7,055	14,162	17,425	1.9	2.9
METH–AME Zion	3	100	490	603	0.1	0.1
METH–C.M.E.	6	675	1,970	2,424	0.3	0.4
METH–Un Methodist	74	21,260	77,049	102,688	11.2	17.0
Missionary Ch	1	10	0	10	0.0	0.0
MJEW–Union Mes Cong	1	NR	NR	NR	-	-
Muslim Est	13	4,279	NR	12,727	1.4	2.1
New Apost Ch	1	NR	NR	NR	-	-
Non-denom Chr Chs	124	55,458	87,034	88,599	9.6	14.6
ORTHE–Ant Orth of NA	1	190	NR	450	0.0	0.1
ORTHE–Orth Ch in Amer	1	125	NR	200	0.0	0.0
ORTHE–Rus Orth Abroad	1	200	NR	650	0.1	0.1
ORTHO–Armen Ap Cilic	1	70	NR	150	0.0	0.0
ORTHO–Armen Ap Etchm	1	125	NR	450	0.0	0.1
ORTHO–Coptic Orth Ch	1	400	NR	596	0.1	0.1
PENT–Apos Faith Msn	1	NR	35	43	0.0	0.0
PENT–Assemb of God	7	1,273	622	1,430	0.2	0.2
PENT–Ch God (Cleve)	11	4,723	13,257	16,312	1.8	2.7
PENT–Ch Lord Jesus Apos	4	NR	NR	NR	-	-
PENT–COGIC	21	1,365	3,587	4,414	0.5	0.7
PENT–Fire Bapt Hol Ch	4	NR	NR	NR	-	-
PENT–Full Gosp Bapt	5	NR	NR	NR	-	-
PENT–Int Foursq Gos	2	46	69	85	0.0	0.0
PENT–Intl Pent Holiness	1	15	20	25	0.0	0.0
PENT–Pent Ch of God	1	70	NR	109	0.0	0.0
PENT–Un Pent Ch Intl	6	NR	NR	NR	-	-
PENT–United Holy Ch	1	NR	NR	NR	-	-
PENT–Vineyard	1	23	35	43	0.0	0.0
PRES–Cumber Presb	1	NR	130	118	0.0	0.0
PRES–Korean Amer Pres	1	NR	NR	NR	-	-
PRES–Korean Pres Amer	1	NR	NR	NR	-	-
PRES–Presb Ch (USA)	27	7,738	23,025	28,330	3.1	4.7
PRES–Presb Ch Amer	10	1,083	993	1,347	0.1	0.2
PRES–Ref Pres of NA	1	28	27	35	0.0	0.0
REF–Christian Ref	1	50	85	105	0.0	0.0
REF–Ref Ch in Am	1	87	199	217	0.0	0.0
Salvation Army	1	201	308	660	0.1	0.1
Sev Day Adv	11	5,549	9,650	11,098	1.2	1.8
Sikh	1	NR	NR	NR	-	-
Tao	1	NR	NR	NR	-	-
Un C of Christ	6	185	705	867	0.1	0.1
Unit Univ	2	235	348	453	0.0	0.1
Zoroastrian	1	NR	NR	52	0.0	0.0

Religious Group	Number of Congrega-tions	Number of Attendees	Number of Communicant, Confirmed, or Full Members	Adherents		
				Number of Adherents	% of Total Pop.	% of Total Adh.
GILMER	**48**	**4,515**	**9,628**	**12,696**	**44.9**	**100.0**
Bahá'í	0	NR	3	3	0.0	0.0
BAPT–So Bapt Conv	15	2,107	4,595	5,533	19.6	43.6
Catholic	1	NR	NR	1,120	4.0	8.8
Chr & Miss Al	1	13	0	13	0.0	0.1
CHR–Chr Ch (Disc)	1	220	423	509	1.8	4.0
CHR–Chs of Christ	3	338	238	432	1.5	3.4
Jehovah's Witness	1	NR	NR	NR	-	-
LDS–L-D Saints	1	NR	NR	345	1.2	2.7
LUTH–E.L.C.A.	1	137	179	231	0.8	1.8
METH–Un Methodist	5	387	1,093	1,230	4.3	9.7
Non-denom Chr Chs	9	985	2,525	2,531	8.9	19.9
PENT–Assemb of God	1	35	20	100	0.4	0.8
PENT–Ch God (Cleve)	2	75	131	158	0.6	1.2
PENT–Ch of God Proph	2	NR	45	54	0.2	0.4
PENT–Intl Pent Holiness	1	70	126	152	0.5	1.2
PENT–Un Pent Ch Intl	1	NR	NR	NR	-	-
PRES–Presb Ch (USA)	1	38	61	73	0.3	0.6
Sev Day Adv	1	90	156	179	0.6	1.4
Unit Univ	1	20	33	33	0.1	0.3
GLASCOCK	**12**	**446**	**1,179**	**1,461**	**47.4**	**100.0**
BAPT–So Bapt Conv	7	278	890	1,118	36.3	76.5
METH–Cong Meth	1	NR	50	63	2.0	4.3
METH–Un Methodist	2	67	98	103	3.3	7.0
PENT–Ch God (Cleve)	2	101	141	177	5.7	12.1
GLYNN	**126**	**13,297**	**28,976**	**43,712**	**54.9**	**100.0**
ANG/EPIS–Episcopal	6	692	1,342	1,638	2.1	3.7
Bahá'í	1	NR	45	45	0.1	0.1
BAPT–Free Will Bapt	1	NR	73	90	0.1	0.2
BAPT–NBC USA	5	190	996	1,225	1.5	2.8
BAPT–So Bapt Conv	25	3,381	8,837	10,870	13.7	24.9
Calv Chpl	1	NR	NR	NR	-	-
Catholic	4	NR	NR	5,210	6.5	11.9
CGOD–Ch God (Ander)	1	0	NR	0	0.0	0.0
Ch of Nazarene	1	30	57	57	0.1	0.1
CHR–Chr Chs & Chs Cr	2	NR	138	170	0.2	0.4
CHR–Chs of Christ	4	156	143	194	0.2	0.4
FRND–Fr Gen Cf	1	NR	0	0	0.0	0.0
HINDU–I/A Temples	1	NR	NR	250	0.3	0.6
Jehovah's Witness	2	NR	NR	NR	-	-
JUD–Reform	1	31	54	146	0.2	0.3
LDS–L-D Saints	2	NR	NR	1,187	1.5	2.7
LUTH–E.L.C.A.	2	188	327	384	0.5	0.9
METH–AME	4	70	460	566	0.7	1.3
METH–C.M.E.	2	60	250	308	0.4	0.7
METH–Un Methodist	16	2,730	5,335	8,642	10.9	19.8
METH–Wesleyan	2	40	52	52	0.1	0.1
Non-denom Chr Chs	12	2,545	3,570	3,913	4.9	9.0
ORTHE–Greek Orthodox	1	30	NR	40	0.1	0.1
PENT–Assemb of God	3	785	1,171	1,182	1.5	2.7
PENT–Ch God (Cleve)	6	1,088	3,325	4,090	5.1	9.4
PENT–Ch of God Proph	2	NR	116	143	0.2	0.3
PENT–COGIC	2	400	750	923	1.2	2.1
PENT–Intl Pent Holiness	1	26	20	25	0.0	0.1
PENT–Un Pent Ch Intl	2	NR	NR	NR	-	-
PRES–Presb Ch (USA)	6	510	1,459	1,795	2.3	4.1
PRES–Presb Ch Amer	2	113	88	112	0.1	0.3
Salvation Army	1	38	58	98	0.1	0.2
Sev Day Adv	3	139	242	278	0.3	0.6
Unit Univ	1	55	68	79	0.1	0.2
GORDON	**89**	**9,451**	**20,628**	**32,427**	**58.8**	**100.0**
ANG/EPIS–Episcopal	1	61	129	168	0.3	0.5
Bahá'í	0	NR	4	4	0.0	0.0
BAPT–So Bapt Conv	38	4,748	11,603	14,677	26.6	45.3
Catholic	1	NR	NR	6,122	11.1	18.9
Ch of Nazarene	1	12	16	23	0.0	0.1
CHR–Chs of Christ	5	498	527	663	1.2	2.0
Jehovah's Witness	1	NR	NR	NR	-	-
LDS–L-D Saints	1	NR	NR	353	0.6	1.1

NR–Not Reported - Represents no adherents reported. Percentages may not total 100 due to rounding.

Table 3: Religious Congregations by County and Group: 2010

Religious Group	Number of Congregations	Number of Attendees	Number of Communicant, Confirmed, or Full Members	Adherents: Number of Adherents	Adherents: % of Total Pop.	Adherents: % of Total Adh.
METH–AME	1	0	100	126	0.2	0.4
METH–Un Methodist	10	668	1,650	2,043	3.7	6.3
Non-denom Chr Chs	7	970	1,045	1,261	2.3	3.9
PENT–Assemb of God	2	79	68	110	0.2	0.3
PENT–Ch God (Cleve)	10	1,402	3,377	4,272	7.7	13.2
PENT–Ch of God Proph	3	NR	457	578	1.0	1.8
PENT–Pent Ch of God	1	70	NR	109	0.2	0.3
PRES–Cumber Presb	1	NR	5	5	0.0	0.0
PRES–Presb Ch (USA)	1	89	161	204	0.4	0.6
Sev Day Adv	5	854	1,486	1,709	3.1	5.3
GRADY	**59**	**4,163**	**10,458**	**13,917**	**55.6**	**100.0**
Bahá'í	0	NR	3	3	0.0	0.0
BAPT–Free Will Bapt	1	NR	73	91	0.4	0.7
BAPT–Natl Mis Bapt Conv	1	0	150	188	0.8	1.4
BAPT–NBC USA	1	0	150	188	0.8	1.4
BAPT–So Bapt Conv	22	2,377	6,282	7,871	31.5	56.6
Catholic	1	NR	NR	615	2.5	4.4
Ch of Nazarene	1	22	74	74	0.3	0.5
CHR–Chr Chs & Chs Cr	1	NR	0	0	0.0	0.0
CHR–Chs of Christ	1	40	38	42	0.2	0.3
Jehovah's Witness	1	NR	NR	NR	-	-
LDS–L-D Saints	1	NR	NR	223	0.9	1.6
METH–AME	6	55	650	814	3.3	5.8
METH–Un Methodist	10	439	1,227	1,404	5.6	10.1
Non-denom Chr Chs	5	470	670	725	2.9	5.2
PENT–Assemb of God	1	80	80	350	1.4	2.5
PENT–Ch God (Cleve)	2	529	874	1,095	4.4	7.9
PENT–Intl Pent Holiness	2	58	79	99	0.4	0.7
PRES–Presb Ch (USA)	1	25	32	40	0.2	0.3
Un C of Christ	1	68	76	95	0.4	0.7
GREENE	**40**	**2,228**	**5,436**	**8,096**	**50.6**	**100.0**
ANG/EPIS–Episcopal	1	62	115	172	1.1	2.1
Bahá'í	0	NR	6	6	0.0	0.1
BAPT–Amer Bapt Assn	1	NR	85	101	0.6	1.2
BAPT–NBC USA	2	125	450	536	3.4	6.6
BAPT–So Bapt Conv	14	1,059	2,524	3,004	18.8	37.1
Catholic	1	NR	NR	1,490	9.3	18.4
CHR–Chr Ch (Disc)	1	0	0	0	0.0	0.0
CHR–Chs of Christ	1	35	32	39	0.2	0.5
Int Cou Comm Ch	1	NR	NR	NR	-	-
Jehovah's Witness	1	NR	NR	NR	-	-
METH–AME	5	70	568	676	4.2	8.3
METH–Un Methodist	5	604	1,261	1,593	10.0	19.7
METH–Wesleyan	1	68	68	88	0.6	1.1
PENT–Ch God (Cleve)	1	29	123	146	0.9	1.8
PENT–Cong Hol Ch	1	86	78	93	0.6	1.1
PRES–Presb Ch (USA)	2	58	101	120	0.8	1.5
PRES–Presb Ch Amer	2	32	25	32	0.2	0.4
GWINNETT	**548**	**122,177**	**204,059**	**366,708**	**45.5**	**100.0**
ANG/EPIS–Anglican NA	2	NR	NR	NR	-	-
ANG/EPIS–Episcopal	5	1,353	3,254	4,038	0.5	1.1
Bahá'í	3	NR	624	624	0.1	0.2
BAPT–Ind Bapt Flwsp Intl	1	NR	NR	NR	-	-
BAPT–NBC USA	2	3,800	5,400	6,976	0.9	1.9
BAPT–Ref Bapt Ch	3	NR	NR	NR	-	-
BAPT–So Bapt Conv	142	36,412	84,087	108,623	13.5	29.6
BRETH–Breth in Chr	1	NR	NR	NR	-	-
BUDD–Mahayana	3	NR	NR	702	0.1	0.2
BUDD–Theravada	1	NR	NR	300	0.0	0.1
Calv Chpl	2	NR	NR	NR	-	-
Catholic	12	NR	NR	67,781	8.4	18.5
CGOD–Ch God (Ander)	2	115	NR	115	0.0	0.0
Ch Cr, Scientst	1	NR	NR	NR	-	-
Ch God (7th Day)	1	NR	NR	NR	-	-
Ch of God Gen Conf	1	NR	30	39	0.0	0.0
Ch of Nazarene	4	667	1,167	1,264	0.2	0.3
Chr & Miss Al	15	1,925	1,401	2,414	0.3	0.7
CHR–Chr Ch (Disc)	6	273	760	982	0.1	0.3
CHR–Chr Chs & Chs Cr	7	NR	1,250	1,615	0.2	0.4
CHR–Chs of Christ	11	3,075	3,193	4,131	0.5	1.1

Religious Group	Number of Congregations	Number of Attendees	Number of Communicant, Confirmed, or Full Members	Adherents: Number of Adherents	Adherents: % of Total Pop.	Adherents: % of Total Adh.
CHR–Int Chs of Christ	1	NR	252	326	0.0	0.1
Christian Brethren	1	NR	NR	NR	-	-
Evan Cov Ch	1	550	0	715	0.1	0.2
Evan Free Ch	1	60	NR	60	0.0	0.0
FRND–Consrv Yr Mtgs	1	NR	0	0	0.0	0.0
HINDU–I/A Temples	6	NR	NR	5,792	0.7	1.6
HINDU–Post Ren	2	NR	NR	75	0.0	0.0
HINDU–Trad Temples	2	NR	NR	107	0.0	0.0
Ind Fund Churches	2	NR	NR	NR	-	-
Jain	1	NR	NR	NR	-	-
Jehovah's Witness	5	NR	NR	NR	-	-
JUD–Orth	1	43	50	60	0.0	0.0
JUD–Reform	1	58	103	278	0.0	0.1
LDS–Comm of Christ	2	NR	236	236	0.0	0.1
LDS–L-D Saints	14	NR	NR	6,799	0.8	1.9
LUTH–Ch Luth Conf	1	NR	NR	NR	-	-
LUTH–E.L.C.A.	9	1,726	3,716	4,772	0.6	1.3
LUTH–Luth-MO Synod	1	124	271	308	0.0	0.1
LUTH–Wisc Ev Luth Syn	1	194	350	432	0.1	0.1
MENN–Menn Br US Conf	1	NR	0	0	0.0	0.0
METH–AME	2	0	250	323	0.0	0.1
METH–AME Zion	2	0	200	258	0.0	0.1
METH–Cong Meth	1	NR	NR	NR	-	-
METH–Un Methodist	37	14,922	39,185	51,680	6.4	14.1
METH–Wesleyan	4	9,343	444	12,146	1.5	3.3
Missionary Ch	2	248	250	288	0.0	0.1
Muslim Est	12	3,388	NR	8,759	1.1	2.4
Non-denom Chr Chs	70	26,005	31,036	34,293	4.3	9.4
ORTHE–Orth Ch in Amer	2	225	NR	800	0.1	0.2
ORTHE–Romania Orth Ar	2	200	NR	1,040	0.1	0.3
ORTHE–Serb Orth USA	1	250	NR	1,600	0.2	0.4
ORTHO–Coptic Orth Ch	1	285	NR	392	0.0	0.1
ORTHO–Malan Syr Orth	1	40	NR	72	0.0	0.0
ORTHO–Syrian Orth Ch	1	50	NR	100	0.0	0.0
PENT–Assemb of God	18	2,487	2,086	3,502	0.4	1.0
PENT–Ch God (Cleve)	16	3,378	7,193	9,292	1.2	2.5
PENT–Ch of God Proph	4	NR	364	470	0.1	0.1
PENT–COGIC	2	550	670	866	0.1	0.2
PENT–Cong Hol Ch	3	117	105	136	0.0	0.0
PENT–Full Gosp Bapt	2	NR	NR	NR	-	-
PENT–Int Foursq Gos	1	0	0	0	0.0	0.0
PENT–Intl Pent Holiness	3	627	1,009	1,303	0.2	0.4
PENT–Open Bible Std	1	0	NR	0	0.0	0.0
PENT–Un Pent Ch Intl	2	NR	NR	NR	-	-
PENT–Vineyard	1	91	100	129	0.0	0.0
PRES–As Ref Pres Ch	3	NR	482	623	0.1	0.2
PRES–Cumber Presb	2	NR	72	72	0.0	0.0
PRES–Kor Pres Abroad	4	NR	NR	NR	-	-
PRES–Korean Amer Pres	4	NR	NR	NR	-	-
PRES–Korean Pres Amer	5	NR	NR	NR	-	-
PRES–Presb Ch (USA)	11	2,101	4,393	5,675	0.7	1.5
PRES–Presb Ch Amer	25	5,519	6,865	9,572	1.2	2.6
PRES–Ref Pres US	1	NR	NR	NR	-	-
REF–Christian Ref	1	31	14	18	0.0	0.0
REF–Ref Ch in Am	1	60	65	65	0.0	0.0
Salvation Army	1	232	288	332	0.0	0.1
Sev Day Adv	17	1,565	2,720	3,130	0.4	0.9
Sikh	1	NR	NR	NR	-	-
Unit Univ	1	88	124	198	0.0	0.1
Unity Ch	1	NR	NR	NR	-	-
Zoroastrian	0	NR	NR	10	0.0	0.0
HABERSHAM	**85**	**8,704**	**19,108**	**27,027**	**62.8**	**100.0**
ANG/EPIS–Anglican NA	1	NR	NR	NR	-	-
ANG/EPIS–Episcopal	1	173	315	315	0.7	1.2
Bahá'í	0	NR	4	4	0.0	0.0
BAPT–So Bapt Conv	34	4,010	12,211	15,065	35.0	55.7
Catholic	1	NR	NR	3,028	7.0	11.2
Chr & Miss Al	2	122	45	162	0.4	0.6
CHR–Chr Chs & Chs Cr	2	NR	374	461	1.1	1.7
CHR–Chs of Christ	1	86	77	94	0.2	0.3
CONG–Cong Chr, NA	1	NR	10	12	0.0	0.0
Jehovah's Witness	1	NR	NR	NR	-	-
LDS–L-D Saints	1	NR	NR	645	1.5	2.4

NR–Not Reported   - Represents no adherents reported.   Percentages may not total 100 due to rounding.

Table 3: Religious Congregations by County and Group: 2010

Religious Group	Number of Congrega-tions	Number of Attendees	Number of Communicant, Confirmed, or Full Members	Adherents		
				Number of Adherents	% of Total Pop.	% of Total Adh.
METH–Un Methodist	9	644	1,734	2,151	5.0	8.0
Non-denom Chr Chs	11	1,335	1,690	1,832	4.3	6.8
PENT–Ch God (Cleve)	5	1,218	1,348	1,663	3.9	6.2
PENT–Cong Hol Ch	7	638	569	702	1.6	2.6
PENT–Int Foursq Gos	2	50	60	74	0.2	0.3
PRES–Presb Ch (USA)	2	277	493	608	1.4	2.2
PRES–Presb Ch Amer	1	41	26	35	0.1	0.1
Sev Day Adv	2	80	138	159	0.4	0.6
Un C of Christ	1	30	14	17	0.0	0.1
HALL	**187**	**40,924**	**80,350**	**136,740**	**76.1**	**100.0**
ANG/EPIS–Anglican NA	1	NR	NR	NR	-	-
ANG/EPIS–Episcopal	2	368	965	987	0.5	0.7
Bahá'í	0	NR	45	45	0.0	0.0
BAPT–Free Will Bapt	1	NR	73	94	0.1	0.1
BAPT–Fund Bapt Flwsp	1	NR	NR	NR	-	-
BAPT–NBC USA	2	0	1,350	1,731	1.0	1.3
BAPT–Ref Bapt Ch	1	NR	NR	NR	-	-
BAPT–So Bapt Conv	67	16,873	40,007	51,292	28.5	37.5
Calv Chpl	1	NR	NR	NR	-	-
Catholic	2	NR	NR	38,311	21.3	28.0
Ch of Nazarene	3	153	333	333	0.2	0.2
CHR–Chr Ch (Disc)	1	0	73	94	0.1	0.1
CHR–Chr Chs & Chs Cr	1	NR	210	269	0.1	0.2
CHR–Chs of Christ	3	181	160	215	0.1	0.2
Jehovah's Witness	2	NR	NR	NR	-	-
LDS–L-D Saints	3	NR	NR	1,522	0.8	1.1
LUTH–E.L.C.A.	2	139	252	252	0.1	0.2
LUTH–Luth–MO Synod	1	174	221	289	0.2	0.2
METH–AME	1	0	100	128	0.1	0.1
METH–C.M.E.	1	0	100	128	0.1	0.1
METH–Un Methodist	23	2,993	7,735	8,874	4.9	6.5
Muslim Est	2	539	NR	1,524	0.8	1.1
Non-denom Chr Chs	27	15,474	23,735	24,218	13.5	17.7
PENT–Assemb of God	6	665	440	793	0.4	0.6
PENT–Ch God (Cleve)	5	381	618	792	0.4	0.6
PENT–Ch Lord Jesus Apos	1	NR	NR	NR	-	-
PENT–Ch of God Proph	2	NR	49	63	0.0	0.0
PENT–Cong Hol Ch	11	1,159	1,187	1,522	0.8	1.1
PENT–Fire Bapt Hol Ch	1	NR	NR	NR	-	-
PENT–Un Pent Ch Intl	3	NR	NR	NR	-	-
PENT–Vineyard	1	51	64	82	0.0	0.1
PRES–Presb Ch (USA)	2	454	918	1,177	0.7	0.9
PRES–Presb Ch Amer	2	949	1,030	1,229	0.7	0.9
Salvation Army	1	101	214	233	0.1	0.2
Sev Day Adv	3	270	471	541	0.3	0.4
Unity Ch	1	NR	NR	NR	-	-
Zoroastrian	0	NR	NR	2	0.0	0.0
HANCOCK	**32**	**710**	**2,866**	**3,321**	**35.2**	**100.0**
Bahá'í	0	NR	6	6	0.1	0.2
BAPT–NBC USA	1	0	150	172	1.8	5.2
BAPT–So Bapt Conv	8	282	577	663	7.0	20.0
CHR–Chs of Christ	1	38	50	68	0.7	2.0
Jehovah's Witness	1	NR	NR	NR	-	-
METH–AME	9	0	1,100	1,263	13.4	38.0
METH–C.M.E.	2	0	300	344	3.6	10.4
METH–Un Methodist	6	130	293	397	4.2	12.0
Non-denom Chr Chs	3	250	350	362	3.8	10.9
PENT–Ch God (Cleve)	1	10	40	46	0.5	1.4
HARALSON	**57**	**5,358**	**11,261**	**14,057**	**48.8**	**100.0**
BAPT–So Bapt Conv	27	3,317	8,012	9,963	34.6	70.9
CHR–Chr Chs & Chs Cr	3	NR	172	214	0.7	1.5
CHR–Chs of Christ	4	365	305	455	1.6	3.2
Jehovah's Witness	1	NR	NR	NR	-	-
LDS–L-D Saints	1	NR	NR	321	1.1	2.3
METH–Un Methodist	9	594	1,464	1,531	5.3	10.9
Non-denom Chr Chs	4	572	655	755	2.6	5.4
PENT–Assemb of God	1	85	75	99	0.3	0.7
PENT–Ch God (Cleve)	3	321	467	581	2.0	4.1
PENT–Cong Hol Ch	1	27	22	27	0.1	0.2
PENT–Intl Pent Holiness	1	59	61	76	0.3	0.5
PRES–Presb Ch (USA)	2	18	28	35	0.1	0.2
HARRIS	**52**	**3,387**	**8,189**	**11,254**	**35.1**	**100.0**
ANG/EPIS–Episcopal	1	79	98	172	0.5	1.5
Bahá'í	0	NR	3	3	0.0	0.0
BAPT–Amer Bapt Assn	1	NR	85	103	0.3	0.9
BAPT–Free Will Bapt	1	NR	73	89	0.3	0.8
BAPT–NBC USA	3	0	450	546	1.7	4.9
BAPT–So Bapt Conv	23	1,898	5,117	6,214	19.4	55.2
Catholic	1	NR	NR	941	2.9	8.4
CHR–Chs of Christ	2	70	70	81	0.3	0.7
LDS–L-D Saints	1	NR	NR	323	1.0	2.9
METH–C.M.E.	2	0	300	364	1.1	3.2
METH–Un Methodist	9	462	1,040	1,248	3.9	11.1
Non-denom Chr Chs	3	290	450	450	1.4	4.0
PENT–Assemb of God	2	320	194	347	1.1	3.1
PENT–Ch God (Cleve)	1	219	255	310	1.0	2.8
PENT–Cong Hol Ch	1	25	13	16	0.0	0.1
Sev Day Adv	1	24	41	47	0.1	0.4
HART	**57**	**4,859**	**13,105**	**18,417**	**73.0**	**100.0**
ANG/EPIS–Episcopal	1	64	95	107	0.4	0.6
Bahá'í	0	NR	1	1	0.0	0.0
BAPT–So Bapt Conv	27	3,372	9,887	11,924	47.3	64.7
Catholic	1	NR	NR	2,650	10.5	14.4
Chr & Miss Al	1	20	25	49	0.2	0.3
CHR–Chr Chs & Chs Cr	1	NR	30	36	0.1	0.2
CHR–Chs of Christ	1	45	35	43	0.2	0.2
Jehovah's Witness	1	NR	NR	NR	-	-
LDS–L-D Saints	1	NR	NR	114	0.5	0.6
LUTH–Luth Cong Msn Chr	1	41	93	112	0.4	0.6
MENN–CG in Cr (Menn)	1	NR	100	121	0.5	0.7
METH–C.M.E.	3	35	420	507	2.0	2.8
METH–Un Methodist	9	799	1,646	1,885	7.5	10.2
Non-denom Chr Chs	3	215	310	310	1.2	1.7
PENT–Ch God (Cleve)	2	159	237	286	1.1	1.6
PENT–Ch of God Proph	1	NR	78	94	0.4	0.5
PENT–Intl Pent Holiness	1	35	35	42	0.2	0.2
PRES–Presb Ch (USA)	2	74	113	136	0.5	0.7
HEARD	**35**	**2,121**	**4,730**	**5,764**	**48.7**	**100.0**
Bahá'í	0	NR	4	4	0.0	0.1
BAPT–So Bapt Conv	15	1,669	3,911	4,843	40.9	84.0
CHR–Chr Chs & Chs Cr	3	NR	0	0	0.0	0.0
CHR–Chs of Christ	2	27	30	36	0.3	0.6
Jehovah's Witness	1	NR	NR	NR	-	-
METH–Un Methodist	7	181	398	438	3.7	7.6
Non-denom Chr Chs	1	100	150	150	1.3	2.6
PENT–Ch God (Cleve)	3	134	232	287	2.4	5.0
PENT–Cong Hol Ch	1	10	5	6	0.1	0.1
PENT–Full Gosp Bapt	1	NR	NR	NR	-	-
PENT–Un Pent Ch Intl	1	NR	NR	NR	-	-
HENRY	**158**	**29,266**	**52,307**	**69,153**	**33.9**	**100.0**
ANG/EPIS–Episcopal	1	146	251	336	0.2	0.5
Bahá'í	0	NR	57	57	0.0	0.1
BAPT–NBC USA	1	200	300	385	0.2	0.6
BAPT–S-D Baptist Gen Con	1	50	41	53	0.0	0.1
BAPT–So Bapt Conv	49	11,867	22,215	28,500	14.0	41.2
Calv Chpl	1	NR	NR	NR	-	-
Catholic	1	NR	NR	3,766	1.8	5.4
Ch of God Gen Conf	1	NR	88	113	0.1	0.2
Ch of Nazarene	1	16	70	70	0.0	0.1
CHR–Chr Ch (Disc)	1	29	45	58	0.0	0.1
CHR–Chr Chs & Chs Cr	4	NR	1,980	2,540	1.2	3.7
CHR–Chs of Christ	4	600	533	715	0.4	1.0
CONG–Cong Chr, NA	1	NR	75	96	0.0	0.1
Jehovah's Witness	2	NR	NR	NR	-	-
LDS–L-D Saints	1	NR	NR	690	0.3	1.0
LUTH–E.L.C.A.	1	61	112	121	0.1	0.2
LUTH–Luth–MO Synod	1	109	158	188	0.1	0.3
LUTH–Wisc Ev Luth Syn	1	33	31	47	0.0	0.1

NR–Not Reported - Represents no adherents reported. Percentages may not total 100 due to rounding.

Table 3: Religious Congregations by County and Group: 2010

Religious Group	Number of Congrega-tions	Number of Attendees	Number of Communicant, Confirmed, or Full Members	Adherents: Number of Adherents	Adherents: % of Total Pop.	Adherents: % of Total Adh.
METH–AME	2	0	250	321	0.2	0.5
METH–Un Methodist	21	3,536	8,808	10,255	5.0	14.8
Non-denom Chr Chs	28	9,795	12,360	14,325	7.0	20.7
PENT–Assemb of God	6	546	407	616	0.3	0.9
PENT–Ch God (Cleve)	7	1,035	1,828	2,345	1.1	3.4
PENT–Ch of God Proph	1	NR	54	69	0.0	0.1
PENT–COGIC	1	60	60	77	0.0	0.1
PENT–Full Gosp Bapt	2	NR	NR	NR	-	-
PENT–Int Foursq Gos	4	348	521	668	0.3	1.0
PENT–Int Pent C Chr	1	94	0	105	0.1	0.2
PENT–Un Pent Ch Intl	3	NR	NR	NR	-	-
PRES–Evan Presby Ch	1	NR	295	378	0.2	0.5
PRES–Presb Ch (USA)	6	669	1,529	1,962	1.0	2.8
PRES–Presb Ch Amer	2	0	113	144	0.1	0.2
Sev Day Adv	1	72	126	145	0.1	0.2
Zoroastrian	0	NR	NR	8	0.0	0.0
HOUSTON	**143**	**19,737**	**46,980**	**73,831**	**52.8**	**100.0**
ANG/EPIS–Episcopal	2	141	320	358	0.3	0.5
Bahá'í	0	NR	156	156	0.1	0.2
BAPT–Free Will Bapt	1	NR	73	92	0.1	0.1
BAPT–Natl Mis Bapt Conv	1	0	0	0	0.0	0.0
BAPT–NBC USA	2	0	400	503	0.4	0.7
BAPT–So Bapt Conv	38	8,866	27,431	34,516	24.7	46.8
Catholic	2	NR	NR	6,124	4.4	8.3
Ch Cr, Scientst	1	NR	NR	NR	-	-
Ch of Nazarene	1	119	205	205	0.1	0.3
Chr & Miss Al	1	20	20	26	0.0	0.0
CHR–Chr Ch (Disc)	1	65	167	210	0.2	0.3
CHR–Chr Chs & Chs Cr	3	NR	370	466	0.3	0.6
CHR–Chs of Christ	5	503	455	595	0.4	0.8
HINDU–I/A Temples	1	NR	NR	1,742	1.2	2.4
Jehovah's Witness	3	NR	NR	NR	-	-
LDS–Comm of Christ	1	NR	118	118	0.1	0.2
LDS–L-D Saints	3	NR	NR	1,812	1.3	2.5
LUTH–E.L.C.A.	1	46	76	80	0.1	0.1
LUTH–Luth–MO Synod	2	406	778	971	0.7	1.3
METH–AME	3	0	400	503	0.4	0.7
METH–C.M.E.	5	315	1,002	1,261	0.9	1.7
METH–Un Methodist	10	4,238	7,618	14,081	10.1	19.1
METH–Wesleyan	1	24	6	31	0.0	0.0
Muslim Est	1	269	NR	762	0.5	1.0
Non-denom Chr Chs	23	2,495	3,650	3,789	2.7	5.1
PENT–Assemb of God	7	777	464	1,276	0.9	1.7
PENT–Ch God (Cleve)	5	528	2,027	2,551	1.8	3.5
PENT–Ch of God by Faith	4	NR	NR	NR	-	-
PENT–Ch of God Proph	1	NR	30	38	0.0	0.1
PENT–Cong Hol Ch	2	145	88	111	0.1	0.2
PENT–Int Foursq Gos	1	95	21	26	0.0	0.0
PENT–Intl Pent Holiness	1	25	67	84	0.1	0.1
PENT–Un Pent Ch Intl	1	NR	NR	NR	-	-
PRES–Presb Ch (USA)	3	60	252	317	0.2	0.4
PRES–Presb Ch Amer	3	440	500	615	0.4	0.8
Salvation Army	1	42	81	174	0.1	0.2
Sev Day Adv	2	118	205	236	0.2	0.3
Zoroastrian	0	NR	NR	2	0.0	0.0
IRWIN	**20**	**1,281**	**3,492**	**4,288**	**45.0**	**100.0**
Bahá'í	0	NR	1	1	0.0	0.0
BAPT–NBC USA	1	0	150	185	1.9	4.3
BAPT–So Bapt Conv	10	731	2,048	2,531	26.5	59.0
CHR–Chs of Christ	1	40	50	60	0.6	1.4
METH–AME	2	0	200	247	2.6	5.8
METH–C.M.E.	1	0	100	124	1.3	2.9
METH–Un Methodist	2	110	309	356	3.7	8.3
Non-denom Chr Chs	1	50	50	62	0.7	1.4
PENT–Ch God (Cleve)	1	350	584	722	7.6	16.8
PENT–Ch of God by Faith	1	NR	NR	NR	-	-
JACKSON	**90**	**7,391**	**17,703**	**22,655**	**37.5**	**100.0**
Bahá'í	0	NR	9	9	0.0	0.0
BAPT–Asc Ref Bap Ch Am	1	NR	NR	NR	-	-
BAPT–Ref Bapt Ch	1	NR	NR	NR	-	-

Religious Group	Number of Congrega-tions	Number of Attendees	Number of Communicant, Confirmed, or Full Members	Adherents: Number of Adherents	Adherents: % of Total Pop.	Adherents: % of Total Adh.
BAPT–So Bapt Conv	38	4,367	10,900	13,765	22.8	60.8
Catholic	1	NR	NR	268	0.4	1.2
CHR–Chr Chs & Chs Cr	2	NR	905	1,143	1.9	5.0
CHR–Chs of Christ	1	56	55	75	0.1	0.3
Jehovah's Witness	2	NR	NR	NR	-	-
LDS–L-D Saints	1	NR	NR	560	0.9	2.5
METH–AME	4	70	488	616	1.0	2.7
METH–C.M.E.	1	0	150	189	0.3	0.8
METH–Un Methodist	18	1,242	2,649	3,096	5.1	13.7
Non-denom Chr Chs	4	924	1,558	1,564	2.6	6.9
PENT–Assemb of God	2	105	15	140	0.2	0.6
PENT–Ch God (Cleve)	1	30	125	158	0.3	0.7
PENT–Ch of God Proph	2	NR	175	221	0.4	1.0
PENT–Cong Hol Ch	5	475	447	564	0.9	2.5
PENT–Fire Bapt Hol Ch	1	NR	NR	NR	-	-
PENT–Un Pent Ch Intl	2	NR	NR	NR	-	-
PRES–Presb Ch (USA)	3	122	227	287	0.5	1.3
JASPER	**28**	**1,750**	**4,051**	**5,005**	**36.0**	**100.0**
Bahá'í	0	NR	9	9	0.1	0.2
BAPT–So Bapt Conv	12	1,025	2,371	2,943	21.2	58.8
CGOD–Ch God (Ander)	1	12	NR	12	0.1	0.2
CHR–Chs of Christ	1	27	20	30	0.2	0.6
Jehovah's Witness	1	NR	NR	NR	-	-
METH–AME	4	130	450	559	4.0	11.2
METH–C.M.E.	2	50	250	310	2.2	6.2
METH–Un Methodist	4	228	540	656	4.7	13.1
Non-denom Chr Chs	2	150	190	212	1.5	4.2
PRES–Presb Ch (USA)	1	128	221	274	2.0	5.5
JEFF DAVIS	**40**	**2,809**	**6,218**	**8,585**	**57.0**	**100.0**
BAPT–Free Will Bapt	1	NR	73	94	0.6	1.1
BAPT–So Bapt Conv	16	1,756	3,805	4,887	32.4	56.9
Catholic	1	NR	NR	463	3.1	5.4
Ch God (7th Day)	1	NR	NR	NR	-	-
Chr & Miss Al	1	29	40	43	0.3	0.5
CHR–Chs of Christ	1	42	30	53	0.4	0.6
LDS–L-D Saints	1	NR	NR	338	2.2	3.9
METH–AME	3	0	400	514	3.4	6.0
METH–C.M.E.	1	0	150	193	1.3	2.2
METH–Un Methodist	2	164	394	398	2.6	4.6
Non-denom Chr Chs	3	220	330	330	2.2	3.8
PENT–Ch God (Cleve)	5	568	940	1,207	8.0	14.1
PENT–Ch of God Proph	1	NR	5	6	0.0	0.1
PENT–Un Pent Ch Intl	1	NR	NR	NR	-	-
Sev Day Adv	2	30	51	59	0.4	0.7
JEFFERSON	**74**	**2,782**	**9,118**	**11,098**	**65.6**	**100.0**
ANG/EPIS–Episcopal	1	17	35	35	0.2	0.3
Bahá'í	0	NR	5	5	0.0	0.0
BAPT–Natl Mis Bapt Conv	3	0	450	559	3.3	5.0
BAPT–NBC USA	1	0	150	186	1.1	1.7
BAPT–So Bapt Conv	17	1,187	3,385	4,204	24.8	37.9
Catholic	1	NR	NR	60	0.4	0.5
CGOD–Ch God (Ander)	1	60	NR	60	0.4	0.5
Ch of Nazarene	1	23	10	28	0.2	0.3
CHR–Chs of Christ	1	30	40	60	0.4	0.5
Jehovah's Witness	1	NR	NR	NR	-	-
MENN–CG in Cr (Menn)	2	NR	296	368	2.2	3.3
METH–AME	12	225	1,682	2,089	12.3	18.8
METH–C.M.E.	3	0	450	559	3.3	5.0
METH–Un Methodist	16	717	1,570	1,633	9.6	14.7
Non-denom Chr Chs	3	230	281	325	1.9	2.9
PENT–Ch God (Cleve)	3	161	260	323	1.9	2.9
PENT–COGIC	1	0	150	186	1.1	1.7
PENT–Un Pent Ch Intl	2	NR	NR	NR	-	-
PRES–As Ref Pres Ch	4	NR	125	155	0.9	1.4
Sev Day Adv	1	132	229	263	1.6	2.4
JENKINS	**25**	**1,528**	**4,107**	**5,269**	**63.2**	**100.0**
Bahá'í	0	NR	3	3	0.0	0.1
BAPT–So Bapt Conv	11	1,096	2,838	3,590	43.0	68.1

NR–Not Reported - Represents no adherents reported. Percentages may not total 100 due to rounding.

Table 3: Religious Congregations by County and Group: 2010

Religious Group	Number of Congregations	Number of Attendees	Number of Communicant, Confirmed, or Full Members	Adherents		
				Number of Adherents	% of Total Pop.	% of Total Adh.
Catholic	1	NR	NR	132	1.6	2.5
CGOD–Ch God (Ander)	1	20	NR	20	0.2	0.4
METH–AME	2	0	300	379	4.5	7.2
METH–Un Methodist	6	304	640	727	8.7	13.8
Non-denom Chr Chs	2	90	85	113	1.4	2.1
PENT–Ch God (Cleve)	1	18	91	115	1.4	2.2
PENT–COGIC	1	0	150	190	2.3	3.6
JOHNSON	**40**	**1,611**	**3,717**	**4,427**	**44.4**	**100.0**
BAPT–Natl Mis Bapt Conv	1	0	150	180	1.8	4.1
BAPT–So Bapt Conv	14	607	1,733	2,074	20.8	46.8
Ch of Nazarene	3	311	482	576	5.8	13.0
CHR–Chr Chs & Chs Cr	2	NR	90	108	1.1	2.4
METH–AME	4	0	400	479	4.8	10.8
METH–Un Methodist	8	199	369	369	3.7	8.3
Non-denom Chr Chs	1	100	150	150	1.5	3.4
PENT–Assemb of God	3	160	67	160	1.6	3.6
PENT–Ch God (Cleve)	2	90	267	320	3.2	7.2
PENT–COGIC	1	125	0	0	0.0	0.0
PENT–Intl Pent Holiness	1	19	9	11	0.1	0.2
JONES	**38**	**3,104**	**8,350**	**10,680**	**37.3**	**100.0**
Bahá'í	0	NR	11	11	0.0	0.1
BAPT–So Bapt Conv	16	2,089	5,543	6,910	24.1	64.7
CHR–Chs of Christ	1	25	18	25	0.1	0.2
Jehovah's Witness	1	NR	NR	NR	-	-
LDS–L-D Saints	1	NR	NR	323	1.1	3.0
METH–AME	10	350	1,265	1,577	5.5	14.8
METH–C.M.E.	1	0	150	187	0.7	1.8
METH–Un Methodist	5	472	1,116	1,338	4.7	12.5
Non-denom Chr Chs	1	70	70	88	0.3	0.8
PENT–Ch God (Cleve)	1	68	120	150	0.5	1.4
PRES–Presb Ch (USA)	1	30	57	71	0.2	0.7
LAMAR	**35**	**1,680**	**9,526**	**11,326**	**61.8**	**100.0**
Bahá'í	0	NR	16	16	0.1	0.1
BAPT–So Bapt Conv	8	821	3,005	3,596	19.6	31.7
Ch of Nazarene	1	112	183	183	1.0	1.6
CHR–Chs of Christ	1	32	65	72	0.4	0.6
Jehovah's Witness	1	NR	NR	NR	-	-
METH–AME	2	0	250	299	1.6	2.6
METH–C.M.E.	1	0	150	179	1.0	1.6
METH–Cong Meth	2	NR	4,138	4,951	27.0	43.7
METH–Un Methodist	9	405	813	920	5.0	8.1
Non-denom Chr Chs	1	60	60	75	0.4	0.7
PENT–Assemb of God	1	90	56	90	0.5	0.8
PENT–Ch God (Cleve)	1	17	103	123	0.7	1.1
PENT–COGIC	3	120	600	718	3.9	6.3
PENT–Intl Pent Holiness	2	23	58	69	0.4	0.6
PENT–Un Pent Ch Intl	1	NR	NR	NR	-	-
PRES–Presb Ch (USA)	1	0	29	35	0.2	0.3
LANIER	**17**	**984**	**2,769**	**3,800**	**37.7**	**100.0**
BAPT–So Bapt Conv	3	351	1,512	1,936	19.2	50.9
Catholic	1	NR	NR	344	3.4	9.1
CHR–Chs of Christ	2	90	85	125	1.2	3.3
Jehovah's Witness	1	NR	NR	NR	-	-
METH–AME	1	0	150	192	1.9	5.1
METH–Un Methodist	3	200	441	506	5.0	13.3
Non-denom Chr Chs	2	130	160	188	1.9	4.9
PENT–Ch God (Cleve)	2	77	184	236	2.3	6.2
Sev Day Adv	2	136	237	273	2.7	7.2
LAURENS	**126**	**9,963**	**22,235**	**28,723**	**59.3**	**100.0**
ANG/EPIS–Episcopal	1	53	97	146	0.3	0.5
Bahá'í	0	NR	7	7	0.0	0.0
BAPT–Free Will Bapt	1	NR	73	91	0.2	0.3
BAPT–Natl Mis Bapt Conv	1	75	100	125	0.3	0.4
BAPT–NBC USA	3	460	710	885	1.8	3.1
BAPT–So Bapt Conv	50	5,595	13,927	17,369	35.9	60.5
Catholic	1	NR	NR	739	1.5	2.6
CGOD–Ch God (Ander)	1	55	NR	55	0.1	0.2

Religious Group	Number of Congregations	Number of Attendees	Number of Communicant, Confirmed, or Full Members	Adherents		
				Number of Adherents	% of Total Pop.	% of Total Adh.
Ch of Nazarene	3	360	603	615	1.3	2.1
CHR–Chr Ch (Disc)	2	0	0	0	0.0	0.0
CHR–Chs of Christ	4	157	142	175	0.4	0.6
Jehovah's Witness	1	NR	NR	NR	-	-
LDS–L-D Saints	1	NR	NR	416	0.9	1.4
METH–AME	5	60	600	748	1.5	2.6
METH–C.M.E.	2	40	250	312	0.6	1.1
METH–Un Methodist	19	1,179	2,996	3,828	7.9	13.3
Non-denom Chr Chs	10	1,090	1,470	1,538	3.2	5.4
PENT–Assemb of God	6	290	209	385	0.8	1.3
PENT–Ch God (Cleve)	3	211	413	515	1.1	1.8
PENT–Ch of God by Faith	1	NR	NR	NR	-	-
PENT–Ch of God Proph	1	NR	39	49	0.1	0.2
PENT–COGIC	1	0	75	94	0.2	0.3
PENT–Cong Hol Ch	2	133	104	130	0.3	0.5
PENT–Full Gosp Bapt	1	NR	NR	NR	-	-
PENT–Un Pent Ch Intl	1	NR	NR	NR	-	-
PRES–Presb Ch (USA)	2	70	185	231	0.5	0.8
Sev Day Adv	3	135	235	270	0.6	0.9
LEE	**25**	**2,221**	**5,236**	**6,422**	**22.7**	**100.0**
Bahá'í	0	NR	26	26	0.1	0.4
BAPT–Ref Bapt Ch	1	NR	NR	NR	-	-
BAPT–So Bapt Conv	8	808	2,759	3,511	12.4	54.7
CHR–Chs of Christ	2	99	128	145	0.5	2.3
Jehovah's Witness	1	NR	NR	NR	-	-
METH–AME	3	0	300	382	1.3	5.9
METH–Un Methodist	3	655	942	1,105	3.9	17.2
Non-denom Chr Chs	3	255	375	375	1.3	5.8
PENT–Ch God (Cleve)	1	249	501	637	2.3	9.9
PENT–Cong Hol Ch	1	12	11	14	0.0	0.2
PENT–Int Foursq Gos	1	51	34	43	0.2	0.7
Sev Day Adv	1	92	160	184	0.7	2.9
LIBERTY	**72**	**5,658**	**11,709**	**17,226**	**27.1**	**100.0**
ANG/EPIS–Episcopal	1	67	115	124	0.2	0.7
Bahá'í	0	NR	12	12	0.0	0.1
BAPT–Amer Bapt Assn	1	NR	150	199	0.3	1.2
BAPT–Natl Mis Bapt Conv	1	0	150	199	0.3	1.2
BAPT–So Bapt Conv	11	1,034	4,101	5,430	8.6	31.5
Catholic	1	NR	NR	1,259	2.0	7.3
CGOD–Ch God (Ander)	1	18	NR	18	0.0	0.1
Ch of Nazarene	1	17	22	28	0.0	0.2
CHR–Chs of Christ	2	185	156	212	0.3	1.2
Jehovah's Witness	1	NR	NR	NR	-	-
LDS–L-D Saints	1	NR	NR	1,129	1.8	6.6
METH–AME	7	590	740	980	1.5	5.7
METH–Un Methodist	4	402	972	1,264	2.0	7.3
Muslim Est	1	10	NR	50	0.1	0.3
Non-denom Chr Chs	18	2,220	2,814	2,968	4.7	17.2
PENT–Assemb of God	2	235	130	256	0.4	1.5
PENT–Ch God (Cleve)	4	654	1,830	2,423	3.8	14.1
PENT–Ch Lord Jesus Apos	1	NR	NR	NR	-	-
PENT–Full Gosp Bapt	4	NR	NR	NR	-	-
PENT–Intl Pent Holiness	1	54	25	33	0.1	0.2
PENT–Un Pent Ch Intl	1	NR	NR	NR	-	-
PRES–Presb Ch (USA)	6	110	357	473	0.7	2.7
Sev Day Adv	1	32	56	64	0.1	0.4
Un C of Christ	1	30	79	105	0.2	0.6
LINCOLN	**24**	**1,312**	**2,798**	**3,510**	**43.9**	**100.0**
Bahá'í	0	NR	3	3	0.0	0.1
BAPT–So Bapt Conv	9	479	1,256	1,483	18.5	42.3
CHR–Chs of Christ	1	30	40	50	0.6	1.4
METH–C.M.E.	2	0	300	354	4.4	10.1
METH–Un Methodist	6	310	727	862	10.8	24.6
Non-denom Chr Chs	1	100	150	150	1.9	4.3
PENT–Assemb of God	1	285	201	466	5.8	13.3
PENT–Ch God (Cleve)	1	5	30	35	0.4	1.0
PENT–Cong Hol Ch	1	91	79	93	1.2	2.6
PENT–Fire Bapt Hol Ch	1	NR	NR	NR	-	-
PRES–Presb Ch (USA)	1	12	12	14	0.2	0.4

NR–Not Reported   - Represents no adherents reported.   Percentages may not total 100 due to rounding.

Table 3: Religious Congregations by County and Group: 2010

Religious Group	Number of Congrega-tions	Number of Attendees	Number of Communicant, Confirmed, or Full Members	Adherents: Number of Adherents	Adherents: % of Total Pop.	Adherents: % of Total Adh.
LONG	**12**	**1,016**	**2,455**	**3,157**	**21.8**	**100.0**
Bahá'í	0	NR	1	1	0.0	0.0
BAPT–So Bapt Conv	7	688	1,888	2,494	17.2	79.0
METH–AME	1	0	100	132	0.9	4.2
METH–Un Methodist	1	51	103	103	0.7	3.3
Non-denom Chr Chs	2	110	165	165	1.1	5.2
PENT–Ch God (Cleve)	1	167	198	262	1.8	8.3
LOWNDES	**166**	**22,856**	**42,940**	**57,669**	**52.8**	**100.0**
ANG/EPIS–Episcopal	3	412	763	982	0.9	1.7
Bahá'í	0	NR	31	31	0.0	0.1
BAPT–Free Will Bapt	2	NR	146	181	0.2	0.3
BAPT–NBC USA	2	85	300	373	0.3	0.6
BAPT–So Bapt Conv	36	7,444	17,212	21,388	19.6	37.1
Catholic	2	NR	NR	3,999	3.7	6.9
CGOD–Ch God (Ander)	1	300	NR	300	0.3	0.5
Ch Cr, Scientst	1	NR	NR	NR	-	-
Ch of Nazarene	1	152	246	246	0.2	0.4
CHR–Chr Ch (Disc)	4	165	467	580	0.5	1.0
CHR–Chr Chs & Chs Cr	1	NR	0	0	0.0	0.0
CHR–Chs of Christ	17	2,675	2,816	3,500	3.2	6.1
Ind Fund Churches	1	NR	NR	NR	-	-
Jehovah's Witness	2	NR	NR	NR	-	-
LDS–L-D Saints	2	NR	NR	1,115	1.0	1.9
LUTH–E.L.C.A.	1	29	29	52	0.0	0.1
LUTH–Luth-MO Synod	1	90	143	159	0.1	0.3
METH–AME	11	625	2,124	2,639	2.4	4.6
METH–C.M.E.	1	45	85	106	0.1	0.2
METH–Un Methodist	10	1,948	5,937	6,835	6.3	11.9
Muslim Est	1	270	NR	762	0.7	1.3
Non-denom Chr Chs	33	6,355	9,154	9,944	9.1	17.2
PENT–Assemb of God	3	185	155	247	0.2	0.4
PENT–Ch God (Cleve)	11	1,222	1,955	2,429	2.2	4.2
PENT–Ch Lord Jesus Apos	1	NR	NR	NR	-	-
PENT–Ch of God by Faith	3	NR	NR	NR	-	-
PENT–Ch of God Proph	2	NR	84	104	0.1	0.2
PENT–COGIC	2	250	300	373	0.3	0.6
PENT–Intl Pent Holiness	1	30	50	62	0.1	0.1
PENT–Un Pent Ch Intl	1	NR	NR	NR	-	-
PRES–Presb Ch (USA)	5	348	566	703	0.6	1.2
PRES–Presb Ch Amer	1	114	158	188	0.2	0.3
Salvation Army	1	21	78	205	0.2	0.4
Sev Day Adv	1	66	116	133	0.1	0.2
Unit Univ	1	25	25	33	0.0	0.1
LUMPKIN	**27**	**2,398**	**4,538**	**7,424**	**24.8**	**100.0**
ANG/EPIS–Episcopal	1	75	110	137	0.5	1.8
Bahá'í	0	NR	4	4	0.0	0.1
BAPT–So Bapt Conv	7	697	1,735	2,070	6.9	27.9
Catholic	1	NR	NR	1,254	4.2	16.9
CHR–Chs of Christ	1	25	21	27	0.1	0.4
Jehovah's Witness	1	NR	NR	NR	-	-
METH–C.M.E.	1	0	150	179	0.6	2.4
METH–Un Methodist	4	696	1,374	2,354	7.9	31.7
Non-denom Chr Chs	4	580	650	775	2.6	10.4
PENT–Assemb of God	1	50	35	80	0.3	1.1
PENT–Ch God (Cleve)	1	83	125	149	0.5	2.0
PENT–Ch of God Proph	1	NR	73	87	0.3	1.2
PENT–Cong Hol Ch	2	117	166	198	0.7	2.7
PRES–Presb Ch (USA)	1	25	34	41	0.1	0.6
Unit Univ	1	50	61	69	0.2	0.9
MCDUFFIE	**44**	**3,485**	**10,542**	**13,644**	**62.4**	**100.0**
ANG/EPIS–Episcopal	1	17	40	82	0.4	0.6
Bahá'í	0	NR	29	29	0.1	0.2
BAPT–NBC USA	2	300	1,279	1,605	7.3	11.8
BAPT–So Bapt Conv	16	2,117	6,341	7,957	36.4	58.3
Catholic	1	NR	NR	573	2.6	4.2
CHR–Chs of Christ	2	101	137	153	0.7	1.1
Jehovah's Witness	1	NR	NR	NR	-	-
METH–AME	4	0	500	627	2.9	4.6
METH–C.M.E.	2	75	240	301	1.4	2.2
METH–Un Methodist	6	463	1,273	1,540	7.0	11.3
Non-denom Chr Chs	3	340	460	475	2.2	3.5
PENT–Ch God (Cleve)	2	57	115	144	0.7	1.1
PENT–Un Pent Ch Intl	1	NR	NR	NR	-	-
PRES–As Ref Pres Ch	1	NR	102	128	0.6	0.9
Sev Day Adv	2	15	26	30	0.1	0.2
MCINTOSH	**23**	**1,069**	**3,079**	**4,354**	**30.4**	**100.0**
ANG/EPIS–Episcopal	2	104	229	272	1.9	6.2
Bahá'í	0	NR	3	3	0.0	0.1
BAPT–So Bapt Conv	5	325	1,304	1,547	10.8	35.5
Catholic	1	NR	NR	397	2.8	9.1
Jehovah's Witness	1	NR	NR	NR	-	-
LDS–L-D Saints	1	NR	NR	256	1.8	5.9
METH–AME	3	0	450	534	3.7	12.3
METH–Un Methodist	2	166	298	412	2.9	9.5
Non-denom Chr Chs	1	110	130	138	1.0	3.2
PENT–Assemb of God	1	15	8	15	0.1	0.3
PENT–Ch God (Cleve)	2	274	465	552	3.9	12.7
PENT–Ch of God Proph	2	NR	89	106	0.7	2.4
PRES–Presb Ch (USA)	2	75	103	122	0.9	2.8
MACON	**40**	**2,372**	**4,936**	**6,169**	**41.9**	**100.0**
ANG/EPIS–Episcopal	1	7	8	8	0.1	0.1
Bahá'í	0	NR	222	222	1.5	3.6
BAPT–NBC USA	2	550	600	719	4.9	11.7
BAPT–So Bapt Conv	9	658	1,829	2,193	14.9	35.5
Catholic	1	NR	NR	210	1.4	3.4
CHR–Chs of Christ	1	15	17	30	0.2	0.5
Jehovah's Witness	1	NR	NR	NR	-	-
LUTH–E.L.C.A.	1	62	87	122	0.8	2.0
MENN–Beachy Amish-Menn	2	442	268	442	3.0	7.2
METH–AME	6	60	700	839	5.7	13.6
METH–C.M.E.	3	30	308	369	2.5	6.0
METH–Un Methodist	6	203	440	494	3.4	8.0
Non-denom Chr Chs	3	255	305	344	2.3	5.6
PENT–Ch of God Proph	1	NR	16	19	0.1	0.3
PENT–Cong Hol Ch	1	35	40	48	0.3	0.8
Sev Day Adv	2	55	96	110	0.7	1.8
MADISON	**47**	**4,072**	**10,162**	**12,335**	**43.9**	**100.0**
Bahá'í	0	NR	1	1	0.0	0.0
BAPT–So Bapt Conv	28	3,126	7,844	9,612	34.2	77.9
CHR–Chr Chs & Chs Cr	2	NR	175	214	0.8	1.7
CHR–Chs of Christ	2	80	113	135	0.5	1.1
Jehovah's Witness	1	NR	NR	NR	-	-
METH–C.M.E.	1	0	150	184	0.7	1.5
METH–Evan Meth Ch	1	NR	NR	NR	-	-
METH–Un Methodist	5	396	1,157	1,372	4.9	11.1
Non-denom Chr Chs	2	200	300	300	1.1	2.4
PENT–Cong Hol Ch	1	46	155	190	0.7	1.5
PENT–Intl Pent Holiness	2	170	188	230	0.8	1.9
PRES–Presb Ch (USA)	2	54	79	97	0.3	0.8
MARION	**23**	**728**	**2,352**	**2,984**	**34.1**	**100.0**
Bahá'í	0	NR	15	15	0.2	0.5
BAPT–Free Will Bapt	2	NR	146	179	2.0	6.0
BAPT–So Bapt Conv	8	424	1,061	1,298	14.8	43.5
Catholic	1	NR	NR	187	2.1	6.3
CHR–Chs of Christ	1	12	12	12	0.1	0.4
METH–AME	4	0	450	550	6.3	18.4
METH–Un Methodist	5	198	442	467	5.3	15.7
PENT–Ch God (Cleve)	1	39	176	215	2.5	7.2
PENT–COGIC	1	55	50	61	0.7	2.0
MERIWETHER	**60**	**3,283**	**8,116**	**9,981**	**45.4**	**100.0**
Bahá'í	0	NR	44	44	0.2	0.4
BAPT–N Am Bapt Conf	1	NR	87	107	0.5	1.1
BAPT–NBC USA	2	140	585	717	3.3	7.2
BAPT–So Bapt Conv	17	1,118	3,401	4,168	19.0	41.8
Catholic	1	NR	NR	145	0.7	1.5
Ch of Nazarene	2	112	213	221	1.0	2.2

NR–Not Reported - Represents no adherents reported. Percentages may not total 100 due to rounding.

Table 3: Religious Congregations by County and Group: 2010

Religious Group	Number of Congregations	Number of Attendees	Number of Communicant, Confirmed, or Full Members	Adherents: Number of Adherents	Adherents: % of Total Pop.	Adherents: % of Total Adh.
CHR–Chs of Christ	2	230	210	378	1.7	3.8
Jehovah's Witness	1	NR	NR	NR	-	-
METH–AME	1	0	100	123	0.6	1.2
METH–C.M.E.	2	0	300	368	1.7	3.7
METH–Un Methodist	14	532	1,338	1,449	6.6	14.5
Non-denom Chr Chs	7	810	975	1,103	5.0	11.1
PENT–Assemb of God	1	120	62	180	0.8	1.8
PENT–Ch God (Cleve)	1	49	55	67	0.3	0.7
PENT–COGIC	3	0	450	552	2.5	5.5
PENT–Cong Hol Ch	1	65	45	55	0.3	0.6
PRES–Presb Ch (USA)	2	37	79	97	0.4	1.0
Sev Day Adv	1	30	51	59	0.3	0.6
Un C of Christ	1	40	121	148	0.7	1.5
MILLER	**19**	**766**	**1,967**	**2,350**	**38.4**	**100.0**
Bahá'í	0	NR	3	3	0.0	0.1
BAPT–Free Will Bapt	7	NR	511	627	10.2	26.7
BAPT–So Bapt Conv	3	297	753	923	15.1	39.3
METH–Un Methodist	2	208	352	387	6.3	16.5
Non-denom Chr Chs	1	100	150	150	2.4	6.4
PENT–Assemb of God	1	50	25	50	0.8	2.1
PENT–Ch God (Cleve)	4	98	150	184	3.0	7.8
Sev Day Adv	1	13	23	26	0.4	1.1
MITCHELL	**53**	**2,954**	**9,890**	**12,274**	**52.2**	**100.0**
ANG/EPIS–Episcopal	1	18	26	26	0.1	0.2
Bahá'í	0	NR	4	4	0.0	0.0
BAPT–Free Will Bapt	3	NR	219	272	1.2	2.2
BAPT–Natl Mis Bapt Conv	3	0	450	560	2.4	4.6
BAPT–NBC USA	3	225	600	746	3.2	6.1
BAPT–So Bapt Conv	20	1,858	6,149	7,648	32.5	62.3
Catholic	1	NR	NR	259	1.1	2.1
CHR–Chr Chs & Chs Cr	1	NR	38	47	0.2	0.4
CHR–Chs of Christ	2	35	32	42	0.2	0.3
Jehovah's Witness	1	NR	NR	NR	-	-
METH–AME	4	0	500	622	2.6	5.1
METH–Un Methodist	7	410	1,081	1,129	4.8	9.2
Non-denom Chr Chs	2	200	365	365	1.6	3.0
PENT–Assemb of God	2	130	93	140	0.6	1.1
PENT–Ch God (Cleve)	2	60	319	397	1.7	3.2
PRES–Presb Ch (USA)	1	18	14	17	0.1	0.1
MONROE	**53**	**2,859**	**8,114**	**9,706**	**36.7**	**100.0**
Bahá'í	0	NR	16	16	0.1	0.2
BAPT–NBC USA	2	0	300	362	1.4	3.7
BAPT–So Bapt Conv	17	1,756	4,525	5,454	20.6	56.2
CHR–Chs of Christ	1	30	32	35	0.1	0.4
HINDU–Post Ren	1	NR	NR	25	0.1	0.3
METH–AME	11	0	1,300	1,567	5.9	16.1
METH–Un Methodist	10	633	1,366	1,522	5.8	15.7
Non-denom Chr Chs	3	185	235	256	1.0	2.6
PENT–Assemb of God	1	40	0	40	0.2	0.4
PENT–Ch God (Cleve)	1	24	43	52	0.2	0.5
PENT–Ch Lord Jesus Apos	1	NR	NR	NR	-	-
PENT–Cong Hol Ch	2	112	213	257	1.0	2.6
PRES–Presb Ch (USA)	1	20	30	36	0.1	0.4
PRES–Presb Ch Amer	1	59	54	84	0.3	0.9
PRES–Ref Pres US	1	NR	NR	NR	-	-
MONTGOMERY	**26**	**1,166**	**3,039**	**3,668**	**40.2**	**100.0**
BAPT–So Bapt Conv	9	737	1,844	2,239	24.5	61.0
METH–AME	4	0	450	546	6.0	14.9
METH–Un Methodist	7	165	278	316	3.5	8.6
PENT–Ch God (Cleve)	4	264	413	501	5.5	13.7
PRES–Presb Ch (USA)	2	0	54	66	0.7	1.8
MORGAN	**37**	**3,170**	**7,441**	**9,414**	**52.7**	**100.0**
ANG/EPIS–Episcopal	1	74	190	190	1.1	2.0
Bahá'í	0	NR	4	4	0.0	0.0
BAPT–NBC USA	1	150	385	474	2.7	5.0
BAPT–So Bapt Conv	14	1,508	3,863	4,752	26.6	50.5
Catholic	1	NR	NR	353	2.0	3.7

Religious Group	Number of Congregations	Number of Attendees	Number of Communicant, Confirmed, or Full Members	Adherents: Number of Adherents	Adherents: % of Total Pop.	Adherents: % of Total Adh.
CHR–Chr Ch (Disc)	1	0	0	0	0.0	0.0
CHR–Chr Chs & Chs Cr	1	NR	0	0	0.0	0.0
CHR–Chs of Christ	1	90	100	168	0.9	1.8
LDS–L-D Saints	1	NR	NR	126	0.7	1.3
METH–AME	1	0	100	123	0.7	1.3
METH–Un Methodist	9	603	1,381	1,562	8.7	16.6
Non-denom Chr Chs	2	410	600	662	3.7	7.0
PENT–Ch God (Cleve)	1	90	259	319	1.8	3.4
PENT–Cong Hol Ch	1	39	35	43	0.2	0.5
PRES–Presb Ch (USA)	1	158	440	541	3.0	5.7
Sev Day Adv	1	48	84	97	0.5	1.0
MURRAY	**43**	**4,031**	**10,866**	**13,636**	**34.4**	**100.0**
BAPT–So Bapt Conv	20	3,037	8,666	10,938	27.6	80.2
CHR–Chs of Christ	2	129	115	145	0.4	1.1
Jehovah's Witness	1	NR	NR	NR	-	-
METH–Un Methodist	7	313	765	938	2.4	6.9
Non-denom Chr Chs	3	280	370	400	1.0	2.9
PENT–Assemb of God	1	0	0	0	0.0	0.0
PENT–Ch God (Cleve)	5	182	466	588	1.5	4.3
PENT–Ch of God Proph	1	NR	174	220	0.6	1.6
PRES–Cumber Presb	1	NR	155	228	0.6	1.7
Sev Day Adv	2	90	155	179	0.5	1.3
MUSCOGEE	**259**	**37,851**	**82,194**	**117,867**	**62.1**	**100.0**
ANG/EPIS–Episcopal	3	438	1,103	1,188	0.6	1.0
Bahá'í	0	NR	37	37	0.0	0.0
BAPT–Amer Bapt USA	2	130	685	855	0.5	0.7
BAPT–Converge/BGC	1	75	NR	90	0.0	0.1
BAPT–Free Will Bapt	3	NR	219	273	0.1	0.2
BAPT–Ind Bapt Flwsp Intl	1	NR	NR	NR	-	-
BAPT–Natl Mis Bapt Conv	1	0	150	187	0.1	0.2
BAPT–NBC Amer	1	600	2,000	2,497	1.3	2.1
BAPT–NBC USA	23	2,595	7,538	9,411	5.0	8.0
BAPT–So Bapt Conv	43	11,504	34,649	43,259	22.8	36.7
Calv Chpl	1	NR	NR	NR	-	-
Catholic	4	NR	NR	8,738	4.6	7.4
CGOD–Ch God (Ander)	1	21	NR	21	0.0	0.0
Ch Cr, Scientst	1	NR	NR	NR	-	-
Ch of Nazarene	3	178	227	249	0.1	0.2
CHR–Chr Ch (Disc)	1	100	300	375	0.2	0.3
CHR–Chr Chs & Chs Cr	1	NR	100	125	0.1	0.1
CHR–Chs of Christ	10	1,257	1,373	1,761	0.9	1.5
Jehovah's Witness	2	NR	NR	NR	-	-
JUD–Conserv	1	56	63	170	0.1	0.1
JUD–Reform	1	60	106	286	0.2	0.2
LDS–L-D Saints	4	NR	NR	2,740	1.4	2.3
LUTH–E.L.C.A.	1	101	169	270	0.1	0.2
LUTH–Luth Cong Msn Chr	1	40	NR	NR	-	-
LUTH–Luth–MO Synod	2	156	300	353	0.2	0.3
METH–AME	14	956	2,720	3,396	1.8	2.9
METH–AME Zion	2	50	210	262	0.1	0.2
METH–C.M.E.	4	400	700	874	0.5	0.7
METH–Free Methodist	1	634	331	634	0.3	0.5
METH–Un Methodist	21	4,404	13,016	15,401	8.1	13.1
Muslim Est	3	809	NR	2,286	1.2	1.9
New Apost Ch	1	NR	NR	NR	-	-
Non-denom Chr Chs	40	6,810	8,497	9,714	5.1	8.2
ORTHE–Greek Orthodox	1	30	NR	80	0.0	0.1
PENT–Apos Faith Msn	1	NR	35	44	0.0	0.0
PENT–Assemb of God	14	3,321	2,475	5,621	3.0	4.8
PENT–Ch God (Cleve)	5	420	954	1,191	0.6	1.0
PENT–Ch Lord Jesus Apos	1	NR	NR	NR	-	-
PENT–Ch of God Proph	3	NR	86	107	0.1	0.1
PENT–COGIC	7	835	1,175	1,467	0.8	1.2
PENT–Cong Hol Ch	1	80	60	75	0.0	0.1
PENT–Full Gosp Bapt	4	NR	NR	NR	-	-
PENT–Int Foursq Gos	1	44	40	50	0.0	0.0
PENT–Intl Pent Holiness	1	11	38	47	0.0	0.0
PENT–Pent Ch of God	2	140	NR	217	0.1	0.2
PENT–Un Pent Ch Intl	2	NR	NR	NR	-	-
PRES–Kor Pres Abroad	1	NR	NR	NR	-	-
PRES–Presb Ch (USA)	9	763	1,536	1,918	1.0	1.6

NR–Not Reported   - Represents no adherents reported.   Percentages may not total 100 due to rounding.

Table 3: Religious Congregations by County and Group: 2010

Religious Group	Number of Congrega-tions	Number of Attendees	Number of Communicant, Confirmed, or Full Members	Adherents		
				Number of Adherents	% of Total Pop.	% of Total Adh.
PRES–Presb Ch Amer	3	240	228	345	0.2	0.3
Salvation Army	1	88	215	262	0.1	0.2
Sev Day Adv	2	465	809	930	0.5	0.8
Un C of Christ	1	0	7	9	0.0	0.0
Unit Univ	1	40	43	48	0.0	0.0
Zoroastrian	0	NR	NR	4	0.0	0.0
NEWTON	**104**	**12,934**	**24,733**	**34,784**	**34.8**	**100.0**
ANG/EPIS–Episcopal	1	150	311	311	0.3	0.9
Bahá'í	0	NR	106	106	0.1	0.3
BAPT–Reg Bapt Gen As	1	NR	NR	NR	-	-
BAPT–So Bapt Conv	34	5,272	11,253	14,484	14.5	41.6
Catholic	1	NR	NR	3,170	3.2	9.1
Ch of Nazarene	1	102	54	174	0.2	0.5
CHR–Chr Chs & Chs Cr	3	NR	1,360	1,750	1.8	5.0
CHR–Chs of Christ	3	180	176	218	0.2	0.6
Jehovah's Witness	1	NR	NR	NR	-	-
LDS–L-D Saints	1	NR	NR	610	0.6	1.8
LUTH–Wisc Ev Luth Syn	1	128	133	176	0.2	0.5
METH–AME	3	225	655	843	0.8	2.4
METH–AME Zion	1	0	150	193	0.2	0.6
METH–Un Methodist	24	2,108	5,090	5,810	5.8	16.7
Non-denom Chr Chs	11	3,895	3,995	5,156	5.2	14.8
PENT–Assemb of God	2	195	235	255	0.3	0.7
PENT–Ch God (Cleve)	1	21	30	39	0.0	0.1
PENT–COGIC	1	0	150	193	0.2	0.6
PENT–Un Pent Ch Intl	3	NR	NR	NR	-	-
PENT–Vineyard	1	52	58	75	0.1	0.2
PRES–As Ref Pres Ch	1	NR	41	53	0.1	0.2
PRES–Presb Ch (USA)	6	339	635	817	0.8	2.3
PRES–Presb Ch Amer	1	181	151	178	0.2	0.5
PRES–Ref Pres US	1	NR	NR	NR	-	-
Sev Day Adv	1	86	150	173	0.2	0.5
OCONEE	**44**	**7,175**	**12,476**	**16,734**	**51.0**	**100.0**
Bahá'í	0	NR	13	13	0.0	0.1
BAPT–NBC USA	1	0	250	318	1.0	1.9
BAPT–So Bapt Conv	11	3,237	6,728	8,547	26.1	51.1
Calv Chpl	1	NR	NR	NR	-	-
CHR–Chr Ch (Disc)	4	292	1,116	1,418	4.3	8.5
CHR–Chs of Christ	2	76	77	104	0.3	0.6
METH–AME	1	0	100	127	0.4	0.8
METH–Un Methodist	7	532	1,252	1,591	4.8	9.5
METH–Wesleyan	1	62	64	81	0.2	0.5
Non-denom Chr Chs	5	750	650	987	3.0	5.9
ORTHE–Greek Orthodox	1	80	NR	200	0.6	1.2
PENT–Assemb of God	1	310	300	865	2.6	5.2
PENT–Ch God (Cleve)	1	956	969	1,231	3.8	7.4
PENT–Cong Hol Ch	1	39	35	44	0.1	0.3
PENT–Full Gosp Bapt	1	NR	NR	NR	-	-
PRES–Presb Ch (USA)	3	393	562	714	2.2	4.3
PRES–Presb Ch Amer	3	448	360	494	1.5	3.0
OGLETHORPE	**29**	**1,156**	**2,789**	**3,347**	**22.5**	**100.0**
Bahá'í	0	NR	34	34	0.2	1.0
BAPT–So Bapt Conv	14	821	2,105	2,565	17.2	76.6
CHR–Chr Chs & Chs Cr	1	NR	0	0	0.0	0.0
CHR–Chs of Christ	1	50	30	50	0.3	1.5
METH–AME	2	0	200	244	1.6	7.3
METH–Evan Meth Ch	1	NR	NR	NR	-	-
METH–Un Methodist	5	103	190	207	1.4	6.2
Non-denom Chr Chs	1	100	150	150	1.0	4.5
PENT–Ch God (Cleve)	1	30	20	24	0.2	0.7
PENT–Cong Hol Ch	2	46	54	66	0.4	2.0
PRES–Presb Ch (USA)	1	6	6	7	0.0	0.2
PAULDING	**88**	**14,545**	**25,644**	**37,569**	**26.4**	**100.0**
ANG/EPIS–Anglican NA	1	NR	NR	NR	-	-
Bahá'í	0	NR	30	30	0.0	0.1
BAPT–Converge/BGC	1	75	NR	90	0.1	0.2
BAPT–Natl Mis Bapt Conv	2	0	300	393	0.3	1.0
BAPT–NBC USA	1	0	150	196	0.1	0.5

Religious Group	Number of Congrega-tions	Number of Attendees	Number of Communicant, Confirmed, or Full Members	Adherents		
				Number of Adherents	% of Total Pop.	% of Total Adh.
BAPT–S-D Baptist Gen Con	1	24	40	52	0.0	0.1
BAPT–So Bapt Conv	34	9,076	15,697	20,539	14.4	54.7
Calv Chpl	1	NR	NR	NR	-	-
Catholic	1	NR	NR	2,714	1.9	7.2
Ch of Nazarene	2	115	51	162	0.1	0.4
CHR–Chr Chs & Chs Cr	2	NR	900	1,178	0.8	3.1
CHR–Chs of Christ	3	360	328	395	0.3	1.1
Jehovah's Witness	1	NR	NR	NR	-	-
LDS–L-D Saints	3	NR	NR	1,133	0.8	3.0
LUTH–E.L.C.A.	1	93	216	216	0.2	0.6
LUTH–Wisc Ev Luth Syn	1	97	136	179	0.1	0.5
METH–AME	1	0	150	196	0.1	0.5
METH–AME Zion	1	0	100	131	0.1	0.3
METH–Un Methodist	12	1,286	3,497	4,728	3.3	12.6
Missionary Ch	1	175	100	175	0.1	0.5
Non-denom Chr Chs	8	2,515	2,775	3,269	2.3	8.7
ORTHE–Ant Orth of NA	1	75	NR	160	0.1	0.4
PENT–Assemb of God	1	166	119	230	0.2	0.6
PENT–Ch God (Cleve)	1	117	390	510	0.4	1.4
PENT–Ch of God Proph	1	NR	37	48	0.0	0.1
PENT–COGIC	1	0	150	196	0.1	0.5
PENT–Cong Hol Ch	1	39	35	46	0.0	0.1
PENT–Un Pent Ch Intl	1	NR	NR	NR	-	-
PRES–Presb Ch (USA)	1	85	148	194	0.1	0.5
PRES–Presb Ch Amer	1	174	168	263	0.2	0.7
Sev Day Adv	1	73	127	146	0.1	0.4
PEACH	**47**	**4,918**	**10,655**	**13,173**	**47.6**	**100.0**
ANG/EPIS–Anglican NA	1	NR	NR	NR	-	-
ANG/EPIS–Episcopal	2	49	97	171	0.6	1.3
Bahá'í	0	NR	121	121	0.4	0.9
BAPT–Free Will Bapt	1	NR	73	89	0.3	0.7
BAPT–NBC USA	1	200	400	486	1.8	3.7
BAPT–So Bapt Conv	7	960	2,726	3,315	12.0	25.2
Calv Chpl	1	NR	NR	NR	-	-
Catholic	1	NR	NR	730	2.6	5.5
CHR–Chs of Christ	2	81	81	101	0.4	0.8
Evan Ch	1	NR	NR	NR	-	-
HINDU–I/A Temples	1	NR	NR	350	1.3	2.7
Jehovah's Witness	2	NR	NR	NR	-	-
METH–AME	5	280	658	800	2.9	6.1
METH–C.M.E.	3	250	921	1,120	4.0	8.5
METH–Un Methodist	6	533	991	1,157	4.2	8.8
Non-denom Chr Chs	6	2,486	4,330	4,375	15.8	33.2
PENT–Assemb of God	1	38	27	80	0.3	0.6
PENT–Ch of God by Faith	2	NR	NR	NR	-	-
PENT–COGIC	1	0	150	182	0.7	1.4
PRES–Presb Ch (USA)	1	23	49	60	0.2	0.5
Sev Day Adv	1	18	31	36	0.1	0.3
Unity Ch	1	NR	NR	NR	-	-
PICKENS	**33**	**2,215**	**4,884**	**7,330**	**24.9**	**100.0**
ANG/EPIS–Episcopal	1	167	212	282	1.0	3.8
Bahá'í	0	NR	8	8	0.0	0.1
BAPT–Prog NBC	1	0	150	182	0.6	2.5
BAPT–So Bapt Conv	7	600	1,515	1,840	6.3	25.1
Catholic	1	NR	NR	1,349	4.6	18.4
Chr & Miss Al	1	99	135	155	0.5	2.1
CHR–Chr Chs & Chs Cr	2	NR	115	140	0.5	1.9
CHR–Chs of Christ	3	147	126	166	0.6	2.3
Jehovah's Witness	1	NR	NR	NR	-	-
LUTH–Luth-MO Synod	1	0	0	0	0.0	0.0
METH–Un Methodist	3	371	1,092	1,489	5.1	20.3
Non-denom Chr Chs	4	525	825	869	3.0	11.9
PENT–Assemb of God	1	27	22	28	0.1	0.4
PENT–Ch God (Cleve)	1	17	199	242	0.8	3.3
PENT–COGIC	1	0	150	182	0.6	2.5
PENT–Cong Hol Ch	1	65	38	46	0.2	0.6
PENT–Un Pent Ch Intl	1	NR	NR	NR	-	-
PRES–Presb Ch (USA)	1	127	174	211	0.7	2.9
PRES–Presb Ch Amer	1	0	0	0	0.0	0.0
Sev Day Adv	1	70	123	141	0.5	1.9

NR–Not Reported - Represents no adherents reported. Percentages may not total 100 due to rounding.

Table 3: Religious Congregations by County and Group: 2010

Religious Group	Number of Congrega-tions	Number of Attendees	Number of Communicant, Confirmed, or Full Members	Adherents		
				Number of Adherents	% of Total Pop.	% of Total Adh.
PIERCE	**41**	**4,007**	**9,047**	**11,108**	**59.2**	**100.0**
BAPT–Free Will Bapt	2	NR	146	183	1.0	1.6
BAPT–NBC USA	1	0	0	0	0.0	0.0
BAPT–So Bapt Conv	16	2,684	6,370	8,001	42.7	72.0
CHR–Chs of Christ	1	25	14	21	0.1	0.2
METH–AME	1	0	100	126	0.7	1.1
METH–Un Methodist	6	285	703	788	4.2	7.1
Non-denom Chr Chs	4	335	415	443	2.4	4.0
PENT–Assemb of God	2	370	474	510	2.7	4.6
PENT–Ch God (Cleve)	5	308	700	879	4.7	7.9
PENT–Ch of God Proph	1	NR	22	28	0.1	0.3
PENT–Un Pent Ch Intl	1	NR	NR	NR	-	-
PRES–Presb Ch (USA)	1	0	103	129	0.7	1.2
PIKE	**37**	**3,121**	**5,719**	**7,089**	**39.7**	**100.0**
Bahá'í	0	NR	25	25	0.1	0.4
BAPT–So Bapt Conv	19	1,520	3,464	4,361	24.4	61.5
Ch of Nazarene	2	118	198	220	1.2	3.1
CHR–Chr Ch (Disc)	1	0	0	0	0.0	0.0
HINDU–Post Ren	1	NR	NR	16	0.1	0.2
METH–AME	1	0	100	126	0.7	1.8
METH–C.M.E.	1	0	150	189	1.1	2.7
METH–Un Methodist	7	274	463	545	3.0	7.7
Non-denom Chr Chs	2	490	835	875	4.9	12.3
PENT–Assemb of God	2	703	461	703	3.9	9.9
PRES–Presb Ch (USA)	1	16	23	29	0.2	0.4
POLK	**78**	**7,285**	**17,586**	**25,472**	**61.4**	**100.0**
ANG/EPIS–Episcopal	1	38	63	97	0.2	0.4
Bahá'í	0	NR	7	7	0.0	0.0
BAPT–NBC USA	2	0	450	572	1.4	2.2
BAPT–So Bapt Conv	35	4,676	12,079	15,349	37.0	60.3
Catholic	1	NR	NR	3,263	7.9	12.8
CHR–Chs of Christ	4	216	272	359	0.9	1.4
Jehovah's Witness	2	NR	NR	NR	-	-
LDS–L-D Saints	1	NR	NR	310	0.7	1.2
METH–AME	3	0	350	445	1.1	1.7
METH–Cong Meth	1	NR	NR	NR	-	-
METH–Un Methodist	8	563	1,805	2,206	5.3	8.7
Non-denom Chr Chs	7	1,151	1,624	1,664	4.0	6.5
PENT–Assemb of God	1	50	42	78	0.2	0.3
PENT–Ch God (Cleve)	3	312	495	629	1.5	2.5
PENT–Ch of God Proph	1	NR	15	19	0.0	0.1
PENT–COGIC	1	31	45	57	0.1	0.2
PENT–Cong Hol Ch	1	72	61	78	0.2	0.3
PENT–Intl Pent Holiness	1	14	14	18	0.0	0.1
PENT–Un Pent Ch Intl	1	NR	NR	NR	-	-
PRES–Presb Ch (USA)	2	107	180	229	0.6	0.9
PRES–Presb Ch Amer	1	23	28	28	0.1	0.1
Sev Day Adv	1	32	56	64	0.2	0.3
PULASKI	**21**	**1,117**	**4,017**	**4,895**	**40.8**	**100.0**
ANG/EPIS–Episcopal	1	57	132	132	1.1	2.7
Bahá'í	0	NR	62	62	0.5	1.3
BAPT–So Bapt Conv	11	757	3,081	3,702	30.8	75.6
Jehovah's Witness	1	NR	NR	NR	-	-
METH–AME	1	0	150	180	1.5	3.7
METH–Un Methodist	1	147	381	562	4.7	11.5
PENT–Assemb of God	1	39	47	59	0.5	1.2
PENT–Ch God (Cleve)	2	47	92	111	0.9	2.3
PENT–Ch of God by Faith	1	NR	NR	NR	-	-
PENT–Cong Hol Ch	1	25	8	10	0.1	0.2
PENT–Intl Pent Holiness	1	45	64	77	0.6	1.6
PUTNAM	**41**	**2,442**	**6,028**	**7,144**	**33.7**	**100.0**
ANG/EPIS–Episcopal	1	23	24	27	0.1	0.4
Bahá'í	0	NR	18	18	0.1	0.3
BAPT–So Bapt Conv	7	920	2,436	2,936	13.8	41.1
CGOD–Ch God (Ander)	1	25	NR	25	0.1	0.3
CHR–Chr Chs & Chs Cr	1	NR	121	146	0.7	2.0
CHR–Chs of Christ	1	25	20	27	0.1	0.4
Jehovah's Witness	1	NR	NR	NR	-	-

Religious Group	Number of Congrega-tions	Number of Attendees	Number of Communicant, Confirmed, or Full Members	Adherents		
				Number of Adherents	% of Total Pop.	% of Total Adh.
LUTH–Luth–MO Synod	1	107	171	178	0.8	2.5
METH–AME	6	0	800	964	4.5	13.5
METH–Un Methodist	9	459	1,268	1,500	7.1	21.0
Non-denom Chr Chs	6	505	625	681	3.2	9.5
PENT–Assemb of God	1	23	0	23	0.1	0.3
PENT–Ch God (Cleve)	1	27	128	154	0.7	2.2
PENT–Ch of God Proph	1	NR	16	19	0.1	0.3
PENT–Intl Pent Holiness	1	65	79	95	0.4	1.3
PRES–Presb Ch (USA)	1	55	77	93	0.4	1.3
PRES–Presb Ch Amer	2	208	245	258	1.2	3.6
QUITMAN	**11**	**323**	**1,111**	**1,342**	**53.4**	**100.0**
Bahá'í	0	NR	1	1	0.0	0.1
BAPT–Natl Mis Bapt Conv	1	0	150	179	7.1	13.3
BAPT–So Bapt Conv	2	139	446	531	21.1	39.6
CHR–Chs of Christ	1	80	110	125	5.0	9.3
METH–AME	3	0	300	357	14.2	26.6
METH–Un Methodist	3	65	69	107	4.3	8.0
PENT–Cong Hol Ch	1	39	35	42	1.7	3.1
RABUN	**49**	**4,019**	**8,645**	**13,486**	**82.9**	**100.0**
ANG/EPIS–Episcopal	1	109	145	145	0.9	1.1
BAPT–So Bapt Conv	21	2,058	5,640	6,652	40.9	49.3
Catholic	1	NR	NR	2,018	12.4	15.0
CHR–Chr Chs & Chs Cr	1	NR	57	67	0.4	0.5
CHR–Chs of Christ	1	40	40	55	0.3	0.4
HINDU–Renaiss	1	NR	NR	1,450	8.9	10.8
Jehovah's Witness	1	NR	NR	NR	-	-
METH–Un Methodist	7	535	1,147	1,313	8.1	9.7
Non-denom Chr Chs	4	620	775	800	4.9	5.9
PENT–Assemb of God	1	60	56	60	0.4	0.4
PENT–Ch God (Cleve)	4	331	478	564	3.5	4.2
PRES–Presb Ch (USA)	5	266	307	362	2.2	2.7
Unity Ch	1	NR	NR	NR	-	-
RANDOLPH	**31**	**724**	**3,461**	**4,194**	**54.3**	**100.0**
Bahá'í	0	NR	68	68	0.9	1.6
BAPT–Free Will Bapt	1	NR	73	88	1.1	2.1
BAPT–Natl Mis Bapt Conv	1	0	150	181	2.3	4.3
BAPT–So Bapt Conv	11	508	1,903	2,298	29.8	54.8
Catholic	1	NR	NR	35	0.5	0.8
CHR–Chr Ch (Disc)	1	15	26	31	0.4	0.7
CHR–Chs of Christ	1	10	10	10	0.1	0.2
Jehovah's Witness	1	NR	NR	NR	-	-
MENN–Cons Menn Conf	1	15	11	13	0.2	0.3
METH–AME	7	0	850	1,027	13.3	24.5
METH–Un Methodist	3	106	289	316	4.1	7.5
PENT–Assemb of God	1	30	0	30	0.4	0.7
PENT–Ch God (Cleve)	1	10	36	43	0.6	1.0
PRES–Presb Ch (USA)	1	30	45	54	0.7	1.3
RICHMOND	**248**	**33,438**	**77,949**	**115,397**	**57.5**	**100.0**
ANG/EPIS–Episcopal	7	1,005	3,048	3,263	1.6	2.8
Bahá'í	0	NR	99	99	0.0	0.1
BAPT–Amer Bapt USA	3	751	929	1,150	0.6	1.0
BAPT–Free Will Bapt	1	NR	73	90	0.0	0.1
BAPT–Natl Mis Bapt Conv	5	75	710	879	0.4	0.8
BAPT–NBC USA	13	5,430	14,190	17,564	8.8	15.2
BAPT–Prog NBC	1	700	800	990	0.5	0.9
BAPT–So Bapt Conv	42	7,658	25,574	31,654	15.8	27.4
BUDD–Mahayana	1	NR	NR	102	0.1	0.1
BUDD–Theravada	1	NR	NR	375	0.2	0.3
Calv Chpl	1	NR	NR	NR	-	-
Catholic	4	NR	NR	15,868	7.9	13.8
CGOD–Ch God (Ander)	2	0	NR	0	0.0	0.0
Ch of Nazarene	1	78	117	117	0.1	0.1
Chr & Miss Al	1	52	48	70	0.0	0.1
CHR–Chr Ch (Disc)	2	84	378	468	0.2	0.4
CHR–Chr Chs & Chs Cr	2	NR	65	80	0.0	0.1
CHR–Chs of Christ	4	596	801	987	0.5	0.9
Christian Brethren	2	NR	NR	NR	-	-
HINDU–Post Ren	1	NR	NR	77	0.0	0.1
Jehovah's Witness	4	NR	NR	NR	-	-

NR–Not Reported - Represents no adherents reported. Percentages may not total 100 due to rounding.

Table 3: Religious Congregations by County and Group: 2010

Religious Group	Number of Congrega-tions	Number of Attendees	Number of Communicant, Confirmed, or Full Members	Adherents: Number of Adherents	Adherents: % of Total Pop.	Adherents: % of Total Adh.
JUD–Conserv	1	142	159	429	0.2	0.4
JUD–Reform	1	81	142	383	0.2	0.3
LDS–L-D Saints	2	NR	NR	1,531	0.8	1.3
LUTH–E.L.C.A.	2	395	1,139	1,711	0.9	1.5
LUTH–Luth Cong Msn Chr	1	85	252	312	0.2	0.3
LUTH–Luth-MO Synod	1	203	433	526	0.3	0.5
METH–AME	5	645	888	1,099	0.5	1.0
METH–AME Zion	1	250	448	555	0.3	0.5
METH–C.M.E.	6	375	1,182	1,463	0.7	1.3
METH–Cong Meth	1	NR	NR	NR	-	-
METH–So Methodist	2	NR	NR	NR	-	-
METH–Un Methodist	23	2,899	8,136	10,546	5.3	9.1
Metro Comm Ch	1	60	128	158	0.1	0.1
Muslim Est	3	609	NR	1,924	1.0	1.7
Non-denom Chr Chs	53	6,554	9,744	10,117	5.0	8.8
ORTHE–Greek Orthodox	1	150	NR	300	0.1	0.3
ORTHO–Malan Syr Orth	1	50	NR	90	0.0	0.1
PENT–Assemb of God	6	472	734	1,012	0.5	0.9
PENT–Ch God (Cleve)	3	435	1,219	1,509	0.8	1.3
PENT–Ch Lord Jesus Apos	4	NR	NR	NR	-	-
PENT–Ch of God Proph	1	NR	54	67	0.0	0.1
PENT–COGIC	5	395	1,121	1,388	0.7	1.2
PENT–Cong Hol Ch	1	87	42	52	0.0	0.0
PENT–Fire Bapt Hol Ch	1	NR	NR	NR	-	-
PENT–Int Foursq Gos	1	17	21	26	0.0	0.0
PENT–Intl Pent Holiness	5	300	637	788	0.4	0.7
PENT–Un Pent Ch Intl	1	NR	NR	NR	-	-
PENT–Vineyard	1	165	220	272	0.1	0.2
PRES–As Ref Pres Ch	1	NR	14	17	0.0	0.0
PRES–Presb Ch (USA)	7	770	1,480	1,832	0.9	1.6
PRES–Presb Ch Amer	3	1,396	2,224	2,450	1.2	2.1
Salvation Army	1	117	143	307	0.2	0.3
Sev Day Adv	1	234	408	469	0.2	0.4
Sikh	1	NR	NR	NR	-	-
Unit Univ	1	123	149	231	0.1	0.2
Unity Ch	1	NR	NR	NR	-	-
ROCKDALE	**98**	**12,379**	**22,983**	**34,911**	**41.0**	**100.0**
ANG/EPIS–Anglican NA	1	NR	NR	NR	-	-
ANG/EPIS–Episcopal	1	96	163	224	0.3	0.6
Bahá'í	0	NR	35	35	0.0	0.1
BAPT–Natl Mis Bapt Conv	1	0	150	188	0.2	0.5
BAPT–So Bapt Conv	27	4,829	9,616	12,037	14.1	34.5
Catholic	2	NR	NR	6,200	7.3	17.8
Chr & Miss Al	2	98	105	126	0.1	0.4
CHR–Chr Chs & Chs Cr	4	NR	565	707	0.8	2.0
CHR–Chs of Christ	2	230	146	239	0.3	0.7
Evan Free Ch	1	40	NR	40	0.0	0.1
Jehovah's Witness	3	NR	NR	NR	-	-
LDS–L-D Saints	2	NR	NR	682	0.8	2.0
LUTH–E.L.C.A.	1	261	537	669	0.8	1.9
METH–AME	1	0	150	188	0.2	0.5
METH–C.M.E.	1	0	100	125	0.1	0.4
METH–Un Methodist	6	1,271	4,087	4,793	5.6	13.7
METH–Wesleyan	1	34	14	44	0.1	0.1
Metro Comm Ch	1	13	24	30	0.0	0.1
Non-denom Chr Chs	19	3,465	4,365	4,813	5.6	13.8
PENT–Assemb of God	4	249	106	309	0.4	0.9
PENT–Ch God (Cleve)	4	883	1,062	1,329	1.6	3.8
PENT–Ch of God Proph	1	NR	54	68	0.1	0.2
PENT–Cong Hol Ch	1	10	5	6	0.0	0.0
PENT–Int Foursq Gos	1	117	135	169	0.2	0.5
PENT–Un Pent Ch Intl	1	NR	NR	NR	-	-
PRES–Free Ch Scot	1	NR	NR	NR	-	-
PRES–Presb Ch (USA)	4	342	852	1,066	1.3	3.1
PRES–Presb Ch Amer	1	75	74	91	0.1	0.3
Sev Day Adv	3	366	638	733	0.9	2.1
Unity Ch	1	NR	NR	NR	-	-
SCHLEY	**11**	**1,025**	**4,073**	**5,239**	**104.6**	**100.0**
Bahá'í	0	NR	23	23	0.5	0.4
BAPT–Free Will Bapt	1	NR	73	95	1.9	1.8
BAPT–So Bapt Conv	4	786	3,381	4,389	87.6	83.8

Religious Group	Number of Congrega-tions	Number of Attendees	Number of Communicant, Confirmed, or Full Members	Adherents: Number of Adherents	Adherents: % of Total Pop.	Adherents: % of Total Adh.
METH–AME	1	0	150	195	3.9	3.7
METH–Un Methodist	5	239	446	537	10.7	10.3
SCREVEN	**65**	**2,604**	**7,016**	**8,454**	**57.9**	**100.0**
Bahá'í	0	NR	3	3	0.0	0.0
BAPT–NBC USA	2	80	175	214	1.5	2.5
BAPT–So Bapt Conv	20	1,228	3,381	4,139	28.4	49.0
Catholic	1	NR	NR	170	1.2	2.0
CGOD–Ch God (Ander)	1	25	NR	25	0.2	0.3
CHR–Chr Ch (Disc)	2	0	59	72	0.5	0.9
CHR–Chr Chs & Chs Cr	3	NR	100	122	0.8	1.4
CHR–Chs of Christ	1	25	25	32	0.2	0.4
Jehovah's Witness	1	NR	NR	NR	-	-
METH–AME	7	25	835	1,022	7.0	12.1
METH–Un Methodist	17	801	1,796	1,918	13.1	22.7
Non-denom Chr Chs	5	420	492	553	3.8	6.5
PENT–COGIC	1	0	150	184	1.3	2.2
PENT–Fire Bapt Hol Ch	3	NR	NR	NR	-	-
PRES–Presb Ch Amer	1	0	0	0	0.0	0.0
SEMINOLE	**32**	**1,676**	**4,910**	**5,909**	**67.7**	**100.0**
Bahá'í	0	NR	1	1	0.0	0.0
BAPT–Free Will Bapt	5	NR	365	444	5.1	7.5
BAPT–So Bapt Conv	7	657	2,258	2,744	31.4	46.4
Catholic	1	NR	NR	69	0.8	1.2
Ch of Nazarene	1	78	72	78	0.9	1.3
CHR–Chs of Christ	2	60	53	68	0.8	1.2
METH–AME	4	0	450	547	6.3	9.3
METH–Un Methodist	4	279	719	764	8.8	12.9
Non-denom Chr Chs	1	100	150	150	1.7	2.5
PENT–Assemb of God	1	36	22	48	0.5	0.8
PENT–Ch God (Cleve)	4	343	471	572	6.6	9.7
PENT–Intl Pent Holiness	1	123	215	261	3.0	4.4
PRES–Presb Ch (USA)	1	0	134	163	1.9	2.8
SPALDING	**112**	**15,598**	**31,146**	**46,817**	**73.1**	**100.0**
ANG/EPIS–Episcopal	1	168	427	495	0.8	1.1
Bahá'í	0	NR	353	353	0.6	0.8
BAPT–Amer Bapt USA	2	550	975	1,218	1.9	2.6
BAPT–NBC USA	1	0	150	187	0.3	0.4
BAPT–Prog NBC	1	0	350	437	0.7	0.9
BAPT–So Bapt Conv	32	4,909	15,470	19,319	30.2	41.3
Catholic	1	NR	NR	1,892	3.0	4.0
Ch of Nazarene	1	74	124	127	0.2	0.3
Chr & Miss Al	1	15	17	20	0.0	0.0
CHR–Chr Ch (Disc)	2	0	150	187	0.3	0.4
CHR–Chs of Christ	3	185	182	242	0.4	0.5
Jehovah's Witness	2	NR	NR	NR	-	-
LDS–L-D Saints	2	NR	NR	997	1.6	2.1
LUTH–E.L.C.A.	1	152	227	275	0.4	0.6
LUTH–Luth-MO Synod	1	35	52	58	0.1	0.1
METH–AME	2	45	470	587	0.9	1.3
METH–C.M.E.	2	100	300	375	0.6	0.8
METH–Cong Meth	1	NR	NR	NR	-	-
METH–Un Methodist	16	1,204	3,500	4,041	6.3	8.6
METH–Wesleyan	1	28	28	36	0.1	0.1
Muslim Est	2	63	NR	105	0.2	0.2
Non-denom Chr Chs	17	2,425	3,080	3,294	5.1	7.0
PENT–Assemb of God	3	4,376	3,484	10,133	15.8	21.6
PENT–Ch God (Cleve)	3	569	890	1,111	1.7	2.4
PENT–Ch of God Proph	1	NR	9	11	0.0	0.0
PENT–Cong Hol Ch	5	341	199	249	0.4	0.5
PENT–Fire Bapt Hol Ch	1	NR	NR	NR	-	-
PENT–Full Gosp Bapt	1	NR	NR	NR	-	-
PENT–Un Pent Ch Intl	1	NR	NR	NR	-	-
PENT–United Holy Ch	1	NR	NR	NR	-	-
PRES–Presb Ch (USA)	1	180	382	477	0.7	1.0
Salvation Army	1	47	97	326	0.5	0.7
Sev Day Adv	2	132	230	265	0.4	0.6
STEPHENS	**54**	**5,680**	**13,190**	**16,754**	**64.0**	**100.0**
ANG/EPIS–Episcopal	1	93	153	196	0.7	1.2
Bahá'í	0	NR	1	1	0.0	0.0

NR–Not Reported - Represents no adherents reported. Percentages may not total 100 due to rounding.

Table 3: Religious Congregations by County and Group: 2010

Religious Group	Number of Congregations	Number of Attendees	Number of Communicant, Confirmed, or Full Members	Adherents		
				Number of Adherents	% of Total Pop.	% of Total Adh.
BAPT–NBC USA	1	185	250	303	1.2	1.8
BAPT–So Bapt Conv	19	2,667	8,649	10,466	40.0	62.5
Catholic	1	NR	NR	537	2.1	3.2
CGOD–Ch God (Ander)	1	24	NR	24	0.1	0.1
Chr & Miss Al	2	513	344	664	2.5	4.0
CHR–Chr Chs & Chs Cr	1	NR	35	42	0.2	0.3
CHR–Chs of Christ	1	30	27	35	0.1	0.2
Jehovah's Witness	1	NR	NR	NR	-	-
LUTH–Luth–MO Synod	1	61	146	184	0.7	1.1
METH–C.M.E.	2	0	320	387	1.5	2.3
METH–Un Methodist	5	466	1,063	1,131	4.3	6.8
Non-denom Chr Chs	4	600	790	859	3.3	5.1
ORTHE–Orth Ch in Amer	1	25	NR	50	0.2	0.3
PENT–Assemb of God	3	286	184	388	1.5	2.3
PENT–Ch God (Cleve)	3	340	819	991	3.8	5.9
PENT–Cong Hol Ch	2	215	149	180	0.7	1.1
PENT–Fire Bapt Hol Ch	1	NR	NR	NR	-	-
PENT–Intl Pent Holiness	1	16	16	19	0.1	0.1
PRES–Presb Ch (USA)	1	73	114	138	0.5	0.8
Salvation Army	1	44	58	76	0.3	0.5
Sev Day Adv	1	42	72	83	0.3	0.5
STEWART	**21**	**468**	**1,745**	**2,007**	**33.1**	**100.0**
Bahá'í	0	NR	84	84	1.4	4.2
BAPT–So Bapt Conv	6	245	654	737	12.2	36.7
CHR–Chs of Christ	1	10	10	10	0.2	0.5
METH–AME	6	0	650	733	12.1	36.5
METH–Un Methodist	7	188	347	408	6.7	20.3
PENT–Assemb of God	1	25	0	35	0.6	1.7
SUMTER	**62**	**6,206**	**13,196**	**17,176**	**52.3**	**100.0**
ANG/EPIS–Episcopal	1	119	248	277	0.8	1.6
Bahá'í	0	NR	78	78	0.2	0.5
BAPT–NBC USA	4	850	1,625	2,018	6.1	11.7
BAPT–So Bapt Conv	18	2,317	5,678	7,051	21.5	41.1
Catholic	1	NR	NR	860	2.6	5.0
CHR–Chs of Christ	3	274	278	351	1.1	2.0
Jehovah's Witness	1	NR	NR	NR	-	-
LDS–L-D Saints	1	NR	NR	521	1.6	3.0
LUTH–E.L.C.A.	1	20	38	41	0.1	0.2
MENN–Mennonite USA	1	65	60	75	0.2	0.4
METH–AME	6	110	695	863	2.6	5.0
METH–Un Methodist	8	848	2,406	2,623	8.0	15.3
METH–Wesleyan	1	29	20	38	0.1	0.2
Non-denom Chr Chs	9	1,105	1,335	1,481	4.5	8.6
PENT–Assemb of God	1	54	26	54	0.2	0.3
PENT–Ch God (Cleve)	1	115	158	196	0.6	1.1
PENT–Ch of God Proph	1	NR	7	9	0.0	0.1
PRES–Presb Ch (USA)	1	67	169	210	0.6	1.2
PRES–Presb Ch Amer	1	63	78	89	0.3	0.5
Sev Day Adv	2	170	297	341	1.0	2.0
TALBOT	**21**	**534**	**2,083**	**2,458**	**35.8**	**100.0**
Bahá'í	0	NR	3	3	0.0	0.1
BAPT–Free Will Bapt	3	NR	219	260	3.8	10.6
BAPT–NBC USA	1	0	150	178	2.6	7.2
BAPT–So Bapt Conv	6	264	1,151	1,368	19.9	55.7
CHR–Chs of Christ	1	43	40	52	0.8	2.1
METH–AME	2	0	200	238	3.5	9.7
METH–Un Methodist	7	107	208	226	3.3	9.2
PENT–Ch God (Cleve)	1	120	112	133	1.9	5.4
TALIAFERRO	**13**	**286**	**511**	**617**	**35.9**	**100.0**
BAPT–So Bapt Conv	6	172	296	346	20.2	56.1
Catholic	1	NR	NR	25	1.5	4.1
METH–C.M.E.	1	0	150	175	10.2	28.4
METH–Un Methodist	3	54	49	53	3.1	8.6
PRES–Presb Ch Amer	2	60	16	18	1.0	2.9
TATTNALL	**56**	**3,091**	**8,185**	**9,922**	**38.9**	**100.0**
Bahá'í	0	NR	1	1	0.0	0.0
BAPT–Amer Bapt Assn	1	NR	85	102	0.4	1.0

Religious Group	Number of Congregations	Number of Attendees	Number of Communicant, Confirmed, or Full Members	Adherents		
				Number of Adherents	% of Total Pop.	% of Total Adh.
BAPT–Free Will Bapt	3	NR	219	262	1.0	2.6
BAPT–Natl Mis Bapt Conv	2	0	300	359	1.4	3.6
BAPT–So Bapt Conv	17	1,475	4,075	4,878	19.1	49.2
Catholic	2	NR	NR	170	0.7	1.7
CGOD–Ch God (Ander)	2	77	NR	77	0.3	0.8
CHR–Chr Ch (Disc)	1	92	301	360	1.4	3.6
Jehovah's Witness	1	NR	NR	NR	-	-
METH–AME	6	0	700	838	3.3	8.4
METH–Un Methodist	9	592	1,341	1,504	5.9	15.2
Non-denom Chr Chs	4	450	540	625	2.4	6.3
PENT–Ch God (Cleve)	4	220	286	342	1.3	3.4
PENT–COGIC	1	0	150	180	0.7	1.8
PENT–Intl Pent Holiness	2	185	187	224	0.9	2.3
PENT–Un Pent Ch Intl	1	NR	NR	NR	-	-
TAYLOR	**29**	**1,013**	**3,358**	**4,104**	**46.1**	**100.0**
Bahá'í	0	NR	30	30	0.3	0.7
BAPT–Free Will Bapt	2	NR	146	178	2.0	4.3
BAPT–So Bapt Conv	12	732	2,112	2,568	28.8	62.6
METH–AME	2	0	200	243	2.7	5.9
METH–Cong Meth	1	NR	239	291	3.3	7.1
METH–Un Methodist	10	276	590	744	8.4	18.1
PENT–Ch God (Cleve)	1	5	41	50	0.6	1.2
PENT–COGIC	1	0	0	0	0.0	0.0
TELFAIR	**61**	**1,823**	**5,349**	**6,535**	**39.6**	**100.0**
Bahá'í	0	NR	4	4	0.0	0.1
BAPT–So Bapt Conv	14	846	2,094	2,479	15.0	37.9
Catholic	1	NR	NR	127	0.8	1.9
CGOD–Ch God (Ander)	1	30	NR	30	0.2	0.5
CHR–Chs of Christ	1	18	17	25	0.2	0.4
Jehovah's Witness	2	NR	NR	NR	-	-
LDS–L-D Saints	1	NR	NR	114	0.7	1.7
METH–AME	2	0	200	237	1.4	3.6
METH–C.M.E.	10	25	1,124	1,331	8.1	20.4
METH–Un Methodist	17	404	989	1,142	6.9	17.5
Non-denom Chr Chs	2	125	350	350	2.1	5.4
ORTHE–Orth Ch in Amer	1	10	NR	20	0.1	0.3
PENT–Ch God (Cleve)	7	365	514	609	3.7	9.3
PENT–Full Gosp Bapt	1	NR	NR	NR	-	-
PRES–Presb Ch (USA)	1	0	57	67	0.4	1.0
TERRELL	**34**	**1,194**	**4,013**	**4,896**	**52.6**	**100.0**
ANG/EPIS–Episcopal	1	18	28	28	0.3	0.6
Bahá'í	0	NR	252	252	2.7	5.1
BAPT–NBC USA	1	0	150	185	2.0	3.8
BAPT–So Bapt Conv	11	648	1,806	2,231	24.0	45.6
CHR–Chs of Christ	2	63	63	107	1.1	2.2
METH–AME	8	0	760	939	10.1	19.2
METH–Un Methodist	7	286	597	647	6.9	13.2
Non-denom Chr Chs	1	100	150	150	1.6	3.1
PENT–Assemb of God	1	25	24	130	1.4	2.7
PENT–Ch God (Cleve)	1	54	151	187	2.0	3.8
PRES–Presb Ch (USA)	1	0	32	40	0.4	0.8
THOMAS	**109**	**9,252**	**21,702**	**27,653**	**61.8**	**100.0**
ANG/EPIS–Anglican NA	1	NR	NR	NR	-	-
ANG/EPIS–Episcopal	3	184	537	675	1.5	2.4
Bahá'í	0	NR	11	11	0.0	0.0
BAPT–Free Will Bapt	1	NR	73	90	0.2	0.3
BAPT–Natl Mis Bapt Conv	3	325	913	1,129	2.5	4.1
BAPT–NBC USA	1	0	150	186	0.4	0.7
BAPT–So Bapt Conv	28	3,130	10,385	12,846	28.7	46.5
Calv Chpl	1	NR	NR	NR	-	-
Catholic	1	NR	NR	851	1.9	3.1
Ch Cr, Scientst	1	NR	NR	NR	-	-
Ch of Nazarene	1	56	78	106	0.2	0.4
CHR–Chr Ch (Disc)	1	0	0	0	0.0	0.0
CHR–Chr Chs & Chs Cr	1	NR	60	74	0.2	0.3
CHR–Chs of Christ	4	408	363	495	1.1	1.8
Jehovah's Witness	1	NR	NR	NR	-	-
LDS–L-D Saints	1	NR	NR	457	1.0	1.7

NR–Not Reported - Represents no adherents reported. Percentages may not total 100 due to rounding.

Table 3: Religious Congregations by County and Group: 2010

Religious Group	Number of Congrega-tions	Number of Attendees	Number of Communicant, Confirmed, or Full Members	Adherents: Number of Adherents	Adherents: % of Total Pop.	Adherents: % of Total Adh.
METH–AME	7	350	1,150	1,422	3.2	5.1
METH–C.M.E.	6	300	1,000	1,237	2.8	4.5
METH–Un Methodist	10	791	1,914	2,147	4.8	7.8
Non-denom Chr Chs	14	2,428	3,005	3,261	7.3	11.8
PENT–Assemb of God	2	88	86	120	0.3	0.4
PENT–Ch God (Cleve)	8	568	835	1,033	2.3	3.7
PENT–Ch Lord Jesus Apos	1	NR	NR	NR	-	-
PENT–Intl Pent Holiness	1	48	58	72	0.2	0.3
PRES–Presb Ch (USA)	5	272	685	847	1.9	3.1
PRES–Presb Ch Amer	1	122	108	135	0.3	0.5
Salvation Army	1	42	67	199	0.4	0.7
Sev Day Adv	3	116	202	233	0.5	0.8
Un C of Christ	1	24	22	27	0.1	0.1
TIFT	**77**	**7,070**	**17,725**	**24,459**	**61.0**	**100.0**
ANG/EPIS–Episcopal	1	141	404	573	1.4	2.3
BAPT–Amer Bapt Assn	3	NR	212	266	0.7	1.1
BAPT–Free Will Bapt	2	NR	146	183	0.5	0.7
BAPT–NBC USA	1	350	450	565	1.4	2.3
BAPT–So Bapt Conv	27	3,339	9,714	12,195	30.4	49.9
Catholic	1	NR	NR	1,374	3.4	5.6
Ch of Nazarene	1	147	131	322	0.8	1.3
CHR–Chs of Christ	2	137	175	245	0.6	1.0
Jehovah's Witness	1	NR	NR	NR	-	-
LDS–L-D Saints	2	NR	NR	1,030	2.6	4.2
LUTH–Luth–MO Synod	1	0	132	132	0.3	0.5
METH–AME	3	0	350	439	1.1	1.8
METH–C.M.E.	1	0	100	126	0.3	0.5
METH–Un Methodist	9	682	2,235	2,622	6.5	10.7
Non-denom Chr Chs	6	875	1,155	1,268	3.2	5.2
PENT–Assemb of God	1	140	160	160	0.4	0.7
PENT–Ch God (Cleve)	9	1,118	2,092	2,626	6.5	10.7
PENT–Ch of God Proph	1	NR	32	40	0.1	0.2
PENT–Un Pent Ch Intl	2	NR	NR	NR	-	-
PRES–Presb Ch (USA)	1	40	103	129	0.3	0.5
PRES–Presb Ch Amer	1	75	89	112	0.3	0.5
Sev Day Adv	1	26	45	52	0.1	0.2
TOOMBS	**81**	**5,931**	**13,436**	**18,620**	**68.4**	**100.0**
ANG/EPIS–Episcopal	1	47	116	171	0.6	0.9
Bahá'í	0	NR	4	4	0.0	0.0
BAPT–Free Will Bapt	3	NR	219	281	1.0	1.5
BAPT–NBC USA	2	0	400	513	1.9	2.8
BAPT–So Bapt Conv	28	3,242	7,473	9,577	35.2	51.4
Catholic	1	NR	NR	992	3.6	5.3
Ch of Nazarene	1	6	16	54	0.2	0.3
CHR–Chs of Christ	2	46	41	57	0.2	0.3
Jehovah's Witness	1	NR	NR	NR	-	-
LDS–L-D Saints	1	NR	NR	445	1.6	2.4
METH–AME	3	90	450	577	2.1	3.1
METH–C.M.E.	1	0	150	192	0.7	1.0
METH–Un Methodist	13	831	1,877	2,259	8.3	12.1
Non-denom Chr Chs	11	1,035	1,341	1,401	5.1	7.5
PENT–Assemb of God	2	232	107	505	1.9	2.7
PENT–Ch God (Cleve)	6	402	890	1,141	4.2	6.1
PENT–Ch of God Proph	1	NR	32	41	0.2	0.2
PENT–Un Pent Ch Intl	1	NR	NR	NR	-	-
PRES–Presb Ch (USA)	3	0	320	410	1.5	2.2
TOWNS	**25**	**2,428**	**4,811**	**5,430**	**51.9**	**100.0**
ANG/EPIS–Anglican NA	1	NR	NR	NR	-	-
Bahá'í	0	NR	1	1	0.0	0.0
BAPT–So Bapt Conv	12	1,018	3,047	3,456	33.0	63.6
Calv Chpl	1	NR	NR	NR	-	-
CHR–Chs of Christ	2	38	38	43	0.4	0.8
Jehovah's Witness	1	NR	NR	NR	-	-
METH–Un Methodist	3	434	730	793	7.6	14.6
Non-denom Chr Chs	2	350	400	462	4.4	8.5
PENT–Ch God (Cleve)	2	463	514	583	5.6	10.7
PRES–Presb Ch (USA)	1	125	81	92	0.9	1.7
TREUTLEN	**18**	**918**	**2,289**	**2,876**	**41.8**	**100.0**
BAPT–NBC Amer	2	230	445	556	8.1	19.3
BAPT–NBC USA	1	0	150	188	2.7	6.5
BAPT–So Bapt Conv	5	351	918	1,148	16.7	39.9
Ch of Nazarene	1	10	15	15	0.2	0.5
CHR–Chs of Christ	1	16	13	16	0.2	0.6
METH–AME	1	0	100	125	1.8	4.3
METH–Un Methodist	3	121	307	339	4.9	11.8
PENT–Assemb of God	1	85	65	143	2.1	5.0
PENT–Ch God (Cleve)	1	90	111	139	2.0	4.8
PENT–COGIC	1	0	150	188	2.7	6.5
PENT–Intl Pent Holiness	1	15	15	19	0.3	0.7
TROUP	**143**	**14,139**	**27,816**	**36,337**	**54.2**	**100.0**
ANG/EPIS–Episcopal	2	116	323	456	0.7	1.3
Bahá'í	0	NR	5	5	0.0	0.0
BAPT–NBC USA	2	550	650	815	1.2	2.2
BAPT–Prog NBC	1	300	400	502	0.7	1.4
BAPT–So Bapt Conv	44	6,036	14,085	17,664	26.3	48.6
Catholic	1	NR	NR	1,064	1.6	2.9
CGOD–Ch God (Ander)	1	99	NR	99	0.1	0.3
CHR–Chr Chs & Chs Cr	1	NR	50	63	0.1	0.2
CHR–Chs of Christ	8	592	527	697	1.0	1.9
CONG–Cong Chr, NA	1	NR	58	73	0.1	0.2
Jehovah's Witness	1	NR	NR	NR	-	-
LDS–L-D Saints	1	NR	NR	352	0.5	1.0
LUTH–E.L.C.A.	1	57	113	139	0.2	0.4
METH–AME	3	0	350	439	0.7	1.2
METH–C.M.E.	3	0	350	439	0.7	1.2
METH–Un Methodist	32	1,946	4,321	5,291	7.9	14.6
Muslim Est	1	25	NR	40	0.1	0.1
Non-denom Chr Chs	21	3,030	4,358	5,240	7.8	14.4
PENT–Assemb of God	2	313	219	393	0.6	1.1
PENT–Ch God (Cleve)	4	423	656	823	1.2	2.3
PENT–Cong Hol Ch	1	25	20	25	0.0	0.1
PENT–Intl Pent Holiness	1	35	22	28	0.0	0.1
PENT–Un Pent Ch Intl	1	NR	NR	NR	-	-
PRES–Orth Pres Ch	1	91	78	119	0.2	0.3
PRES–Presb Ch (USA)	5	381	994	1,247	1.9	3.4
Salvation Army	1	9	23	69	0.1	0.2
Sev Day Adv	2	76	133	153	0.2	0.4
Un C of Christ	1	35	81	102	0.2	0.3
TURNER	**30**	**1,681**	**5,361**	**6,534**	**73.2**	**100.0**
BAPT–Free Will Bapt	1	NR	73	90	1.0	1.4
BAPT–So Bapt Conv	17	1,380	4,394	5,428	60.8	83.1
Ch of Nazarene	1	20	27	43	0.5	0.7
CHR–Chs of Christ	1	32	35	45	0.5	0.7
Jehovah's Witness	1	NR	NR	NR	-	-
METH–AME	1	0	100	124	1.4	1.9
METH–Un Methodist	4	154	439	442	4.9	6.8
PENT–Ch God (Cleve)	1	95	261	322	3.6	4.9
PENT–Ch of God by Faith	1	NR	NR	NR	-	-
PENT–Ch of God Proph	1	NR	32	40	0.4	0.6
PENT–Un Pent Ch Intl	1	NR	NR	NR	-	-
TWIGGS	**20**	**1,400**	**3,747**	**4,401**	**48.8**	**100.0**
Bahá'í	0	NR	5	5	0.1	0.1
BAPT–Amer Bapt Assn	1	NR	85	100	1.1	2.3
BAPT–So Bapt Conv	8	1,176	2,884	3,402	37.7	77.3
METH–C.M.E.	3	0	350	413	4.6	9.4
METH–Un Methodist	5	76	194	195	2.2	4.4
PENT–Assemb of God	1	15	0	15	0.2	0.3
PENT–Ch God (Cleve)	1	95	176	208	2.3	4.7
PENT–Cong Hol Ch	1	38	53	63	0.7	1.4
UNION	**55**	**5,640**	**10,942**	**14,195**	**66.5**	**100.0**
ANG/EPIS–Episcopal	1	75	96	100	0.5	0.7
BAPT–So Bapt Conv	27	3,012	7,225	8,363	39.2	58.9
Catholic	2	NR	NR	1,564	7.3	11.0
Ch of Nazarene	1	60	46	70	0.3	0.5
CHR–Chs of Christ	1	190	170	210	1.0	1.5
Jehovah's Witness	1	NR	NR	NR	-	-
LDS–L-D Saints	1	NR	NR	91	0.4	0.6

NR–Not Reported - Represents no adherents reported. Percentages may not total 100 due to rounding.

Table 3: Religious Congregations by County and Group: 2010

Religious Group	Number of Congrega-tions	Number of Attendees	Number of Communicant, Confirmed, or Full Members	Adherents		
				Number of Adherents	% of Total Pop.	% of Total Adh.
LUTH–E.L.C.A.	1	0	0	0	0.0	0.0
LUTH–Luth-MO Synod	1	128	214	245	1.1	1.7
METH–Un Methodist	6	800	1,445	1,647	7.7	11.6
Non-denom Chr Chs	5	955	1,220	1,308	6.1	9.2
PENT–Assemb of God	1	35	28	48	0.2	0.3
PENT–Ch God (Cleve)	3	149	221	256	1.2	1.8
PENT–Cong Hol Ch	1	39	35	41	0.2	0.3
PRES–Presb Ch Amer	1	158	174	174	0.8	1.2
Sev Day Adv	1	39	68	78	0.4	0.5
Unity Ch	1	NR	NR	NR	-	-
UPSON	**60**	**4,773**	**12,816**	**15,789**	**58.1**	**100.0**
ANG/EPIS–Episcopal	1	7	15	16	0.1	0.1
Bahá'í	0	NR	66	66	0.2	0.4
BAPT–Free Will Bapt	1	NR	73	89	0.3	0.6
BAPT–NBC USA	1	0	350	426	1.6	2.7
BAPT–So Bapt Conv	23	3,284	8,638	10,502	38.7	66.5
CHR–Chs of Christ	4	96	102	115	0.4	0.7
Jehovah's Witness	1	NR	NR	NR	-	-
LDS–L-D Saints	1	NR	NR	347	1.3	2.2
MENN–Beachy Amish-Menn	1	35	15	35	0.1	0.2
METH–AME	6	0	800	973	3.6	6.2
METH–Un Methodist	8	317	1,016	1,167	4.3	7.4
Non-denom Chr Chs	3	385	425	506	1.9	3.2
PENT–Assemb of God	1	200	200	200	0.7	1.3
PENT–Ch God (Cleve)	1	74	466	567	2.1	3.6
PENT–COGIC	1	0	150	182	0.7	1.2
PENT–Intl Pent Holiness	2	230	243	295	1.1	1.9
PENT–Un Pent Ch Intl	1	NR	NR	NR	-	-
PRES–Presb Ch (USA)	1	55	100	122	0.4	0.8
PRES–Presb Ch Amer	1	0	0	0	0.0	0.0
Sev Day Adv	2	90	157	181	0.7	1.1
WALKER	**133**	**15,966**	**30,650**	**38,296**	**55.7**	**100.0**
Bahá'í	0	NR	5	5	0.0	0.0
BAPT–NBC Amer	1	25	68	83	0.1	0.2
BAPT–So Bapt Conv	53	8,933	20,503	25,052	36.4	65.4
Catholic	1	NR	NR	410	0.6	1.1
CGOD–Ch God (Ander)	3	108	NR	108	0.2	0.3
Ch of Nazarene	4	206	371	519	0.8	1.4
CHR–Chs of Christ	10	948	910	1,236	1.8	3.2
Jehovah's Witness	2	NR	NR	NR	-	-
LDS–L-D Saints	1	NR	NR	414	0.6	1.1
METH–AME Zion	2	0	200	244	0.4	0.6
METH–Un Methodist	14	991	2,365	2,862	4.2	7.5
METH–Wesleyan	2	89	80	116	0.2	0.3
Non-denom Chr Chs	11	2,145	2,745	2,926	4.3	7.6
PENT–Assemb of God	3	312	169	330	0.5	0.9
PENT–Ch God (Cleve)	11	1,212	2,050	2,505	3.6	6.5
PENT–Ch God Mtn Asm	1	NR	NR	NR	-	-
PENT–Ch of God Proph	3	NR	88	108	0.2	0.3
PENT–COGIC	1	60	120	147	0.2	0.4
PENT–Un Pent Ch Intl	1	NR	NR	NR	-	-
PRES–Evan Presby Ch	1	NR	73	89	0.1	0.2
PRES–Presb Ch (USA)	2	42	70	86	0.1	0.2
PRES–Presb Ch Amer	4	815	695	897	1.3	2.3
Sev Day Adv	2	80	138	159	0.2	0.4
WALTON	**100**	**13,078**	**24,378**	**33,727**	**40.3**	**100.0**
ANG/EPIS–Anglican NA	1	NR	NR	NR	-	-
ANG/EPIS–Episcopal	1	78	79	84	0.1	0.2
Bahá'í	0	NR	24	24	0.0	0.1
BAPT–Ind Bapt Flwsp Intl	1	NR	NR	NR	-	-
BAPT–So Bapt Conv	26	5,018	10,902	13,754	16.4	40.8
BUDD–Theravada	1	NR	NR	267	0.3	0.8
Catholic	1	NR	NR	1,068	1.3	3.2
Chr & Miss Al	1	60	63	63	0.1	0.2
CHR–Chr Ch (Disc)	2	25	224	283	0.3	0.8
CHR–Chr Chs & Chs Cr	6	NR	1,672	2,109	2.5	6.3
CHR–Chs of Christ	4	170	170	197	0.2	0.6
HINDU–Trad Temples	1	NR	NR	100	0.1	0.3
LDS–L-D Saints	1	NR	NR	553	0.7	1.6
METH–AME	3	0	400	505	0.6	1.5

Religious Group	Number of Congrega-tions	Number of Attendees	Number of Communicant, Confirmed, or Full Members	Adherents		
				Number of Adherents	% of Total Pop.	% of Total Adh.
METH–AME Zion	3	105	400	505	0.6	1.5
METH–Un Methodist	12	1,722	3,299	5,540	6.6	16.4
Non-denom Chr Chs	18	4,234	4,555	5,462	6.5	16.2
PENT–Assemb of God	2	245	369	427	0.5	1.3
PENT–Ch God (Cleve)	5	865	1,485	1,873	2.2	5.6
PENT–Cong Hol Ch	2	199	142	179	0.2	0.5
PENT–Fire Bapt Hol Ch	1	NR	NR	NR	-	-
PENT–Intl Pent Holiness	2	47	55	69	0.1	0.2
PRES–Evan Presby Ch	1	NR	42	53	0.1	0.2
PRES–Presb Ch (USA)	1	100	188	237	0.3	0.7
PRES–Presb Ch Amer	1	50	32	56	0.1	0.2
Sev Day Adv	3	160	277	319	0.4	0.9
WARE	**101**	**7,274**	**17,604**	**23,562**	**64.9**	**100.0**
ANG/EPIS–Episcopal	1	77	148	151	0.4	0.6
Bahá'í	0	NR	6	6	0.0	0.0
BAPT–Free Will Bapt	4	NR	292	357	1.0	1.5
BAPT–Natl Mis Bapt Conv	1	0	150	184	0.5	0.8
BAPT–NBC USA	3	350	1,150	1,407	3.9	6.0
BAPT–Prog NBC	1	75	90	110	0.3	0.5
BAPT–So Bapt Conv	27	3,125	8,686	10,628	29.3	45.1
Catholic	1	NR	NR	1,095	3.0	4.6
Ch of Nazarene	1	43	53	73	0.2	0.3
CHR–Chr Ch (Disc)	1	0	100	122	0.3	0.5
CHR–Chs of Christ	3	152	135	172	0.5	0.7
Jehovah's Witness	1	NR	NR	NR	-	-
LDS–L-D Saints	2	NR	NR	1,117	3.1	4.7
METH–AME	4	0	450	551	1.5	2.3
METH–C.M.E.	1	0	150	184	0.5	0.8
METH–Evan Meth Ch	1	NR	NR	NR	-	-
METH–Un Methodist	12	703	1,966	2,194	6.0	9.3
Non-denom Chr Chs	12	1,505	1,630	1,972	5.4	8.4
PENT–Assemb of God	1	135	229	229	0.6	1.0
PENT–Ch God (Cleve)	8	689	1,074	1,314	3.6	5.6
PENT–Ch of God Proph	6	NR	321	393	1.1	1.7
PENT–COGIC	1	0	150	184	0.5	0.8
PENT–Intl Pent Holiness	4	216	367	449	1.2	1.9
PENT–Un Pent Ch Intl	1	NR	NR	NR	-	-
PRES–Presb Ch (USA)	1	107	254	311	0.9	1.3
Salvation Army	1	23	75	212	0.6	0.9
Sev Day Adv	2	74	128	147	0.4	0.6
WARREN	**25**	**1,054**	**3,312**	**4,004**	**68.6**	**100.0**
BAPT–So Bapt Conv	9	654	1,698	2,072	35.5	51.7
CHR–Chs of Christ	1	60	55	65	1.1	1.6
METH–AME	8	0	850	1,037	17.8	25.9
METH–C.M.E.	1	0	150	183	3.1	4.6
METH–Un Methodist	5	190	409	459	7.9	11.5
Non-denom Chr Chs	1	150	150	188	3.2	4.7
WASHINGTON	**76**	**3,417**	**9,221**	**11,520**	**54.4**	**100.0**
ANG/EPIS–Episcopal	1	14	16	23	0.1	0.2
Bahá'í	0	NR	4	4	0.0	0.0
BAPT–So Bapt Conv	28	1,605	4,531	5,511	26.0	47.8
BUDD–Mahayana	1	NR	NR	38	0.2	0.3
Catholic	1	NR	NR	98	0.5	0.9
CGOD–Ch God (Ander)	1	12	NR	12	0.1	0.1
Ch of Nazarene	2	307	461	555	2.6	4.8
CHR–Chr Ch (Disc)	2	90	185	225	1.1	2.0
CHR–Chr Chs & Chs Cr	3	NR	200	243	1.1	2.1
CHR–Chs of Christ	3	53	60	79	0.4	0.7
Jehovah's Witness	1	NR	NR	NR	-	-
METH–AME	11	0	1,300	1,581	7.5	13.7
METH–C.M.E.	1	0	150	182	0.9	1.6
METH–So Methodist	1	NR	NR	NR	-	-
METH–Un Methodist	10	516	1,319	1,442	6.8	12.5
Non-denom Chr Chs	1	500	250	625	2.9	5.4
PENT–Ch God (Cleve)	4	239	378	460	2.2	4.0
PENT–COGIC	2	0	300	365	1.7	3.2
PENT–Cong Hol Ch	1	66	46	56	0.3	0.5
PENT–Full Gosp Bapt	1	NR	NR	NR	-	-
PRES–Presb Ch Amer	1	15	21	21	0.1	0.2

NR–Not Reported   - Represents no adherents reported.   Percentages may not total 100 due to rounding.

Table 3: Religious Congregations by County and Group: 2010

Religious Group	Number of Congrega-tions	Number of Attendees	Number of Communicant, Confirmed, or Full Members	Adherents: Number of Adherents	Adherents: % of Total Pop.	Adherents: % of Total Adh.
WAYNE	**75**	**6,529**	**15,234**	**19,928**	**66.2**	**100.0**
ANG/EPIS–Episcopal	1	144	155	277	0.9	1.4
Bahá'í	0	NR	1	1	0.0	0.0
BAPT–Amer Bapt Assn	1	NR	85	105	0.3	0.5
BAPT–Asc Ref Bap Ch Am	1	NR	NR	NR	-	-
BAPT–Free Will Bapt	3	NR	219	272	0.9	1.4
BAPT–Ref Bapt Ch	1	NR	NR	NR	-	-
BAPT–So Bapt Conv	25	2,683	8,017	9,941	33.0	49.9
Catholic	1	NR	NR	458	1.5	2.3
CGOD–Ch God (Ander)	1	0	NR	0	0.0	0.0
CHR–Chr Chs & Chs Cr	1	NR	50	62	0.2	0.3
CHR–Chs of Christ	1	4	4	4	0.0	0.0
LDS–L-D Saints	1	NR	NR	491	1.6	2.5
MENN–Unaffil Amish-Menn	1	94	55	94	0.3	0.5
METH–AME	3	0	350	434	1.4	2.2
METH–Un Methodist	7	437	1,037	1,207	4.0	6.1
METH–Wesleyan	1	20	34	26	0.1	0.1
Non-denom Chr Chs	8	1,245	1,225	1,558	5.2	7.8
PENT–Assemb of God	1	70	39	87	0.3	0.4
PENT–Ch God (Cleve)	13	1,748	3,801	4,713	15.7	23.7
PENT–Ch of God Proph	1	NR	42	52	0.2	0.3
PENT–Un Pent Ch Intl	1	NR	NR	NR	-	-
PRES–Presb Ch (USA)	1	66	89	110	0.4	0.6
Sev Day Adv	1	18	31	36	0.1	0.2
WEBSTER	**5**	**226**	**818**	**1,026**	**36.7**	**100.0**
Bahá'í	0	NR	4	4	0.1	0.4
BAPT–So Bapt Conv	2	160	577	720	25.7	70.2
CHR–Chs of Christ	1	29	32	54	1.9	5.3
METH–AME Zion	1	0	150	187	6.7	18.2
METH–Un Methodist	1	37	55	61	2.2	5.9
WHEELER	**17**	**600**	**1,628**	**1,928**	**26.0**	**100.0**
Bahá'í	0	NR	2	2	0.0	0.1
BAPT–So Bapt Conv	7	376	893	1,055	14.2	54.7
CGOD–Ch God (Ander)	2	20	NR	20	0.3	1.0
METH–AME	2	0	250	295	4.0	15.3
METH–C.M.E.	1	0	100	118	1.6	6.1
METH–Un Methodist	3	115	257	289	3.9	15.0
PENT–Ch God (Cleve)	2	89	126	149	2.0	7.7
WHITE	**38**	**4,457**	**7,547**	**10,476**	**38.6**	**100.0**
ANG/EPIS–Episcopal	1	114	193	193	0.7	1.8
Bahá'í	0	NR	3	3	0.0	0.0
BAPT–So Bapt Conv	11	1,647	3,726	4,516	16.6	43.1
Catholic	1	NR	NR	1,502	5.5	14.3
CHR–Chs of Christ	1	40	23	35	0.1	0.3
FRND–Unaffl Mtgs	1	NR	NR	NR	-	-
Grace Gosp Fel	1	NR	NR	NR	-	-
Jehovah's Witness	1	NR	NR	NR	-	-
LUTH–E.L.C.A.	1	41	70	86	0.3	0.8
METH–Un Methodist	8	663	1,459	1,661	6.1	15.9
Non-denom Chr Chs	3	760	900	1,074	4.0	10.3
PENT–Assemb of God	1	45	70	75	0.3	0.7
PENT–Ch God (Cleve)	1	321	162	196	0.7	1.9
PENT–Cong Hol Ch	2	375	292	354	1.3	3.4
PENT–Intl Pent Holiness	1	62	44	53	0.2	0.5
PRES–Presb Ch (USA)	3	336	513	622	2.3	5.9
Sev Day Adv	1	53	92	106	0.4	1.0
WHITFIELD	**139**	**20,986**	**38,371**	**66,703**	**65.0**	**100.0**
ANG/EPIS–Episcopal	1	145	309	360	0.4	0.5
Bahá'í	0	NR	10	10	0.0	0.0
BAPT–NBC USA	2	125	445	573	0.6	0.9
BAPT–So Bapt Conv	49	9,328	18,205	23,456	22.9	35.2
Catholic	1	NR	NR	17,549	17.1	26.3
Ch of Nazarene	3	133	148	151	0.1	0.2
CHR–Chr Chs & Chs Cr	1	NR	0	0	0.0	0.0
CHR–Chs of Christ	9	883	852	1,122	1.1	1.7
Jehovah's Witness	1	NR	NR	NR	-	-
LDS–L-D Saints	2	NR	NR	876	0.9	1.3
LUTH–E.L.C.A.	1	49	211	243	0.2	0.4
METH–AME	1	100	200	258	0.3	0.4

Religious Group	Number of Congrega-tions	Number of Attendees	Number of Communicant, Confirmed, or Full Members	Adherents: Number of Adherents	Adherents: % of Total Pop.	Adherents: % of Total Adh.
METH–Evan Meth Ch	1	NR	NR	NR	-	-
METH–Un Methodist	17	1,634	4,432	5,630	5.5	8.4
Muslim Est	1	270	NR	762	0.7	1.1
Non-denom Chr Chs	18	5,535	8,025	8,504	8.3	12.7
PENT–Assemb of God	5	216	161	377	0.4	0.6
PENT–Ch God (Cleve)	12	1,602	3,477	4,480	4.4	6.7
PENT–Ch God Mtn Asm	1	NR	NR	NR	-	-
PENT–Ch of God Proph	3	NR	81	104	0.1	0.2
PENT–COGIC	1	0	150	193	0.2	0.3
PENT–Un Pent Ch Intl	1	NR	NR	NR	-	-
PRES–Presb Ch (USA)	2	312	625	805	0.8	1.2
PRES–Presb Ch Amer	1	230	277	277	0.3	0.4
Salvation Army	1	26	70	176	0.2	0.3
Sev Day Adv	4	398	693	797	0.8	1.2
WILCOX	**34**	**1,336**	**4,237**	**4,913**	**53.1**	**100.0**
Bahá'í	0	NR	2	2	0.0	0.0
BAPT–Free Will Bapt	1	NR	73	85	0.9	1.7
BAPT–Natl Mis Bapt Conv	1	0	150	176	1.9	3.6
BAPT–So Bapt Conv	21	1,136	3,030	3,547	38.3	72.2
METH–AME	3	0	300	351	3.8	7.1
METH–C.M.E.	1	0	100	117	1.3	2.4
METH–Un Methodist	5	120	304	310	3.3	6.3
PENT–Ch God (Cleve)	1	80	278	325	3.5	6.6
PENT–Ch of God by Faith	1	NR	NR	NR	-	-
WILKES	**37**	**1,905**	**4,550**	**5,763**	**54.4**	**100.0**
ANG/EPIS–Episcopal	1	40	79	80	0.8	1.4
Bahá'í	0	NR	15	15	0.1	0.3
BAPT–So Bapt Conv	14	914	2,712	3,258	30.8	56.5
Catholic	1	NR	NR	305	2.9	5.3
Jehovah's Witness	1	NR	NR	NR	-	-
METH–AME	4	0	450	541	5.1	9.4
METH–Un Methodist	6	301	559	731	6.9	12.7
Non-denom Chr Chs	3	480	550	613	5.8	10.6
PENT–Ch God (Cleve)	1	23	30	36	0.3	0.6
PENT–COGIC	1	75	50	60	0.6	1.0
PENT–Cong Hol Ch	1	10	11	13	0.1	0.2
PENT–Fire Bapt Hol Ch	1	NR	NR	NR	-	-
PRES–Presb Ch (USA)	2	36	48	58	0.5	1.0
Sev Day Adv	1	26	46	53	0.5	0.9
WILKINSON	**32**	**1,291**	**3,747**	**4,554**	**47.6**	**100.0**
Bahá'í	0	NR	11	11	0.1	0.2
BAPT–NBC USA	2	100	215	265	2.8	5.8
BAPT–So Bapt Conv	12	734	1,986	2,447	25.6	53.7
CHR–Chr Chs & Chs Cr	1	NR	50	62	0.6	1.4
CHR–Chs of Christ	2	57	50	64	0.7	1.4
METH–AME	2	40	135	166	1.7	3.6
METH–C.M.E.	1	0	100	123	1.3	2.7
METH–Cong Meth	1	NR	75	92	1.0	2.0
METH–Un Methodist	6	204	465	508	5.3	11.2
Non-denom Chr Chs	2	150	150	188	2.0	4.1
PENT–COGIC	2	0	500	616	6.4	13.5
PENT–Cong Hol Ch	1	6	10	12	0.1	0.3
WORTH	**51**	**3,359**	**8,532**	**10,340**	**47.7**	**100.0**
Bahá'í	0	NR	1	1	0.0	0.0
BAPT–Amer Bapt Assn	1	NR	85	105	0.5	1.0
BAPT–Free Will Bapt	2	NR	146	180	0.8	1.7
BAPT–So Bapt Conv	24	2,346	6,120	7,534	34.8	72.9
CHR–Chs of Christ	1	46	39	52	0.2	0.5
Jehovah's Witness	1	NR	NR	NR	-	-
METH–AME	4	40	340	419	1.9	4.1
METH–C.M.E.	1	0	100	123	0.6	1.2
METH–Un Methodist	8	424	1,009	1,065	4.9	10.3
Non-denom Chr Chs	3	368	425	501	2.3	4.8
PENT–Assemb of God	1	29	0	31	0.1	0.3
PENT–Ch God (Cleve)	2	94	220	271	1.3	2.6
PENT–Ch of God by Faith	1	NR	NR	NR	-	-
PENT–Ch of God Proph	1	NR	33	41	0.2	0.4
PRES–Presb Ch (USA)	1	12	14	17	0.1	0.2

NR–Not Reported - Represents no adherents reported. Percentages may not total 100 due to rounding.

Table 3: Religious Congregations by County and Group: 2010

Religious Group	Number of Congrega-tions	Number of Attendees	Number of Communicant, Confirmed, or Full Members	Adherents		
				Number of Adherents	% of Total Pop.	% of Total Adh.
HAWAII	**1,314**	**111,265**	**129,406**	**561,980**	**41.3**	**100.0**
HAWAII	**274**	**14,394**	**16,820**	**91,526**	**49.5**	**100.0**
ANG/EPIS–Episcopal	5	335	619	686	0.4	0.7
Bahá'í	8	NR	NR	202	0.1	0.2
BAPT–Reg Bapt Gen As	2	NR	NR	NR	-	-
BAPT–So Bapt Conv	20	1,135	1,839	2,231	1.2	2.4
BUDD–Mahayana	37	NR	NR	27,069	14.6	29.6
BUDD–Theravada	1	NR	NR	267	0.1	0.3
BUDD–Vajrayana	3	NR	NR	166	0.1	0.2
Calv Chpl	3	NR	NR	NR	-	-
Catholic	22	NR	NR	30,616	16.5	33.5
Ch Cr, Scientst	2	NR	NR	NR	-	-
Ch of Nazarene	4	225	288	591	0.3	0.6
CHR–Chs of Christ	4	87	61	90	0.0	0.1
CHR–Int Chs of Christ	1	NR	47	57	0.0	0.1
CONG–Cong Chr Add'l	3	NR	266	323	0.2	0.4
Evan Cov Ch	1	221	195	287	0.2	0.3
Evan Free Ch	1	325	NR	325	0.2	0.4
FRND–Indep Yr Mtgs	1	NR	9	11	0.0	0.0
HINDU–I/A Temples	1	NR	NR	250	0.1	0.3
HINDU–Post Ren	6	NR	NR	253	0.1	0.3
HINDU–Renaiss	1	NR	NR	12	0.0	0.0
Jehovah's Witness	9	NR	NR	NR	-	-
JUD–Orth	1	43	50	60	0.0	0.1
LDS–L-D Saints	17	NR	NR	10,422	5.6	11.4
LUTH–E.L.C.A.	1	130	142	155	0.1	0.2
LUTH–Luth–MO Synod	2	149	182	200	0.1	0.2
LUTH–Wisc Ev Luth Syn	1	63	80	103	0.1	0.1
METH–Un Methodist	4	305	333	521	0.3	0.6
Metro Comm Ch	1	30	33	40	0.0	0.0
Missionary Ch	3	194	104	194	0.1	0.2
New Apost Ch	1	NR	NR	NR	-	-
Non-denom Chr Chs	20	2,346	2,897	3,551	1.9	3.9
ORTHE–Orth Ch in Amer	1	25	NR	25	0.0	0.0
PENT–Assemb of God	20	2,705	2,219	3,504	1.9	3.8
PENT–Ch God (Cleve)	6	144	482	585	0.3	0.6
PENT–Int Foursq Gos	12	2,242	2,070	2,511	1.4	2.7
PENT–Intl Pent Holiness	1	80	90	109	0.1	0.1
PENT–Pent Ch of God	1	70	NR	109	0.1	0.1
PENT–Un Pent Ch Intl	6	NR	NR	NR	-	-
PRES–Korean Amer Pres	1	NR	NR	NR	-	-
PRES–Korean Pres Amer	1	NR	NR	NR	-	-
PRES–Presb Ch (USA)	4	1,392	1,382	1,676	0.9	1.8
Salvation Army	3	119	313	609	0.3	0.7
Sev Day Adv	7	623	1,083	1,246	0.7	1.4
Un C of Christ	24	1,406	2,036	2,470	1.3	2.7
Unity Ch	1	NR	NR	NR	-	-
HONOLULU	**744**	**76,130**	**93,222**	**374,560**	**39.3**	**100.0**
ANG/EPIS–Anglican NA	1	NR	NR	NR	-	-
ANG/EPIS–Episcopal	20	1,891	3,720	4,369	0.5	1.2
Bahá'í	7	NR	NR	410	0.0	0.1
BAPT–Amer Bapt Assn	3	NR	165	199	0.0	0.1
BAPT–Amer Bapt USA	3	399	545	658	0.1	0.2
BAPT–Consrv Bapt	1	NR	NR	NR	-	-
BAPT–Converge/BGC	3	225	NR	270	0.0	0.1
BAPT–Free Will Bapt	1	NR	33	40	0.0	0.0
BAPT–Ref Bapt Ch	2	NR	NR	NR	-	-
BAPT–So Bapt Conv	72	5,386	11,804	14,253	1.5	3.8
BRETH–Grace Breth	2	NR	NR	NR	-	-
BUDD–Mahayana	61	NR	NR	24,410	2.6	6.5
BUDD–Theravada	4	NR	NR	3,425	0.4	0.9
BUDD–Vajrayana	3	NR	NR	125	0.0	0.0
Calv Chpl	12	NR	NR	NR	-	-
Catholic	39	NR	NR	173,716	18.2	46.4
CGOD–Ch God (Ander)	1	24	NR	24	0.0	0.0
Ch Cr, Scientst	3	NR	NR	NR	-	-
Ch of Nazarene	17	1,394	1,819	2,853	0.3	0.8
Chr & Miss Al	9	1,194	856	1,591	0.2	0.4
CHR–Chr Ch (Disc)	4	102	179	216	0.0	0.1
CHR–Chr Chs & Chs Cr	8	NR	1,322	1,596	0.2	0.4
CHR–Chs of Christ	8	600	574	711	0.1	0.2
CHR–Int Chs of Christ	1	NR	265	320	0.0	0.1
Evan Cov Ch	1	191	268	248	0.0	0.1
Evan Free Ch	5	925	NR	925	0.1	0.2
FRND–Indep Yr Mtgs	2	NR	87	105	0.0	0.0
HINDU–I/A Temples	2	NR	NR	1,812	0.2	0.5
HINDU–Post Ren	1	NR	NR	25	0.0	0.0
Jehovah's Witness	15	NR	NR	NR	-	-
JUD–Conserv	1	36	40	108	0.0	0.0
JUD–Orth	1	43	50	60	0.0	0.0
JUD–Reform	1	128	226	610	0.1	0.2
LDS–L-D Saints	97	NR	NR	48,750	5.1	13.0
LUTH–E.L.C.A.	8	1,053	1,377	1,944	0.2	0.5
LUTH–Luth–MO Synod	6	629	837	1,088	0.1	0.3
MENN–Mennonite USA	2	23	28	34	0.0	0.0
METH–Un Methodist	22	3,706	5,683	6,850	0.7	1.8
Missionary Ch	8	790	506	798	0.1	0.2
Muslim Est	1	134	NR	308	0.0	0.1
New Apost Ch	1	NR	NR	NR	-	-
Non-denom Chr Chs	74	15,064	18,517	21,359	2.2	5.7
ORTHE–Greek Orthodox	1	115	NR	175	0.0	0.0
ORTHE–Rus Orth Abroad	1	10	NR	25	0.0	0.0
ORTHE–Serb Orth USA	1	30	NR	50	0.0	0.0
ORTHO–Coptic Orth Ch	1	40	NR	50	0.0	0.0
PENT–Assemb of God	51	7,292	4,695	11,935	1.3	3.2
PENT–Ch God (Cleve)	14	627	836	1,009	0.1	0.3
PENT–Ch of God Proph	3	NR	162	196	0.0	0.1
PENT–Int Foursq Gos	29	23,946	21,821	26,348	2.8	7.0
PENT–Intl Pent Holiness	4	338	398	481	0.1	0.1
PENT–Un Pent Ch Intl	8	NR	NR	NR	-	-
PENT–Vineyard	1	43	50	60	0.0	0.0
PRES–Kor Pres Abroad	1	NR	NR	NR	-	-
PRES–Korean Amer Pres	3	NR	NR	NR	-	-
PRES–Korean Pres Amer	5	NR	NR	NR	-	-
PRES–Orth Pres Ch	1	40	23	34	0.0	0.0
PRES–Presb Ch (USA)	2	62	125	151	0.0	0.0
PRES–Presb Ch Amer	3	324	202	287	0.0	0.1
REF–Christian Ref	1	25	41	50	0.0	0.0
REF–Hung Ref Add'l	1	NR	NR	NR	-	-
Salvation Army	4	420	543	1,081	0.1	0.3
Sev Day Adv	19	2,260	3,930	4,520	0.5	1.2
Shinto	2	NR	NR	NR	-	-
Sikh	1	NR	NR	NR	-	-
Un C of Christ	51	6,509	11,363	13,720	1.4	3.7
Unit Univ	1	112	132	174	0.0	0.0
Unity Ch	2	NR	NR	NR	-	-
Zoroastrian	0	NR	NR	4	0.0	0.0
KALAWAO	**1**	**7**	**3**	**3**	**3.3**	**100.0**
Un C of Christ	1	7	3	3	3.3	100.0
KAUAI	**106**	**5,611**	**6,424**	**26,514**	**39.5**	**100.0**
ANG/EPIS–Episcopal	4	360	654	853	1.3	3.2
Bahá'í	5	NR	NR	69	0.1	0.3
BAPT–So Bapt Conv	6	267	597	723	1.1	2.7
BUDD–Mahayana	10	NR	NR	4,091	6.1	15.4
Calv Chpl	3	NR	NR	NR	-	-
Catholic	10	NR	NR	10,108	15.1	38.1
Ch Cr, Scientst	1	NR	NR	NR	-	-
Ch of Nazarene	1	83	77	153	0.2	0.6
CHR–Chr Chs & Chs Cr	2	NR	48	58	0.1	0.2
CHR–Chs of Christ	1	70	46	60	0.1	0.2
CONG–Consrv Cong Chr	1	50	20	24	0.0	0.1
Evan Free Ch	1	90	NR	90	0.1	0.3
FRND–Indep Yr Mtgs	1	NR	0	0	0.0	0.0
Jehovah's Witness	7	NR	NR	NR	-	-
LDS–L-D Saints	6	NR	NR	3,488	5.2	13.2
LUTH–E.L.C.A.	1	148	252	252	0.4	1.0
METH–Un Methodist	2	223	193	350	0.5	1.3
Missionary Ch	5	720	378	720	1.1	2.7
Non-denom Chr Chs	10	1,125	1,321	1,529	2.3	5.8
PENT–Assemb of God	4	628	285	685	1.0	2.6
PENT–Ch God (Cleve)	2	41	88	107	0.2	0.4
PENT–Int Foursq Gos	3	596	568	688	1.0	2.6

NR–Not Reported - Represents no adherents reported. Percentages may not total 100 due to rounding.

Table 3: Religious Congregations by County and Group: 2010

Religious Group	Number of Congrega-tions	Number of Attendees	Number of Communicant, Confirmed, or Full Members	Adherents		
				Number of Adherents	% of Total Pop.	% of Total Adh.
REF–Un Ref Chs N.A.	1	NR	NR	NR	-	-
Salvation Army	2	143	226	463	0.7	1.7
Sev Day Adv	2	212	369	425	0.6	1.6
Un C of Christ	14	855	1,302	1,578	2.4	6.0
Unity Ch	1	NR	NR	NR	-	-
MAUI	**189**	**15,123**	**12,937**	**69,377**	**44.8**	**100.0**
ANG/EPIS–Episcopal	5	470	709	1,024	0.7	1.5
Bahá'í	6	NR	NR	188	0.1	0.3
BAPT–So Bapt Conv	10	1,051	1,078	1,313	0.8	1.9
BUDD–Mahayana	19	NR	NR	6,157	4.0	8.9
BUDD–Vajrayana	2	NR	NR	49	0.0	0.1
Calv Chpl	5	NR	NR	NR	-	-
Catholic	22	NR	NR	35,179	22.7	50.7
Ch Cr, Scientst	1	NR	NR	NR	-	-
Ch of Nazarene	3	148	263	338	0.2	0.5
CHR–Chr Chs & Chs Cr	1	NR	75	91	0.1	0.1
CHR–Chs of Christ	1	60	30	50	0.0	0.1
CHR–Int Chs of Christ	1	NR	25	30	0.0	0.0
CONG–Cong Chr Add'l	2	NR	131	160	0.1	0.2
FRND–Indep Yr Mtgs	1	NR	0	0	0.0	0.0
HINDU–I/A Temples	1	NR	NR	250	0.2	0.4
HINDU–Post Ren	2	NR	NR	177	0.1	0.3
HINDU–Renaiss	1	NR	NR	12	0.0	0.0
Jehovah's Witness	5	NR	NR	NR	-	-
LDS–L-D Saints	14	NR	NR	7,212	4.7	10.4
LUTH–E.L.C.A.	1	173	147	222	0.1	0.3
LUTH–Luth–MO Synod	1	121	160	216	0.1	0.3
METH–Un Methodist	3	403	477	583	0.4	0.8
Muslim Est	1	134	NR	308	0.2	0.4
Non-denom Chr Chs	24	4,525	4,882	5,876	3.8	8.5
ORTHE–Greek Orthodox	1	6	NR	15	0.0	0.0
PENT–Assemb of God	8	6,119	2,147	6,419	4.1	9.3
PENT–Ch God (Cleve)	7	135	451	549	0.4	0.8
PENT–Int Foursq Gos	1	93	107	130	0.1	0.2
PENT–Un Pent Ch Intl	5	NR	NR	NR	-	-
PENT–Vineyard	1	58	93	113	0.1	0.2
Salvation Army	3	148	158	305	0.2	0.4
Sev Day Adv	5	249	433	498	0.3	0.7
Un C of Christ	25	1,230	1,571	1,913	1.2	2.8
Unity Ch	1	NR	NR	NR	-	-
IDAHO	**2,427**	**124,582**	**173,097**	**801,655**	**51.1**	**100.0**
ADA	**355**	**37,013**	**51,384**	**168,829**	**43.0**	**100.0**
ANG/EPIS–Anglican NA	2	NR	NR	NR	-	-
ANG/EPIS–Episcopal	4	749	2,273	2,293	0.6	1.4
Bahá'í	2	NR	209	209	0.1	0.1
BAPT–Amer Bapt Assn	1	NR	19	24	0.0	0.0
BAPT–Amer Bapt USA	7	1,620	2,118	2,673	0.7	1.6
BAPT–Consrv Bapt	1	NR	NR	NR	-	-
BAPT–Converge/BGC	1	75	NR	90	0.0	0.1
BAPT–Free Will Bapt	1	NR	42	53	0.0	0.0
BAPT–Ind Bapt Flwsp Intl	1	NR	NR	NR	-	-
BAPT–Reg Bapt Gen As	4	NR	NR	NR	-	-
BAPT–So Bapt Conv	11	1,198	1,937	2,445	0.6	1.4
BRETH–Ch of Brethren	2	35	150	189	0.0	0.1
BUDD–Mahayana	4	NR	NR	1,271	0.3	0.8
BUDD–Theravada	1	NR	NR	300	0.1	0.2
BUDD–Vajrayana	1	NR	NR	36	0.0	0.0
Calv Chpl	5	NR	NR	NR	-	-
Catholic	9	NR	NR	26,302	6.7	15.6
CGOD–Ch God (Ander)	1	828	NR	828	0.2	0.5
Ch Cr, Scientst	1	NR	NR	NR	-	-
Ch of Nazarene	8	2,444	2,384	3,725	0.9	2.2
Chr & Miss Al	2	40	35	65	0.0	0.0
CHR–Chr Ch (Disc)	3	389	945	1,193	0.3	0.7
CHR–Chr Chs & Chs Cr	8	NR	5,389	6,802	1.7	4.0
CHR–Chs of Christ	3	572	534	800	0.2	0.5
CHR–Int Chs of Christ	1	NR	71	90	0.0	0.1
Christian Brethren	1	NR	NR	NR	-	-
Evan Cov Ch	1	61	44	79	0.0	0.0

Religious Group	Number of Congrega-tions	Number of Attendees	Number of Communicant, Confirmed, or Full Members	Adherents		
				Number of Adherents	% of Total Pop.	% of Total Adh.
Evan Free Ch	1	85	NR	85	0.0	0.1
FRND–Evan Fr Ch Intl	4	372	722	911	0.2	0.5
FRND–Indep Yr Mtgs	1	NR	12	15	0.0	0.0
HINDU–I/A Temples	1	NR	NR	1,562	0.4	0.9
HINDU–Post Ren	1	NR	NR	16	0.0	0.0
Jehovah's Witness	5	NR	NR	NR	-	-
JUD–Orth	1	43	50	60	0.0	0.0
JUD–Reform	1	121	213	575	0.1	0.3
LDS–Comm of Christ	1	NR	128	128	0.0	0.1
LDS–L-D Saints	132	NR	NR	61,860	15.8	36.6
LUTH–E.L.C.A.	5	980	1,859	2,427	0.6	1.4
LUTH–Luth–MO Synod	4	717	1,368	1,887	0.5	1.1
LUTH–Wisc Ev Luth Syn	2	313	349	476	0.1	0.3
MENN–Mennonite USA	2	95	80	101	0.0	0.1
METH–C.M.E.	2	0	200	252	0.1	0.1
METH–Free Methodist	1	401	103	401	0.1	0.2
METH–Un Methodist	8	2,272	4,132	11,234	2.9	6.7
Metro Comm Ch	1	14	19	24	0.0	0.0
Muslim Est	3	402	NR	924	0.2	0.5
New Apost Ch	1	NR	NR	NR	-	-
Non-denom Chr Chs	43	15,809	17,550	22,247	5.7	13.2
ORTHE–Ant Orth of NA	1	30	NR	50	0.0	0.0
ORTHE–Greek Orthodox	1	70	NR	130	0.0	0.1
ORTHE–Rus Orth Abroad	1	35	NR	100	0.0	0.1
ORTHE–Serb Orth USA	1	60	NR	140	0.0	0.1
PENT–Assemb of God	10	1,857	1,004	4,256	1.1	2.5
PENT–Ch of God Proph	1	NR	58	73	0.0	0.0
PENT–Int Foursq Gos	4	394	225	284	0.1	0.2
PENT–Pent Ch of God	1	70	NR	109	0.0	0.1
PENT–Un Pent Ch Intl	3	NR	NR	NR	-	-
PENT–Vineyard	2	2,029	2,650	3,345	0.9	2.0
PRES–Korean Pres Amer	1	NR	NR	NR	-	-
PRES–Orth Pres Ch	1	13	33	46	0.0	0.0
PRES–Presb Ch (USA)	5	851	1,454	1,835	0.5	1.1
PRES–Presb Ch Amer	1	160	137	182	0.0	0.1
REF–Comm Ref Evan	1	NR	NR	NR	-	-
REF–Ref Ch in Am	1	181	153	219	0.1	0.1
REF–Un Ref Chs N.A.	1	NR	NR	NR	-	-
Salvation Army	1	48	106	291	0.1	0.2
Sev Day Adv	8	1,110	1,930	2,219	0.6	1.3
Un Breth in Cr	1	26	24	23	0.0	0.0
Un C of Christ	2	230	418	528	0.1	0.3
Unit Univ	1	214	257	343	0.1	0.2
Zoroastrian	0	NR	NR	4	0.0	0.0
ADAMS	**7**	**314**	**369**	**1,002**	**25.2**	**100.0**
Bahá'í	0	NR	1	1	0.0	0.1
Catholic	1	NR	NR	324	8.1	32.3
Ch of Nazarene	1	56	45	65	1.6	6.5
LDS–L-D Saints	1	NR	NR	183	4.6	18.3
LUTH–Luth–MO Synod	1	15	16	18	0.5	1.8
METH–Un Methodist	1	28	64	130	3.3	13.0
Non-denom Chr Chs	1	150	150	188	4.7	18.8
PENT–Assemb of God	1	65	93	93	2.3	9.3
BANNOCK	**162**	**3,156**	**4,939**	**55,595**	**67.1**	**100.0**
ANG/EPIS–Episcopal	1	53	140	162	0.2	0.3
Bahá'í	1	NR	41	41	0.0	0.1
BAPT–Amer Bapt USA	1	85	244	313	0.4	0.6
BAPT–So Bapt Conv	2	56	435	558	0.7	1.0
Calv Chpl	1	NR	NR	NR	-	-
Catholic	5	NR	NR	5,061	6.1	9.1
Ch of Nazarene	1	327	179	589	0.7	1.1
Chr & Miss Al	1	152	83	269	0.3	0.5
CHR–Chr Ch (Disc)	1	95	359	460	0.6	0.8
CHR–Chr Chs & Chs Cr	1	NR	330	423	0.5	0.8
CHR–Chs of Christ	2	115	104	145	0.2	0.3
FRND–Fr Gen Cf	1	NR	0	0	0.0	0.0
FRND–Indep Yr Mtgs	1	NR	0	0	0.0	0.0
Ind Fund Churches	1	NR	NR	NR	-	-
Jehovah's Witness	1	NR	NR	NR	-	-
LDS–Comm of Christ	1	NR	128	128	0.2	0.2
LDS–L-D Saints	116	NR	NR	43,023	51.9	77.4

NR–Not Reported   - Represents no adherents reported.   Percentages may not total 100 due to rounding.

Table 3: Religious Congregations by County and Group: 2010

Religious Group	Number of Congrega-tions	Number of Attendees	Number of Communicant, Confirmed, or Full Members	Adherents: Number of Adherents	Adherents: % of Total Pop.	Adherents: % of Total Adh.
LUTH–E.L.C.A.	1	66	182	219	0.3	0.4
LUTH–Luth–MO Synod	2	480	854	904	1.1	1.6
METH–Un Methodist	2	167	457	720	0.9	1.3
Muslim Est	1	120	NR	400	0.5	0.7
Non-denom Chr Chs	6	815	730	1,044	1.3	1.9
ORTHE–Greek Orthodox	1	55	NR	85	0.1	0.2
PENT–Assemb of God	2	155	86	318	0.4	0.6
PENT–Ch God (Cleve)	1	16	32	41	0.0	0.1
PENT–Ch of God Proph	1	NR	13	17	0.0	0.0
PENT–Int Foursq Gos	1	81	51	65	0.1	0.1
PENT–Un Pent Ch Intl	1	NR	NR	NR	-	-
PENT–Vineyard	1	50	70	90	0.1	0.2
PRES–Presb Ch (USA)	1	99	189	242	0.3	0.4
Sev Day Adv	1	84	145	167	0.2	0.3
Un C of Christ	1	28	28	36	0.0	0.1
Unit Univ	1	57	59	75	0.1	0.1
BEAR LAKE	**22**	**35**	**73**	**5,251**	**87.7**	**100.0**
Bahá'í	0	NR	4	4	0.1	0.1
Catholic	1	NR	NR	99	1.7	1.9
Jehovah's Witness	1	NR	NR	NR	-	-
LDS–L-D Saints	17	NR	NR	5,060	84.5	96.4
PENT–Int Foursq Gos	1	4	19	24	0.4	0.5
PENT–Vineyard	1	23	40	51	0.9	1.0
PRES–Presb Ch (USA)	1	8	10	13	0.2	0.2
BENEWAH	**22**	**772**	**812**	**5,689**	**61.3**	**100.0**
Bahá'í	0	NR	5	5	0.1	0.1
BAPT–Consrv Bapt	1	NR	NR	NR	-	-
BAPT–So Bapt Conv	1	10	10	12	0.1	0.2
Catholic	3	NR	NR	3,479	37.5	61.2
Ch of Nazarene	1	306	202	736	7.9	12.9
CHR–Chs of Christ	1	12	12	16	0.2	0.3
FRND–Evan Fr Ch Intl	1	10	0	0	0.0	0.0
Jehovah's Witness	1	NR	NR	NR	-	-
LDS–L-D Saints	2	NR	NR	580	6.2	10.2
LUTH–Luth Cong Msn Chr	1	40	80	97	1.0	1.7
Non-denom Chr Chs	4	172	172	215	2.3	3.8
PENT–Assemb of God	2	129	61	227	2.4	4.0
PENT–Int Foursq Gos	1	39	45	55	0.6	1.0
PRES–Presb Ch (USA)	1	0	130	158	1.7	2.8
Sev Day Adv	2	54	95	109	1.2	1.9
BINGHAM	**101**	**733**	**1,416**	**31,043**	**68.1**	**100.0**
ANG/EPIS–Episcopal	2	40	100	130	0.3	0.4
Bahá'í	1	NR	64	64	0.1	0.2
BAPT–Amer Bapt USA	1	103	322	435	1.0	1.4
BAPT–So Bapt Conv	2	149	186	251	0.6	0.8
Calv Chpl	1	NR	NR	NR	-	-
Catholic	5	NR	NR	1,992	4.4	6.4
CHR–Chs of Christ	1	32	30	39	0.1	0.1
Jehovah's Witness	1	NR	NR	NR	-	-
LDS–L-D Saints	73	NR	NR	27,042	59.3	87.1
LUTH–E.L.C.A.	2	77	93	165	0.4	0.5
MENN–Mennonite USA	1	69	226	306	0.7	1.0
METH–Un Methodist	3	140	299	458	1.0	1.5
Non-denom Chr Chs	2	56	44	70	0.2	0.2
PENT–Assemb of God	3	67	52	91	0.2	0.3
PENT–Int Foursq Gos	2	0	0	0	0.0	0.0
PENT–Un Pent Ch Intl	1	NR	NR	NR	-	-
BLAINE	**25**	**926**	**966**	**6,097**	**28.5**	**100.0**
ANG/EPIS–Episcopal	2	228	380	592	2.8	9.7
Bahá'í	0	NR	4	4	0.0	0.1
BAPT–Amer Bapt USA	1	7	7	9	0.0	0.1
BAPT–So Bapt Conv	2	34	31	38	0.2	0.6
BUDD–Theravada	1	NR	NR	266	1.2	4.4
Calv Chpl	1	NR	NR	NR	-	-
Catholic	2	NR	NR	2,075	9.7	34.0
Ch Cr, Scientst	1	NR	NR	NR	-	-
Ind Fund Churches	1	NR	NR	NR	-	-
Jehovah's Witness	2	NR	NR	NR	-	-
LDS–L-D Saints	5	NR	NR	2,275	10.6	37.3
LUTH–Luth–MO Synod	1	47	80	108	0.5	1.8
Non-denom Chr Chs	3	300	235	375	1.8	6.2
PENT–Assemb of God	1	28	0	75	0.4	1.2
PRES–Presb Ch (USA)	1	256	184	228	1.1	3.7
Sev Day Adv	1	26	45	52	0.2	0.9
BOISE	**12**	**325**	**271**	**1,470**	**20.9**	**100.0**
Bahá'í	0	NR	1	1	0.0	0.1
BAPT–So Bapt Conv	1	18	21	25	0.4	1.7
Calv Chpl	1	NR	NR	NR	-	-
Catholic	2	NR	NR	80	1.1	5.4
LDS–L-D Saints	3	NR	NR	872	12.4	59.3
LUTH–E.L.C.A.	1	24	41	58	0.8	3.9
Non-denom Chr Chs	1	120	100	150	2.1	10.2
PENT–Assemb of God	2	129	48	215	3.1	14.6
Sev Day Adv	1	34	60	69	1.0	4.7
BONNER	**58**	**3,253**	**4,164**	**10,533**	**25.8**	**100.0**
ANG/EPIS–Episcopal	1	31	54	54	0.1	0.5
Bahá'í	0	NR	15	15	0.0	0.1
BAPT–Amer Bapt Assn	1	NR	85	102	0.2	1.0
BAPT–Consrv Bapt	2	NR	NR	NR	-	-
BAPT–Reg Bapt Gen As	2	NR	NR	NR	-	-
BAPT–So Bapt Conv	3	81	103	123	0.3	1.2
BUDD–Mahayana	1	NR	NR	28	0.1	0.3
Calv Chpl	1	NR	NR	NR	-	-
Catholic	4	NR	NR	1,953	4.8	18.5
CGOD–Ch God (Ander)	1	47	NR	47	0.1	0.4
Ch Cr, Scientst	1	NR	NR	NR	-	-
Ch of Nazarene	1	181	184	263	0.6	2.5
CHR–Chr Chs & Chs Cr	1	NR	550	657	1.6	6.2
CHR–Chs of Christ	3	69	59	75	0.2	0.7
Evan Free Ch	1	25	NR	25	0.1	0.2
Jehovah's Witness	2	NR	NR	NR	-	-
LDS–Comm of Christ	1	NR	128	128	0.3	1.2
LDS–L-D Saints	6	NR	NR	2,818	6.9	26.8
LUTH–E.L.C.A.	2	208	461	580	1.4	5.5
LUTH–Luth–MO Synod	1	208	214	286	0.7	2.7
METH–Free Methodist	1	48	27	48	0.1	0.5
METH–Un Methodist	2	100	204	282	0.7	2.7
Non-denom Chr Chs	12	1,145	1,180	1,468	3.6	13.9
PENT–Assemb of God	3	676	168	733	1.8	7.0
PENT–Ch God (Cleve)	1	55	64	76	0.2	0.7
PRES–Presb Ch (USA)	1	45	87	104	0.3	1.0
Sev Day Adv	3	334	581	668	1.6	6.3
BONNEVILLE	**185**	**3,543**	**7,344**	**76,103**	**73.0**	**100.0**
ANG/EPIS–Episcopal	1	101	320	346	0.3	0.5
Bahá'í	1	NR	38	38	0.0	0.0
BAPT–Amer Bapt Assn	1	NR	85	114	0.1	0.1
BAPT–Amer Bapt USA	1	81	471	630	0.6	0.8
BAPT–N Am Bapt Conf	1	NR	22	29	0.0	0.0
BAPT–So Bapt Conv	2	187	1,362	1,821	1.7	2.4
BUDD–Mahayana	1	NR	NR	11	0.0	0.0
Calv Chpl	1	NR	NR	NR	-	-
Catholic	2	NR	NR	6,534	6.3	8.6
Ch of Nazarene	1	210	268	268	0.3	0.4
Chr & Miss Al	1	160	95	171	0.2	0.2
CHR–Chr Ch (Disc)	1	0	61	82	0.1	0.1
CHR–Chs of Christ	1	125	132	202	0.2	0.3
FRND–Indep Yr Mtgs	1	NR	15	20	0.0	0.0
HINDU–Post Ren	1	NR	NR	15	0.0	0.0
LDS–L-D Saints	138	NR	NR	59,311	56.9	77.9
LUTH–E.L.C.A.	1	0	0	0	0.0	0.0
LUTH–Luth Cong Msn Chr	1	243	753	1,007	1.0	1.3
LUTH–Luth–MO Synod	2	181	581	785	0.8	1.0
METH–Un Methodist	2	357	704	1,269	1.2	1.7
New Apost Ch	1	NR	NR	NR	-	-
Non-denom Chr Chs	6	970	895	1,282	1.2	1.7
PENT–Assemb of God	3	265	282	483	0.5	0.6
PENT–Ch God (Cleve)	1	10	11	15	0.0	0.0
PENT–COGIC	1	0	150	201	0.2	0.3

NR–Not Reported - Represents no adherents reported. Percentages may not total 100 due to rounding.

Table 3: Religious Congregations by County and Group: 2010

Religious Group	Number of Congrega-tions	Number of Attendees	Number of Communicant, Confirmed, or Full Members	Adherents: Number of Adherents	Adherents: % of Total Pop.	Adherents: % of Total Adh.
PENT–Int Foursq Gos	3	238	281	376	0.4	0.5
PENT–Un Pent Ch Intl	2	NR	NR	NR	-	-
PRES–Orth Pres Ch	1	58	42	57	0.1	0.1
PRES–Presb Ch (USA)	2	213	505	675	0.6	0.9
Salvation Army	1	7	62	111	0.1	0.1
Sev Day Adv	2	82	144	165	0.2	0.2
Unit Univ	1	55	65	80	0.1	0.1
Zoroastrian	0	NR	NR	5	0.0	0.0
BOUNDARY	**22**	**1,137**	**1,971**	**4,148**	**37.8**	**100.0**
ANG/EPIS–Episcopal	1	18	25	25	0.2	0.6
Bahá'í	0	NR	6	6	0.1	0.1
BAPT–So Bapt Conv	2	137	568	703	6.4	16.9
Catholic	1	NR	NR	656	6.0	15.8
Ch of Nazarene	1	56	37	56	0.5	1.4
CHR–Chs of Christ	1	85	55	75	0.7	1.8
Jehovah's Witness	1	NR	NR	NR	-	-
LDS–L-D Saints	2	NR	NR	747	6.8	18.0
LUTH–E.L.C.A.	1	76	3	195	1.8	4.7
MENN–CG in Cr (Menn)	2	NR	328	406	3.7	9.8
METH–Free Methodist	1	77	60	77	0.7	1.9
METH–Un Methodist	1	94	237	277	2.5	6.7
Non-denom Chr Chs	4	380	440	525	4.8	12.7
ORTHE–Ant Orth of NA	1	50	NR	100	0.9	2.4
PENT–Assemb of God	1	60	30	91	0.8	2.2
PRES–Bible Pres	1	NR	NR	NR	-	-
Sev Day Adv	1	104	182	209	1.9	5.0
BUTTE	**14**	**207**	**375**	**2,237**	**77.4**	**100.0**
ANG/EPIS–Episcopal	1	7	15	15	0.5	0.7
Bahá'í	0	NR	1	1	0.0	0.0
BAPT–Amer Bapt USA	1	50	78	99	3.4	4.4
BAPT–So Bapt Conv	2	68	51	65	2.2	2.9
Catholic	1	NR	NR	132	4.6	5.9
LDS–L-D Saints	6	NR	NR	1,634	56.5	73.0
Non-denom Chr Chs	1	50	50	62	2.1	2.8
PENT–COGIC	1	0	150	190	6.6	8.5
PRES–Orth Pres Ch	1	32	30	39	1.3	1.7
CAMAS	**3**	**75**	**110**	**309**	**27.7**	**100.0**
Bahá'í	0	NR	5	5	0.4	1.6
Catholic	1	NR	NR	54	4.8	17.5
LDS–L-D Saints	1	NR	NR	145	13.0	46.9
Non-denom Chr Chs	1	75	105	105	9.4	34.0
CANYON	**204**	**15,585**	**18,712**	**77,144**	**40.8**	**100.0**
ANG/EPIS–Episcopal	2	121	259	328	0.2	0.4
Bahá'í	0	NR	52	52	0.0	0.1
BAPT–Amer Bapt USA	3	169	223	297	0.2	0.4
BAPT–Consrv Bapt	2	NR	NR	NR	-	-
BAPT–Free Will Bapt	1	NR	42	56	0.0	0.1
BAPT–Ref Bapt Ch	1	NR	NR	NR	-	-
BAPT–Reg Bapt Gen As	4	NR	NR	NR	-	-
BAPT–So Bapt Conv	7	422	1,385	1,847	1.0	2.4
BRETH–Ch of Brethren	2	0	332	443	0.2	0.6
Calv Chpl	2	NR	NR	NR	-	-
Catholic	3	NR	NR	17,838	9.4	23.1
CGOD–Ch God (Ander)	1	235	NR	235	0.1	0.3
Ch Cr, Scientst	1	NR	NR	NR	-	-
Ch God (7th Day)	1	NR	NR	NR	-	-
Ch of Nazarene	13	4,250	4,987	7,026	3.7	9.1
Chr & Miss Al	1	245	112	242	0.1	0.3
CHR–Chr Ch (Disc)	2	211	347	463	0.2	0.6
CHR–Chr Chs & Chs Cr	3	NR	400	533	0.3	0.7
CHR–Chs of Christ	5	316	293	362	0.2	0.5
Evan Free Ch	1	110	NR	110	0.1	0.1
FRND–Evan Fr Ch Intl	5	303	625	833	0.4	1.1
Jehovah's Witness	4	NR	NR	NR	-	-
LDS–L-D Saints	63	NR	NR	29,758	15.8	38.6
LUTH–Ch of Luth Br	1	120	105	435	0.2	0.6
LUTH–E.L.C.A.	2	192	447	546	0.3	0.7
LUTH–Luth–MO Synod	2	312	717	940	0.5	1.2
LUTH–Wisc Ev Luth Syn	1	163	205	305	0.2	0.4
MENN–Fel Evg Ch	1	218	83	111	0.1	0.1
MENN–Mennonite USA	1	32	40	53	0.0	0.1
METH–Evan Meth Ch	1	NR	NR	NR	-	-
METH–Free Methodist	4	896	514	896	0.5	1.2
METH–Un Methodist	5	475	828	1,215	0.6	1.6
Non-denom Chr Chs	20	2,503	2,831	3,397	1.8	4.4
PENT–Assemb of God	11	2,187	767	4,896	2.6	6.3
PENT–Ch God (Cleve)	3	162	133	177	0.1	0.2
PENT–Ch of God Proph	4	NR	169	225	0.1	0.3
PENT–Int Foursq Gos	1	77	47	63	0.0	0.1
PENT–Intl Pent Holiness	1	28	18	24	0.0	0.0
PENT–Pent Ch of God	1	70	NR	109	0.1	0.1
PENT–Un Pent Ch Intl	2	NR	NR	NR	-	-
PENT–Vineyard	1	102	175	233	0.1	0.3
PRES–Presb Ch (USA)	4	592	721	961	0.5	1.2
REF–Un Ref Chs N.A.	1	NR	NR	NR	-	-
Salvation Army	2	74	123	134	0.1	0.2
Sev Day Adv	7	965	1,679	1,930	1.0	2.5
Un C of Christ	1	35	53	71	0.0	0.1
CARIBOU	**21**	**99**	**112**	**5,851**	**84.0**	**100.0**
BAPT–So Bapt Conv	1	40	21	27	0.4	0.5
Catholic	2	NR	NR	374	5.4	6.4
LDS–L-D Saints	15	NR	NR	5,327	76.5	91.0
LUTH–Luth–MO Synod	1	10	11	14	0.2	0.2
PENT–Assemb of God	1	15	10	19	0.3	0.3
PRES–Presb Ch (USA)	1	34	70	90	1.3	1.5
CASSIA	**51**	**1,336**	**1,562**	**16,677**	**72.7**	**100.0**
Bahá'í	0	NR	3	3	0.0	0.0
BAPT–Consrv Bapt	1	NR	NR	NR	-	-
BAPT–So Bapt Conv	3	317	622	840	3.7	5.0
Calv Chpl	1	NR	NR	NR	-	-
Catholic	1	NR	NR	2,162	9.4	13.0
CHR–Chr Ch (Disc)	1	0	112	151	0.7	0.9
CHR–Chs of Christ	2	58	56	72	0.3	0.4
Jehovah's Witness	1	NR	NR	NR	-	-
LDS–L-D Saints	32	NR	NR	11,922	51.9	71.5
LUTH–Luth–MO Synod	1	42	49	50	0.2	0.3
METH–Un Methodist	1	101	237	454	2.0	2.7
Non-denom Chr Chs	3	175	195	225	1.0	1.3
PENT–Assemb of God	2	545	132	587	2.6	3.5
PENT–Int Foursq Gos	1	49	45	61	0.3	0.4
PRES–Presb Ch (USA)	1	49	111	150	0.7	0.9
CLARK	**2**	**19**	**50**	**353**	**35.9**	**100.0**
BAPT–Amer Bapt USA	1	19	50	66	6.7	18.7
LDS–L-D Saints	1	NR	NR	287	29.2	81.3
CLEARWATER	**24**	**1,220**	**1,102**	**2,827**	**32.3**	**100.0**
Bahá'í	0	NR	1	1	0.0	0.0
BAPT–So Bapt Conv	2	78	79	91	1.0	3.2
Catholic	1	NR	NR	382	4.4	13.5
CGOD–Ch God (Ander)	1	23	NR	23	0.3	0.8
Ch of Nazarene	1	35	42	61	0.7	2.2
Chr & Miss Al	1	160	59	160	1.8	5.7
CHR–Chr Ch (Disc)	1	33	54	62	0.7	2.2
Jehovah's Witness	1	NR	NR	NR	-	-
LDS–L-D Saints	2	NR	NR	563	6.4	19.9
LUTH–Ch Luth Conf	1	NR	NR	NR	-	-
LUTH–E.L.C.A.	1	37	138	168	1.9	5.9
LUTH–Luth Cong Msn Chr	1	NR	NR	NR	-	-
METH–Un Methodist	2	47	180	223	2.5	7.9
METH–Wesleyan	1	87	40	113	1.3	4.0
Non-denom Chr Chs	2	530	330	663	7.6	23.5
PENT–Assemb of God	1	18	21	26	0.3	0.9
PENT–Pent Ch of God	1	70	NR	109	1.2	3.9
PRES–Presb Ch (USA)	1	20	15	17	0.2	0.6
Sev Day Adv	2	82	143	165	1.9	5.8
Un Breth in Cr	1	0	0	0	0.0	0.0

NR–Not Reported - Represents no adherents reported. Percentages may not total 100 due to rounding.

Table 3: Religious Congregations by County and Group: 2010

Religious Group	Number of Congrega-tions	Number of Attendees	Number of Communicant, Confirmed, or Full Members	Adherents		
				Number of Adherents	% of Total Pop.	% of Total Adh.
CUSTER	**15**	**182**	**135**	**1,757**	**40.2**	**100.0**
ANG/EPIS–Episcopal	1	8	7	7	0.2	0.4
Bahá'í	0	NR	2	2	0.0	0.1
BAPT–So Bapt Conv	1	NR	NR	NR	-	-
Catholic	2	NR	NR	248	5.7	14.1
Jehovah's Witness	1	NR	NR	NR	-	-
LDS–L-D Saints	5	NR	NR	1,189	27.2	67.7
Non-denom Chr Chs	3	120	108	150	3.4	8.5
PENT–Assemb of God	1	48	0	140	3.2	8.0
Un C of Christ	1	6	18	21	0.5	1.2
ELMORE	**41**	**1,823**	**2,830**	**11,454**	**42.4**	**100.0**
ANG/EPIS–Episcopal	2	59	68	82	0.3	0.7
Bahá'í	0	NR	7	7	0.0	0.1
BAPT–Amer Bapt USA	1	79	215	278	1.0	2.4
BAPT–So Bapt Conv	7	327	586	757	2.8	6.6
Calv Chpl	1	NR	NR	NR	-	-
Catholic	3	NR	NR	4,461	16.5	38.9
Ch of Nazarene	1	253	402	461	1.7	4.0
CHR–Chr Ch (Disc)	1	75	241	311	1.2	2.7
CHR–Chs of Christ	1	35	37	40	0.1	0.3
LDS–L-D Saints	9	NR	NR	3,189	11.8	27.8
LUTH–E.L.C.A.	1	46	61	96	0.4	0.8
LUTH–Luth-MO Synod	1	87	258	333	1.2	2.9
METH–Un Methodist	1	0	62	62	0.2	0.5
Non-denom Chr Chs	4	330	289	412	1.5	3.6
PENT–Assemb of God	2	308	180	429	1.6	3.7
PENT–Ch God (Cleve)	1	84	130	168	0.6	1.5
PENT–Ch of God Proph	2	NR	43	56	0.2	0.5
PRES–Presb Ch (USA)	1	9	12	16	0.1	0.1
Sev Day Adv	1	56	97	112	0.4	1.0
Un C of Christ	1	75	142	184	0.7	1.6
FRANKLIN	**39**	**134**	**180**	**12,253**	**95.8**	**100.0**
Catholic	1	NR	NR	627	4.9	5.1
Jehovah's Witness	1	NR	NR	NR	-	-
LDS–L-D Saints	35	NR	NR	11,434	89.4	93.3
Non-denom Chr Chs	1	100	150	150	1.2	1.2
PRES–Presb Ch (USA)	1	34	30	42	0.3	0.3
FREMONT	**33**	**375**	**642**	**10,254**	**77.4**	**100.0**
BAPT–So Bapt Conv	1	20	30	40	0.3	0.4
Catholic	2	NR	NR	970	7.3	9.5
CHR–Chs of Christ	1	30	30	39	0.3	0.4
Jehovah's Witness	1	NR	NR	NR	-	-
LDS–L-D Saints	20	NR	NR	8,586	64.8	83.7
LUTH–Luth-MO Synod	2	77	141	159	1.2	1.6
METH–Un Methodist	1	0	102	102	0.8	1.0
Non-denom Chr Chs	3	200	280	280	2.1	2.7
PENT–Int Foursq Gos	1	18	21	28	0.2	0.3
PRES–Presb Ch (USA)	1	30	38	50	0.4	0.5
GEM	**25**	**911**	**1,039**	**9,423**	**56.4**	**100.0**
ANG/EPIS–Episcopal	1	38	112	112	0.7	1.2
Bahá'í	0	NR	8	8	0.0	0.1
BAPT–Amer Bapt USA	1	65	88	108	0.6	1.1
BAPT–Consrv Bapt	1	NR	NR	NR	-	-
Calv Chpl	1	NR	NR	NR	-	-
Catholic	1	NR	NR	4,989	29.8	52.9
Ch of Nazarene	1	169	214	214	1.3	2.3
CHR–Chs of Christ	1	43	40	52	0.3	0.6
Jehovah's Witness	1	NR	NR	NR	-	-
LDS–L-D Saints	8	NR	NR	3,100	18.5	32.9
LUTH–Luth-MO Synod	1	90	181	228	1.4	2.4
METH–Un Methodist	2	73	91	190	1.1	2.0
PENT–Assemb of God	1	53	0	53	0.3	0.6
PENT–Ch God (Cleve)	1	63	104	128	0.8	1.4
PENT–Int Foursq Gos	1	193	3	4	0.0	0.0
PENT–Vineyard	1	40	60	74	0.4	0.8
PRES–Presb Ch (USA)	1	32	47	58	0.3	0.6
Sev Day Adv	1	52	91	105	0.6	1.1
GOODING	**32**	**812**	**1,256**	**7,285**	**47.1**	**100.0**
ANG/EPIS–Episcopal	1	7	17	17	0.1	0.2
Bahá'í	0	NR	3	3	0.0	0.0
BAPT–Amer Bapt USA	1	18	35	46	0.3	0.6
BAPT–So Bapt Conv	3	63	75	98	0.6	1.3
Calv Chpl	1	NR	NR	NR	-	-
Catholic	3	NR	NR	2,351	15.2	32.3
Ch of Nazarene	1	62	64	107	0.7	1.5
CHR–Chr Chs & Chs Cr	1	NR	0	0	0.0	0.0
CHR–Chs of Christ	3	65	50	70	0.5	1.0
Jehovah's Witness	1	NR	NR	NR	-	-
LDS–Comm of Christ	1	NR	128	128	0.8	1.8
LDS–L-D Saints	8	NR	NR	3,370	21.8	46.3
LUTH–Luth-MO Synod	1	30	25	31	0.2	0.4
METH–Un Methodist	3	128	272	370	2.4	5.1
Non-denom Chr Chs	1	120	200	200	1.3	2.7
PENT–Assemb of God	1	23	23	23	0.1	0.3
PRES–Presb Ch (USA)	1	161	195	254	1.6	3.5
REF–Ref Ch in Am	1	135	169	217	1.4	3.0
IDAHO	**41**	**1,067**	**1,432**	**5,623**	**34.6**	**100.0**
ANG/EPIS–Episcopal	1	15	29	31	0.2	0.6
Bahá'í	0	NR	3	3	0.0	0.1
BAPT–So Bapt Conv	8	241	277	328	2.0	5.8
Calv Chpl	1	NR	NR	NR	-	-
Catholic	7	NR	NR	2,729	16.8	48.5
Ch of Nazarene	2	191	141	239	1.5	4.3
CHR–Chr Chs & Chs Cr	1	NR	250	296	1.8	5.3
Evan Free Ch	1	150	NR	150	0.9	2.7
Ind Fund Churches	1	NR	NR	NR	-	-
Jehovah's Witness	1	NR	NR	NR	-	-
LDS–L-D Saints	2	NR	NR	630	3.9	11.2
LUTH–Luth-MO Synod	1	32	79	84	0.5	1.5
METH–Un Methodist	3	41	201	426	2.6	7.6
METH–Wesleyan	1	25	7	33	0.2	0.6
Non-denom Chr Chs	4	180	210	260	1.6	4.6
PENT–Assemb of God	1	65	38	183	1.1	3.3
PENT–Ch God (Cleve)	2	49	67	79	0.5	1.4
PRES–Presb Ch (USA)	2	29	61	72	0.4	1.3
REF–Christian Ref	1	25	28	33	0.2	0.6
Sev Day Adv	1	24	41	47	0.3	0.8
JEFFERSON	**51**	**189**	**271**	**19,404**	**74.2**	**100.0**
Bahá'í	0	NR	6	6	0.0	0.0
BAPT–Amer Bapt USA	1	20	54	76	0.3	0.4
Catholic	2	NR	NR	132	0.5	0.7
LDS–L-D Saints	44	NR	NR	18,908	72.3	97.4
LUTH–Luth-MO Synod	1	50	70	88	0.3	0.5
Non-denom Chr Chs	1	75	70	94	0.4	0.5
PENT–Int Foursq Gos	1	19	22	31	0.1	0.2
PRES–Presb Ch (USA)	1	25	49	69	0.3	0.4
JEROME	**34**	**928**	**1,339**	**13,330**	**59.6**	**100.0**
ANG/EPIS–Episcopal	1	8	19	19	0.1	0.1
Bahá'í	0	NR	9	9	0.0	0.1
BAPT–Amer Bapt USA	1	54	86	114	0.5	0.9
BAPT–Free Will Bapt	1	NR	42	56	0.3	0.4
BAPT–So Bapt Conv	1	105	69	91	0.4	0.7
Calv Chpl	1	NR	NR	NR	-	-
Catholic	1	NR	NR	6,511	29.1	48.8
CHR–Chr Ch (Disc)	1	0	35	46	0.2	0.3
CHR–Chs of Christ	2	40	35	50	0.2	0.4
Evan Free Ch	1	150	NR	150	0.7	1.1
LDS–L-D Saints	12	NR	NR	4,818	21.5	36.1
LUTH–Luth-MO Synod	3	100	418	492	2.2	3.7
MENN–CG in Cr (Menn)	1	NR	95	126	0.6	0.9
METH–Un Methodist	1	42	84	121	0.5	0.9
Non-denom Chr Chs	1	135	175	175	0.8	1.3
PENT–Assemb of God	2	150	52	267	1.2	2.0
PRES–Presb Ch (USA)	2	125	187	247	1.1	1.9
Sev Day Adv	2	19	33	38	0.2	0.3

NR–Not Reported   - Represents no adherents reported.   Percentages may not total 100 due to rounding.

Table 3: Religious Congregations by County and Group: 2010

Religious Group	Number of Congrega-tions	Number of Attendees	Number of Communicant, Confirmed, or Full Members	Adherents		
				Number of Adherents	% of Total Pop.	% of Total Adh.
KOOTENAI	**123**	**25,496**	**35,360**	**79,972**	**57.7**	**100.0**
ANG/EPIS–Episcopal	1	147	263	439	0.3	0.5
Bahá'í	1	NR	73	73	0.1	0.1
BAPT–Amer Bapt Assn	1	NR	85	105	0.1	0.1
BAPT–Amer Bapt USA	1	59	58	72	0.1	0.1
BAPT–So Bapt Conv	8	575	574	708	0.5	0.9
BUDD–Mahayana	1	NR	NR	102	0.1	0.1
Calv Chpl	4	NR	NR	NR	-	-
Catholic	8	NR	NR	7,597	5.5	9.5
CGOD–Ch God (Ander)	1	30	NR	30	0.0	0.0
Ch Cr, Scientst	1	NR	NR	NR	-	-
Ch of Nazarene	3	468	296	933	0.7	1.2
CHR–Chr Ch (Disc)	2	20	129	159	0.1	0.2
CHR–Chr Chs & Chs Cr	1	NR	8,000	9,872	7.1	12.3
CHR–Chs of Christ	2	320	357	459	0.3	0.6
Evan Free Ch	1	500	NR	500	0.4	0.6
FRND–Evan Fr Ch Intl	3	665	331	408	0.3	0.5
Grace Gosp Fel	1	NR	NR	NR	-	-
Ind Fund Churches	1	NR	NR	NR	-	-
Jehovah's Witness	4	NR	NR	NR	-	-
LDS–Comm of Christ	1	NR	128	128	0.1	0.2
LDS–L-D Saints	14	NR	NR	8,164	5.9	10.2
LUTH–E.L.C.A.	3	391	1,004	1,263	0.9	1.6
LUTH–Luth Cong Msn Chr	2	128	222	274	0.2	0.3
LUTH–Luth-MO Synod	3	549	718	893	0.6	1.1
METH–Free Methodist	1	65	45	65	0.0	0.1
METH–Un Methodist	2	178	365	540	0.4	0.7
METH–Wesleyan	1	21	9	27	0.0	0.0
Non-denom Chr Chs	23	16,780	19,865	21,009	15.2	26.3
ORTHE–Ant Orth of NA	1	85	NR	162	0.1	0.2
PENT–Assemb of God	6	3,022	821	5,253	3.8	6.6
PENT–Int Foursq Gos	2	84	96	118	0.1	0.1
PENT–Open Bible Std	1	13	NR	13	0.0	0.0
PENT–Pent Ch of God	1	70	NR	109	0.1	0.1
PENT–Un Pent Ch Intl	2	NR	NR	NR	-	-
PRES–Presb Ch (USA)	4	341	479	591	0.4	0.7
REF–Comm Ref Evan	1	NR	NR	NR	-	-
Salvation Army	1	159	19	18,269	13.2	22.8
Sev Day Adv	7	806	1,402	1,612	1.2	2.0
Unit Univ	1	20	21	25	0.0	0.0
Unity Ch	1	NR	NR	NR	-	-
LATAH	**66**	**2,968**	**3,638**	**11,003**	**29.5**	**100.0**
ANG/EPIS–Episcopal	1	59	95	129	0.3	1.2
Bahá'í	1	NR	47	47	0.1	0.4
BAPT–Amer Bapt USA	1	48	55	64	0.2	0.6
BAPT–Reg Bapt Gen As	1	NR	NR	NR	-	-
BAPT–So Bapt Conv	1	225	153	179	0.5	1.6
BUDD–Vajrayana	2	NR	NR	70	0.2	0.6
Catholic	4	NR	NR	2,408	6.5	21.9
CGOD–Ch God (Ander)	1	36	NR	36	0.1	0.3
Ch Cr, Scientst	1	NR	NR	NR	-	-
Ch of Nazarene	4	422	554	616	1.7	5.6
CHR–Chr Ch (Disc)	1	0	80	94	0.3	0.9
CHR–Chs of Christ	1	28	30	35	0.1	0.3
Ind Fund Churches	3	NR	NR	NR	-	-
Jehovah's Witness	1	NR	NR	NR	-	-
LDS–L-D Saints	12	NR	NR	3,214	8.6	29.2
LUTH–E.L.C.A.	6	417	822	1,009	2.7	9.2
LUTH–Luth Cong Msn Chr	1	40	76	89	0.2	0.8
MENN–CG in Cr (Menn)	1	NR	52	61	0.2	0.6
METH–Evan Meth Ch	1	NR	NR	NR	-	-
METH–Un Methodist	3	213	403	566	1.5	5.1
Muslim Est	1	134	NR	308	0.8	2.8
Non-denom Chr Chs	6	650	445	845	2.3	7.7
PENT–Assemb of God	2	220	40	299	0.8	2.7
PRES–Presb Ch (USA)	3	199	317	371	1.0	3.4
REF–Comm Ref Evan	2	NR	NR	NR	-	-
Sev Day Adv	3	181	315	362	1.0	3.3
Tao	1	NR	NR	NR	-	-
Unit Univ	1	96	154	201	0.5	1.8

Religious Group	Number of Congrega-tions	Number of Attendees	Number of Communicant, Confirmed, or Full Members	Adherents		
				Number of Adherents	% of Total Pop.	% of Total Adh.
LEMHI	**23**	**749**	**1,317**	**3,638**	**45.8**	**100.0**
ANG/EPIS–Episcopal	1	27	56	90	1.1	2.5
Bahá'í	0	NR	2	2	0.0	0.1
BAPT–So Bapt Conv	2	160	450	529	6.7	14.5
Calv Chpl	1	NR	NR	NR	-	-
Catholic	2	NR	NR	394	5.0	10.8
CHR–Chs of Christ	1	50	42	60	0.8	1.6
Jehovah's Witness	1	NR	NR	NR	-	-
LDS–L-D Saints	4	NR	NR	1,607	20.2	44.2
LUTH–Luth–MO Synod	1	58	87	108	1.4	3.0
METH–Un Methodist	2	50	107	107	1.3	2.9
Non-denom Chr Chs	4	230	335	356	4.5	9.8
PENT–Assemb of God	1	27	10	120	1.5	3.3
PENT–Int Foursq Gos	1	54	75	88	1.1	2.4
PRES–Presb Ch (USA)	1	25	34	40	0.5	1.1
Sev Day Adv	1	68	119	137	1.7	3.8
LEWIS	**22**	**500**	**567**	**1,927**	**50.4**	**100.0**
Bahá'í	0	NR	3	3	0.1	0.2
BAPT–So Bapt Conv	2	46	31	37	1.0	1.9
Catholic	2	NR	NR	373	9.8	19.4
CHR–Chr Chs & Chs Cr	1	NR	57	69	1.8	3.6
FRND–Evan Fr Ch Intl	1	50	34	41	1.1	2.1
Ind Fund Churches	1	NR	NR	NR	-	-
Jehovah's Witness	1	NR	NR	NR	-	-
LDS–L-D Saints	2	NR	NR	734	19.2	38.1
LUTH–E.L.C.A.	2	60	141	140	3.7	7.3
Non-denom Chr Chs	2	90	75	117	3.1	6.1
PENT–Assemb of God	2	76	53	100	2.6	5.2
PENT–Pent Ch of God	1	70	NR	109	2.9	5.7
PRES–Presb Ch (USA)	3	58	87	105	2.7	5.4
Sev Day Adv	1	50	86	99	2.6	5.1
Unity Ch	1	NR	NR	NR	-	-
LINCOLN	**13**	**211**	**300**	**1,892**	**36.3**	**100.0**
ANG/EPIS–Episcopal	1	14	20	24	0.5	1.3
Bahá'í	0	NR	1	1	0.0	0.1
BAPT–Amer Bapt USA	1	35	40	54	1.0	2.9
Catholic	1	NR	NR	165	3.2	8.7
LDS–L-D Saints	4	NR	NR	1,395	26.8	73.7
LUTH–E.L.C.A.	1	0	0	0	0.0	0.0
METH–Un Methodist	2	17	50	52	1.0	2.7
Non-denom Chr Chs	1	100	150	150	2.9	7.9
PENT–Assemb of God	2	45	39	51	1.0	2.7
MADISON	**162**	**118**	**177**	**38,596**	**102.8**	**100.0**
Bahá'í	0	NR	2	2	0.0	0.0
Calv Chpl	1	NR	NR	NR	-	-
Catholic	1	NR	NR	582	1.6	1.5
LDS–L-D Saints	157	NR	NR	37,831	100.8	98.0
Non-denom Chr Chs	2	110	160	162	0.4	0.4
PRES–Presb Ch (USA)	1	8	15	19	0.1	0.0
MINIDOKA	**43**	**1,261**	**2,230**	**14,620**	**72.8**	**100.0**
ANG/EPIS–Episcopal	1	23	54	54	0.3	0.4
BAPT–Free Will Bapt	1	NR	42	54	0.3	0.4
BAPT–N Am Bapt Conf	1	NR	176	227	1.1	1.6
BAPT–So Bapt Conv	2	55	40	51	0.3	0.3
Catholic	1	NR	NR	4,149	20.7	28.4
CHR–Chr Chs & Chs Cr	3	NR	350	451	2.2	3.1
CHR–Chs of Christ	1	40	75	60	0.3	0.4
CONG–Consrv Cong Chr	1	170	144	185	0.9	1.3
LDS–L-D Saints	20	NR	NR	7,714	38.4	52.8
LUTH–Luth–MO Synod	1	151	256	281	1.4	1.9
METH–Un Methodist	2	146	342	469	2.3	3.2
Non-denom Chr Chs	3	425	585	625	3.1	4.3
PENT–Assemb of God	3	200	107	230	1.1	1.6
PENT–Ch God (Cleve)	1	25	15	19	0.1	0.1
PENT–Un Pent Ch Intl	1	NR	NR	NR	-	-
Sev Day Adv	1	26	44	51	0.3	0.3

NR–Not Reported - Represents no adherents reported. Percentages may not total 100 due to rounding.

Association of Statisticians of American Religious Bodies

Standard Denominational Adherents Information for 2011

Name	Statistical Year	Full/Active Members	Other Members	Children	Total	Total Subtractions (Absentees)	Standard Denominational Adherents
Assemblies of God	2010	1,753,881	1,277,063	-	3,030,944	-	3,030,944
Baha'I Faith in the United States	2011	155,231	-	14,023	169,254		169,254
The Brethren Church	2005	10,254	-	-	10,254	-	10,254
The Christian and Missionary Alliance	2003	194,074	206,835	-	400,909	-	400,909
Christian Church (Disciples of Christ)*	2005	462,510	260,333	-	722,843	-	722,843
Church of God (Cleveland, TN)***	2004	6,794,116	-	-	6,794,116	-	6,794,116
The Church of Jesus Christ of Latter-day Saints	2009	6,058,907	-	-	6,058,907		6,058,907
Church of the Nazarene	2010	640,966	9,131	-	650,097	128,522	521,575
Churches of Christ	2011	1,219,735	348,881	-	1,568,616	-	1,568,616
Evangelical Lutheran Church in America	2009	3,444,021	1,099,016	-	4,543,037	-	4,543,037
International Churches of Christ	2009	35,636	-	-	35,636	-	35,636
Int Pentecostal Holiness Church	2005	244,184	59,093	-	303,277	-	303,277
Lutheran Church, Missouri Synod	2010	1,764,024	514,562	-	2,278,586	-	2,278,586
Mennonite Church	2004	111,031	-	-	111,031	-	111,031
Missionary Church	2004	67,395	-	-	67,395	-	67,395
National Assoc. of Free Will Baptists, Inc.	2005	187,193	-	-	187,193	-	187,193
Pentecostal Church of God	2002	45,500	58,500		104,000	-	104,000
Presbyterian Church (U.S.A)**	2010	2,016,091	659,782		2,675,873	-	2,675,873
Presbyterian Church in America	2005	265,080	66,046	-	331,126	-	331,126
Roman Catholic Church	2010	65,390,596	-	-	65,390,596	-	65,390,596
Salvation Army	2007	97,712	290,133	25,183	413,028	-	413,028
Seventh-day Adventist	2010	1,060,386	-	-	1,060,386	-	1,060,386
Southern Baptist Convention	2010	16,136,044	-	-	16,136,044	4,998,598	11,137,446
United Church of Christ	2010	1,058,423	-	-	1,058,423	-	1,058,423
The United Methodist Church	2008	7,774,420	778,060	1,565,327	10,117,807	-	10,117,807
The Wesleyan Church*	2003	119,467	10,992	-	130,459	-	130,459
Wisconsin Evangelical Lutheran Synod	2005	313,553	84,729	-	398,282	-	398,282

*Includes United States and Canada

**Includes Puerto Rico

***Includes foreign figures, US and Canada

Table 3: Religious Congregations by County and Group: 2010

Religious Group	Number of Congregations	Number of Attendees	Number of Communicant, Confirmed, or Full Members	Adherents: Number of Adherents	Adherents: % of Total Pop.	Adherents: % of Total Adh.
NEZ PERCE	**57**	**4,768**	**6,488**	**11,540**	**29.4**	**100.0**
ANG/EPIS–Episcopal	1	81	175	175	0.4	1.5
Bahá'í	2	NR	100	100	0.3	0.9
BAPT–Amer Bapt Assn	1	NR	0	0	0.0	0.0
BAPT–Amer Bapt USA	1	53	68	82	0.2	0.7
BAPT–Asc Ref Bap Ch Am	1	NR	NR	NR	-	-
BAPT–Ref Bapt Ch	1	NR	NR	NR	-	-
BAPT–Reg Bapt Gen As	1	NR	NR	NR	-	-
BAPT–So Bapt Conv	2	257	459	550	1.4	4.8
BUDD–Mahayana	1	NR	NR	102	0.3	0.9
Calv Chpl	1	NR	NR	NR	-	-
Catholic	4	NR	NR	1,468	3.7	12.7
CGOD–Ch God (Ander)	1	0	NR	0	0.0	0.0
Ch of Nazarene	2	278	646	674	1.7	5.8
Chr & Miss Al	1	483	145	503	1.3	4.4
CHR–Chr Chs & Chs Cr	1	NR	100	120	0.3	1.0
CHR–Chs of Christ	1	130	140	150	0.4	1.3
Ind Fund Churches	1	NR	NR	NR	-	-
Jehovah's Witness	1	NR	NR	NR	-	-
LDS–L-D Saints	4	NR	NR	1,961	5.0	17.0
LUTH–E.L.C.A.	3	153	484	553	1.4	4.8
LUTH–Luth–MO Synod	1	54	78	91	0.2	0.8
LUTH–Nor Amer Luth C	1	NR	NR	NR	-	-
METH–Un Methodist	3	186	470	674	1.7	5.8
Non-denom Chr Chs	8	1,805	2,525	2,690	6.9	23.3
PENT–Assemb of God	3	402	112	428	1.1	3.7
PENT–Int Foursq Gos	1	69	68	82	0.2	0.7
PENT–Un Pent Ch Intl	1	NR	NR	NR	-	-
PRES–Presb Ch (USA)	3	298	478	573	1.5	5.0
Salvation Army	1	52	51	114	0.3	1.0
Sev Day Adv	2	196	340	391	1.0	3.4
Un C of Christ	1	271	49	59	0.2	0.5
Unity Ch	1	NR	NR	NR	-	-
ONEIDA	**12**	**41**	**48**	**3,609**	**84.2**	**100.0**
BAPT–So Bapt Conv	1	25	35	45	1.0	1.2
LDS–L-D Saints	10	NR	NR	3,547	82.8	98.3
PRES–Presb Ch (USA)	1	16	13	17	0.4	0.5
OWYHEE	**25**	**544**	**563**	**3,331**	**28.9**	**100.0**
Bahá'í	0	NR	1	1	0.0	0.0
BAPT–So Bapt Conv	1	20	42	54	0.5	1.6
Catholic	6	NR	NR	396	3.4	11.9
CGOD–Ch God (Ander)	1	130	NR	130	1.1	3.9
Ch of Nazarene	1	59	61	70	0.6	2.1
CHR–Chr Ch (Disc)	1	20	56	72	0.6	2.2
CHR–Chs of Christ	1	15	22	15	0.1	0.5
Evan Free Ch	1	55	NR	55	0.5	1.7
FRND–Evan Fr Ch Intl	1	90	80	103	0.9	3.1
LDS–L-D Saints	5	NR	NR	2,013	17.5	60.4
LUTH–Luth–MO Synod	1	50	76	90	0.8	2.7
MENN–CG in Cr (Menn)	1	NR	96	124	1.1	3.7
Non-denom Chr Chs	1	30	32	38	0.3	1.1
PENT–Assemb of God	2	44	34	89	0.8	2.7
PENT–Ch of God Proph	1	NR	35	45	0.4	1.4
PRES–Presb Ch (USA)	1	31	28	36	0.3	1.1
PAYETTE	**40**	**2,027**	**2,612**	**9,472**	**41.9**	**100.0**
ANG/EPIS–Episcopal	1	13	23	23	0.1	0.2
Bahá'í	0	NR	3	3	0.0	0.0
BAPT–Amer Bapt USA	2	362	609	779	3.4	8.2
BAPT–Consrv Bapt	1	NR	NR	NR	-	-
BAPT–So Bapt Conv	2	58	48	61	0.3	0.6
BRETH–Ch of Brethren	1	34	58	74	0.3	0.8
Catholic	1	NR	NR	2,299	10.2	24.3
Ch Cr, Scientst	1	NR	NR	NR	-	-
Ch of Nazarene	3	235	250	317	1.4	3.3
CHR–Chr Chs & Chs Cr	1	NR	43	55	0.2	0.6
CHR–Chs of Christ	2	125	113	141	0.6	1.5
Jehovah's Witness	1	NR	NR	NR	-	-
LDS–Comm of Christ	1	NR	128	128	0.6	1.4
LDS–L-D Saints	7	NR	NR	3,531	15.6	37.3
LUTH–Luth–MO Synod	1	35	45	52	0.2	0.5
MENN–CG in Cr (Menn)	1	NR	83	106	0.5	1.1
METH–Free Methodist	1	127	64	127	0.6	1.3
METH–Un Methodist	2	137	209	250	1.1	2.6
Non-denom Chr Chs	2	90	95	112	0.5	1.2
PENT–Assemb of God	3	546	343	826	3.7	8.7
PENT–Int Foursq Gos	1	36	41	52	0.2	0.5
Sev Day Adv	3	218	380	437	1.9	4.6
Un C of Christ	2	11	77	99	0.4	1.0
POWER	**21**	**559**	**854**	**6,327**	**80.9**	**100.0**
ANG/EPIS–Episcopal	1	5	6	9	0.1	0.1
Bahá'í	0	NR	14	14	0.2	0.2
BAPT–So Bapt Conv	1	25	25	33	0.4	0.5
Catholic	2	NR	NR	2,072	26.5	32.7
CONG–Consrv Cong Chr	1	15	10	13	0.2	0.2
Jehovah's Witness	1	NR	NR	NR	-	-
LDS–L-D Saints	8	NR	NR	3,052	39.0	48.2
LUTH–E.L.C.A.	1	108	404	583	7.5	9.2
LUTH–Luth Cong Msn Chr	1	45	NR	NR	-	-
METH–Un Methodist	1	15	46	89	1.1	1.4
Non-denom Chr Chs	1	100	150	150	1.9	2.4
PENT–Assemb of God	3	246	199	312	4.0	4.9
SHOSHONE	**28**	**954**	**1,355**	**3,229**	**25.3**	**100.0**
ANG/EPIS–Episcopal	1	20	30	36	0.3	1.1
Bahá'í	0	NR	4	4	0.0	0.1
BAPT–Amer Bapt USA	1	45	58	69	0.5	2.1
BAPT–So Bapt Conv	3	181	177	209	1.6	6.5
Catholic	3	NR	NR	704	5.5	21.8
Ch of Nazarene	1	70	59	70	0.5	2.2
CHR–Chs of Christ	1	48	60	70	0.5	2.2
CONG–Consrv Cong Chr	1	70	94	111	0.9	3.4
Evan Free Ch	1	20	NR	20	0.2	0.6
Jehovah's Witness	3	NR	NR	NR	-	-
LDS–L-D Saints	2	NR	NR	683	5.4	21.2
LUTH–E.L.C.A.	1	87	129	169	1.3	5.2
LUTH–Luth Cong Msn Chr	1	62	393	464	3.6	14.4
LUTH–Luth–MO Synod	2	53	97	117	0.9	3.6
METH–Un Methodist	1	15	26	54	0.4	1.7
PENT–Assemb of God	2	99	51	134	1.0	4.1
PENT–Ch God (Cleve)	1	27	40	47	0.4	1.5
PENT–Pent Ch of God	1	70	NR	109	0.9	3.4
Sev Day Adv	1	56	97	112	0.9	3.5
Un C of Christ	1	31	40	47	0.4	1.5
TETON	**14**	**65**	**130**	**3,970**	**39.0**	**100.0**
ANG/EPIS–Episcopal	1	42	106	111	1.1	2.8
Bahá'í	0	NR	2	2	0.0	0.1
Calv Chpl	1	NR	NR	NR	-	-
Catholic	1	NR	NR	388	3.8	9.8
LDS–L-D Saints	10	NR	NR	3,440	33.8	86.6
PENT–Int Foursq Gos	1	23	22	29	0.3	0.7
TWIN FALLS	**128**	**6,412**	**10,166**	**38,659**	**50.1**	**100.0**
ANG/EPIS–Episcopal	2	126	341	450	0.6	1.2
Bahá'í	1	NR	64	64	0.1	0.2
BAPT–Amer Bapt USA	5	444	646	824	1.1	2.1
BAPT–Free Will Bapt	2	NR	84	107	0.1	0.3
BAPT–Reg Bapt Gen As	1	NR	NR	NR	-	-
BAPT–So Bapt Conv	5	239	260	332	0.4	0.9
BRETH–Ch of Brethren	1	35	40	51	0.1	0.1
Calv Chpl	2	NR	NR	NR	-	-
Catholic	2	NR	NR	5,826	7.5	15.1
Ch Cr, Scientst	1	NR	NR	NR	-	-
Ch of Nazarene	4	874	1,084	1,100	1.4	2.8
Chr & Miss Al	1	105	73	163	0.2	0.4
CHR–Chr Ch (Disc)	1	80	132	168	0.2	0.4
CHR–Chr Chs & Chs Cr	4	NR	535	683	0.9	1.8
CHR–Chs of Christ	3	146	145	143	0.2	0.4
Jehovah's Witness	2	NR	NR	NR	-	-
LDS–Comm of Christ	2	NR	256	256	0.3	0.7

NR–Not Reported   - Represents no adherents reported.   Percentages may not total 100 due to rounding.

Table 3: Religious Congregations by County and Group: 2010

Religious Group	Number of Congrega-tions	Number of Attendees	Number of Communicant, Confirmed, or Full Members	Adherents: Number of Adherents	Adherents: % of Total Pop.	Adherents: % of Total Adh.
LDS–L-D Saints	43	NR	NR	19,000	24.6	49.1
LUTH–E.L.C.A.	1	91	138	166	0.2	0.4
LUTH–Luth–MO Synod	5	534	1,312	1,666	2.2	4.3
MENN–CG in Cr (Menn)	2	NR	282	360	0.5	0.9
MENN–Mennonite USA	1	35	75	96	0.1	0.2
METH–Un Methodist	5	290	748	981	1.3	2.5
Muslim Est	1	30	NR	100	0.1	0.3
Non-denom Chr Chs	8	1,469	1,625	1,905	2.5	4.9
ORTHE–Ant Orth of NA	1	28	NR	51	0.1	0.1
PENT–Assemb of God	6	519	445	991	1.3	2.6
PENT–Ch of God Proph	1	NR	19	24	0.0	0.1
PENT–COGIC	1	100	140	179	0.2	0.5
PENT–Int Foursq Gos	1	62	33	42	0.1	0.1
PENT–Pent Ch of God	1	70	NR	109	0.1	0.3
PENT–Un Pent Ch Intl	2	NR	NR	NR	-	-
PRES–Presb Ch (USA)	3	147	321	410	0.5	1.1
REF–Ref Ch in Am	1	753	951	1,633	2.1	4.2
REF–Un Ref Chs N.A.	1	NR	NR	NR	-	-
Salvation Army	1	16	44	350	0.5	0.9
Sev Day Adv	3	199	346	398	0.5	1.0
Unit Univ	1	20	27	31	0.0	0.1
VALLEY	**21**	**850**	**1,089**	**2,840**	**28.8**	**100.0**
ANG/EPIS–Episcopal	1	20	70	70	0.7	2.5
Bahá'í	0	NR	10	10	0.1	0.4
BAPT–So Bapt Conv	2	63	44	52	0.5	1.8
Catholic	2	NR	NR	363	3.7	12.8
Ch of Nazarene	1	86	71	240	2.4	8.5
CHR–Chs of Christ	1	20	20	37	0.4	1.3
Jehovah's Witness	1	NR	NR	NR	-	-
LDS–L-D Saints	3	NR	NR	1,017	10.3	35.8
LUTH–Luth–MO Synod	2	70	131	138	1.4	4.9
Non-denom Chr Chs	4	443	430	553	5.6	19.5
PENT–Assemb of God	1	30	38	38	0.4	1.3
Sev Day Adv	2	56	97	112	1.1	3.9
Un C of Christ	1	62	178	210	2.1	7.4
WASHINGTON	**28**	**890**	**1,347**	**5,089**	**49.9**	**100.0**
ANG/EPIS–Episcopal	1	27	64	64	0.6	1.3
BAPT–Amer Bapt USA	3	126	224	275	2.7	5.4
BAPT–Consrv Bapt	1	NR	NR	NR	-	-
BAPT–So Bapt Conv	1	42	30	37	0.4	0.7
Catholic	2	NR	NR	1,701	16.7	33.4
Ch of Nazarene	1	113	137	137	1.3	2.7
CHR–Chr Chs & Chs Cr	1	NR	150	184	1.8	3.6
CHR–Chs of Christ	2	60	55	60	0.6	1.2
Ind Fund Churches	1	NR	NR	NR	-	-
Jehovah's Witness	1	NR	NR	NR	-	-
LDS–L-D Saints	4	NR	NR	1,731	17.0	34.0
LUTH–Luth–MO Synod	1	18	18	20	0.2	0.4
Non-denom Chr Chs	1	150	150	188	1.8	3.7
PENT–Assemb of God	2	80	26	107	1.0	2.1
PENT–Ch of God Proph	1	NR	27	33	0.3	0.6
PENT–Int Foursq Gos	1	94	166	204	2.0	4.0
PRES–Presb Ch (USA)	1	40	55	67	0.7	1.3
Sev Day Adv	3	140	245	281	2.8	5.5
ILLINOIS	**12,453**	**1,344,758**	**2,204,117**	**7,094,832**	**55.3**	**100.0**
ADAMS	**110**	**14,750**	**26,184**	**52,264**	**77.9**	**100.0**
ANG/EPIS–Anglican NA	1	NR	NR	NR	-	-
Bahá'í	0	NR	25	25	0.0	0.0
BAPT–Amer Bapt USA	2	395	542	659	1.0	1.3
BAPT–NBC USA	1	80	100	122	0.2	0.2
BAPT–Reg Bapt Gen As	3	NR	NR	NR	-	-
BAPT–So Bapt Conv	3	100	515	626	0.9	1.2
BUDD–Theravada	1	NR	NR	15	0.0	0.0
Catholic	8	NR	NR	15,163	22.6	29.0
Ch Cr, Scientst	1	NR	NR	NR	-	-
Ch of Nazarene	1	54	47	125	0.2	0.2
CHR–Chr Ch (Disc)	3	133	387	470	0.7	0.9
CHR–Chr Chs & Chs Cr	7	NR	4,915	5,975	8.9	11.4
CHR–Chs of Christ	2	101	99	128	0.2	0.2
CONG–Cong Chr, NA	1	NR	200	243	0.4	0.5
Evan Free Ch	2	145	NR	145	0.2	0.3
HINDU–Post Ren	1	NR	NR	25	0.0	0.0
Jehovah's Witness	1	NR	NR	NR	-	-
JUD–Reform	1	26	45	122	0.2	0.2
LDS–Comm of Christ	1	NR	119	119	0.2	0.2
LDS–L-D Saints	1	NR	NR	694	1.0	1.3
LUTH–E.L.C.A.	7	565	1,487	2,009	3.0	3.8
LUTH–Luth Cong Msn Chr	1	85	125	152	0.2	0.3
LUTH–Luth–MO Synod	5	836	1,996	2,767	4.1	5.3
MENN–Midw Bchy Am-Menn	1	171	86	171	0.3	0.3
METH–AME	2	0	300	365	0.5	0.7
METH–Un Methodist	16	1,011	2,418	2,831	4.2	5.4
Non-denom Chr Chs	16	8,515	9,339	10,737	16.0	20.5
ORTHE–Orth Ch in Amer	1	24	NR	50	0.1	0.1
PENT–Assemb of God	6	1,733	882	4,227	6.3	8.1
PENT–Un Pent Ch Intl	1	NR	NR	NR	-	-
PRES–Presb Ch (USA)	2	85	130	158	0.2	0.3
Salvation Army	1	83	161	1,385	2.1	2.7
Sev Day Adv	1	30	52	60	0.1	0.1
Un C of Christ	6	523	2,140	2,602	3.9	5.0
Unit Univ	1	55	74	94	0.1	0.2
Unity Ch	2	NR	NR	NR	-	-
ALEXANDER	**29**	**660**	**2,424**	**3,410**	**41.4**	**100.0**
ANG/EPIS–Episcopal	1	13	5	7	0.1	0.2
Bahá'í	0	NR	38	38	0.5	1.1
BAPT–Amer Bapt USA	1	160	240	293	3.6	8.6
BAPT–Free Will Bapt	1	NR	86	105	1.3	3.1
BAPT–NBC USA	1	25	55	67	0.8	2.0
BAPT–So Bapt Conv	8	243	1,422	1,736	21.1	50.9
Catholic	1	NR	NR	473	5.7	13.9
CHR–Chs of Christ	2	25	25	27	0.3	0.8
Jehovah's Witness	1	NR	NR	NR	-	-
LUTH–E.L.C.A.	1	24	40	50	0.6	1.5
METH–AME	1	0	150	183	2.2	5.4
METH–Un Methodist	2	71	89	98	1.2	2.9
Non-denom Chr Chs	1	35	50	50	0.6	1.5
PENT–Assemb of God	2	56	42	62	0.8	1.8
PENT–COGIC	1	0	150	183	2.2	5.4
PENT–Un Pent Ch Intl	3	NR	NR	NR	-	-
PRES–Presb Ch (USA)	1	0	18	22	0.3	0.6
Sev Day Adv	1	8	14	16	0.2	0.5
BOND	**44**	**2,090**	**5,093**	**8,971**	**50.5**	**100.0**
Bahá'í	0	NR	4	4	0.0	0.0
BAPT–Amer Bapt USA	1	68	228	270	1.5	3.0
BAPT–So Bapt Conv	10	431	1,445	1,714	9.6	19.1
BRETH–Ch of Brethren	1	17	14	17	0.1	0.2
Catholic	3	NR	NR	2,380	13.4	26.5
CHR–Chr Chs & Chs Cr	5	NR	1,576	1,870	10.5	20.8
CHR–Chs of Christ	1	60	55	70	0.4	0.8
Jehovah's Witness	1	NR	NR	NR	-	-
LUTH–Luth–MO Synod	1	95	239	330	1.9	3.7
METH–Free Methodist	2	795	464	795	4.5	8.9
METH–Un Methodist	6	253	567	789	4.4	8.8
Non-denom Chr Chs	2	140	215	215	1.2	2.4
PENT–Assemb of God	2	45	31	91	0.5	1.0
PENT–Pent Ch of God	1	70	NR	109	0.6	1.2
PENT–Un Pent Ch Intl	1	NR	NR	NR	-	-
PENT–United Holy Ch	1	NR	NR	NR	-	-
PRES–Cumber Presb	2	NR	40	62	0.3	0.7
PRES–Presb Ch (USA)	3	84	154	183	1.0	2.0
Un C of Christ	1	32	61	72	0.4	0.8
BOONE	**38**	**3,873**	**6,790**	**20,552**	**37.9**	**100.0**
ANG/EPIS–Episcopal	1	35	92	126	0.2	0.6
Ap Chr Ch-Amer	1	71	29	71	0.1	0.3
Bahá'í	0	NR	8	8	0.0	0.0
BAPT–Amer Bapt USA	1	140	206	264	0.5	1.3
BAPT–Converge/BGC	1	75	NR	90	0.2	0.4

NR–Not Reported   - Represents no adherents reported.   Percentages may not total 100 due to rounding.

Table 3: Religious Congregations by County and Group: 2010

Religious Group	Number of Congrega-tions	Number of Attendees	Number of Communicant, Confirmed, or Full Members	Adherents: Number of Adherents	Adherents: % of Total Pop.	Adherents: % of Total Adh.
BAPT–So Bapt Conv	2	32	29	37	0.1	0.2
Catholic	1	NR	NR	10,420	19.2	50.7
CHR–Chs of Christ	1	45	43	58	0.1	0.3
CONG–Cong Chr, NA	1	NR	50	64	0.1	0.3
Evan Cov Ch	1	130	108	169	0.3	0.8
Jehovah's Witness	1	NR	NR	NR	-	-
LDS–L-D Saints	1	NR	NR	246	0.5	1.2
LUTH–E.L.C.A.	4	655	1,430	2,005	3.7	9.8
LUTH–Luth–MO Synod	1	952	1,805	2,584	4.8	12.6
LUTH–Wisc Ev Luth Syn	1	27	31	37	0.1	0.2
METH–Un Methodist	5	556	1,347	2,140	4.0	10.4
Non-denom Chr Chs	4	400	480	525	1.0	2.6
PENT–Assemb of God	2	291	86	291	0.5	1.4
PENT–Open Bible Std	1	50	NR	50	0.1	0.2
PENT–Un Pent Ch Intl	2	NR	NR	NR	-	-
PRES–Presb Ch (USA)	2	237	431	551	1.0	2.7
Salvation Army	1	12	15	58	0.1	0.3
Sev Day Adv	1	42	73	84	0.2	0.4
Un C of Christ	2	123	527	674	1.2	3.3
BROWN	**11**	**267**	**1,194**	**3,020**	**43.5**	**100.0**
Bahá'í	0	NR	4	4	0.1	0.1
BAPT–Amer Bapt USA	1	65	244	278	4.0	9.2
Catholic	1	NR	NR	1,676	24.2	55.5
Ch of Nazarene	1	29	61	70	1.0	2.3
CHR–Chr Ch (Disc)	2	45	216	246	3.5	8.1
CHR–Chr Chs & Chs Cr	3	NR	335	381	5.5	12.6
LUTH–Luth–MO Synod	1	27	57	81	1.2	2.7
METH–Un Methodist	1	61	226	226	3.3	7.5
PRES–Presb Ch (USA)	1	40	51	58	0.8	1.9
BUREAU	**74**	**4,539**	**7,576**	**15,118**	**43.2**	**100.0**
ANG/EPIS–Anglican NA	1	NR	NR	NR	-	-
Bahá'í	0	NR	3	3	0.0	0.0
BAPT–Amer Bapt USA	3	187	206	250	0.7	1.7
BAPT–So Bapt Conv	1	65	204	248	0.7	1.6
Catholic	14	NR	NR	4,564	13.0	30.2
CGOD–Ches God-Gen Con	1	221	333	404	1.2	2.7
Ch of Nazarene	1	244	229	336	1.0	2.2
Chr & Miss Al	1	50	66	72	0.2	0.5
CHR–Chr Ch (Disc)	3	180	460	559	1.6	3.7
CHR–Chs of Christ	1	8	8	8	0.0	0.1
CONG–Consrv Cong Chr	1	40	50	61	0.2	0.4
Evan Assoc RCC	1	NR	NR	NR	-	-
Evan Cov Ch	1	220	275	286	0.8	1.9
Evan Free Ch	1	0	NR	0	0.0	0.0
LDS–L-D Saints	1	NR	NR	85	0.2	0.6
LUTH–E.L.C.A.	4	344	1,196	1,728	4.9	11.4
LUTH–Luth Cong Msn Chr	2	173	740	899	2.6	5.9
LUTH–Luth–MO Synod	1	40	64	68	0.2	0.4
MENN–Mennonite USA	2	115	87	106	0.3	0.7
MENN–Tamp Amish-Menn	1	378	223	378	1.1	2.5
METH–Un Methodist	13	729	2,003	2,528	7.2	16.7
METH–Wesleyan	1	55	27	72	0.2	0.5
Missionary Ch	1	69	55	69	0.2	0.5
Non-denom Chr Chs	5	525	447	680	1.9	4.5
ORTHE–Ant Orth of NA	1	40	NR	70	0.2	0.5
PENT–Assemb of God	3	489	91	555	1.6	3.7
PENT–Pent Ch of God	1	70	NR	109	0.3	0.7
PRES–Presb Ch (USA)	1	38	78	95	0.3	0.6
Sev Day Adv	1	23	40	46	0.1	0.3
Un C of Christ	6	236	691	839	2.4	5.5
CALHOUN	**16**	**338**	**837**	**3,931**	**77.2**	**100.0**
BAPT–So Bapt Conv	2	53	199	237	4.7	6.0
Catholic	2	NR	NR	2,898	56.9	73.7
CHR–Chs of Christ	4	171	143	192	3.8	4.9
LUTH–E.L.C.A.	1	12	48	54	1.1	1.4
LUTH–Luth–MO Synod	3	41	338	419	8.2	10.7
METH–Un Methodist	2	11	21	26	0.5	0.7
PRES–Presb Ch (USA)	2	50	88	105	2.1	2.7
CARROLL	**46**	**2,319**	**5,446**	**8,421**	**54.7**	**100.0**
ANG/EPIS–Episcopal	1	8	9	9	0.1	0.1
Bahá'í	0	NR	2	2	0.0	0.0
BAPT–Amer Bapt USA	2	77	246	290	1.9	3.4
BAPT–So Bapt Conv	1	30	40	47	0.3	0.6
BRETH–Brethren (Ash)	2	NR	160	189	1.2	2.2
BRETH–Ch of Brethren	3	260	483	570	3.7	6.8
Catholic	3	NR	NR	1,508	9.8	17.9
CGOD–Ches God-Gen Con	3	204	329	388	2.5	4.6
CONG–Cong Chr, NA	1	NR	35	41	0.3	0.5
Evan Free Ch	1	80	NR	80	0.5	1.0
Jehovah's Witness	1	NR	NR	NR	-	-
LDS–L-D Saints	1	NR	NR	45	0.3	0.5
LUTH–E.L.C.A.	4	226	818	1,007	6.5	12.0
LUTH–Wisc Ev Luth Syn	2	100	230	283	1.8	3.4
MENN–Mennonite USA	1	40	26	31	0.2	0.4
METH–Un Methodist	10	617	2,017	2,694	17.5	32.0
Non-denom Chr Chs	4	465	575	669	4.3	7.9
PENT–Assemb of God	1	45	30	45	0.3	0.5
PRES–Presb Ch (USA)	2	87	179	211	1.4	2.5
REF–Ref Ch in Am	1	21	33	37	0.2	0.4
Sev Day Adv	1	16	29	33	0.2	0.4
Un C of Christ	1	43	205	242	1.6	2.9
CASS	**40**	**1,572**	**4,863**	**8,767**	**64.3**	**100.0**
Bahá'í	0	NR	1	1	0.0	0.0
BAPT–Amer Bapt USA	1	55	254	313	2.3	3.6
BAPT–So Bapt Conv	3	137	555	684	5.0	7.8
Catholic	4	NR	NR	2,613	19.2	29.8
Ch of Nazarene	3	227	276	349	2.6	4.0
CHR–Chr Ch (Disc)	2	43	122	150	1.1	1.7
CHR–Chr Chs & Chs Cr	3	NR	400	493	3.6	5.6
CONG–Cong Chr, NA	1	NR	35	43	0.3	0.5
Jehovah's Witness	1	NR	NR	NR	-	-
LDS–Comm of Christ	1	NR	82	82	0.6	0.9
LUTH–E.L.C.A.	4	218	756	1,031	7.6	11.8
LUTH–Luth–MO Synod	4	270	985	1,281	9.4	14.6
METH–Un Methodist	6	358	978	1,143	8.4	13.0
Non-denom Chr Chs	2	145	200	206	1.5	2.3
PENT–Assemb of God	2	87	58	119	0.9	1.4
PRES–Cumber Presb	1	NR	34	103	0.8	1.2
PRES–Presb Ch (USA)	2	32	127	156	1.1	1.8
CHAMPAIGN	**211**	**23,250**	**35,985**	**68,972**	**34.3**	**100.0**
ANG/EPIS–Episcopal	3	399	672	910	0.5	1.3
Ap Chr Ch-Amer	1	150	60	150	0.1	0.2
Bahá'í	2	NR	137	137	0.1	0.2
BAPT–Amer Bapt USA	5	813	958	1,129	0.6	1.6
BAPT–Consrv Bapt	1	NR	NR	NR	-	-
BAPT–Converge/BGC	1	75	NR	90	0.0	0.1
BAPT–NBC USA	2	525	850	1,002	0.5	1.5
BAPT–Reg Bapt Gen As	1	NR	NR	NR	-	-
BAPT–So Bapt Conv	11	419	989	1,166	0.6	1.7
BRETH–Ch of Brethren	1	11	57	67	0.0	0.1
BUDD–Mahayana	2	NR	NR	132	0.1	0.2
Catholic	17	NR	NR	15,215	7.6	22.1
CGOD–Ch God (Ander)	1	16	NR	16	0.0	0.0
Ch Cr, Scientst	2	NR	NR	NR	-	-
Ch of Nazarene	6	414	442	613	0.3	0.9
CHR–Chr Ch (Disc)	3	133	425	501	0.2	0.7
CHR–Chr Chs & Chs Cr	10	NR	3,448	4,065	2.0	5.9
CHR–Chs of Christ	3	356	320	448	0.2	0.6
CHR–Int Chs of Christ	1	NR	184	217	0.1	0.3
Christian Brethren	1	NR	NR	NR	-	-
Evan Cov Ch	1	41	0	53	0.0	0.1
Evan Free Ch	2	280	NR	280	0.1	0.4
FRND–Fr Gen Cf	1	NR	113	133	0.1	0.2
HINDU–Post Ren	2	NR	NR	79	0.0	0.1
Jehovah's Witness	2	NR	NR	NR	-	-
JUD–Reform	1	158	278	751	0.4	1.1
LDS–L-D Saints	5	NR	NR	1,682	0.8	2.4
LUTH–Assoc Free Luth	2	NR	NR	NR	-	-
LUTH–E.L.C.A.	5	837	2,189	2,708	1.3	3.9

NR–Not Reported - Represents no adherents reported. Percentages may not total 100 due to rounding.

Table 3: Religious Congregations by County and Group: 2010

Religious Group	Number of Congregations	Number of Attendees	Number of Communicant, Confirmed, or Full Members	Adherents: Number of Adherents	Adherents: % of Total Pop.	Adherents: % of Total Adh.
LUTH–Luth-MO Synod	8	1,416	2,559	3,156	1.6	4.6
LUTH–Nor Amer Luth C	5	NR	NR	NR	-	-
LUTH–Wisc Ev Luth Syn	1	45	69	89	0.0	0.1
MENN–Fel Evg Ch	1	108	102	120	0.1	0.2
MENN–Mennonite USA	2	276	434	512	0.3	0.7
METH–AME	1	135	256	302	0.2	0.4
METH–C.M.E.	1	0	100	118	0.1	0.2
METH–Free Methodist	2	167	129	170	0.1	0.2
METH–Un Methodist	27	3,310	6,104	8,305	4.1	12.0
METH–Wesleyan	1	69	20	90	0.0	0.1
Muslim Est	1	908	NR	3,298	1.6	4.8
Non-denom Chr Chs	27	5,176	6,719	7,377	3.7	10.7
ORTHE–Ant Orth of NA	1	70	NR	120	0.1	0.2
ORTHE–Greek Orthodox	1	125	NR	475	0.2	0.7
PENT–Assemb of God	4	2,012	1,200	4,439	2.2	6.4
PENT–Ch God (Cleve)	1	100	353	416	0.2	0.6
PENT–COGIC	3	25	25	29	0.0	0.0
PENT–Int Foursq Gos	3	189	182	215	0.1	0.3
PENT–Pent Ch of God	1	70	NR	109	0.1	0.2
PENT–Un Pent Ch Intl	4	NR	NR	NR	-	-
PENT–Vineyard	1	2,700	3,500	4,126	2.1	6.0
PRES–Korean Pres Amer	1	NR	NR	NR	-	-
PRES–Presb Ch (USA)	8	1,133	2,044	2,410	1.2	3.5
PRES–Presb Ch Amer	1	0	0	0	0.0	0.0
REF–Christian Ref	1	70	83	98	0.0	0.1
Salvation Army	1	49	62	316	0.2	0.5
Sev Day Adv	3	110	191	220	0.1	0.3
Tao	1	NR	NR	NR	-	-
Un C of Christ	2	183	472	556	0.3	0.8
Unit Univ	1	177	259	359	0.2	0.5
Unity Ch	1	NR	NR	NR	-	-
Zoroastrian	0	NR	NR	3	0.0	0.0
CHRISTIAN	**74**	**3,295**	**9,056**	**16,418**	**47.2**	**100.0**
Bahá'í	0	NR	4	4	0.0	0.0
BAPT–Amer Bapt USA	4	191	681	820	2.4	5.0
BAPT–Reg Bapt Gen As	2	NR	NR	NR	-	-
BAPT–So Bapt Conv	6	236	604	727	2.1	4.4
Catholic	7	NR	NR	5,473	15.7	33.3
CGOD–Ches God-Gen Con	1	90	136	164	0.5	1.0
Ch of Nazarene	2	351	474	474	1.4	2.9
CHR–Chr Ch (Disc)	2	108	321	386	1.1	2.4
CHR–Chr Chs & Chs Cr	7	NR	1,750	2,107	6.1	12.8
CHR–Chs of Christ	1	40	35	45	0.1	0.3
Evan Free Ch	1	150	NR	150	0.4	0.9
Grace Gosp Fel	1	NR	NR	NR	-	-
Jehovah's Witness	1	NR	NR	NR	-	-
LDS–Comm of Christ	2	NR	164	164	0.5	1.0
LUTH–Ch Luth Conf	1	NR	NR	NR	-	-
LUTH–Luth-MO Synod	3	245	966	1,345	3.9	8.2
METH–AME	1	0	150	181	0.5	1.1
METH–Free Methodist	1	36	27	36	0.1	0.2
METH–Un Methodist	13	831	2,286	2,634	7.6	16.0
Non-denom Chr Chs	7	474	586	630	1.8	3.8
PENT–Assemb of God	1	111	85	131	0.4	0.8
PENT–Ch God (Cleve)	2	100	162	195	0.6	1.2
PENT–Un Pent Ch Intl	2	NR	NR	NR	-	-
PRES–Presb Ch (USA)	5	240	482	580	1.7	3.5
Un C of Christ	1	92	143	172	0.5	1.0
CLARK	**50**	**3,069**	**7,561**	**10,354**	**63.4**	**100.0**
BAPT–So Bapt Conv	9	825	2,816	3,398	20.8	32.8
Catholic	2	NR	NR	777	4.8	7.5
CGOD–Ches God-Gen Con	3	213	393	474	2.9	4.6
Ch of Nazarene	3	249	428	863	5.3	8.3
CHR–Chr Ch (Disc)	1	88	298	360	2.2	3.5
CHR–Chr Chs & Chs Cr	4	NR	847	1,022	6.3	9.9
CHR–Chs of Christ	3	145	147	189	1.2	1.8
Ind Fund Churches	1	NR	NR	NR	-	-
Jehovah's Witness	1	NR	NR	NR	-	-
LDS–Comm of Christ	1	NR	82	82	0.5	0.8
LUTH–Luth-MO Synod	1	50	85	102	0.6	1.0
METH–Un Methodist	11	805	1,561	1,927	11.8	18.6

Religious Group	Number of Congregations	Number of Attendees	Number of Communicant, Confirmed, or Full Members	Adherents: Number of Adherents	Adherents: % of Total Pop.	Adherents: % of Total Adh.
METH–Wesleyan	1	36	37	47	0.3	0.5
Non-denom Chr Chs	4	530	696	771	4.7	7.4
PENT–Assemb of God	1	80	23	140	0.9	1.4
PENT–Un Pent Ch Intl	1	NR	NR	NR	-	-
PRES–Cumber Presb	2	NR	81	121	0.7	1.2
Un C of Christ	1	48	67	81	0.5	0.8
CLAY	**53**	**3,365**	**6,437**	**10,985**	**79.5**	**100.0**
Bahá'í	0	NR	2	2	0.0	0.0
BAPT–Amer Bapt USA	1	75	269	327	2.4	3.0
BAPT–So Bapt Conv	10	414	1,277	1,552	11.2	14.1
Catholic	2	NR	NR	2,270	16.4	20.7
CGOD–Ch God (Ander)	1	60	NR	60	0.4	0.5
Ch of Nazarene	1	177	198	243	1.8	2.2
CHR–Chr Chs & Chs Cr	13	NR	1,631	1,983	14.4	18.1
CHR–Chs of Christ	2	65	65	85	0.6	0.8
Jehovah's Witness	1	NR	NR	NR	-	-
LDS–Comm of Christ	2	NR	164	164	1.2	1.5
LUTH–Luth-MO Synod	2	208	496	593	4.3	5.4
MENN–Amish Undif	0	NR	26	76	0.6	0.7
METH–Evan Meth Ch	1	NR	NR	NR	-	-
METH–Un Methodist	7	480	897	1,057	7.7	9.6
Non-denom Chr Chs	3	1,760	1,220	2,200	15.9	20.0
PENT–Assemb of God	1	70	0	140	1.0	1.3
PENT–Ch God (Cleve)	1	36	59	72	0.5	0.7
PENT–Ch of God Proph	1	NR	81	98	0.7	0.9
PENT–Un Pent Ch Intl	2	NR	NR	NR	-	-
PRES–Presb Ch (USA)	1	0	13	16	0.1	0.1
Un C of Christ	1	20	39	47	0.3	0.4
CLINTON	**50**	**1,884**	**4,856**	**26,446**	**70.0**	**100.0**
Bahá'í	0	NR	7	7	0.0	0.0
BAPT–N Am Bapt Conf	1	NR	161	194	0.5	0.7
BAPT–So Bapt Conv	6	389	1,180	1,425	3.8	5.4
Catholic	14	NR	NR	20,300	53.8	76.8
Ch of Nazarene	1	69	84	113	0.3	0.4
CHR–Chr Chs & Chs Cr	2	NR	187	226	0.6	0.9
Jehovah's Witness	1	NR	NR	NR	-	-
LUTH–Luth-MO Synod	4	408	1,134	1,447	3.8	5.5
METH–Un Methodist	9	548	1,042	1,436	3.8	5.4
Non-denom Chr Chs	2	120	120	150	0.4	0.6
PENT–Assemb of God	2	26	14	36	0.1	0.1
PENT–Ch God (Cleve)	1	12	34	41	0.1	0.2
PENT–Un Pent Ch Intl	1	NR	NR	NR	-	-
Salvation Army	1	51	123	141	0.4	0.5
Un C of Christ	5	261	770	930	2.5	3.5
COLES	**80**	**6,247**	**14,674**	**22,690**	**42.1**	**100.0**
ANG/EPIS–Episcopal	1	28	31	31	0.1	0.1
Bahá'í	0	NR	5	5	0.0	0.0
BAPT–Amer Bapt USA	3	457	1,389	1,622	3.0	7.1
BAPT–Natl Mis Bapt Conv	1	0	150	175	0.3	0.8
BAPT–Reg Bapt Gen As	1	NR	NR	NR	-	-
BAPT–So Bapt Conv	6	451	1,552	1,813	3.4	8.0
Catholic	2	NR	NR	3,868	7.2	17.0
CGOD–Ch God (Ander)	2	155	NR	155	0.3	0.7
CGOD–Ches God-Gen Con	3	238	464	542	1.0	2.4
Ch Cr, Scientst	1	NR	NR	NR	-	-
Ch of Nazarene	2	158	256	288	0.5	1.3
Chr & Miss Al	1	78	48	94	0.2	0.4
CHR–Chr Ch (Disc)	2	94	399	466	0.9	2.1
CHR–Chr Chs & Chs Cr	6	NR	2,538	2,965	5.5	13.1
CHR–Chs of Christ	3	134	157	194	0.4	0.9
Ind Fund Churches	1	NR	NR	NR	-	-
Jehovah's Witness	2	NR	NR	NR	-	-
LDS–L-D Saints	1	NR	NR	472	0.9	2.1
LUTH–Luth-MO Synod	3	516	1,704	2,319	4.3	10.2
MENN–Amish Undif	2	NR	100	217	0.4	1.0
METH–AME Zion	1	0	100	117	0.2	0.5
METH–Free Methodist	1	26	36	36	0.1	0.2
METH–Un Methodist	8	744	1,846	2,155	4.0	9.5
Non-denom Chr Chs	15	2,485	3,050	3,751	7.0	16.5
PENT–Assemb of God	2	300	132	380	0.7	1.7

NR–Not Reported - Represents no adherents reported. Percentages may not total 100 due to rounding.

Table 3: Religious Congregations by County and Group: 2010

Religious Group	Number of Congrega-tions	Number of Attendees	Number of Communicant, Confirmed, or Full Members	Adherents		
				Number of Adherents	% of Total Pop.	% of Total Adh.
PENT–Un Pent Ch Intl	2	NR	NR	NR	-	-
PRES–Cumber Presb	1	NR	107	150	0.3	0.7
PRES–Presb Ch (USA)	4	308	497	581	1.1	2.6
Salvation Army	1	38	54	228	0.4	1.0
Sev Day Adv	1	27	47	54	0.1	0.2
Unit Univ	1	10	12	12	0.0	0.1
COOK	**3,354**	**472,950**	**657,957**	**3,097,119**	**59.6**	**100.0**
ANG/EPIS–Anglican NA	8	NR	NR	NR	-	-
ANG/EPIS–Episcopal	60	6,470	15,308	18,854	0.4	0.6
Ap Chr Ch-Amer	1	145	90	145	0.0	0.0
Bahá'í	17	NR	2,781	2,781	0.1	0.1
BAPT–Alliance Bapt	2	NR	NR	NR	-	-
BAPT–Amer Bapt USA	53	8,770	15,923	19,460	0.4	0.6
BAPT–Consrv Bapt	12	NR	NR	NR	-	-
BAPT–Converge/BGC	53	6,000	NR	7,200	0.1	0.2
BAPT–Free Will Bapt	1	NR	86	105	0.0	0.0
BAPT–Fund Bapt Flwsp	1	NR	NR	NR	-	-
BAPT–N Am Bapt Conf	6	NR	637	778	0.0	0.0
BAPT–Natl Mis Bapt Conv	34	2,840	10,112	12,358	0.2	0.4
BAPT–NBC Amer	19	4,030	6,290	7,687	0.1	0.2
BAPT–NBC USA	99	24,496	56,349	68,865	1.3	2.2
BAPT–NT Ind Bapt	2	NR	NR	NR	-	-
BAPT–Prog NBC	41	5,103	12,391	15,143	0.3	0.5
BAPT–Ref Bapt Ch	2	NR	NR	NR	-	-
BAPT–Reg Bapt Gen As	5	NR	NR	NR	-	-
BAPT–So Bapt Conv	181	22,663	40,838	49,909	1.0	1.6
BRETH–Breth in Chr	1	NR	NR	NR	-	-
BRETH–Ch of Brethren	3	47	141	172	0.0	0.0
BUDD–Mahayana	34	NR	NR	17,013	0.3	0.5
BUDD–Theravada	13	NR	NR	5,640	0.1	0.2
BUDD–Vajrayana	11	NR	NR	1,048	0.0	0.0
Calv Chpl	3	NR	NR	NR	-	-
Catholic	371	NR	NR	1,947,223	37.5	62.9
CGOD–Ch God (Ander)	19	2,877	NR	2,877	0.1	0.1
Ch Cr, Scientst	19	NR	NR	NR	-	-
Ch God (7th Day)	4	NR	NR	NR	-	-
Ch of Chr (Hol)	6	NR	NR	NR	-	-
Ch of Nazarene	33	2,762	3,927	5,023	0.1	0.2
Chr & Miss Al	28	1,804	1,436	2,445	0.0	0.1
CHR–Chr Ch (Disc)	15	740	2,324	2,840	0.1	0.1
CHR–Chr Chs & Chs Cr	16	NR	2,632	3,217	0.1	0.1
CHR–Chs of Christ	47	4,649	5,257	6,825	0.1	0.2
CHR–Int Chs of Christ	1	NR	1,062	1,298	0.0	0.0
Christian Brethren	4	NR	NR	NR	-	-
CONG–Cong Chr, NA	6	NR	717	876	0.0	0.0
CONG–Consrv Cong Chr	1	43	97	119	0.0	0.0
Evan Cong Ch	1	NR	0	0	0.0	0.0
Evan Cov Ch	46	6,459	8,931	8,398	0.2	0.3
Evan Free Ch	32	6,198	NR	6,198	0.1	0.2
FRND–Evan Fr Ch Intl	1	55	17	21	0.0	0.0
FRND–Fr Gen Cf	3	NR	210	257	0.0	0.0
FRND–Fr Gen Cf & Un Mtg	1	NR	132	161	0.0	0.0
FRND–Fr Un Mtg	1	NR	28	34	0.0	0.0
FRND–Unaffl Mtgs	2	NR	NR	NR	-	-
Grace Gosp Fel	2	NR	NR	NR	-	-
HINDU–I/A Temples	8	NR	NR	5,234	0.1	0.2
HINDU–Post Ren	17	NR	NR	522	0.0	0.0
HINDU–Renaiss	5	NR	NR	661	0.0	0.0
HINDU–Trad Temples	1	NR	NR	1,900	0.0	0.1
Ind Fund Churches	18	NR	NR	NR	-	-
Int Cou Comm Ch	12	NR	NR	NR	-	-
Jehovah's Witness	60	NR	NR	NR	-	-
JUD–Conserv	14	4,243	4,762	12,857	0.2	0.4
JUD–Orth	57	11,700	4,300	16,250	0.3	0.5
JUD–Reconst	2	676	863	2,330	0.0	0.1
JUD–Reform	19	5,402	9,528	25,726	0.5	0.8
LDS–Comm of Christ	2	NR	242	242	0.0	0.0
LDS–L-D Saints	25	NR	NR	16,508	0.3	0.5
LUTH–E.L.C.A.	145	15,085	39,348	49,925	1.0	1.6
LUTH–Luth–MO Synod	120	15,486	35,960	45,979	0.9	1.5
LUTH–Nor Amer Luth C	1	NR	NR	NR	-	-
LUTH–Wisc Ev Luth Syn	8	664	1,272	1,568	0.0	0.1
MENN–Fel Evg Ch	1	82	59	72	0.0	0.0

Religious Group	Number of Congrega-tions	Number of Attendees	Number of Communicant, Confirmed, or Full Members	Adherents		
				Number of Adherents	% of Total Pop.	% of Total Adh.
MENN–Mennonite USA	17	2,772	2,663	3,255	0.1	0.1
METH–AME	46	3,206	9,221	11,269	0.2	0.4
METH–AME Zion	11	900	2,420	2,958	0.1	0.1
METH–C.M.E.	21	1,889	8,064	9,855	0.2	0.3
METH–Free Methodist	3	682	368	682	0.0	0.0
METH–Un Methodist	121	12,906	26,170	33,584	0.6	1.1
METH–Wesleyan	4	255	232	331	0.0	0.0
Metro Comm Ch	2	118	135	165	0.0	0.0
Missionary Ch	8	454	231	454	0.0	0.0
MJEW–Union Mes Cong	1	NR	NR	NR	-	-
Muslim Est	62	55,313	NR	201,152	3.9	6.5
Nat Spirit Asso	5	NR	NR	NR	-	-
New Apost Ch	8	NR	NR	NR	-	-
Non-denom Chr Chs	486	140,094	187,048	209,195	4.0	6.8
OCATH–Pol Natl Cath	5	NR	NR	NR	-	-
ORTHE–Alban Orth Dio	1	150	NR	350	0.0	0.0
ORTHE–Ant Orth of NA	3	970	NR	4,170	0.1	0.1
ORTHE–Bulgar Orth USA	1	250	NR	425	0.0	0.0
ORTHE–Carp Rus Orth	2	145	NR	450	0.0	0.0
ORTHE–Georgian Orth	1	75	NR	150	0.0	0.0
ORTHE–Greek Orthodox	18	6,965	NR	30,870	0.6	1.0
ORTHE–Macedonian Orth	1	80	NR	200	0.0	0.0
ORTHE–Orth Ch in Amer	11	1,139	NR	3,186	0.1	0.1
ORTHE–Romania Orth Ar	2	230	NR	740	0.0	0.0
ORTHE–Rus Orth Abroad	1	200	NR	500	0.0	0.0
ORTHE–Serb Orth USA	6	1,876	NR	5,533	0.1	0.2
ORTHE–Ukrainian Orth	3	385	NR	1,740	0.0	0.1
ORTHO–Armen Ap Cilic	1	150	NR	1,500	0.0	0.0
ORTHO–Armen Ap Etchm	3	175	NR	850	0.0	0.0
ORTHO–Coptic Orth Ch	1	400	NR	600	0.0	0.0
ORTHO–Eritrean Orth	2	410	NR	610	0.0	0.0
ORTHO–Ethiopian Orth	1	NR	NR	NR	-	-
ORTHO–Malan Dioc Am	4	240	NR	720	0.0	0.0
ORTHO–Malan Syr Orth	3	275	NR	522	0.0	0.0
ORTHO–Syrian Orth Ch	1	75	NR	160	0.0	0.0
PENT–Apos Faith Msn	1	NR	35	43	0.0	0.0
PENT–Assemb of God	64	22,759	20,510	32,646	0.6	1.1
PENT–Ch God (Cleve)	41	3,132	4,704	5,749	0.1	0.2
PENT–Ch Lord Jesus Apos	3	NR	NR	NR	-	-
PENT–Ch of God Proph	4	NR	145	177	0.0	0.0
PENT–COGIC	94	7,046	16,987	20,760	0.4	0.7
PENT–Elim	1	NR	NR	NR	-	-
PENT–Fire Bapt Hol Ch	3	NR	NR	NR	-	-
PENT–Full Gosp Bapt	24	NR	NR	NR	-	-
PENT–Int Foursq Gos	3	753	1,319	1,612	0.0	0.1
PENT–Intl Pent Holiness	1	13	19	23	0.0	0.0
PENT–Open Bible Std	2	131	NR	131	0.0	0.0
PENT–Pent Ch of God	1	70	NR	109	0.0	0.0
PENT–Un Pent Asbl God	4	NR	NR	NR	-	-
PENT–Un Pent Ch Intl	16	NR	NR	NR	-	-
PENT–United Holy Ch	2	NR	NR	NR	-	-
PENT–Vineyard	8	1,402	1,667	2,037	0.0	0.1
PRES–Cum Pres Am	1	NR	NR	NR	-	-
PRES–Cumber Presb	2	NR	53	60	0.0	0.0
PRES–Kor Pres Abroad	5	NR	NR	NR	-	-
PRES–Korean Amer Pres	3	NR	NR	NR	-	-
PRES–Korean Pres Amer	6	NR	NR	NR	-	-
PRES–Orth Pres Ch	5	334	310	405	0.0	0.0
PRES–Presb Ch (USA)	91	9,771	24,987	30,537	0.6	1.0
PRES–Presb Ch Amer	16	1,594	1,587	2,188	0.0	0.1
REF–Christian Ref	27	5,256	7,347	8,979	0.2	0.3
REF–Comm Ref Evan	1	NR	NR	NR	-	-
REF–Hung Ref Add'l	1	NR	NR	NR	-	-
REF–Prot Ref Chs	2	234	155	262	0.0	0.0
REF–Ref Ch in Am	14	2,848	4,762	5,555	0.1	0.2
REF–Un Ref Chs N.A.	3	NR	NR	NR	-	-
Salvation Army	15	1,732	2,017	3,574	0.1	0.1
Sev Day Adv	64	9,357	16,274	18,714	0.4	0.6
Sikh	3	NR	NR	NR	-	-
Swedenborgian	2	NR	NR	NR	-	-
Un C of Christ	101	13,248	32,620	39,866	0.8	1.3
Unit Univ	10	1,002	1,857	2,688	0.1	0.1
Unity Ch	7	NR	NR	NR	-	-
Zoroastrian	1	NR	NR	84	0.0	0.0

NR–Not Reported   - Represents no adherents reported.   Percentages may not total 100 due to rounding.

Table 3: Religious Congregations by County and Group: 2010

Religious Group	Number of Congrega-tions	Number of Attendees	Number of Communicant, Confirmed, or Full Members	Adherents		
				Number of Adherents	% of Total Pop.	% of Total Adh.
CRAWFORD	**58**	**2,476**	**5,520**	**7,502**	**37.9**	**100.0**
ANG/EPIS–Episcopal	1	13	14	19	0.1	0.3
Bahá'í	0	NR	3	3	0.0	0.0
BAPT–Amer Bapt USA	1	28	54	64	0.3	0.9
BAPT–So Bapt Conv	9	738	1,698	2,006	10.1	26.7
Catholic	2	NR	NR	538	2.7	7.2
CGOD–Ches God-Gen Con	1	9	19	22	0.1	0.3
CHR–Chr Ch (Disc)	1	40	132	156	0.8	2.1
CHR–Chr Chs & Chs Cr	8	NR	1,205	1,424	7.2	19.0
CHR–Chs of Christ	2	95	80	105	0.5	1.4
Ind Fund Churches	1	NR	NR	NR	-	-
Jehovah's Witness	1	NR	NR	NR	-	-
LDS–L-D Saints	1	NR	NR	126	0.6	1.7
LUTH–Luth-MO Synod	1	40	60	90	0.5	1.2
MENN–Amish Undif	2	NR	94	248	1.3	3.3
METH–Free Methodist	3	126	103	126	0.6	1.7
METH–Un Methodist	12	625	1,129	1,409	7.1	18.8
METH–Wesleyan	2	118	56	153	0.8	2.0
Non-denom Chr Chs	5	390	535	545	2.8	7.3
PENT–Assemb of God	1	112	51	112	0.6	1.5
PENT–Ch God (Cleve)	1	35	47	56	0.3	0.7
PRES–Cumber Presb	1	NR	20	40	0.2	0.5
PRES–Presb Ch (USA)	1	77	177	209	1.1	2.8
Un C of Christ	1	30	43	51	0.3	0.7
CUMBERLAND	**31**	**1,058**	**2,035**	**3,005**	**27.2**	**100.0**
BAPT–So Bapt Conv	7	429	710	867	7.8	28.9
Catholic	2	NR	NR	483	4.4	16.1
CGOD–Ches God-Gen Con	3	57	85	104	0.9	3.5
CHR–Chr Chs & Chs Cr	2	NR	475	580	5.2	19.3
CHR–Chs of Christ	2	75	70	91	0.8	3.0
METH–Free Methodist	2	121	88	124	1.1	4.1
METH–Un Methodist	7	279	477	598	5.4	19.9
METH–Wesleyan	1	15	15	20	0.2	0.7
Non-denom Chr Chs	1	32	35	40	0.4	1.3
PENT–Un Pent Ch Intl	2	NR	NR	NR	-	-
PRES–Presb Ch (USA)	2	50	80	98	0.9	3.3
DEKALB	**106**	**10,255**	**17,216**	**48,858**	**46.5**	**100.0**
ANG/EPIS–Episcopal	2	125	218	257	0.2	0.5
Bahá'í	0	NR	39	39	0.0	0.1
BAPT–Amer Bapt USA	3	477	945	1,145	1.1	2.3
BAPT–Consrv Bapt	2	NR	NR	NR	-	-
BAPT–Natl Mis Bapt Conv	1	0	150	182	0.2	0.4
BAPT–So Bapt Conv	3	180	578	700	0.7	1.4
Catholic	6	NR	NR	19,447	18.5	39.8
Ch Cr, Scientst	2	NR	NR	NR	-	-
Ch of Nazarene	2	73	159	159	0.2	0.3
CHR–Chr Chs & Chs Cr	1	NR	60	73	0.1	0.1
CHR–Chs of Christ	3	160	151	188	0.2	0.4
CHR–Int Chs of Christ	0	NR	265	321	0.3	0.7
Evan Cov Ch	1	130	152	169	0.2	0.3
Evan Free Ch	1	365	NR	365	0.3	0.7
Ind Fund Churches	1	NR	NR	NR	-	-
Jehovah's Witness	3	NR	NR	NR	-	-
LDS–Comm of Christ	1	NR	121	121	0.1	0.2
LDS–L-D Saints	3	NR	NR	693	0.7	1.4
LUTH–Assoc Free Luth	1	NR	NR	NR	-	-
LUTH–E.L.C.A.	6	1,261	3,122	4,737	4.5	9.7
LUTH–Luth Cong Msn Chr	1	50	203	246	0.2	0.5
LUTH–Luth-MO Synod	4	786	2,096	2,755	2.6	5.6
LUTH–Nor Amer Luth C	1	NR	NR	NR	-	-
METH–Un Methodist	13	1,431	3,744	5,851	5.6	12.0
METH–Wesleyan	2	141	115	183	0.2	0.4
Muslim Est	1	908	NR	3,298	3.1	6.8
Non-denom Chr Chs	12	1,487	1,565	1,908	1.8	3.9
ORTHE–Greek Orthodox	1	50	NR	400	0.4	0.8
PENT–Assemb of God	4	1,107	417	1,414	1.3	2.9
PENT–Ch God (Cleve)	1	185	93	113	0.1	0.2
PENT–Int Foursq Gos	2	304	579	702	0.7	1.4
PENT–Un Pent Ch Intl	3	NR	NR	NR	-	-
PENT–Vineyard	1	40	50	61	0.1	0.1
PRES–Kor Pres Abroad	1	NR	NR	NR	-	-

Religious Group	Number of Congrega-tions	Number of Attendees	Number of Communicant, Confirmed, or Full Members	Adherents		
				Number of Adherents	% of Total Pop.	% of Total Adh.
PRES–Presb Ch (USA)	4	283	625	757	0.7	1.5
Salvation Army	1	40	25	448	0.4	0.9
Sev Day Adv	1	19	33	38	0.0	0.1
Un C of Christ	9	539	1,628	1,972	1.9	4.0
Unit Univ	2	114	83	116	0.1	0.2
DE WITT	**32**	**1,206**	**4,023**	**6,497**	**39.2**	**100.0**
Bahá'í	0	NR	4	4	0.0	0.1
BAPT–So Bapt Conv	2	100	132	160	1.0	2.5
Catholic	3	NR	NR	1,065	6.4	16.4
CGOD–Ch God (Ander)	1	51	NR	51	0.3	0.8
Ch of Nazarene	1	83	163	163	1.0	2.5
CHR–Chr Chs & Chs Cr	7	NR	2,279	2,767	16.7	42.6
CHR–Chs of Christ	1	30	25	40	0.2	0.6
Evan Free Ch	1	140	NR	140	0.8	2.2
Jehovah's Witness	2	NR	NR	NR	-	-
LUTH–Luth-MO Synod	1	59	133	152	0.9	2.3
METH–Un Methodist	6	404	754	1,243	7.5	19.1
Non-denom Chr Chs	1	150	160	188	1.1	2.9
PENT–Assemb of God	1	142	93	187	1.1	2.9
PENT–Ch God (Cleve)	2	47	101	123	0.7	1.9
PENT–Un Pent Ch Intl	1	NR	NR	NR	-	-
PRES–Cumber Presb	1	NR	25	27	0.2	0.4
PRES–Presb Ch (USA)	1	0	154	187	1.1	2.9
DOUGLAS	**69**	**2,545**	**7,684**	**13,331**	**66.7**	**100.0**
Bahá'í	0	NR	3	3	0.0	0.0
BAPT–Amer Bapt USA	6	333	622	782	3.9	5.9
BAPT–So Bapt Conv	3	85	278	349	1.7	2.6
Catholic	3	NR	NR	2,104	10.5	15.8
CGOD–Ch God (Ander)	2	70	NR	70	0.4	0.5
Ch of Nazarene	3	124	140	185	0.9	1.4
CHR–Chr Ch (Disc)	3	140	847	1,064	5.3	8.0
CHR–Chr Chs & Chs Cr	5	NR	1,201	1,509	7.6	11.3
CHR–Chs of Christ	1	70	106	133	0.7	1.0
Jehovah's Witness	1	NR	NR	NR	-	-
LDS–L-D Saints	1	NR	NR	128	0.6	1.0
LUTH–Luth-MO Synod	1	86	290	380	1.9	2.9
MENN–Amish Undif	16	NR	1,094	2,361	11.8	17.7
MENN–Beachy Amish-Menn	1	133	67	133	0.7	1.0
MENN–CG in Cr (Menn)	1	NR	76	95	0.5	0.7
MENN–Cons Menn Conf	1	135	113	142	0.7	1.1
MENN–Mennonite USA	1	140	241	303	1.5	2.3
METH–Un Methodist	9	744	1,640	2,350	11.8	17.6
Non-denom Chr Chs	3	205	260	294	1.5	2.2
PENT–Assemb of God	1	86	69	146	0.7	1.1
PENT–Un Pent Ch Intl	2	NR	NR	NR	-	-
PRES–Presb Ch (USA)	2	35	51	64	0.3	0.5
Un C of Christ	3	159	586	736	3.7	5.5
DUPAGE	**522**	**103,681**	**143,789**	**656,048**	**71.5**	**100.0**
ANG/EPIS–Anglican NA	8	NR	NR	NR	-	-
ANG/EPIS–Episcopal	12	1,631	4,853	5,206	0.6	0.8
Bahá'í	5	NR	400	400	0.0	0.1
BAPT–Amer Bapt USA	7	318	574	706	0.1	0.1
BAPT–Consrv Bapt	3	NR	NR	NR	-	-
BAPT–Converge/BGC	5	700	NR	840	0.1	0.1
BAPT–N Am Bapt Conf	2	NR	230	283	0.0	0.0
BAPT–NT Ind Bapt	1	NR	NR	NR	-	-
BAPT–Reg Bapt Gen As	5	NR	NR	NR	-	-
BAPT–So Bapt Conv	20	1,380	1,753	2,157	0.2	0.3
BRETH–Ch of Brethren	2	134	236	290	0.0	0.0
BUDD–Mahayana	7	NR	NR	2,781	0.3	0.4
BUDD–Theravada	2	NR	NR	1,656	0.2	0.3
Catholic	54	NR	NR	373,823	40.8	57.0
CGOD–Ch God (Ander)	1	68	NR	68	0.0	0.0
Ch Cr, Scientst	5	NR	NR	NR	-	-
Ch God (7th Day)	1	NR	NR	NR	-	-
Ch of Nazarene	4	406	579	589	0.1	0.1
Chr & Miss Al	13	2,293	1,753	3,333	0.4	0.5
CHR–Chr Ch (Disc)	3	214	438	539	0.1	0.1
CHR–Chr Chs & Chs Cr	5	NR	4,730	5,819	0.6	0.9
CHR–Chs of Christ	8	952	918	1,290	0.1	0.2

NR–Not Reported   - Represents no adherents reported.   Percentages may not total 100 due to rounding.

Table 3: Religious Congregations by County and Group: 2010

Religious Group	Number of Congrega-tions	Number of Attendees	Number of Communicant, Confirmed, or Full Members	Adherents		
				Number of Adherents	% of Total Pop.	% of Total Adh.
CHR–Int Chs of Christ	0	NR	530	652	0.1	0.1
Christian Brethren	3	NR	NR	NR	-	-
CONG–Cong Chr, NA	2	NR	138	170	0.0	0.0
Evan Cov Ch	6	1,001	1,081	1,302	0.1	0.2
Evan Free Ch	7	3,659	NR	3,659	0.4	0.6
FRND–Fr Gen Cf & Un Mtg	1	NR	112	138	0.0	0.0
HINDU–I/A Temples	10	NR	NR	3,459	0.4	0.5
HINDU–Post Ren	5	NR	NR	196	0.0	0.0
HINDU–Trad Temples	3	NR	NR	3,100	0.3	0.5
Ind Fund Churches	2	NR	NR	NR	-	-
Jain	1	NR	NR	NR	-	-
Jehovah's Witness	9	NR	NR	NR	-	-
JUD–Orth	1	43	50	60	0.0	0.0
JUD–Reform	1	305	538	1,453	0.2	0.2
LDS–Comm of Christ	2	NR	242	242	0.0	0.0
LDS–L-D Saints	10	NR	NR	3,825	0.4	0.6
LUTH–Assoc Free Luth	1	NR	NR	NR	-	-
LUTH–E.L.C.A.	29	7,635	19,468	24,867	2.7	3.8
LUTH–Evan Luth Syn	1	67	130	166	0.0	0.0
LUTH–Luth-MO Synod	27	8,934	19,178	24,953	2.7	3.8
LUTH–Wisc Ev Luth Syn	2	336	569	752	0.1	0.1
MENN–Mennonite USA	1	132	181	223	0.0	0.0
METH–AME	3	750	2,450	3,014	0.3	0.5
METH–Free Methodist	1	81	0	81	0.0	0.0
METH–Un Methodist	31	4,509	13,160	19,964	2.2	3.0
METH–Wesleyan	2	156	148	203	0.0	0.0
Muslim Est	14	15,011	NR	59,821	6.5	9.1
New Apost Ch	1	NR	NR	NR	-	-
Non-denom Chr Chs	63	30,618	42,673	46,840	5.1	7.1
ORTHE–Ant Orth of NA	1	50	NR	65	0.0	0.0
ORTHE–Greek Orthodox	2	825	NR	3,950	0.4	0.6
ORTHE–Macedonian Orth	1	110	NR	1,200	0.1	0.2
ORTHE–Orth Ch in Amer	2	465	NR	815	0.1	0.1
ORTHE–Rus Orth Abroad	1	50	NR	80	0.0	0.0
ORTHE–Ukrainian Orth	1	30	NR	150	0.0	0.0
ORTHO–Coptic Orth Ch	1	700	NR	1,800	0.2	0.3
ORTHO–Syrian Orth Ch	1	90	NR	400	0.0	0.1
PENT–Assemb of God	8	8,655	1,566	17,088	1.9	2.6
PENT–Ch God (Cleve)	2	111	78	96	0.0	0.0
PENT–Full Gosp Bapt	2	NR	NR	NR	-	-
PENT–Int Foursq Gos	1	49	43	53	0.0	0.0
PENT–Intl Pent Holiness	1	70	65	80	0.0	0.0
PENT–Un Pent Ch Intl	8	NR	NR	NR	-	-
PENT–Vineyard	1	75	35	43	0.0	0.0
PRES–Evan Presby Ch	1	NR	260	320	0.0	0.0
PRES–Korean Pres Amer	1	NR	NR	NR	-	-
PRES–Orth Pres Ch	1	201	154	227	0.0	0.0
PRES–Presb Ch (USA)	18	3,104	7,334	9,023	1.0	1.4
PRES–Presb Ch Amer	6	441	423	504	0.1	0.1
REF–Christian Ref	7	2,006	3,456	4,252	0.5	0.6
REF–Ref Ch in Am	3	299	407	460	0.1	0.1
Salvation Army	1	222	338	1,193	0.1	0.2
Sev Day Adv	15	1,798	3,128	3,597	0.4	0.5
Un C of Christ	20	2,652	8,808	10,836	1.2	1.7
Unit Univ	3	345	582	809	0.1	0.1
Unity Ch	1	NR	NR	NR	-	-
Zoroastrian	0	NR	NR	87	0.0	0.0
EDGAR	**51**	**1,962**	**5,540**	**7,868**	**42.4**	**100.0**
ANG/EPIS–Episcopal	1	4	5	5	0.0	0.1
Bahá'í	0	NR	4	4	0.0	0.1
BAPT–Amer Bapt USA	2	156	301	362	1.9	4.6
BAPT–So Bapt Conv	1	29	33	40	0.2	0.5
Catholic	3	NR	NR	1,128	6.1	14.3
Ch of Nazarene	2	145	211	218	1.2	2.8
CHR–Chr Ch (Disc)	1	180	870	1,047	5.6	13.3
CHR–Chr Chs & Chs Cr	10	NR	1,515	1,824	9.8	23.2
CHR–Chs of Christ	2	85	64	98	0.5	1.2
Grace Gosp Fel	1	NR	NR	NR	-	-
Ind Fund Churches	1	NR	NR	NR	-	-
Jehovah's Witness	1	NR	NR	NR	-	-
LDS–L-D Saints	1	NR	NR	213	1.1	2.7
LUTH–Luth-MO Synod	1	130	291	329	1.8	4.2
METH–AME	1	0	100	120	0.6	1.5
METH–Un Methodist	12	565	1,195	1,361	7.3	17.3
Non-denom Chr Chs	4	445	570	632	3.4	8.0
PENT–Assemb of God	1	45	23	58	0.3	0.7
PENT–Ch God (Cleve)	1	43	85	102	0.5	1.3
PENT–Un Pent Ch Intl	1	NR	NR	NR	-	-
PRES–Presb Ch (USA)	3	117	241	290	1.6	3.7
Sev Day Adv	1	18	32	37	0.2	0.5
EDWARDS	**26**	**1,304**	**3,449**	**4,229**	**62.9**	**100.0**
ANG/EPIS–Episcopal	1	12	16	16	0.2	0.4
BAPT–So Bapt Conv	2	210	641	777	11.6	18.4
CHR–Chr Ch (Disc)	1	50	100	121	1.8	2.9
CHR–Chr Chs & Chs Cr	7	NR	1,241	1,504	22.4	35.6
CHR–Chs of Christ	1	50	40	60	0.9	1.4
CONG–Cong Chr, NA	1	NR	66	80	1.2	1.9
METH–Free Methodist	1	47	48	48	0.7	1.1
METH–Un Methodist	9	401	649	825	12.3	19.5
MORAV–Morav Ch-North	1	96	228	274	4.1	6.5
Non-denom Chr Chs	1	400	400	500	7.4	11.8
PRES–Presb Ch (USA)	1	38	20	24	0.4	0.6
EFFINGHAM	**65**	**4,781**	**10,612**	**23,738**	**69.3**	**100.0**
ANG/EPIS–Episcopal	1	7	3	3	0.0	0.0
BAPT–Free Will Bapt	1	NR	86	106	0.3	0.4
BAPT–So Bapt Conv	8	1,437	3,181	3,915	11.4	16.5
Catholic	10	NR	NR	10,144	29.6	42.7
CGOD–Ch God (Ander)	1	153	NR	153	0.4	0.6
CHR–Chr Chs & Chs Cr	9	NR	1,650	2,031	5.9	8.6
CHR–Chs of Christ	1	85	87	99	0.3	0.4
Jehovah's Witness	1	NR	NR	NR	-	-
LDS–Comm of Christ	1	NR	82	82	0.2	0.3
LDS–L-D Saints	1	NR	NR	205	0.6	0.9
LUTH–E.L.C.A.	3	117	301	347	1.0	1.5
LUTH–Luth-MO Synod	8	1,470	2,636	3,316	9.7	14.0
METH–Un Methodist	11	655	1,478	2,066	6.0	8.7
Non-denom Chr Chs	6	473	734	734	2.1	3.1
PENT–Assemb of God	1	264	152	264	0.8	1.1
PENT–Un Pent Ch Intl	1	NR	NR	NR	-	-
PRES–Presb Ch (USA)	1	120	222	273	0.8	1.2
FAYETTE	**57**	**2,707**	**7,643**	**10,035**	**45.3**	**100.0**
Bahá'í	0	NR	2	2	0.0	0.0
BAPT–So Bapt Conv	15	1,017	3,600	4,343	19.6	43.3
Catholic	3	NR	NR	571	2.6	5.7
CGOD–Ch God (Ander)	2	160	NR	160	0.7	1.6
Ch of Nazarene	2	57	43	128	0.6	1.3
CHR–Chr Ch (Disc)	1	35	100	121	0.5	1.2
CHR–Chr Chs & Chs Cr	7	NR	815	983	4.4	9.8
CHR–Chs of Christ	3	68	77	103	0.5	1.0
Jehovah's Witness	1	NR	NR	NR	-	-
LUTH–E.L.C.A.	1	55	211	221	1.0	2.2
LUTH–Luth-MO Synod	4	547	1,435	1,779	8.0	17.7
METH–Free Methodist	1	53	55	55	0.2	0.5
METH–Un Methodist	8	511	998	1,089	4.9	10.9
PENT–Assemb of God	2	112	41	162	0.7	1.6
PENT–Un Pent Ch Intl	3	NR	NR	NR	-	-
PRES–Cumber Presb	1	NR	8	8	0.0	0.1
PRES–Presb Ch (USA)	1	30	67	81	0.4	0.8
Sev Day Adv	1	12	20	23	0.1	0.2
Un C of Christ	1	50	171	206	0.9	2.1
FORD	**37**	**2,007**	**4,663**	**7,680**	**54.5**	**100.0**
Bahá'í	0	NR	4	4	0.0	0.1
BAPT–So Bapt Conv	2	83	485	592	4.2	7.7
Catholic	5	NR	NR	1,771	12.6	23.1
Ch of Nazarene	2	47	69	104	0.7	1.4
CHR–Chr Ch (Disc)	1	76	292	356	2.5	4.6
CHR–Chr Chs & Chs Cr	1	NR	330	402	2.9	5.2
CHR–Chs of Christ	1	40	35	44	0.3	0.6
CONG–Cong Chr, NA	1	NR	35	43	0.3	0.6
Evan Cov Ch	1	71	191	92	0.7	1.2
LUTH–Assoc Free Luth	1	NR	NR	NR	-	-

NR–Not Reported   - Represents no adherents reported.   Percentages may not total 100 due to rounding.

Table 3: Religious Congregations by County and Group: 2010

Religious Group	Number of Congrega-tions	Number of Attendees	Number of Communicant, Confirmed, or Full Members	Adherents: Number of Adherents	Adherents: % of Total Pop.	Adherents: % of Total Adh.
LUTH–E.L.C.A.	5	340	942	1,223	8.7	15.9
LUTH–Nor Amer Luth C	1	NR	NR	NR	-	-
METH–Un Methodist	7	433	1,341	1,722	12.2	22.4
Non-denom Chr Chs	3	695	600	869	6.2	11.3
PENT–Assemb of God	1	43	29	76	0.5	1.0
PRES–Presb Ch (USA)	3	83	215	262	1.9	3.4
PRES–Presb Ch Amer	1	55	46	60	0.4	0.8
Un C of Christ	1	41	49	60	0.4	0.8
FRANKLIN	**123**	**5,747**	**15,592**	**22,160**	**56.0**	**100.0**
ANG/EPIS–Episcopal	1	20	35	52	0.1	0.2
Bahá'í	0	NR	1	1	0.0	0.0
BAPT–Amer Bapt USA	5	247	518	627	1.6	2.8
BAPT–Free Will Bapt	6	NR	516	624	1.6	2.8
BAPT–Natl Mis Bapt Conv	1	75	125	151	0.4	0.7
BAPT–S-D Baptist Gen Con	1	25	33	40	0.1	0.2
BAPT–So Bapt Conv	40	3,176	8,940	10,815	27.3	48.8
Catholic	5	NR	NR	3,053	7.7	13.8
CGOD–Ch God (Ander)	3	106	NR	106	0.3	0.5
Ch of Nazarene	2	138	188	292	0.7	1.3
CHR–Chr Ch (Disc)	2	92	312	377	1.0	1.7
CHR–Chr Chs & Chs Cr	11	NR	1,620	1,960	5.0	8.8
CHR–Chs of Christ	5	207	191	246	0.6	1.1
Jehovah's Witness	1	NR	NR	NR	-	-
LDS–Comm of Christ	1	NR	82	82	0.2	0.4
LUTH–Luth–MO Synod	1	59	154	182	0.5	0.8
METH–Un Methodist	15	585	1,026	1,288	3.3	5.8
Non-denom Chr Chs	3	200	275	275	0.7	1.2
ORTHE–Orth Ch in Amer	1	40	NR	70	0.2	0.3
PENT–Assemb of God	1	29	0	29	0.1	0.1
PENT–Ch God (Cleve)	7	581	1,274	1,541	3.9	7.0
PENT–Un Pent Ch Intl	7	NR	NR	NR	-	-
PRES–Presb Ch (USA)	1	0	12	15	0.0	0.1
Sev Day Adv	3	167	290	334	0.8	1.5
FULTON	**84**	**4,338**	**9,142**	**13,692**	**36.9**	**100.0**
ANG/EPIS–Anglican NA	1	NR	NR	NR	-	-
ANG/EPIS–Episcopal	1	15	67	67	0.2	0.5
Bahá'í	0	NR	4	4	0.0	0.0
BAPT–Amer Bapt USA	2	188	642	763	2.1	5.6
BAPT–So Bapt Conv	1	66	174	207	0.6	1.5
BRETH–Ch of Brethren	2	71	94	112	0.3	0.8
Catholic	4	NR	NR	1,217	3.3	8.9
CGOD–Ch God (Ander)	1	0	NR	0	0.0	0.0
Ch of Nazarene	9	474	487	673	1.8	4.9
CHR–Chr Ch (Disc)	5	225	1,399	1,662	4.5	12.1
CHR–Chr Chs & Chs Cr	5	NR	730	867	2.3	6.3
CHR–Chs of Christ	1	55	51	67	0.2	0.5
Evan Free Ch	1	350	NR	350	0.9	2.6
Jehovah's Witness	2	NR	NR	NR	-	-
LDS–L-D Saints	1	NR	NR	296	0.8	2.2
LUTH–E.L.C.A.	2	142	426	533	1.4	3.9
LUTH–Luth–MO Synod	1	30	45	65	0.2	0.5
MENN–Amish Undif	1	NR	44	129	0.3	0.9
METH–Free Methodist	1	19	16	19	0.1	0.1
METH–Un Methodist	22	1,113	2,768	3,692	10.0	27.0
Non-denom Chr Chs	7	1,020	1,220	1,457	3.9	10.6
PENT–Assemb of God	3	142	95	228	0.6	1.7
PENT–Un Pent Ch Intl	1	NR	NR	NR	-	-
PRES–Presb Ch (USA)	4	201	419	498	1.3	3.6
REF–Ref Ch in Am	1	45	168	178	0.5	1.3
Salvation Army	1	42	60	325	0.9	2.4
Sev Day Adv	1	36	63	72	0.2	0.5
Un C of Christ	2	59	159	189	0.5	1.4
Unit Univ	1	45	11	22	0.1	0.2
GALLATIN	**23**	**636**	**1,433**	**2,970**	**53.1**	**100.0**
Bahá'í	0	NR	1	1	0.0	0.0
BAPT–So Bapt Conv	4	212	769	916	16.4	30.8
Catholic	4	NR	NR	1,246	22.3	42.0
Ch of Nazarene	1	19	33	94	1.7	3.2
METH–Un Methodist	5	90	106	151	2.7	5.1
Non-denom Chr Chs	1	225	300	300	5.4	10.1

Religious Group	Number of Congrega-tions	Number of Attendees	Number of Communicant, Confirmed, or Full Members	Adherents: Number of Adherents	Adherents: % of Total Pop.	Adherents: % of Total Adh.
PENT–Ch God (Cleve)	3	78	98	117	2.1	3.9
PRES–Cumber Presb	1	NR	26	26	0.5	0.9
PRES–Presb Ch (USA)	4	12	100	119	2.1	4.0
GREENE	**40**	**1,940**	**4,612**	**7,544**	**54.3**	**100.0**
Bahá'í	0	NR	1	1	0.0	0.0
BAPT–Amer Bapt USA	10	758	2,008	2,427	17.5	32.2
BAPT–So Bapt Conv	10	369	1,345	1,626	11.7	21.6
Catholic	3	NR	NR	1,764	12.7	23.4
CHR–Chr Ch (Disc)	1	55	145	175	1.3	2.3
CHR–Chs of Christ	1	14	13	17	0.1	0.2
LUTH–Luth–MO Synod	1	63	193	270	1.9	3.6
MENN–Ber Amish-Menn	1	197	84	197	1.4	2.6
METH–Un Methodist	5	214	523	645	4.6	8.5
Non-denom Chr Chs	3	170	180	212	1.5	2.8
PENT–Assemb of God	1	50	27	98	0.7	1.3
PENT–Un Pent Ch Intl	2	NR	NR	NR	-	-
PRES–Presb Ch (USA)	2	50	93	112	0.8	1.5
GRUNDY	**43**	**3,532**	**6,249**	**20,613**	**41.2**	**100.0**
ANG/EPIS–Episcopal	1	46	66	76	0.2	0.4
Bahá'í	0	NR	7	7	0.0	0.0
BAPT–Amer Bapt Assn	1	NR	85	108	0.2	0.5
BAPT–Amer Bapt USA	1	205	138	175	0.3	0.8
BAPT–Converge/BGC	1	800	NR	960	1.9	4.7
BAPT–Reg Bapt Gen As	1	NR	NR	NR	-	-
BAPT–So Bapt Conv	2	164	441	559	1.1	2.7
Catholic	4	NR	NR	10,700	21.4	51.9
Ch of Nazarene	1	52	49	52	0.1	0.3
CHR–Chr Chs & Chs Cr	3	NR	1,515	1,920	3.8	9.3
CHR–Chs of Christ	1	20	18	20	0.0	0.1
Jehovah's Witness	2	NR	NR	NR	-	-
LDS–L-D Saints	1	NR	NR	365	0.7	1.8
LUTH–Assoc Free Luth	2	NR	NR	NR	-	-
LUTH–E.L.C.A.	2	106	280	374	0.7	1.8
LUTH–Luth–MO Synod	1	151	356	427	0.9	2.1
METH–Un Methodist	8	704	1,832	2,641	5.3	12.8
Non-denom Chr Chs	5	930	670	1,194	2.4	5.8
PENT–Assemb of God	1	60	31	71	0.1	0.3
PENT–Un Pent Ch Intl	1	NR	NR	NR	-	-
PRES–Presb Ch (USA)	3	220	536	679	1.4	3.3
Un C of Christ	1	74	225	285	0.6	1.4
HAMILTON	**31**	**1,138**	**2,844**	**4,666**	**55.2**	**100.0**
ANG/EPIS–Episcopal	1	6	10	12	0.1	0.3
BAPT–So Bapt Conv	13	694	2,132	2,578	30.5	55.3
Catholic	3	NR	NR	1,159	13.7	24.8
CHR–Chr Chs & Chs Cr	2	NR	0	0	0.0	0.0
CHR–Chs of Christ	2	93	81	105	1.2	2.3
MENN–Amish Undif	1	NR	43	121	1.4	2.6
METH–Un Methodist	5	134	248	265	3.1	5.7
PENT–Assemb of God	1	116	89	124	1.5	2.7
PENT–Ch God (Cleve)	1	71	206	249	2.9	5.3
PRES–Cumber Presb	1	NR	5	17	0.2	0.4
PRES–Presb Ch (USA)	1	24	30	36	0.4	0.8
HANCOCK	**66**	**2,383**	**6,195**	**10,135**	**53.1**	**100.0**
ANG/EPIS–Episcopal	1	29	50	76	0.4	0.7
Bahá'í	0	NR	2	2	0.0	0.0
BAPT–Amer Bapt USA	2	72	202	242	1.3	2.4
BAPT–So Bapt Conv	2	51	47	56	0.3	0.6
Calv Chpl	1	NR	NR	NR	-	-
Catholic	5	NR	NR	1,521	8.0	15.0
CHR–Chr Ch (Disc)	1	67	285	342	1.8	3.4
CHR–Chr Chs & Chs Cr	8	NR	970	1,164	6.1	11.5
CONG–Consrv Cong Chr	1	209	216	259	1.4	2.6
Ind Fund Churches	3	NR	NR	NR	-	-
LDS–Comm of Christ	2	NR	238	238	1.2	2.3
LDS–L-D Saints	2	NR	NR	733	3.8	7.2
LUTH–E.L.C.A.	5	332	1,024	1,280	6.7	12.6
LUTH–Luth–MO Synod	2	47	130	153	0.8	1.5
METH–Un Methodist	10	493	1,404	1,860	9.7	18.4

NR–Not Reported - Represents no adherents reported. Percentages may not total 100 due to rounding.

Table 3: Religious Congregations by County and Group: 2010

Religious Group	Number of Congrega-tions	Number of Attendees	Number of Communicant, Confirmed, or Full Members	Adherents		
				Number of Adherents	% of Total Pop.	% of Total Adh.
Non-denom Chr Chs	6	515	499	644	3.4	6.4
PENT–Assemb of God	5	227	153	396	2.1	3.9
PRES–Presb Ch (USA)	7	197	524	629	3.3	6.2
Sev Day Adv	1	8	14	16	0.1	0.2
Un C of Christ	2	136	437	524	2.7	5.2
HARDIN	**10**	**245**	**906**	**1,228**	**28.4**	**100.0**
Bahá'í	0	NR	1	1	0.0	0.1
BAPT–So Bapt Conv	4	148	645	764	17.7	62.2
Catholic	1	NR	NR	150	3.5	12.2
CHR–Chr Chs & Chs Cr	2	NR	140	166	3.8	13.5
CHR–Chs of Christ	2	77	82	96	2.2	7.8
METH–Un Methodist	1	20	38	51	1.2	4.2
HENDERSON	**18**	**689**	**1,822**	**2,437**	**33.2**	**100.0**
Bahá'í	0	NR	1	1	0.0	0.0
BAPT–Amer Bapt USA	1	55	189	223	3.0	9.2
Catholic	1	NR	NR	190	2.6	7.8
Ch of Nazarene	1	40	28	150	2.0	6.2
CHR–Chr Ch (Disc)	1	45	192	226	3.1	9.3
CHR–Chr Chs & Chs Cr	1	NR	150	177	2.4	7.3
LUTH–E.L.C.A.	1	51	132	183	2.5	7.5
METH–Un Methodist	6	334	766	817	11.1	33.5
Non-denom Chr Chs	1	80	80	100	1.4	4.1
PENT–Assemb of God	1	17	13	52	0.7	2.1
PRES–Presb Ch (USA)	3	51	244	287	3.9	11.8
REF–Ref Ch in Am	1	16	27	31	0.4	1.3
HENRY	**90**	**5,063**	**11,891**	**22,819**	**45.2**	**100.0**
ANG/EPIS–Anglican NA	1	NR	NR	NR	-	-
ANG/EPIS–Episcopal	1	23	47	47	0.1	0.2
Bahá'í	0	NR	15	15	0.0	0.1
BAPT–Amer Bapt Assn	1	NR	28	34	0.1	0.1
BAPT–Amer Bapt USA	4	183	607	739	1.5	3.2
BAPT–Converge/BGC	1	75	NR	90	0.2	0.4
BAPT–Free Will Bapt	1	NR	86	105	0.2	0.5
BAPT–Reg Bapt Gen As	1	NR	NR	NR	-	-
BAPT–So Bapt Conv	3	229	440	536	1.1	2.3
Catholic	10	NR	NR	6,390	12.7	28.0
Ch of Nazarene	2	116	176	267	0.5	1.2
CHR–Chr Chs & Chs Cr	3	NR	550	670	1.3	2.9
CHR–Chs of Christ	3	100	79	116	0.2	0.5
CONG–Cong Chr, NA	1	NR	40	49	0.1	0.2
Evan Cong Ch	1	NR	82	100	0.2	0.4
Evan Free Ch	2	405	NR	405	0.8	1.8
Jehovah's Witness	2	NR	NR	NR	-	-
LDS–L-D Saints	2	NR	NR	375	0.7	1.6
LUTH–E.L.C.A.	9	1,010	2,990	4,141	8.2	18.1
LUTH–Luth–MO Synod	5	165	1,031	1,352	2.7	5.9
METH–AME	1	0	100	122	0.2	0.5
METH–Free Methodist	1	13	5	13	0.0	0.1
METH–Un Methodist	14	1,701	3,741	4,904	9.7	21.5
Non-denom Chr Chs	5	316	541	541	1.1	2.4
OCATH–Pol Natl Cath	1	NR	NR	NR	-	-
PENT–Assemb of God	4	165	72	272	0.5	1.2
PENT–Ch God (Cleve)	3	52	95	116	0.2	0.5
PENT–COGIC	1	0	150	183	0.4	0.8
PENT–Un Pent Ch Intl	1	NR	NR	NR	-	-
PRES–Presb Ch (USA)	4	366	566	689	1.4	3.0
Un C of Christ	2	144	450	548	1.1	2.4
IROQUOIS	**76**	**3,899**	**8,666**	**15,708**	**52.9**	**100.0**
Ap Chr Ch-Amer	1	310	180	310	1.0	2.0
Bahá'í	0	NR	1	1	0.0	0.0
BAPT–So Bapt Conv	2	21	61	74	0.2	0.5
Catholic	9	NR	NR	3,890	13.1	24.8
CGOD–Ch God (Ander)	1	0	NR	0	0.0	0.0
Ch of Nazarene	3	92	100	258	0.9	1.6
CHR–Chr Ch (Disc)	2	63	159	192	0.6	1.2
CHR–Chr Chs & Chs Cr	8	NR	1,196	1,448	4.9	9.2
CONG–Cong Chr, NA	1	NR	50	61	0.2	0.4
Evan Free Ch	1	518	NR	518	1.7	3.3
Jehovah's Witness	1	NR	NR	NR	-	-
LDS–L-D Saints	1	NR	NR	92	0.3	0.6
LUTH–Assoc Free Luth	2	NR	NR	NR	-	-
LUTH–E.L.C.A.	3	283	983	1,157	3.9	7.4
LUTH–Luth Ch-Am Asc	1	NR	NR	NR	-	-
LUTH–Luth–MO Synod	11	1,349	3,158	4,077	13.7	26.0
LUTH–Nor Amer Luth C	1	NR	NR	NR	-	-
METH–Un Methodist	16	687	1,901	2,487	8.4	15.8
METH–Wesleyan	1	54	33	70	0.2	0.4
Non-denom Chr Chs	4	295	280	374	1.3	2.4
PENT–Assemb of God	1	23	0	36	0.1	0.2
PRES–Presb Ch (USA)	1	0	28	34	0.1	0.2
REF–Ref Ch in Am	1	74	119	134	0.5	0.9
Un Breth in Cr	1	12	17	11	0.0	0.1
Un C of Christ	3	118	400	484	1.6	3.1
JACKSON	**117**	**8,501**	**17,434**	**29,259**	**48.6**	**100.0**
ANG/EPIS–Episcopal	1	37	65	67	0.1	0.2
Bahá'í	0	NR	47	47	0.1	0.2
BAPT–Amer Bapt USA	8	517	1,042	1,209	2.0	4.1
BAPT–Natl Mis Bapt Conv	1	0	150	174	0.3	0.6
BAPT–NBC Amer	1	80	125	145	0.2	0.5
BAPT–NBC USA	1	0	250	290	0.5	1.0
BAPT–So Bapt Conv	20	1,400	5,730	6,650	11.0	22.7
BUDD–Theravada	1	NR	NR	14	0.0	0.0
Catholic	5	NR	NR	4,220	7.0	14.4
CGOD–Ch God (Ander)	2	25	NR	25	0.0	0.1
Ch Cr, Scientist	2	NR	NR	NR	-	-
Ch of Nazarene	2	125	133	230	0.4	0.8
CHR–Chr Ch (Disc)	1	66	137	159	0.3	0.5
CHR–Chr Chs & Chs Cr	5	NR	1,074	1,246	2.1	4.3
CHR–Chs of Christ	2	170	224	302	0.5	1.0
FRND–Fr Gen Cf	1	NR	12	14	0.0	0.0
HINDU–Post Ren	1	NR	NR	54	0.1	0.2
Jehovah's Witness	2	NR	NR	NR	-	-
LDS–Comm of Christ	1	NR	82	82	0.1	0.3
LDS–L-D Saints	1	NR	NR	661	1.1	2.3
LUTH–E.L.C.A.	5	355	1,022	1,234	2.0	4.2
LUTH–Luth–MO Synod	5	671	1,883	2,414	4.0	8.3
LUTH–Nor Amer Luth C	1	NR	NR	NR	-	-
MENN–Amish Undif	3	NR	117	360	0.6	1.2
METH–AME	2	0	250	290	0.5	1.0
METH–Un Methodist	9	741	1,634	2,005	3.3	6.9
Muslim Est	2	1,816	NR	3,298	5.5	11.3
Non-denom Chr Chs	11	1,568	1,774	2,062	3.4	7.0
PENT–Assemb of God	4	498	478	564	0.9	1.9
PENT–Ch God (Cleve)	1	52	121	140	0.2	0.5
PENT–COGIC	2	0	300	348	0.6	1.2
PENT–Un Pent Ch Intl	4	NR	NR	NR	-	-
PRES–Evan Presby Ch	1	NR	63	73	0.1	0.2
PRES–Presb Ch (USA)	3	161	296	344	0.6	1.2
PRES–Presb Ch Amer	1	37	49	52	0.1	0.2
REF–Comm Ref Evan	1	NR	NR	NR	-	-
Sev Day Adv	1	6	10	12	0.0	0.0
Un C of Christ	2	87	188	218	0.4	0.7
Unit Univ	1	89	178	255	0.4	0.9
Zoroastrian	0	NR	NR	1	0.0	0.0
JASPER	**29**	**879**	**2,251**	**5,060**	**52.2**	**100.0**
Bahá'í	0	NR	2	2	0.0	0.0
BAPT–Amer Bapt USA	1	220	430	520	5.4	10.3
BAPT–So Bapt Conv	3	47	106	128	1.3	2.5
Catholic	2	NR	NR	2,335	24.1	46.1
CHR–Chr Chs & Chs Cr	6	NR	701	848	8.7	16.8
CHR–Chs of Christ	2	88	75	101	1.0	2.0
LUTH–Luth–MO Synod	2	88	180	230	2.4	4.5
METH–Free Methodist	1	65	31	65	0.7	1.3
METH–Un Methodist	6	159	439	451	4.7	8.9
Non-denom Chr Chs	3	165	190	209	2.2	4.1
PENT–Assemb of God	1	23	12	23	0.2	0.5
PRES–Cumber Presb	1	NR	50	106	1.1	2.1
PRES–Presb Ch (USA)	1	24	35	42	0.4	0.8

NR–Not Reported   - Represents no adherents reported.   Percentages may not total 100 due to rounding.

Table 3: Religious Congregations by County and Group: 2010

Religious Group	Number of Congrega-tions	Number of Attendees	Number of Communicant, Confirmed, or Full Members	Adherents: Number of Adherents	Adherents: % of Total Pop.	Adherents: % of Total Adh.
JEFFERSON	**103**	**5,961**	**16,776**	**22,248**	**57.3**	**100.0**
ANG/EPIS–Episcopal	1	45	115	261	0.7	1.2
Bahá'í	0	NR	4	4	0.0	0.0
BAPT–Amer Bapt USA	2	53	90	108	0.3	0.5
BAPT–Free Will Bapt	7	NR	602	725	1.9	3.3
BAPT–Natl Mis Bapt Conv	2	45	347	418	1.1	1.9
BAPT–NBC USA	1	75	250	301	0.8	1.4
BAPT–So Bapt Conv	31	2,224	7,360	8,861	22.8	39.8
Catholic	2	NR	NR	1,409	3.6	6.3
CGOD–Ch God (Ander)	3	140	NR	140	0.4	0.6
Ch of Nazarene	1	45	45	160	0.4	0.7
CHR–Chr Chs & Chs Cr	12	NR	2,690	3,239	8.3	14.6
CHR–Chs of Christ	2	200	195	235	0.6	1.1
Jehovah's Witness	1	NR	NR	NR	-	-
LDS–Comm of Christ	1	NR	82	82	0.2	0.4
LDS–L-D Saints	1	NR	NR	195	0.5	0.9
LUTH–E.L.C.A.	1	31	74	76	0.2	0.3
LUTH–Luth–MO Synod	1	100	247	299	0.8	1.3
MENN–Amish Undif	2	NR	140	345	0.9	1.6
MENN–Mennonite USA	1	NR	NR	NR	-	-
METH–C.M.E.	1	0	100	120	0.3	0.5
METH–Un Methodist	15	621	1,376	1,639	4.2	7.4
Non-denom Chr Chs	6	2,010	2,335	2,722	7.0	12.2
PENT–Assemb of God	1	75	37	85	0.2	0.4
PENT–Ch God (Cleve)	2	116	272	327	0.8	1.5
PENT–COGIC	3	50	205	247	0.6	1.1
PENT–Un Pent Ch Intl	1	NR	NR	NR	-	-
PRES–Presb Ch (USA)	1	94	146	176	0.5	0.8
Sev Day Adv	1	37	64	74	0.2	0.3
JERSEY	**34**	**2,181**	**4,237**	**12,594**	**54.8**	**100.0**
Bahá'í	0	NR	1	1	0.0	0.0
BAPT–Amer Bapt USA	2	299	1,161	1,404	6.1	11.1
BAPT–Reg Bapt Gen As	2	NR	NR	NR	-	-
BAPT–So Bapt Conv	5	545	985	1,191	5.2	9.5
Catholic	6	NR	NR	6,962	30.3	55.3
Ch Cr, Scientst	2	NR	NR	NR	-	-
Ch of Nazarene	1	40	56	101	0.4	0.8
CHR–Chs of Christ	1	70	70	106	0.5	0.8
Jehovah's Witness	1	NR	NR	NR	-	-
LUTH–Luth–MO Synod	1	110	218	290	1.3	2.3
METH–Un Methodist	5	403	651	1,031	4.5	8.2
Non-denom Chr Chs	2	255	350	369	1.6	2.9
PENT–Assemb of God	1	208	130	396	1.7	3.1
PENT–Un Pent Ch Intl	2	NR	NR	NR	-	-
PRES–Presb Ch (USA)	1	78	144	174	0.8	1.4
Un C of Christ	2	173	471	569	2.5	4.5
JO DAVIESS	**46**	**1,868**	**3,815**	**12,919**	**57.0**	**100.0**
ANG/EPIS–Episcopal	1	68	47	126	0.6	1.0
Bahá'í	0	NR	3	3	0.0	0.0
Catholic	10	NR	NR	7,844	34.6	60.7
Ch of Nazarene	1	11	41	41	0.2	0.3
Evan Free Ch	1	250	NR	250	1.1	1.9
Ind Fund Churches	1	NR	NR	NR	-	-
Jehovah's Witness	1	NR	NR	NR	-	-
LDS–L-D Saints	1	NR	NR	38	0.2	0.3
LUTH–E.L.C.A.	7	492	1,245	1,566	6.9	12.1
LUTH–Luth Cong Msn Chr	1	100	154	183	0.8	1.4
LUTH–Luth–MO Synod	1	70	176	216	1.0	1.7
LUTH–Wisc Ev Luth Syn	1	50	71	93	0.4	0.7
METH–Un Methodist	10	503	1,637	1,906	8.4	14.8
Non-denom Chr Chs	1	70	35	88	0.4	0.7
PENT–Assemb of God	1	60	0	80	0.4	0.6
PENT–Un Pent Ch Intl	1	NR	NR	NR	-	-
PRES–Presb Ch (USA)	6	154	339	402	1.8	3.1
Unit Univ	1	40	67	83	0.4	0.6
JOHNSON	**37**	**1,069**	**3,596**	**4,623**	**36.7**	**100.0**
Bahá'í	0	NR	1	1	0.0	0.0
BAPT–Amer Bapt USA	1	52	70	82	0.7	1.8
BAPT–So Bapt Conv	10	548	2,562	3,000	23.8	64.9
Catholic	1	NR	NR	162	1.3	3.5
CHR–Chr Chs & Chs Cr	2	NR	115	135	1.1	2.9
CHR–Chs of Christ	4	104	101	118	0.9	2.6
LDS–Comm of Christ	1	NR	82	82	0.7	1.8
MENN–Amish Undif	1	NR	43	121	1.0	2.6
METH–Un Methodist	8	325	543	653	5.2	14.1
Non-denom Chr Chs	1	10	10	12	0.1	0.3
PENT–Assemb of God	2	30	20	102	0.8	2.2
PENT–Un Pent Ch Intl	5	NR	NR	NR	-	-
PRES–Cumber Presb	1	NR	49	155	1.2	3.4
KANE	**326**	**44,584**	**68,580**	**267,748**	**52.0**	**100.0**
ANG/EPIS–Anglican NA	1	NR	NR	NR	-	-
ANG/EPIS–Episcopal	8	1,185	2,199	2,952	0.6	1.1
Ap Chr Ch-Amer	1	350	180	350	0.1	0.1
Bahá'í	2	NR	176	176	0.0	0.1
BAPT–Amer Bapt USA	10	1,654	3,506	4,526	0.9	1.7
BAPT–Consrv Bapt	1	NR	NR	NR	-	-
BAPT–Converge/BGC	4	1,025	NR	1,230	0.2	0.5
BAPT–Free Will Bapt	2	NR	172	222	0.0	0.1
BAPT–Ind Bapt Flwsp Intl	1	NR	NR	NR	-	-
BAPT–N Am Bapt Conf	1	NR	64	83	0.0	0.0
BAPT–Natl Mis Bapt Conv	1	0	150	194	0.0	0.1
BAPT–NBC USA	1	600	1,000	1,291	0.3	0.5
BAPT–Prog NBC	2	240	500	645	0.1	0.2
BAPT–Ref Bapt Ch	2	NR	NR	NR	-	-
BAPT–Reg Bapt Gen As	2	NR	NR	NR	-	-
BAPT–So Bapt Conv	16	1,550	1,894	2,445	0.5	0.9
BRETH–Ch of Brethren	2	0	414	534	0.1	0.2
BUDD–Mahayana	1	NR	NR	102	0.0	0.0
BUDD–Theravada	2	NR	NR	600	0.1	0.2
Calv Chpl	1	NR	NR	NR	-	-
Catholic	28	NR	NR	155,391	30.2	58.0
CGOD–Ch God (Ander)	2	70	NR	70	0.0	0.0
Ch Cr, Scientst	3	NR	NR	NR	-	-
Ch God (7th Day)	1	NR	NR	NR	-	-
Ch of Nazarene	2	72	108	108	0.0	0.0
Chr & Miss Al	2	179	233	233	0.0	0.1
CHR–Chr Chs & Chs Cr	5	NR	1,025	1,323	0.3	0.5
CHR–Chs of Christ	5	440	379	479	0.1	0.2
CONG–Consrv Cong Chr	1	100	175	226	0.0	0.1
Evan Cov Ch	4	556	578	722	0.1	0.3
Evan Free Ch	2	785	NR	785	0.2	0.3
HINDU–I/A Temples	2	NR	NR	1,048	0.2	0.4
HINDU–Trad Temples	1	NR	NR	1,000	0.2	0.4
Ind Fund Churches	1	NR	NR	NR	-	-
Jehovah's Witness	4	NR	NR	NR	-	-
LDS–Comm of Christ	1	NR	121	121	0.0	0.0
LDS–L-D Saints	6	NR	NR	2,879	0.6	1.1
LUTH–Ch Luth Conf	1	NR	NR	NR	-	-
LUTH–E.L.C.A.	14	2,915	6,181	9,239	1.8	3.5
LUTH–Luth Cong Msn Chr	2	623	2,059	2,658	0.5	1.0
LUTH–Luth–MO Synod	20	4,533	10,040	13,201	2.6	4.9
LUTH–Wisc Ev Luth Syn	2	260	409	435	0.1	0.2
MENN–Mennonite USA	1	NR	125	161	0.0	0.1
METH–AME	3	80	300	387	0.1	0.1
METH–Free Methodist	3	199	263	276	0.1	0.1
METH–Un Methodist	22	3,295	8,924	11,105	2.2	4.1
Metro Comm Ch	1	5	9	12	0.0	0.0
Muslim Est	4	3,632	NR	13,192	2.6	4.9
New Apost Ch	1	NR	NR	NR	-	-
Non-denom Chr Chs	50	12,831	14,451	16,918	3.3	6.3
ORTHE–Greek Orthodox	1	250	NR	1,230	0.2	0.5
ORTHE–Ukrainian Orth	1	150	NR	400	0.1	0.1
PENT–Assemb of God	9	1,933	1,038	2,868	0.6	1.1
PENT–Ch God (Cleve)	8	306	557	719	0.1	0.3
PENT–Ch of God Proph	2	NR	59	76	0.0	0.0
PENT–COGIC	2	450	900	1,162	0.2	0.4
PENT–Full Gosp Bapt	1	NR	NR	NR	-	-
PENT–Int Foursq Gos	1	55	43	56	0.0	0.0
PENT–Open Bible Std	1	125	NR	125	0.0	0.0
PENT–Un Pent Ch Intl	4	NR	NR	NR	-	-
PENT–Vineyard	3	550	630	813	0.2	0.3
PRES–Evan Presby Ch	1	NR	699	902	0.2	0.3

NR–Not Reported - Represents no adherents reported. Percentages may not total 100 due to rounding.

Table 3: Religious Congregations by County and Group: 2010

Religious Group	Number of Congrega-tions	Number of Attendees	Number of Communicant, Confirmed, or Full Members	Adherents		
				Number of Adherents	% of Total Pop.	% of Total Adh.
PRES–Kor Pres Abroad	1	NR	NR	NR	-	-
PRES–Korean Amer Pres	1	NR	NR	NR	-	-
PRES–Korean Pres Amer	1	NR	NR	NR	-	-
PRES–Orth Pres Ch	1	135	106	140	0.0	0.1
PRES–Presb Ch (USA)	5	454	1,293	1,669	0.3	0.6
PRES–Presb Ch Amer	1	191	243	311	0.1	0.1
Salvation Army	3	179	206	850	0.2	0.3
Sev Day Adv	9	704	1,226	1,409	0.3	0.5
Un C of Christ	12	1,652	5,479	7,073	1.4	2.6
Unit Univ	2	271	466	621	0.1	0.2
Unity Ch	1	NR	NR	NR	-	-
Zoroastrian	0	NR	NR	5	0.0	0.0
KANKAKEE	**135**	**12,950**	**21,069**	**56,147**	**49.5**	**100.0**
ANG/EPIS–Episcopal	2	96	201	223	0.2	0.4
Bahá'í	0	NR	10	10	0.0	0.0
BAPT–Amer Bapt USA	1	40	191	237	0.2	0.4
BAPT–Consrv Bapt	1	NR	NR	NR	-	-
BAPT–Free Will Bapt	1	NR	86	107	0.1	0.2
BAPT–Ind Bapt Flwsp Intl	1	NR	NR	NR	-	-
BAPT–N Am Bapt Conf	1	NR	321	399	0.4	0.7
BAPT–Natl Mis Bapt Conv	1	500	500	621	0.5	1.1
BAPT–NBC USA	5	985	1,800	2,237	2.0	4.0
BAPT–Reg Bapt Gen As	1	NR	NR	NR	-	-
BAPT–So Bapt Conv	4	394	1,071	1,331	1.2	2.4
Catholic	18	NR	NR	27,840	24.5	49.6
CGOD–Ch God (Ander)	1	27	NR	27	0.0	0.0
Ch of Nazarene	10	2,955	3,155	4,590	4.0	8.2
CHR–Chr Ch (Disc)	2	64	192	239	0.2	0.4
CHR–Chr Chs & Chs Cr	4	NR	455	565	0.5	1.0
CHR–Chs of Christ	4	208	229	301	0.3	0.5
Evan Free Ch	1	582	NR	582	0.5	1.0
Int Cou Comm Ch	1	NR	NR	NR	-	-
Jehovah's Witness	2	NR	NR	NR	-	-
LDS–L-D Saints	1	NR	NR	390	0.3	0.7
LUTH–E.L.C.A.	3	292	744	930	0.8	1.7
LUTH–Luth–MO Synod	7	1,178	2,706	3,499	3.1	6.2
LUTH–Wisc Ev Luth Syn	2	121	190	235	0.2	0.4
MENN–Mennonite USA	1	20	25	31	0.0	0.1
METH–AME Zion	1	90	200	249	0.2	0.4
METH–Un Methodist	18	1,410	3,170	3,866	3.4	6.9
Non-denom Chr Chs	14	1,985	2,730	2,809	2.5	5.0
ORTHE–Greek Orthodox	1	25	NR	60	0.1	0.1
PENT–Assemb of God	2	65	43	70	0.1	0.1
PENT–Ch God (Cleve)	3	229	366	455	0.4	0.8
PENT–COGIC	1	50	300	373	0.3	0.7
PENT–Full Gosp Bapt	1	NR	NR	NR	-	-
PENT–Int Foursq Gos	1	25	18	22	0.0	0.0
PENT–Open Bible Std	1	322	NR	322	0.3	0.6
PENT–Un Pent Asbl God	1	NR	NR	NR	-	-
PENT–Un Pent Ch Intl	1	NR	NR	NR	-	-
PRES–Orth Pres Ch	1	47	40	56	0.0	0.1
PRES–Presb Ch (USA)	3	122	246	306	0.3	0.5
REF–Ref Ch in Am	4	696	957	1,204	1.1	2.1
Salvation Army	1	47	70	675	0.6	1.2
Sev Day Adv	3	144	250	288	0.3	0.5
Un C of Christ	3	231	803	998	0.9	1.8
KENDALL	**55**	**4,933**	**8,719**	**39,448**	**34.4**	**100.0**
ANG/EPIS–Anglican NA	1	NR	NR	NR	-	-
Bahá'í	0	NR	7	7	0.0	0.0
BAPT–Amer Bapt USA	2	88	226	302	0.3	0.8
BAPT–Converge/BGC	1	75	NR	90	0.1	0.2
BAPT–Reg Bapt Gen As	1	NR	NR	NR	-	-
BAPT–So Bapt Conv	3	122	265	354	0.3	0.9
BRETH–Ch of Brethren	1	40	133	178	0.2	0.5
BUDD–Theravada	1	NR	NR	300	0.3	0.8
BUDD–Vajrayana	1	NR	NR	14	0.0	0.0
Catholic	4	NR	NR	26,089	22.7	66.1
CHR–Chr Chs & Chs Cr	3	NR	378	505	0.4	1.3
CHR–Chs of Christ	1	30	35	35	0.0	0.1
Ind Fund Churches	1	NR	NR	NR	-	-
LDS–Comm of Christ	1	NR	121	121	0.1	0.3

Religious Group	Number of Congrega-tions	Number of Attendees	Number of Communicant, Confirmed, or Full Members	Adherents		
				Number of Adherents	% of Total Pop.	% of Total Adh.
LDS–L-D Saints	1	NR	NR	612	0.5	1.6
LUTH–Assoc Free Luth	4	NR	NR	NR	-	-
LUTH–E.L.C.A.	4	353	844	1,134	1.0	2.9
LUTH–Luth–MO Synod	3	1,043	1,935	2,350	2.0	6.0
MENN–Mennonite USA	1	15	20	27	0.0	0.1
METH–Un Methodist	7	608	1,956	2,514	2.2	6.4
Non-denom Chr Chs	6	985	905	1,259	1.1	3.2
PENT–Assemb of God	2	871	288	1,412	1.2	3.6
PENT–Ch God (Cleve)	2	37	112	150	0.1	0.4
PENT–Vineyard	1	70	105	140	0.1	0.4
PRES–Presb Ch (USA)	2	438	820	1,095	1.0	2.8
Un C of Christ	1	158	569	760	0.7	1.9
KNOX	**93**	**6,164**	**10,403**	**18,655**	**35.3**	**100.0**
ANG/EPIS–Anglican NA	1	NR	NR	NR	-	-
ANG/EPIS–Episcopal	1	14	26	33	0.1	0.2
Bahá'í	0	NR	21	21	0.0	0.1
BAPT–Amer Bapt USA	1	110	321	381	0.7	2.0
BAPT–Converge/BGC	1	800	NR	960	1.8	5.1
BAPT–NBC Amer	1	50	90	107	0.2	0.6
BAPT–Reg Bapt Gen As	1	NR	NR	NR	-	-
BAPT–So Bapt Conv	6	187	350	416	0.8	2.2
Catholic	6	NR	NR	3,347	6.3	17.9
CGOD–Ch God (Ander)	1	140	NR	140	0.3	0.8
Ch Cr, Scientst	1	NR	NR	NR	-	-
Ch of Nazarene	3	301	319	575	1.1	3.1
CHR–Chr Ch (Disc)	3	325	1,083	1,286	2.4	6.9
CHR–Chs of Christ	2	65	60	85	0.2	0.5
CONG–Cong Chr, NA	3	NR	269	319	0.6	1.7
Evan Cov Ch	1	151	258	196	0.4	1.1
Intl Fell Bible Ch	1	NR	NR	NR	-	-
Jehovah's Witness	1	NR	NR	NR	-	-
JUD–Reform	1	16	28	76	0.1	0.4
LDS–Comm of Christ	1	NR	119	119	0.2	0.6
LDS–L-D Saints	1	NR	NR	510	1.0	2.7
LUTH–E.L.C.A.	5	510	1,706	2,535	4.8	13.6
LUTH–Luth–MO Synod	1	140	150	192	0.4	1.0
LUTH–Nor Amer Luth C	1	NR	NR	NR	-	-
METH–AME	1	100	250	297	0.6	1.6
METH–Free Methodist	1	31	35	35	0.1	0.2
METH–Un Methodist	15	1,113	2,560	3,303	6.2	17.7
METH–Wesleyan	1	71	23	92	0.2	0.5
Non-denom Chr Chs	12	905	1,214	1,304	2.5	7.0
PENT–Assemb of God	2	309	132	486	0.9	2.6
PENT–Ch God (Cleve)	1	40	90	107	0.2	0.6
PENT–Ch of God Proph	1	NR	59	70	0.1	0.4
PENT–COGIC	1	30	15	18	0.0	0.1
PENT–Int Foursq Gos	1	72	108	128	0.2	0.7
PENT–Open Bible Std	1	113	NR	113	0.2	0.6
PENT–Un Pent Asbl God	1	NR	NR	NR	-	-
PENT–Un Pent Ch Intl	2	NR	NR	NR	-	-
PRES–Presb Ch (USA)	5	389	811	963	1.8	5.2
Salvation Army	1	74	77	173	0.3	0.9
Sev Day Adv	1	68	118	136	0.3	0.7
Un C of Christ	2	40	111	132	0.2	0.7
LAKE	**402**	**82,970**	**105,067**	**379,104**	**53.9**	**100.0**
ANG/EPIS–Anglican NA	2	NR	NR	NR	-	-
ANG/EPIS–Episcopal	12	2,100	4,505	5,877	0.8	1.6
Bahá'í	7	NR	391	391	0.1	0.1
BAPT–Amer Bapt USA	4	338	534	674	0.1	0.2
BAPT–Converge/BGC	12	2,600	NR	3,120	0.4	0.8
BAPT–N Am Bapt Conf	1	NR	40	50	0.0	0.0
BAPT–Natl Mis Bapt Conv	1	35	500	631	0.1	0.2
BAPT–NBC Amer	1	0	150	189	0.0	0.0
BAPT–NBC USA	6	1,400	4,475	5,647	0.8	1.5
BAPT–Ref Bapt Ch	1	NR	NR	NR	-	-
BAPT–Reg Bapt Gen As	2	NR	NR	NR	-	-
BAPT–So Bapt Conv	22	1,236	2,287	2,886	0.4	0.8
BUDD–Mahayana	1	NR	NR	20	0.0	0.0
Calv Chpl	2	NR	NR	NR	-	-
Catholic	29	NR	NR	211,380	30.0	55.8
Ch Cr, Scientst	5	NR	NR	NR	-	-

NR–Not Reported - Represents no adherents reported. Percentages may not total 100 due to rounding.

Table 3: Religious Congregations by County and Group: 2010

Religious Group	Number of Congrega-tions	Number of Attendees	Number of Communicant, Confirmed, or Full Members	Adherents: Number of Adherents	Adherents: % of Total Pop.	Adherents: % of Total Adh.
Ch God (7th Day)	1	NR	NR	NR	-	-
Ch of Nazarene	5	369	409	540	0.1	0.1
Chr & Miss Al	1	190	160	220	0.0	0.1
CHR–Chr Ch (Disc)	2	156	416	525	0.1	0.1
CHR–Chr Chs & Chs Cr	4	NR	1,190	1,502	0.2	0.4
CHR–Chs of Christ	9	803	667	917	0.1	0.2
CONG–Cong Chr, NA	1	NR	511	645	0.1	0.2
CONG–Consrv Cong Chr	1	65	72	91	0.0	0.0
Evan Assoc RCC	1	NR	NR	NR	-	-
Evan Cong Ch	2	NR	39	49	0.0	0.0
Evan Cov Ch	3	249	281	324	0.0	0.1
Evan Free Ch	13	3,069	NR	3,069	0.4	0.8
FRND–Fr Gen Cf	1	NR	140	177	0.0	0.0
HINDU–I/A Temples	3	NR	NR	450	0.1	0.1
Ind Fund Churches	3	NR	NR	NR	-	-
Jehovah's Witness	8	NR	NR	NR	-	-
JUD–Conserv	5	2,375	2,666	7,198	1.0	1.9
JUD–Orth	5	288	250	400	0.1	0.1
JUD–Reform	8	2,293	4,044	10,919	1.6	2.9
LDS–Comm of Christ	1	NR	121	121	0.0	0.0
LDS–L-D Saints	8	NR	NR	3,686	0.5	1.0
LUTH–E.L.C.A.	19	4,145	9,380	12,702	1.8	3.4
LUTH–Luth Cong Msn Chr	1	460	1,502	1,895	0.3	0.5
LUTH–Luth–MO Synod	10	1,752	4,071	5,277	0.8	1.4
LUTH–Wisc Ev Luth Syn	7	1,145	2,000	2,580	0.4	0.7
MENN–Mennonite USA	1	40	57	72	0.0	0.0
METH–AME	5	0	550	694	0.1	0.2
METH–Free Methodist	1	148	98	148	0.0	0.0
METH–Un Methodist	18	1,895	4,840	6,375	0.9	1.7
METH–Wesleyan	1	73	65	95	0.0	0.0
Missionary Ch	4	1,590	652	1,600	0.2	0.4
MJEW–Union Mes Cong	3	NR	NR	NR	-	-
Muslim Est	3	2,724	NR	9,894	1.4	2.6
New Apost Ch	1	NR	NR	NR	-	-
Non-denom Chr Chs	60	43,332	45,807	54,850	7.8	14.5
ORTHE–Greek Orthodox	2	455	NR	1,390	0.2	0.4
ORTHE–Serb Orth USA	4	740	NR	2,820	0.4	0.7
ORTHO–Armen Ap Cilic	1	35	NR	100	0.0	0.0
ORTHO–Armen Ap Etchm	1	20	NR	300	0.0	0.1
PENT–Assemb of God	9	1,416	611	1,912	0.3	0.5
PENT–Ch God (Cleve)	7	359	477	602	0.1	0.2
PENT–Ch of God Proph	2	NR	134	169	0.0	0.0
PENT–COGIC	3	345	525	663	0.1	0.2
PENT–Int Foursq Gos	2	107	71	90	0.0	0.0
PENT–Un Pent Ch Intl	1	NR	NR	NR	-	-
PENT–Vineyard	2	575	650	820	0.1	0.2
PRES–Evan Presby Ch	1	NR	136	172	0.0	0.0
PRES–Kor Pres Abroad	1	NR	NR	NR	-	-
PRES–Korean Amer Pres	3	NR	NR	NR	-	-
PRES–Korean Pres Amer	3	NR	NR	NR	-	-
PRES–Orth Pres Ch	1	64	40	56	0.0	0.0
PRES–Presb Ch (USA)	9	2,190	5,964	7,526	1.1	2.0
PRES–Presb Ch Amer	2	122	136	163	0.0	0.0
PRES–Ref Pres of NA	1	20	23	30	0.0	0.0
Salvation Army	1	53	58	158	0.0	0.0
Sev Day Adv	5	522	909	1,044	0.1	0.3
Sikh	1	NR	NR	NR	-	-
Un C of Christ	10	862	1,954	2,466	0.4	0.7
Unit Univ	2	215	509	732	0.1	0.2
Unity Ch	1	NR	NR	NR	-	-
Zoroastrian	0	NR	NR	11	0.0	0.0
LASALLE	**154**	**7,793**	**16,648**	**53,555**	**47.0**	**100.0**
ANG/EPIS–Episcopal	3	93	179	179	0.2	0.3
Bahá'í	0	NR	6	6	0.0	0.0
BAPT–Amer Bapt USA	3	112	143	173	0.2	0.3
BAPT–Consrv Bapt	1	NR	NR	NR	-	-
BAPT–Converge/BGC	1	75	NR	90	0.1	0.2
BAPT–Reg Bapt Gen As	2	NR	NR	NR	-	-
BAPT–So Bapt Conv	6	308	785	952	0.8	1.8
Catholic	29	NR	NR	30,429	26.7	56.8
CGOD–Ch God (Ander)	1	40	NR	40	0.0	0.1
Ch Cr, Scientst	1	NR	NR	NR	-	-
Ch of Nazarene	7	1,045	936	1,650	1.4	3.1

Religious Group	Number of Congrega-tions	Number of Attendees	Number of Communicant, Confirmed, or Full Members	Adherents: Number of Adherents	Adherents: % of Total Pop.	Adherents: % of Total Adh.
CHR–Chr Chs & Chs Cr	3	NR	1,180	1,431	1.3	2.7
CHR–Chs of Christ	2	108	101	130	0.1	0.2
Evan Ch	1	NR	NR	NR	-	-
Evan Free Ch	2	135	NR	135	0.1	0.3
Ind Fund Churches	1	NR	NR	NR	-	-
Jehovah's Witness	5	NR	NR	NR	-	-
LDS–Comm of Christ	2	NR	242	242	0.2	0.5
LDS–L-D Saints	1	NR	NR	441	0.4	0.8
LUTH–Assoc Free Luth	4	NR	NR	NR	-	-
LUTH–Ch of Luth Br	1	100	67	260	0.2	0.5
LUTH–E.L.C.A.	10	1,183	3,990	4,995	4.4	9.3
LUTH–Luth Cong Msn Chr	1	80	306	371	0.3	0.7
LUTH–Luth–MO Synod	4	347	747	995	0.9	1.9
METH–Prim Meth Ch	1	NR	NR	NR	-	-
METH–Un Methodist	21	1,443	4,044	5,451	4.8	10.2
Non-denom Chr Chs	12	1,205	1,385	1,607	1.4	3.0
PENT–Assemb of God	5	686	333	855	0.8	1.6
PENT–Ch God (Cleve)	1	24	46	56	0.0	0.1
PENT–Elim	1	NR	NR	NR	-	-
PENT–Int Foursq Gos	2	131	136	165	0.1	0.3
PENT–Open Bible Std	1	80	NR	80	0.1	0.1
PENT–Pent Ch of God	1	70	NR	109	0.1	0.2
PENT–Un Pent Ch Intl	3	NR	NR	NR	-	-
PRES–Presb Ch (USA)	6	132	951	1,154	1.0	2.2
Salvation Army	2	29	65	350	0.3	0.7
Sev Day Adv	3	100	173	199	0.2	0.4
Un C of Christ	4	267	833	1,010	0.9	1.9
LAWRENCE	**53**	**2,042**	**4,650**	**6,718**	**39.9**	**100.0**
BAPT–So Bapt Conv	2	143	580	679	4.0	10.1
BRETH–Ch of Brethren	1	31	58	68	0.4	1.0
Catholic	2	NR	NR	610	3.6	9.1
CGOD–Ch God (Ander)	1	18	NR	18	0.1	0.3
CHR–Chr Ch (Disc)	1	50	246	288	1.7	4.3
CHR–Chr Chs & Chs Cr	8	NR	1,082	1,267	7.5	18.9
CHR–Chs of Christ	2	21	15	20	0.1	0.3
LUTH–Luth–MO Synod	1	28	48	60	0.4	0.9
MENN–Amish Undif	0	NR	3	9	0.1	0.1
METH–AME	1	12	16	19	0.1	0.3
METH–Free Methodist	5	261	229	270	1.6	4.0
METH–Un Methodist	18	814	1,463	2,318	13.8	34.5
METH–Wesleyan	2	109	68	142	0.8	2.1
Non-denom Chr Chs	1	275	450	450	2.7	6.7
PENT–Assemb of God	1	78	70	123	0.7	1.8
PENT–Ch God (Cleve)	2	123	194	227	1.3	3.4
PENT–Un Pent Ch Intl	1	NR	NR	NR	-	-
PRES–Presb Ch (USA)	4	79	128	150	0.9	2.2
LEE	**61**	**3,213**	**8,011**	**18,364**	**51.0**	**100.0**
ANG/EPIS–Episcopal	1	79	101	151	0.4	0.8
Bahá'í	0	NR	3	3	0.0	0.0
BAPT–Amer Bapt USA	3	190	344	409	1.1	2.2
BAPT–So Bapt Conv	3	374	756	900	2.5	4.9
BRETH–Ch of Brethren	2	101	384	457	1.3	2.5
Catholic	9	NR	NR	8,379	23.3	45.6
CGOD–Ch God (Ander)	1	0	NR	0	0.0	0.0
Ch Cr, Scientst	1	NR	NR	NR	-	-
Ch of Nazarene	1	56	33	104	0.3	0.6
Chr & Miss Al	1	109	44	135	0.4	0.7
CHR–Chr Ch (Disc)	1	0	130	155	0.4	0.8
CHR–Chs of Christ	1	28	26	34	0.1	0.2
Evan Cong Ch	2	NR	166	198	0.5	1.1
Evan Free Ch	1	130	NR	130	0.4	0.7
Jehovah's Witness	1	NR	NR	NR	-	-
LUTH–E.L.C.A.	7	680	2,491	3,039	8.4	16.5
LUTH–Luth Cong Msn Chr	2	138	564	671	1.9	3.7
LUTH–Luth–MO Synod	1	81	131	170	0.5	0.9
METH–C.M.E.	1	0	100	119	0.3	0.6
METH–Un Methodist	10	634	1,800	2,161	6.0	11.8
Non-denom Chr Chs	5	395	470	550	1.5	3.0
PENT–Assemb of God	1	125	83	141	0.4	0.8
PENT–Int Foursq Gos	1	28	32	38	0.1	0.2
PRES–Presb Ch (USA)	3	30	249	296	0.8	1.6

NR–Not Reported   - Represents no adherents reported.   Percentages may not total 100 due to rounding.

Table 3: Religious Congregations by County and Group: 2010

Religious Group	Number of Congrega-tions	Number of Attendees	Number of Communicant, Confirmed, or Full Members	Adherents: Number of Adherents	Adherents: % of Total Pop.	Adherents: % of Total Adh.
Un C of Christ	2	35	104	124	0.3	0.7
LIVINGSTON	**74**	**5,744**	**10,640**	**19,270**	**49.5**	**100.0**
ANG/EPIS–Episcopal	1	32	65	89	0.2	0.5
Ap Chr Ch-Amer	2	1,402	642	1,402	3.6	7.3
Bahá'í	0	NR	5	5	0.0	0.0
BAPT–Amer Bapt USA	5	711	1,472	1,773	4.6	9.2
BAPT–Reg Bapt Gen As	2	NR	NR	NR	-	-
Catholic	10	NR	NR	4,564	11.7	23.7
Ch of Nazarene	3	74	107	173	0.4	0.9
CHR–Chr Ch (Disc)	3	102	335	403	1.0	2.1
CHR–Chr Chs & Chs Cr	2	NR	100	120	0.3	0.6
CHR–Chs of Christ	2	91	63	98	0.3	0.5
Jehovah's Witness	1	NR	NR	NR	-	-
LDS–L-D Saints	1	NR	NR	244	0.6	1.3
LUTH–E.L.C.A.	8	709	2,401	2,960	7.6	15.4
LUTH–Luth Cong Msn Chr	1	101	556	670	1.7	3.5
LUTH–Luth-MO Synod	3	230	234	869	2.2	4.5
LUTH–Nor Amer Luth C	2	NR	NR	NR	-	-
MENN–Mennonite USA	1	115	124	149	0.4	0.8
METH–Un Methodist	13	960	2,894	3,630	9.3	18.8
Non-denom Chr Chs	4	660	725	862	2.2	4.5
PENT–Assemb of God	3	224	131	312	0.8	1.6
PENT–Ch God (Cleve)	1	45	57	69	0.2	0.4
PENT–Un Pent Ch Intl	1	NR	NR	NR	-	-
PRES–Presb Ch (USA)	2	187	425	512	1.3	2.7
Un C of Christ	3	101	304	366	0.9	1.9
LOGAN	**59**	**2,740**	**9,886**	**14,062**	**46.4**	**100.0**
ANG/EPIS–Episcopal	1	40	90	104	0.3	0.7
Bahá'í	0	NR	6	6	0.0	0.0
BAPT–Amer Bapt USA	1	95	157	185	0.6	1.3
BAPT–Ind Bapt Flwsp Intl	1	NR	NR	NR	-	-
BAPT–So Bapt Conv	1	40	89	105	0.3	0.7
Catholic	4	NR	NR	2,282	7.5	16.2
Ch of Nazarene	1	46	93	93	0.3	0.7
CHR–Chr Chs & Chs Cr	11	NR	3,293	3,883	12.8	27.6
CHR–Chs of Christ	1	30	20	30	0.1	0.2
Ind Fund Churches	1	NR	NR	NR	-	-
Jehovah's Witness	1	NR	NR	NR	-	-
LUTH–Assoc Free Luth	3	NR	NR	NR	-	-
LUTH–E.L.C.A.	3	219	694	881	2.9	6.3
LUTH–Luth Cong Msn Chr	1	170	662	781	2.6	5.6
LUTH–Luth-MO Synod	5	643	1,516	1,812	6.0	12.9
METH–AME	1	0	150	177	0.6	1.3
METH–Un Methodist	11	433	1,452	1,735	5.7	12.3
Non-denom Chr Chs	5	730	870	981	3.2	7.0
PENT–Assemb of God	1	47	32	66	0.2	0.5
PENT–Ch God (Cleve)	1	70	95	112	0.4	0.8
PENT–Un Pent Ch Intl	1	NR	NR	NR	-	-
PRES–Cumber Presb	1	NR	35	84	0.3	0.6
PRES–Presb Ch (USA)	2	90	212	250	0.8	1.8
Un C of Christ	1	87	420	495	1.6	3.5
MCDONOUGH	**56**	**3,654**	**6,885**	**12,196**	**37.4**	**100.0**
ANG/EPIS–Anglican NA	1	NR	NR	NR	-	-
ANG/EPIS–Episcopal	1	15	22	22	0.1	0.2
Bahá'í	0	NR	11	11	0.0	0.1
BAPT–Amer Bapt USA	3	227	424	485	1.5	4.0
BAPT–Consrv Bapt	1	NR	NR	NR	-	-
BAPT–So Bapt Conv	1	48	105	120	0.4	1.0
Catholic	3	NR	NR	1,445	4.4	11.8
Ch of God Gen Conf	1	NR	41	47	0.1	0.4
Ch of Nazarene	2	76	96	128	0.4	1.0
CHR–Chr Ch (Disc)	2	93	837	958	2.9	7.9
CHR–Chr Chs & Chs Cr	6	NR	1,475	1,688	5.2	13.8
CHR–Chs of Christ	1	85	80	90	0.3	0.7
Ind Fund Churches	1	NR	NR	NR	-	-
Jehovah's Witness	1	NR	NR	NR	-	-
LDS–L-D Saints	1	NR	NR	373	1.1	3.1
LUTH–E.L.C.A.	1	82	170	233	0.7	1.9
LUTH–Luth-MO Synod	1	95	189	220	0.7	1.8
MENN–Amish Undif	2	NR	116	302	0.9	2.5

Religious Group	Number of Congrega-tions	Number of Attendees	Number of Communicant, Confirmed, or Full Members	Adherents: Number of Adherents	Adherents: % of Total Pop.	Adherents: % of Total Adh.
METH–Un Methodist	9	729	1,785	1,927	5.9	15.8
Muslim Est	1	908	NR	1,649	5.1	13.5
Non-denom Chr Chs	3	400	360	501	1.5	4.1
PENT–Assemb of God	3	297	200	592	1.8	4.9
PENT–COGIC	1	0	50	57	0.2	0.5
PENT–Int Foursq Gos	1	109	102	117	0.4	1.0
PENT–Open Bible Std	1	53	NR	53	0.2	0.4
PENT–Vineyard	1	85	100	114	0.3	0.9
PRES–Presb Ch (USA)	5	279	661	756	2.3	6.2
Salvation Army	1	23	16	238	0.7	2.0
Unit Univ	1	50	45	70	0.2	0.6
MCHENRY	**160**	**20,697**	**33,817**	**165,699**	**53.7**	**100.0**
ANG/EPIS–Episcopal	3	270	465	724	0.2	0.4
Bahá'í	1	NR	73	73	0.0	0.0
BAPT–Amer Bapt USA	2	206	533	671	0.2	0.4
BAPT–Converge/BGC	4	1,025	NR	1,230	0.4	0.7
BAPT–Reg Bapt Gen As	1	NR	NR	NR	-	-
BAPT–So Bapt Conv	8	427	620	780	0.3	0.5
Catholic	17	NR	NR	108,465	35.1	65.5
Ch Cr, Scientst	3	NR	NR	NR	-	-
Ch of Nazarene	2	76	121	193	0.1	0.1
Chr & Miss Al	1	149	95	203	0.1	0.1
CHR–Chr Chs & Chs Cr	2	NR	250	315	0.1	0.2
CHR–Chs of Christ	1	100	80	95	0.0	0.1
Evan Cov Ch	1	167	156	217	0.1	0.1
Evan Free Ch	4	1,340	NR	1,340	0.4	0.8
FRND–Fr Gen Cf	1	NR	25	31	0.0	0.0
HINDU–Post Ren	1	NR	NR	77	0.0	0.0
Ind Fund Churches	2	NR	NR	NR	-	-
Jehovah's Witness	4	NR	NR	NR	-	-
JUD–Conserv	1	71	80	216	0.1	0.1
JUD–Reform	1	14	24	65	0.0	0.0
LDS–Comm of Christ	1	NR	121	121	0.0	0.1
LDS–L-D Saints	4	NR	NR	1,449	0.5	0.9
LUTH–E.L.C.A.	13	3,549	9,627	13,277	4.3	8.0
LUTH–Luth-MO Synod	13	2,956	7,339	9,918	3.2	6.0
LUTH–Wisc Ev Luth Syn	1	151	245	337	0.1	0.2
METH–Free Methodist	1	107	165	165	0.1	0.1
METH–Un Methodist	13	1,613	3,880	5,739	1.9	3.5
Muslim Est	2	1,816	NR	6,596	2.1	4.0
Non-denom Chr Chs	13	3,860	4,525	5,461	1.8	3.3
ORTHE–Greek Orthodox	1	50	NR	54	0.0	0.0
PENT–Assemb of God	7	896	413	1,169	0.4	0.7
PENT–Ch of God Proph	1	NR	54	68	0.0	0.0
PENT–Int Foursq Gos	1	89	167	210	0.1	0.1
PENT–Pent Ch of God	2	140	NR	217	0.1	0.1
PENT–Un Pent Ch Intl	6	NR	NR	NR	-	-
PENT–Vineyard	1	48	65	82	0.0	0.0
PRES–Orth Pres Ch	1	0	0	0	0.0	0.0
PRES–Presb Ch (USA)	6	396	1,438	1,810	0.6	1.1
REF–Christian Ref	1	80	36	45	0.0	0.0
Salvation Army	1	49	46	287	0.1	0.2
Sev Day Adv	1	27	47	54	0.0	0.0
Un C of Christ	8	938	2,966	3,733	1.2	2.3
Unit Univ	1	87	161	212	0.1	0.1
Unity Ch	1	NR	NR	NR	-	-
MCLEAN	**181**	**26,085**	**45,354**	**81,774**	**48.2**	**100.0**
ANG/EPIS–Episcopal	2	211	428	702	0.4	0.9
Ap Chr Ch-Amer	2	1,094	667	1,094	0.6	1.3
Bahá'í	1	NR	64	64	0.0	0.1
BAPT–Amer Bapt USA	5	359	752	913	0.5	1.1
BAPT–Converge/BGC	1	75	NR	90	0.1	0.1
BAPT–Natl Mis Bapt Conv	1	150	250	303	0.2	0.4
BAPT–Ref Bapt Ch	1	NR	NR	NR	-	-
BAPT–So Bapt Conv	7	966	1,329	1,613	1.0	2.0
BUDD–Mahayana	2	NR	NR	113	0.1	0.1
Catholic	10	NR	NR	15,215	9.0	18.6
CGOD–Ch God (Ander)	2	273	NR	273	0.2	0.3
Ch Cr, Scientst	1	NR	NR	NR	-	-
Ch of Nazarene	3	326	304	600	0.4	0.7
Chr & Miss Al	1	16	12	43	0.0	0.1

NR–Not Reported - Represents no adherents reported. Percentages may not total 100 due to rounding.

Table 3: Religious Congregations by County and Group: 2010

Religious Group	Number of Congrega-tions	Number of Attendees	Number of Communicant, Confirmed, or Full Members	Adherents: Number of Adherents	Adherents: % of Total Pop.	Adherents: % of Total Adh.
CHR–Chr Ch (Disc)	10	624	2,573	3,122	1.8	3.8
CHR–Chr Chs & Chs Cr	8	NR	6,356	7,713	4.5	9.4
CHR–Chs of Christ	6	518	441	545	0.3	0.7
CHR–Int Chs of Christ	1	NR	87	106	0.1	0.1
Evan Free Ch	1	500	NR	500	0.3	0.6
FRND–Fr Gen Cf	1	NR	14	17	0.0	0.0
HINDU–Post Ren	1	NR	NR	16	0.0	0.0
Jehovah's Witness	2	NR	NR	NR	-	-
JUD–Reform	1	49	86	232	0.1	0.3
LDS–Comm of Christ	1	NR	82	82	0.0	0.1
LDS–L-D Saints	2	NR	NR	1,146	0.7	1.4
LUTH–E.L.C.A.	6	1,367	3,449	4,484	2.6	5.5
LUTH–Luth Cong Msn Chr	2	10	11	13	0.0	0.0
LUTH–Luth–MO Synod	7	1,938	4,080	5,538	3.3	6.8
LUTH–Wisc Ev Luth Syn	1	61	102	120	0.1	0.1
MENN–Fel Evg Ch	3	648	188	228	0.1	0.3
MENN–Mennonite USA	4	348	489	593	0.3	0.7
METH–AME	1	60	125	152	0.1	0.2
METH–C.M.E.	2	0	200	243	0.1	0.3
METH–Un Methodist	21	3,089	7,061	9,881	5.8	12.1
Muslim Est	2	1,816	NR	6,596	3.9	8.1
Nat Spirit Asso	1	NR	NR	NR	-	-
Non-denom Chr Chs	30	8,544	11,513	12,279	7.2	15.0
ORTHE–Orth Ch in Amer	1	34	NR	58	0.0	0.1
PENT–Assemb of God	3	982	465	1,656	1.0	2.0
PENT–Ch God (Cleve)	1	46	98	119	0.1	0.1
PENT–COGIC	1	0	150	182	0.1	0.2
PENT–Int Foursq Gos	1	30	183	222	0.1	0.3
PENT–Un Pent Ch Intl	3	NR	NR	NR	-	-
PENT–Vineyard	1	25	25	30	0.0	0.0
PRES–Presb Ch (USA)	9	1,237	2,834	3,439	2.0	4.2
PRES–Presb Ch Amer	1	292	299	410	0.2	0.5
Salvation Army	1	67	81	316	0.2	0.4
Sev Day Adv	2	68	119	137	0.1	0.2
Un C of Christ	2	158	202	245	0.1	0.3
Unit Univ	1	104	235	331	0.2	0.4
Unity Ch	1	NR	NR	NR	-	-
MACON	**164**	**16,894**	**29,799**	**54,303**	**49.0**	**100.0**
ANG/EPIS–Episcopal	1	94	158	218	0.2	0.4
Bahá'í	1	NR	41	41	0.0	0.1
BAPT–Amer Bapt USA	1	150	554	672	0.6	1.2
BAPT–Free Will Bapt	1	NR	86	104	0.1	0.2
BAPT–NBC USA	2	250	350	425	0.4	0.8
BAPT–NT Ind Bapt	1	NR	NR	NR	-	-
BAPT–Reg Bapt Gen As	3	NR	NR	NR	-	-
BAPT–So Bapt Conv	13	1,323	2,351	2,852	2.6	5.3
BRETH–Ch of Brethren	2	32	139	169	0.2	0.3
BUDD–Vajrayana	1	NR	NR	208	0.2	0.4
Catholic	5	NR	NR	11,451	10.3	21.1
CGOD–Ch God (Ander)	5	256	NR	256	0.2	0.5
CGOD–Ches God-Gen Con	6	1,229	1,390	1,686	1.5	3.1
Ch Cr, Scientist	1	NR	NR	NR	-	-
Ch of Nazarene	5	911	1,108	1,336	1.2	2.5
CHR–Chr Ch (Disc)	7	522	1,928	2,339	2.1	4.3
CHR–Chr Chs & Chs Cr	7	NR	1,972	2,392	2.2	4.4
CHR–Chs of Christ	3	420	590	641	0.6	1.2
FRND–Fr Gen Cf	1	NR	0	0	0.0	0.0
Ind Fund Churches	2	NR	NR	NR	-	-
Jehovah's Witness	1	NR	NR	NR	-	-
LDS–Comm of Christ	1	NR	82	82	0.1	0.2
LDS–L-D Saints	2	NR	NR	804	0.7	1.5
LUTH–E.L.C.A.	2	214	618	778	0.7	1.4
LUTH–Luth–MO Synod	6	1,622	4,102	5,389	4.9	9.9
METH–AME	1	150	300	364	0.3	0.7
METH–C.M.E.	1	75	150	182	0.2	0.3
METH–Free Methodist	1	280	210	280	0.3	0.5
METH–Un Methodist	20	1,666	3,845	5,322	4.8	9.8
METH–Wesleyan	1	24	12	31	0.0	0.1
Muslim Est	1	908	NR	3,298	3.0	6.1
Non-denom Chr Chs	22	4,075	5,060	5,760	5.2	10.6
ORTHE–Greek Orthodox	1	50	NR	125	0.1	0.2
PENT–Assemb of God	4	542	318	846	0.8	1.6
PENT–Ch God (Cleve)	1	54	161	195	0.2	0.4
PENT–COGIC	5	100	600	728	0.7	1.3
PENT–Full Gosp Bapt	5	NR	NR	NR	-	-
PENT–Int Foursq Gos	4	767	1,143	1,387	1.3	2.6
PENT–Un Pent Ch Intl	2	NR	NR	NR	-	-
PRES–Presb Ch (USA)	7	813	1,658	2,011	1.8	3.7
Salvation Army	1	82	120	1,030	0.9	1.9
Sev Day Adv	2	101	176	202	0.2	0.4
Un C of Christ	2	152	529	642	0.6	1.2
Unit Univ	1	32	48	57	0.1	0.1
Unity Ch	2	NR	NR	NR	-	-
MACOUPIN	**112**	**5,111**	**13,746**	**25,600**	**53.6**	**100.0**
ANG/EPIS–Episcopal	2	35	41	69	0.1	0.3
Bahá'í	0	NR	8	8	0.0	0.0
BAPT–Amer Bapt Assn	1	NR	85	103	0.2	0.4
BAPT–Amer Bapt USA	5	223	372	449	0.9	1.8
BAPT–Reg Bapt Gen As	2	NR	NR	NR	-	-
BAPT–So Bapt Conv	20	1,361	3,939	4,756	10.0	18.6
BRETH–Ch of Brethren	2	113	221	267	0.6	1.0
Catholic	9	NR	NR	7,707	16.1	30.1
Ch of Nazarene	2	95	115	134	0.3	0.5
CHR–Chr Ch (Disc)	3	206	786	949	2.0	3.7
CHR–Chr Chs & Chs Cr	9	NR	997	1,204	2.5	4.7
CHR–Chs of Christ	3	29	31	38	0.1	0.1
LDS–Comm of Christ	1	NR	82	82	0.2	0.3
LUTH–E.L.C.A.	5	305	808	1,109	2.3	4.3
LUTH–Luth–MO Synod	6	780	2,386	3,100	6.5	12.1
METH–Un Methodist	17	728	2,063	2,820	5.9	11.0
Non-denom Chr Chs	5	265	290	356	0.7	1.4
ORTHE–Rus Orth Moscow	1	15	NR	40	0.1	0.2
PENT–Assemb of God	6	354	264	672	1.4	2.6
PENT–Int Foursq Gos	1	83	75	91	0.2	0.4
PENT–Pent Ch of God	2	140	NR	217	0.5	0.8
PENT–Un Pent Ch Intl	3	NR	NR	NR	-	-
PRES–Presb Ch (USA)	4	113	187	226	0.5	0.9
Un C of Christ	3	266	996	1,203	2.5	4.7
MADISON	**357**	**34,333**	**69,882**	**131,105**	**48.7**	**100.0**
ANG/EPIS–Episcopal	4	234	521	705	0.3	0.5
Bahá'í	1	NR	139	139	0.1	0.1
BAPT–Amer Bapt Assn	2	NR	150	182	0.1	0.1
BAPT–Amer Bapt USA	15	877	1,723	2,088	0.8	1.6
BAPT–Consrv Bapt	1	NR	NR	NR	-	-
BAPT–Converge/BGC	1	75	NR	90	0.0	0.1
BAPT–Free Will Bapt	3	NR	258	313	0.1	0.2
BAPT–Natl Mis Bapt Conv	2	0	500	606	0.2	0.5
BAPT–NBC USA	4	350	1,325	1,605	0.6	1.2
BAPT–Reg Bapt Gen As	7	NR	NR	NR	-	-
BAPT–So Bapt Conv	48	7,264	19,630	23,784	8.8	18.1
Calv Chpl	2	NR	NR	NR	-	-
Catholic	20	NR	NR	37,243	13.8	28.4
CGOD–Ch God (Ander)	5	237	NR	237	0.1	0.2
Ch Cr, Scientst	2	NR	NR	NR	-	-
Ch of Nazarene	6	412	769	977	0.4	0.7
CHR–Chr Ch (Disc)	3	166	432	523	0.2	0.4
CHR–Chr Chs & Chs Cr	10	NR	1,756	2,128	0.8	1.6
CHR–Chs of Christ	13	1,594	1,450	1,830	0.7	1.4
CONG–Consrv Cong Chr	1	148	238	288	0.1	0.2
Jehovah's Witness	7	NR	NR	NR	-	-
JUD–Reform	1	7	12	32	0.0	0.0
LDS–Comm of Christ	2	NR	220	220	0.1	0.2
LDS–L-D Saints	3	NR	NR	1,460	0.5	1.1
LUTH–E.L.C.A.	4	419	979	1,306	0.5	1.0
LUTH–Luth–MO Synod	22	4,119	10,820	13,677	5.1	10.4
LUTH–Wisc Ev Luth Syn	1	0	0	0	0.0	0.0
METH–AME	7	115	675	818	0.3	0.6
METH–C.M.E.	1	0	100	121	0.0	0.1
METH–Free Methodist	3	406	276	406	0.2	0.3
METH–Un Methodist	23	3,395	6,372	8,168	3.0	6.2
Muslim Est	1	908	NR	3,298	1.2	2.5
Non-denom Chr Chs	40	6,107	8,012	8,797	3.3	6.7
OCATH–Pol Natl Cath	1	NR	NR	NR	-	-
ORTHE–Bulgar Orth USA	1	0	NR	0	0.0	0.0

NR–Not Reported   - Represents no adherents reported.   Percentages may not total 100 due to rounding.

Table 3: Religious Congregations by County and Group: 2010

Religious Group	Number of Congrega-tions	Number of Attendees	Number of Communicant, Confirmed, or Full Members	Adherents: Number of Adherents	Adherents: % of Total Pop.	Adherents: % of Total Adh.
ORTHE–Orth Ch in Amer	2	140	NR	190	0.1	0.1
ORTHO–Armen Ap Cilic	1	60	NR	400	0.1	0.3
PENT–Assemb of God	21	2,396	1,318	3,426	1.3	2.6
PENT–Ch God (Cleve)	5	603	716	868	0.3	0.7
PENT–Ch Lord Jesus Apos	1	NR	NR	NR	-	-
PENT–Ch of God Proph	2	NR	75	91	0.0	0.1
PENT–COGIC	6	250	654	792	0.3	0.6
PENT–Int Foursq Gos	1	72	335	406	0.2	0.3
PENT–Pent Ch of God	3	210	NR	326	0.1	0.2
PENT–Un Pent Ch Intl	8	NR	NR	NR	-	-
PRES–Presb Ch (USA)	13	931	2,013	2,439	0.9	1.9
PRES–Presb Ch Amer	4	378	342	438	0.2	0.3
Salvation Army	2	104	194	1,122	0.4	0.9
Sev Day Adv	1	34	60	69	0.0	0.1
Un C of Christ	17	2,232	7,689	9,316	3.5	7.1
Unit Univ	1	90	129	179	0.1	0.1
Unity Ch	2	NR	NR	NR	-	-
Zoroastrian	0	NR	NR	2	0.0	0.0
MARION	**115**	**6,489**	**14,680**	**24,406**	**61.9**	**100.0**
ANG/EPIS–Episcopal	2	41	83	103	0.3	0.4
Bahá'í	0	NR	6	6	0.0	0.0
BAPT–Amer Bapt USA	1	164	266	323	0.8	1.3
BAPT–Free Will Bapt	2	NR	172	209	0.5	0.9
BAPT–So Bapt Conv	23	1,309	4,185	5,083	12.9	20.8
BRETH–Ch of Brethren	1	0	28	34	0.1	0.1
Catholic	5	NR	NR	2,543	6.4	10.4
CGOD–Ch God (Ander)	2	83	NR	83	0.2	0.3
Ch Cr, Scientst	1	NR	NR	NR	-	-
Ch of Nazarene	1	382	314	540	1.4	2.2
CHR–Chr Ch (Disc)	3	100	446	542	1.4	2.2
CHR–Chr Chs & Chs Cr	14	NR	2,945	3,577	9.1	14.7
CHR–Chs of Christ	4	205	218	273	0.7	1.1
Ind Fund Churches	1	NR	NR	NR	-	-
Jehovah's Witness	2	NR	NR	NR	-	-
JUD–Reform	1	26	45	122	0.3	0.5
LDS–Comm of Christ	2	NR	164	164	0.4	0.7
LDS–L-D Saints	1	NR	NR	435	1.1	1.8
LUTH–E.L.C.A.	1	44	99	119	0.3	0.5
LUTH–Luth–MO Synod	3	663	1,668	1,985	5.0	8.1
METH–AME Zion	1	55	109	132	0.3	0.5
METH–Free Methodist	2	127	125	135	0.3	0.6
METH–Un Methodist	17	811	1,637	2,077	5.3	8.5
Muslim Est	1	908	NR	3,298	8.4	13.5
Non-denom Chr Chs	8	1,140	1,368	1,507	3.8	6.2
PENT–Assemb of God	2	147	102	268	0.7	1.1
PENT–Ch God (Cleve)	2	57	144	175	0.4	0.7
PENT–Un Pent Ch Intl	4	NR	NR	NR	-	-
PRES–Presb Ch (USA)	4	97	279	339	0.9	1.4
Salvation Army	1	5	0	0	0.0	0.0
Sev Day Adv	1	24	41	47	0.1	0.2
Un C of Christ	2	101	236	287	0.7	1.2
MARSHALL	**34**	**1,133**	**3,292**	**6,538**	**51.7**	**100.0**
ANG/EPIS–Anglican NA	1	NR	NR	NR	-	-
Bahá'í	0	NR	1	1	0.0	0.0
BAPT–Amer Bapt USA	1	70	161	192	1.5	2.9
BAPT–Reg Bapt Gen As	1	NR	NR	NR	-	-
Catholic	5	NR	NR	2,282	18.1	34.9
CHR–Chr Ch (Disc)	2	82	476	567	4.5	8.7
CHR–Chr Chs & Chs Cr	2	NR	317	378	3.0	5.8
LUTH–E.L.C.A.	4	216	673	900	7.1	13.8
LUTH–Luth–MO Synod	4	164	496	664	5.3	10.2
METH–Un Methodist	4	191	408	606	4.8	9.3
Non-denom Chr Chs	3	205	205	256	2.0	3.9
PENT–Open Bible Std	1	30	NR	30	0.2	0.5
PENT–Un Pent Ch Intl	1	NR	NR	NR	-	-
PRES–Presb Ch (USA)	4	109	270	322	2.5	4.9
Un C of Christ	1	66	285	340	2.7	5.2
MASON	**32**	**1,564**	**4,498**	**6,580**	**44.9**	**100.0**
ANG/EPIS–Episcopal	1	26	29	84	0.6	1.3
Bahá'í	0	NR	2	2	0.0	0.0

Religious Group	Number of Congrega-tions	Number of Attendees	Number of Communicant, Confirmed, or Full Members	Adherents: Number of Adherents	Adherents: % of Total Pop.	Adherents: % of Total Adh.
BAPT–Amer Bapt USA	2	75	637	763	5.2	11.6
BAPT–Reg Bapt Gen As	1	NR	NR	NR	-	-
BAPT–So Bapt Conv	3	73	406	486	3.3	7.4
Catholic	2	NR	NR	685	4.7	10.4
Ch of Nazarene	1	52	88	140	1.0	2.1
CHR–Chr Ch (Disc)	1	40	267	320	2.2	4.9
CHR–Chr Chs & Chs Cr	2	NR	260	311	2.1	4.7
LDS–L-D Saints	1	NR	NR	94	0.6	1.4
LUTH–Luth–MO Synod	6	541	1,214	1,472	10.0	22.4
METH–Un Methodist	5	284	1,004	1,372	9.4	20.9
Missionary Ch	2	170	150	170	1.2	2.6
Non-denom Chr Chs	2	120	240	240	1.6	3.6
PENT–Assemb of God	2	128	96	315	2.1	4.8
PRES–Presb Ch (USA)	1	55	105	126	0.9	1.9
MASSAC	**53**	**3,227**	**8,013**	**10,284**	**66.7**	**100.0**
Bahá'í	0	NR	7	7	0.0	0.1
BAPT–NBC Amer	1	80	100	121	0.8	1.2
BAPT–So Bapt Conv	14	1,519	4,640	5,626	36.5	54.7
Catholic	1	NR	NR	300	1.9	2.9
CGOD–Ch God (Ander)	1	23	NR	23	0.1	0.2
CHR–Chr Ch (Disc)	1	95	310	376	2.4	3.7
CHR–Chr Chs & Chs Cr	2	NR	235	285	1.8	2.8
CHR–Chs of Christ	6	328	419	566	3.7	5.5
Jehovah's Witness	1	NR	NR	NR	-	-
LDS–Comm of Christ	1	NR	82	82	0.5	0.8
LUTH–Assoc Free Luth	2	NR	NR	NR	-	-
LUTH–E.L.C.A.	2	148	302	420	2.7	4.1
LUTH–Nor Amer Luth C	1	NR	NR	NR	-	-
METH–AME	2	0	200	242	1.6	2.4
METH–Un Methodist	4	266	512	759	4.9	7.4
Non-denom Chr Chs	5	450	550	613	4.0	6.0
PENT–Assemb of God	1	79	62	117	0.8	1.1
PENT–Ch God (Cleve)	2	102	208	252	1.6	2.5
PENT–Un Pent Ch Intl	1	NR	NR	NR	-	-
PRES–Cum Pres Am	1	NR	NR	NR	-	-
PRES–Cumber Presb	1	NR	155	217	1.4	2.1
PRES–Presb Ch (USA)	1	41	42	51	0.3	0.5
Sev Day Adv	1	12	22	25	0.2	0.2
Un C of Christ	1	84	167	202	1.3	2.0
MENARD	**29**	**870**	**3,771**	**5,758**	**45.3**	**100.0**
Bahá'í	0	NR	5	5	0.0	0.1
BAPT–Amer Bapt Assn	1	NR	50	61	0.5	1.1
BAPT–So Bapt Conv	6	259	855	1,038	8.2	18.0
Catholic	2	NR	NR	954	7.5	16.6
CHR–Chr Ch (Disc)	2	125	222	269	2.1	4.7
CHR–Chr Chs & Chs Cr	4	NR	1,100	1,335	10.5	23.2
Evan Free Ch	1	30	NR	30	0.2	0.5
Intl Fell Bible Ch	1	NR	NR	NR	-	-
LUTH–Luth–MO Synod	2	17	416	511	4.0	8.9
METH–Un Methodist	3	208	659	978	7.7	17.0
PENT–Assemb of God	1	31	20	38	0.3	0.7
PENT–Int Foursq Gos	1	20	17	21	0.2	0.4
PENT–Un Pent Ch Intl	1	NR	NR	NR	-	-
PRES–Presb Ch (USA)	4	180	427	518	4.1	9.0
MERCER	**36**	**1,941**	**4,634**	**7,398**	**45.0**	**100.0**
ANG/EPIS–Anglican NA	1	NR	NR	NR	-	-
Bahá'í	0	NR	3	3	0.0	0.0
BAPT–Amer Bapt USA	1	350	538	652	4.0	8.8
BAPT–Converge/BGC	1	75	NR	90	0.5	1.2
BAPT–So Bapt Conv	1	70	289	350	2.1	4.7
Catholic	4	NR	NR	1,521	9.3	20.6
Ch of Nazarene	1	10	0	13	0.1	0.2
CHR–Chr Ch (Disc)	1	80	220	267	1.6	3.6
Evan Free Ch	1	80	NR	80	0.5	1.1
Jehovah's Witness	1	NR	NR	NR	-	-
LUTH–E.L.C.A.	5	219	1,345	1,777	10.8	24.0
METH–Un Methodist	7	418	1,102	1,212	7.4	16.4
Non-denom Chr Chs	2	170	195	213	1.3	2.9
PENT–Assemb of God	2	27	8	86	0.5	1.2
PRES–Presb Ch (USA)	7	324	823	998	6.1	13.5

NR–Not Reported   - Represents no adherents reported.   Percentages may not total 100 due to rounding.

Table 3: Religious Congregations by County and Group: 2010

Religious Group	Number of Congregations	Number of Attendees	Number of Communicant, Confirmed, or Full Members	Adherents: Number of Adherents	Adherents: % of Total Pop.	Adherents: % of Total Adh.
PRES–Presb Ch Amer	1	118	111	136	0.8	1.8
MONROE	**37**	**4,754**	**9,637**	**21,068**	**63.9**	**100.0**
Bahá'í	0	NR	1	1	0.0	0.0
BAPT–So Bapt Conv	4	782	1,540	1,891	5.7	9.0
Catholic	7	NR	NR	9,218	28.0	43.8
CHR–Chr Chs & Chs Cr	1	NR	875	1,075	3.3	5.1
CHR–Chs of Christ	1	20	16	30	0.1	0.1
Jehovah's Witness	1	NR	NR	NR	-	-
LDS–L-D Saints	1	NR	NR	216	0.7	1.0
LUTH–E.L.C.A.	1	135	209	287	0.9	1.4
LUTH–Luth–MO Synod	4	1,353	1,803	2,312	7.0	11.0
METH–Un Methodist	1	135	189	189	0.6	0.9
Non-denom Chr Chs	6	1,076	1,700	1,770	5.4	8.4
PENT–Assemb of God	1	19	8	30	0.1	0.1
PENT–Assm God Intl F	1	NR	NR	NR	-	-
PRES–Presb Ch Amer	1	168	160	198	0.6	0.9
Un C of Christ	7	1,066	3,136	3,851	11.7	18.3
MONTGOMERY	**78**	**3,339**	**9,601**	**13,945**	**46.3**	**100.0**
Bahá'í	0	NR	4	4	0.0	0.0
BAPT–Amer Bapt USA	2	134	333	396	1.3	2.8
BAPT–So Bapt Conv	16	875	2,836	3,373	11.2	24.2
Catholic	5	NR	NR	2,050	6.8	14.7
CHR–Chr Ch (Disc)	3	147	702	835	2.8	6.0
CHR–Chr Chs & Chs Cr	6	NR	632	752	2.5	5.4
CHR–Chs of Christ	1	25	25	25	0.1	0.2
LDS–L-D Saints	1	NR	NR	350	1.2	2.5
LUTH–E.L.C.A.	8	272	961	1,108	3.7	7.9
LUTH–Luth–MO Synod	6	383	1,698	2,162	7.2	15.5
METH–Free Methodist	2	275	209	275	0.9	2.0
METH–Un Methodist	10	462	1,065	1,227	4.1	8.8
Non-denom Chr Chs	3	475	600	644	2.1	4.6
PENT–Assemb of God	3	127	58	177	0.6	1.3
PENT–Un Pent Ch Intl	3	NR	NR	NR	-	-
PRES–Presb Ch (USA)	7	144	435	517	1.7	3.7
Sev Day Adv	1	8	14	16	0.1	0.1
Un C of Christ	1	12	29	34	0.1	0.2
MORGAN	**62**	**3,650**	**9,818**	**17,214**	**48.4**	**100.0**
ANG/EPIS–Episcopal	1	58	79	107	0.3	0.6
Bahá'í	0	NR	117	117	0.3	0.7
BAPT–Amer Bapt Assn	1	NR	42	50	0.1	0.3
BAPT–Amer Bapt USA	3	296	1,260	1,501	4.2	8.7
BAPT–So Bapt Conv	7	445	1,243	1,481	4.2	8.6
Catholic	4	NR	NR	4,495	12.6	26.1
CHR–Chr Ch (Disc)	3	219	961	1,145	3.2	6.7
CHR–Chr Chs & Chs Cr	5	NR	896	1,067	3.0	6.2
CHR–Chs of Christ	2	130	134	151	0.4	0.9
Jehovah's Witness	1	NR	NR	NR	-	-
LDS–Comm of Christ	1	NR	82	82	0.2	0.5
LDS–L-D Saints	1	NR	NR	436	1.2	2.5
LUTH–E.L.C.A.	2	156	302	410	1.2	2.4
LUTH–Luth–MO Synod	5	523	1,186	1,742	4.9	10.1
METH–AME	1	0	150	179	0.5	1.0
METH–Un Methodist	11	645	1,596	1,998	5.6	11.6
Non-denom Chr Chs	5	660	895	913	2.6	5.3
PENT–Assemb of God	1	130	80	174	0.5	1.0
PENT–COGIC	2	100	101	120	0.3	0.7
PENT–Int Foursq Gos	1	5	15	18	0.1	0.1
PENT–Un Pent Ch Intl	1	NR	NR	NR	-	-
PRES–Presb Ch (USA)	2	199	561	668	1.9	3.9
Salvation Army	1	39	30	255	0.7	1.5
Un C of Christ	1	45	88	105	0.3	0.6
MOULTRIE	**41**	**2,154**	**5,354**	**7,884**	**53.1**	**100.0**
Bahá'í	0	NR	3	3	0.0	0.0
BAPT–Amer Bapt USA	1	56	206	255	1.7	3.2
BAPT–So Bapt Conv	2	147	552	684	4.6	8.7
Catholic	2	NR	NR	396	2.7	5.0
CGOD–Ch God (Ander)	2	151	NR	151	1.0	1.9
CHR–Chr Ch (Disc)	2	196	968	1,199	8.1	15.2
CHR–Chr Chs & Chs Cr	3	NR	455	564	3.8	7.2
CHR–Chs of Christ	3	105	110	140	0.9	1.8
LUTH–Luth–MO Synod	1	85	320	409	2.8	5.2
MENN–Amish Undif	9	NR	616	1,260	8.5	16.0
MENN–Beachy Amish-Menn	1	227	119	227	1.5	2.9
METH–Free Methodist	1	28	16	28	0.2	0.4
METH–Un Methodist	5	263	714	853	5.7	10.8
Non-denom Chr Chs	5	863	1,130	1,300	8.8	16.5
PENT–Assemb of God	1	33	24	52	0.4	0.7
PENT–Un Pent Ch Intl	1	NR	NR	NR	-	-
PRES–Cumber Presb	1	NR	97	333	2.2	4.2
PRES–Presb Ch (USA)	1	0	24	30	0.2	0.4
OGLE	**79**	**4,879**	**10,516**	**21,904**	**40.9**	**100.0**
ANG/EPIS–Episcopal	1	41	76	171	0.3	0.8
Bahá'í	0	NR	7	7	0.0	0.0
BAPT–Consrv Bapt	1	NR	NR	NR	-	-
BAPT–Converge/BGC	2	150	NR	180	0.3	0.8
BAPT–NT Ind Bapt	1	NR	NR	NR	-	-
BRETH–Ch of Brethren	3	147	360	441	0.8	2.0
Catholic	4	NR	NR	7,675	14.3	35.0
CGOD–Ch God (Ander)	1	112	NR	112	0.2	0.5
Ch of God Gen Conf	3	NR	184	226	0.4	1.0
Ch of Nazarene	1	11	0	18	0.0	0.1
CHR–Chr Ch (Disc)	1	0	100	123	0.2	0.6
CHR–Chr Chs & Chs Cr	2	NR	70	86	0.2	0.4
CHR–Chs of Christ	1	80	75	97	0.2	0.4
CONG–Consrv Cong Chr	1	28	19	23	0.0	0.1
Evan Cov Ch	1	94	136	122	0.2	0.6
Evan Free Ch	1	200	NR	200	0.4	0.9
Jehovah's Witness	2	NR	NR	NR	-	-
LDS–L-D Saints	1	NR	NR	246	0.5	1.1
LUTH–E.L.C.A.	9	695	2,126	2,749	5.1	12.6
LUTH–Luth Cong Msn Chr	1	119	402	493	0.9	2.3
LUTH–Luth–MO Synod	2	344	685	922	1.7	4.2
METH–Un Methodist	13	869	2,700	3,141	5.9	14.3
Non-denom Chr Chs	8	630	805	861	1.6	3.9
PENT–Assemb of God	4	254	48	663	1.2	3.0
PENT–Ch God (Cleve)	1	29	73	90	0.2	0.4
PENT–Int Foursq Gos	1	62	37	45	0.1	0.2
PENT–Open Bible Std	2	82	NR	82	0.2	0.4
PENT–Un Pent Ch Intl	1	NR	NR	NR	-	-
PRES–Evan Presby Ch	1	NR	471	578	1.1	2.6
PRES–Presb Ch (USA)	2	368	913	1,119	2.1	5.1
PRES–Presb Ch Amer	1	100	131	205	0.4	0.9
REF–Ref Ch in Am	4	330	643	672	1.3	3.1
Sev Day Adv	1	10	17	20	0.0	0.1
Un C of Christ	1	124	438	537	1.0	2.5
PEORIA	**232**	**32,612**	**41,804**	**101,347**	**54.3**	**100.0**
ANG/EPIS–Anglican NA	5	NR	NR	NR	-	-
ANG/EPIS–Episcopal	1	191	372	372	0.2	0.4
Ap Chr Ch-Amer	2	1,457	859	1,457	0.8	1.4
Bahá'í	1	NR	85	85	0.0	0.1
BAPT–Amer Bapt Assn	1	NR	85	104	0.1	0.1
BAPT–Amer Bapt USA	3	359	868	1,066	0.6	1.1
BAPT–Consrv Bapt	2	NR	NR	NR	-	-
BAPT–Converge/BGC	1	75	NR	90	0.0	0.1
BAPT–Free Will Bapt	1	NR	86	106	0.1	0.1
BAPT–Natl Mis Bapt Conv	5	0	600	737	0.4	0.7
BAPT–NBC USA	5	915	1,660	2,039	1.1	2.0
BAPT–So Bapt Conv	12	765	2,218	2,725	1.5	2.7
BRETH–Ch of Brethren	1	85	155	190	0.1	0.2
Catholic	20	NR	NR	26,165	14.0	25.8
CGOD–Ch God (Ander)	4	311	NR	311	0.2	0.3
Ch Cr, Scientst	1	NR	NR	NR	-	-
Ch of Nazarene	4	226	263	491	0.3	0.5
CHR–Chr Ch (Disc)	4	305	1,079	1,326	0.7	1.3
CHR–Chr Chs & Chs Cr	3	NR	1,340	1,646	0.9	1.6
CHR–Chs of Christ	4	415	371	532	0.3	0.5
CONG–Consrv Cong Chr	1	101	202	248	0.1	0.2
Evan Cov Ch	1	83	91	108	0.1	0.1
Evan Free Ch	2	190	NR	190	0.1	0.2

NR–Not Reported   - Represents no adherents reported.   Percentages may not total 100 due to rounding.

Table 3: Religious Congregations by County and Group: 2010

Religious Group	Number of Congregations	Number of Attendees	Number of Communicant, Confirmed, or Full Members	Adherents: Number of Adherents	Adherents: % of Total Pop.	Adherents: % of Total Adh.
HINDU–Post Ren	1	NR	NR	16	0.0	0.0
HINDU–Trad Temples	1	NR	NR	600	0.3	0.6
Jehovah's Witness	1	NR	NR	NR	-	-
JUD–Reform	1	84	148	400	0.2	0.4
LDS–L-D Saints	1	NR	NR	882	0.5	0.9
LUTH–E.L.C.A.	10	1,325	3,611	4,720	2.5	4.7
LUTH–Luth Cong Msn Chr	1	125	159	195	0.1	0.2
LUTH–Luth-MO Synod	6	1,954	4,104	5,385	2.9	5.3
LUTH–Wisc Ev Luth Syn	1	46	59	73	0.0	0.1
MENN–Fel Evg Ch	1	2,572	806	990	0.5	1.0
MENN–Mennonite USA	2	55	80	98	0.1	0.1
METH–AME	1	125	250	307	0.2	0.3
METH–Free Methodist	2	74	73	76	0.0	0.1
METH–Un Methodist	23	2,775	5,379	7,183	3.9	7.1
Missionary Ch	4	248	215	273	0.1	0.3
Muslim Est	6	5,448	NR	19,788	10.6	19.5
New Apost Ch	1	NR	NR	NR	-	-
Non-denom Chr Chs	42	5,893	8,940	9,464	5.1	9.3
ORTHE–Ant Orth of NA	1	35	NR	96	0.1	0.1
ORTHE–Greek Orthodox	1	150	NR	300	0.2	0.3
PENT–Assemb of God	10	2,127	1,116	2,388	1.3	2.4
PENT–Ch God (Cleve)	2	141	269	330	0.2	0.3
PENT–COGIC	3	125	325	399	0.2	0.4
PENT–Full Gosp Bapt	1	NR	NR	NR	-	-
PENT–Un Pent Ch Intl	1	NR	NR	NR	-	-
PRES–Presb Ch (USA)	9	1,300	2,274	2,794	1.5	2.8
PRES–Presb Ch Amer	3	1,611	1,940	1,988	1.1	2.0
Salvation Army	1	70	109	601	0.3	0.6
Sev Day Adv	3	313	544	626	0.3	0.6
Un C of Christ	6	333	718	882	0.5	0.9
Unit Univ	1	205	351	501	0.3	0.5
Unity Ch	1	NR	NR	NR	-	-
Zoroastrian	0	NR	NR	4	0.0	0.0
PERRY	**55**	**3,137**	**8,329**	**12,910**	**57.8**	**100.0**
BAPT–Amer Bapt USA	3	117	158	188	0.8	1.5
BAPT–So Bapt Conv	17	1,582	4,638	5,512	24.7	42.7
Catholic	5	NR	NR	3,029	13.6	23.5
Ch of Nazarene	1	21	61	61	0.3	0.5
CHR–Chr Ch (Disc)	1	50	414	492	2.2	3.8
CHR–Chr Chs & Chs Cr	3	NR	330	392	1.8	3.0
CHR–Chs of Christ	1	16	21	22	0.1	0.2
Jehovah's Witness	1	NR	NR	NR	-	-
LUTH–Luth-MO Synod	3	125	220	270	1.2	2.1
METH–AME Zion	1	0	150	178	0.8	1.4
METH–Un Methodist	3	379	808	945	4.2	7.3
Non-denom Chr Chs	5	535	730	760	3.4	5.9
PENT–Assemb of God	2	97	18	142	0.6	1.1
PENT–Un Pent Ch Intl	3	NR	NR	NR	-	-
PRES–Presb Ch (USA)	2	25	133	158	0.7	1.2
PRES–Presb Ch Amer	1	48	135	152	0.7	1.2
Sev Day Adv	1	14	25	29	0.1	0.2
Un C of Christ	2	128	488	580	2.6	4.5
PIATT	**35**	**1,777**	**4,703**	**6,531**	**39.0**	**100.0**
Bahá'í	0	NR	1	1	0.0	0.0
BAPT–So Bapt Conv	5	318	662	807	4.8	12.4
BRETH–Brethren (Ash)	1	NR	80	98	0.6	1.5
BRETH–Ch of Brethren	2	64	157	191	1.1	2.9
Catholic	2	NR	NR	761	4.5	11.7
CGOD–Ches God-Gen Con	1	84	98	119	0.7	1.8
Ch of Nazarene	2	61	78	186	1.1	2.8
CHR–Chr Ch (Disc)	1	0	81	99	0.6	1.5
CHR–Chr Chs & Chs Cr	2	NR	430	524	3.1	8.0
CHR–Chs of Christ	2	70	76	91	0.5	1.4
Jehovah's Witness	1	NR	NR	NR	-	-
LUTH–E.L.C.A.	1	118	443	443	2.6	6.8
MENN–Fel Evg Ch	1	0	0	0	0.0	0.0
METH–Un Methodist	8	695	1,938	2,441	14.6	37.4
Non-denom Chr Chs	1	70	125	125	0.7	1.9
PENT–Assemb of God	1	24	26	26	0.2	0.4
PENT–Int Foursq Gos	1	102	78	95	0.6	1.5
PRES–Presb Ch (USA)	2	141	265	323	1.9	4.9

Religious Group	Number of Congregations	Number of Attendees	Number of Communicant, Confirmed, or Full Members	Adherents: Number of Adherents	Adherents: % of Total Pop.	Adherents: % of Total Adh.
Un C of Christ	1	30	165	201	1.2	3.1
PIKE	**53**	**2,444**	**4,651**	**6,747**	**41.1**	**100.0**
ANG/EPIS–Episcopal	1	14	24	24	0.1	0.4
BAPT–Amer Bapt USA	2	85	143	173	1.1	2.6
BAPT–Reg Bapt Gen As	2	NR	NR	NR	-	-
BAPT–So Bapt Conv	4	320	872	1,054	6.4	15.6
Catholic	1	NR	NR	364	2.2	5.4
Ch of Nazarene	4	341	396	522	3.2	7.7
CHR–Chr Ch (Disc)	1	0	0	0	0.0	0.0
CHR–Chr Chs & Chs Cr	8	NR	819	990	6.0	14.7
CHR–Chs of Christ	6	277	263	350	2.1	5.2
Evan Ch	1	NR	NR	NR	-	-
LDS–Comm of Christ	1	NR	119	119	0.7	1.8
LDS–L-D Saints	1	NR	NR	103	0.6	1.5
LUTH–Luth-MO Synod	1	45	96	110	0.7	1.6
MENN–Amish Undif	2	NR	90	241	1.5	3.6
METH–Un Methodist	11	507	1,267	1,559	9.5	23.1
Non-denom Chr Chs	3	360	360	478	2.9	7.1
PENT–Assemb of God	2	425	184	529	3.2	7.8
PENT–Pent Ch of God	1	70	NR	109	0.7	1.6
PRES–Presb Ch (USA)	1	0	18	22	0.1	0.3
POPE	**11**	**374**	**1,050**	**1,206**	**27.0**	**100.0**
Bahá'í	0	NR	2	2	0.0	0.2
BAPT–So Bapt Conv	6	170	746	863	19.3	71.6
CHR–Chs of Christ	1	20	19	24	0.5	2.0
LUTH–Luth-MO Synod	1	38	68	77	1.7	6.4
METH–Un Methodist	1	33	63	64	1.4	5.3
PENT–Ch God (Cleve)	1	90	122	141	3.2	11.7
PRES–Presb Ch (USA)	1	23	30	35	0.8	2.9
PULASKI	**31**	**1,408**	**3,448**	**4,412**	**71.6**	**100.0**
Bahá'í	0	NR	49	49	0.8	1.1
BAPT–So Bapt Conv	8	463	1,636	1,985	32.2	45.0
Catholic	2	NR	NR	386	6.3	8.7
CHR–Chr Chs & Chs Cr	1	NR	80	97	1.6	2.2
CHR–Chs of Christ	3	171	160	209	3.4	4.7
CONG–Consrv Cong Chr	2	61	171	208	3.4	4.7
LUTH–Luth-MO Synod	1	18	51	56	0.9	1.3
METH–AME	1	0	150	182	3.0	4.1
METH–Un Methodist	9	281	381	441	7.2	10.0
Non-denom Chr Chs	3	400	750	775	12.6	17.6
PENT–COGIC	1	14	20	24	0.4	0.5
PUTNAM	**12**	**259**	**849**	**2,042**	**34.0**	**100.0**
Catholic	2	NR	NR	1,065	17.7	52.2
CHR–Chr Chs & Chs Cr	1	NR	30	36	0.6	1.8
FRND–Fr Gen Cf	1	NR	68	81	1.3	4.0
JUD–Reform	1	17	30	81	1.3	4.0
LUTH–E.L.C.A.	2	57	175	189	3.1	9.3
METH–Un Methodist	3	100	308	311	5.2	15.2
Non-denom Chr Chs	1	25	30	31	0.5	1.5
Un C of Christ	1	60	208	248	4.1	12.1
RANDOLPH	**76**	**4,599**	**12,075**	**22,403**	**66.9**	**100.0**
Bahá'í	0	NR	5	5	0.0	0.0
BAPT–Amer Bapt USA	1	40	85	100	0.3	0.4
BAPT–Natl Mis Bapt Conv	1	0	150	177	0.5	0.8
BAPT–So Bapt Conv	12	969	2,231	2,629	7.9	11.7
Catholic	10	NR	NR	7,381	22.0	32.9
Ch of Nazarene	1	20	12	20	0.1	0.1
CHR–Chr Chs & Chs Cr	2	NR	110	130	0.4	0.6
CHR–Chs of Christ	1	3	3	4	0.0	0.0
Jehovah's Witness	1	NR	NR	NR	-	-
LDS–Comm of Christ	1	NR	82	82	0.2	0.4
LDS–L-D Saints	1	NR	NR	135	0.4	0.6
LUTH–E.L.C.A.	5	337	1,244	1,545	4.6	6.9
LUTH–Luth-MO Synod	9	1,673	4,784	5,843	17.5	26.1
MENN–Amish Undif	0	NR	4	7	0.0	0.0
METH–AME	1	0	100	118	0.4	0.5
METH–Un Methodist	9	439	1,027	1,334	4.0	6.0

NR–Not Reported   - Represents no adherents reported.   Percentages may not total 100 due to rounding.

Table 3: Religious Congregations by County and Group: 2010

Religious Group	Number of Congrega-tions	Number of Attendees	Number of Communicant, Confirmed, or Full Members	Adherents		
				Number of Adherents	% of Total Pop.	% of Total Adh.
Non-denom Chr Chs	2	430	480	538	1.6	2.4
PENT–Assemb of God	3	95	25	198	0.6	0.9
PENT–COGIC	1	0	350	412	1.2	1.8
PENT–Pent Ch of God	1	70	NR	109	0.3	0.5
PENT–Un Pent Ch Intl	2	NR	NR	NR	-	-
PRES–Evan Presby Ch	1	NR	10	12	0.0	0.1
PRES–Presb Ch (USA)	6	194	648	764	2.3	3.4
PRES–Presb Ch Amer	2	170	177	202	0.6	0.9
PRES–Ref Pres of NA	1	38	31	49	0.1	0.2
Un C of Christ	2	121	517	609	1.8	2.7
RICHLAND	**49**	**2,446**	**4,725**	**9,057**	**55.8**	**100.0**
BAPT–Amer Bapt USA	1	92	128	155	1.0	1.7
BAPT–So Bapt Conv	2	180	670	810	5.0	8.9
BRETH–Ch of Brethren	1	0	35	42	0.3	0.5
Catholic	2	NR	NR	2,692	16.6	29.7
Ch of Nazarene	1	81	82	82	0.5	0.9
CHR–Chr Ch (Disc)	1	30	75	91	0.6	1.0
CHR–Chr Chs & Chs Cr	8	NR	783	946	5.8	10.4
CHR–Chs of Christ	4	150	154	187	1.2	2.1
Grace Gosp Fel	1	NR	NR	NR	-	-
Jehovah's Witness	1	NR	NR	NR	-	-
LDS–L-D Saints	1	NR	NR	375	2.3	4.1
LUTH–E.L.C.A.	1	100	225	547	3.4	6.0
MENN–Amish Undif	1	NR	3	9	0.1	0.1
MENN–Midw Bchy Am-Menn	1	123	52	123	0.8	1.4
METH–Free Methodist	1	136	245	245	1.5	2.7
METH–Un Methodist	11	482	954	1,159	7.1	12.8
Non-denom Chr Chs	6	850	988	1,106	6.8	12.2
PENT–Assemb of God	1	147	96	208	1.3	2.3
PENT–Ch God (Cleve)	1	36	52	63	0.4	0.7
PENT–Un Pent Ch Intl	1	NR	NR	NR	-	-
PRES–Presb Ch (USA)	1	0	115	139	0.9	1.5
Sev Day Adv	1	39	68	78	0.5	0.9
ROCK ISLAND	**179**	**18,203**	**27,985**	**63,088**	**42.8**	**100.0**
ANG/EPIS–Anglican NA	3	NR	NR	NR	-	-
ANG/EPIS–Episcopal	1	62	84	86	0.1	0.1
Bahá'í	0	NR	113	113	0.1	0.2
BAPT–Amer Bapt Assn	2	NR	15	18	0.0	0.0
BAPT–Amer Bapt USA	5	429	683	828	0.6	1.3
BAPT–Asc Ref Bap Ch Am	1	NR	NR	NR	-	-
BAPT–Consrv Bapt	1	NR	NR	NR	-	-
BAPT–Converge/BGC	1	75	NR	90	0.1	0.1
BAPT–Free Will Bapt	2	NR	172	209	0.1	0.3
BAPT–NBC Amer	1	475	500	606	0.4	1.0
BAPT–NBC USA	4	1,010	1,925	2,334	1.6	3.7
BAPT–Ref Bapt Ch	1	NR	NR	NR	-	-
BAPT–Reg Bapt Gen As	3	NR	NR	NR	-	-
BAPT–So Bapt Conv	9	958	1,282	1,554	1.1	2.5
BUDD–Mahayana	1	NR	NR	506	0.3	0.8
Calv Chpl	1	NR	NR	NR	-	-
Catholic	14	NR	NR	18,258	12.4	28.9
Ch Cr, Scientst	1	NR	NR	NR	-	-
Ch of Nazarene	4	224	357	357	0.2	0.6
CHR–Chr Ch (Disc)	4	385	1,851	2,244	1.5	3.6
CHR–Chr Chs & Chs Cr	3	NR	270	327	0.2	0.5
CHR–Chs of Christ	2	195	190	225	0.2	0.4
Christian Brethren	1	NR	NR	NR	-	-
CONG–Cong Chr, NA	1	NR	28	34	0.0	0.1
Evan Cov Ch	2	242	483	314	0.2	0.5
Evan Free Ch	4	805	NR	805	0.5	1.3
HINDU–Trad Temples	1	NR	NR	800	0.5	1.3
Intl Fell Bible Ch	1	NR	NR	NR	-	-
Jehovah's Witness	3	NR	NR	NR	-	-
LDS–Comm of Christ	1	NR	119	119	0.1	0.2
LDS–L-D Saints	2	NR	NR	1,201	0.8	1.9
LUTH–E.L.C.A.	10	1,128	3,753	4,656	3.2	7.4
LUTH–Luth Cong Msn Chr	1	155	589	714	0.5	1.1
LUTH–Luth–MO Synod	7	1,147	2,823	3,542	2.4	5.6
LUTH–Wisc Ev Luth Syn	1	60	147	182	0.1	0.3
MENN–Mennonite USA	1	80	76	92	0.1	0.1
METH–AME	3	70	375	455	0.3	0.7
METH–Un Methodist	17	1,352	3,045	3,777	2.6	6.0
METH–Wesleyan	1	2,682	240	3,487	2.4	5.5
Missionary Ch	1	28	36	36	0.0	0.1
Muslim Est	1	908	NR	3,298	2.2	5.2
New Apost Ch	1	NR	NR	NR	-	-
Non-denom Chr Chs	19	2,851	3,413	3,752	2.5	5.9
ORTHE–Greek Orthodox	2	220	NR	475	0.3	0.8
PENT–Assemb of God	6	851	594	1,500	1.0	2.4
PENT–COGIC	1	0	150	182	0.1	0.3
PENT–Int Foursq Gos	6	386	682	827	0.6	1.3
PENT–Un Pent Ch Intl	3	NR	NR	NR	-	-
PRES–Orth Pres Ch	1	0	0	0	0.0	0.0
PRES–Presb Ch (USA)	10	1,053	2,040	2,473	1.7	3.9
Salvation Army	1	32	35	296	0.2	0.5
Sev Day Adv	1	60	104	120	0.1	0.2
Un C of Christ	4	280	1,811	2,196	1.5	3.5
Unity Ch	1	NR	NR	NR	-	-
ST. CLAIR	**309**	**30,543**	**64,170**	**136,200**	**50.4**	**100.0**
ANG/EPIS–Anglican NA	1	NR	NR	NR	-	-
ANG/EPIS–Episcopal	2	223	550	718	0.3	0.5
Bahá'í	0	NR	152	152	0.1	0.1
BAPT–Amer Bapt USA	6	773	1,306	1,619	0.6	1.2
BAPT–Free Will Bapt	1	NR	86	107	0.0	0.1
BAPT–Natl Mis Bapt Conv	7	15	925	1,147	0.4	0.8
BAPT–NBC USA	5	1,675	3,975	4,928	1.8	3.6
BAPT–Reg Bapt Gen As	1	NR	NR	NR	-	-
BAPT–So Bapt Conv	49	6,723	18,723	23,213	8.6	17.0
Calv Chpl	1	NR	NR	NR	-	-
Catholic	28	NR	NR	46,372	17.2	34.0
CGOD–Ch God (Ander)	7	403	NR	403	0.1	0.3
Ch Cr, Scientst	1	NR	NR	NR	-	-
Ch of Nazarene	7	442	501	643	0.2	0.5
CHR–Chr Ch (Disc)	2	70	154	191	0.1	0.1
CHR–Chr Chs & Chs Cr	6	NR	1,546	1,917	0.7	1.4
CHR–Chs of Christ	6	844	878	1,183	0.4	0.9
Evan Free Ch	1	70	NR	70	0.0	0.1
HINDU–Post Ren	1	NR	NR	25	0.0	0.0
Ind Fund Churches	1	NR	NR	NR	-	-
Jehovah's Witness	4	NR	NR	NR	-	-
LDS–Comm of Christ	2	NR	276	276	0.1	0.2
LDS–L-D Saints	6	NR	NR	2,129	0.8	1.6
LUTH–E.L.C.A.	5	530	1,092	1,492	0.6	1.1
LUTH–Luth–MO Synod	14	1,744	4,032	5,159	1.9	3.8
METH–AME	7	75	770	955	0.4	0.7
METH–AME Zion	2	0	160	198	0.1	0.1
METH–C.M.E.	4	125	525	651	0.2	0.5
METH–Un Methodist	14	4,523	6,481	10,615	3.9	7.8
Muslim Est	1	908	NR	3,298	1.2	2.4
New Apost Ch	1	NR	NR	NR	-	-
Non-denom Chr Chs	43	6,941	10,466	11,175	4.1	8.2
ORTHE–Greek Orthodox	1	75	NR	400	0.1	0.3
ORTHO–Armen Ap Etchm	1	40	NR	1,700	0.6	1.2
PENT–Assemb of God	12	815	427	1,258	0.5	0.9
PENT–Ch God (Cleve)	2	48	312	387	0.1	0.3
PENT–COGIC	12	610	1,945	2,411	0.9	1.8
PENT–Full Gosp Bapt	3	NR	NR	NR	-	-
PENT–Pent Ch of God	1	70	NR	109	0.0	0.1
PENT–Un Pent Ch Intl	9	NR	NR	NR	-	-
PENT–United Holy Ch	1	NR	NR	NR	-	-
PRES–Presb Ch (USA)	2	324	832	1,032	0.4	0.8
PRES–Presb Ch Amer	2	119	186	222	0.1	0.2
Salvation Army	2	45	95	454	0.2	0.3
Sev Day Adv	3	302	525	603	0.2	0.4
Un C of Christ	22	2,011	7,250	8,988	3.3	6.6
SALINE	**84**	**3,943**	**11,644**	**15,588**	**62.6**	**100.0**
ANG/EPIS–Episcopal	1	17	23	27	0.1	0.2
BAPT–Amer Bapt USA	1	40	42	51	0.2	0.3
BAPT–Natl Mis Bapt Conv	1	0	150	181	0.7	1.2
BAPT–S-D Baptist Gen Con	1	5	25	30	0.1	0.2
BAPT–So Bapt Conv	31	2,281	8,392	10,120	40.6	64.9
Catholic	2	NR	NR	847	3.4	5.4

NR–Not Reported - Represents no adherents reported. Percentages may not total 100 due to rounding.

Table 3: Religious Congregations by County and Group: 2010

Religious Group	Number of Congrega-tions	Number of Attendees	Number of Communicant, Confirmed, or Full Members	Adherents		
				Number of Adherents	% of Total Pop.	% of Total Adh.
CGOD–Ch God (Ander)	3	76	NR	76	0.3	0.5
Ch of God Gen Conf	1	NR	25	30	0.1	0.2
CHR–Chr Chs & Chs Cr	2	NR	295	356	1.4	2.3
CHR–Chs of Christ	2	100	99	118	0.5	0.8
Jehovah's Witness	2	NR	NR	NR	-	-
LDS–Comm of Christ	1	NR	82	82	0.3	0.5
LDS–L-D Saints	1	NR	NR	240	1.0	1.5
LUTH–E.L.C.A.	1	14	39	46	0.2	0.3
MENN–Amish Undif	1	NR	49	143	0.6	0.9
MENN–Midw Bchy Am-Menn	1	97	50	97	0.4	0.6
METH–AME	2	7	115	139	0.6	0.9
METH–Un Methodist	6	424	799	1,125	4.5	7.2
Non-denom Chr Chs	9	670	820	913	3.7	5.9
PENT–Ch God (Cleve)	4	134	358	432	1.7	2.8
PENT–Un Pent Ch Intl	3	NR	NR	NR	-	-
PRES–Cumber Presb	5	NR	102	321	1.3	2.1
PRES–Presb Ch (USA)	2	60	148	178	0.7	1.1
Sev Day Adv	1	18	31	36	0.1	0.2
SANGAMON	**225**	**24,883**	**46,707**	**108,076**	**54.7**	**100.0**
ANG/EPIS–Episcopal	3	252	578	704	0.4	0.7
Bahá'í	2	NR	115	115	0.1	0.1
BAPT–Amer Bapt Assn	1	NR	85	104	0.1	0.1
BAPT–Amer Bapt USA	8	1,505	1,745	2,134	1.1	2.0
BAPT–Free Will Bapt	1	NR	86	105	0.1	0.1
BAPT–NBC Amer	1	400	600	734	0.4	0.7
BAPT–NBC USA	2	580	1,970	2,410	1.2	2.2
BAPT–Reg Bapt Gen As	1	NR	NR	NR	-	-
BAPT–So Bapt Conv	18	1,649	4,689	5,736	2.9	5.3
BRETH–Ch of Brethren	1	0	85	104	0.1	0.1
BUDD–Mahayana	1	NR	NR	30	0.0	0.0
Calv Chpl	1	NR	NR	NR	-	-
Catholic	16	NR	NR	31,734	16.1	29.4
CGOD–Ch God (Ander)	4	335	NR	335	0.2	0.3
Ch Cr, Scientst	1	NR	NR	NR	-	-
Ch of Nazarene	4	451	694	983	0.5	0.9
CHR–Chr Ch (Disc)	5	302	1,111	1,359	0.7	1.3
CHR–Chr Chs & Chs Cr	18	NR	7,229	8,843	4.5	8.2
CHR–Chs of Christ	4	350	383	483	0.2	0.4
CHR–Int Chs of Christ	1	NR	44	54	0.0	0.0
Christian Brethren	1	NR	NR	NR	-	-
Evan Free Ch	1	1,200	NR	1,200	0.6	1.1
FRND–Fr Gen Cf	1	NR	0	0	0.0	0.0
HINDU–Trad Temples	1	NR	NR	900	0.5	0.8
Ind Fund Churches	1	NR	NR	NR	-	-
Jehovah's Witness	4	NR	NR	NR	-	-
JUD–Reform	1	91	160	432	0.2	0.4
LDS–Comm of Christ	3	NR	246	246	0.1	0.2
LDS–L-D Saints	2	NR	NR	1,345	0.7	1.2
LUTH–E.L.C.A.	5	887	2,967	3,701	1.9	3.4
LUTH–Luth-MO Synod	13	2,705	5,772	7,632	3.9	7.1
METH–AME	4	250	700	856	0.4	0.8
METH–AME Zion	1	0	60	73	0.0	0.1
METH–Free Methodist	2	77	93	105	0.1	0.1
METH–Un Methodist	27	3,896	7,238	11,252	5.7	10.4
Metro Comm Ch	1	19	25	31	0.0	0.0
MJEW–Union Mes Cong	1	NR	NR	NR	-	-
Muslim Est	1	908	NR	3,298	1.7	3.1
Non-denom Chr Chs	23	4,346	5,281	5,764	2.9	5.3
ORTHE–Greek Orthodox	1	65	NR	280	0.1	0.3
PENT–Assemb of God	7	2,777	475	9,397	4.8	8.7
PENT–Ch God (Cleve)	2	57	257	314	0.2	0.3
PENT–COGIC	5	215	360	440	0.2	0.4
PENT–Int Foursq Gos	2	31	36	44	0.0	0.0
PENT–Un Pent Ch Intl	3	NR	NR	NR	-	-
PENT–Vineyard	1	130	130	159	0.1	0.1
PRES–Orth Pres Ch	1	41	38	61	0.0	0.1
PRES–Presb Ch (USA)	10	1,014	2,673	3,270	1.7	3.0
Salvation Army	1	42	42	370	0.2	0.3
Sev Day Adv	3	141	245	282	0.1	0.3
Un C of Christ	1	53	294	360	0.2	0.3
Unit Univ	1	114	201	291	0.1	0.3
Unity Ch	1	NR	NR	NR	-	-
Zoroastrian	0	NR	NR	6	0.0	0.0

Religious Group	Number of Congrega-tions	Number of Attendees	Number of Communicant, Confirmed, or Full Members	Adherents		
				Number of Adherents	% of Total Pop.	% of Total Adh.
SCHUYLER	**28**	**1,142**	**2,405**	**3,089**	**40.9**	**100.0**
ANG/EPIS–Anglican NA	1	NR	NR	NR	-	-
Bahá'í	0	NR	5	5	0.1	0.2
BAPT–Reg Bapt Gen As	1	NR	NR	NR	-	-
BAPT–So Bapt Conv	1	57	308	366	4.9	11.8
Catholic	1	NR	NR	213	2.8	6.9
Ch of God Gen Conf	1	NR	17	20	0.3	0.6
Ch of Nazarene	1	42	41	49	0.6	1.6
CHR–Chr Ch (Disc)	2	121	400	475	6.3	15.4
CHR–Chr Chs & Chs Cr	3	NR	229	272	3.6	8.8
CHR–Chs of Christ	1	18	17	22	0.3	0.7
LUTH–Luth-MO Synod	1	54	120	180	2.4	5.8
METH–Free Methodist	1	120	130	130	1.7	4.2
METH–Un Methodist	10	411	754	948	12.6	30.7
Non-denom Chr Chs	1	200	250	250	3.3	8.1
PENT–Un Pent Ch Intl	1	NR	NR	NR	-	-
PRES–Presb Ch (USA)	1	109	116	138	1.8	4.5
Sev Day Adv	1	10	18	21	0.3	0.7
SCOTT	**22**	**1,022**	**2,571**	**3,377**	**63.1**	**100.0**
Bahá'í	0	NR	2	2	0.0	0.1
BAPT–Amer Bapt USA	3	221	474	579	10.8	17.1
BAPT–So Bapt Conv	8	419	1,092	1,333	24.9	39.5
Catholic	1	NR	NR	141	2.6	4.2
CHR–Chr Ch (Disc)	1	53	224	273	5.1	8.1
LUTH–E.L.C.A.	1	18	85	96	1.8	2.8
LUTH–Luth-MO Synod	2	107	325	427	8.0	12.6
METH–Un Methodist	5	187	348	500	9.3	14.8
PENT–Assemb of God	1	17	21	26	0.5	0.8
SHELBY	**66**	**3,044**	**7,445**	**11,576**	**51.8**	**100.0**
Bahá'í	0	NR	1	1	0.0	0.0
BAPT–Amer Bapt USA	1	219	422	507	2.3	4.4
BAPT–Reg Bapt Gen As	1	NR	NR	NR	-	-
BAPT–So Bapt Conv	6	261	504	606	2.7	5.2
Catholic	3	NR	NR	2,635	11.8	22.8
CGOD–Ches God-Gen Con	1	12	15	18	0.1	0.2
Ch of Nazarene	1	182	231	275	1.2	2.4
CHR–Chr Chs & Chs Cr	9	NR	2,036	2,448	10.9	21.1
CHR–Chs of Christ	7	226	235	283	1.3	2.4
Jehovah's Witness	1	NR	NR	NR	-	-
JUD–Reform	1	2	4	11	0.0	0.1
LUTH–E.L.C.A.	2	65	92	95	0.4	0.8
LUTH–Luth-MO Synod	5	613	1,416	1,677	7.5	14.5
MENN–Unaffil Amish-Menn	1	11	10	11	0.0	0.1
METH–Free Methodist	2	143	125	143	0.6	1.2
METH–Un Methodist	15	775	1,624	1,937	8.7	16.7
Non-denom Chr Chs	4	420	500	551	2.5	4.8
PENT–Assemb of God	1	73	38	150	0.7	1.3
PENT–Un Pent Ch Intl	2	NR	NR	NR	-	-
PRES–Presb Ch (USA)	1	0	95	114	0.5	1.0
Sev Day Adv	1	27	47	54	0.2	0.5
Un C of Christ	1	15	50	60	0.3	0.5
STARK	**17**	**792**	**1,116**	**2,194**	**36.6**	**100.0**
Ap Chr Ch-Amer	1	272	145	272	4.5	12.4
Bahá'í	0	NR	3	3	0.1	0.1
BAPT–Consrv Bapt	1	NR	NR	NR	-	-
Catholic	2	NR	NR	533	8.9	24.3
Ch of Nazarene	1	58	60	238	4.0	10.8
CONG–Cong Chr, NA	1	NR	75	91	1.5	4.1
LUTH–E.L.C.A.	1	39	90	120	2.0	5.5
METH–Un Methodist	5	248	529	675	11.3	30.8
Non-denom Chr Chs	2	90	90	112	1.9	5.1
PRES–Presb Ch (USA)	1	30	38	46	0.8	2.1
Un C of Christ	2	55	86	104	1.7	4.7
STEPHENSON	**92**	**12,458**	**18,082**	**32,580**	**68.3**	**100.0**
ANG/EPIS–Episcopal	1	40	333	352	0.7	1.1
Bahá'í	0	NR	7	7	0.0	0.0
BAPT–NBC USA	3	270	470	567	1.2	1.7
BAPT–So Bapt Conv	1	57	35	42	0.1	0.1

NR–Not Reported - Represents no adherents reported. Percentages may not total 100 due to rounding.

Table 3: Religious Congregations by County and Group: 2010

Religious Group	Number of Congregations	Number of Attendees	Number of Communicant, Confirmed, or Full Members	Adherents: Number of Adherents	Adherents: % of Total Pop.	Adherents: % of Total Adh.
BRETH–Ch of Brethren	2	64	106	128	0.3	0.4
Catholic	5	NR	NR	5,251	11.0	16.1
CGOD–Ch God (Ander)	1	0	NR	0	0.0	0.0
CGOD–Ches God-Gen Con	1	61	113	136	0.3	0.4
Ch Cr, Scientst	1	NR	NR	NR	-	-
Ch of Nazarene	1	91	162	162	0.3	0.5
CHR–Chs of Christ	1	130	116	170	0.4	0.5
CONG–Consrv Cong Chr	2	267	449	542	1.1	1.7
Evan Cong Ch	2	NR	213	257	0.5	0.8
Evan Free Ch	4	850	NR	850	1.8	2.6
Jehovah's Witness	1	NR	NR	NR	-	-
LDS–L-D Saints	1	NR	NR	268	0.6	0.8
LUTH–E.L.C.A.	5	647	1,546	1,909	4.0	5.9
LUTH–Luth–MO Synod	3	806	1,412	1,760	3.7	5.4
LUTH–Wisc Ev Luth Syn	1	53	76	76	0.2	0.2
MENN–Mennonite USA	1	100	128	154	0.3	0.5
METH–C.M.E.	1	120	177	214	0.4	0.7
METH–Free Methodist	2	203	157	203	0.4	0.6
METH–Un Methodist	17	991	3,074	3,765	7.9	11.6
Non-denom Chr Chs	16	3,740	6,024	6,407	13.4	19.7
ORTHE–Rus Orth Abroad	1	10	NR	15	0.0	0.0
PENT–Assemb of God	1	2,953	1,036	5,485	11.5	16.8
PENT–COGIC	5	175	485	585	1.2	1.8
PENT–Open Bible Std	1	53	NR	53	0.1	0.2
PRES–Presb Ch (USA)	2	97	252	304	0.6	0.9
REF–Christian Ref	1	120	169	204	0.4	0.6
REF–Ref Ch in Am	2	165	306	325	0.7	1.0
Salvation Army	1	31	52	963	2.0	3.0
Sev Day Adv	1	24	42	48	0.1	0.1
Un C of Christ	4	340	1,142	1,378	2.9	4.2
TAZEWELL	**171**	**21,573**	**35,105**	**58,964**	**43.5**	**100.0**
ANG/EPIS–Episcopal	2	66	103	111	0.1	0.2
Ap Chr Ch-Amer	3	1,732	1,021	1,732	1.3	2.9
Bahá'í	0	NR	35	35	0.0	0.1
BAPT–Amer Bapt Assn	1	NR	0	0	0.0	0.0
BAPT–Amer Bapt USA	2	78	353	431	0.3	0.7
BAPT–Consrv Bapt	3	NR	NR	NR	-	-
BAPT–Ind Bapt Flwsp Intl	1	NR	NR	NR	-	-
BAPT–NT Ind Bapt	1	NR	NR	NR	-	-
BAPT–So Bapt Conv	14	924	3,141	3,839	2.8	6.5
Catholic	7	NR	NR	10,650	7.9	18.1
CGOD–Ch God (Ander)	2	438	NR	438	0.3	0.7
Ch of God Gen Conf	1	NR	45	55	0.0	0.1
Ch of Nazarene	6	1,040	1,000	1,788	1.3	3.0
CHR–Chr Ch (Disc)	4	395	872	1,066	0.8	1.8
CHR–Chr Chs & Chs Cr	7	NR	2,040	2,493	1.8	4.2
CHR–Chs of Christ	4	298	316	399	0.3	0.7
Evan Free Ch	1	140	NR	140	0.1	0.2
Ind Fund Churches	3	NR	NR	NR	-	-
Jehovah's Witness	3	NR	NR	NR	-	-
LDS–Comm of Christ	1	NR	119	119	0.1	0.2
LDS–L-D Saints	2	NR	NR	1,000	0.7	1.7
LUTH–E.L.C.A.	4	673	2,147	2,844	2.1	4.8
LUTH–Luth–MO Synod	10	1,805	4,635	6,462	4.8	11.0
MENN–Fel Evg Ch	4	1,071	1,022	1,249	0.9	2.1
MENN–Mennonite USA	8	591	848	1,036	0.8	1.8
METH–Free Methodist	2	114	104	114	0.1	0.2
METH–Un Methodist	15	2,817	5,422	7,702	5.7	13.1
Missionary Ch	3	318	282	321	0.2	0.5
Non-denom Chr Chs	30	6,097	7,756	8,619	6.4	14.6
PENT–Assemb of God	6	1,846	999	2,479	1.8	4.2
PENT–Ch of God Proph	1	NR	70	86	0.1	0.1
PENT–Open Bible Std	1	15	NR	15	0.0	0.0
PENT–Pent Ch of God	1	70	NR	109	0.1	0.2
PENT–Un Pent Ch Intl	2	NR	NR	NR	-	-
PRES–Presb Ch (USA)	5	314	504	616	0.5	1.0
REF–Christian Ref	1	100	35	43	0.0	0.1
REF–Ref Ch in Am	2	152	237	280	0.2	0.5
Salvation Army	1	67	64	329	0.2	0.6
Sev Day Adv	1	5	9	10	0.0	0.0
Un C of Christ	6	407	1,926	2,354	1.7	4.0
UNION	**56**	**2,562**	**8,686**	**11,632**	**65.3**	**100.0**
Bahá'í	0	NR	5	5	0.0	0.0
BAPT–Amer Bapt USA	2	37	64	77	0.4	0.7
BAPT–So Bapt Conv	22	1,530	6,280	7,520	42.2	64.6
Catholic	2	NR	NR	1,200	6.7	10.3
Ch of Nazarene	1	113	179	179	1.0	1.5
CHR–Chr Chs & Chs Cr	1	NR	300	359	2.0	3.1
CHR–Chs of Christ	2	110	89	133	0.7	1.1
Jehovah's Witness	1	NR	NR	NR	-	-
LUTH–E.L.C.A.	2	185	586	726	4.1	6.2
LUTH–Luth Cong Msn Chr	2	144	220	263	1.5	2.3
LUTH–Luth–MO Synod	1	50	120	135	0.8	1.2
METH–Un Methodist	6	291	378	444	2.5	3.8
Non-denom Chr Chs	2	80	90	100	0.6	0.9
PENT–Ch God (Cleve)	1	22	57	68	0.4	0.6
PENT–Un Pent Ch Intl	5	NR	NR	NR	-	-
PRES–Cumber Presb	4	NR	41	91	0.5	0.8
PRES–Evan Presby Ch	1	NR	198	237	1.3	2.0
PRES–Presb Ch (USA)	1	0	79	95	0.5	0.8
VERMILION	**142**	**9,169**	**21,440**	**30,674**	**37.6**	**100.0**
ANG/EPIS–Episcopal	1	45	102	138	0.2	0.4
Bahá'í	0	NR	24	24	0.0	0.1
BAPT–Amer Bapt USA	4	340	921	1,132	1.4	3.7
BAPT–Free Will Bapt	1	NR	86	106	0.1	0.3
BAPT–Natl Mis Bapt Conv	1	0	150	184	0.2	0.6
BAPT–NBC USA	1	100	300	369	0.5	1.2
BAPT–NT Ind Bapt	1	NR	NR	NR	-	-
BAPT–So Bapt Conv	2	77	427	525	0.6	1.7
Catholic	5	NR	NR	3,804	4.7	12.4
CGOD–Ch God (Ander)	2	300	NR	300	0.4	1.0
Ch of Nazarene	10	779	1,179	1,571	1.9	5.1
Chr & Miss Al	2	143	49	267	0.3	0.9
CHR–Chr Ch (Disc)	2	226	752	925	1.1	3.0
CHR–Chr Chs & Chs Cr	24	NR	4,246	5,220	6.4	17.0
CHR–Chs of Christ	3	205	215	270	0.3	0.9
Evan Ch	1	NR	NR	NR	-	-
FRND–Fr Un Mtg	3	NR	236	290	0.4	0.9
Jehovah's Witness	3	NR	NR	NR	-	-
LDS–Comm of Christ	1	NR	82	82	0.1	0.3
LDS–L-D Saints	1	NR	NR	462	0.6	1.5
LUTH–E.L.C.A.	2	111	260	368	0.5	1.2
LUTH–Luth–MO Synod	3	452	1,303	1,703	2.1	5.6
METH–AME	1	65	85	105	0.1	0.3
METH–C.M.E.	2	128	360	443	0.5	1.4
METH–Evan Meth Ch	1	NR	NR	NR	-	-
METH–Un Methodist	24	1,291	3,247	3,752	4.6	12.2
Non-denom Chr Chs	21	4,095	5,886	6,169	7.6	20.1
PENT–Assemb of God	2	230	156	335	0.4	1.1
PENT–Ch God (Cleve)	1	72	77	95	0.1	0.3
PENT–COGIC	1	0	150	184	0.2	0.6
PENT–Full Gosp Bapt	2	NR	NR	NR	-	-
PENT–Int Foursq Gos	1	15	17	21	0.0	0.1
PENT–Pent Ch of God	1	70	NR	109	0.1	0.4
PENT–Un Pent Ch Intl	2	NR	NR	NR	-	-
PRES–Cumber Presb	1	NR	25	90	0.1	0.3
PRES–Presb Ch (USA)	3	214	463	569	0.7	1.9
Salvation Army	1	37	41	329	0.4	1.1
Sev Day Adv	2	45	78	90	0.1	0.3
Un C of Christ	3	129	523	643	0.8	2.1
WABASH	**36**	**1,757**	**3,829**	**6,593**	**55.2**	**100.0**
ANG/EPIS–Episcopal	1	15	42	42	0.4	0.6
BAPT–So Bapt Conv	1	438	743	894	7.5	13.6
Catholic	2	NR	NR	1,984	16.6	30.1
CGOD–Ch God (Ander)	1	139	NR	139	1.2	2.1
Ch of Nazarene	1	28	51	54	0.5	0.8
CHR–Chr Ch (Disc)	2	160	636	765	6.4	11.6
CHR–Chr Chs & Chs Cr	6	NR	735	884	7.4	13.4
CHR–Chs of Christ	1	180	171	216	1.8	3.3
Jehovah's Witness	1	NR	NR	NR	-	-
LUTH–E.L.C.A.	1	27	64	70	0.6	1.1
LUTH–Luth–MO Synod	1	24	60	72	0.6	1.1

NR–Not Reported - Represents no adherents reported. Percentages may not total 100 due to rounding.

Table 3: Religious Congregations by County and Group: 2010

Religious Group	Number of Congregations	Number of Attendees	Number of Communicant, Confirmed, or Full Members	Adherents: Number of Adherents	Adherents: % of Total Pop.	Adherents: % of Total Adh.
METH–Free Methodist	2	87	98	98	0.8	1.5
METH–Un Methodist	11	428	924	1,036	8.7	15.7
Non-denom Chr Chs	2	130	180	188	1.6	2.9
PRES–Presb Ch (USA)	2	80	92	111	0.9	1.7
Un C of Christ	1	21	33	40	0.3	0.6
WARREN	**43**	**2,141**	**5,336**	**7,890**	**44.6**	**100.0**
ANG/EPIS–Anglican NA	1	NR	NR	NR	-	-
Bahá'í	0	NR	10	10	0.1	0.1
BAPT–Amer Bapt USA	2	95	169	204	1.2	2.6
BAPT–Converge/BGC	1	75	NR	90	0.5	1.1
BAPT–So Bapt Conv	1	12	40	48	0.3	0.6
Catholic	2	NR	NR	1,369	7.7	17.4
Ch of Nazarene	3	18	33	42	0.2	0.5
CHR–Chr Ch (Disc)	3	143	575	694	3.9	8.8
CHR–Chr Chs & Chs Cr	2	NR	769	928	5.2	11.8
FRND–Fr Gen Cf	1	NR	9	11	0.1	0.1
Jehovah's Witness	1	NR	NR	NR	-	-
LUTH–E.L.C.A.	1	83	428	515	2.9	6.5
MENN–Amish Undif	1	NR	43	121	0.7	1.5
METH–AME	1	0	150	181	1.0	2.3
METH–Un Methodist	6	412	1,072	1,259	7.1	16.0
Non-denom Chr Chs	8	830	1,000	1,163	6.6	14.7
PENT–Assemb of God	1	30	23	30	0.2	0.4
PENT–Int Foursq Gos	1	72	73	88	0.5	1.1
PRES–Presb Ch (USA)	7	371	942	1,137	6.4	14.4
WASHINGTON	**41**	**2,196**	**5,003**	**10,368**	**70.5**	**100.0**
Bahá'í	0	NR	1	1	0.0	0.0
BAPT–So Bapt Conv	6	315	435	521	3.5	5.0
Catholic	6	NR	NR	4,301	29.2	41.5
CHR–Chr Chs & Chs Cr	1	NR	35	42	0.3	0.4
LUTH–Luth-MO Synod	7	869	2,218	2,754	18.7	26.6
METH–Un Methodist	5	204	495	553	3.8	5.3
Non-denom Chr Chs	1	50	85	85	0.6	0.8
PENT–Assemb of God	1	50	24	62	0.4	0.6
PENT–Int Foursq Gos	1	8	18	22	0.1	0.2
PRES–Presb Ch (USA)	2	70	106	127	0.9	1.2
Un C of Christ	11	630	1,586	1,900	12.9	18.3
WAYNE	**64**	**2,143**	**7,175**	**9,250**	**55.2**	**100.0**
Bahá'í	0	NR	1	1	0.0	0.0
BAPT–Free Will Bapt	3	NR	258	313	1.9	3.4
BAPT–Natl Mis Bapt Conv	1	0	150	182	1.1	2.0
BAPT–So Bapt Conv	18	968	3,539	4,289	25.6	46.4
BRETH–Ch of Brethren	2	125	161	195	1.2	2.1
Catholic	1	NR	NR	297	1.8	3.2
Ch of Nazarene	2	52	99	99	0.6	1.1
CHR–Chr Chs & Chs Cr	8	NR	983	1,191	7.1	12.9
CHR–Chs of Christ	1	65	75	97	0.6	1.0
LDS–Comm of Christ	2	NR	164	164	1.0	1.8
LUTH–Luth-MO Synod	1	14	19	19	0.1	0.2
MENN–Amish Undif	3	NR	68	197	1.2	2.1
METH–Un Methodist	8	330	809	939	5.6	10.2
METH–Wesleyan	1	80	41	104	0.6	1.1
Non-denom Chr Chs	2	215	225	269	1.6	2.9
PENT–Assemb of God	1	150	84	150	0.9	1.6
PENT–Ch God (Cleve)	3	136	136	165	1.0	1.8
PENT–Un Pent Ch Intl	1	NR	NR	NR	-	-
PRES–Cumber Presb	5	NR	349	563	3.4	6.1
Sev Day Adv	1	8	14	16	0.1	0.2
WHITE	**54**	**2,132**	**5,357**	**7,683**	**52.4**	**100.0**
BAPT–So Bapt Conv	12	668	2,053	2,446	16.7	31.8
Catholic	2	NR	NR	960	6.5	12.5
CGOD–Ch God (Ander)	1	25	NR	25	0.2	0.3
Ch of Nazarene	1	57	55	68	0.5	0.9
CHR–Chr Chs & Chs Cr	6	NR	1,252	1,492	10.2	19.4
CHR–Chs of Christ	4	103	97	127	0.9	1.7
Jehovah's Witness	1	NR	NR	NR	-	-
LDS–Comm of Christ	1	NR	82	82	0.6	1.1
LUTH–Luth-MO Synod	1	20	45	51	0.3	0.7

Religious Group	Number of Congregations	Number of Attendees	Number of Communicant, Confirmed, or Full Members	Adherents: Number of Adherents	Adherents: % of Total Pop.	Adherents: % of Total Adh.
METH–Un Methodist	15	568	1,030	1,253	8.5	16.3
Non-denom Chr Chs	1	425	300	531	3.6	6.9
PENT–Assemb of God	1	110	35	116	0.8	1.5
PENT–Ch God (Cleve)	2	115	209	249	1.7	3.2
PRES–Cumber Presb	4	NR	87	150	1.0	2.0
PRES–Presb Ch (USA)	2	41	112	133	0.9	1.7
WHITESIDE	**109**	**9,361**	**20,087**	**34,659**	**59.2**	**100.0**
ANG/EPIS–Episcopal	2	83	164	188	0.3	0.5
Bahá'í	0	NR	31	31	0.1	0.1
BAPT–Amer Bapt USA	4	221	788	959	1.6	2.8
BAPT–Consrv Bapt	1	NR	NR	NR	-	-
BAPT–NT Ind Bapt	1	NR	NR	NR	-	-
BAPT–So Bapt Conv	6	210	1,066	1,297	2.2	3.7
BRETH–Breth in Chr	2	NR	NR	NR	-	-
Catholic	9	NR	NR	10,235	17.5	29.5
CGOD–Ch God (Ander)	2	10	NR	10	0.0	0.0
Ch of Nazarene	2	407	590	591	1.0	1.7
CHR–Chr Ch (Disc)	2	216	516	628	1.1	1.8
CHR–Chr Chs & Chs Cr	5	NR	590	718	1.2	2.1
CHR–Chs of Christ	2	157	148	190	0.3	0.5
Evan Cong Ch	1	NR	0	0	0.0	0.0
Evan Free Ch	1	82	NR	82	0.1	0.2
Jehovah's Witness	1	NR	NR	NR	-	-
LDS–Comm of Christ	1	NR	119	119	0.2	0.3
LDS–L-D Saints	1	NR	NR	355	0.6	1.0
LUTH–E.L.C.A.	6	705	2,615	3,185	5.4	9.2
LUTH–Luth Cong Msn Chr	1	240	425	517	0.9	1.5
LUTH–Luth-MO Synod	4	470	1,580	1,811	3.1	5.2
MENN–Mennonite USA	1	30	104	127	0.2	0.4
MENN–Ref Mennonite	1	NR	39	42	0.1	0.1
METH–Un Methodist	14	1,153	3,227	4,095	7.0	11.8
Non-denom Chr Chs	12	2,910	3,380	3,730	6.4	10.8
PENT–Assemb of God	3	232	133	429	0.7	1.2
PENT–Int Foursq Gos	1	11	63	77	0.1	0.2
PENT–Open Bible Std	1	100	NR	100	0.2	0.3
PENT–Un Pent Ch Intl	1	NR	NR	NR	-	-
PRES–Presb Ch (USA)	4	264	667	812	1.4	2.3
REF–Christian Ref	3	300	572	696	1.2	2.0
REF–Ref Ch in Am	8	1,308	2,811	2,907	5.0	8.4
Salvation Army	1	44	46	257	0.4	0.7
Sev Day Adv	1	24	43	49	0.1	0.1
Un Breth in Cr	1	39	51	34	0.1	0.1
Un C of Christ	3	145	319	388	0.7	1.1
WILL	**342**	**40,215**	**60,151**	**311,505**	**46.0**	**100.0**
ANG/EPIS–Episcopal	4	319	577	656	0.1	0.2
Bahá'í	0	NR	174	174	0.0	0.1
BAPT–Amer Bapt Assn	1	NR	0	0	0.0	0.0
BAPT–Amer Bapt USA	3	295	574	739	0.1	0.2
BAPT–Converge/BGC	5	700	NR	840	0.1	0.3
BAPT–Free Will Bapt	1	NR	86	111	0.0	0.0
BAPT–NBC USA	4	1,475	4,270	5,495	0.8	1.8
BAPT–Reg Bapt Gen As	5	NR	NR	NR	-	-
BAPT–So Bapt Conv	24	1,973	3,671	4,724	0.7	1.5
Calv Chpl	1	NR	NR	NR	-	-
Catholic	39	NR	NR	212,252	31.3	68.1
CGOD–Ch God (Ander)	2	257	NR	257	0.0	0.1
CGOD–Ches God-Gen Con	2	246	35	45	0.0	0.0
Ch of Nazarene	5	267	495	521	0.1	0.2
Chr & Miss Al	2	184	131	213	0.0	0.1
CHR–Chr Chs & Chs Cr	12	NR	2,532	3,258	0.5	1.0
CHR–Chs of Christ	5	395	362	483	0.1	0.2
CONG–Cong Chr, NA	1	NR	113	145	0.0	0.0
CONG–Consrv Cong Chr	1	88	111	143	0.0	0.0
Evan Cov Ch	3	162	118	211	0.0	0.1
Evan Free Ch	6	1,275	NR	1,275	0.2	0.4
HINDU–I/A Temples	1	NR	NR	250	0.0	0.1
Ind Fund Churches	1	NR	NR	NR	-	-
Jehovah's Witness	7	NR	NR	NR	-	-
LDS–Comm of Christ	1	NR	121	121	0.0	0.0
LDS–L-D Saints	5	NR	NR	1,871	0.3	0.6
LUTH–E.L.C.A.	17	3,313	7,210	10,913	1.6	3.5

NR–Not Reported   - Represents no adherents reported.   Percentages may not total 100 due to rounding.

Table 3: Religious Congregations by County and Group: 2010

Religious Group	Number of Congregations	Number of Attendees	Number of Communicant, Confirmed, or Full Members	Adherents: Number of Adherents	Adherents: % of Total Pop.	Adherents: % of Total Adh.
LUTH–Luth Cong Msn Chr	1	400	873	1,123	0.2	0.4
LUTH–Luth–MO Synod	15	2,753	5,880	7,575	1.1	2.4
LUTH–Wisc Ev Luth Syn	3	696	1,347	1,720	0.3	0.6
METH–AME	3	150	550	708	0.1	0.2
METH–C.M.E.	1	0	100	129	0.0	0.0
METH–Free Methodist	1	93	69	93	0.0	0.0
METH–Un Methodist	22	2,971	7,509	11,143	1.6	3.6
METH–Wesleyan	2	77	49	100	0.0	0.0
Muslim Est	3	2,724	NR	9,894	1.5	3.2
Non-denom Chr Chs	51	10,915	12,655	14,384	2.1	4.6
ORTHE–Greek Orthodox	1	200	NR	850	0.1	0.3
ORTHE–Holy Orth in NA	1	42	NR	55	0.0	0.0
ORTHE–Orth Ch in Amer	1	30	NR	100	0.0	0.0
ORTHE–Serb Orth USA	2	160	NR	331	0.0	0.1
ORTHO–Coptic Orth Ch	1	110	NR	200	0.0	0.1
PENT–Assemb of God	10	2,621	633	5,373	0.8	1.7
PENT–Ch God (Cleve)	2	90	147	189	0.0	0.1
PENT–Ch of God Proph	1	NR	57	73	0.0	0.0
PENT–COGIC	6	130	850	1,094	0.2	0.4
PENT–Intl Pent Holiness	2	35	50	64	0.0	0.0
PENT–Un Pent Ch Intl	8	NR	NR	NR	-	-
PENT–United Holy Ch	2	NR	NR	NR	-	-
PENT–Vineyard	1	72	111	143	0.0	0.0
PRES–Orth Pres Ch	1	144	121	162	0.0	0.1
PRES–Presb Ch (USA)	11	786	1,806	2,324	0.3	0.7
PRES–Presb Ch Amer	1	65	47	64	0.0	0.0
REF–Christian Ref	6	1,520	1,570	2,020	0.3	0.6
REF–Prot Ref Chs	1	428	278	485	0.1	0.2
REF–Ref Ch in Am	2	547	727	970	0.1	0.3
REF–Un Ref Chs N.A.	1	NR	NR	NR	-	-
Salvation Army	1	16	35	208	0.0	0.1
Sev Day Adv	4	274	476	547	0.1	0.2
Un C of Christ	13	1,072	3,437	4,423	0.7	1.4
Unit Univ	2	145	194	239	0.0	0.1
Unity Ch	1	NR	NR	NR	-	-
Zoroastrian	0	NR	NR	25	0.0	0.0
WILLIAMSON	**129**	**8,782**	**19,243**	**29,563**	**44.6**	**100.0**
ANG/EPIS–Episcopal	1	20	29	32	0.0	0.1
Bahá'í	0	NR	8	8	0.0	0.0
BAPT–Amer Bapt USA	6	417	774	935	1.4	3.2
BAPT–Free Will Bapt	4	NR	344	416	0.6	1.4
BAPT–Reg Bapt Gen As	2	NR	NR	NR	-	-
BAPT–So Bapt Conv	35	3,438	9,603	11,599	17.5	39.2
Catholic	5	NR	NR	4,788	7.2	16.2
CGOD–Ch God (Ander)	3	521	NR	521	0.8	1.8
Ch of Nazarene	2	62	159	165	0.2	0.6
CHR–Chr Ch (Disc)	1	81	221	267	0.4	0.9
CHR–Chr Chs & Chs Cr	8	NR	1,548	1,870	2.8	6.3
CHR–Chs of Christ	2	245	222	317	0.5	1.1
Jehovah's Witness	1	NR	NR	NR	-	-
JUD–Reform	1	8	14	38	0.1	0.1
LDS–Comm of Christ	1	NR	82	82	0.1	0.3
LDS–L-D Saints	1	NR	NR	556	0.8	1.9
LUTH–E.L.C.A.	1	107	305	327	0.5	1.1
LUTH–Luth–MO Synod	1	110	171	217	0.3	0.7
METH–AME	2	0	200	242	0.4	0.8
METH–Free Methodist	1	34	19	34	0.1	0.1
METH–Un Methodist	16	1,156	2,139	3,004	4.5	10.2
Non-denom Chr Chs	14	1,885	2,159	2,489	3.8	8.4
PENT–Assemb of God	2	145	99	170	0.3	0.6
PENT–Ch God (Cleve)	3	118	316	382	0.6	1.3
PENT–Ch of God Proph	2	NR	107	129	0.2	0.4
PENT–Pent Ch of God	1	70	NR	109	0.2	0.4
PENT–Un Pent Ch Intl	8	NR	NR	NR	-	-
PRES–Presb Ch (USA)	3	162	233	281	0.4	1.0
Sev Day Adv	1	82	142	163	0.2	0.6
Un C of Christ	1	121	349	422	0.6	1.4
WINNEBAGO	**280**	**47,896**	**66,393**	**154,460**	**52.3**	**100.0**
ANG/EPIS–Episcopal	3	204	400	433	0.1	0.3
Bahá'í	1	NR	183	183	0.1	0.1
BAPT–Amer Bapt Assn	2	NR	100	124	0.0	0.1

Religious Group	Number of Congregations	Number of Attendees	Number of Communicant, Confirmed, or Full Members	Adherents: Number of Adherents	Adherents: % of Total Pop.	Adherents: % of Total Adh.
BAPT–Amer Bapt USA	6	730	1,040	1,286	0.4	0.8
BAPT–Asc Ref Bap Ch Am	1	NR	NR	NR	-	-
BAPT–Consrv Bapt	1	NR	NR	NR	-	-
BAPT–Converge/BGC	1	75	NR	90	0.0	0.1
BAPT–Free Will Bapt	1	NR	86	106	0.0	0.1
BAPT–Natl Mis Bapt Conv	3	298	725	896	0.3	0.6
BAPT–NBC Amer	1	150	250	309	0.1	0.2
BAPT–NBC USA	8	1,405	2,870	3,548	1.2	2.3
BAPT–NT Ind Bapt	1	NR	NR	NR	-	-
BAPT–Ref Bapt Ch	1	NR	NR	NR	-	-
BAPT–So Bapt Conv	12	1,191	2,662	3,291	1.1	2.1
BRETH–Ch of Brethren	1	0	64	79	0.0	0.1
BUDD–Mahayana	1	NR	NR	505	0.2	0.3
BUDD–Theravada	3	NR	NR	580	0.2	0.4
Calv Chpl	1	NR	NR	NR	-	-
Catholic	16	NR	NR	59,373	20.1	38.4
CGOD–Ch God (Ander)	3	70	NR	70	0.0	0.0
Ch Cr, Scientst	1	NR	NR	NR	-	-
Ch of God Gen Conf	4	NR	187	231	0.1	0.1
Ch of Nazarene	6	286	486	596	0.2	0.4
CHR–Chr Ch (Disc)	3	305	640	791	0.3	0.5
CHR–Chr Chs & Chs Cr	3	NR	1,635	2,021	0.7	1.3
CHR–Chs of Christ	9	1,090	1,164	1,469	0.5	1.0
CONG–Cong Chr, NA	1	NR	155	192	0.1	0.1
CONG–Consrv Cong Chr	1	80	334	413	0.1	0.3
Evan Cong Ch	1	NR	55	68	0.0	0.0
Evan Cov Ch	5	766	1,042	997	0.3	0.6
Evan Free Ch	7	3,140	NR	3,140	1.1	2.0
FRND–Fr Gen Cf	1	NR	12	15	0.0	0.0
Ind Fund Churches	1	NR	NR	NR	-	-
Jehovah's Witness	6	NR	NR	NR	-	-
JUD–Conserv	1	18	20	54	0.0	0.0
JUD–Reform	1	72	127	343	0.1	0.2
LDS–Comm of Christ	1	NR	138	138	0.0	0.1
LDS–L-D Saints	3	NR	NR	1,380	0.5	0.9
LUTH–E.L.C.A.	22	3,389	10,276	13,657	4.6	8.8
LUTH–Luth Cong Msn Chr	1	170	462	571	0.2	0.4
LUTH–Luth–MO Synod	10	1,498	3,566	4,512	1.5	2.9
LUTH–Wisc Ev Luth Syn	3	264	423	563	0.2	0.4
METH–AME	2	270	405	501	0.2	0.3
METH–C.M.E.	1	0	60	74	0.0	0.0
METH–Free Methodist	1	71	42	71	0.0	0.0
METH–Un Methodist	22	2,633	6,303	8,058	2.7	5.2
METH–Wesleyan	1	35	44	46	0.0	0.0
Muslim Est	1	500	NR	1,000	0.3	0.6
Nat Spirit Asso	2	NR	NR	NR	-	-
Non-denom Chr Chs	45	22,305	23,702	28,641	9.7	18.5
ORTHE–Carp Rus Orth	1	52	NR	143	0.0	0.1
ORTHE–Greek Orthodox	1	115	NR	505	0.2	0.3
ORTHE–Serb Orth USA	1	45	NR	600	0.2	0.4
PENT–Assemb of God	7	3,734	1,552	5,372	1.8	3.5
PENT–Ch God (Cleve)	2	154	155	192	0.1	0.1
PENT–Ch Lord Jesus Apos	1	NR	NR	NR	-	-
PENT–Ch of God Proph	1	NR	8	10	0.0	0.0
PENT–COGIC	2	20	175	216	0.1	0.1
PENT–Int Foursq Gos	1	26	41	51	0.0	0.0
PENT–Intl Pent Holiness	1	43	25	31	0.0	0.0
PENT–Open Bible Std	1	182	NR	182	0.1	0.1
PENT–Pent Ch of God	1	70	NR	109	0.0	0.1
PENT–Un Pent Ch Intl	5	NR	NR	NR	-	-
PRES–Orth Pres Ch	1	41	27	37	0.0	0.0
PRES–Presb Ch (USA)	7	942	2,240	2,769	0.9	1.8
Salvation Army	2	614	509	1,450	0.5	0.9
Sev Day Adv	3	261	453	522	0.2	0.3
Un Breth in Cr	1	16	25	14	0.0	0.0
Un C of Christ	5	395	1,133	1,401	0.5	0.9
Unit Univ	2	171	392	440	0.1	0.3
Unity Ch	1	NR	NR	NR	-	-
Zoroastrian	0	NR	NR	1	0.0	0.0
WOODFORD	**68**	**7,319**	**9,015**	**15,537**	**40.2**	**100.0**
ANG/EPIS–Anglican NA	1	NR	NR	NR	-	-
Ap Chr Ch-Amer	4	2,495	1,492	2,495	6.5	16.1
Bahá'í	0	NR	14	14	0.0	0.1

NR–Not Reported   - Represents no adherents reported.   Percentages may not total 100 due to rounding.

Table 3: Religious Congregations by County and Group: 2010

Religious Group	Number of Congregations	Number of Attendees	Number of Communicant, Confirmed, or Full Members	Adherents: Number of Adherents	Adherents: % of Total Pop.	Adherents: % of Total Adh.
BAPT–Amer Bapt USA	3	194	578	720	1.9	4.6
BAPT–Ref Bapt Ch	1	NR	NR	NR	-	-
BAPT–Reg Bapt Gen As	1	NR	NR	NR	-	-
BRETH–Ch of Brethren	2	0	52	65	0.2	0.4
Catholic	8	NR	NR	3,804	9.8	24.5
Ch of Nazarene	2	156	210	287	0.7	1.8
CHR–Chr Ch (Disc)	1	145	338	421	1.1	2.7
CHR–Chr Chs & Chs Cr	1	NR	0	0	0.0	0.0
CHR–Chs of Christ	2	105	105	124	0.3	0.8
Evan Free Ch	1	45	NR	45	0.1	0.3
Ind Fund Churches	1	NR	NR	NR	-	-
LUTH–E.L.C.A.	2	201	434	706	1.8	4.5
LUTH–Luth–MO Synod	4	336	1,003	1,117	2.9	7.2
LUTH–Nor Amer Luth C	1	NR	NR	NR	-	-
MENN–Fel Evg Ch	3	986	633	789	2.0	5.1
MENN–Mennonite USA	5	525	495	617	1.6	4.0
MENN–Unaffil Amish-Menn	2	169	119	169	0.4	1.1
METH–Un Methodist	9	809	1,678	1,928	5.0	12.4
Non-denom Chr Chs	9	1,002	1,355	1,569	4.1	10.1
PENT–Assemb of God	1	25	0	33	0.1	0.2
PRES–Presb Ch (USA)	2	35	73	91	0.2	0.6
Un C of Christ	2	91	436	543	1.4	3.5
INDIANA	**9,061**	**875,783**	**1,470,855**	**2,874,144**	**44.3**	**100.0**
ADAMS	**111**	**7,814**	**13,200**	**25,182**	**73.2**	**100.0**
ANG/EPIS–Episcopal	1	13	30	30	0.1	0.1
Bahá'í	0	NR	2	2	0.0	0.0
BAPT–Amer Bapt USA	2	87	209	277	0.8	1.1
BRETH–Ch of Brethren	1	241	241	320	0.9	1.3
BRETH–Grace Breth	1	NR	NR	NR	-	-
Catholic	2	NR	NR	3,605	10.5	14.3
CGOD–Ch God (Ander)	1	366	NR	366	1.1	1.5
Ch of Nazarene	4	415	429	661	1.9	2.6
CHR–Chr Chs & Chs Cr	2	NR	160	212	0.6	0.8
CHR–Chs of Christ	1	25	21	29	0.1	0.1
Evan Assoc RCC	2	NR	NR	NR	-	-
Ind Fund Churches	2	NR	NR	NR	-	-
Jehovah's Witness	1	NR	NR	NR	-	-
LDS–L-D Saints	1	NR	NR	305	0.9	1.2
LUTH–Luth–MO Synod	7	1,445	3,077	4,016	11.7	15.9
MENN–Amish Undif	41	NR	2,454	6,343	18.4	25.2
MENN–Beachy Amish-Menn	1	46	25	46	0.1	0.2
MENN–Fel Evg Ch	1	167	133	176	0.5	0.7
MENN–Mennonite USA	2	508	1,147	1,522	4.4	6.0
METH–Un Methodist	9	942	1,645	2,301	6.7	9.1
METH–Wesleyan	1	19	29	25	0.1	0.1
Missionary Ch	4	974	795	979	2.8	3.9
Non-denom Chr Chs	11	1,970	1,895	2,696	7.8	10.7
PENT–Assemb of God	3	215	114	252	0.7	1.0
PENT–Intl Pent Holiness	2	23	61	81	0.2	0.3
PENT–Un Pent Ch Intl	1	NR	NR	NR	-	-
PRES–Presb Ch (USA)	1	37	79	105	0.3	0.4
Un Breth in Cr	3	125	107	107	0.3	0.4
Un C of Christ	3	196	547	726	2.1	2.9
ALLEN	**395**	**66,348**	**90,556**	**190,976**	**53.7**	**100.0**
ANG/EPIS–Episcopal	3	364	739	770	0.2	0.4
Ap Chr Ch-Amer	1	310	157	310	0.1	0.2
Bahá'í	1	NR	84	84	0.0	0.0
BAPT–Amer Bapt USA	8	2,086	3,066	3,878	1.1	2.0
BAPT–Converge/BGC	1	75	NR	90	0.0	0.0
BAPT–Free Will Bapt	2	NR	110	139	0.0	0.1
BAPT–Natl Mis Bapt Conv	1	0	150	190	0.1	0.1
BAPT–NBC Amer	1	0	100	126	0.0	0.1
BAPT–NBC USA	11	2,450	6,841	8,654	2.4	4.5
BAPT–Reg Bapt Gen As	3	NR	NR	NR	-	-
BAPT–So Bapt Conv	15	1,909	3,497	4,424	1.2	2.3
BRETH–Ch of Brethren	3	242	640	810	0.2	0.4
BRETH–Grace Breth	1	NR	NR	NR	-	-
BUDD–Mahayana	1	NR	NR	102	0.0	0.1
BUDD–Theravada	1	NR	NR	292	0.1	0.2

Religious Group	Number of Congregations	Number of Attendees	Number of Communicant, Confirmed, or Full Members	Adherents: Number of Adherents	Adherents: % of Total Pop.	Adherents: % of Total Adh.
Calv Chpl	2	NR	NR	NR	-	-
Catholic	22	NR	NR	56,898	16.0	29.8
CGOD–Ch God (Ander)	5	563	NR	563	0.2	0.3
CGOD–Ches God-Gen Con	5	399	518	655	0.2	0.3
Ch Cr, Scientst	1	NR	NR	NR	-	-
Ch God (7th Day)	1	NR	NR	NR	-	-
Ch of Nazarene	7	1,142	1,405	2,429	0.7	1.3
Chr & Miss Al	2	255	144	336	0.1	0.2
CHR–Chr Ch (Disc)	2	160	457	578	0.2	0.3
CHR–Chr Chs & Chs Cr	12	NR	3,351	4,239	1.2	2.2
CHR–Chs of Christ	6	677	645	835	0.2	0.4
CHR–Int Chs of Christ	1	NR	29	37	0.0	0.0
FRND–Fr Gen Cf	1	NR	0	0	0.0	0.0
FRND–Fr Gen Cf & Un Mtg	1	NR	8	10	0.0	0.0
HINDU–Post Ren	1	NR	NR	25	0.0	0.0
Int Cou Comm Ch	1	NR	NR	NR	-	-
Jehovah's Witness	3	NR	NR	NR	-	-
JUD–Reform	1	104	184	497	0.1	0.3
LDS–Comm of Christ	1	NR	103	103	0.0	0.1
LDS–L-D Saints	3	NR	NR	1,388	0.4	0.7
LUTH–E.L.C.A.	14	2,253	6,137	8,254	2.3	4.3
LUTH–Luth Cong Msn Chr	1	54	68	86	0.0	0.0
LUTH–Luth–MO Synod	35	9,423	18,305	24,019	6.8	12.6
LUTH–Nor Amer Luth C	3	NR	NR	NR	-	-
LUTH–Wisc Ev Luth Syn	2	139	223	288	0.1	0.2
MENN–Amish Undif	19	NR	1,513	3,466	1.0	1.8
MENN–Beachy Amish-Menn	1	76	45	76	0.0	0.0
MENN–Cons Menn Conf	1	140	68	86	0.0	0.0
MENN–Fel Evg Ch	5	1,660	940	1,189	0.3	0.6
MENN–Mennonite USA	5	350	453	573	0.2	0.3
MENN–Unaffil Amish-Menn	2	79	35	79	0.0	0.0
METH–AME	2	150	450	569	0.2	0.3
METH–C.M.E.	1	0	100	126	0.0	0.1
METH–Free Methodist	2	93	61	93	0.0	0.0
METH–Un Methodist	34	6,355	9,529	14,208	4.0	7.4
METH–Wesleyan	4	612	360	796	0.2	0.4
Missionary Ch	18	8,259	2,793	8,291	2.3	4.3
Muslim Est	2	304	NR	1,108	0.3	0.6
New Apost Ch	1	NR	NR	NR	-	-
Non-denom Chr Chs	55	18,820	20,890	25,963	7.3	13.6
ORTHE–Ant Orth of NA	1	59	NR	164	0.0	0.1
ORTHE–Greek Orthodox	1	120	NR	200	0.1	0.1
ORTHE–Orth Ch in Amer	1	140	NR	500	0.1	0.3
ORTHE–Romania Orth Ar	1	25	NR	30	0.0	0.0
ORTHE–Rus Orth Abroad	1	5	NR	37	0.0	0.0
PENT–Assemb of God	7	2,070	1,030	3,960	1.1	2.1
PENT–Ch God (Cleve)	4	260	586	741	0.2	0.4
PENT–Ch of God Proph	1	NR	12	15	0.0	0.0
PENT–COGIC	5	30	350	443	0.1	0.2
PENT–Elim	1	NR	NR	NR	-	-
PENT–Full Gosp Bapt	5	NR	NR	NR	-	-
PENT–Int Foursq Gos	1	658	319	404	0.1	0.2
PENT–Intl Pent Holiness	2	50	45	57	0.0	0.0
PENT–Un Pent Ch Intl	2	NR	NR	NR	-	-
PRES–Presb Ch (USA)	5	334	1,649	2,086	0.6	1.1
PRES–Presb Ch Amer	1	53	37	63	0.0	0.0
REF–Christian Ref	1	60	48	61	0.0	0.0
REF–Ref Ch in Am	1	90	186	202	0.1	0.1
Salvation Army	1	70	96	263	0.1	0.1
Sev Day Adv	3	336	583	671	0.2	0.4
Un Breth in Cr	5	2,053	142	1,748	0.5	0.9
Un C of Christ	5	364	1,166	1,475	0.4	0.8
Unit Univ	1	68	109	124	0.0	0.1
Unity Ch	1	NR	NR	NR	-	-
BARTHOLOMEW	**116**	**11,642**	**24,190**	**37,524**	**48.9**	**100.0**
ANG/EPIS–Episcopal	1	93	180	180	0.2	0.5
Bahá'í	0	NR	17	17	0.0	0.0
BAPT–Amer Bapt Assn	1	NR	85	105	0.1	0.3
BAPT–Amer Bapt USA	5	694	2,703	3,353	4.4	8.9
BAPT–Natl Mis Bapt Conv	1	0	150	186	0.2	0.5
BAPT–So Bapt Conv	6	554	744	923	1.2	2.5
Catholic	1	NR	NR	4,624	6.0	12.3
CGOD–Ch God (Ander)	1	65	NR	65	0.1	0.2

NR–Not Reported   - Represents no adherents reported.   Percentages may not total 100 due to rounding.

Table 3: Religious Congregations by County and Group: 2010

Religious Group	Number of Congrega-tions	Number of Attendees	Number of Communicant, Confirmed, or Full Members	Adherents		
				Number of Adherents	% of Total Pop.	% of Total Adh.
Ch of Nazarene	4	400	535	685	0.9	1.8
Chr & Miss Al	1	44	24	78	0.1	0.2
CHR–Chr Ch (Disc)	1	55	245	304	0.4	0.8
CHR–Chr Chs & Chs Cr	8	NR	5,161	6,401	8.3	17.1
CHR–Chs of Christ	3	275	261	333	0.4	0.9
Christian Un	2	NR	NR	NR	-	-
FRND–Fr Un Mtg	1	NR	129	160	0.2	0.4
HINDU–Post Ren	1	NR	NR	10	0.0	0.0
Jehovah's Witness	1	NR	NR	NR	-	-
JUD–Reform	1	10	17	46	0.1	0.1
LDS–L-D Saints	3	NR	NR	942	1.2	2.5
LUTH–E.L.C.A.	1	150	329	493	0.6	1.3
LUTH–Luth–MO Synod	7	2,519	4,708	6,343	8.3	16.9
METH–Evan Meth Ch	1	NR	NR	NR	-	-
METH–Free Methodist	2	282	278	293	0.4	0.8
METH–Un Methodist	15	1,466	3,028	4,115	5.4	11.0
METH–Wesleyan	7	304	217	396	0.5	1.1
MORAV–Morav Ch-North	1	167	355	487	0.6	1.3
Muslim Est	1	134	NR	308	0.4	0.8
Non-denom Chr Chs	15	3,055	3,089	3,883	5.1	10.3
PENT–Assemb of God	4	456	314	692	0.9	1.8
PENT–Ch God (Cleve)	5	282	545	676	0.9	1.8
PENT–Un Pent Ch Intl	4	NR	NR	NR	-	-
PRES–Pres Ref	1	NR	NR	NR	-	-
PRES–Presb Ch (USA)	3	301	603	748	1.0	2.0
PRES–Ref Pres of NA	1	103	82	121	0.2	0.3
Salvation Army	1	14	38	127	0.2	0.3
Sev Day Adv	2	101	175	202	0.3	0.5
Un Breth in Cr	1	0	0	0	0.0	0.0
Un C of Christ	1	34	72	89	0.1	0.2
Unit Univ	1	84	106	139	0.2	0.4
BENTON	**25**	**652**	**1,832**	**6,971**	**78.7**	**100.0**
BAPT–So Bapt Conv	2	75	219	273	3.1	3.9
Catholic	5	NR	NR	2,708	30.6	38.8
CHR–Chr Ch (Disc)	1	21	17	21	0.2	0.3
CHR–Chr Chs & Chs Cr	4	NR	590	736	8.3	10.6
METH–Free Methodist	1	32	17	32	0.4	0.5
METH–Un Methodist	8	425	844	2,980	33.7	42.7
METH–Wesleyan	1	56	26	73	0.8	1.0
PRES–Presb Ch (USA)	3	43	119	148	1.7	2.1
BLACKFORD	**25**	**1,590**	**2,583**	**3,875**	**30.4**	**100.0**
Bahá'í	0	NR	5	5	0.0	0.1
BAPT–So Bapt Conv	1	50	290	350	2.7	9.0
BRETH–Ch of Brethren	1	23	46	55	0.4	1.4
Catholic	1	NR	NR	400	3.1	10.3
Ch of Nazarene	3	205	318	383	3.0	9.9
CHR–Chr Ch (Disc)	1	55	348	420	3.3	10.8
CHR–Chr Chs & Chs Cr	2	NR	89	107	0.8	2.8
LUTH–E.L.C.A.	1	89	259	292	2.3	7.5
LUTH–Luth–MO Synod	1	21	23	33	0.3	0.9
METH–Un Methodist	6	484	635	946	7.4	24.4
METH–Wesleyan	1	189	99	246	1.9	6.3
Non-denom Chr Chs	2	330	280	412	3.2	10.6
PENT–Assemb of God	1	45	31	50	0.4	1.3
PENT–Un Pent Ch Intl	1	NR	NR	NR	-	-
PRES–Presb Ch (USA)	1	73	111	134	1.0	3.5
Sev Day Adv	1	16	29	33	0.3	0.9
Un Breth in Cr	1	10	20	9	0.1	0.2
BOONE	**63**	**8,119**	**17,301**	**33,547**	**59.2**	**100.0**
ANG/EPIS–Episcopal	2	145	458	532	0.9	1.6
Bahá'í	0	NR	6	6	0.0	0.0
BAPT–Amer Bapt USA	2	313	470	598	1.1	1.8
BAPT–Reg Bapt Gen As	1	NR	NR	NR	-	-
BAPT–So Bapt Conv	1	40	75	95	0.2	0.3
Catholic	2	NR	NR	9,333	16.5	27.8
CGOD–Ch God (Ander)	1	30	NR	30	0.1	0.1
Ch of Nazarene	1	80	152	198	0.3	0.6
Chr & Miss Al	1	651	246	1,085	1.9	3.2
CHR–Chr Ch (Disc)	3	100	1,040	1,323	2.3	3.9
CHR–Chr Chs & Chs Cr	9	NR	5,079	6,462	11.4	19.3

Religious Group	Number of Congrega-tions	Number of Attendees	Number of Communicant, Confirmed, or Full Members	Adherents		
				Number of Adherents	% of Total Pop.	% of Total Adh.
CHR–Chs of Christ	4	285	248	307	0.5	0.9
Evan Free Ch	1	0	NR	0	0.0	0.0
FRND–Unaffl Mtgs	1	NR	NR	NR	-	-
Jehovah's Witness	1	NR	NR	NR	-	-
LDS–L-D Saints	1	NR	NR	281	0.5	0.8
LUTH–Assoc Free Luth	1	NR	NR	NR	-	-
LUTH–E.L.C.A.	2	260	538	775	1.4	2.3
LUTH–Luth–MO Synod	1	310	583	786	1.4	2.3
METH–Un Methodist	8	1,277	2,427	3,735	6.6	11.1
METH–Wesleyan	1	52	35	68	0.1	0.2
Non-denom Chr Chs	8	3,445	3,431	4,394	7.8	13.1
PENT–Assemb of God	1	33	42	65	0.1	0.2
PENT–Ch of God Proph	1	NR	39	50	0.1	0.1
PENT–Pent Ch of God	3	210	NR	326	0.6	1.0
PRES–Presb Ch (USA)	3	812	2,340	2,977	5.3	8.9
Sev Day Adv	1	26	46	53	0.1	0.2
Un C of Christ	1	10	12	15	0.0	0.0
Unit Univ	1	40	34	51	0.1	0.2
Zoroastrian	0	NR	NR	2	0.0	0.0
BROWN	**25**	**1,345**	**2,294**	**3,474**	**22.8**	**100.0**
ANG/EPIS–Anglican NA	3	NR	NR	NR	-	-
Bahá'í	0	NR	7	7	0.0	0.2
BAPT–Amer Bapt USA	2	216	467	551	3.6	15.9
BAPT–So Bapt Conv	3	126	346	408	2.7	11.7
Catholic	1	NR	NR	750	4.9	21.6
Ch Cr, Scientst	1	NR	NR	NR	-	-
Ch of Nazarene	1	185	208	208	1.4	6.0
CHR–Chr Chs & Chs Cr	1	NR	241	284	1.9	8.2
CHR–Chs of Christ	2	60	54	76	0.5	2.2
Jehovah's Witness	1	NR	NR	NR	-	-
METH–Un Methodist	3	191	420	471	3.1	13.6
METH–Wesleyan	1	27	15	35	0.2	1.0
Non-denom Chr Chs	1	400	400	500	3.3	14.4
ORTHE–Bulgar Orth USA	1	15	NR	30	0.2	0.9
PENT–Assemb of God	1	31	44	53	0.3	1.5
PENT–Un Pent Ch Intl	1	NR	NR	NR	-	-
PRES–Presb Ch (USA)	1	0	49	58	0.4	1.7
Salvation Army	1	94	43	43	0.3	1.2
CARROLL	**41**	**2,015**	**4,445**	**7,766**	**38.5**	**100.0**
Bahá'í	0	NR	1	1	0.0	0.0
BAPT–Amer Bapt USA	3	103	231	283	1.4	3.6
BAPT–Reg Bapt Gen As	1	NR	NR	NR	-	-
BAPT–So Bapt Conv	1	75	209	256	1.3	3.3
BRETH–Brethren (Ash)	1	NR	80	98	0.5	1.3
BRETH–Ch of Brethren	3	0	222	272	1.3	3.5
BRETH–Grace Breth	1	NR	NR	NR	-	-
Calv Chpl	1	NR	NR	NR	-	-
Catholic	1	NR	NR	1,870	9.3	24.1
CHR–Chr Ch (Disc)	1	108	375	460	2.3	5.9
CHR–Chr Chs & Chs Cr	4	NR	586	718	3.6	9.2
CHR–Chs of Christ	1	30	15	30	0.1	0.4
LUTH–E.L.C.A.	3	131	359	451	2.2	5.8
METH–Un Methodist	7	741	1,183	1,461	7.2	18.8
METH–Wesleyan	1	55	43	72	0.4	0.9
Non-denom Chr Chs	3	370	521	561	2.8	7.2
PENT–Assemb of God	1	204	124	625	3.1	8.0
PENT–Ch God (Cleve)	1	10	22	27	0.1	0.3
PENT–Un Pent Ch Intl	1	NR	NR	NR	-	-
PRES–Presb Ch (USA)	6	188	474	581	2.9	7.5
CASS	**72**	**5,155**	**9,139**	**17,283**	**44.4**	**100.0**
ANG/EPIS–Episcopal	1	49	100	100	0.3	0.6
Bahá'í	0	NR	17	17	0.0	0.1
BAPT–Amer Bapt USA	4	303	763	949	2.4	5.5
BAPT–NT Ind Bapt	1	NR	NR	NR	-	-
BAPT–So Bapt Conv	3	183	208	259	0.7	1.5
BRETH–Brethren (Ash)	1	NR	80	100	0.3	0.6
BRETH–Ch of Brethren	1	185	245	305	0.8	1.8
Catholic	1	NR	NR	4,583	11.8	26.5
CGOD–Ch God (Ander)	1	85	NR	85	0.2	0.5
Ch of Nazarene	1	138	266	266	0.7	1.5

NR–Not Reported   - Represents no adherents reported.   Percentages may not total 100 due to rounding.

Table 3: Religious Congregations by County and Group: 2010

Religious Group	Number of Congregations	Number of Attendees	Number of Communicant, Confirmed, or Full Members	Adherents: Number of Adherents	Adherents: % of Total Pop.	Adherents: % of Total Adh.
Chr & Miss Al	1	175	138	248	0.6	1.4
CHR–Chr Ch (Disc)	1	91	317	394	1.0	2.3
CHR–Chr Chs & Chs Cr	6	NR	811	1,009	2.6	5.8
CHR–Chs of Christ	3	199	191	231	0.6	1.3
Ind Fund Churches	1	NR	NR	NR	-	-
Jehovah's Witness	1	NR	NR	NR	-	-
LDS–L-D Saints	1	NR	NR	492	1.3	2.8
LUTH–E.L.C.A.	1	28	73	87	0.2	0.5
LUTH–Luth Cong Msn Chr	1	55	271	337	0.9	1.9
LUTH–Luth–MO Synod	1	88	254	336	0.9	1.9
METH–AME	1	0	100	124	0.3	0.7
METH–Un Methodist	15	1,312	2,050	3,045	7.8	17.6
METH–Wesleyan	2	75	33	98	0.3	0.6
Non-denom Chr Chs	11	1,112	1,619	1,814	4.7	10.5
PENT–Assemb of God	2	540	305	540	1.4	3.1
PENT–Ch God (Cleve)	1	117	400	498	1.3	2.9
PENT–Int Foursq Gos	1	39	93	116	0.3	0.7
PENT–Un Pent Ch Intl	1	NR	NR	NR	-	-
PENT–Vineyard	1	80	135	168	0.4	1.0
PRES–Presb Ch (USA)	3	202	525	653	1.7	3.8
Salvation Army	1	36	35	303	0.8	1.8
Sev Day Adv	2	63	110	126	0.3	0.7
CLARK	**136**	**11,531**	**21,862**	**37,618**	**34.1**	**100.0**
ANG/EPIS–Episcopal	1	35	100	100	0.1	0.3
Bahá'í	0	NR	20	20	0.0	0.1
BAPT–Amer Bapt USA	7	398	1,439	1,763	1.6	4.7
BAPT–NBC USA	1	70	114	140	0.1	0.4
BAPT–Reg Bapt Gen As	1	NR	NR	NR	-	-
BAPT–So Bapt Conv	21	2,396	5,711	6,997	6.3	18.6
Catholic	8	NR	NR	10,150	9.2	27.0
CGOD–Ch God (Ander)	4	386	NR	386	0.4	1.0
Ch of Nazarene	3	76	224	264	0.2	0.7
Chr & Miss Al	1	17	11	22	0.0	0.1
CHR–Chr Ch (Disc)	6	346	1,057	1,295	1.2	3.4
CHR–Chr Chs & Chs Cr	11	NR	2,185	2,677	2.4	7.1
CHR–Chs of Christ	12	1,077	1,326	1,670	1.5	4.4
Int Cou Comm Ch	1	NR	NR	NR	-	-
Jehovah's Witness	1	NR	NR	NR	-	-
LDS–L-D Saints	1	NR	NR	320	0.3	0.9
LUTH–E.L.C.A.	1	115	252	344	0.3	0.9
METH–AME	1	75	200	245	0.2	0.7
METH–AME Zion	1	0	100	123	0.1	0.3
METH–Un Methodist	22	1,291	2,514	3,228	2.9	8.6
METH–Wesleyan	1	21	9	27	0.0	0.1
Non-denom Chr Chs	14	4,477	5,420	6,210	5.6	16.5
PENT–Assemb of God	2	252	157	393	0.4	1.0
PENT–Ch God (Cleve)	2	16	10	12	0.0	0.0
PENT–COGIC	1	80	125	153	0.1	0.4
PENT–Un Pent Ch Intl	1	NR	NR	NR	-	-
PRES–Presb Ch (USA)	7	245	540	662	0.6	1.8
Sev Day Adv	3	73	127	146	0.1	0.4
Un C of Christ	1	85	221	271	0.2	0.7
CLAY	**63**	**5,503**	**9,095**	**11,280**	**41.9**	**100.0**
Bahá'í	0	NR	4	4	0.0	0.0
BAPT–Amer Bapt Assn	1	NR	85	104	0.4	0.9
BAPT–Amer Bapt USA	4	565	514	627	2.3	5.6
BAPT–Reg Bapt Gen As	1	NR	NR	NR	-	-
BAPT–So Bapt Conv	1	75	151	184	0.7	1.6
Catholic	1	NR	NR	356	1.3	3.2
Ch of Nazarene	4	402	485	581	2.2	5.2
CHR–Chr Chs & Chs Cr	4	NR	1,330	1,622	6.0	14.4
CHR–Chs of Christ	7	417	435	573	2.1	5.1
Ind Fund Churches	1	NR	NR	NR	-	-
Jehovah's Witness	1	NR	NR	NR	-	-
METH–Un Methodist	17	967	1,544	2,084	7.8	18.5
METH–Wesleyan	1	35	47	46	0.2	0.4
Non-denom Chr Chs	9	2,460	3,438	3,726	13.9	33.0
PENT–Assemb of God	2	81	55	145	0.5	1.3
PENT–Ch God (Cleve)	2	90	129	157	0.6	1.4
PENT–Int Foursq Gos	1	94	80	98	0.4	0.9
PENT–Un Pent Ch Intl	2	NR	NR	NR	-	-
PRES–Presb Ch (USA)	1	150	301	367	1.4	3.3
Un C of Christ	3	167	497	606	2.3	5.4
CLINTON	**63**	**3,690**	**7,253**	**14,645**	**44.1**	**100.0**
Bahá'í	0	NR	2	2	0.0	0.0
BAPT–Amer Bapt USA	4	267	604	763	2.3	5.2
BAPT–Reg Bapt Gen As	1	NR	NR	NR	-	-
BAPT–So Bapt Conv	3	527	1,059	1,338	4.0	9.1
BRETH–Ch of Brethren	1	75	63	80	0.2	0.5
Catholic	1	NR	NR	5,135	15.5	35.1
CGOD–Ch God (Ander)	2	65	NR	65	0.2	0.4
Ch of God Gen Conf	1	NR	33	42	0.1	0.3
Ch of Nazarene	1	336	444	444	1.3	3.0
CHR–Chr Ch (Disc)	1	195	432	546	1.6	3.7
CHR–Chr Chs & Chs Cr	6	NR	1,210	1,529	4.6	10.4
CHR–Chs of Christ	2	99	83	110	0.3	0.8
Evan Free Ch	1	128	NR	128	0.4	0.9
Jehovah's Witness	1	NR	NR	NR	-	-
LDS–L-D Saints	1	NR	NR	139	0.4	0.9
LUTH–E.L.C.A.	2	77	126	158	0.5	1.1
METH–Un Methodist	13	935	1,733	2,157	6.5	14.7
METH–Wesleyan	5	235	217	306	0.9	2.1
Non-denom Chr Chs	5	390	480	515	1.6	3.5
PENT–Assemb of God	3	236	133	391	1.2	2.7
PENT–Un Pent Ch Intl	2	NR	NR	NR	-	-
PRES–Evan Presby Ch	1	NR	287	363	1.1	2.5
PRES–Presb Ch (USA)	3	80	267	337	1.0	2.3
Sev Day Adv	2	25	43	50	0.2	0.3
Un C of Christ	1	20	37	47	0.1	0.3
CRAWFORD	**33**	**1,219**	**2,776**	**3,889**	**36.3**	**100.0**
Bahá'í	0	NR	1	1	0.0	0.0
BAPT–Amer Bapt USA	1	26	53	65	0.6	1.7
BAPT–Reg Bapt Gen As	1	NR	NR	NR	-	-
BAPT–So Bapt Conv	5	127	280	341	3.2	8.8
BRETH–Breth in Chr	1	NR	NR	NR	-	-
Catholic	1	NR	NR	190	1.8	4.9
Ch Christ Chr Union	1	NR	NR	NR	-	-
CHR–Chr Chs & Chs Cr	4	NR	985	1,200	11.2	30.9
CHR–Chs of Christ	1	20	12	18	0.2	0.5
LDS–L-D Saints	1	NR	NR	346	3.2	8.9
MENN–Amish Undif	1	NR	40	111	1.0	2.9
METH–Free Methodist	1	56	40	56	0.5	1.4
METH–Un Methodist	7	276	432	557	5.2	14.3
METH–Wesleyan	3	170	233	221	2.1	5.7
Non-denom Chr Chs	3	490	580	638	6.0	16.4
PRES–Presb Ch (USA)	1	40	96	117	1.1	3.0
Sev Day Adv	1	14	24	28	0.3	0.7
DAVIESS	**89**	**4,496**	**10,105**	**17,545**	**55.4**	**100.0**
ANG/EPIS–Episcopal	1	25	36	36	0.1	0.2
BAPT–Amer Bapt USA	4	315	848	1,095	3.5	6.2
BAPT–Reg Bapt Gen As	1	NR	NR	NR	-	-
BAPT–So Bapt Conv	2	45	275	355	1.1	2.0
Catholic	3	NR	NR	2,688	8.5	15.3
CGOD–Ch God (Ander)	1	21	NR	21	0.1	0.1
CGOD–Ches God-Gen Con	1	55	108	139	0.4	0.8
Ch of Nazarene	2	95	105	264	0.8	1.5
CHR–Chr Ch (Disc)	1	67	182	235	0.7	1.3
CHR–Chr Chs & Chs Cr	10	NR	2,323	3,000	9.5	17.1
CHR–Chs of Christ	3	285	255	332	1.0	1.9
Jehovah's Witness	1	NR	NR	NR	-	-
LDS–Comm of Christ	1	NR	103	103	0.3	0.6
LUTH–Luth Cong Msn Chr	1	43	160	207	0.7	1.2
MENN–Amish Undif	23	NR	1,662	3,708	11.7	21.1
MENN–Beachy Amish-Menn	1	195	126	195	0.6	1.1
MENN–Ber Amish-Menn	1	25	22	25	0.1	0.1
MENN–Cons Menn Conf	2	600	494	638	2.0	3.6
MENN–Unaffil Amish-Menn	3	720	407	720	2.3	4.1
METH–AME	1	0	100	129	0.4	0.7
METH–Free Methodist	1	136	160	160	0.5	0.9
METH–Un Methodist	12	731	1,464	1,880	5.9	10.7
METH–Wesleyan	2	109	89	142	0.4	0.8

NR–Not Reported - Represents no adherents reported. Percentages may not total 100 due to rounding.

Table 3: Religious Congregations by County and Group: 2010

Religious Group	Number of Congregations	Number of Attendees	Number of Communicant, Confirmed, or Full Members	Adherents: Number of Adherents	Adherents: % of Total Pop.	Adherents: % of Total Adh.
Non-denom Chr Chs	5	855	989	1,145	3.6	6.5
PENT–Assemb of God	2	85	30	98	0.3	0.6
PENT–Ch God (Cleve)	1	54	78	101	0.3	0.6
PENT–Un Pent Ch Intl	1	NR	NR	NR	-	-
PRES–Cumber Presb	1	NR	15	33	0.1	0.2
PRES–Presb Ch (USA)	1	35	74	96	0.3	0.5
DEARBORN	**71**	**3,540**	**8,236**	**20,180**	**40.3**	**100.0**
ANG/EPIS–Episcopal	1	38	41	57	0.1	0.3
Bahá'í	0	NR	1	1	0.0	0.0
BAPT–Amer Bapt USA	9	654	1,286	1,592	3.2	7.9
BAPT–Free Will Bapt	1	NR	67	83	0.2	0.4
BAPT–So Bapt Conv	2	75	148	183	0.4	0.9
Catholic	7	NR	NR	9,317	18.6	46.2
Ch of Nazarene	1	31	45	59	0.1	0.3
Chr & Miss Al	1	54	44	76	0.2	0.4
CHR–Chr Chs & Chs Cr	6	NR	1,865	2,308	4.6	11.4
CHR–Chs of Christ	2	67	60	72	0.1	0.4
Christian Un	1	NR	NR	NR	-	-
Jehovah's Witness	2	NR	NR	NR	-	-
LDS–L-D Saints	1	NR	NR	335	0.7	1.7
LUTH–E.L.C.A.	6	369	1,029	1,312	2.6	6.5
LUTH–Luth–MO Synod	4	376	995	1,297	2.6	6.4
METH–Un Methodist	11	685	1,303	1,879	3.8	9.3
METH–Wesleyan	2	49	48	64	0.1	0.3
Non-denom Chr Chs	5	760	830	975	1.9	4.8
PENT–Assemb of God	1	51	68	68	0.1	0.3
PENT–Intl Pent Holiness	1	36	30	37	0.1	0.2
PENT–Vineyard	1	100	0	0	0.0	0.0
PRES–Presb Ch (USA)	4	118	261	323	0.6	1.6
Un C of Christ	2	77	115	142	0.3	0.7
DECATUR	**55**	**2,775**	**6,076**	**14,919**	**58.0**	**100.0**
Bahá'í	0	NR	3	3	0.0	0.0
BAPT–Amer Bapt USA	11	976	2,560	3,191	12.4	21.4
BAPT–So Bapt Conv	2	100	135	168	0.7	1.1
Catholic	4	NR	NR	6,509	25.3	43.6
CGOD–Ch God (Ander)	1	71	NR	71	0.3	0.5
Ch of Nazarene	1	80	75	330	1.3	2.2
CHR–Chr Ch (Disc)	1	30	70	87	0.3	0.6
CHR–Chr Chs & Chs Cr	5	NR	1,080	1,346	5.2	9.0
CHR–Chs of Christ	1	19	16	20	0.1	0.1
Jehovah's Witness	1	NR	NR	NR	-	-
LUTH–E.L.C.A.	1	45	51	54	0.2	0.4
LUTH–Luth–MO Synod	1	46	160	264	1.0	1.8
MENN–Amish Undif	1	NR	44	91	0.4	0.6
METH–Free Methodist	1	30	75	75	0.3	0.5
METH–Un Methodist	12	446	991	1,271	4.9	8.5
METH–Wesleyan	3	172	89	224	0.9	1.5
Non-denom Chr Chs	3	620	410	787	3.1	5.3
PENT–Assemb of God	1	65	26	65	0.3	0.4
PENT–Un Pent Ch Intl	2	NR	NR	NR	-	-
PRES–Presb Ch (USA)	3	75	291	363	1.4	2.4
DEKALB	**76**	**5,891**	**8,054**	**17,165**	**40.7**	**100.0**
Bahá'í	0	NR	1	1	0.0	0.0
BAPT–Amer Bapt USA	1	95	180	226	0.5	1.3
BAPT–Reg Bapt Gen As	1	NR	NR	NR	-	-
BAPT–So Bapt Conv	3	66	101	127	0.3	0.7
BRETH–Breth in Chr	1	NR	NR	NR	-	-
BRETH–Ch of Brethren	3	114	246	308	0.7	1.8
Catholic	3	NR	NR	5,295	12.5	30.8
CGOD–Ch God (Ander)	4	1,101	NR	1,101	2.6	6.4
CGOD–Ches God-Gen Con	2	98	117	147	0.3	0.9
Ch Cr, Scientst	1	NR	NR	NR	-	-
Ch of Nazarene	3	378	448	543	1.3	3.2
Chr & Miss Al	1	125	73	185	0.4	1.1
CHR–Chr Ch (Disc)	1	62	125	157	0.4	0.9
CHR–Chr Chs & Chs Cr	9	NR	1,697	2,126	5.0	12.4
CHR–Chs of Christ	2	90	112	130	0.3	0.8
LUTH–E.L.C.A.	3	66	192	257	0.6	1.5
LUTH–Luth Cong Msn Chr	1	83	125	157	0.4	0.9
LUTH–Luth–MO Synod	3	254	660	853	2.0	5.0
LUTH–Nor Amer Luth C	1	NR	NR	NR	-	-
METH–Un Methodist	16	1,018	1,766	2,380	5.6	13.9
Missionary Ch	1	561	261	561	1.3	3.3
Non-denom Chr Chs	5	1,175	1,175	1,470	3.5	8.6
PENT–Assemb of God	3	254	122	329	0.8	1.9
PENT–Int Pent C Chr	1	25	NR	40	0.1	0.2
PENT–Un Pent Ch Intl	1	NR	NR	NR	-	-
PRES–Evan Presby Ch	1	NR	93	117	0.3	0.7
PRES–Presb Ch (USA)	2	166	387	485	1.1	2.8
Un Breth in Cr	2	139	132	119	0.3	0.7
Un C of Christ	1	21	41	51	0.1	0.3
DELAWARE	**157**	**16,463**	**21,158**	**34,822**	**29.6**	**100.0**
ANG/EPIS–Episcopal	1	66	179	179	0.2	0.5
Bahá'í	1	NR	45	45	0.0	0.1
BAPT–Amer Bapt USA	3	330	468	552	0.5	1.6
BAPT–Natl Mis Bapt Conv	1	0	60	71	0.1	0.2
BAPT–NBC Amer	2	400	950	1,121	1.0	3.2
BAPT–Reg Bapt Gen As	1	NR	NR	NR	-	-
BAPT–So Bapt Conv	7	516	1,608	1,898	1.6	5.5
BRETH–Brethren (Ash)	3	NR	240	283	0.2	0.8
BRETH–Ch of Brethren	2	35	99	117	0.1	0.3
Catholic	3	NR	NR	4,171	3.5	12.0
CGOD–Ch God (Ander)	8	572	NR	572	0.5	1.6
CGOD–Ches God-Gen Con	1	106	185	218	0.2	0.6
Ch Christ Chr Union	1	NR	NR	NR	-	-
Ch of Nazarene	12	1,162	1,574	2,656	2.3	7.6
Chr & Miss Al	1	550	78	608	0.5	1.7
CHR–Chr Ch (Disc)	4	369	901	1,063	0.9	3.1
CHR–Chr Chs & Chs Cr	2	NR	386	456	0.4	1.3
CHR–Chs of Christ	7	570	457	630	0.5	1.8
CONG–Consrv Cong Chr	1	139	201	237	0.2	0.7
CONG–Midw Cong Chr Fel	3	150	127	150	0.1	0.4
FRND–Fr Un Mtg	1	NR	152	179	0.2	0.5
JUD–Reform	1	19	33	89	0.1	0.3
LDS–L-D Saints	3	NR	NR	961	0.8	2.8
LUTH–E.L.C.A.	2	236	550	716	0.6	2.1
LUTH–Luth–MO Synod	1	125	256	314	0.3	0.9
MENN–Mennonite USA	1	20	12	14	0.0	0.0
METH–AME	2	50	250	295	0.3	0.8
METH–Un Methodist	27	4,337	4,301	6,193	5.3	17.8
METH–Wesleyan	3	107	85	140	0.1	0.4
Muslim Est	1	300	NR	600	0.5	1.7
Non-denom Chr Chs	30	4,000	4,928	5,610	4.8	16.1
PENT–Assemb of God	3	874	526	1,371	1.2	3.9
PENT–Ch God Mtn Asm	1	NR	NR	NR	-	-
PENT–Ch of God Proph	1	NR	58	68	0.1	0.2
PENT–COGIC	4	30	215	254	0.2	0.7
PENT–Int Foursq Gos	2	157	442	522	0.4	1.5
PENT–Un Pent Ch Intl	1	NR	NR	NR	-	-
PRES–Presb Ch (USA)	2	324	842	994	0.8	2.9
PRES–Presb Ch Amer	2	673	561	708	0.6	2.0
Salvation Army	1	38	69	339	0.3	1.0
Sev Day Adv	2	57	99	114	0.1	0.3
Un Breth in Cr	1	20	0	17	0.0	0.0
Unit Univ	1	131	221	297	0.3	0.9
DUBOIS	**57**	**3,580**	**6,793**	**31,450**	**75.1**	**100.0**
Bahá'í	0	NR	5	5	0.0	0.0
BAPT–Reg Bapt Gen As	1	NR	NR	NR	-	-
BAPT–So Bapt Conv	5	380	468	581	1.4	1.8
Catholic	11	NR	NR	22,001	52.5	70.0
Ch of Nazarene	2	163	212	431	1.0	1.4
CHR–Chr Chs & Chs Cr	5	NR	820	1,018	2.4	3.2
CHR–Chs of Christ	2	122	92	142	0.3	0.5
Evan Free Ch	1	14	NR	14	0.0	0.0
Jehovah's Witness	1	NR	NR	NR	-	-
LDS–L-D Saints	1	NR	NR	356	0.8	1.1
LUTH–E.L.C.A.	5	565	1,479	1,879	4.5	6.0
LUTH–Luth Cong Msn Chr	1	147	450	559	1.3	1.8
METH–Un Methodist	4	814	1,393	1,655	4.0	5.3
METH–Wesleyan	1	20	12	26	0.1	0.1
Non-denom Chr Chs	2	625	370	782	1.9	2.5

NR–Not Reported - Represents no adherents reported. Percentages may not total 100 due to rounding.

Table 3: Religious Congregations by County and Group: 2010

Religious Group	Number of Congrega-tions	Number of Attendees	Number of Communicant, Confirmed, or Full Members	Adherents		
				Number of Adherents	% of Total Pop.	% of Total Adh.
PENT–Assemb of God	2	136	73	245	0.6	0.8
PENT–Int Foursq Gos	2	68	107	133	0.3	0.4
PENT–Un Pent Ch Intl	2	NR	NR	NR	-	-
PRES–Presb Ch (USA)	1	35	46	57	0.1	0.2
Sev Day Adv	2	38	67	77	0.2	0.2
Un C of Christ	6	453	1,199	1,489	3.6	4.7
ELKHART	**294**	**36,943**	**47,225**	**82,467**	**41.7**	**100.0**
ANG/EPIS–Episcopal	4	252	491	612	0.3	0.7
Bahá'í	0	NR	17	17	0.0	0.0
BAPT–Free Will Bapt	1	NR	55	71	0.0	0.1
BAPT–Natl Mis Bapt Conv	1	275	400	515	0.3	0.6
BAPT–NBC USA	1	0	2,000	2,575	1.3	3.1
BAPT–Reg Bapt Gen As	1	NR	NR	NR	-	-
BAPT–So Bapt Conv	4	119	179	231	0.1	0.3
BRETH–Breth in Chr	2	NR	NR	NR	-	-
BRETH–Brethren (Ash)	7	NR	930	1,198	0.6	1.5
BRETH–Ch of Brethren	17	1,420	2,464	3,173	1.6	3.8
BRETH–Grace Breth	2	NR	NR	NR	-	-
Catholic	4	NR	NR	10,765	5.4	13.1
CGOD–Ch God (Ander)	5	590	NR	590	0.3	0.7
Ch Cr, Scientst	2	NR	NR	NR	-	-
Ch of Nazarene	6	2,234	2,300	4,954	2.5	6.0
Chr & Miss Al	1	95	49	118	0.1	0.1
CHR–Chr Ch (Disc)	2	95	419	540	0.3	0.7
CHR–Chr Chs & Chs Cr	3	NR	250	322	0.2	0.4
CHR–Chs of Christ	2	230	215	286	0.1	0.3
Evan Ch	1	NR	NR	NR	-	-
Evan Free Ch	1	1,200	NR	1,200	0.6	1.5
Ind Fund Churches	2	NR	NR	NR	-	-
Jehovah's Witness	4	NR	NR	NR	-	-
LDS–L-D Saints	3	NR	NR	1,096	0.6	1.3
LUTH–E.L.C.A.	10	1,006	2,164	2,661	1.3	3.2
LUTH–Luth–MO Synod	2	658	970	1,152	0.6	1.4
MENN–Amish Undif	40	NR	2,628	6,244	3.2	7.6
MENN–Beachy Amish-Menn	3	515	344	515	0.3	0.6
MENN–CG in Cr (Menn)	1	NR	24	31	0.0	0.0
MENN–Cons Menn Conf	3	818	808	1,040	0.5	1.3
MENN–Mennonite USA	35	5,170	6,530	8,409	4.3	10.2
METH–AME	1	100	100	129	0.1	0.2
METH–Free Methodist	1	45	41	45	0.0	0.1
METH–Un Methodist	19	3,641	5,088	7,984	4.0	9.7
Missionary Ch	19	5,926	2,782	6,151	3.1	7.5
Non-denom Chr Chs	43	9,375	12,045	13,577	6.9	16.5
ORTHE–Rus Orth Abroad	1	50	NR	168	0.1	0.2
ORTHE–Ukrainian Orth	1	50	NR	80	0.0	0.1
PENT–Assemb of God	8	1,125	669	1,373	0.7	1.7
PENT–Ch God (Cleve)	3	567	594	765	0.4	0.9
PENT–Ch God Mtn Asm	2	NR	NR	NR	-	-
PENT–COGIC	4	130	520	670	0.3	0.8
PENT–Intl Pent Holiness	1	30	40	52	0.0	0.1
PENT–Pent Ch of God	1	70	NR	109	0.1	0.1
PENT–Un Pent Ch Intl	3	NR	NR	NR	-	-
PRES–Evan Presby Ch	1	NR	90	116	0.1	0.1
PRES–Korean Pres Amer	1	NR	NR	NR	-	-
PRES–Presb Ch (USA)	2	322	645	831	0.4	1.0
PRES–Ref Pres of NA	1	55	41	56	0.0	0.1
REF–Christian Ref	1	86	125	161	0.1	0.2
Salvation Army	2	103	169	577	0.3	0.7
Sev Day Adv	3	164	285	328	0.2	0.4
Un Breth in Cr	1	102	61	87	0.0	0.1
Un C of Christ	4	246	580	747	0.4	0.9
Unit Univ	1	79	113	146	0.1	0.2
FAYETTE	**51**	**3,324**	**6,451**	**10,393**	**42.8**	**100.0**
ANG/EPIS–Episcopal	1	15	19	19	0.1	0.2
BAPT–Amer Bapt USA	1	170	361	443	1.8	4.3
BAPT–Ind Bapt Flwsp Intl	2	NR	NR	NR	-	-
BAPT–So Bapt Conv	2	269	583	715	2.9	6.9
Catholic	1	NR	NR	2,060	8.5	19.8
CGOD–Ch God (Ander)	1	76	NR	76	0.3	0.7
Ch Cr, Scientst	1	NR	NR	NR	-	-
Ch of Nazarene	2	96	162	340	1.4	3.3
CHR–Chr Ch (Disc)	2	139	473	580	2.4	5.6
CHR–Chr Chs & Chs Cr	4	NR	480	589	2.4	5.7
CHR–Chs of Christ	3	100	100	127	0.5	1.2
Intl Fell Bible Ch	1	NR	NR	NR	-	-
Jehovah's Witness	1	NR	NR	NR	-	-
LDS–L-D Saints	1	NR	NR	323	1.3	3.1
LUTH–E.L.C.A.	1	12	22	58	0.2	0.6
LUTH–Luth–MO Synod	1	47	40	50	0.2	0.5
LUTH–Nor Amer Luth C	1	NR	NR	NR	-	-
METH–Evan Meth Ch	1	NR	NR	NR	-	-
METH–Un Methodist	8	458	998	1,342	5.5	12.9
Non-denom Chr Chs	11	1,829	2,899	3,087	12.7	29.7
PENT–Assemb of God	1	75	70	200	0.8	1.9
PENT–Ch God (Cleve)	1	12	34	42	0.2	0.4
PRES–Presb Ch (USA)	1	0	120	147	0.6	1.4
Salvation Army	1	14	68	170	0.7	1.6
Sev Day Adv	1	12	22	25	0.1	0.2
FLOYD	**93**	**9,372**	**22,960**	**42,941**	**57.6**	**100.0**
ANG/EPIS–Episcopal	1	82	206	219	0.3	0.5
Bahá'í	0	NR	14	14	0.0	0.0
BAPT–Amer Bapt USA	3	311	851	1,042	1.4	2.4
BAPT–NBC USA	1	150	150	184	0.2	0.4
BAPT–So Bapt Conv	16	2,530	5,139	6,293	8.4	14.7
Catholic	5	NR	NR	12,234	16.4	28.5
CGOD–Ch God (Ander)	2	200	NR	200	0.3	0.5
Ch Cr, Scientst	1	NR	NR	NR	-	-
Ch of Nazarene	3	533	525	1,168	1.6	2.7
CHR–Chr Ch (Disc)	4	411	961	1,177	1.6	2.7
CHR–Chr Chs & Chs Cr	5	NR	6,350	7,775	10.4	18.1
CHR–Chs of Christ	3	500	430	510	0.7	1.2
Jehovah's Witness	1	NR	NR	NR	-	-
LDS–Comm of Christ	2	NR	206	206	0.3	0.5
LDS–L-D Saints	2	NR	NR	1,263	1.7	2.9
LUTH–Luth–MO Synod	2	493	1,106	1,488	2.0	3.5
METH–AME	2	0	300	367	0.5	0.9
METH–AME Zion	1	0	150	184	0.2	0.4
METH–Un Methodist	14	1,505	3,062	4,234	5.7	9.9
METH–Wesleyan	2	38	8	49	0.1	0.1
Muslim Est	1	134	NR	308	0.4	0.7
Non-denom Chr Chs	11	1,765	2,420	2,539	3.4	5.9
PENT–Assemb of God	2	226	120	277	0.4	0.6
PENT–Ch of God Proph	1	NR	48	59	0.1	0.1
PENT–COGIC	1	0	0	0	0.0	0.0
PENT–Un Pent Ch Intl	2	NR	NR	NR	-	-
PRES–Presb Ch (USA)	2	145	263	322	0.4	0.7
Salvation Army	1	57	127	196	0.3	0.5
Sev Day Adv	1	101	176	202	0.3	0.5
Un C of Christ	1	191	348	426	0.6	1.0
Zoroastrian	0	NR	NR	5	0.0	0.0
FOUNTAIN	**38**	**1,805**	**3,823**	**5,458**	**31.7**	**100.0**
BAPT–Reg Bapt Gen As	1	NR	NR	NR	-	-
BAPT–So Bapt Conv	1	18	30	37	0.2	0.7
Catholic	1	NR	NR	600	3.5	11.0
CGOD–Ch God (Ander)	1	102	NR	102	0.6	1.9
Ch of Nazarene	3	409	449	561	3.3	10.3
CHR–Chr Ch (Disc)	3	59	234	286	1.7	5.2
CHR–Chr Chs & Chs Cr	7	NR	1,260	1,540	8.9	28.2
CHR–Chs of Christ	1	35	44	48	0.3	0.9
Jehovah's Witness	1	NR	NR	NR	-	-
LUTH–E.L.C.A.	2	44	160	181	1.0	3.3
METH–Free Methodist	1	94	69	94	0.5	1.7
METH–Un Methodist	6	231	501	635	3.7	11.6
Non-denom Chr Chs	5	555	603	724	4.2	13.3
PENT–Assemb of God	2	206	215	335	1.9	6.1
PENT–Ch God (Cleve)	1	52	82	100	0.6	1.8
PRES–Evan Presby Ch	1	NR	86	105	0.6	1.9
PRES–Presb Ch (USA)	1	0	90	110	0.6	2.0
FRANKLIN	**42**	**1,769**	**4,074**	**9,637**	**41.7**	**100.0**
Bahá'í	0	NR	4	4	0.0	0.0
BAPT–Ind Bapt Flwsp Intl	1	NR	NR	NR	-	-

NR–Not Reported - Represents no adherents reported. Percentages may not total 100 due to rounding.

Table 3: Religious Congregations by County and Group: 2010

Religious Group	Number of Congrega-tions	Number of Attendees	Number of Communicant, Confirmed, or Full Members	Adherents: Number of Adherents	Adherents: % of Total Pop.	Adherents: % of Total Adh.
BAPT–So Bapt Conv	8	521	1,322	1,647	7.1	17.1
Catholic	7	NR	NR	4,743	20.5	49.2
CHR–Chr Chs & Chs Cr	7	NR	356	444	1.9	4.6
LUTH–E.L.C.A.	3	149	447	574	2.5	6.0
METH–Un Methodist	9	626	902	1,000	4.3	10.4
Non-denom Chr Chs	2	200	300	300	1.3	3.1
PENT–Ch God Mtn Asm	1	NR	NR	NR	-	-
PENT–Un Pent Ch Intl	1	NR	NR	NR	-	-
PRES–Presb Ch (USA)	1	25	34	42	0.2	0.4
Un C of Christ	2	248	709	883	3.8	9.2
FULTON	**48**	**3,368**	**4,174**	**7,029**	**33.7**	**100.0**
Bahá'í	0	NR	1	1	0.0	0.0
BAPT–Amer Bapt USA	2	354	507	626	3.0	8.9
BAPT–Reg Bapt Gen As	1	NR	NR	NR	-	-
BAPT–So Bapt Conv	1	65	45	56	0.3	0.8
BRETH–Ch of Brethren	1	18	31	38	0.2	0.5
Catholic	2	NR	NR	1,128	5.4	16.0
CGOD–Ch God (Ander)	2	187	NR	187	0.9	2.7
Ch of Nazarene	1	72	113	113	0.5	1.6
CHR–Chr Ch (Disc)	1	104	330	407	2.0	5.8
CHR–Chr Chs & Chs Cr	1	NR	75	93	0.4	1.3
CHR–Chs of Christ	1	115	104	167	0.8	2.4
Ind Fund Churches	2	NR	NR	NR	-	-
Jehovah's Witness	1	NR	NR	NR	-	-
LUTH–Luth–MO Synod	1	72	251	342	1.6	4.9
MENN–Amish Undif	1	NR	25	71	0.3	1.0
METH–Un Methodist	14	761	1,403	1,816	8.7	25.8
METH–Wesleyan	2	213	6	277	1.3	3.9
Missionary Ch	1	114	43	114	0.5	1.6
Non-denom Chr Chs	7	815	814	1,030	4.9	14.7
PENT–Assemb of God	1	43	34	81	0.4	1.2
PENT–Ch God (Cleve)	1	98	61	75	0.4	1.1
PENT–Int Foursq Gos	1	290	235	290	1.4	4.1
PENT–Un Pent Ch Intl	1	NR	NR	NR	-	-
PRES–Presb Ch (USA)	1	35	75	93	0.4	1.3
Sev Day Adv	1	12	21	24	0.1	0.3
GIBSON	**67**	**3,687**	**5,307**	**13,819**	**41.2**	**100.0**
Bahá'í	0	NR	1	1	0.0	0.0
BAPT–Reg Bapt Gen As	1	NR	NR	NR	-	-
BAPT–So Bapt Conv	3	72	184	226	0.7	1.6
Catholic	6	NR	NR	6,243	18.6	45.2
CGOD–Ch God (Ander)	2	85	NR	85	0.3	0.6
Ch of Nazarene	6	604	676	848	2.5	6.1
CHR–Chr Ch (Disc)	2	79	236	289	0.9	2.1
CHR–Chr Chs & Chs Cr	2	NR	280	343	1.0	2.5
CHR–Chs of Christ	2	70	58	70	0.2	0.5
Ind Fund Churches	1	NR	NR	NR	-	-
Jehovah's Witness	1	NR	NR	NR	-	-
LUTH–E.L.C.A.	1	30	80	89	0.3	0.6
METH–AME	2	0	250	307	0.9	2.2
METH–Un Methodist	15	1,100	1,611	2,114	6.3	15.3
METH–Wesleyan	3	137	89	179	0.5	1.3
Non-denom Chr Chs	3	725	615	931	2.8	6.7
PENT–Assemb of God	3	447	249	837	2.5	6.1
PENT–COGIC	2	0	300	368	1.1	2.7
PENT–Un Pent Ch Intl	1	NR	NR	NR	-	-
PRES–Presb Ch (USA)	6	129	294	361	1.1	2.6
Salvation Army	1	86	75	149	0.4	1.1
Un C of Christ	4	123	309	379	1.1	2.7
GRANT	**130**	**14,255**	**17,704**	**28,060**	**40.1**	**100.0**
ANG/EPIS–Episcopal	2	90	182	195	0.3	0.7
Bahá'í	0	NR	12	12	0.0	0.0
BAPT–Amer Bapt Assn	2	NR	0	0	0.0	0.0
BAPT–Amer Bapt USA	3	186	393	470	0.7	1.7
BAPT–Free Will Bapt	1	NR	55	66	0.1	0.2
BAPT–Natl Mis Bapt Conv	1	0	150	179	0.3	0.6
BAPT–NBC Amer	2	300	400	478	0.7	1.7
BAPT–Ref Bapt Ch	1	NR	NR	NR	-	-
BAPT–Reg Bapt Gen As	1	NR	NR	NR	-	-
BAPT–So Bapt Conv	4	790	1,433	1,714	2.4	6.1

Religious Group	Number of Congrega-tions	Number of Attendees	Number of Communicant, Confirmed, or Full Members	Adherents: Number of Adherents	Adherents: % of Total Pop.	Adherents: % of Total Adh.
BRETH–Ch of Brethren	1	40	49	59	0.1	0.2
Catholic	2	NR	NR	2,328	3.3	8.3
CGOD–Ch God (Ander)	4	296	NR	296	0.4	1.1
Ch of Nazarene	6	267	401	521	0.7	1.9
Chr & Miss Al	2	500	550	650	0.9	2.3
CHR–Chr Ch (Disc)	5	324	1,060	1,268	1.8	4.5
CHR–Chr Chs & Chs Cr	3	NR	150	179	0.3	0.6
CHR–Chs of Christ	4	368	305	353	0.5	1.3
CONG–Cong Chr Add'l	1	NR	104	124	0.2	0.4
Evan Ch	1	NR	NR	NR	-	-
FRND–Fr Un Mtg	9	NR	653	781	1.1	2.8
JUD–Reform	1	11	20	54	0.1	0.2
LDS–L-D Saints	1	NR	NR	462	0.7	1.6
LUTH–E.L.C.A.	1	25	37	39	0.1	0.1
LUTH–Luth–MO Synod	1	224	411	545	0.8	1.9
MENN–Fel Evg Ch	1	590	252	301	0.4	1.1
METH–AME	3	80	510	610	0.9	2.2
METH–Un Methodist	23	2,287	2,614	5,659	8.1	20.2
METH–Wesleyan	17	3,551	2,712	4,616	6.6	16.5
Non-denom Chr Chs	14	3,416	3,983	4,430	6.3	15.8
PENT–Assemb of God	3	440	351	566	0.8	2.0
PENT–Ch God (Cleve)	1	94	171	204	0.3	0.7
PENT–Ch of God Proph	1	NR	54	65	0.1	0.2
PENT–Un Pent Ch Intl	2	NR	NR	NR	-	-
PRES–Presb Ch (USA)	2	136	277	331	0.5	1.2
Salvation Army	1	57	80	114	0.2	0.4
Sev Day Adv	2	132	228	263	0.4	0.9
Un C of Christ	1	51	107	128	0.2	0.5
GREENE	**88**	**4,884**	**8,682**	**12,371**	**37.3**	**100.0**
Bahá'í	0	NR	6	6	0.0	0.0
BAPT–Amer Bapt USA	5	445	696	850	2.6	6.9
BAPT–So Bapt Conv	1	37	42	51	0.2	0.4
Catholic	3	NR	NR	746	2.2	6.0
CGOD–Ch God (Ander)	1	48	NR	48	0.1	0.4
CGOD–Ches God-Gen Con	2	258	152	186	0.6	1.5
Ch of Nazarene	1	14	14	33	0.1	0.3
CHR–Chr Ch (Disc)	2	131	445	543	1.6	4.4
CHR–Chr Chs & Chs Cr	11	NR	2,106	2,571	7.8	20.8
CHR–Chs of Christ	8	540	538	690	2.1	5.6
Grace Gosp Fel	1	NR	NR	NR	-	-
Jehovah's Witness	1	NR	NR	NR	-	-
LDS–L-D Saints	1	NR	NR	368	1.1	3.0
LUTH–E.L.C.A.	1	30	56	71	0.2	0.6
MENN–Amish Undif	0	NR	12	23	0.1	0.2
MENN–Ber Amish-Menn	1	30	18	30	0.1	0.2
MENN–Unaffil Amish-Menn	1	117	39	117	0.4	0.9
METH–Un Methodist	13	564	1,110	1,556	4.7	12.6
METH–Wesleyan	5	170	148	220	0.7	1.8
Non-denom Chr Chs	11	1,520	2,058	2,180	6.6	17.6
PENT–Assemb of God	5	467	338	764	2.3	6.2
PENT–Ch God (Cleve)	4	137	281	343	1.0	2.8
PENT–Ch of God Proph	1	NR	25	31	0.1	0.3
PENT–Pent Ch of God	2	140	NR	217	0.7	1.8
PENT–Un Pent Ch Intl	3	NR	NR	NR	-	-
PRES–Presb Ch (USA)	2	51	92	112	0.3	0.9
Sev Day Adv	1	29	50	58	0.2	0.5
Un C of Christ	1	156	456	557	1.7	4.5
HAMILTON	**190**	**35,945**	**48,062**	**117,070**	**42.6**	**100.0**
ANG/EPIS–Anglican NA	2	NR	NR	NR	-	-
ANG/EPIS–Episcopal	3	486	1,499	1,499	0.5	1.3
Bahá'í	1	NR	57	57	0.0	0.0
BAPT–Amer Bapt Assn	1	NR	120	157	0.1	0.1
BAPT–Amer Bapt USA	2	93	227	298	0.1	0.3
BAPT–Free Will Bapt	1	NR	55	72	0.0	0.1
BAPT–Ref Bapt Ch	1	NR	NR	NR	-	-
BAPT–Reg Bapt Gen As	2	NR	NR	NR	-	-
BAPT–So Bapt Conv	12	455	451	592	0.2	0.5
BRETH–Ch of Brethren	1	124	219	287	0.1	0.2
BUDD–Mahayana	1	NR	NR	103	0.0	0.1
Catholic	8	NR	NR	40,251	14.7	34.4
CGOD–Ch God (Ander)	5	777	NR	777	0.3	0.7

NR–Not Reported - Represents no adherents reported. Percentages may not total 100 due to rounding.

Table 3: Religious Congregations by County and Group: 2010

Religious Group	Number of Congrega-tions	Number of Attendees	Number of Communicant, Confirmed, or Full Members	Adherents: Number of Adherents	Adherents: % of Total Pop.	Adherents: % of Total Adh.
Ch Cr, Scientst	1	NR	NR	NR	-	-
Ch of Nazarene	3	248	444	491	0.2	0.4
Chr & Miss Al	3	269	242	319	0.1	0.3
CHR–Chr Ch (Disc)	5	409	1,714	2,249	0.8	1.9
CHR–Chr Chs & Chs Cr	13	NR	6,214	8,154	3.0	7.0
CHR–Chs of Christ	4	414	490	649	0.2	0.6
Evan Ch	1	NR	NR	NR	-	-
Evan Free Ch	1	4,600	NR	4,600	1.7	3.9
FRND–Central Yr Mtg	1	30	80	105	0.0	0.1
FRND–Fr Un Mtg	7	NR	635	833	0.3	0.7
FRND–Unaffl Mtgs	1	NR	NR	NR	-	-
Jehovah's Witness	2	NR	NR	NR	-	-
JUD–Conserv	1	127	142	383	0.1	0.3
LDS–L-D Saints	6	NR	NR	2,425	0.9	2.1
LUTH–E.L.C.A.	5	1,354	3,379	4,933	1.8	4.2
LUTH–Luth–MO Synod	5	1,769	2,764	3,788	1.4	3.2
LUTH–Nor Amer Luth C	1	NR	NR	NR	-	-
LUTH–Wisc Ev Luth Syn	1	82	120	158	0.1	0.1
METH–AME	1	95	190	249	0.1	0.2
METH–Free Methodist	1	63	49	63	0.0	0.1
METH–Un Methodist	17	3,821	7,301	12,196	4.4	10.4
METH–Wesleyan	7	734	387	956	0.3	0.8
Missionary Ch	2	110	100	110	0.0	0.1
Muslim Est	1	200	NR	1,000	0.4	0.9
Non-denom Chr Chs	31	15,965	17,491	21,214	7.7	18.1
ORTHE–Greek Orthodox	1	450	NR	2,000	0.7	1.7
ORTHO–Coptic Orth Ch	1	270	NR	455	0.2	0.4
PENT–Assemb of God	6	1,063	467	1,443	0.5	1.2
PENT–Ch God (Cleve)	2	70	204	268	0.1	0.2
PENT–Ch of God Proph	2	NR	85	112	0.0	0.1
PENT–Un Pent Ch Intl	4	NR	NR	NR	-	-
PRES–Korean Amer Pres	1	NR	NR	NR	-	-
PRES–Korean Pres Amer	1	NR	NR	NR	-	-
PRES–Orth Pres Ch	1	148	147	185	0.1	0.2
PRES–Presb Ch (USA)	3	592	1,070	1,404	0.5	1.2
PRES–Presb Ch Amer	2	365	332	537	0.2	0.5
REF–Ref Ch in Am	1	136	141	176	0.1	0.2
Sev Day Adv	3	406	706	812	0.3	0.7
Un C of Christ	1	220	540	709	0.3	0.6
Zoroastrian	0	NR	NR	1	0.0	0.0
HANCOCK	**81**	**9,909**	**18,099**	**27,147**	**38.8**	**100.0**
ANG/EPIS–Anglican NA	2	NR	NR	NR	-	-
Bahá'í	0	NR	24	24	0.0	0.1
BAPT–Natl Mis Bapt Conv	1	0	150	188	0.3	0.7
BAPT–Ref Bapt Ch	1	NR	NR	NR	-	-
BAPT–Reg Bapt Gen As	1	NR	NR	NR	-	-
BAPT–So Bapt Conv	4	357	693	867	1.2	3.2
Catholic	2	NR	NR	4,626	6.6	17.0
CGOD–Ch God (Ander)	2	298	NR	298	0.4	1.1
Ch of Nazarene	5	446	721	753	1.1	2.8
CHR–Chr Ch (Disc)	3	318	789	987	1.4	3.6
CHR–Chr Chs & Chs Cr	7	NR	2,820	3,526	5.0	13.0
CHR–Chs of Christ	2	153	143	179	0.3	0.7
FRND–Fr Un Mtg	3	NR	115	144	0.2	0.5
Jehovah's Witness	2	NR	NR	NR	-	-
LUTH–E.L.C.A.	1	187	333	333	0.5	1.2
LUTH–Luth Cong Msn Chr	1	142	309	386	0.6	1.4
LUTH–Luth–MO Synod	2	514	868	1,171	1.7	4.3
LUTH–Nor Amer Luth C	1	NR	NR	NR	-	-
METH–Un Methodist	17	1,408	3,133	4,430	6.3	16.3
METH–Wesleyan	3	305	126	397	0.6	1.5
Non-denom Chr Chs	13	5,065	7,045	7,521	10.7	27.7
PENT–Assemb of God	2	425	278	629	0.9	2.3
PENT–Ch God (Cleve)	2	108	228	285	0.4	1.0
PENT–Un Pent Ch Intl	1	NR	NR	NR	-	-
PENT–Vineyard	1	117	210	263	0.4	1.0
PRES–Presb Ch (USA)	1	48	83	104	0.1	0.4
Sev Day Adv	1	18	31	36	0.1	0.1
HARRISON	**82**	**4,128**	**8,424**	**15,415**	**39.2**	**100.0**
BAPT–So Bapt Conv	7	469	695	848	2.2	5.5
Catholic	6	NR	NR	4,447	11.3	28.8

Religious Group	Number of Congrega-tions	Number of Attendees	Number of Communicant, Confirmed, or Full Members	Adherents: Number of Adherents	Adherents: % of Total Pop.	Adherents: % of Total Adh.
Ch of Nazarene	1	88	82	97	0.2	0.6
CHR–Chr Ch (Disc)	1	45	300	366	0.9	2.4
CHR–Chr Chs & Chs Cr	5	NR	1,425	1,738	4.4	11.3
CHR–Chs of Christ	4	238	260	313	0.8	2.0
Intl Fell Bible Ch	1	NR	NR	NR	-	-
Jehovah's Witness	1	NR	NR	NR	-	-
LDS–L-D Saints	1	NR	NR	289	0.7	1.9
LUTH–E.L.C.A.	2	93	178	182	0.5	1.2
LUTH–Luth–MO Synod	2	17	693	791	2.0	5.1
METH–AME	1	30	45	55	0.1	0.4
METH–Un Methodist	31	1,790	3,231	4,217	10.7	27.4
METH–Wesleyan	1	26	28	34	0.1	0.2
Non-denom Chr Chs	7	720	798	981	2.5	6.4
PENT–Assemb of God	4	388	287	567	1.4	3.7
PENT–Ch of God Proph	1	NR	25	30	0.1	0.2
PRES–Presb Ch (USA)	5	206	337	411	1.0	2.7
Un C of Christ	1	18	40	49	0.1	0.3
HENDRICKS	**124**	**15,571**	**32,236**	**59,295**	**40.8**	**100.0**
ANG/EPIS–Anglican NA	1	NR	NR	NR	-	-
ANG/EPIS–Episcopal	2	157	364	399	0.3	0.7
Bahá'í	0	NR	19	19	0.0	0.0
BAPT–Amer Bapt USA	4	362	871	1,105	0.8	1.9
BAPT–Reg Bapt Gen As	5	NR	NR	NR	-	-
BAPT–So Bapt Conv	3	427	596	756	0.5	1.3
BUDD–Mahayana	2	NR	NR	205	0.1	0.3
Catholic	3	NR	NR	10,861	7.5	18.3
CGOD–Ch God (Ander)	2	147	NR	147	0.1	0.2
Ch of Nazarene	5	699	694	991	0.7	1.7
Chr & Miss Al	1	NR	NR	NR	-	-
CHR–Chr Ch (Disc)	5	392	837	1,062	0.7	1.8
CHR–Chr Chs & Chs Cr	12	NR	12,447	15,790	10.9	26.6
CHR–Chs of Christ	5	806	752	943	0.6	1.6
FRND–Fr Un Mtg	4	NR	493	625	0.4	1.1
HINDU–I/A Temples	1	NR	NR	1,742	1.2	2.9
Jehovah's Witness	1	NR	NR	NR	-	-
LDS–Comm of Christ	1	NR	103	103	0.1	0.2
LDS–L-D Saints	4	NR	NR	2,099	1.4	3.5
LUTH–E.L.C.A.	3	391	288	1,089	0.7	1.8
LUTH–Evan Luth Syn	1	28	42	62	0.0	0.1
LUTH–Luth–MO Synod	3	656	1,015	1,411	1.0	2.4
METH–AME	1	0	150	190	0.1	0.3
METH–AME Zion	1	0	100	127	0.1	0.2
METH–Free Methodist	2	272	230	272	0.2	0.5
METH–Un Methodist	11	2,414	4,616	7,257	5.0	12.2
METH–Wesleyan	1	89	43	116	0.1	0.2
Muslim Est	1	134	NR	308	0.2	0.5
Non-denom Chr Chs	22	7,101	7,430	9,282	6.4	15.7
PENT–Assemb of God	6	1,081	510	1,490	1.0	2.5
PENT–Ch of God Proph	1	NR	37	47	0.0	0.1
PENT–Un Pent Ch Intl	3	NR	NR	NR	-	-
PRES–Presb Ch (USA)	3	152	293	372	0.3	0.6
PRES–Presb Ch Amer	1	90	78	114	0.1	0.2
PRES–Ref Pres of NA	1	60	46	79	0.1	0.1
Sev Day Adv	1	58	102	117	0.1	0.2
Unit Univ	1	55	80	115	0.1	0.2
HENRY	**114**	**7,161**	**14,471**	**19,248**	**38.9**	**100.0**
ANG/EPIS–Episcopal	1	27	50	50	0.1	0.3
Bahá'í	0	NR	2	2	0.0	0.0
BAPT–Amer Bapt USA	1	471	993	1,193	2.4	6.2
BAPT–Free Will Bapt	1	NR	55	66	0.1	0.3
BAPT–Ind Bapt Flwsp Intl	1	NR	NR	NR	-	-
BAPT–So Bapt Conv	5	505	1,669	2,005	4.1	10.4
BRETH–Ch of Brethren	4	161	179	215	0.4	1.1
Catholic	2	NR	NR	626	1.3	3.3
CGOD–Ch God (Ander)	2	299	NR	299	0.6	1.6
Ch Christ Chr Union	1	NR	NR	NR	-	-
Ch of God Gen Conf	1	NR	6	7	0.0	0.0
Ch of Nazarene	10	1,229	1,432	2,017	4.1	10.5
CHR–Chr Ch (Disc)	3	231	1,339	1,609	3.3	8.4
CHR–Chr Chs & Chs Cr	10	NR	1,508	1,812	3.7	9.4
CHR–Chs of Christ	7	282	266	351	0.7	1.8

NR–Not Reported - Represents no adherents reported. Percentages may not total 100 due to rounding.

Table 3: Religious Congregations by County and Group: 2010

Religious Group	Number of Congrega-tions	Number of Attendees	Number of Communicant, Confirmed, or Full Members	Adherents: Number of Adherents	Adherents: % of Total Pop.	Adherents: % of Total Adh.
CONG–Consrv Cong Chr	1	127	97	117	0.2	0.6
CONG–Midw Cong Chr Fel	1	21	24	29	0.1	0.2
Evan Free Ch	1	20	NR	20	0.0	0.1
FRND–Fr Gen Cf	1	NR	11	13	0.0	0.1
FRND–Fr Un Mtg	9	NR	626	752	1.5	3.9
Jehovah's Witness	1	NR	NR	NR	-	-
LDS–L-D Saints	1	NR	NR	273	0.6	1.4
LUTH–E.L.C.A.	1	120	289	374	0.8	1.9
MENN–Amish Undif	1	NR	32	80	0.2	0.4
METH–AME	1	0	150	180	0.4	0.9
METH–Free Methodist	1	44	40	44	0.1	0.2
METH–Un Methodist	14	753	1,465	1,873	3.8	9.7
METH–Wesleyan	5	558	383	725	1.5	3.8
Non-denom Chr Chs	15	1,775	2,475	2,652	5.4	13.8
PENT–Assemb of God	1	122	115	122	0.2	0.6
PENT–Ch God (Cleve)	2	40	20	24	0.0	0.1
PENT–Ch God Mtn Asm	1	NR	NR	NR	-	-
PENT–Int Foursq Gos	1	288	831	999	2.0	5.2
PENT–Un Pent Ch Intl	1	NR	NR	NR	-	-
PRES–Presb Ch (USA)	4	60	373	448	0.9	2.3
Salvation Army	1	16	20	247	0.5	1.3
Sev Day Adv	1	12	21	24	0.0	0.1
HOWARD	**138**	**17,730**	**29,262**	**41,969**	**50.7**	**100.0**
ANG/EPIS–Anglican NA	1	NR	NR	NR	-	-
ANG/EPIS–Episcopal	1	158	200	200	0.2	0.5
Bahá'í	0	NR	45	45	0.1	0.1
BAPT–Amer Bapt Assn	2	NR	100	122	0.1	0.3
BAPT–Amer Bapt USA	2	374	549	670	0.8	1.6
BAPT–N Am Bapt Conf	1	NR	58	71	0.1	0.2
BAPT–Natl Mis Bapt Conv	1	60	100	122	0.1	0.3
BAPT–NBC Amer	1	400	450	549	0.7	1.3
BAPT–Reg Bapt Gen As	3	NR	NR	NR	-	-
BAPT–So Bapt Conv	4	263	565	689	0.8	1.6
BRETH–Ch of Brethren	1	75	113	138	0.2	0.3
BRETH–Grace Breth	1	NR	NR	NR	-	-
Catholic	2	NR	NR	5,200	6.3	12.4
CGOD–Ch God (Ander)	1	295	NR	295	0.4	0.7
Ch Cr, Scientst	1	NR	NR	NR	-	-
Ch of God Gen Conf	1	NR	50	61	0.1	0.1
Ch of Nazarene	3	1,301	1,225	1,361	1.6	3.2
Chr & Miss Al	1	52	37	71	0.1	0.2
CHR–Chr Ch (Disc)	3	299	1,516	1,850	2.2	4.4
CHR–Chr Chs & Chs Cr	8	NR	2,774	3,384	4.1	8.1
CHR–Chs of Christ	2	415	396	489	0.6	1.2
Evan Free Ch	1	60	NR	60	0.1	0.1
FRND–Fr Un Mtg	8	NR	744	908	1.1	2.2
Jehovah's Witness	1	NR	NR	NR	-	-
JUD–Reform	1	12	21	57	0.1	0.1
LDS–L-D Saints	1	NR	NR	593	0.7	1.4
LUTH–E.L.C.A.	1	65	167	183	0.2	0.4
LUTH–Luth-MO Synod	3	519	922	1,152	1.4	2.7
LUTH–Wisc Ev Luth Syn	1	75	106	146	0.2	0.3
MENN–Amish Undif	1	NR	72	117	0.1	0.3
MENN–Beachy Amish-Menn	1	138	90	138	0.2	0.3
MENN–Mennonite USA	2	221	240	293	0.4	0.7
METH–AME	2	100	353	431	0.5	1.0
METH–Free Methodist	2	195	196	201	0.2	0.5
METH–Un Methodist	16	1,550	2,786	4,096	4.9	9.8
METH–Wesleyan	4	313	306	408	0.5	1.0
Muslim Est	1	134	NR	308	0.4	0.7
Non-denom Chr Chs	28	8,675	11,695	12,719	15.4	30.3
ORTHE–Orth Ch in Amer	1	36	NR	85	0.1	0.2
PENT–Assemb of God	4	560	386	816	1.0	1.9
PENT–Ch God (Cleve)	2	201	492	600	0.7	1.4
PENT–Ch God Mtn Asm	1	NR	NR	NR	-	-
PENT–Ch of God Proph	1	NR	43	52	0.1	0.1
PENT–COGIC	2	150	350	427	0.5	1.0
PENT–Int Foursq Gos	1	122	231	282	0.3	0.7
PENT–Pent Ch of God	1	70	NR	109	0.1	0.3
PENT–Un Pent Ch Intl	2	NR	NR	NR	-	-
PRES–Evan Presby Ch	1	NR	432	527	0.6	1.3
PRES–Presb Ch (USA)	2	37	621	758	0.9	1.8
PRES–Ref Pres of NA	1	88	56	89	0.1	0.2

Religious Group	Number of Congrega-tions	Number of Attendees	Number of Communicant, Confirmed, or Full Members	Adherents: Number of Adherents	Adherents: % of Total Pop.	Adherents: % of Total Adh.
Salvation Army	1	60	130	232	0.3	0.6
Sev Day Adv	1	58	100	115	0.1	0.3
Un Breth in Cr	1	427	227	363	0.4	0.9
Un C of Christ	1	156	296	361	0.4	0.9
Unit Univ	1	16	22	22	0.0	0.1
Zoroastrian	0	NR	NR	4	0.0	0.0
HUNTINGTON	**78**	**5,529**	**9,085**	**18,483**	**49.8**	**100.0**
ANG/EPIS–Anglican NA	1	NR	NR	NR	-	-
ANG/EPIS–Episcopal	1	33	108	108	0.3	0.6
Bahá'í	0	NR	3	3	0.0	0.0
BAPT–Amer Bapt USA	2	165	250	304	0.8	1.6
BAPT–Free Will Bapt	2	NR	110	134	0.4	0.7
BAPT–Reg Bapt Gen As	1	NR	NR	NR	-	-
BAPT–So Bapt Conv	3	248	349	425	1.1	2.3
BRETH–Brethren (Ash)	2	NR	160	195	0.5	1.1
BRETH–Ch of Brethren	5	99	439	534	1.4	2.9
Catholic	3	NR	NR	4,876	13.1	26.4
CGOD–Ch God (Ander)	1	137	NR	137	0.4	0.7
Ch of Nazarene	2	539	714	839	2.3	4.5
Chr & Miss Al	2	232	99	327	0.9	1.8
CHR–Chr Ch (Disc)	2	138	407	495	1.3	2.7
CHR–Chr Chs & Chs Cr	2	NR	370	450	1.2	2.4
CHR–Chs of Christ	3	127	116	194	0.5	1.0
Jehovah's Witness	1	NR	NR	NR	-	-
LDS–L-D Saints	2	NR	NR	597	1.6	3.2
LUTH–Luth-MO Synod	2	70	562	780	2.1	4.2
METH–Un Methodist	16	1,274	2,247	2,897	7.8	15.7
METH–Wesleyan	5	215	142	280	0.8	1.5
Non-denom Chr Chs	7	1,020	1,538	1,673	4.5	9.1
PENT–Assemb of God	1	87	48	158	0.4	0.9
PENT–Ch God (Cleve)	1	9	7	9	0.0	0.0
PENT–Ch of God Proph	1	NR	4	5	0.0	0.0
PENT–Un Pent Ch Intl	1	NR	NR	NR	-	-
PRES–Presb Ch (USA)	1	42	59	72	0.2	0.4
Salvation Army	1	33	126	1,908	5.1	10.3
Un Breth in Cr	4	907	973	774	2.1	4.2
Un C of Christ	3	154	254	309	0.8	1.7
JACKSON	**88**	**7,515**	**17,325**	**24,219**	**57.2**	**100.0**
Bahá'í	0	NR	6	6	0.0	0.0
BAPT–Amer Bapt Assn	1	NR	85	105	0.2	0.4
BAPT–Amer Bapt USA	6	572	1,283	1,582	3.7	6.5
BAPT–Natl Mis Bapt Conv	1	150	150	185	0.4	0.8
BAPT–So Bapt Conv	3	446	796	981	2.3	4.1
Catholic	2	NR	NR	1,500	3.5	6.2
CGOD–Ch God (Ander)	1	47	NR	47	0.1	0.2
Ch of Nazarene	7	1,026	1,177	1,974	4.7	8.2
CHR–Chr Ch (Disc)	1	349	1,036	1,277	3.0	5.3
CHR–Chr Chs & Chs Cr	16	NR	3,489	4,302	10.2	17.8
CHR–Chs of Christ	2	95	101	131	0.3	0.5
Jehovah's Witness	1	NR	NR	NR	-	-
LDS–L-D Saints	1	NR	NR	246	0.6	1.0
LUTH–E.L.C.A.	1	228	437	597	1.4	2.5
LUTH–Luth-MO Synod	10	2,826	5,929	7,785	18.4	32.1
MENN–Amish Undif	1	NR	47	120	0.3	0.5
METH–AME	1	0	150	185	0.4	0.8
METH–Free Methodist	1	27	25	27	0.1	0.1
METH–Un Methodist	12	530	1,025	1,233	2.9	5.1
METH–Wesleyan	2	73	50	95	0.2	0.4
Non-denom Chr Chs	8	781	982	1,109	2.6	4.6
PENT–Assemb of God	1	45	0	49	0.1	0.2
PENT–Ch God (Cleve)	2	129	221	272	0.6	1.1
PENT–Un Pent Ch Intl	3	NR	NR	NR	-	-
PRES–Presb Ch (USA)	2	151	271	334	0.8	1.4
Sev Day Adv	1	24	41	47	0.1	0.2
Un C of Christ	1	16	24	30	0.1	0.1
JASPER	**59**	**4,255**	**6,799**	**13,637**	**40.7**	**100.0**
ANG/EPIS–Episcopal	1	6	6	6	0.0	0.0
Ap Chr Ch-Amer	1	152	105	152	0.5	1.1
Bahá'í	0	NR	2	2	0.0	0.0
BAPT–Amer Bapt USA	1	45	162	201	0.6	1.5

NR–Not Reported - Represents no adherents reported. Percentages may not total 100 due to rounding.

Table 3: Religious Congregations by County and Group: 2010

Religious Group	Number of Congrega-tions	Number of Attendees	Number of Communicant, Confirmed, or Full Members	Adherents: Number of Adherents	Adherents: % of Total Pop.	Adherents: % of Total Adh.
BAPT–So Bapt Conv	3	163	298	370	1.1	2.7
Catholic	4	NR	NR	4,341	13.0	31.8
CGOD–Ch God (Ander)	1	27	NR	27	0.1	0.2
Ch of Nazarene	2	111	124	167	0.5	1.2
CHR–Chr Ch (Disc)	1	62	304	377	1.1	2.8
CHR–Chr Chs & Chs Cr	4	NR	680	843	2.5	6.2
CHR–Chs of Christ	2	73	67	84	0.3	0.6
Evan Free Ch	1	115	NR	115	0.3	0.8
Ind Fund Churches	2	NR	NR	NR	-	-
Jehovah's Witness	1	NR	NR	NR	-	-
LDS–L-D Saints	1	NR	NR	153	0.5	1.1
LUTH–Luth-MO Synod	4	280	614	814	2.4	6.0
MENN–Mennonite USA	1	90	71	88	0.3	0.6
METH–Un Methodist	4	523	950	1,366	4.1	10.0
Non-denom Chr Chs	8	712	784	1,071	3.2	7.9
PENT–Assemb of God	4	372	216	536	1.6	3.9
PENT–Ch God (Cleve)	1	14	24	30	0.1	0.2
PENT–Pent Ch of God	2	140	NR	217	0.6	1.6
PENT–Un Pent Ch Intl	2	NR	NR	NR	-	-
PRES–Presb Ch (USA)	1	50	109	135	0.4	1.0
PRES–Presb Ch Amer	1	30	27	27	0.1	0.2
REF–Christian Ref	3	590	817	1,013	3.0	7.4
REF–Ref Ch in Am	2	700	1,439	1,502	4.5	11.0
REF–Un Ref Chs N.A.	1	NR	NR	NR	-	-
JAY	**67**	**2,503**	**3,390**	**8,220**	**38.7**	**100.0**
Bahá'í	0	NR	2	2	0.0	0.0
BAPT–Amer Bapt USA	1	24	28	35	0.2	0.4
BAPT–Reg Bapt Gen As	1	NR	NR	NR	-	-
BAPT–So Bapt Conv	1	16	50	63	0.3	0.8
BRETH–Ch of Brethren	2	0	88	111	0.5	1.4
Catholic	3	NR	NR	1,731	8.1	21.1
Ch of Nazarene	6	481	554	803	3.8	9.8
CHR–Chr Chs & Chs Cr	4	NR	195	245	1.2	3.0
CHR–Chs of Christ	1	50	58	61	0.3	0.7
CONG–Midw Cong Chr Fel	1	35	19	24	0.1	0.3
Evan Ch	1	NR	NR	NR	-	-
FRND–Fr Un Mtg	3	NR	44	55	0.3	0.7
Intl Fell Bible Ch	1	NR	NR	NR	-	-
Jehovah's Witness	1	NR	NR	NR	-	-
LDS–L-D Saints	1	NR	NR	98	0.5	1.2
LUTH–E.L.C.A.	3	150	281	428	2.0	5.2
MENN–Amish Undif	6	NR	334	1,024	4.8	12.5
METH–Evan Meth Ch	1	NR	NR	NR	-	-
METH–Un Methodist	15	820	1,067	2,305	10.8	28.0
METH–Wesleyan	1	120	53	156	0.7	1.9
Missionary Ch	1	342	28	342	1.6	4.2
Non-denom Chr Chs	5	332	345	421	2.0	5.1
PENT–Assemb of God	1	23	11	23	0.1	0.3
PENT–Ch of God Proph	1	NR	16	20	0.1	0.2
PENT–Un Pent Ch Intl	2	NR	NR	NR	-	-
PENT–Vineyard	1	30	0	0	0.0	0.0
PRES–Presb Ch (USA)	1	70	156	196	0.9	2.4
Un C of Christ	2	10	61	77	0.4	0.9
JEFFERSON	**66**	**3,967**	**9,664**	**14,627**	**45.1**	**100.0**
ANG/EPIS–Episcopal	1	63	137	150	0.5	1.0
Bahá'í	0	NR	10	10	0.0	0.1
BAPT–Amer Bapt USA	16	1,197	3,222	3,872	11.9	26.5
BAPT–So Bapt Conv	4	570	1,785	2,145	6.6	14.7
Calv Chpl	1	NR	NR	NR	-	-
Catholic	1	NR	NR	2,500	7.7	17.1
CGOD–Ch God (Ander)	1	19	NR	19	0.1	0.1
Ch of Nazarene	1	37	48	48	0.1	0.3
Chr & Miss Al	1	112	53	137	0.4	0.9
CHR–Chr Ch (Disc)	1	51	172	207	0.6	1.4
CHR–Chr Chs & Chs Cr	7	NR	1,181	1,419	4.4	9.7
CHR–Chs of Christ	1	88	82	107	0.3	0.7
Jehovah's Witness	1	NR	NR	NR	-	-
LDS–L-D Saints	1	NR	NR	332	1.0	2.3
LUTH–E.L.C.A.	1	41	84	98	0.3	0.7
LUTH–Luth-MO Synod	1	70	110	142	0.4	1.0
MENN–Amb Amish-Menn	1	127	57	127	0.4	0.9

Religious Group	Number of Congrega-tions	Number of Attendees	Number of Communicant, Confirmed, or Full Members	Adherents: Number of Adherents	Adherents: % of Total Pop.	Adherents: % of Total Adh.
MENN–Amish Undif	0	NR	35	91	0.3	0.6
METH–AME	1	0	150	180	0.6	1.2
METH–Un Methodist	8	530	1,098	1,235	3.8	8.4
METH–Wesleyan	2	71	59	92	0.3	0.6
Non-denom Chr Chs	6	540	739	755	2.3	5.2
PENT–Assemb of God	1	259	237	360	1.1	2.5
PENT–Un Pent Ch Intl	1	NR	NR	NR	-	-
PRES–Presb Ch (USA)	4	127	240	288	0.9	2.0
Salvation Army	1	29	56	184	0.6	1.3
Sev Day Adv	1	16	28	32	0.1	0.2
Un C of Christ	1	20	81	97	0.3	0.7
JENNINGS	**52**	**3,033**	**6,034**	**10,455**	**36.7**	**100.0**
BAPT–Amer Bapt USA	10	653	1,443	1,798	6.3	17.2
BAPT–So Bapt Conv	5	916	1,714	2,135	7.5	20.4
Catholic	4	NR	NR	2,230	7.8	21.3
CGOD–Ch God (Ander)	4	215	NR	215	0.8	2.1
Ch of Nazarene	1	150	227	227	0.8	2.2
CHR–Chr Chs & Chs Cr	5	NR	1,015	1,264	4.4	12.1
CHR–Chs of Christ	2	85	70	96	0.3	0.9
Jehovah's Witness	1	NR	NR	NR	-	-
LDS–L-D Saints	1	NR	NR	578	2.0	5.5
LUTH–Luth-MO Synod	1	35	80	97	0.3	0.9
METH–Un Methodist	8	398	751	889	3.1	8.5
METH–Wesleyan	1	73	46	95	0.3	0.9
Non-denom Chr Chs	3	270	310	363	1.3	3.5
PENT–Assemb of God	1	50	38	50	0.2	0.5
PENT–Ch God (Cleve)	1	57	152	189	0.7	1.8
PRES–Presb Ch (USA)	3	100	134	167	0.6	1.6
Sev Day Adv	1	31	54	62	0.2	0.6
JOHNSON	**139**	**25,121**	**38,504**	**64,363**	**46.1**	**100.0**
ANG/EPIS–Episcopal	1	78	162	204	0.1	0.3
Bahá'í	0	NR	8	8	0.0	0.0
BAPT–Amer Bapt Assn	4	NR	340	427	0.3	0.7
BAPT–Amer Bapt USA	5	561	1,516	1,905	1.4	3.0
BAPT–Converge/BGC	2	475	NR	570	0.4	0.9
BAPT–Natl Mis Bapt Conv	1	0	150	188	0.1	0.3
BAPT–Ref Bapt Ch	1	NR	NR	NR	-	-
BAPT–Reg Bapt Gen As	2	NR	NR	NR	-	-
BAPT–So Bapt Conv	9	958	2,007	2,522	1.8	3.9
BRETH–Ch of Brethren	1	35	21	26	0.0	0.0
Calv Chpl	1	NR	NR	NR	-	-
Catholic	4	NR	NR	11,589	8.3	18.0
CGOD–Ch God (Ander)	2	110	NR	110	0.1	0.2
Ch of Nazarene	2	202	255	299	0.2	0.5
CHR–Chr Ch (Disc)	6	569	1,774	2,229	1.6	3.5
CHR–Chr Chs & Chs Cr	12	NR	7,484	9,403	6.7	14.6
CHR–Chs of Christ	5	672	701	846	0.6	1.3
CONG–Cong Chr, NA	1	NR	276	347	0.2	0.5
Ind Fund Churches	1	NR	NR	NR	-	-
LDS–L-D Saints	3	NR	NR	1,317	0.9	2.0
LUTH–E.L.C.A.	3	265	501	630	0.5	1.0
LUTH–Luth Cong Msn Chr	1	12	NR	NR	-	-
LUTH–Luth-MO Synod	3	549	1,107	1,408	1.0	2.2
LUTH–Wisc Ev Luth Syn	1	41	37	49	0.0	0.1
METH–AME	1	0	100	126	0.1	0.2
METH–Un Methodist	9	1,530	2,301	3,218	2.3	5.0
METH–Wesleyan	5	141	91	183	0.1	0.3
Non-denom Chr Chs	33	14,021	13,860	17,722	12.7	27.5
ORTHE–Ant Orth of NA	1	16	NR	27	0.0	0.0
PENT–Assemb of God	4	1,561	879	2,520	1.8	3.9
PENT–Ch God (Cleve)	1	35	512	643	0.5	1.0
PENT–Un Pent Ch Intl	3	NR	NR	NR	-	-
PENT–Vineyard	2	2,708	3,067	3,853	2.8	6.0
PRES–Evan Presby Ch	1	NR	180	226	0.2	0.4
PRES–Presb Ch (USA)	5	489	1,033	1,298	0.9	2.0
Salvation Army	1	11	9	307	0.2	0.5
Sev Day Adv	1	26	45	52	0.0	0.1
Un C of Christ	1	56	88	111	0.1	0.2
KNOX	**82**	**5,406**	**8,636**	**18,096**	**47.1**	**100.0**
ANG/EPIS–Episcopal	1	25	23	33	0.1	0.2

NR–Not Reported   - Represents no adherents reported.   Percentages may not total 100 due to rounding.

Table 3: Religious Congregations by County and Group: 2010

Religious Group	Number of Congrega-tions	Number of Attendees	Number of Communicant, Confirmed, or Full Members	Adherents		
				Number of Adherents	% of Total Pop.	% of Total Adh.
Bahá'í	0	NR	12	12	0.0	0.1
BAPT–Amer Bapt USA	4	1,206	1,563	1,867	4.9	10.3
BAPT–So Bapt Conv	4	269	537	641	1.7	3.5
Catholic	6	NR	NR	4,867	12.7	26.9
CGOD–Ch God (Ander)	3	954	NR	954	2.5	5.3
Ch Cr, Scientist	1	NR	NR	NR	-	-
Ch of Nazarene	2	180	355	498	1.3	2.8
CHR–Chr Ch (Disc)	3	196	538	643	1.7	3.6
CHR–Chr Chs & Chs Cr	8	NR	1,060	1,266	3.3	7.0
CHR–Chs of Christ	4	169	179	209	0.5	1.2
Jehovah's Witness	1	NR	NR	NR	-	-
LDS–L-D Saints	1	NR	NR	783	2.0	4.3
LUTH–E.L.C.A.	1	60	199	234	0.6	1.3
LUTH–Luth–MO Synod	2	165	527	702	1.8	3.9
METH–Free Methodist	1	140	132	140	0.4	0.8
METH–Un Methodist	15	852	1,296	1,767	4.6	9.8
METH–Wesleyan	2	127	56	166	0.4	0.9
Non-denom Chr Chs	4	490	943	993	2.6	5.5
PENT–Assemb of God	1	12	12	27	0.1	0.1
PENT–Ch God (Cleve)	1	19	41	49	0.1	0.3
PENT–Ch of God Proph	1	NR	16	19	0.0	0.1
PENT–Int Foursq Gos	1	91	60	72	0.2	0.4
PENT–Un Pent Ch Intl	2	NR	NR	NR	-	-
PRES–Cumber Presb	1	NR	19	19	0.0	0.1
PRES–Presb Ch (USA)	7	201	303	362	0.9	2.0
PRES–Presb Ch Amer	1	0	15	18	0.0	0.1
Salvation Army	1	19	86	962	2.5	5.3
Sev Day Adv	1	0	0	0	0.0	0.0
Un C of Christ	2	231	664	793	2.1	4.4
KOSCIUSKO	**134**	**11,371**	**15,332**	**26,252**	**33.9**	**100.0**
ANG/EPIS–Episcopal	2	159	209	322	0.4	1.2
Ap Chr Ch-Amer	1	150	90	150	0.2	0.6
Bahá'í	0	NR	22	22	0.0	0.1
BAPT–Amer Bapt USA	1	40	65	81	0.1	0.3
BAPT–Free Will Bapt	3	NR	165	206	0.3	0.8
BAPT–Ref Bapt Ch	2	NR	NR	NR	-	-
BAPT–Reg Bapt Gen As	4	NR	NR	NR	-	-
BAPT–So Bapt Conv	2	57	88	110	0.1	0.4
BRETH–Brethren (Ash)	3	NR	240	299	0.4	1.1
BRETH–Ch of Brethren	7	277	558	696	0.9	2.7
BRETH–Grace Breth	4	NR	NR	NR	-	-
Catholic	4	NR	NR	4,356	5.6	16.6
CGOD–Ch God (Ander)	2	1,003	NR	1,003	1.3	3.8
CGOD–Ches God-Gen Con	3	177	367	457	0.6	1.7
Ch Cr, Scientist	1	NR	NR	NR	-	-
Ch of Nazarene	2	86	76	157	0.2	0.6
CHR–Chr Chs & Chs Cr	3	NR	555	692	0.9	2.6
CHR–Chs of Christ	2	120	95	120	0.2	0.5
Evan Free Ch	1	0	NR	0	0.0	0.0
FRND–Fr Un Mtg	1	NR	61	76	0.1	0.3
Ind Fund Churches	1	NR	NR	NR	-	-
Jehovah's Witness	1	NR	NR	NR	-	-
LDS–L-D Saints	1	NR	NR	405	0.5	1.5
LUTH–E.L.C.A.	1	62	125	139	0.2	0.5
LUTH–Luth–MO Synod	2	148	363	478	0.6	1.8
MENN–Amish Undif	17	NR	1,050	2,277	2.9	8.7
MENN–Beachy Amish-Menn	1	166	101	166	0.2	0.6
MENN–Mennonite USA	1	10	26	32	0.0	0.1
MENN–Unaffil Amish-Menn	1	46	33	46	0.1	0.2
METH–Free Methodist	1	153	100	153	0.2	0.6
METH–Un Methodist	21	2,117	3,220	4,821	6.2	18.4
METH–Wesleyan	2	480	418	624	0.8	2.4
Missionary Ch	2	166	73	166	0.2	0.6
Non-denom Chr Chs	19	5,153	6,038	6,510	8.4	24.8
PENT–Assemb of God	3	245	172	291	0.4	1.1
PENT–Ch God (Cleve)	1	17	43	54	0.1	0.2
PENT–COGIC	1	15	15	19	0.0	0.1
PENT–Int Foursq Gos	1	29	33	41	0.1	0.2
PENT–Pent Ch of God	1	70	NR	109	0.1	0.4
PENT–Un Pent Ch Intl	2	NR	NR	NR	-	-
PENT–Vineyard	1	267	308	384	0.5	1.5
PRES–Evan Presby Ch	1	NR	327	408	0.5	1.6
PRES–Presb Ch (USA)	2	97	145	181	0.2	0.7

Religious Group	Number of Congrega-tions	Number of Attendees	Number of Communicant, Confirmed, or Full Members	Adherents		
				Number of Adherents	% of Total Pop.	% of Total Adh.
Salvation Army	1	43	119	164	0.2	0.6
Sev Day Adv	1	18	32	37	0.0	0.1
LAGRANGE	**145**	**3,369**	**10,942**	**21,287**	**57.3**	**100.0**
ANG/EPIS–Episcopal	1	22	68	68	0.2	0.3
BAPT–Amer Bapt USA	2	102	144	198	0.5	0.9
BAPT–Free Will Bapt	1	NR	55	76	0.2	0.4
BAPT–So Bapt Conv	1	29	30	41	0.1	0.2
BRETH–Ch of Brethren	1	0	47	65	0.2	0.3
BRETH–Grace Breth	1	NR	NR	NR	-	-
Calv Chpl	1	NR	NR	NR	-	-
Catholic	2	NR	NR	677	1.8	3.2
CGOD–Ch God (Ander)	2	380	NR	380	1.0	1.8
Ch of Nazarene	1	183	167	216	0.6	1.0
CHR–Chr Chs & Chs Cr	1	NR	500	687	1.9	3.2
CHR–Chs of Christ	1	110	82	120	0.3	0.6
LUTH–E.L.C.A.	1	105	215	253	0.7	1.2
LUTH–Luth–MO Synod	1	85	129	160	0.4	0.8
MENN–Amish Undif	96	NR	6,312	14,011	37.7	65.8
MENN–Beachy Amish-Menn	2	216	124	216	0.6	1.0
MENN–Cons Menn Conf	1	73	78	107	0.3	0.5
MENN–Mennonite USA	5	595	738	1,014	2.7	4.8
MENN–Unaffil Amish-Menn	1	58	27	58	0.2	0.3
METH–Un Methodist	14	852	1,401	1,935	5.2	9.1
Missionary Ch	2	115	66	115	0.3	0.5
Non-denom Chr Chs	3	385	632	647	1.7	3.0
ORTHE–Ant Orth of NA	1	26	NR	72	0.2	0.3
PRES–Presb Ch (USA)	2	24	111	153	0.4	0.7
Sev Day Adv	1	9	16	18	0.0	0.1
LAKE	**519**	**81,026**	**127,707**	**275,161**	**55.5**	**100.0**
ANG/EPIS–Anglican NA	2	NR	NR	NR	-	-
ANG/EPIS–Episcopal	7	348	662	790	0.2	0.3
Bahá'í	0	NR	73	73	0.0	0.0
BAPT–Amer Bapt USA	8	1,114	2,935	3,652	0.7	1.3
BAPT–Converge/BGC	1	75	NR	90	0.0	0.0
BAPT–Natl Mis Bapt Conv	2	35	185	230	0.0	0.1
BAPT–NBC Amer	2	375	535	666	0.1	0.2
BAPT–NBC USA	19	3,285	8,125	10,109	2.0	3.7
BAPT–Prog NBC	8	1,584	3,020	3,757	0.8	1.4
BAPT–Reg Bapt Gen As	10	NR	NR	NR	-	-
BAPT–So Bapt Conv	27	2,037	5,827	7,250	1.5	2.6
BUDD–Mahayana	1	NR	NR	103	0.0	0.0
BUDD–Theravada	1	NR	NR	15	0.0	0.0
Calv Chpl	1	NR	NR	NR	-	-
Catholic	55	NR	NR	101,096	20.4	36.7
CGOD–Ch God (Ander)	6	623	NR	623	0.1	0.2
Ch Cr, Scientist	2	NR	NR	NR	-	-
Ch of Chr (Hol)	3	NR	NR	NR	-	-
Ch of Nazarene	11	923	1,270	2,020	0.4	0.7
CHR–Chr Ch (Disc)	4	110	436	542	0.1	0.2
CHR–Chr Chs & Chs Cr	19	NR	2,983	3,711	0.7	1.3
CHR–Chs of Christ	10	992	971	1,257	0.3	0.5
CONG–Cong Chr, NA	2	NR	90	112	0.0	0.0
Evan Cov Ch	1	40	53	52	0.0	0.0
Evan Free Ch	2	685	NR	685	0.1	0.2
HINDU–I/A Temples	1	NR	NR	250	0.1	0.1
HINDU–Post Ren	1	NR	NR	77	0.0	0.0
Ind Fund Churches	4	NR	NR	NR	-	-
Int Cou Comm Ch	1	NR	NR	NR	-	-
Jehovah's Witness	8	NR	NR	NR	-	-
JUD–Conserv	1	172	193	521	0.1	0.2
JUD–Orth	1	43	50	60	0.0	0.0
JUD–Reform	2	179	316	853	0.2	0.3
LDS–Comm of Christ	1	NR	121	121	0.0	0.0
LDS–L-D Saints	2	NR	NR	1,039	0.2	0.4
LUTH–E.L.C.A.	11	1,283	3,430	4,497	0.9	1.6
LUTH–Evan Luth Syn	1	132	177	221	0.0	0.1
LUTH–Luth–MO Synod	19	2,583	6,476	8,095	1.6	2.9
LUTH–Nor Amer Luth C	1	NR	NR	NR	-	-
LUTH–Wisc Ev Luth Syn	1	59	94	118	0.0	0.0
METH–AME	8	590	1,875	2,333	0.5	0.8
METH–AME Zion	5	190	1,075	1,337	0.3	0.5

NR–Not Reported - Represents no adherents reported. Percentages may not total 100 due to rounding.

Table 3: Religious Congregations by County and Group: 2010

Religious Group	Number of Congrega-tions	Number of Attendees	Number of Communicant, Confirmed, or Full Members	Adherents: Number of Adherents	Adherents: % of Total Pop.	Adherents: % of Total Adh.
METH–C.M.E.	5	900	2,850	3,546	0.7	1.3
METH–Free Methodist	2	86	87	97	0.0	0.0
METH–Un Methodist	21	2,382	4,710	7,844	1.6	2.9
METH–Wesleyan	1	50	28	65	0.0	0.0
Missionary Ch	3	137	111	156	0.0	0.1
Muslim Est	4	920	NR	4,220	0.9	1.5
Nat Spirit Asso	1	NR	NR	NR	-	-
Non-denom Chr Chs	81	43,953	60,052	62,742	12.6	22.8
OCATH–Pol Natl Cath	3	NR	NR	NR	-	-
ORTHE–Ant Orth of NA	1	27	NR	50	0.0	0.0
ORTHE–Carp Rus Orth	2	92	NR	145	0.0	0.1
ORTHE–Greek Orthodox	3	950	NR	6,925	1.4	2.5
ORTHE–Macedonian Orth	1	150	NR	3,500	0.7	1.3
ORTHE–Orth Ch in Amer	2	165	NR	390	0.1	0.1
ORTHE–Serb Orth USA	4	1,065	NR	2,880	0.6	1.0
ORTHE–Ukrainian Orth	1	40	NR	100	0.0	0.0
PENT–Assemb of God	19	2,433	1,310	2,989	0.6	1.1
PENT–Ch God (Cleve)	6	651	1,344	1,672	0.3	0.6
PENT–Ch of God Proph	1	NR	34	42	0.0	0.0
PENT–COGIC	19	1,398	2,798	3,481	0.7	1.3
PENT–Full Gosp Bapt	6	NR	NR	NR	-	-
PENT–Pent Ch of God	3	210	NR	326	0.1	0.1
PENT–Un Pent Ch Intl	9	NR	NR	NR	-	-
PRES–Presb Ch (USA)	12	891	2,141	2,664	0.5	1.0
PRES–Presb Ch Amer	2	84	138	147	0.0	0.1
REF–Christian Ref	8	2,027	2,698	3,357	0.7	1.2
REF–Hung Ref Add'l	1	NR	NR	NR	-	-
REF–Prot Ref Chs	1	108	74	119	0.0	0.0
REF–Ref Ch in Am	4	3,298	5,089	7,062	1.4	2.6
REF–Un Ref Chs N.A.	2	NR	NR	NR	-	-
Salvation Army	2	96	207	621	0.1	0.2
Sev Day Adv	7	879	1,529	1,758	0.4	0.6
Sikh	1	NR	NR	NR	-	-
Un C of Christ	7	495	1,431	1,780	0.4	0.6
Unit Univ	1	82	104	124	0.0	0.0
Unity Ch	1	NR	NR	NR	-	-
Zoroastrian	0	NR	NR	4	0.0	0.0
LAPORTE	**150**	**10,153**	**17,646**	**40,219**	**36.1**	**100.0**
ANG/EPIS–Anglican NA	1	NR	NR	NR	-	-
ANG/EPIS–Episcopal	3	147	343	394	0.4	1.0
Ap Chr Ch-Amer	1	139	83	139	0.1	0.3
Bahá'í	0	NR	7	7	0.0	0.0
BAPT–Amer Bapt Assn	2	NR	170	206	0.2	0.5
BAPT–Amer Bapt USA	3	145	355	430	0.4	1.1
BAPT–Free Will Bapt	1	NR	55	67	0.1	0.2
BAPT–Natl Mis Bapt Conv	3	250	800	968	0.9	2.4
BAPT–NBC Amer	2	75	150	182	0.2	0.5
BAPT–NBC USA	1	0	250	303	0.3	0.8
BAPT–Reg Bapt Gen As	3	NR	NR	NR	-	-
BAPT–So Bapt Conv	3	121	250	303	0.3	0.8
BRETH–Ch of Brethren	1	0	52	63	0.1	0.2
Catholic	13	NR	NR	14,838	13.3	36.9
CGOD–Ch God (Ander)	1	403	NR	403	0.4	1.0
Ch Cr, Scientst	1	NR	NR	NR	-	-
Ch of Nazarene	2	75	103	186	0.2	0.5
CHR–Chr Ch (Disc)	1	40	109	132	0.1	0.3
CHR–Chr Chs & Chs Cr	7	NR	1,244	1,506	1.4	3.7
CHR–Chs of Christ	3	160	155	220	0.2	0.5
CONG–Cong Chr, NA	1	NR	14	17	0.0	0.0
Ind Fund Churches	2	NR	NR	NR	-	-
Jehovah's Witness	1	NR	NR	NR	-	-
JUD–Reform	2	70	123	332	0.3	0.8
LDS–L-D Saints	2	NR	NR	659	0.6	1.6
LUTH–E.L.C.A.	3	846	2,034	2,622	2.4	6.5
LUTH–Luth–MO Synod	8	687	1,950	2,613	2.3	6.5
LUTH–Wisc Ev Luth Syn	1	35	47	70	0.1	0.2
METH–AME	2	65	350	424	0.4	1.1
METH–Free Methodist	2	97	90	97	0.1	0.2
METH–Un Methodist	14	1,399	2,293	3,511	3.1	8.7
METH–Wesleyan	1	48	43	62	0.1	0.2
Missionary Ch	4	273	142	273	0.2	0.7
Muslim Est	2	268	NR	616	0.6	1.5
Nat Spirit Asso	1	NR	NR	NR	-	-
Non-denom Chr Chs	21	2,867	3,470	3,832	3.4	9.5
ORTHE–Rus Orth Abroad	1	2	NR	6	0.0	0.0
ORTHE–Ukrainian Orth	1	20	NR	40	0.0	0.1
PENT–Assemb of God	4	526	259	818	0.7	2.0
PENT–Ch God (Cleve)	2	74	147	178	0.2	0.4
PENT–COGIC	3	90	225	272	0.2	0.7
PENT–Pent Ch of God	2	140	NR	217	0.2	0.5
PENT–Un Pent Ch Intl	4	NR	NR	NR	-	-
PENT–Vineyard	1	225	250	303	0.3	0.8
PRES–Presb Ch (USA)	3	308	754	913	0.8	2.3
PRES–Presb Ch Amer	1	25	25	33	0.0	0.1
Salvation Army	2	73	140	576	0.5	1.4
Sev Day Adv	3	196	340	391	0.4	1.0
Swedenborgian	1	NR	NR	NR	-	-
Un C of Christ	3	264	824	997	0.9	2.5
LAWRENCE	**97**	**6,659**	**14,690**	**20,238**	**43.9**	**100.0**
ANG/EPIS–Episcopal	1	36	111	111	0.2	0.5
Bahá'í	0	NR	5	5	0.0	0.0
BAPT–Amer Bapt Assn	3	NR	285	347	0.8	1.7
BAPT–Amer Bapt USA	9	1,026	2,907	3,544	7.7	17.5
BAPT–Natl Mis Bapt Conv	1	0	150	183	0.4	0.9
BAPT–So Bapt Conv	5	417	430	524	1.1	2.6
Catholic	2	NR	NR	1,875	4.1	9.3
CGOD–Ch God (Ander)	4	565	NR	565	1.2	2.8
Ch of Nazarene	3	230	367	433	0.9	2.1
CHR–Chr Ch (Disc)	2	114	621	757	1.6	3.7
CHR–Chr Chs & Chs Cr	11	NR	2,630	3,206	6.9	15.8
CHR–Chs of Christ	15	1,118	1,084	1,371	3.0	6.8
Grace Gosp Fel	1	NR	NR	NR	-	-
Jehovah's Witness	3	NR	NR	NR	-	-
LDS–L-D Saints	1	NR	NR	507	1.1	2.5
LUTH–Luth–MO Synod	2	96	328	330	0.7	1.6
METH–Free Methodist	1	354	261	354	0.8	1.7
METH–Un Methodist	12	435	878	1,061	2.3	5.2
METH–Wesleyan	2	118	179	153	0.3	0.8
Non-denom Chr Chs	9	1,530	3,530	3,588	7.8	17.7
PENT–Assemb of God	1	281	273	281	0.6	1.4
PENT–Ch God (Cleve)	2	82	151	184	0.4	0.9
PENT–Ch of God Proph	1	NR	54	66	0.1	0.3
PENT–Pent Ch of God	1	70	NR	109	0.2	0.5
PENT–Un Pent Ch Intl	1	NR	NR	NR	-	-
PRES–Presb Ch (USA)	2	106	234	285	0.6	1.4
Salvation Army	1	8	85	253	0.5	1.3
Sev Day Adv	1	73	127	146	0.3	0.7
MADISON	**191**	**19,827**	**26,517**	**48,624**	**36.9**	**100.0**
ANG/EPIS–Anglican NA	4	NR	NR	NR	-	-
ANG/EPIS–Episcopal	2	73	158	171	0.1	0.4
Bahá'í	0	NR	20	20	0.0	0.0
BAPT–Amer Bapt Assn	1	NR	150	182	0.1	0.4
BAPT–Amer Bapt USA	9	982	2,610	3,170	2.4	6.5
BAPT–Natl Mis Bapt Conv	1	0	0	0	0.0	0.0
BAPT–NBC Amer	1	70	80	97	0.1	0.2
BAPT–NBC USA	1	160	250	304	0.2	0.6
BAPT–Ref Bapt Ch	1	NR	NR	NR	-	-
BAPT–So Bapt Conv	10	544	1,145	1,391	1.1	2.9
BRETH–Ch of Brethren	2	70	331	402	0.3	0.8
BUDD–Mahayana	1	NR	NR	102	0.1	0.2
BUDD–Theravada	1	NR	NR	14	0.0	0.0
Catholic	4	NR	NR	7,867	6.0	16.2
CGOD–Ch God (Ander)	15	5,126	NR	5,126	3.9	10.5
Ch Christ Chr Union	3	NR	NR	NR	-	-
Ch of Nazarene	8	1,344	1,798	2,113	1.6	4.3
Chr & Miss Al	2	255	29	310	0.2	0.6
CHR–Chr Ch (Disc)	10	901	3,418	4,151	3.2	8.5
CHR–Chr Chs & Chs Cr	8	NR	1,871	2,272	1.7	4.7
CHR–Chs of Christ	7	693	713	902	0.7	1.9
CONG–Consrv Cong Chr	1	77	167	203	0.2	0.4
FRND–Fr Gen Cf	1	NR	11	13	0.0	0.0
FRND–Fr Un Mtg	3	NR	105	128	0.1	0.3
Jehovah's Witness	4	NR	NR	NR	-	-
LDS–L-D Saints	2	NR	NR	798	0.6	1.6

NR–Not Reported - Represents no adherents reported. Percentages may not total 100 due to rounding.

Table 3: Religious Congregations by County and Group: 2010

Religious Group	Number of Congrega-tions	Number of Attendees	Number of Communicant, Confirmed, or Full Members	Adherents		
				Number of Adherents	% of Total Pop.	% of Total Adh.
LUTH–E.L.C.A.	3	206	523	830	0.6	1.7
LUTH–Luth-MO Synod	1	134	272	395	0.3	0.8
METH–AME	1	0	60	73	0.1	0.2
METH–Free Methodist	1	214	137	214	0.2	0.4
METH–Un Methodist	21	2,092	3,339	4,701	3.6	9.7
METH–Wesleyan	11	725	651	941	0.7	1.9
New Apost Ch	1	NR	NR	NR	-	-
Non-denom Chr Chs	27	4,673	6,703	7,453	5.7	15.3
PENT–Assemb of God	4	678	374	1,598	1.2	3.3
PENT–Ch God (Cleve)	4	315	632	768	0.6	1.6
PENT–Ch of God Proph	1	NR	22	27	0.0	0.1
PENT–COGIC	1	0	25	30	0.0	0.1
PENT–Int Foursq Gos	2	124	131	159	0.1	0.3
PENT–Un Pent Ch Intl	4	NR	NR	NR	-	-
PRES–Presb Ch (USA)	2	191	379	460	0.3	0.9
Salvation Army	1	14	125	907	0.7	1.9
Sev Day Adv	2	166	288	332	0.3	0.7
Un Breth in Cr	1	0	0	0	0.0	0.0
Unity Ch	1	NR	NR	NR	-	-
MARION	**876**	**117,147**	**200,365**	**383,176**	**42.4**	**100.0**
ANG/EPIS–Anglican NA	2	NR	NR	NR	-	-
ANG/EPIS–Episcopal	10	1,506	3,339	3,595	0.4	0.9
Ap Chr Ch-Amer	1	175	103	175	0.0	0.0
Bahá'í	1	NR	243	243	0.0	0.1
BAPT–Alliance Bapt	1	NR	NR	NR	-	-
BAPT–Amer Bapt Assn	1	NR	150	187	0.0	0.0
BAPT–Amer Bapt USA	30	3,982	8,414	10,482	1.2	2.7
BAPT–Converge/BGC	3	2,875	NR	3,450	0.4	0.9
BAPT–Free Will Bapt	1	NR	55	69	0.0	0.0
BAPT–N Am Bapt Conf	1	NR	70	87	0.0	0.0
BAPT–Natl Mis Bapt Conv	5	0	600	747	0.1	0.2
BAPT–NBC Amer	11	2,570	6,650	8,284	0.9	2.2
BAPT–NBC USA	21	3,685	8,794	10,955	1.2	2.9
BAPT–Prog NBC	2	650	1,410	1,756	0.2	0.5
BAPT–Ref Bapt Ch	1	NR	NR	NR	-	-
BAPT–Reg Bapt Gen As	9	NR	NR	NR	-	-
BAPT–So Bapt Conv	50	5,645	11,811	14,713	1.6	3.8
BRETH–Ch of Brethren	1	63	117	146	0.0	0.0
BRETH–Grace Breth	1	NR	NR	NR	-	-
BUDD–Mahayana	5	NR	NR	2,319	0.3	0.6
Calv Chpl	3	NR	NR	NR	-	-
Catholic	40	NR	NR	99,990	11.1	26.1
CGOD–Ch God (Ander)	11	2,419	NR	2,419	0.3	0.6
Ch Cr, Scientst	5	NR	NR	NR	-	-
Ch of Chr (Hol)	1	NR	NR	NR	-	-
Ch of God Gen Conf	1	NR	15	19	0.0	0.0
Ch of Nazarene	18	2,755	3,508	4,531	0.5	1.2
Chr & Miss Al	3	309	0	359	0.0	0.1
CHR–Chr Ch (Disc)	36	4,716	12,219	15,222	1.7	4.0
CHR–Chr Chs & Chs Cr	33	NR	16,494	20,547	2.3	5.4
CHR–Chs of Christ	36	4,998	5,109	6,644	0.7	1.7
CHR–Int Chs of Christ	1	NR	329	410	0.0	0.1
Evan Cov Ch	1	61	114	79	0.0	0.0
Evan Free Ch	4	1,640	NR	1,640	0.2	0.4
FRND–Fr Gen Cf	1	NR	38	47	0.0	0.0
FRND–Fr Un Mtg	6	NR	832	1,036	0.1	0.3
FRND–Unaffl Mtgs	1	NR	NR	NR	-	-
Grace Gosp Fel	1	NR	NR	NR	-	-
HINDU–Post Ren	5	NR	NR	138	0.0	0.0
HINDU–Trad Temples	1	NR	NR	400	0.0	0.1
Int Cou Comm Ch	2	NR	NR	NR	-	-
Jehovah's Witness	10	NR	NR	NR	-	-
JUD–Conserv	0	452	508	1,370	0.2	0.4
JUD–Orth	2	540	200	750	0.1	0.2
JUD–Reconst	0	397	508	1,370	0.2	0.4
JUD–Reform	1	548	967	2,611	0.3	0.7
LDS–Comm of Christ	2	NR	206	206	0.0	0.1
LDS–L-D Saints	9	NR	NR	5,038	0.6	1.3
LUTH–Assoc Free Luth	1	NR	NR	NR	-	-
LUTH–E.L.C.A.	14	1,596	3,527	4,360	0.5	1.1
LUTH–Luth Cong Msn Chr	1	139	224	279	0.0	0.1
LUTH–Luth-MO Synod	13	2,816	5,025	6,890	0.8	1.8
LUTH–Wisc Ev Luth Syn	1	65	115	150	0.0	0.0
MENN–Mennonite USA	3	343	299	372	0.0	0.1
METH–AME	8	1,600	2,446	3,047	0.3	0.8
METH–AME Zion	5	360	850	1,059	0.1	0.3
METH–C.M.E.	8	638	1,885	2,348	0.3	0.6
METH–Free Methodist	8	933	824	969	0.1	0.3
METH–Un Methodist	51	11,076	22,076	36,751	4.1	9.6
METH–Wesleyan	12	949	734	1,234	0.1	0.3
Metro Comm Ch	1	397	370	461	0.1	0.1
MJEW–Assoc Mes Cong	1	NR	NR	NR	-	-
Muslim Est	10	1,412	NR	2,657	0.3	0.7
Nat Spirit Asso	2	NR	NR	NR	-	-
New Apost Ch	1	NR	NR	NR	-	-
Non-denom Chr Chs	181	37,380	51,161	57,433	6.4	15.0
ORTHE–Ant Orth of NA	1	250	NR	700	0.1	0.2
ORTHE–Bulgar Orth USA	2	60	NR	75	0.0	0.0
ORTHE–Greek Orthodox	1	40	NR	90	0.0	0.0
ORTHE–Orth Ch in Amer	2	235	NR	430	0.0	0.1
ORTHE–Serb Orth USA	2	104	NR	404	0.0	0.1
ORTHO–Eritrean Orth	2	275	NR	500	0.1	0.1
ORTHO–Ethiopian Orth	1	NR	NR	NR	-	-
PENT–Assemb of God	22	5,177	3,140	7,866	0.9	2.1
PENT–Ch God (Cleve)	12	841	1,132	1,410	0.2	0.4
PENT–Ch Lord Jesus Apos	5	NR	NR	NR	-	-
PENT–Ch of God Proph	4	NR	156	194	0.0	0.1
PENT–COGIC	21	485	2,608	3,249	0.4	0.8
PENT–Fire Bapt Hol Ch	1	NR	NR	NR	-	-
PENT–Full Gosp Bapt	7	NR	NR	NR	-	-
PENT–Int Foursq Gos	2	63	67	83	0.0	0.0
PENT–Pent Ch of God	2	140	NR	217	0.0	0.1
PENT–Un Pent Ch Intl	11	NR	NR	NR	-	-
PENT–Vineyard	3	802	875	1,090	0.1	0.3
PRES–Cumber Presb	1	NR	8	11	0.0	0.0
PRES–Evan Presby Ch	2	NR	1,436	1,789	0.2	0.5
PRES–Free Pres NA	1	NR	NR	NR	-	-
PRES–Presb Ch (USA)	16	3,536	9,372	11,675	1.3	3.0
PRES–Presb Ch Amer	4	897	634	810	0.1	0.2
PRES–Ref Pres of NA	2	400	317	437	0.0	0.1
REF–Christian Ref	1	40	31	39	0.0	0.0
REF–Ref Ch in Am	1	47	102	119	0.0	0.0
Salvation Army	3	175	307	2,406	0.3	0.6
Sev Day Adv	14	2,092	3,640	4,185	0.5	1.1
Sikh	1	NR	NR	NR	-	-
Un C of Christ	11	1,452	3,506	4,368	0.5	1.1
Unit Univ	4	346	695	979	0.1	0.3
Unity Ch	2	NR	NR	NR	-	-
Zoroastrian	0	NR	NR	6	0.0	0.0
MARSHALL	**92**	**6,976**	**9,320**	**16,275**	**34.6**	**100.0**
ANG/EPIS–Episcopal	2	104	172	212	0.5	1.3
Bahá'í	0	NR	7	7	0.0	0.0
BAPT–Asc Ref Bap Ch Am	1	NR	NR	NR	-	-
BAPT–Ref Bapt Ch	1	NR	NR	NR	-	-
BAPT–Reg Bapt Gen As	3	NR	NR	NR	-	-
BAPT–So Bapt Conv	1	421	410	516	1.1	3.2
BRETH–Ch of Brethren	6	284	792	997	2.1	6.1
Catholic	3	NR	NR	2,044	4.3	12.6
CGOD–Ch God (Ander)	2	130	NR	130	0.3	0.8
Ch of God Gen Conf	3	NR	49	62	0.1	0.4
CHR–Chr Chs & Chs Cr	1	NR	0	0	0.0	0.0
CHR–Chs of Christ	2	45	38	57	0.1	0.4
Evan Cov Ch	1	49	82	64	0.1	0.4
Evan Free Ch	1	280	NR	280	0.6	1.7
Jehovah's Witness	1	NR	NR	NR	-	-
LDS–L-D Saints	1	NR	NR	244	0.5	1.5
LUTH–E.L.C.A.	1	54	151	331	0.7	2.0
LUTH–Luth-MO Synod	3	374	814	1,057	2.2	6.5
MENN–Amish Undif	9	NR	601	1,413	3.0	8.7
MENN–Beachy Amish-Menn	1	76	57	76	0.2	0.5
METH–Un Methodist	14	1,222	2,154	3,218	6.8	19.8
METH–Wesleyan	3	941	591	1,223	2.6	7.5
Missionary Ch	2	299	205	299	0.6	1.8
Non-denom Chr Chs	16	1,938	2,160	2,504	5.3	15.4
PENT–Assemb of God	3	424	228	519	1.1	3.2
PENT–Ch God (Cleve)	1	50	17	21	0.0	0.1

NR–Not Reported - Represents no adherents reported. Percentages may not total 100 due to rounding.

Table 3: Religious Congregations by County and Group: 2010

Religious Group	Number of Congrega-tions	Number of Attendees	Number of Communicant, Confirmed, or Full Members	Adherents: Number of Adherents	Adherents: % of Total Pop.	Adherents: % of Total Adh.
PENT–Open Bible Std	1	9	NR	9	0.0	0.1
PENT–Un Pent Ch Intl	3	NR	NR	NR	-	-
PRES–Presb Ch (USA)	1	48	105	132	0.3	0.8
Sev Day Adv	1	27	47	54	0.1	0.3
Un C of Christ	4	201	640	806	1.7	5.0
MARTIN	**34**	**1,435**	**2,787**	**6,211**	**60.1**	**100.0**
BAPT–So Bapt Conv	2	73	65	80	0.8	1.3
Catholic	4	NR	NR	2,622	25.4	42.2
Ch Christ Chr Union	1	NR	NR	NR	-	-
Ch of Nazarene	1	27	53	53	0.5	0.9
CHR–Chr Chs & Chs Cr	2	NR	500	613	5.9	9.9
CHR–Chs of Christ	5	179	163	214	2.1	3.4
LUTH–E.L.C.A.	1	70	224	300	2.9	4.8
MENN–Amish Undif	3	NR	185	412	4.0	6.6
MENN–Cons Menn Conf	1	300	289	354	3.4	5.7
METH–Un Methodist	7	376	726	932	9.0	15.0
METH–Wesleyan	2	88	110	115	1.1	1.9
Non-denom Chr Chs	3	280	450	460	4.5	7.4
PENT–Assemb of God	2	42	22	56	0.5	0.9
MIAMI	**64**	**4,629**	**8,615**	**13,711**	**37.2**	**100.0**
Bahá'í	0	NR	13	13	0.0	0.1
BAPT–Amer Bapt USA	7	589	1,607	1,942	5.3	14.2
BAPT–Free Will Bapt	1	NR	55	66	0.2	0.5
BAPT–Reg Bapt Gen As	1	NR	NR	NR	-	-
BAPT–So Bapt Conv	1	25	52	63	0.2	0.5
BRETH–Brethren (Ash)	3	NR	240	290	0.8	2.1
BRETH–Ch of Brethren	3	299	426	515	1.4	3.8
Catholic	1	NR	NR	1,118	3.0	8.2
CGOD–Ch God (Ander)	1	30	NR	30	0.1	0.2
Ch of Nazarene	1	114	158	234	0.6	1.7
CHR–Chr Ch (Disc)	1	0	825	997	2.7	7.3
CHR–Chr Chs & Chs Cr	5	NR	1,241	1,499	4.1	10.9
CHR–Chs of Christ	2	34	22	34	0.1	0.2
FRND–Fr Un Mtg	1	NR	102	123	0.3	0.9
Jehovah's Witness	1	NR	NR	NR	-	-
JUD–Reform	1	3	5	14	0.0	0.1
LDS–L-D Saints	1	NR	NR	458	1.2	3.3
LUTH–Luth-MO Synod	1	142	477	652	1.8	4.8
MENN–Amish Undif	2	NR	100	221	0.6	1.6
METH–AME	1	0	150	181	0.5	1.3
METH–Un Methodist	16	1,769	1,376	2,504	6.8	18.3
METH–Wesleyan	1	17	15	22	0.1	0.2
Non-denom Chr Chs	5	875	1,010	1,194	3.2	8.7
PENT–Assemb of God	3	414	281	752	2.0	5.5
PENT–Ch God (Cleve)	1	86	44	53	0.1	0.4
PENT–Int Foursq Gos	1	128	229	277	0.8	2.0
PRES–Presb Ch (USA)	1	60	148	179	0.5	1.3
Salvation Army	1	44	39	280	0.8	2.0
MONROE	**144**	**13,116**	**21,267**	**41,798**	**30.3**	**100.0**
ANG/EPIS–Episcopal	1	266	390	574	0.4	1.4
Bahá'í	1	NR	100	100	0.1	0.2
BAPT–Amer Bapt Assn	1	NR	85	97	0.1	0.2
BAPT–Amer Bapt USA	7	752	1,547	1,774	1.3	4.2
BAPT–NBC Amer	1	150	175	201	0.1	0.5
BAPT–Reg Bapt Gen As	2	NR	NR	NR	-	-
BAPT–So Bapt Conv	4	190	248	284	0.2	0.7
BUDD–Mahayana	2	NR	NR	127	0.1	0.3
BUDD–Vajrayana	2	NR	NR	156	0.1	0.4
Calv Chpl	1	NR	NR	NR	-	-
Catholic	3	NR	NR	10,350	7.5	24.8
CGOD–Ch God (Ander)	2	76	NR	76	0.1	0.2
Ch Cr, Scientst	1	NR	NR	NR	-	-
Ch of Nazarene	5	668	915	1,030	0.7	2.5
CHR–Chr Ch (Disc)	2	234	907	1,040	0.8	2.5
CHR–Chr Chs & Chs Cr	9	NR	4,350	4,988	3.6	11.9
CHR–Chs of Christ	18	1,279	1,454	1,652	1.2	4.0
FRND–Fr Gen Cf	1	NR	74	85	0.1	0.2
HINDU–Post Ren	2	NR	NR	102	0.1	0.2
Jehovah's Witness	1	NR	NR	NR	-	-
JUD–Reform	1	113	199	537	0.4	1.3
LDS–L-D Saints	4	NR	NR	1,723	1.2	4.1
LUTH–E.L.C.A.	1	180	255	333	0.2	0.8
LUTH–Luth-MO Synod	3	402	664	890	0.6	2.1
MENN–Mennonite USA	1	25	12	14	0.0	0.0
METH–AME	1	0	60	69	0.1	0.2
METH–Free Methodist	1	183	207	207	0.2	0.5
METH–Un Methodist	15	1,886	3,529	5,406	3.9	12.9
METH–Wesleyan	2	55	44	72	0.1	0.2
Missionary Ch	1	250	90	250	0.2	0.6
Muslim Est	1	270	NR	600	0.4	1.4
Non-denom Chr Chs	18	3,785	3,532	4,844	3.5	11.6
ORTHE–Ant Orth of NA	1	135	NR	225	0.2	0.5
PENT–Assemb of God	8	959	604	1,390	1.0	3.3
PENT–Ch God (Cleve)	1	85	172	197	0.1	0.5
PENT–Full Gosp Bapt	1	NR	NR	NR	-	-
PENT–Un Pent Ch Intl	9	NR	NR	NR	-	-
PENT–Vineyard	1	124	124	142	0.1	0.3
PRES–Presb Ch (USA)	2	259	495	568	0.4	1.4
PRES–Ref Pres of NA	1	104	77	119	0.1	0.3
Salvation Army	1	35	116	486	0.4	1.2
Sev Day Adv	1	104	180	207	0.2	0.5
Un C of Christ	1	165	210	241	0.2	0.6
Unit Univ	1	382	452	642	0.5	1.5
Unity Ch	1	NR	NR	NR	-	-
MONTGOMERY	**82**	**4,603**	**11,155**	**16,440**	**43.1**	**100.0**
ANG/EPIS–Episcopal	1	85	209	209	0.5	1.3
Bahá'í	0	NR	11	11	0.0	0.1
BAPT–Amer Bapt USA	5	555	1,308	1,600	4.2	9.7
BAPT–Reg Bapt Gen As	1	NR	NR	NR	-	-
BAPT–So Bapt Conv	3	121	224	274	0.7	1.7
Calv Chpl	1	NR	NR	NR	-	-
Catholic	1	NR	NR	2,573	6.7	15.7
CGOD–Ch God (Ander)	1	28	NR	28	0.1	0.2
Ch of Nazarene	2	222	356	356	0.9	2.2
CHR–Chr Ch (Disc)	3	223	1,179	1,442	3.8	8.8
CHR–Chr Chs & Chs Cr	15	NR	2,617	3,200	8.4	19.5
CHR–Chs of Christ	2	153	146	185	0.5	1.1
Christian Un	1	NR	NR	NR	-	-
FRND–Fr Un Mtg	1	NR	6	7	0.0	0.0
Jehovah's Witness	1	NR	NR	NR	-	-
LDS–L-D Saints	1	NR	NR	365	1.0	2.2
LUTH–E.L.C.A.	1	107	31	319	0.8	1.9
LUTH–Luth-MO Synod	1	38	69	74	0.2	0.5
METH–AME	1	0	100	122	0.3	0.7
METH–Un Methodist	12	760	1,650	1,988	5.2	12.1
METH–Wesleyan	1	28	22	36	0.1	0.2
Non-denom Chr Chs	13	1,825	2,735	2,852	7.5	17.3
ORTHE–Carp Rus Orth	1	15	NR	35	0.1	0.2
ORTHE–Orth Ch in Amer	1	45	NR	65	0.2	0.4
PENT–Assemb of God	2	175	84	200	0.5	1.2
PENT–Ch God (Cleve)	2	77	106	130	0.3	0.8
PENT–Un Pent Ch Intl	3	NR	NR	NR	-	-
PRES–Presb Ch (USA)	4	116	261	319	0.8	1.9
Un C of Christ	1	30	41	50	0.1	0.3
MORGAN	**102**	**8,739**	**16,957**	**24,835**	**36.0**	**100.0**
ANG/EPIS–Episcopal	2	70	99	132	0.2	0.5
Bahá'í	0	NR	8	8	0.0	0.0
BAPT–Amer Bapt USA	7	485	1,117	1,379	2.0	5.6
BAPT–So Bapt Conv	8	706	1,576	1,946	2.8	7.8
Catholic	2	NR	NR	3,003	4.4	12.1
CGOD–Ch God (Ander)	3	208	NR	208	0.3	0.8
Ch of Nazarene	6	466	880	948	1.4	3.8
CHR–Chr Ch (Disc)	4	399	1,135	1,401	2.0	5.6
CHR–Chr Chs & Chs Cr	15	NR	3,845	4,747	6.9	19.1
CHR–Chs of Christ	5	263	291	367	0.5	1.5
FRND–Fr Un Mtg	3	NR	157	194	0.3	0.8
Ind Fund Churches	1	NR	NR	NR	-	-
Jehovah's Witness	1	NR	NR	NR	-	-
LDS–Comm of Christ	1	NR	103	103	0.1	0.4
LDS–L-D Saints	1	NR	NR	491	0.7	2.0
LUTH–Luth-MO Synod	3	292	555	766	1.1	3.1

NR–Not Reported - Represents no adherents reported. Percentages may not total 100 due to rounding.

Table 3: Religious Congregations by County and Group: 2010

Religious Group	Number of Congrega-tions	Number of Attendees	Number of Communicant, Confirmed, or Full Members	Adherents		
				Number of Adherents	% of Total Pop.	% of Total Adh.
MENN–Cons Menn Conf	1	60	50	62	0.1	0.2
METH–Evan Meth Ch	1	NR	NR	NR	-	-
METH–Free Methodist	1	56	59	59	0.1	0.2
METH–Un Methodist	8	935	1,582	2,206	3.2	8.9
METH–Wesleyan	4	55	70	72	0.1	0.3
Missionary Ch	2	1,038	336	1,038	1.5	4.2
Non-denom Chr Chs	13	3,118	3,903	4,128	6.0	16.6
PENT–Assemb of God	2	309	380	580	0.8	2.3
PENT–Ch God (Cleve)	3	178	641	791	1.1	3.2
PENT–Un Pent Ch Intl	3	NR	NR	NR	-	-
PRES–Presb Ch (USA)	1	71	118	146	0.2	0.6
Sev Day Adv	1	30	52	60	0.1	0.2
NEWTON	**24**	**1,308**	**2,505**	**5,153**	**36.2**	**100.0**
Bahá'í	0	NR	3	3	0.0	0.1
BAPT–Amer Bapt USA	2	73	287	347	2.4	6.7
BAPT–Converge/BGC	1	75	NR	90	0.6	1.7
BAPT–So Bapt Conv	2	111	261	316	2.2	6.1
Catholic	3	NR	NR	1,996	14.0	38.7
CHR–Chr Ch (Disc)	1	40	142	172	1.2	3.3
CHR–Chr Chs & Chs Cr	1	NR	312	378	2.7	7.3
LUTH–Luth-MO Synod	1	34	75	83	0.6	1.6
METH–Un Methodist	6	334	692	825	5.8	16.0
Non-denom Chr Chs	3	130	126	163	1.1	3.2
PENT–Assemb of God	1	60	45	100	0.7	1.9
PRES–Presb Ch (USA)	2	50	91	110	0.8	2.1
REF–Christian Ref	1	401	471	570	4.0	11.1
NOBLE	**78**	**4,528**	**7,362**	**13,832**	**29.1**	**100.0**
Bahá'í	0	NR	2	2	0.0	0.0
BAPT–Reg Bapt Gen As	1	NR	NR	NR	-	-
BRETH–Ch of Brethren	1	21	15	19	0.0	0.1
Catholic	6	NR	NR	2,901	6.1	21.0
CGOD–Ch God (Ander)	1	65	NR	65	0.1	0.5
Ch of Nazarene	3	237	326	392	0.8	2.8
CHR–Chr Chs & Chs Cr	1	NR	70	88	0.2	0.6
CHR–Chs of Christ	1	45	40	45	0.1	0.3
Evan Ch	2	NR	NR	NR	-	-
Ind Fund Churches	1	NR	NR	NR	-	-
Jehovah's Witness	2	NR	NR	NR	-	-
LDS–L-D Saints	1	NR	NR	371	0.8	2.7
LUTH–E.L.C.A.	4	144	315	377	0.8	2.7
LUTH–Luth-MO Synod	5	637	1,790	2,426	5.1	17.5
MENN–Amish Undif	6	NR	380	1,006	2.1	7.3
METH–Un Methodist	14	1,006	2,107	2,722	5.7	19.7
METH–Wesleyan	3	219	130	286	0.6	2.1
Missionary Ch	1	18	15	18	0.0	0.1
Muslim Est	1	134	NR	308	0.6	2.2
Non-denom Chr Chs	11	1,505	1,612	1,916	4.0	13.9
PENT–Assemb of God	4	293	169	396	0.8	2.9
PENT–Ch God Mtn Asm	1	NR	NR	NR	-	-
PENT–Un Pent Ch Intl	2	NR	NR	NR	-	-
PENT–Vineyard	1	70	95	120	0.3	0.9
PRES–Presb Ch (USA)	4	97	191	241	0.5	1.7
Un C of Christ	1	37	105	133	0.3	1.0
OHIO	**11**	**429**	**1,453**	**1,762**	**28.8**	**100.0**
Bahá'í	0	NR	2	2	0.0	0.1
BAPT–Amer Bapt USA	3	144	326	391	6.4	22.2
BAPT–So Bapt Conv	2	50	200	240	3.9	13.6
Ch of Nazarene	1	31	69	69	1.1	3.9
CHR–Chr Chs & Chs Cr	1	NR	500	600	9.8	34.1
METH–Un Methodist	1	74	119	200	3.3	11.4
METH–Wesleyan	1	7	3	9	0.1	0.5
Non-denom Chr Chs	1	100	150	150	2.4	8.5
Un C of Christ	1	23	84	101	1.6	5.7
ORANGE	**64**	**2,623**	**6,281**	**8,595**	**43.3**	**100.0**
BAPT–Amer Bapt USA	5	507	1,306	1,603	8.1	18.7
BAPT–So Bapt Conv	2	175	187	230	1.2	2.7
Catholic	2	NR	NR	370	1.9	4.3
Ch Christ Chr Union	1	NR	NR	NR	-	-

Religious Group	Number of Congrega-tions	Number of Attendees	Number of Communicant, Confirmed, or Full Members	Adherents		
				Number of Adherents	% of Total Pop.	% of Total Adh.
Ch of Nazarene	2	79	134	135	0.7	1.6
CHR–Chr Ch (Disc)	1	50	164	201	1.0	2.3
CHR–Chr Chs & Chs Cr	9	NR	1,846	2,266	11.4	26.4
CHR–Chs of Christ	7	331	311	391	2.0	4.5
FRND–Fr Un Mtg	4	NR	181	222	1.1	2.6
MENN–Amish Undif	4	NR	241	593	3.0	6.9
MENN–Mennonite USA	1	75	68	83	0.4	1.0
METH–Un Methodist	14	664	1,160	1,347	6.8	15.7
METH–Wesleyan	4	427	211	555	2.8	6.5
Non-denom Chr Chs	2	225	250	306	1.5	3.6
PENT–Assemb of God	1	18	5	28	0.1	0.3
PENT–Ch God (Cleve)	1	24	154	189	1.0	2.2
PENT–Un Pent Ch Intl	2	NR	NR	NR	-	-
PRES–Presb Ch (USA)	1	30	33	41	0.2	0.5
Sev Day Adv	1	18	30	35	0.2	0.4
OWEN	**50**	**2,118**	**3,964**	**5,273**	**24.4**	**100.0**
Bahá'í	0	NR	2	2	0.0	0.0
BAPT–Amer Bapt USA	7	337	775	939	4.4	17.8
BAPT–So Bapt Conv	1	25	42	51	0.2	1.0
Catholic	1	NR	NR	270	1.3	5.1
Ch of Nazarene	4	207	259	371	1.7	7.0
CHR–Chr Chs & Chs Cr	5	NR	640	775	3.6	14.7
CHR–Chs of Christ	6	274	254	331	1.5	6.3
Jehovah's Witness	1	NR	NR	NR	-	-
MENN–Amish Undif	2	NR	63	158	0.7	3.0
METH–Un Methodist	7	362	651	849	3.9	16.1
METH–Wesleyan	1	10	9	13	0.1	0.2
Non-denom Chr Chs	7	702	910	1,003	4.6	19.0
PENT–Assemb of God	1	55	36	127	0.6	2.4
PENT–Ch God (Cleve)	1	8	18	22	0.1	0.4
PENT–Ch of God Proph	1	NR	57	69	0.3	1.3
PENT–Un Pent Ch Intl	2	NR	NR	NR	-	-
PRES–Presb Ch (USA)	2	72	134	162	0.8	3.1
Sev Day Adv	1	66	114	131	0.6	2.5
PARKE	**48**	**1,729**	**4,131**	**5,994**	**34.6**	**100.0**
Bahá'í	0	NR	2	2	0.0	0.0
BAPT–Amer Bapt Assn	1	NR	85	101	0.6	1.7
BAPT–Amer Bapt USA	4	238	255	304	1.8	5.1
BAPT–So Bapt Conv	2	201	370	441	2.5	7.4
Catholic	1	NR	NR	225	1.3	3.8
Ch Cr, Scientst	1	NR	NR	NR	-	-
Ch of Nazarene	1	25	28	30	0.2	0.5
CHR–Chr Ch (Disc)	1	0	421	502	2.9	8.4
CHR–Chr Chs & Chs Cr	6	NR	650	775	4.5	12.9
CHR–Chs of Christ	1	45	45	55	0.3	0.9
FRND–Fr Un Mtg	5	NR	331	395	2.3	6.6
Ind Fund Churches	2	NR	NR	NR	-	-
MENN–Amish Undif	5	NR	309	1,105	6.4	18.4
METH–Un Methodist	7	244	491	623	3.6	10.4
METH–Wesleyan	1	38	25	49	0.3	0.8
Non-denom Chr Chs	5	735	995	1,101	6.3	18.4
PENT–Assemb of God	1	95	55	95	0.5	1.6
PENT–Pent Ch of God	1	70	NR	109	0.6	1.8
PENT–Un Pent Ch Intl	1	NR	NR	NR	-	-
PRES–Presb Ch (USA)	2	38	69	82	0.5	1.4
PERRY	**33**	**1,338**	**2,549**	**9,128**	**47.2**	**100.0**
ANG/EPIS–Episcopal	1	12	15	15	0.1	0.2
Bahá'í	0	NR	2	2	0.0	0.0
BAPT–Amer Bapt USA	4	365	664	795	4.1	8.7
BAPT–So Bapt Conv	1	28	60	72	0.4	0.8
Catholic	8	NR	NR	5,955	30.8	65.2
Ch of Nazarene	1	54	61	83	0.4	0.9
CHR–Chs of Christ	2	210	327	345	1.8	3.8
Jehovah's Witness	1	NR	NR	NR	-	-
LDS–Comm of Christ	1	NR	103	103	0.5	1.1
LDS–L-D Saints	1	NR	NR	202	1.0	2.2
LUTH–Luth-MO Synod	1	87	194	251	1.3	2.7
METH–Un Methodist	6	242	478	563	2.9	6.2
Non-denom Chr Chs	1	150	180	188	1.0	2.1
PENT–Un Pent Ch Intl	2	NR	NR	NR	-	-

NR–Not Reported - Represents no adherents reported. Percentages may not total 100 due to rounding.

Table 3: Religious Congregations by County and Group: 2010

Religious Group	Number of Congregations	Number of Attendees	Number of Communicant, Confirmed, or Full Members	Adherents: Number of Adherents	Adherents: % of Total Pop.	Adherents: % of Total Adh.
Sev Day Adv	1	30	52	60	0.3	0.7
Un C of Christ	2	160	413	494	2.6	5.4
PIKE	**32**	**1,538**	**2,064**	**3,361**	**26.2**	**100.0**
BAPT–Amer Bapt USA	1	275	392	473	3.7	14.1
BAPT–So Bapt Conv	1	80	100	121	0.9	3.6
Catholic	1	NR	NR	373	2.9	11.1
CGOD–Ch God (Ander)	3	185	NR	185	1.4	5.5
Ch of Nazarene	2	118	160	160	1.2	4.8
CHR–Chr Ch (Disc)	1	0	0	0	0.0	0.0
CHR–Chr Chs & Chs Cr	2	NR	200	241	1.9	7.2
CHR–Chs of Christ	3	87	81	103	0.8	3.1
LUTH–Luth Cong Msn Chr	1	75	225	272	2.1	8.1
METH–Free Methodist	2	118	115	122	0.9	3.6
METH–Un Methodist	9	399	607	979	7.6	29.1
METH–Wesleyan	2	55	37	72	0.6	2.1
PENT–Assemb of God	1	90	42	132	1.0	3.9
PENT–Un Pent Ch Intl	1	NR	NR	NR	-	-
PRES–Cumber Presb	1	NR	29	36	0.3	1.1
PRES–Presb Ch (USA)	1	56	76	92	0.7	2.7
PORTER	**134**	**17,727**	**22,452**	**66,076**	**40.2**	**100.0**
ANG/EPIS–Episcopal	2	177	318	451	0.3	0.7
Ap Chr Ch-Amer	1	87	51	87	0.1	0.1
Bahá'í	0	NR	16	16	0.0	0.0
BAPT–Reg Bapt Gen As	6	NR	NR	NR	-	-
BAPT–So Bapt Conv	7	444	989	1,213	0.7	1.8
Calv Chpl	1	NR	NR	NR	-	-
Catholic	8	NR	NR	29,583	18.0	44.8
CGOD–Ch God (Ander)	1	90	NR	90	0.1	0.1
Ch Cr, Scientst	1	NR	NR	NR	-	-
Ch of Nazarene	6	2,659	2,313	4,234	2.6	6.4
CHR–Chr Ch (Disc)	2	224	658	807	0.5	1.2
CHR–Chr Chs & Chs Cr	8	NR	1,263	1,549	0.9	2.3
CHR–Chs of Christ	4	278	271	355	0.2	0.5
Evan Cov Ch	1	95	205	124	0.1	0.2
Evan Free Ch	4	2,116	NR	2,116	1.3	3.2
FRND–Fr Gen Cf	1	NR	17	21	0.0	0.0
Ind Fund Churches	1	NR	NR	NR	-	-
Jehovah's Witness	3	NR	NR	NR	-	-
LDS–L-D Saints	2	NR	NR	1,116	0.7	1.7
LUTH–E.L.C.A.	4	750	2,011	2,660	1.6	4.0
LUTH–Evan Luth Syn	1	59	96	120	0.1	0.2
LUTH–Luth–MO Synod	9	1,604	3,897	4,865	3.0	7.4
MENN–Mennonite USA	2	192	233	286	0.2	0.4
METH–Un Methodist	8	1,581	3,028	4,802	2.9	7.3
METH–Wesleyan	1	189	108	246	0.1	0.4
Metro Comm Ch	1	38	53	65	0.0	0.1
Missionary Ch	1	57	32	57	0.0	0.1
Non-denom Chr Chs	23	4,915	4,230	6,377	3.9	9.7
ORTHE–Greek Orthodox	1	125	NR	800	0.5	1.2
ORTHE–Orth Ch in Amer	1	30	NR	60	0.0	0.1
PENT–Assemb of God	5	1,109	498	1,299	0.8	2.0
PENT–Ch God (Cleve)	2	198	477	585	0.4	0.9
PENT–Ch of God Proph	2	NR	60	74	0.0	0.1
PENT–Un Pent Ch Intl	3	NR	NR	NR	-	-
PRES–Presb Ch (USA)	6	441	1,139	1,397	0.9	2.1
PRES–Presb Ch Amer	1	78	84	110	0.1	0.2
Salvation Army	1	46	49	70	0.0	0.1
Un C of Christ	2	145	356	437	0.3	0.7
Unity Ch	1	NR	NR	NR	-	-
Zoroastrian	0	NR	NR	4	0.0	0.0
POSEY	**48**	**2,583**	**5,766**	**13,198**	**50.9**	**100.0**
ANG/EPIS–Episcopal	2	97	131	189	0.7	1.4
BAPT–So Bapt Conv	2	80	638	774	3.0	5.9
Catholic	5	NR	NR	5,891	22.7	44.6
Ch of Nazarene	3	182	308	452	1.7	3.4
CHR–Chr Ch (Disc)	2	85	386	468	1.8	3.5
CHR–Chr Chs & Chs Cr	4	NR	420	510	2.0	3.9
CHR–Chs of Christ	1	35	28	35	0.1	0.3
Jehovah's Witness	1	NR	NR	NR	-	-
LDS–L-D Saints	1	NR	NR	145	0.6	1.1
METH–AME	2	0	200	243	0.9	1.8
METH–Un Methodist	9	558	1,523	1,779	6.9	13.5
Non-denom Chr Chs	4	672	815	865	3.3	6.6
PENT–Assemb of God	2	390	186	475	1.8	3.6
PENT–Un Pent Ch Intl	1	NR	NR	NR	-	-
PRES–Presb Ch (USA)	2	44	77	93	0.4	0.7
Sev Day Adv	1	3	5	6	0.0	0.0
Un C of Christ	6	437	1,049	1,273	4.9	9.6
PULASKI	**39**	**1,917**	**3,246**	**5,517**	**41.2**	**100.0**
Ap Chr Ch-Amer	1	360	214	360	2.7	6.5
BAPT–Amer Bapt USA	1	28	58	71	0.5	1.3
BAPT–Free Will Bapt	2	NR	110	134	1.0	2.4
BAPT–Reg Bapt Gen As	2	NR	NR	NR	-	-
Catholic	5	NR	NR	1,203	9.0	21.8
Ch of Nazarene	1	183	265	265	2.0	4.8
CHR–Chr Ch (Disc)	2	0	331	404	3.0	7.3
CHR–Chr Chs & Chs Cr	2	NR	470	574	4.3	10.4
CHR–Chs of Christ	1	20	15	25	0.2	0.5
Jehovah's Witness	1	NR	NR	NR	-	-
LUTH–Luth–MO Synod	3	143	309	357	2.7	6.5
METH–Un Methodist	5	307	575	820	6.1	14.9
Non-denom Chr Chs	5	625	605	782	5.8	14.2
PENT–Assemb of God	2	52	17	78	0.6	1.4
PENT–Pent Ch of God	1	70	NR	109	0.8	2.0
PRES–Presb Ch (USA)	2	17	85	104	0.8	1.9
Sev Day Adv	1	24	42	48	0.4	0.9
Un C of Christ	2	88	150	183	1.4	3.3
PUTNAM	**67**	**4,038**	**9,088**	**12,731**	**33.5**	**100.0**
ANG/EPIS–Episcopal	1	48	91	124	0.3	1.0
Bahá'í	0	NR	17	17	0.0	0.1
BAPT–Amer Bapt USA	5	446	1,143	1,355	3.6	10.6
BAPT–Consrv Bapt	1	NR	NR	NR	-	-
BAPT–Ref Bapt Ch	1	NR	NR	NR	-	-
BAPT–Reg Bapt Gen As	1	NR	NR	NR	-	-
BAPT–So Bapt Conv	4	304	787	933	2.5	7.3
BUDD–Mahayana	1	NR	NR	103	0.3	0.8
Calv Chpl	1	NR	NR	NR	-	-
Catholic	1	NR	NR	1,060	2.8	8.3
Ch of Nazarene	2	103	110	286	0.8	2.2
Chr & Miss Al	1	85	82	87	0.2	0.7
CHR–Chr Ch (Disc)	3	209	1,330	1,577	4.2	12.4
CHR–Chr Chs & Chs Cr	8	NR	1,860	2,205	5.8	17.3
CHR–Chs of Christ	5	303	410	511	1.3	4.0
CONG–Cong Chr, NA	1	NR	50	59	0.2	0.5
Evan Free Ch	1	15	NR	15	0.0	0.1
Jehovah's Witness	1	NR	NR	NR	-	-
LDS–L-D Saints	1	NR	NR	252	0.7	2.0
LUTH–Luth–MO Synod	1	99	141	224	0.6	1.8
METH–Un Methodist	9	458	890	1,047	2.8	8.2
Non-denom Chr Chs	8	1,295	1,206	1,644	4.3	12.9
PENT–Assemb of God	2	204	112	214	0.6	1.7
PENT–Ch God (Cleve)	1	22	72	85	0.2	0.7
PENT–Int Foursq Gos	1	153	60	71	0.2	0.6
PENT–Intl Pent Holiness	1	64	120	142	0.4	1.1
PENT–Un Pent Ch Intl	1	NR	NR	NR	-	-
PRES–Presb Ch (USA)	2	114	154	183	0.5	1.4
Sev Day Adv	1	18	30	35	0.1	0.3
Un C of Christ	1	98	423	502	1.3	3.9
RANDOLPH	**75**	**3,122**	**5,636**	**8,601**	**32.9**	**100.0**
Bahá'í	0	NR	1	1	0.0	0.0
BAPT–Reg Bapt Gen As	1	NR	NR	NR	-	-
BAPT–So Bapt Conv	2	97	242	297	1.1	3.5
Catholic	2	NR	NR	698	2.7	8.1
CGOD–Ch God (Ander)	2	97	NR	97	0.4	1.1
Ch of Nazarene	5	258	545	653	2.5	7.6
CHR–Chr Ch (Disc)	4	221	1,003	1,229	4.7	14.3
CHR–Chr Chs & Chs Cr	4	NR	625	766	2.9	8.9
CHR–Chs of Christ	2	75	59	103	0.4	1.2
CONG–Midw Cong Chr Fel	9	574	412	505	1.9	5.9
FRND–Central Yr Mtg	2	140	87	107	0.4	1.2

NR–Not Reported   - Represents no adherents reported.   Percentages may not total 100 due to rounding.

Table 3: Religious Congregations by County and Group: 2010

Religious Group	Number of Congregations	Number of Attendees	Number of Communicant, Confirmed, or Full Members	Adherents		
				Number of Adherents	% of Total Pop.	% of Total Adh.
FRND–Fr Un Mtg	10	NR	716	878	3.4	10.2
Jehovah's Witness	1	NR	NR	NR	-	-
LDS–L-D Saints	1	NR	NR	91	0.3	1.1
LUTH–E.L.C.A.	2	99	171	327	1.2	3.8
MENN–Amish Undif	0	NR	19	41	0.2	0.5
METH–Un Methodist	17	828	1,108	1,846	7.1	21.5
METH–Wesleyan	2	69	45	90	0.3	1.0
Non-denom Chr Chs	3	305	400	405	1.5	4.7
PENT–Assemb of God	2	222	126	276	1.1	3.2
PENT–Open Bible Std	1	97	NR	97	0.4	1.1
PENT–Un Pent Ch Intl	1	NR	NR	NR	-	-
PRES–Presb Ch (USA)	2	40	77	94	0.4	1.1
RIPLEY	**64**	**2,803**	**7,237**	**17,367**	**60.3**	**100.0**
Bahá'í	0	NR	3	3	0.0	0.0
BAPT–Amer Bapt USA	11	837	2,189	2,737	9.5	15.8
BAPT–So Bapt Conv	3	160	420	525	1.8	3.0
Catholic	8	NR	NR	7,843	27.2	45.2
Ch of Nazarene	1	25	35	63	0.2	0.4
CHR–Chr Chs & Chs Cr	8	NR	770	963	3.3	5.5
CHR–Chs of Christ	1	41	40	50	0.2	0.3
LDS–L-D Saints	1	NR	NR	390	1.4	2.2
LUTH–E.L.C.A.	5	434	1,260	1,599	5.5	9.2
LUTH–Luth–MO Synod	1	62	170	212	0.7	1.2
MENN–Amish Undif	1	NR	24	65	0.2	0.4
METH–Un Methodist	10	426	1,112	1,397	4.8	8.0
METH–Wesleyan	3	87	45	113	0.4	0.7
Non-denom Chr Chs	7	415	601	634	2.2	3.7
PENT–Assemb of God	1	93	85	169	0.6	1.0
PENT–Vineyard	1	100	175	219	0.8	1.3
Un C of Christ	2	123	308	385	1.3	2.2
RUSH	**47**	**1,783**	**5,319**	**8,468**	**48.7**	**100.0**
Bahá'í	0	NR	2	2	0.0	0.0
BAPT–Amer Bapt USA	1	145	300	369	2.1	4.4
BAPT–So Bapt Conv	3	163	823	1,012	5.8	12.0
Catholic	1	NR	NR	1,640	9.4	19.4
CGOD–Ch God (Ander)	2	135	NR	135	0.8	1.6
Ch of Nazarene	1	49	110	117	0.7	1.4
CHR–Chr Ch (Disc)	5	312	962	1,183	6.8	14.0
CHR–Chr Chs & Chs Cr	9	NR	1,330	1,635	9.4	19.3
CHR–Chs of Christ	2	75	70	80	0.5	0.9
Christian Un	1	NR	NR	NR	-	-
FRND–Fr Un Mtg	2	NR	34	42	0.2	0.5
Jehovah's Witness	1	NR	NR	NR	-	-
MENN–Amish Undif	3	NR	137	300	1.7	3.5
METH–Un Methodist	5	361	790	1,030	5.9	12.2
METH–Wesleyan	3	85	72	111	0.6	1.3
Non-denom Chr Chs	4	340	474	513	2.9	6.1
PENT–Assemb of God	1	35	0	35	0.2	0.4
PENT–Un Pent Ch Intl	1	NR	NR	NR	-	-
PRES–Presb Ch (USA)	2	83	215	264	1.5	3.1
ST. JOSEPH	**273**	**29,559**	**42,050**	**174,926**	**65.5**	**100.0**
ANG/EPIS–Episcopal	4	386	691	708	0.3	0.4
Ap Chr Ch-Amer	1	57	35	57	0.0	0.0
Bahá'í	3	NR	119	119	0.0	0.1
BAPT–Amer Bapt Assn	1	NR	52	64	0.0	0.0
BAPT–Amer Bapt USA	3	114	142	175	0.1	0.1
BAPT–Natl Mis Bapt Conv	2	150	100	123	0.0	0.1
BAPT–NBC USA	1	0	1,000	1,234	0.5	0.7
BAPT–Reg Bapt Gen As	4	NR	NR	NR	-	-
BAPT–So Bapt Conv	5	1,042	1,601	1,976	0.7	1.1
BRETH–Brethren (Ash)	5	NR	400	494	0.2	0.3
BRETH–Ch of Brethren	6	259	553	683	0.3	0.4
BRETH–Grace Breth	1	NR	NR	NR	-	-
BUDD–Mahayana	1	NR	NR	102	0.0	0.1
Catholic	29	NR	NR	52,666	19.7	30.1
CGOD–Ch God (Ander)	2	193	NR	193	0.1	0.1
Ch Cr, Scientst	1	NR	NR	NR	-	-
Ch of God Gen Conf	2	NR	71	88	0.0	0.1
Ch of Nazarene	3	327	402	502	0.2	0.3
CHR–Chr Ch (Disc)	3	142	588	726	0.3	0.4

Religious Group	Number of Congregations	Number of Attendees	Number of Communicant, Confirmed, or Full Members	Adherents		
				Number of Adherents	% of Total Pop.	% of Total Adh.
CHR–Chr Chs & Chs Cr	7	NR	1,798	2,219	0.8	1.3
CHR–Chs of Christ	3	235	220	280	0.1	0.2
CONG–Cong Chr, NA	1	NR	64	79	0.0	0.0
Evan Cov Ch	1	63	97	82	0.0	0.0
Evan Free Ch	2	760	NR	760	0.3	0.4
FRND–Fr Gen Cf	1	NR	55	68	0.0	0.0
HINDU–Post Ren	1	NR	NR	25	0.0	0.0
Ind Fund Churches	1	NR	NR	NR	-	-
Int Cou Comm Ch	1	NR	NR	NR	-	-
Jehovah's Witness	3	NR	NR	NR	-	-
JUD–Conserv	1	141	158	427	0.2	0.2
JUD–Orth	1	317	110	440	0.2	0.3
JUD–Reform	1	137	241	651	0.2	0.4
LDS–Comm of Christ	1	NR	167	167	0.1	0.1
LDS–L-D Saints	2	NR	NR	1,436	0.5	0.8
LUTH–E.L.C.A.	8	829	2,224	3,257	1.2	1.9
LUTH–Luth–MO Synod	5	420	1,212	1,460	0.5	0.8
LUTH–Wisc Ev Luth Syn	1	115	248	302	0.1	0.2
MENN–Amish Undif	1	NR	49	122	0.0	0.1
MENN–Mennonite USA	2	242	251	310	0.1	0.2
METH–AME	1	0	100	123	0.0	0.1
METH–AME Zion	2	60	265	327	0.1	0.2
METH–C.M.E.	1	0	150	185	0.1	0.1
METH–Free Methodist	1	70	46	70	0.0	0.0
METH–Un Methodist	29	8,914	12,025	77,645	29.1	44.4
METH–Wesleyan	4	324	155	421	0.2	0.2
Missionary Ch	16	2,202	1,113	2,202	0.8	1.3
Muslim Est	3	468	NR	1,116	0.4	0.6
New Apost Ch	1	NR	NR	NR	-	-
Non-denom Chr Chs	35	6,650	8,190	9,476	3.5	5.4
OCATH–Pol Natl Cath	1	NR	NR	NR	-	-
ORTHE–Greek Orthodox	1	200	NR	776	0.3	0.4
ORTHE–Serb Orth USA	2	165	NR	450	0.2	0.3
PENT–Assemb of God	9	979	529	1,217	0.5	0.7
PENT–Ch God (Cleve)	4	242	309	381	0.1	0.2
PENT–Ch of God Proph	1	NR	54	67	0.0	0.0
PENT–COGIC	8	405	1,060	1,308	0.5	0.7
PENT–Int Foursq Gos	1	22	9	11	0.0	0.0
PENT–Pent Ch of God	1	70	NR	109	0.0	0.1
PENT–Un Pent Ch Intl	4	NR	NR	NR	-	-
PENT–Vineyard	1	900	1,100	1,358	0.5	0.8
PRES–Orth Pres Ch	1	37	57	64	0.0	0.0
PRES–Presb Ch (USA)	7	380	1,487	1,835	0.7	1.0
PRES–Presb Ch Amer	1	89	86	120	0.0	0.1
REF–Christian Ref	1	205	288	355	0.1	0.2
Salvation Army	1	61	72	566	0.2	0.3
Sev Day Adv	6	754	1,310	1,507	0.6	0.9
Un Breth in Cr	1	60	46	51	0.0	0.0
Un C of Christ	6	290	830	1,024	0.4	0.6
Unit Univ	1	83	121	166	0.1	0.1
Unity Ch	1	NR	NR	NR	-	-
Zoroastrian	0	NR	NR	1	0.0	0.0
SCOTT	**55**	**2,471**	**7,388**	**9,817**	**40.6**	**100.0**
Bahá'í	0	NR	1	1	0.0	0.0
BAPT–Amer Bapt USA	8	669	1,934	2,364	9.8	24.1
BAPT–So Bapt Conv	3	230	301	368	1.5	3.7
Catholic	1	NR	NR	400	1.7	4.1
CGOD–Ch God (Ander)	1	45	NR	45	0.2	0.5
Ch of Nazarene	1	15	34	46	0.2	0.5
CHR–Chr Chs & Chs Cr	7	NR	2,755	3,367	13.9	34.3
CHR–Chs of Christ	2	123	122	148	0.6	1.5
Jehovah's Witness	1	NR	NR	NR	-	-
LDS–L-D Saints	1	NR	NR	230	1.0	2.3
LUTH–Luth–MO Synod	1	17	28	28	0.1	0.3
METH–Un Methodist	8	248	453	703	2.9	7.2
METH–Wesleyan	2	43	42	56	0.2	0.6
Non-denom Chr Chs	9	741	852	995	4.1	10.1
PENT–Assemb of God	1	17	10	22	0.1	0.2
PENT–Ch God (Cleve)	4	269	691	845	3.5	8.6
PENT–Ch of God Proph	1	NR	31	38	0.2	0.4
PENT–Un Pent Ch Intl	1	NR	NR	NR	-	-
PRES–Presb Ch (USA)	2	31	94	115	0.5	1.2
Sev Day Adv	1	23	40	46	0.2	0.5

NR–Not Reported - Represents no adherents reported. Percentages may not total 100 due to rounding.

Table 3: Religious Congregations by County and Group: 2010

Religious Group	Number of Congrega-tions	Number of Attendees	Number of Communicant, Confirmed, or Full Members	Adherents		
				Number of Adherents	% of Total Pop.	% of Total Adh.
SHELBY	**66**	**4,389**	**9,250**	**15,731**	**35.4**	**100.0**
ANG/EPIS–Episcopal	1	18	25	25	0.1	0.2
Bahá'í	0	NR	2	2	0.0	0.0
BAPT–Amer Bapt USA	9	859	2,433	2,986	6.7	19.0
BAPT–So Bapt Conv	1	52	75	92	0.2	0.6
Catholic	2	NR	NR	3,600	8.1	22.9
CGOD–Ch God (Ander)	1	0	NR	0	0.0	0.0
Ch of Nazarene	2	221	295	457	1.0	2.9
CHR–Chr Ch (Disc)	1	180	400	491	1.1	3.1
CHR–Chr Chs & Chs Cr	7	NR	985	1,209	2.7	7.7
CHR–Chs of Christ	1	18	17	22	0.0	0.1
Christian Un	2	NR	NR	NR	-	-
FRND–Fr Un Mtg	1	NR	36	44	0.1	0.3
Jehovah's Witness	1	NR	NR	NR	-	-
LDS–L-D Saints	1	NR	NR	406	0.9	2.6
LUTH–Luth–MO Synod	1	43	100	154	0.3	1.0
METH–Evan Meth Ch	1	NR	NR	NR	-	-
METH–Un Methodist	15	770	1,923	2,539	5.7	16.1
METH–Wesleyan	4	143	146	186	0.4	1.2
Non-denom Chr Chs	5	1,750	1,800	2,187	4.9	13.9
PENT–Assemb of God	1	22	24	32	0.1	0.2
PENT–Ch God (Cleve)	1	41	95	117	0.3	0.7
PENT–Int Foursq Gos	1	7	8	10	0.0	0.1
PENT–Un Pent Ch Intl	1	NR	NR	NR	-	-
PRES–Presb Ch (USA)	2	65	325	399	0.9	2.5
Salvation Army	1	31	59	162	0.4	1.0
Sev Day Adv	1	44	77	89	0.2	0.6
Un C of Christ	2	125	425	522	1.2	3.3
SPENCER	**52**	**2,205**	**3,891**	**9,893**	**47.2**	**100.0**
ANG/EPIS–Episcopal	1	23	28	28	0.1	0.3
BAPT–Amer Bapt USA	2	120	172	210	1.0	2.1
BAPT–So Bapt Conv	6	373	809	986	4.7	10.0
Catholic	8	NR	NR	4,309	20.6	43.6
Ch of Nazarene	3	141	192	266	1.3	2.7
CHR–Chr Chs & Chs Cr	3	NR	0	0	0.0	0.0
CHR–Chs of Christ	1	30	25	35	0.2	0.4
Ind Fund Churches	1	NR	NR	NR	-	-
Jehovah's Witness	1	NR	NR	NR	-	-
LUTH–E.L.C.A.	1	42	72	90	0.4	0.9
LUTH–Luth–MO Synod	1	123	335	442	2.1	4.5
METH–Free Methodist	1	30	22	30	0.1	0.3
METH–Un Methodist	13	865	1,505	2,645	12.6	26.7
METH–Wesleyan	1	13	0	17	0.1	0.2
Non-denom Chr Chs	2	225	300	306	1.5	3.1
PENT–Assemb of God	1	12	10	16	0.1	0.2
PENT–Un Pent Ch Intl	1	NR	NR	NR	-	-
PRES–Presb Ch (USA)	1	47	59	72	0.3	0.7
Un C of Christ	4	161	362	441	2.1	4.5
STARKE	**30**	**1,320**	**2,712**	**6,177**	**26.4**	**100.0**
Bahá'í	0	NR	7	7	0.0	0.1
BAPT–Free Will Bapt	2	NR	110	134	0.6	2.2
BAPT–Reg Bapt Gen As	1	NR	NR	NR	-	-
BAPT–So Bapt Conv	1	115	136	166	0.7	2.7
Catholic	5	NR	NR	2,291	9.8	37.1
Ch of Nazarene	1	52	83	83	0.4	1.3
CHR–Chr Chs & Chs Cr	2	NR	205	251	1.1	4.1
Ind Fund Churches	1	NR	NR	NR	-	-
Jehovah's Witness	1	NR	NR	NR	-	-
LUTH–Luth–MO Synod	4	235	1,008	1,199	5.1	19.4
METH–Un Methodist	3	290	468	950	4.1	15.4
METH–Wesleyan	1	42	45	55	0.2	0.9
Non-denom Chr Chs	4	440	480	549	2.3	8.9
PENT–Assemb of God	2	71	49	344	1.5	5.6
PENT–Ch God (Cleve)	1	30	25	31	0.1	0.5
Un C of Christ	1	45	96	117	0.5	1.9
STEUBEN	**53**	**4,556**	**5,166**	**11,509**	**33.7**	**100.0**
ANG/EPIS–Episcopal	1	48	74	77	0.2	0.7
Bahá'í	0	NR	11	11	0.0	0.1
Catholic	2	NR	NR	3,354	9.8	29.1
Ch of Nazarene	2	103	146	282	0.8	2.5
CHR–Chr Chs & Chs Cr	6	NR	700	845	2.5	7.3
CHR–Chs of Christ	1	40	36	55	0.2	0.5
Jehovah's Witness	1	NR	NR	NR	-	-
LDS–L-D Saints	1	NR	NR	207	0.6	1.8
LUTH–E.L.C.A.	1	140	352	459	1.3	4.0
LUTH–Luth–MO Synod	4	499	803	969	2.8	8.4
MENN–Amish Undif	2	NR	89	199	0.6	1.7
MENN–Fel Evg Ch	1	650	198	239	0.7	2.1
METH–Un Methodist	9	665	1,055	1,574	4.6	13.7
METH–Wesleyan	1	59	35	77	0.2	0.7
Missionary Ch	3	1,188	466	1,188	3.5	10.3
Muslim Est	1	134	NR	308	0.9	2.7
Non-denom Chr Chs	6	425	525	586	1.7	5.1
PENT–Assemb of God	2	295	142	340	1.0	3.0
PENT–Ch God (Cleve)	1	24	39	47	0.1	0.4
PENT–Pent Ch of God	1	70	NR	109	0.3	0.9
PENT–Un Pent Ch Intl	1	NR	NR	NR	-	-
PRES–Presb Ch (USA)	2	27	146	176	0.5	1.5
Sev Day Adv	1	45	78	90	0.3	0.8
Un Breth in Cr	2	57	49	49	0.1	0.4
Un C of Christ	1	87	222	268	0.8	2.3
SULLIVAN	**59**	**3,019**	**5,878**	**7,773**	**36.2**	**100.0**
Bahá'í	0	NR	1	1	0.0	0.0
BAPT–Amer Bapt USA	3	562	767	915	4.3	11.8
BAPT–Natl Mis Bapt Conv	1	0	150	179	0.8	2.3
BAPT–So Bapt Conv	2	64	270	322	1.5	4.1
Catholic	1	NR	NR	495	2.3	6.4
CGOD–Ches God-Gen Con	1	340	258	308	1.4	4.0
Ch of Nazarene	1	46	64	64	0.3	0.8
CHR–Chr Ch (Disc)	1	96	105	125	0.6	1.6
CHR–Chr Chs & Chs Cr	5	NR	1,645	1,962	9.1	25.2
CHR–Chs of Christ	8	390	366	472	2.2	6.1
Evan Ch	1	NR	NR	NR	-	-
Jehovah's Witness	1	NR	NR	NR	-	-
METH–Evan Meth Ch	1	NR	NR	NR	-	-
METH–Un Methodist	15	506	959	1,310	6.1	16.9
METH–Wesleyan	2	74	45	97	0.5	1.2
Non-denom Chr Chs	5	660	780	900	4.2	11.6
PENT–Assemb of God	2	80	57	133	0.6	1.7
PENT–Ch God (Cleve)	3	143	265	316	1.5	4.1
PENT–Ch God Mtn Asm	1	NR	NR	NR	-	-
PENT–Ch of God Proph	1	NR	2	2	0.0	0.0
PENT–Un Pent Ch Intl	1	NR	NR	NR	-	-
PRES–Presb Ch (USA)	2	58	144	172	0.8	2.2
Un C of Christ	1	0	0	0	0.0	0.0
SWITZERLAND	**28**	**652**	**1,733**	**2,514**	**23.7**	**100.0**
Bahá'í	0	NR	2	2	0.0	0.1
BAPT–Amer Bapt USA	8	297	774	970	9.1	38.6
BAPT–So Bapt Conv	3	137	301	377	3.6	15.0
Catholic	1	NR	NR	90	0.8	3.6
CHR–Chr Chs & Chs Cr	3	NR	150	188	1.8	7.5
MENN–Amish Undif	4	NR	174	469	4.4	18.7
METH–Un Methodist	5	117	244	288	2.7	11.5
METH–Wesleyan	1	8	2	10	0.1	0.4
Non-denom Chr Chs	2	85	75	106	1.0	4.2
PRES–Presb Ch (USA)	1	8	11	14	0.1	0.6
TIPPECANOE	**139**	**14,471**	**23,840**	**56,470**	**32.7**	**100.0**
ANG/EPIS–Episcopal	2	195	408	482	0.3	0.9
Ap Chr Ch-Amer	1	120	78	120	0.1	0.2
Bahá'í	0	NR	40	40	0.0	0.1
BAPT–Amer Bapt USA	2	184	697	833	0.5	1.5
BAPT–Converge/BGC	1	75	NR	90	0.1	0.2
BAPT–Reg Bapt Gen As	1	NR	NR	NR	-	-
BAPT–So Bapt Conv	8	867	1,258	1,503	0.9	2.7
BRETH–Ch of Brethren	1	45	40	48	0.0	0.1
BUDD–Mahayana	1	NR	NR	102	0.1	0.2
BUDD–Theravada	1	NR	NR	15	0.0	0.0
Calv Chpl	2	NR	NR	NR	-	-
Catholic	6	NR	NR	20,011	11.6	35.4

NR–Not Reported - Represents no adherents reported. Percentages may not total 100 due to rounding.

Table 3: Religious Congregations by County and Group: 2010

Religious Group	Number of Congregations	Number of Attendees	Number of Communicant, Confirmed, or Full Members	Adherents: Number of Adherents	Adherents: % of Total Pop.	Adherents: % of Total Adh.
CGOD–Ch God (Ander)	2	80	NR	80	0.0	0.1
Ch Christ Chr Union	1	NR	NR	NR	-	-
Ch Cr, Scientst	1	NR	NR	NR	-	-
Ch of Nazarene	1	221	210	271	0.2	0.5
Chr & Miss Al	2	215	204	254	0.1	0.4
CHR–Chr Ch (Disc)	2	171	1,095	1,308	0.8	2.3
CHR–Chr Chs & Chs Cr	7	NR	1,369	1,635	0.9	2.9
CHR–Chs of Christ	2	425	405	525	0.3	0.9
Evan Cov Ch	2	710	570	923	0.5	1.6
FRND–Fr Gen Cf	1	NR	15	18	0.0	0.0
HINDU–Post Ren	2	NR	NR	35	0.0	0.1
Ind Fund Churches	1	NR	NR	NR	-	-
Jehovah's Witness	1	NR	NR	NR	-	-
JUD–Conserv	1	32	36	97	0.1	0.2
JUD–Reform	1	69	121	327	0.2	0.6
LDS–L-D Saints	5	NR	NR	1,846	1.1	3.3
LUTH–E.L.C.A.	2	290	756	1,000	0.6	1.8
LUTH–Luth-MO Synod	4	892	2,586	3,814	2.2	6.8
LUTH–Wisc Ev Luth Syn	1	0	0	0	0.0	0.0
METH–AME	1	0	100	119	0.1	0.2
METH–Free Methodist	2	39	69	69	0.0	0.1
METH–Un Methodist	18	3,110	4,885	7,074	4.1	12.5
METH–Wesleyan	2	200	136	260	0.2	0.5
Muslim Est	1	134	NR	308	0.2	0.5
Non-denom Chr Chs	15	2,770	3,415	3,949	2.3	7.0
ORTHE–Carp Rus Orth	1	80	NR	135	0.1	0.2
PENT–Assemb of God	5	1,133	737	2,994	1.7	5.3
PENT–Ch God (Cleve)	2	90	78	93	0.1	0.2
PENT–Int Foursq Gos	1	59	51	61	0.0	0.1
PENT–Pent Ch of God	3	210	NR	326	0.2	0.6
PENT–Un Pent Ch Intl	3	NR	NR	NR	-	-
PRES–Evan Presby Ch	1	NR	997	1,191	0.7	2.1
PRES–Presb Ch (USA)	6	579	1,406	1,680	1.0	3.0
PRES–Presb Ch Amer	1	55	48	61	0.0	0.1
PRES–Ref Pres of NA	2	211	153	249	0.1	0.4
REF–Christian Ref	2	329	449	536	0.3	0.9
REF–Ref Ch in Am	2	256	338	426	0.2	0.8
Salvation Army	1	31	45	344	0.2	0.6
Sev Day Adv	1	80	138	159	0.1	0.3
Un Breth in Cr	1	182	158	155	0.1	0.3
Un C of Christ	1	160	568	678	0.4	1.2
Unit Univ	1	172	181	226	0.1	0.4
Unity Ch	1	NR	NR	NR	-	-
TIPTON	**32**	**1,906**	**3,877**	**5,817**	**36.5**	**100.0**
Bahá'í	0	NR	1	1	0.0	0.0
BAPT–Amer Bapt USA	1	75	235	284	1.8	4.9
BAPT–So Bapt Conv	1	25	48	58	0.4	1.0
Catholic	1	NR	NR	1,100	6.9	18.9
Ch of Nazarene	1	53	81	81	0.5	1.4
CHR–Chr Ch (Disc)	2	145	760	918	5.8	15.8
CHR–Chr Chs & Chs Cr	4	NR	549	663	4.2	11.4
CHR–Chs of Christ	2	95	137	172	1.1	3.0
FRND–Fr Un Mtg	1	NR	17	21	0.1	0.4
LUTH–Luth-MO Synod	1	214	399	490	3.1	8.4
METH–Un Methodist	5	243	499	573	3.6	9.9
METH–Wesleyan	3	282	176	367	2.3	6.3
Non-denom Chr Chs	5	650	807	903	5.7	15.5
PENT–Assemb of God	1	60	80	80	0.5	1.4
PENT–Ch God (Cleve)	1	34	36	43	0.3	0.7
PENT–Ch God Mtn Asm	1	NR	NR	NR	-	-
PENT–Un Pent Ch Intl	1	NR	NR	NR	-	-
PRES–Presb Ch (USA)	1	30	52	63	0.4	1.1
UNION	**17**	**786**	**1,613**	**2,564**	**34.1**	**100.0**
Bahá'í	0	NR	1	1	0.0	0.0
BAPT–So Bapt Conv	1	60	217	267	3.6	10.4
BRETH–Ch of Brethren	1	23	28	34	0.5	1.3
Catholic	1	NR	NR	525	7.0	20.5
Ch Christ Chr Union	1	NR	NR	NR	-	-
Ch of Nazarene	2	95	115	140	1.9	5.5
CHR–Chr Chs & Chs Cr	1	NR	200	246	3.3	9.6
FRND–Fr Un Mtg	1	NR	18	22	0.3	0.9
METH–Un Methodist	4	300	619	856	11.4	33.4
Non-denom Chr Chs	4	280	345	387	5.1	15.1
PRES–Presb Ch (USA)	1	28	70	86	1.1	3.4
VANDERBURGH	**212**	**25,496**	**53,349**	**95,361**	**53.1**	**100.0**
ANG/EPIS–Anglican NA	1	NR	NR	NR	-	-
ANG/EPIS–Episcopal	1	144	178	295	0.2	0.3
Bahá'í	0	NR	21	21	0.0	0.0
BAPT–Amer Bapt USA	3	777	1,480	1,792	1.0	1.9
BAPT–Converge/BGC	1	75	NR	90	0.1	0.1
BAPT–Natl Mis Bapt Conv	1	0	0	0	0.0	0.0
BAPT–NBC USA	4	1,390	3,575	4,329	2.4	4.5
BAPT–Reg Bapt Gen As	2	NR	NR	NR	-	-
BAPT–So Bapt Conv	23	3,231	15,039	18,209	10.1	19.1
BUDD–Mahayana	3	NR	NR	124	0.1	0.1
BUDD–Theravada	1	NR	NR	14	0.0	0.0
Calv Chpl	2	NR	NR	NR	-	-
Catholic	20	NR	NR	29,097	16.2	30.5
CGOD–Ch God (Ander)	1	100	NR	100	0.1	0.1
Ch Cr, Scientst	1	NR	NR	NR	-	-
Ch of Nazarene	4	191	304	379	0.2	0.4
CHR–Chr Ch (Disc)	3	241	815	987	0.5	1.0
CHR–Chr Chs & Chs Cr	1	NR	600	726	0.4	0.8
CHR–Chs of Christ	6	815	792	1,038	0.6	1.1
Evan Free Ch	1	150	NR	150	0.1	0.2
FRND–Fr Un Mtg	1	NR	3	4	0.0	0.0
Grace Gosp Fel	2	NR	NR	NR	-	-
Ind Fund Churches	1	NR	NR	NR	-	-
Jehovah's Witness	3	NR	NR	NR	-	-
JUD–Conserv	0	56	63	170	0.1	0.2
JUD–Reform	0	36	63	170	0.1	0.2
LDS–Comm of Christ	1	NR	103	103	0.1	0.1
LDS–L-D Saints	1	NR	NR	811	0.5	0.9
LUTH–E.L.C.A.	5	375	886	1,013	0.6	1.1
LUTH–Luth-MO Synod	8	1,420	2,867	3,540	2.0	3.7
METH–AME	1	0	100	121	0.1	0.1
METH–C.M.E.	1	0	150	182	0.1	0.2
METH–Free Methodist	1	80	81	81	0.0	0.1
METH–Un Methodist	21	3,299	5,955	7,973	4.4	8.4
METH–Wesleyan	4	446	455	580	0.3	0.6
Non-denom Chr Chs	33	8,360	11,983	12,975	7.2	13.6
PENT–Assemb of God	9	1,190	676	1,575	0.9	1.7
PENT–Ch God (Cleve)	3	182	236	286	0.2	0.3
PENT–Ch of God Proph	1	NR	48	58	0.0	0.1
PENT–COGIC	4	400	772	935	0.5	1.0
PENT–Full Gosp Bapt	1	NR	NR	NR	-	-
PENT–Int Foursq Gos	2	187	263	318	0.2	0.3
PENT–Un Pent Ch Intl	1	NR	NR	NR	-	-
PENT–Vineyard	1	82	103	125	0.1	0.1
PRES–Cumber Presb	1	NR	59	84	0.0	0.1
PRES–Evan Presby Ch	1	NR	190	230	0.1	0.2
PRES–Orth Pres Ch	1	68	44	91	0.1	0.1
PRES–Presb Ch (USA)	6	438	771	934	0.5	1.0
Sev Day Adv	4	216	375	431	0.2	0.5
Un C of Christ	13	1,498	4,241	5,135	2.9	5.4
Unit Univ	1	49	58	83	0.0	0.1
Unity Ch	1	NR	NR	NR	-	-
Zoroastrian	0	NR	NR	2	0.0	0.0
VERMILLION	**38**	**1,430**	**3,567**	**6,141**	**37.9**	**100.0**
Bahá'í	0	NR	2	2	0.0	0.0
BAPT–Amer Bapt USA	1	60	297	361	2.2	5.9
BAPT–So Bapt Conv	2	157	304	369	2.3	6.0
Catholic	2	NR	NR	1,010	6.2	16.4
Ch of Nazarene	4	137	143	219	1.4	3.6
CHR–Chr Ch (Disc)	1	80	351	426	2.6	6.9
CHR–Chr Chs & Chs Cr	2	NR	900	1,093	6.7	17.8
CHR–Chs of Christ	1	53	40	52	0.3	0.8
FRND–Fr Un Mtg	2	NR	55	67	0.4	1.1
Jehovah's Witness	1	NR	NR	NR	-	-
LDS–L-D Saints	1	NR	NR	572	3.5	9.3
METH–Un Methodist	10	430	901	1,120	6.9	18.2
Non-denom Chr Chs	4	219	258	318	2.0	5.2

NR–Not Reported   - Represents no adherents reported.   Percentages may not total 100 due to rounding.

Table 3: Religious Congregations by County and Group: 2010

Religious Group	Number of Congrega-tions	Number of Attendees	Number of Communicant, Confirmed, or Full Members	Adherents: Number of Adherents	Adherents: % of Total Pop.	Adherents: % of Total Adh.
PENT–Assemb of God	3	128	45	204	1.3	3.3
PENT–Ch God (Cleve)	1	14	94	114	0.7	1.9
PENT–Int Foursq Gos	1	99	77	93	0.6	1.5
PRES–Presb Ch (USA)	2	53	100	121	0.7	2.0
VIGO	**151**	**13,769**	**20,212**	**35,242**	**32.7**	**100.0**
ANG/EPIS–Episcopal	2	108	229	260	0.2	0.7
Bahá'í	0	NR	41	41	0.0	0.1
BAPT–Amer Bapt USA	7	891	1,763	2,110	2.0	6.0
BAPT–Converge/BGC	1	75	NR	90	0.1	0.3
BAPT–Natl Mis Bapt Conv	2	120	300	359	0.3	1.0
BAPT–NBC USA	1	75	140	168	0.2	0.5
BAPT–Reg Bapt Gen As	2	NR	NR	NR	-	-
BAPT–So Bapt Conv	7	467	1,247	1,493	1.4	4.2
BUDD–Mahayana	1	NR	NR	10	0.0	0.0
Calv Chpl	1	NR	NR	NR	-	-
Catholic	9	NR	NR	7,500	7.0	21.3
CGOD–Ch God (Ander)	1	58	NR	58	0.1	0.2
CGOD–Ches God-Gen Con	1	0	0	0	0.0	0.0
Ch Cr, Scientst	1	NR	NR	NR	-	-
Ch of Nazarene	2	348	407	564	0.5	1.6
Chr & Miss Al	1	60	44	150	0.1	0.4
CHR–Chr Ch (Disc)	1	68	160	192	0.2	0.5
CHR–Chr Chs & Chs Cr	6	NR	2,255	2,699	2.5	7.7
CHR–Chs of Christ	8	616	679	786	0.7	2.2
CONG–Cong Chr, NA	2	NR	75	90	0.1	0.3
FRND–Central Yr Mtg	1	30	18	22	0.0	0.1
HINDU–I/A Temples	1	NR	NR	238	0.2	0.7
Ind Fund Churches	1	NR	NR	NR	-	-
Jehovah's Witness	2	NR	NR	NR	-	-
JUD–Reform	1	23	40	108	0.1	0.3
LDS–L-D Saints	1	NR	NR	576	0.5	1.6
LUTH–E.L.C.A.	3	172	401	578	0.5	1.6
LUTH–Luth–MO Synod	1	152	291	318	0.3	0.9
LUTH–Wisc Ev Luth Syn	1	25	36	46	0.0	0.1
METH–AME	2	0	250	299	0.3	0.8
METH–C.M.E.	1	4	14	17	0.0	0.0
METH–Free Methodist	1	51	21	51	0.0	0.1
METH–Un Methodist	20	1,719	2,981	3,867	3.6	11.0
METH–Wesleyan	8	604	384	786	0.7	2.2
Muslim Est	1	100	NR	150	0.1	0.4
Non-denom Chr Chs	20	5,470	5,935	7,030	6.5	19.9
ORTHE–Ant Orth of NA	1	140	NR	254	0.2	0.7
PENT–Assemb of God	6	1,124	604	1,748	1.6	5.0
PENT–Ch God (Cleve)	2	223	277	332	0.3	0.9
PENT–COGIC	1	125	100	120	0.1	0.3
PENT–Full Gosp Bapt	3	NR	NR	NR	-	-
PENT–Int Foursq Gos	3	324	437	523	0.5	1.5
PENT–Un Pent Ch Intl	4	NR	NR	NR	-	-
PRES–Presb Ch (USA)	2	212	397	475	0.4	1.3
PRES–Ref Pres of NA	1	29	17	24	0.0	0.1
Salvation Army	1	25	77	411	0.4	1.2
Sev Day Adv	3	132	230	265	0.2	0.8
Un C of Christ	2	149	297	356	0.3	1.0
Unit Univ	1	50	65	78	0.1	0.2
WABASH	**80**	**3,758**	**10,185**	**13,755**	**41.8**	**100.0**
Bahá'í	0	NR	1	1	0.0	0.0
BAPT–Free Will Bapt	3	NR	165	198	0.6	1.4
BAPT–Ind Bapt Flwsp Intl	1	NR	NR	NR	-	-
BAPT–Reg Bapt Gen As	2	NR	NR	NR	-	-
BRETH–Brethren (Ash)	5	NR	770	925	2.8	6.7
BRETH–Ch of Brethren	4	322	814	978	3.0	7.1
Catholic	2	NR	NR	1,071	3.3	7.8
CGOD–Ch God (Ander)	1	75	NR	75	0.2	0.5
CGOD–Ches God-Gen Con	1	457	676	812	2.5	5.9
Ch of Nazarene	2	90	193	193	0.6	1.4
Chr & Miss Al	1	130	70	177	0.5	1.3
CHR–Chr Ch (Disc)	1	114	557	669	2.0	4.9
CHR–Chr Chs & Chs Cr	9	NR	1,960	2,355	7.2	17.1
CHR–Chs of Christ	2	90	79	107	0.3	0.8
CONG–Cong Chr, NA	1	NR	185	222	0.7	1.6
FRND–Fr Gen Cf	1	NR	9	11	0.0	0.1
FRND–Fr Un Mtg	1	NR	402	483	1.5	3.5
Ind Fund Churches	1	NR	NR	NR	-	-
LUTH–E.L.C.A.	2	134	614	614	1.9	4.5
LUTH–Luth Cong Msn Chr	1	19	23	28	0.1	0.2
LUTH–Luth–MO Synod	1	70	153	180	0.5	1.3
LUTH–Nor Amer Luth C	1	NR	NR	NR	-	-
METH–C.M.E.	1	0	60	72	0.2	0.5
METH–Un Methodist	18	1,154	2,230	2,872	8.7	20.9
METH–Wesleyan	4	151	56	197	0.6	1.4
Missionary Ch	1	103	85	103	0.3	0.7
Non-denom Chr Chs	4	400	410	499	1.5	3.6
PENT–Assemb of God	3	240	209	355	1.1	2.6
PENT–Ch God (Cleve)	1	46	107	129	0.4	0.9
PENT–Ch God Mtn Asm	1	NR	NR	NR	-	-
PENT–Un Pent Ch Intl	1	NR	NR	NR	-	-
PRES–Presb Ch (USA)	1	67	185	222	0.7	1.6
Un C of Christ	2	96	172	207	0.6	1.5
WARREN	**20**	**658**	**1,956**	**2,505**	**29.4**	**100.0**
Ch of God Gen Conf	1	NR	28	34	0.4	1.4
Ch of Nazarene	1	57	93	93	1.1	3.7
CHR–Chr Chs & Chs Cr	5	NR	863	1,047	12.3	41.8
CHR–Chs of Christ	1	20	15	15	0.2	0.6
LDS–L-D Saints	1	NR	NR	122	1.4	4.9
METH–Un Methodist	7	407	740	923	10.8	36.8
Non-denom Chr Chs	1	80	80	100	1.2	4.0
PENT–Assemb of God	1	28	19	28	0.3	1.1
PRES–Presb Ch (USA)	2	66	118	143	1.7	5.7
WARRICK	**68**	**7,673**	**16,338**	**28,095**	**47.1**	**100.0**
ANG/EPIS–Anglican NA	1	NR	NR	NR	-	-
BAPT–Amer Bapt USA	1	210	250	312	0.5	1.1
BAPT–Free Will Bapt	1	NR	55	69	0.1	0.2
BAPT–Ref Bapt Ch	1	NR	NR	NR	-	-
BAPT–Reg Bapt Gen As	1	NR	NR	NR	-	-
BAPT–So Bapt Conv	6	513	2,052	2,559	4.3	9.1
Catholic	3	NR	NR	6,775	11.4	24.1
Ch of Nazarene	4	196	338	379	0.6	1.3
CHR–Chr Chs & Chs Cr	3	NR	4,509	5,624	9.4	20.0
CHR–Chs of Christ	2	245	215	285	0.5	1.0
Ind Fund Churches	1	NR	NR	NR	-	-
Jehovah's Witness	1	NR	NR	NR	-	-
LDS–L-D Saints	1	NR	NR	707	1.2	2.5
LUTH–E.L.C.A.	1	61	174	183	0.3	0.7
LUTH–Luth–MO Synod	1	72	157	237	0.4	0.8
METH–Free Methodist	1	22	17	22	0.0	0.1
METH–Un Methodist	12	1,083	1,894	2,582	4.3	9.2
METH–Wesleyan	1	51	39	66	0.1	0.2
Muslim Est	1	60	NR	350	0.6	1.2
Non-denom Chr Chs	11	4,125	4,700	5,208	8.7	18.5
PENT–Assemb of God	2	345	252	446	0.7	1.6
PENT–Ch God (Cleve)	1	50	41	51	0.1	0.2
PENT–Un Pent Ch Intl	2	NR	NR	NR	-	-
PRES–Cumber Presb	1	NR	88	360	0.6	1.3
PRES–Presb Ch (USA)	2	144	235	293	0.5	1.0
Salvation Army	1	86	226	226	0.4	0.8
Sev Day Adv	1	38	66	76	0.1	0.3
Un C of Christ	4	372	1,030	1,285	2.2	4.6
WASHINGTON	**73**	**3,706**	**8,748**	**11,489**	**40.7**	**100.0**
Bahá'í	0	NR	6	6	0.0	0.1
BAPT–Amer Bapt USA	9	739	1,654	2,044	7.2	17.8
BAPT–Reg Bapt Gen As	1	NR	NR	NR	-	-
BAPT–S-D Baptist Gen Con	1	15	22	27	0.1	0.2
BAPT–So Bapt Conv	4	455	1,308	1,616	5.7	14.1
Catholic	1	NR	NR	253	0.9	2.2
CGOD–Ch God (Ander)	1	25	NR	25	0.1	0.2
Ch of Nazarene	2	115	180	259	0.9	2.3
CHR–Chr Ch (Disc)	1	110	793	980	3.5	8.5
CHR–Chr Chs & Chs Cr	10	NR	1,870	2,311	8.2	20.1
CHR–Chs of Christ	15	1,337	1,245	1,723	6.1	15.0
FRND–Fr Un Mtg	1	NR	60	74	0.3	0.6
Jehovah's Witness	1	NR	NR	NR	-	-

NR–Not Reported   - Represents no adherents reported.   Percentages may not total 100 due to rounding.

Table 3: Religious Congregations by County and Group: 2010

Religious Group	Number of Congregations	Number of Attendees	Number of Communicant, Confirmed, or Full Members	Adherents: Number of Adherents	Adherents: % of Total Pop.	Adherents: % of Total Adh.
LUTH–Luth–MO Synod	1	30	44	64	0.2	0.6
MENN–Amish Undif	4	NR	167	379	1.3	3.3
MENN–CG in Cr (Menn)	1	NR	125	154	0.5	1.3
METH–Un Methodist	10	402	697	827	2.9	7.2
METH–Wesleyan	1	26	21	34	0.1	0.3
Non-denom Chr Chs	2	210	210	263	0.9	2.3
PENT–Assemb of God	2	158	163	224	0.8	1.9
PENT–Ch God (Cleve)	1	15	17	21	0.1	0.2
PENT–Ch of God Proph	1	NR	18	22	0.1	0.2
PENT–Un Pent Ch Intl	1	NR	NR	NR	-	-
PRES–Presb Ch (USA)	2	69	148	183	0.6	1.6
WAYNE	**121**	**8,706**	**18,148**	**29,566**	**42.9**	**100.0**
ANG/EPIS–Episcopal	1	47	88	88	0.1	0.3
Bahá'í	0	NR	23	23	0.0	0.1
BAPT–Amer Bapt USA	2	289	1,133	1,376	2.0	4.7
BAPT–Natl Mis Bapt Conv	1	120	200	243	0.4	0.8
BAPT–NBC Amer	1	150	250	304	0.4	1.0
BAPT–Reg Bapt Gen As	1	NR	NR	NR	-	-
BAPT–So Bapt Conv	10	805	1,980	2,405	3.5	8.1
BRETH–Ch of Brethren	2	80	130	158	0.2	0.5
Catholic	4	NR	NR	4,854	7.0	16.4
CGOD–Ch God (Ander)	1	22	NR	22	0.0	0.1
Ch Christ Chr Union	1	NR	NR	NR	-	-
Ch of Nazarene	7	445	587	877	1.3	3.0
Chr & Miss Al	1	60	40	82	0.1	0.3
CHR–Chr Ch (Disc)	2	167	828	1,006	1.5	3.4
CHR–Chr Chs & Chs Cr	10	NR	2,455	2,982	4.3	10.1
CHR–Chs of Christ	4	166	139	186	0.3	0.6
Evan Ch	1	NR	NR	NR	-	-
FRND–Central Yr Mtg	1	15	20	24	0.0	0.1
FRND–Fr Gen Cf	1	NR	108	131	0.2	0.4
FRND–Fr Un Mtg	5	NR	311	378	0.5	1.3
FRND–Unaffl Mtgs	1	NR	NR	NR	-	-
HINDU–Post Ren	1	NR	NR	16	0.0	0.1
Jehovah's Witness	1	NR	NR	NR	-	-
JUD–Reform	1	15	27	73	0.1	0.2
LDS–L-D Saints	1	NR	NR	610	0.9	2.1
LUTH–E.L.C.A.	6	635	1,519	2,026	2.9	6.9
MENN–Amish Undif	5	NR	288	625	0.9	2.1
METH–A.W.M.C.	1	26	7	26	0.0	0.1
METH–AME	1	100	400	486	0.7	1.6
METH–Evan Meth Ch	1	NR	NR	NR	-	-
METH–Un Methodist	15	939	2,012	2,715	3.9	9.2
METH–Wesleyan	2	1,111	324	1,444	2.1	4.9
New Apost Ch	1	NR	NR	NR	-	-
Non-denom Chr Chs	14	2,000	2,445	2,723	4.0	9.2
PENT–Assemb of God	4	709	580	944	1.4	3.2
PENT–Ch God (Cleve)	1	275	1,008	1,224	1.8	4.1
PENT–Un Pent Ch Intl	2	NR	NR	NR	-	-
PENT–Vineyard	1	160	400	486	0.7	1.6
PRES–Presb Ch (USA)	2	30	278	338	0.5	1.1
PRES–Presb Ch Amer	1	166	191	201	0.3	0.7
Salvation Army	1	20	89	151	0.2	0.5
Sev Day Adv	1	93	162	186	0.3	0.6
Un C of Christ	1	61	126	153	0.2	0.5
WELLS	**52**	**6,567**	**7,892**	**11,665**	**42.2**	**100.0**
Ap Chr Ch-Amer	2	1,900	1,320	1,900	6.9	16.3
Bahá'í	0	NR	6	6	0.0	0.1
BAPT–Amer Bapt USA	3	215	334	411	1.5	3.5
Catholic	1	NR	NR	219	0.8	1.9
Ch Christ Chr Union	1	NR	NR	NR	-	-
Ch of Nazarene	2	315	402	821	3.0	7.0
CHR–Chr Chs & Chs Cr	3	NR	1,190	1,465	5.3	12.6
CHR–Chs of Christ	1	15	15	20	0.1	0.2
Evan Assoc RCC	1	NR	NR	NR	-	-
FRND–Central Yr Mtg	1	17	18	22	0.1	0.2
Jehovah's Witness	1	NR	NR	NR	-	-
LUTH–E.L.C.A.	3	147	183	475	1.7	4.1
LUTH–Luth–MO Synod	2	277	541	720	2.6	6.2
LUTH–Nor Amer Luth C	1	NR	NR	NR	-	-
MENN–Amish Undif	0	NR	13	40	0.1	0.3

Religious Group	Number of Congregations	Number of Attendees	Number of Communicant, Confirmed, or Full Members	Adherents: Number of Adherents	Adherents: % of Total Pop.	Adherents: % of Total Adh.
METH–Un Methodist	12	876	1,296	1,868	6.8	16.0
METH–Wesleyan	2	333	185	433	1.6	3.7
Missionary Ch	2	968	359	968	3.5	8.3
Non-denom Chr Chs	8	1,130	1,345	1,488	5.4	12.8
PENT–Assemb of God	1	45	33	55	0.2	0.5
PENT–Ch God (Cleve)	1	28	134	165	0.6	1.4
PRES–Presb Ch (USA)	2	218	404	498	1.8	4.3
Sev Day Adv	1	18	30	35	0.1	0.3
Un Breth in Cr	1	65	84	56	0.2	0.5
WHITE	**51**	**3,896**	**6,406**	**10,903**	**44.2**	**100.0**
Ap Chr Ch-Amer	1	167	90	167	0.7	1.5
Bahá'í	0	NR	6	6	0.0	0.1
BAPT–Amer Bapt USA	6	507	1,032	1,264	5.1	11.6
BAPT–So Bapt Conv	1	142	329	403	1.6	3.7
BRETH–Ch of Brethren	4	86	151	185	0.8	1.7
Catholic	2	NR	NR	2,474	10.0	22.7
CGOD–Ches God-Gen Con	2	280	309	379	1.5	3.5
CHR–Chr Ch (Disc)	3	505	757	928	3.8	8.5
CHR–Chr Chs & Chs Cr	3	NR	210	257	1.0	2.4
CHR–Chs of Christ	2	85	93	118	0.5	1.1
Jehovah's Witness	1	NR	NR	NR	-	-
LUTH–E.L.C.A.	1	103	264	287	1.2	2.6
LUTH–Luth–MO Synod	2	30	368	546	2.2	5.0
METH–Un Methodist	9	697	1,304	1,894	7.7	17.4
METH–Wesleyan	1	28	22	36	0.1	0.3
Non-denom Chr Chs	6	680	913	1,025	4.2	9.4
PENT–Assemb of God	2	262	78	350	1.4	3.2
PENT–Ch God (Cleve)	1	65	44	54	0.2	0.5
PRES–Presb Ch (USA)	3	227	381	467	1.9	4.3
Sev Day Adv	1	32	55	63	0.3	0.6
WHITLEY	**63**	**5,608**	**6,964**	**12,418**	**37.3**	**100.0**
Bahá'í	0	NR	1	1	0.0	0.0
BAPT–Free Will Bapt	1	NR	55	68	0.2	0.5
BAPT–Reg Bapt Gen As	3	NR	NR	NR	-	-
BAPT–So Bapt Conv	1	4	5	6	0.0	0.0
BRETH–Ch of Brethren	3	259	336	413	1.2	3.3
BRETH–Grace Breth	1	NR	NR	NR	-	-
Catholic	3	NR	NR	2,120	6.4	17.1
CGOD–Ch God (Ander)	1	223	NR	223	0.7	1.8
CGOD–Ches God-Gen Con	6	1,265	1,303	1,601	4.8	12.9
Ch of Nazarene	3	402	479	657	2.0	5.3
CHR–Chr Chs & Chs Cr	1	NR	40	49	0.1	0.4
CHR–Chs of Christ	1	85	78	100	0.3	0.8
Ind Fund Churches	1	NR	NR	NR	-	-
Jehovah's Witness	1	NR	NR	NR	-	-
LDS–L-D Saints	1	NR	NR	313	0.9	2.5
LUTH–E.L.C.A.	3	279	593	662	2.0	5.3
LUTH–Luth–MO Synod	3	268	744	988	3.0	8.0
MENN–Amish Undif	1	NR	100	219	0.7	1.8
METH–Un Methodist	12	1,271	1,818	2,673	8.0	21.5
METH–Wesleyan	2	428	251	557	1.7	4.5
Missionary Ch	1	39	33	39	0.1	0.3
Non-denom Chr Chs	7	810	805	1,014	3.0	8.2
PENT–Assemb of God	2	163	53	274	0.8	2.2
PENT–Pent Ch of God	1	70	NR	109	0.3	0.9
PRES–Evan Presby Ch	1	NR	143	176	0.5	1.4
PRES–Presb Ch (USA)	1	42	127	156	0.5	1.3
REF–Comm Ref Evan	1	NR	NR	NR	-	-
Un Breth in Cr	1	0	0	0	0.0	0.0
IOWA	**5,107**	**399,246**	**826,253**	**1,642,344**	**53.9**	**100.0**
ADAIR	**19**	**853**	**2,800**	**3,872**	**50.4**	**100.0**
BAPT–So Bapt Conv	1	30	24	29	0.4	0.7
Catholic	2	NR	NR	431	5.6	11.1
CHR–Chr Ch (Disc)	1	30	66	80	1.0	2.1
Evan Free Ch	1	112	NR	112	1.5	2.9
LUTH–E.L.C.A.	1	69	221	306	4.0	7.9
LUTH–Luth Cong Msn Chr	1	171	813	981	12.8	25.3

NR–Not Reported - Represents no adherents reported. Percentages may not total 100 due to rounding.

Table 3: Religious Congregations by County and Group: 2010

Religious Group	Number of Congrega-tions	Number of Attendees	Number of Communicant, Confirmed, or Full Members	Adherents		
				Number of Adherents	% of Total Pop.	% of Total Adh.
LUTH–Luth–MO Synod	3	113	452	538	7.0	13.9
METH–Un Methodist	7	271	1,125	1,276	16.6	33.0
PRES–Presb Ch (USA)	2	57	99	119	1.5	3.1
ADAMS	**15**	**286**	**972**	**1,411**	**35.0**	**100.0**
Bahá'í	0	NR	1	1	0.0	0.1
BAPT–Reg Bapt Gen As	1	NR	NR	NR	-	-
BRETH–Ch of Brethren	2	21	31	37	0.9	2.6
Catholic	1	NR	NR	249	6.2	17.6
CHR–Chr Ch (Disc)	2	0	34	40	1.0	2.8
LUTH–Luth–MO Synod	1	45	168	178	4.4	12.6
METH–Un Methodist	7	168	557	691	17.2	49.0
PRES–Presb Ch (USA)	1	52	181	215	5.3	15.2
ALLAMAKEE	**39**	**1,449**	**4,056**	**9,253**	**64.6**	**100.0**
Bahá'í	0	NR	3	3	0.0	0.0
BAPT–Converge/BGC	2	150	NR	180	1.3	1.9
BUDD–Mahayana	2	NR	NR	525	3.7	5.7
Catholic	9	NR	NR	3,426	23.9	37.0
Evan Free Ch	1	0	NR	0	0.0	0.0
Jehovah's Witness	1	NR	NR	NR	-	-
LUTH–E.L.C.A.	3	445	1,867	2,372	16.6	25.6
LUTH–Evan Luth Syn	1	29	44	50	0.3	0.5
LUTH–Nor Amer Luth C	3	NR	NR	NR	-	-
MENN–Amish Undif	1	NR	59	166	1.2	1.8
METH–Un Methodist	4	170	533	648	4.5	7.0
Non-denom Chr Chs	1	60	60	75	0.5	0.8
PRES–Presb Ch (USA)	7	329	749	910	6.4	9.8
Sev Day Adv	1	22	37	43	0.3	0.5
Un C of Christ	3	244	704	855	6.0	9.2
APPANOOSE	**34**	**1,405**	**2,787**	**5,084**	**39.5**	**100.0**
Bahá'í	0	NR	2	2	0.0	0.0
BAPT–Reg Bapt Gen As	1	NR	NR	NR	-	-
BAPT–So Bapt Conv	2	28	56	68	0.5	1.3
BRETH–Ch of Brethren	1	39	43	52	0.4	1.0
Catholic	1	NR	NR	1,094	8.5	21.5
CGOD–Ch God (Ander)	1	25	NR	25	0.2	0.5
Ch of Nazarene	2	417	281	494	3.8	9.7
CHR–Chr Ch (Disc)	2	40	511	618	4.8	12.2
CHR–Chr Chs & Chs Cr	4	NR	265	320	2.5	6.3
Evan Cov Ch	1	9	42	12	0.1	0.2
LDS–L-D Saints	1	NR	NR	104	0.8	2.0
LUTH–E.L.C.A.	1	45	154	154	1.2	3.0
MENN–Amish Undif	1	NR	45	129	1.0	2.5
MENN–Ber Amish-Menn	1	110	60	110	0.9	2.2
METH–Un Methodist	8	356	975	1,370	10.6	26.9
Non-denom Chr Chs	1	80	75	100	0.8	2.0
PENT–Assemb of God	1	76	42	127	1.0	2.5
PENT–Ch God (Cleve)	1	95	144	174	1.4	3.4
PENT–Open Bible Std	1	22	NR	22	0.2	0.4
PENT–Un Pent Ch Intl	1	NR	NR	NR	-	-
PRES–Presb Ch (USA)	1	40	52	63	0.5	1.2
Sev Day Adv	1	23	40	46	0.4	0.9
AUDUBON	**19**	**982**	**3,239**	**4,823**	**78.8**	**100.0**
BAPT–Reg Bapt Gen As	1	NR	NR	NR	-	-
Catholic	2	NR	NR	646	10.6	13.4
CHR–Chr Ch (Disc)	1	56	250	297	4.9	6.2
CHR–Chr Chs & Chs Cr	1	NR	50	59	1.0	1.2
Evan Free Ch	1	80	NR	80	1.3	1.7
LUTH–E.L.C.A.	6	266	1,190	1,537	25.1	31.9
LUTH–Luth Cong Msn Chr	1	223	580	689	11.3	14.3
LUTH–Luth–MO Synod	1	107	256	347	5.7	7.2
METH–Un Methodist	3	205	729	950	15.5	19.7
PRES–Presb Ch (USA)	1	37	171	203	3.3	4.2
Sev Day Adv	1	8	13	15	0.2	0.3
BENTON	**51**	**2,801**	**7,198**	**13,824**	**53.0**	**100.0**
Bahá'í	0	NR	3	3	0.0	0.0
BAPT–Amer Bapt USA	1	12	24	30	0.1	0.2
Catholic	8	NR	NR	4,201	16.1	30.4
Ch of God Gen Conf	2	NR	54	67	0.3	0.5
CHR–Chr Ch (Disc)	2	87	401	496	1.9	3.6
Evan Free Ch	1	85	NR	85	0.3	0.6
Jehovah's Witness	1	NR	NR	NR	-	-
LDS–L-D Saints	1	NR	NR	117	0.4	0.8
LUTH–E.L.C.A.	2	275	701	946	3.6	6.8
LUTH–Luth–MO Synod	10	1,223	3,479	4,359	16.7	31.5
METH–Un Methodist	10	494	1,416	2,129	8.2	15.4
Non-denom Chr Chs	4	375	395	494	1.9	3.6
PENT–Ch God (Cleve)	1	20	20	25	0.1	0.2
PENT–Int Foursq Gos	1	57	32	40	0.2	0.3
PRES–Presb Ch (USA)	5	147	627	775	3.0	5.6
Swedenborgian	1	NR	NR	NR	-	-
Un C of Christ	1	26	46	57	0.2	0.4
BLACK HAWK	**165**	**22,335**	**37,612**	**71,141**	**54.3**	**100.0**
ANG/EPIS–Episcopal	2	169	474	474	0.4	0.7
Bahá'í	1	NR	41	41	0.0	0.1
BAPT–Amer Bapt USA	4	273	614	740	0.6	1.0
BAPT–Converge/BGC	2	875	NR	1,050	0.8	1.5
BAPT–N Am Bapt Conf	1	NR	40	48	0.0	0.1
BAPT–NBC USA	8	5,940	7,240	8,730	6.7	12.3
BAPT–Reg Bapt Gen As	6	NR	NR	NR	-	-
BAPT–So Bapt Conv	5	236	405	488	0.4	0.7
BRETH–Brethren (Ash)	1	NR	80	96	0.1	0.1
BRETH–Ch of Brethren	2	91	385	464	0.4	0.7
BRETH–Grace Breth	1	NR	NR	NR	-	-
Catholic	11	NR	NR	20,049	15.3	28.2
Ch Cr, Scientst	1	NR	NR	NR	-	-
Ch of God Gen Conf	1	NR	10	12	0.0	0.0
Ch of Nazarene	2	133	238	279	0.2	0.4
CHR–Chr Ch (Disc)	2	183	755	910	0.7	1.3
CHR–Chr Chs & Chs Cr	3	NR	304	367	0.3	0.5
CHR–Chs of Christ	2	148	129	162	0.1	0.2
Christian Brethren	2	NR	NR	NR	-	-
CONG–Consrv Cong Chr	1	128	220	265	0.2	0.4
Evan Free Ch	1	60	NR	60	0.0	0.1
Ind Fund Churches	2	NR	NR	NR	-	-
Jehovah's Witness	1	NR	NR	NR	-	-
JUD–Conserv	1	47	53	143	0.1	0.2
LDS–Comm of Christ	1	NR	119	119	0.1	0.2
LDS–L-D Saints	2	NR	NR	970	0.7	1.4
LUTH–E.L.C.A.	15	3,062	8,437	11,044	8.4	15.5
LUTH–Evan Luth Syn	1	50	93	135	0.1	0.2
LUTH–Luth Ch-Am Asc	2	NR	NR	NR	-	-
LUTH–Luth Cong Msn Chr	1	77	155	187	0.1	0.3
LUTH–Luth–MO Synod	8	865	2,158	2,756	2.1	3.9
MENN–Mennonite USA	1	40	40	48	0.0	0.1
METH–AME	1	150	300	362	0.3	0.5
METH–Free Methodist	1	18	11	18	0.0	0.0
METH–Un Methodist	15	1,289	4,226	5,176	3.9	7.3
METH–Wesleyan	6	945	793	1,228	0.9	1.7
Muslim Est	3	402	NR	924	0.7	1.3
Non-denom Chr Chs	11	1,065	1,540	1,625	1.2	2.3
ORTHE–Greek Orthodox	1	10	NR	60	0.0	0.1
PENT–Assemb of God	4	748	420	1,236	0.9	1.7
PENT–COGIC	1	20	20	24	0.0	0.0
PENT–Full Gosp Bapt	1	NR	NR	NR	-	-
PENT–Int Foursq Gos	1	66	44	53	0.0	0.1
PENT–Open Bible Std	1	375	NR	375	0.3	0.5
PENT–Un Pent Ch Intl	1	NR	NR	NR	-	-
PENT–Vineyard	4	1,695	2,395	2,888	2.2	4.1
PRES–Orth Pres Ch	1	48	39	53	0.0	0.1
PRES–Presb Ch (USA)	9	941	2,200	2,653	2.0	3.7
REF–Ref Ch in Am	3	1,747	2,687	3,266	2.5	4.6
Salvation Army	1	64	79	507	0.4	0.7
Sev Day Adv	2	88	154	177	0.1	0.2
Un C of Christ	3	198	567	684	0.5	1.0
Unit Univ	1	89	147	195	0.1	0.3
BOONE	**48**	**3,438**	**8,066**	**14,008**	**53.3**	**100.0**
ANG/EPIS–Episcopal	1	25	40	101	0.4	0.7
Bahá'í	0	NR	14	14	0.1	0.1

NR–Not Reported   - Represents no adherents reported.   Percentages may not total 100 due to rounding.

Table 3: Religious Congregations by County and Group: 2010

Religious Group	Number of Congrega-tions	Number of Attendees	Number of Communicant, Confirmed, or Full Members	Adherents: Number of Adherents	Adherents: % of Total Pop.	Adherents: % of Total Adh.
BAPT–Amer Bapt USA	1	111	327	398	1.5	2.8
BAPT–NT Ind Bapt	1	NR	NR	NR	-	-
BAPT–So Bapt Conv	1	10	8	10	0.0	0.1
BRETH–Ch of Brethren	1	12	25	30	0.1	0.2
Catholic	3	NR	NR	3,213	12.2	22.9
Ch of Nazarene	1	17	39	60	0.2	0.4
Chr & Miss Al	2	353	224	573	2.2	4.1
CHR–Chr Ch (Disc)	2	70	707	859	3.3	6.1
CHR–Chs of Christ	2	130	100	150	0.6	1.1
Evan Free Ch	2	355	NR	355	1.3	2.5
HINDU–Trad Temples	1	NR	NR	400	1.5	2.9
Jehovah's Witness	1	NR	NR	NR	-	-
LDS–L-D Saints	1	NR	NR	295	1.1	2.1
LUTH–E.L.C.A.	4	523	2,561	2,701	10.3	19.3
LUTH–Luth–MO Synod	3	495	1,189	1,433	5.4	10.2
METH–Un Methodist	9	550	1,785	1,967	7.5	14.0
Non-denom Chr Chs	4	360	410	476	1.8	3.4
PENT–Assemb of God	1	30	0	35	0.1	0.2
PENT–Ch of God Proph	1	NR	37	45	0.2	0.3
PENT–Open Bible Std	1	180	NR	180	0.7	1.3
PRES–Presb Ch (USA)	1	80	273	332	1.3	2.4
Salvation Army	1	49	74	74	0.3	0.5
Sev Day Adv	1	8	13	15	0.1	0.1
Un C of Christ	2	80	240	292	1.1	2.1
BREMER	**48**	**3,836**	**10,474**	**17,052**	**70.2**	**100.0**
ANG/EPIS–Episcopal	1	24	24	39	0.2	0.2
Bahá'í	0	NR	10	10	0.0	0.1
BAPT–Amer Bapt USA	1	59	164	197	0.8	1.2
BAPT–Converge/BGC	2	150	NR	180	0.7	1.1
BAPT–N Am Bapt Conf	1	NR	55	66	0.3	0.4
BAPT–Reg Bapt Gen As	2	NR	NR	NR	-	-
Catholic	2	NR	NR	2,558	10.5	15.0
Ch of Nazarene	1	29	46	178	0.7	1.0
Evan Ch	1	NR	NR	NR	-	-
LDS–L-D Saints	1	NR	NR	130	0.5	0.8
LUTH–E.L.C.A.	10	1,392	5,282	6,867	28.3	40.3
LUTH–Luth Ch-Am Asc	1	NR	NR	NR	-	-
LUTH–Luth–MO Synod	7	649	1,518	1,864	7.7	10.9
LUTH–Nor Amer Luth C	3	NR	NR	NR	-	-
METH–Un Methodist	6	507	2,060	2,872	11.8	16.8
Non-denom Chr Chs	1	80	100	100	0.4	0.6
PENT–Assemb of God	1	12	4	12	0.0	0.1
PENT–Open Bible Std	1	524	NR	524	2.2	3.1
PENT–Vineyard	1	110	130	156	0.6	0.9
Un C of Christ	5	300	1,081	1,299	5.4	7.6
BUCHANAN	**55**	**2,346**	**5,784**	**13,312**	**63.5**	**100.0**
ANG/EPIS–Episcopal	1	13	15	15	0.1	0.1
Bahá'í	0	NR	6	6	0.0	0.0
BAPT–Amer Bapt USA	3	86	125	158	0.8	1.2
BAPT–Converge/BGC	1	75	NR	90	0.4	0.7
BAPT–So Bapt Conv	2	25	43	54	0.3	0.4
Catholic	4	NR	NR	5,191	24.8	39.0
CHR–Chr Chs & Chs Cr	1	NR	40	51	0.2	0.4
Evan Ch	1	NR	NR	NR	-	-
LUTH–Assoc Free Luth	1	NR	NR	NR	-	-
LUTH–E.L.C.A.	3	323	1,260	1,654	7.9	12.4
LUTH–Luth–MO Synod	3	90	244	297	1.4	2.2
MENN–Amish Undif	7	NR	449	1,241	5.9	9.3
METH–Un Methodist	10	564	1,815	2,329	11.1	17.5
METH–Wesleyan	1	130	103	169	0.8	1.3
Non-denom Chr Chs	8	619	828	971	4.6	7.3
PENT–Int Foursq Gos	1	42	138	175	0.8	1.3
PENT–Un Pent Ch Intl	1	NR	NR	NR	-	-
PRES–Orth Pres Ch	1	7	18	23	0.1	0.2
PRES–Presb Ch (USA)	5	254	421	534	2.5	4.0
Un C of Christ	1	118	279	354	1.7	2.7
BUENA VISTA	**48**	**3,191**	**7,041**	**12,663**	**62.5**	**100.0**
ANG/EPIS–Episcopal	1	14	32	32	0.2	0.3
Bahá'í	0	NR	12	12	0.1	0.1
BAPT–Amer Bapt USA	1	44	106	131	0.6	1.0
BAPT–So Bapt Conv	2	145	196	242	1.2	1.9
Catholic	2	NR	NR	3,194	15.8	25.2
CHR–Chr Chs & Chs Cr	2	NR	230	284	1.4	2.2
Evan Cov Ch	1	63	104	82	0.4	0.6
Evan Free Ch	3	730	NR	730	3.6	5.8
Jehovah's Witness	1	NR	NR	NR	-	-
LDS–L-D Saints	1	NR	NR	326	1.6	2.6
LUTH–E.L.C.A.	10	530	2,285	2,635	13.0	20.8
LUTH–Luth–MO Synod	7	701	1,753	2,112	10.4	16.7
METH–Un Methodist	6	382	1,351	1,579	7.8	12.5
Non-denom Chr Chs	1	175	100	219	1.1	1.7
PENT–Assemb of God	1	42	30	67	0.3	0.5
PENT–Int Foursq Gos	1	52	37	46	0.2	0.4
PENT–Un Pent Ch Intl	2	NR	NR	NR	-	-
PRES–Presb Ch (USA)	2	150	471	582	2.9	4.6
PRES–Presb Ch Amer	1	62	96	96	0.5	0.8
Un C of Christ	3	101	238	294	1.5	2.3
BUTLER	**49**	**2,614**	**7,991**	**10,509**	**70.7**	**100.0**
BAPT–N Am Bapt Conf	2	NR	268	328	2.2	3.1
BAPT–Reg Bapt Gen As	3	NR	NR	NR	-	-
BRETH–Ch of Brethren	1	13	32	39	0.3	0.4
Catholic	1	NR	NR	570	3.8	5.4
CHR–Chr Chs & Chs Cr	2	NR	150	183	1.2	1.7
CONG–Consrv Cong Chr	1	186	274	335	2.3	3.2
Ind Fund Churches	1	NR	NR	NR	-	-
Jehovah's Witness	1	NR	NR	NR	-	-
LUTH–E.L.C.A.	6	797	2,673	3,531	23.8	33.6
LUTH–Evan Luth Syn	1	27	60	70	0.5	0.7
LUTH–Luth Cong Msn Chr	1	100	560	685	4.6	6.5
LUTH–Luth–MO Synod	1	16	50	50	0.3	0.5
LUTH–Nor Amer Luth C	2	NR	NR	NR	-	-
METH–Un Methodist	7	224	1,182	1,457	9.8	13.9
METH–Wesleyan	1	15	10	20	0.1	0.2
Non-denom Chr Chs	1	100	90	125	0.8	1.2
PENT–COGIC	1	0	150	183	1.2	1.7
PRES–Presb Ch (USA)	4	137	394	482	3.2	4.6
REF–Christian Ref	2	200	291	356	2.4	3.4
REF–Ref Ch in Am	6	605	1,004	1,113	7.5	10.6
Un C of Christ	4	194	803	982	6.6	9.3
CALHOUN	**36**	**1,759**	**5,659**	**8,582**	**88.7**	**100.0**
BAPT–Amer Bapt USA	1	28	138	165	1.7	1.9
Catholic	5	NR	NR	1,568	16.2	18.3
CHR–Chr Ch (Disc)	2	0	504	601	6.2	7.0
CHR–Chr Chs & Chs Cr	1	NR	150	179	1.9	2.1
Evan Cov Ch	1	112	207	146	1.5	1.7
Evan Free Ch	1	30	NR	30	0.3	0.3
Jehovah's Witness	1	NR	NR	NR	-	-
LUTH–E.L.C.A.	5	544	2,141	2,520	26.1	29.4
LUTH–Luth–MO Synod	5	370	916	1,114	11.5	13.0
MENN–Mennonite USA	1	82	127	151	1.6	1.8
METH–Un Methodist	7	347	1,136	1,395	14.4	16.3
Muslim Est	1	134	NR	308	3.2	3.6
PRES–Presb Ch (USA)	2	56	169	201	2.1	2.3
Sev Day Adv	1	2	4	5	0.1	0.1
Un C of Christ	2	54	167	199	2.1	2.3
CARROLL	**46**	**1,963**	**4,626**	**18,335**	**88.1**	**100.0**
ANG/EPIS–Episcopal	1	8	9	9	0.0	0.0
Bahá'í	0	NR	1	1	0.0	0.0
BAPT–Reg Bapt Gen As	2	NR	NR	NR	-	-
Catholic	14	NR	NR	11,943	57.4	65.1
CHR–Chr Ch (Disc)	1	39	145	178	0.9	1.0
CHR–Chr Chs & Chs Cr	2	NR	125	154	0.7	0.8
Evan Cov Ch	1	8	11	10	0.0	0.1
Ind Fund Churches	1	NR	NR	NR	-	-
LDS–L-D Saints	1	NR	NR	195	0.9	1.1
LUTH–E.L.C.A.	2	137	406	483	2.3	2.6
LUTH–Luth–MO Synod	6	738	1,798	2,358	11.3	12.9
METH–Un Methodist	5	364	1,266	1,712	8.2	9.3
Non-denom Chr Chs	5	430	440	594	2.9	3.2
PENT–Assemb of God	1	145	37	220	1.1	1.2

NR–Not Reported - Represents no adherents reported. Percentages may not total 100 due to rounding.

Table 3: Religious Congregations by County and Group: 2010

Religious Group	Number of Congrega-tions	Number of Attendees	Number of Communicant, Confirmed, or Full Members	Adherents		
				Number of Adherents	% of Total Pop.	% of Total Adh.
PRES–Presb Ch (USA)	4	94	388	478	2.3	2.6
CASS	**42**	**1,905**	**5,356**	**8,578**	**61.5**	**100.0**
BAPT–Amer Bapt USA	1	30	42	51	0.4	0.6
BAPT–Reg Bapt Gen As	1	NR	NR	NR	-	-
Catholic	5	NR	NR	1,403	10.1	16.4
Ch of Nazarene	1	9	40	40	0.3	0.5
CHR–Chr Ch (Disc)	1	0	266	322	2.3	3.8
CHR–Chr Chs & Chs Cr	3	NR	575	697	5.0	8.1
CHR–Chs of Christ	1	40	30	50	0.4	0.6
Evan Free Ch	1	300	NR	300	2.1	3.5
Jehovah's Witness	1	NR	NR	NR	-	-
LDS–L-D Saints	1	NR	NR	273	2.0	3.2
LUTH–E.L.C.A.	2	326	837	999	7.2	11.6
LUTH–Luth-MO Synod	3	257	859	1,022	7.3	11.9
METH–Un Methodist	11	502	1,751	2,223	15.9	25.9
Non-denom Chr Chs	1	35	45	45	0.3	0.5
PENT–Assemb of God	1	100	81	149	1.1	1.7
PENT–Ch of God Proph	1	NR	27	33	0.2	0.4
PRES–Presb Ch (USA)	1	60	190	230	1.6	2.7
Sev Day Adv	1	26	45	52	0.4	0.6
Un C of Christ	5	220	568	689	4.9	8.0
CEDAR	**32**	**1,580**	**5,014**	**8,000**	**43.2**	**100.0**
ANG/EPIS–Anglican NA	1	NR	NR	NR	-	-
ANG/EPIS–Episcopal	1	19	42	42	0.2	0.5
Bahá'í	0	NR	4	4	0.0	0.1
BAPT–Amer Bapt USA	1	20	28	34	0.2	0.4
BAPT–Reg Bapt Gen As	1	NR	NR	NR	-	-
Catholic	3	NR	NR	1,759	9.5	22.0
FRND–Consrv Yr Mtgs	2	NR	88	108	0.6	1.4
FRND–Fr Un Mtg	1	NR	113	138	0.7	1.7
LUTH–E.L.C.A.	3	250	819	1,032	5.6	12.9
LUTH–Luth-MO Synod	3	179	517	622	3.4	7.8
METH–Un Methodist	6	440	1,515	1,935	10.5	24.2
Non-denom Chr Chs	1	75	65	94	0.5	1.2
PENT–Int Foursq Gos	1	121	133	163	0.9	2.0
PENT–Un Pent Ch Intl	1	NR	NR	NR	-	-
PRES–Presb Ch (USA)	2	67	164	201	1.1	2.5
Un C of Christ	5	409	1,526	1,868	10.1	23.4
CERRO GORDO	**71**	**7,558**	**16,319**	**29,944**	**67.8**	**100.0**
ANG/EPIS–Episcopal	1	73	181	206	0.5	0.7
Bahá'í	0	NR	12	12	0.0	0.0
BAPT–Amer Bapt USA	1	144	306	366	0.8	1.2
BAPT–Converge/BGC	1	75	NR	90	0.2	0.3
BAPT–Reg Bapt Gen As	2	NR	NR	NR	-	-
BAPT–So Bapt Conv	1	28	27	32	0.1	0.1
Catholic	5	NR	NR	6,672	15.1	22.3
Ch Cr, Scientst	1	NR	NR	NR	-	-
Ch of Nazarene	1	34	85	85	0.2	0.3
CHR–Chr Ch (Disc)	1	47	141	168	0.4	0.6
CHR–Chr Chs & Chs Cr	2	NR	240	287	0.7	1.0
CHR–Chs of Christ	1	27	34	45	0.1	0.2
CONG–Cong Chr Add'l	1	NR	100	119	0.3	0.4
CONG–Cong Chr, NA	1	NR	262	313	0.7	1.0
Evan Cov Ch	1	203	192	264	0.6	0.9
Evan Free Ch	2	750	NR	750	1.7	2.5
FRND–Fr Un Mtg	1	NR	43	51	0.1	0.2
Jehovah's Witness	1	NR	NR	NR	-	-
LDS–Comm of Christ	1	NR	158	158	0.4	0.5
LDS–L-D Saints	1	NR	NR	480	1.1	1.6
LUTH–E.L.C.A.	8	2,155	6,180	8,272	18.7	27.6
LUTH–Evan Luth Syn	1	28	65	69	0.2	0.2
LUTH–Luth Cong Msn Chr	1	745	1,726	2,062	4.7	6.9
LUTH–Luth-MO Synod	3	428	816	1,080	2.4	3.6
LUTH–Wisc Ev Luth Syn	1	30	91	95	0.2	0.3
METH–Free Methodist	1	44	72	72	0.2	0.2
METH–Un Methodist	12	1,039	3,547	4,856	11.0	16.2
Muslim Est	1	134	NR	308	0.7	1.0
Non-denom Chr Chs	5	650	778	861	2.0	2.9
ORTHE–Greek Orthodox	1	65	NR	200	0.5	0.7
PENT–Assemb of God	1	124	82	185	0.4	0.6

Religious Group	Number of Congrega-tions	Number of Attendees	Number of Communicant, Confirmed, or Full Members	Adherents		
				Number of Adherents	% of Total Pop.	% of Total Adh.
PENT–Open Bible Std	1	90	NR	90	0.2	0.3
PENT–Un Pent Ch Intl	1	NR	NR	NR	-	-
PENT–Vineyard	1	32	48	57	0.1	0.2
PRES–Presb Ch (USA)	1	103	321	384	0.9	1.3
REF–Christian Ref	1	210	244	292	0.7	1.0
REF–Ref Ch in Am	1	120	184	234	0.5	0.8
Salvation Army	1	47	54	341	0.8	1.1
Sev Day Adv	1	57	99	114	0.3	0.4
Un C of Christ	1	64	219	262	0.6	0.9
Unit Univ	1	12	12	12	0.0	0.0
CHEROKEE	**32**	**1,992**	**4,524**	**7,930**	**65.7**	**100.0**
Bahá'í	0	NR	2	2	0.0	0.0
BAPT–Amer Bapt USA	2	46	68	81	0.7	1.0
BAPT–NT Ind Bapt	1	NR	NR	NR	-	-
BAPT–So Bapt Conv	1	30	49	58	0.5	0.7
Calv Chpl	1	NR	NR	NR	-	-
Catholic	2	NR	NR	2,059	17.1	26.0
CHR–Chr Ch (Disc)	1	0	0	0	0.0	0.0
CHR–Chr Chs & Chs Cr	1	NR	0	0	0.0	0.0
CONG–Consrv Cong Chr	1	34	78	93	0.8	1.2
Evan Free Ch	2	373	NR	373	3.1	4.7
Jehovah's Witness	2	NR	NR	NR	-	-
LDS–Comm of Christ	1	NR	189	189	1.6	2.4
LUTH–E.L.C.A.	2	237	900	1,210	10.0	15.3
LUTH–Luth-MO Synod	5	522	1,225	1,459	12.1	18.4
METH–Un Methodist	6	465	1,453	1,774	14.7	22.4
Non-denom Chr Chs	2	120	180	180	1.5	2.3
PRES–Presb Ch (USA)	2	165	380	452	3.7	5.7
CHICKASAW	**28**	**1,286**	**3,800**	**9,590**	**77.1**	**100.0**
Bahá'í	0	NR	1	1	0.0	0.0
BAPT–Amer Bapt USA	1	35	213	261	2.1	2.7
BAPT–Converge/BGC	1	75	NR	90	0.7	0.9
BRETH–Ch of Brethren	1	41	213	261	2.1	2.7
Catholic	7	NR	NR	4,297	34.5	44.8
Jehovah's Witness	1	NR	NR	NR	-	-
LUTH–E.L.C.A.	4	499	1,750	2,529	20.3	26.4
LUTH–Evan Luth Syn	3	136	314	385	3.1	4.0
LUTH–Luth-MO Synod	1	108	234	292	2.3	3.0
METH–Un Methodist	5	240	748	1,074	8.6	11.2
Un C of Christ	4	152	327	400	3.2	4.2
CLARKE	**25**	**888**	**2,589**	**4,515**	**48.6**	**100.0**
BAPT–Reg Bapt Gen As	1	NR	NR	NR	-	-
BAPT–So Bapt Conv	1	18	35	43	0.5	1.0
Catholic	1	NR	NR	546	5.9	12.1
CHR–Chr Ch (Disc)	2	25	744	924	10.0	20.5
CHR–Chr Chs & Chs Cr	2	NR	321	399	4.3	8.8
CHR–Chs of Christ	1	70	62	86	0.9	1.9
Christian Un	1	NR	NR	NR	-	-
Evan Free Ch	1	80	NR	80	0.9	1.8
FRND–Fr Un Mtg	1	NR	31	38	0.4	0.8
Ind Fund Churches	1	NR	NR	NR	-	-
LDS–Comm of Christ	1	NR	158	158	1.7	3.5
LDS–L-D Saints	1	NR	NR	407	4.4	9.0
LUTH–Luth-MO Synod	1	65	115	129	1.4	2.9
MENN–Amish Undif	1	NR	18	57	0.6	1.3
METH–Un Methodist	3	204	675	949	10.2	21.0
Non-denom Chr Chs	2	150	215	215	2.3	4.8
PENT–Assemb of God	2	246	138	393	4.2	8.7
PENT–Ch of God Proph	1	NR	25	31	0.3	0.7
Sev Day Adv	1	30	52	60	0.6	1.3
CLAY	**36**	**2,825**	**7,030**	**11,870**	**71.2**	**100.0**
Bahá'í	0	NR	24	24	0.1	0.2
BAPT–Amer Bapt USA	1	12	20	24	0.1	0.2
BAPT–So Bapt Conv	1	15	53	64	0.4	0.5
Catholic	2	NR	NR	2,485	14.9	20.9
Ch of Nazarene	1	59	36	125	0.7	1.1
CHR–Chr Ch (Disc)	1	99	244	297	1.8	2.5
CHR–Chs of Christ	1	28	28	40	0.2	0.3

NR–Not Reported - Represents no adherents reported. Percentages may not total 100 due to rounding.

Table 3: Religious Congregations by County and Group: 2010

Religious Group	Number of Congrega-tions	Number of Attendees	Number of Communicant, Confirmed, or Full Members	Adherents: Number of Adherents	Adherents: % of Total Pop.	Adherents: % of Total Adh.
CONG–Cong Chr, NA	3	NR	537	653	3.9	5.5
Jehovah's Witness	1	NR	NR	NR	-	-
LDS–L-D Saints	1	NR	NR	306	1.8	2.6
LUTH–E.L.C.A.	3	451	1,655	2,186	13.1	18.4
LUTH–Luth Cong Msn Chr	2	280	619	752	4.5	6.3
LUTH–Luth–MO Synod	2	356	844	1,168	7.0	9.8
METH–Un Methodist	10	537	1,828	2,081	12.5	17.5
Non-denom Chr Chs	3	275	300	369	2.2	3.1
PENT–Assemb of God	1	259	115	470	2.8	4.0
PENT–Un Pent Ch Intl	1	NR	NR	NR	-	-
REF–Ref Ch in Am	1	408	648	735	4.4	6.2
Sev Day Adv	1	46	79	91	0.5	0.8
CLAYTON	**50**	**2,057**	**6,100**	**12,431**	**68.6**	**100.0**
BAPT–Asc Ref Bap Ch Am	1	NR	NR	NR	-	-
Catholic	8	NR	NR	4,351	24.0	35.0
CONG–Cong Chr, NA	1	NR	35	42	0.2	0.3
Evan Free Ch	2	110	NR	110	0.6	0.9
Jehovah's Witness	2	NR	NR	NR	-	-
JUD–Orth	1	180	75	250	1.4	2.0
LUTH–E.L.C.A.	16	957	3,734	4,551	25.1	36.6
LUTH–Luth–MO Synod	2	113	209	259	1.4	2.1
LUTH–Nor Amer Luth C	3	NR	NR	NR	-	-
MENN–Amish Undif	3	NR	152	467	2.6	3.8
METH–Un Methodist	5	288	1,196	1,500	8.3	12.1
Non-denom Chr Chs	4	270	235	338	1.9	2.7
Un C of Christ	2	139	464	563	3.1	4.5
CLINTON	**79**	**5,161**	**11,731**	**25,845**	**52.6**	**100.0**
ANG/EPIS–Episcopal	1	53	132	134	0.3	0.5
Bahá'í	0	NR	17	17	0.0	0.1
BAPT–Amer Bapt USA	2	160	261	318	0.6	1.2
BAPT–So Bapt Conv	3	123	271	331	0.7	1.3
Catholic	11	NR	NR	9,340	19.0	36.1
CGOD–Ch God (Ander)	1	20	NR	20	0.0	0.1
Ch of Nazarene	1	0	0	0	0.0	0.0
CHR–Chr Chs & Chs Cr	1	NR	144	176	0.4	0.7
Evan Free Ch	2	425	NR	425	0.9	1.6
Jehovah's Witness	2	NR	NR	NR	-	-
LDS–Comm of Christ	1	NR	119	119	0.2	0.5
LDS–L-D Saints	2	NR	NR	606	1.2	2.3
LUTH–Assoc Free Luth	1	NR	NR	NR	-	-
LUTH–Ch of Luth Br	1	130	66	176	0.4	0.7
LUTH–E.L.C.A.	12	1,141	3,631	4,840	9.9	18.7
LUTH–Luth–MO Synod	5	940	2,129	2,570	5.2	9.9
METH–AME	1	0	100	122	0.2	0.5
METH–Un Methodist	10	669	2,027	2,896	5.9	11.2
Muslim Est	1	134	NR	308	0.6	1.2
Nat Spirit Asso	2	NR	NR	NR	-	-
Non-denom Chr Chs	5	369	489	514	1.0	2.0
PENT–Assemb of God	2	58	35	128	0.3	0.5
PENT–Int Foursq Gos	1	443	663	809	1.6	3.1
PRES–Presb Ch (USA)	2	53	341	416	0.8	1.6
REF–Ref Ch in Am	1	70	152	177	0.4	0.7
Sev Day Adv	1	19	33	38	0.1	0.1
Un C of Christ	5	345	1,110	1,354	2.8	5.2
Unit Univ	1	9	11	11	0.0	0.0
Unity Ch	1	NR	NR	NR	-	-
CRAWFORD	**39**	**2,404**	**6,472**	**11,156**	**65.3**	**100.0**
ANG/EPIS–Episcopal	1	5	6	11	0.1	0.1
BAPT–Converge/BGC	2	150	NR	180	1.1	1.6
BAPT–So Bapt Conv	1	15	102	128	0.7	1.1
Catholic	5	NR	NR	2,791	16.3	25.0
Evan Free Ch	1	140	NR	140	0.8	1.3
Jehovah's Witness	1	NR	NR	NR	-	-
LDS–Comm of Christ	2	NR	378	378	2.2	3.4
LUTH–E.L.C.A.	1	41	149	187	1.1	1.7
LUTH–Luth–MO Synod	11	1,341	4,268	5,303	31.0	47.5
METH–Un Methodist	4	178	673	785	4.6	7.0
METH–Wesleyan	2	145	104	188	1.1	1.7
Non-denom Chr Chs	1	70	30	88	0.5	0.8
PENT–Assemb of God	1	50	25	50	0.3	0.4

Religious Group	Number of Congrega-tions	Number of Attendees	Number of Communicant, Confirmed, or Full Members	Adherents: Number of Adherents	Adherents: % of Total Pop.	Adherents: % of Total Adh.
PRES–Presb Ch (USA)	4	126	365	459	2.7	4.1
Un C of Christ	2	143	372	468	2.7	4.2
DALLAS	**80**	**14,576**	**20,620**	**36,992**	**55.9**	**100.0**
ANG/EPIS–Episcopal	1	25	51	51	0.1	0.1
Bahá'í	0	NR	14	14	0.0	0.0
BAPT–Reg Bapt Gen As	3	NR	NR	NR	-	-
BAPT–So Bapt Conv	3	337	262	344	0.5	0.9
BRETH–Ch of Brethren	2	92	300	394	0.6	1.1
BRETH–Grace Breth	1	NR	NR	NR	-	-
BRETH–Old Ord Rvr Br	1	NR	44	76	0.1	0.2
Catholic	4	NR	NR	7,733	11.7	20.9
Chr & Miss Al	1	126	49	250	0.4	0.7
CHR–Chr Ch (Disc)	5	237	1,396	1,831	2.8	4.9
CHR–Chr Chs & Chs Cr	1	NR	35	46	0.1	0.1
CHR–Chs of Christ	2	80	50	110	0.2	0.3
Christian Un	1	NR	NR	NR	-	-
Evan Free Ch	2	460	NR	460	0.7	1.2
FRND–Consrv Yr Mtgs	1	NR	78	102	0.2	0.3
FRND–Fr Un Mtg	2	NR	120	157	0.2	0.4
Jehovah's Witness	2	NR	NR	NR	-	-
LDS–L-D Saints	3	NR	NR	733	1.1	2.0
LUTH–E.L.C.A.	5	7,909	7,601	12,108	18.3	32.7
LUTH–Luth Cong Msn Chr	1	306	708	929	1.4	2.5
LUTH–Luth–MO Synod	5	402	1,085	1,312	2.0	3.5
LUTH–Wisc Ev Luth Syn	1	89	97	153	0.2	0.4
METH–Un Methodist	16	1,039	3,387	4,241	6.4	11.5
Non-denom Chr Chs	6	2,825	4,735	4,832	7.3	13.1
PENT–Assemb of God	5	326	103	484	0.7	1.3
PENT–Un Pent Ch Intl	2	NR	NR	NR	-	-
PRES–Presb Ch (USA)	3	130	260	341	0.5	0.9
REF–Ref Ch in Am	1	193	245	291	0.4	0.8
DAVIS	**26**	**736**	**2,541**	**4,233**	**48.4**	**100.0**
Ap Chr Ch-Amer	1	116	61	116	1.3	2.7
BAPT–Reg Bapt Gen As	2	NR	NR	NR	-	-
Catholic	1	NR	NR	111	1.3	2.6
Ch of Nazarene	1	24	40	59	0.7	1.4
CHR–Chr Ch (Disc)	1	100	655	850	9.7	20.1
CHR–Chr Chs & Chs Cr	1	NR	140	182	2.1	4.3
CHR–Chs of Christ	1	10	10	10	0.1	0.2
LUTH–E.L.C.A.	1	23	53	63	0.7	1.5
MENN–Amish Undif	9	NR	520	1,355	15.5	32.0
MENN–CG in Cr (Menn)	1	NR	86	112	1.3	2.6
MENN–Mennonite USA	1	80	119	154	1.8	3.6
METH–Un Methodist	4	287	827	1,117	12.8	26.4
Non-denom Chr Chs	1	30	30	38	0.4	0.9
PENT–Open Bible Std	1	66	NR	66	0.8	1.6
DECATUR	**30**	**730**	**2,005**	**2,840**	**33.6**	**100.0**
Ap Chr Ch-Amer	1	43	14	43	0.5	1.5
BAPT–So Bapt Conv	2	109	260	314	3.7	11.1
Catholic	2	NR	NR	195	2.3	6.9
CHR–Chr Chs & Chs Cr	1	NR	200	242	2.9	8.5
CHR–Chs of Christ	1	20	25	31	0.4	1.1
Ind Fund Churches	1	NR	NR	NR	-	-
LDS–Comm of Christ	4	NR	632	632	7.5	22.3
LUTH–Luth–MO Synod	1	30	64	73	0.9	2.6
MENN–Amish Undif	2	NR	98	259	3.1	9.1
MENN–Beachy Amish-Menn	1	142	89	142	1.7	5.0
MENN–Cons Menn Conf	1	35	14	17	0.2	0.6
METH–Un Methodist	6	106	323	543	6.4	19.1
Non-denom Chr Chs	1	130	150	162	1.9	5.7
PENT–Assemb of God	4	78	64	100	1.2	3.5
PRES–Presb Ch (USA)	2	37	72	87	1.0	3.1
DELAWARE	**31**	**1,072**	**3,609**	**12,453**	**70.1**	**100.0**
Bahá'í	0	NR	1	1	0.0	0.0
BAPT–Consrv Bapt	1	NR	NR	NR	-	-
Catholic	9	NR	NR	7,494	42.2	60.2
Evan Free Ch	1	65	NR	65	0.4	0.5
LDS–L-D Saints	1	NR	NR	187	1.1	1.5

NR–Not Reported   - Represents no adherents reported.   Percentages may not total 100 due to rounding.

Table 3: Religious Congregations by County and Group: 2010

Religious Group	Number of Congrega-tions	Number of Attendees	Number of Communicant, Confirmed, or Full Members	Adherents: Number of Adherents	Adherents: % of Total Pop.	Adherents: % of Total Adh.
LUTH–E.L.C.A.	4	296	1,107	1,414	8.0	11.4
LUTH–Luth–MO Synod	2	173	461	615	3.5	4.9
MENN–Amish Undif	0	NR	2	4	0.0	0.0
METH–Un Methodist	7	311	1,503	1,958	11.0	15.7
PENT–Assemb of God	1	24	13	71	0.4	0.6
PRES–Presb Ch (USA)	2	56	218	269	1.5	2.2
Un C of Christ	3	147	304	375	2.1	3.0
DES MOINES	**67**	**5,239**	**9,766**	**17,575**	**43.6**	**100.0**
ANG/EPIS–Episcopal	1	65	159	231	0.6	1.3
Ap Chr Ch-Amer	1	119	59	119	0.3	0.7
Bahá'í	0	NR	16	16	0.0	0.1
BAPT–Amer Bapt USA	2	344	481	587	1.5	3.3
BAPT–Converge/BGC	1	75	NR	90	0.2	0.5
BAPT–N Am Bapt Conf	2	NR	404	493	1.2	2.8
BAPT–NBC USA	1	0	0	0	0.0	0.0
BAPT–Reg Bapt Gen As	2	NR	NR	NR	-	-
BAPT–So Bapt Conv	2	73	71	87	0.2	0.5
Catholic	3	NR	NR	4,521	11.2	25.7
Ch of Nazarene	2	220	355	402	1.0	2.3
CHR–Chr Ch (Disc)	1	405	819	999	2.5	5.7
CHR–Chr Chs & Chs Cr	1	NR	180	220	0.5	1.3
CHR–Chs of Christ	1	80	73	82	0.2	0.5
CONG–Cong Chr, NA	1	NR	105	128	0.3	0.7
Evan Free Ch	1	38	NR	38	0.1	0.2
LDS–Comm of Christ	1	NR	119	119	0.3	0.7
LDS–L-D Saints	1	NR	NR	463	1.1	2.6
LUTH–E.L.C.A.	6	533	1,405	1,816	4.5	10.3
LUTH–Luth–MO Synod	1	0	87	111	0.3	0.6
LUTH–Wisc Ev Luth Syn	1	29	67	75	0.2	0.4
METH–AME	1	40	60	73	0.2	0.4
METH–Free Methodist	1	24	6	24	0.1	0.1
METH–Un Methodist	11	777	2,190	2,809	7.0	16.0
Non-denom Chr Chs	5	1,305	1,450	1,694	4.2	9.6
PENT–Assemb of God	1	300	110	300	0.7	1.7
PENT–COGIC	1	50	70	85	0.2	0.5
PENT–Int Foursq Gos	1	58	49	60	0.1	0.3
PENT–Open Bible Std	1	90	NR	90	0.2	0.5
PENT–Un Pent Ch Intl	1	NR	NR	NR	-	-
PRES–Cumber Presb	1	NR	27	27	0.1	0.2
PRES–Presb Ch (USA)	3	240	491	599	1.5	3.4
Salvation Army	1	30	49	183	0.5	1.0
Sev Day Adv	1	58	101	116	0.3	0.7
Un C of Christ	5	262	707	862	2.1	4.9
Unit Univ	1	24	56	56	0.1	0.3
DICKINSON	**26**	**3,402**	**6,123**	**12,518**	**75.1**	**100.0**
ANG/EPIS–Episcopal	1	64	119	119	0.7	1.0
Bahá'í	0	NR	7	7	0.0	0.1
BAPT–Converge/BGC	1	75	NR	90	0.5	0.7
Catholic	2	NR	NR	4,340	26.0	34.7
Evan Free Ch	1	450	NR	450	2.7	3.6
FRND–Fr Un Mtg	1	NR	27	32	0.2	0.3
Jehovah's Witness	1	NR	NR	NR	-	-
LUTH–E.L.C.A.	2	674	1,626	2,092	12.6	16.7
LUTH–Luth Cong Msn Chr	1	120	144	169	1.0	1.4
LUTH–Luth–MO Synod	3	341	1,009	1,169	7.0	9.3
LUTH–Wisc Ev Luth Syn	1	30	28	45	0.3	0.4
METH–Un Methodist	5	659	1,740	2,142	12.9	17.1
Non-denom Chr Chs	2	35	45	51	0.3	0.4
PENT–Open Bible Std	1	55	NR	55	0.3	0.4
PRES–Presb Ch (USA)	2	299	641	754	4.5	6.0
REF–Ref Ch in Am	1	516	540	771	4.6	6.2
Un C of Christ	1	84	197	232	1.4	1.9
DUBUQUE	**91**	**5,609**	**9,069**	**64,036**	**68.4**	**100.0**
ANG/EPIS–Episcopal	1	82	155	220	0.2	0.3
Bahá'í	0	NR	12	12	0.0	0.0
BAPT–Amer Bapt USA	1	54	47	58	0.1	0.1
BAPT–So Bapt Conv	3	322	235	288	0.3	0.4
Catholic	29	NR	NR	49,917	53.3	78.0
Ch of Nazarene	1	50	33	100	0.1	0.2
CHR–Chr Ch (Disc)	1	12	38	47	0.1	0.1
CHR–Chr Chs & Chs Cr	1	NR	200	245	0.3	0.4
CHR–Chs of Christ	1	10	8	10	0.0	0.0
Christian Brethren	3	NR	NR	NR	-	-
Evan Free Ch	1	900	NR	900	1.0	1.4
FRND–Fr Gen Cf	1	NR	11	13	0.0	0.0
Ind Fund Churches	1	NR	NR	NR	-	-
Jehovah's Witness	2	NR	NR	NR	-	-
JUD–Reform	1	15	26	70	0.1	0.1
LDS–L-D Saints	1	NR	NR	545	0.6	0.9
LUTH–E.L.C.A.	6	895	2,346	3,130	3.3	4.9
LUTH–Luth–MO Synod	3	370	1,117	1,572	1.7	2.5
METH–Un Methodist	6	695	1,543	2,108	2.3	3.3
Muslim Est	1	134	NR	308	0.3	0.5
Non-denom Chr Chs	10	1,160	1,419	1,594	1.7	2.5
ORTHE–Greek Orthodox	1	25	NR	70	0.1	0.1
PENT–Assemb of God	1	117	56	179	0.2	0.3
PENT–Ch God (Cleve)	1	13	13	16	0.0	0.0
PENT–Un Pent Ch Intl	1	NR	NR	NR	-	-
PENT–United Holy Ch	1	NR	NR	NR	-	-
PRES–Evan Presby Ch	1	NR	145	178	0.2	0.3
PRES–Presb Ch (USA)	3	258	681	834	0.9	1.3
Salvation Army	1	42	28	465	0.5	0.7
Sev Day Adv	1	33	57	66	0.1	0.1
Un C of Christ	5	387	855	1,047	1.1	1.6
Unit Univ	1	35	44	44	0.0	0.1
EMMET	**21**	**1,331**	**4,714**	**7,663**	**74.4**	**100.0**
Bahá'í	0	NR	2	2	0.0	0.0
BAPT–Converge/BGC	1	75	NR	90	0.9	1.2
Catholic	2	NR	NR	1,612	15.6	21.0
Ch of Nazarene	1	9	15	56	0.5	0.7
CHR–Chr Ch (Disc)	1	71	278	336	3.3	4.4
CHR–Chs of Christ	1	45	40	50	0.5	0.7
LUTH–E.L.C.A.	5	545	2,239	2,731	26.5	35.6
LUTH–Luth Cong Msn Chr	1	109	284	344	3.3	4.5
LUTH–Luth–MO Synod	1	112	277	309	3.0	4.0
METH–Free Methodist	1	19	9	19	0.2	0.2
METH–Un Methodist	4	286	1,072	1,511	14.7	19.7
PRES–Presb Ch (USA)	3	60	498	603	5.9	7.9
FAYETTE	**63**	**2,645**	**8,065**	**14,604**	**69.9**	**100.0**
ANG/EPIS–Episcopal	1	14	18	20	0.1	0.1
Ap Chr Ch-Amer	1	96	32	96	0.5	0.7
Bahá'í	0	NR	3	3	0.0	0.0
BAPT–Amer Bapt USA	2	112	219	263	1.3	1.8
BAPT–N Am Bapt Conf	1	NR	149	179	0.9	1.2
BAPT–Reg Bapt Gen As	1	NR	NR	NR	-	-
BAPT–So Bapt Conv	1	18	19	23	0.1	0.2
Catholic	6	NR	NR	4,019	19.2	27.5
CHR–Chr Chs & Chs Cr	2	NR	90	108	0.5	0.7
CHR–Chs of Christ	1	18	12	18	0.1	0.1
Evan Free Ch	2	152	NR	152	0.7	1.0
Jehovah's Witness	1	NR	NR	NR	-	-
LDS–L-D Saints	1	NR	NR	290	1.4	2.0
LUTH–Ch of Luth Br	1	85	140	205	1.0	1.4
LUTH–E.L.C.A.	14	1,204	4,562	5,703	27.3	39.1
LUTH–Luth Ch-Am Asc	1	NR	NR	NR	-	-
LUTH–Luth–MO Synod	4	214	607	716	3.4	4.9
LUTH–Nor Amer Luth C	1	NR	NR	NR	-	-
MENN–Amish Undif	1	NR	6	17	0.1	0.1
MENN–CG in Cr (Menn)	1	NR	56	67	0.3	0.5
METH–Un Methodist	11	437	1,510	1,881	9.0	12.9
METH–Wesleyan	2	99	85	129	0.6	0.9
PENT–Assemb of God	1	15	4	51	0.2	0.3
PENT–Int Foursq Gos	1	51	48	58	0.3	0.4
PRES–Presb Ch (USA)	3	112	475	571	2.7	3.9
Sev Day Adv	1	18	30	35	0.2	0.2
Un Breth in Cr	1	0	0	0	0.0	0.0
FLOYD	**36**	**2,139**	**4,369**	**9,595**	**58.9**	**100.0**
ANG/EPIS–Episcopal	1	9	13	13	0.1	0.1
Bahá'í	0	NR	4	4	0.0	0.0
BAPT–Amer Bapt USA	1	87	215	262	1.6	2.7

NR–Not Reported   - Represents no adherents reported.   Percentages may not total 100 due to rounding.

Table 3: Religious Congregations by County and Group: 2010

Religious Group	Number of Congregations	Number of Attendees	Number of Communicant, Confirmed, or Full Members	Adherents: Number of Adherents	Adherents: % of Total Pop.	Adherents: % of Total Adh.
BAPT–Reg Bapt Gen As	1	NR	NR	NR	-	-
Catholic	3	NR	NR	3,080	18.9	32.1
Chr & Miss Al	1	281	123	423	2.6	4.4
CHR–Chr Ch (Disc)	1	12	38	46	0.3	0.5
Evan Free Ch	1	55	NR	55	0.3	0.6
Jehovah's Witness	2	NR	NR	NR	-	-
LUTH–E.L.C.A.	5	648	1,439	2,328	14.3	24.3
LUTH–Wisc Ev Luth Syn	1	20	25	26	0.2	0.3
METH–Un Methodist	7	379	1,629	2,260	13.9	23.6
METH–Wesleyan	3	112	83	146	0.9	1.5
Non-denom Chr Chs	3	380	500	538	3.3	5.6
PENT–Assemb of God	1	50	0	50	0.3	0.5
PENT–Un Pent Ch Intl	1	NR	NR	NR	-	-
PRES–Presb Ch (USA)	1	41	123	150	0.9	1.6
Sev Day Adv	1	8	15	17	0.1	0.2
Un C of Christ	2	57	162	197	1.2	2.1
FRANKLIN	**30**	**1,679**	**4,599**	**6,902**	**64.6**	**100.0**
BAPT–Converge/BGC	1	75	NR	90	0.8	1.3
BAPT–So Bapt Conv	1	95	118	144	1.3	2.1
Catholic	2	NR	NR	1,129	10.6	16.4
CHR–Chr Ch (Disc)	1	36	191	233	2.2	3.4
CHR–Chr Chs & Chs Cr	1	NR	170	208	1.9	3.0
CHR–Chs of Christ	1	20	23	25	0.2	0.4
LDS–L-D Saints	1	NR	NR	130	1.2	1.9
LUTH–E.L.C.A.	4	269	944	1,285	12.0	18.6
LUTH–Luth Cong Msn Chr	1	150	75	92	0.9	1.3
LUTH–Luth–MO Synod	2	278	652	722	6.8	10.5
METH–Un Methodist	8	319	1,153	1,383	12.9	20.0
Non-denom Chr Chs	1	30	40	40	0.4	0.6
REF–Ref Ch in Am	2	176	513	543	5.1	7.9
Sev Day Adv	1	14	25	29	0.3	0.4
Un C of Christ	3	217	695	849	7.9	12.3
FREMONT	**26**	**565**	**2,069**	**3,147**	**42.3**	**100.0**
BAPT–Amer Bapt USA	1	20	195	235	3.2	7.5
Catholic	2	NR	NR	560	7.5	17.8
Ch of Nazarene	1	72	93	93	1.2	3.0
CHR–Chr Chs & Chs Cr	2	NR	239	288	3.9	9.2
CONG–Cong Chr Add'l	1	NR	75	90	1.2	2.9
LUTH–Luth–MO Synod	1	10	24	24	0.3	0.8
METH–Free Methodist	1	15	11	15	0.2	0.5
METH–Un Methodist	9	224	999	1,302	17.5	41.4
Non-denom Chr Chs	1	50	70	70	0.9	2.2
PENT–Assemb of God	1	18	0	33	0.4	1.0
PRES–Presb Ch (USA)	3	61	149	179	2.4	5.7
Un C of Christ	3	95	214	258	3.5	8.2
GREENE	**28**	**1,482**	**3,652**	**5,253**	**56.3**	**100.0**
BAPT–Amer Bapt USA	2	106	298	361	3.9	6.9
Catholic	4	NR	NR	880	9.4	16.8
CHR–Chr Ch (Disc)	1	90	250	303	3.2	5.8
CHR–Chr Chs & Chs Cr	1	NR	136	165	1.8	3.1
CHR–Chs of Christ	1	40	37	50	0.5	1.0
FRND–Fr Un Mtg	1	NR	0	0	0.0	0.0
Jehovah's Witness	1	NR	NR	NR	-	-
LDS–Comm of Christ	1	NR	158	158	1.7	3.0
LUTH–E.L.C.A.	1	48	121	138	1.5	2.6
LUTH–Luth–MO Synod	1	125	436	557	6.0	10.6
METH–Un Methodist	8	289	1,476	1,672	17.9	31.8
Non-denom Chr Chs	1	130	130	162	1.7	3.1
PENT–Assemb of God	1	390	340	390	4.2	7.4
PENT–Open Bible Std	1	90	NR	90	1.0	1.7
PRES–Presb Ch (USA)	3	174	270	327	3.5	6.2
GRUNDY	**35**	**2,163**	**5,111**	**7,577**	**60.8**	**100.0**
BAPT–Reg Bapt Gen As	3	NR	NR	NR	-	-
BRETH–Ch of Brethren	1	43	146	178	1.4	2.3
Catholic	1	NR	NR	1,064	8.5	14.0
CGOD–Ches God-Gen Con	1	30	80	97	0.8	1.3
LUTH–E.L.C.A.	3	230	552	807	6.5	10.7
LUTH–Luth–MO Synod	2	122	290	350	2.8	4.6

Religious Group	Number of Congregations	Number of Attendees	Number of Communicant, Confirmed, or Full Members	Adherents: Number of Adherents	Adherents: % of Total Pop.	Adherents: % of Total Adh.
METH–Un Methodist	7	367	1,430	1,907	15.3	25.2
Non-denom Chr Chs	1	100	150	150	1.2	2.0
PENT–Assemb of God	1	70	50	122	1.0	1.6
PRES–Presb Ch (USA)	5	395	733	893	7.2	11.8
PRES–Presb Ch Amer	1	138	291	395	3.2	5.2
REF–Christian Ref	3	255	357	435	3.5	5.7
REF–Ref Ch in Am	3	260	452	473	3.8	6.2
REF–Un Ref Chs N.A.	1	NR	NR	NR	-	-
Un C of Christ	2	153	580	706	5.7	9.3
GUTHRIE	**33**	**1,043**	**3,027**	**5,452**	**49.8**	**100.0**
Bahá'í	0	NR	1	1	0.0	0.0
BAPT–Reg Bapt Gen As	1	NR	NR	NR	-	-
BRETH–Ch of Brethren	1	0	53	65	0.6	1.2
Calv Chpl	1	NR	NR	NR	-	-
Catholic	4	NR	NR	1,616	14.8	29.6
CHR–Chr Ch (Disc)	2	127	333	407	3.7	7.5
CHR–Chr Chs & Chs Cr	3	NR	127	155	1.4	2.8
CHR–Chs of Christ	1	16	15	16	0.1	0.3
FRND–Fr Un Mtg	2	NR	97	118	1.1	2.2
LUTH–Luth–MO Synod	3	206	444	582	5.3	10.7
METH–Un Methodist	9	431	1,632	2,042	18.6	37.5
Non-denom Chr Chs	2	175	240	274	2.5	5.0
PENT–Assemb of God	1	24	2	62	0.6	1.1
PENT–Open Bible Std	1	14	NR	14	0.1	0.3
PRES–Presb Ch (USA)	1	38	62	76	0.7	1.4
Sev Day Adv	1	12	21	24	0.2	0.4
HAMILTON	**35**	**1,963**	**6,550**	**9,796**	**62.5**	**100.0**
ANG/EPIS–Episcopal	1	24	52	52	0.3	0.5
Bahá'í	0	NR	2	2	0.0	0.0
BAPT–Amer Bapt USA	1	41	289	354	2.3	3.6
BAPT–Converge/BGC	1	75	NR	90	0.6	0.9
BAPT–Reg Bapt Gen As	1	NR	NR	NR	-	-
Catholic	2	NR	NR	1,433	9.1	14.6
Chr & Miss Al	1	297	172	464	3.0	4.7
CHR–Chr Ch (Disc)	1	0	191	234	1.5	2.4
CHR–Chr Chs & Chs Cr	2	NR	490	601	3.8	6.1
CHR–Chs of Christ	1	10	10	10	0.1	0.1
Christian Brethren	1	NR	NR	NR	-	-
Evan Free Ch	1	14	NR	14	0.1	0.1
Jehovah's Witness	1	NR	NR	NR	-	-
LUTH–Assoc Free Luth	1	NR	NR	NR	-	-
LUTH–E.L.C.A.	3	387	1,574	1,873	12.0	19.1
LUTH–Luth Cong Msn Chr	3	267	885	1,085	6.9	11.1
LUTH–Luth–MO Synod	1	140	324	440	2.8	4.5
LUTH–Nor Amer Luth C	1	NR	NR	NR	-	-
METH–Un Methodist	7	385	1,685	2,123	13.5	21.7
Non-denom Chr Chs	1	140	235	235	1.5	2.4
PRES–Presb Ch (USA)	1	45	78	96	0.6	1.0
Un C of Christ	3	138	563	690	4.4	7.0
HANCOCK	**34**	**2,069**	**4,590**	**7,601**	**67.0**	**100.0**
BAPT–Reg Bapt Gen As	2	NR	NR	NR	-	-
Catholic	3	NR	NR	1,444	12.7	19.0
Ch of Nazarene	1	70	102	225	2.0	3.0
CONG–Consrv Cong Chr	1	180	337	410	3.6	5.4
Evan Free Ch	3	440	NR	440	3.9	5.8
LUTH–E.L.C.A.	6	348	1,024	1,318	11.6	17.3
LUTH–Luth Ch-Am Asc	1	NR	NR	NR	-	-
LUTH–Luth–MO Synod	2	233	792	1,034	9.1	13.6
METH–Un Methodist	7	329	1,563	1,798	15.9	23.7
PRES–Presb Ch (USA)	2	79	103	125	1.1	1.6
REF–Christian Ref	4	340	345	419	3.7	5.5
REF–Ref Ch in U.S.	1	NR	109	127	1.1	1.7
Un C of Christ	1	50	215	261	2.3	3.4
HARDIN	**56**	**3,645**	**8,549**	**11,746**	**67.0**	**100.0**
ANG/EPIS–Episcopal	1	15	28	28	0.2	0.2
Bahá'í	0	NR	4	4	0.0	0.0
BAPT–Amer Bapt USA	1	50	87	105	0.6	0.9
BAPT–Converge/BGC	1	400	NR	480	2.7	4.1

NR–Not Reported - Represents no adherents reported. Percentages may not total 100 due to rounding.

Table 3: Religious Congregations by County and Group: 2010

Religious Group	Number of Congrega-tions	Number of Attendees	Number of Communicant, Confirmed, or Full Members	Adherents		
				Number of Adherents	% of Total Pop.	% of Total Adh.
BAPT–N Am Bapt Conf	1	NR	272	327	1.9	2.8
BAPT–Reg Bapt Gen As	3	NR	NR	NR	-	-
Catholic	2	NR	NR	883	5.0	7.5
CGOD–Ch God (Ander)	1	23	NR	23	0.1	0.2
Ch of Nazarene	1	0	23	23	0.1	0.2
CHR–Chr Ch (Disc)	2	110	228	274	1.6	2.3
CHR–Chr Chs & Chs Cr	1	NR	60	72	0.4	0.6
Evan Free Ch	2	150	NR	150	0.9	1.3
FRND–Fr Un Mtg	2	NR	372	448	2.6	3.8
Jehovah's Witness	1	NR	NR	NR	-	-
LUTH–Assoc Free Luth	2	NR	NR	NR	-	-
LUTH–E.L.C.A.	3	401	982	1,280	7.3	10.9
LUTH–Luth–MO Synod	5	605	1,519	1,862	10.6	15.9
LUTH–Nor Amer Luth C	1	NR	NR	NR	-	-
METH–Un Methodist	9	620	2,358	2,606	14.9	22.2
Non-denom Chr Chs	4	380	525	582	3.3	5.0
PENT–Assemb of God	1	20	22	38	0.2	0.3
PENT–Open Bible Std	1	85	NR	85	0.5	0.7
PRES–Presb Ch (USA)	3	140	356	429	2.4	3.7
PRES–Presb Ch Amer	2	90	171	192	1.1	1.6
REF–Ref Ch in Am	1	80	139	166	0.9	1.4
Un C of Christ	5	476	1,403	1,689	9.6	14.4
HARRISON	**40**	**971**	**4,317**	**7,850**	**52.6**	**100.0**
Bahá'í	0	NR	1	1	0.0	0.0
BAPT–Amer Bapt USA	1	12	44	54	0.4	0.7
Catholic	5	NR	NR	1,969	13.2	25.1
Ch of Nazarene	1	46	93	108	0.7	1.4
Chr & Miss Al	1	57	33	91	0.6	1.2
CHR–Chr Ch (Disc)	1	0	0	0	0.0	0.0
CHR–Chr Chs & Chs Cr	5	NR	765	930	6.2	11.8
Evan Free Ch	1	25	NR	25	0.2	0.3
LDS–Comm of Christ	5	NR	945	945	6.3	12.0
LDS–L-D Saints	1	NR	NR	370	2.5	4.7
LUTH–E.L.C.A.	2	137	493	782	5.2	10.0
LUTH–Luth Cong Msn Chr	1	15	39	47	0.3	0.6
LUTH–Luth–MO Synod	3	276	603	752	5.0	9.6
METH–Un Methodist	10	336	1,189	1,632	10.9	20.8
PENT–Assemb of God	1	22	22	35	0.2	0.4
PRES–Presb Ch (USA)	2	45	90	109	0.7	1.4
HENRY	**49**	**2,222**	**5,188**	**9,322**	**46.3**	**100.0**
ANG/EPIS–Episcopal	1	22	36	36	0.2	0.4
Bahá'í	0	NR	8	8	0.0	0.1
BAPT–Amer Bapt USA	2	129	221	268	1.3	2.9
BAPT–Reg Bapt Gen As	1	NR	NR	NR	-	-
BAPT–So Bapt Conv	2	38	65	79	0.4	0.8
Catholic	1	NR	NR	1,085	5.4	11.6
CGOD–Ches God-Gen Con	1	15	43	52	0.3	0.6
Ch Cr, Scientst	1	NR	NR	NR	-	-
Ch of Nazarene	1	25	13	36	0.2	0.4
CHR–Chr Chs & Chs Cr	2	NR	363	440	2.2	4.7
CONG–Cong Chr, NA	1	NR	13	16	0.1	0.2
Evan Ch	1	NR	NR	NR	-	-
Evan Free Ch	1	120	NR	120	0.6	1.3
FRND–Fr Un Mtg	3	NR	186	226	1.1	2.4
Ind Fund Churches	1	NR	NR	NR	-	-
LDS–Comm of Christ	1	NR	119	119	0.6	1.3
LDS–L-D Saints	1	NR	NR	204	1.0	2.2
LUTH–E.L.C.A.	2	130	486	625	3.1	6.7
LUTH–Luth–MO Synod	1	140	369	407	2.0	4.4
MENN–Mennonite USA	5	503	849	1,030	5.1	11.0
METH–Un Methodist	9	467	1,511	3,250	16.1	34.9
Missionary Ch	1	29	19	29	0.1	0.3
Non-denom Chr Chs	3	138	135	172	0.9	1.8
PENT–Assemb of God	1	52	0	52	0.3	0.6
PENT–Open Bible Std	2	155	NR	155	0.8	1.7
PRES–Presb Ch (USA)	3	233	627	761	3.8	8.2
Un C of Christ	1	26	125	152	0.8	1.6
HOWARD	**27**	**1,054**	**3,225**	**7,950**	**83.1**	**100.0**
Bahá'í	0	NR	2	2	0.0	0.0
BAPT–Amer Bapt USA	1	18	25	31	0.3	0.4

Religious Group	Number of Congrega-tions	Number of Attendees	Number of Communicant, Confirmed, or Full Members	Adherents		
				Number of Adherents	% of Total Pop.	% of Total Adh.
Catholic	5	NR	NR	3,930	41.1	49.4
CONG–Consrv Cong Chr	1	65	80	99	1.0	1.2
LUTH–E.L.C.A.	5	402	1,352	1,727	18.1	21.7
LUTH–Luth–MO Synod	2	119	452	563	5.9	7.1
MENN–Amish Undif	2	NR	68	161	1.7	2.0
MENN–CG in Cr (Menn)	1	NR	121	150	1.6	1.9
METH–Un Methodist	7	318	988	1,131	11.8	14.2
Non-denom Chr Chs	1	90	110	112	1.2	1.4
PENT–Assemb of God	1	17	7	19	0.2	0.2
Un C of Christ	1	25	20	25	0.3	0.3
HUMBOLDT	**19**	**1,335**	**4,831**	**7,671**	**78.2**	**100.0**
BAPT–Amer Bapt USA	1	23	75	91	0.9	1.2
BAPT–Converge/BGC	1	75	NR	90	0.9	1.2
Catholic	2	NR	NR	1,317	13.4	17.2
Jehovah's Witness	1	NR	NR	NR	-	-
LUTH–E.L.C.A.	5	349	1,653	2,132	21.7	27.8
LUTH–Luth Cong Msn Chr	1	87	424	515	5.2	6.7
LUTH–Luth–MO Synod	2	311	841	1,080	11.0	14.1
LUTH–Nor Amer Luth C	2	NR	NR	NR	-	-
METH–Un Methodist	2	390	1,563	2,117	21.6	27.6
Non-denom Chr Chs	1	45	50	56	0.6	0.7
Un C of Christ	1	55	225	273	2.8	3.6
IDA	**21**	**1,455**	**3,949**	**5,971**	**84.2**	**100.0**
BAPT–Converge/BGC	1	75	NR	90	1.3	1.5
BAPT–So Bapt Conv	1	8	18	22	0.3	0.4
Catholic	2	NR	NR	988	13.9	16.5
Evan Free Ch	2	135	NR	135	1.9	2.3
LUTH–E.L.C.A.	1	190	780	951	13.4	15.9
LUTH–Luth Ch-Am Asc	1	NR	NR	NR	-	-
LUTH–Luth–MO Synod	4	538	1,536	1,757	24.8	29.4
METH–Un Methodist	6	342	1,184	1,498	21.1	25.1
Non-denom Chr Chs	1	20	20	25	0.4	0.4
PRES–Presb Ch (USA)	2	147	411	505	7.1	8.5
IOWA	**34**	**2,135**	**5,487**	**9,494**	**58.0**	**100.0**
Amana Ch Soc	1	NR	355	433	2.6	4.6
Bahá'í	0	NR	3	3	0.0	0.0
BAPT–N Am Bapt Conf	1	NR	95	116	0.7	1.2
BAPT–Reg Bapt Gen As	1	NR	NR	NR	-	-
BRETH–Grace Breth	1	NR	NR	NR	-	-
Catholic	4	NR	NR	2,633	16.1	27.7
Ch of Nazarene	1	16	19	19	0.1	0.2
CHR–Chr Ch (Disc)	1	0	180	220	1.3	2.3
Evan Free Ch	1	42	NR	42	0.3	0.4
Jehovah's Witness	1	NR	NR	NR	-	-
LUTH–E.L.C.A.	1	49	109	130	0.8	1.4
LUTH–Luth–MO Synod	8	1,066	2,638	3,179	19.4	33.5
MENN–Mennonite USA	1	200	293	358	2.2	3.8
METH–Un Methodist	8	441	1,066	1,504	9.2	15.8
Non-denom Chr Chs	1	100	150	150	0.9	1.6
PRES–Presb Ch (USA)	2	201	486	593	3.6	6.2
Un C of Christ	1	20	93	114	0.7	1.2
JACKSON	**32**	**1,486**	**4,038**	**11,866**	**59.8**	**100.0**
ANG/EPIS–Episcopal	1	21	42	42	0.2	0.4
Bahá'í	0	NR	3	3	0.0	0.0
BAPT–Amer Bapt USA	1	60	82	99	0.5	0.8
Catholic	9	NR	NR	6,843	34.5	57.7
Jehovah's Witness	1	NR	NR	NR	-	-
LDS–Comm of Christ	1	NR	119	119	0.6	1.0
LUTH–E.L.C.A.	8	805	2,533	3,170	16.0	26.7
METH–Un Methodist	4	229	693	783	3.9	6.6
Non-denom Chr Chs	1	200	105	250	1.3	2.1
PENT–Un Pent Ch Intl	1	NR	NR	NR	-	-
PRES–Presb Ch (USA)	3	84	239	289	1.5	2.4
Un C of Christ	2	87	222	268	1.4	2.3
JASPER	**64**	**5,318**	**10,097**	**16,127**	**43.8**	**100.0**
ANG/EPIS–Episcopal	1	61	102	154	0.4	1.0
Bahá'í	0	NR	4	4	0.0	0.0

NR–Not Reported - Represents no adherents reported. Percentages may not total 100 due to rounding.

Table 3: Religious Congregations by County and Group: 2010

Religious Group	Number of Congrega-tions	Number of Attendees	Number of Communicant, Confirmed, or Full Members	Adherents: Number of Adherents	Adherents: % of Total Pop.	Adherents: % of Total Adh.
BAPT–Amer Bapt USA	1	148	200	242	0.7	1.5
BAPT–Consrv Bapt	1	NR	NR	NR	-	-
BAPT–Reg Bapt Gen As	2	NR	NR	NR	-	-
BAPT–So Bapt Conv	1	16	7	8	0.0	0.0
BRETH–Ch of Brethren	1	62	229	277	0.8	1.7
Catholic	2	NR	NR	2,431	6.6	15.1
Ch of Nazarene	1	37	144	144	0.4	0.9
Chr & Miss Al	1	651	302	1,030	2.8	6.4
CHR–Chr Ch (Disc)	5	276	857	1,038	2.8	6.4
CHR–Chs of Christ	2	48	41	53	0.1	0.3
CONG–Consrv Cong Chr	1	55	149	181	0.5	1.1
Evan Free Ch	1	80	NR	80	0.2	0.5
FRND–Fr Un Mtg	2	NR	305	370	1.0	2.3
Ind Fund Churches	1	NR	NR	NR	-	-
LDS–Comm of Christ	2	NR	316	316	0.9	2.0
LDS–L-D Saints	1	NR	NR	287	0.8	1.8
LUTH–E.L.C.A.	3	200	616	767	2.1	4.8
LUTH–Luth-MO Synod	1	98	273	343	0.9	2.1
METH–Un Methodist	10	798	2,443	3,173	8.6	19.7
Non-denom Chr Chs	5	820	750	1,049	2.8	6.5
PENT–Assemb of God	2	154	94	209	0.6	1.3
PENT–Ch God (Cleve)	1	50	50	61	0.2	0.4
PENT–Int Foursq Gos	1	80	274	332	0.9	2.1
PENT–Un Pent Ch Intl	1	NR	NR	NR	-	-
PENT–Vineyard	1	57	60	73	0.2	0.5
PRES–Presb Ch (USA)	3	239	536	649	1.8	4.0
REF–Christian Ref	3	580	915	1,109	3.0	6.9
REF–Ref Ch in Am	2	600	790	863	2.3	5.4
Salvation Army	1	19	70	195	0.5	1.2
Sev Day Adv	1	14	25	29	0.1	0.2
Un C of Christ	3	175	545	660	1.8	4.1
JEFFERSON	**39**	**1,730**	**3,795**	**6,288**	**37.3**	**100.0**
Bahá'í	1	NR	31	31	0.2	0.5
BAPT–Amer Bapt USA	3	186	201	232	1.4	3.7
BAPT–Ind Bapt Flwsp Intl	1	NR	NR	NR	-	-
BAPT–Reg Bapt Gen As	1	NR	NR	NR	-	-
BAPT–So Bapt Conv	1	12	35	40	0.2	0.6
BRETH–Ch of Brethren	1	17	55	64	0.4	1.0
Catholic	1	NR	NR	1,020	6.1	16.2
Ch of Nazarene	1	38	66	116	0.7	1.8
CHR–Chr Ch (Disc)	2	140	575	664	3.9	10.6
CHR–Chr Chs & Chs Cr	1	NR	0	0	0.0	0.0
FRND–Fr Un Mtg	1	NR	285	329	2.0	5.2
HINDU–I/A Temples	1	NR	NR	238	1.4	3.8
HINDU–Post Ren	3	NR	NR	127	0.8	2.0
LDS–L-D Saints	1	NR	NR	343	2.0	5.5
LUTH–E.L.C.A.	1	105	348	369	2.2	5.9
LUTH–Luth Cong Msn Chr	1	95	121	140	0.8	2.2
LUTH–Luth-MO Synod	1	59	153	185	1.1	2.9
MENN–Amish Undif	1	NR	45	97	0.6	1.5
METH–Free Methodist	1	48	61	61	0.4	1.0
METH–Un Methodist	4	286	764	998	5.9	15.9
Non-denom Chr Chs	6	547	655	739	4.4	11.8
PENT–Assemb of God	1	15	15	50	0.3	0.8
PENT–Int Foursq Gos	1	96	177	204	1.2	3.2
PRES–Presb Ch (USA)	1	76	191	221	1.3	3.5
Sev Day Adv	1	10	17	20	0.1	0.3
Unity Ch	1	NR	NR	NR	-	-
JOHNSON	**110**	**11,043**	**19,053**	**46,278**	**35.4**	**100.0**
ANG/EPIS–Episcopal	2	258	655	655	0.5	1.4
Ap Chr Ch-Amer	1	57	24	57	0.0	0.1
Bahá'í	1	NR	81	81	0.1	0.2
BAPT–Amer Bapt USA	1	30	93	111	0.1	0.2
BAPT–Converge/BGC	2	150	NR	180	0.1	0.4
BAPT–Ind Bapt Flwsp Intl	1	NR	NR	NR	-	-
BAPT–N Am Bapt Conf	1	NR	NR	NR	-	-
BAPT–Reg Bapt Gen As	1	NR	NR	NR	-	-
BAPT–So Bapt Conv	3	390	594	706	0.5	1.5
BUDD–Theravada	1	NR	NR	14	0.0	0.0
BUDD–Vajrayana	1	NR	NR	457	0.3	1.0
Calv Chpl	1	NR	NR	NR	-	-
Catholic	9	NR	NR	15,691	12.0	33.9
Ch Cr, Scientst	2	NR	NR	NR	-	-
Ch of Nazarene	3	172	335	335	0.3	0.7
CHR–Chr Ch (Disc)	1	100	375	446	0.3	1.0
CHR–Chr Chs & Chs Cr	1	NR	183	218	0.2	0.5
CHR–Chs of Christ	1	45	50	65	0.0	0.1
Evan Free Ch	1	1,900	NR	1,900	1.5	4.1
FRND–Consrv Yr Mtgs	1	NR	58	69	0.1	0.1
HINDU–Post Ren	3	NR	NR	118	0.1	0.3
Jehovah's Witness	1	NR	NR	NR	-	-
JUD–Conserv	0	83	93	251	0.2	0.5
JUD–Reform	0	53	93	251	0.2	0.5
LDS–Comm of Christ	1	NR	119	119	0.1	0.3
LDS–L-D Saints	5	NR	NR	1,752	1.3	3.8
LUTH–E.L.C.A.	4	964	2,461	3,584	2.7	7.7
LUTH–Luth-MO Synod	4	522	1,266	1,693	1.3	3.7
MENN–Amish Undif	5	NR	353	858	0.7	1.9
MENN–Beachy Amish-Menn	1	228	135	228	0.2	0.5
MENN–Mennonite USA	1	232	303	360	0.3	0.8
METH–AME	1	0	150	178	0.1	0.4
METH–Free Methodist	1	45	50	50	0.0	0.1
METH–Un Methodist	16	2,080	5,953	8,586	6.6	18.6
Muslim Est	1	134	NR	308	0.2	0.7
Non-denom Chr Chs	11	1,600	2,185	2,250	1.7	4.9
ORTHE–Ant Orth of NA	1	55	NR	120	0.1	0.3
PENT–Assemb of God	2	245	135	448	0.3	1.0
PENT–Int Foursq Gos	1	31	36	43	0.0	0.1
PENT–Un Pent Ch Intl	1	NR	NR	NR	-	-
PENT–Vineyard	1	184	210	250	0.2	0.5
PRES–Presb Ch (USA)	4	665	1,903	2,263	1.7	4.9
PRES–Presb Ch Amer	2	173	143	240	0.2	0.5
REF–Christian Ref	1	85	85	101	0.1	0.2
REF–Ref Ch in Am	1	120	158	241	0.2	0.5
Salvation Army	1	94	82	82	0.1	0.2
Sev Day Adv	1	45	78	90	0.1	0.2
Un C of Christ	3	140	357	424	0.3	0.9
Unit Univ	1	163	257	405	0.3	0.9
JONES	**36**	**1,650**	**4,801**	**9,900**	**48.0**	**100.0**
ANG/EPIS–Episcopal	1	12	19	19	0.1	0.2
Bahá'í	0	NR	7	7	0.0	0.1
BAPT–Amer Bapt USA	1	60	79	95	0.5	1.0
BAPT–Reg Bapt Gen As	1	NR	NR	NR	-	-
BAPT–So Bapt Conv	1	12	89	107	0.5	1.1
Catholic	4	NR	NR	3,463	16.8	35.0
Ch of Nazarene	1	82	61	133	0.6	1.3
CHR–Chr Chs & Chs Cr	1	NR	200	241	1.2	2.4
Jehovah's Witness	1	NR	NR	NR	-	-
LUTH–E.L.C.A.	7	655	2,145	3,157	15.3	31.9
LUTH–Luth-MO Synod	1	100	310	386	1.9	3.9
METH–Un Methodist	7	246	908	1,144	5.5	11.6
Non-denom Chr Chs	1	150	200	200	1.0	2.0
PENT–Assemb of God	1	18	10	18	0.1	0.2
PENT–Int Foursq Gos	1	21	31	37	0.2	0.4
PENT–Un Pent Ch Intl	1	NR	NR	NR	-	-
PRES–Presb Ch (USA)	3	109	270	325	1.6	3.3
Un C of Christ	3	185	472	568	2.8	5.7
KEOKUK	**32**	**831**	**2,143**	**4,418**	**42.0**	**100.0**
Bahá'í	0	NR	2	2	0.0	0.0
BAPT–Amer Bapt USA	2	69	92	112	1.1	2.5
BRETH–Ch of Brethren	1	31	78	95	0.9	2.2
Catholic	3	NR	NR	1,582	15.1	35.8
CHR–Chr Ch (Disc)	4	43	241	292	2.8	6.6
Christian Un	1	NR	NR	NR	-	-
FRND–Fr Un Mtg	2	NR	119	144	1.4	3.3
LUTH–Luth-MO Synod	1	20	44	62	0.6	1.4
MENN–Amish Undif	1	NR	6	17	0.2	0.4
METH–Un Methodist	11	510	1,188	1,676	15.9	37.9
Non-denom Chr Chs	2	100	120	129	1.2	2.9
PRES–Presb Ch (USA)	4	58	253	307	2.9	6.9

NR–Not Reported - Represents no adherents reported. Percentages may not total 100 due to rounding.

Table 3: Religious Congregations by County and Group: 2010

Religious Group	Number of Congrega-tions	Number of Attendees	Number of Communicant, Confirmed, or Full Members	Adherents		
				Number of Adherents	% of Total Pop.	% of Total Adh.
KOSSUTH	**44**	**2,440**	**5,577**	**13,898**	**89.4**	**100.0**
ANG/EPIS–Episcopal	1	20	43	58	0.4	0.4
Bahá'í	0	NR	1	1	0.0	0.0
BAPT–Amer Bapt USA	1	14	23	28	0.2	0.2
BAPT–Consrv Bapt	1	NR	NR	NR	-	-
BAPT–Converge/BGC	1	75	NR	90	0.6	0.6
BAPT–Reg Bapt Gen As	1	NR	NR	NR	-	-
Catholic	7	NR	NR	6,733	43.3	48.4
Evan Free Ch	2	134	NR	134	0.9	1.0
Jehovah's Witness	1	NR	NR	NR	-	-
LUTH–E.L.C.A.	4	354	1,287	1,590	10.2	11.4
LUTH–Luth Cong Msn Chr	1	NR	NR	NR	-	-
LUTH–Luth-MO Synod	7	688	1,901	2,266	14.6	16.3
METH–Un Methodist	6	420	1,278	1,587	10.2	11.4
Non-denom Chr Chs	1	100	85	125	0.8	0.9
PENT–Assemb of God	1	125	66	220	1.4	1.6
PENT–Open Bible Std	1	23	NR	23	0.1	0.2
PRES–Presb Ch (USA)	5	251	410	493	3.2	3.5
PRES–Presb Ch Amer	1	116	166	186	1.2	1.3
REF–Ref Ch in Am	1	75	174	192	1.2	1.4
Un C of Christ	1	45	143	172	1.1	1.2
LEE	**72**	**4,025**	**9,168**	**18,016**	**50.2**	**100.0**
ANG/EPIS–Episcopal	2	54	148	172	0.5	1.0
Bahá'í	0	NR	8	8	0.0	0.0
BAPT–Amer Bapt USA	1	98	507	608	1.7	3.4
BAPT–So Bapt Conv	4	178	410	492	1.4	2.7
Catholic	7	NR	NR	6,389	17.8	35.5
Ch Cr, Scientst	1	NR	NR	NR	-	-
Ch of Nazarene	3	203	273	327	0.9	1.8
CHR–Chr Ch (Disc)	2	753	1,701	2,040	5.7	11.3
CHR–Chr Chs & Chs Cr	2	NR	515	618	1.7	3.4
CHR–Chs of Christ	2	36	34	38	0.1	0.2
Evan Free Ch	1	190	NR	190	0.5	1.1
Jehovah's Witness	2	NR	NR	NR	-	-
LDS–Comm of Christ	2	NR	238	238	0.7	1.3
LDS–L-D Saints	2	NR	NR	479	1.3	2.7
LUTH–E.L.C.A.	2	120	431	542	1.5	3.0
LUTH–Luth-MO Synod	2	44	95	124	0.3	0.7
MENN–Cons Menn Conf	1	25	20	24	0.1	0.1
MENN–Mennonite USA	1	44	127	152	0.4	0.8
METH–Un Methodist	9	428	1,577	1,817	5.1	10.1
Non-denom Chr Chs	8	1,027	1,430	1,480	4.1	8.2
PENT–Assemb of God	2	138	82	196	0.5	1.1
PENT–Int Foursq Gos	2	271	144	173	0.5	1.0
PENT–Un Pent Ch Intl	2	NR	NR	NR	-	-
PRES–Presb Ch (USA)	5	73	371	445	1.2	2.5
Salvation Army	1	17	17	221	0.6	1.2
Sev Day Adv	1	51	89	102	0.3	0.6
Un C of Christ	5	275	951	1,141	3.2	6.3
LINN	**203**	**25,421**	**46,751**	**111,583**	**52.8**	**100.0**
ANG/EPIS–Episcopal	2	236	587	755	0.4	0.7
Bahá'í	1	NR	110	110	0.1	0.1
BAPT–Amer Bapt USA	5	259	569	704	0.3	0.6
BAPT–Consrv Bapt	5	NR	NR	NR	-	-
BAPT–Converge/BGC	2	150	NR	180	0.1	0.2
BAPT–Ind Bapt Flwsp Intl	1	NR	NR	NR	-	-
BAPT–NBC USA	1	200	250	309	0.1	0.3
BAPT–Reg Bapt Gen As	1	NR	NR	NR	-	-
BAPT–So Bapt Conv	4	352	430	532	0.3	0.5
BRETH–Ch of Brethren	2	145	62	77	0.0	0.1
BRETH–Grace Breth	1	NR	NR	NR	-	-
BUDD–Mahayana	1	NR	NR	25	0.0	0.0
Calv Chpl	1	NR	NR	NR	-	-
Catholic	18	NR	NR	40,930	19.4	36.7
CGOD–Ch God (Ander)	1	18	NR	18	0.0	0.0
Ch Cr, Scientst	1	NR	NR	NR	-	-
Ch God (7th Day)	1	NR	NR	NR	-	-
Ch of Nazarene	3	503	626	2,204	1.0	2.0
Chr & Miss Al	1	55	36	101	0.0	0.1
CHR–Chr Ch (Disc)	7	457	1,233	1,525	0.7	1.4
CHR–Chr Chs & Chs Cr	3	NR	1,190	1,471	0.7	1.3
CHR–Chs of Christ	5	350	330	415	0.2	0.4
Christian Brethren	1	NR	NR	NR	-	-
Evan Free Ch	2	780	NR	780	0.4	0.7
FRND–Consrv Yr Mtgs	1	NR	40	49	0.0	0.0
HINDU–Trad Temples	1	NR	NR	800	0.4	0.7
Jehovah's Witness	2	NR	NR	NR	-	-
JUD–Reform	1	65	114	308	0.1	0.3
LDS–Comm of Christ	1	NR	119	119	0.1	0.1
LDS–L-D Saints	4	NR	NR	1,959	0.9	1.8
LUTH–E.L.C.A.	13	3,539	8,632	11,545	5.5	10.3
LUTH–Luth Cong Msn Chr	1	860	2,307	2,852	1.4	2.6
LUTH–Luth-MO Synod	9	1,883	4,387	5,650	2.7	5.1
LUTH–Wisc Ev Luth Syn	1	132	234	300	0.1	0.3
METH–AME	1	100	100	124	0.1	0.1
METH–Free Methodist	2	84	57	84	0.0	0.1
METH–Un Methodist	28	3,702	11,066	14,661	6.9	13.1
METH–Wesleyan	3	521	369	677	0.3	0.6
Muslim Est	3	518	NR	1,416	0.7	1.3
New Apost Ch	1	NR	NR	NR	-	-
Non-denom Chr Chs	21	4,765	6,445	7,070	3.3	6.3
ORTHE–Ant Orth of NA	1	180	NR	380	0.2	0.3
ORTHE–Greek Orthodox	1	40	NR	165	0.1	0.1
PENT–Assemb of God	3	2,069	852	3,726	1.8	3.3
PENT–Ch of God Proph	1	NR	33	41	0.0	0.0
PENT–Int Foursq Gos	1	82	68	84	0.0	0.1
PENT–Open Bible Std	2	300	NR	300	0.1	0.3
PENT–Un Pent Ch Intl	3	NR	NR	NR	-	-
PENT–Vineyard	2	250	350	433	0.2	0.4
PRES–Presb Ch (USA)	14	1,466	3,380	4,179	2.0	3.7
PRES–Presb Ch Amer	1	35	43	48	0.0	0.0
REF–Christian Ref	1	134	243	300	0.1	0.3
REF–Ref Ch in Am	1	421	668	820	0.4	0.7
Salvation Army	1	46	89	1,247	0.6	1.1
Sev Day Adv	2	272	474	545	0.3	0.5
Un C of Christ	4	362	1,078	1,333	0.6	1.2
Unit Univ	1	90	180	232	0.1	0.2
Unity Ch	1	NR	NR	NR	-	-
LOUISA	**23**	**1,207**	**2,471**	**3,886**	**34.1**	**100.0**
Ap Chr Ch-Amer	1	352	200	352	3.1	9.1
BAPT–So Bapt Conv	1	125	163	202	1.8	5.2
Catholic	1	NR	NR	493	4.3	12.7
CGOD–Ches God-Gen Con	1	15	15	19	0.2	0.5
Ch of Nazarene	1	38	47	71	0.6	1.8
Ind Fund Churches	1	NR	NR	NR	-	-
LUTH–Luth-MO Synod	1	46	65	92	0.8	2.4
METH–Free Methodist	1	12	14	14	0.1	0.4
METH–Un Methodist	7	400	1,355	1,863	16.4	47.9
Non-denom Chr Chs	1	25	17	31	0.3	0.8
PENT–Assemb of God	1	15	10	21	0.2	0.5
PRES–Presb Ch (USA)	5	137	525	650	5.7	16.7
PRES–Ref Pres of NA	1	42	60	78	0.7	2.0
LUCAS	**26**	**1,301**	**2,555**	**3,968**	**44.6**	**100.0**
ANG/EPIS–Episcopal	1	10	17	17	0.2	0.4
Bahá'í	0	NR	2	2	0.0	0.1
BAPT–Reg Bapt Gen As	1	NR	NR	NR	-	-
BAPT–So Bapt Conv	1	248	223	273	3.1	6.9
Catholic	1	NR	NR	607	6.8	15.3
Ch of Nazarene	1	93	99	120	1.3	3.0
CHR–Chr Ch (Disc)	1	65	294	360	4.0	9.1
CHR–Chs of Christ	2	44	50	60	0.7	1.5
Christian Un	1	NR	NR	NR	-	-
Jehovah's Witness	1	NR	NR	NR	-	-
LDS–Comm of Christ	1	NR	158	158	1.8	4.0
LUTH–E.L.C.A.	1	82	365	438	4.9	11.0
LUTH–Luth-MO Synod	1	45	63	74	0.8	1.9
MENN–Amish Undif	2	NR	85	214	2.4	5.4
METH–Un Methodist	3	50	654	712	8.0	17.9
Non-denom Chr Chs	3	520	425	654	7.3	16.5
PENT–Assemb of God	1	91	41	182	2.0	4.6
PENT–Ch God (Cleve)	1	6	3	4	0.0	0.1
PENT–Un Pent Ch Intl	1	NR	NR	NR	-	-

NR–Not Reported   - Represents no adherents reported.   Percentages may not total 100 due to rounding.

Table 3: Religious Congregations by County and Group: 2010

Religious Group	Number of Congrega-tions	Number of Attendees	Number of Communicant, Confirmed, or Full Members	Adherents: Number of Adherents	Adherents: % of Total Pop.	Adherents: % of Total Adh.
PRES–Presb Ch (USA)	2	47	76	93	1.0	2.3
LYON	**39**	**4,348**	**6,987**	**10,091**	**87.1**	**100.0**
Ap Chr Ch-Amer	1	745	304	745	6.4	7.4
Bahá'í	0	NR	1	1	0.0	0.0
BAPT–N Am Bapt Conf	3	NR	331	424	3.7	4.2
Catholic	3	NR	NR	1,266	10.9	12.5
CHR–Chr Ch (Disc)	1	30	57	73	0.6	0.7
CONG–Cong Chr Add'l	1	NR	56	72	0.6	0.7
Evan Cov Ch	1	57	60	74	0.6	0.7
LUTH–E.L.C.A.	4	367	1,184	1,421	12.3	14.1
LUTH–Luth Cong Msn Chr	1	46	122	156	1.3	1.5
LUTH–Luth–MO Synod	2	152	322	370	3.2	3.7
METH–Un Methodist	3	320	533	754	6.5	7.5
Non-denom Chr Chs	1	350	325	438	3.8	4.3
PENT–Assemb of God	1	37	26	59	0.5	0.6
PRES–Presb Ch (USA)	4	315	556	711	6.1	7.0
REF–Christian Ref	2	526	586	750	6.5	7.4
REF–Prot Ref Chs	1	159	106	177	1.5	1.8
REF–Ref Ch in Am	7	1,145	2,224	2,352	20.3	23.3
REF–Un Ref Chs N.A.	1	NR	NR	NR	-	-
Un C of Christ	2	99	194	248	2.1	2.5
MADISON	**34**	**1,791**	**3,759**	**6,020**	**38.4**	**100.0**
Bahá'í	0	NR	1	1	0.0	0.0
BAPT–Reg Bapt Gen As	1	NR	NR	NR	-	-
BAPT–So Bapt Conv	1	173	404	513	3.3	8.5
Catholic	2	NR	NR	810	5.2	13.5
Ch of Nazarene	1	33	72	72	0.5	1.2
CHR–Chr Ch (Disc)	3	176	815	1,034	6.6	17.2
CHR–Chr Chs & Chs Cr	2	NR	200	254	1.6	4.2
Evan Free Ch	2	345	NR	345	2.2	5.7
Jehovah's Witness	1	NR	NR	NR	-	-
LDS–L-D Saints	1	NR	NR	132	0.8	2.2
LUTH–E.L.C.A.	1	134	328	435	2.8	7.2
METH–Un Methodist	9	336	1,078	1,435	9.2	23.8
Non-denom Chr Chs	3	385	475	507	3.2	8.4
PENT–Int Foursq Gos	1	66	45	57	0.4	0.9
PENT–Un Pent Ch Intl	1	NR	NR	NR	-	-
PRES–Presb Ch (USA)	3	70	181	230	1.5	3.8
Sev Day Adv	1	41	71	82	0.5	1.4
Un C of Christ	1	32	89	113	0.7	1.9
MAHASKA	**49**	**3,944**	**7,258**	**9,931**	**44.4**	**100.0**
ANG/EPIS–Episcopal	1	26	70	70	0.3	0.7
Bahá'í	0	NR	5	5	0.0	0.1
BAPT–Amer Bapt USA	2	55	94	116	0.5	1.2
BAPT–Reg Bapt Gen As	1	NR	NR	NR	-	-
Catholic	1	NR	NR	1,040	4.6	10.5
Ch of Nazarene	2	296	502	502	2.2	5.1
CHR–Chr Ch (Disc)	1	217	513	633	2.8	6.4
CHR–Chr Chs & Chs Cr	1	NR	40	49	0.2	0.5
CHR–Chs of Christ	1	34	25	39	0.2	0.4
Evan Ch	1	NR	NR	NR	-	-
FRND–Fr Un Mtg	2	NR	233	288	1.3	2.9
LDS–Comm of Christ	1	NR	158	158	0.7	1.6
LDS–L-D Saints	1	NR	NR	192	0.9	1.9
LUTH–Luth–MO Synod	1	78	257	322	1.4	3.2
LUTH–Wisc Ev Luth Syn	1	93	133	165	0.7	1.7
MENN–Amish Undif	1	NR	6	17	0.1	0.2
METH–Evan Meth Ch	1	NR	NR	NR	-	-
METH–Free Methodist	1	62	34	62	0.3	0.6
METH–Un Methodist	8	595	1,784	2,035	9.1	20.5
Non-denom Chr Chs	5	600	725	806	3.6	8.1
PENT–Assemb of God	2	344	232	457	2.0	4.6
PENT–Ch God (Cleve)	1	32	49	60	0.3	0.6
PENT–Open Bible Std	1	55	NR	55	0.2	0.6
PENT–Un Pent Ch Intl	1	NR	NR	NR	-	-
PRES–Presb Ch (USA)	2	112	212	262	1.2	2.6
REF–Christian Ref	5	850	1,219	1,505	6.7	15.2
REF–Ref Ch in Am	2	460	733	804	3.6	8.1
Un C of Christ	2	35	234	289	1.3	2.9
MARION	**71**	**7,888**	**13,294**	**20,064**	**60.2**	**100.0**
Bahá'í	0	NR	4	4	0.0	0.0
BAPT–Amer Bapt USA	2	200	672	832	2.5	4.1
BAPT–Converge/BGC	1	75	NR	90	0.3	0.4
BAPT–Reg Bapt Gen As	2	NR	NR	NR	-	-
BAPT–So Bapt Conv	1	50	11	14	0.0	0.1
Catholic	3	NR	NR	2,368	7.1	11.8
Ch of Nazarene	2	108	211	252	0.8	1.3
CHR–Chr Ch (Disc)	2	109	500	619	1.9	3.1
CHR–Chr Chs & Chs Cr	4	NR	301	372	1.1	1.9
CHR–Chs of Christ	1	50	48	80	0.2	0.4
Evan Free Ch	1	350	NR	350	1.1	1.7
Ind Fund Churches	1	NR	NR	NR	-	-
Jehovah's Witness	1	NR	NR	NR	-	-
LDS–Comm of Christ	1	NR	158	158	0.5	0.8
LDS–L-D Saints	1	NR	NR	212	0.6	1.1
LUTH–E.L.C.A.	2	297	589	820	2.5	4.1
LUTH–Luth–MO Synod	2	146	443	565	1.7	2.8
METH–Free Methodist	1	15	17	17	0.1	0.1
METH–Un Methodist	13	625	1,966	2,568	7.7	12.8
Non-denom Chr Chs	3	155	220	220	0.7	1.1
ORTHE–Orth Ch in Amer	1	25	NR	40	0.1	0.2
PENT–Assemb of God	2	81	16	133	0.4	0.7
PENT–Ch God (Cleve)	1	19	27	33	0.1	0.2
PENT–Int Foursq Gos	1	27	32	40	0.1	0.2
PENT–Open Bible Std	1	60	NR	60	0.2	0.3
PENT–Un Pent Ch Intl	2	NR	NR	NR	-	-
PRES–Orth Pres Ch	1	0	0	0	0.0	0.0
PRES–Presb Ch (USA)	1	45	103	127	0.4	0.6
REF–Christian Ref	7	1,936	2,600	3,217	9.7	16.0
REF–Comm Ref Evan	1	NR	NR	NR	-	-
REF–Ref Ch in Am	7	3,470	5,298	6,783	20.4	33.8
REF–Un Ref Chs N.A.	1	NR	NR	NR	-	-
Sev Day Adv	1	45	78	90	0.3	0.4
MARSHALL	**63**	**4,465**	**10,769**	**21,837**	**53.7**	**100.0**
ANG/EPIS–Episcopal	1	28	60	82	0.2	0.4
Bahá'í	0	NR	23	23	0.1	0.1
BAPT–Amer Bapt USA	2	794	933	1,158	2.8	5.3
BAPT–Reg Bapt Gen As	1	NR	NR	NR	-	-
BAPT–So Bapt Conv	1	38	67	83	0.2	0.4
BRETH–Ch of Brethren	1	0	107	133	0.3	0.6
Catholic	3	NR	NR	7,364	18.1	33.7
CGOD–Ch God (Ander)	1	20	NR	20	0.0	0.1
Ch of Nazarene	1	87	146	252	0.6	1.2
CHR–Chr Ch (Disc)	1	100	532	660	1.6	3.0
CHR–Chr Chs & Chs Cr	2	NR	1,000	1,241	3.1	5.7
CHR–Chs of Christ	2	110	95	135	0.3	0.6
CONG–Cong Chr, NA	2	NR	353	438	1.1	2.0
Evan Free Ch	1	250	NR	250	0.6	1.1
FRND–Fr Un Mtg	3	NR	417	518	1.3	2.4
FRND–Unaffl Mtgs	1	NR	NR	NR	-	-
Jehovah's Witness	1	NR	NR	NR	-	-
LDS–Comm of Christ	1	NR	158	158	0.4	0.7
LDS–L-D Saints	1	NR	NR	403	1.0	1.8
LUTH–E.L.C.A.	4	609	1,493	1,955	4.8	9.0
LUTH–Luth–MO Synod	4	384	920	1,177	2.9	5.4
METH–Un Methodist	9	648	2,506	2,830	7.0	13.0
Non-denom Chr Chs	5	645	847	920	2.3	4.2
PENT–Assemb of God	1	92	0	130	0.3	0.6
PENT–Open Bible Std	1	40	NR	40	0.1	0.2
PENT–Pent Ch of God	1	70	NR	109	0.3	0.5
PENT–Un Pent Ch Intl	1	NR	NR	NR	-	-
PENT–Vineyard	1	60	80	99	0.2	0.5
PRES–Presb Ch (USA)	3	208	445	552	1.4	2.5
Salvation Army	1	32	69	470	1.2	2.2
Sev Day Adv	1	39	68	78	0.2	0.4
Un C of Christ	5	211	450	559	1.4	2.6
MILLS	**27**	**1,068**	**3,147**	**5,876**	**39.0**	**100.0**
ANG/EPIS–Episcopal	1	17	17	17	0.1	0.3
Bahá'í	0	NR	1	1	0.0	0.0
BAPT–Amer Bapt USA	2	97	393	487	3.2	8.3

NR–Not Reported - Represents no adherents reported. Percentages may not total 100 due to rounding.

Table 3: Religious Congregations by County and Group: 2010

Religious Group	Number of Congregations	Number of Attendees	Number of Communicant, Confirmed, or Full Members	Adherents: Number of Adherents	Adherents: % of Total Pop.	Adherents: % of Total Adh.
BAPT–So Bapt Conv	1	51	86	106	0.7	1.8
Catholic	1	NR	NR	1,295	8.6	22.0
Ch of Nazarene	1	0	33	33	0.2	0.6
CHR–Chr Chs & Chs Cr	1	NR	40	50	0.3	0.9
Evan Free Ch	1	125	NR	125	0.8	2.1
LDS–L-D Saints	1	NR	NR	415	2.8	7.1
LUTH–E.L.C.A.	1	85	458	592	3.9	10.1
LUTH–Luth-MO Synod	2	161	423	541	3.6	9.2
METH–Un Methodist	10	346	1,342	1,819	12.1	31.0
Non-denom Chr Chs	2	125	180	181	1.2	3.1
PRES–Presb Ch (USA)	1	10	17	21	0.1	0.4
Sev Day Adv	1	8	14	16	0.1	0.3
Un C of Christ	1	43	143	177	1.2	3.0
MITCHELL	**26**	**1,446**	**3,860**	**7,222**	**67.0**	**100.0**
Bahá'í	0	NR	6	6	0.1	0.1
BAPT–Amer Bapt USA	2	35	135	166	1.5	2.3
BAPT–Reg Bapt Gen As	1	NR	NR	NR	-	-
Catholic	3	NR	NR	2,357	21.9	32.6
Chr & Miss Al	1	94	66	138	1.3	1.9
LUTH–E.L.C.A.	5	672	1,905	2,369	22.0	32.8
LUTH–Evan Luth Syn	1	10	14	14	0.1	0.2
LUTH–Luth-MO Synod	3	255	697	888	8.2	12.3
LUTH–Nor Amer Luth C	1	NR	NR	NR	-	-
MENN–Amish Undif	2	NR	82	223	2.1	3.1
MENN–CG in Cr (Menn)	1	NR	84	103	1.0	1.4
METH–Un Methodist	3	178	556	569	5.3	7.9
Non-denom Chr Chs	1	100	100	125	1.2	1.7
Un C of Christ	2	102	215	264	2.4	3.7
MONONA	**27**	**938**	**3,397**	**5,440**	**58.9**	**100.0**
Bahá'í	0	NR	1	1	0.0	0.0
Catholic	4	NR	NR	1,207	13.1	22.2
CHR–Chr Ch (Disc)	1	45	185	222	2.4	4.1
CHR–Chr Chs & Chs Cr	3	NR	480	575	6.2	10.6
Evan Free Ch	1	100	NR	100	1.1	1.8
Jehovah's Witness	1	NR	NR	NR	-	-
LUTH–E.L.C.A.	3	161	900	1,047	11.3	19.2
LUTH–Luth-MO Synod	2	192	717	889	9.6	16.3
METH–Un Methodist	4	164	590	735	8.0	13.5
Non-denom Chr Chs	2	120	95	150	1.6	2.8
PENT–Un Pent Ch Intl	1	NR	NR	NR	-	-
Un C of Christ	5	156	429	514	5.6	9.4
MONROE	**18**	**843**	**1,721**	**3,802**	**47.7**	**100.0**
ANG/EPIS–Episcopal	1	9	20	22	0.3	0.6
Bahá'í	0	NR	1	1	0.0	0.0
BAPT–Amer Bapt USA	1	25	83	102	1.3	2.7
BAPT–So Bapt Conv	1	25	25	31	0.4	0.8
BRETH–Ch of Brethren	1	0	9	11	0.1	0.3
Catholic	4	NR	NR	1,583	19.9	41.6
CHR–Chr Ch (Disc)	1	105	471	576	7.2	15.1
CHR–Chr Chs & Chs Cr	1	NR	0	0	0.0	0.0
Jehovah's Witness	1	NR	NR	NR	-	-
LUTH–E.L.C.A.	1	48	148	205	2.6	5.4
METH–Un Methodist	2	246	637	793	9.9	20.9
Non-denom Chr Chs	2	240	290	312	3.9	8.2
PENT–Open Bible Std	1	123	NR	123	1.5	3.2
Sev Day Adv	1	22	37	43	0.5	1.1
MONTGOMERY	**30**	**1,516**	**3,863**	**5,682**	**52.9**	**100.0**
ANG/EPIS–Episcopal	1	17	16	16	0.1	0.3
BAPT–Amer Bapt USA	1	36	91	110	1.0	1.9
Catholic	2	NR	NR	605	5.6	10.6
Ch of Nazarene	1	30	33	48	0.4	0.8
Chr & Miss Al	1	250	111	402	3.7	7.1
CHR–Chr Ch (Disc)	1	58	414	501	4.7	8.8
CHR–Chr Chs & Chs Cr	2	NR	175	212	2.0	3.7
Evan Cov Ch	2	111	184	145	1.4	2.6
Jehovah's Witness	1	NR	NR	NR	-	-
LUTH–E.L.C.A.	4	343	1,225	1,578	14.7	27.8
LUTH–Luth-MO Synod	2	103	212	250	2.3	4.4

Religious Group	Number of Congregations	Number of Attendees	Number of Communicant, Confirmed, or Full Members	Adherents: Number of Adherents	Adherents: % of Total Pop.	Adherents: % of Total Adh.
METH–Un Methodist	6	344	1,014	1,311	12.2	23.1
Non-denom Chr Chs	1	65	40	81	0.8	1.4
PENT–Assemb of God	1	18	20	26	0.2	0.5
PRES–Presb Ch (USA)	3	107	251	304	2.8	5.4
Un C of Christ	1	34	77	93	0.9	1.6
MUSCATINE	**65**	**3,583**	**8,047**	**17,603**	**41.2**	**100.0**
ANG/EPIS–Episcopal	1	44	111	124	0.3	0.7
Bahá'í	0	NR	14	14	0.0	0.1
BAPT–Consrv Bapt	2	NR	NR	NR	-	-
BAPT–Converge/BGC	2	150	NR	180	0.4	1.0
BAPT–Reg Bapt Gen As	2	NR	NR	NR	-	-
BAPT–So Bapt Conv	2	84	141	177	0.4	1.0
Catholic	4	NR	NR	6,120	14.3	34.8
Ch of Nazarene	1	0	45	45	0.1	0.3
CHR–Chr Ch (Disc)	3	60	385	482	1.1	2.7
CHR–Chr Chs & Chs Cr	1	NR	40	50	0.1	0.3
CHR–Chs of Christ	1	110	110	150	0.4	0.9
Evan Free Ch	1	200	NR	200	0.5	1.1
FRND–Fr Un Mtg	1	NR	44	55	0.1	0.3
Jehovah's Witness	1	NR	NR	NR	-	-
LDS–Comm of Christ	1	NR	119	119	0.3	0.7
LDS–L-D Saints	1	NR	NR	546	1.3	3.1
LUTH–E.L.C.A.	6	526	1,626	2,071	4.8	11.8
LUTH–Luth-MO Synod	2	261	619	770	1.8	4.4
MENN–Mennonite USA	1	NR	NR	NR	-	-
METH–Un Methodist	12	917	2,708	3,387	7.9	19.2
Non-denom Chr Chs	3	258	310	348	0.8	2.0
PENT–Assemb of God	3	278	121	407	1.0	2.3
PENT–Ch God (Cleve)	1	102	29	36	0.1	0.2
PENT–Int Foursq Gos	1	22	117	147	0.3	0.8
PENT–Open Bible Std	1	0	NR	0	0.0	0.0
PENT–Un Pent Ch Intl	1	NR	NR	NR	-	-
PENT–Vineyard	1	127	170	213	0.5	1.2
PRES–Presb Ch (USA)	4	186	573	718	1.7	4.1
Salvation Army	1	13	42	355	0.8	2.0
Sev Day Adv	1	92	160	184	0.4	1.0
Un C of Christ	3	153	563	705	1.6	4.0
O'BRIEN	**44**	**3,905**	**8,079**	**11,046**	**76.7**	**100.0**
BAPT–NT Ind Bapt	1	NR	NR	NR	-	-
Catholic	5	NR	NR	1,388	9.6	12.6
CGOD–Ches God-Gen Con	1	45	23	28	0.2	0.3
CHR–Chr Chs & Chs Cr	2	NR	170	208	1.4	1.9
Evan Free Ch	2	95	NR	95	0.7	0.9
FRND–Consrv Yr Mtgs	1	NR	75	92	0.6	0.8
LUTH–E.L.C.A.	2	89	206	250	1.7	2.3
LUTH–Luth-MO Synod	6	670	1,746	2,133	14.8	19.3
LUTH–Nor Amer Luth C	1	NR	NR	NR	-	-
METH–Un Methodist	6	571	1,523	1,911	13.3	17.3
Non-denom Chr Chs	1	45	50	56	0.4	0.5
PENT–Assemb of God	1	56	41	81	0.6	0.7
PENT–Intl Pent Holiness	1	60	29	35	0.2	0.3
PRES–Presb Ch (USA)	2	125	267	326	2.3	3.0
REF–Christian Ref	3	725	1,071	1,308	9.1	11.8
REF–Ref Ch in Am	5	1,174	2,253	2,372	16.5	21.5
REF–Un Ref Chs N.A.	1	NR	NR	NR	-	-
Un C of Christ	3	250	625	763	5.3	6.9
OSCEOLA	**22**	**1,428**	**2,805**	**4,635**	**71.7**	**100.0**
BAPT–Consrv Bapt	1	NR	NR	NR	-	-
Catholic	2	NR	NR	835	12.9	18.0
Ind Fund Churches	1	NR	NR	NR	-	-
LUTH–E.L.C.A.	2	195	305	874	13.5	18.9
LUTH–Luth-MO Synod	3	177	387	426	6.6	9.2
METH–Un Methodist	5	123	558	656	10.2	14.2
Non-denom Chr Chs	1	50	35	62	1.0	1.3
PRES–Presb Ch (USA)	2	221	437	529	8.2	11.4
REF–Christian Ref	2	245	372	450	7.0	9.7
REF–Ref Ch in Am	2	385	660	741	11.5	16.0
Un C of Christ	1	32	51	62	1.0	1.3

NR–Not Reported   - Represents no adherents reported.   Percentages may not total 100 due to rounding.

Table 3: Religious Congregations by County and Group: 2010

Religious Group	Number of Congrega-tions	Number of Attendees	Number of Communicant, Confirmed, or Full Members	Adherents		
				Number of Adherents	% of Total Pop.	% of Total Adh.
PAGE	**54**	**2,307**	**6,228**	**9,240**	**58.0**	**100.0**
ANG/EPIS–Episcopal	1	20	43	43	0.3	0.5
Bahá'í	0	NR	1	1	0.0	0.0
BAPT–Amer Bapt USA	2	130	188	224	1.4	2.4
BAPT–So Bapt Conv	2	68	265	315	2.0	3.4
Calv Chpl	1	NR	NR	NR	-	-
Catholic	2	NR	NR	774	4.9	8.4
CGOD–Ches God-Gen Con	1	10	52	62	0.4	0.7
Ch of Nazarene	2	12	46	46	0.3	0.5
Chr & Miss Al	1	95	51	136	0.9	1.5
CHR–Chr Ch (Disc)	3	151	547	651	4.1	7.0
CHR–Chr Chs & Chs Cr	1	NR	50	59	0.4	0.6
CHR–Chs of Christ	1	20	20	20	0.1	0.2
Evan Cov Ch	1	32	71	42	0.3	0.5
Jehovah's Witness	1	NR	NR	NR	-	-
LDS–Comm of Christ	1	NR	189	189	1.2	2.0
LDS–L-D Saints	1	NR	NR	455	2.9	4.9
LUTH–E.L.C.A.	5	230	930	1,138	7.1	12.3
LUTH–Luth-MO Synod	4	432	1,166	1,534	9.6	16.6
LUTH–Wisc Ev Luth Syn	1	14	20	20	0.1	0.2
METH–Free Methodist	1	42	36	42	0.3	0.5
METH–Un Methodist	8	349	1,441	2,013	12.6	21.8
Missionary Ch	2	200	127	200	1.3	2.2
PENT–Assemb of God	2	240	137	265	1.7	2.9
PENT–Ch God (Cleve)	1	23	82	98	0.6	1.1
PENT–Ch of God Proph	1	NR	9	11	0.1	0.1
PENT–Intl Pent Holiness	1	21	19	23	0.1	0.2
PRES–Presb Ch (USA)	5	130	573	681	4.3	7.4
PRES–Ref Pres of NA	1	24	23	29	0.2	0.3
Un C of Christ	1	64	142	169	1.1	1.8
PALO ALTO	**28**	**1,361**	**3,498**	**7,250**	**77.0**	**100.0**
ANG/EPIS–Episcopal	1	8	13	19	0.2	0.3
Ap Chr Ch-Amer	1	461	204	461	4.9	6.4
BAPT–Reg Bapt Gen As	1	NR	NR	NR	-	-
Catholic	7	NR	NR	2,798	29.7	38.6
LUTH–E.L.C.A.	4	266	898	1,097	11.6	15.1
LUTH–Luth-MO Synod	5	302	764	932	9.9	12.9
LUTH–Nor Amer Luth C	1	NR	NR	NR	-	-
METH–Un Methodist	7	290	1,613	1,892	20.1	26.1
PENT–Assemb of God	1	34	6	51	0.5	0.7
PLYMOUTH	**51**	**3,102**	**7,492**	**18,418**	**73.7**	**100.0**
ANG/EPIS–Episcopal	1	4	7	7	0.0	0.0
Bahá'í	0	NR	8	8	0.0	0.0
BAPT–Amer Bapt USA	1	32	25	31	0.1	0.2
BAPT–So Bapt Conv	1	37	40	50	0.2	0.3
Catholic	10	NR	NR	8,529	34.1	46.3
Ch of Nazarene	1	29	40	52	0.2	0.3
CHR–Chr Chs & Chs Cr	2	NR	126	157	0.6	0.9
CHR–Chs of Christ	1	64	55	80	0.3	0.4
Evan Ch	1	NR	NR	NR	-	-
LUTH–E.L.C.A.	11	972	3,036	4,028	16.1	21.9
LUTH–Luth-MO Synod	4	525	1,387	1,764	7.1	9.6
METH–Un Methodist	8	544	1,698	2,280	9.1	12.4
Non-denom Chr Chs	1	400	375	500	2.0	2.7
PENT–Assemb of God	1	76	46	136	0.5	0.7
PRES–Presb Ch (USA)	2	88	173	215	0.9	1.2
REF–Christian Ref	1	NR	165	205	0.8	1.1
REF–Ref Ch in Am	1	144	132	153	0.6	0.8
Un C of Christ	4	187	179	223	0.9	1.2
POCAHONTAS	**24**	**749**	**2,466**	**4,545**	**62.2**	**100.0**
BAPT–Reg Bapt Gen As	1	NR	NR	NR	-	-
BAPT–So Bapt Conv	1	22	20	24	0.3	0.5
Catholic	5	NR	NR	1,721	23.5	37.9
CHR–Chr Ch (Disc)	1	27	137	163	2.2	3.6
LUTH–E.L.C.A.	6	392	1,128	1,333	18.2	29.3
LUTH–Luth Cong Msn Chr	1	40	82	98	1.3	2.2
LUTH–Luth-MO Synod	1	12	28	30	0.4	0.7
LUTH–Nor Amer Luth C	2	NR	NR	NR	-	-
METH–Un Methodist	3	237	914	989	13.5	21.8

Religious Group	Number of Congrega-tions	Number of Attendees	Number of Communicant, Confirmed, or Full Members	Adherents		
				Number of Adherents	% of Total Pop.	% of Total Adh.
PRES–Presb Ch (USA)	2	0	109	130	1.8	2.9
Un C of Christ	1	19	48	57	0.8	1.3
POLK	**402**	**53,160**	**85,956**	**193,762**	**45.0**	**100.0**
ANG/EPIS–Episcopal	6	609	1,638	2,226	0.5	1.1
Bahá'í	1	NR	135	135	0.0	0.1
BAPT–Amer Bapt USA	8	595	985	1,236	0.3	0.6
BAPT–Consrv Bapt	1	NR	NR	NR	-	-
BAPT–Converge/BGC	4	300	NR	360	0.1	0.2
BAPT–Natl Mis Bapt Conv	1	0	150	188	0.0	0.1
BAPT–NBC USA	7	1,075	2,480	3,113	0.7	1.6
BAPT–Reg Bapt Gen As	14	NR	NR	NR	-	-
BAPT–So Bapt Conv	13	2,653	3,896	4,890	1.1	2.5
BRETH–Breth in Chr	1	NR	NR	NR	-	-
BRETH–Ch of Brethren	2	14	116	146	0.0	0.1
BUDD–Mahayana	1	NR	NR	11	0.0	0.0
BUDD–Theravada	3	NR	NR	710	0.2	0.4
Calv Chpl	2	NR	NR	NR	-	-
Catholic	19	NR	NR	62,867	14.6	32.4
CGOD–Ch God (Ander)	1	62	NR	62	0.0	0.0
Ch Cr, Scientst	1	NR	NR	NR	-	-
Ch God (7th Day)	1	NR	NR	NR	-	-
Ch of Nazarene	7	531	771	1,388	0.3	0.7
Chr & Miss Al	2	198	236	340	0.1	0.2
CHR–Chr Ch (Disc)	17	1,999	6,714	8,427	2.0	4.3
CHR–Chr Chs & Chs Cr	7	NR	1,480	1,858	0.4	1.0
CHR–Chs of Christ	8	638	563	725	0.2	0.4
Christian Brethren	1	NR	NR	NR	-	-
CONG–Cong Chr, NA	1	NR	37	46	0.0	0.0
Evan Cov Ch	3	318	289	413	0.1	0.2
Evan Free Ch	12	4,620	NR	4,620	1.1	2.4
FRND–Consrv Yr Mtgs	1	NR	71	89	0.0	0.0
FRND–Fr Un Mtg	1	NR	92	115	0.0	0.1
HINDU–Post Ren	2	NR	NR	101	0.0	0.1
Ind Fund Churches	2	NR	NR	NR	-	-
Int Cou Comm Ch	1	NR	NR	NR	-	-
Jehovah's Witness	5	NR	NR	NR	-	-
JUD–Conserv	1	217	243	656	0.2	0.3
JUD–Orth	2	144	100	200	0.0	0.1
JUD–Reform	1	197	348	940	0.2	0.5
LDS–Comm of Christ	3	NR	474	474	0.1	0.2
LDS–L-D Saints	8	NR	NR	3,822	0.9	2.0
LUTH–E.L.C.A.	17	4,470	12,280	16,540	3.8	8.5
LUTH–Luth Cong Msn Chr	5	1,333	3,287	4,125	1.0	2.1
LUTH–Luth-MO Synod	15	3,049	5,755	7,693	1.8	4.0
LUTH–Wisc Ev Luth Syn	1	96	132	200	0.0	0.1
MENN–Mennonite USA	2	151	131	164	0.0	0.1
METH–AME	3	375	700	879	0.2	0.5
METH–AME Zion	1	80	110	138	0.0	0.1
METH–C.M.E.	1	0	100	126	0.0	0.1
METH–Free Methodist	2	57	78	78	0.0	0.0
METH–Un Methodist	40	5,952	14,133	19,147	4.4	9.9
METH–Wesleyan	2	145	73	188	0.0	0.1
Metro Comm Ch	1	32	55	69	0.0	0.0
Muslim Est	4	502	NR	1,724	0.4	0.9
Non-denom Chr Chs	41	9,476	11,205	12,575	2.9	6.5
ORTHE–Greek Orthodox	1	115	NR	435	0.1	0.2
ORTHE–Serb Orth USA	1	35	NR	140	0.0	0.1
ORTHO–Coptic Orth Ch	1	50	NR	50	0.0	0.0
ORTHO–Malan Dioc Am	1	7	NR	21	0.0	0.0
PENT–Assemb of God	18	5,040	2,069	9,305	2.2	4.8
PENT–Ch God (Cleve)	4	173	179	225	0.1	0.1
PENT–Ch of God Proph	2	NR	88	110	0.0	0.1
PENT–COGIC	5	10	662	831	0.2	0.4
PENT–Full Gosp Bapt	1	NR	NR	NR	-	-
PENT–Int Foursq Gos	1	40	107	134	0.0	0.1
PENT–Open Bible Std	11	1,052	NR	1,052	0.2	0.5
PENT–Pent Ch of God	1	70	NR	109	0.0	0.1
PENT–Un Pent Ch Intl	7	NR	NR	NR	-	-
PENT–Vineyard	1	205	275	345	0.1	0.2
PRES–Cov Ref Pres	1	NR	NR	NR	-	-
PRES–Orth Pres Ch	1	40	47	77	0.0	0.0
PRES–Pres Ref	1	NR	NR	NR	-	-
PRES–Presb Ch (USA)	16	1,578	3,976	4,990	1.2	2.6

NR–Not Reported   - Represents no adherents reported.   Percentages may not total 100 due to rounding.

Table 3: Religious Congregations by County and Group: 2010

Religious Group	Number of Congrega-tions	Number of Attendees	Number of Communicant, Confirmed, or Full Members	Adherents		
				Number of Adherents	% of Total Pop.	% of Total Adh.
PRES–Presb Ch Amer	1	80	69	69	0.0	0.0
REF–Christian Ref	1	250	448	562	0.1	0.3
REF–Ref Ch in Am	4	2,338	3,023	3,651	0.8	1.9
REF–Un Ref Chs N.A.	1	NR	NR	NR	-	-
Salvation Army	2	92	199	464	0.1	0.2
Sev Day Adv	5	728	1,266	1,456	0.3	0.8
Sikh	1	NR	NR	NR	-	-
Un C of Christ	5	1,144	4,282	5,374	1.2	2.8
Unit Univ	1	225	409	557	0.1	0.3
Unity Ch	1	NR	NR	NR	-	-
Zoroastrian	0	NR	NR	1	0.0	0.0
POTTAWATTAMIE	**118**	**7,726**	**19,933**	**36,210**	**38.9**	**100.0**
ANG/EPIS–Episcopal	1	41	71	103	0.1	0.3
Bahá'í	0	NR	21	21	0.0	0.1
BAPT–Amer Bapt USA	2	155	281	346	0.4	1.0
BAPT–Ind Bapt Flwsp Intl	1	NR	NR	NR	-	-
BAPT–Reg Bapt Gen As	2	NR	NR	NR	-	-
BAPT–So Bapt Conv	2	90	205	252	0.3	0.7
BRETH–Ch of Brethren	1	27	66	81	0.1	0.2
Catholic	9	NR	NR	8,947	9.6	24.7
Ch of Nazarene	2	242	328	552	0.6	1.5
Chr & Miss Al	2	201	125	286	0.3	0.8
CHR–Chr Ch (Disc)	2	120	623	767	0.8	2.1
CHR–Chr Chs & Chs Cr	5	NR	2,242	2,759	3.0	7.6
CHR–Chs of Christ	2	280	268	342	0.4	0.9
CONG–Consrv Cong Chr	1	105	250	308	0.3	0.9
Evan Free Ch	1	50	NR	50	0.1	0.1
Grace Gosp Fel	1	NR	NR	NR	-	-
HINDU–Trad Temples	1	NR	NR	25	0.0	0.1
Jehovah's Witness	1	NR	NR	NR	-	-
LDS–Comm of Christ	3	NR	567	567	0.6	1.6
LDS–L-D Saints	4	NR	NR	1,771	1.9	4.9
LUTH–E.L.C.A.	7	915	3,155	4,075	4.4	11.3
LUTH–Luth Cong Msn Chr	1	NR	NR	NR	-	-
LUTH–Luth-MO Synod	6	702	1,828	2,328	2.5	6.4
LUTH–Nor Amer Luth C	1	NR	NR	NR	-	-
METH–Un Methodist	14	1,398	3,893	5,384	5.8	14.9
Missionary Ch	1	30	0	30	0.0	0.1
Non-denom Chr Chs	16	1,951	2,943	3,074	3.3	8.5
ORTHO–Coptic Orth Ch	1	40	NR	80	0.1	0.2
PENT–Assemb of God	4	242	179	446	0.5	1.2
PENT–Ch God (Cleve)	2	138	406	500	0.5	1.4
PENT–Ch of God Proph	1	NR	116	143	0.2	0.4
PENT–Open Bible Std	1	78	NR	78	0.1	0.2
PENT–Un Pent Ch Intl	1	NR	NR	NR	-	-
PRES–Presb Ch (USA)	11	585	1,212	1,492	1.6	4.1
Salvation Army	1	36	51	51	0.1	0.1
Sev Day Adv	1	44	77	89	0.1	0.2
Un C of Christ	6	256	1,026	1,263	1.4	3.5
POWESHIEK	**41**	**1,897**	**5,748**	**9,210**	**48.7**	**100.0**
ANG/EPIS–Episcopal	1	36	76	90	0.5	1.0
Bahá'í	0	NR	8	8	0.0	0.1
BAPT–Amer Bapt USA	1	59	203	241	1.3	2.6
BAPT–Reg Bapt Gen As	1	NR	NR	NR	-	-
Catholic	2	NR	NR	1,615	8.5	17.5
Ch Cr, Scientst	1	NR	NR	NR	-	-
Ch of Nazarene	2	38	38	95	0.5	1.0
Chr & Miss Al	1	89	34	127	0.7	1.4
CHR–Chr Ch (Disc)	1	14	37	44	0.2	0.5
CHR–Chr Chs & Chs Cr	3	NR	1,097	1,302	6.9	14.1
CHR–Chs of Christ	3	100	86	108	0.6	1.2
FRND–Fr Un Mtg	1	NR	152	180	1.0	2.0
LUTH–E.L.C.A.	2	182	525	692	3.7	7.5
LUTH–Luth-MO Synod	2	117	369	431	2.3	4.7
METH–Evan Meth Ch	1	NR	NR	NR	-	-
METH–Un Methodist	8	635	2,086	2,797	14.8	30.4
Non-denom Chr Chs	3	195	260	279	1.5	3.0
PENT–Assemb of God	1	162	52	265	1.4	2.9
PENT–Open Bible Std	1	75	NR	75	0.4	0.8
PRES–Presb Ch (USA)	5	106	475	564	3.0	6.1
Un C of Christ	1	89	250	297	1.6	3.2

Religious Group	Number of Congrega-tions	Number of Attendees	Number of Communicant, Confirmed, or Full Members	Adherents		
				Number of Adherents	% of Total Pop.	% of Total Adh.
RINGGOLD	**26**	**704**	**2,054**	**3,171**	**61.8**	**100.0**
BAPT–Amer Bapt USA	1	109	247	305	5.9	9.6
BAPT–Reg Bapt Gen As	1	NR	NR	NR	-	-
Catholic	1	NR	NR	103	2.0	3.2
CHR–Chr Ch (Disc)	3	72	418	516	10.1	16.3
LDS–Comm of Christ	1	NR	158	158	3.1	5.0
LUTH–Luth-MO Synod	1	13	42	63	1.2	2.0
MENN–Amish Undif	3	NR	131	387	7.5	12.2
METH–Free Methodist	1	16	19	19	0.4	0.6
METH–Un Methodist	9	265	823	1,224	23.9	38.6
Non-denom Chr Chs	1	30	30	38	0.7	1.2
PENT–Assemb of God	2	150	71	216	4.2	6.8
PRES–Presb Ch (USA)	2	49	115	142	2.8	4.5
SAC	**35**	**1,637**	**4,289**	**7,799**	**75.4**	**100.0**
Bahá'í	0	NR	1	1	0.0	0.0
BAPT–Amer Bapt USA	1	15	28	34	0.3	0.4
BAPT–Reg Bapt Gen As	1	NR	NR	NR	-	-
Catholic	6	NR	NR	2,529	24.4	32.4
CHR–Chr Ch (Disc)	1	60	200	241	2.3	3.1
CHR–Chs of Christ	1	14	13	16	0.2	0.2
LUTH–E.L.C.A.	1	64	161	213	2.1	2.7
LUTH–Luth-MO Synod	8	746	1,946	2,331	22.5	29.9
METH–Un Methodist	6	324	1,125	1,446	14.0	18.5
Non-denom Chr Chs	2	105	105	132	1.3	1.7
PRES–Presb Ch (USA)	7	263	565	681	6.6	8.7
Un C of Christ	1	46	145	175	1.7	2.2
SCOTT	**154**	**18,091**	**34,438**	**79,401**	**48.1**	**100.0**
ANG/EPIS–Episcopal	3	265	811	1,056	0.6	1.3
Bahá'í	1	NR	160	160	0.1	0.2
BAPT–Amer Bapt USA	2	200	365	451	0.3	0.6
BAPT–Converge/BGC	5	375	NR	450	0.3	0.6
BAPT–Free Will Bapt	2	NR	76	94	0.1	0.1
BAPT–Ind Bapt Flwsp Intl	1	NR	NR	NR	-	-
BAPT–Natl Mis Bapt Conv	1	400	650	804	0.5	1.0
BAPT–NBC USA	2	625	900	1,113	0.7	1.4
BAPT–Reg Bapt Gen As	2	NR	NR	NR	-	-
BAPT–So Bapt Conv	6	440	1,031	1,274	0.8	1.6
BRETH–Grace Breth	1	NR	NR	NR	-	-
BUDD–Theravada	1	NR	NR	15	0.0	0.0
Catholic	13	NR	NR	30,508	18.5	38.4
Ch Cr, Scientst	1	NR	NR	NR	-	-
Ch of Nazarene	2	116	201	248	0.2	0.3
Chr & Miss Al	2	240	145	245	0.1	0.3
CHR–Chr Ch (Disc)	3	120	519	642	0.4	0.8
CHR–Chr Chs & Chs Cr	3	NR	1,345	1,663	1.0	2.1
CHR–Chs of Christ	2	225	252	344	0.2	0.4
CHR–Int Chs of Christ	1	NR	31	38	0.0	0.0
Evan Free Ch	2	180	NR	180	0.1	0.2
FRND–Fr Un Mtg	2	NR	51	63	0.0	0.1
Jehovah's Witness	2	NR	NR	NR	-	-
JUD–Orth	1	43	50	60	0.0	0.1
JUD–Reform	1	83	146	394	0.2	0.5
LDS–Comm of Christ	3	NR	357	357	0.2	0.4
LDS–L-D Saints	2	NR	NR	1,022	0.6	1.3
LUTH–E.L.C.A.	13	2,959	8,174	10,785	6.5	13.6
LUTH–Luth Cong Msn Chr	1	75	128	158	0.1	0.2
LUTH–Luth-MO Synod	6	1,801	4,149	5,520	3.3	7.0
LUTH–Wisc Ev Luth Syn	1	47	118	157	0.1	0.2
MENN–Mennonite USA	1	35	21	26	0.0	0.0
METH–AME	1	60	114	141	0.1	0.2
METH–Un Methodist	11	1,849	4,027	7,669	4.6	9.7
Metro Comm Ch	1	63	90	111	0.1	0.1
Muslim Est	1	134	NR	308	0.2	0.4
Nat Spirit Asso	2	NR	NR	NR	-	-
Non-denom Chr Chs	19	4,426	4,906	5,850	3.5	7.4
PENT–Assemb of God	4	558	284	711	0.4	0.9
PENT–Ch God (Cleve)	2	82	56	69	0.0	0.1
PENT–Int Foursq Gos	3	207	294	363	0.2	0.5
PENT–Open Bible Std	1	28	NR	28	0.0	0.0
PENT–Un Pent Ch Intl	1	NR	NR	NR	-	-
PENT–Vineyard	2	475	915	1,131	0.7	1.4

NR–Not Reported - Represents no adherents reported. Percentages may not total 100 due to rounding.

Table 3: Religious Congregations by County and Group: 2010

Religious Group	Number of Congrega-tions	Number of Attendees	Number of Communicant, Confirmed, or Full Members	Adherents: Number of Adherents	% of Total Pop.	% of Total Adh.
PRES–Presb Ch (USA)	8	1,090	2,486	3,073	1.9	3.9
REF–Ref Ch in Am	2	347	503	598	0.4	0.8
Salvation Army	1	27	63	268	0.2	0.3
Sev Day Adv	2	194	339	389	0.2	0.5
Sikh	1	NR	NR	NR	-	-
Un C of Christ	2	209	472	583	0.4	0.7
Unit Univ	1	113	209	282	0.2	0.4
SHELBY	**35**	**1,661**	**4,590**	**9,031**	**74.2**	**100.0**
ANG/EPIS–Episcopal	1	12	23	24	0.2	0.3
Bahá'í	0	NR	1	1	0.0	0.0
BAPT–Amer Bapt USA	2	278	419	509	4.2	5.6
BAPT–Consrv Bapt	1	NR	NR	NR	-	-
BAPT–Reg Bapt Gen As	2	NR	NR	NR	-	-
Catholic	6	NR	NR	3,464	28.5	38.4
CHR–Chr Chs & Chs Cr	3	NR	150	182	1.5	2.0
CHR–Chs of Christ	2	125	105	150	1.2	1.7
LDS–Comm of Christ	1	NR	189	189	1.6	2.1
LUTH–Luth Cong Msn Chr	4	529	1,975	2,398	19.7	26.6
LUTH–Luth-MO Synod	1	28	63	91	0.7	1.0
METH–Un Methodist	6	241	981	1,238	10.2	13.7
Non-denom Chr Chs	2	285	400	400	3.3	4.4
PENT–Assemb of God	1	88	55	108	0.9	1.2
PRES–Presb Ch (USA)	1	27	53	64	0.5	0.7
Sev Day Adv	1	8	13	15	0.1	0.2
Un C of Christ	1	40	163	198	1.6	2.2
SIOUX	**79**	**15,877**	**21,624**	**28,776**	**85.4**	**100.0**
ANG/EPIS–Episcopal	1	36	30	30	0.1	0.1
Bahá'í	0	NR	1	1	0.0	0.0
BAPT–Amer Bapt USA	1	64	225	285	0.8	1.0
BAPT–So Bapt Conv	1	46	21	27	0.1	0.1
BRETH–Ch of Brethren	1	18	54	68	0.2	0.2
Catholic	6	NR	NR	2,471	7.3	8.6
Chr & Miss Al	1	186	127	327	1.0	1.1
Evan Free Ch	2	740	NR	740	2.2	2.6
LUTH–E.L.C.A.	4	331	783	1,007	3.0	3.5
LUTH–Luth Cong Msn Chr	2	136	368	466	1.4	1.6
LUTH–Luth-MO Synod	4	409	984	1,276	3.8	4.4
LUTH–Nor Amer Luth C	1	NR	NR	NR	-	-
METH–Un Methodist	3	160	396	537	1.6	1.9
Non-denom Chr Chs	1	100	150	150	0.4	0.5
PENT–Assemb of God	1	35	37	70	0.2	0.2
PRES–Presb Ch (USA)	3	117	230	291	0.9	1.0
PRES–Presb Ch Amer	2	170	135	193	0.6	0.7
REF–Christian Ref	19	6,319	7,036	8,915	26.5	31.0
REF–Heritage Ref	1	NR	75	95	0.3	0.3
REF–Prot Ref Chs	2	565	346	661	2.0	2.3
REF–Ref Ch in Am	19	6,420	10,583	11,112	33.0	38.6
REF–Un Ref Chs N.A.	3	NR	NR	NR	-	-
Un C of Christ	1	25	43	54	0.2	0.2
STORY	**111**	**14,252**	**25,991**	**43,961**	**49.1**	**100.0**
ANG/EPIS–Episcopal	1	140	352	461	0.5	1.0
Bahá'í	1	NR	43	43	0.0	0.1
BAPT–Amer Bapt USA	1	65	181	211	0.2	0.5
BAPT–Reg Bapt Gen As	4	NR	NR	NR	-	-
BAPT–So Bapt Conv	6	2,417	896	1,043	1.2	2.4
BUDD–Vajrayana	1	NR	NR	36	0.0	0.1
Catholic	6	NR	NR	8,825	9.9	20.1
Ch Cr, Scientst	1	NR	NR	NR	-	-
Ch of Nazarene	1	35	56	59	0.1	0.1
CHR–Chr Ch (Disc)	4	146	440	512	0.6	1.2
CHR–Chr Chs & Chs Cr	3	NR	325	378	0.4	0.9
CHR–Chs of Christ	3	72	60	82	0.1	0.2
Evan Free Ch	5	1,465	NR	1,465	1.6	3.3
FRND–Consrv Yr Mtgs	1	NR	21	24	0.0	0.1
Jehovah's Witness	1	NR	NR	NR	-	-
JUD–Reform	1	36	64	173	0.2	0.4
LDS–Comm of Christ	1	NR	158	158	0.2	0.4
LDS–L-D Saints	4	NR	NR	920	1.0	2.1
LUTH–E.L.C.A.	11	1,857	7,062	9,184	10.3	20.9
LUTH–Evan Luth Syn	1	42	37	49	0.1	0.1
LUTH–Luth Ch-Am Asc	1	NR	NR	NR	-	-
LUTH–Luth Cong Msn Chr	6	578	2,103	2,448	2.7	5.6
LUTH–Luth-MO Synod	2	752	1,124	1,526	1.7	3.5
LUTH–Nor Amer Luth C	1	NR	NR	NR	-	-
MENN–Mennonite USA	1	5	6	7	0.0	0.0
METH–Un Methodist	14	1,632	5,083	6,893	7.7	15.7
Muslim Est	1	134	NR	308	0.3	0.7
Non-denom Chr Chs	6	3,355	5,355	5,757	6.4	13.1
ORTHE–Orth Ch in Amer	1	21	NR	21	0.0	0.0
PENT–Assemb of God	3	218	160	383	0.4	0.9
PENT–Int Foursq Gos	1	9	6	7	0.0	0.0
PENT–Open Bible Std	2	31	NR	31	0.0	0.1
PENT–Un Pent Ch Intl	1	NR	NR	NR	-	-
PENT–Vineyard	1	350	400	466	0.5	1.1
PRES–Presb Ch (USA)	5	404	976	1,136	1.3	2.6
PRES–Ref Pres Han	1	NR	NR	NR	-	-
REF–Christian Ref	2	170	292	340	0.4	0.8
Sev Day Adv	2	84	146	168	0.2	0.4
Un C of Christ	1	110	356	414	0.5	0.9
Unit Univ	1	124	289	433	0.5	1.0
Unity Ch	1	NR	NR	NR	-	-
TAMA	**36**	**1,693**	**4,797**	**8,582**	**48.3**	**100.0**
Bahá'í	0	NR	8	8	0.0	0.1
BAPT–Ref Bapt Ch	1	NR	NR	NR	-	-
BAPT–Reg Bapt Gen As	1	NR	NR	NR	-	-
BRETH–Grace Breth	1	NR	NR	NR	-	-
Catholic	4	NR	NR	2,614	14.7	30.5
CHR–Chr Ch (Disc)	1	0	0	0	0.0	0.0
FRND–Fr Un Mtg	1	NR	0	0	0.0	0.0
LUTH–E.L.C.A.	3	259	970	1,077	6.1	12.5
LUTH–Luth Ch-Am Asc	1	NR	NR	NR	-	-
LUTH–Luth-MO Synod	1	28	94	109	0.6	1.3
METH–Un Methodist	10	606	2,265	2,869	16.1	33.4
Non-denom Chr Chs	3	300	400	425	2.4	5.0
PENT–Assemb of God	3	114	19	193	1.1	2.2
PRES–Presb Ch (USA)	3	177	374	462	2.6	5.4
Un C of Christ	3	209	667	825	4.6	9.6
TAYLOR	**29**	**743**	**2,522**	**3,568**	**56.5**	**100.0**
BAPT–Amer Bapt USA	1	91	545	663	10.5	18.6
BAPT–So Bapt Conv	2	44	33	40	0.6	1.1
Catholic	2	NR	NR	244	3.9	6.8
CGOD–Ches God-Gen Con	1	0	0	0	0.0	0.0
Ch of Nazarene	1	0	15	15	0.2	0.4
CHR–Chr Ch (Disc)	3	54	351	427	6.8	12.0
CHR–Chr Chs & Chs Cr	3	NR	235	286	4.5	8.0
CHR–Chs of Christ	2	35	31	39	0.6	1.1
Jehovah's Witness	1	NR	NR	NR	-	-
LDS–L-D Saints	1	NR	NR	196	3.1	5.5
LUTH–Luth-MO Synod	1	16	18	20	0.3	0.6
METH–Un Methodist	5	244	923	1,177	18.6	33.0
Missionary Ch	1	83	58	83	1.3	2.3
Non-denom Chr Chs	1	13	13	16	0.3	0.4
PRES–Presb Ch (USA)	3	137	256	311	4.9	8.7
Sev Day Adv	1	26	44	51	0.8	1.4
UNION	**34**	**1,268**	**3,254**	**5,263**	**42.0**	**100.0**
ANG/EPIS–Episcopal	1	4	3	10	0.1	0.2
Bahá'í	0	NR	1	1	0.0	0.0
BAPT–Amer Bapt USA	1	24	48	59	0.5	1.1
BAPT–Reg Bapt Gen As	1	NR	NR	NR	-	-
BAPT–So Bapt Conv	1	146	295	361	2.9	6.9
Catholic	2	NR	NR	1,157	9.2	22.0
CGOD–Ch God (Ander)	1	20	NR	20	0.2	0.4
Ch Cr, Scientst	1	NR	NR	NR	-	-
Ch of Nazarene	1	0	0	0	0.0	0.0
CHR–Chr Ch (Disc)	1	87	400	490	3.9	9.3
CHR–Chr Chs & Chs Cr	1	NR	20	24	0.2	0.5
Jehovah's Witness	1	NR	NR	NR	-	-
LDS–Comm of Christ	1	NR	158	158	1.3	3.0
LUTH–E.L.C.A.	1	99	334	384	3.1	7.3
LUTH–Luth-MO Synod	1	93	208	258	2.1	4.9

NR–Not Reported - Represents no adherents reported. Percentages may not total 100 due to rounding.

Table 3: Religious Congregations by County and Group: 2010

Religious Group	Number of Congrega-tions	Number of Attendees	Number of Communicant, Confirmed, or Full Members	Adherents: Number of Adherents	Adherents: % of Total Pop.	Adherents: % of Total Adh.
MENN–Amish Undif	0	NR	2	12	0.1	0.2
MENN–Tamp Amish-Menn	1	103	61	103	0.8	2.0
METH–Un Methodist	7	302	889	1,173	9.4	22.3
Non-denom Chr Chs	1	80	100	100	0.8	1.9
PENT–Assemb of God	2	99	53	120	1.0	2.3
PENT–Un Pent Ch Intl	1	NR	NR	NR	-	-
PRES–Presb Ch (USA)	2	107	211	258	2.1	4.9
Sev Day Adv	1	8	15	17	0.1	0.3
Un C of Christ	4	96	456	558	4.5	10.6
VAN BUREN	**30**	**678**	**2,099**	**3,031**	**40.0**	**100.0**
BAPT–Amer Bapt USA	1	6	12	15	0.2	0.5
BAPT–Reg Bapt Gen As	1	NR	NR	NR	-	-
Catholic	1	NR	NR	235	3.1	7.8
Ch of Nazarene	1	0	0	0	0.0	0.0
CHR–Chr Chs & Chs Cr	3	NR	335	410	5.4	13.5
LUTH–Luth-MO Synod	1	15	35	45	0.6	1.5
MENN–Amish Undif	3	NR	216	548	7.2	18.1
METH–Un Methodist	11	320	944	1,122	14.8	37.0
Non-denom Chr Chs	3	210	310	310	4.1	10.2
PENT–Assemb of God	1	55	23	72	1.0	2.4
PRES–Presb Ch (USA)	3	52	174	213	2.8	7.0
Un C of Christ	1	20	50	61	0.8	2.0
WAPELLO	**77**	**4,323**	**7,332**	**14,142**	**39.7**	**100.0**
ANG/EPIS–Episcopal	1	29	48	48	0.1	0.3
Bahá'í	0	NR	11	11	0.0	0.1
BAPT–Amer Bapt USA	3	93	192	233	0.7	1.6
BAPT–Reg Bapt Gen As	1	NR	NR	NR	-	-
BAPT–So Bapt Conv	1	45	285	346	1.0	2.4
BRETH–Ch of Brethren	1	0	53	64	0.2	0.5
Catholic	2	NR	NR	3,325	9.3	23.5
CGOD–Ch God (Ander)	2	99	NR	99	0.3	0.7
Ch of Nazarene	3	172	217	300	0.8	2.1
Chr & Miss Al	1	206	93	266	0.7	1.9
CHR–Chr Ch (Disc)	6	214	904	1,098	3.1	7.8
CHR–Chr Chs & Chs Cr	3	NR	375	456	1.3	3.2
CHR–Chs of Christ	2	100	82	113	0.3	0.8
Jehovah's Witness	1	NR	NR	NR	-	-
JUD–Conserv	1	6	7	19	0.1	0.1
LDS–L-D Saints	1	NR	NR	491	1.4	3.5
LUTH–E.L.C.A.	2	61	163	182	0.5	1.3
LUTH–Luth Cong Msn Chr	1	195	620	753	2.1	5.3
LUTH–Luth-MO Synod	1	91	144	220	0.6	1.6
METH–AME	1	0	100	121	0.3	0.9
METH–Free Methodist	1	66	49	66	0.2	0.5
METH–Un Methodist	9	469	1,576	1,851	5.2	13.1
Non-denom Chr Chs	10	1,335	1,695	1,878	5.3	13.3
PENT–Assemb of God	7	674	109	895	2.5	6.3
PENT–Ch of God Proph	1	NR	23	28	0.1	0.2
PENT–Int Foursq Gos	2	38	43	52	0.1	0.4
PENT–Open Bible Std	3	69	NR	69	0.2	0.5
PENT–Pent Ch of God	1	70	NR	109	0.3	0.8
PENT–Un Pent Ch Intl	1	NR	NR	NR	-	-
PRES–Presb Ch (USA)	3	158	323	392	1.1	2.8
REF–Ref Ch in Am	1	30	40	62	0.2	0.4
Salvation Army	1	28	62	454	1.3	3.2
Sev Day Adv	1	16	28	32	0.1	0.2
Un C of Christ	2	59	90	109	0.3	0.8
WARREN	**66**	**5,059**	**9,342**	**18,322**	**39.6**	**100.0**
Bahá'í	0	NR	6	6	0.0	0.0
BAPT–Amer Bapt USA	1	91	121	151	0.3	0.8
BAPT–Reg Bapt Gen As	4	NR	NR	NR	-	-
BAPT–So Bapt Conv	2	66	170	212	0.5	1.2
Catholic	6	NR	NR	4,646	10.1	25.4
Ch of Nazarene	2	10	17	17	0.0	0.1
CHR–Chr Ch (Disc)	4	190	806	1,006	2.2	5.5
CHR–Chr Chs & Chs Cr	1	NR	200	250	0.5	1.4
CHR–Chs of Christ	1	35	28	35	0.1	0.2
Christian Un	3	NR	NR	NR	-	-
Evan Free Ch	4	1,085	NR	1,085	2.3	5.9
FRND–Fr Un Mtg	4	NR	315	393	0.9	2.1
Jehovah's Witness	1	NR	NR	NR	-	-
LDS–Comm of Christ	1	NR	158	158	0.3	0.9
LDS–L-D Saints	1	NR	NR	167	0.4	0.9
LUTH–E.L.C.A.	3	406	1,215	1,731	3.7	9.4
LUTH–Evan Luth Syn	1	32	41	49	0.1	0.3
LUTH–Luth-MO Synod	4	362	735	991	2.1	5.4
METH–Un Methodist	12	1,147	3,785	4,775	10.3	26.1
Non-denom Chr Chs	4	710	745	889	1.9	4.9
PENT–Assemb of God	1	379	195	694	1.5	3.8
PENT–Un Pent Ch Intl	1	NR	NR	NR	-	-
PRES–Presb Ch (USA)	3	281	589	735	1.6	4.0
REF–Ref Ch in Am	1	240	178	285	0.6	1.6
Un C of Christ	1	25	38	47	0.1	0.3
WASHINGTON	**57**	**3,642**	**6,548**	**12,465**	**57.4**	**100.0**
Bahá'í	0	NR	6	6	0.0	0.0
BAPT–Amer Bapt USA	2	120	264	327	1.5	2.6
BAPT–Converge/BGC	1	75	NR	90	0.4	0.7
BAPT–Reg Bapt Gen As	1	NR	NR	NR	-	-
Catholic	4	NR	NR	3,956	18.2	31.7
CGOD–Ches God-Gen Con	2	73	78	97	0.4	0.8
Ch of Nazarene	1	18	29	29	0.1	0.2
CHR–Chr Ch (Disc)	3	12	113	140	0.6	1.1
Evan Free Ch	1	45	NR	45	0.2	0.4
FRND–Fr Un Mtg	2	NR	88	109	0.5	0.9
Jehovah's Witness	2	NR	NR	NR	-	-
LDS–L-D Saints	1	NR	NR	183	0.8	1.5
LUTH–E.L.C.A.	1	117	469	720	3.3	5.8
LUTH–Luth Ch-Am Asc	1	NR	NR	NR	-	-
LUTH–Luth-MO Synod	1	22	25	39	0.2	0.3
MENN–Amish Undif	4	NR	281	563	2.6	4.5
MENN–Cons Menn Conf	3	455	415	514	2.4	4.1
MENN–Mennonite USA	6	836	1,131	1,401	6.5	11.2
METH–Un Methodist	7	507	1,708	2,019	9.3	16.2
Non-denom Chr Chs	5	970	1,175	1,225	5.6	9.8
PENT–Assemb of God	1	56	21	77	0.4	0.6
PENT–Ch God (Cleve)	1	8	9	11	0.1	0.1
PENT–Un Pent Ch Intl	1	NR	NR	NR	-	-
PRES–Presb Ch (USA)	5	293	690	855	3.9	6.9
PRES–Ref Pres of NA	1	35	46	59	0.3	0.5
WAYNE	**28**	**890**	**2,348**	**3,203**	**50.0**	**100.0**
Bahá'í	0	NR	1	1	0.0	0.0
BAPT–Amer Bapt USA	2	147	282	343	5.4	10.7
BAPT–So Bapt Conv	2	43	217	264	4.1	8.2
Catholic	1	NR	NR	76	1.2	2.4
CHR–Chr Ch (Disc)	3	95	296	360	5.6	11.2
CHR–Chr Chs & Chs Cr	1	NR	100	122	1.9	3.8
CHR–Chs of Christ	1	15	12	18	0.3	0.6
Jehovah's Witness	1	NR	NR	NR	-	-
LDS–Comm of Christ	1	NR	158	158	2.5	4.9
MENN–Amish Undif	2	NR	114	323	5.0	10.1
METH–Un Methodist	9	277	919	1,094	17.1	34.2
Non-denom Chr Chs	1	72	65	90	1.4	2.8
PENT–Assemb of God	3	169	91	241	3.8	7.5
PRES–Presb Ch (USA)	1	72	93	113	1.8	3.5
WEBSTER	**68**	**5,711**	**13,367**	**24,553**	**64.6**	**100.0**
ANG/EPIS–Episcopal	1	34	75	75	0.2	0.3
Bahá'í	0	NR	2	2	0.0	0.0
BAPT–Amer Bapt USA	1	74	391	470	1.2	1.9
BAPT–Converge/BGC	1	75	NR	90	0.2	0.4
BAPT–Ind Bapt Flwsp Intl	1	NR	NR	NR	-	-
BAPT–N Am Bapt Conf	1	NR	28	34	0.1	0.1
BAPT–Reg Bapt Gen As	1	NR	NR	NR	-	-
BAPT–So Bapt Conv	1	90	105	126	0.3	0.5
Catholic	1	NR	NR	7,056	18.6	28.7
Ch of Nazarene	1	47	67	89	0.2	0.4
CHR–Chr Ch (Disc)	1	33	66	79	0.2	0.3
CHR–Chr Chs & Chs Cr	1	NR	125	150	0.4	0.6
CHR–Chs of Christ	1	50	60	80	0.2	0.3
Evan Cov Ch	3	233	324	303	0.8	1.2
Evan Free Ch	1	230	NR	230	0.6	0.9

NR–Not Reported - Represents no adherents reported. Percentages may not total 100 due to rounding.

Table 3: Religious Congregations by County and Group: 2010

Religious Group	Number of Congregations	Number of Attendees	Number of Communicant, Confirmed, or Full Members	Adherents: Number of Adherents	Adherents: % of Total Pop.	Adherents: % of Total Adh.
HINDU–I/A Temples	1	NR	NR	250	0.7	1.0
Jehovah's Witness	1	NR	NR	NR	-	-
LDS–Comm of Christ	1	NR	158	158	0.4	0.6
LDS–L-D Saints	1	NR	NR	483	1.3	2.0
LUTH–E.L.C.A.	10	965	3,271	4,106	10.8	16.7
LUTH–Luth Cong Msn Chr	2	287	891	1,070	2.8	4.4
LUTH–Luth–MO Synod	6	843	2,315	2,973	7.8	12.1
LUTH–Nor Amer Luth C	1	NR	NR	NR	-	-
METH–AME	1	20	60	72	0.2	0.3
METH–Un Methodist	11	766	2,754	3,461	9.1	14.1
Non-denom Chr Chs	6	1,280	1,420	1,653	4.3	6.7
PENT–Assemb of God	1	92	48	127	0.3	0.5
PENT–COGIC	1	30	50	60	0.2	0.2
PENT–Un Pent Ch Intl	1	NR	NR	NR	-	-
PRES–Presb Ch (USA)	3	413	865	1,039	2.7	4.2
Salvation Army	1	23	49	49	0.1	0.2
Sev Day Adv	1	34	58	67	0.2	0.3
Un Breth in Cr	1	19	32	17	0.0	0.1
Un C of Christ	2	73	153	184	0.5	0.7
WINNEBAGO	**32**	**2,067**	**6,447**	**8,979**	**82.6**	**100.0**
Bahá'í	0	NR	5	5	0.0	0.1
BAPT–Converge/BGC	1	75	NR	90	0.8	1.0
BAPT–N Am Bapt Conf	1	NR	82	98	0.9	1.1
BAPT–Reg Bapt Gen As	1	NR	NR	NR	-	-
Catholic	3	NR	NR	810	7.5	9.0
CONG–Consrv Cong Chr	2	102	140	168	1.5	1.9
LUTH–Assoc Free Luth	1	NR	NR	NR	-	-
LUTH–E.L.C.A.	9	1,203	4,308	5,566	51.2	62.0
LUTH–Evan Luth Syn	6	122	284	345	3.2	3.8
LUTH–Luth Ch-Am Asc	1	NR	NR	NR	-	-
METH–Un Methodist	4	330	1,125	1,344	12.4	15.0
Non-denom Chr Chs	1	150	150	188	1.7	2.1
PENT–Int Foursq Gos	1	10	23	28	0.3	0.3
REF–Ref Ch in Am	1	75	330	337	3.1	3.8
WINNESHIEK	**43**	**3,178**	**8,403**	**17,174**	**81.6**	**100.0**
ANG/EPIS–Episcopal	1	17	23	32	0.2	0.2
Bahá'í	0	NR	6	6	0.0	0.0
BAPT–Converge/BGC	1	75	NR	90	0.4	0.5
BAPT–So Bapt Conv	1	14	9	11	0.1	0.1
Catholic	6	NR	NR	6,307	30.0	36.7
CHR–Chs of Christ	1	25	28	30	0.1	0.2
Evan Cov Ch	1	173	76	225	1.1	1.3
FRND–Consrv Yr Mtgs	1	NR	10	12	0.1	0.1
FRND–Fr Un Mtg	1	NR	30	35	0.2	0.2
Jehovah's Witness	1	NR	NR	NR	-	-
LUTH–E.L.C.A.	21	2,549	7,220	9,152	43.5	53.3
LUTH–Evan Luth Syn	1	17	21	24	0.1	0.1
MENN–Amish Undif	0	NR	4	5	0.0	0.0
METH–Un Methodist	3	157	701	878	4.2	5.1
PENT–Assemb of God	1	65	49	103	0.5	0.6
PRES–Presb Ch (USA)	1	0	51	60	0.3	0.3
Un C of Christ	1	52	128	151	0.7	0.9
Unit Univ	1	34	47	53	0.3	0.3
WOODBURY	**143**	**12,514**	**26,457**	**60,423**	**59.1**	**100.0**
ANG/EPIS–Episcopal	3	138	424	800	0.8	1.3
Bahá'í	1	NR	51	51	0.0	0.1
BAPT–Amer Bapt USA	2	68	105	133	0.1	0.2
BAPT–Consrv Bapt	1	NR	NR	NR	-	-
BAPT–Converge/BGC	1	75	NR	90	0.1	0.1
BAPT–Ind Bapt Flwsp Intl	1	NR	NR	NR	-	-
BAPT–So Bapt Conv	4	550	726	917	0.9	1.5
BRETH–Ch of Brethren	1	0	0	0	0.0	0.0
Catholic	13	NR	NR	22,732	22.2	37.6
Ch Cr, Scientst	1	NR	NR	NR	-	-
Ch of Nazarene	3	56	163	186	0.2	0.3
CHR–Chr Ch (Disc)	3	96	282	356	0.3	0.6
CHR–Chr Chs & Chs Cr	3	NR	275	347	0.3	0.6
CHR–Chs of Christ	3	89	90	98	0.1	0.2
Evan Ch	1	NR	NR	NR	-	-
Evan Cov Ch	2	119	144	155	0.2	0.3

Religious Group	Number of Congregations	Number of Attendees	Number of Communicant, Confirmed, or Full Members	Adherents: Number of Adherents	Adherents: % of Total Pop.	Adherents: % of Total Adh.
Evan Free Ch	1	80	NR	80	0.1	0.1
Jehovah's Witness	2	NR	NR	NR	-	-
JUD–Reform	1	78	137	370	0.4	0.6
LDS–Comm of Christ	1	NR	189	189	0.2	0.3
LDS–L-D Saints	2	NR	NR	1,253	1.2	2.1
LUTH–E.L.C.A.	12	1,340	4,324	5,653	5.5	9.4
LUTH–Luth Cong Msn Chr	2	956	3,897	4,921	4.8	8.1
LUTH–Luth–MO Synod	11	1,386	3,833	5,133	5.0	8.5
LUTH–Wisc Ev Luth Syn	1	53	73	102	0.1	0.2
METH–AME	1	0	100	126	0.1	0.2
METH–Un Methodist	21	1,678	5,485	6,997	6.8	11.6
METH–Wesleyan	1	34	26	44	0.0	0.1
Muslim Est	1	134	NR	308	0.3	0.5
New Apost Ch	1	NR	NR	NR	-	-
Non-denom Chr Chs	13	2,090	2,160	2,647	2.6	4.4
ORTHE–Ant Orth of NA	1	80	NR	200	0.2	0.3
ORTHE–Greek Orthodox	1	50	NR	250	0.2	0.4
PENT–Assemb of God	5	838	467	1,730	1.7	2.9
PENT–Ch God (Cleve)	1	30	40	51	0.0	0.1
PENT–Intl Pent Holiness	2	240	143	181	0.2	0.3
PENT–Open Bible Std	1	85	NR	85	0.1	0.1
PENT–Un Pent Ch Intl	1	NR	NR	NR	-	-
PRES–Presb Ch (USA)	7	522	1,151	1,453	1.4	2.4
REF–Christian Ref	2	153	153	193	0.2	0.3
REF–Ref Ch in Am	1	1,116	1,028	1,388	1.4	2.3
Salvation Army	1	41	110	110	0.1	0.2
Sev Day Adv	1	46	80	92	0.1	0.2
Un C of Christ	4	258	739	933	0.9	1.5
Unit Univ	1	35	62	69	0.1	0.1
WORTH	**22**	**1,124**	**2,978**	**5,532**	**72.8**	**100.0**
BAPT–So Bapt Conv	1	28	151	182	2.4	3.3
Catholic	1	NR	NR	390	5.1	7.0
CHR–Chr Chs & Chs Cr	1	NR	150	180	2.4	3.3
LUTH–Ch of Luth Br	1	80	43	98	1.3	1.8
LUTH–E.L.C.A.	9	692	1,763	3,512	46.2	63.5
LUTH–Evan Luth Syn	2	79	96	102	1.3	1.8
LUTH–Luth Cong Msn Chr	1	49	NR	NR	-	-
LUTH–Nor Amer Luth C	2	NR	NR	NR	-	-
MENN–Amish Undif	1	NR	27	59	0.8	1.1
METH–Un Methodist	3	196	748	1,009	13.3	18.2
WRIGHT	**44**	**2,043**	**5,352**	**8,887**	**67.2**	**100.0**
Bahá'í	0	NR	4	4	0.0	0.0
BAPT–Amer Bapt USA	1	40	60	73	0.6	0.8
BAPT–Reg Bapt Gen As	1	NR	NR	NR	-	-
Catholic	3	NR	NR	1,972	14.9	22.2
Ch of Nazarene	1	20	22	61	0.5	0.7
CHR–Chr Chs & Chs Cr	2	NR	320	391	3.0	4.4
Evan Free Ch	2	225	NR	225	1.7	2.5
Jehovah's Witness	1	NR	NR	NR	-	-
LUTH–Assoc Free Luth	1	NR	NR	NR	-	-
LUTH–E.L.C.A.	6	384	1,202	1,614	12.2	18.2
LUTH–Luth Cong Msn Chr	2	158	792	967	7.3	10.9
LUTH–Luth–MO Synod	3	56	122	139	1.1	1.6
LUTH–Nor Amer Luth C	1	NR	NR	NR	-	-
METH–Un Methodist	7	545	1,661	1,950	14.7	21.9
Non-denom Chr Chs	2	165	150	206	1.6	2.3
PENT–Assemb of God	2	58	61	126	1.0	1.4
PRES–Presb Ch (USA)	3	158	285	348	2.6	3.9
REF–Ref Ch in Am	2	107	165	191	1.4	2.1
Un C of Christ	4	127	508	620	4.7	7.0
KANSAS	**4,782**	**381,103**	**729,417**	**1,444,455**	**50.6**	**100.0**
ALLEN	**47**	**2,290**	**4,904**	**8,407**	**62.9**	**100.0**
ANG/EPIS–Episcopal	1	20	35	35	0.3	0.4
Bahá'í	0	NR	2	2	0.0	0.0
BAPT–Amer Bapt USA	2	280	972	1,188	8.9	14.1
BAPT–Reg Bapt Gen As	1	NR	NR	NR	-	-
BAPT–So Bapt Conv	3	235	367	449	3.4	5.3

NR–Not Reported - Represents no adherents reported. Percentages may not total 100 due to rounding.

Table 3: Religious Congregations by County and Group: 2010

Religious Group	Number of Congrega-tions	Number of Attendees	Number of Communicant, Confirmed, or Full Members	Adherents: Number of Adherents	Adherents: % of Total Pop.	Adherents: % of Total Adh.
Catholic	2	NR	NR	1,440	10.8	17.1
Ch of Nazarene	1	24	51	134	1.0	1.6
CHR–Chr Chs & Chs Cr	4	NR	177	216	1.6	2.6
CHR–Chs of Christ	1	24	27	35	0.3	0.4
Evan Cov Ch	1	35	46	46	0.3	0.5
Ind Fund Churches	1	NR	NR	NR	-	-
Jehovah's Witness	1	NR	NR	NR	-	-
LDS–Comm of Christ	1	NR	179	179	1.3	2.1
LDS–L-D Saints	1	NR	NR	423	3.2	5.0
LUTH–E.L.C.A.	1	40	130	181	1.4	2.2
LUTH–Luth–MO Synod	2	191	502	684	5.1	8.1
METH–AME	1	0	150	183	1.4	2.2
METH–Un Methodist	10	442	1,285	1,618	12.1	19.2
Non-denom Chr Chs	5	500	515	651	4.9	7.7
PENT–Assemb of God	6	385	234	663	5.0	7.9
PRES–Presb Ch (USA)	1	90	190	232	1.7	2.8
Sev Day Adv	1	24	42	48	0.4	0.6
ANDERSON	**25**	**768**	**1,831**	**4,270**	**52.7**	**100.0**
Bahá'í	0	NR	1	1	0.0	0.0
BAPT–Amer Bapt USA	2	127	423	529	6.5	12.4
BRETH–Ch of Brethren	1	0	33	41	0.5	1.0
Catholic	5	NR	NR	1,754	21.6	41.1
Ch of Nazarene	1	188	159	331	4.1	7.8
CHR–Chr Chs & Chs Cr	3	NR	395	494	6.1	11.6
CHR–Chs of Christ	1	50	37	60	0.7	1.4
LUTH–Luth–MO Synod	2	125	217	282	3.5	6.6
MENN–Amish Undif	2	NR	73	138	1.7	3.2
METH–Un Methodist	5	196	415	472	5.8	11.1
Non-denom Chr Chs	1	50	40	62	0.8	1.5
PENT–Assemb of God	1	25	17	100	1.2	2.3
Un Breth in Cr	1	7	21	6	0.1	0.1
ATCHISON	**34**	**1,978**	**4,946**	**9,130**	**53.9**	**100.0**
ANG/EPIS–Episcopal	1	55	78	91	0.5	1.0
Bahá'í	0	NR	4	4	0.0	0.0
BAPT–Amer Bapt USA	1	169	381	467	2.8	5.1
Catholic	6	NR	NR	2,720	16.1	29.8
Ch of Nazarene	1	10	21	26	0.2	0.3
CHR–Chr Ch (Disc)	2	302	1,232	1,511	8.9	16.5
CHR–Chr Chs & Chs Cr	2	NR	120	147	0.9	1.6
CHR–Chs of Christ	1	15	15	29	0.2	0.3
LDS–Comm of Christ	1	NR	182	182	1.1	2.0
LUTH–E.L.C.A.	2	76	357	472	2.8	5.2
LUTH–Luth–MO Synod	1	418	945	1,229	7.3	13.5
METH–AME	1	0	100	123	0.7	1.3
METH–Un Methodist	5	207	607	769	4.5	8.4
Non-denom Chr Chs	4	340	445	470	2.8	5.1
PENT–Assemb of God	1	92	44	280	1.7	3.1
PENT–Ch God (Cleve)	1	49	68	83	0.5	0.9
PENT–Pent Ch of God	1	70	NR	109	0.6	1.2
PRES–Presb Ch (USA)	2	121	253	310	1.8	3.4
Sev Day Adv	1	54	94	108	0.6	1.2
BARBER	**22**	**718**	**1,692**	**3,063**	**63.0**	**100.0**
ANG/EPIS–Episcopal	1	12	5	5	0.1	0.2
Ap Chr Ch-Amer	1	59	32	59	1.2	1.9
Bahá'í	0	NR	2	2	0.0	0.1
BAPT–Amer Bapt USA	1	25	50	60	1.2	2.0
BAPT–Ind Bapt Flwsp Intl	1	NR	NR	NR	-	-
BAPT–So Bapt Conv	2	63	151	181	3.7	5.9
Catholic	3	NR	NR	971	20.0	31.7
CHR–Chr Chs & Chs Cr	3	NR	335	401	8.2	13.1
CHR–Chs of Christ	1	20	12	16	0.3	0.5
LUTH–Luth–MO Synod	1	37	94	122	2.5	4.0
METH–Un Methodist	4	226	699	819	16.8	26.7
Non-denom Chr Chs	1	145	170	181	3.7	5.9
PENT–Assemb of God	1	80	25	105	2.2	3.4
PRES–Presb Ch (USA)	1	10	13	16	0.3	0.5
Un C of Christ	1	41	104	125	2.6	4.1
BARTON	**62**	**3,812**	**7,007**	**19,076**	**68.9**	**100.0**
ANG/EPIS–Episcopal	1	17	47	47	0.2	0.2
Bahá'í	0	NR	5	5	0.0	0.0
BAPT–Amer Bapt Assn	1	NR	85	105	0.4	0.6
BAPT–Amer Bapt USA	1	58	171	211	0.8	1.1
BAPT–N Am Bapt Conf	1	NR	276	341	1.2	1.8
BAPT–So Bapt Conv	7	351	613	757	2.7	4.0
Catholic	7	NR	NR	9,300	33.6	48.8
CGOD–Ch God (Ander)	2	165	NR	165	0.6	0.9
Ch of Nazarene	2	191	277	329	1.2	1.7
CHR–Chr Ch (Disc)	1	184	434	536	1.9	2.8
CHR–Chr Chs & Chs Cr	2	NR	215	265	1.0	1.4
CHR–Chs of Christ	1	85	100	118	0.4	0.6
Evan Free Ch	1	400	NR	400	1.4	2.1
Ind Fund Churches	1	NR	NR	NR	-	-
Jehovah's Witness	1	NR	NR	NR	-	-
LDS–L-D Saints	1	NR	NR	390	1.4	2.0
LUTH–E.L.C.A.	4	385	1,022	1,267	4.6	6.6
LUTH–Luth–MO Synod	4	294	622	777	2.8	4.1
METH–AME	1	0	100	123	0.4	0.6
METH–Un Methodist	6	531	1,466	1,816	6.6	9.5
Non-denom Chr Chs	7	536	675	694	2.5	3.6
PENT–Assemb of God	1	325	192	569	2.1	3.0
PENT–Int Foursq Gos	2	52	100	123	0.4	0.6
PENT–Un Pent Ch Intl	1	NR	NR	NR	-	-
PRES–Presb Ch (USA)	1	59	165	204	0.7	1.1
Sev Day Adv	2	80	139	160	0.6	0.8
Swedenborgian	1	NR	NR	NR	-	-
Un C of Christ	2	99	303	374	1.4	2.0
BOURBON	**44**	**2,728**	**5,102**	**8,108**	**53.4**	**100.0**
Ap Chr Ch-Amer	1	82	45	82	0.5	1.0
BAPT–Amer Bapt USA	3	316	901	1,124	7.4	13.9
BAPT–Natl Mis Bapt Conv	1	0	150	187	1.2	2.3
BAPT–So Bapt Conv	1	30	75	94	0.6	1.2
BRETH–Brethren (Ash)	1	NR	80	100	0.7	1.2
BRETH–Ch of Brethren	1	33	11	14	0.1	0.2
Catholic	1	NR	NR	1,600	10.5	19.7
CGOD–Ches God-Gen Con	1	56	64	80	0.5	1.0
Ch of Nazarene	2	282	370	370	2.4	4.6
CHR–Chr Ch (Disc)	1	40	212	265	1.7	3.3
CHR–Chr Chs & Chs Cr	1	NR	0	0	0.0	0.0
CHR–Chs of Christ	2	100	75	103	0.7	1.3
Jehovah's Witness	2	NR	NR	NR	-	-
LDS–Comm of Christ	2	NR	270	270	1.8	3.3
LDS–L-D Saints	1	NR	NR	144	0.9	1.8
LUTH–Luth–MO Synod	1	73	135	164	1.1	2.0
MENN–Amish Undif	1	NR	49	143	0.9	1.8
METH–Un Methodist	8	351	790	1,019	6.7	12.6
Non-denom Chr Chs	8	1,168	1,375	1,537	10.1	19.0
PENT–Assemb of God	1	50	27	226	1.5	2.8
PENT–COGIC	1	0	150	187	1.2	2.3
PENT–Un Pent Ch Intl	1	NR	NR	NR	-	-
PRES–Presb Ch (USA)	1	124	283	353	2.3	4.4
Sev Day Adv	1	23	40	46	0.3	0.6
BROWN	**35**	**1,425**	**3,417**	**5,375**	**53.8**	**100.0**
Bahá'í	0	NR	12	12	0.1	0.2
BAPT–Amer Bapt USA	4	278	863	1,073	10.7	20.0
Catholic	3	NR	NR	900	9.0	16.7
CHR–Chr Ch (Disc)	3	130	346	430	4.3	8.0
CHR–Chr Chs & Chs Cr	1	NR	44	55	0.6	1.0
CHR–Chs of Christ	1	15	15	19	0.2	0.4
LDS–L-D Saints	1	NR	NR	247	2.5	4.6
LUTH–E.L.C.A.	2	104	259	351	3.5	6.5
LUTH–Luth–MO Synod	4	164	343	386	3.9	7.2
MENN–CG in Cr (Menn)	1	NR	77	96	1.0	1.8
METH–AME	1	0	100	124	1.2	2.3
METH–Un Methodist	6	394	842	1,045	10.5	19.4
Non-denom Chr Chs	4	200	309	313	3.1	5.8
PENT–Assemb of God	1	47	27	100	1.0	1.9
PRES–Presb Ch (USA)	1	18	46	57	0.6	1.1
Un C of Christ	2	75	134	167	1.7	3.1

NR–Not Reported - Represents no adherents reported. Percentages may not total 100 due to rounding.

Table 3: Religious Congregations by County and Group: 2010

Religious Group	Number of Congrega-tions	Number of Attendees	Number of Communicant, Confirmed, or Full Members	Adherents		
				Number of Adherents	% of Total Pop.	% of Total Adh.
BUTLER	**88**	**6,975**	**13,577**	**27,835**	**42.3**	**100.0**
ANG/EPIS–Episcopal	1	57	223	244	0.4	0.9
Bahá'í	0	NR	24	24	0.0	0.1
BAPT–Amer Bapt USA	6	608	1,126	1,418	2.2	5.1
BAPT–So Bapt Conv	10	658	3,101	3,905	5.9	14.0
Catholic	3	NR	NR	7,800	11.8	28.0
CGOD–Ch God (Ander)	2	952	NR	952	1.4	3.4
Ch of Nazarene	3	99	141	147	0.2	0.5
CHR–Chr Ch (Disc)	3	50	659	830	1.3	3.0
CHR–Chr Chs & Chs Cr	5	NR	601	757	1.1	2.7
CHR–Chs of Christ	5	311	247	338	0.5	1.2
Evan Cov Ch	1	171	58	222	0.3	0.8
Evan Free Ch	1	0	NR	0	0.0	0.0
FRND–Evan Fr Ch Intl	1	82	156	196	0.3	0.7
Ind Fund Churches	1	NR	NR	NR	-	-
Jehovah's Witness	2	NR	NR	NR	-	-
LDS–Comm of Christ	1	NR	194	194	0.3	0.7
LDS–L-D Saints	1	NR	NR	353	0.5	1.3
LUTH–Luth–MO Synod	3	256	544	666	1.0	2.4
MENN–CG in Cr (Menn)	1	NR	166	209	0.3	0.8
MENN–Mennonite USA	2	258	366	461	0.7	1.7
METH–Un Methodist	14	1,613	3,697	5,946	9.0	21.4
Non-denom Chr Chs	13	1,410	1,647	1,951	3.0	7.0
PENT–Assemb of God	3	370	170	500	0.8	1.8
PENT–Ch of God Proph	1	NR	8	10	0.0	0.0
PENT–Int Foursq Gos	1	13	10	13	0.0	0.0
PRES–Presb Ch (USA)	2	0	340	428	0.6	1.5
Salvation Army	1	21	18	178	0.3	0.6
Sev Day Adv	1	46	81	93	0.1	0.3
CHASE	**9**	**423**	**840**	**1,369**	**49.1**	**100.0**
Bahá'í	0	NR	1	1	0.0	0.1
BAPT–So Bapt Conv	1	43	280	337	12.1	24.6
Catholic	1	NR	NR	390	14.0	28.5
LUTH–Luth–MO Synod	1	41	64	76	2.7	5.6
METH–Un Methodist	3	124	245	256	9.2	18.7
Non-denom Chr Chs	2	180	180	225	8.1	16.4
PRES–Presb Ch (USA)	1	35	70	84	3.0	6.1
CHAUTAUQUA	**18**	**649**	**1,367**	**1,681**	**45.8**	**100.0**
ANG/EPIS–Episcopal	1	37	60	60	1.6	3.6
BAPT–Amer Bapt USA	2	160	545	643	17.5	38.3
BAPT–So Bapt Conv	2	93	264	311	8.5	18.5
Catholic	1	NR	NR	30	0.8	1.8
CHR–Chr Ch (Disc)	1	54	130	153	4.2	9.1
CHR–Chs of Christ	3	109	94	122	3.3	7.3
METH–Un Methodist	5	106	199	257	7.0	15.3
PENT–Assemb of God	2	75	49	75	2.0	4.5
Sev Day Adv	1	15	26	30	0.8	1.8
CHEROKEE	**60**	**2,526**	**6,402**	**12,062**	**55.8**	**100.0**
ANG/EPIS–Episcopal	1	21	30	30	0.1	0.2
BAPT–Amer Bapt USA	1	91	189	234	1.1	1.9
BAPT–So Bapt Conv	10	516	2,567	3,182	14.7	26.4
Catholic	4	NR	NR	3,700	17.1	30.7
Ch of Nazarene	3	126	128	221	1.0	1.8
CHR–Chr Ch (Disc)	2	227	1,013	1,256	5.8	10.4
CHR–Chr Chs & Chs Cr	5	NR	627	777	3.6	6.4
CHR–Chs of Christ	1	53	50	65	0.3	0.5
FRND–Evan Fr Ch Intl	3	285	197	244	1.1	2.0
FRND–Unaffl Mtgs	1	NR	NR	NR	-	-
Jehovah's Witness	2	NR	NR	NR	-	-
LDS–Comm of Christ	1	NR	135	135	0.6	1.1
METH–Un Methodist	9	242	571	786	3.6	6.5
Non-denom Chr Chs	5	295	435	458	2.1	3.8
PENT–Assemb of God	4	492	253	611	2.8	5.1
PENT–Ch of God Proph	1	NR	29	36	0.2	0.3
PENT–COGIC	1	20	20	25	0.1	0.2
PENT–Pent Ch of God	1	70	NR	109	0.5	0.9
PRES–Presb Ch (USA)	4	70	127	157	0.7	1.3
Sev Day Adv	1	18	31	36	0.2	0.3

Religious Group	Number of Congrega-tions	Number of Attendees	Number of Communicant, Confirmed, or Full Members	Adherents		
				Number of Adherents	% of Total Pop.	% of Total Adh.
CHEYENNE	**12**	**453**	**953**	**1,491**	**54.7**	**100.0**
BAPT–So Bapt Conv	2	57	44	52	1.9	3.5
Catholic	2	NR	NR	186	6.8	12.5
CHR–Chs of Christ	1	45	42	55	2.0	3.7
LUTH–Assoc Free Luth	1	NR	NR	NR	-	-
LUTH–E.L.C.A.	2	91	209	262	9.6	17.6
METH–Un Methodist	2	177	583	813	29.8	54.5
METH–Wesleyan	1	63	39	82	3.0	5.5
Sev Day Adv	1	20	36	41	1.5	2.7
CLARK	**14**	**393**	**851**	**1,365**	**61.6**	**100.0**
BAPT–Amer Bapt USA	1	12	33	41	1.9	3.0
Catholic	1	NR	NR	250	11.3	18.3
CGOD–Ch God (Ander)	1	33	NR	33	1.5	2.4
CHR–Chr Chs & Chs Cr	4	NR	239	295	13.3	21.6
CHR–Chs of Christ	1	22	18	25	1.1	1.8
METH–Un Methodist	1	106	228	360	16.3	26.4
Non-denom Chr Chs	2	180	250	250	11.3	18.3
PENT–Assemb of God	1	20	10	20	0.9	1.5
PRES–Presb Ch (USA)	1	0	47	58	2.6	4.2
PRES–Ref Pres of NA	1	20	26	33	1.5	2.4
CLAY	**26**	**1,798**	**3,219**	**5,029**	**58.9**	**100.0**
ANG/EPIS–Episcopal	1	43	76	83	1.0	1.7
Bahá'í	0	NR	1	1	0.0	0.0
BAPT–Amer Bapt USA	1	170	401	490	5.7	9.7
BAPT–So Bapt Conv	1	2	5	6	0.1	0.1
BRETH–Old Ord Rvr Br	1	NR	4	6	0.1	0.1
Catholic	1	NR	NR	561	6.6	11.2
CHR–Chr Chs & Chs Cr	1	NR	140	171	2.0	3.4
Evan Cov Ch	1	451	194	586	6.9	11.7
Jehovah's Witness	1	NR	NR	NR	-	-
LUTH–Luth Cong Msn Chr	1	28	64	78	0.9	1.6
LUTH–Luth–MO Synod	1	193	542	710	8.3	14.1
METH–Un Methodist	9	507	1,263	1,624	19.0	32.3
METH–Wesleyan	1	89	79	116	1.4	2.3
Non-denom Chr Chs	1	30	30	38	0.4	0.8
PENT–Assemb of God	1	27	10	58	0.7	1.2
PRES–Presb Ch (USA)	3	218	371	453	5.3	9.0
PRES–Ref Pres of NA	1	40	39	48	0.6	1.0
CLOUD	**29**	**1,169**	**2,485**	**5,303**	**55.6**	**100.0**
ANG/EPIS–Episcopal	1	13	15	17	0.2	0.3
BAPT–Amer Bapt USA	1	193	364	440	4.6	8.3
Catholic	5	NR	NR	1,894	19.9	35.7
CHR–Chr Chs & Chs Cr	4	NR	261	315	3.3	5.9
Evan Cov Ch	1	73	123	95	1.0	1.8
LDS–L-D Saints	1	NR	NR	205	2.2	3.9
LUTH–E.L.C.A.	2	130	372	491	5.2	9.3
METH–Un Methodist	7	279	941	1,125	11.8	21.2
METH–Wesleyan	2	291	216	379	4.0	7.1
Non-denom Chr Chs	1	50	50	62	0.7	1.2
PENT–Assemb of God	1	74	32	146	1.5	2.8
PENT–Int Foursq Gos	1	23	19	23	0.2	0.4
PRES–Presb Ch (USA)	2	43	92	111	1.2	2.1
COFFEY	**28**	**924**	**2,934**	**4,341**	**50.5**	**100.0**
Bahá'í	0	NR	2	2	0.0	0.0
BAPT–Amer Bapt USA	2	94	369	451	5.2	10.4
BAPT–So Bapt Conv	2	81	249	305	3.5	7.0
BRETH–Ch of Brethren	1	0	7	9	0.1	0.2
Catholic	2	NR	NR	620	7.2	14.3
Ch of Nazarene	1	9	13	22	0.3	0.5
CHR–Chr Chs & Chs Cr	4	NR	645	789	9.2	18.2
CHR–Chs of Christ	3	93	85	115	1.3	2.6
LDS–L-D Saints	1	NR	NR	117	1.4	2.7
LUTH–Luth–MO Synod	1	78	153	208	2.4	4.8
METH–Un Methodist	6	387	1,222	1,399	16.3	32.2
Non-denom Chr Chs	3	72	122	125	1.5	2.9
PENT–Assemb of God	2	110	67	179	2.1	4.1

NR–Not Reported   - Represents no adherents reported.   Percentages may not total 100 due to rounding.

Table 3: Religious Congregations by County and Group: 2010

Religious Group	Number of Congrega-tions	Number of Attendees	Number of Communicant, Confirmed, or Full Members	Adherents		
				Number of Adherents	% of Total Pop.	% of Total Adh.
COMANCHE	**12**	**358**	**1,015**	**1,336**	**70.7**	**100.0**
BAPT–Amer Bapt USA	1	79	127	155	8.2	11.6
BAPT–So Bapt Conv	1	45	100	122	6.5	9.1
Catholic	1	NR	NR	67	3.5	5.0
CHR–Chr Ch (Disc)	1	0	0	0	0.0	0.0
CHR–Chr Chs & Chs Cr	2	NR	296	362	19.1	27.1
METH–Un Methodist	3	140	437	502	26.5	37.6
Non-denom Chr Chs	1	50	30	62	3.3	4.6
PENT–Assemb of God	1	35	0	35	1.9	2.6
PRES–Presb Ch (USA)	1	9	25	31	1.6	2.3
COWLEY	**83**	**4,925**	**11,144**	**17,509**	**48.2**	**100.0**
ANG/EPIS–Episcopal	2	83	190	258	0.7	1.5
Bahá'í	0	NR	41	41	0.1	0.2
BAPT–Amer Bapt USA	3	428	986	1,215	3.3	6.9
BAPT–Free Will Bapt	1	NR	42	52	0.1	0.3
BAPT–Natl Mis Bapt Conv	1	0	150	185	0.5	1.1
BAPT–So Bapt Conv	8	457	2,211	2,724	7.5	15.6
Calv Chpl	1	NR	NR	NR	-	-
Catholic	2	NR	NR	2,500	6.9	14.3
Ch Cr, Scientst	1	NR	NR	NR	-	-
Ch of Nazarene	3	341	432	559	1.5	3.2
CHR–Chr Ch (Disc)	3	216	751	925	2.5	5.3
CHR–Chr Chs & Chs Cr	4	NR	320	394	1.1	2.3
CHR–Chs of Christ	3	241	250	320	0.9	1.8
Evan Free Ch	2	250	NR	250	0.7	1.4
FRND–Evan Fr Ch Intl	2	47	48	59	0.2	0.3
Jehovah's Witness	2	NR	NR	NR	-	-
LDS–L-D Saints	1	NR	NR	461	1.3	2.6
LUTH–Luth–MO Synod	2	355	817	1,205	3.3	6.9
METH–AME	2	55	150	185	0.5	1.1
METH–Un Methodist	12	946	2,675	3,530	9.7	20.2
Non-denom Chr Chs	8	512	702	723	2.0	4.1
PENT–Assemb of God	4	399	255	427	1.2	2.4
PENT–Ch God (Cleve)	2	82	70	86	0.2	0.5
PENT–Ch God Apos Fth	2	NR	NR	NR	-	-
PENT–COGIC	1	50	125	154	0.4	0.9
PENT–Int Foursq Gos	2	138	254	313	0.9	1.8
PENT–Intl Pent Holiness	2	66	59	73	0.2	0.4
PENT–Un Pent Ch Intl	2	NR	NR	NR	-	-
PRES–Presb Ch (USA)	3	220	516	636	1.8	3.6
Salvation Army	1	11	52	179	0.5	1.0
Sev Day Adv	1	28	48	55	0.2	0.3
CRAWFORD	**71**	**4,893**	**9,571**	**18,579**	**47.5**	**100.0**
ANG/EPIS–Episcopal	1	50	104	112	0.3	0.6
Bahá'í	0	NR	21	21	0.1	0.1
BAPT–Amer Bapt USA	4	321	496	601	1.5	3.2
BAPT–So Bapt Conv	5	321	718	870	2.2	4.7
BRETH–Ch of Brethren	1	77	71	86	0.2	0.5
Catholic	4	NR	NR	6,000	15.3	32.3
Ch of Nazarene	3	508	507	980	2.5	5.3
CHR–Chr Ch (Disc)	2	191	986	1,195	3.1	6.4
CHR–Chr Chs & Chs Cr	5	NR	846	1,025	2.6	5.5
CHR–Chs of Christ	2	193	175	206	0.5	1.1
Jehovah's Witness	2	NR	NR	NR	-	-
LDS–Comm of Christ	1	NR	135	135	0.3	0.7
LDS–L-D Saints	1	NR	NR	523	1.3	2.8
LUTH–E.L.C.A.	1	91	178	223	0.6	1.2
LUTH–Luth–MO Synod	3	264	595	746	1.9	4.0
LUTH–Wisc Ev Luth Syn	1	35	69	79	0.2	0.4
METH–Un Methodist	13	645	1,896	2,313	5.9	12.4
Muslim Est	1	20	NR	50	0.1	0.3
Non-denom Chr Chs	13	1,595	2,175	2,326	5.9	12.5
PENT–Assemb of God	1	270	82	360	0.9	1.9
PENT–Ch God (Cleve)	1	68	97	118	0.3	0.6
PRES–Presb Ch (USA)	3	164	245	297	0.8	1.6
Salvation Army	1	18	66	186	0.5	1.0
Sev Day Adv	2	62	109	125	0.3	0.7
Zoroastrian	0	NR	NR	2	0.0	0.0

Religious Group	Number of Congrega-tions	Number of Attendees	Number of Communicant, Confirmed, or Full Members	Adherents		
				Number of Adherents	% of Total Pop.	% of Total Adh.
DECATUR	**21**	**780**	**1,764**	**2,651**	**89.5**	**100.0**
BAPT–Amer Bapt USA	1	52	120	140	4.7	5.3
BAPT–So Bapt Conv	1	5	13	15	0.5	0.6
Catholic	2	NR	NR	342	11.6	12.9
CHR–Chr Ch (Disc)	1	0	104	122	4.1	4.6
CHR–Chs of Christ	1	18	10	20	0.7	0.8
Evan Cov Ch	2	92	64	119	4.0	4.5
LUTH–E.L.C.A.	1	32	132	167	5.6	6.3
LUTH–Luth–MO Synod	1	66	229	328	11.1	12.4
METH–Un Methodist	6	137	624	919	31.0	34.7
Non-denom Chr Chs	3	300	450	450	15.2	17.0
PENT–Assemb of God	1	20	10	20	0.7	0.8
PRES–Presb Ch (USA)	1	58	8	9	0.3	0.3
DICKINSON	**61**	**2,816**	**5,627**	**9,101**	**46.1**	**100.0**
ANG/EPIS–Episcopal	1	30	49	58	0.3	0.6
Bahá'í	0	NR	5	5	0.0	0.1
BAPT–Amer Bapt USA	3	306	300	370	1.9	4.1
BAPT–N Am Bapt Conf	1	NR	59	73	0.4	0.8
BAPT–So Bapt Conv	1	28	81	100	0.5	1.1
BRETH–Breth in Chr	5	NR	NR	NR	-	-
BRETH–Ch of Brethren	1	12	16	20	0.1	0.2
Catholic	6	NR	NR	2,074	10.5	22.8
CGOD–Ch God (Ander)	1	20	NR	20	0.1	0.2
Ch of Nazarene	1	0	21	21	0.1	0.2
CHR–Chr Ch (Disc)	1	0	114	140	0.7	1.5
CHR–Chr Chs & Chs Cr	3	NR	445	548	2.8	6.0
CHR–Chs of Christ	1	17	15	18	0.1	0.2
LUTH–E.L.C.A.	3	228	448	626	3.2	6.9
LUTH–Luth–MO Synod	5	307	750	911	4.6	10.0
METH–Un Methodist	13	1,001	2,014	2,593	13.1	28.5
Non-denom Chr Chs	5	550	660	737	3.7	8.1
PENT–Ch God (Cleve)	1	14	29	36	0.2	0.4
PRES–Evan Presby Ch	1	NR	69	85	0.4	0.9
PRES–Presb Ch (USA)	3	98	187	230	1.2	2.5
Sev Day Adv	1	79	137	158	0.8	1.7
Un Breth in Cr	1	18	15	16	0.1	0.2
Un C of Christ	3	108	213	262	1.3	2.9
DONIPHAN	**29**	**1,009**	**2,547**	**3,762**	**47.4**	**100.0**
Bahá'í	0	NR	2	2	0.0	0.1
BAPT–Amer Bapt USA	2	176	220	265	3.3	7.0
BAPT–So Bapt Conv	4	359	640	769	9.7	20.4
Catholic	5	NR	NR	623	7.8	16.6
CHR–Chr Ch (Disc)	1	65	302	363	4.6	9.6
CHR–Chr Chs & Chs Cr	1	NR	250	301	3.8	8.0
CHR–Chs of Christ	1	28	30	38	0.5	1.0
Jehovah's Witness	1	NR	NR	NR	-	-
LDS–Comm of Christ	1	NR	182	182	2.3	4.8
LUTH–E.L.C.A.	1	43	203	266	3.3	7.1
LUTH–Luth–MO Synod	1	61	140	203	2.6	5.4
METH–AME	1	0	100	120	1.5	3.2
METH–Un Methodist	6	205	383	462	5.8	12.3
PENT–Assemb of God	1	37	21	80	1.0	2.1
PENT–Ch God (Cleve)	1	15	17	20	0.3	0.5
PENT–COGIC	1	20	20	24	0.3	0.6
PRES–Presb Ch (USA)	1	0	37	44	0.6	1.2
DOUGLAS	**113**	**9,564**	**16,467**	**34,583**	**31.2**	**100.0**
ANG/EPIS–Episcopal	2	426	650	1,255	1.1	3.6
Bahá'í	1	NR	86	86	0.1	0.2
BAPT–Amer Bapt Assn	1	NR	85	100	0.1	0.3
BAPT–Amer Bapt USA	2	264	281	331	0.3	1.0
BAPT–Ref Bapt Ch	1	NR	NR	NR	-	-
BAPT–Reg Bapt Gen As	1	NR	NR	NR	-	-
BAPT–So Bapt Conv	4	714	1,739	2,046	1.8	5.9
BRETH–Ch of Brethren	2	47	96	113	0.1	0.3
BUDD–Mahayana	3	NR	NR	229	0.2	0.7
BUDD–Theravada	2	NR	NR	29	0.0	0.1
BUDD–Vajrayana	1	NR	NR	75	0.1	0.2
Calv Chpl	1	NR	NR	NR	-	-
Catholic	5	NR	NR	9,243	8.3	26.7

NR–Not Reported   - Represents no adherents reported.   Percentages may not total 100 due to rounding.

Table 3: Religious Congregations by County and Group: 2010

Religious Group	Number of Congrega-tions	Number of Attendees	Number of Communicant, Confirmed, or Full Members	Adherents: Number of Adherents	Adherents: % of Total Pop.	Adherents: % of Total Adh.
CGOD–Ch God (Ander)	1	60	NR	60	0.1	0.2
Ch of Nazarene	2	218	299	510	0.5	1.5
CHR–Chr Ch (Disc)	1	214	622	732	0.7	2.1
CHR–Chr Chs & Chs Cr	2	NR	310	365	0.3	1.1
CHR–Chs of Christ	8	351	342	431	0.4	1.2
CHR–Int Chs of Christ	1	NR	60	71	0.1	0.2
Christian Brethren	1	NR	NR	NR	-	-
Evan Free Ch	1	205	NR	205	0.2	0.6
FRND–Evan Fr Ch Intl	2	56	81	95	0.1	0.3
FRND–Fr Gen Cf	1	NR	0	0	0.0	0.0
HINDU–Trad Temples	1	NR	NR	20	0.0	0.1
Jehovah's Witness	1	NR	NR	NR	-	-
LDS–Comm of Christ	2	NR	388	388	0.4	1.1
LDS–L-D Saints	4	NR	NR	1,713	1.5	5.0
LUTH–E.L.C.A.	2	305	1,061	1,207	1.1	3.5
LUTH–Luth–MO Synod	2	309	615	834	0.8	2.4
MENN–Mennonite USA	1	55	62	73	0.1	0.2
METH–AME	2	60	225	265	0.2	0.8
METH–Free Methodist	2	789	302	808	0.7	2.3
METH–Un Methodist	13	1,535	3,593	4,655	4.2	13.5
METH–Wesleyan	1	362	166	471	0.4	1.4
Muslim Est	1	134	NR	308	0.3	0.9
Non-denom Chr Chs	15	2,025	2,239	2,753	2.5	8.0
ORTHE–Orth Ch in Amer	1	31	NR	46	0.0	0.1
PENT–Assemb of God	4	392	164	459	0.4	1.3
PENT–COGIC	1	30	27	32	0.0	0.1
PENT–Un Pent Ch Intl	1	NR	NR	NR	-	-
PRES–Evan Presby Ch	1	NR	436	513	0.5	1.5
PRES–Presb Ch (USA)	4	243	789	928	0.8	2.7
PRES–Ref Pres of NA	1	55	55	73	0.1	0.2
Salvation Army	1	47	74	1,113	1.0	3.2
Sev Day Adv	1	24	43	49	0.0	0.1
Un C of Christ	3	505	1,398	1,645	1.5	4.8
Unit Univ	1	108	179	254	0.2	0.7
Unity Ch	1	NR	NR	NR	-	-
EDWARDS	**16**	**430**	**849**	**2,180**	**71.8**	**100.0**
ANG/EPIS–Episcopal	1	7	13	13	0.4	0.6
Bahá'í	0	NR	2	2	0.1	0.1
BAPT–Amer Bapt USA	1	60	41	50	1.6	2.3
Catholic	3	NR	NR	1,091	35.9	50.0
Ch of Nazarene	1	28	16	34	1.1	1.6
CHR–Chr Ch (Disc)	2	36	84	103	3.4	4.7
LUTH–Luth–MO Synod	2	110	191	222	7.3	10.2
METH–Un Methodist	4	134	374	453	14.9	20.8
PENT–Assemb of God	1	31	13	71	2.3	3.3
Un C of Christ	1	24	115	141	4.6	6.5
ELK	**14**	**282**	**792**	**1,079**	**37.4**	**100.0**
BAPT–Amer Bapt USA	3	100	171	203	7.0	18.8
Calv Chpl	1	NR	NR	NR	-	-
Catholic	1	NR	NR	50	1.7	4.6
CHR–Chr Chs & Chs Cr	3	NR	210	249	8.6	23.1
METH–Un Methodist	5	147	369	499	17.3	46.2
PENT–Assemb of God	1	35	42	78	2.7	7.2
ELLIS	**46**	**2,653**	**4,148**	**16,291**	**57.3**	**100.0**
ANG/EPIS–Episcopal	2	37	66	66	0.2	0.4
Bahá'í	0	NR	24	24	0.1	0.1
BAPT–Amer Bapt USA	1	70	105	126	0.4	0.8
BAPT–Reg Bapt Gen As	1	NR	NR	NR	-	-
BAPT–So Bapt Conv	2	195	264	317	1.1	1.9
Catholic	13	NR	NR	10,388	36.5	63.8
Ch of Nazarene	1	53	52	91	0.3	0.6
CHR–Chr Ch (Disc)	1	600	540	648	2.3	4.0
CHR–Chr Chs & Chs Cr	1	NR	57	68	0.2	0.4
CHR–Chs of Christ	1	35	45	50	0.2	0.3
Jehovah's Witness	1	NR	NR	NR	-	-
LDS–L-D Saints	1	NR	NR	345	1.2	2.1
LUTH–E.L.C.A.	3	141	496	560	2.0	3.4
LUTH–Luth Ch-Am Asc	1	NR	NR	NR	-	-
LUTH–Luth–MO Synod	1	152	226	262	0.9	1.6
LUTH–Wisc Ev Luth Syn	1	13	9	10	0.0	0.1

Religious Group	Number of Congrega-tions	Number of Attendees	Number of Communicant, Confirmed, or Full Members	Adherents: Number of Adherents	Adherents: % of Total Pop.	Adherents: % of Total Adh.
MENN–Menn Br US Conf	1	NR	173	208	0.7	1.3
METH–Un Methodist	2	431	1,162	1,720	6.0	10.6
Muslim Est	1	134	NR	308	1.1	1.9
Non-denom Chr Chs	9	641	745	840	3.0	5.2
PENT–Assemb of God	1	52	25	69	0.2	0.4
PRES–Presb Ch (USA)	1	99	159	191	0.7	1.2
ELLSWORTH	**22**	**988**	**1,916**	**3,306**	**50.9**	**100.0**
ANG/EPIS–Episcopal	1	14	26	27	0.4	0.8
BAPT–N Am Bapt Conf	1	NR	138	161	2.5	4.9
BAPT–Reg Bapt Gen As	1	NR	NR	NR	-	-
Catholic	4	NR	NR	789	12.1	23.9
Evan Free Ch	1	90	NR	90	1.4	2.7
Jehovah's Witness	1	NR	NR	NR	-	-
LUTH–E.L.C.A.	2	85	116	133	2.0	4.0
LUTH–Luth–MO Synod	3	350	770	917	14.1	27.7
METH–Un Methodist	4	169	421	606	9.3	18.3
PENT–Assemb of God	1	78	50	124	1.9	3.8
PRES–Presb Ch (USA)	2	147	303	352	5.4	10.6
Un C of Christ	1	55	92	107	1.6	3.2
FINNEY	**53**	**3,433**	**7,516**	**18,446**	**50.2**	**100.0**
ANG/EPIS–Episcopal	1	29	64	77	0.2	0.4
Bahá'í	0	NR	36	36	0.1	0.2
BAPT–Amer Bapt USA	1	50	90	120	0.3	0.7
BAPT–So Bapt Conv	8	478	793	1,061	2.9	5.8
BRETH–Ch of Brethren	1	65	122	163	0.4	0.9
BUDD–Mahayana	1	NR	NR	505	1.4	2.7
Catholic	2	NR	NR	7,064	19.2	38.3
Ch of Nazarene	2	299	484	484	1.3	2.6
CHR–Chr Ch (Disc)	2	75	589	788	2.1	4.3
CHR–Chr Chs & Chs Cr	1	NR	981	1,313	3.6	7.1
CHR–Chs of Christ	1	100	70	125	0.3	0.7
Ind Fund Churches	1	NR	NR	NR	-	-
Jehovah's Witness	1	NR	NR	NR	-	-
LDS–L-D Saints	1	NR	NR	706	1.9	3.8
LUTH–Assoc Free Luth	1	NR	NR	NR	-	-
LUTH–E.L.C.A.	2	123	154	160	0.4	0.9
LUTH–Luth–MO Synod	2	231	425	572	1.6	3.1
MENN–Menn Br US Conf	1	NR	256	343	0.9	1.9
METH–Un Methodist	4	451	1,344	2,007	5.5	10.9
METH–Wesleyan	1	95	146	124	0.3	0.7
Muslim Est	1	134	NR	308	0.8	1.7
Non-denom Chr Chs	7	835	990	1,132	3.1	6.1
ORTHE–Ant Orth of NA	1	20	NR	35	0.1	0.2
PENT–Assemb of God	2	183	162	289	0.8	1.6
PENT–COGIC	1	0	150	201	0.5	1.1
PENT–Intl Pent Holiness	1	31	46	62	0.2	0.3
PRES–Presb Ch (USA)	2	0	208	278	0.8	1.5
Salvation Army	1	57	67	73	0.2	0.4
Sev Day Adv	2	102	178	205	0.6	1.1
Un C of Christ	1	75	161	215	0.6	1.2
FORD	**45**	**3,452**	**6,580**	**22,436**	**66.3**	**100.0**
ANG/EPIS–Episcopal	1	60	153	153	0.5	0.7
Bahá'í	0	NR	8	8	0.0	0.0
BAPT–Amer Bapt USA	1	120	122	162	0.5	0.7
BAPT–Ind Bapt Flwsp Intl	1	NR	NR	NR	-	-
BAPT–So Bapt Conv	3	247	452	599	1.8	2.7
Catholic	3	NR	NR	12,570	37.1	56.0
CGOD–Ch God (Ander)	1	46	NR	46	0.1	0.2
Ch of Nazarene	2	621	800	1,261	3.7	5.6
CHR–Chr Chs & Chs Cr	3	NR	1,060	1,406	4.2	6.3
CHR–Chs of Christ	1	240	206	329	1.0	1.5
FRND–Evan Fr Ch Intl	1	15	17	23	0.1	0.1
Jehovah's Witness	1	NR	NR	NR	-	-
LDS–L-D Saints	2	NR	NR	602	1.8	2.7
LUTH–Luth Cong Msn Chr	1	95	255	338	1.0	1.5
LUTH–Luth–MO Synod	1	139	367	463	1.4	2.1
MENN–CG in Cr (Menn)	1	NR	3	4	0.0	0.0
METH–Free Methodist	1	0	0	0	0.0	0.0
METH–Un Methodist	3	531	1,406	1,798	5.3	8.0
Missionary Ch	1	49	102	102	0.3	0.5

NR–Not Reported   - Represents no adherents reported.   Percentages may not total 100 due to rounding.

Table 3: Religious Congregations by County and Group: 2010

Religious Group	Number of Congrega-tions	Number of Attendees	Number of Communicant, Confirmed, or Full Members	Adherents		
				Number of Adherents	% of Total Pop.	% of Total Adh.
Muslim Est	1	134	NR	308	0.9	1.4
Non-denom Chr Chs	6	760	1,065	1,133	3.3	5.0
PENT–Assemb of God	2	173	124	307	0.9	1.4
PENT–Intl Pent Holiness	2	122	181	240	0.7	1.1
PENT–Un Pent Ch Intl	1	NR	NR	NR	-	-
PRES–Presb Ch (USA)	3	75	204	271	0.8	1.2
Salvation Army	1	19	44	300	0.9	1.3
Sev Day Adv	1	6	11	13	0.0	0.1
FRANKLIN	**58**	**3,559**	**6,485**	**9,910**	**38.1**	**100.0**
ANG/EPIS–Episcopal	1	16	18	18	0.1	0.2
Bahá'í	0	NR	5	5	0.0	0.1
BAPT–Amer Bapt USA	8	652	1,408	1,767	6.8	17.8
BAPT–NBC USA	1	65	57	72	0.3	0.7
BAPT–So Bapt Conv	1	52	75	94	0.4	0.9
BRETH–Ch of Brethren	1	0	94	118	0.5	1.2
Catholic	2	NR	NR	1,350	5.2	13.6
Ch Cr, Scientst	1	NR	NR	NR	-	-
Ch of Nazarene	2	92	177	197	0.8	2.0
CHR–Chr Ch (Disc)	1	61	270	339	1.3	3.4
CHR–Chr Chs & Chs Cr	2	NR	90	113	0.4	1.1
CHR–Chs of Christ	2	150	127	205	0.8	2.1
Ind Fund Churches	1	NR	NR	NR	-	-
Intl Fell Bible Ch	1	NR	NR	NR	-	-
Jehovah's Witness	1	NR	NR	NR	-	-
LDS–Comm of Christ	1	NR	194	194	0.7	2.0
LDS–L-D Saints	1	NR	NR	504	1.9	5.1
LUTH–Luth–MO Synod	1	190	367	557	2.1	5.6
METH–AME	1	0	100	126	0.5	1.3
METH–Un Methodist	10	545	1,333	1,641	6.3	16.6
METH–Wesleyan	1	97	97	126	0.5	1.3
Non-denom Chr Chs	9	1,043	1,285	1,378	5.3	13.9
PENT–Assemb of God	3	309	179	348	1.3	3.5
PENT–Ch God (Cleve)	1	42	68	85	0.3	0.9
PENT–Int Foursq Gos	1	60	108	136	0.5	1.4
PRES–Evan Presby Ch	1	NR	130	163	0.6	1.6
PRES–Presb Ch (USA)	2	150	242	304	1.2	3.1
Sev Day Adv	1	35	61	70	0.3	0.7
GEARY	**51**	**4,330**	**7,437**	**13,160**	**38.3**	**100.0**
ANG/EPIS–Episcopal	1	55	56	195	0.6	1.5
Bahá'í	0	NR	26	26	0.1	0.2
BAPT–Amer Bapt USA	2	281	727	977	2.8	7.4
BAPT–N Am Bapt Conf	1	NR	44	59	0.2	0.4
BAPT–NBC USA	1	200	450	605	1.8	4.6
BAPT–So Bapt Conv	3	266	1,258	1,691	4.9	12.8
Catholic	1	NR	NR	1,355	3.9	10.3
CGOD–Ch God (Ander)	1	250	NR	250	0.7	1.9
Ch of Nazarene	1	372	292	372	1.1	2.8
CHR–Chr Chs & Chs Cr	1	NR	300	403	1.2	3.1
CHR–Chs of Christ	2	61	40	67	0.2	0.5
CONG–Consrv Cong Chr	1	30	28	38	0.1	0.3
Jehovah's Witness	1	NR	NR	NR	-	-
LDS–L-D Saints	2	NR	NR	1,515	4.4	11.5
LUTH–E.L.C.A.	1	38	105	133	0.4	1.0
LUTH–Luth–MO Synod	2	159	334	334	1.0	2.5
METH–AME	1	0	100	134	0.4	1.0
METH–Un Methodist	3	241	641	822	2.4	6.2
METH–Wesleyan	2	35	29	46	0.1	0.3
Muslim Est	2	268	NR	616	1.8	4.7
Non-denom Chr Chs	14	1,550	2,285	2,389	7.0	18.2
PENT–Assemb of God	3	287	90	289	0.8	2.2
PENT–Ch God (Cleve)	1	37	42	56	0.2	0.4
PENT–COGIC	1	125	50	67	0.2	0.5
PRES–Presb Ch (USA)	1	0	418	562	1.6	4.3
Sev Day Adv	1	15	26	30	0.1	0.2
Un C of Christ	1	60	96	129	0.4	1.0
GOVE	**10**	**212**	**638**	**1,539**	**57.1**	**100.0**
BRETH–Ch of Brethren	1	75	224	270	10.0	17.5
Catholic	3	NR	NR	848	31.5	55.1
METH–Un Methodist	4	107	347	354	13.1	23.0
Non-denom Chr Chs	1	15	30	30	1.1	1.9

Religious Group	Number of Congrega-tions	Number of Attendees	Number of Communicant, Confirmed, or Full Members	Adherents		
				Number of Adherents	% of Total Pop.	% of Total Adh.
PRES–Ref Pres of NA	1	15	37	37	1.4	2.4
GRAHAM	**13**	**327**	**758**	**1,244**	**47.9**	**100.0**
Bahá'í	0	NR	4	4	0.2	0.3
BAPT–So Bapt Conv	1	40	50	58	2.2	4.7
Catholic	1	NR	NR	273	10.5	21.9
CGOD–Ch God (Ander)	1	35	NR	35	1.3	2.8
CHR–Chr Chs & Chs Cr	1	NR	150	175	6.7	14.1
Jehovah's Witness	1	NR	NR	NR	-	-
LUTH–Luth–MO Synod	1	21	71	74	2.8	5.9
METH–Un Methodist	3	125	325	383	14.7	30.8
PENT–Assemb of God	2	55	43	108	4.2	8.7
PENT–Ch God (Cleve)	1	16	63	73	2.8	5.9
PRES–Presb Ch (USA)	1	35	52	61	2.3	4.9
GRANT	**23**	**1,142**	**2,315**	**5,209**	**66.5**	**100.0**
ANG/EPIS–Episcopal	1	22	27	27	0.3	0.5
BAPT–Amer Bapt USA	1	140	165	220	2.8	4.2
BAPT–Consrv Bapt	1	NR	NR	NR	-	-
BAPT–Free Will Bapt	1	NR	42	56	0.7	1.1
BAPT–So Bapt Conv	2	240	260	346	4.4	6.6
Catholic	1	NR	NR	1,915	24.5	36.8
CGOD–Ch God (Ander)	1	34	NR	34	0.4	0.7
Ch of Nazarene	1	35	25	66	0.8	1.3
CHR–Chr Ch (Disc)	1	91	311	414	5.3	7.9
CHR–Chs of Christ	1	150	159	220	2.8	4.2
Jehovah's Witness	1	NR	NR	NR	-	-
LDS–L-D Saints	1	NR	NR	254	3.2	4.9
LUTH–Luth–MO Synod	1	30	87	114	1.5	2.2
MENN–CG in Cr (Menn)	1	NR	155	206	2.6	4.0
MENN–Menn Br US Conf	2	NR	112	149	1.9	2.9
METH–Un Methodist	1	125	653	803	10.3	15.4
Non-denom Chr Chs	1	100	150	150	1.9	2.9
PENT–Assemb of God	2	125	87	125	1.6	2.4
PENT–Ch God (Cleve)	1	21	47	63	0.8	1.2
PENT–Intl Pent Holiness	1	29	35	47	0.6	0.9
GRAY	**19**	**658**	**2,328**	**3,563**	**59.3**	**100.0**
Bahá'í	0	NR	1	1	0.0	0.0
BAPT–So Bapt Conv	1	58	110	143	2.4	4.0
Catholic	1	NR	NR	541	9.0	15.2
Ch of Nazarene	1	163	304	304	5.1	8.5
CHR–Chr Chs & Chs Cr	2	NR	160	208	3.5	5.8
Ind Fund Churches	1	NR	NR	NR	-	-
MENN–CG in Cr (Menn)	5	NR	793	1,032	17.2	29.0
MENN–Menn Br US Conf	1	NR	49	64	1.1	1.8
MENN–Mennonite USA	1	30	29	38	0.6	1.1
METH–Un Methodist	4	202	687	976	16.3	27.4
Non-denom Chr Chs	2	205	195	256	4.3	7.2
GREELEY	**7**	**191**	**439**	**836**	**67.0**	**100.0**
Bahá'í	0	NR	1	1	0.1	0.1
BAPT–So Bapt Conv	1	3	8	10	0.8	1.2
Catholic	1	NR	NR	267	21.4	31.9
LDS–Comm of Christ	1	NR	128	128	10.3	15.3
METH–Free Methodist	1	51	8	51	4.1	6.1
METH–Un Methodist	1	87	228	270	21.7	32.3
PENT–Assemb of God	1	50	23	57	4.6	6.8
PRES–Presb Ch (USA)	1	0	43	52	4.2	6.2
GREENWOOD	**32**	**1,093**	**2,168**	**3,314**	**49.5**	**100.0**
Ap Chr Ch-Amer	1	70	40	70	1.0	2.1
Bahá'í	0	NR	2	2	0.0	0.1
BAPT–So Bapt Conv	4	204	639	770	11.5	23.2
Catholic	3	NR	NR	350	5.2	10.6
Ch of Nazarene	1	35	64	91	1.4	2.7
CHR–Chr Ch (Disc)	2	48	213	257	3.8	7.8
CHR–Chr Chs & Chs Cr	2	NR	50	60	0.9	1.8
CHR–Chs of Christ	1	30	20	26	0.4	0.8
Evan Free Ch	1	70	NR	70	1.0	2.1
Jehovah's Witness	1	NR	NR	NR	-	-
LUTH–E.L.C.A.	1	74	211	319	4.8	9.6

NR–Not Reported   - Represents no adherents reported.   Percentages may not total 100 due to rounding.

Table 3: Religious Congregations by County and Group: 2010

Religious Group	Number of Congrega-tions	Number of Attendees	Number of Communicant, Confirmed, or Full Members	Adherents: Number of Adherents	Adherents: % of Total Pop.	Adherents: % of Total Adh.
METH–Un Methodist	8	168	472	570	8.5	17.2
METH–Wesleyan	1	232	101	302	4.5	9.1
Non-denom Chr Chs	1	20	20	25	0.4	0.8
PENT–Assemb of God	1	26	21	26	0.4	0.8
PENT–Intl Pent Holiness	1	22	35	42	0.6	1.3
PRES–Presb Ch (USA)	1	14	13	16	0.2	0.5
Sev Day Adv	1	32	56	64	1.0	1.9
Un C of Christ	1	48	211	254	3.8	7.7
HAMILTON	**9**	**263**	**736**	**1,306**	**48.6**	**100.0**
BAPT–So Bapt Conv	2	52	85	111	4.1	8.5
Catholic	1	NR	NR	340	12.6	26.0
Ch of Nazarene	1	13	18	18	0.7	1.4
CHR–Chr Chs & Chs Cr	1	NR	30	39	1.4	3.0
METH–Un Methodist	2	98	381	543	20.2	41.6
METH–Wesleyan	1	70	96	91	3.4	7.0
PRES–Presb Ch (USA)	1	30	126	164	6.1	12.6
HARPER	**29**	**742**	**2,219**	**3,828**	**63.4**	**100.0**
ANG/EPIS–Episcopal	1	10	18	18	0.3	0.5
Bahá'í	0	NR	2	2	0.0	0.1
BAPT–Amer Bapt USA	2	30	91	111	1.8	2.9
Catholic	1	NR	NR	1,100	18.2	28.7
Ch of Nazarene	1	26	45	53	0.9	1.4
CHR–Chr Chs & Chs Cr	3	NR	670	818	13.6	21.4
CHR–Chs of Christ	4	154	143	202	3.3	5.3
MENN–Mennonite USA	2	110	277	338	5.6	8.8
METH–Un Methodist	5	196	640	715	11.8	18.7
Non-denom Chr Chs	1	35	35	44	0.7	1.1
PENT–Assemb of God	2	103	75	156	2.6	4.1
PENT–Un Pent Ch Intl	1	NR	NR	NR	-	-
PRES–Presb Ch (USA)	3	39	89	109	1.8	2.8
Sev Day Adv	1	14	24	28	0.5	0.7
Un C of Christ	2	25	110	134	2.2	3.5
HARVEY	**74**	**6,817**	**11,772**	**19,470**	**56.1**	**100.0**
ANG/EPIS–Episcopal	1	53	69	123	0.4	0.6
Bahá'í	0	NR	80	80	0.2	0.4
BAPT–Amer Bapt USA	2	122	354	441	1.3	2.3
BAPT–Reg Bapt Gen As	1	NR	NR	NR	-	-
BAPT–So Bapt Conv	1	85	125	156	0.4	0.8
BRETH–Ch of Brethren	1	30	30	37	0.1	0.2
Catholic	3	NR	NR	3,500	10.1	18.0
CGOD–Ch God (Ander)	1	115	NR	115	0.3	0.6
Ch of Nazarene	2	211	322	334	1.0	1.7
CHR–Chr Ch (Disc)	1	71	240	299	0.9	1.5
CHR–Chr Chs & Chs Cr	3	NR	625	778	2.2	4.0
CHR–Chs of Christ	3	162	130	149	0.4	0.8
CONG–Cong Chr, NA	1	NR	101	126	0.4	0.6
Evan Cov Ch	1	140	85	182	0.5	0.9
Evan Free Ch	1	350	NR	350	1.0	1.8
Ind Fund Churches	1	NR	NR	NR	-	-
Jehovah's Witness	1	NR	NR	NR	-	-
LDS–L-D Saints	1	NR	NR	531	1.5	2.7
LUTH–Luth-MO Synod	1	172	357	451	1.3	2.3
MENN–CG in Cr (Menn)	3	NR	535	666	1.9	3.4
MENN–Fel Evg Ch	1	793	412	513	1.5	2.6
MENN–Menn Br US Conf	2	NR	330	411	1.2	2.1
MENN–Mennonite USA	11	2,059	3,486	4,339	12.5	22.3
METH–AME	1	0	100	124	0.4	0.6
METH–Free Methodist	1	22	0	22	0.1	0.1
METH–Un Methodist	10	961	2,452	3,275	9.4	16.8
Missionary Ch	1	105	76	105	0.3	0.5
Non-denom Chr Chs	9	868	1,035	1,148	3.3	5.9
PENT–Assemb of God	1	81	32	117	0.3	0.6
PENT–Int Foursq Gos	1	110	179	223	0.6	1.1
PENT–Pent Ch of God	1	70	NR	109	0.3	0.6
PRES–Presb Ch (USA)	3	166	413	514	1.5	2.6
Sev Day Adv	1	15	26	30	0.1	0.2
Un C of Christ	2	56	178	222	0.6	1.1

Religious Group	Number of Congrega-tions	Number of Attendees	Number of Communicant, Confirmed, or Full Members	Adherents: Number of Adherents	Adherents: % of Total Pop.	Adherents: % of Total Adh.
HASKELL	**11**	**519**	**1,386**	**2,306**	**54.2**	**100.0**
Bahá'í	0	NR	1	1	0.0	0.0
BAPT–So Bapt Conv	3	215	533	697	16.4	30.2
Catholic	1	NR	NR	517	12.1	22.4
CGOD–Ch God (Ander)	1	67	NR	67	1.6	2.9
Ch of Nazarene	1	49	99	99	2.3	4.3
CHR–Chr Chs & Chs Cr	1	NR	250	327	7.7	14.2
CHR–Chs of Christ	2	47	44	57	1.3	2.5
METH–Un Methodist	2	141	459	541	12.7	23.5
HODGEMAN	**10**	**338**	**755**	**1,281**	**66.9**	**100.0**
BAPT–Amer Bapt USA	2	46	122	148	7.7	11.6
BAPT–So Bapt Conv	1	12	82	100	5.2	7.8
Catholic	2	NR	NR	364	19.0	28.4
LUTH–Luth-MO Synod	1	14	14	14	0.7	1.1
MENN–Mennonite USA	1	18	50	61	3.2	4.8
METH–Un Methodist	2	188	410	500	26.1	39.0
PRES–Presb Ch (USA)	1	60	77	94	4.9	7.3
JACKSON	**33**	**1,716**	**3,661**	**5,699**	**42.3**	**100.0**
ANG/EPIS–Episcopal	1	12	19	19	0.1	0.3
Bahá'í	0	NR	4	4	0.0	0.1
BAPT–Amer Bapt USA	4	388	554	693	5.1	12.2
Catholic	2	NR	NR	1,261	9.4	22.1
Ch of Nazarene	1	16	15	20	0.1	0.4
CHR–Chr Ch (Disc)	1	36	100	125	0.9	2.2
CHR–Chr Chs & Chs Cr	4	NR	606	758	5.6	13.3
Jehovah's Witness	2	NR	NR	NR	-	-
LDS–Comm of Christ	1	NR	194	194	1.4	3.4
LUTH–Luth-MO Synod	2	154	273	429	3.2	7.5
METH–Un Methodist	10	686	1,404	1,602	11.9	28.1
Non-denom Chr Chs	3	355	395	475	3.5	8.3
PRES–Presb Ch (USA)	1	18	38	48	0.4	0.8
PRES–Ref Pres of NA	1	51	59	71	0.5	1.2
JEFFERSON	**39**	**2,244**	**3,885**	**7,590**	**39.7**	**100.0**
Bahá'í	0	NR	3	3	0.0	0.0
BAPT–Amer Bapt Assn	1	NR	0	0	0.0	0.0
BAPT–Amer Bapt USA	1	173	375	459	2.4	6.0
BAPT–S-D Baptist Gen Con	1	22	88	108	0.6	1.4
BAPT–So Bapt Conv	1	57	142	174	0.9	2.3
Catholic	5	NR	NR	1,829	9.6	24.1
Ch of Nazarene	1	88	170	170	0.9	2.2
CHR–Chr Chs & Chs Cr	4	NR	300	367	1.9	4.8
CHR–Chs of Christ	1	50	51	63	0.3	0.8
Evan Free Ch	1	100	NR	100	0.5	1.3
Jehovah's Witness	1	NR	NR	NR	-	-
LUTH–E.L.C.A.	1	25	38	48	0.3	0.6
LUTH–Luth-MO Synod	1	111	243	283	1.5	3.7
MENN–Mara Amish-Menn	1	80	41	80	0.4	1.1
METH–Un Methodist	10	583	1,690	2,438	12.7	32.1
Non-denom Chr Chs	4	385	410	505	2.6	6.7
PENT–Assemb of God	3	504	239	850	4.4	11.2
PRES–Presb Ch (USA)	1	16	35	43	0.2	0.6
PRES–Ref Pres of NA	1	50	60	70	0.4	0.9
JEWELL	**20**	**479**	**1,246**	**1,825**	**59.3**	**100.0**
Catholic	2	NR	NR	191	6.2	10.5
Ch of Nazarene	1	18	22	22	0.7	1.2
CHR–Chr Chs & Chs Cr	2	NR	135	156	5.1	8.5
Evan Free Ch	1	25	NR	25	0.8	1.4
FRND–Evan Fr Ch Intl	1	38	89	103	3.3	5.6
LUTH–E.L.C.A.	1	53	147	175	5.7	9.6
LUTH–Luth Cong Msn Chr	1	53	170	197	6.4	10.8
LUTH–Nor Amer Luth C	1	NR	NR	NR	-	-
METH–Un Methodist	7	205	600	847	27.5	46.4
Non-denom Chr Chs	2	78	75	97	3.2	5.3
PENT–Assemb of God	1	9	8	12	0.4	0.7
JOHNSON	**350**	**81,838**	**133,616**	**296,689**	**54.5**	**100.0**
ANG/EPIS–Anglican NA	2	NR	NR	NR	-	-

NR–Not Reported   - Represents no adherents reported.   Percentages may not total 100 due to rounding.

Table 3: Religious Congregations by County and Group: 2010

Religious Group	Number of Congregations	Number of Attendees	Number of Communicant, Confirmed, or Full Members	Adherents: Number of Adherents	Adherents: % of Total Pop.	Adherents: % of Total Adh.
ANG/EPIS–Episcopal	5	1,004	3,245	3,579	0.7	1.2
Bahá'í	1	NR	144	144	0.0	0.0
BAPT–Amer Bapt USA	13	1,661	3,747	4,718	0.9	1.6
BAPT–Asc Ref Bap Ch Am	1	NR	NR	NR	-	-
BAPT–Free Will Bapt	2	NR	105	132	0.0	0.0
BAPT–Natl Mis Bapt Conv	1	0	150	189	0.0	0.1
BAPT–Ref Bapt Ch	1	NR	NR	NR	-	-
BAPT–Reg Bapt Gen As	1	NR	NR	NR	-	-
BAPT–So Bapt Conv	26	13,072	19,474	24,522	4.5	8.3
BRETH–Ch of Brethren	2	19	57	72	0.0	0.0
BUDD–Mahayana	3	NR	NR	3,269	0.6	1.1
BUDD–Theravada	4	NR	NR	343	0.1	0.1
Calv Chpl	2	NR	NR	NR	-	-
Catholic	18	NR	NR	102,131	18.8	34.4
CGOD–Ch God (Ander)	2	890	NR	890	0.2	0.3
Ch Cr, Scientst	2	NR	NR	NR	-	-
Ch of Nazarene	14	5,782	7,411	9,713	1.8	3.3
Chr & Miss Al	1	52	72	72	0.0	0.0
CHR–Chr Ch (Disc)	16	2,217	4,161	5,240	1.0	1.8
CHR–Chr Chs & Chs Cr	9	NR	5,295	6,668	1.2	2.2
CHR–Chs of Christ	8	1,602	1,595	2,282	0.4	0.8
Christian Brethren	1	NR	NR	NR	-	-
Evan Cov Ch	6	1,956	1,920	2,543	0.5	0.9
Evan Free Ch	2	1,631	NR	1,631	0.3	0.5
FRND–Evan Fr Ch Intl	1	15	9	11	0.0	0.0
HINDU–I/A Temples	1	NR	NR	350	0.1	0.1
HINDU–Post Ren	2	NR	NR	92	0.0	0.0
HINDU–Trad Temples	1	NR	NR	1,200	0.2	0.4
Ind Fund Churches	1	NR	NR	NR	-	-
Jain	1	NR	NR	NR	-	-
Jehovah's Witness	4	NR	NR	NR	-	-
JUD–Conserv	2	777	872	2,354	0.4	0.8
JUD–Orth	1	360	170	500	0.1	0.2
JUD–Reform	2	966	1,703	4,598	0.8	1.5
LDS–Comm of Christ	4	NR	776	776	0.1	0.3
LDS–L-D Saints	9	NR	NR	4,966	0.9	1.7
LUTH–E.L.C.A.	12	3,032	5,731	7,503	1.4	2.5
LUTH–Luth–MO Synod	9	3,480	7,460	9,964	1.8	3.4
LUTH–Wisc Ev Luth Syn	1	231	356	458	0.1	0.2
MENN–Menn Br US Conf	2	NR	365	460	0.1	0.2
METH–AME	1	0	150	189	0.0	0.1
METH–Un Methodist	24	11,925	24,949	37,096	6.8	12.5
METH–Wesleyan	4	797	305	1,037	0.2	0.3
MJEW–Union Mes Cong	1	NR	NR	NR	-	-
Muslim Est	3	468	NR	2,616	0.5	0.9
New Apost Ch	1	NR	NR	NR	-	-
Non-denom Chr Chs	62	19,155	28,202	30,513	5.6	10.3
ORTHE–Greek Orthodox	1	115	NR	225	0.0	0.1
ORTHE–Orth Ch in Amer	1	140	NR	320	0.1	0.1
ORTHE–Rus Orth Abroad	1	4	NR	15	0.0	0.0
ORTHE–Serb Orth USA	1	242	NR	410	0.1	0.1
ORTHO–Coptic Orth Ch	1	276	NR	535	0.1	0.2
PENT–Assemb of God	7	3,062	402	3,715	0.7	1.3
PENT–Ch God (Cleve)	2	15	15	19	0.0	0.0
PENT–Ch God Apos Fth	1	NR	NR	NR	-	-
PENT–Ch of God Proph	1	NR	150	189	0.0	0.1
PENT–COGIC	2	0	210	264	0.0	0.1
PENT–Int Foursq Gos	2	12	14	18	0.0	0.0
PENT–Un Pent Ch Intl	1	NR	NR	NR	-	-
PENT–Vineyard	1	877	1,051	1,323	0.2	0.4
PRES–Evan Presby Ch	1	NR	322	405	0.1	0.1
PRES–Orth Pres Ch	1	55	64	93	0.0	0.0
PRES–Presb Ch (USA)	15	3,555	9,766	12,298	2.3	4.1
PRES–Presb Ch Amer	4	861	716	924	0.2	0.3
PRES–Ref Pres of NA	1	102	93	126	0.0	0.0
REF–Christian Ref	1	50	50	63	0.0	0.0
REF–Ref Ch in Am	1	70	87	177	0.0	0.1
Salvation Army	1	63	113	113	0.0	0.0
Sev Day Adv	6	872	1,516	1,743	0.3	0.6
Sikh	1	NR	NR	NR	-	-
Un C of Christ	1	185	363	457	0.1	0.2
Unit Univ	1	190	260	430	0.1	0.1
Unity Ch	2	NR	NR	NR	-	-
Zoroastrian	0	NR	NR	6	0.0	0.0

Religious Group	Number of Congregations	Number of Attendees	Number of Communicant, Confirmed, or Full Members	Adherents: Number of Adherents	Adherents: % of Total Pop.	Adherents: % of Total Adh.
KEARNY	**12**	**463**	**1,029**	**2,838**	**71.4**	**100.0**
ANG/EPIS–Episcopal	1	12	20	32	0.8	1.1
Catholic	2	NR	NR	1,165	29.3	41.1
CHR–Chr Ch (Disc)	1	10	14	18	0.5	0.6
CHR–Chs of Christ	1	65	52	87	2.2	3.1
LUTH–Luth–MO Synod	1	0	156	172	4.3	6.1
MENN–CG in Cr (Menn)	1	NR	110	142	3.6	5.0
METH–Un Methodist	2	174	522	862	21.7	30.4
METH–Wesleyan	1	106	76	138	3.5	4.9
PENT–Assemb of God	1	68	26	154	3.9	5.4
PRES–Presb Ch (USA)	1	28	53	68	1.7	2.4
KINGMAN	**29**	**983**	**2,242**	**4,959**	**63.1**	**100.0**
ANG/EPIS–Episcopal	1	14	41	44	0.6	0.9
BAPT–Amer Bapt USA	2	130	454	553	7.0	11.2
BAPT–Reg Bapt Gen As	1	NR	NR	NR	-	-
Catholic	6	NR	NR	2,100	26.7	42.3
Ch of Nazarene	1	26	47	47	0.6	0.9
CHR–Chr Ch (Disc)	1	56	180	219	2.8	4.4
CHR–Chr Chs & Chs Cr	2	NR	240	292	3.7	5.9
CHR–Chs of Christ	3	165	133	192	2.4	3.9
Jehovah's Witness	1	NR	NR	NR	-	-
LUTH–Luth–MO Synod	1	46	100	127	1.6	2.6
MENN–Mennonite USA	1	96	78	95	1.2	1.9
METH–Un Methodist	7	359	877	1,141	14.5	23.0
PENT–Assemb of God	1	66	27	70	0.9	1.4
PRES–Presb Ch (USA)	1	25	65	79	1.0	1.6
KIOWA	**13**	**765**	**1,527**	**2,087**	**81.7**	**100.0**
Bahá'í	0	NR	1	1	0.0	0.0
BAPT–Amer Bapt USA	1	90	92	108	4.2	5.2
BAPT–So Bapt Conv	1	50	95	112	4.4	5.4
Catholic	1	NR	NR	157	6.1	7.5
CHR–Chs of Christ	1	85	75	90	3.5	4.3
FRND–Evan Fr Ch Intl	1	221	424	500	19.6	24.0
LUTH–Luth–MO Synod	1	17	19	19	0.7	0.9
MENN–CG in Cr (Menn)	1	NR	122	144	5.6	6.9
MENN–Mennonite USA	1	67	78	92	3.6	4.4
METH–Un Methodist	4	206	602	824	32.3	39.5
PENT–Assemb of God	1	29	19	40	1.6	1.9
LABETTE	**64**	**3,007**	**7,352**	**10,874**	**50.3**	**100.0**
ANG/EPIS–Episcopal	1	38	77	135	0.6	1.2
Bahá'í	0	NR	2	2	0.0	0.0
BAPT–Amer Bapt USA	4	448	1,470	1,806	8.4	16.6
BAPT–Free Will Bapt	1	NR	42	52	0.2	0.5
BAPT–Ind Bapt Flwsp Intl	1	NR	NR	NR	-	-
BAPT–So Bapt Conv	7	305	914	1,123	5.2	10.3
BRETH–Ch of Brethren	1	22	43	53	0.2	0.5
Catholic	2	NR	NR	1,000	4.6	9.2
Ch of Nazarene	1	296	367	550	2.5	5.1
CHR–Chr Ch (Disc)	1	105	543	667	3.1	6.1
CHR–Chr Chs & Chs Cr	7	NR	820	1,008	4.7	9.3
CHR–Chs of Christ	1	40	35	60	0.3	0.6
Jehovah's Witness	1	NR	NR	NR	-	-
LDS–L-D Saints	1	NR	NR	256	1.2	2.4
LUTH–Luth–MO Synod	2	48	106	116	0.5	1.1
MENN–Amish Undif	2	NR	59	173	0.8	1.6
MENN–Beachy Amish-Menn	1	43	26	43	0.2	0.4
METH–AME	1	0	100	123	0.6	1.1
METH–Un Methodist	14	564	1,358	1,931	8.9	17.8
Non-denom Chr Chs	5	380	425	503	2.3	4.6
PENT–Assemb of God	3	263	179	307	1.4	2.8
PENT–Ch God (Cleve)	2	45	51	63	0.3	0.6
PENT–Int Foursq Gos	1	264	493	606	2.8	5.6
PENT–Vineyard	1	90	100	123	0.6	1.1
PRES–Presb Ch (USA)	2	56	142	174	0.8	1.6
Un Breth in Cr	1	0	0	0	0.0	0.0
LANE	**6**	**303**	**956**	**1,576**	**90.1**	**100.0**
BAPT–So Bapt Conv	1	58	126	151	8.6	9.6
Catholic	1	NR	NR	317	18.1	20.1

NR–Not Reported - Represents no adherents reported. Percentages may not total 100 due to rounding.

Table 3: Religious Congregations by County and Group: 2010

Religious Group	Number of Congregations	Number of Attendees	Number of Communicant, Confirmed, or Full Members	Adherents		
				Number of Adherents	% of Total Pop.	% of Total Adh.
CHR–Chr Ch (Disc)	1	56	335	400	22.9	25.4
METH–Un Methodist	2	129	435	633	36.2	40.2
Non-denom Chr Chs	1	60	60	75	4.3	4.8
LEAVENWORTH	**82**	**5,725**	**10,715**	**24,816**	**32.6**	**100.0**
ANG/EPIS–Episcopal	1	145	391	398	0.5	1.6
Bahá'í	0	NR	8	8	0.0	0.0
BAPT–Amer Bapt Assn	1	NR	150	187	0.2	0.8
BAPT–Amer Bapt USA	4	685	904	1,125	1.5	4.5
BAPT–Ind Bapt Flwsp Intl	1	NR	NR	NR	-	-
BAPT–NBC USA	1	50	70	87	0.1	0.4
BAPT–So Bapt Conv	7	548	709	883	1.2	3.6
Catholic	7	NR	NR	9,321	12.2	37.6
CGOD–Ch God (Ander)	1	0	NR	0	0.0	0.0
Ch of Nazarene	2	80	153	165	0.2	0.7
CHR–Chr Ch (Disc)	1	130	591	736	1.0	3.0
CHR–Chr Chs & Chs Cr	2	NR	836	1,041	1.4	4.2
CHR–Chs of Christ	4	164	134	200	0.3	0.8
CONG–Cong Chr, NA	1	NR	52	65	0.1	0.3
Evan Free Ch	1	100	NR	100	0.1	0.4
FRND–Evan Fr Ch Intl	3	76	104	129	0.2	0.5
Jehovah's Witness	2	NR	NR	NR	-	-
LDS–Comm of Christ	2	NR	388	388	0.5	1.6
LDS–L-D Saints	2	NR	NR	1,165	1.5	4.7
LUTH–Luth-MO Synod	4	682	1,731	2,348	3.1	9.5
METH–AME	1	160	225	280	0.4	1.1
METH–C.M.E.	1	0	150	187	0.2	0.8
METH–Un Methodist	10	850	1,691	2,364	3.1	9.5
Muslim Est	1	134	NR	308	0.4	1.2
Non-denom Chr Chs	12	1,425	1,579	1,874	2.5	7.6
PENT–Assemb of God	3	267	236	390	0.5	1.6
PENT–COGIC	1	20	20	25	0.0	0.1
PRES–Presb Ch (USA)	1	0	160	199	0.3	0.8
Salvation Army	1	29	49	385	0.5	1.6
Sev Day Adv	2	126	218	251	0.3	1.0
Un C of Christ	1	54	166	207	0.3	0.8
Unity Ch	1	NR	NR	NR	-	-
LINCOLN	**13**	**467**	**1,175**	**1,882**	**58.1**	**100.0**
Bahá'í	0	NR	2	2	0.1	0.1
BAPT–Amer Bapt USA	1	18	43	52	1.6	2.8
Catholic	1	NR	NR	204	6.3	10.8
CHR–Chr Chs & Chs Cr	1	NR	100	122	3.8	6.5
LUTH–E.L.C.A.	1	22	45	50	1.5	2.7
LUTH–Luth-MO Synod	3	195	668	1,028	31.7	54.6
METH–Un Methodist	3	70	172	204	6.3	10.8
METH–Wesleyan	1	25	15	33	1.0	1.8
Non-denom Chr Chs	1	120	100	150	4.6	8.0
PRES–Presb Ch (USA)	1	17	30	37	1.1	2.0
LINN	**25**	**838**	**1,903**	**2,802**	**29.0**	**100.0**
BAPT–Amer Bapt USA	1	45	100	122	1.3	4.4
BAPT–Ind Bapt Flwsp Intl	1	NR	NR	NR	-	-
BAPT–So Bapt Conv	2	101	169	205	2.1	7.3
Catholic	2	NR	NR	380	3.9	13.6
Ch of Nazarene	1	75	89	110	1.1	3.9
CHR–Chr Chs & Chs Cr	4	NR	585	711	7.4	25.4
LDS–L-D Saints	1	NR	NR	134	1.4	4.8
METH–Un Methodist	7	286	582	676	7.0	24.1
Non-denom Chr Chs	4	220	315	319	3.3	11.4
PENT–Assemb of God	1	90	38	115	1.2	4.1
PRES–Presb Ch (USA)	1	21	25	30	0.3	1.1
LOGAN	**12**	**511**	**1,385**	**2,286**	**82.9**	**100.0**
ANG/EPIS–Episcopal	1	10	20	20	0.7	0.9
Catholic	1	NR	NR	577	20.9	25.2
CHR–Chr Chs & Chs Cr	1	NR	325	394	14.3	17.2
CHR–Chs of Christ	1	20	16	23	0.8	1.0
LUTH–E.L.C.A.	1	10	29	41	1.5	1.8
LUTH–Luth-MO Synod	1	60	93	116	4.2	5.1
METH–Un Methodist	2	106	370	564	20.5	24.7
METH–Wesleyan	1	30	32	39	1.4	1.7
Non-denom Chr Chs	3	275	500	512	18.6	22.4
LYON	**62**	**3,822**	**8,080**	**14,842**	**44.1**	**100.0**
ANG/EPIS–Episcopal	1	65	94	179	0.5	1.2
Bahá'í	0	NR	16	16	0.0	0.1
BAPT–Amer Bapt USA	2	115	370	454	1.3	3.1
BAPT–Free Will Bapt	1	NR	42	52	0.2	0.4
BAPT–NBC USA	1	80	100	123	0.4	0.8
BAPT–So Bapt Conv	5	573	402	493	1.5	3.3
Calv Chpl	1	NR	NR	NR	-	-
Catholic	4	NR	NR	3,344	9.9	22.5
Ch of Nazarene	1	178	290	290	0.9	2.0
CHR–Chr Ch (Disc)	1	96	308	378	1.1	2.5
CHR–Chr Chs & Chs Cr	2	NR	184	226	0.7	1.5
CHR–Chs of Christ	1	80	95	100	0.3	0.7
CONG–Cong Chr, NA	1	NR	245	300	0.9	2.0
CONG–Consrv Cong Chr	1	115	245	300	0.9	2.0
FRND–Evan Fr Ch Intl	3	77	126	155	0.5	1.0
Jehovah's Witness	1	NR	NR	NR	-	-
LDS–L-D Saints	1	NR	NR	548	1.6	3.7
LUTH–E.L.C.A.	1	96	303	390	1.2	2.6
LUTH–Luth-MO Synod	2	68	958	1,279	3.8	8.6
METH–AME	1	0	100	123	0.4	0.8
METH–Free Methodist	1	64	44	64	0.2	0.4
METH–Un Methodist	13	875	2,601	3,233	9.6	21.8
Muslim Est	1	134	NR	308	0.9	2.1
Non-denom Chr Chs	7	545	745	788	2.3	5.3
PENT–Assemb of God	2	236	139	571	1.7	3.8
PENT–Ch of God Proph	1	NR	12	15	0.0	0.1
PENT–Int Foursq Gos	1	235	293	359	1.1	2.4
PRES–Presb Ch (USA)	3	138	284	348	1.0	2.3
Salvation Army	1	45	72	392	1.2	2.6
Sev Day Adv	1	7	12	14	0.0	0.1
MCPHERSON	**75**	**6,603**	**13,347**	**18,196**	**62.4**	**100.0**
ANG/EPIS–Episcopal	1	34	62	73	0.3	0.4
Bahá'í	0	NR	8	8	0.0	0.0
BAPT–Amer Bapt USA	3	298	599	731	2.5	4.0
BAPT–So Bapt Conv	2	87	394	481	1.6	2.6
BRETH–Ch of Brethren	2	266	473	577	2.0	3.2
Catholic	2	NR	NR	900	3.1	4.9
Ch of Nazarene	1	21	20	26	0.1	0.1
CHR–Chr Ch (Disc)	3	195	672	820	2.8	4.5
CHR–Chr Chs & Chs Cr	2	NR	250	305	1.0	1.7
CHR–Chs of Christ	2	209	196	269	0.9	1.5
Evan Cov Ch	3	918	738	1,193	4.1	6.6
Evan Free Ch	2	100	NR	100	0.3	0.5
Jehovah's Witness	1	NR	NR	NR	-	-
LUTH–E.L.C.A.	6	771	2,179	2,751	9.4	15.1
LUTH–Luth-MO Synod	3	223	404	515	1.8	2.8
LUTH–Nor Amer Luth C	1	NR	NR	NR	-	-
MENN–CG in Cr (Menn)	6	NR	959	1,170	4.0	6.4
MENN–Menn Br US Conf	1	NR	294	359	1.2	2.0
MENN–Mennonite USA	8	982	2,112	2,576	8.8	14.2
METH–Free Methodist	1	356	350	356	1.2	2.0
METH–Un Methodist	7	682	1,936	2,752	9.4	15.1
Non-denom Chr Chs	10	1,000	935	1,275	4.4	7.0
PENT–Assemb of God	1	100	60	100	0.3	0.5
PENT–Ch God (Cleve)	1	15	11	13	0.0	0.1
PENT–Int Foursq Gos	1	61	120	146	0.5	0.8
PENT–Un Pent Ch Intl	1	NR	NR	NR	-	-
PRES–Presb Ch (USA)	1	118	203	248	0.8	1.4
Sev Day Adv	1	18	31	36	0.1	0.2
Un C of Christ	2	149	341	416	1.4	2.3
MARION	**37**	**1,571**	**5,687**	**7,048**	**55.7**	**100.0**
Bahá'í	0	NR	4	4	0.0	0.1
BAPT–Amer Bapt USA	1	30	118	142	1.1	2.0
BAPT–N Am Bapt Conf	3	NR	316	380	3.0	5.4
Catholic	1	NR	NR	160	1.3	2.3
CHR–Chr Chs & Chs Cr	3	NR	441	530	4.2	7.5
CHR–Chs of Christ	1	10	10	10	0.1	0.1
LUTH–E.L.C.A.	1	18	37	39	0.3	0.6

NR–Not Reported - Represents no adherents reported. Percentages may not total 100 due to rounding.

Table 3: Religious Congregations by County and Group: 2010

Religious Group	Number of Congrega-tions	Number of Attendees	Number of Communicant, Confirmed, or Full Members	Adherents: Number of Adherents	Adherents: % of Total Pop.	Adherents: % of Total Adh.
LUTH–Luth-MO Synod	5	241	461	522	4.1	7.4
MENN–CG in Cr (Menn)	2	NR	193	232	1.8	3.3
MENN–Menn Br US Conf	4	NR	1,240	1,490	11.8	21.1
MENN–Mennonite USA	4	530	1,201	1,443	11.4	20.5
METH–Un Methodist	8	557	1,426	1,753	13.8	24.9
Non-denom Chr Chs	2	165	155	206	1.6	2.9
ORTHE–Ant Orth of NA	1	20	NR	35	0.3	0.5
PRES–Presb Ch (USA)	1	0	85	102	0.8	1.4
MARSHALL	**43**	**1,446**	**3,091**	**6,444**	**63.7**	**100.0**
ANG/EPIS–Episcopal	2	32	82	86	0.9	1.3
Bahá'í	0	NR	1	1	0.0	0.0
BAPT–Amer Bapt USA	1	14	16	20	0.2	0.3
BAPT–Reg Bapt Gen As	3	NR	NR	NR	-	-
Catholic	7	NR	NR	2,072	20.5	32.2
CHR–Chr Ch (Disc)	1	45	175	214	2.1	3.3
CHR–Chr Chs & Chs Cr	1	NR	80	98	1.0	1.5
CHR–Chs of Christ	1	50	45	60	0.6	0.9
Evan Cov Ch	1	22	20	29	0.3	0.5
Jehovah's Witness	1	NR	NR	NR	-	-
LDS–L-D Saints	1	NR	NR	109	1.1	1.7
LUTH–E.L.C.A.	2	118	286	412	4.1	6.4
LUTH–Luth-MO Synod	5	341	712	996	9.8	15.5
METH–Un Methodist	8	372	996	1,294	12.8	20.1
Non-denom Chr Chs	2	225	170	288	2.8	4.5
PENT–Assemb of God	1	123	52	208	2.1	3.2
PRES–Evan Presby Ch	1	NR	66	81	0.8	1.3
PRES–Presb Ch (USA)	4	34	187	228	2.3	3.5
Un C of Christ	1	70	203	248	2.5	3.8
MEADE	**21**	**907**	**1,970**	**3,332**	**72.8**	**100.0**
ANG/EPIS–Episcopal	1	5	8	8	0.2	0.2
BAPT–Amer Bapt USA	2	45	258	329	7.2	9.9
BAPT–So Bapt Conv	1	10	NR	NR	-	-
Catholic	3	NR	NR	834	18.2	25.0
Ch of Nazarene	1	80	125	125	2.7	3.8
CHR–Chr Chs & Chs Cr	1	NR	75	96	2.1	2.9
CHR–Chs of Christ	1	56	42	64	1.4	1.9
FRND–Evan Fr Ch Intl	2	127	112	143	3.1	4.3
LUTH–Luth-MO Synod	1	83	363	530	11.6	15.9
MENN–CG in Cr (Menn)	1	NR	84	107	2.3	3.2
MENN–Fel Evg Bib Ch	1	180	153	180	3.9	5.4
METH–Un Methodist	4	201	575	741	16.2	22.2
Non-denom Chr Chs	2	120	175	175	3.8	5.3
MIAMI	**62**	**3,639**	**6,819**	**16,091**	**49.1**	**100.0**
Bahá'í	0	NR	7	7	0.0	0.0
BAPT–Amer Bapt USA	5	581	988	1,245	3.8	7.7
BAPT–So Bapt Conv	4	176	231	291	0.9	1.8
Catholic	4	NR	NR	5,850	17.8	36.4
Ch of Nazarene	2	94	243	335	1.0	2.1
CHR–Chr Ch (Disc)	2	90	362	456	1.4	2.8
CHR–Chr Chs & Chs Cr	2	NR	132	166	0.5	1.0
CHR–Chs of Christ	3	62	50	77	0.2	0.5
FRND–Evan Fr Ch Intl	1	9	20	25	0.1	0.2
Jehovah's Witness	2	NR	NR	NR	-	-
LDS–Comm of Christ	1	NR	194	194	0.6	1.2
LDS–L-D Saints	2	NR	NR	827	2.5	5.1
LUTH–E.L.C.A.	1	0	0	0	0.0	0.0
LUTH–Luth-MO Synod	3	479	1,256	1,664	5.1	10.3
METH–AME	1	22	28	35	0.1	0.2
METH–Un Methodist	8	479	1,159	1,650	5.0	10.3
METH–Wesleyan	1	35	23	46	0.1	0.3
Non-denom Chr Chs	11	885	1,035	1,156	3.5	7.2
PENT–Assemb of God	3	495	230	984	3.0	6.1
PRES–Evan Presby Ch	2	NR	484	610	1.9	3.8
PRES–Presb Ch (USA)	3	220	356	449	1.4	2.8
Sev Day Adv	1	12	21	24	0.1	0.1
MITCHELL	**22**	**920**	**1,834**	**5,048**	**79.2**	**100.0**
BAPT–Amer Bapt USA	3	45	48	57	0.9	1.1
Catholic	3	NR	NR	2,010	31.5	39.8

Religious Group	Number of Congrega-tions	Number of Attendees	Number of Communicant, Confirmed, or Full Members	Adherents: Number of Adherents	Adherents: % of Total Pop.	Adherents: % of Total Adh.
CHR–Chr Chs & Chs Cr	1	NR	148	177	2.8	3.5
CHR–Chs of Christ	1	54	49	72	1.1	1.4
FRND–Evan Fr Ch Intl	1	52	70	84	1.3	1.7
Jehovah's Witness	1	NR	NR	NR	-	-
LUTH–E.L.C.A.	1	79	246	277	4.3	5.5
LUTH–Luth-MO Synod	1	34	103	141	2.2	2.8
METH–Un Methodist	5	312	697	889	13.9	17.6
Non-denom Chr Chs	2	150	200	212	3.3	4.2
PENT–Assemb of God	1	76	45	856	13.4	17.0
PRES–Presb Ch (USA)	1	44	64	77	1.2	1.5
REF–Christian Ref	1	74	164	196	3.1	3.9
MONTGOMERY	**99**	**5,050**	**11,901**	**19,144**	**54.0**	**100.0**
ANG/EPIS–Episcopal	2	121	206	269	0.8	1.4
Bahá'í	0	NR	27	27	0.1	0.1
BAPT–Amer Bapt USA	4	373	1,213	1,488	4.2	7.8
BAPT–Ind Bapt Flwsp Intl	1	NR	NR	NR	-	-
BAPT–NBC USA	1	15	30	37	0.1	0.2
BAPT–So Bapt Conv	11	656	1,720	2,110	5.9	11.0
BRETH–Ch of Brethren	1	48	144	177	0.5	0.9
Catholic	4	NR	NR	2,900	8.2	15.1
CGOD–Ch God (Ander)	1	77	NR	77	0.2	0.4
Ch of Nazarene	6	474	631	955	2.7	5.0
CHR–Chr Ch (Disc)	2	183	519	637	1.8	3.3
CHR–Chr Chs & Chs Cr	7	NR	2,265	2,779	7.8	14.5
CHR–Chs of Christ	5	310	311	433	1.2	2.3
FRND–Evan Fr Ch Intl	2	68	106	130	0.4	0.7
Ind Fund Churches	1	NR	NR	NR	-	-
Jehovah's Witness	1	NR	NR	NR	-	-
LDS–Comm of Christ	1	NR	135	135	0.4	0.7
LDS–L-D Saints	1	NR	NR	664	1.9	3.5
LUTH–Luth-MO Synod	3	319	740	947	2.7	4.9
METH–AME	2	15	131	161	0.5	0.8
METH–C.M.E.	1	0	40	49	0.1	0.3
METH–Un Methodist	12	725	1,462	2,065	5.8	10.8
METH–Wesleyan	1	17	15	22	0.1	0.1
Non-denom Chr Chs	12	955	1,126	1,270	3.6	6.6
PENT–Assemb of God	3	278	123	646	1.8	3.4
PENT–Ch God (Cleve)	2	129	250	307	0.9	1.6
PENT–COGIC	2	0	150	184	0.5	1.0
PENT–Intl Pent Holiness	2	54	44	54	0.2	0.3
PENT–Un Pent Ch Intl	1	NR	NR	NR	-	-
PRES–Orth Pres Ch	1	19	38	47	0.1	0.2
PRES–Presb Ch (USA)	3	150	363	445	1.3	2.3
Sev Day Adv	3	64	112	129	0.4	0.7
MORRIS	**19**	**823**	**2,098**	**3,421**	**57.8**	**100.0**
BAPT–Amer Bapt USA	1	142	182	217	3.7	6.3
Catholic	1	NR	NR	900	15.2	26.3
CHR–Chr Chs & Chs Cr	3	NR	460	549	9.3	16.0
LUTH–E.L.C.A.	2	55	192	205	3.5	6.0
LUTH–Luth-MO Synod	1	60	79	96	1.6	2.8
METH–Un Methodist	6	290	822	1,045	17.6	30.5
Non-denom Chr Chs	3	220	275	304	5.1	8.9
PRES–Presb Ch (USA)	1	19	35	42	0.7	1.2
Un C of Christ	1	37	53	63	1.1	1.8
MORTON	**14**	**407**	**1,023**	**1,645**	**50.9**	**100.0**
BAPT–So Bapt Conv	2	93	188	237	7.3	14.4
Catholic	1	NR	NR	434	13.4	26.4
CGOD–Ch God (Ander)	2	30	NR	30	0.9	1.8
Ch of Nazarene	1	83	115	115	3.6	7.0
CHR–Chr Chs & Chs Cr	1	NR	100	126	3.9	7.7
CHR–Chs of Christ	1	40	40	45	1.4	2.7
LDS–Comm of Christ	1	NR	156	156	4.8	9.5
LUTH–Luth-MO Synod	1	24	55	55	1.7	3.3
METH–Un Methodist	3	120	341	412	12.7	25.0
PENT–Intl Pent Holiness	1	17	28	35	1.1	2.1
NEMAHA	**29**	**1,900**	**2,418**	**7,728**	**75.9**	**100.0**
Ap Chr Ch-Amer	2	641	342	641	6.3	8.3
Bahá'í	0	NR	1	1	0.0	0.0

NR–Not Reported   - Represents no adherents reported.   Percentages may not total 100 due to rounding.

Table 3: Religious Congregations by County and Group: 2010

Religious Group	Number of Congrega-tions	Number of Attendees	Number of Communicant, Confirmed, or Full Members	Adherents		
				Number of Adherents	% of Total Pop.	% of Total Adh.
BRETH–Ch of Brethren	1	0	30	37	0.4	0.5
Catholic	7	NR	NR	4,166	40.9	53.9
CHR–Chs of Christ	1	45	42	70	0.7	0.9
Evan Free Ch	1	25	NR	25	0.2	0.3
LUTH–Luth–MO Synod	1	79	197	263	2.6	3.4
METH–AME	1	0	100	125	1.2	1.6
METH–Un Methodist	8	318	781	1,160	11.4	15.0
METH–Wesleyan	1	39	43	51	0.5	0.7
Non-denom Chr Chs	3	655	580	819	8.0	10.6
Un Breth in Cr	1	36	30	31	0.3	0.4
Un C of Christ	2	62	272	339	3.3	4.4
NEOSHO	**42**	**2,129**	**5,622**	**9,419**	**57.0**	**100.0**
ANG/EPIS–Episcopal	1	41	54	65	0.4	0.7
BAPT–Amer Bapt USA	3	276	580	717	4.3	7.6
BAPT–Ind Bapt Flwsp Intl	1	NR	NR	NR	-	-
BAPT–So Bapt Conv	1	86	344	425	2.6	4.5
Catholic	3	NR	NR	2,500	15.1	26.5
Ch of Nazarene	1	183	274	274	1.7	2.9
CHR–Chr Ch (Disc)	2	191	907	1,121	6.8	11.9
CHR–Chr Chs & Chs Cr	3	NR	482	596	3.6	6.3
CHR–Chs of Christ	2	57	47	59	0.4	0.6
FRND–Evan Fr Ch Intl	1	41	41	51	0.3	0.5
Jehovah's Witness	1	NR	NR	NR	-	-
LDS–Comm of Christ	1	NR	135	135	0.8	1.4
LUTH–Luth–MO Synod	2	135	415	577	3.5	6.1
MENN–Amish Undif	0	NR	17	51	0.3	0.5
METH–AME	1	0	100	124	0.8	1.3
METH–Un Methodist	6	396	1,176	1,432	8.7	15.2
Non-denom Chr Chs	4	230	280	312	1.9	3.3
PENT–Assemb of God	1	240	175	310	1.9	3.3
PENT–Ch God (Cleve)	1	41	125	155	0.9	1.6
PENT–COGIC	1	0	150	185	1.1	2.0
PENT–Un Pent Ch Intl	1	NR	NR	NR	-	-
PRES–Presb Ch (USA)	2	55	113	140	0.8	1.5
Sev Day Adv	2	50	86	99	0.6	1.1
Un Breth in Cr	1	107	121	91	0.6	1.0
NESS	**18**	**464**	**1,409**	**2,956**	**95.1**	**100.0**
BAPT–Amer Bapt USA	2	102	305	368	11.8	12.4
Catholic	2	NR	NR	1,311	42.2	44.4
Ch of Nazarene	1	35	0	35	1.1	1.2
CHR–Chr Ch (Disc)	1	20	67	81	2.6	2.7
CHR–Chs of Christ	1	20	21	25	0.8	0.8
LUTH–E.L.C.A.	1	15	54	61	2.0	2.1
LUTH–Luth–MO Synod	1	22	50	50	1.6	1.7
MENN–Mennonite USA	1	30	93	112	3.6	3.8
METH–Un Methodist	6	188	775	857	27.6	29.0
PENT–Assemb of God	1	10	6	12	0.4	0.4
Sev Day Adv	1	22	38	44	1.4	1.5
NORTON	**19**	**566**	**2,152**	**3,279**	**57.8**	**100.0**
ANG/EPIS–Episcopal	1	15	20	61	1.1	1.9
Bahá'í	0	NR	4	4	0.1	0.1
BAPT–Amer Bapt USA	1	53	63	74	1.3	2.3
BRETH–Ch of Brethren	1	0	48	56	1.0	1.7
Catholic	2	NR	NR	617	10.9	18.8
CGOD–Ch God (Ander)	2	131	NR	131	2.3	4.0
CHR–Chr Chs & Chs Cr	1	NR	1,131	1,325	23.4	40.4
LUTH–Luth–MO Synod	1	83	133	153	2.7	4.7
LUTH–Wisc Ev Luth Syn	1	32	46	51	0.9	1.6
METH–Un Methodist	5	125	590	633	11.2	19.3
Non-denom Chr Chs	2	100	75	125	2.2	3.8
Sev Day Adv	1	5	9	10	0.2	0.3
Un C of Christ	1	22	33	39	0.7	1.2
OSAGE	**34**	**2,532**	**4,204**	**6,725**	**41.3**	**100.0**
Bahá'í	0	NR	7	7	0.0	0.1
BAPT–Amer Bapt USA	1	120	650	799	4.9	11.9
BAPT–Reg Bapt Gen As	1	NR	NR	NR	-	-
BAPT–So Bapt Conv	1	20	81	100	0.6	1.5
Catholic	2	NR	NR	958	5.9	14.2

Religious Group	Number of Congrega-tions	Number of Attendees	Number of Communicant, Confirmed, or Full Members	Adherents		
				Number of Adherents	% of Total Pop.	% of Total Adh.
CGOD–Ch God (Ander)	1	30	NR	30	0.2	0.4
CHR–Chs of Christ	1	33	35	40	0.2	0.6
Evan Cov Ch	1	133	86	173	1.1	2.6
Ind Fund Churches	1	NR	NR	NR	-	-
Jehovah's Witness	1	NR	NR	NR	-	-
LUTH–E.L.C.A.	1	85	228	332	2.0	4.9
LUTH–Luth–MO Synod	1	80	215	304	1.9	4.5
MENN–Mara Amish-Menn	1	108	60	108	0.7	1.6
METH–Un Methodist	8	493	1,251	1,869	11.5	27.8
METH–Wesleyan	1	28	29	36	0.2	0.5
Non-denom Chr Chs	7	1,220	1,295	1,600	9.8	23.8
PENT–Assemb of God	2	68	27	74	0.5	1.1
PENT–Int Foursq Gos	1	48	88	108	0.7	1.6
PRES–Presb Ch (USA)	1	30	71	87	0.5	1.3
Un C of Christ	1	36	81	100	0.6	1.5
OSBORNE	**20**	**632**	**1,434**	**2,276**	**59.0**	**100.0**
BAPT–Amer Bapt USA	1	41	99	117	3.0	5.1
BRETH–Grace Breth	1	NR	NR	NR	-	-
Catholic	2	NR	NR	368	9.5	16.2
CHR–Chr Chs & Chs Cr	2	NR	100	118	3.1	5.2
FRND–Evan Fr Ch Intl	1	60	64	75	1.9	3.3
LUTH–Luth Cong Msn Chr	1	38	95	112	2.9	4.9
LUTH–Luth–MO Synod	2	149	344	424	11.0	18.6
MENN–Fel Evg Bib Ch	1	15	7	15	0.4	0.7
METH–Free Methodist	1	40	34	40	1.0	1.8
METH–Un Methodist	7	231	658	907	23.5	39.9
PENT–Assemb of God	1	58	33	100	2.6	4.4
OTTAWA	**24**	**919**	**1,659**	**2,467**	**40.5**	**100.0**
ANG/EPIS–Episcopal	1	9	34	34	0.6	1.4
Bahá'í	0	NR	1	1	0.0	0.0
BAPT–Amer Bapt USA	2	82	227	279	4.6	11.3
Catholic	2	NR	NR	443	7.3	18.0
Ch of Nazarene	1	52	52	58	1.0	2.4
LUTH–E.L.C.A.	1	32	101	127	2.1	5.1
METH–Free Methodist	1	21	18	21	0.3	0.9
METH–Un Methodist	6	229	603	689	11.3	27.9
METH–Wesleyan	1	45	28	59	1.0	2.4
Non-denom Chr Chs	5	375	375	486	8.0	19.7
PRES–Presb Ch (USA)	4	74	220	270	4.4	10.9
PAWNEE	**20**	**795**	**1,842**	**3,815**	**54.7**	**100.0**
ANG/EPIS–Episcopal	1	35	40	63	0.9	1.7
Bahá'í	0	NR	3	3	0.0	0.1
BAPT–Amer Bapt USA	2	58	122	145	2.1	3.8
BAPT–So Bapt Conv	1	70	181	215	3.1	5.6
Catholic	1	NR	NR	1,168	16.8	30.6
Ch of Nazarene	1	36	40	50	0.7	1.3
CHR–Chs of Christ	1	40	38	58	0.8	1.5
Jehovah's Witness	1	NR	NR	NR	-	-
LUTH–E.L.C.A.	1	15	36	52	0.7	1.4
LUTH–Luth–MO Synod	1	50	120	147	2.1	3.9
METH–C.M.E.	1	0	100	119	1.7	3.1
METH–Un Methodist	3	144	741	1,119	16.0	29.3
Non-denom Chr Chs	3	130	195	197	2.8	5.2
PENT–Assemb of God	1	146	88	316	4.5	8.3
PRES–Presb Ch (USA)	1	57	113	134	1.9	3.5
Sev Day Adv	1	14	25	29	0.4	0.8
PHILLIPS	**31**	**1,252**	**2,573**	**4,171**	**73.9**	**100.0**
ANG/EPIS–Episcopal	1	10	13	13	0.2	0.3
BAPT–Amer Bapt USA	1	10	120	147	2.6	3.5
BAPT–Reg Bapt Gen As	1	NR	NR	NR	-	-
BAPT–So Bapt Conv	1	4	12	15	0.3	0.4
Catholic	2	NR	NR	433	7.7	10.4
CGOD–Ch God (Ander)	1	71	NR	71	1.3	1.7
CHR–Chr Ch (Disc)	1	107	385	472	8.4	11.3
CHR–Chr Chs & Chs Cr	1	NR	130	159	2.8	3.8
CHR–Chs of Christ	2	34	32	39	0.7	0.9
Jehovah's Witness	1	NR	NR	NR	-	-
LDS–L-D Saints	1	NR	NR	257	4.6	6.2

NR–Not Reported - Represents no adherents reported. Percentages may not total 100 due to rounding.

Table 3: Religious Congregations by County and Group: 2010

Religious Group	Number of Congrega-tions	Number of Attendees	Number of Communicant, Confirmed, or Full Members	Adherents: Number of Adherents	Adherents: % of Total Pop.	Adherents: % of Total Adh.
LUTH–E.L.C.A.	2	133	374	450	8.0	10.8
LUTH–Luth–MO Synod	1	73	197	288	5.1	6.9
METH–Un Methodist	6	175	560	670	11.9	16.1
METH–Wesleyan	2	57	55	75	1.3	1.8
Non-denom Chr Chs	2	200	300	300	5.3	7.2
PENT–Assemb of God	2	208	95	413	7.3	9.9
PRES–Presb Ch (USA)	1	0	75	92	1.6	2.2
REF–Christian Ref	1	105	137	168	3.0	4.0
REF–Ref Ch in Am	1	65	88	109	1.9	2.6
POTTAWATOMIE	**39**	**1,620**	**3,531**	**7,476**	**34.6**	**100.0**
ANG/EPIS–Episcopal	1	45	96	99	0.5	1.3
Bahá'í	0	NR	2	2	0.0	0.0
BAPT–Amer Bapt USA	3	75	180	234	1.1	3.1
BAPT–Reg Bapt Gen As	1	NR	NR	NR	-	-
BAPT–So Bapt Conv	7	268	336	437	2.0	5.8
Catholic	5	NR	NR	2,821	13.1	37.7
CHR–Chr Chs & Chs Cr	2	NR	230	299	1.4	4.0
LUTH–E.L.C.A.	2	96	229	300	1.4	4.0
LUTH–Luth–MO Synod	3	370	767	950	4.4	12.7
METH–Un Methodist	8	395	1,146	1,688	7.8	22.6
Non-denom Chr Chs	2	170	230	238	1.1	3.2
PENT–Assemb of God	1	53	42	53	0.2	0.7
PENT–Ch God (Cleve)	1	8	9	12	0.1	0.2
PRES–Presb Ch (USA)	1	120	202	262	1.2	3.5
Un C of Christ	2	20	62	81	0.4	1.1
PRATT	**27**	**1,654**	**2,763**	**5,301**	**54.9**	**100.0**
ANG/EPIS–Episcopal	1	16	34	45	0.5	0.8
Bahá'í	0	NR	1	1	0.0	0.0
BAPT–Amer Bapt USA	1	94	186	226	2.3	4.3
BAPT–So Bapt Conv	1	275	485	589	6.1	11.1
Catholic	1	NR	NR	1,655	17.1	31.2
Ch of Nazarene	1	25	47	66	0.7	1.2
CHR–Chr Ch (Disc)	2	79	296	359	3.7	6.8
CHR–Chs of Christ	1	70	75	120	1.2	2.3
FRND–Evan Fr Ch Intl	1	67	70	85	0.9	1.6
Ind Fund Churches	1	NR	NR	NR	-	-
Jehovah's Witness	1	NR	NR	NR	-	-
LDS–L-D Saints	1	NR	NR	166	1.7	3.1
METH–Free Methodist	1	40	11	40	0.4	0.8
METH–Un Methodist	7	462	893	1,111	11.5	21.0
Non-denom Chr Chs	3	235	305	321	3.3	6.1
PENT–Assemb of God	1	165	95	195	2.0	3.7
PENT–Intl Pent Holiness	2	61	89	108	1.1	2.0
PRES–Presb Ch (USA)	1	65	176	214	2.2	4.0
RAWLINS	**10**	**375**	**811**	**1,596**	**63.4**	**100.0**
Catholic	3	NR	NR	622	24.7	39.0
CHR–Chr Ch (Disc)	1	38	127	147	5.8	9.2
Evan Cov Ch	1	59	72	77	3.1	4.8
Jehovah's Witness	1	NR	NR	NR	-	-
LUTH–Luth–MO Synod	1	160	306	350	13.9	21.9
METH–Un Methodist	1	78	225	303	12.0	19.0
Non-denom Chr Chs	1	40	40	50	2.0	3.1
Un C of Christ	1	0	41	47	1.9	2.9
RENO	**113**	**12,294**	**21,324**	**34,135**	**52.9**	**100.0**
ANG/EPIS–Episcopal	1	128	400	425	0.7	1.2
Bahá'í	1	NR	41	41	0.1	0.1
BAPT–Amer Bapt USA	3	263	478	586	0.9	1.7
BAPT–Free Will Bapt	1	NR	42	52	0.1	0.2
BAPT–Ind Bapt Flwsp Intl	1	NR	NR	NR	-	-
BAPT–Natl Mis Bapt Conv	1	150	300	368	0.6	1.1
BAPT–So Bapt Conv	4	1,800	2,119	2,600	4.0	7.6
BRETH–Ch of Brethren	2	103	201	247	0.4	0.7
Calv Chpl	1	NR	NR	NR	-	-
Catholic	4	NR	NR	7,000	10.9	20.5
CGOD–Ch God (Ander)	1	105	NR	105	0.2	0.3
Ch Cr, Scientst	1	NR	NR	NR	-	-
Ch of Nazarene	5	1,057	1,265	1,338	2.1	3.9
CHR–Chr Ch (Disc)	2	260	1,186	1,455	2.3	4.3
CHR–Chr Chs & Chs Cr	2	NR	531	651	1.0	1.9
CHR–Chs of Christ	5	615	696	964	1.5	2.8
Christian Brethren	1	NR	NR	NR	-	-
CONG–Cong Chr, NA	1	NR	150	184	0.3	0.5
FRND–Evan Fr Ch Intl	1	93	121	148	0.2	0.4
Ind Fund Churches	1	NR	NR	NR	-	-
Jehovah's Witness	1	NR	NR	NR	-	-
LDS–Comm of Christ	1	NR	194	194	0.3	0.6
LDS–L-D Saints	1	NR	NR	768	1.2	2.2
LUTH–E.L.C.A.	2	335	709	933	1.4	2.7
LUTH–Luth–MO Synod	4	480	1,375	1,632	2.5	4.8
MENN–Amish Undif	5	NR	246	435	0.7	1.3
MENN–Beachy Amish-Menn	3	609	411	609	0.9	1.8
MENN–Cons Menn Conf	2	310	228	280	0.4	0.8
MENN–Menn Br US Conf	1	NR	555	681	1.1	2.0
MENN–Mennonite USA	4	827	1,186	1,455	2.3	4.3
METH–AME	1	35	103	126	0.2	0.4
METH–C.M.E.	1	0	100	123	0.2	0.4
METH–Un Methodist	14	1,350	3,595	4,462	6.9	13.1
METH–Wesleyan	1	46	48	60	0.1	0.2
Non-denom Chr Chs	18	2,754	3,640	4,064	6.3	11.9
PENT–Assemb of God	1	87	45	148	0.2	0.4
PENT–Ch God (Cleve)	1	38	43	53	0.1	0.2
PENT–Intl Pent Holiness	2	165	175	215	0.3	0.6
PENT–Pent Ch of God	1	70	NR	109	0.2	0.3
PENT–Un Pent Ch Intl	1	NR	NR	NR	-	-
PRES–Presb Ch (USA)	3	370	728	893	1.4	2.6
Salvation Army	1	54	105	366	0.6	1.1
Sev Day Adv	2	98	170	196	0.3	0.6
Swedenborgian	1	NR	NR	NR	-	-
Un C of Christ	2	92	138	169	0.3	0.5
REPUBLIC	**24**	**863**	**2,267**	**3,177**	**63.8**	**100.0**
BAPT–Amer Bapt USA	1	40	40	47	0.9	1.5
BAPT–So Bapt Conv	1	30	70	82	1.6	2.6
Catholic	3	NR	NR	437	8.8	13.8
CHR–Chr Chs & Chs Cr	1	NR	230	268	5.4	8.4
Evan Cov Ch	1	54	60	70	1.4	2.2
Evan Free Ch	1	65	NR	65	1.3	2.0
Jehovah's Witness	1	NR	NR	NR	-	-
LUTH–E.L.C.A.	4	161	620	769	15.4	24.2
METH–Un Methodist	5	259	881	1,065	21.4	33.5
METH–Wesleyan	1	71	129	92	1.8	2.9
Non-denom Chr Chs	1	45	50	56	1.1	1.8
PENT–Assemb of God	1	28	19	30	0.6	0.9
PRES–Presb Ch (USA)	3	110	168	196	3.9	6.2
RICE	**36**	**1,648**	**3,711**	**5,937**	**58.9**	**100.0**
ANG/EPIS–Episcopal	1	25	64	64	0.6	1.1
Bahá'í	0	NR	4	4	0.0	0.1
BAPT–Amer Bapt USA	4	211	488	598	5.9	10.1
BAPT–So Bapt Conv	2	17	20	25	0.2	0.4
Catholic	3	NR	NR	1,100	10.9	18.5
Ch of Nazarene	1	29	49	72	0.7	1.2
CHR–Chr Ch (Disc)	1	80	234	287	2.8	4.8
CHR–Chs of Christ	2	95	85	102	1.0	1.7
CONG–Consrv Cong Chr	1	50	145	178	1.8	3.0
LUTH–Luth–MO Synod	1	25	103	315	3.1	5.3
MENN–Fel Evg Ch	1	160	205	251	2.5	4.2
MENN–Mennonite USA	1	20	68	83	0.8	1.4
METH–AME	2	0	200	245	2.4	4.1
METH–Un Methodist	8	507	1,544	1,923	19.1	32.4
Non-denom Chr Chs	1	120	130	150	1.5	2.5
PENT–Assemb of God	2	67	12	84	0.8	1.4
PRES–Presb Ch (USA)	3	125	225	276	2.7	4.6
PRES–Ref Pres of NA	1	70	57	84	0.8	1.4
Un C of Christ	1	47	78	96	1.0	1.6
RILEY	**84**	**7,379**	**12,656**	**24,935**	**35.1**	**100.0**
ANG/EPIS–Episcopal	1	110	231	231	0.3	0.9
Bahá'í	0	NR	23	23	0.0	0.1
BAPT–Amer Bapt USA	2	161	506	598	0.8	2.4
BAPT–Converge/BGC	1	75	NR	90	0.1	0.4

NR–Not Reported - Represents no adherents reported. Percentages may not total 100 due to rounding.

Table 3: Religious Congregations by County and Group: 2010

Religious Group	Number of Congrega-tions	Number of Attendees	Number of Communicant, Confirmed, or Full Members	Adherents: Number of Adherents	Adherents: % of Total Pop.	Adherents: % of Total Adh.
BAPT–Fund Bapt Flwsp	1	NR	NR	NR	-	-
BAPT–So Bapt Conv	5	373	1,222	1,444	2.0	5.8
Calv Chpl	1	NR	NR	NR	-	-
Catholic	4	NR	NR	5,964	8.4	23.9
CGOD–Ch God (Ander)	1	0	NR	0	0.0	0.0
Ch Cr, Scientst	1	NR	NR	NR	-	-
Ch of Nazarene	1	109	128	187	0.3	0.7
CHR–Chr Ch (Disc)	1	106	400	473	0.7	1.9
CHR–Chr Chs & Chs Cr	3	NR	908	1,073	1.5	4.3
CHR–Chs of Christ	2	250	238	350	0.5	1.4
Evan Cov Ch	1	120	55	156	0.2	0.6
Evan Free Ch	2	560	NR	560	0.8	2.2
FRND–Fr Gen Cf	1	NR	7	8	0.0	0.0
HINDU–Post Ren	1	NR	NR	16	0.0	0.1
LDS–Comm of Christ	1	NR	194	194	0.3	0.8
LDS–L-D Saints	3	NR	NR	1,312	1.8	5.3
LUTH–E.L.C.A.	3	462	1,227	1,587	2.2	6.4
LUTH–Luth Cong Msn Chr	1	28	NR	NR	-	-
LUTH–Luth–MO Synod	2	279	729	908	1.3	3.6
LUTH–Wisc Ev Luth Syn	1	45	50	70	0.1	0.3
MENN–Mennonite USA	1	75	90	106	0.1	0.4
METH–AME	1	25	30	35	0.0	0.1
METH–Free Methodist	1	27	13	27	0.0	0.1
METH–Un Methodist	9	879	2,577	3,381	4.8	13.6
METH–Wesleyan	2	656	286	853	1.2	3.4
Muslim Est	1	134	NR	308	0.4	1.2
Non-denom Chr Chs	13	1,945	1,885	2,544	3.6	10.2
ORTHE–Ant Orth of NA	1	15	NR	25	0.0	0.1
PENT–Assemb of God	1	325	139	380	0.5	1.5
PENT–COGIC	2	60	225	266	0.4	1.1
PENT–Vineyard	1	165	210	248	0.3	1.0
PRES–Korean Amer Pres	1	NR	NR	NR	-	-
PRES–Presb Ch (USA)	4	137	830	981	1.4	3.9
PRES–Presb Ch Amer	1	65	29	39	0.1	0.2
Salvation Army	1	5	42	42	0.1	0.2
Sev Day Adv	1	34	58	67	0.1	0.3
Un C of Christ	1	82	223	263	0.4	1.1
Unit Univ	1	72	101	126	0.2	0.5
Unity Ch	1	NR	NR	NR	-	-
ROOKS	**18**	**673**	**1,863**	**3,563**	**68.8**	**100.0**
Bahá'í	0	NR	1	1	0.0	0.0
BAPT–Amer Bapt USA	1	30	21	26	0.5	0.7
BAPT–So Bapt Conv	1	39	312	381	7.4	10.7
Catholic	3	NR	NR	1,219	23.5	34.2
CGOD–Ch God (Ander)	1	49	NR	49	0.9	1.4
Ch of Nazarene	2	101	160	160	3.1	4.5
CHR–Chr Chs & Chs Cr	2	NR	370	452	8.7	12.7
LUTH–Luth–MO Synod	1	35	69	81	1.6	2.3
METH–Un Methodist	4	244	679	892	17.2	25.0
Non-denom Chr Chs	1	100	150	150	2.9	4.2
PENT–Assemb of God	1	60	60	102	2.0	2.9
Un C of Christ	1	15	41	50	1.0	1.4
RUSH	**15**	**367**	**1,158**	**2,529**	**76.5**	**100.0**
Catholic	3	NR	NR	1,178	35.6	46.6
CHR–Chr Chs & Chs Cr	1	NR	55	64	1.9	2.5
LUTH–E.L.C.A.	4	158	483	588	17.8	23.3
METH–Un Methodist	5	99	472	523	15.8	20.7
Non-denom Chr Chs	1	60	60	75	2.3	3.0
Sev Day Adv	1	50	88	101	3.1	4.0
RUSSELL	**29**	**963**	**2,572**	**4,228**	**60.7**	**100.0**
ANG/EPIS–Episcopal	1	3	8	8	0.1	0.2
Bahá'í	0	NR	1	1	0.0	0.0
BAPT–Amer Bapt USA	2	31	49	58	0.8	1.4
BAPT–Reg Bapt Gen As	1	NR	NR	NR	-	-
BAPT–So Bapt Conv	2	38	55	66	0.9	1.6
Catholic	3	NR	NR	1,028	14.7	24.3
Ch of Nazarene	1	0	16	16	0.2	0.4
CHR–Chr Chs & Chs Cr	1	NR	70	84	1.2	2.0
CHR–Chs of Christ	1	34	35	57	0.8	1.3
Jehovah's Witness	1	NR	NR	NR	-	-

Religious Group	Number of Congrega-tions	Number of Attendees	Number of Communicant, Confirmed, or Full Members	Adherents: Number of Adherents	Adherents: % of Total Pop.	Adherents: % of Total Adh.
LUTH–E.L.C.A.	4	356	1,120	1,393	20.0	32.9
METH–Un Methodist	8	374	1,064	1,295	18.6	30.6
Non-denom Chr Chs	1	65	50	81	1.2	1.9
PENT–Assemb of God	1	22	20	41	0.6	1.0
Un C of Christ	2	40	84	100	1.4	2.4
SALINE	**86**	**8,020**	**14,622**	**27,513**	**49.5**	**100.0**
ANG/EPIS–Episcopal	2	134	509	509	0.9	1.9
Bahá'í	0	NR	17	17	0.0	0.1
BAPT–Amer Bapt USA	3	168	665	824	1.5	3.0
BAPT–Free Will Bapt	1	NR	42	52	0.1	0.2
BAPT–Ind Bapt Flwsp Intl	1	NR	NR	NR	-	-
BAPT–NBC USA	1	220	350	434	0.8	1.6
BAPT–So Bapt Conv	5	412	561	695	1.2	2.5
BRETH–Breth in Chr	2	NR	NR	NR	-	-
Catholic	5	NR	NR	7,305	13.1	26.6
CGOD–Ch God (Ander)	1	20	NR	20	0.0	0.1
Ch Cr, Scientst	1	NR	NR	NR	-	-
Ch of Nazarene	2	303	436	437	0.8	1.6
CHR–Chr Ch (Disc)	2	180	462	572	1.0	2.1
CHR–Chr Chs & Chs Cr	1	NR	230	285	0.5	1.0
CHR–Chs of Christ	1	230	269	340	0.6	1.2
Evan Cov Ch	2	984	657	1,279	2.3	4.6
Evan Free Ch	1	35	NR	35	0.1	0.1
FRND–Evan Fr Ch Intl	1	NR	0	0	0.0	0.0
Ind Fund Churches	2	NR	NR	NR	-	-
Jehovah's Witness	1	NR	NR	NR	-	-
LDS–Comm of Christ	1	NR	194	194	0.3	0.7
LDS–L-D Saints	2	NR	NR	905	1.6	3.3
LUTH–E.L.C.A.	7	803	2,227	2,806	5.0	10.2
LUTH–Luth–MO Synod	2	555	1,399	1,818	3.3	6.6
LUTH–Wisc Ev Luth Syn	1	40	54	74	0.1	0.3
MENN–Mennonite USA	1	40	64	79	0.1	0.3
METH–AME	1	0	100	124	0.2	0.5
METH–Free Methodist	1	39	25	39	0.1	0.1
METH–Un Methodist	9	1,448	3,048	4,048	7.3	14.7
Muslim Est	1	134	NR	308	0.6	1.1
Non-denom Chr Chs	12	880	1,110	1,287	2.3	4.7
ORTHE–Ant Orth of NA	1	28	NR	78	0.1	0.3
PENT–Assemb of God	1	165	110	167	0.3	0.6
PENT–Ch God (Cleve)	1	7	48	59	0.1	0.2
PENT–COGIC	1	0	150	186	0.3	0.7
PENT–Int Foursq Gos	2	643	724	897	1.6	3.3
PENT–Un Pent Ch Intl	1	NR	NR	NR	-	-
PRES–Presb Ch (USA)	2	362	842	1,043	1.9	3.8
Salvation Army	1	59	107	336	0.6	1.2
Sev Day Adv	1	94	164	189	0.3	0.7
Un C of Christ	1	9	9	11	0.0	0.0
Unit Univ	1	28	49	61	0.1	0.2
SCOTT	**15**	**891**	**2,688**	**4,289**	**86.9**	**100.0**
ANG/EPIS–Episcopal	1	16	35	35	0.7	0.8
Bahá'í	0	NR	1	1	0.0	0.0
BAPT–Amer Bapt USA	1	344	783	974	19.7	22.7
BAPT–So Bapt Conv	1	50	82	102	2.1	2.4
BRETH–Ch of Brethren	1	54	103	128	2.6	3.0
Catholic	1	NR	NR	767	15.5	17.9
Ch of Nazarene	1	12	21	21	0.4	0.5
CHR–Chr Ch (Disc)	1	130	503	625	12.7	14.6
CHR–Chr Chs & Chs Cr	1	NR	80	99	2.0	2.3
CHR–Chs of Christ	1	36	35	40	0.8	0.9
Jehovah's Witness	1	NR	NR	NR	-	-
LDS–L-D Saints	1	NR	NR	197	4.0	4.6
LUTH–Luth–MO Synod	1	60	184	254	5.1	5.9
MENN–CG in Cr (Menn)	1	NR	123	153	3.1	3.6
METH–Un Methodist	1	179	721	876	17.7	20.4
PENT–Assemb of God	1	10	17	17	0.3	0.4
SEDGWICK	**546**	**61,885**	**124,221**	**254,423**	**51.1**	**100.0**
ANG/EPIS–Episcopal	7	855	1,892	2,465	0.5	1.0
Ap Chr Ch-Amer	1	50	38	50	0.0	0.0
Bahá'í	1	NR	391	391	0.1	0.2
BAPT–Amer Bapt Assn	4	NR	450	572	0.1	0.2

NR–Not Reported - Represents no adherents reported. Percentages may not total 100 due to rounding.

Table 3: Religious Congregations by County and Group: 2010

Religious Group	Number of Congrega-tions	Number of Attendees	Number of Communicant, Confirmed, or Full Members	Adherents: Number of Adherents	Adherents: % of Total Pop.	Adherents: % of Total Adh.
BAPT–Amer Bapt USA	17	1,330	2,497	3,174	0.6	1.2
BAPT–Free Will Bapt	2	NR	84	107	0.0	0.0
BAPT–Ind Bapt Flwsp Intl	5	NR	NR	NR	-	-
BAPT–NBC Amer	4	175	400	509	0.1	0.2
BAPT–NBC USA	5	1,305	6,201	7,883	1.6	3.1
BAPT–Reg Bapt Gen As	1	NR	NR	NR	-	-
BAPT–So Bapt Conv	54	8,047	23,264	29,575	5.9	11.6
BRETH–Brethren (Ash)	2	NR	160	203	0.0	0.1
BRETH–Ch of Brethren	1	85	116	147	0.0	0.1
BRETH–Grace Breth	1	NR	NR	NR	-	-
BUDD–Mahayana	6	NR	NR	2,062	0.4	0.8
BUDD–Theravada	3	NR	NR	1,071	0.2	0.4
BUDD–Vajrayana	3	NR	NR	563	0.1	0.2
Calv Chpl	3	NR	NR	NR	-	-
Catholic	32	NR	NR	74,600	15.0	29.3
CGOD–Ch God (Ander)	8	2,727	NR	2,727	0.5	1.1
Ch Cr, Scientst	1	NR	NR	NR	-	-
Ch God (7th Day)	1	NR	NR	NR	-	-
Ch of Nazarene	16	1,789	3,838	4,032	0.8	1.6
CHR–Chr Ch (Disc)	16	1,361	3,612	4,592	0.9	1.8
CHR–Chr Chs & Chs Cr	17	NR	14,954	19,011	3.8	7.5
CHR–Chs of Christ	22	3,299	3,623	4,516	0.9	1.8
CHR–Int Chs of Christ	1	NR	130	165	0.0	0.1
Christian Brethren	1	NR	NR	NR	-	-
CONG–Cong Chr, NA	1	NR	326	414	0.1	0.2
Evan Cov Ch	1	146	60	190	0.0	0.1
Evan Free Ch	8	2,264	NR	2,264	0.5	0.9
FRND–Evan Fr Ch Intl	6	743	1,139	1,448	0.3	0.6
FRND–Fr Gen Cf & Un Mtg	1	NR	32	41	0.0	0.0
FRND–Fr Un Mtg	1	NR	437	556	0.1	0.2
HINDU–I/A Temples	1	NR	NR	250	0.1	0.1
HINDU–Post Ren	1	NR	NR	77	0.0	0.0
HINDU–Trad Temples	1	NR	NR	350	0.1	0.1
Ind Fund Churches	1	NR	NR	NR	-	-
Jehovah's Witness	7	NR	NR	NR	-	-
LDS–Comm of Christ	3	NR	582	582	0.1	0.2
LDS–L-D Saints	14	NR	NR	6,746	1.4	2.7
LUTH–E.L.C.A.	9	992	2,068	2,488	0.5	1.0
LUTH–Luth–MO Synod	10	2,700	5,305	6,948	1.4	2.7
LUTH–Wisc Ev Luth Syn	1	114	132	169	0.0	0.1
MENN–CG in Cr (Menn)	1	NR	75	95	0.0	0.0
MENN–Menn Br US Conf	2	NR	785	998	0.2	0.4
MENN–Mennonite USA	3	302	601	764	0.2	0.3
METH–AME	2	280	335	426	0.1	0.2
METH–C.M.E.	2	125	450	572	0.1	0.2
METH–Free Methodist	2	151	106	151	0.0	0.1
METH–Un Methodist	42	9,343	21,352	27,680	5.6	10.9
METH–Wesleyan	2	170	69	221	0.0	0.1
Metro Comm Ch	1	117	110	140	0.0	0.1
Missionary Ch	3	200	96	200	0.0	0.1
Muslim Est	4	536	NR	1,232	0.2	0.5
Non-denom Chr Chs	89	12,360	14,710	16,418	3.3	6.5
ORTHE–Ant Orth of NA	3	420	NR	1,241	0.2	0.5
ORTHE–Greek Orthodox	1	55	NR	120	0.0	0.0
PENT–Assemb of God	17	4,001	2,212	6,685	1.3	2.6
PENT–Ch God (Cleve)	6	203	525	667	0.1	0.3
PENT–Ch of God Proph	2	NR	88	112	0.0	0.0
PENT–COGIC	12	492	1,512	1,922	0.4	0.8
PENT–Full Gosp Bapt	3	NR	NR	NR	-	-
PENT–Int Foursq Gos	3	188	373	474	0.1	0.2
PENT–Intl Pent Holiness	3	239	280	356	0.1	0.1
PENT–Pent Ch of God	3	210	NR	326	0.1	0.1
PENT–Un Pent Ch Intl	1	NR	NR	NR	-	-
PENT–Vineyard	1	310	400	509	0.1	0.2
PRES–Presb Ch (USA)	16	2,167	5,177	6,581	1.3	2.6
PRES–Presb Ch Amer	2	463	403	606	0.1	0.2
PRES–Ref Pres of NA	1	39	32	53	0.0	0.0
REF–Comm Ref Evan	1	NR	NR	NR	-	-
REF–Ref Ch in Am	1	132	222	283	0.1	0.1
Salvation Army	2	182	231	1,847	0.4	0.7
Sev Day Adv	7	906	1,575	1,812	0.4	0.7
Un C of Christ	5	242	618	786	0.2	0.3
Unit Univ	1	70	153	205	0.0	0.1
Unity Ch	1	NR	NR	NR	-	-

Religious Group	Number of Congrega-tions	Number of Attendees	Number of Communicant, Confirmed, or Full Members	Adherents: Number of Adherents	Adherents: % of Total Pop.	Adherents: % of Total Adh.
Zoroastrian	0	NR	NR	3	0.0	0.0
SEWARD	**40**	**2,679**	**3,929**	**10,541**	**45.9**	**100.0**
ANG/EPIS–Episcopal	1	27	52	52	0.2	0.5
Bahá'í	0	NR	5	5	0.0	0.0
BAPT–So Bapt Conv	4	369	452	606	2.6	5.7
Catholic	1	NR	NR	5,246	22.9	49.8
CGOD–Ch God (Ander)	2	225	NR	225	1.0	2.1
Ch of Nazarene	1	55	62	90	0.4	0.9
CHR–Chr Ch (Disc)	1	78	217	291	1.3	2.8
CHR–Chr Chs & Chs Cr	1	NR	100	134	0.6	1.3
CHR–Chs of Christ	2	240	230	290	1.3	2.8
FRND–Evan Fr Ch Intl	1	38	69	93	0.4	0.9
Jehovah's Witness	1	NR	NR	NR	-	-
LDS–Comm of Christ	1	NR	156	156	0.7	1.5
LDS–L-D Saints	1	NR	NR	381	1.7	3.6
LUTH–E.L.C.A.	1	11	25	25	0.1	0.2
LUTH–Luth–MO Synod	1	81	227	282	1.2	2.7
MENN–Mennonite USA	1	42	39	52	0.2	0.5
METH–Un Methodist	2	224	556	597	2.6	5.7
Non-denom Chr Chs	12	1,070	1,390	1,478	6.4	14.0
PENT–Assemb of God	2	175	125	241	1.1	2.3
PENT–Ch God (Cleve)	1	0	0	0	0.0	0.0
PENT–COGIC	1	0	150	201	0.9	1.9
PRES–Presb Ch (USA)	1	34	56	75	0.3	0.7
Sev Day Adv	1	10	18	21	0.1	0.2
SHAWNEE	**227**	**22,813**	**42,697**	**84,485**	**47.5**	**100.0**
ANG/EPIS–Episcopal	2	522	1,219	1,219	0.7	1.4
Bahá'í	1	NR	81	81	0.0	0.1
BAPT–Amer Bapt Assn	1	NR	150	186	0.1	0.2
BAPT–Amer Bapt USA	11	956	2,305	2,861	1.6	3.4
BAPT–Free Will Bapt	1	NR	42	52	0.0	0.1
BAPT–Natl Mis Bapt Conv	3	400	1,100	1,365	0.8	1.6
BAPT–NBC Amer	1	0	60	74	0.0	0.1
BAPT–NBC USA	3	300	1,950	2,420	1.4	2.9
BAPT–Ref Bapt Ch	2	NR	NR	NR	-	-
BAPT–Reg Bapt Gen As	1	NR	NR	NR	-	-
BAPT–So Bapt Conv	23	1,912	2,896	3,594	2.0	4.3
BRETH–Ch of Brethren	1	35	130	161	0.1	0.2
Catholic	8	NR	NR	25,280	14.2	29.9
CGOD–Ch God (Ander)	3	110	NR	110	0.1	0.1
Ch Cr, Scientst	1	NR	NR	NR	-	-
Ch God (7th Day)	1	NR	NR	NR	-	-
Ch of Nazarene	6	1,616	1,746	3,414	1.9	4.0
CHR–Chr Ch (Disc)	3	442	1,709	2,121	1.2	2.5
CHR–Chr Chs & Chs Cr	9	NR	2,710	3,363	1.9	4.0
CHR–Chs of Christ	8	948	891	1,239	0.7	1.5
Evan Cov Ch	1	109	154	142	0.1	0.2
Evan Free Ch	1	143	NR	143	0.1	0.2
FRND–Fr Gen Cf	1	NR	35	43	0.0	0.1
HINDU–Post Ren	1	NR	NR	10	0.0	0.0
Jehovah's Witness	3	NR	NR	NR	-	-
JUD–Reform	1	60	105	284	0.2	0.3
LDS–Comm of Christ	1	NR	194	194	0.1	0.2
LDS–L-D Saints	5	NR	NR	3,010	1.7	3.6
LUTH–E.L.C.A.	3	428	1,216	1,602	0.9	1.9
LUTH–Luth–MO Synod	6	1,606	3,521	4,469	2.5	5.3
LUTH–Wisc Ev Luth Syn	1	78	79	104	0.1	0.1
MENN–Menn Br US Conf	1	NR	168	209	0.1	0.2
MENN–Mennonite USA	1	106	110	137	0.1	0.2
METH–AME	3	105	306	380	0.2	0.4
METH–C.M.E.	1	0	150	186	0.1	0.2
METH–Free Methodist	2	82	54	86	0.0	0.1
METH–Un Methodist	23	3,157	6,959	9,501	5.3	11.2
METH–Wesleyan	4	479	288	622	0.3	0.7
Metro Comm Ch	1	72	82	102	0.1	0.1
Muslim Est	1	100	NR	150	0.1	0.2
Non-denom Chr Chs	34	5,220	6,170	7,044	4.0	8.3
ORTHE–Ant Orth of NA	1	40	NR	75	0.0	0.1
PENT–Assemb of God	6	1,064	658	1,504	0.8	1.8
PENT–Ch God (Cleve)	1	38	68	84	0.0	0.1
PENT–Ch Lord Jesus Apos	1	NR	NR	NR	-	-

NR–Not Reported - Represents no adherents reported. Percentages may not total 100 due to rounding.

Table 3: Religious Congregations by County and Group: 2010

Religious Group	Number of Congregations	Number of Attendees	Number of Communicant, Confirmed, or Full Members	Adherents: Number of Adherents	Adherents: % of Total Pop.	Adherents: % of Total Adh.
PENT–Ch of God Proph	1	NR	5	6	0.0	0.0
PENT–COGIC	10	842	1,699	2,109	1.2	2.5
PENT–Int Foursq Gos	1	31	34	42	0.0	0.0
PENT–Un Pent Ch Intl	1	NR	NR	NR	-	-
PRES–Presb Ch (USA)	11	859	1,853	2,300	1.3	2.7
PRES–Ref Pres of NA	1	90	76	93	0.1	0.1
Salvation Army	1	92	128	356	0.2	0.4
Sev Day Adv	4	439	763	878	0.5	1.0
Un C of Christ	2	182	674	837	0.5	1.0
Unit Univ	1	150	159	243	0.1	0.3
Unity Ch	1	NR	NR	NR	-	-
SHERIDAN	**14**	**513**	**916**	**1,918**	**75.0**	**100.0**
Bahá'í	0	NR	1	1	0.0	0.1
BAPT–Amer Bapt USA	1	240	252	310	12.1	16.2
Catholic	4	NR	NR	821	32.1	42.8
CHR–Chr Chs & Chs Cr	1	NR	125	154	6.0	8.0
CHR–Chs of Christ	1	20	20	20	0.8	1.0
LUTH–Luth–MO Synod	1	40	120	141	5.5	7.4
METH–Un Methodist	3	68	203	253	9.9	13.2
Non-denom Chr Chs	2	110	130	138	5.4	7.2
PRES–Presb Ch (USA)	1	35	65	80	3.1	4.2
SHERMAN	**18**	**920**	**1,995**	**3,155**	**52.5**	**100.0**
ANG/EPIS–Episcopal	1	10	15	29	0.5	0.9
BAPT–Amer Bapt USA	1	90	93	113	1.9	3.6
Catholic	1	NR	NR	631	10.5	20.0
Ch of Nazarene	1	23	31	31	0.5	1.0
CHR–Chr Ch (Disc)	1	69	320	389	6.5	12.3
CHR–Chs of Christ	1	40	25	50	0.8	1.6
Evan Free Ch	1	0	NR	0	0.0	0.0
Ind Fund Churches	1	NR	NR	NR	-	-
LUTH–Luth Cong Msn Chr	1	84	376	457	7.6	14.5
METH–Un Methodist	2	212	723	919	15.3	29.1
Non-denom Chr Chs	5	350	350	463	7.7	14.7
PENT–Int Foursq Gos	1	18	21	26	0.4	0.8
Sev Day Adv	1	24	41	47	0.8	1.5
SMITH	**22**	**1,076**	**2,246**	**2,998**	**77.8**	**100.0**
BAPT–Reg Bapt Gen As	1	NR	NR	NR	-	-
Catholic	1	NR	NR	151	3.9	5.0
Ch of Nazarene	2	120	122	216	5.6	7.2
CHR–Chr Ch (Disc)	3	152	417	488	12.7	16.3
CHR–Chr Chs & Chs Cr	3	NR	160	187	4.9	6.2
Evan Free Ch	1	112	NR	112	2.9	3.7
LUTH–E.L.C.A.	2	183	471	563	14.6	18.8
LUTH–Luth Cong Msn Chr	1	75	247	289	7.5	9.6
LUTH–Luth–MO Synod	1	91	145	211	5.5	7.0
METH–Un Methodist	3	168	393	466	12.1	15.5
Non-denom Chr Chs	1	100	150	150	3.9	5.0
PRES–Presb Ch (USA)	1	24	34	40	1.0	1.3
Un C of Christ	2	51	107	125	3.2	4.2
STAFFORD	**19**	**658**	**1,867**	**2,521**	**56.8**	**100.0**
Bahá'í	0	NR	1	1	0.0	0.0
BAPT–Amer Bapt USA	2	81	227	276	6.2	10.9
BAPT–N Am Bapt Conf	1	NR	162	197	4.4	7.8
BAPT–So Bapt Conv	1	15	70	85	1.9	3.4
BRETH–Ch of Brethren	1	80	122	149	3.4	5.9
Catholic	2	NR	NR	327	7.4	13.0
CHR–Chr Ch (Disc)	1	0	273	332	7.5	13.2
CHR–Chs of Christ	2	160	170	218	4.9	8.6
FRND–Evan Fr Ch Intl	1	30	30	37	0.8	1.5
METH–Free Methodist	1	0	0	0	0.0	0.0
METH–Un Methodist	5	192	623	702	15.8	27.8
Non-denom Chr Chs	1	100	150	150	3.4	6.0
PRES–Presb Ch (USA)	1	0	39	47	1.1	1.9
STANTON	**8**	**356**	**669**	**1,436**	**64.3**	**100.0**
BAPT–So Bapt Conv	1	40	40	52	2.3	3.6
Catholic	1	NR	NR	454	20.3	31.6
Ch of Nazarene	2	35	81	104	4.7	7.2
METH–Un Methodist	2	116	449	612	27.4	42.6
METH–Wesleyan	1	145	74	189	8.5	13.2
Non-denom Chr Chs	1	20	25	25	1.1	1.7
STEVENS	**19**	**1,164**	**1,825**	**3,624**	**63.3**	**100.0**
BAPT–Amer Bapt USA	1	65	50	65	1.1	1.8
BAPT–So Bapt Conv	3	106	294	385	6.7	10.6
Catholic	1	NR	NR	1,034	18.1	28.5
CGOD–Ch God (Ander)	1	69	NR	69	1.2	1.9
Ch of Nazarene	1	28	33	33	0.6	0.9
CHR–Chr Chs & Chs Cr	1	NR	300	393	6.9	10.8
CHR–Chs of Christ	1	100	90	120	2.1	3.3
FRND–Evan Fr Ch Intl	2	217	255	334	5.8	9.2
LDS–L-D Saints	1	NR	NR	119	2.1	3.3
LUTH–Luth–MO Synod	1	27	59	59	1.0	1.6
METH–Un Methodist	2	132	410	486	8.5	13.4
Non-denom Chr Chs	2	70	90	92	1.6	2.5
PENT–Assemb of God	1	95	44	173	3.0	4.8
PENT–Intl Pent Holiness	1	255	200	262	4.6	7.2
SUMNER	**63**	**3,259**	**7,728**	**14,841**	**61.5**	**100.0**
ANG/EPIS–Episcopal	1	9	19	19	0.1	0.1
Bahá'í	0	NR	9	9	0.0	0.1
BAPT–Amer Bapt USA	5	227	861	1,073	4.4	7.2
BAPT–Free Will Bapt	1	NR	42	52	0.2	0.4
BAPT–So Bapt Conv	6	372	1,395	1,738	7.2	11.7
Calv Chpl	1	NR	NR	NR	-	-
Catholic	4	NR	NR	4,500	18.6	30.3
CGOD–Ch God (Ander)	1	10	NR	10	0.0	0.1
Ch of Nazarene	1	76	81	199	0.8	1.3
CHR–Chr Ch (Disc)	4	326	1,070	1,333	5.5	9.0
CHR–Chr Chs & Chs Cr	1	NR	50	62	0.3	0.4
CHR–Chs of Christ	5	368	390	495	2.1	3.3
FRND–Evan Fr Ch Intl	1	80	126	157	0.7	1.1
Jehovah's Witness	1	NR	NR	NR	-	-
LDS–L-D Saints	1	NR	NR	341	1.4	2.3
LUTH–E.L.C.A.	1	23	49	87	0.4	0.6
LUTH–Luth–MO Synod	2	111	212	304	1.3	2.0
METH–AME	1	0	150	187	0.8	1.3
METH–Un Methodist	12	1,097	2,512	3,281	13.6	22.1
METH–Wesleyan	1	37	19	48	0.2	0.3
Non-denom Chr Chs	4	240	305	324	1.3	2.2
PENT–Assemb of God	3	220	167	289	1.2	1.9
PRES–Presb Ch (USA)	5	37	225	280	1.2	1.9
Sev Day Adv	1	26	46	53	0.2	0.4
THOMAS	**19**	**1,064**	**1,710**	**4,185**	**53.0**	**100.0**
ANG/EPIS–Episcopal	1	16	30	36	0.5	0.9
Bahá'í	0	NR	2	2	0.0	0.0
BAPT–Amer Bapt USA	1	30	92	112	1.4	2.7
BAPT–So Bapt Conv	1	15	30	36	0.5	0.9
Catholic	1	NR	NR	1,394	17.6	33.3
CHR–Chr Ch (Disc)	1	21	69	84	1.1	2.0
CHR–Chs of Christ	1	49	45	68	0.9	1.6
Jehovah's Witness	1	NR	NR	NR	-	-
LDS–L-D Saints	1	NR	NR	134	1.7	3.2
LUTH–E.L.C.A.	1	17	70	91	1.2	2.2
LUTH–Luth–MO Synod	1	129	176	220	2.8	5.3
METH–Un Methodist	2	236	723	1,202	15.2	28.7
METH–Wesleyan	1	146	75	190	2.4	4.5
Non-denom Chr Chs	3	212	235	290	3.7	6.9
PENT–Assemb of God	1	155	84	230	2.9	5.5
PENT–Un Pent Ch Intl	1	NR	NR	NR	-	-
PRES–Presb Ch (USA)	1	38	79	96	1.2	2.3
TREGO	**13**	**431**	**939**	**1,922**	**64.0**	**100.0**
Bahá'í	0	NR	3	3	0.1	0.2
BAPT–So Bapt Conv	1	18	18	21	0.7	1.1
Catholic	2	NR	NR	648	21.6	33.7
CGOD–Ch God (Ander)	1	115	NR	115	3.8	6.0
CHR–Chr Chs & Chs Cr	1	NR	150	175	5.8	9.1
LUTH–E.L.C.A.	3	126	436	529	17.6	27.5

NR–Not Reported   - Represents no adherents reported.   Percentages may not total 100 due to rounding.

Table 3: Religious Congregations by County and Group: 2010

Religious Group	Number of Congrega-tions	Number of Attendees	Number of Communicant, Confirmed, or Full Members	Adherents		
				Number of Adherents	% of Total Pop.	% of Total Adh.
METH–Un Methodist	2	73	190	277	9.2	14.4
Non-denom Chr Chs	2	75	95	99	3.3	5.2
PRES–Presb Ch (USA)	1	24	47	55	1.8	2.9
WABAUNSEE	**20**	**629**	**1,650**	**2,599**	**36.8**	**100.0**
BAPT–Amer Bapt USA	1	25	25	31	0.4	1.2
BAPT–So Bapt Conv	1	28	60	75	1.1	2.9
Catholic	2	NR	NR	579	8.2	22.3
CHR–Chr Chs & Chs Cr	1	NR	80	100	1.4	3.8
CHR–Chs of Christ	2	68	69	91	1.3	3.5
CONG–Cong Chr, NA	1	NR	95	118	1.7	4.5
Ind Fund Churches	1	NR	NR	NR	-	-
LUTH–Luth–MO Synod	3	315	730	911	12.9	35.1
METH–Un Methodist	6	149	474	548	7.8	21.1
PRES–Presb Ch (USA)	1	10	20	25	0.4	1.0
Un C of Christ	1	34	97	121	1.7	4.7
WALLACE	**9**	**337**	**525**	**998**	**67.2**	**100.0**
BAPT–Amer Bapt USA	1	40	54	66	4.4	6.6
Catholic	2	NR	NR	232	15.6	23.2
Chr & Miss Al	1	80	40	152	10.2	15.2
LUTH–E.L.C.A.	2	29	82	106	7.1	10.6
METH–Un Methodist	2	94	298	320	21.5	32.1
METH–Wesleyan	1	94	51	122	8.2	12.2
WASHINGTON	**33**	**913**	**2,855**	**4,898**	**84.5**	**100.0**
Bahá'í	0	NR	1	1	0.0	0.0
BAPT–So Bapt Conv	1	56	115	139	2.4	2.8
BRETH–Ch of Brethren	1	10	15	18	0.3	0.4
Catholic	5	NR	NR	1,287	22.2	26.3
CHR–Chr Chs & Chs Cr	3	NR	356	430	7.4	8.8
LUTH–E.L.C.A.	5	135	366	418	7.2	8.5
LUTH–Luth Cong Msn Chr	3	96	284	343	5.9	7.0
LUTH–Luth–MO Synod	6	468	1,201	1,443	24.9	29.5
LUTH–Wisc Ev Luth Syn	1	2	2	2	0.0	0.0
METH–Un Methodist	4	95	335	600	10.3	12.2
PENT–Ch of God Proph	1	NR	11	13	0.2	0.3
PRES–Presb Ch (USA)	3	51	169	204	3.5	4.2
WICHITA	**10**	**269**	**571**	**1,443**	**64.6**	**100.0**
BAPT–Amer Bapt USA	1	50	76	96	4.3	6.7
Catholic	2	NR	NR	681	30.5	47.2
METH–Free Methodist	1	38	65	65	2.9	4.5
METH–Un Methodist	2	107	251	337	15.1	23.4
PENT–Assemb of God	1	44	33	80	3.6	5.5
PRES–Evan Presby Ch	1	NR	91	115	5.1	8.0
PRES–Presb Ch (USA)	2	30	55	69	3.1	4.8
WILSON	**34**	**1,093**	**2,937**	**4,718**	**50.1**	**100.0**
ANG/EPIS–Episcopal	1	23	45	73	0.8	1.5
BAPT–Amer Bapt Assn	1	NR	85	104	1.1	2.2
BAPT–Reg Bapt Gen As	1	NR	NR	NR	-	-
BAPT–So Bapt Conv	2	116	239	293	3.1	6.2
Catholic	2	NR	NR	800	8.5	17.0
CGOD–Ch God (Ander)	1	20	NR	20	0.2	0.4
CGOD–Ches God-Gen Con	1	0	0	0	0.0	0.0
Ch of Nazarene	2	158	220	246	2.6	5.2
CHR–Chr Ch (Disc)	2	88	635	778	8.3	16.5
CHR–Chr Chs & Chs Cr	4	NR	411	503	5.3	10.7
CHR–Chs of Christ	1	30	28	36	0.4	0.8
Jehovah's Witness	1	NR	NR	NR	-	-
MENN–CG in Cr (Menn)	1	NR	140	171	1.8	3.6
METH–Un Methodist	6	267	607	843	9.0	17.9
METH–Wesleyan	1	37	90	48	0.5	1.0
Non-denom Chr Chs	2	175	250	250	2.7	5.3
PENT–Assemb of God	1	95	85	431	4.6	9.1
PENT–Ch God (Cleve)	1	30	23	28	0.3	0.6
PENT–Intl Pent Holiness	1	21	32	39	0.4	0.8
PRES–Presb Ch (USA)	1	14	14	17	0.2	0.4
Sev Day Adv	1	19	33	38	0.4	0.8
WOODSON	**13**	**292**	**1,110**	**1,722**	**52.0**	**100.0**
ANG/EPIS–Episcopal	1	7	39	39	1.2	2.3
BAPT–So Bapt Conv	2	69	342	407	12.3	23.6
Catholic	1	NR	NR	400	12.1	23.2
CGOD–Ches God-Gen Con	1	40	74	88	2.7	5.1
CHR–Chr Ch (Disc)	1	0	182	216	6.5	12.5
CHR–Chr Chs & Chs Cr	1	NR	50	59	1.8	3.4
METH–Un Methodist	4	161	389	453	13.7	26.3
PENT–Assemb of God	1	15	0	20	0.6	1.2
PRES–Presb Ch (USA)	1	0	34	40	1.2	2.3
WYANDOTTE	**285**	**23,486**	**38,307**	**77,249**	**49.0**	**100.0**
ANG/EPIS–Episcopal	2	63	177	191	0.1	0.2
Bahá'í	1	NR	95	95	0.1	0.1
BAPT–Amer Bapt Assn	1	NR	85	110	0.1	0.1
BAPT–Amer Bapt USA	17	1,165	2,647	3,413	2.2	4.4
BAPT–Converge/BGC	1	75	NR	90	0.1	0.1
BAPT–Free Will Bapt	1	NR	42	54	0.0	0.1
BAPT–Natl Mis Bapt Conv	4	70	600	774	0.5	1.0
BAPT–NBC Amer	2	875	1,025	1,322	0.8	1.7
BAPT–NBC USA	19	2,719	6,074	7,831	5.0	10.1
BAPT–Reg Bapt Gen As	5	NR	NR	NR	-	-
BAPT–So Bapt Conv	16	765	1,541	1,987	1.3	2.6
BRETH–Ch of Brethren	1	26	51	66	0.0	0.1
BUDD–Mahayana	1	NR	NR	57	0.0	0.1
Catholic	11	NR	NR	24,812	15.8	32.1
CGOD–Ch God (Ander)	5	726	NR	726	0.5	0.9
Ch of Chr (Hol)	1	NR	NR	NR	-	-
Ch of Nazarene	10	1,110	1,265	1,762	1.1	2.3
Chr & Miss Al	3	632	1,047	1,150	0.7	1.5
CHR–Chr Ch (Disc)	12	333	1,131	1,458	0.9	1.9
CHR–Chr Chs & Chs Cr	4	NR	1,010	1,302	0.8	1.7
CHR–Chs of Christ	7	590	627	836	0.5	1.1
CHR–Int Chs of Christ	1	NR	324	418	0.3	0.5
Evan Cov Ch	1	40	32	52	0.0	0.1
Evan Free Ch	1	90	NR	90	0.1	0.1
HINDU–Post Ren	1	NR	NR	25	0.0	0.0
Ind Fund Churches	2	NR	NR	NR	-	-
Jehovah's Witness	2	NR	NR	NR	-	-
LDS–Comm of Christ	3	NR	582	582	0.4	0.8
LDS–L-D Saints	2	NR	NR	2,152	1.4	2.8
LUTH–E.L.C.A.	2	127	323	352	0.2	0.5
LUTH–Luth–MO Synod	6	451	849	1,021	0.6	1.3
LUTH–Wisc Ev Luth Syn	1	0	0	0	0.0	0.0
MENN–Mennonite USA	2	180	266	343	0.2	0.4
METH–AME	9	525	1,625	2,095	1.3	2.7
METH–AME Zion	3	0	350	451	0.3	0.6
METH–C.M.E.	1	150	350	451	0.3	0.6
METH–Free Methodist	1	19	14	19	0.0	0.0
METH–Un Methodist	13	820	1,813	2,419	1.5	3.1
Muslim Est	2	268	NR	616	0.4	0.8
Non-denom Chr Chs	61	8,496	9,310	10,947	7.0	14.2
ORTHE–Ant Orth of NA	1	75	NR	102	0.1	0.1
ORTHE–Serb Orth USA	1	33	NR	120	0.1	0.2
ORTHO–Ethiopian Orth	1	NR	NR	NR	-	-
ORTHO–Malan Dioc Am	1	5	NR	15	0.0	0.0
PENT–Assemb of God	6	845	970	1,477	0.9	1.9
PENT–Ch God (Cleve)	1	0	0	0	0.0	0.0
PENT–Ch God Apos Fth	1	NR	NR	NR	-	-
PENT–Ch of God Proph	2	NR	120	155	0.1	0.2
PENT–COGIC	13	1,070	2,130	2,746	1.7	3.6
PENT–Intl Pent Holiness	3	221	270	348	0.2	0.5
PENT–Un Pent Ch Intl	1	NR	NR	NR	-	-
PRES–Korean Pres Amer	1	NR	NR	NR	-	-
PRES–Presb Ch (USA)	4	131	150	193	0.1	0.2
Salvation Army	1	29	60	421	0.3	0.5
Sev Day Adv	5	599	1,042	1,198	0.8	1.6
Un C of Christ	4	163	310	400	0.3	0.5
Zoroastrian	1	NR	NR	5	0.0	0.0

NR–Not Reported   - Represents no adherents reported.   Percentages may not total 100 due to rounding.

Table 3: Religious Congregations by County and Group: 2010

Religious Group	Number of Congregations	Number of Attendees	Number of Communicant, Confirmed, or Full Members	Adherents: Number of Adherents	Adherents: % of Total Pop.	Adherents: % of Total Adh.
KENTUCKY	**7,745**	**569,674**	**1,470,009**	**2,237,512**	**51.6**	**100.0**
ADAIR	**52**	**2,435**	**5,146**	**6,631**	**35.5**	**100.0**
Bahá'í	0	NR	2	2	0.0	0.0
BAPT–So Bapt Conv	8	575	1,237	1,493	8.0	22.5
BRETH–Breth in Chr	4	NR	NR	NR	-	-
Catholic	1	NR	NR	140	0.8	2.1
CGOD–Ch God (Ander)	1	95	NR	95	0.5	1.4
Ch of Nazarene	3	236	247	352	1.9	5.3
CHR–Chr Chs & Chs Cr	5	NR	856	1,033	5.5	15.6
CHR–Chs of Christ	3	245	225	376	2.0	5.7
MENN–Amish Undif	1	NR	34	104	0.6	1.6
METH–Un Methodist	15	789	1,729	1,965	10.5	29.6
Non-denom Chr Chs	4	265	430	449	2.4	6.8
PENT–Assemb of God	2	139	120	294	1.6	4.4
PENT–Ch God (Cleve)	1	41	116	140	0.8	2.1
PENT–Ch of God Proph	1	NR	21	25	0.1	0.4
PRES–Cumber Presb	1	NR	5	18	0.1	0.3
PRES–Presb Ch (USA)	1	0	38	46	0.2	0.7
Sev Day Adv	1	50	86	99	0.5	1.5
ALLEN	**37**	**2,547**	**5,234**	**6,213**	**31.1**	**100.0**
Bahá'í	0	NR	3	3	0.0	0.0
BAPT–So Bapt Conv	14	1,063	2,698	3,325	16.7	53.5
Catholic	1	NR	NR	102	0.5	1.6
Ch of Nazarene	1	29	101	101	0.5	1.6
CHR–Chs of Christ	2	233	203	253	1.3	4.1
METH–AME	1	0	100	123	0.6	2.0
METH–Free Methodist	1	31	31	31	0.2	0.5
METH–Un Methodist	12	593	1,299	1,383	6.9	22.3
Non-denom Chr Chs	3	585	740	819	4.1	13.2
PENT–Ch of God Proph	1	NR	29	36	0.2	0.6
PENT–Intl Pent Holiness	1	13	30	37	0.2	0.6
ANDERSON	**46**	**3,124**	**9,579**	**12,827**	**59.9**	**100.0**
Bahá'í	0	NR	5	5	0.0	0.0
BAPT–NBC USA	1	100	500	620	2.9	4.8
BAPT–So Bapt Conv	16	1,909	4,981	6,178	28.8	48.2
Catholic	1	NR	NR	850	4.0	6.6
CHR–Chr Ch (Disc)	3	300	950	1,178	5.5	9.2
CHR–Chr Chs & Chs Cr	9	NR	1,962	2,434	11.4	19.0
CHR–Chs of Christ	3	270	255	320	1.5	2.5
Jehovah's Witness	1	NR	NR	NR	-	-
METH–Un Methodist	2	175	567	631	2.9	4.9
Non-denom Chr Chs	1	70	75	88	0.4	0.7
PENT–Assemb of God	2	88	54	95	0.4	0.7
PENT–Ch God (Cleve)	1	29	106	131	0.6	1.0
PENT–Full Gosp Bapt	1	NR	NR	NR	-	-
PENT–Open Bible Std	1	40	NR	40	0.2	0.3
PENT–Pent Ch of God	1	70	NR	109	0.5	0.8
PENT–Un Pent Ch Intl	1	NR	NR	NR	-	-
PRES–Presb Ch (USA)	1	35	58	72	0.3	0.6
Sev Day Adv	1	38	66	76	0.4	0.6
BALLARD	**32**	**1,692**	**5,512**	**6,788**	**82.3**	**100.0**
BAPT–So Bapt Conv	15	1,237	3,968	4,770	57.8	70.3
Catholic	1	NR	NR	175	2.1	2.6
CHR–Chr Ch (Disc)	1	24	14	17	0.2	0.3
CHR–Chs of Christ	1	13	13	13	0.2	0.2
METH–Un Methodist	8	338	698	755	9.2	11.1
Non-denom Chr Chs	1	80	101	101	1.2	1.5
PRES–Cumber Presb	5	NR	718	957	11.6	14.1
BARREN	**82**	**6,471**	**15,462**	**20,101**	**47.7**	**100.0**
ANG/EPIS–Episcopal	1	39	61	82	0.2	0.4
Bahá'í	0	NR	2	2	0.0	0.0
BAPT–Free Will Bapt	2	NR	192	235	0.6	1.2
BAPT–NBC Amer	1	85	250	307	0.7	1.5
BAPT–So Bapt Conv	24	2,716	8,866	10,873	25.8	54.1
Calv Chpl	1	NR	NR	NR	-	-
Catholic	1	NR	NR	704	1.7	3.5
CGOD–Ch God (Ander)	1	0	NR	0	0.0	0.0
Ch of Nazarene	2	151	189	237	0.6	1.2
CHR–Chr Ch (Disc)	1	250	560	687	1.6	3.4
CHR–Chr Chs & Chs Cr	3	NR	586	719	1.7	3.6
CHR–Chs of Christ	12	1,573	1,433	1,778	4.2	8.8
Jehovah's Witness	1	NR	NR	NR	-	-
LDS–L-D Saints	1	NR	NR	382	0.9	1.9
MENN–Amish Undif	3	NR	173	454	1.1	2.3
METH–Un Methodist	16	804	1,859	2,103	5.0	10.5
METH–Wesleyan	1	77	55	100	0.2	0.5
Non-denom Chr Chs	3	470	620	658	1.6	3.3
PENT–Assemb of God	2	155	118	175	0.4	0.9
PENT–Ch God (Cleve)	3	103	338	415	1.0	2.1
PENT–Un Pent Ch Intl	1	NR	NR	NR	-	-
PRES–Presb Ch (USA)	1	0	76	93	0.2	0.5
Sev Day Adv	1	48	84	97	0.2	0.5
BATH	**42**	**1,807**	**2,866**	**4,970**	**42.9**	**100.0**
Bahá'í	0	NR	2	2	0.0	0.0
BAPT–Free Will Bapt	1	NR	96	119	1.0	2.4
BAPT–So Bapt Conv	3	121	279	346	3.0	7.0
Catholic	1	NR	NR	33	0.3	0.7
CGOD–Ch God (Ander)	9	851	NR	851	7.3	17.1
CHR–Chr Ch (Disc)	5	117	537	665	5.7	13.4
CHR–Chr Chs & Chs Cr	6	NR	570	706	6.1	14.2
CHR–Chs of Christ	3	135	127	156	1.3	3.1
Ind Fund Churches	1	NR	NR	NR	-	-
LDS–L-D Saints	1	NR	NR	674	5.8	13.6
MENN–Amish Undif	1	NR	35	103	0.9	2.1
METH–Un Methodist	2	90	312	317	2.7	6.4
Non-denom Chr Chs	4	325	635	662	5.7	13.3
PENT–Assemb of God	1	20	25	29	0.3	0.6
PENT–Ch God (Cleve)	2	148	150	186	1.6	3.7
PRES–Presb Ch (USA)	2	0	98	121	1.0	2.4
BELL	**79**	**5,424**	**17,137**	**21,041**	**73.3**	**100.0**
ANG/EPIS–Episcopal	1	36	59	63	0.2	0.3
Bahá'í	0	NR	2	2	0.0	0.0
BAPT–Amer Bapt USA	1	375	940	1,122	3.9	5.3
BAPT–So Bapt Conv	44	3,730	13,576	16,209	56.5	77.0
Catholic	2	NR	NR	372	1.3	1.8
Ch of Nazarene	2	32	56	56	0.2	0.3
CHR–Chr Ch (Disc)	2	80	329	393	1.4	1.9
CHR–Chr Chs & Chs Cr	1	NR	14	17	0.1	0.1
CHR–Chs of Christ	1	70	65	90	0.3	0.4
METH–AME Zion	1	0	100	119	0.4	0.6
METH–Un Methodist	6	360	801	960	3.3	4.6
Non-denom Chr Chs	2	562	650	775	2.7	3.7
PENT–Assemb of God	1	23	9	31	0.1	0.1
PENT–Ch God (Cleve)	3	74	246	294	1.0	1.4
PENT–Ch God Mtn Asm	3	NR	NR	NR	-	-
PENT–Ch of God Proph	3	NR	113	135	0.5	0.6
PENT–Un Pent Ch Intl	2	NR	NR	NR	-	-
PRES–Presb Ch (USA)	2	37	95	113	0.4	0.5
Salvation Army	1	30	56	260	0.9	1.2
Sev Day Adv	1	15	26	30	0.1	0.1
BOONE	**76**	**11,924**	**29,540**	**59,315**	**49.9**	**100.0**
ANG/EPIS–Episcopal	1	57	110	110	0.1	0.2
Bahá'í	0	NR	17	17	0.0	0.0
BAPT–So Bapt Conv	21	4,992	16,541	21,289	17.9	35.9
BRETH–Ch of Brethren	1	25	66	85	0.1	0.1
Calv Chpl	1	NR	NR	NR	-	-
Catholic	6	NR	NR	19,500	16.4	32.9
CGOD–Ch God (Ander)	1	60	NR	60	0.1	0.1
Ch of Nazarene	1	55	60	79	0.1	0.1
Chr & Miss Al	1	87	51	127	0.1	0.2
CHR–Chr Ch (Disc)	6	467	1,414	1,820	1.5	3.1
CHR–Chr Chs & Chs Cr	4	NR	3,083	3,968	3.3	6.7
CHR–Chs of Christ	4	400	365	440	0.4	0.7
Evan Free Ch	1	1,700	NR	1,700	1.4	2.9
Jehovah's Witness	1	NR	NR	NR	-	-
LUTH–Luth Cong Msn Chr	2	636	1,768	2,275	1.9	3.8

NR–Not Reported   - Represents no adherents reported.   Percentages may not total 100 due to rounding.

Table 3: Religious Congregations by County and Group: 2010

Religious Group	Number of Congregations	Number of Attendees	Number of Communicant, Confirmed, or Full Members	Adherents: Number of Adherents	Adherents: % of Total Pop.	Adherents: % of Total Adh.
LUTH–Luth–MO Synod	1	161	304	390	0.3	0.7
LUTH–Wisc Ev Luth Syn	1	59	81	107	0.1	0.2
METH–Un Methodist	4	699	2,233	2,445	2.1	4.1
METH–Wesleyan	1	26	11	34	0.0	0.1
Muslim Est	3	368	NR	766	0.6	1.3
Non-denom Chr Chs	7	615	1,183	1,206	1.0	2.0
ORTHE–Bulgar Orth USA	1	1	NR	3	0.0	0.0
PENT–Ch God (Cleve)	3	261	386	497	0.4	0.8
PENT–Vineyard	1	1,200	1,600	2,059	1.7	3.5
PRES–Presb Ch (USA)	2	0	232	299	0.3	0.5
PRES–Presb Ch Amer	1	55	35	39	0.0	0.1
BOURBON	**46**	**2,217**	**7,660**	**11,110**	**55.6**	**100.0**
ANG/EPIS–Episcopal	1	61	186	244	1.2	2.2
Bahá'í	0	NR	1	1	0.0	0.0
BAPT–Prog NBC	1	0	150	183	0.9	1.6
BAPT–So Bapt Conv	5	781	2,900	3,548	17.8	31.9
Catholic	1	NR	NR	893	4.5	8.0
CGOD–Ch God (Ander)	2	203	NR	203	1.0	1.8
Ch of Nazarene	3	67	216	332	1.7	3.0
CHR–Chr Ch (Disc)	7	199	1,387	1,697	8.5	15.3
CHR–Chr Chs & Chs Cr	5	NR	995	1,217	6.1	11.0
CHR–Chs of Christ	2	122	114	142	0.7	1.3
LDS–L-D Saints	1	NR	NR	436	2.2	3.9
METH–AME	2	0	300	367	1.8	3.3
METH–Un Methodist	8	337	1,066	1,170	5.9	10.5
METH–Wesleyan	1	8	35	10	0.1	0.1
PENT–Assemb of God	1	333	140	459	2.3	4.1
PENT–Ch God (Cleve)	2	19	17	21	0.1	0.2
PENT–Un Pent Ch Intl	1	NR	NR	NR	-	-
PRES–Presb Ch (USA)	3	87	153	187	0.9	1.7
BOYD	**109**	**7,769**	**21,759**	**29,012**	**58.6**	**100.0**
ANG/EPIS–Episcopal	1	82	171	303	0.6	1.0
Bahá'í	0	NR	3	3	0.0	0.0
BAPT–Enterprise Bapt Assoc	1	NR	NR	NR	-	-
BAPT–Free Will Bapt	15	NR	1,411	1,688	3.4	5.8
BAPT–Ind Bapt Flwsp Intl	1	NR	NR	NR	-	-
BAPT–So Bapt Conv	27	3,089	11,403	13,639	27.5	47.0
Catholic	1	NR	NR	1,950	3.9	6.7
CGOD–Ch God (Ander)	4	794	NR	794	1.6	2.7
Ch of Nazarene	10	919	1,461	1,934	3.9	6.7
CHR–Chr Ch (Disc)	1	236	614	734	1.5	2.5
CHR–Chr Chs & Chs Cr	4	NR	365	437	0.9	1.5
CHR–Chs of Christ	3	127	111	138	0.3	0.5
Jehovah's Witness	1	NR	NR	NR	-	-
LUTH–Luth–MO Synod	1	85	163	199	0.4	0.7
METH–AME	1	0	100	120	0.2	0.4
METH–Un Methodist	14	978	3,823	4,168	8.4	14.4
METH–Wesleyan	3	118	113	154	0.3	0.5
Non-denom Chr Chs	6	674	800	942	1.9	3.2
PENT–Assemb of God	1	38	59	114	0.2	0.4
PENT–Ch God (Cleve)	4	297	591	707	1.4	2.4
PENT–Int Pent C Chr	2	133	7	175	0.4	0.6
PENT–Un Pent Ch Intl	1	NR	NR	NR	-	-
PENT–United Holy Ch	1	NR	NR	NR	-	-
PRES–Presb Ch (USA)	4	100	380	455	0.9	1.6
Salvation Army	1	47	93	253	0.5	0.9
Sev Day Adv	1	52	91	105	0.2	0.4
BOYLE	**70**	**6,477**	**17,920**	**23,769**	**83.6**	**100.0**
ANG/EPIS–Episcopal	1	86	186	224	0.8	0.9
Bahá'í	0	NR	15	15	0.1	0.1
BAPT–NBC USA	1	500	800	955	3.4	4.0
BAPT–So Bapt Conv	27	3,264	11,776	14,051	49.4	59.1
Calv Chpl	1	NR	NR	NR	-	-
Catholic	2	NR	NR	1,439	5.1	6.1
CGOD–Ch God (Ander)	2	265	NR	265	0.9	1.1
Ch of Nazarene	1	49	72	172	0.6	0.7
CHR–Chr Ch (Disc)	3	190	579	691	2.4	2.9
CHR–Chr Chs & Chs Cr	2	NR	967	1,154	4.1	4.9
CHR–Chs of Christ	5	344	344	405	1.4	1.7
Jehovah's Witness	2	NR	NR	NR	-	-
LUTH–Luth–MO Synod	1	57	81	101	0.4	0.4
METH–AME	2	0	250	298	1.0	1.3
METH–Un Methodist	5	467	1,224	1,466	5.2	6.2
METH–Wesleyan	1	28	23	36	0.1	0.2
Muslim Est	1	134	NR	308	1.1	1.3
Non-denom Chr Chs	1	60	80	80	0.3	0.3
PENT–Assemb of God	1	133	88	196	0.7	0.8
PENT–Ch God (Cleve)	4	407	727	867	3.0	3.6
PENT–Pent Ch of God	1	70	NR	109	0.4	0.5
PENT–Un Pent Ch Intl	1	NR	NR	NR	-	-
PRES–Presb Ch (USA)	2	200	512	611	2.1	2.6
PRES–Presb Ch Amer	1	150	97	165	0.6	0.7
Salvation Army	1	71	96	158	0.6	0.7
Sev Day Adv	1	2	3	3	0.0	0.0
BRACKEN	**36**	**671**	**3,006**	**4,479**	**52.8**	**100.0**
BAPT–Free Will Bapt	1	NR	67	83	1.0	1.9
BAPT–So Bapt Conv	7	314	901	1,122	13.2	25.1
Catholic	2	NR	NR	755	8.9	16.9
Ch of Nazarene	1	60	82	92	1.1	2.1
CHR–Chr Ch (Disc)	1	0	0	0	0.0	0.0
CHR–Chr Chs & Chs Cr	10	NR	1,253	1,560	18.4	34.8
LUTH–Luth Ch-Am Asc	1	NR	NR	NR	-	-
METH–Un Methodist	9	271	618	751	8.8	16.8
METH–Wesleyan	1	13	6	17	0.2	0.4
PENT–Assemb of God	1	13	12	16	0.2	0.4
PRES–Presb Ch (USA)	2	0	67	83	1.0	1.9
BREATHITT	**28**	**1,108**	**1,352**	**2,049**	**14.8**	**100.0**
Bahá'í	0	NR	3	3	0.0	0.1
BAPT–So Bapt Conv	4	170	349	419	3.0	20.4
BRETH–Brethren (Ash)	1	NR	80	96	0.7	4.7
BRETH–Grace Breth	2	NR	NR	NR	-	-
Catholic	1	NR	NR	35	0.3	1.7
CGOD–Ch God (Ander)	1	180	NR	180	1.3	8.8
CHR–Chr Chs & Chs Cr	1	NR	100	120	0.9	5.9
CHR–Chs of Christ	1	40	27	45	0.3	2.2
Evan Free Ch	1	55	NR	55	0.4	2.7
Jehovah's Witness	1	NR	NR	NR	-	-
MENN–Cons Menn Conf	3	128	132	159	1.1	7.8
METH–Free Methodist	2	130	25	130	0.9	6.3
METH–Un Methodist	3	191	363	393	2.8	19.2
Non-denom Chr Chs	2	100	40	125	0.9	6.1
PENT–Assemb of God	1	35	45	65	0.5	3.2
PENT–Ch God (Cleve)	1	63	114	137	1.0	6.7
PENT–Open Bible Std	1	0	NR	0	0.0	0.0
PRES–Presb Ch (USA)	1	0	46	55	0.4	2.7
Sev Day Adv	1	16	28	32	0.2	1.6
BRECKINRIDGE	**62**	**2,684**	**6,205**	**10,538**	**52.5**	**100.0**
Bahá'í	0	NR	1	1	0.0	0.0
BAPT–So Bapt Conv	21	1,451	3,774	4,628	23.1	43.9
Catholic	5	NR	NR	2,622	13.1	24.9
CGOD–Ch God (Ander)	1	38	NR	38	0.2	0.4
CHR–Chr Chs & Chs Cr	1	NR	50	61	0.3	0.6
CHR–Chs of Christ	2	60	59	72	0.4	0.7
Jehovah's Witness	1	NR	NR	NR	-	-
MENN–Amish Undif	3	NR	79	273	1.4	2.6
METH–Un Methodist	15	695	1,531	1,695	8.5	16.1
METH–Wesleyan	2	81	43	106	0.5	1.0
Missionary Ch	1	70	21	70	0.3	0.7
Non-denom Chr Chs	3	255	325	387	1.9	3.7
PENT–Ch God (Cleve)	1	34	104	128	0.6	1.2
PRES–Cumber Presb	6	NR	218	457	2.3	4.3
BULLITT	**79**	**7,010**	**17,285**	**24,707**	**33.2**	**100.0**
Bahá'í	0	NR	5	5	0.0	0.0
BAPT–So Bapt Conv	30	4,492	12,140	15,024	20.2	60.8
Catholic	3	NR	NR	3,054	4.1	12.4
Ch of Nazarene	2	143	160	211	0.3	0.9
CHR–Chr Ch (Disc)	1	92	272	337	0.5	1.4
CHR–Chr Chs & Chs Cr	3	NR	616	762	1.0	3.1

NR–Not Reported   - Represents no adherents reported.   Percentages may not total 100 due to rounding.

Table 3: Religious Congregations by County and Group: 2010

Religious Group	Number of Congrega-tions	Number of Attendees	Number of Communicant, Confirmed, or Full Members	Adherents: Number of Adherents	Adherents: % of Total Pop.	Adherents: % of Total Adh.
CHR–Chs of Christ	5	330	275	361	0.5	1.5
Jehovah's Witness	3	NR	NR	NR	-	-
LDS–L-D Saints	1	NR	NR	286	0.4	1.2
LUTH–Luth–MO Synod	1	70	96	141	0.2	0.6
METH–A.W.M.C.	1	46	10	28	0.0	0.1
METH–Un Methodist	8	563	1,391	1,659	2.2	6.7
METH–Wesleyan	1	13	13	17	0.0	0.1
Non-denom Chr Chs	8	670	1,120	1,153	1.6	4.7
PENT–Assemb of God	5	447	463	774	1.0	3.1
PENT–Ch God (Cleve)	2	119	444	549	0.7	2.2
PENT–Ch of God Proph	3	NR	151	187	0.3	0.8
PENT–Int Foursq Gos	1	25	26	32	0.0	0.1
PRES–Presb Ch (USA)	1	0	103	127	0.2	0.5
BUTLER	**51**	**3,067**	**6,839**	**8,749**	**68.9**	**100.0**
BAPT–So Bapt Conv	27	1,898	5,623	6,849	54.0	78.3
Catholic	1	NR	NR	95	0.7	1.1
Ch of Nazarene	1	42	75	75	0.6	0.9
CHR–Chs of Christ	10	431	408	505	4.0	5.8
LDS–L-D Saints	1	NR	NR	230	1.8	2.6
METH–Free Methodist	1	5	4	5	0.0	0.1
METH–Un Methodist	3	58	167	169	1.3	1.9
Non-denom Chr Chs	1	600	500	750	5.9	8.6
PENT–Assemb of God	1	23	15	23	0.2	0.3
PENT–Ch God (Cleve)	1	10	5	6	0.0	0.1
PENT–Un Pent Ch Intl	1	NR	NR	NR	-	-
PRES–Cumber Presb	3	NR	42	42	0.3	0.5
CALDWELL	**43**	**3,135**	**9,370**	**11,815**	**91.0**	**100.0**
BAPT–So Bapt Conv	22	2,458	7,824	9,418	72.5	79.7
Catholic	1	NR	NR	124	1.0	1.0
CHR–Chr Ch (Disc)	2	63	133	160	1.2	1.4
CHR–Chr Chs & Chs Cr	1	NR	90	108	0.8	0.9
CHR–Chs of Christ	1	100	100	110	0.8	0.9
LDS–L-D Saints	1	NR	NR	308	2.4	2.6
MENN–Amb Amish-Menn	1	75	26	75	0.6	0.6
MENN–Amish Undif	0	NR	13	19	0.1	0.2
METH–C.M.E.	1	0	100	120	0.9	1.0
METH–Un Methodist	6	267	625	713	5.5	6.0
Non-denom Chr Chs	1	50	150	150	1.2	1.3
PENT–Assemb of God	1	32	26	56	0.4	0.5
PENT–Un Pent Ch Intl	1	NR	NR	NR	-	-
PRES–Cum Pres Am	1	NR	NR	NR	-	-
PRES–Cumber Presb	2	NR	143	285	2.2	2.4
PRES–Presb Ch (USA)	1	90	140	169	1.3	1.4
CALLOWAY	**88**	**8,540**	**17,506**	**22,018**	**59.2**	**100.0**
ANG/EPIS–Episcopal	1	73	114	114	0.3	0.5
Bahá'í	0	NR	11	11	0.0	0.0
BAPT–Natl Mis Bapt Conv	1	0	150	174	0.5	0.8
BAPT–So Bapt Conv	30	3,635	9,898	11,501	30.9	52.2
Catholic	1	NR	NR	862	2.3	3.9
Ch Cr, Scientst	1	NR	NR	NR	-	-
Ch of Nazarene	1	0	36	36	0.1	0.2
CHR–Chr Ch (Disc)	1	120	190	221	0.6	1.0
CHR–Chs of Christ	17	2,176	2,405	2,943	7.9	13.4
Jehovah's Witness	1	NR	NR	NR	-	-
LDS–L-D Saints	1	NR	NR	440	1.2	2.0
LUTH–Luth–MO Synod	1	116	170	204	0.5	0.9
METH–AME	1	0	100	116	0.3	0.5
METH–Un Methodist	17	1,106	3,113	3,346	9.0	15.2
Non-denom Chr Chs	3	500	540	628	1.7	2.9
PENT–Assemb of God	2	550	385	700	1.9	3.2
PENT–Pent Ch of God	2	140	NR	217	0.6	1.0
PENT–Un Pent Ch Intl	2	NR	NR	NR	-	-
PRES–Cumber Presb	3	NR	182	259	0.7	1.2
PRES–Presb Ch (USA)	1	100	171	199	0.5	0.9
Sev Day Adv	1	24	41	47	0.1	0.2
CAMPBELL	**88**	**6,438**	**16,512**	**44,442**	**49.2**	**100.0**
ANG/EPIS–Episcopal	2	224	698	702	0.8	1.6
Bahá'í	0	NR	8	8	0.0	0.0
BAPT–So Bapt Conv	22	2,816	8,396	10,193	11.3	22.9
Catholic	12	NR	NR	24,500	27.1	55.1
CGOD–Ch God (Ander)	2	17	NR	17	0.0	0.0
Ch of Nazarene	4	194	291	428	0.5	1.0
CHR–Chr Ch (Disc)	1	124	214	260	0.3	0.6
CHR–Chr Chs & Chs Cr	5	NR	430	522	0.6	1.2
CHR–Chs of Christ	1	200	184	256	0.3	0.6
Jehovah's Witness	1	NR	NR	NR	-	-
LUTH–E.L.C.A.	4	204	447	513	0.6	1.2
METH–Un Methodist	9	911	1,941	2,352	2.6	5.3
Non-denom Chr Chs	6	485	820	863	1.0	1.9
PENT–Assemb of God	2	122	91	180	0.2	0.4
PENT–Ch God (Cleve)	6	418	871	1,057	1.2	2.4
PENT–Ch God Mtn Asm	1	NR	NR	NR	-	-
PENT–Un Pent Ch Intl	1	NR	NR	NR	-	-
PENT–Vineyard	1	57	75	91	0.1	0.2
PRES–Presb Ch (USA)	2	141	275	334	0.4	0.8
Salvation Army	1	35	66	96	0.1	0.2
Un C of Christ	5	490	1,705	2,070	2.3	4.7
CARLISLE	**17**	**907**	**2,151**	**2,773**	**54.3**	**100.0**
BAPT–NBC USA	1	0	150	181	3.5	6.5
BAPT–So Bapt Conv	6	607	1,505	1,816	35.6	65.5
Catholic	1	NR	NR	204	4.0	7.4
CHR–Chr Ch (Disc)	2	23	45	54	1.1	1.9
CHR–Chs of Christ	2	112	97	122	2.4	4.4
METH–Un Methodist	4	135	322	355	7.0	12.8
PENT–Assemb of God	1	30	32	41	0.8	1.5
CARROLL	**27**	**1,254**	**3,740**	**5,149**	**47.6**	**100.0**
Bahá'í	0	NR	2	2	0.0	0.0
BAPT–So Bapt Conv	9	564	2,164	2,684	24.8	52.1
Catholic	1	NR	NR	550	5.1	10.7
CHR–Chr Ch (Disc)	2	99	211	262	2.4	5.1
CHR–Chr Chs & Chs Cr	2	NR	180	223	2.1	4.3
CHR–Chs of Christ	1	20	20	22	0.2	0.4
LDS–L-D Saints	1	NR	NR	120	1.1	2.3
LUTH–E.L.C.A.	1	40	73	84	0.8	1.6
MENN–Amish Undif	0	NR	14	40	0.4	0.8
METH–Un Methodist	5	132	493	556	5.1	10.8
METH–Wesleyan	1	74	73	96	0.9	1.9
Non-denom Chr Chs	2	325	510	510	4.7	9.9
PENT–Un Pent Ch Intl	2	NR	NR	NR	-	-
CARTER	**61**	**1,696**	**5,747**	**7,377**	**26.6**	**100.0**
Bahá'í	0	NR	2	2	0.0	0.0
BAPT–Free Will Bapt	9	NR	835	1,017	3.7	13.8
BAPT–Natl Mis Bapt Conv	1	0	150	183	0.7	2.5
BAPT–So Bapt Conv	10	644	1,654	2,014	7.3	27.3
Catholic	1	NR	NR	102	0.4	1.4
Ch of Nazarene	3	151	206	309	1.1	4.2
CHR–Chr Chs & Chs Cr	12	NR	1,535	1,870	6.7	25.3
CHR–Chs of Christ	2	103	85	110	0.4	1.5
LDS–L-D Saints	1	NR	NR	155	0.6	2.1
METH–Un Methodist	7	233	516	621	2.2	8.4
METH–Wesleyan	5	204	157	266	1.0	3.6
Non-denom Chr Chs	3	165	305	324	1.2	4.4
PENT–Assemb of God	1	109	60	109	0.4	1.5
PENT–Ch God (Cleve)	2	87	155	189	0.7	2.6
PENT–Ch of God Proph	1	NR	50	61	0.2	0.8
PENT–Un Pent Ch Intl	2	NR	NR	NR	-	-
PRES–Presb Ch (USA)	1	0	37	45	0.2	0.6
CASEY	**61**	**2,325**	**5,818**	**7,338**	**46.0**	**100.0**
ANG/EPIS–Anglican NA	1	NR	NR	NR	-	-
Bahá'í	0	NR	2	2	0.0	0.0
BAPT–So Bapt Conv	18	1,126	3,372	4,109	25.8	56.0
Catholic	2	NR	NR	312	2.0	4.3
CGOD–Ch God (Ander)	3	105	NR	105	0.7	1.4
Ch of Nazarene	1	25	40	40	0.3	0.5
CHR–Chr Ch (Disc)	2	93	210	256	1.6	3.5
CHR–Chr Chs & Chs Cr	7	NR	405	494	3.1	6.7

NR–Not Reported   - Represents no adherents reported.   Percentages may not total 100 due to rounding.

Table 3: Religious Congregations by County and Group: 2010

Religious Group	Number of Congrega-tions	Number of Attendees	Number of Communicant, Confirmed, or Full Members	Adherents: Number of Adherents	Adherents: % of Total Pop.	Adherents: % of Total Adh.
CHR–Chs of Christ	9	307	288	362	2.3	4.9
MENN–Amish Undif	0	NR	9	27	0.2	0.4
MENN–CG in Cr (Menn)	1	NR	18	22	0.1	0.3
MENN–Midw Bchy Am-Menn	1	135	61	135	0.8	1.8
METH–Un Methodist	11	480	1,265	1,298	8.1	17.7
PENT–Assemb of God	2	19	19	19	0.1	0.3
PENT–Ch God (Cleve)	1	35	129	157	1.0	2.1
PENT–Un Pent Ch Intl	2	NR	NR	NR	-	-
CHRISTIAN	**130**	**10,179**	**27,295**	**39,673**	**53.6**	**100.0**
ANG/EPIS–Episcopal	1	79	197	324	0.4	0.8
Bahá'í	0	NR	10	10	0.0	0.0
BAPT–NBC USA	3	0	1,300	1,702	2.3	4.3
BAPT–Prog NBC	2	0	140	183	0.2	0.5
BAPT–So Bapt Conv	45	6,274	17,302	22,646	30.6	57.1
Catholic	2	NR	NR	3,233	4.4	8.1
Ch of Nazarene	1	46	47	73	0.1	0.2
CHR–Chr Ch (Disc)	8	419	1,193	1,562	2.1	3.9
CHR–Chs of Christ	8	837	783	1,008	1.4	2.5
Jehovah's Witness	1	NR	NR	NR	-	-
LDS–L-D Saints	1	NR	NR	617	0.8	1.6
LUTH–Luth–MO Synod	1	57	142	171	0.2	0.4
MENN–Amish Undif	7	NR	381	1,019	1.4	2.6
METH–C.M.E.	2	0	300	393	0.5	1.0
METH–Un Methodist	19	991	3,041	3,597	4.9	9.1
Non-denom Chr Chs	9	793	1,280	1,361	1.8	3.4
PENT–Assemb of God	3	213	142	341	0.5	0.9
PENT–Ch God (Cleve)	2	92	226	296	0.4	0.7
PENT–Ch of God Proph	1	NR	28	37	0.1	0.1
PENT–COGIC	1	0	0	0	0.0	0.0
PENT–Full Gosp Bapt	1	NR	NR	NR	-	-
PENT–Int Foursq Gos	1	22	20	26	0.0	0.1
PENT–Un Pent Ch Intl	1	NR	NR	NR	-	-
PRES–Cumber Presb	2	NR	128	202	0.3	0.5
PRES–Presb Ch (USA)	3	167	290	380	0.5	1.0
Salvation Army	1	39	102	217	0.3	0.5
Sev Day Adv	3	125	218	250	0.3	0.6
Unit Univ	1	25	25	25	0.0	0.1
CLARK	**71**	**4,091**	**13,584**	**18,611**	**52.3**	**100.0**
ANG/EPIS–Episcopal	2	117	221	463	1.3	2.5
Ap Chr Ch-Amer	1	12	11	12	0.0	0.1
Bahá'í	0	NR	12	12	0.0	0.1
BAPT–Free Will Bapt	1	NR	96	117	0.3	0.6
BAPT–Ind Bapt Flwsp Intl	1	NR	NR	NR	-	-
BAPT–NBC USA	1	150	350	427	1.2	2.3
BAPT–So Bapt Conv	19	1,496	6,029	7,351	20.6	39.5
Catholic	1	NR	NR	730	2.0	3.9
CGOD–Ch God (Ander)	2	408	NR	408	1.1	2.2
Ch of Nazarene	1	45	56	100	0.3	0.5
CHR–Chr Ch (Disc)	3	100	548	668	1.9	3.6
CHR–Chr Chs & Chs Cr	9	NR	2,135	2,603	7.3	14.0
CHR–Chs of Christ	4	285	257	344	1.0	1.8
Jehovah's Witness	1	NR	NR	NR	-	-
LDS–L-D Saints	1	NR	NR	507	1.4	2.7
LUTH–Luth–MO Synod	1	17	45	47	0.1	0.3
METH–AME	1	0	100	122	0.3	0.7
METH–C.M.E.	2	0	200	244	0.7	1.3
METH–Un Methodist	6	667	1,911	2,198	6.2	11.8
METH–Wesleyan	1	24	33	31	0.1	0.2
Non-denom Chr Chs	1	120	35	150	0.4	0.8
PENT–Assemb of God	1	53	45	144	0.4	0.8
PENT–Ch God (Cleve)	4	332	1,130	1,378	3.9	7.4
PENT–Int Foursq Gos	1	18	21	26	0.1	0.1
PENT–Pent Ch of God	1	70	NR	109	0.3	0.6
PENT–Un Pent Ch Intl	2	NR	NR	NR	-	-
PRES–Presb Ch (USA)	2	131	269	328	0.9	1.8
Sev Day Adv	1	46	80	92	0.3	0.5
CLAY	**50**	**2,305**	**8,016**	**9,624**	**44.3**	**100.0**
BAPT–So Bapt Conv	20	1,206	5,517	6,577	30.3	68.3
BRETH–Ch of Brethren	1	56	165	197	0.9	2.0
Catholic	1	NR	NR	69	0.3	0.7

Religious Group	Number of Congrega-tions	Number of Attendees	Number of Communicant, Confirmed, or Full Members	Adherents: Number of Adherents	Adherents: % of Total Pop.	Adherents: % of Total Adh.
CGOD–Ch God (Ander)	1	0	NR	0	0.0	0.0
Chr & Miss Al	1	22	18	34	0.2	0.4
CHR–Chr Chs & Chs Cr	2	NR	140	167	0.8	1.7
CHR–Chs of Christ	3	70	80	100	0.5	1.0
Jehovah's Witness	1	NR	NR	NR	-	-
MENN–Cons Menn Conf	1	0	28	33	0.2	0.3
METH–AME	1	0	100	119	0.5	1.2
METH–Un Methodist	5	104	278	399	1.8	4.1
Non-denom Chr Chs	4	295	525	544	2.5	5.7
PENT–Ch God (Cleve)	3	499	866	1,032	4.7	10.7
PENT–Un Pent Ch Intl	1	NR	NR	NR	-	-
PRES–Evan Presby Ch	1	NR	109	130	0.6	1.4
PRES–Presb Ch (USA)	3	0	98	117	0.5	1.2
Sev Day Adv	1	53	92	106	0.5	1.1
CLINTON	**29**	**1,814**	**4,214**	**5,032**	**49.0**	**100.0**
BAPT–Free Will Bapt	1	NR	96	117	1.1	2.3
BAPT–So Bapt Conv	8	648	1,894	2,311	22.5	45.9
Catholic	1	NR	NR	65	0.6	1.3
Ch of Nazarene	2	295	322	398	3.9	7.9
CHR–Chr Ch (Disc)	1	20	28	34	0.3	0.7
CHR–Chr Chs & Chs Cr	2	NR	181	221	2.2	4.4
CHR–Chs of Christ	1	38	35	46	0.4	0.9
METH–Un Methodist	10	597	1,195	1,343	13.1	26.7
Non-denom Chr Chs	2	190	450	450	4.4	8.9
PENT–Assemb of God	1	26	13	47	0.5	0.9
CRITTENDEN	**37**	**1,492**	**4,304**	**6,029**	**64.7**	**100.0**
BAPT–So Bapt Conv	18	1,220	3,368	4,095	44.0	67.9
Catholic	1	NR	NR	238	2.6	3.9
CGOD–Ch God (Ander)	1	0	NR	0	0.0	0.0
CHR–Chr Ch (Disc)	1	0	50	61	0.7	1.0
CHR–Chs of Christ	1	40	25	45	0.5	0.7
Jehovah's Witness	1	NR	NR	NR	-	-
MENN–Amish Undif	4	NR	219	612	6.6	10.2
METH–Un Methodist	4	168	365	451	4.8	7.5
PENT–Un Pent Ch Intl	1	NR	NR	NR	-	-
PRES–Cumber Presb	3	NR	206	441	4.7	7.3
PRES–Presb Ch (USA)	2	64	71	86	0.9	1.4
CUMBERLAND	**41**	**1,526**	**2,166**	**2,850**	**41.6**	**100.0**
BAPT–So Bapt Conv	3	110	330	397	5.8	13.9
Catholic	1	NR	NR	65	0.9	2.3
CHR–Chr Ch (Disc)	1	0	0	0	0.0	0.0
CHR–Chs of Christ	11	524	499	649	9.5	22.8
Jehovah's Witness	1	NR	NR	NR	-	-
MENN–Unaffil Amish-Menn	1	120	60	120	1.8	4.2
METH–C.M.E.	1	0	100	120	1.8	4.2
METH–Un Methodist	16	542	1,019	1,186	17.3	41.6
Non-denom Chr Chs	2	35	45	49	0.7	1.7
PENT–Assemb of God	1	183	77	220	3.2	7.7
PENT–Un Pent Ch Intl	1	NR	NR	NR	-	-
PRES–Cumber Presb	1	NR	14	19	0.3	0.7
Sev Day Adv	1	12	22	25	0.4	0.9
DAVIESS	**149**	**13,931**	**38,963**	**67,549**	**69.9**	**100.0**
ANG/EPIS–Episcopal	1	169	280	366	0.4	0.5
Bahá'í	0	NR	10	10	0.0	0.0
BAPT–Asc Ref Bap Ch Am	1	NR	NR	NR	-	-
BAPT–Free Will Bapt	1	NR	96	119	0.1	0.2
BAPT–NBC Amer	1	0	0	0	0.0	0.0
BAPT–Ref Bapt Ch	2	NR	NR	NR	-	-
BAPT–So Bapt Conv	53	7,101	24,607	30,394	31.4	45.0
Catholic	17	NR	NR	18,454	19.1	27.3
CGOD–Ch God (Ander)	1	28	NR	28	0.0	0.0
Ch of Nazarene	2	154	215	237	0.2	0.4
CHR–Chr Ch (Disc)	3	333	900	1,112	1.2	1.6
CHR–Chr Chs & Chs Cr	1	NR	2,300	2,841	2.9	4.2
CHR–Chs of Christ	6	570	570	775	0.8	1.1
Jehovah's Witness	1	NR	NR	NR	-	-
JUD–Reform	1	8	14	38	0.0	0.1
LDS–L-D Saints	1	NR	NR	557	0.6	0.8

NR–Not Reported - Represents no adherents reported. Percentages may not total 100 due to rounding.

Table 3: Religious Congregations by County and Group: 2010

Religious Group	Number of Congrega-tions	Number of Attendees	Number of Communicant, Confirmed, or Full Members	Adherents: Number of Adherents	Adherents: % of Total Pop.	Adherents: % of Total Adh.
LUTH–E.L.C.A.	1	43	77	86	0.1	0.1
LUTH–Luth-MO Synod	1	50	89	112	0.1	0.2
METH–AME	1	30	30	37	0.0	0.1
METH–Un Methodist	16	1,575	4,659	5,180	5.4	7.7
METH–Wesleyan	2	163	100	212	0.2	0.3
Muslim Est	1	134	NR	308	0.3	0.5
Non-denom Chr Chs	12	2,242	2,661	3,184	3.3	4.7
PENT–Assemb of God	4	519	294	804	0.8	1.2
PENT–Ch God (Cleve)	3	158	285	352	0.4	0.5
PENT–Ch of God Proph	2	NR	189	233	0.2	0.3
PENT–COGIC	1	55	158	195	0.2	0.3
PENT–Un Pent Ch Intl	1	NR	NR	NR	-	-
PRES–Cumber Presb	3	NR	206	268	0.3	0.4
PRES–Presb Ch (USA)	2	186	389	480	0.5	0.7
PRES–Presb Ch Amer	1	87	98	108	0.1	0.2
Salvation Army	1	64	188	407	0.4	0.6
Sev Day Adv	2	130	227	261	0.3	0.4
Un C of Christ	2	97	269	332	0.3	0.5
Unit Univ	1	35	52	59	0.1	0.1
EDMONSON	**14**	**5,527**	**9,911**	**11,892**	**97.8**	**100.0**
BAPT–So Bapt Conv	9	5,315	9,647	11,507	94.6	96.8
Catholic	1	NR	NR	63	0.5	0.5
CHR–Chs of Christ	3	212	224	261	2.1	2.2
PRES–Cumber Presb	1	NR	40	61	0.5	0.5
ELLIOTT	**8**	**155**	**350**	**403**	**5.1**	**100.0**
BAPT–Enterprise Bapt Assoc	6	NR	NR	NR	-	-
BAPT–So Bapt Conv	1	75	133	158	2.0	39.2
METH–Un Methodist	1	80	217	245	3.1	60.8
ESTILL	**42**	**1,956**	**5,006**	**6,396**	**43.6**	**100.0**
ANG/EPIS–Episcopal	1	5	2	6	0.0	0.1
Bahá'í	0	NR	3	3	0.0	0.0
BAPT–So Bapt Conv	15	873	2,848	3,455	23.5	54.0
Catholic	1	NR	NR	73	0.5	1.1
CGOD–Ch God (Ander)	3	228	NR	228	1.6	3.6
Ch of Nazarene	2	164	211	251	1.7	3.9
CHR–Chr Ch (Disc)	2	82	418	507	3.5	7.9
CHR–Chr Chs & Chs Cr	3	NR	493	598	4.1	9.3
CHR–Chs of Christ	4	95	85	116	0.8	1.8
Jehovah's Witness	1	NR	NR	NR	-	-
METH–Free Methodist	1	52	26	52	0.4	0.8
METH–Un Methodist	4	120	353	384	2.6	6.0
Non-denom Chr Chs	2	260	239	325	2.2	5.1
PENT–Ch God (Cleve)	1	77	322	391	2.7	6.1
PENT–Ch of God Proph	1	NR	6	7	0.0	0.1
PENT–Un Pent Ch Intl	1	NR	NR	NR	-	-
FAYETTE	**266**	**40,999**	**95,924**	**154,462**	**52.2**	**100.0**
ANG/EPIS–Anglican NA	4	NR	NR	NR	-	-
ANG/EPIS–Episcopal	6	988	2,549	2,603	0.9	1.7
Bahá'í	1	NR	81	81	0.0	0.1
BAPT–Amer Bapt Assn	1	NR	65	78	0.0	0.1
BAPT–Free Will Bapt	3	NR	288	347	0.1	0.2
BAPT–Ind Bapt Flwsp Intl	1	NR	NR	NR	-	-
BAPT–NBC Amer	2	200	450	542	0.2	0.4
BAPT–NBC USA	2	600	900	1,083	0.4	0.7
BAPT–Prog NBC	4	1,675	4,000	4,814	1.6	3.1
BAPT–So Bapt Conv	52	12,513	33,655	40,500	13.7	26.2
BUDD–Mahayana	4	NR	NR	282	0.1	0.2
BUDD–Vajrayana	1	NR	NR	52	0.0	0.0
Catholic	8	NR	NR	25,882	8.7	16.8
CGOD–Ch God (Ander)	3	495	NR	495	0.2	0.3
Ch Cr, Scientst	1	NR	NR	NR	-	-
Ch of Nazarene	6	478	716	1,034	0.3	0.7
Chr & Miss Al	5	3,947	223	5,151	1.7	3.3
CHR–Chr Ch (Disc)	14	1,510	4,858	5,846	2.0	3.8
CHR–Chr Chs & Chs Cr	13	NR	16,035	19,296	6.5	12.5
CHR–Chs of Christ	9	1,181	1,179	1,482	0.5	1.0
CHR–Int Chs of Christ	1	NR	50	60	0.0	0.0
Evan Free Ch	1	30	NR	30	0.0	0.0
FRND–Fr Gen Cf	1	NR	53	64	0.0	0.0
HINDU–Post Ren	3	NR	NR	60	0.0	0.0
HINDU–Trad Temples	1	NR	NR	250	0.1	0.2
Jehovah's Witness	3	NR	NR	NR	-	-
JUD–Conserv	2	165	185	500	0.2	0.3
JUD–Reform	1	197	348	940	0.3	0.6
LDS–Comm of Christ	1	NR	103	103	0.0	0.1
LDS–L-D Saints	5	NR	NR	2,209	0.7	1.4
LUTH–E.L.C.A.	3	458	942	1,137	0.4	0.7
LUTH–Luth-MO Synod	3	416	544	792	0.3	0.5
LUTH–Wisc Ev Luth Syn	1	55	62	86	0.0	0.1
MENN–Cons Menn Conf	1	70	33	40	0.0	0.0
METH–AME	3	310	600	722	0.2	0.5
METH–C.M.E.	1	30	100	120	0.0	0.1
METH–Evan Meth Ch	1	NR	NR	NR	-	-
METH–Free Methodist	1	22	15	22	0.0	0.0
METH–Un Methodist	14	4,350	14,086	17,619	6.0	11.4
METH–Wesleyan	2	83	118	108	0.0	0.1
Muslim Est	2	284	NR	533	0.2	0.3
New Apost Ch	1	NR	NR	NR	-	-
Non-denom Chr Chs	23	4,800	4,714	6,705	2.3	4.3
ORTHE–Ant Orth of NA	1	92	NR	255	0.1	0.2
ORTHE–Greek Orthodox	1	110	NR	490	0.2	0.3
ORTHO–Coptic Orth Ch	1	35	NR	35	0.0	0.0
PENT–Assemb of God	9	1,185	772	1,740	0.6	1.1
PENT–Ch God (Cleve)	7	842	1,951	2,348	0.8	1.5
PENT–Ch Lord Jesus Apos	1	NR	NR	NR	-	-
PENT–Ch of God Proph	1	NR	18	22	0.0	0.0
PENT–Full Gosp Bapt	2	NR	NR	NR	-	-
PENT–Pent Ch of God	3	210	NR	326	0.1	0.2
PENT–Un Pent Ch Intl	2	NR	NR	NR	-	-
PENT–Vineyard	1	523	900	1,083	0.4	0.7
PRES–Cumber Presb	1	NR	8	10	0.0	0.0
PRES–Presb Ch (USA)	12	1,603	3,186	3,834	1.3	2.5
PRES–Presb Ch Amer	2	711	708	907	0.3	0.6
Salvation Army	1	136	198	237	0.1	0.2
Sev Day Adv	4	512	891	1,025	0.3	0.7
Un C of Christ	1	23	34	41	0.0	0.0
Unit Univ	1	160	306	437	0.1	0.3
Zoroastrian	0	NR	NR	4	0.0	0.0
FLEMING	**52**	**1,399**	**3,785**	**5,181**	**36.1**	**100.0**
ANG/EPIS–Episcopal	1	16	32	36	0.3	0.7
BAPT–Enterprise Bapt Assoc	1	NR	NR	NR	-	-
BAPT–Free Will Bapt	1	NR	96	118	0.8	2.3
BAPT–So Bapt Conv	4	263	768	943	6.6	18.2
Catholic	1	NR	NR	160	1.1	3.1
CGOD–Ch God (Ander)	3	135	NR	135	0.9	2.6
Ch of Nazarene	1	112	120	120	0.8	2.3
CHR–Chr Ch (Disc)	3	157	546	671	4.7	13.0
CHR–Chr Chs & Chs Cr	14	NR	765	940	6.6	18.1
CHR–Chs of Christ	1	50	50	60	0.4	1.2
MENN–Amish Undif	3	NR	133	394	2.7	7.6
MENN–Menn Chr Fell	1	106	36	106	0.7	2.0
METH–Un Methodist	11	345	885	970	6.8	18.7
METH–Wesleyan	1	13	7	17	0.1	0.3
PENT–Assemb of God	3	126	90	195	1.4	3.8
PENT–Ch God (Cleve)	1	40	98	120	0.8	2.3
PENT–Intl Pent Holiness	1	36	134	165	1.1	3.2
PRES–Presb Ch (USA)	1	0	25	31	0.2	0.6
FLOYD	**81**	**3,921**	**9,484**	**12,453**	**31.6**	**100.0**
ANG/EPIS–Episcopal	1	12	30	30	0.1	0.2
BAPT–Free Will Bapt	17	NR	1,632	1,972	5.0	15.8
BAPT–So Bapt Conv	17	1,493	3,843	4,643	11.8	37.3
Catholic	1	NR	NR	229	0.6	1.8
CGOD–Ch God (Ander)	1	63	NR	63	0.2	0.5
CHR–Chr Chs & Chs Cr	3	NR	300	362	0.9	2.9
CHR–Chs of Christ	11	737	751	990	2.5	7.9
LDS–L-D Saints	1	NR	NR	391	1.0	3.1
METH–Un Methodist	13	888	2,275	2,483	6.3	19.9
Muslim Est	1	134	NR	308	0.8	2.5
Non-denom Chr Chs	2	75	41	94	0.2	0.8

NR–Not Reported   - Represents no adherents reported.   Percentages may not total 100 due to rounding.

Table 3: Religious Congregations by County and Group: 2010

Religious Group	Number of Congrega-tions	Number of Attendees	Number of Communicant, Confirmed, or Full Members	Adherents		
				Number of Adherents	% of Total Pop.	% of Total Adh.
PENT–Assemb of God	2	307	190	382	1.0	3.1
PENT–Ch God (Cleve)	2	83	155	187	0.5	1.5
PENT–Ch of God Proph	4	NR	85	103	0.3	0.8
PENT–Intl Pent Holiness	2	45	55	66	0.2	0.5
PRES–Presb Ch (USA)	2	60	84	101	0.3	0.8
Sev Day Adv	1	24	43	49	0.1	0.4
FRANKLIN	**77**	**7,681**	**21,042**	**28,208**	**57.2**	**100.0**
ANG/EPIS–Episcopal	1	115	329	329	0.7	1.2
Bahá'í	0	NR	39	39	0.1	0.1
BAPT–Natl Mis Bapt Conv	1	0	0	0	0.0	0.0
BAPT–Prog NBC	1	200	0	0	0.0	0.0
BAPT–So Bapt Conv	31	3,805	12,339	14,856	30.1	52.7
Catholic	1	NR	NR	1,911	3.9	6.8
CGOD–Ch God (Ander)	1	100	NR	100	0.2	0.4
Ch of Nazarene	2	201	300	382	0.8	1.4
CHR–Chr Ch (Disc)	5	547	1,924	2,316	4.7	8.2
CHR–Chr Chs & Chs Cr	3	NR	1,065	1,282	2.6	4.5
CHR–Chs of Christ	5	360	332	468	0.9	1.7
Jehovah's Witness	1	NR	NR	NR	-	-
LDS–L-D Saints	1	NR	NR	514	1.0	1.8
LUTH–E.L.C.A.	1	84	113	139	0.3	0.5
METH–AME	1	250	359	432	0.9	1.5
METH–Un Methodist	4	515	2,240	2,411	4.9	8.5
METH–Wesleyan	1	7	10	9	0.0	0.0
Muslim Est	1	35	NR	120	0.2	0.4
Non-denom Chr Chs	2	428	650	725	1.5	2.6
PENT–Assemb of God	3	435	273	613	1.2	2.2
PENT–Ch God (Cleve)	2	133	382	460	0.9	1.6
PENT–Ch of God Proph	1	NR	54	65	0.1	0.2
PENT–Pent Ch of God	2	140	NR	217	0.4	0.8
PENT–Un Pent Ch Intl	1	NR	NR	NR	-	-
PRES–Presb Ch (USA)	2	243	488	588	1.2	2.1
Salvation Army	1	35	61	136	0.3	0.5
Sev Day Adv	2	48	84	96	0.2	0.3
FULTON	**36**	**1,559**	**4,739**	**6,162**	**90.4**	**100.0**
ANG/EPIS–Episcopal	2	32	58	68	1.0	1.1
BAPT–Natl Mis Bapt Conv	1	0	150	178	2.6	2.9
BAPT–So Bapt Conv	11	837	2,861	3,386	49.7	54.9
Catholic	2	NR	NR	223	3.3	3.6
CGOD–Ch God (Ander)	1	0	NR	0	0.0	0.0
Ch of Chr (Hol)	1	NR	NR	NR	-	-
Ch of Nazarene	1	57	87	87	1.3	1.4
CHR–Chr Ch (Disc)	1	20	35	41	0.6	0.7
CHR–Chr Chs & Chs Cr	1	NR	60	71	1.0	1.2
CHR–Chs of Christ	1	130	140	160	2.3	2.6
Jehovah's Witness	1	NR	NR	NR	-	-
LDS–L-D Saints	1	NR	NR	408	6.0	6.6
METH–C.M.E.	2	0	250	296	4.3	4.8
METH–Un Methodist	5	286	859	916	13.4	14.9
Non-denom Chr Chs	2	110	210	219	3.2	3.6
PENT–Assemb of God	2	87	29	109	1.6	1.8
PENT–Un Pent Ch Intl	1	NR	NR	NR	-	-
GALLATIN	**16**	**775**	**2,753**	**3,841**	**44.7**	**100.0**
BAPT–So Bapt Conv	6	429	2,112	2,651	30.9	69.0
Catholic	1	NR	NR	378	4.4	9.8
CGOD–Ch God (Ander)	1	52	NR	52	0.6	1.4
CHR–Chr Ch (Disc)	2	95	262	329	3.8	8.6
CHR–Chr Chs & Chs Cr	1	NR	50	63	0.7	1.6
CHR–Chs of Christ	1	18	17	21	0.2	0.5
METH–Un Methodist	1	85	174	174	2.0	4.5
PENT–Ch God (Cleve)	2	96	138	173	2.0	4.5
PENT–Un Pent Ch Intl	1	NR	NR	NR	-	-
GARRARD	**34**	**2,426**	**7,152**	**8,821**	**52.2**	**100.0**
Bahá'í	0	NR	15	15	0.1	0.2
BAPT–So Bapt Conv	12	1,616	5,124	6,219	36.8	70.5
Catholic	1	NR	NR	131	0.8	1.5
Ch of Nazarene	1	123	207	272	1.6	3.1
CHR–Chr Ch (Disc)	3	53	187	227	1.3	2.6

Religious Group	Number of Congrega-tions	Number of Attendees	Number of Communicant, Confirmed, or Full Members	Adherents		
				Number of Adherents	% of Total Pop.	% of Total Adh.
CHR–Chr Chs & Chs Cr	3	NR	345	419	2.5	4.8
CHR–Chs of Christ	2	95	99	102	0.6	1.2
METH–Un Methodist	6	190	590	655	3.9	7.4
Non-denom Chr Chs	1	50	100	100	0.6	1.1
PENT–Assemb of God	1	169	89	200	1.2	2.3
PENT–Ch God (Cleve)	2	97	321	390	2.3	4.4
PRES–Presb Ch (USA)	2	33	75	91	0.5	1.0
GRANT	**49**	**2,637**	**9,758**	**13,137**	**53.3**	**100.0**
BAPT–So Bapt Conv	23	2,022	6,861	8,767	35.5	66.7
Catholic	1	NR	NR	575	2.3	4.4
Ch of Nazarene	1	15	0	49	0.2	0.4
CHR–Chr Ch (Disc)	2	55	485	620	2.5	4.7
CHR–Chr Chs & Chs Cr	9	NR	1,463	1,869	7.6	14.2
CHR–Chs of Christ	1	38	37	45	0.2	0.3
Jehovah's Witness	1	NR	NR	NR	-	-
LDS–L-D Saints	1	NR	NR	180	0.7	1.4
LUTH–Luth–MO Synod	1	24	55	81	0.3	0.6
METH–Un Methodist	4	202	390	397	1.6	3.0
Non-denom Chr Chs	1	120	180	180	0.7	1.4
PENT–Assemb of God	1	30	25	40	0.2	0.3
PENT–Ch God (Cleve)	1	30	106	135	0.5	1.0
PENT–Vineyard	1	89	126	161	0.7	1.2
PRES–Presb Ch (USA)	1	12	30	38	0.2	0.3
GRAVES	**113**	**9,341**	**20,890**	**28,151**	**75.8**	**100.0**
BAPT–Natl Mis Bapt Conv	1	0	150	185	0.5	0.7
BAPT–So Bapt Conv	45	5,543	14,342	17,676	47.6	62.8
Catholic	2	NR	NR	2,196	5.9	7.8
CGOD–Ch God (Ander)	1	12	NR	12	0.0	0.0
Ch of Nazarene	1	120	151	151	0.4	0.5
CHR–Chr Ch (Disc)	2	146	480	592	1.6	2.1
CHR–Chs of Christ	22	2,066	2,061	2,606	7.0	9.3
Jehovah's Witness	1	NR	NR	NR	-	-
LDS–Comm of Christ	1	NR	156	156	0.4	0.6
LDS–L-D Saints	1	NR	NR	175	0.5	0.6
MENN–Amish Undif	1	NR	66	181	0.5	0.6
MENN–CG in Cr (Menn)	2	NR	260	320	0.9	1.1
MENN–Midw Bchy Am-Menn	1	109	60	109	0.3	0.4
METH–AME	4	0	400	493	1.3	1.8
METH–Un Methodist	15	622	1,482	1,632	4.4	5.8
Non-denom Chr Chs	3	315	480	480	1.3	1.7
PENT–Assemb of God	1	171	221	271	0.7	1.0
PENT–Ch God (Cleve)	1	14	204	251	0.7	0.9
PENT–Intl Pent Holiness	1	88	85	105	0.3	0.4
PENT–Pent Ch of God	1	70	NR	109	0.3	0.4
PENT–Un Pent Ch Intl	1	NR	NR	NR	-	-
PRES–Cum Pres Am	1	NR	NR	NR	-	-
PRES–Cumber Presb	3	NR	147	272	0.7	1.0
PRES–Presb Ch (USA)	1	65	145	179	0.5	0.6
GRAYSON	**65**	**2,598**	**6,843**	**10,657**	**41.4**	**100.0**
Bahá'í	0	NR	3	3	0.0	0.0
BAPT–So Bapt Conv	19	1,151	4,360	5,331	20.7	50.0
Catholic	6	NR	NR	2,100	8.2	19.7
CHR–Chr Chs & Chs Cr	3	NR	405	495	1.9	4.6
CHR–Chs of Christ	11	650	615	796	3.1	7.5
Grace Gosp Fel	1	NR	NR	NR	-	-
LDS–L-D Saints	1	NR	NR	74	0.3	0.7
LUTH–Luth–MO Synod	1	11	22	23	0.1	0.2
MENN–Amb Amish-Menn	1	132	68	132	0.5	1.2
MENN–Amish Undif	1	NR	10	28	0.1	0.3
METH–Un Methodist	8	366	706	787	3.1	7.4
Non-denom Chr Chs	2	192	275	338	1.3	3.2
PENT–Assemb of God	1	42	26	54	0.2	0.5
PENT–Ch God (Cleve)	1	38	167	204	0.8	1.9
PENT–Ch of God Proph	2	NR	61	75	0.3	0.7
PENT–Un Pent Ch Intl	2	NR	NR	NR	-	-
PRES–Cumber Presb	4	NR	98	186	0.7	1.7
Sev Day Adv	1	16	27	31	0.1	0.3

NR–Not Reported - Represents no adherents reported. Percentages may not total 100 due to rounding.

Table 3: Religious Congregations by County and Group: 2010

Religious Group	Number of Congrega-tions	Number of Attendees	Number of Communicant, Confirmed, or Full Members	Adherents		
				Number of Adherents	% of Total Pop.	% of Total Adh.
GREEN	**51**	**3,134**	**7,960**	**9,796**	**87.0**	**100.0**
BAPT–So Bapt Conv	28	2,232	6,212	7,501	66.6	76.6
Catholic	1	NR	NR	62	0.6	0.6
Ch of Nazarene	2	142	137	161	1.4	1.6
CHR–Chr Chs & Chs Cr	1	NR	50	60	0.5	0.6
CHR–Chs of Christ	2	35	30	40	0.4	0.4
MENN–Amb Amish-Menn	1	148	81	148	1.3	1.5
METH–Un Methodist	10	482	1,038	1,177	10.5	12.0
PENT–Un Pent Ch Intl	1	NR	NR	NR	-	-
PRES–Cumber Presb	3	NR	247	448	4.0	4.6
PRES–Presb Ch (USA)	2	95	165	199	1.8	2.0
GREENUP	**82**	**4,931**	**11,825**	**15,449**	**41.9**	**100.0**
Bahá'í	0	NR	2	2	0.0	0.0
BAPT–Enterprise Bapt Assoc	3	NR	NR	NR	-	-
BAPT–Free Will Bapt	6	NR	576	695	1.9	4.5
BAPT–Natl Mis Bapt Conv	2	0	300	362	1.0	2.3
BAPT–So Bapt Conv	13	1,898	3,702	4,469	12.1	28.9
Catholic	1	NR	NR	43	0.1	0.3
CGOD–Ch God (Ander)	3	202	NR	202	0.5	1.3
Ch of Nazarene	6	488	529	970	2.6	6.3
CHR–Chr Chs & Chs Cr	7	NR	2,578	3,112	8.4	20.1
CHR–Chs of Christ	4	258	246	290	0.8	1.9
Jehovah's Witness	1	NR	NR	NR	-	-
LDS–L-D Saints	1	NR	NR	749	2.0	4.8
LUTH–E.L.C.A.	1	20	38	40	0.1	0.3
METH–AME	1	0	100	121	0.3	0.8
METH–Un Methodist	13	790	2,115	2,294	6.2	14.8
METH–Wesleyan	1	12	12	16	0.0	0.1
Non-denom Chr Chs	5	395	660	685	1.9	4.4
PENT–Assemb of God	1	171	149	265	0.7	1.7
PENT–Ch God (Cleve)	6	602	703	849	2.3	5.5
PENT–Ch of God Proph	1	NR	68	82	0.2	0.5
PENT–Int Pent C Chr	1	25	19	60	0.2	0.4
PENT–Pent Ch of God	1	70	NR	109	0.3	0.7
PENT–Un Pent Ch Intl	3	NR	NR	NR	-	-
PRES–Presb Ch (USA)	1	0	28	34	0.1	0.2
HANCOCK	**25**	**1,878**	**6,241**	**8,388**	**97.9**	**100.0**
BAPT–So Bapt Conv	14	1,503	5,174	6,460	75.4	77.0
Catholic	2	NR	NR	733	8.6	8.7
CHR–Chr Chs & Chs Cr	1	NR	50	62	0.7	0.7
CHR–Chs of Christ	1	45	35	50	0.6	0.6
METH–Un Methodist	6	330	953	1,027	12.0	12.2
PRES–Cumber Presb	1	NR	29	56	0.7	0.7
HARDIN	**153**	**13,169**	**33,036**	**50,284**	**47.6**	**100.0**
ANG/EPIS–Anglican NA	1	NR	NR	NR	-	-
ANG/EPIS–Episcopal	1	74	143	143	0.1	0.3
Bahá'í	0	NR	23	23	0.0	0.0
BAPT–Free Will Bapt	1	NR	96	120	0.1	0.2
BAPT–NBC USA	1	200	200	251	0.2	0.5
BAPT–Ref Bapt Ch	1	NR	NR	NR	-	-
BAPT–So Bapt Conv	45	6,331	20,462	25,641	24.3	51.0
Catholic	6	NR	NR	6,986	6.6	13.9
CGOD–Ch God (Ander)	1	175	NR	175	0.2	0.3
Ch of Nazarene	2	58	110	136	0.1	0.3
Chr & Miss Al	3	12	14	14	0.0	0.0
CHR–Chr Ch (Disc)	1	35	60	75	0.1	0.1
CHR–Chr Chs & Chs Cr	8	NR	2,017	2,528	2.4	5.0
CHR–Chs of Christ	7	472	515	607	0.6	1.2
Jehovah's Witness	2	NR	NR	NR	-	-
LDS–L-D Saints	2	NR	NR	1,340	1.3	2.7
LUTH–E.L.C.A.	1	0	0	0	0.0	0.0
LUTH–Luth-MO Synod	2	0	188	219	0.2	0.4
LUTH–Nor Amer Luth C	1	NR	NR	NR	-	-
LUTH–Wisc Ev Luth Syn	1	88	101	170	0.2	0.3
MENN–Amish Undif	3	NR	152	435	0.4	0.9
METH–AME	1	0	150	188	0.2	0.4
METH–Un Methodist	21	1,392	3,892	4,524	4.3	9.0
METH–Wesleyan	2	124	56	161	0.2	0.3
Metro Comm Ch	1	25	22	28	0.0	0.1

Religious Group	Number of Congrega-tions	Number of Attendees	Number of Communicant, Confirmed, or Full Members	Adherents		
				Number of Adherents	% of Total Pop.	% of Total Adh.
Non-denom Chr Chs	12	3,017	3,305	3,987	3.8	7.9
PENT–Assemb of God	7	721	431	1,184	1.1	2.4
PENT–Ch God (Cleve)	4	140	276	346	0.3	0.7
PENT–Ch of God Proph	3	NR	204	256	0.2	0.5
PENT–COGIC	1	0	0	0	0.0	0.0
PENT–Int Foursq Gos	1	7	15	19	0.0	0.0
PENT–Un Pent Ch Intl	2	NR	NR	NR	-	-
PENT–Vineyard	1	160	170	213	0.2	0.4
PRES–Cumber Presb	3	NR	67	67	0.1	0.1
PRES–Presb Ch (USA)	1	0	178	223	0.2	0.4
PRES–Presb Ch Amer	1	60	54	70	0.1	0.1
Sev Day Adv	2	78	135	155	0.1	0.3
HARLAN	**116**	**3,929**	**12,178**	**15,002**	**51.2**	**100.0**
ANG/EPIS–Episcopal	1	22	49	49	0.2	0.3
Bahá'í	0	NR	1	1	0.0	0.0
BAPT–NBC USA	2	80	700	847	2.9	5.6
BAPT–Prim Bapt E Dst	2	50	178	215	0.7	1.4
BAPT–Reg Bapt Gen As	1	NR	NR	NR	-	-
BAPT–So Bapt Conv	44	2,013	6,762	8,182	27.9	54.5
Catholic	3	NR	NR	207	0.7	1.4
CGOD–Ch God (Ander)	1	45	NR	45	0.2	0.3
Ch of Nazarene	2	53	60	72	0.2	0.5
CHR–Chr Ch (Disc)	1	145	264	319	1.1	2.1
CHR–Chr Chs & Chs Cr	5	NR	195	236	0.8	1.6
CHR–Chs of Christ	7	245	238	293	1.0	2.0
Evan Ch	1	NR	NR	NR	-	-
Ind Fund Churches	1	NR	NR	NR	-	-
Jehovah's Witness	1	NR	NR	NR	-	-
LDS–L-D Saints	1	NR	NR	150	0.5	1.0
METH–AME Zion	1	0	100	121	0.4	0.8
METH–Un Methodist	8	228	988	1,062	3.6	7.1
Non-denom Chr Chs	5	277	750	750	2.6	5.0
PENT–Assemb of God	3	96	67	273	0.9	1.8
PENT–Ch God (Cleve)	13	587	1,610	1,948	6.7	13.0
PENT–Ch God Mtn Asm	4	NR	NR	NR	-	-
PENT–Ch of God Proph	3	NR	41	50	0.2	0.3
PRES–Presb Ch (USA)	3	14	78	94	0.3	0.6
Sev Day Adv	1	20	36	41	0.1	0.3
Un Breth in Cr	2	54	61	47	0.2	0.3
HARRISON	**54**	**2,266**	**7,744**	**10,396**	**55.2**	**100.0**
ANG/EPIS–Episcopal	1	28	65	65	0.3	0.6
BAPT–So Bapt Conv	10	686	2,286	2,803	14.9	27.0
Catholic	1	NR	NR	700	3.7	6.7
CGOD–Ch God (Ander)	1	120	NR	120	0.6	1.2
Ch of Nazarene	1	4	7	9	0.0	0.1
CHR–Chr Ch (Disc)	4	304	840	1,030	5.5	9.9
CHR–Chr Chs & Chs Cr	11	NR	2,395	2,937	15.6	28.3
CHR–Chs of Christ	2	115	104	132	0.7	1.3
Jehovah's Witness	1	NR	NR	NR	-	-
MENN–Ber Amish-Menn	1	109	67	109	0.6	1.0
METH–AME	2	40	189	232	1.2	2.2
METH–Un Methodist	10	422	1,374	1,421	7.5	13.7
PENT–Assemb of God	2	156	90	234	1.2	2.3
PENT–Ch God (Cleve)	1	72	89	109	0.6	1.0
PENT–Ch God Mtn Asm	2	NR	NR	NR	-	-
PENT–Pent Ch of God	2	140	NR	217	1.2	2.1
PRES–Presb Ch (USA)	1	0	143	175	0.9	1.7
PRES–Presb Ch Amer	1	70	95	103	0.5	1.0
HART	**65**	**2,224**	**6,731**	**9,192**	**50.5**	**100.0**
BAPT–So Bapt Conv	22	1,253	4,143	5,119	28.1	55.7
Catholic	1	NR	NR	205	1.1	2.2
CHR–Chr Chs & Chs Cr	1	NR	85	105	0.6	1.1
CHR–Chs of Christ	7	314	279	355	2.0	3.9
MENN–Amish Undif	12	NR	696	1,646	9.0	17.9
METH–Un Methodist	12	462	1,130	1,258	6.9	13.7
Non-denom Chr Chs	2	155	240	240	1.3	2.6
PENT–Ch God (Cleve)	1	40	42	52	0.3	0.6
PENT–Ch of God Proph	2	NR	29	36	0.2	0.4
PENT–Un Pent Ch Intl	1	NR	NR	NR	-	-
PRES–Cumber Presb	3	NR	72	157	0.9	1.7

NR–Not Reported   - Represents no adherents reported.   Percentages may not total 100 due to rounding.

Table 3: Religious Congregations by County and Group: 2010

Religious Group	Number of Congrega-tions	Number of Attendees	Number of Communicant, Confirmed, or Full Members	Adherents: Number of Adherents	Adherents: % of Total Pop.	Adherents: % of Total Adh.
PRES–Presb Ch (USA)	1	0	15	19	0.1	0.2
HENDERSON	**67**	**5,648**	**17,920**	**26,633**	**57.6**	**100.0**
ANG/EPIS–Episcopal	1	67	155	155	0.3	0.6
Bahá'í	0	NR	3	3	0.0	0.0
BAPT–Amer Bapt Assn	1	NR	30	37	0.1	0.1
BAPT–NBC USA	1	75	100	122	0.3	0.5
BAPT–Ref Bapt Ch	1	NR	NR	NR	-	-
BAPT–So Bapt Conv	30	2,974	12,459	15,259	33.0	57.3
Catholic	2	NR	NR	4,288	9.3	16.1
Ch of Nazarene	1	91	197	209	0.5	0.8
CHR–Chr Ch (Disc)	2	161	347	425	0.9	1.6
CHR–Chr Chs & Chs Cr	2	NR	40	49	0.1	0.2
CHR–Chs of Christ	1	220	157	253	0.5	0.9
FRND–Fr Gen Cf	1	NR	0	0	0.0	0.0
Jehovah's Witness	1	NR	NR	NR	-	-
LDS–L-D Saints	1	NR	NR	333	0.7	1.3
LUTH–Luth–MO Synod	1	70	127	158	0.3	0.6
METH–AME Zion	1	0	100	122	0.3	0.5
METH–Un Methodist	9	1,101	3,207	3,552	7.7	13.3
Non-denom Chr Chs	1	60	75	75	0.2	0.3
PENT–Assemb of God	4	553	372	899	1.9	3.4
PENT–Ch God (Cleve)	1	20	39	48	0.1	0.2
PENT–Ch of God Proph	1	NR	126	154	0.3	0.6
PRES–Presb Ch (USA)	1	108	181	222	0.5	0.8
Salvation Army	1	81	92	135	0.3	0.5
Sev Day Adv	1	28	48	55	0.1	0.2
Un C of Christ	1	39	65	80	0.2	0.3
HENRY	**44**	**1,637**	**6,587**	**8,305**	**53.9**	**100.0**
BAPT–NBC USA	1	0	681	841	5.5	10.1
BAPT–So Bapt Conv	19	1,160	4,103	5,065	32.9	61.0
Catholic	1	NR	NR	206	1.3	2.5
CHR–Chr Ch (Disc)	10	150	645	796	5.2	9.6
CHR–Chr Chs & Chs Cr	1	NR	250	309	2.0	3.7
MENN–Amish Undif	1	NR	29	81	0.5	1.0
METH–Un Methodist	6	189	663	740	4.8	8.9
PENT–Ch God (Cleve)	1	35	93	115	0.7	1.4
PENT–Intl Pent Holiness	1	75	75	93	0.6	1.1
PENT–Un Pent Ch Intl	2	NR	NR	NR	-	-
PRES–Presb Ch (USA)	1	28	48	59	0.4	0.7
HICKMAN	**32**	**1,712**	**4,116**	**5,223**	**106.5**	**100.0**
Bahá'í	0	NR	5	5	0.1	0.1
BAPT–So Bapt Conv	21	1,331	3,285	3,921	80.0	75.1
Catholic	2	NR	NR	183	3.7	3.5
CHR–Chr Ch (Disc)	1	0	26	31	0.6	0.6
MENN–Amish Undif	1	NR	24	66	1.3	1.3
METH–AME	1	0	150	179	3.7	3.4
METH–Un Methodist	5	204	512	528	10.8	10.1
PENT–Assemb of God	1	177	114	310	6.3	5.9
HOPKINS	**108**	**8,609**	**20,683**	**27,199**	**58.0**	**100.0**
ANG/EPIS–Episcopal	1	51	207	207	0.4	0.8
BAPT–Natl Mis Bapt Conv	1	0	0	0	0.0	0.0
BAPT–NBC USA	1	0	150	183	0.4	0.7
BAPT–So Bapt Conv	38	3,792	12,145	14,796	31.5	54.4
Catholic	3	NR	NR	789	1.7	2.9
CGOD–Ch God (Ander)	1	90	NR	90	0.2	0.3
Ch of Nazarene	1	42	34	46	0.1	0.2
CHR–Chr Ch (Disc)	5	342	928	1,131	2.4	4.2
CHR–Chr Chs & Chs Cr	4	NR	385	469	1.0	1.7
CHR–Chs of Christ	3	359	335	470	1.0	1.7
Jehovah's Witness	1	NR	NR	NR	-	-
LDS–L-D Saints	1	NR	NR	583	1.2	2.1
LUTH–E.L.C.A.	1	35	65	75	0.2	0.3
METH–AME Zion	3	0	350	426	0.9	1.6
METH–C.M.E.	1	65	115	140	0.3	0.5
METH–Un Methodist	11	832	2,233	2,695	5.7	9.9
Non-denom Chr Chs	6	945	970	1,206	2.6	4.4
PENT–Assemb of God	5	763	600	961	2.0	3.5
PENT–Ch God (Cleve)	5	927	1,478	1,801	3.8	6.6

Religious Group	Number of Congrega-tions	Number of Attendees	Number of Communicant, Confirmed, or Full Members	Adherents: Number of Adherents	Adherents: % of Total Pop.	Adherents: % of Total Adh.
PENT–Ch of God Proph	1	NR	33	40	0.1	0.1
PENT–COGIC	2	110	125	152	0.3	0.6
PENT–Pent Ch of God	1	70	NR	109	0.2	0.4
PENT–Un Pent Ch Intl	5	NR	NR	NR	-	-
PRES–Cumber Presb	4	NR	176	397	0.8	1.5
PRES–Presb Ch (USA)	1	112	229	279	0.6	1.0
Salvation Army	1	47	78	100	0.2	0.4
Sev Day Adv	1	27	47	54	0.1	0.2
JACKSON	**34**	**1,224**	**2,833**	**3,564**	**26.4**	**100.0**
BAPT–So Bapt Conv	20	844	2,245	2,738	20.3	76.8
Catholic	1	NR	NR	48	0.4	1.3
CGOD–Ch God (Ander)	1	0	NR	0	0.0	0.0
CHR–Chr Chs & Chs Cr	1	NR	0	0	0.0	0.0
CHR–Chs of Christ	2	54	49	61	0.5	1.7
LDS–L-D Saints	1	NR	NR	33	0.2	0.9
METH–Un Methodist	1	40	40	75	0.6	2.1
Non-denom Chr Chs	1	50	150	150	1.1	4.2
PENT–Ch God (Cleve)	2	76	200	244	1.8	6.8
PENT–Un Pent Ch Intl	1	NR	NR	NR	-	-
REF–Ref Ch in Am	3	160	149	215	1.6	6.0
JEFFERSON	**704**	**84,637**	**218,762**	**405,799**	**54.8**	**100.0**
ANG/EPIS–Anglican NA	2	NR	NR	NR	-	-
ANG/EPIS–Episcopal	18	2,309	5,231	6,448	0.9	1.6
Bahá'í	1	NR	250	250	0.0	0.1
BAPT–Alliance Bapt	2	NR	NR	NR	-	-
BAPT–Amer Bapt USA	3	435	1,507	1,839	0.2	0.5
BAPT–Converge/BGC	1	75	NR	90	0.0	0.0
BAPT–Free Will Bapt	1	NR	96	117	0.0	0.0
BAPT–Natl Mis Bapt Conv	3	0	360	439	0.1	0.1
BAPT–NBC Amer	5	1,185	1,980	2,417	0.3	0.6
BAPT–NBC USA	24	4,245	11,256	13,739	1.9	3.4
BAPT–Prog NBC	6	9,075	12,125	14,799	2.0	3.6
BAPT–Ref Bapt Ch	1	NR	NR	NR	-	-
BAPT–So Bapt Conv	176	32,611	86,766	105,904	14.3	26.1
BUDD–Mahayana	5	NR	NR	2,165	0.3	0.5
BUDD–Vajrayana	1	NR	NR	53	0.0	0.0
Calv Chpl	1	NR	NR	NR	-	-
Catholic	60	NR	NR	120,620	16.3	29.7
CGOD–Ch God (Ander)	5	266	NR	266	0.0	0.1
Ch Cr, Scientist	2	NR	NR	NR	-	-
Ch of Nazarene	6	517	895	1,095	0.1	0.3
Chr & Miss Al	3	413	219	408	0.1	0.1
CHR–Chr Ch (Disc)	12	2,318	7,208	8,798	1.2	2.2
CHR–Chr Chs & Chs Cr	18	NR	36,378	44,402	6.0	10.9
CHR–Chs of Christ	41	4,882	4,852	6,272	0.8	1.5
CHR–Int Chs of Christ	1	NR	150	183	0.0	0.0
Evan Assoc RCC	1	NR	NR	NR	-	-
Evan Free Ch	2	335	NR	335	0.0	0.1
FRND–Fr Gen Cf	1	NR	81	99	0.0	0.0
HINDU–Post Ren	3	NR	NR	118	0.0	0.0
HINDU–Trad Temples	1	NR	NR	160	0.0	0.0
Jain	1	NR	NR	NR	-	-
Jehovah's Witness	12	NR	NR	NR	-	-
JUD–Conserv	2	683	767	2,071	0.3	0.5
JUD–Orth	1	324	120	450	0.1	0.1
JUD–Reform	2	562	992	2,678	0.4	0.7
LDS–Comm of Christ	3	NR	309	309	0.0	0.1
LDS–L-D Saints	8	NR	NR	4,730	0.6	1.2
LUTH–E.L.C.A.	11	990	2,157	2,750	0.4	0.7
LUTH–Luth–MO Synod	5	607	1,193	1,597	0.2	0.4
LUTH–Wisc Ev Luth Syn	1	79	104	131	0.0	0.0
METH–AME	8	465	1,349	1,647	0.2	0.4
METH–AME Zion	7	367	955	1,166	0.2	0.3
METH–C.M.E.	4	299	750	915	0.1	0.2
METH–Free Methodist	1	28	15	28	0.0	0.0
METH–Un Methodist	34	5,421	14,594	17,271	2.3	4.3
METH–Wesleyan	3	87	119	114	0.0	0.0
Metro Comm Ch	1	87	108	132	0.0	0.0
Muslim Est	10	1,301	NR	6,340	0.9	1.6
New Apost Ch	1	NR	NR	NR	-	-
Non-denom Chr Chs	55	5,142	8,376	8,966	1.2	2.2

NR–Not Reported   - Represents no adherents reported.   Percentages may not total 100 due to rounding.

Table 3: Religious Congregations by County and Group: 2010

Religious Group	Number of Congrega-tions	Number of Attendees	Number of Communicant, Confirmed, or Full Members	Adherents: Number of Adherents	Adherents: % of Total Pop.	Adherents: % of Total Adh.
ORTHE–Ant Orth of NA	1	775	NR	950	0.1	0.2
ORTHE–Greek Orthodox	1	100	NR	230	0.0	0.1
ORTHO–Ethiopian Orth	1	NR	NR	NR	-	-
PENT–Assemb of God	13	1,091	655	1,389	0.2	0.3
PENT–Ch God (Cleve)	17	1,681	3,317	4,049	0.5	1.0
PENT–Ch Lord Jesus Apos	1	NR	NR	NR	-	-
PENT–Ch of God Proph	5	NR	392	478	0.1	0.1
PENT–COGIC	2	0	150	183	0.0	0.0
PENT–Full Gosp Bapt	9	NR	NR	NR	-	-
PENT–Int Foursq Gos	1	34	39	48	0.0	0.0
PENT–Un Pent Ch Intl	5	NR	NR	NR	-	-
PENT–Vineyard	2	180	234	286	0.0	0.1
PRES–As Ref Pres Ch	1	NR	35	43	0.0	0.0
PRES–Cum Pres Am	1	NR	NR	NR	-	-
PRES–Cumber Presb	2	NR	171	276	0.0	0.1
PRES–Korean Pres Amer	1	NR	NR	NR	-	-
PRES–Presb Ch (USA)	32	2,611	6,759	8,250	1.1	2.0
PRES–Presb Ch Amer	3	180	215	276	0.0	0.1
Salvation Army	3	174	397	895	0.1	0.2
Sev Day Adv	7	1,250	2,174	2,501	0.3	0.6
Un C of Christ	15	1,126	2,467	3,011	0.4	0.7
Unit Univ	3	327	495	613	0.1	0.2
Unity Ch	2	NR	NR	NR	-	-
Zoroastrian	0	NR	NR	10	0.0	0.0
JESSAMINE	**53**	**4,917**	**9,673**	**13,971**	**28.8**	**100.0**
ANG/EPIS–Anglican NA	2	NR	NR	NR	-	-
ANG/EPIS–Episcopal	1	136	287	298	0.6	2.1
Bahá'í	0	NR	4	4	0.0	0.0
BAPT–NBC USA	1	150	400	501	1.0	3.6
BAPT–So Bapt Conv	8	762	3,018	3,777	7.8	27.0
Catholic	1	NR	NR	820	1.7	5.9
CGOD–Ch God (Ander)	1	30	NR	30	0.1	0.2
Ch of Nazarene	2	45	62	68	0.1	0.5
CHR–Chr Ch (Disc)	4	198	854	1,069	2.2	7.7
CHR–Chr Chs & Chs Cr	3	NR	410	513	1.1	3.7
CHR–Chs of Christ	2	152	117	180	0.4	1.3
Intl Fell Bible Ch	1	NR	NR	NR	-	-
Jehovah's Witness	1	NR	NR	NR	-	-
LDS–L-D Saints	2	NR	NR	1,169	2.4	8.4
METH–AME	1	0	100	125	0.3	0.9
METH–Free Methodist	1	654	473	654	1.3	4.7
METH–Un Methodist	8	937	1,947	1,964	4.0	14.1
Missionary Ch	1	55	31	55	0.1	0.4
Non-denom Chr Chs	7	1,451	1,530	2,000	4.1	14.3
ORTHE–Orth Ch in Amer	1	90	NR	120	0.2	0.9
PENT–Assemb of God	1	72	41	124	0.3	0.9
PENT–Ch God (Cleve)	1	66	222	278	0.6	2.0
PENT–Un Pent Ch Intl	1	NR	NR	NR	-	-
PRES–Presb Ch (USA)	2	119	177	222	0.5	1.6
JOHNSON	**58**	**1,711**	**4,488**	**6,543**	**28.0**	**100.0**
Bahá'í	0	NR	3	3	0.0	0.0
BAPT–Enterprise Bapt Assoc	6	NR	NR	NR	-	-
BAPT–Free Will Bapt	22	NR	2,112	2,552	10.9	39.0
BAPT–So Bapt Conv	3	307	735	888	3.8	13.6
Catholic	1	NR	NR	325	1.4	5.0
CGOD–Ch God (Ander)	5	327	NR	327	1.4	5.0
Ch of Nazarene	1	34	52	116	0.5	1.8
CHR–Chr Chs & Chs Cr	2	NR	125	151	0.6	2.3
CHR–Chs of Christ	7	462	440	558	2.4	8.5
Jehovah's Witness	1	NR	NR	NR	-	-
LDS–L-D Saints	1	NR	NR	313	1.3	4.8
METH–Un Methodist	4	278	763	925	4.0	14.1
PENT–Ch God (Cleve)	2	176	153	185	0.8	2.8
PENT–Int Pent C Chr	2	127	105	200	0.9	3.1
PENT–Un Pent Ch Intl	1	NR	NR	NR	-	-
KENTON	**148**	**9,476**	**25,477**	**77,536**	**48.5**	**100.0**
ANG/EPIS–Anglican NA	2	NR	NR	NR	-	-
ANG/EPIS–Episcopal	1	216	324	696	0.4	0.9
Bahá'í	0	NR	9	9	0.0	0.0
BAPT–Amer Bapt USA	1	0	0	0	0.0	0.0
BAPT–Free Will Bapt	2	NR	134	167	0.1	0.2
BAPT–NBC Amer	1	0	0	0	0.0	0.0
BAPT–So Bapt Conv	33	2,402	9,226	11,481	7.2	14.8
BUDD–Mahayana	1	NR	NR	27	0.0	0.0
Catholic	20	NR	NR	42,500	26.6	54.8
CGOD–Ch God (Ander)	3	255	NR	255	0.2	0.3
Ch of Nazarene	6	546	973	1,360	0.9	1.8
CHR–Chr Ch (Disc)	9	251	962	1,197	0.7	1.5
CHR–Chr Chs & Chs Cr	8	NR	3,215	4,001	2.5	5.2
CHR–Chs of Christ	2	95	97	133	0.1	0.2
Evan Assoc RCC	1	NR	NR	NR	-	-
Jehovah's Witness	2	NR	NR	NR	-	-
LDS–L-D Saints	4	NR	NR	2,422	1.5	3.1
LUTH–E.L.C.A.	1	355	612	813	0.5	1.0
LUTH–Luth–MO Synod	1	68	90	115	0.1	0.1
METH–AME	2	0	300	373	0.2	0.5
METH–AME Zion	1	0	100	124	0.1	0.2
METH–C.M.E.	1	50	80	100	0.1	0.1
METH–Evan Meth Ch	1	NR	NR	NR	-	-
METH–Un Methodist	13	1,306	4,085	5,029	3.1	6.5
METH–Wesleyan	1	45	33	59	0.0	0.1
Muslim Est	1	60	NR	200	0.1	0.3
Non-denom Chr Chs	8	1,820	2,585	2,637	1.7	3.4
PENT–Assemb of God	4	1,009	780	1,520	1.0	2.0
PENT–Ch God (Cleve)	3	246	377	469	0.3	0.6
PENT–Ch God Mtn Asm	1	NR	NR	NR	-	-
PENT–Ch of God Proph	1	NR	45	56	0.0	0.1
PENT–Fire Bapt Hol Ch	1	NR	NR	NR	-	-
PENT–Un Pent Ch Intl	2	NR	NR	NR	-	-
PRES–Evan Presby Ch	1	NR	55	68	0.0	0.1
PRES–Presb Ch (USA)	3	402	817	1,017	0.6	1.3
PRES–Presb Ch Amer	1	38	18	25	0.0	0.0
Salvation Army	1	22	92	133	0.1	0.2
Sev Day Adv	2	199	346	398	0.2	0.5
Un C of Christ	2	91	122	152	0.1	0.2
KNOTT	**13**	**1,335**	**2,834**	**3,576**	**21.9**	**100.0**
Bahá'í	0	NR	1	1	0.0	0.0
BAPT–So Bapt Conv	6	970	2,416	2,890	17.7	80.8
Evan Free Ch	2	85	NR	85	0.5	2.4
Jehovah's Witness	1	NR	NR	NR	-	-
METH–Un Methodist	1	99	136	243	1.5	6.8
Non-denom Chr Chs	2	150	150	200	1.2	5.6
PENT–Ch God (Cleve)	1	31	131	157	1.0	4.4
KNOX	**65**	**3,887**	**13,301**	**16,994**	**53.3**	**100.0**
ANG/EPIS–Episcopal	1	32	41	41	0.1	0.2
BAPT–So Bapt Conv	46	3,345	11,740	14,493	45.5	85.3
Catholic	2	NR	NR	678	2.1	4.0
Ch of Nazarene	1	98	127	127	0.4	0.7
CHR–Chr Ch (Disc)	1	0	100	123	0.4	0.7
CHR–Chr Chs & Chs Cr	3	NR	130	160	0.5	0.9
Jehovah's Witness	1	NR	NR	NR	-	-
METH–AME	1	0	100	123	0.4	0.7
METH–Un Methodist	3	114	586	695	2.2	4.1
Non-denom Chr Chs	1	65	150	150	0.5	0.9
PENT–Ch God (Cleve)	2	233	327	404	1.3	2.4
PENT–Ch God Mtn Asm	2	NR	NR	NR	-	-
PENT–Un Pent Ch Intl	1	NR	NR	NR	-	-
LARUE	**37**	**2,460**	**6,099**	**7,954**	**56.0**	**100.0**
BAPT–So Bapt Conv	21	1,795	4,495	5,486	38.7	69.0
Catholic	1	NR	NR	370	2.6	4.7
Ch of Nazarene	1	68	83	104	0.7	1.3
CHR–Chr Ch (Disc)	1	36	83	101	0.7	1.3
CHR–Chr Chs & Chs Cr	2	NR	396	483	3.4	6.1
CHR–Chs of Christ	2	75	72	93	0.7	1.2
METH–C.M.E.	1	0	100	122	0.9	1.5
METH–Un Methodist	4	231	513	621	4.4	7.8
PENT–Assemb of God	1	49	20	75	0.5	0.9
PENT–Ch God (Cleve)	1	206	233	284	2.0	3.6
PENT–Ch of God Proph	1	NR	32	39	0.3	0.5
PRES–Cumber Presb	1	NR	72	176	1.2	2.2

NR–Not Reported - Represents no adherents reported. Percentages may not total 100 due to rounding.

Table 3: Religious Congregations by County and Group: 2010

Religious Group	Number of Congregations	Number of Attendees	Number of Communicant, Confirmed, or Full Members	Adherents: Number of Adherents	Adherents: % of Total Pop.	Adherents: % of Total Adh.
LAUREL	**93**	**7,960**	**19,747**	**25,653**	**43.6**	**100.0**
Bahá'í	0	NR	1	1	0.0	0.0
BAPT–Natl Mis Bapt Conv	2	85	235	290	0.5	1.1
BAPT–So Bapt Conv	46	4,996	15,021	18,540	31.5	72.3
Catholic	1	NR	NR	512	0.9	2.0
CGOD–Ch God (Ander)	1	30	NR	30	0.1	0.1
Ch of Nazarene	1	45	28	132	0.2	0.5
CHR–Chr Ch (Disc)	2	0	378	467	0.8	1.8
CHR–Chr Chs & Chs Cr	6	NR	504	622	1.1	2.4
CHR–Chs of Christ	7	629	536	711	1.2	2.8
Jehovah's Witness	1	NR	NR	NR	-	-
METH–Un Methodist	5	299	772	896	1.5	3.5
Muslim Est	1	134	NR	308	0.5	1.2
Non-denom Chr Chs	8	769	914	1,135	1.9	4.4
PENT–Assemb of God	2	277	215	600	1.0	2.3
PENT–Ch God (Cleve)	6	597	854	1,054	1.8	4.1
PENT–Un Pent Ch Intl	1	NR	NR	NR	-	-
PRES–Orth Pres Ch	1	57	41	55	0.1	0.2
PRES–Presb Ch (USA)	1	0	175	216	0.4	0.8
Sev Day Adv	1	42	73	84	0.1	0.3
LAWRENCE	**44**	**1,037**	**3,948**	**4,849**	**30.6**	**100.0**
Bahá'í	0	NR	1	1	0.0	0.0
BAPT–Enterprise Bapt Assoc	4	NR	NR	NR	-	-
BAPT–Free Will Bapt	15	NR	1,440	1,754	11.1	36.2
BAPT–Prim Bapt E Dst	1	25	89	108	0.7	2.2
BAPT–So Bapt Conv	7	482	1,086	1,323	8.3	27.3
Catholic	1	NR	NR	86	0.5	1.8
CGOD–Ch God (Ander)	1	40	NR	40	0.3	0.8
CHR–Chr Chs & Chs Cr	2	NR	86	105	0.7	2.2
CHR–Chs of Christ	1	19	19	20	0.1	0.4
Jehovah's Witness	1	NR	NR	NR	-	-
METH–Un Methodist	8	296	728	870	5.5	17.9
Non-denom Chr Chs	2	82	300	300	1.9	6.2
PENT–Ch God (Cleve)	1	93	199	242	1.5	5.0
LEE	**28**	**828**	**1,459**	**2,220**	**28.1**	**100.0**
ANG/EPIS–Episcopal	1	11	27	27	0.3	1.2
Bahá'í	0	NR	2	2	0.0	0.1
BAPT–So Bapt Conv	3	90	446	523	6.6	23.6
Catholic	1	NR	NR	116	1.5	5.2
CGOD–Ch God (Ander)	4	170	NR	170	2.2	7.7
Ch of Nazarene	1	104	144	144	1.8	6.5
CHR–Chr Chs & Chs Cr	1	NR	200	234	3.0	10.5
CHR–Chs of Christ	7	247	287	364	4.6	16.4
Evan Cong Ch	1	NR	41	48	0.6	2.2
Jehovah's Witness	1	NR	NR	NR	-	-
LDS–L-D Saints	1	NR	NR	140	1.8	6.3
METH–Un Methodist	2	50	111	171	2.2	7.7
Non-denom Chr Chs	1	55	46	69	0.9	3.1
PENT–Assemb of God	1	45	24	59	0.7	2.7
PENT–Ch God (Cleve)	2	56	88	103	1.3	4.6
PRES–Presb Ch (USA)	1	0	43	50	0.6	2.3
LESLIE	**27**	**1,128**	**2,739**	**3,481**	**30.8**	**100.0**
BAPT–So Bapt Conv	5	348	1,212	1,449	12.8	41.6
BRETH–Grace Breth	1	NR	NR	NR	-	-
Chr & Miss Al	1	32	0	40	0.4	1.1
CHR–Chs of Christ	7	349	347	411	3.6	11.8
METH–Un Methodist	5	132	362	603	5.3	17.3
PENT–Ch God (Cleve)	5	233	689	824	7.3	23.7
PRES–Presb Ch (USA)	3	34	129	154	1.4	4.4
LETCHER	**49**	**1,945**	**4,903**	**6,187**	**25.2**	**100.0**
BAPT–Prim Bapt E Dst	4	100	356	429	1.7	6.9
BAPT–So Bapt Conv	14	842	3,061	3,692	15.1	59.7
Catholic	2	NR	NR	48	0.2	0.8
CGOD–Ch God (Ander)	1	113	NR	113	0.5	1.8
Ch of Nazarene	1	19	17	58	0.2	0.9
Chr & Miss Al	2	64	41	112	0.5	1.8
CHR–Chs of Christ	11	382	348	438	1.8	7.1
Jehovah's Witness	1	NR	NR	NR	-	-
METH–Un Methodist	4	200	652	724	3.0	11.7
PENT–Assemb of God	1	62	52	110	0.4	1.8
PENT–Ch God (Cleve)	1	60	97	117	0.5	1.9
PENT–Ch God Mtn Asm	1	NR	NR	NR	-	-
PENT–Ch of God Proph	1	NR	66	80	0.3	1.3
PENT–Int Foursq Gos	1	31	27	33	0.1	0.5
PRES–Orth Pres Ch	1	27	16	28	0.1	0.5
PRES–Presb Ch (USA)	3	45	170	205	0.8	3.3
LEWIS	**33**	**535**	**3,225**	**3,877**	**28.0**	**100.0**
BAPT–Free Will Bapt	1	NR	96	117	0.8	3.0
BAPT–So Bapt Conv	3	179	556	678	4.9	17.5
Catholic	1	NR	NR	40	0.3	1.0
Ch Christ Chr Union	1	NR	NR	NR	-	-
Ch of Nazarene	1	22	40	40	0.3	1.0
CHR–Chr Chs & Chs Cr	13	NR	1,411	1,722	12.4	44.4
CHR–Chs of Christ	1	30	30	30	0.2	0.8
MENN–Amish Undif	1	NR	35	103	0.7	2.7
METH–Un Methodist	7	198	799	815	5.9	21.0
PENT–Assemb of God	1	38	17	38	0.3	1.0
PENT–Ch God (Cleve)	2	68	238	290	2.1	7.5
PRES–Presb Ch (USA)	1	0	3	4	0.0	0.1
LINCOLN	**78**	**3,970**	**11,849**	**15,001**	**60.6**	**100.0**
Bahá'í	0	NR	5	5	0.0	0.0
BAPT–So Bapt Conv	32	2,575	8,592	10,605	42.9	70.7
Catholic	1	NR	NR	99	0.4	0.7
CGOD–Ch God (Ander)	5	191	NR	191	0.8	1.3
Ch of Nazarene	1	121	88	121	0.5	0.8
CHR–Chr Ch (Disc)	2	113	228	281	1.1	1.9
CHR–Chr Chs & Chs Cr	6	NR	500	617	2.5	4.1
CHR–Chs of Christ	9	356	335	415	1.7	2.8
Jehovah's Witness	1	NR	NR	NR	-	-
MENN–Amish Undif	4	NR	184	473	1.9	3.2
METH–AME	3	0	300	370	1.5	2.5
METH–Un Methodist	5	325	877	944	3.8	6.3
Non-denom Chr Chs	1	60	150	150	0.6	1.0
PENT–Assemb of God	1	104	90	118	0.5	0.8
PENT–Ch God (Cleve)	4	91	243	300	1.2	2.0
PENT–Ch of God Proph	1	NR	73	90	0.4	0.6
PRES–Presb Ch (USA)	1	0	124	153	0.6	1.0
Sev Day Adv	1	34	60	69	0.3	0.5
LIVINGSTON	**40**	**1,961**	**4,648**	**5,586**	**58.7**	**100.0**
Bahá'í	0	NR	1	1	0.0	0.0
BAPT–Natl Mis Bapt Conv	1	0	150	178	1.9	3.2
BAPT–So Bapt Conv	22	1,481	3,469	4,124	43.3	73.8
Catholic	1	NR	NR	101	1.1	1.8
CHR–Chs of Christ	2	50	55	65	0.7	1.2
MENN–Amish Undif	1	NR	15	41	0.4	0.7
METH–Un Methodist	11	368	763	787	8.3	14.1
Non-denom Chr Chs	1	62	150	150	1.6	2.7
PRES–Cumber Presb	1	NR	45	139	1.5	2.5
LOGAN	**85**	**5,475**	**13,978**	**17,930**	**66.8**	**100.0**
ANG/EPIS–Episcopal	1	24	47	47	0.2	0.3
Bahá'í	0	NR	1	1	0.0	0.0
BAPT–So Bapt Conv	31	3,216	9,530	11,750	43.8	65.5
Catholic	1	NR	NR	500	1.9	2.8
CHR–Chr Ch (Disc)	2	114	271	334	1.2	1.9
CHR–Chr Chs & Chs Cr	2	NR	172	212	0.8	1.2
CHR–Chs of Christ	12	710	724	854	3.2	4.8
Jehovah's Witness	1	NR	NR	NR	-	-
LDS–L-D Saints	1	NR	NR	215	0.8	1.2
MENN–Amish Undif	2	NR	179	502	1.9	2.8
MENN–Beachy Amish-Menn	1	82	45	82	0.3	0.5
METH–AME Zion	3	55	280	345	1.3	1.9
METH–Un Methodist	10	506	1,363	1,482	5.5	8.3
Non-denom Chr Chs	5	618	900	912	3.4	5.1
PENT–Assemb of God	1	14	11	16	0.1	0.1
PENT–Ch God (Cleve)	1	20	13	16	0.1	0.1
PENT–Ch of God Proph	1	NR	12	15	0.1	0.1

NR–Not Reported   - Represents no adherents reported.   Percentages may not total 100 due to rounding.

Table 3: Religious Congregations by County and Group: 2010

Religious Group	Number of Congrega-tions	Number of Attendees	Number of Communicant, Confirmed, or Full Members	Adherents		
				Number of Adherents	% of Total Pop.	% of Total Adh.
PENT–COGIC	1	75	150	185	0.7	1.0
PENT–Un Pent Ch Intl	2	NR	NR	NR	-	-
PRES–Cumber Presb	5	NR	190	351	1.3	2.0
PRES–Presb Ch (USA)	2	41	90	111	0.4	0.6
LYON	**28**	**1,721**	**4,564**	**5,364**	**64.5**	**100.0**
Bahá'í	0	NR	1	1	0.0	0.0
BAPT–So Bapt Conv	17	1,134	3,528	3,992	48.0	74.4
Catholic	1	NR	NR	113	1.4	2.1
CHR–Chs of Christ	2	105	88	107	1.3	2.0
MENN–Amish Undif	1	NR	23	47	0.6	0.9
METH–Un Methodist	6	429	861	1,041	12.5	19.4
PENT–Assemb of God	1	53	63	63	0.8	1.2
MCCRACKEN	**137**	**14,900**	**34,867**	**47,997**	**73.2**	**100.0**
ANG/EPIS–Episcopal	1	157	400	493	0.8	1.0
Bahá'í	0	NR	9	9	0.0	0.0
BAPT–Asc Ref Bap Ch Am	1	NR	NR	NR	-	-
BAPT–Natl Mis Bapt Conv	1	0	150	181	0.3	0.4
BAPT–NBC USA	1	30	30	36	0.1	0.1
BAPT–Prog NBC	1	0	150	181	0.3	0.4
BAPT–So Bapt Conv	41	7,525	21,514	26,017	39.7	54.2
Catholic	4	NR	NR	4,308	6.6	9.0
CGOD–Ch God (Ander)	3	395	NR	395	0.6	0.8
Ch Cr, Scientst	1	NR	NR	NR	-	-
Ch of Nazarene	1	74	60	96	0.1	0.2
CHR–Chr Ch (Disc)	3	185	525	635	1.0	1.3
CHR–Chr Chs & Chs Cr	1	NR	100	121	0.2	0.3
CHR–Chs of Christ	12	2,027	2,250	3,050	4.7	6.4
Evan Cov Ch	1	383	450	498	0.8	1.0
Jehovah's Witness	1	NR	NR	NR	-	-
JUD–Reform	1	16	29	78	0.1	0.2
LDS–L-D Saints	1	NR	NR	713	1.1	1.5
LUTH–E.L.C.A.	1	65	117	128	0.2	0.3
LUTH–Luth Cong Msn Chr	1	35	34	41	0.1	0.1
LUTH–Luth-MO Synod	1	185	409	483	0.7	1.0
METH–AME	3	0	350	423	0.6	0.9
METH–C.M.E.	1	0	60	73	0.1	0.2
METH–Un Methodist	13	1,161	3,750	4,225	6.4	8.8
Metro Comm Ch	1	33	46	56	0.1	0.1
Non-denom Chr Chs	15	1,773	2,373	2,568	3.9	5.4
PENT–Assemb of God	3	261	298	327	0.5	0.7
PENT–Ch God (Cleve)	2	40	197	238	0.4	0.5
PENT–COGIC	1	30	35	42	0.1	0.1
PENT–Cong Hol Ch	1	39	35	42	0.1	0.1
PENT–Full Gosp Bapt	1	NR	NR	NR	-	-
PENT–Pent Ch of God	1	70	NR	109	0.2	0.2
PENT–Un Pent Ch Intl	3	NR	NR	NR	-	-
PRES–As Ref Pres Ch	1	NR	34	41	0.1	0.1
PRES–Cum Pres Am	1	NR	NR	NR	-	-
PRES–Cumber Presb	5	NR	621	1,228	1.9	2.6
PRES–Presb Ch (USA)	3	185	436	527	0.8	1.1
Salvation Army	1	51	97	279	0.4	0.6
Sev Day Adv	2	157	273	314	0.5	0.7
Un C of Christ	1	23	35	42	0.1	0.1
MCCREARY	**24**	**891**	**3,057**	**3,969**	**21.7**	**100.0**
Bahá'í	0	NR	1	1	0.0	0.0
BAPT–So Bapt Conv	11	629	2,503	3,018	16.5	76.0
Catholic	1	NR	NR	42	0.2	1.1
CHR–Chr Ch (Disc)	1	0	0	0	0.0	0.0
CHR–Chs of Christ	1	20	30	35	0.2	0.9
LDS–L-D Saints	1	NR	NR	248	1.4	6.2
METH–Un Methodist	3	121	345	391	2.1	9.9
Non-denom Chr Chs	1	20	0	25	0.1	0.6
PENT–Ch God (Cleve)	1	50	89	107	0.6	2.7
PENT–Ch God Mtn Asm	3	NR	NR	NR	-	-
Sev Day Adv	1	51	89	102	0.6	2.6
MCLEAN	**34**	**1,577**	**5,139**	**6,521**	**68.4**	**100.0**
BAPT–Ref Bapt Ch	1	NR	NR	NR	-	-
BAPT–So Bapt Conv	11	987	3,362	4,093	42.9	62.8
Catholic	2	NR	NR	245	2.6	3.8
CHR–Chr Ch (Disc)	1	44	65	79	0.8	1.2
CHR–Chr Chs & Chs Cr	1	NR	150	183	1.9	2.8
CHR–Chs of Christ	1	55	51	76	0.8	1.2
Jehovah's Witness	1	NR	NR	NR	-	-
METH–Un Methodist	10	460	1,243	1,384	14.5	21.2
METH–Wesleyan	1	31	22	40	0.4	0.6
PENT–Ch of God Proph	2	NR	74	90	0.9	1.4
PRES–Cumber Presb	3	NR	172	331	3.5	5.1
MADISON	**114**	**9,766**	**23,271**	**32,147**	**38.8**	**100.0**
ANG/EPIS–Episcopal	1	50	58	68	0.1	0.2
Bahá'í	0	NR	56	56	0.1	0.2
BAPT–Free Will Bapt	1	NR	96	116	0.1	0.4
BAPT–So Bapt Conv	44	4,842	13,749	16,554	20.0	51.5
Catholic	2	NR	NR	2,005	2.4	6.2
CGOD–Ch God (Ander)	1	122	NR	122	0.1	0.4
Ch Christ Chr Union	1	NR	NR	NR	-	-
Ch of Nazarene	3	145	311	839	1.0	2.6
Chr & Miss Al	1	158	214	397	0.5	1.2
CHR–Chr Ch (Disc)	6	389	1,430	1,722	2.1	5.4
CHR–Chr Chs & Chs Cr	10	NR	1,356	1,633	2.0	5.1
CHR–Chs of Christ	3	470	438	544	0.7	1.7
Christian Brethren	1	NR	NR	NR	-	-
FRND–Fr Gen Cf	1	NR	59	71	0.1	0.2
Jehovah's Witness	2	NR	NR	NR	-	-
LDS–L-D Saints	2	NR	NR	903	1.1	2.8
LUTH–E.L.C.A.	1	41	52	52	0.1	0.2
METH–AME	1	75	150	181	0.2	0.6
METH–Un Methodist	7	765	1,750	2,278	2.7	7.1
METH–Wesleyan	1	76	61	99	0.1	0.3
Muslim Est	1	134	NR	308	0.4	1.0
Non-denom Chr Chs	4	514	730	787	0.9	2.4
PENT–Assemb of God	2	95	58	108	0.1	0.3
PENT–Ch God (Cleve)	7	1,054	1,612	1,941	2.3	6.0
PENT–Int Foursq Gos	1	113	188	226	0.3	0.7
PENT–Un Pent Ch Intl	2	NR	NR	NR	-	-
PENT–Vineyard	2	450	360	433	0.5	1.3
PRES–Presb Ch (USA)	2	123	336	405	0.5	1.3
PRES–Presb Ch Amer	1	55	51	59	0.1	0.2
Salvation Army	1	13	46	106	0.1	0.3
Sev Day Adv	1	38	67	77	0.1	0.2
Unit Univ	1	44	43	57	0.1	0.2
MAGOFFIN	**23**	**1,291**	**2,575**	**3,363**	**25.2**	**100.0**
BAPT–Free Will Bapt	3	NR	288	354	2.7	10.5
BAPT–So Bapt Conv	5	458	1,189	1,460	11.0	43.4
Catholic	1	NR	NR	31	0.2	0.9
CGOD–Ch God (Ander)	1	35	NR	35	0.3	1.0
CHR–Chr Chs & Chs Cr	1	NR	83	102	0.8	3.0
CHR–Chs of Christ	2	105	90	123	0.9	3.7
METH–Un Methodist	1	65	232	249	1.9	7.4
Non-denom Chr Chs	4	390	564	630	4.7	18.7
PENT–Assemb of God	1	43	65	65	0.5	1.9
PENT–Int Pent C Chr	3	125	64	205	1.5	6.1
PENT–Pent Ch of God	1	70	NR	109	0.8	3.2
MARION	**38**	**1,609**	**4,687**	**12,532**	**63.2**	**100.0**
BAPT–Alliance Bapt	1	NR	NR	NR	-	-
BAPT–So Bapt Conv	11	1,002	3,245	3,997	20.2	31.9
Catholic	7	NR	NR	6,511	32.9	52.0
CHR–Chr Ch (Disc)	1	45	67	83	0.4	0.7
CHR–Chr Chs & Chs Cr	4	NR	190	234	1.2	1.9
CHR–Chs of Christ	1	45	45	57	0.3	0.5
LDS–L-D Saints	1	NR	NR	269	1.4	2.1
METH–AME Zion	2	20	132	163	0.8	1.3
METH–Un Methodist	5	297	731	784	4.0	6.3
PENT–Assemb of God	1	116	71	180	0.9	1.4
PENT–Ch God (Cleve)	2	42	108	133	0.7	1.1
PRES–Presb Ch (USA)	2	42	98	121	0.6	1.0
MARSHALL	**70**	**7,546**	**14,750**	**18,520**	**58.9**	**100.0**
ANG/EPIS–Episcopal	1	29	46	46	0.1	0.2

NR–Not Reported - Represents no adherents reported. Percentages may not total 100 due to rounding.

Table 3: Religious Congregations by County and Group: 2010

Religious Group	Number of Congrega-tions	Number of Attendees	Number of Communicant, Confirmed, or Full Members	Adherents: Number of Adherents	Adherents: % of Total Pop.	Adherents: % of Total Adh.
Bahá'í	0	NR	2	2	0.0	0.0
BAPT–So Bapt Conv	25	3,962	9,452	11,218	35.7	60.6
Catholic	2	NR	NR	783	2.5	4.2
Ch of Nazarene	1	36	53	68	0.2	0.4
CHR–Chr Ch (Disc)	1	0	211	250	0.8	1.3
CHR–Chs of Christ	13	1,994	1,912	2,429	7.7	13.1
Jehovah's Witness	1	NR	NR	NR	-	-
LUTH–E.L.C.A.	1	101	185	196	0.6	1.1
METH–Un Methodist	13	1,003	2,089	2,435	7.7	13.1
Non-denom Chr Chs	5	320	430	488	1.6	2.6
PENT–Assemb of God	1	40	48	60	0.2	0.3
PENT–Ch God (Cleve)	1	37	74	88	0.3	0.5
PRES–Cumber Presb	4	NR	205	406	1.3	2.2
PRES–Presb Ch (USA)	1	24	43	51	0.2	0.3
MARTIN	**27**	**819**	**2,433**	**2,871**	**22.2**	**100.0**
BAPT–Free Will Bapt	8	NR	662	791	6.1	27.6
BAPT–Natl Mis Bapt Conv	1	0	150	179	1.4	6.2
BAPT–So Bapt Conv	3	157	616	736	5.7	25.6
BRETH–Ch of Brethren	1	0	10	12	0.1	0.4
Catholic	1	NR	NR	13	0.1	0.5
Ch of Nazarene	3	173	288	306	2.4	10.7
CHR–Chs of Christ	5	276	249	308	2.4	10.7
METH–Un Methodist	2	56	161	171	1.3	6.0
PENT–Ch God (Cleve)	3	157	297	355	2.7	12.4
MASON	**60**	**2,482**	**7,363**	**10,423**	**59.6**	**100.0**
ANG/EPIS–Anglican NA	1	NR	NR	NR	-	-
ANG/EPIS–Episcopal	1	43	98	98	0.6	0.9
Bahá'í	0	NR	2	2	0.0	0.0
BAPT–Natl Mis Bapt Conv	1	0	150	185	1.1	1.8
BAPT–So Bapt Conv	11	711	2,246	2,771	15.8	26.6
Catholic	3	NR	NR	1,200	6.9	11.5
Ch Christ Chr Union	1	NR	NR	NR	-	-
Ch of Nazarene	2	246	334	349	2.0	3.3
CHR–Chr Ch (Disc)	5	270	703	867	5.0	8.3
CHR–Chr Chs & Chs Cr	6	NR	686	846	4.8	8.1
CHR–Chs of Christ	1	18	20	25	0.1	0.2
Jehovah's Witness	1	NR	NR	NR	-	-
LDS–L-D Saints	1	NR	NR	424	2.4	4.1
LUTH–Luth-MO Synod	1	31	45	50	0.3	0.5
MENN–Amish Undif	1	NR	72	203	1.2	1.9
METH–Un Methodist	15	793	2,384	2,683	15.3	25.7
METH–Wesleyan	1	14	31	18	0.1	0.2
Non-denom Chr Chs	2	195	310	325	1.9	3.1
PENT–Assemb of God	3	161	141	203	1.2	1.9
PRES–Presb Ch (USA)	3	0	141	174	1.0	1.7
MEADE	**39**	**3,217**	**9,253**	**16,914**	**59.1**	**100.0**
ANG/EPIS–Episcopal	1	30	38	70	0.2	0.4
Bahá'í	0	NR	2	2	0.0	0.0
BAPT–So Bapt Conv	19	2,330	7,576	9,636	33.7	57.0
Catholic	4	NR	NR	4,227	14.8	25.0
Ch of Nazarene	1	26	31	52	0.2	0.3
CHR–Chr Chs & Chs Cr	1	NR	96	122	0.4	0.7
CHR–Chs of Christ	2	85	63	92	0.3	0.5
LDS–L-D Saints	1	NR	NR	875	3.1	5.2
METH–Un Methodist	3	413	895	1,147	4.0	6.8
Non-denom Chr Chs	3	94	222	225	0.8	1.3
PENT–Assemb of God	1	148	121	200	0.7	1.2
PENT–Ch God (Cleve)	1	79	188	239	0.8	1.4
PENT–Ch God Mtn Asm	1	NR	NR	NR	-	-
PRES–Presb Ch (USA)	1	12	21	27	0.1	0.2
MENIFEE	**9**	**550**	**471**	**742**	**11.8**	**100.0**
BAPT–Consrv Bapt	1	NR	NR	NR	-	-
BAPT–So Bapt Conv	2	95	212	256	4.1	34.5
CGOD–Ch God (Ander)	1	81	NR	81	1.3	10.9
CHR–Chs of Christ	2	80	60	90	1.4	12.1
PENT–Assemb of God	1	84	41	124	2.0	16.7
PENT–Ch God (Cleve)	1	195	130	157	2.5	21.2
PRES–Presb Ch (USA)	1	15	28	34	0.5	4.6
MERCER	**59**	**3,396**	**12,584**	**16,785**	**78.7**	**100.0**
ANG/EPIS–Episcopal	2	40	90	104	0.5	0.6
BAPT–So Bapt Conv	19	2,022	8,212	9,975	46.8	59.4
Catholic	1	NR	NR	848	4.0	5.1
Ch Christ Chr Union	1	NR	NR	NR	-	-
CHR–Chr Ch (Disc)	4	238	671	815	3.8	4.9
CHR–Chr Chs & Chs Cr	7	NR	1,652	2,007	9.4	12.0
CHR–Chs of Christ	4	308	289	363	1.7	2.2
Jehovah's Witness	1	NR	NR	NR	-	-
LDS–L-D Saints	1	NR	NR	503	2.4	3.0
MENN–Menn Chr Fell	1	137	62	137	0.6	0.8
METH–AME	2	50	150	182	0.9	1.1
METH–Un Methodist	4	238	516	548	2.6	3.3
Non-denom Chr Chs	2	171	500	500	2.3	3.0
PENT–Assemb of God	1	21	16	26	0.1	0.2
PENT–Ch God (Cleve)	2	37	197	239	1.1	1.4
PENT–Pent Ch of God	1	70	NR	109	0.5	0.6
PENT–Un Pent Ch Intl	1	NR	NR	NR	-	-
PRES–Cumber Presb	2	NR	35	193	0.9	1.1
PRES–Presb Ch (USA)	3	64	194	236	1.1	1.4
METCALFE	**41**	**1,975**	**5,315**	**7,048**	**69.8**	**100.0**
Bahá'í	0	NR	1	1	0.0	0.0
BAPT–So Bapt Conv	12	960	3,697	4,534	44.9	64.3
Catholic	1	NR	NR	80	0.8	1.1
CHR–Chr Chs & Chs Cr	1	NR	70	86	0.9	1.2
CHR–Chs of Christ	8	532	470	640	6.3	9.1
LDS–L-D Saints	1	NR	NR	389	3.9	5.5
MENN–Amish Undif	1	NR	63	143	1.4	2.0
METH–Un Methodist	9	372	716	781	7.7	11.1
Non-denom Chr Chs	1	85	135	135	1.3	1.9
PENT–Ch God (Cleve)	1	26	19	23	0.2	0.3
PRES–Cumber Presb	6	NR	144	236	2.3	3.3
MONROE	**46**	**2,566**	**4,256**	**5,622**	**51.3**	**100.0**
BAPT–So Bapt Conv	8	666	2,183	2,649	24.2	47.1
Catholic	1	NR	NR	64	0.6	1.1
CHR–Chs of Christ	28	1,705	1,444	1,970	18.0	35.0
Jehovah's Witness	1	NR	NR	NR	-	-
LDS–L-D Saints	1	NR	NR	287	2.6	5.1
MENN–CG in Cr (Menn)	1	NR	107	130	1.2	2.3
METH–Un Methodist	6	195	522	522	4.8	9.3
MONTGOMERY	**48**	**3,660**	**6,468**	**9,276**	**35.0**	**100.0**
ANG/EPIS–Anglican NA	2	NR	NR	NR	-	-
ANG/EPIS–Episcopal	1	45	83	86	0.3	0.9
Bahá'í	0	NR	1	1	0.0	0.0
BAPT–Free Will Bapt	2	NR	163	202	0.8	2.2
BAPT–Ind Bapt Flwsp Intl	1	NR	NR	NR	-	-
BAPT–So Bapt Conv	9	722	2,385	2,951	11.1	31.8
Catholic	1	NR	NR	293	1.1	3.2
CGOD–Ch God (Ander)	4	903	NR	903	3.4	9.7
Ch of Nazarene	1	77	124	124	0.5	1.3
CHR–Chr Ch (Disc)	3	142	820	1,015	3.8	10.9
CHR–Chr Chs & Chs Cr	2	NR	600	742	2.8	8.0
CHR–Chs of Christ	7	625	596	797	3.0	8.6
Jehovah's Witness	1	NR	NR	NR	-	-
METH–C.M.E.	1	0	100	124	0.5	1.3
METH–Un Methodist	4	280	622	730	2.8	7.9
Non-denom Chr Chs	2	310	325	387	1.5	4.2
PENT–Assemb of God	2	425	323	518	2.0	5.6
PENT–Ch God (Cleve)	2	71	168	208	0.8	2.2
PENT–Ch of God Proph	1	NR	30	37	0.1	0.4
PENT–Un Pent Ch Intl	1	NR	NR	NR	-	-
PRES–Presb Ch (USA)	1	60	128	158	0.6	1.7
MORGAN	**36**	**1,256**	**2,420**	**2,968**	**21.3**	**100.0**
Bahá'í	0	NR	1	1	0.0	0.0
BAPT–Enterprise Bapt Assoc	9	NR	NR	NR	-	-
BAPT–So Bapt Conv	5	286	895	1,059	7.6	35.7
Catholic	1	NR	NR	52	0.4	1.8
CGOD–Ch God (Ander)	4	152	NR	152	1.1	5.1

NR–Not Reported - Represents no adherents reported. Percentages may not total 100 due to rounding.

Table 3: Religious Congregations by County and Group: 2010

Religious Group	Number of Congrega-tions	Number of Attendees	Number of Communicant, Confirmed, or Full Members	Adherents: Number of Adherents	Adherents: % of Total Pop.	Adherents: % of Total Adh.
CHR–Chr Ch (Disc)	2	0	85	101	0.7	3.4
CHR–Chr Chs & Chs Cr	1	NR	200	237	1.7	8.0
CHR–Chs of Christ	3	162	140	190	1.4	6.4
Jehovah's Witness	1	NR	NR	NR	-	-
MENN–Mennonite USA	1	22	10	12	0.1	0.4
METH–Un Methodist	1	62	173	173	1.2	5.8
Non-denom Chr Chs	5	472	785	836	6.0	28.2
PENT–Ch God (Cleve)	2	100	96	114	0.8	3.8
PRES–Presb Ch (USA)	1	0	35	41	0.3	1.4
MUHLENBERG	**97**	**5,977**	**18,219**	**22,509**	**71.5**	**100.0**
Bahá'í	0	NR	1	1	0.0	0.0
BAPT–NBC USA	1	86	191	229	0.7	1.0
BAPT–So Bapt Conv	48	4,160	14,751	17,702	56.2	78.6
Catholic	1	NR	NR	245	0.8	1.1
CHR–Chr Ch (Disc)	2	0	54	65	0.2	0.3
CHR–Chr Chs & Chs Cr	1	NR	130	156	0.5	0.7
CHR–Chs of Christ	11	646	630	832	2.6	3.7
Jehovah's Witness	1	NR	NR	NR	-	-
LDS–L-D Saints	1	NR	NR	245	0.8	1.1
METH–AME Zion	2	35	185	222	0.7	1.0
METH–Un Methodist	13	600	1,414	1,677	5.3	7.5
Non-denom Chr Chs	1	110	150	150	0.5	0.7
PENT–Assemb of God	2	89	56	95	0.3	0.4
PENT–Ch God (Cleve)	3	110	286	343	1.1	1.5
PENT–Ch of God Proph	1	NR	69	83	0.3	0.4
PENT–Un Pent Ch Intl	1	NR	NR	NR	-	-
PRES–Cumber Presb	3	NR	117	244	0.8	1.1
PRES–Presb Ch (USA)	4	121	150	180	0.6	0.8
Sev Day Adv	1	20	35	40	0.1	0.2
NELSON	**67**	**4,218**	**10,917**	**23,613**	**54.4**	**100.0**
ANG/EPIS–Episcopal	1	47	84	87	0.2	0.4
Bahá'í	0	NR	1	1	0.0	0.0
BAPT–Amer Bapt USA	1	13	22	28	0.1	0.1
BAPT–NBC USA	1	0	150	188	0.4	0.8
BAPT–So Bapt Conv	22	2,550	6,361	7,965	18.3	33.7
Catholic	9	NR	NR	10,007	23.0	42.4
CHR–Chr Ch (Disc)	5	269	817	1,023	2.4	4.3
CHR–Chr Chs & Chs Cr	4	NR	640	801	1.8	3.4
CHR–Chs of Christ	4	173	179	244	0.6	1.0
Jehovah's Witness	1	NR	NR	NR	-	-
LDS–L-D Saints	1	NR	NR	233	0.5	1.0
LUTH–Luth–MO Synod	1	40	50	53	0.1	0.2
METH–AME Zion	2	87	300	376	0.9	1.6
METH–Un Methodist	6	339	1,049	1,188	2.7	5.0
Non-denom Chr Chs	2	375	650	650	1.5	2.8
PENT–Assemb of God	1	30	25	32	0.1	0.1
PENT–Ch God (Cleve)	2	295	512	641	1.5	2.7
PENT–Ch of God Proph	1	NR	28	35	0.1	0.1
PENT–Un Pent Ch Intl	1	NR	NR	NR	-	-
PRES–Presb Ch (USA)	2	0	49	61	0.1	0.3
NICHOLAS	**23**	**556**	**2,202**	**2,742**	**38.4**	**100.0**
Bahá'í	0	NR	1	1	0.0	0.0
BAPT–So Bapt Conv	3	107	563	690	9.7	25.2
Catholic	1	NR	NR	78	1.1	2.8
CHR–Chr Ch (Disc)	3	12	82	100	1.4	3.6
CHR–Chr Chs & Chs Cr	4	NR	620	760	10.7	27.7
CHR–Chs of Christ	1	30	28	36	0.5	1.3
MENN–Amish Undif	1	NR	25	103	1.4	3.8
METH–Un Methodist	7	366	807	882	12.4	32.2
PENT–Ch God Mtn Asm	1	NR	NR	NR	-	-
PRES–Presb Ch (USA)	1	30	57	70	1.0	2.6
Sev Day Adv	1	11	19	22	0.3	0.8
OHIO	**84**	**3,465**	**11,132**	**14,438**	**60.6**	**100.0**
BAPT–So Bapt Conv	43	2,286	8,393	10,409	43.7	72.1
Catholic	2	NR	NR	530	2.2	3.7
CHR–Chr Chs & Chs Cr	2	NR	400	496	2.1	3.4
CHR–Chs of Christ	7	392	485	562	2.4	3.9
Jehovah's Witness	1	NR	NR	NR	-	-

Religious Group	Number of Congrega-tions	Number of Attendees	Number of Communicant, Confirmed, or Full Members	Adherents: Number of Adherents	Adherents: % of Total Pop.	Adherents: % of Total Adh.
LDS–L-D Saints	1	NR	NR	125	0.5	0.9
MENN–Amish Undif	1	NR	35	103	0.4	0.7
METH–Un Methodist	14	344	869	1,033	4.3	7.2
Non-denom Chr Chs	1	60	60	75	0.3	0.5
PENT–Ch God (Cleve)	4	329	586	727	3.0	5.0
PENT–Ch of God Proph	4	NR	192	238	1.0	1.6
PENT–Un Pent Ch Intl	1	NR	NR	NR	-	-
PRES–Cumber Presb	1	NR	26	40	0.2	0.3
PRES–Presb Ch (USA)	1	8	7	9	0.0	0.1
Sev Day Adv	1	46	79	91	0.4	0.6
OLDHAM	**63**	**5,790**	**15,369**	**27,872**	**46.2**	**100.0**
ANG/EPIS–Episcopal	1	107	221	263	0.4	0.9
Bahá'í	0	NR	16	16	0.0	0.1
BAPT–So Bapt Conv	22	2,815	8,229	10,416	17.3	37.4
Catholic	2	NR	NR	7,464	12.4	26.8
Ch of Nazarene	1	20	42	90	0.1	0.3
CHR–Chr Ch (Disc)	3	249	761	963	1.6	3.5
CHR–Chr Chs & Chs Cr	2	NR	155	196	0.3	0.7
CHR–Chs of Christ	3	115	97	128	0.2	0.5
Evan Free Ch	1	70	NR	70	0.1	0.3
Jehovah's Witness	2	NR	NR	NR	-	-
LDS–L-D Saints	3	NR	NR	1,299	2.2	4.7
LUTH–E.L.C.A.	1	42	43	98	0.2	0.4
LUTH–Luth–MO Synod	1	55	60	68	0.1	0.2
METH–Un Methodist	6	1,454	4,353	5,056	8.4	18.1
Non-denom Chr Chs	3	375	475	513	0.9	1.8
PENT–Assemb of God	3	210	223	375	0.6	1.3
PENT–Ch God (Cleve)	1	5	10	13	0.0	0.0
PENT–Ch of God Proph	1	NR	54	68	0.1	0.2
PENT–Int Foursq Gos	1	121	89	113	0.2	0.4
PENT–Un Pent Ch Intl	1	NR	NR	NR	-	-
PENT–Vineyard	1	0	0	0	0.0	0.0
PRES–Presb Ch (USA)	3	44	353	447	0.7	1.6
Sev Day Adv	1	108	188	216	0.4	0.8
OWEN	**36**	**1,762**	**4,678**	**6,158**	**56.8**	**100.0**
BAPT–So Bapt Conv	22	1,253	3,853	4,759	43.9	77.3
Catholic	1	NR	NR	200	1.8	3.2
CHR–Chr Ch (Disc)	3	99	213	263	2.4	4.3
CHR–Chr Chs & Chs Cr	1	NR	160	198	1.8	3.2
Jehovah's Witness	1	NR	NR	NR	-	-
MENN–Amb Amish-Menn	1	59	27	59	0.5	1.0
METH–Un Methodist	3	60	211	232	2.1	3.8
PENT–Assemb of God	2	181	145	259	2.4	4.2
PENT–Pent Ch of God	1	70	NR	109	1.0	1.8
Sev Day Adv	1	40	69	79	0.7	1.3
OWSLEY	**17**	**466**	**1,165**	**1,581**	**33.2**	**100.0**
BAPT–So Bapt Conv	6	150	566	679	14.3	42.9
Catholic	1	NR	NR	37	0.8	2.3
CHR–Chs of Christ	1	25	20	20	0.4	1.3
METH–Un Methodist	3	130	190	371	7.8	23.5
Non-denom Chr Chs	2	125	125	156	3.3	9.9
PENT–Assemb of God	1	13	10	13	0.3	0.8
PENT–Ch God (Cleve)	1	23	59	71	1.5	4.5
PRES–Presb Ch (USA)	2	0	195	234	4.9	14.8
PENDLETON	**44**	**1,562**	**6,604**	**8,648**	**58.1**	**100.0**
BAPT–So Bapt Conv	20	1,233	4,366	5,340	35.9	61.7
Catholic	3	NR	NR	560	3.8	6.5
CHR–Chr Ch (Disc)	5	121	397	486	3.3	5.6
CHR–Chr Chs & Chs Cr	9	NR	1,470	1,798	12.1	20.8
Jehovah's Witness	1	NR	NR	NR	-	-
METH–Un Methodist	2	71	200	213	1.4	2.5
METH–Wesleyan	1	42	15	55	0.4	0.6
PENT–Assemb of God	1	31	24	35	0.2	0.4
PENT–Ch God (Cleve)	1	34	77	94	0.6	1.1
PRES–Presb Ch (USA)	1	30	55	67	0.5	0.8
PERRY	**74**	**3,090**	**7,477**	**9,705**	**33.8**	**100.0**
ANG/EPIS–Episcopal	1	10	28	28	0.1	0.3

NR–Not Reported   - Represents no adherents reported.   Percentages may not total 100 due to rounding.

Table 3: Religious Congregations by County and Group: 2010

Religious Group	Number of Congrega-tions	Number of Attendees	Number of Communicant, Confirmed, or Full Members	Adherents		
				Number of Adherents	% of Total Pop.	% of Total Adh.
BAPT–Natl Mis Bapt Conv	1	0	150	180	0.6	1.9
BAPT–Reg Bapt Gen As	1	NR	NR	NR	-	-
BAPT–So Bapt Conv	22	1,134	4,386	5,257	18.3	54.2
BRETH–Brethren (Ash)	1	NR	80	96	0.3	1.0
Catholic	1	NR	NR	188	0.7	1.9
CGOD–Ch God (Ander)	1	25	NR	25	0.1	0.3
Ch of Nazarene	1	0	5	30	0.1	0.3
CHR–Chr Ch (Disc)	1	8	23	28	0.1	0.3
CHR–Chr Chs & Chs Cr	2	NR	0	0	0.0	0.0
CHR–Chs of Christ	11	471	495	626	2.2	6.5
Evan Free Ch	2	133	NR	133	0.5	1.4
LDS–L-D Saints	1	NR	NR	301	1.0	3.1
MENN–Cons Menn Conf	1	30	26	31	0.1	0.3
MENN–Mennonite USA	1	50	37	44	0.2	0.5
METH–Un Methodist	3	86	267	307	1.1	3.2
Non-denom Chr Chs	3	475	450	593	2.1	6.1
PENT–Assemb of God	1	17	14	20	0.1	0.2
PENT–Ch God (Cleve)	12	535	1,126	1,350	4.7	13.9
PENT–Ch of God Proph	1	NR	33	40	0.1	0.4
PENT–Un Pent Ch Intl	1	NR	NR	NR	-	-
PRES–Presb Ch (USA)	5	116	357	428	1.5	4.4
PIKE	**123**	**5,518**	**16,635**	**20,633**	**31.7**	**100.0**
Bahá'í	0	NR	3	3	0.0	0.0
BAPT–Free Will Bapt	14	NR	1,291	1,549	2.4	7.5
BAPT–Natl Mis Bapt Conv	1	0	150	180	0.3	0.9
BAPT–So Bapt Conv	26	2,283	8,811	10,575	16.3	51.3
BRETH–Ch of Brethren	1	0	10	12	0.0	0.1
Catholic	3	NR	NR	293	0.5	1.4
CGOD–Ch God (Ander)	4	181	NR	181	0.3	0.9
Chr & Miss Al	3	90	55	152	0.2	0.7
CHR–Chr Ch (Disc)	1	98	203	244	0.4	1.2
CHR–Chr Chs & Chs Cr	10	NR	1,657	1,989	3.1	9.6
CHR–Chs of Christ	25	1,556	1,446	1,802	2.8	8.7
Jehovah's Witness	2	NR	NR	NR	-	-
LDS–L-D Saints	1	NR	NR	210	0.3	1.0
METH–Un Methodist	8	484	1,353	1,408	2.2	6.8
METH–Wesleyan	2	41	41	54	0.1	0.3
Non-denom Chr Chs	3	190	220	238	0.4	1.2
PENT–Assemb of God	2	171	136	234	0.4	1.1
PENT–Ch God (Cleve)	9	404	745	894	1.4	4.3
PENT–Un Pent Ch Intl	1	NR	NR	NR	-	-
PRES–Presb Ch (USA)	6	0	479	575	0.9	2.8
Sev Day Adv	1	20	35	40	0.1	0.2
POWELL	**30**	**1,645**	**3,082**	**4,708**	**37.3**	**100.0**
BAPT–So Bapt Conv	7	540	1,736	2,140	17.0	45.5
BUDD–Mahayana	1	NR	NR	200	1.6	4.2
Catholic	1	NR	NR	78	0.6	1.7
CGOD–Ch God (Ander)	7	624	NR	624	4.9	13.3
CHR–Chr Chs & Chs Cr	2	NR	343	423	3.4	9.0
CHR–Chs of Christ	4	242	218	262	2.1	5.6
METH–Un Methodist	3	125	313	372	2.9	7.9
PENT–Assemb of God	1	38	23	56	0.4	1.2
PENT–Ch God (Cleve)	2	76	229	282	2.2	6.0
PENT–Ch of God Proph	1	NR	133	164	1.3	3.5
PRES–Presb Ch (USA)	1	0	87	107	0.8	2.3
PULASKI	**164**	**11,276**	**29,426**	**36,986**	**58.6**	**100.0**
ANG/EPIS–Episcopal	1	55	158	179	0.3	0.5
Bahá'í	0	NR	2	2	0.0	0.0
BAPT–Amer Bapt Assn	17	NR	2,965	3,599	5.7	9.7
BAPT–Natl Mis Bapt Conv	1	0	150	182	0.3	0.5
BAPT–So Bapt Conv	68	7,196	19,333	23,466	37.2	63.4
Catholic	1	NR	NR	725	1.1	2.0
CGOD–Ch God (Ander)	4	95	NR	95	0.2	0.3
Ch of Nazarene	8	659	913	1,038	1.6	2.8
CHR–Chr Ch (Disc)	2	248	405	492	0.8	1.3
CHR–Chr Chs & Chs Cr	2	NR	300	364	0.6	1.0
CHR–Chs of Christ	15	819	801	1,087	1.7	2.9
Jehovah's Witness	1	NR	NR	NR	-	-
LDS–L-D Saints	1	NR	NR	432	0.7	1.2
LUTH–E.L.C.A.	1	55	90	105	0.2	0.3

Religious Group	Number of Congrega-tions	Number of Attendees	Number of Communicant, Confirmed, or Full Members	Adherents		
				Number of Adherents	% of Total Pop.	% of Total Adh.
METH–AME	1	30	75	91	0.1	0.2
METH–Un Methodist	18	886	2,247	2,484	3.9	6.7
METH–Wesleyan	1	35	15	46	0.1	0.1
Muslim Est	1	40	NR	100	0.2	0.3
Non-denom Chr Chs	4	355	475	538	0.9	1.5
PENT–Assemb of God	1	163	0	163	0.3	0.4
PENT–Ch God (Cleve)	5	428	784	952	1.5	2.6
PENT–Ch God Mtn Asm	1	NR	NR	NR	-	-
PENT–Ch of God Proph	4	NR	240	291	0.5	0.8
PENT–Un Pent Ch Intl	1	NR	NR	NR	-	-
PRES–Cumber Presb	1	NR	43	43	0.1	0.1
PRES–Presb Ch (USA)	2	120	271	329	0.5	0.9
Sev Day Adv	2	92	159	183	0.3	0.5
ROBERTSON	**7**	**149**	**459**	**527**	**23.1**	**100.0**
BAPT–So Bapt Conv	1	42	158	188	8.2	35.7
CHR–Chr Chs & Chs Cr	2	NR	120	142	6.2	26.9
METH–Un Methodist	3	83	172	172	7.5	32.6
PENT–Assemb of God	1	24	9	25	1.1	4.7
ROCKCASTLE	**42**	**2,898**	**7,557**	**9,241**	**54.2**	**100.0**
BAPT–So Bapt Conv	22	2,051	6,309	7,651	44.9	82.8
Catholic	1	NR	NR	48	0.3	0.5
Ch of Nazarene	1	17	40	40	0.2	0.4
CHR–Chr Chs & Chs Cr	4	NR	250	303	1.8	3.3
CHR–Chs of Christ	6	356	340	405	2.4	4.4
Jehovah's Witness	1	NR	NR	NR	-	-
MENN–Amish Undif	0	NR	13	29	0.2	0.3
Non-denom Chr Chs	2	305	315	415	2.4	4.5
PENT–Assemb of God	2	87	98	117	0.7	1.3
PENT–Ch God (Cleve)	2	82	192	233	1.4	2.5
PENT–Un Pent Ch Intl	1	NR	NR	NR	-	-
ROWAN	**35**	**1,937**	**2,691**	**4,640**	**19.9**	**100.0**
ANG/EPIS–Episcopal	1	9	42	43	0.2	0.9
Bahá'í	0	NR	1	1	0.0	0.0
BAPT–Enterprise Bapt Assoc	1	NR	NR	NR	-	-
BAPT–Free Will Bapt	4	NR	384	453	1.9	9.8
BAPT–So Bapt Conv	6	262	863	1,018	4.4	21.9
Catholic	1	NR	NR	365	1.6	7.9
CGOD–Ch God (Ander)	6	680	NR	680	2.9	14.7
Ch of Nazarene	1	93	107	107	0.5	2.3
CHR–Chr Ch (Disc)	1	101	187	221	0.9	4.8
CHR–Chr Chs & Chs Cr	1	NR	100	118	0.5	2.5
CHR–Chs of Christ	1	41	46	55	0.2	1.2
Jehovah's Witness	1	NR	NR	NR	-	-
METH–Un Methodist	1	271	492	657	2.8	14.2
Muslim Est	1	134	NR	308	1.3	6.6
Non-denom Chr Chs	2	150	215	275	1.2	5.9
PENT–Assemb of God	2	82	52	102	0.4	2.2
PENT–Ch God (Cleve)	1	55	109	129	0.6	2.8
PENT–Un Pent Ch Intl	2	NR	NR	NR	-	-
PRES–Presb Ch (USA)	1	25	35	41	0.2	0.9
Sev Day Adv	1	34	58	67	0.3	1.4
RUSSELL	**54**	**3,272**	**6,875**	**8,751**	**49.8**	**100.0**
BAPT–So Bapt Conv	16	1,217	2,559	3,087	17.6	35.3
Catholic	1	NR	NR	167	1.0	1.9
Ch of Nazarene	3	171	263	430	2.4	4.9
CHR–Chr Chs & Chs Cr	5	NR	1,011	1,220	6.9	13.9
CHR–Chs of Christ	3	135	120	155	0.9	1.8
LUTH–E.L.C.A.	1	25	69	100	0.6	1.1
METH–Un Methodist	10	803	1,636	2,048	11.7	23.4
METH–Wesleyan	1	15	4	20	0.1	0.2
Non-denom Chr Chs	4	405	435	587	3.3	6.7
PENT–Ch God (Cleve)	6	475	677	817	4.7	9.3
PENT–Ch of God Proph	2	NR	57	69	0.4	0.8
PENT–Un Pent Ch Intl	1	NR	NR	NR	-	-
Sev Day Adv	1	26	44	51	0.3	0.6
SCOTT	**73**	**5,819**	**12,057**	**19,124**	**40.5**	**100.0**
ANG/EPIS–Episcopal	1	55	147	223	0.5	1.2

NR–Not Reported - Represents no adherents reported. Percentages may not total 100 due to rounding.

Table 3: Religious Congregations by County and Group: 2010

Religious Group	Number of Congregations	Number of Attendees	Number of Communicant, Confirmed, or Full Members	Adherents: Number of Adherents	Adherents: % of Total Pop.	Adherents: % of Total Adh.
Bahá'í	0	NR	1	1	0.0	0.0
BAPT–Free Will Bapt	1	NR	96	122	0.3	0.6
BAPT–Natl Mis Bapt Conv	1	15	20	25	0.1	0.1
BAPT–NBC Amer	1	0	180	228	0.5	1.2
BAPT–So Bapt Conv	17	1,850	4,160	5,277	11.2	27.6
Catholic	1	NR	NR	1,991	4.2	10.4
CGOD–Ch God (Ander)	3	215	NR	215	0.5	1.1
Ch of Nazarene	2	250	440	461	1.0	2.4
CHR–Chr Ch (Disc)	5	305	952	1,208	2.6	6.3
CHR–Chr Chs & Chs Cr	6	NR	1,840	2,334	4.9	12.2
CHR–Chs of Christ	5	217	199	259	0.5	1.4
Evan Free Ch	1	80	NR	80	0.2	0.4
Jehovah's Witness	1	NR	NR	NR	-	-
LDS–L-D Saints	1	NR	NR	597	1.3	3.1
METH–AME	1	0	100	127	0.3	0.7
METH–Un Methodist	6	429	1,088	1,251	2.7	6.5
METH–Wesleyan	1	43	0	56	0.1	0.3
MJEW–Assoc Mes Cong	1	NR	NR	NR	-	-
Non-denom Chr Chs	6	1,805	2,098	2,362	5.0	12.4
PENT–Assemb of God	2	202	244	338	0.7	1.8
PENT–Ch God (Cleve)	2	139	246	312	0.7	1.6
PENT–Ch God Mtn Asm	1	NR	NR	NR	-	-
PENT–Ch of God Proph	1	NR	29	37	0.1	0.2
PENT–Pent Ch of God	2	140	NR	217	0.5	1.1
PENT–Un Pent Ch Intl	1	NR	NR	NR	-	-
PRES–Presb Ch (USA)	2	74	175	222	0.5	1.2
Salvation Army	1	0	42	1,181	2.5	6.2
SHELBY	**66**	**4,871**	**16,712**	**23,318**	**55.4**	**100.0**
ANG/EPIS–Episcopal	1	59	116	116	0.3	0.5
Bahá'í	0	NR	13	13	0.0	0.1
BAPT–So Bapt Conv	28	2,812	10,980	13,592	32.3	58.3
Catholic	1	NR	NR	2,350	5.6	10.1
Ch of Nazarene	1	0	26	26	0.1	0.1
CHR–Chr Ch (Disc)	3	243	858	1,062	2.5	4.6
CHR–Chr Chs & Chs Cr	2	NR	1,200	1,485	3.5	6.4
CHR–Chs of Christ	4	220	207	255	0.6	1.1
Jehovah's Witness	1	NR	NR	NR	-	-
LDS–L-D Saints	1	NR	NR	585	1.4	2.5
LUTH–Luth–MO Synod	1	55	158	209	0.5	0.9
METH–AME	1	0	160	198	0.5	0.8
METH–Un Methodist	9	573	1,700	1,845	4.4	7.9
METH–Wesleyan	1	32	27	42	0.1	0.2
Non-denom Chr Chs	5	642	795	876	2.1	3.8
PENT–Assemb of God	1	55	40	135	0.3	0.6
PENT–Ch God (Cleve)	1	49	69	85	0.2	0.4
PENT–Ch of God Proph	2	NR	84	104	0.2	0.4
PENT–Un Pent Ch Intl	1	NR	NR	NR	-	-
PRES–Presb Ch (USA)	1	95	217	269	0.6	1.2
Sev Day Adv	1	36	62	71	0.2	0.3
SIMPSON	**39**	**3,328**	**7,388**	**9,716**	**56.1**	**100.0**
Bahá'í	0	NR	9	9	0.1	0.1
BAPT–So Bapt Conv	14	1,577	4,772	5,909	34.1	60.8
Catholic	1	NR	NR	500	2.9	5.1
Ch of Nazarene	1	64	65	96	0.6	1.0
CHR–Chs of Christ	7	720	921	1,164	6.7	12.0
Jehovah's Witness	1	NR	NR	NR	-	-
LUTH–E.L.C.A.	1	42	97	125	0.7	1.3
MENN–Beachy Amish-Menn	2	255	164	255	1.5	2.6
METH–AME	1	0	150	186	1.1	1.9
METH–Un Methodist	4	431	947	1,124	6.5	11.6
Non-denom Chr Chs	1	50	45	62	0.4	0.6
PENT–Assemb of God	1	26	10	31	0.2	0.3
PENT–Ch of God Proph	1	NR	30	37	0.2	0.4
PENT–Un Pent Ch Intl	1	NR	NR	NR	-	-
PRES–Presb Ch (USA)	2	147	150	186	1.1	1.9
Sev Day Adv	1	16	28	32	0.2	0.3
SPENCER	**23**	**1,231**	**4,182**	**5,680**	**33.3**	**100.0**
Bahá'í	0	NR	1	1	0.0	0.0
BAPT–So Bapt Conv	9	864	3,085	3,838	22.5	67.6
Catholic	1	NR	NR	420	2.5	7.4

Religious Group	Number of Congregations	Number of Attendees	Number of Communicant, Confirmed, or Full Members	Adherents: Number of Adherents	Adherents: % of Total Pop.	Adherents: % of Total Adh.
CHR–Chr Ch (Disc)	1	48	112	139	0.8	2.4
CHR–Chr Chs & Chs Cr	3	NR	375	467	2.7	8.2
CHR–Chs of Christ	1	55	51	62	0.4	1.1
Ind Fund Churches	1	NR	NR	NR	-	-
LUTH–Luth–MO Synod	1	65	60	70	0.4	1.2
METH–AME	1	0	100	124	0.7	2.2
METH–Un Methodist	1	49	137	165	1.0	2.9
PENT–Assemb of God	1	125	85	175	1.0	3.1
PENT–Ch God (Cleve)	1	25	42	52	0.3	0.9
PENT–Ch of God Proph	1	NR	134	167	1.0	2.9
PENT–Un Pent Ch Intl	1	NR	NR	NR	-	-
TAYLOR	**72**	**5,880**	**12,822**	**17,145**	**69.9**	**100.0**
ANG/EPIS–Episcopal	1	35	75	84	0.3	0.5
Bahá'í	0	NR	3	3	0.0	0.0
BAPT–Ind Bapt Flwsp Intl	1	NR	NR	NR	-	-
BAPT–NBC USA	1	200	250	303	1.2	1.8
BAPT–So Bapt Conv	26	2,778	6,756	8,176	33.4	47.7
Catholic	2	NR	NR	1,015	4.1	5.9
CGOD–Ch God (Ander)	3	201	NR	201	0.8	1.2
Ch of Nazarene	1	41	60	123	0.5	0.7
CHR–Chr Chs & Chs Cr	4	NR	1,030	1,246	5.1	7.3
CHR–Chs of Christ	2	128	135	172	0.7	1.0
Jehovah's Witness	1	NR	NR	NR	-	-
LDS–L-D Saints	1	NR	NR	256	1.0	1.5
MENN–Amish Undif	1	NR	44	142	0.6	0.8
METH–AME	1	60	150	182	0.7	1.1
METH–C.M.E.	1	40	50	61	0.2	0.4
METH–Un Methodist	16	962	2,427	2,780	11.3	16.2
Non-denom Chr Chs	2	1,200	1,220	1,500	6.1	8.7
PENT–Un Pent Ch Intl	1	NR	NR	NR	-	-
PENT–Vineyard	1	225	300	363	1.5	2.1
PRES–Cumber Presb	4	NR	185	373	1.5	2.2
PRES–Presb Ch (USA)	1	0	119	144	0.6	0.8
Sev Day Adv	1	10	18	21	0.1	0.1
TODD	**54**	**2,909**	**7,164**	**9,867**	**79.2**	**100.0**
BAPT–NBC USA	1	35	100	128	1.0	1.3
BAPT–So Bapt Conv	21	1,952	5,516	7,051	56.6	71.5
Catholic	2	NR	NR	373	3.0	3.8
Ch of Nazarene	1	58	88	145	1.2	1.5
CHR–Chr Ch (Disc)	2	40	110	141	1.1	1.4
CHR–Chr Chs & Chs Cr	1	NR	0	0	0.0	0.0
CHR–Chs of Christ	7	365	332	471	3.8	4.8
LDS–L-D Saints	1	NR	NR	198	1.6	2.0
MENN–Amish Undif	3	NR	186	414	3.3	4.2
METH–Un Methodist	12	339	771	797	6.4	8.1
PENT–Assemb of God	1	115	47	115	0.9	1.2
PRES–Cumber Presb	1	NR	7	25	0.2	0.3
PRES–Presb Ch (USA)	1	5	7	9	0.1	0.1
TRIGG	**49**	**3,259**	**8,994**	**11,205**	**78.1**	**100.0**
BAPT–Natl Mis Bapt Conv	1	0	150	181	1.3	1.6
BAPT–So Bapt Conv	25	2,280	6,812	8,219	57.3	73.4
Catholic	1	NR	NR	265	1.8	2.4
CHR–Chr Ch (Disc)	1	110	203	245	1.7	2.2
CHR–Chr Chs & Chs Cr	2	NR	125	151	1.1	1.3
CHR–Chs of Christ	2	151	149	199	1.4	1.8
Jehovah's Witness	1	NR	NR	NR	-	-
MENN–Amish Undif	2	NR	73	215	1.5	1.9
METH–Un Methodist	11	633	1,392	1,624	11.3	14.5
Non-denom Chr Chs	1	85	90	106	0.7	0.9
PENT–Assemb of God	1	0	0	0	0.0	0.0
PENT–Un Pent Ch Intl	1	NR	NR	NR	-	-
TRIMBLE	**20**	**922**	**3,139**	**3,822**	**43.4**	**100.0**
BAPT–So Bapt Conv	8	578	1,904	2,353	26.7	61.6
CHR–Chr Ch (Disc)	1	62	136	168	1.9	4.4
CHR–Chr Chs & Chs Cr	2	NR	380	470	5.3	12.3
METH–Un Methodist	6	192	661	711	8.1	18.6
METH–Wesleyan	2	67	33	87	1.0	2.3
PENT–Assemb of God	1	23	25	33	0.4	0.9

NR–Not Reported   - Represents no adherents reported.   Percentages may not total 100 due to rounding.

Table 3: Religious Congregations by County and Group: 2010

Religious Group	Number of Congregations	Number of Attendees	Number of Communicant, Confirmed, or Full Members	Adherents: Number of Adherents	Adherents: % of Total Pop.	Adherents: % of Total Adh.
UNION	**44**	**1,481**	**5,312**	**9,589**	**63.9**	**100.0**
Bahá'í	0	NR	1	1	0.0	0.0
BAPT–So Bapt Conv	14	856	3,738	4,518	30.1	47.1
Catholic	6	NR	NR	3,159	21.1	32.9
CHR–Chr Ch (Disc)	1	0	0	0	0.0	0.0
CHR–Chr Chs & Chs Cr	3	NR	380	459	3.1	4.8
CHR–Chs of Christ	5	180	181	232	1.5	2.4
METH–C.M.E.	1	45	45	54	0.4	0.6
METH–Un Methodist	6	260	670	706	4.7	7.4
PENT–Assemb of God	1	70	40	70	0.5	0.7
PENT–Ch of God Proph	1	NR	25	30	0.2	0.3
PENT–COGIC	1	25	24	29	0.2	0.3
PRES–Cum Pres Am	1	NR	NR	NR	-	-
PRES–Cumber Presb	2	NR	143	252	1.7	2.6
PRES–Presb Ch (USA)	2	45	65	79	0.5	0.8
WARREN	**162**	**18,249**	**36,857**	**51,344**	**45.1**	**100.0**
ANG/EPIS–Episcopal	1	252	605	661	0.6	1.3
Bahá'í	0	NR	13	13	0.0	0.0
BAPT–Free Will Bapt	2	NR	192	234	0.2	0.5
BAPT–So Bapt Conv	48	8,931	21,742	26,450	23.2	51.5
Catholic	2	NR	NR	4,243	3.7	8.3
Ch of Nazarene	1	129	206	206	0.2	0.4
Chr & Miss Al	2	65	19	82	0.1	0.2
CHR–Chr Ch (Disc)	2	230	840	1,022	0.9	2.0
CHR–Chr Chs & Chs Cr	4	NR	445	541	0.5	1.1
CHR–Chs of Christ	25	3,095	3,080	3,862	3.4	7.5
HINDU–Post Ren	1	NR	NR	16	0.0	0.0
Jehovah's Witness	2	NR	NR	NR	-	-
JUD–Reform	1	12	21	57	0.1	0.1
LDS–L-D Saints	2	NR	NR	1,250	1.1	2.4
LUTH–Luth–MO Synod	1	192	383	467	0.4	0.9
MENN–Amish Undif	1	NR	63	143	0.1	0.3
METH–AME	2	60	200	243	0.2	0.5
METH–Free Methodist	2	73	72	77	0.1	0.1
METH–Un Methodist	23	2,710	5,843	6,482	5.7	12.6
Muslim Est	3	568	NR	1,216	1.1	2.4
Non-denom Chr Chs	6	441	755	761	0.7	1.5
ORTHE–Ant Orth of NA	1	35	NR	50	0.0	0.1
PENT–Assemb of God	4	564	451	581	0.5	1.1
PENT–Ch God (Cleve)	2	127	198	241	0.2	0.5
PENT–Ch of God Proph	1	NR	35	43	0.0	0.1
PENT–Full Gosp Bapt	2	NR	NR	NR	-	-
PENT–Un Pent Ch Intl	4	NR	NR	NR	-	-
PRES–Cum Pres Am	1	NR	NR	NR	-	-
PRES–Cumber Presb	3	NR	222	456	0.4	0.9
PRES–Presb Ch (USA)	6	361	834	1,015	0.9	2.0
PRES–Presb Ch Amer	1	0	0	0	0.0	0.0
Salvation Army	1	37	69	263	0.2	0.5
Sev Day Adv	3	264	459	528	0.5	1.0
Unit Univ	1	103	110	141	0.1	0.3
Unity Ch	1	NR	NR	NR	-	-
WASHINGTON	**38**	**1,873**	**5,351**	**10,261**	**87.6**	**100.0**
BAPT–So Bapt Conv	13	1,207	3,567	4,347	37.1	42.4
Catholic	5	NR	NR	3,723	31.8	36.3
CHR–Chr Chs & Chs Cr	4	NR	625	762	6.5	7.4
CHR–Chs of Christ	4	192	185	228	1.9	2.2
MENN–Amish Undif	1	NR	11	29	0.2	0.3
METH–AME Zion	1	40	60	73	0.6	0.7
METH–Un Methodist	4	85	210	247	2.1	2.4
Non-denom Chr Chs	1	250	250	312	2.7	3.0
PENT–Ch God (Cleve)	2	84	111	135	1.2	1.3
PENT–Ch of God Proph	1	NR	241	294	2.5	2.9
PRES–Presb Ch (USA)	2	15	91	111	0.9	1.1
WAYNE	**51**	**3,205**	**11,224**	**13,688**	**65.8**	**100.0**
Bahá'í	0	NR	1	1	0.0	0.0
BAPT–So Bapt Conv	23	2,068	8,023	9,707	46.6	70.9
Catholic	1	NR	NR	134	0.6	1.0
CGOD–Ch God (Ander)	1	82	NR	82	0.4	0.6
Ch of Nazarene	1	162	230	305	1.5	2.2
CHR–Chr Chs & Chs Cr	2	NR	375	454	2.2	3.3
CHR–Chs of Christ	5	244	224	295	1.4	2.2
Jehovah's Witness	1	NR	NR	NR	-	-
LDS–L-D Saints	1	NR	NR	157	0.8	1.1
MENN–Unaffil Amish-Menn	1	123	65	123	0.6	0.9
METH–AME	2	0	200	242	1.2	1.8
METH–Un Methodist	8	297	955	1,010	4.9	7.4
Non-denom Chr Chs	2	191	1,025	1,025	4.9	7.5
PENT–Assemb of God	1	6	5	7	0.0	0.1
PENT–Ch God (Cleve)	1	20	106	128	0.6	0.9
PENT–Intl Pent Holiness	1	12	15	18	0.1	0.1
WEBSTER	**47**	**1,924**	**5,641**	**7,561**	**55.5**	**100.0**
BAPT–So Bapt Conv	19	1,007	3,853	4,713	34.6	62.3
Catholic	2	NR	NR	500	3.7	6.6
CHR–Chr Ch (Disc)	3	0	172	210	1.5	2.8
CHR–Chs of Christ	4	207	215	259	1.9	3.4
Jehovah's Witness	1	NR	NR	NR	-	-
MENN–Midw Bchy Am-Menn	1	112	57	112	0.8	1.5
METH–Un Methodist	6	412	1,021	1,227	9.0	16.2
Non-denom Chr Chs	1	30	60	60	0.4	0.8
PENT–Assemb of God	2	131	95	205	1.5	2.7
PENT–Ch of God Proph	2	NR	40	49	0.4	0.6
PENT–COGIC	1	25	25	31	0.2	0.4
PRES–Cum Pres Am	1	NR	NR	NR	-	-
PRES–Cumber Presb	4	NR	103	195	1.4	2.6
WHITLEY	**90**	**6,324**	**18,266**	**23,126**	**64.9**	**100.0**
ANG/EPIS–Anglican NA	1	NR	NR	NR	-	-
BAPT–So Bapt Conv	50	4,509	14,019	17,106	48.0	74.0
Catholic	2	NR	NR	92	0.3	0.4
CHR–Chr Ch (Disc)	1	70	93	113	0.3	0.5
CHR–Chr Chs & Chs Cr	5	NR	705	860	2.4	3.7
CHR–Chs of Christ	3	268	244	297	0.8	1.3
Jehovah's Witness	2	NR	NR	NR	-	-
LDS–L-D Saints	1	NR	NR	652	1.8	2.8
METH–Un Methodist	5	575	1,117	1,469	4.1	6.4
Non-denom Chr Chs	1	50	150	150	0.4	0.6
PENT–Assemb of God	2	96	87	130	0.4	0.6
PENT–Ch God (Cleve)	7	744	1,736	2,118	5.9	9.2
PENT–Ch God Mtn Asm	6	NR	NR	NR	-	-
PENT–Un Pent Ch Intl	2	NR	NR	NR	-	-
PRES–Presb Ch (USA)	1	0	94	115	0.3	0.5
Sev Day Adv	1	12	21	24	0.1	0.1
WOLFE	**17**	**773**	**1,116**	**1,570**	**21.3**	**100.0**
Bahá'í	0	NR	1	1	0.0	0.1
BAPT–So Bapt Conv	3	115	315	387	5.3	24.6
Catholic	1	NR	NR	42	0.6	2.7
CGOD–Ch God (Ander)	3	178	NR	178	2.4	11.3
CHR–Chr Ch (Disc)	1	0	0	0	0.0	0.0
CHR–Chs of Christ	1	60	65	85	1.2	5.4
METH–Un Methodist	2	96	228	257	3.5	16.4
Non-denom Chr Chs	5	290	440	538	7.3	34.3
PENT–Ch God (Cleve)	1	34	67	82	1.1	5.2
WOODFORD	**49**	**4,166**	**11,314**	**15,751**	**63.2**	**100.0**
ANG/EPIS–Anglican NA	1	NR	NR	NR	-	-
ANG/EPIS–Episcopal	1	142	327	386	1.5	2.5
BAPT–So Bapt Conv	14	2,410	6,046	7,386	29.6	46.9
Catholic	1	NR	NR	1,763	7.1	11.2
Ch of Nazarene	2	73	115	165	0.7	1.0
CHR–Chr Ch (Disc)	4	318	883	1,079	4.3	6.9
CHR–Chr Chs & Chs Cr	2	NR	830	1,014	4.1	6.4
CHR–Chs of Christ	3	201	176	250	1.0	1.6
Jehovah's Witness	1	NR	NR	NR	-	-
METH–AME	2	0	200	244	1.0	1.5
METH–Un Methodist	6	338	1,486	1,568	6.3	10.0
PENT–Assemb of God	2	375	229	647	2.6	4.1
PENT–Ch God (Cleve)	2	71	158	193	0.8	1.2
PENT–Ch God Mtn Asm	1	NR	NR	NR	-	-
PENT–Ch of God Proph	3	NR	206	252	1.0	1.6
PRES–Presb Ch (USA)	4	238	658	804	3.2	5.1

NR–Not Reported - Represents no adherents reported. Percentages may not total 100 due to rounding.

Table 3: Religious Congregations by County and Group: 2010

Religious Group	Number of Congrega-tions	Number of Attendees	Number of Communicant, Confirmed, or Full Members	Adherents		
				Number of Adherents	% of Total Pop.	% of Total Adh.
LOUISIANA	**5,841**	**515,212**	**1,203,923**	**2,746,897**	**60.6**	**100.0**
ACADIA	**79**	**3,234**	**5,997**	**38,070**	**61.6**	**100.0**
ANG/EPIS–Episcopal	1	25	34	42	0.1	0.1
Bahá'í	0	NR	3	3	0.0	0.0
BAPT–NBC USA	1	0	250	317	0.5	0.8
BAPT–So Bapt Conv	12	972	2,252	2,859	4.6	7.5
Catholic	23	NR	NR	29,701	48.1	78.0
Ch of Nazarene	4	168	247	312	0.5	0.8
CHR–Chr Chs & Chs Cr	2	NR	510	648	1.0	1.7
CHR–Chs of Christ	3	212	218	308	0.5	0.8
Jehovah's Witness	1	NR	NR	NR	-	-
LUTH–Luth–MO Synod	2	60	88	131	0.2	0.3
METH–C.M.E.	3	80	390	495	0.8	1.3
METH–Un Methodist	7	234	662	790	1.3	2.1
Non-denom Chr Chs	6	571	555	715	1.2	1.9
PENT–Assemb of God	4	845	513	1,401	2.3	3.7
PENT–COGIC	1	0	150	190	0.3	0.5
PENT–Intl Pent Holiness	1	42	68	86	0.1	0.2
PENT–Un Pent Ch Intl	7	NR	NR	NR	-	-
PRES–Presb Ch (USA)	1	25	57	72	0.1	0.2
ALLEN	**58**	**2,127**	**6,282**	**12,503**	**48.5**	**100.0**
ANG/EPIS–Episcopal	1	5	7	7	0.0	0.1
BAPT–So Bapt Conv	19	1,304	4,836	5,875	22.8	47.0
Catholic	4	NR	NR	4,650	18.0	37.2
CHR–Chs of Christ	3	157	152	230	0.9	1.8
Ind Fund Churches	1	NR	NR	NR	-	-
Jehovah's Witness	1	NR	NR	NR	-	-
LDS–L-D Saints	1	NR	NR	183	0.7	1.5
METH–AME	3	50	350	425	1.6	3.4
METH–C.M.E.	1	0	100	121	0.5	1.0
METH–Un Methodist	5	103	282	338	1.3	2.7
Non-denom Chr Chs	3	350	475	489	1.9	3.9
PENT–Assemb of God	3	133	55	155	0.6	1.2
PENT–COGIC	2	25	25	30	0.1	0.2
PENT–Un Pent Ch Intl	11	NR	NR	NR	-	-
ASCENSION	**75**	**7,216**	**11,984**	**52,017**	**48.5**	**100.0**
Bahá'í	0	NR	13	13	0.0	0.0
BAPT–Natl Mis Bapt Conv	1	0	150	193	0.2	0.4
BAPT–NBC Amer	1	175	250	322	0.3	0.6
BAPT–NBC USA	1	0	150	193	0.2	0.4
BAPT–Prog NBC	1	0	150	193	0.2	0.4
BAPT–So Bapt Conv	18	2,022	3,951	5,089	4.7	9.8
Catholic	9	NR	NR	36,475	34.0	70.1
CHR–Chs of Christ	2	135	140	202	0.2	0.4
Jehovah's Witness	2	NR	NR	NR	-	-
LDS–L-D Saints	1	NR	NR	988	0.9	1.9
LUTH–Luth–MO Synod	1	62	117	143	0.1	0.3
METH–AME	1	0	100	129	0.1	0.2
METH–Un Methodist	9	663	1,501	1,788	1.7	3.4
Non-denom Chr Chs	10	3,760	4,850	5,328	5.0	10.2
PENT–Assemb of God	2	37	50	136	0.1	0.3
PENT–Ch God (Cleve)	3	153	146	188	0.2	0.4
PENT–COGIC	1	15	15	19	0.0	0.0
PENT–Int Foursq Gos	1	27	13	17	0.0	0.0
PENT–Intl Pent Holiness	1	30	50	64	0.1	0.1
PENT–Pent Ch of God	1	70	NR	109	0.1	0.2
PENT–Un Pent Ch Intl	5	NR	NR	NR	-	-
PRES–Evan Presby Ch	2	NR	235	303	0.3	0.6
PRES–Presb Ch (USA)	1	35	47	61	0.1	0.1
Sev Day Adv	1	32	56	64	0.1	0.1
ASSUMPTION	**22**	**654**	**1,556**	**15,429**	**65.9**	**100.0**
Bahá'í	0	NR	1	1	0.0	0.0
BAPT–NBC USA	2	200	350	429	1.8	2.8
BAPT–So Bapt Conv	3	158	621	761	3.2	4.9
Catholic	7	NR	NR	13,528	57.8	87.7
Jehovah's Witness	1	NR	NR	NR	-	-
METH–AME	1	0	150	184	0.8	1.2
METH–Un Methodist	2	93	161	202	0.9	1.3
Non-denom Chr Chs	1	100	150	150	0.6	1.0
PENT–Assemb of God	1	83	55	91	0.4	0.6
PENT–Ch of God Proph	1	NR	28	34	0.1	0.2
PENT–Intl Pent Holiness	1	20	40	49	0.2	0.3
PENT–Un Pent Ch Intl	2	NR	NR	NR	-	-
AVOYELLES	**63**	**1,779**	**3,925**	**23,442**	**55.7**	**100.0**
ANG/EPIS–Episcopal	1	22	65	77	0.2	0.3
Bahá'í	0	NR	8	8	0.0	0.0
BAPT–Natl Mis Bapt Conv	1	0	150	185	0.4	0.8
BAPT–So Bapt Conv	17	886	2,580	3,180	7.6	13.6
Catholic	22	NR	NR	18,400	43.7	78.5
Ch of Nazarene	1	100	116	127	0.3	0.5
CHR–Chs of Christ	1	55	51	67	0.2	0.3
Jehovah's Witness	2	NR	NR	NR	-	-
LDS–L-D Saints	1	NR	NR	168	0.4	0.7
LUTH–Luth–MO Synod	1	35	41	42	0.1	0.2
METH–Evan Meth Ch	1	NR	NR	NR	-	-
METH–Un Methodist	6	171	304	369	0.9	1.6
Non-denom Chr Chs	2	350	350	438	1.0	1.9
PENT–Assemb of God	1	160	110	196	0.5	0.8
PENT–COGIC	1	0	150	185	0.4	0.8
PENT–Un Pent Ch Intl	5	NR	NR	NR	-	-
BEAUREGARD	**96**	**6,623**	**16,919**	**23,453**	**65.8**	**100.0**
ANG/EPIS–Episcopal	1	25	47	51	0.1	0.2
BAPT–Amer Bapt Assn	1	NR	85	106	0.3	0.5
BAPT–Ind Bapt Flwsp Intl	1	NR	NR	NR	-	-
BAPT–NBC Amer	2	0	335	418	1.2	1.8
BAPT–NBC USA	2	70	165	206	0.6	0.9
BAPT–So Bapt Conv	31	3,280	11,207	13,982	39.2	59.6
Catholic	2	NR	NR	2,380	6.7	10.1
Ch of Nazarene	1	32	64	154	0.4	0.7
CHR–Chs of Christ	9	486	542	723	2.0	3.1
Ind Fund Churches	2	NR	NR	NR	-	-
LUTH–Luth–MO Synod	1	27	78	92	0.3	0.4
MENN–CG in Cr (Menn)	2	NR	287	358	1.0	1.5
METH–AME	1	0	100	125	0.4	0.5
METH–C.M.E.	1	0	100	125	0.4	0.5
METH–Un Methodist	4	282	1,089	1,253	3.5	5.3
New Apost Ch	1	NR	NR	NR	-	-
Non-denom Chr Chs	13	1,872	2,009	2,487	7.0	10.6
PENT–Assemb of God	1	34	59	59	0.2	0.3
PENT–COGIC	4	425	610	761	2.1	3.2
PENT–Un Pent Ch Intl	13	NR	NR	NR	-	-
PRES–Presb Ch (USA)	1	20	29	36	0.1	0.2
PRES–Presb Ch Amer	1	24	33	45	0.1	0.2
Sev Day Adv	1	46	80	92	0.3	0.4
BIENVILLE	**63**	**2,786**	**8,971**	**10,902**	**76.0**	**100.0**
Bahá'í	0	NR	2	2	0.0	0.0
BAPT–Amer Bapt Assn	1	NR	85	103	0.7	0.9
BAPT–Natl Mis Bapt Conv	1	0	150	182	1.3	1.7
BAPT–NBC USA	2	330	1,500	1,823	12.7	16.7
BAPT–So Bapt Conv	31	1,843	5,309	6,452	45.0	59.2
Catholic	1	NR	NR	86	0.6	0.8
CHR–Chs of Christ	2	90	82	116	0.8	1.1
Jehovah's Witness	1	NR	NR	NR	-	-
METH–C.M.E.	7	35	740	899	6.3	8.2
METH–Un Methodist	9	322	889	997	6.9	9.1
Non-denom Chr Chs	1	100	150	150	1.0	1.4
PENT–Assemb of God	3	66	64	92	0.6	0.8
PENT–Un Pent Ch Intl	4	NR	NR	NR	-	-
BOSSIER	**157**	**18,996**	**51,299**	**70,455**	**60.2**	**100.0**
ANG/EPIS–Episcopal	1	89	184	188	0.2	0.3
Bahá'í	0	NR	37	37	0.0	0.1
BAPT–Amer Bapt Assn	3	NR	961	1,205	1.0	1.7
BAPT–Amer Bapt USA	1	500	1,047	1,313	1.1	1.9
BAPT–Ind Bapt Flwsp Intl	1	NR	NR	NR	-	-
BAPT–Natl Mis Bapt Conv	1	0	150	188	0.2	0.3
BAPT–NBC Amer	6	570	1,220	1,530	1.3	2.2

NR–Not Reported - Represents no adherents reported. Percentages may not total 100 due to rounding.

Table 3: Religious Congregations by County and Group: 2010

Religious Group	Number of Congrega-tions	Number of Attendees	Number of Communicant, Confirmed, or Full Members	Adherents: Number of Adherents	Adherents: % of Total Pop.	Adherents: % of Total Adh.
BAPT–NBC USA	2	675	1,410	1,768	1.5	2.5
BAPT–So Bapt Conv	43	7,883	29,620	37,139	31.7	52.7
Catholic	4	NR	NR	5,890	5.0	8.4
CGOD–Ch God (Ander)	2	70	NR	70	0.1	0.1
Ch of Nazarene	2	73	87	107	0.1	0.2
CHR–Chr Ch (Disc)	1	32	42	53	0.0	0.1
CHR–Chs of Christ	7	994	989	1,342	1.1	1.9
Jehovah's Witness	1	NR	NR	NR	-	-
LDS–L-D Saints	1	NR	NR	1,060	0.9	1.5
LUTH–Luth–MO Synod	1	230	369	453	0.4	0.6
METH–AME	1	0	100	125	0.1	0.2
METH–C.M.E.	15	125	1,950	2,445	2.1	3.5
METH–So Methodist	1	NR	NR	NR	-	-
METH–Un Methodist	10	1,732	4,341	5,099	4.4	7.2
METH–Wesleyan	1	30	39	39	0.0	0.1
Muslim Est	1	134	NR	308	0.3	0.4
Non-denom Chr Chs	21	4,510	6,765	7,127	6.1	10.1
PENT–Assemb of God	8	942	937	1,651	1.4	2.3
PENT–Ch God (Cleve)	2	38	35	44	0.0	0.1
PENT–COGIC	4	240	660	828	0.7	1.2
PENT–Full Gosp Bapt	3	NR	NR	NR	-	-
PENT–Un Pent Ch Intl	7	NR	NR	NR	-	-
PRES–Presb Ch (USA)	6	129	356	446	0.4	0.6
CADDO	**316**	**40,731**	**112,722**	**164,003**	**64.3**	**100.0**
ANG/EPIS–Anglican NA	2	NR	NR	NR	-	-
ANG/EPIS–Episcopal	5	867	2,525	3,037	1.2	1.9
Bahá'í	0	NR	94	94	0.0	0.1
BAPT–Amer Bapt Assn	4	NR	288	356	0.1	0.2
BAPT–Asc Ref Bap Ch Am	1	NR	NR	NR	-	-
BAPT–Free Will Bapt	1	NR	92	114	0.0	0.1
BAPT–Ind Bapt Flwsp Intl	1	NR	NR	NR	-	-
BAPT–Natl Mis Bapt Conv	7	0	1,160	1,435	0.6	0.9
BAPT–NBC Amer	12	2,705	5,975	7,393	2.9	4.5
BAPT–NBC USA	18	4,675	10,714	13,257	5.2	8.1
BAPT–So Bapt Conv	73	15,619	56,981	70,507	27.7	43.0
Calv Chpl	1	NR	NR	NR	-	-
Catholic	10	NR	NR	14,397	5.6	8.8
CGOD–Ch God (Ander)	6	484	NR	484	0.2	0.3
Ch Cr, Scientst	1	NR	NR	NR	-	-
Ch of Chr (Hol)	1	NR	NR	NR	-	-
Ch of Nazarene	5	432	734	919	0.4	0.6
CHR–Chr Ch (Disc)	3	385	752	931	0.4	0.6
CHR–Chr Chs & Chs Cr	4	NR	531	657	0.3	0.4
CHR–Chs of Christ	17	1,861	2,108	2,768	1.1	1.7
HINDU–I/A Temples	1	NR	NR	500	0.2	0.3
HINDU–Post Ren	1	NR	NR	16	0.0	0.0
Jehovah's Witness	5	NR	NR	NR	-	-
JUD–Reform	1	122	216	583	0.2	0.4
LDS–L-D Saints	1	NR	NR	1,237	0.5	0.8
LUTH–E.L.C.A.	3	229	405	471	0.2	0.3
LUTH–Luth–MO Synod	3	241	301	349	0.1	0.2
MENN–Beachy Amish-Menn	1	19	6	19	0.0	0.0
METH–AME	5	70	670	829	0.3	0.5
METH–C.M.E.	13	683	2,492	3,084	1.2	1.9
METH–Free Methodist	1	44	57	57	0.0	0.0
METH–Un Methodist	27	4,248	14,255	18,220	7.1	11.1
Muslim Est	2	194	NR	508	0.2	0.3
Non-denom Chr Chs	5	2,770	4,450	4,450	1.7	2.7
ORTHE–Ant Orth of NA	1	50	NR	100	0.0	0.1
ORTHE–Greek Orthodox	1	110	NR	320	0.1	0.2
ORTHO–Coptic Orth Ch	1	15	NR	25	0.0	0.0
PENT–Assemb of God	14	2,639	2,535	9,520	3.7	5.8
PENT–Ch God (Cleve)	1	30	199	246	0.1	0.1
PENT–Ch of God Proph	1	NR	4	5	0.0	0.0
PENT–COGIC	11	180	1,330	1,646	0.6	1.0
PENT–Full Gosp Bapt	12	NR	NR	NR	-	-
PENT–Int Foursq Gos	1	30	31	38	0.0	0.0
PENT–Intl Pent Holiness	2	475	800	990	0.4	0.6
PENT–Un Pent Ch Intl	12	NR	NR	NR	-	-
PENT–Vineyard	1	41	61	75	0.0	0.0
PRES–Presb Ch (USA)	7	485	1,272	1,574	0.6	1.0
PRES–Presb Ch Amer	1	72	79	102	0.0	0.1
Salvation Army	1	146	209	1,061	0.4	0.6
Sev Day Adv	6	728	1,267	1,457	0.6	0.9
Unit Univ	1	82	129	172	0.1	0.1
Unity Ch	1	NR	NR	NR	-	-
CALCASIEU	**239**	**27,351**	**56,403**	**135,566**	**70.3**	**100.0**
ANG/EPIS–Episcopal	4	455	989	1,112	0.6	0.8
Bahá'í	0	NR	54	54	0.0	0.0
BAPT–Ind Bapt Flwsp Intl	1	NR	NR	NR	-	-
BAPT–Natl Mis Bapt Conv	2	0	300	374	0.2	0.3
BAPT–NBC Amer	3	924	1,425	1,775	0.9	1.3
BAPT–NBC USA	6	1,800	3,302	4,113	2.1	3.0
BAPT–Reg Bapt Gen As	1	NR	NR	NR	-	-
BAPT–So Bapt Conv	51	8,689	26,813	33,397	17.3	24.6
Catholic	20	NR	NR	64,050	33.2	47.2
CGOD–Ch God (Ander)	5	926	NR	926	0.5	0.7
Ch Cr, Scientst	1	NR	NR	NR	-	-
Ch of Nazarene	4	153	256	317	0.2	0.2
Chr & Miss Al	1	18	27	27	0.0	0.0
CHR–Chr Ch (Disc)	2	78	293	365	0.2	0.3
CHR–Chr Chs & Chs Cr	2	NR	235	293	0.2	0.2
CHR–Chs of Christ	9	1,050	1,227	1,572	0.8	1.2
Ind Fund Churches	3	NR	NR	NR	-	-
Intl Fell Bible Ch	1	NR	NR	NR	-	-
Jehovah's Witness	6	NR	NR	NR	-	-
JUD–Reform	1	32	57	154	0.1	0.1
LDS–Comm of Christ	1	NR	110	110	0.1	0.1
LDS–L-D Saints	1	NR	NR	901	0.5	0.7
LUTH–E.L.C.A.	1	30	73	83	0.0	0.1
LUTH–Luth–MO Synod	3	205	237	320	0.2	0.2
METH–AME	2	0	250	311	0.2	0.2
METH–C.M.E.	6	310	1,020	1,270	0.7	0.9
METH–Un Methodist	15	2,088	6,003	7,378	3.8	5.4
Muslim Est	1	134	NR	308	0.2	0.2
Non-denom Chr Chs	34	7,790	10,056	10,476	5.4	7.7
ORTHE–Ant Orth of NA	1	12	NR	33	0.0	0.0
PENT–Assemb of God	10	1,340	1,192	2,599	1.3	1.9
PENT–Ch God (Cleve)	3	64	135	168	0.1	0.1
PENT–Ch Lord Jesus Apos	1	NR	NR	NR	-	-
PENT–COGIC	6	430	787	980	0.5	0.7
PENT–Intl Pent Holiness	1	85	170	212	0.1	0.2
PENT–Un Pent Ch Intl	18	NR	NR	NR	-	-
PENT–Vineyard	2	320	480	598	0.3	0.4
PRES–Presb Ch (USA)	3	114	437	544	0.3	0.4
PRES–Presb Ch Amer	2	101	120	141	0.1	0.1
REF–Comm Ref Evan	1	NR	NR	NR	-	-
Salvation Army	1	77	122	331	0.2	0.2
Sev Day Adv	2	96	168	193	0.1	0.1
Un C of Christ	1	30	65	81	0.0	0.1
CALDWELL	**28**	**2,152**	**4,890**	**6,123**	**60.4**	**100.0**
BAPT–So Bapt Conv	15	1,491	3,857	4,727	46.7	77.2
Catholic	1	NR	NR	92	0.9	1.5
CGOD–Ch God (Ander)	1	25	NR	25	0.2	0.4
CHR–Chs of Christ	1	45	42	55	0.5	0.9
METH–Un Methodist	3	127	360	469	4.6	7.7
Non-denom Chr Chs	3	300	515	550	5.4	9.0
PENT–Assemb of God	1	63	0	63	0.6	1.0
PENT–Ch God (Cleve)	2	101	116	142	1.4	2.3
PENT–Un Pent Ch Intl	1	NR	NR	NR	-	-
CAMERON	**16**	**138**	**1,367**	**5,524**	**80.8**	**100.0**
Bahá'í	0	NR	1	1	0.0	0.0
BAPT–So Bapt Conv	4	99	1,233	1,513	22.1	27.4
Catholic	7	NR	NR	3,800	55.6	68.8
METH–Un Methodist	3	39	133	210	3.1	3.8
PENT–Un Pent Ch Intl	2	NR	NR	NR	-	-
CATAHOULA	**42**	**1,729**	**4,739**	**5,916**	**56.8**	**100.0**
BAPT–NBC USA	1	0	150	182	1.7	3.1
BAPT–Ref Bapt Ch	1	NR	NR	NR	-	-
BAPT–So Bapt Conv	26	1,505	4,205	5,106	49.1	86.3
Catholic	1	NR	NR	115	1.1	1.9

NR–Not Reported - Represents no adherents reported. Percentages may not total 100 due to rounding.

Table 3: Religious Congregations by County and Group: 2010

Religious Group	Number of Congrega-tions	Number of Attendees	Number of Communicant, Confirmed, or Full Members	Adherents: Number of Adherents	Adherents: % of Total Pop.	Adherents: % of Total Adh.
CGOD–Ch God (Ander)	1	39	NR	39	0.4	0.7
Jehovah's Witness	1	NR	NR	NR	-	-
METH–Free Methodist	1	20	24	24	0.2	0.4
METH–Un Methodist	3	39	208	221	2.1	3.7
Non-denom Chr Chs	1	50	60	62	0.6	1.0
PENT–Assemb of God	1	40	22	82	0.8	1.4
PENT–Un Pent Ch Intl	4	NR	NR	NR	-	-
PRES–Presb Ch (USA)	1	36	70	85	0.8	1.4
CLAIBORNE	**63**	**1,937**	**6,707**	**7,957**	**46.3**	**100.0**
Bahá'í	0	NR	2	2	0.0	0.0
BAPT–Amer Bapt Assn	2	NR	160	188	1.1	2.4
BAPT–Ind Bapt Flwsp Intl	1	NR	NR	NR	-	-
BAPT–Natl Mis Bapt Conv	1	0	150	176	1.0	2.2
BAPT–So Bapt Conv	13	982	2,819	3,311	19.3	41.6
Catholic	1	NR	NR	86	0.5	1.1
CGOD–Ch God (Ander)	1	0	NR	0	0.0	0.0
CHR–Chs of Christ	5	229	221	299	1.7	3.8
Jehovah's Witness	1	NR	NR	NR	-	-
METH–C.M.E.	15	0	1,750	2,055	12.0	25.8
METH–So Methodist	2	NR	NR	NR	-	-
METH–Un Methodist	8	336	930	979	5.7	12.3
Non-denom Chr Chs	3	175	253	256	1.5	3.2
PENT–Assemb of God	3	180	110	238	1.4	3.0
PENT–COGIC	2	5	170	200	1.2	2.5
PENT–Un Pent Ch Intl	2	NR	NR	NR	-	-
PRES–Presb Ch (USA)	3	30	142	167	1.0	2.1
CONCORDIA	**44**	**2,487**	**6,580**	**8,580**	**41.2**	**100.0**
ANG/EPIS–Episcopal	1	32	41	41	0.2	0.5
Bahá'í	0	NR	1	1	0.0	0.0
BAPT–NBC USA	2	60	230	285	1.4	3.3
BAPT–So Bapt Conv	16	1,548	5,117	6,339	30.4	73.9
Catholic	2	NR	NR	396	1.9	4.6
CGOD–Ch God (Ander)	3	160	NR	160	0.8	1.9
CHR–Chr Ch (Disc)	2	0	0	0	0.0	0.0
CHR–Chr Chs & Chs Cr	1	NR	125	155	0.7	1.8
CHR–Chs of Christ	3	197	185	215	1.0	2.5
Jehovah's Witness	1	NR	NR	NR	-	-
METH–Free Methodist	1	13	7	13	0.1	0.2
METH–Un Methodist	2	111	400	434	2.1	5.1
Non-denom Chr Chs	1	100	150	150	0.7	1.7
PENT–Assemb of God	3	147	148	173	0.8	2.0
PENT–Ch God (Cleve)	1	77	55	68	0.3	0.8
PENT–Un Pent Ch Intl	3	NR	NR	NR	-	-
PRES–Presb Ch (USA)	2	42	121	150	0.7	1.7
DE SOTO	**86**	**3,696**	**10,894**	**14,784**	**55.5**	**100.0**
ANG/EPIS–Episcopal	1	56	74	106	0.4	0.7
Bahá'í	0	NR	30	30	0.1	0.2
BAPT–Amer Bapt Assn	3	NR	170	210	0.8	1.4
BAPT–So Bapt Conv	30	1,984	7,078	8,728	32.7	59.0
Catholic	2	NR	NR	849	3.2	5.7
CGOD–Ch God (Ander)	1	70	NR	70	0.3	0.5
CHR–Chs of Christ	5	153	164	214	0.8	1.4
Jehovah's Witness	1	NR	NR	NR	-	-
LDS–L-D Saints	1	NR	NR	787	3.0	5.3
METH–AME	1	0	100	123	0.5	0.8
METH–C.M.E.	5	0	600	740	2.8	5.0
METH–So Methodist	1	NR	NR	NR	-	-
METH–Un Methodist	12	458	1,107	1,206	4.5	8.2
Non-denom Chr Chs	6	685	955	975	3.7	6.6
PENT–Assemb of God	3	103	95	116	0.4	0.8
PENT–COGIC	3	70	235	290	1.1	2.0
PENT–Un Pent Ch Intl	5	NR	NR	NR	-	-
PRES–Presb Ch (USA)	5	25	127	157	0.6	1.1
Sev Day Adv	1	92	159	183	0.7	1.2
EAST BATON ROUGE	**436**	**78,697**	**160,811**	**296,951**	**67.5**	**100.0**
ANG/EPIS–Anglican NA	2	NR	NR	NR	-	-
ANG/EPIS–Episcopal	9	1,628	4,749	5,901	1.3	2.0
Bahá'í	2	NR	152	152	0.0	0.1

Religious Group	Number of Congrega-tions	Number of Attendees	Number of Communicant, Confirmed, or Full Members	Adherents: Number of Adherents	Adherents: % of Total Pop.	Adherents: % of Total Adh.
BAPT–Amer Bapt Assn	1	NR	40	49	0.0	0.0
BAPT–Amer Bapt USA	2	700	1,635	2,000	0.5	0.7
BAPT–Asc Ref Bap Ch Am	1	NR	NR	NR	-	-
BAPT–Converge/BGC	1	75	NR	90	0.0	0.0
BAPT–Ind Bapt Flwsp Intl	3	NR	NR	NR	-	-
BAPT–Natl Mis Bapt Conv	3	200	650	795	0.2	0.3
BAPT–NBC Amer	6	3,250	6,111	7,477	1.7	2.5
BAPT–NBC USA	32	7,135	19,211	23,505	5.3	7.9
BAPT–Ref Bapt Ch	1	NR	NR	NR	-	-
BAPT–So Bapt Conv	70	12,563	43,512	53,237	12.1	17.9
BUDD–Mahayana	3	NR	NR	1,022	0.2	0.3
Calv Chpl	2	NR	NR	NR	-	-
Catholic	24	NR	NR	97,904	22.2	33.0
CGOD–Ch God (Ander)	2	199	NR	199	0.0	0.1
Ch Cr, Scientst	1	NR	NR	NR	-	-
Ch of Chr (Hol)	1	NR	NR	NR	-	-
Ch of God Gen Conf	1	NR	5	6	0.0	0.0
Ch of Nazarene	2	179	242	346	0.1	0.1
CHR–Chr Ch (Disc)	1	191	812	993	0.2	0.3
CHR–Chr Chs & Chs Cr	2	NR	85	104	0.0	0.0
CHR–Chs of Christ	12	1,580	1,709	2,329	0.5	0.8
FRND–Fr Gen Cf	1	NR	23	28	0.0	0.0
HINDU–I/A Temples	1	NR	NR	1,000	0.2	0.3
HINDU–Post Ren	3	NR	NR	118	0.0	0.0
HINDU–Trad Temples	2	NR	NR	420	0.1	0.1
Jehovah's Witness	6	NR	NR	NR	-	-
JUD–Reform	2	208	367	991	0.2	0.3
LDS–Comm of Christ	1	NR	187	187	0.0	0.1
LDS–L-D Saints	8	NR	NR	3,657	0.8	1.2
LUTH–E.L.C.A.	2	161	383	462	0.1	0.2
LUTH–Luth-MO Synod	4	513	1,017	1,252	0.3	0.4
LUTH–Wisc Ev Luth Syn	1	53	69	91	0.0	0.0
METH–AME	5	280	1,121	1,372	0.3	0.5
METH–AME Zion	1	0	150	184	0.0	0.1
METH–So Methodist	1	NR	NR	NR	-	-
METH–Un Methodist	27	5,178	18,042	21,858	5.0	7.4
Metro Comm Ch	1	70	65	80	0.0	0.0
Muslim Est	5	616	NR	1,532	0.3	0.5
Non-denom Chr Chs	110	39,655	51,039	55,505	12.6	18.7
ORTHE–Greek Orthodox	1	40	NR	97	0.0	0.0
ORTHE–Orth Ch in Amer	2	75	NR	160	0.0	0.1
ORTHO–Armen Ap Etchm	1	50	NR	200	0.0	0.1
PENT–Assemb of God	7	779	633	1,015	0.2	0.3
PENT–Ch God (Cleve)	4	224	1,061	1,298	0.3	0.4
PENT–COGIC	10	200	1,585	1,939	0.4	0.7
PENT–Full Gosp Bapt	7	NR	NR	NR	-	-
PENT–Intl Pent Holiness	5	407	600	734	0.2	0.2
PENT–Un Pent Ch Intl	11	NR	NR	NR	-	-
PENT–Vineyard	1	175	214	262	0.1	0.1
PRES–Evan Presby Ch	1	NR	1,517	1,856	0.4	0.6
PRES–Korean Pres Amer	1	NR	NR	NR	-	-
PRES–Presb Ch (USA)	7	406	1,179	1,443	0.3	0.5
PRES–Presb Ch Amer	4	580	843	984	0.2	0.3
REF–Comm Ref Evan	1	NR	NR	NR	-	-
Salvation Army	1	381	231	231	0.1	0.1
Sev Day Adv	5	680	1,184	1,361	0.3	0.5
Unit Univ	1	266	388	525	0.1	0.2
Unity Ch	1	NR	NR	NR	-	-
EAST CARROLL	**27**	**690**	**3,896**	**5,011**	**64.6**	**100.0**
ANG/EPIS–Episcopal	1	17	27	27	0.3	0.5
BAPT–Free Will Bapt	1	NR	92	115	1.5	2.3
BAPT–Natl Mis Bapt Conv	5	30	600	750	9.7	15.0
BAPT–NBC USA	1	0	500	625	8.1	12.5
BAPT–Prog NBC	1	105	225	281	3.6	5.6
BAPT–So Bapt Conv	8	343	1,861	2,327	30.0	46.4
Catholic	1	NR	NR	154	2.0	3.1
CHR–Chs of Christ	1	75	75	100	1.3	2.0
MENN–CG in Cr (Menn)	1	NR	63	79	1.0	1.6
METH–AME	1	0	100	125	1.6	2.5
METH–Un Methodist	2	72	238	274	3.5	5.5
PENT–Assemb of God	1	12	14	32	0.4	0.6
PENT–Ch God (Cleve)	1	10	20	25	0.3	0.5
PRES–Presb Ch (USA)	1	0	36	45	0.6	0.9

NR–Not Reported - Represents no adherents reported. Percentages may not total 100 due to rounding.

Table 3: Religious Congregations by County and Group: 2010

Religious Group	Number of Congrega-tions	Number of Attendees	Number of Communicant, Confirmed, or Full Members	Adherents: Number of Adherents	Adherents: % of Total Pop.	Adherents: % of Total Adh.
Sev Day Adv	1	26	45	52	0.7	1.0
EAST FELICIANA	**54**	**2,428**	**7,426**	**9,379**	**46.3**	**100.0**
ANG/EPIS–Anglican NA	1	NR	NR	NR	-	-
ANG/EPIS–Episcopal	1	24	102	102	0.5	1.1
Bahá'í	0	NR	2	2	0.0	0.0
BAPT–Asc Ref Bap Ch Am	1	NR	NR	NR	-	-
BAPT–NBC USA	2	0	850	1,007	5.0	10.7
BAPT–Ref Bapt Ch	1	NR	NR	NR	-	-
BAPT–So Bapt Conv	15	1,319	4,317	5,114	25.2	54.5
Catholic	1	NR	NR	275	1.4	2.9
CHR–Chs of Christ	1	50	45	60	0.3	0.6
Jehovah's Witness	1	NR	NR	NR	-	-
LDS–L-D Saints	1	NR	NR	298	1.5	3.2
LUTH–Luth–MO Synod	1	53	91	110	0.5	1.2
METH–AME	2	22	193	229	1.1	2.4
METH–Un Methodist	16	648	1,443	1,721	8.5	18.3
Non-denom Chr Chs	1	80	75	100	0.5	1.1
PENT–Ch God (Cleve)	1	21	25	30	0.1	0.3
PENT–COGIC	1	100	100	118	0.6	1.3
PENT–Intl Pent Holiness	1	30	50	59	0.3	0.6
PENT–Un Pent Ch Intl	2	NR	NR	NR	-	-
PRES–Presb Ch (USA)	3	29	64	76	0.4	0.8
PRES–Presb Ch Amer	1	52	69	78	0.4	0.8
EVANGELINE	**46**	**2,292**	**5,010**	**25,902**	**76.2**	**100.0**
Bahá'í	0	NR	2	2	0.0	0.0
BAPT–NBC Amer	1	150	250	316	0.9	1.2
BAPT–NBC USA	1	0	100	126	0.4	0.5
BAPT–So Bapt Conv	14	1,321	3,604	4,556	13.4	17.6
Catholic	11	NR	NR	19,656	57.8	75.9
CHR–Chr Chs & Chs Cr	2	NR	20	25	0.1	0.1
CHR–Chs of Christ	3	265	263	332	1.0	1.3
Jehovah's Witness	1	NR	NR	NR	-	-
METH–Un Methodist	3	26	31	48	0.1	0.2
Non-denom Chr Chs	2	200	270	275	0.8	1.1
PENT–Assemb of God	1	140	150	161	0.5	0.6
PENT–Ch God (Cleve)	1	15	15	19	0.1	0.1
PENT–Ch Lord Jesus Apos	1	NR	NR	NR	-	-
PENT–Intl Pent Holiness	2	175	305	386	1.1	1.5
PENT–Un Pent Ch Intl	3	NR	NR	NR	-	-
FRANKLIN	**67**	**3,816**	**11,695**	**14,899**	**71.7**	**100.0**
ANG/EPIS–Episcopal	1	13	18	18	0.1	0.1
BAPT–NBC USA	2	70	250	313	1.5	2.1
BAPT–So Bapt Conv	36	2,811	9,917	12,426	59.8	83.4
Catholic	1	NR	NR	276	1.3	1.9
Ch of Chr (Hol)	2	NR	NR	NR	-	-
Ch of Nazarene	1	37	53	53	0.3	0.4
CHR–Chs of Christ	2	125	122	183	0.9	1.2
Jehovah's Witness	1	NR	NR	NR	-	-
LDS–L-D Saints	1	NR	NR	114	0.5	0.8
METH–Free Methodist	1	12	10	12	0.1	0.1
METH–Un Methodist	6	196	603	681	3.3	4.6
Non-denom Chr Chs	3	435	485	562	2.7	3.8
PENT–Assemb of God	3	74	143	148	0.7	1.0
PENT–Un Pent Ch Intl	3	NR	NR	NR	-	-
PRES–Presb Ch (USA)	3	16	47	59	0.3	0.4
Sev Day Adv	1	27	47	54	0.3	0.4
GRANT	**60**	**2,701**	**7,876**	**10,058**	**45.1**	**100.0**
BAPT–So Bapt Conv	30	2,047	6,852	8,326	37.3	82.8
Catholic	3	NR	NR	520	2.3	5.2
CHR–Chs of Christ	5	203	214	280	1.3	2.8
METH–AME	2	80	135	164	0.7	1.6
METH–AME Zion	1	80	35	43	0.2	0.4
METH–Un Methodist	5	132	412	427	1.9	4.2
METH–Wesleyan	1	64	60	83	0.4	0.8
Non-denom Chr Chs	1	10	5	12	0.1	0.1
PENT–Assemb of God	2	78	79	101	0.5	1.0
PENT–Ch God (Cleve)	1	7	23	28	0.1	0.3
PENT–Ch of God Proph	1	NR	61	74	0.3	0.7
PENT–Un Pent Ch Intl	8	NR	NR	NR	-	-
IBERIA	**65**	**4,611**	**10,204**	**51,521**	**70.3**	**100.0**
ANG/EPIS–Episcopal	1	84	239	239	0.3	0.5
Bahá'í	0	NR	5	5	0.0	0.0
BAPT–Ind Bapt Flwsp Intl	2	NR	NR	NR	-	-
BAPT–Natl Mis Bapt Conv	1	0	150	190	0.3	0.4
BAPT–NBC USA	4	300	949	1,202	1.6	2.3
BAPT–So Bapt Conv	10	789	3,300	4,181	5.7	8.1
Catholic	13	NR	NR	38,914	53.1	75.5
Ch of Nazarene	1	70	79	88	0.1	0.2
Chr & Miss Al	1	23	29	34	0.0	0.1
CHR–Chs of Christ	2	180	253	300	0.4	0.6
Jehovah's Witness	1	NR	NR	NR	-	-
JUD–Reform	1	16	28	76	0.1	0.1
LDS–L-D Saints	1	NR	NR	309	0.4	0.6
METH–C.M.E.	1	0	100	127	0.2	0.2
METH–Un Methodist	6	316	1,138	1,324	1.8	2.6
Non-denom Chr Chs	9	1,625	2,190	2,277	3.1	4.4
PENT–Assemb of God	2	855	944	1,248	1.7	2.4
PENT–COGIC	2	200	550	697	1.0	1.4
PENT–Un Pent Ch Intl	2	NR	NR	NR	-	-
PRES–Presb Ch (USA)	1	25	39	49	0.1	0.1
Sev Day Adv	1	30	52	60	0.1	0.1
Un C of Christ	3	98	159	201	0.3	0.4
IBERVILLE	**40**	**8,905**	**12,935**	**24,919**	**74.6**	**100.0**
ANG/EPIS–Episcopal	2	53	149	174	0.5	0.7
Bahá'í	0	NR	13	13	0.0	0.1
BAPT–NBC USA	3	0	450	544	1.6	2.2
BAPT–Prog NBC	1	0	150	181	0.5	0.7
BAPT–So Bapt Conv	8	454	1,458	1,761	5.3	7.1
Catholic	6	NR	NR	11,068	33.2	44.4
CGOD–Ch God (Ander)	1	0	NR	0	0.0	0.0
CHR–Chs of Christ	1	19	12	20	0.1	0.1
Jehovah's Witness	1	NR	NR	NR	-	-
METH–AME	1	0	100	121	0.4	0.5
METH–Un Methodist	8	195	516	594	1.8	2.4
Muslim Est	1	134	NR	308	0.9	1.2
Non-denom Chr Chs	1	8,000	10,000	10,000	30.0	40.1
PENT–Assemb of God	2	50	63	106	0.3	0.4
PENT–Ch of God Proph	1	NR	24	29	0.1	0.1
PENT–COGIC	1	0	0	0	0.0	0.0
PENT–Un Pent Ch Intl	2	NR	NR	NR	-	-
JACKSON	**63**	**3,367**	**8,474**	**10,635**	**65.3**	**100.0**
BAPT–Amer Bapt Assn	1	NR	0	0	0.0	0.0
BAPT–Natl Mis Bapt Conv	3	0	450	548	3.4	5.2
BAPT–So Bapt Conv	24	2,110	6,137	7,478	46.0	70.3
Catholic	1	NR	NR	150	0.9	1.4
CGOD–Ch God (Ander)	3	87	NR	87	0.5	0.8
Ch of Nazarene	1	0	10	10	0.1	0.1
CHR–Chs of Christ	1	95	80	115	0.7	1.1
Jehovah's Witness	1	NR	NR	NR	-	-
LDS–L-D Saints	1	NR	NR	125	0.8	1.2
METH–C.M.E.	2	48	113	138	0.8	1.3
METH–Cong Meth	1	NR	32	39	0.2	0.4
METH–Un Methodist	10	271	749	807	5.0	7.6
Non-denom Chr Chs	2	200	300	300	1.8	2.8
PENT–Assemb of God	2	290	170	315	1.9	3.0
PENT–COGIC	1	35	43	52	0.3	0.5
PENT–Full Gosp Bapt	1	NR	NR	NR	-	-
PENT–Intl Pent Holiness	3	225	360	439	2.7	4.1
PENT–Un Pent Ch Intl	3	NR	NR	NR	-	-
PRES–Cumber Presb	1	NR	19	19	0.1	0.2
Sev Day Adv	1	6	11	13	0.1	0.1
JEFFERSON	**289**	**36,043**	**61,028**	**233,361**	**53.9**	**100.0**
ANG/EPIS–Episcopal	5	448	1,492	2,119	0.5	0.9
Bahá'í	1	NR	124	124	0.0	0.1
BAPT–Ind Bapt Flwsp Intl	1	NR	NR	NR	-	-
BAPT–Natl Mis Bapt Conv	3	100	500	606	0.1	0.3

NR–Not Reported - Represents no adherents reported. Percentages may not total 100 due to rounding.

Table 3: Religious Congregations by County and Group: 2010

Religious Group	Number of Congregations	Number of Attendees	Number of Communicant, Confirmed, or Full Members	Adherents: Number of Adherents	Adherents: % of Total Pop.	Adherents: % of Total Adh.
BAPT–NBC Amer	2	0	300	364	0.1	0.2
BAPT–NBC USA	11	1,975	3,480	4,218	1.0	1.8
BAPT–So Bapt Conv	46	7,760	16,808	20,371	4.7	8.7
BUDD–Mahayana	2	NR	NR	1,041	0.2	0.4
Calv Chpl	1	NR	NR	NR	-	-
Catholic	43	NR	NR	148,827	34.4	63.8
CGOD–Ch God (Ander)	1	50	NR	50	0.0	0.0
Ch of Chr (Hol)	2	NR	NR	NR	-	-
Ch of Nazarene	1	14	21	21	0.0	0.0
Chr & Miss Al	2	48	84	87	0.0	0.0
CHR–Chr Ch (Disc)	1	59	169	205	0.0	0.1
CHR–Chr Chs & Chs Cr	1	NR	200	242	0.1	0.1
CHR–Chs of Christ	2	425	485	625	0.1	0.3
HINDU–Trad Temples	1	NR	NR	500	0.1	0.2
Ind Fund Churches	1	NR	NR	NR	-	-
Jain	1	NR	NR	NR	-	-
Jehovah's Witness	6	NR	NR	NR	-	-
JUD–Conserv	1	210	236	637	0.1	0.3
JUD–Orth	2	443	200	615	0.1	0.3
JUD–Reform	1	251	443	1,196	0.3	0.5
LDS–L-D Saints	3	NR	NR	2,737	0.6	1.2
LUTH–E.L.C.A.	3	261	600	837	0.2	0.4
LUTH–Luth–MO Synod	7	797	1,506	1,892	0.4	0.8
MENN–Mennonite USA	1	80	75	91	0.0	0.0
METH–AME	3	75	650	788	0.2	0.3
METH–C.M.E.	1	0	100	121	0.0	0.1
METH–Un Methodist	11	1,080	4,008	4,926	1.1	2.1
Muslim Est	2	1,034	NR	2,808	0.6	1.2
Non-denom Chr Chs	46	13,445	19,243	20,207	4.7	8.7
ORTHE–Ant Orth of NA	1	90	NR	300	0.1	0.1
PENT–Assemb of God	13	2,992	2,968	7,940	1.8	3.4
PENT–Ch God (Cleve)	8	1,003	1,204	1,459	0.3	0.6
PENT–Ch of God Proph	4	NR	133	161	0.0	0.1
PENT–COGIC	6	252	1,070	1,297	0.3	0.6
PENT–Full Gosp Bapt	6	NR	NR	NR	-	-
PENT–Int Foursq Gos	3	127	133	161	0.0	0.1
PENT–Intl Pent Holiness	1	45	57	69	0.0	0.0
PENT–Un Pent Ch Intl	7	NR	NR	NR	-	-
PENT–Vineyard	1	1,595	2,000	2,424	0.6	1.0
PRES–Cumber Presb	1	NR	6	38	0.0	0.0
PRES–Presb Ch (USA)	7	406	1,021	1,237	0.3	0.5
PRES–Presb Ch Amer	2	120	115	156	0.0	0.1
Salvation Army	1	94	64	64	0.0	0.0
Sev Day Adv	7	604	1,051	1,208	0.3	0.5
Tao	1	NR	NR	NR	-	-
Un C of Christ	3	160	482	584	0.1	0.3
Unity Ch	1	NR	NR	NR	-	-
Zoroastrian	1	NR	NR	8	0.0	0.0
JEFFERSON DAVIS	**50**	**2,462**	**6,270**	**24,233**	**76.7**	**100.0**
ANG/EPIS–Episcopal	1	21	19	27	0.1	0.1
Bahá'í	0	NR	1	1	0.0	0.0
BAPT–Amer Bapt Assn	1	NR	85	107	0.3	0.4
BAPT–NBC USA	1	0	150	189	0.6	0.8
BAPT–So Bapt Conv	10	1,182	3,507	4,408	14.0	18.2
BRETH–Ch of Brethren	1	0	91	114	0.4	0.5
Catholic	11	NR	NR	16,100	51.0	66.4
CHR–Chr Chs & Chs Cr	1	NR	150	189	0.6	0.8
CHR–Chs of Christ	2	195	214	278	0.9	1.1
Jehovah's Witness	1	NR	NR	NR	-	-
LDS–L-D Saints	1	NR	NR	229	0.7	0.9
LUTH–Luth–MO Synod	1	24	73	99	0.3	0.4
METH–C.M.E.	1	0	150	189	0.6	0.8
METH–Un Methodist	8	324	1,172	1,278	4.0	5.3
Non-denom Chr Chs	3	555	525	718	2.3	3.0
PENT–Assemb of God	2	161	20	165	0.5	0.7
PENT–COGIC	1	0	50	63	0.2	0.3
PENT–Un Pent Ch Intl	2	NR	NR	NR	-	-
PRES–Presb Ch (USA)	2	0	63	79	0.3	0.3
LAFAYETTE	**136**	**22,389**	**54,511**	**169,427**	**76.5**	**100.0**
ANG/EPIS–Episcopal	3	523	802	1,314	0.6	0.8
Bahá'í	1	NR	82	82	0.0	0.0

Religious Group	Number of Congregations	Number of Attendees	Number of Communicant, Confirmed, or Full Members	Adherents: Number of Adherents	Adherents: % of Total Pop.	Adherents: % of Total Adh.
BAPT–NBC USA	3	1,200	19,625	24,251	10.9	14.3
BAPT–Ref Bapt Ch	1	NR	NR	NR	-	-
BAPT–So Bapt Conv	20	5,380	11,497	14,207	6.4	8.4
BUDD–Vajrayana	1	NR	NR	53	0.0	0.0
Calv Chpl	1	NR	NR	NR	-	-
Catholic	28	NR	NR	99,935	45.1	59.0
CGOD–Ch God (Ander)	1	12	NR	12	0.0	0.0
Ch Cr, Scientst	1	NR	NR	NR	-	-
CHR–Chr Ch (Disc)	1	0	76	94	0.0	0.1
CHR–Chr Chs & Chs Cr	1	NR	90	111	0.1	0.1
CHR–Chs of Christ	4	547	536	706	0.3	0.4
Christian Brethren	1	NR	NR	NR	-	-
FRND–Fr Gen Cf	1	NR	0	0	0.0	0.0
Jehovah's Witness	4	NR	NR	NR	-	-
JUD–Reform	1	37	65	176	0.1	0.1
LDS–L-D Saints	1	NR	NR	1,208	0.5	0.7
LUTH–E.L.C.A.	1	176	335	476	0.2	0.3
LUTH–Luth–MO Synod	1	56	98	118	0.1	0.1
METH–C.M.E.	4	0	450	556	0.3	0.3
METH–Un Methodist	7	1,315	5,307	6,356	2.9	3.8
Muslim Est	1	134	NR	308	0.1	0.2
Non-denom Chr Chs	24	7,445	10,034	10,747	4.9	6.3
ORTHE–Ant Orth of NA	1	50	NR	130	0.1	0.1
ORTHO–Coptic Orth Ch	1	25	NR	34	0.0	0.0
PENT–Assemb of God	5	3,484	2,232	4,441	2.0	2.6
PENT–Ch God (Cleve)	1	40	138	171	0.1	0.1
PENT–Ch Lord Jesus Apos	1	NR	NR	NR	-	-
PENT–COGIC	2	0	300	371	0.2	0.2
PENT–Intl Pent Holiness	1	1,400	2,000	2,471	1.1	1.5
PENT–Un Pent Ch Intl	3	NR	NR	NR	-	-
PENT–Vineyard	1	150	215	266	0.1	0.2
PRES–Presb Ch (USA)	3	227	365	451	0.2	0.3
PRES–Presb Ch Amer	1	45	43	50	0.0	0.0
Salvation Army	1	20	24	103	0.0	0.1
Sev Day Adv	2	103	179	206	0.1	0.1
Unit Univ	1	20	18	23	0.0	0.0
LAFOURCHE	**71**	**2,927**	**6,780**	**63,861**	**66.3**	**100.0**
ANG/EPIS–Episcopal	1	59	125	256	0.3	0.4
Bahá'í	0	NR	140	140	0.1	0.2
BAPT–Natl Mis Bapt Conv	1	0	150	185	0.2	0.3
BAPT–NBC USA	2	70	130	160	0.2	0.3
BAPT–So Bapt Conv	14	837	3,301	4,075	4.2	6.4
Catholic	19	NR	NR	55,450	57.6	86.8
CHR–Chs of Christ	5	166	166	193	0.2	0.3
Jehovah's Witness	5	NR	NR	NR	-	-
METH–AME	1	0	150	185	0.2	0.3
METH–Un Methodist	5	340	1,057	1,081	1.1	1.7
Non-denom Chr Chs	5	935	1,120	1,244	1.3	1.9
PENT–Assemb of God	4	386	225	626	0.6	1.0
PENT–Int Foursq Gos	1	13	5	6	0.0	0.0
PENT–Un Pent Ch Intl	3	NR	NR	NR	-	-
PRES–Evan Presby Ch	1	NR	0	0	0.0	0.0
PRES–Presb Ch (USA)	3	117	204	252	0.3	0.4
Sev Day Adv	1	4	7	8	0.0	0.0
LA SALLE	**56**	**3,013**	**7,589**	**9,372**	**62.9**	**100.0**
BAPT–Natl Mis Bapt Conv	1	0	150	184	1.2	2.0
BAPT–So Bapt Conv	28	2,496	6,219	7,626	51.2	81.4
Catholic	2	NR	NR	90	0.6	1.0
Ch of Nazarene	2	36	62	106	0.7	1.1
CHR–Chs of Christ	2	60	54	69	0.5	0.7
Jehovah's Witness	1	NR	NR	NR	-	-
METH–C.M.E.	1	0	150	184	1.2	2.0
METH–Free Methodist	2	58	33	58	0.4	0.6
METH–Un Methodist	6	162	588	672	4.5	7.2
Non-denom Chr Chs	1	75	150	150	1.0	1.6
PENT–Assemb of God	3	112	134	173	1.2	1.8
PENT–Ch God (Cleve)	1	14	49	60	0.4	0.6
PENT–Un Pent Ch Intl	6	NR	NR	NR	-	-
LINCOLN	**82**	**6,775**	**17,916**	**23,395**	**50.1**	**100.0**
ANG/EPIS–Episcopal	2	122	213	213	0.5	0.9

NR–Not Reported   - Represents no adherents reported.   Percentages may not total 100 due to rounding.

Table 3: Religious Congregations by County and Group: 2010

Religious Group	Number of Congrega-tions	Number of Attendees	Number of Communicant, Confirmed, or Full Members	Adherents: Number of Adherents	Adherents: % of Total Pop.	Adherents: % of Total Adh.
Bahá'í	0	NR	5	5	0.0	0.0
BAPT–Amer Bapt Assn	1	NR	150	179	0.4	0.8
BAPT–Ind Bapt Flwsp Intl	1	NR	NR	NR	-	-
BAPT–Natl Mis Bapt Conv	2	75	270	321	0.7	1.4
BAPT–NBC USA	6	190	1,025	1,220	2.6	5.2
BAPT–So Bapt Conv	26	3,962	11,437	13,614	29.1	58.2
Catholic	2	NR	NR	1,427	3.1	6.1
CGOD–Ch God (Ander)	1	24	NR	24	0.1	0.1
Ch of Nazarene	1	38	31	112	0.2	0.5
CHR–Chs of Christ	4	276	261	315	0.7	1.3
FRND–Fr Gen Cf	1	NR	0	0	0.0	0.0
Jehovah's Witness	1	NR	NR	NR	-	-
LDS–L-D Saints	1	NR	NR	400	0.9	1.7
LUTH–Luth–MO Synod	1	11	18	18	0.0	0.1
METH–AME	1	0	150	179	0.4	0.8
METH–C.M.E.	4	40	375	446	1.0	1.9
METH–Un Methodist	9	1,220	2,908	3,295	7.1	14.1
Muslim Est	1	134	NR	308	0.7	1.3
PENT–Assemb of God	2	142	162	237	0.5	1.0
PENT–COGIC	2	300	500	595	1.3	2.5
PENT–Full Gosp Bapt	3	NR	NR	NR	-	-
PENT–Intl Pent Holiness	1	55	80	95	0.2	0.4
PENT–Un Pent Ch Intl	6	NR	NR	NR	-	-
PRES–Presb Ch (USA)	2	122	251	299	0.6	1.3
PRES–Presb Ch Amer	1	64	80	93	0.2	0.4
LIVINGSTON	**123**	**14,450**	**36,788**	**63,138**	**49.3**	**100.0**
ANG/EPIS–Episcopal	1	68	126	126	0.1	0.2
Bahá'í	0	NR	10	10	0.0	0.0
BAPT–Ref Bapt Ch	1	NR	NR	NR	-	-
BAPT–So Bapt Conv	57	7,688	24,643	31,412	24.5	49.8
Catholic	4	NR	NR	16,154	12.6	25.6
CGOD–Ch God (Ander)	1	60	NR	60	0.0	0.1
Ch of God Gen Conf	1	NR	115	147	0.1	0.2
Ch of Nazarene	1	0	29	29	0.0	0.0
CHR–Chs of Christ	3	139	129	179	0.1	0.3
Jehovah's Witness	1	NR	NR	NR	-	-
LDS–L-D Saints	2	NR	NR	1,276	1.0	2.0
METH–AME	1	0	100	127	0.1	0.2
METH–Un Methodist	12	1,643	3,783	5,168	4.0	8.2
Non-denom Chr Chs	16	3,920	6,305	6,457	5.0	10.2
PENT–Assemb of God	2	480	740	762	0.6	1.2
PENT–Ch of God Proph	2	NR	40	51	0.0	0.1
PENT–COGIC	3	69	280	357	0.3	0.6
PENT–Intl Pent Holiness	3	170	260	331	0.3	0.5
PENT–Pent Ch of God	2	140	NR	217	0.2	0.3
PENT–Un Pent Ch Intl	8	NR	NR	NR	-	-
PRES–Presb Ch (USA)	1	0	101	129	0.1	0.2
Sev Day Adv	1	73	127	146	0.1	0.2
MADISON	**16**	**556**	**3,854**	**4,822**	**39.9**	**100.0**
ANG/EPIS–Episcopal	1	18	54	54	0.4	1.1
BAPT–NBC USA	3	0	670	826	6.8	17.1
BAPT–So Bapt Conv	4	317	2,445	3,014	24.9	62.5
Catholic	1	NR	NR	94	0.8	1.9
CHR–Chs of Christ	1	30	32	42	0.3	0.9
METH–AME	1	0	100	123	1.0	2.6
METH–AME Zion	1	75	125	154	1.3	3.2
METH–Un Methodist	1	79	314	379	3.1	7.9
PENT–Un Pent Ch Intl	1	NR	NR	NR	-	-
PRES–Presb Ch (USA)	1	0	50	62	0.5	1.3
Sev Day Adv	1	37	64	74	0.6	1.5
MOREHOUSE	**80**	**4,342**	**12,530**	**16,480**	**58.9**	**100.0**
ANG/EPIS–Episcopal	3	112	178	262	0.9	1.6
Bahá'í	0	NR	1	1	0.0	0.0
BAPT–Amer Bapt Assn	2	NR	850	1,053	3.8	6.4
BAPT–Free Will Bapt	1	NR	92	114	0.4	0.7
BAPT–Natl Mis Bapt Conv	4	160	765	948	3.4	5.8
BAPT–NBC Amer	1	175	200	248	0.9	1.5
BAPT–NBC USA	1	50	0	0	0.0	0.0
BAPT–So Bapt Conv	25	1,941	7,075	8,768	31.3	53.2
Catholic	1	NR	NR	393	1.4	2.4
CGOD–Ch God (Ander)	3	164	NR	164	0.6	1.0
CHR–Chs of Christ	3	265	417	514	1.8	3.1
Jehovah's Witness	1	NR	NR	NR	-	-
LDS–L-D Saints	1	NR	NR	330	1.2	2.0
METH–AME	1	0	100	124	0.4	0.8
METH–C.M.E.	4	0	500	620	2.2	3.8
METH–Un Methodist	10	330	949	1,029	3.7	6.2
Non-denom Chr Chs	3	350	500	500	1.8	3.0
PENT–Assemb of God	5	369	364	636	2.3	3.9
PENT–Ch God (Cleve)	2	106	119	147	0.5	0.9
PENT–COGIC	5	250	360	446	1.6	2.7
PENT–Full Gosp Bapt	1	NR	NR	NR	-	-
PENT–Pent Ch of God	1	70	NR	109	0.4	0.7
PENT–Un Pent Ch Intl	1	NR	NR	NR	-	-
PRES–Presb Ch (USA)	1	0	60	74	0.3	0.4
NATCHITOCHES	**113**	**4,988**	**11,992**	**19,562**	**49.4**	**100.0**
ANG/EPIS–Episcopal	1	88	144	157	0.4	0.8
Bahá'í	0	NR	12	12	0.0	0.1
BAPT–Amer Bapt Assn	1	NR	85	105	0.3	0.5
BAPT–Natl Mis Bapt Conv	1	0	150	185	0.5	0.9
BAPT–NBC Amer	1	60	65	80	0.2	0.4
BAPT–So Bapt Conv	40	2,634	7,479	9,243	23.4	47.2
Catholic	15	NR	NR	4,602	11.6	23.5
CGOD–Ch God (Ander)	1	0	NR	0	0.0	0.0
Ch of Nazarene	1	40	47	62	0.2	0.3
CHR–Chs of Christ	2	150	185	260	0.7	1.3
Jehovah's Witness	1	NR	NR	NR	-	-
LDS–L-D Saints	1	NR	NR	375	0.9	1.9
LUTH–Luth–MO Synod	1	54	68	81	0.2	0.4
METH–AME	1	0	100	124	0.3	0.6
METH–Cong Meth	3	NR	105	130	0.3	0.7
METH–Free Methodist	1	30	32	32	0.1	0.2
METH–So Methodist	1	NR	NR	NR	-	-
METH–Un Methodist	10	456	1,495	1,506	3.8	7.7
Muslim Est	1	15	NR	15	0.0	0.1
Non-denom Chr Chs	9	970	1,170	1,300	3.3	6.6
PENT–Assemb of God	4	129	52	301	0.8	1.5
PENT–COGIC	3	200	550	680	1.7	3.5
PENT–Full Gosp Bapt	1	NR	NR	NR	-	-
PENT–Int Foursq Gos	1	10	12	15	0.0	0.1
PENT–Un Pent Ch Intl	7	NR	NR	NR	-	-
PRES–Cumber Presb	1	NR	9	24	0.1	0.1
PRES–Orth Pres Ch	1	17	13	15	0.0	0.1
PRES–Presb Ch (USA)	1	45	64	79	0.2	0.4
Sev Day Adv	2	90	155	179	0.5	0.9
ORLEANS	**331**	**32,048**	**62,505**	**191,588**	**55.7**	**100.0**
ANG/EPIS–Anglican NA	1	NR	NR	NR	-	-
ANG/EPIS–Episcopal	14	1,551	3,466	5,271	1.5	2.8
Bahá'í	1	NR	111	111	0.0	0.1
BAPT–Alliance Bapt	1	NR	NR	NR	-	-
BAPT–Amer Bapt Assn	1	NR	85	102	0.0	0.1
BAPT–Amer Bapt USA	2	580	1,725	2,066	0.6	1.1
BAPT–Converge/BGC	1	75	NR	90	0.0	0.0
BAPT–Natl Mis Bapt Conv	14	0	2,700	3,233	0.9	1.7
BAPT–NBC Amer	8	1,376	3,422	4,098	1.2	2.1
BAPT–NBC USA	23	2,201	7,701	9,221	2.7	4.8
BAPT–Prog NBC	1	500	2,000	2,395	0.7	1.3
BAPT–So Bapt Conv	43	7,810	12,325	14,758	4.3	7.7
BUDD–Mahayana	6	NR	NR	2,412	0.7	1.3
BUDD–Theravada	1	NR	NR	14	0.0	0.0
BUDD–Vajrayana	1	NR	NR	78	0.0	0.0
Catholic	53	NR	NR	106,088	30.9	55.4
Ch Cr, Scientst	2	NR	NR	NR	-	-
Ch of Chr (Hol)	2	NR	NR	NR	-	-
Ch of Nazarene	3	126	174	195	0.1	0.1
CHR–Chr Ch (Disc)	2	14	55	66	0.0	0.0
CHR–Chs of Christ	7	621	536	681	0.2	0.4
CHR–Int Chs of Christ	1	NR	106	127	0.0	0.1
Evan Free Ch	1	120	NR	120	0.0	0.1
FRND–Fr Gen Cf	1	NR	33	40	0.0	0.0
HINDU–I/A Temples	1	NR	NR	1,562	0.5	0.8

NR–Not Reported - Represents no adherents reported. Percentages may not total 100 due to rounding.

Table 3: Religious Congregations by County and Group: 2010

Religious Group	Number of Congregations	Number of Attendees	Number of Communicant, Confirmed, or Full Members	Adherents		
				Number of Adherents	% of Total Pop.	% of Total Adh.
HINDU–Post Ren	1	NR	NR	16	0.0	0.0
Ind Fund Churches	1	NR	NR	NR	-	-
Jehovah's Witness	2	NR	NR	NR	-	-
JUD–Orth	2	162	100	225	0.1	0.1
JUD–Reform	2	694	1,224	3,305	1.0	1.7
LDS–L-D Saints	2	NR	NR	2,252	0.7	1.2
LUTH–E.L.C.A.	3	230	608	717	0.2	0.4
LUTH–Luth-MO Synod	13	713	1,420	1,615	0.5	0.8
LUTH–Wisc Ev Luth Syn	1	58	128	138	0.0	0.1
METH–AME	12	270	1,750	2,095	0.6	1.1
METH–AME Zion	1	0	100	120	0.0	0.1
METH–C.M.E.	1	0	100	120	0.0	0.1
METH–Un Methodist	22	2,147	5,878	6,568	1.9	3.4
Metro Comm Ch	1	57	80	96	0.0	0.1
MJEW–Union Mes Cong	1	NR	NR	NR	-	-
Muslim Est	6	804	NR	1,848	0.5	1.0
Non-denom Chr Chs	3	8,002	9,550	10,050	2.9	5.2
ORTHE–Greek Orthodox	1	150	NR	900	0.3	0.5
ORTHO–Coptic Orth Ch	1	103	NR	119	0.0	0.1
ORTHO–Malan Dioc Am	1	10	NR	30	0.0	0.0
PENT–Assemb of God	7	389	330	638	0.2	0.3
PENT–Ch God (Cleve)	2	294	142	170	0.0	0.1
PENT–Ch Lord Jesus Apos	2	NR	NR	NR	-	-
PENT–COGIC	10	163	851	1,019	0.3	0.5
PENT–Full Gosp Bapt	8	NR	NR	NR	-	-
PENT–Un Pent Ch Intl	6	NR	NR	NR	-	-
PRES–Evan Presby Ch	1	NR	258	309	0.1	0.2
PRES–Presb Ch (USA)	8	514	1,328	1,590	0.5	0.8
PRES–Presb Ch Amer	2	141	148	190	0.1	0.1
Sev Day Adv	6	1,953	3,396	3,906	1.1	2.0
Sikh	1	NR	NR	NR	-	-
Un C of Christ	7	119	535	641	0.2	0.3
Unit Univ	2	101	140	181	0.1	0.1
Unity Ch	1	NR	NR	NR	-	-
Zoroastrian	0	NR	NR	2	0.0	0.0
OUACHITA	**245**	**25,099**	**67,236**	**96,460**	**62.8**	**100.0**
ANG/EPIS–Anglican NA	1	NR	NR	NR	-	-
ANG/EPIS–Episcopal	4	346	989	1,208	0.8	1.3
Bahá'í	0	NR	33	33	0.0	0.0
BAPT–Alliance Bapt	1	NR	NR	NR	-	-
BAPT–Amer Bapt Assn	4	NR	671	843	0.5	0.9
BAPT–Free Will Bapt	1	NR	92	116	0.1	0.1
BAPT–Ind Bapt Flwsp Intl	2	NR	NR	NR	-	-
BAPT–Natl Mis Bapt Conv	3	0	450	565	0.4	0.6
BAPT–NBC Amer	2	140	300	377	0.2	0.4
BAPT–NBC USA	13	1,075	4,325	5,430	3.5	5.6
BAPT–So Bapt Conv	61	11,264	38,074	47,806	31.1	49.6
Catholic	7	NR	NR	10,152	6.6	10.5
CGOD–Ch God (Ander)	4	365	NR	365	0.2	0.4
Ch of Chr (Hol)	1	NR	NR	NR	-	-
Ch of Nazarene	3	64	183	192	0.1	0.2
CHR–Chr Ch (Disc)	1	59	150	188	0.1	0.2
CHR–Chs of Christ	15	2,097	2,267	2,751	1.8	2.9
Jehovah's Witness	2	NR	NR	NR	-	-
JUD–Reform	1	42	74	200	0.1	0.2
LDS–Comm of Christ	2	NR	162	162	0.1	0.2
LDS–L-D Saints	2	NR	NR	1,353	0.9	1.4
LUTH–E.L.C.A.	1	21	50	52	0.0	0.1
LUTH–Luth-MO Synod	1	93	206	268	0.2	0.3
METH–AME	3	0	400	502	0.3	0.5
METH–C.M.E.	6	0	700	879	0.6	0.9
METH–So Methodist	1	NR	NR	NR	-	-
METH–Un Methodist	20	2,417	7,438	8,967	5.8	9.3
METH–Wesleyan	1	71	74	92	0.1	0.1
Muslim Est	2	141	NR	323	0.2	0.3
Non-denom Chr Chs	27	2,960	4,446	4,585	3.0	4.8
ORTHE–Greek Orthodox	1	17	NR	30	0.0	0.0
PENT–Assemb of God	19	2,109	1,505	3,191	2.1	3.3
PENT–Ch God (Cleve)	4	922	2,442	3,066	2.0	3.2
PENT–COGIC	5	455	920	1,155	0.8	1.2
PENT–Fire Bapt Hol Ch	1	NR	NR	NR	-	-
PENT–Full Gosp Bapt	3	NR	NR	NR	-	-
PENT–Intl Pent Holiness	1	100	150	188	0.1	0.2

Religious Group	Number of Congregations	Number of Attendees	Number of Communicant, Confirmed, or Full Members	Adherents		
				Number of Adherents	% of Total Pop.	% of Total Adh.
PENT–Un Pent Ch Intl	8	NR	NR	NR	-	-
PRES–As Ref Pres Ch	1	NR	49	62	0.0	0.1
PRES–Evan Presby Ch	1	NR	152	191	0.1	0.2
PRES–Presb Ch (USA)	3	90	480	603	0.4	0.6
PRES–Presb Ch Amer	1	23	7	9	0.0	0.0
REF–Comm Ref Evan	1	NR	NR	NR	-	-
Salvation Army	1	33	108	166	0.1	0.2
Sev Day Adv	3	195	339	390	0.3	0.4
PLAQUEMINES	**28**	**997**	**3,420**	**13,077**	**56.8**	**100.0**
Bahá'í	0	NR	19	19	0.1	0.1
BAPT–So Bapt Conv	3	186	2,196	2,777	12.1	21.2
Catholic	9	NR	NR	8,790	38.1	67.2
Ch of Nazarene	1	9	25	94	0.4	0.7
CHR–Chs of Christ	1	60	42	60	0.3	0.5
MENN–Mennonite USA	1	22	12	15	0.1	0.1
METH–Un Methodist	2	98	338	409	1.8	3.1
Non-denom Chr Chs	7	540	750	815	3.5	6.2
PENT–Assemb of God	3	82	38	98	0.4	0.7
PENT–Un Pent Ch Intl	1	NR	NR	NR	-	-
POINTE COUPEE	**27**	**716**	**2,249**	**13,507**	**59.2**	**100.0**
ANG/EPIS–Episcopal	3	76	294	320	1.4	2.4
Bahá'í	0	NR	1	1	0.0	0.0
BAPT–NBC USA	2	200	400	489	2.1	3.6
BAPT–So Bapt Conv	8	359	1,291	1,580	6.9	11.7
Catholic	5	NR	NR	10,808	47.4	80.0
Jehovah's Witness	1	NR	NR	NR	-	-
METH–AME	1	0	100	122	0.5	0.9
METH–Un Methodist	5	81	163	187	0.8	1.4
PENT–Un Pent Ch Intl	2	NR	NR	NR	-	-
RAPIDES	**255**	**23,800**	**56,268**	**93,205**	**70.8**	**100.0**
ANG/EPIS–Episcopal	5	396	963	1,097	0.8	1.2
Bahá'í	0	NR	10	10	0.0	0.0
BAPT–Amer Bapt Assn	2	NR	485	606	0.5	0.7
BAPT–Ind Bapt Flwsp Intl	2	NR	NR	NR	-	-
BAPT–Natl Mis Bapt Conv	3	0	450	562	0.4	0.6
BAPT–NBC Amer	4	796	1,625	2,031	1.5	2.2
BAPT–NBC USA	8	990	1,600	2,000	1.5	2.1
BAPT–Ref Bapt Ch	1	NR	NR	NR	-	-
BAPT–So Bapt Conv	91	11,091	36,210	45,258	34.4	48.6
BUDD–Mahayana	1	NR	NR	14	0.0	0.0
Catholic	20	NR	NR	21,160	16.1	22.7
CGOD–Ch God (Ander)	5	170	NR	170	0.1	0.2
Ch Cr, Scientst	1	NR	NR	NR	-	-
Ch of Nazarene	1	34	76	77	0.1	0.1
CHR–Chr Ch (Disc)	1	0	25	31	0.0	0.0
CHR–Chr Chs & Chs Cr	3	NR	110	137	0.1	0.1
CHR–Chs of Christ	7	476	453	640	0.5	0.7
Jehovah's Witness	2	NR	NR	NR	-	-
JUD–Conserv	1	29	32	86	0.1	0.1
JUD–Reform	1	56	98	265	0.2	0.3
LDS–Comm of Christ	1	NR	81	81	0.1	0.1
LDS–L-D Saints	2	NR	NR	1,043	0.8	1.1
LUTH–Luth-MO Synod	3	124	289	348	0.3	0.4
LUTH–Wisc Ev Luth Syn	1	28	54	67	0.1	0.1
METH–A.W.M.C.	1	23	0	23	0.0	0.0
METH–AME	3	0	300	375	0.3	0.4
METH–C.M.E.	1	0	150	187	0.1	0.2
METH–Evan Meth Ch	1	NR	NR	NR	-	-
METH–Free Methodist	3	126	214	214	0.2	0.2
METH–Un Methodist	20	1,335	3,730	4,504	3.4	4.8
METH–Wesleyan	1	137	95	178	0.1	0.2
Muslim Est	1	134	NR	308	0.2	0.3
Non-denom Chr Chs	18	6,775	7,205	9,028	6.9	9.7
PENT–Assemb of God	6	525	410	724	0.6	0.8
PENT–Ch God (Cleve)	1	29	37	46	0.0	0.0
PENT–Ch Lord Jesus Apos	1	NR	NR	NR	-	-
PENT–COGIC	3	20	325	406	0.3	0.4
PENT–Un Pent Ch Intl	19	NR	NR	NR	-	-
PRES–Evan Presby Ch	1	NR	258	322	0.2	0.3
PRES–Orth Pres Ch	1	50	52	62	0.0	0.1

NR–Not Reported - Represents no adherents reported. Percentages may not total 100 due to rounding.

Table 3: Religious Congregations by County and Group: 2010

Religious Group	Number of Congregations	Number of Attendees	Number of Communicant, Confirmed, or Full Members	Adherents: Number of Adherents	Adherents: % of Total Pop.	Adherents: % of Total Adh.
PRES–Presb Ch (USA)	3	33	170	212	0.2	0.2
Salvation Army	1	13	57	124	0.1	0.1
Sev Day Adv	3	402	698	803	0.6	0.9
Unit Univ	1	8	6	6	0.0	0.0
RED RIVER	**26**	**1,274**	**2,727**	**3,679**	**40.5**	**100.0**
Bahá'í	0	NR	3	3	0.0	0.1
BAPT–So Bapt Conv	6	486	1,547	1,928	21.2	52.4
Catholic	1	NR	NR	187	2.1	5.1
CHR–Chs of Christ	1	13	12	16	0.2	0.4
Jehovah's Witness	1	NR	NR	NR	-	-
LDS–L-D Saints	1	NR	NR	204	2.2	5.5
METH–So Methodist	1	NR	NR	NR	-	-
METH–Un Methodist	4	89	279	332	3.7	9.0
Non-denom Chr Chs	5	240	330	338	3.7	9.2
PENT–Assemb of God	1	40	40	40	0.4	1.1
PENT–COGIC	1	200	200	249	2.7	6.8
PENT–Intl Pent Holiness	1	140	200	249	2.7	6.8
PENT–Un Pent Ch Intl	2	NR	NR	NR	-	-
Sev Day Adv	1	66	116	133	1.5	3.6
RICHLAND	**70**	**3,926**	**9,927**	**12,674**	**61.2**	**100.0**
ANG/EPIS–Episcopal	1	19	71	71	0.3	0.6
Bahá'í	0	NR	1	1	0.0	0.0
BAPT–NBC USA	3	350	615	769	3.7	6.1
BAPT–So Bapt Conv	29	2,311	6,580	8,223	39.7	64.9
Catholic	2	NR	NR	325	1.6	2.6
CGOD–Ch God (Ander)	1	17	NR	17	0.1	0.1
CHR–Chs of Christ	4	275	270	356	1.7	2.8
Jehovah's Witness	1	NR	NR	NR	-	-
METH–AME	3	20	300	375	1.8	3.0
METH–C.M.E.	1	0	150	187	0.9	1.5
METH–Un Methodist	7	277	829	907	4.4	7.2
Non-denom Chr Chs	1	150	130	188	0.9	1.5
PENT–Assemb of God	4	174	177	294	1.4	2.3
PENT–Ch God (Cleve)	4	133	160	200	1.0	1.6
PENT–COGIC	2	0	300	375	1.8	3.0
PENT–Un Pent Ch Intl	3	NR	NR	NR	-	-
PRES–Presb Ch (USA)	2	0	25	31	0.1	0.2
PRES–Presb Ch Amer	1	200	319	355	1.7	2.8
Sev Day Adv	1	0	0	0	0.0	0.0
SABINE	**101**	**4,442**	**11,494**	**19,817**	**81.8**	**100.0**
Bahá'í	0	NR	1	1	0.0	0.0
BAPT–Amer Bapt Assn	1	NR	85	105	0.4	0.5
BAPT–Ind Bapt Flwsp Intl	1	NR	NR	NR	-	-
BAPT–NBC USA	1	101	301	371	1.5	1.9
BAPT–So Bapt Conv	55	3,075	9,016	11,121	45.9	56.1
Catholic	4	NR	NR	4,974	20.5	25.1
Ch of Nazarene	4	198	243	597	2.5	3.0
CHR–Chs of Christ	4	107	99	125	0.5	0.6
Jehovah's Witness	1	NR	NR	NR	-	-
LDS–L-D Saints	1	NR	NR	361	1.5	1.8
LUTH–Luth-MO Synod	1	22	28	31	0.1	0.2
METH–AME	2	0	200	247	1.0	1.2
METH–AME Zion	1	0	150	185	0.8	0.9
METH–Cong Meth	3	NR	52	64	0.3	0.3
METH–Un Methodist	7	256	553	644	2.7	3.2
Non-denom Chr Chs	5	575	630	788	3.3	4.0
PENT–Assemb of God	2	108	110	173	0.7	0.9
PENT–Ch of God Proph	1	NR	17	21	0.1	0.1
PENT–Un Pent Ch Intl	6	NR	NR	NR	-	-
PRES–Cumber Presb	1	NR	9	9	0.0	0.0
ST. BERNARD	**25**	**955**	**4,572**	**20,698**	**57.7**	**100.0**
Bahá'í	0	NR	2	2	0.0	0.0
BAPT–So Bapt Conv	4	294	3,041	3,806	10.6	18.4
Calv Chpl	1	NR	NR	NR	-	-
Catholic	6	NR	NR	14,532	40.5	70.2
Ch of Nazarene	1	34	28	34	0.1	0.2
CHR–Chs of Christ	2	83	77	101	0.3	0.5
LUTH–E.L.C.A.	1	65	518	725	2.0	3.5
LUTH–Luth-MO Synod	1	45	320	434	1.2	2.1
METH–Un Methodist	1	45	304	395	1.1	1.9
Muslim Est	1	134	NR	308	0.9	1.5
Non-denom Chr Chs	1	100	150	150	0.4	0.7
PENT–Assemb of God	3	122	94	164	0.5	0.8
PENT–Ch God (Cleve)	1	17	13	16	0.0	0.1
PENT–Un Pent Ch Intl	1	NR	NR	NR	-	-
PRES–Presb Ch (USA)	1	16	25	31	0.1	0.1
ST. CHARLES	**39**	**2,659**	**4,230**	**27,650**	**52.4**	**100.0**
Bahá'í	0	NR	16	16	0.0	0.1
BAPT–NBC USA	5	150	750	943	1.8	3.4
BAPT–So Bapt Conv	9	689	1,324	1,665	3.2	6.0
Catholic	8	NR	NR	21,657	41.0	78.3
CHR–Chs of Christ	1	40	47	55	0.1	0.2
Jehovah's Witness	1	NR	NR	NR	-	-
LDS–L-D Saints	1	NR	NR	312	0.6	1.1
MENN–Mennonite USA	1	60	56	70	0.1	0.3
METH–Un Methodist	3	256	595	813	1.5	2.9
Non-denom Chr Chs	4	940	1,050	1,200	2.3	4.3
PENT–Assemb of God	3	479	315	822	1.6	3.0
PENT–Ch God Mtn Asm	1	NR	NR	NR	-	-
PENT–Full Gosp Bapt	1	NR	NR	NR	-	-
PRES–Presb Ch (USA)	1	45	77	97	0.2	0.4
ST. HELENA	**33**	**1,138**	**4,041**	**5,165**	**46.1**	**100.0**
Bahá'í	0	NR	5	5	0.0	0.1
BAPT–Natl Mis Bapt Conv	1	0	150	185	1.7	3.6
BAPT–So Bapt Conv	16	762	2,369	2,929	26.1	56.7
Catholic	1	NR	NR	200	1.8	3.9
METH–AME	5	220	950	1,174	10.5	22.7
METH–AME Zion	1	0	100	124	1.1	2.4
METH–Un Methodist	7	156	467	548	4.9	10.6
PENT–COGIC	1	0	0	0	0.0	0.0
PENT–Un Pent Ch Intl	1	NR	NR	NR	-	-
ST. JAMES	**19**	**469**	**2,722**	**17,265**	**78.1**	**100.0**
Bahá'í	0	NR	1	1	0.0	0.0
BAPT–Natl Mis Bapt Conv	2	0	300	373	1.7	2.2
BAPT–NBC USA	1	150	2,000	2,484	11.2	14.4
BAPT–So Bapt Conv	1	50	55	68	0.3	0.4
Catholic	6	NR	NR	13,947	63.1	80.8
Jehovah's Witness	1	NR	NR	NR	-	-
METH–Un Methodist	4	85	113	120	0.5	0.7
Non-denom Chr Chs	1	100	150	150	0.7	0.9
PENT–Assemb of God	2	84	103	122	0.6	0.7
PENT–Un Pent Ch Intl	1	NR	NR	NR	-	-
ST. JOHN THE BAPTIST	**26**	**2,072**	**4,106**	**20,417**	**44.5**	**100.0**
ANG/EPIS–Episcopal	1	24	44	44	0.1	0.2
Bahá'í	0	NR	26	26	0.1	0.1
BAPT–NBC Amer	1	0	150	189	0.4	0.9
BAPT–NBC USA	3	110	740	931	2.0	4.6
BAPT–So Bapt Conv	4	377	805	1,013	2.2	5.0
Catholic	6	NR	NR	15,402	33.5	75.4
CHR–Chs of Christ	1	70	50	65	0.1	0.3
Jehovah's Witness	1	NR	NR	NR	-	-
LUTH–E.L.C.A.	1	53	85	112	0.2	0.5
METH–Un Methodist	1	83	281	338	0.7	1.7
Non-denom Chr Chs	2	1,250	1,700	1,862	4.1	9.1
PENT–Assemb of God	1	105	62	230	0.5	1.1
PENT–COGIC	1	0	150	189	0.4	0.9
PENT–Full Gosp Bapt	1	NR	NR	NR	-	-
PENT–Un Pent Ch Intl	1	NR	NR	NR	-	-
PRES–Presb Ch (USA)	1	0	13	16	0.0	0.1
ST. LANDRY	**95**	**3,093**	**7,614**	**59,104**	**70.9**	**100.0**
ANG/EPIS–Episcopal	1	75	151	153	0.2	0.3
BAPT–N Am Bapt Conf	1	NR	105	133	0.2	0.2
BAPT–NBC Amer	1	55	75	95	0.1	0.2
BAPT–NBC USA	3	500	1,100	1,396	1.7	2.4
BAPT–So Bapt Conv	24	1,501	4,201	5,333	6.4	9.0

NR–Not Reported - Represents no adherents reported. Percentages may not total 100 due to rounding.

Table 3: Religious Congregations by County and Group: 2010

Religious Group	Number of Congregations	Number of Attendees	Number of Communicant, Confirmed, or Full Members	Adherents: Number of Adherents	Adherents: % of Total Pop.	Adherents: % of Total Adh.
Catholic	35	NR	NR	49,234	59.0	83.3
CGOD–Ch God (Ander)	1	75	NR	75	0.1	0.1
CHR–Chs of Christ	3	70	94	123	0.1	0.2
Jehovah's Witness	3	NR	NR	NR	-	-
LDS–L-D Saints	1	NR	NR	406	0.5	0.7
METH–Un Methodist	10	361	1,036	1,166	1.4	2.0
Non-denom Chr Chs	2	160	230	230	0.3	0.4
PENT–Assemb of God	1	107	110	110	0.1	0.2
PENT–COGIC	3	189	450	571	0.7	1.0
PENT–Un Pent Ch Intl	5	NR	NR	NR	-	-
PRES–As Ref Pres Ch	1	NR	62	79	0.1	0.1
ST. MARTIN	**31**	**651**	**1,362**	**30,827**	**59.1**	**100.0**
Bahá'í	0	NR	18	18	0.0	0.1
BAPT–So Bapt Conv	6	311	784	984	1.9	3.2
BUDD–Theravada	1	NR	NR	300	0.6	1.0
Catholic	12	NR	NR	28,813	55.2	93.5
CHR–Chs of Christ	1	15	25	34	0.1	0.1
Jehovah's Witness	2	NR	NR	NR	-	-
METH–C.M.E.	1	40	50	63	0.1	0.2
METH–Un Methodist	1	47	106	123	0.2	0.4
Non-denom Chr Chs	3	140	165	182	0.3	0.6
PENT–Assemb of God	1	98	64	122	0.2	0.4
PENT–COGIC	1	0	150	188	0.4	0.6
PENT–Un Pent Ch Intl	2	NR	NR	NR	-	-
ST. MARY	**86**	**4,034**	**9,616**	**29,988**	**54.9**	**100.0**
ANG/EPIS–Episcopal	2	77	150	246	0.5	0.8
Bahá'í	0	NR	2	2	0.0	0.0
BAPT–NBC USA	2	180	562	697	1.3	2.3
BAPT–So Bapt Conv	15	1,016	3,937	4,882	8.9	16.3
Catholic	18	NR	NR	17,834	32.6	59.5
Ch Cr, Scientst	1	NR	NR	NR	-	-
Chr & Miss Al	1	20	20	22	0.0	0.1
CHR–Chs of Christ	3	120	125	168	0.3	0.6
Jehovah's Witness	3	NR	NR	NR	-	-
LDS–L-D Saints	1	NR	NR	341	0.6	1.1
METH–AME	4	100	550	682	1.2	2.3
METH–Un Methodist	11	504	1,477	1,635	3.0	5.5
Non-denom Chr Chs	11	992	1,300	1,384	2.5	4.6
PENT–Assemb of God	4	949	773	1,202	2.2	4.0
PENT–Ch of God Proph	2	NR	84	104	0.2	0.3
PENT–COGIC	4	60	600	744	1.4	2.5
PENT–Un Pent Ch Intl	2	NR	NR	NR	-	-
PRES–Presb Ch (USA)	2	16	36	45	0.1	0.2
ST. TAMMANY	**201**	**24,007**	**46,241**	**117,722**	**50.4**	**100.0**
ANG/EPIS–Episcopal	3	484	1,108	2,005	0.9	1.7
Bahá'í	0	NR	69	69	0.0	0.1
BAPT–Amer Bapt Assn	2	NR	140	174	0.1	0.1
BAPT–Natl Mis Bapt Conv	3	200	550	685	0.3	0.6
BAPT–Ref Bapt Ch	1	NR	NR	NR	-	-
BAPT–So Bapt Conv	44	6,367	17,261	21,507	9.2	18.3
Calv Chpl	1	NR	NR	NR	-	-
Catholic	16	NR	NR	53,149	22.7	45.1
CGOD–Ch God (Ander)	1	53	NR	53	0.0	0.0
Ch Cr, Scientst	2	NR	NR	NR	-	-
Ch of Chr (Hol)	3	NR	NR	NR	-	-
Ch of Nazarene	3	149	258	262	0.1	0.2
CHR–Chr Ch (Disc)	2	105	177	221	0.1	0.2
CHR–Chr Chs & Chs Cr	2	NR	137	171	0.1	0.1
CHR–Chs of Christ	4	540	489	650	0.3	0.6
Christian Brethren	1	NR	NR	NR	-	-
Evan Free Ch	1	250	NR	250	0.1	0.2
Jehovah's Witness	5	NR	NR	NR	-	-
JUD–Reform	1	67	119	321	0.1	0.3
LDS–L-D Saints	2	NR	NR	1,671	0.7	1.4
LUTH–E.L.C.A.	2	318	513	690	0.3	0.6
LUTH–Luth-MO Synod	7	870	1,718	2,369	1.0	2.0
LUTH–Wisc Ev Luth Syn	1	35	59	69	0.0	0.1
METH–AME	7	250	967	1,205	0.5	1.0
METH–Un Methodist	13	3,624	9,171	13,109	5.6	11.1
Muslim Est	1	134	NR	308	0.1	0.3

Religious Group	Number of Congregations	Number of Attendees	Number of Communicant, Confirmed, or Full Members	Adherents: Number of Adherents	Adherents: % of Total Pop.	Adherents: % of Total Adh.
New Apost Ch	1	NR	NR	NR	-	-
Non-denom Chr Chs	15	7,190	7,750	9,156	3.9	7.8
PENT–Assemb of God	11	2,330	2,618	5,782	2.5	4.9
PENT–Ch God (Cleve)	6	308	911	1,135	0.5	1.0
PENT–Ch of God Proph	3	NR	58	72	0.0	0.1
PENT–COGIC	5	0	700	872	0.4	0.7
PENT–Full Gosp Bapt	2	NR	NR	NR	-	-
PENT–Un Pent Ch Intl	15	NR	NR	NR	-	-
PENT–Vineyard	1	75	90	112	0.0	0.1
PRES–Evan Presby Ch	1	NR	97	121	0.1	0.1
PRES–Presb Ch (USA)	5	217	620	773	0.3	0.7
PRES–Presb Ch Amer	2	113	106	125	0.1	0.1
Sev Day Adv	4	288	500	575	0.2	0.5
Unit Univ	1	40	55	61	0.0	0.1
Unity Ch	1	NR	NR	NR	-	-
TANGIPAHOA	**185**	**12,720**	**30,880**	**57,249**	**47.3**	**100.0**
ANG/EPIS–Episcopal	3	155	383	591	0.5	1.0
Bahá'í	0	NR	29	29	0.0	0.1
BAPT–Amer Bapt Assn	3	NR	392	487	0.4	0.9
BAPT–Natl Mis Bapt Conv	2	20	300	372	0.3	0.6
BAPT–So Bapt Conv	52	5,816	15,821	19,638	16.2	34.3
Catholic	6	NR	NR	17,327	14.3	30.3
CGOD–Ch God (Ander)	2	67	NR	67	0.1	0.1
CGOD–Ches God-Gen Con	1	10	10	12	0.0	0.0
Ch Cr, Scientst	1	NR	NR	NR	-	-
Ch of Chr (Hol)	1	NR	NR	NR	-	-
Ch of God Gen Conf	1	NR	40	50	0.0	0.1
CHR–Chr Ch (Disc)	1	46	96	119	0.1	0.2
CHR–Chs of Christ	10	479	505	648	0.5	1.1
Jehovah's Witness	3	NR	NR	NR	-	-
LDS–L-D Saints	3	NR	NR	1,335	1.1	2.3
LUTH–Luth-MO Synod	1	103	163	195	0.2	0.3
METH–AME	19	460	2,641	3,278	2.7	5.7
METH–AME Zion	10	0	1,200	1,490	1.2	2.6
METH–So Methodist	2	NR	NR	NR	-	-
METH–Un Methodist	11	750	2,128	2,665	2.2	4.7
Non-denom Chr Chs	11	3,135	3,425	4,192	3.5	7.3
PENT–Assemb of God	3	592	612	912	0.8	1.6
PENT–Ch God (Cleve)	5	216	290	360	0.3	0.6
PENT–Ch of God Proph	3	NR	179	222	0.2	0.4
PENT–COGIC	11	557	1,725	2,141	1.8	3.7
PENT–Full Gosp Bapt	2	NR	NR	NR	-	-
PENT–Un Pent Ch Intl	13	NR	NR	NR	-	-
PRES–Presb Ch (USA)	3	0	396	492	0.4	0.9
Sev Day Adv	2	314	545	627	0.5	1.1
TENSAS	**18**	**607**	**1,813**	**2,368**	**45.1**	**100.0**
ANG/EPIS–Episcopal	1	21	32	32	0.6	1.4
BAPT–So Bapt Conv	6	451	1,535	1,914	36.4	80.8
Catholic	2	NR	NR	95	1.8	4.0
CGOD–Ch God (Ander)	1	15	NR	15	0.3	0.6
CHR–Chs of Christ	1	25	22	30	0.6	1.3
METH–Un Methodist	2	75	159	181	3.4	7.6
PENT–Assemb of God	1	20	0	20	0.4	0.8
PENT–Un Pent Ch Intl	3	NR	NR	NR	-	-
PRES–Presb Ch (USA)	1	0	65	81	1.5	3.4
TERREBONNE	**91**	**7,150**	**14,357**	**73,645**	**65.8**	**100.0**
ANG/EPIS–Episcopal	2	137	409	604	0.5	0.8
Bahá'í	0	NR	8	8	0.0	0.0
BAPT–NBC USA	7	1,468	2,920	3,662	3.3	5.0
BAPT–So Bapt Conv	13	1,884	5,848	7,333	6.6	10.0
Calv Chpl	1	NR	NR	NR	-	-
Catholic	17	NR	NR	54,640	48.8	74.2
Ch of Nazarene	1	0	6	6	0.0	0.0
CHR–Chs of Christ	4	303	388	550	0.5	0.7
Jehovah's Witness	2	NR	NR	NR	-	-
LDS–L-D Saints	1	NR	NR	829	0.7	1.1
LUTH–Luth-MO Synod	1	75	218	310	0.3	0.4
METH–Un Methodist	5	347	1,157	1,595	1.4	2.2
Non-denom Chr Chs	15	1,125	1,570	1,665	1.5	2.3
PENT–Assemb of God	4	1,032	1,014	1,427	1.3	1.9

NR–Not Reported - Represents no adherents reported. Percentages may not total 100 due to rounding.

Table 3: Religious Congregations by County and Group: 2010

Religious Group	Number of Congregations	Number of Attendees	Number of Communicant, Confirmed, or Full Members	Adherents		
				Number of Adherents	% of Total Pop.	% of Total Adh.
PENT–Ch God (Cleve)	3	72	58	73	0.1	0.1
PENT–Ch of God Proph	1	NR	26	33	0.0	0.0
PENT–Full Gosp Bapt	1	NR	NR	NR	-	-
PENT–Int Foursq Gos	7	639	559	701	0.6	1.0
PENT–Un Pent Ch Intl	3	NR	NR	NR	-	-
PRES–Evan Presby Ch	1	NR	59	74	0.1	0.1
Sev Day Adv	2	68	117	135	0.1	0.2
UNION	**79**	**4,935**	**11,366**	**14,829**	**65.3**	**100.0**
Bahá'í	0	NR	6	6	0.0	0.0
BAPT–So Bapt Conv	40	3,162	9,205	11,239	49.5	75.8
Catholic	1	NR	NR	438	1.9	3.0
CHR–Chs of Christ	15	845	828	1,041	4.6	7.0
Ind Fund Churches	1	NR	NR	NR	-	-
Jehovah's Witness	1	NR	NR	NR	-	-
LDS–L-D Saints	1	NR	NR	196	0.9	1.3
METH–AME	1	0	100	122	0.5	0.8
METH–Un Methodist	7	265	539	672	3.0	4.5
Non-denom Chr Chs	3	205	300	300	1.3	2.0
PENT–Assemb of God	4	458	388	815	3.6	5.5
PENT–Full Gosp Bapt	3	NR	NR	NR	-	-
PENT–Un Pent Ch Intl	2	NR	NR	NR	-	-
VERMILION	**46**	**1,505**	**3,198**	**36,140**	**62.3**	**100.0**
ANG/EPIS–Episcopal	1	33	71	71	0.1	0.2
Bahá'í	0	NR	4	4	0.0	0.0
BAPT–Natl Mis Bapt Conv	1	0	150	190	0.3	0.5
BAPT–So Bapt Conv	7	272	818	1,035	1.8	2.9
Catholic	16	NR	NR	32,259	55.6	89.3
CHR–Chs of Christ	1	46	26	52	0.1	0.1
Jehovah's Witness	1	NR	NR	NR	-	-
METH–Un Methodist	5	140	716	873	1.5	2.4
Non-denom Chr Chs	6	775	952	1,017	1.8	2.8
PENT–Assemb of God	2	185	130	220	0.4	0.6
PENT–Ch God (Cleve)	1	35	50	63	0.1	0.2
PENT–Un Pent Ch Intl	1	NR	NR	NR	-	-
PRES–Presb Ch (USA)	1	19	21	27	0.0	0.1
Un C of Christ	3	0	260	329	0.6	0.9
VERNON	**106**	**7,834**	**20,247**	**28,731**	**54.9**	**100.0**
ANG/EPIS–Episcopal	1	25	24	24	0.0	0.1
Bahá'í	0	NR	12	12	0.0	0.0
BAPT–NBC Amer	1	0	150	194	0.4	0.7
BAPT–NBC USA	1	500	2,000	2,582	4.9	9.0
BAPT–So Bapt Conv	54	4,986	14,404	18,595	35.5	64.7
Catholic	1	NR	NR	782	1.5	2.7
CGOD–Ch God (Ander)	1	40	NR	40	0.1	0.1
Ch of Nazarene	1	0	45	45	0.1	0.2
CHR–Chr Ch (Disc)	1	0	145	187	0.4	0.7
CHR–Chs of Christ	3	235	224	274	0.5	1.0
Jehovah's Witness	1	NR	NR	NR	-	-
LDS–L-D Saints	2	NR	NR	1,295	2.5	4.5
LUTH–Luth-MO Synod	1	39	85	137	0.3	0.5
METH–AME	1	0	150	194	0.4	0.7
METH–Cong Meth	3	NR	163	210	0.4	0.7
METH–Un Methodist	6	180	578	610	1.2	2.1
Muslim Est	1	134	NR	308	0.6	1.1
Non-denom Chr Chs	7	1,055	1,535	1,624	3.1	5.7
PENT–Assemb of God	4	290	224	962	1.8	3.3
PENT–Ch God (Cleve)	1	70	34	44	0.1	0.2
PENT–COGIC	2	280	450	581	1.1	2.0
PENT–Un Pent Ch Intl	12	NR	NR	NR	-	-
PRES–Presb Ch (USA)	1	0	24	31	0.1	0.1
WASHINGTON	**109**	**5,881**	**20,395**	**27,273**	**57.8**	**100.0**
ANG/EPIS–Episcopal	1	58	110	110	0.2	0.4
Bahá'í	0	NR	138	138	0.3	0.5
BAPT–Amer Bapt Assn	8	NR	2,120	2,632	5.6	9.7
BAPT–Natl Mis Bapt Conv	3	220	406	504	1.1	1.8
BAPT–NBC Amer	1	0	150	186	0.4	0.7
BAPT–So Bapt Conv	37	3,460	12,543	15,570	33.0	57.1
Catholic	2	NR	NR	2,099	4.5	7.7

Religious Group	Number of Congregations	Number of Attendees	Number of Communicant, Confirmed, or Full Members	Adherents		
				Number of Adherents	% of Total Pop.	% of Total Adh.
Ch of Chr (Hol)	6	NR	NR	NR	-	-
CHR–Chs of Christ	2	65	56	72	0.2	0.3
Jehovah's Witness	2	NR	NR	NR	-	-
LDS–L-D Saints	1	NR	NR	335	0.7	1.2
LUTH–Luth-MO Synod	1	37	58	65	0.1	0.2
METH–AME	5	90	725	900	1.9	3.3
METH–Un Methodist	12	851	1,513	1,659	3.5	6.1
Non-denom Chr Chs	6	894	1,405	1,464	3.1	5.4
PENT–Assemb of God	1	70	0	91	0.2	0.3
PENT–Ch of God Proph	1	NR	23	29	0.1	0.1
PENT–COGIC	6	25	800	993	2.1	3.6
PENT–Full Gosp Bapt	2	NR	NR	NR	-	-
PENT–Intl Pent Holiness	1	75	120	149	0.3	0.5
PENT–Un Pent Ch Intl	9	NR	NR	NR	-	-
PRES–Presb Ch (USA)	1	0	166	206	0.4	0.8
Sev Day Adv	1	36	62	71	0.2	0.3
WEBSTER	**106**	**6,483**	**21,085**	**26,505**	**64.3**	**100.0**
ANG/EPIS–Episcopal	1	84	229	258	0.6	1.0
Bahá'í	0	NR	2	2	0.0	0.0
BAPT–Amer Bapt Assn	8	NR	1,647	2,011	4.9	7.6
BAPT–NBC USA	4	450	1,175	1,434	3.5	5.4
BAPT–So Bapt Conv	28	2,932	11,698	14,280	34.7	53.9
Catholic	2	NR	NR	642	1.6	2.4
CHR–Chr Ch (Disc)	1	0	30	37	0.1	0.1
CHR–Chr Chs & Chs Cr	1	NR	93	114	0.3	0.4
CHR–Chs of Christ	7	487	431	506	1.2	1.9
Jehovah's Witness	1	NR	NR	NR	-	-
METH–AME	2	45	210	256	0.6	1.0
METH–C.M.E.	11	0	1,570	1,917	4.7	7.2
METH–Un Methodist	13	769	1,951	2,284	5.5	8.6
Non-denom Chr Chs	5	950	1,000	1,190	2.9	4.5
PENT–Assemb of God	7	446	399	678	1.6	2.6
PENT–COGIC	5	130	425	519	1.3	2.0
PENT–Full Gosp Bapt	1	NR	NR	NR	-	-
PENT–Pent Ch of God	1	70	NR	109	0.3	0.4
PENT–Un Pent Ch Intl	5	NR	NR	NR	-	-
PRES–Presb Ch (USA)	1	70	138	168	0.4	0.6
Sev Day Adv	2	50	87	100	0.2	0.4
WEST BATON ROUGE	**15**	**738**	**2,408**	**10,052**	**42.3**	**100.0**
Bahá'í	0	NR	4	4	0.0	0.0
BAPT–So Bapt Conv	5	590	1,926	2,383	10.0	23.7
Catholic	2	NR	NR	7,101	29.9	70.6
Chr & Miss Al	1	20	27	27	0.1	0.3
CHR–Chs of Christ	1	60	84	114	0.5	1.1
Jehovah's Witness	1	NR	NR	NR	-	-
METH–AME	1	0	150	186	0.8	1.9
METH–Un Methodist	1	68	172	181	0.8	1.8
PENT–Un Pent Ch Intl	2	NR	NR	NR	-	-
PRES–Presb Ch (USA)	1	0	45	56	0.2	0.6
WEST CARROLL	**49**	**2,454**	**6,954**	**9,195**	**79.2**	**100.0**
BAPT–Natl Mis Bapt Conv	1	0	150	185	1.6	2.0
BAPT–NBC USA	2	35	215	265	2.3	2.9
BAPT–So Bapt Conv	19	1,371	5,597	6,907	59.5	75.1
Catholic	1	NR	NR	140	1.2	1.5
CGOD–Ch God (Ander)	5	443	NR	443	3.8	4.8
CHR–Chs of Christ	3	126	160	186	1.6	2.0
Jehovah's Witness	1	NR	NR	NR	-	-
METH–AME	1	0	100	123	1.1	1.3
METH–Un Methodist	5	138	301	374	3.2	4.1
PENT–Assemb of God	4	244	287	394	3.4	4.3
PENT–Ch God (Cleve)	4	97	144	178	1.5	1.9
PENT–Un Pent Ch Intl	3	NR	NR	NR	-	-
WEST FELICIANA	**11**	**1,307**	**3,592**	**5,528**	**35.4**	**100.0**
ANG/EPIS–Episcopal	1	141	368	451	2.9	8.2
Bahá'í	0	NR	1	1	0.0	0.0
BAPT–So Bapt Conv	3	263	1,276	1,464	9.4	26.5
Catholic	1	NR	NR	1,057	6.8	19.1
Jehovah's Witness	1	NR	NR	NR	-	-

NR–Not Reported   - Represents no adherents reported.   Percentages may not total 100 due to rounding.

Table 3: Religious Congregations by County and Group: 2010

Religious Group	Number of Congrega-tions	Number of Attendees	Number of Communicant, Confirmed, or Full Members	Adherents		
				Number of Adherents	% of Total Pop.	% of Total Adh.
METH–AME	1	0	100	115	0.7	2.1
METH–Un Methodist	2	203	647	1,064	6.8	19.2
PENT–Intl Pent Holiness	1	700	1,200	1,376	8.8	24.9
PENT–Un Pent Ch Intl	1	NR	NR	NR	-	-
WINN	**67**	**3,130**	**8,478**	**10,889**	**71.1**	**100.0**
ANG/EPIS–Episcopal	1	6	8	8	0.1	0.1
Bahá'í	0	NR	2	2	0.0	0.0
BAPT–Amer Bapt Assn	1	NR	85	103	0.7	0.9
BAPT–Ind Bapt Flwsp Intl	1	NR	NR	NR	-	-
BAPT–Prog NBC	1	0	150	182	1.2	1.7
BAPT–So Bapt Conv	37	2,363	7,052	8,545	55.8	78.5
Catholic	1	NR	NR	184	1.2	1.7
Ch of Nazarene	1	23	36	52	0.3	0.5
CHR–Chs of Christ	4	208	216	285	1.9	2.6
Jehovah's Witness	1	NR	NR	NR	-	-
LDS–L-D Saints	1	NR	NR	252	1.6	2.3
METH–C.M.E.	2	0	200	242	1.6	2.2
METH–Un Methodist	7	207	469	548	3.6	5.0
Non-denom Chr Chs	1	150	150	188	1.2	1.7
PENT–Assemb of God	5	173	85	268	1.8	2.5
PENT–Un Pent Ch Intl	2	NR	NR	NR	-	-
PRES–Presb Ch (USA)	1	0	25	30	0.2	0.3
MAINE	**1,574**	**75,336**	**122,943**	**367,043**	**27.6**	**100.0**
ANDROSCOGGIN	**80**	**5,643**	**9,006**	**37,449**	**34.8**	**100.0**
ANG/EPIS–Episcopal	3	202	351	377	0.4	1.0
Bahá'í	2	NR	49	49	0.0	0.1
BAPT–Amer Bapt USA	6	461	1,431	1,733	1.6	4.6
BAPT–Consrv Bapt	4	NR	NR	NR	-	-
BAPT–Reg Bapt Gen As	1	NR	NR	NR	-	-
BAPT–So Bapt Conv	1	58	78	94	0.1	0.3
BRETH–Ch of Brethren	2	92	72	87	0.1	0.2
Catholic	6	NR	NR	24,480	22.7	65.4
Ch Cr, Scientst	1	NR	NR	NR	-	-
Ch of Nazarene	6	240	266	451	0.4	1.2
CHR–Chs of Christ	1	25	19	25	0.0	0.1
CONG–Cong Chr Add'l	1	NR	2	2	0.0	0.0
FRND–Fr Gen Cf & Un Mtg	2	NR	168	203	0.2	0.5
Jehovah's Witness	2	NR	NR	NR	-	-
LDS–L-D Saints	1	NR	NR	565	0.5	1.5
LUTH–E.L.C.A.	1	97	144	197	0.2	0.5
METH–Un Methodist	6	382	1,317	1,779	1.7	4.8
Muslim Est	1	134	NR	308	0.3	0.8
Non-denom Chr Chs	11	1,575	1,835	2,107	2.0	5.6
ORTHE–Greek Orthodox	1	75	NR	225	0.2	0.6
PENT–Assemb of God	2	370	159	542	0.5	1.4
PENT–Ch God (Cleve)	1	61	138	167	0.2	0.4
PENT–COGIC	1	0	150	182	0.2	0.5
PENT–Un Pent Ch Intl	2	NR	NR	NR	-	-
PENT–Vineyard	3	1,308	1,815	2,198	2.0	5.9
PRES–Presb Ch (USA)	3	70	164	199	0.2	0.5
PRES–Presb Ch Amer	1	40	20	28	0.0	0.1
Salvation Army	1	48	115	572	0.5	1.5
Sev Day Adv	1	56	97	112	0.1	0.3
Un C of Christ	5	229	489	592	0.5	1.6
Unit Univ	1	120	127	175	0.2	0.5
AROOSTOOK	**126**	**5,375**	**7,193**	**33,423**	**46.5**	**100.0**
ANG/EPIS–Episcopal	6	151	294	314	0.4	0.9
Bahá'í	0	NR	16	16	0.0	0.0
BAPT–Amer Bapt USA	13	1,230	1,985	2,330	3.2	7.0
BAPT–Consrv Bapt	1	NR	NR	NR	-	-
BAPT–Converge/BGC	2	150	NR	180	0.3	0.5
BAPT–Free Will Bapt	2	NR	136	160	0.2	0.5
BAPT–So Bapt Conv	2	64	58	68	0.1	0.2
Catholic	27	NR	NR	22,200	30.9	66.4
Ch Cr, Scientst	1	NR	NR	NR	-	-
CHR–Chs of Christ	3	57	58	66	0.1	0.2
Evan Cov Ch	1	45	61	58	0.1	0.2
FRND–Fr Gen Cf & Un Mtg	1	NR	7	8	0.0	0.0
Jehovah's Witness	1	NR	NR	NR	-	-
LDS–L-D Saints	3	NR	NR	885	1.2	2.6
LUTH–E.L.C.A.	3	88	316	412	0.6	1.2
MENN–Amish Undif	2	NR	48	138	0.2	0.4
MENN–CG in Cr (Menn)	1	NR	38	45	0.1	0.1
METH–Un Methodist	11	608	1,701	2,299	3.2	6.9
METH–Wesleyan	6	929	561	1,207	1.7	3.6
Non-denom Chr Chs	16	1,285	1,036	1,609	2.2	4.8
ORTHE–Rus Orth Abroad	1	10	NR	10	0.0	0.0
PENT–Assemb of God	5	402	190	585	0.8	1.8
PENT–Un Pent Ch Intl	7	NR	NR	NR	-	-
Salvation Army	1	31	53	95	0.1	0.3
Sev Day Adv	2	100	174	200	0.3	0.6
Un C of Christ	6	185	411	482	0.7	1.4
Unit Univ	2	40	50	56	0.1	0.2
CUMBERLAND	**247**	**15,976**	**28,934**	**80,252**	**28.5**	**100.0**
ANG/EPIS–Episcopal	10	1,372	4,044	4,870	1.7	6.1
Bahá'í	2	NR	299	299	0.1	0.4
BAPT–Alliance Bapt	1	NR	NR	NR	-	-
BAPT–Amer Bapt USA	14	968	1,666	1,979	0.7	2.5
BAPT–Asc Ref Bap Ch Am	1	NR	NR	NR	-	-
BAPT–Consrv Bapt	5	NR	NR	NR	-	-
BAPT–So Bapt Conv	3	389	731	868	0.3	1.1
BRETH–Ch of Brethren	1	75	54	64	0.0	0.1
BUDD–Mahayana	6	NR	NR	408	0.1	0.5
BUDD–Theravada	1	NR	NR	395	0.1	0.5
BUDD–Vajrayana	2	NR	NR	88	0.0	0.1
Catholic	19	NR	NR	38,243	13.6	47.7
Ch Cr, Scientst	2	NR	NR	NR	-	-
Ch of Nazarene	10	725	685	1,264	0.4	1.6
Chr & Miss Al	3	278	167	360	0.1	0.4
CHR–Chr Chs & Chs Cr	2	NR	6	7	0.0	0.0
CHR–Chs of Christ	3	104	109	138	0.0	0.2
CONG–Cong Chr Add'l	1	NR	261	310	0.1	0.4
CONG–Cong Chr, NA	5	NR	452	537	0.2	0.7
Evan Cov Ch	1	38	51	49	0.0	0.1
Evan Free Ch	1	239	NR	239	0.1	0.3
FRND–Fr Gen Cf & Un Mtg	3	NR	188	223	0.1	0.3
HINDU–Post Ren	4	NR	NR	116	0.0	0.1
Int Cou Comm Ch	1	NR	NR	NR	-	-
Jehovah's Witness	8	NR	NR	NR	-	-
JUD–Conserv	1	276	310	837	0.3	1.0
JUD–Orth	2	122	100	170	0.1	0.2
JUD–Reform	1	213	376	1,015	0.4	1.3
LDS–Comm of Christ	1	NR	102	102	0.0	0.1
LDS–L-D Saints	4	NR	NR	1,834	0.7	2.3
LUTH–E.L.C.A.	6	475	1,127	1,595	0.6	2.0
LUTH–Luth–MO Synod	1	0	197	304	0.1	0.4
LUTH–Wisc Ev Luth Syn	1	7	23	31	0.0	0.0
METH–AME Zion	1	0	150	178	0.1	0.2
METH–Un Methodist	24	1,396	3,268	4,180	1.5	5.2
METH–Wesleyan	1	145	51	189	0.1	0.2
Muslim Est	3	293	NR	924	0.3	1.2
Nat Spirit Asso	1	NR	NR	NR	-	-
Non-denom Chr Chs	23	3,110	3,850	4,388	1.6	5.5
ORTHE–Greek Orthodox	1	140	NR	500	0.2	0.6
PENT–Assemb of God	8	644	312	946	0.3	1.2
PENT–Ch God (Cleve)	3	207	399	474	0.2	0.6
PENT–COGIC	1	60	90	107	0.0	0.1
PENT–I F Chr Assmbl	1	NR	NR	NR	-	-
PENT–Int Foursq Gos	1	12	3	4	0.0	0.0
PENT–Un Pent Ch Intl	3	NR	NR	NR	-	-
PENT–Vineyard	1	368	517	614	0.2	0.8
PRES–Orth Pres Ch	2	116	182	250	0.1	0.3
PRES–Presb Ch Amer	1	82	109	132	0.0	0.2
Salvation Army	2	67	191	437	0.2	0.5
Sev Day Adv	7	624	1,086	1,249	0.4	1.6
Swedenborgian	1	NR	NR	NR	-	-
Un C of Christ	31	2,828	7,016	8,336	3.0	10.4
Unit Univ	4	603	762	999	0.4	1.2
Unity Ch	1	NR	NR	NR	-	-

NR–Not Reported - Represents no adherents reported. Percentages may not total 100 due to rounding.

Table 3: Religious Congregations by County and Group: 2010

Religious Group	Number of Congrega-tions	Number of Attendees	Number of Communicant, Confirmed, or Full Members	Adherents: Number of Adherents	Adherents: % of Total Pop.	Adherents: % of Total Adh.
FRANKLIN	**44**	**1,225**	**2,187**	**7,274**	**23.6**	**100.0**
ANG/EPIS–Episcopal	2	113	174	249	0.8	3.4
Bahá'í	0	NR	7	7	0.0	0.1
BAPT–Amer Bapt USA	3	110	327	384	1.2	5.3
BAPT–Consrv Bapt	2	NR	NR	NR	-	-
BAPT–Reg Bapt Gen As	1	NR	NR	NR	-	-
BAPT–So Bapt Conv	2	126	326	382	1.2	5.3
Catholic	5	NR	NR	3,936	12.8	54.1
Ch of Nazarene	2	48	124	124	0.4	1.7
CHR–Chs of Christ	2	50	34	57	0.2	0.8
CONG–Consrv Cong Chr	1	15	12	14	0.0	0.2
FRND–Fr Gen Cf & Un Mtg	1	NR	17	20	0.1	0.3
FRND–Unaffl Mtgs	1	NR	NR	NR	-	-
Jehovah's Witness	1	NR	NR	NR	-	-
LDS–L-D Saints	1	NR	NR	420	1.4	5.8
METH–Un Methodist	6	215	486	741	2.4	10.2
Non-denom Chr Chs	2	175	90	219	0.7	3.0
PENT–Assemb of God	1	47	23	56	0.2	0.8
PENT–Un Pent Ch Intl	1	NR	NR	NR	-	-
PRES–Presb Ch (USA)	1	40	55	65	0.2	0.9
Sev Day Adv	2	28	48	56	0.2	0.8
Un C of Christ	7	258	464	544	1.8	7.5
HANCOCK	**101**	**3,315**	**5,505**	**9,322**	**17.1**	**100.0**
ANG/EPIS–Episcopal	8	541	955	1,033	1.9	11.1
Bahá'í	0	NR	41	41	0.1	0.4
BAPT–Amer Bapt USA	16	621	914	1,060	1.9	11.4
BAPT–Consrv Bapt	1	NR	NR	NR	-	-
BUDD–Vajrayana	1	NR	NR	35	0.1	0.4
Calv Chpl	1	NR	NR	NR	-	-
Catholic	9	NR	NR	2,523	4.6	27.1
Ch Cr, Scientst	2	NR	NR	NR	-	-
Ch of Nazarene	2	79	98	138	0.3	1.5
CHR–Chs of Christ	1	6	7	12	0.0	0.1
CONG–Cong Chr Add'l	1	NR	82	95	0.2	1.0
CONG–Cong Chr, NA	1	NR	17	20	0.0	0.2
CONG–Consrv Cong Chr	2	94	81	94	0.2	1.0
FRND–Fr Gen Cf & Un Mtg	3	NR	56	65	0.1	0.7
FRND–Unaffl Mtgs	1	NR	NR	NR	-	-
Int Cou Comm Ch	1	NR	NR	NR	-	-
Jehovah's Witness	3	NR	NR	NR	-	-
LDS–Comm of Christ	2	NR	204	204	0.4	2.2
LDS–L-D Saints	1	NR	NR	358	0.7	3.8
LUTH–E.L.C.A.	1	73	131	138	0.3	1.5
METH–Un Methodist	11	298	531	664	1.2	7.1
Non-denom Chr Chs	5	415	510	569	1.0	6.1
PENT–Assemb of God	4	113	57	164	0.3	1.8
PENT–Ch God (Cleve)	4	210	243	282	0.5	3.0
PENT–Un Pent Ch Intl	1	NR	NR	NR	-	-
PRES–Orth Pres Ch	1	0	0	0	0.0	0.0
Sev Day Adv	1	14	25	29	0.1	0.3
Un C of Christ	15	750	1,393	1,616	3.0	17.3
Unit Univ	2	101	160	182	0.3	2.0
KENNEBEC	**144**	**7,516**	**11,541**	**39,052**	**32.0**	**100.0**
ANG/EPIS–Episcopal	6	360	762	885	0.7	2.3
Bahá'í	1	NR	60	60	0.0	0.2
BAPT–Amer Bapt USA	22	1,200	2,294	2,717	2.2	7.0
BAPT–Consrv Bapt	4	NR	NR	NR	-	-
BAPT–Reg Bapt Gen As	1	NR	NR	NR	-	-
BAPT–So Bapt Conv	3	250	146	173	0.1	0.4
BUDD–Mahayana	2	NR	NR	113	0.1	0.3
Catholic	11	NR	NR	21,758	17.8	55.7
Ch Cr, Scientst	1	NR	NR	NR	-	-
Ch of Nazarene	4	240	416	493	0.4	1.3
Chr & Miss Al	1	55	37	65	0.1	0.2
CHR–Chs of Christ	2	93	113	148	0.1	0.4
CONG–Cong Chr Add'l	1	NR	18	21	0.0	0.1
CONG–Cong Chr, NA	1	NR	20	24	0.0	0.1
CONG–Consrv Cong Chr	1	37	39	46	0.0	0.1
Evan Free Ch	1	625	NR	625	0.5	1.6
FRND–Fr Gen Cf & Un Mtg	4	NR	120	142	0.1	0.4
Jehovah's Witness	4	NR	NR	NR	-	-
JUD–Reform	1	61	107	289	0.2	0.7
LDS–L-D Saints	4	NR	NR	1,528	1.3	3.9
LUTH–E.L.C.A.	1	80	469	469	0.4	1.2
LUTH–Luth–MO Synod	1	77	113	144	0.1	0.4
MENN–Fel Evg Ch	1	0	0	0	0.0	0.0
METH–Free Methodist	1	36	29	36	0.0	0.1
METH–Un Methodist	17	1,044	2,570	3,678	3.0	9.4
Nat Spirit Asso	1	NR	NR	NR	-	-
Non-denom Chr Chs	19	1,841	1,986	2,570	2.1	6.6
PENT–Assemb of God	2	370	205	458	0.4	1.2
PENT–Ch God (Cleve)	3	271	228	270	0.2	0.7
PENT–Elim	1	NR	NR	NR	-	-
PENT–Int Foursq Gos	1	93	236	279	0.2	0.7
PENT–Intl Pent Holiness	2	27	40	47	0.0	0.1
PENT–Un Pent Ch Intl	2	NR	NR	NR	-	-
REF–Comm Ref Evan	1	NR	NR	NR	-	-
Salvation Army	2	32	89	247	0.2	0.6
Sev Day Adv	3	114	198	228	0.2	0.6
Un C of Christ	8	326	898	1,063	0.9	2.7
Unit Univ	3	284	348	476	0.4	1.2
KNOX	**62**	**2,905**	**5,249**	**11,122**	**28.0**	**100.0**
ANG/EPIS–Episcopal	3	291	610	740	1.9	6.7
Bahá'í	0	NR	16	16	0.0	0.1
BAPT–Amer Bapt USA	11	559	1,230	1,442	3.6	13.0
BAPT–Consrv Bapt	1	NR	NR	NR	-	-
BAPT–So Bapt Conv	1	35	25	29	0.1	0.3
Catholic	4	NR	NR	4,340	10.9	39.0
Ch Cr, Scientst	2	NR	NR	NR	-	-
Ch of Nazarene	3	55	101	132	0.3	1.2
Christian Brethren	1	NR	NR	NR	-	-
CONG–Cong Chr Add'l	1	NR	15	18	0.0	0.2
CONG–Cong Chr, NA	2	NR	387	454	1.1	4.1
FRND–Fr Gen Cf & Un Mtg	1	NR	0	0	0.0	0.0
Jehovah's Witness	1	NR	NR	NR	-	-
LDS–Comm of Christ	1	NR	102	102	0.3	0.9
LDS–L-D Saints	1	NR	NR	256	0.6	2.3
LUTH–E.L.C.A.	1	79	174	179	0.5	1.6
METH–Un Methodist	7	311	735	1,090	2.7	9.8
Non-denom Chr Chs	10	1,028	1,037	1,300	3.3	11.7
PENT–Assemb of God	1	37	29	46	0.1	0.4
PENT–Ch God (Cleve)	1	50	14	16	0.0	0.1
PENT–Un Pent Ch Intl	2	NR	NR	NR	-	-
PRES–Orth Pres Ch	1	118	104	124	0.3	1.1
Salvation Army	1	24	39	79	0.2	0.7
Sev Day Adv	1	44	76	87	0.2	0.8
Un C of Christ	3	195	407	477	1.2	4.3
Unit Univ	1	79	148	195	0.5	1.8
LINCOLN	**48**	**2,177**	**3,968**	**7,655**	**22.2**	**100.0**
ANG/EPIS–Episcopal	4	284	667	736	2.1	9.6
Bahá'í	0	NR	27	27	0.1	0.4
BAPT–Amer Bapt USA	7	288	512	595	1.7	7.8
BAPT–Consrv Bapt	2	NR	NR	NR	-	-
BAPT–Reg Bapt Gen As	1	NR	NR	NR	-	-
Catholic	3	NR	NR	2,725	7.9	35.6
Ch Cr, Scientst	1	NR	NR	NR	-	-
Ch of Nazarene	2	96	174	195	0.6	2.5
CONG–Cong Chr, NA	1	NR	21	24	0.1	0.3
FRND–Fr Gen Cf & Un Mtg	1	NR	51	59	0.2	0.8
Jehovah's Witness	1	NR	NR	NR	-	-
LDS–L-D Saints	1	NR	NR	175	0.5	2.3
LUTH–E.L.C.A.	1	69	88	103	0.3	1.3
METH–Un Methodist	7	236	692	1,027	3.0	13.4
Non-denom Chr Chs	6	575	729	784	2.3	10.2
PENT–Assemb of God	1	86	48	86	0.2	1.1
Un C of Christ	8	512	897	1,042	3.0	13.6
Unit Univ	1	31	62	77	0.2	1.0
OXFORD	**103**	**3,242**	**5,154**	**10,557**	**18.3**	**100.0**
ANG/EPIS–Episcopal	2	82	173	191	0.3	1.8
Bahá'í	0	NR	35	35	0.1	0.3
BAPT–Amer Bapt Assn	1	NR	85	101	0.2	1.0

NR–Not Reported - Represents no adherents reported. Percentages may not total 100 due to rounding.

Table 3: Religious Congregations by County and Group: 2010

Religious Group	Number of Congregations	Number of Attendees	Number of Communicant, Confirmed, or Full Members	Adherents: Number of Adherents	Adherents: % of Total Pop.	Adherents: % of Total Adh.
BAPT–Amer Bapt USA	9	254	332	393	0.7	3.7
BAPT–Consrv Bapt	1	NR	NR	NR	-	-
BUDD–Mahayana	1	NR	NR	11	0.0	0.1
Catholic	7	NR	NR	3,708	6.4	35.1
Ch Cr, Scientst	2	NR	NR	NR	-	-
Ch of Nazarene	3	81	119	153	0.3	1.4
Chr & Miss Al	2	161	86	253	0.4	2.4
CHR–Chr Chs & Chs Cr	1	NR	30	36	0.1	0.3
CHR–Chs of Christ	1	100	79	110	0.2	1.0
CONG–Cong Chr Add'l	1	NR	28	33	0.1	0.3
CONG–Cong Chr, NA	4	NR	440	521	0.9	4.9
CONG–Consrv Cong Chr	1	15	18	21	0.0	0.2
FRND–Fr Gen Cf & Un Mtg	2	NR	10	12	0.0	0.1
Jehovah's Witness	2	NR	NR	NR	-	-
LDS–Comm of Christ	1	NR	102	102	0.2	1.0
LDS–L-D Saints	1	NR	NR	459	0.8	4.3
LUTH–E.L.C.A.	1	42	79	101	0.2	1.0
MENN–Fel Evg Ch	1	185	80	95	0.2	0.9
METH–Un Methodist	7	164	409	664	1.1	6.3
Nat Spirit Asso	1	NR	NR	NR	-	-
Non-denom Chr Chs	15	1,117	1,379	1,540	2.7	14.6
PENT–Assemb of God	3	110	68	152	0.3	1.4
PENT–Un Pent Ch Intl	3	NR	NR	NR	-	-
PRES–Orth Pres Ch	1	26	0	0	0.0	0.0
PRES–Presb Ch (USA)	1	31	39	46	0.1	0.4
Sev Day Adv	4	292	507	584	1.0	5.5
Swedenborgian	1	NR	NR	NR	-	-
Un C of Christ	18	493	949	1,124	1.9	10.6
Unit Univ	5	89	107	112	0.2	1.1
PENOBSCOT	**177**	**8,589**	**13,730**	**37,055**	**24.1**	**100.0**
ANG/EPIS–Anglican NA	1	NR	NR	NR	-	-
ANG/EPIS–Episcopal	5	294	615	682	0.4	1.8
Bahá'í	0	NR	43	43	0.0	0.1
BAPT–Amer Bapt USA	14	698	1,496	1,759	1.1	4.7
BAPT–Consrv Bapt	5	NR	NR	NR	-	-
BUDD–Mahayana	2	NR	NR	126	0.1	0.3
Calv Chpl	2	NR	NR	NR	-	-
Catholic	15	NR	NR	16,581	10.8	44.7
Ch Cr, Scientst	1	NR	NR	NR	-	-
Ch of Nazarene	5	211	359	359	0.2	1.0
Chr & Miss Al	2	111	77	158	0.1	0.4
CHR–Chs of Christ	3	100	86	120	0.1	0.3
CONG–Cong Chr Add'l	1	NR	16	19	0.0	0.1
CONG–Cong Chr, NA	6	NR	515	606	0.4	1.6
CONG–Consrv Cong Chr	1	45	53	62	0.0	0.2
Evan Cov Ch	1	51	61	66	0.0	0.2
FRND–Fr Gen Cf & Un Mtg	1	NR	21	25	0.0	0.1
Int Cou Comm Ch	1	NR	NR	NR	-	-
Jehovah's Witness	6	NR	NR	NR	-	-
JUD–Conserv	1	101	113	305	0.2	0.8
JUD–Orth	1	36	25	50	0.0	0.1
JUD–Reform	1	90	158	427	0.3	1.2
LDS–Comm of Christ	1	NR	102	102	0.1	0.3
LDS–L-D Saints	4	NR	NR	1,552	1.0	4.2
LUTH–E.L.C.A.	1	100	222	222	0.1	0.6
LUTH–Luth–MO Synod	1	10	22	28	0.0	0.1
METH–Un Methodist	20	1,205	3,429	4,685	3.0	12.6
METH–Wesleyan	2	133	75	173	0.1	0.5
Muslim Est	1	60	NR	100	0.1	0.3
Nat Spirit Asso	1	NR	NR	NR	-	-
New Apost Ch	1	NR	NR	NR	-	-
Non-denom Chr Chs	27	3,245	3,080	4,188	2.7	11.3
ORTHE–Greek Orthodox	1	50	NR	300	0.2	0.8
PENT–Assemb of God	5	489	362	872	0.6	2.4
PENT–Ch God (Cleve)	9	361	472	555	0.4	1.5
PENT–Int Foursq Gos	2	33	95	112	0.1	0.3
PENT–Un Pent Ch Intl	7	NR	NR	NR	-	-
PRES–Orth Pres Ch	1	120	134	172	0.1	0.5
REF–Christian Ref	2	140	113	133	0.1	0.4
Salvation Army	1	47	129	265	0.2	0.7
Sev Day Adv	3	130	226	260	0.2	0.7
Un C of Christ	10	634	1,460	1,717	1.1	4.6
Unit Univ	2	95	171	229	0.1	0.6
Zoroastrian	0	NR	NR	2	0.0	0.0
PISCATAQUIS	**34**	**1,162**	**2,179**	**3,601**	**20.5**	**100.0**
ANG/EPIS–Episcopal	2	49	93	118	0.7	3.3
Bahá'í	0	NR	3	3	0.0	0.1
BAPT–Amer Bapt Assn	2	NR	170	198	1.1	5.5
BAPT–Amer Bapt USA	1	80	334	389	2.2	10.8
BAPT–So Bapt Conv	1	30	23	27	0.2	0.7
Calv Chpl	1	NR	NR	NR	-	-
Catholic	3	NR	NR	320	1.8	8.9
Ch of Nazarene	1	41	69	90	0.5	2.5
Evan Free Ch	2	168	NR	168	1.0	4.7
Jehovah's Witness	3	NR	NR	NR	-	-
LDS–L-D Saints	1	NR	NR	272	1.6	7.6
METH–Un Methodist	6	254	876	1,207	6.9	33.5
Non-denom Chr Chs	2	170	125	213	1.2	5.9
PENT–Assemb of God	2	83	45	83	0.5	2.3
PENT–Intl Pent Holiness	1	65	65	76	0.4	2.1
PENT–Un Pent Ch Intl	1	NR	NR	NR	-	-
Un C of Christ	4	192	339	394	2.2	10.9
Unit Univ	1	30	37	43	0.2	1.2
SAGADAHOC	**41**	**2,580**	**3,175**	**8,572**	**24.3**	**100.0**
ANG/EPIS–Episcopal	2	160	302	472	1.3	5.5
Bahá'í	0	NR	24	24	0.1	0.3
BAPT–Amer Bapt USA	6	334	738	878	2.5	10.2
BAPT–Consrv Bapt	2	NR	NR	NR	-	-
BAPT–Converge/BGC	1	400	NR	480	1.4	5.6
BAPT–Ref Bapt Ch	1	NR	NR	NR	-	-
BAPT–So Bapt Conv	1	55	58	69	0.2	0.8
BUDD–Mahayana	1	NR	NR	10	0.0	0.1
Catholic	3	NR	NR	3,177	9.0	37.1
Ch of Nazarene	5	192	194	272	0.8	3.2
LDS–L-D Saints	1	NR	NR	612	1.7	7.1
METH–Un Methodist	3	325	400	637	1.8	7.4
Non-denom Chr Chs	4	490	510	637	1.8	7.4
ORTHE–Rus Orth Abroad	1	45	NR	88	0.2	1.0
PENT–Assemb of God	1	160	150	174	0.5	2.0
PENT–Int Foursq Gos	1	29	51	61	0.2	0.7
PENT–Un Pent Ch Intl	1	NR	NR	NR	-	-
PRES–Presb Ch (USA)	1	85	115	137	0.4	1.6
Salvation Army	1	45	114	234	0.7	2.7
Sev Day Adv	2	104	180	207	0.6	2.4
Un C of Christ	3	156	339	403	1.1	4.7
SOMERSET	**70**	**2,648**	**4,069**	**9,841**	**18.8**	**100.0**
ANG/EPIS–Episcopal	2	55	86	88	0.2	0.9
Bahá'í	0	NR	32	32	0.1	0.3
BAPT–Amer Bapt USA	6	421	782	930	1.8	9.5
BAPT–Consrv Bapt	3	NR	NR	NR	-	-
Catholic	7	NR	NR	3,694	7.1	37.5
Ch of Nazarene	6	250	359	482	0.9	4.9
Chr & Miss Al	1	20	0	23	0.0	0.2
CHR–Chs of Christ	1	45	40	62	0.1	0.6
CONG–Cong Chr, NA	6	NR	550	654	1.3	6.6
Evan Free Ch	2	171	NR	171	0.3	1.7
FRND–Fr Gen Cf & Un Mtg	1	NR	22	26	0.0	0.3
Jehovah's Witness	1	NR	NR	NR	-	-
LDS–L-D Saints	1	NR	NR	423	0.8	4.3
METH–Un Methodist	6	235	661	1,027	2.0	10.4
Non-denom Chr Chs	6	730	565	913	1.7	9.3
PENT–Assemb of God	2	205	115	298	0.6	3.0
PENT–Ch God (Cleve)	1	45	67	80	0.2	0.8
PENT–Int Foursq Gos	1	49	89	106	0.2	1.1
PENT–Intl Pent Holiness	2	32	43	51	0.1	0.5
PENT–Un Pent Ch Intl	3	NR	NR	NR	-	-
PRES–Orth Pres Ch	1	34	25	40	0.1	0.4
PRES–Presb Ch (USA)	3	21	41	49	0.1	0.5
REF–Christian Ref	1	50	5	6	0.0	0.1
Sev Day Adv	2	160	278	320	0.6	3.3
Un C of Christ	4	100	269	320	0.6	3.3
Unit Univ	1	25	40	46	0.1	0.5

NR–Not Reported   - Represents no adherents reported.   Percentages may not total 100 due to rounding.

Table 3: Religious Congregations by County and Group: 2010

Religious Group	Number of Congrega-tions	Number of Attendees	Number of Communicant, Confirmed, or Full Members	Adherents		
				Number of Adherents	% of Total Pop.	% of Total Adh.
WALDO	**53**	**1,988**	**3,083**	**5,369**	**13.8**	**100.0**
ANG/EPIS–Episcopal	1	96	205	243	0.6	4.5
Bahá'í	0	NR	17	17	0.0	0.3
BAPT–Amer Bapt USA	4	135	480	570	1.5	10.6
BAPT–Consrv Bapt	2	NR	NR	NR	-	-
BAPT–So Bapt Conv	2	135	176	209	0.5	3.9
BUDD–Mahayana	1	NR	NR	11	0.0	0.2
Calv Chpl	2	NR	NR	NR	-	-
Catholic	3	NR	NR	900	2.3	16.8
Ch of Nazarene	1	62	80	143	0.4	2.7
CHR–Chs of Christ	1	60	65	75	0.2	1.4
CONG–Cong Chr Add'l	1	NR	45	53	0.1	1.0
CONG–Cong Chr, NA	2	NR	148	176	0.5	3.3
FRND–Fr Gen Cf & Un Mtg	1	NR	11	13	0.0	0.2
HINDU–Renaiss	1	NR	NR	42	0.1	0.8
Jehovah's Witness	2	NR	NR	NR	-	-
LDS–L-D Saints	1	NR	NR	321	0.8	6.0
MENN–Amish Undif	1	NR	24	65	0.2	1.2
METH–Un Methodist	6	302	511	747	1.9	13.9
Nat Spirit Asso	1	NR	NR	NR	-	-
Non-denom Chr Chs	8	750	622	937	2.4	17.5
PENT–Assemb of God	1	0	0	0	0.0	0.0
PENT–Ch God (Cleve)	1	102	159	189	0.5	3.5
PENT–Ch of God Proph	1	NR	54	64	0.2	1.2
PENT–Un Pent Ch Intl	2	NR	NR	NR	-	-
Sev Day Adv	1	14	25	29	0.1	0.5
Un C of Christ	5	248	338	402	1.0	7.5
Unit Univ	1	84	123	163	0.4	3.0
WASHINGTON	**91**	**1,900**	**3,497**	**6,059**	**18.4**	**100.0**
ANG/EPIS–Episcopal	3	111	195	202	0.6	3.3
Bahá'í	0	NR	33	33	0.1	0.5
BAPT–Amer Bapt USA	3	160	186	218	0.7	3.6
BAPT–Consrv Bapt	1	NR	NR	NR	-	-
BAPT–So Bapt Conv	2	91	104	122	0.4	2.0
BUDD–Mahayana	3	NR	NR	89	0.3	1.5
Catholic	10	NR	NR	1,238	3.8	20.4
Ch Cr, Scientst	1	NR	NR	NR	-	-
CHR–Chr Ch (Disc)	1	42	138	162	0.5	2.7
CHR–Chs of Christ	1	65	50	83	0.3	1.4
CONG–Cong Chr, NA	8	NR	230	270	0.8	4.5
FRND–Fr Gen Cf & Un Mtg	1	NR	23	27	0.1	0.4
Jehovah's Witness	3	NR	NR	NR	-	-
LDS–Comm of Christ	4	NR	408	408	1.2	6.7
LDS–L-D Saints	1	NR	NR	112	0.3	1.8
METH–A.W.M.C.	1	20	0	32	0.1	0.5
METH–Un Methodist	14	354	859	1,409	4.3	23.3
METH–Wesleyan	2	98	76	128	0.4	2.1
Non-denom Chr Chs	10	555	606	773	2.4	12.8
PENT–Assemb of God	3	69	15	82	0.2	1.4
PENT–Ch God (Cleve)	4	99	86	101	0.3	1.7
PENT–Un Pent Ch Intl	5	NR	NR	NR	-	-
Sev Day Adv	2	60	105	121	0.4	2.0
Un C of Christ	7	166	377	443	1.3	7.3
Unit Univ	1	10	6	6	0.0	0.1
YORK	**153**	**9,095**	**14,473**	**60,440**	**30.7**	**100.0**
ANG/EPIS–Episcopal	6	501	1,161	1,342	0.7	2.2
Bahá'í	1	NR	196	196	0.1	0.3
BAPT–Amer Bapt USA	17	1,332	2,634	3,133	1.6	5.2
BAPT–Asc Ref Bap Ch Am	1	NR	NR	NR	-	-
BAPT–Consrv Bapt	3	NR	NR	NR	-	-
BAPT–Ref Bapt Ch	1	NR	NR	NR	-	-
BAPT–Reg Bapt Gen As	2	NR	NR	NR	-	-
BAPT–So Bapt Conv	3	511	538	640	0.3	1.1
BRETH–Ch of Brethren	1	0	0	0	0.0	0.0
BUDD–Mahayana	3	NR	NR	280	0.1	0.5
Catholic	16	NR	NR	40,283	20.4	66.6
Ch Cr, Scientst	2	NR	NR	NR	-	-
Ch of Nazarene	3	36	120	142	0.1	0.2
CHR–Chs of Christ	3	123	117	136	0.1	0.2
CONG–Cong Chr Add'l	2	NR	199	237	0.1	0.4
CONG–Cong Chr, NA	2	NR	57	68	0.0	0.1

Religious Group	Number of Congrega-tions	Number of Attendees	Number of Communicant, Confirmed, or Full Members	Adherents		
				Number of Adherents	% of Total Pop.	% of Total Adh.
CONG–Consrv Cong Chr	4	191	132	157	0.1	0.3
Evan Cov Ch	1	42	0	55	0.0	0.1
Evan Free Ch	1	35	NR	35	0.0	0.1
FRND–Fr Gen Cf & Un Mtg	2	NR	9	11	0.0	0.0
Jehovah's Witness	6	NR	NR	NR	-	-
JUD–Orth	1	25	25	35	0.0	0.1
LDS–L-D Saints	2	NR	NR	912	0.5	1.5
LUTH–E.L.C.A.	1	112	274	375	0.2	0.6
METH–AME Zion	1	0	100	119	0.1	0.2
METH–Un Methodist	14	707	1,966	2,495	1.3	4.1
Non-denom Chr Chs	14	2,326	2,520	2,942	1.5	4.9
ORTHE–Greek Orthodox	1	125	NR	300	0.2	0.5
ORTHE–Holy Orth in NA	1	8	NR	10	0.0	0.0
ORTHE–Serb Orth USA	1	47	NR	315	0.2	0.5
PENT–Assemb of God	6	945	339	1,203	0.6	2.0
PENT–Int Foursq Gos	1	23	10	12	0.0	0.0
PENT–Un Pent Ch Intl	1	NR	NR	NR	-	-
PENT–Vineyard	1	52	70	83	0.0	0.1
PRES–Presb Ch (USA)	1	22	23	27	0.0	0.0
Salvation Army	2	167	343	550	0.3	0.9
Sev Day Adv	3	66	114	131	0.1	0.2
Un C of Christ	19	1,481	3,188	3,792	1.9	6.3
Unit Univ	3	218	338	424	0.2	0.7
MARYLAND	**5,336**	**693,181**	**1,130,888**	**2,415,376**	**41.8**	**100.0**
ALLEGANY	**159**	**9,884**	**20,105**	**35,306**	**47.0**	**100.0**
ANG/EPIS–Anglican NA	1	NR	NR	NR	-	-
ANG/EPIS–Episcopal	6	271	739	930	1.2	2.6
Bahá'í	0	NR	8	8	0.0	0.0
BAPT–Reg Bapt Gen As	1	NR	NR	NR	-	-
BAPT–S-D Baptist Gen Con	1	NR	NR	NR	-	-
BAPT–So Bapt Conv	14	1,268	2,174	2,517	3.4	7.1
BRETH–Ch of Brethren	5	121	421	487	0.6	1.4
Catholic	10	NR	NR	8,838	11.8	25.0
CGOD–Ch God (Ander)	1	25	NR	25	0.0	0.1
Ch of Nazarene	3	206	323	414	0.6	1.2
CHR–Chr Ch (Disc)	1	12	23	27	0.0	0.1
CHR–Chr Chs & Chs Cr	1	NR	150	174	0.2	0.5
CHR–Chs of Christ	1	40	44	64	0.1	0.2
CONG–Cong Chr, NA	1	NR	100	116	0.2	0.3
Jehovah's Witness	3	NR	NR	NR	-	-
JUD–Reform	1	36	64	173	0.2	0.5
LDS–L-D Saints	1	NR	NR	635	0.8	1.8
LUTH–E.L.C.A.	6	604	2,168	2,850	3.8	8.1
LUTH–Luth Cong Msn Chr	1	NR	NR	NR	-	-
LUTH–Luth–MO Synod	1	68	111	123	0.2	0.3
MENN–Mennonite USA	1	85	159	184	0.2	0.5
METH–AME	2	70	250	289	0.4	0.8
METH–Evan Meth Ch	1	NR	NR	NR	-	-
METH–Un Methodist	43	2,302	8,680	9,201	12.3	26.1
METH–Wesleyan	3	63	84	82	0.1	0.2
Muslim Est	1	134	NR	308	0.4	0.9
Non-denom Chr Chs	16	1,954	2,040	2,504	3.3	7.1
PENT–Assemb of God	11	1,503	865	3,229	4.3	9.1
PENT–Ch God (Cleve)	2	256	266	308	0.4	0.9
PENT–Ch of God Proph	1	NR	9	10	0.0	0.0
PENT–Intl Pent Holiness	2	191	208	241	0.3	0.7
PENT–Un Pent Ch Intl	1	NR	NR	NR	-	-
PRES–Presb Ch (USA)	5	260	533	617	0.8	1.7
PRES–Presb Ch Amer	2	82	80	88	0.1	0.2
Salvation Army	1	72	113	292	0.4	0.8
Sev Day Adv	2	136	238	273	0.4	0.8
Un Breth in Cr	1	0	0	0	0.0	0.0
Un C of Christ	4	87	193	223	0.3	0.6
Unit Univ	1	38	62	76	0.1	0.2
ANNE ARUNDEL	**350**	**41,627**	**78,891**	**204,947**	**38.1**	**100.0**
ANG/EPIS–Anglican NA	4	NR	NR	NR	-	-
ANG/EPIS–Episcopal	14	2,146	5,629	7,633	1.4	3.7
Bahá'í	2	NR	150	150	0.0	0.1
BAPT–Alliance Bapt	1	NR	NR	NR	-	-

NR–Not Reported - Represents no adherents reported. Percentages may not total 100 due to rounding.

Table 3: Religious Congregations by County and Group: 2010

Religious Group	Number of Congrega-tions	Number of Attendees	Number of Communicant, Confirmed, or Full Members	Adherents		
				Number of Adherents	% of Total Pop.	% of Total Adh.
BAPT–Amer Bapt Assn	1	NR	85	104	0.0	0.1
BAPT–Amer Bapt USA	2	200	1,215	1,482	0.3	0.7
BAPT–Converge/BGC	1	75	NR	90	0.0	0.0
BAPT–NBC USA	1	0	2,750	3,353	0.6	1.6
BAPT–Ref Bapt Ch	1	NR	NR	NR	-	-
BAPT–Reg Bapt Gen As	2	NR	NR	NR	-	-
BAPT–So Bapt Conv	37	5,507	10,410	12,694	2.4	6.2
BRETH–Ch of Brethren	1	0	114	139	0.0	0.1
BUDD–Mahayana	3	NR	NR	72	0.0	0.0
BUDD–Vajrayana	1	NR	NR	17	0.0	0.0
Catholic	20	NR	NR	95,116	17.7	46.4
CGOD–Ch God (Ander)	2	70	NR	70	0.0	0.0
Ch Cr, Scientst	1	NR	NR	NR	-	-
Ch of Nazarene	7	516	637	683	0.1	0.3
CHR–Chr Chs & Chs Cr	3	NR	1,200	1,463	0.3	0.7
CHR–Chs of Christ	4	510	499	626	0.1	0.3
Evan Cong Ch	1	NR	0	0	0.0	0.0
Evan Free Ch	1	60	NR	60	0.0	0.0
FRND–Fr Gen Cf & Un Mtg	1	NR	80	98	0.0	0.0
HINDU–Post Ren	1	NR	NR	10	0.0	0.0
Ind Fund Churches	1	NR	NR	NR	-	-
Jehovah's Witness	4	NR	NR	NR	-	-
JUD–Conserv	1	107	120	324	0.1	0.2
JUD–Reform	1	185	327	883	0.2	0.4
LDS–L-D Saints	9	NR	NR	3,815	0.7	1.9
LUTH–E.L.C.A.	11	1,580	4,548	6,280	1.2	3.1
LUTH–Luth Cong Msn Chr	2	255	235	287	0.1	0.1
LUTH–Luth-MO Synod	5	1,071	2,423	3,436	0.6	1.7
LUTH–Nor Amer Luth C	2	NR	NR	NR	-	-
METH–AME	7	510	1,610	1,963	0.4	1.0
METH–AME Zion	2	115	240	293	0.1	0.1
METH–Free Methodist	1	37	52	52	0.0	0.0
METH–Un Methodist	69	8,486	24,059	29,254	5.4	14.3
METH–Wesleyan	2	137	146	178	0.0	0.1
Metro Comm Ch	1	18	24	29	0.0	0.0
Muslim Est	3	368	NR	1,116	0.2	0.5
Non-denom Chr Chs	43	10,477	10,891	13,647	2.5	6.7
ORTHE–Ant Orth of NA	1	115	NR	250	0.0	0.1
ORTHE–Greek Orthodox	1	500	NR	3,000	0.6	1.5
PENT–Assemb of God	10	1,781	1,426	3,234	0.6	1.6
PENT–Ch God (Cleve)	13	1,403	1,671	2,038	0.4	1.0
PENT–Ch of God Proph	1	NR	54	66	0.0	0.0
PENT–Elim	1	NR	NR	NR	-	-
PENT–Full Gosp Bapt	1	NR	NR	NR	-	-
PENT–I F Chr Assmbl	1	NR	NR	NR	-	-
PENT–Int Pent C Chr	1	35	48	125	0.0	0.1
PENT–Intl Pent Holiness	1	90	120	146	0.0	0.1
PENT–Pent Ch of God	1	70	NR	109	0.0	0.1
PENT–Un Pent Ch Intl	6	NR	NR	NR	-	-
PENT–Vineyard	1	120	250	305	0.1	0.1
PRES–Korean Pres Amer	1	NR	NR	NR	-	-
PRES–Presb Ch (USA)	7	1,724	3,738	4,558	0.8	2.2
PRES–Presb Ch Amer	10	2,530	2,661	3,817	0.7	1.9
PRES–Ref Pres Han	1	NR	NR	NR	-	-
REF–Comm Ref Evan	1	NR	NR	NR	-	-
Salvation Army	1	28	61	178	0.0	0.1
Sev Day Adv	10	435	757	870	0.2	0.4
Un Breth in Cr	1	34	54	29	0.0	0.0
Un C of Christ	1	60	95	116	0.0	0.1
Unit Univ	1	272	512	674	0.1	0.3
Unity Ch	1	NR	NR	NR	-	-
Zoroastrian	0	NR	NR	15	0.0	0.0
BALTIMORE	**527**	**75,086**	**126,071**	**332,827**	**41.3**	**100.0**
ANG/EPIS–Anglican NA	5	NR	NR	NR	-	-
ANG/EPIS–Episcopal	23	2,144	6,601	8,148	1.0	2.4
Bahá'í	3	NR	340	340	0.0	0.1
BAPT–Alliance Bapt	2	NR	NR	NR	-	-
BAPT–Amer Bapt USA	2	425	728	874	0.1	0.3
BAPT–Converge/BGC	1	75	NR	90	0.0	0.0
BAPT–Ind Bapt Flwsp Intl	1	NR	NR	NR	-	-
BAPT–Natl Mis Bapt Conv	1	0	150	180	0.0	0.1
BAPT–NBC USA	9	3,680	6,170	7,408	0.9	2.2
BAPT–Ref Bapt Ch	1	NR	NR	NR	-	-

Religious Group	Number of Congrega-tions	Number of Attendees	Number of Communicant, Confirmed, or Full Members	Adherents		
				Number of Adherents	% of Total Pop.	% of Total Adh.
BAPT–So Bapt Conv	53	4,440	11,178	13,422	1.7	4.0
BRETH–Breth in Chr	1	NR	NR	NR	-	-
BRETH–Ch of Brethren	4	118	360	432	0.1	0.1
BUDD–Mahayana	3	NR	NR	1,635	0.2	0.5
BUDD–Theravada	1	NR	NR	292	0.0	0.1
BUDD–Vajrayana	1	NR	NR	27	0.0	0.0
Calv Chpl	1	NR	NR	NR	-	-
Catholic	34	NR	NR	153,243	19.0	46.0
CGOD–Ch God (Ander)	3	220	NR	220	0.0	0.1
Ch Cr, Scientst	3	NR	NR	NR	-	-
Ch of Nazarene	4	528	371	591	0.1	0.2
Chr & Miss Al	1	64	50	90	0.0	0.0
CHR–Chr Ch (Disc)	4	142	467	561	0.1	0.2
CHR–Chr Chs & Chs Cr	2	NR	450	540	0.1	0.2
CHR–Chs of Christ	6	508	524	637	0.1	0.2
Christian Brethren	1	NR	NR	NR	-	-
FRND–Fr Gen Cf & Un Mtg	1	NR	109	131	0.0	0.0
Ind Fund Churches	1	NR	NR	NR	-	-
Int Cou Comm Ch	1	NR	NR	NR	-	-
Jehovah's Witness	9	NR	NR	NR	-	-
JUD–Conserv	4	3,082	3,459	9,339	1.2	2.8
JUD–Orth	5	5,040	2,100	7,000	0.9	2.1
JUD–Reform	2	226	398	1,075	0.1	0.3
LDS–Comm of Christ	2	NR	274	274	0.0	0.1
LDS–L-D Saints	2	NR	NR	2,530	0.3	0.8
LUTH–E.L.C.A.	31	3,512	10,341	14,610	1.8	4.4
LUTH–Luth-MO Synod	13	1,188	3,144	3,654	0.5	1.1
LUTH–Nor Amer Luth C	1	NR	NR	NR	-	-
LUTH–Wisc Ev Luth Syn	1	68	116	143	0.0	0.0
MENN–Mennonite USA	1	110	110	132	0.0	0.0
METH–AME	16	2,118	8,248	9,904	1.2	3.0
METH–AME Zion	4	8,000	12,300	14,769	1.8	4.4
METH–Free Methodist	5	304	245	320	0.0	0.1
METH–Un Methodist	87	7,123	21,452	23,327	2.9	7.0
MJEW–Assoc Mes Cong	1	NR	NR	NR	-	-
MJEW–Union Mes Cong	1	NR	NR	NR	-	-
Muslim Est	13	3,608	NR	9,696	1.2	2.9
New Apost Ch	1	NR	NR	NR	-	-
Non-denom Chr Chs	59	17,606	22,161	24,741	3.1	7.4
ORTHE–Ant Orth of NA	1	59	NR	163	0.0	0.0
ORTHE–Greek Orthodox	1	500	NR	1,500	0.2	0.5
ORTHO–Ethiopian Orth	1	NR	NR	NR	-	-
PENT–Assemb of God	12	2,338	1,421	4,632	0.6	1.4
PENT–Ch God (Cleve)	16	3,311	5,088	6,109	0.8	1.8
PENT–Ch Lord Jesus Apos	1	NR	NR	NR	-	-
PENT–Ch of God Proph	1	NR	20	24	0.0	0.0
PENT–COGIC	2	120	151	181	0.0	0.1
PENT–Full Gosp Bapt	4	NR	NR	NR	-	-
PENT–Int Foursq Gos	1	24	33	40	0.0	0.0
PENT–Un Pent Ch Intl	9	NR	NR	NR	-	-
PRES–Evan Presby Ch	1	NR	188	226	0.0	0.1
PRES–Kor Pres Abroad	1	NR	NR	NR	-	-
PRES–Korean Amer Pres	1	NR	NR	NR	-	-
PRES–Korean Pres Amer	4	NR	NR	NR	-	-
PRES–Presb Ch (USA)	9	576	1,059	1,272	0.2	0.4
PRES–Presb Ch Amer	12	2,095	2,811	3,346	0.4	1.0
Salvation Army	3	148	258	1,147	0.1	0.3
Sev Day Adv	6	916	1,592	1,831	0.2	0.6
Sikh	2	NR	NR	NR	-	-
Un C of Christ	7	490	1,300	1,561	0.2	0.5
Unit Univ	1	180	304	412	0.1	0.1
Zoroastrian	0	NR	NR	8	0.0	0.0
BALTIMORE (CITY)	**670**	**123,880**	**168,759**	**293,880**	**47.3**	**100.0**
ANG/EPIS–Anglican NA	2	NR	NR	NR	-	-
ANG/EPIS–Episcopal	27	2,598	6,713	9,901	1.6	3.4
Bahá'í	1	NR	273	273	0.0	0.1
BAPT–Alliance Bapt	1	NR	NR	NR	-	-
BAPT–Amer Bapt USA	15	12,100	7,314	8,789	1.4	3.0
BAPT–Natl Mis Bapt Conv	2	200	450	541	0.1	0.2
BAPT–NBC Amer	7	2,940	4,520	5,432	0.9	1.8
BAPT–NBC USA	27	4,011	11,645	13,994	2.3	4.8
BAPT–Prog NBC	9	1,350	3,994	4,800	0.8	1.6
BAPT–Reg Bapt Gen As	1	NR	NR	NR	-	-

NR–Not Reported - Represents no adherents reported. Percentages may not total 100 due to rounding.

Table 3: Religious Congregations by County and Group: 2010

Religious Group	Number of Congrega-tions	Number of Attendees	Number of Communicant, Confirmed, or Full Members	Adherents		
				Number of Adherents	% of Total Pop.	% of Total Adh.
BAPT–So Bapt Conv	49	3,906	7,338	8,818	1.4	3.0
BRETH–Ch of Brethren	1	14	29	35	0.0	0.0
BUDD–Mahayana	3	NR	NR	33	0.0	0.0
BUDD–Vajrayana	3	NR	NR	530	0.1	0.2
Catholic	55	NR	NR	68,003	11.0	23.1
CGOD–Ch God (Ander)	2	125	NR	125	0.0	0.0
Ch Cr, Scientist	1	NR	NR	NR	-	-
Ch of Nazarene	1	21	51	51	0.0	0.0
Chr & Miss Al	1	97	73	135	0.0	0.0
CHR–Chr Ch (Disc)	4	57	172	207	0.0	0.1
CHR–Chr Chs & Chs Cr	4	NR	242	291	0.0	0.1
CHR–Chs of Christ	3	1,600	2,264	2,572	0.4	0.9
Christian Brethren	1	NR	NR	NR	-	-
Evan Free Ch	3	178	NR	178	0.0	0.1
FRND–Evan Fr Ch Intl	1	125	80	96	0.0	0.0
FRND–Fr Gen Cf & Un Mtg	2	NR	587	705	0.1	0.2
FRND–Unaffl Mtgs	1	NR	NR	NR	-	-
HINDU–Post Ren	2	NR	NR	35	0.0	0.0
Int Cou Comm Ch	1	NR	NR	NR	-	-
Jehovah's Witness	15	NR	NR	NR	-	-
JUD–Conserv	1	349	392	1,058	0.2	0.4
JUD–Orth	25	14,400	5,000	20,000	3.2	6.8
JUD–Reconst	2	118	151	408	0.1	0.1
JUD–Reform	2	1,144	2,017	5,446	0.9	1.9
LDS–Comm of Christ	1	NR	137	137	0.0	0.0
LDS–L-D Saints	3	NR	NR	1,751	0.3	0.6
LUTH–E.L.C.A.	29	2,397	5,185	6,409	1.0	2.2
LUTH–Luth-MO Synod	12	713	1,623	2,223	0.4	0.8
MENN–Mennonite USA	2	182	128	154	0.0	0.1
METH–AME	21	8,215	18,888	22,698	3.7	7.7
METH–AME Zion	6	1,900	2,550	3,064	0.5	1.0
METH–C.M.E.	1	250	400	481	0.1	0.2
METH–Un Methodist	50	4,075	10,702	11,094	1.8	3.8
METH–Wesleyan	2	79	76	103	0.0	0.0
Metro Comm Ch	1	68	74	89	0.0	0.0
Muslim Est	10	1,922	NR	3,414	0.5	1.2
Non-denom Chr Chs	153	48,126	61,020	65,904	10.6	22.4
OCATH–Pol Natl Cath	1	NR	NR	NR	-	-
ORTHE–Greek Orthodox	2	1,150	NR	5,000	0.8	1.7
ORTHE–Orth Ch in Amer	1	85	NR	120	0.0	0.0
ORTHE–Rus Orth Abroad	1	20	NR	50	0.0	0.0
ORTHE–Rus Orth Moscow	1	80	NR	225	0.0	0.1
ORTHE–Ukrainian Orth	1	60	NR	200	0.0	0.1
PENT–Assemb of God	6	1,180	425	1,358	0.2	0.5
PENT–Ch God (Cleve)	8	721	1,119	1,345	0.2	0.5
PENT–Ch of God by Faith	1	NR	NR	NR	-	-
PENT–Ch of God Proph	3	NR	105	126	0.0	0.0
PENT–COGIC	10	1,305	1,715	2,061	0.3	0.7
PENT–Elim	1	NR	NR	NR	-	-
PENT–Fire Bapt Hol Ch	2	NR	NR	NR	-	-
PENT–Full Gosp Bapt	7	NR	NR	NR	-	-
PENT–Int Pent C Chr	1	13	3	17	0.0	0.0
PENT–Intl Pent Holiness	2	403	967	1,162	0.2	0.4
PENT–Un Pent Ch Intl	1	NR	NR	NR	-	-
PENT–United Holy Ch	3	NR	NR	NR	-	-
PRES–Presb Ch (USA)	28	2,991	5,671	6,815	1.1	2.3
PRES–Presb Ch Amer	4	735	751	851	0.1	0.3
Sev Day Adv	10	1,496	2,601	2,992	0.5	1.0
Un C of Christ	8	232	1,088	1,307	0.2	0.4
Unit Univ	1	149	226	264	0.0	0.1
Unity Ch	1	NR	NR	NR	-	-
Zoroastrian	0	NR	NR	10	0.0	0.0
CALVERT	**73**	**7,208**	**12,892**	**55,088**	**62.1**	**100.0**
ANG/EPIS–Episcopal	4	490	837	1,265	1.4	2.3
Bahá'í	0	NR	16	16	0.0	0.0
BAPT–Alliance Bapt	1	NR	NR	NR	-	-
BAPT–Amer Bapt USA	2	63	79	98	0.1	0.2
BAPT–Consrv Bapt	1	NR	NR	NR	-	-
BAPT–Converge/BGC	1	75	NR	90	0.1	0.2
BAPT–So Bapt Conv	8	970	1,256	1,554	1.8	2.8
BRETH–Grace Breth	2	NR	NR	NR	-	-
Catholic	5	NR	NR	39,245	44.2	71.2
CHR–Chs of Christ	2	145	130	200	0.2	0.4
FRND–Fr Gen Cf & Un Mtg	1	NR	24	30	0.0	0.1
Ind Fund Churches	1	NR	NR	NR	-	-
Jehovah's Witness	1	NR	NR	NR	-	-
LDS–L-D Saints	1	NR	NR	752	0.8	1.4
LUTH–E.L.C.A.	1	158	393	532	0.6	1.0
LUTH–Luth-MO Synod	1	246	415	534	0.6	1.0
LUTH–Wisc Ev Luth Syn	1	55	88	117	0.1	0.2
METH–Un Methodist	21	2,370	5,640	6,063	6.8	11.0
METH–Wesleyan	1	20	15	26	0.0	0.0
Muslim Est	1	134	NR	308	0.3	0.6
Non-denom Chr Chs	9	2,120	3,600	3,705	4.2	6.7
PENT–Assemb of God	1	150	70	150	0.2	0.3
PENT–Ch Lord Jesus Apos	2	NR	NR	NR	-	-
PENT–Ch of God Proph	1	NR	54	67	0.1	0.1
PENT–Un Pent Ch Intl	1	NR	NR	NR	-	-
PRES–Presb Ch Amer	1	102	83	115	0.1	0.2
Sev Day Adv	2	110	192	221	0.2	0.4
CAROLINE	**65**	**2,856**	**7,095**	**11,129**	**33.7**	**100.0**
ANG/EPIS–Episcopal	1	45	88	89	0.3	0.8
Bahá'í	0	NR	17	17	0.1	0.2
BAPT–Natl Mis Bapt Conv	2	0	500	621	1.9	5.6
BAPT–So Bapt Conv	2	213	775	963	2.9	8.7
BRETH–Ch of Brethren	2	99	164	204	0.6	1.8
Catholic	3	NR	NR	2,585	7.8	23.2
CGOD–Ch God (Ander)	1	0	NR	0	0.0	0.0
Ch Christ Chr Union	2	NR	NR	NR	-	-
Ch of Nazarene	2	189	297	358	1.1	3.2
CHR–Chr Chs & Chs Cr	1	NR	50	62	0.2	0.6
LUTH–Luth-MO Synod	1	93	265	340	1.0	3.1
METH–AME	5	40	670	832	2.5	7.5
METH–Un Methodist	24	1,020	3,071	3,333	10.1	29.9
METH–Wesleyan	6	467	357	607	1.8	5.5
Non-denom Chr Chs	5	452	522	617	1.9	5.5
PENT–Ch God (Cleve)	2	130	226	281	0.8	2.5
PENT–Ch of God Proph	1	NR	29	36	0.1	0.3
PENT–Pent Ch of God	1	70	NR	109	0.3	1.0
PENT–Un Pent Ch Intl	1	NR	NR	NR	-	-
Sev Day Adv	3	38	64	75	0.2	0.7
CARROLL	**158**	**14,579**	**30,661**	**71,916**	**43.0**	**100.0**
ANG/EPIS–Anglican NA	2	NR	NR	NR	-	-
ANG/EPIS–Episcopal	2	250	736	894	0.5	1.2
Bahá'í	1	NR	54	54	0.0	0.1
BAPT–Converge/BGC	1	75	NR	90	0.1	0.1
BAPT–So Bapt Conv	9	1,854	3,091	3,780	2.3	5.3
BRETH–Brethren (Ash)	1	NR	80	98	0.1	0.1
BRETH–Ch of Brethren	6	422	905	1,107	0.7	1.5
BUDD–Theravada	2	NR	NR	792	0.5	1.1
Catholic	4	NR	NR	30,551	18.3	42.5
CGOD–Ches God-Gen Con	4	200	121	148	0.1	0.2
Ch of Nazarene	3	298	204	350	0.2	0.5
CHR–Chr Chs & Chs Cr	1	NR	125	153	0.1	0.2
CHR–Chs of Christ	2	95	100	140	0.1	0.2
FRND–Fr Gen Cf & Un Mtg	1	NR	31	38	0.0	0.1
Jehovah's Witness	2	NR	NR	NR	-	-
LDS–L-D Saints	3	NR	NR	1,483	0.9	2.1
LUTH–E.L.C.A.	18	1,906	5,610	7,294	4.4	10.1
LUTH–Luth-MO Synod	1	200	176	293	0.2	0.4
MENN–Mennonite USA	1	0	0	0	0.0	0.0
METH–Free Methodist	1	45	16	45	0.0	0.1
METH–Un Methodist	41	3,487	10,939	13,734	8.2	19.1
METH–Wesleyan	1	145	139	189	0.1	0.3
Non-denom Chr Chs	19	3,140	3,355	4,101	2.5	5.7
ORTHE–Ant Orth of NA	1	50	NR	100	0.1	0.1
ORTHO–Malan Syr Orth	1	65	NR	126	0.1	0.2
PENT–Assemb of God	3	321	204	391	0.2	0.5
PENT–Ch God (Cleve)	3	758	746	912	0.5	1.3
PENT–Int Foursq Gos	1	39	33	40	0.0	0.1
PRES–AmPres	1	NR	NR	NR	-	-
PRES–As Ref Pres Ch	3	NR	151	185	0.1	0.3
PRES–Presb Ch (USA)	3	286	527	645	0.4	0.9
PRES–Presb Ch Amer	2	47	1,092	1,450	0.9	2.0

NR–Not Reported   - Represents no adherents reported.   Percentages may not total 100 due to rounding.

Table 3: Religious Congregations by County and Group: 2010

Religious Group	Number of Congrega-tions	Number of Attendees	Number of Communicant, Confirmed, or Full Members	Adherents: Number of Adherents	Adherents: % of Total Pop.	Adherents: % of Total Adh.
PRES–Ref Pres Han	1	NR	NR	NR	-	-
Sev Day Adv	2	146	254	292	0.2	0.4
Un C of Christ	10	677	1,879	2,298	1.4	3.2
Unit Univ	1	73	93	143	0.1	0.2
CECIL	**104**	**8,608**	**16,274**	**31,484**	**31.1**	**100.0**
ANG/EPIS–Anglican NA	1	NR	NR	NR	-	-
ANG/EPIS–Episcopal	5	351	1,076	1,234	1.2	3.9
Bahá'í	0	NR	8	8	0.0	0.0
BAPT–So Bapt Conv	9	1,151	2,899	3,581	3.5	11.4
Catholic	8	NR	NR	9,440	9.3	30.0
Ch of Nazarene	3	249	282	2,095	2.1	6.7
CHR–Chs of Christ	3	73	58	85	0.1	0.3
Jehovah's Witness	1	NR	NR	NR	-	-
LDS–L-D Saints	1	NR	NR	457	0.5	1.5
LUTH–E.L.C.A.	1	75	151	208	0.2	0.7
MENN–Amish Undif	1	NR	61	152	0.2	0.5
METH–AME	6	20	635	784	0.8	2.5
METH–Free Methodist	1	146	68	146	0.1	0.5
METH–Un Methodist	29	2,305	5,661	6,581	6.5	20.9
METH–Wesleyan	2	44	37	57	0.1	0.2
Non-denom Chr Chs	16	3,094	3,720	4,488	4.4	14.3
PENT–Assemb of God	1	212	129	350	0.3	1.1
PENT–Ch God (Cleve)	3	192	362	447	0.4	1.4
PENT–Ch of God Proph	1	NR	36	44	0.0	0.1
PENT–Un Pent Ch Intl	1	NR	NR	NR	-	-
PRES–Orth Pres Ch	1	60	52	72	0.1	0.2
PRES–Presb Ch (USA)	6	425	688	850	0.8	2.7
PRES–Presb Ch Amer	1	32	40	47	0.0	0.1
Sev Day Adv	3	179	311	358	0.4	1.1
CHARLES	**129**	**11,762**	**20,755**	**54,163**	**37.0**	**100.0**
ANG/EPIS–Episcopal	6	485	864	1,483	1.0	2.7
Bahá'í	0	NR	14	14	0.0	0.0
BAPT–Amer Bapt USA	3	209	308	384	0.3	0.7
BAPT–NBC USA	2	200	500	623	0.4	1.2
BAPT–Prog NBC	1	0	60	75	0.1	0.1
BAPT–Reg Bapt Gen As	1	NR	NR	NR	-	-
BAPT–So Bapt Conv	22	3,008	6,853	8,539	5.8	15.8
BRETH–Grace Breth	2	NR	NR	NR	-	-
Calv Chpl	1	NR	NR	NR	-	-
Catholic	12	NR	NR	26,146	17.8	48.3
CGOD–Ch God (Ander)	1	31	NR	31	0.0	0.1
Ch of Nazarene	2	234	238	345	0.2	0.6
CHR–Chs of Christ	2	160	153	210	0.1	0.4
Jehovah's Witness	2	NR	NR	NR	-	-
JUD–Conserv	1	27	30	81	0.1	0.1
JUD–Reform	1	20	36	97	0.1	0.2
LDS–L-D Saints	2	NR	NR	1,012	0.7	1.9
LUTH–E.L.C.A.	1	158	186	245	0.2	0.5
LUTH–Luth-MO Synod	2	211	732	1,096	0.7	2.0
MENN–Amish Undif	4	NR	219	489	0.3	0.9
METH–AME	6	20	635	791	0.5	1.5
METH–So Methodist	1	NR	NR	NR	-	-
METH–Un Methodist	15	1,405	3,999	4,166	2.8	7.7
METH–Wesleyan	3	1,463	765	1,902	1.3	3.5
Muslim Est	1	134	NR	308	0.2	0.6
Non-denom Chr Chs	21	2,947	3,837	4,333	3.0	8.0
ORTHE–Carp Rus Orth	1	50	NR	100	0.1	0.2
PENT–Assemb of God	3	120	108	212	0.1	0.4
PENT–Ch God (Cleve)	1	252	240	299	0.2	0.6
PENT–Int Foursq Gos	1	35	38	47	0.0	0.1
PENT–Intl Pent Holiness	1	115	121	151	0.1	0.3
PENT–Un Pent Ch Intl	1	NR	NR	NR	-	-
PENT–Vineyard	1	40	50	62	0.0	0.1
PRES–Presb Ch (USA)	1	150	253	315	0.2	0.6
PRES–Presb Ch Amer	1	20	50	72	0.0	0.1
Sev Day Adv	3	268	466	535	0.4	1.0
DORCHESTER	**86**	**4,334**	**8,740**	**11,896**	**36.5**	**100.0**
ANG/EPIS–Episcopal	5	192	502	708	2.2	6.0
Bahá'í	0	NR	41	41	0.1	0.3
BAPT–Reg Bapt Gen As	1	NR	NR	NR	-	-

Religious Group	Number of Congrega-tions	Number of Attendees	Number of Communicant, Confirmed, or Full Members	Adherents: Number of Adherents	Adherents: % of Total Pop.	Adherents: % of Total Adh.
BAPT–So Bapt Conv	6	310	629	755	2.3	6.3
Catholic	3	NR	NR	1,217	3.7	10.2
Ch of Nazarene	2	68	80	97	0.3	0.8
Chr & Miss Al	2	172	113	239	0.7	2.0
CHR–Chr Chs & Chs Cr	1	NR	110	132	0.4	1.1
CHR–Chs of Christ	1	75	80	115	0.4	1.0
Jehovah's Witness	1	NR	NR	NR	-	-
LDS–L-D Saints	1	NR	NR	298	0.9	2.5
LUTH–Luth-MO Synod	1	36	57	77	0.2	0.6
METH–AME	2	100	450	540	1.7	4.5
METH–AME Zion	1	0	150	180	0.6	1.5
METH–Un Methodist	41	1,836	4,660	5,256	16.1	44.2
METH–Wesleyan	3	213	171	277	0.8	2.3
Non-denom Chr Chs	6	775	915	1,029	3.2	8.6
PENT–Ch God (Cleve)	3	309	369	443	1.4	3.7
PENT–Un Pent Ch Intl	1	NR	NR	NR	-	-
PRES–Presb Ch Amer	1	56	56	81	0.2	0.7
Salvation Army	1	54	101	108	0.3	0.9
Sev Day Adv	2	54	93	107	0.3	0.9
Un C of Christ	1	84	163	196	0.6	1.6
FREDERICK	**261**	**21,115**	**45,165**	**97,808**	**41.9**	**100.0**
ANG/EPIS–Episcopal	8	643	2,248	2,446	1.0	2.5
Bahá'í	2	NR	101	101	0.0	0.1
BAPT–Amer Bapt Assn	2	NR	116	144	0.1	0.1
BAPT–Amer Bapt USA	2	120	150	186	0.1	0.2
BAPT–Converge/BGC	1	75	NR	90	0.0	0.1
BAPT–Ref Bapt Ch	1	NR	NR	NR	-	-
BAPT–So Bapt Conv	14	1,494	3,315	4,104	1.8	4.2
BRETH–Breth in Chr	1	NR	NR	NR	-	-
BRETH–Ch of Brethren	13	1,736	3,020	3,739	1.6	3.8
BRETH–Grace Breth	1	NR	NR	NR	-	-
BUDD–Vajrayana	1	NR	NR	27	0.0	0.0
Calv Chpl	1	NR	NR	NR	-	-
Catholic	12	NR	NR	36,923	15.8	37.8
CGOD–Ches God-Gen Con	6	268	292	361	0.2	0.4
Ch Cr, Scientst	1	NR	NR	NR	-	-
Ch God (7th Day)	1	NR	NR	NR	-	-
Ch of Nazarene	3	231	255	385	0.2	0.4
Chr & Miss Al	4	172	80	223	0.1	0.2
CHR–Chr Chs & Chs Cr	2	NR	135	167	0.1	0.2
CHR–Chs of Christ	3	335	282	380	0.2	0.4
CHR–Int Chs of Christ	1	NR	58	72	0.0	0.1
Evan Free Ch	1	350	NR	350	0.1	0.4
FRND–Fr Gen Cf & Un Mtg	1	NR	82	102	0.0	0.1
HINDU–Post Ren	1	NR	NR	10	0.0	0.0
Jehovah's Witness	2	NR	NR	NR	-	-
JUD–Orth	1	43	50	60	0.0	0.1
JUD–Reform	1	77	135	364	0.2	0.4
LDS–Comm of Christ	1	NR	137	137	0.1	0.1
LDS–L-D Saints	6	NR	NR	2,631	1.1	2.7
LUTH–E.L.C.A.	31	2,621	10,021	13,673	5.9	14.0
LUTH–Luth Cong Msn Chr	2	30	152	188	0.1	0.2
LUTH–Luth-MO Synod	1	92	113	155	0.1	0.2
LUTH–Nor Amer Luth C	1	NR	NR	NR	-	-
METH–AME	5	311	752	931	0.4	1.0
METH–Un Methodist	47	4,444	12,044	13,890	6.0	14.2
MORAV–Morav Ch-North	1	132	324	395	0.2	0.4
Muslim Est	1	134	NR	308	0.1	0.3
Non-denom Chr Chs	27	3,220	3,765	4,387	1.9	4.5
ORTHE–Ant Orth of NA	1	30	NR	45	0.0	0.0
ORTHE–Greek Orthodox	1	140	NR	500	0.2	0.5
PENT–Assemb of God	7	824	660	1,374	0.6	1.4
PENT–Ch God (Cleve)	3	775	1,734	2,147	0.9	2.2
PENT–Ch of God Proph	2	NR	49	61	0.0	0.1
PENT–Elim	1	NR	NR	NR	-	-
PENT–Int Foursq Gos	2	202	193	239	0.1	0.2
PENT–Pent Ch of God	1	70	NR	109	0.0	0.1
PENT–Un Pent Ch Intl	2	NR	NR	NR	-	-
PRES–As Ref Pres Ch	1	NR	106	131	0.1	0.1
PRES–Orth Pres Ch	1	131	126	161	0.1	0.2
PRES–Presb Ch (USA)	4	186	376	465	0.2	0.5
PRES–Presb Ch Amer	2	250	301	355	0.2	0.4
REF–Ref Ch in Am	1	302	299	299	0.1	0.3

NR–Not Reported - Represents no adherents reported. Percentages may not total 100 due to rounding.

Table 3: Religious Congregations by County and Group: 2010

Religious Group	Number of Congrega-tions	Number of Attendees	Number of Communicant, Confirmed, or Full Members	Adherents: Number of Adherents	Adherents: % of Total Pop.	Adherents: % of Total Adh.
Salvation Army	1	57	146	677	0.3	0.7
Sev Day Adv	5	701	1,219	1,402	0.6	1.4
Un C of Christ	14	814	2,141	2,651	1.1	2.7
Unit Univ	1	105	188	257	0.1	0.3
Unity Ch	1	NR	NR	NR	-	-
Zoroastrian	0	NR	NR	6	0.0	0.0
GARRETT	**96**	**5,452**	**8,000**	**11,015**	**36.6**	**100.0**
ANG/EPIS–Episcopal	2	92	126	295	1.0	2.7
Bahá'í	0	NR	2	2	0.0	0.0
BAPT–So Bapt Conv	5	393	336	400	1.3	3.6
BRETH–Ch of Brethren	12	478	943	1,124	3.7	10.2
BRETH–Grace Breth	1	NR	NR	NR	-	-
Catholic	2	NR	NR	771	2.6	7.0
CGOD–Ches God-Gen Con	1	42	43	51	0.2	0.5
Ch of Nazarene	1	95	94	95	0.3	0.9
CHR–Chr Ch (Disc)	1	0	0	0	0.0	0.0
CHR–Chr Chs & Chs Cr	1	NR	50	60	0.2	0.5
CHR–Chs of Christ	1	43	40	52	0.2	0.5
Evan Free Ch	1	140	NR	140	0.5	1.3
Jehovah's Witness	1	NR	NR	NR	-	-
LDS–L-D Saints	1	NR	NR	202	0.7	1.8
LUTH–E.L.C.A.	9	396	1,063	1,379	4.6	12.5
LUTH–Luth-MO Synod	2	174	471	550	1.8	5.0
MENN–Amish Undif	1	NR	155	261	0.9	2.4
MENN–Cons Menn Conf	1	375	368	439	1.5	4.0
MENN–Menn Chr Fell	1	100	52	100	0.3	0.9
MENN–Mennonite USA	4	241	252	300	1.0	2.7
METH–Un Methodist	21	951	1,830	2,077	6.9	18.9
Non-denom Chr Chs	6	670	885	938	3.1	8.5
PENT–Assemb of God	9	500	364	709	2.4	6.4
PENT–Ch God (Cleve)	4	564	461	549	1.8	5.0
PENT–Ch of God Proph	1	NR	28	33	0.1	0.3
PENT–Un Pent Ch Intl	2	NR	NR	NR	-	-
Sev Day Adv	1	58	100	115	0.4	1.0
Un Breth in Cr	2	115	107	99	0.3	0.9
Un C of Christ	2	25	230	274	0.9	2.5
HARFORD	**192**	**17,728**	**36,611**	**95,771**	**39.1**	**100.0**
ANG/EPIS–Anglican NA	2	NR	NR	NR	-	-
ANG/EPIS–Episcopal	10	719	1,480	1,800	0.7	1.9
Bahá'í	2	NR	54	54	0.0	0.1
BAPT–Free Will Bapt	1	NR	45	55	0.0	0.1
BAPT–NBC Amer	1	0	150	184	0.1	0.2
BAPT–NBC USA	1	0	350	430	0.2	0.4
BAPT–So Bapt Conv	22	2,922	4,899	6,024	2.5	6.3
Catholic	9	NR	NR	44,618	18.2	46.6
Ch Cr, Scientst	1	NR	NR	NR	-	-
Ch of Nazarene	3	519	529	962	0.4	1.0
Chr & Miss Al	2	100	58	173	0.1	0.2
CHR–Chr Chs & Chs Cr	5	NR	3,073	3,779	1.5	3.9
CHR–Chs of Christ	2	165	159	247	0.1	0.3
FRND–Fr Gen Cf & Un Mtg	2	NR	122	150	0.1	0.2
Jehovah's Witness	1	NR	NR	NR	-	-
JUD–Orth	1	43	50	60	0.0	0.1
JUD–Reform	1	101	179	483	0.2	0.5
LDS–L-D Saints	2	NR	NR	1,798	0.7	1.9
LUTH–E.L.C.A.	6	740	2,364	3,175	1.3	3.3
LUTH–Luth Cong Msn Chr	1	865	2,621	3,223	1.3	3.4
LUTH–Luth-MO Synod	2	395	667	960	0.4	1.0
METH–AME	5	100	750	922	0.4	1.0
METH–Un Methodist	35	3,923	9,751	14,141	5.8	14.8
Non-denom Chr Chs	29	3,553	4,476	5,029	2.1	5.3
ORTHE–Greek Orthodox	1	165	NR	750	0.3	0.8
ORTHE–Ukrainian Orth	1	40	NR	150	0.1	0.2
PENT–Assemb of God	4	663	382	967	0.4	1.0
PENT–Ch God (Cleve)	10	633	910	1,119	0.5	1.2
PENT–Ch of God Proph	1	NR	47	58	0.0	0.1
PENT–COGIC	1	75	75	92	0.0	0.1
PENT–Full Gosp Bapt	1	NR	NR	NR	-	-
PENT–Int Foursq Gos	1	87	81	100	0.0	0.1
PENT–Intl Pent Holiness	1	20	36	44	0.0	0.0
PENT–Un Pent Ch Intl	3	NR	NR	NR	-	-

Religious Group	Number of Congrega-tions	Number of Attendees	Number of Communicant, Confirmed, or Full Members	Adherents: Number of Adherents	Adherents: % of Total Pop.	Adherents: % of Total Adh.
PENT–Vineyard	1	65	60	74	0.0	0.1
PRES–Presb Ch (USA)	11	1,141	2,342	2,880	1.2	3.0
PRES–Presb Ch Amer	3	291	240	380	0.2	0.4
Salvation Army	1	41	65	120	0.0	0.1
Sev Day Adv	3	166	288	331	0.1	0.3
Un C of Christ	1	48	129	159	0.1	0.2
Unit Univ	2	148	179	272	0.1	0.3
Zoroastrian	0	NR	NR	8	0.0	0.0
HOWARD	**201**	**28,881**	**47,474**	**123,592**	**43.1**	**100.0**
ANG/EPIS–Episcopal	9	1,277	3,113	5,325	1.9	4.3
Bahá'í	1	NR	415	415	0.1	0.3
BAPT–Amer Bapt USA	2	100	509	631	0.2	0.5
BAPT–NBC USA	3	65	400	496	0.2	0.4
BAPT–So Bapt Conv	30	2,871	5,697	7,067	2.5	5.7
BRETH–Ch of Brethren	1	0	96	119	0.0	0.1
BUDD–Mahayana	2	NR	NR	600	0.2	0.5
Calv Chpl	1	NR	NR	NR	-	-
Catholic	8	NR	NR	54,058	18.8	43.7
CGOD–Ch God (Ander)	4	2,334	NR	2,334	0.8	1.9
Ch Cr, Scientst	1	NR	NR	NR	-	-
Ch of Nazarene	4	816	624	1,363	0.5	1.1
CHR–Chr Ch (Disc)	1	0	110	136	0.0	0.1
CHR–Chs of Christ	1	55	70	90	0.0	0.1
CHR–Int Chs of Christ	1	NR	335	416	0.1	0.3
FRND–Fr Gen Cf & Un Mtg	1	NR	33	41	0.0	0.0
HINDU–Post Ren	2	NR	NR	26	0.0	0.0
Ind Fund Churches	2	NR	NR	NR	-	-
Jehovah's Witness	2	NR	NR	NR	-	-
JUD–Conserv	1	282	317	856	0.3	0.7
JUD–Orth	1	86	100	120	0.0	0.1
JUD–Reconst	1	255	326	880	0.3	0.7
JUD–Reform	2	363	640	1,728	0.6	1.4
LDS–L-D Saints	5	NR	NR	2,522	0.9	2.0
LUTH–E.L.C.A.	9	1,513	2,258	4,985	1.7	4.0
LUTH–Luth-MO Synod	1	90	109	133	0.0	0.1
LUTH–Wisc Ev Luth Syn	1	60	83	109	0.0	0.1
MENN–Mennonite USA	1	55	49	61	0.0	0.0
METH–AME	6	410	1,320	1,638	0.6	1.3
METH–AME Zion	1	0	100	124	0.0	0.1
METH–Un Methodist	30	3,522	9,034	11,250	3.9	9.1
MJEW–Union Mes Cong	1	NR	NR	NR	-	-
Muslim Est	1	134	NR	308	0.1	0.2
Non-denom Chr Chs	25	9,605	15,390	16,344	5.7	13.2
ORTHE–Orth Ch in Amer	1	130	NR	265	0.1	0.2
ORTHO–Coptic Orth Ch	1	225	NR	550	0.2	0.4
ORTHO–Malan Dioc Am	1	170	NR	250	0.1	0.2
PENT–Assemb of God	5	932	529	1,111	0.4	0.9
PENT–COGIC	1	0	60	74	0.0	0.1
PENT–Int Foursq Gos	2	93	88	109	0.0	0.1
PRES–Korean Amer Pres	2	NR	NR	NR	-	-
PRES–Korean Pres Amer	4	NR	NR	NR	-	-
PRES–Orth Pres Ch	2	553	448	716	0.2	0.6
PRES–Presb Ch (USA)	5	749	1,680	2,084	0.7	1.7
PRES–Presb Ch Amer	3	205	240	314	0.1	0.3
Sev Day Adv	8	1,558	2,709	3,117	1.1	2.5
Un C of Christ	1	65	96	119	0.0	0.1
Unit Univ	2	308	496	681	0.2	0.6
Unity Ch	1	NR	NR	NR	-	-
Zoroastrian	0	NR	NR	27	0.0	0.0
KENT	**52**	**2,626**	**6,354**	**10,009**	**49.6**	**100.0**
ANG/EPIS–Anglican NA	1	NR	NR	NR	-	-
ANG/EPIS–Episcopal	5	339	798	930	4.6	9.3
Bahá'í	0	NR	4	4	0.0	0.0
BAPT–So Bapt Conv	1	30	24	28	0.1	0.3
Calv Chpl	1	NR	NR	NR	-	-
Catholic	3	NR	NR	2,588	12.8	25.9
FRND–Fr Gen Cf	1	NR	42	49	0.2	0.5
Jehovah's Witness	1	NR	NR	NR	-	-
LUTH–Luth-MO Synod	1	95	189	261	1.3	2.6
METH–AME	6	0	850	984	4.9	9.8
METH–Un Methodist	20	917	2,858	3,246	16.1	32.4

NR–Not Reported   - Represents no adherents reported.   Percentages may not total 100 due to rounding.

Table 3: Religious Congregations by County and Group: 2010

Religious Group	Number of Congrega-tions	Number of Attendees	Number of Communicant, Confirmed, or Full Members	Adherents: Number of Adherents	Adherents: % of Total Pop.	Adherents: % of Total Adh.
METH–Wesleyan	1	33	21	43	0.2	0.4
Non-denom Chr Chs	3	700	950	988	4.9	9.9
PENT–Assemb of God	1	180	74	260	1.3	2.6
PENT–Ch God (Cleve)	1	30	40	46	0.2	0.5
PENT–Un Pent Ch Intl	2	NR	NR	NR	-	-
PRES–Presb Ch (USA)	1	164	282	326	1.6	3.3
Sev Day Adv	2	94	164	188	0.9	1.9
Unit Univ	1	44	58	68	0.3	0.7
MONTGOMERY	**733**	**99,297**	**163,133**	**384,607**	**39.6**	**100.0**
ANG/EPIS–Anglican NA	3	NR	NR	NR	-	-
ANG/EPIS–Episcopal	24	4,029	9,938	13,626	1.4	3.5
Ap Chr Ch-Amer	1	18	8	18	0.0	0.0
Bahá'í	10	NR	894	894	0.1	0.2
BAPT–Alliance Bapt	5	NR	NR	NR	-	-
BAPT–Amer Bapt USA	35	5,772	13,352	16,373	1.7	4.3
BAPT–Converge/BGC	2	150	NR	180	0.0	0.0
BAPT–NBC USA	1	400	300	368	0.0	0.1
BAPT–So Bapt Conv	99	10,542	22,750	27,897	2.9	7.3
BRETH–Ch of Brethren	2	10	51	63	0.0	0.0
BUDD–Mahayana	11	NR	NR	2,073	0.2	0.5
BUDD–Theravada	4	NR	NR	4,194	0.4	1.1
BUDD–Vajrayana	6	NR	NR	290	0.0	0.1
Catholic	39	NR	NR	122,569	12.6	31.9
CGOD–Ch God (Ander)	5	253	NR	253	0.0	0.1
Ch Cr, Scientst	4	NR	NR	NR	-	-
Ch of Nazarene	6	511	521	761	0.1	0.2
Chr & Miss Al	8	1,042	659	1,369	0.1	0.4
CHR–Chr Ch (Disc)	5	295	903	1,107	0.1	0.3
CHR–Chr Chs & Chs Cr	3	NR	340	417	0.0	0.1
CHR–Chs of Christ	3	435	480	600	0.1	0.2
CHR–Int Chs of Christ	1	NR	342	419	0.0	0.1
Christian Brethren	1	NR	NR	NR	-	-
Evan Free Ch	2	950	NR	950	0.1	0.2
FRND–Fr Gen Cf & Un Mtg	5	NR	948	1,162	0.1	0.3
FRND–Unaffl Mtgs	1	NR	NR	NR	-	-
HINDU–I/A Temples	7	NR	NR	4,053	0.4	1.1
HINDU–Post Ren	11	NR	NR	379	0.0	0.1
HINDU–Renaiss	3	NR	NR	472	0.0	0.1
HINDU–Trad Temples	4	NR	NR	866	0.1	0.2
Int Cou Comm Ch	2	NR	NR	NR	-	-
Jain	1	NR	NR	NR	-	-
Jehovah's Witness	6	NR	NR	NR	-	-
JUD–Conserv	12	5,565	6,246	16,864	1.7	4.4
JUD–Orth	20	4,032	1,800	5,600	0.6	1.5
JUD–Reconst	2	381	486	1,312	0.1	0.3
JUD–Reform	5	1,276	2,250	6,075	0.6	1.6
LDS–L-D Saints	24	NR	NR	12,451	1.3	3.2
LUTH–E.L.C.A.	15	1,896	5,491	6,781	0.7	1.8
LUTH–Luth Ch-Am Asc	1	NR	NR	NR	-	-
LUTH–Luth Cong Msn Chr	1	590	907	1,112	0.1	0.3
LUTH–Luth–MO Synod	7	1,121	2,334	3,036	0.3	0.8
MENN–Mennonite USA	3	190	174	213	0.0	0.1
METH–AME	7	0	900	1,104	0.1	0.3
METH–AME Zion	12	130	1,400	1,717	0.2	0.4
METH–Free Methodist	4	248	233	271	0.0	0.1
METH–Un Methodist	60	7,763	21,738	24,858	2.6	6.5
METH–Wesleyan	3	359	222	468	0.0	0.1
Metro Comm Ch	1	49	84	103	0.0	0.0
Missionary Ch	1	41	54	54	0.0	0.0
MJEW–Union Mes Cong	2	NR	NR	NR	-	-
Muslim Est	10	1,778	NR	12,206	1.3	3.2
New Apost Ch	1	NR	NR	NR	-	-
Non-denom Chr Chs	57	27,006	33,357	36,645	3.8	9.5
ORTHE–Ant Orth of NA	1	350	NR	1,000	0.1	0.3
ORTHE–Carp Rus Orth	1	70	NR	141	0.0	0.0
ORTHE–Georgian Orth	1	40	NR	60	0.0	0.0
ORTHE–Greek Orthodox	1	700	NR	2,750	0.3	0.7
ORTHE–Orth Ch in Amer	3	262	NR	658	0.1	0.2
ORTHE–Serb Orth USA	1	100	NR	2,000	0.2	0.5
ORTHE–Ukrainian Orth	1	150	NR	300	0.0	0.1
ORTHO–Armen Ap Cilic	1	150	NR	2,000	0.2	0.5
ORTHO–Coptic Orth Ch	1	120	NR	200	0.0	0.1
ORTHO–Malan Dioc Am	3	535	NR	780	0.1	0.2
PENT–Assemb of God	14	1,945	1,150	2,718	0.3	0.7
PENT–Ch God (Cleve)	15	1,173	1,333	1,635	0.2	0.4
PENT–Ch Lord Jesus Apos	1	NR	NR	NR	-	-
PENT–Ch of God Proph	1	NR	104	128	0.0	0.0
PENT–Full Gosp Bapt	1	NR	NR	NR	-	-
PENT–Int Foursq Gos	2	1,078	942	1,155	0.1	0.3
PENT–Intl Pent Holiness	6	1,043	890	1,091	0.1	0.3
PENT–Pent Ch of God	1	70	NR	109	0.0	0.0
PENT–Un Pent Ch Intl	5	NR	NR	NR	-	-
PENT–Vineyard	1	80	140	172	0.0	0.0
PRES–As Ref Pres Ch	3	NR	465	570	0.1	0.1
PRES–Evan Presby Ch	1	NR	2,860	3,507	0.4	0.9
PRES–Free Ch Scot	1	NR	NR	NR	-	-
PRES–Korean Amer Pres	1	NR	NR	NR	-	-
PRES–Korean Pres Amer	3	NR	NR	NR	-	-
PRES–Orth Pres Ch	1	94	107	130	0.0	0.0
PRES–Presb Ch (USA)	27	3,214	6,181	7,579	0.8	2.0
PRES–Presb Ch Amer	6	499	587	773	0.1	0.2
REF–Christian Ref	2	120	173	212	0.0	0.1
Salvation Army	1	51	130	133	0.0	0.0
Sev Day Adv	42	8,659	15,057	17,318	1.8	4.5
Sikh	2	NR	NR	NR	-	-
Un C of Christ	6	645	1,670	2,048	0.2	0.5
Unit Univ	5	1,317	2,182	2,921	0.3	0.8
Unity Ch	3	NR	NR	NR	-	-
Zoroastrian	0	NR	NR	296	0.0	0.1
PRINCE GEORGE'S	**750**	**157,807**	**230,013**	**393,431**	**45.6**	**100.0**
ANG/EPIS–Anglican NA	2	NR	NR	NR	-	-
ANG/EPIS–Episcopal	20	2,134	4,234	5,121	0.6	1.3
Bahá'í	4	NR	309	309	0.0	0.1
BAPT–Alliance Bapt	2	NR	NR	NR	-	-
BAPT–Amer Bapt Assn	2	NR	1,350	1,651	0.2	0.4
BAPT–Amer Bapt USA	42	10,838	19,433	23,769	2.8	6.0
BAPT–Consrv Bapt	2	NR	NR	NR	-	-
BAPT–Converge/BGC	12	13,825	NR	16,590	1.9	4.2
BAPT–Natl Mis Bapt Conv	2	0	300	367	0.0	0.1
BAPT–NBC Amer	1	2,200	4,000	4,893	0.6	1.2
BAPT–NBC USA	4	900	2,000	2,446	0.3	0.6
BAPT–Prog NBC	11	2,900	5,860	7,168	0.8	1.8
BAPT–Reg Bapt Gen As	3	NR	NR	NR	-	-
BAPT–S-D Baptist Gen Con	1	34	45	55	0.0	0.0
BAPT–So Bapt Conv	115	13,930	30,076	36,787	4.3	9.4
BRETH–Ch of Brethren	1	0	107	131	0.0	0.0
BRETH–Grace Breth	2	NR	NR	NR	-	-
BUDD–Mahayana	2	NR	NR	2,308	0.3	0.6
BUDD–Theravada	2	NR	NR	750	0.1	0.2
Calv Chpl	1	NR	NR	NR	-	-
Catholic	35	NR	NR	83,959	9.7	21.3
CGOD–Ch God (Ander)	2	95	NR	95	0.0	0.0
Ch Cr, Scientst	2	NR	NR	NR	-	-
Ch God (7th Day)	1	NR	NR	NR	-	-
Ch of Nazarene	10	321	464	635	0.1	0.2
Chr & Miss Al	2	61	52	59	0.0	0.0
CHR–Chr Ch (Disc)	12	337	1,736	2,123	0.2	0.5
CHR–Chr Chs & Chs Cr	1	NR	100	122	0.0	0.0
CHR–Chs of Christ	11	1,632	1,545	2,008	0.2	0.5
Evan Cov Ch	1	43	85	56	0.0	0.0
FRND–Fr Gen Cf & Un Mtg	1	NR	362	443	0.1	0.1
HINDU–I/A Temples	1	NR	NR	1,742	0.2	0.4
HINDU–Trad Temples	3	NR	NR	6,800	0.8	1.7
Ind Fund Churches	4	NR	NR	NR	-	-
Int Cou Comm Ch	1	NR	NR	NR	-	-
Jehovah's Witness	14	NR	NR	NR	-	-
JUD–Conserv	0	58	65	176	0.0	0.0
JUD–Reconst	2	312	398	1,075	0.1	0.3
JUD–Reform	1	108	190	513	0.1	0.1
LDS–Comm of Christ	1	NR	137	137	0.0	0.0
LDS–L-D Saints	10	NR	NR	6,537	0.8	1.7
LUTH–E.L.C.A.	13	860	2,079	2,568	0.3	0.7
LUTH–Luth–MO Synod	10	922	2,141	2,572	0.3	0.7
LUTH–Wisc Ev Luth Syn	1	98	170	248	0.0	0.1
MENN–Mennonite USA	2	499	380	465	0.1	0.1
METH–AME	22	20,980	26,490	32,401	3.8	8.2

NR–Not Reported - Represents no adherents reported. Percentages may not total 100 due to rounding.

Table 3: Religious Congregations by County and Group: 2010

Religious Group	Number of Congrega-tions	Number of Attendees	Number of Communicant, Confirmed, or Full Members	Adherents		
				Number of Adherents	% of Total Pop.	% of Total Adh.
METH–AME Zion	7	65	645	789	0.1	0.2
METH–C.M.E.	2	0	300	367	0.0	0.1
METH–Free Methodist	2	115	145	145	0.0	0.0
METH–Un Methodist	38	4,715	11,865	13,089	1.5	3.3
METH–Wesleyan	3	377	344	491	0.1	0.1
Metro Comm Ch	2	38	57	70	0.0	0.0
MORAV–Morav Ch-North	2	163	272	360	0.0	0.1
Muslim Est	11	3,198	NR	7,896	0.9	2.0
Non-denom Chr Chs	154	60,605	90,726	94,497	10.9	24.0
ORTHE–Greek Orthodox	1	80	NR	500	0.1	0.1
ORTHE–Holy Orth in NA	1	77	NR	100	0.0	0.0
ORTHE–Rus Orth Abroad	1	45	NR	60	0.0	0.0
ORTHO–Eritrean Orth	1	225	NR	450	0.1	0.1
ORTHO–Ethiopian Orth	1	NR	NR	NR	-	-
ORTHO–Malan Syr Orth	1	55	NR	108	0.0	0.0
PENT–Assemb of God	15	3,356	2,793	4,692	0.5	1.2
PENT–Ch God (Cleve)	20	4,021	5,540	6,776	0.8	1.7
PENT–Ch Lord Jesus Apos	4	NR	NR	NR	-	-
PENT–Ch of God Proph	3	NR	252	308	0.0	0.1
PENT–COGIC	5	4	452	553	0.1	0.1
PENT–Fire Bapt Hol Ch	2	NR	NR	NR	-	-
PENT–Full Gosp Bapt	6	NR	NR	NR	-	-
PENT–Int Foursq Gos	4	392	267	327	0.0	0.1
PENT–Intl Pent Holiness	5	473	600	734	0.1	0.2
PENT–Open Bible Std	1	26	NR	26	0.0	0.0
PENT–Pent Ch of God	2	140	NR	217	0.0	0.1
PENT–Un Pent Ch Intl	4	NR	NR	NR	-	-
PENT–United Holy Ch	2	NR	NR	NR	-	-
PRES–Kor Pres Abroad	1	NR	NR	NR	-	-
PRES–Orth Pres Ch	1	52	56	80	0.0	0.0
PRES–Presb Ch (USA)	17	1,285	2,417	2,956	0.3	0.8
PRES–Presb Ch Amer	3	530	636	799	0.1	0.2
PRES–Ref Pres of NA	1	114	89	131	0.0	0.0
Salvation Army	1	43	158	175	0.0	0.0
Sev Day Adv	24	4,251	7,392	8,502	1.0	2.2
Un C of Christ	4	51	535	654	0.1	0.2
Unit Univ	3	224	364	465	0.1	0.1
Unity Ch	1	NR	NR	NR	-	-
Zoroastrian	0	NR	NR	35	0.0	0.0
QUEEN ANNE'S	**62**	**4,109**	**8,485**	**17,566**	**36.8**	**100.0**
ANG/EPIS–Episcopal	3	320	854	924	1.9	5.3
Bahá'í	1	NR	15	15	0.0	0.1
BAPT–So Bapt Conv	3	161	186	227	0.5	1.3
Catholic	3	NR	NR	6,673	14.0	38.0
Ch of Nazarene	1	80	89	89	0.2	0.5
Chr & Miss Al	1	177	103	312	0.7	1.8
CHR–Chs of Christ	1	65	60	80	0.2	0.5
LDS–L-D Saints	1	NR	NR	215	0.4	1.2
LUTH–E.L.C.A.	1	52	85	127	0.3	0.7
LUTH–Luth-MO Synod	1	36	84	101	0.2	0.6
MENN–Beachy Amish-Menn	1	82	42	82	0.2	0.5
METH–AME	4	50	510	622	1.3	3.5
METH–Un Methodist	27	1,825	4,432	5,735	12.0	32.6
Non-denom Chr Chs	5	620	785	810	1.7	4.6
PENT–Assemb of God	2	55	55	91	0.2	0.5
PENT–Ch God (Cleve)	4	174	537	655	1.4	3.7
PENT–COGIC	1	0	150	183	0.4	1.0
PRES–Presb Ch Amer	1	317	333	435	0.9	2.5
Sev Day Adv	1	95	165	190	0.4	1.1
ST. MARY'S	**81**	**6,988**	**10,332**	**38,978**	**37.1**	**100.0**
ANG/EPIS–Anglican NA	1	NR	NR	NR	-	-
ANG/EPIS–Episcopal	7	536	1,251	1,756	1.7	4.5
Bahá'í	1	NR	24	24	0.0	0.1
BAPT–So Bapt Conv	5	844	1,419	1,781	1.7	4.6
BRETH–Grace Breth	1	NR	NR	NR	-	-
Catholic	15	NR	NR	24,014	22.8	61.6
Ch Cr, Scientst	1	NR	NR	NR	-	-
Ch of Nazarene	2	103	165	165	0.2	0.4
CHR–Chr Ch (Disc)	1	16	40	50	0.0	0.1
CHR–Chs of Christ	1	144	146	188	0.2	0.5
Christian Brethren	1	NR	NR	NR	-	-

Religious Group	Number of Congrega-tions	Number of Attendees	Number of Communicant, Confirmed, or Full Members	Adherents		
				Number of Adherents	% of Total Pop.	% of Total Adh.
Jehovah's Witness	1	NR	NR	NR	-	-
LDS–L-D Saints	2	NR	NR	1,075	1.0	2.8
LUTH–E.L.C.A.	1	102	150	222	0.2	0.6
LUTH–Luth-MO Synod	2	281	497	657	0.6	1.7
MENN–Amish Undif	4	NR	273	610	0.6	1.6
METH–AME	2	0	300	377	0.4	1.0
METH–Un Methodist	9	1,452	2,394	3,167	3.0	8.1
METH–Wesleyan	1	204	35	265	0.3	0.7
Non-denom Chr Chs	9	1,805	1,970	2,331	2.2	6.0
PENT–Assemb of God	2	382	313	586	0.6	1.5
PENT–Ch God (Cleve)	1	181	276	346	0.3	0.9
PENT–Ch Lord Jesus Apos	1	NR	NR	NR	-	-
PENT–Int Foursq Gos	1	12	16	20	0.0	0.1
PENT–Un Pent Ch Intl	2	NR	NR	NR	-	-
PRES–Orth Pres Ch	1	104	111	146	0.1	0.4
PRES–Presb Ch (USA)	1	433	487	611	0.6	1.6
PRES–Presb Ch Amer	1	287	277	352	0.3	0.9
Sev Day Adv	1	36	63	72	0.1	0.2
Un C of Christ	1	20	45	56	0.1	0.1
Unit Univ	2	46	80	107	0.1	0.3
SOMERSET	**56**	**2,608**	**5,233**	**5,892**	**22.3**	**100.0**
ANG/EPIS–Episcopal	2	80	127	129	0.5	2.2
Bahá'í	0	NR	53	53	0.2	0.9
BAPT–So Bapt Conv	4	278	541	622	2.3	10.6
BRETH–Ch of Brethren	1	31	71	82	0.3	1.4
Catholic	1	NR	NR	85	0.3	1.4
CHR–Chr Ch (Disc)	1	14	16	18	0.1	0.3
Jehovah's Witness	1	NR	NR	NR	-	-
MENN–Mennonite USA	1	120	130	149	0.6	2.5
METH–AME	1	0	100	115	0.4	2.0
METH–AME Zion	1	0	150	172	0.6	2.9
METH–Un Methodist	32	1,354	3,205	3,485	13.2	59.1
METH–Wesleyan	2	125	129	163	0.6	2.8
Non-denom Chr Chs	1	50	75	75	0.3	1.3
PENT–Assemb of God	1	60	55	77	0.3	1.3
PENT–Ch God (Cleve)	3	446	465	534	2.0	9.1
PENT–Ch of God Proph	1	NR	7	8	0.0	0.1
PENT–Un Pent Ch Intl	1	NR	NR	NR	-	-
PRES–Presb Ch (USA)	2	50	109	125	0.5	2.1
TALBOT	**62**	**4,385**	**9,514**	**16,170**	**42.8**	**100.0**
ANG/EPIS–Anglican NA	1	NR	NR	NR	-	-
ANG/EPIS–Episcopal	7	886	1,953	2,489	6.6	15.4
Bahá'í	0	NR	8	8	0.0	0.0
BAPT–NBC USA	1	0	150	176	0.5	1.1
BAPT–So Bapt Conv	2	306	339	398	1.1	2.5
BRETH–Ch of Brethren	2	167	408	478	1.3	3.0
BRETH–Grace Breth	1	NR	NR	NR	-	-
Catholic	3	NR	NR	4,570	12.1	28.3
Ch Cr, Scientst	1	NR	NR	NR	-	-
Ch of Nazarene	3	147	48	155	0.4	1.0
CHR–Chs of Christ	1	32	34	48	0.1	0.3
FRND–Fr Gen Cf	1	NR	142	167	0.4	1.0
Jehovah's Witness	1	NR	NR	NR	-	-
JUD–Reform	1	73	129	348	0.9	2.2
LUTH–E.L.C.A.	2	180	426	531	1.4	3.3
LUTH–Luth-MO Synod	1	147	221	254	0.7	1.6
METH–AME	3	0	400	469	1.2	2.9
METH–Un Methodist	19	1,152	3,252	3,664	9.7	22.7
METH–Wesleyan	2	208	152	271	0.7	1.7
Non-denom Chr Chs	4	395	545	581	1.5	3.6
PENT–Assemb of God	1	8	0	18	0.0	0.1
PENT–Ch God (Cleve)	1	399	880	1,032	2.7	6.4
PENT–Un Pent Ch Intl	1	NR	NR	NR	-	-
PRES–Presb Ch (USA)	1	115	216	253	0.7	1.6
PRES–Presb Ch Amer	1	75	85	106	0.3	0.7
Unit Univ	1	95	126	154	0.4	1.0
WASHINGTON	**219**	**20,285**	**34,307**	**55,632**	**37.7**	**100.0**
ANG/EPIS–Episcopal	7	514	1,410	1,811	1.2	3.3
Bahá'í	0	NR	26	26	0.0	0.0
BAPT–Amer Bapt Assn	1	NR	85	103	0.1	0.2

NR–Not Reported - Represents no adherents reported. Percentages may not total 100 due to rounding.

Table 3: Religious Congregations by County and Group: 2010

Religious Group	Number of Congregations	Number of Attendees	Number of Communicant, Confirmed, or Full Members	Adherents: Number of Adherents	Adherents: % of Total Pop.	Adherents: % of Total Adh.
BAPT–Reg Bapt Gen As	1	NR	NR	NR	-	-
BAPT–So Bapt Conv	11	974	1,379	1,675	1.1	3.0
BRETH–Breth in Chr	3	NR	NR	NR	-	-
BRETH–Brethren (Ash)	2	NR	160	194	0.1	0.3
BRETH–Ch of Brethren	10	670	1,571	1,908	1.3	3.4
BRETH–Grace Breth	4	NR	NR	NR	-	-
Calv Chpl	1	NR	NR	NR	-	-
Catholic	8	NR	NR	9,350	6.3	16.8
CGOD–Ch God (Ander)	1	25	NR	25	0.0	0.0
CGOD–Ches God-Gen Con	7	463	515	625	0.4	1.1
Ch Cr, Scientst	1	NR	NR	NR	-	-
Ch of Nazarene	5	484	322	722	0.5	1.3
Chr & Miss Al	1	69	32	89	0.1	0.2
CHR–Chr Ch (Disc)	5	546	1,770	2,149	1.5	3.9
CHR–Chr Chs & Chs Cr	3	NR	623	757	0.5	1.4
CHR–Chs of Christ	1	160	200	250	0.2	0.4
Evan Assoc RCC	2	NR	NR	NR	-	-
Evan Free Ch	1	700	NR	700	0.5	1.3
FRND–Fr Gen Cf & Un Mtg	1	NR	0	0	0.0	0.0
HINDU–Post Ren	1	NR	NR	10	0.0	0.0
HINDU–Renaiss	1	NR	NR	12	0.0	0.0
Jehovah's Witness	1	NR	NR	NR	-	-
JUD–Reform	1	59	104	281	0.2	0.5
LDS–L-D Saints	3	NR	NR	1,539	1.0	2.8
LUTH–Assoc Free Luth	2	NR	NR	NR	-	-
LUTH–E.L.C.A.	20	1,610	5,283	6,657	4.5	12.0
LUTH–Luth-MO Synod	2	160	255	350	0.2	0.6
MENN–Mennonite USA	3	182	188	228	0.2	0.4
METH–A.W.M.C.	1	37	10	47	0.0	0.1
METH–AME	1	50	80	97	0.1	0.2
METH–Un Methodist	27	2,811	7,685	8,574	5.8	15.4
Metro Comm Ch	1	54	71	86	0.1	0.2
Missionary Ch	1	26	18	26	0.0	0.0
Muslim Est	1	134	NR	308	0.2	0.6
Non-denom Chr Chs	27	4,656	4,829	5,968	4.0	10.7
ORTHE–Orth Ch in Amer	2	75	NR	163	0.1	0.3
PENT–Assemb of God	7	1,740	795	2,401	1.6	4.3
PENT–Ch God (Cleve)	8	1,712	2,673	3,246	2.2	5.8
PENT–Full Gosp Bapt	1	NR	NR	NR	-	-
PENT–Int Foursq Gos	1	38	21	26	0.0	0.0
PENT–Pent Ch of God	1	70	NR	109	0.1	0.2
PENT–Un Pent Ch Intl	1	NR	NR	NR	-	-
PENT–Vineyard	1	160	240	291	0.2	0.5
PRES–Presb Ch (USA)	5	390	589	715	0.5	1.3
PRES–Presb Ch Amer	2	99	92	120	0.1	0.2
Salvation Army	1	97	125	258	0.2	0.5
Sev Day Adv	8	912	1,585	1,823	1.2	3.3
Un Breth in Cr	1	0	0	0	0.0	0.0
Un C of Christ	9	581	1,519	1,845	1.3	3.3
Unit Univ	1	27	52	68	0.0	0.1
Unity Ch	1	NR	NR	NR	-	-
WICOMICO	**149**	**15,623**	**22,522**	**37,363**	**37.8**	**100.0**
ANG/EPIS–Anglican NA	1	NR	NR	NR	-	-
ANG/EPIS–Episcopal	5	346	833	1,109	1.1	3.0
Bahá'í	1	NR	221	221	0.2	0.6
BAPT–So Bapt Conv	9	2,068	2,398	2,903	2.9	7.8
BRETH–Ch of Brethren	1	61	79	96	0.1	0.3
Calv Chpl	1	NR	NR	NR	-	-
Catholic	2	NR	NR	4,656	4.7	12.5
CGOD–Ch God (Ander)	2	130	NR	130	0.1	0.3
Ch Christ Chr Union	1	NR	NR	NR	-	-
Ch Cr, Scientst	1	NR	NR	NR	-	-
Ch of Nazarene	1	510	489	653	0.7	1.7
CHR–Chr Chs & Chs Cr	4	NR	440	533	0.5	1.4
CHR–Chs of Christ	1	45	58	59	0.1	0.2
FRND–Consrv Yr Mtgs	1	NR	0	0	0.0	0.0
FRND–Fr Gen Cf	1	NR	22	27	0.0	0.1
Jehovah's Witness	3	NR	NR	NR	-	-
JUD–Conserv	1	78	87	235	0.2	0.6
LDS–L-D Saints	2	NR	NR	911	0.9	2.4
LUTH–E.L.C.A.	1	50	89	105	0.1	0.3
LUTH–Luth-MO Synod	1	131	241	275	0.3	0.7
METH–AME	1	0	100	121	0.1	0.3
METH–AME Zion	2	320	500	605	0.6	1.6
METH–Un Methodist	55	4,491	10,732	12,181	12.3	32.6
METH–Wesleyan	5	2,733	819	3,553	3.6	9.5
Muslim Est	1	134	NR	308	0.3	0.8
Non-denom Chr Chs	24	3,265	3,309	4,183	4.2	11.2
PENT–Assemb of God	2	40	6	71	0.1	0.2
PENT–Ch God (Cleve)	3	344	573	694	0.7	1.9
PENT–Ch of God Proph	2	NR	161	195	0.2	0.5
PENT–COGIC	2	25	190	230	0.2	0.6
PENT–Un Pent Ch Intl	2	NR	NR	NR	-	-
PRES–Cumber Presb	1	NR	14	14	0.0	0.0
PRES–Presb Ch (USA)	2	232	340	412	0.4	1.1
PRES–Presb Ch Amer	1	310	261	351	0.4	0.9
Salvation Army	1	42	113	2,018	2.0	5.4
Sev Day Adv	4	220	383	440	0.4	1.2
Unit Univ	1	48	64	72	0.1	0.2
Zoroastrian	0	NR	NR	2	0.0	0.0
WORCESTER	**101**	**6,453**	**13,502**	**24,906**	**48.4**	**100.0**
ANG/EPIS–Anglican NA	1	NR	NR	NR	-	-
ANG/EPIS–Episcopal	5	345	707	790	1.5	3.2
Bahá'í	0	NR	62	62	0.1	0.2
BAPT–So Bapt Conv	12	1,530	3,289	3,809	7.4	15.3
BUDD–Mahayana	1	NR	NR	11	0.0	0.0
Catholic	6	NR	NR	8,120	15.8	32.6
Ch of Nazarene	2	45	16	58	0.1	0.2
Chr & Miss Al	1	10	8	8	0.0	0.0
CHR–Chr Chs & Chs Cr	3	NR	90	104	0.2	0.4
JUD–Reform	1	78	137	370	0.7	1.5
LUTH–E.L.C.A.	1	290	560	744	1.4	3.0
MENN–Mennonite USA	2	43	41	47	0.1	0.2
METH–AME	6	205	675	782	1.5	3.1
METH–Un Methodist	36	2,200	6,081	7,408	14.4	29.7
Non-denom Chr Chs	7	855	884	1,076	2.1	4.3
ORTHE–Greek Orthodox	1	60	NR	150	0.3	0.6
ORTHE–Ukrainian Orth	1	20	NR	35	0.1	0.1
PENT–Assemb of God	2	426	178	435	0.8	1.7
PENT–Ch God (Cleve)	2	117	269	312	0.6	1.3
PENT–Ch of God Proph	1	NR	38	44	0.1	0.2
PENT–Un Pent Ch Intl	1	NR	NR	NR	-	-
PENT–United Holy Ch	1	NR	NR	NR	-	-
PRES–Korean Amer Pres	1	NR	NR	NR	-	-
PRES–Presb Ch (USA)	5	203	421	488	0.9	2.0
Sev Day Adv	2	26	46	53	0.1	0.2
MASSACHUSETTS	**4,200**	**321,917**	**469,787**	**3,748,058**	**57.2**	**100.0**
BARNSTABLE	**167**	**12,004**	**19,710**	**115,360**	**53.4**	**100.0**
ANG/EPIS–Anglican NA	2	NR	NR	NR	-	-
ANG/EPIS–Episcopal	12	1,836	3,981	5,400	2.5	4.7
Bahá'í	1	NR	112	112	0.1	0.1
BAPT–Amer Bapt USA	11	1,107	1,199	1,374	0.6	1.2
BAPT–Consrv Bapt	5	NR	NR	NR	-	-
BAPT–Converge/BGC	2	150	NR	180	0.1	0.2
BAPT–So Bapt Conv	3	72	65	74	0.0	0.1
BUDD–Mahayana	2	NR	NR	126	0.1	0.1
Calv Chpl	1	NR	NR	NR	-	-
Catholic	18	NR	NR	86,370	40.0	74.9
CGOD–Ches God-Gen Con	1	113	32	37	0.0	0.0
Ch Cr, Scientst	5	NR	NR	NR	-	-
Ch of Nazarene	2	128	160	193	0.1	0.2
Chr & Miss Al	2	305	167	411	0.2	0.4
CHR–Chs of Christ	1	80	88	100	0.0	0.1
CONG–Cong Chr, NA	1	NR	366	419	0.2	0.4
Evan Cov Ch	1	142	291	185	0.1	0.2
Evan Free Ch	1	140	NR	140	0.1	0.1
FRND–Fr Gen Cf & Un Mtg	6	NR	166	190	0.1	0.2
HINDU–Post Ren	1	NR	NR	25	0.0	0.0
Int Cou Comm Ch	1	NR	NR	NR	-	-
Jehovah's Witness	5	NR	NR	NR	-	-
JUD–Conserv	1	21	24	65	0.0	0.1
JUD–Orth	1	43	50	60	0.0	0.1

NR–Not Reported - Represents no adherents reported. Percentages may not total 100 due to rounding.

Table 3: Religious Congregations by County and Group: 2010

Religious Group	Number of Congrega-tions	Number of Attendees	Number of Communicant, Confirmed, or Full Members	Adherents: Number of Adherents	Adherents: % of Total Pop.	Adherents: % of Total Adh.
JUD–Reform	2	329	581	1,569	0.7	1.4
LDS–Comm of Christ	1	NR	102	102	0.0	0.1
LDS–L-D Saints	2	NR	NR	723	0.3	0.6
LUTH–E.L.C.A.	3	353	993	1,089	0.5	0.9
LUTH–Evan Luth Syn	1	42	78	88	0.0	0.1
LUTH–Luth-MO Synod	1	12	19	24	0.0	0.0
METH–Un Methodist	16	1,444	3,740	5,423	2.5	4.7
Muslim Est	2	268	NR	616	0.3	0.5
Non-denom Chr Chs	10	997	1,501	1,579	0.7	1.4
ORTHE–Ant Orth of NA	1	80	NR	200	0.1	0.2
ORTHE–Greek Orthodox	1	140	NR	360	0.2	0.3
ORTHO–Armen Ap Etchm	1	12	NR	250	0.1	0.2
PENT–Assemb of God	8	1,305	705	1,633	0.8	1.4
PENT–Int Foursq Gos	1	79	134	154	0.1	0.1
PENT–Un Pent Ch Intl	1	NR	NR	NR	-	-
PRES–Orth Pres Ch	1	84	80	106	0.0	0.1
Salvation Army	1	75	62	214	0.1	0.2
Sev Day Adv	1	82	142	163	0.1	0.1
Swedenborgian	1	NR	NR	NR	-	-
Un C of Christ	18	1,840	3,727	4,270	2.0	3.7
Unit Univ	7	725	1,145	1,332	0.6	1.2
Unity Ch	1	NR	NR	NR	-	-
Zoroastrian	0	NR	NR	4	0.0	0.0
BERKSHIRE	**147**	**5,780**	**11,712**	**67,004**	**51.1**	**100.0**
ANG/EPIS–Episcopal	15	899	1,882	2,721	2.1	4.1
Bahá'í	0	NR	42	42	0.0	0.1
BAPT–Alliance Bapt	1	NR	NR	NR	-	-
BAPT–Amer Bapt USA	10	568	1,567	1,827	1.4	2.7
BAPT–Ref Bapt Ch	1	NR	NR	NR	-	-
BAPT–So Bapt Conv	4	204	198	231	0.2	0.3
BUDD–Mahayana	3	NR	NR	72	0.1	0.1
Calv Chpl	1	NR	NR	NR	-	-
Catholic	32	NR	NR	50,187	38.2	74.9
Ch Cr, Scientst	2	NR	NR	NR	-	-
Ch of Nazarene	1	86	88	103	0.1	0.2
CHR–Chs of Christ	1	80	70	100	0.1	0.1
CONG–Cong Chr Add'l	2	NR	197	230	0.2	0.3
CONG–Cong Chr, NA	7	NR	338	394	0.3	0.6
CONG–Consrv Cong Chr	1	59	54	63	0.0	0.1
Evan Free Ch	1	70	NR	70	0.1	0.1
FRND–Fr Gen Cf & Un Mtg	1	NR	37	43	0.0	0.1
HINDU–Renaiss	1	NR	NR	41	0.0	0.1
Jehovah's Witness	4	NR	NR	NR	-	-
JUD–Conserv	1	292	328	886	0.7	1.3
JUD–Orth	1	43	50	60	0.0	0.1
JUD–Reconst	1	34	44	119	0.1	0.2
JUD–Reform	3	360	635	1,714	1.3	2.6
LDS–L-D Saints	2	NR	NR	545	0.4	0.8
LUTH–E.L.C.A.	2	103	314	441	0.3	0.7
LUTH–Wisc Ev Luth Syn	1	25	65	90	0.1	0.1
METH–AME Zion	2	0	200	233	0.2	0.3
METH–Un Methodist	8	377	1,605	1,811	1.4	2.7
Non-denom Chr Chs	11	1,214	1,446	1,631	1.2	2.4
ORTHE–Greek Orthodox	1	45	NR	170	0.1	0.3
ORTHE–Orth Ch in Amer	1	35	NR	55	0.0	0.1
PENT–Assemb of God	2	190	117	213	0.2	0.3
PENT–Un Pent Ch Intl	1	NR	NR	NR	-	-
Salvation Army	2	52	115	200	0.2	0.3
Sev Day Adv	1	58	101	116	0.1	0.2
Un C of Christ	17	904	2,082	2,428	1.9	3.6
Unit Univ	2	82	137	168	0.1	0.3
BRISTOL	**325**	**21,217**	**30,499**	**333,007**	**60.7**	**100.0**
ANG/EPIS–Anglican NA	3	NR	NR	NR	-	-
ANG/EPIS–Episcopal	15	1,102	2,885	3,948	0.7	1.2
Bahá'í	1	NR	99	99	0.0	0.0
BAPT–Amer Bapt USA	19	1,349	2,999	3,605	0.7	1.1
BAPT–Asc Ref Bap Ch Am	1	NR	NR	NR	-	-
BAPT–Consrv Bapt	6	NR	NR	NR	-	-
BAPT–Converge/BGC	3	550	NR	660	0.1	0.2
BAPT–NBC USA	1	55	65	78	0.0	0.0
BAPT–Ref Bapt Ch	2	NR	NR	NR	-	-
BAPT–So Bapt Conv	7	253	224	269	0.0	0.1
BUDD–Theravada	1	NR	NR	396	0.1	0.1
BUDD–Vajrayana	1	NR	NR	457	0.1	0.1
Catholic	71	NR	NR	286,113	52.2	85.9
Ch Cr, Scientst	2	NR	NR	NR	-	-
Ch of Nazarene	4	562	1,303	1,321	0.2	0.4
Chr & Miss Al	2	221	138	381	0.1	0.1
CHR–Chs of Christ	3	325	265	390	0.1	0.1
Christian Brethren	2	NR	NR	NR	-	-
CONG–Cong Chr, NA	4	NR	748	899	0.2	0.3
CONG–Consrv Cong Chr	5	383	213	256	0.0	0.1
Evan Cov Ch	2	416	630	541	0.1	0.2
FRND–Fr Gen Cf & Un Mtg	6	NR	297	357	0.1	0.1
HINDU–I/A Temples	1	NR	NR	1,742	0.3	0.5
Jehovah's Witness	7	NR	NR	NR	-	-
JUD–Conserv	1	306	343	926	0.2	0.3
JUD–Orth	3	324	175	450	0.1	0.1
JUD–Reconst	1	87	111	300	0.1	0.1
JUD–Reform	1	147	260	702	0.1	0.2
LDS–Comm of Christ	2	NR	204	204	0.0	0.1
LDS–L-D Saints	1	NR	NR	751	0.1	0.2
LUTH–E.L.C.A.	3	311	1,054	1,363	0.2	0.4
LUTH–Luth-MO Synod	1	92	179	256	0.0	0.1
LUTH–Wisc Ev Luth Syn	1	63	113	142	0.0	0.0
METH–AME	3	23	260	313	0.1	0.1
METH–AME Zion	1	0	100	120	0.0	0.0
METH–Free Methodist	2	71	43	71	0.0	0.0
METH–Prim Meth Ch	2	NR	NR	NR	-	-
METH–Un Methodist	14	770	2,393	3,488	0.6	1.0
Muslim Est	3	402	NR	924	0.2	0.3
Nat Spirit Asso	1	NR	NR	NR	-	-
Non-denom Chr Chs	38	7,585	7,890	9,789	1.8	2.9
OCATH–Pol Natl Cath	1	NR	NR	NR	-	-
ORTHE–Greek Orthodox	4	505	NR	1,565	0.3	0.5
PENT–Assemb of God	10	1,698	1,178	2,137	0.4	0.6
PENT–Ch God (Cleve)	9	516	327	393	0.1	0.1
PENT–Ch of God Proph	2	NR	32	38	0.0	0.0
PENT–Elim	1	NR	NR	NR	-	-
PENT–I F Chr Assmbl	4	NR	NR	NR	-	-
PENT–Un Pent Ch Intl	2	NR	NR	NR	-	-
PRES–Orth Pres Ch	1	10	12	12	0.0	0.0
PRES–Presb Ch (USA)	4	158	205	246	0.0	0.1
Salvation Army	3	200	361	759	0.1	0.2
Sev Day Adv	12	675	1,175	1,350	0.2	0.4
Un C of Christ	18	1,633	3,610	4,340	0.8	1.3
Unit Univ	7	425	608	853	0.2	0.3
Zoroastrian	0	NR	NR	3	0.0	0.0
DUKES	**22**	**1,095**	**1,915**	**5,973**	**36.1**	**100.0**
ANG/EPIS–Episcopal	3	319	471	473	2.9	7.9
Bahá'í	0	NR	4	4	0.0	0.1
BAPT–Amer Bapt USA	4	199	390	456	2.8	7.6
BAPT–Converge/BGC	1	75	NR	90	0.5	1.5
BUDD–Vajrayana	1	NR	NR	72	0.4	1.2
Catholic	1	NR	NR	2,896	17.5	48.5
Ch Cr, Scientst	1	NR	NR	NR	-	-
Chr & Miss Al	1	50	49	60	0.4	1.0
CONG–Cong Chr Add'l	1	NR	283	331	2.0	5.5
FRND–Fr Gen Cf & Un Mtg	1	NR	8	9	0.1	0.2
Jehovah's Witness	1	NR	NR	NR	-	-
JUD–Reform	1	194	342	923	5.6	15.5
LDS–L-D Saints	1	NR	NR	84	0.5	1.4
METH–Un Methodist	2	30	126	176	1.1	2.9
PENT–Assemb of God	1	83	34	160	1.0	2.7
Un C of Christ	1	100	141	165	1.0	2.8
Unit Univ	1	45	67	74	0.4	1.2
ESSEX	**434**	**30,495**	**46,158**	**424,453**	**57.1**	**100.0**
ANG/EPIS–Anglican NA	4	NR	NR	NR	-	-
ANG/EPIS–Episcopal	27	2,866	8,867	11,510	1.5	2.7
Bahá'í	1	NR	221	221	0.0	0.1
BAPT–Alliance Bapt	1	NR	NR	NR	-	-
BAPT–Amer Bapt USA	29	2,591	3,981	4,825	0.6	1.1

NR–Not Reported - Represents no adherents reported. Percentages may not total 100 due to rounding.

Table 3: Religious Congregations by County and Group: 2010

Religious Group	Number of Congregations	Number of Attendees	Number of Communicant, Confirmed, or Full Members	Adherents: Number of Adherents	Adherents: % of Total Pop.	Adherents: % of Total Adh.
BAPT–Consrv Bapt	3	NR	NR	NR	-	-
BAPT–Converge/BGC	2	150	NR	180	0.0	0.0
BAPT–Ref Bapt Ch	3	NR	NR	NR	-	-
BAPT–Reg Bapt Gen As	1	NR	NR	NR	-	-
BAPT–So Bapt Conv	10	669	651	789	0.1	0.2
BRETH–Grace Breth	1	NR	NR	NR	-	-
BUDD–Mahayana	4	NR	NR	400	0.1	0.1
BUDD–Theravada	1	NR	NR	395	0.1	0.1
BUDD–Vajrayana	2	NR	NR	71	0.0	0.0
Calv Chpl	2	NR	NR	NR	-	-
Catholic	55	NR	NR	341,970	46.0	80.6
Ch Cr, Scientst	7	NR	NR	NR	-	-
Ch of Nazarene	10	389	464	613	0.1	0.1
Chr & Miss Al	4	232	189	357	0.0	0.1
CHR–Chr Ch (Disc)	1	0	0	0	0.0	0.0
CHR–Chs of Christ	4	110	93	160	0.0	0.0
CHR–Int Chs of Christ	0	NR	423	513	0.1	0.1
Christian Brethren	2	NR	NR	NR	-	-
CONG–Cong Chr, NA	3	NR	232	281	0.0	0.1
CONG–Consrv Cong Chr	13	2,086	2,228	2,700	0.4	0.6
Evan Cov Ch	1	126	190	164	0.0	0.0
FRND–Fr Gen Cf & Un Mtg	3	NR	68	82	0.0	0.0
HINDU–I/A Temples	1	NR	NR	250	0.0	0.1
HINDU–Post Ren	1	NR	NR	10	0.0	0.0
Int Cou Comm Ch	2	NR	NR	NR	-	-
Jehovah's Witness	8	NR	NR	NR	-	-
JUD–Conserv	6	1,292	1,450	3,915	0.5	0.9
JUD–Orth	4	360	200	500	0.1	0.1
JUD–Reconst	1	31	40	108	0.0	0.0
JUD–Reform	4	879	1,550	4,185	0.6	1.0
LDS–L-D Saints	5	NR	NR	2,528	0.3	0.6
LUTH–E.L.C.A.	6	580	1,341	1,862	0.3	0.4
LUTH–Luth Cong Msn Chr	1	50	227	275	0.0	0.1
LUTH–Luth–MO Synod	2	308	438	537	0.1	0.1
METH–AME	1	0	100	121	0.0	0.0
METH–C.M.E.	1	0	150	182	0.0	0.0
METH–Free Methodist	7	813	757	889	0.1	0.2
METH–Prim Meth Ch	2	NR	NR	NR	-	-
METH–Un Methodist	23	1,264	3,891	4,998	0.7	1.2
Missionary Ch	2	89	47	93	0.0	0.0
Muslim Est	2	268	NR	616	0.1	0.1
Nat Spirit Asso	2	NR	NR	NR	-	-
Non-denom Chr Chs	33	3,263	4,078	4,547	0.6	1.1
ORTHE–Ant Orth of NA	1	100	NR	450	0.1	0.1
ORTHE–Greek Orthodox	6	2,230	NR	9,950	1.3	2.3
ORTHE–Holy Orth in NA	1	46	NR	60	0.0	0.0
ORTHE–Orth Ch in Amer	1	45	NR	105	0.0	0.0
ORTHE–Rus Orth Abroad	2	115	NR	250	0.0	0.1
ORTHO–Armen Ap Cilic	1	70	NR	500	0.1	0.1
ORTHO–Armen Ap Etchm	1	50	NR	275	0.0	0.1
PENT–Assemb of God	19	2,586	1,150	5,232	0.7	1.2
PENT–Ch God (Cleve)	5	484	492	596	0.1	0.1
PENT–Ch of God Proph	3	NR	179	217	0.0	0.1
PENT–COGIC	1	0	60	73	0.0	0.0
PENT–I F Chr Assmbl	1	NR	NR	NR	-	-
PENT–Int Foursq Gos	2	80	82	99	0.0	0.0
PENT–Un Pent Ch Intl	3	NR	NR	NR	-	-
PENT–Vineyard	1	142	155	188	0.0	0.0
PRES–Evan Presby Ch	1	NR	1	1	0.0	0.0
PRES–Orth Pres Ch	2	474	387	492	0.1	0.1
PRES–Presb Ch (USA)	3	150	184	223	0.0	0.1
Salvation Army	6	277	552	1,245	0.2	0.3
Sev Day Adv	11	519	904	1,038	0.1	0.2
Un C of Christ	41	3,636	8,193	9,929	1.3	2.3
Unit Univ	13	1,075	1,943	2,674	0.4	0.6
Unity Ch	1	NR	NR	NR	-	-
Zoroastrian	0	NR	NR	9	0.0	0.0
FRANKLIN	**94**	**3,419**	**5,299**	**24,785**	**34.7**	**100.0**
ANG/EPIS–Episcopal	3	169	268	561	0.8	2.3
Bahá'í	0	NR	95	95	0.1	0.4
BAPT–Amer Bapt USA	4	142	519	608	0.9	2.5
BAPT–Converge/BGC	2	150	NR	180	0.3	0.7
BAPT–So Bapt Conv	2	500	301	353	0.5	1.4
BUDD–Mahayana	4	NR	NR	100	0.1	0.4
BUDD–Theravada	2	NR	NR	663	0.9	2.7
BUDD–Vajrayana	1	NR	NR	78	0.1	0.3
Catholic	14	NR	NR	16,509	23.1	66.6
Ch Cr, Scientst	1	NR	NR	NR	-	-
Ch of Nazarene	1	53	55	55	0.1	0.2
Chr & Miss Al	2	283	203	419	0.6	1.7
CHR–Chs of Christ	1	30	28	30	0.0	0.1
CONG–Cong Chr, NA	1	NR	59	69	0.1	0.3
CONG–Consrv Cong Chr	1	80	125	147	0.2	0.6
Evan Cov Ch	1	36	32	47	0.1	0.2
FRND–Fr Gen Cf & Un Mtg	2	NR	155	182	0.3	0.7
HINDU–Post Ren	1	NR	NR	77	0.1	0.3
Jehovah's Witness	3	NR	NR	NR	-	-
LDS–L-D Saints	1	NR	NR	394	0.6	1.6
LUTH–E.L.C.A.	2	120	297	347	0.5	1.4
METH–Un Methodist	5	138	508	615	0.9	2.5
Non-denom Chr Chs	5	350	435	485	0.7	2.0
OCATH–Pol Natl Cath	1	NR	NR	NR	-	-
PENT–Assemb of God	3	154	77	201	0.3	0.8
Salvation Army	1	39	64	121	0.2	0.5
Sev Day Adv	1	20	36	41	0.1	0.2
Sikh	1	NR	NR	NR	-	-
Un C of Christ	21	987	1,907	2,235	3.1	9.0
Unit Univ	6	168	135	173	0.2	0.7
Unity Ch	1	NR	NR	NR	-	-
HAMPDEN	**324**	**21,843**	**34,814**	**280,122**	**60.4**	**100.0**
ANG/EPIS–Episcopal	15	1,238	2,878	3,867	0.8	1.4
Bahá'í	4	NR	263	263	0.1	0.1
BAPT–Amer Bapt USA	22	1,981	4,267	5,185	1.1	1.9
BAPT–Asc Ref Bap Ch Am	1	NR	NR	NR	-	-
BAPT–Consrv Bapt	1	NR	NR	NR	-	-
BAPT–NBC USA	4	355	950	1,154	0.2	0.4
BAPT–Reg Bapt Gen As	1	NR	NR	NR	-	-
BAPT–So Bapt Conv	8	460	527	640	0.1	0.2
BUDD–Mahayana	1	NR	NR	102	0.0	0.0
Catholic	63	NR	NR	223,685	48.3	79.9
CGOD–Ch God (Ander)	1	0	NR	0	0.0	0.0
Ch Cr, Scientst	1	NR	NR	NR	-	-
Ch of Nazarene	2	123	176	176	0.0	0.1
Chr & Miss Al	2	82	71	95	0.0	0.0
CHR–Chs of Christ	2	193	171	230	0.0	0.1
CHR–Int Chs of Christ	1	NR	147	179	0.0	0.1
CONG–Cong Chr, NA	2	NR	103	125	0.0	0.0
CONG–Consrv Cong Chr	1	50	62	75	0.0	0.0
Evan Cov Ch	2	350	348	455	0.1	0.2
Evan Free Ch	1	526	NR	526	0.1	0.2
HINDU–I/A Temples	1	NR	NR	1,742	0.4	0.6
HINDU–Post Ren	1	NR	NR	54	0.0	0.0
Jehovah's Witness	8	NR	NR	NR	-	-
JUD–Conserv	1	510	572	1,544	0.3	0.6
JUD–Orth	2	720	265	1,000	0.2	0.4
JUD–Reform	1	291	513	1,385	0.3	0.5
LDS–L-D Saints	2	NR	NR	1,727	0.4	0.6
LUTH–E.L.C.A.	5	515	1,484	1,967	0.4	0.7
LUTH–Luth–MO Synod	3	308	845	920	0.2	0.3
METH–AME	1	150	350	425	0.1	0.2
METH–AME Zion	1	0	100	122	0.0	0.0
METH–C.M.E.	1	40	80	97	0.0	0.0
METH–Free Methodist	1	0	30	30	0.0	0.0
METH–Un Methodist	13	841	2,402	3,137	0.7	1.1
METH–Wesleyan	2	80	48	104	0.0	0.0
Muslim Est	4	422	NR	994	0.2	0.4
Nat Spirit Asso	1	NR	NR	NR	-	-
New Apost Ch	1	NR	NR	NR	-	-
Non-denom Chr Chs	42	5,105	6,627	7,389	1.6	2.6
OCATH–Pol Natl Cath	2	NR	NR	NR	-	-
ORTHE–Ant Orth of NA	1	40	NR	60	0.0	0.0
ORTHE–Greek Orthodox	4	590	NR	2,510	0.5	0.9
ORTHE–Holy Orth in NA	1	35	NR	45	0.0	0.0
ORTHE–Orth Ch in Amer	1	45	NR	95	0.0	0.0
ORTHE–Rus Orth Abroad	1	30	NR	46	0.0	0.0
ORTHO–Armen Ap Cilic	1	70	NR	400	0.1	0.1

NR–Not Reported   - Represents no adherents reported.   Percentages may not total 100 due to rounding.

Table 3: Religious Congregations by County and Group: 2010

Religious Group	Number of Congrega-tions	Number of Attendees	Number of Communicant, Confirmed, or Full Members	Adherents		
				Number of Adherents	% of Total Pop.	% of Total Adh.
ORTHO–Armen Ap Etchm	1	65	NR	250	0.1	0.1
PENT–Assemb of God	16	2,919	2,140	5,794	1.3	2.1
PENT–Ch God (Cleve)	9	447	779	947	0.2	0.3
PENT–Ch Lord Jesus Apos	1	NR	NR	NR	-	-
PENT–Ch of God Proph	2	NR	55	67	0.0	0.0
PENT–COGIC	6	0	570	693	0.1	0.2
PENT–Fire Bapt Hol Ch	1	NR	NR	NR	-	-
PENT–I F Chr Assmbl	2	NR	NR	NR	-	-
PENT–Un Pent Ch Intl	5	NR	NR	NR	-	-
PENT–United Holy Ch	2	NR	NR	NR	-	-
PRES–Evan Presby Ch	1	NR	54	66	0.0	0.0
PRES–Presb Ch (USA)	3	104	214	260	0.1	0.1
PRES–Presb Ch Amer	1	123	101	142	0.0	0.1
Salvation Army	2	132	221	413	0.1	0.1
Sev Day Adv	4	595	1,035	1,190	0.3	0.4
Un C of Christ	28	2,182	6,107	7,421	1.6	2.6
Unit Univ	3	126	259	326	0.1	0.1
Zoroastrian	0	NR	NR	3	0.0	0.0
HAMPSHIRE	**117**	**5,879**	**10,854**	**66,976**	**42.4**	**100.0**
ANG/EPIS–Anglican NA	1	NR	NR	NR	-	-
ANG/EPIS–Episcopal	5	610	1,287	1,695	1.1	2.5
Bahá'í	4	NR	234	234	0.1	0.3
BAPT–Amer Bapt USA	3	571	555	634	0.4	0.9
BAPT–So Bapt Conv	4	423	316	361	0.2	0.5
BUDD–Mahayana	6	NR	NR	147	0.1	0.2
BUDD–Theravada	1	NR	NR	396	0.3	0.6
BUDD–Vajrayana	3	NR	NR	468	0.3	0.7
Calv Chpl	1	NR	NR	NR	-	-
Catholic	20	NR	NR	50,643	32.0	75.6
Ch Cr, Scientst	1	NR	NR	NR	-	-
CHR–Chs of Christ	1	20	12	25	0.0	0.0
CHR–Int Chs of Christ	0	NR	846	967	0.6	1.4
CONG–Cong Chr, NA	3	NR	286	327	0.2	0.5
FRND–Fr Gen Cf & Un Mtg	1	NR	56	64	0.0	0.1
HINDU–Post Ren	2	NR	NR	102	0.1	0.2
Jehovah's Witness	3	NR	NR	NR	-	-
JUD–Conserv	1	342	384	1,037	0.7	1.5
JUD–Reconst	1	235	300	810	0.5	1.2
JUD–Reform	1	49	87	235	0.1	0.4
LDS–L-D Saints	1	NR	NR	533	0.3	0.8
LUTH–E.L.C.A.	2	129	469	478	0.3	0.7
LUTH–Luth-MO Synod	1	50	201	269	0.2	0.4
METH–AME Zion	1	0	25	29	0.0	0.0
METH–Un Methodist	5	324	917	1,162	0.7	1.7
Muslim Est	1	60	NR	160	0.1	0.2
Non-denom Chr Chs	7	840	675	1,058	0.7	1.6
OCATH–Pol Natl Cath	2	NR	NR	NR	-	-
PENT–Assemb of God	4	236	148	386	0.2	0.6
PENT–Un Pent Ch Intl	1	NR	NR	NR	-	-
PRES–Korean Amer Pres	1	NR	NR	NR	-	-
Sev Day Adv	1	31	54	62	0.0	0.1
Un C of Christ	26	1,577	3,582	4,094	2.6	6.1
Unit Univ	2	382	420	600	0.4	0.9
MIDDLESEX	**915**	**75,902**	**107,364**	**923,929**	**61.5**	**100.0**
ANG/EPIS–Anglican NA	5	NR	NR	NR	-	-
ANG/EPIS–Episcopal	52	4,964	15,401	17,809	1.2	1.9
Bahá'í	11	NR	888	888	0.1	0.1
BAPT–Alliance Bapt	2	NR	NR	NR	-	-
BAPT–Amer Bapt USA	69	5,046	9,395	11,226	0.7	1.2
BAPT–Consrv Bapt	7	NR	NR	NR	-	-
BAPT–Converge/BGC	4	300	NR	360	0.0	0.0
BAPT–NBC USA	1	150	150	179	0.0	0.0
BAPT–Reg Bapt Gen As	1	NR	NR	NR	-	-
BAPT–So Bapt Conv	39	3,731	3,688	4,407	0.3	0.5
BUDD–Mahayana	21	NR	NR	8,745	0.6	0.9
BUDD–Theravada	6	NR	NR	1,934	0.1	0.2
BUDD–Vajrayana	4	NR	NR	311	0.0	0.0
Calv Chpl	1	NR	NR	NR	-	-
Catholic	106	NR	NR	718,209	47.8	77.7
CGOD–Ches God-Gen Con	1	65	53	63	0.0	0.0
Ch Christ Chr Union	1	NR	NR	NR	-	-

Religious Group	Number of Congrega-tions	Number of Attendees	Number of Communicant, Confirmed, or Full Members	Adherents		
				Number of Adherents	% of Total Pop.	% of Total Adh.
Ch Cr, Scientst	12	NR	NR	NR	-	-
Ch God (7th Day)	1	NR	NR	NR	-	-
Ch of Nazarene	19	1,178	1,463	1,815	0.1	0.2
Chr & Miss Al	5	144	106	163	0.0	0.0
CHR–Chr Ch (Disc)	1	0	0	0	0.0	0.0
CHR–Chr Chs & Chs Cr	3	NR	85	102	0.0	0.0
CHR–Chs of Christ	5	345	293	422	0.0	0.0
Christian Brethren	3	NR	NR	NR	-	-
CONG–Cong Chr Add'l	2	NR	556	664	0.0	0.1
CONG–Cong Chr, NA	1	NR	49	59	0.0	0.0
CONG–Consrv Cong Chr	10	1,085	1,216	1,453	0.1	0.2
Evan Cov Ch	6	1,072	440	1,393	0.1	0.2
Evan Free Ch	8	622	NR	622	0.0	0.1
FRND–Fr Gen Cf & Un Mtg	5	NR	642	767	0.1	0.1
HINDU–I/A Temples	5	NR	NR	2,659	0.2	0.3
HINDU–Post Ren	6	NR	NR	249	0.0	0.0
HINDU–Renaiss	2	NR	NR	387	0.0	0.0
HINDU–Trad Temples	2	NR	NR	600	0.0	0.1
Jain	1	NR	NR	NR	-	-
Jehovah's Witness	14	NR	NR	NR	-	-
JUD–Conserv	10	3,047	3,420	9,234	0.6	1.0
JUD–Orth	15	3,168	1,200	4,400	0.3	0.5
JUD–Reconst	2	191	244	659	0.0	0.1
JUD–Reform	14	2,749	4,849	13,092	0.9	1.4
LDS–Comm of Christ	1	NR	102	102	0.0	0.0
LDS–L-D Saints	19	NR	NR	8,420	0.6	0.9
LUTH–E.L.C.A.	15	1,573	3,882	5,493	0.4	0.6
LUTH–Evan Luth Syn	1	62	91	142	0.0	0.0
LUTH–Luth Cong Msn Chr	1	7	25	30	0.0	0.0
LUTH–Luth-MO Synod	2	527	867	1,200	0.1	0.1
MENN–Mennonite USA	1	40	49	59	0.0	0.0
METH–AME	3	525	1,705	2,037	0.1	0.2
METH–AME Zion	1	20	30	36	0.0	0.0
METH–Free Methodist	1	0	0	0	0.0	0.0
METH–Prim Meth Ch	3	NR	NR	NR	-	-
METH–Un Methodist	46	3,460	10,701	15,423	1.0	1.7
Missionary Ch	1	147	116	147	0.0	0.0
Muslim Est	11	1,486	NR	5,580	0.4	0.6
New Apost Ch	2	NR	NR	NR	-	-
Non-denom Chr Chs	62	11,689	13,328	15,674	1.0	1.7
OCATH–Pol Natl Cath	1	NR	NR	NR	-	-
ORTHE–Ant Orth of NA	2	355	NR	1,250	0.1	0.1
ORTHE–Bulgar Orth USA	1	10	NR	116	0.0	0.0
ORTHE–Greek Orthodox	12	2,665	NR	13,310	0.9	1.4
ORTHE–Orth Ch in Amer	2	120	NR	255	0.0	0.0
ORTHE–Romania Orth Ar	1	80	NR	700	0.0	0.1
ORTHE–Rus Orth Abroad	1	27	NR	43	0.0	0.0
ORTHE–Serb Orth USA	1	100	NR	1,000	0.1	0.1
ORTHO–Armen Ap Cilic	1	4,000	NR	400	0.0	0.0
ORTHO–Armen Ap Etchm	4	540	NR	2,275	0.2	0.2
ORTHO–Coptic Orth Ch	1	300	NR	4,000	0.3	0.4
ORTHO–Malan Dioc Am	1	140	NR	220	0.0	0.0
ORTHO–Malan Syr Orth	1	40	NR	72	0.0	0.0
PENT–Assemb of God	28	2,641	1,945	3,703	0.2	0.4
PENT–Ch God (Cleve)	15	890	984	1,176	0.1	0.1
PENT–Ch Lord Jesus Apos	2	NR	NR	NR	-	-
PENT–COGIC	1	25	20	24	0.0	0.0
PENT–Elim	1	NR	NR	NR	-	-
PENT–I F Chr Assmbl	3	NR	NR	NR	-	-
PENT–Int Foursq Gos	6	287	309	369	0.0	0.0
PENT–Un Pent Asbl God	5	NR	NR	NR	-	-
PENT–Un Pent Ch Intl	1	NR	NR	NR	-	-
PENT–Vineyard	4	1,096	1,362	1,627	0.1	0.2
PRES–Cumber Presb	1	NR	35	35	0.0	0.0
PRES–Korean Amer Pres	2	NR	NR	NR	-	-
PRES–Korean Pres Amer	5	NR	NR	NR	-	-
PRES–Orth Pres Ch	2	92	97	120	0.0	0.0
PRES–Presb Ch (USA)	8	761	1,233	1,473	0.1	0.2
PRES–Presb Ch Amer	4	665	520	627	0.0	0.1
PRES–Ref Pres of NA	1	80	68	87	0.0	0.0
REF–Christian Ref	1	30	17	20	0.0	0.0
REF–Ref Ch in Am	1	66	101	106	0.0	0.0
Salvation Army	5	247	474	1,764	0.1	0.2
Sev Day Adv	29	1,845	3,207	3,690	0.2	0.4

NR–Not Reported - Represents no adherents reported. Percentages may not total 100 due to rounding.

Table 3: Religious Congregations by County and Group: 2010

Religious Group	Number of Congrega-tions	Number of Attendees	Number of Communicant, Confirmed, or Full Members	Adherents		
				Number of Adherents	% of Total Pop.	% of Total Adh.
Sikh	2	NR	NR	NR	-	-
Swedenborgian	2	NR	NR	NR	-	-
Tao	2	NR	NR	NR	-	-
Un C of Christ	67	6,595	14,255	17,033	1.1	1.8
Unit Univ	33	4,812	7,703	11,075	0.7	1.2
Unity Ch	1	NR	NR	NR	-	-
Zoroastrian	1	NR	NR	145	0.0	0.0
NANTUCKET	**10**	**496**	**1,128**	**4,065**	**40.0**	**100.0**
ANG/EPIS–Episcopal	1	151	461	461	4.5	11.3
Bahá'í	0	NR	7	7	0.1	0.2
BAPT–Amer Bapt USA	1	120	80	96	0.9	2.4
Catholic	1	NR	NR	2,642	26.0	65.0
Ch Cr, Scientist	1	NR	NR	NR	-	-
CONG–Cong Chr, NA	1	NR	350	421	4.1	10.4
FRND–Fr Gen Cf & Un Mtg	1	NR	0	0	0.0	0.0
METH–Un Methodist	1	49	37	80	0.8	2.0
Non-denom Chr Chs	1	87	12	109	1.1	2.7
PENT–Int Foursq Gos	1	39	41	49	0.5	1.2
Unit Univ	1	50	140	200	2.0	4.9
NORFOLK	**340**	**29,366**	**43,368**	**433,862**	**64.7**	**100.0**
ANG/EPIS–Anglican NA	4	NR	NR	NR	-	-
ANG/EPIS–Episcopal	29	2,550	8,525	11,016	1.6	2.5
Bahá'í	1	NR	198	198	0.0	0.0
BAPT–Amer Bapt USA	19	1,463	2,703	3,268	0.5	0.8
BAPT–Consrv Bapt	5	NR	NR	NR	-	-
BAPT–Converge/BGC	7	525	NR	630	0.1	0.1
BAPT–So Bapt Conv	13	1,285	887	1,072	0.2	0.2
BUDD–Mahayana	3	NR	NR	1,220	0.2	0.3
BUDD–Theravada	1	NR	NR	292	0.0	0.1
BUDD–Vajrayana	3	NR	NR	141	0.0	0.0
Catholic	52	NR	NR	355,321	53.0	81.9
Ch Cr, Scientst	5	NR	NR	NR	-	-
Ch of Nazarene	6	768	880	1,362	0.2	0.3
Chr & Miss Al	1	363	122	572	0.1	0.1
CHR–Chr Ch (Disc)	1	0	0	0	0.0	0.0
CHR–Chs of Christ	1	50	60	77	0.0	0.0
CHR–Int Chs of Christ	0	NR	423	511	0.1	0.1
CONG–Cong Chr Add'l	1	NR	98	118	0.0	0.0
CONG–Cong Chr, NA	6	NR	885	1,070	0.2	0.2
CONG–Consrv Cong Chr	3	344	332	401	0.1	0.1
Evan Cov Ch	2	245	58	319	0.0	0.1
FRND–Fr Gen Cf & Un Mtg	2	NR	185	224	0.0	0.1
HINDU–Post Ren	1	NR	NR	25	0.0	0.0
HINDU–Renaiss	1	NR	NR	12	0.0	0.0
Jain	1	NR	NR	NR	-	-
Jehovah's Witness	2	NR	NR	NR	-	-
JUD–Conserv	9	2,176	2,442	6,593	1.0	1.5
JUD–Orth	12	3,168	1,200	4,400	0.7	1.0
JUD–Reform	8	1,830	3,228	8,716	1.3	2.0
LDS–Comm of Christ	1	NR	102	102	0.0	0.0
LDS–L-D Saints	3	NR	NR	1,160	0.2	0.3
LUTH–E.L.C.A.	5	459	1,305	1,652	0.2	0.4
LUTH–Luth–MO Synod	3	235	458	575	0.1	0.1
METH–Un Methodist	13	702	2,638	3,252	0.5	0.7
MJEW–Union Mes Cong	1	NR	NR	NR	-	-
Muslim Est	3	968	NR	4,616	0.7	1.1
Non-denom Chr Chs	16	1,550	1,830	2,106	0.3	0.5
ORTHE–Ant Orth of NA	3	384	NR	1,339	0.2	0.3
ORTHE–Greek Orthodox	3	675	NR	1,490	0.2	0.3
ORTHE–Holy Orth in NA	2	174	NR	225	0.0	0.1
ORTHO–Eritrean Orth	1	325	NR	485	0.1	0.1
PENT–Assemb of God	10	1,182	828	1,788	0.3	0.4
PENT–Ch God (Cleve)	1	6	17	21	0.0	0.0
PENT–Ch of God Proph	1	NR	35	42	0.0	0.0
PENT–I F Chr Assmbl	1	NR	NR	NR	-	-
PENT–Int Foursq Gos	3	157	154	186	0.0	0.0
PENT–Intl Pent Holiness	1	350	350	423	0.1	0.1
PENT–Vineyard	1	21	21	25	0.0	0.0
PRES–Korean Pres Amer	1	NR	NR	NR	-	-
PRES–Presb Ch (USA)	7	460	989	1,196	0.2	0.3
PRES–Presb Ch Amer	1	0	0	0	0.0	0.0
REF–Christian Ref	1	1,200	425	514	0.1	0.1
Salvation Army	1	53	90	162	0.0	0.0
Sev Day Adv	6	268	467	537	0.1	0.1
Sikh	1	NR	NR	NR	-	-
Un C of Christ	32	4,040	9,339	11,290	1.7	2.6
Unit Univ	17	1,390	2,094	3,102	0.5	0.7
Unity Ch	2	NR	NR	NR	-	-
Zoroastrian	0	NR	NR	16	0.0	0.0
PLYMOUTH	**273**	**17,655**	**31,110**	**210,748**	**42.6**	**100.0**
ANG/EPIS–Anglican NA	2	NR	NR	NR	-	-
ANG/EPIS–Episcopal	12	1,412	4,628	5,950	1.2	2.8
Bahá'í	0	NR	94	94	0.0	0.0
BAPT–Amer Bapt USA	19	1,685	2,371	2,900	0.6	1.4
BAPT–Consrv Bapt	5	NR	NR	NR	-	-
BAPT–Converge/BGC	5	375	NR	450	0.1	0.2
BAPT–Natl Mis Bapt Conv	1	0	150	183	0.0	0.1
BAPT–Ref Bapt Ch	1	NR	NR	NR	-	-
BAPT–Reg Bapt Gen As	1	NR	NR	NR	-	-
BAPT–So Bapt Conv	7	501	476	582	0.1	0.3
BUDD–Mahayana	3	NR	NR	224	0.0	0.1
Calv Chpl	1	NR	NR	NR	-	-
Catholic	35	NR	NR	165,985	33.5	78.8
CGOD–Ches God-Gen Con	1	68	40	49	0.0	0.0
Ch Cr, Scientst	6	NR	NR	NR	-	-
Ch of Nazarene	8	711	1,067	1,279	0.3	0.6
Chr & Miss Al	2	546	245	902	0.2	0.4
CHR–Chs of Christ	1	6	6	6	0.0	0.0
CONG–Cong Chr Add'l	1	NR	197	241	0.0	0.1
CONG–Cong Chr, NA	7	NR	934	1,142	0.2	0.5
CONG–Consrv Cong Chr	3	318	294	360	0.1	0.2
Evan Cov Ch	1	133	134	173	0.0	0.1
Evan Free Ch	1	100	NR	100	0.0	0.0
FRND–Fr Gen Cf & Un Mtg	2	NR	18	22	0.0	0.0
Jehovah's Witness	8	NR	NR	NR	-	-
JUD–Conserv	1	199	223	602	0.1	0.3
JUD–Orth	1	43	50	60	0.0	0.0
JUD–Reconst	1	50	64	173	0.0	0.1
JUD–Reform	2	207	365	986	0.2	0.5
LDS–Comm of Christ	1	NR	102	102	0.0	0.0
LDS–L-D Saints	4	NR	NR	1,810	0.4	0.9
LUTH–E.L.C.A.	7	505	1,889	2,593	0.5	1.2
LUTH–Luth–MO Synod	2	200	349	492	0.1	0.2
METH–AME	2	0	250	306	0.1	0.1
METH–AME Zion	1	0	100	122	0.0	0.1
METH–Un Methodist	19	1,062	2,949	3,953	0.8	1.9
Missionary Ch	1	12	0	12	0.0	0.0
New Apost Ch	1	NR	NR	NR	-	-
Non-denom Chr Chs	23	2,836	3,397	3,889	0.8	1.8
ORTHE–Greek Orthodox	1	225	NR	1,025	0.2	0.5
ORTHE–Holy Orth in NA	1	23	NR	30	0.0	0.0
ORTHE–Orth Ch in Amer	1	45	NR	85	0.0	0.0
PENT–Assemb of God	7	988	600	1,252	0.3	0.6
PENT–Ch God (Cleve)	4	202	352	431	0.1	0.2
PENT–Ch Lord Jesus Apos	1	NR	NR	NR	-	-
PENT–Ch of God Proph	1	NR	25	31	0.0	0.0
PENT–I F Chr Assmbl	1	NR	NR	NR	-	-
PENT–Int Foursq Gos	7	629	728	891	0.2	0.4
PENT–Un Pent Ch Intl	1	NR	NR	NR	-	-
PENT–Vineyard	2	351	571	698	0.1	0.3
Salvation Army	2	141	176	295	0.1	0.1
Sev Day Adv	6	634	1,102	1,267	0.3	0.6
Swedenborgian	2	NR	NR	NR	-	-
Un C of Christ	24	2,543	5,660	6,923	1.4	3.3
Unit Univ	13	905	1,504	2,078	0.4	1.0
SUFFOLK	**450**	**52,563**	**60,019**	**442,649**	**61.3**	**100.0**
ANG/EPIS–Anglican NA	1	NR	NR	NR	-	-
ANG/EPIS–Episcopal	21	2,555	3,730	7,259	1.0	1.6
Bahá'í	1	NR	310	310	0.0	0.1
BAPT–Amer Bapt USA	40	4,464	7,224	8,358	1.2	1.9
BAPT–Consrv Bapt	5	NR	NR	NR	-	-
BAPT–Converge/BGC	2	475	NR	570	0.1	0.1

NR–Not Reported - Represents no adherents reported. Percentages may not total 100 due to rounding.

Table 3: Religious Congregations by County and Group: 2010

Religious Group	Number of Congrega-tions	Number of Attendees	Number of Communicant, Confirmed, or Full Members	Adherents		
				Number of Adherents	% of Total Pop.	% of Total Adh.
BAPT–Natl Mis Bapt Conv	2	0	300	347	0.0	0.1
BAPT–NBC USA	1	0	150	174	0.0	0.0
BAPT–So Bapt Conv	31	2,850	4,021	4,652	0.6	1.1
BUDD–Mahayana	7	NR	NR	4,148	0.6	0.9
BUDD–Theravada	1	NR	NR	396	0.1	0.1
BUDD–Vajrayana	3	NR	NR	99	0.0	0.0
Calv Chpl	1	NR	NR	NR	-	-
Catholic	56	NR	NR	332,744	46.1	75.2
CGOD–Ch God (Ander)	3	6,890	NR	6,890	1.0	1.6
Ch Christ Chr Union	1	NR	NR	NR	-	-
Ch Cr, Scientst	3	NR	NR	NR	-	-
Ch God (7th Day)	1	NR	NR	NR	-	-
Ch of Nazarene	7	488	741	856	0.1	0.2
Chr & Miss Al	4	349	340	493	0.1	0.1
CHR–Chr Ch (Disc)	2	0	0	0	0.0	0.0
CHR–Chr Chs & Chs Cr	1	NR	0	0	0.0	0.0
CHR–Chs of Christ	3	370	360	445	0.1	0.1
CHR–Int Chs of Christ	1	NR	427	494	0.1	0.1
CONG–Consrv Cong Chr	2	2,000	1,391	1,609	0.2	0.4
Evan Cov Ch	2	360	168	468	0.1	0.1
Evan Free Ch	2	395	NR	395	0.1	0.1
FRND–Fr Gen Cf & Un Mtg	2	NR	73	84	0.0	0.0
HINDU–I/A Temples	4	NR	NR	2,201	0.3	0.5
HINDU–Post Ren	4	NR	NR	160	0.0	0.0
HINDU–Renaiss	3	NR	NR	139	0.0	0.0
HINDU–Trad Temples	1	NR	NR	15	0.0	0.0
Int Cou Comm Ch	1	NR	NR	NR	-	-
Jehovah's Witness	9	NR	NR	NR	-	-
JUD–Conserv	1	58	65	176	0.0	0.0
JUD–Orth	7	1,066	400	1,480	0.2	0.3
JUD–Reconst	1	133	170	459	0.1	0.1
JUD–Reform	1	611	1,078	2,911	0.4	0.7
LDS–L-D Saints	5	NR	NR	3,518	0.5	0.8
LUTH–E.L.C.A.	3	104	173	194	0.0	0.0
LUTH–Luth-MO Synod	2	215	453	501	0.1	0.1
METH–AME	6	825	1,800	2,082	0.3	0.5
METH–AME Zion	2	80	500	578	0.1	0.1
METH–Free Methodist	3	125	169	179	0.0	0.0
METH–Un Methodist	11	707	1,275	1,604	0.2	0.4
METH–Wesleyan	1	63	54	82	0.0	0.0
Metro Comm Ch	1	19	20	23	0.0	0.0
Missionary Ch	4	312	218	312	0.0	0.1
Muslim Est	11	2,378	NR	7,646	1.1	1.7
Non-denom Chr Chs	39	11,130	16,171	17,115	2.4	3.9
ORTHE–Alban Orth Dio	1	35	NR	350	0.0	0.1
ORTHE–Ant Orth of NA	1	400	NR	1,250	0.2	0.3
ORTHE–Bulgar Orth USA	1	90	NR	120	0.0	0.0
ORTHE–Greek Orthodox	2	330	NR	750	0.1	0.2
ORTHE–Holy Orth in NA	2	554	NR	720	0.1	0.2
ORTHE–Orth Ch in Amer	5	391	NR	1,903	0.3	0.4
ORTHE–Rus Orth Abroad	1	150	NR	2,000	0.3	0.5
ORTHE–Ukrainian Orth	1	100	NR	200	0.0	0.0
ORTHO–Ethiopian Orth	2	NR	NR	NR	-	-
ORTHO–Syrian Orth Ch	1	200	NR	400	0.1	0.1
PENT–Assemb of God	15	3,498	2,549	4,174	0.6	0.9
PENT–Ch God (Cleve)	10	1,517	1,536	1,777	0.2	0.4
PENT–Ch Lord Jesus Apos	2	NR	NR	NR	-	-
PENT–Ch of God Proph	3	NR	271	314	0.0	0.1
PENT–COGIC	7	275	860	995	0.1	0.2
PENT–Fire Bapt Hol Ch	1	NR	NR	NR	-	-
PENT–I F Chr Assmbl	2	NR	NR	NR	-	-
PENT–Int Foursq Gos	2	266	231	267	0.0	0.1
PENT–Un Pent Ch Intl	3	NR	NR	NR	-	-
PENT–United Holy Ch	3	NR	NR	NR	-	-
PRES–Presb Ch (USA)	6	438	488	565	0.1	0.1
PRES–Presb Ch Amer	3	650	320	373	0.1	0.1
Salvation Army	6	334	563	1,216	0.2	0.3
Sev Day Adv	18	2,668	4,641	5,337	0.7	1.2
Un Breth in Cr	1	50	65	43	0.0	0.0
Un C of Christ	16	1,007	1,982	2,293	0.3	0.5
Unit Univ	9	588	4,732	5,420	0.8	1.2
Zoroastrian	0	NR	NR	16	0.0	0.0

Religious Group	Number of Congrega-tions	Number of Attendees	Number of Communicant, Confirmed, or Full Members	Adherents		
				Number of Adherents	% of Total Pop.	% of Total Adh.
WORCESTER	**582**	**44,203**	**65,837**	**415,125**	**52.0**	**100.0**
ANG/EPIS–Anglican NA	2	NR	NR	NR	-	-
ANG/EPIS–Episcopal	28	2,440	6,448	9,329	1.2	2.2
Bahá'í	1	NR	190	190	0.0	0.0
BAPT–Alliance Bapt	1	NR	NR	NR	-	-
BAPT–Amer Bapt USA	27	2,327	4,370	5,307	0.7	1.3
BAPT–Asc Ref Bap Ch Am	1	NR	NR	NR	-	-
BAPT–Consrv Bapt	8	NR	NR	NR	-	-
BAPT–Converge/BGC	9	1,325	NR	1,590	0.2	0.4
BAPT–Ref Bapt Ch	2	NR	NR	NR	-	-
BAPT–Reg Bapt Gen As	2	NR	NR	NR	-	-
BAPT–So Bapt Conv	19	1,725	1,561	1,896	0.2	0.5
BUDD–Mahayana	2	NR	NR	56	0.0	0.0
BUDD–Theravada	4	NR	NR	6,995	0.9	1.7
Calv Chpl	1	NR	NR	NR	-	-
Catholic	117	NR	NR	306,925	38.4	73.9
Ch Cr, Scientst	2	NR	NR	NR	-	-
Ch of Nazarene	6	489	716	1,135	0.1	0.3
Chr & Miss Al	3	152	161	185	0.0	0.0
CHR–Chr Chs & Chs Cr	4	NR	65	79	0.0	0.0
CHR–Chs of Christ	5	215	210	275	0.0	0.1
CHR–Int Chs of Christ	1	NR	154	187	0.0	0.0
CONG–Consrv Cong Chr	10	563	629	764	0.1	0.2
Evan Cov Ch	3	300	502	390	0.0	0.1
Evan Free Ch	1	26	NR	26	0.0	0.0
FRND–Fr Gen Cf & Un Mtg	1	NR	72	87	0.0	0.0
HINDU–Post Ren	3	NR	NR	118	0.0	0.0
HINDU–Trad Temples	1	NR	NR	1,033	0.1	0.2
Int Cou Comm Ch	1	NR	NR	NR	-	-
Jehovah's Witness	11	NR	NR	NR	-	-
JUD–Conserv	2	408	458	1,237	0.2	0.3
JUD–Orth	3	180	100	250	0.0	0.1
JUD–Reform	3	542	956	2,581	0.3	0.6
LDS–L-D Saints	5	NR	NR	2,772	0.3	0.7
LUTH–Apostolic Luth	2	NR	NR	NR	-	-
LUTH–E.L.C.A.	13	1,688	5,193	6,749	0.8	1.6
LUTH–Luth-MO Synod	3	344	547	700	0.1	0.2
METH–AME	1	0	100	121	0.0	0.0
METH–AME Zion	1	0	100	121	0.0	0.0
METH–Un Methodist	32	1,811	5,802	7,217	0.9	1.7
MJEW–Union Mes Cong	1	NR	NR	NR	-	-
Muslim Est	2	268	NR	616	0.1	0.1
Non-denom Chr Chs	36	8,768	12,445	14,072	1.8	3.4
OCATH–Pol Natl Cath	1	NR	NR	NR	-	-
ORTHE–Ant Orth of NA	2	580	NR	1,475	0.2	0.4
ORTHE–Greek Orthodox	5	885	NR	2,625	0.3	0.6
ORTHE–Orth Ch in Amer	2	340	NR	1,165	0.1	0.3
ORTHE–Romania Orth Ar	2	245	NR	370	0.0	0.1
ORTHO–Armen Ap Cilic	2	140	NR	1,000	0.1	0.2
ORTHO–Armen Ap Etchm	1	200	NR	1,000	0.1	0.2
ORTHO–Syrian Orth Ch	1	110	NR	300	0.0	0.1
PENT–Assemb of God	23	5,408	2,661	6,547	0.8	1.6
PENT–Ch God (Cleve)	11	600	411	499	0.1	0.1
PENT–Ch Lord Jesus Apos	1	NR	NR	NR	-	-
PENT–Ch of God Proph	2	NR	91	111	0.0	0.0
PENT–COGIC	2	101	210	255	0.0	0.1
PENT–Int Foursq Gos	9	906	783	951	0.1	0.2
PENT–Un Pent Ch Intl	2	NR	NR	NR	-	-
PENT–United Holy Ch	1	NR	NR	NR	-	-
PENT–Vineyard	1	125	150	182	0.0	0.0
PRES–Korean Pres Amer	1	NR	NR	NR	-	-
PRES–Orth Pres Ch	1	51	45	60	0.0	0.0
PRES–Presb Ch (USA)	3	228	345	419	0.1	0.1
REF–Christian Ref	3	700	1,014	1,232	0.2	0.3
Salvation Army	5	215	367	491	0.1	0.1
Sev Day Adv	27	3,070	5,338	6,139	0.8	1.5
Sikh	2	NR	NR	NR	-	-
Un C of Christ	65	5,019	11,707	14,218	1.8	3.4
Unit Univ	26	1,709	1,936	3,068	0.4	0.7
Unity Ch	1	NR	NR	NR	-	-
Zoroastrian	0	NR	NR	15	0.0	0.0

NR–Not Reported   - Represents no adherents reported.   Percentages may not total 100 due to rounding.

Table 3: Religious Congregations by County and Group: 2010

Religious Group	Number of Congrega-tions	Number of Attendees	Number of Communicant, Confirmed, or Full Members	Adherents: Number of Adherents	Adherents: % of Total Pop.	Adherents: % of Total Adh.
MICHIGAN	**9,521**	**1,096,974**	**1,632,731**	**4,165,343**	**42.1**	**100.0**
ALCONA	**26**	**1,075**	**1,729**	**2,871**	**26.2**	**100.0**
ANG/EPIS–Episcopal	1	22	37	39	0.4	1.4
Bahá'í	0	NR	1	1	0.0	0.0
BAPT–Amer Bapt USA	1	94	174	194	1.8	6.8
Catholic	4	NR	NR	799	7.3	27.8
FRND–Consrv Yr Mtgs	1	NR	0	0	0.0	0.0
LDS–Comm of Christ	1	NR	167	167	1.5	5.8
LUTH–E.L.C.A.	3	167	343	383	3.5	13.3
LUTH–Luth–MO Synod	2	33	52	54	0.5	1.9
LUTH–Wisc Ev Luth Syn	1	28	79	81	0.7	2.8
METH–Un Methodist	4	144	244	384	3.5	13.4
Non-denom Chr Chs	2	180	181	225	2.1	7.8
PENT–Assemb of God	2	270	209	273	2.5	9.5
PENT–Ch God (Cleve)	1	18	70	78	0.7	2.7
PRES–Presb Ch (USA)	2	97	133	148	1.4	5.2
Sev Day Adv	1	22	39	45	0.4	1.6
ALGER	**25**	**751**	**1,251**	**4,154**	**43.3**	**100.0**
ANG/EPIS–Episcopal	1	18	20	20	0.2	0.5
Bahá'í	0	NR	2	2	0.0	0.0
BAPT–Reg Bapt Gen As	2	NR	NR	NR	-	-
Catholic	4	NR	NR	2,483	25.9	59.8
Jehovah's Witness	1	NR	NR	NR	-	-
LUTH–Assoc Free Luth	2	NR	NR	NR	-	-
LUTH–E.L.C.A.	3	121	296	492	5.1	11.8
LUTH–Luth–MO Synod	2	196	470	519	5.4	12.5
MENN–Mennonite USA	1	30	12	14	0.1	0.3
METH–Un Methodist	3	76	149	192	2.0	4.6
METH–Wesleyan	1	45	34	59	0.6	1.4
Non-denom Chr Chs	3	200	165	255	2.7	6.1
PRES–Presb Ch (USA)	1	35	50	57	0.6	1.4
Sev Day Adv	1	30	53	61	0.6	1.5
ALLEGAN	**132**	**11,222**	**15,220**	**31,768**	**28.5**	**100.0**
ANG/EPIS–Episcopal	3	245	358	499	0.4	1.6
Bahá'í	0	NR	17	17	0.0	0.1
BAPT–Amer Bapt USA	1	70	167	209	0.2	0.7
BAPT–Consrv Bapt	2	NR	NR	NR	-	-
BAPT–NBC USA	1	0	150	188	0.2	0.6
BAPT–Reg Bapt Gen As	4	NR	NR	NR	-	-
BAPT–So Bapt Conv	1	NR	NR	NR	-	-
BUDD–Mahayana	2	NR	NR	1,117	1.0	3.5
Catholic	9	NR	NR	10,071	9.0	31.7
CGOD–Ch God (Ander)	2	220	NR	220	0.2	0.7
Ch Cr, Scientst	1	NR	NR	NR	-	-
CHR–Chr Ch (Disc)	1	70	150	188	0.2	0.6
CHR–Chs of Christ	1	80	90	100	0.1	0.3
CONG–Cong Chr, NA	3	NR	451	564	0.5	1.8
Evan Cov Ch	1	192	256	250	0.2	0.8
Evan Free Ch	1	63	NR	63	0.1	0.2
HINDU–Trad Temples	1	NR	NR	60	0.1	0.2
Ind Fund Churches	5	NR	NR	NR	-	-
Int Cou Comm Ch	1	NR	NR	NR	-	-
Jehovah's Witness	3	NR	NR	NR	-	-
LDS–Comm of Christ	1	NR	167	167	0.1	0.5
LDS–L-D Saints	1	NR	NR	222	0.2	0.7
LUTH–E.L.C.A.	2	131	383	454	0.4	1.4
LUTH–Luth–MO Synod	1	90	140	186	0.2	0.6
LUTH–Wisc Ev Luth Syn	5	523	826	1,044	0.9	3.3
METH–Free Methodist	1	38	29	38	0.0	0.1
METH–Un Methodist	20	1,480	2,247	3,623	3.3	11.4
METH–Wesleyan	4	652	423	847	0.8	2.7
New Apost Ch	1	NR	NR	NR	-	-
Non-denom Chr Chs	12	2,107	2,560	3,173	2.8	10.0
ORTHE–Ant Orth of NA	1	15	NR	42	0.0	0.1
PENT–Assemb of God	4	237	139	346	0.3	1.1
PENT–Ch God (Cleve)	3	99	169	211	0.2	0.7
PENT–COGIC	1	25	35	44	0.0	0.1
PENT–Intl Pent Holiness	1	31	31	39	0.0	0.1
PENT–Un Pent Ch Intl	1	NR	NR	NR	-	-
PRES–Presb Ch (USA)	2	101	112	140	0.1	0.4
REF–Christian Ref	10	1,761	2,058	2,573	2.3	8.1
REF–Ref Ch in Am	11	2,725	3,759	4,465	4.0	14.1
Sev Day Adv	4	112	196	224	0.2	0.7
Un C of Christ	2	155	307	384	0.3	1.2
Unity Ch	1	NR	NR	NR	-	-
ALPENA	**48**	**2,778**	**6,752**	**15,892**	**53.7**	**100.0**
ANG/EPIS–Episcopal	2	129	293	449	1.5	2.8
Bahá'í	0	NR	39	39	0.1	0.2
BAPT–Amer Bapt USA	2	78	66	78	0.3	0.5
BAPT–N Am Bapt Conf	1	NR	289	342	1.2	2.2
BAPT–Reg Bapt Gen As	1	NR	NR	NR	-	-
BAPT–So Bapt Conv	1	54	42	50	0.2	0.3
Catholic	5	NR	NR	6,744	22.8	42.4
CGOD–Ch God (Ander)	1	55	NR	55	0.2	0.3
Ch of Nazarene	1	0	35	35	0.1	0.2
CHR–Chr Chs & Chs Cr	1	NR	20	24	0.1	0.2
CHR–Chs of Christ	1	8	8	12	0.0	0.1
CONG–Cong Chr, NA	1	NR	117	139	0.5	0.9
Jehovah's Witness	1	NR	NR	NR	-	-
JUD–Reform	1	4	7	19	0.1	0.1
LDS–Comm of Christ	2	NR	334	334	1.1	2.1
LDS–L-D Saints	1	NR	NR	162	0.5	1.0
LUTH–E.L.C.A.	5	659	2,173	2,760	9.3	17.4
LUTH–Luth Cong Msn Chr	1	125	148	175	0.6	1.1
LUTH–Luth–MO Synod	3	545	1,606	2,157	7.3	13.6
LUTH–Nor Amer Luth C	1	NR	NR	NR	-	-
MENN–Amish Undif	1	NR	20	51	0.2	0.3
METH–Free Methodist	1	107	82	107	0.4	0.7
METH–Un Methodist	3	268	514	632	2.1	4.0
METH–Wesleyan	1	71	31	92	0.3	0.6
Non-denom Chr Chs	3	400	325	500	1.7	3.1
PENT–Assemb of God	1	116	87	160	0.5	1.0
PENT–Ch of God Proph	1	NR	19	22	0.1	0.1
PENT–Un Pent Ch Intl	1	NR	NR	NR	-	-
PRES–Presb Ch (USA)	1	0	110	130	0.4	0.8
Salvation Army	1	26	33	208	0.7	1.3
Sev Day Adv	1	60	105	121	0.4	0.8
Un C of Christ	1	73	249	295	1.0	1.9
ANTRIM	**46**	**2,274**	**3,059**	**6,569**	**27.9**	**100.0**
ANG/EPIS–Episcopal	1	66	187	187	0.8	2.8
Bahá'í	0	NR	6	6	0.0	0.1
BAPT–Converge/BGC	1	75	NR	90	0.4	1.4
BAPT–Ind Bapt Flwsp Intl	1	NR	NR	NR	-	-
BAPT–Reg Bapt Gen As	2	NR	NR	NR	-	-
BAPT–So Bapt Conv	1	20	35	41	0.2	0.6
BUDD–Mahayana	1	NR	NR	11	0.0	0.2
Catholic	5	NR	NR	2,194	9.3	33.4
Ch of Nazarene	1	28	27	98	0.4	1.5
CHR–Chr Chs & Chs Cr	1	NR	165	196	0.8	3.0
CONG–Cong Chr, NA	1	NR	125	148	0.6	2.3
Jehovah's Witness	2	NR	NR	NR	-	-
LUTH–E.L.C.A.	1	61	90	97	0.4	1.5
LUTH–Luth–MO Synod	3	152	285	309	1.3	4.7
METH–Free Methodist	1	54	29	54	0.2	0.8
METH–Un Methodist	8	355	593	827	3.5	12.6
METH–Wesleyan	2	165	93	215	0.9	3.3
Missionary Ch	1	175	74	175	0.7	2.7
Non-denom Chr Chs	3	250	200	312	1.3	4.7
PENT–Pent Ch of God	2	140	NR	217	0.9	3.3
PRES–Orth Pres Ch	1	40	21	40	0.2	0.6
PRES–Presb Ch (USA)	2	363	651	772	3.3	11.8
REF–Christian Ref	2	185	213	253	1.1	3.9
REF–Ref Ch in Am	1	93	174	222	0.9	3.4
Sev Day Adv	2	52	91	105	0.4	1.6
ARENAC	**35**	**1,316**	**2,245**	**7,482**	**47.1**	**100.0**
ANG/EPIS–Episcopal	1	14	19	22	0.1	0.3
Bahá'í	0	NR	2	2	0.0	0.0
BAPT–Reg Bapt Gen As	1	NR	NR	NR	-	-
BAPT–So Bapt Conv	1	40	45	53	0.3	0.7

NR–Not Reported - Represents no adherents reported. Percentages may not total 100 due to rounding.

Table 3: Religious Congregations by County and Group: 2010

Religious Group	Number of Congrega-tions	Number of Attendees	Number of Communicant, Confirmed, or Full Members	Adherents: Number of Adherents	Adherents: % of Total Pop.	Adherents: % of Total Adh.
Catholic	4	NR	NR	4,520	28.4	60.4
Jehovah's Witness	1	NR	NR	NR	-	-
LDS–Comm of Christ	1	NR	167	167	1.1	2.2
LUTH–E.L.C.A.	1	43	182	182	1.1	2.4
LUTH–Luth Cong Msn Chr	1	13	22	26	0.2	0.3
LUTH–Luth–MO Synod	3	243	604	794	5.0	10.6
LUTH–Wisc Ev Luth Syn	1	58	73	107	0.7	1.4
MENN–Cons Menn Conf	2	145	141	165	1.0	2.2
METH–A.W.M.C.	1	32	0	35	0.2	0.5
METH–Free Methodist	2	61	22	61	0.4	0.8
METH–Un Methodist	6	336	690	885	5.6	11.8
METH–Wesleyan	2	84	55	109	0.7	1.5
Non-denom Chr Chs	3	132	185	193	1.2	2.6
PENT–Assemb of God	1	25	15	25	0.2	0.3
PENT–Pent Ch of God	1	70	NR	109	0.7	1.5
PENT–Un Pent Ch Intl	1	NR	NR	NR	-	-
PRES–Presb Ch (USA)	1	20	23	27	0.2	0.4
BARAGA	**20**	**581**	**1,648**	**4,704**	**53.1**	**100.0**
ANG/EPIS–Anglican NA	1	NR	NR	NR	-	-
Bahá'í	0	NR	1	1	0.0	0.0
BAPT–Reg Bapt Gen As	1	NR	NR	NR	-	-
Catholic	3	NR	NR	2,391	27.0	50.8
Jehovah's Witness	1	NR	NR	NR	-	-
LUTH–Apostolic Luth	1	NR	NR	NR	-	-
LUTH–E.L.C.A.	4	260	864	1,319	14.9	28.0
LUTH–Luth Cong Msn Chr	2	110	314	370	4.2	7.9
LUTH–Luth–MO Synod	1	52	236	270	3.0	5.7
LUTH–Nor Amer Luth C	1	NR	NR	NR	-	-
METH–Un Methodist	2	112	213	289	3.3	6.1
Non-denom Chr Chs	1	40	8	50	0.6	1.1
PENT–Un Pent Ch Intl	1	NR	NR	NR	-	-
Sev Day Adv	1	7	12	14	0.2	0.3
BARRY	**57**	**6,560**	**7,806**	**13,557**	**22.9**	**100.0**
ANG/EPIS–Episcopal	2	83	182	188	0.3	1.4
Bahá'í	0	NR	3	3	0.0	0.0
BAPT–Reg Bapt Gen As	2	NR	NR	NR	-	-
BRETH–Ch of Brethren	1	77	120	147	0.2	1.1
Catholic	4	NR	NR	2,681	4.5	19.8
Ch of Nazarene	2	189	241	288	0.5	2.1
CHR–Chr Ch (Disc)	1	77	120	147	0.2	1.1
CHR–Chs of Christ	1	56	43	60	0.1	0.4
Ind Fund Churches	1	NR	NR	NR	-	-
Jehovah's Witness	1	NR	NR	NR	-	-
LDS–Comm of Christ	1	NR	167	167	0.3	1.2
LDS–L-D Saints	1	NR	NR	356	0.6	2.6
LUTH–E.L.C.A.	2	240	427	540	0.9	4.0
LUTH–Luth–MO Synod	1	45	74	98	0.2	0.7
MENN–Amish Undif	1	NR	35	76	0.1	0.6
METH–Free Methodist	1	222	148	222	0.4	1.6
METH–Un Methodist	13	1,106	1,742	2,422	4.1	17.9
METH–Wesleyan	3	202	193	264	0.4	1.9
Non-denom Chr Chs	10	3,176	2,875	4,009	6.8	29.6
PENT–Assemb of God	2	146	74	261	0.4	1.9
PRES–Presb Ch (USA)	1	176	352	432	0.7	3.2
REF–Christian Ref	1	90	124	152	0.3	1.1
REF–Ref Ch in Am	1	284	509	601	1.0	4.4
Sev Day Adv	2	95	165	190	0.3	1.4
Un Breth in Cr	2	296	212	253	0.4	1.9
BAY	**104**	**9,037**	**18,014**	**57,623**	**53.5**	**100.0**
ANG/EPIS–Episcopal	2	153	392	597	0.6	1.0
Ap Chr Ch-Amer	1	250	143	250	0.2	0.4
Bahá'í	0	NR	12	12	0.0	0.0
BAPT–Amer Bapt USA	2	121	231	278	0.3	0.5
BAPT–N Am Bapt Conf	1	NR	104	125	0.1	0.2
BAPT–NBC USA	1	0	300	361	0.3	0.6
BAPT–Reg Bapt Gen As	3	NR	NR	NR	-	-
BAPT–So Bapt Conv	2	185	148	178	0.2	0.3
Calv Chpl	1	NR	NR	NR	-	-
Catholic	22	NR	NR	33,237	30.8	57.7
CGOD–Ch God (Ander)	2	300	NR	300	0.3	0.5

Religious Group	Number of Congrega-tions	Number of Attendees	Number of Communicant, Confirmed, or Full Members	Adherents: Number of Adherents	Adherents: % of Total Pop.	Adherents: % of Total Adh.
Ch of Nazarene	2	123	123	218	0.2	0.4
Chr & Miss Al	2	76	41	88	0.1	0.2
CHR–Chs of Christ	2	88	79	106	0.1	0.2
Evan Free Ch	1	85	NR	85	0.1	0.1
Int Cou Comm Ch	1	NR	NR	NR	-	-
Jehovah's Witness	2	NR	NR	NR	-	-
JUD–Reform	1	45	80	216	0.2	0.4
LDS–Comm of Christ	2	NR	334	334	0.3	0.6
LDS–L-D Saints	1	NR	NR	378	0.4	0.7
LUTH–E.L.C.A.	1	210	492	633	0.6	1.1
LUTH–Luth–MO Synod	11	3,146	8,581	11,180	10.4	19.4
LUTH–Wisc Ev Luth Syn	5	1,195	2,226	2,900	2.7	5.0
METH–Free Methodist	1	37	21	37	0.0	0.1
METH–Un Methodist	8	724	1,491	2,010	1.9	3.5
METH–Wesleyan	2	105	71	137	0.1	0.2
Missionary Ch	1	87	111	111	0.1	0.2
Non-denom Chr Chs	13	1,462	1,720	1,994	1.9	3.5
PENT–Assemb of God	1	19	11	21	0.0	0.0
PENT–Pent Ch of God	1	70	NR	109	0.1	0.2
PENT–Un Pent Ch Intl	1	NR	NR	NR	-	-
PRES–Presb Ch (USA)	3	410	1,097	1,320	1.2	2.3
Salvation Army	1	58	45	219	0.2	0.4
Sev Day Adv	1	50	87	100	0.1	0.2
Un C of Christ	2	38	74	89	0.1	0.2
Unity Ch	1	NR	NR	NR	-	-
BENZIE	**30**	**1,380**	**2,396**	**3,423**	**19.5**	**100.0**
ANG/EPIS–Episcopal	1	76	111	115	0.7	3.4
Bahá'í	0	NR	3	3	0.0	0.1
BAPT–Reg Bapt Gen As	2	NR	NR	NR	-	-
BAPT–So Bapt Conv	2	65	59	70	0.4	2.0
Catholic	1	NR	NR	465	2.7	13.6
Ch of Nazarene	1	36	49	57	0.3	1.7
CHR–Chr Ch (Disc)	1	0	0	0	0.0	0.0
CHR–Chr Chs & Chs Cr	1	NR	100	119	0.7	3.5
CHR–Chs of Christ	1	37	45	60	0.3	1.8
CONG–Cong Chr, NA	1	NR	150	179	1.0	5.2
CONG–Consrv Cong Chr	1	67	67	80	0.5	2.3
FRND–Fr Gen Cf	1	NR	0	0	0.0	0.0
Ind Fund Churches	1	NR	NR	NR	-	-
Jehovah's Witness	2	NR	NR	NR	-	-
LUTH–E.L.C.A.	2	352	743	788	4.5	23.0
LUTH–Luth–MO Synod	1	66	91	116	0.7	3.4
METH–Un Methodist	3	228	277	447	2.6	13.1
METH–Wesleyan	2	83	49	108	0.6	3.2
Non-denom Chr Chs	2	58	56	78	0.4	2.3
PENT–Assemb of God	1	70	38	75	0.4	2.2
PRES–Presb Ch (USA)	1	128	184	219	1.2	6.4
Sev Day Adv	1	19	33	38	0.2	1.1
Un C of Christ	1	95	341	406	2.3	11.9
BERRIEN	**246**	**23,816**	**37,827**	**73,712**	**47.0**	**100.0**
ANG/EPIS–Episcopal	4	258	483	518	0.3	0.7
Bahá'í	1	NR	62	62	0.0	0.1
BAPT–Amer Bapt Assn	3	NR	164	200	0.1	0.3
BAPT–Amer Bapt USA	2	146	200	243	0.2	0.3
BAPT–Converge/BGC	1	75	NR	90	0.1	0.1
BAPT–Free Will Bapt	1	NR	101	123	0.1	0.2
BAPT–N Am Bapt Conf	5	NR	996	1,212	0.8	1.6
BAPT–Natl Mis Bapt Conv	2	0	150	183	0.1	0.2
BAPT–NBC Amer	2	350	1,000	1,217	0.8	1.7
BAPT–NBC USA	5	670	2,035	2,476	1.6	3.4
BAPT–Reg Bapt Gen As	3	NR	NR	NR	-	-
BAPT–So Bapt Conv	9	433	767	933	0.6	1.3
Calv Chpl	1	NR	NR	NR	-	-
Catholic	11	NR	NR	17,231	11.0	23.4
CGOD–Ch God (Ander)	8	2,046	NR	2,046	1.3	2.8
Ch Cr, Scientist	1	NR	NR	NR	-	-
Ch of Nazarene	2	174	180	306	0.2	0.4
CHR–Chr Ch (Disc)	1	62	119	145	0.1	0.2
CHR–Chr Chs & Chs Cr	5	NR	778	947	0.6	1.3
CHR–Chs of Christ	4	397	409	524	0.3	0.7
CONG–Cong Chr, NA	2	NR	151	184	0.1	0.2

NR–Not Reported - Represents no adherents reported. Percentages may not total 100 due to rounding.

Table 3: Religious Congregations by County and Group: 2010

Religious Group	Number of Congrega-tions	Number of Attendees	Number of Communicant, Confirmed, or Full Members	Adherents		
				Number of Adherents	% of Total Pop.	% of Total Adh.
Evan Cov Ch	1	197	200	256	0.2	0.3
Evan Free Ch	2	768	NR	768	0.5	1.0
HINDU–Post Ren	1	NR	NR	16	0.0	0.0
Ind Fund Churches	5	NR	NR	NR	-	-
Jehovah's Witness	6	NR	NR	NR	-	-
JUD–Conserv	1	82	92	248	0.2	0.3
LDS–Comm of Christ	2	NR	334	334	0.2	0.5
LDS–L-D Saints	2	NR	NR	893	0.6	1.2
LUTH–Ch Luth Conf	1	NR	NR	NR	-	-
LUTH–E.L.C.A.	4	454	878	1,492	1.0	2.0
LUTH–Luth–MO Synod	9	1,948	5,175	6,743	4.3	9.1
LUTH–Nor Amer Luth C	1	NR	NR	NR	-	-
LUTH–Wisc Ev Luth Syn	6	1,352	2,696	3,181	2.0	4.3
METH–AME	3	150	500	608	0.4	0.8
METH–C.M.E.	1	0	100	122	0.1	0.2
METH–Free Methodist	3	202	124	202	0.1	0.3
METH–Un Methodist	23	1,799	3,186	4,642	3.0	6.3
METH–Wesleyan	1	105	16	137	0.1	0.2
Missionary Ch	2	314	164	314	0.2	0.4
Muslim Est	2	822	NR	3,126	2.0	4.2
New Apost Ch	3	NR	NR	NR	-	-
Non-denom Chr Chs	21	2,528	2,047	3,183	2.0	4.3
ORTHE–Greek Orthodox	1	40	NR	100	0.1	0.1
PENT–Assemb of God	5	935	503	1,214	0.8	1.6
PENT–Assm God Intl F	1	NR	NR	NR	-	-
PENT–Ch God (Cleve)	4	181	435	529	0.3	0.7
PENT–Ch of God Proph	3	NR	187	228	0.1	0.3
PENT–COGIC	8	655	1,505	1,831	1.2	2.5
PENT–Int Foursq Gos	2	153	123	150	0.1	0.2
PENT–Pent Ch of God	2	140	NR	217	0.1	0.3
PENT–Un Pent Ch Intl	4	NR	NR	NR	-	-
PRES–Presb Ch (USA)	4	362	868	1,056	0.7	1.4
REF–Christian Ref	1	216	394	479	0.3	0.6
REF–Ref Ch in Am	1	25	33	42	0.0	0.1
Salvation Army	2	45	97	676	0.4	0.9
Sev Day Adv	23	5,010	8,714	10,021	6.4	13.6
Un C of Christ	11	697	1,821	2,216	1.4	3.0
Unit Univ	1	25	40	48	0.0	0.1
BRANCH	**61**	**3,834**	**4,871**	**14,712**	**32.5**	**100.0**
ANG/EPIS–Episcopal	1	74	116	236	0.5	1.6
Bahá'í	0	NR	6	6	0.0	0.0
BAPT–Amer Bapt USA	2	487	428	525	1.2	3.6
BAPT–Reg Bapt Gen As	1	NR	NR	NR	-	-
BAPT–So Bapt Conv	1	38	61	75	0.2	0.5
Catholic	3	NR	NR	5,985	13.2	40.7
Ch of Nazarene	1	150	183	340	0.8	2.3
CHR–Chr Chs & Chs Cr	2	NR	235	288	0.6	2.0
CHR–Chs of Christ	1	40	40	48	0.1	0.3
Jehovah's Witness	2	NR	NR	NR	-	-
LDS–Comm of Christ	1	NR	167	167	0.4	1.1
LDS–L-D Saints	1	NR	NR	364	0.8	2.5
LUTH–E.L.C.A.	1	41	68	74	0.2	0.5
LUTH–Luth–MO Synod	3	192	330	400	0.9	2.7
MENN–Amish Undif	14	NR	675	1,784	3.9	12.1
METH–Free Methodist	2	340	204	340	0.8	2.3
METH–Un Methodist	6	409	839	1,151	2.5	7.8
METH–Wesleyan	2	142	89	185	0.4	1.3
Missionary Ch	3	212	108	212	0.5	1.4
Muslim Est	1	300	NR	500	1.1	3.4
Non-denom Chr Chs	5	805	431	1,007	2.2	6.8
PENT–Assemb of God	2	186	265	267	0.6	1.8
PENT–Ch God (Cleve)	1	21	50	61	0.1	0.4
PRES–Presb Ch (USA)	2	250	350	429	0.9	2.9
Sev Day Adv	1	62	109	125	0.3	0.8
Un Breth in Cr	1	0	0	0	0.0	0.0
Un C of Christ	1	85	117	143	0.3	1.0
CALHOUN	**174**	**15,333**	**21,090**	**44,389**	**32.6**	**100.0**
ANG/EPIS–Episcopal	4	257	531	718	0.5	1.6
Bahá'í	0	NR	21	21	0.0	0.0
BAPT–Amer Bapt USA	8	793	1,355	1,662	1.2	3.7
BAPT–Free Will Bapt	1	NR	101	124	0.1	0.3
BAPT–NBC Amer	1	50	0	0	0.0	0.0
BAPT–NBC USA	3	355	1,070	1,312	1.0	3.0
BAPT–Reg Bapt Gen As	3	NR	NR	NR	-	-
BAPT–S-D Baptist Gen Con	1	59	92	113	0.1	0.3
BAPT–So Bapt Conv	13	529	1,037	1,272	0.9	2.9
Calv Chpl	1	NR	NR	NR	-	-
Catholic	6	NR	NR	11,553	8.5	26.0
CGOD–Ch God (Ander)	3	539	NR	539	0.4	1.2
CGOD–Ches God-Gen Con	1	15	16	20	0.0	0.0
Ch Cr, Scientst	1	NR	NR	NR	-	-
Ch God (7th Day)	1	NR	NR	NR	-	-
Ch of Nazarene	3	235	307	650	0.5	1.5
CHR–Chr Ch (Disc)	1	30	40	49	0.0	0.1
CHR–Chr Chs & Chs Cr	2	NR	260	319	0.2	0.7
CHR–Chs of Christ	6	387	418	545	0.4	1.2
CONG–Cong Chr Add'l	1	NR	40	49	0.0	0.1
FRND–Evan Fr Ch Intl	1	355	152	186	0.1	0.4
FRND–Fr Gen Cf	1	NR	0	0	0.0	0.0
Ind Fund Churches	5	NR	NR	NR	-	-
Jehovah's Witness	4	NR	NR	NR	-	-
JUD–Reform	1	15	26	70	0.1	0.2
LDS–Comm of Christ	1	NR	167	167	0.1	0.4
LDS–L-D Saints	2	NR	NR	1,079	0.8	2.4
LUTH–E.L.C.A.	2	183	398	438	0.3	1.0
LUTH–Luth–MO Synod	6	879	2,091	2,918	2.1	6.6
LUTH–Wisc Ev Luth Syn	1	51	115	162	0.1	0.4
MENN–Amish Undif	2	NR	91	298	0.2	0.7
MENN–Mennonite USA	1	0	45	55	0.0	0.1
METH–AME	2	260	380	466	0.3	1.0
METH–AME Zion	1	0	150	184	0.1	0.4
METH–C.M.E.	1	0	100	123	0.1	0.3
METH–Free Methodist	2	144	121	144	0.1	0.3
METH–Un Methodist	17	1,326	2,499	3,591	2.6	8.1
METH–Wesleyan	4	2,613	814	3,398	2.5	7.7
Missionary Ch	3	141	71	141	0.1	0.3
Non-denom Chr Chs	14	2,768	2,810	3,592	2.6	8.1
ORTHE–Orth Ch in Amer	1	45	NR	80	0.1	0.2
ORTHE–Rus Orth Moscow	1	55	NR	100	0.1	0.2
PENT–Assemb of God	5	521	315	1,316	1.0	3.0
PENT–Ch God (Cleve)	3	490	837	1,026	0.8	2.3
PENT–Ch of God Proph	1	NR	42	52	0.0	0.1
PENT–COGIC	4	225	650	797	0.6	1.8
PENT–Int Foursq Gos	1	28	30	37	0.0	0.1
PENT–Pent Ch of God	1	70	NR	109	0.1	0.2
PENT–Un Pent Ch Intl	3	NR	NR	NR	-	-
PRES–Evan Presby Ch	1	NR	9	11	0.0	0.0
PRES–Korean Pres Amer	1	NR	NR	NR	-	-
PRES–Presb Ch (USA)	6	563	1,279	1,569	1.2	3.5
REF–Christian Ref	1	111	164	201	0.1	0.5
REF–Ref Ch in Am	1	70	84	102	0.1	0.2
Salvation Army	1	79	87	344	0.3	0.8
Sev Day Adv	7	786	1,366	1,572	1.2	3.5
Un C of Christ	4	306	909	1,115	0.8	2.5
Unity Ch	1	NR	NR	NR	-	-
CASS	**56**	**2,489**	**4,196**	**8,390**	**16.0**	**100.0**
ANG/EPIS–Episcopal	1	46	66	74	0.1	0.9
Bahá'í	0	NR	4	4	0.0	0.0
BAPT–Amer Bapt USA	1	51	118	143	0.3	1.7
BAPT–Consrv Bapt	1	NR	NR	NR	-	-
BAPT–NBC USA	1	75	175	212	0.4	2.5
BAPT–So Bapt Conv	1	45	100	121	0.2	1.4
BRETH–Breth in Chr	1	NR	NR	NR	-	-
BRETH–Brethren (Ash)	1	NR	80	97	0.2	1.2
BUDD–Theravada	1	NR	NR	300	0.6	3.6
Catholic	4	NR	NR	2,606	5.0	31.1
CGOD–Ch God (Ander)	3	80	NR	80	0.2	1.0
Ch of Nazarene	1	87	128	178	0.3	2.1
CHR–Chr Ch (Disc)	1	75	150	182	0.3	2.2
CHR–Chr Chs & Chs Cr	2	NR	170	206	0.4	2.5
CHR–Chs of Christ	1	30	20	45	0.1	0.5
Evan Cov Ch	1	49	57	64	0.1	0.8
FRND–Fr Un Mtg	1	NR	81	98	0.2	1.2
Ind Fund Churches	1	NR	NR	NR	-	-

NR–Not Reported - Represents no adherents reported. Percentages may not total 100 due to rounding.

Table 3: Religious Congregations by County and Group: 2010

Religious Group	Number of Congrega-tions	Number of Attendees	Number of Communicant, Confirmed, or Full Members	Adherents		
				Number of Adherents	% of Total Pop.	% of Total Adh.
Jehovah's Witness	2	NR	NR	NR	-	-
LUTH–Luth–MO Synod	1	60	93	113	0.2	1.3
LUTH–Wisc Ev Luth Syn	1	85	276	398	0.8	4.7
MENN–Cons Menn Conf	1	34	30	36	0.1	0.4
METH–AME	3	18	228	277	0.5	3.3
METH–Un Methodist	8	640	1,252	1,575	3.0	18.8
Missionary Ch	3	192	156	192	0.4	2.3
Non-denom Chr Chs	4	445	396	556	1.1	6.6
PENT–Assemb of God	1	27	26	37	0.1	0.4
PENT–Pent Ch of God	1	70	NR	109	0.2	1.3
PENT–Un Pent Ch Intl	1	NR	NR	NR	-	-
PRES–Presb Ch (USA)	2	121	139	169	0.3	2.0
Sev Day Adv	5	259	451	518	1.0	6.2
CHARLEVOIX	**46**	**2,452**	**3,601**	**8,651**	**33.3**	**100.0**
ANG/EPIS–Episcopal	2	80	141	141	0.5	1.6
Bahá'í	0	NR	3	3	0.0	0.0
BAPT–Amer Bapt USA	1	47	90	108	0.4	1.2
BAPT–So Bapt Conv	1	30	45	54	0.2	0.6
BUDD–Vajrayana	1	NR	NR	107	0.4	1.2
Catholic	5	NR	NR	3,324	12.8	38.4
CGOD–Ch God (Ander)	1	44	NR	44	0.2	0.5
Ch Cr, Scientst	1	NR	NR	NR	-	-
Ch of Nazarene	2	70	100	266	1.0	3.1
CHR–Chs of Christ	1	25	25	27	0.1	0.3
Jehovah's Witness	1	NR	NR	NR	-	-
LDS–Comm of Christ	2	NR	334	334	1.3	3.9
LUTH–E.L.C.A.	1	63	106	124	0.5	1.4
LUTH–Evan Luth Syn	1	21	40	50	0.2	0.6
LUTH–Luth–MO Synod	2	225	493	557	2.1	6.4
METH–Free Methodist	1	73	42	73	0.3	0.8
METH–Un Methodist	8	361	553	1,026	4.0	11.9
Missionary Ch	1	236	71	236	0.9	2.7
Nat Spirit Asso	1	NR	NR	NR	-	-
Non-denom Chr Chs	2	280	300	350	1.3	4.0
PENT–Assemb of God	2	111	42	138	0.5	1.6
PENT–Ch God (Cleve)	1	90	106	127	0.5	1.5
PENT–Pent Ch of God	1	70	NR	109	0.4	1.3
PRES–Presb Ch (USA)	3	148	344	413	1.6	4.8
REF–Ref Ch in Am	1	275	441	655	2.5	7.6
Sev Day Adv	1	48	83	95	0.4	1.1
Un C of Christ	2	155	242	290	1.1	3.4
CHEBOYGAN	**42**	**2,797**	**3,254**	**8,332**	**31.9**	**100.0**
ANG/EPIS–Episcopal	2	108	270	270	1.0	3.2
Bahá'í	0	NR	2	2	0.0	0.0
BAPT–Ind Bapt Flwsp Intl	1	NR	NR	NR	-	-
BAPT–Reg Bapt Gen As	2	NR	NR	NR	-	-
BAPT–So Bapt Conv	1	90	105	124	0.5	1.5
Catholic	5	NR	NR	3,714	14.2	44.6
Ch Cr, Scientst	1	NR	NR	NR	-	-
Ch of Nazarene	1	29	30	58	0.2	0.7
CHR–Chr Ch (Disc)	1	55	95	112	0.4	1.3
CHR–Chs of Christ	1	55	55	63	0.2	0.8
Evan Cov Ch	1	177	148	230	0.9	2.8
Jehovah's Witness	2	NR	NR	NR	-	-
LDS–Comm of Christ	1	NR	167	167	0.6	2.0
LDS–L-D Saints	1	NR	NR	167	0.6	2.0
LUTH–E.L.C.A.	1	226	485	636	2.4	7.6
LUTH–Luth–MO Synod	1	147	247	300	1.1	3.6
LUTH–Wisc Ev Luth Syn	1	32	37	50	0.2	0.6
MENN–Mennonite USA	1	33	46	54	0.2	0.6
METH–Free Methodist	1	129	43	129	0.5	1.5
METH–Un Methodist	3	620	724	870	3.3	10.4
METH–Wesleyan	1	46	56	60	0.2	0.7
Non-denom Chr Chs	5	422	395	527	2.0	6.3
PENT–Assemb of God	2	252	109	301	1.2	3.6
PENT–Ch God (Cleve)	1	26	30	35	0.1	0.4
PENT–Pent Ch of God	2	140	NR	217	0.8	2.6
PRES–Presb Ch (USA)	1	132	77	91	0.3	1.1
Sev Day Adv	1	38	65	75	0.3	0.9
Un C of Christ	1	40	68	80	0.3	1.0
CHIPPEWA	**69**	**2,426**	**3,809**	**12,451**	**32.3**	**100.0**
ANG/EPIS–Episcopal	3	74	110	134	0.3	1.1
Bahá'í	0	NR	12	12	0.0	0.1
BAPT–Amer Bapt USA	1	45	51	60	0.2	0.5
BAPT–Ref Bapt Ch	1	NR	NR	NR	-	-
BAPT–Reg Bapt Gen As	1	NR	NR	NR	-	-
BAPT–So Bapt Conv	1	25	16	19	0.0	0.2
Catholic	13	NR	NR	6,665	17.3	53.5
Ch of Nazarene	3	133	99	357	0.9	2.9
CHR–Chr Chs & Chs Cr	2	NR	560	661	1.7	5.3
CHR–Chs of Christ	2	50	36	48	0.1	0.4
Ind Fund Churches	1	NR	NR	NR	-	-
Jehovah's Witness	1	NR	NR	NR	-	-
LDS–Comm of Christ	1	NR	167	167	0.4	1.3
LDS–L-D Saints	1	NR	NR	164	0.4	1.3
LUTH–E.L.C.A.	2	143	378	543	1.4	4.4
LUTH–Luth–MO Synod	6	131	212	272	0.7	2.2
LUTH–Wisc Ev Luth Syn	1	105	158	200	0.5	1.6
METH–Free Methodist	1	51	29	51	0.1	0.4
METH–Un Methodist	5	295	635	832	2.2	6.7
METH–Wesleyan	1	183	66	238	0.6	1.9
Non-denom Chr Chs	4	207	220	271	0.7	2.2
ORTHE–Greek Orthodox	1	25	NR	100	0.3	0.8
PENT–Assemb of God	2	225	97	225	0.6	1.8
PENT–Elim	1	NR	NR	NR	-	-
PENT–Pent Ch of God	1	70	NR	109	0.3	0.9
PENT–Un Pent Ch Intl	1	NR	NR	NR	-	-
PRES–Presb Ch (USA)	8	363	633	748	1.9	6.0
REF–Christian Ref	2	218	216	255	0.7	2.0
Salvation Army	1	53	63	261	0.7	2.1
Sev Day Adv	1	30	51	59	0.2	0.5
CLARE	**48**	**2,772**	**3,508**	**11,961**	**38.7**	**100.0**
Bahá'í	0	NR	3	3	0.0	0.0
BAPT–Amer Bapt Assn	1	NR	20	24	0.1	0.2
BAPT–Reg Bapt Gen As	1	NR	NR	NR	-	-
BAPT–So Bapt Conv	2	84	78	92	0.3	0.8
Catholic	2	NR	NR	4,998	16.2	41.8
CGOD–Ches God-Gen Con	2	61	45	53	0.2	0.4
Ch of Nazarene	2	657	350	2,220	7.2	18.6
CHR–Chr Chs & Chs Cr	2	NR	165	195	0.6	1.6
CHR–Chs of Christ	1	26	23	29	0.1	0.2
Ind Fund Churches	1	NR	NR	NR	-	-
Jehovah's Witness	2	NR	NR	NR	-	-
LDS–Comm of Christ	2	NR	334	334	1.1	2.8
LDS–L-D Saints	1	NR	NR	236	0.8	2.0
LUTH–E.L.C.A.	1	40	89	89	0.3	0.7
LUTH–Luth–MO Synod	2	143	298	350	1.1	2.9
LUTH–Nor Amer Luth C	1	NR	NR	NR	-	-
LUTH–Wisc Ev Luth Syn	2	111	200	213	0.7	1.8
MENN–Amish Undif	5	NR	251	659	2.1	5.5
METH–Un Methodist	2	332	477	663	2.1	5.5
Missionary Ch	1	39	21	39	0.1	0.3
Non-denom Chr Chs	6	415	342	518	1.7	4.3
PENT–Assemb of God	2	238	115	344	1.1	2.9
PENT–Ch God (Cleve)	1	29	86	102	0.3	0.9
Sev Day Adv	1	72	126	145	0.5	1.2
Un Breth in Cr	2	400	219	340	1.1	2.8
Un C of Christ	2	125	266	315	1.0	2.6
Unity Ch	1	NR	NR	NR	-	-
CLINTON	**66**	**4,670**	**6,754**	**24,066**	**31.9**	**100.0**
ANG/EPIS–Anglican NA	1	NR	NR	NR	-	-
ANG/EPIS–Episcopal	2	45	62	77	0.1	0.3
Bahá'í	0	NR	16	16	0.0	0.1
BAPT–Amer Bapt USA	1	30	40	49	0.1	0.2
BAPT–Reg Bapt Gen As	1	NR	NR	NR	-	-
BAPT–So Bapt Conv	1	70	225	276	0.4	1.1
BRETH–Breth in Chr	1	NR	NR	NR	-	-
Catholic	4	NR	NR	13,819	18.3	57.4
CGOD–Ch God (Ander)	1	81	NR	81	0.1	0.3
Ch of Nazarene	2	162	219	442	0.6	1.8
CHR–Chr Chs & Chs Cr	3	NR	175	215	0.3	0.9

NR–Not Reported - Represents no adherents reported. Percentages may not total 100 due to rounding.

Table 3: Religious Congregations by County and Group: 2010

Religious Group	Number of Congregations	Number of Attendees	Number of Communicant, Confirmed, or Full Members	Adherents: Number of Adherents	Adherents: % of Total Pop.	Adherents: % of Total Adh.
CHR–Chs of Christ	2	80	58	108	0.1	0.4
CONG–Cong Chr, NA	1	NR	330	405	0.5	1.7
CONG–Consrv Cong Chr	2	261	289	355	0.5	1.5
Evan Ch	1	NR	NR	NR	-	-
Jehovah's Witness	1	NR	NR	NR	-	-
LDS–Comm of Christ	1	NR	167	167	0.2	0.7
LDS–L-D Saints	1	NR	NR	249	0.3	1.0
LUTH–E.L.C.A.	1	39	44	44	0.1	0.2
LUTH–Luth-MO Synod	4	629	1,013	1,297	1.7	5.4
METH–Free Methodist	2	58	35	58	0.1	0.2
METH–Un Methodist	15	1,310	2,143	3,823	5.1	15.9
METH–Wesleyan	1	70	0	91	0.1	0.4
Non-denom Chr Chs	9	1,345	1,604	1,813	2.4	7.5
PENT–Assemb of God	4	219	157	253	0.3	1.1
PENT–Pent Ch of God	2	140	NR	217	0.3	0.9
Sev Day Adv	1	42	74	85	0.1	0.4
Un C of Christ	1	89	103	126	0.2	0.5
CRAWFORD	**14**	**692**	**1,346**	**2,633**	**18.7**	**100.0**
ANG/EPIS–Episcopal	1	28	45	95	0.7	3.6
Bahá'í	0	NR	2	2	0.0	0.1
BAPT–So Bapt Conv	1	54	79	93	0.7	3.5
Catholic	1	NR	NR	735	5.2	27.9
CHR–Chs of Christ	1	35	30	35	0.2	1.3
Evan Free Ch	1	40	NR	40	0.3	1.5
Jehovah's Witness	1	NR	NR	NR	-	-
LDS–Comm of Christ	1	NR	167	167	1.2	6.3
LUTH–E.L.C.A.	1	44	83	96	0.7	3.6
LUTH–Luth-MO Synod	1	95	253	276	2.0	10.5
METH–Free Methodist	1	197	119	197	1.4	7.5
METH–Un Methodist	1	67	406	677	4.8	25.7
Non-denom Chr Chs	1	40	80	80	0.6	3.0
PENT–Assemb of God	1	58	22	71	0.5	2.7
Sev Day Adv	1	34	60	69	0.5	2.6
DELTA	**58**	**3,532**	**5,649**	**22,455**	**60.6**	**100.0**
ANG/EPIS–Episcopal	2	97	213	537	1.4	2.4
Bahá'í	0	NR	26	26	0.1	0.1
BAPT–Converge/BGC	4	950	NR	1,140	3.1	5.1
BAPT–Reg Bapt Gen As	1	NR	NR	NR	-	-
Catholic	11	NR	NR	13,359	36.0	59.5
Ch Cr, Scientst	1	NR	NR	NR	-	-
Ch of Nazarene	1	22	23	31	0.1	0.1
CHR–Chr Chs & Chs Cr	1	NR	50	59	0.2	0.3
CHR–Chs of Christ	2	80	73	90	0.2	0.4
CONG–Cong Chr, NA	1	NR	102	121	0.3	0.5
Evan Cov Ch	1	96	154	125	0.3	0.6
Ind Fund Churches	1	NR	NR	NR	-	-
Jehovah's Witness	1	NR	NR	NR	-	-
LDS–Comm of Christ	1	NR	167	167	0.5	0.7
LDS–L-D Saints	1	NR	NR	205	0.6	0.9
LUTH–Assoc Free Luth	1	NR	NR	NR	-	-
LUTH–E.L.C.A.	9	843	2,676	3,465	9.3	15.4
LUTH–Luth-MO Synod	1	104	173	177	0.5	0.8
LUTH–Nor Amer Luth C	1	NR	NR	NR	-	-
LUTH–Wisc Ev Luth Syn	2	148	331	390	1.1	1.7
METH–Free Methodist	1	58	19	58	0.2	0.3
METH–Un Methodist	4	351	779	1,028	2.8	4.6
METH–Wesleyan	1	60	6	78	0.2	0.3
Non-denom Chr Chs	2	110	80	138	0.4	0.6
PENT–Assemb of God	1	313	169	313	0.8	1.4
PENT–Ch God (Cleve)	1	39	122	145	0.4	0.6
PENT–Un Pent Ch Intl	1	NR	NR	NR	-	-
PRES–Presb Ch (USA)	1	75	180	214	0.6	1.0
Salvation Army	1	107	169	431	1.2	1.9
Sev Day Adv	2	79	137	158	0.4	0.7
DICKINSON	**47**	**3,410**	**5,606**	**17,921**	**68.5**	**100.0**
ANG/EPIS–Episcopal	1	28	81	82	0.3	0.5
Bahá'í	0	NR	6	6	0.0	0.0
BAPT–Converge/BGC	3	550	NR	660	2.5	3.7
BAPT–Reg Bapt Gen As	1	NR	NR	NR	-	-
BAPT–So Bapt Conv	1	NR	NR	NR	-	-

Religious Group	Number of Congregations	Number of Attendees	Number of Communicant, Confirmed, or Full Members	Adherents: Number of Adherents	Adherents: % of Total Pop.	Adherents: % of Total Adh.
Catholic	8	NR	NR	9,336	35.7	52.1
Chr & Miss Al	1	107	62	195	0.7	1.1
CHR–Chr Chs & Chs Cr	1	NR	40	47	0.2	0.3
CHR–Chs of Christ	1	18	12	26	0.1	0.1
Evan Cov Ch	3	484	405	630	2.4	3.5
Jehovah's Witness	1	NR	NR	NR	-	-
LDS–L-D Saints	1	NR	NR	264	1.0	1.5
LUTH–Assoc Free Luth	1	NR	NR	NR	-	-
LUTH–E.L.C.A.	2	81	263	317	1.2	1.8
LUTH–Luth Cong Msn Chr	3	551	2,458	2,911	11.1	16.2
LUTH–Luth-MO Synod	1	210	460	557	2.1	3.1
LUTH–Wisc Ev Luth Syn	1	65	113	130	0.5	0.7
MENN–Fel Evg Bib Ch	1	15	15	15	0.1	0.1
METH–Un Methodist	5	335	804	1,154	4.4	6.4
Non-denom Chr Chs	4	315	210	394	1.5	2.2
ORTHE–Ant Orth of NA	1	41	NR	114	0.4	0.6
PENT–Assemb of God	1	221	89	390	1.5	2.2
PENT–Ch God (Cleve)	1	8	8	9	0.0	0.1
PENT–Un Pent Ch Intl	1	NR	NR	NR	-	-
PRES–Presb Ch (USA)	2	337	504	597	2.3	3.3
Sev Day Adv	1	44	76	87	0.3	0.5
EATON	**97**	**10,244**	**14,347**	**38,047**	**35.3**	**100.0**
ANG/EPIS–Episcopal	3	203	490	606	0.6	1.6
Bahá'í	0	NR	11	11	0.0	0.0
BAPT–Amer Bapt USA	1	420	531	643	0.6	1.7
BAPT–Converge/BGC	1	75	NR	90	0.1	0.2
BAPT–So Bapt Conv	2	124	113	137	0.1	0.4
Catholic	4	NR	NR	6,420	6.0	16.9
CGOD–Ch God (Ander)	1	68	NR	68	0.1	0.2
Ch of Nazarene	4	151	441	576	0.5	1.5
CHR–Chr Chs & Chs Cr	4	NR	620	751	0.7	2.0
CHR–Chs of Christ	1	27	27	33	0.0	0.1
CONG–Cong Chr, NA	3	NR	343	415	0.4	1.1
Evan Cov Ch	1	67	70	87	0.1	0.2
Ind Fund Churches	5	NR	NR	NR	-	-
Jehovah's Witness	3	NR	NR	NR	-	-
LDS–Comm of Christ	1	NR	167	167	0.2	0.4
LDS–L-D Saints	1	NR	NR	303	0.3	0.8
LUTH–E.L.C.A.	3	345	630	822	0.8	2.2
LUTH–Luth-MO Synod	3	699	1,502	2,008	1.9	5.3
LUTH–Wisc Ev Luth Syn	2	286	567	687	0.6	1.8
MENN–Amish Undif	3	NR	138	308	0.3	0.8
METH–Free Methodist	1	48	30	48	0.0	0.1
METH–Un Methodist	15	1,579	2,726	4,163	3.9	10.9
METH–Wesleyan	1	165	100	215	0.2	0.6
Non-denom Chr Chs	9	1,170	1,160	1,538	1.4	4.0
PENT–Assemb of God	7	3,296	2,196	14,894	13.8	39.1
PENT–Ch God (Cleve)	1	118	143	173	0.2	0.5
PENT–Pent Ch of God	1	70	NR	109	0.1	0.3
PENT–Un Pent Ch Intl	2	NR	NR	NR	-	-
PENT–Vineyard	1	85	120	145	0.1	0.4
PRES–Presb Ch (USA)	1	54	121	147	0.1	0.4
REF–Christian Ref	1	45	62	75	0.1	0.2
Sev Day Adv	3	526	916	1,053	1.0	2.8
Un Breth in Cr	4	355	255	304	0.3	0.8
Un C of Christ	4	268	868	1,051	1.0	2.8
EMMET	**52**	**3,323**	**4,441**	**12,318**	**37.7**	**100.0**
ANG/EPIS–Anglican NA	1	NR	NR	NR	-	-
ANG/EPIS–Episcopal	1	116	269	279	0.9	2.3
Bahá'í	0	NR	4	4	0.0	0.0
BAPT–Reg Bapt Gen As	1	NR	NR	NR	-	-
BAPT–So Bapt Conv	2	55	136	163	0.5	1.3
BUDD–Mahayana	1	NR	NR	11	0.0	0.1
Catholic	7	NR	NR	5,671	17.3	46.0
Ch Cr, Scientst	1	NR	NR	NR	-	-
Ch of Nazarene	2	224	255	398	1.2	3.2
CHR–Chr Ch (Disc)	1	66	195	234	0.7	1.9
CHR–Chs of Christ	1	80	80	100	0.3	0.8
Ind Fund Churches	2	NR	NR	NR	-	-
Jehovah's Witness	2	NR	NR	NR	-	-
JUD–Reform	1	67	118	319	1.0	2.6

NR–Not Reported - Represents no adherents reported. Percentages may not total 100 due to rounding.

Table 3: Religious Congregations by County and Group: 2010

Religious Group	Number of Congregations	Number of Attendees	Number of Communicant, Confirmed, or Full Members	Adherents: Number of Adherents	Adherents: % of Total Pop.	Adherents: % of Total Adh.
LDS–L-D Saints	1	NR	NR	289	0.9	2.3
LUTH–E.L.C.A.	1	94	229	330	1.0	2.7
LUTH–Luth–MO Synod	1	225	380	440	1.3	3.6
LUTH–Wisc Ev Luth Syn	1	54	70	91	0.3	0.7
MENN–Mennonite USA	2	270	139	167	0.5	1.4
METH–Un Methodist	5	503	837	1,386	4.2	11.3
Missionary Ch	2	280	124	280	0.9	2.3
Non-denom Chr Chs	8	728	755	978	3.0	7.9
PENT–Assemb of God	1	55	30	55	0.2	0.4
PENT–Pent Ch of God	1	70	NR	109	0.3	0.9
PRES–Presb Ch (USA)	2	222	586	704	2.2	5.7
Salvation Army	1	65	54	101	0.3	0.8
Sev Day Adv	2	83	144	166	0.5	1.3
Un C of Christ	1	66	36	43	0.1	0.3
GENESEE	**456**	**52,803**	**75,408**	**167,763**	**39.4**	**100.0**
ANG/EPIS–Anglican NA	2	NR	NR	NR	-	-
ANG/EPIS–Episcopal	6	525	1,240	1,578	0.4	0.9
Bahá'í	1	NR	169	169	0.0	0.1
BAPT–Alliance Bapt	1	NR	NR	NR	-	-
BAPT–Amer Bapt Assn	2	NR	225	278	0.1	0.2
BAPT–Amer Bapt USA	11	1,832	2,309	2,850	0.7	1.7
BAPT–Consrv Bapt	1	NR	NR	NR	-	-
BAPT–Free Will Bapt	3	NR	303	374	0.1	0.2
BAPT–Ind Bapt Flwsp Intl	2	NR	NR	NR	-	-
BAPT–Natl Mis Bapt Conv	7	370	1,090	1,345	0.3	0.8
BAPT–NBC USA	19	5,080	10,780	13,304	3.1	7.9
BAPT–Prog NBC	1	27	37	46	0.0	0.0
BAPT–Reg Bapt Gen As	6	NR	NR	NR	-	-
BAPT–So Bapt Conv	29	2,383	6,050	7,466	1.8	4.5
BRETH–Breth in Chr	1	NR	NR	NR	-	-
BRETH–Ch of Brethren	1	12	27	33	0.0	0.0
Calv Chpl	1	NR	NR	NR	-	-
Catholic	25	NR	NR	45,566	10.7	27.2
CGOD–Ch God (Ander)	9	991	NR	991	0.2	0.6
Ch Christ Chr Union	2	NR	NR	NR	-	-
Ch Cr, Scientst	2	NR	NR	NR	-	-
Ch of Nazarene	15	3,708	3,458	4,554	1.1	2.7
CHR–Chr Ch (Disc)	5	200	423	522	0.1	0.3
CHR–Chr Chs & Chs Cr	3	NR	205	253	0.1	0.2
CHR–Chs of Christ	12	1,962	2,471	3,185	0.7	1.9
CONG–Consrv Cong Chr	1	100	100	123	0.0	0.1
FRND–Consrv Yr Mtgs	1	NR	12	15	0.0	0.0
HINDU–I/A Temples	1	NR	NR	250	0.1	0.1
HINDU–Trad Temples	1	NR	NR	3,000	0.7	1.8
Ind Fund Churches	3	NR	NR	NR	-	-
Jehovah's Witness	10	NR	NR	NR	-	-
JUD–Conserv	1	105	118	319	0.1	0.2
JUD–Reform	1	74	131	354	0.1	0.2
LDS–Comm of Christ	4	NR	668	668	0.2	0.4
LDS–L-D Saints	4	NR	NR	1,865	0.4	1.1
LUTH–E.L.C.A.	6	547	1,025	1,360	0.3	0.8
LUTH–Luth–MO Synod	18	3,590	7,792	10,920	2.6	6.5
LUTH–Wisc Ev Luth Syn	7	569	1,175	1,465	0.3	0.9
MENN–Cons Menn Conf	1	30	22	27	0.0	0.0
METH–AME	3	350	601	742	0.2	0.4
METH–AME Zion	1	70	100	123	0.0	0.1
METH–C.M.E.	4	180	700	864	0.2	0.5
METH–Free Methodist	12	1,759	779	1,762	0.4	1.1
METH–Un Methodist	37	3,922	7,589	11,034	2.6	6.6
METH–Wesleyan	7	598	461	779	0.2	0.5
Metro Comm Ch	1	28	36	44	0.0	0.0
Missionary Ch	4	581	321	585	0.1	0.3
Muslim Est	9	3,157	NR	11,029	2.6	6.6
New Apost Ch	1	NR	NR	NR	-	-
Non-denom Chr Chs	45	10,043	12,396	14,506	3.4	8.6
ORTHE–Ant Orth of NA	1	175	NR	717	0.2	0.4
ORTHE–Greek Orthodox	1	100	NR	230	0.1	0.1
ORTHE–Orth Ch in Amer	2	172	NR	445	0.1	0.3
PENT–Assemb of God	16	3,625	1,347	5,964	1.4	3.6
PENT–Ch God (Cleve)	7	387	539	665	0.2	0.4
PENT–Ch Lord Jesus Apos	3	NR	NR	NR	-	-
PENT–Ch of God Proph	1	NR	44	54	0.0	0.0
PENT–COGIC	18	1,325	3,520	4,344	1.0	2.6
PENT–Full Gosp Bapt	4	NR	NR	NR	-	-
PENT–Int Foursq Gos	2	436	287	354	0.1	0.2
PENT–Int Pent C Chr	1	79	36	118	0.0	0.1
PENT–Intl Pent Holiness	1	30	30	37	0.0	0.0
PENT–Pent Ch of God	10	700	NR	1,087	0.3	0.6
PENT–Un Pent Ch Intl	6	NR	NR	NR	-	-
PRES–Evan Presby Ch	2	NR	481	594	0.1	0.4
PRES–Presb Ch (USA)	11	1,270	3,390	4,184	1.0	2.5
PRES–Presb Ch Amer	1	249	369	369	0.1	0.2
REF–Christian Ref	1	45	57	70	0.0	0.0
REF–Ref Ch in Am	1	110	240	254	0.1	0.2
Salvation Army	2	224	259	1,626	0.4	1.0
Sev Day Adv	8	613	1,066	1,226	0.3	0.7
Un Breth in Cr	2	170	193	145	0.0	0.1
Un C of Christ	3	235	607	749	0.2	0.4
Unit Univ	1	65	130	170	0.0	0.1
Unity Ch	1	NR	NR	NR	-	-
Zoroastrian	0	NR	NR	13	0.0	0.0
GLADWIN	**38**	**2,097**	**3,754**	**8,234**	**32.0**	**100.0**
ANG/EPIS–Episcopal	1	57	92	92	0.4	1.1
Bahá'í	0	NR	2	2	0.0	0.0
BAPT–Converge/BGC	1	75	NR	90	0.4	1.1
BAPT–N Am Bapt Conf	1	NR	182	214	0.8	2.6
BRETH–Ch of Brethren	1	0	114	134	0.5	1.6
Catholic	2	NR	NR	2,857	11.1	34.7
CGOD–Ch God (Ander)	1	45	NR	45	0.2	0.5
Ch of Nazarene	2	134	207	218	0.8	2.6
CHR–Chs of Christ	1	75	90	124	0.5	1.5
Jehovah's Witness	1	NR	NR	NR	-	-
LDS–Comm of Christ	2	NR	334	334	1.3	4.1
LUTH–E.L.C.A.	2	192	598	965	3.8	11.7
LUTH–Luth–MO Synod	1	247	601	654	2.5	7.9
LUTH–Wisc Ev Luth Syn	2	104	203	249	1.0	3.0
MENN–Amish Undif	4	NR	211	561	2.2	6.8
METH–Free Methodist	1	143	81	143	0.6	1.7
METH–Un Methodist	5	275	416	543	2.1	6.6
Missionary Ch	1	35	23	35	0.1	0.4
Non-denom Chr Chs	4	450	365	561	2.2	6.8
PENT–Assemb of God	2	177	98	254	1.0	3.1
PRES–Presb Ch (USA)	1	40	53	62	0.2	0.8
Sev Day Adv	2	48	84	97	0.4	1.2
GOGEBIC	**34**	**2,032**	**3,225**	**9,824**	**59.8**	**100.0**
ANG/EPIS–Episcopal	1	14	15	54	0.3	0.5
BAPT–Converge/BGC	1	800	NR	960	5.8	9.8
BAPT–Reg Bapt Gen As	2	NR	NR	NR	-	-
Catholic	5	NR	NR	4,781	29.1	48.7
CHR–Chs of Christ	1	8	4	8	0.0	0.1
Jehovah's Witness	2	NR	NR	NR	-	-
LUTH–Apostolic Luth	1	NR	NR	NR	-	-
LUTH–E.L.C.A.	6	419	1,597	2,053	12.5	20.9
LUTH–Luth–MO Synod	5	391	989	1,240	7.5	12.6
METH–Un Methodist	2	73	179	221	1.3	2.2
Non-denom Chr Chs	3	241	349	365	2.2	3.7
ORTHE–Ant Orth of NA	1	8	NR	22	0.1	0.2
PENT–Assemb of God	1	39	23	40	0.2	0.4
PRES–Presb Ch (USA)	2	13	25	29	0.2	0.3
Sev Day Adv	1	26	44	51	0.3	0.5
GRAND TRAVERSE	**82**	**10,337**	**13,063**	**34,264**	**39.4**	**100.0**
ANG/EPIS–Anglican NA	1	NR	NR	NR	-	-
ANG/EPIS–Episcopal	1	235	362	566	0.7	1.7
Bahá'í	0	NR	38	38	0.0	0.1
BAPT–Amer Bapt USA	1	43	67	80	0.1	0.2
BAPT–Reg Bapt Gen As	2	NR	NR	NR	-	-
BAPT–So Bapt Conv	1	76	73	88	0.1	0.3
Catholic	7	NR	NR	13,969	16.1	40.8
CGOD–Ch God (Ander)	1	120	NR	120	0.1	0.4
Ch Cr, Scientst	1	NR	NR	NR	-	-
Ch of Nazarene	2	210	170	386	0.4	1.1
CHR–Chr Ch (Disc)	1	135	248	298	0.3	0.9
CHR–Chr Chs & Chs Cr	2	NR	100	120	0.1	0.4

NR–Not Reported   - Represents no adherents reported.   Percentages may not total 100 due to rounding.

Table 3: Religious Congregations by County and Group: 2010

Religious Group	Number of Congrega-tions	Number of Attendees	Number of Communicant, Confirmed, or Full Members	Adherents: Number of Adherents	Adherents: % of Total Pop.	Adherents: % of Total Adh.
CHR–Chs of Christ	1	130	105	125	0.1	0.4
Evan Cov Ch	1	54	59	70	0.1	0.2
FRND–Fr Un Mtg	2	NR	68	82	0.1	0.2
Ind Fund Churches	2	NR	NR	NR	-	-
Jehovah's Witness	2	NR	NR	NR	-	-
JUD–Reform	1	29	52	140	0.2	0.4
LDS–Comm of Christ	2	NR	334	334	0.4	1.0
LDS–L-D Saints	1	NR	NR	639	0.7	1.9
LUTH–E.L.C.A.	2	293	889	1,156	1.3	3.4
LUTH–Luth Cong Msn Chr	1	45	NR	NR	-	-
LUTH–Luth–MO Synod	3	785	1,754	2,438	2.8	7.1
LUTH–Wisc Ev Luth Syn	1	107	159	217	0.2	0.6
METH–Free Methodist	1	7	12	12	0.0	0.0
METH–Un Methodist	9	1,184	1,946	2,708	3.1	7.9
METH–Wesleyan	2	343	237	446	0.5	1.3
Missionary Ch	1	47	20	47	0.1	0.1
Non-denom Chr Chs	13	4,109	3,155	5,135	5.9	15.0
ORTHE–Greek Orthodox	1	15	NR	70	0.1	0.2
PENT–Assemb of God	1	325	99	437	0.5	1.3
PENT–Ch God (Cleve)	1	55	132	159	0.2	0.5
PENT–Pent Ch of God	2	140	NR	217	0.2	0.6
PENT–Un Pent Ch Intl	1	NR	NR	NR	-	-
PRES–Presb Ch (USA)	1	496	1,189	1,428	1.6	4.2
PRES–Presb Ch Amer	1	100	95	133	0.2	0.4
REF–Christian Ref	2	155	85	102	0.1	0.3
REF–Ref Ch in Am	1	764	1,101	1,700	2.0	5.0
Salvation Army	1	76	75	254	0.3	0.7
Sev Day Adv	1	116	203	233	0.3	0.7
Un Breth in Cr	1	0	0	0	0.0	0.0
Un C of Christ	1	35	79	95	0.1	0.3
Unit Univ	1	108	157	222	0.3	0.6
Unity Ch	1	NR	NR	NR	-	-
GRATIOT	**79**	**3,931**	**5,832**	**13,269**	**31.2**	**100.0**
ANG/EPIS–Episcopal	1	35	70	99	0.2	0.7
Bahá'í	0	NR	4	4	0.0	0.0
BAPT–Amer Bapt USA	1	19	25	30	0.1	0.2
BAPT–Reg Bapt Gen As	3	NR	NR	NR	-	-
BAPT–So Bapt Conv	2	54	64	76	0.2	0.6
BRETH–Ch of Brethren	1	105	135	161	0.4	1.2
Catholic	6	NR	NR	4,689	11.0	35.3
CGOD–Ch God (Ander)	4	675	NR	675	1.6	5.1
CGOD–Ches God-Gen Con	2	180	110	131	0.3	1.0
Ch Cr, Scientst	1	NR	NR	NR	-	-
Ch of Nazarene	3	185	226	269	0.6	2.0
CHR–Chr Chs & Chs Cr	4	NR	1,010	1,207	2.8	9.1
Jehovah's Witness	1	NR	NR	NR	-	-
LDS–Comm of Christ	1	NR	167	167	0.4	1.3
LDS–L-D Saints	1	NR	NR	192	0.5	1.4
LUTH–Luth–MO Synod	2	131	538	695	1.6	5.2
LUTH–Wisc Ev Luth Syn	1	158	275	321	0.8	2.4
MENN–Amish Undif	0	NR	5	19	0.0	0.1
MENN–CG in Cr (Menn)	2	NR	272	325	0.8	2.4
METH–Free Methodist	3	181	120	181	0.4	1.4
METH–Un Methodist	12	625	1,185	1,469	3.5	11.1
METH–Wesleyan	4	191	135	248	0.6	1.9
Non-denom Chr Chs	3	418	368	522	1.2	3.9
PENT–Assemb of God	3	179	65	239	0.6	1.8
PENT–Int Foursq Gos	1	24	18	22	0.1	0.2
PENT–Intl Pent Holiness	1	9	13	16	0.0	0.1
PENT–Pent Ch of God	2	140	NR	217	0.5	1.6
PENT–Vineyard	1	27	12	14	0.0	0.1
PRES–Presb Ch (USA)	5	180	450	538	1.3	4.1
Salvation Army	1	24	41	232	0.5	1.7
Sev Day Adv	3	112	194	223	0.5	1.7
Un Breth in Cr	3	254	271	217	0.5	1.6
Un C of Christ	1	25	59	71	0.2	0.5
HILLSDALE	**76**	**4,694**	**5,428**	**11,057**	**23.7**	**100.0**
ANG/EPIS–Episcopal	1	22	41	42	0.1	0.4
Bahá'í	0	NR	17	17	0.0	0.2
BAPT–Amer Bapt USA	1	55	102	124	0.3	1.1
BAPT–Converge/BGC	1	75	NR	90	0.2	0.8

Religious Group	Number of Congrega-tions	Number of Attendees	Number of Communicant, Confirmed, or Full Members	Adherents: Number of Adherents	Adherents: % of Total Pop.	Adherents: % of Total Adh.
BAPT–Free Will Bapt	1	NR	101	123	0.3	1.1
BAPT–Reg Bapt Gen As	2	NR	NR	NR	-	-
BAPT–So Bapt Conv	2	246	457	557	1.2	5.0
Catholic	1	NR	NR	2,198	4.7	19.9
Ch Cr, Scientst	1	NR	NR	NR	-	-
Ch of Nazarene	2	87	118	156	0.3	1.4
CHR–Chr Chs & Chs Cr	2	NR	85	104	0.2	0.9
CHR–Chs of Christ	1	36	35	40	0.1	0.4
CONG–Cong Chr, NA	2	NR	155	189	0.4	1.7
Ind Fund Churches	3	NR	NR	NR	-	-
Jehovah's Witness	1	NR	NR	NR	-	-
LDS–L-D Saints	1	NR	NR	349	0.7	3.2
LUTH–E.L.C.A.	1	74	144	171	0.4	1.5
LUTH–Luth–MO Synod	1	189	327	411	0.9	3.7
MENN–Amish Undif	7	NR	250	681	1.5	6.2
MENN–Mennonite USA	2	92	92	112	0.2	1.0
METH–Free Methodist	2	364	203	364	0.8	3.3
METH–Un Methodist	12	565	853	1,268	2.7	11.5
METH–Wesleyan	2	101	73	132	0.3	1.2
Missionary Ch	1	170	106	170	0.4	1.5
New Apost Ch	1	NR	NR	NR	-	-
Non-denom Chr Chs	9	985	1,176	1,381	3.0	12.5
PENT–Assemb of God	2	199	121	328	0.7	3.0
PENT–Pent Ch of God	4	280	NR	435	0.9	3.9
PRES–Orth Pres Ch	1	69	36	47	0.1	0.4
PRES–Presb Ch (USA)	3	152	322	393	0.8	3.6
Salvation Army	1	24	61	310	0.7	2.8
Sev Day Adv	2	78	137	157	0.3	1.4
Un Breth in Cr	3	831	416	708	1.5	6.4
HOUGHTON	**67**	**2,684**	**5,318**	**15,697**	**42.9**	**100.0**
ANG/EPIS–Episcopal	2	60	87	117	0.3	0.7
Bahá'í	0	NR	23	23	0.1	0.1
BAPT–Reg Bapt Gen As	2	NR	NR	NR	-	-
BAPT–So Bapt Conv	1	160	335	400	1.1	2.5
Catholic	9	NR	NR	8,374	22.9	53.3
Ch Cr, Scientst	1	NR	NR	NR	-	-
Ch of Nazarene	1	5	5	8	0.0	0.1
CHR–Chr Chs & Chs Cr	1	NR	60	72	0.2	0.5
CHR–Chs of Christ	1	25	25	25	0.1	0.2
FRND–Fr Gen Cf	1	NR	15	18	0.0	0.1
HINDU–Post Ren	1	NR	NR	10	0.0	0.1
Jehovah's Witness	1	NR	NR	NR	-	-
JUD–Reform	1	9	16	43	0.1	0.3
LDS–L-D Saints	1	NR	NR	181	0.5	1.2
LUTH–Apostolic Luth	8	NR	NR	NR	-	-
LUTH–Assoc Free Luth	2	NR	NR	NR	-	-
LUTH–E.L.C.A.	7	592	2,032	2,527	6.9	16.1
LUTH–Luth–MO Synod	3	383	693	791	2.2	5.0
LUTH–Wisc Ev Luth Syn	2	127	226	343	0.9	2.2
METH–Un Methodist	7	398	989	1,240	3.4	7.9
Non-denom Chr Chs	5	633	453	816	2.2	5.2
ORTHE–Rus Orth Abroad	1	20	NR	100	0.3	0.6
PENT–Assemb of God	1	111	49	252	0.7	1.6
PENT–Un Pent Ch Intl	1	NR	NR	NR	-	-
PRES–Presb Ch (USA)	1	16	30	36	0.1	0.2
Salvation Army	1	10	48	48	0.1	0.3
Sev Day Adv	1	43	75	86	0.2	0.5
Un C of Christ	2	38	74	88	0.2	0.6
Unit Univ	1	54	83	99	0.3	0.6
Unity Ch	1	NR	NR	NR	-	-
HURON	**82**	**4,334**	**8,119**	**17,490**	**52.8**	**100.0**
ANG/EPIS–Episcopal	2	42	91	91	0.3	0.5
Bahá'í	0	NR	1	1	0.0	0.0
BAPT–Ind Bapt Flwsp Intl	1	NR	NR	NR	-	-
BAPT–Reg Bapt Gen As	1	NR	NR	NR	-	-
Catholic	16	NR	NR	6,765	20.4	38.7
Ch of Nazarene	2	39	44	57	0.2	0.3
CHR–Chs of Christ	1	20	24	28	0.1	0.2
Jehovah's Witness	1	NR	NR	NR	-	-
LDS–Comm of Christ	3	NR	501	501	1.5	2.9
LDS–L-D Saints	1	NR	NR	78	0.2	0.4

NR–Not Reported - Represents no adherents reported. Percentages may not total 100 due to rounding.

Table 3: Religious Congregations by County and Group: 2010

Religious Group	Number of Congrega-tions	Number of Attendees	Number of Communicant, Confirmed, or Full Members	Adherents: Number of Adherents	Adherents: % of Total Pop.	Adherents: % of Total Adh.
LUTH–Luth Cong Msn Chr	1	10	7	8	0.0	0.0
LUTH–Luth-MO Synod	9	1,433	3,387	4,450	13.4	25.4
LUTH–Nor Amer Luth C	1	NR	NR	NR	-	-
LUTH–Wisc Ev Luth Syn	3	326	648	788	2.4	4.5
MENN–Amish Undif	0	NR	23	63	0.2	0.4
MENN–Cons Menn Conf	3	340	369	436	1.3	2.5
MENN–Mennonite USA	1	65	107	126	0.4	0.7
METH–Free Methodist	2	287	128	287	0.9	1.6
METH–Un Methodist	17	1,010	1,904	2,583	7.8	14.8
METH–Wesleyan	1	37	54	48	0.1	0.3
Missionary Ch	2	168	139	168	0.5	1.0
Non-denom Chr Chs	3	147	196	215	0.6	1.2
PENT–Assemb of God	3	238	127	350	1.1	2.0
PENT–Un Pent Ch Intl	1	NR	NR	NR	-	-
PRES–Presb Ch (USA)	5	75	187	221	0.7	1.3
PRES–Presb Ch Amer	1	75	145	183	0.6	1.0
Sev Day Adv	1	22	37	43	0.1	0.2
INGHAM	**269**	**30,836**	**46,091**	**112,439**	**40.0**	**100.0**
ANG/EPIS–Episcopal	5	522	1,505	1,710	0.6	1.5
Bahá'í	3	NR	196	196	0.1	0.2
BAPT–Amer Bapt Assn	1	NR	85	101	0.0	0.1
BAPT–Amer Bapt USA	11	1,148	2,477	2,953	1.1	2.6
BAPT–Converge/BGC	3	550	NR	660	0.2	0.6
BAPT–Ind Bapt Flwsp Intl	1	NR	NR	NR	-	-
BAPT–N Am Bapt Conf	1	NR	172	205	0.1	0.2
BAPT–NBC USA	1	400	600	715	0.3	0.6
BAPT–Reg Bapt Gen As	3	NR	NR	NR	-	-
BAPT–So Bapt Conv	10	652	1,109	1,322	0.5	1.2
BRETH–Ch of Brethren	1	24	50	60	0.0	0.1
BUDD–Mahayana	3	NR	NR	604	0.2	0.5
Calv Chpl	1	NR	NR	NR	-	-
Catholic	16	NR	NR	44,637	15.9	39.7
CGOD–Ch God (Ander)	2	217	NR	217	0.1	0.2
Ch Cr, Scientst	1	NR	NR	NR	-	-
Ch of Nazarene	9	826	1,121	1,449	0.5	1.3
Chr & Miss Al	1	105	172	172	0.1	0.2
CHR–Chr Ch (Disc)	1	95	198	236	0.1	0.2
CHR–Chr Chs & Chs Cr	4	NR	490	584	0.2	0.5
CHR–Chs of Christ	5	417	439	512	0.2	0.5
CHR–Int Chs of Christ	1	NR	42	50	0.0	0.0
CONG–Cong Chr, NA	3	NR	423	504	0.2	0.4
Evan Free Ch	1	85	NR	85	0.0	0.1
FRND–Fr Gen Cf	1	NR	34	41	0.0	0.0
HINDU–I/A Temples	1	NR	NR	50	0.0	0.0
HINDU–Post Ren	3	NR	NR	51	0.0	0.0
HINDU–Trad Temples	1	NR	NR	100	0.0	0.1
Jain	1	NR	NR	NR	-	-
Jehovah's Witness	4	NR	NR	NR	-	-
JUD–Reconst	1	110	140	378	0.1	0.3
JUD–Reform	1	131	231	624	0.2	0.6
LDS–Comm of Christ	3	NR	501	501	0.2	0.4
LDS–L-D Saints	4	NR	NR	1,985	0.7	1.8
LUTH–E.L.C.A.	8	970	2,030	3,106	1.1	2.8
LUTH–Luth-MO Synod	9	1,173	2,122	2,741	1.0	2.4
LUTH–Wisc Ev Luth Syn	4	582	1,455	1,885	0.7	1.7
MENN–Mennonite USA	1	40	40	48	0.0	0.0
METH–AME	2	270	850	1,013	0.4	0.9
METH–C.M.E.	1	0	78	93	0.0	0.1
METH–Free Methodist	6	747	455	765	0.3	0.7
METH–Un Methodist	24	2,819	5,160	6,993	2.5	6.2
METH–Wesleyan	4	887	414	1,153	0.4	1.0
Missionary Ch	1	49	35	49	0.0	0.0
Muslim Est	2	615	NR	4,050	1.4	3.6
Nat Spirit Asso	1	NR	NR	NR	-	-
Non-denom Chr Chs	23	9,980	13,205	14,679	5.2	13.1
ORTHE–Ant Orth of NA	1	30	NR	35	0.0	0.0
ORTHE–Greek Orthodox	1	200	NR	600	0.2	0.5
ORTHE–Rus Orth Abroad	1	10	NR	25	0.0	0.0
ORTHE–Rus Orth Moscow	1	65	NR	85	0.0	0.1
ORTHO–Armen Ap Etchm	2	45	NR	95	0.0	0.1
PENT–Assemb of God	10	1,484	537	2,318	0.8	2.1
PENT–Ch God (Cleve)	5	240	388	463	0.2	0.4
PENT–Ch of God Proph	1	NR	9	11	0.0	0.0
PENT–COGIC	4	740	1,375	1,639	0.6	1.5
PENT–Pent Ch of God	1	70	NR	109	0.0	0.1
PENT–Un Pent Ch Intl	3	NR	NR	NR	-	-
PENT–Vineyard	2	169	238	284	0.1	0.3
PRES–Orth Pres Ch	1	19	26	32	0.0	0.0
PRES–Presb Ch (USA)	12	1,208	2,534	3,021	1.1	2.7
PRES–Presb Ch Amer	1	47	36	53	0.0	0.0
REF–Christian Ref	2	592	678	808	0.3	0.7
REF–Ref Ch in Am	2	587	656	782	0.3	0.7
Salvation Army	2	86	110	432	0.2	0.4
Sev Day Adv	7	443	770	886	0.3	0.8
Sikh	3	NR	NR	NR	-	-
Swedenborgian	1	NR	NR	NR	-	-
Un Breth in Cr	3	359	277	307	0.1	0.3
Un C of Christ	6	818	2,278	2,716	1.0	2.4
Unit Univ	1	210	350	453	0.2	0.4
Unity Ch	2	NR	NR	NR	-	-
Zoroastrian	0	NR	NR	8	0.0	0.0
IONIA	**81**	**5,352**	**6,048**	**22,080**	**34.6**	**100.0**
ANG/EPIS–Episcopal	1	22	71	71	0.1	0.3
Bahá'í	0	NR	5	5	0.0	0.0
BAPT–Amer Bapt USA	2	92	88	108	0.2	0.5
BAPT–Consrv Bapt	1	NR	NR	NR	-	-
BAPT–Reg Bapt Gen As	5	NR	NR	NR	-	-
BRETH–Grace Breth	1	NR	NR	NR	-	-
Catholic	8	NR	NR	12,410	19.4	56.2
CGOD–Ch God (Ander)	1	68	NR	68	0.1	0.3
Ch of Nazarene	3	229	186	412	0.6	1.9
CHR–Chr Ch (Disc)	2	62	154	189	0.3	0.9
CHR–Chr Chs & Chs Cr	1	NR	100	123	0.2	0.6
CONG–Cong Chr, NA	2	NR	233	286	0.4	1.3
Evan Cov Ch	1	113	247	147	0.2	0.7
Ind Fund Churches	2	NR	NR	NR	-	-
Jehovah's Witness	1	NR	NR	NR	-	-
LDS–L-D Saints	1	NR	NR	258	0.4	1.2
LUTH–Luth-MO Synod	3	179	414	569	0.9	2.6
LUTH–Wisc Ev Luth Syn	1	19	43	57	0.1	0.3
MENN–Cons Menn Conf	1	70	41	50	0.1	0.2
METH–Free Methodist	4	141	125	155	0.2	0.7
METH–Un Methodist	11	870	1,303	2,437	3.8	11.0
METH–Wesleyan	4	450	80	586	0.9	2.7
Non-denom Chr Chs	10	2,122	1,875	2,652	4.1	12.0
ORTHE–Rus Orth Abroad	1	15	NR	30	0.0	0.1
PENT–Assemb of God	3	247	153	352	0.6	1.6
PENT–Ch God (Cleve)	2	78	122	150	0.2	0.7
PENT–Open Bible Std	1	15	NR	15	0.0	0.1
PRES–Presb Ch (USA)	2	95	136	167	0.3	0.8
REF–Christian Ref	2	299	421	517	0.8	2.3
Sev Day Adv	2	72	126	145	0.2	0.7
Un Breth in Cr	1	36	52	31	0.0	0.1
Un C of Christ	1	58	73	90	0.1	0.4
IOSCO	**45**	**2,983**	**4,604**	**10,180**	**39.3**	**100.0**
ANG/EPIS–Anglican NA	1	NR	NR	NR	-	-
ANG/EPIS–Episcopal	2	69	221	227	0.9	2.2
Bahá'í	0	NR	9	9	0.0	0.1
BAPT–Amer Bapt USA	1	105	123	141	0.5	1.4
BAPT–Converge/BGC	1	400	NR	480	1.9	4.7
BAPT–Reg Bapt Gen As	1	NR	NR	NR	-	-
BAPT–So Bapt Conv	1	50	95	109	0.4	1.1
Catholic	4	NR	NR	3,070	11.9	30.2
Ch of Nazarene	2	96	95	160	0.6	1.6
CHR–Chs of Christ	1	45	40	50	0.2	0.5
Jehovah's Witness	2	NR	NR	NR	-	-
LDS–Comm of Christ	1	NR	167	167	0.6	1.6
LDS–L-D Saints	1	NR	NR	233	0.9	2.3
LUTH–E.L.C.A.	2	101	204	239	0.9	2.3
LUTH–Luth-MO Synod	3	340	1,092	1,367	5.3	13.4
LUTH–Wisc Ev Luth Syn	1	198	490	589	2.3	5.8
MENN–Amish Undif	1	NR	14	22	0.1	0.2
METH–Un Methodist	6	514	1,004	1,811	7.0	17.8
Non-denom Chr Chs	6	745	710	993	3.8	9.8

NR–Not Reported - Represents no adherents reported. Percentages may not total 100 due to rounding.

Table 3: Religious Congregations by County and Group: 2010

Religious Group	Number of Congrega-tions	Number of Attendees	Number of Communicant, Confirmed, or Full Members	Adherents		
				Number of Adherents	% of Total Pop.	% of Total Adh.
PENT–Assemb of God	3	196	99	235	0.9	2.3
PENT–Intl Pent Holiness	1	8	17	20	0.1	0.2
PENT–Un Pent Ch Intl	1	NR	NR	NR	-	-
PRES–Evan Presby Ch	1	NR	45	52	0.2	0.5
PRES–Presb Ch (USA)	1	100	152	175	0.7	1.7
Sev Day Adv	1	16	27	31	0.1	0.3
IRON	**26**	**855**	**1,810**	**6,045**	**51.2**	**100.0**
ANG/EPIS–Episcopal	2	33	55	55	0.5	0.9
Bahá'í	0	NR	1	1	0.0	0.0
BAPT–Converge/BGC	1	75	NR	90	0.8	1.5
BAPT–Reg Bapt Gen As	1	NR	NR	NR	-	-
Calv Chpl	1	NR	NR	NR	-	-
Catholic	3	NR	NR	3,451	29.2	57.1
Ch of Nazarene	1	26	30	43	0.4	0.7
Evan Cov Ch	1	136	177	177	1.5	2.9
Ind Fund Churches	1	NR	NR	NR	-	-
Jehovah's Witness	1	NR	NR	NR	-	-
LUTH–Ch Luth Conf	1	NR	NR	NR	-	-
LUTH–E.L.C.A.	4	268	1,021	1,434	12.1	23.7
LUTH–Luth-MO Synod	2	68	126	141	1.2	2.3
LUTH–Wisc Ev Luth Syn	1	20	38	41	0.3	0.7
METH–Un Methodist	3	108	235	380	3.2	6.3
PENT–Assemb of God	1	55	0	87	0.7	1.4
PRES–Presb Ch (USA)	1	50	98	112	0.9	1.9
Sev Day Adv	1	16	29	33	0.3	0.5
ISABELLA	**70**	**4,719**	**6,806**	**21,646**	**30.8**	**100.0**
ANG/EPIS–Episcopal	1	71	175	175	0.2	0.8
Bahá'í	0	NR	23	23	0.0	0.1
BAPT–Converge/BGC	1	75	NR	90	0.1	0.4
BAPT–Reg Bapt Gen As	2	NR	NR	NR	-	-
BAPT–So Bapt Conv	1	15	16	19	0.0	0.1
BRETH–Ch of Brethren	1	80	102	119	0.2	0.5
BUDD–Mahayana	1	NR	NR	17	0.0	0.1
Catholic	7	NR	NR	10,176	14.5	47.0
CGOD–Ch God (Ander)	1	25	NR	25	0.0	0.1
Ch of God Gen Conf	1	NR	60	70	0.1	0.3
Ch of Nazarene	3	312	171	421	0.6	1.9
CHR–Chr Chs & Chs Cr	4	NR	416	484	0.7	2.2
CHR–Chs of Christ	2	166	172	215	0.3	1.0
FRND–Fr Gen Cf	1	NR	16	19	0.0	0.1
Jehovah's Witness	1	NR	NR	NR	-	-
JUD–Reform	1	16	28	76	0.1	0.4
LDS–Comm of Christ	1	NR	167	167	0.2	0.8
LDS–L-D Saints	1	NR	NR	483	0.7	2.2
LUTH–E.L.C.A.	1	137	407	507	0.7	2.3
LUTH–Luth-MO Synod	1	204	458	559	0.8	2.6
LUTH–Wisc Ev Luth Syn	2	253	295	368	0.5	1.7
MENN–Amish Undif	2	NR	87	277	0.4	1.3
METH–Free Methodist	1	82	57	82	0.1	0.4
METH–Un Methodist	11	673	1,253	1,676	2.4	7.7
METH–Wesleyan	2	115	43	150	0.2	0.7
Muslim Est	1	411	NR	1,563	2.2	7.2
Non-denom Chr Chs	8	1,460	1,507	1,975	2.8	9.1
PENT–Assemb of God	1	120	56	265	0.4	1.2
PENT–Ch God (Cleve)	1	105	44	51	0.1	0.2
PENT–Pent Ch of God	1	70	NR	109	0.2	0.5
PENT–Un Pent Ch Intl	1	NR	NR	NR	-	-
PRES–Evan Presby Ch	1	NR	671	781	1.1	3.6
PRES–Presb Ch (USA)	2	137	321	374	0.5	1.7
Salvation Army	1	14	23	41	0.1	0.2
Sev Day Adv	1	88	153	176	0.3	0.8
Un Breth in Cr	1	22	22	19	0.0	0.1
Unit Univ	1	68	63	94	0.1	0.4
JACKSON	**162**	**13,995**	**19,865**	**48,756**	**30.4**	**100.0**
ANG/EPIS–Episcopal	6	245	409	623	0.4	1.3
Bahá'í	0	NR	87	87	0.1	0.2
BAPT–Amer Bapt Assn	1	NR	85	103	0.1	0.2
BAPT–Amer Bapt USA	4	368	683	829	0.5	1.7
BAPT–Consrv Bapt	3	NR	NR	NR	-	-
BAPT–Converge/BGC	1	75	NR	90	0.1	0.2
BAPT–Ind Bapt Flwsp Intl	2	NR	NR	NR	-	-
BAPT–Natl Mis Bapt Conv	1	20	15	18	0.0	0.0
BAPT–NBC USA	2	200	850	1,032	0.6	2.1
BAPT–Reg Bapt Gen As	7	NR	NR	NR	-	-
BAPT–So Bapt Conv	8	919	1,677	2,036	1.3	4.2
Catholic	8	NR	NR	19,651	12.3	40.3
CGOD–Ch God (Ander)	4	293	NR	293	0.2	0.6
Ch Cr, Scientst	1	NR	NR	NR	-	-
Ch of Nazarene	3	1,367	705	1,560	1.0	3.2
CHR–Chr Chs & Chs Cr	1	NR	385	467	0.3	1.0
CHR–Chs of Christ	4	255	305	368	0.2	0.8
CONG–Cong Chr, NA	3	NR	340	413	0.3	0.8
HINDU–I/A Temples	1	NR	NR	250	0.2	0.5
Ind Fund Churches	1	NR	NR	NR	-	-
Int Cou Comm Ch	1	NR	NR	NR	-	-
Jehovah's Witness	2	NR	NR	NR	-	-
JUD–Reform	1	40	71	192	0.1	0.4
LDS–Comm of Christ	1	NR	167	167	0.1	0.3
LDS–L-D Saints	1	NR	NR	836	0.5	1.7
LUTH–E.L.C.A.	3	331	878	1,156	0.7	2.4
LUTH–Luth-MO Synod	3	655	2,008	2,575	1.6	5.3
LUTH–Wisc Ev Luth Syn	2	103	228	281	0.2	0.6
METH–AME	1	30	80	97	0.1	0.2
METH–C.M.E.	1	0	150	182	0.1	0.4
METH–Free Methodist	5	2,184	1,644	2,184	1.4	4.5
METH–Un Methodist	17	903	2,281	3,380	2.1	6.9
METH–Wesleyan	5	642	312	835	0.5	1.7
Missionary Ch	3	198	105	198	0.1	0.4
New Apost Ch	1	NR	NR	NR	-	-
Non-denom Chr Chs	19	2,655	2,923	3,533	2.2	7.2
ORTHE–Orth Ch in Amer	2	80	NR	112	0.1	0.2
PENT–Assemb of God	5	578	242	825	0.5	1.7
PENT–Ch God (Cleve)	1	104	201	244	0.2	0.5
PENT–Ch Lord Jesus Apos	1	NR	NR	NR	-	-
PENT–Ch of God Proph	1	NR	32	39	0.0	0.1
PENT–COGIC	3	230	380	461	0.3	0.9
PENT–Pent Ch of God	2	140	NR	217	0.1	0.4
PENT–Un Pent Ch Intl	4	NR	NR	NR	-	-
PRES–Presb Ch (USA)	4	504	1,172	1,423	0.9	2.9
REF–Christian Ref	1	80	60	73	0.0	0.1
Salvation Army	1	48	84	407	0.3	0.8
Sev Day Adv	2	174	303	349	0.2	0.7
Un Breth in Cr	2	272	237	232	0.1	0.5
Un C of Christ	4	256	676	821	0.5	1.7
Unit Univ	1	46	90	117	0.1	0.2
Unity Ch	1	NR	NR	NR	-	-
KALAMAZOO	**226**	**36,512**	**51,943**	**95,754**	**38.3**	**100.0**
ANG/EPIS–Episcopal	5	504	975	1,528	0.6	1.6
Bahá'í	1	NR	74	74	0.0	0.1
BAPT–Amer Bapt Assn	1	NR	0	0	0.0	0.0
BAPT–Amer Bapt USA	3	690	1,383	1,679	0.7	1.8
BAPT–Converge/BGC	2	150	NR	180	0.1	0.2
BAPT–Free Will Bapt	2	NR	202	245	0.1	0.3
BAPT–NBC Amer	1	950	1,600	1,943	0.8	2.0
BAPT–NBC USA	2	600	900	1,093	0.4	1.1
BAPT–Ref Bapt Ch	1	NR	NR	NR	-	-
BAPT–Reg Bapt Gen As	2	NR	NR	NR	-	-
BAPT–So Bapt Conv	6	279	469	570	0.2	0.6
BRETH–Ch of Brethren	1	0	66	80	0.0	0.1
BUDD–Vajrayana	2	NR	NR	102	0.0	0.1
Calv Chpl	1	NR	NR	NR	-	-
Catholic	9	NR	NR	23,876	9.5	24.9
CGOD–Ch God (Ander)	2	200	NR	200	0.1	0.2
Ch Cr, Scientst	1	NR	NR	NR	-	-
Ch of Nazarene	3	516	801	803	0.3	0.8
CHR–Chr Ch (Disc)	1	45	115	140	0.1	0.1
CHR–Chr Chs & Chs Cr	3	NR	790	959	0.4	1.0
CHR–Chs of Christ	5	358	420	500	0.2	0.5
CONG–Cong Chr, NA	1	NR	79	96	0.0	0.1
Evan Cov Ch	2	132	204	171	0.1	0.2
Evan Free Ch	2	307	NR	307	0.1	0.3
FRND–Fr Gen Cf	1	NR	43	52	0.0	0.1
HINDU–I/A Temples	1	NR	NR	350	0.1	0.4

NR–Not Reported - Represents no adherents reported. Percentages may not total 100 due to rounding.

Table 3: Religious Congregations by County and Group: 2010

Religious Group	Number of Congrega-tions	Number of Attendees	Number of Communicant, Confirmed, or Full Members	Adherents: Number of Adherents	Adherents: % of Total Pop.	Adherents: % of Total Adh.
HINDU–Post Ren	1	NR	NR	77	0.0	0.1
HINDU–Trad Temples	1	NR	NR	577	0.2	0.6
Ind Fund Churches	4	NR	NR	NR	-	-
Jehovah's Witness	5	NR	NR	NR	-	-
JUD–Conserv	1	99	111	300	0.1	0.3
JUD–Reform	1	53	93	251	0.1	0.3
LDS–Comm of Christ	1	NR	167	167	0.1	0.2
LDS–L-D Saints	4	NR	NR	1,443	0.6	1.5
LUTH–E.L.C.A.	4	655	1,644	2,045	0.8	2.1
LUTH–Luth–MO Synod	3	870	1,646	2,357	0.9	2.5
LUTH–Wisc Ev Luth Syn	1	108	191	252	0.1	0.3
MENN–Fel Evg Ch	1	0	0	0	0.0	0.0
MENN–Mennonite USA	1	10	NR	NR	-	-
METH–AME	2	100	250	304	0.1	0.3
METH–Free Methodist	2	447	295	447	0.2	0.5
METH–Un Methodist	18	2,335	4,574	6,757	2.7	7.1
METH–Wesleyan	2	445	292	579	0.2	0.6
Missionary Ch	2	220	143	220	0.1	0.2
MJEW–Assoc Mes Cong	1	NR	NR	NR	-	-
Muslim Est	2	661	NR	2,563	1.0	2.7
New Apost Ch	2	NR	NR	NR	-	-
Non-denom Chr Chs	31	15,182	18,553	21,643	8.6	22.6
ORTHE–Greek Orthodox	1	60	NR	275	0.1	0.3
PENT–Assemb of God	5	558	300	709	0.3	0.7
PENT–Ch God (Cleve)	1	186	247	300	0.1	0.3
PENT–Ch of God Proph	1	NR	54	66	0.0	0.1
PENT–COGIC	5	180	659	800	0.3	0.8
PENT–Int Foursq Gos	2	234	63	77	0.0	0.1
PENT–Un Pent Ch Intl	3	NR	NR	NR	-	-
PENT–Vineyard	1	50	59	72	0.0	0.1
PRES–Korean Pres Amer	1	NR	NR	NR	-	-
PRES–Orth Pres Ch	1	23	21	28	0.0	0.0
PRES–Presb Ch (USA)	6	769	1,645	1,998	0.8	2.1
REF–Christian Ref	13	2,695	3,767	4,574	1.8	4.8
REF–Prot Ref Chs	1	62	44	67	0.0	0.1
REF–Ref Ch in Am	16	4,383	6,666	8,414	3.4	8.8
REF–Un Ref Chs N.A.	1	NR	NR	NR	-	-
Salvation Army	1	63	107	720	0.3	0.8
Sev Day Adv	7	438	761	876	0.3	0.9
Sikh	1	NR	NR	NR	-	-
Un C of Christ	5	617	1,191	1,446	0.6	1.5
Unit Univ	2	278	279	399	0.2	0.4
Unity Ch	1	NR	NR	NR	-	-
Zoroastrian	0	NR	NR	3	0.0	0.0
KALKASKA	**22**	**860**	**1,630**	**3,070**	**17.9**	**100.0**
Bahá'í	0	NR	3	3	0.0	0.1
BAPT–Reg Bapt Gen As	1	NR	NR	NR	-	-
BAPT–So Bapt Conv	1	50	125	151	0.9	4.9
Catholic	1	NR	NR	779	4.5	25.4
Ch of Nazarene	1	74	82	160	0.9	5.2
CHR–Chr Chs & Chs Cr	3	NR	445	538	3.1	17.5
CHR–Chs of Christ	1	25	30	35	0.2	1.1
Ind Fund Churches	1	NR	NR	NR	-	-
Jehovah's Witness	1	NR	NR	NR	-	-
LDS–L-D Saints	1	NR	NR	159	0.9	5.2
LUTH–Luth–MO Synod	1	100	245	346	2.0	11.3
METH–Un Methodist	3	201	324	324	1.9	10.6
Non-denom Chr Chs	3	235	205	297	1.7	9.7
PENT–Assemb of God	2	100	20	100	0.6	3.3
PENT–Ch God (Cleve)	1	39	88	106	0.6	3.5
Sev Day Adv	1	36	63	72	0.4	2.3
KENT	**566**	**117,207**	**152,605**	**329,532**	**54.7**	**100.0**
ANG/EPIS–Episcopal	7	766	1,942	2,225	0.4	0.7
Ap Chr Ch-Amer	1	229	92	229	0.0	0.1
Bahá'í	2	NR	127	127	0.0	0.0
BAPT–Amer Bapt Assn	1	NR	95	119	0.0	0.0
BAPT–Amer Bapt USA	2	23	68	85	0.0	0.0
BAPT–Consrv Bapt	2	NR	NR	NR	-	-
BAPT–Converge/BGC	7	850	NR	1,020	0.2	0.3
BAPT–NBC Amer	2	1,500	5,100	6,402	1.1	1.9
BAPT–NBC USA	1	250	600	753	0.1	0.2
BAPT–Prog NBC	1	70	100	126	0.0	0.0
BAPT–Ref Bapt Ch	1	NR	NR	NR	-	-
BAPT–Reg Bapt Gen As	27	NR	NR	NR	-	-
BAPT–S-D Baptist Gen Con	1	15	16	20	0.0	0.0
BAPT–So Bapt Conv	5	231	209	262	0.0	0.1
BRETH–Ch of Brethren	1	0	94	118	0.0	0.0
BUDD–Mahayana	2	NR	NR	538	0.1	0.2
Calv Chpl	2	NR	NR	NR	-	-
Catholic	37	NR	NR	114,437	19.0	34.7
CGOD–Ch God (Ander)	7	516	NR	516	0.1	0.2
Ch Cr, Scientst	2	NR	NR	NR	-	-
Ch of God Gen Conf	4	NR	167	210	0.0	0.1
Ch of Nazarene	7	1,292	842	1,984	0.3	0.6
Chr & Miss Al	2	100	51	131	0.0	0.0
CHR–Chr Ch (Disc)	2	362	767	963	0.2	0.3
CHR–Chr Chs & Chs Cr	5	NR	1,000	1,255	0.2	0.4
CHR–Chs of Christ	7	656	746	1,030	0.2	0.3
CHR–Int Chs of Christ	1	NR	40	50	0.0	0.0
Christian Brethren	2	NR	NR	NR	-	-
CONG–Cong Chr, NA	2	NR	878	1,102	0.2	0.3
Evan Cov Ch	6	1,679	1,345	2,182	0.4	0.7
Evan Free Ch	2	265	NR	265	0.0	0.1
FRND–Fr Gen Cf	1	NR	23	29	0.0	0.0
Grace Gosp Fel	6	NR	NR	NR	-	-
HINDU–Post Ren	1	NR	NR	16	0.0	0.0
HINDU–Trad Temples	1	NR	NR	2,100	0.3	0.6
Ind Fund Churches	15	NR	NR	NR	-	-
Int Cou Comm Ch	1	NR	NR	NR	-	-
Jehovah's Witness	11	NR	NR	NR	-	-
JUD–Conserv	1	102	115	310	0.1	0.1
JUD–Orth	1	43	50	60	0.0	0.0
JUD–Reform	1	157	277	748	0.1	0.2
LDS–Comm of Christ	5	NR	835	835	0.1	0.3
LDS–L-D Saints	4	NR	NR	2,541	0.4	0.8
LUTH–E.L.C.A.	13	2,382	5,587	7,256	1.2	2.2
LUTH–Luth–MO Synod	17	2,426	4,865	6,472	1.1	2.0
LUTH–Wisc Ev Luth Syn	3	513	802	1,041	0.2	0.3
METH–AME	1	200	350	439	0.1	0.1
METH–AME Zion	2	0	200	251	0.0	0.1
METH–Free Methodist	5	437	297	492	0.1	0.1
METH–Un Methodist	33	5,179	7,807	13,286	2.2	4.0
METH–Wesleyan	16	6,307	1,121	8,201	1.4	2.5
Metro Comm Ch	1	43	33	41	0.0	0.0
Missionary Ch	1	54	48	54	0.0	0.0
Muslim Est	5	1,944	NR	8,252	1.4	2.5
New Apost Ch	1	NR	NR	NR	-	-
Non-denom Chr Chs	50	42,340	50,344	56,337	9.3	17.1
ORTHE–Ant Orth of NA	2	320	NR	900	0.1	0.3
ORTHE–Greek Orthodox	1	115	NR	600	0.1	0.2
ORTHE–Orth Ch in Amer	1	50	NR	100	0.0	0.0
ORTHE–Rus Orth Moscow	1	65	NR	85	0.0	0.0
ORTHO–Coptic Orth Ch	1	30	NR	45	0.0	0.0
PENT–Assemb of God	12	3,083	3,796	5,084	0.8	1.5
PENT–Ch God (Cleve)	3	144	436	547	0.1	0.2
PENT–Ch of God Proph	1	NR	34	43	0.0	0.0
PENT–COGIC	4	165	385	483	0.1	0.1
PENT–Int Foursq Gos	1	21	43	54	0.0	0.0
PENT–Un Pent Ch Intl	6	NR	NR	NR	-	-
PENT–Vineyard	2	450	613	769	0.1	0.2
PRES–Orth Pres Ch	6	1,115	857	1,354	0.2	0.4
PRES–Presb Ch (USA)	7	1,297	2,746	3,447	0.6	1.0
PRES–Presb Ch Amer	1	277	285	381	0.1	0.1
PRES–Ref Pres of NA	1	46	42	59	0.0	0.0
REF–Can Amer Ref	1	NR	NR	NR	-	-
REF–Christian Ref	80	25,424	34,377	43,152	7.2	13.1
REF–Free Ref NA	1	NR	NR	NR	-	-
REF–Heritage Ref	1	NR	447	561	0.1	0.2
REF–Prot Ref Chs	6	1,858	1,250	2,062	0.3	0.6
REF–Ref Ch in Am	38	7,841	13,233	14,993	2.5	4.5
REF–Un Ref Chs N.A.	7	NR	NR	NR	-	-
Salvation Army	2	157	218	1,584	0.3	0.5
Sev Day Adv	16	1,577	2,741	3,154	0.5	1.0
Sikh	1	NR	NR	NR	-	-
Un Breth in Cr	3	649	404	553	0.1	0.2

NR–Not Reported   - Represents no adherents reported.   Percentages may not total 100 due to rounding.

Table 3: Religious Congregations by County and Group: 2010

Religious Group	Number of Congrega-tions	Number of Attendees	Number of Communicant, Confirmed, or Full Members	Adherents		
				Number of Adherents	% of Total Pop.	% of Total Adh.
Un C of Christ	10	1,536	3,557	4,465	0.7	1.4
Unit Univ	1	56	108	139	0.0	0.0
Unity Ch	2	NR	NR	NR	-	-
Zoroastrian	0	NR	NR	8	0.0	0.0
KEWEENAW	**5**	**146**	**313**	**629**	**29.2**	**100.0**
ANG/EPIS–Episcopal	1	40	7	7	0.3	1.1
Bahá'í	0	NR	2	2	0.1	0.3
Catholic	1	NR	NR	257	11.9	40.9
CONG–Consrv Cong Chr	1	0	0	0	0.0	0.0
LUTH–E.L.C.A.	1	84	266	325	15.1	51.7
METH–Un Methodist	1	22	38	38	1.8	6.0
LAKE	**21**	**804**	**860**	**2,116**	**18.3**	**100.0**
Bahá'í	0	NR	3	3	0.0	0.1
BAPT–Reg Bapt Gen As	1	NR	NR	NR	-	-
Catholic	3	NR	NR	824	7.1	38.9
CHR–Chr Ch (Disc)	1	0	0	0	0.0	0.0
CHR–Chs of Christ	1	39	25	35	0.3	1.7
Ind Fund Churches	2	NR	NR	NR	-	-
Jehovah's Witness	1	NR	NR	NR	-	-
LUTH–Luth–MO Synod	1	48	97	106	0.9	5.0
METH–AME	1	20	100	116	1.0	5.5
METH–Un Methodist	3	85	111	178	1.5	8.4
METH–Wesleyan	1	101	66	131	1.1	6.2
Non-denom Chr Chs	2	270	185	350	3.0	16.5
PENT–Assemb of God	1	51	26	87	0.8	4.1
PRES–Presb Ch (USA)	1	120	127	147	1.3	6.9
Sev Day Adv	2	70	120	139	1.2	6.6
LAPEER	**79**	**6,433**	**9,225**	**27,090**	**30.7**	**100.0**
ANG/EPIS–Anglican NA	1	NR	NR	NR	-	-
ANG/EPIS–Episcopal	3	125	209	233	0.3	0.9
Bahá'í	0	NR	4	4	0.0	0.0
BAPT–Amer Bapt USA	1	65	18	22	0.0	0.1
BAPT–Reg Bapt Gen As	2	NR	NR	NR	-	-
BAPT–So Bapt Conv	1	150	140	170	0.2	0.6
Catholic	5	NR	NR	13,538	15.3	50.0
Ch of Nazarene	3	170	187	224	0.3	0.8
CHR–Chr Chs & Chs Cr	2	NR	775	941	1.1	3.5
CHR–Chs of Christ	2	267	287	410	0.5	1.5
Ind Fund Churches	3	NR	NR	NR	-	-
Jehovah's Witness	2	NR	NR	NR	-	-
LDS–Comm of Christ	2	NR	334	334	0.4	1.2
LDS–L-D Saints	1	NR	NR	501	0.6	1.8
LUTH–E.L.C.A.	2	275	507	604	0.7	2.2
LUTH–Luth–MO Synod	4	691	1,591	2,239	2.5	8.3
LUTH–Wisc Ev Luth Syn	2	109	237	288	0.3	1.1
MENN–Amish Undif	0	NR	2	7	0.0	0.0
METH–Free Methodist	1	120	123	123	0.1	0.5
METH–Un Methodist	11	949	1,305	2,298	2.6	8.5
METH–Wesleyan	2	425	243	553	0.6	2.0
Missionary Ch	1	52	45	52	0.1	0.2
New Apost Ch	1	NR	NR	NR	-	-
Non-denom Chr Chs	13	1,620	1,525	2,051	2.3	7.6
PENT–Assemb of God	3	757	398	925	1.0	3.4
PENT–Ch God (Cleve)	1	80	224	272	0.3	1.0
PENT–Elim	1	NR	NR	NR	-	-
PENT–Un Pent Ch Intl	2	NR	NR	NR	-	-
PENT–Vineyard	1	150	170	206	0.2	0.8
PRES–Orth Pres Ch	1	65	64	89	0.1	0.3
PRES–Presb Ch (USA)	1	107	379	460	0.5	1.7
REF–Christian Ref	1	125	198	240	0.3	0.9
Sev Day Adv	2	91	158	182	0.2	0.7
Un C of Christ	1	40	102	124	0.1	0.5
LEELANAU	**28**	**1,232**	**2,318**	**9,087**	**41.9**	**100.0**
ANG/EPIS–Episcopal	1	30	33	39	0.2	0.4
Bahá'í	0	NR	7	7	0.0	0.1
BAPT–So Bapt Conv	1	12	15	17	0.1	0.2
Catholic	8	NR	NR	5,861	27.0	64.5
Ch Cr, Scientst	1	NR	NR	NR	-	-
CHR–Chr Chs & Chs Cr	1	NR	80	93	0.4	1.0
CONG–Cong Chr, NA	1	NR	224	261	1.2	2.9
Evan Cov Ch	1	73	58	95	0.4	1.0
Jehovah's Witness	1	NR	NR	NR	-	-
LUTH–E.L.C.A.	2	153	392	536	2.5	5.9
LUTH–Evan Luth Syn	1	112	203	230	1.1	2.5
LUTH–Luth–MO Synod	3	217	366	429	2.0	4.7
METH–Un Methodist	4	355	557	1,075	5.0	11.8
PRES–Presb Ch (USA)	1	90	31	36	0.2	0.4
REF–Ref Ch in Am	1	115	190	220	1.0	2.4
Un C of Christ	1	75	162	188	0.9	2.1
LENAWEE	**129**	**11,963**	**16,661**	**37,108**	**37.1**	**100.0**
ANG/EPIS–Episcopal	2	48	255	258	0.3	0.7
Bahá'í	0	NR	27	27	0.0	0.1
BAPT–Amer Bapt USA	2	153	312	377	0.4	1.0
BAPT–Free Will Bapt	2	NR	202	244	0.2	0.7
BAPT–Ref Bapt Ch	1	NR	NR	NR	-	-
BAPT–Reg Bapt Gen As	3	NR	NR	NR	-	-
BAPT–So Bapt Conv	6	317	1,287	1,556	1.6	4.2
BRETH–Ch of Brethren	1	24	20	24	0.0	0.1
Catholic	9	NR	NR	13,558	13.6	36.5
Ch Cr, Scientst	1	NR	NR	NR	-	-
Ch of Nazarene	5	836	963	1,103	1.1	3.0
Chr & Miss Al	1	NR	NR	NR	-	-
CHR–Chr Ch (Disc)	1	41	100	121	0.1	0.3
CHR–Chs of Christ	2	365	329	425	0.4	1.1
CONG–Cong Chr, NA	4	NR	225	272	0.3	0.7
Evan Free Ch	2	900	NR	900	0.9	2.4
FRND–Evan Fr Ch Intl	4	247	174	210	0.2	0.6
Ind Fund Churches	2	NR	NR	NR	-	-
Jehovah's Witness	3	NR	NR	NR	-	-
LDS–L-D Saints	1	NR	NR	621	0.6	1.7
LUTH–E.L.C.A.	5	591	1,217	1,809	1.8	4.9
LUTH–Luth–MO Synod	5	744	1,461	1,821	1.8	4.9
LUTH–Wisc Ev Luth Syn	4	502	994	1,178	1.2	3.2
MENN–Fel Evg Ch	1	38	37	45	0.0	0.1
METH–AME	1	0	150	181	0.2	0.5
METH–Free Methodist	1	52	48	52	0.1	0.1
METH–Un Methodist	15	1,000	2,553	3,631	3.6	9.8
METH–Wesleyan	1	64	36	83	0.1	0.2
Missionary Ch	1	48	25	48	0.0	0.1
New Apost Ch	1	NR	NR	NR	-	-
Non-denom Chr Chs	16	3,012	3,340	3,852	3.9	10.4
PENT–Assemb of God	3	1,316	539	1,397	1.4	3.8
PENT–Ch God (Cleve)	4	215	537	649	0.6	1.7
PENT–Ch of God Proph	1	NR	21	25	0.0	0.1
PENT–Intl Pent Holiness	1	160	250	302	0.3	0.8
PENT–Pent Ch of God	1	70	NR	109	0.1	0.3
PENT–Un Pent Ch Intl	2	NR	NR	NR	-	-
PRES–Presb Ch (USA)	6	503	892	1,079	1.1	2.9
Salvation Army	1	39	53	322	0.3	0.9
Sev Day Adv	2	102	178	204	0.2	0.5
Un Breth in Cr	3	460	243	392	0.4	1.1
Un C of Christ	2	116	193	233	0.2	0.6
LIVINGSTON	**101**	**14,228**	**21,452**	**68,590**	**37.9**	**100.0**
ANG/EPIS–Episcopal	3	204	466	495	0.3	0.7
Bahá'í	0	NR	11	11	0.0	0.0
BAPT–Amer Bapt USA	3	293	643	793	0.4	1.2
BAPT–Converge/BGC	1	75	NR	90	0.0	0.1
BAPT–Reg Bapt Gen As	3	NR	NR	NR	-	-
BAPT–So Bapt Conv	3	155	267	329	0.2	0.5
Catholic	9	NR	NR	36,976	20.4	53.9
CGOD–Ch God (Ander)	1	85	NR	85	0.0	0.1
Ch of Nazarene	5	1,415	1,333	3,010	1.7	4.4
CHR–Chr Chs & Chs Cr	2	NR	100	123	0.1	0.2
CHR–Chs of Christ	3	402	319	475	0.3	0.7
Evan Free Ch	1	200	NR	200	0.1	0.3
Jehovah's Witness	3	NR	NR	NR	-	-
LDS–Comm of Christ	1	NR	167	167	0.1	0.2
LDS–L-D Saints	2	NR	NR	968	0.5	1.4
LUTH–Apostolic Luth	1	NR	NR	NR	-	-

NR–Not Reported   - Represents no adherents reported.   Percentages may not total 100 due to rounding.

Table 3: Religious Congregations by County and Group: 2010

Religious Group	Number of Congrega- tions	Number of Attendees	Number of Communicant, Confirmed, or Full Members	Adherents		
				Number of Adherents	% of Total Pop.	% of Total Adh.
LUTH–E.L.C.A.	6	1,438	2,844	3,999	2.2	5.8
LUTH–Luth-MO Synod	6	1,639	3,162	4,219	2.3	6.2
LUTH–Wisc Ev Luth Syn	1	89	225	287	0.2	0.4
MENN–Mennonite USA	1	13	9	11	0.0	0.0
METH–AME	1	0	100	123	0.1	0.2
METH–Free Methodist	2	108	69	108	0.1	0.2
METH–Un Methodist	9	1,139	2,141	3,443	1.9	5.0
METH–Wesleyan	1	71	38	92	0.1	0.1
Non-denom Chr Chs	12	4,550	4,615	5,707	3.2	8.3
PENT–Assemb of God	3	678	365	974	0.5	1.4
PENT–Ch God (Cleve)	2	112	295	364	0.2	0.5
PENT–Int Foursq Gos	1	0	24	30	0.0	0.0
PENT–Un Pent Ch Intl	2	NR	NR	NR	-	-
PRES–Evan Presby Ch	2	NR	2,129	2,626	1.5	3.8
PRES–Orth Pres Ch	1	54	47	59	0.0	0.1
PRES–Presb Ch (USA)	3	560	1,231	1,518	0.8	2.2
PRES–Presb Ch Amer	1	89	52	81	0.0	0.1
REF–Comm Ref Evan	1	NR	NR	NR	-	-
Salvation Army	1	50	66	230	0.1	0.3
Sev Day Adv	1	49	85	98	0.1	0.1
Un Breth in Cr	1	565	326	481	0.3	0.7
Un C of Christ	1	140	255	315	0.2	0.5
Unit Univ	1	55	68	102	0.1	0.1
Zoroastrian	0	NR	NR	1	0.0	0.0
LUCE	**16**	**662**	**851**	**1,958**	**29.5**	**100.0**
ANG/EPIS–Episcopal	1	10	31	31	0.5	1.6
Bahá'í	0	NR	1	1	0.0	0.1
BAPT–Reg Bapt Gen As	1	NR	NR	NR	-	-
BAPT–So Bapt Conv	1	35	47	54	0.8	2.8
Catholic	1	NR	NR	593	8.9	30.3
CHR–Chs of Christ	1	25	25	30	0.5	1.5
Jehovah's Witness	1	NR	NR	NR	-	-
LUTH–E.L.C.A.	1	57	248	370	5.6	18.9
LUTH–Luth-MO Synod	1	50	51	150	2.3	7.7
METH–Un Methodist	2	65	137	186	2.8	9.5
Non-denom Chr Chs	2	180	180	226	3.4	11.5
PENT–Assemb of God	1	100	37	100	1.5	5.1
PENT–Pent Ch of God	1	70	NR	109	1.6	5.6
PRES–Presb Ch (USA)	1	54	67	77	1.2	3.9
Sev Day Adv	1	16	27	31	0.5	1.6
MACKINAC	**35**	**1,334**	**1,534**	**6,332**	**57.0**	**100.0**
ANG/EPIS–Episcopal	4	89	51	57	0.5	0.9
Bahá'í	0	NR	1	1	0.0	0.0
BAPT–Reg Bapt Gen As	2	NR	NR	NR	-	-
Catholic	6	NR	NR	4,046	36.4	63.9
CONG–Cong Chr, NA	1	NR	83	96	0.9	1.5
Evan Free Ch	1	43	NR	43	0.4	0.7
Jehovah's Witness	1	NR	NR	NR	-	-
LUTH–E.L.C.A.	4	160	354	459	4.1	7.2
LUTH–Luth-MO Synod	1	71	140	149	1.3	2.4
LUTH–Wisc Ev Luth Syn	1	6	12	15	0.1	0.2
MENN–Amish Undif	1	NR	24	65	0.6	1.0
MENN–Mennonite USA	3	153	115	133	1.2	2.1
METH–Un Methodist	2	125	232	397	3.6	6.3
Non-denom Chr Chs	5	600	445	750	6.7	11.8
PENT–Assemb of God	1	32	16	51	0.5	0.8
PRES–Presb Ch (USA)	2	55	61	70	0.6	1.1
MACOMB	**356**	**48,417**	**72,849**	**362,120**	**43.1**	**100.0**
ANG/EPIS–Anglican NA	1	NR	NR	NR	-	-
ANG/EPIS–Episcopal	5	298	464	1,003	0.1	0.3
Bahá'í	0	NR	91	91	0.0	0.0
BAPT–Amer Bapt Assn	3	NR	200	242	0.0	0.1
BAPT–Amer Bapt USA	2	220	235	284	0.0	0.1
BAPT–Consrv Bapt	1	NR	NR	NR	-	-
BAPT–Free Will Bapt	3	NR	303	367	0.0	0.1
BAPT–Ind Bapt Flwsp Intl	2	NR	NR	NR	-	-
BAPT–N Am Bapt Conf	6	NR	953	1,154	0.1	0.3
BAPT–Natl Mis Bapt Conv	1	75	105	127	0.0	0.0
BAPT–NBC USA	2	180	300	363	0.0	0.1
BAPT–So Bapt Conv	22	2,918	5,566	6,738	0.8	1.9

Religious Group	Number of Congrega- tions	Number of Attendees	Number of Communicant, Confirmed, or Full Members	Adherents		
				Number of Adherents	% of Total Pop.	% of Total Adh.
BUDD–Mahayana	3	NR	NR	741	0.1	0.2
BUDD–Theravada	1	NR	NR	1,364	0.2	0.4
Calv Chpl	1	NR	NR	NR	-	-
Catholic	56	NR	NR	249,439	29.7	68.9
CGOD–Ch God (Ander)	4	180	NR	180	0.0	0.0
Ch Christ Chr Union	1	NR	NR	NR	-	-
Ch of Nazarene	7	2,046	2,091	3,095	0.4	0.9
Chr & Miss Al	3	639	668	780	0.1	0.2
CHR–Chr Chs & Chs Cr	1	NR	600	726	0.1	0.2
CHR–Chs of Christ	10	1,600	1,700	2,078	0.2	0.6
Christian Brethren	2	NR	NR	NR	-	-
CONG–Consrv Cong Chr	1	31	51	62	0.0	0.0
HINDU–Trad Temples	1	NR	NR	450	0.1	0.1
Jehovah's Witness	7	NR	NR	NR	-	-
LDS–Comm of Christ	2	NR	334	334	0.0	0.1
LDS–L-D Saints	3	NR	NR	1,628	0.2	0.4
LUTH–E.L.C.A.	20	2,412	7,629	9,668	1.1	2.7
LUTH–Luth Ch-Am Asc	1	NR	NR	NR	-	-
LUTH–Luth Cong Msn Chr	1	230	719	870	0.1	0.2
LUTH–Luth-MO Synod	26	10,850	21,508	29,359	3.5	8.1
LUTH–Wisc Ev Luth Syn	3	316	544	708	0.1	0.2
METH–AME	4	75	500	605	0.1	0.2
METH–AME Zion	1	0	150	182	0.0	0.1
METH–C.M.E.	1	100	150	182	0.0	0.1
METH–Un Methodist	18	1,847	3,608	5,251	0.6	1.5
METH–Wesleyan	2	883	288	1,148	0.1	0.3
Missionary Ch	6	829	306	829	0.1	0.2
Muslim Est	4	1,511	NR	2,863	0.3	0.8
New Apost Ch	5	NR	NR	NR	-	-
Non-denom Chr Chs	38	13,448	14,905	17,213	2.0	4.8
OCATH–Pol Natl Cath	1	NR	NR	NR	-	-
ORTHE–Bulgar Orth USA	1	40	NR	100	0.0	0.0
ORTHE–Greek Orthodox	2	800	NR	4,500	0.5	1.2
ORTHE–Macedonian Orth	1	325	NR	2,975	0.4	0.8
ORTHE–Orth Ch in Amer	1	400	NR	1,000	0.1	0.3
ORTHE–Serb Orth USA	1	120	NR	350	0.0	0.1
PENT–Assemb of God	17	2,665	1,378	4,011	0.5	1.1
PENT–Ch God (Cleve)	4	496	1,354	1,639	0.2	0.5
PENT–Ch of God Proph	1	NR	49	59	0.0	0.0
PENT–COGIC	2	200	1,000	1,211	0.1	0.3
PENT–Elim	2	NR	NR	NR	-	-
PENT–Full Gosp Bapt	1	NR	NR	NR	-	-
PENT–I F Chr Assmbl	3	NR	NR	NR	-	-
PENT–Int Foursq Gos	2	142	83	100	0.0	0.0
PENT–Un Pent Ch Intl	5	NR	NR	NR	-	-
PENT–Vineyard	1	200	200	242	0.0	0.1
PRES–Cumber Presb	1	NR	6	18	0.0	0.0
PRES–Presb Ch (USA)	10	1,268	2,333	2,824	0.3	0.8
PRES–Presb Ch Amer	1	0	0	0	0.0	0.0
REF–Ref Ch in Am	1	32	59	75	0.0	0.0
Salvation Army	2	133	175	194	0.0	0.1
Sev Day Adv	4	286	496	571	0.1	0.2
Un C of Christ	9	622	1,748	2,116	0.3	0.6
Unity Ch	2	NR	NR	NR	-	-
Zoroastrian	0	NR	NR	11	0.0	0.0
MANISTEE	**40**	**1,883**	**3,295**	**10,091**	**40.8**	**100.0**
ANG/EPIS–Episcopal	1	42	112	116	0.5	1.1
Bahá'í	0	NR	5	5	0.0	0.0
BAPT–Converge/BGC	1	75	NR	90	0.4	0.9
BAPT–Reg Bapt Gen As	2	NR	NR	NR	-	-
BRETH–Ch of Brethren	3	111	181	211	0.9	2.1
Catholic	5	NR	NR	5,106	20.6	50.6
CHR–Chr Ch (Disc)	1	155	260	303	1.2	3.0
CHR–Chr Chs & Chs Cr	1	NR	24	28	0.1	0.3
Evan Cov Ch	1	283	194	368	1.5	3.6
Jehovah's Witness	2	NR	NR	NR	-	-
LDS–L-D Saints	1	NR	NR	106	0.4	1.1
LUTH–E.L.C.A.	2	181	483	733	3.0	7.3
LUTH–Luth-MO Synod	5	380	1,019	1,405	5.7	13.9
LUTH–Nor Amer Luth C	1	NR	NR	NR	-	-
LUTH–Wisc Ev Luth Syn	1	38	67	74	0.3	0.7
METH–Un Methodist	4	293	490	898	3.6	8.9
Non-denom Chr Chs	2	95	85	122	0.5	1.2

NR–Not Reported - Represents no adherents reported. Percentages may not total 100 due to rounding.

Table 3: Religious Congregations by County and Group: 2010

Religious Group	Number of Congrega-tions	Number of Attendees	Number of Communicant, Confirmed, or Full Members	Adherents: Number of Adherents	Adherents: % of Total Pop.	Adherents: % of Total Adh.
PENT–Assemb of God	1	38	30	128	0.5	1.3
PENT–Un Pent Ch Intl	1	NR	NR	NR	-	-
PRES–Orth Pres Ch	1	17	11	15	0.1	0.1
Salvation Army	1	28	34	34	0.1	0.3
Sev Day Adv	1	35	61	70	0.3	0.7
Un C of Christ	2	112	239	279	1.1	2.8
MARQUETTE	**96**	**4,965**	**11,842**	**32,136**	**47.9**	**100.0**
ANG/EPIS–Episcopal	5	127	459	517	0.8	1.6
Bahá'í	1	NR	65	65	0.1	0.2
BAPT–Converge/BGC	3	225	NR	270	0.4	0.8
BAPT–Free Will Bapt	1	NR	101	118	0.2	0.4
BAPT–Reg Bapt Gen As	1	NR	NR	NR	-	-
BAPT–So Bapt Conv	3	97	119	139	0.2	0.4
BUDD–Mahayana	1	NR	NR	102	0.2	0.3
Catholic	13	NR	NR	15,626	23.3	48.6
Ch of Nazarene	1	28	14	36	0.1	0.1
CHR–Chr Chs & Chs Cr	1	NR	450	524	0.8	1.6
CHR–Chs of Christ	1	95	74	123	0.2	0.4
Evan Cov Ch	2	102	152	133	0.2	0.4
FRND–Fr Gen Cf	1	NR	8	9	0.0	0.0
Ind Fund Churches	1	NR	NR	NR	-	-
Jehovah's Witness	2	NR	NR	NR	-	-
JUD–Reform	1	22	39	105	0.2	0.3
LDS–L-D Saints	1	NR	NR	447	0.7	1.4
LUTH–Apostolic Luth	3	NR	NR	NR	-	-
LUTH–Assoc Free Luth	1	NR	NR	NR	-	-
LUTH–Ch Luth Conf	1	NR	NR	NR	-	-
LUTH–E.L.C.A.	13	1,420	5,383	6,536	9.7	20.3
LUTH–Luth Cong Msn Chr	1	40	56	65	0.1	0.2
LUTH–Luth–MO Synod	3	704	1,548	2,197	3.3	6.8
LUTH–Wisc Ev Luth Syn	2	34	106	113	0.2	0.4
METH–Un Methodist	9	663	1,761	2,542	3.8	7.9
Missionary Ch	1	55	27	55	0.1	0.2
New Apost Ch	1	NR	NR	NR	-	-
Non-denom Chr Chs	7	516	530	644	1.0	2.0
ORTHE–Greek Orthodox	1	10	NR	45	0.1	0.1
PENT–Assemb of God	2	394	218	497	0.7	1.5
PENT–Ch God (Cleve)	1	8	16	19	0.0	0.1
PENT–Un Pent Ch Intl	2	NR	NR	NR	-	-
PRES–Presb Ch (USA)	3	238	437	509	0.8	1.6
REF–Christian Ref	1	50	50	58	0.1	0.2
Salvation Army	2	55	104	478	0.7	1.5
Sev Day Adv	1	35	61	70	0.1	0.2
Unit Univ	1	47	64	94	0.1	0.3
Unity Ch	1	NR	NR	NR	-	-
MASON	**56**	**3,638**	**5,323**	**12,700**	**44.2**	**100.0**
ANG/EPIS–Anglican NA	1	NR	NR	NR	-	-
ANG/EPIS–Episcopal	1	32	51	59	0.2	0.5
Bahá'í	0	NR	38	38	0.1	0.3
BAPT–Converge/BGC	3	550	NR	660	2.3	5.2
BAPT–Reg Bapt Gen As	2	NR	NR	NR	-	-
BAPT–So Bapt Conv	1	15	40	48	0.2	0.4
BRETH–Ch of Brethren	1	40	42	50	0.2	0.4
BUDD–Mahayana	1	NR	NR	20	0.1	0.2
Calv Chpl	1	NR	NR	NR	-	-
Catholic	6	NR	NR	4,385	15.3	34.5
Ch Cr, Scientst	1	NR	NR	NR	-	-
Ch of Nazarene	1	0	81	81	0.3	0.6
CHR–Chr Chs & Chs Cr	1	NR	50	60	0.2	0.5
CHR–Chs of Christ	1	70	65	80	0.3	0.6
CONG–Cong Chr Add'l	1	NR	559	667	2.3	5.3
Evan Cov Ch	2	161	139	209	0.7	1.6
Evan Free Ch	1	160	NR	160	0.6	1.3
Jehovah's Witness	1	NR	NR	NR	-	-
LDS–Comm of Christ	1	NR	167	167	0.6	1.3
LDS–L-D Saints	1	NR	NR	205	0.7	1.6
LUTH–E.L.C.A.	3	216	545	864	3.0	6.8
LUTH–Luth–MO Synod	3	362	948	1,177	4.1	9.3
LUTH–Wisc Ev Luth Syn	1	25	79	97	0.3	0.8
MENN–Amish Undif	1	NR	11	38	0.1	0.3
METH–Free Methodist	1	68	58	68	0.2	0.5
METH–Un Methodist	5	457	757	1,341	4.7	10.6
METH–Wesleyan	1	30	14	39	0.1	0.3
Non-denom Chr Chs	6	770	840	1,037	3.6	8.2
PENT–Assemb of God	1	120	63	150	0.5	1.2
PENT–Un Pent Ch Intl	1	NR	NR	NR	-	-
REF–Christian Ref	1	70	51	61	0.2	0.5
REF–Ref Ch in Am	1	358	529	650	2.3	5.1
Salvation Army	1	26	46	125	0.4	1.0
Sev Day Adv	1	42	72	83	0.3	0.7
Unit Univ	1	66	78	81	0.3	0.6
MECOSTA	**59**	**4,095**	**5,653**	**13,098**	**30.6**	**100.0**
ANG/EPIS–Episcopal	1	22	35	43	0.1	0.3
Bahá'í	0	NR	16	16	0.0	0.1
BAPT–Consrv Bapt	1	NR	NR	NR	-	-
BAPT–Reg Bapt Gen As	2	NR	NR	NR	-	-
BAPT–So Bapt Conv	1	65	98	116	0.3	0.9
BRETH–Ch of Brethren	1	0	0	0	0.0	0.0
Catholic	4	NR	NR	4,796	11.2	36.6
CGOD–Ch God (Ander)	2	146	NR	146	0.3	1.1
Ch of Nazarene	1	41	40	58	0.1	0.4
CHR–Chr Chs & Chs Cr	3	NR	190	224	0.5	1.7
CHR–Chs of Christ	1	25	25	30	0.1	0.2
Evan Free Ch	1	556	NR	556	1.3	4.2
Jehovah's Witness	2	NR	NR	NR	-	-
LDS–Comm of Christ	1	NR	167	167	0.4	1.3
LDS–L-D Saints	1	NR	NR	267	0.6	2.0
LUTH–E.L.C.A.	1	101	204	235	0.5	1.8
LUTH–Luth–MO Synod	2	511	975	1,268	3.0	9.7
LUTH–Wisc Ev Luth Syn	2	112	213	283	0.7	2.2
MENN–Amish Undif	5	NR	316	719	1.7	5.5
METH–Free Methodist	4	258	191	258	0.6	2.0
METH–Un Methodist	8	682	1,265	1,458	3.4	11.1
METH–Wesleyan	2	156	108	203	0.5	1.5
Non-denom Chr Chs	4	811	811	1,014	2.4	7.7
PENT–Assemb of God	2	110	66	146	0.3	1.1
PENT–Ch God (Cleve)	1	68	135	159	0.4	1.2
PENT–Un Pent Ch Intl	1	NR	NR	NR	-	-
PRES–Presb Ch (USA)	1	134	207	244	0.6	1.9
REF–Christian Ref	1	120	135	159	0.4	1.2
Salvation Army	1	14	23	23	0.1	0.2
Sev Day Adv	1	29	50	58	0.1	0.4
Un C of Christ	1	134	383	452	1.1	3.5
MENOMINEE	**40**	**2,273**	**3,947**	**14,154**	**58.9**	**100.0**
ANG/EPIS–Episcopal	2	24	50	76	0.3	0.5
Bahá'í	0	NR	2	2	0.0	0.0
BAPT–Converge/BGC	1	400	NR	480	2.0	3.4
BAPT–So Bapt Conv	1	20	30	36	0.1	0.3
Catholic	7	NR	NR	8,038	33.5	56.8
CHR–Chs of Christ	1	15	15	18	0.1	0.1
Evan Cov Ch	4	188	239	245	1.0	1.7
Evan Free Ch	1	175	NR	175	0.7	1.2
Jehovah's Witness	1	NR	NR	NR	-	-
LDS–L-D Saints	1	NR	NR	229	1.0	1.6
LUTH–E.L.C.A.	5	475	1,896	2,598	10.8	18.4
LUTH–Wisc Ev Luth Syn	4	265	610	753	3.1	5.3
METH–Un Methodist	3	169	400	469	2.0	3.3
MORAV–Morav Ch-North	1	29	38	38	0.2	0.3
Non-denom Chr Chs	2	170	75	213	0.9	1.5
PENT–Assemb of God	2	99	44	143	0.6	1.0
PENT–Ch God (Cleve)	1	9	47	56	0.2	0.4
PRES–Presb Ch (USA)	1	87	243	288	1.2	2.0
Sev Day Adv	2	148	258	297	1.2	2.1
MIDLAND	**93**	**12,030**	**16,579**	**38,960**	**46.6**	**100.0**
ANG/EPIS–Episcopal	2	225	611	611	0.7	1.6
Bahá'í	1	NR	28	28	0.0	0.1
BAPT–Amer Bapt USA	1	159	420	510	0.6	1.3
BAPT–Ind Bapt Flwsp Intl	1	NR	NR	NR	-	-
BAPT–Reg Bapt Gen As	2	NR	NR	NR	-	-
BAPT–So Bapt Conv	3	254	426	517	0.6	1.3
BRETH–Ch of Brethren	1	37	39	47	0.1	0.1

NR–Not Reported   - Represents no adherents reported.   Percentages may not total 100 due to rounding.

Table 3: Religious Congregations by County and Group: 2010

Religious Group	Number of Congregations	Number of Attendees	Number of Communicant, Confirmed, or Full Members	Adherents: Number of Adherents	Adherents: % of Total Pop.	Adherents: % of Total Adh.
Catholic	6	NR	NR	12,271	14.7	31.5
CGOD–Ch God (Ander)	6	695	NR	695	0.8	1.8
Ch Cr, Scientist	1	NR	NR	NR	-	-
Ch of Nazarene	3	251	349	377	0.5	1.0
CHR–Chr Chs & Chs Cr	1	NR	198	240	0.3	0.6
CHR–Chs of Christ	1	160	165	189	0.2	0.5
Evan Free Ch	2	1,560	NR	1,560	1.9	4.0
Grace Gosp Fel	1	NR	NR	NR	-	-
Jehovah's Witness	1	NR	NR	NR	-	-
LDS–Comm of Christ	3	NR	501	501	0.6	1.3
LDS–L-D Saints	2	NR	NR	879	1.1	2.3
LUTH–E.L.C.A.	2	521	1,488	1,902	2.3	4.9
LUTH–Evan Luth Syn	1	87	242	320	0.4	0.8
LUTH–Luth-MO Synod	5	1,462	2,571	3,834	4.6	9.8
LUTH–Wisc Ev Luth Syn	1	154	336	416	0.5	1.1
MENN–Mennonite USA	1	62	60	73	0.1	0.2
METH–Free Methodist	2	448	184	448	0.5	1.1
METH–Un Methodist	11	1,277	3,292	4,784	5.7	12.3
METH–Wesleyan	4	416	257	542	0.6	1.4
Metro Comm Ch	1	10	15	18	0.0	0.0
Missionary Ch	1	124	65	124	0.1	0.3
Non-denom Chr Chs	8	1,415	1,385	1,779	2.1	4.6
PENT–Assemb of God	3	1,036	513	1,583	1.9	4.1
PENT–Ch God (Cleve)	1	100	398	483	0.6	1.2
PENT–Pent Ch of God	2	140	NR	217	0.3	0.6
PENT–Un Pent Ch Intl	2	NR	NR	NR	-	-
PENT–Vineyard	1	325	450	546	0.7	1.4
PRES–Presb Ch (USA)	2	460	1,444	1,753	2.1	4.5
PRES–Presb Ch Amer	1	68	75	89	0.1	0.2
REF–Ref Ch in Am	1	185	269	349	0.4	0.9
Salvation Army	1	39	69	394	0.5	1.0
Sev Day Adv	2	166	287	331	0.4	0.8
Un C of Christ	1	115	315	382	0.5	1.0
Unit Univ	1	79	127	168	0.2	0.4
MISSAUKEE	**28**	**2,590**	**3,726**	**5,735**	**38.6**	**100.0**
Bahá'í	0	NR	1	1	0.0	0.0
BAPT–Reg Bapt Gen As	1	NR	NR	NR	-	-
BAPT–So Bapt Conv	1	25	16	19	0.1	0.3
Catholic	1	NR	NR	830	5.6	14.5
CHR–Chr Chs & Chs Cr	1	NR	60	73	0.5	1.3
Jehovah's Witness	1	NR	NR	NR	-	-
LUTH–E.L.C.A.	1	91	280	375	2.5	6.5
MENN–Amish Undif	1	NR	61	196	1.3	3.4
METH–Free Methodist	1	23	18	23	0.2	0.4
METH–Un Methodist	3	191	302	549	3.7	9.6
Non-denom Chr Chs	2	430	395	538	3.6	9.4
PENT–Assemb of God	1	30	17	33	0.2	0.6
PRES–Evan Presby Ch	1	NR	59	72	0.5	1.3
PRES–Presb Ch (USA)	2	68	92	112	0.8	2.0
REF–Christian Ref	7	1,265	1,650	2,010	13.5	35.0
REF–Ref Ch in Am	3	437	724	845	5.7	14.7
Sev Day Adv	1	30	51	59	0.4	1.0
MONROE	**150**	**15,086**	**25,568**	**69,122**	**45.5**	**100.0**
ANG/EPIS–Episcopal	1	39	71	73	0.0	0.1
Bahá'í	0	NR	13	13	0.0	0.0
BAPT–Amer Bapt USA	3	418	486	593	0.4	0.9
BAPT–Converge/BGC	2	150	NR	180	0.1	0.3
BAPT–Free Will Bapt	1	NR	101	123	0.1	0.2
BAPT–Natl Mis Bapt Conv	1	0	150	183	0.1	0.3
BAPT–Reg Bapt Gen As	2	NR	NR	NR	-	-
BAPT–So Bapt Conv	23	2,567	5,348	6,523	4.3	9.4
Catholic	14	NR	NR	31,981	21.0	46.3
CGOD–Ch God (Ander)	1	45	NR	45	0.0	0.1
Ch Cr, Scientist	1	NR	NR	NR	-	-
Ch God (7th Day)	1	NR	NR	NR	-	-
Ch of Nazarene	3	408	436	561	0.4	0.8
Chr & Miss Al	3	670	341	1,020	0.7	1.5
CHR–Chr Chs & Chs Cr	2	NR	250	305	0.2	0.4
CHR–Chs of Christ	3	230	225	285	0.2	0.4
Jehovah's Witness	3	NR	NR	NR	-	-
LDS–Comm of Christ	1	NR	167	167	0.1	0.2
LDS–L-D Saints	1	NR	NR	566	0.4	0.8
LUTH–E.L.C.A.	9	1,091	3,041	3,982	2.6	5.8
LUTH–Luth Cong Msn Chr	2	316	945	1,153	0.8	1.7
LUTH–Luth-MO Synod	8	1,333	3,449	4,438	2.9	6.4
LUTH–Wisc Ev Luth Syn	3	355	783	969	0.6	1.4
METH–AME	1	0	100	122	0.1	0.2
METH–Free Methodist	2	1,410	422	1,410	0.9	2.0
METH–Un Methodist	17	1,316	2,819	4,122	2.7	6.0
METH–Wesleyan	3	294	233	382	0.3	0.6
Muslim Est	1	411	NR	1,563	1.0	2.3
Non-denom Chr Chs	11	1,408	2,008	2,137	1.4	3.1
OCATH–Pol Natl Cath	1	NR	NR	NR	-	-
ORTHE–Serb Orth USA	1	32	NR	140	0.1	0.2
PENT–Assemb of God	4	879	371	1,049	0.7	1.5
PENT–Ch God (Cleve)	4	816	2,499	3,048	2.0	4.4
PENT–Ch God Mtn Asm	2	NR	NR	NR	-	-
PENT–COGIC	1	0	150	183	0.1	0.3
PENT–Open Bible Std	2	388	NR	388	0.3	0.6
PENT–Un Pent Ch Intl	2	NR	NR	NR	-	-
PENT–Vineyard	2	260	400	488	0.3	0.7
PRES–Presb Ch (USA)	4	51	483	589	0.4	0.9
Salvation Army	1	65	82	122	0.1	0.2
Sev Day Adv	2	91	158	182	0.1	0.3
Un Breth in Cr	1	43	37	37	0.0	0.1
MONTCALM	**102**	**6,739**	**8,946**	**19,557**	**30.9**	**100.0**
ANG/EPIS–Episcopal	1	50	70	115	0.2	0.6
Bahá'í	0	NR	3	3	0.0	0.0
BAPT–Amer Bapt USA	1	15	50	61	0.1	0.3
BAPT–Reg Bapt Gen As	6	NR	NR	NR	-	-
BRETH–Ch of Brethren	1	27	30	37	0.1	0.2
Catholic	8	NR	NR	5,258	8.3	26.9
CGOD–Ch God (Ander)	3	239	NR	239	0.4	1.2
CGOD–Ches God-Gen Con	1	60	45	55	0.1	0.3
Ch of Nazarene	1	56	69	102	0.2	0.5
CHR–Chr Ch (Disc)	1	53	89	109	0.2	0.6
CHR–Chr Chs & Chs Cr	3	NR	125	153	0.2	0.8
CHR–Chs of Christ	2	18	20	22	0.0	0.1
CONG–Cong Chr, NA	3	NR	597	730	1.2	3.7
Evan Assoc RCC	1	NR	NR	NR	-	-
Evan Free Ch	1	240	NR	240	0.4	1.2
Ind Fund Churches	3	NR	NR	NR	-	-
Jehovah's Witness	3	NR	NR	NR	-	-
LDS–Comm of Christ	2	NR	334	334	0.5	1.7
LDS–L-D Saints	1	NR	NR	610	1.0	3.1
LUTH–E.L.C.A.	5	331	896	1,191	1.9	6.1
LUTH–Luth-MO Synod	5	363	645	796	1.3	4.1
LUTH–Nor Amer Luth C	1	NR	NR	NR	-	-
MENN–Amish Undif	6	NR	146	394	0.6	2.0
MENN–CG in Cr (Menn)	1	NR	106	130	0.2	0.7
MENN–Mennonite USA	1	45	46	56	0.1	0.3
METH–Free Methodist	2	168	110	168	0.3	0.9
METH–Un Methodist	10	985	1,905	2,785	4.4	14.2
METH–Wesleyan	4	994	360	1,293	2.0	6.6
Missionary Ch	1	16	19	19	0.0	0.1
Non-denom Chr Chs	8	1,840	1,390	2,300	3.6	11.8
PENT–Assemb of God	2	78	43	135	0.2	0.7
PENT–Ch God (Cleve)	1	17	70	86	0.1	0.4
PENT–Int Pent C Chr	1	29	18	39	0.1	0.2
PENT–Intl Pent Holiness	1	139	188	230	0.4	1.2
PENT–Pent Ch of God	1	70	NR	109	0.2	0.6
REF–Christian Ref	1	220	325	397	0.6	2.0
REF–Comm Ref Evan	1	NR	NR	NR	-	-
Sev Day Adv	5	436	757	871	1.4	4.5
Un Breth in Cr	1	90	152	77	0.1	0.4
Un C of Christ	2	160	338	413	0.7	2.1
MONTMORENCY	**21**	**964**	**1,609**	**2,756**	**28.2**	**100.0**
ANG/EPIS–Episcopal	2	45	100	124	1.3	4.5
Bahá'í	0	NR	1	1	0.0	0.0
BAPT–So Bapt Conv	2	41	57	65	0.7	2.4
Catholic	3	NR	NR	764	7.8	27.7
CHR–Chs of Christ	1	50	55	68	0.7	2.5

NR–Not Reported - Represents no adherents reported. Percentages may not total 100 due to rounding.

Table 3: Religious Congregations by County and Group: 2010

Religious Group	Number of Congrega-tions	Number of Attendees	Number of Communicant, Confirmed, or Full Members	Adherents: Number of Adherents	Adherents: % of Total Pop.	Adherents: % of Total Adh.
CONG–Consrv Cong Chr	1	90	125	143	1.5	5.2
Jehovah's Witness	1	NR	NR	NR	-	-
LUTH–Evan Luth Syn	1	35	47	67	0.7	2.4
LUTH–Luth-MO Synod	2	266	687	824	8.4	29.9
METH–Free Methodist	2	67	60	67	0.7	2.4
METH–Un Methodist	1	59	117	168	1.7	6.1
Non-denom Chr Chs	2	110	100	138	1.4	5.0
PENT–Assemb of God	1	60	45	80	0.8	2.9
Un C of Christ	2	141	215	247	2.5	9.0
MUSKEGON	**187**	**18,236**	**25,547**	**51,929**	**30.2**	**100.0**
ANG/EPIS–Episcopal	4	229	517	532	0.3	1.0
Bahá'í	0	NR	97	97	0.1	0.2
BAPT–Amer Bapt USA	3	308	662	817	0.5	1.6
BAPT–Consrv Bapt	1	NR	NR	NR	-	-
BAPT–Converge/BGC	9	675	NR	810	0.5	1.6
BAPT–NBC Amer	3	700	1,350	1,666	1.0	3.2
BAPT–NBC USA	1	225	500	617	0.4	1.2
BAPT–NT Ind Bapt	1	NR	NR	NR	-	-
BAPT–Reg Bapt Gen As	6	NR	NR	NR	-	-
BAPT–So Bapt Conv	1	15	30	37	0.0	0.1
BRETH–Ch of Brethren	1	24	28	35	0.0	0.1
Calv Chpl	1	NR	NR	NR	-	-
Catholic	11	NR	NR	13,687	7.9	26.4
CGOD–Ch God (Ander)	2	124	NR	124	0.1	0.2
Ch Cr, Scientst	1	NR	NR	NR	-	-
Ch of Nazarene	3	433	562	650	0.4	1.3
Chr & Miss Al	2	80	95	145	0.1	0.3
CHR–Chr Ch (Disc)	2	83	192	237	0.1	0.5
CHR–Chr Chs & Chs Cr	2	NR	415	512	0.3	1.0
CHR–Chs of Christ	2	170	160	215	0.1	0.4
Christian Brethren	1	NR	NR	NR	-	-
CONG–Cong Chr, NA	2	NR	171	211	0.1	0.4
CONG–Consrv Cong Chr	1	99	94	116	0.1	0.2
Evan Cov Ch	5	1,326	1,058	1,723	1.0	3.3
Evan Free Ch	1	300	NR	300	0.2	0.6
Grace Gosp Fel	2	NR	NR	NR	-	-
Ind Fund Churches	5	NR	NR	NR	-	-
Jehovah's Witness	3	NR	NR	NR	-	-
JUD–Reform	1	35	61	165	0.1	0.3
LDS–Comm of Christ	1	NR	167	167	0.1	0.3
LDS–L-D Saints	1	NR	NR	394	0.2	0.8
LUTH–E.L.C.A.	8	818	1,943	2,678	1.6	5.2
LUTH–Evan Luth Syn	1	20	70	88	0.1	0.2
LUTH–Luth-MO Synod	5	930	2,355	3,163	1.8	6.1
LUTH–Wisc Ev Luth Syn	1	96	188	271	0.2	0.5
MENN–Amish Undif	2	NR	65	160	0.1	0.3
METH–AME	1	100	200	247	0.1	0.5
METH–AME Zion	1	0	60	74	0.0	0.1
METH–Free Methodist	3	305	253	323	0.2	0.6
METH–Un Methodist	13	1,398	2,563	3,181	1.8	6.1
METH–Wesleyan	5	432	223	561	0.3	1.1
Missionary Ch	1	90	88	90	0.1	0.2
Muslim Est	1	411	NR	1,563	0.9	3.0
Non-denom Chr Chs	16	2,570	2,050	3,277	1.9	6.3
ORTHE–Greek Orthodox	1	120	NR	350	0.2	0.7
PENT–Assemb of God	6	871	458	1,605	0.9	3.1
PENT–Ch God (Cleve)	2	441	669	826	0.5	1.6
PENT–COGIC	4	150	575	710	0.4	1.4
PENT–Full Gosp Bapt	1	NR	NR	NR	-	-
PENT–Un Pent Ch Intl	4	NR	NR	NR	-	-
PENT–Vineyard	1	103	125	154	0.1	0.3
PRES–Evan Presby Ch	1	NR	34	42	0.0	0.1
PRES–Presb Ch (USA)	1	122	288	355	0.2	0.7
REF–Christian Ref	8	1,256	1,615	1,993	1.2	3.8
REF–Ref Ch in Am	13	2,515	4,228	4,997	2.9	9.6
Salvation Army	1	53	116	482	0.3	0.9
Sev Day Adv	2	180	314	361	0.2	0.7
Un C of Christ	3	381	845	1,043	0.6	2.0
Unit Univ	1	48	63	78	0.0	0.2
Unity Ch	1	NR	NR	NR	-	-
NEWAYGO	**72**	**5,701**	**6,963**	**13,728**	**28.3**	**100.0**
ANG/EPIS–Episcopal	2	93	173	187	0.4	1.4
Bahá'í	0	NR	8	8	0.0	0.1
BAPT–Reg Bapt Gen As	4	NR	NR	NR	-	-
BAPT–S-D Baptist Gen Con	1	57	57	70	0.1	0.5
BAPT–So Bapt Conv	2	20	20	25	0.1	0.2
Catholic	5	NR	NR	3,242	6.7	23.6
Ch of Nazarene	1	43	30	43	0.1	0.3
CHR–Chr Ch (Disc)	1	58	152	187	0.4	1.4
CHR–Chr Chs & Chs Cr	1	NR	150	184	0.4	1.3
CHR–Chs of Christ	1	27	22	30	0.1	0.2
Evan Free Ch	1	90	NR	90	0.2	0.7
FRND–Fr Gen Cf	1	NR	0	0	0.0	0.0
Grace Gosp Fel	5	NR	NR	NR	-	-
Ind Fund Churches	3	NR	NR	NR	-	-
Jehovah's Witness	1	NR	NR	NR	-	-
LDS–L-D Saints	1	NR	NR	258	0.5	1.9
LUTH–Luth-MO Synod	2	159	287	438	0.9	3.2
MENN–Amish Undif	2	NR	118	290	0.6	2.1
METH–Un Methodist	6	471	839	1,600	3.3	11.7
METH–Wesleyan	4	762	376	991	2.0	7.2
Non-denom Chr Chs	9	1,485	1,535	1,883	3.9	13.7
PENT–Assemb of God	3	294	134	498	1.0	3.6
PENT–Ch God (Cleve)	1	105	208	256	0.5	1.9
PENT–Un Pent Ch Intl	1	NR	NR	NR	-	-
PRES–Orth Pres Ch	1	39	22	32	0.1	0.2
REF–Christian Ref	7	1,332	1,672	2,056	4.2	15.0
REF–Ref Ch in Am	3	475	810	936	1.9	6.8
Sev Day Adv	1	42	74	85	0.2	0.6
Un C of Christ	2	149	276	339	0.7	2.5
OAKLAND	**717**	**141,256**	**206,801**	**607,575**	**50.5**	**100.0**
ANG/EPIS–Episcopal	19	2,012	4,853	6,603	0.5	1.1
Bahá'í	5	NR	394	394	0.0	0.1
BAPT–Amer Bapt USA	12	1,294	3,128	3,797	0.3	0.6
BAPT–Consrv Bapt	2	NR	NR	NR	-	-
BAPT–Converge/BGC	4	300	NR	360	0.0	0.1
BAPT–Free Will Bapt	6	NR	606	736	0.1	0.1
BAPT–Fund Bapt Flwsp	1	NR	NR	NR	-	-
BAPT–Ind Bapt Flwsp Intl	2	NR	NR	NR	-	-
BAPT–N Am Bapt Conf	2	NR	212	257	0.0	0.0
BAPT–Natl Mis Bapt Conv	4	3,000	6,800	8,254	0.7	1.4
BAPT–NBC Amer	1	3	3	4	0.0	0.0
BAPT–NBC USA	13	2,025	5,400	6,554	0.5	1.1
BAPT–Reg Bapt Gen As	6	NR	NR	NR	-	-
BAPT–So Bapt Conv	38	3,207	7,505	9,109	0.8	1.5
BRETH–Breth in Chr	1	NR	NR	NR	-	-
BRETH–Ch of Brethren	1	70	83	101	0.0	0.0
BUDD–Mahayana	6	NR	NR	3,266	0.3	0.5
BUDD–Theravada	2	NR	NR	1,382	0.1	0.2
Calv Chpl	1	NR	NR	NR	-	-
Catholic	64	NR	NR	289,116	24.0	47.6
CGOD–Ch God (Ander)	8	1,131	NR	1,131	0.1	0.2
Ch Cr, Scientst	6	NR	NR	NR	-	-
Ch of Nazarene	11	1,722	2,326	3,014	0.3	0.5
Chr & Miss Al	6	958	855	1,237	0.1	0.2
CHR–Chr Ch (Disc)	3	233	457	555	0.0	0.1
CHR–Chr Chs & Chs Cr	4	NR	275	334	0.0	0.1
CHR–Chs of Christ	20	3,859	3,864	5,232	0.4	0.9
CONG–Cong Chr, NA	7	NR	1,826	2,216	0.2	0.4
CONG–Consrv Cong Chr	2	154	282	342	0.0	0.1
Evan Cov Ch	3	680	431	883	0.1	0.1
Evan Free Ch	1	90	NR	90	0.0	0.0
FRND–Fr Gen Cf	2	NR	33	40	0.0	0.0
HINDU–I/A Temples	4	NR	NR	440	0.0	0.1
HINDU–Post Ren	5	NR	NR	143	0.0	0.0
HINDU–Trad Temples	2	NR	NR	1,150	0.1	0.2
Ind Fund Churches	2	NR	NR	NR	-	-
Int Cou Comm Ch	1	NR	NR	NR	-	-
Jain	1	NR	NR	NR	-	-
Jehovah's Witness	14	NR	NR	NR	-	-
JUD–Conserv	3	1,942	2,180	5,886	0.5	1.0
JUD–Orth	20	8,892	2,750	12,350	1.0	2.0

NR–Not Reported   - Represents no adherents reported.   Percentages may not total 100 due to rounding.

Table 3: Religious Congregations by County and Group: 2010

Religious Group	Number of Congrega-tions	Number of Attendees	Number of Communicant, Confirmed, or Full Members	Adherents: Number of Adherents	Adherents: % of Total Pop.	Adherents: % of Total Adh.
JUD–Reconst	1	29	37	100	0.0	0.0
JUD–Reform	6	3,744	6,604	17,831	1.5	2.9
LDS–Comm of Christ	3	NR	501	501	0.0	0.1
LDS–L-D Saints	11	NR	NR	4,378	0.4	0.7
LUTH–Ch Luth Conf	1	NR	NR	NR	-	-
LUTH–E.L.C.A.	25	3,493	7,550	10,566	0.9	1.7
LUTH–Luth-MO Synod	33	7,786	16,539	21,616	1.8	3.6
LUTH–Wisc Ev Luth Syn	3	331	544	703	0.1	0.1
METH–AME	3	200	785	953	0.1	0.2
METH–AME Zion	2	0	250	303	0.0	0.0
METH–C.M.E.	1	0	100	121	0.0	0.0
METH–Free Methodist	6	793	804	909	0.1	0.1
METH–Un Methodist	51	9,701	23,389	34,739	2.9	5.7
METH–Wesleyan	2	527	317	685	0.1	0.1
Metro Comm Ch	2	169	175	212	0.0	0.0
Missionary Ch	4	331	251	331	0.0	0.1
Muslim Est	6	2,755	NR	9,378	0.8	1.5
Nat Spirit Asso	2	NR	NR	NR	-	-
New Apost Ch	1	NR	NR	NR	-	-
Non-denom Chr Chs	72	62,929	82,602	91,287	7.6	15.0
ORTHE–Ant Orth of NA	2	300	NR	1,600	0.1	0.3
ORTHE–Greek Orthodox	3	1,020	NR	3,000	0.2	0.5
ORTHE–Macedonian Orth	1	45	NR	300	0.0	0.0
ORTHE–Orth Ch in Amer	4	420	NR	1,565	0.1	0.3
ORTHE–Romania Orth Ar	1	120	NR	400	0.0	0.1
ORTHE–Rus Orth Abroad	1	60	NR	120	0.0	0.0
ORTHE–Serb Orth USA	1	150	NR	550	0.0	0.1
ORTHE–Ukrainian Orth	1	175	NR	500	0.0	0.1
ORTHO–Armen Ap Etchm	1	290	NR	2,500	0.2	0.4
ORTHO–Coptic Orth Ch	1	650	NR	1,670	0.1	0.3
ORTHO–Ethiopian Orth	3	NR	NR	NR	-	-
ORTHO–Malan Dioc Am	2	165	NR	495	0.0	0.1
ORTHO–Malan Syr Orth	1	75	NR	144	0.0	0.0
ORTHO–Syrian Orth Ch	1	375	NR	1,000	0.1	0.2
PENT–Assemb of God	24	4,763	2,735	8,762	0.7	1.4
PENT–Ch God (Cleve)	10	624	1,949	2,366	0.2	0.4
PENT–Ch Lord Jesus Apos	2	NR	NR	NR	-	-
PENT–Ch of God Proph	1	NR	135	164	0.0	0.0
PENT–COGIC	4	320	525	637	0.1	0.1
PENT–Elim	2	NR	NR	NR	-	-
PENT–Full Gosp Bapt	5	NR	NR	NR	-	-
PENT–I F Chr Assmbl	1	NR	NR	NR	-	-
PENT–Int Foursq Gos	3	320	106	129	0.0	0.0
PENT–Intl Pent Holiness	1	30	30	36	0.0	0.0
PENT–Open Bible Std	1	105	NR	105	0.0	0.0
PENT–Un Pent Ch Intl	6	NR	NR	NR	-	-
PENT–Vineyard	1	108	125	152	0.0	0.0
PRES–Evan Presby Ch	5	NR	771	936	0.1	0.2
PRES–Kor Pres Abroad	1	NR	NR	NR	-	-
PRES–Korean Amer Pres	1	NR	NR	NR	-	-
PRES–Korean Pres Amer	1	NR	NR	NR	-	-
PRES–Orth Pres Ch	2	243	193	251	0.0	0.0
PRES–Presb Ch (USA)	29	4,002	10,635	12,909	1.1	2.1
PRES–Ref Pres of NA	1	55	39	64	0.0	0.0
REF–Christian Ref	2	251	298	362	0.0	0.1
Salvation Army	3	284	457	2,174	0.2	0.4
Sev Day Adv	11	984	1,710	1,968	0.2	0.3
Sikh	3	NR	NR	NR	-	-
Swedenborgian	1	NR	NR	NR	-	-
Un C of Christ	8	435	1,430	1,736	0.1	0.3
Unit Univ	6	527	952	1,289	0.1	0.2
Unity Ch	8	NR	NR	NR	-	-
Zoroastrian	1	NR	NR	102	0.0	0.0
OCEANA	**48**	**2,389**	**3,057**	**9,580**	**36.1**	**100.0**
ANG/EPIS–Episcopal	1	23	44	47	0.2	0.5
Bahá'í	0	NR	25	25	0.1	0.3
BAPT–Converge/BGC	1	75	NR	90	0.3	0.9
BAPT–Reg Bapt Gen As	3	NR	NR	NR	-	-
Catholic	6	NR	NR	5,084	19.1	53.1
Ch of Nazarene	1	0	26	26	0.1	0.3
Ind Fund Churches	1	NR	NR	NR	-	-
Jehovah's Witness	1	NR	NR	NR	-	-
LDS–L-D Saints	1	NR	NR	217	0.8	2.3
LUTH–E.L.C.A.	1	122	276	358	1.3	3.7
LUTH–Luth-MO Synod	2	120	153	191	0.7	2.0
LUTH–Wisc Ev Luth Syn	1	35	74	102	0.4	1.1
MENN–Amish Undif	0	NR	19	53	0.2	0.6
MENN–Ref Mennonite	1	NR	27	30	0.1	0.3
METH–Un Methodist	7	558	605	884	3.3	9.2
METH–Wesleyan	6	320	183	415	1.6	4.3
Missionary Ch	1	29	29	29	0.1	0.3
Non-denom Chr Chs	3	345	223	431	1.6	4.5
PENT–Assemb of God	1	20	14	25	0.1	0.3
PRES–Presb Ch (USA)	1	62	76	94	0.4	1.0
REF–Christian Ref	2	197	239	295	1.1	3.1
REF–Comm Ref Evan	1	NR	NR	NR	-	-
REF–Ref Ch in Am	2	260	520	546	2.1	5.7
Sev Day Adv	2	66	114	132	0.5	1.4
Un C of Christ	2	157	410	506	1.9	5.3
OGEMAW	**33**	**2,039**	**2,519**	**6,822**	**31.4**	**100.0**
ANG/EPIS–Episcopal	2	53	112	135	0.6	2.0
BAPT–So Bapt Conv	2	70	59	69	0.3	1.0
BRETH–Ch of Brethren	1	65	48	56	0.3	0.8
Catholic	3	NR	NR	2,839	13.1	41.6
CGOD–Ch God (Ander)	1	0	NR	0	0.0	0.0
Ch of Nazarene	1	33	50	50	0.2	0.7
CHR–Chs of Christ	2	38	36	44	0.2	0.6
FRND–Evan Fr Ch Intl	1	77	45	53	0.2	0.8
Jehovah's Witness	1	NR	NR	NR	-	-
LDS–Comm of Christ	1	NR	167	167	0.8	2.4
LDS–L-D Saints	1	NR	NR	139	0.6	2.0
LUTH–E.L.C.A.	1	93	196	246	1.1	3.6
LUTH–Luth-MO Synod	3	130	611	715	3.3	10.5
METH–Free Methodist	1	355	187	355	1.6	5.2
METH–Un Methodist	3	288	503	720	3.3	10.6
Non-denom Chr Chs	3	310	380	438	2.0	6.4
PENT–Assemb of God	2	460	0	650	3.0	9.5
PENT–Ch God (Cleve)	1	45	87	102	0.5	1.5
PENT–Un Pent Ch Intl	1	NR	NR	NR	-	-
Sev Day Adv	1	22	38	44	0.2	0.6
Unity Ch	1	NR	NR	NR	-	-
ONTONAGON	**32**	**637**	**1,649**	**3,610**	**53.2**	**100.0**
Bahá'í	0	NR	1	1	0.0	0.0
BAPT–Reg Bapt Gen As	1	NR	NR	NR	-	-
Catholic	5	NR	NR	1,416	20.9	39.2
Jehovah's Witness	2	NR	NR	NR	-	-
LUTH–Apostolic Luth	1	NR	NR	NR	-	-
LUTH–Assoc Free Luth	1	NR	NR	NR	-	-
LUTH–E.L.C.A.	7	210	782	826	12.2	22.9
LUTH–Luth-MO Synod	2	120	335	480	7.1	13.3
LUTH–Wisc Ev Luth Syn	1	27	72	83	1.2	2.3
METH–Un Methodist	6	144	369	543	8.0	15.0
METH–Wesleyan	1	40	0	52	0.8	1.4
Non-denom Chr Chs	1	25	10	31	0.5	0.9
PENT–Assemb of God	2	53	38	130	1.9	3.6
PRES–Presb Ch (USA)	1	0	11	12	0.2	0.3
Sev Day Adv	1	18	31	36	0.5	1.0
OSCEOLA	**54**	**2,960**	**3,928**	**8,369**	**35.6**	**100.0**
BAPT–Converge/BGC	1	75	NR	90	0.4	1.1
BAPT–Reg Bapt Gen As	2	NR	NR	NR	-	-
Catholic	3	NR	NR	1,503	6.4	18.0
CGOD–Ch God (Ander)	1	90	NR	90	0.4	1.1
Ch of Nazarene	1	315	186	568	2.4	6.8
CONG–Consrv Cong Chr	1	9	7	9	0.0	0.1
Evan Cov Ch	2	186	219	242	1.0	2.9
Evan Free Ch	1	220	NR	220	0.9	2.6
FRND–Fr Gen Cf	1	NR	0	0	0.0	0.0
Ind Fund Churches	1	NR	NR	NR	-	-
Jehovah's Witness	1	NR	NR	NR	-	-
LDS–Comm of Christ	1	NR	167	167	0.7	2.0
LUTH–E.L.C.A.	3	245	540	784	3.3	9.4
LUTH–Luth-MO Synod	1	200	501	597	2.5	7.1
LUTH–Nor Amer Luth C	1	NR	NR	NR	-	-

NR–Not Reported - Represents no adherents reported. Percentages may not total 100 due to rounding.

Table 3: Religious Congregations by County and Group: 2010

Religious Group	Number of Congrega-tions	Number of Attendees	Number of Communicant, Confirmed, or Full Members	Adherents		
				Number of Adherents	% of Total Pop.	% of Total Adh.
MENN–Amish Undif	5	NR	226	593	2.5	7.1
METH–Free Methodist	3	197	139	197	0.8	2.4
METH–Un Methodist	11	506	883	1,770	7.5	21.1
METH–Wesleyan	3	166	98	216	0.9	2.6
Non-denom Chr Chs	2	180	180	225	1.0	2.7
PENT–Assemb of God	2	149	92	260	1.1	3.1
PENT–Ch God (Cleve)	1	19	23	28	0.1	0.3
PRES–Presb Ch (USA)	1	88	10	12	0.1	0.1
REF–Christian Ref	1	261	477	585	2.5	7.0
Sev Day Adv	3	54	94	108	0.5	1.3
Un C of Christ	1	0	86	105	0.4	1.3
OSCODA	**17**	**775**	**948**	**2,514**	**29.1**	**100.0**
ANG/EPIS–Episcopal	1	26	46	46	0.5	1.8
Bahá'í	0	NR	1	1	0.0	0.0
BAPT–So Bapt Conv	1	17	30	35	0.4	1.4
Catholic	1	NR	NR	837	9.7	33.3
CGOD–Ch God (Ander)	1	255	NR	255	3.0	10.1
CHR–Chs of Christ	1	55	51	67	0.8	2.7
Jehovah's Witness	1	NR	NR	NR	-	-
LUTH–Luth-MO Synod	1	32	59	60	0.7	2.4
LUTH–Wisc Ev Luth Syn	1	21	51	51	0.6	2.0
MENN–Amish Undif	3	NR	179	424	4.9	16.9
METH–Un Methodist	1	63	184	296	3.4	11.8
Non-denom Chr Chs	2	185	195	235	2.7	9.3
PENT–Assemb of God	1	47	43	81	0.9	3.2
PENT–Int Foursq Gos	1	28	30	35	0.4	1.4
Sev Day Adv	1	46	79	91	1.1	3.6
OTSEGO	**29**	**2,257**	**2,264**	**9,932**	**41.1**	**100.0**
ANG/EPIS–Episcopal	1	26	59	66	0.3	0.7
Bahá'í	0	NR	5	5	0.0	0.1
BAPT–So Bapt Conv	3	98	91	110	0.5	1.1
Catholic	2	NR	NR	5,800	24.0	58.4
Ch of Nazarene	1	43	66	83	0.3	0.8
CHR–Chs of Christ	1	70	70	100	0.4	1.0
Evan Free Ch	2	676	NR	676	2.8	6.8
HINDU–Post Ren	1	NR	NR	77	0.3	0.8
Jehovah's Witness	2	NR	NR	NR	-	-
LDS–L-D Saints	1	NR	NR	223	0.9	2.2
LUTH–E.L.C.A.	1	115	227	317	1.3	3.2
LUTH–Luth-MO Synod	1	110	253	289	1.2	2.9
LUTH–Wisc Ev Luth Syn	1	34	35	50	0.2	0.5
METH–Free Methodist	1	109	50	109	0.5	1.1
METH–Un Methodist	1	259	591	887	3.7	8.9
New Apost Ch	1	NR	NR	NR	-	-
Non-denom Chr Chs	2	330	335	413	1.7	4.2
PENT–Assemb of God	1	150	75	240	1.0	2.4
PENT–Un Pent Ch Intl	1	NR	NR	NR	-	-
PRES–Presb Ch (USA)	1	80	149	180	0.7	1.8
PRES–Ref Pres of NA	1	11	8	9	0.0	0.1
REF–Christian Ref	1	60	69	83	0.3	0.8
Sev Day Adv	1	31	54	62	0.3	0.6
Un C of Christ	1	55	127	153	0.6	1.5
OTTAWA	**281**	**64,256**	**88,679**	**139,186**	**52.8**	**100.0**
ANG/EPIS–Episcopal	2	320	781	1,038	0.4	0.7
Bahá'í	1	NR	60	60	0.0	0.0
BAPT–Consrv Bapt	1	NR	NR	NR	-	-
BAPT–Converge/BGC	1	75	NR	90	0.0	0.1
BAPT–Ref Bapt Ch	1	NR	NR	NR	-	-
BAPT–Reg Bapt Gen As	4	NR	NR	NR	-	-
BAPT–So Bapt Conv	1	80	61	76	0.0	0.1
BUDD–Theravada	1	NR	NR	300	0.1	0.2
Catholic	11	NR	NR	24,710	9.4	17.8
Ch Cr, Scientst	1	NR	NR	NR	-	-
Ch God (7th Day)	3	NR	NR	NR	-	-
Ch of Nazarene	2	208	273	393	0.1	0.3
Chr & Miss Al	1	85	0	81	0.0	0.1
CHR–Chr Chs & Chs Cr	3	NR	690	863	0.3	0.6
CHR–Chs of Christ	4	276	234	300	0.1	0.2
Christian Brethren	2	NR	NR	NR	-	-
Evan Cov Ch	1	76	89	99	0.0	0.1
Evan Free Ch	1	100	NR	100	0.0	0.1
FRND–Fr Gen Cf	1	NR	4	5	0.0	0.0
Grace Gosp Fel	5	NR	NR	NR	-	-
Ind Fund Churches	5	NR	NR	NR	-	-
Jehovah's Witness	4	NR	NR	NR	-	-
LDS–Comm of Christ	1	NR	167	167	0.1	0.1
LDS–L-D Saints	2	NR	NR	1,317	0.5	0.9
LUTH–Ch Luth Conf	1	NR	NR	NR	-	-
LUTH–E.L.C.A.	3	239	508	739	0.3	0.5
LUTH–Evan Luth Syn	1	23	24	69	0.0	0.0
LUTH–Luth-MO Synod	12	2,210	4,618	5,859	2.2	4.2
MENN–Mennonite USA	1	80	70	88	0.0	0.1
METH–Free Methodist	1	71	54	71	0.0	0.1
METH–Un Methodist	5	1,129	2,137	2,959	1.1	2.1
METH–Wesleyan	8	6,604	2,661	8,587	3.3	6.2
Missionary Ch	1	15	0	15	0.0	0.0
New Apost Ch	2	NR	NR	NR	-	-
Non-denom Chr Chs	28	9,876	10,486	12,970	4.9	9.3
PENT–Assemb of God	7	996	661	1,498	0.6	1.1
PENT–Ch God (Cleve)	3	124	492	615	0.2	0.4
PENT–Ch of God Proph	2	NR	83	104	0.0	0.1
PENT–Un Pent Asbl God	1	NR	NR	NR	-	-
PENT–Un Pent Ch Intl	2	NR	NR	NR	-	-
PENT–Vineyard	2	391	400	500	0.2	0.4
PRES–Orth Pres Ch	3	463	329	515	0.2	0.4
PRES–Presb Ch (USA)	4	1,070	2,423	3,029	1.1	2.2
PRES–Presb Ch Amer	1	195	212	257	0.1	0.2
REF–Christian Ref	67	18,633	26,956	33,697	12.8	24.2
REF–Prot Ref Chs	7	2,240	1,482	2,510	1.0	1.8
REF–Ref Ch in Am	47	17,905	31,297	33,297	12.6	23.9
REF–Un Ref Chs N.A.	4	NR	NR	NR	-	-
Salvation Army	2	146	248	809	0.3	0.6
Sev Day Adv	5	434	755	868	0.3	0.6
Un C of Christ	2	192	424	530	0.2	0.4
Zoroastrian	0	NR	NR	1	0.0	0.0
PRESQUE ISLE	**34**	**1,906**	**3,466**	**8,236**	**61.6**	**100.0**
ANG/EPIS–Episcopal	1	13	26	26	0.2	0.3
Bahá'í	0	NR	1	1	0.0	0.0
BAPT–So Bapt Conv	2	69	69	79	0.6	1.0
Catholic	4	NR	NR	3,872	28.9	47.0
CHR–Chs of Christ	1	25	24	28	0.2	0.3
Jehovah's Witness	1	NR	NR	NR	-	-
LDS–Comm of Christ	1	NR	167	167	1.2	2.0
LUTH–Assoc Free Luth	1	NR	NR	NR	-	-
LUTH–E.L.C.A.	3	134	250	320	2.4	3.9
LUTH–Evan Luth Syn	1	88	135	154	1.2	1.9
LUTH–Luth-MO Synod	7	662	1,631	2,016	15.1	24.5
METH–Un Methodist	2	126	274	376	2.8	4.6
Non-denom Chr Chs	6	580	600	806	6.0	9.8
PENT–Assemb of God	2	94	53	119	0.9	1.4
PRES–Presb Ch (USA)	1	73	164	189	1.4	2.3
Sev Day Adv	1	42	72	83	0.6	1.0
ROSCOMMON	**35**	**2,071**	**2,988**	**5,872**	**24.0**	**100.0**
ANG/EPIS–Episcopal	1	54	82	135	0.6	2.3
BAPT–Amer Bapt USA	2	318	411	465	1.9	7.9
BAPT–Reg Bapt Gen As	2	NR	NR	NR	-	-
BAPT–So Bapt Conv	3	193	235	266	1.1	4.5
Catholic	5	NR	NR	1,956	8.0	33.3
CHR–Chs of Christ	1	50	40	50	0.2	0.9
CONG–Cong Chr, NA	1	NR	150	170	0.7	2.9
Jehovah's Witness	2	NR	NR	NR	-	-
LDS–Comm of Christ	1	NR	167	167	0.7	2.8
LDS–L-D Saints	1	NR	NR	107	0.4	1.8
LUTH–E.L.C.A.	1	110	166	184	0.8	3.1
LUTH–Luth-MO Synod	2	310	577	636	2.6	10.8
LUTH–Wisc Ev Luth Syn	1	29	58	58	0.2	1.0
METH–Free Methodist	1	30	16	30	0.1	0.5
METH–Un Methodist	2	346	583	831	3.4	14.2
METH–Wesleyan	1	158	90	205	0.8	3.5
Non-denom Chr Chs	2	220	190	276	1.1	4.7
PENT–Assemb of God	3	152	80	174	0.7	3.0

NR–Not Reported - Represents no adherents reported. Percentages may not total 100 due to rounding.

Table 3: Religious Congregations by County and Group: 2010

Religious Group	Number of Congregations	Number of Attendees	Number of Communicant, Confirmed, or Full Members	Adherents: Number of Adherents	Adherents: % of Total Pop.	Adherents: % of Total Adh.
PENT–Ch God (Cleve)	1	51	59	67	0.3	1.1
PRES–Presb Ch (USA)	1	30	48	54	0.2	0.9
Sev Day Adv	1	20	36	41	0.2	0.7
SAGINAW	**216**	**19,840**	**42,635**	**92,066**	**46.0**	**100.0**
ANG/EPIS–Episcopal	4	244	512	534	0.3	0.6
Bahá'í	0	NR	46	46	0.0	0.0
BAPT–Amer Bapt USA	5	412	724	878	0.4	1.0
BAPT–Natl Mis Bapt Conv	2	0	300	364	0.2	0.4
BAPT–NBC USA	12	2,265	6,170	7,486	3.7	8.1
BAPT–Reg Bapt Gen As	4	NR	NR	NR	-	-
BAPT–So Bapt Conv	3	103	122	148	0.1	0.2
BRETH–Breth in Chr	1	NR	NR	NR	-	-
BRETH–Ch of Brethren	1	22	20	24	0.0	0.0
Calv Chpl	1	NR	NR	NR	-	-
Catholic	29	NR	NR	35,873	17.9	39.0
CGOD–Ch God (Ander)	1	26	NR	26	0.0	0.0
Ch God (7th Day)	2	NR	NR	NR	-	-
Ch of Nazarene	7	502	571	771	0.4	0.8
Chr & Miss Al	2	423	457	457	0.2	0.5
CHR–Chr Ch (Disc)	1	22	60	73	0.0	0.1
CHR–Chr Chs & Chs Cr	1	NR	120	146	0.1	0.2
CHR–Chs of Christ	3	205	194	247	0.1	0.3
CONG–Cong Chr, NA	1	NR	40	49	0.0	0.1
Ind Fund Churches	1	NR	NR	NR	-	-
Int Cou Comm Ch	1	NR	NR	NR	-	-
Jehovah's Witness	4	NR	NR	NR	-	-
LDS–Comm of Christ	3	NR	501	501	0.3	0.5
LDS–L-D Saints	1	NR	NR	676	0.3	0.7
LUTH–Ch Luth Conf	1	NR	NR	NR	-	-
LUTH–E.L.C.A.	10	1,096	3,828	4,933	2.5	5.4
LUTH–Evan Luth Syn	2	194	481	573	0.3	0.6
LUTH–Luth-MO Synod	15	4,778	12,219	15,264	7.6	16.6
LUTH–Wisc Ev Luth Syn	11	1,786	3,512	4,358	2.2	4.7
MENN–Mennonite USA	2	31	108	131	0.1	0.1
METH–AME	2	20	130	158	0.1	0.2
METH–C.M.E.	1	0	340	413	0.2	0.4
METH–Free Methodist	1	60	41	60	0.0	0.1
METH–Un Methodist	16	1,644	3,373	4,818	2.4	5.2
METH–Wesleyan	4	428	306	557	0.3	0.6
Muslim Est	1	50	NR	100	0.0	0.1
Non-denom Chr Chs	16	2,910	3,977	4,623	2.3	5.0
ORTHE–Greek Orthodox	1	125	NR	350	0.2	0.4
PENT–Assemb of God	7	816	468	1,265	0.6	1.4
PENT–Ch God (Cleve)	2	50	143	174	0.1	0.2
PENT–Ch Lord Jesus Apos	1	NR	NR	NR	-	-
PENT–COGIC	8	60	1,345	1,632	0.8	1.8
PENT–Full Gosp Bapt	2	NR	NR	NR	-	-
PENT–Intl Pent Holiness	1	15	25	30	0.0	0.0
PENT–Pent Ch of God	4	280	NR	435	0.2	0.5
PENT–Un Pent Ch Intl	2	NR	NR	NR	-	-
PRES–Presb Ch (USA)	6	621	1,282	1,556	0.8	1.7
REF–Christian Ref	1	40	48	58	0.0	0.1
Salvation Army	1	35	23	947	0.5	1.0
Sev Day Adv	4	292	509	585	0.3	0.6
Un Breth in Cr	1	130	116	111	0.1	0.1
Un C of Christ	3	155	524	636	0.3	0.7
ST. CLAIR	**131**	**13,376**	**18,303**	**61,525**	**37.7**	**100.0**
ANG/EPIS–Episcopal	6	409	1,081	1,153	0.7	1.9
Bahá'í	0	NR	26	26	0.0	0.0
BAPT–Amer Bapt USA	3	191	303	368	0.2	0.6
BAPT–Prog NBC	1	75	100	121	0.1	0.2
BAPT–Reg Bapt Gen As	1	NR	NR	NR	-	-
BAPT–So Bapt Conv	2	25	35	42	0.0	0.1
Catholic	11	NR	NR	32,248	19.8	52.4
Ch Cr, Scientst	1	NR	NR	NR	-	-
Ch of Nazarene	2	82	136	142	0.1	0.2
CHR–Chr Chs & Chs Cr	1	NR	120	146	0.1	0.2
CHR–Chs of Christ	2	141	132	180	0.1	0.3
CONG–Cong Chr Add'l	1	NR	188	228	0.1	0.4
CONG–Cong Chr, NA	1	NR	53	64	0.0	0.1
Evan Free Ch	1	300	NR	300	0.2	0.5
HINDU–Trad Temples	1	NR	NR	40	0.0	0.1
Ind Fund Churches	1	NR	NR	NR	-	-
Int Cou Comm Ch	2	NR	NR	NR	-	-
Jehovah's Witness	3	NR	NR	NR	-	-
LDS–Comm of Christ	3	NR	501	501	0.3	0.8
LDS–L-D Saints	1	NR	NR	530	0.3	0.9
LUTH–E.L.C.A.	8	885	2,308	3,414	2.1	5.5
LUTH–Luth-MO Synod	8	1,198	2,983	3,958	2.4	6.4
LUTH–Wisc Ev Luth Syn	2	170	350	418	0.3	0.7
METH–AME	1	25	65	79	0.0	0.1
METH–Free Methodist	2	199	212	230	0.1	0.4
METH–Un Methodist	19	1,392	2,705	3,878	2.4	6.3
METH–Wesleyan	5	597	172	776	0.5	1.3
Missionary Ch	4	2,108	700	2,108	1.3	3.4
Muslim Est	1	411	NR	1,563	1.0	2.5
Non-denom Chr Chs	15	2,919	3,540	4,097	2.5	6.7
ORTHE–Greek Orthodox	1	40	NR	49	0.0	0.1
ORTHE–Serb Orth USA	1	70	NR	225	0.1	0.4
PENT–Assemb of God	3	1,047	334	1,280	0.8	2.1
PENT–Ch God (Cleve)	2	272	324	393	0.2	0.6
PENT–Intl Pent Holiness	1	74	48	58	0.0	0.1
PENT–Un Pent Ch Intl	2	NR	NR	NR	-	-
PRES–Presb Ch (USA)	4	252	783	951	0.6	1.5
Salvation Army	1	142	222	895	0.5	1.5
Sev Day Adv	1	62	107	123	0.1	0.2
Un C of Christ	5	290	775	941	0.6	1.5
Unity Ch	1	NR	NR	NR	-	-
ST. JOSEPH	**111**	**8,253**	**11,312**	**25,924**	**42.3**	**100.0**
ANG/EPIS–Episcopal	2	135	261	283	0.5	1.1
Bahá'í	0	NR	8	8	0.0	0.0
BAPT–Amer Bapt Assn	1	NR	80	100	0.2	0.4
BAPT–Amer Bapt USA	2	202	290	362	0.6	1.4
BAPT–Converge/BGC	1	75	NR	90	0.1	0.3
BAPT–Ind Bapt Flwsp Intl	1	NR	NR	NR	-	-
BAPT–NBC USA	2	250	500	624	1.0	2.4
BAPT–Reg Bapt Gen As	1	NR	NR	NR	-	-
BRETH–Ch of Brethren	1	0	63	79	0.1	0.3
Catholic	6	NR	NR	9,460	15.4	36.5
CGOD–Ch God (Ander)	2	90	NR	90	0.1	0.3
Ch Cr, Scientst	1	NR	NR	NR	-	-
Ch of Nazarene	3	309	535	858	1.4	3.3
CHR–Chr Chs & Chs Cr	3	NR	238	297	0.5	1.1
CHR–Chs of Christ	1	35	36	39	0.1	0.2
Evan Ch	1	NR	NR	NR	-	-
Ind Fund Churches	4	NR	NR	NR	-	-
Jehovah's Witness	2	NR	NR	NR	-	-
LDS–L-D Saints	1	NR	NR	427	0.7	1.6
LUTH–E.L.C.A.	2	125	312	347	0.6	1.3
LUTH–Luth-MO Synod	6	642	1,119	1,410	2.3	5.4
LUTH–Wisc Ev Luth Syn	1	116	188	231	0.4	0.9
MENN–Amish Undif	11	NR	691	1,533	2.5	5.9
MENN–Beachy Amish-Menn	1	111	67	111	0.2	0.4
MENN–Cons Menn Conf	1	100	60	75	0.1	0.3
MENN–Mennonite USA	3	218	315	393	0.6	1.5
METH–AME	1	0	100	125	0.2	0.5
METH–Un Methodist	12	766	1,630	2,218	3.6	8.6
METH–Wesleyan	3	460	291	599	1.0	2.3
Missionary Ch	5	546	263	546	0.9	2.1
Non-denom Chr Chs	14	2,999	3,049	3,758	6.1	14.5
PENT–Assemb of God	2	242	104	369	0.6	1.4
PENT–Ch God (Cleve)	1	29	12	15	0.0	0.1
PENT–COGIC	1	40	65	81	0.1	0.3
PENT–Int Foursq Gos	1	80	92	115	0.2	0.4
PENT–Intl Pent Holiness	1	70	37	46	0.1	0.2
PENT–Pent Ch of God	1	70	NR	109	0.2	0.4
PENT–Un Pent Ch Intl	1	NR	NR	NR	-	-
PRES–Presb Ch (USA)	3	336	593	740	1.2	2.9
REF–Christian Ref	1	50	50	62	0.1	0.2
Salvation Army	1	34	47	66	0.1	0.3
Sev Day Adv	2	92	160	184	0.3	0.7
Un C of Christ	1	31	56	70	0.1	0.3
Zoroastrian	0	NR	NR	4	0.0	0.0

NR–Not Reported   - Represents no adherents reported.   Percentages may not total 100 due to rounding.

Table 3: Religious Congregations by County and Group: 2010

Religious Group	Number of Congrega-tions	Number of Attendees	Number of Communicant, Confirmed, or Full Members	Adherents: Number of Adherents	Adherents: % of Total Pop.	Adherents: % of Total Adh.
SANILAC	**88**	**4,447**	**6,869**	**17,728**	**41.1**	**100.0**
ANG/EPIS–Episcopal	2	88	169	193	0.4	1.1
Bahá'í	0	NR	3	3	0.0	0.0
BAPT–Amer Bapt USA	1	62	42	51	0.1	0.3
BAPT–Ind Bapt Flwsp Intl	1	NR	NR	NR	-	-
BAPT–Reg Bapt Gen As	1	NR	NR	NR	-	-
BRETH–Breth in Chr	1	NR	NR	NR	-	-
BUDD–Mahayana	1	NR	NR	20	0.0	0.1
Catholic	10	NR	NR	7,460	17.3	42.1
Ch of Nazarene	1	41	48	48	0.1	0.3
Chr & Miss Al	1	75	42	123	0.3	0.7
CHR–Chs of Christ	1	20	12	20	0.0	0.1
Evan Free Ch	1	80	NR	80	0.2	0.5
Ind Fund Churches	2	NR	NR	NR	-	-
Jehovah's Witness	1	NR	NR	NR	-	-
LDS–Comm of Christ	4	NR	668	668	1.5	3.8
LDS–L-D Saints	1	NR	NR	122	0.3	0.7
LUTH–E.L.C.A.	2	84	210	252	0.6	1.4
LUTH–Luth-MO Synod	7	625	1,628	1,982	4.6	11.2
MENN–Amish Undif	4	NR	207	550	1.3	3.1
METH–Free Methodist	2	375	356	383	0.9	2.2
METH–Un Methodist	21	1,249	1,878	3,124	7.2	17.6
METH–Wesleyan	2	442	262	575	1.3	3.2
Missionary Ch	5	534	388	576	1.3	3.2
Non-denom Chr Chs	4	365	330	457	1.1	2.6
PENT–Assemb of God	3	92	60	245	0.6	1.4
PENT–Ch God (Cleve)	1	16	70	85	0.2	0.5
PENT–Pent Ch of God	1	70	NR	109	0.3	0.6
PENT–Un Pent Ch Intl	1	NR	NR	NR	-	-
PRES–Korean Pres Amer	1	NR	NR	NR	-	-
PRES–Presb Ch (USA)	5	229	496	602	1.4	3.4
SCHOOLCRAFT	**21**	**809**	**1,532**	**4,702**	**55.4**	**100.0**
ANG/EPIS–Episcopal	1	12	37	37	0.4	0.8
Bahá'í	0	NR	1	1	0.0	0.0
BAPT–Amer Bapt USA	1	118	286	335	3.9	7.1
Catholic	4	NR	NR	2,750	32.4	58.5
Jehovah's Witness	1	NR	NR	NR	-	-
LDS–Comm of Christ	1	NR	167	167	2.0	3.6
LUTH–E.L.C.A.	1	127	207	336	4.0	7.1
LUTH–Luth-MO Synod	1	53	96	116	1.4	2.5
MENN–Cons Menn Conf	1	30	21	25	0.3	0.5
MENN–Mennonite USA	2	72	53	62	0.7	1.3
METH–Un Methodist	2	82	172	195	2.3	4.1
Non-denom Chr Chs	2	135	306	352	4.1	7.5
PENT–Int Foursq Gos	1	36	61	72	0.8	1.5
PENT–Pent Ch of God	1	70	NR	109	1.3	2.3
PRES–Presb Ch (USA)	1	50	84	98	1.2	2.1
Sev Day Adv	1	24	41	47	0.6	1.0
SHIAWASSEE	**99**	**6,041**	**8,463**	**23,458**	**33.2**	**100.0**
ANG/EPIS–Episcopal	2	71	133	210	0.3	0.9
Bahá'í	0	NR	5	5	0.0	0.0
BAPT–Amer Bapt USA	2	86	157	191	0.3	0.8
BAPT–Reg Bapt Gen As	2	NR	NR	NR	-	-
BAPT–So Bapt Conv	2	48	203	247	0.3	1.1
BUDD–Theravada	2	NR	NR	389	0.6	1.7
Catholic	5	NR	NR	9,009	12.8	38.4
CGOD–Ch God (Ander)	1	98	NR	98	0.1	0.4
Ch God (7th Day)	1	NR	NR	NR	-	-
Ch of Nazarene	6	1,350	1,106	3,393	4.8	14.5
CHR–Chr Chs & Chs Cr	3	NR	54	66	0.1	0.3
CHR–Chs of Christ	1	25	30	30	0.0	0.1
CONG–Cong Chr, NA	3	NR	456	555	0.8	2.4
CONG–Consrv Cong Chr	2	116	135	164	0.2	0.7
Evan Free Ch	1	60	NR	60	0.1	0.3
Ind Fund Churches	2	NR	NR	NR	-	-
Jehovah's Witness	4	NR	NR	NR	-	-
LDS–Comm of Christ	1	NR	167	167	0.2	0.7
LDS–L-D Saints	1	NR	NR	397	0.6	1.7
LUTH–Luth Cong Msn Chr	1	136	26	32	0.0	0.1
LUTH–Luth-MO Synod	1	0	98	117	0.2	0.5
LUTH–Nor Amer Luth C	1	NR	NR	NR	-	-
LUTH–Wisc Ev Luth Syn	3	446	1,177	1,441	2.0	6.1
METH–Free Methodist	3	148	153	157	0.2	0.7
METH–Un Methodist	20	1,033	1,921	2,969	4.2	12.7
METH–Wesleyan	2	397	290	516	0.7	2.2
Non-denom Chr Chs	11	1,158	1,321	1,591	2.3	6.8
PENT–Assemb of God	4	125	93	198	0.3	0.8
PENT–Ch God (Cleve)	2	194	189	230	0.3	1.0
PENT–Pent Ch of God	3	210	NR	326	0.5	1.4
PENT–Un Pent Ch Intl	1	NR	NR	NR	-	-
PENT–Vineyard	1	79	110	134	0.2	0.6
PRES–Evan Presby Ch	1	NR	111	135	0.2	0.6
Salvation Army	1	10	0	0	0.0	0.0
Sev Day Adv	1	102	178	205	0.3	0.9
Un C of Christ	2	149	350	426	0.6	1.8
TUSCOLA	**93**	**7,558**	**13,409**	**23,195**	**41.6**	**100.0**
Bahá'í	0	NR	5	5	0.0	0.0
BAPT–Amer Bapt USA	1	42	30	36	0.1	0.2
BAPT–Reg Bapt Gen As	3	NR	NR	NR	-	-
BAPT–So Bapt Conv	1	55	33	40	0.1	0.2
Calv Chpl	1	NR	NR	NR	-	-
Catholic	7	NR	NR	4,756	8.5	20.5
CGOD–Ch God (Ander)	1	220	NR	220	0.4	0.9
Ch of Nazarene	7	497	485	665	1.2	2.9
CHR–Chr Chs & Chs Cr	2	NR	303	366	0.7	1.6
CHR–Chs of Christ	3	90	106	137	0.2	0.6
Evan Free Ch	1	50	NR	50	0.1	0.2
Ind Fund Churches	3	NR	NR	NR	-	-
Jehovah's Witness	1	NR	NR	NR	-	-
LDS–Comm of Christ	3	NR	501	501	0.9	2.2
LDS–L-D Saints	1	NR	NR	172	0.3	0.7
LUTH–E.L.C.A.	2	98	292	337	0.6	1.5
LUTH–Luth Cong Msn Chr	1	188	920	1,110	2.0	4.8
LUTH–Luth-MO Synod	7	2,030	5,203	6,601	11.8	28.5
LUTH–Wisc Ev Luth Syn	2	356	767	1,033	1.9	4.5
MENN–Amish Undif	1	NR	46	137	0.2	0.6
MENN–Cons Menn Conf	1	52	43	52	0.1	0.2
METH–Free Methodist	1	57	52	57	0.1	0.2
METH–Un Methodist	15	1,145	2,177	3,092	5.5	13.3
METH–Wesleyan	1	129	146	168	0.3	0.7
Missionary Ch	3	178	90	178	0.3	0.8
MORAV–Morav Ch-North	1	91	245	292	0.5	1.3
Non-denom Chr Chs	8	1,030	933	1,290	2.3	5.6
PENT–Assemb of God	5	319	182	544	1.0	2.3
PENT–Ch God (Cleve)	2	119	115	139	0.2	0.6
PRES–Presb Ch (USA)	4	183	500	603	1.1	2.6
REF–Comm Ref Evan	1	NR	NR	NR	-	-
Sev Day Adv	2	68	119	137	0.2	0.6
Un Breth in Cr	1	561	116	477	0.9	2.1
VAN BUREN	**117**	**6,524**	**9,599**	**26,926**	**35.3**	**100.0**
ANG/EPIS–Anglican NA	1	NR	NR	NR	-	-
ANG/EPIS–Episcopal	2	83	79	139	0.2	0.5
Bahá'í	0	NR	16	16	0.0	0.1
BAPT–Amer Bapt Assn	3	NR	280	346	0.5	1.3
BAPT–Amer Bapt USA	1	182	184	227	0.3	0.8
BAPT–Converge/BGC	1	75	NR	90	0.1	0.3
BAPT–Free Will Bapt	1	NR	101	125	0.2	0.5
BAPT–Natl Mis Bapt Conv	1	30	30	37	0.0	0.1
BAPT–NBC USA	2	125	220	272	0.4	1.0
BAPT–Reg Bapt Gen As	3	NR	NR	NR	-	-
BAPT–So Bapt Conv	3	66	77	95	0.1	0.4
Catholic	7	NR	NR	12,943	17.0	48.1
CGOD–Ch God (Ander)	2	46	NR	46	0.1	0.2
Ch Cr, Scientst	1	NR	NR	NR	-	-
Ch of Nazarene	1	44	31	56	0.1	0.2
CHR–Chr Ch (Disc)	1	0	12	15	0.0	0.1
CHR–Chr Chs & Chs Cr	1	NR	150	185	0.2	0.7
CHR–Chs of Christ	2	85	90	115	0.2	0.4
CONG–Cong Chr, NA	1	NR	23	28	0.0	0.1
CONG–Consrv Cong Chr	3	123	139	172	0.2	0.6
HINDU–Renaiss	1	NR	NR	12	0.0	0.0
Ind Fund Churches	3	NR	NR	NR	-	-

NR–Not Reported   - Represents no adherents reported.   Percentages may not total 100 due to rounding.

Table 3: Religious Congregations by County and Group: 2010

Religious Group	Number of Congrega-tions	Number of Attendees	Number of Communicant, Confirmed, or Full Members	Adherents: Number of Adherents	Adherents: % of Total Pop.	Adherents: % of Total Adh.
Int Cou Comm Ch	2	NR	NR	NR	-	-
Jehovah's Witness	4	NR	NR	NR	-	-
LDS–L-D Saints	2	NR	NR	549	0.7	2.0
LUTH–Ch Luth Conf	1	NR	NR	NR	-	-
LUTH–E.L.C.A.	1	305	662	786	1.0	2.9
LUTH–Luth-MO Synod	1	235	1,176	1,310	1.7	4.9
LUTH–Wisc Ev Luth Syn	3	250	437	571	0.7	2.1
MENN–Amish Undif	1	NR	22	45	0.1	0.2
MENN–Fel Evg Ch	1	287	141	174	0.2	0.6
METH–Free Methodist	1	40	40	40	0.1	0.1
METH–Un Methodist	14	823	1,532	2,395	3.1	8.9
Missionary Ch	1	105	82	105	0.1	0.4
New Apost Ch	1	NR	NR	NR	-	-
Non-denom Chr Chs	14	1,575	1,381	2,070	2.7	7.7
PENT–Assemb of God	2	106	71	175	0.2	0.6
PENT–Ch God (Cleve)	1	22	30	37	0.0	0.1
PENT–COGIC	1	0	150	185	0.2	0.7
PENT–Int Pent C Chr	1	72	68	167	0.2	0.6
PENT–Intl Pent Holiness	2	108	118	146	0.2	0.5
PENT–Pent Ch of God	3	210	NR	326	0.4	1.2
PENT–Un Pent Ch Intl	3	NR	NR	NR	-	-
PRES–Presb Ch (USA)	3	193	431	533	0.7	2.0
REF–Christian Ref	2	197	200	247	0.3	0.9
REF–Ref Ch in Am	3	562	606	954	1.3	3.5
Sev Day Adv	7	466	810	932	1.2	3.5
Un C of Christ	1	109	210	260	0.3	1.0
WASHTENAW	**273**	**28,748**	**45,146**	**113,196**	**32.8**	**100.0**
ANG/EPIS–Episcopal	8	869	1,994	2,264	0.7	2.0
Bahá'í	3	NR	358	358	0.1	0.3
BAPT–Amer Bapt USA	7	946	1,487	1,770	0.5	1.6
BAPT–Converge/BGC	1	75	NR	90	0.0	0.1
BAPT–Free Will Bapt	5	NR	505	601	0.2	0.5
BAPT–Ind Bapt Flwsp Intl	1	NR	NR	NR	-	-
BAPT–NBC USA	5	700	1,160	1,381	0.4	1.2
BAPT–Prog NBC	1	160	200	238	0.1	0.2
BAPT–Reg Bapt Gen As	1	NR	NR	NR	-	-
BAPT–So Bapt Conv	12	1,311	2,267	2,699	0.8	2.4
BRETH–Ch of Brethren	1	70	42	50	0.0	0.0
BUDD–Mahayana	4	NR	NR	300	0.1	0.3
BUDD–Theravada	3	NR	NR	295	0.1	0.3
BUDD–Vajrayana	2	NR	NR	180	0.1	0.2
Calv Chpl	1	NR	NR	NR	-	-
Catholic	14	NR	NR	42,603	12.4	37.6
CGOD–Ch God (Ander)	2	510	NR	510	0.1	0.5
Ch Cr, Scientst	1	NR	NR	NR	-	-
Ch of Nazarene	4	115	135	192	0.1	0.2
Chr & Miss Al	2	74	26	104	0.0	0.1
CHR–Chr Ch (Disc)	1	38	87	104	0.0	0.1
CHR–Chr Chs & Chs Cr	1	NR	35	42	0.0	0.0
CHR–Chs of Christ	6	635	629	825	0.2	0.7
CONG–Cong Chr, NA	1	NR	753	896	0.3	0.8
Evan Cov Ch	1	99	41	129	0.0	0.1
FRND–Evan Fr Ch Intl	1	89	40	48	0.0	0.0
FRND–Fr Gen Cf	2	NR	132	157	0.0	0.1
HINDU–I/A Temples	1	NR	NR	250	0.1	0.2
HINDU–Post Ren	3	NR	NR	112	0.0	0.1
Ind Fund Churches	2	NR	NR	NR	-	-
Jehovah's Witness	6	NR	NR	NR	-	-
JUD–Conserv	1	407	457	1,234	0.4	1.1
JUD–Reconst	1	37	47	127	0.0	0.1
JUD–Reform	1	380	670	1,809	0.5	1.6
LDS–Comm of Christ	1	NR	167	167	0.0	0.1
LDS–L-D Saints	7	NR	NR	2,929	0.8	2.6
LUTH–E.L.C.A.	8	1,150	3,129	4,079	1.2	3.6
LUTH–Luth Cong Msn Chr	1	105	NR	NR	-	-
LUTH–Luth-MO Synod	9	2,346	3,228	4,287	1.2	3.8
LUTH–Wisc Ev Luth Syn	6	585	1,257	1,535	0.4	1.4
MENN–Mennonite USA	2	95	52	62	0.0	0.1
METH–AME	5	600	1,175	1,399	0.4	1.2
METH–Free Methodist	5	807	701	846	0.2	0.7
METH–Un Methodist	17	2,869	5,867	9,039	2.6	8.0
METH–Wesleyan	2	699	130	908	0.3	0.8
Metro Comm Ch	1	9	15	18	0.0	0.0
MJEW–Union Mes Cong	1	NR	NR	NR	-	-
Muslim Est	3	1,481	NR	4,463	1.3	3.9
New Apost Ch	1	NR	NR	NR	-	-
Non-denom Chr Chs	19	3,980	4,655	5,418	1.6	4.8
ORTHE–Ant Orth of NA	1	23	NR	63	0.0	0.1
ORTHE–Greek Orthodox	1	275	NR	400	0.1	0.4
ORTHE–Rus Orth Abroad	1	91	NR	300	0.1	0.3
ORTHO–Armen Ap Etchm	1	10	NR	30	0.0	0.0
ORTHO–Coptic Orth Ch	1	50	NR	125	0.0	0.1
PENT–Assemb of God	13	854	565	1,375	0.4	1.2
PENT–Ch God (Cleve)	2	347	1,036	1,233	0.4	1.1
PENT–Ch Lord Jesus Apos	1	NR	NR	NR	-	-
PENT–Ch of God Proph	1	NR	15	18	0.0	0.0
PENT–COGIC	11	935	1,979	2,356	0.7	2.1
PENT–Pent Ch of God	3	210	NR	326	0.1	0.3
PENT–Un Pent Ch Intl	3	NR	NR	NR	-	-
PENT–Vineyard	1	626	1,065	1,268	0.4	1.1
PRES–Evan Presby Ch	2	NR	635	756	0.2	0.7
PRES–Presb Ch (USA)	7	1,200	3,029	3,606	1.0	3.2
PRES–Presb Ch Amer	1	55	49	69	0.0	0.1
REF–Christian Ref	4	620	781	930	0.3	0.8
REF–Ref Ch in Am	1	165	121	241	0.1	0.2
Salvation Army	2	89	79	270	0.1	0.2
Sev Day Adv	5	374	651	748	0.2	0.7
Un C of Christ	13	1,113	3,110	3,702	1.1	3.3
Unit Univ	2	470	590	849	0.2	0.8
Unity Ch	2	NR	NR	NR	-	-
Zoroastrian	0	NR	NR	13	0.0	0.0
WAYNE	**1,330**	**197,567**	**314,872**	**788,507**	**43.3**	**100.0**
ANG/EPIS–Anglican NA	2	NR	NR	NR	-	-
ANG/EPIS–Episcopal	33	2,932	6,676	7,711	0.4	1.0
Ap Chr Ch-Amer	1	200	112	200	0.0	0.0
Bahá'í	3	NR	547	547	0.0	0.1
BAPT–Amer Bapt Assn	1	NR	0	0	0.0	0.0
BAPT–Amer Bapt USA	32	11,669	22,682	28,021	1.5	3.6
BAPT–Converge/BGC	6	450	NR	540	0.0	0.1
BAPT–Free Will Bapt	16	NR	1,616	1,996	0.1	0.3
BAPT–Ind Bapt Flwsp Intl	7	NR	NR	NR	-	-
BAPT–N Am Bapt Conf	2	NR	763	943	0.1	0.1
BAPT–Natl Mis Bapt Conv	14	1,270	5,305	6,554	0.4	0.8
BAPT–NBC Amer	4	880	1,400	1,730	0.1	0.2
BAPT–NBC USA	110	28,802	61,861	76,422	4.2	9.7
BAPT–Prog NBC	14	1,985	3,973	4,908	0.3	0.6
BAPT–Ref Bapt Ch	1	NR	NR	NR	-	-
BAPT–Reg Bapt Gen As	4	NR	NR	NR	-	-
BAPT–So Bapt Conv	42	3,337	6,592	8,144	0.4	1.0
BRETH–Ch of Brethren	1	29	55	68	0.0	0.0
BUDD–Mahayana	1	NR	NR	102	0.0	0.0
BUDD–Theravada	1	NR	NR	300	0.0	0.0
Calv Chpl	1	NR	NR	NR	-	-
Catholic	149	NR	NR	297,283	16.3	37.7
CGOD–Ch God (Ander)	13	1,094	NR	1,094	0.1	0.1
Ch Christ Chr Union	1	NR	NR	NR	-	-
Ch Cr, Scientst	6	NR	NR	NR	-	-
Ch of Chr (Hol)	4	NR	NR	NR	-	-
Ch of Nazarene	9	679	898	1,014	0.1	0.1
Chr & Miss Al	7	324	104	503	0.0	0.1
CHR–Chr Ch (Disc)	6	250	526	650	0.0	0.1
CHR–Chr Chs & Chs Cr	9	NR	3,357	4,147	0.2	0.5
CHR–Chs of Christ	36	5,662	6,328	8,182	0.4	1.0
CHR–Int Chs of Christ	1	NR	224	277	0.0	0.0
Christian Brethren	4	NR	NR	NR	-	-
CONG–Cong Chr, NA	5	NR	827	1,022	0.1	0.1
Evan Cov Ch	9	2,080	1,694	2,704	0.1	0.3
Evan Free Ch	1	175	NR	175	0.0	0.0
FRND–Fr Gen Cf	1	NR	17	21	0.0	0.0
FRND–Unaffl Mtgs	1	NR	NR	NR	-	-
HINDU–I/A Temples	2	NR	NR	3,304	0.2	0.4
HINDU–Post Ren	2	NR	NR	104	0.0	0.0
HINDU–Renaiss	2	NR	NR	24	0.0	0.0
HINDU–Trad Temples	1	NR	NR	1,000	0.1	0.1
Ind Fund Churches	1	NR	NR	NR	-	-
Int Cou Comm Ch	3	NR	NR	NR	-	-

NR–Not Reported - Represents no adherents reported. Percentages may not total 100 due to rounding.

Table 3: Religious Congregations by County and Group: 2010

Religious Group	Number of Congregations	Number of Attendees	Number of Communicant, Confirmed, or Full Members	Adherents: Number of Adherents	Adherents: % of Total Pop.	Adherents: % of Total Adh.
Jehovah's Witness	30	NR	NR	NR	-	-
JUD–Reconst	1	16	21	57	0.0	0.0
JUD–Reform	1	11	19	51	0.0	0.0
LDS–Comm of Christ	4	NR	668	668	0.0	0.1
LDS–L-D Saints	11	NR	NR	5,591	0.3	0.7
LUTH–Apostolic Luth	1	NR	NR	NR	-	-
LUTH–E.L.C.A.	37	3,372	9,259	12,328	0.7	1.6
LUTH–Luth Cong Msn Chr	2	800	1,906	2,355	0.1	0.3
LUTH–Luth-MO Synod	52	9,091	17,148	22,687	1.2	2.9
LUTH–Wisc Ev Luth Syn	12	1,210	2,838	3,672	0.2	0.5
MENN–Mennonite USA	2	32	561	693	0.0	0.1
METH–AME	29	4,706	10,684	13,199	0.7	1.7
METH–AME Zion	8	485	1,850	2,285	0.1	0.3
METH–C.M.E.	14	663	2,664	3,291	0.2	0.4
METH–Free Methodist	9	870	764	933	0.1	0.1
METH–Un Methodist	53	5,411	11,672	14,689	0.8	1.9
METH–Wesleyan	5	336	198	437	0.0	0.1
Missionary Ch	3	262	259	272	0.0	0.0
MORAV–Morav Ch-North	1	44	66	93	0.0	0.0
Muslim Est	38	16,707	NR	67,775	3.7	8.6
New Apost Ch	2	NR	NR	NR	-	-
Non-denom Chr Chs	144	62,105	80,241	92,394	5.1	11.7
OCATH–Pol Natl Cath	2	NR	NR	NR	-	-
ORTHE–Ant Orth of NA	2	524	NR	2,435	0.1	0.3
ORTHE–Bulgar Orth USA	2	165	NR	570	0.0	0.1
ORTHE–Greek Orthodox	4	900	NR	3,075	0.2	0.4
ORTHE–Orth Ch in Amer	7	747	NR	1,285	0.1	0.2
ORTHE–Romania Orth Ar	1	60	NR	300	0.0	0.0
ORTHE–Rus Orth Moscow	2	130	NR	265	0.0	0.0
ORTHE–Serb Orth USA	1	1,230	NR	6,500	0.4	0.8
ORTHE–Ukrainian Orth	1	20	NR	40	0.0	0.0
ORTHO–Armen Ap Cilic	1	200	NR	3,000	0.2	0.4
ORTHO–Eritrean Orth	1	30	NR	50	0.0	0.0
ORTHO–Malan Dioc Am	1	20	NR	60	0.0	0.0
PENT–Assemb of God	30	5,383	2,409	8,201	0.5	1.0
PENT–Ch God (Cleve)	22	1,963	4,036	4,986	0.3	0.6
PENT–Ch God Mtn Asm	4	NR	NR	NR	-	-
PENT–Ch Lord Jesus Apos	8	NR	NR	NR	-	-
PENT–Ch of God by Faith	1	NR	NR	NR	-	-
PENT–Ch of God Proph	5	NR	376	465	0.0	0.1
PENT–COGIC	66	7,643	12,986	16,043	0.9	2.0
PENT–Fire Bapt Hol Ch	2	NR	NR	NR	-	-
PENT–Full Gosp Bapt	13	NR	NR	NR	-	-
PENT–I F Chr Assmbl	1	NR	NR	NR	-	-
PENT–Intl Pent Holiness	1	30	55	68	0.0	0.0
PENT–Pent Ch of God	2	140	NR	217	0.0	0.0
PENT–Un Pent Ch Intl	15	NR	NR	NR	-	-
PENT–United Holy Ch	1	NR	NR	NR	-	-
PRES–Cum Pres Am	1	NR	NR	NR	-	-
PRES–Cumber Presb	1	NR	12	29	0.0	0.0
PRES–Evan Presby Ch	4	NR	4,086	5,048	0.3	0.6
PRES–Free Ch Scot	1	NR	NR	NR	-	-
PRES–Presb Ch (USA)	36	4,440	11,419	14,107	0.8	1.8
REF–Christian Ref	2	335	514	635	0.0	0.1
REF–Hung Ref Add'l	1	NR	NR	NR	-	-
REF–Ref Ch in Am	4	392	400	604	0.0	0.1
Salvation Army	8	468	837	3,827	0.2	0.5
Sev Day Adv	19	3,540	6,155	7,079	0.4	0.9
Sikh	2	NR	NR	NR	-	-
Un C of Christ	18	1,101	4,971	6,141	0.3	0.8
Unit Univ	2	167	241	303	0.0	0.0
Unity Ch	7	NR	NR	NR	-	-
Zoroastrian	0	NR	NR	14	0.0	0.0
WEXFORD	**68**	**4,851**	**7,263**	**12,243**	**37.4**	**100.0**
ANG/EPIS–Episcopal	1	36	43	51	0.2	0.4
Bahá'í	0	NR	10	10	0.0	0.1
BAPT–Amer Bapt USA	1	461	504	620	1.9	5.1
BAPT–Converge/BGC	1	75	NR	90	0.3	0.7
BAPT–Reg Bapt Gen As	1	NR	NR	NR	-	-
BAPT–So Bapt Conv	2	75	145	178	0.5	1.5
Catholic	3	NR	NR	2,015	6.2	16.5
CGOD–Ch God (Ander)	1	65	NR	65	0.2	0.5
Ch of Nazarene	4	314	393	604	1.8	4.9
CHR–Chr Ch (Disc)	3	56	209	257	0.8	2.1
CHR–Chs of Christ	1	39	52	59	0.2	0.5
Evan Cov Ch	1	51	85	66	0.2	0.5
Grace Gosp Fel	1	NR	NR	NR	-	-
Ind Fund Churches	3	NR	NR	NR	-	-
Jehovah's Witness	1	NR	NR	NR	-	-
LDS–Comm of Christ	1	NR	167	167	0.5	1.4
LDS–L-D Saints	1	NR	NR	293	0.9	2.4
LUTH–Ch Luth Conf	1	NR	NR	NR	-	-
LUTH–E.L.C.A.	2	240	406	489	1.5	4.0
LUTH–Luth-MO Synod	2	237	458	598	1.8	4.9
LUTH–Wisc Ev Luth Syn	1	40	61	76	0.2	0.6
MENN–Amish Undif	2	NR	70	215	0.7	1.8
METH–Free Methodist	4	155	97	155	0.5	1.3
METH–Un Methodist	5	447	784	1,303	4.0	10.6
METH–Wesleyan	1	31	13	40	0.1	0.3
Non-denom Chr Chs	10	1,688	2,555	3,179	9.7	26.0
PENT–Assemb of God	1	67	54	67	0.2	0.5
PENT–Ch God (Cleve)	1	14	5	6	0.0	0.0
PENT–Int Foursq Gos	2	30	40	49	0.1	0.4
PENT–Pent Ch of God	1	70	NR	109	0.3	0.9
PENT–Un Pent Ch Intl	1	NR	NR	NR	-	-
PRES–Presb Ch (USA)	1	108	258	318	1.0	2.6
REF–Christian Ref	1	255	363	447	1.4	3.7
Salvation Army	1	53	64	217	0.7	1.8
Sev Day Adv	4	187	325	374	1.1	3.1
Un C of Christ	1	57	102	126	0.4	1.0
MINNESOTA	**5,967**	**676,954**	**1,220,415**	**2,989,600**	**56.3**	**100.0**
AITKIN	**43**	**1,467**	**3,524**	**6,504**	**40.1**	**100.0**
ANG/EPIS–Episcopal	1	16	12	12	0.1	0.2
Bahá'í	0	NR	4	4	0.0	0.1
BAPT–Consrv Bapt	1	NR	NR	NR	-	-
BAPT–Converge/BGC	1	75	NR	90	0.6	1.4
BAPT–So Bapt Conv	1	30	40	46	0.3	0.7
Catholic	4	NR	NR	1,357	8.4	20.9
Chr & Miss Al	2	23	8	28	0.2	0.4
CHR–Chr Chs & Chs Cr	1	NR	45	52	0.3	0.8
Jehovah's Witness	1	NR	NR	NR	-	-
LDS–L-D Saints	1	NR	NR	217	1.3	3.3
LUTH–Assoc Free Luth	1	NR	NR	NR	-	-
LUTH–Ch of Luth Br	2	52	35	63	0.4	1.0
LUTH–E.L.C.A.	7	558	1,850	2,398	14.8	36.9
LUTH–Luth-MO Synod	5	270	846	1,100	6.8	16.9
METH–Un Methodist	6	194	409	665	4.1	10.2
PENT–Assemb of God	4	171	103	274	1.7	4.2
PRES–Presb Ch (USA)	3	23	84	97	0.6	1.5
Sev Day Adv	1	36	63	72	0.4	1.1
Un C of Christ	1	19	25	29	0.2	0.4
ANOKA	**169**	**43,455**	**43,411**	**164,167**	**49.6**	**100.0**
ANG/EPIS–Anglican NA	1	NR	NR	NR	-	-
ANG/EPIS–Episcopal	1	83	270	270	0.1	0.2
Bahá'í	1	NR	74	74	0.0	0.0
BAPT–Consrv Bapt	2	NR	NR	NR	-	-
BAPT–Converge/BGC	15	16,375	NR	19,650	5.9	12.0
BAPT–NT Ind Bapt	3	NR	NR	NR	-	-
BAPT–Reg Bapt Gen As	1	NR	NR	NR	-	-
BAPT–So Bapt Conv	3	392	579	722	0.2	0.4
BUDD–Theravada	2	NR	NR	591	0.2	0.4
Catholic	12	NR	NR	75,535	22.8	46.0
Ch of Nazarene	2	278	209	568	0.2	0.3
Chr & Miss Al	5	905	661	1,711	0.5	1.0
CHR–Chr Chs & Chs Cr	2	NR	265	330	0.1	0.2
Christian Brethren	1	NR	NR	NR	-	-
Evan Ch	1	NR	NR	NR	-	-
Evan Cov Ch	3	324	345	421	0.1	0.3
Evan Free Ch	6	2,385	NR	2,385	0.7	1.5
HINDU–Post Ren	1	NR	NR	25	0.0	0.0
Jehovah's Witness	2	NR	NR	NR	-	-
LDS–L-D Saints	2	NR	NR	757	0.2	0.5

NR–Not Reported - Represents no adherents reported. Percentages may not total 100 due to rounding.

Table 3: Religious Congregations by County and Group: 2010

Religious Group	Number of Congrega-tions	Number of Attendees	Number of Communicant, Confirmed, or Full Members	Adherents		
				Number of Adherents	% of Total Pop.	% of Total Adh.
LUTH–Assoc Free Luth	2	NR	NR	NR	-	-
LUTH–E.L.C.A.	20	7,606	22,209	30,954	9.4	18.9
LUTH–Luth Cong Msn Chr	5	1,541	2,630	3,279	1.0	2.0
LUTH–Luth–MO Synod	10	2,844	6,275	8,466	2.6	5.2
LUTH–Wisc Ev Luth Syn	2	309	581	760	0.2	0.5
MENN–Mennonite USA	1	30	57	71	0.0	0.0
METH–Un Methodist	9	1,388	2,757	4,365	1.3	2.7
METH–Wesleyan	5	518	261	674	0.2	0.4
Muslim Est	2	268	NR	616	0.2	0.4
Non-denom Chr Chs	19	3,230	3,473	4,152	1.3	2.5
ORTHE–Orth Ch in Amer	2	120	NR	135	0.0	0.1
ORTHE–Rus Orth Abroad	1	20	NR	60	0.0	0.0
PENT–Assemb of God	9	3,795	1,173	5,656	1.7	3.4
PENT–Ch God (Cleve)	2	105	180	224	0.1	0.1
PENT–Ch of God Proph	1	NR	33	41	0.0	0.0
PENT–Intl Pent Holiness	2	115	58	72	0.0	0.0
PENT–Un Pent Ch Intl	3	NR	NR	NR	-	-
PRES–Presb Ch (USA)	2	320	424	529	0.2	0.3
Salvation Army	1	37	66	84	0.0	0.1
Sev Day Adv	2	222	386	443	0.1	0.3
Un C of Christ	1	166	346	431	0.1	0.3
Unit Univ	1	79	99	116	0.0	0.1
Unity Ch	1	NR	NR	NR	-	-
BECKER	**69**	**5,057**	**10,587**	**21,824**	**67.1**	**100.0**
ANG/EPIS–Episcopal	3	84	184	264	0.8	1.2
Bahá'í	0	NR	1	1	0.0	0.0
BAPT–Consrv Bapt	2	NR	NR	NR	-	-
Catholic	15	NR	NR	7,400	22.8	33.9
Chr & Miss Al	2	419	159	654	2.0	3.0
Evan Free Ch	1	80	NR	80	0.2	0.4
Jehovah's Witness	1	NR	NR	NR	-	-
LDS–L-D Saints	1	NR	NR	217	0.7	1.0
LUTH–Apostolic Luth	1	NR	NR	NR	-	-
LUTH–Ch Luth Conf	2	NR	NR	NR	-	-
LUTH–E.L.C.A.	15	1,747	5,009	6,541	20.1	30.0
LUTH–Evan Luth Syn	1	64	100	118	0.4	0.5
LUTH–Luth Cong Msn Chr	2	110	150	186	0.6	0.9
LUTH–Luth–MO Synod	7	761	2,387	3,066	9.4	14.0
MENN–Amish Undif	1	NR	39	114	0.4	0.5
MENN–Mennonite USA	2	95	85	106	0.3	0.5
METH–Un Methodist	2	217	437	454	1.4	2.1
Non-denom Chr Chs	4	595	620	757	2.3	3.5
PENT–Assemb of God	4	195	95	244	0.8	1.1
PENT–Vineyard	1	494	950	1,179	3.6	5.4
Sev Day Adv	1	114	198	228	0.7	1.0
Un C of Christ	1	82	173	215	0.7	1.0
BELTRAMI	**68**	**4,747**	**7,982**	**18,975**	**42.7**	**100.0**
ANG/EPIS–Episcopal	3	56	144	171	0.4	0.9
Bahá'í	1	NR	53	53	0.1	0.3
BAPT–Consrv Bapt	1	NR	NR	NR	-	-
BAPT–Converge/BGC	1	75	NR	90	0.2	0.5
BAPT–Reg Bapt Gen As	1	NR	NR	NR	-	-
BAPT–So Bapt Conv	1	35	37	46	0.1	0.2
Calv Chpl	1	NR	NR	NR	-	-
Catholic	12	NR	NR	7,200	16.2	37.9
Ch Cr, Scientst	1	NR	NR	NR	-	-
Ch of Nazarene	1	29	40	52	0.1	0.3
Chr & Miss Al	1	85	0	112	0.3	0.6
CHR–Chr Chs & Chs Cr	1	NR	50	62	0.1	0.3
Evan Cov Ch	1	612	250	796	1.8	4.2
Evan Free Ch	3	600	NR	600	1.4	3.2
FRND–Fr Gen Cf	1	NR	0	0	0.0	0.0
Ind Fund Churches	1	NR	NR	NR	-	-
Jehovah's Witness	1	NR	NR	NR	-	-
LDS–L-D Saints	1	NR	NR	575	1.3	3.0
LUTH–Assoc Free Luth	3	NR	NR	NR	-	-
LUTH–E.L.C.A.	12	1,394	4,642	5,406	12.2	28.5
LUTH–Luth Ch-Am Asc	1	NR	NR	NR	-	-
LUTH–Luth–MO Synod	2	208	643	804	1.8	4.2
LUTH–Wisc Ev Luth Syn	1	106	179	244	0.5	1.3
METH–Un Methodist	1	165	363	661	1.5	3.5

Religious Group	Number of Congrega-tions	Number of Attendees	Number of Communicant, Confirmed, or Full Members	Adherents		
				Number of Adherents	% of Total Pop.	% of Total Adh.
Non-denom Chr Chs	5	850	955	1,082	2.4	5.7
PENT–Assemb of God	3	297	125	393	0.9	2.1
PENT–Un Pent Ch Intl	1	NR	NR	NR	-	-
PRES–Evan Presby Ch	1	NR	44	55	0.1	0.3
PRES–Presb Ch (USA)	3	123	283	353	0.8	1.9
Sev Day Adv	1	68	117	135	0.3	0.7
Unit Univ	1	44	57	85	0.2	0.4
BENTON	**37**	**2,991**	**6,180**	**19,567**	**50.9**	**100.0**
Bahá'í	0	NR	6	6	0.0	0.0
BAPT–Consrv Bapt	1	NR	NR	NR	-	-
Catholic	8	NR	NR	10,539	27.4	53.9
Chr & Miss Al	1	160	90	260	0.7	1.3
CHR–Chr Chs & Chs Cr	1	NR	15	19	0.0	0.1
Evan Cov Ch	1	71	64	92	0.2	0.5
Evan Free Ch	1	120	NR	120	0.3	0.6
LUTH–E.L.C.A.	6	871	2,740	3,932	10.2	20.1
LUTH–Luth–MO Synod	7	874	2,090	2,682	7.0	13.7
LUTH–Wisc Ev Luth Syn	1	148	233	308	0.8	1.6
METH–Un Methodist	1	69	205	312	0.8	1.6
Non-denom Chr Chs	2	300	325	387	1.0	2.0
PENT–Assemb of God	2	211	85	347	0.9	1.8
PENT–Un Pent Ch Intl	1	NR	NR	NR	-	-
PRES–Presb Ch (USA)	1	94	160	199	0.5	1.0
Salvation Army	1	25	76	258	0.7	1.3
Sev Day Adv	1	48	84	97	0.3	0.5
Un C of Christ	1	0	7	9	0.0	0.0
BIG STONE	**29**	**1,022**	**2,607**	**4,506**	**85.5**	**100.0**
BAPT–Consrv Bapt	1	NR	NR	NR	-	-
BAPT–Converge/BGC	1	75	NR	90	1.7	2.0
Catholic	3	NR	NR	1,408	26.7	31.2
Jehovah's Witness	1	NR	NR	NR	-	-
LUTH–Assoc Free Luth	2	NR	NR	NR	-	-
LUTH–E.L.C.A.	5	373	1,262	1,431	27.2	31.8
LUTH–Luth–MO Synod	4	228	681	805	15.3	17.9
LUTH–Wisc Ev Luth Syn	2	128	210	268	5.1	5.9
MENN–Hutt Breth	2	NR	NR	NR	-	-
METH–Un Methodist	4	105	310	310	5.9	6.9
PENT–Assemb of God	1	55	41	74	1.4	1.6
Sev Day Adv	1	34	58	67	1.3	1.5
Un C of Christ	2	24	45	53	1.0	1.2
BLUE EARTH	**75**	**7,968**	**17,057**	**37,719**	**58.9**	**100.0**
ANG/EPIS–Episcopal	1	85	115	220	0.3	0.6
Bahá'í	0	NR	21	21	0.0	0.1
BAPT–Amer Bapt USA	1	50	130	154	0.2	0.4
BAPT–Consrv Bapt	1	NR	NR	NR	-	-
BAPT–Converge/BGC	1	400	NR	480	0.7	1.3
BAPT–So Bapt Conv	1	50	30	35	0.1	0.1
Catholic	9	NR	NR	13,093	20.5	34.7
Ch of Nazarene	1	0	33	33	0.1	0.1
CHR–Chr Ch (Disc)	2	60	180	213	0.3	0.6
CHR–Chr Chs & Chs Cr	2	NR	110	130	0.2	0.3
CHR–Chs of Christ	1	50	56	87	0.1	0.2
Evan Free Ch	1	240	NR	240	0.4	0.6
LDS–L-D Saints	1	NR	NR	630	1.0	1.7
LUTH–Assoc Free Luth	1	NR	NR	NR	-	-
LUTH–Ch Luth Conf	2	NR	NR	NR	-	-
LUTH–E.L.C.A.	12	1,928	6,691	8,497	13.3	22.5
LUTH–Evan Luth Syn	1	501	665	943	1.5	2.5
LUTH–Luth Cong Msn Chr	1	40	NR	NR	-	-
LUTH–Luth–MO Synod	9	1,962	4,807	6,953	10.9	18.4
LUTH–Wisc Ev Luth Syn	1	145	201	259	0.4	0.7
METH–Un Methodist	6	579	1,348	1,756	2.7	4.7
Muslim Est	2	268	NR	616	1.0	1.6
Non-denom Chr Chs	5	440	605	630	1.0	1.7
PENT–Assemb of God	1	270	81	302	0.5	0.8
PENT–Un Pent Ch Intl	1	NR	NR	NR	-	-
PENT–Vineyard	1	110	190	224	0.3	0.6
PRES–Presb Ch (USA)	4	388	1,038	1,226	1.9	3.3
PRES–Presb Ch Amer	1	50	57	61	0.1	0.2
Salvation Army	1	33	70	126	0.2	0.3

NR–Not Reported   - Represents no adherents reported.   Percentages may not total 100 due to rounding.

Table 3: Religious Congregations by County and Group: 2010

Religious Group	Number of Congrega-tions	Number of Attendees	Number of Communicant, Confirmed, or Full Members	Adherents: Number of Adherents	Adherents: % of Total Pop.	Adherents: % of Total Adh.
Sev Day Adv	1	74	128	147	0.2	0.4
Un C of Christ	2	160	374	442	0.7	1.2
Unit Univ	1	85	127	201	0.3	0.5
BROWN	**40**	**3,818**	**9,793**	**23,150**	**89.4**	**100.0**
ANG/EPIS–Episcopal	1	10	11	11	0.0	0.0
BAPT–NT Ind Bapt	1	NR	NR	NR	-	-
Catholic	7	NR	NR	10,778	41.6	46.6
Chr & Miss Al	1	NR	NR	NR	-	-
CHR–Chr Chs & Chs Cr	1	NR	0	0	0.0	0.0
Jehovah's Witness	1	NR	NR	NR	-	-
LUTH–Ch Luth Conf	2	NR	NR	NR	-	-
LUTH–E.L.C.A.	9	1,045	3,504	4,633	17.9	20.0
LUTH–Luth Cong Msn Chr	4	487	1,673	2,011	7.8	8.7
LUTH–Luth–MO Synod	2	222	563	721	2.8	3.1
LUTH–Wisc Ev Luth Syn	3	1,546	3,034	3,700	14.3	16.0
METH–Un Methodist	4	338	691	869	3.4	3.8
Non-denom Chr Chs	1	40	50	50	0.2	0.2
PENT–Assemb of God	1	25	12	65	0.3	0.3
Un C of Christ	1	65	197	237	0.9	1.0
Unit Univ	1	40	58	75	0.3	0.3
CARLTON	**57**	**4,028**	**6,956**	**15,995**	**45.2**	**100.0**
ANG/EPIS–Episcopal	2	22	34	34	0.1	0.2
Bahá'í	0	NR	11	11	0.0	0.1
BAPT–Converge/BGC	2	475	NR	570	1.6	3.6
Catholic	6	NR	NR	5,632	15.9	35.2
Chr & Miss Al	1	47	23	79	0.2	0.5
Evan Cov Ch	4	443	281	575	1.6	3.6
Evan Free Ch	1	25	NR	25	0.1	0.2
Jehovah's Witness	2	NR	NR	NR	-	-
LDS–L-D Saints	1	NR	NR	127	0.4	0.8
LUTH–Apostolic Luth	2	NR	NR	NR	-	-
LUTH–Assoc Free Luth	1	NR	NR	NR	-	-
LUTH–E.L.C.A.	9	1,164	3,396	4,785	13.5	29.9
LUTH–Luth Cong Msn Chr	1	40	127	155	0.4	1.0
LUTH–Luth–MO Synod	7	581	1,656	2,104	5.9	13.2
LUTH–Nor Amer Luth C	1	NR	NR	NR	-	-
METH–Un Methodist	4	251	297	433	1.2	2.7
Non-denom Chr Chs	5	860	869	1,100	3.1	6.9
PENT–Assemb of God	2	42	26	83	0.2	0.5
PENT–Un Pent Ch Intl	1	NR	NR	NR	-	-
PRES–Presb Ch (USA)	3	52	191	233	0.7	1.5
Salvation Army	1	12	21	21	0.1	0.1
Sev Day Adv	1	14	24	28	0.1	0.2
CARVER	**60**	**8,324**	**15,813**	**38,539**	**42.3**	**100.0**
Bahá'í	1	NR	28	28	0.0	0.1
BAPT–Converge/BGC	2	150	NR	180	0.2	0.5
BAPT–N Am Bapt Conf	1	NR	80	104	0.1	0.3
BUDD–Mahayana	1	NR	NR	536	0.6	1.4
Catholic	8	NR	NR	14,887	16.4	38.6
Ch of Nazarene	1	48	61	61	0.1	0.2
Chr & Miss Al	4	766	244	1,014	1.1	2.6
CONG–Consrv Cong Chr	1	45	101	131	0.1	0.3
Evan Free Ch	2	475	NR	475	0.5	1.2
HINDU–I/A Temples	1	NR	NR	250	0.3	0.6
Jehovah's Witness	2	NR	NR	NR	-	-
LDS–L-D Saints	1	NR	NR	305	0.3	0.8
LUTH–E.L.C.A.	7	2,023	5,610	7,959	8.7	20.7
LUTH–Luth Cong Msn Chr	1	73	111	144	0.2	0.4
LUTH–Luth–MO Synod	13	3,936	8,018	10,440	11.5	27.1
METH–Un Methodist	2	110	207	313	0.3	0.8
MORAV–Morav Ch-North	3	202	497	575	0.6	1.5
Non-denom Chr Chs	2	220	275	275	0.3	0.7
PENT–Assemb of God	2	131	30	180	0.2	0.5
PRES–Presb Ch (USA)	1	45	73	95	0.1	0.2
REF–Ref Ch in U.S.	1	NR	211	240	0.3	0.6
Un C of Christ	3	100	267	347	0.4	0.9
CASS	**53**	**3,338**	**5,151**	**10,657**	**37.3**	**100.0**
ANG/EPIS–Episcopal	2	31	134	202	0.7	1.9
Bahá'í	0	NR	13	13	0.0	0.1
BAPT–Converge/BGC	3	225	NR	270	0.9	2.5
Catholic	8	NR	NR	2,820	9.9	26.5
Ch of Nazarene	1	102	72	162	0.6	1.5
Chr & Miss Al	5	116	96	204	0.7	1.9
CONG–Cong Chr, NA	1	NR	44	53	0.2	0.5
Evan Free Ch	2	295	NR	295	1.0	2.8
LUTH–E.L.C.A.	13	1,211	2,593	3,621	12.7	34.0
LUTH–Luth Cong Msn Chr	1	50	285	342	1.2	3.2
LUTH–Luth–MO Synod	3	189	360	455	1.6	4.3
METH–Un Methodist	1	38	41	82	0.3	0.8
Non-denom Chr Chs	6	580	540	726	2.5	6.8
PENT–Assemb of God	2	175	72	225	0.8	2.1
PENT–Ch God (Cleve)	1	63	117	140	0.5	1.3
PENT–Pent Ch of God	1	70	NR	109	0.4	1.0
Sev Day Adv	1	44	77	89	0.3	0.8
Un C of Christ	2	149	707	849	3.0	8.0
CHIPPEWA	**29**	**2,503**	**7,493**	**10,688**	**85.9**	**100.0**
Bahá'í	0	NR	7	7	0.1	0.1
BAPT–Converge/BGC	1	75	NR	90	0.7	0.8
BAPT–Reg Bapt Gen As	1	NR	NR	NR	-	-
Catholic	2	NR	NR	1,531	12.3	14.3
Evan Ch	1	NR	NR	NR	-	-
Jehovah's Witness	1	NR	NR	NR	-	-
LUTH–E.L.C.A.	12	1,282	5,144	6,343	51.0	59.3
LUTH–Evan Luth Syn	1	32	46	53	0.4	0.5
LUTH–Luth Cong Msn Chr	1	40	91	111	0.9	1.0
LUTH–Luth–MO Synod	3	183	570	693	5.6	6.5
METH–Un Methodist	1	114	281	355	2.9	3.3
PRES–Presb Ch (USA)	1	12	11	13	0.1	0.1
REF–Christian Ref	1	300	346	420	3.4	3.9
REF–Ref Ch in Am	2	435	912	969	7.8	9.1
Un C of Christ	1	30	85	103	0.8	1.0
CHISAGO	**54**	**6,432**	**10,001**	**23,415**	**43.5**	**100.0**
Bahá'í	0	NR	6	6	0.0	0.0
BAPT–Consrv Bapt	1	NR	NR	NR	-	-
BAPT–Converge/BGC	4	300	NR	360	0.7	1.5
BAPT–NT Ind Bapt	2	NR	NR	NR	-	-
Catholic	4	NR	NR	6,089	11.3	26.0
Evan Cov Ch	3	269	262	349	0.6	1.5
Evan Free Ch	4	924	NR	924	1.7	3.9
Jehovah's Witness	1	NR	NR	NR	-	-
LDS–L-D Saints	1	NR	NR	466	0.9	2.0
LUTH–Assoc Free Luth	1	NR	NR	NR	-	-
LUTH–E.L.C.A.	12	2,042	6,894	9,017	16.7	38.5
LUTH–Luth Cong Msn Chr	2	222	555	689	1.3	2.9
LUTH–Luth–MO Synod	3	230	506	631	1.2	2.7
METH–Un Methodist	4	511	613	754	1.4	3.2
Non-denom Chr Chs	5	435	529	593	1.1	2.5
ORTHE–Orth Ch in Amer	2	30	NR	55	0.1	0.2
PENT–Assemb of God	3	1,469	636	3,482	6.5	14.9
PENT–Un Pent Ch Intl	2	NR	NR	NR	-	-
CLAY	**74**	**7,095**	**17,677**	**35,938**	**60.9**	**100.0**
ANG/EPIS–Episcopal	1	54	265	265	0.4	0.7
Bahá'í	0	NR	24	24	0.0	0.1
BAPT–Consrv Bapt	1	NR	NR	NR	-	-
BAPT–Converge/BGC	1	75	NR	90	0.2	0.3
BAPT–NT Ind Bapt	1	NR	NR	NR	-	-
BAPT–Reg Bapt Gen As	1	NR	NR	NR	-	-
Catholic	11	NR	NR	9,900	16.8	27.5
Ch of Nazarene	1	37	35	44	0.1	0.1
Chr & Miss Al	1	199	110	333	0.6	0.9
CHR–Chr Chs & Chs Cr	1	NR	115	141	0.2	0.4
CHR–Chs of Christ	1	20	15	16	0.0	0.0
Jehovah's Witness	1	NR	NR	NR	-	-
LUTH–Assoc Free Luth	2	NR	NR	NR	-	-
LUTH–Ch of Luth Br	2	1,013	506	3,083	5.2	8.6
LUTH–E.L.C.A.	22	3,739	11,953	16,160	27.4	45.0
LUTH–Evan Luth Syn	1	28	50	63	0.1	0.2
LUTH–Luth Cong Msn Chr	3	360	1,640	2,008	3.4	5.6

NR–Not Reported - Represents no adherents reported. Percentages may not total 100 due to rounding.

Table 3: Religious Congregations by County and Group: 2010

Religious Group	Number of Congregations	Number of Attendees	Number of Communicant, Confirmed, or Full Members	Adherents		
				Number of Adherents	% of Total Pop.	% of Total Adh.
LUTH–Luth–MO Synod	3	509	1,070	1,280	2.2	3.6
LUTH–Wisc Ev Luth Syn	1	52	141	167	0.3	0.5
MENN–Hutt Breth	1	NR	NR	NR	-	-
METH–Un Methodist	2	141	340	418	0.7	1.2
Non-denom Chr Chs	5	350	345	437	0.7	1.2
PENT–Assemb of God	2	155	99	326	0.6	0.9
PENT–Un Pent Ch Intl	1	NR	NR	NR	-	-
PRES–Presb Ch (USA)	3	104	284	348	0.6	1.0
Sev Day Adv	1	34	58	67	0.1	0.2
Un C of Christ	4	225	627	768	1.3	2.1
CLEARWATER	**29**	**1,391**	**3,118**	**4,463**	**51.3**	**100.0**
ANG/EPIS–Episcopal	1	19	40	110	1.3	2.5
Bahá'í	0	NR	1	1	0.0	0.0
BAPT–Converge/BGC	1	75	NR	90	1.0	2.0
Catholic	1	NR	NR	360	4.1	8.1
Evan Free Ch	1	85	NR	85	1.0	1.9
Jehovah's Witness	2	NR	NR	NR	-	-
LDS–L-D Saints	1	NR	NR	215	2.5	4.8
LUTH–Assoc Free Luth	4	NR	NR	NR	-	-
LUTH–Ch of Luth Br	1	89	104	187	2.2	4.2
LUTH–E.L.C.A.	7	434	1,925	2,041	23.5	45.7
LUTH–Evan Luth Syn	1	28	121	136	1.6	3.0
LUTH–Luth–MO Synod	1	54	130	173	2.0	3.9
LUTH–Nor Amer Luth C	2	NR	NR	NR	-	-
MENN–Amish Undif	1	NR	51	105	1.2	2.4
Non-denom Chr Chs	4	565	725	894	10.3	20.0
PENT–Assemb of God	1	42	21	66	0.8	1.5
COOK	**15**	**1,039**	**1,236**	**2,664**	**51.5**	**100.0**
Bahá'í	0	NR	1	1	0.0	0.0
BAPT–Converge/BGC	2	475	NR	570	11.0	21.4
Catholic	2	NR	NR	432	8.3	16.2
Evan Free Ch	1	100	NR	100	1.9	3.8
Jehovah's Witness	1	NR	NR	NR	-	-
LUTH–E.L.C.A.	3	236	636	892	17.2	33.5
LUTH–Luth Cong Msn Chr	1	42	151	172	3.3	6.5
LUTH–Luth–MO Synod	1	0	0	0	0.0	0.0
Non-denom Chr Chs	1	100	150	150	2.9	5.6
PENT–Assemb of God	1	7	5	13	0.3	0.5
Sev Day Adv	1	4	8	9	0.2	0.3
Un C of Christ	1	75	285	325	6.3	12.2
COTTONWOOD	**41**	**2,826**	**5,629**	**9,461**	**81.0**	**100.0**
ANG/EPIS–Episcopal	1	9	22	22	0.2	0.2
BAPT–Consrv Bapt	2	NR	NR	NR	-	-
BAPT–NT Ind Bapt	1	NR	NR	NR	-	-
Catholic	2	NR	NR	1,834	15.7	19.4
Chr & Miss Al	1	326	150	530	4.5	5.6
Evan Free Ch	1	280	NR	280	2.4	3.0
LUTH–Assoc Free Luth	1	NR	NR	NR	-	-
LUTH–E.L.C.A.	8	773	2,775	3,454	29.6	36.5
LUTH–Luth–MO Synod	2	357	996	1,260	10.8	13.3
MENN–Fel Evg Bib Ch	3	198	162	198	1.7	2.1
MENN–Hutt Breth	2	NR	NR	NR	-	-
MENN–Menn Br US Conf	1	NR	92	112	1.0	1.2
MENN–Mennonite USA	2	182	379	463	4.0	4.9
METH–Un Methodist	4	255	444	539	4.6	5.7
Non-denom Chr Chs	4	275	290	344	2.9	3.6
PENT–Assemb of God	1	55	28	72	0.6	0.8
PENT–Ch of God Proph	1	NR	35	43	0.4	0.5
PRES–Presb Ch (USA)	3	96	222	271	2.3	2.9
Sev Day Adv	1	20	34	39	0.3	0.4
CROW WING	**89**	**8,934**	**14,812**	**33,898**	**54.2**	**100.0**
ANG/EPIS–Episcopal	1	32	65	79	0.1	0.2
Bahá'í	0	NR	11	11	0.0	0.0
BAPT–Consrv Bapt	1	NR	NR	NR	-	-
BAPT–Converge/BGC	4	1,025	NR	1,230	2.0	3.6
BAPT–NT Ind Bapt	2	NR	NR	NR	-	-
BAPT–Reg Bapt Gen As	1	NR	NR	NR	-	-
BAPT–So Bapt Conv	2	61	25	30	0.0	0.1
Catholic	13	NR	NR	10,751	17.2	31.7
Ch Cr, Scientst	1	NR	NR	NR	-	-
Ch of Nazarene	2	169	286	293	0.5	0.9
Chr & Miss Al	2	175	96	300	0.5	0.9
CHR–Chr Chs & Chs Cr	1	NR	40	49	0.1	0.1
CHR–Chs of Christ	1	30	25	27	0.0	0.1
Evan Free Ch	4	1,165	NR	1,165	1.9	3.4
FRND–Fr Gen Cf	1	NR	14	17	0.0	0.1
Jehovah's Witness	1	NR	NR	NR	-	-
LDS–L-D Saints	1	NR	NR	563	0.9	1.7
LUTH–Assoc Free Luth	1	NR	NR	NR	-	-
LUTH–E.L.C.A.	11	2,924	8,787	11,323	18.1	33.4
LUTH–Luth Cong Msn Chr	2	273	753	917	1.5	2.7
LUTH–Luth–MO Synod	7	572	1,647	2,070	3.3	6.1
LUTH–Nor Amer Luth C	1	NR	NR	NR	-	-
LUTH–Wisc Ev Luth Syn	1	120	222	249	0.4	0.7
METH–Un Methodist	5	484	929	1,400	2.2	4.1
METH–Wesleyan	1	89	47	116	0.2	0.3
Non-denom Chr Chs	8	732	807	939	1.5	2.8
PENT–Assemb of God	3	609	284	1,282	2.1	3.8
PENT–Ch God (Cleve)	1	3	3	4	0.0	0.0
PENT–Un Pent Ch Intl	1	NR	NR	NR	-	-
PRES–Orth Pres Ch	1	33	13	28	0.0	0.1
PRES–Presb Ch (USA)	4	232	323	393	0.6	1.2
Salvation Army	1	48	67	226	0.4	0.7
Sev Day Adv	1	74	129	148	0.2	0.4
Un C of Christ	1	77	226	275	0.4	0.8
Unit Univ	1	7	13	13	0.0	0.0
DAKOTA	**219**	**47,481**	**66,880**	**232,928**	**58.4**	**100.0**
ANG/EPIS–Episcopal	5	443	1,065	1,222	0.3	0.5
Ap Chr Ch-Amer	1	130	41	130	0.0	0.1
Bahá'í	0	NR	114	114	0.0	0.0
BAPT–Amer Bapt USA	1	50	91	114	0.0	0.0
BAPT–Consrv Bapt	1	NR	NR	NR	-	-
BAPT–Converge/BGC	9	3,975	NR	4,770	1.2	2.0
BAPT–N Am Bapt Conf	3	NR	434	544	0.1	0.2
BAPT–NT Ind Bapt	1	NR	NR	NR	-	-
BAPT–So Bapt Conv	3	207	419	525	0.1	0.2
BRETH–Ch of Brethren	1	0	81	102	0.0	0.0
BUDD–Theravada	2	NR	NR	696	0.2	0.3
Catholic	18	NR	NR	112,264	28.2	48.2
Ch Cr, Scientst	1	NR	NR	NR	-	-
Ch of Nazarene	2	66	73	75	0.0	0.0
Chr & Miss Al	4	899	434	1,379	0.3	0.6
CHR–Chr Ch (Disc)	1	81	71	89	0.0	0.0
CHR–Chr Chs & Chs Cr	1	NR	400	501	0.1	0.2
CHR–Chs of Christ	2	115	105	135	0.0	0.1
CONG–Cong Chr, NA	1	NR	67	84	0.0	0.0
CONG–Consrv Cong Chr	1	38	20	25	0.0	0.0
Evan Cov Ch	3	867	665	1,127	0.3	0.5
Evan Free Ch	5	1,750	NR	1,750	0.4	0.8
HINDU–I/A Temples	1	NR	NR	160	0.0	0.1
HINDU–Trad Temples	1	NR	NR	30	0.0	0.0
Jehovah's Witness	4	NR	NR	NR	-	-
JUD–Conserv	2	315	354	956	0.2	0.4
LDS–Comm of Christ	1	NR	138	138	0.0	0.1
LDS–L-D Saints	8	NR	NR	2,662	0.7	1.1
LUTH–Assoc Free Luth	2	NR	NR	NR	-	-
LUTH–Ch Luth Conf	1	NR	NR	NR	-	-
LUTH–Ch of Luth Br	1	130	100	230	0.1	0.1
LUTH–E.L.C.A.	27	11,591	31,913	45,852	11.5	19.7
LUTH–Evan Luth Syn	2	196	203	293	0.1	0.1
LUTH–Luth Cong Msn Chr	2	5,281	6,278	7,869	2.0	3.4
LUTH–Luth–MO Synod	11	2,078	4,138	5,351	1.3	2.3
LUTH–Wisc Ev Luth Syn	7	1,586	2,984	3,807	1.0	1.6
MENN–Fel Evg Ch	1	98	130	163	0.0	0.1
MENN–Menn Br US Conf	1	NR	110	138	0.0	0.1
METH–AME	1	0	100	125	0.0	0.1
METH–Un Methodist	14	2,412	4,327	6,751	1.7	2.9
METH–Wesleyan	1	58	34	75	0.0	0.0
Muslim Est	5	670	NR	1,540	0.4	0.7
Non-denom Chr Chs	17	5,510	7,386	8,200	2.1	3.5
ORTHE–Ant Orth of NA	1	115	NR	333	0.1	0.1

NR–Not Reported   - Represents no adherents reported.   Percentages may not total 100 due to rounding.

Table 3: Religious Congregations by County and Group: 2010

Religious Group	Number of Congrega-tions	Number of Attendees	Number of Communicant, Confirmed, or Full Members	Adherents: Number of Adherents	Adherents: % of Total Pop.	Adherents: % of Total Adh.
ORTHE–Orth Ch in Amer	1	50	NR	50	0.0	0.0
ORTHE–Romania Orth Ar	1	60	NR	200	0.1	0.1
ORTHE–Serb Orth USA	1	30	NR	40	0.0	0.0
ORTHO–Coptic Orth Ch	1	300	NR	550	0.1	0.2
PENT–Assemb of God	17	6,731	1,678	18,200	4.6	7.8
PENT–COGIC	1	0	150	188	0.0	0.1
PENT–Intl Pent Holiness	1	180	100	125	0.0	0.1
PENT–Un Pent Ch Intl	3	NR	NR	NR	-	-
PENT–Vineyard	3	515	784	983	0.2	0.4
PRES–Kor Pres Abroad	1	NR	NR	NR	-	-
PRES–Presb Ch (USA)	4	226	460	577	0.1	0.2
PRES–Presb Ch Amer	1	40	31	48	0.0	0.0
REF–Christian Ref	1	50	96	120	0.0	0.1
REF–Ref Ch in Am	1	366	778	897	0.2	0.4
Sev Day Adv	1	171	297	342	0.1	0.1
Un C of Christ	2	84	211	264	0.1	0.1
Unit Univ	1	17	20	20	0.0	0.0
Zoroastrian	1	NR	NR	5	0.0	0.0
DODGE	**38**	**2,745**	**6,122**	**13,889**	**69.1**	**100.0**
ANG/EPIS–Episcopal	1	27	54	95	0.5	0.7
Bahá'í	0	NR	10	10	0.0	0.1
BAPT–Consrv Bapt	1	NR	NR	NR	-	-
BAPT–Converge/BGC	1	75	NR	90	0.4	0.6
BAPT–Reg Bapt Gen As	1	NR	NR	NR	-	-
BAPT–S-D Baptist Gen Con	1	48	90	116	0.6	0.8
Catholic	5	NR	NR	3,819	19.0	27.5
CHR–Chr Chs & Chs Cr	2	NR	235	303	1.5	2.2
CONG–Consrv Cong Chr	1	57	117	151	0.8	1.1
LDS–L-D Saints	1	NR	NR	112	0.6	0.8
LUTH–Assoc Free Luth	1	NR	NR	NR	-	-
LUTH–E.L.C.A.	4	1,043	2,652	4,782	23.8	34.4
LUTH–Luth Ch-Am Asc	1	NR	NR	NR	-	-
LUTH–Luth Cong Msn Chr	1	130	721	929	4.6	6.7
LUTH–Luth–MO Synod	3	195	497	613	3.1	4.4
LUTH–Wisc Ev Luth Syn	1	86	119	162	0.8	1.2
METH–Un Methodist	4	174	509	721	3.6	5.2
Non-denom Chr Chs	1	55	60	69	0.3	0.5
PENT–Assemb of God	2	475	147	764	3.8	5.5
PRES–Presb Ch (USA)	3	189	442	570	2.8	4.1
Sev Day Adv	1	91	158	182	0.9	1.3
Un C of Christ	2	100	311	401	2.0	2.9
DOUGLAS	**64**	**6,264**	**13,371**	**25,307**	**70.3**	**100.0**
ANG/EPIS–Episcopal	1	26	43	43	0.1	0.2
Bahá'í	0	NR	10	10	0.0	0.0
BAPT–Converge/BGC	2	150	NR	180	0.5	0.7
Catholic	6	NR	NR	6,636	18.4	26.2
CHR–Chr Chs & Chs Cr	1	NR	375	451	1.3	1.8
Evan Cov Ch	4	871	504	1,132	3.1	4.5
Evan Free Ch	2	325	NR	325	0.9	1.3
Jehovah's Witness	1	NR	NR	NR	-	-
LDS–L-D Saints	1	NR	NR	304	0.8	1.2
LUTH–Assoc Free Luth	1	NR	NR	NR	-	-
LUTH–Ch of Luth Br	1	80	40	155	0.4	0.6
LUTH–E.L.C.A.	16	2,337	7,717	10,027	27.8	39.6
LUTH–Luth Cong Msn Chr	6	486	924	1,112	3.1	4.4
LUTH–Luth–MO Synod	9	1,010	2,178	2,751	7.6	10.9
LUTH–Wisc Ev Luth Syn	1	81	157	195	0.5	0.8
MENN–CG in Cr (Menn)	1	NR	75	90	0.2	0.4
METH–Free Methodist	1	25	28	28	0.1	0.1
METH–Un Methodist	2	192	510	708	2.0	2.8
Non-denom Chr Chs	3	420	325	525	1.5	2.1
PENT–Assemb of God	1	95	63	129	0.4	0.5
PENT–Un Pent Ch Intl	1	NR	NR	NR	-	-
PRES–Presb Ch (USA)	1	46	98	118	0.3	0.5
Sev Day Adv	1	20	36	41	0.1	0.2
Un C of Christ	1	100	288	347	1.0	1.4
FARIBAULT	**44**	**2,429**	**6,550**	**12,125**	**83.3**	**100.0**
BAPT–Amer Bapt USA	1	80	180	215	1.5	1.8
BAPT–Consrv Bapt	1	NR	NR	NR	-	-
Catholic	5	NR	NR	3,583	24.6	29.6
Evan Cov Ch	1	74	53	96	0.7	0.8
Evan Free Ch	1	75	NR	75	0.5	0.6
Jehovah's Witness	1	NR	NR	NR	-	-
LUTH–Assoc Free Luth	1	NR	NR	NR	-	-
LUTH–Ch of Luth Br	1	30	34	49	0.3	0.4
LUTH–E.L.C.A.	12	993	3,362	4,281	29.4	35.3
LUTH–Luth–MO Synod	7	441	1,279	1,513	10.4	12.5
METH–Un Methodist	6	314	933	1,247	8.6	10.3
Non-denom Chr Chs	1	50	50	62	0.4	0.5
PENT–Assemb of God	2	154	76	306	2.1	2.5
PRES–Presb Ch (USA)	2	120	253	303	2.1	2.5
Un C of Christ	2	98	330	395	2.7	3.3
FILLMORE	**74**	**3,681**	**11,705**	**19,914**	**95.4**	**100.0**
ANG/EPIS–Episcopal	2	41	80	106	0.5	0.5
Bahá'í	0	NR	4	4	0.0	0.0
BAPT–NT Ind Bapt	2	NR	NR	NR	-	-
BAPT–Reg Bapt Gen As	1	NR	NR	NR	-	-
BRETH–Ch of Brethren	1	0	45	55	0.3	0.3
Catholic	8	NR	NR	4,223	20.2	21.2
Chr & Miss Al	1	152	100	172	0.8	0.9
LDS–L-D Saints	1	NR	NR	75	0.4	0.4
LUTH–Ch Luth Conf	1	NR	NR	NR	-	-
LUTH–E.L.C.A.	26	1,746	6,725	8,861	42.5	44.5
LUTH–Luth Cong Msn Chr	1	217	971	1,193	5.7	6.0
LUTH–Luth–MO Synod	5	476	1,441	1,677	8.0	8.4
MENN–Amish Undif	8	NR	376	978	4.7	4.9
METH–Free Methodist	1	170	87	170	0.8	0.9
METH–Un Methodist	9	348	1,087	1,395	6.7	7.0
Non-denom Chr Chs	2	105	130	131	0.6	0.7
PENT–Assemb of God	1	150	78	220	1.1	1.1
PRES–Presb Ch (USA)	3	84	208	256	1.2	1.3
REF–Ref Ch in Am	1	192	373	398	1.9	2.0
FREEBORN	**62**	**5,397**	**15,345**	**26,382**	**84.4**	**100.0**
ANG/EPIS–Episcopal	1	25	65	68	0.2	0.3
Bahá'í	0	NR	1	1	0.0	0.0
BAPT–Amer Bapt USA	3	291	739	890	2.8	3.4
BAPT–Reg Bapt Gen As	2	NR	NR	NR	-	-
Catholic	3	NR	NR	5,388	17.2	20.4
CHR–Chr Chs & Chs Cr	1	NR	150	181	0.6	0.7
CHR–Chs of Christ	1	40	30	39	0.1	0.1
CONG–Consrv Cong Chr	1	24	35	42	0.1	0.2
Evan Free Ch	1	700	NR	700	2.2	2.7
Jehovah's Witness	1	NR	NR	NR	-	-
LDS–L-D Saints	1	NR	NR	167	0.5	0.6
LUTH–E.L.C.A.	24	2,550	10,436	13,724	43.9	52.0
LUTH–Evan Luth Syn	3	174	600	786	2.5	3.0
LUTH–Luth Cong Msn Chr	1	55	195	235	0.8	0.9
LUTH–Luth–MO Synod	2	241	614	771	2.5	2.9
LUTH–Nor Amer Luth C	1	NR	NR	NR	-	-
METH–Free Methodist	1	35	39	39	0.1	0.1
METH–Un Methodist	4	267	667	902	2.9	3.4
Non-denom Chr Chs	2	130	220	220	0.7	0.8
PENT–Assemb of God	1	130	89	385	1.2	1.5
PENT–Un Pent Ch Intl	1	NR	NR	NR	-	-
PENT–Vineyard	1	160	220	265	0.8	1.0
PRES–Presb Ch (USA)	1	240	599	721	2.3	2.7
REF–Christian Ref	1	130	210	253	0.8	1.0
REF–Ref Ch in Am	1	120	188	200	0.6	0.8
Salvation Army	1	59	116	248	0.8	0.9
Sev Day Adv	1	26	46	53	0.2	0.2
Un C of Christ	1	0	86	104	0.3	0.4
GOODHUE	**87**	**6,684**	**17,985**	**30,515**	**66.1**	**100.0**
ANG/EPIS–Episcopal	4	149	389	421	0.9	1.4
Bahá'í	0	NR	5	5	0.0	0.0
BAPT–Consrv Bapt	1	NR	NR	NR	-	-
BAPT–Converge/BGC	2	150	NR	180	0.4	0.6
BAPT–NT Ind Bapt	1	NR	NR	NR	-	-
BAPT–So Bapt Conv	1	45	101	123	0.3	0.4
Calv Chpl	1	NR	NR	NR	-	-
Catholic	8	NR	NR	5,805	12.6	19.0

NR–Not Reported - Represents no adherents reported. Percentages may not total 100 due to rounding.

Table 3: Religious Congregations by County and Group: 2010

Religious Group	Number of Congrega-tions	Number of Attendees	Number of Communicant, Confirmed, or Full Members	Adherents: Number of Adherents	Adherents: % of Total Pop.	Adherents: % of Total Adh.
CHR–Chr Chs & Chs Cr	1	NR	20	24	0.1	0.1
CHR–Chs of Christ	1	28	17	28	0.1	0.1
Evan Cov Ch	1	237	251	308	0.7	1.0
Evan Free Ch	1	70	NR	70	0.2	0.2
Jehovah's Witness	1	NR	NR	NR	-	-
LDS–Comm of Christ	1	NR	138	138	0.3	0.5
LDS–L-D Saints	1	NR	NR	346	0.7	1.1
LUTH–Assoc Free Luth	4	NR	NR	NR	-	-
LUTH–Ch Luth Conf	1	NR	NR	NR	-	-
LUTH–E.L.C.A.	25	3,318	11,580	15,837	34.3	51.9
LUTH–Luth Cong Msn Chr	1	27	79	96	0.2	0.3
LUTH–Luth–MO Synod	3	165	745	864	1.9	2.8
LUTH–Wisc Ev Luth Syn	9	1,196	2,710	3,308	7.2	10.8
MENN–Fel Evg Ch	1	60	32	39	0.1	0.1
METH–Un Methodist	4	297	937	1,338	2.9	4.4
METH–Wesleyan	1	19	13	25	0.1	0.1
Non-denom Chr Chs	1	95	70	119	0.3	0.4
PENT–Assemb of God	5	552	216	614	1.3	2.0
PENT–Un Pent Ch Intl	2	NR	NR	NR	-	-
PRES–Presb Ch (USA)	1	135	350	427	0.9	1.4
Sev Day Adv	2	52	89	103	0.2	0.3
Un C of Christ	2	89	243	297	0.6	1.0
GRANT	**25**	**1,461**	**3,527**	**5,507**	**91.5**	**100.0**
Bahá'í	0	NR	4	4	0.1	0.1
Catholic	2	NR	NR	519	8.6	9.4
Evan Free Ch	1	137	NR	137	2.3	2.5
LUTH–E.L.C.A.	10	706	2,213	3,389	56.3	61.5
LUTH–Luth Cong Msn Chr	1	68	164	196	3.3	3.6
LUTH–Luth–MO Synod	3	120	376	426	7.1	7.7
METH–Un Methodist	2	60	133	144	2.4	2.6
Non-denom Chr Chs	2	300	415	415	6.9	7.5
PENT–Assemb of God	1	15	8	26	0.4	0.5
PRES–Presb Ch (USA)	2	30	166	198	3.3	3.6
REF–Ref Ch in Am	1	25	48	53	0.9	1.0
HENNEPIN	**838**	**168,215**	**271,405**	**626,233**	**54.3**	**100.0**
ANG/EPIS–Anglican NA	3	NR	NR	NR	-	-
ANG/EPIS–Episcopal	18	2,450	7,476	8,209	0.7	1.3
Bahá'í	6	NR	634	634	0.1	0.1
BAPT–Alliance Bapt	2	NR	NR	NR	-	-
BAPT–Amer Bapt USA	11	1,341	3,686	4,480	0.4	0.7
BAPT–Consrv Bapt	3	NR	NR	NR	-	-
BAPT–Converge/BGC	26	13,525	NR	16,230	1.4	2.6
BAPT–N Am Bapt Conf	3	NR	780	948	0.1	0.2
BAPT–Natl Mis Bapt Conv	2	400	510	620	0.1	0.1
BAPT–NBC Amer	3	1,350	5,150	6,259	0.5	1.0
BAPT–NBC USA	4	825	1,200	1,458	0.1	0.2
BAPT–NT Ind Bapt	5	NR	NR	NR	-	-
BAPT–Ref Bapt Ch	1	NR	NR	NR	-	-
BAPT–So Bapt Conv	11	900	1,232	1,497	0.1	0.2
BRETH–Ch of Brethren	1	15	6	7	0.0	0.0
BRETH–Grace Breth	1	NR	NR	NR	-	-
BUDD–Mahayana	9	NR	NR	893	0.1	0.1
BUDD–Theravada	3	NR	NR	44	0.0	0.0
BUDD–Vajrayana	9	NR	NR	502	0.0	0.1
Calv Chpl	1	NR	NR	NR	-	-
Catholic	73	NR	NR	215,205	18.7	34.4
CGOD–Ch God (Ander)	1	30	NR	30	0.0	0.0
Ch Cr, Scientst	4	NR	NR	NR	-	-
Ch of God Gen Conf	2	NR	81	98	0.0	0.0
Ch of Nazarene	7	494	614	784	0.1	0.1
Chr & Miss Al	9	1,663	1,353	2,444	0.2	0.4
CHR–Chr Ch (Disc)	4	102	550	668	0.1	0.1
CHR–Chr Chs & Chs Cr	3	NR	250	304	0.0	0.0
CHR–Chs of Christ	4	605	579	725	0.1	0.1
CHR–Int Chs of Christ	1	NR	205	249	0.0	0.0
CONG–Cong Chr, NA	2	NR	4,109	4,994	0.4	0.8
CONG–Consrv Cong Chr	4	5,837	4,735	5,755	0.5	0.9
Evan Ch	2	NR	NR	NR	-	-
Evan Cov Ch	21	4,472	3,513	5,816	0.5	0.9
Evan Free Ch	19	8,547	NR	8,547	0.7	1.4
FRND–Fr Gen Cf	1	NR	149	181	0.0	0.0
FRND–Unaffl Mtgs	1	NR	NR	NR	-	-
HINDU–I/A Temples	2	NR	NR	1,842	0.2	0.3
HINDU–Post Ren	3	NR	NR	103	0.0	0.0
HINDU–Renaiss	2	NR	NR	24	0.0	0.0
HINDU–Trad Temples	4	NR	NR	1,545	0.1	0.2
Int Cou Comm Ch	2	NR	NR	NR	-	-
Jain	1	NR	NR	NR	-	-
Jehovah's Witness	7	NR	NR	NR	-	-
JUD–Conserv	3	2,342	2,629	7,098	0.6	1.1
JUD–Orth	5	1,152	500	1,600	0.1	0.3
JUD–Reconst	1	44	56	151	0.0	0.0
JUD–Reform	3	1,808	3,188	8,608	0.7	1.4
LDS–Comm of Christ	1	NR	138	138	0.0	0.0
LDS–L-D Saints	15	NR	NR	7,888	0.7	1.3
LUTH–Apostolic Luth	2	NR	NR	NR	-	-
LUTH–Assoc Free Luth	5	NR	NR	NR	-	-
LUTH–Ch Luth Conf	2	NR	NR	NR	-	-
LUTH–Ch of Luth Br	2	292	329	428	0.0	0.1
LUTH–E.L.C.A.	106	35,173	94,278	124,732	10.8	19.9
LUTH–Evan Luth Syn	2	486	678	907	0.1	0.1
LUTH–Luth Ch-Am Asc	1	NR	NR	NR	-	-
LUTH–Luth Cong Msn Chr	6	1,606	5,687	6,912	0.6	1.1
LUTH–Luth–MO Synod	34	6,713	14,710	18,836	1.6	3.0
LUTH–Wisc Ev Luth Syn	12	2,121	3,781	4,734	0.4	0.8
MENN–Mennonite USA	3	160	204	248	0.0	0.0
METH–AME	3	350	1,100	1,337	0.1	0.2
METH–C.M.E.	1	20	31	38	0.0	0.0
METH–Free Methodist	2	64	55	64	0.0	0.0
METH–Un Methodist	42	6,708	14,098	20,286	1.8	3.2
METH–Wesleyan	1	87	79	113	0.0	0.0
Metro Comm Ch	1	239	332	404	0.0	0.1
Muslim Est	23	4,330	NR	7,760	0.7	1.2
New Apost Ch	1	NR	NR	NR	-	-
Non-denom Chr Chs	103	42,501	55,113	59,811	5.2	9.6
OCATH–Pol Natl Cath	1	NR	NR	NR	-	-
ORTHE–Greek Orthodox	1	350	NR	1,545	0.1	0.2
ORTHE–Orth Ch in Amer	2	380	NR	1,292	0.1	0.2
ORTHE–Rus Orth Abroad	1	100	NR	100	0.0	0.0
ORTHE–Ukrainian Orth	1	120	NR	400	0.0	0.1
ORTHO–Ethiopian Orth	1	NR	NR	NR	-	-
PENT–Apos Faith Msn	1	NR	35	43	0.0	0.0
PENT–Assemb of God	32	5,298	2,851	16,128	1.4	2.6
PENT–Ch God (Cleve)	5	851	1,118	1,359	0.1	0.2
PENT–Ch of God Proph	2	NR	48	58	0.0	0.0
PENT–COGIC	8	865	905	1,100	0.1	0.2
PENT–Int Foursq Gos	6	291	380	462	0.0	0.1
PENT–Intl Pent Holiness	3	180	91	111	0.0	0.0
PENT–Open Bible Std	1	48	NR	48	0.0	0.0
PENT–Pent Ch of God	2	140	NR	217	0.0	0.0
PENT–Un Pent Ch Intl	3	NR	NR	NR	-	-
PENT–Vineyard	4	673	797	969	0.1	0.2
PRES–Presb Ch (USA)	21	3,366	13,939	16,941	1.5	2.7
PRES–Presb Ch Amer	1	119	146	170	0.0	0.0
REF–Christian Ref	2	391	530	644	0.1	0.1
REF–Comm Ref Evan	1	NR	NR	NR	-	-
REF–Ref Ch in Am	2	211	220	296	0.0	0.0
REF–Ref Ch in U.S.	1	NR	111	183	0.0	0.0
Salvation Army	3	222	294	1,270	0.1	0.2
Sev Day Adv	24	2,472	4,299	4,945	0.4	0.8
Sikh	1	NR	NR	NR	-	-
Un C of Christ	20	2,333	10,126	12,307	1.1	2.0
Unit Univ	5	1,053	1,717	2,449	0.2	0.4
Unity Ch	2	NR	NR	NR	-	-
Zoroastrian	0	NR	NR	8	0.0	0.0
HOUSTON	**33**	**3,017**	**6,103**	**13,537**	**71.1**	**100.0**
Bahá'í	0	NR	2	2	0.0	0.0
BAPT–Converge/BGC	1	400	NR	480	2.5	3.5
Catholic	5	NR	NR	4,848	25.5	35.8
Evan Free Ch	3	335	NR	335	1.8	2.5
Jehovah's Witness	1	NR	NR	NR	-	-
LUTH–E.L.C.A.	6	984	3,514	4,613	24.2	34.1
LUTH–Luth Cong Msn Chr	1	67	199	240	1.3	1.8
LUTH–Luth–MO Synod	1	50	79	101	0.5	0.7

NR–Not Reported - Represents no adherents reported. Percentages may not total 100 due to rounding.

Table 3: Religious Congregations by County and Group: 2010

Religious Group	Number of Congrega-tions	Number of Attendees	Number of Communicant, Confirmed, or Full Members	Adherents: Number of Adherents	Adherents: % of Total Pop.	Adherents: % of Total Adh.
LUTH–Wisc Ev Luth Syn	5	618	1,211	1,503	7.9	11.1
METH–Un Methodist	6	302	561	757	4.0	5.6
MORAV–Morav Ch-North	1	61	92	116	0.6	0.9
Non-denom Chr Chs	2	115	115	144	0.8	1.1
Un C of Christ	1	85	330	398	2.1	2.9
HUBBARD	**32**	**2,209**	**4,413**	**8,102**	**39.7**	**100.0**
ANG/EPIS–Episcopal	1	43	34	34	0.2	0.4
Bahá'í	0	NR	6	6	0.0	0.1
BAPT–Consrv Bapt	2	NR	NR	NR	-	-
Catholic	4	NR	NR	2,100	10.3	25.9
Ch of Nazarene	1	40	18	125	0.6	1.5
CHR–Chr Chs & Chs Cr	2	NR	85	102	0.5	1.3
CHR–Chs of Christ	1	60	64	88	0.4	1.1
Jehovah's Witness	1	NR	NR	NR	-	-
LUTH–E.L.C.A.	5	779	1,800	2,326	11.4	28.7
LUTH–Luth Cong Msn Chr	1	70	NR	NR	-	-
LUTH–Luth-MO Synod	4	537	1,375	1,821	8.9	22.5
METH–Free Methodist	1	37	21	37	0.2	0.5
METH–Un Methodist	3	354	735	911	4.5	11.2
Non-denom Chr Chs	3	170	155	213	1.0	2.6
PENT–Assemb of God	1	90	52	259	1.3	3.2
PRES–Presb Ch (USA)	1	0	18	22	0.1	0.3
Sev Day Adv	1	29	50	58	0.3	0.7
ISANTI	**34**	**3,137**	**5,830**	**11,758**	**31.1**	**100.0**
Bahá'í	0	NR	3	3	0.0	0.0
BAPT–Converge/BGC	8	600	NR	720	1.9	6.1
BAPT–Reg Bapt Gen As	1	NR	NR	NR	-	-
BAPT–So Bapt Conv	1	140	101	126	0.3	1.1
Catholic	3	NR	NR	3,166	8.4	26.9
Evan Cov Ch	1	88	58	114	0.3	1.0
Evan Free Ch	2	170	NR	170	0.4	1.4
Jehovah's Witness	1	NR	NR	NR	-	-
LUTH–E.L.C.A.	6	1,288	4,262	5,809	15.4	49.4
LUTH–Luth Cong Msn Chr	1	6	7	9	0.0	0.1
LUTH–Luth-MO Synod	2	235	530	618	1.6	5.3
LUTH–Wisc Ev Luth Syn	1	83	145	171	0.5	1.5
METH–Un Methodist	1	139	338	340	0.9	2.9
Non-denom Chr Chs	2	220	300	300	0.8	2.6
PENT–Assemb of God	2	142	40	159	0.4	1.4
PENT–Un Pent Ch Intl	1	NR	NR	NR	-	-
Sev Day Adv	1	26	46	53	0.1	0.5
ITASCA	**97**	**5,178**	**8,796**	**21,711**	**48.2**	**100.0**
ANG/EPIS–Episcopal	2	41	143	159	0.4	0.7
Bahá'í	0	NR	25	25	0.1	0.1
BAPT–Consrv Bapt	1	NR	NR	NR	-	-
BAPT–Converge/BGC	2	150	NR	180	0.4	0.8
BAPT–NT Ind Bapt	1	NR	NR	NR	-	-
BAPT–So Bapt Conv	2	78	62	74	0.2	0.3
Calv Chpl	2	NR	NR	NR	-	-
Catholic	13	NR	NR	8,485	18.8	39.1
CGOD–Ch God (Ander)	1	75	NR	75	0.2	0.3
Ch of Nazarene	1	31	81	81	0.2	0.4
Chr & Miss Al	5	540	356	851	1.9	3.9
CHR–Chr Chs & Chs Cr	1	NR	0	0	0.0	0.0
Evan Cov Ch	1	25	6	32	0.1	0.1
Evan Free Ch	2	247	NR	247	0.5	1.1
FRND–Fr Gen Cf	1	NR	0	0	0.0	0.0
Ind Fund Churches	1	NR	NR	NR	-	-
Jehovah's Witness	2	NR	NR	NR	-	-
LDS–L-D Saints	1	NR	NR	291	0.6	1.3
LUTH–Apostolic Luth	1	NR	NR	NR	-	-
LUTH–Ch of Luth Br	1	55	51	84	0.2	0.4
LUTH–E.L.C.A.	13	1,064	3,289	4,397	9.8	20.3
LUTH–Luth Cong Msn Chr	1	17	15	18	0.0	0.1
LUTH–Luth-MO Synod	6	603	1,890	2,527	5.6	11.6
LUTH–Wisc Ev Luth Syn	1	38	70	123	0.3	0.6
MENN–Cons Menn Conf	1	42	37	44	0.1	0.2
METH–Un Methodist	5	240	524	843	1.9	3.9
Non-denom Chr Chs	10	1,100	982	1,400	3.1	6.4
ORTHE–Orth Ch in Amer	1	25	NR	30	0.1	0.1

Religious Group	Number of Congrega-tions	Number of Attendees	Number of Communicant, Confirmed, or Full Members	Adherents: Number of Adherents	Adherents: % of Total Pop.	Adherents: % of Total Adh.
PENT–Assemb of God	3	259	126	390	0.9	1.8
PENT–Ch God (Cleve)	2	127	229	274	0.6	1.3
PENT–Un Pent Ch Intl	1	NR	NR	NR	-	-
PRES–Presb Ch (USA)	9	363	814	975	2.2	4.5
Sev Day Adv	2	41	72	82	0.2	0.4
Unit Univ	1	17	24	24	0.1	0.1
JACKSON	**27**	**1,502**	**4,671**	**7,805**	**76.0**	**100.0**
BAPT–Consrv Bapt	1	NR	NR	NR	-	-
Catholic	3	NR	NR	2,016	19.6	25.8
Jehovah's Witness	1	NR	NR	NR	-	-
LUTH–Ch Luth Conf	1	NR	NR	NR	-	-
LUTH–E.L.C.A.	7	609	2,235	2,797	27.2	35.8
LUTH–Luth-MO Synod	9	698	1,890	2,313	22.5	29.6
METH–Un Methodist	3	127	399	477	4.6	6.1
PENT–Assemb of God	1	14	0	25	0.2	0.3
PRES–Presb Ch (USA)	1	54	147	177	1.7	2.3
KANABEC	**21**	**1,957**	**2,883**	**6,118**	**37.7**	**100.0**
Bahá'í	0	NR	2	2	0.0	0.0
BAPT–Converge/BGC	3	550	NR	660	4.1	10.8
Catholic	2	NR	NR	1,320	8.1	21.6
Ch of Nazarene	1	28	25	37	0.2	0.6
Evan Cov Ch	1	186	132	242	1.5	4.0
Jehovah's Witness	1	NR	NR	NR	-	-
LUTH–Assoc Free Luth	1	NR	NR	NR	-	-
LUTH–E.L.C.A.	5	543	1,624	2,338	14.4	38.2
LUTH–Luth-MO Synod	2	283	640	807	5.0	13.2
METH–Un Methodist	2	81	277	383	2.4	6.3
PENT–Assemb of God	1	130	53	170	1.0	2.8
PRES–Presb Ch (USA)	1	76	94	115	0.7	1.9
REF–Christian Ref	1	80	36	44	0.3	0.7
KANDIYOHI	**76**	**10,080**	**17,431**	**31,080**	**73.6**	**100.0**
ANG/EPIS–Episcopal	1	12	25	31	0.1	0.1
Bahá'í	0	NR	9	9	0.0	0.0
BAPT–Converge/BGC	3	550	NR	660	1.6	2.1
BAPT–NT Ind Bapt	1	NR	NR	NR	-	-
BAPT–So Bapt Conv	1	21	14	17	0.0	0.1
Catholic	4	NR	NR	5,376	12.7	17.3
CGOD–Ch God (Ander)	1	108	NR	108	0.3	0.3
Ch of Nazarene	1	45	61	61	0.1	0.2
CHR–Chs of Christ	1	55	40	70	0.2	0.2
Evan Cov Ch	3	657	678	854	2.0	2.7
Evan Free Ch	2	972	NR	972	2.3	3.1
FRND–Fr Gen Cf	1	NR	0	0	0.0	0.0
Jehovah's Witness	1	NR	NR	NR	-	-
LDS–L-D Saints	1	NR	NR	225	0.5	0.7
LUTH–Assoc Free Luth	3	NR	NR	NR	-	-
LUTH–E.L.C.A.	22	3,787	11,110	14,040	33.2	45.2
LUTH–Luth-MO Synod	3	435	1,012	1,565	3.7	5.0
LUTH–Wisc Ev Luth Syn	1	133	245	295	0.7	0.9
METH–Un Methodist	6	389	875	1,322	3.1	4.3
Non-denom Chr Chs	2	275	282	344	0.8	1.1
PENT–Assemb of God	2	1,074	520	2,043	4.8	6.6
PENT–Int Foursq Gos	1	102	62	76	0.2	0.2
PENT–Un Pent Ch Intl	1	NR	NR	NR	-	-
PRES–Presb Ch (USA)	3	185	602	738	1.7	2.4
REF–Christian Ref	4	868	1,185	1,453	3.4	4.7
REF–Ref Ch in Am	2	284	472	537	1.3	1.7
REF–Un Ref Chs N.A.	1	NR	NR	NR	-	-
Salvation Army	1	23	59	77	0.2	0.2
Sev Day Adv	2	79	137	158	0.4	0.5
Unit Univ	1	26	43	49	0.1	0.2
KITTSON	**23**	**1,125**	**2,421**	**4,141**	**91.0**	**100.0**
ANG/EPIS–Episcopal	1	12	9	9	0.2	0.2
BAPT–Converge/BGC	1	75	NR	90	2.0	2.2
BAPT–So Bapt Conv	1	15	108	129	2.8	3.1
Catholic	3	NR	NR	500	11.0	12.1
Evan Cov Ch	3	222	190	289	6.3	7.0
LUTH–E.L.C.A.	8	489	1,756	2,584	56.8	62.4

NR–Not Reported - Represents no adherents reported. Percentages may not total 100 due to rounding.

Table 3: Religious Congregations by County and Group: 2010

Religious Group	Number of Congrega-tions	Number of Attendees	Number of Communicant, Confirmed, or Full Members	Adherents: Number of Adherents	Adherents: % of Total Pop.	Adherents: % of Total Adh.
LUTH–Luth Cong Msn Chr	1	38	55	66	1.4	1.6
Non-denom Chr Chs	1	110	75	138	3.0	3.3
PENT–Assemb of God	2	71	47	122	2.7	2.9
PRES–Presb Ch (USA)	1	65	133	159	3.5	3.8
Sev Day Adv	1	28	48	55	1.2	1.3
KOOCHICHING	**31**	**1,272**	**2,464**	**6,553**	**49.2**	**100.0**
ANG/EPIS–Episcopal	1	27	50	87	0.7	1.3
Bahá'í	0	NR	6	6	0.0	0.1
BAPT–Converge/BGC	1	75	NR	90	0.7	1.4
BAPT–So Bapt Conv	1	20	18	21	0.2	0.3
Catholic	3	NR	NR	2,799	21.0	42.7
Ch of Nazarene	1	0	0	0	0.0	0.0
Chr & Miss Al	1	28	12	21	0.2	0.3
CHR–Chs of Christ	1	10	10	10	0.1	0.2
Evan Cov Ch	3	287	219	372	2.8	5.7
Evan Free Ch	1	10	NR	10	0.1	0.2
Jehovah's Witness	1	NR	NR	NR	-	-
LDS–L-D Saints	1	NR	NR	117	0.9	1.8
LUTH–Assoc Free Luth	2	NR	NR	NR	-	-
LUTH–E.L.C.A.	4	381	1,400	2,102	15.8	32.1
LUTH–Luth–MO Synod	1	84	222	226	1.7	3.4
Non-denom Chr Chs	2	145	199	224	1.7	3.4
PENT–Assemb of God	1	56	50	153	1.1	2.3
PENT–Un Pent Ch Intl	1	NR	NR	NR	-	-
Salvation Army	1	20	66	66	0.5	1.0
Sev Day Adv	2	26	46	53	0.4	0.8
Un C of Christ	2	103	166	196	1.5	3.0
LAC QUI PARLE	**30**	**1,531**	**4,577**	**6,952**	**95.8**	**100.0**
BAPT–Converge/BGC	1	75	NR	90	1.2	1.3
Catholic	4	NR	NR	1,046	14.4	15.0
Evan Cov Ch	1	91	102	118	1.6	1.7
LUTH–E.L.C.A.	12	986	3,204	4,132	56.9	59.4
LUTH–Luth Cong Msn Chr	1	40	50	59	0.8	0.8
LUTH–Luth–MO Synod	5	249	974	1,220	16.8	17.5
LUTH–Wisc Ev Luth Syn	2	32	49	55	0.8	0.8
METH–Un Methodist	2	10	56	63	0.9	0.9
PRES–Presb Ch (USA)	1	28	74	88	1.2	1.3
Un C of Christ	1	20	68	81	1.1	1.2
LAKE	**29**	**1,330**	**5,639**	**8,493**	**78.2**	**100.0**
Bahá'í	0	NR	3	3	0.0	0.0
BAPT–Amer Bapt USA	1	65	185	216	2.0	2.5
BAPT–Consrv Bapt	2	NR	NR	NR	-	-
BAPT–Converge/BGC	1	75	NR	90	0.8	1.1
Catholic	2	NR	NR	1,393	12.8	16.4
CHR–Chr Ch (Disc)	1	60	2,088	2,437	22.4	28.7
Evan Free Ch	1	50	NR	50	0.5	0.6
Jehovah's Witness	3	NR	NR	NR	-	-
LUTH–E.L.C.A.	5	469	2,070	2,725	25.1	32.1
LUTH–Luth Cong Msn Chr	2	96	256	299	2.8	3.5
LUTH–Luth–MO Synod	2	79	122	153	1.4	1.8
METH–Un Methodist	2	90	288	288	2.7	3.4
Non-denom Chr Chs	1	25	20	31	0.3	0.4
PENT–Assemb of God	2	71	78	191	1.8	2.2
PENT–Vineyard	1	170	211	246	2.3	2.9
PRES–Presb Ch (USA)	2	35	126	147	1.4	1.7
Un C of Christ	1	45	192	224	2.1	2.6
LAKE OF THE WOODS	**16**	**586**	**1,538**	**2,576**	**63.7**	**100.0**
Bahá'í	0	NR	4	4	0.1	0.2
Catholic	3	NR	NR	350	8.7	13.6
Evan Cov Ch	1	49	21	64	1.6	2.5
Jehovah's Witness	1	NR	NR	NR	-	-
LUTH–E.L.C.A.	5	361	1,199	1,758	43.5	68.2
LUTH–Luth–MO Synod	1	0	88	103	2.5	4.0
Non-denom Chr Chs	1	40	75	75	1.9	2.9
PENT–Assemb of God	1	75	33	85	2.1	3.3
Sev Day Adv	1	16	28	32	0.8	1.2
Un C of Christ	2	45	90	105	2.6	4.1

Religious Group	Number of Congrega-tions	Number of Attendees	Number of Communicant, Confirmed, or Full Members	Adherents: Number of Adherents	Adherents: % of Total Pop.	Adherents: % of Total Adh.
LE SUEUR	**39**	**1,859**	**5,256**	**12,024**	**43.4**	**100.0**
ANG/EPIS–Episcopal	2	16	20	25	0.1	0.2
Bahá'í	0	NR	2	2	0.0	0.0
BAPT–NT Ind Bapt	1	NR	NR	NR	-	-
Catholic	14	NR	NR	4,711	17.0	39.2
CHR–Chr Chs & Chs Cr	1	NR	150	187	0.7	1.6
LUTH–Ch of Luth Br	1	195	80	594	2.1	4.9
LUTH–E.L.C.A.	5	653	2,453	3,235	11.7	26.9
LUTH–Luth–MO Synod	3	257	746	918	3.3	7.6
LUTH–Wisc Ev Luth Syn	2	214	399	487	1.8	4.1
METH–Un Methodist	4	235	609	873	3.2	7.3
Non-denom Chr Chs	1	30	40	40	0.1	0.3
PENT–Assemb of God	1	14	3	17	0.1	0.1
PRES–Presb Ch (USA)	2	73	246	306	1.1	2.5
Sev Day Adv	1	16	29	33	0.1	0.3
Un C of Christ	1	156	479	596	2.2	5.0
LINCOLN	**23**	**1,080**	**2,211**	**4,511**	**76.5**	**100.0**
Bahá'í	0	NR	1	1	0.0	0.0
BAPT–NT Ind Bapt	1	NR	NR	NR	-	-
Catholic	4	NR	NR	1,673	28.4	37.1
Chr & Miss Al	1	50	28	100	1.7	2.2
Jehovah's Witness	1	NR	NR	NR	-	-
LUTH–Assoc Free Luth	1	NR	NR	NR	-	-
LUTH–Ch of Luth Br	1	48	43	86	1.5	1.9
LUTH–E.L.C.A.	6	592	1,570	1,884	32.0	41.8
LUTH–Wisc Ev Luth Syn	3	210	432	535	9.1	11.9
MENN–Hutt Breth	1	NR	NR	NR	-	-
METH–Un Methodist	3	90	137	142	2.4	3.1
PENT–Assemb of God	1	90	0	90	1.5	2.0
LYON	**48**	**3,355**	**6,822**	**16,788**	**64.9**	**100.0**
ANG/EPIS–Episcopal	1	17	35	48	0.2	0.3
Bahá'í	0	NR	5	5	0.0	0.0
BAPT–So Bapt Conv	1	75	50	62	0.2	0.4
Calv Chpl	1	NR	NR	NR	-	-
Catholic	6	NR	NR	7,457	28.8	44.4
Chr & Miss Al	3	254	266	390	1.5	2.3
CHR–Chr Chs & Chs Cr	1	NR	0	0	0.0	0.0
CHR–Chs of Christ	1	14	10	18	0.1	0.1
CONG–Consrv Cong Chr	1	33	57	70	0.3	0.4
Evan Free Ch	2	317	NR	317	1.2	1.9
Jehovah's Witness	2	NR	NR	NR	-	-
LDS–L-D Saints	1	NR	NR	293	1.1	1.7
LUTH–E.L.C.A.	8	1,119	3,403	4,322	16.7	25.7
LUTH–Evan Luth Syn	2	88	283	351	1.4	2.1
LUTH–Luth Cong Msn Chr	2	295	400	494	1.9	2.9
LUTH–Wisc Ev Luth Syn	3	321	677	848	3.3	5.1
METH–Un Methodist	4	331	798	1,115	4.3	6.6
Non-denom Chr Chs	3	325	500	500	1.9	3.0
PENT–Assemb of God	2	60	0	82	0.3	0.5
PRES–Presb Ch (USA)	3	92	313	386	1.5	2.3
Sev Day Adv	1	14	25	29	0.1	0.2
Zoroastrian	0	NR	NR	1	0.0	0.0
MCLEOD	**55**	**6,146**	**16,852**	**29,923**	**81.6**	**100.0**
Bahá'í	0	NR	2	2	0.0	0.0
BAPT–Converge/BGC	2	150	NR	180	0.5	0.6
BAPT–N Am Bapt Conf	1	NR	54	67	0.2	0.2
BAPT–NT Ind Bapt	1	NR	NR	NR	-	-
Catholic	5	NR	NR	8,020	21.9	26.8
Ch of God Gen Conf	1	NR	28	35	0.1	0.1
CONG–Consrv Cong Chr	2	79	164	204	0.6	0.7
Evan Cov Ch	1	146	107	190	0.5	0.6
Evan Free Ch	2	262	NR	262	0.7	0.9
Jehovah's Witness	2	NR	NR	NR	-	-
LDS–L-D Saints	1	NR	NR	302	0.8	1.0
LUTH–E.L.C.A.	5	423	1,390	1,761	4.8	5.9
LUTH–Luth Cong Msn Chr	3	1,259	4,952	6,152	16.8	20.6
LUTH–Luth–MO Synod	10	2,121	7,185	8,954	24.4	29.9
LUTH–Wisc Ev Luth Syn	4	369	726	862	2.4	2.9
METH–Free Methodist	1	30	4	30	0.1	0.1

NR–Not Reported   - Represents no adherents reported.   Percentages may not total 100 due to rounding.

Table 3: Religious Congregations by County and Group: 2010

Religious Group	Number of Congrega-tions	Number of Attendees	Number of Communicant, Confirmed, or Full Members	Adherents: Number of Adherents	Adherents: % of Total Pop.	Adherents: % of Total Adh.
METH–Un Methodist	2	221	554	656	1.8	2.2
Non-denom Chr Chs	1	25	19	31	0.1	0.1
PENT–Assemb of God	2	405	207	432	1.2	1.4
PENT–Intl Pent Holiness	1	100	50	62	0.2	0.2
PENT–Un Pent Ch Intl	1	NR	NR	NR	-	-
PRES–Presb Ch (USA)	1	80	158	196	0.5	0.7
Sev Day Adv	1	185	322	370	1.0	1.2
Un C of Christ	5	291	930	1,155	3.2	3.9
MAHNOMEN	**15**	**432**	**901**	**3,026**	**55.9**	**100.0**
ANG/EPIS–Episcopal	1	17	75	104	1.9	3.4
Bahá'í	0	NR	2	2	0.0	0.1
BAPT–Converge/BGC	1	75	NR	90	1.7	3.0
Catholic	6	NR	NR	1,800	33.3	59.5
LUTH–E.L.C.A.	4	179	449	551	10.2	18.2
LUTH–Luth–MO Synod	2	108	200	250	4.6	8.3
Un C of Christ	1	53	175	229	4.2	7.6
MARSHALL	**52**	**1,436**	**3,370**	**6,566**	**69.6**	**100.0**
BAPT–Converge/BGC	1	75	NR	90	1.0	1.4
Catholic	13	NR	NR	2,000	21.2	30.5
Chr & Miss Al	1	35	10	42	0.4	0.6
Evan Cov Ch	2	99	110	128	1.4	1.9
Evan Free Ch	1	135	NR	135	1.4	2.1
LUTH–Assoc Free Luth	4	NR	NR	NR	-	-
LUTH–E.L.C.A.	20	914	2,912	3,714	39.3	56.6
LUTH–Evan Luth Syn	1	29	33	58	0.6	0.9
LUTH–Luth Ch-Am Asc	2	NR	NR	NR	-	-
LUTH–Luth–MO Synod	2	68	175	234	2.5	3.6
LUTH–Nor Amer Luth C	1	NR	NR	NR	-	-
METH–Un Methodist	1	28	77	77	0.8	1.2
PENT–Assemb of God	1	15	0	21	0.2	0.3
PRES–Presb Ch (USA)	1	18	32	39	0.4	0.6
PRES–Presb Ch Amer	1	20	21	28	0.3	0.4
MARTIN	**52**	**4,468**	**10,553**	**17,518**	**84.1**	**100.0**
ANG/EPIS–Episcopal	1	39	67	73	0.4	0.4
Bahá'í	0	NR	1	1	0.0	0.0
BAPT–Amer Bapt USA	1	23	50	60	0.3	0.3
Catholic	4	NR	NR	3,776	18.1	21.6
CHR–Chr Chs & Chs Cr	3	NR	182	219	1.1	1.3
Evan Cov Ch	2	271	310	352	1.7	2.0
Evan Free Ch	2	600	NR	600	2.9	3.4
Jehovah's Witness	1	NR	NR	NR	-	-
LDS–L-D Saints	1	NR	NR	185	0.9	1.1
LUTH–E.L.C.A.	9	1,021	3,835	4,409	21.2	25.2
LUTH–Luth–MO Synod	12	1,559	4,153	5,001	24.0	28.5
LUTH–Wisc Ev Luth Syn	1	58	89	115	0.6	0.7
METH–Un Methodist	4	286	785	1,116	5.4	6.4
Non-denom Chr Chs	2	141	135	176	0.8	1.0
PENT–Assemb of God	2	130	63	150	0.7	0.9
PENT–Un Pent Ch Intl	1	NR	NR	NR	-	-
Salvation Army	1	22	26	254	1.2	1.4
Sev Day Adv	1	1	2	2	0.0	0.0
Un C of Christ	4	317	855	1,029	4.9	5.9
MEEKER	**44**	**3,092**	**8,009**	**16,176**	**69.4**	**100.0**
ANG/EPIS–Episcopal	1	21	33	37	0.2	0.2
BAPT–Converge/BGC	2	150	NR	180	0.8	1.1
Catholic	7	NR	NR	5,946	25.5	36.8
Ch of God Gen Conf	2	NR	81	101	0.4	0.6
Ch of Nazarene	1	72	89	130	0.6	0.8
CHR–Chr Chs & Chs Cr	2	NR	220	274	1.2	1.7
Evan Cov Ch	2	216	372	281	1.2	1.7
Evan Free Ch	2	145	NR	145	0.6	0.9
Jehovah's Witness	1	NR	NR	NR	-	-
LUTH–Apostolic Luth	1	NR	NR	NR	-	-
LUTH–E.L.C.A.	10	1,485	5,280	6,641	28.5	41.1
LUTH–Luth–MO Synod	2	159	463	569	2.4	3.5
LUTH–Wisc Ev Luth Syn	2	233	617	713	3.1	4.4
MENN–Beachy Amish-Menn	1	108	64	108	0.5	0.7
METH–Un Methodist	1	109	261	369	1.6	2.3

Religious Group	Number of Congrega-tions	Number of Attendees	Number of Communicant, Confirmed, or Full Members	Adherents: Number of Adherents	Adherents: % of Total Pop.	Adherents: % of Total Adh.
Non-denom Chr Chs	2	220	250	300	1.3	1.9
PENT–Assemb of God	1	39	0	39	0.2	0.2
PRES–Presb Ch (USA)	1	55	78	97	0.4	0.6
Sev Day Adv	1	24	43	49	0.2	0.3
Un C of Christ	2	56	158	197	0.8	1.2
MILLE LACS	**48**	**4,912**	**7,233**	**18,624**	**71.4**	**100.0**
Bahá'í	0	NR	15	15	0.1	0.1
BAPT–Converge/BGC	4	300	NR	360	1.4	1.9
Catholic	6	NR	NR	5,987	22.9	32.1
Chr & Miss Al	3	241	94	299	1.1	1.6
Evan Cov Ch	1	134	95	174	0.7	0.9
Evan Free Ch	4	464	NR	464	1.8	2.5
Jehovah's Witness	2	NR	NR	NR	-	-
LDS–L-D Saints	1	NR	NR	540	2.1	2.9
LUTH–E.L.C.A.	8	1,227	3,805	5,074	19.4	27.2
LUTH–Evan Luth Syn	1	83	193	246	0.9	1.3
LUTH–Luth–MO Synod	3	196	669	832	3.2	4.5
METH–Un Methodist	5	264	570	793	3.0	4.3
Non-denom Chr Chs	3	450	460	562	2.2	3.0
PENT–Assemb of God	3	899	342	2,046	7.8	11.0
PRES–Presb Ch (USA)	1	75	138	172	0.7	0.9
REF–Christian Ref	2	525	729	907	3.5	4.9
Un C of Christ	1	54	123	153	0.6	0.8
MORRISON	**53**	**2,904**	**4,332**	**22,360**	**67.4**	**100.0**
ANG/EPIS–Episcopal	1	15	40	40	0.1	0.2
Bahá'í	0	NR	1	1	0.0	0.0
BAPT–Converge/BGC	1	75	NR	90	0.3	0.4
Catholic	19	NR	NR	15,614	47.0	69.8
Ch of Nazarene	1	0	4	4	0.0	0.0
Chr & Miss Al	3	268	189	410	1.2	1.8
CONG–Consrv Cong Chr	1	99	61	75	0.2	0.3
Evan Cov Ch	2	386	328	502	1.5	2.2
Evan Free Ch	1	170	NR	170	0.5	0.8
Jehovah's Witness	1	NR	NR	NR	-	-
LUTH–Assoc Free Luth	1	NR	NR	NR	-	-
LUTH–E.L.C.A.	5	542	1,459	2,083	6.3	9.3
LUTH–Luth Cong Msn Chr	1	177	292	360	1.1	1.6
LUTH–Luth–MO Synod	7	399	1,010	1,209	3.6	5.4
LUTH–Wisc Ev Luth Syn	1	56	121	142	0.4	0.6
METH–Free Methodist	1	200	68	200	0.6	0.9
METH–Un Methodist	2	131	316	434	1.3	1.9
Non-denom Chr Chs	1	45	55	56	0.2	0.3
PENT–Assemb of God	1	200	108	624	1.9	2.8
PENT–Ch God (Cleve)	1	31	26	32	0.1	0.1
PRES–Presb Ch (USA)	1	56	101	125	0.4	0.6
Un C of Christ	1	54	153	189	0.6	0.8
MOWER	**68**	**4,545**	**11,480**	**25,984**	**66.3**	**100.0**
ANG/EPIS–Episcopal	1	46	143	180	0.5	0.7
Bahá'í	0	NR	17	17	0.0	0.1
BAPT–Reg Bapt Gen As	3	NR	NR	NR	-	-
BAPT–So Bapt Conv	1	13	36	45	0.1	0.2
Catholic	10	NR	NR	9,399	24.0	36.2
CHR–Chr Chs & Chs Cr	1	NR	125	155	0.4	0.6
CHR–Chs of Christ	1	32	32	46	0.1	0.2
Evan Free Ch	1	413	NR	413	1.1	1.6
Jehovah's Witness	1	NR	NR	NR	-	-
LDS–L-D Saints	1	NR	NR	299	0.8	1.2
LUTH–Assoc Free Luth	1	NR	NR	NR	-	-
LUTH–Ch Luth Conf	1	NR	NR	NR	-	-
LUTH–E.L.C.A.	16	1,943	7,629	10,155	25.9	39.1
LUTH–Luth–MO Synod	6	404	1,113	1,321	3.4	5.1
LUTH–Wisc Ev Luth Syn	2	86	193	213	0.5	0.8
MENN–Hutt Breth	1	NR	NR	NR	-	-
METH–Free Methodist	1	134	109	134	0.3	0.5
METH–Un Methodist	9	393	1,109	1,454	3.7	5.6
METH–Wesleyan	1	201	43	261	0.7	1.0
Non-denom Chr Chs	1	35	40	44	0.1	0.2
PENT–Assemb of God	1	450	90	460	1.2	1.8
PENT–Open Bible Std	1	48	NR	48	0.1	0.2
PENT–Un Pent Ch Intl	2	NR	NR	NR	-	-

NR–Not Reported   - Represents no adherents reported.   Percentages may not total 100 due to rounding.

Table 3: Religious Congregations by County and Group: 2010

Religious Group	Number of Congregations	Number of Attendees	Number of Communicant, Confirmed, or Full Members	Adherents		
				Number of Adherents	% of Total Pop.	% of Total Adh.
PRES–Presb Ch (USA)	2	217	528	657	1.7	2.5
Salvation Army	1	62	71	432	1.1	1.7
Un C of Christ	2	68	202	251	0.6	1.0
MURRAY	**26**	**1,663**	**3,368**	**6,686**	**76.6**	**100.0**
BAPT–Converge/BGC	1	75	NR	90	1.0	1.3
Catholic	5	NR	NR	2,330	26.7	34.8
Evan Free Ch	1	125	NR	125	1.4	1.9
LUTH–E.L.C.A.	8	605	1,764	2,220	25.4	33.2
LUTH–Luth–MO Synod	2	270	630	760	8.7	11.4
METH–Un Methodist	2	78	178	235	2.7	3.5
PRES–Presb Ch (USA)	4	129	294	353	4.0	5.3
REF–Christian Ref	1	125	159	191	2.2	2.9
REF–Ref Ch in Am	2	256	343	382	4.4	5.7
NICOLLET	**29**	**4,430**	**8,275**	**17,699**	**54.1**	**100.0**
ANG/EPIS–Episcopal	1	26	37	105	0.3	0.6
Bahá'í	0	NR	10	10	0.0	0.1
Catholic	5	NR	NR	5,741	17.5	32.4
Chr & Miss Al	1	54	28	83	0.3	0.5
Evan Cov Ch	1	846	434	1,100	3.4	6.2
FRND–Unaffl Mtgs	1	NR	NR	NR	-	-
Jehovah's Witness	1	NR	NR	NR	-	-
LUTH–E.L.C.A.	6	1,196	3,681	5,104	15.6	28.8
LUTH–Evan Luth Syn	2	289	430	574	1.8	3.2
LUTH–Luth–MO Synod	2	295	579	802	2.5	4.5
LUTH–Wisc Ev Luth Syn	5	1,036	2,167	2,583	7.9	14.6
METH–Un Methodist	1	232	516	741	2.3	4.2
Non-denom Chr Chs	1	30	37	38	0.1	0.2
PENT–Assemb of God	1	327	152	570	1.7	3.2
PRES–Presb Ch (USA)	1	99	204	248	0.8	1.4
NOBLES	**48**	**3,358**	**7,052**	**14,793**	**69.2**	**100.0**
BAPT–Consrv Bapt	1	NR	NR	NR	-	-
BAPT–Converge/BGC	1	75	NR	90	0.4	0.6
BAPT–NT Ind Bapt	1	NR	NR	NR	-	-
BRETH–Ch of Brethren	1	21	54	68	0.3	0.5
Catholic	7	NR	NR	5,620	26.3	38.0
CHR–Chr Chs & Chs Cr	1	NR	400	500	2.3	3.4
Evan Cov Ch	1	93	108	121	0.6	0.8
Evan Free Ch	1	65	NR	65	0.3	0.4
Jehovah's Witness	1	NR	NR	NR	-	-
LDS–L-D Saints	1	NR	NR	245	1.1	1.7
LUTH–E.L.C.A.	4	612	2,083	2,638	12.3	17.8
LUTH–Luth–MO Synod	4	476	1,198	1,423	6.7	9.6
METH–Un Methodist	3	224	508	626	2.9	4.2
Non-denom Chr Chs	2	43	70	70	0.3	0.5
PENT–Assemb of God	1	189	88	240	1.1	1.6
PENT–Ch of God Proph	1	NR	50	63	0.3	0.4
PENT–Intl Pent Holiness	1	270	135	169	0.8	1.1
PENT–Un Pent Ch Intl	1	NR	NR	NR	-	-
PRES–Evan Presby Ch	1	NR	95	119	0.6	0.8
PRES–Presb Ch (USA)	8	404	951	1,189	5.6	8.0
REF–Christian Ref	4	529	787	984	4.6	6.7
REF–Ref Ch in Am	2	357	525	563	2.6	3.8
NORMAN	**31**	**1,181**	**3,614**	**5,120**	**74.7**	**100.0**
Catholic	5	NR	NR	700	10.2	13.7
Evan Free Ch	1	65	NR	65	0.9	1.3
LUTH–Assoc Free Luth	1	NR	NR	NR	-	-
LUTH–Ch of Luth Br	1	40	51	68	1.0	1.3
LUTH–E.L.C.A.	17	830	2,878	3,406	49.7	66.5
LUTH–Luth–MO Synod	3	167	528	685	10.0	13.4
METH–Un Methodist	1	25	105	120	1.8	2.3
Non-denom Chr Chs	1	25	15	31	0.5	0.6
Un C of Christ	1	29	37	45	0.7	0.9
OLMSTED	**139**	**22,227**	**39,613**	**92,269**	**64.0**	**100.0**
ANG/EPIS–Episcopal	2	300	1,044	1,269	0.9	1.4
Bahá'í	1	NR	52	52	0.0	0.1
BAPT–Converge/BGC	3	225	NR	270	0.2	0.3
BAPT–NT Ind Bapt	1	NR	NR	NR	-	-
BAPT–Reg Bapt Gen As	1	NR	NR	NR	-	-
BAPT–So Bapt Conv	7	387	517	646	0.4	0.7
BUDD–Theravada	1	NR	NR	395	0.3	0.4
Calv Chpl	1	NR	NR	NR	-	-
Catholic	10	NR	NR	33,236	23.0	36.0
Ch of Nazarene	3	111	204	244	0.2	0.3
Chr & Miss Al	2	1,474	653	3,643	2.5	3.9
CHR–Chr Ch (Disc)	1	22	0	0	0.0	0.0
CHR–Chr Chs & Chs Cr	4	NR	695	868	0.6	0.9
CHR–Chs of Christ	3	110	85	130	0.1	0.1
Evan Cov Ch	3	456	365	593	0.4	0.6
Evan Free Ch	5	1,642	NR	1,642	1.1	1.8
FRND–Fr Gen Cf	1	NR	0	0	0.0	0.0
Jehovah's Witness	1	NR	NR	NR	-	-
JUD–Orth	1	43	50	60	0.0	0.1
JUD–Reform	1	69	121	327	0.2	0.4
LDS–Comm of Christ	1	NR	138	138	0.1	0.1
LDS–L-D Saints	5	NR	NR	1,844	1.3	2.0
LUTH–Ch of Luth Br	1	135	78	256	0.2	0.3
LUTH–E.L.C.A.	14	4,454	14,193	18,955	13.1	20.5
LUTH–Luth–MO Synod	9	2,025	4,177	5,078	3.5	5.5
LUTH–Wisc Ev Luth Syn	4	844	1,327	1,674	1.2	1.8
MENN–CG in Cr (Menn)	1	NR	2	2	0.0	0.0
MENN–Mennonite USA	1	30	22	27	0.0	0.0
METH–Un Methodist	12	1,746	3,958	5,176	3.6	5.6
METH–Wesleyan	1	44	49	57	0.0	0.1
Metro Comm Ch	1	19	24	30	0.0	0.0
Muslim Est	2	234	NR	488	0.3	0.5
Nat Spirit Asso	1	NR	NR	NR	-	-
Non-denom Chr Chs	14	5,086	7,930	8,569	5.9	9.3
ORTHE–Greek Orthodox	1	100	NR	200	0.1	0.2
PENT–Assemb of God	3	1,005	235	1,522	1.1	1.6
PENT–COGIC	1	60	50	62	0.0	0.1
PENT–Int Foursq Gos	1	27	13	16	0.0	0.0
PENT–Un Pent Ch Intl	2	NR	NR	NR	-	-
PRES–Presb Ch (USA)	3	385	984	1,229	0.9	1.3
PRES–Presb Ch Amer	1	175	179	247	0.2	0.3
REF–Ref Ch in Am	1	69	148	160	0.1	0.2
Salvation Army	1	142	159	486	0.3	0.5
Sev Day Adv	2	198	343	395	0.3	0.4
Un C of Christ	3	436	1,446	1,806	1.3	2.0
Unit Univ	1	174	372	477	0.3	0.5
OTTER TAIL	**126**	**10,601**	**22,776**	**40,599**	**70.8**	**100.0**
ANG/EPIS–Episcopal	1	28	53	75	0.1	0.2
Bahá'í	0	NR	5	5	0.0	0.0
BAPT–Amer Bapt USA	1	15	14	17	0.0	0.0
BAPT–Consrv Bapt	1	NR	NR	NR	-	-
BAPT–Converge/BGC	5	375	NR	450	0.8	1.1
BAPT–Reg Bapt Gen As	1	NR	NR	NR	-	-
BAPT–So Bapt Conv	1	3	3	4	0.0	0.0
Catholic	14	NR	NR	7,813	13.6	19.2
Ch of Nazarene	1	569	445	711	1.2	1.8
Chr & Miss Al	2	266	133	443	0.8	1.1
CHR–Chs of Christ	1	30	22	35	0.1	0.1
Evan Free Ch	2	210	NR	210	0.4	0.5
Jehovah's Witness	1	NR	NR	NR	-	-
LDS–Comm of Christ	1	NR	138	138	0.2	0.3
LUTH–Apostolic Luth	1	NR	NR	NR	-	-
LUTH–Assoc Free Luth	4	NR	NR	NR	-	-
LUTH–Ch of Luth Br	6	937	919	3,276	5.7	8.1
LUTH–E.L.C.A.	30	3,487	11,939	15,304	26.7	37.7
LUTH–Luth Cong Msn Chr	5	371	958	1,146	2.0	2.8
LUTH–Luth–MO Synod	20	2,020	5,307	6,572	11.5	16.2
MENN–Amish Undif	2	NR	60	170	0.3	0.4
METH–Un Methodist	9	561	1,017	1,538	2.7	3.8
Non-denom Chr Chs	2	740	595	925	1.6	2.3
PENT–Assemb of God	4	265	123	299	0.5	0.7
PRES–Presb Ch (USA)	3	270	555	664	1.2	1.6
Salvation Army	1	77	43	275	0.5	0.7
Sev Day Adv	1	26	46	53	0.1	0.1
Un C of Christ	5	306	351	420	0.7	1.0
Unit Univ	1	45	50	56	0.1	0.1

NR–Not Reported   - Represents no adherents reported.   Percentages may not total 100 due to rounding.

Table 3: Religious Congregations by County and Group: 2010

Religious Group	Number of Congrega-tions	Number of Attendees	Number of Communicant, Confirmed, or Full Members	Adherents: Number of Adherents	Adherents: % of Total Pop.	Adherents: % of Total Adh.
PENNINGTON	**30**	**1,774**	**5,291**	**9,468**	**68.0**	**100.0**
Bahá'í	0	NR	1	1	0.0	0.0
BAPT–Converge/BGC	2	150	NR	180	1.3	1.9
Catholic	3	NR	NR	2,100	15.1	22.2
CHR–Chs of Christ	1	5	5	5	0.0	0.1
Evan Cov Ch	1	83	69	108	0.8	1.1
Evan Free Ch	1	252	NR	252	1.8	2.7
LUTH–Assoc Free Luth	3	NR	NR	NR	-	-
LUTH–Ch of Luth Br	2	60	52	162	1.2	1.7
LUTH–E.L.C.A.	11	875	4,519	5,865	42.1	61.9
LUTH–Luth–MO Synod	1	68	230	287	2.1	3.0
METH–Un Methodist	1	114	184	248	1.8	2.6
Non-denom Chr Chs	1	70	100	100	0.7	1.1
PENT–Assemb of God	1	34	21	34	0.2	0.4
Sev Day Adv	2	63	110	126	0.9	1.3
PINE	**58**	**3,211**	**5,797**	**13,419**	**45.1**	**100.0**
ANG/EPIS–Episcopal	1	14	33	44	0.1	0.3
Bahá'í	0	NR	11	11	0.0	0.1
BAPT–Converge/BGC	2	150	NR	180	0.6	1.3
BAPT–NT Ind Bapt	1	NR	NR	NR	-	-
BAPT–Reg Bapt Gen As	1	NR	NR	NR	-	-
Catholic	8	NR	NR	4,553	15.3	33.9
CHR–Chs of Christ	1	14	17	28	0.1	0.2
Evan Free Ch	4	583	NR	583	2.0	4.3
Jehovah's Witness	1	NR	NR	NR	-	-
LDS–L-D Saints	2	NR	NR	440	1.5	3.3
LUTH–Apostolic Luth	1	NR	NR	NR	-	-
LUTH–Assoc Free Luth	1	NR	NR	NR	-	-
LUTH–E.L.C.A.	10	805	2,826	3,815	12.8	28.4
LUTH–Luth–MO Synod	6	442	1,418	1,811	6.1	13.5
LUTH–Nor Amer Luth C	1	NR	NR	NR	-	-
METH–Free Methodist	1	70	45	70	0.2	0.5
METH–Un Methodist	1	25	34	39	0.1	0.3
Non-denom Chr Chs	8	805	803	1,032	3.5	7.7
PENT–Assemb of God	2	81	43	132	0.4	1.0
PENT–Ch God (Cleve)	1	78	300	362	1.2	2.7
PRES–Presb Ch (USA)	2	17	88	106	0.4	0.8
PRES–Presb Ch Amer	1	70	82	99	0.3	0.7
Sev Day Adv	1	27	47	54	0.2	0.4
Un C of Christ	1	30	50	60	0.2	0.4
PIPESTONE	**30**	**2,687**	**5,117**	**8,625**	**89.9**	**100.0**
BAPT–Converge/BGC	1	75	NR	90	0.9	1.0
Catholic	2	NR	NR	1,949	20.3	22.6
Evan Free Ch	2	140	NR	140	1.5	1.6
LDS–L-D Saints	1	NR	NR	183	1.9	2.1
LUTH–Assoc Free Luth	1	NR	NR	NR	-	-
LUTH–E.L.C.A.	3	214	1,103	1,375	14.3	15.9
LUTH–Luth–MO Synod	4	330	908	1,107	11.5	12.8
LUTH–Wisc Ev Luth Syn	1	21	43	68	0.7	0.8
METH–Un Methodist	3	108	337	492	5.1	5.7
Non-denom Chr Chs	1	70	100	100	1.0	1.2
PRES–Presb Ch (USA)	3	172	421	520	5.4	6.0
REF–Christian Ref	4	925	1,261	1,558	16.2	18.1
REF–Prot Ref Chs	1	75	49	84	0.9	1.0
REF–Ref Ch in Am	2	525	840	896	9.3	10.4
Sev Day Adv	1	32	55	63	0.7	0.7
POLK	**93**	**3,677**	**10,022**	**19,685**	**62.3**	**100.0**
Bahá'í	0	NR	7	7	0.0	0.0
BAPT–Converge/BGC	1	75	NR	90	0.3	0.5
BAPT–So Bapt Conv	1	14	11	13	0.0	0.1
BUDD–Theravada	1	NR	NR	267	0.8	1.4
Catholic	13	NR	NR	6,500	20.6	33.0
CHR–Chr Chs & Chs Cr	1	NR	55	67	0.2	0.3
CHR–Chs of Christ	1	8	6	8	0.0	0.0
Evan Cov Ch	1	84	52	109	0.3	0.6
Evan Free Ch	1	70	NR	70	0.2	0.4
Jehovah's Witness	4	NR	NR	NR	-	-
LUTH–Assoc Free Luth	9	NR	NR	NR	-	-
LUTH–E.L.C.A.	28	2,063	6,818	8,732	27.6	44.4
LUTH–Evan Luth Syn	4	146	263	348	1.1	1.8
LUTH–Luth Ch-Am Asc	1	NR	NR	NR	-	-
LUTH–Luth Cong Msn Chr	2	201	746	911	2.9	4.6
LUTH–Luth–MO Synod	6	330	811	958	3.0	4.9
LUTH–Nor Amer Luth C	2	NR	NR	NR	-	-
MENN–Amish Undif	2	NR	70	206	0.7	1.0
MENN–Hutt Breth	1	NR	NR	NR	-	-
METH–Un Methodist	4	88	270	321	1.0	1.6
Non-denom Chr Chs	2	320	375	400	1.3	2.0
PENT–Assemb of God	1	40	20	52	0.2	0.3
PRES–Presb Ch (USA)	3	180	433	529	1.7	2.7
REF–Christian Ref	2	20	21	26	0.1	0.1
Sev Day Adv	1	26	46	53	0.2	0.3
Unit Univ	1	12	18	18	0.1	0.1
POPE	**28**	**1,801**	**4,737**	**7,491**	**68.1**	**100.0**
Bahá'í	0	NR	2	2	0.0	0.0
BAPT–Converge/BGC	1	75	NR	90	0.8	1.2
Catholic	3	NR	NR	1,339	12.2	17.9
Evan Cov Ch	1	40	41	52	0.5	0.7
Evan Free Ch	1	180	NR	180	1.6	2.4
Jehovah's Witness	1	NR	NR	NR	-	-
LUTH–Assoc Free Luth	2	NR	NR	NR	-	-
LUTH–E.L.C.A.	11	1,074	3,899	4,799	43.6	64.1
LUTH–Luth Cong Msn Chr	2	95	101	121	1.1	1.6
LUTH–Luth–MO Synod	1	72	257	311	2.8	4.2
LUTH–Wisc Ev Luth Syn	1	53	85	106	1.0	1.4
METH–Un Methodist	2	102	205	248	2.3	3.3
PENT–Assemb of God	1	78	42	118	1.1	1.6
Un C of Christ	1	32	105	125	1.1	1.7
RAMSEY	**381**	**48,303**	**86,707**	**256,240**	**50.4**	**100.0**
ANG/EPIS–Episcopal	12	1,673	4,332	5,395	1.1	2.1
Bahá'í	3	NR	324	324	0.1	0.1
BAPT–Amer Bapt USA	13	1,778	2,923	3,566	0.7	1.4
BAPT–Consrv Bapt	3	NR	NR	NR	-	-
BAPT–Converge/BGC	16	2,250	NR	2,700	0.5	1.1
BAPT–NBC Amer	1	500	700	854	0.2	0.3
BAPT–NBC USA	1	350	2,100	2,562	0.5	1.0
BAPT–NT Ind Bapt	2	NR	NR	NR	-	-
BAPT–So Bapt Conv	7	709	666	813	0.2	0.3
BUDD–Mahayana	3	NR	NR	3,188	0.6	1.2
BUDD–Theravada	1	NR	NR	14	0.0	0.0
Calv Chpl	1	NR	NR	NR	-	-
Catholic	44	NR	NR	124,823	24.5	48.7
Ch Cr, Scientst	3	NR	NR	NR	-	-
Ch God (7th Day)	1	NR	NR	NR	-	-
Ch of Nazarene	2	121	133	158	0.0	0.1
Chr & Miss Al	11	3,578	6,141	6,823	1.3	2.7
CHR–Chr Chs & Chs Cr	2	NR	260	317	0.1	0.1
CHR–Chs of Christ	3	205	170	217	0.0	0.1
Evan Cov Ch	8	1,686	1,952	2,193	0.4	0.9
Evan Free Ch	4	825	NR	825	0.2	0.3
FRND–Fr Gen Cf	2	NR	153	187	0.0	0.1
HINDU–Post Ren	2	NR	NR	50	0.0	0.0
Jehovah's Witness	6	NR	NR	NR	-	-
JUD–Conserv	1	862	967	2,611	0.5	1.0
JUD–Orth	1	43	50	60	0.0	0.0
JUD–Reform	1	397	701	1,893	0.4	0.7
LDS–Comm of Christ	1	NR	138	138	0.0	0.1
LDS–L-D Saints	6	NR	NR	3,501	0.7	1.4
LUTH–E.L.C.A.	54	10,742	30,712	39,691	7.8	15.5
LUTH–Luth Ch-Am Asc	1	NR	NR	NR	-	-
LUTH–Luth Cong Msn Chr	2	765	2,192	2,674	0.5	1.0
LUTH–Luth–MO Synod	14	2,496	5,296	7,193	1.4	2.8
LUTH–Wisc Ev Luth Syn	8	1,219	2,299	3,035	0.6	1.2
MENN–Mennonite USA	2	15	19	23	0.0	0.0
METH–AME	2	0	400	488	0.1	0.2
METH–Free Methodist	1	0	0	0	0.0	0.0
METH–Un Methodist	18	3,014	5,111	7,423	1.5	2.9
Muslim Est	5	1,236	NR	4,232	0.8	1.7
Nat Spirit Asso	1	NR	NR	NR	-	-
Non-denom Chr Chs	26	5,628	6,433	7,856	1.5	3.1

NR–Not Reported   - Represents no adherents reported.   Percentages may not total 100 due to rounding.

Table 3: Religious Congregations by County and Group: 2010

Religious Group	Number of Congrega-tions	Number of Attendees	Number of Communicant, Confirmed, or Full Members	Adherents: Number of Adherents	Adherents: % of Total Pop.	Adherents: % of Total Adh.
ORTHE–Greek Orthodox	1	150	NR	450	0.1	0.2
ORTHE–Holy Orth in NA	1	35	NR	45	0.0	0.0
ORTHE–Orth Ch in Amer	2	130	NR	350	0.1	0.1
ORTHE–Serb Orth USA	1	58	NR	300	0.1	0.1
ORTHE–Ukrainian Orth	1	80	NR	350	0.1	0.1
ORTHO–Armen Ap Etchm	1	25	NR	75	0.0	0.0
ORTHO–Eritrean Orth	1	50	NR	500	0.1	0.2
ORTHO–Ethiopian Orth	1	NR	NR	NR	-	-
PENT–Assemb of God	20	2,657	2,214	3,617	0.7	1.4
PENT–Ch God (Cleve)	2	63	66	81	0.0	0.0
PENT–Ch Lord Jesus Apos	1	NR	NR	NR	-	-
PENT–COGIC	8	235	925	1,128	0.2	0.4
PENT–Pent Ch of God	1	70	NR	109	0.0	0.0
PENT–Un Pent Ch Intl	3	NR	NR	NR	-	-
PENT–Vineyard	1	15	20	24	0.0	0.0
PRES–Orth Pres Ch	1	55	39	55	0.0	0.0
PRES–Presb Ch (USA)	14	1,656	4,464	5,446	1.1	2.1
PRES–Presb Ch Amer	1	0	0	0	0.0	0.0
REF–Christian Ref	2	438	483	589	0.1	0.2
Salvation Army	3	256	366	2,226	0.4	0.9
Sev Day Adv	6	304	529	609	0.1	0.2
Swedenborgian	1	NR	NR	NR	-	-
Un C of Christ	10	1,103	2,484	3,030	0.6	1.2
Unit Univ	2	831	945	1,427	0.3	0.6
Unity Ch	1	NR	NR	NR	-	-
Zoroastrian	0	NR	NR	2	0.0	0.0
RED LAKE	**14**	**572**	**1,644**	**3,907**	**95.5**	**100.0**
Catholic	4	NR	NR	1,800	44.0	46.1
LUTH–E.L.C.A.	5	316	922	1,185	29.0	30.3
LUTH–Evan Luth Syn	1	70	105	147	3.6	3.8
LUTH–Luth Cong Msn Chr	1	75	331	411	10.1	10.5
LUTH–Luth–MO Synod	2	86	229	293	7.2	7.5
PRES–Presb Ch (USA)	1	25	57	71	1.7	1.8
REDWOOD	**50**	**2,601**	**6,514**	**12,848**	**80.0**	**100.0**
ANG/EPIS–Episcopal	1	27	212	313	1.9	2.4
Bahá'í	0	NR	2	2	0.0	0.0
BAPT–NT Ind Bapt	1	NR	NR	NR	-	-
Catholic	9	NR	NR	4,432	27.6	34.5
Chr & Miss Al	1	74	47	113	0.7	0.9
CHR–Chr Chs & Chs Cr	2	NR	140	173	1.1	1.3
Evan Free Ch	1	80	NR	80	0.5	0.6
Jehovah's Witness	1	NR	NR	NR	-	-
LUTH–E.L.C.A.	11	776	2,570	3,326	20.7	25.9
LUTH–Evan Luth Syn	2	69	164	229	1.4	1.8
LUTH–Luth Cong Msn Chr	3	211	721	893	5.6	7.0
LUTH–Luth–MO Synod	2	45	90	94	0.6	0.7
LUTH–Wisc Ev Luth Syn	4	628	1,347	1,583	9.9	12.3
METH–Un Methodist	6	387	847	1,021	6.4	7.9
Non-denom Chr Chs	1	25	20	31	0.2	0.2
PENT–Assemb of God	1	90	64	90	0.6	0.7
PENT–Pent Ch of God	1	70	NR	109	0.7	0.8
PRES–Presb Ch (USA)	2	113	280	347	2.2	2.7
Sev Day Adv	1	6	10	12	0.1	0.1
RENVILLE	**44**	**2,638**	**6,712**	**12,250**	**77.9**	**100.0**
Catholic	7	NR	NR	3,859	24.5	31.5
Ch of God Gen Conf	1	NR	6	7	0.0	0.1
Ch of Nazarene	1	0	0	0	0.0	0.0
Evan Cov Ch	1	79	107	103	0.7	0.8
Evan Free Ch	2	165	NR	165	1.0	1.3
LUTH–E.L.C.A.	13	1,190	3,987	4,987	31.7	40.7
LUTH–Wisc Ev Luth Syn	7	552	1,188	1,379	8.8	11.3
METH–Un Methodist	9	437	1,004	1,273	8.1	10.4
Non-denom Chr Chs	1	100	150	150	1.0	1.2
PRES–Presb Ch (USA)	1	65	136	165	1.0	1.3
REF–Christian Ref	1	50	134	162	1.0	1.3
RICE	**69**	**7,472**	**12,770**	**32,148**	**50.1**	**100.0**
ANG/EPIS–Episcopal	2	139	327	327	0.5	1.0
Bahá'í	0	NR	18	18	0.0	0.1

Religious Group	Number of Congrega-tions	Number of Attendees	Number of Communicant, Confirmed, or Full Members	Adherents: Number of Adherents	Adherents: % of Total Pop.	Adherents: % of Total Adh.
BAPT–Converge/BGC	2	800	NR	960	1.5	3.0
BAPT–Reg Bapt Gen As	2	NR	NR	NR	-	-
BAPT–So Bapt Conv	1	35	28	34	0.1	0.1
Catholic	6	NR	NR	12,337	19.2	38.4
Chr & Miss Al	1	107	78	184	0.3	0.6
CHR–Chr Chs & Chs Cr	1	NR	80	98	0.2	0.3
CHR–Chs of Christ	1	15	20	25	0.0	0.1
Evan Free Ch	2	295	NR	295	0.5	0.9
FRND–Fr Gen Cf	1	NR	20	24	0.0	0.1
Jehovah's Witness	2	NR	NR	NR	-	-
LDS–L-D Saints	2	NR	NR	449	0.7	1.4
LUTH–Ch of Luth Br	1	63	59	200	0.3	0.6
LUTH–E.L.C.A.	10	2,407	6,206	9,230	14.4	28.7
LUTH–Luth Cong Msn Chr	1	272	NR	NR	-	-
LUTH–Luth–MO Synod	7	983	2,803	3,570	5.6	11.1
MENN–Fel Evg Ch	1	0	0	0	0.0	0.0
METH–Un Methodist	7	651	1,536	1,955	3.0	6.1
MORAV–Morav Ch-North	1	39	88	121	0.2	0.4
Muslim Est	2	604	NR	312	0.5	1.0
Non-denom Chr Chs	3	290	465	487	0.8	1.5
PENT–Assemb of God	6	316	132	405	0.6	1.3
PENT–Ch God (Cleve)	1	106	107	131	0.2	0.4
Sev Day Adv	1	36	63	72	0.1	0.2
Un C of Christ	3	274	699	853	1.3	2.7
Unit Univ	1	40	41	61	0.1	0.2
Unity Ch	1	NR	NR	NR	-	-
ROCK	**21**	**2,330**	**5,159**	**8,324**	**85.9**	**100.0**
ANG/EPIS–Episcopal	1	13	13	14	0.1	0.2
Bahá'í	0	NR	3	3	0.0	0.0
BAPT–Consrv Bapt	1	NR	NR	NR	-	-
Catholic	2	NR	NR	1,943	20.1	23.3
Jehovah's Witness	1	NR	NR	NR	-	-
LUTH–E.L.C.A.	3	471	1,508	2,012	20.8	24.2
LUTH–Evan Luth Syn	1	75	259	273	2.8	3.3
LUTH–Luth–MO Synod	3	364	821	1,004	10.4	12.1
METH–Un Methodist	2	152	304	439	4.5	5.3
PENT–Assemb of God	1	57	18	64	0.7	0.8
PRES–Presb Ch (USA)	2	197	632	790	8.2	9.5
REF–Christian Ref	1	280	362	453	4.7	5.4
REF–Ref Ch in Am	2	721	1,239	1,329	13.7	16.0
REF–Un Ref Chs N.A.	1	NR	NR	NR	-	-
ROSEAU	**45**	**2,075**	**4,084**	**8,129**	**52.0**	**100.0**
ANG/EPIS–Episcopal	1	15	26	26	0.2	0.3
Bahá'í	0	NR	3	3	0.0	0.0
BAPT–Converge/BGC	2	150	NR	180	1.2	2.2
BAPT–So Bapt Conv	2	29	22	27	0.2	0.3
Catholic	6	NR	NR	2,100	13.4	25.8
CHR–Chr Chs & Chs Cr	1	NR	10	12	0.1	0.1
CONG–Cong Chr, NA	1	NR	55	68	0.4	0.8
Evan Cov Ch	1	137	139	178	1.1	2.2
LDS–L-D Saints	1	NR	NR	219	1.4	2.7
LUTH–Assoc Free Luth	7	NR	NR	NR	-	-
LUTH–E.L.C.A.	11	861	2,838	3,726	23.8	45.8
LUTH–Evan Luth Syn	1	9	9	12	0.1	0.1
LUTH–Luth Cong Msn Chr	2	202	397	493	3.2	6.1
LUTH–Luth–MO Synod	1	32	49	49	0.3	0.6
LUTH–Nor Amer Luth C	2	NR	NR	NR	-	-
Non-denom Chr Chs	3	455	281	568	3.6	7.0
PENT–Assemb of God	2	179	244	455	2.9	5.6
Sev Day Adv	1	6	11	13	0.1	0.2
ST. LOUIS	**272**	**19,250**	**36,563**	**93,830**	**46.9**	**100.0**
ANG/EPIS–Episcopal	7	373	917	1,240	0.6	1.3
Bahá'í	1	NR	102	102	0.1	0.1
BAPT–Amer Bapt USA	2	50	113	133	0.1	0.1
BAPT–Converge/BGC	13	975	NR	1,170	0.6	1.2
BAPT–NT Ind Bapt	2	NR	NR	NR	-	-
BAPT–Reg Bapt Gen As	4	NR	NR	NR	-	-
BAPT–So Bapt Conv	4	74	61	72	0.0	0.1
BUDD–Theravada	1	NR	NR	14	0.0	0.0
Catholic	35	NR	NR	38,757	19.4	41.3

NR–Not Reported   - Represents no adherents reported.   Percentages may not total 100 due to rounding.

Table 3: Religious Congregations by County and Group: 2010

Religious Group	Number of Congrega-tions	Number of Attendees	Number of Communicant, Confirmed, or Full Members	Adherents		
				Number of Adherents	% of Total Pop.	% of Total Adh.
Ch Cr, Scientst	1	NR	NR	NR	-	-
Ch of Nazarene	1	0	0	0	0.0	0.0
Chr & Miss Al	3	237	111	375	0.2	0.4
CHR–Chr Ch (Disc)	1	0	45	53	0.0	0.1
CHR–Chr Chs & Chs Cr	1	NR	0	0	0.0	0.0
CHR–Chs of Christ	5	155	177	220	0.1	0.2
CONG–Cong Chr, NA	1	NR	79	93	0.0	0.1
CONG–Consrv Cong Chr	3	122	370	436	0.2	0.5
Evan Ch	1	NR	NR	NR	-	-
Evan Cov Ch	9	1,216	944	1,581	0.8	1.7
Evan Free Ch	5	782	NR	782	0.4	0.8
FRND–Fr Gen Cf	1	NR	18	21	0.0	0.0
Int Cou Comm Ch	1	NR	NR	NR	-	-
Jehovah's Witness	7	NR	NR	NR	-	-
JUD–Orth	1	72	75	100	0.0	0.1
JUD–Reconst	0	69	88	238	0.1	0.3
JUD–Reform	0	50	88	238	0.1	0.3
LDS–Comm of Christ	1	NR	138	138	0.1	0.1
LDS–L-D Saints	3	NR	NR	1,329	0.7	1.4
LUTH–Apostolic Luth	2	NR	NR	NR	-	-
LUTH–Assoc Free Luth	3	NR	NR	NR	-	-
LUTH–E.L.C.A.	46	4,741	17,730	22,945	11.5	24.5
LUTH–Luth Ch-Am Asc	1	NR	NR	NR	-	-
LUTH–Luth Cong Msn Chr	4	191	554	652	0.3	0.7
LUTH–Luth–MO Synod	11	966	2,269	3,100	1.5	3.3
LUTH–Wisc Ev Luth Syn	1	127	143	199	0.1	0.2
METH–AME	1	0	150	177	0.1	0.2
METH–Un Methodist	18	1,131	2,993	4,346	2.2	4.6
METH–Wesleyan	1	32	2	42	0.0	0.0
Muslim Est	1	134	NR	308	0.2	0.3
Nat Spirit Asso	1	NR	NR	NR	-	-
New Apost Ch	1	NR	NR	NR	-	-
Non-denom Chr Chs	21	2,190	2,315	2,889	1.4	3.1
OCATH–Pol Natl Cath	1	NR	NR	NR	-	-
ORTHE–Greek Orthodox	1	100	NR	175	0.1	0.2
ORTHE–Orth Ch in Amer	1	4	NR	4	0.0	0.0
ORTHE–Serb Orth USA	4	448	NR	797	0.4	0.8
PENT–Assemb of God	14	1,672	588	2,560	1.3	2.7
PENT–Un Pent Ch Intl	1	NR	NR	NR	-	-
PENT–Vineyard	2	1,901	3,000	3,533	1.8	3.8
PRES–Presb Ch (USA)	10	541	1,726	2,032	1.0	2.2
PRES–Presb Ch Amer	1	18	25	28	0.0	0.0
Salvation Army	3	125	193	1,133	0.6	1.2
Sev Day Adv	2	122	213	245	0.1	0.3
Un C of Christ	4	482	1,087	1,280	0.6	1.4
Unit Univ	2	150	249	293	0.1	0.3
SCOTT	**75**	**11,105**	**17,657**	**66,060**	**50.8**	**100.0**
Bahá'í	0	NR	8	8	0.0	0.0
BAPT–Converge/BGC	2	875	NR	1,050	0.8	1.6
BAPT–N Am Bapt Conf	1	NR	23	30	0.0	0.0
BAPT–NT Ind Bapt	2	NR	NR	NR	-	-
Catholic	12	NR	NR	39,912	30.7	60.4
Chr & Miss Al	3	323	161	494	0.4	0.7
Evan Ch	1	NR	NR	NR	-	-
Evan Free Ch	1	45	NR	45	0.0	0.1
Grace Gosp Fel	1	NR	NR	NR	-	-
Jehovah's Witness	1	NR	NR	NR	-	-
LUTH–Assoc Free Luth	2	NR	NR	NR	-	-
LUTH–E.L.C.A.	12	3,122	7,930	12,835	9.9	19.4
LUTH–Luth Cong Msn Chr	1	450	NR	NR	-	-
LUTH–Luth–MO Synod	4	640	1,485	1,943	1.5	2.9
LUTH–Wisc Ev Luth Syn	5	788	1,703	2,095	1.6	3.2
METH–Un Methodist	7	481	719	1,157	0.9	1.8
Non-denom Chr Chs	9	3,630	4,905	5,275	4.1	8.0
PENT–Assemb of God	3	329	165	467	0.4	0.7
PENT–Open Bible Std	1	32	NR	32	0.0	0.0
PRES–Presb Ch (USA)	2	130	216	284	0.2	0.4
REF–Christian Ref	1	157	155	204	0.2	0.3
Sev Day Adv	2	63	109	126	0.1	0.2
Un C of Christ	1	40	78	103	0.1	0.2
Unity Ch	1	NR	NR	NR	-	-

Religious Group	Number of Congrega-tions	Number of Attendees	Number of Communicant, Confirmed, or Full Members	Adherents		
				Number of Adherents	% of Total Pop.	% of Total Adh.
SHERBURNE	**53**	**7,906**	**12,603**	**33,779**	**38.2**	**100.0**
ANG/EPIS–Episcopal	1	34	78	78	0.1	0.2
Bahá'í	0	NR	21	21	0.0	0.1
BAPT–Amer Bapt Assn	1	NR	85	110	0.1	0.3
BAPT–Converge/BGC	4	300	NR	360	0.4	1.1
BAPT–NT Ind Bapt	1	NR	NR	NR	-	-
Catholic	4	NR	NR	11,772	13.3	34.9
Chr & Miss Al	2	1,535	520	3,002	3.4	8.9
Evan Cov Ch	1	36	24	47	0.1	0.1
Evan Free Ch	4	1,403	NR	1,403	1.6	4.2
LDS–L-D Saints	1	NR	NR	510	0.6	1.5
LUTH–E.L.C.A.	6	1,202	2,978	4,222	4.8	12.5
LUTH–Evan Luth Syn	1	73	156	204	0.2	0.6
LUTH–Luth Cong Msn Chr	1	980	4,238	5,486	6.2	16.2
LUTH–Luth–MO Synod	6	677	1,647	2,141	2.4	6.3
LUTH–Wisc Ev Luth Syn	1	106	146	173	0.2	0.5
MENN–Menn Br US Conf	1	NR	789	1,021	1.2	3.0
METH–Un Methodist	3	281	448	1,043	1.2	3.1
Non-denom Chr Chs	7	600	730	862	1.0	2.6
PENT–Assemb of God	4	461	205	523	0.6	1.5
PENT–Ch of God Proph	1	NR	31	40	0.0	0.1
PENT–Pent Ch of God	1	70	NR	109	0.1	0.3
Sev Day Adv	1	18	32	37	0.0	0.1
Un C of Christ	1	130	475	615	0.7	1.8
SIBLEY	**41**	**2,786**	**6,480**	**10,466**	**68.7**	**100.0**
Ap Chr Ch-Amer	1	125	66	125	0.8	1.2
Bahá'í	0	NR	7	7	0.0	0.1
BAPT–Converge/BGC	1	75	NR	90	0.6	0.9
Catholic	7	NR	NR	2,354	15.5	22.5
Chr & Miss Al	1	50	23	80	0.5	0.8
Evan Cov Ch	1	100	97	130	0.9	1.2
Jehovah's Witness	1	NR	NR	NR	-	-
LUTH–E.L.C.A.	9	790	2,287	2,830	18.6	27.0
LUTH–Evan Luth Syn	1	31	90	99	0.7	0.9
LUTH–Luth–MO Synod	8	808	2,149	2,508	16.5	24.0
LUTH–Wisc Ev Luth Syn	3	526	1,076	1,304	8.6	12.5
MENN–Hutt Breth	2	NR	NR	NR	-	-
METH–Un Methodist	1	108	156	206	1.4	2.0
PENT–Assemb of God	1	29	0	75	0.5	0.7
Sev Day Adv	1	19	33	38	0.2	0.4
Un C of Christ	3	125	496	620	4.1	5.9
STEARNS	**131**	**11,250**	**19,236**	**93,064**	**61.8**	**100.0**
ANG/EPIS–Episcopal	3	96	154	200	0.1	0.2
Bahá'í	1	NR	49	49	0.0	0.1
BAPT–Converge/BGC	3	550	NR	660	0.4	0.7
BAPT–NT Ind Bapt	1	NR	NR	NR	-	-
BAPT–Reg Bapt Gen As	2	NR	NR	NR	-	-
BAPT–So Bapt Conv	1	25	50	61	0.0	0.1
Calv Chpl	1	NR	NR	NR	-	-
Catholic	48	NR	NR	62,565	41.5	67.2
Ch of God Gen Conf	1	NR	10	12	0.0	0.0
CHR–Chr Chs & Chs Cr	1	NR	190	232	0.2	0.2
CHR–Chs of Christ	1	80	50	80	0.1	0.1
CONG–Consrv Cong Chr	1	150	76	93	0.1	0.1
Evan Cov Ch	1	155	161	202	0.1	0.2
Evan Free Ch	4	810	NR	810	0.5	0.9
Jehovah's Witness	2	NR	NR	NR	-	-
LDS–L-D Saints	2	NR	NR	839	0.6	0.9
LUTH–E.L.C.A.	16	3,296	10,294	14,075	9.3	15.1
LUTH–Evan Luth Syn	1	90	171	214	0.1	0.2
LUTH–Luth Cong Msn Chr	1	55	NR	NR	-	-
LUTH–Luth–MO Synod	9	1,328	3,213	4,072	2.7	4.4
METH–Un Methodist	5	693	1,544	2,171	1.4	2.3
Non-denom Chr Chs	8	1,510	1,620	1,936	1.3	2.1
ORTHE–Orth Ch in Amer	1	15	NR	21	0.0	0.0
PENT–Assemb of God	9	2,003	587	3,469	2.3	3.7
PRES–Evan Presby Ch	1	NR	112	137	0.1	0.1
PRES–Presb Ch (USA)	2	161	541	660	0.4	0.7
REF–Christian Ref	1	63	76	93	0.1	0.1
Un C of Christ	2	117	272	332	0.2	0.4
Unit Univ	1	53	66	81	0.1	0.1

NR–Not Reported   - Represents no adherents reported.   Percentages may not total 100 due to rounding.

Table 3: Religious Congregations by County and Group: 2010

Religious Group	Number of Congrega-tions	Number of Attendees	Number of Communicant, Confirmed, or Full Members	Adherents: Number of Adherents	Adherents: % of Total Pop.	Adherents: % of Total Adh.
Unity Ch	1	NR	NR	NR	-	-
STEELE	**51**	**5,730**	**12,168**	**26,337**	**72.0**	**100.0**
ANG/EPIS–Episcopal	1	68	232	305	0.8	1.2
Bahá'í	0	NR	4	4	0.0	0.0
BAPT–Amer Bapt USA	1	50	126	158	0.4	0.6
BAPT–Converge/BGC	1	400	NR	480	1.3	1.8
BAPT–NT Ind Bapt	1	NR	NR	NR	-	-
Catholic	7	NR	NR	9,225	25.2	35.0
CHR–Chr Chs & Chs Cr	1	NR	60	75	0.2	0.3
CHR–Chs of Christ	1	60	40	65	0.2	0.2
Evan Cov Ch	1	49	49	64	0.2	0.2
Evan Free Ch	1	170	NR	170	0.5	0.6
Jehovah's Witness	2	NR	NR	NR	-	-
LUTH–Assoc Free Luth	1	NR	NR	NR	-	-
LUTH–E.L.C.A.	11	2,060	7,566	10,021	27.4	38.0
LUTH–Luth–MO Synod	3	602	1,193	1,546	4.2	5.9
LUTH–Wisc Ev Luth Syn	1	76	164	193	0.5	0.7
METH–Un Methodist	3	301	638	839	2.3	3.2
Muslim Est	2	268	NR	616	1.7	2.3
Non-denom Chr Chs	5	950	1,220	1,326	3.6	5.0
PENT–Assemb of God	2	270	144	335	0.9	1.3
PENT–Ch God (Cleve)	1	35	5	6	0.0	0.0
PENT–Un Pent Ch Intl	1	NR	NR	NR	-	-
PRES–Presb Ch (USA)	1	160	264	331	0.9	1.3
Sev Day Adv	1	19	33	38	0.1	0.1
Un C of Christ	2	192	430	540	1.5	2.1
STEVENS	**23**	**2,615**	**3,907**	**7,036**	**72.3**	**100.0**
Ap Chr Ch-Amer	2	750	367	750	7.7	10.7
Bahá'í	0	NR	1	1	0.0	0.0
BAPT–NT Ind Bapt	1	NR	NR	NR	-	-
Catholic	2	NR	NR	1,546	15.9	22.0
Ch of Nazarene	1	28	58	58	0.6	0.8
Evan Free Ch	1	242	NR	242	2.5	3.4
LUTH–Ch Luth Conf	1	NR	NR	NR	-	-
LUTH–E.L.C.A.	7	979	2,526	3,253	33.4	46.2
LUTH–Luth Cong Msn Chr	1	130	112	134	1.4	1.9
LUTH–Luth–MO Synod	1	95	238	288	3.0	4.1
LUTH–Wisc Ev Luth Syn	1	55	113	131	1.3	1.9
METH–Un Methodist	1	88	112	112	1.2	1.6
PENT–Assemb of God	1	75	29	100	1.0	1.4
REF–Christian Ref	1	72	100	120	1.2	1.7
Un C of Christ	2	101	251	301	3.1	4.3
SWIFT	**29**	**1,830**	**4,475**	**8,054**	**82.3**	**100.0**
Bahá'í	0	NR	1	1	0.0	0.0
BAPT–Converge/BGC	2	150	NR	180	1.8	2.2
Catholic	5	NR	NR	2,399	24.5	29.8
Evan Free Ch	2	245	NR	245	2.5	3.0
LUTH–E.L.C.A.	9	860	3,004	3,490	35.7	43.3
LUTH–Luth–MO Synod	5	368	1,039	1,205	12.3	15.0
METH–Un Methodist	1	20	57	60	0.6	0.7
Non-denom Chr Chs	1	50	75	75	0.8	0.9
PENT–Assemb of God	1	45	30	76	0.8	0.9
PRES–Presb Ch (USA)	1	24	44	53	0.5	0.7
Un C of Christ	2	68	225	270	2.8	3.4
TODD	**56**	**2,910**	**6,075**	**14,599**	**58.6**	**100.0**
Bahá'í	0	NR	7	7	0.0	0.0
BAPT–Consrv Bapt	1	NR	NR	NR	-	-
BAPT–Converge/BGC	1	75	NR	90	0.4	0.6
Catholic	7	NR	NR	5,498	22.1	37.7
CGOD–Ch God (Ander)	1	164	NR	164	0.7	1.1
Ch of Nazarene	2	55	73	73	0.3	0.5
Chr & Miss Al	1	203	88	363	1.5	2.5
CHR–Chr Chs & Chs Cr	1	NR	100	123	0.5	0.8
CONG–Consrv Cong Chr	1	12	16	20	0.1	0.1
Evan Cov Ch	1	61	47	79	0.3	0.5
Evan Free Ch	1	15	NR	15	0.1	0.1
LUTH–Ch of Luth Br	1	104	89	197	0.8	1.3
LUTH–E.L.C.A.	6	573	1,799	2,276	9.1	15.6
LUTH–Luth Cong Msn Chr	1	189	764	941	3.8	6.4

Religious Group	Number of Congrega-tions	Number of Attendees	Number of Communicant, Confirmed, or Full Members	Adherents: Number of Adherents	Adherents: % of Total Pop.	Adherents: % of Total Adh.
LUTH–Luth–MO Synod	8	611	1,740	2,258	9.1	15.5
MENN–Amish Undif	7	NR	321	822	3.3	5.6
METH–Un Methodist	7	340	500	810	3.3	5.5
Non-denom Chr Chs	2	145	215	215	0.9	1.5
PENT–Assemb of God	3	225	120	411	1.7	2.8
Sev Day Adv	1	30	53	61	0.2	0.4
Un C of Christ	3	108	143	176	0.7	1.2
TRAVERSE	**28**	**1,162**	**3,294**	**6,300**	**177.1**	**200.0**
ANG/EPIS–Episcopal	2	74	160	542	15.2	17.2
Catholic	6	NR	NR	1,904	53.5	60.4
Evan Cov Ch	2	158	184	206	5.8	6.5
Jehovah's Witness	2	NR	NR	NR	-	-
LUTH–E.L.C.A.	4	316	1,020	1,278	35.9	40.6
LUTH–Luth–MO Synod	6	444	1,534	1,904	53.5	60.4
METH–Un Methodist	2	60	140	162	4.6	5.1
PRES–Presb Ch (USA)	4	110	256	304	8.5	9.7
WABASHA	**40**	**2,868**	**6,555**	**15,997**	**73.8**	**100.0**
ANG/EPIS–Episcopal	2	44	181	181	0.8	1.1
Bahá'í	0	NR	2	2	0.0	0.0
BAPT–Converge/BGC	1	400	NR	480	2.2	3.0
Catholic	8	NR	NR	6,439	29.7	40.3
CHR–Chr Chs & Chs Cr	1	NR	175	212	1.0	1.3
Christian Brethren	1	NR	NR	NR	-	-
Evan Free Ch	2	230	NR	230	1.1	1.4
LUTH–E.L.C.A.	3	600	1,006	2,195	10.1	13.7
LUTH–Luth–MO Synod	5	498	1,791	2,208	10.2	13.8
LUTH–Wisc Ev Luth Syn	6	557	2,134	2,376	11.0	14.9
METH–Un Methodist	5	262	451	677	3.1	4.2
Non-denom Chr Chs	1	65	60	81	0.4	0.5
PRES–Presb Ch (USA)	1	0	149	181	0.8	1.1
Un C of Christ	4	212	606	735	3.4	4.6
WADENA	**45**	**2,162**	**4,515**	**8,374**	**60.5**	**100.0**
ANG/EPIS–Episcopal	1	20	67	67	0.5	0.8
BAPT–Amer Bapt Assn	1	NR	15	18	0.1	0.2
BAPT–Reg Bapt Gen As	1	NR	NR	NR	-	-
Catholic	4	NR	NR	1,812	13.1	21.6
Chr & Miss Al	4	440	260	610	4.4	7.3
CHR–Chs of Christ	1	12	11	16	0.1	0.2
Evan Ch	1	NR	NR	NR	-	-
Jehovah's Witness	1	NR	NR	NR	-	-
LDS–L-D Saints	1	NR	NR	126	0.9	1.5
LUTH–Apostolic Luth	1	NR	NR	NR	-	-
LUTH–Assoc Free Luth	2	NR	NR	NR	-	-
LUTH–E.L.C.A.	4	406	1,455	1,946	14.1	23.2
LUTH–Luth Cong Msn Chr	3	178	659	806	5.8	9.6
LUTH–Luth–MO Synod	6	378	1,186	1,542	11.1	18.4
METH–Un Methodist	6	304	404	637	4.6	7.6
Non-denom Chr Chs	2	108	161	161	1.2	1.9
PENT–Assemb of God	3	197	69	362	2.6	4.3
Sev Day Adv	1	61	106	122	0.9	1.5
Un C of Christ	2	58	122	149	1.1	1.8
WASECA	**39**	**2,962**	**7,173**	**14,470**	**75.6**	**100.0**
Bahá'í	0	NR	7	7	0.0	0.0
BAPT–NT Ind Bapt	1	NR	NR	NR	-	-
BAPT–So Bapt Conv	2	10	7	9	0.0	0.1
Catholic	4	NR	NR	4,574	23.9	31.6
CONG–Cong Chr, NA	2	NR	171	210	1.1	1.5
Evan Cov Ch	2	137	176	179	0.9	1.2
Evan Free Ch	1	300	NR	300	1.6	2.1
LDS–L-D Saints	1	NR	NR	92	0.5	0.6
LUTH–E.L.C.A.	9	958	3,410	4,633	24.2	32.0
LUTH–Luth–MO Synod	5	940	2,364	3,050	15.9	21.1
LUTH–Wisc Ev Luth Syn	2	126	232	267	1.4	1.8
METH–Un Methodist	3	196	501	667	3.5	4.6
METH–Wesleyan	1	14	20	18	0.1	0.1
Non-denom Chr Chs	3	145	145	181	0.9	1.3
PENT–Assemb of God	2	116	67	193	1.0	1.3
Un C of Christ	1	20	73	90	0.5	0.6

NR–Not Reported   - Represents no adherents reported.   Percentages may not total 100 due to rounding.

Table 3: Religious Congregations by County and Group: 2010

Religious Group	Number of Congrega-tions	Number of Attendees	Number of Communicant, Confirmed, or Full Members	Adherents		
				Number of Adherents	% of Total Pop.	% of Total Adh.
WASHINGTON	**129**	**27,722**	**48,456**	**137,242**	**57.6**	**100.0**
ANG/EPIS–Episcopal	3	386	884	1,050	0.4	0.8
Bahá'í	1	NR	70	70	0.0	0.1
BAPT–Consrv Bapt	1	NR	NR	NR	-	-
BAPT–Converge/BGC	6	450	NR	540	0.2	0.4
BAPT–N Am Bapt Conf	1	NR	131	164	0.1	0.1
BAPT–NT Ind Bapt	3	NR	NR	NR	-	-
BAPT–So Bapt Conv	1	8	12	15	0.0	0.0
BUDD–Theravada	1	NR	NR	300	0.1	0.2
Catholic	9	NR	NR	64,157	26.9	46.7
CGOD–Ch God (Ander)	1	120	NR	120	0.1	0.1
Ch Cr, Scientst	1	NR	NR	NR	-	-
Chr & Miss Al	5	337	339	689	0.3	0.5
CHR–Chr Ch (Disc)	1	70	233	292	0.1	0.2
CHR–Chr Chs & Chs Cr	2	NR	288	361	0.2	0.3
CHR–Chs of Christ	2	277	257	332	0.1	0.2
Christian Brethren	1	NR	NR	NR	-	-
CONG–Cong Chr, NA	1	NR	163	204	0.1	0.1
CONG–Consrv Cong Chr	2	257	241	302	0.1	0.2
Evan Cov Ch	5	2,640	1,268	3,432	1.4	2.5
Evan Free Ch	4	2,590	NR	2,590	1.1	1.9
FRND–Fr Gen Cf	1	NR	15	19	0.0	0.0
HINDU–Post Ren	1	NR	NR	10	0.0	0.0
Jehovah's Witness	3	NR	NR	NR	-	-
LDS–L-D Saints	5	NR	NR	2,280	1.0	1.7
LUTH–E.L.C.A.	19	8,344	22,684	33,016	13.9	24.1
LUTH–Luth Cong Msn Chr	1	1,150	2,500	3,134	1.3	2.3
LUTH–Luth-MO Synod	9	2,372	4,342	6,021	2.5	4.4
LUTH–Wisc Ev Luth Syn	6	680	1,297	1,463	0.6	1.1
METH–Un Methodist	7	1,174	2,546	3,544	1.5	2.6
METH–Wesleyan	1	87	31	113	0.0	0.1
Non-denom Chr Chs	9	4,960	8,615	9,105	3.8	6.6
PENT–Assemb of God	3	448	125	610	0.3	0.4
PENT–Pent Ch of God	1	70	NR	109	0.0	0.1
PENT–Un Pent Ch Intl	2	NR	NR	NR	-	-
PENT–Vineyard	1	45	30	38	0.0	0.0
PRES–Presb Ch (USA)	3	483	1,133	1,420	0.6	1.0
Sev Day Adv	2	18	31	36	0.0	0.0
Un C of Christ	3	156	532	667	0.3	0.5
Unit Univ	1	600	689	1,039	0.4	0.8
WATONWAN	**34**	**2,025**	**5,218**	**8,966**	**80.0**	**100.0**
Catholic	2	NR	NR	2,514	22.4	28.0
CHR–Chr Chs & Chs Cr	1	NR	35	43	0.4	0.5
Jehovah's Witness	1	NR	NR	NR	-	-
LUTH–Assoc Free Luth	1	NR	NR	NR	-	-
LUTH–E.L.C.A.	11	878	3,048	3,806	33.9	42.4
LUTH–Luth Cong Msn Chr	1	70	196	242	2.2	2.7
LUTH–Luth-MO Synod	4	298	540	631	5.6	7.0
LUTH–Nor Amer Luth C	1	NR	NR	NR	-	-
LUTH–Wisc Ev Luth Syn	3	269	564	669	6.0	7.5
METH–Un Methodist	2	104	230	243	2.2	2.7
Non-denom Chr Chs	3	205	190	257	2.3	2.9
PENT–Assemb of God	1	45	32	89	0.8	1.0
PENT–Un Pent Ch Intl	1	NR	NR	NR	-	-
PRES–Presb Ch (USA)	2	156	383	472	4.2	5.3
WILKIN	**19**	**980**	**2,551**	**4,871**	**74.1**	**100.0**
Bahá'í	0	NR	1	1	0.0	0.0
BAPT–Amer Bapt USA	1	30	108	131	2.0	2.7
BAPT–Consrv Bapt	1	NR	NR	NR	-	-
BAPT–Converge/BGC	1	75	NR	90	1.4	1.8
Catholic	2	NR	NR	1,503	22.9	30.9
Jehovah's Witness	1	NR	NR	NR	-	-
LUTH–Ch of Luth Br	1	85	57	134	2.0	2.8
LUTH–E.L.C.A.	6	470	1,705	2,141	32.6	44.0
LUTH–Luth-MO Synod	2	112	294	327	5.0	6.7
METH–Un Methodist	1	85	242	330	5.0	6.8
Non-denom Chr Chs	1	100	70	125	1.9	2.6
PRES–Presb Ch (USA)	1	23	49	59	0.9	1.2
Un C of Christ	1	0	25	30	0.5	0.6

Religious Group	Number of Congrega-tions	Number of Attendees	Number of Communicant, Confirmed, or Full Members	Adherents		
				Number of Adherents	% of Total Pop.	% of Total Adh.
WINONA	**76**	**5,440**	**11,647**	**28,421**	**55.2**	**100.0**
ANG/EPIS–Episcopal	1	58	95	95	0.2	0.3
Bahá'í	0	NR	19	19	0.0	0.1
BAPT–Amer Bapt USA	1	32	72	84	0.2	0.3
BAPT–NT Ind Bapt	1	NR	NR	NR	-	-
BAPT–Ref Bapt Ch	1	NR	NR	NR	-	-
BAPT–So Bapt Conv	2	94	108	127	0.2	0.4
BRETH–Ch of Brethren	1	39	94	110	0.2	0.4
BUDD–Theravada	1	NR	NR	15	0.0	0.1
Catholic	13	NR	NR	11,470	22.3	40.4
Ch of Nazarene	1	66	70	114	0.2	0.4
Chr & Miss Al	1	30	37	37	0.1	0.1
CHR–Chr Chs & Chs Cr	1	NR	40	47	0.1	0.2
CHR–Chs of Christ	2	42	38	49	0.1	0.2
Evan Free Ch	1	850	NR	850	1.7	3.0
FRND–Fr Gen Cf	1	NR	8	9	0.0	0.0
Ind Fund Churches	1	NR	NR	NR	-	-
Jehovah's Witness	1	NR	NR	NR	-	-
LDS–L-D Saints	1	NR	NR	263	0.5	0.9
LUTH–E.L.C.A.	5	837	3,155	4,203	8.2	14.8
LUTH–Luth-MO Synod	5	501	2,463	3,206	6.2	11.3
LUTH–Wisc Ev Luth Syn	9	1,464	3,207	4,012	7.8	14.1
MENN–Amish Undif	2	NR	129	370	0.7	1.3
METH–Un Methodist	7	350	884	1,166	2.3	4.1
MORAV–Morav Ch-North	2	128	234	307	0.6	1.1
Muslim Est	1	134	NR	308	0.6	1.1
Non-denom Chr Chs	3	325	280	406	0.8	1.4
PENT–Assemb of God	2	159	24	334	0.6	1.2
PENT–Un Pent Ch Intl	1	NR	NR	NR	-	-
PRES–Presb Ch (USA)	3	95	202	237	0.5	0.8
Sev Day Adv	1	34	58	67	0.1	0.2
Un C of Christ	3	167	381	447	0.9	1.6
Unit Univ	1	35	49	69	0.1	0.2
WRIGHT	**102**	**13,658**	**21,390**	**55,051**	**44.1**	**100.0**
ANG/EPIS–Episcopal	1	22	9	9	0.0	0.0
Bahá'í	0	NR	10	10	0.0	0.0
BAPT–Converge/BGC	3	2,150	NR	2,580	2.1	4.7
BAPT–So Bapt Conv	1	23	71	93	0.1	0.2
BUDD–Theravada	1	NR	NR	300	0.2	0.5
Catholic	13	NR	NR	18,699	15.0	34.0
Ch of Nazarene	1	76	63	105	0.1	0.2
Chr & Miss Al	2	168	110	260	0.2	0.5
CHR–Chr Chs & Chs Cr	2	NR	155	203	0.2	0.4
CHR–Chs of Christ	1	14	10	14	0.0	0.0
Evan Cov Ch	8	1,494	868	1,941	1.6	3.5
Evan Free Ch	7	1,595	NR	1,595	1.3	2.9
Jehovah's Witness	3	NR	NR	NR	-	-
LDS–L-D Saints	1	NR	NR	405	0.3	0.7
LUTH–Assoc Free Luth	2	NR	NR	NR	-	-
LUTH–E.L.C.A.	14	2,769	8,854	13,093	10.5	23.8
LUTH–Luth Cong Msn Chr	6	1,351	3,412	4,477	3.6	8.1
LUTH–Luth-MO Synod	10	1,593	3,846	5,369	4.3	9.8
LUTH–Wisc Ev Luth Syn	6	673	1,576	1,968	1.6	3.6
METH–Un Methodist	7	776	1,401	2,198	1.8	4.0
Non-denom Chr Chs	2	225	150	282	0.2	0.5
PENT–Assemb of God	4	360	171	576	0.5	1.0
PRES–Presb Ch (USA)	3	163	308	404	0.3	0.7
REF–Ref Ch in Am	1	65	88	97	0.1	0.2
Sev Day Adv	1	16	27	31	0.0	0.1
Un C of Christ	2	125	261	342	0.3	0.6
YELLOW MEDICINE	**34**	**2,047**	**5,498**	**9,727**	**93.2**	**100.0**
BAPT–Consrv Bapt	1	NR	NR	NR	-	-
Catholic	3	NR	NR	2,274	21.8	23.4
Chr & Miss Al	2	86	47	137	1.3	1.4
CHR–Chr Chs & Chs Cr	1	NR	80	97	0.9	1.0
Evan Free Ch	1	85	NR	85	0.8	0.9
LUTH–E.L.C.A.	12	1,135	3,907	5,226	50.1	53.7
LUTH–Luth Cong Msn Chr	2	82	NR	NR	-	-
LUTH–Luth-MO Synod	3	226	665	828	7.9	8.5
LUTH–Wisc Ev Luth Syn	2	188	374	465	4.5	4.8
METH–Un Methodist	1	23	78	83	0.8	0.9

NR–Not Reported - Represents no adherents reported. Percentages may not total 100 due to rounding.

Table 3: Religious Congregations by County and Group: 2010

Religious Group	Number of Congrega-tions	Number of Attendees	Number of Communicant, Confirmed, or Full Members	Adherents		
				Number of Adherents	% of Total Pop.	% of Total Adh.
Non-denom Chr Chs	1	67	25	84	0.8	0.9
PENT–Assemb of God	2	71	44	110	1.1	1.1
PRES–Presb Ch (USA)	2	54	149	181	1.7	1.9
Un C of Christ	1	30	129	157	1.5	1.6
MISSISSIPPI	**6,765**	**525,212**	**1,303,304**	**1,742,916**	**58.7**	**100.0**
ADAMS	**71**	**6,461**	**16,130**	**22,242**	**68.9**	**100.0**
ANG/EPIS–Episcopal	1	79	305	374	1.2	1.7
Bahá'í	0	NR	4	4	0.0	0.0
BAPT–NBC USA	3	1,975	2,700	3,256	10.1	14.6
BAPT–So Bapt Conv	14	1,667	7,309	8,813	27.3	39.6
Catholic	4	NR	NR	2,017	6.2	9.1
CGOD–Ch God (Ander)	2	238	NR	238	0.7	1.1
CHR–Chs of Christ	3	383	554	683	2.1	3.1
Evan Cov Ch	1	60	90	78	0.2	0.4
Jehovah's Witness	1	NR	NR	NR	-	-
JUD–Reform	1	9	16	43	0.1	0.2
LDS–L-D Saints	1	NR	NR	325	1.0	1.5
LUTH–Luth-MO Synod	1	24	32	36	0.1	0.2
METH–AME	9	195	1,230	1,483	4.6	6.7
METH–Un Methodist	6	474	1,422	1,738	5.4	7.8
Non-denom Chr Chs	6	510	525	649	2.0	2.9
PENT–Assemb of God	6	288	156	360	1.1	1.6
PENT–Ch God (Cleve)	2	237	727	877	2.7	3.9
PENT–Ch of God Proph	1	NR	30	36	0.1	0.2
PENT–COGIC	2	0	500	603	1.9	2.7
PENT–Full Gosp Bapt	1	NR	NR	NR	-	-
PENT–Un Pent Ch Intl	1	NR	NR	NR	-	-
PRES–Evan Presby Ch	1	NR	30	36	0.1	0.2
PRES–Presb Ch (USA)	2	190	301	363	1.1	1.6
PRES–Presb Ch Amer	1	40	39	46	0.1	0.2
Sev Day Adv	1	92	160	184	0.6	0.8
ALCORN	**107**	**9,354**	**19,369**	**24,483**	**66.1**	**100.0**
ANG/EPIS–Episcopal	1	56	98	98	0.3	0.4
Bahá'í	0	NR	3	3	0.0	0.0
BAPT–Amer Bapt Assn	2	NR	350	432	1.2	1.8
BAPT–Free Will Bapt	2	NR	108	133	0.4	0.5
BAPT–Natl Mis Bapt Conv	1	85	125	154	0.4	0.6
BAPT–NBC USA	1	0	0	0	0.0	0.0
BAPT–So Bapt Conv	32	5,141	11,450	14,134	38.1	57.7
Catholic	1	NR	NR	443	1.2	1.8
CHR–Chr Chs & Chs Cr	5	NR	672	830	2.2	3.4
CHR–Chs of Christ	20	1,705	1,579	2,018	5.4	8.2
Jehovah's Witness	1	NR	NR	NR	-	-
LDS–L-D Saints	1	NR	NR	486	1.3	2.0
LUTH–Luth-MO Synod	1	12	20	20	0.1	0.1
METH–C.M.E.	4	125	609	752	2.0	3.1
METH–Un Methodist	12	652	2,045	2,264	6.1	9.2
Non-denom Chr Chs	8	1,290	1,515	1,668	4.5	6.8
PENT–Assemb of God	2	121	77	165	0.4	0.7
PENT–Ch God (Cleve)	1	5	8	10	0.0	0.0
PENT–Un Pent Ch Intl	6	NR	NR	NR	-	-
PRES–Cumber Presb	1	NR	31	31	0.1	0.1
PRES–Evan Presby Ch	1	NR	468	578	1.6	2.4
PRES–Presb Ch (USA)	2	40	80	99	0.3	0.4
PRES–Presb Ch Amer	1	60	23	41	0.1	0.2
Sev Day Adv	1	62	108	124	0.3	0.5
AMITE	**44**	**1,607**	**5,182**	**6,691**	**51.0**	**100.0**
BAPT–Natl Mis Bapt Conv	2	0	300	363	2.8	5.4
BAPT–So Bapt Conv	22	1,361	3,698	4,474	34.1	66.9
Catholic	1	NR	NR	48	0.4	0.7
Ch of Nazarene	1	36	56	56	0.4	0.8
Jehovah's Witness	1	NR	NR	NR	-	-
LDS–L-D Saints	1	NR	NR	397	3.0	5.9
METH–AME	1	0	100	121	0.9	1.8
METH–C.M.E.	4	0	450	544	4.1	8.1
METH–Un Methodist	3	92	142	166	1.3	2.5
PENT–Assemb of God	1	25	27	28	0.2	0.4

Religious Group	Number of Congrega-tions	Number of Attendees	Number of Communicant, Confirmed, or Full Members	Adherents		
				Number of Adherents	% of Total Pop.	% of Total Adh.
PENT–Ch God (Cleve)	1	33	77	93	0.7	1.4
PENT–Ch of God Proph	2	NR	53	64	0.5	1.0
PENT–COGIC	2	50	250	302	2.3	4.5
PRES–Presb Ch (USA)	2	10	29	35	0.3	0.5
ATTALA	**68**	**3,600**	**8,629**	**11,053**	**56.5**	**100.0**
ANG/EPIS–Episcopal	1	12	27	39	0.2	0.4
BAPT–Natl Mis Bapt Conv	2	0	300	376	1.9	3.4
BAPT–So Bapt Conv	24	2,000	5,640	7,072	36.1	64.0
Catholic	1	NR	NR	194	1.0	1.8
CGOD–Ch God (Ander)	1	50	NR	50	0.3	0.5
Ch of Nazarene	1	10	9	10	0.1	0.1
CHR–Chs of Christ	4	245	243	296	1.5	2.7
LDS–L-D Saints	1	NR	NR	150	0.8	1.4
LUTH–E.L.C.A.	1	20	23	28	0.1	0.3
METH–AME Zion	1	0	100	125	0.6	1.1
METH–Cong Meth	3	NR	134	168	0.9	1.5
METH–Un Methodist	15	668	1,173	1,291	6.6	11.7
Non-denom Chr Chs	2	175	185	223	1.1	2.0
PENT–Assemb of God	1	184	101	205	1.0	1.9
PENT–Ch God (Cleve)	2	55	93	117	0.6	1.1
PENT–Ch of God Proph	1	NR	39	49	0.3	0.4
PENT–COGIC	1	0	150	188	1.0	1.7
PENT–Un Pent Ch Intl	2	NR	NR	NR	-	-
PRES–Presb Ch (USA)	2	35	73	92	0.5	0.8
PRES–Presb Ch Amer	2	146	339	380	1.9	3.4
BENTON	**31**	**1,984**	**4,301**	**5,658**	**64.8**	**100.0**
ANG/EPIS–Episcopal	1	13	27	27	0.3	0.5
BAPT–So Bapt Conv	12	1,009	3,096	3,828	43.9	67.7
CHR–Chs of Christ	5	441	416	577	6.6	10.2
METH–C.M.E.	2	0	200	247	2.8	4.4
METH–Un Methodist	5	177	253	279	3.2	4.9
Muslim Est	1	134	NR	308	3.5	5.4
Non-denom Chr Chs	2	200	200	250	2.9	4.4
PENT–COGIC	1	0	60	74	0.8	1.3
PRES–Cumber Presb	1	NR	24	37	0.4	0.7
PRES–Presb Ch (USA)	1	10	25	31	0.4	0.5
BOLIVAR	**99**	**5,224**	**12,852**	**17,274**	**50.6**	**100.0**
ANG/EPIS–Episcopal	2	74	136	162	0.5	0.9
Bahá'í	0	NR	9	9	0.0	0.1
BAPT–Natl Mis Bapt Conv	1	200	180	225	0.7	1.3
BAPT–NBC USA	10	335	1,293	1,613	4.7	9.3
BAPT–So Bapt Conv	23	1,466	5,439	6,786	19.9	39.3
Catholic	5	NR	NR	928	2.7	5.4
Ch of Chr (Hol)	1	NR	NR	NR	-	-
Ch of Nazarene	2	85	217	217	0.6	1.3
CHR–Chr Ch (Disc)	2	15	42	52	0.2	0.3
CHR–Chs of Christ	6	613	828	1,024	3.0	5.9
Evan Cov Ch	1	56	42	73	0.2	0.4
Jehovah's Witness	2	NR	NR	NR	-	-
JUD–Reform	1	13	23	62	0.2	0.4
LUTH–Luth-MO Synod	1	17	29	34	0.1	0.2
METH–AME	6	0	625	780	2.3	4.5
METH–AME Zion	1	0	100	125	0.4	0.7
METH–Un Methodist	12	521	1,298	1,521	4.5	8.8
Muslim Est	2	268	NR	616	1.8	3.6
Non-denom Chr Chs	7	790	1,055	1,112	3.3	6.4
PENT–Assemb of God	3	209	171	304	0.9	1.8
PENT–Ch God (Cleve)	1	74	168	210	0.6	1.2
PENT–Ch of God Proph	1	NR	17	21	0.1	0.1
PENT–COGIC	3	0	450	561	1.6	3.2
PENT–Full Gosp Bapt	1	NR	NR	NR	-	-
PRES–Presb Ch (USA)	3	122	247	308	0.9	1.8
PRES–Presb Ch Amer	1	325	412	449	1.3	2.6
Sev Day Adv	1	41	71	82	0.2	0.5
CALHOUN	**71**	**3,481**	**9,860**	**12,298**	**82.2**	**100.0**
BAPT–Free Will Bapt	1	NR	54	67	0.4	0.5
BAPT–So Bapt Conv	48	3,108	8,122	10,080	67.4	82.0
Catholic	1	NR	NR	85	0.6	0.7

NR–Not Reported - Represents no adherents reported. Percentages may not total 100 due to rounding.

Table 3: Religious Congregations by County and Group: 2010

Religious Group	Number of Congregations	Number of Attendees	Number of Communicant, Confirmed, or Full Members	Adherents: Number of Adherents	Adherents: % of Total Pop.	Adherents: % of Total Adh.
Ch of Nazarene	1	15	24	28	0.2	0.2
CHR–Chs of Christ	2	47	42	59	0.4	0.5
METH–AME	2	0	210	261	1.7	2.1
METH–C.M.E.	5	0	500	621	4.2	5.0
METH–Un Methodist	6	210	673	805	5.4	6.5
PENT–Ch God (Cleve)	2	101	185	230	1.5	1.9
PENT–Ch of God Proph	2	NR	50	62	0.4	0.5
PENT–Full Gosp Bapt	1	NR	NR	NR	-	-
CARROLL	**41**	**1,592**	**4,664**	**5,513**	**52.0**	**100.0**
ANG/EPIS–Episcopal	1	16	18	18	0.2	0.3
Bahá'í	0	NR	2	2	0.0	0.0
BAPT–So Bapt Conv	17	1,125	2,817	3,374	31.8	61.2
CHR–Chr Ch (Disc)	1	55	60	72	0.7	1.3
CHR–Chs of Christ	1	35	35	40	0.4	0.7
METH–AME	1	0	100	120	1.1	2.2
METH–C.M.E.	7	0	750	898	8.5	16.3
METH–Un Methodist	9	306	594	620	5.9	11.2
PENT–COGIC	1	0	150	180	1.7	3.3
PRES–Presb Ch Amer	3	55	138	189	1.8	3.4
CHICKASAW	**91**	**4,578**	**13,072**	**16,493**	**94.8**	**100.0**
ANG/EPIS–Episcopal	1	10	7	7	0.0	0.0
Bahá'í	0	NR	1	1	0.0	0.0
BAPT–Free Will Bapt	1	NR	54	68	0.4	0.4
BAPT–Natl Mis Bapt Conv	2	0	300	375	2.2	2.3
BAPT–NBC Amer	1	0	0	0	0.0	0.0
BAPT–NBC USA	3	180	450	563	3.2	3.4
BAPT–So Bapt Conv	26	2,708	8,633	10,803	62.1	65.5
Catholic	2	NR	NR	409	2.4	2.5
Ch of Nazarene	3	212	252	305	1.8	1.8
CHR–Chr Chs & Chs Cr	1	NR	20	25	0.1	0.2
CHR–Chs of Christ	7	410	390	506	2.9	3.1
Jehovah's Witness	1	NR	NR	NR	-	-
MENN–CG in Cr (Menn)	1	NR	111	139	0.8	0.8
METH–C.M.E.	6	0	650	813	4.7	4.9
METH–Un Methodist	15	528	1,403	1,469	8.4	8.9
Non-denom Chr Chs	3	220	230	276	1.6	1.7
PENT–Assemb of God	1	20	6	32	0.2	0.2
PENT–Ch God (Cleve)	4	195	281	352	2.0	2.1
PENT–Ch of God Proph	4	NR	106	133	0.8	0.8
PENT–COGIC	1	35	65	81	0.5	0.5
PENT–Un Pent Ch Intl	2	NR	NR	NR	-	-
PRES–Presb Ch (USA)	4	16	59	74	0.4	0.4
PRES–Presb Ch Amer	2	44	54	62	0.4	0.4
CHOCTAW	**34**	**1,580**	**3,921**	**4,818**	**56.4**	**100.0**
BAPT–So Bapt Conv	13	892	2,444	2,998	35.1	62.2
Catholic	1	NR	NR	40	0.5	0.8
CHR–Chs of Christ	1	100	93	127	1.5	2.6
METH–Un Methodist	6	302	555	573	6.7	11.9
Non-denom Chr Chs	2	138	210	210	2.5	4.4
PENT–Ch God (Cleve)	1	78	106	130	1.5	2.7
PENT–COGIC	1	0	150	184	2.2	3.8
PENT–Pent Ch of God	1	70	NR	109	1.3	2.3
PRES–As Ref Pres Ch	1	NR	58	71	0.8	1.5
PRES–Cumber Presb	1	NR	184	236	2.8	4.9
PRES–Presb Ch (USA)	5	0	83	102	1.2	2.1
PRES–Presb Ch Amer	1	0	38	38	0.4	0.8
CLAIBORNE	**37**	**638**	**2,501**	**3,082**	**32.1**	**100.0**
ANG/EPIS–Episcopal	1	26	82	82	0.9	2.7
Bahá'í	0	NR	1	1	0.0	0.0
BAPT–Natl Mis Bapt Conv	1	0	150	183	1.9	5.9
BAPT–NBC USA	1	0	150	183	1.9	5.9
BAPT–So Bapt Conv	4	103	305	372	3.9	12.1
Catholic	1	NR	NR	78	0.8	2.5
Ch of Chr (Hol)	1	NR	NR	NR	-	-
CHR–Chr Ch (Disc)	12	113	674	822	8.6	26.7
CHR–Chs of Christ	2	30	25	45	0.5	1.5
Jehovah's Witness	1	NR	NR	NR	-	-
METH–AME	4	0	500	610	6.4	19.8
METH–Un Methodist	4	61	214	258	2.7	8.4
Non-denom Chr Chs	2	130	180	188	2.0	6.1
PENT–Un Pent Ch Intl	1	NR	NR	NR	-	-
PRES–Presb Ch (USA)	1	110	107	130	1.4	4.2
Sev Day Adv	1	65	113	130	1.4	4.2
CLARKE	**88**	**4,659**	**10,563**	**12,683**	**75.8**	**100.0**
ANG/EPIS–Episcopal	1	12	12	12	0.1	0.1
BAPT–NBC USA	1	0	150	185	1.1	1.5
BAPT–So Bapt Conv	31	2,451	6,667	8,224	49.2	64.8
CGOD–Ch God (Ander)	5	82	NR	82	0.5	0.6
Ch of Nazarene	1	78	319	319	1.9	2.5
CHR–Chs of Christ	2	90	73	102	0.6	0.8
METH–AME	3	0	350	432	2.6	3.4
METH–Cong Meth	1	NR	17	21	0.1	0.2
METH–Un Methodist	26	1,145	2,157	2,207	13.2	17.4
Non-denom Chr Chs	2	160	300	300	1.8	2.4
PENT–Assemb of God	5	260	137	332	2.0	2.6
PENT–Ch God (Cleve)	1	15	15	19	0.1	0.1
PENT–Intl Pent Holiness	7	346	330	407	2.4	3.2
PENT–Un Pent Ch Intl	1	NR	NR	NR	-	-
Sev Day Adv	1	20	36	41	0.2	0.3
CLAY	**54**	**3,486**	**9,094**	**11,920**	**57.8**	**100.0**
ANG/EPIS–Episcopal	1	64	107	119	0.6	1.0
BAPT–NBC USA	1	250	275	342	1.7	2.9
BAPT–So Bapt Conv	17	1,700	5,417	6,739	32.7	56.5
Catholic	1	NR	NR	215	1.0	1.8
CHR–Chr Ch (Disc)	3	280	533	663	3.2	5.6
CHR–Chs of Christ	4	156	141	164	0.8	1.4
LDS–L-D Saints	1	NR	NR	474	2.3	4.0
MENN–CG in Cr (Menn)	1	NR	122	152	0.7	1.3
METH–AME	2	0	200	249	1.2	2.1
METH–C.M.E.	1	0	150	187	0.9	1.6
METH–Un Methodist	7	444	1,137	1,319	6.4	11.1
Non-denom Chr Chs	5	370	475	513	2.5	4.3
PENT–Ch God (Cleve)	2	116	239	297	1.4	2.5
PENT–Ch of God Proph	1	NR	9	11	0.1	0.1
PENT–Pent Ch of God	1	70	NR	109	0.5	0.9
PENT–Un Pent Ch Intl	1	NR	NR	NR	-	-
PRES–Cumber Presb	1	NR	8	23	0.1	0.2
PRES–Evan Presby Ch	1	NR	171	213	1.0	1.8
PRES–Presb Ch (USA)	2	0	48	60	0.3	0.5
Sev Day Adv	1	36	62	71	0.3	0.6
COAHOMA	**52**	**2,193**	**11,563**	**15,428**	**59.0**	**100.0**
ANG/EPIS–Episcopal	1	74	161	207	0.8	1.3
Bahá'í	0	NR	35	35	0.1	0.2
BAPT–Natl Mis Bapt Conv	1	0	150	193	0.7	1.3
BAPT–NBC USA	8	180	3,360	4,332	16.6	28.1
BAPT–So Bapt Conv	12	821	4,039	5,208	19.9	33.8
Catholic	2	NR	NR	935	3.6	6.1
CGOD–Ch God (Ander)	1	65	NR	65	0.2	0.4
Ch of Nazarene	1	23	23	36	0.1	0.2
CHR–Chr Ch (Disc)	1	0	618	797	3.0	5.2
CHR–Chr Chs & Chs Cr	1	NR	30	39	0.1	0.3
CHR–Chs of Christ	2	103	119	155	0.6	1.0
Jehovah's Witness	1	NR	NR	NR	-	-
MENN–CG in Cr (Menn)	1	NR	153	197	0.8	1.3
METH–AME	3	110	400	516	2.0	3.3
METH–AME Zion	1	0	100	129	0.5	0.8
METH–C.M.E.	1	0	100	129	0.5	0.8
METH–Un Methodist	5	374	1,299	1,371	5.2	8.9
Non-denom Chr Chs	4	280	410	413	1.6	2.7
PENT–Assemb of God	1	35	50	53	0.2	0.3
PENT–Ch God (Cleve)	1	14	60	77	0.3	0.5
PENT–COGIC	1	0	120	155	0.6	1.0
PENT–Un Pent Ch Intl	1	NR	NR	NR	-	-
PRES–Presb Ch Amer	1	100	311	357	1.4	2.3
Sev Day Adv	1	14	25	29	0.1	0.2

NR–Not Reported   - Represents no adherents reported.   Percentages may not total 100 due to rounding.

Table 3: Religious Congregations by County and Group: 2010

Religious Group	Number of Congregations	Number of Attendees	Number of Communicant, Confirmed, or Full Members	Adherents		
				Number of Adherents	% of Total Pop.	% of Total Adh.
COPIAH	**108**	**5,414**	**14,704**	**18,355**	**62.3**	**100.0**
ANG/EPIS–Episcopal	1	18	31	31	0.1	0.2
Bahá'í	0	NR	3	3	0.0	0.0
BAPT–Natl Mis Bapt Conv	1	0	150	186	0.6	1.0
BAPT–NBC USA	2	0	300	372	1.3	2.0
BAPT–So Bapt Conv	31	3,005	8,504	10,536	35.8	57.4
Catholic	2	NR	NR	280	1.0	1.5
Ch of Chr (Hol)	6	NR	NR	NR	-	-
Ch of Nazarene	2	25	55	71	0.2	0.4
CHR–Chr Ch (Disc)	2	0	106	131	0.4	0.7
CHR–Chs of Christ	2	59	41	80	0.3	0.4
Jehovah's Witness	2	NR	NR	NR	-	-
LDS–L-D Saints	2	NR	NR	507	1.7	2.8
METH–AME	7	0	700	867	2.9	4.7
METH–AME Zion	2	0	250	310	1.1	1.7
METH–C.M.E.	4	0	400	496	1.7	2.7
METH–So Methodist	1	NR	NR	NR	-	-
METH–Un Methodist	24	1,152	2,398	2,542	8.6	13.8
Non-denom Chr Chs	5	650	900	912	3.1	5.0
PENT–Assemb of God	1	15	4	16	0.1	0.1
PENT–COGIC	1	80	0	0	0.0	0.0
PENT–Intl Pent Holiness	1	212	450	558	1.9	3.0
PENT–Un Pent Ch Intl	5	NR	NR	NR	-	-
PRES–Presb Ch Amer	3	97	236	255	0.9	1.4
Sev Day Adv	1	101	176	202	0.7	1.1
COVINGTON	**51**	**2,841**	**7,767**	**9,705**	**49.6**	**100.0**
ANG/EPIS–Episcopal	1	25	41	41	0.2	0.4
Bahá'í	0	NR	2	2	0.0	0.0
BAPT–Amer Bapt Assn	1	NR	100	125	0.6	1.3
BAPT–Natl Mis Bapt Conv	1	0	150	187	1.0	1.9
BAPT–So Bapt Conv	20	1,931	5,347	6,674	34.1	68.8
CHR–Chs of Christ	3	83	72	106	0.5	1.1
LDS–L-D Saints	1	NR	NR	291	1.5	3.0
METH–C.M.E.	4	0	450	562	2.9	5.8
METH–Un Methodist	8	324	846	908	4.6	9.4
Non-denom Chr Chs	3	310	535	535	2.7	5.5
PENT–COGIC	1	20	0	0	0.0	0.0
PENT–Full Gosp Bapt	1	NR	NR	NR	-	-
PENT–Un Pent Ch Intl	3	NR	NR	NR	-	-
PRES–Presb Ch Amer	4	148	224	274	1.4	2.8
DESOTO	**180**	**25,944**	**61,258**	**85,106**	**52.8**	**100.0**
ANG/EPIS–Anglican NA	1	NR	NR	NR	-	-
ANG/EPIS–Episcopal	2	181	715	740	0.5	0.9
Bahá'í	0	NR	15	15	0.0	0.0
BAPT–Free Will Bapt	1	NR	54	69	0.0	0.1
BAPT–NBC USA	6	3,300	5,250	6,716	4.2	7.9
BAPT–Ref Bapt Ch	2	NR	NR	NR	-	-
BAPT–So Bapt Conv	48	11,083	34,193	43,740	27.1	51.4
Catholic	3	NR	NR	5,928	3.7	7.0
Ch of Nazarene	2	62	70	85	0.1	0.1
CHR–Chr Ch (Disc)	1	60	155	198	0.1	0.2
CHR–Chr Chs & Chs Cr	3	NR	155	198	0.1	0.2
CHR–Chs of Christ	14	2,649	2,982	3,941	2.4	4.6
Jehovah's Witness	2	NR	NR	NR	-	-
LDS–L-D Saints	1	NR	NR	810	0.5	1.0
LUTH–Luth-MO Synod	3	242	403	491	0.3	0.6
METH–AME	3	50	275	352	0.2	0.4
METH–AME Zion	1	0	100	128	0.1	0.2
METH–C.M.E.	13	0	1,600	2,047	1.3	2.4
METH–Cong Meth	1	NR	NR	NR	-	-
METH–Un Methodist	17	2,524	6,885	8,142	5.0	9.6
Non-denom Chr Chs	24	2,740	4,655	4,820	3.0	5.7
PENT–Assemb of God	6	2,068	1,247	3,535	2.2	4.2
PENT–Ch God (Cleve)	6	383	873	1,117	0.7	1.3
PENT–Ch of God Proph	1	NR	25	32	0.0	0.0
PENT–COGIC	1	17	20	26	0.0	0.0
PENT–Intl Pent Holiness	2	78	122	156	0.1	0.2
PENT–Un Pent Ch Intl	4	NR	NR	NR	-	-
PRES–As Ref Pres Ch	2	NR	114	146	0.1	0.2
PRES–Cumber Presb	1	NR	348	485	0.3	0.6
PRES–Presb Ch (USA)	6	241	568	727	0.5	0.9
PRES–Presb Ch Amer	2	165	258	258	0.2	0.3
Sev Day Adv	1	101	176	202	0.1	0.2
Zoroastrian	0	NR	NR	2	0.0	0.0
FORREST	**137**	**16,525**	**35,477**	**51,184**	**68.3**	**100.0**
ANG/EPIS–Episcopal	2	251	738	774	1.0	1.5
Bahá'í	0	NR	16	16	0.0	0.0
BAPT–Alliance Bapt	1	NR	NR	NR	-	-
BAPT–Amer Bapt Assn	2	NR	305	375	0.5	0.7
BAPT–NBC Amer	1	0	0	0	0.0	0.0
BAPT–So Bapt Conv	40	8,147	18,650	22,904	30.6	44.7
Catholic	3	NR	NR	6,613	8.8	12.9
CGOD–Ch God (Ander)	2	45	NR	45	0.1	0.1
Ch Cr, Scientst	1	NR	NR	NR	-	-
Ch of Nazarene	1	53	85	89	0.1	0.2
CHR–Chr Ch (Disc)	1	19	85	104	0.1	0.2
CHR–Chs of Christ	3	378	444	592	0.8	1.2
Jehovah's Witness	4	NR	NR	NR	-	-
JUD–Reform	1	26	46	124	0.2	0.2
LDS–L-D Saints	4	NR	NR	1,751	2.3	3.4
LUTH–Luth-MO Synod	1	125	215	256	0.3	0.5
METH–AME	3	0	350	430	0.6	0.8
METH–C.M.E.	2	0	200	246	0.3	0.5
METH–So Methodist	1	NR	NR	NR	-	-
METH–Un Methodist	16	1,849	5,607	6,226	8.3	12.2
Muslim Est	2	268	NR	616	0.8	1.2
Non-denom Chr Chs	14	3,760	5,560	5,854	7.8	11.4
PENT–Assemb of God	5	220	120	314	0.4	0.6
PENT–Ch God (Cleve)	3	348	735	903	1.2	1.8
PENT–Ch Lord Jesus Apos	1	NR	NR	NR	-	-
PENT–Ch of God Proph	1	NR	19	23	0.0	0.0
PENT–COGIC	2	0	150	184	0.2	0.4
PENT–Full Gosp Bapt	4	NR	NR	NR	-	-
PENT–Int Foursq Gos	1	30	30	37	0.0	0.1
PENT–Un Pent Ch Intl	4	NR	NR	NR	-	-
PRES–Presb Ch (USA)	2	0	245	301	0.4	0.6
PRES–Presb Ch Amer	4	614	1,213	1,502	2.0	2.9
Salvation Army	1	89	147	315	0.4	0.6
Sev Day Adv	3	282	492	565	0.8	1.1
Unit Univ	1	21	25	25	0.0	0.0
FRANKLIN	**38**	**1,693**	**4,334**	**5,365**	**66.1**	**100.0**
BAPT–So Bapt Conv	18	1,071	3,056	3,809	46.9	71.0
Catholic	1	NR	NR	32	0.4	0.6
CHR–Chs of Christ	2	70	50	82	1.0	1.5
METH–AME	1	0	100	125	1.5	2.3
METH–Un Methodist	8	185	394	449	5.5	8.4
Non-denom Chr Chs	1	100	150	150	1.8	2.8
PENT–Ch God (Cleve)	3	234	389	485	6.0	9.0
PENT–COGIC	1	0	150	187	2.3	3.5
PENT–Un Pent Ch Intl	1	NR	NR	NR	-	-
PRES–Presb Ch Amer	2	33	45	46	0.6	0.9
GEORGE	**60**	**3,807**	**8,810**	**11,613**	**51.4**	**100.0**
Bahá'í	0	NR	13	13	0.1	0.1
BAPT–Natl Mis Bapt Conv	1	125	165	208	0.9	1.8
BAPT–NBC Amer	1	0	150	189	0.8	1.6
BAPT–So Bapt Conv	15	1,687	5,264	6,642	29.4	57.2
Catholic	1	NR	NR	369	1.6	3.2
Ch of Nazarene	1	13	39	39	0.2	0.3
CHR–Chs of Christ	2	80	71	82	0.4	0.7
Jehovah's Witness	1	NR	NR	NR	-	-
LDS–L-D Saints	1	NR	NR	233	1.0	2.0
METH–Un Methodist	16	699	1,610	1,945	8.6	16.7
Non-denom Chr Chs	5	500	750	750	3.3	6.5
PENT–Assemb of God	6	387	319	602	2.7	5.2
PENT–Ch God (Cleve)	3	251	373	471	2.1	4.1
PENT–Intl Pent Holiness	2	49	36	45	0.2	0.4
PENT–Un Pent Ch Intl	4	NR	NR	NR	-	-
PRES–Presb Ch (USA)	1	16	20	25	0.1	0.2

NR–Not Reported   - Represents no adherents reported.   Percentages may not total 100 due to rounding.

Table 3: Religious Congregations by County and Group: 2010

Religious Group	Number of Congregations	Number of Attendees	Number of Communicant, Confirmed, or Full Members	Adherents		
				Number of Adherents	% of Total Pop.	% of Total Adh.
GREENE	**43**	**1,448**	**3,396**	**4,196**	**29.1**	**100.0**
BAPT–Natl Mis Bapt Conv	1	0	150	180	1.3	4.3
BAPT–So Bapt Conv	18	915	2,512	3,014	20.9	71.8
Catholic	1	NR	NR	26	0.2	0.6
CGOD–Ch God (Ander)	1	2	NR	2	0.0	0.0
CHR–Chs of Christ	3	88	83	109	0.8	2.6
METH–Cong Meth	2	NR	22	26	0.2	0.6
METH–Un Methodist	3	60	103	110	0.8	2.6
PENT–Assemb of God	3	181	111	243	1.7	5.8
PENT–Ch God (Cleve)	4	202	240	288	2.0	6.9
PENT–Un Pent Ch Intl	4	NR	NR	NR	-	-
PRES–As Ref Pres Ch	1	NR	60	72	0.5	1.7
PRES–Presb Ch (USA)	1	0	55	66	0.5	1.6
PRES–Presb Ch Amer	1	0	60	60	0.4	1.4
GRENADA	**66**	**4,783**	**11,829**	**14,755**	**67.4**	**100.0**
ANG/EPIS–Episcopal	1	64	135	167	0.8	1.1
Bahá'í	0	NR	1	1	0.0	0.0
BAPT–Amer Bapt Assn	1	NR	85	104	0.5	0.7
BAPT–Natl Mis Bapt Conv	1	0	0	0	0.0	0.0
BAPT–NBC USA	1	150	560	687	3.1	4.7
BAPT–So Bapt Conv	21	2,541	6,925	8,501	38.8	57.6
Catholic	1	NR	NR	360	1.6	2.4
Ch of Nazarene	1	51	100	102	0.5	0.7
CHR–Chs of Christ	4	405	408	531	2.4	3.6
Jehovah's Witness	2	NR	NR	NR	-	-
METH–AME	7	150	840	1,031	4.7	7.0
METH–Un Methodist	8	462	1,105	1,329	6.1	9.0
Non-denom Chr Chs	4	540	920	920	4.2	6.2
PENT–Ch God (Cleve)	4	293	447	549	2.5	3.7
PENT–Ch of God Proph	2	NR	46	56	0.3	0.4
PENT–COGIC	1	0	150	184	0.8	1.2
PENT–Full Gosp Bapt	3	NR	NR	NR	-	-
PENT–Pent Ch of God	1	70	NR	109	0.5	0.7
PENT–Un Pent Ch Intl	1	NR	NR	NR	-	-
PRES–Presb Ch (USA)	1	32	41	50	0.2	0.3
PRES–Presb Ch Amer	1	25	66	74	0.3	0.5
HANCOCK	**52**	**3,345**	**6,050**	**13,302**	**30.3**	**100.0**
ANG/EPIS–Episcopal	2	159	277	387	0.9	2.9
Bahá'í	0	NR	3	3	0.0	0.0
BAPT–So Bapt Conv	12	1,230	2,752	3,356	7.6	25.2
Calv Chpl	1	NR	NR	NR	-	-
Catholic	6	NR	NR	5,392	12.3	40.5
Chr & Miss Al	1	NR	NR	NR	-	-
CHR–Chr Chs & Chs Cr	1	NR	0	0	0.0	0.0
CHR–Chs of Christ	2	110	104	162	0.4	1.2
Jehovah's Witness	1	NR	NR	NR	-	-
LDS–L-D Saints	1	NR	NR	608	1.4	4.6
LUTH–Luth–MO Synod	1	102	136	136	0.3	1.0
METH–AME	2	50	175	213	0.5	1.6
METH–Un Methodist	8	408	1,026	1,117	2.5	8.4
Non-denom Chr Chs	5	740	1,035	1,110	2.5	8.3
PENT–Assemb of God	2	175	50	225	0.5	1.7
PENT–Ch God (Cleve)	2	40	95	116	0.3	0.9
PENT–Un Pent Ch Intl	1	NR	NR	NR	-	-
PRES–Presb Ch (USA)	2	267	328	400	0.9	3.0
PRES–Presb Ch Amer	1	50	44	48	0.1	0.4
Sev Day Adv	1	14	25	29	0.1	0.2
HARRISON	**222**	**19,954**	**47,586**	**93,068**	**49.7**	**100.0**
ANG/EPIS–Episcopal	5	691	1,662	2,351	1.3	2.5
Bahá'í	0	NR	84	84	0.0	0.1
BAPT–Amer Bapt Assn	2	NR	170	210	0.1	0.2
BAPT–Free Will Bapt	1	NR	54	67	0.0	0.1
BAPT–Natl Mis Bapt Conv	2	225	500	619	0.3	0.7
BAPT–NBC Amer	5	600	760	941	0.5	1.0
BAPT–NBC USA	5	1,050	2,460	3,045	1.6	3.3
BAPT–Ref Bapt Ch	1	NR	NR	NR	-	-
BAPT–So Bapt Conv	51	7,088	23,696	29,329	15.7	31.5
Calv Chpl	1	NR	NR	NR	-	-
Catholic	20	NR	NR	30,667	16.4	33.0
CGOD–Ch God (Ander)	1	66	NR	66	0.0	0.1
Ch Cr, Scientst	1	NR	NR	NR	-	-
Ch of Nazarene	3	115	183	193	0.1	0.2
Chr & Miss Al	1	NR	NR	NR	-	-
CHR–Chr Ch (Disc)	1	0	66	82	0.0	0.1
CHR–Chr Chs & Chs Cr	1	NR	25	31	0.0	0.0
CHR–Chs of Christ	7	566	584	830	0.4	0.9
Jehovah's Witness	6	NR	NR	NR	-	-
JUD–Conserv	1	41	46	124	0.1	0.1
LDS–Comm of Christ	1	NR	187	187	0.1	0.2
LDS–L-D Saints	3	NR	NR	3,120	1.7	3.4
LUTH–E.L.C.A.	2	135	348	387	0.2	0.4
LUTH–Luth–MO Synod	3	40	437	442	0.2	0.5
MENN–Mennonite USA	1	150	200	248	0.1	0.3
METH–AME	3	0	400	495	0.3	0.5
METH–C.M.E.	1	0	150	186	0.1	0.2
METH–Free Methodist	1	13	9	13	0.0	0.0
METH–Un Methodist	27	3,175	8,693	9,613	5.1	10.3
Muslim Est	1	75	NR	200	0.1	0.2
Non-denom Chr Chs	26	2,830	3,539	3,809	2.0	4.1
ORTHE–Greek Orthodox	1	35	NR	85	0.0	0.1
PENT–Assemb of God	7	1,662	897	2,568	1.4	2.8
PENT–Ch God (Cleve)	6	279	555	687	0.4	0.7
PENT–Ch of God Proph	1	NR	12	15	0.0	0.0
PENT–COGIC	3	50	350	433	0.2	0.5
PENT–Full Gosp Bapt	2	NR	NR	NR	-	-
PENT–Int Foursq Gos	1	0	0	0	0.0	0.0
PENT–Un Pent Ch Intl	4	NR	NR	NR	-	-
PRES–Presb Ch (USA)	4	353	351	434	0.2	0.5
PRES–Presb Ch Amer	3	328	470	568	0.3	0.6
Salvation Army	1	42	98	248	0.1	0.3
Sev Day Adv	3	336	583	671	0.4	0.7
Unit Univ	1	9	17	20	0.0	0.0
Unity Ch	1	NR	NR	NR	-	-
HINDS	**405**	**51,655**	**127,891**	**164,492**	**67.1**	**100.0**
ANG/EPIS–Episcopal	10	1,244	4,333	5,085	2.1	3.1
Bahá'í	2	NR	143	143	0.1	0.1
BAPT–Alliance Bapt	2	NR	NR	NR	-	-
BAPT–Asc Ref Bap Ch Am	1	NR	NR	NR	-	-
BAPT–Ind Bapt Flwsp Intl	1	NR	NR	NR	-	-
BAPT–Natl Mis Bapt Conv	10	65	1,450	1,821	0.7	1.1
BAPT–NBC USA	37	3,745	14,409	18,094	7.4	11.0
BAPT–Prog NBC	1	0	150	188	0.1	0.1
BAPT–Ref Bapt Ch	1	NR	NR	NR	-	-
BAPT–So Bapt Conv	70	12,018	39,309	49,361	20.1	30.0
BUDD–Theravada	1	NR	NR	14	0.0	0.0
Catholic	9	NR	NR	7,293	3.0	4.4
CGOD–Ch God (Ander)	2	150	NR	150	0.1	0.1
Ch of Chr (Hol)	14	NR	NR	NR	-	-
Ch of Nazarene	3	446	374	787	0.3	0.5
CHR–Chr Ch (Disc)	4	153	429	539	0.2	0.3
CHR–Chr Chs & Chs Cr	1	NR	40	50	0.0	0.0
CHR–Chs of Christ	15	2,359	2,991	3,656	1.5	2.2
CHR–Int Chs of Christ	1	NR	7	9	0.0	0.0
HINDU–I/A Temples	1	NR	NR	1,742	0.7	1.1
HINDU–Post Ren	1	NR	NR	25	0.0	0.0
HINDU–Trad Temples	1	NR	NR	200	0.1	0.1
Jehovah's Witness	6	NR	NR	NR	-	-
JUD–Reform	1	121	214	578	0.2	0.4
LDS–Comm of Christ	1	NR	187	187	0.1	0.1
LDS–L-D Saints	2	NR	NR	898	0.4	0.5
LUTH–E.L.C.A.	2	122	230	289	0.1	0.2
LUTH–Luth–MO Synod	3	254	471	572	0.2	0.3
MENN–Mennonite USA	1	40	24	30	0.0	0.0
METH–AME	9	2,037	4,338	5,447	2.2	3.3
METH–AME Zion	4	90	453	569	0.2	0.3
METH–C.M.E.	7	0	1,520	1,909	0.8	1.2
METH–Cong Meth	2	NR	759	953	0.4	0.6
METH–Un Methodist	38	6,292	19,899	22,068	9.0	13.4
METH–Wesleyan	1	62	76	81	0.0	0.0
Muslim Est	2	284	NR	808	0.3	0.5
Non-denom Chr Chs	63	16,560	24,710	26,270	10.7	16.0
ORTHE–Greek Orthodox	1	85	NR	370	0.2	0.2

NR–Not Reported - Represents no adherents reported. Percentages may not total 100 due to rounding.

Table 3: Religious Congregations by County and Group: 2010

Religious Group	Number of Congrega-tions	Number of Attendees	Number of Communicant, Confirmed, or Full Members	Adherents		
				Number of Adherents	% of Total Pop.	% of Total Adh.
ORTHE–Orth Ch in Amer	1	75	NR	150	0.1	0.1
PENT–Assemb of God	6	772	589	1,049	0.4	0.6
PENT–Ch God (Cleve)	3	81	411	516	0.2	0.3
PENT–Ch Lord Jesus Apos	2	NR	NR	NR	-	-
PENT–Ch of God Proph	2	NR	77	97	0.0	0.1
PENT–COGIC	20	635	3,055	3,836	1.6	2.3
PENT–Full Gosp Bapt	6	NR	NR	NR	-	-
PENT–Intl Pent Holiness	3	70	82	103	0.0	0.1
PENT–Un Pent Ch Intl	6	NR	NR	NR	-	-
PRES–Evan Presby Ch	1	NR	376	472	0.2	0.3
PRES–Presb Ch (USA)	4	366	892	1,120	0.5	0.7
PRES–Presb Ch Amer	13	2,373	3,965	4,742	1.9	2.9
REF–Comm Ref Evan	1	NR	NR	NR	-	-
Salvation Army	1	186	243	283	0.1	0.2
Sev Day Adv	3	930	1,618	1,861	0.8	1.1
Sikh	1	NR	NR	NR	-	-
Unit Univ	1	40	67	77	0.0	0.0
HOLMES	**93**	**2,740**	**8,231**	**10,236**	**53.3**	**100.0**
ANG/EPIS–Episcopal	1	16	40	41	0.2	0.4
Bahá'í	0	NR	5	5	0.0	0.0
BAPT–Natl Mis Bapt Conv	2	50	250	322	1.7	3.1
BAPT–NBC USA	1	0	250	322	1.7	3.1
BAPT–So Bapt Conv	26	1,019	3,312	4,263	22.2	41.6
Catholic	1	NR	NR	41	0.2	0.4
CGOD–Ch God (Ander)	1	0	NR	0	0.0	0.0
Ch of Chr (Hol)	2	NR	NR	NR	-	-
CHR–Chs of Christ	3	68	50	64	0.3	0.6
Jehovah's Witness	1	NR	NR	NR	-	-
JUD–Reform	1	9	16	43	0.2	0.4
METH–AME	3	0	300	386	2.0	3.8
METH–AME Zion	2	0	250	322	1.7	3.1
METH–C.M.E.	7	0	750	965	5.0	9.4
METH–Un Methodist	22	685	1,374	1,550	8.1	15.1
New Apost Ch	1	NR	NR	NR	-	-
Non-denom Chr Chs	5	435	625	644	3.4	6.3
PENT–Ch God (Cleve)	1	57	50	64	0.3	0.6
PENT–COGIC	6	290	760	978	5.1	9.6
PENT–Un Pent Ch Intl	1	NR	NR	NR	-	-
PRES–Presb Ch Amer	5	97	174	197	1.0	1.9
Sev Day Adv	1	14	25	29	0.2	0.3
HUMPHREYS	**30**	**889**	**3,221**	**4,071**	**43.4**	**100.0**
ANG/EPIS–Episcopal	1	8	21	23	0.2	0.6
Bahá'í	0	NR	7	7	0.1	0.2
BAPT–Natl Mis Bapt Conv	2	0	300	388	4.1	9.5
BAPT–NBC USA	1	0	0	0	0.0	0.0
BAPT–So Bapt Conv	7	413	1,525	1,970	21.0	48.4
Catholic	1	NR	NR	49	0.5	1.2
CGOD–Ch God (Ander)	1	30	NR	30	0.3	0.7
CHR–Chs of Christ	2	58	57	73	0.8	1.8
Jehovah's Witness	1	NR	NR	NR	-	-
METH–AME	2	0	200	258	2.8	6.3
METH–Un Methodist	5	208	444	454	4.8	11.2
PENT–Ch God (Cleve)	2	46	45	58	0.6	1.4
PENT–COGIC	2	0	300	388	4.1	9.5
PENT–Un Pent Ch Intl	1	NR	NR	NR	-	-
PRES–Presb Ch Amer	1	100	278	322	3.4	7.9
Sev Day Adv	1	26	44	51	0.5	1.3
ISSAQUENA	**2**	**55**	**129**	**159**	**11.3**	**100.0**
BAPT–So Bapt Conv	1	45	118	138	9.8	86.8
METH–Un Methodist	1	10	11	21	1.5	13.2
ITAWAMBA	**70**	**3,461**	**8,763**	**10,342**	**44.2**	**100.0**
Bahá'í	0	NR	1	1	0.0	0.0
BAPT–Free Will Bapt	2	NR	108	131	0.6	1.3
BAPT–So Bapt Conv	19	1,663	4,545	5,510	23.5	53.3
Catholic	1	NR	NR	67	0.3	0.6
CHR–Chr Chs & Chs Cr	2	NR	260	315	1.3	3.0
CHR–Chs of Christ	11	643	657	777	3.3	7.5
LDS–Comm of Christ	1	NR	156	156	0.7	1.5
METH–C.M.E.	4	0	550	667	2.9	6.4
METH–Un Methodist	15	712	1,904	2,053	8.8	19.9
Non-denom Chr Chs	3	209	269	286	1.2	2.8
PENT–Ch God (Cleve)	4	234	151	183	0.8	1.8
PENT–Ch of God Proph	5	NR	162	196	0.8	1.9
PENT–Un Pent Ch Intl	3	NR	NR	NR	-	-
JACKSON	**195**	**19,975**	**46,240**	**70,757**	**50.7**	**100.0**
ANG/EPIS–Episcopal	3	405	999	1,111	0.8	1.6
Bahá'í	0	NR	15	15	0.0	0.0
BAPT–Amer Bapt Assn	4	NR	255	317	0.2	0.4
BAPT–Natl Mis Bapt Conv	2	0	300	373	0.3	0.5
BAPT–NBC Amer	1	150	250	311	0.2	0.4
BAPT–NBC USA	4	830	1,433	1,781	1.3	2.5
BAPT–So Bapt Conv	46	6,700	24,415	30,352	21.7	42.9
Catholic	11	NR	NR	12,438	8.9	17.6
CGOD–Ch God (Ander)	2	47	NR	47	0.0	0.1
Ch of Nazarene	2	315	439	439	0.3	0.6
CHR–Chr Ch (Disc)	2	0	90	112	0.1	0.2
CHR–Chs of Christ	10	857	934	1,217	0.9	1.7
Jehovah's Witness	5	NR	NR	NR	-	-
LDS–Comm of Christ	3	NR	561	561	0.4	0.8
LDS–L-D Saints	1	NR	NR	678	0.5	1.0
LUTH–E.L.C.A.	1	131	474	569	0.4	0.8
LUTH–Luth–MO Synod	1	68	174	269	0.2	0.4
METH–AME Zion	2	0	300	373	0.3	0.5
METH–Un Methodist	26	3,008	7,966	9,063	6.5	12.8
Non-denom Chr Chs	25	3,753	4,250	4,974	3.6	7.0
PENT–Assemb of God	19	2,512	1,466	3,329	2.4	4.7
PENT–Ch God (Cleve)	4	118	219	272	0.2	0.4
PENT–Ch Lord Jesus Apos	2	NR	NR	NR	-	-
PENT–Ch of God Proph	1	NR	16	20	0.0	0.0
PENT–COGIC	2	375	350	435	0.3	0.6
PENT–Intl Pent Holiness	3	146	221	275	0.2	0.4
PENT–Un Pent Ch Intl	6	NR	NR	NR	-	-
PRES–As Ref Pres Ch	1	NR	28	35	0.0	0.0
PRES–Presb Ch (USA)	3	472	918	1,141	0.8	1.6
PRES–Presb Ch Amer	1	24	34	36	0.0	0.1
Salvation Army	1	25	65	136	0.1	0.2
Sev Day Adv	1	39	68	78	0.1	0.1
JASPER	**67**	**2,858**	**6,662**	**7,967**	**46.7**	**100.0**
BAPT–NBC USA	2	0	400	489	2.9	6.1
BAPT–So Bapt Conv	27	1,549	4,093	5,006	29.3	62.8
Catholic	1	NR	NR	50	0.3	0.6
CGOD–Ch God (Ander)	1	40	NR	40	0.2	0.5
CHR–Chs of Christ	1	30	20	30	0.2	0.4
Jehovah's Witness	3	NR	NR	NR	-	-
METH–AME	1	60	120	147	0.9	1.8
METH–Cong Meth	2	NR	107	131	0.8	1.6
METH–Un Methodist	19	704	1,341	1,400	8.2	17.6
Non-denom Chr Chs	2	165	235	235	1.4	2.9
PENT–Assemb of God	1	115	75	115	0.7	1.4
PENT–COGIC	1	100	125	153	0.9	1.9
PRES–Presb Ch (USA)	4	47	74	91	0.5	1.1
PRES–Presb Ch Amer	2	48	72	80	0.5	1.0
JEFFERSON	**28**	**785**	**2,432**	**2,987**	**38.7**	**100.0**
Bahá'í	0	NR	1	1	0.0	0.0
BAPT–Natl Mis Bapt Conv	2	0	300	363	4.7	12.2
BAPT–NBC Amer	1	200	250	303	3.9	10.1
BAPT–So Bapt Conv	6	179	458	554	7.2	18.5
Catholic	1	NR	NR	109	1.4	3.6
CHR–Chr Ch (Disc)	2	10	215	260	3.4	8.7
Jehovah's Witness	1	NR	NR	NR	-	-
METH–AME	5	0	500	605	7.8	20.3
METH–Un Methodist	7	262	543	573	7.4	19.2
Non-denom Chr Chs	1	50	25	62	0.8	2.1
PRES–Presb Ch Amer	1	20	30	30	0.4	1.0
Sev Day Adv	1	64	110	127	1.6	4.3

NR–Not Reported   - Represents no adherents reported.   Percentages may not total 100 due to rounding.

Table 3: Religious Congregations by County and Group: 2010

Religious Group	Number of Congrega-tions	Number of Attendees	Number of Communicant, Confirmed, or Full Members	Adherents: Number of Adherents	Adherents: % of Total Pop.	Adherents: % of Total Adh.
JEFFERSON DAVIS	**35**	**1,302**	**4,536**	**5,598**	**44.8**	**100.0**
Bahá'í	0	NR	38	38	0.3	0.7
BAPT–Amer Bapt Assn	1	NR	50	60	0.5	1.1
BAPT–NBC Amer	1	0	150	181	1.4	3.2
BAPT–So Bapt Conv	11	860	2,519	3,044	24.4	54.4
Catholic	2	NR	NR	230	1.8	4.1
Ch of Chr (Hol)	2	NR	NR	NR	-	-
Ch of Nazarene	1	17	55	55	0.4	1.0
CHR–Chs of Christ	1	38	35	45	0.4	0.8
Jehovah's Witness	1	NR	NR	NR	-	-
METH–C.M.E.	6	0	800	967	7.7	17.3
METH–Un Methodist	5	127	371	384	3.1	6.9
Non-denom Chr Chs	2	160	210	225	1.8	4.0
PENT–COGIC	1	0	150	181	1.4	3.2
PRES–Presb Ch Amer	1	100	158	188	1.5	3.4
JONES	**163**	**14,206**	**33,622**	**43,669**	**64.4**	**100.0**
ANG/EPIS–Episcopal	1	135	176	176	0.3	0.4
Bahá'í	0	NR	4	4	0.0	0.0
BAPT–Ind Bapt Flwsp Intl	1	NR	NR	NR	-	-
BAPT–Natl Mis Bapt Conv	2	70	350	439	0.6	1.0
BAPT–NBC Amer	2	50	250	314	0.5	0.7
BAPT–NBC USA	3	480	1,075	1,348	2.0	3.1
BAPT–Ref Bapt Ch	1	NR	NR	NR	-	-
BAPT–So Bapt Conv	59	7,769	22,794	28,589	42.2	65.5
Catholic	1	NR	NR	1,350	2.0	3.1
CGOD–Ch God (Ander)	5	238	NR	238	0.4	0.5
Ch of Nazarene	2	86	108	109	0.2	0.2
CHR–Chs of Christ	3	255	297	427	0.6	1.0
Jehovah's Witness	1	NR	NR	NR	-	-
LDS–L-D Saints	1	NR	NR	395	0.6	0.9
LUTH–Luth–MO Synod	1	14	20	22	0.0	0.1
METH–AME	4	60	500	627	0.9	1.4
METH–Cong Meth	8	NR	298	374	0.6	0.9
METH–Un Methodist	23	1,245	3,034	3,390	5.0	7.8
Non-denom Chr Chs	17	2,485	2,841	3,218	4.7	7.4
PENT–Assemb of God	7	535	289	632	0.9	1.4
PENT–Ch God (Cleve)	3	326	522	655	1.0	1.5
PENT–Un Pent Ch Intl	7	NR	NR	NR	-	-
PRES–Evan Presby Ch	1	NR	248	311	0.5	0.7
PRES–Presb Ch (USA)	2	84	195	245	0.4	0.6
PRES–Presb Ch Amer	2	75	75	89	0.1	0.2
Salvation Army	1	43	118	227	0.3	0.5
Sev Day Adv	4	231	402	462	0.7	1.1
Unit Univ	1	25	26	28	0.0	0.1
KEMPER	**50**	**1,607**	**3,340**	**3,873**	**37.0**	**100.0**
BAPT–Free Will Bapt	1	NR	54	66	0.6	1.7
BAPT–So Bapt Conv	14	394	1,141	1,390	13.3	35.9
CGOD–Ch God (Ander)	1	0	NR	0	0.0	0.0
CHR–Chs of Christ	1	33	25	34	0.3	0.9
Jehovah's Witness	1	NR	NR	NR	-	-
METH–Cong Meth	1	NR	NR	NR	-	-
METH–Un Methodist	25	983	1,910	2,104	20.1	54.3
PENT–Assemb of God	1	102	83	133	1.3	3.4
PENT–Un Pent Ch Intl	2	NR	NR	NR	-	-
PRES–Presb Ch Amer	3	95	127	146	1.4	3.8
LAFAYETTE	**80**	**6,554**	**14,450**	**19,129**	**40.4**	**100.0**
ANG/EPIS–Anglican NA	1	NR	NR	NR	-	-
ANG/EPIS–Episcopal	1	299	627	738	1.6	3.9
Bahá'í	0	NR	7	7	0.0	0.0
BAPT–Amer Bapt Assn	1	NR	100	117	0.2	0.6
BAPT–Free Will Bapt	2	NR	108	126	0.3	0.7
BAPT–Natl Mis Bapt Conv	1	0	150	176	0.4	0.9
BAPT–NBC USA	4	370	1,240	1,452	3.1	7.6
BAPT–So Bapt Conv	23	2,428	5,952	6,971	14.7	36.4
Catholic	1	NR	NR	1,104	2.3	5.8
Ch of Nazarene	1	68	62	162	0.3	0.8
CHR–Chs of Christ	7	479	487	601	1.3	3.1
FRND–Fr Gen Cf	1	NR	10	12	0.0	0.1
Jehovah's Witness	1	NR	NR	NR	-	-
LDS–L-D Saints	1	NR	NR	442	0.9	2.3
LUTH–Luth–MO Synod	1	35	48	58	0.1	0.3
METH–AME	1	0	150	176	0.4	0.9
METH–C.M.E.	4	70	503	589	1.2	3.1
METH–Un Methodist	18	1,300	3,237	4,002	8.5	20.9
Muslim Est	1	134	NR	308	0.7	1.6
Non-denom Chr Chs	4	420	470	551	1.2	2.9
PENT–Assemb of God	1	160	178	206	0.4	1.1
PRES–Presb Ch (USA)	2	330	722	846	1.8	4.4
PRES–Presb Ch Amer	2	425	334	402	0.8	2.1
Unit Univ	1	36	65	83	0.2	0.4
LAMAR	**54**	**8,935**	**23,608**	**30,009**	**53.9**	**100.0**
BAPT–So Bapt Conv	27	7,021	20,089	25,299	45.5	84.3
Catholic	1	NR	NR	419	0.8	1.4
CHR–Chs of Christ	2	65	70	82	0.1	0.3
LUTH–E.L.C.A.	1	10	25	25	0.0	0.1
METH–Un Methodist	12	1,219	2,665	2,986	5.4	10.0
Muslim Est	1	134	NR	308	0.6	1.0
Non-denom Chr Chs	2	175	225	244	0.4	0.8
PENT–Ch God (Cleve)	4	173	293	369	0.7	1.2
PENT–Full Gosp Bapt	1	NR	NR	NR	-	-
PENT–Un Pent Ch Intl	2	NR	NR	NR	-	-
Sev Day Adv	1	138	241	277	0.5	0.9
LAUDERDALE	**200**	**17,073**	**44,368**	**57,533**	**71.7**	**100.0**
ANG/EPIS–Episcopal	2	300	729	749	0.9	1.3
Bahá'í	0	NR	42	42	0.1	0.1
BAPT–Free Will Bapt	1	NR	54	67	0.1	0.1
BAPT–Natl Mis Bapt Conv	1	0	150	186	0.2	0.3
BAPT–NBC USA	15	1,275	5,740	7,110	8.9	12.4
BAPT–So Bapt Conv	47	6,423	22,315	27,641	34.4	48.0
Calv Chpl	2	NR	NR	NR	-	-
Catholic	2	NR	NR	1,828	2.3	3.2
CGOD–Ch God (Ander)	8	806	NR	806	1.0	1.4
CGOD–Ches God-Gen Con	2	49	0	0	0.0	0.0
Ch of Nazarene	2	339	584	632	0.8	1.1
CHR–Chr Ch (Disc)	1	240	535	663	0.8	1.2
CHR–Chs of Christ	6	354	329	442	0.6	0.8
Jehovah's Witness	1	NR	NR	NR	-	-
JUD–Reform	1	18	31	84	0.1	0.1
LDS–L-D Saints	1	NR	NR	808	1.0	1.4
LUTH–Luth–MO Synod	1	73	110	135	0.2	0.2
MENN–Mennonite USA	1	90	75	93	0.1	0.2
METH–AME	2	0	300	372	0.5	0.6
METH–AME Zion	2	0	250	310	0.4	0.5
METH–C.M.E.	4	40	420	520	0.6	0.9
METH–Cong Meth	1	NR	25	31	0.0	0.1
METH–So Methodist	3	NR	NR	NR	-	-
METH–Un Methodist	43	2,430	5,923	6,666	8.3	11.6
Muslim Est	1	134	NR	308	0.4	0.5
Non-denom Chr Chs	18	2,690	3,740	4,025	5.0	7.0
PENT–Assemb of God	6	533	334	643	0.8	1.1
PENT–Ch God (Cleve)	2	230	661	819	1.0	1.4
PENT–Ch of God Proph	2	NR	48	59	0.1	0.1
PENT–COGIC	1	0	0	0	0.0	0.0
PENT–Full Gosp Bapt	1	NR	NR	NR	-	-
PENT–Int Foursq Gos	1	57	79	98	0.1	0.2
PENT–Intl Pent Holiness	3	166	158	196	0.2	0.3
PENT–Un Pent Ch Intl	3	NR	NR	NR	-	-
PRES–Evan Presby Ch	1	NR	428	530	0.7	0.9
PRES–Presb Ch (USA)	4	161	211	261	0.3	0.5
PRES–Presb Ch Amer	4	173	178	232	0.3	0.4
Salvation Army	1	26	108	245	0.3	0.4
Sev Day Adv	3	466	811	932	1.2	1.6
LAWRENCE	**44**	**2,911**	**7,069**	**9,015**	**69.7**	**100.0**
Bahá'í	0	NR	3	3	0.0	0.0
BAPT–So Bapt Conv	22	2,150	5,679	7,031	54.4	78.0
Catholic	1	NR	NR	22	0.2	0.2
CGOD–Ch God (Ander)	1	38	NR	38	0.3	0.4
Ch of Chr (Hol)	3	NR	NR	NR	-	-
CHR–Chs of Christ	3	75	72	83	0.6	0.9

NR–Not Reported - Represents no adherents reported. Percentages may not total 100 due to rounding.

Table 3: Religious Congregations by County and Group: 2010

Religious Group	Number of Congregations	Number of Attendees	Number of Communicant, Confirmed, or Full Members	Adherents: Number of Adherents	Adherents: % of Total Pop.	Adherents: % of Total Adh.
METH–Un Methodist	5	357	844	947	7.3	10.5
Muslim Est	1	134	NR	308	2.4	3.4
PENT–Ch God (Cleve)	1	7	19	24	0.2	0.3
PENT–Ch of God Proph	1	NR	52	64	0.5	0.7
PENT–COGIC	2	150	400	495	3.8	5.5
PENT–Un Pent Ch Intl	4	NR	NR	NR	-	-
LEAKE	**82**	**3,905**	**9,519**	**13,237**	**55.6**	**100.0**
BAPT–NBC USA	2	0	400	515	2.2	3.9
BAPT–So Bapt Conv	39	2,598	6,646	8,550	35.9	64.6
Catholic	1	NR	NR	900	3.8	6.8
CGOD–Ch God (Ander)	2	183	NR	183	0.8	1.4
CHR–Chr Ch (Disc)	1	0	30	39	0.2	0.3
CHR–Chr Chs & Chs Cr	1	NR	40	51	0.2	0.4
CHR–Chs of Christ	1	20	18	22	0.1	0.2
Jehovah's Witness	1	NR	NR	NR	-	-
LDS–L-D Saints	1	NR	NR	102	0.4	0.8
METH–AME	1	0	100	129	0.5	1.0
METH–AME Zion	1	0	100	129	0.5	1.0
METH–Cong Meth	3	NR	156	201	0.8	1.5
METH–Un Methodist	12	483	964	1,066	4.5	8.1
Non-denom Chr Chs	2	160	200	225	0.9	1.7
PENT–Assemb of God	2	80	25	80	0.3	0.6
PENT–Ch God (Cleve)	2	251	438	563	2.4	4.3
PENT–COGIC	1	0	150	193	0.8	1.5
PENT–Un Pent Ch Intl	5	NR	NR	NR	-	-
PRES–Cumber Presb	1	NR	30	58	0.2	0.4
PRES–Presb Ch Amer	3	130	222	231	1.0	1.7
LEE	**180**	**17,863**	**39,574**	**51,466**	**62.1**	**100.0**
ANG/EPIS–Episcopal	1	172	339	401	0.5	0.8
Bahá'í	0	NR	3	3	0.0	0.0
BAPT–Amer Bapt Assn	1	NR	85	107	0.1	0.2
BAPT–Free Will Bapt	3	NR	162	204	0.2	0.4
BAPT–Natl Mis Bapt Conv	2	0	300	378	0.5	0.7
BAPT–NBC Amer	3	380	550	693	0.8	1.3
BAPT–NBC USA	2	0	300	378	0.5	0.7
BAPT–So Bapt Conv	51	7,541	21,479	27,074	32.7	52.6
Catholic	2	NR	NR	2,031	2.4	3.9
CGOD–Ch God (Ander)	1	18	NR	18	0.0	0.0
Ch of Nazarene	1	30	78	78	0.1	0.2
CHR–Chr Ch (Disc)	1	0	134	169	0.2	0.3
CHR–Chr Chs & Chs Cr	5	NR	533	672	0.8	1.3
CHR–Chs of Christ	11	1,695	1,709	2,189	2.6	4.3
HINDU–Post Ren	1	NR	NR	10	0.0	0.0
LDS–L-D Saints	1	NR	NR	723	0.9	1.4
LUTH–E.L.C.A.	1	33	63	96	0.1	0.2
LUTH–Luth-MO Synod	1	62	131	153	0.2	0.3
METH–C.M.E.	11	340	1,280	1,613	1.9	3.1
METH–Un Methodist	30	4,482	7,422	8,371	10.1	16.3
Non-denom Chr Chs	14	1,855	2,411	2,560	3.1	5.0
PENT–Assemb of God	6	186	95	228	0.3	0.4
PENT–Ch God (Cleve)	3	344	773	974	1.2	1.9
PENT–Ch Lord Jesus Apos	1	NR	NR	NR	-	-
PENT–Ch of God Proph	6	NR	253	319	0.4	0.6
PENT–COGIC	1	100	150	189	0.2	0.4
PENT–Full Gosp Bapt	1	NR	NR	NR	-	-
PENT–Un Pent Ch Intl	6	NR	NR	NR	-	-
PRES–As Ref Pres Ch	2	NR	79	100	0.1	0.2
PRES–Presb Ch (USA)	5	252	664	837	1.0	1.6
PRES–Presb Ch Amer	2	238	385	458	0.6	0.9
Salvation Army	1	75	97	328	0.4	0.6
Sev Day Adv	2	38	66	76	0.1	0.1
Unit Univ	1	22	33	36	0.0	0.1
LEFLORE	**72**	**4,320**	**13,585**	**17,976**	**55.6**	**100.0**
ANG/EPIS–Episcopal	1	143	306	306	0.9	1.7
Bahá'í	0	NR	130	130	0.4	0.7
BAPT–Amer Bapt Assn	1	NR	85	108	0.3	0.6
BAPT–NBC USA	4	0	925	1,173	3.6	6.5
BAPT–Prog NBC	1	0	150	190	0.6	1.1
BAPT–So Bapt Conv	17	1,686	5,825	7,387	22.9	41.1
Catholic	2	NR	NR	620	1.9	3.4

Religious Group	Number of Congregations	Number of Attendees	Number of Communicant, Confirmed, or Full Members	Adherents: Number of Adherents	Adherents: % of Total Pop.	Adherents: % of Total Adh.
CHR–Chr Ch (Disc)	2	70	340	431	1.3	2.4
CHR–Chs of Christ	2	255	360	460	1.4	2.6
LDS–L-D Saints	1	NR	NR	370	1.1	2.1
LUTH–Luth-MO Synod	1	4	3	3	0.0	0.0
METH–AME	2	0	250	317	1.0	1.8
METH–C.M.E.	3	0	550	697	2.2	3.9
METH–Un Methodist	10	599	1,663	1,765	5.5	9.8
Non-denom Chr Chs	6	805	810	1,094	3.4	6.1
PENT–Assemb of God	1	8	9	25	0.1	0.1
PENT–Ch God (Cleve)	2	125	175	222	0.7	1.2
PENT–Ch of God Proph	1	NR	104	132	0.4	0.7
PENT–COGIC	6	0	853	1,082	3.3	6.0
PENT–Pent Ch of God	2	140	NR	217	0.7	1.2
PENT–Un Pent Ch Intl	1	NR	NR	NR	-	-
PRES–Presb Ch (USA)	1	165	440	558	1.7	3.1
PRES–Presb Ch Amer	2	155	236	266	0.8	1.5
Salvation Army	1	23	123	138	0.4	0.8
Sev Day Adv	2	142	248	285	0.9	1.6
LINCOLN	**102**	**8,142**	**21,281**	**27,291**	**78.3**	**100.0**
ANG/EPIS–Episcopal	1	67	172	172	0.5	0.6
Bahá'í	0	NR	4	4	0.0	0.0
BAPT–Natl Mis Bapt Conv	3	0	450	563	1.6	2.1
BAPT–NBC Amer	1	0	300	375	1.1	1.4
BAPT–So Bapt Conv	41	5,341	15,131	18,927	54.3	69.4
Catholic	1	NR	NR	405	1.2	1.5
Ch of Chr (Hol)	1	NR	NR	NR	-	-
Ch of Nazarene	1	44	52	54	0.2	0.2
CHR–Chs of Christ	14	1,069	1,238	1,699	4.9	6.2
Jehovah's Witness	1	NR	NR	NR	-	-
LDS–L-D Saints	1	NR	NR	320	0.9	1.2
METH–AME	5	0	600	751	2.2	2.8
METH–Cong Meth	1	NR	31	39	0.1	0.1
METH–Un Methodist	15	692	1,806	2,136	6.1	7.8
Non-denom Chr Chs	6	435	640	662	1.9	2.4
PENT–Assemb of God	2	175	121	285	0.8	1.0
PENT–Ch God (Cleve)	1	41	55	69	0.2	0.3
PENT–COGIC	1	0	150	188	0.5	0.7
PENT–Un Pent Ch Intl	2	NR	NR	NR	-	-
PRES–Presb Ch (USA)	1	10	18	23	0.1	0.1
PRES–Presb Ch Amer	1	219	428	521	1.5	1.9
Sev Day Adv	2	49	85	98	0.3	0.4
LOWNDES	**140**	**13,295**	**30,405**	**39,883**	**66.7**	**100.0**
ANG/EPIS–Episcopal	2	171	388	483	0.8	1.2
Bahá'í	0	NR	2	2	0.0	0.0
BAPT–Free Will Bapt	1	NR	104	129	0.2	0.3
BAPT–Natl Mis Bapt Conv	3	0	300	373	0.6	0.9
BAPT–NBC USA	9	1,389	2,978	3,698	6.2	9.3
BAPT–Ref Bapt Ch	1	NR	NR	NR	-	-
BAPT–So Bapt Conv	29	5,857	15,325	19,032	31.8	47.7
Catholic	1	NR	NR	1,245	2.1	3.1
Ch Cr, Scientst	1	NR	NR	NR	-	-
Ch of Nazarene	1	24	105	105	0.2	0.3
CHR–Chr Chs & Chs Cr	1	NR	0	0	0.0	0.0
CHR–Chs of Christ	11	1,106	1,340	1,789	3.0	4.5
Jehovah's Witness	2	NR	NR	NR	-	-
JUD–Reform	1	10	17	46	0.1	0.1
LDS–L-D Saints	1	NR	NR	538	0.9	1.3
LUTH–Luth-MO Synod	1	46	56	63	0.1	0.2
LUTH–Wisc Ev Luth Syn	1	9	10	10	0.0	0.0
METH–AME	1	0	150	186	0.3	0.5
METH–C.M.E.	8	115	1,175	1,459	2.4	3.7
METH–Un Methodist	19	1,260	4,073	4,632	7.7	11.6
Non-denom Chr Chs	13	1,795	2,165	2,429	4.1	6.1
PENT–Assemb of God	4	543	333	888	1.5	2.2
PENT–Ch God (Cleve)	3	178	395	491	0.8	1.2
PENT–Ch of God by Faith	1	NR	NR	NR	-	-
PENT–COGIC	3	240	410	509	0.9	1.3
PENT–Full Gosp Bapt	10	NR	NR	NR	-	-
PENT–Pent Ch of God	2	140	NR	217	0.4	0.5
PENT–Un Pent Ch Intl	1	NR	NR	NR	-	-
PRES–Cumber Presb	3	NR	248	403	0.7	1.0

NR–Not Reported - Represents no adherents reported. Percentages may not total 100 due to rounding.

Table 3: Religious Congregations by County and Group: 2010

Religious Group	Number of Congrega-tions	Number of Attendees	Number of Communicant, Confirmed, or Full Members	Adherents		
				Number of Adherents	% of Total Pop.	% of Total Adh.
PRES–Evan Presby Ch	1	NR	48	60	0.1	0.2
PRES–Presb Ch (USA)	1	0	128	159	0.3	0.4
PRES–Presb Ch Amer	1	200	249	316	0.5	0.8
Salvation Army	1	50	125	298	0.5	0.7
Sev Day Adv	2	162	281	323	0.5	0.8
MADISON	**116**	**13,911**	**34,830**	**49,710**	**52.2**	**100.0**
ANG/EPIS–Anglican NA	1	NR	NR	NR	-	-
ANG/EPIS–Episcopal	3	488	1,256	1,378	1.4	2.8
Bahá'í	0	NR	64	64	0.1	0.1
BAPT–Amer Bapt Assn	1	NR	150	189	0.2	0.4
BAPT–Natl Mis Bapt Conv	1	0	150	189	0.2	0.4
BAPT–NBC USA	6	350	1,325	1,673	1.8	3.4
BAPT–Prog NBC	1	150	300	379	0.4	0.8
BAPT–So Bapt Conv	26	7,037	18,062	22,812	24.0	45.9
Catholic	5	NR	NR	5,242	5.5	10.5
CGOD–Ch God (Ander)	2	163	NR	163	0.2	0.3
Ch Cr, Scientst	1	NR	NR	NR	-	-
Ch of Chr (Hol)	2	NR	NR	NR	-	-
CHR–Chr Ch (Disc)	2	15	63	80	0.1	0.2
CHR–Chs of Christ	5	421	516	667	0.7	1.3
Jehovah's Witness	1	NR	NR	NR	-	-
LDS–L-D Saints	1	NR	NR	765	0.8	1.5
METH–AME	3	175	500	631	0.7	1.3
METH–AME Zion	12	0	1,500	1,894	2.0	3.8
METH–C.M.E.	2	0	200	253	0.3	0.5
METH–Un Methodist	13	2,071	5,966	7,000	7.4	14.1
Muslim Est	2	268	NR	616	0.6	1.2
Non-denom Chr Chs	5	1,000	2,150	2,150	2.3	4.3
ORTHE–Ant Orth of NA	1	80	NR	135	0.1	0.3
PENT–Assemb of God	1	57	42	57	0.1	0.1
PENT–Ch God (Cleve)	1	42	48	61	0.1	0.1
PENT–Ch Lord Jesus Apos	1	NR	NR	NR	-	-
PENT–COGIC	4	100	500	631	0.7	1.3
PENT–Full Gosp Bapt	1	NR	NR	NR	-	-
PENT–Un Pent Ch Intl	3	NR	NR	NR	-	-
PRES–Evan Presby Ch	1	NR	224	283	0.3	0.6
PRES–Presb Ch (USA)	1	65	100	126	0.1	0.3
PRES–Presb Ch Amer	5	1,395	1,617	2,156	2.3	4.3
Sev Day Adv	1	34	60	69	0.1	0.1
Un C of Christ	1	0	37	47	0.0	0.1
MARION	**84**	**5,364**	**15,227**	**19,057**	**70.4**	**100.0**
ANG/EPIS–Episcopal	1	36	57	57	0.2	0.3
Bahá'í	0	NR	1	1	0.0	0.0
BAPT–Natl Mis Bapt Conv	1	0	150	187	0.7	1.0
BAPT–NBC Amer	3	0	300	375	1.4	2.0
BAPT–NBC USA	1	0	150	187	0.7	1.0
BAPT–So Bapt Conv	24	2,908	9,878	12,336	45.5	64.7
Catholic	1	NR	NR	226	0.8	1.2
Ch of Nazarene	1	8	15	23	0.1	0.1
CHR–Chs of Christ	2	60	75	98	0.4	0.5
Jehovah's Witness	1	NR	NR	NR	-	-
LDS–L-D Saints	1	NR	NR	442	1.6	2.3
METH–C.M.E.	2	0	250	312	1.2	1.6
METH–Cong Meth	1	NR	52	65	0.2	0.3
METH–Un Methodist	23	1,081	2,304	2,355	8.7	12.4
Non-denom Chr Chs	5	410	605	645	2.4	3.4
PENT–Assemb of God	1	65	63	100	0.4	0.5
PENT–Ch God (Cleve)	9	667	1,160	1,449	5.3	7.6
PENT–COGIC	1	50	60	75	0.3	0.4
PENT–Un Pent Ch Intl	3	NR	NR	NR	-	-
PRES–Presb Ch Amer	1	45	48	56	0.2	0.3
Sev Day Adv	2	34	59	68	0.3	0.4
MARSHALL	**94**	**5,047**	**14,734**	**17,914**	**48.2**	**100.0**
ANG/EPIS–Episcopal	1	36	72	133	0.4	0.7
Bahá'í	0	NR	1	1	0.0	0.0
BAPT–So Bapt Conv	25	3,013	8,129	9,908	26.7	55.3
Catholic	1	NR	NR	264	0.7	1.5
CHR–Chs of Christ	5	320	424	523	1.4	2.9
Jehovah's Witness	1	NR	NR	NR	-	-
LUTH–Luth-MO Synod	1	12	15	15	0.0	0.1
METH–C.M.E.	26	450	3,270	3,986	10.7	22.3
METH–Un Methodist	18	635	1,659	1,763	4.7	9.8
Non-denom Chr Chs	5	420	620	625	1.7	3.5
PENT–Assemb of God	2	110	106	162	0.4	0.9
PENT–COGIC	2	0	300	366	1.0	2.0
PENT–Un Pent Ch Intl	4	NR	NR	NR	-	-
PRES–Presb Ch (USA)	3	51	138	168	0.5	0.9
MONROE	**122**	**7,442**	**16,841**	**20,742**	**56.1**	**100.0**
ANG/EPIS–Episcopal	1	29	68	112	0.3	0.5
Bahá'í	0	NR	3	3	0.0	0.0
BAPT–Amer Bapt Assn	2	NR	235	289	0.8	1.4
BAPT–Free Will Bapt	6	NR	474	582	1.6	2.8
BAPT–Natl Mis Bapt Conv	2	0	0	0	0.0	0.0
BAPT–So Bapt Conv	35	3,876	9,199	11,296	30.5	54.5
Catholic	2	NR	NR	229	0.6	1.1
CHR–Chr Chs & Chs Cr	1	NR	125	153	0.4	0.7
CHR–Chs of Christ	13	1,127	1,121	1,431	3.9	6.9
Jehovah's Witness	2	NR	NR	NR	-	-
METH–C.M.E.	4	0	450	553	1.5	2.7
METH–Un Methodist	28	1,493	3,514	4,102	11.1	19.8
Non-denom Chr Chs	4	410	510	537	1.5	2.6
PENT–Assemb of God	3	195	133	208	0.6	1.0
PENT–Ch God (Cleve)	4	112	174	214	0.6	1.0
PENT–Ch of God Proph	4	NR	116	142	0.4	0.7
PENT–COGIC	2	100	450	553	1.5	2.7
PENT–Full Gosp Bapt	1	NR	NR	NR	-	-
PENT–Un Pent Ch Intl	3	NR	NR	NR	-	-
PRES–Presb Ch (USA)	3	0	154	189	0.5	0.9
PRES–Presb Ch Amer	1	70	62	88	0.2	0.4
Sev Day Adv	1	30	53	61	0.2	0.3
MONTGOMERY	**47**	**2,914**	**7,231**	**8,622**	**78.9**	**100.0**
BAPT–Prog NBC	1	225	325	399	3.7	4.6
BAPT–So Bapt Conv	18	1,523	4,283	5,263	48.2	61.0
Catholic	1	NR	NR	60	0.5	0.7
CHR–Chs of Christ	3	223	200	243	2.2	2.8
Jehovah's Witness	1	NR	NR	NR	-	-
METH–AME	2	0	200	246	2.3	2.9
METH–Un Methodist	15	766	1,701	1,789	16.4	20.7
PENT–Ch God (Cleve)	3	127	213	262	2.4	3.0
PENT–COGIC	2	15	200	246	2.3	2.9
PRES–Presb Ch Amer	1	35	109	114	1.0	1.3
NESHOBA	**108**	**5,987**	**13,679**	**18,402**	**62.0**	**100.0**
ANG/EPIS–Episcopal	1	22	43	43	0.1	0.2
Bahá'í	0	NR	9	9	0.0	0.0
BAPT–Natl Mis Bapt Conv	1	0	150	194	0.7	1.1
BAPT–NBC USA	1	0	150	194	0.7	1.1
BAPT–So Bapt Conv	43	3,545	9,256	11,955	40.3	65.0
Catholic	3	NR	NR	691	2.3	3.8
CGOD–Ch God (Ander)	6	216	NR	216	0.7	1.2
Ch of Nazarene	1	20	27	27	0.1	0.1
CHR–Chs of Christ	3	147	141	174	0.6	0.9
LDS–L-D Saints	1	NR	NR	243	0.8	1.3
MENN–Mennonite USA	2	35	36	46	0.2	0.2
METH–Cong Meth	2	NR	27	35	0.1	0.2
METH–Un Methodist	19	1,097	2,483	2,777	9.4	15.1
Non-denom Chr Chs	2	260	350	350	1.2	1.9
PENT–Assemb of God	4	90	79	121	0.4	0.7
PENT–Ch God (Cleve)	6	338	557	719	2.4	3.9
PENT–COGIC	1	0	150	194	0.7	1.1
PENT–Intl Pent Holiness	1	48	45	58	0.2	0.3
PENT–Pent Ch of God	1	70	NR	109	0.4	0.6
PENT–Un Pent Ch Intl	6	NR	NR	NR	-	-
PRES–Cumber Presb	1	NR	46	89	0.3	0.5
PRES–Presb Ch (USA)	1	14	19	25	0.1	0.1
PRES–Presb Ch Amer	2	85	111	133	0.4	0.7
NEWTON	**64**	**4,088**	**10,089**	**12,583**	**57.9**	**100.0**
ANG/EPIS–Episcopal	1	6	5	5	0.0	0.0
Bahá'í	0	NR	1	1	0.0	0.0

NR–Not Reported   - Represents no adherents reported.   Percentages may not total 100 due to rounding.

Table 3: Religious Congregations by County and Group: 2010

Religious Group	Number of Congregations	Number of Attendees	Number of Communicant, Confirmed, or Full Members	Adherents: Number of Adherents	Adherents: % of Total Pop.	Adherents: % of Total Adh.
BAPT–Natl Mis Bapt Conv	1	250	250	312	1.4	2.5
BAPT–NBC USA	1	0	150	188	0.9	1.5
BAPT–So Bapt Conv	34	3,199	7,644	9,555	44.0	75.9
Catholic	2	NR	NR	121	0.6	1.0
CHR–Chr Chs & Chs Cr	2	NR	235	294	1.4	2.3
CHR–Chs of Christ	3	140	112	222	1.0	1.8
Jehovah's Witness	1	NR	NR	NR	-	-
METH–Cong Meth	2	NR	80	100	0.5	0.8
METH–Un Methodist	10	395	1,164	1,251	5.8	9.9
PENT–Ch God (Cleve)	2	84	142	178	0.8	1.4
PENT–COGIC	1	0	150	188	0.9	1.5
PENT–Full Gosp Bapt	1	NR	NR	NR	-	-
PRES–Cumber Presb	1	NR	96	96	0.4	0.8
PRES–Presb Ch (USA)	1	14	17	21	0.1	0.2
PRES–Presb Ch Amer	1	0	43	51	0.2	0.4
NOXUBEE	**47**	**1,495**	**4,595**	**5,735**	**49.7**	**100.0**
ANG/EPIS–Episcopal	1	8	7	7	0.1	0.1
Bahá'í	0	NR	4	4	0.0	0.1
BAPT–Natl Mis Bapt Conv	5	0	650	820	7.1	14.3
BAPT–NBC USA	1	125	150	189	1.6	3.3
BAPT–So Bapt Conv	9	650	1,336	1,685	14.6	29.4
Catholic	1	NR	NR	60	0.5	1.0
CGOD–Ch God (Ander)	2	39	NR	39	0.3	0.7
CHR–Chs of Christ	2	65	63	80	0.7	1.4
Jehovah's Witness	1	NR	NR	NR	-	-
MENN–CG in Cr (Menn)	3	NR	401	506	4.4	8.8
MENN–Mennonite USA	2	100	107	135	1.2	2.4
METH–AME Zion	1	0	100	126	1.1	2.2
METH–C.M.E.	6	0	650	820	7.1	14.3
METH–Un Methodist	7	383	788	851	7.4	14.8
Non-denom Chr Chs	1	85	100	106	0.9	1.8
PENT–Assemb of God	1	5	0	5	0.0	0.1
PENT–COGIC	1	0	150	189	1.6	3.3
PRES–Cumber Presb	2	NR	26	37	0.3	0.6
PRES–Presb Ch Amer	1	35	63	76	0.7	1.3
OKTIBBEHA	**87**	**8,350**	**18,437**	**22,714**	**47.6**	**100.0**
ANG/EPIS–Episcopal	1	135	325	325	0.7	1.4
Bahá'í	0	NR	10	10	0.0	0.0
BAPT–Amer Bapt Assn	1	NR	16	19	0.0	0.1
BAPT–Natl Mis Bapt Conv	1	0	150	176	0.4	0.8
BAPT–NBC USA	5	350	1,200	1,405	2.9	6.2
BAPT–So Bapt Conv	28	3,785	9,586	11,222	23.5	49.4
BUDD–Mahayana	2	NR	NR	204	0.4	0.9
Catholic	1	NR	NR	1,219	2.6	5.4
Ch of Chr (Hol)	4	NR	NR	NR	-	-
Ch of Nazarene	1	26	27	46	0.1	0.2
CHR–Chr Ch (Disc)	1	11	8	9	0.0	0.0
CHR–Chs of Christ	4	492	457	605	1.3	2.7
Jehovah's Witness	1	NR	NR	NR	-	-
LUTH–Luth–MO Synod	1	30	60	67	0.1	0.3
METH–Un Methodist	20	1,818	4,351	4,451	9.3	19.6
Muslim Est	1	134	NR	308	0.6	1.4
Non-denom Chr Chs	3	450	600	625	1.3	2.8
PENT–Assemb of God	2	85	40	121	0.3	0.5
PENT–Ch God (Cleve)	2	252	440	515	1.1	2.3
PENT–COGIC	1	300	300	351	0.7	1.5
PENT–Full Gosp Bapt	1	NR	NR	NR	-	-
PENT–Un Pent Ch Intl	1	NR	NR	NR	-	-
PRES–Presb Ch (USA)	3	322	744	871	1.8	3.8
PRES–Presb Ch Amer	2	160	123	165	0.3	0.7
PANOLA	**115**	**5,619**	**16,289**	**20,788**	**59.9**	**100.0**
ANG/EPIS–Episcopal	1	27	64	111	0.3	0.5
Bahá'í	0	NR	3	3	0.0	0.0
BAPT–Amer Bapt Assn	1	NR	85	107	0.3	0.5
BAPT–Natl Mis Bapt Conv	1	0	150	189	0.5	0.9
BAPT–NBC Amer	1	0	150	189	0.5	0.9
BAPT–NBC USA	4	200	1,550	1,952	5.6	9.4
BAPT–So Bapt Conv	33	2,654	7,400	9,318	26.8	44.8
BUDD–Mahayana	1	NR	NR	25	0.1	0.1
Catholic	2	NR	NR	360	1.0	1.7
CGOD–Ch God (Ander)	2	243	NR	243	0.7	1.2
Ch of Nazarene	1	0	21	21	0.1	0.1
CHR–Chs of Christ	8	555	540	670	1.9	3.2
Jehovah's Witness	1	NR	NR	NR	-	-
METH–AME Zion	8	100	1,000	1,259	3.6	6.1
METH–C.M.E.	12	0	1,450	1,826	5.3	8.8
METH–Un Methodist	21	962	2,434	2,724	7.8	13.1
Non-denom Chr Chs	2	465	595	675	1.9	3.2
PENT–Assemb of God	3	95	36	109	0.3	0.5
PENT–Ch God (Cleve)	3	90	241	303	0.9	1.5
PENT–COGIC	2	42	32	40	0.1	0.2
PENT–Un Pent Ch Intl	3	NR	NR	NR	-	-
PRES–Presb Ch (USA)	3	140	454	572	1.6	2.8
PRES–Presb Ch Amer	1	20	40	41	0.1	0.2
Sev Day Adv	1	26	44	51	0.1	0.2
PEARL RIVER	**86**	**8,928**	**24,681**	**36,022**	**64.5**	**100.0**
ANG/EPIS–Episcopal	1	30	79	79	0.1	0.2
Bahá'í	0	NR	4	4	0.0	0.0
BAPT–Amer Bapt Assn	1	NR	85	105	0.2	0.3
BAPT–NBC Amer	2	225	450	555	1.0	1.5
BAPT–So Bapt Conv	37	4,502	17,650	21,769	39.0	60.4
Catholic	2	NR	NR	4,079	7.3	11.3
CHR–Chs of Christ	2	155	124	167	0.3	0.5
HINDU–I/A Temples	1	NR	NR	1,562	2.8	4.3
HINDU–Trad Temples	1	NR	NR	100	0.2	0.3
Jehovah's Witness	2	NR	NR	NR	-	-
LDS–L-D Saints	1	NR	NR	594	1.1	1.6
LUTH–Luth Cong Msn Chr	1	NR	NR	NR	-	-
LUTH–Luth–MO Synod	1	74	114	134	0.2	0.4
METH–AME	1	0	150	185	0.3	0.5
METH–Un Methodist	8	596	1,679	1,816	3.3	5.0
Non-denom Chr Chs	5	2,400	3,100	3,100	5.6	8.6
PENT–Assemb of God	3	318	160	434	0.8	1.2
PENT–Ch God (Cleve)	6	276	666	821	1.5	2.3
PENT–Ch of God Proph	1	NR	11	14	0.0	0.0
PENT–COGIC	1	250	300	370	0.7	1.0
PENT–Full Gosp Bapt	2	NR	NR	NR	-	-
PENT–Intl Pent Holiness	1	37	34	42	0.1	0.1
PENT–Un Pent Ch Intl	4	NR	NR	NR	-	-
PRES–Presb Ch (USA)	1	20	19	23	0.0	0.1
PRES–Presb Ch Amer	1	45	56	69	0.1	0.2
PERRY	**45**	**1,990**	**5,213**	**6,465**	**52.8**	**100.0**
BAPT–Free Will Bapt	6	NR	324	400	3.3	6.2
BAPT–So Bapt Conv	18	1,389	4,061	5,010	40.9	77.5
CGOD–Ch God (Ander)	1	0	NR	0	0.0	0.0
CHR–Chs of Christ	2	55	40	60	0.5	0.9
METH–Cong Meth	2	NR	51	63	0.5	1.0
METH–Un Methodist	7	272	472	514	4.2	8.0
PENT–Assemb of God	1	110	22	120	1.0	1.9
PENT–Ch God (Cleve)	5	149	215	265	2.2	4.1
PENT–Ch of God Proph	1	NR	14	17	0.1	0.3
PENT–Un Pent Ch Intl	1	NR	NR	NR	-	-
PRES–Presb Ch Amer	1	15	14	16	0.1	0.2
PIKE	**94**	**7,067**	**18,985**	**25,493**	**63.1**	**100.0**
ANG/EPIS–Episcopal	1	61	120	120	0.3	0.5
Bahá'í	0	NR	5	5	0.0	0.0
BAPT–Natl Mis Bapt Conv	5	0	750	950	2.4	3.7
BAPT–NBC USA	2	0	750	950	2.4	3.7
BAPT–S-D Baptist Gen Con	1	10	NR	NR	-	-
BAPT–So Bapt Conv	29	4,426	12,353	15,652	38.7	61.4
Catholic	3	NR	NR	1,453	3.6	5.7
Ch of Chr (Hol)	3	NR	NR	NR	-	-
Ch of Nazarene	3	127	336	354	0.9	1.4
CHR–Chr Ch (Disc)	1	53	120	152	0.4	0.6
CHR–Chs of Christ	5	462	388	613	1.5	2.4
Jehovah's Witness	1	NR	NR	NR	-	-
LDS–L-D Saints	1	NR	NR	302	0.7	1.2
LUTH–Luth–MO Synod	1	14	18	18	0.0	0.1
METH–AME	4	0	450	570	1.4	2.2
METH–Un Methodist	11	675	1,886	2,131	5.3	8.4

NR–Not Reported   - Represents no adherents reported.   Percentages may not total 100 due to rounding.

Table 3: Religious Congregations by County and Group: 2010

Religious Group	Number of Congrega-tions	Number of Attendees	Number of Communicant, Confirmed, or Full Members	Adherents		
				Number of Adherents	% of Total Pop.	% of Total Adh.
Non-denom Chr Chs	5	600	760	825	2.0	3.2
ORTHE–Orth Ch in Amer	1	25	NR	50	0.1	0.2
PENT–Assemb of God	2	196	137	223	0.6	0.9
PENT–Ch God (Cleve)	2	65	67	85	0.2	0.3
PENT–Ch of God Proph	1	NR	20	25	0.1	0.1
PENT–COGIC	3	70	375	475	1.2	1.9
PENT–Full Gosp Bapt	1	NR	NR	NR	-	-
PENT–Un Pent Ch Intl	1	NR	NR	NR	-	-
PRES–Presb Ch (USA)	3	95	169	214	0.5	0.8
PRES–Presb Ch Amer	1	90	128	151	0.4	0.6
Salvation Army	1	14	7	7	0.0	0.0
Sev Day Adv	2	84	146	168	0.4	0.7
PONTOTOC	**93**	**6,606**	**15,618**	**19,837**	**66.2**	**100.0**
BAPT–Free Will Bapt	3	NR	162	204	0.7	1.0
BAPT–So Bapt Conv	49	5,152	12,843	16,199	54.1	81.7
Catholic	1	NR	NR	325	1.1	1.6
Ch of Nazarene	2	6	20	20	0.1	0.1
CHR–Chs of Christ	5	312	254	399	1.3	2.0
Jehovah's Witness	1	NR	NR	NR	-	-
MENN–Amish Undif	1	NR	65	175	0.6	0.9
METH–C.M.E.	3	35	270	341	1.1	1.7
METH–Un Methodist	17	816	1,607	1,674	5.6	8.4
Non-denom Chr Chs	2	190	185	237	0.8	1.2
PENT–Assemb of God	1	8	9	14	0.0	0.1
PENT–Ch God (Cleve)	1	12	77	97	0.3	0.5
PENT–Ch of God Proph	1	NR	24	30	0.1	0.2
PENT–Un Pent Ch Intl	2	NR	NR	NR	-	-
PRES–Presb Ch (USA)	3	51	74	93	0.3	0.5
PRES–Presb Ch Amer	1	24	28	29	0.1	0.1
PRENTISS	**85**	**6,889**	**14,696**	**17,942**	**71.0**	**100.0**
Bahá'í	0	NR	1	1	0.0	0.0
BAPT–Amer Bapt Assn	1	NR	85	104	0.4	0.6
BAPT–Free Will Bapt	7	NR	378	461	1.8	2.6
BAPT–So Bapt Conv	30	3,718	9,263	11,294	44.7	62.9
Catholic	1	NR	NR	70	0.3	0.4
CHR–Chs of Christ	15	1,369	1,232	1,579	6.2	8.8
LDS–L-D Saints	1	NR	NR	407	1.6	2.3
METH–C.M.E.	1	60	170	207	0.8	1.2
METH–Un Methodist	17	1,054	2,655	2,805	11.1	15.6
Non-denom Chr Chs	4	500	650	700	2.8	3.9
PENT–Assemb of God	1	65	65	73	0.3	0.4
PENT–Ch God (Cleve)	2	73	68	83	0.3	0.5
PENT–Ch of God Proph	1	NR	16	20	0.1	0.1
PENT–COGIC	1	50	100	122	0.5	0.7
PENT–Un Pent Ch Intl	2	NR	NR	NR	-	-
PRES–Presb Ch (USA)	1	0	13	16	0.1	0.1
QUITMAN	**31**	**1,276**	**4,327**	**6,777**	**82.4**	**100.0**
BAPT–Amer Bapt USA	1	100	150	187	2.3	2.8
BAPT–NBC Amer	1	60	250	312	3.8	4.6
BAPT–NBC USA	1	0	150	187	2.3	2.8
BAPT–So Bapt Conv	9	494	2,050	2,557	31.1	37.7
CHR–Chs of Christ	2	110	120	150	1.8	2.2
Jehovah's Witness	1	NR	NR	NR	-	-
METH–AME	1	0	100	125	1.5	1.8
METH–AME Zion	1	0	100	125	1.5	1.8
METH–Un Methodist	3	208	601	2,129	25.9	31.4
Non-denom Chr Chs	1	100	150	150	1.8	2.2
PENT–Assemb of God	1	52	0	52	0.6	0.8
PENT–Ch God (Cleve)	2	77	117	146	1.8	2.2
PENT–COGIC	4	15	470	586	7.1	8.6
PENT–Un Pent Ch Intl	2	NR	NR	NR	-	-
PRES–Presb Ch Amer	1	60	69	71	0.9	1.0
RANKIN	**177**	**33,640**	**70,914**	**91,437**	**64.6**	**100.0**
ANG/EPIS–Anglican NA	1	NR	NR	NR	-	-
ANG/EPIS–Episcopal	2	164	341	387	0.3	0.4
Bahá'í	0	NR	12	12	0.0	0.0
BAPT–Amer Bapt Assn	1	NR	150	187	0.1	0.2
BAPT–Free Will Bapt	1	NR	54	67	0.0	0.1

Religious Group	Number of Congrega-tions	Number of Attendees	Number of Communicant, Confirmed, or Full Members	Adherents		
				Number of Adherents	% of Total Pop.	% of Total Adh.
BAPT–Natl Mis Bapt Conv	1	0	150	187	0.1	0.2
BAPT–NBC USA	4	600	1,200	1,494	1.1	1.6
BAPT–So Bapt Conv	58	18,209	43,477	54,112	38.2	59.2
Calv Chpl	1	NR	NR	NR	-	-
Catholic	2	NR	NR	4,096	2.9	4.5
CGOD–Ch God (Ander)	1	38	NR	38	0.0	0.0
Ch of Chr (Hol)	3	NR	NR	NR	-	-
Ch of Nazarene	1	86	78	88	0.1	0.1
CHR–Chs of Christ	5	435	385	493	0.3	0.5
HINDU–Trad Temples	1	NR	NR	750	0.5	0.8
Jehovah's Witness	2	NR	NR	NR	-	-
LDS–L-D Saints	3	NR	NR	1,675	1.2	1.8
LUTH–E.L.C.A.	1	73	177	177	0.1	0.2
LUTH–Luth-MO Synod	1	101	121	150	0.1	0.2
METH–C.M.E.	3	0	350	436	0.3	0.5
METH–Cong Meth	1	NR	198	246	0.2	0.3
METH–Un Methodist	30	3,192	8,421	9,554	6.7	10.4
Non-denom Chr Chs	18	8,805	11,295	11,438	8.1	12.5
PENT–Assemb of God	9	585	473	805	0.6	0.9
PENT–Ch God (Cleve)	4	427	1,318	1,640	1.2	1.8
PENT–Ch of God Proph	1	NR	36	45	0.0	0.0
PENT–COGIC	4	0	600	747	0.5	0.8
PENT–Intl Pent Holiness	2	33	42	52	0.0	0.1
PENT–Pent Ch of God	1	70	NR	109	0.1	0.1
PENT–Un Pent Ch Intl	7	NR	NR	NR	-	-
PENT–Vineyard	1	100	115	143	0.1	0.2
PRES–Evan Presby Ch	1	NR	497	619	0.4	0.7
PRES–Presb Ch Amer	3	408	578	689	0.5	0.8
Sev Day Adv	2	314	546	628	0.4	0.7
Un C of Christ	1	0	300	373	0.3	0.4
SCOTT	**93**	**5,759**	**14,739**	**19,144**	**67.7**	**100.0**
ANG/EPIS–Episcopal	1	5	7	7	0.0	0.0
BAPT–Natl Mis Bapt Conv	2	0	300	380	1.3	2.0
BAPT–NBC USA	1	0	150	190	0.7	1.0
BAPT–So Bapt Conv	50	3,809	10,547	13,342	47.2	69.7
Catholic	2	NR	NR	1,000	3.5	5.2
CHR–Chr Chs & Chs Cr	1	NR	45	57	0.2	0.3
CHR–Chs of Christ	2	95	82	120	0.4	0.6
Jehovah's Witness	1	NR	NR	NR	-	-
LUTH–E.L.C.A.	1	33	31	53	0.2	0.3
METH–Un Methodist	21	975	2,629	2,868	10.1	15.0
Non-denom Chr Chs	2	180	250	250	0.9	1.3
PENT–Ch God (Cleve)	3	563	562	711	2.5	3.7
PENT–Un Pent Ch Intl	2	NR	NR	NR	-	-
PRES–Cumber Presb	2	NR	17	21	0.1	0.1
PRES–Presb Ch Amer	1	60	51	67	0.2	0.3
Sev Day Adv	1	39	68	78	0.3	0.4
SHARKEY	**18**	**855**	**2,471**	**3,030**	**61.6**	**100.0**
ANG/EPIS–Episcopal	1	24	75	75	1.5	2.5
BAPT–NBC USA	1	100	214	264	5.4	8.7
BAPT–So Bapt Conv	5	319	1,361	1,681	34.2	55.5
Catholic	1	NR	NR	35	0.7	1.2
CHR–Chs of Christ	1	25	22	50	1.0	1.7
METH–C.M.E.	1	0	100	124	2.5	4.1
METH–Un Methodist	3	153	349	431	8.8	14.2
Non-denom Chr Chs	2	210	280	288	5.9	9.5
PENT–Ch of God Proph	2	NR	27	33	0.7	1.1
Sev Day Adv	1	24	43	49	1.0	1.6
SIMPSON	**89**	**6,322**	**17,327**	**21,627**	**78.6**	**100.0**
Bahá'í	0	NR	6	6	0.0	0.0
BAPT–Natl Mis Bapt Conv	1	0	150	188	0.7	0.9
BAPT–NBC USA	1	400	525	659	2.4	3.0
BAPT–So Bapt Conv	53	4,567	13,899	17,436	63.4	80.6
Catholic	1	NR	NR	132	0.5	0.6
Ch of Chr (Hol)	1	NR	NR	NR	-	-
CHR–Chs of Christ	2	55	52	71	0.3	0.3
Jehovah's Witness	1	NR	NR	NR	-	-
METH–C.M.E.	2	0	300	376	1.4	1.7
METH–Cong Meth	1	NR	23	29	0.1	0.1
METH–Un Methodist	8	476	951	1,052	3.8	4.9

NR–Not Reported - Represents no adherents reported. Percentages may not total 100 due to rounding.

Table 3: Religious Congregations by County and Group: 2010

Religious Group	Number of Congrega-tions	Number of Attendees	Number of Communicant, Confirmed, or Full Members	Adherents: Number of Adherents	Adherents: % of Total Pop.	Adherents: % of Total Adh.
Non-denom Chr Chs	4	425	570	606	2.2	2.8
PENT–Assemb of God	2	72	61	92	0.3	0.4
PENT–Ch God (Cleve)	4	142	420	527	1.9	2.4
PENT–COGIC	3	85	250	314	1.1	1.5
PENT–Full Gosp Bapt	1	NR	NR	NR	-	-
PENT–Un Pent Ch Intl	2	NR	NR	NR	-	-
PRES–Presb Ch Amer	2	100	120	139	0.5	0.6
SMITH	**46**	**2,220**	**5,001**	**6,100**	**37.0**	**100.0**
Bahá'í	0	NR	1	1	0.0	0.0
BAPT–So Bapt Conv	22	1,747	3,895	4,853	29.4	79.6
CHR–Chr Chs & Chs Cr	1	NR	60	75	0.5	1.2
CHR–Chs of Christ	1	20	11	20	0.1	0.3
Jehovah's Witness	1	NR	NR	NR	-	-
LUTH–E.L.C.A.	1	6	11	12	0.1	0.2
MENN–CG in Cr (Menn)	1	NR	35	44	0.3	0.7
METH–C.M.E.	1	0	150	187	1.1	3.1
METH–Un Methodist	9	267	513	532	3.2	8.7
PENT–Assemb of God	1	10	8	11	0.1	0.2
PENT–Ch God (Cleve)	2	90	177	221	1.3	3.6
PENT–Un Pent Ch Intl	3	NR	NR	NR	-	-
PRES–Presb Ch Amer	2	64	111	111	0.7	1.8
Sev Day Adv	1	16	29	33	0.2	0.5
STONE	**29**	**1,735**	**4,666**	**6,315**	**35.5**	**100.0**
Bahá'í	0	NR	1	1	0.0	0.0
BAPT–Amer Bapt Assn	2	NR	285	350	2.0	5.5
BAPT–Natl Mis Bapt Conv	1	0	150	184	1.0	2.9
BAPT–Ref Bapt Ch	1	NR	NR	NR	-	-
BAPT–So Bapt Conv	10	1,072	2,850	3,501	19.7	55.4
Catholic	1	NR	NR	372	2.1	5.9
CHR–Chs of Christ	1	25	42	57	0.3	0.9
Jehovah's Witness	1	NR	NR	NR	-	-
LDS–L-D Saints	1	NR	NR	327	1.8	5.2
METH–Un Methodist	3	324	898	1,008	5.7	16.0
Non-denom Chr Chs	2	160	275	275	1.5	4.4
PENT–Assemb of God	1	30	0	40	0.2	0.6
PENT–Ch God (Cleve)	1	75	88	108	0.6	1.7
PENT–Full Gosp Bapt	1	NR	NR	NR	-	-
PENT–Un Pent Ch Intl	1	NR	NR	NR	-	-
PRES–Presb Ch (USA)	1	33	49	60	0.3	1.0
Sev Day Adv	1	16	28	32	0.2	0.5
SUNFLOWER	**71**	**2,783**	**8,793**	**10,770**	**36.6**	**100.0**
ANG/EPIS–Episcopal	2	60	115	115	0.4	1.1
Bahá'í	0	NR	5	5	0.0	0.0
BAPT–NBC USA	5	0	1,364	1,683	5.7	15.6
BAPT–So Bapt Conv	20	1,161	4,018	4,959	16.8	46.0
Catholic	2	NR	NR	212	0.7	2.0
CGOD–Ch God (Ander)	1	29	NR	29	0.1	0.3
Ch of Chr (Hol)	3	NR	NR	NR	-	-
Ch of Nazarene	1	17	25	25	0.1	0.2
CHR–Chr Ch (Disc)	2	0	60	74	0.3	0.7
CHR–Chs of Christ	4	245	284	429	1.5	4.0
Jehovah's Witness	1	NR	NR	NR	-	-
METH–AME	2	0	200	247	0.8	2.3
METH–C.M.E.	1	0	150	185	0.6	1.7
METH–Un Methodist	12	601	1,691	1,822	6.2	16.9
Non-denom Chr Chs	3	260	390	390	1.3	3.6
PENT–Assemb of God	1	25	25	43	0.1	0.4
PENT–Ch God (Cleve)	4	92	186	230	0.8	2.1
PENT–Ch of God by Faith	1	NR	NR	NR	-	-
PENT–COGIC	3	150	30	37	0.1	0.3
PENT–Full Gosp Bapt	1	NR	NR	NR	-	-
PRES–Presb Ch Amer	1	45	80	89	0.3	0.8
Sev Day Adv	1	98	170	196	0.7	1.8
TALLAHATCHIE	**47**	**1,279**	**4,519**	**5,420**	**35.2**	**100.0**
ANG/EPIS–Episcopal	1	30	87	87	0.6	1.6
Bahá'í	0	NR	1	1	0.0	0.0
BAPT–NBC USA	2	0	300	361	2.3	6.7
BAPT–So Bapt Conv	11	579	2,338	2,817	18.3	52.0
Catholic	1	NR	NR	31	0.2	0.6
Ch of Nazarene	1	58	69	72	0.5	1.3
CHR–Chs of Christ	6	187	207	280	1.8	5.2
METH–AME	1	0	100	120	0.8	2.2
METH–AME Zion	1	0	100	120	0.8	2.2
METH–C.M.E.	3	0	300	361	2.3	6.7
METH–Un Methodist	6	144	405	422	2.7	7.8
PENT–Ch God (Cleve)	5	198	289	348	2.3	6.4
PENT–Ch of God Proph	5	NR	152	183	1.2	3.4
PENT–COGIC	1	0	0	0	0.0	0.0
PRES–Presb Ch (USA)	2	18	65	78	0.5	1.4
PRES–Presb Ch Amer	1	65	106	139	0.9	2.6
TATE	**74**	**5,761**	**13,308**	**17,439**	**60.4**	**100.0**
Bahá'í	0	NR	3	3	0.0	0.0
BAPT–NBC USA	3	120	600	749	2.6	4.3
BAPT–So Bapt Conv	19	2,968	7,886	9,840	34.1	56.4
Catholic	1	NR	NR	260	0.9	1.5
Ch of Nazarene	1	34	48	49	0.2	0.3
CHR–Chs of Christ	15	1,350	1,613	2,080	7.2	11.9
Jehovah's Witness	1	NR	NR	NR	-	-
LDS–L-D Saints	1	NR	NR	620	2.1	3.6
METH–AME	5	75	550	686	2.4	3.9
METH–C.M.E.	7	0	800	998	3.5	5.7
METH–Un Methodist	11	537	1,058	1,230	4.3	7.1
Non-denom Chr Chs	1	170	175	212	0.7	1.2
PENT–Assemb of God	2	230	228	280	1.0	1.6
PENT–Ch God (Cleve)	1	84	6	7	0.0	0.0
PENT–COGIC	2	95	176	220	0.8	1.3
PENT–Intl Pent Holiness	1	17	21	26	0.1	0.1
PENT–Un Pent Ch Intl	1	NR	NR	NR	-	-
PRES–Presb Ch (USA)	1	75	133	166	0.6	1.0
Sev Day Adv	1	6	11	13	0.0	0.1
TIPPAH	**78**	**5,278**	**11,656**	**14,681**	**66.0**	**100.0**
BAPT–So Bapt Conv	33	3,387	8,687	10,840	48.8	73.8
Catholic	1	NR	NR	250	1.1	1.7
CHR–Chs of Christ	8	804	791	957	4.3	6.5
Jehovah's Witness	1	NR	NR	NR	-	-
METH–Cong Meth	1	NR	42	52	0.2	0.4
METH–Un Methodist	19	685	1,509	1,720	7.7	11.7
Non-denom Chr Chs	2	120	180	180	0.8	1.2
PENT–Assemb of God	2	72	52	112	0.5	0.8
PENT–Ch God (Cleve)	1	20	55	69	0.3	0.5
PENT–Un Pent Ch Intl	3	NR	NR	NR	-	-
PRES–As Ref Pres Ch	1	NR	29	36	0.2	0.2
PRES–Cumber Presb	1	NR	78	179	0.8	1.2
PRES–Presb Ch (USA)	4	160	201	251	1.1	1.7
PRES–Presb Ch Amer	1	30	32	35	0.2	0.2
TISHOMINGO	**73**	**3,876**	**8,499**	**10,190**	**52.0**	**100.0**
BAPT–Amer Bapt Assn	3	NR	255	309	1.6	3.0
BAPT–Free Will Bapt	5	NR	270	327	1.7	3.2
BAPT–So Bapt Conv	23	1,842	4,945	5,996	30.6	58.8
Catholic	2	NR	NR	42	0.2	0.4
CHR–Chs of Christ	8	860	855	1,035	5.3	10.2
Jehovah's Witness	1	NR	NR	NR	-	-
METH–C.M.E.	2	0	200	243	1.2	2.4
METH–Un Methodist	17	740	1,508	1,639	8.4	16.1
Non-denom Chr Chs	5	350	350	437	2.2	4.3
PENT–Assemb of God	1	15	0	21	0.1	0.2
PENT–Ch God (Cleve)	1	69	89	108	0.6	1.1
PENT–Ch of God Proph	1	NR	27	33	0.2	0.3
PENT–Un Pent Ch Intl	4	NR	NR	NR	-	-
TUNICA	**16**	**473**	**1,523**	**1,872**	**17.4**	**100.0**
ANG/EPIS–Episcopal	1	28	73	73	0.7	3.9
Bahá'í	0	NR	1	1	0.0	0.1
BAPT–So Bapt Conv	5	225	608	797	7.4	42.6
CHR–Chs of Christ	2	75	89	115	1.1	6.1
METH–AME	1	0	100	131	1.2	7.0
METH–C.M.E.	1	0	100	131	1.2	7.0

NR–Not Reported   - Represents no adherents reported.   Percentages may not total 100 due to rounding.

Table 3: Religious Congregations by County and Group: 2010

Religious Group	Number of Congrega-tions	Number of Attendees	Number of Communicant, Confirmed, or Full Members	Adherents		
				Number of Adherents	% of Total Pop.	% of Total Adh.
METH–Un Methodist	1	95	290	295	2.7	15.8
PENT–Ch of God Proph	1	NR	37	48	0.4	2.6
PENT–Un Pent Ch Intl	1	NR	NR	NR	-	-
PRES–Evan Presby Ch	1	NR	125	164	1.5	8.8
PRES–Presb Ch (USA)	1	0	13	17	0.2	0.9
Sev Day Adv	1	50	87	100	0.9	5.3
UNION	**88**	**7,627**	**18,710**	**23,351**	**86.1**	**100.0**
BAPT–Natl Mis Bapt Conv	1	0	150	188	0.7	0.8
BAPT–NBC Amer	1	107	250	313	1.2	1.3
BAPT–So Bapt Conv	42	4,869	13,214	16,520	60.9	70.7
Catholic	1	NR	NR	398	1.5	1.7
Ch of Nazarene	1	32	23	37	0.1	0.2
CHR–Chs of Christ	5	405	391	477	1.8	2.0
Jehovah's Witness	1	NR	NR	NR	-	-
LDS–L-D Saints	1	NR	NR	186	0.7	0.8
METH–C.M.E.	2	0	200	250	0.9	1.1
METH–Un Methodist	19	1,461	3,000	3,289	12.1	14.1
Non-denom Chr Chs	3	290	400	412	1.5	1.8
PENT–Assemb of God	1	150	235	235	0.9	1.0
PENT–Ch God (Cleve)	2	188	249	311	1.1	1.3
PENT–COGIC	1	0	150	188	0.7	0.8
PENT–Un Pent Ch Intl	2	NR	NR	NR	-	-
PRES–As Ref Pres Ch	3	NR	253	316	1.2	1.4
PRES–Presb Ch (USA)	1	55	72	90	0.3	0.4
Sev Day Adv	1	70	123	141	0.5	0.6
WALTHALL	**24**	**1,789**	**5,080**	**6,565**	**42.5**	**100.0**
BAPT–So Bapt Conv	16	1,366	4,373	5,494	35.6	83.7
Catholic	1	NR	NR	205	1.3	3.1
Ch of Chr (Hol)	1	NR	NR	NR	-	-
CHR–Chs of Christ	1	18	12	20	0.1	0.3
METH–Un Methodist	1	80	230	243	1.6	3.7
Non-denom Chr Chs	2	325	315	415	2.7	6.3
PENT–COGIC	1	0	150	188	1.2	2.9
PENT–Un Pent Ch Intl	1	NR	NR	NR	-	-
WARREN	**85**	**6,668**	**22,630**	**31,669**	**64.9**	**100.0**
ANG/EPIS–Anglican NA	1	NR	NR	NR	-	-
ANG/EPIS–Episcopal	4	230	647	653	1.3	2.1
Bahá'í	1	NR	36	36	0.1	0.1
BAPT–Natl Mis Bapt Conv	3	0	450	562	1.2	1.8
BAPT–NBC USA	8	0	2,200	2,747	5.6	8.7
BAPT–Prog NBC	1	45	0	0	0.0	0.0
BAPT–So Bapt Conv	14	2,447	11,317	14,129	29.0	44.6
Catholic	3	NR	NR	2,789	5.7	8.8
Ch of Chr (Hol)	1	NR	NR	NR	-	-
Ch of Nazarene	1	66	127	130	0.3	0.4
CHR–Chr Ch (Disc)	1	46	134	167	0.3	0.5
CHR–Chs of Christ	6	479	467	606	1.2	1.9
Jehovah's Witness	1	NR	NR	NR	-	-
JUD–Reform	1	15	26	70	0.1	0.2
LDS–L-D Saints	1	NR	NR	677	1.4	2.1
LUTH–Luth-MO Synod	1	28	33	46	0.1	0.1
METH–AME	3	0	350	437	0.9	1.4
METH–Un Methodist	10	746	3,373	3,859	7.9	12.2
Muslim Est	1	134	NR	308	0.6	1.0
Non-denom Chr Chs	8	1,580	1,950	2,214	4.5	7.0
ORTHE–Ant Orth of NA	1	90	NR	185	0.4	0.6
PENT–Assemb of God	1	53	48	118	0.2	0.4
PENT–Ch God (Cleve)	1	59	140	175	0.4	0.6
PENT–Ch of God Proph	1	NR	51	64	0.1	0.2
PENT–COGIC	2	0	300	375	0.8	1.2
PENT–Pent Ch of God	1	70	NR	109	0.2	0.3
PENT–Un Pent Ch Intl	1	NR	NR	NR	-	-
PENT–Vineyard	1	15	15	19	0.0	0.1
PRES–Presb Ch (USA)	2	250	379	473	1.0	1.5
PRES–Presb Ch Amer	1	74	121	144	0.3	0.5
Salvation Army	1	28	95	151	0.3	0.5
Sev Day Adv	2	213	371	426	0.9	1.3
WASHINGTON	**115**	**7,698**	**24,498**	**33,193**	**64.9**	**100.0**
ANG/EPIS–Episcopal	4	162	348	367	0.7	1.1
Bahá'í	0	NR	3	3	0.0	0.0
BAPT–Natl Mis Bapt Conv	2	0	300	381	0.7	1.1
BAPT–NBC USA	19	1,100	4,625	5,869	11.5	17.7
BAPT–Prog NBC	2	0	150	190	0.4	0.6
BAPT–So Bapt Conv	22	2,144	10,564	13,406	26.2	40.4
Catholic	4	NR	NR	1,893	3.7	5.7
Ch of Chr (Hol)	1	NR	NR	NR	-	-
Ch of Nazarene	1	9	22	22	0.0	0.1
CHR–Chs of Christ	5	355	468	584	1.1	1.8
Jehovah's Witness	2	NR	NR	NR	-	-
JUD–Reform	1	24	42	113	0.2	0.3
LDS–L-D Saints	1	NR	NR	553	1.1	1.7
LUTH–Luth-MO Synod	1	17	21	25	0.0	0.1
MENN–CG in Cr (Menn)	1	NR	151	192	0.4	0.6
METH–AME	5	225	850	1,079	2.1	3.3
METH–Un Methodist	8	548	1,523	1,829	3.6	5.5
Non-denom Chr Chs	15	2,091	3,170	3,530	6.9	10.6
PENT–Assemb of God	4	146	103	175	0.3	0.5
PENT–Ch God (Cleve)	4	194	579	735	1.4	2.2
PENT–Ch of God Proph	1	NR	29	37	0.1	0.1
PENT–COGIC	2	0	300	381	0.7	1.1
PENT–Pent Ch of God	1	70	NR	109	0.2	0.3
PENT–Un Pent Ch Intl	1	NR	NR	NR	-	-
PRES–Presb Ch (USA)	4	233	585	742	1.5	2.2
PRES–Presb Ch Amer	1	60	68	71	0.1	0.2
Salvation Army	1	44	118	356	0.7	1.1
Sev Day Adv	2	276	479	551	1.1	1.7
WAYNE	**84**	**4,395**	**9,226**	**11,696**	**56.4**	**100.0**
Bahá'í	0	NR	1	1	0.0	0.0
BAPT–Free Will Bapt	6	NR	324	404	1.9	3.5
BAPT–Natl Mis Bapt Conv	1	0	0	0	0.0	0.0
BAPT–NBC USA	1	0	0	0	0.0	0.0
BAPT–So Bapt Conv	28	2,540	6,287	7,848	37.8	67.1
Catholic	1	NR	NR	86	0.4	0.7
Ch of Nazarene	1	37	48	52	0.3	0.4
CHR–Chs of Christ	2	87	81	104	0.5	0.9
Jehovah's Witness	1	NR	NR	NR	-	-
METH–AME	1	0	100	125	0.6	1.1
METH–So Methodist	3	NR	NR	NR	-	-
METH–Un Methodist	22	765	1,684	1,829	8.8	15.6
PENT–Assemb of God	11	625	256	707	3.4	6.0
PENT–Ch God (Cleve)	2	275	379	473	2.3	4.0
PENT–Un Pent Ch Intl	1	NR	NR	NR	-	-
PRES–Presb Ch Amer	3	66	66	67	0.3	0.6
WEBSTER	**50**	**2,452**	**5,830**	**7,238**	**70.6**	**100.0**
Bahá'í	0	NR	1	1	0.0	0.0
BAPT–Free Will Bapt	1	NR	54	67	0.7	0.9
BAPT–Natl Mis Bapt Conv	1	0	150	186	1.8	2.6
BAPT–So Bapt Conv	25	1,625	4,198	5,218	50.9	72.1
Catholic	1	NR	NR	65	0.6	0.9
CHR–Chs of Christ	1	70	80	90	0.9	1.2
Jehovah's Witness	1	NR	NR	NR	-	-
METH–C.M.E.	1	0	100	124	1.2	1.7
METH–Cong Meth	1	NR	34	42	0.4	0.6
METH–Un Methodist	9	342	746	863	8.4	11.9
Non-denom Chr Chs	1	150	150	188	1.8	2.6
PENT–Ch God (Cleve)	5	265	255	317	3.1	4.4
PENT–Ch of God Proph	2	NR	62	77	0.8	1.1
PENT–Full Gosp Bapt	1	NR	NR	NR	-	-
WILKINSON	**34**	**1,356**	**3,997**	**4,966**	**50.3**	**100.0**
ANG/EPIS–Episcopal	1	17	29	120	1.2	2.4
Bahá'í	0	NR	1	1	0.0	0.0
BAPT–NBC USA	1	0	150	183	1.9	3.7
BAPT–So Bapt Conv	8	701	2,046	2,490	25.2	50.1
Catholic	2	NR	NR	113	1.1	2.3
CHR–Chs of Christ	3	200	213	308	3.1	6.2
Jehovah's Witness	1	NR	NR	NR	-	-

NR–Not Reported   - Represents no adherents reported.   Percentages may not total 100 due to rounding.

Table 3: Religious Congregations by County and Group: 2010

Religious Group	Number of Congregations	Number of Attendees	Number of Communicant, Confirmed, or Full Members	Adherents: Number of Adherents	Adherents: % of Total Pop.	Adherents: % of Total Adh.
METH–AME	2	0	200	243	2.5	4.9
METH–C.M.E.	2	0	250	304	3.1	6.1
METH–Un Methodist	6	210	724	776	7.9	15.6
Non-denom Chr Chs	1	150	250	250	2.5	5.0
PENT–Un Pent Ch Intl	3	NR	NR	NR	-	-
PRES–Presb Ch Amer	3	60	104	143	1.4	2.9
Sev Day Adv	1	18	30	35	0.4	0.7
WINSTON	**82**	**4,259**	**12,010**	**14,943**	**77.8**	**100.0**
Bahá'í	0	NR	2	2	0.0	0.0
BAPT–Natl Mis Bapt Conv	4	0	600	744	3.9	5.0
BAPT–NBC USA	6	160	1,150	1,426	7.4	9.5
BAPT–So Bapt Conv	34	2,480	7,186	8,909	46.4	59.6
Catholic	1	NR	NR	71	0.4	0.5
Ch of Chr (Hol)	1	NR	NR	NR	-	-
CHR–Chs of Christ	1	30	28	36	0.2	0.2
Jehovah's Witness	1	NR	NR	NR	-	-
LUTH–E.L.C.A.	2	23	20	24	0.1	0.2
METH–C.M.E.	2	0	200	248	1.3	1.7
METH–Un Methodist	17	967	2,061	2,182	11.4	14.6
Non-denom Chr Chs	1	120	20	150	0.8	1.0
PENT–Assemb of God	5	209	75	307	1.6	2.1
PENT–COGIC	4	150	505	626	3.3	4.2
PENT–Un Pent Ch Intl	2	NR	NR	NR	-	-
PRES–Presb Ch Amer	1	120	163	218	1.1	1.5
YALOBUSHA	**61**	**3,850**	**10,927**	**13,383**	**105.6**	**100.0**
BAPT–Natl Mis Bapt Conv	1	0	150	184	1.5	1.4
BAPT–NBC USA	1	0	300	368	2.9	2.7
BAPT–So Bapt Conv	27	3,012	8,120	9,959	78.6	74.4
CHR–Chr Chs & Chs Cr	1	NR	0	0	0.0	0.0
CHR–Chs of Christ	4	233	308	413	3.3	3.1
METH–AME Zion	2	0	250	307	2.4	2.3
METH–C.M.E.	5	0	650	797	6.3	6.0
METH–Cong Meth	1	NR	33	40	0.3	0.3
METH–Un Methodist	7	317	635	729	5.8	5.4
Non-denom Chr Chs	2	110	110	137	1.1	1.0
PENT–Assemb of God	1	10	10	15	0.1	0.1
PENT–Ch God (Cleve)	3	78	157	193	1.5	1.4
PENT–Ch of God Proph	1	NR	37	45	0.4	0.3
PENT–Un Pent Ch Intl	1	NR	NR	NR	-	-
PRES–Presb Ch (USA)	1	0	40	49	0.4	0.4
PRES–Presb Ch Amer	2	53	63	73	0.6	0.5
Sev Day Adv	1	37	64	74	0.6	0.6
YAZOO	**76**	**3,442**	**9,670**	**13,109**	**46.7**	**100.0**
ANG/EPIS–Episcopal	1	43	64	64	0.2	0.5
Bahá'í	0	NR	39	39	0.1	0.3
BAPT–Amer Bapt Assn	2	NR	230	286	1.0	2.2
BAPT–Natl Mis Bapt Conv	1	0	150	186	0.7	1.4
BAPT–NBC USA	4	0	600	746	2.7	5.7
BAPT–So Bapt Conv	26	1,598	4,754	5,907	21.0	45.1
Catholic	2	NR	NR	779	2.8	5.9
CGOD–Ch God (Ander)	1	388	NR	388	1.4	3.0
Ch of Chr (Hol)	1	NR	NR	NR	-	-
CHR–Chs of Christ	2	94	105	139	0.5	1.1
Jehovah's Witness	1	NR	NR	NR	-	-
METH–AME	6	0	750	932	3.3	7.1
METH–C.M.E.	2	0	200	249	0.9	1.9
METH–Un Methodist	15	666	1,796	1,968	7.0	15.0
Non-denom Chr Chs	2	215	260	298	1.1	2.3
PENT–Ch God (Cleve)	1	20	34	42	0.1	0.3
PENT–Ch of God Proph	1	NR	53	66	0.2	0.5
PENT–COGIC	2	0	300	373	1.3	2.8
PENT–Pent Ch of God	2	140	NR	217	0.8	1.7
PENT–Un Pent Ch Intl	1	NR	NR	NR	-	-
PRES–Presb Ch Amer	2	230	252	335	1.2	2.6
Sev Day Adv	1	48	83	95	0.3	0.7

Religious Group	Number of Congregations	Number of Attendees	Number of Communicant, Confirmed, or Full Members	Adherents: Number of Adherents	Adherents: % of Total Pop.	Adherents: % of Total Adh.
MISSOURI	**9,001**	**799,394**	**1,627,977**	**2,950,894**	**49.3**	**100.0**
ADAIR	**53**	**3,709**	**6,615**	**11,006**	**43.0**	**100.0**
ANG/EPIS–Episcopal	1	46	59	74	0.3	0.7
Bahá'í	0	NR	5	5	0.0	0.0
BAPT–Free Will Bapt	2	NR	126	148	0.6	1.3
BAPT–So Bapt Conv	9	877	1,848	2,171	8.5	19.7
BUDD–Theravada	1	NR	NR	15	0.1	0.1
Catholic	2	NR	NR	1,400	5.5	12.7
CGOD–Ch God (Ander)	1	62	NR	62	0.2	0.6
Ch of Nazarene	1	235	258	332	1.3	3.0
CHR–Chr Ch (Disc)	1	102	659	774	3.0	7.0
CHR–Chr Chs & Chs Cr	3	NR	611	718	2.8	6.5
CHR–Chs of Christ	2	218	186	256	1.0	2.3
Evan Ch	2	NR	NR	NR	-	-
Evan Free Ch	1	200	NR	200	0.8	1.8
Jehovah's Witness	1	NR	NR	NR	-	-
LDS–L-D Saints	2	NR	NR	841	3.3	7.6
LUTH–Luth–MO Synod	1	195	222	268	1.0	2.4
MENN–Amish Undif	2	NR	73	170	0.7	1.5
METH–Un Methodist	7	508	1,101	1,571	6.1	14.3
Non-denom Chr Chs	6	955	1,060	1,357	5.3	12.3
PENT–Assemb of God	3	201	108	251	1.0	2.3
PENT–Ch of God Proph	1	NR	13	15	0.1	0.1
PENT–Un Pent Ch Intl	1	NR	NR	NR	-	-
PRES–Presb Ch (USA)	1	70	173	203	0.8	1.8
Salvation Army	1	25	87	145	0.6	1.3
Sev Day Adv	1	15	26	30	0.1	0.3
ANDREW	**25**	**1,390**	**4,169**	**5,616**	**32.5**	**100.0**
ANG/EPIS–Episcopal	1	8	19	19	0.1	0.3
Bahá'í	0	NR	11	11	0.1	0.2
BAPT–So Bapt Conv	5	421	1,773	2,169	12.5	38.6
Catholic	1	NR	NR	476	2.8	8.5
CHR–Chr Ch (Disc)	2	171	453	554	3.2	9.9
CHR–Chr Chs & Chs Cr	2	NR	100	122	0.7	2.2
CHR–Chs of Christ	2	85	72	103	0.6	1.8
Jehovah's Witness	1	NR	NR	NR	-	-
METH–Un Methodist	6	326	874	1,187	6.9	21.1
Non-denom Chr Chs	2	208	385	385	2.2	6.9
PENT–Ch God (Cleve)	1	30	105	128	0.7	2.3
PRES–Presb Ch (USA)	1	17	25	31	0.2	0.6
Un C of Christ	1	124	352	431	2.5	7.7
ATCHISON	**25**	**817**	**3,182**	**3,922**	**69.0**	**100.0**
ANG/EPIS–Episcopal	1	7	12	12	0.2	0.3
Bahá'í	0	NR	4	4	0.1	0.1
BAPT–So Bapt Conv	3	114	477	562	9.9	14.3
Catholic	2	NR	NR	141	2.5	3.6
CHR–Chr Ch (Disc)	3	70	413	487	8.6	12.4
Jehovah's Witness	1	NR	NR	NR	-	-
LUTH–E.L.C.A.	1	64	324	360	6.3	9.2
LUTH–Luth Cong Msn Chr	2	178	737	869	15.3	22.2
LUTH–Nor Amer Luth C	2	NR	NR	NR	-	-
METH–Un Methodist	5	232	966	1,174	20.7	29.9
Non-denom Chr Chs	1	46	45	58	1.0	1.5
PENT–Assemb of God	1	60	39	60	1.1	1.5
PENT–Ch God (Cleve)	1	20	10	12	0.2	0.3
PRES–Presb Ch (USA)	2	26	155	183	3.2	4.7
AUDRAIN	**72**	**2,626**	**9,911**	**15,139**	**59.3**	**100.0**
ANG/EPIS–Episcopal	1	25	35	36	0.1	0.2
Bahá'í	0	NR	6	6	0.0	0.0
BAPT–NBC USA	1	0	250	307	1.2	2.0
BAPT–So Bapt Conv	16	1,128	4,440	5,460	21.4	36.1
Catholic	4	NR	NR	1,900	7.4	12.6
Ch of Nazarene	2	125	129	259	1.0	1.7
CHR–Chr Ch (Disc)	4	205	821	1,010	4.0	6.7
CHR–Chr Chs & Chs Cr	9	NR	995	1,224	4.8	8.1
CHR–Chs of Christ	1	25	15	30	0.1	0.2
Int Cou Comm Ch	1	NR	NR	NR	-	-
Jehovah's Witness	2	NR	NR	NR	-	-

NR–Not Reported   - Represents no adherents reported.   Percentages may not total 100 due to rounding.

Table 3: Religious Congregations by County and Group: 2010

Religious Group	Number of Congregations	Number of Attendees	Number of Communicant, Confirmed, or Full Members	Adherents: Number of Adherents	Adherents: % of Total Pop.	Adherents: % of Total Adh.
LDS–L-D Saints	1	NR	NR	361	1.4	2.4
LUTH–Luth–MO Synod	2	179	355	446	1.7	2.9
MENN–Amish Undif	6	NR	299	833	3.3	5.5
MENN–Tamp Amish-Menn	1	77	39	77	0.3	0.5
METH–AME	1	0	150	184	0.7	1.2
METH–C.M.E.	1	0	150	184	0.7	1.2
METH–Un Methodist	4	261	686	840	3.3	5.5
METH–Wesleyan	1	10	2	13	0.1	0.1
Non-denom Chr Chs	1	170	200	212	0.8	1.4
PENT–Assemb of God	2	34	16	133	0.5	0.9
PENT–COGIC	2	0	300	369	1.4	2.4
PENT–Un Pent Ch Intl	1	NR	NR	NR	-	-
PRES–Presb Ch (USA)	7	365	985	1,211	4.7	8.0
Sev Day Adv	1	22	38	44	0.2	0.3
BARRY	**105**	**5,262**	**12,306**	**19,308**	**54.2**	**100.0**
ANG/EPIS–Episcopal	2	59	87	87	0.2	0.5
Bahá'í	0	NR	9	9	0.0	0.0
BAPT–Free Will Bapt	6	NR	378	463	1.3	2.4
BAPT–So Bapt Conv	33	2,465	7,924	9,707	27.3	50.3
Calv Chpl	1	NR	NR	NR	-	-
Catholic	4	NR	NR	3,719	10.4	19.3
Ch of Nazarene	4	190	299	370	1.0	1.9
CHR–Chr Ch (Disc)	1	40	101	124	0.3	0.6
CHR–Chr Chs & Chs Cr	4	NR	286	350	1.0	1.8
CHR–Chs of Christ	10	694	681	794	2.2	4.1
Jehovah's Witness	3	NR	NR	NR	-	-
LDS–L-D Saints	1	NR	NR	261	0.7	1.4
LUTH–E.L.C.A.	1	34	46	48	0.1	0.2
LUTH–Luth–MO Synod	4	301	624	694	1.9	3.6
METH–Un Methodist	7	418	772	901	2.5	4.7
METH–Wesleyan	1	18	13	23	0.1	0.1
Non-denom Chr Chs	6	505	660	751	2.1	3.9
PENT–Assemb of God	8	406	215	639	1.8	3.3
PENT–Ch God Apos Fth	2	NR	NR	NR	-	-
PENT–Pent Ch of God	1	70	NR	109	0.3	0.6
PENT–Un Pent Ch Intl	3	NR	NR	NR	-	-
PRES–Presb Ch (USA)	2	60	207	254	0.7	1.3
Sev Day Adv	1	2	4	5	0.0	0.0
BARTON	**39**	**2,169**	**4,708**	**6,649**	**53.6**	**100.0**
Ap Chr Ch-Amer	1	130	74	130	1.0	2.0
BAPT–Free Will Bapt	3	NR	189	236	1.9	3.5
BAPT–So Bapt Conv	7	575	1,552	1,940	15.6	29.2
Catholic	1	NR	NR	225	1.8	3.4
Ch of Nazarene	1	33	32	33	0.3	0.5
CHR–Chr Ch (Disc)	1	0	0	0	0.0	0.0
CHR–Chr Chs & Chs Cr	3	NR	690	862	7.0	13.0
CHR–Chs of Christ	1	80	85	108	0.9	1.6
Jehovah's Witness	1	NR	NR	NR	-	-
LDS–Comm of Christ	1	NR	135	135	1.1	2.0
LUTH–Luth–MO Synod	1	0	132	168	1.4	2.5
MENN–Amish Undif	1	NR	67	162	1.3	2.4
MENN–Menn Chr Fell	1	112	56	112	0.9	1.7
METH–Un Methodist	5	853	1,144	1,768	14.3	26.6
Non-denom Chr Chs	3	285	325	381	3.1	5.7
PENT–Assemb of God	2	60	53	185	1.5	2.8
PENT–Ch God (Cleve)	1	22	57	71	0.6	1.1
PENT–Ch of God Proph	1	NR	26	32	0.3	0.5
PENT–Un Pent Ch Intl	1	NR	NR	NR	-	-
PRES–Cumber Presb	1	NR	39	39	0.3	0.6
PRES–Presb Ch (USA)	1	0	19	24	0.2	0.4
Sev Day Adv	1	19	33	38	0.3	0.6
BATES	**50**	**1,883**	**6,614**	**8,855**	**51.9**	**100.0**
Bahá'í	0	NR	2	2	0.0	0.0
BAPT–Reg Bapt Gen As	1	NR	NR	NR	-	-
BAPT–So Bapt Conv	11	599	2,450	3,029	17.8	34.2
Catholic	1	NR	NR	424	2.5	4.8
Ch of Nazarene	1	62	81	169	1.0	1.9
CHR–Chr Ch (Disc)	1	115	567	701	4.1	7.9
CHR–Chr Chs & Chs Cr	8	NR	1,037	1,282	7.5	14.5
CHR–Chs of Christ	3	150	153	184	1.1	2.1

Religious Group	Number of Congregations	Number of Attendees	Number of Communicant, Confirmed, or Full Members	Adherents: Number of Adherents	Adherents: % of Total Pop.	Adherents: % of Total Adh.
Jehovah's Witness	1	NR	NR	NR	-	-
LDS–Comm of Christ	2	NR	358	358	2.1	4.0
LUTH–E.L.C.A.	1	28	56	80	0.5	0.9
LUTH–Luth–MO Synod	1	107	210	264	1.5	3.0
MENN–CG in Cr (Menn)	1	NR	158	195	1.1	2.2
METH–AME	1	0	100	124	0.7	1.4
METH–Un Methodist	10	450	1,095	1,397	8.2	15.8
Non-denom Chr Chs	1	30	40	40	0.2	0.5
PENT–Assemb of God	3	262	155	419	2.5	4.7
PRES–Presb Ch (USA)	2	60	112	138	0.8	1.6
Un C of Christ	1	20	40	49	0.3	0.6
BENTON	**43**	**2,795**	**6,738**	**8,634**	**45.3**	**100.0**
BAPT–So Bapt Conv	11	675	2,890	3,343	17.5	38.7
BRETH–Ch of Brethren	2	23	38	44	0.2	0.5
Catholic	2	NR	NR	360	1.9	4.2
Ch of Nazarene	1	48	60	60	0.3	0.7
CHR–Chs of Christ	2	55	50	65	0.3	0.8
Jehovah's Witness	1	NR	NR	NR	-	-
LDS–Comm of Christ	1	NR	179	179	0.9	2.1
LUTH–E.L.C.A.	2	200	497	591	3.1	6.8
LUTH–Luth–MO Synod	7	636	1,321	1,646	8.6	19.1
MENN–Amish Undif	0	NR	31	76	0.4	0.9
MENN–Unaffil Amish-Menn	1	108	68	108	0.6	1.3
METH–Un Methodist	6	400	895	1,251	6.6	14.5
Non-denom Chr Chs	4	525	670	707	3.7	8.2
PENT–Assemb of God	1	55	39	95	0.5	1.1
PENT–Pent Ch of God	1	70	NR	109	0.6	1.3
Unity Ch	1	NR	NR	NR	-	-
BOLLINGER	**36**	**1,094**	**2,958**	**4,864**	**39.3**	**100.0**
Bahá'í	0	NR	1	1	0.0	0.0
BAPT–Free Will Bapt	1	NR	63	77	0.6	1.6
BAPT–So Bapt Conv	10	487	1,697	2,064	16.7	42.4
Catholic	2	NR	NR	1,225	9.9	25.2
CHR–Chs of Christ	1	27	27	35	0.3	0.7
LUTH–E.L.C.A.	2	54	138	205	1.7	4.2
METH–Cong Meth	3	NR	172	209	1.7	4.3
METH–Un Methodist	7	254	405	509	4.1	10.5
Non-denom Chr Chs	3	185	345	369	3.0	7.6
PENT–Assemb of God	2	34	23	64	0.5	1.3
PENT–Ch God (Cleve)	1	15	15	18	0.1	0.4
PENT–Un Pent Ch Intl	1	NR	NR	NR	-	-
PRES–Presb Ch (USA)	3	38	72	88	0.7	1.8
BOONE	**167**	**18,190**	**40,737**	**63,949**	**39.3**	**100.0**
ANG/EPIS–Anglican NA	1	NR	NR	NR	-	-
ANG/EPIS–Episcopal	2	213	631	844	0.5	1.3
Bahá'í	2	NR	111	111	0.1	0.2
BAPT–Alliance Bapt	1	NR	NR	NR	-	-
BAPT–Amer Bapt Assn	1	NR	85	102	0.1	0.2
BAPT–Amer Bapt USA	2	267	683	819	0.5	1.3
BAPT–Free Will Bapt	1	NR	63	76	0.0	0.1
BAPT–N Am Bapt Conf	1	NR	NR	NR	-	-
BAPT–Natl Mis Bapt Conv	1	0	0	0	0.0	0.0
BAPT–Prog NBC	1	0	150	180	0.1	0.3
BAPT–So Bapt Conv	29	4,811	11,100	13,307	8.2	20.8
BUDD–Mahayana	1	NR	NR	102	0.1	0.2
BUDD–Theravada	3	NR	NR	44	0.0	0.1
Catholic	4	NR	NR	10,684	6.6	16.7
Ch Cr, Scientst	1	NR	NR	NR	-	-
Ch of Nazarene	3	143	146	215	0.1	0.3
CHR–Chr Ch (Disc)	12	1,074	5,047	6,051	3.7	9.5
CHR–Chr Chs & Chs Cr	8	NR	1,615	1,936	1.2	3.0
CHR–Chs of Christ	7	661	637	843	0.5	1.3
CHR–Int Chs of Christ	1	NR	83	100	0.1	0.2
Evan Free Ch	2	365	NR	365	0.2	0.6
FRND–Fr Gen Cf	1	NR	30	36	0.0	0.1
HINDU–Post Ren	2	NR	NR	50	0.0	0.1
HINDU–Renaiss	1	NR	NR	12	0.0	0.0
Jehovah's Witness	1	NR	NR	NR	-	-
JUD–Reform	1	92	163	440	0.3	0.7
LDS–Comm of Christ	2	NR	276	276	0.2	0.4

NR–Not Reported   - Represents no adherents reported.   Percentages may not total 100 due to rounding.

Table 3: Religious Congregations by County and Group: 2010

Religious Group	Number of Congrega-tions	Number of Attendees	Number of Communicant, Confirmed, or Full Members	Adherents: Number of Adherents	Adherents: % of Total Pop.	Adherents: % of Total Adh.
LDS–L-D Saints	6	NR	NR	1,941	1.2	3.0
LUTH–E.L.C.A.	1	235	606	752	0.5	1.2
LUTH–Luth–MO Synod	5	989	1,539	2,083	1.3	3.3
LUTH–Wisc Ev Luth Syn	1	30	32	40	0.0	0.1
MENN–Mennonite USA	1	NR	NR	NR	-	-
METH–AME	3	20	195	234	0.1	0.4
METH–AME Zion	1	0	100	120	0.1	0.2
METH–C.M.E.	1	0	100	120	0.1	0.2
METH–Un Methodist	16	1,986	4,371	5,723	3.5	8.9
Muslim Est	1	400	NR	600	0.4	0.9
Non-denom Chr Chs	15	4,013	8,230	8,463	5.2	13.2
ORTHE–Greek Orthodox	1	70	NR	200	0.1	0.3
ORTHE–Rus Orth Abroad	1	18	NR	18	0.0	0.0
PENT–Assemb of God	5	1,164	345	1,560	1.0	2.4
PENT–COGIC	1	35	50	60	0.0	0.1
PENT–Pent Ch of God	2	140	NR	217	0.1	0.3
PENT–Un Pent Ch Intl	1	NR	NR	NR	-	-
PRES–Evan Presby Ch	1	NR	1,300	1,558	1.0	2.4
PRES–Presb Ch (USA)	2	379	1,025	1,229	0.8	1.9
PRES–Presb Ch Amer	3	144	150	165	0.1	0.3
Salvation Army	1	51	87	138	0.1	0.2
Sev Day Adv	2	510	886	1,019	0.6	1.6
Un C of Christ	2	234	683	819	0.5	1.3
Unit Univ	1	146	218	297	0.2	0.5
Unity Ch	1	NR	NR	NR	-	-
BUCHANAN	**115**	**13,064**	**27,033**	**43,895**	**49.2**	**100.0**
ANG/EPIS–Episcopal	1	66	151	151	0.2	0.3
Bahá'í	1	NR	32	32	0.0	0.1
BAPT–NBC USA	1	130	140	171	0.2	0.4
BAPT–So Bapt Conv	23	2,871	8,957	10,955	12.3	25.0
BRETH–Ch of Brethren	1	16	28	34	0.0	0.1
Calv Chpl	1	NR	NR	NR	-	-
Catholic	9	NR	NR	8,934	10.0	20.4
Ch Cr, Scientst	1	NR	NR	NR	-	-
Ch God (7th Day)	1	NR	NR	NR	-	-
Ch of Nazarene	2	160	322	419	0.5	1.0
CHR–Chr Ch (Disc)	4	623	1,433	1,753	2.0	4.0
CHR–Chr Chs & Chs Cr	5	NR	1,320	1,614	1.8	3.7
CHR–Chs of Christ	1	85	70	90	0.1	0.2
Jehovah's Witness	2	NR	NR	NR	-	-
JUD–Reform	1	13	23	62	0.1	0.1
LDS–Comm of Christ	2	NR	364	364	0.4	0.8
LDS–L-D Saints	2	NR	NR	1,532	1.7	3.5
LUTH–E.L.C.A.	1	141	259	310	0.3	0.7
LUTH–Luth–MO Synod	2	508	944	1,208	1.4	2.8
METH–AME	2	0	200	245	0.3	0.6
METH–Un Methodist	14	1,247	3,241	4,155	4.7	9.5
METH–Wesleyan	1	55	0	72	0.1	0.2
Muslim Est	1	134	NR	308	0.3	0.7
Non-denom Chr Chs	10	5,115	6,840	7,001	7.8	15.9
PENT–Assemb of God	4	722	794	1,262	1.4	2.9
PENT–Ch God (Cleve)	3	143	343	420	0.5	1.0
PENT–Int Foursq Gos	1	23	26	32	0.0	0.1
PENT–Pent Ch of God	2	140	NR	217	0.2	0.5
PENT–Un Pent Ch Intl	2	NR	NR	NR	-	-
PRES–Cumber Presb	1	NR	16	35	0.0	0.1
PRES–Presb Ch (USA)	7	447	764	934	1.0	2.1
Salvation Army	1	39	136	808	0.9	1.8
Sev Day Adv	2	281	489	562	0.6	1.3
Un Breth in Cr	1	50	0	43	0.0	0.1
Un C of Christ	1	55	141	172	0.2	0.4
Unity Ch	1	NR	NR	NR	-	-
BUTLER	**77**	**6,576**	**11,907**	**17,973**	**42.0**	**100.0**
ANG/EPIS–Episcopal	1	32	36	97	0.2	0.5
Bahá'í	0	NR	2	2	0.0	0.0
BAPT–Free Will Bapt	1	NR	63	77	0.2	0.4
BAPT–Natl Mis Bapt Conv	2	0	300	367	0.9	2.0
BAPT–So Bapt Conv	22	1,794	5,350	6,541	15.3	36.4
Catholic	1	NR	NR	2,143	5.0	11.9
CGOD–Ch God (Ander)	2	247	NR	247	0.6	1.4
Ch of Nazarene	1	64	71	100	0.2	0.6
CHR–Chr Ch (Disc)	2	110	518	633	1.5	3.5
CHR–Chs of Christ	7	447	413	519	1.2	2.9
HINDU–Post Ren	1	NR	NR	25	0.1	0.1
Jehovah's Witness	1	NR	NR	NR	-	-
LDS–L-D Saints	1	NR	NR	638	1.5	3.5
LUTH–E.L.C.A.	1	25	55	69	0.2	0.4
LUTH–Luth–MO Synod	1	70	286	343	0.8	1.9
METH–AME	1	0	150	183	0.4	1.0
METH–Un Methodist	6	458	864	1,016	2.4	5.7
Muslim Est	1	134	NR	308	0.7	1.7
Non-denom Chr Chs	9	2,015	2,360	2,631	6.1	14.6
PENT–Assemb of God	5	243	127	330	0.8	1.8
PENT–Ch God (Cleve)	1	554	861	1,053	2.5	5.9
PENT–Ch of God Proph	1	NR	21	26	0.1	0.1
PENT–Intl Pent Holiness	2	125	126	154	0.4	0.9
PENT–Pent Ch of God	1	70	NR	109	0.3	0.6
PENT–Un Pent Ch Intl	2	NR	NR	NR	-	-
PRES–Presb Ch (USA)	2	85	116	142	0.3	0.8
Sev Day Adv	1	78	135	155	0.4	0.9
Un C of Christ	1	25	53	65	0.2	0.4
CALDWELL	**30**	**996**	**3,258**	**4,196**	**44.5**	**100.0**
BAPT–So Bapt Conv	9	498	1,764	2,186	23.2	52.1
Catholic	1	NR	NR	104	1.1	2.5
Ch of Nazarene	1	77	92	99	1.1	2.4
CHR–Chr Ch (Disc)	1	0	0	0	0.0	0.0
CHR–Chr Chs & Chs Cr	2	NR	100	124	1.3	3.0
CHR–Chs of Christ	2	55	51	63	0.7	1.5
Christian Un	3	NR	NR	NR	-	-
LDS–Comm of Christ	1	NR	182	182	1.9	4.3
METH–Un Methodist	7	298	909	1,184	12.6	28.2
PENT–Assemb of God	2	68	35	99	1.1	2.4
Un C of Christ	1	0	125	155	1.6	3.7
CALLAWAY	**72**	**3,886**	**10,405**	**15,662**	**35.3**	**100.0**
ANG/EPIS–Episcopal	2	34	87	118	0.3	0.8
Bahá'í	0	NR	11	11	0.0	0.1
BAPT–Natl Mis Bapt Conv	1	0	150	181	0.4	1.2
BAPT–So Bapt Conv	20	1,637	5,399	6,516	14.7	41.6
Catholic	3	NR	NR	2,193	4.9	14.0
Ch of Nazarene	1	148	242	357	0.8	2.3
CHR–Chr Ch (Disc)	8	250	1,112	1,342	3.0	8.6
CHR–Chr Chs & Chs Cr	1	NR	330	398	0.9	2.5
CHR–Chs of Christ	1	70	90	110	0.2	0.7
Jehovah's Witness	2	NR	NR	NR	-	-
LDS–Comm of Christ	1	NR	138	138	0.3	0.9
LDS–L-D Saints	1	NR	NR	488	1.1	3.1
LUTH–Luth–MO Synod	2	189	375	489	1.1	3.1
METH–AME	1	0	100	121	0.3	0.8
METH–Un Methodist	15	581	1,128	1,474	3.3	9.4
Non-denom Chr Chs	3	520	575	663	1.5	4.2
PENT–Assemb of God	2	98	55	216	0.5	1.4
PENT–Pent Ch of God	1	70	NR	109	0.2	0.7
PRES–Presb Ch (USA)	5	247	531	641	1.4	4.1
Sev Day Adv	1	22	38	44	0.1	0.3
Un C of Christ	1	20	44	53	0.1	0.3
CAMDEN	**69**	**6,213**	**11,332**	**17,045**	**38.7**	**100.0**
ANG/EPIS–Episcopal	1	68	102	105	0.2	0.6
Bahá'í	0	NR	6	6	0.0	0.0
BAPT–So Bapt Conv	17	1,684	4,829	5,641	12.8	33.1
Catholic	2	NR	NR	1,950	4.4	11.4
Ch of Nazarene	1	124	112	170	0.4	1.0
CHR–Chr Ch (Disc)	3	194	985	1,151	2.6	6.8
CHR–Chr Chs & Chs Cr	2	NR	50	58	0.1	0.3
CHR–Chs of Christ	5	190	190	231	0.5	1.4
Evan Free Ch	1	45	NR	45	0.1	0.3
Jehovah's Witness	1	NR	NR	NR	-	-
LDS–Comm of Christ	1	NR	179	179	0.4	1.1
LDS–L-D Saints	2	NR	NR	900	2.0	5.3
LUTH–E.L.C.A.	2	211	447	574	1.3	3.4
LUTH–Luth Cong Msn Chr	1	42	35	41	0.1	0.2
LUTH–Luth–MO Synod	3	473	801	925	2.1	5.4

NR–Not Reported - Represents no adherents reported. Percentages may not total 100 due to rounding.

Table 3: Religious Congregations by County and Group: 2010

Religious Group	Number of Congrega-tions	Number of Attendees	Number of Communicant, Confirmed, or Full Members	Adherents: Number of Adherents	Adherents: % of Total Pop.	Adherents: % of Total Adh.
METH–Free Methodist	1	31	2	31	0.1	0.2
METH–Un Methodist	4	391	935	1,172	2.7	6.9
Non-denom Chr Chs	11	1,660	2,070	2,372	5.4	13.9
PENT–Assemb of God	5	819	303	1,051	2.4	6.2
PENT–Int Foursq Gos	1	68	76	89	0.2	0.5
PENT–Pent Ch of God	1	70	NR	109	0.2	0.6
PRES–Presb Ch (USA)	2	125	179	209	0.5	1.2
Sev Day Adv	1	18	31	36	0.1	0.2
Unity Ch	1	NR	NR	NR	-	-
CAPE GIRARDEAU	**116**	**16,750**	**29,197**	**58,180**	**76.9**	**100.0**
ANG/EPIS–Episcopal	1	64	140	150	0.2	0.3
Bahá'í	0	NR	11	11	0.0	0.0
BAPT–Amer Bapt Assn	1	NR	20	24	0.0	0.0
BAPT–Free Will Bapt	2	NR	126	152	0.2	0.3
BAPT–So Bapt Conv	22	3,870	7,831	9,440	12.5	16.2
Catholic	4	NR	NR	11,162	14.8	19.2
CGOD–Ch God (Ander)	2	99	NR	99	0.1	0.2
Ch Cr, Scientist	1	NR	NR	NR	-	-
Ch of Nazarene	2	105	284	395	0.5	0.7
CHR–Chr Ch (Disc)	1	107	372	448	0.6	0.8
CHR–Chr Chs & Chs Cr	1	NR	195	235	0.3	0.4
CHR–Chs of Christ	5	391	371	524	0.7	0.9
Jehovah's Witness	3	NR	NR	NR	-	-
LDS–L-D Saints	3	NR	NR	787	1.0	1.4
LUTH–E.L.C.A.	1	87	138	204	0.3	0.4
LUTH–Evan Luth Syn	1	0	81	101	0.1	0.2
LUTH–Luth Ch-Am Asc	1	NR	NR	NR	-	-
LUTH–Luth–MO Synod	16	3,839	7,830	9,647	12.7	16.6
METH–AME	2	0	250	301	0.4	0.5
METH–Cong Meth	1	NR	25	30	0.0	0.1
METH–Un Methodist	16	3,429	4,773	6,658	8.8	11.4
Muslim Est	1	30	NR	90	0.1	0.2
Non-denom Chr Chs	5	1,530	4,055	4,178	5.5	7.2
ORTHE–Ant Orth of NA	1	19	NR	27	0.0	0.0
PENT–Assemb of God	6	2,470	731	11,130	14.7	19.1
PENT–Ch God (Cleve)	1	15	125	151	0.2	0.3
PENT–Ch of God Proph	1	NR	29	35	0.0	0.1
PENT–COGIC	2	30	190	229	0.3	0.4
PENT–Un Pent Ch Intl	3	NR	NR	NR	-	-
PRES–Presb Ch (USA)	3	240	528	636	0.8	1.1
Salvation Army	1	89	97	142	0.2	0.2
Sev Day Adv	2	56	98	113	0.1	0.2
Un C of Christ	4	280	897	1,081	1.4	1.9
CARROLL	**32**	**1,288**	**5,407**	**6,969**	**75.0**	**100.0**
Bahá'í	0	NR	1	1	0.0	0.0
BAPT–So Bapt Conv	13	531	3,203	3,884	41.8	55.7
Catholic	2	NR	NR	419	4.5	6.0
Ch of Nazarene	1	26	56	56	0.6	0.8
CHR–Chr Ch (Disc)	3	137	520	631	6.8	9.1
CHR–Chs of Christ	1	30	32	35	0.4	0.5
Jehovah's Witness	1	NR	NR	NR	-	-
LUTH–Luth–MO Synod	2	228	545	675	7.3	9.7
MENN–Amish Undif	1	NR	58	145	1.6	2.1
METH–AME	1	0	100	121	1.3	1.7
METH–Un Methodist	5	191	684	767	8.3	11.0
Non-denom Chr Chs	1	100	150	150	1.6	2.2
PENT–Assemb of God	1	45	58	85	0.9	1.2
CARTER	**23**	**744**	**1,669**	**2,218**	**35.4**	**100.0**
Bahá'í	0	NR	5	5	0.1	0.2
BAPT–Free Will Bapt	2	NR	126	155	2.5	7.0
BAPT–So Bapt Conv	5	245	993	1,218	19.4	54.9
Catholic	1	NR	NR	98	1.6	4.4
CGOD–Ch God (Ander)	1	45	NR	45	0.7	2.0
CHR–Chs of Christ	1	34	30	38	0.6	1.7
Jehovah's Witness	1	NR	NR	NR	-	-
METH–Un Methodist	4	109	146	199	3.2	9.0
Non-denom Chr Chs	1	100	150	150	2.4	6.8
PENT–Assemb of God	2	204	173	254	4.1	11.5
PENT–Ch of God Proph	3	NR	37	45	0.7	2.0
PENT–Un Pent Ch Intl	1	NR	NR	NR	-	-

Religious Group	Number of Congrega-tions	Number of Attendees	Number of Communicant, Confirmed, or Full Members	Adherents: Number of Adherents	Adherents: % of Total Pop.	Adherents: % of Total Adh.
Un C of Christ	1	7	9	11	0.2	0.5
CASS	**106**	**10,912**	**22,690**	**36,175**	**36.4**	**100.0**
ANG/EPIS–Episcopal	1	25	100	100	0.1	0.3
Bahá'í	0	NR	5	5	0.0	0.0
BAPT–Amer Bapt Assn	1	NR	150	188	0.2	0.5
BAPT–Free Will Bapt	2	NR	126	158	0.2	0.4
BAPT–Ind Bapt Flwsp Intl	1	NR	NR	NR	-	-
BAPT–So Bapt Conv	27	4,127	12,585	15,812	15.9	43.7
Catholic	3	NR	NR	6,301	6.3	17.4
Ch of God Gen Conf	1	NR	54	68	0.1	0.2
Ch of Nazarene	5	514	593	732	0.7	2.0
CHR–Chr Ch (Disc)	7	547	1,713	2,152	2.2	5.9
CHR–Chr Chs & Chs Cr	1	NR	0	0	0.0	0.0
CHR–Chs of Christ	7	389	369	465	0.5	1.3
Evan Free Ch	4	445	NR	445	0.4	1.2
Ind Fund Churches	1	NR	NR	NR	-	-
Jehovah's Witness	3	NR	NR	NR	-	-
LDS–Comm of Christ	2	NR	358	358	0.4	1.0
LUTH–E.L.C.A.	1	70	96	113	0.1	0.3
LUTH–Luth–MO Synod	2	394	779	1,046	1.1	2.9
LUTH–Wisc Ev Luth Syn	1	62	86	112	0.1	0.3
MENN–Fel Evg Ch	2	351	250	314	0.3	0.9
METH–Free Methodist	1	13	0	13	0.0	0.0
METH–Un Methodist	8	1,222	2,875	4,005	4.0	11.1
Non-denom Chr Chs	12	1,670	1,947	2,245	2.3	6.2
PENT–Assemb of God	7	912	366	1,244	1.3	3.4
PENT–COGIC	1	10	6	8	0.0	0.0
PENT–Un Pent Ch Intl	1	NR	NR	NR	-	-
PRES–Presb Ch (USA)	4	161	232	291	0.3	0.8
CEDAR	**36**	**1,781**	**4,513**	**6,694**	**47.9**	**100.0**
Bahá'í	0	NR	4	4	0.0	0.1
BAPT–Free Will Bapt	2	NR	126	154	1.1	2.3
BAPT–So Bapt Conv	6	439	1,921	2,344	16.8	35.0
Catholic	2	NR	NR	230	1.6	3.4
Ch of Nazarene	1	62	60	86	0.6	1.3
CHR–Chr Ch (Disc)	1	53	140	171	1.2	2.6
CHR–Chr Chs & Chs Cr	5	NR	630	769	5.5	11.5
CHR–Chs of Christ	2	165	170	190	1.4	2.8
Jehovah's Witness	1	NR	NR	NR	-	-
LDS–Comm of Christ	2	NR	314	314	2.2	4.7
LDS–L-D Saints	1	NR	NR	447	3.2	6.7
LUTH–Luth–MO Synod	1	50	101	122	0.9	1.8
MENN–Amish Undif	1	NR	36	132	0.9	2.0
METH–Free Methodist	1	14	14	14	0.1	0.2
METH–Un Methodist	4	229	496	638	4.6	9.5
Non-denom Chr Chs	2	300	350	400	2.9	6.0
PENT–Assemb of God	2	444	119	640	4.6	9.6
PRES–Presb Ch (USA)	2	25	32	39	0.3	0.6
CHARITON	**37**	**976**	**3,205**	**6,066**	**77.5**	**100.0**
BAPT–NBC USA	1	25	30	36	0.5	0.6
BAPT–So Bapt Conv	6	253	1,089	1,318	16.8	21.7
Catholic	5	NR	NR	2,135	27.3	35.2
CHR–Chr Ch (Disc)	5	30	135	163	2.1	2.7
CHR–Chr Chs & Chs Cr	1	NR	96	116	1.5	1.9
LUTH–E.L.C.A.	1	19	43	43	0.5	0.7
LUTH–Luth–MO Synod	3	277	664	828	10.6	13.6
MENN–Amish Undif	1	NR	49	143	1.8	2.4
METH–AME	2	0	200	242	3.1	4.0
METH–Un Methodist	12	372	899	1,042	13.3	17.2
CHRISTIAN	**99**	**18,081**	**18,620**	**44,992**	**58.1**	**100.0**
Bahá'í	0	NR	9	9	0.0	0.0
BAPT–Free Will Bapt	2	NR	126	160	0.2	0.4
BAPT–Ref Bapt Ch	1	NR	NR	NR	-	-
BAPT–So Bapt Conv	41	4,951	10,716	13,638	17.6	30.3
Catholic	3	NR	NR	2,709	3.5	6.0
Ch of Nazarene	2	155	301	312	0.4	0.7
CHR–Chr Ch (Disc)	5	182	805	1,025	1.3	2.3
CHR–Chr Chs & Chs Cr	2	NR	300	382	0.5	0.8

NR–Not Reported - Represents no adherents reported. Percentages may not total 100 due to rounding.

Table 3: Religious Congregations by County and Group: 2010

Religious Group	Number of Congregations	Number of Attendees	Number of Communicant, Confirmed, or Full Members	Adherents: Number of Adherents	Adherents: % of Total Pop.	Adherents: % of Total Adh.
CHR–Chs of Christ	8	881	868	1,007	1.3	2.2
Christian Un	1	NR	NR	NR	-	-
Jehovah's Witness	2	NR	NR	NR	-	-
LUTH–Luth-MO Synod	1	100	71	95	0.1	0.2
METH–Free Methodist	1	17	0	17	0.0	0.0
METH–Un Methodist	9	1,176	1,543	2,395	3.1	5.3
Non-denom Chr Chs	6	735	855	968	1.3	2.2
PENT–Assemb of God	7	9,581	2,454	21,528	27.8	47.8
PENT–Int Foursq Gos	1	32	33	42	0.1	0.1
PENT–Un Pent Ch Intl	2	NR	NR	NR	-	-
PRES–Evan Presby Ch	1	NR	0	0	0.0	0.0
PRES–Presb Ch (USA)	1	63	96	122	0.2	0.3
PRES–Presb Ch Amer	1	85	250	350	0.5	0.8
Sev Day Adv	1	55	96	110	0.1	0.2
Un C of Christ	1	68	97	123	0.2	0.3
CLARK	**26**	**829**	**2,478**	**3,375**	**47.3**	**100.0**
BAPT–So Bapt Conv	5	209	1,007	1,233	17.3	36.5
Catholic	3	NR	NR	240	3.4	7.1
CHR–Chr Ch (Disc)	3	125	451	552	7.7	16.4
CHR–Chs of Christ	1	35	35	40	0.6	1.2
MENN–Amish Undif	1	NR	41	117	1.6	3.5
METH–Un Methodist	7	137	349	467	6.5	13.8
Non-denom Chr Chs	2	90	90	112	1.6	3.3
PRES–Presb Ch (USA)	2	49	88	108	1.5	3.2
Sev Day Adv	1	34	59	68	1.0	2.0
Un C of Christ	1	150	358	438	6.1	13.0
CLAY	**215**	**31,611**	**57,117**	**105,280**	**47.4**	**100.0**
ANG/EPIS–Episcopal	3	325	689	737	0.3	0.7
Bahá'í	0	NR	25	25	0.0	0.0
BAPT–Amer Bapt Assn	2	NR	200	251	0.1	0.2
BAPT–Free Will Bapt	1	NR	63	79	0.0	0.1
BAPT–Ind Bapt Flwsp Intl	1	NR	NR	NR	-	-
BAPT–So Bapt Conv	44	7,797	18,742	23,504	10.6	22.3
Calv Chpl	1	NR	NR	NR	-	-
Catholic	9	NR	NR	23,511	10.6	22.3
CGOD–Ch God (Ander)	1	50	NR	50	0.0	0.0
Ch Cr, Scientst	1	NR	NR	NR	-	-
Ch of Nazarene	5	655	680	1,085	0.5	1.0
CHR–Chr Ch (Disc)	13	1,268	4,312	5,408	2.4	5.1
CHR–Chr Chs & Chs Cr	6	NR	379	475	0.2	0.5
CHR–Chs of Christ	9	1,052	938	1,184	0.5	1.1
Christian Un	2	NR	NR	NR	-	-
Evan Cov Ch	2	215	220	280	0.1	0.3
Evan Free Ch	1	80	NR	80	0.0	0.1
Ind Fund Churches	1	NR	NR	NR	-	-
Int Cou Comm Ch	1	NR	NR	NR	-	-
Jehovah's Witness	5	NR	NR	NR	-	-
LDS–Comm of Christ	4	NR	764	764	0.3	0.7
LDS–L-D Saints	9	NR	NR	3,741	1.7	3.6
LUTH–E.L.C.A.	3	434	874	1,125	0.5	1.1
LUTH–Luth Cong Msn Chr	1	30	30	38	0.0	0.0
LUTH–Luth-MO Synod	5	1,047	2,188	2,806	1.3	2.7
METH–AME	1	0	100	125	0.1	0.1
METH–Un Methodist	17	3,406	7,844	12,219	5.5	11.6
METH–Wesleyan	1	32	24	42	0.0	0.0
Muslim Est	3	402	NR	924	0.4	0.9
Non-denom Chr Chs	27	9,160	12,295	13,338	6.0	12.7
ORTHE–Orth Ch in Amer	1	29	NR	44	0.0	0.0
PENT–Assemb of God	11	1,955	1,060	5,883	2.7	5.6
PENT–Ch God (Cleve)	1	15	39	49	0.0	0.0
PENT–Ch of God Proph	1	NR	36	45	0.0	0.0
PENT–Intl Pent Holiness	1	25	42	53	0.0	0.1
PENT–Open Bible Std	1	15	NR	15	0.0	0.0
PENT–Pent Ch of God	4	280	NR	435	0.2	0.4
PENT–Un Pent Ch Intl	5	NR	NR	NR	-	-
PENT–Vineyard	2	2,829	4,130	5,179	2.3	4.9
PRES–Evan Presby Ch	1	NR	563	706	0.3	0.7
PRES–Presb Ch (USA)	3	206	329	413	0.2	0.4
PRES–Presb Ch Amer	1	60	63	77	0.0	0.1
Salvation Army	1	88	138	163	0.1	0.2
Sev Day Adv	1	68	118	136	0.1	0.1
Un C of Christ	1	88	232	291	0.1	0.3
Unity Ch	1	NR	NR	NR	-	-
CLINTON	**40**	**2,282**	**6,626**	**10,607**	**51.1**	**100.0**
Bahá'í	0	NR	4	4	0.0	0.0
BAPT–NBC USA	1	35	50	62	0.3	0.6
BAPT–So Bapt Conv	7	960	2,897	3,566	17.2	33.6
Catholic	3	NR	NR	1,314	6.3	12.4
CHR–Chr Ch (Disc)	4	353	1,682	2,070	10.0	19.5
CHR–Chr Chs & Chs Cr	1	NR	93	114	0.5	1.1
CHR–Chs of Christ	2	75	82	102	0.5	1.0
Jehovah's Witness	2	NR	NR	NR	-	-
LDS–Comm of Christ	2	NR	364	364	1.8	3.4
LDS–L-D Saints	3	NR	NR	783	3.8	7.4
LUTH–Luth-MO Synod	1	63	140	188	0.9	1.8
METH–Un Methodist	5	413	1,001	1,321	6.4	12.5
Non-denom Chr Chs	1	100	150	150	0.7	1.4
PENT–Assemb of God	2	128	62	336	1.6	3.2
PENT–Ch God (Cleve)	2	41	49	60	0.3	0.6
PENT–Pent Ch of God	1	70	NR	109	0.5	1.0
PENT–Un Pent Ch Intl	1	NR	NR	NR	-	-
PRES–Presb Ch (USA)	2	44	52	64	0.3	0.6
COLE	**93**	**10,979**	**22,816**	**52,877**	**69.6**	**100.0**
ANG/EPIS–Episcopal	1	140	400	426	0.6	0.8
Bahá'í	0	NR	25	25	0.0	0.0
BAPT–NBC USA	1	150	300	368	0.5	0.7
BAPT–So Bapt Conv	21	2,900	9,738	11,941	15.7	22.6
BUDD–Theravada	2	NR	NR	314	0.4	0.6
Catholic	9	NR	NR	20,145	26.5	38.1
CGOD–Ch God (Ander)	1	120	NR	120	0.2	0.2
Ch of Nazarene	1	88	105	145	0.2	0.3
CHR–Chr Ch (Disc)	3	318	1,042	1,278	1.7	2.4
CHR–Chr Chs & Chs Cr	4	NR	570	699	0.9	1.3
CHR–Chs of Christ	3	481	456	610	0.8	1.2
Christian Un	1	NR	NR	NR	-	-
Evan Free Ch	1	200	NR	200	0.3	0.4
Jehovah's Witness	1	NR	NR	NR	-	-
JUD–Reform	1	15	26	70	0.1	0.1
LDS–Comm of Christ	1	NR	138	138	0.2	0.3
LDS–L-D Saints	1	NR	NR	718	0.9	1.4
LUTH–E.L.C.A.	3	321	744	950	1.3	1.8
LUTH–Evan Luth Syn	1	54	71	89	0.1	0.2
LUTH–Luth-MO Synod	5	1,208	2,940	3,892	5.1	7.4
METH–AME	1	0	150	184	0.2	0.3
METH–AME Zion	1	0	100	123	0.2	0.2
METH–Free Methodist	1	11	17	17	0.0	0.0
METH–Un Methodist	5	725	1,747	2,187	2.9	4.1
Muslim Est	1	134	NR	308	0.4	0.6
New Apost Ch	1	NR	NR	NR	-	-
Non-denom Chr Chs	7	1,250	1,454	1,613	2.1	3.1
PENT–Assemb of God	3	889	458	1,306	1.7	2.5
PENT–COGIC	1	0	150	184	0.2	0.3
PENT–Pent Ch of God	2	1,270	NR	1,973	2.6	3.7
PENT–Un Pent Ch Intl	2	NR	NR	NR	-	-
PRES–Presb Ch (USA)	1	310	902	1,106	1.5	2.1
Salvation Army	1	49	78	279	0.4	0.5
Sev Day Adv	1	59	103	118	0.2	0.2
Un C of Christ	2	247	1,060	1,300	1.7	2.5
Unit Univ	1	40	42	51	0.1	0.1
Unity Ch	1	NR	NR	NR	-	-
COOPER	**53**	**2,099**	**5,841**	**9,553**	**54.3**	**100.0**
ANG/EPIS–Episcopal	1	19	33	33	0.2	0.3
Bahá'í	0	NR	3	3	0.0	0.0
BAPT–So Bapt Conv	14	576	2,234	2,700	15.3	28.3
BUDD–Mahayana	1	NR	NR	16	0.1	0.2
Catholic	4	NR	NR	2,117	12.0	22.2
CHR–Chr Ch (Disc)	2	105	318	384	2.2	4.0
CHR–Chr Chs & Chs Cr	1	NR	210	254	1.4	2.7
CHR–Chs of Christ	2	51	49	64	0.4	0.7
Jehovah's Witness	1	NR	NR	NR	-	-
LDS–Comm of Christ	1	NR	138	138	0.8	1.4

NR–Not Reported   - Represents no adherents reported.   Percentages may not total 100 due to rounding.

Table 3: Religious Congregations by County and Group: 2010

Religious Group	Number of Congrega-tions	Number of Attendees	Number of Communicant, Confirmed, or Full Members	Adherents: Number of Adherents	Adherents: % of Total Pop.	Adherents: % of Total Adh.
LUTH–Luth–MO Synod	4	283	815	1,036	5.9	10.8
MENN–Amish Undif	2	NR	86	242	1.4	2.5
METH–AME	2	60	185	224	1.3	2.3
METH–Un Methodist	4	249	736	836	4.7	8.8
Non-denom Chr Chs	2	140	200	200	1.1	2.1
PENT–Assemb of God	1	68	28	85	0.5	0.9
PENT–Ch of God Proph	1	NR	46	56	0.3	0.6
PENT–Int Foursq Gos	1	84	159	192	1.1	2.0
PENT–Open Bible Std	1	140	NR	140	0.8	1.5
PENT–Pent Ch of God	1	70	NR	109	0.6	1.1
PENT–Un Pent Ch Intl	1	NR	NR	NR	-	-
PRES–Presb Ch (USA)	3	108	213	257	1.5	2.7
Sev Day Adv	1	22	39	45	0.3	0.5
Un C of Christ	2	124	349	422	2.4	4.4
CRAWFORD	**49**	**2,672**	**4,982**	**8,094**	**32.8**	**100.0**
Bahá'í	0	NR	8	8	0.0	0.1
BAPT–Free Will Bapt	2	NR	126	155	0.6	1.9
BAPT–So Bapt Conv	15	858	2,542	3,131	12.7	38.7
Catholic	3	NR	NR	1,134	4.6	14.0
CHR–Chr Chs & Chs Cr	1	NR	50	62	0.3	0.8
CHR–Chs of Christ	1	80	78	92	0.4	1.1
Evan Free Ch	1	200	NR	200	0.8	2.5
Jehovah's Witness	1	NR	NR	NR	-	-
LUTH–Luth–MO Synod	2	135	404	534	2.2	6.6
METH–Un Methodist	2	141	291	439	1.8	5.4
Non-denom Chr Chs	3	350	475	488	2.0	6.0
PENT–Assemb of God	8	509	164	706	2.9	8.7
PENT–Ch God (Cleve)	2	158	552	680	2.8	8.4
PENT–Pent Ch of God	1	70	NR	109	0.4	1.3
PENT–Un Pent Ch Intl	3	NR	NR	NR	-	-
PRES–Presb Ch (USA)	3	142	242	298	1.2	3.7
Sev Day Adv	1	29	50	58	0.2	0.7
DADE	**39**	**1,570**	**3,710**	**5,295**	**67.2**	**100.0**
BAPT–So Bapt Conv	14	715	2,259	2,711	34.4	51.2
Catholic	1	NR	NR	88	1.1	1.7
Ch of God Gen Conf	1	NR	5	6	0.1	0.1
CHR–Chr Ch (Disc)	2	70	150	180	2.3	3.4
CHR–Chr Chs & Chs Cr	3	NR	250	300	3.8	5.7
CHR–Chs of Christ	4	188	173	224	2.8	4.2
LDS–L-D Saints	1	NR	NR	664	8.4	12.5
LUTH–Luth–MO Synod	1	305	485	610	7.7	11.5
METH–Un Methodist	4	153	273	313	4.0	5.9
ORTHE–Serb Orth USA	1	3	NR	3	0.0	0.1
PENT–Assemb of God	2	85	46	114	1.4	2.2
PRES–Cumber Presb	1	NR	4	4	0.1	0.1
PRES–Presb Ch (USA)	4	51	65	78	1.0	1.5
DALLAS	**31**	**2,305**	**4,005**	**5,518**	**32.9**	**100.0**
Bahá'í	0	NR	9	9	0.1	0.2
BAPT–Free Will Bapt	4	NR	252	311	1.9	5.6
BAPT–So Bapt Conv	10	599	1,957	2,412	14.4	43.7
Catholic	1	NR	NR	129	0.8	2.3
Ch God (7th Day)	1	NR	NR	NR	-	-
CHR–Chr Ch (Disc)	1	89	208	256	1.5	4.6
CHR–Chr Chs & Chs Cr	2	NR	125	154	0.9	2.8
CHR–Chs of Christ	2	120	117	157	0.9	2.8
Jehovah's Witness	1	NR	NR	NR	-	-
LUTH–Luth–MO Synod	1	15	38	42	0.3	0.8
MENN–Tamp Amish-Menn	1	950	536	950	5.7	17.2
METH–Un Methodist	2	141	276	402	2.4	7.3
Non-denom Chr Chs	3	240	340	350	2.1	6.3
PENT–Assemb of God	2	151	147	346	2.1	6.3
DAVIESS	**36**	**1,209**	**3,836**	**5,631**	**66.8**	**100.0**
Bahá'í	0	NR	1	1	0.0	0.0
BAPT–So Bapt Conv	9	461	2,056	2,596	30.8	46.1
Catholic	1	NR	NR	92	1.1	1.6
CHR–Chr Ch (Disc)	3	182	609	769	9.1	13.7
CHR–Chs of Christ	3	60	42	69	0.8	1.2
LDS–L-D Saints	1	NR	NR	351	4.2	6.2

Religious Group	Number of Congrega-tions	Number of Attendees	Number of Communicant, Confirmed, or Full Members	Adherents: Number of Adherents	Adherents: % of Total Pop.	Adherents: % of Total Adh.
MENN–Amish Undif	6	NR	255	596	7.1	10.6
MENN–CG in Cr (Menn)	1	NR	76	96	1.1	1.7
METH–Un Methodist	6	140	407	496	5.9	8.8
Non-denom Chr Chs	2	264	250	330	3.9	5.9
PENT–Assemb of God	2	75	64	144	1.7	2.6
PRES–Presb Ch (USA)	1	0	29	37	0.4	0.7
Sev Day Adv	1	27	47	54	0.6	1.0
DEKALB	**28**	**1,005**	**2,962**	**3,683**	**28.6**	**100.0**
BAPT–Free Will Bapt	1	NR	63	73	0.6	2.0
BAPT–So Bapt Conv	8	330	1,194	1,386	10.8	37.6
Catholic	1	NR	NR	146	1.1	4.0
Ch of Nazarene	1	119	177	177	1.4	4.8
CHR–Chr Ch (Disc)	2	27	182	211	1.6	5.7
CHR–Chr Chs & Chs Cr	1	NR	0	0	0.0	0.0
CHR–Chs of Christ	1	25	24	28	0.2	0.8
LDS–Comm of Christ	3	NR	546	546	4.2	14.8
MENN–Menn Chr Fell	1	88	46	88	0.7	2.4
METH–Un Methodist	7	256	599	732	5.7	19.9
PENT–Assemb of God	1	160	113	275	2.1	7.5
PRES–Presb Ch (USA)	1	0	18	21	0.2	0.6
DENT	**36**	**3,026**	**6,006**	**8,448**	**54.0**	**100.0**
BAPT–Free Will Bapt	1	NR	63	77	0.5	0.9
BAPT–So Bapt Conv	13	1,766	4,501	5,487	35.0	65.0
Catholic	1	NR	NR	456	2.9	5.4
CGOD–Ch God (Ander)	1	13	NR	13	0.1	0.2
CHR–Chr Chs & Chs Cr	1	NR	200	244	1.6	2.9
CHR–Chs of Christ	3	255	239	299	1.9	3.5
LDS–L-D Saints	1	NR	NR	178	1.1	2.1
LUTH–E.L.C.A.	1	33	35	51	0.3	0.6
LUTH–Luth–MO Synod	1	70	150	191	1.2	2.3
MENN–Ber Amish-Menn	1	139	74	139	0.9	1.6
METH–Un Methodist	4	204	404	408	2.6	4.8
Non-denom Chr Chs	2	95	95	119	0.8	1.4
PENT–Assemb of God	2	343	156	575	3.7	6.8
PENT–Pent Ch of God	1	70	NR	109	0.7	1.3
PENT–Un Pent Ch Intl	1	NR	NR	NR	-	-
PRES–Cumber Presb	1	NR	23	26	0.2	0.3
Sev Day Adv	1	38	66	76	0.5	0.9
DOUGLAS	**20**	**1,072**	**1,538**	**2,915**	**21.3**	**100.0**
Bahá'í	0	NR	1	1	0.0	0.0
BAPT–Free Will Bapt	2	NR	126	152	1.1	5.2
BAPT–So Bapt Conv	4	187	538	648	4.7	22.2
Catholic	1	NR	NR	245	1.8	8.4
CGOD–Ch God (Ander)	1	0	NR	0	0.0	0.0
Ch of Nazarene	3	316	356	594	4.3	20.4
CHR–Chs of Christ	4	210	190	254	1.9	8.7
LDS–L-D Saints	1	NR	NR	491	3.6	16.8
LUTH–Nor Amer Luth C	1	NR	NR	NR	-	-
METH–Un Methodist	1	96	184	230	1.7	7.9
PENT–Assemb of God	1	225	78	225	1.6	7.7
Sev Day Adv	1	38	65	75	0.5	2.6
DUNKLIN	**86**	**4,505**	**11,307**	**16,542**	**51.8**	**100.0**
BAPT–So Bapt Conv	27	2,042	7,968	9,906	31.0	59.9
Calv Chpl	1	NR	NR	NR	-	-
Catholic	3	NR	NR	1,620	5.1	9.8
CGOD–Ch God (Ander)	1	38	NR	38	0.1	0.2
Ch of Nazarene	1	40	65	65	0.2	0.4
CHR–Chr Ch (Disc)	1	69	164	204	0.6	1.2
CHR–Chr Chs & Chs Cr	2	NR	295	367	1.1	2.2
CHR–Chs of Christ	12	792	798	1,016	3.2	6.1
Jehovah's Witness	1	NR	NR	NR	-	-
LUTH–Luth–MO Synod	2	21	38	48	0.2	0.3
METH–AME	1	0	100	124	0.4	0.7
METH–Un Methodist	10	404	924	1,080	3.4	6.5
PENT–Assemb of God	8	589	132	944	3.0	5.7
PENT–Ch God (Cleve)	2	38	167	208	0.7	1.3
PENT–COGIC	2	20	150	186	0.6	1.1
PENT–Intl Pent Holiness	2	285	315	392	1.2	2.4

NR–Not Reported - Represents no adherents reported. Percentages may not total 100 due to rounding.

Table 3: Religious Congregations by County and Group: 2010

Religious Group	Number of Congrega-tions	Number of Attendees	Number of Communicant, Confirmed, or Full Members	Adherents: Number of Adherents	% of Total Pop.	% of Total Adh.
PENT–Pent Ch of God	1	70	NR	109	0.3	0.7
PENT–Un Pent Ch Intl	5	NR	NR	NR	-	-
PRES–Presb Ch (USA)	3	81	164	204	0.6	1.2
Sev Day Adv	1	16	27	31	0.1	0.2
FRANKLIN	**177**	**10,631**	**23,446**	**48,833**	**48.1**	**100.0**
ANG/EPIS–Episcopal	1	7	17	17	0.0	0.0
Bahá'í	0	NR	15	15	0.0	0.0
BAPT–Amer Bapt Assn	2	NR	485	598	0.6	1.2
BAPT–Free Will Bapt	2	NR	126	155	0.2	0.3
BAPT–Ind Bapt Flwsp Intl	2	NR	NR	NR	-	-
BAPT–So Bapt Conv	35	3,266	8,440	10,413	10.3	21.3
Catholic	17	NR	NR	18,173	17.9	37.2
Ch Cr, Scientst	2	NR	NR	NR	-	-
Ch of Nazarene	3	159	247	363	0.4	0.7
CHR–Chr Ch (Disc)	1	40	65	80	0.1	0.2
CHR–Chr Chs & Chs Cr	6	NR	1,961	2,420	2.4	5.0
CHR–Chs of Christ	4	275	231	305	0.3	0.6
Christian Brethren	1	NR	NR	NR	-	-
Evan Free Ch	1	74	NR	74	0.1	0.2
Jehovah's Witness	2	NR	NR	NR	-	-
LDS–L-D Saints	2	NR	NR	961	0.9	2.0
LUTH–E.L.C.A.	2	108	271	317	0.3	0.6
LUTH–Luth–MO Synod	10	1,450	2,883	3,788	3.7	7.8
METH–AME	1	0	100	123	0.1	0.3
METH–Un Methodist	15	753	1,681	2,076	2.0	4.3
METH–Wesleyan	1	20	20	26	0.0	0.1
New Apost Ch	1	NR	NR	NR	-	-
Non-denom Chr Chs	19	2,175	2,706	2,940	2.9	6.0
PENT–Assemb of God	11	667	443	1,152	1.1	2.4
PENT–Ch God (Cleve)	3	108	24	30	0.0	0.1
PENT–COGIC	2	0	300	370	0.4	0.8
PENT–Pent Ch of God	2	140	NR	217	0.2	0.4
PENT–Un Pent Ch Intl	5	NR	NR	NR	-	-
PRES–Presb Ch (USA)	6	299	498	614	0.6	1.3
PRES–Presb Ch Amer	2	90	106	126	0.1	0.3
Sev Day Adv	2	60	103	119	0.1	0.2
Un C of Christ	14	940	2,724	3,361	3.3	6.9
GASCONADE	**50**	**2,282**	**5,346**	**8,958**	**58.8**	**100.0**
Bahá'í	0	NR	1	1	0.0	0.0
BAPT–So Bapt Conv	10	629	1,988	2,388	15.7	26.7
Catholic	3	NR	NR	2,022	13.3	22.6
CHR–Chr Chs & Chs Cr	3	NR	405	487	3.2	5.4
CHR–Chs of Christ	1	72	62	87	0.6	1.0
Evan Free Ch	3	245	NR	245	1.6	2.7
Ind Fund Churches	1	NR	NR	NR	-	-
Jehovah's Witness	1	NR	NR	NR	-	-
LUTH–Luth–MO Synod	4	258	619	750	4.9	8.4
METH–Un Methodist	6	214	466	627	4.1	7.0
Non-denom Chr Chs	1	100	150	150	1.0	1.7
PENT–Assemb of God	1	65	30	145	1.0	1.6
PENT–Pent Ch of God	1	70	NR	109	0.7	1.2
PENT–Un Pent Ch Intl	3	NR	NR	NR	-	-
PRES–Presb Ch (USA)	1	25	73	88	0.6	1.0
PRES–Presb Ch Amer	2	45	38	41	0.3	0.5
Sev Day Adv	1	10	18	21	0.1	0.2
Un C of Christ	8	549	1,496	1,797	11.8	20.1
GENTRY	**29**	**1,205**	**3,640**	**5,291**	**78.5**	**100.0**
Bahá'í	0	NR	1	1	0.0	0.0
BAPT–So Bapt Conv	7	585	1,993	2,449	36.3	46.3
Catholic	1	NR	NR	338	5.0	6.4
Ch God (7th Day)	1	NR	NR	NR	-	-
CHR–Chr Ch (Disc)	4	123	565	694	10.3	13.1
CHR–Chs of Christ	3	103	103	127	1.9	2.4
LDS–L-D Saints	1	NR	NR	244	3.6	4.6
MENN–Amish Undif	2	NR	93	279	4.1	5.3
METH–Un Methodist	5	321	737	963	14.3	18.2
PENT–Assemb of God	2	28	18	37	0.5	0.7
PRES–Presb Ch (USA)	2	35	112	138	2.0	2.6
Sev Day Adv	1	10	18	21	0.3	0.4

Religious Group	Number of Congrega-tions	Number of Attendees	Number of Communicant, Confirmed, or Full Members	Adherents: Number of Adherents	% of Total Pop.	% of Total Adh.
GREENE	**355**	**52,511**	**92,731**	**143,541**	**52.2**	**100.0**
ANG/EPIS–Anglican NA	3	NR	NR	NR	-	-
ANG/EPIS–Episcopal	4	518	1,299	1,649	0.6	1.1
Bahá'í	1	NR	93	93	0.0	0.1
BAPT–Amer Bapt Assn	1	NR	75	90	0.0	0.1
BAPT–Amer Bapt USA	1	238	919	1,102	0.4	0.8
BAPT–Free Will Bapt	8	NR	504	604	0.2	0.4
BAPT–Ind Bapt Flwsp Intl	2	NR	NR	NR	-	-
BAPT–Natl Mis Bapt Conv	1	0	150	180	0.1	0.1
BAPT–NBC USA	1	115	170	204	0.1	0.1
BAPT–Ref Bapt Ch	1	NR	NR	NR	-	-
BAPT–S-D Baptist Gen Con	1	NR	NR	NR	-	-
BAPT–So Bapt Conv	85	15,153	44,385	53,214	19.3	37.1
BUDD–Theravada	2	NR	NR	29	0.0	0.0
Calv Chpl	2	NR	NR	NR	-	-
Catholic	6	NR	NR	15,294	5.6	10.7
CGOD–Ch God (Ander)	3	239	NR	239	0.1	0.2
Ch Cr, Scientst	1	NR	NR	NR	-	-
Ch God (7th Day)	1	NR	NR	NR	-	-
Ch of God Gen Conf	1	NR	5	6	0.0	0.0
Ch of Nazarene	8	540	642	1,007	0.4	0.7
Chr & Miss Al	1	40	95	95	0.0	0.1
CHR–Chr Ch (Disc)	10	1,052	2,417	2,898	1.1	2.0
CHR–Chr Chs & Chs Cr	8	NR	1,887	2,262	0.8	1.6
CHR–Chs of Christ	18	3,512	3,703	4,499	1.6	3.1
CHR–Int Chs of Christ	1	NR	33	40	0.0	0.0
Christian Brethren	1	NR	NR	NR	-	-
Evan Cov Ch	1	96	73	125	0.0	0.1
Evan Free Ch	1	600	NR	600	0.2	0.4
FRND–Fr Gen Cf	1	NR	15	18	0.0	0.0
Ind Fund Churches	1	NR	NR	NR	-	-
Jehovah's Witness	6	NR	NR	NR	-	-
JUD–Reform	1	62	110	297	0.1	0.2
LDS–Comm of Christ	2	NR	270	270	0.1	0.2
LDS–L-D Saints	8	NR	NR	4,622	1.7	3.2
LUTH–Assoc Free Luth	1	NR	NR	NR	-	-
LUTH–E.L.C.A.	2	437	1,126	1,394	0.5	1.0
LUTH–Luth–MO Synod	4	1,446	2,798	3,521	1.3	2.5
LUTH–Wisc Ev Luth Syn	1	50	75	90	0.0	0.1
METH–AME	1	0	150	180	0.1	0.1
METH–Free Methodist	1	10	14	14	0.0	0.0
METH–Un Methodist	28	4,859	10,556	14,145	5.1	9.9
METH–Wesleyan	1	14	0	18	0.0	0.0
Muslim Est	1	134	NR	308	0.1	0.2
New Apost Ch	1	NR	NR	NR	-	-
Non-denom Chr Chs	39	9,475	12,169	13,035	4.7	9.1
ORTHE–Orth Ch in Amer	2	65	NR	121	0.0	0.1
PENT–Assemb of God	42	11,561	3,801	14,846	5.4	10.3
PENT–Ch God (Cleve)	2	168	563	675	0.2	0.5
PENT–Ch God Apos Fth	1	NR	NR	NR	-	-
PENT–Ch of God Proph	1	NR	30	36	0.0	0.0
PENT–COGIC	1	85	50	60	0.0	0.0
PENT–Int Foursq Gos	4	256	267	320	0.1	0.2
PENT–Un Pent Ch Intl	5	NR	NR	NR	-	-
PENT–Vineyard	1	66	97	116	0.0	0.1
PRES–As Ref Pres Ch	1	NR	0	0	0.0	0.0
PRES–Cumber Presb	1	NR	70	175	0.1	0.1
PRES–Presb Ch (USA)	11	1,173	3,040	3,645	1.3	2.5
REF–Comm Ref Evan	1	NR	NR	NR	-	-
Salvation Army	1	60	161	317	0.1	0.2
Sev Day Adv	3	288	502	577	0.2	0.4
Un C of Christ	2	101	333	399	0.1	0.3
Unit Univ	1	98	84	109	0.0	0.1
Unity Ch	2	NR	NR	NR	-	-
Zoroastrian	0	NR	NR	3	0.0	0.0
GRUNDY	**50**	**2,230**	**6,785**	**9,255**	**90.2**	**100.0**
ANG/EPIS–Episcopal	1	10	13	30	0.3	0.3
BAPT–So Bapt Conv	15	1,046	3,744	4,615	45.0	49.9
Catholic	2	NR	NR	329	3.2	3.6
Ch of Nazarene	1	52	123	123	1.2	1.3
CHR–Chr Ch (Disc)	4	132	522	643	6.3	6.9
CHR–Chr Chs & Chs Cr	4	NR	447	551	5.4	6.0

NR–Not Reported - Represents no adherents reported. Percentages may not total 100 due to rounding.

Table 3: Religious Congregations by County and Group: 2010

Religious Group	Number of Congrega-tions	Number of Attendees	Number of Communicant, Confirmed, or Full Members	Adherents: Number of Adherents	Adherents: % of Total Pop.	Adherents: % of Total Adh.
CHR–Chs of Christ	1	30	30	40	0.4	0.4
Jehovah's Witness	1	NR	NR	NR	-	-
LDS–L-D Saints	1	NR	NR	296	2.9	3.2
LUTH–Luth–MO Synod	1	38	80	104	1.0	1.1
MENN–Amish Undif	4	NR	153	348	3.4	3.8
METH–Un Methodist	8	409	880	1,250	12.2	13.5
Non-denom Chr Chs	3	230	350	350	3.4	3.8
PENT–Assemb of God	1	195	201	277	2.7	3.0
PENT–Int Foursq Gos	1	7	7	9	0.1	0.1
PENT–Un Pent Ch Intl	1	NR	NR	NR	-	-
PRES–Presb Ch (USA)	1	81	235	290	2.8	3.1
HARRISON	**45**	**1,353**	**4,346**	**5,581**	**62.3**	**100.0**
Bahá'í	0	NR	3	3	0.0	0.1
BAPT–So Bapt Conv	13	660	1,975	2,462	27.5	44.1
Calv Chpl	1	NR	NR	NR	-	-
Catholic	1	NR	NR	137	1.5	2.5
CHR–Chr Ch (Disc)	5	57	773	964	10.8	17.3
CHR–Chr Chs & Chs Cr	2	NR	170	212	2.4	3.8
CHR–Chs of Christ	3	109	91	132	1.5	2.4
Christian Un	1	NR	NR	NR	-	-
Jehovah's Witness	1	NR	NR	NR	-	-
LDS–Comm of Christ	2	NR	316	316	3.5	5.7
LUTH–Luth–MO Synod	1	19	18	23	0.3	0.4
MENN–Amish Undif	1	NR	82	243	2.7	4.4
METH–Un Methodist	11	384	804	965	10.8	17.3
PENT–Assemb of God	3	124	114	124	1.4	2.2
HENRY	**66**	**3,362**	**9,318**	**13,852**	**62.2**	**100.0**
ANG/EPIS–Episcopal	1	18	54	73	0.3	0.5
Bahá'í	0	NR	4	4	0.0	0.0
BAPT–Natl Mis Bapt Conv	1	0	150	182	0.8	1.3
BAPT–So Bapt Conv	24	1,695	5,849	7,080	31.8	51.1
BRETH–Ch of Brethren	1	15	41	50	0.2	0.4
Catholic	5	NR	NR	1,548	7.0	11.2
Ch of Nazarene	2	79	107	179	0.8	1.3
CHR–Chr Ch (Disc)	5	215	766	927	4.2	6.7
CHR–Chs of Christ	2	115	150	196	0.9	1.4
LDS–Comm of Christ	1	NR	179	179	0.8	1.3
LDS–L-D Saints	1	NR	NR	573	2.6	4.1
LUTH–Luth–MO Synod	2	149	282	355	1.6	2.6
MENN–Amish Undif	1	NR	34	75	0.3	0.5
METH–Un Methodist	8	594	1,207	1,515	6.8	10.9
Non-denom Chr Chs	1	100	150	150	0.7	1.1
PENT–Assemb of God	1	115	0	200	0.9	1.4
PENT–Intl Pent Holiness	1	21	19	23	0.1	0.2
PENT–Pent Ch of God	1	70	NR	109	0.5	0.8
PENT–Un Pent Ch Intl	1	NR	NR	NR	-	-
PRES–Cumber Presb	2	NR	10	62	0.3	0.4
PRES–Presb Ch (USA)	4	76	143	173	0.8	1.2
Sev Day Adv	1	100	173	199	0.9	1.4
HICKORY	**26**	**1,497**	**2,744**	**3,700**	**38.4**	**100.0**
BAPT–So Bapt Conv	8	728	1,666	1,917	19.9	51.8
Catholic	1	NR	NR	230	2.4	6.2
Ch of God Gen Conf	1	NR	10	12	0.1	0.3
Ch of Nazarene	1	39	29	39	0.4	1.1
CHR–Chr Ch (Disc)	2	78	125	144	1.5	3.9
CHR–Chr Chs & Chs Cr	1	NR	70	81	0.8	2.2
Jehovah's Witness	1	NR	NR	NR	-	-
LUTH–Luth–MO Synod	1	24	37	40	0.4	1.1
MENN–Amish Undif	2	NR	24	75	0.8	2.0
METH–Un Methodist	3	271	453	664	6.9	17.9
Non-denom Chr Chs	1	150	115	188	2.0	5.1
PENT–Assemb of God	3	207	195	287	3.0	7.8
Un C of Christ	1	0	20	23	0.2	0.6
HOLT	**34**	**736**	**3,001**	**3,671**	**74.7**	**100.0**
BAPT–So Bapt Conv	5	193	578	684	13.9	18.6
Catholic	1	NR	NR	50	1.0	1.4
CGOD–Ch God (Ander)	1	20	NR	20	0.4	0.5
Ch of Nazarene	3	41	86	88	1.8	2.4
CHR–Chr Ch (Disc)	2	85	300	355	7.2	9.7
CHR–Chr Chs & Chs Cr	5	NR	619	732	14.9	19.9
LDS–Comm of Christ	1	NR	182	182	3.7	5.0
LUTH–Luth–MO Synod	3	93	238	277	5.6	7.5
METH–Un Methodist	6	219	834	1,102	22.4	30.0
Non-denom Chr Chs	1	45	70	70	1.4	1.9
PENT–Un Pent Ch Intl	1	NR	NR	NR	-	-
PRES–Presb Ch (USA)	5	40	94	111	2.3	3.0
HOWARD	**31**	**1,547**	**3,680**	**5,078**	**50.1**	**100.0**
ANG/EPIS–Episcopal	1	15	17	17	0.2	0.3
Bahá'í	0	NR	3	3	0.0	0.1
BAPT–So Bapt Conv	7	226	956	1,148	11.3	22.6
Catholic	2	NR	NR	790	7.8	15.6
CHR–Chr Ch (Disc)	4	112	604	725	7.1	14.3
CHR–Chs of Christ	1	35	30	43	0.4	0.8
LDS–L-D Saints	1	NR	NR	117	1.2	2.3
LUTH–Luth–MO Synod	1	35	85	109	1.1	2.1
METH–AME	1	0	100	120	1.2	2.4
METH–Un Methodist	5	338	808	814	8.0	16.0
Non-denom Chr Chs	4	670	835	900	8.9	17.7
PENT–Assemb of God	1	15	16	20	0.2	0.4
PENT–Int Foursq Gos	1	49	3	4	0.0	0.1
PRES–Presb Ch (USA)	1	12	18	22	0.2	0.4
Un C of Christ	1	40	205	246	2.4	4.8
HOWELL	**93**	**5,509**	**11,723**	**17,034**	**42.2**	**100.0**
ANG/EPIS–Episcopal	1	33	73	73	0.2	0.4
Bahá'í	1	NR	14	14	0.0	0.1
BAPT–Amer Bapt Assn	1	NR	85	106	0.3	0.6
BAPT–Free Will Bapt	4	NR	252	313	0.8	1.8
BAPT–Natl Mis Bapt Conv	1	0	150	186	0.5	1.1
BAPT–So Bapt Conv	19	1,672	6,334	7,864	19.5	46.2
BRETH–Ch of Brethren	1	53	74	92	0.2	0.5
Catholic	4	NR	NR	1,180	2.9	6.9
CGOD–Ch God (Ander)	6	248	NR	248	0.6	1.5
Ch of Nazarene	3	97	105	136	0.3	0.8
CHR–Chr Chs & Chs Cr	3	NR	805	1,000	2.5	5.9
CHR–Chs of Christ	14	1,298	1,206	1,480	3.7	8.7
HINDU–Post Ren	1	NR	NR	54	0.1	0.3
Jehovah's Witness	2	NR	NR	NR	-	-
LDS–Comm of Christ	1	NR	135	135	0.3	0.8
LDS–L-D Saints	1	NR	NR	604	1.5	3.5
LUTH–E.L.C.A.	1	52	95	111	0.3	0.7
LUTH–Luth Cong Msn Chr	1	30	75	93	0.2	0.5
LUTH–Luth–MO Synod	1	52	124	161	0.4	0.9
LUTH–Wisc Ev Luth Syn	1	9	9	10	0.0	0.1
METH–Un Methodist	3	524	736	1,005	2.5	5.9
Non-denom Chr Chs	6	745	900	981	2.4	5.8
PENT–Assemb of God	5	408	217	573	1.4	3.4
PENT–Ch of God Proph	1	NR	17	21	0.1	0.1
PENT–Intl Pent Holiness	1	15	26	32	0.1	0.2
PENT–Pent Ch of God	2	140	NR	217	0.5	1.3
PENT–Un Pent Ch Intl	2	NR	NR	NR	-	-
PRES–Cumber Presb	1	NR	20	21	0.1	0.1
PRES–Presb Ch (USA)	3	53	133	165	0.4	1.0
Sev Day Adv	2	80	138	159	0.4	0.9
IRON	**35**	**1,399**	**3,478**	**4,840**	**45.5**	**100.0**
ANG/EPIS–Episcopal	1	19	34	43	0.4	0.9
Bahá'í	0	NR	1	1	0.0	0.0
BAPT–Free Will Bapt	1	NR	63	76	0.7	1.6
BAPT–So Bapt Conv	12	672	2,564	3,094	29.1	63.9
Catholic	2	NR	NR	354	3.3	7.3
Ch of Nazarene	2	86	102	134	1.3	2.8
CHR–Chs of Christ	1	50	54	60	0.6	1.2
Jehovah's Witness	1	NR	NR	NR	-	-
LUTH–Luth–MO Synod	2	35	81	83	0.8	1.7
METH–Un Methodist	3	157	294	390	3.7	8.1
Non-denom Chr Chs	1	50	100	100	0.9	2.1
PENT–Assemb of God	6	248	168	375	3.5	7.7
PENT–Pent Ch of God	1	70	NR	109	1.0	2.3
PENT–Un Pent Ch Intl	1	NR	NR	NR	-	-

NR–Not Reported - Represents no adherents reported. Percentages may not total 100 due to rounding.

Table 3: Religious Congregations by County and Group: 2010

Religious Group	Number of Congrega-tions	Number of Attendees	Number of Communicant, Confirmed, or Full Members	Adherents		
				Number of Adherents	% of Total Pop.	% of Total Adh.
PRES–Presb Ch (USA)	1	12	17	21	0.2	0.4
JACKSON	**812**	**101,515**	**212,059**	**355,967**	**52.8**	**100.0**
ANG/EPIS–Episcopal	14	1,744	4,475	5,254	0.8	1.5
Ap Chr Ch-Amer	1	80	50	80	0.0	0.0
Bahá'í	3	NR	459	459	0.1	0.1
BAPT–Alliance Bapt	2	NR	NR	NR	-	-
BAPT–Amer Bapt USA	11	1,176	1,864	2,308	0.3	0.6
BAPT–Converge/BGC	3	550	NR	660	0.1	0.2
BAPT–Free Will Bapt	5	NR	315	390	0.1	0.1
BAPT–Ind Bapt Flwsp Intl	1	NR	NR	NR	-	-
BAPT–Natl Mis Bapt Conv	6	170	710	879	0.1	0.2
BAPT–NBC Amer	7	2,525	4,760	5,895	0.9	1.7
BAPT–NBC USA	22	4,650	8,951	11,085	1.6	3.1
BAPT–Prog NBC	7	730	3,140	3,889	0.6	1.1
BAPT–Reg Bapt Gen As	4	NR	NR	NR	-	-
BAPT–So Bapt Conv	111	14,769	51,635	63,946	9.5	18.0
BRETH–Ch of Brethren	1	0	45	56	0.0	0.0
BUDD–Mahayana	2	NR	NR	517	0.1	0.1
BUDD–Theravada	3	NR	NR	43	0.0	0.0
BUDD–Vajrayana	1	NR	NR	25	0.0	0.0
Catholic	52	NR	NR	69,441	10.3	19.5
CGOD–Ch God (Ander)	5	345	NR	345	0.1	0.1
CGOD–Ches God-Gen Con	1	0	0	0	0.0	0.0
Ch Cr, Scientst	3	NR	NR	NR	-	-
Ch God (7th Day)	1	NR	NR	NR	-	-
Ch of Chr (Hol)	2	NR	NR	NR	-	-
Ch of Nazarene	21	2,584	4,466	5,104	0.8	1.4
CHR–Chr Ch (Disc)	32	2,962	11,629	14,402	2.1	4.0
CHR–Chr Chs & Chs Cr	10	NR	1,851	2,292	0.3	0.6
CHR–Chs of Christ	25	3,108	3,181	3,972	0.6	1.1
Christian Brethren	1	NR	NR	NR	-	-
Christian Un	1	NR	NR	NR	-	-
Evan Cov Ch	3	387	259	503	0.1	0.1
Evan Free Ch	5	160	NR	160	0.0	0.0
FRND–Consrv Yr Mtgs	1	NR	70	87	0.0	0.0
FRND–Evan Fr Ch Intl	1	49	85	105	0.0	0.0
HINDU–I/A Temples	1	NR	NR	1,562	0.2	0.4
HINDU–Renaiss	2	NR	NR	96	0.0	0.0
Ind Fund Churches	2	NR	NR	NR	-	-
Int Cou Comm Ch	1	NR	NR	NR	-	-
Jehovah's Witness	11	NR	NR	NR	-	-
JUD–Orth	1	43	50	60	0.0	0.0
JUD–Reform	1	159	281	759	0.1	0.2
LDS–Comm of Christ	42	NR	15,794	15,794	2.3	4.4
LDS–L-D Saints	19	NR	NR	12,365	1.8	3.5
LUTH–E.L.C.A.	8	552	989	1,409	0.2	0.4
LUTH–Luth-MO Synod	15	3,068	6,972	9,238	1.4	2.6
LUTH–Wisc Ev Luth Syn	1	93	132	178	0.0	0.1
MENN–Menn Br US Conf	1	NR	10	12	0.0	0.0
METH–AME	16	1,025	3,630	4,495	0.7	1.3
METH–AME Zion	2	200	502	622	0.1	0.2
METH–C.M.E.	4	355	804	996	0.1	0.3
METH–Free Methodist	1	78	54	78	0.0	0.0
METH–Un Methodist	56	9,880	20,451	28,482	4.2	8.0
METH–Wesleyan	2	41	14	53	0.0	0.0
Metro Comm Ch	1	149	176	218	0.0	0.1
Muslim Est	9	1,172	NR	2,614	0.4	0.7
New Apost Ch	1	NR	NR	NR	-	-
Non-denom Chr Chs	98	27,177	35,406	41,006	6.1	11.5
ORTHE–Greek Orthodox	1	220	NR	1,000	0.1	0.3
ORTHE–Serb Orth USA	1	98	NR	150	0.0	0.0
ORTHO–Armen Ap Etchm	1	30	NR	85	0.0	0.0
PENT–Assemb of God	36	11,239	9,418	16,253	2.4	4.6
PENT–Ch God (Cleve)	5	217	422	523	0.1	0.1
PENT–Ch Lord Jesus Apos	1	NR	NR	NR	-	-
PENT–COGIC	18	3,640	5,540	6,861	1.0	1.9
PENT–Full Gosp Bapt	1	NR	NR	NR	-	-
PENT–Int Foursq Gos	4	282	330	409	0.1	0.1
PENT–Intl Pent Holiness	3	264	234	290	0.0	0.1
PENT–Pent Ch of God	5	350	NR	544	0.1	0.2
PENT–Un Pent Ch Intl	8	NR	NR	NR	-	-
PENT–Vineyard	1	39	75	93	0.0	0.0
PRES–Cumber Presb	1	NR	13	13	0.0	0.0
PRES–Evan Presby Ch	1	NR	1,608	1,991	0.3	0.6
PRES–Free Pres NA	1	NR	NR	NR	-	-
PRES–Presb Ch (USA)	26	2,417	6,133	7,595	1.1	2.1
PRES–Presb Ch Amer	1	40	27	45	0.0	0.0
REF–Christian Ref	1	NR	0	0	0.0	0.0
REF–Un Ref Chs N.A.	1	NR	NR	NR	-	-
Salvation Army	5	440	487	2,737	0.4	0.8
Sev Day Adv	8	1,614	2,806	3,227	0.5	0.9
Sikh	2	NR	NR	NR	-	-
Un C of Christ	8	363	1,317	1,631	0.2	0.5
Unit Univ	2	281	439	586	0.1	0.2
Unity Ch	7	NR	NR	NR	-	-
JASPER	**209**	**18,506**	**47,669**	**67,991**	**57.9**	**100.0**
ANG/EPIS–Anglican NA	1	NR	NR	NR	-	-
ANG/EPIS–Episcopal	2	325	909	1,082	0.9	1.6
Bahá'í	1	NR	35	35	0.0	0.1
BAPT–Amer Bapt Assn	1	NR	85	107	0.1	0.2
BAPT–Free Will Bapt	2	NR	126	158	0.1	0.2
BAPT–Ind Bapt Flwsp Intl	1	NR	NR	NR	-	-
BAPT–NBC USA	1	0	250	314	0.3	0.5
BAPT–Ref Bapt Ch	1	NR	NR	NR	-	-
BAPT–Reg Bapt Gen As	1	NR	NR	NR	-	-
BAPT–So Bapt Conv	39	5,654	17,658	22,176	18.9	32.6
BUDD–Theravada	1	NR	NR	15	0.0	0.0
Calv Chpl	1	NR	NR	NR	-	-
Catholic	5	NR	NR	6,024	5.1	8.9
CGOD–Ch God (Ander)	3	187	NR	187	0.2	0.3
Ch Cr, Scientst	1	NR	NR	NR	-	-
Ch God (7th Day)	1	NR	NR	NR	-	-
Ch of Nazarene	6	717	1,120	1,867	1.6	2.7
CHR–Chr Ch (Disc)	2	187	350	440	0.4	0.6
CHR–Chr Chs & Chs Cr	27	NR	8,761	11,003	9.4	16.2
CHR–Chs of Christ	5	690	612	805	0.7	1.2
CONG–Cong Chr, NA	1	NR	150	188	0.2	0.3
Evan Cov Ch	1	106	105	138	0.1	0.2
FRND–Evan Fr Ch Intl	1	65	121	152	0.1	0.2
Ind Fund Churches	1	NR	NR	NR	-	-
Jehovah's Witness	5	NR	NR	NR	-	-
JUD–Reform	1	19	34	92	0.1	0.1
LDS–Comm of Christ	3	NR	405	405	0.3	0.6
LDS–L-D Saints	4	NR	NR	2,445	2.1	3.6
LUTH–E.L.C.A.	1	52	90	111	0.1	0.2
LUTH–Evan Luth Syn	1	60	85	98	0.1	0.1
LUTH–Luth-MO Synod	2	230	735	923	0.8	1.4
METH–AME	1	0	150	188	0.2	0.3
METH–Free Methodist	1	15	14	15	0.0	0.0
METH–Un Methodist	22	2,364	4,365	5,355	4.6	7.9
Metro Comm Ch	1	20	21	26	0.0	0.0
Muslim Est	1	20	NR	60	0.1	0.1
Non-denom Chr Chs	22	5,470	9,240	9,588	8.2	14.1
PENT–Assemb of God	12	1,080	664	1,472	1.3	2.2
PENT–Ch God (Cleve)	2	90	323	406	0.3	0.6
PENT–Ch of God Proph	2	NR	65	82	0.1	0.1
PENT–Int Foursq Gos	1	317	101	127	0.1	0.2
PENT–Pent Ch of God	4	280	NR	435	0.4	0.6
PENT–Un Pent Ch Intl	4	NR	NR	NR	-	-
PRES–Evan Presby Ch	1	NR	50	63	0.1	0.1
PRES–Presb Ch (USA)	5	298	653	820	0.7	1.2
PRES–Presb Ch Amer	1	55	63	75	0.1	0.1
Salvation Army	2	109	136	285	0.2	0.4
Sev Day Adv	2	76	131	151	0.1	0.2
Un C of Christ	1	20	62	78	0.1	0.1
Unity Ch	1	NR	NR	NR	-	-
JEFFERSON	**162**	**16,118**	**37,194**	**79,939**	**36.5**	**100.0**
ANG/EPIS–Episcopal	1	18	28	32	0.0	0.0
Bahá'í	0	NR	43	43	0.0	0.1
BAPT–Amer Bapt Assn	1	NR	85	106	0.0	0.1
BAPT–Amer Bapt USA	1	69	123	153	0.1	0.2
BAPT–Free Will Bapt	2	NR	126	156	0.1	0.2
BAPT–Natl Mis Bapt Conv	1	0	150	186	0.1	0.2
BAPT–Ref Bapt Ch	1	NR	NR	NR	-	-

NR–Not Reported   - Represents no adherents reported.   Percentages may not total 100 due to rounding.

Table 3: Religious Congregations by County and Group: 2010

Religious Group	Number of Congregations	Number of Attendees	Number of Communicant, Confirmed, or Full Members	Adherents: Number of Adherents	Adherents: % of Total Pop.	Adherents: % of Total Adh.
BAPT–So Bapt Conv	39	7,048	22,036	27,355	12.5	34.2
Calv Chpl	1	NR	NR	NR	-	-
Catholic	11	NR	NR	30,495	13.9	38.1
CGOD–Ch God (Ander)	1	113	NR	113	0.1	0.1
Ch of God Gen Conf	1	NR	35	43	0.0	0.1
Ch of Nazarene	5	255	346	572	0.3	0.7
CHR–Chr Ch (Disc)	2	170	419	520	0.2	0.7
CHR–Chr Chs & Chs Cr	3	NR	420	521	0.2	0.7
CHR–Chs of Christ	6	718	856	1,024	0.5	1.3
Ind Fund Churches	1	NR	NR	NR	-	-
Jehovah's Witness	4	NR	NR	NR	-	-
LDS–Comm of Christ	2	NR	276	276	0.1	0.3
LDS–L-D Saints	2	NR	NR	606	0.3	0.8
LUTH–E.L.C.A.	2	176	431	560	0.3	0.7
LUTH–Luth–MO Synod	11	2,176	4,068	5,528	2.5	6.9
METH–AME	2	0	250	310	0.1	0.4
METH–Un Methodist	15	1,137	2,261	3,110	1.4	3.9
METH–Wesleyan	1	105	0	137	0.1	0.2
New Apost Ch	1	NR	NR	NR	-	-
Non-denom Chr Chs	10	1,590	2,110	2,238	1.0	2.8
ORTHE–Rus Orth Abroad	1	75	NR	260	0.1	0.3
PENT–Assemb of God	10	1,494	697	2,371	1.1	3.0
PENT–Ch God (Cleve)	4	177	295	366	0.2	0.5
PENT–Int Foursq Gos	2	37	25	31	0.0	0.0
PENT–Pent Ch of God	1	70	NR	109	0.0	0.1
PENT–Un Pent Ch Intl	6	NR	NR	NR	-	-
PRES–Presb Ch (USA)	5	180	386	479	0.2	0.6
Salvation Army	1	36	66	176	0.1	0.2
Un C of Christ	5	474	1,662	2,063	0.9	2.6
JOHNSON	**81**	**5,134**	**14,063**	**20,354**	**38.7**	**100.0**
ANG/EPIS–Episcopal	1	28	131	174	0.3	0.9
Bahá'í	0	NR	22	22	0.0	0.1
BAPT–NBC USA	1	0	150	183	0.3	0.9
BAPT–So Bapt Conv	27	2,914	7,791	9,499	18.1	46.7
BRETH–Ch of Brethren	1	40	42	51	0.1	0.3
Catholic	2	NR	NR	1,815	3.5	8.9
Ch of Nazarene	2	171	154	332	0.6	1.6
CHR–Chr Ch (Disc)	2	235	594	724	1.4	3.6
CHR–Chr Chs & Chs Cr	4	NR	1,410	1,719	3.3	8.4
CHR–Chs of Christ	2	137	114	186	0.4	0.9
Evan Free Ch	1	30	NR	30	0.1	0.1
Jehovah's Witness	1	NR	NR	NR	-	-
LDS–Comm of Christ	3	NR	537	537	1.0	2.6
LDS–L-D Saints	2	NR	NR	784	1.5	3.9
LUTH–Luth–MO Synod	2	195	368	477	0.9	2.3
MENN–Amish Undif	1	NR	66	131	0.2	0.6
METH–C.M.E.	1	0	100	122	0.2	0.6
METH–Un Methodist	8	575	1,503	1,763	3.4	8.7
Muslim Est	1	134	NR	308	0.6	1.5
Non-denom Chr Chs	5	390	505	549	1.0	2.7
PENT–Assemb of God	1	95	55	183	0.3	0.9
PENT–COGIC	1	15	25	30	0.1	0.1
PENT–Pent Ch of God	1	70	NR	109	0.2	0.5
PENT–Un Pent Ch Intl	1	NR	NR	NR	-	-
PRES–Cumber Presb	3	NR	89	140	0.3	0.7
PRES–Presb Ch (USA)	5	27	271	330	0.6	1.6
Sev Day Adv	2	78	136	156	0.3	0.8
KNOX	**21**	**597**	**1,522**	**2,371**	**57.4**	**100.0**
BAPT–So Bapt Conv	8	266	709	880	21.3	37.1
Catholic	2	NR	NR	450	10.9	19.0
Ch of Nazarene	1	10	32	40	1.0	1.7
CHR–Chr Ch (Disc)	2	62	121	150	3.6	6.3
CHR–Chr Chs & Chs Cr	2	NR	165	205	5.0	8.6
METH–Un Methodist	4	129	351	358	8.7	15.1
PENT–Assemb of God	2	130	144	288	7.0	12.1
LACLEDE	**85**	**6,052**	**13,460**	**18,666**	**52.5**	**100.0**
ANG/EPIS–Episcopal	1	18	32	32	0.1	0.2
Bahá'í	0	NR	13	13	0.0	0.1
BAPT–Free Will Bapt	10	NR	630	782	2.2	4.2
BAPT–So Bapt Conv	24	1,800	5,487	6,814	19.2	36.5
Catholic	2	NR	NR	1,488	4.2	8.0
CGOD–Ch God (Ander)	3	198	NR	198	0.6	1.1
Ch of Nazarene	1	173	256	310	0.9	1.7
CHR–Chr Ch (Disc)	2	98	275	341	1.0	1.8
CHR–Chr Chs & Chs Cr	4	NR	1,060	1,316	3.7	7.1
CHR–Chs of Christ	4	385	351	459	1.3	2.5
Ind Fund Churches	2	NR	NR	NR	-	-
Jehovah's Witness	1	NR	NR	NR	-	-
LDS–Comm of Christ	1	NR	135	135	0.4	0.7
LDS–L-D Saints	1	NR	NR	529	1.5	2.8
LUTH–Luth–MO Synod	2	180	228	306	0.9	1.6
METH–Un Methodist	9	511	1,392	1,536	4.3	8.2
METH–Wesleyan	1	12	0	16	0.0	0.1
Non-denom Chr Chs	6	1,965	3,025	3,182	8.9	17.0
PENT–Assemb of God	4	556	224	616	1.7	3.3
PENT–Pent Ch of God	1	70	NR	109	0.3	0.6
PENT–Un Pent Ch Intl	2	NR	NR	NR	-	-
PRES–Cumber Presb	2	NR	151	240	0.7	1.3
Sev Day Adv	1	32	55	63	0.2	0.3
Un C of Christ	1	54	146	181	0.5	1.0
LAFAYETTE	**86**	**5,643**	**14,884**	**21,332**	**63.9**	**100.0**
ANG/EPIS–Episcopal	1	27	49	106	0.3	0.5
Bahá'í	0	NR	7	7	0.0	0.0
BAPT–Free Will Bapt	1	NR	63	77	0.2	0.4
BAPT–NBC USA	1	10	20	25	0.1	0.1
BAPT–So Bapt Conv	16	1,614	5,351	6,565	19.7	30.8
Catholic	3	NR	NR	1,378	4.1	6.5
CHR–Chr Ch (Disc)	5	202	650	797	2.4	3.7
CHR–Chr Chs & Chs Cr	2	NR	290	356	1.1	1.7
CHR–Chs of Christ	3	145	123	196	0.6	0.9
Evan Free Ch	1	135	NR	135	0.4	0.6
Jehovah's Witness	1	NR	NR	NR	-	-
LDS–Comm of Christ	2	NR	358	358	1.1	1.7
LDS–L-D Saints	3	NR	NR	1,368	4.1	6.4
LUTH–Ch Luth Conf	1	NR	NR	NR	-	-
LUTH–Luth–MO Synod	8	1,608	3,291	3,984	11.9	18.7
METH–AME	5	0	600	736	2.2	3.5
METH–Un Methodist	11	553	1,554	1,863	5.6	8.7
Non-denom Chr Chs	6	562	770	802	2.4	3.8
PENT–Assemb of God	5	282	121	577	1.7	2.7
PRES–Cumber Presb	2	NR	39	41	0.1	0.2
PRES–Presb Ch (USA)	4	56	192	236	0.7	1.1
Un C of Christ	5	449	1,406	1,725	5.2	8.1
LAWRENCE	**108**	**7,559**	**15,376**	**23,572**	**61.0**	**100.0**
Bahá'í	0	NR	2	2	0.0	0.0
BAPT–So Bapt Conv	30	3,254	9,060	11,375	29.4	48.3
Catholic	4	NR	NR	2,474	6.4	10.5
CGOD–Ches God-Gen Con	1	11	8	10	0.0	0.0
Ch of Nazarene	3	115	132	179	0.5	0.8
CHR–Chr Ch (Disc)	4	129	558	701	1.8	3.0
CHR–Chr Chs & Chs Cr	6	NR	649	815	2.1	3.5
CHR–Chs of Christ	4	435	372	426	1.1	1.8
Christian Un	2	NR	NR	NR	-	-
Evan Free Ch	1	35	NR	35	0.1	0.1
Jehovah's Witness	2	NR	NR	NR	-	-
LDS–Comm of Christ	1	NR	135	135	0.3	0.6
LDS–L-D Saints	2	NR	NR	904	2.3	3.8
LUTH–Luth–MO Synod	2	260	499	644	1.7	2.7
MENN–Amish Undif	3	NR	172	430	1.1	1.8
MENN–Menn Chr Fell	1	154	62	154	0.4	0.7
MENN–Tamp Amish-Menn	1	185	81	185	0.5	0.8
METH–Free Methodist	2	65	47	65	0.2	0.3
METH–Un Methodist	13	779	1,652	2,020	5.2	8.6
Non-denom Chr Chs	9	1,658	1,503	2,100	5.4	8.9
PENT–Assemb of God	7	283	117	508	1.3	2.2
PENT–Ch God (Cleve)	1	55	35	44	0.1	0.2
PENT–Un Pent Ch Intl	4	NR	NR	NR	-	-
PRES–Presb Ch (USA)	3	99	216	271	0.7	1.1
Un C of Christ	2	42	76	95	0.2	0.4

NR–Not Reported - Represents no adherents reported. Percentages may not total 100 due to rounding.

Table 3: Religious Congregations by County and Group: 2010

Religious Group	Number of Congregations	Number of Attendees	Number of Communicant, Confirmed, or Full Members	Adherents: Number of Adherents	Adherents: % of Total Pop.	Adherents: % of Total Adh.
LEWIS	**37**	**1,208**	**4,172**	**5,906**	**57.8**	**100.0**
BAPT–Reg Bapt Gen As	1	NR	NR	NR	-	-
BAPT–So Bapt Conv	14	638	2,525	3,081	30.2	52.2
Catholic	3	NR	NR	440	4.3	7.5
CHR–Chr Ch (Disc)	3	118	497	606	5.9	10.3
CHR–Chr Chs & Chs Cr	1	NR	160	195	1.9	3.3
LUTH–Luth–MO Synod	1	72	208	267	2.6	4.5
MENN–Amish Undif	3	NR	128	376	3.7	6.4
METH–Un Methodist	6	235	466	647	6.3	11.0
Non-denom Chr Chs	1	85	150	150	1.5	2.5
PENT–Assemb of God	2	56	30	135	1.3	2.3
PENT–Un Pent Ch Intl	1	NR	NR	NR	-	-
Sev Day Adv	1	4	8	9	0.1	0.2
LINCOLN	**66**	**3,807**	**7,861**	**16,004**	**30.4**	**100.0**
Bahá'í	0	NR	5	5	0.0	0.0
BAPT–Free Will Bapt	1	NR	63	80	0.2	0.5
BAPT–Ind Bapt Flwsp Intl	1	NR	NR	NR	-	-
BAPT–So Bapt Conv	13	1,388	3,400	4,338	8.3	27.1
Calv Chpl	2	NR	NR	NR	-	-
Catholic	5	NR	NR	5,670	10.8	35.4
CHR–Chr Ch (Disc)	3	274	850	1,084	2.1	6.8
CHR–Chr Chs & Chs Cr	3	NR	300	383	0.7	2.4
CHR–Chs of Christ	2	205	170	195	0.4	1.2
Jehovah's Witness	1	NR	NR	NR	-	-
LUTH–Luth–MO Synod	1	202	471	625	1.2	3.9
METH–Un Methodist	11	680	1,281	1,714	3.3	10.7
METH–Wesleyan	1	100	57	130	0.2	0.8
Non-denom Chr Chs	5	357	425	472	0.9	2.9
PENT–Assemb of God	4	298	150	428	0.8	2.7
PENT–Ch God (Cleve)	1	13	17	22	0.0	0.1
PENT–Un Pent Ch Intl	2	NR	NR	NR	-	-
PRES–As Ref Pres Ch	2	NR	25	32	0.1	0.2
PRES–Presb Ch (USA)	4	124	213	272	0.5	1.7
PRES–Ref Pres GA	1	NR	NR	NR	-	-
Un C of Christ	3	166	434	554	1.1	3.5
LINN	**50**	**2,500**	**6,063**	**8,633**	**67.7**	**100.0**
Bahá'í	0	NR	8	8	0.1	0.1
BAPT–So Bapt Conv	16	952	3,100	3,819	29.9	44.2
Catholic	2	NR	NR	994	7.8	11.5
Ch of Nazarene	1	42	78	78	0.6	0.9
CHR–Chr Ch (Disc)	3	237	735	906	7.1	10.5
CHR–Chr Chs & Chs Cr	1	NR	35	43	0.3	0.5
CHR–Chs of Christ	4	150	154	193	1.5	2.2
Jehovah's Witness	2	NR	NR	NR	-	-
LDS–L-D Saints	1	NR	NR	111	0.9	1.3
LUTH–Luth–MO Synod	1	0	14	15	0.1	0.2
MENN–Beachy Amish-Menn	1	16	13	16	0.1	0.2
MENN–Mara Amish-Menn	1	79	30	79	0.6	0.9
METH–Un Methodist	11	769	1,600	1,954	15.3	22.6
Non-denom Chr Chs	1	60	50	75	0.6	0.9
PENT–Assemb of God	3	153	135	207	1.6	2.4
PRES–Presb Ch (USA)	1	30	89	110	0.9	1.3
Sev Day Adv	1	12	22	25	0.2	0.3
LIVINGSTON	**41**	**2,293**	**7,532**	**10,897**	**71.7**	**100.0**
ANG/EPIS–Episcopal	1	34	43	53	0.3	0.5
Bahá'í	0	NR	1	1	0.0	0.0
BAPT–Amer Bapt USA	1	7	30	36	0.2	0.3
BAPT–So Bapt Conv	13	963	4,762	5,731	37.7	52.6
Catholic	1	NR	NR	1,092	7.2	10.0
CHR–Chr Ch (Disc)	3	119	265	319	2.1	2.9
CHR–Chs of Christ	1	78	70	95	0.6	0.9
Jehovah's Witness	1	NR	NR	NR	-	-
LDS–Comm of Christ	1	NR	182	182	1.2	1.7
LDS–L-D Saints	1	NR	NR	210	1.4	1.9
LUTH–Luth–MO Synod	1	42	64	73	0.5	0.7
MENN–Amish Undif	0	NR	47	99	0.7	0.9
METH–AME	1	0	100	120	0.8	1.1
METH–Free Methodist	1	65	144	144	0.9	1.3
METH–Un Methodist	4	463	1,167	1,776	11.7	16.3
Non-denom Chr Chs	2	125	180	181	1.2	1.7
PENT–Assemb of God	1	91	45	123	0.8	1.1
PENT–Ch God (Cleve)	1	137	118	142	0.9	1.3
PENT–Pent Ch of God	1	70	NR	109	0.7	1.0
PENT–Un Pent Ch Intl	1	NR	NR	NR	-	-
PRES–Presb Ch (USA)	2	40	108	130	0.9	1.2
Salvation Army	1	29	24	65	0.4	0.6
Sev Day Adv	1	30	53	61	0.4	0.6
Un C of Christ	1	0	129	155	1.0	1.4
MCDONALD	**47**	**2,260**	**5,040**	**7,400**	**32.1**	**100.0**
ANG/EPIS–Episcopal	1	32	75	106	0.5	1.4
Bahá'í	0	NR	12	12	0.1	0.2
BAPT–Free Will Bapt	1	NR	63	80	0.3	1.1
BAPT–So Bapt Conv	16	998	2,744	3,498	15.2	47.3
Catholic	1	NR	NR	567	2.5	7.7
Ch of Nazarene	3	251	287	435	1.9	5.9
CHR–Chr Chs & Chs Cr	2	NR	260	331	1.4	4.5
CHR–Chs of Christ	2	40	36	48	0.2	0.6
LDS–L-D Saints	1	NR	NR	322	1.4	4.4
METH–Un Methodist	9	280	587	916	4.0	12.4
Non-denom Chr Chs	5	460	775	794	3.4	10.7
PENT–Assemb of God	3	95	80	147	0.6	2.0
PENT–Ch God Apos Fth	1	NR	NR	NR	-	-
PENT–Intl Pent Holiness	1	54	35	45	0.2	0.6
Sev Day Adv	1	50	86	99	0.4	1.3
MACON	**59**	**2,675**	**8,347**	**11,078**	**71.2**	**100.0**
Bahá'í	0	NR	1	1	0.0	0.0
BAPT–So Bapt Conv	16	1,224	4,657	5,729	36.8	51.7
Catholic	2	NR	NR	180	1.2	1.6
Ch of Nazarene	1	85	108	151	1.0	1.4
CHR–Chr Ch (Disc)	2	135	385	474	3.0	4.3
CHR–Chr Chs & Chs Cr	5	NR	815	1,003	6.4	9.1
CHR–Chs of Christ	2	70	63	96	0.6	0.9
LDS–Comm of Christ	1	NR	138	138	0.9	1.2
LDS–L-D Saints	1	NR	NR	185	1.2	1.7
LUTH–Luth–MO Synod	1	128	314	387	2.5	3.5
MENN–Amish Undif	6	NR	244	606	3.9	5.5
METH–AME	1	0	100	123	0.8	1.1
METH–Un Methodist	8	361	676	941	6.0	8.5
Non-denom Chr Chs	2	390	375	488	3.1	4.4
PENT–Assemb of God	2	70	64	81	0.5	0.7
PRES–Presb Ch (USA)	5	133	268	330	2.1	3.0
Sev Day Adv	2	42	73	84	0.5	0.8
Un C of Christ	2	37	66	81	0.5	0.7
MADISON	**44**	**2,095**	**4,159**	**5,710**	**46.7**	**100.0**
BAPT–Free Will Bapt	7	NR	441	539	4.4	9.4
BAPT–So Bapt Conv	10	1,216	2,182	2,666	21.8	46.7
Catholic	1	NR	NR	436	3.6	7.6
CGOD–Ches God-Gen Con	1	41	28	34	0.3	0.6
Ch of God Gen Conf	1	NR	15	18	0.1	0.3
Ch of Nazarene	1	95	75	145	1.2	2.5
CHR–Chr Ch (Disc)	1	70	265	324	2.7	5.7
CHR–Chr Chs & Chs Cr	1	NR	0	0	0.0	0.0
CHR–Chs of Christ	5	235	258	293	2.4	5.1
Jehovah's Witness	1	NR	NR	NR	-	-
LDS–L-D Saints	1	NR	NR	190	1.6	3.3
LUTH–Luth–MO Synod	2	90	142	188	1.5	3.3
METH–Cong Meth	1	NR	49	60	0.5	1.1
METH–Un Methodist	5	181	450	501	4.1	8.8
Non-denom Chr Chs	1	100	150	150	1.2	2.6
PENT–Assemb of God	1	29	0	40	0.3	0.7
PENT–Ch of God Proph	1	NR	30	37	0.3	0.6
PENT–Un Pent Ch Intl	1	NR	NR	NR	-	-
PRES–Presb Ch (USA)	1	20	44	54	0.4	0.9
Sev Day Adv	1	18	30	35	0.3	0.6
MARIES	**26**	**952**	**2,603**	**4,185**	**45.6**	**100.0**
Bahá'í	0	NR	1	1	0.0	0.0
BAPT–So Bapt Conv	8	426	1,664	2,033	22.2	48.6

NR–Not Reported - Represents no adherents reported. Percentages may not total 100 due to rounding.

Table 3: Religious Congregations by County and Group: 2010

Religious Group	Number of Congregations	Number of Attendees	Number of Communicant, Confirmed, or Full Members	Adherents: Number of Adherents	Adherents: % of Total Pop.	Adherents: % of Total Adh.
Catholic	3	NR	NR	706	7.7	16.9
Ch of Nazarene	1	22	19	23	0.3	0.5
CHR–Chr Chs & Chs Cr	1	NR	150	183	2.0	4.4
CHR–Chs of Christ	1	65	58	89	1.0	2.1
LDS–Comm of Christ	1	NR	138	138	1.5	3.3
LUTH–Luth–MO Synod	1	42	90	109	1.2	2.6
METH–Un Methodist	4	221	420	706	7.7	16.9
PENT–Assemb of God	3	176	63	197	2.1	4.7
PENT–Un Pent Ch Intl	3	NR	NR	NR	-	-
MARION	**70**	**4,912**	**10,936**	**17,222**	**59.8**	**100.0**
ANG/EPIS–Episcopal	2	51	70	133	0.5	0.8
Ap Chr Ch-Amer	1	220	103	220	0.8	1.3
Bahá'í	0	NR	3	3	0.0	0.0
BAPT–Free Will Bapt	1	NR	63	78	0.3	0.5
BAPT–So Bapt Conv	16	1,294	3,932	4,845	16.8	28.1
Catholic	2	NR	NR	2,721	9.5	15.8
Ch of Nazarene	2	131	202	251	0.9	1.5
CHR–Chr Ch (Disc)	5	247	1,078	1,328	4.6	7.7
CHR–Chr Chs & Chs Cr	2	NR	790	973	3.4	5.6
CHR–Chs of Christ	6	158	137	176	0.6	1.0
Evan Free Ch	1	95	NR	95	0.3	0.6
Jehovah's Witness	1	NR	NR	NR	-	-
LDS–Comm of Christ	1	NR	119	119	0.4	0.7
LDS–L-D Saints	1	NR	NR	428	1.5	2.5
LUTH–Luth–MO Synod	3	505	1,277	1,676	5.8	9.7
MENN–Fel Evg Ch	1	82	80	99	0.3	0.6
METH–AME	1	0	100	123	0.4	0.7
METH–Free Methodist	1	44	16	44	0.2	0.3
METH–Un Methodist	7	421	1,018	1,442	5.0	8.4
Non-denom Chr Chs	5	845	970	1,081	3.8	6.3
PENT–Assemb of God	4	549	472	767	2.7	4.5
PENT–Un Pent Ch Intl	2	NR	NR	NR	-	-
PRES–Presb Ch (USA)	3	234	462	569	2.0	3.3
Salvation Army	1	10	0	0	0.0	0.0
Sev Day Adv	1	26	44	51	0.2	0.3
MERCER	**18**	**664**	**2,053**	**2,688**	**71.0**	**100.0**
Bahá'í	0	NR	1	1	0.0	0.0
BAPT–So Bapt Conv	5	310	1,399	1,744	46.1	64.9
Catholic	1	NR	NR	50	1.3	1.9
CHR–Chr Ch (Disc)	1	75	168	209	5.5	7.8
CHR–Chr Chs & Chs Cr	1	NR	0	0	0.0	0.0
CHR–Chs of Christ	1	25	25	30	0.8	1.1
LUTH–Luth–MO Synod	1	20	30	34	0.9	1.3
MENN–Amish Undif	3	NR	57	156	4.1	5.8
METH–Un Methodist	2	108	226	290	7.7	10.8
Non-denom Chr Chs	1	60	101	101	2.7	3.8
PENT–Assemb of God	2	66	46	73	1.9	2.7
MILLER	**56**	**3,122**	**7,639**	**13,962**	**56.4**	**100.0**
Bahá'í	0	NR	3	3	0.0	0.0
BAPT–So Bapt Conv	22	1,634	5,028	6,225	25.2	44.6
Calv Chpl	1	NR	NR	NR	-	-
Catholic	5	NR	NR	4,192	16.9	30.0
Ch of Nazarene	2	200	312	347	1.4	2.5
CHR–Chr Ch (Disc)	1	87	372	461	1.9	3.3
CHR–Chr Chs & Chs Cr	3	NR	655	811	3.3	5.8
CHR–Chs of Christ	8	362	346	434	1.8	3.1
CONG–Cong Chr, NA	1	NR	50	62	0.3	0.4
Jehovah's Witness	1	NR	NR	NR	-	-
LUTH–Luth–MO Synod	1	0	120	150	0.6	1.1
METH–Un Methodist	2	107	255	281	1.1	2.0
Non-denom Chr Chs	3	180	230	250	1.0	1.8
PENT–Assemb of God	4	465	222	580	2.3	4.2
PENT–Pent Ch of God	1	70	NR	109	0.4	0.8
Un C of Christ	1	17	46	57	0.2	0.4
MISSISSIPPI	**37**	**1,608**	**4,902**	**6,350**	**44.2**	**100.0**
BAPT–Free Will Bapt	1	NR	63	76	0.5	1.2
BAPT–Natl Mis Bapt Conv	1	0	150	182	1.3	2.9
BAPT–So Bapt Conv	10	574	2,537	3,071	21.4	48.4

Religious Group	Number of Congregations	Number of Attendees	Number of Communicant, Confirmed, or Full Members	Adherents: Number of Adherents	Adherents: % of Total Pop.	Adherents: % of Total Adh.
Catholic	1	NR	NR	353	2.5	5.6
CGOD–Ch God (Ander)	1	160	NR	160	1.1	2.5
Ch of Nazarene	1	0	0	0	0.0	0.0
CHR–Chr Chs & Chs Cr	2	NR	277	335	2.3	5.3
CHR–Chs of Christ	2	42	48	55	0.4	0.9
Jehovah's Witness	1	NR	NR	NR	-	-
METH–AME	2	0	250	303	2.1	4.8
METH–Un Methodist	4	255	658	716	5.0	11.3
Non-denom Chr Chs	4	300	400	424	3.0	6.7
PENT–Assemb of God	2	112	72	147	1.0	2.3
PENT–Ch of God Proph	1	NR	48	58	0.4	0.9
PENT–COGIC	1	0	150	182	1.3	2.9
PENT–Intl Pent Holiness	1	45	40	48	0.3	0.8
PENT–Un Pent Ch Intl	1	NR	NR	NR	-	-
Sev Day Adv	1	120	209	240	1.7	3.8
MONITEAU	**40**	**1,834**	**5,667**	**9,470**	**60.7**	**100.0**
BAPT–So Bapt Conv	17	996	3,561	4,429	28.4	46.8
Catholic	2	NR	NR	1,700	10.9	18.0
CHR–Chr Ch (Disc)	3	110	292	363	2.3	3.8
CHR–Chs of Christ	1	40	37	48	0.3	0.5
Evan Assoc RCC	2	NR	NR	NR	-	-
Jehovah's Witness	1	NR	NR	NR	-	-
LDS–L-D Saints	1	NR	NR	290	1.9	3.1
LUTH–Luth–MO Synod	2	10	467	706	4.5	7.5
MENN–Fel Evg Ch	1	145	253	315	2.0	3.3
METH–Un Methodist	3	154	391	501	3.2	5.3
PENT–Assemb of God	3	129	84	285	1.8	3.0
PENT–Ch of God Proph	1	NR	38	47	0.3	0.5
PENT–Pent Ch of God	1	70	NR	109	0.7	1.2
Un C of Christ	2	180	544	677	4.3	7.1
MONROE	**36**	**1,839**	**3,981**	**6,215**	**70.3**	**100.0**
Bahá'í	0	NR	2	2	0.0	0.0
BAPT–So Bapt Conv	9	511	1,463	1,780	20.1	28.6
Catholic	3	NR	NR	942	10.7	15.2
CHR–Chr Ch (Disc)	8	492	1,160	1,411	16.0	22.7
LUTH–Luth–MO Synod	1	41	113	150	1.7	2.4
MENN–Amish Undif	3	NR	113	301	3.4	4.8
MENN–Ber Amish-Menn	1	20	12	20	0.2	0.3
METH–AME	1	0	100	122	1.4	2.0
METH–Un Methodist	4	183	452	727	8.2	11.7
Non-denom Chr Chs	3	480	490	603	6.8	9.7
PENT–Assemb of God	1	35	0	65	0.7	1.0
PRES–Presb Ch (USA)	2	77	76	92	1.0	1.5
MONTGOMERY	**42**	**1,360**	**3,450**	**5,659**	**46.2**	**100.0**
Bahá'í	0	NR	3	3	0.0	0.1
BAPT–So Bapt Conv	10	362	1,241	1,515	12.4	26.8
Catholic	4	NR	NR	1,439	11.8	25.4
Ch of Nazarene	1	30	28	98	0.8	1.7
CHR–Chr Ch (Disc)	3	84	350	427	3.5	7.5
CHR–Chr Chs & Chs Cr	3	NR	165	201	1.6	3.6
CHR–Chs of Christ	1	50	50	64	0.5	1.1
LUTH–Luth–MO Synod	3	242	464	629	5.1	11.1
METH–Un Methodist	9	358	736	802	6.6	14.2
Non-denom Chr Chs	1	100	150	150	1.2	2.7
PENT–Assemb of God	1	15	12	25	0.2	0.4
PENT–Un Pent Ch Intl	2	NR	NR	NR	-	-
PRES–Presb Ch (USA)	3	64	124	151	1.2	2.7
Un C of Christ	1	55	127	155	1.3	2.7
MORGAN	**52**	**2,651**	**6,353**	**9,283**	**45.1**	**100.0**
Bahá'í	0	NR	1	1	0.0	0.0
BAPT–So Bapt Conv	18	1,023	3,326	4,003	19.5	43.1
Catholic	2	NR	NR	1,278	6.2	13.8
CGOD–Ch God (Ander)	1	27	NR	27	0.1	0.3
CHR–Chr Ch (Disc)	2	173	335	403	2.0	4.3
CHR–Chr Chs & Chs Cr	1	NR	150	181	0.9	1.9
CHR–Chs of Christ	1	45	28	36	0.2	0.4
Jehovah's Witness	1	NR	NR	NR	-	-
LUTH–Assoc Free Luth	1	NR	NR	NR	-	-

NR–Not Reported   - Represents no adherents reported.   Percentages may not total 100 due to rounding.

Table 3: Religious Congregations by County and Group: 2010

Religious Group	Number of Congregations	Number of Attendees	Number of Communicant, Confirmed, or Full Members	Adherents: Number of Adherents	Adherents: % of Total Pop.	Adherents: % of Total Adh.
LUTH–E.L.C.A.	1	35	48	62	0.3	0.7
LUTH–Luth–MO Synod	3	224	427	570	2.8	6.1
MENN–CG in Cr (Menn)	3	NR	302	363	1.8	3.9
METH–Un Methodist	7	460	1,178	1,423	6.9	15.3
Non-denom Chr Chs	2	150	180	187	0.9	2.0
PENT–Assemb of God	3	337	188	411	2.0	4.4
PENT–Pent Ch of God	1	70	NR	109	0.5	1.2
PENT–Un Pent Ch Intl	1	NR	NR	NR	-	-
PRES–Presb Ch (USA)	3	71	123	148	0.7	1.6
Un C of Christ	1	36	67	81	0.4	0.9
NEW MADRID	**51**	**2,045**	**6,660**	**9,819**	**51.8**	**100.0**
BAPT–Amer Bapt Assn	2	NR	185	227	1.2	2.3
BAPT–So Bapt Conv	16	905	4,723	5,796	30.6	59.0
BRETH–Ch of Brethren	1	14	27	33	0.2	0.3
Catholic	2	NR	NR	1,303	6.9	13.3
CGOD–Ch God (Ander)	2	129	NR	129	0.7	1.3
Ch of Nazarene	1	14	15	20	0.1	0.2
CHR–Chr Ch (Disc)	1	27	42	52	0.3	0.5
CHR–Chs of Christ	6	260	248	310	1.6	3.2
METH–C.M.E.	1	0	100	123	0.6	1.3
METH–Cong Meth	1	NR	33	40	0.2	0.4
METH–Un Methodist	7	242	427	508	2.7	5.2
Non-denom Chr Chs	1	40	50	50	0.3	0.5
PENT–Assemb of God	4	340	181	456	2.4	4.6
PENT–Ch God (Cleve)	1	49	285	350	1.8	3.6
PENT–COGIC	2	0	300	368	1.9	3.7
PENT–Un Pent Ch Intl	2	NR	NR	NR	-	-
PRES–Presb Ch (USA)	1	25	44	54	0.3	0.5
NEWTON	**100**	**8,649**	**20,258**	**27,743**	**47.7**	**100.0**
ANG/EPIS–Episcopal	1	12	30	36	0.1	0.1
Bahá'í	0	NR	12	12	0.0	0.0
BAPT–Free Will Bapt	2	NR	126	156	0.3	0.6
BAPT–So Bapt Conv	39	3,598	12,999	16,129	27.8	58.1
Catholic	2	NR	NR	1,005	1.7	3.6
CGOD–Ch God (Ander)	1	109	NR	109	0.2	0.4
Ch of Nazarene	2	162	219	247	0.4	0.9
Chr & Miss Al	1	58	109	109	0.2	0.4
CHR–Chr Ch (Disc)	1	125	510	633	1.1	2.3
CHR–Chr Chs & Chs Cr	6	NR	1,165	1,446	2.5	5.2
CHR–Chs of Christ	15	1,418	1,304	1,709	2.9	6.2
CONG–Cong Chr, NA	1	NR	100	124	0.2	0.4
Jehovah's Witness	3	NR	NR	NR	-	-
LDS–Comm of Christ	1	NR	135	135	0.2	0.5
LDS–L-D Saints	2	NR	NR	780	1.3	2.8
LUTH–Luth–MO Synod	1	90	208	208	0.4	0.7
MENN–Menn Chr Fell	1	127	61	127	0.2	0.5
METH–Un Methodist	5	963	2,031	2,425	4.2	8.7
Non-denom Chr Chs	5	865	810	1,080	1.9	3.9
PENT–Assemb of God	6	987	336	1,038	1.8	3.7
PENT–Pent Ch of God	1	70	NR	109	0.2	0.4
PENT–Un Pent Ch Intl	2	NR	NR	NR	-	-
PRES–Presb Ch (USA)	1	50	77	96	0.2	0.3
Sev Day Adv	1	15	26	30	0.1	0.1
NODAWAY	**43**	**2,019**	**6,945**	**12,335**	**52.8**	**100.0**
ANG/EPIS–Episcopal	1	21	26	26	0.1	0.2
Bahá'í	0	NR	10	10	0.0	0.1
BAPT–So Bapt Conv	4	644	2,178	2,529	10.8	20.5
Calv Chpl	1	NR	NR	NR	-	-
Catholic	3	NR	NR	3,403	14.6	27.6
Ch of Nazarene	1	62	60	79	0.3	0.6
CHR–Chr Ch (Disc)	6	208	1,592	1,849	7.9	15.0
CHR–Chr Chs & Chs Cr	5	NR	702	815	3.5	6.6
CHR–Chs of Christ	2	78	80	104	0.4	0.8
Jehovah's Witness	1	NR	NR	NR	-	-
LDS–Comm of Christ	1	NR	182	182	0.8	1.5
LDS–L-D Saints	1	NR	NR	303	1.3	2.5
LUTH–Luth–MO Synod	1	95	126	151	0.6	1.2
MENN–Amish Undif	0	NR	21	39	0.2	0.3
MENN–Menn Chr Fell	1	97	35	97	0.4	0.8
METH–Un Methodist	12	512	1,601	2,185	9.3	17.7

Religious Group	Number of Congregations	Number of Attendees	Number of Communicant, Confirmed, or Full Members	Adherents: Number of Adherents	Adherents: % of Total Pop.	Adherents: % of Total Adh.
Non-denom Chr Chs	1	140	150	175	0.7	1.4
PENT–Assemb of God	1	115	80	270	1.2	2.2
PRES–Presb Ch (USA)	1	47	102	118	0.5	1.0
OREGON	**52**	**1,170**	**3,963**	**5,023**	**46.2**	**100.0**
BAPT–Free Will Bapt	20	NR	1,260	1,510	13.9	30.1
BAPT–So Bapt Conv	12	403	1,929	2,311	21.2	46.0
Catholic	1	NR	NR	136	1.2	2.7
CGOD–Ch God (Ander)	1	46	NR	46	0.4	0.9
CHR–Chs of Christ	6	398	367	457	4.2	9.1
Jehovah's Witness	1	NR	NR	NR	-	-
METH–Un Methodist	4	139	321	350	3.2	7.0
PENT–Assemb of God	4	184	73	197	1.8	3.9
PENT–Ch of God Proph	1	NR	13	16	0.1	0.3
PENT–Un Pent Ch Intl	2	NR	NR	NR	-	-
OSAGE	**36**	**596**	**2,038**	**9,863**	**71.1**	**100.0**
Bahá'í	0	NR	2	2	0.0	0.0
BAPT–So Bapt Conv	6	215	741	917	6.6	9.3
Catholic	12	NR	NR	7,298	52.6	74.0
CHR–Chr Chs & Chs Cr	5	NR	417	516	3.7	5.2
LDS–Comm of Christ	1	NR	138	138	1.0	1.4
LDS–L-D Saints	1	NR	NR	71	0.5	0.7
LUTH–Luth–MO Synod	2	22	119	148	1.1	1.5
MENN–Unaffil Amish-Menn	1	87	54	87	0.6	0.9
METH–Un Methodist	2	91	259	274	2.0	2.8
Non-denom Chr Chs	1	100	150	150	1.1	1.5
PENT–Assemb of God	1	32	25	97	0.7	1.0
PENT–Un Pent Ch Intl	1	NR	NR	NR	-	-
Un C of Christ	3	49	133	165	1.2	1.7
OZARK	**22**	**1,087**	**1,349**	**1,988**	**20.4**	**100.0**
Bahá'í	0	NR	3	3	0.0	0.2
BAPT–Amer Bapt Assn	1	NR	85	100	1.0	5.0
BAPT–So Bapt Conv	1	90	185	218	2.2	11.0
Catholic	1	NR	NR	151	1.6	7.6
CGOD–Ch God (Ander)	1	0	NR	0	0.0	0.0
CHR–Chr Ch (Disc)	1	82	253	299	3.1	15.0
CHR–Chs of Christ	10	579	545	666	6.8	33.5
Jehovah's Witness	1	NR	NR	NR	-	-
LUTH–Luth–MO Synod	1	12	17	19	0.2	1.0
METH–Un Methodist	1	66	127	183	1.9	9.2
PENT–Assemb of God	3	242	107	318	3.3	16.0
Sev Day Adv	1	16	27	31	0.3	1.6
PEMISCOT	**58**	**2,681**	**8,296**	**11,172**	**61.1**	**100.0**
Bahá'í	0	NR	1	1	0.0	0.0
BAPT–Natl Mis Bapt Conv	2	0	300	381	2.1	3.4
BAPT–So Bapt Conv	16	893	5,462	6,936	37.9	62.1
Catholic	1	NR	NR	263	1.4	2.4
Ch of Nazarene	2	11	24	41	0.2	0.4
CHR–Chr Chs & Chs Cr	1	NR	60	76	0.4	0.7
CHR–Chs of Christ	9	537	489	613	3.4	5.5
METH–AME	1	0	100	127	0.7	1.1
METH–Un Methodist	6	210	611	744	4.1	6.7
METH–Wesleyan	1	83	48	108	0.6	1.0
Non-denom Chr Chs	2	180	250	250	1.4	2.2
PENT–Assemb of God	3	121	40	166	0.9	1.5
PENT–Ch God (Cleve)	3	199	344	437	2.4	3.9
PENT–COGIC	2	0	150	190	1.0	1.7
PENT–Intl Pent Holiness	2	76	114	145	0.8	1.3
PENT–Pent Ch of God	3	210	NR	326	1.8	2.9
PENT–Un Pent Ch Intl	2	NR	NR	NR	-	-
PRES–Presb Ch (USA)	1	77	158	201	1.1	1.8
Sev Day Adv	1	84	145	167	0.9	1.5
PERRY	**31**	**2,263**	**4,326**	**12,435**	**65.5**	**100.0**
Bahá'í	0	NR	1	1	0.0	0.0
BAPT–So Bapt Conv	5	409	1,109	1,376	7.3	11.1
Catholic	8	NR	NR	6,940	36.6	55.8
CGOD–Ch God (Ander)	1	44	NR	44	0.2	0.4
Ch of Nazarene	1	0	0	0	0.0	0.0

NR–Not Reported   - Represents no adherents reported.   Percentages may not total 100 due to rounding.

Table 3: Religious Congregations by County and Group: 2010

Religious Group	Number of Congrega-tions	Number of Attendees	Number of Communicant, Confirmed, or Full Members	Adherents		
				Number of Adherents	% of Total Pop.	% of Total Adh.
CHR–Chs of Christ	1	17	10	15	0.1	0.1
Jehovah's Witness	1	NR	NR	NR	-	-
LUTH–Luth-MO Synod	6	1,443	2,709	3,465	18.3	27.9
METH–Un Methodist	2	85	166	189	1.0	1.5
Non-denom Chr Chs	2	150	195	212	1.1	1.7
PENT–Assemb of God	1	60	41	75	0.4	0.6
PENT–Un Pent Ch Intl	1	NR	NR	NR	-	-
PRES–Presb Ch (USA)	2	55	95	118	0.6	0.9
PETTIS	**92**	**6,562**	**16,851**	**25,105**	**59.5**	**100.0**
ANG/EPIS–Episcopal	1	55	138	138	0.3	0.5
Bahá'í	0	NR	9	9	0.0	0.0
BAPT–Amer Bapt Assn	1	NR	50	63	0.1	0.3
BAPT–Free Will Bapt	1	NR	63	79	0.2	0.3
BAPT–NBC USA	1	0	91	114	0.3	0.5
BAPT–So Bapt Conv	26	2,175	8,529	10,669	25.3	42.5
Catholic	3	NR	NR	2,902	6.9	11.6
Ch Cr, Scientst	1	NR	NR	NR	-	-
Ch of Nazarene	1	11	18	18	0.0	0.1
CHR–Chr Ch (Disc)	1	175	710	888	2.1	3.5
CHR–Chr Chs & Chs Cr	1	NR	475	594	1.4	2.4
CHR–Chs of Christ	1	65	54	84	0.2	0.3
Jehovah's Witness	1	NR	NR	NR	-	-
LDS–Comm of Christ	1	NR	179	179	0.4	0.7
LDS–L-D Saints	1	NR	NR	611	1.4	2.4
LUTH–E.L.C.A.	2	81	180	259	0.6	1.0
LUTH–Luth-MO Synod	3	226	1,042	1,403	3.3	5.6
MENN–Amish Undif	1	NR	34	59	0.1	0.2
MENN–Tamp Amish-Menn	1	419	225	419	1.0	1.7
METH–AME	1	0	100	125	0.3	0.5
METH–Un Methodist	15	1,384	2,469	2,907	6.9	11.6
New Apost Ch	1	NR	NR	NR	-	-
Non-denom Chr Chs	8	900	1,394	1,439	3.4	5.7
PENT–Assemb of God	3	335	68	469	1.1	1.9
PENT–Ch God (Cleve)	2	49	59	74	0.2	0.3
PENT–COGIC	1	25	25	31	0.1	0.1
PENT–Int Foursq Gos	1	43	29	36	0.1	0.1
PENT–Open Bible Std	2	154	NR	154	0.4	0.6
PENT–Pent Ch of God	1	70	NR	109	0.3	0.4
PENT–Un Pent Ch Intl	2	NR	NR	NR	-	-
PRES–Presb Ch (USA)	3	167	445	557	1.3	2.2
Salvation Army	1	23	43	214	0.5	0.9
Sev Day Adv	2	147	256	294	0.7	1.2
Un C of Christ	1	58	166	208	0.5	0.8
PHELPS	**80**	**4,993**	**11,719**	**18,673**	**41.4**	**100.0**
ANG/EPIS–Episcopal	2	149	327	327	0.7	1.8
Bahá'í	1	NR	44	44	0.1	0.2
BAPT–Free Will Bapt	1	NR	63	76	0.2	0.4
BAPT–So Bapt Conv	23	1,386	5,216	6,253	13.8	33.5
Catholic	3	NR	NR	2,334	5.2	12.5
CGOD–Ch God (Ander)	3	309	NR	309	0.7	1.7
Ch of Nazarene	1	44	60	62	0.1	0.3
CHR–Chr Ch (Disc)	1	0	43	52	0.1	0.3
CHR–Chr Chs & Chs Cr	6	NR	2,180	2,614	5.8	14.0
CHR–Chs of Christ	7	603	557	724	1.6	3.9
FRND–Fr Gen Cf	1	NR	0	0	0.0	0.0
Ind Fund Churches	1	NR	NR	NR	-	-
Jehovah's Witness	2	NR	NR	NR	-	-
LDS–Comm of Christ	1	NR	138	138	0.3	0.7
LDS–L-D Saints	1	NR	NR	806	1.8	4.3
LUTH–E.L.C.A.	1	22	32	33	0.1	0.2
LUTH–Luth-MO Synod	4	382	855	1,042	2.3	5.6
METH–Un Methodist	3	388	831	1,139	2.5	6.1
Muslim Est	1	134	NR	308	0.7	1.6
New Apost Ch	1	NR	NR	NR	-	-
Non-denom Chr Chs	4	310	402	437	1.0	2.3
PENT–Assemb of God	5	832	420	1,214	2.7	6.5
PENT–Pent Ch of God	1	70	NR	109	0.2	0.6
PENT–Un Pent Ch Intl	2	NR	NR	NR	-	-
PENT–Vineyard	1	183	262	314	0.7	1.7
PRES–Presb Ch (USA)	1	97	147	176	0.4	0.9
Sev Day Adv	1	76	132	152	0.3	0.8

Religious Group	Number of Congrega-tions	Number of Attendees	Number of Communicant, Confirmed, or Full Members	Adherents		
				Number of Adherents	% of Total Pop.	% of Total Adh.
Unit Univ	1	8	10	10	0.0	0.1
PIKE	**70**	**2,361**	**7,088**	**10,005**	**54.0**	**100.0**
ANG/EPIS–Episcopal	2	24	37	40	0.2	0.4
Bahá'í	0	NR	2	2	0.0	0.0
BAPT–So Bapt Conv	24	1,354	4,499	5,420	29.3	54.2
Catholic	3	NR	NR	1,250	6.8	12.5
Ch of Nazarene	1	101	131	230	1.2	2.3
CHR–Chr Ch (Disc)	10	181	683	823	4.4	8.2
CHR–Chr Chs & Chs Cr	1	NR	0	0	0.0	0.0
CHR–Chs of Christ	1	25	28	30	0.2	0.3
Jehovah's Witness	1	NR	NR	NR	-	-
LUTH–Luth-MO Synod	2	66	160	214	1.2	2.1
MENN–Amish Undif	3	NR	159	377	2.0	3.8
METH–AME	2	0	250	301	1.6	3.0
METH–Free Methodist	1	27	19	27	0.1	0.3
METH–Un Methodist	5	124	267	308	1.7	3.1
New Apost Ch	1	NR	NR	NR	-	-
Non-denom Chr Chs	3	200	275	287	1.6	2.9
PENT–Un Pent Ch Intl	1	NR	NR	NR	-	-
PRES–Presb Ch (USA)	9	259	578	696	3.8	7.0
PLATTE	**75**	**8,152**	**14,982**	**32,380**	**36.3**	**100.0**
ANG/EPIS–Episcopal	1	136	500	599	0.7	1.8
Bahá'í	0	NR	15	15	0.0	0.0
BAPT–Amer Bapt Assn	1	NR	120	148	0.2	0.5
BAPT–Free Will Bapt	1	NR	63	78	0.1	0.2
BAPT–N Am Bapt Conf	1	NR	124	153	0.2	0.5
BAPT–So Bapt Conv	18	3,246	4,377	5,391	6.0	16.6
Catholic	3	NR	NR	11,380	12.7	35.1
Ch of Nazarene	1	56	101	101	0.1	0.3
CHR–Chr Ch (Disc)	13	459	1,719	2,117	2.4	6.5
CHR–Chr Chs & Chs Cr	3	NR	337	415	0.5	1.3
CHR–Chs of Christ	1	230	257	401	0.4	1.2
Jehovah's Witness	4	NR	NR	NR	-	-
LDS–L-D Saints	5	NR	NR	1,959	2.2	6.1
LUTH–E.L.C.A.	1	255	525	682	0.8	2.1
LUTH–Luth-MO Synod	3	502	965	1,323	1.5	4.1
LUTH–Nor Amer Luth C	1	NR	NR	NR	-	-
LUTH–Wisc Ev Luth Syn	1	64	97	134	0.2	0.4
METH–C.M.E.	1	0	150	185	0.2	0.6
METH–Un Methodist	5	1,179	3,595	4,472	5.0	13.8
Non-denom Chr Chs	5	1,445	1,435	1,873	2.1	5.8
PENT–Assemb of God	2	388	212	463	0.5	1.4
PENT–Un Pent Ch Intl	2	NR	NR	NR	-	-
PRES–Presb Ch (USA)	1	192	334	411	0.5	1.3
REF–Ref Ch in U.S.	1	NR	56	80	0.1	0.2
POLK	**60**	**5,905**	**8,189**	**12,167**	**39.1**	**100.0**
ANG/EPIS–Episcopal	1	48	65	65	0.2	0.5
Bahá'í	0	NR	8	8	0.0	0.1
BAPT–So Bapt Conv	18	2,805	4,556	5,592	18.0	46.0
Catholic	2	NR	NR	633	2.0	5.2
Ch of God Gen Conf	1	NR	25	31	0.1	0.3
Ch of Nazarene	1	95	86	95	0.3	0.8
CHR–Chr Ch (Disc)	2	116	357	438	1.4	3.6
CHR–Chr Chs & Chs Cr	2	NR	55	68	0.2	0.6
CHR–Chs of Christ	3	225	208	266	0.9	2.2
Jehovah's Witness	2	NR	NR	NR	-	-
LUTH–Luth-MO Synod	1	70	171	209	0.7	1.7
MENN–Amish Undif	1	NR	69	186	0.6	1.5
METH–Un Methodist	7	480	1,117	1,458	4.7	12.0
Non-denom Chr Chs	7	500	719	729	2.3	6.0
PENT–Assemb of God	7	1,470	651	2,168	7.0	17.8
PENT–Pent Ch of God	1	70	NR	109	0.4	0.9
PENT–Un Pent Ch Intl	1	NR	NR	NR	-	-
PRES–Cumber Presb	2	NR	58	61	0.2	0.5
Sev Day Adv	1	26	44	51	0.2	0.4
PULASKI	**88**	**5,424**	**13,452**	**18,800**	**36.0**	**100.0**
Bahá'í	0	NR	16	16	0.0	0.1
BAPT–Free Will Bapt	2	NR	126	155	0.3	0.8

NR–Not Reported   - Represents no adherents reported.   Percentages may not total 100 due to rounding.

Table 3: Religious Congregations by County and Group: 2010

Religious Group	Number of Congrega-tions	Number of Attendees	Number of Communicant, Confirmed, or Full Members	Adherents		
				Number of Adherents	% of Total Pop.	% of Total Adh.
BAPT–NBC Amer	1	200	146	180	0.3	1.0
BAPT–So Bapt Conv	33	2,587	9,266	11,427	21.9	60.8
Catholic	4	NR	NR	452	0.9	2.4
CGOD–Ch God (Ander)	4	183	NR	183	0.4	1.0
Ch of Nazarene	1	86	95	102	0.2	0.5
CHR–Chr Ch (Disc)	1	38	110	136	0.3	0.7
CHR–Chr Chs & Chs Cr	6	NR	1,075	1,326	2.5	7.1
CHR–Chs of Christ	8	394	401	488	0.9	2.6
Christian Un	2	NR	NR	NR	-	-
Jehovah's Witness	1	NR	NR	NR	-	-
LDS–L-D Saints	2	NR	NR	1,311	2.5	7.0
LUTH–Luth–MO Synod	1	98	202	256	0.5	1.4
MENN–Amish Undif	1	NR	25	79	0.2	0.4
METH–Un Methodist	3	316	580	727	1.4	3.9
Non-denom Chr Chs	6	995	1,075	1,244	2.4	6.6
PENT–Assemb of God	5	328	159	395	0.8	2.1
PENT–Ch God (Cleve)	1	64	49	60	0.1	0.3
PENT–Pent Ch of God	1	70	NR	109	0.2	0.6
PENT–Un Pent Ch Intl	2	NR	NR	NR	-	-
PRES–Presb Ch (USA)	1	46	94	116	0.2	0.6
PRES–Presb Ch Amer	1	0	0	0	0.0	0.0
Sev Day Adv	1	19	33	38	0.1	0.2
PUTNAM	**18**	**613**	**1,786**	**2,512**	**50.5**	**100.0**
BAPT–So Bapt Conv	5	342	925	1,129	22.7	44.9
Catholic	1	NR	NR	65	1.3	2.6
CHR–Chr Chs & Chs Cr	4	NR	505	616	12.4	24.5
CHR–Chs of Christ	3	88	78	104	2.1	4.1
Grace Gosp Fel	1	NR	NR	NR	-	-
MENN–Amish Undif	1	NR	50	143	2.9	5.7
METH–Un Methodist	1	63	193	296	5.9	11.8
PENT–Assemb of God	1	50	35	50	1.0	2.0
PENT–Pent Ch of God	1	70	NR	109	2.2	4.3
RALLS	**17**	**788**	**3,093**	**4,057**	**39.9**	**100.0**
BAPT–So Bapt Conv	6	445	1,844	2,245	22.1	55.3
Catholic	1	NR	NR	353	3.5	8.7
CHR–Chr Ch (Disc)	4	113	627	763	7.5	18.8
CHR–Chr Chs & Chs Cr	1	NR	125	152	1.5	3.7
LUTH–Luth–MO Synod	1	12	23	33	0.3	0.8
METH–Un Methodist	3	194	428	455	4.5	11.2
PRES–Presb Ch (USA)	1	24	46	56	0.6	1.4
RANDOLPH	**57**	**3,453**	**10,129**	**14,243**	**56.0**	**100.0**
Bahá'í	0	NR	3	3	0.0	0.0
BAPT–Reg Bapt Gen As	1	NR	NR	NR	-	-
BAPT–So Bapt Conv	11	815	3,805	4,640	18.3	32.6
Catholic	1	NR	NR	1,634	6.4	11.5
CGOD–Ch God (Ander)	1	24	NR	24	0.1	0.2
Ch of Nazarene	1	68	72	171	0.7	1.2
CHR–Chr Ch (Disc)	8	203	1,196	1,459	5.7	10.2
CHR–Chr Chs & Chs Cr	3	NR	585	713	2.8	5.0
CHR–Chs of Christ	3	121	120	144	0.6	1.0
Jehovah's Witness	1	NR	NR	NR	-	-
LDS–L-D Saints	1	NR	NR	415	1.6	2.9
LUTH–Luth–MO Synod	1	75	223	256	1.0	1.8
MENN–Amish Undif	1	NR	65	191	0.8	1.3
METH–AME	2	0	250	305	1.2	2.1
METH–Un Methodist	5	321	652	814	3.2	5.7
Non-denom Chr Chs	9	1,425	2,519	2,561	10.1	18.0
PENT–Assemb of God	2	163	68	222	0.9	1.6
PENT–COGIC	2	10	160	195	0.8	1.4
PENT–Un Pent Ch Intl	1	NR	NR	NR	-	-
PRES–Cumber Presb	1	NR	13	28	0.1	0.2
PRES–Presb Ch (USA)	1	90	157	191	0.8	1.3
Sev Day Adv	1	138	241	277	1.1	1.9
RAY	**53**	**3,002**	**7,184**	**9,247**	**39.4**	**100.0**
Bahá'í	0	NR	2	2	0.0	0.0
BAPT–So Bapt Conv	14	1,327	3,979	4,905	20.9	53.0
BRETH–Ch of Brethren	1	43	37	46	0.2	0.5
Catholic	1	NR	NR	291	1.2	3.1

Religious Group	Number of Congrega-tions	Number of Attendees	Number of Communicant, Confirmed, or Full Members	Adherents		
				Number of Adherents	% of Total Pop.	% of Total Adh.
CGOD–Ches God-Gen Con	1	40	83	102	0.4	1.1
Ch of Nazarene	2	66	150	150	0.6	1.6
CHR–Chr Ch (Disc)	4	126	382	471	2.0	5.1
CHR–Chr Chs & Chs Cr	1	NR	60	74	0.3	0.8
CHR–Chs of Christ	2	85	70	90	0.4	1.0
Christian Un	5	NR	NR	NR	-	-
Jehovah's Witness	1	NR	NR	NR	-	-
LDS–Comm of Christ	1	NR	179	179	0.8	1.9
LUTH–Luth–MO Synod	1	54	120	145	0.6	1.6
MENN–Menn Chr Fell	1	92	52	92	0.4	1.0
METH–AME	1	0	100	123	0.5	1.3
METH–C.M.E.	1	50	100	123	0.5	1.3
METH–Un Methodist	7	389	1,163	1,224	5.2	13.2
Non-denom Chr Chs	2	268	370	400	1.7	4.3
PENT–Assemb of God	2	322	166	510	2.2	5.5
PENT–Intl Pent Holiness	1	25	54	67	0.3	0.7
PENT–Pent Ch of God	1	70	NR	109	0.5	1.2
PENT–Un Pent Ch Intl	1	NR	NR	NR	-	-
PRES–Presb Ch (USA)	2	45	117	144	0.6	1.6
REYNOLDS	**23**	**1,127**	**2,881**	**3,613**	**54.0**	**100.0**
Bahá'í	0	NR	1	1	0.0	0.0
BAPT–So Bapt Conv	11	772	2,411	2,903	43.4	80.3
Catholic	2	NR	NR	83	1.2	2.3
Ch of Nazarene	1	34	30	38	0.6	1.1
CHR–Chs of Christ	1	20	13	17	0.3	0.5
LDS–Comm of Christ	1	NR	138	138	2.1	3.8
METH–Un Methodist	1	56	99	139	2.1	3.8
Non-denom Chr Chs	2	135	135	169	2.5	4.7
PENT–Assemb of God	4	110	54	125	1.9	3.5
RIPLEY	**38**	**1,504**	**2,619**	**3,665**	**26.0**	**100.0**
BAPT–Free Will Bapt	2	NR	126	153	1.1	4.2
BAPT–Natl Mis Bapt Conv	1	0	150	182	1.3	5.0
BAPT–S-D Baptist Gen Con	1	22	20	24	0.2	0.7
BAPT–So Bapt Conv	5	306	1,246	1,514	10.7	41.3
Catholic	1	NR	NR	208	1.5	5.7
CGOD–Ch God (Ander)	4	263	NR	263	1.9	7.2
Ch of God Gen Conf	1	NR	5	6	0.0	0.2
CHR–Chr Ch (Disc)	1	36	75	91	0.6	2.5
CHR–Chr Chs & Chs Cr	1	NR	0	0	0.0	0.0
CHR–Chs of Christ	7	310	317	368	2.6	10.0
Jehovah's Witness	1	NR	NR	NR	-	-
LUTH–Luth–MO Synod	1	31	42	46	0.3	1.3
METH–Un Methodist	2	89	146	150	1.1	4.1
Non-denom Chr Chs	3	320	350	425	3.0	11.6
PENT–Assemb of God	1	54	33	107	0.8	2.9
PENT–Ch God (Cleve)	1	25	37	45	0.3	1.2
PENT–Un Pent Ch Intl	2	NR	NR	NR	-	-
PRES–Orth Pres Ch	1	24	15	17	0.1	0.5
PRES–Presb Ch (USA)	1	0	15	18	0.1	0.5
Sev Day Adv	1	24	42	48	0.3	1.3
ST. CHARLES	**224**	**42,939**	**66,601**	**186,493**	**51.7**	**100.0**
ANG/EPIS–Anglican NA	1	NR	NR	NR	-	-
ANG/EPIS–Episcopal	2	240	604	788	0.2	0.4
Ap Chr Ch-Amer	1	16	12	16	0.0	0.0
Bahá'í	3	NR	81	81	0.0	0.0
BAPT–Amer Bapt Assn	1	NR	85	106	0.0	0.1
BAPT–Free Will Bapt	2	NR	126	157	0.0	0.1
BAPT–Natl Mis Bapt Conv	1	0	150	187	0.1	0.1
BAPT–So Bapt Conv	31	6,623	18,039	22,527	6.2	12.1
BUDD–Mahayana	2	NR	NR	252	0.1	0.1
Catholic	20	NR	NR	85,536	23.7	45.9
CGOD–Ch God (Ander)	3	86	NR	86	0.0	0.0
Ch Cr, Scientst	2	NR	NR	NR	-	-
Ch of Nazarene	3	507	390	1,032	0.3	0.6
Chr & Miss Al	1	65	0	80	0.0	0.0
CHR–Chr Ch (Disc)	4	93	292	365	0.1	0.2
CHR–Chr Chs & Chs Cr	6	NR	4,369	5,456	1.5	2.9
CHR–Chs of Christ	11	1,064	1,037	1,356	0.4	0.7
Evan Free Ch	1	3,500	NR	3,500	1.0	1.9
HINDU–Post Ren	1	NR	NR	77	0.0	0.0

NR–Not Reported - Represents no adherents reported. Percentages may not total 100 due to rounding.

Table 3: Religious Congregations by County and Group: 2010

Religious Group	Number of Congrega-tions	Number of Attendees	Number of Communicant, Confirmed, or Full Members	Adherents: Number of Adherents	Adherents: % of Total Pop.	Adherents: % of Total Adh.
Ind Fund Churches	1	NR	NR	NR	-	-
Jehovah's Witness	2	NR	NR	NR	-	-
JUD–Reform	1	20	36	97	0.0	0.1
LDS–Comm of Christ	1	NR	138	138	0.0	0.1
LDS–L-D Saints	8	NR	NR	3,281	0.9	1.8
LUTH–E.L.C.A.	5	1,056	1,718	2,363	0.7	1.3
LUTH–Luth Cong Msn Chr	1	175	209	261	0.1	0.1
LUTH–Luth–MO Synod	12	5,181	10,868	14,851	4.1	8.0
LUTH–Wisc Ev Luth Syn	2	159	277	367	0.1	0.2
METH–AME	2	45	175	219	0.1	0.1
METH–Un Methodist	10	4,920	5,735	13,478	3.7	7.2
METH–Wesleyan	1	92	58	120	0.0	0.1
Non-denom Chr Chs	36	14,356	14,270	18,336	5.1	9.8
PENT–Assemb of God	9	1,789	997	2,307	0.6	1.2
PENT–Ch God (Cleve)	2	83	180	225	0.1	0.1
PENT–Ch of God Proph	1	NR	54	67	0.0	0.0
PENT–Int Foursq Gos	1	28	28	35	0.0	0.0
PENT–Pent Ch of God	1	70	NR	109	0.0	0.1
PENT–Un Pent Ch Intl	7	NR	NR	NR	-	-
PRES–Evan Presby Ch	1	NR	35	44	0.0	0.0
PRES–Presb Ch (USA)	3	789	1,846	2,305	0.6	1.2
PRES–Presb Ch Amer	2	330	299	402	0.1	0.2
REF–Ref Ch in Am	1	173	281	336	0.1	0.2
Salvation Army	2	91	137	482	0.1	0.3
Sev Day Adv	1	144	250	288	0.1	0.2
Sikh	1	NR	NR	NR	-	-
Un C of Christ	13	1,244	3,825	4,777	1.3	2.6
Unity Ch	1	NR	NR	NR	-	-
Zoroastrian	0	NR	NR	3	0.0	0.0
ST. CLAIR	**30**	**1,125**	**3,634**	**4,542**	**46.3**	**100.0**
BAPT–So Bapt Conv	11	645	2,472	2,909	29.7	64.0
BRETH–Ch of Brethren	1	25	43	51	0.5	1.1
Catholic	1	NR	NR	80	0.8	1.8
Ch of Nazarene	1	16	18	47	0.5	1.0
CHR–Chr Ch (Disc)	2	0	145	171	1.7	3.8
CHR–Chr Chs & Chs Cr	4	NR	233	274	2.8	6.0
LUTH–Luth–MO Synod	1	75	119	142	1.4	3.1
MENN–Amish Undif	1	NR	54	131	1.3	2.9
METH–Un Methodist	5	199	403	505	5.2	11.1
PENT–Assemb of God	1	125	69	140	1.4	3.1
PRES–Presb Ch (USA)	1	10	16	19	0.2	0.4
Un C of Christ	1	30	62	73	0.7	1.6
STE. GENEVIEVE	**27**	**843**	**2,450**	**9,326**	**51.4**	**100.0**
ANG/EPIS–Episcopal	1	22	5	5	0.0	0.1
Bahá'í	0	NR	1	1	0.0	0.0
BAPT–So Bapt Conv	12	534	1,901	2,306	12.7	24.7
Catholic	9	NR	NR	6,434	35.5	69.0
Jehovah's Witness	1	NR	NR	NR	-	-
LUTH–Luth–MO Synod	1	57	143	159	0.9	1.7
Non-denom Chr Chs	2	175	300	300	1.7	3.2
PRES–Presb Ch (USA)	1	55	100	121	0.7	1.3
ST. FRANCOIS	**126**	**7,807**	**19,374**	**28,737**	**44.0**	**100.0**
ANG/EPIS–Episcopal	1	16	41	41	0.1	0.1
Bahá'í	0	NR	10	10	0.0	0.0
BAPT–Free Will Bapt	10	NR	630	760	1.2	2.6
BAPT–So Bapt Conv	32	2,706	10,510	12,686	19.4	44.1
Calv Chpl	1	NR	NR	NR	-	-
Catholic	5	NR	NR	2,991	4.6	10.4
CGOD–Ch God (Ander)	3	182	NR	182	0.3	0.6
CGOD–Ches God-Gen Con	4	225	403	486	0.7	1.7
Ch of God Gen Conf	1	NR	45	54	0.1	0.2
Ch of Nazarene	3	267	397	412	0.6	1.4
CHR–Chr Ch (Disc)	3	0	338	408	0.6	1.4
CHR–Chr Chs & Chs Cr	3	NR	222	268	0.4	0.9
CHR–Chs of Christ	4	275	276	343	0.5	1.2
Evan Free Ch	1	40	NR	40	0.1	0.1
Jehovah's Witness	2	NR	NR	NR	-	-
LDS–Comm of Christ	1	NR	138	138	0.2	0.5
LDS–L-D Saints	2	NR	NR	705	1.1	2.5
LUTH–Luth–MO Synod	4	483	1,273	1,663	2.5	5.8

Religious Group	Number of Congrega-tions	Number of Attendees	Number of Communicant, Confirmed, or Full Members	Adherents: Number of Adherents	Adherents: % of Total Pop.	Adherents: % of Total Adh.
METH–Un Methodist	11	941	1,777	2,422	3.7	8.4
Non-denom Chr Chs	6	661	810	866	1.3	3.0
ORTHE–Orth Ch in Amer	1	20	NR	40	0.1	0.1
PENT–Assemb of God	9	1,212	542	1,747	2.7	6.1
PENT–Ch God (Cleve)	10	647	1,679	2,027	3.1	7.1
PENT–Pent Ch of God	1	70	NR	109	0.2	0.4
PENT–Un Pent Ch Intl	3	NR	NR	NR	-	-
PRES–Presb Ch (USA)	2	0	173	209	0.3	0.7
Sev Day Adv	1	27	47	54	0.1	0.2
Un C of Christ	1	35	63	76	0.1	0.3
Unity Ch	1	NR	NR	NR	-	-
ST. LOUIS	**730**	**116,311**	**202,309**	**516,073**	**51.7**	**100.0**
ANG/EPIS–Anglican NA	2	NR	NR	NR	-	-
ANG/EPIS–Episcopal	16	2,383	7,180	7,763	0.8	1.5
Bahá'í	3	NR	373	373	0.0	0.1
BAPT–Alliance Bapt	1	NR	NR	NR	-	-
BAPT–Amer Bapt Assn	1	NR	0	0	0.0	0.0
BAPT–Amer Bapt USA	1	7,567	8,029	9,739	1.0	1.9
BAPT–Converge/BGC	3	550	NR	660	0.1	0.1
BAPT–Free Will Bapt	3	NR	189	229	0.0	0.0
BAPT–Natl Mis Bapt Conv	6	0	750	910	0.1	0.2
BAPT–NBC Amer	2	45	225	273	0.0	0.1
BAPT–NBC USA	8	1,010	2,455	2,978	0.3	0.6
BAPT–Prog NBC	1	0	150	182	0.0	0.0
BAPT–Reg Bapt Gen As	1	NR	NR	NR	-	-
BAPT–So Bapt Conv	74	10,381	32,486	39,405	3.9	7.6
BUDD–Mahayana	5	NR	NR	3,257	0.3	0.6
BUDD–Theravada	2	NR	NR	1,378	0.1	0.3
Calv Chpl	1	NR	NR	NR	-	-
Catholic	74	NR	NR	230,488	23.1	44.7
CGOD–Ch God (Ander)	8	539	NR	539	0.1	0.1
Ch Cr, Scientst	8	NR	NR	NR	-	-
Ch of Nazarene	11	1,202	1,633	2,301	0.2	0.4
Chr & Miss Al	2	98	63	168	0.0	0.0
CHR–Chr Ch (Disc)	10	685	1,831	2,221	0.2	0.4
CHR–Chr Chs & Chs Cr	11	NR	4,060	4,925	0.5	1.0
CHR–Chs of Christ	20	2,914	2,848	3,608	0.4	0.7
CHR–Int Chs of Christ	1	NR	314	381	0.0	0.1
Christian Brethren	1	NR	NR	NR	-	-
CONG–Cong Chr, NA	1	NR	14	17	0.0	0.0
Evan Assoc RCC	1	NR	NR	NR	-	-
Evan Cov Ch	3	591	320	769	0.1	0.1
Evan Free Ch	8	2,720	NR	2,720	0.3	0.5
HINDU–I/A Temples	3	NR	NR	2,659	0.3	0.5
HINDU–Post Ren	2	NR	NR	35	0.0	0.0
HINDU–Renaiss	1	NR	NR	85	0.0	0.0
HINDU–Trad Temples	1	NR	NR	500	0.1	0.1
Ind Fund Churches	5	NR	NR	NR	-	-
Jain	1	NR	NR	NR	-	-
Jehovah's Witness	11	NR	NR	NR	-	-
JUD–Conserv	3	1,207	1,355	3,659	0.4	0.7
JUD–Orth	8	1,692	700	2,350	0.2	0.5
JUD–Reconst	1	9	12	32	0.0	0.0
JUD–Reform	6	2,563	4,520	12,204	1.2	2.4
LDS–Comm of Christ	3	NR	414	414	0.0	0.1
LDS–L-D Saints	16	NR	NR	7,275	0.7	1.4
LUTH–Assoc Free Luth	1	NR	NR	NR	-	-
LUTH–Ch Luth Conf	1	NR	NR	NR	-	-
LUTH–E.L.C.A.	17	2,723	6,571	8,286	0.8	1.6
LUTH–Luth–MO Synod	39	14,241	29,182	38,950	3.9	7.5
LUTH–Wisc Ev Luth Syn	1	105	163	242	0.0	0.0
METH–AME	11	150	1,178	1,429	0.1	0.3
METH–AME Zion	2	75	240	291	0.0	0.1
METH–C.M.E.	4	300	1,226	1,487	0.1	0.3
METH–Free Methodist	1	35	29	35	0.0	0.0
METH–Un Methodist	33	6,935	16,043	23,057	2.3	4.5
METH–Wesleyan	1	26	34	34	0.0	0.0
Muslim Est	7	938	NR	1,908	0.2	0.4
Non-denom Chr Chs	86	32,643	40,853	44,442	4.4	8.6
ORTHE–Ant Orth of NA	1	60	NR	100	0.0	0.0
ORTHE–Greek Orthodox	1	200	NR	1,500	0.2	0.3
ORTHE–Holy Orth in NA	1	15	NR	20	0.0	0.0
ORTHE–Serb Orth USA	1	38	NR	82	0.0	0.0

NR–Not Reported   - Represents no adherents reported.   Percentages may not total 100 due to rounding.

Table 3: Religious Congregations by County and Group: 2010

Religious Group	Number of Congrega-tions	Number of Attendees	Number of Communicant, Confirmed, or Full Members	Adherents: Number of Adherents	Adherents: % of Total Pop.	Adherents: % of Total Adh.
ORTHO–Coptic Orth Ch	1	150	NR	250	0.0	0.0
ORTHO–Ethiopian Orth	1	NR	NR	NR	-	-
ORTHO–Malan Dioc Am	1	30	NR	90	0.0	0.0
PENT–Apos Faith Msn	1	NR	35	42	0.0	0.0
PENT–Assemb of God	27	2,493	1,631	3,299	0.3	0.6
PENT–Ch God (Cleve)	3	2,870	2,814	3,413	0.3	0.7
PENT–Ch Lord Jesus Apos	1	NR	NR	NR	-	-
PENT–COGIC	8	975	1,500	1,819	0.2	0.4
PENT–Full Gosp Bapt	3	NR	NR	NR	-	-
PENT–Int Foursq Gos	6	360	475	576	0.1	0.1
PENT–Intl Pent Holiness	1	96	120	146	0.0	0.0
PENT–Pent Ch of God	2	140	NR	217	0.0	0.0
PENT–Un Pent Ch Intl	16	NR	NR	NR	-	-
PENT–United Holy Ch	2	NR	NR	NR	-	-
PENT–Vineyard	2	282	377	457	0.0	0.1
PRES–Evan Presby Ch	5	NR	2,397	2,908	0.3	0.6
PRES–Free Ch Scot	1	NR	NR	NR	-	-
PRES–Korean Amer Pres	1	NR	NR	NR	-	-
PRES–Korean Pres Amer	2	NR	NR	NR	-	-
PRES–Orth Pres Ch	2	98	88	117	0.0	0.0
PRES–Presb Ch (USA)	21	3,178	9,008	10,927	1.1	2.1
PRES–Presb Ch Amer	16	4,955	4,592	5,919	0.6	1.1
REF–Christian Ref	1	75	77	93	0.0	0.0
Salvation Army	4	362	456	3,274	0.3	0.6
Sev Day Adv	8	1,372	2,388	2,745	0.3	0.5
Sikh	1	NR	NR	NR	-	-
Swedenborgian	1	NR	NR	NR	-	-
Un C of Christ	30	3,725	10,218	12,394	1.2	2.4
Unit Univ	2	510	693	1,013	0.1	0.2
Unity Ch	2	NR	NR	NR	-	-
Zoroastrian	0	NR	NR	14	0.0	0.0
ST. LOUIS (CITY)	**411**	**47,134**	**71,669**	**147,353**	**46.1**	**100.0**
ANG/EPIS–Episcopal	6	617	1,162	1,578	0.5	1.1
Bahá'í	1	NR	159	159	0.0	0.1
BAPT–Alliance Bapt	1	NR	NR	NR	-	-
BAPT–Amer Bapt USA	10	2,282	4,884	5,834	1.8	4.0
BAPT–Converge/BGC	1	75	NR	90	0.0	0.1
BAPT–Free Will Bapt	1	NR	63	75	0.0	0.1
BAPT–Natl Mis Bapt Conv	11	285	1,485	1,774	0.6	1.2
BAPT–NBC Amer	3	400	600	717	0.2	0.5
BAPT–NBC USA	32	12,310	17,183	20,526	6.4	13.9
BAPT–Prog NBC	9	565	1,935	2,311	0.7	1.6
BAPT–Reg Bapt Gen As	1	NR	NR	NR	-	-
BAPT–So Bapt Conv	37	4,294	6,693	7,995	2.5	5.4
BUDD–Mahayana	6	NR	NR	986	0.3	0.7
BUDD–Theravada	1	NR	NR	15	0.0	0.0
BUDD–Vajrayana	1	NR	NR	62	0.0	0.0
Catholic	39	NR	NR	49,014	15.4	33.3
CGOD–Ch God (Ander)	3	630	NR	630	0.2	0.4
Ch Cr, Scientst	2	NR	NR	NR	-	-
Ch of Chr (Hol)	4	NR	NR	NR	-	-
Ch of Nazarene	4	96	124	243	0.1	0.2
CHR–Chr Ch (Disc)	6	379	822	982	0.3	0.7
CHR–Chr Chs & Chs Cr	2	NR	23	27	0.0	0.0
CHR–Chs of Christ	6	525	513	592	0.2	0.4
Christian Brethren	3	NR	NR	NR	-	-
Evan Free Ch	2	157	NR	157	0.0	0.1
FRND–Fr Gen Cf	1	NR	107	128	0.0	0.1
Grace Gosp Fel	2	NR	NR	NR	-	-
HINDU–I/A Temples	3	NR	NR	2,050	0.6	1.4
HINDU–Post Ren	2	NR	NR	41	0.0	0.0
Jehovah's Witness	6	NR	NR	NR	-	-
JUD–Orth	1	43	50	60	0.0	0.0
JUD–Reform	1	419	739	1,995	0.6	1.4
LDS–L-D Saints	1	NR	NR	685	0.2	0.5
LUTH–E.L.C.A.	4	290	519	648	0.2	0.4
LUTH–Luth-MO Synod	25	2,525	5,115	6,967	2.2	4.7
MENN–Mennonite USA	2	65	119	142	0.0	0.1
METH–AME	11	1,820	4,011	4,791	1.5	3.3
METH–AME Zion	3	45	300	358	0.1	0.2
METH–C.M.E.	4	825	1,550	1,852	0.6	1.3
METH–Free Methodist	2	51	55	61	0.0	0.0
METH–Un Methodist	14	1,621	2,673	3,768	1.2	2.6

Religious Group	Number of Congrega-tions	Number of Attendees	Number of Communicant, Confirmed, or Full Members	Adherents: Number of Adherents	Adherents: % of Total Pop.	Adherents: % of Total Adh.
Metro Comm Ch	1	260	379	453	0.1	0.3
Muslim Est	10	1,488	NR	3,356	1.1	2.3
Nat Spirit Asso	1	NR	NR	NR	-	-
Non-denom Chr Chs	44	10,797	12,912	14,233	4.5	9.7
OCATH–Pol Natl Cath	1	NR	NR	NR	-	-
ORTHE–Greek Orthodox	1	275	NR	2,000	0.6	1.4
ORTHE–Orth Ch in Amer	2	60	NR	85	0.0	0.1
ORTHE–Rus Orth Abroad	1	70	NR	118	0.0	0.1
ORTHE–Serb Orth USA	1	120	NR	550	0.2	0.4
PENT–Assemb of God	6	221	96	325	0.1	0.2
PENT–Ch God (Cleve)	2	175	328	392	0.1	0.3
PENT–Ch Lord Jesus Apos	3	NR	NR	NR	-	-
PENT–COGIC	15	960	1,870	2,234	0.7	1.5
PENT–Full Gosp Bapt	5	NR	NR	NR	-	-
PENT–Pent Ch of God	1	70	NR	109	0.0	0.1
PENT–Un Pent Ch Intl	2	NR	NR	NR	-	-
PENT–United Holy Ch	1	NR	NR	NR	-	-
PRES–Evan Presby Ch	1	NR	24	29	0.0	0.0
PRES–Presb Ch (USA)	14	598	1,633	1,951	0.6	1.3
PRES–Presb Ch Amer	4	370	550	615	0.2	0.4
Sev Day Adv	2	491	854	982	0.3	0.7
Sikh	1	NR	NR	NR	-	-
Un C of Christ	15	707	1,829	2,185	0.7	1.5
Unit Univ	1	153	310	423	0.1	0.3
Unity Ch	1	NR	NR	NR	-	-
Zoroastrian	1	NR	NR	NR	-	-
SALINE	**74**	**2,851**	**8,651**	**12,903**	**55.2**	**100.0**
ANG/EPIS–Episcopal	1	7	4	13	0.1	0.1
Bahá'í	0	NR	14	14	0.1	0.1
BAPT–Free Will Bapt	1	NR	63	77	0.3	0.6
BAPT–So Bapt Conv	15	773	3,310	4,024	17.2	31.2
Catholic	3	NR	NR	2,009	8.6	15.6
CGOD–Ch God (Ander)	1	5	NR	5	0.0	0.0
Ch of Nazarene	1	90	189	189	0.8	1.5
CHR–Chr Ch (Disc)	5	0	614	746	3.2	5.8
CHR–Chr Chs & Chs Cr	1	NR	30	36	0.2	0.3
CHR–Chs of Christ	3	98	110	133	0.6	1.0
Ind Fund Churches	1	NR	NR	NR	-	-
Jehovah's Witness	1	NR	NR	NR	-	-
LDS–Comm of Christ	1	NR	179	179	0.8	1.4
LDS–L-D Saints	1	NR	NR	260	1.1	2.0
LUTH–Luth-MO Synod	7	466	1,098	1,318	5.6	10.2
METH–AME	2	75	250	304	1.3	2.4
METH–Un Methodist	10	374	1,179	1,564	6.7	12.1
Non-denom Chr Chs	4	425	600	612	2.6	4.7
PENT–Assemb of God	4	229	126	283	1.2	2.2
PENT–COGIC	2	50	200	243	1.0	1.9
PENT–Un Pent Ch Intl	1	NR	NR	NR	-	-
PRES–Cumber Presb	1	NR	102	187	0.8	1.4
PRES–Presb Ch (USA)	5	176	375	456	2.0	3.5
Sev Day Adv	1	20	34	39	0.2	0.3
Un C of Christ	2	63	174	212	0.9	1.6
SCHUYLER	**17**	**382**	**1,550**	**2,118**	**47.8**	**100.0**
Bahá'í	0	NR	1	1	0.0	0.0
BAPT–So Bapt Conv	4	131	565	702	15.8	33.1
CHR–Chr Chs & Chs Cr	3	NR	540	671	15.1	31.7
LUTH–E.L.C.A.	1	27	47	68	1.5	3.2
MENN–Amish Undif	2	NR	90	256	5.8	12.1
METH–Un Methodist	3	85	127	180	4.1	8.5
Non-denom Chr Chs	3	119	180	180	4.1	8.5
PENT–Assemb of God	1	20	0	60	1.4	2.8
SCOTLAND	**18**	**455**	**1,004**	**1,420**	**29.3**	**100.0**
BAPT–So Bapt Conv	5	183	298	383	7.9	27.0
Catholic	1	NR	NR	123	2.5	8.7
CHR–Chr Ch (Disc)	1	33	45	58	1.2	4.1
CHR–Chr Chs & Chs Cr	1	NR	150	193	4.0	13.6
CHR–Chs of Christ	2	45	45	55	1.1	3.9
Jehovah's Witness	1	NR	NR	NR	-	-
LUTH–Luth-MO Synod	1	24	28	38	0.8	2.7
METH–Un Methodist	5	140	381	497	10.3	35.0

NR–Not Reported   - Represents no adherents reported.   Percentages may not total 100 due to rounding.

Table 3: Religious Congregations by County and Group: 2010

Religious Group	Number of Congrega-tions	Number of Attendees	Number of Communicant, Confirmed, or Full Members	Adherents		
				Number of Adherents	% of Total Pop.	% of Total Adh.
PRES–Presb Ch (USA)	1	30	57	73	1.5	5.1
SCOTT	**92**	**5,748**	**12,911**	**23,315**	**59.5**	**100.0**
ANG/EPIS–Anglican NA	1	NR	NR	NR	-	-
ANG/EPIS–Episcopal	1	28	35	63	0.2	0.3
Bahá'í	0	NR	1	1	0.0	0.0
BAPT–Amer Bapt Assn	1	NR	60	74	0.2	0.3
BAPT–NBC USA	1	30	50	62	0.2	0.3
BAPT–So Bapt Conv	20	1,765	6,272	7,765	19.8	33.3
Catholic	7	NR	NR	6,531	16.7	28.0
CGOD–Ch God (Ander)	2	225	NR	225	0.6	1.0
Ch of Nazarene	2	93	206	206	0.5	0.9
CHR–Chr Ch (Disc)	2	133	287	355	0.9	1.5
CHR–Chr Chs & Chs Cr	3	NR	590	730	1.9	3.1
CHR–Chs of Christ	6	657	672	884	2.3	3.8
Jehovah's Witness	1	NR	NR	NR	-	-
LDS–Comm of Christ	1	NR	82	82	0.2	0.4
LDS–L-D Saints	1	NR	NR	500	1.3	2.1
LUTH–Luth–MO Synod	3	215	565	635	1.6	2.7
METH–AME	1	0	100	124	0.3	0.5
METH–Un Methodist	10	687	1,581	1,957	5.0	8.4
METH–Wesleyan	1	29	42	38	0.1	0.2
Muslim Est	1	134	NR	308	0.8	1.3
Non-denom Chr Chs	12	1,112	1,500	1,638	4.2	7.0
PENT–Assemb of God	4	327	310	452	1.2	1.9
PENT–Ch God (Cleve)	1	75	198	245	0.6	1.1
PENT–Ch of God Proph	1	NR	20	25	0.1	0.1
PENT–COGIC	1	100	136	168	0.4	0.7
PENT–Intl Pent Holiness	1	25	19	24	0.1	0.1
PENT–Un Pent Ch Intl	5	NR	NR	NR	-	-
PRES–Presb Ch (USA)	1	75	119	147	0.4	0.6
Sev Day Adv	1	38	66	76	0.2	0.3
SHANNON	**26**	**570**	**1,389**	**2,039**	**24.2**	**100.0**
BAPT–So Bapt Conv	6	284	812	987	11.7	48.4
Catholic	1	NR	NR	42	0.5	2.1
CHR–Chr Chs & Chs Cr	1	NR	100	122	1.4	6.0
CHR–Chs of Christ	2	45	43	55	0.7	2.7
Jehovah's Witness	1	NR	NR	NR	-	-
LDS–L-D Saints	1	NR	NR	183	2.2	9.0
MENN–Mennonite USA	1	15	21	26	0.3	1.3
METH–Un Methodist	4	105	203	321	3.8	15.7
PENT–Assemb of God	3	91	36	91	1.1	4.5
PENT–Ch of God Proph	5	NR	148	180	2.1	8.8
Un C of Christ	1	30	26	32	0.4	1.6
SHELBY	**32**	**1,017**	**3,062**	**4,370**	**68.6**	**100.0**
BAPT–Reg Bapt Gen As	1	NR	NR	NR	-	-
BAPT–So Bapt Conv	9	477	1,112	1,370	21.5	31.4
Catholic	2	NR	NR	544	8.5	12.4
Ch of Nazarene	1	23	20	75	1.2	1.7
CHR–Chr Ch (Disc)	1	20	24	30	0.5	0.7
CHR–Chr Chs & Chs Cr	5	NR	1,185	1,460	22.9	33.4
CHR–Chs of Christ	1	14	9	20	0.3	0.5
Evan Free Ch	1	45	NR	45	0.7	1.0
LUTH–Luth–MO Synod	1	14	43	56	0.9	1.3
MENN–Mennonite USA	1	55	58	71	1.1	1.6
MENN–Tamp Amish-Menn	1	70	43	70	1.1	1.6
METH–Un Methodist	7	269	534	591	9.3	13.5
Non-denom Chr Chs	1	30	34	38	0.6	0.9
STODDARD	**69**	**4,056**	**7,088**	**9,771**	**32.6**	**100.0**
Bahá'í	0	NR	1	1	0.0	0.0
BAPT–Amer Bapt Assn	2	NR	170	206	0.7	2.1
BAPT–Natl Mis Bapt Conv	1	0	150	181	0.6	1.9
BAPT–So Bapt Conv	17	1,232	3,346	4,048	13.5	41.4
BRETH–Ch of Brethren	1	14	37	45	0.2	0.5
Catholic	2	NR	NR	610	2.0	6.2
CGOD–Ch God (Ander)	1	45	NR	45	0.2	0.5
Ch of Nazarene	3	110	228	272	0.9	2.8
CHR–Chr Ch (Disc)	1	95	206	249	0.8	2.5
CHR–Chr Chs & Chs Cr	3	NR	99	120	0.4	1.2
CHR–Chs of Christ	8	693	680	798	2.7	8.2
Evan Free Ch	1	15	NR	15	0.1	0.2
Jehovah's Witness	2	NR	NR	NR	-	-
LDS–Comm of Christ	1	NR	135	135	0.5	1.4
LUTH–Luth–MO Synod	1	55	80	130	0.4	1.3
MENN–Amb Amish-Menn	1	136	70	136	0.5	1.4
METH–Un Methodist	7	553	905	1,266	4.2	13.0
Non-denom Chr Chs	4	325	450	475	1.6	4.9
PENT–Assemb of God	7	716	345	814	2.7	8.3
PENT–Ch God (Cleve)	1	27	142	172	0.6	1.8
PENT–Un Pent Ch Intl	4	NR	NR	NR	-	-
PRES–Presb Ch (USA)	1	40	44	53	0.2	0.5
STONE	**48**	**3,254**	**6,212**	**8,994**	**27.9**	**100.0**
ANG/EPIS–Episcopal	1	37	36	36	0.1	0.4
Bahá'í	0	NR	6	6	0.0	0.1
BAPT–Free Will Bapt	1	NR	92	107	0.3	1.2
BAPT–So Bapt Conv	15	1,724	3,678	4,268	13.3	47.5
Catholic	1	NR	NR	1,620	5.0	18.0
Ch of Nazarene	1	54	62	62	0.2	0.7
CHR–Chr Chs & Chs Cr	2	NR	330	383	1.2	4.3
CHR–Chs of Christ	4	222	217	263	0.8	2.9
Christian Un	1	NR	NR	NR	-	-
Jehovah's Witness	1	NR	NR	NR	-	-
LUTH–Luth–MO Synod	1	138	337	350	1.1	3.9
METH–Un Methodist	2	457	728	971	3.0	10.8
Non-denom Chr Chs	3	55	95	95	0.3	1.1
PENT–Assemb of God	5	295	218	358	1.1	4.0
PENT–Ch God (Cleve)	2	108	158	183	0.6	2.0
PENT–Ch God Apos Fth	1	NR	NR	NR	-	-
PENT–Un Pent Ch Intl	3	NR	NR	NR	-	-
PRES–Cumber Presb	1	NR	17	17	0.1	0.2
PRES–Presb Ch (USA)	2	140	196	227	0.7	2.5
Sev Day Adv	1	24	42	48	0.1	0.5
SULLIVAN	**25**	**763**	**1,981**	**2,864**	**42.7**	**100.0**
Bahá'í	0	NR	3	3	0.0	0.1
BAPT–So Bapt Conv	7	309	1,040	1,274	19.0	44.5
Catholic	1	NR	NR	320	4.8	11.2
CGOD–Ch God (Ander)	1	0	NR	0	0.0	0.0
CHR–Chr Ch (Disc)	1	0	2	2	0.0	0.1
CHR–Chr Chs & Chs Cr	3	NR	395	484	7.2	16.9
CHR–Chs of Christ	3	83	81	104	1.5	3.6
LUTH–Luth–MO Synod	1	27	38	44	0.7	1.5
METH–Un Methodist	2	84	196	217	3.2	7.6
Non-denom Chr Chs	1	100	150	150	2.2	5.2
PENT–Assemb of God	2	73	35	107	1.6	3.7
PENT–Pent Ch of God	1	70	NR	109	1.6	3.8
PRES–Presb Ch (USA)	2	17	41	50	0.7	1.7
TANEY	**81**	**8,485**	**12,647**	**19,782**	**38.3**	**100.0**
ANG/EPIS–Episcopal	1	34	54	61	0.1	0.3
Bahá'í	0	NR	13	13	0.0	0.1
BAPT–Amer Bapt Assn	2	NR	170	205	0.4	1.0
BAPT–Free Will Bapt	1	NR	63	76	0.1	0.4
BAPT–So Bapt Conv	14	3,058	5,989	7,224	14.0	36.5
Calv Chpl	1	NR	NR	NR	-	-
Catholic	2	NR	NR	2,135	4.1	10.8
Ch Cr, Scientst	1	NR	NR	NR	-	-
Ch of Nazarene	3	149	199	225	0.4	1.1
CHR–Chr Ch (Disc)	2	53	399	481	0.9	2.4
CHR–Chr Chs & Chs Cr	3	NR	275	332	0.6	1.7
CHR–Chs of Christ	6	542	337	465	0.9	2.4
Evan Free Ch	1	190	NR	190	0.4	1.0
Ind Fund Churches	1	NR	NR	NR	-	-
Jehovah's Witness	3	NR	NR	NR	-	-
LDS–Comm of Christ	1	NR	135	135	0.3	0.7
LDS–L-D Saints	4	NR	NR	1,541	3.0	7.8
LUTH–E.L.C.A.	1	110	262	266	0.5	1.3
LUTH–Luth–MO Synod	2	437	601	753	1.5	3.8
METH–Un Methodist	2	449	673	828	1.6	4.2
Missionary Ch	1	13	8	13	0.0	0.1
Non-denom Chr Chs	13	2,395	2,430	3,075	6.0	15.5

NR–Not Reported - Represents no adherents reported. Percentages may not total 100 due to rounding.

Table 3: Religious Congregations by County and Group: 2010

Religious Group	Number of Congrega-tions	Number of Attendees	Number of Communicant, Confirmed, or Full Members	Adherents		
				Number of Adherents	% of Total Pop.	% of Total Adh.
PENT–Assemb of God	6	700	489	1,115	2.2	5.6
PENT–Ch God Apos Fth	2	NR	NR	NR	-	-
PENT–Un Pent Ch Intl	1	NR	NR	NR	-	-
PRES–Presb Ch (USA)	4	288	435	525	1.0	2.7
Salvation Army	1	33	57	57	0.1	0.3
Sev Day Adv	1	34	58	67	0.1	0.3
Unity Ch	1	NR	NR	NR	-	-
TEXAS	**97**	**4,097**	**11,419**	**14,622**	**56.2**	**100.0**
BAPT–Free Will Bapt	10	NR	630	757	2.9	5.2
BAPT–So Bapt Conv	33	2,071	7,031	8,449	32.5	57.8
BRETH–Ch of Brethren	2	46	66	79	0.3	0.5
Catholic	4	NR	NR	316	1.2	2.2
CGOD–Ch God (Ander)	2	35	NR	35	0.1	0.2
CHR–Chr Chs & Chs Cr	7	NR	980	1,178	4.5	8.1
CHR–Chs of Christ	7	393	387	500	1.9	3.4
Jehovah's Witness	3	NR	NR	NR	-	-
LDS–L-D Saints	1	NR	NR	360	1.4	2.5
LUTH–Luth–MO Synod	1	60	114	158	0.6	1.1
MENN–Amish Undif	2	NR	44	126	0.5	0.9
METH–Un Methodist	5	324	700	807	3.1	5.5
Non-denom Chr Chs	4	375	625	644	2.5	4.4
PENT–Assemb of God	7	274	158	393	1.5	2.7
PENT–Ch of God Proph	2	NR	21	25	0.1	0.2
PENT–Intl Pent Holiness	5	501	632	759	2.9	5.2
PENT–Un Pent Ch Intl	1	NR	NR	NR	-	-
Sev Day Adv	1	18	31	36	0.1	0.2
VERNON	**52**	**2,248**	**7,244**	**9,922**	**46.9**	**100.0**
ANG/EPIS–Episcopal	1	42	111	122	0.6	1.2
Bahá'í	0	NR	1	1	0.0	0.0
BAPT–Free Will Bapt	1	NR	63	78	0.4	0.8
BAPT–So Bapt Conv	13	1,020	3,501	4,333	20.5	43.7
Catholic	2	NR	NR	542	2.6	5.5
Ch of Nazarene	1	73	148	148	0.7	1.5
CHR–Chr Ch (Disc)	1	20	29	36	0.2	0.4
CHR–Chr Chs & Chs Cr	9	NR	1,225	1,516	7.2	15.3
CHR–Chs of Christ	2	110	118	148	0.7	1.5
Evan Free Ch	1	50	NR	50	0.2	0.5
Jehovah's Witness	1	NR	NR	NR	-	-
LDS–Comm of Christ	1	NR	135	135	0.6	1.4
LDS–L-D Saints	1	NR	NR	386	1.8	3.9
LUTH–E.L.C.A.	1	60	178	216	1.0	2.2
LUTH–Luth–MO Synod	1	25	53	61	0.3	0.6
MENN–Amish Undif	1	NR	38	77	0.4	0.8
MENN–CG in Cr (Menn)	1	NR	104	129	0.6	1.3
METH–Un Methodist	7	258	827	1,048	5.0	10.6
Non-denom Chr Chs	3	389	399	486	2.3	4.9
PENT–Assemb of God	1	65	47	89	0.4	0.9
PENT–Un Pent Ch Intl	1	NR	NR	NR	-	-
PRES–Presb Ch (USA)	1	74	158	196	0.9	2.0
Sev Day Adv	1	62	109	125	0.6	1.3
WARREN	**38**	**3,961**	**6,307**	**12,118**	**37.3**	**100.0**
Bahá'í	0	NR	4	4	0.0	0.0
BAPT–Converge/BGC	1	75	NR	90	0.3	0.7
BAPT–So Bapt Conv	5	539	1,174	1,457	4.5	12.0
Catholic	3	NR	NR	3,288	10.1	27.1
Ch of Nazarene	1	85	93	93	0.3	0.8
CHR–Chr Chs & Chs Cr	1	NR	280	347	1.1	2.9
CHR–Chs of Christ	3	190	143	198	0.6	1.6
Jehovah's Witness	2	NR	NR	NR	-	-
LDS–L-D Saints	1	NR	NR	520	1.6	4.3
LUTH–Luth–MO Synod	1	159	391	516	1.6	4.3
METH–Un Methodist	8	480	937	1,374	4.2	11.3
METH–Wesleyan	1	164	94	213	0.7	1.8
Non-denom Chr Chs	4	1,630	1,595	2,038	6.3	16.8
PENT–Ch God (Cleve)	1	63	56	69	0.2	0.6
PENT–Un Pent Ch Intl	1	NR	NR	NR	-	-
Un C of Christ	5	576	1,540	1,911	5.9	15.8

Religious Group	Number of Congrega-tions	Number of Attendees	Number of Communicant, Confirmed, or Full Members	Adherents		
				Number of Adherents	% of Total Pop.	% of Total Adh.
WASHINGTON	**43**	**1,748**	**3,562**	**6,444**	**25.6**	**100.0**
Bahá'í	0	NR	8	8	0.0	0.1
BAPT–Free Will Bapt	2	NR	126	155	0.6	2.4
BAPT–Natl Mis Bapt Conv	1	0	150	184	0.7	2.9
BAPT–So Bapt Conv	9	604	1,732	2,129	8.5	33.0
Catholic	4	NR	NR	1,707	6.8	26.5
CGOD–Ches God-Gen Con	3	60	66	81	0.3	1.3
Ch of Nazarene	2	29	27	45	0.2	0.7
CHR–Chs of Christ	1	18	20	22	0.1	0.3
Jehovah's Witness	1	NR	NR	NR	-	-
LUTH–Luth–MO Synod	1	18	28	28	0.1	0.4
METH–Un Methodist	5	245	452	563	2.2	8.7
Non-denom Chr Chs	1	75	75	94	0.4	1.5
PENT–Assemb of God	4	230	119	278	1.1	4.3
PENT–Ch God (Cleve)	4	329	681	837	3.3	13.0
PENT–Ch of God Proph	1	NR	61	75	0.3	1.2
PENT–Pent Ch of God	2	140	NR	217	0.9	3.4
PENT–Un Pent Ch Intl	1	NR	NR	NR	-	-
PRES–Presb Ch (USA)	1	0	17	21	0.1	0.3
WAYNE	**42**	**1,861**	**2,717**	**3,945**	**29.2**	**100.0**
Bahá'í	0	NR	1	1	0.0	0.0
BAPT–Reg Bapt Gen As	1	NR	NR	NR	-	-
BAPT–So Bapt Conv	13	417	1,261	1,493	11.0	37.8
Catholic	2	NR	NR	154	1.1	3.9
Ch of Nazarene	1	49	91	91	0.7	2.3
CHR–Chr Chs & Chs Cr	1	NR	57	67	0.5	1.7
CHR–Chs of Christ	3	83	65	89	0.7	2.3
LUTH–Evan Luth Syn	1	7	11	16	0.1	0.4
METH–Un Methodist	6	350	476	614	4.5	15.6
Non-denom Chr Chs	5	625	665	816	6.0	20.7
PENT–Assemb of God	5	190	90	387	2.9	9.8
PENT–Pent Ch of God	2	140	NR	217	1.6	5.5
PENT–Un Pent Ch Intl	2	NR	NR	NR	-	-
WEBSTER	**97**	**6,178**	**13,162**	**19,539**	**54.0**	**100.0**
Bahá'í	0	NR	9	9	0.0	0.0
BAPT–Free Will Bapt	11	NR	693	883	2.4	4.5
BAPT–So Bapt Conv	25	2,128	6,063	7,723	21.3	39.5
Catholic	1	NR	NR	504	1.4	2.6
Ch of Nazarene	3	760	582	1,116	3.1	5.7
CHR–Chr Ch (Disc)	4	127	596	759	2.1	3.9
CHR–Chr Chs & Chs Cr	2	NR	465	592	1.6	3.0
CHR–Chs of Christ	9	433	435	568	1.6	2.9
LDS–L-D Saints	1	NR	NR	482	1.3	2.5
LUTH–Luth–MO Synod	3	319	557	764	2.1	3.9
LUTH–Wisc Ev Luth Syn	1	39	79	88	0.2	0.5
MENN–Amish Undif	12	NR	758	2,252	6.2	11.5
METH–Evan Meth Ch	1	NR	NR	NR	-	-
METH–Un Methodist	9	588	950	1,276	3.5	6.5
Non-denom Chr Chs	6	1,375	1,720	1,820	5.0	9.3
ORTHE–Orth Ch in Amer	1	2	NR	2	0.0	0.0
PENT–Assemb of God	2	253	129	425	1.2	2.2
PENT–Ch God (Cleve)	2	32	8	10	0.0	0.1
PENT–Pent Ch of God	1	70	NR	109	0.3	0.6
PRES–Cumber Presb	2	NR	28	53	0.1	0.3
Sev Day Adv	1	52	90	104	0.3	0.5
WORTH	**14**	**320**	**1,401**	**1,756**	**80.9**	**100.0**
BAPT–So Bapt Conv	4	144	629	744	34.3	42.4
CHR–Chr Ch (Disc)	1	0	192	227	10.5	12.9
CHR–Chr Chs & Chs Cr	3	NR	300	355	16.4	20.2
CHR–Chs of Christ	1	25	25	32	1.5	1.8
METH–Un Methodist	3	69	206	244	11.2	13.9
PENT–Assemb of God	1	82	38	141	6.5	8.0
PRES–Presb Ch (USA)	1	0	11	13	0.6	0.7
WRIGHT	**69**	**3,315**	**8,204**	**11,290**	**60.0**	**100.0**
ANG/EPIS–Episcopal	1	20	43	45	0.2	0.4
BAPT–Free Will Bapt	14	NR	882	1,104	5.9	9.8
BAPT–So Bapt Conv	19	1,624	5,013	6,273	33.3	55.6
Catholic	2	NR	NR	304	1.6	2.7

NR–Not Reported   - Represents no adherents reported.   Percentages may not total 100 due to rounding.

Table 3: Religious Congregations by County and Group: 2010

Religious Group	Number of Congrega-tions	Number of Attendees	Number of Communicant, Confirmed, or Full Members	Adherents: Number of Adherents	Adherents: % of Total Pop.	Adherents: % of Total Adh.
CGOD–Ch God (Ander)	2	67	NR	67	0.4	0.6
Ch of Nazarene	3	177	226	309	1.6	2.7
CHR–Chr Ch (Disc)	1	0	37	46	0.2	0.4
CHR–Chr Chs & Chs Cr	2	NR	260	325	1.7	2.9
CHR–Chs of Christ	5	218	214	264	1.4	2.3
Jehovah's Witness	1	NR	NR	NR	-	-
LDS–L-D Saints	1	NR	NR	361	1.9	3.2
MENN–Amish Undif	2	NR	79	182	1.0	1.6
MENN–CG in Cr (Menn)	1	NR	78	98	0.5	0.9
METH–Un Methodist	3	105	373	418	2.2	3.7
Non-denom Chr Chs	3	640	660	800	4.3	7.1
PENT–Assemb of God	5	426	235	554	2.9	4.9
PENT–Un Pent Ch Intl	2	NR	NR	NR	-	-
PRES–Cumber Presb	1	NR	39	65	0.3	0.6
Sev Day Adv	1	38	65	75	0.4	0.7
MONTANA	**1,778**	**95,105**	**143,149**	**376,976**	**38.1**	**100.0**
BEAVERHEAD	**23**	**794**	**947**	**2,945**	**31.9**	**100.0**
ANG/EPIS–Episcopal	1	26	33	57	0.6	1.9
Bahá'í	0	NR	1	1	0.0	0.0
BAPT–Amer Bapt Assn	1	NR	10	12	0.1	0.4
BAPT–So Bapt Conv	1	30	27	32	0.3	1.1
Catholic	3	NR	NR	650	7.0	22.1
FRND–Indep Yr Mtgs	1	NR	0	0	0.0	0.0
Jehovah's Witness	1	NR	NR	NR	-	-
LDS–L-D Saints	4	NR	NR	1,051	11.4	35.7
LUTH–Assoc Free Luth	1	NR	NR	NR	-	-
METH–Un Methodist	1	38	82	99	1.1	3.4
Non-denom Chr Chs	3	250	290	337	3.6	11.4
PENT–Assemb of God	2	106	67	194	2.1	6.6
PENT–Vineyard	1	245	275	322	3.5	10.9
PRES–Presb Ch (USA)	2	92	150	176	1.9	6.0
Sev Day Adv	1	7	12	14	0.2	0.5
BIG HORN	**39**	**1,227**	**1,488**	**8,408**	**65.4**	**100.0**
Bahá'í	0	NR	23	23	0.2	0.3
BAPT–Amer Bapt USA	5	222	322	437	3.4	5.2
BAPT–Consrv Bapt	1	NR	NR	NR	-	-
BAPT–So Bapt Conv	1	37	90	122	0.9	1.5
Catholic	6	NR	NR	5,102	39.7	60.7
Chr & Miss Al	1	26	24	48	0.4	0.6
CONG–Consrv Cong Chr	1	61	175	237	1.8	2.8
Jehovah's Witness	1	NR	NR	NR	-	-
LDS–L-D Saints	1	NR	NR	802	6.2	9.5
LUTH–E.L.C.A.	1	34	77	97	0.8	1.2
LUTH–Luth–MO Synod	2	33	148	230	1.8	2.7
MENN–CG in Cr (Menn)	1	NR	62	84	0.7	1.0
MENN–Hutt Breth	1	NR	NR	NR	-	-
MENN–Mennonite USA	1	27	58	79	0.6	0.9
METH–Un Methodist	1	30	41	101	0.8	1.2
New Apost Ch	2	NR	NR	NR	-	-
Non-denom Chr Chs	3	170	170	212	1.6	2.5
PENT–Assemb of God	2	58	30	66	0.5	0.8
PENT–Int Foursq Gos	1	193	183	248	1.9	2.9
PENT–Open Bible Std	1	85	NR	85	0.7	1.0
PENT–Pent Ch of God	3	210	NR	326	2.5	3.9
PENT–Un Pent Ch Intl	1	NR	NR	NR	-	-
Sev Day Adv	1	16	29	33	0.3	0.4
Un C of Christ	1	25	56	76	0.6	0.9
BLAINE	**30**	**531**	**862**	**3,948**	**60.8**	**100.0**
Bahá'í	0	NR	5	5	0.1	0.1
BAPT–So Bapt Conv	2	50	50	66	1.0	1.7
Catholic	6	NR	NR	2,580	39.7	65.3
Chr & Miss Al	1	73	39	98	1.5	2.5
CHR–Chr Chs & Chs Cr	1	NR	86	113	1.7	2.9
CHR–Chs of Christ	1	11	10	13	0.2	0.3
Evan Ch	1	NR	NR	NR	-	-
Jehovah's Witness	1	NR	NR	NR	-	-
LDS–L-D Saints	1	NR	NR	168	2.6	4.3

Religious Group	Number of Congrega-tions	Number of Attendees	Number of Communicant, Confirmed, or Full Members	Adherents: Number of Adherents	Adherents: % of Total Pop.	Adherents: % of Total Adh.
LUTH–E.L.C.A.	4	127	329	367	5.7	9.3
LUTH–Luth–MO Synod	1	39	66	93	1.4	2.4
MENN–Hutt Breth	2	NR	NR	NR	-	-
METH–Un Methodist	2	29	111	171	2.6	4.3
PENT–Assemb of God	4	154	90	177	2.7	4.5
PRES–Presb Ch (USA)	2	37	57	75	1.2	1.9
Sev Day Adv	1	11	19	22	0.3	0.6
BROADWATER	**12**	**377**	**664**	**1,683**	**30.0**	**100.0**
ANG/EPIS–Episcopal	1	10	10	22	0.4	1.3
Bahá'í	0	NR	6	6	0.1	0.4
BAPT–So Bapt Conv	2	16	137	164	2.9	9.7
Catholic	1	NR	NR	390	6.9	23.2
Chr & Miss Al	1	98	60	91	1.6	5.4
LDS–L-D Saints	1	NR	NR	397	7.1	23.6
LUTH–E.L.C.A.	1	40	204	264	4.7	15.7
LUTH–Luth Cong Msn Chr	1	11	11	13	0.2	0.8
METH–Un Methodist	1	47	101	136	2.4	8.1
Non-denom Chr Chs	1	125	100	156	2.8	9.3
PENT–Assemb of God	1	21	19	26	0.5	1.5
Sev Day Adv	1	9	16	18	0.3	1.1
CARBON	**29**	**811**	**1,214**	**4,154**	**41.2**	**100.0**
ANG/EPIS–Episcopal	2	44	62	84	0.8	2.0
Bahá'í	0	NR	6	6	0.1	0.1
BAPT–So Bapt Conv	6	117	95	111	1.1	2.7
Catholic	4	NR	NR	1,967	19.5	47.4
Chr & Miss Al	1	54	38	80	0.8	1.9
CHR–Chr Ch (Disc)	1	17	23	27	0.3	0.6
CHR–Chs of Christ	1	22	24	30	0.3	0.7
LDS–L-D Saints	2	NR	NR	400	4.0	9.6
LUTH–E.L.C.A.	2	116	236	284	2.8	6.8
LUTH–Luth–MO Synod	2	64	128	252	2.5	6.1
METH–Un Methodist	3	97	235	417	4.1	10.0
METH–Wesleyan	1	88	48	114	1.1	2.7
Non-denom Chr Chs	1	65	60	81	0.8	1.9
PENT–Int Foursq Gos	1	0	0	0	0.0	0.0
Sev Day Adv	1	38	66	76	0.8	1.8
Un C of Christ	1	89	193	225	2.2	5.4
CARTER	**6**	**135**	**231**	**471**	**40.6**	**100.0**
BAPT–So Bapt Conv	1	18	24	27	2.3	5.7
Catholic	1	NR	NR	97	8.4	20.6
LDS–L-D Saints	1	NR	NR	86	7.4	18.3
LUTH–E.L.C.A.	1	27	72	99	8.5	21.0
LUTH–Luth Cong Msn Chr	1	15	60	68	5.9	14.4
Non-denom Chr Chs	1	75	75	94	8.1	20.0
CASCADE	**110**	**7,862**	**12,333**	**30,609**	**37.6**	**100.0**
ANG/EPIS–Episcopal	1	49	225	225	0.3	0.7
Bahá'í	0	NR	45	45	0.1	0.1
BAPT–Amer Bapt Assn	1	NR	10	12	0.0	0.0
BAPT–Amer Bapt USA	1	79	102	124	0.2	0.4
BAPT–Converge/BGC	1	75	NR	90	0.1	0.3
BAPT–NT Ind Bapt	2	NR	NR	NR	-	-
BAPT–So Bapt Conv	7	444	635	771	0.9	2.5
Calv Chpl	1	NR	NR	NR	-	-
Catholic	12	NR	NR	9,375	11.5	30.6
CGOD–Ch God (Ander)	1	35	NR	35	0.0	0.1
Ch Cr, Scientst	1	NR	NR	NR	-	-
Ch of Nazarene	1	86	187	187	0.2	0.6
Chr & Miss Al	1	193	117	294	0.4	1.0
CHR–Chr Ch (Disc)	1	88	395	480	0.6	1.6
CHR–Chr Chs & Chs Cr	2	NR	90	109	0.1	0.4
CHR–Chs of Christ	1	245	210	275	0.3	0.9
CHR–Int Chs of Christ	1	NR	14	17	0.0	0.1
Evan Ch	1	NR	NR	NR	-	-
Evan Free Ch	1	300	NR	300	0.4	1.0
FRND–Indep Yr Mtgs	1	NR	0	0	0.0	0.0
Jehovah's Witness	2	NR	NR	NR	-	-
JUD–Reform	1	16	28	76	0.1	0.2
LDS–Comm of Christ	1	NR	128	128	0.2	0.4

NR–Not Reported   - Represents no adherents reported.   Percentages may not total 100 due to rounding.

Table 3: Religious Congregations by County and Group: 2010

Religious Group	Number of Congrega-tions	Number of Attendees	Number of Communicant, Confirmed, or Full Members	Adherents		
				Number of Adherents	% of Total Pop.	% of Total Adh.
LDS–L-D Saints	10	NR	NR	4,125	5.1	13.5
LUTH–Ch of Luth Br	1	42	25	57	0.1	0.2
LUTH–E.L.C.A.	6	637	1,790	2,387	2.9	7.8
LUTH–Luth Cong Msn Chr	1	208	1,260	1,531	1.9	5.0
LUTH–Luth–MO Synod	3	225	736	923	1.1	3.0
LUTH–Wisc Ev Luth Syn	1	34	65	77	0.1	0.3
MENN–Hutt Breth	4	NR	NR	NR	-	-
METH–AME	1	40	60	73	0.1	0.2
METH–Un Methodist	8	439	812	1,061	1.3	3.5
Metro Comm Ch	1	36	58	70	0.1	0.2
New Apost Ch	1	NR	NR	NR	-	-
Non-denom Chr Chs	16	2,405	2,813	3,132	3.9	10.2
ORTHE–Greek Orthodox	1	20	NR	80	0.1	0.3
PENT–Assemb of God	2	886	440	1,900	2.3	6.2
PENT–Ch God (Cleve)	1	17	19	23	0.0	0.1
PENT–Int Foursq Gos	1	522	409	497	0.6	1.6
PENT–Un Pent Ch Intl	2	NR	NR	NR	-	-
PENT–Vineyard	1	135	207	251	0.3	0.8
PRES–Kor Pres Abroad	1	NR	NR	NR	-	-
PRES–Presb Ch (USA)	2	249	659	801	1.0	2.6
REF–Ref Ch in Am	1	32	45	52	0.1	0.2
Salvation Army	1	40	51	195	0.2	0.6
Sev Day Adv	1	146	254	292	0.4	1.0
Un C of Christ	1	139	444	539	0.7	1.8
CHOUTEAU	**18**	**464**	**897**	**4,977**	**85.6**	**100.0**
ANG/EPIS–Episcopal	1	5	12	12	0.2	0.2
Bahá'í	0	NR	1	1	0.0	0.0
BAPT–So Bapt Conv	1	68	68	85	1.5	1.7
Catholic	3	NR	NR	3,435	59.1	69.0
CGOD–Ch God (Ander)	1	0	NR	0	0.0	0.0
CHR–Chr Chs & Chs Cr	1	NR	200	251	4.3	5.0
Evan Free Ch	1	160	NR	160	2.8	3.2
LDS–L-D Saints	1	NR	NR	167	2.9	3.4
LUTH–E.L.C.A.	1	46	240	324	5.6	6.5
LUTH–Luth Cong Msn Chr	1	NR	NR	NR	-	-
LUTH–Luth–MO Synod	1	18	34	34	0.6	0.7
MENN–Hutt Breth	1	NR	NR	NR	-	-
METH–Un Methodist	5	167	342	508	8.7	10.2
CUSTER	**18**	**1,438**	**2,219**	**5,356**	**45.8**	**100.0**
ANG/EPIS–Episcopal	1	2	3	3	0.0	0.1
Bahá'í	0	NR	3	3	0.0	0.1
BAPT–Amer Bapt USA	1	93	109	131	1.1	2.4
BAPT–So Bapt Conv	1	60	126	152	1.3	2.8
Catholic	1	NR	NR	1,580	13.5	29.5
CHR–Chr Ch (Disc)	1	45	103	124	1.1	2.3
CHR–Chs of Christ	2	46	37	41	0.4	0.8
LDS–L-D Saints	1	NR	NR	480	4.1	9.0
LUTH–E.L.C.A.	1	91	389	545	4.7	10.2
LUTH–Luth–MO Synod	1	115	317	429	3.7	8.0
METH–Un Methodist	1	130	337	642	5.5	12.0
METH–Wesleyan	1	96	30	125	1.1	2.3
Non-denom Chr Chs	1	500	400	625	5.3	11.7
PENT–Assemb of God	1	75	36	85	0.7	1.6
PENT–Int Foursq Gos	1	44	36	43	0.4	0.8
PRES–Presb Ch (USA)	1	49	110	132	1.1	2.5
Sev Day Adv	1	47	82	94	0.8	1.8
Un C of Christ	1	45	101	122	1.0	2.3
DANIELS	**8**	**219**	**1,066**	**1,733**	**99.0**	**100.0**
Catholic	1	NR	NR	425	24.3	24.5
Chr & Miss Al	1	40	30	65	3.7	3.8
LUTH–Luth Cong Msn Chr	4	133	983	1,169	66.8	67.5
METH–Un Methodist	1	16	30	36	2.1	2.1
PENT–Assemb of God	1	30	23	38	2.2	2.2
DAWSON	**24**	**1,118**	**2,194**	**5,562**	**62.0**	**100.0**
Bahá'í	0	NR	2	2	0.0	0.0
BAPT–So Bapt Conv	1	45	62	74	0.8	1.3
Catholic	2	NR	NR	1,978	22.1	35.6
Chr & Miss Al	2	311	126	475	5.3	8.5

Religious Group	Number of Congrega-tions	Number of Attendees	Number of Communicant, Confirmed, or Full Members	Adherents		
				Number of Adherents	% of Total Pop.	% of Total Adh.
CHR–Chs of Christ	1	27	25	25	0.3	0.4
Evan Ch	1	NR	NR	NR	-	-
Jehovah's Witness	1	NR	NR	NR	-	-
LDS–L-D Saints	1	NR	NR	411	4.6	7.4
LUTH–E.L.C.A.	2	165	459	575	6.4	10.3
LUTH–Luth–MO Synod	1	186	858	1,108	12.4	19.9
MENN–Mennonite USA	3	69	116	138	1.5	2.5
METH–Un Methodist	3	71	205	248	2.8	4.5
Non-denom Chr Chs	2	140	150	188	2.1	3.4
PENT–Assemb of God	1	68	42	165	1.8	3.0
PENT–Un Pent Ch Intl	1	NR	NR	NR	-	-
Sev Day Adv	1	36	62	71	0.8	1.3
Un C of Christ	1	0	87	104	1.2	1.9
DEER LODGE	**14**	**448**	**683**	**4,188**	**45.0**	**100.0**
ANG/EPIS–Episcopal	1	27	60	60	0.6	1.4
Bahá'í	0	NR	13	13	0.1	0.3
BAPT–Converge/BGC	1	75	NR	90	1.0	2.1
BAPT–So Bapt Conv	2	69	184	212	2.3	5.1
Catholic	2	NR	NR	2,600	28.0	62.1
CHR–Chs of Christ	1	55	48	75	0.8	1.8
Jehovah's Witness	1	NR	NR	NR	-	-
LDS–L-D Saints	1	NR	NR	542	5.8	12.9
LUTH–E.L.C.A.	1	65	203	261	2.8	6.2
LUTH–Luth–MO Synod	1	8	13	13	0.1	0.3
METH–Un Methodist	1	33	71	95	1.0	2.3
PENT–Assemb of God	1	73	33	160	1.7	3.8
PRES–Presb Ch (USA)	1	43	58	67	0.7	1.6
FALLON	**11**	**392**	**858**	**1,810**	**62.6**	**100.0**
BAPT–N Am Bapt Conf	1	NR	85	104	3.6	5.7
BAPT–Reg Bapt Gen As	1	NR	NR	NR	-	-
BAPT–So Bapt Conv	1	30	44	54	1.9	3.0
Catholic	2	NR	NR	455	15.7	25.1
Evan Free Ch	1	65	NR	65	2.2	3.6
LUTH–E.L.C.A.	2	154	637	893	30.9	49.3
METH–Wesleyan	1	28	26	36	1.2	2.0
PENT–Assemb of God	1	90	0	122	4.2	6.7
Un C of Christ	1	25	66	81	2.8	4.5
FERGUS	**38**	**1,233**	**2,454**	**5,667**	**48.9**	**100.0**
ANG/EPIS–Episcopal	1	18	61	61	0.5	1.1
Bahá'í	0	NR	2	2	0.0	0.0
BAPT–So Bapt Conv	1	112	101	119	1.0	2.1
Catholic	6	NR	NR	1,954	16.9	34.5
Ch of Nazarene	1	20	36	36	0.3	0.6
Chr & Miss Al	1	54	0	54	0.5	1.0
CHR–Chr Chs & Chs Cr	1	NR	225	265	2.3	4.7
Jehovah's Witness	1	NR	NR	NR	-	-
LDS–L-D Saints	1	NR	NR	468	4.0	8.3
LUTH–E.L.C.A.	1	162	463	611	5.3	10.8
LUTH–Luth Cong Msn Chr	1	45	218	257	2.2	4.5
LUTH–Luth–MO Synod	2	77	120	133	1.1	2.3
LUTH–Wisc Ev Luth Syn	1	14	41	50	0.4	0.9
MENN–Amish Undif	1	NR	24	65	0.6	1.1
MENN–Hutt Breth	4	NR	NR	NR	-	-
METH–Un Methodist	6	219	456	590	5.1	10.4
Non-denom Chr Chs	3	210	210	288	2.5	5.1
PENT–Assemb of God	1	155	69	212	1.8	3.7
PENT–Int Foursq Gos	1	106	125	147	1.3	2.6
PENT–Un Pent Ch Intl	1	NR	NR	NR	-	-
PRES–Presb Ch (USA)	2	0	232	273	2.4	4.8
Sev Day Adv	1	41	71	82	0.7	1.4
FLATHEAD	**127**	**11,417**	**14,419**	**29,456**	**32.4**	**100.0**
ANG/EPIS–Episcopal	2	134	257	343	0.4	1.2
Bahá'í	0	NR	35	35	0.0	0.1
BAPT–Amer Bapt Assn	3	NR	255	311	0.3	1.1
BAPT–Amer Bapt USA	1	42	59	72	0.1	0.2
BAPT–Converge/BGC	1	75	NR	90	0.1	0.3
BAPT–Natl Mis Bapt Conv	1	25	12	15	0.0	0.1
BAPT–Reg Bapt Gen As	6	NR	NR	NR	-	-

NR–Not Reported   - Represents no adherents reported.   Percentages may not total 100 due to rounding.

Table 3: Religious Congregations by County and Group: 2010

Religious Group	Number of Congrega-tions	Number of Attendees	Number of Communicant, Confirmed, or Full Members	Adherents: Number of Adherents	Adherents: % of Total Pop.	Adherents: % of Total Adh.
BAPT–So Bapt Conv	6	933	998	1,217	1.3	4.1
BUDD–Mahayana	3	NR	NR	141	0.2	0.5
Calv Chpl	4	NR	NR	NR	-	-
Catholic	6	NR	NR	4,933	5.4	16.7
CGOD–Ch God (Ander)	3	220	NR	220	0.2	0.7
Ch Cr, Scientst	1	NR	NR	NR	-	-
Ch of Nazarene	3	373	448	635	0.7	2.2
Chr & Miss Al	4	400	233	572	0.6	1.9
CHR–Chr Ch (Disc)	1	39	57	70	0.1	0.2
CHR–Chr Chs & Chs Cr	2	NR	353	430	0.5	1.5
CHR–Chs of Christ	3	247	237	282	0.3	1.0
FRND–Indep Yr Mtgs	1	NR	0	0	0.0	0.0
Jehovah's Witness	5	NR	NR	NR	-	-
JUD–Reform	1	20	35	94	0.1	0.3
LDS–L-D Saints	9	NR	NR	4,011	4.4	13.6
LUTH–Assoc Free Luth	2	NR	NR	NR	-	-
LUTH–E.L.C.A.	4	570	1,588	1,870	2.1	6.3
LUTH–Luth Cong Msn Chr	3	535	1,149	1,401	1.5	4.8
LUTH–Luth-MO Synod	4	791	1,510	2,078	2.3	7.1
MENN–Mennonite USA	1	62	95	116	0.1	0.4
METH–Un Methodist	5	572	934	1,636	1.8	5.6
Non-denom Chr Chs	18	3,870	4,131	4,920	5.4	16.7
PENT–Assemb of God	7	1,766	838	2,364	2.6	8.0
PENT–Ch God (Cleve)	1	59	77	94	0.1	0.3
PENT–Ch of God Proph	1	NR	6	7	0.0	0.0
PENT–Int Foursq Gos	3	122	122	149	0.2	0.5
PENT–Un Pent Ch Intl	1	NR	NR	NR	-	-
PRES–Bible Pres	1	NR	NR	NR	-	-
PRES–Presb Ch (USA)	2	205	435	530	0.6	1.8
PRES–Presb Ch Amer	1	0	0	0	0.0	0.0
Salvation Army	1	46	53	207	0.2	0.7
Sev Day Adv	4	226	393	451	0.5	1.5
Un C of Christ	1	40	60	73	0.1	0.2
Unit Univ	1	45	49	89	0.1	0.3
GALLATIN	**108**	**9,750**	**11,719**	**28,911**	**32.3**	**100.0**
ANG/EPIS–Episcopal	3	252	637	770	0.9	2.7
Bahá'í	0	NR	28	28	0.0	0.1
BAPT–Amer Bapt USA	2	248	261	313	0.3	1.1
BAPT–So Bapt Conv	6	407	498	598	0.7	2.1
BUDD–Mahayana	1	NR	NR	26	0.0	0.1
BUDD–Vajrayana	1	NR	NR	41	0.0	0.1
Calv Chpl	2	NR	NR	NR	-	-
Catholic	6	NR	NR	6,400	7.1	22.1
Ch Cr, Scientst	1	NR	NR	NR	-	-
Ch of Nazarene	1	51	156	156	0.2	0.5
Chr & Miss Al	2	397	190	566	0.6	2.0
CHR–Chr Ch (Disc)	1	45	172	207	0.2	0.7
CHR–Chr Chs & Chs Cr	3	NR	213	256	0.3	0.9
CHR–Chs of Christ	4	341	325	435	0.5	1.5
CHR–Int Chs of Christ	1	NR	11	13	0.0	0.0
Evan Ch	1	NR	NR	NR	-	-
Evan Free Ch	2	714	NR	714	0.8	2.5
FRND–Indep Yr Mtgs	1	NR	15	18	0.0	0.1
Jehovah's Witness	2	NR	NR	NR	-	-
JUD–Orth	1	43	50	60	0.1	0.2
JUD–Reform	1	47	83	224	0.3	0.8
LDS–L-D Saints	9	NR	NR	3,582	4.0	12.4
LUTH–E.L.C.A.	3	518	1,410	1,936	2.2	6.7
LUTH–Luth Cong Msn Chr	1	95	413	496	0.6	1.7
LUTH–Luth-MO Synod	3	292	640	753	0.8	2.6
LUTH–Wisc Ev Luth Syn	1	63	83	91	0.1	0.3
METH–AME	1	0	100	120	0.1	0.4
METH–Un Methodist	3	524	872	1,752	2.0	6.1
Muslim Est	1	134	NR	308	0.3	1.1
New Apost Ch	1	NR	NR	NR	-	-
Non-denom Chr Chs	12	2,735	1,893	3,510	3.9	12.1
ORTHE–Orth Ch in Amer	1	45	NR	50	0.1	0.2
PENT–Assemb of God	5	589	321	1,303	1.5	4.5
PENT–Ch God (Cleve)	1	14	20	24	0.0	0.1
PENT–Int Foursq Gos	1	46	50	60	0.1	0.2
PENT–Un Pent Ch Intl	1	NR	NR	NR	-	-
PENT–Vineyard	2	60	80	96	0.1	0.3
PRES–Evan Presby Ch	1	NR	220	264	0.3	0.9
PRES–Presb Ch (USA)	3	259	415	498	0.6	1.7
PRES–Presb Ch Amer	1	218	165	219	0.2	0.8
REF–Christian Ref	5	1,012	1,328	1,595	1.8	5.5
REF–Un Ref Chs N.A.	1	NR	NR	NR	-	-
Salvation Army	1	15	20	182	0.2	0.6
Sev Day Adv	4	384	668	768	0.9	2.7
Sikh	1	NR	NR	NR	-	-
Un C of Christ	1	100	282	339	0.4	1.2
Unit Univ	1	102	100	140	0.2	0.5
Unity Ch	1	NR	NR	NR	-	-
GARFIELD	**8**	**110**	**205**	**441**	**36.6**	**100.0**
BAPT–So Bapt Conv	1	28	34	42	3.5	9.5
Catholic	1	NR	NR	110	9.1	24.9
CHR–Chs of Christ	1	4	6	10	0.8	2.3
LDS–L-D Saints	1	NR	NR	58	4.8	13.2
LUTH–E.L.C.A.	1	17	75	92	7.6	20.9
PENT–Assemb of God	1	24	10	33	2.7	7.5
PRES–Presb Ch (USA)	1	21	53	65	5.4	14.7
Sev Day Adv	1	16	27	31	2.6	7.0
GLACIER	**23**	**681**	**1,238**	**9,336**	**69.7**	**100.0**
Bahá'í	0	NR	20	20	0.1	0.2
BAPT–So Bapt Conv	2	40	117	156	1.2	1.7
Catholic	5	NR	NR	7,400	55.2	79.3
LDS–L-D Saints	1	NR	NR	294	2.2	3.1
LUTH–E.L.C.A.	1	75	547	547	4.1	5.9
LUTH–Luth Cong Msn Chr	1	50	75	100	0.7	1.1
MENN–Hutt Breth	6	NR	NR	NR	-	-
METH–Un Methodist	2	46	48	57	0.4	0.6
Non-denom Chr Chs	2	240	230	325	2.4	3.5
PENT–Assemb of God	2	187	76	270	2.0	2.9
PRES–Presb Ch (USA)	1	43	125	167	1.2	1.8
GOLDEN VALLEY	**6**	**36**	**39**	**217**	**24.5**	**100.0**
BAPT–So Bapt Conv	1	15	27	32	3.6	14.7
Catholic	1	NR	NR	162	18.3	74.7
LUTH–E.L.C.A.	1	6	6	6	0.7	2.8
MENN–Hutt Breth	1	NR	NR	NR	-	-
METH–Un Methodist	2	15	6	17	1.9	7.8
GRANITE	**9**	**90**	**128**	**727**	**23.6**	**100.0**
ANG/EPIS–Episcopal	1	8	21	22	0.7	3.0
Bahá'í	0	NR	2	2	0.1	0.3
Catholic	2	NR	NR	250	8.1	34.4
LDS–L-D Saints	2	NR	NR	303	9.8	41.7
METH–Un Methodist	2	22	27	49	1.6	6.7
Non-denom Chr Chs	1	60	55	75	2.4	10.3
PRES–Presb Ch (USA)	1	0	23	26	0.8	3.6
HILL	**39**	**1,182**	**2,377**	**6,075**	**37.7**	**100.0**
ANG/EPIS–Episcopal	1	10	40	44	0.3	0.7
Bahá'í	0	NR	10	10	0.1	0.2
BAPT–Amer Bapt USA	2	63	56	71	0.4	1.2
BAPT–So Bapt Conv	1	55	58	73	0.5	1.2
Catholic	5	NR	NR	1,820	11.3	30.0
Ch of Nazarene	1	14	20	70	0.4	1.2
Chr & Miss Al	1	70	34	100	0.6	1.6
CHR–Chr Chs & Chs Cr	1	NR	450	569	3.5	9.4
Evan Ch	1	NR	NR	NR	-	-
Jehovah's Witness	1	NR	NR	NR	-	-
LDS–L-D Saints	1	NR	NR	591	3.7	9.7
LUTH–E.L.C.A.	8	392	1,065	1,476	9.2	24.3
LUTH–Luth Cong Msn Chr	1	80	NR	NR	-	-
LUTH–Luth-MO Synod	1	57	91	119	0.7	2.0
MENN–Hutt Breth	5	NR	NR	NR	-	-
METH–Un Methodist	2	107	296	377	2.3	6.2
PENT–Assemb of God	2	213	112	579	3.6	9.5
PENT–Int Foursq Gos	2	46	21	27	0.2	0.4
PENT–Un Pent Ch Intl	1	NR	NR	NR	-	-
PRES–Presb Ch (USA)	1	36	56	71	0.4	1.2
Sev Day Adv	1	39	68	78	0.5	1.3

NR–Not Reported   - Represents no adherents reported.   Percentages may not total 100 due to rounding.

Table 3: Religious Congregations by County and Group: 2010

Religious Group	Number of Congrega-tions	Number of Attendees	Number of Communicant, Confirmed, or Full Members	Adherents		
				Number of Adherents	% of Total Pop.	% of Total Adh.
JEFFERSON	**21**	**563**	**733**	**2,536**	**22.2**	**100.0**
Bahá'í	0	NR	5	5	0.0	0.2
BAPT–So Bapt Conv	3	155	201	241	2.1	9.5
Catholic	3	NR	NR	990	8.7	39.0
Ch of Nazarene	1	19	12	45	0.4	1.8
LDS–Comm of Christ	1	NR	128	128	1.1	5.0
LDS–L-D Saints	2	NR	NR	444	3.9	17.5
LUTH–E.L.C.A.	1	6	7	7	0.1	0.3
LUTH–Luth–MO Synod	2	34	96	121	1.1	4.8
METH–Un Methodist	3	115	145	227	2.0	9.0
Non-denom Chr Chs	1	100	80	125	1.1	4.9
PENT–Assemb of God	2	114	24	163	1.4	6.4
Sev Day Adv	2	20	35	40	0.4	1.6
JUDITH BASIN	**11**	**118**	**210**	**1,208**	**58.3**	**100.0**
Bahá'í	0	NR	3	3	0.1	0.2
BAPT–So Bapt Conv	1	13	4	5	0.2	0.4
Catholic	4	NR	NR	978	47.2	81.0
LUTH–Luth–MO Synod	1	24	51	57	2.8	4.7
MENN–Hutt Breth	2	NR	NR	NR	-	-
METH–Un Methodist	1	38	80	80	3.9	6.6
PRES–Presb Ch (USA)	2	43	72	85	4.1	7.0
LAKE	**53**	**1,915**	**3,072**	**11,291**	**39.3**	**100.0**
ANG/EPIS–Episcopal	2	70	165	182	0.6	1.6
Bahá'í	0	NR	34	34	0.1	0.3
BAPT–Reg Bapt Gen As	2	NR	NR	NR	-	-
BAPT–So Bapt Conv	5	138	121	151	0.5	1.3
Catholic	7	NR	NR	5,100	17.7	45.2
Ch of Nazarene	1	47	59	136	0.5	1.2
Chr & Miss Al	4	272	153	482	1.7	4.3
CHR–Chr Ch (Disc)	1	35	74	92	0.3	0.8
CHR–Chr Chs & Chs Cr	3	NR	305	380	1.3	3.4
CHR–Chs of Christ	2	83	61	98	0.3	0.9
FRND–Indep Yr Mtgs	1	NR	0	0	0.0	0.0
Jehovah's Witness	2	NR	NR	NR	-	-
LDS–L-D Saints	3	NR	NR	1,415	4.9	12.5
LUTH–E.L.C.A.	3	226	966	1,191	4.1	10.5
LUTH–Luth–MO Synod	3	146	187	237	0.8	2.1
MENN–Amish Undif	1	NR	71	140	0.5	1.2
MENN–CG in Cr (Menn)	1	NR	73	91	0.3	0.8
METH–Un Methodist	2	115	180	285	1.0	2.5
PENT–Assemb of God	3	478	227	798	2.8	7.1
PENT–Int Foursq Gos	2	82	56	70	0.2	0.6
PENT–Un Pent Ch Intl	2	NR	NR	NR	-	-
PRES–Presb Ch (USA)	2	136	189	235	0.8	2.1
Sev Day Adv	1	87	151	174	0.6	1.5
LEWIS AND CLARK	**83**	**6,223**	**8,534**	**24,523**	**38.7**	**100.0**
ANG/EPIS–Episcopal	2	138	355	550	0.9	2.2
Bahá'í	1	NR	33	33	0.1	0.1
BAPT–Amer Bapt Assn	1	NR	85	103	0.2	0.4
BAPT–Amer Bapt USA	1	72	92	112	0.2	0.5
BAPT–NT Ind Bapt	1	NR	NR	NR	-	-
BAPT–Ref Bapt Ch	1	NR	NR	NR	-	-
BAPT–So Bapt Conv	7	344	1,046	1,268	2.0	5.2
BUDD–Mahayana	1	NR	NR	11	0.0	0.0
Calv Chpl	1	NR	NR	NR	-	-
Catholic	8	NR	NR	8,800	13.9	35.9
Ch Cr, Scientst	1	NR	NR	NR	-	-
Ch of Nazarene	1	75	69	120	0.2	0.5
Chr & Miss Al	1	137	108	202	0.3	0.8
CHR–Chr Ch (Disc)	1	110	180	218	0.3	0.9
CHR–Chr Chs & Chs Cr	1	NR	45	55	0.1	0.2
CHR–Chs of Christ	3	230	205	290	0.5	1.2
Christian Brethren	1	NR	NR	NR	-	-
Evan Cov Ch	2	419	188	544	0.9	2.2
FRND–Indep Yr Mtgs	1	NR	3	4	0.0	0.0
Jehovah's Witness	2	NR	NR	NR	-	-
LDS–Comm of Christ	1	NR	128	128	0.2	0.5
LDS–L-D Saints	6	NR	NR	2,965	4.7	12.1
LUTH–E.L.C.A.	3	699	1,579	2,685	4.2	10.9
LUTH–Luth–MO Synod	1	333	509	679	1.1	2.8
LUTH–Wisc Ev Luth Syn	1	47	78	99	0.2	0.4
MENN–Hutt Breth	2	NR	NR	NR	-	-
METH–Un Methodist	4	476	796	904	1.4	3.7
Non-denom Chr Chs	10	1,240	1,345	1,587	2.5	6.5
ORTHE–Orth Ch in Amer	1	12	NR	15	0.0	0.1
PENT–Assemb of God	2	827	428	1,500	2.4	6.1
PENT–Int Foursq Gos	2	450	334	405	0.6	1.7
PENT–Intl Pent Holiness	2	60	57	69	0.1	0.3
PENT–Un Pent Ch Intl	1	NR	NR	NR	-	-
PENT–Vineyard	1	65	77	93	0.1	0.4
PRES–Presb Ch (USA)	1	227	346	419	0.7	1.7
PRES–Presb Ch Amer	1	0	0	0	0.0	0.0
REF–Christian Ref	1	50	38	46	0.1	0.2
REF–Comm Ref Evan	1	NR	NR	NR	-	-
Salvation Army	1	19	29	161	0.3	0.7
Sev Day Adv	1	76	131	151	0.2	0.6
Un C of Christ	1	72	200	242	0.4	1.0
Unit Univ	1	45	50	65	0.1	0.3
LIBERTY	**10**	**191**	**451**	**1,235**	**52.8**	**100.0**
Catholic	1	NR	NR	585	25.0	47.4
Chr & Miss Al	1	47	28	84	3.6	6.8
LDS–L-D Saints	1	NR	NR	56	2.4	4.5
LUTH–E.L.C.A.	1	12	20	20	0.9	1.6
LUTH–Luth Cong Msn Chr	1	80	308	368	15.7	29.8
MENN–Hutt Breth	3	NR	NR	NR	-	-
METH–Un Methodist	1	34	86	111	4.7	9.0
PRES–Presb Ch (USA)	1	18	9	11	0.5	0.9
LINCOLN	**46**	**1,926**	**3,384**	**6,462**	**32.8**	**100.0**
ANG/EPIS–Episcopal	3	48	64	64	0.3	1.0
Bahá'í	0	NR	16	16	0.1	0.2
BAPT–Amer Bapt Assn	1	NR	85	100	0.5	1.5
BAPT–Amer Bapt USA	1	80	200	235	1.2	3.6
BAPT–Reg Bapt Gen As	1	NR	NR	NR	-	-
BAPT–So Bapt Conv	3	225	658	772	3.9	11.9
Catholic	3	NR	NR	650	3.3	10.1
CGOD–Ch God (Ander)	3	77	NR	77	0.4	1.2
Ch of Nazarene	1	82	94	137	0.7	2.1
Chr & Miss Al	1	93	54	93	0.5	1.4
CHR–Chr Chs & Chs Cr	1	NR	600	704	3.6	10.9
CHR–Chs of Christ	2	43	40	56	0.3	0.9
Evan Free Ch	1	67	NR	67	0.3	1.0
FRND–Indep Yr Mtgs	1	NR	0	0	0.0	0.0
Jehovah's Witness	3	NR	NR	NR	-	-
LDS–L-D Saints	3	NR	NR	981	5.0	15.2
LUTH–E.L.C.A.	1	146	100	476	2.4	7.4
LUTH–Luth–MO Synod	2	158	274	346	1.8	5.4
MENN–Amish Undif	1	NR	33	69	0.4	1.1
METH–Un Methodist	2	94	187	264	1.3	4.1
Non-denom Chr Chs	4	245	370	425	2.2	6.6
PENT–Assemb of God	2	206	103	341	1.7	5.3
PENT–Ch God (Cleve)	1	177	220	258	1.3	4.0
PENT–Int Foursq Gos	2	43	43	50	0.3	0.8
PRES–Presb Ch (USA)	1	14	22	26	0.1	0.4
Sev Day Adv	2	128	221	255	1.3	3.9
MCCONE	**8**	**201**	**531**	**990**	**57.1**	**100.0**
BAPT–Amer Bapt USA	1	36	41	48	2.8	4.8
BAPT–So Bapt Conv	1	35	45	53	3.1	5.4
Catholic	2	NR	NR	300	17.3	30.3
Evan Ch	1	NR	NR	NR	-	-
LUTH–E.L.C.A.	1	90	397	517	29.8	52.2
LUTH–Wisc Ev Luth Syn	1	17	30	39	2.2	3.9
PENT–Assemb of God	1	23	18	33	1.9	3.3
MADISON	**23**	**493**	**580**	**1,920**	**25.0**	**100.0**
ANG/EPIS–Episcopal	3	112	155	170	2.2	8.9
Bahá'í	0	NR	3	3	0.0	0.2
BAPT–Consrv Bapt	1	NR	NR	NR	-	-
BAPT–NT Ind Bapt	1	NR	NR	NR	-	-

NR–Not Reported - Represents no adherents reported. Percentages may not total 100 due to rounding.

Table 3: Religious Congregations by County and Group: 2010

Religious Group	Number of Congrega-tions	Number of Attendees	Number of Communicant, Confirmed, or Full Members	Adherents: Number of Adherents	Adherents: % of Total Pop.	Adherents: % of Total Adh.
BAPT–So Bapt Conv	2	88	93	107	1.4	5.6
Catholic	4	NR	NR	600	7.8	31.3
Ch Cr, Scientst	1	NR	NR	NR	-	-
CHR–Chs of Christ	1	16	12	18	0.2	0.9
Jehovah's Witness	1	NR	NR	NR	-	-
LDS–L-D Saints	2	NR	NR	407	5.3	21.2
LUTH–Luth–MO Synod	1	25	51	68	0.9	3.5
METH–Un Methodist	2	92	110	248	3.2	12.9
Non-denom Chr Chs	1	35	50	50	0.7	2.6
PENT–Assemb of God	2	90	22	152	2.0	7.9
PRES–Presb Ch (USA)	1	35	84	97	1.3	5.1
MEAGHER	**8**	**133**	**167**	**527**	**27.9**	**100.0**
BAPT–So Bapt Conv	1	37	34	39	2.1	7.4
Catholic	1	NR	NR	250	13.2	47.4
Chr & Miss Al	1	37	33	66	3.5	12.5
LDS–L-D Saints	1	NR	NR	48	2.5	9.1
LUTH–E.L.C.A.	1	50	84	106	5.6	20.1
MENN–Hutt Breth	2	NR	NR	NR	-	-
PRES–Presb Ch (USA)	1	9	16	18	1.0	3.4
MINERAL	**15**	**294**	**325**	**903**	**21.4**	**100.0**
Bahá'í	0	NR	3	3	0.1	0.3
BAPT–So Bapt Conv	2	3	4	5	0.1	0.6
Catholic	2	NR	NR	150	3.6	16.6
CHR–Chs of Christ	1	7	12	20	0.5	2.2
Evan Free Ch	1	60	NR	60	1.4	6.6
Jehovah's Witness	1	NR	NR	NR	-	-
LDS–L-D Saints	1	NR	NR	209	4.9	23.1
LUTH–Luth–MO Synod	1	40	77	100	2.4	11.1
METH–A.W.M.C.	1	48	54	59	1.4	6.5
METH–Un Methodist	2	54	81	135	3.2	15.0
Non-denom Chr Chs	1	6	20	20	0.5	2.2
PENT–Assemb of God	1	50	30	91	2.2	10.1
Sev Day Adv	1	26	44	51	1.2	5.6
MISSOULA	**101**	**8,071**	**10,594**	**31,181**	**28.5**	**100.0**
ANG/EPIS–Episcopal	1	185	731	930	0.9	3.0
Bahá'í	2	NR	117	117	0.1	0.4
BAPT–Amer Bapt Assn	1	NR	85	101	0.1	0.3
BAPT–Amer Bapt USA	1	86	178	211	0.2	0.7
BAPT–N Am Bapt Conf	1	NR	90	107	0.1	0.3
BAPT–Reg Bapt Gen As	1	NR	NR	NR	-	-
BAPT–So Bapt Conv	8	712	382	452	0.4	1.4
BUDD–Mahayana	3	NR	NR	163	0.1	0.5
BUDD–Theravada	1	NR	NR	267	0.2	0.9
BUDD–Vajrayana	1	NR	NR	209	0.2	0.7
Catholic	8	NR	NR	9,800	9.0	31.4
Ch Cr, Scientst	1	NR	NR	NR	-	-
Ch of Nazarene	1	90	125	127	0.1	0.4
Chr & Miss Al	4	1,114	550	1,659	1.5	5.3
CHR–Chr Ch (Disc)	2	61	180	213	0.2	0.7
CHR–Chr Chs & Chs Cr	1	NR	130	154	0.1	0.5
CHR–Chs of Christ	1	220	220	250	0.2	0.8
CHR–Int Chs of Christ	1	NR	64	76	0.1	0.2
Evan Ch	1	NR	NR	NR	-	-
Evan Free Ch	1	75	NR	75	0.1	0.2
FRND–Indep Yr Mtgs	1	NR	44	52	0.0	0.2
HINDU–Post Ren	1	NR	NR	25	0.0	0.1
Jehovah's Witness	1	NR	NR	NR	-	-
JUD–Reform	1	44	78	211	0.2	0.7
LDS–L-D Saints	9	NR	NR	4,879	4.5	15.6
LUTH–E.L.C.A.	6	696	2,016	2,912	2.7	9.3
LUTH–Luth–MO Synod	4	405	849	1,034	0.9	3.3
LUTH–Wisc Ev Luth Syn	1	57	86	105	0.1	0.3
METH–A.W.M.C.	1	24	15	29	0.0	0.1
METH–Free Methodist	1	29	23	29	0.0	0.1
METH–Un Methodist	2	204	424	533	0.5	1.7
Non-denom Chr Chs	9	1,625	1,775	2,056	1.9	6.6
ORTHE–Greek Orthodox	1	45	NR	120	0.1	0.4
PENT–Assemb of God	4	1,080	450	1,565	1.4	5.0
PENT–Int Foursq Gos	4	446	221	262	0.2	0.8
PENT–Pent Ch of God	2	140	NR	217	0.2	0.7

Religious Group	Number of Congrega-tions	Number of Attendees	Number of Communicant, Confirmed, or Full Members	Adherents: Number of Adherents	Adherents: % of Total Pop.	Adherents: % of Total Adh.
PENT–Un Pent Ch Intl	1	NR	NR	NR	-	-
PENT–Vineyard	1	10	10	12	0.0	0.0
PRES–Presb Ch (USA)	3	307	599	709	0.6	2.3
PRES–Presb Ch Amer	1	0	0	0	0.0	0.0
REF–Comm Ref Evan	1	NR	NR	NR	-	-
Salvation Army	1	27	72	243	0.2	0.8
Sev Day Adv	1	192	333	383	0.4	1.2
Un C of Christ	1	174	717	849	0.8	2.7
Unit Univ	1	23	30	45	0.0	0.1
Unity Ch	1	NR	NR	NR	-	-
MUSSELSHELL	**19**	**336**	**392**	**1,509**	**33.3**	**100.0**
Bahá'í	0	NR	3	3	0.1	0.2
BAPT–Amer Bapt USA	1	74	54	64	1.4	4.2
BAPT–So Bapt Conv	1	6	16	19	0.4	1.3
Catholic	3	NR	NR	751	16.5	49.8
CHR–Chs of Christ	1	38	27	41	0.9	2.7
Evan Ch	1	NR	NR	NR	-	-
Jehovah's Witness	1	NR	NR	NR	-	-
LDS–L-D Saints	1	NR	NR	270	5.9	17.9
LUTH–E.L.C.A.	1	41	88	117	2.6	7.8
LUTH–Luth–MO Synod	1	10	10	12	0.3	0.8
LUTH–Wisc Ev Luth Syn	1	21	20	20	0.4	1.3
MENN–Hutt Breth	2	NR	NR	NR	-	-
METH–Un Methodist	1	25	43	51	1.1	3.4
Non-denom Chr Chs	2	55	60	71	1.6	4.7
PENT–Assemb of God	1	42	29	42	0.9	2.8
Sev Day Adv	1	24	42	48	1.1	3.2
PARK	**30**	**1,385**	**2,146**	**4,619**	**29.5**	**100.0**
ANG/EPIS–Episcopal	2	77	204	204	1.3	4.4
Bahá'í	0	NR	14	14	0.1	0.3
BAPT–Amer Bapt USA	1	50	69	81	0.5	1.8
BAPT–So Bapt Conv	2	46	37	44	0.3	1.0
Catholic	3	NR	NR	1,504	9.6	32.6
Ch of Nazarene	1	27	48	48	0.3	1.0
CHR–Chs of Christ	1	63	56	81	0.5	1.8
Jehovah's Witness	1	NR	NR	NR	-	-
LDS–L-D Saints	2	NR	NR	640	4.1	13.9
LUTH–E.L.C.A.	3	142	474	541	3.5	11.7
LUTH–Wisc Ev Luth Syn	1	52	73	80	0.5	1.7
METH–Un Methodist	4	171	377	409	2.6	8.9
Non-denom Chr Chs	6	568	580	715	4.6	15.5
PENT–Assemb of God	1	121	95	121	0.8	2.6
PENT–Ch God (Cleve)	1	14	24	28	0.2	0.6
Sev Day Adv	1	54	95	109	0.7	2.4
PETROLEUM	**1**	**NR**	**NR**	**158**	**32.0**	**100.0**
Catholic	1	NR	NR	158	32.0	100.0
PHILLIPS	**24**	**564**	**859**	**2,156**	**50.7**	**100.0**
Bahá'í	0	NR	2	2	0.0	0.1
BAPT–So Bapt Conv	2	54	55	66	1.6	3.1
Catholic	5	NR	NR	655	15.4	30.4
CHR–Chr Chs & Chs Cr	1	NR	35	42	1.0	1.9
Evan Free Ch	1	45	NR	45	1.1	2.1
Jehovah's Witness	1	NR	NR	NR	-	-
LDS–L-D Saints	1	NR	NR	138	3.2	6.4
LUTH–Ch of Luth Br	1	100	58	166	3.9	7.7
LUTH–E.L.C.A.	5	154	528	749	17.6	34.7
MENN–Hutt Breth	2	NR	NR	NR	-	-
METH–Un Methodist	1	10	14	14	0.3	0.6
Non-denom Chr Chs	1	80	80	100	2.4	4.6
PENT–Assemb of God	2	121	87	179	4.2	8.3
PENT–Un Pent Ch Intl	1	NR	NR	NR	-	-
PONDERA	**28**	**676**	**1,384**	**2,998**	**48.7**	**100.0**
BAPT–So Bapt Conv	2	44	107	132	2.1	4.4
Catholic	3	NR	NR	900	14.6	30.0
Jehovah's Witness	3	NR	NR	NR	-	-
LDS–L-D Saints	1	NR	NR	276	4.5	9.2
LUTH–Luth Cong Msn Chr	4	141	624	771	12.5	25.7

NR–Not Reported - Represents no adherents reported. Percentages may not total 100 due to rounding.

Table 3: Religious Congregations by County and Group: 2010

Religious Group	Number of Congrega-tions	Number of Attendees	Number of Communicant, Confirmed, or Full Members	Adherents: Number of Adherents	% of Total Pop.	% of Total Adh.
MENN–Hutt Breth	5	NR	NR	NR	-	-
METH–Un Methodist	3	47	119	152	2.5	5.1
Non-denom Chr Chs	2	220	220	275	4.5	9.2
PENT–Assemb of God	2	72	11	118	1.9	3.9
PENT–Un Pent Ch Intl	1	NR	NR	NR	-	-
PRES–Presb Ch (USA)	1	82	225	278	4.5	9.3
REF–Christian Ref	1	70	78	96	1.6	3.2
POWDER RIVER	**7**	**102**	**208**	**658**	**37.8**	**100.0**
Bahá'í	0	NR	1	1	0.1	0.2
BAPT–Consrv Bapt	1	NR	NR	NR	-	-
Catholic	1	NR	NR	375	21.5	57.0
LDS–L-D Saints	1	NR	NR	32	1.8	4.9
LUTH–E.L.C.A.	1	22	91	91	5.2	13.8
METH–Wesleyan	1	21	10	27	1.5	4.1
PENT–Assemb of God	1	22	32	46	2.6	7.0
Un C of Christ	1	37	74	86	4.9	13.1
POWELL	**15**	**482**	**556**	**1,691**	**24.1**	**100.0**
ANG/EPIS–Episcopal	1	20	71	71	1.0	4.2
Bahá'í	0	NR	8	8	0.1	0.5
BAPT–So Bapt Conv	2	117	109	124	1.8	7.3
Catholic	3	NR	NR	435	6.2	25.7
Evan Free Ch	1	50	NR	50	0.7	3.0
Jehovah's Witness	1	NR	NR	NR	-	-
LDS–Comm of Christ	1	NR	128	128	1.8	7.6
LDS–L-D Saints	1	NR	NR	434	6.2	25.7
LUTH–Luth–MO Synod	1	42	64	89	1.3	5.3
MENN–Menn Chr Fell	1	81	35	81	1.2	4.8
PENT–Assemb of God	1	87	35	150	2.1	8.9
PENT–Vineyard	1	50	70	80	1.1	4.7
PRES–Presb Ch (USA)	1	35	36	41	0.6	2.4
PRAIRIE	**7**	**142**	**257**	**503**	**42.7**	**100.0**
Catholic	1	NR	NR	174	14.8	34.6
Evan Ch	1	NR	NR	NR	-	-
LUTH–E.L.C.A.	1	15	60	70	5.9	13.9
LUTH–Luth–MO Synod	1	18	28	31	2.6	6.2
LUTH–Wisc Ev Luth Syn	1	21	49	58	4.9	11.5
METH–Wesleyan	1	38	16	49	4.2	9.7
PRES–Presb Ch (USA)	1	50	104	121	10.3	24.1
RAVALLI	**63**	**3,905**	**4,778**	**11,709**	**29.1**	**100.0**
ANG/EPIS–Episcopal	2	57	141	141	0.4	1.2
Bahá'í	0	NR	22	22	0.1	0.2
BAPT–Amer Bapt USA	3	244	346	414	1.0	3.5
BAPT–N Am Bapt Conf	1	NR	36	43	0.1	0.4
BAPT–NT Ind Bapt	1	NR	NR	NR	-	-
BAPT–So Bapt Conv	5	377	543	650	1.6	5.6
Calv Chpl	1	NR	NR	NR	-	-
Catholic	4	NR	NR	2,225	5.5	19.0
Ch Cr, Scientst	1	NR	NR	NR	-	-
Ch of Nazarene	1	147	102	163	0.4	1.4
Chr & Miss Al	1	277	101	420	1.0	3.6
CHR–Chr Ch (Disc)	1	28	64	77	0.2	0.7
CHR–Chs of Christ	2	120	91	113	0.3	1.0
HINDU–Post Ren	1	NR	NR	16	0.0	0.1
Jehovah's Witness	2	NR	NR	NR	-	-
LDS–L-D Saints	6	NR	NR	2,606	6.5	22.3
LUTH–E.L.C.A.	1	129	664	920	2.3	7.9
LUTH–Luth–MO Synod	2	198	393	475	1.2	4.1
METH–Un Methodist	3	298	476	805	2.0	6.9
METH–Wesleyan	2	89	50	116	0.3	1.0
MJEW–Union Mes Cong	1	NR	NR	NR	-	-
Non-denom Chr Chs	10	1,100	890	1,390	3.5	11.9
PENT–Assemb of God	2	258	171	304	0.8	2.6
PENT–Int Foursq Gos	4	230	151	181	0.5	1.5
PENT–Intl Pent Holiness	1	63	70	84	0.2	0.7
PRES–Presb Ch (USA)	1	100	138	165	0.4	1.4
Sev Day Adv	4	190	329	379	0.9	3.2

Religious Group	Number of Congrega-tions	Number of Attendees	Number of Communicant, Confirmed, or Full Members	Adherents: Number of Adherents	% of Total Pop.	% of Total Adh.
RICHLAND	**31**	**1,259**	**2,710**	**5,652**	**58.0**	**100.0**
ANG/EPIS–Episcopal	1	17	42	58	0.6	1.0
Bahá'í	0	NR	2	2	0.0	0.0
BAPT–So Bapt Conv	1	92	101	123	1.3	2.2
Catholic	5	NR	NR	1,539	15.8	27.2
Ch of Nazarene	1	24	31	45	0.5	0.8
Chr & Miss Al	4	218	130	378	3.9	6.7
CHR–Chs of Christ	1	45	35	45	0.5	0.8
CONG–Consrv Cong Chr	1	80	79	96	1.0	1.7
LDS–L-D Saints	1	NR	NR	287	2.9	5.1
LUTH–Ch of Luth Br	1	88	91	300	3.1	5.3
LUTH–E.L.C.A.	5	306	1,305	1,653	17.0	29.2
LUTH–Luth Ch-Am Asc	1	NR	NR	NR	-	-
LUTH–Luth–MO Synod	2	103	338	411	4.2	7.3
METH–Un Methodist	1	50	182	182	1.9	3.2
Non-denom Chr Chs	1	65	65	81	0.8	1.4
PENT–Assemb of God	1	105	101	200	2.1	3.5
PRES–Presb Ch (USA)	1	9	15	18	0.2	0.3
Sev Day Adv	1	10	17	20	0.2	0.4
Un C of Christ	2	47	176	214	2.2	3.8
ROOSEVELT	**45**	**929**	**2,367**	**6,551**	**62.8**	**100.0**
Bahá'í	0	NR	20	20	0.2	0.3
BAPT–Amer Bapt USA	1	23	21	28	0.3	0.4
BAPT–So Bapt Conv	4	83	105	139	1.3	2.1
BRETH–Ch of Brethren	1	23	15	20	0.2	0.3
Catholic	5	NR	NR	2,375	22.8	36.3
Ch of Nazarene	1	9	11	41	0.4	0.6
CHR–Chs of Christ	1	15	9	11	0.1	0.2
LDS–Comm of Christ	1	NR	128	128	1.2	2.0
LDS–L-D Saints	2	NR	NR	898	8.6	13.7
LUTH–Assoc Free Luth	2	NR	NR	NR	-	-
LUTH–E.L.C.A.	7	273	1,194	1,534	14.7	23.4
LUTH–Luth Cong Msn Chr	1	31	57	76	0.7	1.2
LUTH–Luth–MO Synod	1	14	48	56	0.5	0.9
LUTH–Wisc Ev Luth Syn	1	13	9	15	0.1	0.2
MENN–Fel Evg Bib Ch	1	20	10	20	0.2	0.3
MENN–Hutt Breth	1	NR	NR	NR	-	-
MENN–Menn Br US Conf	1	NR	51	68	0.7	1.0
METH–Un Methodist	1	20	97	97	0.9	1.5
Non-denom Chr Chs	1	50	15	62	0.6	0.9
PENT–Assemb of God	3	202	125	259	2.5	4.0
PENT–Pent Ch of God	1	70	NR	109	1.0	1.7
PRES–Presb Ch (USA)	6	60	410	544	5.2	8.3
Sev Day Adv	1	13	23	26	0.2	0.4
Un C of Christ	1	10	19	25	0.2	0.4
ROSEBUD	**30**	**813**	**1,195**	**5,134**	**55.6**	**100.0**
ANG/EPIS–Episcopal	1	10	15	16	0.2	0.3
Bahá'í	0	NR	17	17	0.2	0.3
BAPT–So Bapt Conv	3	190	410	531	5.8	10.3
Catholic	4	NR	NR	2,573	27.9	50.1
Chr & Miss Al	2	54	81	126	1.4	2.5
CHR–Chs of Christ	1	15	11	18	0.2	0.4
Evan Free Ch	1	75	NR	75	0.8	1.5
Jehovah's Witness	1	NR	NR	NR	-	-
LDS–L-D Saints	2	NR	NR	607	6.6	11.8
LUTH–Luth–MO Synod	4	129	366	479	5.2	9.3
MENN–Amish Undif	1	NR	35	89	1.0	1.7
MENN–Mennonite USA	2	8	68	88	1.0	1.7
METH–Wesleyan	1	34	19	44	0.5	0.9
PENT–Assemb of God	2	151	15	157	1.7	3.1
PENT–Int Foursq Gos	1	2	2	3	0.0	0.1
PENT–Pent Ch of God	1	70	NR	109	1.2	2.1
PRES–Presb Ch (USA)	2	40	136	176	1.9	3.4
Un C of Christ	1	35	20	26	0.3	0.5
SANDERS	**35**	**1,078**	**1,012**	**2,673**	**23.4**	**100.0**
Bahá'í	0	NR	3	3	0.0	0.1
BAPT–Reg Bapt Gen As	1	NR	NR	NR	-	-
BAPT–So Bapt Conv	3	81	81	95	0.8	3.6
Catholic	4	NR	NR	350	3.1	13.1

NR–Not Reported - Represents no adherents reported. Percentages may not total 100 due to rounding.

Table 3: Religious Congregations by County and Group: 2010

Religious Group	Number of Congrega-tions	Number of Attendees	Number of Communicant, Confirmed, or Full Members	Adherents		
				Number of Adherents	% of Total Pop.	% of Total Adh.
CGOD–Ch God (Ander)	1	60	NR	60	0.5	2.2
Chr & Miss Al	1	151	64	215	1.9	8.0
CHR–Chr Chs & Chs Cr	1	NR	0	0	0.0	0.0
CHR–Chs of Christ	1	10	10	10	0.1	0.4
CONG–Consrv Cong Chr	1	48	127	149	1.3	5.6
Jehovah's Witness	2	NR	NR	NR	-	-
LDS–L-D Saints	2	NR	NR	540	4.7	20.2
LUTH–E.L.C.A.	3	106	216	254	2.2	9.5
LUTH–Luth Cong Msn Chr	1	NR	NR	NR	-	-
METH–Un Methodist	5	90	104	172	1.5	6.4
Non-denom Chr Chs	3	180	205	225	2.0	8.4
PENT–Assemb of God	2	205	70	339	3.0	12.7
PENT–Pent Ch of God	1	70	NR	109	1.0	4.1
PRES–Presb Ch (USA)	1	11	18	21	0.2	0.8
Sev Day Adv	2	66	114	131	1.1	4.9
SHERIDAN	**26**	**686**	**2,238**	**3,678**	**108.7**	**100.0**
BAPT–So Bapt Conv	1	25	20	23	0.7	0.6
Catholic	2	NR	NR	784	23.2	21.3
CHR–Chs of Christ	1	62	60	68	2.0	1.8
LDS–L-D Saints	1	NR	NR	86	2.5	2.3
LUTH–E.L.C.A.	7	269	962	1,306	38.6	35.5
LUTH–Luth Cong Msn Chr	5	155	935	1,088	32.2	29.6
LUTH–Luth-MO Synod	1	23	60	73	2.2	2.0
MENN–Mennonite USA	1	24	25	29	0.9	0.8
METH–Un Methodist	2	19	29	37	1.1	1.0
PENT–Assemb of God	2	60	40	60	1.8	1.6
Sev Day Adv	1	9	16	18	0.5	0.5
Un C of Christ	2	40	91	106	3.1	2.9
SILVER BOW	**41**	**1,739**	**2,840**	**14,491**	**42.4**	**100.0**
ANG/EPIS–Anglican NA	1	NR	NR	NR	-	-
ANG/EPIS–Episcopal	1	50	345	345	1.0	2.4
Bahá'í	1	NR	16	16	0.0	0.1
BAPT–Amer Bapt USA	2	52	39	46	0.1	0.3
BAPT–So Bapt Conv	2	128	501	596	1.7	4.1
Catholic	8	NR	NR	9,050	26.5	62.5
Ch Cr, Scientst	1	NR	NR	NR	-	-
Ch of Nazarene	1	20	37	37	0.1	0.3
CHR–Chr Ch (Disc)	1	14	15	18	0.1	0.1
CHR–Chr Chs & Chs Cr	1	NR	25	30	0.1	0.2
CHR–Chs of Christ	1	45	52	69	0.2	0.5
Evan Free Ch	1	100	NR	100	0.3	0.7
Jehovah's Witness	1	NR	NR	NR	-	-
JUD–Reform	1	10	17	46	0.1	0.3
LDS–L-D Saints	2	NR	NR	1,726	5.0	11.9
LUTH–E.L.C.A.	2	226	710	819	2.4	5.7
LUTH–Luth-MO Synod	1	55	127	159	0.5	1.1
METH–Un Methodist	2	125	186	193	0.6	1.3
Non-denom Chr Chs	1	100	150	150	0.4	1.0
ORTHE–Serb Orth USA	1	45	NR	200	0.6	1.4
PENT–Assemb of God	1	162	62	230	0.7	1.6
PENT–Ch God (Cleve)	1	362	253	301	0.9	2.1
PENT–Int Foursq Gos	1	51	55	65	0.2	0.4
PENT–Intl Pent Holiness	1	35	8	10	0.0	0.1
PENT–Un Pent Ch Intl	1	NR	NR	NR	-	-
PRES–Presb Ch (USA)	1	75	103	123	0.4	0.8
Sev Day Adv	1	57	99	114	0.3	0.8
Un C of Christ	1	27	40	48	0.1	0.3
Unity Ch	1	NR	NR	NR	-	-
STILLWATER	**21**	**586**	**1,044**	**2,264**	**24.8**	**100.0**
ANG/EPIS–Episcopal	1	16	26	32	0.4	1.4
Bahá'í	0	NR	1	1	0.0	0.0
BAPT–So Bapt Conv	2	157	296	358	3.9	15.8
Catholic	2	NR	NR	688	7.5	30.4
CGOD–Ch God (Ander)	1	50	NR	50	0.5	2.2
Evan Ch	4	NR	NR	NR	-	-
Jehovah's Witness	1	NR	NR	NR	-	-
LDS–L-D Saints	1	NR	NR	228	2.5	10.1
LUTH–E.L.C.A.	2	131	298	387	4.2	17.1
LUTH–Luth-MO Synod	1	45	118	141	1.5	6.2
METH–Un Methodist	1	13	21	27	0.3	1.2
PENT–Assemb of God	1	25	23	36	0.4	1.6
PENT–Int Foursq Gos	1	43	80	97	1.1	4.3
Un C of Christ	3	106	181	219	2.4	9.7
SWEET GRASS	**11**	**278**	**689**	**1,118**	**30.6**	**100.0**
ANG/EPIS–Episcopal	1	17	74	74	2.0	6.6
BAPT–So Bapt Conv	1	35	44	53	1.5	4.7
Catholic	1	NR	NR	148	4.1	13.2
CHR–Chs of Christ	1	13	11	13	0.4	1.2
Evan Ch	1	NR	NR	NR	-	-
LDS–L-D Saints	1	NR	NR	111	3.0	9.9
LUTH–E.L.C.A.	1	104	299	407	11.1	36.4
LUTH–Luth Cong Msn Chr	1	43	115	138	3.8	12.3
PENT–Ch God (Cleve)	1	9	38	46	1.3	4.1
Sev Day Adv	1	16	29	33	0.9	3.0
Un C of Christ	1	41	79	95	2.6	8.5
TETON	**26**	**862**	**1,785**	**3,815**	**62.8**	**100.0**
Bahá'í	0	NR	2	2	0.0	0.1
BAPT–So Bapt Conv	1	86	148	178	2.9	4.7
Catholic	4	NR	NR	1,100	18.1	28.8
CHR–Chs of Christ	1	25	25	30	0.5	0.8
LDS–L-D Saints	2	NR	NR	538	8.9	14.1
LUTH–E.L.C.A.	4	220	691	903	14.9	23.7
LUTH–Luth Cong Msn Chr	1	40	127	153	2.5	4.0
LUTH–Luth-MO Synod	2	76	128	152	2.5	4.0
MENN–Hutt Breth	3	NR	NR	NR	-	-
METH–Un Methodist	2	61	219	219	3.6	5.7
Non-denom Chr Chs	1	90	70	112	1.8	2.9
PENT–Assemb of God	2	169	193	214	3.5	5.6
Sev Day Adv	1	55	96	110	1.8	2.9
Un C of Christ	2	40	86	104	1.7	2.7
TOOLE	**18**	**504**	**1,059**	**2,498**	**46.9**	**100.0**
BAPT–So Bapt Conv	2	135	212	250	4.7	10.0
Catholic	2	NR	NR	650	12.2	26.0
CHR–Chs of Christ	1	10	10	10	0.2	0.4
LDS–L-D Saints	1	NR	NR	282	5.3	11.3
LUTH–E.L.C.A.	4	207	659	1,008	18.9	40.4
LUTH–Luth Ch-Am Asc	1	NR	NR	NR	-	-
MENN–Hutt Breth	3	NR	NR	NR	-	-
METH–Un Methodist	2	52	126	148	2.8	5.9
PENT–Assemb of God	1	70	0	90	1.7	3.6
Sev Day Adv	1	30	52	60	1.1	2.4
TREASURE	**4**	**63**	**140**	**442**	**61.6**	**100.0**
BAPT–So Bapt Conv	1	18	12	14	1.9	3.2
Catholic	1	NR	NR	284	39.6	64.3
LUTH–Luth-MO Synod	1	15	54	60	8.4	13.6
PRES–Presb Ch (USA)	1	30	74	84	11.7	19.0
VALLEY	**33**	**741**	**1,513**	**3,440**	**46.7**	**100.0**
ANG/EPIS–Episcopal	1	17	33	39	0.5	1.1
Bahá'í	0	NR	5	5	0.1	0.1
BAPT–Consrv Bapt	1	NR	NR	NR	-	-
BAPT–So Bapt Conv	4	59	121	146	2.0	4.2
Catholic	6	NR	NR	1,010	13.7	29.4
CHR–Chs of Christ	1	20	19	23	0.3	0.7
Evan Ch	1	NR	NR	NR	-	-
Jehovah's Witness	2	NR	NR	NR	-	-
LDS–L-D Saints	1	NR	NR	200	2.7	5.8
LUTH–E.L.C.A.	6	260	985	1,359	18.4	39.5
LUTH–Luth Cong Msn Chr	1	NR	NR	NR	-	-
LUTH–Luth-MO Synod	1	18	26	29	0.4	0.8
MENN–Fel Evg Bib Ch	1	95	33	95	1.3	2.8
MENN–Menn Br US Conf	1	NR	75	91	1.2	2.6
METH–Un Methodist	2	36	87	98	1.3	2.8
PENT–Assemb of God	1	150	74	170	2.3	4.9
PENT–Pent Ch of God	1	70	NR	109	1.5	3.2
PRES–Presb Ch (USA)	1	0	16	19	0.3	0.6
Un C of Christ	1	16	39	47	0.6	1.4

NR–Not Reported - Represents no adherents reported. Percentages may not total 100 due to rounding.

Table 3: Religious Congregations by County and Group: 2010

Religious Group	Number of Congregations	Number of Attendees	Number of Communicant, Confirmed, or Full Members	Adherents: Number of Adherents	Adherents: % of Total Pop.	Adherents: % of Total Adh.
WHEATLAND	**15**	**284**	**373**	**970**	**44.7**	**100.0**
Bahá'í	0	NR	1	1	0.0	0.1
Catholic	3	NR	NR	200	9.2	20.6
LDS–L-D Saints	1	NR	NR	105	4.8	10.8
LUTH–E.L.C.A.	3	108	194	305	14.1	31.4
LUTH–Luth–MO Synod	1	14	27	29	1.3	3.0
MENN–Hutt Breth	2	NR	NR	NR	-	-
METH–Un Methodist	2	44	69	89	4.1	9.2
METH–Wesleyan	1	43	24	56	2.6	5.8
PENT–Assemb of God	1	75	38	161	7.4	16.6
PRES–Presb Ch (USA)	1	0	20	24	1.1	2.5
WIBAUX	**5**	**140**	**159**	**895**	**88.0**	**100.0**
Catholic	2	NR	NR	663	65.2	74.1
LUTH–E.L.C.A.	1	38	91	103	10.1	11.5
Non-denom Chr Chs	1	60	50	75	7.4	8.4
PENT–Assemb of God	1	42	18	54	5.3	6.0
YELLOWSTONE	**164**	**17,108**	**26,629**	**57,904**	**39.1**	**100.0**
ANG/EPIS–Episcopal	3	221	529	718	0.5	1.2
Bahá'í	2	NR	130	130	0.1	0.2
BAPT–Amer Bapt Assn	1	NR	4	5	0.0	0.0
BAPT–Amer Bapt USA	2	175	143	175	0.1	0.3
BAPT–Consrv Bapt	1	NR	NR	NR	-	-
BAPT–NT Ind Bapt	1	NR	NR	NR	-	-
BAPT–So Bapt Conv	15	1,559	2,280	2,796	1.9	4.8
Calv Chpl	1	NR	NR	NR	-	-
Catholic	12	NR	NR	17,155	11.6	29.6
Ch Cr, Scientst	1	NR	NR	NR	-	-
Ch of Nazarene	4	166	226	317	0.2	0.5
Chr & Miss Al	1	170	81	230	0.2	0.4
CHR–Chr Ch (Disc)	3	139	325	398	0.3	0.7
CHR–Chr Chs & Chs Cr	2	NR	90	110	0.1	0.2
CHR–Chs of Christ	1	235	220	280	0.2	0.5
Evan Ch	6	NR	NR	NR	-	-
Evan Free Ch	1	67	NR	67	0.0	0.1
FRND–Indep Yr Mtgs	1	NR	3	4	0.0	0.0
Jehovah's Witness	5	NR	NR	NR	-	-
JUD–Reform	1	28	50	135	0.1	0.2
LDS–Comm of Christ	2	NR	256	256	0.2	0.4
LDS–L-D Saints	14	NR	NR	7,140	4.8	12.3
LUTH–Ch of Luth Br	1	72	56	201	0.1	0.3
LUTH–E.L.C.A.	11	1,541	4,695	5,591	3.8	9.7
LUTH–Luth Ch-Am Asc	1	NR	NR	NR	-	-
LUTH–Luth Cong Msn Chr	2	45	NR	NR	-	-
LUTH–Luth–MO Synod	7	973	2,375	3,084	2.1	5.3
LUTH–Wisc Ev Luth Syn	1	160	221	291	0.2	0.5
MENN–Hutt Breth	1	NR	NR	NR	-	-
METH–AME	1	0	100	123	0.1	0.2
METH–Un Methodist	7	870	2,212	2,772	1.9	4.8
METH–Wesleyan	2	104	55	135	0.1	0.2
Muslim Est	1	5	NR	25	0.0	0.0
New Apost Ch	1	NR	NR	NR	-	-
Non-denom Chr Chs	12	3,929	5,535	5,908	4.0	10.2
ORTHE–Orth Ch in Amer	1	75	NR	100	0.1	0.2
PENT–Assemb of God	7	717	373	1,310	0.9	2.3
PENT–Ch of God Proph	2	NR	52	64	0.0	0.1
PENT–Int Foursq Gos	4	4,255	3,813	4,675	3.2	8.1
PENT–Open Bible Std	2	130	NR	130	0.1	0.2
PENT–Pent Ch of God	1	70	NR	109	0.1	0.2
PENT–Un Pent Ch Intl	2	NR	NR	NR	-	-
PENT–Vineyard	1	110	130	159	0.1	0.3
PRES–Korean Pres Amer	1	NR	NR	NR	-	-
PRES–Presb Ch (USA)	2	163	419	514	0.3	0.9
PRES–Presb Ch Amer	1	300	326	412	0.3	0.7
REF–Comm Ref Evan	1	NR	NR	NR	-	-
Salvation Army	1	46	72	131	0.1	0.2
Sev Day Adv	2	216	375	431	0.3	0.7
Un C of Christ	6	510	1,426	1,748	1.2	3.0
Unit Univ	1	57	57	75	0.1	0.1
Unity Ch	1	NR	NR	NR	-	-

Religious Group	Number of Congregations	Number of Attendees	Number of Communicant, Confirmed, or Full Members	Adherents: Number of Adherents	Adherents: % of Total Pop.	Adherents: % of Total Adh.
NEBRASKA	**2,860**	**224,555**	**433,726**	**1,016,529**	**55.7**	**100.0**
ADAMS	**46**	**4,730**	**9,747**	**18,600**	**59.3**	**100.0**
ANG/EPIS–Episcopal	1	55	217	217	0.7	1.2
Bahá'í	0	NR	7	7	0.0	0.0
BAPT–Amer Bapt USA	2	96	144	177	0.6	1.0
BAPT–So Bapt Conv	1	35	25	31	0.1	0.2
Catholic	5	NR	NR	4,881	15.6	26.2
CGOD–Ch God (Ander)	1	12	NR	12	0.0	0.1
Ch of Nazarene	1	238	282	414	1.3	2.2
CHR–Chr Ch (Disc)	1	0	184	226	0.7	1.2
CHR–Chr Chs & Chs Cr	1	NR	60	74	0.2	0.4
CHR–Chs of Christ	1	76	75	100	0.3	0.5
Evan Free Ch	1	575	NR	575	1.8	3.1
Jehovah's Witness	1	NR	NR	NR	-	-
LDS–L-D Saints	1	NR	NR	524	1.7	2.8
LUTH–E.L.C.A.	4	779	2,011	2,680	8.5	14.4
LUTH–Luth–MO Synod	8	1,053	3,137	3,961	12.6	21.3
LUTH–Wisc Ev Luth Syn	1	57	103	124	0.4	0.7
METH–Un Methodist	5	610	1,814	2,076	6.6	11.2
Non-denom Chr Chs	1	150	150	188	0.6	1.0
PENT–Assemb of God	2	555	208	728	2.3	3.9
PENT–COGIC	1	0	60	74	0.2	0.4
PENT–Un Pent Ch Intl	1	NR	NR	NR	-	-
PRES–Presb Ch (USA)	3	308	919	1,129	3.6	6.1
Salvation Army	1	38	112	112	0.4	0.6
Sev Day Adv	1	33	57	66	0.2	0.4
Un C of Christ	1	60	182	224	0.7	1.2
ANTELOPE	**26**	**837**	**2,209**	**4,973**	**74.4**	**100.0**
Catholic	5	NR	NR	2,082	31.1	41.9
Chr & Miss Al	1	68	42	95	1.4	1.9
CHR–Chr Chs & Chs Cr	2	NR	200	245	3.7	4.9
CONG–Cong Chr, NA	1	NR	60	73	1.1	1.5
Evan Free Ch	1	80	NR	80	1.2	1.6
LDS–Comm of Christ	1	NR	189	189	2.8	3.8
LUTH–Luth–MO Synod	5	334	890	1,064	15.9	21.4
METH–Un Methodist	6	243	552	812	12.1	16.3
Sev Day Adv	1	34	60	69	1.0	1.4
Un C of Christ	3	78	216	264	3.9	5.3
ARTHUR	**1**	**88**	**244**	**314**	**68.3**	**100.0**
BAPT–Amer Bapt USA	1	88	244	314	68.3	100.0
BANNER	**2**	**59**	**66**	**78**	**11.3**	**100.0**
ANG/EPIS–Episcopal	1	9	16	16	2.3	20.5
Non-denom Chr Chs	1	50	50	62	9.0	79.5
BLAINE	**5**	**137**	**260**	**326**	**68.2**	**100.0**
LUTH–Wisc Ev Luth Syn	1	20	39	50	10.5	15.3
Non-denom Chr Chs	1	50	150	150	31.4	46.0
PENT–Open Bible Std	1	40	NR	40	8.4	12.3
Un C of Christ	2	27	71	86	18.0	26.4
BOONE	**22**	**788**	**1,848**	**4,323**	**78.5**	**100.0**
BAPT–Amer Bapt USA	2	85	70	85	1.5	2.0
Catholic	5	NR	NR	1,937	35.2	44.8
CHR–Chs of Christ	1	20	25	30	0.5	0.7
Evan Free Ch	1	50	NR	50	0.9	1.2
LUTH–E.L.C.A.	2	278	805	964	17.5	22.3
LUTH–Luth–MO Synod	2	88	178	207	3.8	4.8
METH–Un Methodist	5	213	668	911	16.5	21.1
PENT–Assemb of God	1	17	6	23	0.4	0.5
PRES–Presb Ch (USA)	2	23	47	57	1.0	1.3
Un C of Christ	1	14	49	59	1.1	1.4
BOX BUTTE	**22**	**1,036**	**2,218**	**5,568**	**49.2**	**100.0**
ANG/EPIS–Episcopal	1	71	75	102	0.9	1.8
Bahá'í	0	NR	1	1	0.0	0.0
BAPT–Amer Bapt USA	1	46	60	74	0.7	1.3

NR–Not Reported - Represents no adherents reported. Percentages may not total 100 due to rounding.

Table 3: Religious Congregations by County and Group: 2010

Religious Group	Number of Congrega-tions	Number of Attendees	Number of Communicant, Confirmed, or Full Members	Adherents		
				Number of Adherents	% of Total Pop.	% of Total Adh.
Catholic	2	NR	NR	2,301	20.3	41.3
CGOD–Ch God (Ander)	1	40	NR	40	0.4	0.7
CHR–Chr Ch (Disc)	1	0	0	0	0.0	0.0
CHR–Chr Chs & Chs Cr	1	NR	50	62	0.5	1.1
CHR–Chs of Christ	1	25	23	30	0.3	0.5
CONG–Cong Chr, NA	1	NR	20	25	0.2	0.4
Evan Free Ch	1	75	NR	75	0.7	1.3
LDS–L-D Saints	1	NR	NR	251	2.2	4.5
LUTH–E.L.C.A.	1	133	498	617	5.5	11.1
LUTH–Luth–MO Synod	1	105	529	708	6.3	12.7
METH–Un Methodist	3	303	637	797	7.0	14.3
New Apost Ch	1	NR	NR	NR	-	-
PENT–Assemb of God	1	75	0	94	0.8	1.7
PENT–Un Pent Ch Intl	1	NR	NR	NR	-	-
PRES–Presb Ch (USA)	1	89	197	244	2.2	4.4
Sev Day Adv	2	74	128	147	1.3	2.6
BOYD	**17**	**492**	**927**	**1,704**	**81.2**	**100.0**
Catholic	1	NR	NR	543	25.9	31.9
Evan Cov Ch	1	19	48	25	1.2	1.5
LUTH–E.L.C.A.	2	73	168	168	8.0	9.9
LUTH–Luth–MO Synod	4	156	324	449	21.4	26.3
LUTH–Wisc Ev Luth Syn	1	20	54	65	3.1	3.8
METH–Un Methodist	3	45	120	174	8.3	10.2
METH–Wesleyan	2	51	40	67	3.2	3.9
Non-denom Chr Chs	1	65	75	81	3.9	4.8
PENT–Assemb of God	1	48	27	48	2.3	2.8
Un C of Christ	1	15	71	84	4.0	4.9
BROWN	**11**	**575**	**1,125**	**2,114**	**67.2**	**100.0**
Bahá'í	0	NR	1	1	0.0	0.0
Catholic	1	NR	NR	400	12.7	18.9
Ch of Nazarene	1	89	128	193	6.1	9.1
Evan Free Ch	1	115	NR	115	3.7	5.4
LUTH–Luth–MO Synod	1	108	403	523	16.6	24.7
METH–Un Methodist	3	167	437	661	21.0	31.3
New Apost Ch	1	NR	NR	NR	-	-
Non-denom Chr Chs	1	35	40	44	1.4	2.1
PENT–Assemb of God	1	38	33	78	2.5	3.7
Un C of Christ	1	23	83	99	3.1	4.7
BUFFALO	**64**	**7,103**	**12,067**	**27,564**	**59.8**	**100.0**
ANG/EPIS–Episcopal	1	104	215	215	0.5	0.8
Bahá'í	0	NR	16	16	0.0	0.1
BAPT–Amer Bapt USA	2	518	1,247	1,535	3.3	5.6
BAPT–Converge/BGC	1	75	NR	90	0.2	0.3
BAPT–So Bapt Conv	1	27	23	28	0.1	0.1
Catholic	7	NR	NR	9,043	19.6	32.8
CGOD–Ch God (Ander)	1	36	NR	36	0.1	0.1
Ch God (7th Day)	2	NR	NR	NR	-	-
Ch of Nazarene	1	46	73	73	0.2	0.3
CHR–Chr Ch (Disc)	1	65	172	212	0.5	0.8
CHR–Chr Chs & Chs Cr	3	NR	302	372	0.8	1.3
CHR–Chs of Christ	2	120	127	165	0.4	0.6
Evan Free Ch	3	1,295	NR	1,295	2.8	4.7
FRND–Fr Un Mtg	1	NR	0	0	0.0	0.0
Jehovah's Witness	1	NR	NR	NR	-	-
LDS–L-D Saints	1	NR	NR	587	1.3	2.1
LUTH–E.L.C.A.	2	601	1,905	2,292	5.0	8.3
LUTH–Luth–MO Synod	7	1,250	2,733	3,637	7.9	13.2
LUTH–Wisc Ev Luth Syn	1	58	73	96	0.2	0.3
METH–Un Methodist	11	1,318	3,587	4,898	10.6	17.8
Non-denom Chr Chs	3	445	610	625	1.4	2.3
ORTHE–Ant Orth of NA	1	45	NR	90	0.2	0.3
PENT–Assemb of God	2	629	298	1,173	2.5	4.3
PENT–Ch of God Proph	2	NR	48	59	0.1	0.2
PENT–Int Foursq Gos	1	40	75	92	0.2	0.3
PENT–Open Bible Std	1	171	NR	171	0.4	0.6
PRES–Presb Ch (USA)	1	125	287	353	0.8	1.3
PRES–Presb Ch Amer	1	80	143	143	0.3	0.5
Salvation Army	1	19	60	186	0.4	0.7
Sev Day Adv	1	36	63	72	0.2	0.3
Unit Univ	1	0	10	10	0.0	0.0

Religious Group	Number of Congrega-tions	Number of Attendees	Number of Communicant, Confirmed, or Full Members	Adherents		
				Number of Adherents	% of Total Pop.	% of Total Adh.
BURT	**26**	**1,197**	**3,321**	**5,109**	**74.5**	**100.0**
BAPT–Amer Bapt USA	2	81	402	485	7.1	9.5
BAPT–Converge/BGC	1	75	NR	90	1.3	1.8
BAPT–So Bapt Conv	1	42	28	34	0.5	0.7
Catholic	3	NR	NR	712	10.4	13.9
Evan Cov Ch	1	64	101	83	1.2	1.6
Evan Free Ch	1	120	NR	120	1.7	2.3
LUTH–E.L.C.A.	2	142	475	573	8.4	11.2
LUTH–Luth Cong Msn Chr	1	178	869	1,048	15.3	20.5
LUTH–Luth–MO Synod	2	76	249	292	4.3	5.7
METH–Un Methodist	6	220	776	1,106	16.1	21.6
Non-denom Chr Chs	1	24	24	30	0.4	0.6
PENT–Assemb of God	1	20	21	83	1.2	1.6
PRES–Presb Ch (USA)	3	148	364	439	6.4	8.6
Sev Day Adv	1	7	12	14	0.2	0.3
BUTLER	**22**	**510**	**1,297**	**5,220**	**62.2**	**100.0**
BAPT–So Bapt Conv	1	15	20	25	0.3	0.5
Catholic	11	NR	NR	3,654	43.5	70.0
CHR–Chr Ch (Disc)	1	0	13	16	0.2	0.3
LUTH–E.L.C.A.	1	33	144	144	1.7	2.8
LUTH–Luth–MO Synod	2	171	440	554	6.6	10.6
LUTH–Wisc Ev Luth Syn	1	92	151	187	2.2	3.6
METH–Un Methodist	4	179	522	631	7.5	12.1
Un C of Christ	1	20	7	9	0.1	0.2
CASS	**44**	**2,015**	**4,458**	**8,752**	**34.7**	**100.0**
ANG/EPIS–Episcopal	1	35	104	104	0.4	1.2
Bahá'í	0	NR	6	6	0.0	0.1
BAPT–Amer Bapt USA	1	12	19	24	0.1	0.3
BAPT–So Bapt Conv	2	133	103	128	0.5	1.5
Catholic	4	NR	NR	2,557	10.1	29.2
CHR–Chr Ch (Disc)	5	176	482	597	2.4	6.8
CHR–Chr Chs & Chs Cr	1	NR	30	37	0.1	0.4
CHR–Chs of Christ	1	11	11	19	0.1	0.2
Jehovah's Witness	1	NR	NR	NR	-	-
LDS–L-D Saints	1	NR	NR	296	1.2	3.4
LUTH–E.L.C.A.	2	133	358	458	1.8	5.2
LUTH–Luth–MO Synod	5	497	1,137	1,429	5.7	16.3
METH–Un Methodist	11	535	1,384	2,013	8.0	23.0
METH–Wesleyan	1	18	0	23	0.1	0.3
Missionary Ch	1	73	34	73	0.3	0.8
Non-denom Chr Chs	1	100	130	130	0.5	1.5
PENT–Assemb of God	1	25	6	47	0.2	0.5
PRES–Presb Ch (USA)	2	180	279	346	1.4	4.0
Un C of Christ	3	87	375	465	1.8	5.3
CEDAR	**22**	**643**	**2,177**	**7,468**	**84.4**	**100.0**
Bahá'í	0	NR	6	6	0.1	0.1
Catholic	9	NR	NR	4,775	53.9	63.9
LUTH–Assoc Free Luth	1	NR	NR	NR	-	-
LUTH–E.L.C.A.	3	316	1,190	1,430	16.2	19.1
LUTH–Luth–MO Synod	1	74	212	273	3.1	3.7
METH–Un Methodist	3	160	398	504	5.7	6.7
PENT–Assemb of God	1	17	6	29	0.3	0.4
PRES–Presb Ch (USA)	2	26	148	183	2.1	2.5
Un C of Christ	2	50	217	268	3.0	3.6
CHASE	**15**	**802**	**1,519**	**2,695**	**68.0**	**100.0**
BAPT–So Bapt Conv	1	16	16	20	0.5	0.7
BRETH–Ch of Brethren	1	0	14	17	0.4	0.6
Catholic	2	NR	NR	658	16.6	24.4
CHR–Chs of Christ	3	60	65	76	1.9	2.8
Jehovah's Witness	1	NR	NR	NR	-	-
LUTH–Luth–MO Synod	3	305	784	953	24.0	35.4
METH–Un Methodist	2	212	543	703	17.7	26.1
METH–Wesleyan	1	129	42	168	4.2	6.2
Non-denom Chr Chs	1	80	55	100	2.5	3.7
CHERRY	**19**	**800**	**1,193**	**2,704**	**47.3**	**100.0**
ANG/EPIS–Episcopal	1	14	36	38	0.7	1.4

NR–Not Reported - Represents no adherents reported. Percentages may not total 100 due to rounding.

Table 3: Religious Congregations by County and Group: 2010

Religious Group	Number of Congrega-tions	Number of Attendees	Number of Communicant, Confirmed, or Full Members	Adherents: Number of Adherents	Adherents: % of Total Pop.	Adherents: % of Total Adh.
Bahá'í	0	NR	6	6	0.1	0.2
BAPT–So Bapt Conv	1	6	71	85	1.5	3.1
Catholic	2	NR	NR	800	14.0	29.6
Evan Free Ch	1	100	NR	100	1.8	3.7
LDS–L-D Saints	1	NR	NR	123	2.2	4.5
LUTH–Ch Luth Conf	1	NR	NR	NR	-	-
LUTH–Luth–MO Synod	3	77	166	205	3.6	7.6
LUTH–Wisc Ev Luth Syn	1	88	206	282	4.9	10.4
METH–Un Methodist	3	156	271	455	8.0	16.8
Non-denom Chr Chs	1	55	50	69	1.2	2.6
PENT–Assemb of God	1	140	50	140	2.5	5.2
PRES–Presb Ch (USA)	1	75	224	268	4.7	9.9
REF–Christian Ref	1	65	72	86	1.5	3.2
Sev Day Adv	1	24	41	47	0.8	1.7
CHEYENNE	**35**	**1,570**	**2,943**	**5,952**	**59.5**	**100.0**
ANG/EPIS–Episcopal	1	23	32	32	0.3	0.5
Bahá'í	0	NR	2	2	0.0	0.0
BAPT–So Bapt Conv	3	36	48	59	0.6	1.0
Catholic	3	NR	NR	1,500	15.0	25.2
Ch of Nazarene	1	47	16	69	0.7	1.2
CHR–Chr Ch (Disc)	1	45	86	106	1.1	1.8
CHR–Chr Chs & Chs Cr	1	NR	0	0	0.0	0.0
CHR–Chs of Christ	2	44	38	44	0.4	0.7
Evan Free Ch	1	275	NR	275	2.8	4.6
Jehovah's Witness	1	NR	NR	NR	-	-
LDS–L-D Saints	1	NR	NR	398	4.0	6.7
LUTH–E.L.C.A.	6	405	1,031	1,290	12.9	21.7
LUTH–Luth–MO Synod	4	256	641	759	7.6	12.8
METH–Un Methodist	3	241	644	903	9.0	15.2
PENT–Assemb of God	2	58	44	75	0.8	1.3
PENT–Int Foursq Gos	1	26	106	131	1.3	2.2
PRES–Presb Ch (USA)	2	65	195	240	2.4	4.0
PRES–Presb Ch Amer	1	15	1	1	0.0	0.0
Sev Day Adv	1	34	59	68	0.7	1.1
CLAY	**28**	**705**	**2,598**	**4,061**	**62.1**	**100.0**
ANG/EPIS–Episcopal	1	8	13	13	0.2	0.3
Catholic	3	NR	NR	864	13.2	21.3
CHR–Chr Ch (Disc)	1	0	0	0	0.0	0.0
CHR–Chr Chs & Chs Cr	4	NR	435	538	8.2	13.2
LUTH–E.L.C.A.	3	213	610	770	11.8	19.0
LUTH–Luth–MO Synod	1	9	12	12	0.2	0.3
LUTH–Wisc Ev Luth Syn	1	20	46	55	0.8	1.4
METH–Un Methodist	5	133	404	474	7.2	11.7
PRES–Presb Ch (USA)	3	100	246	304	4.6	7.5
REF–Ref Ch in U.S.	2	NR	305	381	5.8	9.4
Sev Day Adv	1	14	24	28	0.4	0.7
Un C of Christ	3	208	503	622	9.5	15.3
COLFAX	**16**	**521**	**1,458**	**6,308**	**60.0**	**100.0**
Catholic	5	NR	NR	4,457	42.4	70.7
Jehovah's Witness	1	NR	NR	NR	-	-
LUTH–E.L.C.A.	2	140	424	552	5.2	8.8
LUTH–Luth–MO Synod	4	181	505	637	6.1	10.1
METH–Un Methodist	2	18	111	118	1.1	1.9
PRES–Presb Ch (USA)	2	182	418	544	5.2	8.6
CUMING	**30**	**1,348**	**3,467**	**8,187**	**89.6**	**100.0**
Bahá'í	0	NR	4	4	0.0	0.0
BAPT–Converge/BGC	1	75	NR	90	1.0	1.1
BAPT–So Bapt Conv	1	9	8	10	0.1	0.1
Catholic	8	NR	NR	3,790	41.5	46.3
CHR–Chs of Christ	1	30	17	30	0.3	0.4
Jehovah's Witness	2	NR	NR	NR	-	-
LUTH–E.L.C.A.	2	250	700	887	9.7	10.8
LUTH–Luth–MO Synod	7	753	2,155	2,604	28.5	31.8
MENN–Mennonite USA	1	65	138	170	1.9	2.1
METH–Un Methodist	3	67	211	269	2.9	3.3
PENT–Assemb of God	1	48	21	70	0.8	0.9
PRES–Presb Ch (USA)	1	0	47	58	0.6	0.7
Un C of Christ	2	51	166	205	2.2	2.5

Religious Group	Number of Congrega-tions	Number of Attendees	Number of Communicant, Confirmed, or Full Members	Adherents: Number of Adherents	Adherents: % of Total Pop.	Adherents: % of Total Adh.
CUSTER	**45**	**1,774**	**3,366**	**5,717**	**52.3**	**100.0**
ANG/EPIS–Episcopal	1	14	37	54	0.5	0.9
Bahá'í	0	NR	2	2	0.0	0.0
BAPT–Amer Bapt USA	4	267	313	382	3.5	6.7
BAPT–Converge/BGC	1	75	NR	90	0.8	1.6
Catholic	4	NR	NR	809	7.4	14.2
CGOD–Ch God (Ander)	2	72	NR	72	0.7	1.3
Ch of Nazarene	1	22	24	26	0.2	0.5
CHR–Chr Chs & Chs Cr	4	NR	481	587	5.4	10.3
CHR–Chs of Christ	1	82	80	116	1.1	2.0
Evan Free Ch	2	170	NR	170	1.6	3.0
Jehovah's Witness	1	NR	NR	NR	-	-
LDS–L-D Saints	1	NR	NR	163	1.5	2.9
LUTH–E.L.C.A.	2	55	224	309	2.8	5.4
LUTH–Luth–MO Synod	3	66	128	155	1.4	2.7
LUTH–Wisc Ev Luth Syn	1	47	99	121	1.1	2.1
METH–Un Methodist	10	561	1,517	2,068	18.9	36.2
Non-denom Chr Chs	4	175	200	221	2.0	3.9
PENT–Assemb of God	1	63	41	108	1.0	1.9
PRES–Presb Ch (USA)	1	67	155	189	1.7	3.3
Sev Day Adv	1	38	65	75	0.7	1.3
DAKOTA	**28**	**1,661**	**3,669**	**10,300**	**49.0**	**100.0**
Bahá'í	0	NR	5	5	0.0	0.0
BAPT–So Bapt Conv	1	45	60	78	0.4	0.8
Catholic	7	NR	NR	4,598	21.9	44.6
CHR–Chr Chs & Chs Cr	1	NR	130	170	0.8	1.7
Evan Ch	1	NR	NR	NR	-	-
Evan Free Ch	2	65	NR	65	0.3	0.6
LUTH–E.L.C.A.	6	734	2,001	2,478	11.8	24.1
LUTH–Luth–MO Synod	1	111	482	590	2.8	5.7
METH–Un Methodist	3	168	545	714	3.4	6.9
Muslim Est	1	134	NR	308	1.5	3.0
Non-denom Chr Chs	2	180	180	226	1.1	2.2
PENT–Assemb of God	2	144	69	810	3.9	7.9
PRES–Presb Ch (USA)	1	80	197	258	1.2	2.5
DAWES	**24**	**1,089**	**1,955**	**4,186**	**45.6**	**100.0**
ANG/EPIS–Episcopal	1	39	67	67	0.7	1.6
Bahá'í	0	NR	2	2	0.0	0.0
BAPT–Amer Bapt USA	1	100	223	260	2.8	6.2
BAPT–So Bapt Conv	1	35	39	46	0.5	1.1
Catholic	2	NR	NR	1,205	13.1	28.8
Ch of Nazarene	2	23	30	37	0.4	0.9
CHR–Chr Chs & Chs Cr	1	NR	75	88	1.0	2.1
CHR–Chs of Christ	1	21	19	21	0.2	0.5
LDS–Comm of Christ	1	NR	128	128	1.4	3.1
LDS–L-D Saints	1	NR	NR	228	2.5	5.4
LUTH–E.L.C.A.	1	60	169	255	2.8	6.1
LUTH–Luth–MO Synod	2	126	347	435	4.7	10.4
METH–Un Methodist	3	199	514	773	8.4	18.5
METH–Wesleyan	1	23	0	30	0.3	0.7
Non-denom Chr Chs	1	150	150	188	2.0	4.5
PENT–Assemb of God	2	189	0	200	2.2	4.8
Sev Day Adv	2	64	111	128	1.4	3.1
Un C of Christ	1	60	81	95	1.0	2.3
DAWSON	**59**	**3,274**	**6,728**	**15,219**	**62.6**	**100.0**
ANG/EPIS–Episcopal	2	24	30	39	0.2	0.3
BAPT–Converge/BGC	1	75	NR	90	0.4	0.6
BAPT–So Bapt Conv	1	297	174	224	0.9	1.5
Catholic	5	NR	NR	4,949	20.3	32.5
CGOD–Ch God (Ander)	1	20	NR	20	0.1	0.1
Ch of Nazarene	2	110	145	145	0.6	1.0
CHR–Chr Ch (Disc)	1	0	0	0	0.0	0.0
CHR–Chr Chs & Chs Cr	5	NR	581	748	3.1	4.9
CHR–Chs of Christ	2	37	41	47	0.2	0.3
Evan Free Ch	3	348	NR	348	1.4	2.3
Jehovah's Witness	1	NR	NR	NR	-	-
LDS–L-D Saints	1	NR	NR	471	1.9	3.1
LUTH–E.L.C.A.	5	492	1,985	2,603	10.7	17.1
LUTH–Luth Cong Msn Chr	1	101	127	163	0.7	1.1

NR–Not Reported - Represents no adherents reported. Percentages may not total 100 due to rounding.

Table 3: Religious Congregations by County and Group: 2010

Religious Group	Number of Congrega-tions	Number of Attendees	Number of Communicant, Confirmed, or Full Members	Adherents: Number of Adherents	Adherents: % of Total Pop.	Adherents: % of Total Adh.
LUTH–Luth-MO Synod	3	236	733	978	4.0	6.4
LUTH–Nor Amer Luth C	1	NR	NR	NR	-	-
METH–Un Methodist	7	530	1,640	2,286	9.4	15.0
Muslim Est	1	134	NR	308	1.3	2.0
Non-denom Chr Chs	3	240	274	300	1.2	2.0
PENT–Assemb of God	5	275	171	454	1.9	3.0
PENT–Ch God (Cleve)	1	28	44	57	0.2	0.4
PENT–Ch of God Proph	1	NR	88	113	0.5	0.7
PRES–Presb Ch (USA)	4	250	561	722	3.0	4.7
Sev Day Adv	2	77	134	154	0.6	1.0
DEUEL	**10**	**357**	**727**	**1,206**	**62.1**	**100.0**
Catholic	1	NR	NR	210	10.8	17.4
LUTH–E.L.C.A.	2	58	101	147	7.6	12.2
LUTH–Luth-MO Synod	2	34	187	209	10.8	17.3
METH–Un Methodist	2	107	310	398	20.5	33.0
PENT–Assemb of God	2	150	104	212	10.9	17.6
PENT–Int Foursq Gos	1	8	25	30	1.5	2.5
DIXON	**21**	**1,172**	**2,078**	**3,770**	**62.8**	**100.0**
Bahá'í	0	NR	1	1	0.0	0.0
Catholic	3	NR	NR	975	16.3	25.9
CHR–Chr Chs & Chs Cr	1	NR	50	62	1.0	1.6
Evan Cov Ch	1	76	115	99	1.7	2.6
Evan Free Ch	2	235	NR	235	3.9	6.2
LUTH–E.L.C.A.	5	432	996	1,276	21.3	33.8
LUTH–Luth-MO Synod	4	227	474	545	9.1	14.5
METH–Un Methodist	2	98	303	404	6.7	10.7
Non-denom Chr Chs	1	60	60	75	1.3	2.0
PRES–Presb Ch (USA)	1	24	38	47	0.8	1.2
Un C of Christ	1	20	41	51	0.9	1.4
DODGE	**54**	**5,590**	**11,582**	**18,218**	**49.7**	**100.0**
ANG/EPIS–Episcopal	1	41	102	117	0.3	0.6
Bahá'í	0	NR	4	4	0.0	0.0
BAPT–Amer Bapt USA	1	180	388	476	1.3	2.6
BAPT–Converge/BGC	1	75	NR	90	0.2	0.5
BAPT–So Bapt Conv	1	45	40	49	0.1	0.3
Catholic	5	NR	NR	1,698	4.6	9.3
Ch of Nazarene	1	385	350	828	2.3	4.5
Chr & Miss Al	1	388	254	742	2.0	4.1
CHR–Chr Ch (Disc)	1	43	145	178	0.5	1.0
CHR–Chs of Christ	1	50	60	70	0.2	0.4
Evan Free Ch	1	350	NR	350	1.0	1.9
Jehovah's Witness	1	NR	NR	NR	-	-
LDS–Comm of Christ	1	NR	189	189	0.5	1.0
LDS–L-D Saints	1	NR	NR	515	1.4	2.8
LUTH–E.L.C.A.	11	1,582	4,134	5,329	14.5	29.3
LUTH–Luth Cong Msn Chr	2	129	180	221	0.6	1.2
LUTH–Luth-MO Synod	8	1,058	3,177	4,113	11.2	22.6
LUTH–Wisc Ev Luth Syn	1	7	10	11	0.0	0.1
METH–Un Methodist	3	359	881	1,144	3.1	6.3
Non-denom Chr Chs	3	290	360	392	1.1	2.2
PENT–Assemb of God	1	90	56	170	0.5	0.9
PENT–Ch God (Cleve)	1	3	4	5	0.0	0.0
PENT–Un Pent Ch Intl	1	NR	NR	NR	-	-
PRES–Presb Ch (USA)	2	325	734	900	2.5	4.9
Sev Day Adv	1	27	47	54	0.1	0.3
Un C of Christ	3	163	467	573	1.6	3.1
DOUGLAS	**422**	**53,618**	**89,295**	**274,980**	**53.2**	**100.0**
ANG/EPIS–Anglican NA	1	NR	NR	NR	-	-
ANG/EPIS–Episcopal	6	972	2,276	2,742	0.5	1.0
Bahá'í	1	NR	155	155	0.0	0.1
BAPT–Amer Bapt USA	12	1,178	1,948	2,455	0.5	0.9
BAPT–Consrv Bapt	2	NR	NR	NR	-	-
BAPT–Converge/BGC	5	700	NR	840	0.2	0.3
BAPT–Ind Bapt Flwsp Intl	3	NR	NR	NR	-	-
BAPT–Natl Mis Bapt Conv	1	0	150	189	0.0	0.1
BAPT–NBC Amer	2	150	250	315	0.1	0.1
BAPT–NBC USA	12	1,600	7,025	8,852	1.7	3.2
BAPT–Reg Bapt Gen As	7	NR	NR	NR	-	-

Religious Group	Number of Congrega-tions	Number of Attendees	Number of Communicant, Confirmed, or Full Members	Adherents: Number of Adherents	Adherents: % of Total Pop.	Adherents: % of Total Adh.
BAPT–So Bapt Conv	22	2,705	6,205	7,819	1.5	2.8
BUDD–Mahayana	5	NR	NR	3,392	0.7	1.2
BUDD–Theravada	1	NR	NR	15	0.0	0.0
Calv Chpl	1	NR	NR	NR	-	-
Catholic	50	NR	NR	123,962	24.0	45.1
CGOD–Ch God (Ander)	1	65	NR	65	0.0	0.0
Ch Cr, Scientst	3	NR	NR	NR	-	-
Ch of Chr (Hol)	1	NR	NR	NR	-	-
Ch of God Gen Conf	1	NR	90	113	0.0	0.0
Ch of Nazarene	4	323	372	422	0.1	0.2
Chr & Miss Al	6	3,459	2,624	10,322	2.0	3.8
CHR–Chr Ch (Disc)	4	383	736	927	0.2	0.3
CHR–Chr Chs & Chs Cr	7	NR	2,325	2,930	0.6	1.1
CHR–Chs of Christ	4	772	752	948	0.2	0.3
CHR–Int Chs of Christ	1	NR	88	111	0.0	0.0
Christian Brethren	1	NR	NR	NR	-	-
Evan Cov Ch	4	570	838	741	0.1	0.3
Evan Free Ch	3	1,300	NR	1,300	0.3	0.5
FRND–Consrv Yr Mtgs	1	NR	12	15	0.0	0.0
HINDU–Post Ren	2	NR	NR	177	0.0	0.1
HINDU–Trad Temples	1	NR	NR	500	0.1	0.2
Jehovah's Witness	8	NR	NR	NR	-	-
JUD–Conserv	1	455	511	1,380	0.3	0.5
JUD–Orth	2	310	150	430	0.1	0.2
JUD–Reform	1	412	727	1,963	0.4	0.7
LDS–Comm of Christ	2	NR	378	378	0.1	0.1
LDS–L-D Saints	17	NR	NR	7,138	1.4	2.6
LUTH–Assoc Free Luth	1	NR	NR	NR	-	-
LUTH–E.L.C.A.	28	6,652	15,454	21,108	4.1	7.7
LUTH–Luth Cong Msn Chr	2	1,112	2,688	3,387	0.7	1.2
LUTH–Luth-MO Synod	18	5,425	9,091	12,758	2.5	4.6
LUTH–Wisc Ev Luth Syn	3	600	839	1,157	0.2	0.4
MENN–Fel Evg Bib Ch	2	525	455	525	0.1	0.2
MENN–Menn Br US Conf	3	NR	115	145	0.0	0.1
MENN–Mennonite USA	1	5	8	10	0.0	0.0
METH–AME	4	100	550	693	0.1	0.3
METH–AME Zion	2	0	200	252	0.0	0.1
METH–C.M.E.	1	0	100	126	0.0	0.0
METH–Free Methodist	1	39	48	48	0.0	0.0
METH–Un Methodist	20	4,211	8,335	13,611	2.6	4.9
Metro Comm Ch	1	145	125	158	0.0	0.1
Muslim Est	3	768	NR	4,616	0.9	1.7
Nat Spirit Asso	1	NR	NR	NR	-	-
New Apost Ch	1	NR	NR	NR	-	-
Non-denom Chr Chs	32	8,148	7,936	10,754	2.1	3.9
ORTHE–Ant Orth of NA	2	181	NR	385	0.1	0.1
ORTHE–Greek Orthodox	2	225	NR	425	0.1	0.2
ORTHE–Orth Ch in Amer	1	15	NR	25	0.0	0.0
PENT–Assemb of God	12	2,531	871	4,039	0.8	1.5
PENT–Ch God (Cleve)	3	187	297	374	0.1	0.1
PENT–COGIC	15	440	1,775	2,237	0.4	0.8
PENT–Full Gosp Bapt	2	NR	NR	NR	-	-
PENT–Int Foursq Gos	1	130	160	202	0.0	0.1
PENT–Intl Pent Holiness	3	235	133	168	0.0	0.1
PENT–Open Bible Std	1	45	NR	45	0.0	0.0
PENT–Un Pent Ch Intl	2	NR	NR	NR	-	-
PENT–Vineyard	1	160	205	258	0.0	0.1
PRES–Evan Presby Ch	1	NR	850	1,071	0.2	0.4
PRES–Presb Ch (USA)	21	3,281	5,781	7,284	1.4	2.6
PRES–Presb Ch Amer	2	317	230	339	0.1	0.1
REF–Christian Ref	1	120	132	166	0.0	0.1
REF–Ref Ch in Am	1	383	573	675	0.1	0.2
Salvation Army	4	300	398	2,010	0.4	0.7
Sev Day Adv	7	860	1,495	1,719	0.3	0.6
Sikh	1	NR	NR	NR	-	-
Tao	1	NR	NR	NR	-	-
Un C of Christ	4	937	2,496	3,145	0.6	1.1
Unit Univ	2	187	343	467	0.1	0.2
Unity Ch	2	NR	NR	NR	-	-
Zoroastrian	0	NR	NR	2	0.0	0.0
DUNDY	**8**	**255**	**768**	**1,105**	**55.0**	**100.0**
BAPT–So Bapt Conv	1	50	37	44	2.2	4.0
Catholic	1	NR	NR	135	6.7	12.2

NR–Not Reported - Represents no adherents reported. Percentages may not total 100 due to rounding.

Table 3: Religious Congregations by County and Group: 2010

Religious Group	Number of Congregations	Number of Attendees	Number of Communicant, Confirmed, or Full Members	Adherents: Number of Adherents	Adherents: % of Total Pop.	Adherents: % of Total Adh.
LUTH–E.L.C.A.	2	110	436	531	26.4	48.1
METH–Un Methodist	3	95	264	358	17.8	32.4
PRES–Presb Ch (USA)	1	0	31	37	1.8	3.3
FILLMORE	**22**	**1,003**	**2,157**	**4,406**	**74.8**	**100.0**
Catholic	5	NR	NR	1,442	24.5	32.7
Evan Free Ch	1	167	NR	167	2.8	3.8
LUTH–E.L.C.A.	3	150	429	569	9.7	12.9
LUTH–Luth–MO Synod	1	29	57	61	1.0	1.4
LUTH–Wisc Ev Luth Syn	2	95	163	194	3.3	4.4
MENN–Mennonite USA	1	109	183	220	3.7	5.0
METH–Un Methodist	6	329	1,038	1,348	22.9	30.6
PENT–Assemb of God	1	38	12	75	1.3	1.7
Un C of Christ	2	86	275	330	5.6	7.5
FRANKLIN	**15**	**626**	**1,516**	**2,286**	**70.9**	**100.0**
Catholic	2	NR	NR	216	6.7	9.4
Evan Free Ch	1	49	NR	49	1.5	2.1
LUTH–E.L.C.A.	2	171	653	776	24.1	33.9
LUTH–Luth–MO Synod	2	81	165	194	6.0	8.5
METH–Un Methodist	3	102	320	565	17.5	24.7
METH–Wesleyan	1	46	36	60	1.9	2.6
Missionary Ch	1	55	31	55	1.7	2.4
PRES–Presb Ch (USA)	1	70	117	140	4.3	6.1
Un C of Christ	2	52	194	231	7.2	10.1
FRONTIER	**12**	**431**	**1,402**	**1,815**	**65.9**	**100.0**
Bahá'í	0	NR	2	2	0.1	0.1
Catholic	1	NR	NR	120	4.4	6.6
CHR–Chr Chs & Chs Cr	1	NR	50	60	2.2	3.3
LUTH–E.L.C.A.	1	83	500	581	21.1	32.0
LUTH–Luth–MO Synod	1	70	250	316	11.5	17.4
METH–Un Methodist	5	201	484	598	21.7	32.9
PENT–Vineyard	1	50	85	101	3.7	5.6
Un C of Christ	2	27	31	37	1.3	2.0
FURNAS	**26**	**1,212**	**2,636**	**4,272**	**86.1**	**100.0**
ANG/EPIS–Episcopal	1	20	32	41	0.8	1.0
BAPT–Amer Bapt USA	3	190	342	413	8.3	9.7
BAPT–Converge/BGC	1	75	NR	90	1.8	2.1
Catholic	3	NR	NR	729	14.7	17.1
CHR–Chr Ch (Disc)	1	50	50	60	1.2	1.4
CHR–Chr Chs & Chs Cr	3	NR	255	308	6.2	7.2
Evan Free Ch	2	100	NR	100	2.0	2.3
LUTH–Luth–MO Synod	3	318	840	1,019	20.5	23.9
METH–Free Methodist	1	30	17	30	0.6	0.7
METH–Un Methodist	5	296	812	1,136	22.9	26.6
PRES–Presb Ch (USA)	1	62	96	116	2.3	2.7
Sev Day Adv	1	16	28	32	0.6	0.7
Un C of Christ	1	55	164	198	4.0	4.6
GAGE	**59**	**4,357**	**10,733**	**15,751**	**70.6**	**100.0**
ANG/EPIS–Episcopal	2	34	52	165	0.7	1.0
Bahá'í	0	NR	4	4	0.0	0.0
BAPT–Amer Bapt USA	1	49	154	187	0.8	1.2
BAPT–N Am Bapt Conf	1	NR	29	35	0.2	0.2
BAPT–So Bapt Conv	1	20	16	19	0.1	0.1
BRETH–Ch of Brethren	1	43	74	90	0.4	0.6
Catholic	5	NR	NR	1,631	7.3	10.4
Ch of Nazarene	1	25	29	47	0.2	0.3
CHR–Chr Ch (Disc)	1	125	353	428	1.9	2.7
CHR–Chr Chs & Chs Cr	2	NR	500	607	2.7	3.9
CHR–Chs of Christ	2	69	57	82	0.4	0.5
Jehovah's Witness	2	NR	NR	NR	-	-
LDS–L-D Saints	1	NR	NR	264	1.2	1.7
LUTH–E.L.C.A.	10	1,607	4,591	5,897	26.4	37.4
LUTH–Luth Cong Msn Chr	1	21	113	137	0.6	0.9
LUTH–Luth–MO Synod	4	506	1,313	1,622	7.3	10.3
LUTH–Wisc Ev Luth Syn	3	172	302	370	1.7	2.3
MENN–Mennonite USA	2	184	355	431	1.9	2.7
METH–Un Methodist	8	391	1,263	1,634	7.3	10.4
Non-denom Chr Chs	2	700	800	900	4.0	5.7

Religious Group	Number of Congregations	Number of Attendees	Number of Communicant, Confirmed, or Full Members	Adherents: Number of Adherents	Adherents: % of Total Pop.	Adherents: % of Total Adh.
PENT–Assemb of God	1	96	38	174	0.8	1.1
PENT–Un Pent Ch Intl	1	NR	NR	NR	-	-
PRES–Presb Ch (USA)	3	147	379	460	2.1	2.9
REF–Ref Ch in Am	1	96	169	182	0.8	1.2
Salvation Army	1	16	37	259	1.2	1.6
Sev Day Adv	1	16	27	31	0.1	0.2
Un C of Christ	1	40	78	95	0.4	0.6
GARDEN	**13**	**295**	**693**	**1,058**	**51.4**	**100.0**
ANG/EPIS–Episcopal	1	12	18	18	0.9	1.7
Catholic	2	NR	NR	220	10.7	20.8
CHR–Chs of Christ	1	3	2	5	0.2	0.5
LUTH–E.L.C.A.	2	73	258	299	14.5	28.3
METH–Un Methodist	2	92	306	342	16.6	32.3
METH–Wesleyan	2	62	63	81	3.9	7.7
PENT–Assemb of God	1	21	10	52	2.5	4.9
PRES–Presb Ch (USA)	1	30	33	38	1.8	3.6
Sev Day Adv	1	2	3	3	0.1	0.3
GARFIELD	**8**	**359**	**973**	**1,738**	**84.8**	**100.0**
BAPT–So Bapt Conv	1	85	216	255	12.4	14.7
Catholic	1	NR	NR	500	24.4	28.8
CHR–Chr Chs & Chs Cr	1	NR	150	177	8.6	10.2
LUTH–Luth–MO Synod	1	70	178	220	10.7	12.7
METH–Un Methodist	2	135	233	338	16.5	19.4
PENT–Assemb of God	1	30	15	35	1.7	2.0
Un C of Christ	1	39	181	213	10.4	12.3
GOSPER	**6**	**326**	**1,207**	**1,590**	**77.8**	**100.0**
Catholic	1	NR	NR	75	3.7	4.7
CHR–Chr Ch (Disc)	1	21	100	120	5.9	7.5
LUTH–Luth Cong Msn Chr	1	131	547	657	32.1	41.3
LUTH–Luth–MO Synod	1	108	416	515	25.2	32.4
METH–Un Methodist	2	66	144	223	10.9	14.0
GRANT	**7**	**59**	**262**	**433**	**70.5**	**100.0**
ANG/EPIS–Episcopal	1	20	30	62	10.1	14.3
Bahá'í	0	NR	2	2	0.3	0.5
Catholic	1	NR	NR	60	9.8	13.9
CONG–Cong Chr, NA	2	NR	141	166	27.0	38.3
LDS–L-D Saints	1	NR	NR	46	7.5	10.6
LUTH–Luth–MO Synod	1	23	61	65	10.6	15.0
Sev Day Adv	1	16	28	32	5.2	7.4
GREELEY	**9**	**243**	**664**	**2,011**	**79.2**	**100.0**
Catholic	2	NR	NR	1,214	47.8	60.4
LUTH–E.L.C.A.	1	69	269	269	10.6	13.4
LUTH–Luth–MO Synod	1	70	122	152	6.0	7.6
MENN–CG in Cr (Menn)	1	NR	69	85	3.3	4.2
METH–Un Methodist	4	104	204	291	11.5	14.5
HALL	**70**	**7,458**	**14,580**	**34,431**	**58.7**	**100.0**
ANG/EPIS–Episcopal	1	58	298	298	0.5	0.9
Bahá'í	0	NR	15	15	0.0	0.0
BAPT–Amer Bapt USA	1	60	98	125	0.2	0.4
BAPT–Converge/BGC	2	150	NR	180	0.3	0.5
BAPT–Ind Bapt Flwsp Intl	1	NR	NR	NR	-	-
BAPT–Reg Bapt Gen As	1	NR	NR	NR	-	-
BAPT–So Bapt Conv	1	12	6	8	0.0	0.0
Catholic	6	NR	NR	12,037	20.5	35.0
Ch Cr, Scientst	1	NR	NR	NR	-	-
Ch of Nazarene	2	150	122	262	0.4	0.8
Chr & Miss Al	1	187	75	255	0.4	0.7
CHR–Chr Ch (Disc)	1	0	228	290	0.5	0.8
CHR–Chr Chs & Chs Cr	1	NR	850	1,082	1.8	3.1
CHR–Chs of Christ	1	60	63	70	0.1	0.2
Evan Free Ch	1	940	NR	940	1.6	2.7
Jehovah's Witness	1	NR	NR	NR	-	-
LDS–Comm of Christ	1	NR	189	189	0.3	0.5
LDS–L-D Saints	3	NR	NR	1,078	1.8	3.1
LUTH–E.L.C.A.	3	602	2,683	3,368	5.7	9.8

NR–Not Reported - Represents no adherents reported. Percentages may not total 100 due to rounding.

Table 3: Religious Congregations by County and Group: 2010

Religious Group	Number of Congrega-tions	Number of Attendees	Number of Communicant, Confirmed, or Full Members	Adherents: Number of Adherents	Adherents: % of Total Pop.	Adherents: % of Total Adh.
LUTH–Luth–MO Synod	7	1,621	3,601	4,752	8.1	13.8
LUTH–Wisc Ev Luth Syn	1	92	140	213	0.4	0.6
MENN–Mennonite USA	1	80	72	92	0.2	0.3
METH–Un Methodist	8	1,069	3,241	4,695	8.0	13.6
Non-denom Chr Chs	6	955	1,081	1,219	2.1	3.5
ORTHE–Greek Orthodox	1	7	NR	30	0.1	0.1
PENT–Assemb of God	4	655	274	1,311	2.2	3.8
PENT–Ch God (Cleve)	2	153	213	271	0.5	0.8
PENT–Ch of God Proph	1	NR	18	23	0.0	0.1
PENT–Int Foursq Gos	1	39	43	55	0.1	0.2
PENT–Un Pent Ch Intl	1	NR	NR	NR	-	-
PRES–Presb Ch (USA)	2	233	626	797	1.4	2.3
PRES–Presb Ch Amer	1	55	57	72	0.1	0.2
Salvation Army	1	20	38	38	0.1	0.1
Sev Day Adv	2	155	269	310	0.5	0.9
Un C of Christ	1	105	280	356	0.6	1.0
Unity Ch	1	NR	NR	NR	-	-
HAMILTON	**28**	**1,992**	**3,288**	**5,610**	**61.5**	**100.0**
Bahá'í	1	NR	23	23	0.3	0.4
BAPT–Converge/BGC	1	75	NR	90	1.0	1.6
Catholic	2	NR	NR	591	6.5	10.5
CHR–Chr Ch (Disc)	1	0	195	241	2.6	4.3
Evan Cov Ch	1	60	109	78	0.9	1.4
Evan Free Ch	3	380	NR	380	4.2	6.8
LDS–L-D Saints	1	NR	NR	250	2.7	4.5
LUTH–E.L.C.A.	4	439	829	1,048	11.5	18.7
LUTH–Luth–MO Synod	3	266	554	711	7.8	12.7
LUTH–Wisc Ev Luth Syn	1	44	51	77	0.8	1.4
METH–Un Methodist	3	321	1,065	1,485	16.3	26.5
Non-denom Chr Chs	3	292	270	365	4.0	6.5
PENT–Assemb of God	1	25	0	38	0.4	0.7
PRES–Presb Ch (USA)	1	32	74	91	1.0	1.6
Sev Day Adv	1	26	45	52	0.6	0.9
Un C of Christ	1	32	73	90	1.0	1.6
HARLAN	**16**	**622**	**1,103**	**1,756**	**51.3**	**100.0**
Catholic	2	NR	NR	248	7.2	14.1
CHR–Chr Ch (Disc)	1	0	55	65	1.9	3.7
Evan Free Ch	2	149	NR	149	4.4	8.5
LUTH–E.L.C.A.	1	64	101	130	3.8	7.4
LUTH–Luth Cong Msn Chr	2	125	372	441	12.9	25.1
METH–Free Methodist	1	27	38	38	1.1	2.2
METH–Un Methodist	5	184	452	588	17.2	33.5
Non-denom Chr Chs	1	45	50	56	1.6	3.2
PRES–Presb Ch (USA)	1	28	35	41	1.2	2.3
HAYES	**3**	**105**	**51**	**161**	**16.6**	**100.0**
BAPT–Converge/BGC	1	75	NR	90	9.3	55.9
CHR–Chs of Christ	1	8	4	15	1.6	9.3
Un C of Christ	1	22	47	56	5.8	34.8
HITCHCOCK	**16**	**607**	**947**	**1,793**	**61.7**	**100.0**
Catholic	3	NR	NR	292	10.0	16.3
CGOD–Ch God (Ander)	1	65	NR	65	2.2	3.6
Chr & Miss Al	2	190	105	307	10.6	17.1
CHR–Chs of Christ	1	30	28	36	1.2	2.0
LUTH–Luth–MO Synod	2	60	230	307	10.6	17.1
METH–Un Methodist	4	190	518	688	23.7	38.4
Missionary Ch	1	45	22	45	1.5	2.5
Non-denom Chr Chs	1	12	12	15	0.5	0.8
Un C of Christ	1	15	32	38	1.3	2.1
HOLT	**35**	**1,757**	**3,041**	**7,222**	**69.2**	**100.0**
BAPT–So Bapt Conv	1	14	35	42	0.4	0.6
Catholic	6	NR	NR	3,044	29.2	42.1
CHR–Chr Chs & Chs Cr	1	NR	21	25	0.2	0.3
Jehovah's Witness	1	NR	NR	NR	-	-
LDS–L-D Saints	1	NR	NR	134	1.3	1.9
LUTH–E.L.C.A.	1	68	270	322	3.1	4.5
LUTH–Luth–MO Synod	3	285	648	810	7.8	11.2
LUTH–Wisc Ev Luth Syn	1	27	33	47	0.5	0.7

Religious Group	Number of Congrega-tions	Number of Attendees	Number of Communicant, Confirmed, or Full Members	Adherents: Number of Adherents	Adherents: % of Total Pop.	Adherents: % of Total Adh.
MENN–Amish Undif	1	NR	36	107	1.0	1.5
METH–Un Methodist	6	229	682	905	8.7	12.5
METH–Wesleyan	2	178	149	231	2.2	3.2
Non-denom Chr Chs	2	575	625	744	7.1	10.3
PENT–Assemb of God	4	212	147	332	3.2	4.6
PRES–Presb Ch (USA)	5	169	395	479	4.6	6.6
HOOKER	**5**	**146**	**274**	**436**	**59.2**	**100.0**
ANG/EPIS–Episcopal	1	15	42	42	5.7	9.6
Catholic	1	NR	NR	70	9.5	16.1
METH–Un Methodist	1	38	110	188	25.5	43.1
Non-denom Chr Chs	1	75	100	100	13.6	22.9
PENT–Assemb of God	1	18	22	36	4.9	8.3
HOWARD	**17**	**702**	**1,323**	**3,445**	**54.9**	**100.0**
Bahá'í	0	NR	1	1	0.0	0.0
BAPT–Converge/BGC	2	150	NR	180	2.9	5.2
Catholic	3	NR	NR	1,467	23.4	42.6
LUTH–Assoc Free Luth	1	NR	NR	NR	-	-
LUTH–E.L.C.A.	2	92	274	323	5.1	9.4
LUTH–Luth–MO Synod	2	234	598	793	12.6	23.0
LUTH–Nor Amer Luth C	1	NR	NR	NR	-	-
METH–Un Methodist	4	123	347	504	8.0	14.6
PENT–Assemb of God	1	65	32	90	1.4	2.6
PRES–Presb Ch (USA)	1	38	71	87	1.4	2.5
JEFFERSON	**28**	**1,649**	**3,778**	**5,505**	**72.9**	**100.0**
ANG/EPIS–Episcopal	1	13	33	54	0.7	1.0
Bahá'í	0	NR	1	1	0.0	0.0
BAPT–Amer Bapt USA	1	89	189	226	3.0	4.1
Catholic	1	NR	NR	794	10.5	14.4
CGOD–Ch God (Ander)	1	29	NR	29	0.4	0.5
CHR–Chr Ch (Disc)	1	35	106	127	1.7	2.3
Jehovah's Witness	1	NR	NR	NR	-	-
LUTH–Assoc Free Luth	1	NR	NR	NR	-	-
LUTH–E.L.C.A.	4	320	855	1,106	14.7	20.1
LUTH–Luth–MO Synod	4	349	1,008	1,174	15.6	21.3
LUTH–Wisc Ev Luth Syn	1	188	288	350	4.6	6.4
MENN–Fel Evg Bib Ch	1	113	95	113	1.5	2.1
METH–Un Methodist	4	156	499	655	8.7	11.9
PENT–Assemb of God	1	62	27	67	0.9	1.2
PENT–Int Foursq Gos	1	48	99	119	1.6	2.2
PRES–Presb Ch (USA)	2	132	339	406	5.4	7.4
Sev Day Adv	1	26	46	53	0.7	1.0
Un C of Christ	2	89	193	231	3.1	4.2
JOHNSON	**16**	**663**	**1,704**	**3,633**	**69.6**	**100.0**
ANG/EPIS–Episcopal	1	3	6	9	0.2	0.2
Bahá'í	0	NR	3	3	0.1	0.1
BAPT–Reg Bapt Gen As	1	NR	NR	NR	-	-
BUDD–Mahayana	1	NR	NR	25	0.5	0.7
Catholic	2	NR	NR	1,508	28.9	41.5
LUTH–E.L.C.A.	1	65	234	282	5.4	7.8
LUTH–Luth Cong Msn Chr	2	149	517	607	11.6	16.7
LUTH–Luth–MO Synod	3	277	533	674	12.9	18.6
METH–Un Methodist	3	118	289	382	7.3	10.5
PRES–Presb Ch (USA)	1	15	30	35	0.7	1.0
Un C of Christ	1	36	92	108	2.1	3.0
KEARNEY	**18**	**1,232**	**2,878**	**4,253**	**65.5**	**100.0**
Bahá'í	0	NR	2	2	0.0	0.0
Catholic	2	NR	NR	446	6.9	10.5
CHR–Chr Ch (Disc)	1	48	206	252	3.9	5.9
Evan Free Ch	3	320	NR	320	4.9	7.5
LUTH–E.L.C.A.	3	253	858	1,045	16.1	24.6
LUTH–Luth Cong Msn Chr	1	70	295	362	5.6	8.5
LUTH–Luth–MO Synod	2	220	555	659	10.2	15.5
METH–Un Methodist	4	196	566	682	10.5	16.0
PRES–Presb Ch (USA)	2	125	396	485	7.5	11.4

NR–Not Reported   - Represents no adherents reported.   Percentages may not total 100 due to rounding.

Table 3: Religious Congregations by County and Group: 2010

Religious Group	Number of Congrega-tions	Number of Attendees	Number of Communicant, Confirmed, or Full Members	Adherents		
				Number of Adherents	% of Total Pop.	% of Total Adh.
KEITH	**24**	**1,599**	**2,316**	**5,385**	**64.4**	**100.0**
ANG/EPIS–Episcopal	1	15	76	82	1.0	1.5
BAPT–Converge/BGC	1	400	NR	480	5.7	8.9
BAPT–So Bapt Conv	1	15	8	10	0.1	0.2
Catholic	2	NR	NR	1,300	15.5	24.1
CHR–Chs of Christ	1	80	70	90	1.1	1.7
Evan Free Ch	1	300	NR	300	3.6	5.6
LDS–Comm of Christ	1	NR	128	128	1.5	2.4
LUTH–E.L.C.A.	1	46	2	212	2.5	3.9
LUTH–Luth Cong Msn Chr	1	33	45	54	0.6	1.0
LUTH–Luth-MO Synod	4	332	910	1,253	15.0	23.3
LUTH–Nor Amer Luth C	1	NR	NR	NR	-	-
MENN–CG in Cr (Menn)	1	NR	49	59	0.7	1.1
METH–Un Methodist	2	226	692	978	11.7	18.2
PENT–Assemb of God	1	43	24	67	0.8	1.2
PRES–Presb Ch (USA)	2	20	16	19	0.2	0.4
Sev Day Adv	1	16	29	33	0.4	0.6
Un C of Christ	2	73	267	320	3.8	5.9
KEYA PAHA	**7**	**264**	**340**	**468**	**56.8**	**100.0**
LUTH–Luth-MO Synod	1	28	58	67	8.1	14.3
METH–Un Methodist	2	41	144	164	19.9	35.0
Non-denom Chr Chs	2	125	120	156	18.9	33.3
PENT–Assemb of God	1	60	0	60	7.3	12.8
Sev Day Adv	1	10	18	21	2.5	4.5
KIMBALL	**13**	**490**	**810**	**1,452**	**38.0**	**100.0**
ANG/EPIS–Episcopal	1	11	26	26	0.7	1.8
BAPT–So Bapt Conv	1	12	19	23	0.6	1.6
Catholic	1	NR	NR	300	7.9	20.7
Ch of Nazarene	1	12	24	43	1.1	3.0
Evan Free Ch	1	140	NR	140	3.7	9.6
Jehovah's Witness	1	NR	NR	NR	-	-
LUTH–E.L.C.A.	1	65	205	239	6.3	16.5
LUTH–Luth-MO Synod	1	51	107	136	3.6	9.4
METH–Un Methodist	2	120	338	416	10.9	28.7
Non-denom Chr Chs	1	30	25	38	1.0	2.6
PENT–Assemb of God	1	19	12	26	0.7	1.8
PRES–Presb Ch (USA)	1	30	54	65	1.7	4.5
KNOX	**32**	**1,268**	**3,653**	**6,684**	**76.8**	**100.0**
ANG/EPIS–Episcopal	3	51	239	254	2.9	3.8
Bahá'í	0	NR	4	4	0.0	0.1
Catholic	5	NR	NR	2,128	24.5	31.8
Evan Cov Ch	1	81	120	105	1.2	1.6
Ind Fund Churches	1	NR	NR	NR	-	-
LUTH–E.L.C.A.	6	517	1,670	2,153	24.7	32.2
LUTH–Luth-MO Synod	4	275	754	900	10.3	13.5
MENN–Amish Undif	1	NR	24	65	0.7	1.0
METH–Un Methodist	4	193	497	662	7.6	9.9
Non-denom Chr Chs	1	70	80	88	1.0	1.3
PRES–Presb Ch (USA)	2	15	72	88	1.0	1.3
Un C of Christ	4	66	193	237	2.7	3.5
LANCASTER	**236**	**35,255**	**61,237**	**133,827**	**46.9**	**100.0**
ANG/EPIS–Episcopal	4	445	1,000	1,111	0.4	0.8
Bahá'í	1	NR	204	204	0.1	0.2
BAPT–Amer Bapt Assn	1	NR	150	184	0.1	0.1
BAPT–Amer Bapt USA	3	210	316	387	0.1	0.3
BAPT–NBC USA	1	0	150	184	0.1	0.1
BAPT–Reg Bapt Gen As	1	NR	NR	NR	-	-
BAPT–S-D Baptist Gen Con	1	20	12	15	0.0	0.0
BAPT–So Bapt Conv	7	869	1,730	2,120	0.7	1.6
BRETH–Ch of Brethren	1	51	78	96	0.0	0.1
BUDD–Mahayana	5	NR	NR	684	0.2	0.5
BUDD–Vajrayana	1	NR	NR	107	0.0	0.1
Calv Chpl	1	NR	NR	NR	-	-
Catholic	16	NR	NR	42,609	14.9	31.8
CGOD–Ch God (Ander)	1	79	NR	79	0.0	0.1
Ch Cr, Scientst	2	NR	NR	NR	-	-
Ch of Nazarene	2	254	314	356	0.1	0.3
Chr & Miss Al	6	848	428	856	0.3	0.6
CHR–Chr Ch (Disc)	9	563	1,783	2,185	0.8	1.6
CHR–Chr Chs & Chs Cr	2	NR	1,212	1,486	0.5	1.1
CHR–Chs of Christ	4	620	558	679	0.2	0.5
Evan Cov Ch	2	270	367	351	0.1	0.3
Evan Free Ch	5	1,579	NR	1,579	0.6	1.2
FRND–Consrv Yr Mtgs	1	NR	24	29	0.0	0.0
HINDU–Post Ren	2	NR	NR	41	0.0	0.0
Jehovah's Witness	3	NR	NR	NR	-	-
JUD–Conserv	1	92	103	278	0.1	0.2
JUD–Reform	1	57	101	273	0.1	0.2
LDS–Comm of Christ	1	NR	189	189	0.1	0.1
LDS–L-D Saints	7	NR	NR	3,369	1.2	2.5
LUTH–E.L.C.A.	15	5,208	10,874	14,216	5.0	10.6
LUTH–Luth Cong Msn Chr	1	84	155	190	0.1	0.1
LUTH–Luth-MO Synod	14	5,766	9,562	13,043	4.6	9.7
LUTH–Wisc Ev Luth Syn	2	339	430	568	0.2	0.4
MENN–Fel Evg Bib Ch	1	85	78	85	0.0	0.1
MENN–Menn Br US Conf	2	NR	138	169	0.1	0.1
MENN–Mennonite USA	1	91	100	123	0.0	0.1
METH–AME	1	0	100	123	0.0	0.1
METH–Free Methodist	2	83	69	83	0.0	0.1
METH–Un Methodist	29	5,005	11,847	17,595	6.2	13.1
Missionary Ch	1	43	34	43	0.0	0.0
Muslim Est	2	268	NR	616	0.2	0.5
Non-denom Chr Chs	24	4,313	4,854	5,775	2.0	4.3
ORTHE–Greek Orthodox	1	70	NR	200	0.1	0.1
ORTHE–Orth Ch in Amer	1	30	NR	45	0.0	0.0
PENT–Assemb of God	3	1,546	497	3,954	1.4	3.0
PENT–Ch God (Cleve)	2	98	126	154	0.1	0.1
PENT–COGIC	1	30	50	61	0.0	0.0
PENT–Int Foursq Gos	1	0	22	27	0.0	0.0
PENT–Open Bible Std	1	0	NR	0	0.0	0.0
PENT–Un Pent Ch Intl	3	NR	NR	NR	-	-
PRES–Orth Pres Ch	1	55	69	82	0.0	0.1
PRES–Presb Ch (USA)	10	1,400	3,870	4,744	1.7	3.5
PRES–Presb Ch Amer	3	575	497	573	0.2	0.4
REF–Christian Ref	1	100	41	50	0.0	0.0
REF–Ref Ch in Am	3	596	914	1,077	0.4	0.8
REF–Ref Ch in U.S.	1	NR	97	128	0.0	0.1
Salvation Army	1	68	172	1,181	0.4	0.9
Sev Day Adv	8	1,992	3,464	3,984	1.4	3.0
Un C of Christ	6	1,294	4,150	5,087	1.8	3.8
Unit Univ	1	159	308	391	0.1	0.3
Unity Ch	1	NR	NR	NR	-	-
Zoroastrian	0	NR	NR	9	0.0	0.0
LINCOLN	**55**	**4,563**	**8,024**	**20,246**	**55.8**	**100.0**
ANG/EPIS–Episcopal	1	80	146	197	0.5	1.0
Bahá'í	0	NR	24	24	0.1	0.1
BAPT–Amer Bapt USA	1	133	773	961	2.6	4.7
BAPT–Converge/BGC	1	75	NR	90	0.2	0.4
BAPT–So Bapt Conv	3	137	325	404	1.1	2.0
Catholic	6	NR	NR	6,983	19.2	34.5
CGOD–Ch God (Ander)	1	14	NR	14	0.0	0.1
Ch of Nazarene	1	127	218	218	0.6	1.1
CHR–Chr Ch (Disc)	1	84	400	497	1.4	2.5
CHR–Chr Chs & Chs Cr	1	NR	110	137	0.4	0.7
CHR–Chs of Christ	1	100	95	125	0.3	0.6
Evan Cov Ch	1	25	24	32	0.1	0.2
Evan Free Ch	3	669	NR	669	1.8	3.3
Jehovah's Witness	1	NR	NR	NR	-	-
LDS–Comm of Christ	1	NR	128	128	0.4	0.6
LDS–L-D Saints	3	NR	NR	1,016	2.8	5.0
LUTH–E.L.C.A.	4	463	1,586	2,276	6.3	11.2
LUTH–Luth-MO Synod	2	333	1,080	1,487	4.1	7.3
LUTH–Wisc Ev Luth Syn	1	36	72	94	0.3	0.5
METH–Un Methodist	6	583	1,505	2,136	5.9	10.6
METH–Wesleyan	1	637	270	828	2.3	4.1
Non-denom Chr Chs	4	355	402	469	1.3	2.3
PENT–Assemb of God	4	251	174	351	1.0	1.7
PENT–Ch God (Cleve)	1	42	22	27	0.1	0.1
PENT–Int Foursq Gos	1	109	85	106	0.3	0.5
PENT–Un Pent Ch Intl	1	NR	NR	NR	-	-
PRES–Presb Ch (USA)	2	145	365	454	1.3	2.2

NR–Not Reported   - Represents no adherents reported.   Percentages may not total 100 due to rounding.

Table 3: Religious Congregations by County and Group: 2010

Religious Group	Number of Congrega-tions	Number of Attendees	Number of Communicant, Confirmed, or Full Members	Adherents		
				Number of Adherents	% of Total Pop.	% of Total Adh.
Salvation Army	1	87	84	367	1.0	1.8
Sev Day Adv	1	78	136	156	0.4	0.8
LOGAN	**3**	**76**	**67**	**434**	**56.9**	**100.0**
Catholic	2	NR	NR	351	46.0	80.9
PRES–Presb Ch (USA)	1	76	67	83	10.9	19.1
LOUP	**2**	**80**	**28**	**80**	**12.7**	**100.0**
Evan Free Ch	1	25	NR	25	4.0	31.3
PENT–Assemb of God	1	55	28	55	8.7	68.8
MCPHERSON	**2**	**76**	**77**	**121**	**22.4**	**100.0**
METH–Free Methodist	1	60	39	60	11.1	49.6
METH–Un Methodist	1	16	38	61	11.3	50.4
MADISON	**57**	**5,851**	**13,303**	**27,139**	**77.8**	**100.0**
ANG/EPIS–Episcopal	1	40	170	217	0.6	0.8
Bahá'í	0	NR	6	6	0.0	0.0
BAPT–Amer Bapt USA	1	129	232	288	0.8	1.1
BAPT–Ind Bapt Flwsp Intl	1	NR	NR	NR	-	-
BAPT–So Bapt Conv	4	256	318	395	1.1	1.5
Catholic	4	NR	NR	9,364	26.8	34.5
Ch of Nazarene	1	6	12	12	0.0	0.0
CHR–Chr Chs & Chs Cr	2	NR	640	794	2.3	2.9
CHR–Chs of Christ	1	71	59	108	0.3	0.4
CONG–Consrv Cong Chr	1	40	37	46	0.1	0.2
Evan Free Ch	2	160	NR	160	0.5	0.6
LDS–L-D Saints	1	NR	NR	413	1.2	1.5
LUTH–E.L.C.A.	6	484	1,368	1,662	4.8	6.1
LUTH–Luth Cong Msn Chr	1	125	357	443	1.3	1.6
LUTH–Luth–MO Synod	10	2,501	6,294	8,250	23.7	30.4
LUTH–Wisc Ev Luth Syn	2	328	640	792	2.3	2.9
METH–Un Methodist	6	449	1,487	1,903	5.5	7.0
Muslim Est	1	134	NR	308	0.9	1.1
Non-denom Chr Chs	4	595	720	752	2.2	2.8
PENT–Assemb of God	2	220	192	285	0.8	1.1
PENT–Ch God (Cleve)	1	4	29	36	0.1	0.1
PRES–Presb Ch (USA)	1	125	273	339	1.0	1.2
Salvation Army	1	43	39	39	0.1	0.1
Sev Day Adv	1	46	79	91	0.3	0.3
Un C of Christ	2	95	351	436	1.3	1.6
MERRICK	**27**	**1,156**	**2,175**	**4,329**	**55.2**	**100.0**
ANG/EPIS–Episcopal	1	8	15	36	0.5	0.8
Bahá'í	0	NR	3	3	0.0	0.1
BAPT–Amer Bapt USA	1	25	92	113	1.4	2.6
BAPT–So Bapt Conv	2	14	14	17	0.2	0.4
Catholic	3	NR	NR	948	12.1	21.9
CHR–Chr Chs & Chs Cr	2	NR	100	123	1.6	2.8
CONG–Consrv Cong Chr	1	16	2	2	0.0	0.0
Evan Free Ch	1	350	NR	350	4.5	8.1
FRND–Fr Gen Cf & Un Mtg	1	NR	54	66	0.8	1.5
Jehovah's Witness	1	NR	NR	NR	-	-
LUTH–E.L.C.A.	1	50	171	197	2.5	4.6
LUTH–Luth–MO Synod	2	160	398	496	6.3	11.5
METH–Un Methodist	8	444	1,169	1,788	22.8	41.3
METH–Wesleyan	1	24	18	31	0.4	0.7
Non-denom Chr Chs	1	25	50	50	0.6	1.2
PRES–Presb Ch (USA)	1	40	89	109	1.4	2.5
MORRILL	**17**	**692**	**1,499**	**2,494**	**49.5**	**100.0**
Bahá'í	0	NR	1	1	0.0	0.0
BAPT–Amer Bapt USA	1	85	98	121	2.4	4.9
Catholic	1	NR	NR	550	10.9	22.1
CHR–Chr Chs & Chs Cr	2	NR	275	338	6.7	13.6
CONG–Consrv Cong Chr	1	30	149	183	3.6	7.3
LUTH–E.L.C.A.	1	24	94	94	1.9	3.8
LUTH–Luth–MO Synod	2	113	311	407	8.1	16.3
METH–Un Methodist	1	0	0	0	0.0	0.0
Non-denom Chr Chs	2	180	220	250	5.0	10.0
ORTHE–Greek Orthodox	1	32	NR	70	1.4	2.8

Religious Group	Number of Congrega-tions	Number of Attendees	Number of Communicant, Confirmed, or Full Members	Adherents		
				Number of Adherents	% of Total Pop.	% of Total Adh.
PENT–Assemb of God	2	95	42	100	2.0	4.0
PRES–Presb Ch (USA)	1	90	189	233	4.6	9.3
Sev Day Adv	1	5	9	10	0.2	0.4
Un C of Christ	1	38	111	137	2.7	5.5
NANCE	**9**	**278**	**859**	**2,256**	**60.4**	**100.0**
Bahá'í	0	NR	2	2	0.1	0.1
BAPT–Reg Bapt Gen As	1	NR	NR	NR	-	-
Catholic	3	NR	NR	1,275	34.1	56.5
LUTH–E.L.C.A.	1	95	324	326	8.7	14.5
LUTH–Luth–MO Synod	1	58	164	224	6.0	9.9
METH–Un Methodist	2	81	250	284	7.6	12.6
PRES–Presb Ch (USA)	1	44	119	145	3.9	6.4
NEMAHA	**30**	**1,175**	**2,998**	**6,849**	**94.5**	**100.0**
Bahá'í	0	NR	7	7	0.1	0.1
BAPT–So Bapt Conv	1	15	14	17	0.2	0.2
Catholic	3	NR	NR	3,150	43.5	46.0
CHR–Chr Ch (Disc)	4	0	52	62	0.9	0.9
CHR–Chr Chs & Chs Cr	1	NR	250	299	4.1	4.4
CHR–Chs of Christ	1	20	16	23	0.3	0.3
Jehovah's Witness	1	NR	NR	NR	-	-
LUTH–E.L.C.A.	7	472	1,307	1,650	22.8	24.1
LUTH–Luth Cong Msn Chr	1	85	243	290	4.0	4.2
LUTH–Luth–MO Synod	1	117	223	269	3.7	3.9
METH–Un Methodist	6	187	511	623	8.6	9.1
Non-denom Chr Chs	2	165	250	250	3.4	3.7
PENT–Assemb of God	1	61	30	95	1.3	1.4
PRES–Presb Ch (USA)	1	53	95	114	1.6	1.7
NUCKOLLS	**20**	**682**	**1,800**	**2,945**	**65.4**	**100.0**
Bahá'í	0	NR	3	3	0.1	0.1
BAPT–Amer Bapt USA	1	35	80	95	2.1	3.2
Catholic	4	NR	NR	739	16.4	25.1
Ch of Nazarene	1	40	22	53	1.2	1.8
CHR–Chr Chs & Chs Cr	2	NR	168	200	4.4	6.8
CHR–Chs of Christ	1	14	12	15	0.3	0.5
Evan Free Ch	1	45	NR	45	1.0	1.5
LUTH–E.L.C.A.	4	169	541	604	13.4	20.5
LUTH–Luth–MO Synod	2	151	364	435	9.7	14.8
METH–Un Methodist	1	86	252	341	7.6	11.6
Non-denom Chr Chs	1	35	60	60	1.3	2.0
PRES–Presb Ch (USA)	1	53	109	130	2.9	4.4
Un C of Christ	1	54	189	225	5.0	7.6
OTOE	**49**	**2,179**	**5,369**	**11,388**	**72.4**	**100.0**
ANG/EPIS–Episcopal	1	20	53	85	0.5	0.7
Bahá'í	1	NR	13	13	0.1	0.1
BAPT–Converge/BGC	1	75	NR	90	0.6	0.8
BAPT–Reg Bapt Gen As	1	NR	NR	NR	-	-
BAPT–So Bapt Conv	1	25	47	58	0.4	0.5
Catholic	6	NR	NR	3,496	22.2	30.7
CHR–Chr Ch (Disc)	2	0	416	510	3.2	4.5
CHR–Chr Chs & Chs Cr	2	NR	138	169	1.1	1.5
CHR–Chs of Christ	2	44	51	59	0.4	0.5
Evan Free Ch	2	207	NR	207	1.3	1.8
Jehovah's Witness	1	NR	NR	NR	-	-
LDS–Comm of Christ	1	NR	189	189	1.2	1.7
LDS–L-D Saints	1	NR	NR	344	2.2	3.0
LUTH–E.L.C.A.	8	777	2,139	2,767	17.6	24.3
LUTH–Luth–MO Synod	1	31	77	89	0.6	0.8
METH–Un Methodist	6	407	979	1,663	10.6	14.6
PENT–Assemb of God	1	97	0	97	0.6	0.9
PENT–Un Pent Ch Intl	1	NR	NR	NR	-	-
PRES–Presb Ch (USA)	4	164	353	433	2.8	3.8
Sev Day Adv	1	14	24	28	0.2	0.2
Un C of Christ	5	318	890	1,091	6.9	9.6
PAWNEE	**13**	**354**	**893**	**1,879**	**67.8**	**100.0**
Bahá'í	0	NR	3	3	0.1	0.2
Catholic	2	NR	NR	696	25.1	37.0
CHR–Chr Ch (Disc)	1	30	98	117	4.2	6.2

NR–Not Reported - Represents no adherents reported. Percentages may not total 100 due to rounding.

Table 3: Religious Congregations by County and Group: 2010

Religious Group	Number of Congregations	Number of Attendees	Number of Communicant, Confirmed, or Full Members	Adherents: Number of Adherents	Adherents: % of Total Pop.	Adherents: % of Total Adh.
CHR–Chr Chs & Chs Cr	1	NR	35	42	1.5	2.2
CHR–Chs of Christ	1	4	4	5	0.2	0.3
LUTH–Luth-MO Synod	1	50	115	158	5.7	8.4
MENN–Amish Undif	1	NR	35	103	3.7	5.5
METH–Un Methodist	3	67	193	296	10.7	15.8
Non-denom Chr Chs	1	100	150	150	5.4	8.0
PRES–Presb Ch (USA)	1	47	101	120	4.3	6.4
Un C of Christ	1	56	159	189	6.8	10.1
PERKINS	**12**	**552**	**1,082**	**2,386**	**80.3**	**100.0**
Catholic	2	NR	NR	802	27.0	33.6
Evan Free Ch	1	200	NR	200	6.7	8.4
LUTH–Luth-MO Synod	2	120	310	356	12.0	14.9
MENN–CG in Cr (Menn)	1	NR	171	212	7.1	8.9
MENN–Menn Br US Conf	1	NR	42	52	1.8	2.2
METH–Un Methodist	3	171	463	659	22.2	27.6
Non-denom Chr Chs	1	30	60	60	2.0	2.5
Un C of Christ	1	31	36	45	1.5	1.9
PHELPS	**26**	**2,223**	**3,984**	**6,307**	**68.6**	**100.0**
ANG/EPIS–Episcopal	1	31	78	87	0.9	1.4
Bahá'í	0	NR	2	2	0.0	0.0
BAPT–Amer Bapt USA	1	138	289	356	3.9	5.6
Catholic	1	NR	NR	527	5.7	8.4
Ch of Nazarene	1	0	43	43	0.5	0.7
Evan Cov Ch	1	45	62	58	0.6	0.9
Evan Free Ch	5	815	NR	815	8.9	12.9
Jehovah's Witness	1	NR	NR	NR	-	-
LDS–L-D Saints	1	NR	NR	122	1.3	1.9
LUTH–Assoc Free Luth	1	NR	NR	NR	-	-
LUTH–E.L.C.A.	4	363	961	1,163	12.7	18.4
LUTH–Luth Cong Msn Chr	2	229	1,169	1,438	15.7	22.8
LUTH–Luth-MO Synod	2	251	435	598	6.5	9.5
METH–Un Methodist	2	186	674	699	7.6	11.1
PENT–Assemb of God	1	52	52	132	1.4	2.1
PRES–Presb Ch (USA)	1	95	187	230	2.5	3.6
Sev Day Adv	1	18	32	37	0.4	0.6
PIERCE	**16**	**1,359**	**3,622**	**5,708**	**78.6**	**100.0**
Catholic	3	NR	NR	1,148	15.8	20.1
LUTH–E.L.C.A.	2	192	562	666	9.2	11.7
LUTH–Luth-MO Synod	5	804	2,123	2,705	37.2	47.4
LUTH–Wisc Ev Luth Syn	1	100	158	182	2.5	3.2
METH–Un Methodist	3	188	553	727	10.0	12.7
Un C of Christ	2	75	226	280	3.9	4.9
PLATTE	**46**	**4,406**	**9,097**	**26,643**	**82.6**	**100.0**
ANG/EPIS–Episcopal	1	25	66	71	0.2	0.3
Bahá'í	0	NR	1	1	0.0	0.0
BAPT–Amer Bapt USA	1	89	189	238	0.7	0.9
BAPT–N Am Bapt Conf	2	NR	100	126	0.4	0.5
BAPT–So Bapt Conv	1	100	135	170	0.5	0.6
Catholic	10	NR	NR	13,543	42.0	50.8
Ch of Nazarene	1	16	5	25	0.1	0.1
CHR–Chs of Christ	1	60	52	84	0.3	0.3
Evan Free Ch	1	700	NR	700	2.2	2.6
Jehovah's Witness	1	NR	NR	NR	-	-
LDS–Comm of Christ	1	NR	189	189	0.6	0.7
LDS–L-D Saints	1	NR	NR	369	1.1	1.4
LUTH–E.L.C.A.	5	234	722	848	2.6	3.2
LUTH–Luth Cong Msn Chr	1	525	1,926	2,421	7.5	9.1
LUTH–Luth-MO Synod	7	1,570	3,241	4,276	13.3	16.0
METH–Un Methodist	3	438	1,140	1,753	5.4	6.6
Non-denom Chr Chs	2	100	100	126	0.4	0.5
PENT–Assemb of God	1	110	48	226	0.7	0.8
PENT–Int Foursq Gos	1	53	49	62	0.2	0.2
PRES–Presb Ch (USA)	1	0	295	371	1.2	1.4
Sev Day Adv	2	56	97	111	0.3	0.4
Un C of Christ	2	330	742	933	2.9	3.5
POLK	**18**	**943**	**1,641**	**3,051**	**56.4**	**100.0**
BAPT–Converge/BGC	2	150	NR	180	3.3	5.9

Religious Group	Number of Congregations	Number of Attendees	Number of Communicant, Confirmed, or Full Members	Adherents: Number of Adherents	Adherents: % of Total Pop.	Adherents: % of Total Adh.
Catholic	3	NR	NR	806	14.9	26.4
Evan Cov Ch	1	54	234	70	1.3	2.3
Evan Free Ch	2	254	NR	254	4.7	8.3
LUTH–E.L.C.A.	3	179	538	604	11.2	19.8
LUTH–Luth Cong Msn Chr	1	NR	NR	NR	-	-
LUTH–Luth-MO Synod	1	60	140	165	3.1	5.4
METH–Un Methodist	4	206	694	922	17.1	30.2
Non-denom Chr Chs	1	40	35	50	0.9	1.6
RED WILLOW	**28**	**1,425**	**2,914**	**8,538**	**77.2**	**100.0**
ANG/EPIS–Episcopal	1	62	123	175	1.6	2.0
BAPT–Amer Bapt USA	1	32	77	93	0.8	1.1
BAPT–So Bapt Conv	1	NR	NR	NR	-	-
Catholic	4	NR	NR	3,787	34.3	44.4
CGOD–Ch God (Ander)	1	20	NR	20	0.2	0.2
Ch Cr, Scientst	1	NR	NR	NR	-	-
Ch of Nazarene	1	70	49	151	1.4	1.8
CHR–Chr Chs & Chs Cr	3	NR	550	667	6.0	7.8
CHR–Chs of Christ	1	52	48	77	0.7	0.9
CONG–Cong Chr, NA	1	NR	150	182	1.6	2.1
Evan Free Ch	1	355	NR	355	3.2	4.2
Jehovah's Witness	1	NR	NR	NR	-	-
LDS–L-D Saints	1	NR	NR	319	2.9	3.7
LUTH–E.L.C.A.	1	65	216	311	2.8	3.6
LUTH–Luth-MO Synod	2	269	623	756	6.8	8.9
LUTH–Wisc Ev Luth Syn	1	10	14	16	0.1	0.2
METH–Un Methodist	2	355	925	1,400	12.7	16.4
PENT–Assemb of God	1	81	59	135	1.2	1.6
PRES–Presb Ch (USA)	2	30	37	45	0.4	0.5
Sev Day Adv	1	24	43	49	0.4	0.6
RICHARDSON	**36**	**1,177**	**3,012**	**5,296**	**63.3**	**100.0**
ANG/EPIS–Episcopal	1	13	18	20	0.2	0.4
Bahá'í	0	NR	2	2	0.0	0.0
BAPT–Amer Bapt USA	1	21	25	30	0.4	0.6
BAPT–So Bapt Conv	1	18	24	29	0.3	0.5
BRETH–Brethren (Ash)	1	NR	80	95	1.1	1.8
Catholic	5	NR	NR	1,660	19.8	31.3
Ch of Nazarene	1	59	88	118	1.4	2.2
CHR–Chr Ch (Disc)	4	75	642	764	9.1	14.4
CHR–Chs of Christ	1	40	37	40	0.5	0.8
Jehovah's Witness	1	NR	NR	NR	-	-
LUTH–E.L.C.A.	3	171	419	546	6.5	10.3
LUTH–Luth-MO Synod	3	210	536	666	8.0	12.6
METH–Un Methodist	7	271	654	756	9.0	14.3
Non-denom Chr Chs	2	145	250	250	3.0	4.7
PENT–Assemb of God	1	71	59	109	1.3	2.1
PRES–Presb Ch (USA)	2	40	70	83	1.0	1.6
Sev Day Adv	1	8	13	15	0.2	0.3
Un C of Christ	1	35	95	113	1.4	2.1
ROCK	**6**	**200**	**486**	**716**	**46.9**	**100.0**
ANG/EPIS–Episcopal	1	25	47	47	3.1	6.6
Catholic	1	NR	NR	100	6.6	14.0
LUTH–E.L.C.A.	1	66	223	269	17.6	37.6
METH–Un Methodist	1	54	158	234	15.3	32.7
Non-denom Chr Chs	1	30	40	40	2.6	5.6
PENT–Assemb of God	1	25	18	26	1.7	3.6
SALINE	**32**	**1,547**	**3,951**	**7,358**	**51.8**	**100.0**
ANG/EPIS–Episcopal	2	20	30	45	0.3	0.6
Bahá'í	0	NR	7	7	0.0	0.1
BAPT–Ind Bapt Flwsp Intl	1	NR	NR	NR	-	-
BAPT–So Bapt Conv	1	12	9	11	0.1	0.1
Catholic	5	NR	NR	2,111	14.9	28.7
Jehovah's Witness	1	NR	NR	NR	-	-
LDS–L-D Saints	1	NR	NR	171	1.2	2.3
LUTH–E.L.C.A.	2	205	655	806	5.7	11.0
LUTH–Luth-MO Synod	3	496	1,423	1,746	12.3	23.7
METH–Un Methodist	8	325	849	1,170	8.2	15.9
Non-denom Chr Chs	2	195	200	244	1.7	3.3
PENT–Assemb of God	1	95	34	130	0.9	1.8

NR–Not Reported   - Represents no adherents reported.   Percentages may not total 100 due to rounding.

Table 3: Religious Congregations by County and Group: 2010

Religious Group	Number of Congrega-tions	Number of Attendees	Number of Communicant, Confirmed, or Full Members	Adherents		
				Number of Adherents	% of Total Pop.	% of Total Adh.
PENT–Ch God (Cleve)	1	13	13	16	0.1	0.2
Un C of Christ	4	186	731	901	6.3	12.2
SARPY	**90**	**11,692**	**19,953**	**66,399**	**41.8**	**100.0**
ANG/EPIS–Episcopal	2	203	394	508	0.3	0.8
Bahá'í	1	NR	42	42	0.0	0.1
BAPT–Amer Bapt USA	2	116	115	149	0.1	0.2
BAPT–Asc Ref Bap Ch Am	1	NR	NR	NR	-	-
BAPT–Converge/BGC	2	150	NR	180	0.1	0.3
BAPT–Ind Bapt Flwsp Intl	1	NR	NR	NR	-	-
BAPT–Ref Bapt Ch	1	NR	NR	NR	-	-
BAPT–Reg Bapt Gen As	3	NR	NR	NR	-	-
BAPT–So Bapt Conv	8	1,958	3,027	3,923	2.5	5.9
Calv Chpl	1	NR	NR	NR	-	-
Catholic	8	NR	NR	34,059	21.4	51.3
Ch of Nazarene	1	242	241	250	0.2	0.4
Chr & Miss Al	3	582	137	816	0.5	1.2
CHR–Chr Ch (Disc)	1	0	91	118	0.1	0.2
CHR–Chr Chs & Chs Cr	2	NR	1,200	1,555	1.0	2.3
CHR–Chs of Christ	2	265	263	362	0.2	0.5
Evan Cov Ch	1	211	163	274	0.2	0.4
Evan Free Ch	1	85	NR	85	0.1	0.1
HINDU–Post Ren	1	NR	NR	10	0.0	0.0
Jehovah's Witness	2	NR	NR	NR	-	-
LDS–L-D Saints	6	NR	NR	3,030	1.9	4.6
LUTH–E.L.C.A.	4	1,260	2,576	3,485	2.2	5.2
LUTH–Luth Cong Msn Chr	2	940	1,777	2,303	1.4	3.5
LUTH–Luth–MO Synod	5	1,080	4,235	5,816	3.7	8.8
MENN–Menn Br US Conf	1	NR	186	241	0.2	0.4
METH–Un Methodist	5	1,220	2,300	3,563	2.2	5.4
Non-denom Chr Chs	7	700	860	945	0.6	1.4
ORTHE–Serb Orth USA	1	122	NR	223	0.1	0.3
PENT–Assemb of God	3	1,361	523	2,150	1.4	3.2
PENT–Ch God (Cleve)	1	231	231	299	0.2	0.5
PENT–Int Foursq Gos	1	57	75	97	0.1	0.1
PENT–Intl Pent Holiness	1	69	38	49	0.0	0.1
PENT–Un Pent Ch Intl	3	NR	NR	NR	-	-
PRES–Presb Ch (USA)	3	644	1,139	1,476	0.9	2.2
PRES–Presb Ch Amer	1	0	0	0	0.0	0.0
Sev Day Adv	2	196	340	391	0.2	0.6
SAUNDERS	**48**	**2,094**	**4,537**	**12,274**	**59.1**	**100.0**
Bahá'í	0	NR	9	9	0.0	0.1
BAPT–Converge/BGC	2	150	NR	180	0.9	1.5
Catholic	13	NR	NR	5,866	28.2	47.8
Chr & Miss Al	1	67	31	107	0.5	0.9
CHR–Chr Ch (Disc)	1	60	257	320	1.5	2.6
CHR–Chr Chs & Chs Cr	1	NR	40	50	0.2	0.4
CONG–Cong Chr, NA	1	NR	42	52	0.3	0.4
Evan Cov Ch	3	220	194	286	1.4	2.3
Evan Free Ch	1	180	NR	180	0.9	1.5
Jehovah's Witness	2	NR	NR	NR	-	-
LDS–L-D Saints	1	NR	NR	102	0.5	0.8
LUTH–E.L.C.A.	8	613	1,988	2,640	12.7	21.5
LUTH–Luth Cong Msn Chr	2	105	311	387	1.9	3.2
LUTH–Luth–MO Synod	2	178	428	527	2.5	4.3
METH–Un Methodist	5	310	713	916	4.4	7.5
PRES–Presb Ch (USA)	4	181	442	550	2.6	4.5
Un C of Christ	1	30	82	102	0.5	0.8
SCOTTS BLUFF	**71**	**4,516**	**8,517**	**18,535**	**50.1**	**100.0**
ANG/EPIS–Episcopal	2	105	276	311	0.8	1.7
Bahá'í	0	NR	34	34	0.1	0.2
BAPT–Amer Bapt USA	1	125	375	465	1.3	2.5
BAPT–Converge/BGC	1	75	NR	90	0.2	0.5
BAPT–So Bapt Conv	1	55	122	151	0.4	0.8
Calv Chpl	1	NR	NR	NR	-	-
Catholic	6	NR	NR	6,036	16.3	32.6
CGOD–Ch God (Ander)	2	47	NR	47	0.1	0.3
Ch Cr, Scientst	1	NR	NR	NR	-	-
Ch of Nazarene	1	60	58	82	0.2	0.4
CHR–Chr Ch (Disc)	1	77	200	248	0.7	1.3
CHR–Chr Chs & Chs Cr	6	NR	1,066	1,321	3.6	7.1
CHR–Chs of Christ	1	45	61	78	0.2	0.4
CONG–Consrv Cong Chr	5	599	1,389	1,721	4.7	9.3
Evan Free Ch	2	270	NR	270	0.7	1.5
Jehovah's Witness	1	NR	NR	NR	-	-
LDS–Comm of Christ	1	NR	128	128	0.3	0.7
LDS–L-D Saints	2	NR	NR	754	2.0	4.1
LUTH–E.L.C.A.	3	294	664	874	2.4	4.7
LUTH–Luth–MO Synod	4	385	1,012	1,242	3.4	6.7
LUTH–Wisc Ev Luth Syn	1	15	35	47	0.1	0.3
METH–Un Methodist	6	463	1,291	1,909	5.2	10.3
METH–Wesleyan	1	52	41	68	0.2	0.4
Non-denom Chr Chs	6	996	866	1,266	3.4	6.8
PENT–Assemb of God	5	335	172	518	1.4	2.8
PENT–Ch God (Cleve)	1	30	58	72	0.2	0.4
PENT–Int Foursq Gos	1	183	27	33	0.1	0.2
PENT–Open Bible Std	1	0	NR	0	0.0	0.0
PENT–Un Pent Ch Intl	1	NR	NR	NR	-	-
PRES–Presb Ch (USA)	2	112	274	340	0.9	1.8
Sev Day Adv	3	166	288	331	0.9	1.8
Un C of Christ	1	27	80	99	0.3	0.5
SEWARD	**41**	**3,864**	**7,259**	**11,475**	**68.5**	**100.0**
ANG/EPIS–Episcopal	1	40	62	62	0.4	0.5
Bahá'í	0	NR	3	3	0.0	0.0
Catholic	4	NR	NR	1,993	11.9	17.4
Ch of Nazarene	1	77	82	125	0.7	1.1
CHR–Chs of Christ	1	35	38	40	0.2	0.3
Evan Free Ch	1	300	NR	300	1.8	2.6
Jehovah's Witness	1	NR	NR	NR	-	-
LUTH–E.L.C.A.	2	165	518	688	4.1	6.0
LUTH–Luth Ch-Am Asc	1	NR	NR	NR	-	-
LUTH–Luth Cong Msn Chr	2	164	216	263	1.6	2.3
LUTH–Luth–MO Synod	10	1,771	4,042	5,075	30.3	44.2
LUTH–Wisc Ev Luth Syn	1	37	48	60	0.4	0.5
MENN–Mennonite USA	3	350	522	636	3.8	5.5
METH–Un Methodist	7	570	1,391	1,731	10.3	15.1
Missionary Ch	1	130	55	130	0.8	1.1
Non-denom Chr Chs	1	70	85	88	0.5	0.8
PENT–Assemb of God	1	74	47	98	0.6	0.9
PENT–Un Pent Ch Intl	1	NR	NR	NR	-	-
Un C of Christ	2	81	150	183	1.1	1.6
SHERIDAN	**26**	**624**	**1,442**	**2,471**	**45.2**	**100.0**
ANG/EPIS–Episcopal	2	27	49	87	1.6	3.5
Bahá'í	0	NR	6	6	0.1	0.2
BAPT–Amer Bapt Assn	1	NR	85	104	1.9	4.2
Catholic	3	NR	NR	400	7.3	16.2
CGOD–Ch God (Ander)	1	60	NR	60	1.1	2.4
FRND–Evan Fr Ch Intl	1	15	37	45	0.8	1.8
Jehovah's Witness	1	NR	NR	NR	-	-
LDS–L-D Saints	1	NR	NR	125	2.3	5.1
LUTH–E.L.C.A.	2	36	126	139	2.5	5.6
LUTH–Luth–MO Synod	4	117	389	443	8.1	17.9
LUTH–Wisc Ev Luth Syn	1	8	17	17	0.3	0.7
METH–Un Methodist	4	183	495	708	12.9	28.7
METH–Wesleyan	1	71	37	92	1.7	3.7
Non-denom Chr Chs	1	30	30	38	0.7	1.5
PENT–Assemb of God	1	15	18	22	0.4	0.9
PRES–Presb Ch (USA)	1	50	131	160	2.9	6.5
Sev Day Adv	1	12	22	25	0.5	1.0
SHERMAN	**14**	**240**	**512**	**2,346**	**74.4**	**100.0**
BAPT–Reg Bapt Gen As	2	NR	NR	NR	-	-
BAPT–So Bapt Conv	1	11	28	34	1.1	1.4
Catholic	3	NR	NR	1,540	48.9	65.6
CHR–Chr Chs & Chs Cr	1	NR	50	60	1.9	2.6
LUTH–Luth–MO Synod	2	145	263	343	10.9	14.6
METH–Un Methodist	3	81	140	332	10.5	14.2
PRES–Presb Ch (USA)	1	0	26	31	1.0	1.3
Un C of Christ	1	3	5	6	0.2	0.3

NR–Not Reported - Represents no adherents reported. Percentages may not total 100 due to rounding.

Table 3: Religious Congregations by County and Group: 2010

Religious Group	Number of Congrega-tions	Number of Attendees	Number of Communicant, Confirmed, or Full Members	Adherents: Number of Adherents	Adherents: % of Total Pop.	Adherents: % of Total Adh.
SIOUX	**3**	**52**	**105**	**281**	**21.4**	**100.0**
Catholic	1	NR	NR	100	7.6	35.6
LUTH–Luth–MO Synod	1	17	39	45	3.4	16.0
METH–Un Methodist	1	35	66	136	10.4	48.4
STANTON	**10**	**606**	**1,363**	**2,203**	**35.9**	**100.0**
Bahá'í	0	NR	1	1	0.0	0.0
Catholic	1	NR	NR	357	5.8	16.2
Evan Free Ch	1	140	NR	140	2.3	6.4
LUTH–E.L.C.A.	2	81	208	240	3.9	10.9
LUTH–Luth–MO Synod	2	166	567	700	11.4	31.8
LUTH–Wisc Ev Luth Syn	1	93	182	226	3.7	10.3
METH–Un Methodist	2	86	216	299	4.9	13.6
Un C of Christ	1	40	189	240	3.9	10.9
THAYER	**34**	**1,591**	**3,905**	**5,148**	**98.5**	**100.0**
BRETH–Ch of Brethren	1	0	77	92	1.8	1.8
Catholic	2	NR	NR	450	8.6	8.7
CHR–Chr Ch (Disc)	1	0	0	0	0.0	0.0
CHR–Chr Chs & Chs Cr	2	NR	248	296	5.7	5.7
CHR–Chs of Christ	1	40	37	48	0.9	0.9
LUTH–Assoc Free Luth	1	NR	NR	NR	-	-
LUTH–E.L.C.A.	8	517	1,438	1,695	32.4	32.9
LUTH–Luth Cong Msn Chr	1	166	460	549	10.5	10.7
LUTH–Luth–MO Synod	6	472	909	1,100	21.0	21.4
MENN–Fel Evg Bib Ch	1	35	40	35	0.7	0.7
METH–Un Methodist	5	213	462	600	11.5	11.7
Non-denom Chr Chs	1	50	68	68	1.3	1.3
PENT–Assemb of God	1	29	16	36	0.7	0.7
PRES–Presb Ch (USA)	2	50	119	142	2.7	2.8
Un C of Christ	1	19	31	37	0.7	0.7
THOMAS	**6**	**102**	**192**	**325**	**50.2**	**100.0**
Catholic	1	NR	NR	50	7.7	15.4
LUTH–Luth–MO Synod	1	10	24	35	5.4	10.8
PENT–Assemb of God	1	49	44	90	13.9	27.7
Un C of Christ	3	43	124	150	23.2	46.2
THURSTON	**19**	**710**	**1,985**	**3,269**	**47.1**	**100.0**
Bahá'í	0	NR	28	28	0.4	0.9
Catholic	1	NR	NR	283	4.1	8.7
Evan Cov Ch	1	28	32	36	0.5	1.1
LDS–Comm of Christ	1	NR	189	189	2.7	5.8
LDS–L-D Saints	1	NR	NR	516	7.4	15.8
LUTH–E.L.C.A.	3	230	692	834	12.0	25.5
LUTH–Luth–MO Synod	2	158	381	462	6.7	14.1
METH–Un Methodist	3	78	171	296	4.3	9.1
Non-denom Chr Chs	1	100	150	150	2.2	4.6
PENT–Assemb of God	2	57	33	113	1.6	3.5
PRES–Presb Ch (USA)	3	19	121	169	2.4	5.2
REF–Ref Ch in Am	1	40	188	193	2.8	5.9
VALLEY	**13**	**519**	**1,181**	**2,837**	**66.6**	**100.0**
BAPT–Converge/BGC	1	75	NR	90	2.1	3.2
BAPT–S-D Baptist Gen Con	1	NR	141	170	4.0	6.0
Catholic	1	NR	NR	970	22.8	34.2
CHR–Chr Chs & Chs Cr	1	NR	150	181	4.2	6.4
Evan Free Ch	1	62	NR	62	1.5	2.2
LUTH–E.L.C.A.	1	50	172	172	4.0	6.1
LUTH–Luth–MO Synod	1	74	184	256	6.0	9.0
METH–Un Methodist	4	222	511	816	19.2	28.8
PENT–Assemb of God	1	36	0	92	2.2	3.2
PRES–Presb Ch (USA)	1	0	23	28	0.7	1.0
WASHINGTON	**26**	**2,578**	**4,863**	**15,312**	**75.7**	**100.0**
ANG/EPIS–Episcopal	1	51	115	115	0.6	0.8
Bahá'í	0	NR	1	1	0.0	0.0
BAPT–Amer Bapt USA	1	45	60	74	0.4	0.5
BAPT–Converge/BGC	1	75	NR	90	0.4	0.6
BAPT–So Bapt Conv	1	15	8	10	0.0	0.1
Catholic	3	NR	NR	8,421	41.6	55.0
CHR–Chr Chs & Chs Cr	1	NR	125	154	0.8	1.0
CHR–Chs of Christ	1	35	40	45	0.2	0.3
Jehovah's Witness	1	NR	NR	NR	-	-
LDS–L-D Saints	1	NR	NR	282	1.4	1.8
LUTH–E.L.C.A.	4	740	1,729	2,462	12.2	16.1
LUTH–Luth Cong Msn Chr	1	35	NR	NR	-	-
LUTH–Luth–MO Synod	2	378	903	1,175	5.8	7.7
METH–Un Methodist	2	249	755	958	4.7	6.3
Non-denom Chr Chs	2	675	575	844	4.2	5.5
PENT–Assemb of God	1	40	40	50	0.2	0.3
PRES–Presb Ch (USA)	1	110	229	282	1.4	1.8
Un C of Christ	2	130	283	349	1.7	2.3
WAYNE	**17**	**1,090**	**3,675**	**5,701**	**59.4**	**100.0**
Bahá'í	0	NR	7	7	0.1	0.1
BAPT–Amer Bapt USA	1	45	63	74	0.8	1.3
Catholic	1	NR	NR	984	10.3	17.3
CHR–Chr Chs & Chs Cr	1	NR	275	323	3.4	5.7
Evan Free Ch	1	80	NR	80	0.8	1.4
LUTH–E.L.C.A.	2	244	1,182	1,567	16.3	27.5
LUTH–Luth–MO Synod	4	373	1,119	1,407	14.7	24.7
LUTH–Wisc Ev Luth Syn	1	85	204	234	2.4	4.1
METH–Un Methodist	3	179	689	833	8.7	14.6
PENT–Assemb of God	1	19	0	32	0.3	0.6
PRES–Presb Ch (USA)	2	65	136	160	1.7	2.8
WEBSTER	**16**	**623**	**1,551**	**2,736**	**71.8**	**100.0**
BAPT–Amer Bapt USA	1	9	9	11	0.3	0.4
Catholic	2	NR	NR	758	19.9	27.7
CHR–Chr Chs & Chs Cr	1	NR	50	60	1.6	2.2
Jehovah's Witness	1	NR	NR	NR	-	-
LUTH–Luth Cong Msn Chr	1	90	276	331	8.7	12.1
LUTH–Luth–MO Synod	3	244	538	676	17.7	24.7
METH–Un Methodist	5	219	621	796	20.9	29.1
METH–Wesleyan	1	36	32	47	1.2	1.7
PENT–Assemb of God	1	25	25	57	1.5	2.1
WHEELER	**4**	**79**	**124**	**319**	**39.0**	**100.0**
BAPT–So Bapt Conv	1	27	30	36	4.4	11.3
Catholic	1	NR	NR	100	12.2	31.3
LUTH–Luth–MO Synod	1	22	42	51	6.2	16.0
METH–Un Methodist	1	30	52	132	16.1	41.4
YORK	**33**	**3,115**	**6,805**	**10,593**	**77.5**	**100.0**
BAPT–Amer Bapt USA	1	20	5	6	0.0	0.1
BAPT–Converge/BGC	1	75	NR	90	0.7	0.8
BAPT–So Bapt Conv	1	2	5	6	0.0	0.1
Catholic	2	NR	NR	1,899	13.9	17.9
Ch of Nazarene	1	88	60	289	2.1	2.7
CHR–Chr Ch (Disc)	1	0	115	138	1.0	1.3
CHR–Chs of Christ	1	530	381	526	3.8	5.0
Evan Free Ch	1	60	NR	60	0.4	0.6
LUTH–E.L.C.A.	3	212	682	829	6.1	7.8
LUTH–Luth–MO Synod	6	834	2,440	2,656	19.4	25.1
LUTH–Wisc Ev Luth Syn	1	86	90	109	0.8	1.0
MENN–Fel Evg Bib Ch	1	129	68	129	0.9	1.2
MENN–Menn Br US Conf	1	NR	140	169	1.2	1.6
MENN–Mennonite USA	1	400	1,128	1,358	9.9	12.8
METH–Un Methodist	5	394	1,123	1,520	11.1	14.3
Non-denom Chr Chs	1	67	72	84	0.6	0.8
PENT–Assemb of God	1	150	77	221	1.6	2.1
PRES–Presb Ch (USA)	2	24	340	409	3.0	3.9
Un C of Christ	2	44	79	95	0.7	0.9
NEVADA	**1,392**	**138,199**	**209,396**	**929,055**	**34.4**	**100.0**
CARSON CITY (CITY)	**40**	**3,638**	**5,171**	**14,916**	**27.0**	**100.0**
ANG/EPIS–Episcopal	1	100	135	199	0.4	1.3
Bahá'í	1	NR	31	31	0.1	0.2
BAPT–Amer Bapt USA	1	28	60	72	0.1	0.5

NR–Not Reported   - Represents no adherents reported.   Percentages may not total 100 due to rounding.

Table 3: Religious Congregations by County and Group: 2010

Religious Group	Number of Congregations	Number of Attendees	Number of Communicant, Confirmed, or Full Members	Adherents: Number of Adherents	Adherents: % of Total Pop.	Adherents: % of Total Adh.
BAPT–Consrv Bapt	1	NR	NR	NR	-	-
BAPT–So Bapt Conv	3	160	598	715	1.3	4.8
Calv Chpl	1	NR	NR	NR	-	-
Catholic	2	NR	NR	2,578	4.7	17.3
Ch Cr, Scientst	1	NR	NR	NR	-	-
Ch of Nazarene	1	95	0	106	0.2	0.7
CHR–Chr Chs & Chs Cr	1	NR	350	419	0.8	2.8
CHR–Chs of Christ	1	68	60	90	0.2	0.6
Jehovah's Witness	1	NR	NR	NR	-	-
LDS–L-D Saints	7	NR	NR	2,869	5.2	19.2
LUTH–E.L.C.A.	1	136	243	272	0.5	1.8
LUTH–Luth–MO Synod	1	143	261	261	0.5	1.7
METH–Un Methodist	1	270	486	862	1.6	5.8
METH–Wesleyan	1	199	126	259	0.5	1.7
Muslim Est	1	17	NR	308	0.6	2.1
Non-denom Chr Chs	5	1,025	1,825	1,844	3.3	12.4
ORTHO–Armen Ap Etchm	1	50	NR	600	1.1	4.0
PENT–Assemb of God	1	947	270	2,500	4.5	16.8
PENT–Int Foursq Gos	1	4	5	6	0.0	0.0
PENT–Intl Pent Holiness	1	85	100	120	0.2	0.8
PRES–Presb Ch (USA)	1	126	332	397	0.7	2.7
Salvation Army	1	24	9	86	0.2	0.6
Sev Day Adv	1	161	280	322	0.6	2.2
Unity Ch	1	NR	NR	NR	-	-
CHURCHILL	**31**	**1,754**	**2,199**	**8,816**	**35.4**	**100.0**
ANG/EPIS–Episcopal	1	28	75	79	0.3	0.9
Bahá'í	1	NR	17	17	0.1	0.2
BAPT–So Bapt Conv	4	240	906	1,120	4.5	12.7
Catholic	1	NR	NR	2,460	9.9	27.9
Ch of Nazarene	1	417	50	417	1.7	4.7
Chr & Miss Al	1	65	25	65	0.3	0.7
CHR–Chs of Christ	1	50	43	62	0.2	0.7
Ind Fund Churches	1	NR	NR	NR	-	-
Jehovah's Witness	1	NR	NR	NR	-	-
LDS–L-D Saints	7	NR	NR	2,786	11.2	31.6
LUTH–Luth–MO Synod	1	73	146	174	0.7	2.0
METH–Un Methodist	1	128	264	489	2.0	5.5
Non-denom Chr Chs	3	255	250	318	1.3	3.6
PENT–Assemb of God	3	328	250	521	2.1	5.9
PENT–Pent Ch of God	1	70	NR	109	0.4	1.2
PENT–Un Pent Ch Intl	1	NR	NR	NR	-	-
REF–Comm Ref Evan	1	NR	NR	NR	-	-
Sev Day Adv	1	100	173	199	0.8	2.3
CLARK	**806**	**96,872**	**152,687**	**697,799**	**35.8**	**100.0**
ANG/EPIS–Anglican NA	1	NR	NR	NR	-	-
ANG/EPIS–Episcopal	9	1,235	2,568	2,670	0.1	0.4
Bahá'í	9	NR	1,250	1,250	0.1	0.2
BAPT–Amer Bapt Assn	3	NR	305	379	0.0	0.1
BAPT–Amer Bapt USA	11	1,670	3,877	4,818	0.2	0.7
BAPT–Consrv Bapt	2	NR	NR	NR	-	-
BAPT–Ind Bapt Flwsp Intl	3	NR	NR	NR	-	-
BAPT–Natl Mis Bapt Conv	4	20	490	609	0.0	0.1
BAPT–NBC Amer	1	0	150	186	0.0	0.0
BAPT–NBC USA	3	505	775	963	0.0	0.1
BAPT–Prog NBC	1	0	0	0	0.0	0.0
BAPT–Reg Bapt Gen As	1	NR	NR	NR	-	-
BAPT–So Bapt Conv	90	12,820	25,182	31,297	1.6	4.5
BUDD–Mahayana	15	NR	NR	9,947	0.5	1.4
BUDD–Theravada	6	NR	NR	4,016	0.2	0.6
BUDD–Vajrayana	4	NR	NR	155	0.0	0.0
Calv Chpl	10	NR	NR	NR	-	-
Catholic	32	NR	NR	354,110	18.1	50.7
CGOD–Ch God (Ander)	1	100	NR	100	0.0	0.0
Ch Cr, Scientst	2	NR	NR	NR	-	-
Ch God (7th Day)	2	NR	NR	NR	-	-
Ch of Chr (Hol)	2	NR	NR	NR	-	-
Ch of Nazarene	5	426	479	736	0.0	0.1
Chr & Miss Al	3	1,115	580	2,289	0.1	0.3
CHR–Chr Ch (Disc)	6	223	636	790	0.0	0.1
CHR–Chr Chs & Chs Cr	4	NR	13,780	17,126	0.9	2.5
CHR–Chs of Christ	13	1,441	1,384	1,885	0.1	0.3

Religious Group	Number of Congregations	Number of Attendees	Number of Communicant, Confirmed, or Full Members	Adherents: Number of Adherents	Adherents: % of Total Pop.	Adherents: % of Total Adh.
CHR–Int Chs of Christ	1	NR	204	254	0.0	0.0
Evan Cov Ch	1	55	50	72	0.0	0.0
Evan Free Ch	1	85	NR	85	0.0	0.0
FRND–Evan Fr Ch Intl	1	250	90	112	0.0	0.0
FRND–Indep Yr Mtgs	1	NR	0	0	0.0	0.0
HINDU–Post Ren	4	NR	NR	101	0.0	0.0
HINDU–Renaiss	1	NR	NR	12	0.0	0.0
HINDU–Trad Temples	1	NR	NR	2,000	0.1	0.3
Ind Fund Churches	1	NR	NR	NR	-	-
Jain	1	NR	NR	NR	-	-
Jehovah's Witness	13	NR	NR	NR	-	-
JUD–Conserv	2	557	625	1,688	0.1	0.2
JUD–Orth	7	1,224	600	1,700	0.1	0.2
JUD–Reconst	1	53	68	184	0.0	0.0
JUD–Reform	2	507	895	2,416	0.1	0.3
LDS–Comm of Christ	1	NR	159	159	0.0	0.0
LDS–L-D Saints	218	NR	NR	124,291	6.4	17.8
LUTH–E.L.C.A.	13	3,345	5,861	8,409	0.4	1.2
LUTH–Luth Ch-Am Asc	1	NR	NR	NR	-	-
LUTH–Luth Cong Msn Chr	1	30	49	61	0.0	0.0
LUTH–Luth–MO Synod	10	2,300	2,822	4,261	0.2	0.6
LUTH–Wisc Ev Luth Syn	6	882	1,269	1,741	0.1	0.2
METH–AME	3	270	850	1,056	0.1	0.2
METH–C.M.E.	1	25	35	43	0.0	0.0
METH–Un Methodist	17	2,747	3,462	6,812	0.3	1.0
Metro Comm Ch	1	155	90	112	0.0	0.0
MJEW–Union Mes Cong	1	NR	NR	NR	-	-
Muslim Est	5	763	NR	1,084	0.1	0.2
Nat Spirit Asso	1	NR	NR	NR	-	-
New Apost Ch	1	NR	NR	NR	-	-
Non-denom Chr Chs	94	41,184	53,653	60,415	3.1	8.7
ORTHE–Ant Orth of NA	1	79	NR	217	0.0	0.0
ORTHE–Greek Orthodox	1	500	NR	5,000	0.3	0.7
ORTHE–Orth Ch in Amer	2	225	NR	800	0.0	0.1
ORTHE–Romania Orth Ar	1	50	NR	200	0.0	0.0
ORTHE–Serb Orth USA	1	100	NR	1,300	0.1	0.2
ORTHO–Armen Ap Cilic	1	65	NR	260	0.0	0.0
ORTHO–Eritrean Orth	1	250	NR	150	0.0	0.0
ORTHO–Ethiopian Orth	1	NR	NR	NR	-	-
ORTHO–Malan Dioc Am	1	8	NR	24	0.0	0.0
ORTHO–Syrian Orth Ch	1	55	NR	240	0.0	0.0
PENT–Assemb of God	29	11,249	14,423	19,025	1.0	2.7
PENT–Ch God (Cleve)	6	541	754	937	0.0	0.1
PENT–Ch of God Proph	4	NR	98	122	0.0	0.0
PENT–COGIC	21	1,883	4,581	5,693	0.3	0.8
PENT–Full Gosp Bapt	7	NR	NR	NR	-	-
PENT–Int Foursq Gos	19	2,775	3,002	3,731	0.2	0.5
PENT–Un Pent Ch Intl	4	NR	NR	NR	-	-
PENT–United Holy Ch	1	NR	NR	NR	-	-
PRES–Kor Pres Abroad	2	NR	NR	NR	-	-
PRES–Korean Pres Amer	3	NR	NR	NR	-	-
PRES–Presb Ch (USA)	7	1,311	2,303	2,862	0.1	0.4
PRES–Presb Ch Amer	3	261	230	267	0.0	0.0
REF–Christian Ref	5	503	351	436	0.0	0.1
REF–Hung Ref Add'l	1	NR	NR	NR	-	-
Salvation Army	4	625	517	1,252	0.1	0.2
Sev Day Adv	13	2,063	3,589	4,126	0.2	0.6
Sikh	2	NR	NR	NR	-	-
Un C of Christ	6	253	482	599	0.0	0.1
Unit Univ	1	89	119	156	0.0	0.0
Unity Ch	2	NR	NR	NR	-	-
Zoroastrian	0	NR	NR	8	0.0	0.0
DOUGLAS	**30**	**3,945**	**5,746**	**13,899**	**29.6**	**100.0**
ANG/EPIS–Episcopal	2	51	100	163	0.3	1.2
Bahá'í	0	NR	10	10	0.0	0.1
BAPT–Consrv Bapt	1	NR	NR	NR	-	-
BAPT–Ref Bapt Ch	1	NR	NR	NR	-	-
BAPT–So Bapt Conv	4	217	247	291	0.6	2.1
BUDD–Vajrayana	1	NR	NR	52	0.1	0.4
Calv Chpl	1	NR	NR	NR	-	-
Catholic	2	NR	NR	4,999	10.6	36.0
Ch of Nazarene	1	132	108	405	0.9	2.9
Jehovah's Witness	1	NR	NR	NR	-	-

NR–Not Reported - Represents no adherents reported. Percentages may not total 100 due to rounding.

Table 3: Religious Congregations by County and Group: 2010

Religious Group	Number of Congrega-tions	Number of Attendees	Number of Communicant, Confirmed, or Full Members	Adherents		
				Number of Adherents	% of Total Pop.	% of Total Adh.
JUD–Reform	1	54	95	256	0.5	1.8
LDS–L-D Saints	3	NR	NR	1,710	3.6	12.3
LUTH–Luth–MO Synod	2	372	549	627	1.3	4.5
METH–Un Methodist	1	160	420	954	2.0	6.9
Non-denom Chr Chs	4	2,515	3,950	3,950	8.4	28.4
PENT–Assemb of God	1	50	36	101	0.2	0.7
PENT–Int Foursq Gos	2	287	195	230	0.5	1.7
PENT–Pent Ch of God	1	70	NR	109	0.2	0.8
PRES–Presb Ch (USA)	1	37	36	42	0.1	0.3
ELKO	**59**	**2,032**	**3,504**	**19,323**	**39.6**	**100.0**
ANG/EPIS–Episcopal	2	39	279	279	0.6	1.4
Bahá'í	0	NR	22	22	0.0	0.1
BAPT–Amer Bapt USA	1	60	92	119	0.2	0.6
BAPT–So Bapt Conv	12	662	1,565	2,023	4.1	10.5
Calv Chpl	2	NR	NR	NR	-	-
Catholic	4	NR	NR	6,768	13.9	35.0
Ch of Nazarene	1	53	53	95	0.2	0.5
CHR–Chs of Christ	1	35	33	57	0.1	0.3
Jehovah's Witness	1	NR	NR	NR	-	-
LDS–L-D Saints	18	NR	NR	7,952	16.3	41.2
LUTH–E.L.C.A.	1	45	252	252	0.5	1.3
LUTH–Luth–MO Synod	1	106	165	213	0.4	1.1
METH–Un Methodist	2	48	69	85	0.2	0.4
Non-denom Chr Chs	4	485	460	637	1.3	3.3
PENT–Assemb of God	2	136	70	145	0.3	0.8
PENT–Int Foursq Gos	1	35	30	39	0.1	0.2
PENT–Pent Ch of God	1	70	NR	109	0.2	0.6
PRES–Presb Ch (USA)	4	230	365	472	1.0	2.4
Sev Day Adv	1	28	49	56	0.1	0.3
ESMERALDA	**1**	**21**	**21**	**24**	**3.1**	**100.0**
Bahá'í	0	NR	1	1	0.1	4.2
BAPT–So Bapt Conv	1	21	20	23	2.9	95.8
EUREKA	**6**	**89**	**157**	**1,452**	**73.1**	**100.0**
Bahá'í	0	NR	1	1	0.1	0.1
BAPT–So Bapt Conv	4	89	156	191	9.6	13.2
Catholic	1	NR	NR	1,080	54.4	74.4
LDS–L-D Saints	1	NR	NR	180	9.1	12.4
HUMBOLDT	**22**	**861**	**1,156**	**7,712**	**46.7**	**100.0**
Bahá'í	0	NR	20	20	0.1	0.3
BAPT–So Bapt Conv	3	238	341	433	2.6	5.6
Calv Chpl	1	NR	NR	NR	-	-
Catholic	3	NR	NR	4,096	24.8	53.1
CHR–Chs of Christ	1	11	11	14	0.1	0.2
Ind Fund Churches	1	NR	NR	NR	-	-
LDS–L-D Saints	4	NR	NR	2,028	12.3	26.3
LUTH–Luth–MO Synod	1	60	153	217	1.3	2.8
METH–Un Methodist	1	70	105	189	1.1	2.5
Non-denom Chr Chs	2	206	240	258	1.6	3.3
PENT–Assemb of God	3	185	109	245	1.5	3.2
PENT–Int Foursq Gos	1	30	71	90	0.5	1.2
Sev Day Adv	1	61	106	122	0.7	1.6
LANDER	**20**	**331**	**860**	**2,935**	**50.8**	**100.0**
ANG/EPIS–Episcopal	1	7	10	10	0.2	0.3
Bahá'í	0	NR	4	4	0.1	0.1
BAPT–So Bapt Conv	8	163	672	851	14.7	29.0
Calv Chpl	1	NR	NR	NR	-	-
Catholic	1	NR	NR	883	15.3	30.1
CHR–Chs of Christ	1	30	24	45	0.8	1.5
LDS–L-D Saints	3	NR	NR	904	15.7	30.8
LUTH–Luth–MO Synod	1	12	17	20	0.3	0.7
METH–Un Methodist	1	17	26	26	0.5	0.9
PENT–Assemb of God	1	38	21	73	1.3	2.5
PENT–Int Foursq Gos	1	41	47	60	1.0	2.0
PRES–Orth Pres Ch	1	23	39	59	1.0	2.0

Religious Group	Number of Congrega-tions	Number of Attendees	Number of Communicant, Confirmed, or Full Members	Adherents		
				Number of Adherents	% of Total Pop.	% of Total Adh.
LINCOLN	**14**	**227**	**276**	**2,942**	**55.0**	**100.0**
ANG/EPIS–Episcopal	1	11	38	38	0.7	1.3
Bahá'í	0	NR	1	1	0.0	0.0
BAPT–So Bapt Conv	2	84	137	169	3.2	5.7
Catholic	1	NR	NR	214	4.0	7.3
LDS–L-D Saints	6	NR	NR	2,323	43.5	79.0
METH–Un Methodist	1	52	44	79	1.5	2.7
Non-denom Chr Chs	2	45	55	60	1.1	2.0
PENT–Assemb of God	1	35	1	58	1.1	2.0
LYON	**47**	**1,708**	**2,642**	**10,852**	**20.9**	**100.0**
ANG/EPIS–Episcopal	1	8	6	6	0.0	0.1
Bahá'í	0	NR	22	22	0.0	0.2
BAPT–So Bapt Conv	7	352	1,082	1,333	2.6	12.3
Calv Chpl	2	NR	NR	NR	-	-
Catholic	4	NR	NR	3,724	7.2	34.3
CGOD–Ch God (Ander)	1	60	NR	60	0.1	0.6
Ch of Nazarene	2	105	145	174	0.3	1.6
CHR–Chs of Christ	1	25	20	28	0.1	0.3
Jehovah's Witness	3	NR	NR	NR	-	-
LDS–L-D Saints	6	NR	NR	3,598	6.9	33.2
LUTH–E.L.C.A.	1	33	32	32	0.1	0.3
LUTH–Luth–MO Synod	2	70	75	94	0.2	0.9
METH–Free Methodist	1	23	22	23	0.0	0.2
METH–Un Methodist	2	94	171	301	0.6	2.8
Non-denom Chr Chs	4	400	493	525	1.0	4.8
PENT–Assemb of God	4	181	84	282	0.5	2.6
PENT–Ch God (Cleve)	1	19	12	15	0.0	0.1
PENT–Int Foursq Gos	1	34	43	53	0.1	0.5
PENT–Open Bible Std	1	56	NR	56	0.1	0.5
PENT–Vineyard	1	185	325	400	0.8	3.7
Sev Day Adv	2	63	110	126	0.2	1.2
MINERAL	**16**	**309**	**611**	**1,466**	**30.7**	**100.0**
Bahá'í	0	NR	4	4	0.1	0.3
BAPT–Reg Bapt Gen As	1	NR	NR	NR	-	-
BAPT–So Bapt Conv	3	94	266	306	6.4	20.9
Catholic	1	NR	NR	171	3.6	11.7
CHR–Chs of Christ	1	12	12	12	0.3	0.8
Jehovah's Witness	1	NR	NR	NR	-	-
LDS–L-D Saints	2	NR	NR	539	11.3	36.8
LUTH–Luth–MO Synod	1	22	13	14	0.3	1.0
METH–Un Methodist	1	30	36	44	0.9	3.0
Non-denom Chr Chs	1	25	40	40	0.8	2.7
PENT–Assemb of God	1	88	38	103	2.2	7.0
PENT–COGIC	1	0	150	173	3.6	11.8
PRES–Presb Ch (USA)	1	27	33	38	0.8	2.6
Sev Day Adv	1	11	19	22	0.5	1.5
NYE	**54**	**2,451**	**3,669**	**13,631**	**31.0**	**100.0**
ANG/EPIS–Episcopal	2	50	78	88	0.2	0.6
Bahá'í	0	NR	13	13	0.0	0.1
BAPT–Amer Bapt USA	1	46	40	47	0.1	0.3
BAPT–So Bapt Conv	12	602	1,533	1,814	4.1	13.3
Calv Chpl	2	NR	NR	NR	-	-
Catholic	5	NR	NR	5,875	13.4	43.1
CHR–Chs of Christ	2	52	49	62	0.1	0.5
Ind Fund Churches	1	NR	NR	NR	-	-
Jehovah's Witness	1	NR	NR	NR	-	-
LDS–L-D Saints	8	NR	NR	3,370	7.7	24.7
LUTH–E.L.C.A.	1	68	185	204	0.5	1.5
LUTH–Luth–MO Synod	1	153	127	142	0.3	1.0
METH–Un Methodist	1	94	135	139	0.3	1.0
MJEW–Union Mes Cong	1	NR	NR	NR	-	-
Non-denom Chr Chs	3	830	930	1,062	2.4	7.8
PENT–Assemb of God	3	173	98	271	0.6	2.0
PENT–Ch God (Cleve)	1	35	0	0	0.0	0.0
PENT–Ch of God Proph	1	NR	12	14	0.0	0.1
PENT–Int Foursq Gos	2	146	152	180	0.4	1.3
PENT–Un Pent Ch Intl	1	NR	NR	NR	-	-
PENT–Vineyard	1	88	100	118	0.3	0.9
PRES–Presb Ch (USA)	1	0	7	8	0.0	0.1

NR–Not Reported - Represents no adherents reported. Percentages may not total 100 due to rounding.

Table 3: Religious Congregations by County and Group: 2010

Religious Group	Number of Congrega-tions	Number of Attendees	Number of Communicant, Confirmed, or Full Members	Adherents: Number of Adherents	Adherents: % of Total Pop.	Adherents: % of Total Adh.
Salvation Army	1	61	118	118	0.3	0.9
Sev Day Adv	2	53	92	106	0.2	0.8
PERSHING	**12**	**260**	**325**	**1,628**	**24.1**	**100.0**
ANG/EPIS–Episcopal	1	18	13	13	0.2	0.8
Bahá'í	0	NR	25	25	0.4	1.5
BAPT–So Bapt Conv	4	131	203	239	3.5	14.7
Catholic	1	NR	NR	707	10.5	43.4
CHR–Chs of Christ	1	18	11	22	0.3	1.4
LDS–L-D Saints	1	NR	NR	475	7.0	29.2
LUTH–Wisc Ev Luth Syn	1	15	14	19	0.3	1.2
METH–Un Methodist	1	12	19	52	0.8	3.2
Non-denom Chr Chs	1	30	40	40	0.6	2.5
PENT–Assemb of God	1	36	0	36	0.5	2.2
STOREY	**4**	**68**	**86**	**1,022**	**25.5**	**100.0**
ANG/EPIS–Episcopal	1	13	28	28	0.7	2.7
BAPT–So Bapt Conv	1	25	25	29	0.7	2.8
Catholic	1	NR	NR	927	23.1	90.7
PRES–Presb Ch (USA)	1	30	33	38	0.9	3.7
WASHOE	**214**	**23,412**	**29,982**	**124,506**	**29.5**	**100.0**
ANG/EPIS–Anglican NA	3	NR	NR	NR	-	-
ANG/EPIS–Episcopal	7	576	1,549	1,600	0.4	1.3
Bahá'í	3	NR	299	299	0.1	0.2
BAPT–Amer Bapt USA	3	383	415	508	0.1	0.4
BAPT–Consrv Bapt	2	NR	NR	NR	-	-
BAPT–NBC USA	1	175	370	453	0.1	0.4
BAPT–Ref Bapt Ch	1	NR	NR	NR	-	-
BAPT–Reg Bapt Gen As	1	NR	NR	NR	-	-
BAPT–So Bapt Conv	26	2,812	3,728	4,561	1.1	3.7
BUDD–Mahayana	3	NR	NR	557	0.1	0.4
Calv Chpl	2	NR	NR	NR	-	-
Catholic	13	NR	NR	60,509	14.4	48.6
CGOD–Ch God (Ander)	2	65	NR	65	0.0	0.1
Ch Cr, Scientst	1	NR	NR	NR	-	-
Ch of Nazarene	5	555	675	1,058	0.3	0.8
Chr & Miss Al	1	65	60	70	0.0	0.1
CHR–Chr Ch (Disc)	1	40	42	51	0.0	0.0
CHR–Chr Chs & Chs Cr	2	NR	149	182	0.0	0.1
CHR–Chs of Christ	7	402	335	552	0.1	0.4
CHR–Int Chs of Christ	1	NR	49	60	0.0	0.0
Evan Free Ch	3	743	NR	743	0.2	0.6
FRND–Indep Yr Mtgs	1	NR	20	24	0.0	0.0
HINDU–Post Ren	2	NR	NR	35	0.0	0.0
Ind Fund Churches	1	NR	NR	NR	-	-
Jehovah's Witness	5	NR	NR	NR	-	-
JUD–Conserv	1	57	64	173	0.0	0.1
JUD–Orth	1	43	50	60	0.0	0.0
JUD–Reform	1	87	153	413	0.1	0.3
LDS–Comm of Christ	1	NR	158	158	0.0	0.1
LDS–L-D Saints	33	NR	NR	19,436	4.6	15.6
LUTH–E.L.C.A.	4	472	1,174	1,407	0.3	1.1
LUTH–Luth-MO Synod	2	460	1,112	1,716	0.4	1.4
LUTH–Wisc Ev Luth Syn	2	149	168	231	0.1	0.2
METH–AME	1	125	200	245	0.1	0.2
METH–Un Methodist	5	910	2,029	3,002	0.7	2.4
MJEW–Assoc Mes Cong	1	NR	NR	NR	-	-
Muslim Est	1	134	NR	308	0.1	0.2
Nat Spirit Asso	1	NR	NR	NR	-	-
Non-denom Chr Chs	17	10,080	12,375	13,462	3.2	10.8
ORTHE–Greek Orthodox	1	125	NR	375	0.1	0.3
ORTHE–Rus Orth Abroad	1	30	NR	60	0.0	0.0
ORTHE–Serb Orth USA	1	35	NR	55	0.0	0.0
PENT–Assemb of God	10	2,018	774	7,141	1.7	5.7
PENT–Ch God (Cleve)	2	70	53	65	0.0	0.1
PENT–COGIC	2	155	270	330	0.1	0.3
PENT–Int Foursq Gos	7	390	492	602	0.1	0.5
PENT–Intl Pent Holiness	1	93	54	66	0.0	0.1
PENT–Un Pent Ch Intl	2	NR	NR	NR	-	-
PENT–Vineyard	1	180	205	251	0.1	0.2
PRES–Kor Pres Abroad	2	NR	NR	NR	-	-
PRES–Orth Pres Ch	1	46	46	66	0.0	0.1

Religious Group	Number of Congrega-tions	Number of Attendees	Number of Communicant, Confirmed, or Full Members	Adherents: Number of Adherents	Adherents: % of Total Pop.	Adherents: % of Total Adh.
PRES–Presb Ch (USA)	5	751	1,033	1,264	0.3	1.0
Salvation Army	1	146	58	130	0.0	0.1
Sev Day Adv	4	768	1,336	1,536	0.4	1.2
Sikh	1	NR	NR	NR	-	-
Un C of Christ	2	155	276	338	0.1	0.3
Unit Univ	1	117	211	289	0.1	0.2
Unity Ch	1	NR	NR	NR	-	-
WHITE PINE	**16**	**221**	**304**	**6,132**	**61.1**	**100.0**
ANG/EPIS–Episcopal	1	33	62	62	0.6	1.0
Bahá'í	0	NR	3	3	0.0	0.0
BAPT–So Bapt Conv	2	110	117	140	1.4	2.3
Catholic	2	NR	NR	3,069	30.6	50.0
Ch of Nazarene	1	0	0	0	0.0	0.0
LDS–L-D Saints	6	NR	NR	2,688	26.8	43.8
METH–Un Methodist	2	48	100	114	1.1	1.9
PENT–Assemb of God	1	20	12	44	0.4	0.7
PENT–Int Foursq Gos	1	10	10	12	0.1	0.2
NEW HAMPSHIRE	**1,025**	**61,434**	**101,108**	**462,772**	**35.2**	**100.0**
BELKNAP	**58**	**2,768**	**4,934**	**19,857**	**33.0**	**100.0**
ANG/EPIS–Episcopal	3	168	255	378	0.6	1.9
Bahá'í	0	NR	53	53	0.1	0.3
BAPT–Amer Bapt USA	10	829	1,847	2,184	3.6	11.0
BAPT–Consrv Bapt	2	NR	NR	NR	-	-
BAPT–So Bapt Conv	1	35	25	30	0.0	0.2
Catholic	8	NR	NR	12,810	21.3	64.5
Ch Cr, Scientst	1	NR	NR	NR	-	-
Chr & Miss Al	1	16	18	20	0.0	0.1
CHR–Chs of Christ	1	52	44	55	0.1	0.3
CONG–Cong Chr, NA	4	NR	162	192	0.3	1.0
JUD–Reform	1	41	73	197	0.3	1.0
LDS–L-D Saints	1	NR	NR	463	0.8	2.3
LUTH–E.L.C.A.	1	66	157	182	0.3	0.9
METH–Un Methodist	3	189	504	868	1.4	4.4
Non-denom Chr Chs	5	355	397	456	0.8	2.3
ORTHE–Greek Orthodox	1	30	NR	120	0.2	0.6
PENT–Assemb of God	4	173	97	226	0.4	1.1
PENT–Un Pent Ch Intl	1	NR	NR	NR	-	-
PENT–Vineyard	1	200	155	183	0.3	0.9
PRES–Presb Ch Amer	1	70	95	131	0.2	0.7
Salvation Army	1	49	48	131	0.2	0.7
Sev Day Adv	1	42	72	83	0.1	0.4
Un C of Christ	5	411	858	1,015	1.7	5.1
Unit Univ	1	42	74	80	0.1	0.4
CARROLL	**51**	**2,637**	**4,561**	**10,177**	**21.3**	**100.0**
ANG/EPIS–Episcopal	4	325	616	978	2.0	9.6
Bahá'í	0	NR	40	40	0.1	0.4
BAPT–Amer Bapt Assn	1	NR	150	174	0.4	1.7
BAPT–Amer Bapt USA	6	328	613	709	1.5	7.0
BAPT–Reg Bapt Gen As	1	NR	NR	NR	-	-
BAPT–So Bapt Conv	1	200	120	139	0.3	1.4
BUDD–Vajrayana	1	NR	NR	35	0.1	0.3
Catholic	2	NR	NR	4,304	9.0	42.3
Ch Cr, Scientst	1	NR	NR	NR	-	-
Ch of Nazarene	1	24	16	25	0.1	0.2
Chr & Miss Al	1	68	44	108	0.2	1.1
CHR–Chs of Christ	1	120	100	135	0.3	1.3
CONG–Consrv Cong Chr	1	200	127	147	0.3	1.4
FRND–Fr Gen Cf & Un Mtg	1	NR	21	24	0.1	0.2
Jehovah's Witness	1	NR	NR	NR	-	-
LDS–L-D Saints	1	NR	NR	165	0.3	1.6
LUTH–E.L.C.A.	1	69	222	302	0.6	3.0
METH–Un Methodist	8	307	719	837	1.8	8.2
Non-denom Chr Chs	5	235	260	300	0.6	2.9
PENT–Assemb of God	1	115	90	115	0.2	1.1
Sev Day Adv	1	49	85	98	0.2	1.0
Un C of Christ	10	540	1,224	1,416	3.0	13.9
Unit Univ	1	57	114	126	0.3	1.2

NR–Not Reported   - Represents no adherents reported.   Percentages may not total 100 due to rounding.

Table 3: Religious Congregations by County and Group: 2010

Religious Group	Number of Congrega-tions	Number of Attendees	Number of Communicant, Confirmed, or Full Members	Adherents: Number of Adherents	Adherents: % of Total Pop.	Adherents: % of Total Adh.
CHESHIRE	**85**	**4,339**	**6,116**	**18,675**	**24.2**	**100.0**
ANG/EPIS–Episcopal	2	166	263	322	0.4	1.7
Bahá'í	1	NR	39	39	0.1	0.2
BAPT–Amer Bapt USA	3	112	264	309	0.4	1.7
BAPT–Ref Bapt Ch	1	NR	NR	NR	-	-
BUDD–Mahayana	3	NR	NR	33	0.0	0.2
Catholic	9	NR	NR	9,237	12.0	49.5
Ch Cr, Scientst	1	NR	NR	NR	-	-
Ch of Nazarene	1	76	75	196	0.3	1.0
Chr & Miss Al	1	219	182	219	0.3	1.2
CHR–Chs of Christ	1	35	41	55	0.1	0.3
Christian Brethren	1	NR	NR	NR	-	-
CONG–Cong Chr Add'l	1	NR	5	6	0.0	0.0
CONG–Cong Chr, NA	2	NR	95	111	0.1	0.6
Evan Cov Ch	1	272	171	354	0.5	1.9
Evan Free Ch	1	300	NR	300	0.4	1.6
FRND–Fr Gen Cf & Un Mtg	2	NR	73	85	0.1	0.5
Jehovah's Witness	1	NR	NR	NR	-	-
JUD–Reconst	1	80	102	275	0.4	1.5
LDS–L-D Saints	1	NR	NR	612	0.8	3.3
LUTH–E.L.C.A.	1	35	95	102	0.1	0.5
LUTH–Luth-MO Synod	2	200	519	646	0.8	3.5
METH–Un Methodist	10	168	450	609	0.8	3.3
Non-denom Chr Chs	7	965	855	1,241	1.6	6.6
ORTHE–Greek Orthodox	1	100	NR	250	0.3	1.3
PENT–Assemb of God	3	124	71	241	0.3	1.3
PENT–Int Foursq Gos	2	219	199	233	0.3	1.2
PRES–Orth Pres Ch	1	48	46	69	0.1	0.4
Salvation Army	1	22	46	130	0.2	0.7
Sev Day Adv	2	98	171	197	0.3	1.1
Un C of Christ	16	886	2,111	2,471	3.2	13.2
Unit Univ	5	214	243	333	0.4	1.8
COOS	**50**	**1,412**	**2,292**	**16,130**	**48.8**	**100.0**
ANG/EPIS–Episcopal	3	122	182	267	0.8	1.7
Bahá'í	0	NR	10	10	0.0	0.1
BAPT–Amer Bapt USA	3	92	149	173	0.5	1.1
BAPT–So Bapt Conv	1	22	41	48	0.1	0.3
Catholic	5	NR	NR	12,710	38.5	78.8
Ch Cr, Scientst	1	NR	NR	NR	-	-
CHR–Chs of Christ	1	25	36	60	0.2	0.4
CONG–Consrv Cong Chr	1	60	38	44	0.1	0.3
FRND–Fr Gen Cf & Un Mtg	1	NR	0	0	0.0	0.0
Jehovah's Witness	4	NR	NR	NR	-	-
LDS–L-D Saints	2	NR	NR	313	0.9	1.9
LUTH–E.L.C.A.	1	53	122	248	0.8	1.5
METH–Un Methodist	9	239	751	939	2.8	5.8
Non-denom Chr Chs	4	225	220	280	0.8	1.7
ORTHE–Orth Ch in Amer	1	15	NR	26	0.1	0.2
PENT–Assemb of God	3	162	102	228	0.7	1.4
PENT–Int Foursq Gos	1	117	109	126	0.4	0.8
PRES–Presb Ch Amer	1	38	20	28	0.1	0.2
Salvation Army	1	25	66	113	0.3	0.7
Sev Day Adv	1	20	34	39	0.1	0.2
Un C of Christ	6	197	412	478	1.4	3.0
GRAFTON	**109**	**4,032**	**7,537**	**20,149**	**22.6**	**100.0**
ANG/EPIS–Anglican NA	1	NR	NR	NR	-	-
ANG/EPIS–Episcopal	7	423	989	1,246	1.4	6.2
Bahá'í	0	NR	91	91	0.1	0.5
BAPT–Amer Bapt USA	12	586	1,084	1,256	1.4	6.2
BAPT–Consrv Bapt	3	NR	NR	NR	-	-
BAPT–Converge/BGC	1	75	NR	90	0.1	0.4
BAPT–Ref Bapt Ch	1	NR	NR	NR	-	-
BAPT–So Bapt Conv	2	47	49	57	0.1	0.3
Catholic	12	NR	NR	9,503	10.7	47.2
Ch Cr, Scientst	2	NR	NR	NR	-	-
Ch of Nazarene	2	76	84	86	0.1	0.4
Chr & Miss Al	1	40	30	78	0.1	0.4
CONG–Cong Chr, NA	1	NR	55	64	0.1	0.3
CONG–Consrv Cong Chr	1	60	36	42	0.0	0.2
FRND–Fr Gen Cf & Un Mtg	2	NR	204	236	0.3	1.2
Jehovah's Witness	5	NR	NR	NR	-	-
LDS–L-D Saints	3	NR	NR	1,036	1.2	5.1
LUTH–E.L.C.A.	2	171	383	514	0.6	2.6
METH–Un Methodist	15	612	1,363	1,824	2.0	9.1
Non-denom Chr Chs	5	403	283	506	0.6	2.5
PENT–Assemb of God	6	296	213	406	0.5	2.0
PENT–Ch God (Cleve)	2	69	56	65	0.1	0.3
PENT–Un Pent Ch Intl	2	NR	NR	NR	-	-
PRES–Korean Pres Amer	1	NR	NR	NR	-	-
Sev Day Adv	1	82	143	164	0.2	0.8
Un C of Christ	18	1,009	2,323	2,692	3.0	13.4
Unit Univ	1	83	151	193	0.2	1.0
HILLSBOROUGH	**246**	**19,423**	**30,623**	**173,730**	**43.4**	**100.0**
ANG/EPIS–Anglican NA	1	NR	NR	NR	-	-
ANG/EPIS–Episcopal	8	994	3,205	3,819	1.0	2.2
Bahá'í	3	NR	190	190	0.0	0.1
BAPT–Amer Bapt USA	12	671	1,253	1,523	0.4	0.9
BAPT–Consrv Bapt	6	NR	NR	NR	-	-
BAPT–So Bapt Conv	8	328	591	718	0.2	0.4
BUDD–Mahayana	1	NR	NR	11	0.0	0.0
Calv Chpl	3	NR	NR	NR	-	-
Catholic	39	NR	NR	124,993	31.2	71.9
Ch Cr, Scientst	4	NR	NR	NR	-	-
Ch of Nazarene	3	453	374	706	0.2	0.4
Chr & Miss Al	2	142	60	217	0.1	0.1
CHR–Chr Chs & Chs Cr	6	NR	2,088	2,538	0.6	1.5
CHR–Chs of Christ	3	310	301	437	0.1	0.3
CHR–Int Chs of Christ	1	NR	190	231	0.1	0.1
CONG–Cong Chr Add'l	1	NR	45	55	0.0	0.0
CONG–Consrv Cong Chr	2	225	213	259	0.1	0.1
Evan Cov Ch	4	644	624	837	0.2	0.5
HINDU–Post Ren	3	NR	NR	118	0.0	0.1
Jehovah's Witness	5	NR	NR	NR	-	-
JUD–Conserv	2	323	362	977	0.2	0.6
JUD–Orth	1	43	50	60	0.0	0.0
JUD–Reform	2	206	364	983	0.2	0.6
LDS–L-D Saints	6	NR	NR	2,517	0.6	1.4
LUTH–Apostolic Luth	1	NR	NR	NR	-	-
LUTH–E.L.C.A.	3	267	652	954	0.2	0.5
LUTH–Luth-MO Synod	4	403	749	932	0.2	0.5
LUTH–Wisc Ev Luth Syn	1	66	103	142	0.0	0.1
METH–Un Methodist	10	865	2,634	3,922	1.0	2.3
Muslim Est	2	384	NR	1,308	0.3	0.8
New Apost Ch	1	NR	NR	NR	-	-
Non-denom Chr Chs	27	7,571	7,705	9,559	2.4	5.5
OCATH–Pol Natl Cath	1	NR	NR	NR	-	-
ORTHE–Greek Orthodox	4	695	NR	2,210	0.6	1.3
ORTHE–Orth Ch in Amer	1	23	NR	50	0.0	0.0
ORTHE–Rus Orth Moscow	1	50	NR	120	0.0	0.1
ORTHO–Coptic Orth Ch	1	310	NR	610	0.2	0.4
PENT–Assemb of God	7	494	198	713	0.2	0.4
PENT–Ch God (Cleve)	1	59	126	153	0.0	0.1
PENT–Ch of God Proph	1	NR	19	23	0.0	0.0
PENT–Int Foursq Gos	9	569	552	671	0.2	0.4
PENT–Un Pent Ch Intl	1	NR	NR	NR	-	-
PENT–United Holy Ch	1	NR	NR	NR	-	-
PENT–Vineyard	1	205	230	280	0.1	0.2
PRES–Free Pres NA	1	NR	NR	NR	-	-
PRES–Korean Pres Amer	1	NR	NR	NR	-	-
PRES–Orth Pres Ch	1	75	81	119	0.0	0.1
PRES–Presb Ch (USA)	6	354	1,063	1,292	0.3	0.7
PRES–Presb Ch Amer	2	93	64	80	0.0	0.0
Salvation Army	2	74	236	1,621	0.4	0.9
Sev Day Adv	4	176	305	352	0.1	0.2
Un C of Christ	20	1,864	5,125	6,229	1.6	3.6
Unit Univ	5	487	871	1,195	0.3	0.7
Zoroastrian	0	NR	NR	6	0.0	0.0
MERRIMACK	**111**	**8,200**	**14,419**	**45,317**	**30.9**	**100.0**
ANG/EPIS–Episcopal	6	728	2,481	2,769	1.9	6.1
Bahá'í	1	NR	80	80	0.1	0.2
BAPT–Amer Bapt USA	12	765	2,627	3,133	2.1	6.9
BAPT–Consrv Bapt	5	NR	NR	NR	-	-

NR–Not Reported   - Represents no adherents reported.   Percentages may not total 100 due to rounding.

Table 3: Religious Congregations by County and Group: 2010

Religious Group	Number of Congregations	Number of Attendees	Number of Communicant, Confirmed, or Full Members	Adherents		
				Number of Adherents	% of Total Pop.	% of Total Adh.
BAPT–Ref Bapt Ch	2	NR	NR	NR	-	-
BAPT–So Bapt Conv	4	171	153	182	0.1	0.4
BUDD–Vajrayana	1	NR	NR	17	0.0	0.0
Catholic	7	NR	NR	24,654	16.8	54.4
Ch Cr, Scientst	2	NR	NR	NR	-	-
Ch of Nazarene	3	236	222	261	0.2	0.6
CHR–Chr Chs & Chs Cr	1	NR	0	0	0.0	0.0
CHR–Chs of Christ	1	85	71	116	0.1	0.3
Christian Brethren	1	NR	NR	NR	-	-
CONG–Cong Chr, NA	2	NR	254	303	0.2	0.7
CONG–Consrv Cong Chr	2	150	142	169	0.1	0.4
Evan Cov Ch	1	0	0	0	0.0	0.0
Evan Free Ch	1	400	NR	400	0.3	0.9
FRND–Fr Gen Cf & Un Mtg	2	NR	74	88	0.1	0.2
HINDU–I/A Temples	1	NR	NR	25	0.0	0.1
Jehovah's Witness	4	NR	NR	NR	-	-
JUD–Reform	1	105	186	502	0.3	1.1
LDS–L-D Saints	2	NR	NR	1,026	0.7	2.3
LUTH–E.L.C.A.	1	81	242	369	0.3	0.8
METH–Un Methodist	6	485	1,406	2,293	1.6	5.1
Non-denom Chr Chs	6	1,770	1,693	2,213	1.5	4.9
ORTHE–Greek Orthodox	1	100	NR	530	0.4	1.2
ORTHE–Holy Orth in NA	1	39	NR	50	0.0	0.1
PENT–Assemb of God	2	203	91	219	0.1	0.5
PENT–Ch God (Cleve)	2	88	112	134	0.1	0.3
PENT–Int Foursq Gos	2	866	642	766	0.5	1.7
PRES–Presb Ch (USA)	1	127	265	316	0.2	0.7
PRES–Presb Ch Amer	1	49	44	68	0.0	0.2
Salvation Army	1	66	200	512	0.3	1.1
Sev Day Adv	1	78	135	155	0.1	0.3
Un C of Christ	21	1,353	2,952	3,520	2.4	7.8
Unit Univ	3	255	347	447	0.3	1.0
ROCKINGHAM	**184**	**11,352**	**20,654**	**114,915**	**38.9**	**100.0**
ANG/EPIS–Anglican NA	1	NR	NR	NR	-	-
ANG/EPIS–Episcopal	8	939	2,441	3,858	1.3	3.4
Bahá'í	1	NR	114	114	0.0	0.1
BAPT–Amer Bapt USA	19	1,350	3,211	3,859	1.3	3.4
BAPT–Consrv Bapt	3	NR	NR	NR	-	-
BAPT–Ref Bapt Ch	1	NR	NR	NR	-	-
BAPT–So Bapt Conv	9	896	800	961	0.3	0.8
BUDD–Mahayana	5	NR	NR	185	0.1	0.2
Calv Chpl	1	NR	NR	NR	-	-
Catholic	24	NR	NR	84,697	28.7	73.7
Ch Cr, Scientst	2	NR	NR	NR	-	-
Ch of Nazarene	2	106	88	170	0.1	0.1
CHR–Chr Chs & Chs Cr	3	NR	464	558	0.2	0.5
CHR–Chs of Christ	3	72	69	92	0.0	0.1
CONG–Cong Chr, NA	2	NR	328	394	0.1	0.3
CONG–Consrv Cong Chr	3	125	244	293	0.1	0.3
Evan Free Ch	3	83	NR	83	0.0	0.1
FRND–Fr Gen Cf & Un Mtg	2	NR	0	0	0.0	0.0
Jehovah's Witness	2	NR	NR	NR	-	-
JUD–Conserv	1	241	270	729	0.2	0.6
JUD–Reform	1	43	76	205	0.1	0.2
LDS–L-D Saints	3	NR	NR	1,430	0.5	1.2
LUTH–E.L.C.A.	3	423	840	1,003	0.3	0.9
LUTH–Luth-MO Synod	1	117	247	334	0.1	0.3
METH–Un Methodist	18	1,357	3,221	4,319	1.5	3.8
Non-denom Chr Chs	14	1,700	1,595	2,178	0.7	1.9
ORTHE–Greek Orthodox	1	100	NR	200	0.1	0.2
PENT–Assemb of God	7	1,091	545	1,679	0.6	1.5
PENT–Vineyard	1	72	93	112	0.0	0.1
PRES–Evan Presby Ch	1	NR	285	343	0.1	0.3
PRES–Presb Ch (USA)	2	228	313	376	0.1	0.3
PRES–Presb Ch Amer	2	109	107	129	0.0	0.1
REF–Christian Ref	1	30	27	32	0.0	0.0
Salvation Army	3	58	136	287	0.1	0.2
Sev Day Adv	2	102	178	205	0.1	0.2
Un C of Christ	24	1,758	4,379	5,263	1.8	4.6
Unit Univ	5	352	583	825	0.3	0.7
Zoroastrian	0	NR	NR	2	0.0	0.0

Religious Group	Number of Congregations	Number of Attendees	Number of Communicant, Confirmed, or Full Members	Adherents		
				Number of Adherents	% of Total Pop.	% of Total Adh.
STRAFFORD	**84**	**5,360**	**6,737**	**33,633**	**27.3**	**100.0**
ANG/EPIS–Anglican NA	1	NR	NR	NR	-	-
ANG/EPIS–Episcopal	2	187	456	605	0.5	1.8
Bahá'í	1	NR	73	73	0.1	0.2
BAPT–Amer Bapt USA	4	217	304	361	0.3	1.1
BAPT–Consrv Bapt	6	NR	NR	NR	-	-
BAPT–Free Will Bapt	1	NR	101	120	0.1	0.4
BAPT–So Bapt Conv	2	85	109	130	0.1	0.4
BUDD–Vajrayana	1	NR	NR	36	0.0	0.1
Catholic	11	NR	NR	22,112	18.0	65.7
CGOD–Ch God (Ander)	1	0	NR	0	0.0	0.0
Ch Cr, Scientst	1	NR	NR	NR	-	-
CHR–Chs of Christ	2	110	80	125	0.1	0.4
CONG–Consrv Cong Chr	2	140	119	141	0.1	0.4
Evan Free Ch	1	596	NR	596	0.5	1.8
FRND–Fr Gen Cf & Un Mtg	2	NR	88	105	0.1	0.3
HINDU–Trad Temples	1	NR	NR	40	0.0	0.1
Jehovah's Witness	3	NR	NR	NR	-	-
JUD–Reform	1	62	109	294	0.2	0.9
LDS–L-D Saints	2	NR	NR	669	0.5	2.0
METH–Un Methodist	3	429	1,144	1,763	1.4	5.2
Muslim Est	1	134	NR	308	0.3	0.9
Non-denom Chr Chs	6	1,225	1,291	1,535	1.2	4.6
ORTHE–Greek Orthodox	2	145	NR	575	0.5	1.7
PENT–Assemb of God	5	643	292	843	0.7	2.5
PENT–Ch God (Cleve)	2	35	30	36	0.0	0.1
PENT–Int Foursq Gos	1	82	81	96	0.1	0.3
PRES–Orth Pres Ch	1	36	28	40	0.0	0.1
PRES–Presb Ch (USA)	1	130	142	169	0.1	0.5
REF–Christian Ref	1	70	64	76	0.1	0.2
REF–Comm Ref Evan	1	NR	NR	NR	-	-
Salvation Army	1	23	61	204	0.2	0.6
Sev Day Adv	3	100	174	201	0.2	0.6
Un C of Christ	9	911	1,932	2,296	1.9	6.8
Unit Univ	1	0	59	84	0.1	0.2
Unity Ch	1	NR	NR	NR	-	-
SULLIVAN	**47**	**1,911**	**3,235**	**10,189**	**23.3**	**100.0**
ANG/EPIS–Anglican NA	1	NR	NR	NR	-	-
ANG/EPIS–Episcopal	4	112	226	321	0.7	3.2
Bahá'í	0	NR	11	11	0.0	0.1
BAPT–Amer Bapt USA	7	410	747	889	2.0	8.7
BAPT–Consrv Bapt	2	NR	NR	NR	-	-
BAPT–So Bapt Conv	1	15	19	23	0.1	0.2
Catholic	1	NR	NR	6,008	13.7	59.0
CONG–Cong Chr Add'l	1	NR	92	109	0.2	1.1
CONG–Cong Chr, NA	1	NR	75	89	0.2	0.9
Evan Free Ch	1	14	NR	14	0.0	0.1
FRND–Fr Gen Cf & Un Mtg	1	NR	19	23	0.1	0.2
LUTH–E.L.C.A.	1	40	72	91	0.2	0.9
METH–Un Methodist	6	177	523	655	1.5	6.4
New Apost Ch	1	NR	NR	NR	-	-
Non-denom Chr Chs	4	350	395	473	1.1	4.6
ORTHE–Greek Orthodox	1	24	NR	100	0.2	1.0
ORTHE–Orth Ch in Amer	1	40	NR	85	0.2	0.8
PENT–Assemb of God	1	52	19	70	0.2	0.7
PENT–Int Foursq Gos	1	246	147	175	0.4	1.7
PENT–Intl Pent Holiness	1	13	18	21	0.0	0.2
Sev Day Adv	2	36	63	73	0.2	0.7
Un C of Christ	7	382	791	941	2.2	9.2
Unit Univ	1	0	18	18	0.0	0.2
NEW JERSEY	**6,114**	**640,935**	**841,292**	**4,809,520**	**54.7**	**100.0**
ATLANTIC	**231**	**21,024**	**25,603**	**117,189**	**42.7**	**100.0**
ANG/EPIS–Anglican NA	1	NR	NR	NR	-	-
ANG/EPIS–Episcopal	7	501	814	1,062	0.4	0.9
Bahá'í	0	NR	47	47	0.0	0.0
BAPT–Amer Bapt USA	2	275	633	767	0.3	0.7
BAPT–NBC USA	3	2,500	3,300	3,999	1.5	3.4
BAPT–Prog NBC	1	0	150	182	0.1	0.2
BAPT–Reg Bapt Gen As	3	NR	NR	NR	-	-

NR–Not Reported - Represents no adherents reported. Percentages may not total 100 due to rounding.

Table 3: Religious Congregations by County and Group: 2010

Religious Group	Number of Congregations	Number of Attendees	Number of Communicant, Confirmed, or Full Members	Adherents: Number of Adherents	Adherents: % of Total Pop.	Adherents: % of Total Adh.
BAPT–So Bapt Conv	5	220	249	302	0.1	0.3
Calv Chpl	1	NR	NR	NR	-	-
Catholic	23	NR	NR	65,867	24.0	56.2
CGOD–Ch God (Ander)	1	45	NR	45	0.0	0.0
Ch Cr, Scientst	1	NR	NR	NR	-	-
Ch of Nazarene	1	61	103	148	0.1	0.1
Chr & Miss Al	4	420	298	601	0.2	0.5
CHR–Chr Ch (Disc)	1	0	0	0	0.0	0.0
CHR–Chr Chs & Chs Cr	2	NR	0	0	0.0	0.0
CHR–Chs of Christ	2	70	70	85	0.0	0.1
Christian Brethren	1	NR	NR	NR	-	-
CONG–Cong Chr, NA	1	NR	40	48	0.0	0.0
Evan Free Ch	1	550	NR	550	0.2	0.5
FRND–Fr Gen Cf	1	NR	23	28	0.0	0.0
HINDU–I/A Temples	1	NR	NR	1,742	0.6	1.5
HINDU–Post Ren	2	NR	NR	41	0.0	0.0
HINDU–Trad Temples	1	NR	NR	230	0.1	0.2
Ind Fund Churches	1	NR	NR	NR	-	-
Jehovah's Witness	5	NR	NR	NR	-	-
JUD–Conserv	3	732	821	2,217	0.8	1.9
JUD–Orth	4	310	150	430	0.2	0.4
JUD–Reconst	1	25	32	86	0.0	0.1
JUD–Reform	1	247	435	1,174	0.4	1.0
LDS–L-D Saints	2	NR	NR	1,037	0.4	0.9
LUTH–E.L.C.A.	7	682	1,369	3,175	1.2	2.7
LUTH–Luth–MO Synod	1	87	125	150	0.1	0.1
LUTH–Nor Amer Luth C	1	NR	NR	NR	-	-
METH–AME	6	300	1,000	1,212	0.4	1.0
METH–AME Zion	3	0	550	667	0.2	0.6
METH–Un Methodist	27	2,119	3,612	5,768	2.1	4.9
METH–Wesleyan	3	206	174	268	0.1	0.2
MORAV–Morav Ch-North	1	83	278	371	0.1	0.3
Muslim Est	4	1,860	NR	9,422	3.4	8.0
New Apost Ch	1	NR	NR	NR	-	-
Non-denom Chr Chs	32	5,815	6,769	7,570	2.8	6.5
ORTHE–Greek Orthodox	2	310	NR	1,420	0.5	1.2
ORTHE–Orth Ch in Amer	2	31	NR	60	0.0	0.1
ORTHO–Coptic Orth Ch	1	25	NR	40	0.0	0.0
PENT–Assemb of God	18	2,031	1,529	2,615	1.0	2.2
PENT–Ch God (Cleve)	2	110	64	78	0.0	0.1
PENT–Ch Lord Jesus Apos	1	NR	NR	NR	-	-
PENT–Ch of God Proph	3	NR	87	105	0.0	0.1
PENT–COGIC	3	5	215	261	0.1	0.2
PENT–Elim	1	NR	NR	NR	-	-
PENT–Fire Bapt Hol Ch	1	NR	NR	NR	-	-
PENT–Full Gosp Bapt	1	NR	NR	NR	-	-
PENT–I F Chr Assmbl	1	NR	NR	NR	-	-
PENT–Int Foursq Gos	1	133	111	135	0.0	0.1
PENT–Un Pent Ch Intl	4	NR	NR	NR	-	-
PENT–United Holy Ch	1	NR	NR	NR	-	-
PRES–Korean Pres Amer	1	NR	NR	NR	-	-
PRES–Presb Ch (USA)	8	521	1,051	1,274	0.5	1.1
PRES–Presb Ch Amer	2	14	18	19	0.0	0.0
Salvation Army	1	41	96	236	0.1	0.2
Sev Day Adv	5	377	655	754	0.3	0.6
Un C of Christ	2	230	625	757	0.3	0.6
Unit Univ	1	88	110	144	0.1	0.1
BERGEN	**681**	**66,734**	**80,897**	**583,426**	**64.5**	**100.0**
ANG/EPIS–Episcopal	34	2,404	6,003	8,128	0.9	1.4
Bahá'í	2	NR	232	232	0.0	0.0
BAPT–Amer Bapt USA	21	1,464	2,647	3,191	0.4	0.5
BAPT–Consrv Bapt	2	NR	NR	NR	-	-
BAPT–NBC USA	6	655	4,100	4,942	0.5	0.8
BAPT–Ref Bapt Ch	2	NR	NR	NR	-	-
BAPT–Reg Bapt Gen As	3	NR	NR	NR	-	-
BAPT–So Bapt Conv	14	901	1,032	1,244	0.1	0.2
BUDD–Mahayana	6	NR	NR	1,114	0.1	0.2
BUDD–Vajrayana	1	NR	NR	25	0.0	0.0
Calv Chpl	1	NR	NR	NR	-	-
Catholic	79	NR	NR	430,007	47.5	73.7
CGOD–Ch God (Ander)	1	60	NR	60	0.0	0.0
Ch Cr, Scientst	3	NR	NR	NR	-	-
Ch of Nazarene	7	651	984	1,041	0.1	0.2
Chr & Miss Al	15	1,262	1,285	1,529	0.2	0.3
CHR–Chr Chs & Chs Cr	1	NR	0	0	0.0	0.0
CHR–Chs of Christ	3	145	151	195	0.0	0.0
Christian Brethren	4	NR	NR	NR	-	-
Evan Cov Ch	1	409	271	532	0.1	0.1
Evan Free Ch	6	841	NR	841	0.1	0.1
FRND–Fr Gen Cf & Un Mtg	1	NR	69	83	0.0	0.0
Grace Gosp Fel	1	NR	NR	NR	-	-
HINDU–I/A Temples	4	NR	NR	1,800	0.2	0.3
HINDU–Post Ren	5	NR	NR	80	0.0	0.0
HINDU–Renaiss	1	NR	NR	12	0.0	0.0
HINDU–Trad Temples	3	NR	NR	5,150	0.6	0.9
Ind Fund Churches	3	NR	NR	NR	-	-
Int Cou Comm Ch	1	NR	NR	NR	-	-
Jehovah's Witness	10	NR	NR	NR	-	-
JUD–Conserv	13	3,531	3,963	10,700	1.2	1.8
JUD–Orth	44	13,320	5,000	18,500	2.0	3.2
JUD–Reconst	1	42	54	146	0.0	0.0
JUD–Reform	9	1,843	3,250	8,775	1.0	1.5
LDS–Comm of Christ	1	NR	161	161	0.0	0.0
LDS–L-D Saints	4	NR	NR	1,430	0.2	0.2
LUTH–Ch of Luth Br	2	123	118	271	0.0	0.0
LUTH–E.L.C.A.	28	1,592	5,146	6,360	0.7	1.1
LUTH–Luth–MO Synod	12	1,036	2,839	3,605	0.4	0.6
METH–AME	1	0	150	181	0.0	0.0
METH–AME Zion	6	233	905	1,091	0.1	0.2
METH–Un Methodist	35	3,888	6,644	8,128	0.9	1.4
Muslim Est	7	2,439	NR	4,799	0.5	0.8
New Apost Ch	1	NR	NR	NR	-	-
Non-denom Chr Chs	58	11,216	12,447	14,717	1.6	2.5
OCATH–Pol Natl Cath	1	NR	NR	NR	-	-
ORTHE–Ant Orth of NA	1	150	NR	450	0.0	0.1
ORTHE–Greek Orthodox	4	1,350	NR	4,850	0.5	0.8
ORTHE–Orth Ch in Amer	2	160	NR	219	0.0	0.0
ORTHE–Rus Orth Moscow	1	165	NR	800	0.1	0.1
ORTHO–Armen Ap Cilic	1	200	NR	3,000	0.3	0.5
ORTHO–Armen Ap Etchm	2	225	NR	1,240	0.1	0.2
ORTHO–Coptic Orth Ch	1	175	NR	650	0.1	0.1
ORTHO–Ethiopian Orth	1	NR	NR	NR	-	-
ORTHO–Malan Dioc Am	2	240	NR	360	0.0	0.1
ORTHO–Malan Syr Orth	1	75	NR	144	0.0	0.0
ORTHO–Syrian Orth Ch	4	850	NR	2,660	0.3	0.5
PENT–Assemb of God	28	3,169	2,031	4,124	0.5	0.7
PENT–Ch God (Cleve)	6	266	227	274	0.0	0.0
PENT–Ch of God Proph	2	NR	128	154	0.0	0.0
PENT–COGIC	3	0	60	72	0.0	0.0
PENT–Fire Bapt Hol Ch	1	NR	NR	NR	-	-
PENT–United Holy Ch	1	NR	NR	NR	-	-
PENT–Vineyard	2	570	765	922	0.1	0.2
PRES–As Ref Pres Ch	1	NR	52	63	0.0	0.0
PRES–Kor Pres Abroad	14	NR	NR	NR	-	-
PRES–Korean Amer Pres	8	NR	NR	NR	-	-
PRES–Korean Pres Amer	17	NR	NR	NR	-	-
PRES–Orth Pres Ch	1	50	58	81	0.0	0.0
PRES–Presb Ch (USA)	42	5,163	9,348	11,269	1.2	1.9
PRES–Presb Ch Amer	3	325	220	309	0.0	0.1
PRES–Ref Pres of NA	1	27	30	34	0.0	0.0
REF–Christian Ref	6	900	1,509	1,819	0.2	0.3
REF–Hung Ref Add'l	1	NR	NR	NR	-	-
REF–Ref Ch in Am	37	3,144	6,028	6,989	0.8	1.2
Salvation Army	2	72	122	299	0.0	0.1
Sev Day Adv	6	652	1,134	1,305	0.1	0.2
Sikh	1	NR	NR	NR	-	-
Un C of Christ	10	468	1,215	1,465	0.2	0.3
Unit Univ	3	283	519	722	0.1	0.1
Unity Ch	1	NR	NR	NR	-	-
Zoroastrian	0	NR	NR	82	0.0	0.0
BURLINGTON	**318**	**28,947**	**43,449**	**186,274**	**41.5**	**100.0**
ANG/EPIS–Anglican NA	1	NR	NR	NR	-	-
ANG/EPIS–Episcopal	17	1,540	3,453	4,267	1.0	2.3
Bahá'í	0	NR	106	106	0.0	0.1
BAPT–Amer Bapt USA	17	1,669	2,376	2,880	0.6	1.5
BAPT–NBC USA	7	1,635	3,852	4,670	1.0	2.5

NR–Not Reported   - Represents no adherents reported.   Percentages may not total 100 due to rounding.

Table 3: Religious Congregations by County and Group: 2010

Religious Group	Number of Congregations	Number of Attendees	Number of Communicant, Confirmed, or Full Members	Adherents: Number of Adherents	Adherents: % of Total Pop.	Adherents: % of Total Adh.
BAPT–Ref Bapt Ch	1	NR	NR	NR	-	-
BAPT–Reg Bapt Gen As	5	NR	NR	NR	-	-
BAPT–So Bapt Conv	7	704	1,157	1,403	0.3	0.8
BUDD–Vajrayana	1	NR	NR	72	0.0	0.0
Calv Chpl	2	NR	NR	NR	-	-
Catholic	22	NR	NR	111,334	24.8	59.8
CGOD–Ch God (Ander)	1	0	NR	0	0.0	0.0
Ch Cr, Scientst	1	NR	NR	NR	-	-
Ch of Nazarene	1	71	64	131	0.0	0.1
Chr & Miss Al	3	1,849	1,721	2,587	0.6	1.4
CHR–Chr Ch (Disc)	3	0	0	0	0.0	0.0
CHR–Chs of Christ	2	258	240	320	0.1	0.2
Evan Free Ch	1	100	NR	100	0.0	0.1
FRND–Fr Gen Cf	11	NR	841	1,019	0.2	0.5
HINDU–I/A Temples	1	NR	NR	350	0.1	0.2
HINDU–Post Ren	2	NR	NR	75	0.0	0.0
Ind Fund Churches	1	NR	NR	NR	-	-
Int Cou Comm Ch	1	NR	NR	NR	-	-
Jehovah's Witness	6	NR	NR	NR	-	-
JUD–Conserv	2	303	340	918	0.2	0.5
JUD–Orth	1	43	50	60	0.0	0.0
JUD–Reconst	1	70	89	240	0.1	0.1
JUD–Reform	1	287	507	1,369	0.3	0.7
LDS–L-D Saints	5	NR	NR	2,953	0.7	1.6
LUTH–Ch of Luth Br	1	74	56	179	0.0	0.1
LUTH–E.L.C.A.	10	1,620	3,803	6,149	1.4	3.3
LUTH–Luth-MO Synod	3	257	390	625	0.1	0.3
METH–AME	13	500	1,820	2,206	0.5	1.2
METH–AME Zion	2	0	300	364	0.1	0.2
METH–C.M.E.	1	35	52	63	0.0	0.0
METH–Un Methodist	37	3,431	6,601	9,806	2.2	5.3
METH–Wesleyan	2	109	48	142	0.0	0.1
MORAV–Morav Ch-North	2	122	309	391	0.1	0.2
Muslim Est	6	2,139	NR	7,770	1.7	4.2
New Apost Ch	1	NR	NR	NR	-	-
Non-denom Chr Chs	39	6,042	8,267	9,153	2.0	4.9
ORTHE–Orth Ch in Amer	1	70	NR	120	0.0	0.1
ORTHO–Coptic Orth Ch	1	200	NR	500	0.1	0.3
PENT–Assemb of God	18	3,309	2,110	7,979	1.8	4.3
PENT–Ch God (Cleve)	4	246	247	299	0.1	0.2
PENT–Ch Lord Jesus Apos	2	NR	NR	NR	-	-
PENT–COGIC	2	0	0	0	0.0	0.0
PENT–Elim	2	NR	NR	NR	-	-
PENT–Fire Bapt Hol Ch	1	NR	NR	NR	-	-
PENT–Full Gosp Bapt	3	NR	NR	NR	-	-
PENT–I F Chr Assmbl	1	NR	NR	NR	-	-
PENT–Un Pent Ch Intl	3	NR	NR	NR	-	-
PENT–United Holy Ch	2	NR	NR	NR	-	-
PRES–AmPres	1	NR	NR	NR	-	-
PRES–Kor Pres Abroad	1	NR	NR	NR	-	-
PRES–Korean Pres Amer	1	NR	NR	NR	-	-
PRES–Orth Pres Ch	1	44	35	51	0.0	0.0
PRES–Presb Ch (USA)	17	1,688	3,771	4,571	1.0	2.5
PRES–Presb Ch Amer	3	212	198	267	0.1	0.1
REF–Christian Ref	1	20	17	21	0.0	0.0
REF–Hung Ref Add'l	1	NR	NR	NR	-	-
Sev Day Adv	5	247	429	494	0.1	0.3
Sikh	2	NR	NR	NR	-	-
Un C of Christ	2	20	155	188	0.0	0.1
Unit Univ	1	33	45	55	0.0	0.0
Unity Ch	1	NR	NR	NR	-	-
Zoroastrian	0	NR	NR	27	0.0	0.0
CAMDEN	**372**	**35,038**	**51,512**	**275,475**	**53.6**	**100.0**
ANG/EPIS–Episcopal	17	1,365	2,577	4,813	0.9	1.7
Bahá'í	1	NR	62	62	0.0	0.0
BAPT–Amer Bapt USA	19	2,704	5,525	6,786	1.3	2.5
BAPT–Consrv Bapt	3	NR	NR	NR	-	-
BAPT–NBC USA	5	880	1,735	2,131	0.4	0.8
BAPT–Prog NBC	1	400	500	614	0.1	0.2
BAPT–Ref Bapt Ch	1	NR	NR	NR	-	-
BAPT–Reg Bapt Gen As	5	NR	NR	NR	-	-
BAPT–So Bapt Conv	7	465	670	823	0.2	0.3
BRETH–Breth in Chr	1	NR	NR	NR	-	-
BUDD–Mahayana	6	NR	NR	3,206	0.6	1.2
BUDD–Theravada	1	NR	NR	396	0.1	0.1
Calv Chpl	1	NR	NR	NR	-	-
Catholic	55	NR	NR	180,343	35.1	65.5
CGOD–Ch God (Ander)	3	144	NR	144	0.0	0.1
Ch Cr, Scientst	2	NR	NR	NR	-	-
Ch of Nazarene	1	69	48	173	0.0	0.1
Chr & Miss Al	5	742	376	981	0.2	0.4
CHR–Chs of Christ	3	228	237	291	0.1	0.1
Christian Brethren	1	NR	NR	NR	-	-
Evan Free Ch	1	60	NR	60	0.0	0.0
FRND–Fr Gen Cf	2	NR	271	333	0.1	0.1
HINDU–I/A Temples	2	NR	NR	1,992	0.4	0.7
HINDU–Post Ren	2	NR	NR	41	0.0	0.0
Ind Fund Churches	4	NR	NR	NR	-	-
Jain	1	NR	NR	NR	-	-
Jehovah's Witness	6	NR	NR	NR	-	-
JUD–Conserv	2	1,518	1,704	4,601	0.9	1.7
JUD–Orth	4	842	350	1,170	0.2	0.4
JUD–Reform	2	978	1,724	4,655	0.9	1.7
LDS–L-D Saints	2	NR	NR	593	0.1	0.2
LUTH–E.L.C.A.	16	1,489	4,301	6,584	1.3	2.4
LUTH–Luth-MO Synod	2	244	558	708	0.1	0.3
MENN–Mennonite USA	3	120	99	122	0.0	0.0
METH–AME	14	305	2,057	2,526	0.5	0.9
METH–AME Zion	4	80	422	518	0.1	0.2
METH–Un Methodist	47	4,857	8,290	13,954	2.7	5.1
METH–Wesleyan	2	51	40	66	0.0	0.0
Muslim Est	7	2,599	NR	9,970	1.9	3.6
Non-denom Chr Chs	47	8,290	10,294	11,379	2.2	4.1
ORTHE–Greek Orthodox	1	500	NR	2,500	0.5	0.9
PENT–Assemb of God	15	2,833	2,087	3,182	0.6	1.2
PENT–Ch God (Cleve)	3	109	157	193	0.0	0.1
PENT–Ch Lord Jesus Apos	2	NR	NR	NR	-	-
PENT–Ch of God Proph	1	NR	48	59	0.0	0.0
PENT–COGIC	6	190	925	1,136	0.2	0.4
PENT–Elim	1	NR	NR	NR	-	-
PENT–Fire Bapt Hol Ch	2	NR	NR	NR	-	-
PENT–Int Foursq Gos	1	77	103	127	0.0	0.0
PRES–Evan Presby Ch	2	NR	206	253	0.0	0.1
PRES–Kor Pres Abroad	1	NR	NR	NR	-	-
PRES–Korean Amer Pres	1	NR	NR	NR	-	-
PRES–Korean Pres Amer	2	NR	NR	NR	-	-
PRES–Orth Pres Ch	4	282	289	387	0.1	0.1
PRES–Presb Ch (USA)	14	1,550	4,110	5,048	1.0	1.8
PRES–Presb Ch Amer	1	260	319	413	0.1	0.1
Salvation Army	1	35	92	510	0.1	0.2
Sev Day Adv	5	588	1,023	1,177	0.2	0.4
Unit Univ	1	184	313	413	0.1	0.1
Zoroastrian	0	NR	NR	42	0.0	0.0
CAPE MAY	**101**	**8,931**	**11,573**	**53,136**	**54.6**	**100.0**
ANG/EPIS–Episcopal	6	592	930	1,302	1.3	2.5
Bahá'í	0	NR	28	28	0.0	0.1
BAPT–Amer Bapt USA	5	392	679	788	0.8	1.5
BAPT–NBC USA	3	185	200	232	0.2	0.4
BAPT–So Bapt Conv	2	29	37	43	0.0	0.1
Calv Chpl	1	NR	NR	NR	-	-
Catholic	14	NR	NR	35,541	36.5	66.9
Ch of Nazarene	1	302	231	430	0.4	0.8
Chr & Miss Al	1	723	153	1,500	1.5	2.8
CHR–Chs of Christ	1	54	35	45	0.0	0.1
FRND–Fr Gen Cf	1	NR	45	52	0.1	0.1
HINDU–Post Ren	1	NR	NR	20	0.0	0.0
Jehovah's Witness	2	NR	NR	NR	-	-
LDS–L-D Saints	1	NR	NR	291	0.3	0.5
LUTH–E.L.C.A.	6	552	1,529	2,155	2.2	4.1
MENN–Bible Flwshp	1	32	NR	43	0.0	0.1
METH–AME	4	15	420	487	0.5	0.9
METH–Un Methodist	23	1,952	3,389	4,408	4.5	8.3
Non-denom Chr Chs	12	3,040	2,855	3,862	4.0	7.3
ORTHE–Greek Orthodox	1	50	NR	500	0.5	0.9
PENT–Assemb of God	4	358	271	476	0.5	0.9
PRES–Orth Pres Ch	2	88	83	125	0.1	0.2

NR–Not Reported - Represents no adherents reported. Percentages may not total 100 due to rounding.

Table 3: Religious Congregations by County and Group: 2010

Religious Group	Number of Congregations	Number of Attendees	Number of Communicant, Confirmed, or Full Members	Adherents: Number of Adherents	Adherents: % of Total Pop.	Adherents: % of Total Adh.
PRES–Presb Ch (USA)	4	373	440	510	0.5	1.0
PRES–Presb Ch Amer	2	92	72	95	0.1	0.2
Sev Day Adv	3	102	176	203	0.2	0.4
CUMBERLAND	**184**	**13,352**	**18,878**	**54,912**	**35.0**	**100.0**
ANG/EPIS–Anglican NA	1	NR	NR	NR	-	-
ANG/EPIS–Episcopal	4	128	330	330	0.2	0.6
Bahá'í	0	NR	21	21	0.0	0.0
BAPT–Amer Bapt USA	8	758	1,756	2,158	1.4	3.9
BAPT–Free Will Bapt	2	NR	80	98	0.1	0.2
BAPT–NBC USA	1	0	100	123	0.1	0.2
BAPT–Reg Bapt Gen As	1	NR	NR	NR	-	-
BAPT–S-D Baptist Gen Con	2	148	383	471	0.3	0.9
BAPT–So Bapt Conv	3	210	261	321	0.2	0.6
BRETH–Breth in Chr	1	NR	NR	NR	-	-
BUDD–Mahayana	1	NR	NR	1,250	0.8	2.3
Calv Chpl	1	NR	NR	NR	-	-
Catholic	12	NR	NR	23,944	15.3	43.6
Ch of Nazarene	4	721	682	1,302	0.8	2.4
Chr & Miss Al	1	620	208	765	0.5	1.4
CHR–Chr Chs & Chs Cr	1	NR	75	92	0.1	0.2
FRND–Fr Gen Cf	2	NR	54	66	0.0	0.1
Ind Fund Churches	2	NR	NR	NR	-	-
Jehovah's Witness	5	NR	NR	NR	-	-
JUD–Conserv	1	168	189	510	0.3	0.9
JUD–Orth	1	43	50	60	0.0	0.1
JUD–Reform	1	46	82	221	0.1	0.4
LDS–L-D Saints	3	NR	NR	1,042	0.7	1.9
LUTH–E.L.C.A.	3	265	894	1,088	0.7	2.0
LUTH–Luth-MO Synod	1	60	188	253	0.2	0.5
MENN–Mennonite USA	1	45	65	80	0.1	0.1
METH–AME	6	120	810	995	0.6	1.8
METH–AME Zion	3	0	300	369	0.2	0.7
METH–Un Methodist	35	2,155	3,727	5,888	3.8	10.7
METH–Wesleyan	4	266	175	347	0.2	0.6
Muslim Est	1	419	NR	1,474	0.9	2.7
Non-denom Chr Chs	21	2,985	3,849	4,228	2.7	7.7
ORTHE–Greek Orthodox	1	115	NR	235	0.1	0.4
ORTHE–Rus Orth Abroad	2	70	NR	120	0.1	0.2
ORTHE–Ukrainian Orth	1	35	NR	85	0.1	0.2
PENT–Assemb of God	9	1,836	1,100	2,700	1.7	4.9
PENT–Ch God (Cleve)	7	358	303	372	0.2	0.7
PENT–Ch Lord Jesus Apos	2	NR	NR	NR	-	-
PENT–Ch of God Proph	1	NR	12	15	0.0	0.0
PENT–COGIC	2	75	300	369	0.2	0.7
PENT–Fire Bapt Hol Ch	2	NR	NR	NR	-	-
PENT–Un Pent Ch Intl	3	NR	NR	NR	-	-
PRES–Orth Pres Ch	3	211	168	216	0.1	0.4
PRES–Presb Ch (USA)	9	469	988	1,214	0.8	2.2
PRES–Presb Ch Amer	1	90	122	148	0.1	0.3
Salvation Army	2	102	155	273	0.2	0.5
Sev Day Adv	6	834	1,451	1,669	1.1	3.0
ESSEX	**608**	**69,625**	**99,714**	**444,696**	**56.7**	**100.0**
ANG/EPIS–Anglican NA	1	NR	NR	NR	-	-
ANG/EPIS–Episcopal	22	2,172	6,047	7,240	0.9	1.6
Bahá'í	3	NR	220	220	0.0	0.0
BAPT–Amer Bapt USA	50	6,029	13,400	16,585	2.1	3.7
BAPT–Consrv Bapt	4	NR	NR	NR	-	-
BAPT–Converge/BGC	2	150	NR	180	0.0	0.0
BAPT–N Am Bapt Conf	1	NR	35	43	0.0	0.0
BAPT–Natl Mis Bapt Conv	4	100	1,250	1,547	0.2	0.3
BAPT–NBC Amer	2	375	580	718	0.1	0.2
BAPT–NBC USA	33	7,410	15,446	19,117	2.4	4.3
BAPT–Prog NBC	3	170	550	681	0.1	0.2
BAPT–Ref Bapt Ch	1	NR	NR	NR	-	-
BAPT–Reg Bapt Gen As	1	NR	NR	NR	-	-
BAPT–So Bapt Conv	16	1,543	1,640	2,030	0.3	0.5
BUDD–Mahayana	5	NR	NR	8,762	1.1	2.0
BUDD–Vajrayana	1	NR	NR	457	0.1	0.1
Calv Chpl	1	NR	NR	NR	-	-
Catholic	65	NR	NR	261,966	33.4	58.9
CGOD–Ch God (Ander)	1	60	NR	60	0.0	0.0
Ch Cr, Scientst	1	NR	NR	NR	-	-
Ch of Nazarene	4	487	607	633	0.1	0.1
Chr & Miss Al	7	644	551	847	0.1	0.2
CHR–Chr Ch (Disc)	10	75	140	173	0.0	0.0
CHR–Chr Chs & Chs Cr	1	NR	0	0	0.0	0.0
CHR–Chs of Christ	6	999	1,212	1,437	0.2	0.3
Christian Brethren	1	NR	NR	NR	-	-
Evan Cov Ch	2	61	120	79	0.0	0.0
Evan Free Ch	3	370	NR	370	0.0	0.1
FRND–Fr Gen Cf & Un Mtg	1	NR	111	137	0.0	0.0
HINDU–I/A Temples	1	NR	NR	50	0.0	0.0
HINDU–Post Ren	1	NR	NR	25	0.0	0.0
Int Cou Comm Ch	1	NR	NR	NR	-	-
Jain	1	NR	NR	NR	-	-
Jehovah's Witness	15	NR	NR	NR	-	-
JUD–Conserv	9	3,372	3,785	10,220	1.3	2.3
JUD–Orth	10	2,880	1,200	4,000	0.5	0.9
JUD–Reconst	1	186	238	643	0.1	0.1
JUD–Reform	5	1,791	3,159	8,529	1.1	1.9
LDS–L-D Saints	7	NR	NR	4,522	0.6	1.0
LUTH–E.L.C.A.	6	314	859	1,069	0.1	0.2
LUTH–Luth-MO Synod	5	265	525	658	0.1	0.1
MENN–Bible Flwshp	1	52	NR	70	0.0	0.0
METH–AME	15	4,515	10,105	12,507	1.6	2.8
METH–AME Zion	3	200	650	804	0.1	0.2
METH–C.M.E.	1	250	565	699	0.1	0.2
METH–Free Methodist	2	128	136	136	0.0	0.0
METH–Un Methodist	23	1,645	3,348	4,227	0.5	1.0
METH–Wesleyan	1	85	65	111	0.0	0.0
Missionary Ch	1	110	97	110	0.0	0.0
MJEW–Assoc Mes Cong	1	NR	NR	NR	-	-
Muslim Est	17	8,150	NR	23,743	3.0	5.3
Non-denom Chr Chs	44	8,830	9,246	12,350	1.6	2.8
ORTHE–Greek Orthodox	1	175	NR	2,000	0.3	0.4
ORTHE–Macedonian Orth	1	125	NR	2,000	0.3	0.4
ORTHE–Rus Orth Abroad	2	70	NR	110	0.0	0.0
ORTHE–Ukrainian Orth	2	57	NR	240	0.0	0.1
ORTHO–Armen Ap Etchm	1	225	NR	600	0.1	0.1
ORTHO–Coptic Orth Ch	2	800	NR	1,010	0.1	0.2
ORTHO–Ethiopian Orth	1	NR	NR	NR	-	-
ORTHO–Malan Dioc Am	1	90	NR	120	0.0	0.0
ORTHO–Malan Syr Orth	1	55	NR	108	0.0	0.0
PENT–Assemb of God	32	3,820	2,832	4,681	0.6	1.1
PENT–Ch God (Cleve)	16	1,758	1,977	2,447	0.3	0.6
PENT–Ch Lord Jesus Apos	3	NR	NR	NR	-	-
PENT–Ch of God by Faith	1	NR	NR	NR	-	-
PENT–Ch of God Proph	3	NR	120	149	0.0	0.0
PENT–COGIC	10	1,025	2,112	2,614	0.3	0.6
PENT–Full Gosp Bapt	4	NR	NR	NR	-	-
PENT–I F Chr Assmbl	1	NR	NR	NR	-	-
PENT–Int Foursq Gos	1	308	360	446	0.1	0.1
PENT–Pent Ch of God	1	70	NR	109	0.0	0.0
PENT–Un Pent Ch Intl	2	NR	NR	NR	-	-
PENT–United Holy Ch	10	NR	NR	NR	-	-
PRES–Kor Pres Abroad	1	NR	NR	NR	-	-
PRES–Korean Amer Pres	1	NR	NR	NR	-	-
PRES–Presb Ch (USA)	38	2,168	6,931	8,578	1.1	1.9
PRES–Presb Ch Amer	4	475	374	517	0.1	0.1
REF–Ref Ch in Am	9	330	402	559	0.1	0.1
Salvation Army	5	387	501	814	0.1	0.2
Sev Day Adv	17	3,194	5,554	6,389	0.8	1.4
Un C of Christ	11	847	2,239	2,771	0.4	0.6
Unit Univ	2	228	425	669	0.1	0.2
Unity Ch	1	NR	NR	NR	-	-
Zoroastrian	0	NR	NR	10	0.0	0.0
GLOUCESTER	**216**	**37,050**	**47,406**	**139,398**	**48.4**	**100.0**
ANG/EPIS–Episcopal	11	1,025	2,588	3,521	1.2	2.5
Bahá'í	0	NR	54	54	0.0	0.0
BAPT–Amer Bapt Assn	1	NR	25	31	0.0	0.0
BAPT–Amer Bapt USA	7	324	830	1,018	0.4	0.7
BAPT–Consrv Bapt	5	NR	NR	NR	-	-
BAPT–NBC USA	4	9,180	8,495	10,419	3.6	7.5
BAPT–Reg Bapt Gen As	2	NR	NR	NR	-	-

NR–Not Reported   - Represents no adherents reported.   Percentages may not total 100 due to rounding.

Table 3: Religious Congregations by County and Group: 2010

Religious Group	Number of Congregations	Number of Attendees	Number of Communicant, Confirmed, or Full Members	Adherents: Number of Adherents	Adherents: % of Total Pop.	Adherents: % of Total Adh.
BAPT–So Bapt Conv	4	8,576	12,062	14,793	5.1	10.6
BUDD–Mahayana	1	NR	NR	102	0.0	0.1
Catholic	21	NR	NR	75,218	26.1	54.0
Ch of Nazarene	1	59	81	300	0.1	0.2
Chr & Miss Al	3	424	193	706	0.2	0.5
CHR–Chr Chs & Chs Cr	1	NR	250	307	0.1	0.2
CHR–Chs of Christ	2	328	295	337	0.1	0.2
Evan Free Ch	2	475	NR	475	0.2	0.3
FRND–Fr Gen Cf	3	NR	154	189	0.1	0.1
Ind Fund Churches	2	NR	NR	NR	-	-
Jehovah's Witness	4	NR	NR	NR	-	-
JUD–Orth	1	43	50	60	0.0	0.0
LDS–Comm of Christ	1	NR	161	161	0.1	0.1
LDS–L-D Saints	2	NR	NR	660	0.2	0.5
LUTH–E.L.C.A.	4	469	1,165	1,886	0.7	1.4
MENN–Bible Flwshp	1	110	NR	149	0.1	0.1
METH–AME	9	155	1,100	1,349	0.5	1.0
METH–Un Methodist	45	4,349	6,808	10,154	3.5	7.3
METH–Wesleyan	1	22	27	29	0.0	0.0
Muslim Est	1	419	NR	1,474	0.5	1.1
Nat Spirit Asso	1	NR	NR	NR	-	-
Non-denom Chr Chs	33	8,030	9,567	10,701	3.7	7.7
PENT–Assemb of God	14	1,751	935	2,198	0.8	1.6
PENT–Ch God (Cleve)	1	45	40	49	0.0	0.0
PENT–COGIC	3	0	270	331	0.1	0.2
PENT–Un Pent Ch Intl	2	NR	NR	NR	-	-
PRES–Orth Pres Ch	1	29	33	40	0.0	0.0
PRES–Presb Ch (USA)	13	888	1,639	2,010	0.7	1.4
PRES–Presb Ch Amer	2	27	20	24	0.0	0.0
Sev Day Adv	5	288	501	576	0.2	0.4
Sikh	1	NR	NR	NR	-	-
Un C of Christ	1	34	63	77	0.0	0.1
HUDSON	**380**	**31,117**	**36,845**	**370,621**	**58.4**	**100.0**
ANG/EPIS–Anglican NA	1	NR	NR	NR	-	-
ANG/EPIS–Episcopal	12	721	1,729	1,864	0.3	0.5
Bahá'í	1	NR	109	109	0.0	0.0
BAPT–Amer Bapt USA	18	2,023	4,299	5,126	0.8	1.4
BAPT–Consrv Bapt	1	NR	NR	NR	-	-
BAPT–N Am Bapt Conf	1	NR	82	98	0.0	0.0
BAPT–NBC USA	11	2,000	8,621	10,280	1.6	2.8
BAPT–Ref Bapt Ch	1	NR	NR	NR	-	-
BAPT–So Bapt Conv	13	1,965	2,153	2,567	0.4	0.7
BUDD–Mahayana	4	NR	NR	1,050	0.2	0.3
Calv Chpl	1	NR	NR	NR	-	-
Catholic	53	NR	NR	280,930	44.3	75.8
CGOD–Ch God (Ander)	1	54	NR	54	0.0	0.0
CGOD–Ches God-Gen Con	1	0	0	0	0.0	0.0
Ch Cr, Scientst	1	NR	NR	NR	-	-
Ch of Nazarene	4	329	377	482	0.1	0.1
Chr & Miss Al	8	284	200	282	0.0	0.1
CHR–Chr Ch (Disc)	2	0	0	0	0.0	0.0
CHR–Chs of Christ	1	20	20	25	0.0	0.0
Evan Free Ch	2	170	NR	170	0.0	0.0
HINDU–I/A Temples	9	NR	NR	6,532	1.0	1.8
HINDU–Post Ren	1	NR	NR	25	0.0	0.0
HINDU–Renaiss	1	NR	NR	12	0.0	0.0
HINDU–Trad Temples	5	NR	NR	1,590	0.3	0.4
Jehovah's Witness	11	NR	NR	NR	-	-
JUD–Conserv	3	350	393	1,061	0.2	0.3
JUD–Orth	6	1,620	700	2,250	0.4	0.6
JUD–Reform	2	107	189	510	0.1	0.1
LDS–L-D Saints	5	NR	NR	4,124	0.7	1.1
LUTH–E.L.C.A.	22	958	1,793	2,739	0.4	0.7
LUTH–Luth-MO Synod	3	82	97	115	0.0	0.0
METH–AME	2	300	700	835	0.1	0.2
METH–AME Zion	2	100	400	477	0.1	0.1
METH–C.M.E.	1	100	150	179	0.0	0.0
METH–Free Methodist	1	282	417	417	0.1	0.1
METH–Prim Meth Ch	1	NR	NR	NR	-	-
METH–Un Methodist	19	670	1,056	1,519	0.2	0.4
METH–Wesleyan	2	173	117	225	0.0	0.1
Missionary Ch	2	120	94	120	0.0	0.0
Muslim Est	13	5,820	NR	21,042	3.3	5.7
New Apost Ch	1	NR	NR	NR	-	-
Non-denom Chr Chs	22	3,300	4,860	4,994	0.8	1.3
ORTHE–Carp Rus Orth	1	23	NR	30	0.0	0.0
ORTHE–Greek Orthodox	2	220	NR	1,030	0.2	0.3
ORTHE–Orth Ch in Amer	2	110	NR	298	0.0	0.1
ORTHE–Rus Orth Moscow	1	50	NR	100	0.0	0.0
ORTHE–Ukrainian Orth	1	40	NR	150	0.0	0.0
ORTHO–Armen Ap Etchm	1	40	NR	150	0.0	0.0
ORTHO–Coptic Orth Ch	4	2,230	NR	4,560	0.7	1.2
PENT–Assemb of God	27	3,529	2,702	4,795	0.8	1.3
PENT–Ch God (Cleve)	7	316	284	339	0.1	0.1
PENT–Ch Lord Jesus Apos	2	NR	NR	NR	-	-
PENT–Ch of God Proph	3	NR	226	270	0.0	0.1
PENT–COGIC	3	125	450	537	0.1	0.1
PENT–Fire Bapt Hol Ch	2	NR	NR	NR	-	-
PENT–Int Foursq Gos	2	187	174	207	0.0	0.1
PENT–Intl Pent Holiness	1	12	12	14	0.0	0.0
PENT–Un Pent Ch Intl	1	NR	NR	NR	-	-
PENT–United Holy Ch	5	NR	NR	NR	-	-
PENT–Vineyard	1	30	40	48	0.0	0.0
PRES–Presb Ch (USA)	9	359	610	727	0.1	0.2
PRES–Presb Ch Amer	2	115	152	156	0.0	0.0
REF–Christian Ref	3	155	142	169	0.0	0.0
REF–Ref Ch in Am	11	379	544	878	0.1	0.2
Salvation Army	3	128	308	1,301	0.2	0.4
Sev Day Adv	15	1,521	2,645	3,042	0.5	0.8
Zoroastrian	0	NR	NR	17	0.0	0.0
HUNTERDON	**111**	**6,633**	**12,751**	**65,514**	**51.0**	**100.0**
ANG/EPIS–Episcopal	4	396	1,199	1,496	1.2	2.3
Bahá'í	0	NR	21	21	0.0	0.0
BAPT–Amer Bapt USA	6	307	551	666	0.5	1.0
BAPT–Consrv Bapt	2	NR	NR	NR	-	-
BAPT–Ref Bapt Ch	1	NR	NR	NR	-	-
BAPT–So Bapt Conv	1	65	52	63	0.0	0.1
BRETH–Ch of Brethren	1	0	124	150	0.1	0.2
BUDD–Mahayana	1	NR	NR	11	0.0	0.0
Calv Chpl	1	NR	NR	NR	-	-
Catholic	10	NR	NR	47,122	36.7	71.9
Ch of Nazarene	1	70	39	120	0.1	0.2
CHR–Chr Chs & Chs Cr	1	NR	130	157	0.1	0.2
Evan Free Ch	1	200	NR	200	0.2	0.3
FRND–Fr Gen Cf	1	NR	31	37	0.0	0.1
HINDU–Post Ren	1	NR	NR	50	0.0	0.1
Ind Fund Churches	1	NR	NR	NR	-	-
Jehovah's Witness	3	NR	NR	NR	-	-
JUD–Orth	1	43	50	60	0.0	0.1
JUD–Reform	1	79	140	378	0.3	0.6
LDS–L-D Saints	1	NR	NR	447	0.3	0.7
LUTH–E.L.C.A.	3	349	846	1,113	0.9	1.7
LUTH–Luth-MO Synod	2	282	1,139	1,465	1.1	2.2
METH–Un Methodist	22	999	2,269	3,293	2.6	5.0
METH–Wesleyan	2	369	70	479	0.4	0.7
Muslim Est	1	60	NR	150	0.1	0.2
Non-denom Chr Chs	5	680	597	926	0.7	1.4
ORTHE–Greek Orthodox	1	65	NR	300	0.2	0.5
ORTHE–Orth Ch in Amer	1	35	NR	62	0.0	0.1
PENT–Assemb of God	4	419	259	506	0.4	0.8
PENT–Un Pent Ch Intl	1	NR	NR	NR	-	-
PRES–Orth Pres Ch	1	43	30	41	0.0	0.1
PRES–Presb Ch (USA)	16	1,419	3,145	3,802	3.0	5.8
PRES–Presb Ch Amer	1	14	15	18	0.0	0.0
REF–Ref Ch in Am	8	585	1,654	1,827	1.4	2.8
Salvation Army	1	48	57	97	0.1	0.1
Un C of Christ	1	41	197	238	0.2	0.4
Unit Univ	1	65	136	206	0.2	0.3
Unity Ch	1	NR	NR	NR	-	-
Zoroastrian	0	NR	NR	13	0.0	0.0
MERCER	**276**	**28,657**	**43,000**	**192,783**	**52.6**	**100.0**
ANG/EPIS–Episcopal	12	1,663	4,113	6,290	1.7	3.3
Bahá'í	2	NR	182	182	0.0	0.1
BAPT–Alliance Bapt	1	NR	NR	NR	-	-

NR–Not Reported   - Represents no adherents reported.   Percentages may not total 100 due to rounding.

Table 3: Religious Congregations by County and Group: 2010

Religious Group	Number of Congrega-tions	Number of Attendees	Number of Communicant, Confirmed, or Full Members	Adherents		
				Number of Adherents	% of Total Pop.	% of Total Adh.
BAPT–Amer Bapt USA	19	2,780	4,829	5,836	1.6	3.0
BAPT–Consrv Bapt	3	NR	NR	NR	-	-
BAPT–Natl Mis Bapt Conv	1	150	150	181	0.0	0.1
BAPT–NBC Amer	1	35	150	181	0.0	0.1
BAPT–NBC USA	6	1,530	2,500	3,021	0.8	1.6
BAPT–Reg Bapt Gen As	1	NR	NR	NR	-	-
BAPT–So Bapt Conv	3	75	85	103	0.0	0.1
BUDD–Mahayana	6	NR	NR	277	0.1	0.1
BUDD–Vajrayana	2	NR	NR	495	0.1	0.3
Calv Chpl	1	NR	NR	NR	-	-
Catholic	25	NR	NR	121,650	33.2	63.1
CGOD–Ch God (Ander)	1	40	NR	40	0.0	0.0
Ch Cr, Scientst	2	NR	NR	NR	-	-
Ch of Nazarene	2	247	138	267	0.1	0.1
Chr & Miss Al	4	230	139	323	0.1	0.2
CHR–Chr Ch (Disc)	1	0	3	4	0.0	0.0
CHR–Chr Chs & Chs Cr	1	NR	300	363	0.1	0.2
CHR–Chs of Christ	3	390	375	475	0.1	0.2
Christian Brethren	1	NR	NR	NR	-	-
Evan Free Ch	1	100	NR	100	0.0	0.1
FRND–Fr Gen Cf	2	NR	301	364	0.1	0.2
HINDU–Post Ren	2	NR	NR	41	0.0	0.0
HINDU–Trad Temples	1	NR	NR	500	0.1	0.3
Ind Fund Churches	1	NR	NR	NR	-	-
Int Cou Comm Ch	1	NR	NR	NR	-	-
Jehovah's Witness	2	NR	NR	NR	-	-
JUD–Conserv	3	1,093	1,227	3,313	0.9	1.7
JUD–Orth	3	1,188	475	1,650	0.5	0.9
JUD–Reconst	1	33	42	113	0.0	0.1
JUD–Reform	2	625	1,103	2,978	0.8	1.5
LDS–L-D Saints	3	NR	NR	1,533	0.4	0.8
LUTH–Ch of Luth Br	1	78	49	141	0.0	0.1
LUTH–E.L.C.A.	11	1,124	2,382	3,346	0.9	1.7
LUTH–Luth-MO Synod	3	200	427	569	0.2	0.3
MENN–Mennonite USA	2	75	40	48	0.0	0.0
METH–AME	7	350	1,299	1,570	0.4	0.8
METH–AME Zion	2	0	160	193	0.1	0.1
METH–Un Methodist	16	1,506	3,553	5,840	1.6	3.0
METH–Wesleyan	2	125	78	163	0.0	0.1
Muslim Est	5	1,509	NR	5,122	1.4	2.7
New Apost Ch	1	NR	NR	NR	-	-
Non-denom Chr Chs	21	6,191	6,901	8,165	2.2	4.2
OCATH–Pol Natl Cath	1	NR	NR	NR	-	-
ORTHE–Greek Orthodox	1	200	NR	1,200	0.3	0.6
ORTHE–Orth Ch in Amer	2	150	NR	310	0.1	0.2
ORTHE–Ukrainian Orth	2	210	NR	450	0.1	0.2
PENT–Assemb of God	16	1,392	1,863	2,939	0.8	1.5
PENT–Ch God (Cleve)	7	1,462	1,155	1,396	0.4	0.7
PENT–Ch Lord Jesus Apos	5	NR	NR	NR	-	-
PENT–Ch of God Proph	1	NR	160	193	0.1	0.1
PENT–COGIC	1	0	0	0	0.0	0.0
PENT–Un Pent Ch Intl	2	NR	NR	NR	-	-
PENT–United Holy Ch	7	NR	NR	NR	-	-
PRES–Kor Pres Abroad	2	NR	NR	NR	-	-
PRES–Orth Pres Ch	1	32	29	41	0.0	0.0
PRES–Presb Ch (USA)	20	2,278	6,314	7,631	2.1	4.0
PRES–Presb Ch Amer	2	275	216	307	0.1	0.2
REF–Hung Ref Add'l	1	NR	NR	NR	-	-
REF–Ref Ch in Am	1	48	147	181	0.0	0.1
Salvation Army	1	63	46	123	0.0	0.1
Sev Day Adv	8	759	1,321	1,518	0.4	0.8
Sikh	1	NR	NR	NR	-	-
Un C of Christ	1	0	121	146	0.0	0.1
Unit Univ	2	451	627	862	0.2	0.4
Zoroastrian	0	NR	NR	49	0.0	0.0
MIDDLESEX	**421**	**45,225**	**60,950**	**455,416**	**56.2**	**100.0**
ANG/EPIS–Anglican NA	1	NR	NR	NR	-	-
ANG/EPIS–Episcopal	15	1,369	3,598	4,460	0.6	1.0
Bahá'í	0	NR	88	88	0.0	0.0
BAPT–Amer Bapt USA	17	2,384	9,034	10,953	1.4	2.4
BAPT–Consrv Bapt	4	NR	NR	NR	-	-
BAPT–Natl Mis Bapt Conv	2	100	200	242	0.0	0.1
BAPT–NBC Amer	1	50	50	61	0.0	0.0

Religious Group	Number of Congrega-tions	Number of Attendees	Number of Communicant, Confirmed, or Full Members	Adherents		
				Number of Adherents	% of Total Pop.	% of Total Adh.
BAPT–NBC USA	6	1,000	2,450	2,970	0.4	0.7
BAPT–NT Ind Bapt	1	NR	NR	NR	-	-
BAPT–Ref Bapt Ch	1	NR	NR	NR	-	-
BAPT–So Bapt Conv	9	464	581	704	0.1	0.2
BUDD–Mahayana	5	NR	NR	3,041	0.4	0.7
Calv Chpl	3	NR	NR	NR	-	-
Catholic	72	NR	NR	322,340	39.8	70.8
Ch of Nazarene	2	97	150	165	0.0	0.0
Chr & Miss Al	6	2,313	1,611	5,010	0.6	1.1
CHR–Chr Ch (Disc)	2	0	1,800	2,182	0.3	0.5
CHR–Chs of Christ	2	130	84	164	0.0	0.0
CHR–Int Chs of Christ	1	NR	253	307	0.0	0.1
Christian Brethren	1	NR	NR	NR	-	-
Evan Cov Ch	2	65	140	85	0.0	0.0
FRND–Fr Gen Cf & Un Mtg	1	NR	38	46	0.0	0.0
HINDU–I/A Temples	8	NR	NR	7,180	0.9	1.6
HINDU–Post Ren	7	NR	NR	118	0.0	0.0
HINDU–Renaiss	1	NR	NR	12	0.0	0.0
HINDU–Trad Temples	4	NR	NR	3,550	0.4	0.8
Ind Fund Churches	1	NR	NR	NR	-	-
Jain	1	NR	NR	NR	-	-
Jehovah's Witness	7	NR	NR	NR	-	-
JUD–Conserv	6	1,770	1,987	5,365	0.7	1.2
JUD–Orth	12	4,320	1,700	6,000	0.7	1.3
JUD–Reform	4	737	1,300	3,510	0.4	0.8
LDS–Comm of Christ	1	NR	161	161	0.0	0.0
LDS–L-D Saints	3	NR	NR	1,619	0.2	0.4
LUTH–E.L.C.A.	15	788	2,816	3,552	0.4	0.8
LUTH–Luth-MO Synod	4	506	929	1,158	0.1	0.3
LUTH–Wisc Ev Luth Syn	1	37	81	114	0.0	0.0
MENN–Bible Flwshp	2	196	NR	264	0.0	0.1
METH–AME	3	1,000	1,650	2,000	0.2	0.4
METH–AME Zion	2	100	350	424	0.1	0.1
METH–Un Methodist	19	2,313	4,552	6,090	0.8	1.3
Metro Comm Ch	1	30	31	38	0.0	0.0
Muslim Est	9	4,170	NR	17,723	2.2	3.9
New Apost Ch	1	NR	NR	NR	-	-
Non-denom Chr Chs	41	11,831	14,054	15,782	1.9	3.5
OCATH–Pol Natl Cath	2	NR	NR	NR	-	-
ORTHE–Ant Orth of NA	1	120	NR	200	0.0	0.0
ORTHE–Carp Rus Orth	1	150	NR	325	0.0	0.1
ORTHE–Greek Orthodox	2	695	NR	7,400	0.9	1.6
ORTHE–Orth Ch in Amer	2	170	NR	800	0.1	0.2
ORTHE–Rus Orth Abroad	1	30	NR	60	0.0	0.0
ORTHE–Ukrainian Orth	2	185	NR	810	0.1	0.2
ORTHO–Coptic Orth Ch	2	1,200	NR	3,380	0.4	0.7
ORTHO–Malan Dioc Am	1	165	NR	250	0.0	0.1
ORTHO–Malan Syr Orth	1	115	NR	216	0.0	0.0
ORTHO–Syrian Orth Ch	1	40	NR	50	0.0	0.0
PENT–Assemb of God	17	1,855	1,264	2,225	0.3	0.5
PENT–Ch God (Cleve)	3	179	192	233	0.0	0.1
PENT–Ch Lord Jesus Apos	1	NR	NR	NR	-	-
PENT–COGIC	1	0	150	182	0.0	0.0
PENT–Full Gosp Bapt	1	NR	NR	NR	-	-
PENT–Int Foursq Gos	1	0	0	0	0.0	0.0
PENT–Intl Pent Holiness	1	74	80	97	0.0	0.0
PENT–Un Pent Ch Intl	1	NR	NR	NR	-	-
PRES–Kor Pres Abroad	2	NR	NR	NR	-	-
PRES–Korean Amer Pres	1	NR	NR	NR	-	-
PRES–Korean Pres Amer	3	NR	NR	NR	-	-
PRES–Presb Ch (USA)	24	1,735	4,428	5,368	0.7	1.2
PRES–Presb Ch Amer	2	70	56	78	0.0	0.0
REF–Christian Ref	1	250	99	120	0.0	0.0
REF–Hung Ref Add'l	2	NR	NR	NR	-	-
REF–Ref Ch in Am	10	704	1,568	1,874	0.2	0.4
Salvation Army	2	259	304	485	0.1	0.1
Sev Day Adv	13	1,145	1,992	2,290	0.3	0.5
Sikh	2	NR	NR	NR	-	-
Un Breth in Cr	1	17	22	15	0.0	0.0
Un C of Christ	7	177	932	1,130	0.1	0.2
Unit Univ	1	120	175	243	0.0	0.1
Zoroastrian	1	NR	NR	107	0.0	0.0

NR–Not Reported   - Represents no adherents reported.   Percentages may not total 100 due to rounding.

Table 3: Religious Congregations by County and Group: 2010

Religious Group	Number of Congregations	Number of Attendees	Number of Communicant, Confirmed, or Full Members	Adherents		
				Number of Adherents	% of Total Pop.	% of Total Adh.
MONMOUTH	**397**	**39,431**	**50,304**	**360,391**	**57.2**	**100.0**
ANG/EPIS–Episcopal	22	2,070	4,561	6,504	1.0	1.8
Bahá'í	0	NR	111	111	0.0	0.0
BAPT–Amer Bapt Assn	1	NR	20	24	0.0	0.0
BAPT–Amer Bapt USA	19	1,625	3,731	4,538	0.7	1.3
BAPT–Consrv Bapt	5	NR	NR	NR	-	-
BAPT–NBC USA	6	725	2,125	2,585	0.4	0.7
BAPT–Prog NBC	1	150	300	365	0.1	0.1
BAPT–So Bapt Conv	5	575	642	781	0.1	0.2
BUDD–Mahayana	3	NR	NR	572	0.1	0.2
BUDD–Theravada	1	NR	NR	167	0.0	0.0
BUDD–Vajrayana	1	NR	NR	78	0.0	0.0
Calv Chpl	3	NR	NR	NR	-	-
Catholic	47	NR	NR	262,031	41.6	72.7
CGOD–Ch God (Ander)	1	0	NR	0	0.0	0.0
Ch Cr, Scientist	2	NR	NR	NR	-	-
Ch of Nazarene	1	20	39	39	0.0	0.0
CHR–Chs of Christ	3	222	194	232	0.0	0.1
Christian Brethren	1	NR	NR	NR	-	-
Evan Cov Ch	1	57	0	74	0.0	0.0
Evan Free Ch	2	295	NR	295	0.0	0.1
FRND–Fr Gen Cf & Un Mtg	2	NR	79	96	0.0	0.0
HINDU–I/A Temples	1	NR	NR	238	0.0	0.1
HINDU–Post Ren	3	NR	NR	202	0.0	0.1
Ind Fund Churches	1	NR	NR	NR	-	-
Jehovah's Witness	10	NR	NR	NR	-	-
JUD–Conserv	5	1,873	2,102	5,675	0.9	1.6
JUD–Orth	28	7,200	2,500	10,000	1.6	2.8
JUD–Reform	5	1,123	1,980	5,346	0.8	1.5
LDS–L-D Saints	3	NR	NR	1,562	0.2	0.4
LUTH–E.L.C.A.	11	1,174	3,619	5,194	0.8	1.4
LUTH–Luth-MO Synod	3	311	734	881	0.1	0.2
MENN–Bible Flwshp	1	40	NR	54	0.0	0.0
METH–AME	8	350	1,425	1,733	0.3	0.5
METH–AME Zion	9	290	1,050	1,277	0.2	0.4
METH–Free Methodist	1	90	104	104	0.0	0.0
METH–Un Methodist	45	3,487	7,307	12,139	1.9	3.4
Muslim Est	5	2,080	NR	7,397	1.2	2.1
New Apost Ch	1	NR	NR	NR	-	-
Non-denom Chr Chs	33	4,797	5,100	6,240	1.0	1.7
OCATH–Pol Natl Cath	1	NR	NR	NR	-	-
ORTHE–Carp Rus Orth	1	60	NR	72	0.0	0.0
ORTHE–Greek Orthodox	2	685	NR	2,100	0.3	0.6
ORTHE–Rus Orth Abroad	3	250	NR	440	0.1	0.1
ORTHO–Armen Ap Etchm	1	130	NR	500	0.1	0.1
ORTHO–Coptic Orth Ch	2	1,250	NR	3,265	0.5	0.9
PENT–Assemb of God	23	3,974	2,419	4,989	0.8	1.4
PENT–Ch God (Cleve)	6	635	520	633	0.1	0.2
PENT–Ch Lord Jesus Apos	3	NR	NR	NR	-	-
PENT–Ch of God Proph	2	NR	108	131	0.0	0.0
PENT–COGIC	3	75	450	547	0.1	0.2
PENT–Full Gosp Bapt	1	NR	NR	NR	-	-
PENT–Int Pent C Chr	1	14	69	69	0.0	0.0
PENT–United Holy Ch	2	NR	NR	NR	-	-
PRES–Cumber Presb	1	NR	36	40	0.0	0.0
PRES–Kor Pres Abroad	1	NR	NR	NR	-	-
PRES–Presb Ch (USA)	21	2,162	5,509	6,701	1.1	1.9
PRES–Presb Ch Amer	2	195	160	223	0.0	0.1
PRES–Ref Pres Han	1	NR	NR	NR	-	-
REF–Ref Ch in Am	9	670	1,792	2,082	0.3	0.6
Salvation Army	2	146	325	561	0.1	0.2
Sev Day Adv	5	328	570	655	0.1	0.2
Un C of Christ	2	145	331	403	0.1	0.1
Unit Univ	1	158	292	425	0.1	0.1
Unity Ch	1	NR	NR	NR	-	-
Zoroastrian	0	NR	NR	21	0.0	0.0
MORRIS	**310**	**32,504**	**49,307**	**293,864**	**59.7**	**100.0**
ANG/EPIS–Episcopal	20	1,781	4,266	5,649	1.1	1.9
Bahá'í	0	NR	75	75	0.0	0.0
BAPT–Amer Bapt USA	8	524	804	980	0.2	0.3
BAPT–Consrv Bapt	1	NR	NR	NR	-	-
BAPT–NBC USA	2	1,000	2,000	2,439	0.5	0.8
BAPT–Ref Bapt Ch	1	NR	NR	NR	-	-
BAPT–Reg Bapt Gen As	1	NR	NR	NR	-	-
BAPT–So Bapt Conv	4	478	444	541	0.1	0.2
BUDD–Mahayana	3	NR	NR	307	0.1	0.1
BUDD–Vajrayana	1	NR	NR	27	0.0	0.0
Calv Chpl	1	NR	NR	NR	-	-
Catholic	49	NR	NR	206,700	42.0	70.3
Ch Cr, Scientst	1	NR	NR	NR	-	-
Ch of Nazarene	2	120	169	225	0.0	0.1
Chr & Miss Al	9	1,767	1,193	3,037	0.6	1.0
CHR–Chr Chs & Chs Cr	1	NR	120	146	0.0	0.0
CHR–Chs of Christ	5	224	212	287	0.1	0.1
CHR–Int Chs of Christ	0	NR	108	132	0.0	0.0
Evan Free Ch	2	415	NR	415	0.1	0.1
FRND–Fr Gen Cf & Un Mtg	2	NR	179	218	0.0	0.1
HINDU–I/A Temples	5	NR	NR	6,988	1.4	2.4
HINDU–Post Ren	3	NR	NR	109	0.0	0.0
HINDU–Trad Temples	1	NR	NR	150	0.0	0.1
Ind Fund Churches	2	NR	NR	NR	-	-
Int Cou Comm Ch	1	NR	NR	NR	-	-
Jehovah's Witness	4	NR	NR	NR	-	-
JUD–Conserv	5	1,286	1,443	3,896	0.8	1.3
JUD–Orth	5	360	200	500	0.1	0.2
JUD–Reform	4	739	1,304	3,521	0.7	1.2
LDS–L-D Saints	4	NR	NR	1,842	0.4	0.6
LUTH–Ch of Luth Br	1	257	138	846	0.2	0.3
LUTH–E.L.C.A.	12	1,246	3,199	4,238	0.9	1.4
LUTH–Luth-MO Synod	4	318	669	785	0.2	0.3
LUTH–Wisc Ev Luth Syn	1	55	99	123	0.0	0.0
MENN–Bible Flwshp	1	50	NR	68	0.0	0.0
MENN–Mennonite USA	1	30	20	24	0.0	0.0
METH–AME	4	140	440	537	0.1	0.2
METH–Free Methodist	1	18	12	18	0.0	0.0
METH–Un Methodist	29	2,325	5,988	9,363	1.9	3.2
Muslim Est	3	1,519	NR	4,474	0.9	1.5
New Apost Ch	2	NR	NR	NR	-	-
Non-denom Chr Chs	23	11,513	13,972	16,212	3.3	5.5
ORTHE–Carp Rus Orth	1	65	NR	125	0.0	0.0
ORTHE–Greek Orthodox	1	300	NR	2,310	0.5	0.8
ORTHE–Orth Ch in Amer	2	175	NR	450	0.1	0.2
ORTHO–Coptic Orth Ch	1	55	NR	110	0.0	0.0
ORTHO–Malan Dioc Am	1	100	NR	150	0.0	0.1
PENT–Assemb of God	13	1,113	636	1,576	0.3	0.5
PENT–Ch God (Cleve)	2	59	64	78	0.0	0.0
PENT–Ch of God Proph	1	NR	31	38	0.0	0.0
PENT–COGIC	1	200	250	305	0.1	0.1
PENT–Intl Pent Holiness	1	55	65	79	0.0	0.0
PENT–Vineyard	1	80	90	110	0.0	0.0
PRES–Korean Amer Pres	1	NR	NR	NR	-	-
PRES–Orth Pres Ch	1	34	34	41	0.0	0.0
PRES–Presb Ch (USA)	31	2,560	7,581	9,245	1.9	3.1
PRES–Presb Ch Amer	2	103	107	150	0.0	0.1
REF–Christian Ref	2	117	138	168	0.0	0.1
REF–Free Ref NA	1	NR	NR	NR	-	-
REF–Heritage Ref	1	NR	94	115	0.0	0.0
REF–Ref Ch in Am	5	502	1,232	1,381	0.3	0.5
REF–Un Ref Chs N.A.	1	NR	NR	NR	-	-
Salvation Army	2	91	150	303	0.1	0.1
Sev Day Adv	4	227	395	454	0.1	0.2
Un C of Christ	3	210	1,049	1,279	0.3	0.4
Unit Univ	1	293	337	467	0.1	0.2
Unity Ch	1	NR	NR	NR	-	-
Zoroastrian	0	NR	NR	58	0.0	0.0
OCEAN	**302**	**56,285**	**44,637**	**275,856**	**47.8**	**100.0**
ANG/EPIS–Episcopal	12	1,316	2,641	3,889	0.7	1.4
Bahá'í	0	NR	56	56	0.0	0.0
BAPT–Amer Bapt USA	5	315	549	672	0.1	0.2
BAPT–Consrv Bapt	7	NR	NR	NR	-	-
BAPT–NBC USA	3	240	550	673	0.1	0.2
BAPT–Reg Bapt Gen As	1	NR	NR	NR	-	-
BAPT–So Bapt Conv	3	91	78	95	0.0	0.0
BUDD–Mahayana	1	NR	NR	102	0.0	0.0
Calv Chpl	3	NR	NR	NR	-	-

NR–Not Reported - Represents no adherents reported. Percentages may not total 100 due to rounding.

Table 3: Religious Congregations by County and Group: 2010

Religious Group	Number of Congrega-tions	Number of Attendees	Number of Communicant, Confirmed, or Full Members	Adherents: Number of Adherents	Adherents: % of Total Pop.	Adherents: % of Total Adh.
Catholic	26	NR	NR	173,318	30.1	62.8
Ch Cr, Scientst	1	NR	NR	NR	-	-
Ch of Nazarene	1	140	153	153	0.0	0.1
Chr & Miss Al	6	1,134	1,230	1,863	0.3	0.7
CHR–Chr Chs & Chs Cr	1	NR	55	67	0.0	0.0
CHR–Chs of Christ	2	106	95	158	0.0	0.1
Christian Brethren	1	NR	NR	NR	-	-
CONG–Cong Chr, NA	1	NR	55	67	0.0	0.0
Evan Cong Ch	1	NR	147	180	0.0	0.1
Evan Free Ch	1	115	NR	115	0.0	0.0
FRND–Fr Gen Cf	2	NR	40	49	0.0	0.0
HINDU–Trad Temples	1	NR	NR	21	0.0	0.0
Int Cou Comm Ch	1	NR	NR	NR	-	-
Jehovah's Witness	5	NR	NR	NR	-	-
JUD–Conserv	2	431	484	1,307	0.2	0.5
JUD–Orth	90	36,000	12,500	50,000	8.7	18.1
JUD–Reform	1	153	270	729	0.1	0.3
LDS–L-D Saints	3	NR	NR	1,191	0.2	0.4
LUTH–E.L.C.A.	10	1,244	3,562	4,847	0.8	1.8
LUTH–Luth Cong Msn Chr	1	40	56	69	0.0	0.0
LUTH–Luth-MO Synod	3	455	1,037	1,141	0.2	0.4
MENN–Bible Flwshp	1	26	NR	35	0.0	0.0
METH–AME	3	0	400	490	0.1	0.2
METH–AME Zion	2	40	156	191	0.0	0.1
METH–Un Methodist	27	2,803	5,970	11,319	2.0	4.1
Muslim Est	2	838	NR	2,949	0.5	1.1
New Apost Ch	1	NR	NR	NR	-	-
Non-denom Chr Chs	29	4,808	4,986	6,384	1.1	2.3
ORTHE–Greek Orthodox	1	300	NR	750	0.1	0.3
ORTHE–Orth Ch in Amer	2	165	NR	400	0.1	0.1
ORTHE–Rus Orth Abroad	1	70	NR	130	0.0	0.0
PENT–Assemb of God	11	1,872	2,024	3,141	0.5	1.1
PENT–Ch God (Cleve)	2	42	141	173	0.0	0.1
PENT–COGIC	3	400	775	949	0.2	0.3
PENT–Vineyard	1	200	250	306	0.1	0.1
PRES–Orth Pres Ch	1	46	41	57	0.0	0.0
PRES–Presb Ch (USA)	12	2,085	5,036	6,164	1.1	2.2
REF–Ref Ch in Am	3	484	781	929	0.2	0.3
Salvation Army	1	65	100	233	0.0	0.1
Sev Day Adv	2	170	295	340	0.1	0.1
Un C of Christ	1	54	76	93	0.0	0.0
Unit Univ	1	37	48	48	0.0	0.0
Zoroastrian	0	NR	NR	13	0.0	0.0
PASSAIC	**330**	**36,465**	**32,415**	**289,272**	**57.7**	**100.0**
ANG/EPIS–Episcopal	10	723	1,523	1,887	0.4	0.7
Bahá'í	1	NR	119	119	0.0	0.0
BAPT–Amer Bapt USA	22	1,710	2,954	3,652	0.7	1.3
BAPT–Consrv Bapt	1	NR	NR	NR	-	-
BAPT–NBC USA	5	450	1,850	2,287	0.5	0.8
BAPT–So Bapt Conv	4	600	516	638	0.1	0.2
BUDD–Mahayana	1	NR	NR	102	0.0	0.0
Calv Chpl	1	NR	NR	NR	-	-
Catholic	52	NR	NR	199,315	39.8	68.9
CGOD–Ch God (Ander)	2	90	NR	90	0.0	0.0
Ch Cr, Scientst	1	NR	NR	NR	-	-
Ch God (7th Day)	1	NR	NR	NR	-	-
Ch of Nazarene	4	423	330	429	0.1	0.1
Chr & Miss Al	3	279	182	378	0.1	0.1
Evan Free Ch	1	83	NR	83	0.0	0.0
Grace Gosp Fel	2	NR	NR	NR	-	-
HINDU–I/A Temples	2	NR	NR	1,992	0.4	0.7
HINDU–Trad Temples	1	NR	NR	1,200	0.2	0.4
Ind Fund Churches	1	NR	NR	NR	-	-
Jehovah's Witness	6	NR	NR	NR	-	-
JUD–Conserv	3	302	339	915	0.2	0.3
JUD–Orth	15	5,760	2,000	8,000	1.6	2.8
JUD–Reform	1	233	411	1,110	0.2	0.4
LDS–L-D Saints	3	NR	NR	3,012	0.6	1.0
LUTH–E.L.C.A.	3	315	675	1,031	0.2	0.4
LUTH–Luth-MO Synod	4	329	839	1,047	0.2	0.4
METH–AME	2	0	450	556	0.1	0.2
METH–AME Zion	3	215	471	582	0.1	0.2
METH–Free Methodist	5	888	939	1,025	0.2	0.4

Religious Group	Number of Congrega-tions	Number of Attendees	Number of Communicant, Confirmed, or Full Members	Adherents: Number of Adherents	Adherents: % of Total Pop.	Adherents: % of Total Adh.
METH–Un Methodist	16	2,068	3,487	4,106	0.8	1.4
Missionary Ch	1	65	55	65	0.0	0.0
Muslim Est	14	7,420	NR	27,915	5.6	9.7
New Apost Ch	2	NR	NR	NR	-	-
Non-denom Chr Chs	21	5,037	4,437	6,603	1.3	2.3
OCATH–Pol Natl Cath	4	NR	NR	NR	-	-
ORTHE–Ant Orth of NA	1	300	NR	1,500	0.3	0.5
ORTHE–Greek Orthodox	1	400	NR	1,500	0.3	0.5
ORTHE–Macedonian Orth	1	75	NR	300	0.1	0.1
ORTHE–Orth Ch in Amer	3	247	NR	595	0.1	0.2
ORTHE–Rus Orth Abroad	2	105	NR	205	0.0	0.1
ORTHE–Rus Orth Moscow	2	200	NR	750	0.1	0.3
ORTHE–Serb Orth USA	1	85	NR	610	0.1	0.2
ORTHE–Ukrainian Orth	2	90	NR	350	0.1	0.1
ORTHO–Malan Dioc Am	1	110	NR	180	0.0	0.1
PENT–Assemb of God	22	3,151	1,942	4,263	0.9	1.5
PENT–Ch God (Cleve)	8	1,030	967	1,196	0.2	0.4
PENT–Ch Lord Jesus Apos	2	NR	NR	NR	-	-
PENT–Ch of God Proph	2	NR	302	373	0.1	0.1
PENT–COGIC	1	0	150	185	0.0	0.1
PENT–Fire Bapt Hol Ch	2	NR	NR	NR	-	-
PENT–Pent Ch of God	1	70	NR	109	0.0	0.0
PENT–Un Pent Ch Intl	2	NR	NR	NR	-	-
PENT–United Holy Ch	3	NR	NR	NR	-	-
PRES–Kor Pres Abroad	1	NR	NR	NR	-	-
PRES–Korean Pres Amer	1	NR	NR	NR	-	-
PRES–Presb Ch (USA)	12	188	1,659	2,051	0.4	0.7
REF–Christian Ref	10	1,075	1,551	1,918	0.4	0.7
REF–Ref Ch in Am	18	1,219	2,211	2,531	0.5	0.9
REF–Un Ref Chs N.A.	1	NR	NR	NR	-	-
Salvation Army	2	188	283	444	0.1	0.2
Sev Day Adv	7	752	1,307	1,503	0.3	0.5
Un C of Christ	2	160	435	538	0.1	0.2
Unit Univ	1	30	31	31	0.0	0.0
Zoroastrian	0	NR	NR	1	0.0	0.0
SALEM	**96**	**6,241**	**9,682**	**20,855**	**31.6**	**100.0**
ANG/EPIS–Episcopal	4	169	296	436	0.7	2.1
Bahá'í	0	NR	3	3	0.0	0.0
BAPT–Amer Bapt USA	5	323	1,020	1,236	1.9	5.9
BAPT–Consrv Bapt	2	NR	NR	NR	-	-
BAPT–Free Will Bapt	1	NR	35	42	0.1	0.2
BAPT–NBC USA	3	175	460	558	0.8	2.7
BAPT–So Bapt Conv	1	75	190	230	0.3	1.1
Catholic	6	NR	NR	6,959	10.5	33.4
Ch Cr, Scientst	1	NR	NR	NR	-	-
Ch of Nazarene	3	152	223	277	0.4	1.3
FRND–Fr Gen Cf	3	NR	280	339	0.5	1.6
Jehovah's Witness	1	NR	NR	NR	-	-
LDS–L-D Saints	1	NR	NR	324	0.5	1.6
LUTH–E.L.C.A.	2	131	329	395	0.6	1.9
LUTH–Luth-MO Synod	1	33	36	55	0.1	0.3
MENN–Mara Amish-Menn	1	55	21	55	0.1	0.3
MENN–Mennonite USA	1	42	40	48	0.1	0.2
METH–AME	7	120	750	909	1.4	4.4
METH–Un Methodist	23	2,095	2,979	4,594	7.0	22.0
METH–Wesleyan	2	65	70	85	0.1	0.4
Non-denom Chr Chs	12	1,305	1,447	1,851	2.8	8.9
PENT–Assemb of God	5	725	284	943	1.4	4.5
PENT–Ch God (Cleve)	1	40	19	23	0.0	0.1
PENT–Un Pent Ch Intl	1	NR	NR	NR	-	-
PRES–Orth Pres Ch	2	178	224	320	0.5	1.5
PRES–Presb Ch (USA)	5	468	819	993	1.5	4.8
Sev Day Adv	2	90	157	180	0.3	0.9
SOMERSET	**196**	**19,550**	**35,460**	**156,935**	**48.5**	**100.0**
ANG/EPIS–Anglican NA	2	NR	NR	NR	-	-
ANG/EPIS–Episcopal	9	976	2,672	3,131	1.0	2.0
Bahá'í	2	NR	71	71	0.0	0.0
BAPT–Amer Bapt USA	4	2,224	5,493	6,771	2.1	4.3
BAPT–Consrv Bapt	2	NR	NR	NR	-	-
BAPT–NBC Amer	1	0	150	185	0.1	0.1
BAPT–NBC USA	1	110	173	213	0.1	0.1

NR–Not Reported   - Represents no adherents reported.   Percentages may not total 100 due to rounding.

Table 3: Religious Congregations by County and Group: 2010

Religious Group	Number of Congrega-tions	Number of Attendees	Number of Communicant, Confirmed, or Full Members	Adherents: Number of Adherents	Adherents: % of Total Pop.	Adherents: % of Total Adh.
BAPT–S-D Baptist Gen Con	1	5	17	21	0.0	0.0
BAPT–So Bapt Conv	4	436	622	767	0.2	0.5
BUDD–Mahayana	3	NR	NR	304	0.1	0.2
Calv Chpl	2	NR	NR	NR	-	-
Catholic	29	NR	NR	98,951	30.6	63.1
Ch Cr, Scientst	2	NR	NR	NR	-	-
Ch of Nazarene	1	25	36	36	0.0	0.0
Chr & Miss Al	2	581	282	999	0.3	0.6
CHR–Chr Ch (Disc)	2	0	222	274	0.1	0.2
CHR–Chs of Christ	1	110	95	125	0.0	0.1
CHR–Int Chs of Christ	0	NR	108	133	0.0	0.1
Christian Brethren	1	NR	NR	NR	-	-
CONG–Cong Chr, NA	2	NR	283	349	0.1	0.2
Evan Free Ch	1	312	NR	312	0.1	0.2
HINDU–I/A Temples	1	NR	NR	2,333	0.7	1.5
HINDU–Post Ren	3	NR	NR	66	0.0	0.0
HINDU–Trad Temples	3	NR	NR	3,325	1.0	2.1
Ind Fund Churches	1	NR	NR	NR	-	-
Int Cou Comm Ch	1	NR	NR	NR	-	-
Jehovah's Witness	3	NR	NR	NR	-	-
JUD–Conserv	3	651	731	1,974	0.6	1.3
JUD–Orth	2	86	100	120	0.0	0.1
JUD–Reconst	1	177	226	610	0.2	0.4
JUD–Reform	2	471	830	2,241	0.7	1.4
LDS–L-D Saints	1	NR	NR	522	0.2	0.3
LUTH–E.L.C.A.	3	416	1,122	1,503	0.5	1.0
LUTH–Luth-MO Synod	4	330	699	907	0.3	0.6
METH–AME	4	0	450	555	0.2	0.4
METH–AME Zion	1	0	100	123	0.0	0.1
METH–Un Methodist	14	1,040	2,559	3,615	1.1	2.3
METH–Wesleyan	1	75	0	98	0.0	0.1
Muslim Est	5	849	NR	3,274	1.0	2.1
Non-denom Chr Chs	15	4,290	5,635	6,001	1.9	3.8
ORTHE–Carp Rus Orth	1	60	NR	125	0.0	0.1
ORTHE–Georgian Orth	1	80	NR	150	0.0	0.1
ORTHE–Orth Ch in Amer	1	80	NR	145	0.0	0.1
ORTHE–Rus Orth Abroad	1	45	NR	80	0.0	0.1
ORTHE–Ukrainian Orth	1	125	NR	400	0.1	0.3
ORTHO–Coptic Orth Ch	1	250	NR	300	0.1	0.2
PENT–Assemb of God	6	1,240	669	1,460	0.5	0.9
PENT–Ch God (Cleve)	1	8	10	12	0.0	0.0
PENT–Intl Pent Holiness	1	92	107	132	0.0	0.1
Pillar of Fire	1	NR	1,500	1,500	0.5	1.0
PRES–Orth Pres Ch	1	70	96	103	0.0	0.1
PRES–Presb Ch (USA)	16	2,476	5,551	6,842	2.1	4.4
PRES–Presb Ch Amer	2	123	88	123	0.0	0.1
REF–Ref Ch in Am	15	1,323	4,219	4,843	1.5	3.1
Salvation Army	1	112	125	220	0.1	0.1
Sev Day Adv	2	104	182	209	0.1	0.1
Sikh	1	NR	NR	NR	-	-
Un C of Christ	2	94	117	144	0.0	0.1
Unit Univ	1	104	120	177	0.1	0.1
Zoroastrian	0	NR	NR	61	0.0	0.0
SUSSEX	**97**	**5,878**	**10,087**	**71,806**	**48.1**	**100.0**
ANG/EPIS–Episcopal	4	454	909	1,269	0.9	1.8
Bahá'í	0	NR	8	8	0.0	0.0
BAPT–Amer Bapt USA	3	86	229	278	0.2	0.4
BAPT–Asc Ref Bap Ch Am	1	NR	NR	NR	-	-
BAPT–Consrv Bapt	2	NR	NR	NR	-	-
BAPT–NBC USA	1	0	150	182	0.1	0.3
BAPT–Ref Bapt Ch	1	NR	NR	NR	-	-
BAPT–Reg Bapt Gen As	1	NR	NR	NR	-	-
BAPT–So Bapt Conv	1	12	12	15	0.0	0.0
BUDD–Mahayana	3	NR	NR	757	0.5	1.1
Catholic	16	NR	NR	56,400	37.8	78.5
Ch Cr, Scientst	1	NR	NR	NR	-	-
Ch of Nazarene	1	7	4	17	0.0	0.0
Chr & Miss Al	1	76	25	103	0.1	0.1
CHR–Chr Chs & Chs Cr	1	NR	68	83	0.1	0.1
CONG–Cong Chr, NA	1	NR	170	206	0.1	0.3
Evan Free Ch	2	585	NR	585	0.4	0.8
Jehovah's Witness	3	NR	NR	NR	-	-
JUD–Orth	1	43	50	60	0.0	0.1

Religious Group	Number of Congrega-tions	Number of Attendees	Number of Communicant, Confirmed, or Full Members	Adherents: Number of Adherents	Adherents: % of Total Pop.	Adherents: % of Total Adh.
LDS–L-D Saints	1	NR	NR	448	0.3	0.6
LUTH–E.L.C.A.	2	304	977	1,294	0.9	1.8
LUTH–Luth-MO Synod	3	285	616	847	0.6	1.2
METH–Un Methodist	14	1,030	2,122	3,538	2.4	4.9
METH–Wesleyan	1	26	24	34	0.0	0.0
New Apost Ch	1	NR	NR	NR	-	-
Non-denom Chr Chs	6	1,330	1,780	1,813	1.2	2.5
ORTHE–Orth Ch in Amer	1	65	NR	300	0.2	0.4
PENT–Assemb of God	4	166	130	187	0.1	0.3
PRES–Evan Presby Ch	1	NR	57	69	0.0	0.1
PRES–Presb Ch (USA)	11	934	2,081	2,526	1.7	3.5
REF–Christian Ref	1	250	289	351	0.2	0.5
REF–Ref Ch in Am	1	52	98	100	0.1	0.1
REF–Un Ref Chs N.A.	1	NR	NR	NR	-	-
Sev Day Adv	3	132	230	264	0.2	0.4
Unit Univ	1	41	58	69	0.0	0.1
Unity Ch	1	NR	NR	NR	-	-
Zoroastrian	0	NR	NR	3	0.0	0.0
UNION	**382**	**45,266**	**65,410**	**354,958**	**66.2**	**100.0**
ANG/EPIS–Anglican NA	1	NR	NR	NR	-	-
ANG/EPIS–Episcopal	14	1,566	5,025	6,735	1.3	1.9
Bahá'í	0	NR	70	70	0.0	0.0
BAPT–Amer Bapt USA	27	5,216	9,121	11,239	2.1	3.2
BAPT–Consrv Bapt	4	NR	NR	NR	-	-
BAPT–NBC Amer	1	0	150	185	0.0	0.1
BAPT–NBC USA	9	1,325	2,650	3,265	0.6	0.9
BAPT–Prog NBC	2	800	950	1,171	0.2	0.3
BAPT–S-D Baptist Gen Con	1	30	59	73	0.0	0.0
BAPT–So Bapt Conv	8	745	879	1,083	0.2	0.3
BUDD–Theravada	1	NR	NR	292	0.1	0.1
BUDD–Vajrayana	1	NR	NR	16	0.0	0.0
Catholic	42	NR	NR	247,240	46.1	69.7
CGOD–Ch God (Ander)	2	150	NR	150	0.0	0.0
Ch Cr, Scientst	1	NR	NR	NR	-	-
Ch God (7th Day)	1	NR	NR	NR	-	-
Ch of Nazarene	2	190	271	281	0.1	0.1
Chr & Miss Al	5	365	257	465	0.1	0.1
CHR–Chr Ch (Disc)	2	0	0	0	0.0	0.0
CHR–Chr Chs & Chs Cr	1	NR	60	74	0.0	0.0
CHR–Chs of Christ	2	95	94	113	0.0	0.0
Christian Brethren	4	NR	NR	NR	-	-
FRND–Fr Gen Cf & Un Mtg	1	NR	118	145	0.0	0.0
HINDU–I/A Temples	1	NR	NR	250	0.0	0.1
HINDU–Post Ren	1	NR	NR	25	0.0	0.0
Jehovah's Witness	10	NR	NR	NR	-	-
JUD–Conserv	5	1,385	1,554	4,196	0.8	1.2
JUD–Orth	10	2,880	1,000	4,000	0.7	1.1
JUD–Reconst	1	101	129	348	0.1	0.1
JUD–Reform	4	1,151	2,030	5,481	1.0	1.5
LDS–L-D Saints	5	NR	NR	2,521	0.5	0.7
LUTH–E.L.C.A.	10	848	2,377	3,025	0.6	0.9
LUTH–Luth-MO Synod	5	397	831	1,022	0.2	0.3
METH–AME	8	1,035	1,850	2,280	0.4	0.6
METH–AME Zion	4	150	446	550	0.1	0.2
METH–Un Methodist	20	1,330	2,941	3,992	0.7	1.1
METH–Wesleyan	1	0	19	0	0.0	0.0
MORAV–Morav Ch-North	1	30	37	52	0.0	0.0
Muslim Est	8	3,070	NR	10,494	2.0	3.0
New Apost Ch	2	NR	NR	NR	-	-
Non-denom Chr Chs	35	11,077	16,779	17,396	3.2	4.9
OCATH–Pol Natl Cath	2	NR	NR	NR	-	-
ORTHE–Carp Rus Orth	2	130	NR	297	0.1	0.1
ORTHE–Greek Orthodox	3	770	NR	4,275	0.8	1.2
ORTHE–Orth Ch in Amer	1	35	NR	45	0.0	0.0
ORTHE–Rus Orth Moscow	1	60	NR	400	0.1	0.1
ORTHE–Serb Orth USA	2	90	NR	490	0.1	0.1
ORTHO–Coptic Orth Ch	1	110	NR	210	0.0	0.1
PENT–Apos Faith Msn	1	NR	35	43	0.0	0.0
PENT–Assemb of God	19	4,190	3,029	5,172	1.0	1.5
PENT–Ch God (Cleve)	4	394	347	428	0.1	0.1
PENT–Ch Lord Jesus Apos	2	NR	NR	NR	-	-
PENT–Ch of God Proph	5	NR	310	382	0.1	0.1
PENT–COGIC	4	60	330	407	0.1	0.1

NR–Not Reported   - Represents no adherents reported.   Percentages may not total 100 due to rounding.

Table 3: Religious Congregations by County and Group: 2010

Religious Group	Number of Congregations	Number of Attendees	Number of Communicant, Confirmed, or Full Members	Adherents: Number of Adherents	% of Total Pop.	% of Total Adh.
PENT–Elim	1	NR	NR	NR	-	-
PENT–Fire Bapt Hol Ch	2	NR	NR	NR	-	-
PENT–Full Gosp Bapt	2	NR	NR	NR	-	-
PENT–Int Foursq Gos	4	351	455	561	0.1	0.2
PENT–Intl Pent Holiness	1	517	341	420	0.1	0.1
PENT–Un Pent Ch Intl	2	NR	NR	NR	-	-
PENT–United Holy Ch	6	NR	NR	NR	-	-
PRES–Kor Pres Abroad	1	NR	NR	NR	-	-
PRES–Korean Pres Amer	1	NR	NR	NR	-	-
PRES–Orth Pres Ch	1	65	97	124	0.0	0.0
PRES–Presb Ch (USA)	27	2,583	6,762	8,332	1.6	2.3
PRES–Presb Ch Amer	1	0	0	0	0.0	0.0
REF–Ref Ch in Am	2	60	174	192	0.0	0.1
Salvation Army	2	127	116	345	0.1	0.1
Sev Day Adv	12	996	1,731	1,991	0.4	0.6
Un C of Christ	5	500	1,299	1,601	0.3	0.5
Unit Univ	2	292	687	1,000	0.2	0.3
Zoroastrian	0	NR	NR	14	0.0	0.0
WARREN	**105**	**6,982**	**11,412**	**46,743**	**43.0**	**100.0**
ANG/EPIS–Episcopal	6	397	930	1,117	1.0	2.4
Bahá'í	0	NR	15	15	0.0	0.0
BAPT–Consrv Bapt	2	NR	NR	NR	-	-
BAPT–Reg Bapt Gen As	2	NR	NR	NR	-	-
BRETH–Grace Breth	1	NR	NR	NR	-	-
BUDD–Vajrayana	1	NR	NR	78	0.1	0.2
Catholic	11	NR	NR	28,114	25.9	60.1
Ch of Nazarene	1	83	37	83	0.1	0.2
Chr & Miss Al	2	595	289	903	0.8	1.9
CHR–Chs of Christ	1	90	74	100	0.1	0.2
Evan Free Ch	1	352	NR	352	0.3	0.8
HINDU–Trad Temples	1	NR	NR	200	0.2	0.4
Ind Fund Churches	2	NR	NR	NR	-	-
Jain	1	NR	NR	NR	-	-
Jehovah's Witness	3	NR	NR	NR	-	-
JUD–Reform	1	43	76	205	0.2	0.4
LUTH–E.L.C.A.	5	424	1,423	1,901	1.7	4.1
LUTH–Luth–MO Synod	2	151	354	431	0.4	0.9
MENN–Bible Flwshp	1	38	NR	51	0.0	0.1
MENN–Mennonite USA	1	42	38	46	0.0	0.1
METH–AME	1	0	100	122	0.1	0.3
METH–Un Methodist	21	1,693	4,008	6,311	5.8	13.5
Muslim Est	1	420	NR	1,474	1.4	3.2
New Apost Ch	1	NR	NR	NR	-	-
Non-denom Chr Chs	5	550	555	688	0.6	1.5
ORTHE–Orth Ch in Amer	1	35	NR	50	0.0	0.1
ORTHE–Rus Orth Moscow	1	20	NR	100	0.1	0.2
PENT–Assemb of God	2	228	120	279	0.3	0.6
PENT–Elim	1	NR	NR	NR	-	-
PENT–Int Foursq Gos	1	31	47	57	0.1	0.1
PRES–Orth Pres Ch	3	381	317	382	0.4	0.8
PRES–Presb Ch (USA)	15	1,053	2,491	3,029	2.8	6.5
PRES–Presb Ch Amer	1	80	102	123	0.1	0.3
Sev Day Adv	4	155	270	310	0.3	0.7
Un C of Christ	1	85	127	154	0.1	0.3
Unit Univ	1	36	39	64	0.1	0.1
Zoroastrian	0	NR	NR	4	0.0	0.0
NEW MEXICO	**2,447**	**171,458**	**272,647**	**1,031,198**	**50.1**	**100.0**
BERNALILLO	**412**	**66,111**	**83,027**	**312,701**	**47.2**	**100.0**
ANG/EPIS–Anglican NA	4	NR	NR	NR	-	-
ANG/EPIS–Episcopal	8	1,314	3,631	4,634	0.7	1.5
Bahá'í	2	NR	773	773	0.1	0.2
BAPT–Amer Bapt Assn	1	NR	60	74	0.0	0.0
BAPT–Amer Bapt USA	2	168	301	371	0.1	0.1
BAPT–Consrv Bapt	1	NR	NR	NR	-	-
BAPT–Free Will Bapt	1	NR	6	7	0.0	0.0
BAPT–Natl Mis Bapt Conv	1	55	85	105	0.0	0.0
BAPT–NBC Amer	2	125	400	492	0.1	0.2
BAPT–NBC USA	1	0	125	154	0.0	0.0
BAPT–Ref Bapt Ch	1	NR	NR	NR	-	-
BAPT–Reg Bapt Gen As	1	NR	NR	NR	-	-
BAPT–S-D Baptist Gen Con	1	6	8	10	0.0	0.0
BAPT–So Bapt Conv	47	12,489	14,073	17,325	2.6	5.5
BRETH–Breth in Chr	1	NR	NR	NR	-	-
BRETH–Grace Breth	1	NR	NR	NR	-	-
BUDD–Mahayana	8	NR	NR	3,276	0.5	1.0
BUDD–Theravada	3	NR	NR	3,029	0.5	1.0
BUDD–Vajrayana	5	NR	NR	185	0.0	0.1
Calv Chpl	3	NR	NR	NR	-	-
Catholic	44	NR	NR	175,266	26.5	56.0
CGOD–Ch God (Ander)	1	700	NR	700	0.1	0.2
Ch Cr, Scientst	1	NR	NR	NR	-	-
Ch God (7th Day)	1	NR	NR	NR	-	-
Ch of Nazarene	7	1,413	1,992	3,015	0.5	1.0
CHR–Chr Ch (Disc)	5	424	1,034	1,273	0.2	0.4
CHR–Chr Chs & Chs Cr	5	NR	1,065	1,311	0.2	0.4
CHR–Chs of Christ	15	2,347	2,253	2,896	0.4	0.9
CHR–Int Chs of Christ	1	NR	110	135	0.0	0.0
Evan Free Ch	2	500	NR	500	0.1	0.2
FRND–Fr Gen Cf	1	NR	144	177	0.0	0.1
HINDU–Post Ren	6	NR	NR	291	0.0	0.1
HINDU–Renaiss	2	NR	NR	24	0.0	0.0
HINDU–Trad Temples	1	NR	NR	500	0.1	0.2
Ind Fund Churches	2	NR	NR	NR	-	-
Jehovah's Witness	7	NR	NR	NR	-	-
JUD–Conserv	1	223	250	675	0.1	0.2
JUD–Orth	1	43	50	60	0.0	0.0
JUD–Reform	1	378	667	1,801	0.3	0.6
LDS–Comm of Christ	1	NR	61	61	0.0	0.0
LDS–L-D Saints	25	NR	NR	14,184	2.1	4.5
LUTH–E.L.C.A.	8	1,037	2,466	2,912	0.4	0.9
LUTH–Luth Ch-Am Asc	1	NR	NR	NR	-	-
LUTH–Luth Cong Msn Chr	1	1,137	2,193	2,700	0.4	0.9
LUTH–Luth–MO Synod	7	909	1,644	2,030	0.3	0.6
LUTH–Wisc Ev Luth Syn	1	161	247	332	0.1	0.1
MENN–CG in Cr (Menn)	1	NR	7	9	0.0	0.0
MENN–Cons Menn Conf	1	90	55	68	0.0	0.0
MENN–Mennonite USA	1	100	70	86	0.0	0.0
METH–AME	1	95	225	277	0.0	0.1
METH–C.M.E.	1	0	150	185	0.0	0.1
METH–Un Methodist	18	3,730	7,658	9,592	1.4	3.1
METH–Wesleyan	2	61	40	79	0.0	0.0
Metro Comm Ch	1	108	154	190	0.0	0.1
MJEW–Union Mes Cong	1	NR	NR	NR	-	-
Muslim Est	2	634	NR	1,808	0.3	0.6
New Apost Ch	1	NR	NR	NR	-	-
Non-denom Chr Chs	51	25,156	26,551	33,054	5.0	10.6
ORTHE–Greek Orthodox	1	300	NR	1,500	0.2	0.5
ORTHE–Orth Ch in Amer	1	85	NR	120	0.0	0.0
ORTHO–Coptic Orth Ch	1	15	NR	24	0.0	0.0
PENT–Assemb of God	22	6,865	3,673	9,602	1.4	3.1
PENT–Ch God (Cleve)	3	113	312	384	0.1	0.1
PENT–Ch of God Proph	2	NR	57	70	0.0	0.0
PENT–COGIC	3	20	335	412	0.1	0.1
PENT–Full Gosp Bapt	3	NR	NR	NR	-	-
PENT–Int Foursq Gos	4	211	214	263	0.0	0.1
PENT–Intl Pent Holiness	2	222	179	220	0.0	0.1
PENT–Pent Ch of God	2	140	NR	217	0.0	0.1
PENT–Un Pent Ch Intl	4	NR	NR	NR	-	-
PENT–Vineyard	3	157	191	235	0.0	0.1
PRES–Cumber Presb	1	NR	1,069	2,527	0.4	0.8
PRES–Orth Pres Ch	1	25	29	38	0.0	0.0
PRES–Presb Ch (USA)	11	1,933	4,092	5,037	0.8	1.6
PRES–Presb Ch Amer	2	95	54	79	0.0	0.0
REF–Christian Ref	3	182	231	284	0.0	0.1
Salvation Army	2	108	153	448	0.1	0.1
Sev Day Adv	8	1,386	2,410	2,772	0.4	0.9
Sikh	2	NR	NR	NR	-	-
Un C of Christ	4	356	686	845	0.1	0.3
Unit Univ	2	495	794	994	0.2	0.3
Unity Ch	2	NR	NR	NR	-	-
Zoroastrian	0	NR	NR	4	0.0	0.0

NR–Not Reported   - Represents no adherents reported.   Percentages may not total 100 due to rounding.

Table 3: Religious Congregations by County and Group: 2010

Religious Group	Number of Congrega-tions	Number of Attendees	Number of Communicant, Confirmed, or Full Members	Adherents		
				Number of Adherents	% of Total Pop.	% of Total Adh.
CATRON	**18**	**234**	**369**	**1,066**	**28.6**	**100.0**
Bahá'í	0	NR	4	4	0.1	0.4
BAPT–So Bapt Conv	5	130	231	260	7.0	24.4
Catholic	5	NR	NR	300	8.1	28.1
CHR–Chs of Christ	1	15	14	18	0.5	1.7
LDS–L-D Saints	2	NR	NR	347	9.3	32.6
PRES–Presb Ch (USA)	3	49	50	56	1.5	5.3
Sev Day Adv	2	40	70	81	2.2	7.6
CHAVES	**89**	**7,729**	**16,287**	**35,097**	**53.5**	**100.0**
ANG/EPIS–Anglican NA	2	NR	NR	NR	-	-
ANG/EPIS–Episcopal	1	106	255	255	0.4	0.7
Bahá'í	1	NR	48	48	0.1	0.1
BAPT–Amer Bapt Assn	1	NR	80	102	0.2	0.3
BAPT–Ind Bapt Flwsp Intl	2	NR	NR	NR	-	-
BAPT–NBC USA	1	50	50	64	0.1	0.2
BAPT–So Bapt Conv	18	1,151	5,486	7,011	10.7	20.0
Calv Chpl	1	NR	NR	NR	-	-
Catholic	6	NR	NR	14,031	21.4	40.0
Ch Cr, Scientst	1	NR	NR	NR	-	-
Ch of Nazarene	3	412	528	746	1.1	2.1
CHR–Chs of Christ	8	694	815	1,053	1.6	3.0
Jehovah's Witness	4	NR	NR	NR	-	-
LDS–L-D Saints	3	NR	NR	1,351	2.1	3.8
LUTH–E.L.C.A.	1	57	79	92	0.1	0.3
LUTH–Luth–MO Synod	1	122	226	305	0.5	0.9
LUTH–Wisc Ev Luth Syn	1	14	23	36	0.1	0.1
METH–AME	1	0	150	192	0.3	0.5
METH–Un Methodist	5	367	1,095	1,238	1.9	3.5
New Apost Ch	1	NR	NR	NR	-	-
Non-denom Chr Chs	8	3,679	5,999	6,149	9.4	17.5
PENT–Assemb of God	4	455	403	837	1.3	2.4
PENT–Ch God (Cleve)	2	50	43	55	0.1	0.2
PENT–Ch of God Proph	1	NR	54	69	0.1	0.2
PENT–COGIC	1	0	150	192	0.3	0.5
PENT–Int Foursq Gos	1	18	21	27	0.0	0.1
PENT–Pent Ch of God	1	70	NR	109	0.2	0.3
PENT–Un Pent Ch Intl	1	NR	NR	NR	-	-
PRES–Presb Ch (USA)	4	304	476	608	0.9	1.7
Salvation Army	1	36	57	240	0.4	0.7
Sev Day Adv	3	144	249	287	0.4	0.8
CIBOLA	**53**	**1,582**	**2,054**	**13,313**	**48.9**	**100.0**
ANG/EPIS–Episcopal	1	31	116	117	0.4	0.9
Bahá'í	1	NR	35	35	0.1	0.3
BAPT–So Bapt Conv	6	314	662	819	3.0	6.2
BUDD–Vajrayana	1	NR	NR	25	0.1	0.2
Catholic	13	NR	NR	9,000	33.1	67.6
Ch of Nazarene	4	117	144	392	1.4	2.9
CHR–Chs of Christ	1	225	210	273	1.0	2.1
Jehovah's Witness	1	NR	NR	NR	-	-
LDS–L-D Saints	3	NR	NR	1,219	4.5	9.2
LUTH–Luth–MO Synod	1	16	22	22	0.1	0.2
METH–A.W.M.C.	2	7	5	7	0.0	0.1
METH–Un Methodist	1	57	128	168	0.6	1.3
Non-denom Chr Chs	4	375	450	510	1.9	3.8
PENT–Assemb of God	4	100	55	126	0.5	0.9
PENT–Ch God (Cleve)	4	90	158	195	0.7	1.5
PENT–Pent Ch of God	3	210	NR	326	1.2	2.4
PENT–Un Pent Ch Intl	2	NR	NR	NR	-	-
Sev Day Adv	1	40	69	79	0.3	0.6
COLFAX	**37**	**983**	**2,737**	**7,275**	**52.9**	**100.0**
ANG/EPIS–Episcopal	1	22	60	60	0.4	0.8
Bahá'í	0	NR	3	3	0.0	0.0
BAPT–So Bapt Conv	7	492	1,538	1,821	13.2	25.0
Catholic	9	NR	NR	3,426	24.9	47.1
CHR–Chr Ch (Disc)	1	0	200	237	1.7	3.3
CHR–Chs of Christ	3	126	72	99	0.7	1.4
Jehovah's Witness	1	NR	NR	NR	-	-
LDS–L-D Saints	1	NR	NR	461	3.4	6.3
LUTH–Luth–MO Synod	2	29	26	31	0.2	0.4
METH–Un Methodist	4	122	389	482	3.5	6.6
PENT–Assemb of God	2	110	53	188	1.4	2.6
PENT–Ch of God Proph	1	NR	54	64	0.5	0.9
PENT–Int Foursq Gos	1	14	17	20	0.1	0.3
PRES–Presb Ch (USA)	2	0	62	73	0.5	1.0
Sev Day Adv	1	16	29	33	0.2	0.5
Un C of Christ	1	52	234	277	2.0	3.8
CURRY	**74**	**6,509**	**12,787**	**27,193**	**56.2**	**100.0**
ANG/EPIS–Episcopal	1	71	103	103	0.2	0.4
Bahá'í	0	NR	11	11	0.0	0.0
BAPT–Amer Bapt Assn	1	NR	85	110	0.2	0.4
BAPT–Ind Bapt Flwsp Intl	1	NR	NR	NR	-	-
BAPT–NBC USA	1	0	150	194	0.4	0.7
BAPT–So Bapt Conv	15	2,005	6,191	8,011	16.6	29.5
BRETH–Ch of Brethren	1	0	83	107	0.2	0.4
Catholic	4	NR	NR	9,861	20.4	36.3
CGOD–Ch God (Ander)	1	50	NR	50	0.1	0.2
Ch of Nazarene	2	388	603	603	1.2	2.2
CHR–Chr Chs & Chs Cr	2	NR	350	453	0.9	1.7
CHR–Chs of Christ	8	900	916	1,200	2.5	4.4
Jehovah's Witness	1	NR	NR	NR	-	-
LDS–Comm of Christ	1	NR	61	61	0.1	0.2
LDS–L-D Saints	1	NR	NR	912	1.9	3.4
LUTH–E.L.C.A.	1	38	70	83	0.2	0.3
LUTH–Luth Cong Msn Chr	1	NR	NR	NR	-	-
LUTH–Luth–MO Synod	1	58	82	101	0.2	0.4
METH–C.M.E.	1	0	100	129	0.3	0.5
METH–Un Methodist	6	520	1,397	1,742	3.6	6.4
Metro Comm Ch	1	16	22	28	0.1	0.1
Non-denom Chr Chs	7	2,015	2,070	2,600	5.4	9.6
PENT–Assemb of God	4	265	142	417	0.9	1.5
PENT–Ch God (Cleve)	1	9	52	67	0.1	0.2
PENT–Ch of God Proph	1	NR	20	26	0.1	0.1
PENT–COGIC	1	0	0	0	0.0	0.0
PENT–Full Gosp Bapt	3	NR	NR	NR	-	-
PENT–Un Pent Ch Intl	2	NR	NR	NR	-	-
PRES–Presb Ch (USA)	2	78	88	114	0.2	0.4
Salvation Army	1	24	67	67	0.1	0.2
Sev Day Adv	1	72	124	143	0.3	0.5
DE BACA	**8**	**345**	**985**	**1,985**	**98.2**	**100.0**
ANG/EPIS–Episcopal	1	8	22	22	1.1	1.1
Bahá'í	0	NR	1	1	0.0	0.1
BAPT–So Bapt Conv	1	100	526	636	31.5	32.0
Catholic	1	NR	NR	705	34.9	35.5
CHR–Chs of Christ	1	100	150	195	9.6	9.8
LDS–L-D Saints	1	NR	NR	47	2.3	2.4
MENN–CG in Cr (Menn)	1	NR	48	58	2.9	2.9
METH–Un Methodist	1	67	168	233	11.5	11.7
Non-denom Chr Chs	1	70	70	88	4.4	4.4
DOÑA ANA	**186**	**13,499**	**22,319**	**102,339**	**48.9**	**100.0**
ANG/EPIS–Anglican NA	1	NR	NR	NR	-	-
ANG/EPIS–Episcopal	3	449	908	1,039	0.5	1.0
Bahá'í	1	NR	498	498	0.2	0.5
BAPT–NBC USA	1	45	80	101	0.0	0.1
BAPT–Ref Bapt Ch	2	NR	NR	NR	-	-
BAPT–So Bapt Conv	31	3,213	8,514	10,712	5.1	10.5
BUDD–Mahayana	1	NR	NR	11	0.0	0.0
Calv Chpl	3	NR	NR	NR	-	-
Catholic	26	NR	NR	66,491	31.8	65.0
CGOD–Ch God (Ander)	1	40	NR	40	0.0	0.0
Ch Cr, Scientst	1	NR	NR	NR	-	-
Ch of Nazarene	3	170	258	324	0.2	0.3
CHR–Chr Ch (Disc)	1	75	126	159	0.1	0.2
CHR–Chr Chs & Chs Cr	2	NR	130	164	0.1	0.2
CHR–Chs of Christ	8	756	862	997	0.5	1.0
Christian Brethren	1	NR	NR	NR	-	-
Evan Free Ch	1	230	NR	230	0.1	0.2
FRND–Fr Gen Cf	1	NR	25	31	0.0	0.0
HINDU–I/A Temples	1	NR	NR	250	0.1	0.2
HINDU–Post Ren	1	NR	NR	77	0.0	0.1

NR–Not Reported - Represents no adherents reported. Percentages may not total 100 due to rounding.

Table 3: Religious Congregations by County and Group: 2010

Religious Group	Number of Congrega-tions	Number of Attendees	Number of Communicant, Confirmed, or Full Members	Adherents: Number of Adherents	Adherents: % of Total Pop.	Adherents: % of Total Adh.
Jehovah's Witness	3	NR	NR	NR	-	-
JUD–Orth	1	43	50	60	0.0	0.1
JUD–Reform	1	95	168	454	0.2	0.4
LDS–Comm of Christ	1	NR	61	61	0.0	0.1
LDS–L-D Saints	10	NR	NR	4,436	2.1	4.3
LUTH–E.L.C.A.	2	266	471	560	0.3	0.5
LUTH–Luth–MO Synod	2	183	263	373	0.2	0.4
LUTH–Wisc Ev Luth Syn	1	71	113	139	0.1	0.1
MENN–Bible Flwshp	1	24	NR	32	0.0	0.0
METH–C.M.E.	1	0	100	126	0.1	0.1
METH–Un Methodist	6	956	3,012	3,956	1.9	3.9
Muslim Est	2	314	NR	618	0.3	0.6
Non-denom Chr Chs	9	1,875	2,200	2,558	1.2	2.5
ORTHE–Ukrainian Orth	1	25	NR	30	0.0	0.0
PENT–Assemb of God	19	2,772	1,635	4,250	2.0	4.2
PENT–Ch God (Cleve)	5	213	242	304	0.1	0.3
PENT–Ch of God Proph	2	NR	55	69	0.0	0.1
PENT–COGIC	1	15	100	126	0.1	0.1
PENT–Int Foursq Gos	3	256	287	361	0.2	0.4
PENT–Intl Pent Holiness	6	292	299	376	0.2	0.4
PENT–Pent Ch of God	1	70	NR	109	0.1	0.1
PENT–Un Pent Ch Intl	3	NR	NR	NR	-	-
PENT–Vineyard	1	100	45	57	0.0	0.1
PRES–Presb Ch (USA)	3	240	585	736	0.4	0.7
PRES–Presb Ch Amer	2	202	420	460	0.2	0.4
Salvation Army	1	20	41	50	0.0	0.0
Sev Day Adv	5	258	447	515	0.2	0.5
Un C of Christ	1	75	126	159	0.1	0.2
Unit Univ	1	156	198	240	0.1	0.2
Unity Ch	1	NR	NR	NR	-	-
EDDY	**92**	**5,908**	**15,479**	**35,008**	**65.0**	**100.0**
ANG/EPIS–Episcopal	2	80	181	230	0.4	0.7
Bahá'í	0	NR	86	86	0.2	0.2
BAPT–Free Will Bapt	1	NR	6	8	0.0	0.0
BAPT–Ind Bapt Flwsp Intl	2	NR	NR	NR	-	-
BAPT–NBC USA	2	80	100	125	0.2	0.4
BAPT–So Bapt Conv	16	1,562	8,533	10,694	19.9	30.5
Catholic	6	NR	NR	13,254	24.6	37.9
Ch of Nazarene	3	161	279	295	0.5	0.8
CHR–Chr Ch (Disc)	2	75	240	301	0.6	0.9
CHR–Chr Chs & Chs Cr	2	NR	135	169	0.3	0.5
CHR–Chs of Christ	10	1,035	1,070	1,356	2.5	3.9
FRND–Fr Gen Cf	1	NR	0	0	0.0	0.0
Jehovah's Witness	3	NR	NR	NR	-	-
LDS–Comm of Christ	1	NR	61	61	0.1	0.2
LDS–L-D Saints	3	NR	NR	1,457	2.7	4.2
LUTH–E.L.C.A.	1	49	89	98	0.2	0.3
LUTH–Luth–MO Synod	2	73	139	159	0.3	0.5
MENN–Mennonite USA	1	30	25	31	0.1	0.1
METH–C.M.E.	2	0	200	251	0.5	0.7
METH–Un Methodist	7	604	1,610	2,092	3.9	6.0
Non-denom Chr Chs	6	1,170	1,575	1,750	3.3	5.0
PENT–Assemb of God	8	698	409	1,668	3.1	4.8
PENT–Ch God (Cleve)	4	132	287	360	0.7	1.0
PENT–Ch of God Proph	1	NR	6	8	0.0	0.0
PENT–COGIC	1	0	150	188	0.3	0.5
PENT–Un Pent Ch Intl	2	NR	NR	NR	-	-
PRES–Presb Ch (USA)	2	123	236	296	0.5	0.8
Sev Day Adv	1	36	62	71	0.1	0.2
GRANT	**60**	**1,632**	**2,699**	**14,747**	**50.0**	**100.0**
ANG/EPIS–Anglican NA	1	NR	NR	NR	-	-
ANG/EPIS–Episcopal	1	67	148	148	0.5	1.0
Bahá'í	0	NR	20	20	0.1	0.1
BAPT–So Bapt Conv	9	446	1,106	1,329	4.5	9.0
BUDD–Mahayana	1	NR	NR	11	0.0	0.1
BUDD–Vajrayana	2	NR	NR	40	0.1	0.3
Calv Chpl	1	NR	NR	NR	-	-
Catholic	13	NR	NR	9,587	32.5	65.0
Ch of Nazarene	1	38	24	38	0.1	0.3
CHR–Chs of Christ	4	226	200	283	1.0	1.9
FRND–Fr Gen Cf	1	NR	27	32	0.1	0.2
Jehovah's Witness	2	NR	NR	NR	-	-
LDS–L-D Saints	6	NR	NR	1,638	5.5	11.1
LUTH–Luth–MO Synod	1	44	67	80	0.3	0.5
METH–Un Methodist	2	131	338	384	1.3	2.6
Non-denom Chr Chs	3	165	165	220	0.7	1.5
PENT–Assemb of God	5	269	207	473	1.6	3.2
PENT–Int Foursq Gos	1	20	24	29	0.1	0.2
PRES–Presb Ch (USA)	2	125	212	255	0.9	1.7
Sev Day Adv	1	39	68	78	0.3	0.5
Swedenborgian	1	NR	NR	NR	-	-
Un C of Christ	1	29	45	54	0.2	0.4
Unit Univ	1	33	48	48	0.2	0.3
GUADALUPE	**19**	**148**	**136**	**4,208**	**89.8**	**100.0**
BAPT–So Bapt Conv	1	22	38	46	1.0	1.1
Catholic	13	NR	NR	4,000	85.3	95.1
CHR–Chs of Christ	2	55	36	71	1.5	1.7
Jehovah's Witness	1	NR	NR	NR	-	-
METH–Un Methodist	1	16	22	28	0.6	0.7
PENT–Assemb of God	1	55	40	63	1.3	1.5
HARDING	**6**	**54**	**217**	**858**	**123.5**	**100.0**
BAPT–So Bapt Conv	1	30	177	197	28.3	23.0
Catholic	3	NR	NR	608	87.5	70.9
CHR–Chr Ch (Disc)	1	12	20	22	3.2	2.6
METH–Un Methodist	1	12	20	31	4.5	3.6
HIDALGO	**15**	**248**	**374**	**3,830**	**78.3**	**100.0**
Bahá'í	0	NR	12	12	0.2	0.3
BAPT–So Bapt Conv	3	78	181	223	4.6	5.8
Catholic	3	NR	NR	2,871	58.7	75.0
CHR–Chr Chs & Chs Cr	1	NR	0	0	0.0	0.0
CHR–Chs of Christ	1	5	5	5	0.1	0.1
Jehovah's Witness	1	NR	NR	NR	-	-
LDS–L-D Saints	3	NR	NR	448	9.2	11.7
METH–Un Methodist	1	35	108	116	2.4	3.0
Non-denom Chr Chs	1	40	35	50	1.0	1.3
PENT–Assemb of God	1	90	33	105	2.1	2.7
LEA	**111**	**8,279**	**18,155**	**35,411**	**54.7**	**100.0**
ANG/EPIS–Anglican NA	1	NR	NR	NR	-	-
ANG/EPIS–Episcopal	2	29	64	64	0.1	0.2
Bahá'í	1	NR	156	156	0.2	0.4
BAPT–Amer Bapt Assn	1	NR	60	78	0.1	0.2
BAPT–Free Will Bapt	1	NR	6	8	0.0	0.0
BAPT–So Bapt Conv	27	2,547	10,451	13,641	21.1	38.5
Catholic	6	NR	NR	10,274	15.9	29.0
Ch of Nazarene	2	180	154	301	0.5	0.9
CHR–Chr Chs & Chs Cr	3	NR	345	450	0.7	1.3
CHR–Chs of Christ	13	1,133	1,501	1,969	3.0	5.6
Jehovah's Witness	1	NR	NR	NR	-	-
LDS–L-D Saints	2	NR	NR	958	1.5	2.7
LUTH–E.L.C.A.	1	36	86	95	0.1	0.3
LUTH–Luth–MO Synod	2	70	104	125	0.2	0.4
METH–C.M.E.	1	25	50	65	0.1	0.2
METH–Un Methodist	6	554	1,498	1,811	2.8	5.1
Non-denom Chr Chs	12	2,360	2,395	3,111	4.8	8.8
PENT–Assemb of God	9	870	353	1,109	1.7	3.1
PENT–Ch God (Cleve)	6	195	319	416	0.6	1.2
PENT–Ch of God Proph	2	NR	45	59	0.1	0.2
PENT–COGIC	3	60	120	157	0.2	0.4
PENT–Intl Pent Holiness	1	70	70	91	0.1	0.3
PENT–Un Pent Ch Intl	2	NR	NR	NR	-	-
PRES–Presb Ch (USA)	2	20	137	179	0.3	0.5
Salvation Army	1	13	38	60	0.1	0.2
Sev Day Adv	3	117	203	234	0.4	0.7
LINCOLN	**46**	**2,384**	**4,187**	**8,007**	**39.1**	**100.0**
ANG/EPIS–Anglican NA	1	NR	NR	NR	-	-
ANG/EPIS–Episcopal	1	101	190	190	0.9	2.4
Bahá'í	0	NR	31	31	0.2	0.4
BAPT–So Bapt Conv	7	702	1,510	1,762	8.6	22.0

NR–Not Reported   - Represents no adherents reported.   Percentages may not total 100 due to rounding.

Table 3: Religious Congregations by County and Group: 2010

Religious Group	Number of Congregations	Number of Attendees	Number of Communicant, Confirmed, or Full Members	Adherents		
				Number of Adherents	% of Total Pop.	% of Total Adh.
Calv Chpl	1	NR	NR	NR	-	-
Catholic	9	NR	NR	2,745	13.4	34.3
Ch of Nazarene	1	182	244	340	1.7	4.2
CHR–Chr Ch (Disc)	1	135	286	334	1.6	4.2
CHR–Chs of Christ	3	297	323	380	1.9	4.7
FRND–Fr Gen Cf	1	NR	0	0	0.0	0.0
Jehovah's Witness	1	NR	NR	NR	-	-
LDS–L-D Saints	1	NR	NR	426	2.1	5.3
LUTH–Luth–MO Synod	1	49	90	91	0.4	1.1
METH–Un Methodist	3	255	416	477	2.3	6.0
Non-denom Chr Chs	6	440	790	790	3.9	9.9
PENT–Assemb of God	2	62	41	131	0.6	1.6
PENT–Int Foursq Gos	1	18	52	61	0.3	0.8
PENT–Un Pent Ch Intl	1	NR	NR	NR	-	-
PRES–Presb Ch (USA)	4	115	165	193	0.9	2.4
Sev Day Adv	1	28	49	56	0.3	0.7
LOS ALAMOS	**35**	**2,538**	**6,017**	**12,093**	**67.4**	**100.0**
ANG/EPIS–Episcopal	1	144	264	428	2.4	3.5
Bahá'í	1	NR	66	66	0.4	0.5
BAPT–Amer Bapt USA	1	166	301	367	2.0	3.0
BAPT–So Bapt Conv	2	487	2,064	2,515	14.0	20.8
BUDD–Mahayana	1	NR	NR	103	0.6	0.9
Calv Chpl	1	NR	NR	NR	-	-
Catholic	2	NR	NR	2,870	16.0	23.7
Ch Cr, Scientst	1	NR	NR	NR	-	-
Ch of Nazarene	1	16	57	57	0.3	0.5
Chr & Miss Al	1	355	186	505	2.8	4.2
CHR–Chr Ch (Disc)	1	166	301	367	2.0	3.0
CHR–Chr Chs & Chs Cr	1	NR	175	213	1.2	1.8
CHR–Chs of Christ	1	195	224	310	1.7	2.6
Christian Brethren	1	NR	NR	NR	-	-
FRND–Fr Gen Cf	1	NR	0	0	0.0	0.0
Jehovah's Witness	1	NR	NR	NR	-	-
LDS–L-D Saints	2	NR	NR	1,011	5.6	8.4
LUTH–E.L.C.A.	1	185	396	634	3.5	5.2
LUTH–Luth–MO Synod	1	32	2	44	0.2	0.4
METH–Un Methodist	2	241	807	1,074	6.0	8.9
ORTHE–Orth Ch in Amer	1	21	NR	34	0.2	0.3
PENT–Assemb of God	1	74	34	93	0.5	0.8
PENT–Un Pent Ch Intl	1	NR	NR	NR	-	-
PENT–Vineyard	1	65	93	113	0.6	0.9
PRES–Presb Ch (USA)	2	40	113	138	0.8	1.1
PRES–Presb Ch Amer	1	53	66	76	0.4	0.6
REF–Ref Ch in Am	1	40	50	55	0.3	0.5
Sev Day Adv	1	12	21	24	0.1	0.2
Un C of Christ	1	159	642	782	4.4	6.5
Unit Univ	1	87	155	214	1.2	1.8
LUNA	**34**	**1,573**	**2,591**	**10,788**	**43.0**	**100.0**
ANG/EPIS–Anglican NA	1	NR	NR	NR	-	-
ANG/EPIS–Episcopal	1	25	41	41	0.2	0.4
Bahá'í	0	NR	79	79	0.3	0.7
BAPT–So Bapt Conv	4	367	808	1,012	4.0	9.4
Calv Chpl	1	NR	NR	NR	-	-
Catholic	3	NR	NR	6,323	25.2	58.6
Ch of Nazarene	1	52	82	82	0.3	0.8
CHR–Chr Chs & Chs Cr	1	NR	135	169	0.7	1.6
CHR–Chs of Christ	3	130	118	161	0.6	1.5
HINDU–Post Ren	1	NR	NR	100	0.4	0.9
Jehovah's Witness	1	NR	NR	NR	-	-
LDS–L-D Saints	3	NR	NR	914	3.6	8.5
LUTH–Luth–MO Synod	1	46	64	65	0.3	0.6
METH–Un Methodist	1	201	471	739	2.9	6.9
Non-denom Chr Chs	3	410	580	592	2.4	5.5
PENT–Assemb of God	2	150	25	178	0.7	1.6
PENT–Ch God (Cleve)	1	20	27	34	0.1	0.3
PENT–Pent Ch of God	1	70	NR	109	0.4	1.0
PENT–Un Pent Ch Intl	1	NR	NR	NR	-	-
PRES–Presb Ch (USA)	1	34	42	53	0.2	0.5
Sev Day Adv	2	68	119	137	0.5	1.3
Unity Ch	1	NR	NR	NR	-	-

Religious Group	Number of Congregations	Number of Attendees	Number of Communicant, Confirmed, or Full Members	Adherents		
				Number of Adherents	% of Total Pop.	% of Total Adh.
MCKINLEY	**105**	**4,240**	**6,809**	**32,490**	**45.4**	**100.0**
ANG/EPIS–Anglican NA	1	NR	NR	NR	-	-
ANG/EPIS–Episcopal	1	25	63	63	0.1	0.2
Bahá'í	1	NR	168	168	0.2	0.5
BAPT–Amer Bapt Assn	3	NR	255	334	0.5	1.0
BAPT–Consrv Bapt	2	NR	NR	NR	-	-
BAPT–Reg Bapt Gen As	1	NR	NR	NR	-	-
BAPT–So Bapt Conv	11	656	2,004	2,628	3.7	8.1
Calv Chpl	1	NR	NR	NR	-	-
Catholic	12	NR	NR	13,200	18.5	40.6
CGOD–Ches God-Gen Con	2	54	0	0	0.0	0.0
Ch of Nazarene	3	111	158	204	0.3	0.6
CHR–Chr Chs & Chs Cr	2	NR	100	131	0.2	0.4
CHR–Chs of Christ	3	120	148	195	0.3	0.6
FRND–Fr Gen Cf	1	NR	0	0	0.0	0.0
Jehovah's Witness	1	NR	NR	NR	-	-
LDS–L-D Saints	11	NR	NR	9,434	13.2	29.0
LUTH–Luth–MO Synod	2	55	74	105	0.1	0.3
METH–AME	1	0	100	131	0.2	0.4
METH–Un Methodist	1	123	429	445	0.6	1.4
Muslim Est	1	134	NR	308	0.4	0.9
New Apost Ch	1	NR	NR	NR	-	-
Non-denom Chr Chs	5	850	920	1,086	1.5	3.3
PENT–Assemb of God	7	420	216	687	1.0	2.1
PENT–Ch God (Cleve)	14	451	776	1,018	1.4	3.1
PENT–Pent Ch of God	5	350	NR	544	0.8	1.7
PENT–Un Pent Ch Intl	2	NR	NR	NR	-	-
PRES–Presb Ch (USA)	1	35	50	66	0.1	0.2
REF–Christian Ref	8	768	1,194	1,566	2.2	4.8
Sev Day Adv	1	88	154	177	0.2	0.5
MORA	**33**	**266**	**222**	**3,178**	**65.1**	**100.0**
Bahá'í	0	NR	1	1	0.0	0.0
BAPT–So Bapt Conv	2	55	40	48	1.0	1.5
BUDD–Vajrayana	1	NR	NR	13	0.3	0.4
Catholic	22	NR	NR	2,795	57.3	87.9
CHR–Chs of Christ	4	110	101	134	2.7	4.2
PENT–Assemb of God	1	50	15	110	2.3	3.5
PRES–Presb Ch (USA)	2	43	52	62	1.3	2.0
Sev Day Adv	1	8	13	15	0.3	0.5
OTERO	**94**	**6,088**	**8,659**	**25,900**	**40.6**	**100.0**
ANG/EPIS–Anglican NA	2	NR	NR	NR	-	-
ANG/EPIS–Episcopal	2	65	209	209	0.3	0.8
Bahá'í	1	NR	145	145	0.2	0.6
BAPT–Consrv Bapt	1	NR	NR	NR	-	-
BAPT–NBC USA	1	90	125	155	0.2	0.6
BAPT–Reg Bapt Gen As	1	NR	NR	NR	-	-
BAPT–So Bapt Conv	18	1,314	2,541	3,160	5.0	12.2
BUDD–Vajrayana	1	NR	NR	25	0.0	0.1
Calv Chpl	1	NR	NR	NR	-	-
Catholic	11	NR	NR	11,862	18.6	45.8
Ch Cr, Scientst	1	NR	NR	NR	-	-
Ch of Nazarene	2	117	152	152	0.2	0.6
CHR–Chr Ch (Disc)	1	0	35	44	0.1	0.2
CHR–Chr Chs & Chs Cr	1	NR	45	56	0.1	0.2
CHR–Chs of Christ	12	443	476	605	0.9	2.3
Jehovah's Witness	3	NR	NR	NR	-	-
LDS–Comm of Christ	1	NR	61	61	0.1	0.2
LDS–L-D Saints	3	NR	NR	1,426	2.2	5.5
LUTH–E.L.C.A.	1	112	292	355	0.6	1.4
LUTH–Luth–MO Synod	1	103	144	172	0.3	0.7
METH–AME	1	0	100	124	0.2	0.5
METH–Un Methodist	6	620	1,580	1,986	3.1	7.7
Non-denom Chr Chs	6	1,038	1,032	1,359	2.1	5.2
PENT–Assemb of God	5	1,740	937	3,052	4.8	11.8
PENT–Ch God (Cleve)	1	29	47	58	0.1	0.2
PENT–COGIC	1	80	150	187	0.3	0.7
PENT–Full Gosp Bapt	2	NR	NR	NR	-	-
PENT–Un Pent Ch Intl	1	NR	NR	NR	-	-
PRES–Presb Ch (USA)	1	43	57	71	0.1	0.3
PRES–Presb Ch Amer	1	81	90	100	0.2	0.4
REF–Ref Ch in Am	1	87	218	248	0.4	1.0

NR–Not Reported - Represents no adherents reported. Percentages may not total 100 due to rounding.

Table 3: Religious Congregations by County and Group: 2010

Religious Group	Number of Congrega-tions	Number of Attendees	Number of Communicant, Confirmed, or Full Members	Adherents: Number of Adherents	Adherents: % of Total Pop.	Adherents: % of Total Adh.
Salvation Army	1	8	30	57	0.1	0.2
Sev Day Adv	1	88	153	176	0.3	0.7
Unit Univ	1	30	40	55	0.1	0.2
QUAY	**32**	**1,197**	**3,995**	**8,734**	**96.6**	**100.0**
ANG/EPIS–Episcopal	1	18	43	43	0.5	0.5
Bahá'í	0	NR	7	7	0.1	0.1
BAPT–So Bapt Conv	8	497	2,938	3,521	38.9	40.3
Catholic	5	NR	NR	3,510	38.8	40.2
CHR–Chr Chs & Chs Cr	1	NR	80	96	1.1	1.1
CHR–Chs of Christ	3	105	100	131	1.4	1.5
Jehovah's Witness	1	NR	NR	NR	-	-
LDS–L-D Saints	1	NR	NR	263	2.9	3.0
METH–Un Methodist	4	208	456	562	6.2	6.4
Non-denom Chr Chs	2	70	110	112	1.2	1.3
PENT–Assemb of God	4	247	182	396	4.4	4.5
PRES–Presb Ch (USA)	1	30	42	50	0.6	0.6
Sev Day Adv	1	22	37	43	0.5	0.5
RIO ARRIBA	**86**	**2,917**	**2,380**	**26,106**	**64.9**	**100.0**
ANG/EPIS–Episcopal	2	39	59	69	0.2	0.3
Bahá'í	0	NR	41	41	0.1	0.2
BAPT–So Bapt Conv	5	158	300	370	0.9	1.4
BRETH–Ch of Brethren	1	12	14	17	0.0	0.1
Calv Chpl	1	NR	NR	NR	-	-
Catholic	41	NR	NR	21,305	52.9	81.6
CHR–Chs of Christ	3	121	113	145	0.4	0.6
Jehovah's Witness	1	NR	NR	NR	-	-
LDS–L-D Saints	3	NR	NR	765	1.9	2.9
METH–Un Methodist	3	160	251	325	0.8	1.2
Muslim Est	1	134	NR	308	0.8	1.2
Non-denom Chr Chs	3	340	400	450	1.1	1.7
ORTHE–Orth Ch in Amer	1	5	NR	5	0.0	0.0
PENT–Assemb of God	8	982	379	1,107	2.8	4.2
PENT–Int Foursq Gos	2	566	325	401	1.0	1.5
PENT–Pent Ch of God	2	140	NR	217	0.5	0.8
PENT–Un Pent Ch Intl	1	NR	NR	NR	-	-
PRES–Presb Ch (USA)	3	69	148	183	0.5	0.7
REF–Ref Ch in Am	1	65	130	145	0.4	0.6
Sev Day Adv	3	126	220	253	0.6	1.0
Sikh	1	NR	NR	NR	-	-
ROOSEVELT	**41**	**2,793**	**5,621**	**10,760**	**54.2**	**100.0**
ANG/EPIS–Episcopal	1	8	8	8	0.0	0.1
Bahá'í	0	NR	33	33	0.2	0.3
BAPT–So Bapt Conv	12	1,045	3,134	3,944	19.9	36.7
Catholic	2	NR	NR	3,349	16.9	31.1
Ch of Nazarene	1	75	68	75	0.4	0.7
CHR–Chr Chs & Chs Cr	1	NR	0	0	0.0	0.0
CHR–Chs of Christ	8	689	712	858	4.3	8.0
Jehovah's Witness	1	NR	NR	NR	-	-
LDS–L-D Saints	2	NR	NR	568	2.9	5.3
LUTH–Luth-MO Synod	1	29	37	48	0.2	0.4
METH–Un Methodist	3	215	793	893	4.5	8.3
Non-denom Chr Chs	3	505	580	631	3.2	5.9
PENT–Assemb of God	1	57	29	70	0.4	0.7
PENT–Ch God (Cleve)	1	120	101	127	0.6	1.2
PENT–Ch of God Proph	1	NR	30	38	0.2	0.4
PENT–Un Pent Ch Intl	1	NR	NR	NR	-	-
PRES–Presb Ch (USA)	1	35	70	88	0.4	0.8
Sev Day Adv	1	15	26	30	0.2	0.3
SANDOVAL	**97**	**6,130**	**9,129**	**55,784**	**42.4**	**100.0**
ANG/EPIS–Episcopal	1	47	188	198	0.2	0.4
Bahá'í	2	NR	124	124	0.1	0.2
BAPT–Natl Mis Bapt Conv	1	0	150	189	0.1	0.3
BAPT–Reg Bapt Gen As	1	NR	NR	NR	-	-
BAPT–So Bapt Conv	14	1,506	2,435	3,067	2.3	5.5
BUDD–Mahayana	2	NR	NR	39	0.0	0.1
Calv Chpl	1	NR	NR	NR	-	-
Catholic	25	NR	NR	40,035	30.4	71.8
Ch Cr, Scientst	1	NR	NR	NR	-	-
CHR–Chr Chs & Chs Cr	2	NR	405	510	0.4	0.9
CHR–Chs of Christ	2	152	188	243	0.2	0.4
Evan Free Ch	1	250	NR	250	0.2	0.4
Jehovah's Witness	3	NR	NR	NR	-	-
LDS–L-D Saints	9	NR	NR	4,143	3.1	7.4
LUTH–Ch Luth Conf	1	NR	NR	NR	-	-
LUTH–E.L.C.A.	1	162	225	298	0.2	0.5
LUTH–Luth-MO Synod	2	119	177	218	0.2	0.4
LUTH–Wisc Ev Luth Syn	1	44	68	74	0.1	0.1
MENN–Cons Menn Conf	1	25	27	34	0.0	0.1
METH–Un Methodist	3	335	477	662	0.5	1.2
Non-denom Chr Chs	7	1,730	2,220	2,544	1.9	4.6
PENT–Assemb of God	3	570	531	905	0.7	1.6
PENT–Ch God (Cleve)	1	18	11	14	0.0	0.0
PENT–Int Foursq Gos	1	59	46	58	0.0	0.1
PENT–Un Pent Ch Intl	1	NR	NR	NR	-	-
PRES–Cumber Presb	1	NR	46	46	0.0	0.1
PRES–Orth Pres Ch	1	66	39	46	0.0	0.1
PRES–Presb Ch (USA)	4	289	463	583	0.4	1.0
Sev Day Adv	3	706	1,228	1,412	1.1	2.5
Unit Univ	1	52	81	87	0.1	0.2
Zoroastrian	0	NR	NR	5	0.0	0.0
SAN JUAN	**173**	**11,140**	**18,695**	**52,628**	**40.5**	**100.0**
ANG/EPIS–Anglican NA	1	NR	NR	NR	-	-
ANG/EPIS–Episcopal	3	144	439	460	0.4	0.9
Bahá'í	2	NR	138	138	0.1	0.3
BAPT–Amer Bapt Assn	2	NR	85	110	0.1	0.2
BAPT–Amer Bapt USA	1	7	12	16	0.0	0.0
BAPT–Ind Bapt Flwsp Intl	2	NR	NR	NR	-	-
BAPT–NT Ind Bapt	1	NR	NR	NR	-	-
BAPT–So Bapt Conv	29	2,403	6,672	8,633	6.6	16.4
BRETH–Breth in Chr	2	NR	NR	NR	-	-
Calv Chpl	1	NR	NR	NR	-	-
Catholic	11	NR	NR	12,500	9.6	23.8
Ch Cr, Scientst	1	NR	NR	NR	-	-
Ch of Nazarene	3	624	663	956	0.7	1.8
CHR–Chr Ch (Disc)	1	109	243	314	0.2	0.6
CHR–Chr Chs & Chs Cr	3	NR	175	226	0.2	0.4
CHR–Chs of Christ	9	613	804	1,014	0.8	1.9
Jehovah's Witness	2	NR	NR	NR	-	-
LDS–Comm of Christ	1	NR	128	128	0.1	0.2
LDS–L-D Saints	24	NR	NR	14,690	11.3	27.9
LUTH–E.L.C.A.	1	100	278	357	0.3	0.7
LUTH–Luth-MO Synod	1	124	199	241	0.2	0.5
LUTH–Wisc Ev Luth Syn	1	78	101	166	0.1	0.3
MENN–Mennonite USA	1	40	40	52	0.0	0.1
METH–Cong Meth	1	NR	16	21	0.0	0.0
METH–Un Methodist	8	797	2,701	3,449	2.7	6.6
Non-denom Chr Chs	20	3,290	3,529	4,261	3.3	8.1
PENT–Assemb of God	11	1,513	772	2,587	2.0	4.9
PENT–Ch God (Cleve)	8	222	216	279	0.2	0.5
PENT–Ch God Apos Fth	1	NR	NR	NR	-	-
PENT–Int Foursq Gos	2	101	66	85	0.1	0.2
PENT–Pent Ch of God	1	70	NR	109	0.1	0.2
PENT–Un Pent Ch Intl	3	NR	NR	NR	-	-
PRES–Presb Ch (USA)	2	209	484	626	0.5	1.2
PRES–Presb Ch Amer	1	70	58	87	0.1	0.2
REF–Christian Ref	5	261	299	387	0.3	0.7
Salvation Army	1	18	21	87	0.1	0.2
Sev Day Adv	5	302	526	604	0.5	1.1
Unit Univ	1	45	30	45	0.0	0.1
SAN MIGUEL	**67**	**973**	**1,578**	**23,899**	**81.3**	**100.0**
ANG/EPIS–Episcopal	1	39	73	73	0.2	0.3
Bahá'í	0	NR	12	12	0.0	0.1
BAPT–So Bapt Conv	4	175	619	738	2.5	3.1
BUDD–Vajrayana	1	NR	NR	14	0.0	0.1
Calv Chpl	1	NR	NR	NR	-	-
Catholic	38	NR	NR	21,688	73.8	90.7
CHR–Chr Chs & Chs Cr	1	NR	0	0	0.0	0.0
CHR–Chs of Christ	4	255	208	287	1.0	1.2
FRND–Fr Gen Cf	1	NR	0	0	0.0	0.0

NR–Not Reported - Represents no adherents reported. Percentages may not total 100 due to rounding.

Table 3: Religious Congregations by County and Group: 2010

Religious Group	Number of Congregations	Number of Attendees	Number of Communicant, Confirmed, or Full Members	Adherents: Number of Adherents	Adherents: % of Total Pop.	Adherents: % of Total Adh.
Jehovah's Witness	1	NR	NR	NR	-	-
LDS–L-D Saints	1	NR	NR	258	0.9	1.1
LUTH–E.L.C.A.	1	39	62	73	0.2	0.3
LUTH–Luth–MO Synod	1	7	20	27	0.1	0.1
MENN–CG in Cr (Menn)	1	NR	31	37	0.1	0.2
METH–Un Methodist	1	45	61	78	0.3	0.3
Non-denom Chr Chs	2	155	250	250	0.9	1.0
PENT–Assemb of God	4	157	91	187	0.6	0.8
PENT–Int Foursq Gos	1	8	7	8	0.0	0.0
PENT–Un Pent Ch Intl	1	NR	NR	NR	-	-
PRES–Presb Ch (USA)	1	65	95	113	0.4	0.5
Sev Day Adv	1	28	49	56	0.2	0.2
SANTA FE	**134**	**6,850**	**10,444**	**87,490**	**60.7**	**100.0**
ANG/EPIS–Episcopal	5	553	1,204	1,463	1.0	1.7
Bahá'í	2	NR	177	177	0.1	0.2
BAPT–So Bapt Conv	8	1,025	1,932	2,305	1.6	2.6
BUDD–Mahayana	4	NR	NR	163	0.1	0.2
BUDD–Vajrayana	6	NR	NR	761	0.5	0.9
Calv Chpl	1	NR	NR	NR	-	-
Catholic	23	NR	NR	69,552	48.2	79.5
Ch Cr, Scientst	1	NR	NR	NR	-	-
Ch God (7th Day)	1	NR	NR	NR	-	-
Ch of Nazarene	2	84	35	95	0.1	0.1
CHR–Chr Ch (Disc)	2	58	65	78	0.1	0.1
CHR–Chr Chs & Chs Cr	2	NR	305	364	0.3	0.4
CHR–Chs of Christ	4	167	161	190	0.1	0.2
FRND–Fr Gen Cf	2	NR	89	106	0.1	0.1
HINDU–Post Ren	5	NR	NR	205	0.1	0.2
HINDU–Renaiss	2	NR	NR	53	0.0	0.1
Jehovah's Witness	4	NR	NR	NR	-	-
JUD–Orth	2	86	100	120	0.1	0.1
JUD–Reform	1	210	371	1,002	0.7	1.1
LDS–Comm of Christ	1	NR	61	61	0.0	0.1
LDS–L-D Saints	4	NR	NR	2,247	1.6	2.6
LUTH–E.L.C.A.	2	176	261	279	0.2	0.3
LUTH–Luth–MO Synod	2	156	299	361	0.3	0.4
METH–Un Methodist	3	380	1,219	1,387	1.0	1.6
Muslim Est	2	169	NR	458	0.3	0.5
Non-denom Chr Chs	13	1,670	1,770	2,178	1.5	2.5
ORTHE–Ant Orth of NA	1	80	NR	112	0.1	0.1
ORTHE–Greek Orthodox	1	45	NR	95	0.1	0.1
ORTHE–Rus Orth Abroad	1	32	NR	75	0.1	0.1
PENT–Assemb of God	5	543	395	866	0.6	1.0
PENT–Ch God (Cleve)	2	41	58	69	0.0	0.1
PENT–Int Foursq Gos	1	46	45	54	0.0	0.1
PENT–Intl Pent Holiness	1	92	70	83	0.1	0.1
PENT–Pent Ch of God	1	70	NR	109	0.1	0.1
PENT–Un Pent Ch Intl	2	NR	NR	NR	-	-
PENT–Vineyard	1	225	215	256	0.2	0.3
PRES–Presb Ch (USA)	3	266	462	551	0.4	0.6
PRES–Presb Ch Amer	1	0	0	0	0.0	0.0
REF–Comm Ref Evan	1	NR	NR	NR	-	-
Salvation Army	1	29	0	255	0.2	0.3
Sev Day Adv	4	327	568	654	0.5	0.7
Un C of Christ	1	169	320	382	0.3	0.4
Unit Univ	1	151	262	324	0.2	0.4
Unity Ch	2	NR	NR	NR	-	-
SIERRA	**34**	**802**	**1,295**	**3,269**	**27.3**	**100.0**
ANG/EPIS–Episcopal	2	39	72	113	0.9	3.5
Bahá'í	0	NR	13	13	0.1	0.4
BAPT–So Bapt Conv	2	284	818	933	7.8	28.5
BUDD–Mahayana	1	NR	NR	11	0.1	0.3
Catholic	11	NR	NR	1,021	8.5	31.2
CGOD–Ch God (Ander)	1	0	NR	0	0.0	0.0
Ch of Nazarene	1	23	15	35	0.3	1.1
Chr & Miss Al	1	60	20	94	0.8	2.9
CHR–Chr Chs & Chs Cr	1	NR	40	46	0.4	1.4
CHR–Chs of Christ	2	75	81	86	0.7	2.6
Jehovah's Witness	1	NR	NR	NR	-	-
LDS–Comm of Christ	1	NR	61	61	0.5	1.9
LDS–L-D Saints	1	NR	NR	366	3.1	11.2
LUTH–Luth Ch-Am Asc	1	NR	NR	NR	-	-
LUTH–Luth–MO Synod	1	0	10	10	0.1	0.3
METH–Un Methodist	1	50	67	86	0.7	2.6
Non-denom Chr Chs	1	15	30	30	0.3	0.9
PENT–Assemb of God	2	203	0	286	2.4	8.7
PENT–Int Foursq Gos	1	34	35	40	0.3	1.2
PENT–Un Pent Ch Intl	1	NR	NR	NR	-	-
Sev Day Adv	1	19	33	38	0.3	1.2
SOCORRO	**40**	**1,037**	**1,285**	**9,571**	**53.6**	**100.0**
ANG/EPIS–Episcopal	1	55	95	95	0.5	1.0
Bahá'í	0	NR	40	40	0.2	0.4
BAPT–Ind Bapt Flwsp Intl	1	NR	NR	NR	-	-
BAPT–So Bapt Conv	3	248	568	698	3.9	7.3
Calv Chpl	1	NR	NR	NR	-	-
Catholic	15	NR	NR	7,036	39.4	73.5
Ch God (7th Day)	1	NR	NR	NR	-	-
CHR–Chs of Christ	1	30	25	35	0.2	0.4
FRND–Fr Gen Cf	1	NR	0	0	0.0	0.0
Jehovah's Witness	1	NR	NR	NR	-	-
LDS–L-D Saints	2	NR	NR	556	3.1	5.8
LUTH–Luth–MO Synod	1	30	22	22	0.1	0.2
METH–Un Methodist	2	42	74	107	0.6	1.1
METH–Wesleyan	1	38	46	49	0.3	0.5
Muslim Est	1	134	NR	308	1.7	3.2
Non-denom Chr Chs	2	175	250	250	1.4	2.6
PENT–Assemb of God	2	114	38	114	0.6	1.2
PENT–Pent Ch of God	1	70	NR	109	0.6	1.1
PRES–Presb Ch (USA)	2	73	78	96	0.5	1.0
Sev Day Adv	1	28	49	56	0.3	0.6
TAOS	**83**	**1,791**	**2,134**	**22,584**	**68.6**	**100.0**
ANG/EPIS–Episcopal	1	120	332	332	1.0	1.5
Bahá'í	0	NR	65	65	0.2	0.3
BAPT–So Bapt Conv	5	144	321	382	1.2	1.7
BRETH–Grace Breth	1	NR	NR	NR	-	-
BUDD–Mahayana	4	NR	NR	235	0.7	1.0
BUDD–Vajrayana	1	NR	NR	208	0.6	0.9
Calv Chpl	1	NR	NR	NR	-	-
Catholic	33	NR	NR	17,986	54.6	79.6
Ch Cr, Scientst	1	NR	NR	NR	-	-
CHR–Chs of Christ	3	110	122	151	0.5	0.7
FRND–Fr Gen Cf	1	NR	0	0	0.0	0.0
HINDU–Post Ren	1	NR	NR	77	0.2	0.3
HINDU–Trad Temples	1	NR	NR	300	0.9	1.3
Jehovah's Witness	3	NR	NR	NR	-	-
JUD–Orth	1	43	50	60	0.2	0.3
LDS–L-D Saints	3	NR	NR	599	1.8	2.7
LUTH–Luth–MO Synod	1	23	17	17	0.1	0.1
METH–Un Methodist	1	50	54	147	0.4	0.7
Muslim Est	1	134	NR	308	0.9	1.4
Non-denom Chr Chs	5	475	650	675	2.0	3.0
PENT–Assemb of God	4	192	106	225	0.7	1.0
PENT–Int Foursq Gos	3	64	89	106	0.3	0.5
PENT–Pent Ch of God	3	210	NR	326	1.0	1.4
PRES–Presb Ch (USA)	3	147	191	227	0.7	1.0
Sev Day Adv	2	79	137	158	0.5	0.7
TORRANCE	**38**	**1,226**	**2,109**	**7,245**	**44.2**	**100.0**
Bahá'í	0	NR	20	20	0.1	0.3
BAPT–Ref Bapt Ch	1	NR	NR	NR	-	-
BAPT–So Bapt Conv	4	367	1,126	1,373	8.4	19.0
BUDD–Mahayana	1	NR	NR	20	0.1	0.3
Calv Chpl	1	NR	NR	NR	-	-
Catholic	12	NR	NR	4,055	24.8	56.0
Ch of Nazarene	2	87	125	133	0.8	1.8
CHR–Chs of Christ	3	189	141	222	1.4	3.1
Jehovah's Witness	1	NR	NR	NR	-	-
LDS–L-D Saints	1	NR	NR	421	2.6	5.8
METH–Un Methodist	3	178	355	428	2.6	5.9
Non-denom Chr Chs	4	215	300	306	1.9	4.2
PENT–Assemb of God	3	120	42	158	1.0	2.2
PENT–Pent Ch of God	1	70	NR	109	0.7	1.5

NR–Not Reported   - Represents no adherents reported.   Percentages may not total 100 due to rounding.

Table 3: Religious Congregations by County and Group: 2010

Religious Group	Number of Congrega-tions	Number of Attendees	Number of Communicant, Confirmed, or Full Members	Adherents		
				Number of Adherents	% of Total Pop.	% of Total Adh.
PENT–Un Pent Ch Intl	1	NR	NR	NR	-	-
UNION	**19**	**542**	**1,131**	**3,285**	**72.2**	**100.0**
BAPT–So Bapt Conv	2	101	362	428	9.4	13.0
Catholic	4	NR	NR	1,851	40.7	56.3
CHR–Chs of Christ	1	66	65	70	1.5	2.1
Jehovah's Witness	2	NR	NR	NR	-	-
METH–Un Methodist	3	129	369	556	12.2	16.9
Non-denom Chr Chs	3	199	264	274	6.0	8.3
PENT–Assemb of God	1	24	19	45	1.0	1.4
PENT–Ch God (Cleve)	1	9	27	32	0.7	1.0
PENT–Un Pent Ch Intl	1	NR	NR	NR	-	-
Sev Day Adv	1	14	25	29	0.6	0.9
VALENCIA	**76**	**3,710**	**6,741**	**32,356**	**42.3**	**100.0**
ANG/EPIS–Episcopal	2	96	189	189	0.2	0.6
Bahá'í	3	NR	77	77	0.1	0.2
BAPT–Ind Bapt Flwsp Intl	1	NR	NR	NR	-	-
BAPT–NT Ind Bapt	1	NR	NR	NR	-	-
BAPT–So Bapt Conv	10	890	2,563	3,210	4.2	9.9
BUDD–Mahayana	1	NR	NR	11	0.0	0.0
Calv Chpl	2	NR	NR	NR	-	-
Catholic	12	NR	NR	21,584	28.2	66.7
Ch of Nazarene	3	219	203	402	0.5	1.2
CHR–Chr Chs & Chs Cr	2	NR	270	338	0.4	1.0
CHR–Chs of Christ	4	250	238	296	0.4	0.9
Jehovah's Witness	3	NR	NR	NR	-	-
LDS–L-D Saints	4	NR	NR	2,092	2.7	6.5
LUTH–E.L.C.A.	1	55	140	155	0.2	0.5
LUTH–Luth–MO Synod	1	45	78	115	0.2	0.4
METH–Un Methodist	2	441	870	1,150	1.5	3.6
Non-denom Chr Chs	10	1,070	1,277	1,475	1.9	4.6
PENT–Assemb of God	4	293	110	397	0.5	1.2
PENT–Ch God (Cleve)	2	74	89	111	0.1	0.3
PENT–Ch of God Proph	1	NR	48	60	0.1	0.2
PENT–Un Pent Ch Intl	1	NR	NR	NR	-	-
PRES–Presb Ch (USA)	3	35	167	209	0.3	0.6
Sev Day Adv	3	242	422	485	0.6	1.5
NEW YORK	**14,110**	**1,567,789**	**1,872,223**	**9,923,512**	**51.2**	**100.0**
ALBANY	**230**	**20,585**	**30,396**	**137,564**	**45.2**	**100.0**
ANG/EPIS–Episcopal	12	1,069	2,229	2,783	0.9	2.0
Bahá'í	1	NR	89	89	0.0	0.1
BAPT–Amer Bapt USA	8	260	852	1,001	0.3	0.7
BAPT–Consrv Bapt	2	NR	NR	NR	-	-
BAPT–Converge/BGC	2	150	NR	180	0.1	0.1
BAPT–Natl Mis Bapt Conv	1	0	150	176	0.1	0.1
BAPT–NBC USA	5	500	1,500	1,763	0.6	1.3
BAPT–Ref Bapt Ch	1	NR	NR	NR	-	-
BAPT–Reg Bapt Gen As	2	NR	NR	NR	-	-
BAPT–So Bapt Conv	5	511	300	353	0.1	0.3
BUDD–Mahayana	3	NR	NR	164	0.1	0.1
BUDD–Vajrayana	3	NR	NR	129	0.0	0.1
Catholic	28	NR	NR	85,267	28.0	62.0
Ch Cr, Scientst	1	NR	NR	NR	-	-
Ch of Nazarene	2	41	62	136	0.0	0.1
Chr & Miss Al	3	239	201	318	0.1	0.2
CHR–Chr Chs & Chs Cr	1	NR	300	353	0.1	0.3
CHR–Chs of Christ	1	155	133	168	0.1	0.1
CHR–Int Chs of Christ	1	NR	29	34	0.0	0.0
Christian Brethren	1	NR	NR	NR	-	-
CONG–Cong Chr, NA	1	NR	110	129	0.0	0.1
CONG–Consrv Cong Chr	2	115	86	101	0.0	0.1
Evan Free Ch	1	34	NR	34	0.0	0.0
FRND–Fr Gen Cf & Un Mtg	1	NR	63	74	0.0	0.1
HINDU–I/A Temples	1	NR	NR	1,742	0.6	1.3
HINDU–Post Ren	4	NR	NR	166	0.1	0.1
HINDU–Trad Temples	1	NR	NR	800	0.3	0.6
Jain	1	NR	NR	NR	-	-
Jehovah's Witness	3	NR	NR	NR	-	-
JUD–Conserv	2	678	761	2,055	0.7	1.5
JUD–Orth	2	266	100	370	0.1	0.3
JUD–Reform	2	547	964	2,603	0.9	1.9
LDS–L-D Saints	2	NR	NR	1,247	0.4	0.9
LUTH–E.L.C.A.	6	436	1,395	1,921	0.6	1.4
LUTH–Luth–MO Synod	6	872	1,457	1,990	0.7	1.4
MENN–Bruderhof Comm	1	33	11	18	0.0	0.0
METH–AME	1	150	420	494	0.2	0.4
METH–AME Zion	2	20	200	235	0.1	0.2
METH–Un Methodist	15	1,228	4,435	5,181	1.7	3.8
Muslim Est	3	1,218	NR	4,567	1.5	3.3
Non-denom Chr Chs	21	7,296	7,110	9,294	3.1	6.8
OCATH–Pol Natl Cath	1	NR	NR	NR	-	-
ORTHE–Ant Orth of NA	1	31	NR	85	0.0	0.1
ORTHE–Greek Orthodox	1	325	NR	1,000	0.3	0.7
ORTHE–Orth Ch in Amer	2	170	NR	325	0.1	0.2
ORTHE–Rus Orth Abroad	1	60	NR	120	0.0	0.1
ORTHO–Armen Ap Etchm	1	60	NR	225	0.1	0.2
ORTHO–Coptic Orth Ch	1	70	NR	135	0.0	0.1
ORTHO–Eritrean Orth	1	225	NR	55	0.0	0.0
ORTHO–Malan Dioc Am	1	50	NR	80	0.0	0.1
PENT–Assemb of God	13	1,114	542	1,392	0.5	1.0
PENT–Ch God (Cleve)	1	60	75	88	0.0	0.1
PENT–Ch of God Proph	1	NR	279	328	0.1	0.2
PENT–COGIC	1	0	60	71	0.0	0.1
PENT–Full Gosp Bapt	1	NR	NR	NR	-	-
PENT–Vineyard	1	60	75	88	0.0	0.1
PRES–Presb Ch (USA)	13	649	1,722	2,024	0.7	1.5
REF–Ref Ch in Am	17	1,151	3,208	3,729	1.2	2.7
Salvation Army	2	52	178	288	0.1	0.2
Sev Day Adv	2	355	618	710	0.2	0.5
Un C of Christ	5	178	294	346	0.1	0.3
Unit Univ	1	157	388	528	0.2	0.4
Unity Ch	1	NR	NR	NR	-	-
Zoroastrian	0	NR	NR	12	0.0	0.0
ALLEGANY	**99**	**4,625**	**6,636**	**14,236**	**29.1**	**100.0**
ANG/EPIS–Episcopal	5	98	108	114	0.2	0.8
Bahá'í	0	NR	11	11	0.0	0.1
BAPT–Amer Bapt USA	5	322	697	833	1.7	5.9
BAPT–Reg Bapt Gen As	5	NR	NR	NR	-	-
BAPT–S-D Baptist Gen Con	3	114	177	211	0.4	1.5
BAPT–So Bapt Conv	1	20	20	24	0.0	0.2
Catholic	10	NR	NR	4,313	8.8	30.3
Ch Christ Chr Union	1	NR	NR	NR	-	-
Chr & Miss Al	3	214	102	278	0.6	2.0
CHR–Chr Ch (Disc)	1	40	116	139	0.3	1.0
CHR–Chr Chs & Chs Cr	3	NR	58	69	0.1	0.5
FRND–Fr Gen Cf & Un Mtg	1	NR	17	20	0.0	0.1
Jehovah's Witness	2	NR	NR	NR	-	-
LDS–L-D Saints	1	NR	NR	221	0.5	1.6
LUTH–E.L.C.A.	1	30	33	47	0.1	0.3
LUTH–Luth–MO Synod	2	133	305	351	0.7	2.5
MENN–Amish Undif	5	NR	217	483	1.0	3.4
MENN–Mennonite USA	2	140	135	161	0.3	1.1
METH–Evan Meth Ch	1	NR	NR	NR	-	-
METH–Free Methodist	1	50	33	50	0.1	0.4
METH–Un Methodist	22	929	2,598	3,386	6.9	23.8
METH–Wesleyan	6	1,079	646	1,403	2.9	9.9
Non-denom Chr Chs	7	1,110	857	1,386	2.8	9.7
PENT–Assemb of God	2	120	96	189	0.4	1.3
PENT–Elim	1	NR	NR	NR	-	-
PRES–Presb Ch (USA)	3	71	108	129	0.3	0.9
PRES–Presb Ch Amer	1	50	49	59	0.1	0.4
Salvation Army	1	48	54	127	0.3	0.9
Sev Day Adv	1	45	78	90	0.2	0.6
Un C of Christ	1	0	109	130	0.3	0.9
Unit Univ	1	12	12	12	0.0	0.1
BRONX	**619**	**71,507**	**83,380**	**518,003**	**37.4**	**100.0**
ANG/EPIS–Anglican NA	3	NR	NR	NR	-	-
ANG/EPIS–Episcopal	23	2,290	3,974	5,103	0.4	1.0
BAPT–Amer Bapt USA	27	6,041	8,088	10,142	0.7	2.0

NR–Not Reported   - Represents no adherents reported.   Percentages may not total 100 due to rounding.

Table 3: Religious Congregations by County and Group: 2010

Religious Group	Number of Congregations	Number of Attendees	Number of Communicant, Confirmed, or Full Members	Adherents: Number of Adherents	Adherents: % of Total Pop.	Adherents: % of Total Adh.
BAPT–Consrv Bapt	2	NR	NR	NR	-	-
BAPT–Natl Mis Bapt Conv	1	0	150	188	0.0	0.0
BAPT–NBC Amer	2	400	675	846	0.1	0.2
BAPT–NBC USA	28	3,694	7,120	8,928	0.6	1.7
BAPT–Reg Bapt Gen As	2	NR	NR	NR	-	-
BAPT–S-D Baptist Gen Con	1	24	31	39	0.0	0.0
BAPT–So Bapt Conv	15	1,062	1,697	2,128	0.2	0.4
BRETH–Breth in Chr	1	NR	NR	NR	-	-
BUDD–Mahayana	4	NR	NR	1,363	0.1	0.3
BUDD–Theravada	2	NR	NR	1,761	0.1	0.3
Calv Chpl	1	NR	NR	NR	-	-
Catholic	71	NR	NR	353,098	25.5	68.2
CGOD–Ch God (Ander)	2	31	NR	31	0.0	0.0
Ch of Nazarene	6	794	928	1,133	0.1	0.2
Chr & Miss Al	9	786	613	947	0.1	0.2
CHR–Chr Ch (Disc)	4	100	120	150	0.0	0.0
CHR–Chr Chs & Chs Cr	2	NR	220	276	0.0	0.1
CHR–Chs of Christ	4	120	96	158	0.0	0.0
CHR–Int Chs of Christ	0	NR	216	271	0.0	0.1
CONG–Consrv Cong Chr	2	92	53	66	0.0	0.0
Evan Cov Ch	2	322	250	418	0.0	0.1
HINDU–I/A Temples	1	NR	NR	40	0.0	0.0
HINDU–Post Ren	3	NR	NR	69	0.0	0.0
HINDU–Trad Temples	2	NR	NR	1,093	0.1	0.2
Int Cou Comm Ch	1	NR	NR	NR	-	-
Jehovah's Witness	16	NR	NR	NR	-	-
JUD–Conserv	1	366	426	1,108	0.1	0.2
JUD–Orth	20	8,640	3,000	12,000	0.9	2.3
JUD–Reform	1	118	217	564	0.0	0.1
LDS–L-D Saints	5	NR	NR	5,629	0.4	1.1
LUTH–E.L.C.A.	16	859	1,662	2,211	0.2	0.4
LUTH–Luth Cong Msn Chr	1	NR	NR	NR	-	-
LUTH–Luth–MO Synod	4	377	641	850	0.1	0.2
MENN–Mennonite USA	6	263	223	280	0.0	0.1
METH–AME	4	330	685	859	0.1	0.2
METH–AME Zion	4	40	470	589	0.0	0.1
METH–C.M.E.	2	180	330	414	0.0	0.1
METH–Free Methodist	3	139	129	143	0.0	0.0
METH–Un Methodist	17	2,141	6,054	7,503	0.5	1.4
METH–Wesleyan	2	70	66	91	0.0	0.0
Missionary Ch	2	80	60	90	0.0	0.0
MORAV–Morav Ch-North	1	78	141	244	0.0	0.0
Muslim Est	24	10,752	NR	38,506	2.8	7.4
New Apost Ch	2	NR	NR	NR	-	-
Non-denom Chr Chs	72	12,042	22,803	25,209	1.8	4.9
OCATH–Pol Natl Cath	1	NR	NR	NR	-	-
ORTHE–Greek Orthodox	2	370	NR	1,600	0.1	0.3
ORTHO–Ethiopian Orth	1	NR	NR	NR	-	-
ORTHO–Malan Dioc Am	1	500	NR	750	0.1	0.1
PENT–Apos Faith Msn	2	NR	70	88	0.0	0.0
PENT–Assemb of God	46	7,874	5,391	10,441	0.8	2.0
PENT–Ch God (Cleve)	35	3,574	3,816	4,785	0.3	0.9
PENT–Ch Lord Jesus Apos	5	NR	NR	NR	-	-
PENT–Ch of God Proph	7	NR	572	717	0.1	0.1
PENT–COGIC	4	300	360	451	0.0	0.1
PENT–I F Chr Assmbl	1	NR	NR	NR	-	-
PENT–Intl Pent Holiness	1	118	325	408	0.0	0.1
PENT–Pent Ch of God	1	70	NR	109	0.0	0.0
PENT–Un Pent Asbl God	1	NR	NR	NR	-	-
PENT–Un Pent Ch Intl	5	NR	NR	NR	-	-
PRES–Korean Amer Pres	1	NR	NR	NR	-	-
PRES–Korean Pres Amer	1	NR	NR	NR	-	-
PRES–Presb Ch (USA)	18	867	1,688	2,117	0.2	0.4
PRES–Presb Ch Amer	1	0	0	0	0.0	0.0
REF–Ref Ch in Am	5	337	308	392	0.0	0.1
Salvation Army	2	167	311	817	0.1	0.2
Sev Day Adv	40	4,976	8,655	9,951	0.7	1.9
Un Breth in Cr	1	98	149	84	0.0	0.0
Un C of Christ	11	25	597	749	0.1	0.1
Unity Ch	2	NR	NR	NR	-	-
Zoroastrian	0	NR	NR	6	0.0	0.0
BROOME	**229**	**17,119**	**29,185**	**105,064**	**52.4**	**100.0**
ANG/EPIS–Anglican NA	2	NR	NR	NR	-	-

Religious Group	Number of Congregations	Number of Attendees	Number of Communicant, Confirmed, or Full Members	Adherents: Number of Adherents	Adherents: % of Total Pop.	Adherents: % of Total Adh.
ANG/EPIS–Episcopal	7	626	1,117	1,573	0.8	1.5
Bahá'í	0	NR	38	38	0.0	0.0
BAPT–Amer Bapt USA	7	443	871	1,027	0.5	1.0
BAPT–Reg Bapt Gen As	13	NR	NR	NR	-	-
BAPT–So Bapt Conv	4	307	329	388	0.2	0.4
BUDD–Mahayana	1	NR	NR	505	0.3	0.5
BUDD–Theravada	1	NR	NR	300	0.1	0.3
Catholic	33	NR	NR	62,220	31.0	59.2
Ch Christ Chr Union	3	NR	NR	NR	-	-
Ch Cr, Scientist	1	NR	NR	NR	-	-
Ch of Nazarene	2	320	323	413	0.2	0.4
Chr & Miss Al	5	282	203	433	0.2	0.4
CHR–Chr Ch (Disc)	1	0	0	0	0.0	0.0
CHR–Chr Chs & Chs Cr	2	NR	190	224	0.1	0.2
CHR–Chs of Christ	1	70	64	90	0.0	0.1
Evan Free Ch	1	70	NR	70	0.0	0.1
FRND–Fr Gen Cf & Un Mtg	1	NR	14	17	0.0	0.0
HINDU–Post Ren	1	NR	NR	54	0.0	0.1
Jehovah's Witness	5	NR	NR	NR	-	-
JUD–Conserv	1	180	202	545	0.3	0.5
JUD–Orth	1	533	200	740	0.4	0.7
JUD–Reform	1	128	226	610	0.3	0.6
LDS–Comm of Christ	1	NR	161	161	0.1	0.2
LDS–L-D Saints	1	NR	NR	813	0.4	0.8
LUTH–E.L.C.A.	5	385	1,326	2,406	1.2	2.3
LUTH–Luth–MO Synod	2	87	274	310	0.2	0.3
METH–AME Zion	1	30	100	118	0.1	0.1
METH–Free Methodist	2	1,545	2,243	2,305	1.1	2.2
METH–Prim Meth Ch	1	NR	NR	NR	-	-
METH–Un Methodist	41	2,653	11,399	14,039	7.0	13.4
METH–Wesleyan	2	224	84	292	0.1	0.3
Muslim Est	1	500	NR	800	0.4	0.8
New Apost Ch	1	NR	NR	NR	-	-
Non-denom Chr Chs	31	4,344	5,455	6,006	3.0	5.7
OCATH–Pol Natl Cath	1	NR	NR	NR	-	-
ORTHE–Carp Rus Orth	2	390	NR	885	0.4	0.8
ORTHE–Greek Orthodox	2	199	NR	555	0.3	0.5
ORTHE–Orth Ch in Amer	2	120	NR	225	0.1	0.2
ORTHE–Rus Orth Abroad	1	30	NR	35	0.0	0.0
ORTHE–Ukrainian Orth	1	165	NR	500	0.2	0.5
ORTHO–Armen Ap Etchm	1	40	NR	85	0.0	0.1
PENT–Assemb of God	4	1,846	1,040	2,211	1.1	2.1
PENT–Ch God (Cleve)	1	45	45	53	0.0	0.1
PENT–Ch of God Proph	1	NR	9	11	0.0	0.0
PENT–COGIC	1	0	150	177	0.1	0.2
PENT–Un Pent Ch Intl	1	NR	NR	NR	-	-
PRES–Presb Ch (USA)	14	829	1,907	2,249	1.1	2.1
PRES–Presb Ch Amer	1	110	51	63	0.0	0.1
PRES–Ref Pres of NA	1	19	14	22	0.0	0.0
REF–Christian Ref	1	100	154	182	0.1	0.2
Salvation Army	1	26	138	271	0.1	0.3
Sev Day Adv	2	98	171	197	0.1	0.2
Un C of Christ	6	204	434	512	0.3	0.5
Unit Univ	1	171	253	334	0.2	0.3
Unity Ch	1	NR	NR	NR	-	-
CATTARAUGUS	**146**	**6,021**	**10,348**	**29,512**	**36.7**	**100.0**
ANG/EPIS–Episcopal	6	193	346	436	0.5	1.5
Bahá'í	1	NR	46	46	0.1	0.2
BAPT–Amer Bapt USA	3	210	636	774	1.0	2.6
BAPT–Consrv Bapt	1	NR	NR	NR	-	-
BAPT–Reg Bapt Gen As	10	NR	NR	NR	-	-
BAPT–So Bapt Conv	2	92	140	170	0.2	0.6
Catholic	12	NR	NR	12,351	15.4	41.9
Ch of Nazarene	1	18	41	56	0.1	0.2
Chr & Miss Al	3	76	58	134	0.2	0.5
CHR–Chs of Christ	1	15	14	18	0.0	0.1
CONG–Cong Chr, NA	1	NR	72	88	0.1	0.3
FRND–Fr Gen Cf & Un Mtg	1	NR	0	0	0.0	0.0
Jehovah's Witness	4	NR	NR	NR	-	-
JUD–Reform	1	18	31	84	0.1	0.3
LDS–L-D Saints	3	NR	NR	1,191	1.5	4.0
LUTH–E.L.C.A.	2	119	319	395	0.5	1.3
LUTH–Luth–MO Synod	7	476	1,017	1,646	2.0	5.6

NR–Not Reported   - Represents no adherents reported.   Percentages may not total 100 due to rounding.

Table 3: Religious Congregations by County and Group: 2010

Religious Group	Number of Congrega-tions	Number of Attendees	Number of Communicant, Confirmed, or Full Members	Adherents		
				Number of Adherents	% of Total Pop.	% of Total Adh.
MENN–Amish Undif	12	NR	630	1,437	1.8	4.9
METH–AME	1	0	100	122	0.2	0.4
METH–Free Methodist	9	1,152	539	1,160	1.4	3.9
METH–Un Methodist	26	1,231	3,480	4,190	5.2	14.2
METH–Wesleyan	4	198	195	258	0.3	0.9
Muslim Est	1	406	NR	1,522	1.9	5.2
New Apost Ch	2	NR	NR	NR	-	-
Non-denom Chr Chs	13	1,225	1,250	1,562	1.9	5.3
PENT–Assemb of God	1	120	40	120	0.1	0.4
PENT–Ch of God Proph	1	NR	35	43	0.1	0.1
PENT–COGIC	1	0	150	183	0.2	0.6
PENT–Un Pent Ch Intl	1	NR	NR	NR	-	-
PRES–Presb Ch (USA)	8	264	778	947	1.2	3.2
Salvation Army	1	27	57	135	0.2	0.5
Sev Day Adv	4	92	160	184	0.2	0.6
Un C of Christ	2	89	214	260	0.3	0.9
CAYUGA	**86**	**3,620**	**7,656**	**34,056**	**42.6**	**100.0**
ANG/EPIS–Episcopal	3	188	286	438	0.5	1.3
Bahá'í	0	NR	7	7	0.0	0.0
BAPT–Amer Bapt Assn	2	NR	85	101	0.1	0.3
BAPT–Amer Bapt USA	8	416	1,016	1,211	1.5	3.6
BAPT–Consrv Bapt	2	NR	NR	NR	-	-
BAPT–Ref Bapt Ch	2	NR	NR	NR	-	-
BAPT–Reg Bapt Gen As	1	NR	NR	NR	-	-
BAPT–So Bapt Conv	2	45	70	83	0.1	0.2
Calv Chpl	1	NR	NR	NR	-	-
Catholic	10	NR	NR	23,937	29.9	70.3
Ch Christ Chr Union	1	NR	NR	NR	-	-
Ch of Nazarene	2	150	204	204	0.3	0.6
Chr & Miss Al	1	259	134	398	0.5	1.2
CHR–Chr Ch (Disc)	1	0	198	236	0.3	0.7
FRND–Fr Gen Cf & Un Mtg	1	NR	85	101	0.1	0.3
Jehovah's Witness	1	NR	NR	NR	-	-
JUD–Conserv	1	15	17	46	0.1	0.1
LDS–L-D Saints	1	NR	NR	404	0.5	1.2
LUTH–Luth–MO Synod	1	25	36	36	0.0	0.1
MENN–Amish Undif	1	NR	43	121	0.2	0.4
MENN–CG in Cr (Menn)	1	NR	41	49	0.1	0.1
METH–AME Zion	1	0	100	119	0.1	0.3
METH–Un Methodist	13	720	2,724	3,214	4.0	9.4
New Apost Ch	1	NR	NR	NR	-	-
Non-denom Chr Chs	7	770	993	1,088	1.4	3.2
ORTHE–Orth Ch in Amer	1	60	NR	150	0.2	0.4
PENT–Assemb of God	3	136	46	192	0.2	0.6
PENT–Ch God (Cleve)	1	45	73	87	0.1	0.3
PRES–Presb Ch (USA)	8	339	685	816	1.0	2.4
REF–Ref Ch in Am	1	70	139	154	0.2	0.5
Salvation Army	1	55	110	208	0.3	0.6
Sev Day Adv	2	160	277	319	0.4	0.9
Un C of Christ	3	143	245	292	0.4	0.9
Unit Univ	1	24	42	45	0.1	0.1
CHAUTAUQUA	**226**	**13,233**	**21,620**	**53,980**	**40.0**	**100.0**
ANG/EPIS–Anglican NA	1	NR	NR	NR	-	-
ANG/EPIS–Episcopal	6	356	768	956	0.7	1.8
Bahá'í	0	NR	50	50	0.0	0.1
BAPT–Amer Bapt USA	8	476	714	855	0.6	1.6
BAPT–Converge/BGC	4	300	NR	360	0.3	0.7
BAPT–Reg Bapt Gen As	8	NR	NR	NR	-	-
BAPT–So Bapt Conv	5	180	173	207	0.2	0.4
Catholic	13	NR	NR	20,912	15.5	38.7
CGOD–Ch God (Ander)	4	397	NR	397	0.3	0.7
Ch Cr, Scientst	1	NR	NR	NR	-	-
Ch of Nazarene	1	80	66	80	0.1	0.1
Chr & Miss Al	4	210	167	346	0.3	0.6
CHR–Chs of Christ	1	77	79	119	0.1	0.2
CONG–Consrv Cong Chr	5	482	617	739	0.5	1.4
Evan Cov Ch	3	602	731	783	0.6	1.5
FRND–Fr Gen Cf & Un Mtg	2	NR	29	35	0.0	0.1
HINDU–Post Ren	1	NR	NR	100	0.1	0.2
Int Cou Comm Ch	1	NR	NR	NR	-	-
Jehovah's Witness	5	NR	NR	NR	-	-
JUD–Reform	1	18	31	84	0.1	0.2
LDS–L-D Saints	2	NR	NR	962	0.7	1.8
LUTH–E.L.C.A.	12	830	3,416	4,114	3.0	7.6
LUTH–Luth Cong Msn Chr	1	30	NR	NR	-	-
LUTH–Luth–MO Synod	3	143	264	337	0.2	0.6
MENN–Amish Undif	12	NR	696	1,672	1.2	3.1
METH–A.W.M.C.	2	60	20	68	0.1	0.1
METH–AME Zion	1	0	100	120	0.1	0.2
METH–Free Methodist	4	809	265	816	0.6	1.5
METH–Un Methodist	45	3,137	7,780	10,407	7.7	19.3
METH–Wesleyan	5	515	284	670	0.5	1.2
Muslim Est	1	406	NR	1,522	1.1	2.8
Nat Spirit Asso	2	NR	NR	NR	-	-
New Apost Ch	2	NR	NR	NR	-	-
Non-denom Chr Chs	21	2,153	2,302	2,778	2.1	5.1
ORTHE–Greek Orthodox	1	75	NR	150	0.1	0.3
ORTHE–Orth Ch in Amer	1	20	NR	80	0.1	0.1
PENT–Assemb of God	8	630	388	882	0.7	1.6
PENT–Ch God (Cleve)	1	66	98	117	0.1	0.2
PENT–Elim	1	NR	NR	NR	-	-
PENT–I F Chr Assmbl	2	NR	NR	NR	-	-
PENT–Int Foursq Gos	1	26	30	36	0.0	0.1
PENT–Intl Pent Holiness	1	65	65	78	0.1	0.1
PENT–Open Bible Std	1	0	NR	0	0.0	0.0
PENT–Un Pent Ch Intl	1	NR	NR	NR	-	-
PRES–Korean Pres Amer	1	NR	NR	NR	-	-
PRES–Presb Ch (USA)	7	307	1,251	1,498	1.1	2.8
REF–Ref Ch in Am	2	216	469	534	0.4	1.0
Salvation Army	2	135	265	528	0.4	1.0
Sev Day Adv	2	81	141	162	0.1	0.3
Un C of Christ	3	122	217	260	0.2	0.5
Unit Univ	3	229	144	166	0.1	0.3
Unity Ch	1	NR	NR	NR	-	-
CHEMUNG	**110**	**7,044**	**11,563**	**32,633**	**36.7**	**100.0**
ANG/EPIS–Anglican NA	1	NR	NR	NR	-	-
ANG/EPIS–Episcopal	6	236	463	1,077	1.2	3.3
Bahá'í	0	NR	10	10	0.0	0.0
BAPT–Amer Bapt USA	5	310	903	1,089	1.2	3.3
BAPT–Reg Bapt Gen As	3	NR	NR	NR	-	-
BAPT–So Bapt Conv	6	296	369	445	0.5	1.4
Calv Chpl	1	NR	NR	NR	-	-
Catholic	5	NR	NR	14,593	16.4	44.7
CGOD–Ches God-Gen Con	1	116	45	54	0.1	0.2
Ch Cr, Scientst	1	NR	NR	NR	-	-
Ch of Nazarene	3	160	214	277	0.3	0.8
Chr & Miss Al	2	393	229	656	0.7	2.0
CHR–Chr Ch (Disc)	1	35	55	66	0.1	0.2
CHR–Chs of Christ	1	55	49	70	0.1	0.2
Evan Free Ch	1	85	NR	85	0.1	0.3
FRND–Fr Gen Cf & Un Mtg	1	NR	23	28	0.0	0.1
Jain	1	NR	NR	NR	-	-
Jehovah's Witness	1	NR	NR	NR	-	-
LDS–L-D Saints	1	NR	NR	659	0.7	2.0
LUTH–E.L.C.A.	3	158	467	514	0.6	1.6
METH–AME Zion	1	0	150	181	0.2	0.6
METH–Free Methodist	1	63	36	63	0.1	0.2
METH–Un Methodist	22	1,169	3,726	4,479	5.0	13.7
METH–Wesleyan	3	427	186	555	0.6	1.7
Muslim Est	2	456	NR	1,662	1.9	5.1
New Apost Ch	1	NR	NR	NR	-	-
Non-denom Chr Chs	11	1,459	2,025	2,135	2.4	6.5
ORTHE–Greek Orthodox	1	15	NR	80	0.1	0.2
ORTHE–Orth Ch in Amer	1	50	NR	150	0.2	0.5
PENT–Assemb of God	5	530	263	814	0.9	2.5
PENT–COGIC	2	300	650	784	0.9	2.4
PENT–Elim	1	NR	NR	NR	-	-
PENT–Int Foursq Gos	1	33	17	21	0.0	0.1
PENT–Un Pent Ch Intl	1	NR	NR	NR	-	-
PRES–Presb Ch (USA)	6	407	1,018	1,228	1.4	3.8
Salvation Army	1	19	80	160	0.2	0.5
Sev Day Adv	3	134	234	269	0.3	0.8
Un C of Christ	2	98	299	361	0.4	1.1
Unit Univ	1	40	52	68	0.1	0.2

NR–Not Reported   - Represents no adherents reported.   Percentages may not total 100 due to rounding.

Table 3: Religious Congregations by County and Group: 2010

Religious Group	Number of Congregations	Number of Attendees	Number of Communicant, Confirmed, or Full Members	Adherents		
				Number of Adherents	% of Total Pop.	% of Total Adh.
CHENANGO	**77**	**2,704**	**6,217**	**14,306**	**28.3**	**100.0**
ANG/EPIS–Episcopal	8	295	830	1,444	2.9	10.1
Bahá'í	0	NR	4	4	0.0	0.0
BAPT–Amer Bapt USA	7	301	790	949	1.9	6.6
BAPT–Ref Bapt Ch	1	NR	NR	NR	-	-
BAPT–Reg Bapt Gen As	7	NR	NR	NR	-	-
BAPT–So Bapt Conv	3	97	83	100	0.2	0.7
BUDD–Vajrayana	1	NR	NR	40	0.1	0.3
Catholic	8	NR	NR	5,528	11.0	38.6
Chr & Miss Al	1	39	31	52	0.1	0.4
CHR–Chs of Christ	1	25	20	35	0.1	0.2
CONG–Cong Chr, NA	1	NR	20	24	0.0	0.2
FRND–Fr Gen Cf & Un Mtg	1	NR	27	32	0.1	0.2
Jehovah's Witness	1	NR	NR	NR	-	-
LDS–L-D Saints	2	NR	NR	427	0.8	3.0
LUTH–E.L.C.A.	1	35	301	385	0.8	2.7
MENN–Amish Undif	1	NR	9	24	0.0	0.2
METH–Free Methodist	1	109	86	109	0.2	0.8
METH–Un Methodist	12	549	2,368	2,884	5.7	20.2
New Apost Ch	1	NR	NR	NR	-	-
Non-denom Chr Chs	7	760	700	1,007	2.0	7.0
PENT–Assemb of God	2	107	36	169	0.3	1.2
PRES–Presb Ch (USA)	3	71	166	199	0.4	1.4
Sev Day Adv	1	34	58	67	0.1	0.5
Un C of Christ	6	282	688	827	1.6	5.8
CLINTON	**80**	**3,257**	**4,188**	**35,416**	**43.1**	**100.0**
ANG/EPIS–Episcopal	2	111	307	353	0.4	1.0
Bahá'í	0	NR	26	26	0.0	0.1
BAPT–Amer Bapt USA	1	22	65	76	0.1	0.2
BAPT–So Bapt Conv	2	75	105	123	0.1	0.3
Catholic	31	NR	NR	27,695	33.7	78.2
Ch of Nazarene	2	294	192	323	0.4	0.9
Chr & Miss Al	1	145	95	204	0.2	0.6
CHR–Chs of Christ	1	35	19	50	0.1	0.1
FRND–Fr Gen Cf & Un Mtg	1	NR	0	0	0.0	0.0
Jehovah's Witness	2	NR	NR	NR	-	-
JUD–Reform	1	45	79	213	0.3	0.6
LDS–L-D Saints	1	NR	NR	380	0.5	1.1
LUTH–E.L.C.A.	1	43	82	106	0.1	0.3
METH–Un Methodist	12	531	1,578	1,815	2.2	5.1
METH–Wesleyan	6	440	235	573	0.7	1.6
Muslim Est	1	406	NR	1,522	1.9	4.3
New Apost Ch	1	NR	NR	NR	-	-
Non-denom Chr Chs	3	450	470	600	0.7	1.7
PENT–Assemb of God	1	186	111	336	0.4	0.9
PENT–Ch God (Cleve)	1	25	40	47	0.1	0.1
PENT–Un Pent Ch Intl	1	NR	NR	NR	-	-
PRES–Presb Ch (USA)	4	316	589	688	0.8	1.9
Salvation Army	1	16	29	74	0.1	0.2
Sev Day Adv	2	44	76	87	0.1	0.2
Unit Univ	1	73	90	125	0.2	0.4
COLUMBIA	**92**	**2,501**	**6,919**	**24,699**	**39.1**	**100.0**
ANG/EPIS–Episcopal	7	283	541	834	1.3	3.4
Bahá'í	0	NR	11	11	0.0	0.0
BAPT–Amer Bapt USA	1	20	100	117	0.2	0.5
BAPT–NBC USA	1	0	500	586	0.9	2.4
BAPT–So Bapt Conv	1	30	10	12	0.0	0.0
BUDD–Mahayana	3	NR	NR	129	0.2	0.5
BUDD–Vajrayana	3	NR	NR	166	0.3	0.7
Catholic	11	NR	NR	15,375	24.4	62.2
CONG–Consrv Cong Chr	1	35	31	36	0.1	0.1
FRND–Fr Gen Cf & Un Mtg	2	NR	59	69	0.1	0.3
LDS–L-D Saints	1	NR	NR	207	0.3	0.8
LUTH–E.L.C.A.	9	269	1,216	1,755	2.8	7.1
LUTH–Luth–MO Synod	2	122	191	221	0.4	0.9
METH–AME	1	25	62	73	0.1	0.3
METH–AME Zion	1	0	100	117	0.2	0.5
METH–Un Methodist	15	268	1,693	2,009	3.2	8.1
Non-denom Chr Chs	6	475	640	731	1.2	3.0
ORTHE–Holy Orth in NA	1	8	NR	10	0.0	0.0
ORTHE–Ukrainian Orth	1	35	NR	60	0.1	0.2
PENT–Assemb of God	1	50	30	125	0.2	0.5
PENT–Ch God (Cleve)	1	44	36	42	0.1	0.2
PENT–Un Pent Ch Intl	1	NR	NR	NR	-	-
PRES–Presb Ch (USA)	5	164	364	427	0.7	1.7
REF–Ref Ch in Am	13	583	1,155	1,379	2.2	5.6
Salvation Army	1	3	0	0	0.0	0.0
Sev Day Adv	2	81	141	162	0.3	0.7
Un C of Christ	1	6	39	46	0.1	0.2
CORTLAND	**65**	**2,957**	**4,822**	**13,908**	**28.2**	**100.0**
ANG/EPIS–Episcopal	2	99	211	296	0.6	2.1
Bahá'í	0	NR	7	7	0.0	0.1
BAPT–Amer Bapt USA	2	104	337	401	0.8	2.9
BAPT–Reg Bapt Gen As	5	NR	NR	NR	-	-
BAPT–So Bapt Conv	1	113	98	117	0.2	0.8
Catholic	5	NR	NR	6,378	12.9	45.9
Ch Christ Chr Union	2	NR	NR	NR	-	-
Ch Cr, Scientist	1	NR	NR	NR	-	-
Chr & Miss Al	1	40	17	51	0.1	0.4
CHR–Chr Chs & Chs Cr	1	NR	35	42	0.1	0.3
Jehovah's Witness	2	NR	NR	NR	-	-
LDS–L-D Saints	1	NR	NR	404	0.8	2.9
LUTH–E.L.C.A.	1	12	125	125	0.3	0.9
LUTH–Luth–MO Synod	1	109	161	195	0.4	1.4
MENN–Amish Undif	1	NR	23	63	0.1	0.5
METH–Free Methodist	1	56	29	56	0.1	0.4
METH–Un Methodist	13	664	1,833	2,747	5.6	19.8
METH–Wesleyan	2	69	14	89	0.2	0.6
New Apost Ch	1	NR	NR	NR	-	-
Non-denom Chr Chs	6	965	610	1,216	2.5	8.7
PENT–Assemb of God	2	145	53	148	0.3	1.1
PENT–Elim	1	NR	NR	NR	-	-
PENT–Un Pent Ch Intl	1	NR	NR	NR	-	-
PRES–Presb Ch (USA)	4	254	467	556	1.1	4.0
PRES–Presb Ch Amer	2	0	0	0	0.0	0.0
Salvation Army	1	24	112	196	0.4	1.4
Sev Day Adv	1	59	103	118	0.2	0.8
Un C of Christ	3	206	530	631	1.3	4.5
Unit Univ	1	38	57	72	0.1	0.5
DELAWARE	**115**	**4,157**	**8,147**	**21,153**	**44.1**	**100.0**
ANG/EPIS–Episcopal	10	273	510	616	1.3	2.9
Bahá'í	0	NR	4	4	0.0	0.0
BAPT–Amer Bapt USA	5	257	379	443	0.9	2.1
BAPT–Consrv Bapt	2	NR	NR	NR	-	-
BAPT–Reg Bapt Gen As	3	NR	NR	NR	-	-
BAPT–So Bapt Conv	1	49	58	68	0.1	0.3
BUDD–Vajrayana	3	NR	NR	150	0.3	0.7
Catholic	9	NR	NR	8,538	17.8	40.4
Chr & Miss Al	4	318	248	550	1.1	2.6
CHR–Chs of Christ	1	10	10	13	0.0	0.1
Ind Fund Churches	1	NR	NR	NR	-	-
Int Cou Comm Ch	2	NR	NR	NR	-	-
Jehovah's Witness	4	NR	NR	NR	-	-
JUD–Conserv	1	149	167	451	0.9	2.1
LDS–L-D Saints	1	NR	NR	200	0.4	0.9
LUTH–E.L.C.A.	1	50	256	259	0.5	1.2
LUTH–Luth–MO Synod	2	91	208	263	0.5	1.2
METH–Free Methodist	1	135	131	135	0.3	0.6
METH–Un Methodist	27	847	3,564	4,198	8.7	19.8
Muslim Est	1	406	NR	1,522	3.2	7.2
Non-denom Chr Chs	5	387	422	510	1.1	2.4
ORTHE–Rus Orth Moscow	1	12	NR	12	0.0	0.1
PENT–Assemb of God	5	219	131	355	0.7	1.7
PRES–Presb Ch (USA)	17	539	1,203	1,405	2.9	6.6
PRES–Ref Pres of NA	1	50	45	50	0.1	0.2
REF–Ref Ch in Am	1	60	203	233	0.5	1.1
Salvation Army	4	222	462	1,007	2.1	4.8
Un C of Christ	2	83	146	171	0.4	0.8
DUTCHESS	**222**	**17,259**	**28,458**	**159,189**	**53.5**	**100.0**
ANG/EPIS–Episcopal	24	1,696	3,543	4,915	1.7	3.1
Bahá'í	0	NR	96	96	0.0	0.1

NR–Not Reported   - Represents no adherents reported.   Percentages may not total 100 due to rounding.

Table 3: Religious Congregations by County and Group: 2010

Religious Group	Number of Congrega-tions	Number of Attendees	Number of Communicant, Confirmed, or Full Members	Adherents		
				Number of Adherents	% of Total Pop.	% of Total Adh.
BAPT–Amer Bapt USA	8	367	992	1,185	0.4	0.7
BAPT–Consrv Bapt	1	NR	NR	NR	-	-
BAPT–NBC USA	4	785	1,151	1,375	0.5	0.9
BAPT–Prog NBC	1	40	0	0	0.0	0.0
BAPT–Reg Bapt Gen As	1	NR	NR	NR	-	-
BAPT–So Bapt Conv	3	100	166	198	0.1	0.1
BUDD–Mahayana	1	NR	NR	11	0.0	0.0
BUDD–Vajrayana	3	NR	NR	104	0.0	0.1
Calv Chpl	1	NR	NR	NR	-	-
Catholic	22	NR	NR	111,112	37.4	69.8
Ch Cr, Scientst	1	NR	NR	NR	-	-
Ch of Nazarene	4	333	272	410	0.1	0.3
Chr & Miss Al	3	418	159	733	0.2	0.5
CHR–Chs of Christ	3	163	132	163	0.1	0.1
Evan Free Ch	1	135	NR	135	0.0	0.1
FRND–Fr Gen Cf & Un Mtg	3	NR	150	179	0.1	0.1
HINDU–Post Ren	1	NR	NR	25	0.0	0.0
HINDU–Trad Temples	1	NR	NR	200	0.1	0.1
Ind Fund Churches	1	NR	NR	NR	-	-
Jehovah's Witness	8	NR	NR	NR	-	-
JUD–Conserv	2	413	464	1,253	0.4	0.8
JUD–Orth	2	310	150	430	0.1	0.3
JUD–Reform	2	167	295	796	0.3	0.5
LDS–L-D Saints	2	NR	NR	839	0.3	0.5
LUTH–E.L.C.A.	5	390	1,464	1,775	0.6	1.1
LUTH–Luth-MO Synod	4	392	1,031	1,387	0.5	0.9
MENN–Bible Flwshp	2	101	NR	136	0.0	0.1
METH–AME Zion	3	0	675	806	0.3	0.5
METH–Un Methodist	22	1,417	5,115	6,804	2.3	4.3
Muslim Est	3	1,112	NR	7,044	2.4	4.4
Non-denom Chr Chs	24	3,534	4,238	4,841	1.6	3.0
ORTHE–Ant Orth of NA	1	9	NR	24	0.0	0.0
ORTHE–Greek Orthodox	1	200	NR	500	0.2	0.3
ORTHE–Orth Ch in Amer	1	120	NR	200	0.1	0.1
ORTHE–Rus Orth Abroad	1	30	NR	60	0.0	0.0
ORTHO–Malan Dioc Am	1	40	NR	70	0.0	0.0
PENT–Assemb of God	6	1,754	1,087	2,482	0.8	1.6
PENT–Ch God (Cleve)	2	112	135	161	0.1	0.1
PENT–Ch of God Proph	1	NR	170	203	0.1	0.1
PENT–COGIC	3	230	600	717	0.2	0.5
PENT–Fire Bapt Hol Ch	1	NR	NR	NR	-	-
PENT–Vineyard	1	151	204	244	0.1	0.2
PRES–Presb Ch (USA)	12	610	1,499	1,791	0.6	1.1
REF–Christian Ref	1	54	70	84	0.0	0.1
REF–Hung Ref Add'l	1	NR	NR	NR	-	-
REF–Ref Ch in Am	10	1,177	2,926	3,588	1.2	2.3
Salvation Army	2	96	212	382	0.1	0.2
Sev Day Adv	7	620	1,079	1,240	0.4	0.8
Sikh	1	NR	NR	NR	-	-
Un C of Christ	2	123	267	319	0.1	0.2
Unit Univ	1	60	116	154	0.1	0.1
Zoroastrian	0	NR	NR	18	0.0	0.0
ERIE	**689**	**64,557**	**109,993**	**527,375**	**57.4**	**100.0**
ANG/EPIS–Anglican NA	4	NR	NR	NR	-	-
ANG/EPIS–Episcopal	30	2,243	5,072	7,048	0.8	1.3
Bahá'í	3	NR	407	407	0.0	0.1
BAPT–Alliance Bapt	1	NR	NR	NR	-	-
BAPT–Amer Bapt USA	25	4,447	6,541	7,803	0.8	1.5
BAPT–Consrv Bapt	4	NR	NR	NR	-	-
BAPT–N Am Bapt Conf	3	NR	555	662	0.1	0.1
BAPT–Natl Mis Bapt Conv	1	0	150	179	0.0	0.0
BAPT–NBC Amer	1	125	200	239	0.0	0.0
BAPT–NBC USA	15	4,270	8,640	10,307	1.1	2.0
BAPT–Prog NBC	1	2,000	5,000	5,964	0.6	1.1
BAPT–Ref Bapt Ch	1	NR	NR	NR	-	-
BAPT–Reg Bapt Gen As	10	NR	NR	NR	-	-
BAPT–So Bapt Conv	17	1,308	1,188	1,417	0.2	0.3
BUDD–Mahayana	4	NR	NR	2,321	0.3	0.4
BUDD–Vajrayana	2	NR	NR	105	0.0	0.0
Calv Chpl	1	NR	NR	NR	-	-
Catholic	109	NR	NR	352,894	38.4	66.9
CGOD–Ch God (Ander)	1	0	NR	0	0.0	0.0
Ch Cr, Scientst	4	NR	NR	NR	-	-

Religious Group	Number of Congrega-tions	Number of Attendees	Number of Communicant, Confirmed, or Full Members	Adherents		
				Number of Adherents	% of Total Pop.	% of Total Adh.
Ch of Nazarene	3	183	142	349	0.0	0.1
Chr & Miss Al	4	857	343	1,076	0.1	0.2
CHR–Chr Ch (Disc)	7	123	455	543	0.1	0.1
CHR–Chr Chs & Chs Cr	3	NR	480	573	0.1	0.1
CHR–Chs of Christ	5	587	702	688	0.1	0.1
CONG–Consrv Cong Chr	2	35	54	64	0.0	0.0
Evan Cov Ch	1	62	76	81	0.0	0.0
Evan Free Ch	2	165	NR	165	0.0	0.0
FRND–Fr Gen Cf & Un Mtg	3	NR	130	155	0.0	0.0
HINDU–I/A Temples	1	NR	NR	250	0.0	0.0
HINDU–Post Ren	3	NR	NR	1,102	0.1	0.2
HINDU–Trad Temples	2	NR	NR	1,600	0.2	0.3
Int Cou Comm Ch	2	NR	NR	NR	-	-
Jain	2	NR	NR	NR	-	-
Jehovah's Witness	13	NR	NR	NR	-	-
JUD–Conserv	2	575	645	1,742	0.2	0.3
JUD–Orth	7	720	300	1,000	0.1	0.2
JUD–Reconst	1	270	345	932	0.1	0.2
JUD–Reform	3	892	1,574	4,250	0.5	0.8
LDS–Comm of Christ	1	NR	158	158	0.0	0.0
LDS–L-D Saints	4	NR	NR	2,248	0.2	0.4
LUTH–E.L.C.A.	34	3,715	10,666	15,244	1.7	2.9
LUTH–Luth Cong Msn Chr	4	138	600	716	0.1	0.1
LUTH–Luth-MO Synod	23	2,426	6,755	8,704	0.9	1.7
LUTH–Nor Amer Luth C	1	NR	NR	NR	-	-
LUTH–Wisc Ev Luth Syn	1	65	115	162	0.0	0.0
MENN–Mennonite USA	2	213	241	287	0.0	0.1
METH–AME	6	300	700	835	0.1	0.2
METH–AME Zion	7	605	1,555	1,855	0.2	0.4
METH–C.M.E.	1	0	525	626	0.1	0.1
METH–Free Methodist	5	707	448	707	0.1	0.1
METH–Un Methodist	44	3,500	11,811	14,760	1.6	2.8
METH–Wesleyan	10	4,989	1,001	6,486	0.7	1.2
Muslim Est	13	4,800	NR	16,961	1.8	3.2
Nat Spirit Asso	1	NR	NR	NR	-	-
New Apost Ch	3	NR	NR	NR	-	-
Non-denom Chr Chs	61	13,514	17,204	18,962	2.1	3.6
OCATH–Pol Natl Cath	2	NR	NR	NR	-	-
ORTHE–Carp Rus Orth	1	50	NR	85	0.0	0.0
ORTHE–Greek Orthodox	1	350	NR	2,200	0.2	0.4
ORTHE–Holy Orth in NA	1	12	NR	15	0.0	0.0
ORTHE–Macedonian Orth	1	45	NR	398	0.0	0.1
ORTHE–Orth Ch in Amer	2	80	NR	150	0.0	0.0
ORTHE–Rus Orth Abroad	1	40	NR	75	0.0	0.0
ORTHE–Serb Orth USA	1	170	NR	930	0.1	0.2
ORTHE–Ukrainian Orth	1	55	NR	250	0.0	0.0
PENT–Assemb of God	20	3,326	4,864	6,313	0.7	1.2
PENT–Ch God (Cleve)	4	187	216	258	0.0	0.0
PENT–Ch Lord Jesus Apos	4	NR	NR	NR	-	-
PENT–Ch of God by Faith	1	NR	NR	NR	-	-
PENT–Ch of God Proph	1	NR	80	95	0.0	0.0
PENT–COGIC	23	600	3,510	4,187	0.5	0.8
PENT–Elim	3	NR	NR	NR	-	-
PENT–Fire Bapt Hol Ch	1	NR	NR	NR	-	-
PENT–Full Gosp Bapt	9	NR	NR	NR	-	-
PENT–I F Chr Assmbl	1	NR	NR	NR	-	-
PENT–Un Pent Ch Intl	1	NR	NR	NR	-	-
PENT–United Holy Ch	1	NR	NR	NR	-	-
PENT–Vineyard	1	29	39	47	0.0	0.0
PRES–Bible Pres	1	NR	NR	NR	-	-
PRES–Evan Presby Ch	1	NR	489	583	0.1	0.1
PRES–Free Pres NA	1	NR	NR	NR	-	-
PRES–Presb Ch (USA)	34	2,514	7,449	8,886	1.0	1.7
PRES–Presb Ch Amer	1	221	159	159	0.0	0.0
Sev Day Adv	4	440	766	881	0.1	0.2
Sikh	2	NR	NR	NR	-	-
Tao	1	NR	NR	NR	-	-
Un C of Christ	32	2,024	6,904	8,236	0.9	1.6
Unit Univ	4	580	739	991	0.1	0.2
Unity Ch	3	NR	NR	NR	-	-
Zoroastrian	0	NR	NR	9	0.0	0.0
ESSEX	**67**	**2,198**	**3,791**	**13,352**	**33.9**	**100.0**
ANG/EPIS–Episcopal	5	224	369	452	1.1	3.4

NR–Not Reported - Represents no adherents reported. Percentages may not total 100 due to rounding.

Table 3: Religious Congregations by County and Group: 2010

Religious Group	Number of Congregations	Number of Attendees	Number of Communicant, Confirmed, or Full Members	Adherents: Number of Adherents	Adherents: % of Total Pop.	Adherents: % of Total Adh.
Bahá'í	0	NR	18	18	0.0	0.1
BAPT–Amer Bapt USA	3	101	172	200	0.5	1.5
BAPT–Reg Bapt Gen As	2	NR	NR	NR	-	-
BAPT–So Bapt Conv	3	199	173	201	0.5	1.5
Catholic	17	NR	NR	8,467	21.5	63.4
Ch of Nazarene	2	60	91	91	0.2	0.7
Chr & Miss Al	1	49	25	49	0.1	0.4
CHR–Chs of Christ	1	18	17	22	0.1	0.2
CONG–Cong Chr, NA	1	NR	32	37	0.1	0.3
FRND–Fr Gen Cf & Un Mtg	1	NR	0	0	0.0	0.0
Jehovah's Witness	2	NR	NR	NR	-	-
LDS–L-D Saints	2	NR	NR	310	0.8	2.3
METH–Un Methodist	15	651	1,838	2,213	5.6	16.6
Non-denom Chr Chs	3	630	640	788	2.0	5.9
PENT–Assemb of God	1	28	22	46	0.1	0.3
PRES–Presb Ch (USA)	1	15	22	26	0.1	0.2
Un C of Christ	7	223	372	432	1.1	3.2
FRANKLIN	**70**	**1,904**	**3,491**	**22,909**	**44.4**	**100.0**
ANG/EPIS–Episcopal	5	205	364	413	0.8	1.8
Bahá'í	0	NR	26	26	0.1	0.1
BAPT–Amer Bapt USA	2	135	130	154	0.3	0.7
BAPT–So Bapt Conv	6	270	251	297	0.6	1.3
Catholic	20	NR	NR	17,735	34.4	77.4
Ch of Nazarene	1	33	31	33	0.1	0.1
Chr & Miss Al	1	43	43	71	0.1	0.3
FRND–Fr Gen Cf & Un Mtg	1	NR	23	27	0.1	0.1
Jehovah's Witness	2	NR	NR	NR	-	-
LDS–L-D Saints	1	NR	NR	178	0.3	0.8
MENN–Amish Undif	1	NR	64	181	0.4	0.8
METH–Free Methodist	1	34	13	34	0.1	0.1
METH–Un Methodist	12	452	1,597	1,833	3.6	8.0
METH–Wesleyan	3	120	87	156	0.3	0.7
Non-denom Chr Chs	2	320	299	400	0.8	1.7
OCATH–Un Cath Ch	1	NR	NR	702	1.4	3.1
PENT–Assemb of God	1	25	20	27	0.1	0.1
PRES–Presb Ch (USA)	5	123	219	259	0.5	1.1
Sev Day Adv	3	39	68	78	0.2	0.3
Un C of Christ	1	65	216	256	0.5	1.1
Unit Univ	1	40	40	49	0.1	0.2
FULTON	**53**	**2,292**	**4,769**	**14,557**	**26.2**	**100.0**
ANG/EPIS–Episcopal	1	91	313	391	0.7	2.7
Bahá'í	0	NR	5	5	0.0	0.0
BAPT–Consrv Bapt	2	NR	NR	NR	-	-
BAPT–Reg Bapt Gen As	2	NR	NR	NR	-	-
BUDD–Mahayana	1	NR	NR	102	0.2	0.7
Catholic	4	NR	NR	7,963	14.3	54.7
Ch of Nazarene	1	31	14	59	0.1	0.4
CHR–Chr Ch (Disc)	1	0	22	26	0.0	0.2
CHR–Chs of Christ	1	90	74	120	0.2	0.8
CONG–Consrv Cong Chr	1	25	17	20	0.0	0.1
FRND–Fr Gen Cf & Un Mtg	1	NR	0	0	0.0	0.0
Jehovah's Witness	1	NR	NR	NR	-	-
JUD–Conserv	1	79	89	240	0.4	1.6
LDS–L-D Saints	1	NR	NR	446	0.8	3.1
LUTH–E.L.C.A.	2	28	97	136	0.2	0.9
METH–AME Zion	2	18	130	156	0.3	1.1
METH–Free Methodist	2	75	62	75	0.1	0.5
METH–Un Methodist	9	622	2,311	2,681	4.8	18.4
METH–Wesleyan	1	56	49	73	0.1	0.5
Non-denom Chr Chs	7	603	585	756	1.4	5.2
ORTHE–Greek Orthodox	1	7	NR	30	0.1	0.2
PENT–Assemb of God	1	71	54	90	0.2	0.6
PRES–Presb Ch (USA)	6	346	659	789	1.4	5.4
REF–Ref Ch in Am	1	80	125	152	0.3	1.0
Salvation Army	1	11	48	111	0.2	0.8
Sev Day Adv	1	24	41	47	0.1	0.3
Un C of Christ	1	35	74	89	0.2	0.6
GENESEE	**77**	**4,670**	**7,487**	**26,423**	**44.0**	**100.0**
ANG/EPIS–Anglican NA	1	NR	NR	NR	-	-
ANG/EPIS–Episcopal	3	155	408	528	0.9	2.0

Religious Group	Number of Congregations	Number of Attendees	Number of Communicant, Confirmed, or Full Members	Adherents: Number of Adherents	Adherents: % of Total Pop.	Adherents: % of Total Adh.
Bahá'í	0	NR	9	9	0.0	0.0
BAPT–Amer Bapt USA	6	284	615	736	1.2	2.8
BAPT–Consrv Bapt	2	NR	NR	NR	-	-
BAPT–Natl Mis Bapt Conv	1	0	150	179	0.3	0.7
BAPT–Reg Bapt Gen As	3	NR	NR	NR	-	-
BAPT–So Bapt Conv	2	425	325	389	0.6	1.5
Catholic	9	NR	NR	15,455	25.7	58.5
Chr & Miss Al	1	15	15	26	0.0	0.1
CHR–Chr Ch (Disc)	2	0	0	0	0.0	0.0
Ind Fund Churches	1	NR	NR	NR	-	-
Jehovah's Witness	1	NR	NR	NR	-	-
LDS–L-D Saints	1	NR	NR	312	0.5	1.2
LUTH–Luth–MO Synod	1	168	459	571	1.0	2.2
METH–Free Methodist	1	815	339	815	1.4	3.1
METH–Un Methodist	13	728	2,247	3,033	5.0	11.5
New Apost Ch	1	NR	NR	NR	-	-
Non-denom Chr Chs	8	1,110	1,225	1,449	2.4	5.5
PENT–Assemb of God	2	228	121	364	0.6	1.4
PENT–Ch of God by Faith	1	NR	NR	NR	-	-
PENT–Elim	1	NR	NR	NR	-	-
PENT–Un Pent Ch Intl	1	NR	NR	NR	-	-
PRES–Presb Ch (USA)	11	598	1,298	1,553	2.6	5.9
Salvation Army	1	26	59	748	1.2	2.8
Sev Day Adv	1	53	92	106	0.2	0.4
Un C of Christ	2	65	125	150	0.2	0.6
GREENE	**72**	**2,806**	**6,182**	**18,359**	**37.3**	**100.0**
ANG/EPIS–Episcopal	5	135	337	389	0.8	2.1
Bahá'í	0	NR	12	12	0.0	0.1
BAPT–Amer Bapt USA	1	16	47	55	0.1	0.3
BAPT–Consrv Bapt	2	NR	NR	NR	-	-
BAPT–Ref Bapt Ch	1	NR	NR	NR	-	-
BAPT–So Bapt Conv	2	70	68	79	0.2	0.4
BUDD–Vajrayana	2	NR	NR	87	0.2	0.5
Catholic	9	NR	NR	9,935	20.2	54.1
CHR–Chr Chs & Chs Cr	1	NR	0	0	0.0	0.0
CONG–Consrv Cong Chr	1	20	30	35	0.1	0.2
HINDU–Post Ren	1	NR	NR	50	0.1	0.3
Jehovah's Witness	2	NR	NR	NR	-	-
JUD–Reform	1	45	80	216	0.4	1.2
LDS–L-D Saints	1	NR	NR	155	0.3	0.8
LUTH–E.L.C.A.	2	55	416	416	0.8	2.3
LUTH–Luth–MO Synod	1	176	446	546	1.1	3.0
MENN–Bruderhof Comm	1	262	133	212	0.4	1.2
METH–AME	1	0	100	116	0.2	0.6
METH–AME Zion	1	0	100	116	0.2	0.6
METH–Free Methodist	1	36	17	36	0.1	0.2
METH–Un Methodist	16	714	2,552	3,392	6.9	18.5
METH–Wesleyan	1	64	38	83	0.2	0.5
Non-denom Chr Chs	7	770	877	1,012	2.1	5.5
ORTHE–Greek Orthodox	1	60	NR	280	0.6	1.5
PENT–Assemb of God	1	45	27	60	0.1	0.3
PRES–Presb Ch (USA)	1	37	28	33	0.1	0.2
REF–Ref Ch in Am	8	286	852	1,018	2.1	5.5
Un C of Christ	1	15	22	26	0.1	0.1
HAMILTON	**24**	**1,127**	**518**	**3,140**	**64.9**	**100.0**
ANG/EPIS–Episcopal	2	64	33	37	0.8	1.2
Bahá'í	0	NR	1	1	0.0	0.0
BAPT–Consrv Bapt	1	NR	NR	NR	-	-
BAPT–Reg Bapt Gen As	1	NR	NR	NR	-	-
BAPT–So Bapt Conv	1	55	20	23	0.5	0.7
Catholic	6	NR	NR	1,629	33.7	51.9
CONG–Consrv Cong Chr	1	175	127	145	3.0	4.6
Evan Free Ch	1	135	NR	135	2.8	4.3
FRND–Fr Gen Cf & Un Mtg	1	NR	0	0	0.0	0.0
METH–Un Methodist	5	152	252	252	5.2	8.0
METH–Wesleyan	2	84	46	110	2.3	3.5
Muslim Est	1	406	NR	761	15.7	24.2
Non-denom Chr Chs	1	26	26	32	0.7	1.0
PRES–Presb Ch (USA)	1	30	13	15	0.3	0.5

NR–Not Reported - Represents no adherents reported. Percentages may not total 100 due to rounding.

Table 3: Religious Congregations by County and Group: 2010

Religious Group	Number of Congrega-tions	Number of Attendees	Number of Communicant, Confirmed, or Full Members	Adherents		
				Number of Adherents	% of Total Pop.	% of Total Adh.
HERKIMER	**85**	**2,923**	**6,786**	**24,805**	**38.4**	**100.0**
ANG/EPIS–Episcopal	5	289	510	710	1.1	2.9
Bahá'í	0	NR	5	5	0.0	0.0
BAPT–Amer Bapt USA	8	301	1,074	1,287	2.0	5.2
BAPT–Consrv Bapt	2	NR	NR	NR	-	-
BAPT–Ref Bapt Ch	1	NR	NR	NR	-	-
BAPT–Reg Bapt Gen As	1	NR	NR	NR	-	-
BAPT–So Bapt Conv	1	29	29	35	0.1	0.1
Catholic	11	NR	NR	15,425	23.9	62.2
Chr & Miss Al	1	65	37	74	0.1	0.3
Jehovah's Witness	1	NR	NR	NR	-	-
JUD–Conserv	1	37	41	111	0.2	0.4
LDS–L-D Saints	1	NR	NR	261	0.4	1.1
LUTH–E.L.C.A.	3	152	812	1,003	1.6	4.0
MENN–Amish Undif	3	NR	148	401	0.6	1.6
MENN–Bruderhof Comm	1	32	7	17	0.0	0.1
METH–Free Methodist	1	135	104	135	0.2	0.5
METH–Un Methodist	19	572	2,375	2,878	4.5	11.6
Non-denom Chr Chs	4	340	395	451	0.7	1.8
OCATH–Pol Natl Cath	1	NR	NR	NR	-	-
ORTHE–Orth Ch in Amer	1	75	NR	150	0.2	0.6
ORTHE–Rus Orth Abroad	2	154	NR	84	0.1	0.3
ORTHE–Ukrainian Orth	1	40	NR	100	0.2	0.4
PENT–Assemb of God	3	195	109	217	0.3	0.9
PENT–Elim	2	NR	NR	NR	-	-
PRES–Presb Ch (USA)	4	177	467	560	0.9	2.3
REF–Ref Ch in Am	2	218	494	626	1.0	2.5
Salvation Army	1	27	36	103	0.2	0.4
Sev Day Adv	1	14	24	28	0.0	0.1
Un C of Christ	1	64	59	71	0.1	0.3
Unit Univ	2	7	60	73	0.1	0.3
JEFFERSON	**149**	**7,107**	**11,048**	**39,538**	**34.0**	**100.0**
ANG/EPIS–Episcopal	9	394	863	1,102	0.9	2.8
Bahá'í	0	NR	18	18	0.0	0.0
BAPT–Amer Bapt USA	9	782	867	1,087	0.9	2.7
BAPT–Consrv Bapt	1	NR	NR	NR	-	-
BAPT–S-D Baptist Gen Con	1	12	2	3	0.0	0.0
BAPT–So Bapt Conv	6	678	649	814	0.7	2.1
Catholic	23	NR	NR	21,194	18.2	53.6
Ch of Nazarene	3	406	418	618	0.5	1.6
Chr & Miss Al	2	371	110	662	0.6	1.7
CHR–Chr Ch (Disc)	1	0	40	50	0.0	0.1
CHR–Chs of Christ	1	41	36	50	0.0	0.1
Jehovah's Witness	3	NR	NR	NR	-	-
JUD–Conserv	1	34	38	103	0.1	0.3
LDS–L-D Saints	2	NR	NR	1,466	1.3	3.7
LUTH–E.L.C.A.	3	169	417	700	0.6	1.8
LUTH–Wisc Ev Luth Syn	1	0	0	0	0.0	0.0
MENN–Amish Undif	2	NR	58	176	0.2	0.4
MENN–Beachy Amish-Menn	1	98	53	98	0.1	0.2
MENN–Mennonite USA	1	75	65	82	0.1	0.2
METH–AME Zion	1	7	13	16	0.0	0.0
METH–Un Methodist	34	1,336	3,963	4,757	4.1	12.0
METH–Wesleyan	1	31	25	40	0.0	0.1
Muslim Est	1	406	NR	1,522	1.3	3.8
Non-denom Chr Chs	8	686	686	951	0.8	2.4
ORTHE–Greek Orthodox	1	30	NR	140	0.1	0.4
PENT–Assemb of God	5	515	329	824	0.7	2.1
PENT–Ch God (Cleve)	2	122	162	203	0.2	0.5
PENT–Elim	1	NR	NR	NR	-	-
PENT–I F Chr Assmbl	2	NR	NR	NR	-	-
PENT–Un Pent Ch Intl	1	NR	NR	NR	-	-
PRES–Presb Ch (USA)	10	390	1,019	1,278	1.1	3.2
REF–Ref Ch in Am	1	83	295	350	0.3	0.9
Salvation Army	1	48	71	181	0.2	0.5
Sev Day Adv	3	93	162	186	0.2	0.5
Un C of Christ	6	262	638	800	0.7	2.0
Unit Univ	1	38	51	67	0.1	0.2
KINGS	**1,426**	**358,673**	**280,376**	**1,291,850**	**51.6**	**100.0**
ANG/EPIS–Anglican NA	1	NR	NR	NR	-	-
ANG/EPIS–Episcopal	33	4,995	10,689	16,370	0.7	1.3

Religious Group	Number of Congrega-tions	Number of Attendees	Number of Communicant, Confirmed, or Full Members	Adherents		
				Number of Adherents	% of Total Pop.	% of Total Adh.
BAPT–Amer Bapt USA	54	22,320	38,246	46,868	1.9	3.6
BAPT–Consrv Bapt	10	NR	NR	NR	-	-
BAPT–Converge/BGC	8	600	NR	720	0.0	0.1
BAPT–Natl Mis Bapt Conv	3	46	205	251	0.0	0.0
BAPT–NBC USA	29	2,840	7,325	8,976	0.4	0.7
BAPT–Prog NBC	15	4,445	11,525	14,123	0.6	1.1
BAPT–Reg Bapt Gen As	1	NR	NR	NR	-	-
BAPT–S-D Baptist Gen Con	1	74	74	91	0.0	0.0
BAPT–So Bapt Conv	34	2,660	3,298	4,041	0.2	0.3
BRETH–Ch of Brethren	3	39	238	292	0.0	0.0
BUDD–Mahayana	11	NR	NR	778	0.0	0.1
BUDD–Theravada	3	NR	NR	854	0.0	0.1
BUDD–Vajrayana	3	NR	NR	516	0.0	0.0
Calv Chpl	1	NR	NR	NR	-	-
Catholic	107	NR	NR	623,796	24.9	48.3
CGOD–Ch God (Ander)	7	699	NR	699	0.0	0.1
CGOD–Ches God-Gen Con	1	41	63	77	0.0	0.0
Ch Christ Chr Union	1	NR	NR	NR	-	-
Ch Cr, Scientst	1	NR	NR	NR	-	-
Ch God (7th Day)	2	NR	NR	NR	-	-
Ch of Nazarene	16	2,383	3,169	3,300	0.1	0.3
Chr & Miss Al	13	1,019	1,080	1,348	0.1	0.1
CHR–Chr Ch (Disc)	28	1,130	2,720	3,333	0.1	0.3
CHR–Chr Chs & Chs Cr	11	NR	386	473	0.0	0.0
CHR–Chs of Christ	6	655	715	942	0.0	0.1
CHR–Int Chs of Christ	0	NR	216	265	0.0	0.0
CONG–Cong Chr Add'l	1	NR	37	45	0.0	0.0
CONG–Cong Chr, NA	4	NR	541	663	0.0	0.1
Evan Cov Ch	1	60	95	78	0.0	0.0
Evan Free Ch	5	580	NR	580	0.0	0.0
FRND–Evan Fr Ch Intl	1	NR	0	0	0.0	0.0
FRND–Fr Gen Cf & Un Mtg	1	NR	222	272	0.0	0.0
HINDU–I/A Temples	1	NR	NR	1,562	0.1	0.1
HINDU–Post Ren	2	NR	NR	35	0.0	0.0
HINDU–Trad Temples	5	NR	NR	835	0.0	0.1
Int Cou Comm Ch	1	NR	NR	NR	-	-
Jehovah's Witness	29	NR	NR	NR	-	-
JUD–Conserv	9	1,486	1,732	4,503	0.2	0.3
JUD–Orth	325	201,600	70,000	280,000	11.2	21.7
JUD–Reform	5	771	1,413	3,674	0.1	0.3
LDS–L-D Saints	11	NR	NR	9,096	0.4	0.7
LUTH–Ch of Luth Br	1	171	139	368	0.0	0.0
LUTH–E.L.C.A.	28	1,447	2,895	3,999	0.2	0.3
LUTH–Luth Cong Msn Chr	3	167	350	429	0.0	0.0
LUTH–Luth–MO Synod	8	471	729	1,087	0.0	0.1
MENN–Bible Flwshp	1	25	NR	34	0.0	0.0
MENN–Mennonite USA	6	483	450	551	0.0	0.0
METH–AME	13	935	5,611	6,876	0.3	0.5
METH–AME Zion	6	800	2,000	2,451	0.1	0.2
METH–C.M.E.	2	0	300	368	0.0	0.0
METH–Free Methodist	4	357	365	374	0.0	0.0
METH–Un Methodist	30	2,666	6,901	8,915	0.4	0.7
METH–Wesleyan	6	1,108	928	1,441	0.1	0.1
Missionary Ch	3	250	380	380	0.0	0.0
MORAV–Morav Ch-North	2	298	363	474	0.0	0.0
Muslim Est	60	24,926	NR	95,126	3.8	7.4
New Apost Ch	1	NR	NR	NR	-	-
Non-denom Chr Chs	129	42,702	57,866	61,291	2.4	4.7
OCATH–Pol Natl Cath	1	NR	NR	NR	-	-
ORTHE–Ant Orth of NA	2	375	NR	1,350	0.1	0.1
ORTHE–Greek Orthodox	4	2,150	NR	8,500	0.3	0.7
ORTHE–Orth Ch in Amer	2	120	NR	350	0.0	0.0
ORTHE–Rus Orth Abroad	2	200	NR	500	0.0	0.0
ORTHE–Ukrainian Orth	2	445	NR	2,500	0.1	0.2
ORTHO–Armen Ap Etchm	1	30	NR	130	0.0	0.0
ORTHO–Coptic Orth Ch	1	700	NR	2,400	0.1	0.2
ORTHO–Malan Dioc Am	1	50	NR	75	0.0	0.0
ORTHO–Syrian Orth Ch	1	40	NR	140	0.0	0.0
PENT–Apos Faith Msn	3	NR	105	129	0.0	0.0
PENT–Assemb of God	53	5,864	5,834	10,472	0.4	0.8
PENT–Ch God (Cleve)	37	4,145	5,695	6,979	0.3	0.5
PENT–Ch Lord Jesus Apos	4	NR	NR	NR	-	-
PENT–Ch of God Proph	12	NR	1,435	1,758	0.1	0.1
PENT–COGIC	22	1,305	4,059	4,974	0.2	0.4

NR–Not Reported - Represents no adherents reported. Percentages may not total 100 due to rounding.

Table 3: Religious Congregations by County and Group: 2010

Religious Group	Number of Congrega-tions	Number of Attendees	Number of Communicant, Confirmed, or Full Members	Adherents: Number of Adherents	Adherents: % of Total Pop.	Adherents: % of Total Adh.
PENT–Fire Bapt Hol Ch	5	NR	NR	NR	-	-
PENT–Full Gosp Bapt	7	NR	NR	NR	-	-
PENT–I F Chr Assmbl	2	NR	NR	NR	-	-
PENT–Intl Pent Holiness	4	1,482	2,226	2,728	0.1	0.2
PENT–Open Bible Std	1	100	NR	100	0.0	0.0
PENT–Pent Ch of God	4	280	NR	435	0.0	0.0
PENT–Un Pent Ch Intl	6	NR	NR	NR	-	-
PENT–United Holy Ch	5	NR	NR	NR	-	-
PENT–Vineyard	1	87	105	129	0.0	0.0
PRES–Kor Pres Abroad	4	NR	NR	NR	-	-
PRES–Korean Pres Amer	1	NR	NR	NR	-	-
PRES–Presb Ch (USA)	23	1,350	2,072	2,539	0.1	0.2
PRES–Presb Ch Amer	1	0	0	0	0.0	0.0
REF–Comm Ref Evan	1	NR	NR	NR	-	-
REF–Ref Ch in Am	13	641	1,080	1,314	0.1	0.1
Salvation Army	5	347	947	3,557	0.1	0.3
Sev Day Adv	74	13,113	22,800	26,226	1.0	2.0
Sikh	1	NR	NR	NR	-	-
Un Breth in Cr	1	0	0	0	0.0	0.0
Un C of Christ	8	380	528	647	0.0	0.1
Unit Univ	2	220	224	290	0.0	0.0
Unity Ch	2	NR	NR	NR	-	-
Zoroastrian	0	NR	NR	8	0.0	0.0
LEWIS	**64**	**4,568**	**3,748**	**11,406**	**42.1**	**100.0**
ANG/EPIS–Episcopal	4	97	186	192	0.7	1.7
Ap Chr Ch-Amer	1	120	39	120	0.4	1.1
Bahá'í	0	NR	2	2	0.0	0.0
BAPT–Amer Bapt USA	3	134	193	237	0.9	2.1
BAPT–So Bapt Conv	2	115	66	81	0.3	0.7
Catholic	17	NR	NR	6,443	23.8	56.5
Ch of Nazarene	1	85	91	120	0.4	1.1
CHR–Chr Ch (Disc)	1	0	0	0	0.0	0.0
LDS–L-D Saints	1	NR	NR	113	0.4	1.0
MENN–Amish Undif	2	NR	65	188	0.7	1.6
MENN–Cons Menn Conf	6	945	817	1,005	3.7	8.8
MENN–Mennonite USA	3	407	581	715	2.6	6.3
METH–Un Methodist	11	2,091	994	1,242	4.6	10.9
METH–Wesleyan	1	30	28	39	0.1	0.3
Non-denom Chr Chs	4	300	277	375	1.4	3.3
PENT–Assemb of God	1	50	0	50	0.2	0.4
PRES–Presb Ch (USA)	2	119	216	266	1.0	2.3
REF–Ref Ch in Am	1	25	90	91	0.3	0.8
Un C of Christ	3	50	103	127	0.5	1.1
LIVINGSTON	**83**	**5,336**	**7,700**	**25,866**	**39.6**	**100.0**
ANG/EPIS–Episcopal	4	181	275	411	0.6	1.6
Bahá'í	0	NR	8	8	0.0	0.0
BAPT–Amer Bapt USA	2	110	177	208	0.3	0.8
BAPT–Consrv Bapt	2	NR	NR	NR	-	-
BAPT–Ref Bapt Ch	1	NR	NR	NR	-	-
BAPT–So Bapt Conv	1	30	62	73	0.1	0.3
BUDD–Mahayana	1	NR	NR	28	0.0	0.1
Catholic	6	NR	NR	14,916	22.8	57.7
CGOD–Ch God (Ander)	1	20	NR	20	0.0	0.1
Ch of Nazarene	1	138	170	178	0.3	0.7
CHR–Chs of Christ	1	11	12	13	0.0	0.1
Evan Free Ch	1	20	NR	20	0.0	0.1
FRND–Fr Gen Cf & Un Mtg	1	NR	0	0	0.0	0.0
Jain	1	NR	NR	NR	-	-
Jehovah's Witness	3	NR	NR	NR	-	-
LDS–L-D Saints	1	NR	NR	402	0.6	1.6
LUTH–E.L.C.A.	2	150	372	422	0.6	1.6
LUTH–Luth–MO Synod	1	49	92	94	0.1	0.4
MENN–Amish Undif	1	NR	9	24	0.0	0.1
METH–Free Methodist	1	75	61	75	0.1	0.3
METH–Un Methodist	13	850	2,084	3,168	4.8	12.2
METH–Wesleyan	2	336	150	437	0.7	1.7
Non-denom Chr Chs	11	2,355	2,324	3,019	4.6	11.7
PENT–Assemb of God	3	116	48	165	0.3	0.6
PENT–Elim	2	NR	NR	NR	-	-
PENT–Int Foursq Gos	1	85	88	104	0.2	0.4
PENT–Vineyard	1	55	73	86	0.1	0.3
PRES–Presb Ch (USA)	16	660	1,545	1,818	2.8	7.0
Un C of Christ	2	95	150	177	0.3	0.7
MADISON	**88**	**3,942**	**8,355**	**22,008**	**30.0**	**100.0**
ANG/EPIS–Episcopal	5	278	626	953	1.3	4.3
Bahá'í	0	NR	5	5	0.0	0.0
BAPT–Amer Bapt USA	10	629	1,223	1,460	2.0	6.6
BAPT–Reg Bapt Gen As	2	NR	NR	NR	-	-
BAPT–S-D Baptist Gen Con	1	25	38	45	0.1	0.2
BAPT–So Bapt Conv	2	32	44	53	0.1	0.2
Catholic	9	NR	NR	10,810	14.7	49.1
Ch Cr, Scientst	1	NR	NR	NR	-	-
Ch of Nazarene	1	66	103	152	0.2	0.7
Chr & Miss Al	1	189	124	326	0.4	1.5
CHR–Chs of Christ	1	16	8	18	0.0	0.1
CONG–Cong Chr Add'l	1	NR	106	127	0.2	0.6
Jehovah's Witness	3	NR	NR	NR	-	-
LDS–L-D Saints	2	NR	NR	353	0.5	1.6
LUTH–Luth–MO Synod	2	103	179	222	0.3	1.0
MENN–Amish Undif	2	NR	68	217	0.3	1.0
MENN–Menn Chr Fell	1	125	85	125	0.2	0.6
METH–Free Methodist	1	313	201	313	0.4	1.4
METH–Un Methodist	22	760	3,650	4,249	5.8	19.3
Non-denom Chr Chs	5	750	680	963	1.3	4.4
PENT–Assemb of God	2	95	48	135	0.2	0.6
PENT–Elim	3	NR	NR	NR	-	-
PENT–I F Chr Assmbl	1	NR	NR	NR	-	-
PRES–Presb Ch (USA)	5	460	1,025	1,223	1.7	5.6
Salvation Army	1	22	42	142	0.2	0.6
Sev Day Adv	2	34	60	69	0.1	0.3
Un C of Christ	2	45	40	48	0.1	0.2
MONROE	**571**	**66,589**	**96,938**	**345,007**	**46.4**	**100.0**
ANG/EPIS–Anglican NA	1	NR	NR	NR	-	-
ANG/EPIS–Episcopal	20	2,043	4,807	5,455	0.7	1.6
Bahá'í	7	NR	455	455	0.1	0.1
BAPT–Alliance Bapt	1	NR	NR	NR	-	-
BAPT–Amer Bapt USA	29	3,722	9,601	11,572	1.6	3.4
BAPT–Consrv Bapt	1	NR	NR	NR	-	-
BAPT–Converge/BGC	2	875	NR	1,050	0.1	0.3
BAPT–N Am Bapt Conf	2	NR	332	400	0.1	0.1
BAPT–Natl Mis Bapt Conv	4	0	600	723	0.1	0.2
BAPT–NBC USA	6	1,275	3,425	4,128	0.6	1.2
BAPT–Ref Bapt Ch	2	NR	NR	NR	-	-
BAPT–Reg Bapt Gen As	5	NR	NR	NR	-	-
BAPT–So Bapt Conv	12	591	679	818	0.1	0.2
BUDD–Mahayana	6	NR	NR	1,135	0.2	0.3
BUDD–Theravada	3	NR	NR	996	0.1	0.3
BUDD–Vajrayana	3	NR	NR	69	0.0	0.0
Calv Chpl	5	NR	NR	NR	-	-
Catholic	64	NR	NR	191,112	25.7	55.4
CGOD–Ch God (Ander)	2	104	NR	104	0.0	0.0
Ch Cr, Scientst	2	NR	NR	NR	-	-
Ch of Nazarene	6	800	743	1,323	0.2	0.4
Chr & Miss Al	2	174	134	302	0.0	0.1
CHR–Chr Ch (Disc)	2	94	306	369	0.0	0.1
CHR–Chr Chs & Chs Cr	2	NR	225	271	0.0	0.1
CHR–Chs of Christ	6	1,225	1,197	1,615	0.2	0.5
Christian Brethren	2	NR	NR	NR	-	-
Evan Cov Ch	1	91	42	118	0.0	0.0
Evan Free Ch	2	184	NR	184	0.0	0.1
FRND–Fr Gen Cf & Un Mtg	1	NR	117	141	0.0	0.0
HINDU–Post Ren	2	NR	NR	35	0.0	0.0
HINDU–Trad Temples	2	NR	NR	500	0.1	0.1
Ind Fund Churches	1	NR	NR	NR	-	-
Jehovah's Witness	11	NR	NR	NR	-	-
JUD–Conserv	3	926	1,039	2,805	0.4	0.8
JUD–Orth	5	1,872	700	2,600	0.3	0.8
JUD–Reform	4	1,040	1,834	4,952	0.7	1.4
LDS–Comm of Christ	1	NR	158	158	0.0	0.0
LDS–L-D Saints	8	NR	NR	4,260	0.6	1.2
LUTH–E.L.C.A.	19	2,041	6,405	8,513	1.1	2.5
LUTH–Luth–MO Synod	11	2,628	5,249	7,146	1.0	2.1

NR–Not Reported   - Represents no adherents reported.   Percentages may not total 100 due to rounding.

Table 3: Religious Congregations by County and Group: 2010

Religious Group	Number of Congrega-tions	Number of Attendees	Number of Communicant, Confirmed, or Full Members	Adherents		
				Number of Adherents	% of Total Pop.	% of Total Adh.
LUTH–Nor Amer Luth C	1	NR	NR	NR	-	-
LUTH–Wisc Ev Luth Syn	1	47	81	106	0.0	0.0
MENN–Amish Undif	7	NR	474	1,183	0.2	0.3
MENN–Mennonite USA	2	61	49	59	0.0	0.0
METH–AME	1	500	1,053	1,269	0.2	0.4
METH–AME Zion	1	300	500	603	0.1	0.2
METH–C.M.E.	2	500	1,350	1,627	0.2	0.5
METH–Free Methodist	9	2,081	1,644	2,084	0.3	0.6
METH–Un Methodist	30	3,491	10,603	13,572	1.8	3.9
METH–Wesleyan	5	397	249	516	0.1	0.1
Metro Comm Ch	1	64	83	100	0.0	0.0
MJEW–Union Mes Cong	1	NR	NR	NR	-	-
Muslim Est	6	2,436	NR	9,133	1.2	2.6
Nat Spirit Asso	1	NR	NR	NR	-	-
New Apost Ch	1	NR	NR	NR	-	-
Non-denom Chr Chs	96	25,850	24,644	36,038	4.8	10.4
OCATH–Pol Natl Cath	1	NR	NR	NR	-	-
ORTHE–Greek Orthodox	2	375	NR	675	0.1	0.2
ORTHE–Macedonian Orth	1	85	NR	340	0.0	0.1
ORTHE–Orth Ch in Amer	1	60	NR	100	0.0	0.0
ORTHE–Rus Orth Abroad	1	126	NR	166	0.0	0.0
ORTHE–Ukrainian Orth	1	120	NR	250	0.0	0.1
ORTHO–Armen Ap Etchm	1	40	NR	75	0.0	0.0
ORTHO–Coptic Orth Ch	2	102	NR	272	0.0	0.1
ORTHO–Eritrean Orth	1	250	NR	100	0.0	0.0
ORTHO–Malan Dioc Am	1	45	NR	60	0.0	0.0
PENT–Assemb of God	14	1,779	1,003	2,390	0.3	0.7
PENT–Ch God (Cleve)	6	310	395	476	0.1	0.1
PENT–Ch Lord Jesus Apos	4	NR	NR	NR	-	-
PENT–Ch of God by Faith	4	NR	NR	NR	-	-
PENT–Ch of God Proph	1	NR	129	155	0.0	0.0
PENT–COGIC	6	435	920	1,109	0.1	0.3
PENT–Elim	5	NR	NR	NR	-	-
PENT–Full Gosp Bapt	6	NR	NR	NR	-	-
PENT–I F Chr Assmbl	2	NR	NR	NR	-	-
PENT–Intl Pent Holiness	1	121	144	174	0.0	0.1
PENT–Un Pent Ch Intl	1	NR	NR	NR	-	-
PENT–Vineyard	2	173	263	317	0.0	0.1
PRES–As Ref Pres Ch	1	NR	0	0	0.0	0.0
PRES–Orth Pres Ch	2	143	153	215	0.0	0.1
PRES–Presb Ch (USA)	31	3,011	8,121	9,788	1.3	2.8
PRES–Presb Ch Amer	1	150	152	233	0.0	0.1
PRES–Ref Pres of NA	1	64	52	85	0.0	0.0
REF–Christian Ref	2	360	494	595	0.1	0.2
REF–Hung Ref Add'l	1	NR	NR	NR	-	-
REF–Ref Ch in Am	3	273	487	596	0.1	0.2
Salvation Army	3	221	439	691	0.1	0.2
Sev Day Adv	8	868	1,511	1,737	0.2	0.5
Sikh	4	NR	NR	NR	-	-
Un C of Christ	13	1,286	2,785	3,357	0.5	1.0
Unit Univ	2	780	1,112	1,444	0.2	0.4
Unity Ch	2	NR	NR	NR	-	-
Zoroastrian	0	NR	NR	8	0.0	0.0
MONTGOMERY	**73**	**2,682**	**5,678**	**21,942**	**43.7**	**100.0**
ANG/EPIS–Episcopal	2	71	182	323	0.6	1.5
Bahá'í	0	NR	5	5	0.0	0.0
BAPT–Amer Bapt USA	1	48	279	339	0.7	1.5
BAPT–Reg Bapt Gen As	1	NR	NR	NR	-	-
BAPT–So Bapt Conv	2	80	140	170	0.3	0.8
BUDD–Mahayana	1	NR	NR	25	0.0	0.1
Catholic	11	NR	NR	13,946	27.8	63.6
Chr & Miss Al	1	48	40	95	0.2	0.4
HINDU–Post Ren	1	NR	NR	10	0.0	0.0
Ind Fund Churches	1	NR	NR	NR	-	-
Jehovah's Witness	2	NR	NR	NR	-	-
JUD–Conserv	1	32	36	97	0.2	0.4
LUTH–E.L.C.A.	8	351	1,240	2,217	4.4	10.1
MENN–Mennonite USA	1	NR	29	35	0.1	0.2
METH–Un Methodist	10	235	1,146	1,312	2.6	6.0
Non-denom Chr Chs	5	825	835	1,056	2.1	4.8
OCATH–Pol Natl Cath	1	NR	NR	NR	-	-
PENT–Assemb of God	2	138	55	151	0.3	0.7
PENT–Ch God (Cleve)	1	30	14	17	0.0	0.1
PENT–Ch of God Proph	1	NR	21	26	0.1	0.1
PENT–Elim	1	NR	NR	NR	-	-
PRES–Orth Pres Ch	1	71	57	74	0.1	0.3
PRES–Presb Ch (USA)	2	70	242	294	0.6	1.3
REF–Ref Ch in Am	13	580	1,172	1,420	2.8	6.5
Salvation Army	1	19	39	162	0.3	0.7
Sev Day Adv	2	84	146	168	0.3	0.8
NASSAU	**743**	**90,493**	**106,556**	**899,212**	**67.1**	**100.0**
ANG/EPIS–Episcopal	40	3,129	8,853	11,741	0.9	1.3
Bahá'í	3	NR	286	286	0.0	0.0
BAPT–Amer Bapt USA	12	1,577	2,345	2,834	0.2	0.3
BAPT–Asc Ref Bap Ch Am	1	NR	NR	NR	-	-
BAPT–Converge/BGC	4	625	NR	750	0.1	0.1
BAPT–N Am Bapt Conf	1	NR	200	242	0.0	0.0
BAPT–NBC Amer	3	185	325	393	0.0	0.0
BAPT–NBC USA	13	1,255	6,455	7,802	0.6	0.9
BAPT–Ref Bapt Ch	1	NR	NR	NR	-	-
BAPT–Reg Bapt Gen As	2	NR	NR	NR	-	-
BAPT–So Bapt Conv	5	354	380	459	0.0	0.1
BUDD–Mahayana	4	NR	NR	752	0.1	0.1
Catholic	72	NR	NR	677,149	50.6	75.3
CGOD–Ch God (Ander)	3	255	NR	255	0.0	0.0
Ch Cr, Scientst	4	NR	NR	NR	-	-
Ch God (7th Day)	1	NR	NR	NR	-	-
Ch of Nazarene	13	1,181	1,102	1,862	0.1	0.2
Chr & Miss Al	9	1,077	621	728	0.1	0.1
CHR–Chr Ch (Disc)	5	0	200	242	0.0	0.0
CHR–Chr Chs & Chs Cr	5	NR	686	829	0.1	0.1
CHR–Chs of Christ	4	518	748	615	0.0	0.1
Christian Brethren	1	NR	NR	NR	-	-
CONG–Consrv Cong Chr	1	20	12	15	0.0	0.0
Evan Free Ch	2	139	NR	139	0.0	0.0
FRND–Fr Gen Cf & Un Mtg	5	NR	272	329	0.0	0.0
HINDU–I/A Temples	3	NR	NR	1,622	0.1	0.2
HINDU–Post Ren	4	NR	NR	221	0.0	0.0
HINDU–Trad Temples	1	NR	NR	400	0.0	0.0
Int Cou Comm Ch	2	NR	NR	NR	-	-
Jehovah's Witness	8	NR	NR	NR	-	-
JUD–Conserv	28	7,144	8,326	21,648	1.6	2.4
JUD–Orth	60	28,800	10,000	40,000	3.0	4.4
JUD–Reconst	2	363	482	1,253	0.1	0.1
JUD–Reform	19	3,538	6,480	16,848	1.3	1.9
LDS–L-D Saints	6	NR	NR	1,996	0.1	0.2
LUTH–E.L.C.A.	37	3,432	10,553	14,973	1.1	1.7
LUTH–Luth Ch-Am Asc	1	NR	NR	NR	-	-
LUTH–Luth Cong Msn Chr	2	118	233	282	0.0	0.0
LUTH–Luth–MO Synod	8	1,264	3,365	4,018	0.3	0.4
METH–AME	9	351	1,786	2,159	0.2	0.2
METH–AME Zion	8	300	1,350	1,632	0.1	0.2
METH–Un Methodist	40	2,951	9,455	11,941	0.9	1.3
Missionary Ch	2	170	175	195	0.0	0.0
MJEW–Union Mes Cong	2	NR	NR	NR	-	-
Muslim Est	11	4,517	NR	15,690	1.2	1.7
Nat Spirit Asso	1	NR	NR	NR	-	-
New Apost Ch	2	NR	NR	NR	-	-
Non-denom Chr Chs	66	10,364	13,976	15,154	1.1	1.7
OCATH–Pol Natl Cath	1	NR	NR	NR	-	-
ORTHE–Ant Orth of NA	1	100	NR	375	0.0	0.0
ORTHE–Carp Rus Orth	1	45	NR	135	0.0	0.0
ORTHE–Greek Orthodox	7	2,500	NR	12,300	0.9	1.4
ORTHE–Orth Ch in Amer	2	125	NR	225	0.0	0.0
ORTHE–Rus Orth Abroad	2	120	NR	210	0.0	0.0
ORTHE–Ukrainian Orth	1	40	NR	150	0.0	0.0
ORTHO–Coptic Orth Ch	1	650	NR	1,500	0.1	0.2
ORTHO–Malan Dioc Am	4	660	NR	1,105	0.1	0.1
ORTHO–Malan Syr Orth	2	295	NR	558	0.0	0.1
ORTHO–Syrian Orth Ch	1	60	NR	200	0.0	0.0
PENT–Apos Faith Msn	1	NR	35	42	0.0	0.0
PENT–Assemb of God	33	4,621	2,456	5,259	0.4	0.6
PENT–Ch God (Cleve)	19	1,232	1,722	2,081	0.2	0.2
PENT–Ch Lord Jesus Apos	3	NR	NR	NR	-	-
PENT–Ch of God Proph	7	NR	550	665	0.0	0.1
PENT–COGIC	8	110	995	1,203	0.1	0.1

NR–Not Reported   - Represents no adherents reported.   Percentages may not total 100 due to rounding.

Table 3: Religious Congregations by County and Group: 2010

Religious Group	Number of Congrega-tions	Number of Attendees	Number of Communicant, Confirmed, or Full Members	Adherents		
				Number of Adherents	% of Total Pop.	% of Total Adh.
PENT–Fire Bapt Hol Ch	1	NR	NR	NR	-	-
PENT–Full Gosp Bapt	1	NR	NR	NR	-	-
PENT–I F Chr Assmbl	3	NR	NR	NR	-	-
PENT–Un Pent Ch Intl	4	NR	NR	NR	-	-
PENT–Vineyard	1	500	575	695	0.1	0.1
PRES–As Ref Pres Ch	2	NR	36	44	0.0	0.0
PRES–Bible Pres	1	NR	NR	NR	-	-
PRES–Kor Pres Abroad	4	NR	NR	NR	-	-
PRES–Korean Amer Pres	4	NR	NR	NR	-	-
PRES–Korean Pres Amer	6	NR	NR	NR	-	-
PRES–Orth Pres Ch	2	245	267	338	0.0	0.0
PRES–Presb Ch (USA)	21	1,428	2,733	3,303	0.2	0.4
PRES–Presb Ch Amer	4	167	229	327	0.0	0.0
REF–Ref Ch in Am	11	942	1,632	1,858	0.1	0.2
Salvation Army	3	364	443	1,633	0.1	0.2
Sev Day Adv	24	1,648	2,866	3,296	0.2	0.4
Sikh	3	NR	NR	NR	-	-
Un C of Christ	11	616	2,449	2,960	0.2	0.3
Unit Univ	4	398	902	1,201	0.1	0.1
Unity Ch	3	NR	NR	NR	-	-
Zoroastrian	0	NR	NR	95	0.0	0.0
NEW YORK	**865**	**148,591**	**171,505**	**698,097**	**44.0**	**100.0**
ANG/EPIS–Anglican NA	3	NR	NR	NR	-	-
ANG/EPIS–Episcopal	46	7,484	18,385	26,178	1.7	3.7
Bahá'í	1	NR	1,942	1,942	0.1	0.3
BAPT–Alliance Bapt	2	NR	NR	NR	-	-
BAPT–Amer Bapt USA	41	14,093	22,139	25,048	1.6	3.6
BAPT–Consrv Bapt	4	NR	NR	NR	-	-
BAPT–Converge/BGC	1	400	NR	480	0.0	0.1
BAPT–Fund Bapt Flwsp	1	NR	NR	NR	-	-
BAPT–Natl Mis Bapt Conv	1	0	0	0	0.0	0.0
BAPT–NBC USA	17	1,770	4,040	4,571	0.3	0.7
BAPT–Prog NBC	3	805	1,410	1,595	0.1	0.2
BAPT–Reg Bapt Gen As	1	NR	NR	NR	-	-
BAPT–So Bapt Conv	25	3,108	2,971	3,361	0.2	0.5
BRETH–Grace Breth	1	NR	NR	NR	-	-
BUDD–Mahayana	35	NR	NR	23,982	1.5	3.4
BUDD–Vajrayana	22	NR	NR	2,192	0.1	0.3
Calv Chpl	1	NR	NR	NR	-	-
Catholic	109	NR	NR	323,325	20.4	46.3
CGOD–Ch God (Ander)	2	0	NR	0	0.0	0.0
Ch Cr, Scientst	8	NR	NR	NR	-	-
Ch of Chr (Hol)	1	NR	NR	NR	-	-
Ch of Nazarene	1	85	113	113	0.0	0.0
Chr & Miss Al	6	1,134	906	1,605	0.1	0.2
CHR–Chr Ch (Disc)	7	196	564	638	0.0	0.1
CHR–Chr Chs & Chs Cr	6	NR	105	119	0.0	0.0
CHR–Chs of Christ	7	780	933	1,109	0.1	0.2
CHR–Int Chs of Christ	1	NR	648	733	0.0	0.1
Christian Brethren	2	NR	NR	NR	-	-
CONG–Consrv Cong Chr	1	45	23	26	0.0	0.0
Evan Cov Ch	1	66	0	86	0.0	0.0
FRND–Fr Gen Cf & Un Mtg	4	NR	261	295	0.0	0.0
HINDU–I/A Temples	7	NR	NR	3,791	0.2	0.5
HINDU–Post Ren	20	NR	NR	941	0.1	0.1
HINDU–Renaiss	8	NR	NR	337	0.0	0.0
HINDU–Trad Temples	1	NR	NR	0	0.0	0.0
Int Cou Comm Ch	1	NR	NR	NR	-	-
Jain	1	NR	NR	NR	-	-
Jehovah's Witness	11	NR	NR	NR	-	-
JUD–Conserv	9	2,996	3,492	9,079	0.6	1.3
JUD–Orth	77	46,080	16,000	64,000	4.0	9.2
JUD–Reconst	2	418	555	1,443	0.1	0.2
JUD–Reform	10	5,153	9,437	24,536	1.5	3.5
LDS–L-D Saints	14	NR	NR	8,354	0.5	1.2
LUTH–E.L.C.A.	17	1,447	3,135	4,039	0.3	0.6
LUTH–Luth-MO Synod	5	221	356	489	0.0	0.1
MENN–Bruderhof Comm	1	26	8	11	0.0	0.0
MENN–CG in Cr (Menn)	1	NR	4	5	0.0	0.0
MENN–Mennonite USA	2	70	97	110	0.0	0.0
METH–AME	13	1,750	3,700	4,186	0.3	0.6
METH–AME Zion	3	400	800	905	0.1	0.1
METH–C.M.E.	1	200	400	453	0.0	0.1
METH–Free Methodist	1	100	134	134	0.0	0.0
METH–Un Methodist	20	2,419	5,610	7,232	0.5	1.0
Metro Comm Ch	1	387	521	589	0.0	0.1
MJEW–Union Mes Cong	2	NR	NR	NR	-	-
MORAV–Morav Ch-North	2	220	501	738	0.0	0.1
Muslim Est	21	10,278	NR	42,545	2.7	6.1
New Apost Ch	1	NR	NR	NR	-	-
Non-denom Chr Chs	54	27,505	37,755	42,502	2.7	6.1
ORTHE–Bulgar Orth USA	1	50	NR	100	0.0	0.0
ORTHE–Carp Rus Orth	2	85	NR	260	0.0	0.0
ORTHE–Greek Orthodox	10	805	NR	3,980	0.3	0.6
ORTHE–Orth Ch in Amer	5	388	NR	720	0.0	0.1
ORTHE–Rus Orth Abroad	2	175	NR	1,530	0.1	0.2
ORTHE–Rus Orth Moscow	2	250	NR	6,200	0.4	0.9
ORTHE–Serb Orth USA	1	150	NR	2,600	0.2	0.4
ORTHE–Ukrainian Orth	3	257	NR	1,400	0.1	0.2
ORTHO–Armen Ap Cilic	1	150	NR	3,000	0.2	0.4
ORTHO–Armen Ap Etchm	2	180	NR	1,570	0.1	0.2
ORTHO–Coptic Orth Ch	1	125	NR	200	0.0	0.0
ORTHO–Eritrean Orth	2	345	NR	300	0.0	0.0
ORTHO–Ethiopian Orth	1	NR	NR	NR	-	-
ORTHO–Malan Dioc Am	1	30	NR	50	0.0	0.0
PENT–Assemb of God	32	3,290	3,150	4,991	0.3	0.7
PENT–Ch God (Cleve)	8	750	741	838	0.1	0.1
PENT–Ch Lord Jesus Apos	7	NR	NR	NR	-	-
PENT–Ch of God Proph	2	NR	103	117	0.0	0.0
PENT–COGIC	5	190	645	730	0.0	0.1
PENT–Fire Bapt Hol Ch	1	NR	NR	NR	-	-
PENT–I F Chr Assmbl	1	NR	NR	NR	-	-
PENT–Int Foursq Gos	1	183	210	238	0.0	0.0
PENT–Intl Pent Holiness	2	110	120	136	0.0	0.0
PENT–Un Pent Asbl God	1	NR	NR	NR	-	-
PENT–Un Pent Ch Intl	1	NR	NR	NR	-	-
PENT–United Holy Ch	2	NR	NR	NR	-	-
PENT–Vineyard	1	316	135	153	0.0	0.0
PRES–Korean Amer Pres	2	NR	NR	NR	-	-
PRES–Korean Pres Amer	1	NR	NR	NR	-	-
PRES–Presb Ch (USA)	30	2,304	9,283	10,503	0.7	1.5
PRES–Presb Ch Amer	5	2,436	2,222	2,646	0.2	0.4
REF–Christian Ref	2	75	16	18	0.0	0.0
REF–Hung Ref Add'l	1	NR	NR	NR	-	-
REF–Ref Ch in Am	10	1,901	7,827	10,268	0.6	1.5
REF–Un Ref Chs N.A.	1	NR	NR	NR	-	-
Salvation Army	5	414	679	798	0.1	0.1
Sev Day Adv	21	2,696	4,690	5,393	0.3	0.8
Shinto	1	NR	NR	NR	-	-
Sikh	2	NR	NR	NR	-	-
Swedenborgian	2	NR	NR	NR	-	-
Tao	1	NR	NR	NR	-	-
Un C of Christ	10	1,133	2,841	3,214	0.2	0.5
Unit Univ	3	167	1,898	2,261	0.1	0.3
Unity Ch	3	NR	NR	NR	-	-
Zoroastrian	0	NR	NR	66	0.0	0.0
NIAGARA	**212**	**13,982**	**28,573**	**93,820**	**43.3**	**100.0**
ANG/EPIS–Episcopal	9	616	1,359	1,564	0.7	1.7
Bahá'í	0	NR	38	38	0.0	0.0
BAPT–Amer Bapt USA	9	756	1,436	1,711	0.8	1.8
BAPT–NBC USA	1	0	500	596	0.3	0.6
BAPT–Reg Bapt Gen As	2	NR	NR	NR	-	-
BAPT–So Bapt Conv	5	119	117	139	0.1	0.1
Catholic	29	NR	NR	51,948	24.0	55.4
CGOD–Ch God (Ander)	1	260	NR	260	0.1	0.3
Ch Cr, Scientst	1	NR	NR	NR	-	-
Ch of Nazarene	2	82	113	113	0.1	0.1
Chr & Miss Al	2	394	200	566	0.3	0.6
CHR–Chr Ch (Disc)	2	0	130	155	0.1	0.2
CHR–Chs of Christ	2	135	160	199	0.1	0.2
CONG–Cong Chr, NA	1	NR	96	114	0.1	0.1
FRND–Fr Gen Cf & Un Mtg	1	NR	4	5	0.0	0.0
HINDU–Post Ren	1	NR	NR	100	0.0	0.1
Jehovah's Witness	7	NR	NR	NR	-	-
JUD–Conserv	1	30	34	92	0.0	0.1
JUD–Reform	1	14	25	68	0.0	0.1

NR–Not Reported   - Represents no adherents reported.   Percentages may not total 100 due to rounding.

Table 3: Religious Congregations by County and Group: 2010

Religious Group	Number of Congrega-tions	Number of Attendees	Number of Communicant, Confirmed, or Full Members	Adherents		
				Number of Adherents	% of Total Pop.	% of Total Adh.
LDS–Comm of Christ	1	NR	158	158	0.1	0.2
LDS–L-D Saints	2	NR	NR	1,125	0.5	1.2
LUTH–E.L.C.A.	11	779	2,085	3,232	1.5	3.4
LUTH–Luth Cong Msn Chr	3	401	986	1,175	0.5	1.3
LUTH–Luth–MO Synod	16	1,995	6,357	8,260	3.8	8.8
METH–AME	2	215	660	787	0.4	0.8
METH–AME Zion	1	0	100	119	0.1	0.1
METH–Free Methodist	4	373	248	373	0.2	0.4
METH–Un Methodist	19	1,732	5,596	7,978	3.7	8.5
METH–Wesleyan	2	204	81	266	0.1	0.3
Muslim Est	1	406	NR	1,522	0.7	1.6
New Apost Ch	1	NR	NR	NR	-	-
Non-denom Chr Chs	25	3,085	3,346	4,010	1.9	4.3
OCATH–Pol Natl Cath	1	NR	NR	NR	-	-
ORTHE–Ant Orth of NA	1	140	NR	500	0.2	0.5
ORTHE–Holy Orth in NA	1	15	NR	20	0.0	0.0
ORTHO–Armen Ap Cilic	1	40	NR	100	0.0	0.1
ORTHO–Armen Ap Etchm	1	30	NR	100	0.0	0.1
ORTHO–Coptic Orth Ch	1	70	NR	90	0.0	0.1
PENT–Assemb of God	4	473	340	822	0.4	0.9
PENT–Ch God (Cleve)	2	151	146	174	0.1	0.2
PENT–Ch Lord Jesus Apos	3	NR	NR	NR	-	-
PENT–COGIC	3	20	330	393	0.2	0.4
PENT–Elim	1	NR	NR	NR	-	-
PENT–Full Gosp Bapt	1	NR	NR	NR	-	-
PENT–I F Chr Assmbl	1	NR	NR	NR	-	-
PENT–Vineyard	1	94	120	143	0.1	0.2
PRES–Evan Presby Ch	1	NR	74	88	0.0	0.1
PRES–Presb Ch (USA)	12	873	2,253	2,685	1.2	2.9
Salvation Army	2	65	149	451	0.2	0.5
Sev Day Adv	2	68	118	135	0.1	0.1
Un C of Christ	7	317	1,168	1,392	0.6	1.5
Unit Univ	1	30	46	54	0.0	0.1
ONEIDA	**244**	**11,748**	**22,278**	**119,669**	**50.9**	**100.0**
ANG/EPIS–Episcopal	13	621	1,319	2,200	0.9	1.8
Bahá'í	0	NR	40	40	0.0	0.0
BAPT–Amer Bapt Assn	1	NR	85	102	0.0	0.1
BAPT–Amer Bapt USA	11	990	1,981	2,371	1.0	2.0
BAPT–Consrv Bapt	5	NR	NR	NR	-	-
BAPT–Ind Bapt Flwsp Intl	1	NR	NR	NR	-	-
BAPT–Reg Bapt Gen As	3	NR	NR	NR	-	-
BAPT–S-D Baptist Gen Con	2	106	149	178	0.1	0.1
BAPT–So Bapt Conv	5	323	363	435	0.2	0.4
Catholic	49	NR	NR	86,750	36.9	72.5
Ch Cr, Scientst	1	NR	NR	NR	-	-
Ch of Nazarene	1	14	27	56	0.0	0.0
Chr & Miss Al	6	394	191	573	0.2	0.5
CHR–Chs of Christ	2	105	112	137	0.1	0.1
FRND–Fr Gen Cf & Un Mtg	1	NR	20	24	0.0	0.0
Jehovah's Witness	6	NR	NR	NR	-	-
JUD–Conserv	1	98	110	297	0.1	0.2
JUD–Reform	1	90	159	429	0.2	0.4
LDS–L-D Saints	2	NR	NR	1,037	0.4	0.9
LUTH–E.L.C.A.	3	303	1,603	2,306	1.0	1.9
LUTH–Luth–MO Synod	2	264	526	760	0.3	0.6
MENN–Amish Undif	1	NR	11	29	0.0	0.0
METH–AME	1	0	150	180	0.1	0.2
METH–AME Zion	1	0	150	180	0.1	0.2
METH–Free Methodist	1	110	83	110	0.0	0.1
METH–Un Methodist	38	1,715	6,872	8,054	3.4	6.7
METH–Wesleyan	2	300	71	391	0.2	0.3
Muslim Est	2	556	NR	2,422	1.0	2.0
New Apost Ch	1	NR	NR	NR	-	-
Non-denom Chr Chs	22	3,390	3,810	4,390	1.9	3.7
OCATH–Pol Natl Cath	2	NR	NR	NR	-	-
ORTHE–Ant Orth of NA	1	60	NR	130	0.1	0.1
ORTHE–Rus Orth Abroad	1	30	NR	60	0.0	0.1
ORTHE–Ukrainian Orth	1	25	NR	80	0.0	0.1
PENT–Assemb of God	5	460	252	657	0.3	0.5
PENT–COGIC	2	0	120	144	0.1	0.1
PENT–Elim	3	NR	NR	NR	-	-
PENT–Int Foursq Gos	2	132	133	159	0.1	0.1
PENT–Un Pent Ch Intl	1	NR	NR	NR	-	-

Religious Group	Number of Congrega-tions	Number of Attendees	Number of Communicant, Confirmed, or Full Members	Adherents		
				Number of Adherents	% of Total Pop.	% of Total Adh.
PRES–Presb Ch (USA)	22	938	2,435	2,915	1.2	2.4
PRES–Ref Pres of NA	1	55	38	60	0.0	0.1
Salvation Army	2	77	270	583	0.2	0.5
Sev Day Adv	7	250	433	499	0.2	0.4
Un C of Christ	7	248	618	740	0.3	0.6
Unit Univ	2	94	147	189	0.1	0.2
Zoroastrian	0	NR	NR	2	0.0	0.0
ONONDAGA	**399**	**34,189**	**58,542**	**259,503**	**55.6**	**100.0**
ANG/EPIS–Anglican NA	2	NR	NR	NR	-	-
ANG/EPIS–Episcopal	15	1,345	3,679	4,789	1.0	1.8
Bahá'í	1	NR	90	90	0.0	0.0
BAPT–Amer Bapt USA	21	2,587	4,261	5,154	1.1	2.0
BAPT–Consrv Bapt	2	NR	NR	NR	-	-
BAPT–Ind Bapt Flwsp Intl	1	NR	NR	NR	-	-
BAPT–Natl Mis Bapt Conv	4	0	600	726	0.2	0.3
BAPT–NBC USA	4	825	1,174	1,420	0.3	0.5
BAPT–Ref Bapt Ch	1	NR	NR	NR	-	-
BAPT–Reg Bapt Gen As	4	NR	NR	NR	-	-
BAPT–So Bapt Conv	14	2,187	2,219	2,684	0.6	1.0
BUDD–Mahayana	2	NR	NR	534	0.1	0.2
BUDD–Vajrayana	2	NR	NR	70	0.0	0.0
Calv Chpl	2	NR	NR	NR	-	-
Catholic	58	NR	NR	163,488	35.0	63.0
Ch Christ Chr Union	1	NR	NR	NR	-	-
Ch Cr, Scientst	1	NR	NR	NR	-	-
Ch of Nazarene	3	393	392	944	0.2	0.4
Chr & Miss Al	6	664	552	1,029	0.2	0.4
CHR–Chr Ch (Disc)	1	25	50	60	0.0	0.0
CHR–Chr Chs & Chs Cr	4	NR	600	726	0.2	0.3
CHR–Chs of Christ	3	429	400	495	0.1	0.2
CHR–Int Chs of Christ	1	NR	24	29	0.0	0.0
CONG–Consrv Cong Chr	2	182	193	233	0.0	0.1
Evan Cov Ch	3	356	178	463	0.1	0.2
FRND–Fr Gen Cf & Un Mtg	1	NR	71	86	0.0	0.0
HINDU–I/A Temples	1	NR	NR	1,742	0.4	0.7
HINDU–Post Ren	1	NR	NR	25	0.0	0.0
HINDU–Trad Temples	1	NR	NR	3,200	0.7	1.2
Int Cou Comm Ch	2	NR	NR	NR	-	-
Jain	1	NR	NR	NR	-	-
Jehovah's Witness	4	NR	NR	NR	-	-
JUD–Conserv	2	779	874	2,360	0.5	0.9
JUD–Orth	2	266	100	370	0.1	0.1
JUD–Reform	1	277	489	1,320	0.3	0.5
LDS–L-D Saints	4	NR	NR	1,799	0.4	0.7
LUTH–E.L.C.A.	12	1,449	5,421	7,368	1.6	2.8
LUTH–Luth–MO Synod	1	50	233	329	0.1	0.1
LUTH–Wisc Ev Luth Syn	1	51	56	73	0.0	0.0
METH–AME	1	0	100	121	0.0	0.0
METH–AME Zion	1	220	451	545	0.1	0.2
METH–C.M.E.	1	200	500	605	0.1	0.2
METH–Free Methodist	2	404	319	463	0.1	0.2
METH–Un Methodist	45	3,329	15,576	18,796	4.0	7.2
METH–Wesleyan	6	712	288	925	0.2	0.4
Muslim Est	4	1,918	NR	6,566	1.4	2.5
New Apost Ch	1	NR	NR	NR	-	-
Non-denom Chr Chs	39	7,269	7,470	9,853	2.1	3.8
OCATH–Pol Natl Cath	1	NR	NR	NR	-	-
ORTHE–Ant Orth of NA	1	140	NR	402	0.1	0.2
ORTHE–Bulgar Orth USA	1	45	NR	70	0.0	0.0
ORTHE–Greek Orthodox	1	150	NR	2,400	0.5	0.9
ORTHE–Macedonian Orth	1	70	NR	600	0.1	0.2
ORTHE–Orth Ch in Amer	1	50	NR	100	0.0	0.0
ORTHE–Romania Orth Ar	1	40	NR	120	0.0	0.0
ORTHE–Rus Orth Abroad	1	50	NR	70	0.0	0.0
ORTHE–Ukrainian Orth	1	60	NR	100	0.0	0.0
ORTHO–Armen Ap Cilic	1	25	NR	50	0.0	0.0
ORTHO–Armen Ap Etchm	1	30	NR	100	0.0	0.0
ORTHO–Coptic Orth Ch	1	25	NR	90	0.0	0.0
ORTHO–Malan Dioc Am	1	30	NR	50	0.0	0.0
PENT–Assemb of God	15	2,218	1,274	2,566	0.5	1.0
PENT–Ch God (Cleve)	2	64	81	98	0.0	0.0
PENT–Ch Lord Jesus Apos	2	NR	NR	NR	-	-
PENT–Ch of God by Faith	1	NR	NR	NR	-	-

NR–Not Reported   - Represents no adherents reported.   Percentages may not total 100 due to rounding.

Table 3: Religious Congregations by County and Group: 2010

Religious Group	Number of Congrega-tions	Number of Attendees	Number of Communicant, Confirmed, or Full Members	Adherents		
				Number of Adherents	% of Total Pop.	% of Total Adh.
PENT–Ch of God Proph	1	NR	54	65	0.0	0.0
PENT–COGIC	15	990	1,879	2,273	0.5	0.9
PENT–Elim	1	NR	NR	NR	-	-
PENT–I F Chr Assmbl	2	NR	NR	NR	-	-
PENT–Int Foursq Gos	1	33	38	46	0.0	0.0
PENT–Un Pent Ch Intl	1	NR	NR	NR	-	-
PENT–Vineyard	2	1,063	1,611	1,948	0.4	0.8
PRES–Evan Presby Ch	1	NR	143	173	0.0	0.1
PRES–Orth Pres Ch	1	28	23	28	0.0	0.0
PRES–Presb Ch (USA)	23	1,272	3,401	4,113	0.9	1.6
PRES–Ref Pres of NA	2	205	203	247	0.1	0.1
REF–Christian Ref	1	50	51	62	0.0	0.0
REF–Ref Ch in Am	2	127	307	384	0.1	0.1
Salvation Army	3	241	428	619	0.1	0.2
Sev Day Adv	5	626	1,088	1,251	0.3	0.5
Sikh	1	NR	NR	NR	-	-
Tao	1	NR	NR	NR	-	-
Un C of Christ	7	443	1,244	1,505	0.3	0.6
Unit Univ	2	197	357	469	0.1	0.2
Unity Ch	2	NR	NR	NR	-	-
Zoroastrian	0	NR	NR	24	0.0	0.0
ONTARIO	**111**	**7,705**	**13,702**	**45,557**	**42.2**	**100.0**
ANG/EPIS–Episcopal	5	371	704	923	0.9	2.0
Bahá'í	1	NR	70	70	0.1	0.2
BAPT–Amer Bapt USA	7	682	1,183	1,421	1.3	3.1
BAPT–Consrv Bapt	2	NR	NR	NR	-	-
BAPT–Prog NBC	1	0	150	180	0.2	0.4
BAPT–Reg Bapt Gen As	2	NR	NR	NR	-	-
BAPT–So Bapt Conv	2	156	245	294	0.3	0.6
Calv Chpl	1	NR	NR	NR	-	-
Catholic	9	NR	NR	25,433	23.6	55.8
Ch Cr, Scientst	1	NR	NR	NR	-	-
Ch of Nazarene	1	0	43	43	0.0	0.1
Chr & Miss Al	1	18	38	43	0.0	0.1
CHR–Chr Chs & Chs Cr	1	NR	130	156	0.1	0.3
CONG–Cong Chr, NA	1	NR	54	65	0.1	0.1
FRND–Fr Gen Cf & Un Mtg	2	NR	144	173	0.2	0.4
Ind Fund Churches	1	NR	NR	NR	-	-
Jehovah's Witness	3	NR	NR	NR	-	-
JUD–Reform	1	34	60	162	0.2	0.4
LDS–L-D Saints	1	NR	NR	556	0.5	1.2
LUTH–E.L.C.A.	2	136	334	441	0.4	1.0
LUTH–Luth-MO Synod	2	352	827	1,059	1.0	2.3
METH–Un Methodist	20	1,647	4,921	6,312	5.8	13.9
METH–Wesleyan	2	1,177	130	1,530	1.4	3.4
New Apost Ch	1	NR	NR	NR	-	-
Non-denom Chr Chs	12	1,070	1,180	1,424	1.3	3.1
ORTHE–Ant Orth of NA	1	60	NR	350	0.3	0.8
ORTHE–Romania Orth Ar	1	85	NR	400	0.4	0.9
PENT–Assemb of God	2	102	43	108	0.1	0.2
PENT–Ch God (Cleve)	2	96	73	88	0.1	0.2
PENT–Elim	3	NR	NR	NR	-	-
PENT–Un Pent Ch Intl	1	NR	NR	NR	-	-
PRES–Presb Ch (USA)	9	1,010	1,750	2,102	1.9	4.6
Salvation Army	2	106	178	499	0.5	1.1
Sev Day Adv	1	61	106	122	0.1	0.3
Un C of Christ	6	500	1,259	1,513	1.4	3.3
Unit Univ	1	42	80	90	0.1	0.2
ORANGE	**285**	**30,489**	**31,221**	**197,976**	**53.1**	**100.0**
ANG/EPIS–Episcopal	18	1,135	2,822	3,700	1.0	1.9
Bahá'í	0	NR	63	63	0.0	0.0
BAPT–Amer Bapt USA	5	323	787	994	0.3	0.5
BAPT–Consrv Bapt	5	NR	NR	NR	-	-
BAPT–NBC USA	2	325	650	821	0.2	0.4
BAPT–Ref Bapt Ch	1	NR	NR	NR	-	-
BAPT–Reg Bapt Gen As	2	NR	NR	NR	-	-
BAPT–So Bapt Conv	3	114	132	167	0.0	0.1
BUDD–Mahayana	5	NR	NR	680	0.2	0.3
BUDD–Vajrayana	1	NR	NR	167	0.0	0.1
Calv Chpl	1	NR	NR	NR	-	-
Catholic	45	NR	NR	131,308	35.2	66.3

Religious Group	Number of Congrega-tions	Number of Attendees	Number of Communicant, Confirmed, or Full Members	Adherents		
				Number of Adherents	% of Total Pop.	% of Total Adh.
Ch Cr, Scientst	1	NR	NR	NR	-	-
Ch of Nazarene	3	115	151	181	0.0	0.1
Chr & Miss Al	2	165	135	187	0.1	0.1
CHR–Chr Ch (Disc)	1	0	0	0	0.0	0.0
CHR–Chs of Christ	3	140	124	185	0.0	0.1
CHR–Int Chs of Christ	0	NR	214	270	0.1	0.1
CONG–Consrv Cong Chr	1	70	185	234	0.1	0.1
Evan Free Ch	1	65	NR	65	0.0	0.0
FRND–Fr Gen Cf & Un Mtg	1	NR	38	48	0.0	0.0
HINDU–Post Ren	1	NR	NR	15	0.0	0.0
HINDU–Renaiss	1	NR	NR	12	0.0	0.0
Jehovah's Witness	9	NR	NR	NR	-	-
JUD–Conserv	4	477	535	1,444	0.4	0.7
JUD–Orth	8	15,120	3,500	21,000	5.6	10.6
JUD–Reform	3	338	597	1,612	0.4	0.8
LDS–L-D Saints	4	NR	NR	1,455	0.4	0.7
LUTH–E.L.C.A.	5	531	1,620	2,135	0.6	1.1
LUTH–Luth-MO Synod	5	788	1,559	2,475	0.7	1.3
MENN–Bruderhof Comm	2	494	213	394	0.1	0.2
METH–AME	1	0	150	189	0.1	0.1
METH–AME Zion	3	50	254	321	0.1	0.2
METH–Un Methodist	26	1,538	5,436	7,242	1.9	3.7
METH–Wesleyan	1	226	68	294	0.1	0.1
Muslim Est	3	987	NR	3,644	1.0	1.8
Non-denom Chr Chs	22	2,138	2,549	2,947	0.8	1.5
ORTHE–Ant Orth of NA	1	50	NR	70	0.0	0.0
ORTHE–Greek Orthodox	2	230	NR	750	0.2	0.4
ORTHE–Orth Ch in Amer	1	10	NR	100	0.0	0.1
ORTHE–Romania Orth Ar	1	3	NR	3	0.0	0.0
ORTHE–Rus Orth Moscow	1	25	NR	50	0.0	0.0
PENT–Assemb of God	14	1,575	991	1,725	0.5	0.9
PENT–Ch God (Cleve)	5	686	1,396	1,763	0.5	0.9
PENT–Ch of God by Faith	1	NR	NR	NR	-	-
PENT–Ch of God Proph	3	NR	117	148	0.0	0.1
PENT–COGIC	1	75	301	380	0.1	0.2
PENT–Elim	1	NR	NR	NR	-	-
PENT–Fire Bapt Hol Ch	1	NR	NR	NR	-	-
PENT–Un Pent Ch Intl	1	NR	NR	NR	-	-
PENT–United Holy Ch	2	NR	NR	NR	-	-
PRES–Evan Presby Ch	3	NR	771	974	0.3	0.5
PRES–Korean Amer Pres	1	NR	NR	NR	-	-
PRES–Presb Ch (USA)	22	1,176	2,990	3,776	1.0	1.9
PRES–Presb Ch Amer	1	120	192	228	0.1	0.1
PRES–Ref Pres of NA	1	25	31	37	0.0	0.0
REF–Christian Ref	1	200	233	294	0.1	0.1
REF–Ref Ch in Am	8	536	1,058	1,215	0.3	0.6
REF–Un Ref Chs N.A.	1	NR	NR	NR	-	-
Salvation Army	3	154	449	1,121	0.3	0.6
Sev Day Adv	6	374	650	748	0.2	0.4
Un C of Christ	2	53	171	216	0.1	0.1
Unit Univ	2	58	89	107	0.0	0.1
Zoroastrian	0	NR	NR	22	0.0	0.0
ORLEANS	**57**	**2,951**	**7,715**	**16,491**	**38.5**	**100.0**
ANG/EPIS–Episcopal	3	59	159	159	0.4	1.0
Bahá'í	0	NR	9	9	0.0	0.1
BAPT–Amer Bapt USA	5	356	2,576	3,079	7.2	18.7
BAPT–N Am Bapt Conf	1	NR	76	91	0.2	0.6
BAPT–NBC USA	3	0	300	359	0.8	2.2
BAPT–Reg Bapt Gen As	1	NR	NR	NR	-	-
BAPT–So Bapt Conv	1	78	70	84	0.2	0.5
Catholic	4	NR	NR	6,819	15.9	41.3
Chr & Miss Al	2	94	55	203	0.5	1.2
Jehovah's Witness	1	NR	NR	NR	-	-
LUTH–E.L.C.A.	3	153	521	761	1.8	4.6
LUTH–Luth-MO Synod	1	86	190	225	0.5	1.4
MENN–Amish Undif	2	NR	61	137	0.3	0.8
METH–Free Methodist	1	170	113	170	0.4	1.0
METH–Un Methodist	11	652	1,944	2,338	5.5	14.2
METH–Wesleyan	1	26	59	34	0.1	0.2
Non-denom Chr Chs	6	595	625	793	1.8	4.8
PENT–Assemb of God	4	335	219	354	0.8	2.1
PRES–Presb Ch (USA)	4	265	592	708	1.7	4.3
Sev Day Adv	1	36	63	72	0.2	0.4

NR–Not Reported - Represents no adherents reported. Percentages may not total 100 due to rounding.

Table 3: Religious Congregations by County and Group: 2010

Religious Group	Number of Congrega-tions	Number of Attendees	Number of Communicant, Confirmed, or Full Members	Adherents		
				Number of Adherents	% of Total Pop.	% of Total Adh.
Un C of Christ	1	31	61	73	0.2	0.4
Unit Univ	1	15	22	23	0.1	0.1
OSWEGO	**136**	**6,032**	**11,163**	**42,167**	**34.5**	**100.0**
ANG/EPIS–Episcopal	5	186	372	562	0.5	1.3
Bahá'í	0	NR	17	17	0.0	0.0
BAPT–Amer Bapt USA	7	260	618	746	0.6	1.8
BAPT–NT Ind Bapt	1	NR	NR	NR	-	-
BAPT–Reg Bapt Gen As	4	NR	NR	NR	-	-
BAPT–So Bapt Conv	2	33	26	31	0.0	0.1
Catholic	17	NR	NR	25,395	20.8	60.2
Ch Cr, Scientst	1	NR	NR	NR	-	-
Ch of Nazarene	2	128	163	233	0.2	0.6
Chr & Miss Al	3	622	380	870	0.7	2.1
CHR–Chr Chs & Chs Cr	3	NR	183	221	0.2	0.5
CHR–Chs of Christ	1	90	90	100	0.1	0.2
Jehovah's Witness	1	NR	NR	NR	-	-
LDS–L-D Saints	2	NR	NR	799	0.7	1.9
LUTH–E.L.C.A.	2	117	551	715	0.6	1.7
MENN–Amish Undif	1	NR	36	107	0.1	0.3
METH–Un Methodist	35	1,537	5,464	7,662	6.3	18.2
METH–Wesleyan	5	494	291	643	0.5	1.5
Non-denom Chr Chs	15	1,545	1,590	2,029	1.7	4.8
PENT–Assemb of God	4	207	88	217	0.2	0.5
PENT–Ch God (Cleve)	1	180	200	241	0.2	0.6
PENT–Elim	2	NR	NR	NR	-	-
PENT–Int Foursq Gos	1	10	12	14	0.0	0.0
PENT–Un Pent Ch Intl	1	NR	NR	NR	-	-
PRES–Presb Ch (USA)	5	118	177	214	0.2	0.5
PRES–Ref Pres of NA	2	95	81	102	0.1	0.2
Salvation Army	2	51	128	424	0.3	1.0
Sev Day Adv	3	136	236	272	0.2	0.6
Sikh	1	NR	NR	NR	-	-
Un C of Christ	6	188	422	509	0.4	1.2
Unit Univ	1	35	38	44	0.0	0.1
OTSEGO	**111**	**3,741**	**9,207**	**24,184**	**38.8**	**100.0**
ANG/EPIS–Episcopal	11	559	1,077	1,331	2.1	5.5
Bahá'í	0	NR	17	17	0.0	0.1
BAPT–Amer Bapt USA	7	383	891	1,030	1.7	4.3
BAPT–Consrv Bapt	4	NR	NR	NR	-	-
BAPT–Reg Bapt Gen As	1	NR	NR	NR	-	-
BAPT–So Bapt Conv	1	10	20	23	0.0	0.1
BUDD–Mahayana	1	NR	NR	115	0.2	0.5
BUDD–Vajrayana	2	NR	NR	244	0.4	1.0
Catholic	6	NR	NR	11,599	18.6	48.0
Ch Cr, Scientst	1	NR	NR	NR	-	-
CHR–Chs of Christ	1	21	13	23	0.0	0.1
FRND–Fr Gen Cf & Un Mtg	4	NR	46	53	0.1	0.2
Jehovah's Witness	2	NR	NR	NR	-	-
JUD–Conserv	1	72	81	219	0.4	0.9
LDS–L-D Saints	1	NR	NR	301	0.5	1.2
LUTH–E.L.C.A.	4	122	601	840	1.3	3.5
MENN–Amish Undif	2	NR	103	223	0.4	0.9
METH–Un Methodist	31	919	4,164	5,307	8.5	21.9
METH–Wesleyan	1	59	38	77	0.1	0.3
Non-denom Chr Chs	9	805	815	1,013	1.6	4.2
ORTHE–Orth Ch in Amer	1	12	NR	25	0.0	0.1
PENT–Assemb of God	3	175	101	205	0.3	0.8
PENT–Elim	1	NR	NR	NR	-	-
PRES–Presb Ch (USA)	12	385	931	1,076	1.7	4.4
REF–Christian Ref	1	16	40	46	0.1	0.2
Salvation Army	1	93	59	163	0.3	0.7
Sev Day Adv	1	28	49	56	0.1	0.2
Unit Univ	1	82	161	198	0.3	0.8
PUTNAM	**55**	**1,971**	**4,103**	**48,378**	**48.5**	**100.0**
ANG/EPIS–Episcopal	5	311	711	1,006	1.0	2.1
Bahá'í	0	NR	13	13	0.0	0.0
BAPT–Amer Bapt USA	2	60	403	488	0.5	1.0
BAPT–Consrv Bapt	2	NR	NR	NR	-	-
BAPT–Ref Bapt Ch	1	NR	NR	NR	-	-
BAPT–So Bapt Conv	1	30	21	25	0.0	0.1
BUDD–Mahayana	1	NR	NR	250	0.3	0.5
BUDD–Vajrayana	1	NR	NR	167	0.2	0.3
Catholic	9	NR	NR	41,420	41.5	85.6
Chr & Miss Al	1	85	57	117	0.1	0.2
CHR–Chs of Christ	1	30	28	36	0.0	0.1
FRND–Fr Gen Cf & Un Mtg	1	NR	0	0	0.0	0.0
Int Cou Comm Ch	1	NR	NR	NR	-	-
Jehovah's Witness	1	NR	NR	NR	-	-
JUD–Conserv	1	118	132	356	0.4	0.7
JUD–Orth	1	43	50	60	0.1	0.1
JUD–Reform	2	156	275	742	0.7	1.5
LUTH–E.L.C.A.	1	120	406	561	0.6	1.2
LUTH–Luth-MO Synod	1	110	310	636	0.6	1.3
MENN–Bible Flwshp	1	20	NR	27	0.0	0.1
METH–Un Methodist	8	298	922	1,201	1.2	2.5
Non-denom Chr Chs	1	50	50	62	0.1	0.1
ORTHE–Greek Orthodox	1	25	NR	45	0.0	0.1
ORTHE–Rus Orth Abroad	1	40	NR	100	0.1	0.2
PENT–Assemb of God	2	136	97	196	0.2	0.4
PENT–Elim	1	NR	NR	NR	-	-
PENT–Pent Ch of God	1	70	NR	109	0.1	0.2
PRES–Presb Ch (USA)	5	269	628	761	0.8	1.6
Sev Day Adv	1	0	0	0	0.0	0.0
QUEENS	**1,306**	**199,076**	**165,776**	**1,102,518**	**49.4**	**100.0**
ANG/EPIS–Episcopal	28	3,402	7,099	9,241	0.4	0.8
BAPT–Amer Bapt USA	33	17,171	10,099	12,003	0.5	1.1
BAPT–Consrv Bapt	17	NR	NR	NR	-	-
BAPT–Natl Mis Bapt Conv	2	0	300	357	0.0	0.0
BAPT–NBC Amer	2	125	200	238	0.0	0.0
BAPT–NBC USA	18	3,530	6,109	7,261	0.3	0.7
BAPT–Prog NBC	2	850	1,350	1,605	0.1	0.1
BAPT–Reg Bapt Gen As	1	NR	NR	NR	-	-
BAPT–S-D Baptist Gen Con	1	67	62	74	0.0	0.0
BAPT–So Bapt Conv	50	3,549	3,949	4,694	0.2	0.4
BUDD–Mahayana	26	NR	NR	12,957	0.6	1.2
BUDD–Theravada	2	NR	NR	1,381	0.1	0.1
BUDD–Vajrayana	3	NR	NR	548	0.0	0.0
Calv Chpl	1	NR	NR	NR	-	-
Catholic	100	NR	NR	677,520	30.4	61.5
CGOD–Ch God (Ander)	6	468	NR	468	0.0	0.0
Ch Cr, Scientst	3	NR	NR	NR	-	-
Ch God (7th Day)	2	NR	NR	NR	-	-
Ch of Nazarene	21	1,414	1,811	1,985	0.1	0.2
Chr & Miss Al	22	3,105	2,333	3,585	0.2	0.3
CHR–Chr Ch (Disc)	6	60	173	206	0.0	0.0
CHR–Chr Chs & Chs Cr	4	NR	224	266	0.0	0.0
CHR–Chs of Christ	14	940	730	1,057	0.0	0.1
CHR–Int Chs of Christ	0	NR	216	257	0.0	0.0
CONG–Cong Chr, NA	1	NR	280	333	0.0	0.0
Evan Cov Ch	1	59	28	77	0.0	0.0
Evan Free Ch	1	100	NR	100	0.0	0.0
FRND–Fr Gen Cf & Un Mtg	2	NR	33	39	0.0	0.0
HINDU–I/A Temples	13	NR	NR	2,756	0.1	0.2
HINDU–Post Ren	14	NR	NR	2,364	0.1	0.2
HINDU–Renaiss	1	NR	NR	40	0.0	0.0
HINDU–Trad Temples	18	NR	NR	16,775	0.8	1.5
Int Cou Comm Ch	3	NR	NR	NR	-	-
Intl Fell Bible Ch	4	NR	NR	NR	-	-
Jain	1	NR	NR	NR	-	-
Jehovah's Witness	21	NR	NR	NR	-	-
JUD–Conserv	12	2,057	2,398	6,235	0.3	0.6
JUD–Orth	110	57,600	20,000	80,000	3.6	7.3
JUD–Reform	3	289	529	1,375	0.1	0.1
LDS–L-D Saints	14	NR	NR	10,463	0.5	0.9
LUTH–E.L.C.A.	34	2,180	5,092	7,210	0.3	0.7
LUTH–Luth-MO Synod	24	1,260	2,091	2,686	0.1	0.2
LUTH–Wisc Ev Luth Syn	1	54	57	76	0.0	0.0
MENN–Mennonite USA	2	80	39	46	0.0	0.0
METH–AME	14	17,175	23,630	28,085	1.3	2.5
METH–AME Zion	6	600	1,370	1,628	0.1	0.1
METH–C.M.E.	3	120	425	505	0.0	0.0
METH–Free Methodist	2	50	39	52	0.0	0.0
METH–Un Methodist	27	3,775	6,386	6,932	0.3	0.6

NR–Not Reported   - Represents no adherents reported.   Percentages may not total 100 due to rounding.

Table 3: Religious Congregations by County and Group: 2010

Religious Group	Number of Congrega-tions	Number of Attendees	Number of Communicant, Confirmed, or Full Members	Adherents		
				Number of Adherents	% of Total Pop.	% of Total Adh.
METH–Wesleyan	3	273	413	355	0.0	0.0
Missionary Ch	5	172	139	186	0.0	0.0
MJEW–Union Mes Cong	1	NR	NR	NR	-	-
MORAV–Morav Ch-North	1	116	151	258	0.0	0.0
Muslim Est	57	21,634	NR	81,456	3.7	7.4
New Apost Ch	6	NR	NR	NR	-	-
Non-denom Chr Chs	129	23,259	29,538	33,325	1.5	3.0
ORTHE–Greek Orthodox	6	4,110	NR	24,250	1.1	2.2
ORTHE–Holy Orth in NA	1	35	NR	45	0.0	0.0
ORTHE–Macedonian Orth	1	30	NR	500	0.0	0.0
ORTHE–Orth Ch in Amer	7	330	NR	950	0.0	0.1
ORTHE–Romania Orth Ar	3	260	NR	2,950	0.1	0.3
ORTHE–Rus Orth Abroad	1	30	NR	60	0.0	0.0
ORTHE–Rus Orth Moscow	1	6	NR	15	0.0	0.0
ORTHE–Ukrainian Orth	3	47	NR	170	0.0	0.0
ORTHO–Armen Ap Cilic	1	125	NR	2,000	0.1	0.2
ORTHO–Armen Ap Etchm	1	150	NR	300	0.0	0.0
ORTHO–Coptic Orth Ch	2	1,425	NR	3,425	0.2	0.3
ORTHO–Malan Dioc Am	4	690	NR	1,100	0.0	0.1
PENT–Assemb of God	59	9,792	10,063	13,989	0.6	1.3
PENT–Ch God (Cleve)	24	1,640	1,903	2,262	0.1	0.2
PENT–Ch Lord Jesus Apos	8	NR	NR	NR	-	-
PENT–Ch of God Proph	4	NR	401	477	0.0	0.0
PENT–COGIC	10	410	800	951	0.0	0.1
PENT–Elim	1	NR	NR	NR	-	-
PENT–Fire Bapt Hol Ch	1	NR	NR	NR	-	-
PENT–Full Gosp Bapt	4	NR	NR	NR	-	-
PENT–I F Chr Assmbl	2	NR	NR	NR	-	-
PENT–Int Foursq Gos	4	78	99	118	0.0	0.0
PENT–Intl Pent Holiness	2	141	157	187	0.0	0.0
PENT–Open Bible Std	1	150	NR	150	0.0	0.0
PENT–Pent Ch of God	1	70	NR	109	0.0	0.0
PENT–Un Pent Ch Intl	7	NR	NR	NR	-	-
PENT–United Holy Ch	1	NR	NR	NR	-	-
PENT–Vineyard	1	150	180	214	0.0	0.0
PRES–As Ref Pres Ch	12	NR	1,156	1,374	0.1	0.1
PRES–Cumber Presb	2	NR	137	167	0.0	0.0
PRES–Kor Pres Abroad	23	NR	NR	NR	-	-
PRES–Korean Amer Pres	19	NR	NR	NR	-	-
PRES–Korean Pres Amer	42	NR	NR	NR	-	-
PRES–Orth Pres Ch	2	47	13	15	0.0	0.0
PRES–Presb Ch (USA)	35	2,049	4,284	5,092	0.2	0.5
PRES–Presb Ch Amer	10	827	1,036	1,165	0.1	0.1
REF–Christian Ref	2	117	157	187	0.0	0.0
REF–Ref Ch in Am	23	2,358	2,954	3,445	0.2	0.3
Salvation Army	5	702	1,110	1,473	0.1	0.1
Sev Day Adv	45	6,754	11,745	13,507	0.6	1.2
Sikh	5	NR	NR	NR	-	-
Swedenborgian	1	NR	NR	NR	-	-
Tao	2	NR	NR	NR	-	-
Un C of Christ	14	969	2,243	2,666	0.1	0.2
Unit Univ	1	50	45	67	0.0	0.0
Unity Ch	4	NR	NR	NR	-	-
Zoroastrian	0	NR	NR	78	0.0	0.0
RENSSELAER	**146**	**6,494**	**13,931**	**63,516**	**39.8**	**100.0**
ANG/EPIS–Episcopal	8	417	963	1,282	0.8	2.0
Bahá'í	0	NR	36	36	0.0	0.1
BAPT–Amer Bapt USA	8	355	969	1,154	0.7	1.8
BAPT–Consrv Bapt	2	NR	NR	NR	-	-
BAPT–Converge/BGC	1	75	NR	90	0.1	0.1
BAPT–NBC USA	1	199	350	417	0.3	0.7
BAPT–S-D Baptist Gen Con	1	90	132	157	0.1	0.2
BAPT–So Bapt Conv	3	183	156	186	0.1	0.3
BUDD–Mahayana	1	NR	NR	50	0.0	0.1
BUDD–Vajrayana	1	NR	NR	53	0.0	0.1
Catholic	21	NR	NR	44,756	28.1	70.5
Chr & Miss Al	3	198	101	330	0.2	0.5
CHR–Chr Ch (Disc)	2	0	0	0	0.0	0.0
CHR–Chr Chs & Chs Cr	1	NR	30	36	0.0	0.1
CHR–Chs of Christ	2	60	55	69	0.0	0.1
Evan Cov Ch	1	23	23	30	0.0	0.0
HINDU–Post Ren	2	NR	NR	26	0.0	0.0
Jehovah's Witness	4	NR	NR	NR	-	-

Religious Group	Number of Congrega-tions	Number of Attendees	Number of Communicant, Confirmed, or Full Members	Adherents		
				Number of Adherents	% of Total Pop.	% of Total Adh.
JUD–Conserv	1	65	73	197	0.1	0.3
JUD–Orth	1	43	50	60	0.0	0.1
JUD–Reform	1	89	157	424	0.3	0.7
LUTH–E.L.C.A.	9	471	1,714	2,384	1.5	3.8
LUTH–Luth–MO Synod	1	46	59	86	0.1	0.1
METH–AME Zion	1	75	240	286	0.2	0.5
METH–Un Methodist	24	990	4,083	5,096	3.2	8.0
Non-denom Chr Chs	12	1,465	1,790	2,001	1.3	3.2
ORTHE–Greek Orthodox	1	65	NR	290	0.2	0.5
ORTHE–Ukrainian Orth	1	70	NR	150	0.1	0.2
ORTHO–Armen Ap Cilic	1	60	NR	300	0.2	0.5
PENT–Assemb of God	4	96	76	198	0.1	0.3
PENT–Ch God (Cleve)	1	84	59	70	0.0	0.1
PENT–COGIC	1	0	150	179	0.1	0.3
PENT–Elim	1	NR	NR	NR	-	-
PRES–Presb Ch (USA)	9	690	954	1,136	0.7	1.8
REF–Fed Ref Ch	1	NR	NR	NR	-	-
REF–Ref Ch in Am	7	396	1,321	1,495	0.9	2.4
Salvation Army	1	42	71	113	0.1	0.2
Sev Day Adv	2	29	50	58	0.0	0.1
Sikh	1	NR	NR	NR	-	-
Un C of Christ	3	118	269	320	0.2	0.5
Zoroastrian	0	NR	NR	1	0.0	0.0
RICHMOND	**199**	**23,877**	**21,101**	**306,682**	**65.4**	**100.0**
ANG/EPIS–Episcopal	10	707	1,369	1,734	0.4	0.6
BAPT–Amer Bapt USA	2	1,085	2,450	2,975	0.6	1.0
BAPT–Consrv Bapt	3	NR	NR	NR	-	-
BAPT–Reg Bapt Gen As	1	NR	NR	NR	-	-
BAPT–So Bapt Conv	7	438	592	719	0.2	0.2
BUDD–Mahayana	1	NR	NR	103	0.0	0.0
Calv Chpl	1	NR	NR	NR	-	-
Catholic	41	NR	NR	254,170	54.2	82.9
Chr & Miss Al	3	132	47	182	0.0	0.1
CHR–Chr Chs & Chs Cr	1	NR	65	79	0.0	0.0
CHR–Chs of Christ	2	100	90	126	0.0	0.0
CHR–Int Chs of Christ	0	NR	216	262	0.1	0.1
CONG–Cong Chr, NA	1	NR	98	119	0.0	0.0
Evan Free Ch	3	390	NR	390	0.1	0.1
FRND–Fr Gen Cf & Un Mtg	1	NR	4	5	0.0	0.0
HINDU–Post Ren	2	NR	NR	93	0.0	0.0
HINDU–Trad Temples	1	NR	NR	1,000	0.2	0.3
Jehovah's Witness	4	NR	NR	NR	-	-
JUD–Conserv	1	123	143	372	0.1	0.1
JUD–Orth	10	4,320	1,500	6,000	1.3	2.0
JUD–Reform	1	90	164	426	0.1	0.1
LDS–L-D Saints	2	NR	NR	1,328	0.3	0.4
LUTH–Ch of Luth Br	1	140	100	331	0.1	0.1
LUTH–E.L.C.A.	8	598	2,059	2,941	0.6	1.0
LUTH–Luth–MO Synod	3	436	807	931	0.2	0.3
METH–AME	1	69	69	84	0.0	0.0
METH–AME Zion	2	25	153	186	0.0	0.1
METH–Un Methodist	10	725	1,954	2,255	0.5	0.7
MORAV–Morav Ch-North	4	269	622	792	0.2	0.3
Muslim Est	6	2,150	NR	8,115	1.7	2.6
Non-denom Chr Chs	16	4,609	5,133	5,966	1.3	1.9
ORTHE–Greek Orthodox	1	400	NR	4,000	0.9	1.3
ORTHE–Orth Ch in Amer	1	20	NR	50	0.0	0.0
ORTHO–Coptic Orth Ch	2	920	NR	2,425	0.5	0.8
ORTHO–Malan Dioc Am	3	390	NR	620	0.1	0.2
ORTHO–Malan Syr Orth	2	115	NR	216	0.0	0.1
PENT–Assemb of God	11	4,487	1,491	5,012	1.1	1.6
PENT–Ch God (Cleve)	1	40	24	29	0.0	0.0
PENT–Ch Lord Jesus Apos	2	NR	NR	NR	-	-
PENT–COGIC	1	0	50	61	0.0	0.0
PENT–Elim	1	NR	NR	NR	-	-
PENT–Full Gosp Bapt	1	NR	NR	NR	-	-
PENT–I F Chr Assmbl	1	NR	NR	NR	-	-
PENT–Pent Ch of God	1	70	NR	109	0.0	0.0
PENT–Un Pent Ch Intl	1	NR	NR	NR	-	-
PENT–United Holy Ch	1	NR	NR	NR	-	-
PRES–Korean Pres Amer	1	NR	NR	NR	-	-
PRES–Presb Ch (USA)	3	105	272	330	0.1	0.1
REF–Christian Ref	1	118	116	141	0.0	0.0

NR–Not Reported   - Represents no adherents reported.   Percentages may not total 100 due to rounding.

Table 3: Religious Congregations by County and Group: 2010

Religious Group	Number of Congrega-tions	Number of Attendees	Number of Communicant, Confirmed, or Full Members	Adherents		
				Number of Adherents	% of Total Pop.	% of Total Adh.
REF–Hung Ref Add'l	1	NR	NR	NR	-	-
REF–Ref Ch in Am	5	390	505	624	0.1	0.2
Salvation Army	2	75	194	425	0.1	0.1
Sev Day Adv	5	284	494	568	0.1	0.2
Un C of Christ	1	0	216	262	0.1	0.1
Unit Univ	1	57	104	124	0.0	0.0
Zoroastrian	0	NR	NR	2	0.0	0.0
ROCKLAND	**311**	**64,498**	**40,322**	**214,485**	**68.8**	**100.0**
ANG/EPIS–Episcopal	10	696	1,588	2,319	0.7	1.1
Bahá'í	0	NR	52	52	0.0	0.0
BAPT–Amer Bapt USA	3	172	152	194	0.1	0.1
BAPT–Consrv Bapt	2	NR	NR	NR	-	-
BAPT–NBC USA	4	900	1,510	1,929	0.6	0.9
BAPT–So Bapt Conv	7	1,458	1,386	1,770	0.6	0.8
BUDD–Mahayana	3	NR	NR	322	0.1	0.2
Catholic	21	NR	NR	109,386	35.1	51.0
Ch of Nazarene	2	132	171	183	0.1	0.1
Chr & Miss Al	12	1,010	773	1,362	0.4	0.6
CHR–Int Chs of Christ	0	NR	214	273	0.1	0.1
CONG–Consrv Cong Chr	1	42	55	70	0.0	0.0
Evan Free Ch	1	90	NR	90	0.0	0.0
FRND–Evan Fr Ch Intl	1	60	58	74	0.0	0.0
FRND–Fr Gen Cf & Un Mtg	1	NR	56	72	0.0	0.0
HINDU–Post Ren	1	NR	NR	10	0.0	0.0
HINDU–Trad Temples	1	NR	NR	300	0.1	0.1
Jehovah's Witness	3	NR	NR	NR	-	-
JUD–Conserv	5	1,659	1,862	5,027	1.6	2.3
JUD–Orth	110	43,200	15,000	60,000	19.3	28.0
JUD–Reform	4	771	1,359	3,669	1.2	1.7
LDS–L-D Saints	1	NR	NR	417	0.1	0.2
LUTH–Ch of Luth Br	1	37	38	54	0.0	0.0
LUTH–E.L.C.A.	4	396	1,202	1,632	0.5	0.8
LUTH–Luth-MO Synod	1	62	94	117	0.0	0.1
METH–AME Zion	4	270	557	711	0.2	0.3
METH–Un Methodist	13	418	1,308	1,603	0.5	0.7
METH–Wesleyan	1	140	121	182	0.1	0.1
MJEW–Union Mes Cong	1	NR	NR	NR	-	-
Muslim Est	3	1,218	NR	4,566	1.5	2.1
New Apost Ch	1	NR	NR	NR	-	-
Non-denom Chr Chs	20	6,505	7,755	8,613	2.8	4.0
ORTHE–Greek Orthodox	1	120	NR	290	0.1	0.1
ORTHE–Orth Ch in Amer	2	45	NR	128	0.0	0.1
ORTHE–Rus Orth Abroad	2	275	NR	400	0.1	0.2
ORTHO–Coptic Orth Ch	1	400	NR	800	0.3	0.4
ORTHO–Malan Dioc Am	4	440	NR	715	0.2	0.3
ORTHO–Malan Syr Orth	4	300	NR	576	0.2	0.3
PENT–Assemb of God	9	1,170	819	1,464	0.5	0.7
PENT–Ch God (Cleve)	7	609	602	769	0.2	0.4
PENT–Ch of God Proph	1	NR	118	151	0.0	0.1
PENT–Intl Pent Holiness	1	20	20	26	0.0	0.0
PENT–Un Pent Ch Intl	1	NR	NR	NR	-	-
PENT–Vineyard	1	30	36	46	0.0	0.0
PRES–Kor Pres Abroad	1	NR	NR	NR	-	-
PRES–Korean Amer Pres	1	NR	NR	NR	-	-
PRES–Korean Pres Amer	1	NR	NR	NR	-	-
PRES–Presb Ch (USA)	10	444	977	1,248	0.4	0.6
PRES–Presb Ch Amer	2	15	11	14	0.0	0.0
REF–Ref Ch in Am	6	290	592	702	0.2	0.3
Salvation Army	2	140	241	278	0.1	0.1
Sev Day Adv	8	842	1,465	1,685	0.5	0.8
Un C of Christ	1	72	64	82	0.0	0.0
Unit Univ	1	50	66	104	0.0	0.0
Zoroastrian	2	NR	NR	10	0.0	0.0
ST. LAWRENCE	**171**	**5,306**	**9,772**	**40,189**	**35.9**	**100.0**
ANG/EPIS–Episcopal	10	446	931	1,250	1.1	3.1
Bahá'í	0	NR	37	37	0.0	0.1
BAPT–Amer Bapt USA	3	135	236	282	0.3	0.7
BAPT–Ref Bapt Ch	1	NR	NR	NR	-	-
BAPT–Reg Bapt Gen As	1	NR	NR	NR	-	-
BAPT–So Bapt Conv	9	563	606	725	0.6	1.8
Catholic	32	NR	NR	24,478	21.9	60.9
Ch Cr, Scientst	1	NR	NR	NR	-	-
Ch of Nazarene	2	145	170	215	0.2	0.5
CHR–Chs of Christ	2	71	53	84	0.1	0.2
CONG–Cong Chr Add'l	1	NR	79	94	0.1	0.2
FRND–Fr Gen Cf & Un Mtg	1	NR	8	10	0.0	0.0
HINDU–Post Ren	2	NR	NR	93	0.1	0.2
HINDU–Renaiss	1	NR	NR	0	0.0	0.0
HINDU–Trad Temples	1	NR	NR	1,033	0.9	2.6
Jehovah's Witness	3	NR	NR	NR	-	-
LDS–L-D Saints	2	NR	NR	622	0.6	1.5
MENN–Amish Undif	13	NR	676	1,840	1.6	4.6
METH–AME Zion	1	0	150	179	0.2	0.4
METH–Free Methodist	1	31	20	31	0.0	0.1
METH–Un Methodist	32	990	3,418	4,105	3.7	10.2
METH–Wesleyan	8	436	252	567	0.5	1.4
Non-denom Chr Chs	7	995	670	1,291	1.2	3.2
PENT–Assemb of God	3	147	31	191	0.2	0.5
PENT–Elim	1	NR	NR	NR	-	-
PRES–Orth Pres Ch	1	43	36	57	0.1	0.1
PRES–Presb Ch (USA)	18	682	1,256	1,502	1.3	3.7
PRES–Ref Pres of NA	1	55	33	66	0.1	0.2
Salvation Army	2	52	83	173	0.2	0.4
Sev Day Adv	3	62	108	124	0.1	0.3
Un C of Christ	7	308	696	832	0.7	2.1
Unit Univ	1	145	223	308	0.3	0.8
SARATOGA	**146**	**14,322**	**22,318**	**86,057**	**39.2**	**100.0**
ANG/EPIS–Episcopal	8	1,006	2,578	4,073	1.9	4.7
Bahá'í	0	NR	49	49	0.0	0.1
BAPT–Amer Bapt USA	7	386	723	873	0.4	1.0
BAPT–Asc Ref Bap Ch Am	1	NR	NR	NR	-	-
BAPT–Consrv Bapt	2	NR	NR	NR	-	-
BAPT–Converge/BGC	1	800	NR	960	0.4	1.1
BAPT–Ref Bapt Ch	3	NR	NR	NR	-	-
BAPT–So Bapt Conv	5	426	265	320	0.1	0.4
BUDD–Mahayana	1	NR	NR	11	0.0	0.0
Calv Chpl	1	NR	NR	NR	-	-
Catholic	16	NR	NR	52,507	23.9	61.0
Ch Cr, Scientst	1	NR	NR	NR	-	-
Chr & Miss Al	3	1,078	464	1,984	0.9	2.3
CHR–Chs of Christ	2	100	95	113	0.1	0.1
CONG–Consrv Cong Chr	1	50	41	50	0.0	0.1
Evan Cov Ch	1	112	162	146	0.1	0.2
FRND–Fr Gen Cf & Un Mtg	2	NR	90	109	0.0	0.1
HINDU–Post Ren	1	NR	NR	16	0.0	0.0
Jehovah's Witness	3	NR	NR	NR	-	-
JUD–Conserv	1	90	101	273	0.1	0.3
JUD–Orth	2	72	75	100	0.0	0.1
JUD–Reform	1	105	186	502	0.2	0.6
LDS–L-D Saints	3	NR	NR	1,677	0.8	1.9
LUTH–E.L.C.A.	3	336	1,063	1,416	0.6	1.6
LUTH–Luth-MO Synod	1	241	594	1,010	0.5	1.2
LUTH–Wisc Ev Luth Syn	1	124	172	232	0.1	0.3
METH–AME Zion	1	0	20	24	0.0	0.0
METH–Free Methodist	3	103	63	103	0.0	0.1
METH–Un Methodist	23	1,897	7,067	8,800	4.0	10.2
METH–Wesleyan	2	155	95	202	0.1	0.2
Non-denom Chr Chs	18	5,265	5,668	6,756	3.1	7.9
ORTHE–Ant Orth of NA	1	50	NR	110	0.1	0.1
ORTHE–Orth Ch in Amer	1	50	NR	100	0.0	0.1
PENT–Assemb of God	5	168	76	268	0.1	0.3
PENT–Ch God (Cleve)	1	84	211	255	0.1	0.3
PENT–Un Pent Ch Intl	1	NR	NR	NR	-	-
PRES–As Ref Pres Ch	1	NR	176	213	0.1	0.2
PRES–Presb Ch (USA)	9	732	927	1,120	0.5	1.3
PRES–Presb Ch Amer	1	80	83	126	0.1	0.1
REF–Ref Ch in Am	4	377	820	934	0.4	1.1
Salvation Army	1	17	62	125	0.1	0.1
Sev Day Adv	1	56	98	113	0.1	0.1
Un C of Christ	1	250	155	187	0.1	0.2
Unit Univ	1	112	139	200	0.1	0.2

NR–Not Reported   - Represents no adherents reported.   Percentages may not total 100 due to rounding.

Table 3: Religious Congregations by County and Group: 2010

Religious Group	Number of Congrega-tions	Number of Attendees	Number of Communicant, Confirmed, or Full Members	Adherents: Number of Adherents	Adherents: % of Total Pop.	Adherents: % of Total Adh.
SCHENECTADY	**122**	**10,133**	**16,884**	**72,846**	**47.1**	**100.0**
ANG/EPIS–Episcopal	6	481	1,218	1,436	0.9	2.0
Bahá'í	1	NR	46	46	0.0	0.1
BAPT–Amer Bapt USA	7	263	1,212	1,465	0.9	2.0
BAPT–NBC USA	1	0	200	242	0.2	0.3
BAPT–So Bapt Conv	3	359	423	511	0.3	0.7
BUDD–Mahayana	1	NR	NR	11	0.0	0.0
BUDD–Vajrayana	1	NR	NR	71	0.0	0.1
Catholic	16	NR	NR	44,178	28.6	60.6
Ch Cr, Scientst	1	NR	NR	NR	-	-
Ch of Nazarene	1	61	63	172	0.1	0.2
Chr & Miss Al	1	19	17	28	0.0	0.0
CHR–Chs of Christ	2	40	50	54	0.0	0.1
Christian Brethren	1	NR	NR	NR	-	-
CONG–Consrv Cong Chr	2	273	299	362	0.2	0.5
Evan Free Ch	1	47	NR	47	0.0	0.1
FRND–Fr Gen Cf & Un Mtg	2	NR	43	52	0.0	0.1
HINDU–Post Ren	1	NR	NR	10	0.0	0.0
Jehovah's Witness	2	NR	NR	NR	-	-
JUD–Conserv	1	282	316	853	0.6	1.2
JUD–Orth	1	266	100	370	0.2	0.5
JUD–Reform	1	237	418	1,129	0.7	1.5
LUTH–E.L.C.A.	4	418	1,375	1,842	1.2	2.5
LUTH–Luth–MO Synod	3	378	1,024	1,458	0.9	2.0
METH–AME	1	100	125	151	0.1	0.2
METH–AME Zion	1	100	150	181	0.1	0.2
METH–Un Methodist	12	606	2,455	2,824	1.8	3.9
METH–Wesleyan	1	108	64	140	0.1	0.2
Muslim Est	4	1,624	NR	6,089	3.9	8.4
New Apost Ch	1	NR	NR	NR	-	-
Non-denom Chr Chs	9	850	1,010	1,151	0.7	1.6
OCATH–Pol Natl Cath	1	NR	NR	NR	-	-
ORTHE–Greek Orthodox	1	100	NR	215	0.1	0.3
PENT–Assemb of God	1	690	401	690	0.4	0.9
PENT–Ch God (Cleve)	2	272	136	164	0.1	0.2
PENT–COGIC	3	0	450	544	0.4	0.7
PENT–Elim	1	NR	NR	NR	-	-
PENT–Un Pent Ch Intl	1	NR	NR	NR	-	-
PRES–Evan Presby Ch	1	NR	279	337	0.2	0.5
PRES–Orth Pres Ch	1	77	93	118	0.1	0.2
PRES–Presb Ch (USA)	5	384	609	736	0.5	1.0
PRES–Presb Ch Amer	2	485	500	527	0.3	0.7
REF–Ref Ch in Am	9	1,101	3,029	3,597	2.3	4.9
Salvation Army	1	87	166	239	0.2	0.3
Sev Day Adv	2	89	155	178	0.1	0.2
Un C of Christ	1	86	65	79	0.1	0.1
Unit Univ	1	250	393	548	0.4	0.8
Zoroastrian	0	NR	NR	1	0.0	0.0
SCHOHARIE	**60**	**2,036**	**4,094**	**12,836**	**39.2**	**100.0**
ANG/EPIS–Episcopal	2	41	56	62	0.2	0.5
Bahá'í	0	NR	5	5	0.0	0.0
BAPT–Amer Bapt USA	1	110	154	180	0.5	1.4
BAPT–Consrv Bapt	1	NR	NR	NR	-	-
BAPT–Reg Bapt Gen As	1	NR	NR	NR	-	-
BAPT–So Bapt Conv	2	55	28	33	0.1	0.3
Calv Chpl	1	NR	NR	NR	-	-
Catholic	3	NR	NR	6,768	20.7	52.7
Chr & Miss Al	1	44	41	58	0.2	0.5
Jehovah's Witness	1	NR	NR	NR	-	-
LDS–L-D Saints	1	NR	NR	386	1.2	3.0
LUTH–E.L.C.A.	4	193	860	1,506	4.6	11.7
LUTH–Luth Cong Msn Chr	1	37	NR	NR	-	-
LUTH–Nor Amer Luth C	2	NR	NR	NR	-	-
METH–Un Methodist	19	485	1,677	2,048	6.3	16.0
METH–Wesleyan	1	190	86	247	0.8	1.9
Non-denom Chr Chs	6	403	403	532	1.6	4.1
PENT–Assemb of God	2	140	102	211	0.6	1.6
PENT–Ch God (Cleve)	1	12	15	18	0.1	0.1
PRES–Presb Ch (USA)	4	93	179	210	0.6	1.6
REF–Ref Ch in Am	5	215	456	534	1.6	4.2
Un C of Christ	1	18	32	38	0.1	0.3

Religious Group	Number of Congrega-tions	Number of Attendees	Number of Communicant, Confirmed, or Full Members	Adherents: Number of Adherents	Adherents: % of Total Pop.	Adherents: % of Total Adh.
SCHUYLER	**35**	**1,003**	**2,233**	**5,057**	**27.6**	**100.0**
ANG/EPIS–Episcopal	3	69	117	145	0.8	2.9
Bahá'í	0	NR	4	4	0.0	0.1
BAPT–Amer Bapt USA	5	156	501	592	3.2	11.7
BAPT–Reg Bapt Gen As	3	NR	NR	NR	-	-
BUDD–Mahayana	1	NR	NR	11	0.1	0.2
Catholic	2	NR	NR	2,359	12.9	46.6
Ch of Nazarene	1	5	30	30	0.2	0.6
Jehovah's Witness	2	NR	NR	NR	-	-
MENN–Amish Undif	1	NR	6	19	0.1	0.4
METH–Un Methodist	9	329	990	1,121	6.1	22.2
METH–Wesleyan	1	32	20	42	0.2	0.8
Non-denom Chr Chs	1	110	100	138	0.8	2.7
PENT–Assemb of God	1	80	45	100	0.5	2.0
PRES–Presb Ch (USA)	5	222	420	496	2.7	9.8
SENECA	**42**	**1,373**	**3,192**	**5,520**	**15.7**	**100.0**
ANG/EPIS–Episcopal	4	139	375	399	1.1	7.2
Bahá'í	0	NR	20	20	0.1	0.4
BAPT–Consrv Bapt	3	NR	NR	NR	-	-
Calv Chpl	1	NR	NR	NR	-	-
Catholic	2	NR	NR	943	2.7	17.1
CHR–Chr Chs & Chs Cr	1	NR	180	214	0.6	3.9
Jehovah's Witness	2	NR	NR	NR	-	-
LDS–L-D Saints	1	NR	NR	486	1.4	8.8
LUTH–Luth–MO Synod	2	146	213	266	0.8	4.8
MENN–Amish Undif	5	NR	297	731	2.1	13.2
METH–Un Methodist	5	244	1,004	1,093	3.1	19.8
METH–Wesleyan	1	41	33	53	0.2	1.0
Non-denom Chr Chs	5	465	445	584	1.7	10.6
PENT–Assemb of God	1	40	32	45	0.1	0.8
PRES–Presb Ch (USA)	6	217	403	479	1.4	8.7
REF–Ref Ch in Am	2	81	190	207	0.6	3.8
Un C of Christ	1	0	0	0	0.0	0.0
STEUBEN	**162**	**8,815**	**13,353**	**34,809**	**35.2**	**100.0**
ANG/EPIS–Episcopal	6	332	705	873	0.9	2.5
Bahá'í	0	NR	8	8	0.0	0.0
BAPT–Amer Bapt USA	11	585	1,188	1,441	1.5	4.1
BAPT–Consrv Bapt	1	NR	NR	NR	-	-
BAPT–Reg Bapt Gen As	6	NR	NR	NR	-	-
BAPT–So Bapt Conv	1	125	200	243	0.2	0.7
Catholic	11	NR	NR	13,963	14.1	40.1
Ch of Nazarene	1	51	70	132	0.1	0.4
Chr & Miss Al	2	320	172	342	0.3	1.0
CHR–Chr Chs & Chs Cr	2	NR	83	101	0.1	0.3
CHR–Chs of Christ	1	10	10	10	0.0	0.0
Jehovah's Witness	3	NR	NR	NR	-	-
JUD–Conserv	1	5	6	16	0.0	0.0
LDS–Comm of Christ	1	NR	158	158	0.2	0.5
LDS–L-D Saints	3	NR	NR	675	0.7	1.9
LUTH–E.L.C.A.	2	59	190	204	0.2	0.6
LUTH–Luth–MO Synod	2	86	175	237	0.2	0.7
MENN–Amish Undif	10	NR	575	1,317	1.3	3.8
MENN–Mennonite USA	3	125	128	155	0.2	0.4
METH–Free Methodist	1	41	56	56	0.1	0.2
METH–Un Methodist	32	1,422	4,687	6,292	6.4	18.1
METH–Wesleyan	8	2,247	721	2,921	3.0	8.4
Non-denom Chr Chs	22	1,895	2,044	2,473	2.5	7.1
ORTHE–Carp Rus Orth	1	30	NR	65	0.1	0.2
PENT–Assemb of God	6	449	343	657	0.7	1.9
PENT–Elim	1	NR	NR	NR	-	-
PENT–Un Pent Ch Intl	1	NR	NR	NR	-	-
PRES–Presb Ch (USA)	15	669	1,244	1,509	1.5	4.3
Salvation Army	2	114	135	421	0.4	1.2
Sev Day Adv	2	104	180	207	0.2	0.6
Un C of Christ	4	146	275	333	0.3	1.0
SUFFOLK	**704**	**68,596**	**113,066**	**1,076,830**	**72.1**	**100.0**
ANG/EPIS–Episcopal	42	3,655	9,147	12,287	0.8	1.1
Bahá'í	5	NR	278	278	0.0	0.0
BAPT–Amer Bapt USA	10	663	1,719	2,095	0.1	0.2

NR–Not Reported - Represents no adherents reported. Percentages may not total 100 due to rounding.

Table 3: Religious Congregations by County and Group: 2010

Religious Group	Number of Congrega-tions	Number of Attendees	Number of Communicant, Confirmed, or Full Members	Adherents		
				Number of Adherents	% of Total Pop.	% of Total Adh.
BAPT–Asc Ref Bap Ch Am	1	NR	NR	NR	-	-
BAPT–Consrv Bapt	6	NR	NR	NR	-	-
BAPT–N Am Bapt Conf	1	NR	33	40	0.0	0.0
BAPT–Natl Mis Bapt Conv	1	0	150	183	0.0	0.0
BAPT–NBC Amer	2	500	1,050	1,280	0.1	0.1
BAPT–NBC USA	9	900	1,820	2,218	0.1	0.2
BAPT–Prog NBC	1	0	150	183	0.0	0.0
BAPT–Ref Bapt Ch	2	NR	NR	NR	-	-
BAPT–Reg Bapt Gen As	3	NR	NR	NR	-	-
BAPT–So Bapt Conv	7	343	517	630	0.0	0.1
BUDD–Mahayana	5	NR	NR	2,783	0.2	0.3
BUDD–Theravada	1	NR	NR	1,364	0.1	0.1
BUDD–Vajrayana	2	NR	NR	913	0.1	0.1
Calv Chpl	3	NR	NR	NR	-	-
Catholic	74	NR	NR	879,457	58.9	81.7
CGOD–Ch God (Ander)	1	0	NR	0	0.0	0.0
Ch Cr, Scientst	6	NR	NR	NR	-	-
Ch of Nazarene	15	926	1,081	1,291	0.1	0.1
Chr & Miss Al	2	240	167	244	0.0	0.0
CHR–Chr Chs & Chs Cr	7	NR	1,365	1,664	0.1	0.2
CHR–Chs of Christ	8	1,035	950	1,261	0.1	0.1
CHR–Int Chs of Christ	0	NR	216	263	0.0	0.0
Christian Brethren	2	NR	NR	NR	-	-
CONG–Cong Chr Add'l	1	NR	342	417	0.0	0.0
Evan Cov Ch	1	20	36	26	0.0	0.0
Evan Free Ch	7	938	NR	938	0.1	0.1
FRND–Fr Gen Cf & Un Mtg	4	NR	64	78	0.0	0.0
Grace Gosp Fel	1	NR	NR	NR	-	-
HINDU–I/A Temples	1	NR	NR	863	0.1	0.1
HINDU–Post Ren	1	NR	NR	16	0.0	0.0
Intl Fell Bible Ch	1	NR	NR	NR	-	-
Jehovah's Witness	28	NR	NR	NR	-	-
JUD–Conserv	11	1,929	2,248	5,845	0.4	0.5
JUD–Orth	14	3,456	1,300	4,800	0.3	0.4
JUD–Reconst	1	141	187	486	0.0	0.0
JUD–Reform	10	1,930	3,534	9,188	0.6	0.9
LDS–L-D Saints	8	NR	NR	3,392	0.2	0.3
LUTH–Ch of Luth Br	2	142	100	289	0.0	0.0
LUTH–E.L.C.A.	24	4,073	13,604	19,066	1.3	1.8
LUTH–Luth Cong Msn Chr	2	189	404	492	0.0	0.0
LUTH–Luth–MO Synod	15	2,589	8,706	12,767	0.9	1.2
LUTH–Wisc Ev Luth Syn	1	31	43	58	0.0	0.0
MENN–Menn Br US Conf	1	NR	0	0	0.0	0.0
METH–AME	9	365	1,722	2,099	0.1	0.2
METH–AME Zion	10	125	1,140	1,390	0.1	0.1
METH–Un Methodist	47	2,891	16,367	20,975	1.4	1.9
METH–Wesleyan	1	200	171	260	0.0	0.0
Muslim Est	14	6,242	NR	19,887	1.3	1.8
Nat Spirit Asso	3	NR	NR	NR	-	-
New Apost Ch	5	NR	NR	NR	-	-
Non-denom Chr Chs	75	17,752	20,349	23,981	1.6	2.2
OCATH–Pol Natl Cath	1	NR	NR	NR	-	-
ORTHE–Ant Orth of NA	1	20	NR	25	0.0	0.0
ORTHE–Greek Orthodox	6	1,720	NR	9,740	0.7	0.9
ORTHE–Orth Ch in Amer	2	100	NR	175	0.0	0.0
ORTHO–Malan Dioc Am	1	160	NR	250	0.0	0.0
PENT–Assemb of God	31	3,556	2,350	4,357	0.3	0.4
PENT–Ch God (Cleve)	27	4,220	5,347	6,518	0.4	0.6
PENT–Ch Lord Jesus Apos	3	NR	NR	NR	-	-
PENT–Ch of God Proph	3	NR	314	383	0.0	0.0
PENT–COGIC	10	450	775	945	0.1	0.1
PENT–Fire Bapt Hol Ch	1	NR	NR	NR	-	-
PENT–Full Gosp Bapt	2	NR	NR	NR	-	-
PENT–I F Chr Assmbl	1	NR	NR	NR	-	-
PENT–Un Pent Ch Intl	1	NR	NR	NR	-	-
PENT–United Holy Ch	2	NR	NR	NR	-	-
PENT–Vineyard	2	90	108	132	0.0	0.0
PRES–Korean Amer Pres	2	NR	NR	NR	-	-
PRES–Korean Pres Amer	2	NR	NR	NR	-	-
PRES–Orth Pres Ch	1	48	67	90	0.0	0.0
PRES–Presb Ch (USA)	38	3,725	8,495	10,355	0.7	1.0
PRES–Presb Ch Amer	1	20	8	16	0.0	0.0
REF–Christian Ref	1	50	67	82	0.0	0.0
REF–Comm Ref Evan	1	NR	NR	NR	-	-
REF–Ref Ch in Am	4	375	594	754	0.1	0.1
REF–Un Ref Chs N.A.	1	NR	NR	NR	-	-
Salvation Army	3	115	189	220	0.0	0.0
Sev Day Adv	21	1,454	2,528	2,907	0.2	0.3
Un C of Christ	12	864	2,607	3,178	0.2	0.3
Unit Univ	7	354	657	937	0.1	0.1
Unity Ch	2	NR	NR	NR	-	-
Zoroastrian	0	NR	NR	19	0.0	0.0
SULLIVAN	**116**	**6,034**	**5,823**	**31,575**	**40.7**	**100.0**
ANG/EPIS–Episcopal	3	71	83	178	0.2	0.6
Bahá'í	0	NR	16	16	0.0	0.1
BAPT–So Bapt Conv	1	30	75	90	0.1	0.3
BUDD–Mahayana	2	NR	NR	328	0.4	1.0
BUDD–Vajrayana	3	NR	NR	532	0.7	1.7
Catholic	21	NR	NR	15,352	19.8	48.6
CGOD–Ch God (Ander)	1	45	NR	45	0.1	0.1
Ch of Nazarene	1	76	116	140	0.2	0.4
FRND–Fr Gen Cf & Un Mtg	1	NR	15	18	0.0	0.1
HINDU–Renaiss	3	NR	NR	274	0.4	0.9
HINDU–Trad Temples	2	NR	NR	1,083	1.4	3.4
Jehovah's Witness	3	NR	NR	NR	-	-
JUD–Conserv	1	22	25	68	0.1	0.2
JUD–Orth	11	2,664	1,000	3,700	4.8	11.7
JUD–Reform	2	116	205	554	0.7	1.8
LDS–L-D Saints	1	NR	NR	189	0.2	0.6
LUTH–E.L.C.A.	3	103	370	566	0.7	1.8
METH–Free Methodist	3	242	163	242	0.3	0.8
METH–Un Methodist	23	748	2,239	3,140	4.0	9.9
Muslim Est	2	812	NR	3,044	3.9	9.6
Non-denom Chr Chs	1	100	150	150	0.2	0.5
ORTHE–Greek Orthodox	1	0	NR	0	0.0	0.0
ORTHE–Ukrainian Orth	1	20	NR	60	0.1	0.2
PENT–Assemb of God	7	388	208	430	0.6	1.4
PENT–Ch God (Cleve)	2	105	113	136	0.2	0.4
PRES–Presb Ch (USA)	8	170	367	443	0.6	1.4
PRES–Ref Pres of NA	1	85	87	106	0.1	0.3
REF–Ref Ch in Am	4	141	390	445	0.6	1.4
Sev Day Adv	1	30	52	60	0.1	0.2
Un C of Christ	2	48	130	157	0.2	0.5
Unit Univ	1	18	19	29	0.0	0.1
TIOGA	**72**	**3,492**	**7,464**	**15,985**	**31.3**	**100.0**
ANG/EPIS–Episcopal	3	110	216	309	0.6	1.9
Bahá'í	0	NR	5	5	0.0	0.0
BAPT–Amer Bapt USA	3	261	718	872	1.7	5.5
BAPT–Consrv Bapt	1	NR	NR	NR	-	-
BAPT–Reg Bapt Gen As	3	NR	NR	NR	-	-
BAPT–So Bapt Conv	3	150	200	243	0.5	1.5
BUDD–Mahayana	1	NR	NR	29	0.1	0.2
Catholic	2	NR	NR	5,831	11.4	36.5
Ch Christ Chr Union	1	NR	NR	NR	-	-
Ch of Nazarene	2	373	424	424	0.8	2.7
Chr & Miss Al	5	328	184	508	1.0	3.2
CHR–Chs of Christ	1	10	10	10	0.0	0.1
CONG–Cong Chr, NA	1	NR	20	24	0.0	0.2
CONG–Consrv Cong Chr	1	75	100	121	0.2	0.8
Jehovah's Witness	2	NR	NR	NR	-	-
LDS–L-D Saints	1	NR	NR	332	0.6	2.1
LUTH–E.L.C.A.	1	15	44	44	0.1	0.3
LUTH–Luth–MO Synod	1	70	136	237	0.5	1.5
METH–Un Methodist	22	943	4,074	5,269	10.3	33.0
Non-denom Chr Chs	8	810	805	1,065	2.1	6.7
PENT–Assemb of God	2	15	0	15	0.0	0.1
PRES–Presb Ch (USA)	4	257	434	527	1.0	3.3
PRES–Ref Pres of NA	1	22	13	24	0.0	0.2
Sev Day Adv	1	13	23	26	0.1	0.2
Un C of Christ	2	40	58	70	0.1	0.4
TOMPKINS	**92**	**6,263**	**9,873**	**23,155**	**22.8**	**100.0**
ANG/EPIS–Episcopal	4	203	438	514	0.5	2.2
Bahá'í	1	NR	101	101	0.1	0.4
BAPT–Amer Bapt USA	7	424	639	727	0.7	3.1

NR–Not Reported - Represents no adherents reported. Percentages may not total 100 due to rounding.

Table 3: Religious Congregations by County and Group: 2010

Religious Group	Number of Congrega-tions	Number of Attendees	Number of Communicant, Confirmed, or Full Members	Adherents: Number of Adherents	Adherents: % of Total Pop.	Adherents: % of Total Adh.
BAPT–Consrv Bapt	1	NR	NR	NR	-	-
BAPT–Reg Bapt Gen As	3	NR	NR	NR	-	-
BAPT–So Bapt Conv	1	45	40	46	0.0	0.2
BUDD–Mahayana	1	NR	NR	10	0.0	0.0
BUDD–Vajrayana	2	NR	NR	98	0.1	0.4
Calv Chpl	1	NR	NR	NR	-	-
Catholic	7	NR	NR	7,344	7.2	31.7
Ch Cr, Scientst	1	NR	NR	NR	-	-
Ch of Nazarene	1	25	65	65	0.1	0.3
Chr & Miss Al	1	51	37	77	0.1	0.3
CHR–Chs of Christ	2	105	88	130	0.1	0.6
Evan Free Ch	1	150	NR	150	0.1	0.6
FRND–Fr Gen Cf & Un Mtg	2	NR	149	170	0.2	0.7
HINDU–Post Ren	1	NR	NR	25	0.0	0.1
Jehovah's Witness	1	NR	NR	NR	-	-
JUD–Conserv	1	220	247	667	0.7	2.9
JUD–Reform	1	65	114	308	0.3	1.3
LDS–L-D Saints	3	NR	NR	1,064	1.0	4.6
LUTH–E.L.C.A.	1	163	656	919	0.9	4.0
LUTH–Luth–MO Synod	1	83	263	345	0.3	1.5
METH–AME Zion	1	65	50	57	0.1	0.2
METH–Un Methodist	11	882	2,659	3,866	3.8	16.7
Non-denom Chr Chs	11	1,670	1,396	2,112	2.1	9.1
ORTHE–Greek Orthodox	1	50	NR	215	0.2	0.9
PENT–Assemb of God	4	637	292	956	0.9	4.1
PENT–Elim	1	NR	NR	NR	-	-
PENT–Un Pent Ch Intl	1	NR	NR	NR	-	-
PENT–Vineyard	1	210	300	341	0.3	1.5
PRES–Kor Pres Abroad	1	NR	NR	NR	-	-
PRES–Korean Pres Amer	1	NR	NR	NR	-	-
PRES–Presb Ch (USA)	3	324	752	856	0.8	3.7
PRES–Presb Ch Amer	1	115	50	75	0.1	0.3
REF–Fed Ref Ch	1	NR	NR	NR	-	-
Salvation Army	1	147	118	260	0.3	1.1
Sev Day Adv	1	46	80	92	0.1	0.4
Un C of Christ	6	380	923	1,050	1.0	4.5
Unit Univ	1	203	416	511	0.5	2.2
Zoroastrian	0	NR	NR	4	0.0	0.0
ULSTER	**185**	**8,518**	**16,855**	**75,147**	**41.2**	**100.0**
ANG/EPIS–Episcopal	9	544	1,193	1,297	0.7	1.7
Bahá'í	0	NR	47	47	0.0	0.1
BAPT–Amer Bapt USA	1	140	186	219	0.1	0.3
BAPT–NBC USA	3	190	305	358	0.2	0.5
BAPT–So Bapt Conv	2	120	16	19	0.0	0.0
BUDD–Mahayana	5	NR	NR	149	0.1	0.2
Catholic	27	NR	NR	50,256	27.5	66.9
Ch Cr, Scientst	2	NR	NR	NR	-	-
Ch God (7th Day)	1	NR	NR	NR	-	-
Ch of Nazarene	2	90	104	125	0.1	0.2
Chr & Miss Al	1	33	27	80	0.0	0.1
CHR–Chs of Christ	2	55	47	57	0.0	0.1
CONG–Cong Chr, NA	1	NR	100	118	0.1	0.2
Evan Free Ch	2	383	NR	383	0.2	0.5
FRND–Evan Fr Ch Intl	1	140	100	118	0.1	0.2
FRND–Fr Gen Cf & Un Mtg	1	NR	39	46	0.0	0.1
FRND–Unaffl Mtgs	1	NR	NR	NR	-	-
HINDU–Post Ren	5	NR	NR	191	0.1	0.3
HINDU–Renaiss	1	NR	NR	84	0.0	0.1
Ind Fund Churches	1	NR	NR	NR	-	-
Int Cou Comm Ch	1	NR	NR	NR	-	-
Jehovah's Witness	7	NR	NR	NR	-	-
JUD–Conserv	1	95	107	289	0.2	0.4
JUD–Orth	2	72	75	100	0.1	0.1
JUD–Reconst	1	101	129	348	0.2	0.5
JUD–Reform	1	133	235	634	0.3	0.8
LDS–L-D Saints	2	NR	NR	722	0.4	1.0
LUTH–E.L.C.A.	8	498	1,894	2,566	1.4	3.4
LUTH–Luth–MO Synod	1	30	58	67	0.0	0.1
MENN–Bruderhof Comm	3	803	359	688	0.4	0.9
METH–AME	1	0	100	118	0.1	0.2
METH–AME Zion	2	0	250	294	0.2	0.4
METH–Un Methodist	27	1,036	4,473	5,708	3.1	7.6
METH–Wesleyan	3	86	63	112	0.1	0.1

Religious Group	Number of Congrega-tions	Number of Attendees	Number of Communicant, Confirmed, or Full Members	Adherents: Number of Adherents	Adherents: % of Total Pop.	Adherents: % of Total Adh.
Muslim Est	1	406	NR	1,522	0.8	2.0
New Apost Ch	1	NR	NR	NR	-	-
Non-denom Chr Chs	10	1,153	1,250	1,567	0.9	2.1
ORTHE–Greek Orthodox	1	40	NR	150	0.1	0.2
PENT–Assemb of God	5	245	176	390	0.2	0.5
PENT–Ch God (Cleve)	2	41	58	68	0.0	0.1
PENT–COGIC	1	200	250	294	0.2	0.4
PENT–Elim	1	NR	NR	NR	-	-
PRES–Presb Ch (USA)	4	131	315	370	0.2	0.5
REF–Ref Ch in Am	25	1,460	4,379	4,987	2.7	6.6
Salvation Army	1	49	161	161	0.1	0.2
Sev Day Adv	4	134	234	269	0.1	0.4
Unit Univ	1	110	125	162	0.1	0.2
Zoroastrian	0	NR	NR	14	0.0	0.0
WARREN	**70**	**3,503**	**6,396**	**23,392**	**35.6**	**100.0**
ANG/EPIS–Episcopal	7	504	939	1,089	1.7	4.7
Bahá'í	0	NR	15	15	0.0	0.1
BAPT–Amer Bapt USA	5	133	333	393	0.6	1.7
BAPT–NBC USA	1	35	96	113	0.2	0.5
BAPT–Reg Bapt Gen As	1	NR	NR	NR	-	-
BAPT–So Bapt Conv	1	300	229	270	0.4	1.2
Catholic	10	NR	NR	14,546	22.1	62.2
Ch Cr, Scientst	1	NR	NR	NR	-	-
CHR–Chs of Christ	1	40	37	48	0.1	0.2
Jehovah's Witness	2	NR	NR	NR	-	-
JUD–Conserv	1	79	89	240	0.4	1.0
JUD–Reform	1	57	101	273	0.4	1.2
LDS–L-D Saints	1	NR	NR	571	0.9	2.4
LUTH–Luth–MO Synod	2	137	479	605	0.9	2.6
METH–Free Methodist	1	78	96	96	0.1	0.4
METH–Un Methodist	12	471	1,837	2,093	3.2	8.9
METH–Wesleyan	6	396	262	517	0.8	2.2
Non-denom Chr Chs	4	365	375	461	0.7	2.0
PENT–Assemb of God	3	183	106	287	0.4	1.2
PRES–Presb Ch (USA)	6	531	1,105	1,303	2.0	5.6
PRES–Presb Ch Amer	1	50	34	47	0.1	0.2
Salvation Army	1	60	147	280	0.4	1.2
Sev Day Adv	1	18	30	35	0.1	0.1
Unit Univ	1	66	86	110	0.2	0.5
WASHINGTON	**90**	**2,868**	**6,536**	**22,092**	**34.9**	**100.0**
ANG/EPIS–Episcopal	8	210	361	475	0.8	2.2
Bahá'í	0	NR	11	11	0.0	0.0
BAPT–Amer Bapt USA	11	368	1,243	1,475	2.3	6.7
BAPT–Consrv Bapt	1	NR	NR	NR	-	-
BAPT–So Bapt Conv	2	54	50	59	0.1	0.3
Catholic	10	NR	NR	13,581	21.5	61.5
CHR–Chs of Christ	1	25	20	25	0.0	0.1
CONG–Consrv Cong Chr	1	75	72	85	0.1	0.4
FRND–Fr Gen Cf & Un Mtg	1	NR	49	58	0.1	0.3
Ind Fund Churches	1	NR	NR	NR	-	-
Jehovah's Witness	3	NR	NR	NR	-	-
LDS–L-D Saints	1	NR	NR	245	0.4	1.1
METH–Un Methodist	22	715	2,668	3,311	5.2	15.0
METH–Wesleyan	2	69	69	90	0.1	0.4
Non-denom Chr Chs	6	555	698	774	1.2	3.5
ORTHE–Orth Ch in Amer	3	55	NR	140	0.2	0.6
PENT–Assemb of God	3	330	171	448	0.7	2.0
PRES–Evan Presby Ch	1	NR	224	266	0.4	1.2
PRES–Presb Ch (USA)	10	298	650	771	1.2	3.5
REF–Ref Ch in Am	1	60	143	155	0.2	0.7
Sev Day Adv	1	54	95	109	0.2	0.5
Un C of Christ	1	0	12	14	0.0	0.1
WAYNE	**116**	**6,752**	**11,607**	**31,678**	**33.8**	**100.0**
ANG/EPIS–Episcopal	4	160	266	326	0.3	1.0
Bahá'í	0	NR	83	83	0.1	0.3
BAPT–Amer Bapt USA	12	564	1,801	2,188	2.3	6.9
BAPT–Reg Bapt Gen As	1	NR	NR	NR	-	-
BAPT–So Bapt Conv	2	35	44	53	0.1	0.2
Calv Chpl	1	NR	NR	NR	-	-
Catholic	8	NR	NR	15,422	16.4	48.7

NR–Not Reported - Represents no adherents reported. Percentages may not total 100 due to rounding.

Table 3: Religious Congregations by County and Group: 2010

Religious Group	Number of Congrega-tions	Number of Attendees	Number of Communicant, Confirmed, or Full Members	Adherents: Number of Adherents	Adherents: % of Total Pop.	Adherents: % of Total Adh.
CGOD–Ch God (Ander)	1	20	NR	20	0.0	0.1
Chr & Miss Al	1	98	65	159	0.2	0.5
CHR–Chs of Christ	2	52	39	50	0.1	0.2
Jehovah's Witness	3	NR	NR	NR	-	-
LDS–L-D Saints	2	NR	NR	1,171	1.2	3.7
LUTH–E.L.C.A.	1	33	114	154	0.2	0.5
LUTH–Luth-MO Synod	2	46	110	120	0.1	0.4
MENN–Amish Undif	1	NR	69	183	0.2	0.6
MENN–Mennonite USA	1	20	20	24	0.0	0.1
METH–Free Methodist	5	1,052	465	1,052	1.1	3.3
METH–Un Methodist	20	1,093	3,933	4,868	5.2	15.4
Non-denom Chr Chs	12	1,480	1,580	1,927	2.1	6.1
PENT–Assemb of God	7	735	411	767	0.8	2.4
PENT–Ch God (Cleve)	1	68	68	83	0.1	0.3
PENT–Ch of God by Faith	1	NR	NR	NR	-	-
PENT–COGIC	2	150	0	0	0.0	0.0
PENT–Elim	3	NR	NR	NR	-	-
PRES–Presb Ch (USA)	12	528	1,356	1,647	1.8	5.2
REF–Christian Ref	1	125	175	213	0.2	0.7
REF–Ref Ch in Am	6	383	828	955	1.0	3.0
Sev Day Adv	2	46	80	92	0.1	0.3
Un C of Christ	2	64	100	121	0.1	0.4
WESTCHESTER	**653**	**61,203**	**92,469**	**609,660**	**64.2**	**100.0**
ANG/EPIS–Episcopal	49	4,095	11,879	14,016	1.5	2.3
Bahá'í	5	NR	338	338	0.0	0.1
BAPT–Amer Bapt USA	22	1,744	4,966	6,071	0.6	1.0
BAPT–Consrv Bapt	5	NR	NR	NR	-	-
BAPT–Ind Bapt Flwsp Intl	2	NR	NR	NR	-	-
BAPT–NBC USA	11	3,600	6,150	7,518	0.8	1.2
BAPT–Prog NBC	1	65	85	104	0.0	0.0
BAPT–So Bapt Conv	13	1,033	843	1,031	0.1	0.2
BUDD–Mahayana	10	NR	NR	3,730	0.4	0.6
BUDD–Theravada	1	NR	NR	1,364	0.1	0.2
BUDD–Vajrayana	1	NR	NR	456	0.0	0.1
Calv Chpl	2	NR	NR	NR	-	-
Catholic	100	NR	NR	435,590	45.9	71.4
CGOD–Ch God (Ander)	1	80	NR	80	0.0	0.0
Ch Cr, Scientst	4	NR	NR	NR	-	-
Ch of Nazarene	7	527	460	611	0.1	0.1
Chr & Miss Al	8	1,168	686	1,775	0.2	0.3
CHR–Chr Ch (Disc)	3	0	0	0	0.0	0.0
CHR–Chr Chs & Chs Cr	1	NR	50	61	0.0	0.0
CHR–Chs of Christ	3	245	251	337	0.0	0.1
CHR–Int Chs of Christ	0	NR	431	527	0.1	0.1
Christian Brethren	1	NR	NR	NR	-	-
Evan Cov Ch	3	274	702	357	0.0	0.1
FRND–Fr Gen Cf & Un Mtg	5	NR	357	436	0.0	0.1
HINDU–I/A Temples	2	NR	NR	1,792	0.2	0.3
HINDU–Post Ren	4	NR	NR	122	0.0	0.0
Intl Fell Bible Ch	1	NR	NR	NR	-	-
Jehovah's Witness	8	NR	NR	NR	-	-
JUD–Conserv	16	4,017	4,682	12,173	1.3	2.0
JUD–Orth	17	7,776	2,700	10,800	1.1	1.8
JUD–Reconst	4	443	588	1,529	0.2	0.3
JUD–Reform	18	5,158	8,899	24,561	2.6	4.0
LDS–L-D Saints	7	NR	NR	3,257	0.3	0.5
LUTH–Ch of Luth Br	1	165	58	352	0.0	0.1
LUTH–E.L.C.A.	16	1,332	3,964	5,163	0.5	0.8
LUTH–Luth Cong Msn Chr	1	55	94	115	0.0	0.0
LUTH–Luth-MO Synod	8	602	1,537	2,269	0.2	0.4
METH–AME	6	108	650	795	0.1	0.1
METH–AME Zion	11	2,500	6,160	7,530	0.8	1.2
METH–C.M.E.	1	125	173	211	0.0	0.0
METH–Free Methodist	2	45	53	55	0.0	0.0
METH–Un Methodist	33	1,583	6,190	7,664	0.8	1.3
METH–Wesleyan	1	40	70	52	0.0	0.0
Missionary Ch	1	120	98	120	0.0	0.0
Muslim Est	10	3,472	NR	13,715	1.4	2.2
New Apost Ch	1	NR	NR	NR	-	-
Non-denom Chr Chs	43	6,645	7,030	8,861	0.9	1.5
ORTHE–Ant Orth of NA	1	120	NR	300	0.0	0.0
ORTHE–Carp Rus Orth	1	25	NR	94	0.0	0.0
ORTHE–Greek Orthodox	3	975	NR	2,650	0.3	0.4
ORTHE–Orth Ch in Amer	1	120	NR	250	0.0	0.0
ORTHO–Armen Ap Etchm	1	105	NR	290	0.0	0.0
ORTHO–Coptic Orth Ch	1	50	NR	60	0.0	0.0
ORTHO–Ethiopian Orth	1	NR	NR	NR	-	-
ORTHO–Malan Dioc Am	6	1,100	NR	1,670	0.2	0.3
ORTHO–Malan Syr Orth	1	75	NR	144	0.0	0.0
PENT–Assemb of God	31	2,623	2,250	4,172	0.4	0.7
PENT–Ch God (Cleve)	14	1,139	1,600	1,956	0.2	0.3
PENT–Ch Lord Jesus Apos	5	NR	NR	NR	-	-
PENT–Ch of God Proph	4	NR	240	293	0.0	0.0
PENT–COGIC	3	530	1,355	1,656	0.2	0.3
PENT–Elim	1	NR	NR	NR	-	-
PENT–Fire Bapt Hol Ch	4	NR	NR	NR	-	-
PENT–I F Chr Assmbl	2	NR	NR	NR	-	-
PENT–Int Foursq Gos	1	41	34	42	0.0	0.0
PENT–Intl Pent Holiness	1	35	32	39	0.0	0.0
PENT–Un Pent Ch Intl	6	NR	NR	NR	-	-
PENT–Vineyard	2	155	210	257	0.0	0.0
PRES–Kor Pres Abroad	2	NR	NR	NR	-	-
PRES–Korean Amer Pres	2	NR	NR	NR	-	-
PRES–Korean Pres Amer	1	NR	NR	NR	-	-
PRES–Orth Pres Ch	1	23	26	28	0.0	0.0
PRES–Presb Ch (USA)	26	2,450	6,910	8,447	0.9	1.4
PRES–Presb Ch Amer	3	239	151	220	0.0	0.0
REF–Ref Ch in Am	11	1,071	3,022	3,244	0.3	0.5
Salvation Army	6	287	516	1,027	0.1	0.2
Sev Day Adv	23	2,126	3,697	4,253	0.4	0.7
Sikh	1	NR	NR	NR	-	-
Un Breth in Cr	1	29	42	25	0.0	0.0
Un C of Christ	11	501	1,483	1,813	0.2	0.3
Unit Univ	5	367	757	1,104	0.1	0.2
Zoroastrian	0	NR	NR	88	0.0	0.0
WYOMING	**62**	**2,289**	**4,549**	**14,455**	**34.3**	**100.0**
ANG/EPIS–Episcopal	3	119	180	418	1.0	2.9
Bahá'í	0	NR	3	3	0.0	0.0
BAPT–Amer Bapt USA	3	150	194	229	0.5	1.6
BAPT–Consrv Bapt	4	NR	NR	NR	-	-
BAPT–N Am Bapt Conf	1	NR	58	69	0.2	0.5
BAPT–NBC Amer	1	70	300	354	0.8	2.4
BAPT–So Bapt Conv	1	25	4	5	0.0	0.0
Catholic	5	NR	NR	7,968	18.9	55.1
Ch of Nazarene	1	74	36	74	0.2	0.5
Chr & Miss Al	1	17	13	22	0.1	0.2
CHR–Chr Chs & Chs Cr	1	NR	12	14	0.0	0.1
CHR–Chs of Christ	1	17	9	15	0.0	0.1
Jehovah's Witness	1	NR	NR	NR	-	-
LDS–L-D Saints	1	NR	NR	246	0.6	1.7
LUTH–E.L.C.A.	1	97	198	269	0.6	1.9
MENN–Amish Undif	0	NR	14	31	0.1	0.2
MENN–Beachy Amish-Menn	1	64	46	64	0.2	0.4
METH–Free Methodist	2	240	133	240	0.6	1.7
METH–Un Methodist	10	392	1,268	1,981	4.7	13.7
Non-denom Chr Chs	4	387	435	510	1.2	3.5
PENT–Ch God (Cleve)	1	77	55	65	0.2	0.4
PENT–Elim	5	NR	NR	NR	-	-
PRES–Presb Ch (USA)	5	132	333	393	0.9	2.7
Sev Day Adv	1	30	51	59	0.1	0.4
Un C of Christ	8	398	1,207	1,426	3.4	9.9
YATES	**45**	**1,483**	**3,649**	**7,718**	**30.4**	**100.0**
ANG/EPIS–Episcopal	2	81	114	142	0.6	1.8
Bahá'í	0	NR	4	4	0.0	0.1
BAPT–Amer Bapt USA	7	243	810	992	3.9	12.9
BAPT–Consrv Bapt	1	NR	NR	NR	-	-
BAPT–Reg Bapt Gen As	2	NR	NR	NR	-	-
BAPT–So Bapt Conv	1	10	12	15	0.1	0.2
Catholic	4	NR	NR	2,870	11.3	37.2
Ch of Nazarene	1	20	9	55	0.2	0.7
Ind Fund Churches	1	NR	NR	NR	-	-
Jehovah's Witness	1	NR	NR	NR	-	-
LDS–L-D Saints	1	NR	NR	183	0.7	2.4
LUTH–E.L.C.A.	2	112	410	491	1.9	6.4

NR–Not Reported - Represents no adherents reported. Percentages may not total 100 due to rounding.

Table 3: Religious Congregations by County and Group: 2010

Religious Group	Number of Congregations	Number of Attendees	Number of Communicant, Confirmed, or Full Members	Adherents		
				Number of Adherents	% of Total Pop.	% of Total Adh.
MENN–Beachy Amish-Menn	1	82	47	82	0.3	1.1
METH–Un Methodist	12	457	1,616	2,095	8.3	27.1
Non-denom Chr Chs	1	160	175	200	0.8	2.6
PENT–Assemb of God	1	80	36	80	0.3	1.0
PRES–Presb Ch (USA)	5	174	354	433	1.7	5.6
Un C of Christ	2	64	62	76	0.3	1.0
NORTH CAROLINA	**15,737**	**1,609,384**	**3,250,513**	**4,530,365**	**47.5**	**100.0**
ALAMANCE	**239**	**23,713**	**49,128**	**63,493**	**42.0**	**100.0**
ANG/EPIS–Episcopal	2	230	725	725	0.5	1.1
Bahá'í	2	NR	39	39	0.0	0.1
BAPT–NBC USA	2	305	400	489	0.3	0.8
BAPT–Prog NBC	1	0	175	214	0.1	0.3
BAPT–Ref Bapt Ch	2	NR	NR	NR	-	-
BAPT–So Bapt Conv	46	4,665	12,932	15,808	10.5	24.9
Catholic	1	NR	NR	3,068	2.0	4.8
Ch of Nazarene	4	314	573	598	0.4	0.9
CHR–Chr Ch (Disc)	2	0	0	0	0.0	0.0
CHR–Chr Chs & Chs Cr	1	NR	85	104	0.1	0.2
CHR–Chs of Christ	4	202	222	275	0.2	0.4
Christian Brethren	1	NR	NR	NR	-	-
CONG–Cong Chr, NA	1	NR	35	43	0.0	0.1
CONG–Consrv Cong Chr	2	286	650	795	0.5	1.3
Evan Assoc RCC	2	NR	NR	NR	-	-
FRND–Consrv Yr Mtgs	1	NR	21	26	0.0	0.0
FRND–Evan Fr Ch Intl	2	232	94	115	0.1	0.2
FRND–Fr Gen Cf & Un Mtg	1	NR	28	34	0.0	0.1
FRND–Fr Un Mtg	3	NR	445	544	0.4	0.9
FRND–Unaffl Mtgs	1	NR	NR	NR	-	-
Jehovah's Witness	2	NR	NR	NR	-	-
LDS–L-D Saints	4	NR	NR	1,329	0.9	2.1
LUTH–E.L.C.A.	3	397	886	1,068	0.7	1.7
LUTH–Luth–MO Synod	1	33	60	70	0.0	0.1
METH–AME	14	100	1,975	2,414	1.6	3.8
METH–AME Zion	1	0	100	122	0.1	0.2
METH–Evan Meth Ch	1	NR	NR	NR	-	-
METH–Un Methodist	26	3,038	10,582	11,901	7.9	18.7
METH–Wesleyan	5	194	232	252	0.2	0.4
Non-denom Chr Chs	40	8,645	9,325	11,320	7.5	17.8
ORTHE–Greek Orthodox	1	50	NR	95	0.1	0.1
ORTHE–Rus Orth Abroad	1	8	NR	14	0.0	0.0
PENT–Assemb of God	6	564	323	615	0.4	1.0
PENT–Ch God (Cleve)	6	672	750	917	0.6	1.4
PENT–Ch Lord Jesus Apos	1	NR	NR	NR	-	-
PENT–Ch of God Proph	4	NR	180	220	0.1	0.3
PENT–COGIC	1	100	175	214	0.1	0.3
PENT–Intl Pent Holiness	3	705	885	1,082	0.7	1.7
PENT–United Holy Ch	1	NR	NR	NR	-	-
PRES–As Ref Pres Ch	2	NR	230	281	0.2	0.4
PRES–Presb Ch (USA)	12	1,217	3,112	3,804	2.5	6.0
PRES–Presb Ch Amer	1	48	92	98	0.1	0.2
PRES–Ref Pres US	1	NR	NR	NR	-	-
Salvation Army	1	43	84	281	0.2	0.4
Sev Day Adv	3	162	281	324	0.2	0.5
Un C of Christ	17	1,503	3,432	4,195	2.8	6.6
ALEXANDER	**69**	**8,826**	**17,812**	**21,614**	**58.1**	**100.0**
Bahá'í	0	NR	2	2	0.0	0.0
BAPT–So Bapt Conv	35	5,960	12,259	14,824	39.9	68.6
Catholic	1	NR	NR	147	0.4	0.7
CHR–Chs of Christ	1	70	60	70	0.2	0.3
LUTH–E.L.C.A.	5	889	1,932	2,355	6.3	10.9
LUTH–Luth–MO Synod	1	170	390	425	1.1	2.0
MENN–Beachy Amish-Menn	1	45	32	45	0.1	0.2
METH–AME Zion	1	0	100	121	0.3	0.6
METH–Un Methodist	10	764	1,771	2,050	5.5	9.5
METH–Wesleyan	2	118	116	154	0.4	0.7
Non-denom Chr Chs	3	520	530	651	1.8	3.0
PENT–Assemb of God	1	20	0	21	0.1	0.1
PENT–Ch God (Cleve)	2	162	149	180	0.5	0.8
PENT–Fire Bapt Hol Ch	1	NR	NR	NR	-	-

Religious Group	Number of Congregations	Number of Attendees	Number of Communicant, Confirmed, or Full Members	Adherents		
				Number of Adherents	% of Total Pop.	% of Total Adh.
PENT–United Holy Ch	1	NR	NR	NR	-	-
PRES–As Ref Pres Ch	2	NR	270	326	0.9	1.5
PRES–Presb Ch (USA)	2	108	201	243	0.7	1.1
ALLEGHANY	**33**	**1,793**	**3,613**	**4,537**	**40.7**	**100.0**
ANG/EPIS–Episcopal	1	69	76	93	0.8	2.0
BAPT–Free Will Bapt	1	NR	52	61	0.5	1.3
BAPT–So Bapt Conv	14	867	2,087	2,452	22.0	54.0
BRETH–Ch of Brethren	3	30	202	237	2.1	5.2
Catholic	1	NR	NR	120	1.1	2.6
Ch Christ Chr Union	1	NR	NR	NR	-	-
Jehovah's Witness	1	NR	NR	NR	-	-
LDS–L-D Saints	1	NR	NR	74	0.7	1.6
METH–Un Methodist	5	243	550	705	6.3	15.5
Non-denom Chr Chs	3	450	450	564	5.1	12.4
PENT–Ch God (Cleve)	1	84	101	119	1.1	2.6
PRES–Presb Ch (USA)	1	50	95	112	1.0	2.5
ANSON	**100**	**3,949**	**11,683**	**14,000**	**52.0**	**100.0**
ANG/EPIS–Episcopal	2	59	133	141	0.5	1.0
Bahá'í	0	NR	25	25	0.1	0.2
BAPT–Natl Mis Bapt Conv	1	0	150	180	0.7	1.3
BAPT–Orig Free Will Bapt	1	90	123	148	0.5	1.1
BAPT–So Bapt Conv	26	1,942	5,499	6,601	24.5	47.2
Catholic	1	NR	NR	121	0.4	0.9
CGOD–Ch God (Ander)	1	50	NR	50	0.2	0.4
CHR–Chs of Christ	1	30	28	36	0.1	0.3
Jehovah's Witness	1	NR	NR	NR	-	-
MENN–CG in Cr (Menn)	1	NR	17	20	0.1	0.1
METH–AME Zion	20	122	2,473	2,969	11.0	21.2
METH–Un Methodist	23	716	1,664	1,910	7.1	13.6
Non-denom Chr Chs	7	710	895	988	3.7	7.1
PENT–Ch God (Cleve)	3	122	184	221	0.8	1.6
PENT–Ch Lord Jesus Apos	1	NR	NR	NR	-	-
PENT–Ch of God Proph	4	NR	135	162	0.6	1.2
PENT–COGIC	1	0	150	180	0.7	1.3
PENT–Intl Pent Holiness	1	12	12	14	0.1	0.1
PRES–Presb Ch (USA)	5	96	195	234	0.9	1.7
ASHE	**90**	**4,928**	**10,386**	**13,068**	**47.9**	**100.0**
ANG/EPIS–Episcopal	1	70	65	96	0.4	0.7
Bahá'í	0	NR	7	7	0.0	0.1
BAPT–So Bapt Conv	50	3,414	7,526	8,861	32.5	67.8
BRETH–Ch of Brethren	1	0	69	81	0.3	0.6
Catholic	1	NR	NR	593	2.2	4.5
Ch Christ Chr Union	3	NR	NR	NR	-	-
Ch of Nazarene	1	31	39	39	0.1	0.3
CHR–Chr Chs & Chs Cr	1	NR	125	147	0.5	1.1
CHR–Chs of Christ	2	72	79	99	0.4	0.8
FRND–Fr Gen Cf	1	NR	0	0	0.0	0.0
METH–Un Methodist	17	789	1,677	2,190	8.0	16.8
Non-denom Chr Chs	2	185	271	298	1.1	2.3
PENT–Assemb of God	1	45	35	56	0.2	0.4
PENT–Ch of God Proph	1	NR	17	20	0.1	0.2
PENT–Int Pent C Chr	1	18	NR	30	0.1	0.2
PRES–Presb Ch (USA)	5	232	372	438	1.6	3.4
PRES–Presb Ch Amer	1	40	49	50	0.2	0.4
Sev Day Adv	1	32	55	63	0.2	0.5
AVERY	**64**	**3,192**	**5,983**	**7,593**	**42.7**	**100.0**
ANG/EPIS–Episcopal	1	21	5	12	0.1	0.2
Bahá'í	0	NR	11	11	0.1	0.1
BAPT–Free Will Bapt	1	NR	114	131	0.7	1.7
BAPT–Natl Mis Bapt Conv	1	0	150	172	1.0	2.3
BAPT–So Bapt Conv	29	1,994	3,673	4,212	23.7	55.5
Catholic	1	NR	NR	634	3.6	8.3
CHR–Chr Chs & Chs Cr	3	NR	300	344	1.9	4.5
CHR–Chs of Christ	3	61	62	71	0.4	0.9
Jehovah's Witness	1	NR	NR	NR	-	-
LDS–L-D Saints	1	NR	NR	85	0.5	1.1
LUTH–E.L.C.A.	1	22	10	10	0.1	0.1
LUTH–Luth Cong Msn Chr	1	120	311	357	2.0	4.7

NR–Not Reported - Represents no adherents reported. Percentages may not total 100 due to rounding.

Table 3: Religious Congregations by County and Group: 2010

Religious Group	Number of Congregations	Number of Attendees	Number of Communicant, Confirmed, or Full Members	Adherents: Number of Adherents	Adherents: % of Total Pop.	Adherents: % of Total Adh.
LUTH–Luth-MO Synod	1	63	56	56	0.3	0.7
METH–Evan Meth Ch	1	NR	NR	NR	-	-
METH–Un Methodist	3	86	160	192	1.1	2.5
Non-denom Chr Chs	2	90	90	115	0.6	1.5
PENT–Ch God (Cleve)	1	39	37	42	0.2	0.6
PRES–Evan Presby Ch	2	NR	104	119	0.7	1.6
PRES–Presb Ch (USA)	8	529	668	766	4.3	10.1
PRES–Presb Ch Amer	2	75	73	81	0.5	1.1
Sev Day Adv	1	92	159	183	1.0	2.4
BEAUFORT	**167**	**7,438**	**20,492**	**25,978**	**54.4**	**100.0**
ANG/EPIS–Anglican NA	1	NR	NR	NR	-	-
ANG/EPIS–Episcopal	9	530	1,081	1,303	2.7	5.0
Bahá'í	0	NR	62	62	0.1	0.2
BAPT–Free Will Bapt	8	NR	912	1,099	2.3	4.2
BAPT–Natl Mis Bapt Conv	5	175	850	1,024	2.1	3.9
BAPT–Orig Free Will Bapt	11	990	1,353	1,630	3.4	6.3
BAPT–So Bapt Conv	14	1,261	2,676	3,223	6.7	12.4
Catholic	1	NR	NR	1,020	2.1	3.9
CHR–Chr Ch (Disc)	21	278	1,222	1,472	3.1	5.7
CHR–Chr Chs & Chs Cr	19	NR	4,268	5,141	10.8	19.8
CHR–Chs of Christ	3	295	272	352	0.7	1.4
Jehovah's Witness	2	NR	NR	NR	-	-
LDS–L-D Saints	1	NR	NR	333	0.7	1.3
LUTH–E.L.C.A.	1	44	47	51	0.1	0.2
METH–AME Zion	8	35	850	1,024	2.1	3.9
METH–C.M.E.	1	20	20	24	0.1	0.1
METH–Un Methodist	14	706	2,588	3,123	6.5	12.0
Non-denom Chr Chs	13	1,280	1,750	1,868	3.9	7.2
PENT–Assemb of God	3	353	155	368	0.8	1.4
PENT–Ch God (Cleve)	9	656	963	1,160	2.4	4.5
PENT–Ch of God Proph	1	NR	15	18	0.0	0.1
PENT–COGIC	1	100	100	120	0.3	0.5
PENT–Full Gosp Bapt	2	NR	NR	NR	-	-
PENT–Intl Pent Holiness	7	224	263	317	0.7	1.2
PENT–Pent FW Bapt	1	NR	NR	NR	-	-
PENT–Un Pent Ch Intl	1	NR	NR	NR	-	-
PENT–United Holy Ch	2	NR	NR	NR	-	-
PRES–Presb Ch (USA)	2	275	618	744	1.6	2.9
PRES–Presb Ch Amer	1	48	87	87	0.2	0.3
REF–Christian Ref	1	100	120	145	0.3	0.6
REF–Un Ref Chs N.A.	1	NR	NR	NR	-	-
Salvation Army	1	7	114	148	0.3	0.6
Sev Day Adv	2	61	106	122	0.3	0.5
BERTIE	**52**	**2,512**	**6,344**	**8,015**	**37.7**	**100.0**
ANG/EPIS–Episcopal	3	73	130	206	1.0	2.6
Bahá'í	0	NR	24	24	0.1	0.3
BAPT–Natl Mis Bapt Conv	1	0	150	177	0.8	2.2
BAPT–NBC USA	5	40	600	710	3.3	8.9
BAPT–So Bapt Conv	23	1,206	3,739	4,424	20.8	55.2
Catholic	1	NR	NR	76	0.4	0.9
CHR–Chr Ch (Disc)	2	0	0	0	0.0	0.0
Jehovah's Witness	1	NR	NR	NR	-	-
METH–Un Methodist	4	147	341	409	1.9	5.1
Non-denom Chr Chs	2	350	400	462	2.2	5.8
PENT–Assemb of God	5	494	303	750	3.5	9.4
PENT–COGIC	3	100	400	473	2.2	5.9
PENT–Intl Pent Holiness	2	102	257	304	1.4	3.8
BLADEN	**120**	**5,524**	**15,521**	**18,933**	**53.8**	**100.0**
ANG/EPIS–Episcopal	1	17	34	34	0.1	0.2
Bahá'í	0	NR	14	14	0.0	0.1
BAPT–Free Will Bapt	1	NR	38	46	0.1	0.2
BAPT–Orig Free Will Bapt	2	180	246	298	0.8	1.6
BAPT–So Bapt Conv	39	3,182	7,534	9,138	26.0	48.3
Catholic	1	NR	NR	222	0.6	1.2
CHR–Chs of Christ	1	10	10	15	0.0	0.1
Jehovah's Witness	1	NR	NR	NR	-	-
METH–AME	2	0	300	364	1.0	1.9
METH–AME Zion	26	295	3,685	4,470	12.7	23.6
METH–Un Methodist	12	811	1,993	2,350	6.7	12.4
Non-denom Chr Chs	3	300	450	450	1.3	2.4

Religious Group	Number of Congregations	Number of Attendees	Number of Communicant, Confirmed, or Full Members	Adherents: Number of Adherents	Adherents: % of Total Pop.	Adherents: % of Total Adh.
PENT–Assemb of God	1	120	41	120	0.3	0.6
PENT–Ch God (Cleve)	3	66	136	165	0.5	0.9
PENT–Ch of God Proph	2	NR	82	99	0.3	0.5
PENT–Fire Bapt Hol Ch	3	NR	NR	NR	-	-
PENT–Intl Pent Holiness	4	165	201	244	0.7	1.3
PENT–Pent FW Bapt	7	NR	NR	NR	-	-
PENT–Un Pent Ch Intl	1	NR	NR	NR	-	-
PENT–United Holy Ch	1	NR	NR	NR	-	-
PRES–Presb Ch (USA)	7	252	537	651	1.8	3.4
Sev Day Adv	2	126	220	253	0.7	1.3
BRUNSWICK	**152**	**12,319**	**26,067**	**38,216**	**35.6**	**100.0**
ANG/EPIS–Episcopal	3	437	908	1,001	0.9	2.6
Bahá'í	0	NR	23	23	0.0	0.1
BAPT–Orig Free Will Bapt	1	90	123	144	0.1	0.4
BAPT–So Bapt Conv	58	4,781	12,312	14,428	13.4	37.8
BUDD–Theravada	1	NR	NR	375	0.3	1.0
Catholic	2	NR	NR	5,782	5.4	15.1
Ch of Nazarene	1	38	27	56	0.1	0.1
Chr & Miss Al	1	50	28	78	0.1	0.2
CHR–Chs of Christ	3	139	93	121	0.1	0.3
Jehovah's Witness	2	NR	NR	NR	-	-
LDS–L-D Saints	3	NR	NR	1,105	1.0	2.9
LUTH–E.L.C.A.	2	347	563	602	0.6	1.6
METH–AME	8	0	1,050	1,230	1.1	3.2
METH–AME Zion	9	0	1,350	1,582	1.5	4.1
METH–Un Methodist	13	2,440	4,910	5,900	5.5	15.4
METH–Wesleyan	1	137	0	178	0.2	0.5
Non-denom Chr Chs	16	2,420	2,794	3,227	3.0	8.4
PENT–Assemb of God	3	362	189	393	0.4	1.0
PENT–Ch God (Cleve)	5	151	237	278	0.3	0.7
PENT–Ch of God Proph	1	NR	5	6	0.0	0.0
PENT–Fire Bapt Hol Ch	2	NR	NR	NR	-	-
PENT–Full Gosp Bapt	1	NR	NR	NR	-	-
PENT–Intl Pent Holiness	3	102	112	131	0.1	0.3
PENT–Pent FW Bapt	4	NR	NR	NR	-	-
PENT–United Holy Ch	1	NR	NR	NR	-	-
PENT–Vineyard	1	64	70	82	0.1	0.2
PRES–As Ref Pres Ch	1	NR	0	0	0.0	0.0
PRES–Presb Ch (USA)	6	761	1,273	1,492	1.4	3.9
Zoroastrian	0	NR	NR	2	0.0	0.0
BUNCOMBE	**382**	**40,615**	**91,198**	**122,565**	**51.4**	**100.0**
ANG/EPIS–Anglican NA	7	NR	NR	NR	-	-
ANG/EPIS–Episcopal	10	1,367	3,318	3,532	1.5	2.9
Bahá'í	2	NR	257	257	0.1	0.2
BAPT–Alliance Bapt	2	NR	NR	NR	-	-
BAPT–Amer Bapt Assn	1	NR	60	71	0.0	0.1
BAPT–Amer Bapt USA	2	275	460	546	0.2	0.4
BAPT–Free Will Bapt	9	NR	1,026	1,219	0.5	1.0
BAPT–Natl Mis Bapt Conv	2	50	200	238	0.1	0.2
BAPT–NBC USA	2	0	210	249	0.1	0.2
BAPT–Prog NBC	1	0	150	178	0.1	0.1
BAPT–S-D Baptist Gen Con	1	12	13	15	0.0	0.0
BAPT–So Bapt Conv	116	18,584	50,025	59,419	24.9	48.5
BUDD–Mahayana	5	NR	NR	244	0.1	0.2
BUDD–Vajrayana	2	NR	NR	92	0.0	0.1
Calv Chpl	1	NR	NR	NR	-	-
Catholic	5	NR	NR	9,014	3.8	7.4
CGOD–Ch God (Ander)	4	131	NR	131	0.1	0.1
Ch Cr, Scientst	1	NR	NR	NR	-	-
Ch of Nazarene	2	103	153	243	0.1	0.2
Chr & Miss Al	1	55	64	125	0.1	0.1
CHR–Chr Ch (Disc)	4	8	193	229	0.1	0.2
CHR–Chr Chs & Chs Cr	4	NR	348	413	0.2	0.3
CHR–Chs of Christ	6	432	400	515	0.2	0.4
Christian Brethren	1	NR	NR	NR	-	-
FRND–Fr Gen Cf	2	NR	67	80	0.0	0.1
HINDU–Post Ren	3	NR	NR	147	0.1	0.1
Jehovah's Witness	4	NR	NR	NR	-	-
JUD–Conserv	1	110	123	332	0.1	0.3
JUD–Orth	1	43	50	60	0.0	0.0
JUD–Reform	1	151	267	721	0.3	0.6

NR–Not Reported   - Represents no adherents reported.   Percentages may not total 100 due to rounding.

Table 3: Religious Congregations by County and Group: 2010

Religious Group	Number of Congregations	Number of Attendees	Number of Communicant, Confirmed, or Full Members	Adherents: Number of Adherents	Adherents: % of Total Pop.	Adherents: % of Total Adh.
LDS–L-D Saints	3	NR	NR	1,764	0.7	1.4
LUTH–E.L.C.A.	3	616	1,067	1,335	0.6	1.1
LUTH–Luth–MO Synod	1	270	424	546	0.2	0.4
LUTH–Wisc Ev Luth Syn	1	136	193	243	0.1	0.2
MENN–Mennonite USA	1	52	57	68	0.0	0.1
METH–AME	1	100	210	249	0.1	0.2
METH–AME Zion	5	0	600	713	0.3	0.6
METH–C.M.E.	1	150	330	392	0.2	0.3
METH–Un Methodist	49	4,032	11,133	13,809	5.8	11.3
METH–Wesleyan	3	139	132	181	0.1	0.1
Missionary Ch	1	125	0	125	0.1	0.1
Muslim Est	1	75	NR	150	0.1	0.1
Non-denom Chr Chs	33	6,850	8,605	9,989	4.2	8.1
ORTHE–Carp Rus Orth	1	30	NR	79	0.0	0.1
ORTHE–Greek Orthodox	1	75	NR	325	0.1	0.3
ORTHE–Orth Ch in Amer	1	25	NR	40	0.0	0.0
PENT–Assemb of God	5	697	437	1,752	0.7	1.4
PENT–Ch God (Cleve)	10	513	815	968	0.4	0.8
PENT–Ch of God Proph	1	NR	83	99	0.0	0.1
PENT–COGIC	1	0	0	0	0.0	0.0
PENT–Fire Bapt Hol Ch	3	NR	NR	NR	-	-
PENT–Intl Pent Holiness	5	324	525	624	0.3	0.5
PENT–Un Pent Ch Intl	1	NR	NR	NR	-	-
PENT–Vineyard	2	45	80	95	0.0	0.1
PRES–As Ref Pres Ch	2	NR	6	7	0.0	0.0
PRES–Evan Presby Ch	2	NR	612	727	0.3	0.6
PRES–Orth Pres Ch	1	20	16	31	0.0	0.0
PRES–Presb Ch (USA)	16	1,545	3,130	3,718	1.6	3.0
PRES–Presb Ch Amer	10	1,534	1,986	2,447	1.0	2.0
Salvation Army	1	115	151	184	0.1	0.2
Sev Day Adv	9	1,230	2,137	2,459	1.0	2.0
Un C of Christ	2	196	400	475	0.2	0.4
Unit Univ	2	400	685	901	0.4	0.7
BURKE	**202**	**18,067**	**44,060**	**55,195**	**60.7**	**100.0**
ANG/EPIS–Episcopal	4	231	550	591	0.7	1.1
Bahá'í	0	NR	81	81	0.1	0.1
BAPT–Free Will Bapt	5	NR	570	682	0.8	1.2
BAPT–NBC USA	1	100	125	150	0.2	0.3
BAPT–So Bapt Conv	92	10,879	29,368	35,161	38.7	63.7
Catholic	1	NR	NR	794	0.9	1.4
CGOD–Ch God (Ander)	4	380	NR	380	0.4	0.7
Chr & Miss Al	1	125	222	222	0.2	0.4
CHR–Chr Ch (Disc)	1	30	38	45	0.0	0.1
CHR–Chr Chs & Chs Cr	1	NR	45	54	0.1	0.1
CHR–Chs of Christ	1	59	47	66	0.1	0.1
Jehovah's Witness	2	NR	NR	NR	-	-
LDS–L-D Saints	1	NR	NR	764	0.8	1.4
LUTH–E.L.C.A.	2	207	580	618	0.7	1.1
MENN–Menn Br US Conf	1	NR	12	14	0.0	0.0
METH–AME	9	99	1,150	1,377	1.5	2.5
METH–AME Zion	2	100	400	479	0.5	0.9
METH–Evan Meth Ch	3	NR	NR	NR	-	-
METH–Un Methodist	30	2,275	5,808	6,922	7.6	12.5
METH–Wesleyan	3	189	201	246	0.3	0.4
Muslim Est	1	134	NR	308	0.3	0.6
New Apost Ch	1	NR	NR	NR	-	-
Non-denom Chr Chs	12	1,375	2,020	2,189	2.4	4.0
PENT–Assemb of God	6	720	162	851	0.9	1.5
PENT–Ch God (Cleve)	4	272	876	1,049	1.2	1.9
PENT–Ch of God Proph	2	NR	21	25	0.0	0.0
PENT–Intl Pent Holiness	2	41	55	66	0.1	0.1
PENT–Un Pent Ch Intl	1	NR	NR	NR	-	-
PRES–Presb Ch (USA)	6	578	1,341	1,606	1.8	2.9
PRES–Presb Ch Amer	1	83	58	76	0.1	0.1
Sev Day Adv	2	190	330	379	0.4	0.7
CABARRUS	**282**	**39,900**	**65,157**	**94,526**	**53.1**	**100.0**
ANG/EPIS–Anglican NA	1	NR	NR	NR	-	-
ANG/EPIS–Episcopal	1	239	535	560	0.3	0.6
Bahá'í	0	NR	45	45	0.0	0.0
BAPT–Amer Bapt USA	1	175	175	222	0.1	0.2
BAPT–Free Will Bapt	2	NR	228	290	0.2	0.3

Religious Group	Number of Congregations	Number of Attendees	Number of Communicant, Confirmed, or Full Members	Adherents: Number of Adherents	Adherents: % of Total Pop.	Adherents: % of Total Adh.
BAPT–NBC USA	1	200	300	381	0.2	0.4
BAPT–Orig Free Will Bapt	1	90	123	156	0.1	0.2
BAPT–So Bapt Conv	77	12,090	22,744	28,900	16.2	30.6
BRETH–Ch of Brethren	1	46	61	78	0.0	0.1
Catholic	2	NR	NR	4,425	2.5	4.7
CGOD–Ch God (Ander)	3	368	NR	368	0.2	0.4
Ch of Nazarene	2	150	190	224	0.1	0.2
CHR–Chr Ch (Disc)	1	0	150	191	0.1	0.2
CHR–Chr Chs & Chs Cr	1	NR	720	915	0.5	1.0
CHR–Chs of Christ	3	500	460	582	0.3	0.6
Evan Assoc RCC	1	NR	NR	NR	-	-
Jehovah's Witness	2	NR	NR	NR	-	-
LDS–L-D Saints	2	NR	NR	1,290	0.7	1.4
LUTH–E.L.C.A.	15	1,690	3,552	4,372	2.5	4.6
LUTH–Luth–MO Synod	3	305	408	573	0.3	0.6
LUTH–Nor Amer Luth C	2	NR	NR	NR	-	-
METH–AME Zion	14	505	2,107	2,677	1.5	2.8
METH–Evan Meth Ch	1	NR	NR	NR	-	-
METH–Un Methodist	30	5,842	11,639	17,276	9.7	18.3
METH–Wesleyan	5	561	760	730	0.4	0.8
Missionary Ch	1	2	0	2	0.0	0.0
Non-denom Chr Chs	43	9,001	10,139	11,766	6.6	12.4
PENT–Assemb of God	3	3,192	1,501	6,585	3.7	7.0
PENT–Ch God (Cleve)	12	1,376	2,436	3,095	1.7	3.3
PENT–Ch Lord Jesus Apos	1	NR	NR	NR	-	-
PENT–Ch of God Proph	4	NR	179	227	0.1	0.2
PENT–COGIC	1	0	0	0	0.0	0.0
PENT–Cong Hol Ch	1	9	8	10	0.0	0.0
PENT–Fire Bapt Hol Ch	2	NR	NR	NR	-	-
PENT–Full Gosp Bapt	2	NR	NR	NR	-	-
PENT–Int Foursq Gos	7	1,044	1,255	1,595	0.9	1.7
PENT–Intl Pent Holiness	4	263	536	681	0.4	0.7
PENT–Un Pent Ch Intl	1	NR	NR	NR	-	-
PRES–As Ref Pres Ch	1	NR	56	71	0.0	0.1
PRES–Presb Ch (USA)	17	1,590	3,829	4,865	2.7	5.1
PRES–Presb Ch Amer	2	365	331	445	0.2	0.5
REF–Comm Ref Evan	1	NR	NR	NR	-	-
Salvation Army	1	43	96	199	0.1	0.2
Sev Day Adv	2	119	207	238	0.1	0.3
Un C of Christ	4	135	387	492	0.3	0.5
CALDWELL	**153**	**16,875**	**39,416**	**48,345**	**58.2**	**100.0**
ANG/EPIS–Episcopal	1	78	169	224	0.3	0.5
Bahá'í	0	NR	12	12	0.0	0.0
BAPT–Free Will Bapt	1	NR	114	138	0.2	0.3
BAPT–So Bapt Conv	72	10,899	28,477	34,351	41.4	71.1
Catholic	1	NR	NR	653	0.8	1.4
CGOD–Ch God (Ander)	1	200	NR	200	0.2	0.4
Ch of God Gen Conf	1	NR	74	89	0.1	0.2
CHR–Chr Chs & Chs Cr	2	NR	80	97	0.1	0.2
CHR–Chs of Christ	2	116	132	152	0.2	0.3
LDS–L-D Saints	1	NR	NR	320	0.4	0.7
LUTH–E.L.C.A.	6	472	867	1,078	1.3	2.2
LUTH–Nor Amer Luth C	1	NR	NR	NR	-	-
MENN–Menn Br US Conf	3	NR	172	207	0.2	0.4
METH–AME	5	150	573	691	0.8	1.4
METH–Un Methodist	25	1,757	4,291	5,025	6.1	10.4
METH–Wesleyan	1	68	73	88	0.1	0.2
Non-denom Chr Chs	11	1,335	1,855	1,956	2.4	4.0
PENT–Assemb of God	1	75	60	94	0.1	0.2
PENT–Ch God (Cleve)	7	285	622	750	0.9	1.6
PENT–Ch of God Proph	1	NR	41	49	0.1	0.1
PENT–Intl Pent Holiness	3	809	757	913	1.1	1.9
PRES–Presb Ch (USA)	5	541	893	1,077	1.3	2.2
Sev Day Adv	1	50	86	99	0.1	0.2
Un C of Christ	1	40	68	82	0.1	0.2
CAMDEN	**19**	**1,101**	**2,670**	**3,356**	**33.6**	**100.0**
ANG/EPIS–Anglican NA	1	NR	NR	NR	-	-
BAPT–NBC USA	2	270	300	372	3.7	11.1
BAPT–So Bapt Conv	2	158	699	866	8.7	25.8
CHR–Chr Chs & Chs Cr	2	NR	310	384	3.8	11.4
METH–AME Zion	2	0	250	310	3.1	9.2

NR–Not Reported   - Represents no adherents reported.   Percentages may not total 100 due to rounding.

Table 3: Religious Congregations by County and Group: 2010

Religious Group	Number of Congrega-tions	Number of Attendees	Number of Communicant, Confirmed, or Full Members	Adherents: Number of Adherents	Adherents: % of Total Pop.	Adherents: % of Total Adh.
METH–Un Methodist	5	273	607	775	7.8	23.1
PENT–Assemb of God	1	20	0	24	0.2	0.7
PENT–COGIC	2	300	450	558	5.6	16.6
PENT–Intl Pent Holiness	1	35	9	11	0.1	0.3
PENT–Vineyard	1	45	45	56	0.6	1.7
CARTERET	**121**	**10,568**	**21,649**	**29,372**	**44.2**	**100.0**
ANG/EPIS–Anglican NA	1	NR	NR	NR	-	-
ANG/EPIS–Episcopal	3	429	958	994	1.5	3.4
Bahá'í	0	NR	6	6	0.0	0.0
BAPT–Free Will Bapt	4	NR	456	532	0.8	1.8
BAPT–Natl Mis Bapt Conv	2	0	150	175	0.3	0.6
BAPT–Orig Free Will Bapt	12	1,080	1,476	1,722	2.6	5.9
BAPT–So Bapt Conv	24	2,555	6,644	7,749	11.7	26.4
Catholic	1	NR	NR	2,345	3.5	8.0
Ch of Nazarene	2	238	160	275	0.4	0.9
CHR–Chr Ch (Disc)	2	82	347	405	0.6	1.4
CHR–Chs of Christ	2	105	100	160	0.2	0.5
Evan Assoc RCC	1	NR	NR	NR	-	-
FRND–Fr Gen Cf	1	NR	6	7	0.0	0.0
Jehovah's Witness	2	NR	NR	NR	-	-
LDS–L-D Saints	2	NR	NR	1,057	1.6	3.6
LUTH–E.L.C.A.	1	126	234	280	0.4	1.0
METH–AME Zion	5	250	547	638	1.0	2.2
METH–Un Methodist	23	1,999	5,384	6,523	9.8	22.2
METH–Wesleyan	1	102	59	133	0.2	0.5
Non-denom Chr Chs	10	1,539	1,532	2,007	3.0	6.8
PENT–Assemb of God	2	148	153	363	0.5	1.2
PENT–Ch God (Cleve)	3	252	559	652	1.0	2.2
PENT–Ch of God Proph	1	NR	80	93	0.1	0.3
PENT–Intl Pent Holiness	8	1,192	1,839	2,145	3.2	7.3
PENT–Un Pent Ch Intl	1	NR	NR	NR	-	-
PRES–Presb Ch (USA)	4	394	825	962	1.4	3.3
Salvation Army	1	34	65	65	0.1	0.2
Unit Univ	1	43	69	84	0.1	0.3
Unity Ch	1	NR	NR	NR	-	-
CASWELL	**53**	**2,883**	**6,455**	**7,522**	**31.7**	**100.0**
ANG/EPIS–Episcopal	1	10	18	18	0.1	0.2
BAPT–NBC USA	1	250	475	562	2.4	7.5
BAPT–Ref Bapt Ch	1	NR	NR	NR	-	-
BAPT–So Bapt Conv	14	1,134	2,632	3,116	13.1	41.4
Jehovah's Witness	1	NR	NR	NR	-	-
METH–AME	3	0	400	473	2.0	6.3
METH–Un Methodist	16	642	1,517	1,825	7.7	24.3
Non-denom Chr Chs	6	631	960	992	4.2	13.2
PENT–Full Gosp Bapt	1	NR	NR	NR	-	-
PENT–Intl Pent Holiness	1	50	62	73	0.3	1.0
PRES–Presb Ch (USA)	7	129	346	410	1.7	5.5
Un C of Christ	1	37	45	53	0.2	0.7
CATAWBA	**281**	**35,408**	**68,443**	**93,104**	**60.3**	**100.0**
ANG/EPIS–Anglican NA	2	NR	NR	NR	-	-
ANG/EPIS–Episcopal	3	339	1,177	1,252	0.8	1.3
Bahá'í	0	NR	57	57	0.0	0.1
BAPT–Amer Bapt USA	1	350	600	734	0.5	0.8
BAPT–Converge/BGC	1	75	NR	90	0.1	0.1
BAPT–Free Will Bapt	2	NR	228	279	0.2	0.3
BAPT–Natl Mis Bapt Conv	1	0	0	0	0.0	0.0
BAPT–So Bapt Conv	83	11,080	25,848	31,641	20.5	34.0
Catholic	2	NR	NR	3,840	2.5	4.1
CGOD–Ch God (Ander)	3	367	NR	367	0.2	0.4
Ch Cr, Scientst	1	NR	NR	NR	-	-
Ch God (7th Day)	1	NR	NR	NR	-	-
Ch of Nazarene	1	45	37	45	0.0	0.0
Chr & Miss Al	1	188	412	436	0.3	0.5
CHR–Chr Chs & Chs Cr	1	NR	48	59	0.0	0.1
CHR–Chs of Christ	4	295	295	463	0.3	0.5
Evan Assoc RCC	1	NR	NR	NR	-	-
Evan Cov Ch	1	0	12	0	0.0	0.0
FRND–Fr Gen Cf	1	NR	0	0	0.0	0.0
Jehovah's Witness	2	NR	NR	NR	-	-
JUD–Reform	1	32	56	151	0.1	0.2

Religious Group	Number of Congrega-tions	Number of Attendees	Number of Communicant, Confirmed, or Full Members	Adherents: Number of Adherents	Adherents: % of Total Pop.	Adherents: % of Total Adh.
LDS–L-D Saints	3	NR	NR	1,700	1.1	1.8
LUTH–E.L.C.A.	21	2,905	6,376	7,835	5.1	8.4
LUTH–Luth–MO Synod	12	3,002	5,968	7,493	4.9	8.0
LUTH–Nor Amer Luth C	7	NR	NR	NR	-	-
MENN–Mennonite USA	3	205	225	275	0.2	0.3
METH–AME	1	0	350	428	0.3	0.5
METH–AME Zion	10	285	1,210	1,481	1.0	1.6
METH–Un Methodist	34	6,519	12,523	17,815	11.5	19.1
METH–Wesleyan	4	256	276	333	0.2	0.4
MORAV–Morav Ch-South	1	72	115	134	0.1	0.1
Non-denom Chr Chs	24	3,483	4,280	4,692	3.0	5.0
PENT–Assemb of God	7	1,607	582	1,905	1.2	2.0
PENT–Ch God (Cleve)	9	677	1,442	1,765	1.1	1.9
PENT–COGIC	2	450	300	367	0.2	0.4
PENT–Fire Bapt Hol Ch	2	NR	NR	NR	-	-
PENT–Intl Pent Holiness	5	574	957	1,171	0.8	1.3
PENT–Un Pent Ch Intl	2	NR	NR	NR	-	-
PRES–Orth Pres Ch	1	45	43	52	0.0	0.1
PRES–Presb Ch (USA)	5	964	1,733	2,121	1.4	2.3
PRES–Presb Ch Amer	1	168	136	220	0.1	0.2
Salvation Army	1	137	165	265	0.2	0.3
Sev Day Adv	3	341	593	682	0.4	0.7
Un C of Christ	9	897	2,336	2,860	1.9	3.1
Unit Univ	1	50	63	96	0.1	0.1
CHATHAM	**128**	**8,020**	**21,042**	**26,665**	**42.0**	**100.0**
ANG/EPIS–Anglican NA	1	NR	NR	NR	-	-
ANG/EPIS–Episcopal	1	103	184	184	0.3	0.7
Bahá'í	1	NR	44	44	0.1	0.2
BAPT–Free Will Bapt	1	NR	114	138	0.2	0.5
BAPT–So Bapt Conv	40	4,664	10,953	13,231	20.8	49.6
BUDD–Mahayana	1	NR	NR	29	0.0	0.1
Catholic	1	NR	NR	1,066	1.7	4.0
CGOD–Ch God (Ander)	1	30	NR	30	0.0	0.1
Ch of Nazarene	1	36	35	36	0.1	0.1
CHR–Chr Ch (Disc)	1	0	0	0	0.0	0.0
CHR–Chs of Christ	1	35	34	34	0.1	0.1
FRND–Evan Fr Ch Intl	1	31	22	27	0.0	0.1
FRND–Fr Un Mtg	3	NR	288	348	0.5	1.3
Jehovah's Witness	1	NR	NR	NR	-	-
LDS–L-D Saints	1	NR	NR	141	0.2	0.5
LUTH–E.L.C.A.	1	27	0	0	0.0	0.0
METH–AME	2	0	250	302	0.5	1.1
METH–AME Zion	18	85	3,025	3,654	5.8	13.7
METH–C.M.E.	1	0	150	181	0.3	0.7
METH–Un Methodist	23	1,483	3,507	4,234	6.7	15.9
METH–Wesleyan	2	122	104	158	0.2	0.6
Non-denom Chr Chs	8	781	895	1,068	1.7	4.0
PENT–Assemb of God	1	85	47	85	0.1	0.3
PENT–Ch God (Cleve)	2	172	168	203	0.3	0.8
PENT–Ch of God Proph	3	NR	116	140	0.2	0.5
PENT–Intl Pent Holiness	1	166	249	301	0.5	1.1
PRES–Presb Ch (USA)	5	128	391	472	0.7	1.8
Sev Day Adv	1	42	73	84	0.1	0.3
Un C of Christ	4	30	393	475	0.7	1.8
CHEROKEE	**75**	**4,289**	**9,429**	**12,587**	**45.9**	**100.0**
ANG/EPIS–Episcopal	1	70	175	175	0.6	1.4
Bahá'í	0	NR	2	2	0.0	0.0
BAPT–So Bapt Conv	37	2,440	6,421	7,506	27.4	59.6
Calv Chpl	1	NR	NR	NR	-	-
Catholic	2	NR	NR	1,007	3.7	8.0
CGOD–Ch God (Ander)	1	0	NR	0	0.0	0.0
CHR–Chs of Christ	2	83	74	84	0.3	0.7
Evan Free Ch	1	50	NR	50	0.2	0.4
Jehovah's Witness	1	NR	NR	NR	-	-
LDS–L-D Saints	1	NR	NR	327	1.2	2.6
LUTH–E.L.C.A.	1	57	89	104	0.4	0.8
METH–Free Methodist	1	34	26	34	0.1	0.3
METH–Un Methodist	8	550	1,478	1,806	6.6	14.3
Non-denom Chr Chs	5	405	446	506	1.8	4.0
ORTHE–Carp Rus Orth	1	8	NR	20	0.1	0.2
PENT–Assemb of God	2	121	82	209	0.8	1.7

NR–Not Reported   - Represents no adherents reported.   Percentages may not total 100 due to rounding.

Table 3: Religious Congregations by County and Group: 2010

Religious Group	Number of Congregations	Number of Attendees	Number of Communicant, Confirmed, or Full Members	Adherents: Number of Adherents	Adherents: % of Total Pop.	Adherents: % of Total Adh.
PENT–Ch God (Cleve)	4	238	232	271	1.0	2.2
PENT–Ch of God Proph	1	NR	30	35	0.1	0.3
PRES–Evan Presby Ch	1	NR	69	81	0.3	0.6
PRES–Presb Ch Amer	2	115	100	134	0.5	1.1
Sev Day Adv	2	118	205	236	0.9	1.9
CHOWAN	**35**	**2,184**	**5,508**	**7,180**	**48.5**	**100.0**
ANG/EPIS–Episcopal	2	340	775	775	5.2	10.8
Bahá'í	0	NR	6	6	0.0	0.1
BAPT–So Bapt Conv	6	928	2,428	2,928	19.8	40.8
Catholic	1	NR	NR	549	3.7	7.6
CHR–Chr Ch (Disc)	1	0	0	0	0.0	0.0
CHR–Chr Chs & Chs Cr	3	NR	200	241	1.6	3.4
CHR–Chs of Christ	1	50	75	80	0.5	1.1
Jehovah's Witness	1	NR	NR	NR	-	-
LDS–L-D Saints	1	NR	NR	233	1.6	3.2
METH–AME Zion	7	120	665	802	5.4	11.2
METH–Un Methodist	2	252	659	733	5.0	10.2
Non-denom Chr Chs	2	130	200	205	1.4	2.9
ORTHE–Orth Ch in Amer	1	9	NR	12	0.1	0.2
PENT–Assemb of God	1	77	53	77	0.5	1.1
PENT–Ch God (Cleve)	1	22	59	71	0.5	1.0
PENT–Intl Pent Holiness	4	208	324	391	2.6	5.4
PRES–Presb Ch (USA)	1	48	64	77	0.5	1.1
CLAY	**45**	**3,332**	**7,870**	**10,024**	**94.7**	**100.0**
ANG/EPIS–Episcopal	1	153	256	256	2.4	2.6
BAPT–Free Will Bapt	1	NR	73	85	0.8	0.8
BAPT–So Bapt Conv	24	2,153	6,163	7,183	67.8	71.7
Catholic	1	NR	NR	704	6.6	7.0
Ch of Nazarene	1	30	31	31	0.3	0.3
CHR–Chs of Christ	3	95	82	118	1.1	1.2
METH–Un Methodist	5	375	792	903	8.5	9.0
Non-denom Chr Chs	1	250	150	312	2.9	3.1
PENT–Assemb of God	2	70	30	90	0.9	0.9
PENT–Ch God (Cleve)	5	182	263	307	2.9	3.1
PRES–Presb Ch (USA)	1	24	30	35	0.3	0.3
CLEVELAND	**237**	**22,096**	**49,111**	**60,451**	**61.6**	**100.0**
ANG/EPIS–Episcopal	1	92	172	172	0.2	0.3
Bahá'í	0	NR	205	205	0.2	0.3
BAPT–Free Will Bapt	2	NR	228	277	0.3	0.5
BAPT–Natl Mis Bapt Conv	1	0	150	182	0.2	0.3
BAPT–NBC USA	8	1,275	2,590	3,146	3.2	5.2
BAPT–Prog NBC	1	0	150	182	0.2	0.3
BAPT–So Bapt Conv	104	12,401	30,336	36,854	37.6	61.0
BUDD–Theravada	1	NR	NR	300	0.3	0.5
Catholic	2	NR	NR	792	0.8	1.3
Ch of Nazarene	2	227	266	274	0.3	0.5
CHR–Chs of Christ	2	88	85	100	0.1	0.2
Jehovah's Witness	1	NR	NR	NR	-	-
LDS–L-D Saints	1	NR	NR	455	0.5	0.8
LUTH–E.L.C.A.	3	265	683	775	0.8	1.3
LUTH–Nor Amer Luth C	1	NR	NR	NR	-	-
METH–AME Zion	10	100	1,290	1,567	1.6	2.6
METH–C.M.E.	2	100	176	214	0.2	0.4
METH–Evan Meth Ch	1	NR	NR	NR	-	-
METH–Un Methodist	37	2,472	5,994	6,921	7.1	11.4
METH–Wesleyan	4	474	486	616	0.6	1.0
Non-denom Chr Chs	24	2,906	3,368	3,848	3.9	6.4
PENT–Assemb of God	1	50	35	50	0.1	0.1
PENT–Ch God (Cleve)	7	573	862	1,047	1.1	1.7
PENT–Fire Bapt Hol Ch	1	NR	NR	NR	-	-
PENT–Int Foursq Gos	3	306	245	298	0.3	0.5
PENT–Intl Pent Holiness	3	148	145	176	0.2	0.3
PENT–Un Pent Ch Intl	1	NR	NR	NR	-	-
PRES–As Ref Pres Ch	2	NR	178	216	0.2	0.4
PRES–Presb Ch (USA)	7	507	1,270	1,543	1.6	2.6
PRES–Presb Ch Amer	1	0	0	0	0.0	0.0
Salvation Army	1	28	52	74	0.1	0.1
Sev Day Adv	2	84	145	167	0.2	0.3
COLUMBUS	**179**	**10,835**	**26,816**	**33,660**	**57.9**	**100.0**
ANG/EPIS–Episcopal	1	37	70	70	0.1	0.2
Bahá'í	0	NR	215	215	0.4	0.6
BAPT–Free Will Bapt	2	NR	76	92	0.2	0.3
BAPT–Natl Mis Bapt Conv	3	60	410	499	0.9	1.5
BAPT–Orig Free Will Bapt	11	990	1,353	1,645	2.8	4.9
BAPT–So Bapt Conv	70	6,004	16,129	19,615	33.8	58.3
Catholic	2	NR	NR	1,063	1.8	3.2
Chr & Miss Al	1	66	33	89	0.2	0.3
CHR–Chs of Christ	1	55	60	70	0.1	0.2
Jehovah's Witness	2	NR	NR	NR	-	-
LDS–L-D Saints	2	NR	NR	350	0.6	1.0
LUTH–E.L.C.A.	1	4	8	8	0.0	0.0
METH–AME	6	0	800	973	1.7	2.9
METH–AME Zion	12	280	1,608	1,956	3.4	5.8
METH–Un Methodist	18	863	2,249	2,559	4.4	7.6
METH–Wesleyan	1	117	137	152	0.3	0.5
Non-denom Chr Chs	12	1,160	1,485	1,606	2.8	4.8
PENT–Assemb of God	2	300	276	391	0.7	1.2
PENT–Ch God (Cleve)	8	350	611	743	1.3	2.2
PENT–Ch of God Proph	1	NR	41	50	0.1	0.1
PENT–COGIC	1	0	150	182	0.3	0.5
PENT–Fire Bapt Hol Ch	1	NR	NR	NR	-	-
PENT–Full Gosp Bapt	1	NR	NR	NR	-	-
PENT–Intl Pent Holiness	3	259	517	629	1.1	1.9
PENT–Pent FW Bapt	5	NR	NR	NR	-	-
PENT–United Holy Ch	3	NR	NR	NR	-	-
PRES–Presb Ch (USA)	5	192	417	507	0.9	1.5
Sev Day Adv	4	98	171	196	0.3	0.6
CRAVEN	**185**	**15,811**	**33,515**	**49,079**	**47.4**	**100.0**
ANG/EPIS–Anglican NA	1	NR	NR	NR	-	-
ANG/EPIS–Episcopal	5	426	648	1,170	1.1	2.4
Bahá'í	0	NR	28	28	0.0	0.1
BAPT–Free Will Bapt	6	NR	684	840	0.8	1.7
BAPT–Natl Mis Bapt Conv	3	110	430	528	0.5	1.1
BAPT–Orig Free Will Bapt	15	1,350	1,844	2,264	2.2	4.6
BAPT–So Bapt Conv	19	3,982	9,352	11,480	11.1	23.4
Catholic	2	NR	NR	6,394	6.2	13.0
Ch Cr, Scientst	1	NR	NR	NR	-	-
Ch of Nazarene	1	58	43	58	0.1	0.1
CHR–Chr Ch (Disc)	16	217	777	954	0.9	1.9
CHR–Chr Chs & Chs Cr	2	NR	300	368	0.4	0.7
CHR–Chs of Christ	3	240	217	245	0.2	0.5
Jehovah's Witness	1	NR	NR	NR	-	-
JUD–Reform	1	35	62	167	0.2	0.3
LDS–L-D Saints	2	NR	NR	1,547	1.5	3.2
LUTH–E.L.C.A.	2	245	387	446	0.4	0.9
LUTH–Luth–MO Synod	1	108	150	181	0.2	0.4
LUTH–Nor Amer Luth C	1	NR	NR	NR	-	-
METH–AME	1	11	17	21	0.0	0.0
METH–AME Zion	18	310	3,191	3,917	3.8	8.0
METH–Un Methodist	19	2,690	6,626	8,237	8.0	16.8
Non-denom Chr Chs	23	3,465	4,290	4,718	4.6	9.6
PENT–Assemb of God	2	253	210	331	0.3	0.7
PENT–Ch God (Cleve)	3	564	882	1,083	1.0	2.2
PENT–Ch Lord Jesus Apos	1	NR	NR	NR	-	-
PENT–Ch of God Proph	1	NR	24	29	0.0	0.1
PENT–Full Gosp Bapt	5	NR	NR	NR	-	-
PENT–Intl Pent Holiness	11	535	824	1,011	1.0	2.1
PENT–Pent FW Bapt	1	NR	NR	NR	-	-
PENT–Un Pent Ch Intl	1	NR	NR	NR	-	-
PENT–United Holy Ch	2	NR	NR	NR	-	-
PRES–Orth Pres Ch	1	50	71	101	0.1	0.2
PRES–Presb Ch (USA)	6	647	1,490	1,829	1.8	3.7
PRES–Presb Ch Amer	1	53	84	90	0.1	0.2
Salvation Army	1	44	110	148	0.1	0.3
Sev Day Adv	4	363	631	726	0.7	1.5
Un C of Christ	1	0	85	104	0.1	0.2
Unit Univ	1	55	58	64	0.1	0.1
CUMBERLAND	**440**	**60,277**	**110,435**	**148,417**	**46.5**	**100.0**
ANG/EPIS–Anglican NA	1	NR	NR	NR	-	-

NR–Not Reported - Represents no adherents reported. Percentages may not total 100 due to rounding.

Table 3: Religious Congregations by County and Group: 2010

Religious Group	Number of Congrega-tions	Number of Attendees	Number of Communicant, Confirmed, or Full Members	Adherents: Number of Adherents	Adherents: % of Total Pop.	Adherents: % of Total Adh.
ANG/EPIS–Episcopal	6	459	1,325	1,639	0.5	1.1
Bahá'í	0	NR	105	105	0.0	0.1
BAPT–Amer Bapt USA	1	2,800	4,216	5,351	1.7	3.6
BAPT–Natl Mis Bapt Conv	4	155	380	482	0.2	0.3
BAPT–NBC USA	2	1,600	3,101	3,936	1.2	2.7
BAPT–Orig Free Will Bapt	2	180	246	312	0.1	0.2
BAPT–Prog NBC	1	300	450	571	0.2	0.4
BAPT–Ref Bapt Ch	1	NR	NR	NR	-	-
BAPT–So Bapt Conv	86	10,790	27,124	34,428	10.8	23.2
BUDD–Theravada	1	NR	NR	375	0.1	0.3
Calv Chpl	1	NR	NR	NR	-	-
Catholic	7	NR	NR	8,926	2.8	6.0
Ch of Nazarene	1	99	105	160	0.1	0.1
Chr & Miss Al	1	80	43	88	0.0	0.1
CHR–Chr Ch (Disc)	8	101	998	1,267	0.4	0.9
CHR–Chr Chs & Chs Cr	1	NR	450	571	0.2	0.4
CHR–Chs of Christ	4	640	546	806	0.3	0.5
CHR–Int Chs of Christ	1	NR	120	152	0.0	0.1
FRND–Consrv Yr Mtgs	1	NR	8	10	0.0	0.0
FRND–Fr Gen Cf	1	NR	8	10	0.0	0.0
Jehovah's Witness	8	NR	NR	NR	-	-
LDS–L-D Saints	8	NR	NR	5,277	1.7	3.6
LUTH–E.L.C.A.	1	147	277	383	0.1	0.3
LUTH–Luth Ch-Am Asc	1	NR	NR	NR	-	-
LUTH–Luth-MO Synod	1	91	169	273	0.1	0.2
LUTH–Wisc Ev Luth Syn	1	38	38	57	0.0	0.0
METH–AME	1	650	800	1,015	0.3	0.7
METH–AME Zion	23	2,160	6,107	7,752	2.4	5.2
METH–C.M.E.	1	0	150	190	0.1	0.1
METH–Free Methodist	1	20	30	30	0.0	0.0
METH–Un Methodist	28	2,912	10,452	11,722	3.7	7.9
METH–Wesleyan	1	6	58	8	0.0	0.0
Muslim Est	2	184	NR	408	0.1	0.3
New Apost Ch	1	NR	NR	NR	-	-
Non-denom Chr Chs	111	25,769	34,192	36,256	11.4	24.4
ORTHE–Greek Orthodox	1	175	NR	400	0.1	0.3
ORTHE–Orth Ch in Amer	1	30	NR	40	0.0	0.0
PENT–Assemb of God	14	1,490	1,016	2,697	0.8	1.8
PENT–Ch God (Cleve)	21	2,401	3,785	4,804	1.5	3.2
PENT–Ch Lord Jesus Apos	2	NR	NR	NR	-	-
PENT–Ch of God Proph	4	NR	472	599	0.2	0.4
PENT–COGIC	8	240	595	755	0.2	0.5
PENT–Full Gosp Bapt	2	NR	NR	NR	-	-
PENT–Intl Pent Holiness	20	3,733	6,591	8,366	2.6	5.6
PENT–Pent FW Bapt	3	NR	NR	NR	-	-
PENT–Un Pent Ch Intl	4	NR	NR	NR	-	-
PENT–United Holy Ch	2	NR	NR	NR	-	-
PRES–As Ref Pres Ch	1	NR	70	89	0.0	0.1
PRES–Bible Pres	1	NR	NR	NR	-	-
PRES–Presb Ch (USA)	26	1,919	4,995	6,340	2.0	4.3
PRES–Presb Ch Amer	3	310	170	257	0.1	0.2
Salvation Army	1	49	74	143	0.0	0.1
Sev Day Adv	3	562	977	1,123	0.4	0.8
Un C of Christ	3	187	192	244	0.1	0.2
CURRITUCK	**35**	**2,188**	**5,481**	**7,041**	**29.9**	**100.0**
ANG/EPIS–Episcopal	1	26	38	38	0.2	0.5
Bahá'í	0	NR	6	6	0.0	0.1
BAPT–NBC USA	1	0	150	182	0.8	2.6
BAPT–So Bapt Conv	10	1,278	2,802	3,403	14.5	48.3
Catholic	1	NR	NR	290	1.2	4.1
CHR–Chr Ch (Disc)	3	0	0	0	0.0	0.0
CHR–Chr Chs & Chs Cr	2	NR	325	395	1.7	5.6
CHR–Chs of Christ	1	25	25	28	0.1	0.4
METH–AME Zion	3	0	350	425	1.8	6.0
METH–Un Methodist	7	422	1,339	1,573	6.7	22.3
Non-denom Chr Chs	2	180	176	250	1.1	3.6
ORTHE–Carp Rus Orth	1	20	NR	25	0.1	0.4
PENT–Assemb of God	2	147	107	228	1.0	3.2
PENT–Intl Pent Holiness	1	90	163	198	0.8	2.8
DARE	**63**	**5,386**	**8,649**	**12,632**	**37.2**	**100.0**
ANG/EPIS–Anglican NA	1	NR	NR	NR	-	-

Religious Group	Number of Congrega-tions	Number of Attendees	Number of Communicant, Confirmed, or Full Members	Adherents: Number of Adherents	Adherents: % of Total Pop.	Adherents: % of Total Adh.
ANG/EPIS–Episcopal	2	370	757	786	2.3	6.2
Bahá'í	0	NR	5	5	0.0	0.0
BAPT–So Bapt Conv	8	762	1,015	1,199	3.5	9.5
Calv Chpl	1	NR	NR	NR	-	-
Catholic	3	NR	NR	1,747	5.2	13.8
Ch Cr, Scientst	1	NR	NR	NR	-	-
CHR–Chr Ch (Disc)	1	0	0	0	0.0	0.0
CHR–Chr Chs & Chs Cr	2	NR	115	136	0.4	1.1
Jehovah's Witness	1	NR	NR	NR	-	-
LDS–L-D Saints	1	NR	NR	390	1.1	3.1
LUTH–E.L.C.A.	1	0	0	0	0.0	0.0
LUTH–Luth-MO Synod	1	110	165	195	0.6	1.5
METH–Un Methodist	15	2,025	4,514	5,287	15.6	41.9
Non-denom Chr Chs	7	810	1,080	1,200	3.5	9.5
PENT–Assemb of God	8	913	530	1,096	3.2	8.7
PENT–Ch God (Cleve)	1	32	22	26	0.1	0.2
PENT–Ch of God Proph	2	NR	40	47	0.1	0.4
PENT–Cong Hol Ch	1	25	7	8	0.0	0.1
PENT–Int Pent C Chr	2	62	38	76	0.2	0.6
PENT–Intl Pent Holiness	1	65	34	40	0.1	0.3
PRES–Presb Ch (USA)	2	161	285	337	1.0	2.7
Unit Univ	1	51	42	57	0.2	0.5
DAVIDSON	**251**	**26,838**	**51,032**	**64,659**	**39.7**	**100.0**
ANG/EPIS–Episcopal	2	117	310	325	0.2	0.5
Bahá'í	0	NR	41	41	0.0	0.1
BAPT–Free Will Bapt	7	NR	722	884	0.5	1.4
BAPT–Natl Mis Bapt Conv	1	0	150	184	0.1	0.3
BAPT–NBC USA	2	300	500	612	0.4	0.9
BAPT–Orig Free Will Bapt	2	180	246	301	0.2	0.5
BAPT–Prog NBC	1	200	280	343	0.2	0.5
BAPT–So Bapt Conv	49	6,258	14,433	17,677	10.9	27.3
BRETH–Ch of Brethren	1	20	72	88	0.1	0.1
BUDD–Theravada	1	NR	NR	396	0.2	0.6
Catholic	2	NR	NR	1,284	0.8	2.0
Ch of Nazarene	1	40	38	40	0.0	0.1
Chr & Miss Al	2	342	292	565	0.3	0.9
CHR–Chs of Christ	5	303	284	385	0.2	0.6
Evan Assoc RCC	1	NR	NR	NR	-	-
FRND–Fr Un Mtg	1	NR	54	66	0.0	0.1
Jehovah's Witness	3	NR	NR	NR	-	-
LDS–Comm of Christ	1	NR	137	137	0.1	0.2
LUTH–E.L.C.A.	9	832	1,738	2,379	1.5	3.7
METH–AME Zion	5	0	632	774	0.5	1.2
METH–Evan Meth Ch	1	NR	NR	NR	-	-
METH–Un Methodist	59	7,104	16,529	19,949	12.2	30.9
METH–Wesleyan	9	1,485	1,229	1,931	1.2	3.0
MORAV–Morav Ch-South	1	51	67	79	0.0	0.1
Non-denom Chr Chs	36	6,120	6,578	7,786	4.8	12.0
PENT–Assemb of God	5	451	435	661	0.4	1.0
PENT–Ch God (Cleve)	5	411	613	751	0.5	1.2
PENT–Ch Lord Jesus Apos	1	NR	NR	NR	-	-
PENT–Ch of God Proph	4	NR	137	168	0.1	0.3
PENT–Cong Hol Ch	1	14	13	16	0.0	0.0
PENT–Fire Bapt Hol Ch	3	NR	NR	NR	-	-
PENT–Intl Pent Holiness	3	349	600	735	0.5	1.1
PENT–Un Pent Ch Intl	1	NR	NR	NR	-	-
PRES–Presb Ch (USA)	5	377	790	968	0.6	1.5
PRES–Presb Ch Amer	1	363	347	450	0.3	0.7
Salvation Army	1	24	75	181	0.1	0.3
Sev Day Adv	3	118	206	236	0.1	0.4
Un C of Christ	16	1,379	3,484	4,267	2.6	6.6
DAVIE	**85**	**7,981**	**16,189**	**20,376**	**49.4**	**100.0**
ANG/EPIS–Episcopal	2	49	73	77	0.2	0.4
Bahá'í	0	NR	12	12	0.0	0.1
BAPT–So Bapt Conv	19	1,851	4,738	5,769	14.0	28.3
Catholic	1	NR	NR	1,080	2.6	5.3
CHR–Chs of Christ	3	309	311	432	1.0	2.1
Jehovah's Witness	2	NR	NR	NR	-	-
LUTH–E.L.C.A.	1	31	58	62	0.2	0.3
METH–AME Zion	6	0	948	1,154	2.8	5.7
METH–C.M.E.	1	0	150	183	0.4	0.9

NR–Not Reported   - Represents no adherents reported.   Percentages may not total 100 due to rounding.

Table 3: Religious Congregations by County and Group: 2010

Religious Group	Number of Congrega-tions	Number of Attendees	Number of Communicant, Confirmed, or Full Members	Adherents		
				Number of Adherents	% of Total Pop.	% of Total Adh.
METH–Un Methodist	25	2,408	5,223	6,200	15.0	30.4
METH–Wesleyan	1	17	24	22	0.1	0.1
MORAV–Morav Ch-South	1	125	211	249	0.6	1.2
Non-denom Chr Chs	10	2,485	2,985	3,340	8.1	16.4
PENT–Assemb of God	1	20	16	46	0.1	0.2
PENT–Ch God (Cleve)	4	138	365	444	1.1	2.2
PENT–Ch of God Proph	1	NR	25	30	0.1	0.1
PENT–Intl Pent Holiness	1	227	180	219	0.5	1.1
PRES–Presb Ch (USA)	5	303	838	1,020	2.5	5.0
Sev Day Adv	1	18	32	37	0.1	0.2
DUPLIN	**147**	**6,934**	**14,397**	**18,661**	**31.9**	**100.0**
Bahá'í	0	NR	8	8	0.0	0.0
BAPT–Amer Bapt USA	1	150	307	384	0.7	2.1
BAPT–Free Will Bapt	2	NR	228	285	0.5	1.5
BAPT–Natl Mis Bapt Conv	1	225	350	438	0.7	2.3
BAPT–Orig Free Will Bapt	12	1,080	1,476	1,846	3.2	9.9
BAPT–So Bapt Conv	29	2,158	5,065	6,335	10.8	33.9
Catholic	3	NR	NR	315	0.5	1.7
Ch of Nazarene	1	22	17	22	0.0	0.1
CHR–Chr Ch (Disc)	6	0	0	0	0.0	0.0
CHR–Chs of Christ	2	40	29	34	0.1	0.2
Jehovah's Witness	1	NR	NR	NR	-	-
LDS–L-D Saints	1	NR	NR	277	0.5	1.5
METH–AME	8	0	950	1,188	2.0	6.4
METH–AME Zion	6	0	750	938	1.6	5.0
METH–Un Methodist	14	717	1,775	2,116	3.6	11.3
METH–Wesleyan	1	84	70	109	0.2	0.6
Non-denom Chr Chs	7	770	790	1,039	1.8	5.6
PENT–Assemb of God	2	132	100	228	0.4	1.2
PENT–Ch God (Cleve)	1	102	248	310	0.5	1.7
PENT–Cong Hol Ch	3	117	105	131	0.2	0.7
PENT–Intl Pent Holiness	7	557	689	862	1.5	4.6
PENT–Pent FW Bapt	12	NR	NR	NR	-	-
PENT–United Holy Ch	8	NR	NR	NR	-	-
PRES–Presb Ch (USA)	16	714	1,340	1,676	2.9	9.0
Sev Day Adv	2	40	71	81	0.1	0.4
Unit Univ	1	26	29	39	0.1	0.2
DURHAM	**306**	**43,824**	**78,192**	**112,093**	**41.9**	**100.0**
ANG/EPIS–Anglican NA	1	NR	NR	NR	-	-
ANG/EPIS–Episcopal	6	864	1,763	2,644	1.0	2.4
Bahá'í	2	NR	281	281	0.1	0.3
BAPT–Alliance Bapt	1	NR	NR	NR	-	-
BAPT–Amer Bapt USA	9	2,850	7,085	8,651	3.2	7.7
BAPT–Converge/BGC	1	75	NR	90	0.0	0.1
BAPT–Free Will Bapt	4	NR	456	557	0.2	0.5
BAPT–NBC USA	3	225	425	519	0.2	0.5
BAPT–Orig Free Will Bapt	4	360	492	601	0.2	0.5
BAPT–So Bapt Conv	62	10,418	21,246	25,941	9.7	23.1
BRETH–Ch of Brethren	1	19	50	61	0.0	0.1
BUDD–Mahayana	2	NR	NR	113	0.0	0.1
BUDD–Vajrayana	1	NR	NR	52	0.0	0.0
Catholic	4	NR	NR	10,471	3.9	9.3
CGOD–Ch God (Ander)	1	0	NR	0	0.0	0.0
Ch Cr, Scientst	1	NR	NR	NR	-	-
Ch of Nazarene	1	180	206	206	0.1	0.2
Chr & Miss Al	2	78	58	97	0.0	0.1
CHR–Chr Ch (Disc)	2	0	0	0	0.0	0.0
CHR–Chr Chs & Chs Cr	1	NR	80	98	0.0	0.1
CHR–Chs of Christ	4	775	865	1,154	0.4	1.0
Christian Brethren	2	NR	NR	NR	-	-
FRND–Consrv Yr Mtgs	1	NR	147	179	0.1	0.2
FRND–Fr Gen Cf	1	NR	147	179	0.1	0.2
HINDU–Post Ren	1	NR	NR	1,000	0.4	0.9
Jehovah's Witness	4	NR	NR	NR	-	-
JUD–Conserv	1	215	241	651	0.2	0.6
JUD–Orth	1	18	18	25	0.0	0.0
JUD–Reform	1	337	595	1,606	0.6	1.4
LDS–L-D Saints	4	NR	NR	1,761	0.7	1.6
LUTH–E.L.C.A.	4	411	924	1,188	0.4	1.1
LUTH–Luth-MO Synod	1	136	314	373	0.1	0.3
MENN–Mennonite USA	1	38	40	49	0.0	0.0
METH–AME	4	400	1,810	2,210	0.8	2.0
METH–AME Zion	4	475	965	1,178	0.4	1.1
METH–C.M.E.	2	300	500	610	0.2	0.5
METH–Un Methodist	29	2,689	8,509	10,157	3.8	9.1
METH–Wesleyan	2	1,280	646	1,664	0.6	1.5
Metro Comm Ch	1	17	31	38	0.0	0.0
MORAV–Morav Ch-South	1	166	136	219	0.1	0.2
Muslim Est	5	1,042	NR	2,004	0.7	1.8
Non-denom Chr Chs	61	14,473	19,243	21,434	8.0	19.1
ORTHE–Greek Orthodox	1	150	NR	275	0.1	0.2
ORTHE–Orth Ch in Amer	1	50	NR	100	0.0	0.1
PENT–Assemb of God	5	421	546	877	0.3	0.8
PENT–Ch God (Cleve)	2	72	328	400	0.1	0.4
PENT–Ch Lord Jesus Apos	4	NR	NR	NR	-	-
PENT–Ch of God Proph	3	NR	438	535	0.2	0.5
PENT–COGIC	3	715	1,825	2,228	0.8	2.0
PENT–Full Gosp Bapt	1	NR	NR	NR	-	-
PENT–Int Foursq Gos	1	12	9	11	0.0	0.0
PENT–Intl Pent Holiness	3	345	312	381	0.1	0.3
PENT–United Holy Ch	6	NR	NR	NR	-	-
PENT–Vineyard	1	10	10	12	0.0	0.0
PRES–As Ref Pres Ch	1	NR	12	15	0.0	0.0
PRES–Evan Presby Ch	1	NR	29	35	0.0	0.0
PRES–Presb Ch (USA)	10	1,931	3,825	4,670	1.7	4.2
PRES–Presb Ch Amer	1	707	752	1,040	0.4	0.9
PRES–Ref Pres of NA	1	53	49	85	0.0	0.1
Salvation Army	2	100	147	154	0.1	0.1
Sev Day Adv	6	577	1,004	1,154	0.4	1.0
Sikh	2	NR	NR	NR	-	-
Un C of Christ	4	450	1,064	1,299	0.5	1.2
Unit Univ	2	390	569	758	0.3	0.7
Unity Ch	1	NR	NR	NR	-	-
Zoroastrian	0	NR	NR	3	0.0	0.0
EDGECOMBE	**129**	**10,168**	**18,609**	**22,652**	**40.1**	**100.0**
ANG/EPIS–Episcopal	6	209	530	533	0.9	2.4
Bahá'í	0	NR	18	18	0.0	0.1
BAPT–Alliance Bapt	1	NR	NR	NR	-	-
BAPT–Free Will Bapt	1	NR	114	140	0.2	0.6
BAPT–Natl Mis Bapt Conv	1	0	150	184	0.3	0.8
BAPT–NBC USA	1	0	150	184	0.3	0.8
BAPT–Orig Free Will Bapt	4	360	492	604	1.1	2.7
BAPT–Prog NBC	1	300	375	460	0.8	2.0
BAPT–So Bapt Conv	17	1,669	4,804	5,896	10.4	26.0
Calv Chpl	1	NR	NR	NR	-	-
Catholic	2	NR	NR	461	0.8	2.0
CHR–Chr Ch (Disc)	5	50	236	290	0.5	1.3
CHR–Chr Chs & Chs Cr	1	NR	115	141	0.2	0.6
Jehovah's Witness	2	NR	NR	NR	-	-
MENN–Mennonite USA	1	80	133	163	0.3	0.7
METH–AME	1	135	215	264	0.5	1.2
METH–AME Zion	2	0	250	307	0.5	1.4
METH–Un Methodist	8	388	1,189	1,392	2.5	6.1
Muslim Est	1	134	NR	308	0.5	1.4
Non-denom Chr Chs	47	5,508	7,138	7,941	14.0	35.1
PENT–Assemb of God	1	175	250	250	0.4	1.1
PENT–Ch God (Cleve)	5	510	1,245	1,528	2.7	6.7
PENT–Ch Lord Jesus Apos	1	NR	NR	NR	-	-
PENT–Intl Pent Holiness	3	227	513	630	1.1	2.8
PENT–Pent Ch of God	1	70	NR	109	0.2	0.5
PENT–United Holy Ch	7	NR	NR	NR	-	-
PRES–Presb Ch (USA)	7	353	692	849	1.5	3.7
Un C of Christ	1	0	0	0	0.0	0.0
FORSYTH	**437**	**70,470**	**137,607**	**189,864**	**54.1**	**100.0**
ANG/EPIS–Anglican NA	1	NR	NR	NR	-	-
ANG/EPIS–Episcopal	6	1,241	3,773	4,577	1.3	2.4
Bahá'í	1	NR	195	195	0.1	0.1
BAPT–Alliance Bapt	1	NR	NR	NR	-	-
BAPT–Amer Bapt USA	5	2,370	4,102	5,063	1.4	2.7
BAPT–Natl Mis Bapt Conv	1	0	0	0	0.0	0.0
BAPT–NBC USA	7	1,400	3,430	4,234	1.2	2.2
BAPT–Orig Free Will Bapt	1	90	123	152	0.0	0.1

NR–Not Reported - Represents no adherents reported. Percentages may not total 100 due to rounding.

Table 3: Religious Congregations by County and Group: 2010

Religious Group	Number of Congregations	Number of Attendees	Number of Communicant, Confirmed, or Full Members	Adherents		
				Number of Adherents	% of Total Pop.	% of Total Adh.
BAPT–Prog NBC	1	125	150	185	0.1	0.1
BAPT–Ref Bapt Ch	1	NR	NR	NR	-	-
BAPT–So Bapt Conv	68	13,059	29,291	36,155	10.3	19.0
BRETH–Breth in Chr	1	NR	NR	NR	-	-
BRETH–Ch of Brethren	1	98	168	207	0.1	0.1
BUDD–Vajrayana	1	NR	NR	35	0.0	0.0
Calv Chpl	1	NR	NR	NR	-	-
Catholic	6	NR	NR	14,165	4.0	7.5
CGOD–Ch God (Ander)	1	0	NR	0	0.0	0.0
Ch of Nazarene	3	87	79	126	0.0	0.1
Chr & Miss Al	3	754	753	1,214	0.3	0.6
CHR–Chr Ch (Disc)	8	173	706	871	0.2	0.5
CHR–Chr Chs & Chs Cr	8	NR	4,946	6,105	1.7	3.2
CHR–Chs of Christ	12	1,756	1,964	2,522	0.7	1.3
FRND–Fr Gen Cf	1	NR	0	0	0.0	0.0
FRND–Fr Gen Cf & Un Mtg	1	NR	106	131	0.0	0.1
FRND–Fr Un Mtg	3	NR	200	247	0.1	0.1
HINDU–Post Ren	1	NR	NR	16	0.0	0.0
Jehovah's Witness	5	NR	NR	NR	-	-
JUD–Reform	1	147	260	702	0.2	0.4
LDS–Comm of Christ	1	NR	118	118	0.0	0.1
LDS–L-D Saints	5	NR	NR	3,042	0.9	1.6
LUTH–E.L.C.A.	5	598	1,303	1,591	0.5	0.8
LUTH–Luth-MO Synod	3	633	1,279	1,650	0.5	0.9
LUTH–Wisc Ev Luth Syn	1	60	97	131	0.0	0.1
METH–AME	2	0	300	370	0.1	0.2
METH–AME Zion	10	590	2,170	2,679	0.8	1.4
METH–C.M.E.	4	275	770	950	0.3	0.5
METH–Evan Meth Ch	1	NR	NR	NR	-	-
METH–Un Methodist	57	8,631	23,833	30,003	8.6	15.8
METH–Wesleyan	7	937	908	1,219	0.3	0.6
Metro Comm Ch	1	62	79	98	0.0	0.1
MORAV–Morav Ch-South	31	4,234	9,235	10,860	3.1	5.7
Muslim Est	3	443	NR	1,516	0.4	0.8
New Apost Ch	1	NR	NR	NR	-	-
Non-denom Chr Chs	82	23,750	33,022	35,617	10.2	18.8
ORTHE–Greek Orthodox	1	350	NR	800	0.2	0.4
ORTHE–Serb Orth USA	1	167	NR	420	0.1	0.2
PENT–Assemb of God	10	3,138	2,907	8,038	2.3	4.2
PENT–Ch God (Cleve)	10	363	640	790	0.2	0.4
PENT–Ch Lord Jesus Apos	1	NR	NR	NR	-	-
PENT–Ch of God Proph	1	NR	118	146	0.0	0.1
PENT–COGIC	1	0	150	185	0.1	0.1
PENT–Fire Bapt Hol Ch	1	NR	NR	NR	-	-
PENT–Full Gosp Bapt	1	NR	NR	NR	-	-
PENT–Intl Pent Holiness	6	475	721	890	0.3	0.5
PENT–Un Pent Ch Intl	3	NR	NR	NR	-	-
PRES–As Ref Pres Ch	2	NR	74	91	0.0	0.0
PRES–Evan Presby Ch	2	NR	1,634	2,017	0.6	1.1
PRES–Free Pres NA	1	NR	NR	NR	-	-
PRES–Presb Ch (USA)	12	1,882	4,311	5,321	1.5	2.8
PRES–Presb Ch Amer	6	1,077	858	998	0.3	0.5
Salvation Army	3	174	235	323	0.1	0.2
Sev Day Adv	4	1,018	1,769	2,035	0.6	1.1
Un C of Christ	5	174	521	643	0.2	0.3
Unit Univ	1	139	309	419	0.1	0.2
Unity Ch	1	NR	NR	NR	-	-
Zoroastrian	0	NR	NR	2	0.0	0.0
FRANKLIN	**90**	**9,232**	**19,241**	**22,975**	**37.9**	**100.0**
ANG/EPIS–Episcopal	2	50	83	101	0.2	0.4
Bahá'í	0	NR	7	7	0.0	0.0
BAPT–Amer Bapt USA	1	55	30	37	0.1	0.2
BAPT–Natl Mis Bapt Conv	3	0	450	556	0.9	2.4
BAPT–NBC USA	1	0	150	185	0.3	0.8
BAPT–So Bapt Conv	40	4,484	9,668	11,939	19.7	52.0
Catholic	1	NR	NR	521	0.9	2.3
CHR–Chr Ch (Disc)	1	0	0	0	0.0	0.0
Jehovah's Witness	2	NR	NR	NR	-	-
METH–AME Zion	1	0	150	185	0.3	0.8
METH–Un Methodist	10	469	1,504	1,733	2.9	7.5
Non-denom Chr Chs	10	3,439	5,996	6,230	10.3	27.1
PENT–Ch God (Cleve)	6	436	391	483	0.8	2.1
PENT–Ch of God Proph	2	NR	82	101	0.2	0.4
PENT–COGIC	1	150	100	123	0.2	0.5
PENT–Int Foursq Gos	1	16	15	19	0.0	0.1
PENT–Intl Pent Holiness	1	47	98	121	0.2	0.5
PENT–United Holy Ch	1	NR	NR	NR	-	-
PRES–Presb Ch (USA)	1	22	69	85	0.1	0.4
Sev Day Adv	1	29	50	58	0.1	0.3
Un C of Christ	4	35	398	491	0.8	2.1
GASTON	**393**	**40,937**	**92,462**	**117,714**	**57.1**	**100.0**
ANG/EPIS–Anglican NA	2	NR	NR	NR	-	-
ANG/EPIS–Episcopal	3	262	736	878	0.4	0.7
Bahá'í	0	NR	48	48	0.0	0.0
BAPT–Free Will Bapt	20	NR	2,128	2,607	1.3	2.2
BAPT–Natl Mis Bapt Conv	1	0	150	184	0.1	0.2
BAPT–NBC Amer	1	325	560	686	0.3	0.6
BAPT–NBC USA	6	825	1,900	2,328	1.1	2.0
BAPT–Ref Bapt Ch	1	NR	NR	NR	-	-
BAPT–So Bapt Conv	131	18,106	46,239	56,643	27.5	48.1
Catholic	3	NR	NR	4,159	2.0	3.5
Ch of Nazarene	2	50	42	76	0.0	0.1
CHR–Chr Ch (Disc)	1	0	0	0	0.0	0.0
CHR–Chr Chs & Chs Cr	1	NR	65	80	0.0	0.1
CHR–Chs of Christ	1	141	151	200	0.1	0.2
Jehovah's Witness	4	NR	NR	NR	-	-
JUD–Reform	1	42	74	200	0.1	0.2
LDS–L-D Saints	1	NR	NR	1,185	0.6	1.0
LUTH–E.L.C.A.	11	1,294	3,120	3,839	1.9	3.3
LUTH–Luth Cong Msn Chr	1	43	84	103	0.0	0.1
LUTH–Nor Amer Luth C	4	NR	NR	NR	-	-
METH–AME Zion	18	435	2,233	2,735	1.3	2.3
METH–C.M.E.	1	0	100	123	0.1	0.1
METH–Un Methodist	31	3,404	9,544	11,358	5.5	9.6
METH–Wesleyan	10	1,108	1,374	1,441	0.7	1.2
Muslim Est	1	134	NR	308	0.1	0.3
Non-denom Chr Chs	44	6,617	8,751	9,371	4.5	8.0
PENT–Assemb of God	5	640	628	1,458	0.7	1.2
PENT–Ch God (Cleve)	32	4,164	6,463	7,917	3.8	6.7
PENT–Ch Lord Jesus Apos	1	NR	NR	NR	-	-
PENT–Ch of God Proph	2	NR	60	74	0.0	0.1
PENT–Cong Hol Ch	2	69	46	56	0.0	0.0
PENT–Fire Bapt Hol Ch	6	NR	NR	NR	-	-
PENT–Int Foursq Gos	4	485	710	870	0.4	0.7
PENT–Intl Pent Holiness	4	521	772	946	0.5	0.8
PENT–Pent FW Bapt	1	NR	NR	NR	-	-
PENT–Un Pent Ch Intl	1	NR	NR	NR	-	-
PRES–As Ref Pres Ch	9	NR	1,673	2,049	1.0	1.7
PRES–Evan Presby Ch	2	NR	104	127	0.1	0.1
PRES–Orth Pres Ch	1	0	0	0	0.0	0.0
PRES–Presb Ch (USA)	15	1,607	3,671	4,497	2.2	3.8
PRES–Presb Ch Amer	3	340	538	615	0.3	0.5
Salvation Army	1	140	179	180	0.1	0.2
Sev Day Adv	3	140	242	279	0.1	0.2
Un C of Christ	1	45	77	94	0.0	0.1
GATES	**36**	**2,030**	**5,122**	**6,433**	**52.7**	**100.0**
ANG/EPIS–Episcopal	2	20	55	61	0.5	0.9
Bahá'í	0	NR	2	2	0.0	0.0
BAPT–So Bapt Conv	17	1,283	3,627	4,399	36.1	68.4
CONG–Cong Chr Add'l	1	NR	163	198	1.6	3.1
METH–AME Zion	5	120	512	621	5.1	9.7
METH–Un Methodist	6	148	413	493	4.0	7.7
Non-denom Chr Chs	2	300	350	400	3.3	6.2
PENT–Assemb of God	3	159	0	259	2.1	4.0
GRAHAM	**19**	**1,167**	**2,590**	**3,205**	**36.2**	**100.0**
ANG/EPIS–Episcopal	1	26	29	29	0.3	0.9
BAPT–So Bapt Conv	13	967	2,305	2,774	31.3	86.6
Catholic	1	NR	NR	63	0.7	2.0
LUTH–E.L.C.A.	1	26	12	12	0.1	0.4
METH–Un Methodist	1	87	183	252	2.8	7.9
Non-denom Chr Chs	1	50	50	62	0.7	1.9
PENT–Ch God (Cleve)	1	11	11	13	0.1	0.4

NR–Not Reported   - Represents no adherents reported.   Percentages may not total 100 due to rounding.

Table 3: Religious Congregations by County and Group: 2010

Religious Group	Number of Congrega-tions	Number of Attendees	Number of Communicant, Confirmed, or Full Members	Adherents: Number of Adherents	Adherents: % of Total Pop.	Adherents: % of Total Adh.
GRANVILLE	**86**	**11,427**	**20,565**	**25,179**	**42.0**	**100.0**
ANG/EPIS–Episcopal	2	139	249	249	0.4	1.0
Bahá'í	0	NR	11	11	0.0	0.0
BAPT–Amer Bapt USA	1	65	163	196	0.3	0.8
BAPT–NBC USA	1	125	250	300	0.5	1.2
BAPT–So Bapt Conv	34	3,865	10,098	12,138	20.3	48.2
Catholic	1	NR	NR	595	1.0	2.4
Jehovah's Witness	1	NR	NR	NR	-	-
METH–AME Zion	4	20	400	481	0.8	1.9
METH–Un Methodist	13	892	2,089	2,437	4.1	9.7
Non-denom Chr Chs	14	5,910	6,350	7,625	12.7	30.3
PENT–Ch God (Cleve)	3	144	345	415	0.7	1.6
PENT–Ch Lord Jesus Apos	1	NR	NR	NR	-	-
PENT–Ch of God Proph	1	NR	26	31	0.1	0.1
PENT–COGIC	1	0	150	180	0.3	0.7
PENT–United Holy Ch	1	NR	NR	NR	-	-
PRES–Presb Ch (USA)	6	192	289	347	0.6	1.4
Un C of Christ	2	75	145	174	0.3	0.7
GREENE	**52**	**2,203**	**5,010**	**5,782**	**27.1**	**100.0**
Bahá'í	0	NR	7	7	0.0	0.1
BAPT–Free Will Bapt	1	NR	114	140	0.7	2.4
BAPT–Natl Mis Bapt Conv	1	0	150	184	0.9	3.2
BAPT–Orig Free Will Bapt	8	720	983	1,203	5.6	20.8
BAPT–So Bapt Conv	2	152	366	448	2.1	7.7
CHR–Chr Ch (Disc)	5	21	174	213	1.0	3.7
Jehovah's Witness	2	NR	NR	NR	-	-
METH–AME	1	0	150	184	0.9	3.2
METH–AME Zion	7	95	680	832	3.9	14.4
METH–Un Methodist	6	302	997	1,117	5.2	19.3
Non-denom Chr Chs	6	700	1,100	1,100	5.1	19.0
PENT–Ch God (Cleve)	1	40	108	132	0.6	2.3
PENT–Intl Pent Holiness	2	126	116	142	0.7	2.5
PENT–Pent FW Bapt	2	NR	NR	NR	-	-
PENT–United Holy Ch	6	NR	NR	NR	-	-
PRES–Presb Ch (USA)	2	47	65	80	0.4	1.4
GUILFORD	**683**	**89,039**	**170,815**	**236,061**	**48.3**	**100.0**
ANG/EPIS–Anglican NA	3	NR	NR	NR	-	-
ANG/EPIS–Episcopal	10	1,490	5,112	5,704	1.2	2.4
Bahá'í	3	NR	303	303	0.1	0.1
BAPT–Alliance Bapt	1	NR	NR	NR	-	-
BAPT–Amer Bapt USA	2	200	322	393	0.1	0.2
BAPT–Free Will Bapt	4	NR	456	556	0.1	0.2
BAPT–Natl Mis Bapt Conv	1	0	150	183	0.0	0.1
BAPT–NBC Amer	1	45	80	98	0.0	0.0
BAPT–NBC USA	6	2,040	3,480	4,246	0.9	1.8
BAPT–Orig Free Will Bapt	1	90	123	150	0.0	0.1
BAPT–Prog NBC	1	400	400	488	0.1	0.2
BAPT–So Bapt Conv	113	16,101	38,585	47,080	9.6	19.9
BUDD–Mahayana	3	NR	NR	1,021	0.2	0.4
BUDD–Theravada	1	NR	NR	300	0.1	0.1
BUDD–Vajrayana	2	NR	NR	89	0.0	0.0
Calv Chpl	1	NR	NR	NR	-	-
Catholic	7	NR	NR	17,582	3.6	7.4
CGOD–Ch God (Ander)	3	310	NR	310	0.1	0.1
Ch Cr, Scientst	1	NR	NR	NR	-	-
Ch God (7th Day)	1	NR	NR	NR	-	-
Ch of Nazarene	5	264	296	334	0.1	0.1
Chr & Miss Al	7	417	231	563	0.1	0.2
CHR–Chr Ch (Disc)	8	221	1,252	1,528	0.3	0.6
CHR–Chr Chs & Chs Cr	4	NR	544	664	0.1	0.3
CHR–Chs of Christ	9	1,466	1,767	2,474	0.5	1.0
CHR–Int Chs of Christ	1	NR	100	122	0.0	0.1
Christian Brethren	1	NR	NR	NR	-	-
Evan Assoc RCC	1	NR	NR	NR	-	-
Evan Cov Ch	2	472	529	614	0.1	0.3
Evan Free Ch	1	1,000	NR	1,000	0.2	0.4
FRND–Consrv Yr Mtgs	1	NR	114	139	0.0	0.1
FRND–Evan Fr Ch Intl	2	44	44	54	0.0	0.0
FRND–Fr Gen Cf	1	NR	114	139	0.0	0.1
FRND–Fr Gen Cf & Un Mtg	1	NR	0	0	0.0	0.0
FRND–Fr Un Mtg	13	NR	1,374	1,677	0.3	0.7
HINDU–I/A Temples	1	NR	NR	238	0.0	0.1
HINDU–Post Ren	1	NR	NR	25	0.0	0.0
Jehovah's Witness	8	NR	NR	NR	-	-
JUD–Conserv	1	343	385	1,040	0.2	0.4
JUD–Orth	1	43	50	60	0.0	0.0
JUD–Reform	2	388	684	1,847	0.4	0.8
LDS–L-D Saints	8	NR	NR	4,978	1.0	2.1
LUTH–Apostolic Luth	1	NR	NR	NR	-	-
LUTH–E.L.C.A.	15	1,395	2,967	3,860	0.8	1.6
LUTH–Luth–MO Synod	5	476	724	841	0.2	0.4
MENN–Mennonite USA	1	36	22	27	0.0	0.0
METH–AME	13	450	2,475	3,020	0.6	1.3
METH–AME Zion	6	765	872	1,064	0.2	0.5
METH–C.M.E.	2	975	1,400	1,708	0.3	0.7
METH–Evan Meth Ch	4	NR	NR	NR	-	-
METH–Un Methodist	84	12,802	34,205	42,284	8.7	17.9
METH–Wesleyan	20	3,338	3,255	4,343	0.9	1.8
MORAV–Morav Ch-South	2	141	289	367	0.1	0.2
Muslim Est	5	1,072	NR	3,984	0.8	1.7
Non-denom Chr Chs	145	28,785	40,707	42,845	8.8	18.1
ORTHE–Greek Orthodox	2	185	NR	420	0.1	0.2
ORTHE–Orth Ch in Amer	1	75	NR	120	0.0	0.1
ORTHO–Ethiopian Orth	1	NR	NR	NR	-	-
PENT–Assemb of God	13	1,942	1,044	2,988	0.6	1.3
PENT–Assm God Intl F	1	NR	NR	NR	-	-
PENT–Ch God (Cleve)	13	476	860	1,049	0.2	0.4
PENT–Ch Lord Jesus Apos	1	NR	NR	NR	-	-
PENT–Ch of God Proph	6	NR	678	827	0.2	0.4
PENT–COGIC	7	2,205	4,465	5,448	1.1	2.3
PENT–Cong Hol Ch	1	39	35	43	0.0	0.0
PENT–Full Gosp Bapt	3	NR	NR	NR	-	-
PENT–Int Foursq Gos	4	163	447	545	0.1	0.2
PENT–Intl Pent Holiness	10	860	1,398	1,706	0.3	0.7
PENT–Pent FW Bapt	1	NR	NR	NR	-	-
PENT–Un Pent Ch Intl	4	NR	NR	NR	-	-
PENT–United Holy Ch	3	NR	NR	NR	-	-
PENT–Vineyard	1	125	125	153	0.0	0.1
PRES–As Ref Pres Ch	8	NR	452	552	0.1	0.2
PRES–Korean Amer Pres	1	NR	NR	NR	-	-
PRES–Korean Pres Amer	1	NR	NR	NR	-	-
PRES–Orth Pres Ch	1	77	59	70	0.0	0.0
PRES–Presb Ch (USA)	28	4,688	12,618	15,396	3.2	6.5
PRES–Presb Ch Amer	3	370	450	590	0.1	0.2
Salvation Army	2	92	240	424	0.1	0.2
Sev Day Adv	5	1,157	2,013	2,314	0.5	1.0
Un C of Christ	13	865	2,291	2,795	0.6	1.2
Unit Univ	1	151	229	279	0.1	0.1
Unity Ch	1	NR	NR	NR	-	-
HALIFAX	**133**	**8,470**	**20,842**	**25,842**	**47.3**	**100.0**
ANG/EPIS–Episcopal	6	172	309	383	0.7	1.5
Bahá'í	0	NR	7	7	0.0	0.0
BAPT–Amer Bapt USA	2	325	420	508	0.9	2.0
BAPT–Free Will Bapt	2	NR	228	276	0.5	1.1
BAPT–Natl Mis Bapt Conv	2	0	300	363	0.7	1.4
BAPT–NBC Amer	1	500	1,200	1,452	2.7	5.6
BAPT–NBC USA	4	0	1,210	1,464	2.7	5.7
BAPT–Orig Free Will Bapt	2	180	246	298	0.5	1.2
BAPT–So Bapt Conv	35	2,394	7,101	8,592	15.7	33.2
Catholic	2	NR	NR	458	0.8	1.8
CHR–Chr Chs & Chs Cr	6	NR	1,131	1,368	2.5	5.3
CHR–Chs of Christ	2	40	40	45	0.1	0.2
Jehovah's Witness	3	NR	NR	NR	-	-
LDS–L-D Saints	1	NR	NR	344	0.6	1.3
METH–AME	3	0	400	484	0.9	1.9
METH–Un Methodist	19	994	3,504	3,832	7.0	14.8
Non-denom Chr Chs	17	2,890	3,230	4,037	7.4	15.6
PENT–Assemb of God	1	53	58	60	0.1	0.2
PENT–Ch God (Cleve)	3	145	391	473	0.9	1.8
PENT–Ch Lord Jesus Apos	2	NR	NR	NR	-	-
PENT–COGIC	1	0	60	73	0.1	0.3
PENT–Intl Pent Holiness	9	551	751	909	1.7	3.5
PENT–Pent Ch of God	1	70	NR	109	0.2	0.4
PENT–Un Pent Ch Intl	1	NR	NR	NR	-	-

NR–Not Reported - Represents no adherents reported. Percentages may not total 100 due to rounding.

Table 3: Religious Congregations by County and Group: 2010

Religious Group	Number of Congrega-tions	Number of Attendees	Number of Communicant, Confirmed, or Full Members	Adherents: Number of Adherents	Adherents: % of Total Pop.	Adherents: % of Total Adh.
PENT–United Holy Ch	4	NR	NR	NR	-	-
PRES–Presb Ch (USA)	3	129	209	253	0.5	1.0
Sev Day Adv	1	27	47	54	0.1	0.2
HARNETT	**180**	**15,007**	**30,672**	**39,594**	**34.5**	**100.0**
ANG/EPIS–Episcopal	2	499	681	687	0.6	1.7
Bahá'í	0	NR	25	25	0.0	0.1
BAPT–Free Will Bapt	4	NR	456	585	0.5	1.5
BAPT–Natl Mis Bapt Conv	1	0	150	192	0.2	0.5
BAPT–NBC USA	1	0	95	122	0.1	0.3
BAPT–Orig Free Will Bapt	4	360	492	631	0.6	1.6
BAPT–So Bapt Conv	45	6,073	13,199	16,923	14.8	42.7
Catholic	1	NR	NR	895	0.8	2.3
Chr & Miss Al	1	60	46	68	0.1	0.2
CHR–Chr Ch (Disc)	3	55	98	126	0.1	0.3
CHR–Chs of Christ	1	35	32	38	0.0	0.1
FRND–Fr Un Mtg	1	NR	82	105	0.1	0.3
Jehovah's Witness	2	NR	NR	NR	-	-
LDS–L-D Saints	1	NR	NR	508	0.4	1.3
METH–AME Zion	15	295	2,175	2,789	2.4	7.0
METH–Un Methodist	16	1,481	4,105	4,386	3.8	11.1
Non-denom Chr Chs	17	3,310	3,582	4,449	3.9	11.2
PENT–Assemb of God	3	379	396	600	0.5	1.5
PENT–Ch God (Cleve)	8	454	905	1,160	1.0	2.9
PENT–Ch Lord Jesus Apos	1	NR	NR	NR	-	-
PENT–Ch of God Proph	7	NR	246	315	0.3	0.8
PENT–COGIC	2	0	300	385	0.3	1.0
PENT–Intl Pent Holiness	5	779	1,167	1,496	1.3	3.8
PENT–Pent FW Bapt	17	NR	NR	NR	-	-
PENT–Un Pent Ch Intl	1	NR	NR	NR	-	-
PENT–United Holy Ch	1	NR	NR	NR	-	-
PRES–Presb Ch (USA)	18	1,111	2,258	2,895	2.5	7.3
PRES–Presb Ch Amer	1	60	84	101	0.1	0.3
Sev Day Adv	1	56	98	113	0.1	0.3
HAYWOOD	**146**	**12,622**	**33,606**	**42,216**	**71.5**	**100.0**
ANG/EPIS–Episcopal	2	182	456	471	0.8	1.1
Bahá'í	0	NR	9	9	0.0	0.0
BAPT–Free Will Bapt	6	NR	684	802	1.4	1.9
BAPT–Ref Bapt Ch	1	NR	NR	NR	-	-
BAPT–So Bapt Conv	68	6,872	22,315	26,169	44.3	62.0
BUDD–Mahayana	1	NR	NR	11	0.0	0.0
Calv Chpl	1	NR	NR	NR	-	-
Catholic	3	NR	NR	1,248	2.1	3.0
Ch of Nazarene	1	43	60	93	0.2	0.2
CHR–Chs of Christ	1	95	100	120	0.2	0.3
Jehovah's Witness	1	NR	NR	NR	-	-
LDS–L-D Saints	1	NR	NR	400	0.7	0.9
LUTH–Luth–MO Synod	1	82	122	137	0.2	0.3
METH–AME Zion	2	45	112	131	0.2	0.3
METH–Free Methodist	1	15	15	15	0.0	0.0
METH–Un Methodist	28	2,803	6,682	8,789	14.9	20.8
METH–Wesleyan	3	132	204	172	0.3	0.4
Non-denom Chr Chs	9	1,653	1,800	2,127	3.6	5.0
PENT–Assemb of God	1	100	0	115	0.2	0.3
PENT–Ch God (Cleve)	4	171	318	373	0.6	0.9
PENT–Ch of God Proph	2	NR	73	86	0.1	0.2
PENT–Pent Ch of God	1	70	NR	109	0.2	0.3
PRES–Evan Presby Ch	1	NR	83	97	0.2	0.2
PRES–Presb Ch (USA)	2	123	179	210	0.4	0.5
PRES–Presb Ch Amer	2	99	117	122	0.2	0.3
Salvation Army	2	52	129	240	0.4	0.6
Sev Day Adv	1	85	148	170	0.3	0.4
HENDERSON	**154**	**20,297**	**40,872**	**53,081**	**49.7**	**100.0**
ANG/EPIS–Anglican NA	1	NR	NR	NR	-	-
ANG/EPIS–Episcopal	7	929	2,025	2,135	2.0	4.0
Bahá'í	1	NR	33	33	0.0	0.1
BAPT–Ref Bapt Ch	3	NR	NR	NR	-	-
BAPT–So Bapt Conv	59	9,496	21,753	25,936	24.3	48.9
BRETH–Ch of Brethren	1	93	68	81	0.1	0.2
Catholic	1	NR	NR	4,347	4.1	8.2
Ch Cr, Scientst	1	NR	NR	NR	-	-

Religious Group	Number of Congrega-tions	Number of Attendees	Number of Communicant, Confirmed, or Full Members	Adherents: Number of Adherents	Adherents: % of Total Pop.	Adherents: % of Total Adh.
Ch of God Gen Conf	1	NR	18	21	0.0	0.0
Ch of Nazarene	1	226	601	601	0.6	1.1
Chr & Miss Al	1	88	74	141	0.1	0.3
CHR–Chr Chs & Chs Cr	1	NR	75	89	0.1	0.2
CHR–Chs of Christ	1	210	225	307	0.3	0.6
Jehovah's Witness	2	NR	NR	NR	-	-
JUD–Reform	1	60	106	286	0.3	0.5
LDS–L-D Saints	1	NR	NR	762	0.7	1.4
LUTH–E.L.C.A.	1	469	877	1,016	1.0	1.9
LUTH–Luth–MO Synod	1	115	217	232	0.2	0.4
LUTH–Nor Amer Luth C	1	NR	NR	NR	-	-
METH–AME Zion	3	55	301	359	0.3	0.7
METH–Un Methodist	13	1,943	4,944	5,488	5.1	10.3
METH–Wesleyan	4	220	244	286	0.3	0.5
Metro Comm Ch	1	30	44	52	0.0	0.1
Missionary Ch	1	130	80	130	0.1	0.2
Non-denom Chr Chs	13	1,545	2,457	2,746	2.6	5.2
ORTHE–Rus Orth Abroad	1	30	NR	65	0.1	0.1
PENT–Assemb of God	2	100	25	133	0.1	0.3
PENT–Ch God (Cleve)	4	232	379	452	0.4	0.9
PENT–COGIC	1	0	150	179	0.2	0.3
PENT–Fire Bapt Hol Ch	1	NR	NR	NR	-	-
PENT–Int Foursq Gos	1	126	219	261	0.2	0.5
PENT–Intl Pent Holiness	1	464	491	585	0.5	1.1
PENT–Un Pent Ch Intl	1	NR	NR	NR	-	-
PRES–As Ref Pres Ch	3	NR	402	479	0.4	0.9
PRES–Orth Pres Ch	1	15	12	12	0.0	0.0
PRES–Presb Ch (USA)	6	894	1,666	1,986	1.9	3.7
PRES–Presb Ch Amer	2	1,446	1,004	1,019	1.0	1.9
Salvation Army	1	69	86	178	0.2	0.3
Sev Day Adv	5	1,074	1,867	2,147	2.0	4.0
Un C of Christ	1	113	224	267	0.3	0.5
Unit Univ	1	125	205	270	0.3	0.5
Unity Ch	1	NR	NR	NR	-	-
HERTFORD	**49**	**2,587**	**7,238**	**8,851**	**35.9**	**100.0**
ANG/EPIS–Episcopal	1	43	140	148	0.6	1.7
BAPT–Free Will Bapt	2	NR	228	272	1.1	3.1
BAPT–Natl Mis Bapt Conv	1	0	150	179	0.7	2.0
BAPT–NBC USA	1	0	150	179	0.7	2.0
BAPT–Orig Free Will Bapt	1	90	123	147	0.6	1.7
BAPT–So Bapt Conv	21	1,307	4,389	5,230	21.2	59.1
Catholic	1	NR	NR	125	0.5	1.4
CHR–Chr Chs & Chs Cr	1	NR	15	18	0.1	0.2
Jehovah's Witness	1	NR	NR	NR	-	-
LDS–L-D Saints	1	NR	NR	126	0.5	1.4
METH–AME Zion	1	0	100	119	0.5	1.3
METH–Un Methodist	4	128	665	743	3.0	8.4
Non-denom Chr Chs	6	360	485	515	2.1	5.8
PENT–Assemb of God	3	520	518	729	3.0	8.2
PENT–Ch God (Cleve)	1	43	38	45	0.2	0.5
PENT–COGIC	1	0	75	89	0.4	1.0
PRES–Presb Ch (USA)	1	26	39	46	0.2	0.5
Sev Day Adv	1	70	123	141	0.6	1.6
HOKE	**52**	**3,853**	**7,869**	**10,781**	**23.0**	**100.0**
Bahá'í	0	NR	3	3	0.0	0.0
BAPT–Natl Mis Bapt Conv	1	0	150	199	0.4	1.8
BAPT–So Bapt Conv	10	1,117	2,777	3,690	7.9	34.2
Catholic	1	NR	NR	729	1.6	6.8
Jehovah's Witness	1	NR	NR	NR	-	-
METH–AME Zion	4	375	775	1,030	2.2	9.6
METH–Evan Meth Ch	1	NR	NR	NR	-	-
METH–Un Methodist	6	326	849	1,046	2.2	9.7
Muslim Est	1	134	NR	308	0.7	2.9
Non-denom Chr Chs	8	1,240	2,160	2,160	4.6	20.0
PENT–Assemb of God	3	112	90	209	0.4	1.9
PENT–Ch God (Cleve)	4	133	207	275	0.6	2.6
PENT–Ch of God Proph	1	NR	29	39	0.1	0.4
PENT–Intl Pent Holiness	3	135	155	206	0.4	1.9
PENT–Un Pent Ch Intl	1	NR	NR	NR	-	-
PRES–Presb Ch (USA)	6	253	626	832	1.8	7.7
Sev Day Adv	1	28	48	55	0.1	0.5

NR–Not Reported   - Represents no adherents reported.   Percentages may not total 100 due to rounding.

Table 3: Religious Congregations by County and Group: 2010

Religious Group	Number of Congrega-tions	Number of Attendees	Number of Communicant, Confirmed, or Full Members	Adherents		
				Number of Adherents	% of Total Pop.	% of Total Adh.
HYDE	**27**	**388**	**781**	**1,071**	**18.4**	**100.0**
ANG/EPIS–Episcopal	1	28	106	136	2.3	12.7
Bahá'í	0	NR	1	1	0.0	0.1
BAPT–So Bapt Conv	4	20	30	35	0.6	3.3
CHR–Chr Ch (Disc)	7	0	0	0	0.0	0.0
CHR–Chr Chs & Chs Cr	5	NR	125	145	2.5	13.5
CHR–Chs of Christ	1	30	20	35	0.6	3.3
METH–Un Methodist	5	181	397	555	9.6	51.8
PENT–Assemb of God	2	61	36	88	1.5	8.2
PENT–Intl Pent Holiness	1	43	27	31	0.5	2.9
PRES–Presb Ch (USA)	1	25	39	45	0.8	4.2
IREDELL	**263**	**27,546**	**56,736**	**81,136**	**50.9**	**100.0**
ANG/EPIS–Episcopal	3	293	575	612	0.4	0.8
Bahá'í	0	NR	32	32	0.0	0.0
BAPT–Alliance Bapt	1	NR	NR	NR	-	-
BAPT–Free Will Bapt	1	NR	114	141	0.1	0.2
BAPT–Natl Mis Bapt Conv	1	0	150	186	0.1	0.2
BAPT–NBC USA	2	225	695	862	0.5	1.1
BAPT–So Bapt Conv	60	8,605	22,142	27,466	17.2	33.9
Catholic	2	NR	NR	8,734	5.5	10.8
CGOD–Ch God (Ander)	1	275	NR	275	0.2	0.3
Ch of Nazarene	2	232	188	245	0.2	0.3
Chr & Miss Al	2	152	193	266	0.2	0.3
CHR–Chr Chs & Chs Cr	1	NR	37	46	0.0	0.1
CHR–Chs of Christ	5	760	833	1,224	0.8	1.5
FRND–Fr Un Mtg	2	NR	87	108	0.1	0.1
HINDU–Post Ren	1	NR	NR	10	0.0	0.0
Jehovah's Witness	2	NR	NR	NR	-	-
JUD–Conserv	1	53	60	162	0.1	0.2
LDS–L-D Saints	3	NR	NR	1,840	1.2	2.3
LUTH–E.L.C.A.	3	391	902	1,155	0.7	1.4
LUTH–Luth Cong Msn Chr	1	75	80	99	0.1	0.1
LUTH–Luth–MO Synod	1	92	112	125	0.1	0.2
LUTH–Nor Amer Luth C	4	NR	NR	NR	-	-
MENN–Amish Undif	1	NR	57	110	0.1	0.1
METH–AME Zion	14	296	1,775	2,202	1.4	2.7
METH–Evan Meth Ch	1	NR	NR	NR	-	-
METH–Un Methodist	45	5,337	12,113	15,489	9.7	19.1
METH–Wesleyan	5	227	305	296	0.2	0.4
Muslim Est	1	134	NR	308	0.2	0.4
Non-denom Chr Chs	31	6,965	9,080	9,711	6.1	12.0
ORTHE–Greek Orthodox	1	90	NR	360	0.2	0.4
PENT–Assemb of God	7	411	385	598	0.4	0.7
PENT–Ch God (Cleve)	9	866	1,391	1,725	1.1	2.1
PENT–Ch Lord Jesus Apos	1	NR	NR	NR	-	-
PENT–Ch of God Proph	1	NR	26	32	0.0	0.0
PENT–Fire Bapt Hol Ch	1	NR	NR	NR	-	-
PENT–Int Foursq Gos	3	350	305	378	0.2	0.5
PENT–Intl Pent Holiness	1	14	35	43	0.0	0.1
PENT–Un Pent Ch Intl	2	NR	NR	NR	-	-
PRES–As Ref Pres Ch	11	NR	1,151	1,428	0.9	1.8
PRES–Presb Ch (USA)	20	1,308	3,132	3,885	2.4	4.8
PRES–Presb Ch Amer	3	184	276	338	0.2	0.4
Salvation Army	1	36	71	118	0.1	0.1
Sev Day Adv	1	70	121	139	0.1	0.2
Un C of Christ	4	105	313	388	0.2	0.5
JACKSON	**100**	**6,625**	**14,315**	**18,563**	**46.1**	**100.0**
ANG/EPIS–Anglican NA	1	NR	NR	NR	-	-
ANG/EPIS–Episcopal	3	257	773	792	2.0	4.3
Bahá'í	0	NR	13	13	0.0	0.1
BAPT–So Bapt Conv	51	3,354	9,688	11,250	27.9	60.6
Catholic	1	NR	NR	413	1.0	2.2
Chr & Miss Al	2	138	47	197	0.5	1.1
CHR–Chs of Christ	2	185	174	244	0.6	1.3
Jehovah's Witness	2	NR	NR	NR	-	-
LDS–L-D Saints	1	NR	NR	536	1.3	2.9
LUTH–E.L.C.A.	1	40	77	83	0.2	0.4
METH–AME Zion	1	0	100	116	0.3	0.6
METH–Un Methodist	11	979	1,790	2,701	6.7	14.6
METH–Wesleyan	3	92	79	119	0.3	0.6
Non-denom Chr Chs	8	1,015	945	1,331	3.3	7.2

Religious Group	Number of Congrega-tions	Number of Attendees	Number of Communicant, Confirmed, or Full Members	Adherents		
				Number of Adherents	% of Total Pop.	% of Total Adh.
PENT–Assemb of God	2	43	15	58	0.1	0.3
PENT–Ch God (Cleve)	6	276	336	390	1.0	2.1
PRES–Presb Ch (USA)	3	168	214	249	0.6	1.3
PRES–Presb Ch Amer	1	50	15	15	0.0	0.1
Sev Day Adv	1	28	49	56	0.1	0.3
JOHNSTON	**259**	**24,970**	**43,960**	**61,554**	**36.4**	**100.0**
ANG/EPIS–Episcopal	3	190	434	524	0.3	0.9
Bahá'í	0	NR	45	45	0.0	0.1
BAPT–Free Will Bapt	5	NR	570	730	0.4	1.2
BAPT–Natl Mis Bapt Conv	1	150	100	128	0.1	0.2
BAPT–Orig Free Will Bapt	25	2,250	3,074	3,938	2.3	6.4
BAPT–So Bapt Conv	53	7,325	15,426	19,761	11.7	32.1
Calv Chpl	1	NR	NR	NR	-	-
Catholic	1	NR	NR	4,263	2.5	6.9
CGOD–Ch God (Ander)	1	0	NR	0	0.0	0.0
CHR–Chr Ch (Disc)	20	366	1,348	1,727	1.0	2.8
CHR–Chs of Christ	2	105	122	133	0.1	0.2
CONG–Cong Chr, NA	1	NR	367	470	0.3	0.8
HINDU–Post Ren	1	NR	NR	54	0.0	0.1
Jehovah's Witness	2	NR	NR	NR	-	-
LDS–L-D Saints	3	NR	NR	993	0.6	1.6
LUTH–Luth–MO Synod	1	340	520	722	0.4	1.2
METH–AME	11	102	1,150	1,473	0.9	2.4
METH–AME Zion	3	0	350	448	0.3	0.7
METH–Un Methodist	21	2,121	5,621	8,253	4.9	13.4
Non-denom Chr Chs	21	6,627	8,019	8,754	5.2	14.2
PENT–Assemb of God	7	608	291	705	0.4	1.1
PENT–Ch God (Cleve)	12	978	1,400	1,793	1.1	2.9
PENT–Ch of God Proph	10	NR	470	602	0.4	1.0
PENT–Intl Pent Holiness	18	2,804	2,876	3,684	2.2	6.0
PENT–Pent FW Bapt	11	NR	NR	NR	-	-
PENT–United Holy Ch	5	NR	NR	NR	-	-
PRES–As Ref Pres Ch	1	NR	70	90	0.1	0.1
PRES–Presb Ch (USA)	13	711	1,299	1,664	1.0	2.7
PRES–Presb Ch Amer	1	91	73	97	0.1	0.2
Salvation Army	1	31	55	166	0.1	0.3
Sev Day Adv	3	96	166	191	0.1	0.3
Un C of Christ	1	75	114	146	0.1	0.2
JONES	**36**	**1,258**	**3,239**	**3,874**	**38.2**	**100.0**
ANG/EPIS–Episcopal	1	9	10	12	0.1	0.3
BAPT–Free Will Bapt	1	NR	114	137	1.3	3.5
BAPT–Natl Mis Bapt Conv	2	15	170	204	2.0	5.3
BAPT–Orig Free Will Bapt	2	180	246	295	2.9	7.6
BAPT–So Bapt Conv	4	221	538	646	6.4	16.7
CHR–Chr Ch (Disc)	2	0	85	102	1.0	2.6
METH–AME Zion	6	15	685	823	8.1	21.2
METH–Un Methodist	6	197	431	562	5.5	14.5
Non-denom Chr Chs	6	556	681	758	7.5	19.6
PENT–COGIC	1	0	150	180	1.8	4.6
PENT–Pent FW Bapt	2	NR	NR	NR	-	-
PENT–United Holy Ch	2	NR	NR	NR	-	-
PRES–Presb Ch (USA)	1	65	129	155	1.5	4.0
LEE	**126**	**10,502**	**21,198**	**30,170**	**52.1**	**100.0**
ANG/EPIS–Episcopal	1	126	377	377	0.7	1.2
Bahá'í	0	NR	7	7	0.0	0.0
BAPT–Free Will Bapt	1	NR	114	143	0.2	0.5
BAPT–So Bapt Conv	21	2,516	6,109	7,645	13.2	25.3
Catholic	1	NR	NR	3,402	5.9	11.3
CHR–Chr Ch (Disc)	1	65	213	267	0.5	0.9
CHR–Chr Chs & Chs Cr	1	NR	11	14	0.0	0.0
CHR–Chs of Christ	2	80	64	80	0.1	0.3
Jehovah's Witness	1	NR	NR	NR	-	-
LDS–L-D Saints	2	NR	NR	1,169	2.0	3.9
LUTH–E.L.C.A.	1	99	233	263	0.5	0.9
METH–AME	2	90	165	206	0.4	0.7
METH–AME Zion	14	355	1,876	2,348	4.1	7.8
METH–Un Methodist	10	1,014	3,510	4,160	7.2	13.8
METH–Wesleyan	1	60	62	78	0.1	0.3
Non-denom Chr Chs	28	3,975	4,875	5,438	9.4	18.0
PENT–Assemb of God	3	337	198	351	0.6	1.2

NR–Not Reported   - Represents no adherents reported.   Percentages may not total 100 due to rounding.

Table 3: Religious Congregations by County and Group: 2010

Religious Group	Number of Congrega-tions	Number of Attendees	Number of Communicant, Confirmed, or Full Members	Adherents: Number of Adherents	Adherents: % of Total Pop.	Adherents: % of Total Adh.
PENT–Ch God (Cleve)	2	383	378	473	0.8	1.6
PENT–Ch of God Proph	2	NR	83	104	0.2	0.3
PENT–Intl Pent Holiness	4	220	400	501	0.9	1.7
PENT–Pent FW Bapt	3	NR	NR	NR	-	-
PENT–Un Pent Ch Intl	2	NR	NR	NR	-	-
PENT–United Holy Ch	2	NR	NR	NR	-	-
PRES–Presb Ch (USA)	14	874	1,862	2,330	4.0	7.7
Salvation Army	1	14	16	16	0.0	0.1
Sev Day Adv	2	51	89	102	0.2	0.3
Un C of Christ	4	243	556	696	1.2	2.3
LENOIR	**183**	**11,388**	**25,271**	**33,394**	**56.1**	**100.0**
ANG/EPIS–Episcopal	3	220	468	602	1.0	1.8
Bahá'í	0	NR	107	107	0.2	0.3
BAPT–Free Will Bapt	7	NR	798	975	1.6	2.9
BAPT–Natl Mis Bapt Conv	2	125	425	520	0.9	1.6
BAPT–Orig Free Will Bapt	13	1,170	1,599	1,955	3.3	5.9
BAPT–So Bapt Conv	18	1,478	4,192	5,124	8.6	15.3
BUDD–Mahayana	1	NR	NR	1,247	2.1	3.7
Catholic	1	NR	NR	464	0.8	1.4
Ch Cr, Scientst	1	NR	NR	NR	-	-
CHR–Chr Ch (Disc)	23	814	2,430	2,970	5.0	8.9
CHR–Chs of Christ	2	40	42	51	0.1	0.2
Jehovah's Witness	1	NR	NR	NR	-	-
JUD–Reform	1	9	15	40	0.1	0.1
LDS–L-D Saints	3	NR	NR	1,473	2.5	4.4
LUTH–E.L.C.A.	1	21	41	41	0.1	0.1
LUTH–Luth–MO Synod	1	61	113	121	0.2	0.4
METH–AME	1	200	400	489	0.8	1.5
METH–AME Zion	9	0	971	1,187	2.0	3.6
METH–Un Methodist	14	971	2,554	3,019	5.1	9.0
Muslim Est	1	134	NR	308	0.5	0.9
Non-denom Chr Chs	37	3,976	7,272	7,595	12.8	22.7
PENT–Assemb of God	3	131	82	171	0.3	0.5
PENT–Ch God (Cleve)	5	797	1,412	1,726	2.9	5.2
PENT–Ch of God Proph	1	NR	28	34	0.1	0.1
PENT–Cong Hol Ch	1	39	35	43	0.1	0.1
PENT–Intl Pent Holiness	5	630	1,275	1,559	2.6	4.7
PENT–Pent FW Bapt	7	NR	NR	NR	-	-
PENT–Un Pent Ch Intl	1	NR	NR	NR	-	-
PENT–United Holy Ch	8	NR	NR	NR	-	-
PRES–Presb Ch (USA)	7	327	584	714	1.2	2.1
Salvation Army	1	55	86	464	0.8	1.4
Sev Day Adv	3	190	330	380	0.6	1.1
Un C of Christ	1	0	12	15	0.0	0.0
LINCOLN	**160**	**15,296**	**32,809**	**42,506**	**54.3**	**100.0**
ANG/EPIS–Episcopal	3	275	531	722	0.9	1.7
Bahá'í	0	NR	3	3	0.0	0.0
BAPT–Free Will Bapt	2	NR	228	278	0.4	0.7
BAPT–Natl Mis Bapt Conv	1	0	150	183	0.2	0.4
BAPT–NBC USA	1	0	100	122	0.2	0.3
BAPT–So Bapt Conv	55	7,101	16,160	19,694	25.2	46.3
Catholic	2	NR	NR	2,203	2.8	5.2
CHR–Chr Ch (Disc)	1	0	80	97	0.1	0.2
CHR–Chs of Christ	1	30	30	38	0.0	0.1
Jehovah's Witness	1	NR	NR	NR	-	-
LDS–L-D Saints	1	NR	NR	650	0.8	1.5
LUTH–E.L.C.A.	9	909	2,271	2,676	3.4	6.3
LUTH–Luth–MO Synod	1	123	174	218	0.3	0.5
LUTH–Nor Amer Luth C	1	NR	NR	NR	-	-
METH–AME Zion	5	15	570	695	0.9	1.6
METH–Evan Meth Ch	1	NR	NR	NR	-	-
METH–Un Methodist	35	3,431	8,037	9,520	12.2	22.4
METH–Wesleyan	5	584	497	760	1.0	1.8
Non-denom Chr Chs	10	1,271	1,633	1,788	2.3	4.2
PENT–Assemb of God	1	24	8	24	0.0	0.1
PENT–Ch God (Cleve)	7	677	845	1,030	1.3	2.4
PENT–Ch of God Proph	1	NR	30	37	0.0	0.1
PENT–Fire Bapt Hol Ch	1	NR	NR	NR	-	-
PENT–Int Foursq Gos	2	46	79	96	0.1	0.2
PENT–Intl Pent Holiness	2	137	202	246	0.3	0.6
PENT–Un Pent Ch Intl	1	NR	NR	NR	-	-

Religious Group	Number of Congrega-tions	Number of Attendees	Number of Communicant, Confirmed, or Full Members	Adherents: Number of Adherents	Adherents: % of Total Pop.	Adherents: % of Total Adh.
PRES–As Ref Pres Ch	1	NR	41	50	0.1	0.1
PRES–Presb Ch (USA)	3	412	784	955	1.2	2.2
PRES–Presb Ch Amer	2	150	135	158	0.2	0.4
Sev Day Adv	2	51	89	102	0.1	0.2
Un C of Christ	2	60	132	161	0.2	0.4
MCDOWELL	**107**	**7,413**	**15,363**	**19,173**	**42.6**	**100.0**
ANG/EPIS–Episcopal	1	72	116	116	0.3	0.6
Bahá'í	0	NR	28	28	0.1	0.1
BAPT–Free Will Bapt	11	NR	1,254	1,507	3.3	7.9
BAPT–So Bapt Conv	36	3,926	8,740	10,502	23.3	54.8
Catholic	1	NR	NR	267	0.6	1.4
Chr & Miss Al	1	105	78	189	0.4	1.0
CHR–Chr Chs & Chs Cr	2	NR	110	132	0.3	0.7
CHR–Chs of Christ	3	114	109	140	0.3	0.7
Jehovah's Witness	1	NR	NR	NR	-	-
LDS–L-D Saints	1	NR	NR	398	0.9	2.1
LUTH–Luth–MO Synod	1	19	42	44	0.1	0.2
METH–AME	1	0	150	180	0.4	0.9
METH–AME Zion	2	0	200	240	0.5	1.3
METH–Un Methodist	17	995	1,770	2,077	4.6	10.8
METH–Wesleyan	2	133	149	173	0.4	0.9
Non-denom Chr Chs	6	1,130	1,300	1,500	3.3	7.8
PENT–Assemb of God	1	80	32	144	0.3	0.8
PENT–Ch God (Cleve)	6	386	551	662	1.5	3.5
PENT–Ch God Mtn Asm	1	NR	NR	NR	-	-
PENT–Ch of God Proph	1	NR	11	13	0.0	0.1
PENT–Intl Pent Holiness	4	130	222	267	0.6	1.4
PRES–Presb Ch (USA)	5	95	177	213	0.5	1.1
PRES–Presb Ch Amer	2	181	242	287	0.6	1.5
Sev Day Adv	1	47	82	94	0.2	0.5
MACON	**107**	**8,006**	**17,041**	**22,713**	**67.0**	**100.0**
ANG/EPIS–Episcopal	4	342	375	561	1.7	2.5
Bahá'í	0	NR	5	5	0.0	0.0
BAPT–So Bapt Conv	47	3,833	10,851	12,726	37.5	56.0
Catholic	2	NR	NR	1,205	3.6	5.3
Ch Cr, Scientst	1	NR	NR	NR	-	-
Ch of Nazarene	1	23	26	27	0.1	0.1
Chr & Miss Al	1	281	228	502	1.5	2.2
CHR–Chr Chs & Chs Cr	1	NR	0	0	0.0	0.0
CHR–Chs of Christ	2	115	92	123	0.4	0.5
Jehovah's Witness	1	NR	NR	NR	-	-
LDS–Comm of Christ	1	NR	118	118	0.3	0.5
LDS–L-D Saints	1	NR	NR	313	0.9	1.4
LUTH–E.L.C.A.	1	18	35	37	0.1	0.2
LUTH–Luth Ch-Am Asc	1	NR	NR	NR	-	-
LUTH–Luth–MO Synod	1	95	135	144	0.4	0.6
METH–Un Methodist	16	1,201	2,550	3,395	10.0	14.9
Non-denom Chr Chs	5	570	885	910	2.7	4.0
PENT–Assemb of God	6	413	212	858	2.5	3.8
PENT–Ch God (Cleve)	6	606	697	817	2.4	3.6
PENT–Un Pent Ch Intl	1	NR	NR	NR	-	-
PRES–Evan Presby Ch	2	NR	155	182	0.5	0.8
PRES–Presb Ch (USA)	3	349	439	515	1.5	2.3
PRES–Presb Ch Amer	1	30	26	34	0.1	0.1
Sev Day Adv	1	82	142	163	0.5	0.7
Unit Univ	1	48	70	78	0.2	0.3
MADISON	**83**	**3,811**	**10,493**	**12,917**	**62.2**	**100.0**
ANG/EPIS–Episcopal	1	89	146	146	0.7	1.1
Bahá'í	0	NR	2	2	0.0	0.0
BAPT–Alliance Bapt	1	NR	NR	NR	-	-
BAPT–Free Will Bapt	3	NR	306	361	1.7	2.8
BAPT–So Bapt Conv	59	3,095	9,148	10,782	51.9	83.5
Catholic	1	NR	NR	269	1.3	2.1
CGOD–Ch God (Ander)	7	150	NR	150	0.7	1.2
METH–Un Methodist	4	146	338	553	2.7	4.3
Non-denom Chr Chs	1	40	50	50	0.2	0.4
PENT–Ch God (Cleve)	2	133	266	314	1.5	2.4
PRES–Presb Ch (USA)	3	85	154	182	0.9	1.4
Salvation Army	1	73	83	108	0.5	0.8

NR–Not Reported - Represents no adherents reported. Percentages may not total 100 due to rounding.

Table 3: Religious Congregations by County and Group: 2010

Religious Group	Number of Congrega-tions	Number of Attendees	Number of Communicant, Confirmed, or Full Members	Adherents: Number of Adherents	Adherents: % of Total Pop.	Adherents: % of Total Adh.
MARTIN	**80**	**3,432**	**9,968**	**12,240**	**49.9**	**100.0**
ANG/EPIS–Episcopal	1	44	119	146	0.6	1.2
Bahá'í	0	NR	22	22	0.1	0.2
BAPT–Free Will Bapt	1	NR	114	137	0.6	1.1
BAPT–Natl Mis Bapt Conv	1	100	200	240	1.0	2.0
BAPT–Orig Free Will Bapt	2	180	246	295	1.2	2.4
BAPT–So Bapt Conv	11	1,066	2,829	3,398	13.9	27.8
Catholic	1	NR	NR	381	1.6	3.1
CHR–Chr Ch (Disc)	17	232	1,256	1,509	6.2	12.3
CHR–Chr Chs & Chs Cr	12	NR	1,914	2,299	9.4	18.8
CHR–Chs of Christ	1	29	20	20	0.1	0.2
METH–AME Zion	3	35	255	306	1.2	2.5
METH–Un Methodist	6	180	504	581	2.4	4.7
Non-denom Chr Chs	5	725	1,010	1,081	4.4	8.8
PENT–Assemb of God	1	49	0	49	0.2	0.4
PENT–Ch God (Cleve)	1	73	79	95	0.4	0.8
PENT–COGIC	2	100	350	420	1.7	3.4
PENT–Full Gosp Bapt	1	NR	NR	NR	-	-
PENT–Intl Pent Holiness	8	551	892	1,071	4.4	8.8
PENT–Pent FW Bapt	1	NR	NR	NR	-	-
PENT–Un Pent Ch Intl	1	NR	NR	NR	-	-
PENT–United Holy Ch	1	NR	NR	NR	-	-
PRES–Presb Ch (USA)	3	68	158	190	0.8	1.6
MECKLENBURG	**847**	**161,804**	**297,187**	**477,366**	**51.9**	**100.0**
ANG/EPIS–Anglican NA	7	NR	NR	NR	-	-
ANG/EPIS–Episcopal	11	2,671	9,481	11,020	1.2	2.3
Bahá'í	3	NR	819	819	0.1	0.2
BAPT–Alliance Bapt	6	NR	NR	NR	-	-
BAPT–Amer Bapt USA	9	8,233	16,577	20,752	2.3	4.3
BAPT–Converge/BGC	1	2,000	NR	2,400	0.3	0.5
BAPT–Free Will Bapt	1	NR	114	143	0.0	0.0
BAPT–N Am Bapt Conf	1	NR	70	88	0.0	0.0
BAPT–Natl Mis Bapt Conv	2	45	206	258	0.0	0.1
BAPT–NBC USA	12	4,855	8,951	11,205	1.2	2.3
BAPT–So Bapt Conv	161	23,376	66,363	83,078	9.0	17.4
BUDD–Mahayana	5	NR	NR	1,190	0.1	0.2
BUDD–Theravada	2	NR	NR	696	0.1	0.1
Calv Chpl	2	NR	NR	NR	-	-
Catholic	15	NR	NR	78,021	8.5	16.3
CGOD–Ch God (Ander)	4	322	NR	322	0.0	0.1
Ch Cr, Scientst	2	NR	NR	NR	-	-
Ch of Nazarene	8	919	1,377	1,686	0.2	0.4
Chr & Miss Al	7	657	653	976	0.1	0.2
CHR–Chr Ch (Disc)	4	120	442	553	0.1	0.1
CHR–Chr Chs & Chs Cr	3	NR	195	244	0.0	0.1
CHR–Chs of Christ	11	2,245	2,382	3,202	0.3	0.7
Christian Brethren	1	NR	NR	NR	-	-
Evan Free Ch	1	1,410	NR	1,410	0.2	0.3
FRND–Consrv Yr Mtgs	1	NR	17	21	0.0	0.0
FRND–Fr Gen Cf	2	NR	102	128	0.0	0.0
HINDU–I/A Temples	1	NR	NR	129	0.0	0.0
HINDU–Post Ren	4	NR	NR	105	0.0	0.0
HINDU–Trad Temples	1	NR	NR	1,033	0.1	0.2
Jain	2	NR	NR	NR	-	-
Jehovah's Witness	10	NR	NR	NR	-	-
JUD–Conserv	1	629	706	1,906	0.2	0.4
JUD–Orth	2	86	100	120	0.0	0.0
JUD–Reconst	1	24	31	84	0.0	0.0
JUD–Reform	2	652	1,150	3,105	0.3	0.7
LDS–Comm of Christ	1	NR	118	118	0.0	0.0
LDS–L-D Saints	12	NR	NR	7,600	0.8	1.6
LUTH–E.L.C.A.	15	3,484	5,664	8,031	0.9	1.7
LUTH–Luth Cong Msn Chr	3	458	906	1,134	0.1	0.2
LUTH–Luth–MO Synod	8	1,001	1,820	2,608	0.3	0.5
LUTH–Wisc Ev Luth Syn	1	84	148	202	0.0	0.0
METH–AME	7	500	1,468	1,838	0.2	0.4
METH–AME Zion	36	3,045	7,723	9,668	1.1	2.0
METH–C.M.E.	4	270	1,240	1,552	0.2	0.3
METH–Un Methodist	61	16,362	41,499	58,637	6.4	12.3
METH–Wesleyan	2	192	275	249	0.0	0.1
Metro Comm Ch	2	133	158	198	0.0	0.0
Missionary Ch	1	95	45	95	0.0	0.0
MJEW–Assoc Mes Cong	1	NR	NR	NR	-	-
MORAV–Morav Ch-South	3	312	527	646	0.1	0.1
Muslim Est	10	1,356	NR	2,972	0.3	0.6
New Apost Ch	1	NR	NR	NR	-	-
Non-denom Chr Chs	136	50,126	64,715	71,033	7.7	14.9
ORTHE–Greek Orthodox	2	1,050	NR	7,500	0.8	1.6
ORTHE–Orth Ch in Amer	1	120	NR	150	0.0	0.0
ORTHE–Rus Orth Abroad	1	35	NR	100	0.0	0.0
ORTHE–Serb Orth USA	1	45	NR	180	0.0	0.0
ORTHO–Armen Ap Etchm	1	65	NR	300	0.0	0.1
ORTHO–Coptic Orth Ch	1	125	NR	240	0.0	0.1
ORTHO–Eritrean Orth	2	55	NR	200	0.0	0.0
ORTHO–Ethiopian Orth	2	NR	NR	NR	-	-
ORTHO–Malan Syr Orth	1	30	NR	54	0.0	0.0
PENT–Assemb of God	17	1,566	1,140	1,906	0.2	0.4
PENT–Ch God (Cleve)	32	8,581	11,934	14,940	1.6	3.1
PENT–Ch Lord Jesus Apos	1	NR	NR	NR	-	-
PENT–Ch of God Proph	3	NR	262	328	0.0	0.1
PENT–COGIC	7	960	1,670	2,091	0.2	0.4
PENT–Fire Bapt Hol Ch	4	NR	NR	NR	-	-
PENT–Full Gosp Bapt	4	NR	NR	NR	-	-
PENT–Int Foursq Gos	6	2,801	2,513	3,146	0.3	0.7
PENT–Intl Pent Holiness	4	361	373	467	0.1	0.1
PENT–Un Pent Ch Intl	4	NR	NR	NR	-	-
PENT–Vineyard	1	89	115	144	0.0	0.0
PRES–As Ref Pres Ch	16	NR	1,412	1,768	0.2	0.4
PRES–Bible Pres	1	NR	NR	NR	-	-
PRES–Evan Presby Ch	6	NR	1,748	2,188	0.2	0.5
PRES–Korean Pres Amer	1	NR	NR	NR	-	-
PRES–Orth Pres Ch	2	397	301	411	0.0	0.1
PRES–Pres Ref	1	NR	NR	NR	-	-
PRES–Presb Ch (USA)	72	13,593	30,594	38,300	4.2	8.0
PRES–Presb Ch Amer	16	3,216	3,791	5,129	0.6	1.1
PRES–Ref Pres Han	1	NR	NR	NR	-	-
Salvation Army	3	126	204	489	0.1	0.1
Sev Day Adv	13	2,240	3,896	4,480	0.5	0.9
Sikh	2	NR	NR	NR	-	-
Un C of Christ	3	144	382	478	0.1	0.1
Unit Univ	3	543	810	1,096	0.1	0.2
Unity Ch	2	NR	NR	NR	-	-
Zoroastrian	0	NR	NR	6	0.0	0.0
MITCHELL	**61**	**3,995**	**9,121**	**11,186**	**71.8**	**100.0**
ANG/EPIS–Episcopal	1	44	108	201	1.3	1.8
Bahá'í	0	NR	1	1	0.0	0.0
BAPT–Free Will Bapt	2	NR	192	225	1.4	2.0
BAPT–So Bapt Conv	34	2,756	7,248	8,502	54.6	76.0
BRETH–Ch of Brethren	3	54	110	129	0.8	1.2
Catholic	1	NR	NR	231	1.5	2.1
CGOD–Ch God (Ander)	1	0	NR	0	0.0	0.0
CHR–Chs of Christ	1	50	41	67	0.4	0.6
METH–Un Methodist	6	228	510	681	4.4	6.1
Non-denom Chr Chs	3	445	525	587	3.8	5.2
PENT–Assemb of God	2	205	91	216	1.4	1.9
PENT–Ch God (Cleve)	2	65	67	79	0.5	0.7
PRES–Presb Ch (USA)	5	148	228	267	1.7	2.4
MONTGOMERY	**99**	**4,422**	**10,762**	**13,480**	**48.5**	**100.0**
Bahá'í	0	NR	3	3	0.0	0.0
BAPT–Natl Mis Bapt Conv	1	0	150	184	0.7	1.4
BAPT–So Bapt Conv	26	1,346	3,739	4,582	16.5	34.0
Catholic	1	NR	NR	632	2.3	4.7
CHR–Chs of Christ	1	30	30	46	0.2	0.3
Jehovah's Witness	1	NR	NR	NR	-	-
METH–AME	1	0	150	184	0.7	1.4
METH–AME Zion	12	0	1,500	1,838	6.6	13.6
METH–Un Methodist	21	869	2,259	2,466	8.9	18.3
METH–Wesleyan	3	326	372	425	1.5	3.2
Non-denom Chr Chs	7	825	950	1,100	4.0	8.2
ORTHE–Greek Orthodox	1	50	NR	56	0.2	0.4
PENT–Ch God (Cleve)	6	373	446	547	2.0	4.1
PENT–Ch Lord Jesus Apos	1	NR	NR	NR	-	-
PENT–Ch of God Proph	1	NR	54	66	0.2	0.5

NR–Not Reported - Represents no adherents reported. Percentages may not total 100 due to rounding.

Table 3: Religious Congregations by County and Group: 2010

Religious Group	Number of Congrega-tions	Number of Attendees	Number of Communicant, Confirmed, or Full Members	Adherents: Number of Adherents	Adherents: % of Total Pop.	Adherents: % of Total Adh.
PENT–COGIC	1	50	100	123	0.4	0.9
PENT–Intl Pent Holiness	5	231	395	484	1.7	3.6
PRES–Presb Ch (USA)	6	249	475	582	2.1	4.3
PRES–Presb Ch Amer	1	0	0	0	0.0	0.0
Sev Day Adv	1	62	107	123	0.4	0.9
Un C of Christ	2	11	32	39	0.1	0.3
MOORE	**170**	**15,967**	**32,104**	**44,765**	**50.7**	**100.0**
ANG/EPIS–Anglican NA	1	NR	NR	NR	-	-
ANG/EPIS–Episcopal	2	441	800	861	1.0	1.9
Bahá'í	0	NR	8	8	0.0	0.0
BAPT–Natl Mis Bapt Conv	2	250	650	781	0.9	1.7
BAPT–So Bapt Conv	39	4,435	10,685	12,835	14.5	28.7
Calv Chpl	1	NR	NR	NR	-	-
Catholic	3	NR	NR	5,653	6.4	12.6
Ch Cr, Scientst	1	NR	NR	NR	-	-
Chr & Miss Al	1	105	42	150	0.2	0.3
CHR–Chr Ch (Disc)	1	0	0	0	0.0	0.0
CHR–Chs of Christ	1	50	35	46	0.1	0.1
CONG–Cong Chr, NA	1	NR	50	60	0.1	0.1
Evan Free Ch	1	400	NR	400	0.5	0.9
FRND–Evan Fr Ch Intl	3	147	102	123	0.1	0.3
FRND–Fr Un Mtg	2	NR	112	135	0.2	0.3
FRND–Unaffl Mtgs	1	NR	NR	NR	-	-
Jehovah's Witness	1	NR	NR	NR	-	-
JUD–Reform	1	48	84	227	0.3	0.5
LDS–L-D Saints	1	NR	NR	636	0.7	1.4
LUTH–E.L.C.A.	1	291	616	720	0.8	1.6
LUTH–Luth–MO Synod	2	101	182	205	0.2	0.5
METH–AME	1	0	100	120	0.1	0.3
METH–AME Zion	20	110	2,625	3,153	3.6	7.0
METH–Un Methodist	18	1,941	4,754	5,473	6.2	12.2
METH–Wesleyan	1	74	71	96	0.1	0.2
Non-denom Chr Chs	24	4,885	5,864	6,549	7.4	14.6
PENT–Assemb of God	2	118	99	200	0.2	0.4
PENT–Ch God (Cleve)	4	134	181	217	0.2	0.5
PENT–Ch Lord Jesus Apos	1	NR	NR	NR	-	-
PENT–Ch of God Proph	4	NR	82	99	0.1	0.2
PENT–COGIC	1	15	15	18	0.0	0.0
PENT–Intl Pent Holiness	1	47	52	62	0.1	0.1
PENT–Un Pent Ch Intl	1	NR	NR	NR	-	-
PRES–Evan Presby Ch	1	NR	62	74	0.1	0.2
PRES–Presb Ch (USA)	20	1,881	4,178	5,019	5.7	11.2
PRES–Presb Ch Amer	1	319	255	364	0.4	0.8
Sev Day Adv	1	35	61	70	0.1	0.2
Un C of Christ	3	140	339	407	0.5	0.9
Zoroastrian	0	NR	NR	4	0.0	0.0
NASH	**167**	**13,930**	**32,583**	**40,751**	**42.5**	**100.0**
ANG/EPIS–Episcopal	2	314	847	952	1.0	2.3
Bahá'í	0	NR	6	6	0.0	0.0
BAPT–Free Will Bapt	3	NR	342	418	0.4	1.0
BAPT–NBC USA	2	0	300	367	0.4	0.9
BAPT–Orig Free Will Bapt	8	720	984	1,203	1.3	3.0
BAPT–Ref Bapt Ch	1	NR	NR	NR	-	-
BAPT–So Bapt Conv	60	7,412	17,150	20,959	21.9	51.4
Catholic	1	NR	NR	1,400	1.5	3.4
Ch Cr, Scientst	1	NR	NR	NR	-	-
Ch of Nazarene	1	104	205	234	0.2	0.6
CHR–Chr Ch (Disc)	4	75	183	224	0.2	0.5
CHR–Chr Chs & Chs Cr	3	NR	83	101	0.1	0.2
CHR–Chs of Christ	2	110	95	121	0.1	0.3
Jehovah's Witness	2	NR	NR	NR	-	-
JUD–Reform	1	6	10	27	0.0	0.1
LDS–L-D Saints	1	NR	NR	526	0.5	1.3
LUTH–E.L.C.A.	1	69	122	166	0.2	0.4
METH–AME	5	0	500	611	0.6	1.5
METH–Un Methodist	17	1,623	5,353	5,817	6.1	14.3
Non-denom Chr Chs	5	690	900	937	1.0	2.3
PENT–Apos Faith Msn	1	NR	35	43	0.0	0.1
PENT–Assemb of God	3	661	1,211	1,320	1.4	3.2
PENT–Ch God (Cleve)	11	874	1,809	2,211	2.3	5.4
PENT–Ch Lord Jesus Apos	2	NR	NR	NR	-	-

Religious Group	Number of Congrega-tions	Number of Attendees	Number of Communicant, Confirmed, or Full Members	Adherents: Number of Adherents	Adherents: % of Total Pop.	Adherents: % of Total Adh.
PENT–Ch of God Proph	5	NR	277	339	0.4	0.8
PENT–COGIC	1	0	150	183	0.2	0.4
PENT–Full Gosp Bapt	1	NR	NR	NR	-	-
PENT–Intl Pent Holiness	7	489	577	705	0.7	1.7
PENT–Pent FW Bapt	1	NR	NR	NR	-	-
PENT–Un Pent Ch Intl	1	NR	NR	NR	-	-
PENT–United Holy Ch	4	NR	NR	NR	-	-
PENT–Vineyard	1	120	181	221	0.2	0.5
PRES–Presb Ch (USA)	5	465	951	1,162	1.2	2.9
Salvation Army	1	58	74	228	0.2	0.6
Sev Day Adv	2	112	195	225	0.2	0.6
Unit Univ	1	28	43	45	0.0	0.1
NEW HANOVER	**225**	**30,527**	**67,260**	**95,869**	**47.3**	**100.0**
ANG/EPIS–Anglican NA	1	NR	NR	NR	-	-
ANG/EPIS–Episcopal	8	1,526	4,245	4,661	2.3	4.9
Bahá'í	1	NR	55	55	0.0	0.1
BAPT–Free Will Bapt	1	NR	114	135	0.1	0.1
BAPT–NBC USA	2	325	450	533	0.3	0.6
BAPT–Prog NBC	1	140	287	340	0.2	0.4
BAPT–So Bapt Conv	41	8,224	23,366	27,688	13.7	28.9
Calv Chpl	1	NR	NR	NR	-	-
Catholic	5	NR	NR	14,671	7.2	15.3
Ch Cr, Scientst	1	NR	NR	NR	-	-
Ch God (7th Day)	1	NR	NR	NR	-	-
Ch of Nazarene	1	86	135	135	0.1	0.1
Chr & Miss Al	1	45	0	79	0.0	0.1
CHR–Chr Ch (Disc)	2	172	444	526	0.3	0.5
CHR–Chr Chs & Chs Cr	2	NR	80	95	0.0	0.1
CHR–Chs of Christ	3	328	304	401	0.2	0.4
Christian Brethren	1	NR	NR	NR	-	-
FRND–Consrv Yr Mtgs	1	NR	48	57	0.0	0.1
HINDU–Post Ren	1	NR	NR	77	0.0	0.1
Jehovah's Witness	4	NR	NR	NR	-	-
JUD–Orth	1	43	50	60	0.0	0.1
JUD–Reform	1	95	167	451	0.2	0.5
LDS–Comm of Christ	1	NR	118	118	0.1	0.1
LDS–L-D Saints	2	NR	NR	1,710	0.8	1.8
LUTH–E.L.C.A.	5	972	2,116	2,513	1.2	2.6
LUTH–Luth–MO Synod	1	114	140	159	0.1	0.2
METH–AME	12	605	2,402	2,846	1.4	3.0
METH–AME Zion	8	650	1,570	1,860	0.9	1.9
METH–Un Methodist	12	3,366	10,201	11,977	5.9	12.5
METH–Wesleyan	2	145	79	189	0.1	0.2
Metro Comm Ch	1	103	115	136	0.1	0.1
MORAV–Morav Ch-South	1	39	100	122	0.1	0.1
Muslim Est	3	318	NR	924	0.5	1.0
Non-denom Chr Chs	40	9,230	11,546	12,099	6.0	12.6
ORTHE–Greek Orthodox	1	130	NR	325	0.2	0.3
ORTHE–Orth Ch in Amer	1	25	NR	50	0.0	0.1
PENT–Assemb of God	2	58	41	58	0.0	0.1
PENT–Ch God (Cleve)	4	534	1,208	1,431	0.7	1.5
PENT–Ch of God Proph	2	NR	84	100	0.0	0.1
PENT–COGIC	1	400	700	829	0.4	0.9
PENT–Fire Bapt Hol Ch	1	NR	NR	NR	-	-
PENT–Full Gosp Bapt	6	NR	NR	NR	-	-
PENT–Intl Pent Holiness	4	302	437	518	0.3	0.5
PENT–Pent FW Bapt	2	NR	NR	NR	-	-
PENT–Un Pent Ch Intl	2	NR	NR	NR	-	-
PENT–United Holy Ch	4	NR	NR	NR	-	-
PRES–As Ref Pres Ch	1	NR	27	32	0.0	0.0
PRES–Evan Presby Ch	2	NR	754	893	0.4	0.9
PRES–Orth Pres Ch	1	0	0	0	0.0	0.0
PRES–Presb Ch (USA)	13	1,756	4,613	5,466	2.7	5.7
PRES–Presb Ch Amer	1	0	0	0	0.0	0.0
Salvation Army	1	80	189	206	0.1	0.2
Sev Day Adv	4	444	771	887	0.4	0.9
Un C of Christ	1	30	63	75	0.0	0.1
Unit Univ	1	242	241	382	0.2	0.4
Unity Ch	1	NR	NR	NR	-	-
NORTHAMPTON	**45**	**1,884**	**5,573**	**6,531**	**29.6**	**100.0**
ANG/EPIS–Episcopal	1	24	53	53	0.2	0.8

NR–Not Reported - Represents no adherents reported. Percentages may not total 100 due to rounding.

Table 3: Religious Congregations by County and Group: 2010

Religious Group	Number of Congrega-tions	Number of Attendees	Number of Communicant, Confirmed, or Full Members	Adherents		
				Number of Adherents	% of Total Pop.	% of Total Adh.
Bahá'í	0	NR	4	4	0.0	0.1
BAPT–NBC USA	2	450	550	651	2.9	10.0
BAPT–So Bapt Conv	14	725	2,477	2,932	13.3	44.9
CHR–Chr Chs & Chs Cr	1	NR	60	71	0.3	1.1
FRND–Consrv Yr Mtgs	1	NR	54	64	0.3	1.0
Jehovah's Witness	2	NR	NR	NR	-	-
METH–AME	5	120	760	900	4.1	13.8
METH–Un Methodist	16	480	1,560	1,743	7.9	26.7
Non-denom Chr Chs	1	50	55	62	0.3	0.9
PENT–Assemb of God	1	35	0	51	0.2	0.8
PENT–United Holy Ch	1	NR	NR	NR	-	-
ONSLOW	**158**	**17,988**	**32,765**	**51,397**	**28.9**	**100.0**
ANG/EPIS–Episcopal	3	299	549	879	0.5	1.7
Bahá'í	1	NR	45	45	0.0	0.1
BAPT–Free Will Bapt	6	NR	684	865	0.5	1.7
BAPT–Natl Mis Bapt Conv	2	150	350	443	0.2	0.9
BAPT–Orig Free Will Bapt	3	270	369	467	0.3	0.9
BAPT–Ref Bapt Ch	1	NR	NR	NR	-	-
BAPT–So Bapt Conv	28	6,049	13,706	17,337	9.8	33.7
Calv Chpl	1	NR	NR	NR	-	-
Catholic	2	NR	NR	7,579	4.3	14.7
CGOD–Ch God (Ander)	3	417	NR	417	0.2	0.8
Ch of Nazarene	2	85	125	177	0.1	0.3
CHR–Chr Ch (Disc)	3	220	566	716	0.4	1.4
CHR–Chr Chs & Chs Cr	2	NR	215	272	0.2	0.5
CHR–Chs of Christ	4	454	532	628	0.4	1.2
Jehovah's Witness	3	NR	NR	NR	-	-
LDS–L-D Saints	2	NR	NR	2,351	1.3	4.6
LUTH–E.L.C.A.	1	105	122	139	0.1	0.3
LUTH–Luth–MO Synod	1	0	191	231	0.1	0.4
LUTH–Wisc Ev Luth Syn	1	57	68	104	0.1	0.2
METH–AME	2	0	250	316	0.2	0.6
METH–AME Zion	6	170	745	942	0.5	1.8
METH–Un Methodist	12	1,830	4,963	6,057	3.4	11.8
Muslim Est	1	134	NR	308	0.2	0.6
Non-denom Chr Chs	34	6,265	7,315	8,232	4.6	16.0
PENT–Assemb of God	3	565	132	598	0.3	1.2
PENT–Ch God (Cleve)	3	165	436	552	0.3	1.1
PENT–COGIC	1	0	150	190	0.1	0.4
PENT–Int Foursq Gos	1	18	76	96	0.1	0.2
PENT–Intl Pent Holiness	4	151	234	296	0.2	0.6
PENT–Pent FW Bapt	7	NR	NR	NR	-	-
PENT–Un Pent Ch Intl	1	NR	NR	NR	-	-
PENT–United Holy Ch	6	NR	NR	NR	-	-
PRES–As Ref Pres Ch	1	NR	77	97	0.1	0.2
PRES–Presb Ch (USA)	3	306	480	607	0.3	1.2
PRES–Presb Ch Amer	1	95	96	130	0.1	0.3
Salvation Army	1	43	46	46	0.0	0.1
Sev Day Adv	2	140	243	280	0.2	0.5
ORANGE	**160**	**14,939**	**34,101**	**58,863**	**44.0**	**100.0**
ANG/EPIS–Episcopal	4	1,136	2,782	3,136	2.3	5.3
Bahá'í	4	NR	298	298	0.2	0.5
BAPT–Alliance Bapt	2	NR	NR	NR	-	-
BAPT–Amer Bapt USA	2	395	774	921	0.7	1.6
BAPT–So Bapt Conv	26	2,368	7,309	8,699	6.5	14.8
BUDD–Mahayana	3	NR	NR	205	0.2	0.3
BUDD–Vajrayana	3	NR	NR	564	0.4	1.0
Calv Chpl	1	NR	NR	NR	-	-
Catholic	3	NR	NR	13,432	10.0	22.8
CGOD–Ch God (Ander)	1	23	NR	23	0.0	0.0
Ch Cr, Scientst	1	NR	NR	NR	-	-
Ch of Nazarene	1	32	58	58	0.0	0.1
CHR–Chr Ch (Disc)	1	0	52	62	0.0	0.1
CHR–Int Chs of Christ	1	NR	285	339	0.3	0.6
FRND–Fr Gen Cf	1	NR	0	0	0.0	0.0
HINDU–I/A Temples	1	NR	NR	1,562	1.2	2.7
HINDU–Post Ren	1	NR	NR	77	0.1	0.1
Jehovah's Witness	1	NR	NR	NR	-	-
JUD–Reconst	1	146	187	505	0.4	0.9
LDS–L-D Saints	4	NR	NR	1,783	1.3	3.0
LUTH–E.L.C.A.	1	266	505	814	0.6	1.4
LUTH–Luth–MO Synod	1	69	106	130	0.1	0.2
MENN–Mennonite USA	1	65	35	42	0.0	0.1
METH–AME	10	400	1,865	2,220	1.7	3.8
METH–AME Zion	2	0	200	238	0.2	0.4
METH–C.M.E.	2	110	300	357	0.3	0.6
METH–Un Methodist	27	3,377	9,163	11,336	8.5	19.3
METH–Wesleyan	2	132	68	172	0.1	0.3
Muslim Est	1	134	NR	308	0.2	0.5
Non-denom Chr Chs	18	3,712	4,772	5,057	3.8	8.6
PENT–Assemb of God	1	65	50	65	0.0	0.1
PENT–Ch God (Cleve)	2	117	748	890	0.7	1.5
PENT–Ch of God Proph	2	NR	65	77	0.1	0.1
PENT–Intl Pent Holiness	1	25	35	42	0.0	0.1
PENT–United Holy Ch	4	NR	NR	NR	-	-
PENT–Vineyard	1	30	49	58	0.0	0.1
PRES–As Ref Pres Ch	1	NR	27	32	0.0	0.1
PRES–Presb Ch (USA)	10	1,258	2,527	3,008	2.2	5.1
PRES–Presb Ch Amer	2	254	292	378	0.3	0.6
Sev Day Adv	2	88	154	177	0.1	0.3
Un C of Christ	3	477	962	1,145	0.9	1.9
Unit Univ	2	260	433	647	0.5	1.1
Unity Ch	2	NR	NR	NR	-	-
Zoroastrian	0	NR	NR	6	0.0	0.0
PAMLICO	**56**	**2,336**	**5,111**	**6,042**	**46.0**	**100.0**
ANG/EPIS–Episcopal	1	73	164	177	1.3	2.9
Bahá'í	0	NR	2	2	0.0	0.0
BAPT–Natl Mis Bapt Conv	4	125	500	579	4.4	9.6
BAPT–Orig Free Will Bapt	8	720	983	1,138	8.7	18.8
BAPT–So Bapt Conv	2	115	232	269	2.0	4.5
Catholic	1	NR	NR	187	1.4	3.1
CHR–Chr Ch (Disc)	8	30	159	184	1.4	3.0
CHR–Chr Chs & Chs Cr	1	NR	56	65	0.5	1.1
METH–AME Zion	6	0	700	811	6.2	13.4
METH–Un Methodist	9	539	1,188	1,378	10.5	22.8
Non-denom Chr Chs	4	490	602	637	4.8	10.5
PENT–Assemb of God	1	30	20	30	0.2	0.5
PENT–Ch God (Cleve)	1	47	38	44	0.3	0.7
PENT–Ch of God Proph	1	NR	7	8	0.1	0.1
PENT–Intl Pent Holiness	4	102	94	109	0.8	1.8
PRES–Presb Ch Amer	1	24	31	36	0.3	0.6
Un C of Christ	4	41	335	388	3.0	6.4
PASQUOTANK	**79**	**6,159**	**12,957**	**17,997**	**44.3**	**100.0**
ANG/EPIS–Episcopal	1	130	443	443	1.1	2.5
Bahá'í	0	NR	8	8	0.0	0.0
BAPT–Natl Mis Bapt Conv	1	0	150	182	0.4	1.0
BAPT–Orig Free Will Bapt	1	90	123	149	0.4	0.8
BAPT–So Bapt Conv	12	1,242	3,920	4,761	11.7	26.5
Calv Chpl	1	NR	NR	NR	-	-
Catholic	1	NR	NR	1,545	3.8	8.6
Ch of Nazarene	1	66	81	81	0.2	0.5
CHR–Chr Ch (Disc)	3	0	233	283	0.7	1.6
CHR–Chr Chs & Chs Cr	3	NR	365	443	1.1	2.5
CHR–Chs of Christ	1	30	21	36	0.1	0.2
Jehovah's Witness	1	NR	NR	NR	-	-
LDS–L-D Saints	2	NR	NR	938	2.3	5.2
LUTH–E.L.C.A.	1	93	130	159	0.4	0.9
METH–AME Zion	11	100	1,225	1,488	3.7	8.3
METH–Evan Meth Ch	1	NR	NR	NR	-	-
METH–Un Methodist	7	669	2,275	2,656	6.5	14.8
Non-denom Chr Chs	20	2,320	2,800	3,113	7.7	17.3
PENT–Assemb of God	1	175	150	275	0.7	1.5
PENT–Ch God (Cleve)	1	570	173	210	0.5	1.2
PENT–Ch of God Proph	1	NR	29	35	0.1	0.2
PENT–Int Pent C Chr	1	75	NR	125	0.3	0.7
PENT–Intl Pent Holiness	2	396	453	550	1.4	3.1
PENT–Un Pent Ch Intl	1	NR	NR	NR	-	-
PENT–United Holy Ch	1	NR	NR	NR	-	-
PRES–Presb Ch (USA)	1	46	121	147	0.4	0.8
Salvation Army	1	74	113	204	0.5	1.1
Sev Day Adv	1	83	144	166	0.4	0.9

NR–Not Reported   - Represents no adherents reported.   Percentages may not total 100 due to rounding.

Table 3: Religious Congregations by County and Group: 2010

Religious Group	Number of Congrega-tions	Number of Attendees	Number of Communicant, Confirmed, or Full Members	Adherents: Number of Adherents	Adherents: % of Total Pop.	Adherents: % of Total Adh.
PENDER	**99**	**5,605**	**13,480**	**18,964**	**36.3**	**100.0**
ANG/EPIS–Episcopal	2	104	157	160	0.3	0.8
Bahá'í	0	NR	8	8	0.0	0.0
BAPT–Free Will Bapt	2	NR	228	276	0.5	1.5
BAPT–Natl Mis Bapt Conv	1	0	150	181	0.3	1.0
BAPT–So Bapt Conv	26	2,340	6,188	7,483	14.3	39.5
Catholic	3	NR	NR	2,008	3.8	10.6
CHR–Chr Ch (Disc)	1	0	0	0	0.0	0.0
CHR–Chs of Christ	1	10	5	10	0.0	0.1
Jehovah's Witness	1	NR	NR	NR	-	-
LDS–L-D Saints	2	NR	NR	734	1.4	3.9
METH–AME	12	275	1,510	1,826	3.5	9.6
METH–AME Zion	1	0	100	121	0.2	0.6
METH–Un Methodist	9	1,218	2,607	3,306	6.3	17.4
Non-denom Chr Chs	10	1,020	1,368	1,438	2.8	7.6
PENT–Assemb of God	1	35	25	42	0.1	0.2
PENT–Ch God (Cleve)	2	80	77	93	0.2	0.5
PENT–Full Gosp Bapt	1	NR	NR	NR	-	-
PENT–Intl Pent Holiness	1	63	109	132	0.3	0.7
PENT–Pent FW Bapt	6	NR	NR	NR	-	-
PENT–United Holy Ch	7	NR	NR	NR	-	-
PRES–Evan Presby Ch	1	NR	58	70	0.1	0.4
PRES–Presb Ch (USA)	8	454	879	1,063	2.0	5.6
Sev Day Adv	1	6	11	13	0.0	0.1
PERQUIMANS	**40**	**1,857**	**4,826**	**5,718**	**42.5**	**100.0**
ANG/EPIS–Episcopal	1	84	125	125	0.9	2.2
Bahá'í	0	NR	2	2	0.0	0.0
BAPT–NBC USA	1	0	0	0	0.0	0.0
BAPT–So Bapt Conv	8	493	1,471	1,747	13.0	30.6
CHR–Chr Ch (Disc)	1	0	0	0	0.0	0.0
CHR–Chr Chs & Chs Cr	2	NR	148	176	1.3	3.1
FRND–Fr Un Mtg	2	NR	174	207	1.5	3.6
Jehovah's Witness	1	NR	NR	NR	-	-
METH–AME Zion	7	0	700	831	6.2	14.5
METH–Un Methodist	8	503	1,348	1,579	11.7	27.6
METH–Wesleyan	1	138	93	179	1.3	3.1
Non-denom Chr Chs	3	450	600	612	4.5	10.7
PENT–Assemb of God	2	102	70	131	1.0	2.3
PENT–Int Pent C Chr	1	16	15	34	0.3	0.6
PENT–Intl Pent Holiness	2	71	80	95	0.7	1.7
PERSON	**59**	**5,425**	**12,509**	**15,888**	**40.3**	**100.0**
ANG/EPIS–Episcopal	1	49	91	91	0.2	0.6
Bahá'í	0	NR	6	6	0.0	0.0
BAPT–NBC USA	3	675	1,100	1,335	3.4	8.4
BAPT–So Bapt Conv	22	2,672	6,221	7,548	19.1	47.5
Catholic	1	NR	NR	640	1.6	4.0
CHR–Chs of Christ	1	43	40	49	0.1	0.3
LDS–L-D Saints	1	NR	NR	265	0.7	1.7
METH–AME	3	25	325	394	1.0	2.5
METH–Un Methodist	14	1,220	3,226	3,813	9.7	24.0
Non-denom Chr Chs	5	625	765	856	2.2	5.4
PENT–Ch God (Cleve)	2	76	316	383	1.0	2.4
PENT–COGIC	2	0	300	364	0.9	2.3
PENT–Full Gosp Bapt	1	NR	NR	NR	-	-
PENT–United Holy Ch	2	NR	NR	NR	-	-
PRES–Presb Ch (USA)	1	40	119	144	0.4	0.9
PITT	**248**	**24,767**	**45,209**	**69,469**	**41.3**	**100.0**
ANG/EPIS–Episcopal	4	418	1,097	1,435	0.9	2.1
Bahá'í	0	NR	122	122	0.1	0.2
BAPT–Amer Bapt USA	1	600	600	729	0.4	1.0
BAPT–Free Will Bapt	13	NR	1,482	1,801	1.1	2.6
BAPT–Natl Mis Bapt Conv	5	300	1,016	1,235	0.7	1.8
BAPT–Orig Free Will Bapt	21	1,890	2,582	3,138	1.9	4.5
BAPT–So Bapt Conv	23	1,980	5,551	6,746	4.0	9.7
BUDD–Vajrayana	1	NR	NR	71	0.0	0.1
Catholic	3	NR	NR	5,489	3.3	7.9
Ch God (7th Day)	1	NR	NR	NR	-	-
CHR–Chr Ch (Disc)	19	673	2,069	2,514	1.5	3.6
CHR–Chr Chs & Chs Cr	6	NR	960	1,167	0.7	1.7
CHR–Chs of Christ	3	224	210	270	0.2	0.4
CHR–Int Chs of Christ	1	NR	4	5	0.0	0.0
FRND–Consrv Yr Mtgs	1	NR	7	9	0.0	0.0
HINDU–Trad Temples	1	NR	NR	50	0.0	0.1
Jehovah's Witness	3	NR	NR	NR	-	-
JUD–Conserv	0	21	24	65	0.0	0.1
JUD–Reform	0	14	24	65	0.0	0.1
LDS–L-D Saints	3	NR	NR	1,003	0.6	1.4
LUTH–E.L.C.A.	1	79	99	127	0.1	0.2
LUTH–Luth–MO Synod	1	0	0	0	0.0	0.0
MENN–CG in Cr (Menn)	1	NR	134	163	0.1	0.2
METH–AME	1	25	40	49	0.0	0.1
METH–AME Zion	8	100	1,025	1,246	0.7	1.8
METH–Un Methodist	15	3,978	8,816	16,530	9.8	23.8
METH–Wesleyan	1	45	18	59	0.0	0.1
Muslim Est	2	170	NR	350	0.2	0.5
Non-denom Chr Chs	44	10,470	13,450	16,917	10.1	24.4
ORTHE–Greek Orthodox	1	25	NR	50	0.0	0.1
PENT–Assemb of God	2	431	449	1,224	0.7	1.8
PENT–Ch God (Cleve)	7	684	978	1,188	0.7	1.7
PENT–Ch Lord Jesus Apos	5	NR	NR	NR	-	-
PENT–COGIC	1	0	150	182	0.1	0.3
PENT–Full Gosp Bapt	1	NR	NR	NR	-	-
PENT–Int Foursq Gos	2	43	69	84	0.0	0.1
PENT–Intl Pent Holiness	19	1,270	1,883	2,288	1.4	3.3
PENT–Pent FW Bapt	1	NR	NR	NR	-	-
PENT–Un Pent Ch Intl	2	NR	NR	NR	-	-
PENT–United Holy Ch	11	NR	NR	NR	-	-
PRES–Presb Ch (USA)	7	726	1,394	1,694	1.0	2.4
PRES–Presb Ch Amer	1	243	371	495	0.3	0.7
Salvation Army	1	47	58	289	0.2	0.4
Sev Day Adv	3	246	427	491	0.3	0.7
Unit Univ	1	65	100	125	0.1	0.2
Zoroastrian	0	NR	NR	4	0.0	0.0
POLK	**58**	**3,560**	**8,291**	**10,735**	**52.3**	**100.0**
ANG/EPIS–Episcopal	3	270	461	482	2.4	4.5
Bahá'í	0	NR	7	7	0.0	0.1
BAPT–So Bapt Conv	25	1,885	4,742	5,535	27.0	51.6
BRETH–Ch of Brethren	2	83	345	403	2.0	3.8
Catholic	1	NR	NR	1,039	5.1	9.7
Ch Cr, Scientst	1	NR	NR	NR	-	-
CHR–Chs of Christ	1	20	20	28	0.1	0.3
Jehovah's Witness	1	NR	NR	NR	-	-
LUTH–Luth–MO Synod	1	41	67	73	0.4	0.7
METH–C.M.E.	2	0	300	350	1.7	3.3
METH–Un Methodist	7	354	704	885	4.3	8.2
Non-denom Chr Chs	3	240	245	299	1.5	2.8
PENT–Assemb of God	1	10	10	21	0.1	0.2
PENT–Ch God (Cleve)	1	49	47	55	0.3	0.5
PENT–Intl Pent Holiness	2	33	59	69	0.3	0.6
PRES–As Ref Pres Ch	1	NR	72	84	0.4	0.8
PRES–Presb Ch (USA)	3	274	497	580	2.8	5.4
Sev Day Adv	1	150	262	301	1.5	2.8
Un C of Christ	1	120	425	496	2.4	4.6
Unit Univ	1	31	28	28	0.1	0.3
RANDOLPH	**269**	**20,812**	**38,739**	**49,682**	**35.0**	**100.0**
ANG/EPIS–Anglican NA	2	NR	NR	NR	-	-
ANG/EPIS–Episcopal	1	97	176	218	0.2	0.4
Bahá'í	0	NR	15	15	0.0	0.0
BAPT–Free Will Bapt	2	NR	228	281	0.2	0.6
BAPT–Natl Mis Bapt Conv	1	0	150	185	0.1	0.4
BAPT–So Bapt Conv	61	6,368	13,514	16,662	11.8	33.5
Catholic	1	NR	NR	688	0.5	1.4
CGOD–Ch God (Ander)	1	0	NR	0	0.0	0.0
Ch of Nazarene	2	133	245	438	0.3	0.9
CHR–Chr Chs & Chs Cr	1	NR	85	105	0.1	0.2
CHR–Chs of Christ	1	80	65	80	0.1	0.2
CONG–Cong Chr Add'l	1	NR	382	471	0.3	0.9
CONG–Consrv Cong Chr	1	31	31	38	0.0	0.1
Evan Cov Ch	1	570	307	741	0.5	1.5
FRND–Fr Un Mtg	14	NR	2,372	2,924	2.1	5.9

NR–Not Reported   - Represents no adherents reported.   Percentages may not total 100 due to rounding.

Table 3: Religious Congregations by County and Group: 2010

Religious Group	Number of Congregations	Number of Attendees	Number of Communicant, Confirmed, or Full Members	Adherents: Number of Adherents	Adherents: % of Total Pop.	Adherents: % of Total Adh.
Jehovah's Witness	4	NR	NR	NR	-	-
LDS–L-D Saints	1	NR	NR	581	0.4	1.2
LUTH–E.L.C.A.	1	34	50	57	0.0	0.1
LUTH–Nor Amer Luth C	1	NR	NR	NR	-	-
METH–AME	2	0	200	247	0.2	0.5
METH–AME Zion	2	0	250	308	0.2	0.6
METH–Evan Meth Ch	1	NR	NR	NR	-	-
METH–Un Methodist	68	4,503	10,237	12,429	8.8	25.0
METH–Wesleyan	25	2,111	2,045	2,745	1.9	5.5
Muslim Est	1	134	NR	308	0.2	0.6
Non-denom Chr Chs	34	4,135	4,748	5,537	3.9	11.1
PENT–Assemb of God	3	360	196	364	0.3	0.7
PENT–Ch God (Cleve)	11	1,210	1,402	1,729	1.2	3.5
PENT–Ch of God Proph	4	NR	166	205	0.1	0.4
PENT–COGIC	1	50	60	74	0.1	0.1
PENT–Fire Bapt Hol Ch	1	NR	NR	NR	-	-
PENT–Int Foursq Gos	1	21	24	30	0.0	0.1
PENT–Intl Pent Holiness	5	403	394	486	0.3	1.0
PENT–Un Pent Ch Intl	1	NR	NR	NR	-	-
PRES–Presb Ch (USA)	2	297	726	895	0.6	1.8
PRES–Presb Ch Amer	1	90	69	92	0.1	0.2
Salvation Army	1	20	23	42	0.0	0.1
Sev Day Adv	1	44	76	87	0.1	0.2
Un C of Christ	7	121	503	620	0.4	1.2
RICHMOND	**167**	**8,449**	**21,403**	**26,602**	**57.0**	**100.0**
ANG/EPIS–Episcopal	2	35	98	98	0.2	0.4
Bahá'í	0	NR	24	24	0.1	0.1
BAPT–Free Will Bapt	7	NR	722	888	1.9	3.3
BAPT–Natl Mis Bapt Conv	3	210	375	461	1.0	1.7
BAPT–Orig Free Will Bapt	5	450	614	755	1.6	2.8
BAPT–Prog NBC	2	50	260	320	0.7	1.2
BAPT–So Bapt Conv	31	2,666	7,461	9,180	19.7	34.5
Catholic	1	NR	NR	321	0.7	1.2
CHR–Chr Chs & Chs Cr	1	NR	5	6	0.0	0.0
CHR–Chs of Christ	2	120	98	140	0.3	0.5
Jehovah's Witness	1	NR	NR	NR	-	-
LDS–L-D Saints	1	NR	NR	297	0.6	1.1
LUTH–E.L.C.A.	1	34	88	99	0.2	0.4
METH–AME Zion	18	95	1,802	2,217	4.8	8.3
METH–Un Methodist	24	1,304	3,927	4,400	9.4	16.5
METH–Wesleyan	3	140	131	182	0.4	0.7
Muslim Est	1	134	NR	308	0.7	1.2
Non-denom Chr Chs	16	1,713	2,213	2,350	5.0	8.8
PENT–Assemb of God	1	180	0	180	0.4	0.7
PENT–Ch God (Cleve)	5	228	260	320	0.7	1.2
PENT–Ch of God Proph	6	NR	427	525	1.1	2.0
PENT–COGIC	5	75	750	923	2.0	3.5
PENT–Cong Hol Ch	3	64	58	71	0.2	0.3
PENT–Intl Pent Holiness	8	271	321	395	0.8	1.5
PENT–Un Pent Ch Intl	1	NR	NR	NR	-	-
PRES–Evan Presby Ch	2	NR	142	175	0.4	0.7
PRES–Presb Ch (USA)	10	271	982	1,208	2.6	4.5
PRES–Presb Ch Amer	4	241	365	430	0.9	1.6
Sev Day Adv	2	113	196	226	0.5	0.8
Un C of Christ	1	55	84	103	0.2	0.4
ROBESON	**316**	**23,137**	**45,753**	**60,027**	**44.7**	**100.0**
ANG/EPIS–Episcopal	1	93	265	355	0.3	0.6
Bahá'í	0	NR	440	440	0.3	0.7
BAPT–Natl Mis Bapt Conv	2	0	300	379	0.3	0.6
BAPT–So Bapt Conv	125	11,737	25,006	31,588	23.5	52.6
BUDD–Mahayana	1	NR	NR	11	0.0	0.0
Catholic	2	NR	NR	1,415	1.1	2.4
Chr & Miss Al	2	98	108	135	0.1	0.2
CHR–Chs of Christ	2	152	116	168	0.1	0.3
Jehovah's Witness	4	NR	NR	NR	-	-
LDS–L-D Saints	3	NR	NR	1,197	0.9	2.0
LUTH–E.L.C.A.	1	34	61	67	0.0	0.1
METH–AME	9	145	1,115	1,408	1.0	2.3
METH–AME Zion	16	225	2,200	2,779	2.1	4.6
METH–Un Methodist	33	2,195	5,926	6,813	5.1	11.3
Non-denom Chr Chs	22	2,795	3,820	4,032	3.0	6.7

Religious Group	Number of Congregations	Number of Attendees	Number of Communicant, Confirmed, or Full Members	Adherents: Number of Adherents	Adherents: % of Total Pop.	Adherents: % of Total Adh.
PENT–Assemb of God	18	1,604	664	2,018	1.5	3.4
PENT–Ch God (Cleve)	27	1,966	1,956	2,471	1.8	4.1
PENT–Ch of God Proph	1	NR	47	59	0.0	0.1
PENT–Intl Pent Holiness	13	1,375	1,655	2,091	1.6	3.5
PENT–Un Pent Ch Intl	6	NR	NR	NR	-	-
PENT–United Holy Ch	3	NR	NR	NR	-	-
PRES–Presb Ch (USA)	22	624	1,911	2,414	1.8	4.0
Sev Day Adv	3	94	163	187	0.1	0.3
ROCKINGHAM	**203**	**15,989**	**30,610**	**38,543**	**41.2**	**100.0**
ANG/EPIS–Episcopal	4	221	432	448	0.5	1.2
Bahá'í	0	NR	8	8	0.0	0.0
BAPT–Free Will Bapt	1	NR	114	137	0.1	0.4
BAPT–Natl Mis Bapt Conv	1	45	40	48	0.1	0.1
BAPT–NBC USA	4	690	1,116	1,341	1.4	3.5
BAPT–Orig Free Will Bapt	1	90	123	148	0.2	0.4
BAPT–Ref Bapt Ch	1	NR	NR	NR	-	-
BAPT–So Bapt Conv	40	5,163	11,547	13,874	14.8	36.0
BRETH–Ch of Brethren	1	87	152	183	0.2	0.5
BRETH–Grace Breth	1	NR	NR	NR	-	-
Catholic	2	NR	NR	1,172	1.3	3.0
Chr & Miss Al	1	79	52	153	0.2	0.4
CHR–Chr Ch (Disc)	7	161	498	598	0.6	1.6
CHR–Chr Chs & Chs Cr	7	NR	1,080	1,298	1.4	3.4
CHR–Chs of Christ	2	55	53	82	0.1	0.2
Christian Brethren	1	NR	NR	NR	-	-
Evan Cov Ch	1	95	115	124	0.1	0.3
FRND–Evan Fr Ch Intl	1	81	64	77	0.1	0.2
FRND–Fr Gen Cf & Un Mtg	1	NR	45	54	0.1	0.1
Jehovah's Witness	3	NR	NR	NR	-	-
LDS–L-D Saints	1	NR	NR	479	0.5	1.2
LUTH–E.L.C.A.	1	26	30	40	0.0	0.1
METH–AME	1	0	150	180	0.2	0.5
METH–Evan Meth Ch	1	NR	NR	NR	-	-
METH–Un Methodist	38	2,531	5,925	6,960	7.4	18.1
METH–Wesleyan	6	955	954	1,242	1.3	3.2
MORAV–Morav Ch-South	2	119	242	286	0.3	0.7
Muslim Est	1	134	NR	308	0.3	0.8
Non-denom Chr Chs	31	4,065	4,855	5,429	5.8	14.1
PENT–Assemb of God	5	391	343	578	0.6	1.5
PENT–Ch God (Cleve)	8	357	369	443	0.5	1.1
PENT–Ch Lord Jesus Apos	1	NR	NR	NR	-	-
PENT–Ch of God Proph	2	NR	142	171	0.2	0.4
PENT–COGIC	2	0	150	180	0.2	0.5
PENT–Full Gosp Bapt	1	NR	NR	NR	-	-
PENT–Intl Pent Holiness	7	288	622	747	0.8	1.9
PENT–Un Pent Ch Intl	1	NR	NR	NR	-	-
PENT–United Holy Ch	1	NR	NR	NR	-	-
PRES–Presb Ch (USA)	11	305	1,282	1,540	1.6	4.0
Salvation Army	1	23	59	160	0.2	0.4
Sev Day Adv	1	28	48	55	0.1	0.1
ROWAN	**253**	**24,820**	**49,785**	**63,971**	**46.2**	**100.0**
ANG/EPIS–Episcopal	4	286	794	798	0.6	1.2
Bahá'í	0	NR	28	28	0.0	0.0
BAPT–Free Will Bapt	1	NR	114	140	0.1	0.2
BAPT–So Bapt Conv	61	8,231	17,204	21,079	15.2	33.0
Catholic	1	NR	NR	2,377	1.7	3.7
CGOD–Ch God (Ander)	1	25	NR	25	0.0	0.0
Ch Cr, Scientst	1	NR	NR	NR	-	-
Ch of Nazarene	1	39	68	68	0.0	0.1
CHR–Chr Chs & Chs Cr	2	NR	145	178	0.1	0.3
CHR–Chs of Christ	7	393	448	544	0.4	0.9
Evan Assoc RCC	2	NR	NR	NR	-	-
Jehovah's Witness	3	NR	NR	NR	-	-
LDS–L-D Saints	1	NR	NR	487	0.4	0.8
LUTH–E.L.C.A.	23	2,457	5,308	6,847	4.9	10.7
LUTH–Luth Cong Msn Chr	5	1,122	3,032	3,715	2.7	5.8
LUTH–Luth-MO Synod	1	50	75	125	0.1	0.2
LUTH–Nor Amer Luth C	8	NR	NR	NR	-	-
LUTH–Wisc Ev Luth Syn	1	32	64	76	0.1	0.1
METH–AME Zion	13	210	1,550	1,899	1.4	3.0
METH–Un Methodist	33	3,199	7,848	9,708	7.0	15.2

NR–Not Reported   - Represents no adherents reported.   Percentages may not total 100 due to rounding.

Table 3: Religious Congregations by County and Group: 2010

Religious Group	Number of Congrega-tions	Number of Attendees	Number of Communicant, Confirmed, or Full Members	Adherents: Number of Adherents	Adherents: % of Total Pop.	Adherents: % of Total Adh.
METH–Wesleyan	3	412	389	535	0.4	0.8
Non-denom Chr Chs	32	5,154	6,165	7,303	5.3	11.4
PENT–Assemb of God	3	235	224	325	0.2	0.5
PENT–Ch God (Cleve)	9	630	1,086	1,331	1.0	2.1
PENT–Ch of God Proph	3	NR	78	96	0.1	0.2
PENT–Fire Bapt Hol Ch	1	NR	NR	NR	-	-
PENT–Int Foursq Gos	3	353	387	474	0.3	0.7
PRES–As Ref Pres Ch	2	NR	87	107	0.1	0.2
PRES–Presb Ch (USA)	15	1,136	2,441	2,991	2.2	4.7
PRES–Presb Ch Amer	2	182	275	307	0.2	0.5
Salvation Army	1	76	119	151	0.1	0.2
Sev Day Adv	2	131	228	262	0.2	0.4
Un C of Christ	8	467	1,628	1,995	1.4	3.1
RUTHERFORD	**194**	**15,580**	**41,025**	**50,341**	**74.2**	**100.0**
ANG/EPIS–Episcopal	2	137	192	193	0.3	0.4
Bahá'í	0	NR	8	8	0.0	0.0
BAPT–Amer Bapt USA	1	95	86	104	0.2	0.2
BAPT–Free Will Bapt	2	NR	228	275	0.4	0.5
BAPT–Natl Mis Bapt Conv	2	30	516	622	0.9	1.2
BAPT–NBC USA	1	0	110	133	0.2	0.3
BAPT–Prog NBC	1	150	250	301	0.4	0.6
BAPT–So Bapt Conv	102	10,829	29,565	35,623	52.5	70.8
BRETH–Ch of Brethren	1	65	182	219	0.3	0.4
Catholic	1	NR	NR	658	1.0	1.3
Ch of Nazarene	1	79	62	93	0.1	0.2
CHR–Chs of Christ	1	40	50	65	0.1	0.1
Jehovah's Witness	1	NR	NR	NR	-	-
LDS–L-D Saints	1	NR	NR	388	0.6	0.8
LUTH–E.L.C.A.	1	45	72	82	0.1	0.2
METH–AME Zion	13	0	1,550	1,868	2.8	3.7
METH–C.M.E.	4	80	384	463	0.7	0.9
METH–Un Methodist	26	1,601	4,551	5,594	8.2	11.1
METH–Wesleyan	3	199	257	260	0.4	0.5
Non-denom Chr Chs	8	1,240	1,640	1,794	2.6	3.6
PENT–Assemb of God	1	30	25	40	0.1	0.1
PENT–Ch God (Cleve)	4	185	195	235	0.3	0.5
PENT–Cong Hol Ch	5	320	257	310	0.5	0.6
PENT–Fire Bapt Hol Ch	2	NR	NR	NR	-	-
PENT–Int Foursq Gos	1	172	180	217	0.3	0.4
PRES–Presb Ch (USA)	7	223	561	676	1.0	1.3
Sev Day Adv	2	60	104	120	0.2	0.2
SAMPSON	**207**	**10,226**	**26,043**	**35,640**	**56.2**	**100.0**
ANG/EPIS–Episcopal	1	47	129	129	0.2	0.4
Bahá'í	0	NR	4	4	0.0	0.0
BAPT–Free Will Bapt	1	NR	114	142	0.2	0.4
BAPT–Natl Mis Bapt Conv	1	0	150	187	0.3	0.5
BAPT–NBC USA	1	250	400	499	0.8	1.4
BAPT–Orig Free Will Bapt	5	450	615	767	1.2	2.2
BAPT–So Bapt Conv	63	5,127	14,191	17,699	27.9	49.7
Catholic	3	NR	NR	3,485	5.5	9.8
CHR–Chr Ch (Disc)	17	345	1,504	1,876	3.0	5.3
CHR–Chs of Christ	1	25	23	36	0.1	0.1
Jehovah's Witness	1	NR	NR	NR	-	-
LDS–L-D Saints	1	NR	NR	342	0.5	1.0
LUTH–E.L.C.A.	1	0	0	0	0.0	0.0
METH–AME	2	0	300	374	0.6	1.0
METH–AME Zion	11	75	1,473	1,837	2.9	5.2
METH–Un Methodist	22	1,104	2,671	3,041	4.8	8.5
Non-denom Chr Chs	10	1,000	1,500	1,500	2.4	4.2
PENT–Assemb of God	1	25	16	44	0.1	0.1
PENT–Ch God (Cleve)	6	310	481	600	0.9	1.7
PENT–Ch of God Proph	8	NR	266	332	0.5	0.9
PENT–Full Gosp Bapt	1	NR	NR	NR	-	-
PENT–Intl Pent Holiness	12	1,136	1,598	1,993	3.1	5.6
PENT–Pent FW Bapt	20	NR	NR	NR	-	-
PENT–Un Pent Ch Intl	1	NR	NR	NR	-	-
PENT–United Holy Ch	9	NR	NR	NR	-	-
PRES–Presb Ch (USA)	5	270	508	634	1.0	1.8
Sev Day Adv	2	50	86	99	0.2	0.3
Unit Univ	1	12	14	20	0.0	0.1

Religious Group	Number of Congrega-tions	Number of Attendees	Number of Communicant, Confirmed, or Full Members	Adherents: Number of Adherents	Adherents: % of Total Pop.	Adherents: % of Total Adh.
SCOTLAND	**85**	**5,096**	**11,531**	**14,481**	**40.1**	**100.0**
ANG/EPIS–Episcopal	1	26	57	65	0.2	0.4
Bahá'í	0	NR	63	63	0.2	0.4
BAPT–Free Will Bapt	1	NR	114	141	0.4	1.0
BAPT–Natl Mis Bapt Conv	1	0	150	185	0.5	1.3
BAPT–Prog NBC	1	120	300	370	1.0	2.6
BAPT–So Bapt Conv	14	1,149	2,519	3,110	8.6	21.5
Catholic	1	NR	NR	442	1.2	3.1
Ch of Nazarene	1	18	30	30	0.1	0.2
CHR–Chr Ch (Disc)	1	0	0	0	0.0	0.0
CHR–Chr Chs & Chs Cr	1	NR	60	74	0.2	0.5
CHR–Chs of Christ	1	20	15	25	0.1	0.2
FRND–Fr Gen Cf	1	NR	0	0	0.0	0.0
Jehovah's Witness	1	NR	NR	NR	-	-
LUTH–E.L.C.A.	1	50	78	106	0.3	0.7
METH–AME	3	0	450	556	1.5	3.8
METH–AME Zion	6	40	725	895	2.5	6.2
METH–Un Methodist	11	929	2,998	3,514	9.7	24.3
METH–Wesleyan	1	81	49	105	0.3	0.7
Non-denom Chr Chs	7	595	880	900	2.5	6.2
PENT–Assemb of God	3	232	104	280	0.8	1.9
PENT–Ch God (Cleve)	5	613	797	984	2.7	6.8
PENT–Ch of God Proph	2	NR	55	68	0.2	0.5
PENT–Fire Bapt Hol Ch	1	NR	NR	NR	-	-
PENT–Full Gosp Bapt	1	NR	NR	NR	-	-
PENT–Intl Pent Holiness	9	767	619	764	2.1	5.3
PENT–Un Pent Ch Intl	1	NR	NR	NR	-	-
PRES–As Ref Pres Ch	0	NR	145	179	0.5	1.2
PRES–Presb Ch (USA)	8	396	1,219	1,505	4.2	10.4
Sev Day Adv	1	60	104	120	0.3	0.8
STANLY	**150**	**15,149**	**30,431**	**40,447**	**66.8**	**100.0**
ANG/EPIS–Episcopal	1	85	117	173	0.3	0.4
Bahá'í	0	NR	6	6	0.0	0.0
BAPT–Orig Free Will Bapt	2	180	246	297	0.5	0.7
BAPT–So Bapt Conv	62	7,341	16,950	20,485	33.8	50.6
Catholic	1	NR	NR	375	0.6	0.9
Ch of Nazarene	1	72	109	111	0.2	0.3
CHR–Chs of Christ	1	53	52	68	0.1	0.2
Jehovah's Witness	2	NR	NR	NR	-	-
LDS–L-D Saints	1	NR	NR	622	1.0	1.5
LUTH–E.L.C.A.	4	429	1,018	1,209	2.0	3.0
LUTH–Luth Cong Msn Chr	1	24	22	27	0.0	0.1
METH–AME Zion	6	50	790	955	1.6	2.4
METH–Un Methodist	30	2,843	5,958	9,562	15.8	23.6
METH–Wesleyan	1	92	114	120	0.2	0.3
Non-denom Chr Chs	13	1,835	2,255	2,505	4.1	6.2
PENT–Assemb of God	1	575	275	940	1.6	2.3
PENT–Ch God (Cleve)	5	479	530	641	1.1	1.6
PENT–Ch of God Proph	1	NR	37	45	0.1	0.1
PENT–Fire Bapt Hol Ch	1	NR	NR	NR	-	-
PENT–Int Foursq Gos	1	38	28	34	0.1	0.1
PENT–Intl Pent Holiness	4	193	231	279	0.5	0.7
PRES–As Ref Pres Ch	1	NR	48	58	0.1	0.1
PRES–Presb Ch (USA)	6	348	940	1,136	1.9	2.8
PRES–Presb Ch Amer	2	394	421	462	0.8	1.1
Sev Day Adv	1	55	96	110	0.2	0.3
Un C of Christ	1	63	188	227	0.4	0.6
STOKES	**81**	**6,163**	**13,472**	**16,568**	**35.0**	**100.0**
ANG/EPIS–Episcopal	2	43	96	97	0.2	0.6
Bahá'í	0	NR	2	2	0.0	0.0
BAPT–So Bapt Conv	22	2,645	5,870	7,026	14.8	42.4
Catholic	1	NR	NR	664	1.4	4.0
CHR–Chr Ch (Disc)	1	70	239	286	0.6	1.7
CHR–Chr Chs & Chs Cr	6	NR	1,563	1,871	3.9	11.3
CHR–Chs of Christ	1	58	70	70	0.1	0.4
Jehovah's Witness	2	NR	NR	NR	-	-
METH–AME Zion	1	0	150	180	0.4	1.1
METH–Un Methodist	18	943	2,041	2,448	5.2	14.8
MORAV–Morav Ch-South	2	256	438	550	1.2	3.3
Non-denom Chr Chs	12	1,693	2,086	2,276	4.8	13.7
ORTHE–Greek Orthodox	1	0	NR	0	0.0	0.0

NR–Not Reported   - Represents no adherents reported.   Percentages may not total 100 due to rounding.

Table 3: Religious Congregations by County and Group: 2010

Religious Group	Number of Congregations	Number of Attendees	Number of Communicant, Confirmed, or Full Members	Adherents		
				Number of Adherents	% of Total Pop.	% of Total Adh.
PENT–Ch God (Cleve)	5	222	519	621	1.3	3.7
PENT–Intl Pent Holiness	1	41	74	89	0.2	0.5
PRES–Presb Ch (USA)	6	192	324	388	0.8	2.3
SURRY	**178**	**15,136**	**30,276**	**39,434**	**53.5**	**100.0**
ANG/EPIS–Episcopal	2	99	181	261	0.4	0.7
Bahá'í	0	NR	29	29	0.0	0.1
BAPT–Natl Mis Bapt Conv	1	0	150	183	0.2	0.5
BAPT–So Bapt Conv	76	8,072	18,594	22,625	30.7	57.4
BRETH–Ch of Brethren	2	86	247	301	0.4	0.8
Catholic	1	NR	NR	446	0.6	1.1
CHR–Chr Ch (Disc)	1	70	184	224	0.3	0.6
CHR–Chr Chs & Chs Cr	4	NR	490	596	0.8	1.5
CHR–Chs of Christ	3	135	126	163	0.2	0.4
FRND–Fr Un Mtg	8	NR	423	515	0.7	1.3
Jehovah's Witness	2	NR	NR	NR	-	-
LDS–L-D Saints	3	NR	NR	1,397	1.9	3.5
LUTH–E.L.C.A.	1	48	49	68	0.1	0.2
METH–AME	1	0	100	122	0.2	0.3
METH–AME Zion	1	0	100	122	0.2	0.3
METH–Un Methodist	26	1,575	3,675	4,754	6.5	12.1
METH–Wesleyan	4	470	323	612	0.8	1.6
MORAV–Morav Ch-South	1	165	351	403	0.5	1.0
Non-denom Chr Chs	16	3,135	3,290	3,955	5.4	10.0
PENT–Assemb of God	2	105	55	198	0.3	0.5
PENT–Ch God (Cleve)	4	163	334	406	0.6	1.0
PENT–Ch of God Proph	1	NR	10	12	0.0	0.0
PENT–Intl Pent Holiness	7	504	674	820	1.1	2.1
PENT–Un Pent Ch Intl	1	NR	NR	NR	-	-
PENT–United Holy Ch	1	NR	NR	NR	-	-
PRES–Orth Pres Ch	1	68	54	82	0.1	0.2
PRES–Presb Ch (USA)	7	388	718	874	1.2	2.2
Salvation Army	1	53	119	266	0.4	0.7
SWAIN	**42**	**2,181**	**3,905**	**5,327**	**38.1**	**100.0**
ANG/EPIS–Episcopal	1	18	40	44	0.3	0.8
Bahá'í	0	NR	20	20	0.1	0.4
BAPT–Free Will Bapt	1	NR	114	139	1.0	2.6
BAPT–So Bapt Conv	19	1,143	2,657	3,234	23.1	60.7
Catholic	2	NR	NR	338	2.4	6.3
Ch of Nazarene	1	7	17	72	0.5	1.4
CHR–Chs of Christ	1	30	20	30	0.2	0.6
LUTH–E.L.C.A.	1	15	26	26	0.2	0.5
METH–Un Methodist	1	85	251	273	2.0	5.1
METH–Wesleyan	2	85	42	110	0.8	2.1
Non-denom Chr Chs	3	210	320	329	2.4	6.2
PENT–Assemb of God	1	20	13	28	0.2	0.5
PENT–Ch God (Cleve)	3	280	221	269	1.9	5.0
PENT–Intl Pent Holiness	2	52	41	50	0.4	0.9
PENT–Pent Ch of God	2	140	NR	217	1.6	4.1
PRES–Presb Ch (USA)	1	84	103	125	0.9	2.3
Sev Day Adv	1	12	20	23	0.2	0.4
TRANSYLVANIA	**65**	**5,032**	**12,598**	**17,485**	**52.8**	**100.0**
ANG/EPIS–Anglican NA	1	NR	NR	NR	-	-
ANG/EPIS–Episcopal	1	215	448	554	1.7	3.2
Bahá'í	0	NR	8	8	0.0	0.0
BAPT–Ref Bapt Ch	1	NR	NR	NR	-	-
BAPT–So Bapt Conv	33	2,921	9,268	10,688	32.3	61.1
BUDD–Mahayana	1	NR	NR	11	0.0	0.1
Catholic	2	NR	NR	2,429	7.3	13.9
Ch Cr, Scientst	1	NR	NR	NR	-	-
Ch of Nazarene	1	14	10	14	0.0	0.1
CHR–Chs of Christ	1	41	38	40	0.1	0.2
FRND–Fr Gen Cf	1	NR	39	45	0.1	0.3
Jehovah's Witness	1	NR	NR	NR	-	-
LDS–L-D Saints	1	NR	NR	230	0.7	1.3
LUTH–E.L.C.A.	1	130	210	226	0.7	1.3
METH–Un Methodist	6	630	1,397	1,699	5.1	9.7
METH–Wesleyan	1	205	211	267	0.8	1.5
Non-denom Chr Chs	4	425	325	532	1.6	3.0
PENT–Assemb of God	1	55	40	55	0.2	0.3
PENT–Ch God (Cleve)	3	146	270	311	0.9	1.8

Religious Group	Number of Congregations	Number of Attendees	Number of Communicant, Confirmed, or Full Members	Adherents		
				Number of Adherents	% of Total Pop.	% of Total Adh.
PENT–Ch of God Proph	1	NR	16	18	0.1	0.1
PRES–Presb Ch Amer	1	108	105	117	0.4	0.7
Sev Day Adv	1	26	46	53	0.2	0.3
Unit Univ	1	116	167	188	0.6	1.1
TYRRELL	**21**	**527**	**1,410**	**1,680**	**38.1**	**100.0**
ANG/EPIS–Episcopal	2	24	39	42	1.0	2.5
Bahá'í	0	NR	1	1	0.0	0.1
BAPT–Free Will Bapt	1	NR	114	132	3.0	7.9
BAPT–Orig Free Will Bapt	3	270	369	429	9.7	25.5
BAPT–So Bapt Conv	2	85	263	306	6.9	18.2
Catholic	1	NR	NR	22	0.5	1.3
CHR–Chr Ch (Disc)	3	20	24	28	0.6	1.7
CHR–Chr Chs & Chs Cr	3	NR	205	238	5.4	14.2
METH–AME Zion	2	0	200	232	5.3	13.8
METH–Un Methodist	3	85	170	170	3.9	10.1
PENT–Assemb of God	1	43	25	80	1.8	4.8
UNION	**241**	**34,768**	**68,097**	**94,121**	**46.8**	**100.0**
ANG/EPIS–Episcopal	2	416	796	880	0.4	0.9
Bahá'í	0	NR	54	54	0.0	0.1
BAPT–Free Will Bapt	2	NR	152	199	0.1	0.2
BAPT–Natl Mis Bapt Conv	1	0	150	196	0.1	0.2
BAPT–NBC USA	4	275	600	785	0.4	0.8
BAPT–Ref Bapt Ch	1	NR	NR	NR	-	-
BAPT–So Bapt Conv	80	14,152	30,680	40,155	19.9	42.7
Calv Chpl	1	NR	NR	NR	-	-
Catholic	1	NR	NR	3,054	1.5	3.2
CGOD–Ch God (Ander)	2	126	NR	126	0.1	0.1
Ch of Nazarene	2	131	175	175	0.1	0.2
Chr & Miss Al	1	33	12	30	0.0	0.0
CHR–Chs of Christ	3	185	191	224	0.1	0.2
Evan Free Ch	2	430	NR	430	0.2	0.5
FRND–Fr Un Mtg	1	NR	13	17	0.0	0.0
Jehovah's Witness	3	NR	NR	NR	-	-
LDS–L-D Saints	2	NR	NR	1,168	0.6	1.2
LUTH–E.L.C.A.	3	215	271	332	0.2	0.4
LUTH–Luth Cong Msn Chr	2	381	844	1,105	0.5	1.2
METH–AME Zion	17	550	2,435	3,187	1.6	3.4
METH–C.M.E.	1	0	150	196	0.1	0.2
METH–Un Methodist	33	4,181	11,053	18,721	9.3	19.9
METH–Wesleyan	1	74	60	96	0.0	0.1
Missionary Ch	1	700	2,100	2,100	1.0	2.2
Non-denom Chr Chs	33	10,307	13,815	14,970	7.4	15.9
PENT–Assemb of God	1	45	40	99	0.0	0.1
PENT–Ch God (Cleve)	8	371	901	1,179	0.6	1.3
PENT–Int Foursq Gos	1	80	32	42	0.0	0.0
PENT–Intl Pent Holiness	4	180	161	211	0.1	0.2
PENT–Un Pent Ch Intl	1	NR	NR	NR	-	-
PRES–As Ref Pres Ch	3	NR	105	137	0.1	0.1
PRES–Presb Ch (USA)	17	1,390	2,630	3,442	1.7	3.7
PRES–Presb Ch Amer	3	384	394	486	0.2	0.5
Sev Day Adv	4	162	283	325	0.2	0.3
VANCE	**107**	**7,944**	**17,339**	**22,209**	**48.9**	**100.0**
ANG/EPIS–Episcopal	3	134	272	368	0.8	1.7
Bahá'í	0	NR	122	122	0.3	0.5
BAPT–Alliance Bapt	1	NR	NR	NR	-	-
BAPT–Free Will Bapt	1	NR	114	141	0.3	0.6
BAPT–Ind Bapt Flwsp Intl	1	NR	NR	NR	-	-
BAPT–NBC Amer	1	325	380	471	1.0	2.1
BAPT–NBC USA	2	0	300	372	0.8	1.7
BAPT–Prog NBC	1	130	380	471	1.0	2.1
BAPT–So Bapt Conv	22	2,419	6,053	7,505	16.5	33.8
Catholic	1	NR	NR	850	1.9	3.8
CHR–Chs of Christ	2	95	83	103	0.2	0.5
Evan Assoc RCC	1	NR	NR	NR	-	-
Jehovah's Witness	1	NR	NR	NR	-	-
LDS–L-D Saints	1	NR	NR	433	1.0	1.9
METH–AME Zion	7	135	773	958	2.1	4.3
METH–Un Methodist	18	1,057	2,766	3,023	6.7	13.6
Non-denom Chr Chs	11	1,085	1,578	1,604	3.5	7.2
PENT–Ch God (Cleve)	4	1,150	1,720	2,133	4.7	9.6

NR–Not Reported   - Represents no adherents reported.   Percentages may not total 100 due to rounding.

Table 3: Religious Congregations by County and Group: 2010

Religious Group	Number of Congrega-tions	Number of Attendees	Number of Communicant, Confirmed, or Full Members	Adherents		
				Number of Adherents	% of Total Pop.	% of Total Adh.
PENT–Ch Lord Jesus Apos	3	NR	NR	NR	-	-
PENT–Ch of God Proph	1	NR	19	24	0.1	0.1
PENT–COGIC	1	150	300	372	0.8	1.7
PENT–Intl Pent Holiness	4	638	942	1,168	2.6	5.3
PENT–United Holy Ch	5	NR	NR	NR	-	-
PRES–Presb Ch (USA)	6	228	389	482	1.1	2.2
PRES–Presb Ch Amer	1	60	102	114	0.3	0.5
Salvation Army	1	82	46	267	0.6	1.2
Sev Day Adv	2	73	127	146	0.3	0.7
Un C of Christ	5	183	873	1,082	2.4	4.9
WAKE	**712**	**133,429**	**229,023**	**418,188**	**46.4**	**100.0**
ANG/EPIS–Anglican NA	5	NR	NR	NR	-	-
ANG/EPIS–Episcopal	13	2,947	7,715	10,059	1.1	2.4
Bahá'í	3	NR	554	554	0.1	0.1
BAPT–Alliance Bapt	4	NR	NR	NR	-	-
BAPT–Amer Bapt USA	4	1,950	2,760	3,475	0.4	0.8
BAPT–Converge/BGC	2	150	NR	180	0.0	0.0
BAPT–Free Will Bapt	5	NR	570	718	0.1	0.2
BAPT–Natl Mis Bapt Conv	1	0	150	189	0.0	0.0
BAPT–NBC Amer	1	250	300	378	0.0	0.1
BAPT–NBC USA	8	2,200	3,950	4,973	0.6	1.2
BAPT–Orig Free Will Bapt	5	450	615	774	0.1	0.2
BAPT–Prog NBC	2	0	300	378	0.0	0.1
BAPT–So Bapt Conv	160	34,964	64,322	80,987	9.0	19.4
BRETH–Breth in Chr	1	NR	NR	NR	-	-
BUDD–Mahayana	6	NR	NR	5,801	0.6	1.4
BUDD–Vajrayana	1	NR	NR	208	0.0	0.0
Calv Chpl	3	NR	NR	NR	-	-
Catholic	17	NR	NR	99,126	11.0	23.7
CGOD–Ch God (Ander)	3	96	NR	96	0.0	0.0
Ch Cr, Scientst	2	NR	NR	NR	-	-
Ch of Nazarene	6	1,188	1,243	1,471	0.2	0.4
Chr & Miss Al	9	1,341	1,073	1,783	0.2	0.4
CHR–Chr Ch (Disc)	14	561	1,492	1,879	0.2	0.4
CHR–Chr Chs & Chs Cr	6	NR	1,340	1,687	0.2	0.4
CHR–Chs of Christ	9	1,592	1,545	2,126	0.2	0.5
Christian Brethren	2	NR	NR	NR	-	-
Evan Assoc RCC	1	NR	NR	NR	-	-
Evan Cov Ch	1	156	97	203	0.0	0.0
Evan Free Ch	1	70	NR	70	0.0	0.0
FRND–Fr Gen Cf	1	NR	0	0	0.0	0.0
HINDU–I/A Temples	3	NR	NR	2,342	0.3	0.6
HINDU–Post Ren	4	NR	NR	105	0.0	0.0
HINDU–Trad Temples	2	NR	NR	3,300	0.4	0.8
Int Cou Comm Ch	1	NR	NR	NR	-	-
Jain	1	NR	NR	NR	-	-
Jehovah's Witness	9	NR	NR	NR	-	-
JUD–Conserv	1	383	430	1,161	0.1	0.3
JUD–Orth	3	288	175	400	0.0	0.1
JUD–Reform	2	398	702	1,895	0.2	0.5
LDS–Comm of Christ	2	NR	236	236	0.0	0.1
LDS–L-D Saints	20	NR	NR	8,660	1.0	2.1
LUTH–E.L.C.A.	8	2,104	3,926	5,505	0.6	1.3
LUTH–Luth–MO Synod	4	1,504	2,715	3,779	0.4	0.9
LUTH–Wisc Ev Luth Syn	2	156	199	257	0.0	0.1
MENN–Mennonite USA	1	75	60	76	0.0	0.0
METH–AME	9	400	1,585	1,996	0.2	0.5
METH–AME Zion	7	975	2,390	3,009	0.3	0.7
METH–C.M.E.	4	230	660	831	0.1	0.2
METH–Un Methodist	46	14,938	47,291	57,196	6.3	13.7
METH–Wesleyan	1	75	66	98	0.0	0.0
Metro Comm Ch	1	136	137	172	0.0	0.0
MJEW–Union Mes Cong	1	NR	NR	NR	-	-
MORAV–Morav Ch-South	1	189	418	507	0.1	0.1
Muslim Est	7	4,842	NR	10,299	1.1	2.5
New Apost Ch	1	NR	NR	NR	-	-
Non-denom Chr Chs	115	38,653	48,223	52,583	5.8	12.6
ORTHE–Ant Orth of NA	1	180	NR	500	0.1	0.1
ORTHE–Greek Orthodox	1	310	NR	1,390	0.2	0.3
ORTHE–Orth Ch in Amer	1	85	NR	150	0.0	0.0
ORTHO–Coptic Orth Ch	1	350	NR	535	0.1	0.1
ORTHO–Malan Dioc Am	1	25	NR	75	0.0	0.0
PENT–Assemb of God	15	3,522	1,313	5,042	0.6	1.2
PENT–Ch God (Cleve)	20	1,812	2,887	3,635	0.4	0.9
PENT–Ch Lord Jesus Apos	1	NR	NR	NR	-	-
PENT–Ch of God Proph	7	NR	574	723	0.1	0.2
PENT–COGIC	6	3,200	3,750	4,722	0.5	1.1
PENT–Elim	1	NR	NR	NR	-	-
PENT–Fire Bapt Hol Ch	1	NR	NR	NR	-	-
PENT–Full Gosp Bapt	1	NR	NR	NR	-	-
PENT–Int Foursq Gos	4	882	1,004	1,264	0.1	0.3
PENT–Intl Pent Holiness	14	1,316	1,388	1,748	0.2	0.4
PENT–Pent FW Bapt	3	NR	NR	NR	-	-
PENT–Un Pent Ch Intl	6	NR	NR	NR	-	-
PENT–United Holy Ch	2	NR	NR	NR	-	-
PENT–Vineyard	4	529	614	773	0.1	0.2
PRES–As Ref Pres Ch	3	NR	137	172	0.0	0.0
PRES–Evan Presby Ch	2	NR	176	222	0.0	0.1
PRES–Korean Pres Amer	1	NR	NR	NR	-	-
PRES–Orth Pres Ch	2	139	148	222	0.0	0.1
PRES–Presb Ch (USA)	24	5,128	14,159	17,827	2.0	4.3
PRES–Presb Ch Amer	11	563	1,001	1,398	0.2	0.3
REF–Comm Ref Evan	1	NR	NR	NR	-	-
REF–Ref Ch in Am	1	104	175	197	0.0	0.0
Salvation Army	1	182	185	745	0.1	0.2
Sev Day Adv	7	914	1,590	1,829	0.2	0.4
Un C of Christ	13	640	2,137	2,691	0.3	0.6
Unit Univ	2	287	546	793	0.1	0.2
Unity Ch	2	NR	NR	NR	-	-
Zoroastrian	0	NR	NR	13	0.0	0.0
WARREN	**43**	**2,549**	**6,125**	**7,192**	**34.3**	**100.0**
ANG/EPIS–Episcopal	3	44	71	75	0.4	1.0
Bahá'í	0	NR	12	12	0.1	0.2
BAPT–So Bapt Conv	10	1,019	2,584	3,048	14.5	42.4
Catholic	1	NR	NR	138	0.7	1.9
Jehovah's Witness	1	NR	NR	NR	-	-
LUTH–E.L.C.A.	1	139	243	263	1.3	3.7
LUTH–Luth–MO Synod	1	106	206	244	1.2	3.4
METH–AME	1	0	100	118	0.6	1.6
METH–Un Methodist	9	367	1,065	1,139	5.4	15.8
Non-denom Chr Chs	5	610	750	864	4.1	12.0
PENT–Ch God (Cleve)	1	61	53	63	0.3	0.9
PENT–Ch Lord Jesus Apos	1	NR	NR	NR	-	-
PENT–Ch of God Proph	1	NR	5	6	0.0	0.1
PENT–Intl Pent Holiness	1	47	123	145	0.7	2.0
PENT–United Holy Ch	1	NR	NR	NR	-	-
PRES–Presb Ch (USA)	2	30	45	53	0.3	0.7
Un C of Christ	4	126	868	1,024	4.9	14.2
WASHINGTON	**56**	**1,839**	**5,670**	**6,836**	**51.7**	**100.0**
ANG/EPIS–Episcopal	3	65	116	118	0.9	1.7
Bahá'í	0	NR	207	207	1.6	3.0
BAPT–Free Will Bapt	2	NR	228	277	2.1	4.1
BAPT–NBC USA	1	75	150	182	1.4	2.7
BAPT–Orig Free Will Bapt	4	360	492	597	4.5	8.7
BAPT–So Bapt Conv	5	260	779	945	7.1	13.8
Catholic	1	NR	NR	205	1.5	3.0
Ch of Nazarene	1	83	135	142	1.1	2.1
CHR–Chr Ch (Disc)	7	79	208	252	1.9	3.7
CHR–Chr Chs & Chs Cr	8	NR	1,394	1,692	12.8	24.8
CHR–Chs of Christ	1	25	19	24	0.2	0.4
Jehovah's Witness	1	NR	NR	NR	-	-
METH–AME Zion	4	0	450	546	4.1	8.0
METH–Un Methodist	6	160	509	553	4.2	8.1
Non-denom Chr Chs	4	480	595	625	4.7	9.1
PENT–Ch God (Cleve)	3	92	115	140	1.1	2.0
PENT–COGIC	2	0	60	73	0.6	1.1
PENT–Intl Pent Holiness	3	160	213	258	2.0	3.8
WATAUGA	**94**	**9,005**	**16,338**	**21,055**	**41.2**	**100.0**
ANG/EPIS–Anglican NA	1	NR	NR	NR	-	-
ANG/EPIS–Episcopal	3	449	914	1,089	2.1	5.2
Bahá'í	1	NR	55	55	0.1	0.3
BAPT–So Bapt Conv	45	4,490	9,404	10,512	20.6	49.9
Catholic	2	NR	NR	685	1.3	3.3

NR–Not Reported   - Represents no adherents reported.   Percentages may not total 100 due to rounding.

Table 3: Religious Congregations by County and Group: 2010

Religious Group	Number of Congregations	Number of Attendees	Number of Communicant, Confirmed, or Full Members	Adherents: Number of Adherents	Adherents: % of Total Pop.	Adherents: % of Total Adh.
Ch Cr, Scientst	1	NR	NR	NR	-	-
Ch of Nazarene	1	16	20	22	0.0	0.1
Chr & Miss Al	1	950	335	1,085	2.1	5.2
CHR–Chr Chs & Chs Cr	2	NR	190	212	0.4	1.0
CHR–Chs of Christ	1	72	59	76	0.1	0.4
Jehovah's Witness	1	NR	NR	NR	-	-
LDS–L-D Saints	1	NR	NR	421	0.8	2.0
LUTH–E.L.C.A.	3	456	1,184	1,484	2.9	7.0
MENN–Menn Br US Conf	1	NR	42	47	0.1	0.2
METH–Un Methodist	13	1,197	2,373	3,222	6.3	15.3
Non-denom Chr Chs	4	490	530	643	1.3	3.1
ORTHE–Ant Orth of NA	1	18	NR	24	0.0	0.1
PENT–Assemb of God	2	90	55	90	0.2	0.4
PENT–Int Foursq Gos	1	44	68	76	0.1	0.4
PRES–As Ref Pres Ch	1	NR	25	28	0.1	0.1
PRES–Presb Ch (USA)	3	442	695	777	1.5	3.7
PRES–Presb Ch Amer	2	95	37	62	0.1	0.3
Sev Day Adv	1	36	63	72	0.1	0.3
Un C of Christ	1	90	204	228	0.4	1.1
Unit Univ	1	70	85	145	0.3	0.7
WAYNE	**267**	**19,530**	**37,232**	**49,647**	**40.5**	**100.0**
ANG/EPIS–Episcopal	3	240	526	526	0.4	1.1
Bahá'í	0	NR	78	78	0.1	0.2
BAPT–Free Will Bapt	4	NR	456	566	0.5	1.1
BAPT–Natl Mis Bapt Conv	3	0	450	559	0.5	1.1
BAPT–Orig Free Will Bapt	18	1,620	2,211	2,745	2.2	5.5
BAPT–So Bapt Conv	30	2,537	6,736	8,363	6.8	16.8
Catholic	2	NR	NR	2,800	2.3	5.6
Chr & Miss Al	1	70	44	106	0.1	0.2
CHR–Chr Ch (Disc)	21	252	1,069	1,327	1.1	2.7
CHR–Chs of Christ	2	258	236	325	0.3	0.7
FRND–Fr Un Mtg	6	NR	442	549	0.4	1.1
Jehovah's Witness	2	NR	NR	NR	-	-
JUD–Reform	1	9	15	40	0.0	0.1
LDS–L-D Saints	5	NR	NR	2,270	1.9	4.6
LUTH–E.L.C.A.	1	106	332	357	0.3	0.7
LUTH–Luth-MO Synod	1	33	65	87	0.1	0.2
METH–AME	1	0	150	186	0.2	0.4
METH–AME Zion	9	190	1,170	1,453	1.2	2.9
METH–Un Methodist	26	2,577	6,867	8,001	6.5	16.1
METH–Wesleyan	1	96	69	125	0.1	0.3
Muslim Est	1	50	NR	50	0.0	0.1
New Apost Ch	1	NR	NR	NR	-	-
Non-denom Chr Chs	46	7,845	10,728	12,082	9.9	24.3
PENT–Assemb of God	3	333	250	351	0.3	0.7
PENT–Ch God (Cleve)	6	572	952	1,182	1.0	2.4
PENT–Ch Lord Jesus Apos	1	NR	NR	NR	-	-
PENT–Ch of God Proph	5	NR	130	161	0.1	0.3
PENT–COGIC	1	0	150	186	0.2	0.4
PENT–Fire Bapt Hol Ch	1	NR	NR	NR	-	-
PENT–Full Gosp Bapt	1	NR	NR	NR	-	-
PENT–Intl Pent Holiness	16	1,758	1,917	2,380	1.9	4.8
PENT–Pent FW Bapt	13	NR	NR	NR	-	-
PENT–Un Pent Ch Intl	1	NR	NR	NR	-	-
PENT–United Holy Ch	18	NR	NR	NR	-	-
PRES–Presb Ch (USA)	6	473	1,264	1,569	1.3	3.2
PRES–Presb Ch Amer	2	103	137	157	0.1	0.3
Salvation Army	1	59	128	295	0.2	0.6
Sev Day Adv	6	309	537	618	0.5	1.2
Un C of Christ	1	40	123	153	0.1	0.3
WILKES	**146**	**13,419**	**32,542**	**40,013**	**57.7**	**100.0**
ANG/EPIS–Episcopal	1	149	427	532	0.8	1.3
Bahá'í	0	NR	6	6	0.0	0.0
BAPT–Natl Mis Bapt Conv	1	0	150	181	0.3	0.5
BAPT–So Bapt Conv	86	9,824	25,635	30,932	44.6	77.3
BRETH–Ch of Brethren	1	0	71	86	0.1	0.2
Catholic	1	NR	NR	329	0.5	0.8
CHR–Chs of Christ	3	225	179	250	0.4	0.6
FRND–Fr Gen Cf	2	NR	0	0	0.0	0.0
Jehovah's Witness	2	NR	NR	NR	-	-
LDS–L-D Saints	1	NR	NR	510	0.7	1.3
LUTH–Luth Cong Msn Chr	1	55	240	290	0.4	0.7
LUTH–Nor Amer Luth C	1	NR	NR	NR	-	-
MENN–Amish Undif	0	NR	4	7	0.0	0.0
MENN–Menn Br US Conf	1	NR	14	17	0.0	0.0
METH–AME Zion	3	20	325	392	0.6	1.0
METH–Un Methodist	17	1,174	2,700	3,129	4.5	7.8
Non-denom Chr Chs	9	1,384	1,639	1,901	2.7	4.8
PENT–Assemb of God	2	88	65	143	0.2	0.4
PENT–Ch God (Cleve)	4	150	213	257	0.4	0.6
PENT–Ch of God Proph	1	NR	20	24	0.0	0.1
PENT–Fire Bapt Hol Ch	1	NR	NR	NR	-	-
PENT–Intl Pent Holiness	3	125	178	215	0.3	0.5
PRES–As Ref Pres Ch	1	NR	0	0	0.0	0.0
PRES–Presb Ch (USA)	2	187	609	735	1.1	1.8
Sev Day Adv	2	38	67	77	0.1	0.2
WILSON	**164**	**12,655**	**25,991**	**34,022**	**41.9**	**100.0**
ANG/EPIS–Anglican NA	1	NR	NR	NR	-	-
ANG/EPIS–Episcopal	3	292	833	1,551	1.9	4.6
Bahá'í	0	NR	129	129	0.2	0.4
BAPT–Amer Bapt USA	1	190	362	447	0.6	1.3
BAPT–Free Will Bapt	5	NR	570	704	0.9	2.1
BAPT–Natl Mis Bapt Conv	1	0	150	185	0.2	0.5
BAPT–NBC USA	1	200	300	371	0.5	1.1
BAPT–Orig Free Will Bapt	17	1,530	2,088	2,579	3.2	7.6
BAPT–So Bapt Conv	19	2,506	6,775	8,369	10.3	24.6
Catholic	1	NR	NR	1,510	1.9	4.4
CGOD–Ch God (Ander)	1	15	NR	15	0.0	0.0
CHR–Chr Ch (Disc)	13	200	920	1,137	1.4	3.3
CHR–Chr Chs & Chs Cr	1	NR	150	185	0.2	0.5
CHR–Chs of Christ	2	71	61	77	0.1	0.2
Jehovah's Witness	1	NR	NR	NR	-	-
LDS–L-D Saints	1	NR	NR	458	0.6	1.3
LUTH–E.L.C.A.	1	55	112	132	0.2	0.4
LUTH–Luth-MO Synod	1	74	50	100	0.1	0.3
METH–AME	1	0	150	185	0.2	0.5
METH–AME Zion	6	150	850	1,050	1.3	3.1
METH–Un Methodist	12	1,166	4,193	5,122	6.3	15.1
Non-denom Chr Chs	24	3,575	4,405	4,923	6.1	14.5
PENT–Assemb of God	1	70	50	90	0.1	0.3
PENT–Ch God (Cleve)	5	1,044	1,068	1,319	1.6	3.9
PENT–Ch of God Proph	2	NR	29	36	0.0	0.1
PENT–Full Gosp Bapt	3	NR	NR	NR	-	-
PENT–Intl Pent Holiness	13	764	1,036	1,280	1.6	3.8
PENT–Un Pent Ch Intl	1	NR	NR	NR	-	-
PENT–United Holy Ch	10	NR	NR	NR	-	-
PRES–As Ref Pres Ch	1	NR	18	22	0.0	0.1
PRES–Evan Presby Ch	1	NR	87	107	0.1	0.3
PRES–Presb Ch (USA)	7	465	1,062	1,312	1.6	3.9
PRES–Presb Ch Amer	1	80	59	78	0.1	0.2
Salvation Army	1	60	113	113	0.1	0.3
Sev Day Adv	4	148	257	295	0.4	0.9
Un C of Christ	1	0	114	141	0.2	0.4
YADKIN	**96**	**8,541**	**17,880**	**22,717**	**59.1**	**100.0**
Bahá'í	0	NR	11	11	0.0	0.0
BAPT–Natl Mis Bapt Conv	1	0	150	182	0.5	0.8
BAPT–So Bapt Conv	33	4,123	10,070	12,235	31.9	53.9
Catholic	2	NR	NR	1,194	3.1	5.3
CHR–Chs of Christ	3	225	185	263	0.7	1.2
FRND–Fr Un Mtg	9	NR	847	1,029	2.7	4.5
Jehovah's Witness	1	NR	NR	NR	-	-
LUTH–E.L.C.A.	1	30	36	37	0.1	0.2
MENN–Amish Undif	0	NR	6	10	0.0	0.0
METH–AME Zion	3	0	400	486	1.3	2.1
METH–Evan Meth Ch	1	NR	NR	NR	-	-
METH–Un Methodist	18	1,149	2,515	2,978	7.8	13.1
Non-denom Chr Chs	13	2,623	3,010	3,455	9.0	15.2
PENT–Assemb of God	2	141	89	156	0.4	0.7
PENT–Ch God (Cleve)	2	76	149	181	0.5	0.8
PENT–Intl Pent Holiness	4	134	296	360	0.9	1.6
PRES–Presb Ch (USA)	2	40	44	53	0.1	0.2
Un C of Christ	1	0	72	87	0.2	0.4

NR–Not Reported   - Represents no adherents reported.   Percentages may not total 100 due to rounding.

Table 3: Religious Congregations by County and Group: 2010

Religious Group	Number of Congrega-tions	Number of Attendees	Number of Communicant, Confirmed, or Full Members	Adherents: Number of Adherents	Adherents: % of Total Pop.	Adherents: % of Total Adh.
YANCEY	**49**	**2,493**	**5,419**	**6,618**	**37.1**	**100.0**
ANG/EPIS–Episcopal	1	53	88	90	0.5	1.4
Bahá'í	0	NR	9	9	0.1	0.1
BAPT–So Bapt Conv	24	1,478	3,712	4,364	24.5	65.9
Catholic	1	NR	NR	171	1.0	2.6
CHR–Chs of Christ	1	29	19	24	0.1	0.4
FRND–Fr Gen Cf	1	NR	32	38	0.2	0.6
Jehovah's Witness	1	NR	NR	NR	-	-
LUTH–E.L.C.A.	1	15	35	35	0.2	0.5
METH–AME Zion	1	0	100	118	0.7	1.8
METH–Un Methodist	7	428	775	966	5.4	14.6
Non-denom Chr Chs	1	150	125	188	1.1	2.8
PENT–Ch God (Cleve)	1	106	100	118	0.7	1.8
PENT–Ch of God Proph	1	NR	44	52	0.3	0.8
PRES–Presb Ch (USA)	7	203	326	383	2.1	5.8
Sev Day Adv	1	31	54	62	0.3	0.9
NORTH DAKOTA	**1,498**	**82,047**	**199,790**	**451,456**	**67.1**	**100.0**
ADAMS	**15**	**573**	**1,118**	**2,383**	**101.7**	**100.0**
BAPT–So Bapt Conv	1	51	37	43	1.8	1.8
Catholic	2	NR	NR	726	31.0	30.5
Evan Free Ch	1	32	NR	32	1.4	1.3
LUTH–E.L.C.A.	6	198	895	1,044	44.6	43.8
METH–Un Methodist	1	60	115	176	7.5	7.4
PENT–Assemb of God	2	212	22	305	13.0	12.8
Un C of Christ	2	20	49	57	2.4	2.4
BARNES	**38**	**1,550**	**4,073**	**7,039**	**63.6**	**100.0**
ANG/EPIS–Episcopal	1	10	14	20	0.2	0.3
Bahá'í	0	NR	3	3	0.0	0.0
BAPT–N Am Bapt Conf	1	NR	96	114	1.0	1.6
BAPT–So Bapt Conv	1	5	5	6	0.1	0.1
Catholic	6	NR	NR	1,700	15.4	24.2
Ch of Nazarene	1	186	230	405	3.7	5.8
Evan Free Ch	1	55	NR	55	0.5	0.8
Jehovah's Witness	2	NR	NR	NR	-	-
LUTH–Assoc Free Luth	2	NR	NR	NR	-	-
LUTH–E.L.C.A.	14	895	2,829	3,518	31.8	50.0
LUTH–Luth-MO Synod	1	27	129	163	1.5	2.3
LUTH–Wisc Ev Luth Syn	1	32	64	85	0.8	1.2
METH–Un Methodist	2	181	484	635	5.7	9.0
PENT–Assemb of God	2	99	54	140	1.3	2.0
PENT–Un Pent Ch Intl	1	NR	NR	NR	-	-
REF–Ref Ch in Am	1	24	31	36	0.3	0.5
Un C of Christ	1	36	134	159	1.4	2.3
BENSON	**28**	**512**	**1,585**	**5,689**	**85.4**	**100.0**
ANG/EPIS–Episcopal	1	12	80	97	1.5	1.7
Bahá'í	0	NR	18	18	0.3	0.3
BAPT–So Bapt Conv	1	25	57	78	1.2	1.4
Catholic	8	NR	NR	3,638	54.6	63.9
Evan Free Ch	1	37	NR	37	0.6	0.7
LUTH–Assoc Free Luth	2	NR	NR	NR	-	-
LUTH–Ch of Luth Br	1	25	22	147	2.2	2.6
LUTH–E.L.C.A.	11	377	1,349	1,580	23.7	27.8
PENT–Assemb of God	1	30	19	39	0.6	0.7
PRES–Presb Ch (USA)	2	6	40	55	0.8	1.0
BILLINGS	**3**	**65**	**37**	**77**	**9.8**	**100.0**
Catholic	1	NR	NR	35	4.5	45.5
LUTH–E.L.C.A.	1	30	32	36	4.6	46.8
Un C of Christ	1	35	5	6	0.8	7.8
BOTTINEAU	**26**	**1,221**	**2,764**	**4,536**	**70.6**	**100.0**
Bahá'í	0	NR	10	10	0.2	0.2
BAPT–Amer Bapt USA	1	22	39	45	0.7	1.0
Catholic	4	NR	NR	822	12.8	18.1
Evan Free Ch	1	70	NR	70	1.1	1.5
Jehovah's Witness	1	NR	NR	NR	-	-
LUTH–Ch of Luth Br	2	205	146	509	7.9	11.2
LUTH–E.L.C.A.	9	523	1,854	2,247	35.0	49.5
LUTH–Luth-MO Synod	3	171	436	518	8.1	11.4
METH–Un Methodist	2	94	112	121	1.9	2.7
PRES–Presb Ch (USA)	2	110	121	141	2.2	3.1
Sev Day Adv	1	26	46	53	0.8	1.2
BOWMAN	**13**	**461**	**1,399**	**3,597**	**114.2**	**100.0**
Catholic	3	NR	NR	1,610	51.1	44.8
LUTH–E.L.C.A.	5	282	1,087	1,510	47.9	42.0
METH–Un Methodist	1	85	151	247	7.8	6.9
PENT–Assemb of God	1	70	44	91	2.9	2.5
PRES–Presb Ch (USA)	1	0	3	4	0.1	0.1
Sev Day Adv	1	24	41	47	1.5	1.3
Un C of Christ	1	0	73	88	2.8	2.4
BURKE	**18**	**464**	**1,399**	**2,124**	**107.9**	**100.0**
BAPT–Amer Bapt USA	1	70	125	149	7.6	7.0
Catholic	3	NR	NR	342	17.4	16.1
Jehovah's Witness	2	NR	NR	NR	-	-
LUTH–E.L.C.A.	6	252	1,103	1,415	71.9	66.6
LUTH–Luth Ch-Am Asc	1	NR	NR	NR	-	-
LUTH–Luth-MO Synod	1	17	34	36	1.8	1.7
METH–Un Methodist	1	44	75	75	3.8	3.5
PENT–Assemb of God	1	64	35	75	3.8	3.5
PENT–Ch God (Cleve)	1	13	23	27	1.4	1.3
PRES–Presb Ch (USA)	1	4	4	5	0.3	0.2
BURLEIGH	**72**	**9,521**	**21,558**	**52,035**	**64.0**	**100.0**
ANG/EPIS–Episcopal	1	107	300	375	0.5	0.7
Bahá'í	0	NR	37	37	0.0	0.1
BAPT–Amer Bapt USA	1	82	348	422	0.5	0.8
BAPT–N Am Bapt Conf	2	NR	1,037	1,259	1.5	2.4
BAPT–So Bapt Conv	4	141	143	174	0.2	0.3
Calv Chpl	1	NR	NR	NR	-	-
Catholic	6	NR	NR	20,169	24.8	38.8
Ch of Nazarene	1	79	126	126	0.2	0.2
CHR–Chs of Christ	1	50	47	62	0.1	0.1
Evan Ch	1	NR	NR	NR	-	-
Evan Free Ch	1	643	NR	643	0.8	1.2
FRND–Fr Gen Cf	1	NR	6	7	0.0	0.0
LDS–L-D Saints	1	NR	NR	986	1.2	1.9
LUTH–Assoc Free Luth	1	NR	NR	NR	-	-
LUTH–Ch Luth Conf	1	NR	NR	NR	-	-
LUTH–Ch of Luth Br	1	122	110	280	0.3	0.5
LUTH–E.L.C.A.	11	3,078	10,904	14,300	17.6	27.5
LUTH–Luth Cong Msn Chr	1	680	1,000	1,214	1.5	2.3
LUTH–Luth-MO Synod	3	450	1,978	2,671	3.3	5.1
LUTH–Wisc Ev Luth Syn	1	68	139	166	0.2	0.3
METH–Un Methodist	5	829	1,921	2,574	3.2	4.9
METH–Wesleyan	1	107	51	139	0.2	0.3
Muslim Est	1	134	NR	308	0.4	0.6
Non-denom Chr Chs	4	385	405	482	0.6	0.9
PENT–Assemb of God	7	1,262	435	2,101	2.6	4.0
PENT–Ch God (Cleve)	2	101	81	98	0.1	0.2
PENT–Ch of God Proph	1	NR	15	18	0.0	0.0
PENT–Int Foursq Gos	1	355	408	495	0.6	1.0
PENT–Open Bible Std	1	81	NR	81	0.1	0.2
PENT–Un Pent Ch Intl	1	NR	NR	NR	-	-
PRES–Presb Ch (USA)	2	187	633	768	0.9	1.5
REF–Ref Ch in Am	1	160	518	628	0.8	1.2
Salvation Army	1	42	69	437	0.5	0.8
Sev Day Adv	2	191	332	382	0.5	0.7
Un C of Christ	1	127	438	532	0.7	1.0
Unit Univ	1	60	77	101	0.1	0.2
CASS	**140**	**18,220**	**41,168**	**89,055**	**59.5**	**100.0**
ANG/EPIS–Anglican NA	1	NR	NR	NR	-	-
ANG/EPIS–Episcopal	2	234	394	608	0.4	0.7
Bahá'í	1	NR	45	45	0.0	0.1
BAPT–Amer Bapt USA	1	32	110	133	0.1	0.1
BAPT–Asc Ref Bap Ch Am	1	NR	NR	NR	-	-

NR–Not Reported - Represents no adherents reported. Percentages may not total 100 due to rounding.

Table 3: Religious Congregations by County and Group: 2010

Religious Group	Number of Congregations	Number of Attendees	Number of Communicant, Confirmed, or Full Members	Adherents: Number of Adherents	Adherents: % of Total Pop.	Adherents: % of Total Adh.
BAPT–N Am Bapt Conf	1	NR	157	190	0.1	0.2
BAPT–Ref Bapt Ch	1	NR	NR	NR	-	-
BAPT–So Bapt Conv	5	143	251	304	0.2	0.3
Calv Chpl	1	NR	NR	NR	-	-
Catholic	14	NR	NR	26,438	17.7	29.7
Ch Cr, Scientst	1	NR	NR	NR	-	-
Ch God (7th Day)	1	NR	NR	NR	-	-
Ch of Nazarene	1	505	130	1,200	0.8	1.3
CHR–Chs of Christ	1	30	32	40	0.0	0.0
Christian Brethren	1	NR	NR	NR	-	-
Evan Cov Ch	1	91	93	118	0.1	0.1
Evan Free Ch	4	2,609	NR	2,609	1.7	2.9
Jehovah's Witness	1	NR	NR	NR	-	-
JUD–Reform	1	16	28	76	0.1	0.1
LDS–Comm of Christ	1	NR	138	138	0.1	0.2
LDS–L-D Saints	3	NR	NR	1,162	0.8	1.3
LUTH–Assoc Free Luth	2	NR	NR	NR	-	-
LUTH–Ch Luth Conf	1	NR	NR	NR	-	-
LUTH–Ch of Luth Br	1	77	68	297	0.2	0.3
LUTH–E.L.C.A.	41	8,627	29,135	39,119	26.1	43.9
LUTH–Luth Cong Msn Chr	1	673	1,768	2,139	1.4	2.4
LUTH–Luth-MO Synod	5	981	2,491	3,387	2.3	3.8
LUTH–Wisc Ev Luth Syn	1	95	115	175	0.1	0.2
METH–Free Methodist	1	22	7	22	0.0	0.0
METH–Un Methodist	10	1,160	2,011	3,315	2.2	3.7
MORAV–Morav Ch-North	4	159	407	502	0.3	0.6
Muslim Est	1	134	NR	308	0.2	0.3
Non-denom Chr Chs	3	465	380	587	0.4	0.7
ORTHE–Orth Ch in Amer	1	35	NR	50	0.0	0.1
PENT–Assemb of God	3	1,172	785	2,846	1.9	3.2
PENT–Ch God (Cleve)	2	33	49	59	0.0	0.1
PENT–Un Pent Ch Intl	1	NR	NR	NR	-	-
PRES–Orth Pres Ch	1	11	11	11	0.0	0.0
PRES–Presb Ch (USA)	8	460	1,459	1,765	1.2	2.0
REF–Ref Ch in Am	1	85	63	79	0.1	0.1
Salvation Army	1	64	60	150	0.1	0.2
Sev Day Adv	2	92	160	184	0.1	0.2
Un C of Christ	4	171	763	923	0.6	1.0
Unit Univ	1	44	58	76	0.1	0.1
CAVALIER	**20**	**491**	**1,409**	**3,145**	**78.8**	**100.0**
BAPT–So Bapt Conv	1	25	40	47	1.2	1.5
Catholic	4	NR	NR	1,293	32.4	41.1
Evan Ch	1	NR	NR	NR	-	-
LUTH–E.L.C.A.	5	248	945	1,201	30.1	38.2
LUTH–Luth-MO Synod	2	52	86	110	2.8	3.5
MENN–Mennonite USA	1	20	21	24	0.6	0.8
METH–Un Methodist	1	37	134	250	6.3	7.9
PENT–Assemb of God	1	28	19	29	0.7	0.9
PRES–Presb Ch (USA)	4	81	164	191	4.8	6.1
DICKEY	**27**	**1,198**	**2,458**	**3,907**	**73.9**	**100.0**
ANG/EPIS–Episcopal	1	8	25	25	0.5	0.6
BAPT–Amer Bapt USA	1	45	20	24	0.5	0.6
Catholic	3	NR	NR	808	15.3	20.7
Ch of Nazarene	2	255	238	287	5.4	7.3
Jehovah's Witness	1	NR	NR	NR	-	-
LUTH–E.L.C.A.	4	220	908	1,148	21.7	29.4
LUTH–Luth-MO Synod	3	316	712	822	15.5	21.0
MENN–Hutt Breth	2	NR	NR	NR	-	-
METH–Un Methodist	4	172	363	508	9.6	13.0
PENT–Assemb of God	2	123	92	166	3.1	4.2
PENT–Assm God Intl F	1	NR	NR	NR	-	-
PRES–Presb Ch (USA)	2	36	60	73	1.4	1.9
Sev Day Adv	1	23	40	46	0.9	1.2
DIVIDE	**10**	**302**	**950**	**1,463**	**70.6**	**100.0**
Bahá'í	0	NR	1	1	0.0	0.1
Catholic	2	NR	NR	207	10.0	14.1
LUTH–E.L.C.A.	7	261	930	1,179	56.9	80.6
PENT–Assemb of God	1	41	19	76	3.7	5.2

Religious Group	Number of Congregations	Number of Attendees	Number of Communicant, Confirmed, or Full Members	Adherents: Number of Adherents	Adherents: % of Total Pop.	Adherents: % of Total Adh.
DUNN	**13**	**243**	**1,122**	**3,670**	**103.8**	**100.0**
Bahá'í	0	NR	27	27	0.8	0.7
Catholic	5	NR	NR	2,379	67.3	64.8
LUTH–Assoc Free Luth	1	NR	NR	NR	-	-
LUTH–E.L.C.A.	4	166	935	1,081	30.6	29.5
LUTH–Luth Cong Msn Chr	1	50	95	113	3.2	3.1
PENT–Assemb of God	1	18	37	37	1.0	1.0
Un C of Christ	1	9	28	33	0.9	0.9
EDDY	**9**	**339**	**1,029**	**1,725**	**72.3**	**100.0**
Catholic	1	NR	NR	500	21.0	29.0
CONG–Consrv Cong Chr	1	29	46	55	2.3	3.2
Evan Free Ch	1	30	NR	30	1.3	1.7
LUTH–E.L.C.A.	4	241	923	1,070	44.9	62.0
LUTH–Luth-MO Synod	1	14	17	18	0.8	1.0
METH–Un Methodist	1	25	43	52	2.2	3.0
EMMONS	**16**	**435**	**1,177**	**3,627**	**102.2**	**100.0**
BAPT–N Am Bapt Conf	1	NR	110	130	3.7	3.6
Catholic	6	NR	NR	2,233	62.9	61.6
LUTH–E.L.C.A.	1	97	267	348	9.8	9.6
LUTH–Luth Cong Msn Chr	1	100	349	411	11.6	11.3
LUTH–Wisc Ev Luth Syn	1	43	83	91	2.6	2.5
METH–Un Methodist	1	50	142	142	4.0	3.9
PENT–Assemb of God	1	15	0	15	0.4	0.4
PRES–Presb Ch (USA)	1	0	20	24	0.7	0.7
REF–Christian Ref	1	47	75	88	2.5	2.4
REF–Ref Ch in Am	2	83	131	145	4.1	4.0
FOSTER	**15**	**956**	**3,292**	**4,726**	**141.4**	**100.0**
Bahá'í	0	NR	1	1	0.0	0.0
BAPT–N Am Bapt Conf	1	NR	92	110	3.3	2.3
Catholic	2	NR	NR	706	21.1	14.9
Ch of Nazarene	1	27	63	63	1.9	1.3
Evan Free Ch	1	11	NR	11	0.3	0.2
LUTH–E.L.C.A.	4	321	1,214	1,507	45.1	31.9
LUTH–Luth Cong Msn Chr	2	321	1,518	1,812	54.2	38.3
LUTH–Luth-MO Synod	1	60	208	261	7.8	5.5
METH–Un Methodist	1	85	84	84	2.5	1.8
PENT–Assemb of God	1	56	22	64	1.9	1.4
Un C of Christ	1	75	90	107	3.2	2.3
GOLDEN VALLEY	**8**	**147**	**396**	**1,534**	**91.3**	**100.0**
Bahá'í	0	NR	1	1	0.1	0.1
Catholic	2	NR	NR	1,056	62.9	68.8
Evan Ch	1	NR	NR	NR	-	-
LUTH–E.L.C.A.	2	87	237	286	17.0	18.6
LUTH–Luth-MO Synod	1	54	115	141	8.4	9.2
METH–Un Methodist	1	6	6	6	0.4	0.4
Un C of Christ	1	0	37	44	2.6	2.9
GRAND FORKS	**77**	**7,055**	**15,386**	**35,953**	**53.8**	**100.0**
ANG/EPIS–Episcopal	1	65	221	221	0.3	0.6
Bahá'í	0	NR	29	29	0.0	0.1
BAPT–N Am Bapt Conf	1	NR	337	400	0.6	1.1
BAPT–So Bapt Conv	3	50	64	76	0.1	0.2
BUDD–Theravada	1	NR	NR	15	0.0	0.0
Catholic	8	NR	NR	11,769	17.6	32.7
CGOD–Ch God (Ander)	1	50	NR	50	0.1	0.1
Ch of Nazarene	2	148	85	181	0.3	0.5
CHR–Chs of Christ	1	50	40	70	0.1	0.2
Evan Cov Ch	1	847	180	1,101	1.6	3.1
Evan Free Ch	1	378	NR	378	0.6	1.1
JUD–Reform	1	21	37	100	0.1	0.3
LDS–Comm of Christ	1	NR	138	138	0.2	0.4
LDS–L-D Saints	1	NR	NR	970	1.5	2.7
LUTH–Assoc Free Luth	4	NR	NR	NR	-	-
LUTH–Ch of Luth Br	1	135	83	236	0.4	0.7
LUTH–E.L.C.A.	22	3,233	10,982	15,552	23.3	43.3
LUTH–Luth-MO Synod	4	330	814	985	1.5	2.7
METH–Un Methodist	4	382	920	1,207	1.8	3.4

NR–Not Reported - Represents no adherents reported. Percentages may not total 100 due to rounding.

Table 3: Religious Congregations by County and Group: 2010

Religious Group	Number of Congregations	Number of Attendees	Number of Communicant, Confirmed, or Full Members	Adherents		
				Number of Adherents	% of Total Pop.	% of Total Adh.
Non-denom Chr Chs	4	576	562	721	1.1	2.0
PENT–Assemb of God	3	324	74	573	0.9	1.6
PENT–Ch God (Cleve)	1	36	30	36	0.1	0.1
PENT–Int Foursq Gos	1	43	29	34	0.1	0.1
PENT–Un Pent Ch Intl	1	NR	NR	NR	-	-
PRES–Presb Ch (USA)	5	181	302	359	0.5	1.0
Salvation Army	1	42	67	293	0.4	0.8
Sev Day Adv	1	114	197	227	0.3	0.6
Un C of Christ	2	50	195	232	0.3	0.6
GRANT	**19**	**359**	**867**	**1,723**	**72.0**	**100.0**
BAPT–N Am Bapt Conf	1	NR	85	98	4.1	5.7
BAPT–So Bapt Conv	1	18	22	25	1.0	1.5
Catholic	4	NR	NR	679	28.4	39.4
CONG–Consrv Cong Chr	1	30	53	61	2.5	3.5
LUTH–Assoc Free Luth	1	NR	NR	NR	-	-
LUTH–E.L.C.A.	2	131	413	478	20.0	27.7
LUTH–Wisc Ev Luth Syn	3	51	146	167	7.0	9.7
MENN–Hutt Breth	1	NR	NR	NR	-	-
METH–Un Methodist	1	26	39	56	2.3	3.3
PENT–Assemb of God	1	41	43	81	3.4	4.7
PRES–Orth Pres Ch	1	37	31	38	1.6	2.2
Un C of Christ	2	25	35	40	1.7	2.3
GRIGGS	**18**	**602**	**949**	**1,505**	**62.2**	**100.0**
Bahá'í	0	NR	3	3	0.1	0.2
Catholic	2	NR	NR	225	9.3	15.0
Evan Free Ch	2	110	NR	110	4.5	7.3
LUTH–Assoc Free Luth	1	NR	NR	NR	-	-
LUTH–Ch of Luth Br	1	62	68	129	5.3	8.6
LUTH–E.L.C.A.	7	323	680	811	33.5	53.9
LUTH–Luth Cong Msn Chr	1	25	36	42	1.7	2.8
LUTH–Luth–MO Synod	2	43	102	108	4.5	7.2
PENT–Assemb of God	1	20	25	36	1.5	2.4
PRES–Presb Ch (USA)	1	19	35	41	1.7	2.7
HETTINGER	**15**	**359**	**699**	**2,449**	**98.9**	**100.0**
Catholic	3	NR	NR	1,483	59.9	60.6
CONG–Consrv Cong Chr	1	51	83	96	3.9	3.9
Evan Free Ch	1	65	NR	65	2.6	2.7
LUTH–Assoc Free Luth	1	NR	NR	NR	-	-
LUTH–E.L.C.A.	3	133	397	531	21.4	21.7
LUTH–Luth Cong Msn Chr	2	38	92	107	4.3	4.4
PENT–Assemb of God	1	35	16	38	1.5	1.6
Un C of Christ	3	37	111	129	5.2	5.3
KIDDER	**15**	**465**	**1,326**	**2,027**	**83.2**	**100.0**
Catholic	2	NR	NR	325	13.3	16.0
Ch of Nazarene	1	24	36	47	1.9	2.3
LUTH–E.L.C.A.	4	155	582	701	28.8	34.6
LUTH–Luth–MO Synod	1	30	188	223	9.2	11.0
LUTH–Wisc Ev Luth Syn	1	67	213	250	10.3	12.3
METH–Un Methodist	4	150	256	420	17.2	20.7
PRES–Presb Ch (USA)	1	31	19	23	0.9	1.1
Un C of Christ	1	8	32	38	1.6	1.9
LAMOURE	**34**	**1,081**	**2,165**	**3,839**	**92.8**	**100.0**
BAPT–Converge/BGC	1	75	NR	90	2.2	2.3
Catholic	5	NR	NR	979	23.7	25.5
Ch God (7th Day)	1	NR	NR	NR	-	-
Ch of Nazarene	1	65	70	204	4.9	5.3
CONG–Consrv Cong Chr	1	85	100	119	2.9	3.1
LUTH–E.L.C.A.	8	316	1,023	1,214	29.3	31.6
LUTH–Luth Cong Msn Chr	1	35	100	119	2.9	3.1
LUTH–Luth–MO Synod	2	166	363	413	10.0	10.8
MENN–Hutt Breth	2	NR	NR	NR	-	-
METH–Un Methodist	6	139	277	347	8.4	9.0
PENT–Assemb of God	1	100	34	128	3.1	3.3
PRES–Presb Ch (USA)	2	20	58	69	1.7	1.8
REF–Ref Ch in Am	1	34	60	65	1.6	1.7
Sev Day Adv	2	46	80	92	2.2	2.4

Religious Group	Number of Congregations	Number of Attendees	Number of Communicant, Confirmed, or Full Members	Adherents		
				Number of Adherents	% of Total Pop.	% of Total Adh.
LOGAN	**12**	**263**	**768**	**1,632**	**82.0**	**100.0**
BAPT–N Am Bapt Conf	3	NR	120	142	7.1	8.7
Catholic	1	NR	NR	654	32.9	40.1
LUTH–E.L.C.A.	4	198	522	665	33.4	40.7
LUTH–Luth–MO Synod	1	8	23	28	1.4	1.7
METH–Un Methodist	1	31	56	77	3.9	4.7
PENT–Assemb of God	1	10	0	10	0.5	0.6
Un C of Christ	1	16	47	56	2.8	3.4
MCHENRY	**28**	**700**	**2,459**	**4,665**	**86.5**	**100.0**
Bahá'í	0	NR	3	3	0.1	0.1
BAPT–Amer Bapt USA	2	85	119	142	2.6	3.0
BAPT–N Am Bapt Conf	1	NR	98	117	2.2	2.5
BAPT–So Bapt Conv	1	4	4	5	0.1	0.1
Catholic	5	NR	NR	1,370	25.4	29.4
LUTH–E.L.C.A.	10	401	1,786	2,501	46.4	53.6
LUTH–Luth–MO Synod	4	132	295	354	6.6	7.6
METH–Un Methodist	2	30	46	48	0.9	1.0
PRES–Presb Ch (USA)	1	18	18	21	0.4	0.5
REF–Ref Ch in U.S.	1	NR	21	22	0.4	0.5
Un C of Christ	1	30	69	82	1.5	1.8
MCINTOSH	**20**	**553**	**2,042**	**2,809**	**100.0**	**100.0**
Bahá'í	0	NR	1	1	0.0	0.0
BAPT–N Am Bapt Conf	4	NR	436	505	18.0	18.0
Catholic	3	NR	NR	464	16.5	16.5
LUTH–E.L.C.A.	2	290	1,063	1,191	42.4	42.4
LUTH–Luth–MO Synod	1	25	40	40	1.4	1.4
LUTH–Wisc Ev Luth Syn	1	19	30	35	1.2	1.2
METH–Un Methodist	4	90	189	234	8.3	8.3
PENT–Assemb of God	1	25	6	25	0.9	0.9
PENT–Un Pent Ch Intl	1	NR	NR	NR	-	-
REF–Ref Ch in U.S.	1	NR	44	45	1.6	1.6
Sev Day Adv	1	19	33	38	1.4	1.4
Un C of Christ	1	85	200	231	8.2	8.2
MCKENZIE	**26**	**789**	**1,661**	**2,689**	**42.3**	**100.0**
Bahá'í	0	NR	4	4	0.1	0.1
BAPT–So Bapt Conv	3	50	112	141	2.2	5.2
Catholic	2	NR	NR	574	9.0	21.3
Ch of Nazarene	1	8	7	11	0.2	0.4
LUTH–Ch of Luth Br	1	38	29	48	0.8	1.8
LUTH–E.L.C.A.	10	319	1,114	1,287	20.2	47.9
LUTH–Luth–MO Synod	1	12	80	80	1.3	3.0
METH–Wesleyan	2	102	66	133	2.1	4.9
PENT–Assemb of God	1	200	75	200	3.1	7.4
PRES–Presb Ch (USA)	1	0	25	32	0.5	1.2
Sev Day Adv	2	50	86	99	1.6	3.7
Un C of Christ	2	10	63	80	1.3	3.0
MCLEAN	**43**	**1,512**	**4,764**	**8,182**	**91.3**	**100.0**
ANG/EPIS–Episcopal	1	18	86	86	1.0	1.1
Bahá'í	0	NR	1	1	0.0	0.0
BAPT–N Am Bapt Conf	3	NR	284	333	3.7	4.1
Catholic	8	NR	NR	2,230	24.9	27.3
Evan Free Ch	2	120	NR	120	1.3	1.5
LUTH–E.L.C.A.	12	792	2,479	3,083	34.4	37.7
LUTH–Luth Cong Msn Chr	1	125	803	943	10.5	11.5
LUTH–Luth–MO Synod	3	121	432	549	6.1	6.7
LUTH–Nor Amer Luth C	1	NR	NR	NR	-	-
METH–Un Methodist	3	84	233	259	2.9	3.2
ORTHE–Ukrainian Orth	1	10	NR	10	0.1	0.1
PENT–Assemb of God	2	57	46	100	1.1	1.2
PENT–Ch God (Cleve)	1	51	42	49	0.5	0.6
PRES–Presb Ch (USA)	1	35	41	48	0.5	0.6
Sev Day Adv	2	29	50	58	0.6	0.7
Un C of Christ	2	70	267	313	3.5	3.8
MERCER	**29**	**1,464**	**3,511**	**6,757**	**80.2**	**100.0**
BAPT–N Am Bapt Conf	1	NR	189	224	2.7	3.3
BAPT–So Bapt Conv	1	51	88	104	1.2	1.5

NR–Not Reported   - Represents no adherents reported.   Percentages may not total 100 due to rounding.

Table 3: Religious Congregations by County and Group: 2010

Religious Group	Number of Congrega-tions	Number of Attendees	Number of Communicant, Confirmed, or Full Members	Adherents: Number of Adherents	Adherents: % of Total Pop.	Adherents: % of Total Adh.
Catholic	2	NR	NR	1,157	13.7	17.1
Ch of Nazarene	1	47	62	76	0.9	1.1
CONG–Consrv Cong Chr	2	117	241	285	3.4	4.2
Evan Free Ch	1	50	NR	50	0.6	0.7
LDS–L-D Saints	1	NR	NR	118	1.4	1.7
LUTH–Assoc Free Luth	3	NR	NR	NR	-	-
LUTH–E.L.C.A.	4	320	495	1,723	20.5	25.5
LUTH–Luth Cong Msn Chr	1	178	1,183	1,401	16.6	20.7
LUTH–Luth-MO Synod	4	296	810	970	11.5	14.4
METH–Un Methodist	2	62	175	203	2.4	3.0
Non-denom Chr Chs	1	25	30	31	0.4	0.5
PENT–Assemb of God	2	239	110	265	3.1	3.9
PENT–Ch God (Cleve)	1	48	74	88	1.0	1.3
PENT–Un Pent Ch Intl	1	NR	NR	NR	-	-
Sev Day Adv	1	31	54	62	0.7	0.9
MORTON	**47**	**2,072**	**6,274**	**22,446**	**81.7**	**100.0**
Bahá'í	0	NR	5	5	0.0	0.0
BAPT–N Am Bapt Conf	1	NR	143	175	0.6	0.8
BAPT–So Bapt Conv	2	95	336	412	1.5	1.8
Catholic	12	NR	NR	14,554	53.0	64.8
Ch of Nazarene	2	260	236	397	1.4	1.8
CHR–Chs of Christ	1	45	32	66	0.2	0.3
CONG–Consrv Cong Chr	1	35	35	43	0.2	0.2
Jehovah's Witness	3	NR	NR	NR	-	-
LUTH–E.L.C.A.	6	613	2,848	3,557	12.9	15.8
LUTH–Luth Ch-Am Asc	1	NR	NR	NR	-	-
LUTH–Luth-MO Synod	4	283	705	906	3.3	4.0
LUTH–Wisc Ev Luth Syn	1	115	224	279	1.0	1.2
METH–Un Methodist	2	110	254	328	1.2	1.5
Non-denom Chr Chs	1	131	552	552	2.0	2.5
PENT–Assemb of God	2	85	62	148	0.5	0.7
PRES–Presb Ch (USA)	1	66	173	212	0.8	0.9
Sev Day Adv	1	64	112	129	0.5	0.6
Un C of Christ	6	170	557	683	2.5	3.0
MOUNTRAIL	**27**	**542**	**1,583**	**4,734**	**61.7**	**100.0**
Bahá'í	0	NR	9	9	0.1	0.2
BAPT–Amer Bapt USA	1	24	22	27	0.4	0.6
BAPT–So Bapt Conv	1	30	13	16	0.2	0.3
Catholic	4	NR	NR	2,449	31.9	51.7
LDS–L-D Saints	1	NR	NR	382	5.0	8.1
LUTH–Apostolic Luth	1	NR	NR	NR	-	-
LUTH–Assoc Free Luth	2	NR	NR	NR	-	-
LUTH–E.L.C.A.	8	364	1,343	1,577	20.6	33.3
LUTH–Luth Ch-Am Asc	2	NR	NR	NR	-	-
PENT–Assemb of God	1	68	31	71	0.9	1.5
PENT–Ch God (Cleve)	1	13	30	37	0.5	0.8
PENT–Un Pent Ch Intl	1	NR	NR	NR	-	-
Un C of Christ	4	43	135	166	2.2	3.5
NELSON	**23**	**645**	**2,123**	**3,010**	**96.3**	**100.0**
ANG/EPIS–Episcopal	1	5	8	8	0.3	0.3
Bahá'í	0	NR	1	1	0.0	0.0
Catholic	4	NR	NR	429	13.7	14.3
LUTH–Assoc Free Luth	1	NR	NR	NR	-	-
LUTH–E.L.C.A.	12	488	1,932	2,338	74.8	77.7
LUTH–Luth-MO Synod	1	15	21	24	0.8	0.8
Non-denom Chr Chs	2	115	105	144	4.6	4.8
PENT–Un Pent Ch Intl	1	NR	NR	NR	-	-
Un C of Christ	1	22	56	65	2.1	2.2
Zoroastrian	0	NR	NR	1	0.0	0.0
OLIVER	**3**	**85**	**398**	**830**	**45.0**	**100.0**
Catholic	1	NR	NR	417	22.6	50.2
LUTH–E.L.C.A.	1	70	349	359	19.4	43.3
METH–Un Methodist	1	15	49	54	2.9	6.5
PEMBINA	**41**	**1,178**	**3,143**	**5,203**	**70.2**	**100.0**
ANG/EPIS–Episcopal	1	11	11	11	0.1	0.2
Bahá'í	0	NR	2	2	0.0	0.0
BAPT–Consrv Bapt	1	NR	NR	NR	-	-
Catholic	7	NR	NR	1,238	16.7	23.8
Evan Cov Ch	1	23	28	30	0.4	0.6
Evan Free Ch	2	145	NR	145	2.0	2.8
LUTH–E.L.C.A.	9	418	1,904	2,313	31.2	44.5
LUTH–Luth-MO Synod	4	156	450	515	6.9	9.9
METH–Un Methodist	9	202	404	447	6.0	8.6
PENT–Assemb of God	3	121	59	162	2.2	3.1
PRES–Presb Ch (USA)	4	102	285	340	4.6	6.5
PIERCE	**15**	**513**	**1,247**	**3,375**	**77.5**	**100.0**
Bahá'í	0	NR	1	1	0.0	0.0
Catholic	3	NR	NR	1,562	35.9	46.3
Evan Free Ch	1	85	NR	85	2.0	2.5
Jehovah's Witness	1	NR	NR	NR	-	-
LUTH–E.L.C.A.	5	280	959	1,360	31.2	40.3
LUTH–Luth-MO Synod	1	50	175	203	4.7	6.0
MENN–Mennonite USA	1	45	58	69	1.6	2.0
METH–Un Methodist	1	10	14	14	0.3	0.4
PENT–Assemb of God	1	43	30	69	1.6	2.0
PRES–Presb Ch (USA)	1	0	10	12	0.3	0.4
RAMSEY	**27**	**1,289**	**3,038**	**6,860**	**59.9**	**100.0**
ANG/EPIS–Episcopal	1	9	23	24	0.2	0.3
Bahá'í	0	NR	7	7	0.1	0.1
Catholic	2	NR	NR	2,439	21.3	35.6
Ch God (7th Day)	1	NR	NR	NR	-	-
Evan Free Ch	1	200	NR	200	1.7	2.9
Jehovah's Witness	1	NR	NR	NR	-	-
LDS–L-D Saints	1	NR	NR	127	1.1	1.9
LUTH–Assoc Free Luth	4	NR	NR	NR	-	-
LUTH–E.L.C.A.	8	764	2,448	3,204	28.0	46.7
LUTH–Luth-MO Synod	1	50	187	205	1.8	3.0
LUTH–Nor Amer Luth C	1	NR	NR	NR	-	-
METH–Un Methodist	2	100	213	355	3.1	5.2
Non-denom Chr Chs	1	30	20	38	0.3	0.6
PENT–Assemb of God	1	94	67	173	1.5	2.5
PRES–Presb Ch (USA)	2	42	73	88	0.8	1.3
RANSOM	**21**	**745**	**2,922**	**4,604**	**84.4**	**100.0**
Bahá'í	0	NR	2	2	0.0	0.0
BAPT–Amer Bapt USA	1	20	31	38	0.7	0.8
Catholic	3	NR	NR	839	15.4	18.2
Jehovah's Witness	1	NR	NR	NR	-	-
LUTH–Assoc Free Luth	1	NR	NR	NR	-	-
LUTH–E.L.C.A.	7	462	2,229	2,921	53.5	63.4
LUTH–Luth Cong Msn Chr	2	77	298	361	6.6	7.8
LUTH–Luth-MO Synod	1	52	137	150	2.7	3.3
METH–Un Methodist	3	81	205	230	4.2	5.0
PENT–Assemb of God	1	39	0	39	0.7	0.8
PRES–Presb Ch (USA)	1	14	20	24	0.4	0.5
RENVILLE	**15**	**440**	**1,568**	**2,332**	**94.4**	**100.0**
BAPT–Amer Bapt USA	1	28	56	67	2.7	2.9
Catholic	3	NR	NR	423	17.1	18.1
Ch of Nazarene	1	45	22	79	3.2	3.4
LUTH–E.L.C.A.	6	270	1,302	1,509	61.1	64.7
LUTH–Luth Cong Msn Chr	1	25	33	39	1.6	1.7
LUTH–Luth-MO Synod	1	27	53	58	2.3	2.5
METH–Un Methodist	2	45	102	157	6.4	6.7
RICHLAND	**45**	**1,986**	**5,786**	**11,755**	**72.0**	**100.0**
Bahá'í	0	NR	2	2	0.0	0.0
Catholic	7	NR	NR	4,423	27.1	37.6
CONG–Cong Chr Add'l	1	NR	22	27	0.2	0.2
Evan Free Ch	2	291	NR	291	1.8	2.5
LDS–L-D Saints	1	NR	NR	143	0.9	1.2
LUTH–Assoc Free Luth	1	NR	NR	NR	-	-
LUTH–E.L.C.A.	12	606	2,903	3,175	19.5	27.0
LUTH–Luth-MO Synod	8	527	1,760	2,114	13.0	18.0
METH–Un Methodist	5	220	483	692	4.2	5.9
Non-denom Chr Chs	1	20	20	25	0.2	0.2
PENT–Assemb of God	1	143	78	244	1.5	2.1

NR–Not Reported - Represents no adherents reported. Percentages may not total 100 due to rounding.

Table 3: Religious Congregations by County and Group: 2010

Religious Group	Number of Congrega-tions	Number of Attendees	Number of Communicant, Confirmed, or Full Members	Adherents: Number of Adherents	Adherents: % of Total Pop.	Adherents: % of Total Adh.
PENT–Ch God (Cleve)	1	31	39	47	0.3	0.4
PENT–Un Pent Ch Intl	1	NR	NR	NR	-	-
Sev Day Adv	1	60	105	121	0.7	1.0
Un C of Christ	3	88	374	451	2.8	3.8
ROLETTE	**25**	**784**	**1,363**	**16,239**	**116.5**	**100.0**
ANG/EPIS–Episcopal	1	10	38	38	0.3	0.2
Bahá'í	0	NR	26	26	0.2	0.2
BAPT–So Bapt Conv	1	22	15	20	0.1	0.1
Catholic	7	NR	NR	13,931	100.0	85.8
Chr & Miss Al	1	54	0	54	0.4	0.3
LDS–L-D Saints	1	NR	NR	101	0.7	0.6
LUTH–Ch of Luth Br	1	45	50	173	1.2	1.1
LUTH–E.L.C.A.	3	175	782	983	7.1	6.1
LUTH–Luth–MO Synod	1	47	176	220	1.6	1.4
METH–Un Methodist	2	31	87	114	0.8	0.7
PENT–Assemb of God	3	109	30	147	1.1	0.9
PENT–Ch God (Cleve)	1	71	8	11	0.1	0.1
PENT–Pent Ch of God	2	140	NR	217	1.6	1.3
PRES–Presb Ch (USA)	1	80	151	204	1.5	1.3
SARGENT	**17**	**568**	**2,123**	**3,495**	**91.3**	**100.0**
BAPT–Amer Bapt USA	1	12	4	5	0.1	0.1
Catholic	5	NR	NR	790	20.6	22.6
LUTH–E.L.C.A.	6	360	1,780	2,222	58.0	63.6
LUTH–Luth–MO Synod	2	143	255	362	9.5	10.4
MENN–Hutt Breth	1	NR	NR	NR	-	-
METH–Un Methodist	1	32	74	90	2.4	2.6
PENT–Assemb of God	1	21	10	26	0.7	0.7
SHERIDAN	**14**	**282**	**902**	**1,131**	**85.6**	**100.0**
BAPT–N Am Bapt Conf	3	NR	203	228	17.3	20.2
Catholic	1	NR	NR	30	2.3	2.7
LUTH–E.L.C.A.	3	104	397	447	33.8	39.5
LUTH–Luth–MO Synod	1	53	138	163	12.3	14.4
METH–Un Methodist	3	68	96	153	11.6	13.5
PENT–Assemb of God	1	35	29	65	4.9	5.7
Sev Day Adv	2	22	39	45	3.4	4.0
SIOUX	**11**	**81**	**291**	**3,168**	**76.3**	**100.0**
ANG/EPIS–Episcopal	3	41	186	431	10.4	13.6
Bahá'í	0	NR	36	36	0.9	1.1
BAPT–So Bapt Conv	2	40	69	98	2.4	3.1
Catholic	5	NR	NR	2,161	52.0	68.2
LDS–L-D Saints	1	NR	NR	442	10.6	14.0
SLOPE	**2**	**25**	**88**	**222**	**30.5**	**100.0**
Catholic	1	NR	NR	44	6.1	19.8
LUTH–E.L.C.A.	1	25	88	178	24.5	80.2
STARK	**43**	**2,164**	**3,233**	**17,249**	**71.3**	**100.0**
ANG/EPIS–Episcopal	1	24	31	31	0.1	0.2
Bahá'í	0	NR	3	3	0.0	0.0
BAPT–Amer Bapt USA	1	25	13	16	0.1	0.1
BAPT–N Am Bapt Conf	1	NR	175	210	0.9	1.2
BAPT–So Bapt Conv	3	76	63	76	0.3	0.4
Calv Chpl	1	NR	NR	NR	-	-
Catholic	12	NR	NR	12,110	50.0	70.2
Ch of Nazarene	1	57	45	106	0.4	0.6
CHR–Chs of Christ	1	30	25	35	0.1	0.2
CONG–Consrv Cong Chr	1	350	129	155	0.6	0.9
Jehovah's Witness	1	NR	NR	NR	-	-
LDS–L-D Saints	1	NR	NR	376	1.6	2.2
LUTH–Assoc Free Luth	2	NR	NR	NR	-	-
LUTH–Ch of Luth Br	1	140	42	272	1.1	1.6
LUTH–E.L.C.A.	5	611	1,676	2,120	8.8	12.3
LUTH–Luth–MO Synod	2	142	270	336	1.4	1.9
METH–Un Methodist	1	130	240	429	1.8	2.5
Non-denom Chr Chs	3	300	205	385	1.6	2.2
PENT–Assemb of God	1	200	82	310	1.3	1.8
PENT–Ch God (Cleve)	1	26	15	18	0.1	0.1
PENT–Un Pent Ch Intl	1	NR	NR	NR	-	-
Sev Day Adv	1	23	40	46	0.2	0.3
Un C of Christ	1	30	179	215	0.9	1.2
STEELE	**15**	**423**	**1,118**	**1,564**	**79.2**	**100.0**
Bahá'í	0	NR	3	3	0.2	0.2
BAPT–So Bapt Conv	1	10	16	19	1.0	1.2
Catholic	2	NR	NR	178	9.0	11.4
LUTH–E.L.C.A.	7	300	941	1,156	58.5	73.9
LUTH–Luth–MO Synod	1	26	58	65	3.3	4.2
METH–Un Methodist	1	16	15	15	0.8	1.0
PENT–Assemb of God	1	33	22	54	2.7	3.5
PRES–Presb Ch (USA)	1	25	41	48	2.4	3.1
Un C of Christ	1	13	22	26	1.3	1.7
STUTSMAN	**49**	**2,847**	**8,266**	**13,721**	**65.0**	**100.0**
ANG/EPIS–Episcopal	1	64	123	128	0.6	0.9
Bahá'í	0	NR	13	13	0.1	0.1
BAPT–Converge/BGC	1	75	NR	90	0.4	0.7
BAPT–N Am Bapt Conf	2	NR	265	314	1.5	2.3
Catholic	6	NR	NR	2,663	12.6	19.4
Ch of Nazarene	1	148	209	210	1.0	1.5
Evan Ch	1	NR	NR	NR	-	-
Jehovah's Witness	1	NR	NR	NR	-	-
LDS–L-D Saints	1	NR	NR	292	1.4	2.1
LUTH–Assoc Free Luth	1	NR	NR	NR	-	-
LUTH–Ch Luth Conf	1	NR	NR	NR	-	-
LUTH–Ch of Luth Br	1	200	85	315	1.5	2.3
LUTH–E.L.C.A.	9	1,049	4,650	5,856	27.8	42.7
LUTH–Luth–MO Synod	4	271	841	1,047	5.0	7.6
LUTH–Wisc Ev Luth Syn	1	8	20	23	0.1	0.2
METH–Free Methodist	1	11	10	11	0.1	0.1
METH–Un Methodist	6	425	976	1,351	6.4	9.8
Non-denom Chr Chs	1	12	15	15	0.1	0.1
PENT–Assemb of God	2	177	121	252	1.2	1.8
PENT–Un Pent Ch Intl	1	NR	NR	NR	-	-
PRES–Presb Ch (USA)	1	196	333	395	1.9	2.9
Salvation Army	1	17	43	88	0.4	0.6
Sev Day Adv	2	144	251	289	1.4	2.1
Un C of Christ	3	50	311	369	1.7	2.7
TOWNER	**10**	**247**	**635**	**1,247**	**55.5**	**100.0**
Catholic	3	NR	NR	460	20.5	36.9
LUTH–Assoc Free Luth	1	NR	NR	NR	-	-
LUTH–E.L.C.A.	2	120	290	367	16.3	29.4
LUTH–Luth–MO Synod	1	33	193	225	10.0	18.0
METH–Un Methodist	2	46	114	147	6.5	11.8
PENT–Assemb of God	1	48	38	48	2.1	3.8
TRAILL	**31**	**1,530**	**4,239**	**6,105**	**75.2**	**100.0**
Bahá'í	0	NR	4	4	0.0	0.1
Catholic	2	NR	NR	652	8.0	10.7
Evan Free Ch	1	120	NR	120	1.5	2.0
LUTH–Assoc Free Luth	3	NR	NR	NR	-	-
LUTH–Ch of Luth Br	1	84	48	145	1.8	2.4
LUTH–E.L.C.A.	19	1,090	3,769	4,716	58.1	77.2
LUTH–Luth Cong Msn Chr	1	80	8	10	0.1	0.2
LUTH–Luth–MO Synod	1	85	230	252	3.1	4.1
METH–Un Methodist	1	18	54	54	0.7	0.9
Un C of Christ	2	53	126	152	1.9	2.5
WALSH	**41**	**1,302**	**4,076**	**8,320**	**74.8**	**100.0**
Bahá'í	0	NR	1	1	0.0	0.0
BAPT–Converge/BGC	1	75	NR	90	0.8	1.1
Catholic	9	NR	NR	3,320	29.9	39.9
Evan Free Ch	1	20	NR	20	0.2	0.2
Jehovah's Witness	1	NR	NR	NR	-	-
LUTH–Assoc Free Luth	3	NR	NR	NR	-	-
LUTH–E.L.C.A.	12	831	3,351	3,991	35.9	48.0
LUTH–Luth–MO Synod	1	68	181	224	2.0	2.7
MENN–CG in Cr (Menn)	1	NR	104	125	1.1	1.5
MENN–Hutt Breth	1	NR	NR	NR	-	-

NR–Not Reported - Represents no adherents reported. Percentages may not total 100 due to rounding.

Table 3: Religious Congregations by County and Group: 2010

Religious Group	Number of Congregations	Number of Attendees	Number of Communicant, Confirmed, or Full Members	Adherents: Number of Adherents	Adherents: % of Total Pop.	Adherents: % of Total Adh.
METH–Un Methodist	3	81	72	83	0.7	1.0
Non-denom Chr Chs	1	90	140	140	1.3	1.7
PENT–Assemb of God	1	58	27	85	0.8	1.0
PENT–Un Pent Ch Intl	1	NR	NR	NR	-	-
PRES–Presb Ch (USA)	5	79	200	241	2.2	2.9
WARD	**89**	**6,568**	**13,369**	**32,697**	**53.0**	**100.0**
ANG/EPIS–Episcopal	1	40	82	86	0.1	0.3
Bahá'í	0	NR	29	29	0.0	0.1
BAPT–Amer Bapt USA	2	202	320	394	0.6	1.2
BAPT–N Am Bapt Conf	1	NR	418	515	0.8	1.6
BAPT–So Bapt Conv	3	133	218	269	0.4	0.8
Calv Chpl	1	NR	NR	NR	-	-
Catholic	10	NR	NR	11,445	18.6	35.0
Ch of Nazarene	4	228	284	392	0.6	1.2
Chr & Miss Al	1	51	36	74	0.1	0.2
CHR–Chs of Christ	1	140	140	210	0.3	0.6
Evan Free Ch	1	150	NR	150	0.2	0.5
Jehovah's Witness	1	NR	NR	NR	-	-
LDS–L-D Saints	2	NR	NR	1,152	1.9	3.5
LUTH–Assoc Free Luth	1	NR	NR	NR	-	-
LUTH–Ch of Luth Br	1	530	365	1,302	2.1	4.0
LUTH–E.L.C.A.	22	2,210	6,530	9,109	14.8	27.9
LUTH–Luth Ch-Am Asc	1	NR	NR	NR	-	-
LUTH–Luth Cong Msn Chr	1	150	200	246	0.4	0.8
LUTH–Luth-MO Synod	4	546	1,949	2,655	4.3	8.1
LUTH–Wisc Ev Luth Syn	1	14	8	12	0.0	0.0
MENN–Menn Br US Conf	1	NR	66	81	0.1	0.2
METH–Un Methodist	5	417	802	1,175	1.9	3.6
Muslim Est	1	15	NR	20	0.0	0.1
Non-denom Chr Chs	8	515	585	676	1.1	2.1
ORTHE–Orth Ch in Amer	1	25	NR	60	0.1	0.2
PENT–Assemb of God	3	807	265	1,135	1.8	3.5
PENT–Ch God (Cleve)	3	241	333	410	0.7	1.3
PENT–Ch of God Proph	1	NR	39	48	0.1	0.1
PENT–Un Pent Ch Intl	1	NR	NR	NR	-	-
PRES–Presb Ch (USA)	2	40	281	346	0.6	1.1
REF–Ref Ch in U.S.	1	NR	17	26	0.0	0.1
Salvation Army	1	24	36	241	0.4	0.7
Sev Day Adv	1	90	157	181	0.3	0.6
Un C of Christ	1	0	209	258	0.4	0.8
WELLS	**29**	**879**	**2,169**	**3,690**	**87.7**	**100.0**
BAPT–N Am Bapt Conf	2	NR	135	156	3.7	4.2
BAPT–So Bapt Conv	1	65	50	58	1.4	1.6
Catholic	4	NR	NR	973	23.1	26.4
CGOD–Ch God (Ander)	1	55	NR	55	1.3	1.5
Ch of Nazarene	1	10	32	32	0.8	0.9
LUTH–Assoc Free Luth	1	NR	NR	NR	-	-
LUTH–E.L.C.A.	7	393	1,172	1,443	34.3	39.1
LUTH–Luth Cong Msn Chr	1	105	231	267	6.3	7.2
LUTH–Luth-MO Synod	1	13	86	105	2.5	2.8
MENN–Menn Br US Conf	1	NR	118	137	3.3	3.7
METH–Un Methodist	2	36	57	82	1.9	2.2
Non-denom Chr Chs	1	5	7	7	0.2	0.2
PENT–Assemb of God	1	35	0	52	1.2	1.4
PENT–Un Pent Ch Intl	1	NR	NR	NR	-	-
Sev Day Adv	4	162	281	323	7.7	8.8
WILLIAMS	**51**	**2,952**	**6,305**	**12,897**	**57.6**	**100.0**
ANG/EPIS–Episcopal	1	29	64	90	0.4	0.7
Bahá'í	0	NR	2	2	0.0	0.0
BAPT–So Bapt Conv	1	110	148	180	0.8	1.4
Catholic	5	NR	NR	3,248	14.5	25.2
Ch of Nazarene	1	26	60	80	0.4	0.6
Chr & Miss Al	1	35	11	43	0.2	0.3
CHR–Chs of Christ	1	50	40	55	0.2	0.4
Evan Free Ch	1	115	NR	115	0.5	0.9
Jehovah's Witness	1	NR	NR	NR	-	-
LDS–L-D Saints	1	NR	NR	679	3.0	5.3
LUTH–Assoc Free Luth	4	NR	NR	NR	-	-
LUTH–Ch of Luth Br	1	154	130	285	1.3	2.2
LUTH–E.L.C.A.	19	1,127	4,700	5,982	26.7	46.4
LUTH–Luth Ch-Am Asc	2	NR	NR	NR	-	-
LUTH–Luth Cong Msn Chr	1	20	28	34	0.2	0.3
LUTH–Luth-MO Synod	1	75	212	297	1.3	2.3
METH–Un Methodist	1	111	330	330	1.5	2.6
METH–Wesleyan	1	520	154	676	3.0	5.2
Non-denom Chr Chs	2	230	200	288	1.3	2.2
PENT–Assemb of God	2	261	138	318	1.4	2.5
PENT–Ch God (Cleve)	1	51	60	73	0.3	0.6
PENT–Un Pent Ch Intl	1	NR	NR	NR	-	-
Salvation Army	1	38	28	122	0.5	0.9
Sev Day Adv	1	0	0	0	0.0	0.0
OHIO	**13,606**	**1,265,197**	**2,160,933**	**5,071,684**	**44.0**	**100.0**
ADAMS	**84**	**2,809**	**4,518**	**6,965**	**24.4**	**100.0**
Bahá'í	0	NR	9	9	0.0	0.1
BAPT–So Bapt Conv	6	254	314	389	1.4	5.6
Catholic	2	NR	NR	500	1.8	7.2
CGOD–Ch God (Ander)	1	70	NR	70	0.2	1.0
Ch Christ Chr Union	7	NR	NR	NR	-	-
Ch of Nazarene	3	152	203	298	1.0	4.3
CHR–Chr Chs & Chs Cr	8	NR	1,099	1,363	4.8	19.6
CHR–Chs of Christ	2	70	61	82	0.3	1.2
Christian Un	10	NR	NR	NR	-	-
LDS–L-D Saints	1	NR	NR	313	1.1	4.5
MENN–Amish Undif	4	NR	246	471	1.6	6.8
METH–Un Methodist	18	726	913	1,260	4.4	18.1
Non-denom Chr Chs	9	1,237	1,197	1,547	5.4	22.2
PENT–Assemb of God	1	64	0	79	0.3	1.1
PENT–Ch God (Cleve)	3	59	66	82	0.3	1.2
PRES–Presb Ch (USA)	7	135	338	419	1.5	6.0
Sev Day Adv	2	42	72	83	0.3	1.2
ALLEN	**156**	**14,702**	**25,898**	**55,482**	**52.2**	**100.0**
ANG/EPIS–Anglican NA	1	NR	NR	NR	-	-
Bahá'í	0	NR	20	20	0.0	0.0
BAPT–Amer Bapt USA	4	290	952	1,167	1.1	2.1
BAPT–Free Will Bapt	1	NR	67	82	0.1	0.1
BAPT–Natl Mis Bapt Conv	2	0	300	368	0.3	0.7
BAPT–NBC USA	4	600	2,800	3,431	3.2	6.2
BAPT–Reg Bapt Gen As	3	NR	NR	NR	-	-
BAPT–So Bapt Conv	4	699	1,313	1,609	1.5	2.9
BRETH–Ch of Brethren	4	176	578	708	0.7	1.3
Calv Chpl	1	NR	NR	NR	-	-
Catholic	8	NR	NR	17,946	16.9	32.3
CGOD–Ch God (Ander)	1	0	NR	0	0.0	0.0
Ch Cr, Scientst	1	NR	NR	NR	-	-
Ch of Nazarene	3	2,156	1,588	3,774	3.5	6.8
Chr & Miss Al	2	243	250	545	0.5	1.0
CHR–Chr Ch (Disc)	2	328	1,053	1,290	1.2	2.3
CHR–Chr Chs & Chs Cr	3	NR	390	478	0.4	0.9
CHR–Chs of Christ	5	262	317	401	0.4	0.7
Christian Un	2	NR	NR	NR	-	-
CONG–Cong Chr, NA	1	NR	92	113	0.1	0.2
CONG–Consrv Cong Chr	1	116	222	272	0.3	0.5
Evan Assoc RCC	1	NR	NR	NR	-	-
Evan Free Ch	1	290	NR	290	0.3	0.5
FRND–Fr Gen Cf	1	NR	7	9	0.0	0.0
FRND–Fr Un Mtg	1	NR	18	22	0.0	0.0
Jehovah's Witness	2	NR	NR	NR	-	-
JUD–Reform	1	33	58	157	0.1	0.3
LDS–Comm of Christ	1	NR	133	133	0.1	0.2
LUTH–E.L.C.A.	7	741	2,241	3,068	2.9	5.5
LUTH–Luth-MO Synod	1	94	158	175	0.2	0.3
MENN–Mennonite USA	4	469	740	907	0.9	1.6
MENN–Ref Mennonite	1	NR	30	33	0.0	0.1
METH–AME	1	0	150	184	0.2	0.3
METH–Un Methodist	27	2,600	5,051	7,302	6.9	13.2
METH–Wesleyan	2	133	118	173	0.2	0.3
Missionary Ch	4	341	259	353	0.3	0.6
Muslim Est	2	268	NR	616	0.6	1.1
Non-denom Chr Chs	20	3,690	4,520	5,102	4.8	9.2

NR–Not Reported - Represents no adherents reported. Percentages may not total 100 due to rounding.

Table 3: Religious Congregations by County and Group: 2010

Religious Group	Number of Congregations	Number of Attendees	Number of Communicant, Confirmed, or Full Members	Adherents: Number of Adherents	Adherents: % of Total Pop.	Adherents: % of Total Adh.
PENT–Assemb of God	3	330	191	577	0.5	1.0
PENT–Assm God Intl F	1	NR	NR	NR	-	-
PENT–COGIC	2	0	300	368	0.3	0.7
PENT–Fire Bapt Hol Ch	1	NR	NR	NR	-	-
PENT–Pent Ch of God	1	70	NR	109	0.1	0.2
PENT–Un Pent Ch Intl	1	NR	NR	NR	-	-
PRES–Presb Ch (USA)	5	153	550	674	0.6	1.2
Salvation Army	1	38	116	1,443	1.4	2.6
Sev Day Adv	2	84	145	167	0.2	0.3
Un Breth in Cr	2	120	95	103	0.1	0.2
Un C of Christ	6	358	1,052	1,289	1.2	2.3
Unit Univ	1	20	24	24	0.0	0.0
ASHLAND	**110**	**10,581**	**11,273**	**23,221**	**43.7**	**100.0**
ANG/EPIS–Episcopal	1	41	76	76	0.1	0.3
Bahá'í	0	NR	4	4	0.0	0.0
BAPT–Amer Bapt USA	2	175	570	697	1.3	3.0
BAPT–Converge/BGC	2	4,000	NR	4,800	9.0	20.7
BAPT–Ind Bapt Flwsp Intl	3	NR	NR	NR	-	-
BAPT–Reg Bapt Gen As	2	NR	NR	NR	-	-
BAPT–So Bapt Conv	3	111	103	126	0.2	0.5
BRETH–Breth in Chr	1	NR	NR	NR	-	-
BRETH–Brethren (Ash)	5	NR	770	941	1.8	4.1
BRETH–Ch of Brethren	3	370	491	600	1.1	2.6
BRETH–Grace Breth	2	NR	NR	NR	-	-
Catholic	2	NR	NR	1,509	2.8	6.5
CGOD–Ch God (Ander)	2	70	NR	70	0.1	0.3
CGOD–Ches God-Gen Con	1	26	37	45	0.1	0.2
Ch of Nazarene	2	143	228	246	0.5	1.1
CHR–Chr Ch (Disc)	1	135	340	415	0.8	1.8
CHR–Chr Chs & Chs Cr	3	NR	370	452	0.9	1.9
CHR–Chs of Christ	2	259	290	357	0.7	1.5
CONG–Cong Chr, NA	1	NR	49	60	0.1	0.3
Evan Free Ch	1	148	NR	148	0.3	0.6
Jehovah's Witness	1	NR	NR	NR	-	-
LDS–L-D Saints	1	NR	NR	256	0.5	1.1
LUTH–E.L.C.A.	6	490	1,113	1,589	3.0	6.8
LUTH–Luth Cong Msn Chr	1	73	67	82	0.2	0.4
LUTH–Nor Amer Luth C	2	NR	NR	NR	-	-
MENN–Amish Undif	12	NR	678	1,661	3.1	7.2
MENN–CG in Cr (Menn)	1	NR	75	92	0.2	0.4
METH–Un Methodist	17	1,130	3,035	3,773	7.1	16.2
Muslim Est	1	134	NR	308	0.6	1.3
Non-denom Chr Chs	13	2,455	1,847	3,119	5.9	13.4
ORTHE–Greek Orthodox	1	35	NR	42	0.1	0.2
PENT–Assemb of God	1	307	164	539	1.0	2.3
PENT–Ch God (Cleve)	3	81	246	301	0.6	1.3
PENT–COGIC	1	100	50	61	0.1	0.3
PENT–Intl Pent Holiness	1	10	13	16	0.0	0.1
PENT–Open Bible Std	1	25	NR	25	0.0	0.1
PENT–Un Pent Ch Intl	1	NR	NR	NR	-	-
PRES–Presb Ch (USA)	5	209	395	483	0.9	2.1
Salvation Army	1	54	78	103	0.2	0.4
Un C of Christ	1	0	184	225	0.4	1.0
ASHTABULA	**160**	**8,133**	**16,425**	**36,683**	**36.1**	**100.0**
ANG/EPIS–Episcopal	2	134	308	318	0.3	0.9
Bahá'í	0	NR	11	11	0.0	0.0
BAPT–Amer Bapt USA	7	648	1,369	1,668	1.6	4.5
BAPT–Free Will Bapt	1	NR	67	82	0.1	0.2
BAPT–Natl Mis Bapt Conv	1	0	150	183	0.2	0.5
BAPT–NBC USA	1	350	500	609	0.6	1.7
BAPT–Reg Bapt Gen As	2	NR	NR	NR	-	-
BAPT–So Bapt Conv	8	268	291	355	0.3	1.0
Catholic	11	NR	NR	14,134	13.9	38.5
CGOD–Ch God (Ander)	1	69	NR	69	0.1	0.2
Ch of Nazarene	7	793	1,197	1,334	1.3	3.6
Chr & Miss Al	2	289	187	457	0.5	1.2
CHR–Chr Ch (Disc)	1	0	0	0	0.0	0.0
CHR–Chr Chs & Chs Cr	5	NR	525	640	0.6	1.7
CHR–Chs of Christ	2	175	170	215	0.2	0.6
CONG–Cong Chr, NA	1	NR	45	55	0.1	0.1
Evan Cov Ch	1	43	32	56	0.1	0.2
Grace Gosp Fel	1	NR	NR	NR	-	-
Jehovah's Witness	2	NR	NR	NR	-	-
JUD–Reform	1	7	12	32	0.0	0.1
LDS–L-D Saints	1	NR	NR	516	0.5	1.4
LUTH–E.L.C.A.	5	508	1,583	1,891	1.9	5.2
LUTH–Luth–MO Synod	3	220	439	627	0.6	1.7
MENN–Amish Undif	16	NR	889	2,203	2.2	6.0
METH–A.W.M.C.	2	42	21	58	0.1	0.2
METH–AME	1	0	100	122	0.1	0.3
METH–Un Methodist	23	1,598	3,638	4,850	4.8	13.2
METH–Wesleyan	1	35	68	46	0.0	0.1
Nat Spirit Asso	1	NR	NR	NR	-	-
New Apost Ch	2	NR	NR	NR	-	-
Non-denom Chr Chs	12	998	1,194	1,332	1.3	3.6
PENT–Assemb of God	6	650	448	843	0.8	2.3
PENT–Ch God (Cleve)	5	315	636	775	0.8	2.1
PENT–Ch of God Proph	1	NR	14	17	0.0	0.0
PENT–COGIC	1	0	150	183	0.2	0.5
PENT–Int Foursq Gos	1	34	26	32	0.0	0.1
PENT–Intl Pent Holiness	1	18	25	30	0.0	0.1
PENT–Pent Ch of God	1	70	NR	109	0.1	0.3
PENT–Un Pent Ch Intl	1	NR	NR	NR	-	-
PRES–Presb Ch (USA)	9	540	1,077	1,312	1.3	3.6
Sev Day Adv	2	69	120	138	0.1	0.4
Un C of Christ	8	260	1,133	1,381	1.4	3.8
ATHENS	**97**	**4,666**	**7,733**	**13,103**	**20.2**	**100.0**
ANG/EPIS–Episcopal	2	105	183	183	0.3	1.4
Bahá'í	0	NR	7	7	0.0	0.1
BAPT–Amer Bapt USA	2	122	509	579	0.9	4.4
BAPT–Reg Bapt Gen As	3	NR	NR	NR	-	-
BAPT–So Bapt Conv	4	106	165	188	0.3	1.4
BUDD–Vajrayana	1	NR	NR	71	0.1	0.5
Catholic	5	NR	NR	1,946	3.0	14.9
CGOD–Ch God (Ander)	2	36	NR	36	0.1	0.3
Ch of Nazarene	2	109	167	213	0.3	1.6
Chr & Miss Al	1	120	39	181	0.3	1.4
CHR–Chr Ch (Disc)	7	93	349	397	0.6	3.0
CHR–Chr Chs & Chs Cr	9	NR	1,273	1,449	2.2	11.1
CHR–Chs of Christ	1	88	85	100	0.2	0.8
FRND–Fr Gen Cf	1	NR	69	79	0.1	0.6
Jehovah's Witness	1	NR	NR	NR	-	-
LDS–L-D Saints	1	NR	NR	429	0.7	3.3
LUTH–E.L.C.A.	1	132	319	450	0.7	3.4
METH–A.W.M.C.	1	5	0	9	0.0	0.1
METH–Un Methodist	24	1,342	1,883	3,027	4.7	23.1
METH–Wesleyan	6	677	509	880	1.4	6.7
Muslim Est	1	134	NR	308	0.5	2.4
Non-denom Chr Chs	11	1,324	1,636	1,803	2.8	13.8
PENT–Assemb of God	1	85	0	140	0.2	1.1
PENT–Ch of God Proph	1	NR	16	18	0.0	0.1
PENT–Un Pent Ch Intl	2	NR	NR	NR	-	-
PRES–Presb Ch (USA)	5	111	403	459	0.7	3.5
Sev Day Adv	1	38	66	76	0.1	0.6
Unit Univ	1	39	55	75	0.1	0.6
AUGLAIZE	**70**	**6,002**	**9,740**	**26,884**	**58.5**	**100.0**
BAPT–Amer Bapt USA	2	183	364	452	1.0	1.7
BAPT–Reg Bapt Gen As	1	NR	NR	NR	-	-
BAPT–So Bapt Conv	2	135	255	316	0.7	1.2
Calv Chpl	1	NR	NR	NR	-	-
Catholic	7	NR	NR	11,646	25.3	43.3
CGOD–Ch God (Ander)	2	530	NR	530	1.2	2.0
CGOD–Ches God-Gen Con	1	41	43	53	0.1	0.2
Ch of Nazarene	4	399	522	656	1.4	2.4
Chr & Miss Al	2	903	439	1,654	3.6	6.2
CHR–Chs of Christ	1	80	61	95	0.2	0.4
Christian Un	2	NR	NR	NR	-	-
CONG–Consrv Cong Chr	1	50	118	146	0.3	0.5
FRND–Fr Un Mtg	1	NR	17	21	0.0	0.1
Jehovah's Witness	2	NR	NR	NR	-	-
LDS–L-D Saints	2	NR	NR	802	1.7	3.0
LUTH–E.L.C.A.	4	626	1,765	2,408	5.2	9.0

NR–Not Reported - Represents no adherents reported. Percentages may not total 100 due to rounding.

Table 3: Religious Congregations by County and Group: 2010

Religious Group	Number of Congregations	Number of Attendees	Number of Communicant, Confirmed, or Full Members	Adherents		
				Number of Adherents	% of Total Pop.	% of Total Adh.
LUTH–Luth–MO Synod	1	53	63	69	0.2	0.3
LUTH–Nor Amer Luth C	1	NR	NR	NR	-	-
METH–Un Methodist	13	1,244	2,373	3,236	7.0	12.0
METH–Wesleyan	1	30	28	39	0.1	0.1
Missionary Ch	1	95	49	95	0.2	0.4
Non-denom Chr Chs	6	365	571	615	1.3	2.3
ORTHE–Orth Ch in Amer	1	35	NR	60	0.1	0.2
PENT–Assemb of God	2	333	207	430	0.9	1.6
PENT–Ch God Mtn Asm	1	NR	NR	NR	-	-
PENT–Open Bible Std	1	10	NR	10	0.0	0.0
PRES–Presb Ch (USA)	1	0	1	1	0.0	0.0
Un Breth in Cr	1	13	13	12	0.0	0.0
Un C of Christ	5	877	2,851	3,538	7.7	13.2
BELMONT	**144**	**6,875**	**14,892**	**26,764**	**38.0**	**100.0**
ANG/EPIS–Episcopal	1	27	40	55	0.1	0.2
Bahá'í	0	NR	5	5	0.0	0.0
BAPT–Amer Bapt USA	1	68	163	191	0.3	0.7
BAPT–So Bapt Conv	4	245	527	618	0.9	2.3
Catholic	16	NR	NR	8,179	11.6	30.6
CGOD–Ch God (Ander)	1	96	NR	96	0.1	0.4
Ch of Nazarene	5	200	251	426	0.6	1.6
Chr & Miss Al	1	100	96	166	0.2	0.6
CHR–Chr Ch (Disc)	3	88	235	276	0.4	1.0
CHR–Chr Chs & Chs Cr	7	NR	1,802	2,113	3.0	7.9
CHR–Chs of Christ	14	790	958	1,288	1.8	4.8
FRND–Consrv Yr Mtgs	2	NR	170	199	0.3	0.7
FRND–Evan Fr Ch Intl	1	769	540	633	0.9	2.4
Jehovah's Witness	3	NR	NR	NR	-	-
LDS–Comm of Christ	1	NR	118	118	0.2	0.4
LUTH–E.L.C.A.	4	257	914	1,078	1.5	4.0
MENN–Amish Undif	1	NR	35	95	0.1	0.4
MENN–Mennonite USA	1	45	54	63	0.1	0.2
METH–AME	1	0	150	176	0.3	0.7
METH–Un Methodist	37	1,686	5,173	5,930	8.4	22.2
METH–Wesleyan	1	41	41	53	0.1	0.2
Non-denom Chr Chs	8	940	1,130	1,253	1.8	4.7
ORTHE–Carp Rus Orth	1	90	NR	123	0.2	0.5
ORTHE–Greek Orthodox	1	75	NR	335	0.5	1.3
ORTHE–Orth Ch in Amer	1	5	NR	5	0.0	0.0
PENT–Assemb of God	3	398	231	551	0.8	2.1
PENT–Ch God (Cleve)	1	10	12	14	0.0	0.1
PENT–Elim	1	NR	NR	NR	-	-
PENT–Un Pent Ch Intl	1	NR	NR	NR	-	-
PRES–Presb Ch (USA)	20	839	2,116	2,482	3.5	9.3
Salvation Army	1	76	64	164	0.2	0.6
Unit Univ	1	30	67	79	0.1	0.3
BROWN	**69**	**3,602**	**9,861**	**14,805**	**33.0**	**100.0**
Bahá'í	0	NR	4	4	0.0	0.0
BAPT–Amer Bapt USA	1	30	30	37	0.1	0.2
BAPT–So Bapt Conv	11	848	2,122	2,608	5.8	17.6
Catholic	5	NR	NR	2,870	6.4	19.4
Ch Christ Chr Union	1	NR	NR	NR	-	-
Ch of Nazarene	3	293	287	351	0.8	2.4
CHR–Chr Chs & Chs Cr	10	NR	1,640	2,016	4.5	13.6
CHR–Chs of Christ	2	70	65	96	0.2	0.6
Jehovah's Witness	1	NR	NR	NR	-	-
LDS–L-D Saints	1	NR	NR	376	0.8	2.5
LUTH–E.L.C.A.	1	120	399	447	1.0	3.0
MENN–Beachy Amish-Menn	1	156	78	156	0.3	1.1
METH–AME	1	0	100	123	0.3	0.8
METH–C.M.E.	1	0	100	123	0.3	0.8
METH–Un Methodist	14	665	916	1,290	2.9	8.7
METH–Wesleyan	1	77	82	100	0.2	0.7
Non-denom Chr Chs	5	970	3,575	3,587	8.0	24.2
PENT–Assemb of God	1	29	16	53	0.1	0.4
PENT–Ch God (Cleve)	1	6	6	7	0.0	0.0
PENT–Ch God Mtn Asm	1	NR	NR	NR	-	-
PRES–Presb Ch (USA)	5	100	178	219	0.5	1.5
PRES–Presb Ch Amer	1	204	203	268	0.6	1.8
Un C of Christ	1	34	60	74	0.2	0.5

Religious Group	Number of Congregations	Number of Attendees	Number of Communicant, Confirmed, or Full Members	Adherents		
				Number of Adherents	% of Total Pop.	% of Total Adh.
BUTLER	**333**	**39,421**	**66,191**	**138,939**	**37.7**	**100.0**
ANG/EPIS–Episcopal	4	558	1,123	1,215	0.3	0.9
Bahá'í	1	NR	43	43	0.0	0.0
BAPT–Amer Bapt Assn	2	NR	85	106	0.0	0.1
BAPT–Amer Bapt USA	4	845	2,059	2,559	0.7	1.8
BAPT–Converge/BGC	1	75	NR	90	0.0	0.1
BAPT–Enterprise Bapt Assoc	1	NR	NR	NR	-	-
BAPT–Ind Bapt Flwsp Intl	6	NR	NR	NR	-	-
BAPT–Natl Mis Bapt Conv	3	0	450	559	0.2	0.4
BAPT–NBC USA	1	0	500	621	0.2	0.4
BAPT–Reg Bapt Gen As	1	NR	NR	NR	-	-
BAPT–So Bapt Conv	47	4,388	13,074	16,247	4.4	11.7
BUDD–Mahayana	1	NR	NR	28	0.0	0.0
Calv Chpl	1	NR	NR	NR	-	-
Catholic	13	NR	NR	44,417	12.1	32.0
CGOD–Ch God (Ander)	17	2,822	NR	2,822	0.8	2.0
Ch Cr, Scientst	1	NR	NR	NR	-	-
Ch of Nazarene	10	1,810	2,914	3,383	0.9	2.4
Chr & Miss Al	3	167	69	230	0.1	0.2
CHR–Chr Ch (Disc)	4	171	396	492	0.1	0.4
CHR–Chr Chs & Chs Cr	11	NR	4,800	5,965	1.6	4.3
CHR–Chs of Christ	8	580	598	716	0.2	0.5
Evan Cov Ch	1	144	177	187	0.1	0.1
Evan Free Ch	1	600	NR	600	0.2	0.4
FRND–Fr Gen Cf	1	NR	15	19	0.0	0.0
Jain	1	NR	NR	NR	-	-
Jehovah's Witness	6	NR	NR	NR	-	-
JUD–Conserv	1	101	113	305	0.1	0.2
JUD–Reform	1	31	55	148	0.0	0.1
LDS–Comm of Christ	1	NR	133	133	0.0	0.1
LDS–L-D Saints	8	NR	NR	3,911	1.1	2.8
LUTH–E.L.C.A.	10	1,191	3,109	4,100	1.1	3.0
LUTH–Luth–MO Synod	3	569	852	1,150	0.3	0.8
MENN–Mennonite USA	1	35	68	85	0.0	0.1
METH–AME	4	120	525	652	0.2	0.5
METH–C.M.E.	2	75	325	404	0.1	0.3
METH–Un Methodist	26	4,002	6,329	9,294	2.5	6.7
METH–Wesleyan	3	240	163	312	0.1	0.2
Missionary Ch	2	83	62	83	0.0	0.1
Muslim Est	1	600	NR	2,000	0.5	1.4
Non-denom Chr Chs	43	11,785	14,246	16,144	4.4	11.6
ORTHE–Greek Orthodox	1	45	NR	90	0.0	0.1
PENT–Assemb of God	9	1,700	723	2,410	0.7	1.7
PENT–Ch God (Cleve)	14	3,354	7,132	8,863	2.4	6.4
PENT–Ch of God Proph	2	NR	60	75	0.0	0.1
PENT–COGIC	2	0	300	373	0.1	0.3
PENT–Fire Bapt Hol Ch	1	NR	NR	NR	-	-
PENT–Intl Pent Holiness	2	176	135	168	0.0	0.1
PENT–Pent Ch of God	2	140	NR	217	0.1	0.2
PENT–Un Pent Ch Intl	5	NR	NR	NR	-	-
PENT–United Holy Ch	1	NR	NR	NR	-	-
PENT–Vineyard	3	950	1,150	1,429	0.4	1.0
PRES–Evan Presby Ch	1	NR	135	168	0.0	0.1
PRES–Presb Ch (USA)	15	1,467	2,690	3,343	0.9	2.4
Salvation Army	3	92	298	1,215	0.3	0.9
Sev Day Adv	6	212	367	423	0.1	0.3
Sikh	2	NR	NR	NR	-	-
Un C of Christ	4	265	858	1,066	0.3	0.8
Unit Univ	1	28	60	64	0.0	0.0
Unity Ch	2	NR	NR	NR	-	-
Zoroastrian	1	NR	NR	15	0.0	0.0
CARROLL	**47**	**2,102**	**4,729**	**8,505**	**29.5**	**100.0**
Bahá'í	0	NR	1	1	0.0	0.0
Catholic	4	NR	NR	1,826	6.3	21.5
Ch of Nazarene	2	90	78	104	0.4	1.2
CHR–Chr Ch (Disc)	1	150	329	398	1.4	4.7
CHR–Chr Chs & Chs Cr	3	NR	430	520	1.8	6.1
CHR–Chs of Christ	1	50	47	60	0.2	0.7
Jehovah's Witness	1	NR	NR	NR	-	-
LUTH–E.L.C.A.	3	206	672	1,166	4.0	13.7
MENN–Amish Undif	5	NR	256	614	2.1	7.2
METH–Un Methodist	13	923	2,058	2,595	9.0	30.5

NR–Not Reported   - Represents no adherents reported.   Percentages may not total 100 due to rounding.

Table 3: Religious Congregations by County and Group: 2010

Religious Group	Number of Congrega-tions	Number of Attendees	Number of Communicant, Confirmed, or Full Members	Adherents		
				Number of Adherents	% of Total Pop.	% of Total Adh.
METH–Wesleyan	1	31	21	40	0.1	0.5
Non-denom Chr Chs	4	485	458	606	2.1	7.1
PENT–Assemb of God	2	110	68	200	0.7	2.4
PRES–Presb Ch (USA)	6	45	289	350	1.2	4.1
Sev Day Adv	1	12	22	25	0.1	0.3
CHAMPAIGN	**72**	**4,547**	**7,550**	**11,408**	**28.5**	**100.0**
ANG/EPIS–Episcopal	2	68	139	149	0.4	1.3
Bahá'í	0	NR	7	7	0.0	0.1
BAPT–Amer Bapt USA	5	294	809	997	2.5	8.7
BAPT–Free Will Bapt	3	NR	201	248	0.6	2.2
BAPT–NBC USA	1	0	150	185	0.5	1.6
BAPT–So Bapt Conv	2	50	72	89	0.2	0.8
Catholic	4	NR	NR	1,488	3.7	13.0
CGOD–Ch God (Ander)	3	182	NR	182	0.5	1.6
Ch Christ Chr Union	4	NR	NR	NR	-	-
Ch of God Gen Conf	1	NR	9	11	0.0	0.1
Ch of Nazarene	3	303	359	832	2.1	7.3
CHR–Chr Chs & Chs Cr	1	NR	100	123	0.3	1.1
CHR–Chs of Christ	1	45	40	70	0.2	0.6
FRND–Evan Fr Ch Intl	2	168	88	108	0.3	0.9
Jehovah's Witness	1	NR	NR	NR	-	-
LUTH–E.L.C.A.	2	166	537	662	1.7	5.8
MENN–Cons Menn Conf	1	230	175	216	0.5	1.9
METH–AME	2	0	200	246	0.6	2.2
METH–Un Methodist	14	1,160	2,366	3,099	7.7	27.2
Missionary Ch	1	104	42	104	0.3	0.9
Non-denom Chr Chs	11	1,490	1,750	1,962	4.9	17.2
ORTHE–Rus Orth Abroad	1	20	NR	25	0.1	0.2
PENT–Assemb of God	1	60	80	80	0.2	0.7
PENT–Ch of God Proph	2	NR	44	54	0.1	0.5
PENT–Vineyard	1	70	65	80	0.2	0.7
PRES–Presb Ch (USA)	2	137	317	391	1.0	3.4
Swedenborgian	1	NR	NR	NR	-	-
CLARK	**184**	**12,975**	**25,304**	**43,489**	**31.4**	**100.0**
ANG/EPIS–Episcopal	1	137	251	357	0.3	0.8
Bahá'í	0	NR	15	15	0.0	0.0
BAPT–Amer Bapt USA	3	550	1,122	1,369	1.0	3.1
BAPT–Enterprise Bapt Assoc	1	NR	NR	NR	-	-
BAPT–Free Will Bapt	6	NR	402	491	0.4	1.1
BAPT–NBC USA	1	225	350	427	0.3	1.0
BAPT–Reg Bapt Gen As	1	NR	NR	NR	-	-
BAPT–So Bapt Conv	11	925	2,168	2,645	1.9	6.1
BRETH–Breth in Chr	2	NR	NR	NR	-	-
BRETH–Ch of Brethren	3	196	731	892	0.6	2.1
BRETH–Grace Breth	1	NR	NR	NR	-	-
Catholic	6	NR	NR	9,130	6.6	21.0
CGOD–Ch God (Ander)	7	1,141	NR	1,141	0.8	2.6
Ch Christ Chr Union	5	NR	NR	NR	-	-
Ch Cr, Scientst	1	NR	NR	NR	-	-
Ch of God Gen Conf	2	NR	158	193	0.1	0.4
Ch of Nazarene	6	965	1,443	1,626	1.2	3.7
CHR–Chr Ch (Disc)	2	7	367	448	0.3	1.0
CHR–Chr Chs & Chs Cr	6	NR	3,155	3,850	2.8	8.9
CHR–Chs of Christ	5	380	403	480	0.3	1.1
CONG–Cong Chr, NA	1	NR	18	22	0.0	0.1
Ind Fund Churches	1	NR	NR	NR	-	-
Int Cou Comm Ch	1	NR	NR	NR	-	-
Jehovah's Witness	2	NR	NR	NR	-	-
JUD–Reform	1	44	77	208	0.2	0.5
LDS–L-D Saints	1	NR	NR	937	0.7	2.2
LUTH–E.L.C.A.	10	783	2,388	2,991	2.2	6.9
LUTH–Luth-MO Synod	1	130	253	365	0.3	0.8
LUTH–Nor Amer Luth C	3	NR	NR	NR	-	-
LUTH–Wisc Ev Luth Syn	1	71	98	122	0.1	0.3
MENN–Mennonite USA	2	117	85	104	0.1	0.2
METH–AME	3	50	370	451	0.3	1.0
METH–C.M.E.	1	0	180	220	0.2	0.5
METH–Un Methodist	23	1,960	3,639	5,223	3.8	12.0
Missionary Ch	4	184	87	189	0.1	0.4
Muslim Est	2	154	NR	348	0.3	0.8
New Apost Ch	1	NR	NR	NR	-	-

Religious Group	Number of Congrega-tions	Number of Attendees	Number of Communicant, Confirmed, or Full Members	Adherents		
				Number of Adherents	% of Total Pop.	% of Total Adh.
Non-denom Chr Chs	20	2,817	3,455	3,754	2.7	8.6
ORTHE–Greek Orthodox	1	50	NR	225	0.2	0.5
PENT–Assemb of God	3	171	120	296	0.2	0.7
PENT–Ch God (Cleve)	2	115	416	508	0.4	1.2
PENT–Ch of God Proph	1	NR	31	38	0.0	0.1
PENT–COGIC	2	0	150	183	0.1	0.4
PENT–Fire Bapt Hol Ch	1	NR	NR	NR	-	-
PENT–Int Foursq Gos	1	69	138	168	0.1	0.4
PENT–Int Pent C Chr	4	133	114	140	0.1	0.3
PENT–Open Bible Std	1	101	NR	101	0.1	0.2
PENT–Pent Ch of God	1	70	NR	109	0.1	0.3
PENT–Un Pent Ch Intl	1	NR	NR	NR	-	-
PENT–United Holy Ch	1	NR	NR	NR	-	-
PENT–Vineyard	2	300	446	544	0.4	1.3
PRES–Presb Ch (USA)	5	528	979	1,195	0.9	2.7
Salvation Army	1	38	290	312	0.2	0.7
Sev Day Adv	3	196	341	392	0.3	0.9
Un Breth in Cr	1	25	33	22	0.0	0.1
Un C of Christ	5	343	1,031	1,258	0.9	2.9
CLERMONT	**176**	**15,584**	**28,901**	**71,619**	**36.3**	**100.0**
ANG/EPIS–Episcopal	1	25	49	49	0.0	0.1
Bahá'í	1	NR	27	27	0.0	0.0
BAPT–Amer Bapt Assn	2	NR	145	181	0.1	0.3
BAPT–Amer Bapt USA	1	0	0	0	0.0	0.0
BAPT–Free Will Bapt	2	NR	134	167	0.1	0.2
BAPT–Ind Bapt Flwsp Intl	2	NR	NR	NR	-	-
BAPT–NBC USA	1	60	60	75	0.0	0.1
BAPT–So Bapt Conv	25	1,903	5,817	7,267	3.7	10.1
BRETH–Ch of Brethren	1	0	52	65	0.0	0.1
BRETH–Grace Breth	1	NR	NR	NR	-	-
BUDD–Mahayana	1	NR	NR	11	0.0	0.0
Catholic	13	NR	NR	31,460	15.9	43.9
CGOD–Ch God (Ander)	3	82	NR	82	0.0	0.1
Ch of Nazarene	10	629	968	1,293	0.7	1.8
CHR–Chr Chs & Chs Cr	19	NR	6,002	7,498	3.8	10.5
CHR–Chs of Christ	3	593	490	689	0.3	1.0
Evan Free Ch	1	1,000	NR	1,000	0.5	1.4
Jehovah's Witness	3	NR	NR	NR	-	-
LDS–Comm of Christ	1	NR	133	133	0.1	0.2
LUTH–E.L.C.A.	2	171	284	411	0.2	0.6
LUTH–Luth-MO Synod	1	247	535	697	0.4	1.0
METH–AME	1	0	150	187	0.1	0.3
METH–Un Methodist	27	3,409	5,616	8,947	4.5	12.5
METH–Wesleyan	2	169	139	220	0.1	0.3
Muslim Est	1	20	NR	100	0.1	0.1
Non-denom Chr Chs	20	5,106	5,160	6,586	3.3	9.2
ORTHE–Ant Orth of NA	1	80	NR	239	0.1	0.3
PENT–Assemb of God	7	545	439	753	0.4	1.1
PENT–Ch God (Cleve)	7	364	885	1,106	0.6	1.5
PENT–Ch God Mtn Asm	4	NR	NR	NR	-	-
PENT–Un Pent Ch Intl	1	NR	NR	NR	-	-
PENT–Vineyard	2	845	1,200	1,499	0.8	2.1
PRES–Presb Ch (USA)	6	242	467	583	0.3	0.8
Salvation Army	1	26	46	168	0.1	0.2
Sev Day Adv	1	36	63	72	0.0	0.1
Un C of Christ	1	32	40	50	0.0	0.1
Zoroastrian	0	NR	NR	4	0.0	0.0
CLINTON	**71**	**4,449**	**9,485**	**14,787**	**35.2**	**100.0**
Bahá'í	0	NR	2	2	0.0	0.0
BAPT–Amer Bapt USA	2	88	374	461	1.1	3.1
BAPT–Free Will Bapt	1	NR	67	83	0.2	0.6
BAPT–Natl Mis Bapt Conv	1	0	150	185	0.4	1.3
BAPT–Prim Bapt E Dst	1	25	89	110	0.3	0.7
BAPT–So Bapt Conv	6	377	985	1,214	2.9	8.2
Catholic	1	NR	NR	2,179	5.2	14.7
CGOD–Ch God (Ander)	3	211	NR	211	0.5	1.4
Ch Christ Chr Union	1	NR	NR	NR	-	-
Ch of Nazarene	2	287	422	541	1.3	3.7
CHR–Chr Ch (Disc)	1	107	379	467	1.1	3.2
CHR–Chr Chs & Chs Cr	7	NR	1,820	2,243	5.3	15.2
CHR–Chs of Christ	3	64	62	74	0.2	0.5

NR–Not Reported   - Represents no adherents reported.   Percentages may not total 100 due to rounding.

Table 3: Religious Congregations by County and Group: 2010

Religious Group	Number of Congregations	Number of Attendees	Number of Communicant, Confirmed, or Full Members	Adherents: Number of Adherents	Adherents: % of Total Pop.	Adherents: % of Total Adh.
Evan Free Ch	1	0	NR	0	0.0	0.0
FRND–Fr Gen Cf & Un Mtg	1	NR	32	39	0.1	0.3
FRND–Fr Un Mtg	10	NR	591	728	1.7	4.9
Jehovah's Witness	2	NR	NR	NR	-	-
LDS–L-D Saints	1	NR	NR	349	0.8	2.4
LUTH–E.L.C.A.	1	92	204	269	0.6	1.8
METH–AME	1	0	150	185	0.4	1.3
METH–Un Methodist	10	598	1,347	1,776	4.2	12.0
METH–Wesleyan	1	55	10	72	0.2	0.5
Non-denom Chr Chs	8	1,944	1,899	2,431	5.8	16.4
PENT–Assemb of God	1	131	88	172	0.4	1.2
PENT–Ch God (Cleve)	2	264	324	399	0.9	2.7
PRES–Presb Ch (USA)	1	120	340	419	1.0	2.8
Sev Day Adv	1	47	82	94	0.2	0.6
Un C of Christ	1	39	68	84	0.2	0.6
COLUMBIANA	**191**	**13,458**	**25,241**	**42,923**	**39.8**	**100.0**
ANG/EPIS–Anglican NA	1	NR	NR	NR	-	-
ANG/EPIS–Episcopal	3	85	133	216	0.2	0.5
Bahá'í	0	NR	6	6	0.0	0.0
BAPT–Amer Bapt USA	2	142	308	369	0.3	0.9
BAPT–Converge/BGC	2	150	NR	180	0.2	0.4
BAPT–Ind Bapt Flwsp Intl	1	NR	NR	NR	-	-
BAPT–NBC USA	3	80	470	562	0.5	1.3
BAPT–Reg Bapt Gen As	2	NR	NR	NR	-	-
BAPT–So Bapt Conv	2	90	298	357	0.3	0.8
BRETH–Brethren (Ash)	1	NR	80	96	0.1	0.2
BRETH–Ch of Brethren	1	36	72	86	0.1	0.2
Catholic	10	NR	NR	9,658	9.0	22.5
CGOD–Ch God (Ander)	1	0	NR	0	0.0	0.0
Ch of Nazarene	9	736	1,400	1,423	1.3	3.3
CHR–Chr Ch (Disc)	3	80	1,395	1,669	1.5	3.9
CHR–Chr Chs & Chs Cr	13	NR	2,502	2,994	2.8	7.0
CHR–Chs of Christ	7	514	471	606	0.6	1.4
CONG–Cong Chr, NA	1	NR	208	249	0.2	0.6
FRND–Consrv Yr Mtgs	3	NR	204	244	0.2	0.6
FRND–Evan Fr Ch Intl	5	1,644	1,165	1,394	1.3	3.2
Grace Gosp Fel	1	NR	NR	NR	-	-
Jehovah's Witness	6	NR	NR	NR	-	-
JUD–Reform	1	6	11	30	0.0	0.1
LDS–L-D Saints	1	NR	NR	577	0.5	1.3
LUTH–E.L.C.A.	9	631	2,468	3,120	2.9	7.3
MENN–Beachy Amish-Menn	1	63	43	63	0.1	0.1
MENN–CG in Cr (Menn)	1	NR	119	142	0.1	0.3
MENN–Mennonite USA	2	180	227	272	0.3	0.6
METH–A.W.M.C.	1	205	113	234	0.2	0.5
METH–AME	2	30	181	217	0.2	0.5
METH–AME Zion	1	0	150	180	0.2	0.4
METH–Free Methodist	3	216	174	226	0.2	0.5
METH–Un Methodist	30	2,136	5,403	6,917	6.4	16.1
Non-denom Chr Chs	20	3,790	3,435	4,803	4.5	11.2
PENT–Assemb of God	6	920	431	1,305	1.2	3.0
PENT–Ch God (Cleve)	2	124	259	310	0.3	0.7
PENT–Fire Bapt Hol Ch	1	NR	NR	NR	-	-
PENT–Un Pent Ch Intl	2	NR	NR	NR	-	-
PRES–Evan Presby Ch	1	NR	137	164	0.2	0.4
PRES–Presb Ch (USA)	23	1,177	2,496	2,987	2.8	7.0
PRES–Presb Ch Amer	1	140	156	187	0.2	0.4
Salvation Army	2	54	214	452	0.4	1.1
Sev Day Adv	1	6	10	12	0.0	0.0
Un Breth in Cr	1	125	77	107	0.1	0.2
Un C of Christ	2	98	425	509	0.5	1.2
COSHOCTON	**87**	**4,802**	**10,346**	**15,161**	**41.1**	**100.0**
ANG/EPIS–Episcopal	1	30	81	81	0.2	0.5
Bahá'í	0	NR	1	1	0.0	0.0
BAPT–Amer Bapt USA	3	410	748	917	2.5	6.0
BAPT–Reg Bapt Gen As	1	NR	NR	NR	-	-
BAPT–So Bapt Conv	2	190	345	423	1.1	2.8
Catholic	1	NR	NR	1,350	3.7	8.9
CGOD–Ch God (Ander)	1	35	NR	35	0.1	0.2
Ch of Nazarene	4	533	769	774	2.1	5.1
Chr & Miss Al	1	41	30	60	0.2	0.4

Religious Group	Number of Congregations	Number of Attendees	Number of Communicant, Confirmed, or Full Members	Adherents: Number of Adherents	Adherents: % of Total Pop.	Adherents: % of Total Adh.
CHR–Chr Ch (Disc)	1	60	199	244	0.7	1.6
CHR–Chr Chs & Chs Cr	2	NR	130	159	0.4	1.0
CHR–Chs of Christ	5	193	175	233	0.6	1.5
Jehovah's Witness	1	NR	NR	NR	-	-
LDS–L-D Saints	1	NR	NR	148	0.4	1.0
LUTH–E.L.C.A.	1	70	322	322	0.9	2.1
MENN–Amish Undif	13	NR	812	1,760	4.8	11.6
MENN–Beachy Amish-Menn	1	116	71	116	0.3	0.8
MENN–Mennonite USA	1	25	30	37	0.1	0.2
METH–AME	1	24	38	47	0.1	0.3
METH–Un Methodist	21	1,293	4,096	4,988	13.5	32.9
METH–Wesleyan	2	124	121	161	0.4	1.1
Non-denom Chr Chs	9	1,100	1,253	1,449	3.9	9.6
PENT–Assemb of God	1	24	10	37	0.1	0.2
PENT–Int Foursq Gos	1	74	71	87	0.2	0.6
PENT–Pent Ch of God	2	140	NR	217	0.6	1.4
PENT–Un Pent Ch Intl	1	NR	NR	NR	-	-
PRES–Presb Ch (USA)	5	206	569	698	1.9	4.6
Salvation Army	1	41	151	422	1.1	2.8
Sev Day Adv	1	13	23	26	0.1	0.2
Un C of Christ	2	60	301	369	1.0	2.4
CRAWFORD	**97**	**6,593**	**12,856**	**22,195**	**50.7**	**100.0**
Bahá'í	0	NR	5	5	0.0	0.0
BAPT–Amer Bapt USA	1	50	110	133	0.3	0.6
BAPT–Free Will Bapt	2	NR	134	163	0.4	0.7
BAPT–Ind Bapt Flwsp Intl	1	NR	NR	NR	-	-
BAPT–Reg Bapt Gen As	1	NR	NR	NR	-	-
BAPT–So Bapt Conv	2	60	79	96	0.2	0.4
Catholic	4	NR	NR	5,812	13.3	26.2
Ch Christ Chr Union	2	NR	NR	NR	-	-
Ch of Nazarene	3	983	1,038	1,056	2.4	4.8
Chr & Miss Al	2	261	186	309	0.7	1.4
CHR–Chr Ch (Disc)	1	24	154	187	0.4	0.8
CHR–Chr Chs & Chs Cr	4	NR	310	376	0.9	1.7
CHR–Chs of Christ	2	107	110	130	0.3	0.6
Jehovah's Witness	2	NR	NR	NR	-	-
LDS–L-D Saints	1	NR	NR	437	1.0	2.0
LUTH–E.L.C.A.	10	889	2,993	3,727	8.5	16.8
LUTH–Luth Cong Msn Chr	3	250	722	876	2.0	3.9
LUTH–Nor Amer Luth C	2	NR	NR	NR	-	-
METH–AME	1	0	100	121	0.3	0.5
METH–Free Methodist	1	279	197	279	0.6	1.3
METH–Un Methodist	14	1,104	2,731	3,408	7.8	15.4
METH–Wesleyan	1	19	10	25	0.1	0.1
Non-denom Chr Chs	12	1,617	1,855	2,127	4.9	9.6
ORTHE–Greek Orthodox	1	3	NR	3	0.0	0.0
PENT–Assemb of God	2	95	77	174	0.4	0.8
PENT–Ch God (Cleve)	3	84	187	227	0.5	1.0
PENT–Ch of God Proph	2	NR	59	72	0.2	0.3
PENT–Int Foursq Gos	1	27	55	67	0.2	0.3
PENT–Int Pent C Chr	2	25	NR	40	0.1	0.2
PENT–Pent Ch of God	1	70	NR	109	0.2	0.5
PENT–Un Pent Ch Intl	1	NR	NR	NR	-	-
PRES–Presb Ch (USA)	3	147	232	281	0.6	1.3
Salvation Army	1	21	32	171	0.4	0.8
Sev Day Adv	3	108	188	217	0.5	1.0
Un C of Christ	5	370	1,292	1,567	3.6	7.1
CUYAHOGA	**955**	**122,325**	**198,602**	**674,791**	**52.7**	**100.0**
ANG/EPIS–Anglican NA	3	NR	NR	NR	-	-
ANG/EPIS–Episcopal	21	2,550	6,718	8,142	0.6	1.2
Bahá'í	4	NR	395	395	0.0	0.1
BAPT–Amer Bapt Assn	1	NR	85	102	0.0	0.0
BAPT–Amer Bapt USA	31	8,016	17,494	21,077	1.6	3.1
BAPT–Asc Ref Bap Ch Am	1	NR	NR	NR	-	-
BAPT–Converge/BGC	1	400	NR	480	0.0	0.1
BAPT–Free Will Bapt	5	NR	335	404	0.0	0.1
BAPT–N Am Bapt Conf	3	NR	1,084	1,306	0.1	0.2
BAPT–Natl Mis Bapt Conv	11	50	1,800	2,169	0.2	0.3
BAPT–NBC Amer	3	170	300	361	0.0	0.1
BAPT–NBC USA	44	5,667	20,810	25,072	2.0	3.7
BAPT–Prog NBC	4	1,395	2,580	3,108	0.2	0.5

NR–Not Reported   - Represents no adherents reported.   Percentages may not total 100 due to rounding.

Table 3: Religious Congregations by County and Group: 2010

Religious Group	Number of Congrega-tions	Number of Attendees	Number of Communicant, Confirmed, or Full Members	Adherents		
				Number of Adherents	% of Total Pop.	% of Total Adh.
BAPT–Ref Bapt Ch	1	NR	NR	NR	-	-
BAPT–Reg Bapt Gen As	12	NR	NR	NR	-	-
BAPT–So Bapt Conv	29	4,315	4,708	5,672	0.4	0.8
BRETH–Ch of Brethren	1	80	194	234	0.0	0.0
BRETH–Grace Breth	1	NR	NR	NR	-	-
BUDD–Mahayana	7	NR	NR	3,504	0.3	0.5
BUDD–Theravada	2	NR	NR	410	0.0	0.1
BUDD–Vajrayana	2	NR	NR	159	0.0	0.0
Calv Chpl	1	NR	NR	NR	-	-
Catholic	108	NR	NR	366,464	28.6	54.3
CGOD–Ch God (Ander)	10	839	NR	839	0.1	0.1
Ch Cr, Scientst	4	NR	NR	NR	-	-
Ch of Chr (Hol)	2	NR	NR	NR	-	-
Ch of God Gen Conf	1	NR	27	33	0.0	0.0
Ch of Nazarene	10	749	1,012	4,744	0.4	0.7
Chr & Miss Al	11	3,766	1,984	6,277	0.5	0.9
CHR–Chr Ch (Disc)	18	1,206	3,773	4,546	0.4	0.7
CHR–Chr Chs & Chs Cr	6	NR	449	541	0.0	0.1
CHR–Chs of Christ	13	1,387	1,467	2,153	0.2	0.3
CHR–Int Chs of Christ	1	NR	213	257	0.0	0.0
CONG–Cong Chr, NA	1	NR	70	84	0.0	0.0
CONG–Consrv Cong Chr	1	61	68	82	0.0	0.0
Evan Assoc RCC	1	NR	NR	NR	-	-
Evan Cov Ch	2	124	157	161	0.0	0.0
Evan Free Ch	2	530	NR	530	0.0	0.1
FRND–Consrv Yr Mtgs	1	NR	0	0	0.0	0.0
FRND–Evan Fr Ch Intl	5	1,805	605	729	0.1	0.1
FRND–Fr Gen Cf	1	NR	59	71	0.0	0.0
HINDU–I/A Temples	3	NR	NR	2,150	0.2	0.3
HINDU–Post Ren	5	NR	NR	141	0.0	0.0
HINDU–Trad Temples	3	NR	NR	2,590	0.2	0.4
Int Cou Comm Ch	2	NR	NR	NR	-	-
Jain	1	NR	NR	NR	-	-
Jehovah's Witness	23	NR	NR	NR	-	-
JUD–Conserv	3	2,389	2,681	7,239	0.6	1.1
JUD–Orth	22	8,640	3,000	12,000	0.9	1.8
JUD–Reconst	1	83	106	286	0.0	0.0
JUD–Reform	6	2,374	4,187	11,305	0.9	1.7
LDS–L-D Saints	10	NR	NR	4,546	0.4	0.7
LUTH–Assoc Free Luth	1	NR	NR	NR	-	-
LUTH–E.L.C.A.	37	4,335	10,735	13,691	1.1	2.0
LUTH–Luth Cong Msn Chr	1	25	63	76	0.0	0.0
LUTH–Luth–MO Synod	38	6,584	14,244	18,445	1.4	2.7
LUTH–Nor Amer Luth C	1	NR	NR	NR	-	-
LUTH–Wisc Ev Luth Syn	1	76	144	173	0.0	0.0
MENN–Fel Evg Ch	1	157	47	57	0.0	0.0
MENN–Mennonite USA	3	327	529	637	0.0	0.1
METH–AME	16	930	3,635	4,380	0.3	0.6
METH–AME Zion	4	280	564	680	0.1	0.1
METH–C.M.E.	4	275	720	867	0.1	0.1
METH–Free Methodist	4	609	699	715	0.1	0.1
METH–Un Methodist	52	7,176	18,729	24,308	1.9	3.6
METH–Wesleyan	2	335	113	435	0.0	0.1
Missionary Ch	1	152	67	152	0.0	0.0
MJEW–Union Mes Cong	1	NR	NR	NR	-	-
Muslim Est	13	1,986	NR	3,342	0.3	0.5
New Apost Ch	2	NR	NR	NR	-	-
Non-denom Chr Chs	69	30,970	35,501	41,873	3.3	6.2
OCATH–Pol Natl Cath	2	NR	NR	NR	-	-
ORTHE–Ant Orth of NA	3	430	NR	1,586	0.1	0.2
ORTHE–Carp Rus Orth	1	22	NR	54	0.0	0.0
ORTHE–Greek Orthodox	6	1,600	NR	5,651	0.4	0.8
ORTHE–Orth Ch in Amer	8	1,230	NR	3,349	0.3	0.5
ORTHE–Romania Orth Ar	1	140	NR	650	0.1	0.1
ORTHE–Rus Orth Abroad	1	90	NR	300	0.0	0.0
ORTHE–Serb Orth USA	2	360	NR	1,500	0.1	0.2
ORTHE–Ukrainian Orth	4	332	NR	1,567	0.1	0.2
ORTHO–Armen Ap Cilic	1	40	NR	100	0.0	0.0
ORTHO–Armen Ap Etchm	1	30	NR	100	0.0	0.0
ORTHO–Coptic Orth Ch	1	800	NR	1,500	0.1	0.2
ORTHO–Malan Dioc Am	1	15	NR	45	0.0	0.0
ORTHO–Malan Syr Orth	1	30	NR	54	0.0	0.0
PENT–Assemb of God	21	2,759	1,519	3,904	0.3	0.6
PENT–Ch God (Cleve)	10	1,266	3,087	3,719	0.3	0.6
PENT–Ch God Mtn Asm	1	NR	NR	NR	-	-
PENT–Ch Lord Jesus Apos	6	NR	NR	NR	-	-
PENT–Ch of God Proph	5	NR	389	469	0.0	0.1
PENT–COGIC	24	795	3,435	4,139	0.3	0.6
PENT–Fire Bapt Hol Ch	1	NR	NR	NR	-	-
PENT–Full Gosp Bapt	7	NR	NR	NR	-	-
PENT–I F Chr Assmbl	1	NR	NR	NR	-	-
PENT–Int Foursq Gos	4	221	380	458	0.0	0.1
PENT–Un Pent Ch Intl	7	NR	NR	NR	-	-
PENT–United Holy Ch	4	NR	NR	NR	-	-
PENT–Vineyard	1	250	350	422	0.0	0.1
PRES–Cum Pres Am	2	NR	NR	NR	-	-
PRES–Evan Presby Ch	1	NR	1,890	2,277	0.2	0.3
PRES–Kor Pres Abroad	1	NR	NR	NR	-	-
PRES–Korean Amer Pres	1	NR	NR	NR	-	-
PRES–Presb Ch (USA)	28	3,573	7,411	8,929	0.7	1.3
PRES–Presb Ch Amer	1	25	20	24	0.0	0.0
REF–Christian Ref	2	107	198	239	0.0	0.0
REF–Ref Ch in Am	3	210	421	527	0.0	0.1
Salvation Army	8	507	644	2,982	0.2	0.4
Sev Day Adv	15	2,438	4,239	4,876	0.4	0.7
Sikh	3	NR	NR	NR	-	-
Swedenborgian	1	NR	NR	NR	-	-
Un C of Christ	38	3,547	11,290	13,602	1.1	2.0
Unit Univ	5	695	1,178	1,560	0.1	0.2
Unity Ch	5	NR	NR	NR	-	-
Zoroastrian	0	NR	NR	14	0.0	0.0
DARKE	**93**	**7,121**	**10,894**	**22,120**	**41.8**	**100.0**
ANG/EPIS–Episcopal	1	40	91	91	0.2	0.4
Bahá'í	0	NR	1	1	0.0	0.0
BAPT–Reg Bapt Gen As	2	NR	NR	NR	-	-
BAPT–So Bapt Conv	7	308	1,053	1,303	2.5	5.9
BRETH–Ch of Brethren	10	995	1,846	2,284	4.3	10.3
BRETH–Grace Breth	2	NR	NR	NR	-	-
Catholic	5	NR	NR	7,097	13.4	32.1
CGOD–Ch God (Ander)	1	280	NR	280	0.5	1.3
Ch of Nazarene	2	75	143	240	0.5	1.1
Chr & Miss Al	1	60	37	75	0.1	0.3
CHR–Chr Chs & Chs Cr	2	NR	440	544	1.0	2.5
CHR–Chs of Christ	1	35	35	40	0.1	0.2
CONG–Consrv Cong Chr	1	100	200	247	0.5	1.1
CONG–Midw Cong Chr Fel	8	266	238	294	0.6	1.3
Jehovah's Witness	1	NR	NR	NR	-	-
JUD–Reform	1	13	23	62	0.1	0.3
LDS–L-D Saints	1	NR	NR	225	0.4	1.0
LUTH–E.L.C.A.	5	291	963	1,286	2.4	5.8
LUTH–Luth Cong Msn Chr	1	167	662	819	1.5	3.7
LUTH–Nor Amer Luth C	1	NR	NR	NR	-	-
METH–Un Methodist	16	1,903	2,394	3,447	6.5	15.6
METH–Wesleyan	2	209	142	272	0.5	1.2
Missionary Ch	2	533	234	533	1.0	2.4
New Apost Ch	1	NR	NR	NR	-	-
Non-denom Chr Chs	11	1,400	1,569	1,864	3.5	8.4
PENT–Assemb of God	1	152	100	206	0.4	0.9
PENT–Ch God (Cleve)	1	75	270	334	0.6	1.5
PENT–Ch God Mtn Asm	1	NR	NR	NR	-	-
PENT–Open Bible Std	1	21	NR	21	0.0	0.1
PRES–Presb Ch (USA)	2	148	338	418	0.8	1.9
Un C of Christ	1	30	92	114	0.2	0.5
Unit Univ	1	20	23	23	0.0	0.1
DEFIANCE	**74**	**6,163**	**12,107**	**24,485**	**62.7**	**100.0**
ANG/EPIS–Episcopal	1	34	54	66	0.2	0.3
Ap Chr Ch-Amer	1	217	103	217	0.6	0.9
Bahá'í	0	NR	3	3	0.0	0.0
BAPT–Reg Bapt Gen As	1	NR	NR	NR	-	-
BAPT–So Bapt Conv	8	367	648	800	2.0	3.3
BRETH–Ch of Brethren	2	0	174	215	0.6	0.9
Catholic	5	NR	NR	7,984	20.5	32.6
CGOD–Ch God (Ander)	1	270	NR	270	0.7	1.1
CGOD–Ches God-Gen Con	1	138	116	143	0.4	0.6
Ch of Nazarene	2	204	263	609	1.6	2.5

NR–Not Reported   - Represents no adherents reported.   Percentages may not total 100 due to rounding.

Table 3: Religious Congregations by County and Group: 2010

Religious Group	Number of Congrega-tions	Number of Attendees	Number of Communicant, Confirmed, or Full Members	Adherents		
				Number of Adherents	% of Total Pop.	% of Total Adh.
CHR–Chr Chs & Chs Cr	4	NR	1,009	1,246	3.2	5.1
CHR–Chs of Christ	1	67	80	104	0.3	0.4
LUTH–E.L.C.A.	6	708	2,093	2,645	6.8	10.8
LUTH–Luth Ch-Am Asc	1	NR	NR	NR	-	-
LUTH–Luth–MO Synod	4	808	2,569	3,491	8.9	14.3
MENN–Amish Undif	1	NR	51	124	0.3	0.5
MENN–Beachy Amish-Menn	1	33	25	33	0.1	0.1
MENN–Cons Menn Conf	1	180	155	191	0.5	0.8
METH–Free Methodist	1	8	8	8	0.0	0.0
METH–Un Methodist	12	871	2,445	2,939	7.5	12.0
Missionary Ch	1	135	0	135	0.3	0.6
Non-denom Chr Chs	5	1,445	1,426	1,832	4.7	7.5
PENT–Assemb of God	3	178	105	242	0.6	1.0
PENT–Ch God (Cleve)	1	47	68	84	0.2	0.3
PENT–Open Bible Std	1	16	NR	16	0.0	0.1
PENT–Pent Ch of God	2	140	NR	217	0.6	0.9
PENT–Un Pent Ch Intl	1	NR	NR	NR	-	-
PRES–Presb Ch (USA)	2	126	216	267	0.7	1.1
Sev Day Adv	2	64	110	127	0.3	0.5
Un C of Christ	2	107	386	477	1.2	1.9
DELAWARE	**126**	**12,442**	**20,028**	**58,096**	**33.3**	**100.0**
ANG/EPIS–Anglican NA	1	NR	NR	NR	-	-
ANG/EPIS–Episcopal	1	102	180	217	0.1	0.4
Bahá'í	0	NR	24	24	0.0	0.0
BAPT–Amer Bapt USA	4	344	373	484	0.3	0.8
BAPT–Converge/BGC	1	75	NR	90	0.1	0.2
BAPT–Free Will Bapt	2	NR	134	174	0.1	0.3
BAPT–Ind Bapt Flwsp Intl	1	NR	NR	NR	-	-
BAPT–Reg Bapt Gen As	1	NR	NR	NR	-	-
BAPT–So Bapt Conv	4	1,487	1,561	2,027	1.2	3.5
BRETH–Grace Breth	2	NR	NR	NR	-	-
BUDD–Mahayana	2	NR	NR	1,011	0.6	1.7
Catholic	5	NR	NR	22,100	12.7	38.0
CGOD–Ch God (Ander)	1	50	NR	50	0.0	0.1
Ch Christ Chr Union	3	NR	NR	NR	-	-
Ch Cr, Scientst	1	NR	NR	NR	-	-
Ch of Nazarene	3	642	466	1,352	0.8	2.3
CHR–Chr Chs & Chs Cr	4	NR	870	1,130	0.6	1.9
CHR–Chs of Christ	5	338	319	419	0.2	0.7
Christian Un	1	NR	NR	NR	-	-
Evan Cov Ch	1	183	248	238	0.1	0.4
FRND–Evan Fr Ch Intl	2	179	151	196	0.1	0.3
FRND–Fr Gen Cf	1	NR	8	10	0.0	0.0
HINDU–I/A Temples	3	NR	NR	2,333	1.3	4.0
HINDU–Trad Temples	1	NR	NR	4,000	2.3	6.9
Jehovah's Witness	1	NR	NR	NR	-	-
LDS–Comm of Christ	1	NR	133	133	0.1	0.2
LDS–L-D Saints	3	NR	NR	1,168	0.7	2.0
LUTH–E.L.C.A.	2	440	1,110	1,505	0.9	2.6
LUTH–Luth–MO Synod	2	215	276	360	0.2	0.6
LUTH–Wisc Ev Luth Syn	1	109	182	228	0.1	0.4
METH–AME	1	50	107	139	0.1	0.2
METH–Un Methodist	17	2,809	5,538	7,261	4.2	12.5
METH–Wesleyan	2	47	35	61	0.0	0.1
MORAV–Morav Ch-North	1	42	42	48	0.0	0.1
Nat Spirit Asso	2	NR	NR	NR	-	-
Non-denom Chr Chs	11	2,206	2,500	2,917	1.7	5.0
ORTHE–Ant Orth of NA	1	53	NR	114	0.1	0.2
PENT–Assemb of God	4	170	96	219	0.1	0.4
PENT–Ch God (Cleve)	2	41	84	109	0.1	0.2
PENT–Un Pent Ch Intl	2	NR	NR	NR	-	-
PENT–Vineyard	2	885	1,350	1,753	1.0	3.0
PRES–Presb Ch (USA)	8	712	2,083	2,705	1.6	4.7
REF–Ref Ch in Am	2	561	863	1,210	0.7	2.1
Salvation Army	1	33	46	623	0.4	1.1
Sev Day Adv	3	100	175	201	0.1	0.3
Un Breth in Cr	1	103	0	88	0.1	0.2
Un C of Christ	3	375	921	1,196	0.7	2.1
Unit Univ	2	91	153	195	0.1	0.3
Unity Ch	1	NR	NR	NR	-	-
Zoroastrian	0	NR	NR	8	0.0	0.0

Religious Group	Number of Congrega-tions	Number of Attendees	Number of Communicant, Confirmed, or Full Members	Adherents		
				Number of Adherents	% of Total Pop.	% of Total Adh.
ERIE	**103**	**8,735**	**18,184**	**42,922**	**55.7**	**100.0**
ANG/EPIS–Anglican NA	1	NR	NR	NR	-	-
ANG/EPIS–Episcopal	2	129	438	475	0.6	1.1
Bahá'í	0	NR	3	3	0.0	0.0
BAPT–Amer Bapt USA	1	60	88	105	0.1	0.2
BAPT–Free Will Bapt	1	NR	67	80	0.1	0.2
BAPT–Natl Mis Bapt Conv	1	0	150	180	0.2	0.4
BAPT–NBC USA	3	380	575	689	0.9	1.6
BAPT–Reg Bapt Gen As	1	NR	NR	NR	-	-
BAPT–So Bapt Conv	5	245	927	1,111	1.4	2.6
Catholic	7	NR	NR	19,734	25.6	46.0
Ch of Nazarene	2	385	414	472	0.6	1.1
CHR–Chr Chs & Chs Cr	1	NR	200	240	0.3	0.6
CHR–Chs of Christ	3	250	255	310	0.4	0.7
CONG–Consrv Cong Chr	1	92	247	296	0.4	0.7
FRND–Evan Fr Ch Intl	1	NR	0	0	0.0	0.0
FRND–Fr Gen Cf	1	NR	0	0	0.0	0.0
Jehovah's Witness	2	NR	NR	NR	-	-
JUD–Reform	1	24	42	113	0.1	0.3
LDS–Comm of Christ	1	NR	133	133	0.2	0.3
LDS–L-D Saints	1	NR	NR	575	0.7	1.3
LUTH–E.L.C.A.	9	1,185	3,312	4,228	5.5	9.9
LUTH–Luth Cong Msn Chr	1	55	98	117	0.2	0.3
LUTH–Luth–MO Synod	1	90	178	200	0.3	0.5
METH–AME	1	0	150	180	0.2	0.4
METH–AME Zion	1	0	100	120	0.2	0.3
METH–C.M.E.	1	0	150	180	0.2	0.4
METH–Un Methodist	10	720	2,015	2,397	3.1	5.6
Non-denom Chr Chs	14	3,425	4,050	4,624	6.0	10.8
ORTHE–Rus Orth Abroad	1	12	NR	20	0.0	0.0
PENT–Assemb of God	5	560	343	1,141	1.5	2.7
PENT–Ch God (Cleve)	3	233	622	745	1.0	1.7
PENT–Ch God Mtn Asm	1	NR	NR	NR	-	-
PENT–Ch of God Proph	2	NR	48	58	0.1	0.1
PENT–COGIC	1	0	150	180	0.2	0.4
PENT–Int Foursq Gos	1	206	214	256	0.3	0.6
PRES–Orth Pres Ch	1	0	0	0	0.0	0.0
PRES–Presb Ch (USA)	3	67	373	447	0.6	1.0
Salvation Army	2	12	23	137	0.2	0.3
Sev Day Adv	1	24	43	49	0.1	0.1
Un C of Christ	7	556	2,753	3,299	4.3	7.7
Unit Univ	1	25	23	28	0.0	0.1
FAIRFIELD	**163**	**15,604**	**28,231**	**57,159**	**39.1**	**100.0**
ANG/EPIS–Episcopal	2	164	310	379	0.3	0.7
Bahá'í	0	NR	10	10	0.0	0.0
BAPT–Amer Bapt USA	1	28	35	44	0.0	0.1
BAPT–Free Will Bapt	2	NR	134	167	0.1	0.3
BAPT–Ind Bapt Flwsp Intl	1	NR	NR	NR	-	-
BAPT–Reg Bapt Gen As	4	NR	NR	NR	-	-
BAPT–So Bapt Conv	9	1,635	2,488	3,107	2.1	5.4
BRETH–Grace Breth	1	NR	NR	NR	-	-
Catholic	6	NR	NR	17,500	12.0	30.6
CGOD–Ch God (Ander)	2	219	NR	219	0.1	0.4
Ch Christ Chr Union	3	NR	NR	NR	-	-
Ch Cr, Scientst	1	NR	NR	NR	-	-
Ch of Nazarene	3	610	491	1,032	0.7	1.8
CHR–Chr Chs & Chs Cr	5	NR	4,220	5,270	3.6	9.2
CHR–Chs of Christ	4	570	523	789	0.5	1.4
Christian Un	2	NR	NR	NR	-	-
Jehovah's Witness	3	NR	NR	NR	-	-
LDS–Comm of Christ	1	NR	133	133	0.1	0.2
LDS–L-D Saints	4	NR	NR	1,773	1.2	3.1
LUTH–E.L.C.A.	16	1,286	3,617	4,732	3.2	8.3
LUTH–Luth–MO Synod	3	286	748	925	0.6	1.6
MENN–Amish Undif	1	NR	47	127	0.1	0.2
MENN–Beachy Amish-Menn	1	73	33	73	0.0	0.1
MENN–Fel Evg Ch	1	0	0	0	0.0	0.0
METH–Un Methodist	33	3,574	6,966	9,738	6.7	17.0
METH–Wesleyan	1	20	33	26	0.0	0.0
Non-denom Chr Chs	24	4,052	4,440	5,501	3.8	9.6
PENT–Assemb of God	3	629	174	1,106	0.8	1.9
PENT–Ch God (Cleve)	3	623	581	726	0.5	1.3

NR–Not Reported - Represents no adherents reported. Percentages may not total 100 due to rounding.

Table 3: Religious Congregations by County and Group: 2010

Religious Group	Number of Congrega-tions	Number of Attendees	Number of Communicant, Confirmed, or Full Members	Adherents		
				Number of Adherents	% of Total Pop.	% of Total Adh.
PENT–Intl Pent Holiness	1	28	35	44	0.0	0.1
PENT–Un Pent Ch Intl	3	NR	NR	NR	-	-
PENT–Vineyard	2	715	890	1,111	0.8	1.9
PRES–Presb Ch (USA)	6	444	868	1,084	0.7	1.9
Salvation Army	1	55	136	139	0.1	0.2
Sev Day Adv	1	84	147	169	0.1	0.3
Un Breth in Cr	3	246	352	211	0.1	0.4
Un C of Christ	5	263	820	1,024	0.7	1.8
Unity Ch	1	NR	NR	NR	-	-
FAYETTE	**55**	**2,893**	**5,235**	**7,354**	**25.3**	**100.0**
ANG/EPIS–Episcopal	1	47	214	226	0.8	3.1
Bahá'í	0	NR	3	3	0.0	0.0
BAPT–Amer Bapt USA	3	130	392	484	1.7	6.6
BAPT–Free Will Bapt	1	NR	67	83	0.3	1.1
BAPT–Ind Bapt Flwsp Intl	1	NR	NR	NR	-	-
BAPT–So Bapt Conv	1	29	73	90	0.3	1.2
Catholic	1	NR	NR	625	2.2	8.5
CGOD–Ch God (Ander)	2	72	NR	72	0.2	1.0
Ch Christ Chr Union	4	NR	NR	NR	-	-
Ch Cr, Scientst	1	NR	NR	NR	-	-
Ch of Nazarene	1	79	78	126	0.4	1.7
CHR–Chr Chs & Chs Cr	5	NR	820	1,013	3.5	13.8
CHR–Chs of Christ	2	126	95	121	0.4	1.6
Jehovah's Witness	1	NR	NR	NR	-	-
LDS–L-D Saints	1	NR	NR	78	0.3	1.1
LUTH–E.L.C.A.	1	49	95	110	0.4	1.5
METH–AME	1	50	30	37	0.1	0.5
METH–Un Methodist	12	728	1,483	1,983	6.8	27.0
Non-denom Chr Chs	9	1,305	1,465	1,707	5.9	23.2
PENT–Assemb of God	1	120	55	120	0.4	1.6
PENT–Ch God (Cleve)	1	30	21	26	0.1	0.4
PENT–Int Pent C Chr	1	0	NR	25	0.1	0.3
PENT–Un Pent Ch Intl	1	NR	NR	NR	-	-
PRES–Presb Ch (USA)	3	128	344	425	1.5	5.8
FRANKLIN	**910**	**137,972**	**210,299**	**470,287**	**40.4**	**100.0**
ANG/EPIS–Anglican NA	1	NR	NR	NR	-	-
ANG/EPIS–Episcopal	12	1,666	4,109	4,958	0.4	1.1
Ap Chr Ch-Amer	1	38	17	38	0.0	0.0
Bahá'í	4	NR	445	445	0.0	0.1
BAPT–Alliance Bapt	1	NR	NR	NR	-	-
BAPT–Amer Bapt USA	30	5,500	9,303	11,460	1.0	2.4
BAPT–Converge/BGC	3	225	NR	270	0.0	0.1
BAPT–Enterprise Bapt Assoc	4	NR	NR	NR	-	-
BAPT–Free Will Bapt	16	NR	1,072	1,321	0.1	0.3
BAPT–Ind Bapt Flwsp Intl	2	NR	NR	NR	-	-
BAPT–Natl Mis Bapt Conv	3	600	1,200	1,478	0.1	0.3
BAPT–NBC Amer	1	300	2,300	2,833	0.2	0.6
BAPT–NBC USA	13	2,115	7,139	8,794	0.8	1.9
BAPT–Reg Bapt Gen As	8	NR	NR	NR	-	-
BAPT–So Bapt Conv	62	6,822	14,750	18,170	1.6	3.9
BRETH–Brethren (Ash)	2	NR	160	197	0.0	0.0
BRETH–Ch of Brethren	1	5	9	11	0.0	0.0
BRETH–Grace Breth	12	NR	NR	NR	-	-
BUDD–Mahayana	7	NR	NR	3,319	0.3	0.7
BUDD–Theravada	3	NR	NR	710	0.1	0.2
BUDD–Vajrayana	2	NR	NR	124	0.0	0.0
Calv Chpl	1	NR	NR	NR	-	-
Catholic	51	NR	NR	153,400	13.2	32.6
CGOD–Ch God (Ander)	11	4,962	NR	4,962	0.4	1.1
CGOD–Ches God-Gen Con	1	0	0	0	0.0	0.0
Ch Christ Chr Union	21	NR	NR	NR	-	-
Ch Cr, Scientst	4	NR	NR	NR	-	-
Ch of Nazarene	19	6,765	6,953	9,754	0.8	2.1
Chr & Miss Al	8	680	663	1,252	0.1	0.3
CHR–Chr Ch (Disc)	12	1,844	5,366	6,610	0.6	1.4
CHR–Chr Chs & Chs Cr	21	NR	6,046	7,448	0.6	1.6
CHR–Chs of Christ	21	2,526	2,301	3,187	0.3	0.7
CHR–Int Chs of Christ	1	NR	115	142	0.0	0.0
Christian Un	1	NR	NR	NR	-	-
CONG–Cong Chr, NA	1	NR	150	185	0.0	0.0
Evan Cov Ch	3	431	161	561	0.0	0.1

Religious Group	Number of Congrega-tions	Number of Attendees	Number of Communicant, Confirmed, or Full Members	Adherents		
				Number of Adherents	% of Total Pop.	% of Total Adh.
Evan Free Ch	2	125	NR	125	0.0	0.0
FRND–Evan Fr Ch Intl	2	109	68	84	0.0	0.0
FRND–Fr Gen Cf	1	NR	80	99	0.0	0.0
HINDU–I/A Temples	3	NR	NR	2,876	0.2	0.6
HINDU–Post Ren	5	NR	NR	153	0.0	0.0
HINDU–Trad Temples	1	NR	NR	27	0.0	0.0
Ind Fund Churches	2	NR	NR	NR	-	-
Int Cou Comm Ch	2	NR	NR	NR	-	-
Jehovah's Witness	15	NR	NR	NR	-	-
JUD–Conserv	2	1,132	1,271	3,432	0.3	0.7
JUD–Orth	4	1,800	700	2,500	0.2	0.5
JUD–Reconst	1	39	50	135	0.0	0.0
JUD–Reform	3	813	1,433	3,869	0.3	0.8
LDS–Comm of Christ	4	NR	532	532	0.0	0.1
LDS–L-D Saints	18	NR	NR	7,980	0.7	1.7
LUTH–Assoc Free Luth	1	NR	NR	NR	-	-
LUTH–E.L.C.A.	34	6,682	13,925	18,648	1.6	4.0
LUTH–Luth Cong Msn Chr	1	1,909	6,113	7,530	0.6	1.6
LUTH–Luth–MO Synod	9	1,153	2,128	2,692	0.2	0.6
LUTH–Nor Amer Luth C	7	NR	NR	NR	-	-
LUTH–Wisc Ev Luth Syn	3	379	668	850	0.1	0.2
MENN–Cons Menn Conf	3	434	256	315	0.0	0.1
MENN–Fel Evg Ch	1	410	0	0	0.0	0.0
MENN–Mennonite USA	2	186	149	184	0.0	0.0
METH–A.W.M.C.	1	56	0	65	0.0	0.0
METH–AME	5	775	2,760	3,400	0.3	0.7
METH–AME Zion	1	230	380	468	0.0	0.1
METH–C.M.E.	1	0	100	123	0.0	0.0
METH–Free Methodist	1	75	75	75	0.0	0.0
METH–Un Methodist	75	15,470	28,411	40,980	3.5	8.7
METH–Wesleyan	8	2,783	938	3,618	0.3	0.8
Metro Comm Ch	1	35	45	55	0.0	0.0
Missionary Ch	1	12	0	12	0.0	0.0
MJEW–Union Mes Cong	1	NR	NR	NR	-	-
MORAV–Morav Ch-North	1	48	69	80	0.0	0.0
Muslim Est	17	3,859	NR	15,578	1.3	3.3
New Apost Ch	1	NR	NR	NR	-	-
Non-denom Chr Chs	110	37,291	43,283	51,038	4.4	10.9
ORTHE–Carp Rus Orth	1	30	NR	50	0.0	0.0
ORTHE–Greek Orthodox	1	800	NR	2,700	0.2	0.6
ORTHE–Macedonian Orth	1	100	NR	1,000	0.1	0.2
ORTHE–Orth Ch in Amer	2	132	NR	220	0.0	0.0
ORTHE–Rus Orth Abroad	1	20	NR	50	0.0	0.0
ORTHE–Serb Orth USA	1	75	NR	250	0.0	0.1
ORTHO–Armen Ap Etchm	1	25	NR	40	0.0	0.0
ORTHO–Coptic Orth Ch	1	500	NR	500	0.0	0.1
ORTHO–Eritrean Orth	1	75	NR	550	0.0	0.1
ORTHO–Ethiopian Orth	1	NR	NR	NR	-	-
PENT–Assemb of God	19	2,379	2,136	3,600	0.3	0.8
PENT–Ch God (Cleve)	13	2,724	3,190	3,930	0.3	0.8
PENT–Ch God Mtn Asm	2	NR	NR	NR	-	-
PENT–Ch Lord Jesus Apos	6	NR	NR	NR	-	-
PENT–Ch of God Proph	2	NR	140	172	0.0	0.0
PENT–COGIC	13	405	1,840	2,267	0.2	0.5
PENT–Fire Bapt Hol Ch	1	NR	NR	NR	-	-
PENT–Full Gosp Bapt	8	NR	NR	NR	-	-
PENT–Int Foursq Gos	1	86	103	127	0.0	0.0
PENT–Int Pent C Chr	2	51	25	86	0.0	0.0
PENT–Intl Pent Holiness	1	43	25	31	0.0	0.0
PENT–Pent Ch of God	1	70	NR	109	0.0	0.0
PENT–Un Pent Ch Intl	14	NR	NR	NR	-	-
PENT–United Holy Ch	3	NR	NR	NR	-	-
PENT–Vineyard	11	10,853	12,584	15,502	1.3	3.3
PRES–Kor Pres Abroad	1	NR	NR	NR	-	-
PRES–Orth Pres Ch	1	171	244	354	0.0	0.1
PRES–Presb Ch (USA)	36	2,943	10,090	12,429	1.1	2.6
PRES–Presb Ch Amer	3	351	400	501	0.0	0.1
REF–Christian Ref	1	55	93	115	0.0	0.0
REF–Ref Ch in Am	1	64	71	99	0.0	0.0
Salvation Army	4	213	523	758	0.1	0.2
Sev Day Adv	18	2,338	4,064	4,676	0.4	1.0
Sikh	4	NR	NR	NR	-	-
Un Breth in Cr	5	331	448	285	0.0	0.1
Un C of Christ	11	2,404	7,999	9,854	0.8	2.1

NR–Not Reported - Represents no adherents reported. Percentages may not total 100 due to rounding.

Table 3: Religious Congregations by County and Group: 2010

Religious Group	Number of Congrega-tions	Number of Attendees	Number of Communicant, Confirmed, or Full Members	Adherents		
				Number of Adherents	% of Total Pop.	% of Total Adh.
Unit Univ	2	450	631	870	0.1	0.2
Unity Ch	1	NR	NR	NR	-	-
Zoroastrian	0	NR	NR	10	0.0	0.0
FULTON	**79**	**7,682**	**12,367**	**24,348**	**57.0**	**100.0**
Bahá'í	0	NR	3	3	0.0	0.0
BAPT–Reg Bapt Gen As	1	NR	NR	NR	-	-
BAPT–So Bapt Conv	2	96	182	226	0.5	0.9
BRETH–Ch of Brethren	2	14	23	29	0.1	0.1
Catholic	5	NR	NR	7,621	17.8	31.3
CGOD–Ch God (Ander)	1	150	NR	150	0.4	0.6
Ch of Nazarene	4	421	631	969	2.3	4.0
Chr & Miss Al	1	102	69	196	0.5	0.8
CHR–Chr Ch (Disc)	5	286	1,314	1,630	3.8	6.7
CHR–Chr Chs & Chs Cr	5	NR	591	733	1.7	3.0
CHR–Chs of Christ	1	21	17	26	0.1	0.1
Christian Un	2	NR	NR	NR	-	-
Evan Assoc RCC	1	NR	NR	NR	-	-
Jehovah's Witness	1	NR	NR	NR	-	-
LDS–L-D Saints	1	NR	NR	217	0.5	0.9
LUTH–E.L.C.A.	5	729	1,921	2,384	5.6	9.8
LUTH–Luth–MO Synod	3	329	1,000	1,231	2.9	5.1
MENN–Fel Evg Ch	2	1,132	1,267	1,571	3.7	6.5
MENN–Mennonite USA	7	1,332	1,874	2,324	5.4	9.5
MENN–Ref Mennonite	1	NR	15	17	0.0	0.1
METH–Un Methodist	11	663	1,535	1,978	4.6	8.1
Missionary Ch	3	762	534	762	1.8	3.1
Non-denom Chr Chs	6	1,135	1,045	1,443	3.4	5.9
PENT–Assemb of God	3	384	106	544	1.3	2.2
PENT–Un Pent Ch Intl	1	NR	NR	NR	-	-
Sev Day Adv	2	26	46	53	0.1	0.2
Un C of Christ	2	70	146	181	0.4	0.7
Unit Univ	1	30	48	60	0.1	0.2
GALLIA	**66**	**3,226**	**5,610**	**8,418**	**27.2**	**100.0**
ANG/EPIS–Episcopal	1	22	60	65	0.2	0.8
Bahá'í	0	NR	1	1	0.0	0.0
BAPT–Amer Bapt USA	4	611	1,226	1,499	4.8	17.8
BAPT–Enterprise Bapt Assoc	2	NR	NR	NR	-	-
BAPT–Free Will Bapt	1	NR	67	82	0.3	1.0
BAPT–Natl Mis Bapt Conv	1	75	0	0	0.0	0.0
BAPT–Reg Bapt Gen As	3	NR	NR	NR	-	-
BAPT–So Bapt Conv	4	175	500	611	2.0	7.3
Catholic	1	NR	NR	482	1.6	5.7
CGOD–Ch God (Ander)	1	132	NR	132	0.4	1.6
Ch Christ Chr Union	4	NR	NR	NR	-	-
Ch of Nazarene	1	205	360	360	1.2	4.3
CHR–Chr Chs & Chs Cr	4	NR	455	556	1.8	6.6
CHR–Chs of Christ	2	155	171	250	0.8	3.0
CONG–Cong Chr, NA	1	NR	15	18	0.1	0.2
FRND–Fr Gen Cf	1	NR	0	0	0.0	0.0
Jehovah's Witness	1	NR	NR	NR	-	-
LDS–L-D Saints	1	NR	NR	354	1.1	4.2
LUTH–E.L.C.A.	1	62	140	165	0.5	2.0
LUTH–Nor Amer Luth C	1	NR	NR	NR	-	-
MENN–Amish Undif	5	NR	274	733	2.4	8.7
MENN–Mennonite USA	1	25	NR	NR	-	-
METH–Un Methodist	11	632	1,033	1,437	4.6	17.1
METH–Wesleyan	2	91	78	119	0.4	1.4
Non-denom Chr Chs	6	790	789	1,013	3.3	12.0
PENT–Assemb of God	1	20	17	21	0.1	0.2
PENT–Ch God (Cleve)	2	162	229	280	0.9	3.3
PENT–Ch of God Proph	1	NR	31	38	0.1	0.5
PENT–Un Pent Ch Intl	1	NR	NR	NR	-	-
PRES–Presb Ch (USA)	1	69	164	200	0.6	2.4
Zoroastrian	0	NR	NR	2	0.0	0.0
GEAUGA	**130**	**5,943**	**13,436**	**52,988**	**56.7**	**100.0**
ANG/EPIS–Anglican NA	1	NR	NR	NR	-	-
ANG/EPIS–Episcopal	1	53	222	222	0.2	0.4
Bahá'í	0	NR	17	17	0.0	0.0
BAPT–Amer Bapt USA	1	75	185	229	0.2	0.4
BAPT–Converge/BGC	1	75	NR	90	0.1	0.2

Religious Group	Number of Congrega-tions	Number of Attendees	Number of Communicant, Confirmed, or Full Members	Adherents		
				Number of Adherents	% of Total Pop.	% of Total Adh.
BAPT–Natl Mis Bapt Conv	1	0	150	185	0.2	0.3
BAPT–Reg Bapt Gen As	2	NR	NR	NR	-	-
BAPT–So Bapt Conv	3	225	392	484	0.5	0.9
Catholic	9	NR	NR	30,880	33.1	58.3
Ch Christ Chr Union	1	NR	NR	NR	-	-
Ch Cr, Scientst	1	NR	NR	NR	-	-
Ch of Nazarene	1	59	0	85	0.1	0.2
Chr & Miss Al	2	275	110	428	0.5	0.8
CHR–Chr Ch (Disc)	2	122	320	395	0.4	0.7
CHR–Chr Chs & Chs Cr	3	NR	280	346	0.4	0.7
CHR–Chs of Christ	1	17	16	20	0.0	0.0
CONG–Consrv Cong Chr	3	291	463	572	0.6	1.1
FRND–Evan Fr Ch Intl	1	302	68	84	0.1	0.2
Jehovah's Witness	4	NR	NR	NR	-	-
LDS–L-D Saints	1	NR	NR	233	0.2	0.4
LUTH–E.L.C.A.	2	451	1,017	1,391	1.5	2.6
LUTH–Luth–MO Synod	3	308	580	721	0.8	1.4
MENN–Amish Undif	53	NR	3,588	8,537	9.1	16.1
MENN–Beachy Amish-Menn	1	133	72	133	0.1	0.3
MENN–Cons Menn Conf	1	150	112	138	0.1	0.3
MENN–Mennonite USA	1	64	50	62	0.1	0.1
METH–Un Methodist	5	1,116	2,505	3,354	3.6	6.3
Non-denom Chr Chs	9	859	913	1,126	1.2	2.1
PENT–Assemb of God	4	514	334	744	0.8	1.4
PENT–Ch God (Cleve)	1	55	4	5	0.0	0.0
PRES–Presb Ch (USA)	2	241	459	567	0.6	1.1
Sev Day Adv	1	80	139	160	0.2	0.3
Un C of Christ	7	478	1,440	1,780	1.9	3.4
Unity Ch	1	NR	NR	NR	-	-
GREENE	**181**	**16,343**	**29,554**	**57,395**	**35.5**	**100.0**
ANG/EPIS–Episcopal	2	99	187	235	0.1	0.4
Bahá'í	1	NR	119	119	0.1	0.2
BAPT–Amer Bapt USA	3	25	107	128	0.1	0.2
BAPT–Asc Ref Bap Ch Am	1	NR	NR	NR	-	-
BAPT–Enterprise Bapt Assoc	2	NR	NR	NR	-	-
BAPT–Free Will Bapt	3	NR	201	241	0.1	0.4
BAPT–Ind Bapt Flwsp Intl	3	NR	NR	NR	-	-
BAPT–N Am Bapt Conf	1	NR	124	149	0.1	0.3
BAPT–NBC USA	2	0	350	419	0.3	0.7
BAPT–Prim Bapt E Dst	2	50	178	213	0.1	0.4
BAPT–Ref Bapt Ch	1	NR	NR	NR	-	-
BAPT–Reg Bapt Gen As	3	NR	NR	NR	-	-
BAPT–So Bapt Conv	14	2,035	6,096	7,305	4.5	12.7
BRETH–Ch of Brethren	1	64	144	173	0.1	0.3
Calv Chpl	1	NR	NR	NR	-	-
Catholic	5	NR	NR	14,064	8.7	24.5
CGOD–Ch God (Ander)	7	537	NR	537	0.3	0.9
Ch Christ Chr Union	2	NR	NR	NR	-	-
Ch Cr, Scientst	1	NR	NR	NR	-	-
Ch of Nazarene	5	1,795	1,738	2,296	1.4	4.0
CHR–Chr Ch (Disc)	1	40	101	121	0.1	0.2
CHR–Chr Chs & Chs Cr	7	NR	1,825	2,187	1.4	3.8
CHR–Chs of Christ	6	683	682	834	0.5	1.5
CONG–Consrv Cong Chr	1	412	787	943	0.6	1.6
FRND–Fr Gen Cf	1	NR	122	146	0.1	0.3
FRND–Fr Un Mtg	3	NR	173	207	0.1	0.4
HINDU–Trad Temples	1	NR	NR	4,000	2.5	7.0
Jehovah's Witness	2	NR	NR	NR	-	-
LDS–Comm of Christ	1	NR	133	133	0.1	0.2
LDS–L-D Saints	4	NR	NR	2,002	1.2	3.5
LUTH–E.L.C.A.	5	1,013	1,951	2,497	1.5	4.4
LUTH–Luth Cong Msn Chr	1	56	87	104	0.1	0.2
LUTH–Luth–MO Synod	1	172	325	407	0.3	0.7
METH–AME	5	225	800	959	0.6	1.7
METH–Un Methodist	19	1,663	3,239	4,844	3.0	8.4
Missionary Ch	4	361	270	361	0.2	0.6
Muslim Est	1	40	NR	50	0.0	0.1
New Apost Ch	1	NR	NR	NR	-	-
Non-denom Chr Chs	27	4,695	5,595	6,291	3.9	11.0
PENT–Assemb of God	3	295	156	415	0.3	0.7
PENT–Ch God (Cleve)	4	366	629	754	0.5	1.3
PENT–Int Pent C Chr	1	20	30	50	0.0	0.1
PENT–Open Bible Std	1	130	NR	130	0.1	0.2

NR–Not Reported   - Represents no adherents reported.   Percentages may not total 100 due to rounding.

Table 3: Religious Congregations by County and Group: 2010

Religious Group	Number of Congrega-tions	Number of Attendees	Number of Communicant, Confirmed, or Full Members	Adherents		
				Number of Adherents	% of Total Pop.	% of Total Adh.
PENT–Un Pent Ch Intl	1	NR	NR	NR	-	-
PRES–Korean Amer Pres	1	NR	NR	NR	-	-
PRES–Presb Ch (USA)	11	962	1,702	2,040	1.3	3.6
Sev Day Adv	1	22	39	45	0.0	0.1
Sikh	2	NR	NR	NR	-	-
Un C of Christ	4	524	1,583	1,897	1.2	3.3
Unit Univ	1	59	81	97	0.1	0.2
Zoroastrian	0	NR	NR	2	0.0	0.0
GUERNSEY	**92**	**4,620**	**8,106**	**13,588**	**33.9**	**100.0**
ANG/EPIS–Episcopal	1	22	37	53	0.1	0.4
Bahá'í	0	NR	5	5	0.0	0.0
BAPT–Amer Bapt USA	5	312	592	722	1.8	5.3
BAPT–Reg Bapt Gen As	3	NR	NR	NR	-	-
BAPT–So Bapt Conv	4	300	790	964	2.4	7.1
Catholic	4	NR	NR	2,112	5.3	15.5
CGOD–Ch God (Ander)	1	6	NR	6	0.0	0.0
Ch Christ Chr Union	2	NR	NR	NR	-	-
Ch of Nazarene	1	121	179	179	0.4	1.3
CHR–Chr Ch (Disc)	1	97	391	477	1.2	3.5
CHR–Chr Chs & Chs Cr	1	NR	40	49	0.1	0.4
CHR–Chs of Christ	6	785	650	915	2.3	6.7
Jehovah's Witness	1	NR	NR	NR	-	-
LUTH–E.L.C.A.	4	182	358	507	1.3	3.7
LUTH–Luth–MO Synod	1	19	33	50	0.1	0.4
MENN–Amish Undif	4	NR	227	552	1.4	4.1
MENN–Beachy Amish-Menn	1	236	114	236	0.6	1.7
METH–AME	1	0	100	122	0.3	0.9
METH–C.M.E.	1	0	150	183	0.5	1.3
METH–Free Methodist	1	47	19	47	0.1	0.3
METH–Un Methodist	23	1,301	2,860	3,875	9.7	28.5
METH–Wesleyan	1	41	23	53	0.1	0.4
Non-denom Chr Chs	7	408	480	549	1.4	4.0
ORTHE–Orth Ch in Amer	1	0	NR	0	0.0	0.0
PENT–Assemb of God	1	190	89	299	0.7	2.2
PENT–Ch God (Cleve)	1	47	36	44	0.1	0.3
PENT–Ch of God Proph	1	NR	79	96	0.2	0.7
PENT–Int Foursq Gos	1	54	76	93	0.2	0.7
PENT–Open Bible Std	1	76	NR	76	0.2	0.6
PENT–Pent Ch of God	1	70	NR	109	0.3	0.8
PENT–Un Pent Ch Intl	1	NR	NR	NR	-	-
PRES–Presb Ch (USA)	9	285	680	829	2.1	6.1
Salvation Army	1	21	98	386	1.0	2.8
HAMILTON	**666**	**88,778**	**153,627**	**421,006**	**52.5**	**100.0**
ANG/EPIS–Anglican NA	2	NR	NR	NR	-	-
ANG/EPIS–Episcopal	20	2,665	7,192	8,438	1.1	2.0
Bahá'í	1	NR	148	148	0.0	0.0
BAPT–Amer Bapt USA	17	5,095	8,488	10,374	1.3	2.5
BAPT–Consrv Bapt	2	NR	NR	NR	-	-
BAPT–Converge/BGC	1	75	NR	90	0.0	0.0
BAPT–Ind Bapt Flwsp Intl	3	NR	NR	NR	-	-
BAPT–Natl Mis Bapt Conv	1	0	150	183	0.0	0.0
BAPT–NBC Amer	4	950	2,600	3,178	0.4	0.8
BAPT–NBC USA	17	4,875	8,600	10,511	1.3	2.5
BAPT–Prog NBC	2	250	550	672	0.1	0.2
BAPT–Reg Bapt Gen As	1	NR	NR	NR	-	-
BAPT–So Bapt Conv	43	3,213	7,760	9,485	1.2	2.3
BRETH–Breth in Chr	1	NR	NR	NR	-	-
BRETH–Ch of Brethren	1	0	28	34	0.0	0.0
BUDD–Mahayana	1	NR	NR	28	0.0	0.0
BUDD–Theravada	2	NR	NR	411	0.1	0.1
Catholic	83	NR	NR	205,094	25.6	48.7
CGOD–Ch God (Ander)	11	926	NR	926	0.1	0.2
Ch Cr, Scientst	4	NR	NR	NR	-	-
Ch of Nazarene	18	1,991	2,795	4,102	0.5	1.0
Chr & Miss Al	1	167	155	230	0.0	0.1
CHR–Chr Ch (Disc)	12	838	2,157	2,636	0.3	0.6
CHR–Chr Chs & Chs Cr	27	NR	8,148	9,959	1.2	2.4
CHR–Chs of Christ	15	2,201	1,965	3,021	0.4	0.7
CHR–Int Chs of Christ	1	NR	315	385	0.0	0.1
Christian Brethren	1	NR	NR	NR	-	-
CONG–Cong Chr, NA	1	NR	60	73	0.0	0.0
Evan Cov Ch	1	110	208	143	0.0	0.0
Evan Free Ch	2	268	NR	268	0.0	0.1
FRND–Fr Gen Cf	1	NR	77	94	0.0	0.0
FRND–Fr Gen Cf & Un Mtg	1	NR	41	50	0.0	0.0
FRND–Fr Un Mtg	1	NR	69	84	0.0	0.0
HINDU–I/A Temples	1	NR	NR	350	0.0	0.1
HINDU–Post Ren	3	NR	NR	50	0.0	0.0
HINDU–Trad Temples	1	NR	NR	2,000	0.2	0.5
Int Cou Comm Ch	1	NR	NR	NR	-	-
Jehovah's Witness	12	NR	NR	NR	-	-
JUD–Conserv	3	927	1,040	2,808	0.3	0.7
JUD–Orth	8	1,440	600	2,000	0.2	0.5
JUD–Reform	5	1,264	2,230	6,021	0.8	1.4
LDS–Comm of Christ	1	NR	133	133	0.0	0.0
LDS–L-D Saints	10	NR	NR	4,917	0.6	1.2
LUTH–E.L.C.A.	12	2,003	3,839	5,153	0.6	1.2
LUTH–Luth Cong Msn Chr	1	100	288	352	0.0	0.1
LUTH–Luth–MO Synod	10	1,248	2,278	2,751	0.3	0.7
LUTH–Wisc Ev Luth Syn	1	276	321	468	0.1	0.1
MENN–Cons Menn Conf	1	18	22	27	0.0	0.0
MENN–Mennonite USA	2	103	93	114	0.0	0.0
METH–AME	10	1,360	2,700	3,300	0.4	0.8
METH–AME Zion	3	0	300	367	0.0	0.1
METH–C.M.E.	4	100	450	550	0.1	0.1
METH–Free Methodist	1	32	6	32	0.0	0.0
METH–Un Methodist	51	8,264	16,212	31,193	3.9	7.4
METH–Wesleyan	4	164	91	214	0.0	0.1
Metro Comm Ch	1	24	17	21	0.0	0.0
Muslim Est	4	709	NR	1,724	0.2	0.4
New Apost Ch	1	NR	NR	NR	-	-
Non-denom Chr Chs	69	27,407	37,616	39,553	4.9	9.4
ORTHE–Greek Orthodox	1	500	NR	2,500	0.3	0.6
ORTHE–Macedonian Orth	1	50	NR	150	0.0	0.0
ORTHE–Orth Ch in Amer	1	140	NR	200	0.0	0.0
ORTHE–Rus Orth Abroad	1	75	NR	250	0.0	0.1
ORTHE–Serb Orth USA	1	114	NR	509	0.1	0.1
ORTHO–Eritrean Orth	2	260	NR	270	0.0	0.1
PENT–Assemb of God	6	1,166	614	1,646	0.2	0.4
PENT–Ch God (Cleve)	13	894	1,583	1,935	0.2	0.5
PENT–Ch God Mtn Asm	2	NR	NR	NR	-	-
PENT–Ch Lord Jesus Apos	1	NR	NR	NR	-	-
PENT–Ch of God Proph	1	NR	53	65	0.0	0.0
PENT–COGIC	10	615	1,680	2,053	0.3	0.5
PENT–Fire Bapt Hol Ch	1	NR	NR	NR	-	-
PENT–Full Gosp Bapt	3	NR	NR	NR	-	-
PENT–Un Pent Ch Intl	3	NR	NR	NR	-	-
PENT–Vineyard	7	7,442	12,103	14,793	1.8	3.5
Pillar of Fire	1	NR	125	125	0.0	0.0
PRES–Bible Pres	1	NR	NR	NR	-	-
PRES–Evan Presby Ch	1	NR	195	238	0.0	0.1
PRES–Presb Ch (USA)	44	5,120	10,592	12,946	1.6	3.1
PRES–Presb Ch Amer	4	315	357	380	0.0	0.1
Salvation Army	3	180	311	475	0.1	0.1
Sev Day Adv	6	678	1,179	1,355	0.2	0.3
Swedenborgian	1	NR	NR	NR	-	-
Un C of Christ	26	1,636	4,330	5,292	0.7	1.3
Unit Univ	4	530	763	1,090	0.1	0.3
Unity Ch	2	NR	NR	NR	-	-
Zoroastrian	0	NR	NR	19	0.0	0.0
HANCOCK	**93**	**10,006**	**17,456**	**33,754**	**45.1**	**100.0**
ANG/EPIS–Episcopal	1	86	225	240	0.3	0.7
Bahá'í	0	NR	14	14	0.0	0.0
BAPT–Reg Bapt Gen As	1	NR	NR	NR	-	-
BAPT–So Bapt Conv	1	135	135	165	0.2	0.5
BRETH–Brethren (Ash)	1	NR	80	98	0.1	0.3
Catholic	1	NR	NR	9,434	12.6	27.9
CGOD–Ch God (Ander)	2	330	NR	330	0.4	1.0
CGOD–Ches God-Gen Con	4	682	603	735	1.0	2.2
Ch Cr, Scientst	1	NR	NR	NR	-	-
Ch of Nazarene	2	260	336	567	0.8	1.7
CHR–Chr Ch (Disc)	1	60	325	396	0.5	1.2
CHR–Chr Chs & Chs Cr	4	NR	795	969	1.3	2.9
CHR–Chs of Christ	2	140	127	198	0.3	0.6

NR–Not Reported   - Represents no adherents reported.   Percentages may not total 100 due to rounding.

Table 3: Religious Congregations by County and Group: 2010

Religious Group	Number of Congregations	Number of Attendees	Number of Communicant, Confirmed, or Full Members	Adherents		
				Number of Adherents	% of Total Pop.	% of Total Adh.
Evan Free Ch	1	575	NR	575	0.8	1.7
FRND–Fr Gen Cf	1	NR	7	9	0.0	0.0
Jehovah's Witness	1	NR	NR	NR	-	-
LDS–L-D Saints	1	NR	NR	593	0.8	1.8
LUTH–E.L.C.A.	7	1,152	3,266	4,330	5.8	12.8
LUTH–Luth Cong Msn Chr	1	22	18	22	0.0	0.1
LUTH–Luth–MO Synod	1	67	112	142	0.2	0.4
LUTH–Wisc Ev Luth Syn	2	511	823	1,038	1.4	3.1
METH–AME	1	35	50	61	0.1	0.2
METH–Un Methodist	31	2,859	5,963	7,615	10.2	22.6
Non-denom Chr Chs	9	1,470	1,680	1,913	2.6	5.7
PENT–Assemb of God	2	563	306	729	1.0	2.2
PENT–Ch God (Cleve)	1	299	385	469	0.6	1.4
PENT–Pent Ch of God	1	70	NR	109	0.1	0.3
PRES–Evan Presby Ch	1	NR	580	707	0.9	2.1
PRES–Presb Ch (USA)	5	339	1,185	1,445	1.9	4.3
Salvation Army	1	28	122	443	0.6	1.3
Sev Day Adv	1	54	95	109	0.1	0.3
Un Breth in Cr	2	210	121	179	0.2	0.5
Un C of Christ	1	38	78	95	0.1	0.3
Unit Univ	1	21	25	25	0.0	0.1
HARDIN	**74**	**3,126**	**6,966**	**11,528**	**36.0**	**100.0**
BAPT–Amer Bapt USA	1	102	80	98	0.3	0.9
BAPT–Free Will Bapt	2	NR	134	164	0.5	1.4
BAPT–Reg Bapt Gen As	1	NR	NR	NR	-	-
Catholic	2	NR	NR	1,800	5.6	15.6
CGOD–Ch God (Ander)	2	67	NR	67	0.2	0.6
Ch of Nazarene	1	72	137	137	0.4	1.2
Chr & Miss Al	1	97	55	145	0.5	1.3
CHR–Chr Ch (Disc)	2	0	70	86	0.3	0.7
CHR–Chr Chs & Chs Cr	6	NR	820	1,003	3.1	8.7
CHR–Chs of Christ	1	38	31	31	0.1	0.3
Christian Un	1	NR	NR	NR	-	-
Grace Gosp Fel	1	NR	NR	NR	-	-
Jehovah's Witness	1	NR	NR	NR	-	-
LUTH–E.L.C.A.	3	131	447	532	1.7	4.6
LUTH–Wisc Ev Luth Syn	1	30	77	102	0.3	0.9
MENN–Amish Undif	8	NR	348	939	2.9	8.1
METH–AME	1	35	50	61	0.2	0.5
METH–Un Methodist	18	1,166	2,828	3,383	10.6	29.3
Non-denom Chr Chs	4	330	335	420	1.3	3.6
PENT–Assemb of God	3	345	168	431	1.3	3.7
PENT–Intl Pent Holiness	1	20	20	24	0.1	0.2
PENT–Pent Ch of God	4	280	NR	435	1.4	3.8
PENT–Un Pent Ch Intl	1	NR	NR	NR	-	-
PRES–Presb Ch (USA)	4	125	195	238	0.7	2.1
Un C of Christ	4	288	1,171	1,432	4.5	12.4
HARRISON	**50**	**1,393**	**3,053**	**4,430**	**27.9**	**100.0**
BAPT–So Bapt Conv	1	30	30	36	0.2	0.8
Catholic	3	NR	NR	535	3.4	12.1
CGOD–Ch God (Ander)	1	31	NR	31	0.2	0.7
Ch of Nazarene	3	40	108	114	0.7	2.6
CHR–Chr Chs & Chs Cr	3	NR	305	366	2.3	8.3
CHR–Chs of Christ	3	129	141	177	1.1	4.0
FRND–Consrv Yr Mtgs	1	NR	60	72	0.5	1.6
Jehovah's Witness	1	NR	NR	NR	-	-
LUTH–E.L.C.A.	1	38	79	136	0.9	3.1
MENN–Amish Undif	3	NR	111	305	1.9	6.9
METH–AME	1	0	150	180	1.1	4.1
METH–Un Methodist	17	875	1,568	1,870	11.8	42.2
PENT–Assemb of God	1	8	9	17	0.1	0.4
PENT–Un Pent Ch Intl	2	NR	NR	NR	-	-
PRES–Presb Ch (USA)	9	242	492	591	3.7	13.3
HENRY	**58**	**5,152**	**12,141**	**19,029**	**67.4**	**100.0**
ANG/EPIS–Episcopal	1	28	32	32	0.1	0.2
BAPT–So Bapt Conv	3	132	805	996	3.5	5.2
BRETH–Ch of Brethren	0	7	2	2	0.0	0.0
Calv Chpl	1	NR	NR	NR	-	-
Catholic	4	NR	NR	3,435	12.2	18.1
CGOD–Ches God-Gen Con	1	25	29	36	0.1	0.2

Religious Group	Number of Congregations	Number of Attendees	Number of Communicant, Confirmed, or Full Members	Adherents		
				Number of Adherents	% of Total Pop.	% of Total Adh.
Ch of Nazarene	1	363	328	658	2.3	3.5
CHR–Chr Chs & Chs Cr	1	NR	130	161	0.6	0.8
Christian Un	1	NR	NR	NR	-	-
Evan Assoc RCC	1	NR	NR	NR	-	-
Grace Gosp Fel	1	NR	NR	NR	-	-
Jehovah's Witness	1	NR	NR	NR	-	-
LUTH–E.L.C.A.	9	1,006	2,845	3,550	12.6	18.7
LUTH–Evan Luth Syn	1	131	332	427	1.5	2.2
LUTH–Luth Ch-Am Asc	1	NR	NR	NR	-	-
LUTH–Luth–MO Synod	9	2,004	4,429	5,635	20.0	29.6
MENN–Fel Evg Ch	1	0	0	0	0.0	0.0
METH–Un Methodist	12	739	1,990	2,722	9.6	14.3
METH–Wesleyan	1	20	19	26	0.1	0.1
Non-denom Chr Chs	3	400	550	550	1.9	2.9
PRES–Evan Presby Ch	1	NR	15	19	0.1	0.1
PRES–Presb Ch (USA)	1	85	133	165	0.6	0.9
REF–Ref Ch in U.S.	1	NR	73	92	0.3	0.5
Un Breth in Cr	1	40	34	34	0.1	0.2
Un C of Christ	1	172	395	489	1.7	2.6
HIGHLAND	**105**	**4,864**	**11,146**	**14,205**	**32.6**	**100.0**
ANG/EPIS–Episcopal	1	52	95	95	0.2	0.7
Bahá'í	0	NR	2	2	0.0	0.0
BAPT–Amer Bapt USA	4	387	828	1,032	2.4	7.3
BAPT–Free Will Bapt	2	NR	134	167	0.4	1.2
BAPT–So Bapt Conv	4	210	551	686	1.6	4.8
BRETH–Ch of Brethren	1	0	3	4	0.0	0.0
Catholic	2	NR	NR	780	1.8	5.5
CGOD–Ch God (Ander)	1	13	NR	13	0.0	0.1
Ch Christ Chr Union	5	NR	NR	NR	-	-
Ch Cr, Scientst	1	NR	NR	NR	-	-
Ch of Nazarene	2	188	266	266	0.6	1.9
CHR–Chr Chs & Chs Cr	15	NR	2,165	2,697	6.2	19.0
CHR–Chs of Christ	3	293	250	342	0.8	2.4
Christian Un	2	NR	NR	NR	-	-
Evan Free Ch	1	80	NR	80	0.2	0.6
FRND–Fr Un Mtg	5	NR	367	457	1.0	3.2
Jehovah's Witness	2	NR	NR	NR	-	-
LDS–L-D Saints	1	NR	NR	123	0.3	0.9
LUTH–E.L.C.A.	2	59	103	120	0.3	0.8
MENN–Amish Undif	2	NR	93	269	0.6	1.9
MENN–Beachy Amish-Menn	1	99	54	99	0.2	0.7
MENN–CG in Cr (Menn)	1	NR	52	65	0.1	0.5
METH–AME	2	0	300	374	0.9	2.6
METH–Un Methodist	16	981	2,047	2,259	5.2	15.9
METH–Wesleyan	1	22	25	29	0.1	0.2
Non-denom Chr Chs	11	1,800	2,635	2,733	6.3	19.2
PENT–Assemb of God	1	55	41	100	0.2	0.7
PENT–Ch God (Cleve)	3	256	421	524	1.2	3.7
PENT–Ch God Mtn Asm	2	NR	NR	NR	-	-
PENT–Ch of God Proph	1	NR	47	59	0.1	0.4
PENT–Int Pent C Chr	2	45	13	63	0.1	0.4
PENT–Intl Pent Holiness	1	12	40	50	0.1	0.4
PENT–Un Pent Ch Intl	1	NR	NR	NR	-	-
PRES–Presb Ch (USA)	4	142	423	527	1.2	3.7
Sev Day Adv	1	40	69	79	0.2	0.6
Un Breth in Cr	1	130	122	111	0.3	0.8
HOCKING	**62**	**3,075**	**4,764**	**7,479**	**25.5**	**100.0**
ANG/EPIS–Episcopal	1	17	32	33	0.1	0.4
BAPT–Free Will Bapt	1	NR	67	82	0.3	1.1
BAPT–So Bapt Conv	3	235	530	648	2.2	8.7
Catholic	1	NR	NR	1,000	3.4	13.4
CGOD–Ch God (Ander)	1	100	NR	100	0.3	1.3
Ch Christ Chr Union	2	NR	NR	NR	-	-
Ch of Nazarene	1	291	310	310	1.1	4.1
Chr & Miss Al	1	178	81	319	1.1	4.3
CHR–Chr Ch (Disc)	1	30	65	80	0.3	1.1
CHR–Chr Chs & Chs Cr	2	NR	250	306	1.0	4.1
CHR–Chs of Christ	2	110	72	109	0.4	1.5
Jehovah's Witness	1	NR	NR	NR	-	-
LDS–Comm of Christ	1	NR	118	118	0.4	1.6
LUTH–E.L.C.A.	3	159	515	560	1.9	7.5

NR–Not Reported - Represents no adherents reported. Percentages may not total 100 due to rounding.

Table 3: Religious Congregations by County and Group: 2010

Religious Group	Number of Congrega-tions	Number of Attendees	Number of Communicant, Confirmed, or Full Members	Adherents: Number of Adherents	Adherents: % of Total Pop.	Adherents: % of Total Adh.
LUTH–Luth–MO Synod	1	96	97	133	0.5	1.8
MENN–Amish Undif	0	NR	6	17	0.1	0.2
MENN–Cons Menn Conf	1	70	50	61	0.2	0.8
MENN–Mennonite USA	1	22	20	24	0.1	0.3
METH–Un Methodist	26	949	1,482	2,282	7.8	30.5
METH–Wesleyan	2	40	8	52	0.2	0.7
Non-denom Chr Chs	4	440	500	575	2.0	7.7
PENT–Ch God (Cleve)	1	81	250	306	1.0	4.1
PENT–Un Pent Ch Intl	1	NR	NR	NR	-	-
PENT–Vineyard	1	37	15	18	0.1	0.2
PRES–Presb Ch (USA)	1	91	192	235	0.8	3.1
Un Breth in Cr	2	129	104	111	0.4	1.5
HOLMES	**203**	**5,524**	**16,730**	**28,949**	**68.3**	**100.0**
Bahá'í	0	NR	3	3	0.0	0.0
BAPT–Reg Bapt Gen As	1	NR	NR	NR	-	-
BRETH–Ch of Brethren	1	21	51	70	0.2	0.2
BRETH–Grace Breth	1	NR	NR	NR	-	-
Catholic	1	NR	NR	625	1.5	2.2
CGOD–Ches God-Gen Con	1	16	25	34	0.1	0.1
Chr & Miss Al	1	57	40	90	0.2	0.3
CHR–Chr Chs & Chs Cr	9	NR	1,384	1,895	4.5	6.5
CHR–Chs of Christ	2	145	125	150	0.4	0.5
Evan Cov Ch	1	96	197	125	0.3	0.4
LUTH–E.L.C.A.	2	112	296	346	0.8	1.2
LUTH–Luth–MO Synod	1	40	83	97	0.2	0.3
LUTH–Nor Amer Luth C	1	NR	NR	NR	-	-
MENN–Amish Undif	140	NR	8,839	17,654	41.7	61.0
MENN–Beachy Amish-Menn	3	563	325	563	1.3	1.9
MENN–Ber Amish-Menn	2	160	92	160	0.4	0.6
MENN–Cons Menn Conf	5	1,213	923	1,264	3.0	4.4
MENN–Mennonite USA	6	1,224	1,457	1,995	4.7	6.9
MENN–Unaffil Amish-Menn	1	130	92	130	0.3	0.4
METH–Un Methodist	7	417	1,163	1,452	3.4	5.0
METH–Wesleyan	1	85	89	111	0.3	0.4
Non-denom Chr Chs	7	930	885	1,206	2.8	4.2
PENT–Ch God (Cleve)	1	45	77	105	0.2	0.4
PENT–Pent Ch of God	1	70	NR	109	0.3	0.4
PENT–Un Pent Ch Intl	2	NR	NR	NR	-	-
PRES–Presb Ch (USA)	1	75	146	200	0.5	0.7
PRES–Presb Ch Amer	1	77	141	170	0.4	0.6
Sev Day Adv	1	33	57	66	0.2	0.2
Un C of Christ	2	15	240	329	0.8	1.1
HURON	**88**	**5,726**	**9,455**	**27,552**	**46.2**	**100.0**
ANG/EPIS–Episcopal	1	31	54	66	0.1	0.2
Bahá'í	0	NR	1	1	0.0	0.0
BAPT–Amer Bapt USA	2	200	647	808	1.4	2.9
BAPT–Free Will Bapt	1	NR	67	84	0.1	0.3
BAPT–Ind Bapt Flwsp Intl	2	NR	NR	NR	-	-
BAPT–Reg Bapt Gen As	1	NR	NR	NR	-	-
BAPT–So Bapt Conv	3	195	534	667	1.1	2.4
Catholic	9	NR	NR	13,950	23.4	50.6
Ch Cr, Scientst	1	NR	NR	NR	-	-
Ch of Nazarene	1	82	153	328	0.6	1.2
Chr & Miss Al	4	1,041	484	1,686	2.8	6.1
CHR–Chr Chs & Chs Cr	2	NR	20	25	0.0	0.1
CHR–Chs of Christ	4	195	155	217	0.4	0.8
Jehovah's Witness	2	NR	NR	NR	-	-
LUTH–E.L.C.A.	3	605	1,424	2,291	3.8	8.3
LUTH–Nor Amer Luth C	3	NR	NR	NR	-	-
MENN–Amish Undif	1	NR	47	103	0.2	0.4
METH–Un Methodist	14	1,193	2,518	3,194	5.4	11.6
Non-denom Chr Chs	11	1,062	1,325	1,471	2.5	5.3
PENT–Assemb of God	4	218	152	276	0.5	1.0
PENT–Ch God (Cleve)	3	195	524	655	1.1	2.4
PENT–Ch God Mtn Asm	1	NR	NR	NR	-	-
PENT–Ch of God Proph	1	NR	79	99	0.2	0.4
PENT–Full Gosp Bapt	1	NR	NR	NR	-	-
PENT–Un Pent Ch Intl	1	NR	NR	NR	-	-
PRES–Presb Ch (USA)	1	214	364	455	0.8	1.7
REF–Christian Ref	1	200	193	241	0.4	0.9
Salvation Army	1	37	48	113	0.2	0.4

Religious Group	Number of Congrega-tions	Number of Attendees	Number of Communicant, Confirmed, or Full Members	Adherents: Number of Adherents	Adherents: % of Total Pop.	Adherents: % of Total Adh.
Sev Day Adv	4	57	99	114	0.2	0.4
Un C of Christ	5	201	567	708	1.2	2.6
JACKSON	**85**	**3,539**	**7,107**	**9,474**	**28.5**	**100.0**
Bahá'í	0	NR	2	2	0.0	0.0
BAPT–Amer Bapt USA	2	240	351	433	1.3	4.6
BAPT–Free Will Bapt	7	NR	469	579	1.7	6.1
BAPT–Ind Bapt Flwsp Intl	1	NR	NR	NR	-	-
BAPT–So Bapt Conv	4	153	464	573	1.7	6.0
Catholic	2	NR	NR	350	1.1	3.7
Ch Christ Chr Union	4	NR	NR	NR	-	-
Ch of Nazarene	3	386	386	522	1.6	5.5
CHR–Chr Ch (Disc)	1	35	150	185	0.6	2.0
CHR–Chr Chs & Chs Cr	4	NR	162	200	0.6	2.1
CHR–Chs of Christ	3	75	73	87	0.3	0.9
Evan Ch	1	NR	NR	NR	-	-
Jehovah's Witness	1	NR	NR	NR	-	-
LDS–Comm of Christ	3	NR	354	354	1.1	3.7
LDS–L-D Saints	1	NR	NR	282	0.8	3.0
LUTH–E.L.C.A.	1	42	91	104	0.3	1.1
MENN–Amish Undif	2	NR	138	339	1.0	3.6
MENN–Beachy Amish-Menn	1	35	20	35	0.1	0.4
MENN–Mennonite USA	1	25	30	37	0.1	0.4
METH–Un Methodist	12	925	1,974	2,628	7.9	27.7
METH–Wesleyan	2	241	252	313	0.9	3.3
Non-denom Chr Chs	14	1,140	1,621	1,692	5.1	17.9
PENT–Assemb of God	1	40	13	66	0.2	0.7
PENT–Ch God (Cleve)	1	30	57	70	0.2	0.7
PENT–Ch of God Proph	1	NR	50	62	0.2	0.7
PENT–Int Pent C Chr	1	35	33	50	0.2	0.5
PENT–Intl Pent Holiness	1	28	30	37	0.1	0.4
PENT–Un Pent Ch Intl	2	NR	NR	NR	-	-
PRES–Presb Ch (USA)	7	85	344	425	1.3	4.5
Sev Day Adv	1	24	43	49	0.1	0.5
JEFFERSON	**153**	**6,441**	**12,985**	**32,169**	**46.1**	**100.0**
ANG/EPIS–Episcopal	2	58	218	218	0.3	0.7
BAPT–Amer Bapt USA	2	48	151	178	0.3	0.6
BAPT–NBC USA	1	185	200	236	0.3	0.7
BAPT–So Bapt Conv	3	93	270	318	0.5	1.0
Catholic	16	NR	NR	13,851	19.9	43.1
CGOD–Ch God (Ander)	3	230	NR	230	0.3	0.7
Ch Christ Chr Union	2	NR	NR	NR	-	-
Ch Cr, Scientst	1	NR	NR	NR	-	-
Ch of Nazarene	5	185	374	427	0.6	1.3
CHR–Chr Ch (Disc)	3	70	190	224	0.3	0.7
CHR–Chr Chs & Chs Cr	8	NR	1,349	1,589	2.3	4.9
CHR–Chs of Christ	2	105	100	115	0.2	0.4
Evan Ch	1	NR	NR	NR	-	-
FRND–Evan Fr Ch Intl	2	119	93	110	0.2	0.3
Jehovah's Witness	2	NR	NR	NR	-	-
JUD–Reform	1	27	48	130	0.2	0.4
LDS–L-D Saints	1	NR	NR	482	0.7	1.5
LUTH–E.L.C.A.	1	98	177	259	0.4	0.8
LUTH–Luth–MO Synod	1	47	121	170	0.2	0.5
MENN–Amish Undif	1	NR	47	120	0.2	0.4
METH–AME	3	0	275	324	0.5	1.0
METH–AME Zion	1	0	100	118	0.2	0.4
METH–C.M.E.	1	0	100	118	0.2	0.4
METH–Un Methodist	44	2,626	5,731	7,214	10.3	22.4
METH–Wesleyan	1	27	21	35	0.1	0.1
Non-denom Chr Chs	13	950	1,247	1,318	1.9	4.1
ORTHE–Greek Orthodox	1	100	NR	350	0.5	1.1
ORTHE–Orth Ch in Amer	3	88	NR	162	0.2	0.5
ORTHE–Serb Orth USA	1	75	NR	577	0.8	1.8
PENT–Assemb of God	3	167	192	296	0.4	0.9
PENT–COGIC	1	150	0	0	0.0	0.0
PENT–Un Pent Ch Intl	1	NR	NR	NR	-	-
PRES–Evan Presby Ch	1	NR	36	42	0.1	0.1
PRES–Presb Ch (USA)	18	893	1,768	2,082	3.0	6.5
Salvation Army	1	42	47	724	1.0	2.3
Sev Day Adv	1	27	47	54	0.1	0.2
Un C of Christ	1	31	83	98	0.1	0.3

NR–Not Reported   - Represents no adherents reported.   Percentages may not total 100 due to rounding.

Table 3: Religious Congregations by County and Group: 2010

Religious Group	Number of Congrega-tions	Number of Attendees	Number of Communicant, Confirmed, or Full Members	Adherents		
				Number of Adherents	% of Total Pop.	% of Total Adh.
KNOX	**120**	**7,800**	**14,535**	**23,165**	**38.0**	**100.0**
ANG/EPIS–Episcopal	2	147	211	276	0.5	1.2
Bahá'í	0	NR	4	4	0.0	0.0
BAPT–Amer Bapt USA	4	353	774	949	1.6	4.1
BAPT–Enterprise Bapt Assoc	1	NR	NR	NR	-	-
BAPT–Free Will Bapt	1	NR	67	82	0.1	0.4
BAPT–Ind Bapt Flwsp Intl	1	NR	NR	NR	-	-
BAPT–Ref Bapt Ch	1	NR	NR	NR	-	-
BAPT–Reg Bapt Gen As	1	NR	NR	NR	-	-
BAPT–So Bapt Conv	5	137	401	492	0.8	2.1
BRETH–Ch of Brethren	2	346	294	361	0.6	1.6
BRETH–Grace Breth	2	NR	NR	NR	-	-
Catholic	2	NR	NR	3,250	5.3	14.0
CGOD–Ch God (Ander)	2	142	NR	142	0.2	0.6
Ch of Nazarene	6	1,259	1,368	1,787	2.9	7.7
Chr & Miss Al	3	517	261	668	1.1	2.9
CHR–Chr Ch (Disc)	1	41	78	96	0.2	0.4
CHR–Chr Chs & Chs Cr	12	NR	2,145	2,631	4.3	11.4
CHR–Chs of Christ	3	180	183	220	0.4	0.9
Ind Fund Churches	1	NR	NR	NR	-	-
Jehovah's Witness	1	NR	NR	NR	-	-
LDS–L-D Saints	1	NR	NR	385	0.6	1.7
LUTH–E.L.C.A.	3	216	568	729	1.2	3.1
MENN–Amish Undif	16	NR	893	2,111	3.5	9.1
MENN–Cons Menn Conf	1	60	55	67	0.1	0.3
METH–AME	1	0	100	123	0.2	0.5
METH–Un Methodist	24	1,463	3,087	3,616	5.9	15.6
Non-denom Chr Chs	7	1,109	1,225	1,450	2.4	6.3
PENT–Assemb of God	2	279	171	522	0.9	2.3
PENT–Ch God (Cleve)	2	287	516	633	1.0	2.7
PENT–Int Foursq Gos	1	55	113	139	0.2	0.6
PENT–Un Pent Ch Intl	1	NR	NR	NR	-	-
PENT–Vineyard	1	190	225	276	0.5	1.2
PRES–Presb Ch (USA)	2	178	246	302	0.5	1.3
Salvation Army	1	71	166	243	0.4	1.0
Sev Day Adv	5	660	1,146	1,319	2.2	5.7
Un C of Christ	1	110	238	292	0.5	1.3
LAKE	**167**	**14,507**	**23,354**	**113,707**	**49.4**	**100.0**
ANG/EPIS–Anglican NA	2	NR	NR	NR	-	-
ANG/EPIS–Episcopal	5	513	916	966	0.4	0.8
Bahá'í	1	NR	52	52	0.0	0.0
BAPT–Amer Bapt USA	4	381	647	777	0.3	0.7
BAPT–Consrv Bapt	1	NR	NR	NR	-	-
BAPT–Converge/BGC	1	75	NR	90	0.0	0.1
BAPT–NBC USA	2	175	250	300	0.1	0.3
BAPT–Reg Bapt Gen As	6	NR	NR	NR	-	-
BAPT–So Bapt Conv	6	932	978	1,175	0.5	1.0
BRETH–Ch of Brethren	1	76	153	184	0.1	0.2
Catholic	16	NR	NR	80,869	35.2	71.1
CGOD–Ch God (Ander)	1	46	NR	46	0.0	0.0
Ch Cr, Scientst	1	NR	NR	NR	-	-
Ch of God Gen Conf	1	NR	5	6	0.0	0.0
Ch of Nazarene	3	297	385	408	0.2	0.4
Chr & Miss Al	4	181	128	256	0.1	0.2
CHR–Chr Ch (Disc)	5	130	235	282	0.1	0.2
CHR–Chr Chs & Chs Cr	3	NR	225	270	0.1	0.2
CHR–Chs of Christ	4	310	281	363	0.2	0.3
Evan Cov Ch	1	25	56	32	0.0	0.0
FRND–Evan Fr Ch Intl	1	386	121	145	0.1	0.1
Jehovah's Witness	7	NR	NR	NR	-	-
JUD–Reform	1	26	45	122	0.1	0.1
LDS–Comm of Christ	1	NR	158	158	0.1	0.1
LDS–L-D Saints	3	NR	NR	1,126	0.5	1.0
LUTH–Ch of Luth Br	1	355	227	602	0.3	0.5
LUTH–E.L.C.A.	4	417	1,054	1,346	0.6	1.2
LUTH–Luth Cong Msn Chr	1	143	415	499	0.2	0.4
LUTH–Luth-MO Synod	8	1,008	2,282	2,905	1.3	2.6
LUTH–Wisc Ev Luth Syn	1	42	89	117	0.1	0.1
METH–C.M.E.	1	0	150	180	0.1	0.2
METH–Un Methodist	11	2,269	6,540	8,667	3.8	7.6
Non-denom Chr Chs	22	3,418	3,188	4,510	2.0	4.0
ORTHE–Orth Ch in Amer	1	140	NR	216	0.1	0.2
PENT–Assemb of God	10	1,221	734	2,045	0.9	1.8
PENT–Ch God (Cleve)	4	641	1,094	1,314	0.6	1.2
PENT–COGIC	1	60	60	72	0.0	0.1
PENT–Un Pent Ch Intl	1	NR	NR	NR	-	-
PENT–United Holy Ch	2	NR	NR	NR	-	-
PENT–Vineyard	1	199	210	252	0.1	0.2
PRES–Orth Pres Ch	1	0	0	0	0.0	0.0
PRES–Presb Ch (USA)	3	222	483	580	0.3	0.5
Salvation Army	1	56	87	238	0.1	0.2
Sev Day Adv	2	70	122	141	0.1	0.1
Un C of Christ	8	609	1,780	2,139	0.9	1.9
Unit Univ	1	84	204	252	0.1	0.2
Zoroastrian	1	NR	NR	5	0.0	0.0
LAWRENCE	**92**	**5,083**	**10,190**	**14,404**	**23.1**	**100.0**
ANG/EPIS–Episcopal	1	25	54	86	0.1	0.6
Bahá'í	0	NR	7	7	0.0	0.0
BAPT–Amer Bapt Assn	2	NR	335	408	0.7	2.8
BAPT–Amer Bapt USA	2	297	896	1,091	1.7	7.6
BAPT–Enterprise Bapt Assoc	2	NR	NR	NR	-	-
BAPT–Free Will Bapt	10	NR	699	851	1.4	5.9
BAPT–Natl Mis Bapt Conv	2	250	400	487	0.8	3.4
BAPT–NBC USA	1	0	0	0	0.0	0.0
BAPT–So Bapt Conv	7	794	1,542	1,878	3.0	13.0
Catholic	4	NR	NR	1,928	3.1	13.4
CGOD–Ch God (Ander)	1	21	NR	21	0.0	0.1
Ch of Nazarene	7	561	899	1,007	1.6	7.0
CHR–Chr Chs & Chs Cr	3	NR	1,305	1,589	2.5	11.0
CHR–Chs of Christ	9	676	638	835	1.3	5.8
Jehovah's Witness	2	NR	NR	NR	-	-
LDS–Comm of Christ	1	NR	118	118	0.2	0.8
LUTH–E.L.C.A.	1	56	129	185	0.3	1.3
MENN–Mennonite USA	1	20	35	43	0.1	0.3
METH–AME	1	25	40	49	0.1	0.3
METH–Un Methodist	17	913	1,430	1,784	2.9	12.4
Non-denom Chr Chs	9	1,140	1,275	1,513	2.4	10.5
PENT–Assemb of God	1	22	15	51	0.1	0.4
PENT–Ch God (Cleve)	1	197	195	237	0.4	1.6
PENT–Ch of God Proph	1	NR	54	66	0.1	0.5
PENT–Int Pent C Chr	1	11	1	20	0.0	0.1
PENT–Intl Pent Holiness	1	28	30	37	0.1	0.3
PENT–Un Pent Ch Intl	2	NR	NR	NR	-	-
PRES–Presb Ch (USA)	2	47	93	113	0.2	0.8
LICKING	**195**	**17,403**	**30,942**	**56,932**	**34.2**	**100.0**
ANG/EPIS–Episcopal	2	244	539	546	0.3	1.0
Bahá'í	0	NR	37	37	0.0	0.1
BAPT–Alliance Bapt	1	NR	NR	NR	-	-
BAPT–Amer Bapt USA	11	723	1,287	1,588	1.0	2.8
BAPT–Free Will Bapt	1	NR	67	83	0.0	0.1
BAPT–Ind Bapt Flwsp Intl	1	NR	NR	NR	-	-
BAPT–NBC USA	1	200	500	617	0.4	1.1
BAPT–Ref Bapt Ch	1	NR	NR	NR	-	-
BAPT–Reg Bapt Gen As	3	NR	NR	NR	-	-
BAPT–S-D Baptist Gen Con	1	37	53	65	0.0	0.1
BAPT–So Bapt Conv	12	3,717	5,612	6,926	4.2	12.2
BRETH–Brethren (Ash)	1	NR	80	99	0.1	0.2
BRETH–Grace Breth	1	NR	NR	NR	-	-
Catholic	7	NR	NR	16,000	9.6	28.1
CGOD–Ch God (Ander)	1	59	NR	59	0.0	0.1
Ch Christ Chr Union	3	NR	NR	NR	-	-
Ch of Nazarene	5	1,306	933	1,757	1.1	3.1
CHR–Chr Ch (Disc)	3	213	430	531	0.3	0.9
CHR–Chr Chs & Chs Cr	15	NR	3,588	4,428	2.7	7.8
CHR–Chs of Christ	6	462	481	600	0.4	1.1
Christian Un	4	NR	NR	NR	-	-
FRND–Fr Gen Cf	1	NR	25	31	0.0	0.1
HINDU–Post Ren	1	NR	NR	16	0.0	0.0
Jehovah's Witness	2	NR	NR	NR	-	-
JUD–Reform	1	14	24	65	0.0	0.1
LDS–L-D Saints	2	NR	NR	1,049	0.6	1.8
LUTH–Assoc Free Luth	1	NR	NR	NR	-	-
LUTH–E.L.C.A.	6	582	1,567	1,986	1.2	3.5

NR–Not Reported   - Represents no adherents reported.   Percentages may not total 100 due to rounding.

Table 3: Religious Congregations by County and Group: 2010

Religious Group	Number of Congrega-tions	Number of Attendees	Number of Communicant, Confirmed, or Full Members	Adherents		
				Number of Adherents	% of Total Pop.	% of Total Adh.
LUTH–Luth–MO Synod	2	130	179	245	0.1	0.4
MENN–Amish Undif	0	NR	14	38	0.0	0.1
MENN–Beachy Amish-Menn	1	165	89	165	0.1	0.3
METH–AME	1	0	35	43	0.0	0.1
METH–Un Methodist	41	3,619	6,370	8,923	5.4	15.7
METH–Wesleyan	1	230	128	299	0.2	0.5
Non-denom Chr Chs	18	2,415	3,448	3,597	2.2	6.3
PENT–Assemb of God	2	173	74	303	0.2	0.5
PENT–Ch God (Cleve)	2	105	265	327	0.2	0.6
PENT–COGIC	1	35	30	37	0.0	0.1
PENT–Int Foursq Gos	1	37	46	57	0.0	0.1
PENT–Open Bible Std	1	52	NR	52	0.0	0.1
PENT–Pent Ch of God	1	70	NR	109	0.1	0.2
PENT–Un Pent Ch Intl	3	NR	NR	NR	-	-
PENT–Vineyard	4	1,295	1,561	1,927	1.2	3.4
PRES–Evan Presby Ch	1	NR	127	157	0.1	0.3
PRES–Orth Pres Ch	1	92	69	87	0.1	0.2
PRES–Presb Ch (USA)	12	956	1,831	2,260	1.4	4.0
PRES–Presb Ch Amer	1	0	0	0	0.0	0.0
Salvation Army	1	57	127	208	0.1	0.4
Sev Day Adv	2	146	253	291	0.2	0.5
Un C of Christ	4	269	1,073	1,324	0.8	2.3
LOGAN	**87**	**5,505**	**8,437**	**14,600**	**31.8**	**100.0**
ANG/EPIS–Episcopal	1	20	27	56	0.1	0.4
Bahá'í	0	NR	2	2	0.0	0.0
BAPT–Amer Bapt USA	1	23	55	68	0.1	0.5
BAPT–Reg Bapt Gen As	2	NR	NR	NR	-	-
BAPT–So Bapt Conv	4	276	398	493	1.1	3.4
BRETH–Brethren (Ash)	1	NR	80	99	0.2	0.7
BRETH–Ch of Brethren	2	125	117	145	0.3	1.0
Catholic	2	NR	NR	2,250	4.9	15.4
CGOD–Ch God (Ander)	3	624	NR	624	1.4	4.3
Ch Christ Chr Union	2	NR	NR	NR	-	-
Ch of Nazarene	3	247	221	589	1.3	4.0
CHR–Chr Ch (Disc)	2	100	532	660	1.4	4.5
CHR–Chr Chs & Chs Cr	5	NR	692	858	1.9	5.9
CHR–Chs of Christ	2	105	103	125	0.3	0.9
FRND–Evan Fr Ch Intl	3	107	87	108	0.2	0.7
Jehovah's Witness	1	NR	NR	NR	-	-
LDS–L-D Saints	1	NR	NR	397	0.9	2.7
LUTH–E.L.C.A.	4	280	603	852	1.9	5.8
MENN–Amish Undif	5	NR	302	640	1.4	4.4
MENN–Cons Menn Conf	1	25	14	17	0.0	0.1
MENN–Mennonite USA	4	447	430	533	1.2	3.7
METH–AME	1	25	84	104	0.2	0.7
METH–Un Methodist	19	1,517	2,501	3,201	7.0	21.9
Missionary Ch	1	25	11	25	0.1	0.2
Non-denom Chr Chs	5	645	675	834	1.8	5.7
PENT–Assemb of God	1	45	27	60	0.1	0.4
PENT–Open Bible Std	1	26	NR	26	0.1	0.2
PENT–Vineyard	2	343	425	527	1.1	3.6
PRES–Presb Ch (USA)	5	346	684	848	1.8	5.8
PRES–Ref Pres of NA	1	35	30	44	0.1	0.3
Sev Day Adv	1	19	33	38	0.1	0.3
Un C of Christ	1	100	304	377	0.8	2.6
LORAIN	**291**	**26,736**	**45,727**	**132,752**	**44.1**	**100.0**
ANG/EPIS–Episcopal	3	216	458	586	0.2	0.4
Bahá'í	0	NR	32	32	0.0	0.0
BAPT–Alliance Bapt	1	NR	NR	NR	-	-
BAPT–Amer Bapt USA	7	459	796	972	0.3	0.7
BAPT–Converge/BGC	2	150	NR	180	0.1	0.1
BAPT–Enterprise Bapt Assoc	1	NR	NR	NR	-	-
BAPT–Free Will Bapt	4	NR	268	327	0.1	0.2
BAPT–Natl Mis Bapt Conv	1	60	0	0	0.0	0.0
BAPT–NBC Amer	1	50	100	122	0.0	0.1
BAPT–NBC USA	5	850	1,250	1,527	0.5	1.2
BAPT–Reg Bapt Gen As	13	NR	NR	NR	-	-
BAPT–So Bapt Conv	23	1,879	5,036	6,151	2.0	4.6
BRETH–Ch of Brethren	1	33	27	33	0.0	0.0
Catholic	27	NR	NR	73,443	24.4	55.3
CGOD–Ch God (Ander)	1	220	NR	220	0.1	0.2
Ch Christ Chr Union	1	NR	NR	NR	-	-
Ch Cr, Scientst	1	NR	NR	NR	-	-
Ch God (7th Day)	1	NR	NR	NR	-	-
Ch of Nazarene	4	387	508	655	0.2	0.5
Chr & Miss Al	2	140	152	184	0.1	0.1
CHR–Chr Ch (Disc)	4	426	1,612	1,969	0.7	1.5
CHR–Chr Chs & Chs Cr	1	NR	500	611	0.2	0.5
CHR–Chs of Christ	6	622	614	860	0.3	0.6
CONG–Consrv Cong Chr	3	272	280	342	0.1	0.3
Evan Free Ch	3	1,131	NR	1,131	0.4	0.9
FRND–Fr Gen Cf	1	NR	21	26	0.0	0.0
Grace Gosp Fel	1	NR	NR	NR	-	-
Jehovah's Witness	7	NR	NR	NR	-	-
JUD–Reform	1	29	51	138	0.0	0.1
LDS–Comm of Christ	1	NR	158	158	0.1	0.1
LDS–L-D Saints	2	NR	NR	1,172	0.4	0.9
LUTH–E.L.C.A.	6	616	1,385	2,240	0.7	1.7
LUTH–Luth–MO Synod	13	954	2,481	3,301	1.1	2.5
MENN–Fel Evg Ch	1	0	0	0	0.0	0.0
MENN–Mennonite USA	1	55	51	62	0.0	0.0
METH–AME	3	80	500	611	0.2	0.5
METH–Free Methodist	1	58	31	58	0.0	0.0
METH–Un Methodist	25	2,320	6,183	6,898	2.3	5.2
METH–Wesleyan	2	169	116	220	0.1	0.2
Missionary Ch	1	43	0	43	0.0	0.0
Muslim Est	1	30	NR	50	0.0	0.0
New Apost Ch	1	NR	NR	NR	-	-
Non-denom Chr Chs	39	10,010	13,682	14,751	4.9	11.1
ORTHE–Greek Orthodox	1	100	NR	250	0.1	0.2
ORTHE–Macedonian Orth	1	50	NR	150	0.0	0.1
ORTHE–Orth Ch in Amer	2	119	NR	180	0.1	0.1
ORTHE–Serb Orth USA	2	58	NR	111	0.0	0.1
ORTHE–Ukrainian Orth	1	45	NR	100	0.0	0.1
PENT–Assemb of God	9	1,488	1,066	1,849	0.6	1.4
PENT–Ch God (Cleve)	9	659	1,035	1,264	0.4	1.0
PENT–Ch God Mtn Asm	1	NR	NR	NR	-	-
PENT–Ch of God Proph	1	NR	76	93	0.0	0.1
PENT–COGIC	3	40	50	61	0.0	0.0
PENT–Int Foursq Gos	7	453	326	398	0.1	0.3
PENT–Intl Pent Holiness	1	57	91	111	0.0	0.1
PENT–Pent Ch of God	1	70	NR	109	0.0	0.1
PENT–Un Pent Ch Intl	1	NR	NR	NR	-	-
PRES–Presb Ch (USA)	4	310	776	948	0.3	0.7
Salvation Army	2	94	233	1,013	0.3	0.8
Sev Day Adv	4	200	348	400	0.1	0.3
Un C of Christ	17	1,695	5,389	6,582	2.2	5.0
Unit Univ	1	39	45	60	0.0	0.0
LUCAS	**372**	**42,526**	**73,338**	**197,938**	**44.8**	**100.0**
ANG/EPIS–Anglican NA	1	NR	NR	NR	-	-
ANG/EPIS–Episcopal	8	864	1,843	2,242	0.5	1.1
Ap Chr Ch-Amer	1	53	29	53	0.0	0.0
Bahá'í	1	NR	70	70	0.0	0.0
BAPT–Amer Bapt USA	12	1,218	1,684	2,064	0.5	1.0
BAPT–Converge/BGC	1	75	NR	90	0.0	0.0
BAPT–Free Will Bapt	1	NR	67	82	0.0	0.0
BAPT–Ind Bapt Flwsp Intl	2	NR	NR	NR	-	-
BAPT–N Am Bapt Conf	1	NR	971	1,190	0.3	0.6
BAPT–Natl Mis Bapt Conv	4	145	240	294	0.1	0.1
BAPT–NBC Amer	1	75	150	184	0.0	0.1
BAPT–NBC USA	15	2,143	8,035	9,846	2.2	5.0
BAPT–Ref Bapt Ch	1	NR	NR	NR	-	-
BAPT–Reg Bapt Gen As	2	NR	NR	NR	-	-
BAPT–So Bapt Conv	13	581	1,010	1,238	0.3	0.6
BRETH–Ch of Brethren	1	24	32	39	0.0	0.0
BRETH–Grace Breth	2	NR	NR	NR	-	-
BUDD–Mahayana	2	NR	NR	31	0.0	0.0
Calv Chpl	1	NR	NR	NR	-	-
Catholic	35	NR	NR	92,283	20.9	46.6
CGOD–Ch God (Ander)	5	1,198	NR	1,198	0.3	0.6
CGOD–Ches God-Gen Con	3	248	210	257	0.1	0.1
Ch Cr, Scientst	3	NR	NR	NR	-	-
Ch God (7th Day)	1	NR	NR	NR	-	-
Ch of Chr (Hol)	1	NR	NR	NR	-	-

NR–Not Reported - Represents no adherents reported. Percentages may not total 100 due to rounding.

Table 3: Religious Congregations by County and Group: 2010

Religious Group	Number of Congrega-tions	Number of Attendees	Number of Communicant, Confirmed, or Full Members	Adherents: Number of Adherents	Adherents: % of Total Pop.	Adherents: % of Total Adh.
Ch of Nazarene	5	495	630	846	0.2	0.4
Chr & Miss Al	9	2,362	1,804	4,251	1.0	2.1
CHR–Chr Ch (Disc)	5	669	1,135	1,391	0.3	0.7
CHR–Chr Chs & Chs Cr	4	NR	1,300	1,593	0.4	0.8
CHR–Chs of Christ	5	929	959	1,223	0.3	0.6
CHR–Int Chs of Christ	1	NR	61	75	0.0	0.0
CONG–Cong Chr, NA	5	NR	1,095	1,342	0.3	0.7
Evan Cov Ch	1	196	152	255	0.1	0.1
FRND–Fr Gen Cf	1	NR	7	9	0.0	0.0
HINDU–Post Ren	2	NR	NR	26	0.0	0.0
HINDU–Trad Temples	1	NR	NR	300	0.1	0.2
Int Cou Comm Ch	1	NR	NR	NR	-	-
Jain	1	NR	NR	NR	-	-
Jehovah's Witness	4	NR	NR	NR	-	-
JUD–Conserv	1	267	300	810	0.2	0.4
JUD–Orth	2	720	315	1,000	0.2	0.5
JUD–Reform	1	293	516	1,393	0.3	0.7
LDS–Comm of Christ	2	NR	266	266	0.1	0.1
LDS–L-D Saints	2	NR	NR	1,441	0.3	0.7
LUTH–E.L.C.A.	34	4,336	13,571	18,207	4.1	9.2
LUTH–Luth Cong Msn Chr	1	650	1,769	2,168	0.5	1.1
LUTH–Luth–MO Synod	10	1,240	2,449	3,196	0.7	1.6
LUTH–Wisc Ev Luth Syn	5	250	514	611	0.1	0.3
MENN–Mennonite USA	2	82	113	138	0.0	0.1
METH–AME	3	320	550	674	0.2	0.3
METH–AME Zion	4	200	700	858	0.2	0.4
METH–C.M.E.	1	150	500	613	0.1	0.3
METH–Free Methodist	2	183	142	183	0.0	0.1
METH–Un Methodist	29	3,630	7,150	10,000	2.3	5.1
METH–Wesleyan	2	32	49	42	0.0	0.0
Missionary Ch	1	27	26	27	0.0	0.0
Muslim Est	3	694	NR	1,908	0.4	1.0
New Apost Ch	1	NR	NR	NR	-	-
Non-denom Chr Chs	33	9,980	10,807	13,071	3.0	6.6
ORTHE–Ant Orth of NA	2	265	NR	1,000	0.2	0.5
ORTHE–Greek Orthodox	1	250	NR	1,500	0.3	0.8
ORTHO–Coptic Orth Ch	1	150	NR	180	0.0	0.1
PENT–Assemb of God	6	1,646	864	2,401	0.5	1.2
PENT–Ch God (Cleve)	4	1,672	3,021	3,702	0.8	1.9
PENT–Ch Lord Jesus Apos	1	NR	NR	NR	-	-
PENT–Ch of God Proph	2	NR	43	53	0.0	0.0
PENT–COGIC	7	1,085	2,175	2,665	0.6	1.3
PENT–Full Gosp Bapt	7	NR	NR	NR	-	-
PENT–Int Foursq Gos	1	76	43	53	0.0	0.0
PENT–Intl Pent Holiness	6	268	625	766	0.2	0.4
PENT–Open Bible Std	1	0	NR	0	0.0	0.0
PENT–Un Pent Ch Intl	2	NR	NR	NR	-	-
PENT–United Holy Ch	1	NR	NR	NR	-	-
PENT–Vineyard	1	122	130	159	0.0	0.1
PRES–Presb Ch (USA)	9	911	1,856	2,274	0.5	1.1
PRES–Presb Ch Amer	1	180	94	117	0.0	0.1
REF–Christian Ref	1	150	110	135	0.0	0.1
Salvation Army	1	70	181	248	0.1	0.1
Sev Day Adv	2	406	706	812	0.2	0.4
Sikh	1	NR	NR	NR	-	-
Un Breth in Cr	1	0	0	0	0.0	0.0
Un C of Christ	9	776	2,009	2,462	0.6	1.2
Unit Univ	1	170	260	333	0.1	0.2
Unity Ch	1	NR	NR	NR	-	-
MADISON	**73**	**4,373**	**7,250**	**13,768**	**31.7**	**100.0**
ANG/EPIS–Episcopal	1	35	77	79	0.2	0.6
BAPT–Amer Bapt USA	1	60	199	240	0.6	1.7
BAPT–Enterprise Bapt Assoc	1	NR	NR	NR	-	-
BAPT–Free Will Bapt	4	NR	268	323	0.7	2.3
BAPT–Reg Bapt Gen As	1	NR	NR	NR	-	-
BAPT–So Bapt Conv	4	409	882	1,062	2.4	7.7
BRETH–Grace Breth	3	NR	NR	NR	-	-
Catholic	2	NR	NR	2,500	5.8	18.2
CGOD–Ch God (Ander)	1	17	NR	17	0.0	0.1
Ch Christ Chr Union	8	NR	NR	NR	-	-
Ch of Nazarene	3	465	640	725	1.7	5.3
CHR–Chr Chs & Chs Cr	1	NR	75	90	0.2	0.7
CHR–Chs of Christ	1	35	25	40	0.1	0.3
HINDU–I/A Temples	1	NR	NR	1,742	4.0	12.7
Jehovah's Witness	2	NR	NR	NR	-	-
LDS–L-D Saints	1	NR	NR	271	0.6	2.0
LUTH–E.L.C.A.	2	220	452	590	1.4	4.3
LUTH–Nor Amer Luth C	1	NR	NR	NR	-	-
MENN–Amish Undif	1	NR	7	7	0.0	0.1
MENN–Beachy Amish-Menn	3	435	285	435	1.0	3.2
MENN–Cons Menn Conf	3	509	366	441	1.0	3.2
MENN–Mennonite USA	2	223	257	309	0.7	2.2
METH–AME	1	0	21	25	0.1	0.2
METH–Un Methodist	8	693	1,660	2,389	5.5	17.4
Non-denom Chr Chs	6	470	620	662	1.5	4.8
PENT–Assemb of God	1	135	42	160	0.4	1.2
PENT–Ch God (Cleve)	1	30	73	88	0.2	0.6
PENT–Int Pent C Chr	1	0	NR	6	0.0	0.0
PENT–Un Pent Ch Intl	2	NR	NR	NR	-	-
PENT–Vineyard	2	310	450	542	1.2	3.9
PRES–Presb Ch (USA)	3	327	662	797	1.8	5.8
Un C of Christ	1	0	189	228	0.5	1.7
MAHONING	**321**	**25,166**	**45,701**	**136,813**	**57.3**	**100.0**
ANG/EPIS–Episcopal	3	188	408	509	0.2	0.4
Bahá'í	0	NR	34	34	0.0	0.0
BAPT–Amer Bapt USA	6	620	1,326	1,580	0.7	1.2
BAPT–Converge/BGC	3	950	NR	1,140	0.5	0.8
BAPT–Free Will Bapt	1	NR	67	80	0.0	0.1
BAPT–Natl Mis Bapt Conv	1	0	150	179	0.1	0.1
BAPT–NBC USA	13	2,010	6,400	7,626	3.2	5.6
BAPT–Reg Bapt Gen As	4	NR	NR	NR	-	-
BAPT–So Bapt Conv	16	888	1,433	1,707	0.7	1.2
BRETH–Ch of Brethren	3	197	300	357	0.1	0.3
Catholic	45	NR	NR	71,180	29.8	52.0
CGOD–Ch God (Ander)	4	395	NR	395	0.2	0.3
Ch Cr, Scientst	1	NR	NR	NR	-	-
Ch of Nazarene	5	417	817	830	0.3	0.6
Chr & Miss Al	1	35	38	50	0.0	0.0
CHR–Chr Ch (Disc)	6	307	1,127	1,343	0.6	1.0
CHR–Chr Chs & Chs Cr	8	NR	3,114	3,710	1.6	2.7
CHR–Chs of Christ	6	412	500	682	0.3	0.5
Evan Cong Ch	1	NR	92	110	0.0	0.1
Evan Cov Ch	3	458	871	595	0.2	0.4
FRND–Evan Fr Ch Intl	4	419	259	309	0.1	0.2
Jehovah's Witness	6	NR	NR	NR	-	-
JUD–Orth	1	144	55	200	0.1	0.1
JUD–Reform	1	156	276	745	0.3	0.5
LUTH–Assoc Free Luth	1	NR	NR	NR	-	-
LUTH–E.L.C.A.	16	1,612	4,956	6,782	2.8	5.0
LUTH–Luth Cong Msn Chr	2	102	312	372	0.2	0.3
LUTH–Luth–MO Synod	6	347	864	1,130	0.5	0.8
MENN–Mennonite USA	2	124	121	144	0.1	0.1
METH–A.W.M.C.	1	12	7	15	0.0	0.0
METH–AME	4	0	550	655	0.3	0.5
METH–AME Zion	2	70	200	238	0.1	0.2
METH–C.M.E.	2	100	310	369	0.2	0.3
METH–Free Methodist	2	205	191	215	0.1	0.2
METH–Prim Meth Ch	1	NR	NR	NR	-	-
METH–Un Methodist	22	2,126	5,538	6,671	2.8	4.9
Muslim Est	1	134	NR	308	0.1	0.2
Non-denom Chr Chs	33	3,676	4,868	5,310	2.2	3.9
OCATH–Pol Natl Cath	1	NR	NR	NR	-	-
ORTHE–Ant Orth of NA	1	90	NR	140	0.1	0.1
ORTHE–Carp Rus Orth	1	37	NR	150	0.1	0.1
ORTHE–Greek Orthodox	3	490	NR	2,700	1.1	2.0
ORTHE–Orth Ch in Amer	3	199	NR	347	0.1	0.3
ORTHE–Rus Orth Moscow	1	45	NR	80	0.0	0.1
ORTHE–Serb Orth USA	2	75	NR	220	0.1	0.2
ORTHE–Ukrainian Orth	1	120	NR	400	0.2	0.3
PENT–Assemb of God	16	4,953	3,184	8,240	3.5	6.0
PENT–Ch God (Cleve)	3	91	210	250	0.1	0.2
PENT–Ch Lord Jesus Apos	2	NR	NR	NR	-	-
PENT–COGIC	6	300	490	584	0.2	0.4
PENT–Fire Bapt Hol Ch	1	NR	NR	NR	-	-
PENT–Full Gosp Bapt	1	NR	NR	NR	-	-
PENT–I F Chr Assmbl	1	NR	NR	NR	-	-

NR–Not Reported - Represents no adherents reported. Percentages may not total 100 due to rounding.

Table 3: Religious Congregations by County and Group: 2010

Religious Group	Number of Congregations	Number of Attendees	Number of Communicant, Confirmed, or Full Members	Adherents: Number of Adherents	Adherents: % of Total Pop.	Adherents: % of Total Adh.
PENT–Int Foursq Gos	2	93	110	131	0.1	0.1
PENT–United Holy Ch	2	NR	NR	NR	-	-
PRES–Evan Presby Ch	1	NR	406	484	0.2	0.4
PRES–Presb Ch (USA)	24	1,655	3,940	4,695	2.0	3.4
PRES–Presb Ch Amer	1	67	108	130	0.1	0.1
REF–Hung Ref Add'l	1	NR	NR	NR	-	-
Salvation Army	2	79	277	572	0.2	0.4
Sev Day Adv	3	302	525	603	0.3	0.4
Un C of Christ	4	414	1,147	1,367	0.6	1.0
Unit Univ	1	52	120	150	0.1	0.1
MARION	**95**	**7,541**	**13,529**	**20,127**	**30.3**	**100.0**
ANG/EPIS–Episcopal	1	22	28	104	0.2	0.5
Bahá'í	0	NR	3	3	0.0	0.0
BAPT–Amer Bapt USA	6	564	1,023	1,230	1.8	6.1
BAPT–Converge/BGC	1	75	NR	90	0.1	0.4
BAPT–Enterprise Bapt Assoc	3	NR	NR	NR	-	-
BAPT–Free Will Bapt	2	NR	134	161	0.2	0.8
BAPT–Ind Bapt Flwsp Intl	2	NR	NR	NR	-	-
BAPT–Natl Mis Bapt Conv	1	0	150	180	0.3	0.9
BAPT–Reg Bapt Gen As	2	NR	NR	NR	-	-
BAPT–So Bapt Conv	2	140	230	277	0.4	1.4
BRETH–Ch of Brethren	1	0	43	52	0.1	0.3
BRETH–Grace Breth	1	NR	NR	NR	-	-
Catholic	1	NR	NR	2,500	3.8	12.4
CGOD–Ch God (Ander)	1	37	NR	37	0.1	0.2
CGOD–Ches God-Gen Con	1	47	51	61	0.1	0.3
Ch Christ Chr Union	1	NR	NR	NR	-	-
Ch of Nazarene	3	1,229	1,188	1,311	2.0	6.5
Chr & Miss Al	1	283	182	476	0.7	2.4
CHR–Chr Ch (Disc)	1	64	521	627	0.9	3.1
CHR–Chr Chs & Chs Cr	3	NR	495	595	0.9	3.0
CHR–Chs of Christ	1	270	325	350	0.5	1.7
CONG–Consrv Cong Chr	2	127	124	149	0.2	0.7
Jehovah's Witness	1	NR	NR	NR	-	-
JUD–Reform	1	19	33	89	0.1	0.4
LDS–L-D Saints	1	NR	NR	474	0.7	2.4
LUTH–E.L.C.A.	7	934	2,222	2,823	4.2	14.0
LUTH–Luth–MO Synod	1	45	79	112	0.2	0.6
MENN–Amish Undif	0	NR	22	60	0.1	0.3
METH–A.W.M.C.	1	94	15	123	0.2	0.6
METH–AME	1	0	150	180	0.3	0.9
METH–Un Methodist	17	1,328	2,943	3,366	5.1	16.7
METH–Wesleyan	1	366	262	476	0.7	2.4
Non-denom Chr Chs	11	1,135	1,395	1,523	2.3	7.6
PENT–Assemb of God	1	160	69	160	0.2	0.8
PENT–Ch God (Cleve)	1	88	464	558	0.8	2.8
PENT–Ch of God Proph	1	NR	32	38	0.1	0.2
PENT–COGIC	2	0	120	144	0.2	0.7
PENT–Int Foursq Gos	1	54	45	54	0.1	0.3
PENT–Int Pent C Chr	1	36	12	144	0.2	0.7
PENT–Pent Ch of God	1	70	NR	109	0.2	0.5
PENT–Un Pent Ch Intl	1	NR	NR	NR	-	-
PRES–Presb Ch (USA)	3	43	437	526	0.8	2.6
Salvation Army	1	80	76	182	0.3	0.9
Sev Day Adv	1	66	114	131	0.2	0.7
Un C of Christ	2	165	542	652	1.0	3.2
MEDINA	**144**	**15,544**	**29,916**	**89,004**	**51.6**	**100.0**
ANG/EPIS–Episcopal	3	213	551	646	0.4	0.7
Ap Chr Ch-Amer	1	233	119	233	0.1	0.3
Bahá'í	0	NR	14	14	0.0	0.0
BAPT–Amer Bapt USA	1	8	8	10	0.0	0.0
BAPT–Ind Bapt Flwsp Intl	3	NR	NR	NR	-	-
BAPT–N Am Bapt Conf	1	NR	NR	NR	-	-
BAPT–NBC Amer	1	35	50	62	0.0	0.1
BAPT–NBC USA	1	0	150	186	0.1	0.2
BAPT–Reg Bapt Gen As	5	NR	NR	NR	-	-
BAPT–So Bapt Conv	5	300	604	747	0.4	0.8
BRETH–Brethren (Ash)	1	NR	80	99	0.1	0.1
BRETH–Ch of Brethren	1	67	90	111	0.1	0.1
BRETH–Grace Breth	2	NR	NR	NR	-	-
Catholic	9	NR	NR	48,514	28.2	54.5

Religious Group	Number of Congregations	Number of Attendees	Number of Communicant, Confirmed, or Full Members	Adherents: Number of Adherents	Adherents: % of Total Pop.	Adherents: % of Total Adh.
Ch Cr, Scientst	1	NR	NR	NR	-	-
Ch of Nazarene	3	309	402	584	0.3	0.7
Chr & Miss Al	3	905	356	1,305	0.8	1.5
CHR–Chr Ch (Disc)	4	611	1,908	2,360	1.4	2.7
CHR–Chr Chs & Chs Cr	3	NR	2,089	2,584	1.5	2.9
CHR–Chs of Christ	3	260	236	288	0.2	0.3
CONG–Consrv Cong Chr	1	91	80	99	0.1	0.1
Evan Free Ch	1	0	NR	0	0.0	0.0
FRND–Evan Fr Ch Intl	1	54	36	45	0.0	0.1
HINDU–I/A Temples	1	NR	NR	1,742	1.0	2.0
Jehovah's Witness	3	NR	NR	NR	-	-
LDS–L-D Saints	2	NR	NR	828	0.5	0.9
LUTH–E.L.C.A.	9	1,286	3,742	4,799	2.8	5.4
LUTH–Luth–MO Synod	4	560	1,738	2,268	1.3	2.5
MENN–Amish Undif	4	NR	221	616	0.4	0.7
MENN–Mennonite USA	1	50	110	136	0.1	0.2
METH–Un Methodist	18	2,139	6,236	7,472	4.3	8.4
METH–Wesleyan	1	187	129	243	0.1	0.3
Non-denom Chr Chs	18	5,047	6,181	6,711	3.9	7.5
ORTHE–Ukrainian Orth	1	10	NR	40	0.0	0.0
PENT–Assemb of God	6	615	350	737	0.4	0.8
PENT–Ch God (Cleve)	2	90	124	153	0.1	0.2
PENT–Ch God Mtn Asm	1	NR	NR	NR	-	-
PENT–Int Foursq Gos	2	969	850	1,051	0.6	1.2
PRES–Presb Ch (USA)	3	150	286	354	0.2	0.4
PRES–Presb Ch Amer	1	209	190	254	0.1	0.3
REF–Ref Ch in Am	1	376	658	797	0.5	0.9
Salvation Army	2	60	87	158	0.1	0.2
Sev Day Adv	1	58	101	116	0.1	0.1
Un C of Christ	7	638	2,117	2,619	1.5	2.9
Unit Univ	1	14	23	23	0.0	0.0
Unity Ch	1	NR	NR	NR	-	-
MEIGS	**75**	**2,679**	**4,839**	**6,425**	**27.0**	**100.0**
ANG/EPIS–Episcopal	1	18	48	68	0.3	1.1
BAPT–Amer Bapt USA	2	58	73	89	0.4	1.4
BAPT–Free Will Bapt	1	NR	67	81	0.3	1.3
BAPT–So Bapt Conv	2	126	335	406	1.7	6.3
Catholic	1	NR	NR	283	1.2	4.4
CGOD–Ch God (Ander)	1	20	NR	20	0.1	0.3
Ch of Nazarene	7	321	399	667	2.8	10.4
CHR–Chr Chs & Chs Cr	7	NR	697	845	3.6	13.2
CHR–Chs of Christ	7	280	267	338	1.4	5.3
CONG–Cong Chr, NA	1	NR	160	194	0.8	3.0
Jehovah's Witness	1	NR	NR	NR	-	-
LDS–Comm of Christ	1	NR	118	118	0.5	1.8
LUTH–E.L.C.A.	2	41	71	87	0.4	1.4
MENN–Amish Undif	1	NR	34	92	0.4	1.4
METH–Free Methodist	1	29	24	29	0.1	0.5
METH–Un Methodist	23	782	1,188	1,637	6.9	25.5
Non-denom Chr Chs	10	795	992	1,080	4.5	16.8
PENT–Ch God (Cleve)	2	92	219	266	1.1	4.1
PRES–Presb Ch (USA)	2	18	33	40	0.2	0.6
Un Breth in Cr	2	99	114	85	0.4	1.3
MERCER	**71**	**4,050**	**7,259**	**32,703**	**80.1**	**100.0**
Bahá'í	0	NR	1	1	0.0	0.0
BAPT–So Bapt Conv	1	40	40	50	0.1	0.2
BRETH–Ch of Brethren	1	0	32	40	0.1	0.1
Catholic	20	NR	NR	23,728	58.1	72.6
CGOD–Ches God-Gen Con	6	592	606	759	1.9	2.3
Ch of Nazarene	2	184	332	488	1.2	1.5
CHR–Chr Chs & Chs Cr	2	NR	255	319	0.8	1.0
CHR–Chs of Christ	1	37	23	41	0.1	0.1
CONG–Midw Cong Chr Fel	2	42	52	65	0.2	0.2
FRND–Fr Un Mtg	1	NR	4	5	0.0	0.0
Jehovah's Witness	1	NR	NR	NR	-	-
LUTH–E.L.C.A.	6	619	1,896	2,397	5.9	7.3
LUTH–Nor Amer Luth C	2	NR	NR	NR	-	-
MENN–Amish Undif	0	NR	25	95	0.2	0.3
METH–Un Methodist	13	1,115	2,276	2,770	6.8	8.5
Missionary Ch	1	196	211	211	0.5	0.6
Non-denom Chr Chs	6	750	935	1,025	2.5	3.1

NR–Not Reported   - Represents no adherents reported.   Percentages may not total 100 due to rounding.

Table 3: Religious Congregations by County and Group: 2010

Religious Group	Number of Congrega-tions	Number of Attendees	Number of Communicant, Confirmed, or Full Members	Adherents		
				Number of Adherents	% of Total Pop.	% of Total Adh.
PENT–Ch God (Cleve)	1	94	60	75	0.2	0.2
PENT–Un Pent Ch Intl	1	NR	NR	NR	-	-
PRES–Presb Ch (USA)	1	59	89	111	0.3	0.3
Un Breth in Cr	2	242	170	207	0.5	0.6
Un C of Christ	1	80	252	316	0.8	1.0
MIAMI	**132**	**14,481**	**18,423**	**38,159**	**37.2**	**100.0**
ANG/EPIS–Episcopal	2	115	276	276	0.3	0.7
Bahá'í	0	NR	6	6	0.0	0.0
BAPT–Amer Bapt USA	5	614	1,379	1,689	1.6	4.4
BAPT–Free Will Bapt	2	NR	134	164	0.2	0.4
BAPT–Ind Bapt Flwsp Intl	2	NR	NR	NR	-	-
BAPT–NBC USA	1	50	75	92	0.1	0.2
BAPT–Reg Bapt Gen As	1	NR	NR	NR	-	-
BAPT–So Bapt Conv	5	543	1,055	1,292	1.3	3.4
BRETH–Breth in Chr	2	NR	NR	NR	-	-
BRETH–Brethren (Ash)	1	NR	80	98	0.1	0.3
BRETH–Ch of Brethren	9	563	1,553	1,903	1.9	5.0
BRETH–Grace Breth	3	NR	NR	NR	-	-
Catholic	7	NR	NR	10,860	10.6	28.5
CGOD–Ch God (Ander)	2	50	NR	50	0.0	0.1
Ch of God Gen Conf	3	NR	183	224	0.2	0.6
Ch of Nazarene	5	1,156	1,094	1,625	1.6	4.3
CHR–Chr Chs & Chs Cr	2	NR	620	760	0.7	2.0
CHR–Chs of Christ	3	330	350	435	0.4	1.1
Evan Assoc RCC	1	NR	NR	NR	-	-
FRND–Fr Un Mtg	2	NR	44	54	0.1	0.1
Grace Gosp Fel	1	NR	NR	NR	-	-
Ind Fund Churches	1	NR	NR	NR	-	-
Jehovah's Witness	2	NR	NR	NR	-	-
LDS–L-D Saints	1	NR	NR	550	0.5	1.4
LUTH–E.L.C.A.	6	436	1,294	1,527	1.5	4.0
LUTH–Luth Ch-Am Asc	1	NR	NR	NR	-	-
LUTH–Nor Amer Luth C	1	NR	NR	NR	-	-
METH–AME	2	0	140	172	0.2	0.5
METH–Un Methodist	14	6,304	4,307	8,884	8.7	23.3
METH–Wesleyan	1	50	42	65	0.1	0.2
Missionary Ch	3	219	61	219	0.2	0.6
Non-denom Chr Chs	17	2,895	3,197	3,888	3.8	10.2
PENT–Assemb of God	3	140	58	150	0.1	0.4
PENT–Ch God Mtn Asm	2	NR	NR	NR	-	-
PENT–Open Bible Std	1	41	NR	41	0.0	0.1
PENT–Un Pent Ch Intl	3	NR	NR	NR	-	-
PRES–Presb Ch (USA)	4	391	730	894	0.9	2.3
PRES–Presb Ch Amer	1	0	0	0	0.0	0.0
Salvation Army	1	50	117	251	0.2	0.7
Sev Day Adv	1	34	58	67	0.1	0.2
Un C of Christ	8	500	1,570	1,923	1.9	5.0
MONROE	**76**	**2,650**	**5,172**	**7,507**	**51.3**	**100.0**
Ap Chr Ch-Amer	1	75	48	75	0.5	1.0
BAPT–Amer Bapt USA	1	30	80	95	0.6	1.3
BAPT–So Bapt Conv	3	151	719	858	5.9	11.4
Catholic	4	NR	NR	756	5.2	10.1
CGOD–Ch God (Ander)	1	20	NR	20	0.1	0.3
Ch of Nazarene	1	10	83	83	0.6	1.1
CHR–Chr Chs & Chs Cr	3	NR	352	420	2.9	5.6
CHR–Chs of Christ	26	1,394	1,398	1,881	12.8	25.1
CONG–Consrv Cong Chr	1	30	92	110	0.8	1.5
MENN–Amish Undif	5	NR	240	542	3.7	7.2
METH–Free Methodist	1	54	47	54	0.4	0.7
METH–Un Methodist	19	504	1,254	1,583	10.8	21.1
Non-denom Chr Chs	1	100	100	125	0.9	1.7
PENT–Un Pent Ch Intl	1	NR	NR	NR	-	-
PRES–Presb Ch (USA)	3	44	63	75	0.5	1.0
Un C of Christ	5	238	696	830	5.7	11.1
MONTGOMERY	**583**	**78,189**	**123,913**	**259,795**	**48.5**	**100.0**
ANG/EPIS–Anglican NA	2	NR	NR	NR	-	-
ANG/EPIS–Episcopal	6	747	2,157	2,455	0.5	0.9
Bahá'í	2	NR	144	144	0.0	0.1
BAPT–Alliance Bapt	1	NR	NR	NR	-	-
BAPT–Amer Bapt Assn	0	NR	60	73	0.0	0.0

Religious Group	Number of Congrega-tions	Number of Attendees	Number of Communicant, Confirmed, or Full Members	Adherents		
				Number of Adherents	% of Total Pop.	% of Total Adh.
BAPT–Amer Bapt USA	14	4,304	8,914	10,828	2.0	4.2
BAPT–Enterprise Bapt Assoc	1	NR	NR	NR	-	-
BAPT–Free Will Bapt	3	NR	230	279	0.1	0.1
BAPT–Fund Bapt Flwsp	1	NR	NR	NR	-	-
BAPT–Ind Bapt Flwsp Intl	7	NR	NR	NR	-	-
BAPT–Natl Mis Bapt Conv	10	200	1,130	1,373	0.3	0.5
BAPT–NBC USA	25	5,065	11,150	13,544	2.5	5.2
BAPT–Prim Bapt E Dst	1	25	89	108	0.0	0.0
BAPT–Prog NBC	1	0	0	0	0.0	0.0
BAPT–Reg Bapt Gen As	5	NR	NR	NR	-	-
BAPT–So Bapt Conv	60	10,621	20,415	24,798	4.6	9.5
BRETH–Breth in Chr	3	NR	NR	NR	-	-
BRETH–Brethren (Ash)	2	NR	160	194	0.0	0.1
BRETH–Ch of Brethren	11	648	1,686	2,048	0.4	0.8
BRETH–Grace Breth	10	NR	NR	NR	-	-
BUDD–Mahayana	1	NR	NR	1,255	0.2	0.5
BUDD–Vajrayana	2	NR	NR	61	0.0	0.0
Catholic	34	NR	NR	78,909	14.7	30.4
CGOD–Ch God (Ander)	17	2,438	NR	2,438	0.5	0.9
Ch Christ Chr Union	1	NR	NR	NR	-	-
Ch Cr, Scientist	3	NR	NR	NR	-	-
Ch of Nazarene	21	2,642	3,031	3,711	0.7	1.4
Chr & Miss Al	9	5,887	1,943	8,516	1.6	3.3
CHR–Chr Ch (Disc)	5	386	929	1,128	0.2	0.4
CHR–Chr Chs & Chs Cr	7	NR	4,940	6,001	1.1	2.3
CHR–Chs of Christ	24	2,439	2,596	3,347	0.6	1.3
CHR–Int Chs of Christ	1	NR	51	62	0.0	0.0
Christian Brethren	1	NR	NR	NR	-	-
Christian Un	1	NR	NR	NR	-	-
FRND–Fr Gen Cf	1	NR	14	17	0.0	0.0
FRND–Fr Un Mtg	1	NR	15	18	0.0	0.0
HINDU–I/A Temples	2	NR	NR	1,980	0.4	0.8
HINDU–Post Ren	3	NR	NR	109	0.0	0.0
HINDU–Trad Temples	1	NR	NR	2,000	0.4	0.8
Int Cou Comm Ch	1	NR	NR	NR	-	-
Jehovah's Witness	8	NR	NR	NR	-	-
JUD–Conserv	1	261	293	791	0.1	0.3
JUD–Orth	1	43	50	60	0.0	0.0
JUD–Reform	2	387	683	1,844	0.3	0.7
LDS–Comm of Christ	1	NR	133	133	0.0	0.1
LDS–L-D Saints	7	NR	NR	3,817	0.7	1.5
LUTH–E.L.C.A.	29	2,926	8,047	9,576	1.8	3.7
LUTH–Luth Cong Msn Chr	2	150	415	504	0.1	0.2
LUTH–Luth–MO Synod	5	616	1,083	1,369	0.3	0.5
LUTH–Nor Amer Luth C	1	NR	NR	NR	-	-
LUTH–Wisc Ev Luth Syn	1	60	130	161	0.0	0.1
METH–AME	5	600	1,798	2,184	0.4	0.8
METH–AME Zion	3	75	402	488	0.1	0.2
METH–C.M.E.	2	1,260	2,250	2,733	0.5	1.1
METH–Free Methodist	2	106	94	123	0.0	0.0
METH–Un Methodist	45	6,449	10,760	15,761	2.9	6.1
METH–Wesleyan	6	258	244	336	0.1	0.1
Metro Comm Ch	1	48	60	73	0.0	0.0
Missionary Ch	1	24	12	24	0.0	0.0
Muslim Est	4	784	NR	1,678	0.3	0.6
Nat Spirit Asso	1	NR	NR	NR	-	-
Non-denom Chr Chs	56	17,295	22,050	24,610	4.6	9.5
ORTHE–Greek Orthodox	1	275	NR	3,500	0.7	1.3
ORTHE–Orth Ch in Amer	1	100	NR	170	0.0	0.1
ORTHO–Coptic Orth Ch	1	276	NR	535	0.1	0.2
PENT–Assemb of God	10	3,817	1,586	5,643	1.1	2.2
PENT–Ch God (Cleve)	11	593	2,053	2,494	0.5	1.0
PENT–Ch God Mtn Asm	1	NR	NR	NR	-	-
PENT–Ch of God Proph	2	NR	42	51	0.0	0.0
PENT–COGIC	8	275	775	941	0.2	0.4
PENT–Full Gosp Bapt	1	NR	NR	NR	-	-
PENT–Intl Pent Holiness	3	65	101	123	0.0	0.0
PENT–Open Bible Std	6	661	NR	661	0.1	0.3
PENT–Pent Ch of God	1	70	NR	109	0.0	0.0
PENT–Un Pent Ch Intl	1	NR	NR	NR	-	-
PENT–United Holy Ch	1	NR	NR	NR	-	-
PENT–Vineyard	4	208	287	349	0.1	0.1
PRES–Orth Pres Ch	2	269	239	331	0.1	0.1
PRES–Presb Ch (USA)	11	1,060	2,037	2,474	0.5	1.0

NR–Not Reported - Represents no adherents reported. Percentages may not total 100 due to rounding.

Table 3: Religious Congregations by County and Group: 2010

Religious Group	Number of Congrega-tions	Number of Attendees	Number of Communicant, Confirmed, or Full Members	Adherents: Number of Adherents	% of Total Pop.	% of Total Adh.
Salvation Army	1	94	301	847	0.2	0.3
Sev Day Adv	10	1,992	3,463	3,983	0.7	1.5
Un Breth in Cr	2	47	48	41	0.0	0.0
Un C of Christ	18	1,476	4,636	5,631	1.1	2.2
Unit Univ	1	167	187	245	0.0	0.1
Unity Ch	1	NR	NR	NR	-	-
Zoroastrian	0	NR	NR	6	0.0	0.0
MORGAN	**44**	**1,407**	**3,083**	**3,740**	**24.8**	**100.0**
Bahá'í	0	NR	2	2	0.0	0.1
Catholic	1	NR	NR	129	0.9	3.4
Ch of Nazarene	2	70	87	97	0.6	2.6
CHR–Chr Chs & Chs Cr	6	NR	895	1,086	7.2	29.0
CHR–Chs of Christ	6	260	240	301	2.0	8.0
FRND–Consrv Yr Mtgs	1	NR	21	25	0.2	0.7
Jehovah's Witness	1	NR	NR	NR	-	-
LUTH–E.L.C.A.	1	13	39	50	0.3	1.3
MENN–Amish Undif	1	NR	35	95	0.6	2.5
MENN–Beachy Amish-Menn	1	136	88	136	0.9	3.6
METH–Un Methodist	18	674	1,331	1,446	9.6	38.7
Non-denom Chr Chs	3	150	200	212	1.4	5.7
PRES–Presb Ch (USA)	2	49	94	114	0.8	3.0
Un Breth in Cr	1	55	51	47	0.3	1.3
MORROW	**62**	**3,103**	**5,468**	**8,331**	**23.9**	**100.0**
Bahá'í	0	NR	7	7	0.0	0.1
BAPT–Amer Bapt USA	3	198	374	465	1.3	5.6
BAPT–Enterprise Bapt Assoc	1	NR	NR	NR	-	-
BAPT–Free Will Bapt	2	NR	134	167	0.5	2.0
BAPT–Ind Bapt Flwsp Intl	1	NR	NR	NR	-	-
BAPT–So Bapt Conv	4	123	201	250	0.7	3.0
BRETH–Grace Breth	1	NR	NR	NR	-	-
Catholic	1	NR	NR	425	1.2	5.1
Ch of Nazarene	3	193	198	328	0.9	3.9
Chr & Miss Al	1	548	231	805	2.3	9.7
CHR–Chr Chs & Chs Cr	5	NR	563	700	2.0	8.4
FRND–Evan Fr Ch Intl	2	452	332	413	1.2	5.0
LUTH–Luth Cong Msn Chr	2	61	161	200	0.6	2.4
MENN–Amish Undif	4	NR	214	590	1.7	7.1
MENN–Mennonite USA	1	50	51	63	0.2	0.8
METH–Un Methodist	19	861	2,090	2,872	8.2	34.5
METH–Wesleyan	1	43	41	56	0.2	0.7
Non-denom Chr Chs	5	470	630	662	1.9	7.9
PENT–Assemb of God	1	45	30	66	0.2	0.8
PENT–Intl Pent Holiness	1	1	1	1	0.0	0.0
PENT–Un Pent Ch Intl	1	NR	NR	NR	-	-
PRES–Presb Ch (USA)	2	58	165	205	0.6	2.5
Un C of Christ	1	0	45	56	0.2	0.7
MUSKINGUM	**148**	**9,707**	**18,582**	**31,630**	**36.7**	**100.0**
ANG/EPIS–Episcopal	1	67	137	182	0.2	0.6
Bahá'í	0	NR	9	9	0.0	0.0
BAPT–Amer Bapt USA	6	428	867	1,060	1.2	3.4
BAPT–NBC USA	1	0	0	0	0.0	0.0
BAPT–Reg Bapt Gen As	1	NR	NR	NR	-	-
BAPT–So Bapt Conv	4	138	378	462	0.5	1.5
BRETH–Ch of Brethren	1	55	83	101	0.1	0.3
Calv Chpl	1	NR	NR	NR	-	-
Catholic	4	NR	NR	5,170	6.0	16.3
CGOD–Ch God (Ander)	1	135	NR	135	0.2	0.4
Ch Cr, Scientst	1	NR	NR	NR	-	-
Ch of Nazarene	5	434	484	574	0.7	1.8
Chr & Miss Al	3	328	163	537	0.6	1.7
CHR–Chr Ch (Disc)	1	304	755	923	1.1	2.9
CHR–Chr Chs & Chs Cr	4	NR	1,960	2,397	2.8	7.6
CHR–Chs of Christ	7	599	654	863	1.0	2.7
FRND–Evan Fr Ch Intl	1	172	61	75	0.1	0.2
Jehovah's Witness	2	NR	NR	NR	-	-
LDS–L-D Saints	2	NR	NR	1,043	1.2	3.3
LUTH–E.L.C.A.	8	351	1,037	1,377	1.6	4.4
LUTH–Luth–MO Synod	1	295	469	688	0.8	2.2
MENN–Amish Undif	2	NR	113	293	0.3	0.9
METH–AME	1	70	150	183	0.2	0.6

Religious Group	Number of Congrega-tions	Number of Attendees	Number of Communicant, Confirmed, or Full Members	Adherents: Number of Adherents	% of Total Pop.	% of Total Adh.
METH–Free Methodist	3	125	85	125	0.1	0.4
METH–Un Methodist	40	3,001	6,391	8,971	10.4	28.4
METH–Wesleyan	1	61	44	79	0.1	0.2
Non-denom Chr Chs	16	1,770	2,187	2,431	2.8	7.7
PENT–Assemb of God	2	152	83	186	0.2	0.6
PENT–Ch God (Cleve)	1	176	299	366	0.4	1.2
PENT–Int Pent C Chr	1	0	0	125	0.1	0.4
PENT–Open Bible Std	1	107	NR	107	0.1	0.3
PENT–Pent Ch of God	1	70	NR	109	0.1	0.3
PENT–Un Pent Ch Intl	3	NR	NR	NR	-	-
PENT–Vineyard	1	150	200	245	0.3	0.8
PRES–Presb Ch (USA)	16	451	1,285	1,571	1.8	5.0
Salvation Army	1	45	68	499	0.6	1.6
Sev Day Adv	2	120	209	241	0.3	0.8
Un C of Christ	1	103	411	503	0.6	1.6
NOBLE	**33**	**1,325**	**2,005**	**4,012**	**27.4**	**100.0**
Bahá'í	0	NR	1	1	0.0	0.0
BAPT–Reg Bapt Gen As	1	NR	NR	NR	-	-
BAPT–So Bapt Conv	1	110	203	237	1.6	5.9
Catholic	5	NR	NR	1,542	10.5	38.4
Ch of Nazarene	1	74	90	110	0.8	2.7
CHR–Chr Chs & Chs Cr	1	NR	250	292	2.0	7.3
CHR–Chs of Christ	6	450	460	594	4.1	14.8
Jehovah's Witness	1	NR	NR	NR	-	-
METH–Free Methodist	3	209	173	209	1.4	5.2
METH–Un Methodist	13	427	763	951	6.5	23.7
PRES–Presb Ch (USA)	1	55	65	76	0.5	1.9
OTTAWA	**55**	**4,103**	**9,785**	**21,020**	**50.7**	**100.0**
ANG/EPIS–Episcopal	2	59	81	106	0.3	0.5
Bahá'í	0	NR	8	8	0.0	0.0
BAPT–Amer Bapt USA	1	35	103	122	0.3	0.6
BAPT–Reg Bapt Gen As	1	NR	NR	NR	-	-
BAPT–So Bapt Conv	2	60	391	463	1.1	2.2
Catholic	6	NR	NR	7,243	17.5	34.5
CGOD–Ch God (Ander)	1	74	NR	74	0.2	0.4
Ch of Nazarene	1	69	56	249	0.6	1.2
Chr & Miss Al	1	135	70	200	0.5	1.0
CHR–Chr Ch (Disc)	1	0	47	56	0.1	0.3
CHR–Chs of Christ	2	60	54	68	0.2	0.3
Jehovah's Witness	1	NR	NR	NR	-	-
LUTH–E.L.C.A.	10	1,348	4,370	6,558	15.8	31.2
LUTH–Luth–MO Synod	1	95	193	377	0.9	1.8
LUTH–Nor Amer Luth C	1	NR	NR	NR	-	-
METH–Un Methodist	8	664	1,635	1,957	4.7	9.3
Non-denom Chr Chs	2	215	270	281	0.7	1.3
ORTHE–Orth Ch in Amer	1	25	NR	38	0.1	0.2
PENT–Assemb of God	1	170	85	206	0.5	1.0
PENT–Ch God (Cleve)	1	11	28	33	0.1	0.2
PENT–Ch of God Proph	1	NR	24	28	0.1	0.1
PENT–Pent Ch of God	1	70	NR	109	0.3	0.5
PRES–Presb Ch (USA)	2	85	167	198	0.5	0.9
Un Breth in Cr	2	298	181	254	0.6	1.2
Un C of Christ	5	630	2,022	2,392	5.8	11.4
PAULDING	**43**	**2,598**	**4,002**	**10,250**	**52.3**	**100.0**
Ap Chr Ch-Amer	1	520	260	520	2.7	5.1
Bahá'í	0	NR	2	2	0.0	0.0
BAPT–Reg Bapt Gen As	1	NR	NR	NR	-	-
BAPT–So Bapt Conv	1	135	200	248	1.3	2.4
Catholic	4	NR	NR	4,532	23.1	44.2
CGOD–Ch God (Ander)	2	138	NR	138	0.7	1.3
Ch of Nazarene	4	370	449	722	3.7	7.0
CHR–Chr Ch (Disc)	1	110	323	400	2.0	3.9
CHR–Chr Chs & Chs Cr	2	NR	110	136	0.7	1.3
CHR–Chs of Christ	1	70	75	100	0.5	1.0
Christian Un	1	NR	NR	NR	-	-
Jehovah's Witness	1	NR	NR	NR	-	-
LUTH–E.L.C.A.	2	141	502	583	3.0	5.7
LUTH–Luth–MO Synod	1	62	193	282	1.4	2.8
LUTH–Nor Amer Luth C	1	NR	NR	NR	-	-
METH–Un Methodist	11	725	1,267	1,834	9.4	17.9

NR–Not Reported   - Represents no adherents reported.   Percentages may not total 100 due to rounding.

Table 3: Religious Congregations by County and Group: 2010

Religious Group	Number of Congrega-tions	Number of Attendees	Number of Communicant, Confirmed, or Full Members	Adherents: Number of Adherents	Adherents: % of Total Pop.	Adherents: % of Total Adh.
Non-denom Chr Chs	4	265	305	361	1.8	3.5
PENT–Ch God (Cleve)	1	12	99	123	0.6	1.2
PRES–Evan Presby Ch	1	NR	96	119	0.6	1.2
PRES–Presb Ch (USA)	2	25	58	72	0.4	0.7
Un C of Christ	1	25	63	78	0.4	0.8
PERRY	**75**	**3,115**	**4,934**	**9,503**	**26.4**	**100.0**
Bahá'í	0	NR	1	1	0.0	0.0
BAPT–Amer Bapt USA	1	52	50	62	0.2	0.7
BAPT–Free Will Bapt	1	NR	67	83	0.2	0.9
BAPT–So Bapt Conv	4	461	580	721	2.0	7.6
BRETH–Ch of Brethren	1	40	108	134	0.4	1.4
Catholic	6	NR	NR	3,000	8.3	31.6
CGOD–Ch God (Ander)	1	35	NR	35	0.1	0.4
Ch Christ Chr Union	2	NR	NR	NR	-	-
Ch of Nazarene	1	92	211	211	0.6	2.2
CHR–Chr Ch (Disc)	2	0	0	0	0.0	0.0
CHR–Chr Chs & Chs Cr	1	NR	0	0	0.0	0.0
CHR–Chs of Christ	6	280	269	350	1.0	3.7
Christian Un	2	NR	NR	NR	-	-
Jehovah's Witness	2	NR	NR	NR	-	-
LUTH–E.L.C.A.	4	191	479	646	1.8	6.8
LUTH–Nor Amer Luth C	1	NR	NR	NR	-	-
MENN–Amish Undif	1	NR	17	50	0.1	0.5
MENN–Menn Chr Fell	1	83	42	83	0.2	0.9
METH–Free Methodist	1	29	30	30	0.1	0.3
METH–Un Methodist	19	800	1,641	2,472	6.9	26.0
METH–Wesleyan	2	74	38	96	0.3	1.0
Non-denom Chr Chs	6	680	900	950	2.6	10.0
PENT–Un Pent Ch Intl	3	NR	NR	NR	-	-
PRES–Presb Ch (USA)	2	72	106	132	0.4	1.4
Un Breth in Cr	2	97	103	84	0.2	0.9
Un C of Christ	3	129	292	363	1.0	3.8
PICKAWAY	**72**	**4,939**	**7,652**	**11,584**	**20.8**	**100.0**
ANG/EPIS–Anglican NA	1	NR	NR	NR	-	-
ANG/EPIS–Episcopal	1	67	134	136	0.2	1.2
Bahá'í	0	NR	6	6	0.0	0.1
BAPT–Ind Bapt Flwsp Intl	1	NR	NR	NR	-	-
BAPT–Reg Bapt Gen As	1	NR	NR	NR	-	-
BAPT–So Bapt Conv	4	368	1,055	1,284	2.3	11.1
BRETH–Ch of Brethren	1	0	69	84	0.2	0.7
Catholic	2	NR	NR	1,750	3.1	15.1
CGOD–Ch God (Ander)	2	122	NR	122	0.2	1.1
Ch Christ Chr Union	7	NR	NR	NR	-	-
Ch of Nazarene	3	694	672	873	1.6	7.5
CHR–Chr Chs & Chs Cr	3	NR	265	322	0.6	2.8
CHR–Chs of Christ	1	175	193	288	0.5	2.5
FRND–Fr Gen Cf	1	NR	0	0	0.0	0.0
Jehovah's Witness	1	NR	NR	NR	-	-
LUTH–E.L.C.A.	4	487	889	1,160	2.1	10.0
MENN–Amish Undif	1	NR	20	53	0.1	0.5
METH–AME	1	0	150	182	0.3	1.6
METH–Free Methodist	1	28	2	28	0.1	0.2
METH–Un Methodist	24	1,892	2,882	3,641	6.5	31.4
Non-denom Chr Chs	6	560	750	800	1.4	6.9
PENT–Assemb of God	1	259	75	259	0.5	2.2
PENT–Ch God (Cleve)	2	134	195	237	0.4	2.0
PENT–Un Pent Ch Intl	1	NR	NR	NR	-	-
PRES–Presb Ch (USA)	2	153	295	359	0.6	3.1
PIKE	**55**	**1,757**	**4,396**	**5,681**	**19.8**	**100.0**
Bahá'í	0	NR	7	7	0.0	0.1
BAPT–Enterprise Bapt Assoc	1	NR	NR	NR	-	-
BAPT–Free Will Bapt	2	NR	134	165	0.6	2.9
BAPT–Ref Bapt Ch	1	NR	NR	NR	-	-
BAPT–So Bapt Conv	2	340	2,012	2,484	8.7	43.7
Catholic	1	NR	NR	275	1.0	4.8
Ch Christ Chr Union	10	NR	NR	NR	-	-
Ch of Nazarene	1	26	35	35	0.1	0.6
CHR–Chr Chs & Chs Cr	2	NR	175	216	0.8	3.8
CHR–Chs of Christ	4	316	256	372	1.3	6.5
Christian Un	9	NR	NR	NR	-	-

Religious Group	Number of Congrega-tions	Number of Attendees	Number of Communicant, Confirmed, or Full Members	Adherents: Number of Adherents	Adherents: % of Total Pop.	Adherents: % of Total Adh.
Jehovah's Witness	1	NR	NR	NR	-	-
MENN–Amish Undif	1	NR	40	97	0.3	1.7
METH–AME	1	0	150	185	0.6	3.3
METH–Un Methodist	9	433	603	791	2.8	13.9
Non-denom Chr Chs	8	557	795	821	2.9	14.5
PENT–Ch God (Cleve)	1	16	74	91	0.3	1.6
PRES–Presb Ch (USA)	1	69	115	142	0.5	2.5
PORTAGE	**136**	**10,305**	**17,507**	**44,659**	**27.7**	**100.0**
ANG/EPIS–Anglican NA	1	NR	NR	NR	-	-
ANG/EPIS–Episcopal	2	139	294	395	0.2	0.9
Bahá'í	0	NR	25	25	0.0	0.1
BAPT–Amer Bapt USA	1	90	175	207	0.1	0.5
BAPT–Free Will Bapt	1	NR	67	79	0.0	0.2
BAPT–Ind Bapt Flwsp Intl	1	NR	NR	NR	-	-
BAPT–NBC USA	1	0	0	0	0.0	0.0
BAPT–Reg Bapt Gen As	3	NR	NR	NR	-	-
BAPT–So Bapt Conv	4	156	410	486	0.3	1.1
BRETH–Breth in Chr	1	NR	NR	NR	-	-
BRETH–Ch of Brethren	1	20	38	45	0.0	0.1
Catholic	10	NR	NR	19,905	12.3	44.6
CGOD–Ch God (Ander)	4	385	NR	385	0.2	0.9
Ch of Nazarene	4	219	266	373	0.2	0.8
Chr & Miss Al	2	243	204	467	0.3	1.0
CHR–Chr Ch (Disc)	6	366	1,517	1,797	1.1	4.0
CHR–Chr Chs & Chs Cr	2	NR	485	575	0.4	1.3
CHR–Chs of Christ	4	322	271	391	0.2	0.9
Evan Free Ch	1	100	NR	100	0.1	0.2
FRND–Evan Fr Ch Intl	2	190	79	94	0.1	0.2
FRND–Fr Gen Cf	1	NR	21	25	0.0	0.1
Grace Gosp Fel	1	NR	NR	NR	-	-
Int Cou Comm Ch	2	NR	NR	NR	-	-
Jehovah's Witness	4	NR	NR	NR	-	-
LDS–L-D Saints	2	NR	NR	847	0.5	1.9
LUTH–E.L.C.A.	2	283	720	960	0.6	2.1
LUTH–Luth–MO Synod	4	339	793	1,004	0.6	2.2
MENN–Amish Undif	2	NR	163	387	0.2	0.9
MENN–Mennonite USA	1	71	46	55	0.0	0.1
METH–AME	2	65	292	346	0.2	0.8
METH–Free Methodist	1	85	71	85	0.1	0.2
METH–Prim Meth Ch	1	NR	NR	NR	-	-
METH–Un Methodist	15	1,815	4,168	5,993	3.7	13.4
Muslim Est	1	134	NR	308	0.2	0.7
Non-denom Chr Chs	21	3,226	4,135	4,693	2.9	10.5
ORTHE–Orth Ch in Amer	2	147	NR	222	0.1	0.5
PENT–Assemb of God	4	664	331	828	0.5	1.9
PENT–Ch God (Cleve)	2	243	335	397	0.2	0.9
PENT–Ch God Mtn Asm	1	NR	NR	NR	-	-
PENT–Ch Lord Jesus Apos	1	NR	NR	NR	-	-
PENT–COGIC	3	80	310	367	0.2	0.8
PRES–Presb Ch (USA)	1	131	154	182	0.1	0.4
PRES–Ref Pres of NA	1	30	20	24	0.0	0.1
Salvation Army	1	25	28	80	0.0	0.2
Sev Day Adv	1	20	36	41	0.0	0.1
Un C of Christ	7	604	1,855	2,198	1.4	4.9
Unit Univ	1	113	198	293	0.2	0.7
PREBLE	**79**	**4,880**	**9,339**	**13,078**	**30.9**	**100.0**
BAPT–Ind Bapt Flwsp Intl	3	NR	NR	NR	-	-
BAPT–So Bapt Conv	10	808	2,660	3,267	7.7	25.0
BRETH–Brethren (Ash)	2	NR	160	196	0.5	1.5
BRETH–Ch of Brethren	5	584	820	1,007	2.4	7.7
BRETH–Grace Breth	1	NR	NR	NR	-	-
Catholic	3	NR	NR	845	2.0	6.5
CGOD–Ch God (Ander)	3	465	NR	465	1.1	3.6
Ch of Nazarene	1	65	106	106	0.3	0.8
CHR–Chr Chs & Chs Cr	2	NR	125	154	0.4	1.2
CHR–Chs of Christ	2	80	86	131	0.3	1.0
FRND–Central Yr Mtg	1	25	0	0	0.0	0.0
FRND–Fr Un Mtg	1	NR	22	27	0.1	0.2
Jehovah's Witness	1	NR	NR	NR	-	-
LDS–L-D Saints	1	NR	NR	287	0.7	2.2
LUTH–E.L.C.A.	6	401	1,079	1,473	3.5	11.3

NR–Not Reported - Represents no adherents reported. Percentages may not total 100 due to rounding.

Table 3: Religious Congregations by County and Group: 2010

Religious Group	Number of Congrega-tions	Number of Attendees	Number of Communicant, Confirmed, or Full Members	Adherents: Number of Adherents	Adherents: % of Total Pop.	Adherents: % of Total Adh.
LUTH–Nor Amer Luth C	1	NR	NR	NR	-	-
METH–Un Methodist	12	972	1,439	1,781	4.2	13.6
Non-denom Chr Chs	9	820	1,050	1,145	2.7	8.8
PENT–Ch God (Cleve)	4	158	382	469	1.1	3.6
PENT–Un Pent Ch Intl	1	NR	NR	NR	-	-
PRES–Presb Ch (USA)	3	219	489	601	1.4	4.6
Un C of Christ	6	263	889	1,092	2.6	8.3
Unit Univ	1	20	32	32	0.1	0.2
PUTNAM	**49**	**3,415**	**4,669**	**27,086**	**78.5**	**100.0**
BAPT–So Bapt Conv	2	89	217	272	0.8	1.0
BRETH–Ch of Brethren	1	261	477	598	1.7	2.2
Catholic	11	NR	NR	20,794	60.3	76.8
CGOD–Ch God (Ander)	2	387	NR	387	1.1	1.4
Ch Christ Chr Union	1	NR	NR	NR	-	-
Ch of Nazarene	2	140	118	245	0.7	0.9
CHR–Chr Ch (Disc)	1	84	168	211	0.6	0.8
CHR–Chr Chs & Chs Cr	1	NR	50	63	0.2	0.2
LUTH–E.L.C.A.	3	212	400	539	1.6	2.0
LUTH–Nor Amer Luth C	1	NR	NR	NR	-	-
MENN–Mennonite USA	3	762	726	911	2.6	3.4
METH–Un Methodist	10	602	1,398	1,719	5.0	6.3
Missionary Ch	2	130	117	130	0.4	0.5
Non-denom Chr Chs	5	490	760	834	2.4	3.1
PENT–Assemb of God	1	112	109	112	0.3	0.4
PENT–Pent Ch of God	1	70	NR	109	0.3	0.4
PRES–Presb Ch (USA)	2	76	129	162	0.5	0.6
RICHLAND	**198**	**22,050**	**30,451**	**52,681**	**42.3**	**100.0**
ANG/EPIS–Episcopal	2	111	340	438	0.4	0.8
Ap Chr Ch-Amer	1	375	170	375	0.3	0.7
Bahá'í	1	NR	72	72	0.1	0.1
BAPT–Amer Bapt USA	2	148	259	313	0.3	0.6
BAPT–Consrv Bapt	1	NR	NR	NR	-	-
BAPT–Converge/BGC	2	2,075	NR	2,490	2.0	4.7
BAPT–Free Will Bapt	9	NR	603	728	0.6	1.4
BAPT–Ind Bapt Flwsp Intl	3	NR	NR	NR	-	-
BAPT–NBC USA	2	300	677	817	0.7	1.6
BAPT–So Bapt Conv	8	501	983	1,186	1.0	2.3
BRETH–Ch of Brethren	2	68	79	95	0.1	0.2
BRETH–Grace Breth	2	NR	NR	NR	-	-
Calv Chpl	1	NR	NR	NR	-	-
Catholic	5	NR	NR	9,658	7.8	18.3
CGOD–Ch God (Ander)	3	421	NR	421	0.3	0.8
CGOD–Ches God-Gen Con	1	87	125	151	0.1	0.3
Ch Christ Chr Union	2	NR	NR	NR	-	-
Ch Cr, Scientst	1	NR	NR	NR	-	-
Ch of Nazarene	4	301	398	514	0.4	1.0
Chr & Miss Al	5	716	469	1,104	0.9	2.1
CHR–Chr Ch (Disc)	3	192	512	618	0.5	1.2
CHR–Chr Chs & Chs Cr	5	NR	907	1,095	0.9	2.1
CHR–Chs of Christ	5	227	236	324	0.3	0.6
Christian Brethren	1	NR	NR	NR	-	-
CONG–Cong Chr, NA	3	NR	1,059	1,278	1.0	2.4
CONG–Consrv Cong Chr	1	25	35	42	0.0	0.1
Evan Ch	1	NR	NR	NR	-	-
Evan Free Ch	2	280	NR	280	0.2	0.5
FRND–Evan Fr Ch Intl	1	31	28	34	0.0	0.1
Jain	1	NR	NR	NR	-	-
Jehovah's Witness	3	NR	NR	NR	-	-
JUD–Reform	1	27	48	130	0.1	0.2
LDS–Comm of Christ	1	NR	133	133	0.1	0.3
LDS–L-D Saints	1	NR	NR	631	0.5	1.2
LUTH–E.L.C.A.	14	1,071	2,520	3,015	2.4	5.7
LUTH–Luth Cong Msn Chr	2	299	779	940	0.8	1.8
LUTH–Luth–MO Synod	1	20	40	42	0.0	0.1
LUTH–Nor Amer Luth C	5	NR	NR	NR	-	-
MENN–Amish Undif	3	NR	183	464	0.4	0.9
METH–AME	1	80	151	182	0.1	0.3
METH–Free Methodist	1	150	113	150	0.1	0.3
METH–Un Methodist	18	1,516	3,836	5,072	4.1	9.6
METH–Wesleyan	3	431	242	560	0.4	1.1
Muslim Est	1	30	NR	50	0.0	0.1

Religious Group	Number of Congrega-tions	Number of Attendees	Number of Communicant, Confirmed, or Full Members	Adherents: Number of Adherents	Adherents: % of Total Pop.	Adherents: % of Total Adh.
Non-denom Chr Chs	31	10,012	11,412	12,988	10.4	24.7
ORTHE–Greek Orthodox	1	45	NR	100	0.1	0.2
PENT–Assemb of God	2	559	20	1,098	0.9	2.1
PENT–Ch God (Cleve)	3	528	1,365	1,648	1.3	3.1
PENT–Ch of God Proph	1	NR	96	116	0.1	0.2
PENT–COGIC	2	400	550	664	0.5	1.3
PENT–Full Gosp Bapt	2	NR	NR	NR	-	-
PENT–Int Foursq Gos	2	126	108	130	0.1	0.2
PENT–Int Pent C Chr	1	0	0	80	0.1	0.2
PENT–Intl Pent Holiness	1	7	13	16	0.0	0.0
PENT–Open Bible Std	1	112	NR	112	0.1	0.2
PENT–Un Pent Ch Intl	1	NR	NR	NR	-	-
PRES–Orth Pres Ch	1	97	134	162	0.1	0.3
PRES–Presb Ch (USA)	7	223	736	888	0.7	1.7
Salvation Army	1	44	57	133	0.1	0.3
Sev Day Adv	2	178	308	355	0.3	0.7
Un C of Christ	2	185	607	733	0.6	1.4
Unit Univ	1	52	48	56	0.0	0.1
Unity Ch	1	NR	NR	NR	-	-
ROSS	**116**	**7,936**	**13,470**	**20,070**	**25.7**	**100.0**
ANG/EPIS–Anglican NA	1	NR	NR	NR	-	-
ANG/EPIS–Episcopal	1	35	93	93	0.1	0.5
Bahá'í	0	NR	2	2	0.0	0.0
BAPT–Amer Bapt USA	1	465	994	1,200	1.5	6.0
BAPT–Enterprise Bapt Assoc	1	NR	NR	NR	-	-
BAPT–Free Will Bapt	2	NR	134	162	0.2	0.8
BAPT–Ref Bapt Ch	1	NR	NR	NR	-	-
BAPT–Reg Bapt Gen As	1	NR	NR	NR	-	-
BAPT–So Bapt Conv	4	560	2,002	2,416	3.1	12.0
BRETH–Ch of Brethren	1	0	36	43	0.1	0.2
Catholic	2	NR	NR	2,750	3.5	13.7
CGOD–Ch God (Ander)	3	378	NR	378	0.5	1.9
Ch Christ Chr Union	14	NR	NR	NR	-	-
Ch Cr, Scientst	1	NR	NR	NR	-	-
Ch of Nazarene	2	141	275	275	0.4	1.4
CHR–Chr Ch (Disc)	1	42	76	92	0.1	0.5
CHR–Chr Chs & Chs Cr	3	NR	445	537	0.7	2.7
CHR–Chs of Christ	2	175	153	214	0.3	1.1
Christian Un	6	NR	NR	NR	-	-
FRND–Fr Un Mtg	1	NR	2	2	0.0	0.0
Jehovah's Witness	2	NR	NR	NR	-	-
LDS–Comm of Christ	1	NR	118	118	0.2	0.6
LDS–L-D Saints	1	NR	NR	418	0.5	2.1
LUTH–E.L.C.A.	1	162	358	487	0.6	2.4
LUTH–Luth–MO Synod	1	54	90	125	0.2	0.6
MENN–Amish Undif	1	NR	35	103	0.1	0.5
MENN–Menn Chr Fell	1	58	24	58	0.1	0.3
METH–AME	2	40	150	181	0.2	0.9
METH–Un Methodist	23	1,712	3,052	4,139	5.3	20.6
METH–Wesleyan	2	495	579	644	0.8	3.2
Non-denom Chr Chs	15	2,450	3,050	3,302	4.2	16.5
PENT–Assemb of God	2	158	76	186	0.2	0.9
PENT–Ch God (Cleve)	4	256	384	463	0.6	2.3
PENT–COGIC	1	75	90	109	0.1	0.5
PENT–Int Pent C Chr	1	31	36	50	0.1	0.2
PENT–Un Pent Ch Intl	1	NR	NR	NR	-	-
PENT–Vineyard	1	175	200	241	0.3	1.2
PRES–Presb Ch (USA)	5	302	695	839	1.1	4.2
Salvation Army	1	39	89	172	0.2	0.9
Sev Day Adv	1	90	156	179	0.2	0.9
Un C of Christ	1	43	76	92	0.1	0.5
SANDUSKY	**81**	**6,482**	**11,951**	**28,891**	**47.4**	**100.0**
ANG/EPIS–Episcopal	2	70	132	267	0.4	0.9
Bahá'í	0	NR	7	7	0.0	0.0
BAPT–Amer Bapt Assn	1	NR	85	104	0.2	0.4
BAPT–Free Will Bapt	1	NR	67	82	0.1	0.3
BAPT–Ind Bapt Flwsp Intl	1	NR	NR	NR	-	-
BAPT–So Bapt Conv	4	134	235	288	0.5	1.0
BRETH–Brethren (Ash)	1	NR	80	98	0.2	0.3
BRETH–Grace Breth	1	NR	NR	NR	-	-
Catholic	6	NR	NR	12,396	20.3	42.9

NR–Not Reported - Represents no adherents reported. Percentages may not total 100 due to rounding.

Table 3: Religious Congregations by County and Group: 2010

Religious Group	Number of Congregations	Number of Attendees	Number of Communicant, Confirmed, or Full Members	Adherents: Number of Adherents	Adherents: % of Total Pop.	Adherents: % of Total Adh.
Ch of Nazarene	2	112	140	263	0.4	0.9
Chr & Miss Al	1	174	153	311	0.5	1.1
CHR–Chr Ch (Disc)	1	41	94	115	0.2	0.4
CHR–Chs of Christ	3	118	118	152	0.2	0.5
Jehovah's Witness	1	NR	NR	NR	-	-
LDS–L-D Saints	1	NR	NR	341	0.6	1.2
LUTH–E.L.C.A.	10	1,349	3,730	5,154	8.5	17.8
LUTH–Luth Cong Msn Chr	1	160	830	1,019	1.7	3.5
LUTH–Nor Amer Luth C	2	NR	NR	NR	-	-
MENN–Mennonite USA	1	24	19	23	0.0	0.1
METH–AME	1	12	20	25	0.0	0.1
METH–Un Methodist	15	1,323	2,902	3,744	6.1	13.0
Missionary Ch	1	45	37	45	0.1	0.2
New Apost Ch	1	NR	NR	NR	-	-
Non-denom Chr Chs	8	1,972	1,843	2,484	4.1	8.6
PENT–Assemb of God	4	247	148	365	0.6	1.3
PENT–Ch God (Cleve)	2	53	72	88	0.1	0.3
PENT–COGIC	1	150	200	245	0.4	0.8
PENT–Un Pent Ch Intl	1	NR	NR	NR	-	-
PENT–Vineyard	1	200	250	307	0.5	1.1
PRES–Presb Ch (USA)	3	160	333	409	0.7	1.4
Sev Day Adv	1	6	11	13	0.0	0.0
Un C of Christ	2	132	445	546	0.9	1.9
SCIOTO	**166**	**7,027**	**12,605**	**19,646**	**24.7**	**100.0**
ANG/EPIS–Episcopal	1	77	126	210	0.3	1.1
Bahá'í	0	NR	4	4	0.0	0.0
BAPT–Amer Bapt USA	1	66	73	89	0.1	0.5
BAPT–Enterprise Bapt Assoc	2	NR	NR	NR	-	-
BAPT–Free Will Bapt	24	NR	1,608	1,951	2.5	9.9
BAPT–Ind Bapt Flwsp Intl	4	NR	NR	NR	-	-
BAPT–Natl Mis Bapt Conv	1	85	85	103	0.1	0.5
BAPT–Reg Bapt Gen As	4	NR	NR	NR	-	-
BAPT–So Bapt Conv	2	110	132	160	0.2	0.8
Calv Chpl	1	NR	NR	NR	-	-
Catholic	7	NR	NR	3,250	4.1	16.5
CGOD–Ch God (Ander)	3	0	NR	0	0.0	0.0
CGOD–Ches God-Gen Con	1	43	170	206	0.3	1.0
Ch Christ Chr Union	10	NR	NR	NR	-	-
Ch of Nazarene	8	1,093	1,158	1,337	1.7	6.8
Chr & Miss Al	1	NR	NR	NR	-	-
CHR–Chr Ch (Disc)	1	30	96	116	0.1	0.6
CHR–Chr Chs & Chs Cr	7	NR	1,232	1,495	1.9	7.6
CHR–Chs of Christ	6	437	369	510	0.6	2.6
Christian Un	3	NR	NR	NR	-	-
Jehovah's Witness	2	NR	NR	NR	-	-
JUD–Reform	1	7	13	35	0.0	0.2
LDS–Comm of Christ	4	NR	472	472	0.6	2.4
LDS–L-D Saints	1	NR	NR	404	0.5	2.1
LUTH–E.L.C.A.	2	100	269	371	0.5	1.9
MENN–Mennonite USA	1	52	40	49	0.1	0.2
METH–AME	1	0	100	121	0.2	0.6
METH–Un Methodist	33	1,373	2,168	2,950	3.7	15.0
METH–Wesleyan	2	52	70	68	0.1	0.3
Non-denom Chr Chs	16	2,910	3,020	3,813	4.8	19.4
PENT–Assemb of God	1	33	23	100	0.1	0.5
PENT–Ch God (Cleve)	5	220	557	676	0.9	3.4
PENT–Ch of God Proph	1	NR	23	28	0.0	0.1
PENT–Int Pent C Chr	1	74	57	110	0.1	0.6
PENT–Un Pent Ch Intl	2	NR	NR	NR	-	-
PRES–Presb Ch (USA)	3	138	422	512	0.6	2.6
Salvation Army	1	22	86	230	0.3	1.2
Sev Day Adv	1	53	92	106	0.1	0.5
Un C of Christ	1	52	140	170	0.2	0.9
SENECA	**84**	**4,064**	**8,946**	**30,756**	**54.2**	**100.0**
ANG/EPIS–Episcopal	1	32	60	81	0.1	0.3
Bahá'í	0	NR	4	4	0.0	0.0
BAPT–Amer Bapt USA	1	15	38	46	0.1	0.1
BAPT–Free Will Bapt	1	NR	67	82	0.1	0.3
BAPT–Ind Bapt Flwsp Intl	2	NR	NR	NR	-	-
BAPT–NBC USA	1	90	125	153	0.3	0.5
BAPT–Reg Bapt Gen As	1	NR	NR	NR	-	-
BAPT–So Bapt Conv	2	81	146	178	0.3	0.6
BRETH–Ch of Brethren	1	11	26	32	0.1	0.1
Catholic	8	NR	NR	18,803	33.1	61.1
CGOD–Ches God-Gen Con	1	85	111	136	0.2	0.4
Ch of Nazarene	2	185	303	342	0.6	1.1
Chr & Miss Al	1	75	43	106	0.2	0.3
CHR–Chr Ch (Disc)	2	114	243	297	0.5	1.0
CHR–Chr Chs & Chs Cr	1	NR	395	483	0.9	1.6
CHR–Chs of Christ	1	60	77	100	0.2	0.3
Jehovah's Witness	2	NR	NR	NR	-	-
LDS–L-D Saints	1	NR	NR	218	0.4	0.7
LUTH–E.L.C.A.	4	354	1,061	1,529	2.7	5.0
LUTH–Luth Cong Msn Chr	1	125	NR	NR	-	-
LUTH–Luth–MO Synod	1	65	110	160	0.3	0.5
METH–AME	1	0	350	428	0.8	1.4
METH–Un Methodist	18	1,169	2,708	3,159	5.6	10.3
Non-denom Chr Chs	1	25	25	31	0.1	0.1
PENT–Assemb of God	2	236	142	511	0.9	1.7
PENT–Ch God (Cleve)	3	127	167	204	0.4	0.7
PENT–Ch of God Proph	1	NR	31	38	0.1	0.1
PENT–Int Foursq Gos	2	49	54	66	0.1	0.2
PENT–Pent Ch of God	2	140	NR	217	0.4	0.7
PENT–Un Pent Ch Intl	1	NR	NR	NR	-	-
PRES–Presb Ch (USA)	2	144	269	329	0.6	1.1
Salvation Army	1	30	69	163	0.3	0.5
Un Breth in Cr	1	93	46	80	0.1	0.3
Un C of Christ	14	759	2,276	2,780	4.9	9.0
SHELBY	**65**	**7,040**	**10,278**	**28,254**	**57.2**	**100.0**
ANG/EPIS–Episcopal	1	39	51	52	0.1	0.2
Bahá'í	0	NR	6	6	0.0	0.0
BAPT–Amer Bapt USA	2	146	332	421	0.9	1.5
BAPT–NBC USA	1	40	100	127	0.3	0.4
BAPT–Reg Bapt Gen As	1	NR	NR	NR	-	-
BAPT–So Bapt Conv	4	249	656	832	1.7	2.9
BRETH–Ch of Brethren	1	43	86	109	0.2	0.4
Catholic	7	NR	NR	13,353	27.0	47.3
CGOD–Ch God (Ander)	1	220	NR	220	0.4	0.8
Ch of Nazarene	2	223	306	440	0.9	1.6
CHR–Chr Ch (Disc)	1	0	85	108	0.2	0.4
CONG–Midw Cong Chr Fel	1	55	115	146	0.3	0.5
FRND–Fr Gen Cf	1	NR	7	9	0.0	0.0
Jehovah's Witness	1	NR	NR	NR	-	-
LDS–L-D Saints	1	NR	NR	318	0.6	1.1
LUTH–E.L.C.A.	7	998	2,443	3,456	7.0	12.2
LUTH–Luth–MO Synod	1	75	124	160	0.3	0.6
LUTH–Nor Amer Luth C	1	NR	NR	NR	-	-
METH–Un Methodist	11	1,841	2,338	2,901	5.9	10.3
METH–Wesleyan	1	46	26	60	0.1	0.2
Missionary Ch	1	33	35	35	0.1	0.1
Non-denom Chr Chs	6	2,310	1,912	2,971	6.0	10.5
PENT–Assemb of God	1	100	45	100	0.2	0.4
PENT–Ch God (Cleve)	1	66	312	396	0.8	1.4
PENT–Ch God Mtn Asm	1	NR	NR	NR	-	-
PENT–COGIC	1	140	199	252	0.5	0.9
PENT–Open Bible Std	1	0	NR	0	0.0	0.0
PENT–Un Pent Ch Intl	1	NR	NR	NR	-	-
PRES–Presb Ch (USA)	1	60	168	213	0.4	0.8
Salvation Army	1	62	79	488	1.0	1.7
Un C of Christ	4	294	853	1,081	2.2	3.8
STARK	**436**	**49,243**	**90,406**	**176,398**	**47.0**	**100.0**
ANG/EPIS–Episcopal	5	433	905	1,246	0.3	0.7
Bahá'í	0	NR	25	25	0.0	0.0
BAPT–Amer Bapt USA	8	950	2,492	3,014	0.8	1.7
BAPT–Consrv Bapt	1	NR	NR	NR	-	-
BAPT–Free Will Bapt	1	NR	67	81	0.0	0.0
BAPT–Ind Bapt Flwsp Intl	2	NR	NR	NR	-	-
BAPT–Natl Mis Bapt Conv	1	0	150	181	0.0	0.1
BAPT–NBC USA	6	925	1,875	2,268	0.6	1.3
BAPT–Prog NBC	1	180	200	242	0.1	0.1
BAPT–Reg Bapt Gen As	6	NR	NR	NR	-	-
BAPT–So Bapt Conv	6	265	563	681	0.2	0.4

NR–Not Reported   - Represents no adherents reported.   Percentages may not total 100 due to rounding.

Table 3: Religious Congregations by County and Group: 2010

Religious Group	Number of Congrega-tions	Number of Attendees	Number of Communicant, Confirmed, or Full Members	Adherents		
				Number of Adherents	% of Total Pop.	% of Total Adh.
BRETH–Breth in Chr	3	NR	NR	NR	-	-
BRETH–Brethren (Ash)	2	NR	160	193	0.1	0.1
BRETH–Ch of Brethren	6	352	716	866	0.2	0.5
BRETH–Grace Breth	3	NR	NR	NR	-	-
Catholic	28	NR	NR	55,831	14.9	31.7
CGOD–Ch God (Ander)	12	1,016	NR	1,016	0.3	0.6
Ch Cr, Scientst	2	NR	NR	NR	-	-
Ch of Nazarene	10	1,056	1,873	2,025	0.5	1.1
Chr & Miss Al	4	484	370	723	0.2	0.4
CHR–Chr Ch (Disc)	4	508	1,570	1,899	0.5	1.1
CHR–Chr Chs & Chs Cr	19	NR	9,169	11,088	3.0	6.3
CHR–Chs of Christ	15	1,787	1,991	2,446	0.7	1.4
CONG–Cong Chr, NA	1	NR	304	368	0.1	0.2
CONG–Consrv Cong Chr	3	166	379	458	0.1	0.3
Evan Cong Ch	1	NR	58	70	0.0	0.0
FRND–Evan Fr Ch Intl	5	2,677	1,634	1,976	0.5	1.1
Grace Gosp Fel	2	NR	NR	NR	-	-
HINDU–Post Ren	1	NR	NR	25	0.0	0.0
Jehovah's Witness	10	NR	NR	NR	-	-
JUD–Conserv	1	100	112	302	0.1	0.2
JUD–Orth	1	133	50	185	0.0	0.1
JUD–Reform	1	215	380	1,026	0.3	0.6
LDS–L-D Saints	3	NR	NR	1,695	0.5	1.0
LUTH–E.L.C.A.	23	2,786	7,532	9,685	2.6	5.5
LUTH–Luth–MO Synod	2	537	945	1,371	0.4	0.8
MENN–Amish Undif	3	NR	178	447	0.1	0.3
MENN–Beachy Amish-Menn	2	143	97	143	0.0	0.1
MENN–Cons Menn Conf	3	533	493	596	0.2	0.3
MENN–Mennonite USA	7	947	1,281	1,549	0.4	0.9
METH–A.W.M.C.	7	257	121	275	0.1	0.2
METH–AME	3	130	450	544	0.1	0.3
METH–AME Zion	1	0	350	423	0.1	0.2
METH–C.M.E.	1	0	100	121	0.0	0.1
METH–Free Methodist	2	229	164	229	0.1	0.1
METH–Un Methodist	55	5,737	15,334	18,955	5.0	10.7
Muslim Est	2	268	NR	616	0.2	0.3
New Apost Ch	1	NR	NR	NR	-	-
Non-denom Chr Chs	60	18,979	24,353	27,998	7.5	15.9
ORTHE–Ant Orth of NA	1	100	NR	282	0.1	0.2
ORTHE–Greek Orthodox	3	1,000	NR	4,200	1.1	2.4
ORTHE–Orth Ch in Amer	3	185	NR	350	0.1	0.2
ORTHE–Serb Orth USA	1	40	NR	182	0.0	0.1
PENT–Assemb of God	11	1,126	787	1,568	0.4	0.9
PENT–Ch God (Cleve)	10	1,058	2,500	3,023	0.8	1.7
PENT–Ch of God Proph	1	NR	19	23	0.0	0.0
PENT–COGIC	10	525	1,280	1,548	0.4	0.9
PENT–Int Foursq Gos	4	155	286	346	0.1	0.2
PENT–Int Pent C Chr	1	13	28	49	0.0	0.0
PENT–Open Bible Std	2	120	NR	120	0.0	0.1
PENT–Pent Ch of God	1	70	NR	109	0.0	0.1
PENT–Un Pent Ch Intl	4	NR	NR	NR	-	-
PENT–United Holy Ch	2	NR	NR	NR	-	-
PRES–Presb Ch (USA)	11	1,022	2,874	3,476	0.9	2.0
REF–Fed Ref Ch	1	NR	NR	NR	-	-
Salvation Army	3	176	446	1,293	0.3	0.7
Sev Day Adv	2	98	170	195	0.1	0.1
Un C of Christ	17	1,716	5,538	6,697	1.8	3.8
Unit Univ	1	46	37	55	0.0	0.0
Unity Ch	1	NR	NR	NR	-	-
SUMMIT	**486**	**65,082**	**99,210**	**254,754**	**47.0**	**100.0**
ANG/EPIS–Anglican NA	4	NR	NR	NR	-	-
ANG/EPIS–Episcopal	10	1,490	3,736	5,016	0.9	2.0
Bahá'í	0	NR	71	71	0.0	0.0
BAPT–Amer Bapt USA	8	864	1,815	2,192	0.4	0.9
BAPT–Consrv Bapt	1	NR	NR	NR	-	-
BAPT–Free Will Bapt	3	NR	201	243	0.0	0.1
BAPT–Ind Bapt Flwsp Intl	3	NR	NR	NR	-	-
BAPT–Natl Mis Bapt Conv	2	225	425	513	0.1	0.2
BAPT–NBC Amer	1	200	300	362	0.1	0.1
BAPT–NBC USA	5	815	1,400	1,691	0.3	0.7
BAPT–Prog NBC	3	75	500	604	0.1	0.2
BAPT–Reg Bapt Gen As	8	NR	NR	NR	-	-
BAPT–So Bapt Conv	16	1,158	1,329	1,605	0.3	0.6
BRETH–Ch of Brethren	3	260	454	548	0.1	0.2
BRETH–Grace Breth	5	NR	NR	NR	-	-
BUDD–Mahayana	2	NR	NR	114	0.0	0.0
BUDD–Theravada	1	NR	NR	300	0.1	0.1
BUDD–Vajrayana	2	NR	NR	94	0.0	0.0
Calv Chpl	1	NR	NR	NR	-	-
Catholic	33	NR	NR	116,941	21.6	45.9
CGOD–Ch God (Ander)	8	1,819	NR	1,819	0.3	0.7
Ch Cr, Scientst	2	NR	NR	NR	-	-
Ch of Nazarene	15	1,156	1,772	2,140	0.4	0.8
Chr & Miss Al	13	2,139	1,753	3,831	0.7	1.5
CHR–Chr Ch (Disc)	10	745	2,756	3,329	0.6	1.3
CHR–Chr Chs & Chs Cr	13	NR	3,210	3,877	0.7	1.5
CHR–Chs of Christ	16	1,612	1,741	2,221	0.4	0.9
CONG–Cong Chr, NA	2	NR	630	761	0.1	0.3
Evan Cong Ch	2	NR	252	304	0.1	0.1
Evan Cov Ch	1	60	40	78	0.0	0.0
Evan Free Ch	1	60	NR	60	0.0	0.0
FRND–Evan Fr Ch Intl	3	137	86	104	0.0	0.0
FRND–Fr Gen Cf	1	NR	5	6	0.0	0.0
HINDU–Post Ren	1	NR	NR	77	0.0	0.0
Int Cou Comm Ch	1	NR	NR	NR	-	-
Jehovah's Witness	9	NR	NR	NR	-	-
JUD–Conserv	1	300	337	910	0.2	0.4
JUD–Orth	1	86	100	120	0.0	0.0
JUD–Reform	2	290	511	1,380	0.3	0.5
LDS–Comm of Christ	2	NR	316	316	0.1	0.1
LDS–L-D Saints	3	NR	NR	1,782	0.3	0.7
LUTH–E.L.C.A.	14	1,568	3,795	5,093	0.9	2.0
LUTH–Luth Cong Msn Chr	2	111	294	355	0.1	0.1
LUTH–Luth–MO Synod	12	1,762	3,718	4,679	0.9	1.8
MENN–Mennonite USA	1	22	22	27	0.0	0.0
METH–A.W.M.C.	3	49	22	71	0.0	0.0
METH–AME	4	0	510	616	0.1	0.2
METH–AME Zion	1	150	420	507	0.1	0.2
METH–C.M.E.	2	200	500	604	0.1	0.2
METH–Free Methodist	2	689	517	689	0.1	0.3
METH–Un Methodist	41	5,464	14,539	18,708	3.5	7.3
METH–Wesleyan	2	109	104	141	0.0	0.1
Muslim Est	2	634	NR	1,808	0.3	0.7
New Apost Ch	2	NR	NR	NR	-	-
Non-denom Chr Chs	75	31,574	36,211	43,422	8.0	17.0
ORTHE–Ant Orth of NA	1	140	NR	300	0.1	0.1
ORTHE–Bulgar Orth USA	2	110	NR	205	0.0	0.1
ORTHE–Carp Rus Orth	1	15	NR	25	0.0	0.0
ORTHE–Greek Orthodox	1	375	NR	1,660	0.3	0.7
ORTHE–Macedonian Orth	1	120	NR	240	0.0	0.1
ORTHE–Orth Ch in Amer	2	180	NR	440	0.1	0.2
ORTHE–Serb Orth USA	4	249	NR	1,360	0.3	0.5
PENT–Assemb of God	15	1,754	966	2,962	0.5	1.2
PENT–Ch God (Cleve)	6	448	913	1,103	0.2	0.4
PENT–Ch God Mtn Asm	1	NR	NR	NR	-	-
PENT–Ch of God Proph	1	NR	85	103	0.0	0.0
PENT–COGIC	6	445	1,020	1,232	0.2	0.5
PENT–Full Gosp Bapt	1	NR	NR	NR	-	-
PENT–I F Chr Assmbl	1	NR	NR	NR	-	-
PENT–Int Foursq Gos	1	76	87	105	0.0	0.0
PENT–Int Pent C Chr	1	0	0	175	0.0	0.1
PENT–Open Bible Std	1	27	NR	27	0.0	0.0
PENT–Un Pent Ch Intl	5	NR	NR	NR	-	-
PENT–United Holy Ch	1	NR	NR	NR	-	-
PENT–Vineyard	1	68	68	82	0.0	0.0
PRES–Evan Presby Ch	1	NR	250	302	0.1	0.1
PRES–Presb Ch (USA)	14	1,361	2,518	3,041	0.6	1.2
PRES–Presb Ch Amer	3	395	398	534	0.1	0.2
REF–Christian Ref	1	117	98	118	0.0	0.0
Salvation Army	3	141	283	771	0.1	0.3
Sev Day Adv	5	545	948	1,090	0.2	0.4
Sikh	1	NR	NR	NR	-	-
Un C of Christ	21	2,461	6,934	8,375	1.5	3.3
Unit Univ	1	232	250	371	0.1	0.1
Unity Ch	2	NR	NR	NR	-	-
Zoroastrian	0	NR	NR	4	0.0	0.0

NR–Not Reported - Represents no adherents reported. Percentages may not total 100 due to rounding.

Table 3: Religious Congregations by County and Group: 2010

Religious Group	Number of Congrega-tions	Number of Attendees	Number of Communicant, Confirmed, or Full Members	Adherents: Number of Adherents	Adherents: % of Total Pop.	Adherents: % of Total Adh.
TRUMBULL	**286**	**20,545**	**39,810**	**96,400**	**45.8**	**100.0**
ANG/EPIS–Episcopal	2	168	496	496	0.2	0.5
Bahá'í	1	NR	43	43	0.0	0.0
BAPT–Amer Bapt USA	5	225	519	623	0.3	0.6
BAPT–Converge/BGC	1	75	NR	90	0.0	0.1
BAPT–Free Will Bapt	2	NR	134	161	0.1	0.2
BAPT–Ind Bapt Flwsp Intl	2	NR	NR	NR	-	-
BAPT–Natl Mis Bapt Conv	2	15	165	198	0.1	0.2
BAPT–NBC USA	2	370	510	612	0.3	0.6
BAPT–Reg Bapt Gen As	6	NR	NR	NR	-	-
BAPT–So Bapt Conv	12	554	1,600	1,919	0.9	2.0
BRETH–Ch of Brethren	1	81	86	103	0.0	0.1
Catholic	22	NR	NR	39,749	18.9	41.2
CGOD–Ch God (Ander)	9	675	NR	675	0.3	0.7
Ch of Nazarene	9	855	1,218	1,634	0.8	1.7
Chr & Miss Al	2	914	529	1,232	0.6	1.3
CHR–Chr Ch (Disc)	14	1,152	3,950	4,739	2.3	4.9
CHR–Chr Chs & Chs Cr	6	NR	1,375	1,650	0.8	1.7
CHR–Chs of Christ	3	187	173	210	0.1	0.2
CONG–Cong Chr, NA	1	NR	270	324	0.2	0.3
Evan Cong Ch	1	NR	52	62	0.0	0.1
HINDU–Trad Temples	1	NR	NR	65	0.0	0.1
Int Cou Comm Ch	1	NR	NR	NR	-	-
Jehovah's Witness	7	NR	NR	NR	-	-
JUD–Conserv	1	56	63	170	0.1	0.2
LDS–L-D Saints	2	NR	NR	1,605	0.8	1.7
LUTH–E.L.C.A.	12	844	2,757	3,334	1.6	3.5
LUTH–Luth-MO Synod	1	35	131	154	0.1	0.2
LUTH–Wisc Ev Luth Syn	1	13	25	26	0.0	0.0
MENN–Amish Undif	24	NR	1,623	3,864	1.8	4.0
METH–A.W.M.C.	1	14	11	16	0.0	0.0
METH–AME	1	210	440	528	0.3	0.5
METH–Free Methodist	1	65	53	65	0.0	0.1
METH–Un Methodist	37	3,034	9,212	10,783	5.1	11.2
Muslim Est	1	134	NR	308	0.1	0.3
New Apost Ch	1	NR	NR	NR	-	-
Non-denom Chr Chs	34	6,360	7,500	8,722	4.1	9.0
OCATH–Pol Natl Cath	1	NR	NR	NR	-	-
ORTHE–Carp Rus Orth	1	98	NR	200	0.1	0.2
ORTHE–Greek Orthodox	1	100	NR	2,000	1.0	2.1
ORTHE–Orth Ch in Amer	2	155	NR	253	0.1	0.3
ORTHE–Serb Orth USA	1	40	NR	40	0.0	0.0
PENT–Assemb of God	12	1,683	907	2,248	1.1	2.3
PENT–Ch God (Cleve)	5	613	1,235	1,482	0.7	1.5
PENT–Ch of God Proph	1	NR	43	52	0.0	0.1
PENT–COGIC	7	745	1,785	2,141	1.0	2.2
PENT–Full Gosp Bapt	1	NR	NR	NR	-	-
PENT–I F Chr Assmbl	2	NR	NR	NR	-	-
PENT–Un Pent Ch Intl	2	NR	NR	NR	-	-
PENT–United Holy Ch	1	NR	NR	NR	-	-
PRES–Presb Ch (USA)	11	638	1,481	1,777	0.8	1.8
Salvation Army	1	51	121	497	0.2	0.5
Sev Day Adv	2	146	254	293	0.1	0.3
Un C of Christ	4	240	1,042	1,250	0.6	1.3
Unit Univ	1	0	7	7	0.0	0.0
Unity Ch	1	NR	NR	NR	-	-
TUSCARAWAS	**185**	**14,717**	**25,573**	**45,489**	**49.1**	**100.0**
ANG/EPIS–Episcopal	1	43	115	115	0.1	0.3
Bahá'í	0	NR	3	3	0.0	0.0
BAPT–Consrv Bapt	1	NR	NR	NR	-	-
BAPT–Natl Mis Bapt Conv	1	0	25	31	0.0	0.1
BAPT–Reg Bapt Gen As	2	NR	NR	NR	-	-
BAPT–So Bapt Conv	6	234	334	408	0.4	0.9
BRETH–Ch of Brethren	2	104	139	170	0.2	0.4
Catholic	5	NR	NR	8,750	9.5	19.2
CGOD–Ch God (Ander)	4	302	NR	302	0.3	0.7
Ch Christ Chr Union	1	NR	NR	NR	-	-
Ch of Nazarene	7	759	1,185	1,353	1.5	3.0
Chr & Miss Al	1	255	166	435	0.5	1.0
CHR–Chr Ch (Disc)	1	73	187	228	0.2	0.5
CHR–Chr Chs & Chs Cr	4	NR	1,500	1,831	2.0	4.0
CHR–Chs of Christ	6	456	406	562	0.6	1.2
Evan Assoc RCC	2	NR	NR	NR	-	-
FRND–Evan Fr Ch Intl	1	31	10	12	0.0	0.0
Jehovah's Witness	3	NR	NR	NR	-	-
LDS–Comm of Christ	1	NR	158	158	0.2	0.3
LDS–L-D Saints	1	NR	NR	385	0.4	0.8
LUTH–E.L.C.A.	11	790	2,981	3,508	3.8	7.7
LUTH–Nor Amer Luth C	3	NR	NR	NR	-	-
MENN–Amish Undif	19	NR	1,160	2,370	2.6	5.2
MENN–Beachy Amish-Menn	3	345	223	345	0.4	0.8
MENN–Cons Menn Conf	1	210	159	194	0.2	0.4
MENN–Mennonite USA	2	155	120	146	0.2	0.3
MENN–Unaffil Amish-Menn	1	32	18	32	0.0	0.1
METH–AME Zion	1	10	25	31	0.0	0.1
METH–Free Methodist	1	3,521	705	3,521	3.8	7.7
METH–Un Methodist	33	2,415	6,343	8,466	9.1	18.6
METH–Wesleyan	1	164	94	213	0.2	0.5
MORAV–Morav Ch-North	6	602	1,295	1,544	1.7	3.4
Non-denom Chr Chs	18	1,935	2,485	2,752	3.0	6.0
PENT–Assemb of God	4	355	362	712	0.8	1.6
PENT–Ch God (Cleve)	5	284	646	788	0.9	1.7
PENT–COGIC	1	25	25	31	0.0	0.1
PENT–Int Foursq Gos	4	466	439	536	0.6	1.2
PENT–Int Pent C Chr	2	63	13	85	0.1	0.2
PENT–Un Pent Ch Intl	3	NR	NR	NR	-	-
PRES–Presb Ch (USA)	3	190	352	430	0.5	0.9
Salvation Army	1	45	90	394	0.4	0.9
Sev Day Adv	1	16	27	31	0.0	0.1
Un C of Christ	11	837	3,783	4,617	5.0	10.1
UNION	**62**	**4,303**	**10,085**	**16,247**	**31.1**	**100.0**
Bahá'í	0	NR	13	13	0.0	0.1
BAPT–Amer Bapt Assn	1	NR	85	108	0.2	0.7
BAPT–Amer Bapt USA	3	129	329	417	0.8	2.6
BAPT–Free Will Bapt	2	NR	134	170	0.3	1.0
BAPT–Reg Bapt Gen As	1	NR	NR	NR	-	-
BAPT–So Bapt Conv	3	52	59	75	0.1	0.5
BRETH–Grace Breth	1	NR	NR	NR	-	-
Catholic	2	NR	NR	2,500	4.8	15.4
CGOD–Ch God (Ander)	2	60	NR	60	0.1	0.4
Ch Christ Chr Union	2	NR	NR	NR	-	-
Ch of Nazarene	1	346	445	445	0.9	2.7
CHR–Chr Chs & Chs Cr	3	NR	840	1,065	2.0	6.6
CHR–Chs of Christ	2	360	291	445	0.9	2.7
FRND–Evan Fr Ch Intl	3	345	192	243	0.5	1.5
Jehovah's Witness	1	NR	NR	NR	-	-
LDS–L-D Saints	1	NR	NR	441	0.8	2.7
LUTH–E.L.C.A.	2	478	1,477	1,501	2.9	9.2
LUTH–Luth-MO Synod	2	180	1,364	1,775	3.4	10.9
LUTH–Nor Amer Luth C	1	NR	NR	NR	-	-
METH–AME	1	0	31	39	0.1	0.2
METH–Un Methodist	15	1,444	3,237	5,040	9.6	31.0
Non-denom Chr Chs	4	300	348	376	0.7	2.3
PENT–Assemb of God	1	83	138	138	0.3	0.8
PENT–Ch God (Cleve)	1	135	315	399	0.8	2.5
PENT–Ch of God Proph	1	NR	22	28	0.1	0.2
PENT–Int Foursq Gos	1	34	42	53	0.1	0.3
PENT–Un Pent Ch Intl	1	NR	NR	NR	-	-
PENT–Vineyard	1	210	170	215	0.4	1.3
PRES–Presb Ch (USA)	2	94	450	570	1.1	3.5
Un C of Christ	1	53	103	131	0.3	0.8
VAN WERT	**50**	**4,910**	**7,726**	**12,132**	**42.2**	**100.0**
Bahá'í	0	NR	4	4	0.0	0.0
BAPT–Amer Bapt Assn	1	NR	30	37	0.1	0.3
Catholic	1	NR	NR	2,410	8.4	19.9
CGOD–Ch God (Ander)	1	90	NR	90	0.3	0.7
CGOD–Ches God-Gen Con	3	543	892	1,099	3.8	9.1
Ch of Nazarene	2	29	30	44	0.2	0.4
CHR–Chr Chs & Chs Cr	1	NR	0	0	0.0	0.0
FRND–Evan Fr Ch Intl	1	440	237	292	1.0	2.4
FRND–Fr Un Mtg	2	NR	31	38	0.1	0.3
Jehovah's Witness	1	NR	NR	NR	-	-
LUTH–E.L.C.A.	4	327	835	1,200	4.2	9.9

NR–Not Reported - Represents no adherents reported. Percentages may not total 100 due to rounding.

Table 3: Religious Congregations by County and Group: 2010

Religious Group	Number of Congregations	Number of Attendees	Number of Communicant, Confirmed, or Full Members	Adherents: Number of Adherents	Adherents: % of Total Pop.	Adherents: % of Total Adh.
LUTH–Luth–MO Synod	4	448	1,027	1,360	4.7	11.2
METH–Un Methodist	11	1,236	2,478	2,918	10.2	24.1
Non-denom Chr Chs	5	845	1,155	1,282	4.5	10.6
PENT–Assemb of God	1	91	50	180	0.6	1.5
PENT–Ch God (Cleve)	1	53	40	49	0.2	0.4
PENT–Pent Ch of God	1	70	NR	109	0.4	0.9
PENT–Un Pent Ch Intl	1	NR	NR	NR	-	-
PENT–Vineyard	1	250	0	0	0.0	0.0
PRES–Presb Ch (USA)	2	110	416	513	1.8	4.2
REF–Ref Ch in Am	1	72	178	185	0.6	1.5
Salvation Army	1	44	77	92	0.3	0.8
Sev Day Adv	1	5	9	10	0.0	0.1
Un Breth in Cr	3	257	237	220	0.8	1.8
VINTON	**34**	**1,024**	**1,953**	**2,731**	**20.3**	**100.0**
ANG/EPIS–Episcopal	1	16	30	30	0.2	1.1
Bahá'í	0	NR	1	1	0.0	0.0
BAPT–Amer Bapt USA	1	0	13	16	0.1	0.6
BAPT–Free Will Bapt	3	NR	201	247	1.8	9.0
BAPT–So Bapt Conv	2	117	418	513	3.8	18.8
Catholic	1	NR	NR	200	1.5	7.3
Ch Christ Chr Union	1	NR	NR	NR	-	-
Ch of Nazarene	2	53	92	138	1.0	5.1
CHR–Chr Ch (Disc)	3	0	130	160	1.2	5.9
CHR–Chs of Christ	2	50	46	59	0.4	2.2
Christian Un	1	NR	NR	NR	-	-
LDS–Comm of Christ	1	NR	118	118	0.9	4.3
MENN–Amish Undif	1	NR	44	120	0.9	4.4
METH–Un Methodist	9	352	435	584	4.3	21.4
Non-denom Chr Chs	2	190	210	262	2.0	9.6
PENT–Assemb of God	1	80	50	80	0.6	2.9
PENT–Ch God (Cleve)	1	140	121	149	1.1	5.5
PRES–Presb Ch (USA)	2	26	44	54	0.4	2.0
WARREN	**162**	**19,865**	**30,488**	**62,230**	**29.3**	**100.0**
ANG/EPIS–Anglican NA	2	NR	NR	NR	-	-
ANG/EPIS–Episcopal	4	266	390	406	0.2	0.7
Bahá'í	0	NR	23	23	0.0	0.0
BAPT–Amer Bapt USA	2	280	434	552	0.3	0.9
BAPT–Free Will Bapt	1	NR	67	85	0.0	0.1
BAPT–Ind Bapt Flwsp Intl	2	NR	NR	NR	-	-
BAPT–So Bapt Conv	20	3,544	7,183	9,140	4.3	14.7
BRETH–Brethren (Ash)	1	NR	80	102	0.0	0.2
Catholic	5	NR	NR	19,509	9.2	31.3
CGOD–Ch God (Ander)	12	1,409	NR	1,409	0.7	2.3
Ch of Nazarene	6	606	577	848	0.4	1.4
CHR–Chr Ch (Disc)	1	145	310	394	0.2	0.6
CHR–Chr Chs & Chs Cr	10	NR	5,235	6,661	3.1	10.7
CHR–Chs of Christ	7	725	742	871	0.4	1.4
Christian Un	1	NR	NR	NR	-	-
CONG–Consrv Cong Chr	1	35	105	134	0.1	0.2
Evan Free Ch	2	1,300	NR	1,300	0.6	2.1
FRND–Fr Gen Cf	1	NR	52	66	0.0	0.1
Jehovah's Witness	2	NR	NR	NR	-	-
JUD–Reconst	1	20	25	68	0.0	0.1
LUTH–E.L.C.A.	2	243	468	637	0.3	1.0
LUTH–Luth Cong Msn Chr	1	415	NR	NR	-	-
LUTH–Luth–MO Synod	2	387	654	960	0.5	1.5
LUTH–Nor Amer Luth C	1	NR	NR	NR	-	-
LUTH–Wisc Ev Luth Syn	1	81	108	138	0.1	0.2
METH–AME	1	0	150	191	0.1	0.3
METH–Un Methodist	16	1,968	3,708	5,828	2.7	9.4
Non-denom Chr Chs	29	4,880	5,000	6,122	2.9	9.8
PENT–Assemb of God	2	451	305	451	0.2	0.7
PENT–Ch God (Cleve)	5	623	1,045	1,330	0.6	2.1
PENT–Ch God Mtn Asm	1	NR	NR	NR	-	-
PENT–Ch of God Proph	2	NR	76	97	0.0	0.2
PENT–Pent Ch of God	1	70	NR	109	0.1	0.2
PENT–Un Pent Ch Intl	3	NR	NR	NR	-	-
PENT–Vineyard	2	820	900	1,145	0.5	1.8
PRES–Presb Ch (USA)	6	1,081	2,030	2,583	1.2	4.2
PRES–Presb Ch Amer	1	287	398	540	0.3	0.9
Sev Day Adv	1	58	102	117	0.1	0.2
Un C of Christ	3	171	321	408	0.2	0.7
Unit Univ	1	NR	NR	NR	-	-
Zoroastrian	0	NR	NR	6	0.0	0.0
WASHINGTON	**137**	**7,918**	**14,452**	**23,702**	**38.4**	**100.0**
ANG/EPIS–Episcopal	1	51	79	224	0.4	0.9
Bahá'í	0	NR	5	5	0.0	0.0
BAPT–Amer Bapt USA	10	1,262	2,647	3,142	5.1	13.3
BAPT–Ind Bapt Flwsp Intl	1	NR	NR	NR	-	-
BAPT–Reg Bapt Gen As	2	NR	NR	NR	-	-
BAPT–So Bapt Conv	4	340	854	1,014	1.6	4.3
Catholic	6	NR	NR	5,424	8.8	22.9
Ch of Nazarene	4	372	562	603	1.0	2.5
Chr & Miss Al	1	61	37	107	0.2	0.5
CHR–Chr Ch (Disc)	1	14	41	49	0.1	0.2
CHR–Chr Chs & Chs Cr	7	NR	858	1,018	1.6	4.3
CHR–Chs of Christ	14	1,461	1,427	1,863	3.0	7.9
Christian Un	3	NR	NR	NR	-	-
CONG–Consrv Cong Chr	2	92	165	196	0.3	0.8
FRND–Fr Gen Cf	1	NR	9	11	0.0	0.0
Jehovah's Witness	2	NR	NR	NR	-	-
LDS–L-D Saints	1	NR	NR	378	0.6	1.6
LUTH–E.L.C.A.	1	159	431	595	1.0	2.5
LUTH–Wisc Ev Luth Syn	1	56	89	109	0.2	0.5
METH–AME	1	0	150	178	0.3	0.8
METH–Evan Meth Ch	1	NR	NR	NR	-	-
METH–Un Methodist	34	1,662	3,252	4,278	6.9	18.0
METH–Wesleyan	1	14	21	18	0.0	0.1
Non-denom Chr Chs	16	1,565	1,935	2,129	3.4	9.0
PENT–Assemb of God	1	42	33	65	0.1	0.3
PENT–Ch God (Cleve)	3	144	166	197	0.3	0.8
PENT–Intl Pent Holiness	2	74	387	459	0.7	1.9
PENT–Un Pent Ch Intl	2	NR	NR	NR	-	-
PRES–Presb Ch (USA)	7	316	623	739	1.2	3.1
Salvation Army	1	18	70	179	0.3	0.8
Sev Day Adv	1	12	21	24	0.0	0.1
Un C of Christ	4	123	472	560	0.9	2.4
Unit Univ	1	80	118	138	0.2	0.6
WAYNE	**234**	**19,920**	**35,296**	**62,771**	**54.8**	**100.0**
ANG/EPIS–Episcopal	1	101	255	258	0.2	0.4
Ap Chr Ch-Amer	2	1,517	725	1,517	1.3	2.4
Bahá'í	0	NR	7	7	0.0	0.0
BAPT–Converge/BGC	1	2,000	NR	2,400	2.1	3.8
BAPT–Free Will Bapt	2	NR	134	167	0.1	0.3
BAPT–Ind Bapt Flwsp Intl	1	NR	NR	NR	-	-
BAPT–Natl Mis Bapt Conv	1	0	150	186	0.2	0.3
BAPT–NBC USA	1	0	150	186	0.2	0.3
BAPT–Reg Bapt Gen As	2	NR	NR	NR	-	-
BAPT–So Bapt Conv	5	279	761	946	0.8	1.5
BRETH–Brethren (Ash)	2	NR	160	199	0.2	0.3
BRETH–Ch of Brethren	4	176	703	874	0.8	1.4
BRETH–Grace Breth	2	NR	NR	NR	-	-
BUDD–Mahayana	1	NR	NR	28	0.0	0.0
Catholic	5	NR	NR	9,031	7.9	14.4
CGOD–Ch God (Ander)	2	132	NR	132	0.1	0.2
CGOD–Ches God-Gen Con	2	191	315	392	0.3	0.6
Ch Cr, Scientst	1	NR	NR	NR	-	-
Ch of Nazarene	3	1,373	1,131	2,684	2.3	4.3
Chr & Miss Al	3	497	370	753	0.7	1.2
CHR–Chr Ch (Disc)	2	30	1,047	1,302	1.1	2.1
CHR–Chr Chs & Chs Cr	6	NR	1,366	1,698	1.5	2.7
CHR–Chs of Christ	5	335	296	382	0.3	0.6
Evan Assoc RCC	1	NR	NR	NR	-	-
FRND–Fr Gen Cf	1	NR	26	32	0.0	0.1
Jehovah's Witness	2	NR	NR	NR	-	-
JUD–Reconst	1	34	43	116	0.1	0.2
LDS–L-D Saints	1	NR	NR	342	0.3	0.5
LUTH–E.L.C.A.	9	858	2,585	3,308	2.9	5.3
LUTH–Luth Cong Msn Chr	2	NR	NR	NR	-	-
LUTH–Luth–MO Synod	1	22	31	37	0.0	0.1
LUTH–Nor Amer Luth C	1	NR	NR	NR	-	-
MENN–Amish Undif	65	NR	4,087	9,283	8.1	14.8

NR–Not Reported   - Represents no adherents reported.   Percentages may not total 100 due to rounding.

Table 3: Religious Congregations by County and Group: 2010

Religious Group	Number of Congrega-tions	Number of Attendees	Number of Communicant, Confirmed, or Full Members	Adherents: Number of Adherents	Adherents: % of Total Pop.	Adherents: % of Total Adh.
MENN–CG in Cr (Menn)	1	NR	165	205	0.2	0.3
MENN–Cons Menn Conf	2	664	474	589	0.5	0.9
MENN–Mennonite USA	12	1,681	2,607	3,241	2.8	5.2
MENN–Ref Mennonite	1	NR	18	20	0.0	0.0
METH–Free Methodist	1	598	390	598	0.5	1.0
METH–Un Methodist	24	2,001	5,263	6,267	5.5	10.0
METH–Wesleyan	1	30	38	39	0.0	0.1
Non-denom Chr Chs	22	4,703	5,642	6,436	5.6	10.3
PENT–Assemb of God	2	279	119	369	0.3	0.6
PENT–Ch God (Cleve)	4	242	453	563	0.5	0.9
PENT–Ch God Mtn Asm	1	NR	NR	NR	-	-
PENT–Int Foursq Gos	2	78	346	430	0.4	0.7
PENT–Un Pent Ch Intl	2	NR	NR	NR	-	-
PRES–Presb Ch (USA)	13	1,360	3,178	3,951	3.5	6.3
Salvation Army	1	24	115	1,098	1.0	1.7
Sev Day Adv	1	40	70	81	0.1	0.1
Un C of Christ	5	538	1,888	2,347	2.0	3.7
Unit Univ	1	137	188	277	0.2	0.4
WILLIAMS	**76**	**4,735**	**8,616**	**15,458**	**41.1**	**100.0**
Bahá'í	0	NR	2	2	0.0	0.0
BAPT–Ind Bapt Flwsp Intl	1	NR	NR	NR	-	-
BAPT–Reg Bapt Gen As	1	NR	NR	NR	-	-
BAPT–So Bapt Conv	2	140	297	363	1.0	2.3
BRETH–Brethren (Ash)	1	NR	80	98	0.3	0.6
BRETH–Ch of Brethren	2	100	120	147	0.4	1.0
Catholic	4	NR	NR	3,881	10.3	25.1
CGOD–Ches God-Gen Con	2	64	58	71	0.2	0.5
Ch of Nazarene	3	204	340	598	1.6	3.9
Chr & Miss Al	2	70	44	98	0.3	0.6
CHR–Chr Chs & Chs Cr	6	NR	1,185	1,448	3.8	9.4
Christian Un	2	NR	NR	NR	-	-
Jehovah's Witness	1	NR	NR	NR	-	-
LDS–L-D Saints	1	NR	NR	254	0.7	1.6
LUTH–E.L.C.A.	4	410	1,230	1,666	4.4	10.8
LUTH–Luth Cong Msn Chr	1	25	66	81	0.2	0.5
LUTH–Luth-MO Synod	1	48	198	228	0.6	1.5
LUTH–Nor Amer Luth C	1	NR	NR	NR	-	-
MENN–Amish Undif	0	NR	28	63	0.2	0.4
MENN–Fel Evg Ch	1	289	0	0	0.0	0.0
MENN–Mennonite USA	3	501	576	704	1.9	4.6
METH–Free Methodist	1	103	63	103	0.3	0.7
METH–Un Methodist	15	1,055	2,295	3,073	8.2	19.9
Missionary Ch	1	35	11	35	0.1	0.2
Non-denom Chr Chs	6	1,100	1,100	1,376	3.7	8.9
PENT–Assemb of God	1	35	17	63	0.2	0.4
PENT–Pent Ch of God	1	70	NR	109	0.3	0.7
PENT–Un Pent Ch Intl	1	NR	NR	NR	-	-
PRES–Presb Ch (USA)	5	262	658	804	2.1	5.2
Un Breth in Cr	6	224	248	193	0.5	1.2
WOOD	**146**	**20,584**	**30,484**	**65,902**	**52.5**	**100.0**
ANG/EPIS–Episcopal	2	110	254	308	0.2	0.5
Bahá'í	0	NR	27	27	0.0	0.0
BAPT–Amer Bapt USA	1	60	102	122	0.1	0.2
BAPT–Free Will Bapt	1	NR	67	80	0.1	0.1
BAPT–Natl Mis Bapt Conv	2	0	300	359	0.3	0.5
BAPT–Reg Bapt Gen As	1	NR	NR	NR	-	-
BAPT–So Bapt Conv	5	165	302	361	0.3	0.5
BRETH–Ch of Brethren	1	58	73	87	0.1	0.1
BRETH–Grace Breth	2	NR	NR	NR	-	-
Catholic	13	NR	NR	21,564	17.2	32.7
CGOD–Ch God (Ander)	2	116	NR	116	0.1	0.2
CGOD–Ches God-Gen Con	1	121	107	128	0.1	0.2
Ch of Nazarene	2	169	205	283	0.2	0.4
Chr & Miss Al	2	332	271	543	0.4	0.8
CHR–Chr Ch (Disc)	3	140	499	597	0.5	0.9
CHR–Chr Chs & Chs Cr	7	NR	1,177	1,408	1.1	2.1
CHR–Chs of Christ	1	70	50	80	0.1	0.1
CONG–Cong Chr, NA	3	NR	154	184	0.1	0.3
Evan Free Ch	1	200	NR	200	0.2	0.3
Jehovah's Witness	2	NR	NR	NR	-	-
LDS–L-D Saints	3	NR	NR	1,107	0.9	1.7

Religious Group	Number of Congrega-tions	Number of Attendees	Number of Communicant, Confirmed, or Full Members	Adherents: Number of Adherents	Adherents: % of Total Pop.	Adherents: % of Total Adh.
LUTH–E.L.C.A.	19	2,750	7,933	10,189	8.1	15.5
LUTH–Evan Luth Syn	2	120	209	321	0.3	0.5
LUTH–Luth-MO Synod	1	60	140	181	0.1	0.3
MENN–Fel Evg Ch	1	120	78	93	0.1	0.1
METH–AME	1	0	100	120	0.1	0.2
METH–Un Methodist	31	2,607	5,358	7,318	5.8	11.1
METH–Wesleyan	1	62	30	81	0.1	0.1
Muslim Est	1	500	NR	2,000	1.6	3.0
Non-denom Chr Chs	10	9,818	10,092	12,373	9.9	18.8
ORTHE–Orth Ch in Amer	1	60	NR	85	0.1	0.1
PENT–Assemb of God	3	1,115	524	2,206	1.8	3.3
PENT–Ch God (Cleve)	1	54	302	361	0.3	0.5
PENT–Pent Ch of God	2	140	NR	217	0.2	0.3
PENT–Un Pent Ch Intl	1	NR	NR	NR	-	-
PENT–Vineyard	2	285	509	609	0.5	0.9
PRES–Evan Presby Ch	1	NR	42	50	0.0	0.1
PRES–Presb Ch (USA)	5	184	682	816	0.7	1.2
Salvation Army	1	48	71	97	0.1	0.1
Sev Day Adv	2	36	61	71	0.1	0.1
Un Breth in Cr	2	919	450	782	0.6	1.2
Un C of Christ	2	130	227	272	0.2	0.4
Unit Univ	1	35	88	106	0.1	0.2
WYANDOT	**45**	**2,871**	**6,160**	**12,340**	**54.6**	**100.0**
BAPT–Amer Bapt USA	1	15	15	18	0.1	0.1
BAPT–Free Will Bapt	1	NR	67	82	0.4	0.7
BAPT–So Bapt Conv	1	37	123	151	0.7	1.2
Catholic	3	NR	NR	4,737	20.9	38.4
CGOD–Ches God-Gen Con	1	108	166	204	0.9	1.7
Ch of Nazarene	2	106	285	285	1.3	2.3
CHR–Chs of Christ	1	22	21	27	0.1	0.2
Jehovah's Witness	1	NR	NR	NR	-	-
LUTH–E.L.C.A.	5	443	1,817	2,184	9.7	17.7
METH–Un Methodist	16	1,369	2,224	2,731	12.1	22.1
METH–Wesleyan	1	45	28	59	0.3	0.5
Non-denom Chr Chs	2	235	270	294	1.3	2.4
PENT–Assemb of God	1	45	28	89	0.4	0.7
PENT–Ch God (Cleve)	1	58	66	81	0.4	0.7
PENT–Ch of God Proph	1	NR	23	28	0.1	0.2
PENT–Pent Ch of God	1	70	NR	109	0.5	0.9
PENT–Un Pent Ch Intl	1	NR	NR	NR	-	-
PRES–Presb Ch (USA)	2	105	194	238	1.1	1.9
Un C of Christ	3	213	833	1,023	4.5	8.3
OKLAHOMA	**7,057**	**690,853**	**1,550,418**	**2,226,379**	**59.3**	**100.0**
ADAIR	**56**	**3,730**	**8,323**	**11,102**	**48.9**	**100.0**
Bahá'í	0	NR	36	36	0.2	0.3
BAPT–Amer Bapt Assn	2	NR	170	217	1.0	2.0
BAPT–So Bapt Conv	26	1,565	5,461	6,979	30.8	62.9
CHR–Chr Chs & Chs Cr	1	NR	120	153	0.7	1.4
CHR–Chs of Christ	6	328	294	393	1.7	3.5
METH–Un Methodist	3	98	687	741	3.3	6.7
Non-denom Chr Chs	6	805	845	1,045	4.6	9.4
PENT–Assemb of God	7	626	212	800	3.5	7.2
PENT–Intl Pent Holiness	2	204	438	560	2.5	5.0
PENT–Pent Ch of God	1	70	NR	109	0.5	1.0
PENT–Un Pent Ch Intl	1	NR	NR	NR	-	-
Sev Day Adv	1	34	60	69	0.3	0.6
ALFALFA	**30**	**886**	**3,244**	**4,021**	**71.3**	**100.0**
BAPT–N Am Bapt Conf	1	NR	34	39	0.7	1.0
BAPT–So Bapt Conv	3	228	810	939	16.6	23.4
BRETH–Ch of Brethren	1	8	25	29	0.5	0.7
Catholic	2	NR	NR	272	4.8	6.8
Ch of Nazarene	2	33	59	59	1.0	1.5
CHR–Chr Ch (Disc)	4	134	493	571	10.1	14.2
CHR–Chr Chs & Chs Cr	2	NR	165	191	3.4	4.8
CHR–Chs of Christ	2	125	102	130	2.3	3.2
Christian Un	1	NR	NR	NR	-	-
FRND–Evan Fr Ch Intl	1	25	57	66	1.2	1.6

NR–Not Reported   - Represents no adherents reported.   Percentages may not total 100 due to rounding.

Table 3: Religious Congregations by County and Group: 2010

Religious Group	Number of Congregations	Number of Attendees	Number of Communicant, Confirmed, or Full Members	Adherents: Number of Adherents	Adherents: % of Total Pop.	Adherents: % of Total Adh.
MENN–CG in Cr (Menn)	1	NR	94	109	1.9	2.7
METH–Free Methodist	1	9	12	12	0.2	0.3
METH–Un Methodist	6	278	1,341	1,538	27.3	38.2
Non-denom Chr Chs	1	30	30	38	0.7	0.9
PENT–Assemb of God	1	8	6	9	0.2	0.2
Un C of Christ	1	8	16	19	0.3	0.5
ATOKA	**54**	**2,828**	**7,679**	**9,718**	**68.5**	**100.0**
Bahá'í	0	NR	1	1	0.0	0.0
BAPT–Free Will Bapt	4	NR	380	464	3.3	4.8
BAPT–So Bapt Conv	23	1,424	5,517	6,735	47.5	69.3
Catholic	1	NR	NR	100	0.7	1.0
Ch of Nazarene	1	24	38	78	0.5	0.8
CHR–Chs of Christ	7	363	384	477	3.4	4.9
Jehovah's Witness	1	NR	NR	NR	-	-
METH–C.M.E.	1	0	100	122	0.9	1.3
METH–Un Methodist	4	87	249	358	2.5	3.7
Non-denom Chr Chs	3	715	875	932	6.6	9.6
PENT–Assemb of God	3	82	35	178	1.3	1.8
PENT–Intl Pent Holiness	2	63	83	101	0.7	1.0
PENT–Pent Ch of God	1	70	NR	109	0.8	1.1
PENT–Un Pent Ch Intl	1	NR	NR	NR	-	-
PRES–Cumber Presb	2	NR	17	63	0.4	0.6
BEAVER	**27**	**911**	**2,607**	**3,367**	**59.7**	**100.0**
BAPT–So Bapt Conv	7	397	1,022	1,278	22.7	38.0
Catholic	1	NR	NR	39	0.7	1.2
Ch of Nazarene	1	18	15	18	0.3	0.5
CHR–Chr Chs & Chs Cr	2	NR	160	200	3.5	5.9
CHR–Chs of Christ	3	83	87	114	2.0	3.4
FRND–Evan Fr Ch Intl	1	22	81	101	1.8	3.0
LUTH–Luth-MO Synod	1	15	38	38	0.7	1.1
MENN–Menn Br US Conf	1	NR	73	91	1.6	2.7
MENN–Mennonite USA	1	66	102	128	2.3	3.8
METH–Un Methodist	7	258	994	1,237	21.9	36.7
PENT–Assemb of God	1	34	17	100	1.8	3.0
PRES–Presb Ch (USA)	1	18	18	23	0.4	0.7
BECKHAM	**55**	**4,553**	**10,025**	**15,071**	**68.1**	**100.0**
Bahá'í	0	NR	1	1	0.0	0.0
BAPT–So Bapt Conv	16	1,369	5,843	7,240	32.7	48.0
Catholic	1	NR	NR	1,125	5.1	7.5
Ch of Nazarene	2	101	162	226	1.0	1.5
CHR–Chr Ch (Disc)	2	145	271	336	1.5	2.2
CHR–Chr Chs & Chs Cr	3	NR	60	74	0.3	0.5
CHR–Chs of Christ	6	665	828	1,072	4.8	7.1
Jehovah's Witness	1	NR	NR	NR	-	-
LUTH–Luth-MO Synod	1	25	27	32	0.1	0.2
METH–Free Methodist	1	62	0	62	0.3	0.4
METH–Un Methodist	4	386	1,094	1,563	7.1	10.4
Non-denom Chr Chs	7	1,025	1,395	1,414	6.4	9.4
PENT–Assemb of God	6	738	122	1,652	7.5	11.0
PENT–Ch of God Proph	1	NR	40	50	0.2	0.3
PENT–Intl Pent Holiness	1	30	30	37	0.2	0.2
PENT–Un Pent Ch Intl	1	NR	NR	NR	-	-
PRES–Presb Ch (USA)	1	0	140	173	0.8	1.1
Sev Day Adv	1	7	12	14	0.1	0.1
BLAINE	**51**	**2,031**	**4,734**	**6,249**	**52.3**	**100.0**
ANG/EPIS–Episcopal	1	19	55	55	0.5	0.9
Bahá'í	0	NR	14	14	0.1	0.2
BAPT–Amer Bapt USA	2	43	38	46	0.4	0.7
BAPT–N Am Bapt Conf	1	NR	46	55	0.5	0.9
BAPT–So Bapt Conv	10	559	1,313	1,576	13.2	25.2
Catholic	2	NR	NR	300	2.5	4.8
Ch of Nazarene	1	103	152	199	1.7	3.2
CHR–Chr Ch (Disc)	2	70	208	250	2.1	4.0
CHR–Chr Chs & Chs Cr	3	NR	584	701	5.9	11.2
CHR–Chs of Christ	4	178	217	262	2.2	4.2
Jehovah's Witness	1	NR	NR	NR	-	-
LDS–Comm of Christ	1	NR	156	156	1.3	2.5
LUTH–Luth-MO Synod	1	35	93	93	0.8	1.5

Religious Group	Number of Congregations	Number of Attendees	Number of Communicant, Confirmed, or Full Members	Adherents: Number of Adherents	Adherents: % of Total Pop.	Adherents: % of Total Adh.
MENN–Menn Br US Conf	1	NR	45	54	0.5	0.9
METH–Free Methodist	2	263	15	267	2.2	4.3
METH–Un Methodist	6	237	1,148	1,432	12.0	22.9
METH–Wesleyan	1	35	13	46	0.4	0.7
Non-denom Chr Chs	3	240	340	350	2.9	5.6
PENT–Assemb of God	4	129	112	178	1.5	2.8
PENT–Intl Pent Holiness	2	40	47	56	0.5	0.9
Sev Day Adv	2	71	124	142	1.2	2.3
Un C of Christ	1	9	14	17	0.1	0.3
BRYAN	**95**	**8,518**	**22,092**	**27,713**	**65.3**	**100.0**
ANG/EPIS–Episcopal	1	36	63	83	0.2	0.3
Bahá'í	0	NR	2	2	0.0	0.0
BAPT–Amer Bapt Assn	1	NR	120	147	0.3	0.5
BAPT–Free Will Bapt	1	NR	95	116	0.3	0.4
BAPT–So Bapt Conv	40	3,521	14,078	17,225	40.6	62.2
Catholic	1	NR	NR	250	0.6	0.9
Ch of Nazarene	3	229	367	402	0.9	1.5
CHR–Chr Ch (Disc)	1	75	160	196	0.5	0.7
CHR–Chr Chs & Chs Cr	2	NR	165	202	0.5	0.7
CHR–Chs of Christ	12	864	846	1,088	2.6	3.9
Jehovah's Witness	3	NR	NR	NR	-	-
LDS–L-D Saints	1	NR	NR	682	1.6	2.5
LUTH–Assoc Free Luth	1	NR	NR	NR	-	-
LUTH–E.L.C.A.	1	37	79	88	0.2	0.3
METH–Un Methodist	8	341	1,001	1,401	3.3	5.1
Non-denom Chr Chs	3	2,660	4,350	4,350	10.3	15.7
PENT–Assemb of God	5	221	132	276	0.7	1.0
PENT–Intl Pent Holiness	1	135	355	434	1.0	1.6
PENT–Pent Ch of God	4	280	NR	435	1.0	1.6
PENT–Un Pent Ch Intl	2	NR	NR	NR	-	-
PRES–Presb Ch (USA)	3	80	211	258	0.6	0.9
Sev Day Adv	1	39	68	78	0.2	0.3
CADDO	**114**	**5,746**	**17,785**	**23,176**	**78.3**	**100.0**
Bahá'í	0	NR	18	18	0.1	0.1
BAPT–Amer Bapt Assn	3	NR	222	276	0.9	1.2
BAPT–Amer Bapt USA	3	121	260	323	1.1	1.4
BAPT–Ind Bapt Flwsp Intl	1	NR	NR	NR	-	-
BAPT–So Bapt Conv	27	2,099	10,892	13,522	45.7	58.3
Catholic	5	NR	NR	300	1.0	1.3
Ch of Nazarene	3	140	209	299	1.0	1.3
CHR–Chr Ch (Disc)	3	143	314	390	1.3	1.7
CHR–Chr Chs & Chs Cr	6	NR	348	432	1.5	1.9
CHR–Chs of Christ	10	734	746	994	3.4	4.3
Jehovah's Witness	1	NR	NR	NR	-	-
LDS–L-D Saints	1	NR	NR	530	1.8	2.3
LUTH–E.L.C.A.	2	20	45	95	0.3	0.4
LUTH–Luth-MO Synod	2	55	114	116	0.4	0.5
MENN–Mennonite USA	3	276	333	413	1.4	1.8
METH–Un Methodist	20	790	2,555	2,968	10.0	12.8
Non-denom Chr Chs	3	300	399	399	1.3	1.7
PENT–Assemb of God	9	445	255	579	2.0	2.5
PENT–Ch God (Cleve)	2	114	239	297	1.0	1.3
PENT–Intl Pent Holiness	7	350	665	826	2.8	3.6
PENT–Pent Ch of God	2	140	NR	217	0.7	0.9
REF–Ref Ch in Am	1	19	171	182	0.6	0.8
CANADIAN	**134**	**15,304**	**31,706**	**50,792**	**44.0**	**100.0**
ANG/EPIS–Episcopal	2	46	129	137	0.1	0.3
Bahá'í	1	NR	49	49	0.0	0.1
BAPT–Free Will Bapt	4	NR	380	481	0.4	0.9
BAPT–So Bapt Conv	26	5,177	14,632	18,522	16.0	36.5
Catholic	7	NR	NR	6,622	5.7	13.0
CGOD–Ch God (Ander)	1	25	NR	25	0.0	0.0
Ch of Nazarene	7	811	1,270	1,594	1.4	3.1
CHR–Chr Ch (Disc)	5	372	959	1,214	1.1	2.4
CHR–Chr Chs & Chs Cr	3	NR	976	1,235	1.1	2.4
CHR–Chs of Christ	14	1,523	1,481	2,001	1.7	3.9
Jehovah's Witness	3	NR	NR	NR	-	-
LDS–L-D Saints	4	NR	NR	2,512	2.2	4.9
LUTH–E.L.C.A.	1	129	325	449	0.4	0.9
LUTH–Luth-MO Synod	2	257	548	702	0.6	1.4

NR–Not Reported   - Represents no adherents reported.   Percentages may not total 100 due to rounding.

Table 3: Religious Congregations by County and Group: 2010

Religious Group	Number of Congrega-tions	Number of Attendees	Number of Communicant, Confirmed, or Full Members	Adherents: Number of Adherents	Adherents: % of Total Pop.	Adherents: % of Total Adh.
METH–AME	1	0	100	127	0.1	0.3
METH–C.M.E.	1	0	100	127	0.1	0.3
METH–Free Methodist	1	10	0	10	0.0	0.0
METH–Un Methodist	12	1,622	5,870	7,367	6.4	14.5
Non-denom Chr Chs	17	3,141	3,350	4,022	3.5	7.9
PENT–Assemb of God	7	1,583	1,056	2,668	2.3	5.3
PENT–Ch God (Cleve)	3	108	120	152	0.1	0.3
PENT–Intl Pent Holiness	3	226	145	184	0.2	0.4
PENT–Pent Ch of God	3	210	NR	326	0.3	0.6
PENT–Un Pent Ch Intl	3	NR	NR	NR	-	-
PRES–Presb Ch (USA)	2	26	151	191	0.2	0.4
Sev Day Adv	1	38	65	75	0.1	0.1
CARTER	**125**	**9,982**	**24,110**	**32,137**	**67.6**	**100.0**
ANG/EPIS–Episcopal	1	127	425	428	0.9	1.3
Bahá'í	0	NR	1	1	0.0	0.0
BAPT–Amer Bapt Assn	3	NR	170	213	0.4	0.7
BAPT–Free Will Bapt	7	NR	665	833	1.8	2.6
BAPT–Ind Bapt Flwsp Intl	2	NR	NR	NR	-	-
BAPT–Natl Mis Bapt Conv	1	0	150	188	0.4	0.6
BAPT–NBC Amer	1	80	120	150	0.3	0.5
BAPT–So Bapt Conv	33	3,512	11,892	14,893	31.3	46.3
Catholic	1	NR	NR	856	1.8	2.7
Ch of Nazarene	2	102	212	228	0.5	0.7
CHR–Chr Ch (Disc)	2	140	390	488	1.0	1.5
CHR–Chr Chs & Chs Cr	2	NR	50	63	0.1	0.2
CHR–Chs of Christ	13	1,050	1,170	1,473	3.1	4.6
Jehovah's Witness	1	NR	NR	NR	-	-
LDS–Comm of Christ	1	NR	156	156	0.3	0.5
LDS–L-D Saints	1	NR	NR	555	1.2	1.7
LUTH–Luth-MO Synod	1	53	83	110	0.2	0.3
METH–AME	1	0	100	125	0.3	0.4
METH–Un Methodist	8	964	5,109	5,575	11.7	17.3
Muslim Est	1	134	NR	308	0.6	1.0
Non-denom Chr Chs	15	1,650	1,963	2,215	4.7	6.9
PENT–Assemb of God	7	1,001	371	1,072	2.3	3.3
PENT–Ch God (Cleve)	1	143	200	250	0.5	0.8
PENT–COGIC	1	0	150	188	0.4	0.6
PENT–Intl Pent Holiness	5	178	217	272	0.6	0.8
PENT–Pent Ch of God	7	490	NR	761	1.6	2.4
PENT–Un Pent Ch Intl	4	NR	NR	NR	-	-
PRES–Presb Ch (USA)	1	120	249	312	0.7	1.0
Salvation Army	1	136	89	219	0.5	0.7
Sev Day Adv	1	102	178	205	0.4	0.6
CHEROKEE	**82**	**5,869**	**11,463**	**16,092**	**34.2**	**100.0**
ANG/EPIS–Episcopal	1	39	62	68	0.1	0.4
Bahá'í	0	NR	60	60	0.1	0.4
BAPT–Amer Bapt Assn	1	NR	85	104	0.2	0.6
BAPT–Free Will Bapt	3	NR	285	349	0.7	2.2
BAPT–Ind Bapt Flwsp Intl	2	NR	NR	NR	-	-
BAPT–So Bapt Conv	26	2,413	6,259	7,675	16.3	47.7
Catholic	2	NR	NR	800	1.7	5.0
CGOD–Ch God (Ander)	1	0	NR	0	0.0	0.0
Ch God (7th Day)	1	NR	NR	NR	-	-
Ch of Nazarene	1	35	118	118	0.3	0.7
CHR–Chr Ch (Disc)	1	52	85	104	0.2	0.6
CHR–Chr Chs & Chs Cr	1	NR	40	49	0.1	0.3
CHR–Chs of Christ	7	561	508	650	1.4	4.0
Evan Free Ch	1	87	NR	87	0.2	0.5
Int Cou Comm Ch	1	NR	NR	NR	-	-
Jehovah's Witness	1	NR	NR	NR	-	-
LDS–L-D Saints	1	NR	NR	718	1.5	4.5
LUTH–Luth-MO Synod	1	52	102	108	0.2	0.7
MENN–Fel Evg Bib Ch	1	54	50	54	0.1	0.3
METH–Un Methodist	7	454	2,050	2,365	5.0	14.7
Non-denom Chr Chs	7	987	1,052	1,266	2.7	7.9
PENT–Assemb of God	3	556	312	722	1.5	4.5
PENT–Ch God (Cleve)	2	60	46	56	0.1	0.3
PENT–Intl Pent Holiness	2	175	96	118	0.3	0.7
PENT–Pent Ch of God	3	210	NR	326	0.7	2.0
PENT–Un Pent Ch Intl	1	NR	NR	NR	-	-
PRES–Presb Ch (USA)	2	83	147	180	0.4	1.1
Sev Day Adv	1	26	44	51	0.1	0.3
Unit Univ	1	25	62	64	0.1	0.4
CHOCTAW	**58**	**6,514**	**14,193**	**16,396**	**107.8**	**100.0**
ANG/EPIS–Episcopal	1	20	57	57	0.4	0.3
BAPT–So Bapt Conv	20	1,347	5,306	6,564	43.2	40.0
Catholic	2	NR	NR	100	0.7	0.6
Ch of Nazarene	1	55	56	144	0.9	0.9
CHR–Chr Ch (Disc)	1	35	59	73	0.5	0.4
CHR–Chs of Christ	8	346	367	448	2.9	2.7
HINDU–I/A Temples	1	NR	NR	250	1.6	1.5
Jehovah's Witness	1	NR	NR	NR	-	-
METH–C.M.E.	1	0	100	124	0.8	0.8
METH–Un Methodist	9	204	573	652	4.3	4.0
Non-denom Chr Chs	2	4,250	7,250	7,312	48.1	44.6
PENT–Assemb of God	4	193	113	278	1.8	1.7
PENT–Ch God (Cleve)	1	36	159	197	1.3	1.2
PENT–Un Pent Ch Intl	1	NR	NR	NR	-	-
PRES–Cumber Presb	1	NR	7	21	0.1	0.1
PRES–Presb Ch (USA)	3	0	97	120	0.8	0.7
Sev Day Adv	1	28	49	56	0.4	0.3
CIMARRON	**20**	**594**	**1,750**	**2,220**	**89.7**	**100.0**
BAPT–So Bapt Conv	8	297	836	1,045	42.2	47.1
Catholic	1	NR	NR	98	4.0	4.4
CHR–Chr Chs & Chs Cr	1	NR	114	142	5.7	6.4
CHR–Chs of Christ	2	60	56	74	3.0	3.3
LUTH–Luth-MO Synod	1	15	30	30	1.2	1.4
METH–Un Methodist	5	170	672	779	31.5	35.1
PENT–Intl Pent Holiness	2	52	42	52	2.1	2.3
CLEVELAND	**237**	**38,935**	**79,124**	**110,195**	**43.1**	**100.0**
ANG/EPIS–Anglican NA	1	NR	NR	NR	-	-
ANG/EPIS–Episcopal	2	398	917	1,272	0.5	1.2
Bahá'í	2	NR	178	178	0.1	0.2
BAPT–Amer Bapt Assn	2	NR	235	287	0.1	0.3
BAPT–Free Will Bapt	9	NR	855	1,046	0.4	0.9
BAPT–So Bapt Conv	65	11,026	31,129	38,074	14.9	34.6
BUDD–Mahayana	1	NR	NR	11	0.0	0.0
Calv Chpl	1	NR	NR	NR	-	-
Catholic	5	NR	NR	9,479	3.7	8.6
CGOD–Ch God (Ander)	1	330	NR	330	0.1	0.3
CGOD–Ches God-Gen Con	1	38	48	59	0.0	0.1
Ch Cr, Scientst	1	NR	NR	NR	-	-
Ch of Nazarene	8	458	1,039	1,264	0.5	1.1
CHR–Chr Ch (Disc)	3	642	1,689	2,066	0.8	1.9
CHR–Chr Chs & Chs Cr	3	NR	600	734	0.3	0.7
CHR–Chs of Christ	14	2,806	2,620	3,893	1.5	3.5
Evan Cov Ch	2	4,636	4,964	6,026	2.4	5.5
FRND–Fr Gen Cf	1	NR	0	0	0.0	0.0
HINDU–Post Ren	1	NR	NR	10	0.0	0.0
Jehovah's Witness	3	NR	NR	NR	-	-
LDS–L-D Saints	9	NR	NR	3,889	1.5	3.5
LUTH–E.L.C.A.	1	141	311	347	0.1	0.3
LUTH–Luth-MO Synod	2	400	963	1,215	0.5	1.1
LUTH–Wisc Ev Luth Syn	2	115	192	255	0.1	0.2
METH–Free Methodist	1	27	0	27	0.0	0.0
METH–Un Methodist	12	2,844	12,615	14,560	5.7	13.2
METH–Wesleyan	1	32	24	42	0.0	0.0
Muslim Est	1	134	NR	308	0.1	0.3
Non-denom Chr Chs	39	10,978	16,330	17,124	6.7	15.5
ORTHE–Ant Orth of NA	1	75	NR	87	0.0	0.1
PENT–Assemb of God	14	1,794	1,100	3,134	1.2	2.8
PENT–Ch God (Cleve)	3	316	610	746	0.3	0.7
PENT–Int Foursq Gos	1	48	55	67	0.0	0.1
PENT–Intl Pent Holiness	6	734	887	1,085	0.4	1.0
PENT–Pent Ch of God	4	280	NR	435	0.2	0.4
PENT–Un Pent Ch Intl	3	NR	NR	NR	-	-
PRES–Orth Pres Ch	1	23	28	33	0.0	0.0
PRES–Presb Ch (USA)	3	326	1,190	1,455	0.6	1.3
PRES–Presb Ch Amer	1	140	195	232	0.1	0.2
Salvation Army	1	18	54	80	0.0	0.1
Sev Day Adv	3	156	272	313	0.1	0.3

NR–Not Reported   - Represents no adherents reported.   Percentages may not total 100 due to rounding.

Table 3: Religious Congregations by County and Group: 2010

Religious Group	Number of Congregations	Number of Attendees	Number of Communicant, Confirmed, or Full Members	Adherents: Number of Adherents	Adherents: % of Total Pop.	Adherents: % of Total Adh.
Unit Univ	1	20	24	32	0.0	0.0
Unity Ch	1	NR	NR	NR	-	-
COAL	**22**	**884**	**2,990**	**3,850**	**65.0**	**100.0**
ANG/EPIS–Episcopal	1	10	14	16	0.3	0.4
Bahá'í	0	NR	1	1	0.0	0.0
BAPT–So Bapt Conv	7	404	2,118	2,625	44.3	68.2
Ch of Nazarene	1	37	78	78	1.3	2.0
CHR–Chs of Christ	3	143	133	184	3.1	4.8
MENN–Amish Undif	1	NR	42	100	1.7	2.6
METH–Un Methodist	2	100	467	577	9.7	15.0
Non-denom Chr Chs	1	40	40	50	0.8	1.3
PENT–Assemb of God	1	38	35	38	0.6	1.0
PENT–Intl Pent Holiness	1	29	9	11	0.2	0.3
PENT–Pent Ch of God	1	70	NR	109	1.8	2.8
PRES–Cumber Presb	1	NR	9	9	0.2	0.2
PRES–Presb Ch (USA)	1	0	21	26	0.4	0.7
Sev Day Adv	1	13	23	26	0.4	0.7
COMANCHE	**189**	**15,742**	**43,704**	**63,240**	**51.0**	**100.0**
ANG/EPIS–Episcopal	1	84	225	231	0.2	0.4
Bahá'í	0	NR	88	88	0.1	0.1
BAPT–Amer Bapt Assn	2	NR	125	156	0.1	0.2
BAPT–Amer Bapt USA	1	42	200	250	0.2	0.4
BAPT–Free Will Bapt	3	NR	285	356	0.3	0.6
BAPT–NBC USA	3	843	1,450	1,809	1.5	2.9
BAPT–So Bapt Conv	47	5,497	25,250	31,501	25.4	49.8
Catholic	3	NR	NR	4,748	3.8	7.5
Ch of Nazarene	5	206	482	627	0.5	1.0
Chr & Miss Al	1	16	16	16	0.0	0.0
CHR–Chr Ch (Disc)	3	193	414	516	0.4	0.8
CHR–Chr Chs & Chs Cr	4	NR	650	811	0.7	1.3
CHR–Chs of Christ	15	1,334	1,286	1,654	1.3	2.6
Grace Gosp Fel	2	NR	NR	NR	-	-
HINDU–I/A Temples	1	NR	NR	250	0.2	0.4
Jehovah's Witness	3	NR	NR	NR	-	-
LDS–L-D Saints	2	NR	NR	2,421	2.0	3.8
LUTH–E.L.C.A.	1	34	57	76	0.1	0.1
LUTH–Luth–MO Synod	2	325	598	850	0.7	1.3
MENN–Menn Br US Conf	2	NR	115	143	0.1	0.2
METH–AME	3	100	400	499	0.4	0.8
METH–C.M.E.	1	0	100	125	0.1	0.2
METH–Un Methodist	21	1,507	5,536	6,409	5.2	10.1
Muslim Est	2	184	NR	358	0.3	0.6
Non-denom Chr Chs	16	1,883	2,464	2,603	2.1	4.1
ORTHO–Coptic Orth Ch	1	7	NR	15	0.0	0.0
PENT–Assemb of God	14	2,460	2,132	3,607	2.9	5.7
PENT–Ch God (Cleve)	7	248	316	394	0.3	0.6
PENT–COGIC	2	50	225	281	0.2	0.4
PENT–Full Gosp Bapt	2	NR	NR	NR	-	-
PENT–Intl Pent Holiness	2	126	76	95	0.1	0.2
PENT–Pent Ch of God	2	140	NR	217	0.2	0.3
PENT–Un Pent Ch Intl	1	NR	NR	NR	-	-
PRES–Korean Amer Pres	1	NR	NR	NR	-	-
PRES–Presb Ch (USA)	4	144	425	530	0.4	0.8
PRES–Presb Ch Amer	2	65	67	72	0.1	0.1
REF–Ref Ch in Am	1	60	129	141	0.1	0.2
Salvation Army	1	36	180	896	0.7	1.4
Sev Day Adv	2	113	196	226	0.2	0.4
Un C of Christ	2	45	171	213	0.2	0.3
Unit Univ	1	0	46	56	0.0	0.1
COTTON	**28**	**1,480**	**4,403**	**5,427**	**87.6**	**100.0**
BAPT–Amer Bapt USA	1	35	80	98	1.6	1.8
BAPT–So Bapt Conv	11	785	3,003	3,691	59.6	68.0
Catholic	1	NR	NR	35	0.6	0.6
Ch of Nazarene	2	92	180	202	3.3	3.7
CHR–Chr Ch (Disc)	1	20	52	64	1.0	1.2
CHR–Chs of Christ	3	160	159	195	3.1	3.6
METH–Un Methodist	2	113	520	610	9.8	11.2
Non-denom Chr Chs	1	90	100	112	1.8	2.1
PENT–Assemb of God	2	68	58	113	1.8	2.1
PENT–Ch God (Cleve)	1	98	206	253	4.1	4.7

Religious Group	Number of Congregations	Number of Attendees	Number of Communicant, Confirmed, or Full Members	Adherents: Number of Adherents	Adherents: % of Total Pop.	Adherents: % of Total Adh.
PRES–Presb Ch (USA)	2	9	28	34	0.5	0.6
Sev Day Adv	1	10	17	20	0.3	0.4
CRAIG	**51**	**3,151**	**7,940**	**9,900**	**65.9**	**100.0**
ANG/EPIS–Episcopal	1	25	39	49	0.3	0.5
Bahá'í	0	NR	21	21	0.1	0.2
BAPT–Free Will Bapt	1	NR	95	115	0.8	1.2
BAPT–Natl Mis Bapt Conv	1	0	150	181	1.2	1.8
BAPT–So Bapt Conv	16	1,029	4,046	4,889	32.5	49.4
Catholic	2	NR	NR	190	1.3	1.9
CGOD–Ch God (Ander)	1	124	NR	124	0.8	1.3
Ch Cr, Scientst	1	NR	NR	NR	-	-
Ch of Nazarene	1	41	65	65	0.4	0.7
CHR–Chr Chs & Chs Cr	3	NR	355	429	2.9	4.3
CHR–Chs of Christ	2	169	183	233	1.6	2.4
Jehovah's Witness	1	NR	NR	NR	-	-
LDS–Comm of Christ	1	NR	135	135	0.9	1.4
LUTH–Luth–MO Synod	1	11	27	28	0.2	0.3
MENN–Amish Undif	1	NR	6	17	0.1	0.2
METH–AME	1	0	100	121	0.8	1.2
METH–Un Methodist	5	282	1,131	1,186	7.9	12.0
Non-denom Chr Chs	2	800	900	1,000	6.7	10.1
PENT–Assemb of God	3	218	127	454	3.0	4.6
PENT–Int Foursq Gos	2	178	162	196	1.3	2.0
PENT–Un Pent Ch Intl	1	NR	NR	NR	-	-
PENT–Vineyard	1	95	95	115	0.8	1.2
PRES–Presb Ch (USA)	1	35	54	65	0.4	0.7
Sev Day Adv	2	144	249	287	1.9	2.9
CREEK	**134**	**9,271**	**23,963**	**33,815**	**48.3**	**100.0**
ANG/EPIS–Episcopal	1	64	195	195	0.3	0.6
Bahá'í	0	NR	21	21	0.0	0.1
BAPT–Free Will Bapt	9	NR	855	1,056	1.5	3.1
BAPT–So Bapt Conv	35	3,553	14,280	17,632	25.2	52.1
BUDD–Mahayana	1	NR	NR	10	0.0	0.0
Catholic	3	NR	NR	700	1.0	2.1
CGOD–Ch God (Ander)	2	325	NR	325	0.5	1.0
Ch of Nazarene	4	381	592	906	1.3	2.7
CHR–Chr Ch (Disc)	4	109	173	214	0.3	0.6
CHR–Chr Chs & Chs Cr	5	NR	535	661	0.9	2.0
CHR–Chs of Christ	8	459	494	639	0.9	1.9
Jehovah's Witness	2	NR	NR	NR	-	-
LDS–L-D Saints	1	NR	NR	686	1.0	2.0
METH–AME	2	18	31	38	0.1	0.1
METH–C.M.E.	1	0	100	123	0.2	0.4
METH–Free Methodist	1	47	16	47	0.1	0.1
METH–Un Methodist	11	624	2,532	2,838	4.1	8.4
Muslim Est	1	134	NR	308	0.4	0.9
Non-denom Chr Chs	18	1,714	2,105	2,362	3.4	7.0
PENT–Assemb of God	9	1,244	644	1,784	2.5	5.3
PENT–Ch God Apos Fth	1	NR	NR	NR	-	-
PENT–Ch of God Proph	1	NR	76	94	0.1	0.3
PENT–COGIC	1	0	350	432	0.6	1.3
PENT–Intl Pent Holiness	2	73	137	169	0.2	0.5
PENT–Pent Ch of God	1	70	NR	109	0.2	0.3
PENT–Un Pent Ch Intl	3	NR	NR	NR	-	-
PRES–Presb Ch (USA)	2	225	384	474	0.7	1.4
Salvation Army	2	63	151	1,656	2.4	4.9
Sev Day Adv	3	168	292	336	0.5	1.0
CUSTER	**84**	**5,212**	**14,797**	**20,531**	**74.7**	**100.0**
ANG/EPIS–Episcopal	1	13	30	46	0.2	0.2
Bahá'í	0	NR	14	14	0.1	0.1
BAPT–Amer Bapt Assn	4	NR	340	416	1.5	2.0
BAPT–Free Will Bapt	3	NR	285	349	1.3	1.7
BAPT–Ind Bapt Flwsp Intl	1	NR	NR	NR	-	-
BAPT–NBC USA	1	0	150	184	0.7	0.9
BAPT–So Bapt Conv	12	1,868	6,826	8,360	30.4	40.7
BRETH–Breth in Chr	1	NR	NR	NR	-	-
Catholic	4	NR	NR	1,261	4.6	6.1
Ch of Nazarene	3	84	146	168	0.6	0.8
Chr & Miss Al	1	26	14	37	0.1	0.2
CHR–Chr Ch (Disc)	2	95	286	350	1.3	1.7

NR–Not Reported - Represents no adherents reported. Percentages may not total 100 due to rounding.

Table 3: Religious Congregations by County and Group: 2010

Religious Group	Number of Congrega-tions	Number of Attendees	Number of Communicant, Confirmed, or Full Members	Adherents: Number of Adherents	Adherents: % of Total Pop.	Adherents: % of Total Adh.
CHR–Chr Chs & Chs Cr	5	NR	781	957	3.5	4.7
CHR–Chs of Christ	6	700	796	1,128	4.1	5.5
Evan Free Ch	1	70	NR	70	0.3	0.3
Jehovah's Witness	1	NR	NR	NR	-	-
LDS–L-D Saints	1	NR	NR	593	2.2	2.9
LUTH–E.L.C.A.	2	83	202	223	0.8	1.1
MENN–Beachy Amish-Menn	1	58	27	58	0.2	0.3
MENN–CG in Cr (Menn)	1	NR	39	48	0.2	0.2
MENN–Menn Br US Conf	1	NR	382	468	1.7	2.3
MENN–Mennonite USA	2	80	83	102	0.4	0.5
METH–Un Methodist	8	564	2,895	3,152	11.5	15.4
Non-denom Chr Chs	4	545	700	731	2.7	3.6
PENT–Assemb of God	6	717	338	888	3.2	4.3
PENT–Intl Pent Holiness	2	38	53	65	0.2	0.3
PENT–Pent Ch of God	3	210	NR	326	1.2	1.6
PENT–Un Pent Ch Intl	2	NR	NR	NR	-	-
PRES–Cumber Presb	1	NR	64	115	0.4	0.6
PRES–Presb Ch (USA)	2	0	135	165	0.6	0.8
Sev Day Adv	1	14	25	29	0.1	0.1
Un C of Christ	1	47	186	228	0.8	1.1
DELAWARE	**88**	**6,000**	**12,675**	**16,280**	**39.2**	**100.0**
ANG/EPIS–Episcopal	1	90	164	164	0.4	1.0
Bahá'í	0	NR	72	72	0.2	0.4
BAPT–Free Will Bapt	1	NR	95	114	0.3	0.7
BAPT–Ind Bapt Flwsp Intl	1	NR	NR	NR	-	-
BAPT–So Bapt Conv	38	2,464	6,886	8,293	20.0	50.9
Catholic	1	NR	NR	190	0.5	1.2
Ch of Nazarene	1	24	28	125	0.3	0.8
Chr & Miss Al	1	95	64	118	0.3	0.7
CHR–Chr Chs & Chs Cr	2	NR	510	614	1.5	3.8
CHR–Chs of Christ	5	468	444	589	1.4	3.6
Ind Fund Churches	1	NR	NR	NR	-	-
Jehovah's Witness	2	NR	NR	NR	-	-
LDS–Comm of Christ	1	NR	135	135	0.3	0.8
LDS–L-D Saints	1	NR	NR	453	1.1	2.8
LUTH–E.L.C.A.	1	41	79	153	0.4	0.9
LUTH–Luth-MO Synod	1	32	40	49	0.1	0.3
METH–Evan Meth Ch	1	NR	NR	NR	-	-
METH–Un Methodist	3	513	1,322	1,636	3.9	10.0
Non-denom Chr Chs	11	1,306	1,464	1,731	4.2	10.6
PENT–Assemb of God	5	362	180	439	1.1	2.7
PENT–Ch God (Cleve)	1	33	63	76	0.2	0.5
PENT–Ch God Apos Fth	2	NR	NR	NR	-	-
PENT–Intl Pent Holiness	2	257	516	621	1.5	3.8
PENT–Un Pent Ch Intl	2	NR	NR	NR	-	-
PRES–Presb Ch (USA)	1	0	65	78	0.2	0.5
Sev Day Adv	2	315	548	630	1.5	3.9
DEWEY	**29**	**1,039**	**3,143**	**4,127**	**85.8**	**100.0**
BAPT–So Bapt Conv	5	303	936	1,162	24.2	28.2
BRETH–Breth in Chr	1	NR	NR	NR	-	-
Catholic	1	NR	NR	100	2.1	2.4
Ch of Nazarene	2	112	157	187	3.9	4.5
CHR–Chr Ch (Disc)	3	118	250	310	6.4	7.5
CHR–Chr Chs & Chs Cr	6	NR	820	1,018	21.2	24.7
CHR–Chs of Christ	3	145	133	176	3.7	4.3
MENN–Mennonite USA	1	4	12	15	0.3	0.4
METH–Un Methodist	4	207	720	963	20.0	23.3
Non-denom Chr Chs	1	60	60	75	1.6	1.8
PENT–Assemb of God	2	90	55	121	2.5	2.9
ELLIS	**24**	**862**	**2,557**	**3,186**	**76.8**	**100.0**
BAPT–N Am Bapt Conf	1	NR	41	51	1.2	1.6
BAPT–So Bapt Conv	4	253	1,188	1,471	35.4	46.2
Catholic	1	NR	NR	50	1.2	1.6
Ch of Nazarene	3	85	113	124	3.0	3.9
CHR–Chr Ch (Disc)	2	51	110	136	3.3	4.3
CHR–Chr Chs & Chs Cr	1	NR	100	124	3.0	3.9
CHR–Chs of Christ	3	105	100	114	2.7	3.6
LUTH–Luth-MO Synod	1	30	43	44	1.1	1.4
METH–Un Methodist	4	213	723	901	21.7	28.3
Non-denom Chr Chs	1	70	80	88	2.1	2.8

Religious Group	Number of Congrega-tions	Number of Attendees	Number of Communicant, Confirmed, or Full Members	Adherents: Number of Adherents	Adherents: % of Total Pop.	Adherents: % of Total Adh.
PENT–Assemb of God	2	27	10	27	0.7	0.8
Sev Day Adv	1	28	49	56	1.3	1.8
GARFIELD	**124**	**10,890**	**23,657**	**34,676**	**57.2**	**100.0**
ANG/EPIS–Episcopal	1	76	162	209	0.3	0.6
Bahá'í	1	NR	49	49	0.1	0.1
BAPT–Amer Bapt Assn	1	NR	85	106	0.2	0.3
BAPT–Ind Bapt Flwsp Intl	2	NR	NR	NR	-	-
BAPT–NBC USA	2	0	300	374	0.6	1.1
BAPT–Reg Bapt Gen As	1	NR	NR	NR	-	-
BAPT–So Bapt Conv	20	3,418	7,977	9,940	16.4	28.7
BRETH–Ch of Brethren	1	45	39	49	0.1	0.1
Calv Chpl	1	NR	NR	NR	-	-
Catholic	3	NR	NR	3,743	6.2	10.8
Ch of Nazarene	2	211	517	540	0.9	1.6
Chr & Miss Al	1	36	35	50	0.1	0.1
CHR–Chr Ch (Disc)	9	798	1,984	2,472	4.1	7.1
CHR–Chr Chs & Chs Cr	2	NR	700	872	1.4	2.5
CHR–Chs of Christ	4	546	523	709	1.2	2.0
Christian Un	3	NR	NR	NR	-	-
Evan Free Ch	1	40	NR	40	0.1	0.1
Jehovah's Witness	1	NR	NR	NR	-	-
LDS–L-D Saints	2	NR	NR	1,172	1.9	3.4
LUTH–E.L.C.A.	1	28	38	39	0.1	0.1
LUTH–Luth-MO Synod	8	671	2,035	2,687	4.4	7.7
MENN–Menn Br US Conf	1	NR	310	386	0.6	1.1
MENN–Mennonite USA	1	60	76	95	0.2	0.3
METH–AME	1	15	23	29	0.0	0.1
METH–Free Methodist	1	16	28	28	0.0	0.1
METH–Un Methodist	12	1,256	4,377	5,206	8.6	15.0
METH–Wesleyan	2	160	98	208	0.3	0.6
Non-denom Chr Chs	17	1,785	2,280	2,511	4.1	7.2
PENT–Assemb of God	6	1,074	730	1,407	2.3	4.1
PENT–Ch God (Cleve)	1	5	8	10	0.0	0.0
PENT–Ch of God Proph	1	NR	13	16	0.0	0.0
PENT–COGIC	2	0	300	374	0.6	1.1
PENT–Intl Pent Holiness	2	66	55	69	0.1	0.2
PENT–Pent Ch of God	1	70	NR	109	0.2	0.3
PENT–Un Pent Ch Intl	1	NR	NR	NR	-	-
PRES–Presb Ch (USA)	1	200	312	389	0.6	1.1
PRES–Ref Pres of NA	1	30	12	23	0.0	0.1
Salvation Army	1	114	99	173	0.3	0.5
Sev Day Adv	2	128	222	256	0.4	0.7
Un C of Christ	3	42	270	336	0.6	1.0
GARVIN	**90**	**6,282**	**15,856**	**20,433**	**74.1**	**100.0**
ANG/EPIS–Episcopal	2	18	32	32	0.1	0.2
Bahá'í	0	NR	3	3	0.0	0.0
BAPT–Free Will Bapt	1	NR	95	117	0.4	0.6
BAPT–Ind Bapt Flwsp Intl	1	NR	NR	NR	-	-
BAPT–NBC USA	1	0	60	74	0.3	0.4
BAPT–Ref Bapt Ch	1	NR	NR	NR	-	-
BAPT–So Bapt Conv	25	2,887	10,362	12,785	46.4	62.6
Catholic	3	NR	NR	410	1.5	2.0
CGOD–Ch God (Ander)	1	84	NR	84	0.3	0.4
Ch of Nazarene	1	47	82	82	0.3	0.4
CHR–Chr Ch (Disc)	2	89	186	230	0.8	1.1
CHR–Chr Chs & Chs Cr	1	NR	40	49	0.2	0.2
CHR–Chs of Christ	13	987	1,062	1,365	4.9	6.7
Jehovah's Witness	2	NR	NR	NR	-	-
LDS–L-D Saints	1	NR	NR	358	1.3	1.8
METH–Un Methodist	8	472	1,935	2,234	8.1	10.9
Non-denom Chr Chs	12	992	1,439	1,526	5.5	7.5
PENT–Assemb of God	4	278	126	337	1.2	1.6
PENT–Ch God (Cleve)	1	41	37	46	0.2	0.2
PENT–Intl Pent Holiness	2	141	143	176	0.6	0.9
PENT–Pent Ch of God	2	140	NR	217	0.8	1.1
PENT–Un Pent Ch Intl	4	NR	NR	NR	-	-
PRES–Presb Ch (USA)	1	70	192	237	0.9	1.2
Sev Day Adv	1	36	62	71	0.3	0.3
GRADY	**86**	**7,015**	**18,735**	**24,500**	**46.7**	**100.0**
ANG/EPIS–Episcopal	1	35	67	75	0.1	0.3

NR–Not Reported   - Represents no adherents reported.   Percentages may not total 100 due to rounding.

Table 3: Religious Congregations by County and Group: 2010

Religious Group	Number of Congregations	Number of Attendees	Number of Communicant, Confirmed, or Full Members	Adherents		
				Number of Adherents	% of Total Pop.	% of Total Adh.
Bahá'í	0	NR	23	23	0.0	0.1
BAPT–Free Will Bapt	2	NR	190	236	0.5	1.0
BAPT–Ind Bapt Flwsp Intl	1	NR	NR	NR	-	-
BAPT–NBC USA	1	65	125	155	0.3	0.6
BAPT–So Bapt Conv	24	3,010	11,083	13,769	26.3	56.2
Catholic	1	NR	NR	420	0.8	1.7
Ch of Nazarene	2	76	125	125	0.2	0.5
CHR–Chr Ch (Disc)	2	165	675	839	1.6	3.4
CHR–Chr Chs & Chs Cr	3	NR	615	764	1.5	3.1
CHR–Chs of Christ	13	1,389	1,440	1,771	3.4	7.2
Jehovah's Witness	1	NR	NR	NR	-	-
LDS–L-D Saints	1	NR	NR	268	0.5	1.1
LUTH–E.L.C.A.	1	30	41	57	0.1	0.2
LUTH–Luth–MO Synod	1	60	100	129	0.2	0.5
MENN–CG in Cr (Menn)	2	NR	211	262	0.5	1.1
METH–Un Methodist	8	445	2,533	2,854	5.4	11.6
Non-denom Chr Chs	5	555	705	770	1.5	3.1
PENT–Assemb of God	8	828	448	1,297	2.5	5.3
PENT–Ch God (Cleve)	1	42	57	71	0.1	0.3
PENT–Intl Pent Holiness	1	35	71	88	0.2	0.4
PENT–Pent Ch of God	2	140	NR	217	0.4	0.9
PENT–Un Pent Ch Intl	1	NR	NR	NR	-	-
PRES–Presb Ch (USA)	1	40	68	84	0.2	0.3
PRES–Presb Ch Amer	1	30	39	47	0.1	0.2
Salvation Army	1	34	57	108	0.2	0.4
Sev Day Adv	1	36	62	71	0.1	0.3
GRANT	**31**	**1,176**	**3,434**	**4,295**	**94.9**	**100.0**
Bahá'í	0	NR	3	3	0.1	0.1
BAPT–So Bapt Conv	6	358	1,090	1,312	29.0	30.5
Catholic	2	NR	NR	170	3.8	4.0
Ch of Nazarene	1	24	20	44	1.0	1.0
CHR–Chr Ch (Disc)	5	295	744	895	19.8	20.8
CHR–Chr Chs & Chs Cr	3	NR	280	337	7.4	7.8
CHR–Chs of Christ	2	137	112	152	3.4	3.5
LUTH–Luth–MO Synod	1	25	33	40	0.9	0.9
METH–Un Methodist	7	283	1,098	1,273	28.1	29.6
PENT–Assemb of God	4	54	54	69	1.5	1.6
GREER	**26**	**1,297**	**3,663**	**4,624**	**74.1**	**100.0**
Bahá'í	0	NR	1	1	0.0	0.0
BAPT–Amer Bapt Assn	1	NR	85	100	1.6	2.2
BAPT–So Bapt Conv	8	386	2,272	2,684	43.0	58.0
Catholic	1	NR	NR	140	2.2	3.0
Ch of Nazarene	1	16	36	44	0.7	1.0
CHR–Chr Chs & Chs Cr	1	NR	0	0	0.0	0.0
CHR–Chs of Christ	4	355	433	535	8.6	11.6
LUTH–Luth–MO Synod	1	78	87	130	2.1	2.8
METH–Un Methodist	3	179	540	552	8.8	11.9
Non-denom Chr Chs	1	100	100	125	2.0	2.7
PENT–Assemb of God	2	150	22	217	3.5	4.7
PENT–Ch God (Cleve)	1	33	48	57	0.9	1.2
PENT–Un Pent Ch Intl	1	NR	NR	NR	-	-
PRES–Cumber Presb	1	NR	39	39	0.6	0.8
HARMON	**13**	**775**	**3,193**	**4,124**	**141.1**	**100.0**
Bahá'í	0	NR	4	4	0.1	0.1
BAPT–So Bapt Conv	4	438	2,773	3,487	119.3	84.6
Catholic	1	NR	NR	78	2.7	1.9
Ch of Nazarene	1	25	34	38	1.3	0.9
CHR–Chs of Christ	4	202	167	245	8.4	5.9
METH–Un Methodist	2	60	204	218	7.5	5.3
PENT–Assemb of God	1	50	11	54	1.8	1.3
HARPER	**15**	**535**	**2,366**	**3,072**	**83.4**	**100.0**
BAPT–So Bapt Conv	2	200	1,191	1,481	40.2	48.2
Catholic	1	NR	NR	154	4.2	5.0
CHR–Chr Ch (Disc)	1	32	65	81	2.2	2.6
CHR–Chr Chs & Chs Cr	2	NR	235	292	7.9	9.5
CHR–Chs of Christ	2	54	63	74	2.0	2.4
LUTH–Luth–MO Synod	1	0	93	101	2.7	3.3
METH–Un Methodist	3	175	663	778	21.1	25.3
Non-denom Chr Chs	1	25	21	31	0.8	1.0
PENT–Assemb of God	2	49	35	80	2.2	2.6
HASKELL	**54**	**2,485**	**5,789**	**7,579**	**59.4**	**100.0**
BAPT–Free Will Bapt	11	NR	1,045	1,303	10.2	17.2
BAPT–So Bapt Conv	16	917	3,069	3,828	30.0	50.5
Catholic	1	NR	NR	62	0.5	0.8
CHR–Chr Ch (Disc)	1	27	55	69	0.5	0.9
CHR–Chr Chs & Chs Cr	1	NR	50	62	0.5	0.8
CHR–Chs of Christ	3	148	173	208	1.6	2.7
Jehovah's Witness	1	NR	NR	NR	-	-
METH–Un Methodist	3	117	342	362	2.8	4.8
Non-denom Chr Chs	8	610	735	813	6.4	10.7
PENT–Assemb of God	6	605	278	820	6.4	10.8
PENT–Intl Pent Holiness	1	61	42	52	0.4	0.7
PENT–Un Pent Ch Intl	1	NR	NR	NR	-	-
Sev Day Adv	1	0	0	0	0.0	0.0
HUGHES	**59**	**2,378**	**6,175**	**7,596**	**54.2**	**100.0**
ANG/EPIS–Episcopal	1	12	20	20	0.1	0.3
Bahá'í	0	NR	14	14	0.1	0.2
BAPT–Amer Bapt Assn	1	NR	85	103	0.7	1.4
BAPT–Free Will Bapt	4	NR	380	458	3.3	6.0
BAPT–So Bapt Conv	21	1,079	3,802	4,586	32.8	60.4
Catholic	1	NR	NR	38	0.3	0.5
CGOD–Ch God (Ander)	1	60	NR	60	0.4	0.8
Ch of Nazarene	2	113	146	188	1.3	2.5
CHR–Chr Ch (Disc)	1	15	35	42	0.3	0.6
CHR–Chs of Christ	8	310	350	422	3.0	5.6
METH–Free Methodist	1	16	30	30	0.2	0.4
METH–Un Methodist	11	199	802	892	6.4	11.7
Non-denom Chr Chs	1	30	30	38	0.3	0.5
PENT–Assemb of God	3	312	218	388	2.8	5.1
PENT–Intl Pent Holiness	2	232	263	317	2.3	4.2
PENT–Un Pent Ch Intl	1	NR	NR	NR	-	-
JACKSON	**58**	**4,863**	**11,494**	**14,706**	**55.6**	**100.0**
ANG/EPIS–Episcopal	1	32	56	56	0.2	0.4
Bahá'í	0	NR	14	14	0.1	0.1
BAPT–Amer Bapt Assn	2	NR	170	214	0.8	1.5
BAPT–So Bapt Conv	15	2,252	5,511	6,922	26.2	47.1
Catholic	1	NR	NR	450	1.7	3.1
Ch of Nazarene	2	46	80	80	0.3	0.5
CHR–Chr Ch (Disc)	1	70	118	148	0.6	1.0
CHR–Chs of Christ	9	674	739	977	3.7	6.6
Jehovah's Witness	1	NR	NR	NR	-	-
LDS–L-D Saints	1	NR	NR	557	2.1	3.8
LUTH–Luth–MO Synod	1	31	20	25	0.1	0.2
METH–Un Methodist	7	602	3,386	3,552	13.4	24.2
Non-denom Chr Chs	6	700	955	992	3.8	6.7
PENT–Assemb of God	5	275	170	351	1.3	2.4
PENT–Ch God (Cleve)	1	79	57	72	0.3	0.5
PENT–Ch of God Proph	1	NR	3	4	0.0	0.0
PENT–Un Pent Ch Intl	1	NR	NR	NR	-	-
PRES–Presb Ch (USA)	1	36	67	84	0.3	0.6
Salvation Army	1	39	101	154	0.6	1.0
Sev Day Adv	1	27	47	54	0.2	0.4
JEFFERSON	**26**	**1,640**	**4,669**	**5,854**	**90.5**	**100.0**
BAPT–Amer Bapt Assn	1	NR	150	185	2.9	3.2
BAPT–So Bapt Conv	10	840	3,267	4,029	62.3	68.8
Catholic	1	NR	NR	35	0.5	0.6
Ch of Nazarene	1	8	28	28	0.4	0.5
CHR–Chr Ch (Disc)	1	55	150	185	2.9	3.2
CHR–Chs of Christ	4	365	351	463	7.2	7.9
METH–Un Methodist	3	200	568	683	10.6	11.7
PENT–Assemb of God	5	172	155	246	3.8	4.2
JOHNSTON	**43**	**2,045**	**5,136**	**6,599**	**60.2**	**100.0**
Bahá'í	0	NR	2	2	0.0	0.0
BAPT–Free Will Bapt	2	NR	190	234	2.1	3.5
BAPT–So Bapt Conv	16	936	3,581	4,411	40.3	66.8

NR–Not Reported   - Represents no adherents reported.   Percentages may not total 100 due to rounding.

Table 3: Religious Congregations by County and Group: 2010

Religious Group	Number of Congrega-tions	Number of Attendees	Number of Communicant, Confirmed, or Full Members	Adherents: Number of Adherents	Adherents: % of Total Pop.	Adherents: % of Total Adh.
Catholic	1	NR	NR	20	0.2	0.3
Ch of Nazarene	2	151	252	352	3.2	5.3
CHR–Chs of Christ	7	400	359	436	4.0	6.6
Jehovah's Witness	1	NR	NR	NR	-	-
METH–Un Methodist	4	175	418	451	4.1	6.8
PENT–Assemb of God	2	170	95	290	2.6	4.4
PENT–Ch God (Cleve)	3	87	134	165	1.5	2.5
PENT–Ch of God Proph	1	NR	33	41	0.4	0.6
PENT–Intl Pent Holiness	1	44	45	55	0.5	0.8
PENT–Pent Ch of God	1	70	NR	109	1.0	1.7
PENT–Un Pent Ch Intl	1	NR	NR	NR	-	-
PRES–Presb Ch (USA)	1	12	27	33	0.3	0.5
KAY	**102**	**7,223**	**19,490**	**28,439**	**61.1**	**100.0**
ANG/EPIS–Episcopal	1	105	220	287	0.6	1.0
Bahá'í	0	NR	23	23	0.0	0.1
BAPT–Amer Bapt Assn	1	NR	0	0	0.0	0.0
BAPT–Free Will Bapt	2	NR	190	236	0.5	0.8
BAPT–So Bapt Conv	21	1,970	8,016	9,963	21.4	35.0
Catholic	5	NR	NR	2,979	6.4	10.5
CGOD–Ch God (Ander)	2	66	NR	66	0.1	0.2
Ch of Nazarene	5	298	656	656	1.4	2.3
CHR–Chr Ch (Disc)	7	529	1,749	2,174	4.7	7.6
CHR–Chr Chs & Chs Cr	3	NR	190	236	0.5	0.8
CHR–Chs of Christ	5	574	605	778	1.7	2.7
Ind Fund Churches	1	NR	NR	NR	-	-
Jehovah's Witness	2	NR	NR	NR	-	-
JUD–Reform	1	8	14	38	0.1	0.1
LDS–L-D Saints	2	NR	NR	745	1.6	2.6
LUTH–E.L.C.A.	1	30	56	62	0.1	0.2
LUTH–Luth–MO Synod	4	377	779	1,192	2.6	4.2
METH–AME	1	0	150	186	0.4	0.7
METH–Un Methodist	11	1,102	4,931	5,538	11.9	19.5
METH–Wesleyan	2	86	72	112	0.2	0.4
Non-denom Chr Chs	8	725	910	987	2.1	3.5
PENT–Assemb of God	5	612	207	858	1.8	3.0
PENT–Int Foursq Gos	1	272	190	236	0.5	0.8
PENT–Intl Pent Holiness	2	84	62	77	0.2	0.3
PENT–Pent Ch of God	2	140	NR	217	0.5	0.8
PENT–Un Pent Ch Intl	1	NR	NR	NR	-	-
PRES–Presb Ch (USA)	4	212	379	471	1.0	1.7
Salvation Army	1	19	67	294	0.6	1.0
Sev Day Adv	1	14	24	28	0.1	0.1
KINGFISHER	**39**	**2,349**	**7,267**	**11,487**	**76.4**	**100.0**
Bahá'í	0	NR	15	15	0.1	0.1
BAPT–N Am Bapt Conf	1	NR	101	127	0.8	1.1
BAPT–So Bapt Conv	8	784	2,940	3,702	24.6	32.2
Catholic	3	NR	NR	2,546	16.9	22.2
Ch of Nazarene	2	118	386	386	2.6	3.4
CHR–Chr Ch (Disc)	3	171	683	860	5.7	7.5
CHR–Chr Chs & Chs Cr	2	NR	150	189	1.3	1.6
CHR–Chs of Christ	2	120	128	159	1.1	1.4
Christian Un	1	NR	NR	NR	-	-
Evan Assoc RCC	1	NR	NR	NR	-	-
LUTH–Luth–MO Synod	2	229	632	801	5.3	7.0
METH–Un Methodist	4	327	1,505	1,795	11.9	15.6
Non-denom Chr Chs	2	105	256	256	1.7	2.2
PENT–Assemb of God	3	82	33	100	0.7	0.9
PENT–Ch God (Cleve)	1	30	34	43	0.3	0.4
PENT–Intl Pent Holiness	2	147	177	223	1.5	1.9
PRES–Presb Ch (USA)	1	118	117	147	1.0	1.3
Un C of Christ	1	118	110	138	0.9	1.2
KIOWA	**39**	**2,037**	**6,044**	**7,789**	**82.5**	**100.0**
Bahá'í	0	NR	1	1	0.0	0.0
BAPT–Amer Bapt Assn	1	NR	85	103	1.1	1.3
BAPT–Amer Bapt USA	2	88	198	241	2.6	3.1
BAPT–Ind Bapt Flwsp Intl	1	NR	NR	NR	-	-
BAPT–So Bapt Conv	9	725	3,823	4,652	49.2	59.7
Catholic	1	NR	NR	172	1.8	2.2
Ch of Nazarene	1	13	9	24	0.3	0.3
CHR–Chr Ch (Disc)	1	41	79	96	1.0	1.2

Religious Group	Number of Congrega-tions	Number of Attendees	Number of Communicant, Confirmed, or Full Members	Adherents: Number of Adherents	Adherents: % of Total Pop.	Adherents: % of Total Adh.
CHR–Chr Chs & Chs Cr	1	NR	102	124	1.3	1.6
CHR–Chs of Christ	5	388	399	518	5.5	6.7
Jehovah's Witness	1	NR	NR	NR	-	-
LUTH–E.L.C.A.	1	24	42	55	0.6	0.7
LUTH–Luth–MO Synod	1	34	60	65	0.7	0.8
METH–Un Methodist	4	223	905	1,027	10.9	13.2
Non-denom Chr Chs	1	100	150	150	1.6	1.9
PENT–Assemb of God	4	175	85	215	2.3	2.8
PENT–Intl Pent Holiness	1	71	76	92	1.0	1.2
PENT–Pent Ch of God	2	140	NR	217	2.3	2.8
PENT–Un Pent Ch Intl	1	NR	NR	NR	-	-
PRES–Presb Ch (USA)	1	15	30	37	0.4	0.5
LATIMER	**42**	**1,771**	**5,750**	**7,544**	**67.6**	**100.0**
BAPT–Free Will Bapt	5	NR	475	581	5.2	7.7
BAPT–So Bapt Conv	18	1,046	4,612	5,638	50.5	74.7
Catholic	1	NR	NR	180	1.6	2.4
CHR–Chr Chs & Chs Cr	2	NR	25	31	0.3	0.4
CHR–Chs of Christ	4	149	142	179	1.6	2.4
Jehovah's Witness	1	NR	NR	NR	-	-
METH–Un Methodist	2	101	218	232	2.1	3.1
Non-denom Chr Chs	1	100	100	125	1.1	1.7
PENT–Assemb of God	6	340	99	486	4.4	6.4
PRES–Presb Ch (USA)	1	0	18	22	0.2	0.3
Sev Day Adv	1	35	61	70	0.6	0.9
LE FLORE	**161**	**8,869**	**20,393**	**28,703**	**57.0**	**100.0**
Bahá'í	0	NR	13	13	0.0	0.0
BAPT–Amer Bapt Assn	4	NR	670	829	1.6	2.9
BAPT–Free Will Bapt	12	NR	1,140	1,411	2.8	4.9
BAPT–NBC USA	1	0	150	186	0.4	0.6
BAPT–So Bapt Conv	58	4,329	13,383	16,563	32.9	57.7
Catholic	3	NR	NR	303	0.6	1.1
CGOD–Ches God-Gen Con	2	45	63	78	0.2	0.3
Ch God (7th Day)	1	NR	NR	NR	-	-
Ch of Nazarene	6	217	415	602	1.2	2.1
CHR–Chr Ch (Disc)	1	18	22	27	0.1	0.1
CHR–Chr Chs & Chs Cr	4	NR	144	178	0.4	0.6
CHR–Chs of Christ	11	669	581	793	1.6	2.8
Jehovah's Witness	1	NR	NR	NR	-	-
LDS–Comm of Christ	1	NR	156	156	0.3	0.5
LDS–L-D Saints	2	NR	NR	673	1.3	2.3
METH–Un Methodist	12	503	1,545	1,753	3.5	6.1
Non-denom Chr Chs	9	865	1,055	1,182	2.3	4.1
PENT–Assemb of God	20	1,781	885	3,077	6.1	10.7
PENT–Ch of God Proph	2	NR	78	97	0.2	0.3
PENT–Pent Ch of God	6	420	NR	652	1.3	2.3
PENT–Un Pent Ch Intl	2	NR	NR	NR	-	-
PRES–Cumber Presb	1	NR	3	19	0.0	0.1
PRES–Presb Ch (USA)	2	22	90	111	0.2	0.4
LINCOLN	**85**	**4,991**	**12,625**	**16,813**	**49.1**	**100.0**
Bahá'í	0	NR	5	5	0.0	0.0
BAPT–Amer Bapt Assn	2	NR	335	415	1.2	2.5
BAPT–Free Will Bapt	2	NR	190	235	0.7	1.4
BAPT–So Bapt Conv	20	2,152	7,334	9,083	26.5	54.0
Catholic	4	NR	NR	532	1.6	3.2
Ch of Nazarene	4	127	321	325	0.9	1.9
CHR–Chr Ch (Disc)	5	225	476	590	1.7	3.5
CHR–Chr Chs & Chs Cr	6	NR	453	561	1.6	3.3
CHR–Chs of Christ	6	250	251	290	0.8	1.7
Christian Un	1	NR	NR	NR	-	-
FRND–Evan Fr Ch Intl	1	130	160	198	0.6	1.2
Jehovah's Witness	1	NR	NR	NR	-	-
LUTH–E.L.C.A.	1	28	55	58	0.2	0.3
LUTH–Luth–MO Synod	1	47	113	170	0.5	1.0
METH–AME	1	0	100	124	0.4	0.7
METH–C.M.E.	1	0	150	186	0.5	1.1
METH–Un Methodist	8	443	1,497	1,563	4.6	9.3
Non-denom Chr Chs	5	500	655	680	2.0	4.0
PENT–Assemb of God	10	1,003	445	1,587	4.6	9.4
PENT–Pent Ch of God	1	70	NR	109	0.3	0.6
PENT–Un Pent Ch Intl	2	NR	NR	NR	-	-

NR–Not Reported - Represents no adherents reported. Percentages may not total 100 due to rounding.

Table 3: Religious Congregations by County and Group: 2010

Religious Group	Number of Congrega-tions	Number of Attendees	Number of Communicant, Confirmed, or Full Members	Adherents		
				Number of Adherents	% of Total Pop.	% of Total Adh.
PRES–Presb Ch (USA)	2	0	56	69	0.2	0.4
Sev Day Adv	1	16	29	33	0.1	0.2
LOGAN	**69**	**3,690**	**10,150**	**14,084**	**33.7**	**100.0**
ANG/EPIS–Episcopal	2	52	99	125	0.3	0.9
Bahá'í	0	NR	44	44	0.1	0.3
BAPT–NBC USA	1	0	150	186	0.4	1.3
BAPT–So Bapt Conv	18	1,442	4,789	5,937	14.2	42.2
Catholic	2	NR	NR	871	2.1	6.2
Ch of Nazarene	3	174	324	325	0.8	2.3
CHR–Chr Ch (Disc)	1	307	830	1,029	2.5	7.3
CHR–Chr Chs & Chs Cr	5	NR	412	511	1.2	3.6
CHR–Chs of Christ	5	191	196	216	0.5	1.5
Jehovah's Witness	1	NR	NR	NR	-	-
LDS–L-D Saints	2	NR	NR	843	2.0	6.0
LUTH–Luth–MO Synod	2	75	138	165	0.4	1.2
METH–AME	2	0	250	310	0.7	2.2
METH–C.M.E.	1	0	100	124	0.3	0.9
METH–Free Methodist	1	20	26	26	0.1	0.2
METH–Un Methodist	5	263	1,245	1,331	3.2	9.5
Non-denom Chr Chs	5	450	630	638	1.5	4.5
PENT–Assemb of God	4	560	355	708	1.7	5.0
PENT–Ch God (Cleve)	2	59	80	99	0.2	0.7
PENT–Ch of God Proph	1	NR	21	26	0.1	0.2
PENT–COGIC	2	0	300	372	0.9	2.6
PENT–Un Pent Ch Intl	1	NR	NR	NR	-	-
PRES–Presb Ch (USA)	1	73	111	138	0.3	1.0
Sev Day Adv	1	12	22	25	0.1	0.2
Un C of Christ	1	12	28	35	0.1	0.2
LOVE	**23**	**1,761**	**5,749**	**7,420**	**78.7**	**100.0**
BAPT–So Bapt Conv	11	943	4,425	5,457	57.9	73.5
Catholic	1	NR	NR	410	4.4	5.5
CHR–Chr Ch (Disc)	1	40	90	111	1.2	1.5
CHR–Chs of Christ	2	350	400	495	5.3	6.7
METH–Un Methodist	3	113	429	513	5.4	6.9
Non-denom Chr Chs	2	160	200	200	2.1	2.7
PENT–Assemb of God	1	50	80	80	0.8	1.1
PENT–Intl Pent Holiness	2	105	125	154	1.6	2.1
MCCLAIN	**76**	**5,772**	**12,855**	**17,542**	**50.8**	**100.0**
Bahá'í	0	NR	1	1	0.0	0.0
BAPT–Free Will Bapt	6	NR	570	718	2.1	4.1
BAPT–So Bapt Conv	25	3,398	8,244	10,381	30.1	59.2
Catholic	1	NR	NR	878	2.5	5.0
Ch of Nazarene	2	40	36	52	0.2	0.3
CHR–Chr Ch (Disc)	2	44	73	92	0.3	0.5
CHR–Chr Chs & Chs Cr	1	NR	155	195	0.6	1.1
CHR–Chs of Christ	7	324	329	392	1.1	2.2
Evan Cov Ch	1	304	89	395	1.1	2.3
HINDU–Post Ren	1	NR	NR	10	0.0	0.1
Jehovah's Witness	1	NR	NR	NR	-	-
LDS–L-D Saints	1	NR	NR	251	0.7	1.4
METH–AME	1	0	100	126	0.4	0.7
METH–Un Methodist	6	481	1,999	2,245	6.5	12.8
Non-denom Chr Chs	5	349	450	487	1.4	2.8
PENT–Assemb of God	4	253	160	285	0.8	1.6
PENT–Intl Pent Holiness	6	432	622	783	2.3	4.5
PENT–Pent Ch of God	2	140	NR	217	0.6	1.2
PENT–Un Pent Ch Intl	2	NR	NR	NR	-	-
PRES–Presb Ch (USA)	2	7	27	34	0.1	0.2
MCCURTAIN	**135**	**5,665**	**13,077**	**17,959**	**54.2**	**100.0**
ANG/EPIS–Episcopal	1	8	18	23	0.1	0.1
Bahá'í	0	NR	3	3	0.0	0.0
BAPT–Amer Bapt Assn	10	NR	1,299	1,625	4.9	9.0
BAPT–Free Will Bapt	2	NR	190	238	0.7	1.3
BAPT–Natl Mis Bapt Conv	1	0	150	188	0.6	1.0
BAPT–NBC USA	1	65	70	88	0.3	0.5
BAPT–So Bapt Conv	27	2,027	6,384	7,985	24.1	44.5
Catholic	1	NR	NR	215	0.6	1.2
Ch of Nazarene	1	14	46	46	0.1	0.3
CHR–Chr Ch (Disc)	1	16	25	31	0.1	0.2
CHR–Chr Chs & Chs Cr	4	NR	103	129	0.4	0.7
CHR–Chs of Christ	19	994	970	1,196	3.6	6.7
Jehovah's Witness	4	NR	NR	NR	-	-
LDS–L-D Saints	1	NR	NR	378	1.1	2.1
METH–C.M.E.	2	0	250	313	0.9	1.7
METH–Un Methodist	16	537	1,798	2,092	6.3	11.6
Non-denom Chr Chs	3	310	505	536	1.6	3.0
PENT–Assemb of God	15	1,203	635	1,969	5.9	11.0
PENT–Ch God (Cleve)	7	297	368	460	1.4	2.6
PENT–Pent Ch of God	1	70	NR	109	0.3	0.6
PENT–Un Pent Ch Intl	3	NR	NR	NR	-	-
PRES–Cumber Presb	2	NR	42	59	0.2	0.3
PRES–Presb Ch (USA)	13	124	221	276	0.8	1.5
MCINTOSH	**56**	**2,637**	**6,642**	**8,587**	**42.4**	**100.0**
ANG/EPIS–Episcopal	1	14	29	73	0.4	0.9
Bahá'í	0	NR	7	7	0.0	0.1
BAPT–Amer Bapt Assn	1	NR	85	101	0.5	1.2
BAPT–Free Will Bapt	3	NR	285	338	1.7	3.9
BAPT–Ind Bapt Flwsp Intl	1	NR	NR	NR	-	-
BAPT–So Bapt Conv	22	1,356	4,435	5,267	26.0	61.3
Catholic	1	NR	NR	132	0.7	1.5
CGOD–Ches God-Gen Con	1	39	47	56	0.3	0.7
Ch of Nazarene	1	19	30	30	0.1	0.3
CHR–Chr Ch (Disc)	1	21	15	18	0.1	0.2
CHR–Chr Chs & Chs Cr	2	NR	80	95	0.5	1.1
CHR–Chs of Christ	6	393	474	622	3.1	7.2
Jehovah's Witness	1	NR	NR	NR	-	-
LUTH–Luth–MO Synod	1	20	28	28	0.1	0.3
METH–AME	1	0	100	119	0.6	1.4
METH–Un Methodist	2	196	704	878	4.3	10.2
Non-denom Chr Chs	1	100	100	125	0.6	1.5
PENT–Assemb of God	3	325	106	449	2.2	5.2
PENT–Ch God (Cleve)	1	31	88	105	0.5	1.2
PENT–COGIC	1	20	0	0	0.0	0.0
PENT–Intl Pent Holiness	1	26	19	23	0.1	0.3
PENT–Pent Ch of God	1	70	NR	109	0.5	1.3
PENT–Un Pent Ch Intl	2	NR	NR	NR	-	-
PRES–Presb Ch (USA)	1	7	10	12	0.1	0.1
MAJOR	**35**	**1,664**	**4,233**	**5,293**	**70.3**	**100.0**
BAPT–So Bapt Conv	7	436	1,421	1,730	23.0	32.7
Catholic	1	NR	NR	53	0.7	1.0
Ch God (7th Day)	1	NR	NR	NR	-	-
Ch of Nazarene	4	241	264	342	4.5	6.5
CHR–Chr Ch (Disc)	4	161	391	476	6.3	9.0
CHR–Chr Chs & Chs Cr	1	NR	75	91	1.2	1.7
CHR–Chs of Christ	2	100	93	121	1.6	2.3
Christian Un	1	NR	NR	NR	-	-
MENN–CG in Cr (Menn)	1	NR	150	183	2.4	3.5
MENN–Fel Evg Bib Ch	1	30	35	30	0.4	0.6
MENN–Menn Br US Conf	2	NR	703	856	11.4	16.2
METH–Un Methodist	5	276	701	909	12.1	17.2
METH–Wesleyan	1	45	46	59	0.8	1.1
Non-denom Chr Chs	1	200	250	250	3.3	4.7
PENT–Assemb of God	3	175	104	193	2.6	3.6
MARSHALL	**40**	**2,572**	**6,436**	**8,779**	**55.4**	**100.0**
BAPT–Ind Bapt Flwsp Intl	1	NR	NR	NR	-	-
BAPT–So Bapt Conv	20	1,657	4,530	5,542	35.0	63.1
Catholic	1	NR	NR	956	6.0	10.9
Ch of Nazarene	1	34	114	114	0.7	1.3
CHR–Chs of Christ	7	449	506	639	4.0	7.3
METH–Un Methodist	3	267	1,053	1,137	7.2	13.0
PENT–Assemb of God	2	112	38	152	1.0	1.7
PENT–COGIC	1	0	150	184	1.2	2.1
PENT–Intl Pent Holiness	1	53	45	55	0.3	0.6
PENT–Un Pent Ch Intl	3	NR	NR	NR	-	-
MAYES	**117**	**6,787**	**15,074**	**20,646**	**50.0**	**100.0**
ANG/EPIS–Episcopal	1	31	60	61	0.1	0.3

NR–Not Reported   - Represents no adherents reported.   Percentages may not total 100 due to rounding.

Table 3: Religious Congregations by County and Group: 2010

Religious Group	Number of Congregations	Number of Attendees	Number of Communicant, Confirmed, or Full Members	Adherents: Number of Adherents	Adherents: % of Total Pop.	Adherents: % of Total Adh.
Bahá'í	0	NR	46	46	0.1	0.2
BAPT–Amer Bapt Assn	2	NR	170	211	0.5	1.0
BAPT–Free Will Bapt	10	NR	950	1,181	2.9	5.7
BAPT–So Bapt Conv	37	3,168	8,309	10,325	25.0	50.0
Catholic	2	NR	NR	900	2.2	4.4
CGOD–Ch God (Ander)	1	254	NR	254	0.6	1.2
Ch of Nazarene	2	78	118	148	0.4	0.7
CHR–Chr Ch (Disc)	3	211	480	596	1.4	2.9
CHR–Chr Chs & Chs Cr	5	NR	466	579	1.4	2.8
CHR–Chs of Christ	5	412	418	504	1.2	2.4
Evan Free Ch	1	80	NR	80	0.2	0.4
Jehovah's Witness	1	NR	NR	NR	-	-
LDS–Comm of Christ	1	NR	135	135	0.3	0.7
LDS–L-D Saints	1	NR	NR	390	0.9	1.9
LUTH–Luth-MO Synod	2	118	197	262	0.6	1.3
MENN–Amish Undif	3	NR	151	272	0.7	1.3
MENN–CG in Cr (Menn)	1	NR	33	41	0.1	0.2
MENN–Cons Menn Conf	2	175	162	201	0.5	1.0
METH–Un Methodist	6	505	1,523	1,848	4.5	9.0
Non-denom Chr Chs	11	925	1,125	1,240	3.0	6.0
PENT–Assemb of God	8	448	270	693	1.7	3.4
PENT–Ch God (Cleve)	3	234	279	347	0.8	1.7
PENT–Ch God Apos Fth	1	NR	NR	NR	-	-
PENT–Ch of God Proph	1	NR	61	76	0.2	0.4
PENT–Pent Ch of God	1	70	NR	109	0.3	0.5
PENT–Un Pent Ch Intl	2	NR	NR	NR	-	-
PRES–Cumber Presb	1	NR	13	14	0.0	0.1
PRES–Presb Ch (USA)	2	70	95	118	0.3	0.6
Sev Day Adv	1	8	13	15	0.0	0.1
MURRAY	**38**	**2,652**	**5,991**	**7,477**	**55.4**	**100.0**
Bahá'í	0	NR	2	2	0.0	0.0
BAPT–Free Will Bapt	2	NR	190	234	1.7	3.1
BAPT–So Bapt Conv	10	976	3,280	4,041	30.0	54.0
Catholic	1	NR	NR	246	1.8	3.3
CHR–Chr Ch (Disc)	1	70	141	174	1.3	2.3
CHR–Chr Chs & Chs Cr	1	NR	75	92	0.7	1.2
CHR–Chs of Christ	5	395	392	450	3.3	6.0
Jehovah's Witness	1	NR	NR	NR	-	-
LUTH–Luth-MO Synod	1	8	18	21	0.2	0.3
METH–Un Methodist	2	244	712	886	6.6	11.8
Non-denom Chr Chs	4	750	915	977	7.2	13.1
PENT–Assemb of God	2	51	23	62	0.5	0.8
PENT–Intl Pent Holiness	2	104	94	116	0.9	1.6
PENT–Un Pent Ch Intl	3	NR	NR	NR	-	-
PRES–Presb Ch (USA)	2	0	56	69	0.5	0.9
Sev Day Adv	1	54	93	107	0.8	1.4
MUSKOGEE	**178**	**15,101**	**38,587**	**51,789**	**73.0**	**100.0**
ANG/EPIS–Episcopal	1	89	171	236	0.3	0.5
Bahá'í	0	NR	79	79	0.1	0.2
BAPT–Amer Bapt USA	1	60	123	152	0.2	0.3
BAPT–Free Will Bapt	6	NR	570	706	1.0	1.4
BAPT–Ind Bapt Flwsp Intl	1	NR	NR	NR	-	-
BAPT–Natl Mis Bapt Conv	4	0	360	446	0.6	0.9
BAPT–NBC Amer	1	100	200	248	0.3	0.5
BAPT–NBC USA	5	290	1,270	1,573	2.2	3.0
BAPT–S-D Baptist Gen Con	1	NR	NR	NR	-	-
BAPT–So Bapt Conv	47	4,957	18,696	23,152	32.6	44.7
Catholic	2	NR	NR	2,500	3.5	4.8
CGOD–Ches God-Gen Con	1	14	13	16	0.0	0.0
Ch of Nazarene	1	133	175	256	0.4	0.5
CHR–Chr Ch (Disc)	1	14	20	25	0.0	0.0
CHR–Chr Chs & Chs Cr	5	NR	1,455	1,802	2.5	3.5
CHR–Chs of Christ	17	1,607	1,591	2,106	3.0	4.1
Evan Free Ch	1	60	NR	60	0.1	0.1
Jehovah's Witness	1	NR	NR	NR	-	-
JUD–Reform	1	8	14	38	0.1	0.1
LDS–L-D Saints	2	NR	NR	1,356	1.9	2.6
LUTH–Luth-MO Synod	1	34	130	159	0.2	0.3
METH–AME	4	75	380	471	0.7	0.9
METH–C.M.E.	2	0	200	248	0.3	0.5
METH–Un Methodist	12	875	5,166	5,762	8.1	11.1

Religious Group	Number of Congregations	Number of Attendees	Number of Communicant, Confirmed, or Full Members	Adherents: Number of Adherents	Adherents: % of Total Pop.	Adherents: % of Total Adh.
Muslim Est	1	134	NR	308	0.4	0.6
Non-denom Chr Chs	22	3,439	4,760	4,906	6.9	9.5
PENT–Assemb of God	15	2,254	2,171	3,353	4.7	6.5
PENT–Ch God (Cleve)	2	65	69	85	0.1	0.2
PENT–Ch of God Proph	1	NR	17	21	0.0	0.0
PENT–Intl Pent Holiness	4	226	205	254	0.4	0.5
PENT–Pent Ch of God	4	280	NR	435	0.6	0.8
PENT–Un Pent Ch Intl	3	NR	NR	NR	-	-
PRES–Presb Ch (USA)	4	169	356	441	0.6	0.9
Salvation Army	1	50	105	260	0.4	0.5
Sev Day Adv	2	168	291	335	0.5	0.6
Unity Ch	1	NR	NR	NR	-	-
NOBLE	**34**	**1,897**	**6,040**	**7,994**	**69.1**	**100.0**
ANG/EPIS–Episcopal	1	19	28	28	0.2	0.4
BAPT–Amer Bapt Assn	1	NR	85	106	0.9	1.3
BAPT–Ind Bapt Flwsp Intl	1	NR	NR	NR	-	-
BAPT–So Bapt Conv	7	625	2,462	3,057	26.4	38.2
BRETH–Ch of Brethren	1	0	166	206	1.8	2.6
Catholic	2	NR	NR	350	3.0	4.4
Ch of Nazarene	1	126	211	211	1.8	2.6
CHR–Chr Ch (Disc)	3	207	1,020	1,267	11.0	15.8
CHR–Chr Chs & Chs Cr	2	NR	50	62	0.5	0.8
CHR–Chs of Christ	1	115	127	193	1.7	2.4
Jehovah's Witness	1	NR	NR	NR	-	-
LUTH–E.L.C.A.	1	70	97	114	1.0	1.4
LUTH–Luth-MO Synod	1	90	457	619	5.4	7.7
METH–AME	1	0	150	186	1.6	2.3
METH–Un Methodist	6	266	808	936	8.1	11.7
Non-denom Chr Chs	1	120	120	150	1.3	1.9
PENT–Assemb of God	2	155	20	212	1.8	2.7
PRES–Presb Ch (USA)	1	104	239	297	2.6	3.7
NOWATA	**25**	**1,195**	**2,955**	**3,591**	**34.1**	**100.0**
Bahá'í	0	NR	6	6	0.1	0.2
BAPT–So Bapt Conv	6	320	1,074	1,314	12.5	36.6
Catholic	1	NR	NR	50	0.5	1.4
CGOD–Ch God (Ander)	1	30	NR	30	0.3	0.8
Ch of Nazarene	1	16	32	32	0.3	0.9
CHR–Chr Ch (Disc)	1	50	143	175	1.7	4.9
CHR–Chr Chs & Chs Cr	1	NR	220	269	2.6	7.5
CHR–Chs of Christ	2	65	79	97	0.9	2.7
Jehovah's Witness	1	NR	NR	NR	-	-
METH–Un Methodist	4	146	703	761	7.2	21.2
Non-denom Chr Chs	2	370	470	500	4.7	13.9
PENT–Assemb of God	1	40	21	107	1.0	3.0
PENT–Ch God (Cleve)	1	82	100	122	1.2	3.4
PENT–Intl Pent Holiness	1	50	34	42	0.4	1.2
PRES–Presb Ch (USA)	1	0	27	33	0.3	0.9
Sev Day Adv	1	26	46	53	0.5	1.5
OKFUSKEE	**37**	**1,527**	**4,872**	**6,084**	**49.9**	**100.0**
Bahá'í	0	NR	4	4	0.0	0.1
BAPT–Amer Bapt Assn	2	NR	135	164	1.3	2.7
BAPT–Free Will Bapt	3	NR	285	346	2.8	5.7
BAPT–NBC Amer	1	40	40	49	0.4	0.8
BAPT–So Bapt Conv	12	911	3,340	4,060	33.3	66.7
Catholic	1	NR	NR	15	0.1	0.2
CGOD–Ch God (Ander)	1	0	NR	0	0.0	0.0
CHR–Chr Ch (Disc)	2	41	90	109	0.9	1.8
CHR–Chr Chs & Chs Cr	1	NR	30	36	0.3	0.6
CHR–Chs of Christ	3	208	190	243	2.0	4.0
METH–AME	2	0	250	304	2.5	5.0
METH–C.M.E.	1	5	10	12	0.1	0.2
METH–Un Methodist	1	95	309	373	3.1	6.1
Non-denom Chr Chs	1	80	100	100	0.8	1.6
PENT–Assemb of God	3	126	64	236	1.9	3.9
PENT–Full Gosp Bapt	1	NR	NR	NR	-	-
PENT–Intl Pent Holiness	1	21	25	30	0.2	0.5
PENT–Un Pent Ch Intl	1	NR	NR	NR	-	-
Zoroastrian	0	NR	NR	3	0.0	0.0

NR–Not Reported - Represents no adherents reported. Percentages may not total 100 due to rounding.

Table 3: Religious Congregations by County and Group: 2010

Religious Group	Number of Congregations	Number of Attendees	Number of Communicant, Confirmed, or Full Members	Adherents: Number of Adherents	Adherents: % of Total Pop.	Adherents: % of Total Adh.
OKLAHOMA	**905**	**181,216**	**320,010**	**520,992**	**72.5**	**100.0**
ANG/EPIS–Anglican NA	1	NR	NR	NR	-	-
ANG/EPIS–Episcopal	12	1,931	4,117	5,226	0.7	1.0
Bahá'í	3	NR	388	388	0.1	0.1
BAPT–Amer Bapt Assn	6	NR	585	732	0.1	0.1
BAPT–Amer Bapt USA	1	850	2,000	2,503	0.3	0.5
BAPT–Free Will Bapt	13	NR	1,235	1,546	0.2	0.3
BAPT–Ind Bapt Flwsp Intl	4	NR	NR	NR	-	-
BAPT–Natl Mis Bapt Conv	4	0	600	751	0.1	0.1
BAPT–NBC Amer	5	890	1,885	2,359	0.3	0.5
BAPT–NBC USA	11	2,901	5,751	7,197	1.0	1.4
BAPT–Prog NBC	9	1,655	4,950	6,195	0.9	1.2
BAPT–Ref Bapt Ch	2	NR	NR	NR	-	-
BAPT–So Bapt Conv	181	31,754	118,626	148,461	20.7	28.5
BUDD–Mahayana	12	NR	NR	6,952	1.0	1.3
BUDD–Theravada	4	NR	NR	2,054	0.3	0.4
BUDD–Vajrayana	1	NR	NR	36	0.0	0.0
Calv Chpl	2	NR	NR	NR	-	-
Catholic	27	NR	NR	61,318	8.5	11.8
CGOD–Ch God (Ander)	5	4,699	NR	4,699	0.7	0.9
Ch Cr, Scientst	5	NR	NR	NR	-	-
Ch God (7th Day)	2	NR	NR	NR	-	-
Ch of Nazarene	32	7,773	12,691	14,413	2.0	2.8
Chr & Miss Al	2	53	29	84	0.0	0.0
CHR–Chr Ch (Disc)	23	3,081	7,771	9,725	1.4	1.9
CHR–Chr Chs & Chs Cr	10	NR	2,210	2,766	0.4	0.5
CHR–Chs of Christ	56	13,296	13,577	17,894	2.5	3.4
CHR–Int Chs of Christ	1	NR	58	73	0.0	0.0
Christian Brethren	2	NR	NR	NR	-	-
CONG–Cong Chr, NA	1	NR	30	38	0.0	0.0
Evan Cov Ch	2	28,193	4,455	36,651	5.1	7.0
Evan Free Ch	2	0	NR	0	0.0	0.0
FRND–Evan Fr Ch Intl	1	24	22	28	0.0	0.0
FRND–Fr Gen Cf	1	NR	28	35	0.0	0.0
HINDU–I/A Temples	1	NR	NR	416	0.1	0.1
HINDU–Post Ren	5	NR	NR	230	0.0	0.0
HINDU–Trad Temples	1	NR	NR	4,200	0.6	0.8
Intl Fell Bible Ch	1	NR	NR	NR	-	-
Jehovah's Witness	13	NR	NR	NR	-	-
JUD–Conserv	1	138	155	418	0.1	0.1
JUD–Reform	1	175	309	834	0.1	0.2
LDS–Comm of Christ	3	NR	468	468	0.1	0.1
LDS–L-D Saints	12	NR	NR	7,713	1.1	1.5
LUTH–Assoc Free Luth	1	NR	NR	NR	-	-
LUTH–E.L.C.A.	8	623	1,263	1,577	0.2	0.3
LUTH–Luth Cong Msn Chr	1	NR	NR	NR	-	-
LUTH–Luth-MO Synod	9	1,126	2,997	3,912	0.5	0.8
LUTH–Nor Amer Luth C	1	NR	NR	NR	-	-
LUTH–Wisc Ev Luth Syn	1	94	133	169	0.0	0.0
MENN–Menn Br US Conf	1	NR	163	204	0.0	0.0
MENN–Mennonite USA	2	20	16	20	0.0	0.0
METH–AME	9	150	1,550	1,940	0.3	0.4
METH–AME Zion	1	0	100	125	0.0	0.0
METH–C.M.E.	7	205	1,150	1,439	0.2	0.3
METH–Free Methodist	20	1,249	914	1,626	0.2	0.3
METH–Un Methodist	55	10,473	47,619	55,343	7.7	10.6
METH–Wesleyan	1	45	56	59	0.0	0.0
Muslim Est	5	1,436	NR	2,232	0.3	0.4
Nat Spirit Asso	1	NR	NR	NR	-	-
New Apost Ch	1	NR	NR	NR	-	-
Non-denom Chr Chs	128	46,837	57,634	65,046	9.1	12.5
ORTHE–Ant Orth of NA	3	437	NR	1,024	0.1	0.2
ORTHE–Greek Orthodox	1	100	NR	250	0.0	0.0
ORTHE–Rus Orth Abroad	1	48	NR	94	0.0	0.0
ORTHE–Ukrainian Orth	1	35	NR	75	0.0	0.0
ORTHO–Armen Ap Etchm	1	45	NR	100	0.0	0.0
ORTHO–Ethiopian Orth	1	NR	NR	NR	-	-
ORTHO–Malan Dioc Am	1	40	NR	120	0.0	0.0
ORTHO–Malan Syr Orth	1	75	NR	144	0.0	0.0
PENT–Assemb of God	43	11,100	6,295	16,004	2.2	3.1
PENT–Ch God (Cleve)	7	554	503	630	0.1	0.1
PENT–Ch God Apos Fth	2	NR	NR	NR	-	-
PENT–Ch of God Proph	3	NR	195	244	0.0	0.0
PENT–COGIC	14	520	1,870	2,340	0.3	0.4
PENT–Full Gosp Bapt	4	NR	NR	NR	-	-
PENT–Int Foursq Gos	2	153	222	278	0.0	0.1
PENT–Intl Pent Holiness	26	3,397	4,189	5,243	0.7	1.0
PENT–Pent Ch of God	5	350	NR	544	0.1	0.1
PENT–Un Pent Ch Intl	8	NR	NR	NR	-	-
PENT–Vineyard	1	73	50	63	0.0	0.0
PRES–Cumber Presb	2	NR	77	166	0.0	0.0
PRES–Korean Amer Pres	1	NR	NR	NR	-	-
PRES–Korean Pres Amer	1	NR	NR	NR	-	-
PRES–Orth Pres Ch	1	14	30	38	0.0	0.0
PRES–Presb Ch (USA)	16	1,534	5,667	7,092	1.0	1.4
PRES–Presb Ch Amer	2	263	245	271	0.0	0.1
REF–Ref Ch in Am	1	292	393	491	0.1	0.1
Salvation Army	1	63	174	225	0.0	0.0
Sev Day Adv	14	1,576	2,740	3,152	0.4	0.6
Sikh	1	NR	NR	NR	-	-
Un C of Christ	4	615	1,329	1,663	0.2	0.3
Unit Univ	2	261	496	641	0.1	0.1
Unity Ch	1	NR	NR	NR	-	-
Zoroastrian	0	NR	NR	5	0.0	0.0
OKMULGEE	**93**	**6,445**	**20,175**	**26,575**	**66.3**	**100.0**
ANG/EPIS–Episcopal	1	17	28	47	0.1	0.2
Bahá'í	0	NR	11	11	0.0	0.0
BAPT–Free Will Bapt	3	NR	285	352	0.9	1.3
BAPT–NBC Amer	1	75	90	111	0.3	0.4
BAPT–So Bapt Conv	23	2,746	12,283	15,171	37.9	57.1
Catholic	2	NR	NR	1,150	2.9	4.3
Ch of Nazarene	2	317	513	565	1.4	2.1
CHR–Chr Ch (Disc)	4	113	571	705	1.8	2.7
CHR–Chr Chs & Chs Cr	1	NR	168	208	0.5	0.8
CHR–Chs of Christ	8	553	626	762	1.9	2.9
Jehovah's Witness	1	NR	NR	NR	-	-
LDS–Comm of Christ	1	NR	156	156	0.4	0.6
LDS–L-D Saints	1	NR	NR	553	1.4	2.1
LUTH–Luth-MO Synod	1	47	148	187	0.5	0.7
METH–AME	2	30	135	167	0.4	0.6
METH–AME Zion	1	0	150	185	0.5	0.7
METH–C.M.E.	1	20	50	62	0.2	0.2
METH–Free Methodist	1	5	5	5	0.0	0.0
METH–Un Methodist	6	459	2,014	2,319	5.8	8.7
Non-denom Chr Chs	11	927	1,207	1,297	3.2	4.9
PENT–Assemb of God	7	532	241	731	1.8	2.8
PENT–Ch God (Cleve)	1	6	25	31	0.1	0.1
PENT–Ch of God Proph	1	NR	75	93	0.2	0.3
PENT–COGIC	1	0	150	185	0.5	0.7
PENT–Int Foursq Gos	1	54	46	57	0.1	0.2
PENT–Intl Pent Holiness	3	415	909	1,123	2.8	4.2
PENT–Un Pent Ch Intl	4	NR	NR	NR	-	-
PRES–Presb Ch (USA)	2	35	124	153	0.4	0.6
Sev Day Adv	2	94	165	189	0.5	0.7
OSAGE	**80**	**3,589**	**11,285**	**15,979**	**33.7**	**100.0**
ANG/EPIS–Episcopal	1	28	48	48	0.1	0.3
Bahá'í	0	NR	6	6	0.0	0.0
BAPT–Free Will Bapt	1	NR	95	117	0.2	0.7
BAPT–NBC USA	1	10	20	25	0.1	0.2
BAPT–So Bapt Conv	21	1,555	7,768	9,545	20.1	59.7
Catholic	7	NR	NR	1,500	3.2	9.4
Ch of Nazarene	4	164	254	320	0.7	2.0
CHR–Chr Ch (Disc)	3	67	279	343	0.7	2.1
CHR–Chr Chs & Chs Cr	3	NR	285	350	0.7	2.2
CHR–Chs of Christ	6	283	229	340	0.7	2.1
FRND–Fr Un Mtg	1	NR	81	100	0.2	0.6
Jehovah's Witness	1	NR	NR	NR	-	-
LDS–L-D Saints	1	NR	NR	144	0.3	0.9
METH–Un Methodist	8	238	957	1,176	2.5	7.4
Non-denom Chr Chs	6	455	605	634	1.3	4.0
PENT–Assemb of God	9	631	380	880	1.9	5.5
PENT–Ch God (Cleve)	1	23	22	27	0.1	0.2
PENT–Ch God Apos Fth	1	NR	NR	NR	-	-
PENT–COGIC	1	0	150	184	0.4	1.2
PENT–Intl Pent Holiness	1	8	12	15	0.0	0.1

NR–Not Reported   - Represents no adherents reported.   Percentages may not total 100 due to rounding.

Table 3: Religious Congregations by County and Group: 2010

Religious Group	Number of Congrega-tions	Number of Attendees	Number of Communicant, Confirmed, or Full Members	Adherents		
				Number of Adherents	% of Total Pop.	% of Total Adh.
PENT–Pent Ch of God	1	70	NR	109	0.2	0.7
PRES–Presb Ch (USA)	2	57	94	116	0.2	0.7
OTTAWA	**84**	**4,989**	**17,436**	**23,127**	**72.6**	**100.0**
ANG/EPIS–Episcopal	1	35	94	110	0.3	0.5
Bahá'í	0	NR	16	16	0.1	0.1
BAPT–Amer Bapt Assn	1	NR	85	105	0.3	0.5
BAPT–Free Will Bapt	1	NR	95	118	0.4	0.5
BAPT–So Bapt Conv	29	2,148	11,119	13,758	43.2	59.5
Catholic	1	NR	NR	1,000	3.1	4.3
Ch of Nazarene	1	112	198	198	0.6	0.9
CHR–Chr Ch (Disc)	1	62	198	245	0.8	1.1
CHR–Chr Chs & Chs Cr	8	NR	1,320	1,633	5.1	7.1
CHR–Chs of Christ	4	190	179	234	0.7	1.0
FRND–Evan Fr Ch Intl	2	103	8	10	0.0	0.0
FRND–Fr Un Mtg	1	NR	3	4	0.0	0.0
Jehovah's Witness	1	NR	NR	NR	-	-
LDS–Comm of Christ	1	NR	135	135	0.4	0.6
LDS–L-D Saints	1	NR	NR	495	1.6	2.1
LUTH–Luth-MO Synod	2	139	278	348	1.1	1.5
METH–Un Methodist	6	334	1,910	2,075	6.5	9.0
Non-denom Chr Chs	6	650	920	920	2.9	4.0
PENT–Assemb of God	13	1,060	688	1,381	4.3	6.0
PENT–Pent Ch of God	1	70	NR	109	0.3	0.5
PENT–Un Pent Ch Intl	1	NR	NR	NR	-	-
PRES–Presb Ch (USA)	1	68	158	196	0.6	0.8
Sev Day Adv	1	18	32	37	0.1	0.2
PAWNEE	**44**	**2,079**	**6,845**	**8,860**	**53.4**	**100.0**
ANG/EPIS–Episcopal	2	25	29	66	0.4	0.7
Bahá'í	0	NR	3	3	0.0	0.0
BAPT–Free Will Bapt	2	NR	190	234	1.4	2.6
BAPT–So Bapt Conv	9	863	4,241	5,229	31.5	59.0
Catholic	1	NR	NR	22	0.1	0.2
Ch of Nazarene	1	70	134	233	1.4	2.6
CHR–Chr Ch (Disc)	1	89	190	234	1.4	2.6
CHR–Chr Chs & Chs Cr	2	NR	335	413	2.5	4.7
CHR–Chs of Christ	3	160	170	205	1.2	2.3
Ind Fund Churches	1	NR	NR	NR	-	-
Jehovah's Witness	2	NR	NR	NR	-	-
LDS–L-D Saints	1	NR	NR	373	2.3	4.2
METH–Un Methodist	6	189	751	871	5.3	9.8
Non-denom Chr Chs	4	263	385	385	2.3	4.3
PENT–Assemb of God	4	289	254	396	2.4	4.5
PENT–Ch of God Proph	1	NR	9	11	0.1	0.1
PENT–Intl Pent Holiness	1	89	62	76	0.5	0.9
PENT–Un Pent Ch Intl	1	NR	NR	NR	-	-
PRES–Presb Ch (USA)	1	18	49	60	0.4	0.7
Sev Day Adv	1	24	43	49	0.3	0.6
PAYNE	**120**	**10,590**	**26,875**	**37,393**	**48.3**	**100.0**
ANG/EPIS–Episcopal	2	129	372	387	0.5	1.0
Bahá'í	1	NR	26	26	0.0	0.1
BAPT–Amer Bapt Assn	1	NR	85	100	0.1	0.3
BAPT–Free Will Bapt	3	NR	285	336	0.4	0.9
BAPT–Natl Mis Bapt Conv	1	0	150	177	0.2	0.5
BAPT–So Bapt Conv	26	3,793	12,846	15,131	19.6	40.5
BRETH–Ch of Brethren	1	55	121	143	0.2	0.4
BUDD–Mahayana	1	NR	NR	11	0.0	0.0
BUDD–Theravada	1	NR	NR	15	0.0	0.0
Catholic	3	NR	NR	3,000	3.9	8.0
CGOD–Ch God (Ander)	2	22	NR	22	0.0	0.1
Ch Cr, Scientst	1	NR	NR	NR	-	-
Ch of Nazarene	2	99	207	248	0.3	0.7
Chr & Miss Al	1	59	33	77	0.1	0.2
CHR–Chr Ch (Disc)	2	366	1,315	1,549	2.0	4.1
CHR–Chr Chs & Chs Cr	6	NR	1,796	2,116	2.7	5.7
CHR–Chs of Christ	9	1,020	1,010	1,358	1.8	3.6
Evan Free Ch	1	40	NR	40	0.1	0.1
FRND–Evan Fr Ch Intl	1	28	39	46	0.1	0.1
FRND–Fr Gen Cf	1	NR	35	41	0.1	0.1
Jehovah's Witness	2	NR	NR	NR	-	-
LDS–Comm of Christ	1	NR	156	156	0.2	0.4
LDS–L-D Saints	4	NR	NR	1,472	1.9	3.9
LUTH–E.L.C.A.	1	111	184	263	0.3	0.7
LUTH–Luth-MO Synod	2	197	372	470	0.6	1.3
METH–Free Methodist	2	61	52	62	0.1	0.2
METH–Un Methodist	8	1,261	4,255	5,284	6.8	14.1
Muslim Est	1	134	NR	308	0.4	0.8
Non-denom Chr Chs	11	1,720	2,085	2,256	2.9	6.0
PENT–Assemb of God	8	745	498	914	1.2	2.4
PENT–Ch God (Cleve)	1	15	36	42	0.1	0.1
PENT–COGIC	1	20	12	14	0.0	0.0
PENT–Intl Pent Holiness	1	33	33	39	0.1	0.1
PENT–Pent Ch of God	2	140	NR	217	0.3	0.6
PENT–Un Pent Ch Intl	2	NR	NR	NR	-	-
PRES–Presb Ch (USA)	2	294	625	736	1.0	2.0
PRES–Presb Ch Amer	1	100	65	78	0.1	0.2
PRES–Ref Pres of NA	1	54	48	75	0.1	0.2
Salvation Army	1	30	44	70	0.1	0.2
Sev Day Adv	1	34	58	67	0.1	0.2
Unit Univ	1	30	32	46	0.1	0.1
Zoroastrian	0	NR	NR	1	0.0	0.0
PITTSBURG	**135**	**7,072**	**23,849**	**30,689**	**67.0**	**100.0**
ANG/EPIS–Episcopal	1	64	117	118	0.3	0.4
Bahá'í	0	NR	7	7	0.0	0.0
BAPT–Amer Bapt Assn	1	NR	85	103	0.2	0.3
BAPT–Free Will Bapt	8	NR	760	916	2.0	3.0
BAPT–Ind Bapt Flwsp Intl	1	NR	NR	NR	-	-
BAPT–Natl Mis Bapt Conv	1	0	150	181	0.4	0.6
BAPT–NBC USA	1	0	350	422	0.9	1.4
BAPT–So Bapt Conv	43	2,721	14,432	17,403	38.0	56.7
Catholic	1	NR	NR	1,500	3.3	4.9
CGOD–Ches God-Gen Con	1	25	31	37	0.1	0.1
Ch God (7th Day)	1	NR	NR	NR	-	-
Ch of Nazarene	3	218	320	378	0.8	1.2
CHR–Chr Ch (Disc)	2	79	152	183	0.4	0.6
CHR–Chr Chs & Chs Cr	6	NR	543	655	1.4	2.1
CHR–Chs of Christ	13	963	964	1,166	2.5	3.8
FRND–Fr Gen Cf	1	NR	0	0	0.0	0.0
Jehovah's Witness	2	NR	NR	NR	-	-
LDS–Comm of Christ	2	NR	312	312	0.7	1.0
LDS–L-D Saints	1	NR	NR	589	1.3	1.9
LUTH–Luth-MO Synod	1	45	147	179	0.4	0.6
METH–AME	1	0	100	121	0.3	0.4
METH–Un Methodist	11	482	2,087	2,240	4.9	7.3
Non-denom Chr Chs	9	1,450	2,150	2,175	4.7	7.1
ORTHE–Orth Ch in Amer	1	12	NR	12	0.0	0.0
PENT–Assemb of God	9	463	292	689	1.5	2.2
PENT–Ch God (Cleve)	1	56	152	183	0.4	0.6
PENT–Ch of God Proph	1	NR	7	8	0.0	0.0
PENT–Int Foursq Gos	1	37	25	30	0.1	0.1
PENT–Intl Pent Holiness	3	117	134	162	0.4	0.5
PENT–Pent Ch of God	2	140	NR	217	0.5	0.7
PENT–Un Pent Ch Intl	2	NR	NR	NR	-	-
PRES–Presb Ch (USA)	1	145	417	503	1.1	1.6
Salvation Army	1	24	61	138	0.3	0.4
Sev Day Adv	2	31	54	62	0.1	0.2
PONTOTOC	**103**	**7,523**	**16,558**	**21,657**	**57.8**	**100.0**
ANG/EPIS–Episcopal	1	80	158	180	0.5	0.8
Bahá'í	0	NR	31	31	0.1	0.1
BAPT–Amer Bapt Assn	1	NR	85	104	0.3	0.5
BAPT–Free Will Bapt	12	NR	1,140	1,398	3.7	6.5
BAPT–NBC USA	1	0	500	613	1.6	2.8
BAPT–Ref Bapt Ch	1	NR	NR	NR	-	-
BAPT–So Bapt Conv	28	3,328	8,106	9,941	26.5	45.9
Catholic	1	NR	NR	574	1.5	2.7
Ch of Nazarene	1	110	182	182	0.5	0.8
CHR–Chr Ch (Disc)	1	60	270	331	0.9	1.5
CHR–Chr Chs & Chs Cr	1	NR	105	129	0.3	0.6
CHR–Chs of Christ	11	1,263	1,249	1,590	4.2	7.3
Jehovah's Witness	1	NR	NR	NR	-	-
JUD–Reform	1	9	15	40	0.1	0.2
LDS–L-D Saints	1	NR	NR	511	1.4	2.4

NR–Not Reported - Represents no adherents reported. Percentages may not total 100 due to rounding.

Table 3: Religious Congregations by County and Group: 2010

Religious Group	Number of Congrega-tions	Number of Attendees	Number of Communicant, Confirmed, or Full Members	Adherents		
				Number of Adherents	% of Total Pop.	% of Total Adh.
LUTH–Luth–MO Synod	1	44	89	107	0.3	0.5
METH–Un Methodist	8	489	2,095	2,352	6.3	10.9
Muslim Est	1	134	NR	308	0.8	1.4
Non-denom Chr Chs	8	1,010	1,185	1,350	3.6	6.2
PENT–Assemb of God	6	237	100	308	0.8	1.4
PENT–Ch God (Cleve)	1	118	204	250	0.7	1.2
PENT–Ch of God Proph	2	NR	47	58	0.2	0.3
PENT–COGIC	1	0	0	0	0.0	0.0
PENT–Int Foursq Gos	1	124	103	126	0.3	0.6
PENT–Intl Pent Holiness	5	337	503	617	1.6	2.8
PENT–Pent Ch of God	1	70	NR	109	0.3	0.5
PENT–Un Pent Ch Intl	2	NR	NR	NR	-	-
PRES–Cumber Presb	1	NR	90	100	0.3	0.5
PRES–Presb Ch (USA)	1	64	174	213	0.6	1.0
Salvation Army	1	16	75	75	0.2	0.3
Sev Day Adv	1	30	52	60	0.2	0.3
POTTAWATOMIE	**140**	**12,157**	**34,368**	**44,594**	**64.2**	**100.0**
ANG/EPIS–Episcopal	1	102	186	303	0.4	0.7
Bahá'í	0	NR	25	25	0.0	0.1
BAPT–Amer Bapt Assn	2	NR	235	292	0.4	0.7
BAPT–Free Will Bapt	7	NR	665	826	1.2	1.9
BAPT–Natl Mis Bapt Conv	1	0	150	186	0.3	0.4
BAPT–So Bapt Conv	42	5,708	22,771	28,269	40.7	63.4
Catholic	3	NR	NR	1,534	2.2	3.4
CGOD–Ch God (Ander)	1	156	NR	156	0.2	0.3
CGOD–Ches God-Gen Con	1	50	130	161	0.2	0.4
Ch Cr, Scientst	1	NR	NR	NR	-	-
Ch God (7th Day)	1	NR	NR	NR	-	-
Ch of Nazarene	2	127	403	426	0.6	1.0
CHR–Chr Ch (Disc)	2	138	449	557	0.8	1.2
CHR–Chr Chs & Chs Cr	2	NR	108	134	0.2	0.3
CHR–Chs of Christ	16	1,541	1,428	1,845	2.7	4.1
FRND–Evan Fr Ch Intl	1	28	19	24	0.0	0.1
Jehovah's Witness	2	NR	NR	NR	-	-
LDS–L-D Saints	1	NR	NR	10	0.0	0.0
LUTH–E.L.C.A.	1	89	112	137	0.2	0.3
LUTH–Luth–MO Synod	1	125	164	204	0.3	0.5
METH–AME	1	14	14	17	0.0	0.0
METH–C.M.E.	1	0	100	124	0.2	0.3
METH–Free Methodist	3	75	86	157	0.2	0.4
METH–Un Methodist	11	591	3,436	3,806	5.5	8.5
Non-denom Chr Chs	10	1,615	2,510	2,563	3.7	5.7
PENT–Assemb of God	9	766	352	911	1.3	2.0
PENT–Ch God (Cleve)	4	263	323	401	0.6	0.9
PENT–Intl Pent Holiness	3	333	355	441	0.6	1.0
PENT–Pent Ch of God	4	280	NR	435	0.6	1.0
PENT–Un Pent Ch Intl	2	NR	NR	NR	-	-
PRES–Presb Ch (USA)	2	38	135	168	0.2	0.4
Salvation Army	1	66	121	377	0.5	0.8
Sev Day Adv	1	52	91	105	0.2	0.2
PUSHMATAHA	**52**	**2,211**	**6,007**	**7,940**	**68.6**	**100.0**
ANG/EPIS–Episcopal	1	22	47	47	0.4	0.6
BAPT–Amer Bapt Assn	1	NR	150	181	1.6	2.3
BAPT–Free Will Bapt	3	NR	285	344	3.0	4.3
BAPT–So Bapt Conv	16	988	4,221	5,100	44.1	64.2
Catholic	1	NR	NR	60	0.5	0.8
Ch of Nazarene	1	67	80	97	0.8	1.2
CHR–Chr Chs & Chs Cr	4	NR	135	163	1.4	2.1
CHR–Chs of Christ	6	315	276	394	3.4	5.0
Jehovah's Witness	2	NR	NR	NR	-	-
METH–Un Methodist	6	124	421	476	4.1	6.0
Non-denom Chr Chs	2	100	110	124	1.1	1.6
PENT–Assemb of God	6	543	190	848	7.3	10.7
PENT–Un Pent Ch Intl	1	NR	NR	NR	-	-
PRES–Presb Ch (USA)	1	6	11	13	0.1	0.2
Sev Day Adv	1	46	81	93	0.8	1.2
ROGER MILLS	**23**	**1,043**	**2,726**	**3,588**	**98.4**	**100.0**
BAPT–So Bapt Conv	10	414	1,769	2,212	60.7	61.6
CHR–Chs of Christ	6	226	231	291	8.0	8.1
METH–Un Methodist	2	101	503	610	16.7	17.0

Religious Group	Number of Congrega-tions	Number of Attendees	Number of Communicant, Confirmed, or Full Members	Adherents		
				Number of Adherents	% of Total Pop.	% of Total Adh.
Non-denom Chr Chs	1	100	150	150	4.1	4.2
PENT–Assemb of God	2	144	0	234	6.4	6.5
PENT–Intl Pent Holiness	2	58	73	91	2.5	2.5
ROGERS	**116**	**10,226**	**27,963**	**38,468**	**44.3**	**100.0**
ANG/EPIS–Episcopal	1	60	100	133	0.2	0.3
Bahá'í	0	NR	8	8	0.0	0.0
BAPT–Amer Bapt Assn	2	NR	170	212	0.2	0.6
BAPT–Free Will Bapt	4	NR	380	473	0.5	1.2
BAPT–So Bapt Conv	39	4,473	17,006	21,180	24.4	55.1
Catholic	1	NR	NR	2,000	2.3	5.2
CGOD–Ch God (Ander)	1	65	NR	65	0.1	0.2
Ch God (7th Day)	1	NR	NR	NR	-	-
Ch of Nazarene	2	195	272	275	0.3	0.7
CHR–Chr Ch (Disc)	1	110	560	697	0.8	1.8
CHR–Chr Chs & Chs Cr	4	NR	650	810	0.9	2.1
CHR–Chs of Christ	8	765	764	934	1.1	2.4
Jehovah's Witness	2	NR	NR	NR	-	-
LDS–L-D Saints	1	NR	NR	706	0.8	1.8
LUTH–Luth–MO Synod	2	142	281	341	0.4	0.9
MENN–Amish Undif	1	NR	74	134	0.2	0.3
MENN–Mennonite USA	1	120	202	252	0.3	0.7
METH–AME	1	0	100	125	0.1	0.3
METH–Free Methodist	2	484	0	484	0.6	1.3
METH–Un Methodist	10	1,416	4,792	5,857	6.7	15.2
Non-denom Chr Chs	7	755	985	1,081	1.2	2.8
PENT–Assemb of God	11	1,228	848	1,648	1.9	4.3
PENT–Ch God (Cleve)	1	52	54	67	0.1	0.2
PENT–Ch of God Proph	1	NR	17	21	0.0	0.1
PENT–COGIC	2	55	200	249	0.3	0.6
PENT–Intl Pent Holiness	1	38	20	25	0.0	0.1
PENT–Pent Ch of God	1	70	NR	109	0.1	0.3
PENT–Un Pent Ch Intl	4	NR	NR	NR	-	-
PRES–Presb Ch (USA)	2	103	315	392	0.5	1.0
PRES–Presb Ch Amer	1	0	0	0	0.0	0.0
Sev Day Adv	1	95	165	190	0.2	0.5
SEMINOLE	**89**	**3,989**	**11,689**	**16,029**	**62.9**	**100.0**
ANG/EPIS–Episcopal	1	8	15	27	0.1	0.2
Bahá'í	0	NR	45	45	0.2	0.3
BAPT–Amer Bapt Assn	3	NR	370	462	1.8	2.9
BAPT–Free Will Bapt	3	NR	285	356	1.4	2.2
BAPT–So Bapt Conv	21	1,421	6,912	8,630	33.9	53.8
Catholic	3	NR	NR	483	1.9	3.0
CGOD–Ch God (Ander)	1	47	NR	47	0.2	0.3
Ch of Nazarene	3	60	94	140	0.5	0.9
CHR–Chr Ch (Disc)	2	32	112	140	0.5	0.9
CHR–Chs of Christ	9	635	667	789	3.1	4.9
Jehovah's Witness	1	NR	NR	NR	-	-
LDS–Comm of Christ	1	NR	156	156	0.6	1.0
LDS–L-D Saints	1	NR	NR	404	1.6	2.5
METH–AME	1	0	100	125	0.5	0.8
METH–AME Zion	1	0	100	125	0.5	0.8
METH–C.M.E.	1	0	100	125	0.5	0.8
METH–Cong Meth	1	NR	17	21	0.1	0.1
METH–Un Methodist	7	257	1,357	1,503	5.9	9.4
Non-denom Chr Chs	4	470	620	637	2.5	4.0
PENT–Assemb of God	10	737	269	1,121	4.4	7.0
PENT–Ch God (Cleve)	1	30	33	41	0.2	0.3
PENT–Intl Pent Holiness	6	206	272	340	1.3	2.1
PENT–Pent Ch of God	1	70	NR	109	0.4	0.7
PENT–Un Pent Ch Intl	1	NR	NR	NR	-	-
PRES–Presb Ch (USA)	5	0	137	171	0.7	1.1
Sev Day Adv	1	16	28	32	0.1	0.2
SEQUOYAH	**87**	**4,917**	**10,876**	**15,436**	**36.4**	**100.0**
Bahá'í	0	NR	5	5	0.0	0.0
BAPT–Amer Bapt Assn	4	NR	345	430	1.0	2.8
BAPT–Free Will Bapt	3	NR	282	351	0.8	2.3
BAPT–Natl Mis Bapt Conv	1	0	150	187	0.4	1.2
BAPT–So Bapt Conv	29	1,570	6,404	7,976	18.8	51.7
Catholic	2	NR	NR	220	0.5	1.4
Ch of Nazarene	2	135	227	257	0.6	1.7

NR–Not Reported   - Represents no adherents reported.   Percentages may not total 100 due to rounding.

Table 3: Religious Congregations by County and Group: 2010

Religious Group	Number of Congrega-tions	Number of Attendees	Number of Communicant, Confirmed, or Full Members	Adherents: Number of Adherents	Adherents: % of Total Pop.	Adherents: % of Total Adh.
CHR–Chs of Christ	8	417	377	465	1.1	3.0
Christian Un	1	NR	NR	NR	-	-
Ind Fund Churches	1	NR	NR	NR	-	-
Jehovah's Witness	1	NR	NR	NR	-	-
LDS–Comm of Christ	1	NR	156	156	0.4	1.0
LDS–L-D Saints	1	NR	NR	331	0.8	2.1
LUTH–Luth–MO Synod	1	32	40	52	0.1	0.3
METH–Evan Meth Ch	1	NR	NR	NR	-	-
METH–Free Methodist	1	0	0	0	0.0	0.0
METH–Un Methodist	5	405	1,393	1,701	4.0	11.0
Non-denom Chr Chs	6	650	557	839	2.0	5.4
PENT–Assemb of God	11	1,309	651	1,794	4.2	11.6
PENT–Ch God (Cleve)	1	33	48	60	0.1	0.4
PENT–Intl Pent Holiness	1	25	11	14	0.0	0.1
PENT–Pent Ch of God	3	210	NR	326	0.8	2.1
PENT–Un Pent Ch Intl	1	NR	NR	NR	-	-
PRES–Presb Ch (USA)	1	40	72	90	0.2	0.6
Sev Day Adv	1	91	158	182	0.4	1.2
STEPHENS	**101**	**9,174**	**22,301**	**29,313**	**65.1**	**100.0**
ANG/EPIS–Episcopal	1	61	136	154	0.3	0.5
Bahá'í	0	NR	10	10	0.0	0.0
BAPT–Amer Bapt Assn	5	NR	836	1,029	2.3	3.5
BAPT–Free Will Bapt	2	NR	190	234	0.5	0.8
BAPT–Ref Bapt Ch	1	NR	NR	NR	-	-
BAPT–So Bapt Conv	30	4,851	13,487	16,607	36.9	56.7
Catholic	2	NR	NR	644	1.4	2.2
Ch of Nazarene	2	113	318	345	0.8	1.2
CHR–Chr Ch (Disc)	2	322	926	1,140	2.5	3.9
CHR–Chr Chs & Chs Cr	2	NR	74	91	0.2	0.3
CHR–Chs of Christ	11	1,206	1,397	1,566	3.5	5.3
Intl Fell Bible Ch	1	NR	NR	NR	-	-
Jehovah's Witness	1	NR	NR	NR	-	-
LDS–L-D Saints	1	NR	NR	473	1.0	1.6
LUTH–Luth–MO Synod	1	40	95	110	0.2	0.4
METH–C.M.E.	1	0	100	123	0.3	0.4
METH–Un Methodist	7	502	2,461	2,800	6.2	9.6
Non-denom Chr Chs	13	1,010	1,295	1,395	3.1	4.8
PENT–Assemb of God	8	728	224	1,582	3.5	5.4
PENT–Ch God (Cleve)	2	144	351	432	1.0	1.5
PENT–COGIC	1	35	30	37	0.1	0.1
PENT–Int Foursq Gos	1	57	80	99	0.2	0.3
PENT–Pent Ch of God	1	70	NR	109	0.2	0.4
PENT–Un Pent Ch Intl	2	NR	NR	NR	-	-
PRES–Cumber Presb	1	NR	89	89	0.2	0.3
PRES–Presb Ch (USA)	1	0	141	174	0.4	0.6
Sev Day Adv	1	35	61	70	0.2	0.2
TEXAS	**63**	**3,942**	**7,649**	**11,562**	**56.0**	**100.0**
ANG/EPIS–Episcopal	1	12	17	20	0.1	0.2
Bahá'í	0	NR	2	2	0.0	0.0
BAPT–Free Will Bapt	1	NR	95	123	0.6	1.1
BAPT–So Bapt Conv	15	1,105	2,185	2,840	13.8	24.6
Catholic	2	NR	NR	1,814	8.8	15.7
CGOD–Ch God (Ander)	1	23	NR	23	0.1	0.2
Ch of Nazarene	2	342	500	632	3.1	5.5
CHR–Chr Ch (Disc)	3	96	281	365	1.8	3.2
CHR–Chr Chs & Chs Cr	1	NR	285	370	1.8	3.2
CHR–Chs of Christ	6	475	405	616	3.0	5.3
Jehovah's Witness	1	NR	NR	NR	-	-
LDS–L-D Saints	1	NR	NR	187	0.9	1.6
LUTH–Luth–MO Synod	3	230	392	519	2.5	4.5
MENN–Fel Evg Bib Ch	1	75	50	75	0.4	0.6
MENN–Menn Br US Conf	1	NR	40	52	0.3	0.4
METH–Un Methodist	7	533	2,174	2,375	11.5	20.5
Non-denom Chr Chs	6	570	738	774	3.8	6.7
PENT–Assemb of God	2	160	96	170	0.8	1.5
PENT–Int Foursq Gos	1	93	2	3	0.0	0.0
PENT–Intl Pent Holiness	2	54	174	226	1.1	2.0
PENT–Pent Ch of God	1	70	NR	109	0.5	0.9
PENT–Un Pent Ch Intl	2	NR	NR	NR	-	-
PRES–Presb Ch (USA)	1	68	151	196	0.9	1.7
Sev Day Adv	2	36	62	71	0.3	0.6

Religious Group	Number of Congrega-tions	Number of Attendees	Number of Communicant, Confirmed, or Full Members	Adherents: Number of Adherents	Adherents: % of Total Pop.	Adherents: % of Total Adh.
TILLMAN	**31**	**1,855**	**6,005**	**7,543**	**94.4**	**100.0**
Bahá'í	0	NR	17	17	0.2	0.2
BAPT–Amer Bapt Assn	1	NR	85	105	1.3	1.4
BAPT–So Bapt Conv	12	959	4,165	5,126	64.1	68.0
Catholic	1	NR	NR	150	1.9	2.0
CHR–Chr Ch (Disc)	1	79	196	241	3.0	3.2
CHR–Chs of Christ	5	391	414	494	6.2	6.5
METH–AME	1	0	100	123	1.5	1.6
METH–Un Methodist	5	241	908	989	12.4	13.1
PENT–Assemb of God	3	155	89	260	3.3	3.4
PENT–Intl Pent Holiness	1	22	14	17	0.2	0.2
PRES–Presb Ch (USA)	1	8	17	21	0.3	0.3
TULSA	**754**	**124,757**	**252,721**	**378,323**	**62.7**	**100.0**
ANG/EPIS–Anglican NA	3	NR	NR	NR	-	-
ANG/EPIS–Episcopal	10	1,393	4,080	4,582	0.8	1.2
Bahá'í	1	NR	196	196	0.0	0.1
BAPT–Amer Bapt Assn	6	NR	965	1,208	0.2	0.3
BAPT–Amer Bapt USA	4	865	1,619	2,027	0.3	0.5
BAPT–Free Will Bapt	23	NR	2,185	2,736	0.5	0.7
BAPT–Ind Bapt Flwsp Intl	1	NR	NR	NR	-	-
BAPT–NBC USA	12	2,265	5,481	6,862	1.1	1.8
BAPT–Prog NBC	1	200	275	344	0.1	0.1
BAPT–Ref Bapt Ch	4	NR	NR	NR	-	-
BAPT–S-D Baptist Gen Con	1	NR	NR	NR	-	-
BAPT–So Bapt Conv	140	24,598	72,037	90,187	14.9	23.8
BUDD–Mahayana	1	NR	NR	506	0.1	0.1
BUDD–Theravada	1	NR	NR	14	0.0	0.0
BUDD–Vajrayana	1	NR	NR	10	0.0	0.0
Calv Chpl	1	NR	NR	NR	-	-
Catholic	23	NR	NR	49,144	8.1	13.0
CGOD–Ch God (Ander)	5	611	NR	611	0.1	0.2
CGOD–Ches God-Gen Con	2	160	300	376	0.1	0.1
Ch Cr, Scientst	2	NR	NR	NR	-	-
Ch God (7th Day)	1	NR	NR	NR	-	-
Ch of Nazarene	17	2,534	3,225	4,777	0.8	1.3
Chr & Miss Al	2	436	730	751	0.1	0.2
CHR–Chr Ch (Disc)	19	1,623	4,001	5,009	0.8	1.3
CHR–Chr Chs & Chs Cr	21	NR	6,515	8,156	1.4	2.2
CHR–Chs of Christ	31	6,498	6,312	8,206	1.4	2.2
CHR–Int Chs of Christ	1	NR	47	59	0.0	0.0
Evan Cov Ch	1	642	782	835	0.1	0.2
Evan Free Ch	1	125	NR	125	0.0	0.0
FRND–Fr Gen Cf	1	NR	25	31	0.0	0.0
HINDU–Trad Temples	1	NR	NR	160	0.0	0.0
Ind Fund Churches	1	NR	NR	NR	-	-
Jain	1	NR	NR	NR	-	-
Jehovah's Witness	10	NR	NR	NR	-	-
JUD–Conserv	1	442	496	1,339	0.2	0.4
JUD–Reform	1	224	395	1,066	0.2	0.3
LDS–Comm of Christ	6	NR	936	936	0.2	0.2
LDS–L-D Saints	12	NR	NR	7,407	1.2	2.0
LUTH–E.L.C.A.	7	857	2,143	2,331	0.4	0.6
LUTH–Luth Cong Msn Chr	1	NR	NR	NR	-	-
LUTH–Luth–MO Synod	9	1,917	2,807	4,163	0.7	1.1
LUTH–Wisc Ev Luth Syn	1	66	99	130	0.0	0.0
MENN–Menn Br US Conf	2	NR	515	645	0.1	0.2
METH–AME	3	50	2,450	3,067	0.5	0.8
METH–AME Zion	2	0	250	313	0.1	0.1
METH–C.M.E.	3	0	450	563	0.1	0.1
METH–Free Methodist	9	570	54	570	0.1	0.2
METH–Un Methodist	44	13,282	53,116	64,194	10.6	17.0
METH–Wesleyan	1	26	36	34	0.0	0.0
Metro Comm Ch	1	21	35	44	0.0	0.0
Muslim Est	5	1,167	NR	2,954	0.5	0.8
New Apost Ch	1	NR	NR	NR	-	-
Non-denom Chr Chs	150	48,127	55,029	64,535	10.7	17.1
ORTHE–Ant Orth of NA	1	92	NR	253	0.0	0.1
ORTHE–Greek Orthodox	1	120	NR	265	0.0	0.1
ORTHE–Orth Ch in Amer	1	65	NR	100	0.0	0.0
ORTHO–Armen Ap Etchm	1	35	NR	60	0.0	0.0
ORTHO–Coptic Orth Ch	1	67	NR	100	0.0	0.0
PENT–Assemb of God	48	8,771	6,470	12,845	2.1	3.4

NR–Not Reported - Represents no adherents reported. Percentages may not total 100 due to rounding.

Table 3: Religious Congregations by County and Group: 2010

Religious Group	Number of Congrega-tions	Number of Attendees	Number of Communicant, Confirmed, or Full Members	Adherents		
				Number of Adherents	% of Total Pop.	% of Total Adh.
PENT–Ch God (Cleve)	7	498	616	771	0.1	0.2
PENT–Ch God Apos Fth	2	NR	NR	NR	-	-
PENT–Ch of God Proph	6	NR	475	595	0.1	0.2
PENT–COGIC	7	180	860	1,077	0.2	0.3
PENT–Int Foursq Gos	8	340	565	707	0.1	0.2
PENT–Intl Pent Holiness	5	843	3,301	4,133	0.7	1.1
PENT–Pent Ch of God	1	70	NR	109	0.0	0.0
PENT–Un Pent Ch Intl	17	NR	NR	NR	-	-
PENT–Vineyard	1	65	80	100	0.0	0.0
PRES–Cum Pres Am	1	NR	NR	NR	-	-
PRES–Cumber Presb	1	NR	60	72	0.0	0.0
PRES–Evan Presby Ch	1	NR	2,125	2,660	0.4	0.7
PRES–Presb Ch (USA)	15	1,696	5,244	6,565	1.1	1.7
PRES–Presb Ch Amer	2	430	533	661	0.1	0.2
Salvation Army	3	391	209	348	0.1	0.1
Sev Day Adv	8	1,255	2,183	2,510	0.4	0.7
Un C of Christ	2	131	373	467	0.1	0.1
Unit Univ	3	1,009	2,041	2,715	0.4	0.7
Unity Ch	2	NR	NR	NR	-	-
Zoroastrian	0	NR	NR	7	0.0	0.0
WAGONER	**75**	**4,718**	**14,289**	**18,886**	**25.8**	**100.0**
ANG/EPIS–Episcopal	1	8	13	13	0.0	0.1
Bahá'í	0	NR	73	73	0.1	0.4
BAPT–Free Will Bapt	8	NR	760	959	1.3	5.1
BAPT–So Bapt Conv	14	1,458	6,962	8,789	12.0	46.5
Catholic	2	NR	NR	319	0.4	1.7
Ch of Nazarene	2	90	119	195	0.3	1.0
CHR–Chr Ch (Disc)	1	115	305	385	0.5	2.0
CHR–Chr Chs & Chs Cr	3	NR	215	271	0.4	1.4
CHR–Chs of Christ	8	525	546	663	0.9	3.5
Ind Fund Churches	1	NR	NR	NR	-	-
Jehovah's Witness	2	NR	NR	NR	-	-
METH–C.M.E.	3	0	400	505	0.7	2.7
METH–Un Methodist	7	691	2,423	2,935	4.0	15.5
Non-denom Chr Chs	8	785	1,180	1,214	1.7	6.4
PENT–Assemb of God	3	767	503	1,464	2.0	7.8
PENT–Ch God (Cleve)	1	106	169	213	0.3	1.1
PENT–Ch of God Proph	3	NR	307	388	0.5	2.1
PENT–COGIC	1	0	150	189	0.3	1.0
PENT–Intl Pent Holiness	2	48	55	69	0.1	0.4
PENT–Pent Ch of God	1	70	NR	109	0.1	0.6
PENT–Un Pent Ch Intl	1	NR	NR	NR	-	-
PRES–Presb Ch (USA)	1	35	74	93	0.1	0.5
Sev Day Adv	2	20	35	40	0.1	0.2
WASHINGTON	**99**	**9,684**	**26,330**	**35,793**	**70.2**	**100.0**
ANG/EPIS–Anglican NA	1	NR	NR	NR	-	-
ANG/EPIS–Episcopal	1	121	391	391	0.8	1.1
Bahá'í	0	NR	26	26	0.1	0.1
BAPT–Amer Bapt Assn	1	NR	85	104	0.2	0.3
BAPT–Asc Ref Bap Ch Am	1	NR	NR	NR	-	-
BAPT–Free Will Bapt	2	NR	190	232	0.5	0.6
BAPT–Ref Bapt Ch	1	NR	NR	NR	-	-
BAPT–So Bapt Conv	22	2,462	11,303	13,813	27.1	38.6
Catholic	3	NR	NR	2,381	4.7	6.7
CGOD–Ch God (Ander)	1	43	NR	43	0.1	0.1
Ch Cr, Scientst	1	NR	NR	NR	-	-
Ch of Nazarene	2	439	792	1,039	2.0	2.9
CHR–Chr Ch (Disc)	2	197	559	683	1.3	1.9
CHR–Chr Chs & Chs Cr	5	NR	828	1,012	2.0	2.8
CHR–Chs of Christ	3	690	785	945	1.9	2.6
FRND–Evan Fr Ch Intl	2	35	35	43	0.1	0.1
Jehovah's Witness	1	NR	NR	NR	-	-
LDS–Comm of Christ	1	NR	156	156	0.3	0.4
LDS–L-D Saints	3	NR	NR	1,169	2.3	3.3
LUTH–E.L.C.A.	1	37	59	72	0.1	0.2
LUTH–Luth–MO Synod	1	160	355	441	0.9	1.2
METH–AME	1	0	150	183	0.4	0.5
METH–Un Methodist	8	1,043	5,715	6,075	11.9	17.0
METH–Wesleyan	4	1,091	716	1,418	2.8	4.0
Non-denom Chr Chs	12	2,170	2,540	2,825	5.5	7.9
PENT–Assemb of God	4	732	422	1,186	2.3	3.3
PENT–Ch God Apos Fth	1	NR	NR	NR	-	-
PENT–Ch of God Proph	1	NR	39	48	0.1	0.1
PENT–COGIC	1	0	0	0	0.0	0.0
PENT–Int Foursq Gos	1	24	24	29	0.1	0.1
PENT–Intl Pent Holiness	4	116	135	165	0.3	0.5
PENT–Un Pent Ch Intl	1	NR	NR	NR	-	-
PRES–Orth Pres Ch	1	34	34	37	0.1	0.1
PRES–Presb Ch (USA)	2	167	701	857	1.7	2.4
Salvation Army	1	46	168	277	0.5	0.8
Sev Day Adv	1	47	82	94	0.2	0.3
Unit Univ	1	30	40	49	0.1	0.1
WASHITA	**39**	**1,948**	**5,949**	**7,806**	**67.1**	**100.0**
BAPT–Amer Bapt Assn	1	NR	80	100	0.9	1.3
BAPT–N Am Bapt Conf	1	NR	97	122	1.0	1.6
BAPT–So Bapt Conv	9	671	3,374	4,237	36.4	54.3
Catholic	1	NR	NR	81	0.7	1.0
CHR–Chr Chs & Chs Cr	1	NR	0	0	0.0	0.0
CHR–Chs of Christ	8	519	524	646	5.6	8.3
LUTH–E.L.C.A.	1	53	175	230	2.0	2.9
MENN–Menn Br US Conf	2	NR	464	583	5.0	7.5
MENN–Mennonite USA	2	100	130	163	1.4	2.1
METH–Un Methodist	4	148	666	726	6.2	9.3
Non-denom Chr Chs	1	60	100	100	0.9	1.3
PENT–Assemb of God	3	229	87	416	3.6	5.3
PENT–Intl Pent Holiness	1	45	60	75	0.6	1.0
PENT–Pent Ch of God	1	70	NR	109	0.9	1.4
PRES–Cumber Presb	1	NR	90	90	0.8	1.2
PRES–Presb Ch (USA)	2	53	102	128	1.1	1.6
WOODS	**34**	**1,842**	**4,552**	**6,063**	**68.3**	**100.0**
Bahá'í	0	NR	3	3	0.0	0.0
BAPT–So Bapt Conv	3	306	1,264	1,487	16.7	24.5
Catholic	2	NR	NR	148	1.7	2.4
CGOD–Ch God (Ander)	2	115	NR	115	1.3	1.9
Ch of Nazarene	1	99	134	233	2.6	3.8
CHR–Chr Ch (Disc)	2	112	215	253	2.8	4.2
CHR–Chr Chs & Chs Cr	2	NR	75	88	1.0	1.5
CHR–Chs of Christ	4	295	292	399	4.5	6.6
FRND–Evan Fr Ch Intl	1	35	88	104	1.2	1.7
Jehovah's Witness	1	NR	NR	NR	-	-
LDS–L-D Saints	1	NR	NR	127	1.4	2.1
LUTH–Luth–MO Synod	1	100	361	468	5.3	7.7
METH–Un Methodist	6	337	1,684	2,030	22.9	33.5
METH–Wesleyan	3	244	223	317	3.6	5.2
Non-denom Chr Chs	1	60	60	75	0.8	1.2
PENT–Assemb of God	2	65	40	84	0.9	1.4
PRES–Presb Ch (USA)	1	50	72	85	1.0	1.4
Sev Day Adv	1	24	41	47	0.5	0.8
WOODWARD	**47**	**3,304**	**10,556**	**15,080**	**75.1**	**100.0**
ANG/EPIS–Episcopal	1	27	71	77	0.4	0.5
Bahá'í	0	NR	3	3	0.0	0.0
BAPT–Free Will Bapt	1	NR	95	117	0.6	0.8
BAPT–Ind Bapt Flwsp Intl	1	NR	NR	NR	-	-
BAPT–So Bapt Conv	12	1,103	5,117	6,328	31.5	42.0
Catholic	3	NR	NR	1,765	8.8	11.7
Ch of Nazarene	1	136	144	144	0.7	1.0
CHR–Chr Ch (Disc)	3	201	852	1,054	5.2	7.0
CHR–Chr Chs & Chs Cr	1	NR	79	98	0.5	0.6
CHR–Chs of Christ	1	280	310	364	1.8	2.4
LDS–Comm of Christ	1	NR	156	156	0.8	1.0
LDS–L-D Saints	1	NR	NR	339	1.7	2.2
LUTH–Luth–MO Synod	1	40	89	112	0.6	0.7
METH–Free Methodist	3	53	18	54	0.3	0.4
METH–Un Methodist	7	604	2,819	3,168	15.8	21.0
Non-denom Chr Chs	4	395	465	498	2.5	3.3
PENT–Assemb of God	2	332	138	565	2.8	3.7
PENT–Ch God (Cleve)	1	38	47	58	0.3	0.4
PENT–Un Pent Ch Intl	1	NR	NR	NR	-	-
PRES–Presb Ch (USA)	1	35	48	59	0.3	0.4
Sev Day Adv	1	60	105	121	0.6	0.8

NR–Not Reported - Represents no adherents reported. Percentages may not total 100 due to rounding.

Table 3: Religious Congregations by County and Group: 2010

Religious Group	Number of Congrega-tions	Number of Attendees	Number of Communicant, Confirmed, or Full Members	Adherents		
				Number of Adherents	% of Total Pop.	% of Total Adh.
OREGON	**4,026**	**324,981**	**455,240**	**1,194,793**	**31.2**	**100.0**
BAKER	**38**	**1,120**	**1,691**	**5,084**	**31.5**	**100.0**
ANG/EPIS–Episcopal	1	26	50	104	0.6	2.0
Bahá'í	0	NR	24	24	0.1	0.5
BAPT–Consrv Bapt	4	NR	NR	NR	-	-
BAPT–So Bapt Conv	1	50	17	20	0.1	0.4
Calv Chpl	1	NR	NR	NR	-	-
Catholic	3	NR	NR	1,196	7.4	23.5
Ch Cr, Scientst	1	NR	NR	NR	-	-
Ch of Nazarene	2	404	357	574	3.6	11.3
CHR–Chr Chs & Chs Cr	2	NR	300	353	2.2	6.9
CHR–Chs of Christ	2	39	32	44	0.3	0.9
Jehovah's Witness	2	NR	NR	NR	-	-
LDS–Comm of Christ	1	NR	128	128	0.8	2.5
LDS–L-D Saints	4	NR	NR	1,363	8.4	26.8
LUTH–Nor Amer Luth C	1	NR	NR	NR	-	-
METH–Un Methodist	3	98	216	286	1.8	5.6
Non-denom Chr Chs	1	70	70	88	0.5	1.7
PENT–Assemb of God	3	196	107	341	2.1	6.7
PENT–Int Foursq Gos	1	23	26	31	0.2	0.6
PENT–Pent Ch of God	1	70	NR	109	0.7	2.1
PRES–Presb Ch (USA)	2	35	174	205	1.3	4.0
Sev Day Adv	2	109	190	218	1.4	4.3
BENTON	**84**	**6,135**	**8,611**	**22,224**	**26.0**	**100.0**
ANG/EPIS–Episcopal	1	239	330	656	0.8	3.0
Bahá'í	3	NR	210	210	0.2	0.9
BAPT–Consrv Bapt	6	NR	NR	NR	-	-
BAPT–So Bapt Conv	2	331	657	758	0.9	3.4
BUDD–Mahayana	3	NR	NR	149	0.2	0.7
BUDD–Vajrayana	2	NR	NR	89	0.1	0.4
Calv Chpl	1	NR	NR	NR	-	-
Catholic	2	NR	NR	7,077	8.3	31.8
Ch Cr, Scientst	1	NR	NR	NR	-	-
Ch of Nazarene	2	315	278	319	0.4	1.4
CHR–Chr Ch (Disc)	1	105	297	343	0.4	1.5
CHR–Chr Chs & Chs Cr	2	NR	601	694	0.8	3.1
CHR–Chs of Christ	2	230	266	334	0.4	1.5
Evan Ch	1	NR	NR	NR	-	-
Evan Cov Ch	1	125	35	162	0.2	0.7
Evan Free Ch	1	30	NR	30	0.0	0.1
FRND–Indep Yr Mtgs	1	NR	28	32	0.0	0.1
HINDU–Post Ren	1	NR	NR	77	0.1	0.3
Jehovah's Witness	1	NR	NR	NR	-	-
LDS–L-D Saints	6	NR	NR	2,892	3.4	13.0
LUTH–E.L.C.A.	1	154	332	411	0.5	1.8
LUTH–Luth-MO Synod	3	231	548	634	0.7	2.9
LUTH–Wisc Ev Luth Syn	1	31	45	45	0.1	0.2
MENN–Mennonite USA	1	65	65	75	0.1	0.3
METH–Free Methodist	1	63	21	63	0.1	0.3
METH–Un Methodist	3	275	789	1,175	1.4	5.3
Muslim Est	1	134	NR	308	0.4	1.4
Non-denom Chr Chs	9	1,758	1,695	2,201	2.6	9.9
ORTHE–Orth Ch in Amer	1	80	NR	80	0.1	0.4
ORTHE–Rus Orth Abroad	1	45	NR	80	0.1	0.4
PENT–Assemb of God	3	284	162	417	0.5	1.9
PENT–Ch God (Cleve)	1	14	6	7	0.0	0.0
PENT–Int Foursq Gos	3	270	280	323	0.4	1.5
PENT–Pent Ch of God	2	140	NR	217	0.3	1.0
PENT–Un Pent Ch Intl	4	NR	NR	NR	-	-
PRES–Orth Pres Ch	1	134	93	120	0.1	0.5
PRES–Presb Ch (USA)	3	400	900	1,039	1.2	4.7
REF–Christian Ref	1	55	48	55	0.1	0.2
Sev Day Adv	1	132	230	265	0.3	1.2
Un Breth in Cr	1	45	48	39	0.0	0.2
Un C of Christ	1	150	354	409	0.5	1.8
Unit Univ	1	300	293	434	0.5	2.0
Zoroastrian	0	NR	NR	5	0.0	0.0
CLACKAMAS	**312**	**36,239**	**51,794**	**109,797**	**29.2**	**100.0**
ANG/EPIS–Anglican NA	1	NR	NR	NR	-	-
ANG/EPIS–Episcopal	5	755	2,149	2,600	0.7	2.4
Ap Chr Ch-Amer	1	52	31	52	0.0	0.0
Bahá'í	6	NR	410	410	0.1	0.4
BAPT–Amer Bapt Assn	1	NR	85	103	0.0	0.1
BAPT–Amer Bapt USA	3	550	739	899	0.2	0.8
BAPT–Consrv Bapt	15	NR	NR	NR	-	-
BAPT–Converge/BGC	2	150	NR	180	0.0	0.2
BAPT–Free Will Bapt	1	NR	41	50	0.0	0.0
BAPT–N Am Bapt Conf	2	NR	169	206	0.1	0.2
BAPT–So Bapt Conv	8	938	1,520	1,849	0.5	1.7
BUDD–Theravada	1	NR	NR	396	0.1	0.4
Calv Chpl	2	NR	NR	NR	-	-
Catholic	13	NR	NR	27,128	7.2	24.7
CGOD–Ch God (Ander)	2	50	NR	50	0.0	0.0
Ch Cr, Scientst	2	NR	NR	NR	-	-
Ch of Nazarene	7	680	1,016	1,273	0.3	1.2
Chr & Miss Al	1	308	170	608	0.2	0.6
CHR–Chr Chs & Chs Cr	12	NR	3,966	4,825	1.3	4.4
CHR–Chs of Christ	10	551	471	658	0.2	0.6
Evan Ch	11	NR	NR	NR	-	-
Evan Cov Ch	3	768	479	998	0.3	0.9
Evan Free Ch	3	365	NR	365	0.1	0.3
FRND–Evan Fr Ch Intl	2	85	100	122	0.0	0.1
Jehovah's Witness	9	NR	NR	NR	-	-
JUD–Reform	1	53	93	251	0.1	0.2
LDS–L-D Saints	29	NR	NR	14,058	3.7	12.8
LUTH–E.L.C.A.	14	1,670	4,003	5,075	1.3	4.6
LUTH–Luth Cong Msn Chr	1	140	160	195	0.1	0.2
LUTH–Luth-MO Synod	7	1,009	1,667	2,098	0.6	1.9
LUTH–Wisc Ev Luth Syn	1	81	150	224	0.1	0.2
MENN–Mennonite USA	2	79	80	97	0.0	0.1
METH–Evan Meth Ch	1	NR	NR	NR	-	-
METH–Free Methodist	1	70	50	70	0.0	0.1
METH–Un Methodist	12	954	1,815	2,741	0.7	2.5
METH–Wesleyan	1	40	34	52	0.0	0.0
Missionary Ch	1	21	30	30	0.0	0.0
Non-denom Chr Chs	45	15,739	18,000	21,736	5.8	19.8
ORTHE–Orth Ch in Amer	2	300	NR	525	0.1	0.5
ORTHE–Rus Orth Abroad	1	75	NR	450	0.1	0.4
ORTHE–Serb Orth USA	1	50	NR	500	0.1	0.5
ORTHO–Armen Ap Etchm	1	75	NR	800	0.2	0.7
PENT–Assemb of God	13	1,493	1,034	2,099	0.6	1.9
PENT–Ch God (Cleve)	1	42	173	210	0.1	0.2
PENT–Ch God Apos Fth	1	NR	NR	NR	-	-
PENT–Int Foursq Gos	14	4,343	5,672	6,901	1.8	6.3
PENT–Intl Pent Holiness	1	46	35	43	0.0	0.0
PENT–Un Pent Ch Intl	3	NR	NR	NR	-	-
PRES–Korean Amer Pres	1	NR	NR	NR	-	-
PRES–Korean Pres Amer	1	NR	NR	NR	-	-
PRES–Presb Ch (USA)	8	1,711	2,355	2,865	0.8	2.6
REF–Christian Ref	1	70	54	66	0.0	0.1
REF–Comm Ref Evan	1	NR	NR	NR	-	-
REF–Un Ref Chs N.A.	1	NR	NR	NR	-	-
Sev Day Adv	12	2,334	4,060	4,669	1.2	4.3
Un C of Christ	7	420	771	938	0.2	0.9
Unit Univ	2	172	212	327	0.1	0.3
Unity Ch	1	NR	NR	NR	-	-
Zoroastrian	0	NR	NR	5	0.0	0.0
CLATSOP	**56**	**2,573**	**4,169**	**10,202**	**27.5**	**100.0**
ANG/EPIS–Episcopal	2	93	219	226	0.6	2.2
Bahá'í	2	NR	77	77	0.2	0.8
BAPT–Amer Bapt USA	1	50	65	77	0.2	0.8
BAPT–Consrv Bapt	4	NR	NR	NR	-	-
BAPT–Reg Bapt Gen As	1	NR	NR	NR	-	-
Calv Chpl	1	NR	NR	NR	-	-
Catholic	3	NR	NR	3,595	9.7	35.2
Ch Cr, Scientst	2	NR	NR	NR	-	-
Ch of Nazarene	2	63	74	89	0.2	0.9
CHR–Chr Chs & Chs Cr	3	NR	560	664	1.8	6.5
CHR–Chs of Christ	2	24	17	26	0.1	0.3
FRND–Evan Fr Ch Intl	1	40	51	60	0.2	0.6
Ind Fund Churches	2	NR	NR	NR	-	-
Jehovah's Witness	2	NR	NR	NR	-	-

NR–Not Reported - Represents no adherents reported. Percentages may not total 100 due to rounding.

Table 3: Religious Congregations by County and Group: 2010

Religious Group	Number of Congrega-tions	Number of Attendees	Number of Communicant, Confirmed, or Full Members	Adherents: Number of Adherents	Adherents: % of Total Pop.	Adherents: % of Total Adh.
LDS–L-D Saints	2	NR	NR	1,483	4.0	14.5
LUTH–Apostolic Luth	1	NR	NR	NR	-	-
LUTH–Assoc Free Luth	1	NR	NR	NR	-	-
LUTH–E.L.C.A.	3	259	804	910	2.5	8.9
METH–Un Methodist	3	129	250	347	0.9	3.4
Non-denom Chr Chs	6	1,320	1,423	1,658	4.5	16.3
PENT–Assemb of God	4	247	141	414	1.1	4.1
PENT–Un Pent Ch Intl	1	NR	NR	NR	-	-
PRES–Presb Ch (USA)	3	243	307	364	1.0	3.6
Sev Day Adv	2	82	143	164	0.4	1.6
Un C of Christ	1	0	15	18	0.0	0.2
Unit Univ	1	23	23	30	0.1	0.3
COLUMBIA	**71**	**3,694**	**3,785**	**9,823**	**19.9**	**100.0**
ANG/EPIS–Episcopal	1	43	103	111	0.2	1.1
Bahá'í	1	NR	41	41	0.1	0.4
BAPT–Consrv Bapt	3	NR	NR	NR	-	-
BAPT–Converge/BGC	2	150	NR	180	0.4	1.8
BAPT–So Bapt Conv	5	201	224	273	0.6	2.8
BUDD–Mahayana	2	NR	NR	317	0.6	3.2
Catholic	4	NR	NR	1,377	2.8	14.0
CGOD–Ch God (Ander)	3	327	NR	327	0.7	3.3
Ch of Nazarene	1	36	30	60	0.1	0.6
CHR–Chr Chs & Chs Cr	2	NR	145	176	0.4	1.8
CHR–Chs of Christ	2	120	119	151	0.3	1.5
Ind Fund Churches	3	NR	NR	NR	-	-
Jehovah's Witness	3	NR	NR	NR	-	-
LDS–L-D Saints	5	NR	NR	2,477	5.0	25.2
LUTH–Apostolic Luth	1	NR	NR	NR	-	-
LUTH–E.L.C.A.	3	263	595	726	1.5	7.4
LUTH–Evan Luth Syn	1	12	29	42	0.1	0.4
LUTH–Luth-MO Synod	2	123	187	242	0.5	2.5
METH–Un Methodist	3	95	202	296	0.6	3.0
Non-denom Chr Chs	10	1,257	1,179	1,596	3.2	16.2
PENT–Assemb of God	6	390	238	604	1.2	6.1
PENT–Int Foursq Gos	3	449	279	340	0.7	3.5
PRES–Bible Pres	1	NR	NR	NR	-	-
PRES–Presb Ch (USA)	2	89	172	209	0.4	2.1
Sev Day Adv	2	139	242	278	0.6	2.8
COOS	**101**	**5,309**	**7,744**	**15,320**	**24.3**	**100.0**
ANG/EPIS–Episcopal	4	154	323	359	0.6	2.3
Bahá'í	0	NR	76	76	0.1	0.5
BAPT–Amer Bapt Assn	2	NR	105	123	0.2	0.8
BAPT–Amer Bapt USA	2	145	160	187	0.3	1.2
BAPT–Consrv Bapt	5	NR	NR	NR	-	-
BAPT–Ref Bapt Ch	1	NR	NR	NR	-	-
BAPT–So Bapt Conv	1	76	145	169	0.3	1.1
BUDD–Vajrayana	1	NR	NR	32	0.1	0.2
Calv Chpl	2	NR	NR	NR	-	-
Catholic	5	NR	NR	2,658	4.2	17.3
CGOD–Ch God (Ander)	3	90	NR	90	0.1	0.6
Ch Cr, Scientst	1	NR	NR	NR	-	-
Ch of Nazarene	3	359	464	539	0.9	3.5
CHR–Chr Ch (Disc)	1	30	50	58	0.1	0.4
CHR–Chr Chs & Chs Cr	4	NR	472	551	0.9	3.6
CHR–Chs of Christ	3	257	272	310	0.5	2.0
Jehovah's Witness	5	NR	NR	NR	-	-
LDS–Comm of Christ	1	NR	167	167	0.3	1.1
LDS–L-D Saints	4	NR	NR	2,626	4.2	17.1
LUTH–E.L.C.A.	3	240	863	961	1.5	6.3
LUTH–Evan Luth Syn	1	16	34	43	0.1	0.3
LUTH–Luth-MO Synod	2	82	138	184	0.3	1.2
LUTH–Wisc Ev Luth Syn	1	6	4	4	0.0	0.0
METH–Un Methodist	3	163	331	413	0.7	2.7
Non-denom Chr Chs	14	2,321	2,291	2,956	4.7	19.3
PENT–Assemb of God	8	414	296	575	0.9	3.8
PENT–Ch God (Cleve)	3	211	284	332	0.5	2.2
PENT–Int Foursq Gos	4	115	189	221	0.4	1.4
PENT–Pent Ch of God	1	70	NR	109	0.2	0.7
PENT–Un Pent Ch Intl	1	NR	NR	NR	-	-
PRES–Presb Ch (USA)	5	122	344	402	0.6	2.6
Salvation Army	1	42	56	397	0.6	2.6

Religious Group	Number of Congrega-tions	Number of Attendees	Number of Communicant, Confirmed, or Full Members	Adherents: Number of Adherents	Adherents: % of Total Pop.	Adherents: % of Total Adh.
Sev Day Adv	3	374	650	748	1.2	4.9
Unit Univ	1	22	30	30	0.0	0.2
Unity Ch	2	NR	NR	NR	-	-
CROOK	**24**	**1,221**	**2,269**	**4,964**	**23.7**	**100.0**
ANG/EPIS–Episcopal	1	30	61	61	0.3	1.2
Bahá'í	0	NR	52	52	0.2	1.0
BAPT–Consrv Bapt	1	NR	NR	NR	-	-
BAPT–So Bapt Conv	1	65	150	180	0.9	3.6
Calv Chpl	1	NR	NR	NR	-	-
Catholic	1	NR	NR	1,035	4.9	20.9
CGOD–Ch God (Ander)	1	20	NR	20	0.1	0.4
Ch of Nazarene	1	130	124	203	1.0	4.1
CHR–Chr Chs & Chs Cr	2	NR	663	797	3.8	16.1
CHR–Chs of Christ	1	100	75	150	0.7	3.0
Jehovah's Witness	1	NR	NR	NR	-	-
LDS–L-D Saints	2	NR	NR	1,027	4.9	20.7
LUTH–E.L.C.A.	1	95	145	160	0.8	3.2
Non-denom Chr Chs	2	275	400	400	1.9	8.1
PENT–Assemb of God	1	58	43	108	0.5	2.2
PENT–Ch of God Proph	1	NR	29	35	0.2	0.7
PENT–COGIC	1	0	150	180	0.9	3.6
PENT–Int Foursq Gos	1	255	198	238	1.1	4.8
PENT–Pent Ch of God	1	70	NR	109	0.5	2.2
PENT–Un Pent Ch Intl	1	NR	NR	NR	-	-
PRES–Presb Ch (USA)	1	51	53	64	0.3	1.3
Sev Day Adv	1	72	126	145	0.7	2.9
CURRY	**43**	**1,768**	**1,934**	**5,581**	**25.0**	**100.0**
ANG/EPIS–Episcopal	3	131	162	208	0.9	3.7
Bahá'í	0	NR	24	24	0.1	0.4
BAPT–Consrv Bapt	1	NR	NR	NR	-	-
BAPT–So Bapt Conv	1	30	72	81	0.4	1.5
Calv Chpl	2	NR	NR	NR	-	-
Catholic	3	NR	NR	1,560	7.0	28.0
Ch Cr, Scientst	1	NR	NR	NR	-	-
Ch of Nazarene	1	242	165	242	1.1	4.3
CHR–Chr Chs & Chs Cr	1	NR	70	79	0.4	1.4
CHR–Chs of Christ	2	103	92	126	0.6	2.3
HINDU–I/A Temples	1	NR	NR	250	1.1	4.5
Ind Fund Churches	1	NR	NR	NR	-	-
Jehovah's Witness	2	NR	NR	NR	-	-
LDS–L-D Saints	3	NR	NR	994	4.4	17.8
LUTH–Assoc Free Luth	1	NR	NR	NR	-	-
LUTH–E.L.C.A.	2	80	181	308	1.4	5.5
Non-denom Chr Chs	5	395	460	500	2.2	9.0
PENT–Assemb of God	5	378	128	549	2.5	9.8
PENT–Int Foursq Gos	2	101	142	160	0.7	2.9
PENT–Un Pent Ch Intl	1	NR	NR	NR	-	-
PRES–Presb Ch (USA)	2	155	172	194	0.9	3.5
Sev Day Adv	2	153	266	306	1.4	5.5
Unity Ch	1	NR	NR	NR	-	-
DESCHUTES	**146**	**14,403**	**16,338**	**40,314**	**25.6**	**100.0**
ANG/EPIS–Episcopal	4	504	792	1,009	0.6	2.5
Bahá'í	2	NR	145	145	0.1	0.4
BAPT–Amer Bapt Assn	1	NR	35	43	0.0	0.1
BAPT–Consrv Bapt	5	NR	NR	NR	-	-
BAPT–Converge/BGC	1	75	NR	90	0.1	0.2
BAPT–So Bapt Conv	8	300	474	576	0.4	1.4
BUDD–Theravada	1	NR	NR	267	0.2	0.7
BUDD–Vajrayana	2	NR	NR	74	0.0	0.2
Calv Chpl	4	NR	NR	NR	-	-
Catholic	5	NR	NR	11,643	7.4	28.9
CGOD–Ch God (Ander)	1	0	NR	0	0.0	0.0
Ch Cr, Scientst	1	NR	NR	NR	-	-
Ch God (7th Day)	1	NR	NR	NR	-	-
Ch of Nazarene	5	733	500	1,086	0.7	2.7
CHR–Chr Chs & Chs Cr	5	NR	1,290	1,568	1.0	3.9
CHR–Chs of Christ	4	348	297	488	0.3	1.2
Evan Ch	1	NR	NR	NR	-	-
Evan Free Ch	1	120	NR	120	0.1	0.3
FRND–Evan Fr Ch Intl	1	NR	0	0	0.0	0.0

NR–Not Reported - Represents no adherents reported. Percentages may not total 100 due to rounding.

Table 3: Religious Congregations by County and Group: 2010

Religious Group	Number of Congregations	Number of Attendees	Number of Communicant, Confirmed, or Full Members	Adherents		
				Number of Adherents	% of Total Pop.	% of Total Adh.
FRND–Indep Yr Mtgs	1	NR	7	9	0.0	0.0
HINDU–Post Ren	1	NR	NR	54	0.0	0.1
Jehovah's Witness	6	NR	NR	NR	-	-
JUD–Reform	1	35	61	165	0.1	0.4
LDS–Comm of Christ	2	NR	334	334	0.2	0.8
LDS–L-D Saints	9	NR	NR	5,174	3.3	12.8
LUTH–E.L.C.A.	5	706	1,223	1,765	1.1	4.4
LUTH–Luth–MO Synod	3	94	581	987	0.6	2.4
LUTH–Wisc Ev Luth Syn	1	11	38	47	0.0	0.1
MENN–Mennonite USA	1	25	0	0	0.0	0.0
METH–Free Methodist	3	696	774	846	0.5	2.1
METH–Un Methodist	1	220	505	870	0.6	2.2
MJEW–Union Mes Cong	1	NR	NR	NR	-	-
Non-denom Chr Chs	22	4,272	4,446	5,453	3.5	13.5
ORTHE–Orth Ch in Amer	1	14	NR	26	0.0	0.1
PENT–Assemb of God	9	787	461	1,238	0.8	3.1
PENT–Ch God (Cleve)	2	174	177	215	0.1	0.5
PENT–Int Foursq Gos	4	2,849	2,163	2,628	1.7	6.5
PENT–Intl Pent Holiness	1	228	60	73	0.0	0.2
PENT–Open Bible Std	2	671	NR	671	0.4	1.7
PENT–Pent Ch of God	2	140	NR	217	0.1	0.5
PENT–Un Pent Ch Intl	2	NR	NR	NR	-	-
PRES–Orth Pres Ch	1	60	85	91	0.1	0.2
PRES–Presb Ch (USA)	2	807	1,027	1,248	0.8	3.1
Salvation Army	1	18	16	89	0.1	0.2
Sev Day Adv	5	402	699	803	0.5	2.0
Sikh	1	NR	NR	NR	-	-
Un C of Christ	1	14	17	21	0.0	0.1
Unit Univ	1	100	131	181	0.1	0.4
Unity Ch	1	NR	NR	NR	-	-
DOUGLAS	**183**	**11,412**	**16,969**	**29,491**	**27.4**	**100.0**
ANG/EPIS–Episcopal	5	113	303	303	0.3	1.0
Bahá'í	1	NR	145	145	0.1	0.5
BAPT–Amer Bapt Assn	5	NR	425	502	0.5	1.7
BAPT–Amer Bapt USA	1	60	39	46	0.0	0.2
BAPT–Consrv Bapt	5	NR	NR	NR	-	-
BAPT–So Bapt Conv	8	448	2,346	2,771	2.6	9.4
BUDD–Mahayana	1	NR	NR	11	0.0	0.0
Calv Chpl	4	NR	NR	NR	-	-
Catholic	5	NR	NR	2,443	2.3	8.3
CGOD–Ch God (Ander)	3	503	NR	503	0.5	1.7
Ch Cr, Scientst	1	NR	NR	NR	-	-
Ch of Nazarene	4	373	426	543	0.5	1.8
Chr & Miss Al	2	244	141	506	0.5	1.7
CHR–Chr Chs & Chs Cr	13	NR	1,238	1,462	1.4	5.0
CHR–Chs of Christ	8	521	532	728	0.7	2.5
Evan Free Ch	2	228	NR	228	0.2	0.8
FRND–Indep Yr Mtgs	1	NR	0	0	0.0	0.0
Ind Fund Churches	1	NR	NR	NR	-	-
Jehovah's Witness	11	NR	NR	NR	-	-
LDS–Comm of Christ	1	NR	167	167	0.2	0.6
LDS–L-D Saints	7	NR	NR	4,540	4.2	15.4
LUTH–E.L.C.A.	1	100	240	284	0.3	1.0
LUTH–Evan Luth Syn	2	55	95	108	0.1	0.4
LUTH–Luth–MO Synod	3	265	368	430	0.4	1.5
METH–Free Methodist	2	169	106	169	0.2	0.6
METH–Un Methodist	12	409	683	1,033	1.0	3.5
Missionary Ch	3	213	128	215	0.2	0.7
Muslim Est	1	134	NR	308	0.3	1.0
Non-denom Chr Chs	22	4,210	5,429	6,394	5.9	21.7
PENT–Apos Faith Msn	1	NR	35	41	0.0	0.1
PENT–Assemb of God	12	575	358	853	0.8	2.9
PENT–Ch God (Cleve)	4	539	646	763	0.7	2.6
PENT–Ch of God Proph	2	NR	64	76	0.1	0.3
PENT–Int Foursq Gos	5	672	616	727	0.7	2.5
PENT–Open Bible Std	2	192	NR	192	0.2	0.7
PENT–Pent Ch of God	1	70	NR	109	0.1	0.4
PENT–Un Pent Ch Intl	2	NR	NR	NR	-	-
PRES–Orth Pres Ch	1	37	0	0	0.0	0.0
PRES–Presb Ch (USA)	5	172	457	540	0.5	1.8
Salvation Army	1	20	31	105	0.1	0.4
Sev Day Adv	10	1,090	1,894	2,179	2.0	7.4
Unit Univ	1	0	57	67	0.1	0.2

Religious Group	Number of Congregations	Number of Attendees	Number of Communicant, Confirmed, or Full Members	Adherents		
				Number of Adherents	% of Total Pop.	% of Total Adh.
Unity Ch	1	NR	NR	NR	-	-
GILLIAM	**7**	**147**	**189**	**492**	**26.3**	**100.0**
Bahá'í	0	NR	4	4	0.2	0.8
BAPT–Consrv Bapt	1	NR	NR	NR	-	-
Catholic	2	NR	NR	142	7.6	28.9
Ch of Nazarene	1	49	21	113	6.0	23.0
METH–Un Methodist	1	55	73	128	6.8	26.0
Sev Day Adv	1	4	8	9	0.5	1.8
Un C of Christ	1	39	83	96	5.1	19.5
GRANT	**28**	**508**	**768**	**1,839**	**24.7**	**100.0**
ANG/EPIS–Episcopal	1	18	62	62	0.8	3.4
Bahá'í	0	NR	11	11	0.1	0.6
BAPT–Consrv Bapt	2	NR	NR	NR	-	-
BAPT–Ind Bapt Flwsp Intl	1	NR	NR	NR	-	-
Calv Chpl	1	NR	NR	NR	-	-
Catholic	4	NR	NR	405	5.4	22.0
Ch of Nazarene	1	101	87	143	1.9	7.8
CHR–Chr Ch (Disc)	1	0	60	70	0.9	3.8
CHR–Chs of Christ	1	10	7	8	0.1	0.4
Jehovah's Witness	1	NR	NR	NR	-	-
LDS–L-D Saints	2	NR	NR	462	6.2	25.1
LUTH–Luth–MO Synod	1	18	36	36	0.5	2.0
METH–Evan Meth Ch	1	NR	NR	NR	-	-
METH–Un Methodist	1	42	80	147	2.0	8.0
Non-denom Chr Chs	2	150	210	212	2.8	11.5
PENT–Assemb of God	2	46	25	64	0.9	3.5
PRES–Presb Ch (USA)	3	37	41	48	0.6	2.6
Sev Day Adv	3	86	149	171	2.3	9.3
HARNEY	**19**	**282**	**589**	**2,068**	**27.9**	**100.0**
ANG/EPIS–Episcopal	1	27	21	21	0.3	1.0
Bahá'í	0	NR	19	19	0.3	0.9
BAPT–Consrv Bapt	1	NR	NR	NR	-	-
Calv Chpl	1	NR	NR	NR	-	-
Catholic	3	NR	NR	689	9.3	33.3
Ch of Nazarene	1	96	93	104	1.4	5.0
CHR–Chr Chs & Chs Cr	1	NR	90	107	1.4	5.2
CHR–Chs of Christ	1	8	7	8	0.1	0.4
Jehovah's Witness	1	NR	NR	NR	-	-
LDS–L-D Saints	2	NR	NR	678	9.1	32.8
LUTH–E.L.C.A.	2	22	41	66	0.9	3.2
LUTH–Luth–MO Synod	1	12	24	27	0.4	1.3
MENN–CG in Cr (Menn)	1	NR	17	20	0.3	1.0
PENT–Int Foursq Gos	1	40	136	162	2.2	7.8
PRES–Presb Ch (USA)	1	51	96	115	1.5	5.6
Sev Day Adv	1	26	45	52	0.7	2.5
HOOD RIVER	**35**	**1,957**	**3,153**	**8,587**	**38.4**	**100.0**
ANG/EPIS–Episcopal	1	68	109	193	0.9	2.2
Bahá'í	0	NR	51	51	0.2	0.6
BAPT–Consrv Bapt	1	NR	NR	NR	-	-
BAPT–So Bapt Conv	3	115	222	277	1.2	3.2
Catholic	1	NR	NR	3,693	16.5	43.0
Ch of Nazarene	2	109	122	135	0.6	1.6
Chr & Miss Al	2	130	80	180	0.8	2.1
CHR–Chr Ch (Disc)	1	100	500	625	2.8	7.3
CHR–Chs of Christ	3	155	129	187	0.8	2.2
Jehovah's Witness	1	NR	NR	NR	-	-
LDS–L-D Saints	1	NR	NR	689	3.1	8.0
LUTH–E.L.C.A.	1	51	104	117	0.5	1.4
LUTH–Evan Luth Syn	1	18	25	31	0.1	0.4
METH–Un Methodist	2	59	155	214	1.0	2.5
Non-denom Chr Chs	5	462	650	728	3.3	8.5
PENT–Assemb of God	2	212	124	363	1.6	4.2
PENT–Int Foursq Gos	1	0	0	0	0.0	0.0
PENT–Un Pent Ch Intl	1	NR	NR	NR	-	-
PENT–Vineyard	1	250	350	437	2.0	5.1
PRES–Presb Ch (USA)	1	0	68	85	0.4	1.0
Sev Day Adv	2	104	180	207	0.9	2.4
Un C of Christ	1	80	217	271	1.2	3.2

NR–Not Reported   - Represents no adherents reported.   Percentages may not total 100 due to rounding.

Table 3: Religious Congregations by County and Group: 2010

Religious Group	Number of Congrega-tions	Number of Attendees	Number of Communicant, Confirmed, or Full Members	Adherents: Number of Adherents	Adherents: % of Total Pop.	Adherents: % of Total Adh.
Unit Univ	1	44	67	104	0.5	1.2
JACKSON	**197**	**17,622**	**24,715**	**57,864**	**28.5**	**100.0**
ANG/EPIS–Anglican NA	1	NR	NR	NR	-	-
ANG/EPIS–Episcopal	4	346	694	782	0.4	1.4
Bahá'í	3	NR	345	345	0.2	0.6
BAPT–Amer Bapt USA	2	342	421	505	0.2	0.9
BAPT–Consrv Bapt	4	NR	NR	NR	-	-
BAPT–So Bapt Conv	10	435	926	1,110	0.5	1.9
BUDD–Mahayana	6	NR	NR	66	0.0	0.1
BUDD–Vajrayana	2	NR	NR	83	0.0	0.1
Calv Chpl	4	NR	NR	NR	-	-
Catholic	6	NR	NR	16,565	8.2	28.6
CGOD–Ch God (Ander)	1	65	NR	65	0.0	0.1
Ch Cr, Scientst	2	NR	NR	NR	-	-
Ch of Nazarene	6	1,079	1,409	1,913	0.9	3.3
Chr & Miss Al	2	214	161	325	0.2	0.6
CHR–Chr Ch (Disc)	1	71	222	266	0.1	0.5
CHR–Chr Chs & Chs Cr	7	NR	675	809	0.4	1.4
CHR–Chs of Christ	8	507	432	555	0.3	1.0
FRND–Evan Fr Ch Intl	2	145	187	224	0.1	0.4
FRND–Indep Yr Mtgs	1	NR	37	44	0.0	0.1
HINDU–Post Ren	2	NR	NR	102	0.1	0.2
HINDU–Renaiss	2	NR	NR	54	0.0	0.1
Ind Fund Churches	1	NR	NR	NR	-	-
Jehovah's Witness	5	NR	NR	NR	-	-
JUD–Orth	1	43	50	60	0.0	0.1
JUD–Reform	1	98	173	467	0.2	0.8
LDS–Comm of Christ	1	NR	167	167	0.1	0.3
LDS–L-D Saints	15	NR	NR	8,471	4.2	14.6
LUTH–E.L.C.A.	2	215	138	703	0.3	1.2
LUTH–Evan Luth Syn	1	39	50	70	0.0	0.1
LUTH–Luth-MO Synod	5	480	810	966	0.5	1.7
METH–Un Methodist	5	476	798	1,080	0.5	1.9
METH–Wesleyan	2	62	31	81	0.0	0.1
New Apost Ch	1	NR	NR	NR	-	-
Non-denom Chr Chs	29	8,440	11,419	12,432	6.1	21.5
ORTHE–Orth Ch in Amer	1	35	NR	70	0.0	0.1
ORTHE–Rus Orth Abroad	1	24	NR	30	0.0	0.1
PENT–Apos Faith Msn	1	NR	200	240	0.1	0.4
PENT–Assemb of God	14	1,438	698	3,217	1.6	5.6
PENT–Ch God (Cleve)	1	29	109	131	0.1	0.2
PENT–Int Foursq Gos	4	447	358	429	0.2	0.7
PENT–Pent Ch of God	4	280	NR	435	0.2	0.8
PENT–Un Pent Ch Intl	2	NR	NR	NR	-	-
PRES–Evan Presby Ch	2	NR	404	484	0.2	0.8
PRES–Orth Pres Ch	1	80	71	91	0.0	0.2
PRES–Presb Ch (USA)	6	693	1,219	1,462	0.7	2.5
Salvation Army	1	17	33	71	0.0	0.1
Sev Day Adv	9	1,121	1,949	2,242	1.1	3.9
Un C of Christ	2	248	342	410	0.2	0.7
Unit Univ	1	153	187	238	0.1	0.4
Unity Ch	2	NR	NR	NR	-	-
Zoroastrian	0	NR	NR	4	0.0	0.0
JEFFERSON	**30**	**1,652**	**3,038**	**5,763**	**26.5**	**100.0**
ANG/EPIS–Episcopal	1	37	16	18	0.1	0.3
Bahá'í	0	NR	65	65	0.3	1.1
BAPT–Amer Bapt Assn	1	NR	85	106	0.5	1.8
BAPT–Consrv Bapt	2	NR	NR	NR	-	-
BAPT–Natl Mis Bapt Conv	1	0	150	187	0.9	3.2
BAPT–So Bapt Conv	3	508	1,443	1,795	8.3	31.1
Catholic	2	NR	NR	1,156	5.3	20.1
Ch of Nazarene	1	20	41	41	0.2	0.7
CHR–Chr Chs & Chs Cr	2	NR	155	193	0.9	3.3
CHR–Chs of Christ	1	35	40	55	0.3	1.0
FRND–Evan Fr Ch Intl	1	100	112	139	0.6	2.4
Jehovah's Witness	2	NR	NR	NR	-	-
LDS–L-D Saints	1	NR	NR	584	2.7	10.1
LUTH–E.L.C.A.	1	37	73	130	0.6	2.3
METH–Free Methodist	1	92	49	92	0.4	1.6
METH–Un Methodist	1	75	182	279	1.3	4.8
Non-denom Chr Chs	2	120	160	175	0.8	3.0

Religious Group	Number of Congrega-tions	Number of Attendees	Number of Communicant, Confirmed, or Full Members	Adherents: Number of Adherents	Adherents: % of Total Pop.	Adherents: % of Total Adh.
PENT–Assemb of God	1	273	162	273	1.3	4.7
PENT–Int Foursq Gos	2	151	104	129	0.6	2.2
PENT–Intl Pent Holiness	1	56	26	32	0.1	0.6
PENT–Pent Ch of God	1	70	NR	109	0.5	1.9
PRES–Presb Ch (USA)	1	0	40	50	0.2	0.9
Sev Day Adv	1	78	135	155	0.7	2.7
JOSEPHINE	**90**	**7,133**	**10,245**	**21,499**	**26.0**	**100.0**
ANG/EPIS–Episcopal	2	54	261	267	0.3	1.2
Bahá'í	2	NR	114	114	0.1	0.5
BAPT–Amer Bapt Assn	1	NR	60	71	0.1	0.3
BAPT–Amer Bapt USA	2	225	296	349	0.4	1.6
BAPT–Consrv Bapt	1	NR	NR	NR	-	-
BAPT–Reg Bapt Gen As	1	NR	NR	NR	-	-
BAPT–So Bapt Conv	3	135	179	211	0.3	1.0
BRETH–Breth in Chr	1	NR	NR	NR	-	-
BRETH–Ch of Brethren	1	4	16	19	0.0	0.1
BUDD–Vajrayana	1	NR	NR	20	0.0	0.1
Calv Chpl	1	NR	NR	NR	-	-
Catholic	2	NR	NR	3,891	4.7	18.1
Ch Cr, Scientst	1	NR	NR	NR	-	-
Ch of Nazarene	3	97	87	286	0.3	1.3
Chr & Miss Al	2	32	23	63	0.1	0.3
CHR–Chr Ch (Disc)	1	160	314	370	0.4	1.7
CHR–Chr Chs & Chs Cr	1	NR	450	531	0.6	2.5
CHR–Chs of Christ	4	230	248	283	0.3	1.3
Evan Free Ch	1	65	NR	65	0.1	0.3
FRND–Evan Fr Ch Intl	1	5	0	0	0.0	0.0
Grace Gosp Fel	1	NR	NR	NR	-	-
HINDU–Post Ren	1	NR	NR	25	0.0	0.1
Ind Fund Churches	1	NR	NR	NR	-	-
Jehovah's Witness	3	NR	NR	NR	-	-
LDS–L-D Saints	7	NR	NR	4,143	5.0	19.3
LUTH–E.L.C.A.	2	209	579	619	0.7	2.9
LUTH–Evan Luth Syn	1	41	63	70	0.1	0.3
LUTH–Luth-MO Synod	1	123	247	289	0.3	1.3
MENN–Menn Br US Conf	1	NR	43	51	0.1	0.2
METH–Un Methodist	3	217	409	603	0.7	2.8
Non-denom Chr Chs	17	3,170	3,919	4,338	5.2	20.2
PENT–Apos Faith Msn	1	NR	35	41	0.0	0.2
PENT–Assemb of God	4	886	398	1,732	2.1	8.1
PENT–Ch God (Cleve)	1	40	60	71	0.1	0.3
PENT–Int Foursq Gos	1	111	500	590	0.7	2.7
PENT–Pent Ch of God	1	70	NR	109	0.1	0.5
PENT–Un Pent Ch Intl	1	NR	NR	NR	-	-
PENT–Vineyard	1	298	345	407	0.5	1.9
PRES–Orth Pres Ch	1	82	132	173	0.2	0.8
PRES–Presb Ch (USA)	1	111	177	209	0.3	1.0
Salvation Army	1	50	45	64	0.1	0.3
Sev Day Adv	5	690	1,199	1,379	1.7	6.4
Unit Univ	1	28	46	46	0.1	0.2
Unity Ch	1	NR	NR	NR	-	-
KLAMATH	**99**	**5,939**	**7,376**	**18,330**	**27.6**	**100.0**
ANG/EPIS–Episcopal	2	63	117	183	0.3	1.0
Bahá'í	1	NR	44	44	0.1	0.2
BAPT–Amer Bapt Assn	1	NR	85	102	0.2	0.6
BAPT–Consrv Bapt	3	NR	NR	NR	-	-
BAPT–Ind Bapt Flwsp Intl	1	NR	NR	NR	-	-
BAPT–So Bapt Conv	4	234	996	1,199	1.8	6.5
Calv Chpl	4	NR	NR	NR	-	-
Catholic	7	NR	NR	4,460	6.7	24.3
CGOD–Ch God (Ander)	1	142	NR	142	0.2	0.8
Ch Cr, Scientst	1	NR	NR	NR	-	-
Ch of Nazarene	2	117	143	165	0.2	0.9
Chr & Miss Al	1	40	22	61	0.1	0.3
CHR–Chr Chs & Chs Cr	3	NR	750	903	1.4	4.9
CHR–Chs of Christ	3	110	132	184	0.3	1.0
Evan Free Ch	1	250	NR	250	0.4	1.4
FRND–Evan Fr Ch Intl	2	61	107	129	0.2	0.7
Ind Fund Churches	1	NR	NR	NR	-	-
Jehovah's Witness	1	NR	NR	NR	-	-
LDS–Comm of Christ	1	NR	167	167	0.3	0.9

NR–Not Reported   - Represents no adherents reported.   Percentages may not total 100 due to rounding.

Table 3: Religious Congregations by County and Group: 2010

Religious Group	Number of Congrega-tions	Number of Attendees	Number of Communicant, Confirmed, or Full Members	Adherents		
				Number of Adherents	% of Total Pop.	% of Total Adh.
LDS–L-D Saints	8	NR	NR	3,133	4.7	17.1
LUTH–E.L.C.A.	2	185	694	866	1.3	4.7
LUTH–Evan Luth Syn	1	35	48	57	0.1	0.3
LUTH–Luth–MO Synod	2	134	158	189	0.3	1.0
METH–Un Methodist	4	110	248	362	0.5	2.0
METH–Wesleyan	1	34	21	44	0.1	0.2
Muslim Est	1	134	NR	308	0.5	1.7
Non-denom Chr Chs	13	1,285	1,516	1,735	2.6	9.5
PENT–Assemb of God	7	829	364	1,305	2.0	7.1
PENT–Ch God (Cleve)	1	117	80	96	0.1	0.5
PENT–COGIC	1	35	25	30	0.0	0.2
PENT–Int Foursq Gos	3	756	393	473	0.7	2.6
PENT–Open Bible Std	2	135	NR	135	0.2	0.7
PENT–Pent Ch of God	1	70	NR	109	0.2	0.6
PENT–Un Pent Ch Intl	1	NR	NR	NR	-	-
PENT–Vineyard	1	70	110	132	0.2	0.7
PRES–Presb Ch (USA)	5	689	647	779	1.2	4.2
Sev Day Adv	3	268	466	535	0.8	2.9
Un C of Christ	1	18	23	28	0.0	0.2
Unit Univ	1	18	20	25	0.0	0.1
LAKE	**26**	**522**	**511**	**1,745**	**22.1**	**100.0**
ANG/EPIS–Episcopal	1	11	10	14	0.2	0.8
Bahá'í	0	NR	5	5	0.1	0.3
BAPT–Consrv Bapt	1	NR	NR	NR	-	-
BAPT–So Bapt Conv	1	15	44	51	0.6	2.9
Calv Chpl	1	NR	NR	NR	-	-
Catholic	5	NR	NR	548	6.9	31.4
Ch of Nazarene	1	21	14	53	0.7	3.0
Jehovah's Witness	1	NR	NR	NR	-	-
LDS–L-D Saints	2	NR	NR	412	5.2	23.6
LUTH–Luth–MO Synod	1	15	20	24	0.3	1.4
METH–Un Methodist	2	34	48	104	1.3	6.0
Non-denom Chr Chs	2	140	160	190	2.4	10.9
PENT–Assemb of God	2	99	50	129	1.6	7.4
PENT–Ch God (Cleve)	1	34	12	14	0.2	0.8
PENT–Int Foursq Gos	1	32	11	13	0.2	0.7
PENT–Open Bible Std	1	30	NR	30	0.4	1.7
PRES–Presb Ch (USA)	1	45	56	65	0.8	3.7
Sev Day Adv	2	46	81	93	1.2	5.3
LANE	**357**	**24,919**	**37,354**	**87,756**	**25.0**	**100.0**
ANG/EPIS–Episcopal	7	671	1,326	1,380	0.4	1.6
Bahá'í	4	NR	497	497	0.1	0.6
BAPT–Amer Bapt Assn	1	NR	85	100	0.0	0.1
BAPT–Amer Bapt USA	4	227	556	655	0.2	0.7
BAPT–Consrv Bapt	12	NR	NR	NR	-	-
BAPT–Free Will Bapt	1	NR	41	48	0.0	0.1
BAPT–Natl Mis Bapt Conv	1	0	150	177	0.1	0.2
BAPT–Reg Bapt Gen As	1	NR	NR	NR	-	-
BAPT–So Bapt Conv	12	1,191	2,749	3,239	0.9	3.7
BRETH–Ch of Brethren	1	17	27	32	0.0	0.0
BUDD–Mahayana	5	NR	NR	1,839	0.5	2.1
BUDD–Vajrayana	5	NR	NR	189	0.1	0.2
Calv Chpl	6	NR	NR	NR	-	-
Catholic	15	NR	NR	21,785	6.2	24.8
CGOD–Ch God (Ander)	3	503	NR	503	0.1	0.6
Ch Cr, Scientst	3	NR	NR	NR	-	-
Ch God (7th Day)	1	NR	NR	NR	-	-
Ch of Nazarene	9	1,099	1,288	1,534	0.4	1.7
Chr & Miss Al	2	157	97	228	0.1	0.3
CHR–Chr Ch (Disc)	7	814	1,423	1,677	0.5	1.9
CHR–Chr Chs & Chs Cr	25	NR	3,536	4,166	1.2	4.7
CHR–Chs of Christ	12	722	682	857	0.2	1.0
Evan Ch	5	NR	NR	NR	-	-
Evan Cov Ch	2	173	192	225	0.1	0.3
Evan Free Ch	2	115	NR	115	0.0	0.1
FRND–Evan Fr Ch Intl	2	108	147	173	0.0	0.2
FRND–Indep Yr Mtgs	2	NR	107	126	0.0	0.1
HINDU–I/A Temples	1	NR	NR	1,562	0.4	1.8
HINDU–Post Ren	4	NR	NR	161	0.0	0.2
HINDU–Renaiss	1	NR	NR	12	0.0	0.0
Jehovah's Witness	13	NR	NR	NR	-	-

Religious Group	Number of Congrega-tions	Number of Attendees	Number of Communicant, Confirmed, or Full Members	Adherents		
				Number of Adherents	% of Total Pop.	% of Total Adh.
JUD–Orth	2	180	100	250	0.1	0.3
JUD–Reconst	1	286	365	986	0.3	1.1
LDS–Comm of Christ	2	NR	334	334	0.1	0.4
LDS–L-D Saints	24	NR	NR	12,687	3.6	14.5
LUTH–Assoc Free Luth	1	NR	NR	NR	-	-
LUTH–Ch of Luth Br	1	35	25	60	0.0	0.1
LUTH–E.L.C.A.	10	1,108	2,788	3,641	1.0	4.1
LUTH–Luth Cong Msn Chr	1	NR	NR	NR	-	-
LUTH–Luth–MO Synod	9	569	922	1,101	0.3	1.3
LUTH–Wisc Ev Luth Syn	1	44	62	71	0.0	0.1
MENN–Menn Br US Conf	1	NR	20	24	0.0	0.0
MENN–Mennonite USA	1	17	26	31	0.0	0.0
METH–C.M.E.	1	0	100	118	0.0	0.1
METH–Evan Meth Ch	1	NR	NR	NR	-	-
METH–Free Methodist	3	170	115	170	0.0	0.2
METH–Un Methodist	12	957	1,764	2,564	0.7	2.9
METH–Wesleyan	1	37	25	48	0.0	0.1
Muslim Est	1	134	NR	308	0.1	0.4
New Apost Ch	1	NR	NR	NR	-	-
Non-denom Chr Chs	24	5,275	5,970	6,744	1.9	7.7
ORTHE–Greek Orthodox	1	85	NR	100	0.0	0.1
ORTHE–Serb Orth USA	1	80	NR	140	0.0	0.2
PENT–Assemb of God	20	2,108	1,154	2,959	0.8	3.4
PENT–Ch God (Cleve)	2	87	62	73	0.0	0.1
PENT–Ch of God Proph	1	NR	25	29	0.0	0.0
PENT–Int Foursq Gos	15	4,093	5,916	6,970	2.0	7.9
PENT–Intl Pent Holiness	1	90	84	99	0.0	0.1
PENT–Open Bible Std	10	1,006	NR	1,006	0.3	1.1
PENT–Pent Ch of God	4	280	NR	435	0.1	0.5
PENT–Un Pent Ch Intl	6	NR	NR	NR	-	-
PRES–Kor Pres Abroad	1	NR	NR	NR	-	-
PRES–Presb Ch (USA)	7	597	956	1,126	0.3	1.3
PRES–Presb Ch Amer	1	0	105	130	0.0	0.1
REF–Comm Ref Evan	1	NR	NR	NR	-	-
Salvation Army	2	98	149	287	0.1	0.3
Sev Day Adv	11	1,297	2,256	2,594	0.7	3.0
Sikh	1	NR	NR	NR	-	-
Tao	1	NR	NR	NR	-	-
Un C of Christ	1	289	775	913	0.3	1.0
Unit Univ	2	200	353	478	0.1	0.5
Unity Ch	1	NR	NR	NR	-	-
LINCOLN	**78**	**3,641**	**4,643**	**9,980**	**21.7**	**100.0**
ANG/EPIS–Episcopal	4	161	271	293	0.6	2.9
Bahá'í	0	NR	72	72	0.2	0.7
BAPT–Amer Bapt Assn	1	NR	85	98	0.2	1.0
BAPT–Amer Bapt USA	1	35	66	76	0.2	0.8
BAPT–Consrv Bapt	2	NR	NR	NR	-	-
BAPT–So Bapt Conv	6	309	426	491	1.1	4.9
BUDD–Mahayana	1	NR	NR	20	0.0	0.2
Calv Chpl	1	NR	NR	NR	-	-
Catholic	4	NR	NR	2,524	5.5	25.3
Ch Cr, Scientst	1	NR	NR	NR	-	-
Ch of Nazarene	2	454	370	472	1.0	4.7
CHR–Chr Chs & Chs Cr	4	NR	285	328	0.7	3.3
CHR–Chs of Christ	3	90	78	103	0.2	1.0
Evan Ch	1	NR	NR	NR	-	-
Jehovah's Witness	2	NR	NR	NR	-	-
LDS–L-D Saints	3	NR	NR	1,563	3.4	15.7
LUTH–E.L.C.A.	1	94	216	243	0.5	2.4
LUTH–Luth–MO Synod	3	180	265	282	0.6	2.8
LUTH–Wisc Ev Luth Syn	1	0	0	0	0.0	0.0
MENN–Mennonite USA	1	60	60	69	0.1	0.7
METH–Un Methodist	1	0	134	169	0.4	1.7
Non-denom Chr Chs	8	426	516	595	1.3	6.0
PENT–Assemb of God	7	310	146	575	1.2	5.8
PENT–Int Foursq Gos	5	498	298	343	0.7	3.4
PENT–Pent Ch of God	1	70	NR	109	0.2	1.1
PENT–Un Pent Ch Intl	1	NR	NR	NR	-	-
PENT–Vineyard	2	238	295	340	0.7	3.4
PRES–Presb Ch (USA)	4	369	437	503	1.1	5.0
Sev Day Adv	3	249	433	498	1.1	5.0
Un C of Christ	1	78	156	180	0.4	1.8
Unit Univ	1	20	34	34	0.1	0.3

NR–Not Reported   - Represents no adherents reported.   Percentages may not total 100 due to rounding.

Table 3: Religious Congregations by County and Group: 2010

Religious Group	Number of Congrega-tions	Number of Attendees	Number of Communicant, Confirmed, or Full Members	Adherents		
				Number of Adherents	% of Total Pop.	% of Total Adh.
Unity Ch	2	NR	NR	NR	-	-
LINN	**156**	**10,672**	**15,099**	**32,118**	**27.5**	**100.0**
ANG/EPIS–Episcopal	3	132	211	293	0.3	0.9
Bahá'í	1	NR	124	124	0.1	0.4
BAPT–Amer Bapt Assn	1	NR	100	123	0.1	0.4
BAPT–Asc Ref Bap Ch Am	1	NR	NR	NR	-	-
BAPT–Consrv Bapt	11	NR	NR	NR	-	-
BAPT–Ref Bapt Ch	2	NR	NR	NR	-	-
BAPT–Reg Bapt Gen As	1	NR	NR	NR	-	-
BAPT–So Bapt Conv	5	323	815	1,003	0.9	3.1
Calv Chpl	3	NR	NR	NR	-	-
Catholic	8	NR	NR	7,690	6.6	23.9
CGOD–Ch God (Ander)	3	323	NR	323	0.3	1.0
Ch Cr, Scientst	1	NR	NR	NR	-	-
Ch God (7th Day)	1	NR	NR	NR	-	-
Ch of Nazarene	3	346	408	568	0.5	1.8
CHR–Chr Ch (Disc)	2	233	743	914	0.8	2.8
CHR–Chr Chs & Chs Cr	10	NR	1,770	2,178	1.9	6.8
CHR–Chs of Christ	6	329	296	361	0.3	1.1
Evan Ch	5	NR	NR	NR	-	-
Ind Fund Churches	1	NR	NR	NR	-	-
Jehovah's Witness	5	NR	NR	NR	-	-
LDS–L-D Saints	11	NR	NR	4,224	3.6	13.2
LUTH–E.L.C.A.	4	350	906	1,118	1.0	3.5
LUTH–Luth Cong Msn Chr	1	99	150	185	0.2	0.6
LUTH–Luth–MO Synod	4	212	400	544	0.5	1.7
MENN–CG in Cr (Menn)	1	NR	125	154	0.1	0.5
MENN–Cons Menn Conf	1	200	196	241	0.2	0.8
MENN–Mennonite USA	4	609	551	678	0.6	2.1
METH–Free Methodist	2	88	106	113	0.1	0.4
METH–Un Methodist	5	259	657	797	0.7	2.5
Missionary Ch	1	92	80	92	0.1	0.3
Non-denom Chr Chs	18	3,810	4,395	4,884	4.2	15.2
PENT–Assemb of God	8	1,463	1,060	2,627	2.3	8.2
PENT–Ch God (Cleve)	3	157	156	192	0.2	0.6
PENT–Int Foursq Gos	4	534	569	700	0.6	2.2
PENT–Intl Pent Holiness	1	28	22	27	0.0	0.1
PENT–Pent Ch of God	4	280	NR	435	0.4	1.4
PENT–Un Pent Ch Intl	2	NR	NR	NR	-	-
PENT–Vineyard	1	122	171	210	0.2	0.7
PRES–Presb Ch (USA)	3	332	467	575	0.5	1.8
Salvation Army	1	19	44	81	0.1	0.3
Sev Day Adv	4	332	577	664	0.6	2.1
MALHEUR	**66**	**2,289**	**3,216**	**18,183**	**58.1**	**100.0**
ANG/EPIS–Episcopal	2	65	194	202	0.6	1.1
Bahá'í	0	NR	24	24	0.1	0.1
BAPT–Amer Bapt Assn	1	NR	85	106	0.3	0.6
BAPT–Amer Bapt USA	1	183	220	275	0.9	1.5
BAPT–Consrv Bapt	3	NR	NR	NR	-	-
BAPT–So Bapt Conv	1	75	75	94	0.3	0.5
BUDD–Mahayana	1	NR	NR	1,250	4.0	6.9
BUDD–Vajrayana	1	NR	NR	53	0.2	0.3
Calv Chpl	1	NR	NR	NR	-	-
Catholic	7	NR	NR	8,060	25.7	44.3
CGOD–Ch God (Ander)	1	185	NR	185	0.6	1.0
Ch Cr, Scientst	1	NR	NR	NR	-	-
Ch of Nazarene	4	481	435	786	2.5	4.3
CHR–Chr Ch (Disc)	1	51	150	187	0.6	1.0
CHR–Chr Chs & Chs Cr	3	NR	381	476	1.5	2.6
CHR–Chs of Christ	1	110	65	100	0.3	0.5
Jehovah's Witness	2	NR	NR	NR	-	-
LDS–L-D Saints	13	NR	NR	4,284	13.7	23.6
LUTH–E.L.C.A.	2	81	241	254	0.8	1.4
LUTH–Luth–MO Synod	1	90	216	286	0.9	1.6
METH–Un Methodist	5	74	193	230	0.7	1.3
Non-denom Chr Chs	5	520	533	675	2.2	3.7
PENT–Assemb of God	4	176	94	287	0.9	1.6
PENT–Ch of God Proph	1	NR	10	12	0.0	0.1
PRES–Presb Ch (USA)	2	98	125	156	0.5	0.9
Sev Day Adv	2	100	175	201	0.6	1.1
MARION	**289**	**30,574**	**40,091**	**133,875**	**42.5**	**100.0**
ANG/EPIS–Episcopal	5	571	1,208	1,404	0.4	1.0
Ap Chr Ch-Amer	1	389	171	389	0.1	0.3
Bahá'í	2	NR	393	393	0.1	0.3
BAPT–Amer Bapt Assn	1	NR	85	107	0.0	0.1
BAPT–Amer Bapt USA	2	206	371	467	0.1	0.3
BAPT–Consrv Bapt	12	NR	NR	NR	-	-
BAPT–Free Will Bapt	1	NR	41	52	0.0	0.0
BAPT–Ind Bapt Flwsp Intl	1	NR	NR	NR	-	-
BAPT–Reg Bapt Gen As	2	NR	NR	NR	-	-
BAPT–So Bapt Conv	4	373	482	607	0.2	0.5
BRETH–Breth in Chr	1	NR	NR	NR	-	-
BUDD–Mahayana	1	NR	NR	34	0.0	0.0
Calv Chpl	3	NR	NR	NR	-	-
Catholic	15	NR	NR	62,607	19.9	46.8
CGOD–Ch God (Ander)	3	364	NR	364	0.1	0.3
Ch Cr, Scientst	2	NR	NR	NR	-	-
Ch God (7th Day)	1	NR	NR	NR	-	-
Ch of Nazarene	8	1,531	2,969	3,159	1.0	2.4
Chr & Miss Al	3	2,904	1,534	7,439	2.4	5.6
CHR–Chr Ch (Disc)	5	618	1,704	2,146	0.7	1.6
CHR–Chr Chs & Chs Cr	7	NR	1,791	2,255	0.7	1.7
CHR–Chs of Christ	7	688	613	841	0.3	0.6
Evan Ch	6	NR	NR	NR	-	-
Evan Cov Ch	1	272	279	354	0.1	0.3
Evan Free Ch	2	325	NR	325	0.1	0.2
FRND–Evan Fr Ch Intl	6	373	414	521	0.2	0.4
FRND–Indep Yr Mtgs	1	NR	28	35	0.0	0.0
FRND–Unaffl Mtgs	1	NR	NR	NR	-	-
Grace Gosp Fel	1	NR	NR	NR	-	-
HINDU–Post Ren	1	NR	NR	25	0.0	0.0
Ind Fund Churches	2	NR	NR	NR	-	-
Jehovah's Witness	9	NR	NR	NR	-	-
JUD–Reconst	1	105	134	362	0.1	0.3
LDS–Comm of Christ	2	NR	334	334	0.1	0.2
LDS–L-D Saints	25	NR	NR	10,201	3.2	7.6
LUTH–Ch of Luth Br	1	82	35	121	0.0	0.1
LUTH–E.L.C.A.	9	976	2,579	3,501	1.1	2.6
LUTH–Luth–MO Synod	7	661	1,278	1,561	0.5	1.2
LUTH–Nor Amer Luth C	1	NR	NR	NR	-	-
LUTH–Wisc Ev Luth Syn	1	118	231	290	0.1	0.2
MENN–Menn Br US Conf	2	NR	1,000	1,259	0.4	0.9
MENN–Mennonite USA	6	589	654	824	0.3	0.6
METH–AME Zion	1	0	150	189	0.1	0.1
METH–Free Methodist	3	474	382	474	0.2	0.4
METH–Un Methodist	10	976	2,126	2,920	0.9	2.2
METH–Wesleyan	3	389	213	506	0.2	0.4
Non-denom Chr Chs	28	7,436	8,784	9,883	3.1	7.4
PENT–Assemb of God	16	4,638	2,110	7,644	2.4	5.7
PENT–Ch God (Cleve)	5	208	341	429	0.1	0.3
PENT–Ch of God Proph	7	NR	221	278	0.1	0.2
PENT–Int Foursq Gos	8	1,241	1,283	1,616	0.5	1.2
PENT–Intl Pent Holiness	2	116	90	113	0.0	0.1
PENT–Open Bible Std	2	115	NR	115	0.0	0.1
PENT–Pent Ch of God	3	210	NR	326	0.1	0.2
PENT–Un Pent Ch Intl	4	NR	NR	NR	-	-
PRES–Presb Ch (USA)	6	790	1,429	1,799	0.6	1.3
PRES–Presb Ch Amer	1	78	39	49	0.0	0.0
REF–Christian Ref	1	140	214	269	0.1	0.2
REF–Un Ref Chs N.A.	1	NR	NR	NR	-	-
Salvation Army	1	217	223	404	0.1	0.3
Sev Day Adv	10	2,022	3,517	4,045	1.3	3.0
Sikh	1	NR	NR	NR	-	-
Un C of Christ	2	229	417	525	0.2	0.4
Unit Univ	1	150	224	314	0.1	0.2
Unity Ch	1	NR	NR	NR	-	-
MORROW	**27**	**675**	**1,017**	**5,419**	**48.5**	**100.0**
ANG/EPIS–Episcopal	1	28	43	106	0.9	2.0
Bahá'í	0	NR	9	9	0.1	0.2
BAPT–Amer Bapt USA	1	12	10	13	0.1	0.2
BAPT–Consrv Bapt	1	NR	NR	NR	-	-
BAPT–Reg Bapt Gen As	1	NR	NR	NR	-	-

NR–Not Reported - Represents no adherents reported. Percentages may not total 100 due to rounding.

Table 3: Religious Congregations by County and Group: 2010

Religious Group	Number of Congrega-tions	Number of Attendees	Number of Communicant, Confirmed, or Full Members	Adherents		
				Number of Adherents	% of Total Pop.	% of Total Adh.
BAPT–So Bapt Conv	1	65	54	69	0.6	1.3
Catholic	3	NR	NR	3,084	27.6	56.9
Ch of Nazarene	1	12	18	38	0.3	0.7
CHR–Chr Ch (Disc)	1	38	68	87	0.8	1.6
CHR–Chr Chs & Chs Cr	1	NR	95	121	1.1	2.2
CONG–Cong Chr, NA	1	NR	99	126	1.1	2.3
LDS–L-D Saints	2	NR	NR	785	7.0	14.5
LUTH–E.L.C.A.	2	45	89	89	0.8	1.6
LUTH–Luth Cong Msn Chr	1	35	74	94	0.8	1.7
METH–Un Methodist	1	44	79	149	1.3	2.7
Non-denom Chr Chs	3	100	130	132	1.2	2.4
PENT–Assemb of God	2	170	49	277	2.5	5.1
PENT–Intl Pent Holiness	1	18	7	9	0.1	0.2
Sev Day Adv	2	70	122	140	1.3	2.6
Un C of Christ	1	38	71	91	0.8	1.7
MULTNOMAH	**626**	**60,758**	**90,109**	**263,934**	**35.9**	**100.0**
ANG/EPIS–Anglican NA	2	NR	NR	NR	-	-
ANG/EPIS–Episcopal	14	1,831	3,926	5,051	0.7	1.9
Bahá'í	3	NR	1,117	1,117	0.2	0.4
BAPT–Amer Bapt Assn	1	NR	85	102	0.0	0.0
BAPT–Amer Bapt USA	17	3,208	4,870	5,817	0.8	2.2
BAPT–Consrv Bapt	25	NR	NR	NR	-	-
BAPT–Converge/BGC	5	375	NR	450	0.1	0.2
BAPT–N Am Bapt Conf	3	NR	414	495	0.1	0.2
BAPT–Natl Mis Bapt Conv	1	0	150	179	0.0	0.1
BAPT–NBC Amer	2	225	400	478	0.1	0.2
BAPT–Ref Bapt Ch	1	NR	NR	NR	-	-
BAPT–Reg Bapt Gen As	1	NR	NR	NR	-	-
BAPT–S-D Baptist Gen Con	1	30	28	33	0.0	0.0
BAPT–So Bapt Conv	24	2,630	2,874	3,433	0.5	1.3
BRETH–Ch of Brethren	1	30	52	62	0.0	0.0
BUDD–Mahayana	16	NR	NR	7,314	1.0	2.8
BUDD–Theravada	2	NR	NR	592	0.1	0.2
BUDD–Vajrayana	12	NR	NR	998	0.1	0.4
Calv Chpl	1	NR	NR	NR	-	-
Catholic	42	NR	NR	111,678	15.2	42.3
CGOD–Ch God (Ander)	12	1,241	NR	1,241	0.2	0.5
Ch Cr, Scientst	5	NR	NR	NR	-	-
Ch God (7th Day)	1	NR	NR	NR	-	-
Ch of Nazarene	7	926	1,242	1,714	0.2	0.6
Chr & Miss Al	6	1,539	1,164	2,532	0.3	1.0
CHR–Chr Ch (Disc)	7	567	1,253	1,497	0.2	0.6
CHR–Chr Chs & Chs Cr	11	NR	3,520	4,205	0.6	1.6
CHR–Chs of Christ	9	1,480	1,160	1,690	0.2	0.6
Evan Ch	4	NR	NR	NR	-	-
Evan Cov Ch	6	590	545	768	0.1	0.3
FRND–Evan Fr Ch Intl	5	333	462	552	0.1	0.2
FRND–Indep Yr Mtgs	2	NR	153	183	0.0	0.1
HINDU–I/A Temples	1	NR	NR	1,562	0.2	0.6
HINDU–Post Ren	7	NR	NR	263	0.0	0.1
HINDU–Renaiss	4	NR	NR	120	0.0	0.0
Int Cou Comm Ch	1	NR	NR	NR	-	-
Intl Fell Bible Ch	1	NR	NR	NR	-	-
Jain	2	NR	NR	NR	-	-
Jehovah's Witness	11	NR	NR	NR	-	-
JUD–Conserv	1	864	970	2,619	0.4	1.0
JUD–Orth	4	443	200	615	0.1	0.2
JUD–Reconst	1	252	322	869	0.1	0.3
JUD–Reform	1	459	810	2,187	0.3	0.8
LDS–Comm of Christ	1	NR	167	167	0.0	0.1
LDS–L-D Saints	25	NR	NR	16,721	2.3	6.3
LUTH–Apostolic Luth	1	NR	NR	NR	-	-
LUTH–Ch of Luth Br	1	76	49	122	0.0	0.0
LUTH–E.L.C.A.	25	2,356	5,056	6,453	0.9	2.4
LUTH–Evan Luth Syn	1	51	106	138	0.0	0.1
LUTH–Luth-MO Synod	14	1,330	2,002	2,676	0.4	1.0
LUTH–Wisc Ev Luth Syn	1	130	266	315	0.0	0.1
MENN–Menn Br US Conf	4	NR	2,284	2,728	0.4	1.0
MENN–Mennonite USA	4	361	423	505	0.1	0.2
METH–AME	2	275	400	478	0.1	0.2
METH–AME Zion	1	0	100	119	0.0	0.0
METH–C.M.E.	2	100	250	299	0.0	0.1
METH–Free Methodist	4	312	209	312	0.0	0.1

Religious Group	Number of Congrega-tions	Number of Attendees	Number of Communicant, Confirmed, or Full Members	Adherents		
				Number of Adherents	% of Total Pop.	% of Total Adh.
METH–Un Methodist	26	1,674	3,511	4,972	0.7	1.9
METH–Wesleyan	3	233	141	304	0.0	0.1
Metro Comm Ch	1	203	251	300	0.0	0.1
Muslim Est	6	1,170	NR	2,140	0.3	0.8
New Apost Ch	1	NR	NR	NR	-	-
Non-denom Chr Chs	63	15,377	20,505	22,656	3.1	8.6
OCATH–Un Cath Ch	1	NR	NR	702	0.1	0.3
ORTHE–Ant Orth of NA	1	175	NR	500	0.1	0.2
ORTHE–Greek Orthodox	1	350	NR	2,100	0.3	0.8
ORTHE–Holy Orth in NA	1	77	NR	100	0.0	0.0
ORTHE–Orth Ch in Amer	2	220	NR	510	0.1	0.2
ORTHE–Ukrainian Orth	1	65	NR	120	0.0	0.0
ORTHO–Coptic Orth Ch	1	50	NR	100	0.0	0.0
ORTHO–Eritrean Orth	2	325	NR	205	0.0	0.1
ORTHO–Ethiopian Orth	1	NR	NR	NR	-	-
ORTHO–Syrian Orth Ch	1	85	NR	280	0.0	0.1
PENT–Apos Faith Msn	1	NR	650	776	0.1	0.3
PENT–Assemb of God	18	4,275	3,599	6,132	0.8	2.3
PENT–Ch God (Cleve)	9	629	1,077	1,286	0.2	0.5
PENT–Ch of God Proph	4	NR	151	180	0.0	0.1
PENT–COGIC	10	800	1,705	2,037	0.3	0.8
PENT–Full Gosp Bapt	4	NR	NR	NR	-	-
PENT–Int Foursq Gos	15	3,555	7,095	8,475	1.2	3.2
PENT–Intl Pent Holiness	1	48	35	42	0.0	0.0
PENT–Open Bible Std	3	303	NR	303	0.0	0.1
PENT–Pent Ch of God	1	70	NR	109	0.0	0.0
PENT–Un Pent Ch Intl	6	NR	NR	NR	-	-
PENT–Vineyard	1	140	152	182	0.0	0.1
PRES–Evan Presby Ch	1	NR	57	68	0.0	0.0
PRES–Korean Amer Pres	1	NR	NR	NR	-	-
PRES–Korean Pres Amer	1	NR	NR	NR	-	-
PRES–Orth Pres Ch	1	155	128	172	0.0	0.1
PRES–Presb Ch (USA)	25	2,108	4,555	5,441	0.7	2.1
PRES–Presb Ch Amer	2	225	191	207	0.0	0.1
REF–Christian Ref	1	120	151	180	0.0	0.1
Salvation Army	3	261	354	1,369	0.2	0.5
Sev Day Adv	21	3,476	6,042	6,951	0.9	2.6
Sikh	2	NR	NR	NR	-	-
Un C of Christ	9	1,373	1,532	1,830	0.2	0.7
Unit Univ	3	1,202	1,198	1,756	0.2	0.7
Unity Ch	2	NR	NR	NR	-	-
POLK	**85**	**6,588**	**7,550**	**17,903**	**23.7**	**100.0**
ANG/EPIS–Episcopal	3	147	310	341	0.5	1.9
Bahá'í	0	NR	50	50	0.1	0.3
BAPT–Consrv Bapt	3	NR	NR	NR	-	-
BAPT–N Am Bapt Conf	2	NR	413	508	0.7	2.8
BAPT–Reg Bapt Gen As	1	NR	NR	NR	-	-
BAPT–So Bapt Conv	2	172	192	236	0.3	1.3
BUDD–Mahayana	1	NR	NR	11	0.0	0.1
Calv Chpl	2	NR	NR	NR	-	-
Catholic	2	NR	NR	2,522	3.3	14.1
Ch of Nazarene	3	192	81	315	0.4	1.8
Chr & Miss Al	1	189	136	230	0.3	1.3
CHR–Chr Ch (Disc)	1	77	338	415	0.6	2.3
CHR–Chr Chs & Chs Cr	3	NR	510	627	0.8	3.5
CHR–Chs of Christ	3	125	95	170	0.2	0.9
Evan Ch	1	NR	NR	NR	-	-
Evan Free Ch	1	400	NR	400	0.5	2.2
HINDU–Post Ren	1	NR	NR	25	0.0	0.1
Jehovah's Witness	3	NR	NR	NR	-	-
LDS–L-D Saints	11	NR	NR	4,648	6.2	26.0
LUTH–E.L.C.A.	1	190	612	741	1.0	4.1
LUTH–Luth-MO Synod	2	120	214	254	0.3	1.4
MENN–Fel Evg Bib Ch	1	504	504	504	0.7	2.8
MENN–Menn Br US Conf	1	NR	130	160	0.2	0.9
MENN–Mennonite USA	2	90	105	129	0.2	0.7
METH–Free Methodist	1	47	10	47	0.1	0.3
METH–Un Methodist	5	200	327	491	0.7	2.7
Non-denom Chr Chs	9	1,245	1,680	1,764	2.3	9.9
PENT–Apos Faith Msn	1	NR	35	43	0.1	0.2
PENT–Assemb of God	6	1,020	301	1,330	1.8	7.4
PENT–Ch God (Cleve)	1	107	57	70	0.1	0.4
PENT–Ch of God Proph	1	NR	13	16	0.0	0.1

NR–Not Reported - Represents no adherents reported. Percentages may not total 100 due to rounding.

Table 3: Religious Congregations by County and Group: 2010

Religious Group	Number of Congrega-tions	Number of Attendees	Number of Communicant, Confirmed, or Full Members	Adherents: Number of Adherents	Adherents: % of Total Pop.	Adherents: % of Total Adh.
PENT–Int Foursq Gos	3	1,233	702	863	1.1	4.8
PENT–Open Bible Std	1	0	NR	0	0.0	0.0
PENT–Pent Ch of God	1	70	NR	109	0.1	0.6
PENT–Vineyard	1	229	365	449	0.6	2.5
PRES–Presb Ch (USA)	2	83	113	139	0.2	0.8
Sev Day Adv	2	148	257	296	0.4	1.7
SHERMAN	**7**	**91**	**184**	**303**	**17.2**	**100.0**
Bahá'í	0	NR	7	7	0.4	2.3
BAPT–Consrv Bapt	2	NR	NR	NR	-	-
BAPT–So Bapt Conv	1	21	34	40	2.3	13.2
Catholic	1	NR	NR	30	1.7	9.9
CHR–Chr Chs & Chs Cr	1	NR	30	35	2.0	11.6
METH–Un Methodist	1	30	54	121	6.9	39.9
PRES–Presb Ch (USA)	1	40	59	70	4.0	23.1
TILLAMOOK	**37**	**1,870**	**2,977**	**7,080**	**28.0**	**100.0**
ANG/EPIS–Episcopal	2	122	261	321	1.3	4.5
Bahá'í	1	NR	30	30	0.1	0.4
BAPT–Asc Ref Bap Ch Am	1	NR	NR	NR	-	-
BAPT–Consrv Bapt	1	NR	NR	NR	-	-
BAPT–Ref Bapt Ch	1	NR	NR	NR	-	-
BAPT–So Bapt Conv	1	20	29	34	0.1	0.5
Catholic	2	NR	NR	2,196	8.7	31.0
Ch of Nazarene	2	313	370	443	1.8	6.3
CHR–Chr Chs & Chs Cr	3	NR	533	627	2.5	8.9
CHR–Chs of Christ	1	35	27	37	0.1	0.5
FRND–Evan Fr Ch Intl	1	32	86	101	0.4	1.4
Ind Fund Churches	1	NR	NR	NR	-	-
LDS–L-D Saints	2	NR	NR	879	3.5	12.4
LUTH–E.L.C.A.	1	34	43	50	0.2	0.7
LUTH–Luth–MO Synod	1	60	54	64	0.3	0.9
METH–Un Methodist	3	154	338	415	1.6	5.9
Non-denom Chr Chs	5	605	570	782	3.1	11.0
PENT–Assemb of God	4	175	96	477	1.9	6.7
PRES–Presb Ch (USA)	1	46	64	75	0.3	1.1
Sev Day Adv	2	237	412	474	1.9	6.7
Un C of Christ	1	37	64	75	0.3	1.1
UMATILLA	**122**	**6,286**	**9,639**	**29,900**	**39.4**	**100.0**
ANG/EPIS–Episcopal	3	110	254	297	0.4	1.0
Bahá'í	1	NR	121	121	0.2	0.4
BAPT–Amer Bapt Assn	1	NR	85	107	0.1	0.4
BAPT–Amer Bapt USA	2	111	530	668	0.9	2.2
BAPT–Consrv Bapt	6	NR	NR	NR	-	-
BAPT–Reg Bapt Gen As	1	NR	NR	NR	-	-
BAPT–So Bapt Conv	4	245	341	430	0.6	1.4
BRETH–Ch of Brethren	1	0	117	148	0.2	0.5
Calv Chpl	2	NR	NR	NR	-	-
Catholic	6	NR	NR	11,402	15.0	38.1
CGOD–Ch God (Ander)	2	185	NR	185	0.2	0.6
Ch of Nazarene	3	230	283	391	0.5	1.3
CHR–Chr Ch (Disc)	2	131	248	313	0.4	1.0
CHR–Chr Chs & Chs Cr	3	NR	555	700	0.9	2.3
CHR–Chs of Christ	3	90	86	117	0.2	0.4
CONG–Cong Chr, NA	1	NR	100	126	0.2	0.4
HINDU–I/A Temples	1	NR	NR	238	0.3	0.8
Jehovah's Witness	2	NR	NR	NR	-	-
LDS–L-D Saints	13	NR	NR	4,748	6.3	15.9
LUTH–E.L.C.A.	3	226	603	844	1.1	2.8
LUTH–Luth Cong Msn Chr	1	85	138	174	0.2	0.6
LUTH–Luth–MO Synod	1	68	154	188	0.2	0.6
LUTH–Wisc Ev Luth Syn	1	9	21	26	0.0	0.1
MENN–Hutt Breth	1	NR	NR	NR	-	-
METH–Free Methodist	2	325	167	325	0.4	1.1
METH–Un Methodist	5	184	508	675	0.9	2.3
METH–Wesleyan	1	32	18	42	0.1	0.1
Non-denom Chr Chs	6	379	425	506	0.7	1.7
PENT–Assemb of God	13	1,080	537	1,893	2.5	6.3
PENT–Ch God (Cleve)	2	298	243	306	0.4	1.0
PENT–Ch of God Proph	3	NR	49	62	0.1	0.2
PENT–Cong Hol Ch	1	39	35	44	0.1	0.1
PENT–Int Foursq Gos	2	224	184	232	0.3	0.8

Religious Group	Number of Congrega-tions	Number of Attendees	Number of Communicant, Confirmed, or Full Members	Adherents: Number of Adherents	Adherents: % of Total Pop.	Adherents: % of Total Adh.
PENT–Pent Ch of God	1	70	NR	109	0.1	0.4
PENT–Un Pent Ch Intl	1	NR	NR	NR	-	-
PENT–Vineyard	1	135	184	232	0.3	0.8
PRES–Presb Ch (USA)	8	276	517	652	0.9	2.2
Salvation Army	1	48	170	186	0.2	0.6
Sev Day Adv	11	1,706	2,966	3,413	4.5	11.4
UNION	**49**	**2,319**	**3,032**	**7,911**	**30.7**	**100.0**
ANG/EPIS–Episcopal	1	40	88	88	0.3	1.1
Bahá'í	0	NR	37	37	0.1	0.5
BAPT–Consrv Bapt	2	NR	NR	NR	-	-
BAPT–Ref Bapt Ch	1	NR	NR	NR	-	-
BAPT–So Bapt Conv	2	35	181	219	0.9	2.8
Calv Chpl	1	NR	NR	NR	-	-
Catholic	4	NR	NR	1,257	4.9	15.9
CGOD–Ch God (Ander)	1	58	NR	58	0.2	0.7
Ch of Nazarene	2	264	238	517	2.0	6.5
CHR–Chr Ch (Disc)	1	82	278	336	1.3	4.2
CHR–Chr Chs & Chs Cr	2	NR	190	230	0.9	2.9
CHR–Chs of Christ	1	60	50	70	0.3	0.9
FRND–Evan Fr Ch Intl	1	NR	0	0	0.0	0.0
Jehovah's Witness	1	NR	NR	NR	-	-
LDS–L-D Saints	7	NR	NR	2,348	9.1	29.7
LUTH–E.L.C.A.	1	63	123	123	0.5	1.6
LUTH–Luth Cong Msn Chr	1	30	NR	NR	-	-
LUTH–Luth–MO Synod	1	60	108	139	0.5	1.8
METH–Free Methodist	1	55	20	55	0.2	0.7
METH–Un Methodist	5	129	215	349	1.4	4.4
Non-denom Chr Chs	5	605	665	783	3.0	9.9
PENT–Assemb of God	2	137	57	271	1.1	3.4
PENT–Int Foursq Gos	1	322	202	245	1.0	3.1
PENT–Pent Ch of God	1	70	NR	109	0.4	1.4
PRES–Presb Ch (USA)	1	80	181	219	0.9	2.8
Sev Day Adv	3	229	399	458	1.8	5.8
WALLOWA	**25**	**451**	**957**	**1,976**	**28.2**	**100.0**
ANG/EPIS–Episcopal	1	11	23	28	0.4	1.4
Bahá'í	0	NR	27	27	0.4	1.4
BAPT–Consrv Bapt	2	NR	NR	NR	-	-
BUDD–Mahayana	1	NR	NR	28	0.4	1.4
Catholic	2	NR	NR	250	3.6	12.7
Ch of Nazarene	1	22	30	36	0.5	1.8
CHR–Chr Chs & Chs Cr	3	NR	325	380	5.4	19.2
CHR–Chs of Christ	1	30	35	40	0.6	2.0
HINDU–Post Ren	1	NR	NR	77	1.1	3.9
Jehovah's Witness	1	NR	NR	NR	-	-
LDS–L-D Saints	1	NR	NR	330	4.7	16.7
LUTH–E.L.C.A.	1	22	28	29	0.4	1.5
METH–Un Methodist	2	61	93	156	2.2	7.9
Non-denom Chr Chs	2	65	80	88	1.3	4.5
PENT–Assemb of God	2	115	53	202	2.9	10.2
PRES–Presb Ch (USA)	1	25	54	63	0.9	3.2
REF–Comm Ref Evan	1	NR	NR	NR	-	-
Sev Day Adv	1	70	123	141	2.0	7.1
Un C of Christ	1	30	86	101	1.4	5.1
WASCO	**39**	**1,797**	**2,813**	**10,310**	**40.9**	**100.0**
ANG/EPIS–Episcopal	1	67	117	205	0.8	2.0
Bahá'í	1	NR	81	81	0.3	0.8
BAPT–Consrv Bapt	2	NR	NR	NR	-	-
BAPT–So Bapt Conv	1	118	342	417	1.7	4.0
Calv Chpl	1	NR	NR	NR	-	-
Catholic	3	NR	NR	5,192	20.6	50.4
CGOD–Ch God (Ander)	1	35	NR	35	0.1	0.3
Ch Cr, Scientst	1	NR	NR	NR	-	-
Ch of Nazarene	1	56	68	78	0.3	0.8
CHR–Chr Ch (Disc)	1	0	35	43	0.2	0.4
CHR–Chr Chs & Chs Cr	1	NR	500	609	2.4	5.9
Evan Ch	2	NR	NR	NR	-	-
FRND–Indep Yr Mtgs	1	NR	0	0	0.0	0.0
Jehovah's Witness	2	NR	NR	NR	-	-
LDS–L-D Saints	2	NR	NR	1,084	4.3	10.5
LUTH–E.L.C.A.	1	114	263	283	1.1	2.7

NR–Not Reported - Represents no adherents reported. Percentages may not total 100 due to rounding.

Table 3: Religious Congregations by County and Group: 2010

Religious Group	Number of Congrega-tions	Number of Attendees	Number of Communicant, Confirmed, or Full Members	Adherents: Number of Adherents	Adherents: % of Total Pop.	Adherents: % of Total Adh.
LUTH–Evan Luth Syn	1	30	64	98	0.4	1.0
LUTH–Luth–MO Synod	1	50	111	125	0.5	1.2
METH–Un Methodist	3	91	154	233	0.9	2.3
Non-denom Chr Chs	3	360	255	458	1.8	4.4
ORTHE–Serb Orth USA	1	30	NR	50	0.2	0.5
PENT–Assemb of God	3	260	199	517	2.1	5.0
PENT–Int Foursq Gos	1	77	49	60	0.2	0.6
PRES–Presb Ch (USA)	1	327	271	330	1.3	3.2
Salvation Army	1	37	54	118	0.5	1.1
Sev Day Adv	1	92	159	183	0.7	1.8
Un C of Christ	1	53	91	111	0.4	1.1
WASHINGTON	**342**	**43,057**	**58,363**	**163,415**	**30.8**	**100.0**
ANG/EPIS–Episcopal	7	796	1,895	2,699	0.5	1.7
Bahá'í	8	NR	740	740	0.1	0.5
BAPT–Amer Bapt Assn	1	NR	85	106	0.0	0.1
BAPT–Amer Bapt USA	1	164	457	572	0.1	0.4
BAPT–Consrv Bapt	12	NR	NR	NR	-	-
BAPT–Converge/BGC	5	375	NR	450	0.1	0.3
BAPT–N Am Bapt Conf	4	NR	561	702	0.1	0.4
BAPT–Reg Bapt Gen As	2	NR	NR	NR	-	-
BAPT–So Bapt Conv	19	1,634	3,689	4,617	0.9	2.8
BRETH–Grace Breth	1	NR	NR	NR	-	-
BUDD–Mahayana	3	NR	NR	953	0.2	0.6
Calv Chpl	3	NR	NR	NR	-	-
Catholic	11	NR	NR	55,886	10.6	34.2
CGOD–Ch God (Ander)	4	351	NR	351	0.1	0.2
Ch Cr, Scientst	2	NR	NR	NR	-	-
Ch of Nazarene	4	687	862	1,105	0.2	0.7
Chr & Miss Al	1	66	82	82	0.0	0.1
CHR–Chr Ch (Disc)	3	393	1,131	1,416	0.3	0.9
CHR–Chr Chs & Chs Cr	8	NR	2,556	3,199	0.6	2.0
CHR–Chs of Christ	9	1,625	1,636	1,942	0.4	1.2
Evan Ch	2	NR	NR	NR	-	-
Evan Cov Ch	4	1,069	562	1,390	0.3	0.9
FRND–Evan Fr Ch Intl	5	356	383	479	0.1	0.3
FRND–Indep Yr Mtgs	1	NR	0	0	0.0	0.0
HINDU–I/A Temples	2	NR	NR	1,992	0.4	1.2
HINDU–Post Ren	2	NR	NR	50	0.0	0.0
HINDU–Trad Temples	1	NR	NR	2,000	0.4	1.2
Ind Fund Churches	2	NR	NR	NR	-	-
Jehovah's Witness	7	NR	NR	NR	-	-
JUD–Orth	1	43	50	60	0.0	0.0
LDS–Comm of Christ	1	NR	167	167	0.0	0.1
LDS–L-D Saints	45	NR	NR	23,763	4.5	14.5
LUTH–E.L.C.A.	10	1,630	3,395	4,803	0.9	2.9
LUTH–Luth–MO Synod	10	2,025	3,337	4,403	0.8	2.7
LUTH–Wisc Ev Luth Syn	2	86	136	168	0.0	0.1
MENN–Menn Br US Conf	1	NR	0	0	0.0	0.0
METH–Free Methodist	2	250	192	252	0.0	0.2
METH–Un Methodist	15	1,206	2,627	3,974	0.8	2.4
Muslim Est	2	268	NR	616	0.1	0.4
Non-denom Chr Chs	45	16,625	19,143	22,717	4.3	13.9
ORTHE–Greek Orthodox	1	180	NR	550	0.1	0.3
PENT–Assemb of God	13	2,659	1,354	4,641	0.9	2.8
PENT–Ch of God Proph	1	NR	34	43	0.0	0.0
PENT–Int Foursq Gos	9	5,437	3,708	4,641	0.9	2.8
PENT–Intl Pent Holiness	1	22	13	16	0.0	0.0
PENT–Pent Ch of God	1	70	NR	109	0.0	0.1
PENT–Un Pent Ch Intl	6	NR	NR	NR	-	-
PENT–Vineyard	3	290	345	432	0.1	0.3
PRES–Evan Presby Ch	1	NR	1,443	1,806	0.3	1.1
PRES–Korean Pres Amer	1	NR	NR	NR	-	-
PRES–Presb Ch (USA)	11	1,293	2,165	2,710	0.5	1.7
PRES–Presb Ch Amer	2	300	259	286	0.1	0.2
REF–Christian Ref	3	205	278	348	0.1	0.2
Salvation Army	2	71	85	229	0.0	0.1
Sev Day Adv	12	2,119	3,686	4,238	0.8	2.6
Un C of Christ	4	519	983	1,230	0.2	0.8
Unit Univ	2	243	324	474	0.1	0.3
Unity Ch	1	NR	NR	NR	-	-
Zoroastrian	0	NR	NR	8	0.0	0.0

Religious Group	Number of Congrega-tions	Number of Attendees	Number of Communicant, Confirmed, or Full Members	Adherents: Number of Adherents	Adherents: % of Total Pop.	Adherents: % of Total Adh.
WHEELER	**7**	**148**	**146**	**340**	**23.6**	**100.0**
Bahá'í	0	NR	1	1	0.1	0.3
Catholic	1	NR	NR	40	2.8	11.8
Jehovah's Witness	1	NR	NR	NR	-	-
LDS–L-D Saints	1	NR	NR	48	3.3	14.1
METH–Un Methodist	1	45	41	85	5.9	25.0
Non-denom Chr Chs	1	20	25	25	1.7	7.4
PENT–Assemb of God	2	83	79	141	9.8	41.5
YAMHILL	**125**	**9,210**	**12,162**	**33,403**	**33.7**	**100.0**
ANG/EPIS–Episcopal	2	188	278	463	0.5	1.4
Bahá'í	3	NR	89	89	0.1	0.3
BAPT–Amer Bapt USA	2	252	585	723	0.7	2.2
BAPT–Consrv Bapt	5	NR	NR	NR	-	-
BAPT–Converge/BGC	1	75	NR	90	0.1	0.3
BAPT–Ref Bapt Ch	2	NR	NR	NR	-	-
BAPT–So Bapt Conv	5	236	547	676	0.7	2.0
Calv Chpl	3	NR	NR	NR	-	-
Catholic	6	NR	NR	11,274	11.4	33.8
CGOD–Ch God (Ander)	1	75	NR	75	0.1	0.2
Ch Cr, Scientst	1	NR	NR	NR	-	-
Ch of Nazarene	3	1,336	1,146	2,407	2.4	7.2
CHR–Chr Ch (Disc)	1	32	83	103	0.1	0.3
CHR–Chr Chs & Chs Cr	6	NR	1,435	1,775	1.8	5.3
CHR–Chs of Christ	3	227	209	332	0.3	1.0
Evan Ch	2	NR	NR	NR	-	-
Evan Cov Ch	2	320	306	416	0.4	1.2
FRND–Evan Fr Ch Intl	7	1,000	1,655	2,047	2.1	6.1
Jehovah's Witness	5	NR	NR	NR	-	-
LDS–L-D Saints	10	NR	NR	4,446	4.5	13.3
LUTH–E.L.C.A.	3	338	374	491	0.5	1.5
LUTH–Luth Cong Msn Chr	1	96	203	251	0.3	0.8
LUTH–Luth–MO Synod	2	151	290	363	0.4	1.1
MENN–Mennonite USA	2	60	52	64	0.1	0.2
METH–Free Methodist	3	572	135	572	0.6	1.7
METH–Un Methodist	7	508	693	1,028	1.0	3.1
Non-denom Chr Chs	12	1,755	1,865	2,264	2.3	6.8
PENT–Assemb of God	7	651	391	1,238	1.2	3.7
PENT–Int Foursq Gos	2	464	129	160	0.2	0.5
PENT–Open Bible Std	1	0	NR	0	0.0	0.0
PENT–Un Pent Ch Intl	1	NR	NR	NR	-	-
PRES–Orth Pres Ch	1	56	57	71	0.1	0.2
PRES–Presb Ch (USA)	2	78	409	506	0.5	1.5
PRES–Presb Ch Amer	1	0	0	0	0.0	0.0
REF–Christian Ref	1	50	79	98	0.1	0.3
Salvation Army	1	15	25	75	0.1	0.2
Sev Day Adv	7	624	1,084	1,248	1.3	3.7
Unit Univ	1	51	43	58	0.1	0.2
PENNSYLVANIA	**15,359**	**1,280,678**	**2,268,785**	**6,838,440**	**53.8**	**100.0**
ADAMS	**138**	**11,611**	**20,494**	**45,550**	**44.9**	**100.0**
ANG/EPIS–Episcopal	1	125	253	331	0.3	0.7
Bahá'í	0	NR	12	12	0.0	0.0
BAPT–Amer Bapt Assn	1	NR	75	90	0.1	0.2
BAPT–Amer Bapt USA	2	272	385	462	0.5	1.0
BAPT–Consrv Bapt	1	NR	NR	NR	-	-
BAPT–Free Will Bapt	1	NR	45	54	0.1	0.1
BAPT–N Am Bapt Conf	1	NR	111	133	0.1	0.3
BAPT–So Bapt Conv	5	372	1,336	1,603	1.6	3.5
BRETH–Breth in Chr	4	NR	NR	NR	-	-
BRETH–Ch of Brethren	4	475	518	621	0.6	1.4
Catholic	7	NR	NR	15,049	14.8	33.0
CGOD–Ch God (Ander)	1	104	NR	104	0.1	0.2
Ch of Nazarene	1	30	63	63	0.1	0.1
CHR–Chs of Christ	1	155	115	175	0.2	0.4
Evan Cong Ch	1	NR	51	61	0.1	0.1
FRND–Fr Gen Cf & Un Mtg	2	NR	57	68	0.1	0.1
Jehovah's Witness	2	NR	NR	NR	-	-
LDS–L-D Saints	3	NR	NR	878	0.9	1.9
LUTH–E.L.C.A.	27	2,218	7,838	10,902	10.8	23.9
MENN–Bible Flwshp	1	47	NR	63	0.1	0.1

NR–Not Reported   - Represents no adherents reported.   Percentages may not total 100 due to rounding.

Table 3: Religious Congregations by County and Group: 2010

Religious Group	Number of Congrega-tions	Number of Attendees	Number of Communicant, Confirmed, or Full Members	Adherents: Number of Adherents	Adherents: % of Total Pop.	Adherents: % of Total Adh.
MENN–Mennonite USA	2	98	134	161	0.2	0.4
METH–AME Zion	1	0	150	180	0.2	0.4
METH–Un Methodist	15	796	1,922	2,525	2.5	5.5
Non-denom Chr Chs	10	1,085	1,125	1,371	1.4	3.0
PENT–Assemb of God	12	3,201	1,207	4,677	4.6	10.3
PENT–Ch God (Cleve)	2	134	384	461	0.5	1.0
PENT–Ch of God Proph	2	NR	79	95	0.1	0.2
PENT–Elim	1	NR	NR	NR	-	-
PENT–Int Foursq Gos	2	349	263	316	0.3	0.7
PENT–United Holy Ch	1	NR	NR	NR	-	-
PRES–Orth Pres Ch	1	41	39	46	0.0	0.1
PRES–Presb Ch (USA)	3	625	1,066	1,279	1.3	2.8
Sev Day Adv	2	104	180	208	0.2	0.5
Un Breth in Cr	3	244	291	208	0.2	0.5
Un C of Christ	14	1,100	2,740	3,287	3.2	7.2
Unit Univ	1	36	55	67	0.1	0.1
ALLEGHENY	**1,148**	**101,196**	**189,660**	**740,979**	**60.6**	**100.0**
ANG/EPIS–Anglican NA	24	NR	NR	NR	-	-
ANG/EPIS–Episcopal	19	1,997	6,189	7,780	0.6	1.0
Bahá'í	2	NR	179	179	0.0	0.0
BAPT–Amer Bapt USA	42	8,795	14,592	17,148	1.4	2.3
BAPT–Consrv Bapt	3	NR	NR	NR	-	-
BAPT–Converge/BGC	3	225	NR	270	0.0	0.0
BAPT–Fund Bapt Flwsp	1	NR	NR	NR	-	-
BAPT–Ind Bapt Flwsp Intl	1	NR	NR	NR	-	-
BAPT–N Am Bapt Conf	2	NR	131	154	0.0	0.0
BAPT–NBC USA	12	1,575	2,863	3,365	0.3	0.5
BAPT–Prog NBC	1	0	60	71	0.0	0.0
BAPT–Reg Bapt Gen As	1	NR	NR	NR	-	-
BAPT–So Bapt Conv	32	1,314	1,943	2,283	0.2	0.3
BRETH–Ch of Brethren	3	29	250	294	0.0	0.0
BUDD–Mahayana	5	NR	NR	1,523	0.1	0.2
BUDD–Vajrayana	3	NR	NR	96	0.0	0.0
Calv Chpl	1	NR	NR	NR	-	-
Catholic	179	NR	NR	460,672	37.7	62.2
CGOD–Ch God (Ander)	4	276	NR	276	0.0	0.0
CGOD–Ches God-Gen Con	1	28	28	33	0.0	0.0
Ch Cr, Scientst	3	NR	NR	NR	-	-
Ch of Nazarene	10	628	959	1,167	0.1	0.2
Chr & Miss Al	18	3,822	2,568	6,171	0.5	0.8
CHR–Chr Ch (Disc)	6	207	677	796	0.1	0.1
CHR–Chr Chs & Chs Cr	18	NR	2,768	3,253	0.3	0.4
CHR–Chs of Christ	8	730	684	947	0.1	0.1
CHR–Int Chs of Christ	1	NR	86	101	0.0	0.0
Christian Brethren	2	NR	NR	NR	-	-
CONG–Cong Chr, NA	3	NR	178	209	0.0	0.0
Evan Cov Ch	3	171	207	223	0.0	0.0
Evan Free Ch	2	950	NR	950	0.1	0.1
FRND–Fr Gen Cf	2	NR	171	201	0.0	0.0
HINDU–I/A Temples	3	NR	NR	700	0.1	0.1
HINDU–Post Ren	4	NR	NR	1,051	0.1	0.1
HINDU–Trad Temples	2	NR	NR	6,700	0.5	0.9
Int Cou Comm Ch	1	NR	NR	NR	-	-
Jain	1	NR	NR	NR	-	-
Jehovah's Witness	19	NR	NR	NR	-	-
JUD–Conserv	3	1,320	1,482	4,001	0.3	0.5
JUD–Orth	12	2,664	1,000	3,700	0.3	0.5
JUD–Reconst	1	159	203	548	0.0	0.1
JUD–Reform	6	1,782	3,142	8,483	0.7	1.1
LDS–Comm of Christ	3	NR	474	474	0.0	0.1
LDS–L-D Saints	10	NR	NR	4,370	0.4	0.6
LUTH–Assoc Free Luth	1	NR	NR	NR	-	-
LUTH–E.L.C.A.	77	5,892	19,688	24,718	2.0	3.3
LUTH–Luth–MO Synod	21	1,347	3,169	4,104	0.3	0.6
LUTH–Nor Amer Luth C	4	NR	NR	NR	-	-
LUTH–Wisc Ev Luth Syn	1	50	74	97	0.0	0.0
MENN–Mennonite USA	1	85	72	85	0.0	0.0
METH–A.W.M.C.	1	22	17	36	0.0	0.0
METH–AME	22	1,789	5,425	6,375	0.5	0.9
METH–AME Zion	12	491	1,450	1,704	0.1	0.2
METH–C.M.E.	2	0	300	353	0.0	0.0
METH–Free Methodist	3	172	147	200	0.0	0.0
METH–Prim Meth Ch	6	NR	NR	NR	-	-

Religious Group	Number of Congrega-tions	Number of Attendees	Number of Communicant, Confirmed, or Full Members	Adherents: Number of Adherents	Adherents: % of Total Pop.	Adherents: % of Total Adh.
METH–Un Methodist	100	10,728	34,728	44,204	3.6	6.0
METH–Wesleyan	1	22	46	29	0.0	0.0
Metro Comm Ch	1	24	38	45	0.0	0.0
MJEW–Union Mes Cong	1	NR	NR	NR	-	-
Muslim Est	10	2,064	NR	5,822	0.5	0.8
Nat Spirit Asso	1	NR	NR	NR	-	-
New Apost Ch	2	NR	NR	NR	-	-
Non-denom Chr Chs	85	20,908	30,388	33,103	2.7	4.5
OCATH–Pol Natl Cath	4	NR	NR	NR	-	-
ORTHE–Ant Orth of NA	2	518	NR	1,725	0.1	0.2
ORTHE–Carp Rus Orth	5	527	NR	898	0.1	0.1
ORTHE–Greek Orthodox	7	1,295	NR	2,990	0.2	0.4
ORTHE–Orth Ch in Amer	8	494	NR	894	0.1	0.1
ORTHE–Rus Orth Abroad	1	30	NR	60	0.0	0.0
ORTHE–Serb Orth USA	3	344	NR	2,189	0.2	0.3
ORTHE–Ukrainian Orth	3	350	NR	850	0.1	0.1
PENT–Assemb of God	30	7,684	4,792	12,398	1.0	1.7
PENT–Ch God (Cleve)	6	304	585	687	0.1	0.1
PENT–Ch Lord Jesus Apos	6	NR	NR	NR	-	-
PENT–COGIC	15	617	2,042	2,400	0.2	0.3
PENT–Fire Bapt Hol Ch	1	NR	NR	NR	-	-
PENT–Full Gosp Bapt	4	NR	NR	NR	-	-
PENT–I F Chr Assmbl	2	NR	NR	NR	-	-
PENT–Intl Pent Holiness	1	30	46	54	0.0	0.0
PENT–Open Bible Std	3	161	NR	161	0.0	0.0
PENT–Un Pent Ch Intl	4	NR	NR	NR	-	-
PENT–United Holy Ch	1	NR	NR	NR	-	-
PENT–Vineyard	2	173	235	276	0.0	0.0
PRES–As Ref Pres Ch	2	NR	108	127	0.0	0.0
PRES–Bible Pres	1	NR	NR	NR	-	-
PRES–Evan Presby Ch	5	NR	2,468	2,900	0.2	0.4
PRES–Orth Pres Ch	3	140	91	128	0.0	0.0
PRES–Presb Ch (USA)	145	14,706	36,452	42,838	3.5	5.8
PRES–Presb Ch Amer	8	1,033	1,136	1,451	0.1	0.2
PRES–Ref Pres of NA	4	412	370	501	0.0	0.1
REF–Hung Ref Add'l	2	NR	NR	NR	-	-
Salvation Army	9	388	1,052	3,715	0.3	0.5
Sev Day Adv	6	964	1,676	1,927	0.2	0.3
Sikh	1	NR	NR	NR	-	-
Un C of Christ	16	488	1,372	1,612	0.1	0.2
Unit Univ	4	272	859	1,028	0.1	0.1
Unity Ch	1	NR	NR	NR	-	-
Zoroastrian	1	NR	NR	106	0.0	0.0
ARMSTRONG	**154**	**9,209**	**17,592**	**36,756**	**53.3**	**100.0**
ANG/EPIS–Anglican NA	3	NR	NR	NR	-	-
ANG/EPIS–Episcopal	1	33	109	146	0.2	0.4
BAPT–Amer Bapt USA	5	522	1,092	1,289	1.9	3.5
BAPT–Reg Bapt Gen As	1	NR	NR	NR	-	-
BRETH–Brethren (Ash)	1	NR	80	94	0.1	0.3
BRETH–Ch of Brethren	3	223	447	528	0.8	1.4
BRETH–Grace Breth	1	NR	NR	NR	-	-
Catholic	11	NR	NR	11,961	17.3	32.5
CGOD–Ch God (Ander)	5	1,374	NR	1,374	2.0	3.7
CGOD–Ches God-Gen Con	4	247	357	421	0.6	1.1
Ch of Nazarene	2	60	65	68	0.1	0.2
Chr & Miss Al	1	53	42	92	0.1	0.3
CHR–Chs of Christ	1	100	122	168	0.2	0.5
CONG–Consrv Cong Chr	3	223	304	359	0.5	1.0
Evan Assoc RCC	1	NR	NR	NR	-	-
Jehovah's Witness	2	NR	NR	NR	-	-
LUTH–E.L.C.A.	17	872	3,840	5,676	8.2	15.4
LUTH–Nor Amer Luth C	4	NR	NR	NR	-	-
MENN–Amish Undif	2	NR	97	236	0.3	0.6
METH–A.W.M.C.	3	57	38	99	0.1	0.3
METH–Free Methodist	3	356	272	364	0.5	1.0
METH–Un Methodist	22	1,083	3,689	4,652	6.7	12.7
Non-denom Chr Chs	12	1,345	1,164	1,769	2.6	4.8
PENT–Assemb of God	5	411	252	672	1.0	1.8
PENT–Ch God (Cleve)	1	158	100	118	0.2	0.3
PENT–Ch of God Proph	2	NR	96	113	0.2	0.3
PENT–Elim	1	NR	NR	NR	-	-
PENT–Intl Pent Holiness	1	10	10	12	0.0	0.0
PRES–Presb Ch (USA)	27	1,720	3,885	4,586	6.7	12.5

NR–Not Reported   - Represents no adherents reported.   Percentages may not total 100 due to rounding.

Table 3: Religious Congregations by County and Group: 2010

Religious Group	Number of Congrega-tions	Number of Attendees	Number of Communicant, Confirmed, or Full Members	Adherents: Number of Adherents	Adherents: % of Total Pop.	Adherents: % of Total Adh.
PRES–Presb Ch Amer	2	69	118	135	0.2	0.4
Salvation Army	1	29	79	250	0.4	0.7
Sev Day Adv	1	18	32	37	0.1	0.1
Un C of Christ	5	246	1,302	1,537	2.2	4.2
BEAVER	**232**	**16,219**	**28,475**	**88,734**	**52.0**	**100.0**
ANG/EPIS–Anglican NA	5	NR	NR	NR	-	-
Bahá'í	0	NR	8	8	0.0	0.0
BAPT–Amer Bapt USA	4	220	532	628	0.4	0.7
BAPT–Ind Bapt Flwsp Intl	1	NR	NR	NR	-	-
BAPT–NBC USA	4	350	1,100	1,299	0.8	1.5
BAPT–So Bapt Conv	8	425	490	578	0.3	0.7
Catholic	22	NR	NR	46,096	27.0	51.9
CGOD–Ch God (Ander)	1	42	NR	42	0.0	0.0
CGOD–Ches God-Gen Con	1	41	57	67	0.0	0.1
Ch of Nazarene	5	307	369	505	0.3	0.6
Chr & Miss Al	9	763	588	1,127	0.7	1.3
CHR–Chr Ch (Disc)	1	0	95	112	0.1	0.1
CHR–Chr Chs & Chs Cr	2	NR	250	295	0.2	0.3
CHR–Chs of Christ	3	250	210	310	0.2	0.3
Evan Free Ch	2	1,630	NR	1,630	1.0	1.8
Jehovah's Witness	6	NR	NR	NR	-	-
LDS–L-D Saints	1	NR	NR	544	0.3	0.6
LUTH–Assoc Free Luth	1	NR	NR	NR	-	-
LUTH–E.L.C.A.	17	1,156	4,848	6,560	3.8	7.4
LUTH–Luth Cong Msn Chr	1	48	51	60	0.0	0.1
LUTH–Luth–MO Synod	2	254	587	744	0.4	0.8
MENN–Amish Undif	0	NR	9	24	0.0	0.0
METH–A.W.M.C.	3	76	38	103	0.1	0.1
METH–AME	4	150	620	732	0.4	0.8
METH–AME Zion	1	100	200	236	0.1	0.3
METH–Free Methodist	6	549	533	588	0.3	0.7
METH–Prim Meth Ch	1	NR	NR	NR	-	-
METH–Un Methodist	28	2,580	7,834	10,096	5.9	11.4
METH–Wesleyan	2	120	89	156	0.1	0.2
Muslim Est	1	30	NR	812	0.5	0.9
Non-denom Chr Chs	14	1,374	1,630	1,866	1.1	2.1
ORTHE–Ant Orth of NA	1	30	NR	50	0.0	0.1
ORTHE–Carp Rus Orth	1	75	NR	134	0.1	0.2
ORTHE–Greek Orthodox	2	275	NR	800	0.5	0.9
ORTHE–Orth Ch in Amer	1	150	NR	260	0.2	0.3
ORTHE–Serb Orth USA	2	135	NR	920	0.5	1.0
ORTHE–Ukrainian Orth	1	110	NR	400	0.2	0.5
ORTHO–Coptic Orth Ch	1	140	NR	270	0.2	0.3
PENT–Assemb of God	5	394	296	632	0.4	0.7
PENT–Ch God (Cleve)	2	35	127	150	0.1	0.2
PENT–COGIC	6	570	720	850	0.5	1.0
PENT–I F Chr Assmbl	2	NR	NR	NR	-	-
PENT–Int Foursq Gos	1	81	56	66	0.0	0.1
PRES–Evan Presby Ch	2	NR	216	255	0.1	0.3
PRES–Presb Ch (USA)	35	2,533	5,507	6,501	3.8	7.3
PRES–Presb Ch Amer	5	523	597	771	0.5	0.9
PRES–Ref Pres of NA	4	522	426	549	0.3	0.6
Salvation Army	3	132	304	803	0.5	0.9
Sev Day Adv	1	34	60	69	0.0	0.1
Un C of Christ	1	15	28	33	0.0	0.0
Zoroastrian	0	NR	NR	3	0.0	0.0
BEDFORD	**152**	**8,773**	**15,569**	**22,368**	**44.9**	**100.0**
ANG/EPIS–Episcopal	1	30	48	48	0.1	0.2
Bahá'í	0	NR	5	5	0.0	0.0
BAPT–S-D Baptist Gen Con	1	40	50	60	0.1	0.3
BAPT–So Bapt Conv	2	80	97	116	0.2	0.5
BRETH–Breth in Chr	6	NR	NR	NR	-	-
BRETH–Brethren (Ash)	1	NR	80	96	0.2	0.4
BRETH–Ch of Brethren	19	1,155	2,765	3,304	6.6	14.8
BRETH–Grace Breth	4	NR	NR	NR	-	-
Catholic	3	NR	NR	1,780	3.6	8.0
CGOD–Ches God-Gen Con	5	269	391	467	0.9	2.1
Ch of Nazarene	2	124	154	190	0.4	0.8
Chr & Miss Al	1	85	57	102	0.2	0.5
CHR–Chr Chs & Chs Cr	1	NR	120	143	0.3	0.6
CONG–Consrv Cong Chr	2	77	133	159	0.3	0.7
FRND–Fr Gen Cf & Un Mtg	1	NR	53	63	0.1	0.3
Grace Gosp Fel	1	NR	NR	NR	-	-
Jehovah's Witness	2	NR	NR	NR	-	-
LDS–L-D Saints	1	NR	NR	235	0.5	1.1
LUTH–E.L.C.A.	15	617	1,892	2,499	5.0	11.2
LUTH–Luth Cong Msn Chr	1	30	59	71	0.1	0.3
METH–AME Zion	1	15	20	24	0.0	0.1
METH–Un Methodist	35	2,010	3,557	4,901	9.8	21.9
Non-denom Chr Chs	19	2,420	2,930	3,588	7.2	16.0
ORTHE–Carp Rus Orth	1	15	NR	30	0.1	0.1
PENT–Assemb of God	8	562	268	1,039	2.1	4.6
PENT–Ch God (Cleve)	5	585	994	1,188	2.4	5.3
PRES–Presb Ch (USA)	2	132	354	423	0.9	1.9
Sev Day Adv	1	66	114	131	0.3	0.6
Un C of Christ	11	461	1,428	1,706	3.4	7.6
BERKS	**402**	**41,256**	**83,747**	**196,956**	**47.9**	**100.0**
ANG/EPIS–Episcopal	6	542	1,074	1,591	0.4	0.8
Bahá'í	1	NR	64	64	0.0	0.0
BAPT–Amer Bapt USA	2	81	313	382	0.1	0.2
BAPT–Consrv Bapt	1	NR	NR	NR	-	-
BAPT–Prog NBC	1	0	150	183	0.0	0.1
BAPT–So Bapt Conv	6	281	314	383	0.1	0.2
BRETH–Breth in Chr	1	NR	NR	NR	-	-
BRETH–Ch of Brethren	5	420	628	767	0.2	0.4
BUDD–Mahayana	1	NR	NR	10	0.0	0.0
Catholic	21	NR	NR	75,672	18.4	38.4
CGOD–Ch God (Ander)	3	200	NR	200	0.0	0.1
CGOD–Ches God-Gen Con	1	0	0	0	0.0	0.0
Ch Cr, Scientst	1	NR	NR	NR	-	-
Ch of Nazarene	4	257	402	621	0.2	0.3
CHR–Chr Chs & Chs Cr	1	NR	68	83	0.0	0.0
CHR–Chs of Christ	4	206	184	258	0.1	0.1
Christian Brethren	2	NR	NR	NR	-	-
Evan Assoc RCC	3	NR	NR	NR	-	-
Evan Cong Ch	14	NR	2,546	3,109	0.8	1.6
Evan Free Ch	3	1,267	NR	1,267	0.3	0.6
FRND–Fr Gen Cf	3	NR	117	143	0.0	0.1
Ind Fund Churches	2	NR	NR	NR	-	-
Jehovah's Witness	8	NR	NR	NR	-	-
JUD–Conserv	1	188	211	570	0.1	0.3
JUD–Orth	1	43	50	60	0.0	0.0
JUD–Reform	1	130	229	618	0.2	0.3
LDS–L-D Saints	3	NR	NR	1,618	0.4	0.8
LUTH–Assoc Free Luth	3	NR	NR	NR	-	-
LUTH–E.L.C.A.	80	9,040	32,431	42,411	10.3	21.5
MENN–Amish Undif	0	NR	14	31	0.0	0.0
MENN–Bible Flwshp	7	2,013	NR	2,718	0.7	1.4
MENN–CG in Cr (Menn)	1	NR	131	160	0.0	0.1
MENN–Mennonite USA	18	1,229	1,049	1,281	0.3	0.7
METH–AME	2	150	450	549	0.1	0.3
METH–Free Methodist	1	30	23	30	0.0	0.0
METH–Un Methodist	20	2,130	6,027	7,777	1.9	3.9
METH–Wesleyan	1	65	62	85	0.0	0.0
Missionary Ch	1	490	283	490	0.1	0.2
MORAV–Morav Ch-North	1	46	80	116	0.0	0.1
Muslim Est	1	260	NR	812	0.2	0.4
New Apost Ch	1	NR	NR	NR	-	-
Non-denom Chr Chs	42	6,421	6,938	8,565	2.1	4.3
OCATH–Pol Natl Cath	1	NR	NR	NR	-	-
ORTHE–Greek Orthodox	2	340	NR	1,695	0.4	0.9
ORTHE–Orth Ch in Amer	1	95	NR	180	0.0	0.1
ORTHE–Romania Orth Ar	1	40	NR	200	0.0	0.1
ORTHE–Rus Orth Moscow	1	80	NR	200	0.0	0.1
PENT–Assemb of God	13	5,056	1,692	7,373	1.8	3.7
PENT–Ch God (Cleve)	7	1,768	1,668	2,037	0.5	1.0
PENT–COGIC	3	200	270	330	0.1	0.2
PENT–Un Pent Ch Intl	3	NR	NR	NR	-	-
PENT–United Holy Ch	1	NR	NR	NR	-	-
PRES–Orth Pres Ch	2	197	223	248	0.1	0.1
PRES–Presb Ch (USA)	4	352	816	996	0.2	0.5
PRES–Presb Ch Amer	1	42	30	54	0.0	0.0
Salvation Army	3	127	199	643	0.2	0.3
Sev Day Adv	15	1,486	2,587	2,973	0.7	1.5

NR–Not Reported   - Represents no adherents reported.   Percentages may not total 100 due to rounding.

Table 3: Religious Congregations by County and Group: 2010

Religious Group	Number of Congregations	Number of Attendees	Number of Communicant, Confirmed, or Full Members	Adherents: Number of Adherents	Adherents: % of Total Pop.	Adherents: % of Total Adh.
Sikh	2	NR	NR	NR	-	-
Un C of Christ	61	5,869	22,244	27,159	6.6	13.8
Unit Univ	1	115	180	235	0.1	0.1
Unity Ch	1	NR	NR	NR	-	-
Zoroastrian	0	NR	NR	9	0.0	0.0
BLAIR	**222**	**15,495**	**27,430**	**66,633**	**52.4**	**100.0**
ANG/EPIS–Episcopal	3	162	262	374	0.3	0.6
Bahá'í	0	NR	24	24	0.0	0.0
BAPT–Amer Bapt USA	3	185	472	563	0.4	0.8
BAPT–Consrv Bapt	1	NR	NR	NR	-	-
BAPT–So Bapt Conv	9	443	599	715	0.6	1.1
BRETH–Breth in Chr	3	NR	NR	NR	-	-
BRETH–Ch of Brethren	19	1,135	3,134	3,739	2.9	5.6
BRETH–Grace Breth	5	NR	NR	NR	-	-
Catholic	21	NR	NR	27,606	21.7	41.4
CGOD–Ches God-Gen Con	8	419	670	799	0.6	1.2
Chr & Miss Al	7	690	415	1,053	0.8	1.6
CHR–Chr Chs & Chs Cr	1	NR	600	716	0.6	1.1
CHR–Chs of Christ	2	93	88	112	0.1	0.2
CONG–Consrv Cong Chr	1	79	130	155	0.1	0.2
Grace Gosp Fel	2	NR	NR	NR	-	-
Jehovah's Witness	1	NR	NR	NR	-	-
JUD–Conserv	1	90	101	273	0.2	0.4
JUD–Orth	1	43	50	60	0.0	0.1
JUD–Reform	1	41	72	194	0.2	0.3
LDS–L-D Saints	1	NR	NR	567	0.4	0.9
LUTH–E.L.C.A.	23	1,710	6,277	8,207	6.5	12.3
MENN–Amish Undif	1	NR	78	205	0.2	0.3
MENN–Mennonite USA	4	197	245	292	0.2	0.4
METH–A.W.M.C.	1	17	0	22	0.0	0.0
METH–AME	1	0	100	119	0.1	0.2
METH–Un Methodist	40	3,007	6,569	9,099	7.2	13.7
Missionary Ch	4	275	200	291	0.2	0.4
Muslim Est	1	260	NR	812	0.6	1.2
Non-denom Chr Chs	23	3,560	3,988	4,792	3.8	7.2
ORTHE–Ant Orth of NA	1	80	NR	120	0.1	0.2
ORTHE–Greek Orthodox	1	35	NR	160	0.1	0.2
ORTHE–Orth Ch in Amer	2	13	NR	28	0.0	0.0
ORTHO–Coptic Orth Ch	1	45	NR	60	0.0	0.1
PENT–Assemb of God	6	1,507	936	2,486	2.0	3.7
PENT–Ch God (Cleve)	3	475	763	910	0.7	1.4
PENT–COGIC	1	0	60	72	0.1	0.1
PENT–Un Pent Ch Intl	1	NR	NR	NR	-	-
PRES–Orth Pres Ch	1	213	213	272	0.2	0.4
PRES–Presb Ch (USA)	8	448	810	966	0.8	1.4
Salvation Army	1	65	107	213	0.2	0.3
Sev Day Adv	1	9	16	18	0.0	0.0
Un C of Christ	7	199	451	538	0.4	0.8
Zoroastrian	0	NR	NR	1	0.0	0.0
BRADFORD	**129**	**6,871**	**11,983**	**23,042**	**36.8**	**100.0**
ANG/EPIS–Episcopal	4	150	408	496	0.8	2.2
Bahá'í	0	NR	9	9	0.0	0.0
BAPT–Amer Bapt USA	12	746	1,330	1,605	2.6	7.0
BAPT–Consrv Bapt	1	NR	NR	NR	-	-
BAPT–Reg Bapt Gen As	1	NR	NR	NR	-	-
BAPT–So Bapt Conv	1	42	19	23	0.0	0.1
Catholic	7	NR	NR	6,600	10.5	28.6
CGOD–Ch God (Ander)	1	45	NR	45	0.1	0.2
Chr & Miss Al	2	101	36	157	0.3	0.7
CHR–Chr Ch (Disc)	5	266	1,367	1,650	2.6	7.2
CHR–Chr Chs & Chs Cr	3	NR	300	362	0.6	1.6
CONG–Cong Chr, NA	1	NR	14	17	0.0	0.1
CONG–Consrv Cong Chr	1	48	64	77	0.1	0.3
FRND–Fr Gen Cf	1	NR	11	13	0.0	0.1
Jehovah's Witness	1	NR	NR	NR	-	-
LDS–L-D Saints	1	NR	NR	339	0.5	1.5
LUTH–E.L.C.A.	2	143	553	702	1.1	3.0
MENN–Amish Undif	2	NR	102	273	0.4	1.2
MENN–Cons Menn Conf	1	150	115	139	0.2	0.6
MENN–Mennonite USA	1	0	26	31	0.0	0.1
METH–Un Methodist	38	1,385	3,839	4,878	7.8	21.2
METH–Wesleyan	6	952	511	1,238	2.0	5.4
Non-denom Chr Chs	16	1,920	1,829	2,474	4.0	10.7
PENT–Assemb of God	2	225	88	243	0.4	1.1
PENT–Elim	1	NR	NR	NR	-	-
PRES–Presb Ch (USA)	12	500	1,062	1,282	2.0	5.6
Salvation Army	1	24	18	53	0.1	0.2
Sev Day Adv	2	52	90	104	0.2	0.5
Un C of Christ	1	75	144	174	0.3	0.8
Unit Univ	2	47	48	58	0.1	0.3
BUCKS	**394**	**40,090**	**72,409**	**429,943**	**68.8**	**100.0**
ANG/EPIS–Anglican NA	2	NR	NR	NR	-	-
ANG/EPIS–Episcopal	18	1,423	3,393	3,951	0.6	0.9
Bahá'í	0	NR	87	87	0.0	0.0
BAPT–Amer Bapt USA	6	610	881	1,063	0.2	0.2
BAPT–Consrv Bapt	8	NR	NR	NR	-	-
BAPT–Converge/BGC	1	75	NR	90	0.0	0.0
BAPT–N Am Bapt Conf	1	NR	99	119	0.0	0.0
BAPT–NBC USA	1	0	65	78	0.0	0.0
BAPT–Reg Bapt Gen As	2	NR	NR	NR	-	-
BAPT–So Bapt Conv	10	903	801	967	0.2	0.2
BRETH–Breth in Chr	1	NR	NR	NR	-	-
BRETH–Brethren (Ash)	1	NR	80	97	0.0	0.0
BRETH–Ch of Brethren	2	175	212	256	0.0	0.1
BUDD–Mahayana	5	NR	NR	1,179	0.2	0.3
BUDD–Theravada	1	NR	NR	1,365	0.2	0.3
Calv Chpl	2	NR	NR	NR	-	-
Catholic	41	NR	NR	321,963	51.5	74.9
CGOD–Ch God (Ander)	3	335	NR	335	0.1	0.1
Ch Cr, Scientst	1	NR	NR	NR	-	-
Ch of Nazarene	1	23	23	31	0.0	0.0
Chr & Miss Al	3	70	49	100	0.0	0.0
CHR–Chr Ch (Disc)	1	80	122	147	0.0	0.0
CHR–Chr Chs & Chs Cr	2	NR	286	345	0.1	0.1
CHR–Chs of Christ	3	333	321	449	0.1	0.1
Christian Brethren	2	NR	NR	NR	-	-
Evan Ch	1	NR	NR	NR	-	-
Evan Cov Ch	1	65	164	84	0.0	0.0
Evan Free Ch	2	655	NR	655	0.1	0.2
FRND–Fr Gen Cf	14	NR	1,597	1,927	0.3	0.4
HINDU–I/A Temples	1	NR	NR	250	0.0	0.1
HINDU–Post Ren	2	NR	NR	41	0.0	0.0
HINDU–Trad Temples	1	NR	NR	500	0.1	0.1
Ind Fund Churches	2	NR	NR	NR	-	-
Jehovah's Witness	10	NR	NR	NR	-	-
JUD–Conserv	4	1,079	1,211	3,270	0.5	0.8
JUD–Orth	5	529	300	735	0.1	0.2
JUD–Reconst	3	430	549	1,482	0.2	0.3
JUD–Reform	3	668	1,178	3,181	0.5	0.7
LDS–Comm of Christ	1	NR	161	161	0.0	0.0
LDS–L-D Saints	3	NR	NR	1,399	0.2	0.3
LUTH–E.L.C.A.	39	4,716	14,883	19,148	3.1	4.5
LUTH–Luth–MO Synod	3	272	743	893	0.1	0.2
MENN–Bible Flwshp	1	271	NR	366	0.1	0.1
MENN–Mennonite USA	12	1,734	2,652	3,200	0.5	0.7
METH–AME	3	20	220	265	0.0	0.1
METH–AME Zion	1	40	50	60	0.0	0.0
METH–Prim Meth Ch	2	NR	NR	NR	-	-
METH–Un Methodist	33	4,611	11,269	16,238	2.6	3.8
METH–Wesleyan	1	64	37	83	0.0	0.0
Muslim Est	3	722	NR	2,026	0.3	0.5
New Apost Ch	1	NR	NR	NR	-	-
Non-denom Chr Chs	38	8,881	11,772	13,716	2.2	3.2
ORTHE–Carp Rus Orth	1	24	NR	57	0.0	0.0
ORTHE–Orth Ch in Amer	1	35	NR	60	0.0	0.0
ORTHO–Malan Dioc Am	2	410	NR	660	0.1	0.2
PENT–Assemb of God	14	3,907	1,712	5,417	0.9	1.3
PENT–Ch God (Cleve)	4	242	343	414	0.1	0.1
PENT–Fire Bapt Hol Ch	1	NR	NR	NR	-	-
PENT–I F Chr Assmbl	1	NR	NR	NR	-	-
PENT–Un Pent Ch Intl	1	NR	NR	NR	-	-
PENT–United Holy Ch	1	NR	NR	NR	-	-
PRES–Korean Pres Amer	2	NR	NR	NR	-	-
PRES–Orth Pres Ch	2	45	34	37	0.0	0.0

NR–Not Reported - Represents no adherents reported. Percentages may not total 100 due to rounding.

Table 3: Religious Congregations by County and Group: 2010

Religious Group	Number of Congregations	Number of Attendees	Number of Communicant, Confirmed, or Full Members	Adherents: Number of Adherents	Adherents: % of Total Pop.	Adherents: % of Total Adh.
PRES–Presb Ch (USA)	18	2,928	8,379	10,112	1.6	2.4
PRES–Presb Ch Amer	6	919	955	1,231	0.2	0.3
REF–Ref Ch in Am	7	676	1,333	1,535	0.2	0.4
Salvation Army	1	63	132	380	0.1	0.1
Sev Day Adv	1	111	193	222	0.0	0.1
Un C of Christ	21	1,724	5,828	7,033	1.1	1.6
Unit Univ	2	222	295	470	0.1	0.1
Zoroastrian	0	NR	NR	13	0.0	0.0
BUTLER	**227**	**21,334**	**34,845**	**109,133**	**59.4**	**100.0**
ANG/EPIS–Anglican NA	4	NR	NR	NR	-	-
Bahá'í	0	NR	7	7	0.0	0.0
BAPT–Amer Bapt USA	2	76	157	189	0.1	0.2
BAPT–Consrv Bapt	1	NR	NR	NR	-	-
BAPT–Converge/BGC	1	75	NR	90	0.0	0.1
BAPT–Free Will Bapt	1	NR	67	81	0.0	0.1
BAPT–Ind Bapt Flwsp Intl	1	NR	NR	NR	-	-
BAPT–Ref Bapt Ch	1	NR	NR	NR	-	-
BAPT–Reg Bapt Gen As	1	NR	NR	NR	-	-
BAPT–So Bapt Conv	4	100	90	108	0.1	0.1
BRETH–Brethren (Ash)	1	NR	80	96	0.1	0.1
BRETH–Ch of Brethren	1	0	93	112	0.1	0.1
Catholic	25	NR	NR	54,600	29.7	50.0
CGOD–Ch God (Ander)	1	317	NR	317	0.2	0.3
CGOD–Ches God-Gen Con	1	70	96	115	0.1	0.1
Ch Cr, Scientst	1	NR	NR	NR	-	-
Ch of Nazarene	5	346	434	695	0.4	0.6
Chr & Miss Al	8	2,200	1,341	4,940	2.7	4.5
CHR–Chr Ch (Disc)	1	51	146	176	0.1	0.2
CHR–Chr Chs & Chs Cr	2	NR	400	481	0.3	0.4
CHR–Chs of Christ	2	82	76	99	0.1	0.1
CONG–Consrv Cong Chr	1	300	412	496	0.3	0.5
Evan Free Ch	2	165	NR	165	0.1	0.2
FRND–Fr Gen Cf	1	NR	0	0	0.0	0.0
HINDU–I/A Temples	1	NR	NR	3,000	1.6	2.7
Jehovah's Witness	5	NR	NR	NR	-	-
LDS–L-D Saints	3	NR	NR	1,248	0.7	1.1
LUTH–Assoc Free Luth	1	NR	NR	NR	-	-
LUTH–E.L.C.A.	18	1,989	5,958	8,651	4.7	7.9
LUTH–Luth–MO Synod	3	553	1,285	1,719	0.9	1.6
LUTH–Nor Amer Luth C	4	NR	NR	NR	-	-
METH–A.W.M.C.	3	101	40	136	0.1	0.1
METH–Free Methodist	2	120	113	120	0.1	0.1
METH–Un Methodist	28	3,627	8,991	11,132	6.1	10.2
Non-denom Chr Chs	24	6,550	6,060	8,298	4.5	7.6
ORTHE–Ant Orth of NA	1	28	NR	37	0.0	0.0
ORTHE–Greek Orthodox	1	25	NR	13	0.0	0.0
ORTHE–Orth Ch in Amer	1	65	NR	110	0.1	0.1
ORTHE–Ukrainian Orth	1	75	NR	150	0.1	0.1
PENT–Assemb of God	5	762	422	1,173	0.6	1.1
PENT–Ch of God Proph	2	NR	80	96	0.1	0.1
PENT–Vineyard	1	11	11	13	0.0	0.0
PRES–Evan Presby Ch	1	NR	186	224	0.1	0.2
PRES–Orth Pres Ch	1	109	106	148	0.1	0.1
PRES–Presb Ch (USA)	43	2,796	7,040	8,470	4.6	7.8
PRES–Presb Ch Amer	4	574	781	915	0.5	0.8
Salvation Army	1	34	94	381	0.2	0.3
Sev Day Adv	2	41	71	82	0.0	0.1
Un C of Christ	2	70	180	217	0.1	0.2
Unit Univ	1	22	28	33	0.0	0.0
CAMBRIA	**247**	**12,132**	**28,370**	**103,114**	**71.8**	**100.0**
ANG/EPIS–Anglican NA	2	NR	NR	NR	-	-
ANG/EPIS–Episcopal	1	64	127	157	0.1	0.2
Bahá'í	0	NR	4	4	0.0	0.0
BAPT–Amer Bapt USA	5	238	543	638	0.4	0.6
BAPT–NBC USA	3	120	1,400	1,644	1.1	1.6
BAPT–So Bapt Conv	2	97	122	143	0.1	0.1
BRETH–Breth in Chr	1	NR	NR	NR	-	-
BRETH–Brethren (Ash)	2	NR	160	188	0.1	0.2
BRETH–Ch of Brethren	11	804	1,898	2,229	1.6	2.2
BRETH–Grace Breth	6	NR	NR	NR	-	-
Catholic	54	NR	NR	64,831	45.1	62.9
CGOD–Ch God (Ander)	3	166	NR	166	0.1	0.2
CGOD–Ches God-Gen Con	3	223	170	200	0.1	0.2
Ch of Nazarene	5	195	192	342	0.2	0.3
Chr & Miss Al	10	605	370	986	0.7	1.0
CHR–Chr Ch (Disc)	3	30	178	209	0.1	0.2
CHR–Chr Chs & Chs Cr	1	NR	125	147	0.1	0.1
CHR–Chs of Christ	1	55	70	90	0.1	0.1
Jehovah's Witness	4	NR	NR	NR	-	-
LDS–L-D Saints	1	NR	NR	605	0.4	0.6
LUTH–E.L.C.A.	15	1,271	4,281	5,930	4.1	5.8
LUTH–Luth–MO Synod	1	35	68	68	0.0	0.1
LUTH–Nor Amer Luth C	1	NR	NR	NR	-	-
MENN–Amish Undif	1	NR	45	115	0.1	0.1
MENN–Mennonite USA	2	170	164	193	0.1	0.2
METH–A.W.M.C.	1	16	12	20	0.0	0.0
METH–AME	1	0	150	176	0.1	0.2
METH–AME Zion	1	40	60	70	0.0	0.1
METH–Un Methodist	55	3,754	12,594	15,503	10.8	15.0
Non-denom Chr Chs	11	2,235	2,445	2,908	2.0	2.8
OCATH–Pol Natl Cath	2	NR	NR	NR	-	-
ORTHE–Ant Orth of NA	1	90	NR	300	0.2	0.3
ORTHE–Carp Rus Orth	1	225	NR	495	0.3	0.5
ORTHE–Greek Orthodox	1	15	NR	72	0.1	0.1
ORTHE–Orth Ch in Amer	5	122	NR	304	0.2	0.3
ORTHE–Serb Orth USA	1	40	NR	200	0.1	0.2
ORTHE–Ukrainian Orth	3	105	NR	210	0.1	0.2
PENT–Assemb of God	4	182	161	294	0.2	0.3
PENT–Ch God (Cleve)	2	212	497	584	0.4	0.6
PENT–COGIC	1	0	150	176	0.1	0.2
PRES–Presb Ch (USA)	11	642	1,501	1,762	1.2	1.7
PRES–Presb Ch Amer	1	90	83	111	0.1	0.1
Salvation Army	1	67	151	285	0.2	0.3
Sev Day Adv	1	70	121	139	0.1	0.1
Un C of Christ	5	154	528	620	0.4	0.6
CAMERON	**17**	**725**	**1,237**	**3,502**	**68.9**	**100.0**
ANG/EPIS–Episcopal	1	37	81	81	1.6	2.3
BAPT–Amer Bapt USA	1	70	118	136	2.7	3.9
BAPT–So Bapt Conv	2	51	201	232	4.6	6.6
Catholic	2	NR	NR	1,838	36.1	52.5
Chr & Miss Al	1	107	62	198	3.9	5.7
Jehovah's Witness	1	NR	NR	NR	-	-
LUTH–E.L.C.A.	1	28	80	115	2.3	3.3
MENN–Mennonite USA	1	70	70	81	1.6	2.3
METH–Free Methodist	1	65	30	65	1.3	1.9
METH–Un Methodist	3	128	361	506	10.0	14.4
METH–Wesleyan	1	21	21	27	0.5	0.8
Non-denom Chr Chs	1	100	150	150	2.9	4.3
PRES–Presb Ch (USA)	1	48	63	73	1.4	2.1
CARBON	**89**	**4,333**	**12,402**	**29,400**	**45.1**	**100.0**
ANG/EPIS–Episcopal	4	190	514	601	0.9	2.0
Bahá'í	0	NR	1	1	0.0	0.0
BAPT–Amer Bapt USA	2	38	85	101	0.2	0.3
BRETH–Ch of Brethren	1	24	47	56	0.1	0.2
Calv Chpl	1	NR	NR	NR	-	-
Catholic	14	NR	NR	12,418	19.0	42.2
CHR–Chs of Christ	1	9	9	9	0.0	0.0
Evan Cong Ch	5	NR	465	552	0.8	1.9
Evan Free Ch	2	269	NR	269	0.4	0.9
Grace Gosp Fel	1	NR	NR	NR	-	-
Jehovah's Witness	2	NR	NR	NR	-	-
LDS–L-D Saints	1	NR	NR	161	0.2	0.5
LUTH–E.L.C.A.	24	1,496	6,256	8,845	13.6	30.1
MENN–Bible Flwshp	1	93	NR	126	0.2	0.4
METH–Un Methodist	7	445	1,060	1,278	2.0	4.3
Non-denom Chr Chs	6	695	775	931	1.4	3.2
ORTHE–Carp Rus Orth	2	110	NR	264	0.4	0.9
PRES–Presb Ch (USA)	3	108	348	413	0.6	1.4
Un C of Christ	12	856	2,842	3,375	5.2	11.5
CENTRE	**192**	**13,835**	**25,977**	**57,774**	**37.5**	**100.0**
ANG/EPIS–Episcopal	3	470	959	1,344	0.9	2.3

NR–Not Reported - Represents no adherents reported. Percentages may not total 100 due to rounding.

Table 3: Religious Congregations by County and Group: 2010

Religious Group	Number of Congrega-tions	Number of Attendees	Number of Communicant, Confirmed, or Full Members	Adherents: Number of Adherents	Adherents: % of Total Pop.	Adherents: % of Total Adh.
Bahá'í	0	NR	37	37	0.0	0.1
BAPT–Amer Bapt USA	3	265	780	888	0.6	1.5
BAPT–Consrv Bapt	3	NR	NR	NR	-	-
BAPT–Converge/BGC	1	800	NR	960	0.6	1.7
BAPT–Ref Bapt Ch	1	NR	NR	NR	-	-
BAPT–Reg Bapt Gen As	1	NR	NR	NR	-	-
BAPT–So Bapt Conv	1	12	26	30	0.0	0.1
BRETH–Breth in Chr	3	NR	NR	NR	-	-
BRETH–Brethren (Ash)	1	NR	80	91	0.1	0.2
BRETH–Ch of Brethren	1	0	509	580	0.4	1.0
Catholic	8	NR	NR	19,203	12.5	33.2
Ch Christ Chr Union	1	NR	NR	NR	-	-
Ch Cr, Scientst	1	NR	NR	NR	-	-
Ch of Nazarene	1	19	30	30	0.0	0.1
Chr & Miss Al	9	1,598	834	2,185	1.4	3.8
CHR–Chr Chs & Chs Cr	6	NR	1,319	1,502	1.0	2.6
CHR–Chs of Christ	5	170	144	195	0.1	0.3
CHR–Int Chs of Christ	1	NR	28	32	0.0	0.1
Evan Free Ch	1	150	NR	150	0.1	0.3
FRND–Fr Gen Cf & Un Mtg	1	NR	224	255	0.2	0.4
Intl Fell Bible Ch	1	NR	NR	NR	-	-
Jehovah's Witness	3	NR	NR	NR	-	-
JUD–Reform	1	111	196	529	0.3	0.9
LDS–L-D Saints	4	NR	NR	1,212	0.8	2.1
LUTH–E.L.C.A.	18	1,689	5,503	6,548	4.3	11.3
LUTH–Luth–MO Synod	1	106	122	151	0.1	0.3
MENN–Amish Undif	11	NR	678	1,764	1.1	3.1
MENN–Mennonite USA	1	120	105	120	0.1	0.2
METH–AME	1	0	150	171	0.1	0.3
METH–Free Methodist	2	109	62	109	0.1	0.2
METH–Un Methodist	46	3,333	8,317	11,098	7.2	19.2
METH–Wesleyan	3	213	229	277	0.2	0.5
Muslim Est	1	150	NR	400	0.3	0.7
Non-denom Chr Chs	11	1,050	1,075	1,355	0.9	2.3
ORTHE–Orth Ch in Amer	2	160	NR	229	0.1	0.4
PENT–Assemb of God	4	1,050	419	1,503	1.0	2.6
PENT–Ch God (Cleve)	1	58	101	115	0.1	0.2
PENT–Un Pent Ch Intl	1	NR	NR	NR	-	-
PRES–Korean Pres Amer	1	NR	NR	NR	-	-
PRES–Presb Ch (USA)	7	826	1,829	2,083	1.4	3.6
PRES–Presb Ch Amer	2	321	205	273	0.2	0.5
PRES–Ref Pres of NA	1	98	84	132	0.1	0.2
Salvation Army	1	19	30	36	0.0	0.1
Sev Day Adv	1	37	64	74	0.0	0.1
Un C of Christ	14	729	1,564	1,781	1.2	3.1
Unit Univ	1	172	274	332	0.2	0.6
CHESTER	**410**	**41,502**	**74,951**	**315,590**	**63.3**	**100.0**
ANG/EPIS–Anglican NA	2	NR	NR	NR	-	-
ANG/EPIS–Episcopal	15	2,453	5,731	6,765	1.4	2.1
Ap Chr Ch-Amer	1	76	37	76	0.0	0.0
Bahá'í	1	NR	149	149	0.0	0.0
BAPT–Amer Bapt USA	15	1,925	3,254	4,015	0.8	1.3
BAPT–Natl Mis Bapt Conv	1	0	0	0	0.0	0.0
BAPT–NBC Amer	3	325	700	864	0.2	0.3
BAPT–NBC USA	1	300	500	617	0.1	0.2
BAPT–Ref Bapt Ch	3	NR	NR	NR	-	-
BAPT–So Bapt Conv	9	995	1,003	1,238	0.2	0.4
BRETH–Breth in Chr	1	NR	NR	NR	-	-
BRETH–Ch of Brethren	4	392	494	610	0.1	0.2
BRETH–Grace Breth	4	NR	NR	NR	-	-
BUDD–Vajrayana	1	NR	NR	20	0.0	0.0
Calv Chpl	1	NR	NR	NR	-	-
Catholic	33	NR	NR	212,113	42.5	67.2
Ch Cr, Scientst	3	NR	NR	NR	-	-
Ch of Nazarene	3	381	408	911	0.2	0.3
Chr & Miss Al	2	71	115	161	0.0	0.1
CHR–Chs of Christ	6	321	307	418	0.1	0.1
CHR–Int Chs of Christ	1	NR	25	31	0.0	0.0
Christian Brethren	2	NR	NR	NR	-	-
Evan Free Ch	3	830	NR	830	0.2	0.3
FRND–Fr Gen Cf	17	NR	1,836	2,266	0.5	0.7
FRND–Fr Gen Cf & Un Mtg	1	NR	77	95	0.0	0.0
Ind Fund Churches	3	NR	NR	NR	-	-
Int Cou Comm Ch	1	NR	NR	NR	-	-
Jehovah's Witness	5	NR	NR	NR	-	-
JUD–Conserv	4	626	703	1,898	0.4	0.6
JUD–Orth	1	43	50	60	0.0	0.0
JUD–Reform	1	92	162	437	0.1	0.1
LDS–L-D Saints	2	NR	NR	1,213	0.2	0.4
LUTH–E.L.C.A.	16	2,953	8,378	11,169	2.2	3.5
LUTH–Luth–MO Synod	1	180	337	468	0.1	0.1
MENN–Amish Undif	16	NR	1,126	2,580	0.5	0.8
MENN–Bible Flwshp	1	99	NR	134	0.0	0.0
MENN–Mennonite USA	7	743	716	884	0.2	0.3
METH–AME	11	320	1,302	1,607	0.3	0.5
METH–AME Zion	4	40	399	492	0.1	0.2
METH–Un Methodist	46	4,528	13,541	18,931	3.8	6.0
Muslim Est	2	661	NR	913	0.2	0.3
Non-denom Chr Chs	63	12,194	13,809	17,153	3.4	5.4
ORTHE–Ant Orth of NA	1	80	NR	100	0.0	0.0
ORTHE–Carp Rus Orth	1	175	NR	325	0.1	0.1
ORTHE–Orth Ch in Amer	1	25	NR	50	0.0	0.0
ORTHE–Ukrainian Orth	1	120	NR	200	0.0	0.1
PENT–Assemb of God	10	1,253	643	1,707	0.3	0.5
PENT–Ch God (Cleve)	3	130	203	250	0.1	0.1
PENT–Ch Lord Jesus Apos	1	NR	NR	NR	-	-
PENT–COGIC	3	205	560	691	0.1	0.2
PENT–Fire Bapt Hol Ch	1	NR	NR	NR	-	-
PENT–Full Gosp Bapt	1	NR	NR	NR	-	-
PENT–Un Pent Ch Intl	2	NR	NR	NR	-	-
PENT–Vineyard	2	587	865	1,067	0.2	0.3
PRES–Evan Presby Ch	3	NR	727	897	0.2	0.3
PRES–Free Pres NA	1	NR	NR	NR	-	-
PRES–Orth Pres Ch	1	82	105	151	0.0	0.0
PRES–Presb Ch (USA)	28	5,190	11,547	14,248	2.9	4.5
PRES–Presb Ch Amer	8	1,119	1,014	1,431	0.3	0.5
REF–Christian Ref	1	40	25	31	0.0	0.0
Salvation Army	2	94	66	227	0.0	0.1
Sev Day Adv	4	132	230	265	0.1	0.1
Swedenborgian	1	NR	NR	NR	-	-
Un C of Christ	13	1,000	2,781	3,432	0.7	1.1
Unit Univ	4	722	1,026	1,378	0.3	0.4
Zoroastrian	0	NR	NR	22	0.0	0.0
CLARION	**111**	**5,843**	**9,733**	**22,414**	**56.1**	**100.0**
ANG/EPIS–Episcopal	1	24	34	67	0.2	0.3
Bahá'í	0	NR	4	4	0.0	0.0
BAPT–Amer Bapt USA	1	75	48	56	0.1	0.2
BAPT–Consrv Bapt	1	NR	NR	NR	-	-
BAPT–So Bapt Conv	2	855	1,089	1,273	3.2	5.7
Catholic	8	NR	NR	9,079	22.7	40.5
CGOD–Ch God (Ander)	5	466	NR	466	1.2	2.1
Ch of Nazarene	5	171	193	343	0.9	1.5
Chr & Miss Al	1	47	2	61	0.2	0.3
CHR–Chs of Christ	2	70	74	110	0.3	0.5
Evan Cong Ch	4	NR	292	341	0.9	1.5
Jehovah's Witness	3	NR	NR	NR	-	-
LDS–L-D Saints	1	NR	NR	162	0.4	0.7
LUTH–E.L.C.A.	8	389	1,085	1,482	3.7	6.6
MENN–Amish Undif	3	NR	107	302	0.8	1.3
METH–A.W.M.C.	2	145	58	157	0.4	0.7
METH–Free Methodist	2	43	33	43	0.1	0.2
METH–Un Methodist	31	1,436	3,613	4,593	11.5	20.5
METH–Wesleyan	2	67	46	87	0.2	0.4
Non-denom Chr Chs	7	1,151	1,251	1,560	3.9	7.0
PENT–Assemb of God	1	100	50	180	0.5	0.8
PENT–Ch God (Cleve)	1	39	53	62	0.2	0.3
PENT–Ch of God Proph	3	NR	99	116	0.3	0.5
PRES–Presb Ch (USA)	11	547	1,164	1,361	3.4	6.1
PRES–Ref Pres of NA	1	23	20	20	0.1	0.1
Un C of Christ	5	195	418	489	1.2	2.2
CLEARFIELD	**203**	**9,583**	**15,939**	**42,597**	**52.2**	**100.0**
ANG/EPIS–Episcopal	5	135	261	345	0.4	0.8
Bahá'í	0	NR	3	3	0.0	0.0
BAPT–Amer Bapt USA	2	80	133	156	0.2	0.4

NR–Not Reported - Represents no adherents reported. Percentages may not total 100 due to rounding.

Table 3: Religious Congregations by County and Group: 2010

Religious Group	Number of Congregations	Number of Attendees	Number of Communicant, Confirmed, or Full Members	Adherents		
				Number of Adherents	% of Total Pop.	% of Total Adh.
BAPT–Consrv Bapt	1	NR	NR	NR	-	-
BAPT–So Bapt Conv	2	141	128	150	0.2	0.4
BRETH–Ch of Brethren	3	63	80	94	0.1	0.2
Catholic	20	NR	NR	19,331	23.7	45.4
CGOD–Ch God (Ander)	2	960	NR	960	1.2	2.3
CGOD–Ches God-Gen Con	3	159	140	164	0.2	0.4
Ch of Nazarene	3	101	145	190	0.2	0.4
Chr & Miss Al	12	1,080	776	1,687	2.1	4.0
CHR–Chs of Christ	8	228	200	260	0.3	0.6
Evan Cov Ch	1	63	97	82	0.1	0.2
Evan Free Ch	1	130	NR	130	0.2	0.3
FRND–Fr Gen Cf & Un Mtg	1	NR	112	131	0.2	0.3
Jehovah's Witness	2	NR	NR	NR	-	-
JUD–Reform	1	10	18	49	0.1	0.1
LUTH–E.L.C.A.	12	613	2,292	2,936	3.6	6.9
LUTH–Luth–MO Synod	1	60	193	247	0.3	0.6
MENN–Amish Undif	5	NR	290	820	1.0	1.9
METH–AME	1	0	100	117	0.1	0.3
METH–Free Methodist	5	295	199	319	0.4	0.7
METH–Prim Meth Ch	2	NR	NR	NR	-	-
METH–Un Methodist	62	2,939	7,489	9,535	11.7	22.4
METH–Wesleyan	2	284	164	370	0.5	0.9
Non-denom Chr Chs	10	825	970	1,095	1.3	2.6
OCATH–Pol Natl Cath	1	NR	NR	NR	-	-
ORTHE–Carp Rus Orth	1	75	NR	158	0.2	0.4
ORTHE–Orth Ch in Amer	4	145	NR	211	0.3	0.5
ORTHE–Ukrainian Orth	1	30	NR	150	0.2	0.4
PENT–Assemb of God	4	271	222	423	0.5	1.0
PENT–Ch God (Cleve)	1	26	31	36	0.0	0.1
PENT–Pent FW Bapt	1	NR	NR	NR	-	-
PRES–Presb Ch (USA)	15	700	1,432	1,681	2.1	3.9
PRES–Presb Ch Amer	1	15	11	14	0.0	0.0
Salvation Army	2	78	198	454	0.6	1.1
Sev Day Adv	1	9	16	18	0.0	0.0
Un C of Christ	4	68	239	281	0.3	0.7
CLINTON	**81**	**3,211**	**7,281**	**12,714**	**32.4**	**100.0**
ANG/EPIS–Episcopal	2	44	76	76	0.2	0.6
Bahá'í	0	NR	1	1	0.0	0.0
BAPT–So Bapt Conv	1	230	108	128	0.3	1.0
BRETH–Breth in Chr	1	NR	NR	NR	-	-
BRETH–Ch of Brethren	1	62	76	90	0.2	0.7
BRETH–Grace Breth	1	NR	NR	NR	-	-
Catholic	3	NR	NR	2,620	6.7	20.6
Chr & Miss Al	2	64	30	98	0.2	0.8
CHR–Chr Chs & Chs Cr	3	NR	880	1,047	2.7	8.2
CHR–Chs of Christ	4	89	75	101	0.3	0.8
Ind Fund Churches	1	NR	NR	NR	-	-
Jehovah's Witness	1	NR	NR	NR	-	-
JUD–Reform	1	11	19	51	0.1	0.4
LDS–L-D Saints	1	NR	NR	181	0.5	1.4
LUTH–E.L.C.A.	7	269	925	1,034	2.6	8.1
MENN–Amish Undif	8	NR	559	1,315	3.4	10.3
METH–Free Methodist	1	23	21	23	0.1	0.2
METH–Un Methodist	23	1,235	2,848	3,638	9.3	28.6
METH–Wesleyan	4	337	240	439	1.1	3.5
Non-denom Chr Chs	5	375	480	532	1.4	4.2
PENT–Assemb of God	2	27	25	70	0.2	0.6
PRES–Presb Ch (USA)	3	159	321	382	1.0	3.0
Salvation Army	1	39	144	351	0.9	2.8
Sev Day Adv	1	29	50	58	0.1	0.5
Un C of Christ	4	218	403	479	1.2	3.8
COLUMBIA	**125**	**7,295**	**18,507**	**31,278**	**46.5**	**100.0**
ANG/EPIS–Episcopal	3	112	240	259	0.4	0.8
Bahá'í	0	NR	8	8	0.0	0.0
BAPT–Amer Bapt USA	2	210	448	521	0.8	1.7
BAPT–Asc Ref Bap Ch Am	1	NR	NR	NR	-	-
BAPT–Consrv Bapt	1	NR	NR	NR	-	-
BAPT–So Bapt Conv	1	60	80	93	0.1	0.3
Catholic	7	NR	NR	8,035	11.9	25.7
Ch Cr, Scientst	1	NR	NR	NR	-	-
Chr & Miss Al	1	133	81	159	0.2	0.5

Religious Group	Number of Congregations	Number of Attendees	Number of Communicant, Confirmed, or Full Members	Adherents		
				Number of Adherents	% of Total Pop.	% of Total Adh.
CHR–Chr Ch (Disc)	2	87	594	690	1.0	2.2
CHR–Chr Chs & Chs Cr	7	NR	1,223	1,422	2.1	4.5
FRND–Fr Gen Cf	1	NR	60	70	0.1	0.2
Jehovah's Witness	1	NR	NR	NR	-	-
LDS–Comm of Christ	1	NR	161	161	0.2	0.5
LDS–L-D Saints	1	NR	NR	524	0.8	1.7
LUTH–E.L.C.A.	12	1,012	3,760	4,889	7.3	15.6
LUTH–Luth–MO Synod	1	15	19	20	0.0	0.1
MENN–Amish Undif	1	NR	55	121	0.2	0.4
METH–Un Methodist	45	2,474	7,243	8,572	12.7	27.4
Non-denom Chr Chs	14	2,162	2,258	2,810	4.2	9.0
ORTHE–Orth Ch in Amer	1	60	NR	120	0.2	0.4
PENT–Assemb of God	4	342	531	637	0.9	2.0
PENT–Un Pent Ch Intl	1	NR	NR	NR	-	-
PRES–Presb Ch (USA)	5	230	514	597	0.9	1.9
Salvation Army	1	26	90	243	0.4	0.8
Sev Day Adv	1	34	58	67	0.1	0.2
Un C of Christ	9	338	1,084	1,260	1.9	4.0
CRAWFORD	**205**	**10,255**	**17,218**	**39,112**	**44.1**	**100.0**
ANG/EPIS–Episcopal	2	102	154	218	0.2	0.6
Bahá'í	0	NR	4	4	0.0	0.0
BAPT–Amer Bapt USA	10	1,025	1,267	1,523	1.7	3.9
BAPT–Converge/BGC	1	75	NR	90	0.1	0.2
BAPT–Fund Bapt Flwsp	1	NR	NR	NR	-	-
BAPT–So Bapt Conv	1	85	40	48	0.1	0.1
Catholic	15	NR	NR	13,272	15.0	33.9
CGOD–Ch God (Ander)	7	1,124	NR	1,124	1.3	2.9
Ch of Nazarene	6	188	238	434	0.5	1.1
Chr & Miss Al	7	615	367	803	0.9	2.1
CHR–Chr Chs & Chs Cr	4	NR	600	721	0.8	1.8
CHR–Chs of Christ	2	50	55	63	0.1	0.2
Evan Free Ch	2	155	NR	155	0.2	0.4
Jehovah's Witness	3	NR	NR	NR	-	-
LDS–Comm of Christ	1	NR	158	158	0.2	0.4
LDS–L-D Saints	1	NR	NR	447	0.5	1.1
LUTH–E.L.C.A.	6	297	1,396	1,611	1.8	4.1
MENN–Amish Undif	26	NR	1,415	3,506	3.9	9.0
MENN–Beachy Amish-Menn	2	126	95	126	0.1	0.3
MENN–Mennonite USA	2	151	159	191	0.2	0.5
METH–A.W.M.C.	4	164	79	204	0.2	0.5
METH–AME	1	0	150	180	0.2	0.5
METH–Free Methodist	2	239	18	239	0.3	0.6
METH–Un Methodist	44	2,294	5,592	7,401	8.3	18.9
New Apost Ch	1	NR	NR	NR	-	-
Non-denom Chr Chs	27	1,995	2,376	2,758	3.1	7.1
PENT–Assemb of God	2	130	76	159	0.2	0.4
PENT–Full Gosp Bapt	1	NR	NR	NR	-	-
PENT–Open Bible Std	2	40	NR	40	0.0	0.1
PENT–Un Pent Ch Intl	1	NR	NR	NR	-	-
PRES–Presb Ch (USA)	13	963	2,131	2,562	2.9	6.6
PRES–Ref Pres of NA	1	29	25	36	0.0	0.1
Salvation Army	1	19	60	109	0.1	0.3
Un Breth in Cr	2	261	175	223	0.3	0.6
Un C of Christ	3	48	463	557	0.6	1.4
Unit Univ	1	80	125	150	0.2	0.4
CUMBERLAND	**288**	**37,361**	**59,181**	**124,182**	**52.8**	**100.0**
ANG/EPIS–Anglican NA	1	NR	NR	NR	-	-
ANG/EPIS–Episcopal	4	640	1,552	1,750	0.7	1.4
Bahá'í	0	NR	53	53	0.0	0.0
BAPT–Amer Bapt USA	1	145	325	386	0.2	0.3
BAPT–Asc Ref Bap Ch Am	1	NR	NR	NR	-	-
BAPT–Consrv Bapt	1	NR	NR	NR	-	-
BAPT–Ref Bapt Ch	1	NR	NR	NR	-	-
BAPT–So Bapt Conv	7	586	726	862	0.4	0.7
BRETH–Breth in Chr	15	NR	NR	NR	-	-
BRETH–Ch of Brethren	7	565	1,107	1,315	0.6	1.1
Catholic	8	NR	NR	36,186	15.4	29.1
CGOD–Ch God (Ander)	2	92	NR	92	0.0	0.1
CGOD–Ches God-Gen Con	26	3,118	4,056	4,817	2.0	3.9
Ch of Nazarene	3	319	311	433	0.2	0.3
Chr & Miss Al	9	1,999	1,211	2,430	1.0	2.0

NR–Not Reported   - Represents no adherents reported.   Percentages may not total 100 due to rounding.

Table 3: Religious Congregations by County and Group: 2010

Religious Group	Number of Congrega-tions	Number of Attendees	Number of Communicant, Confirmed, or Full Members	Adherents		
				Number of Adherents	% of Total Pop.	% of Total Adh.
CHR–Chr Ch (Disc)	1	40	347	412	0.2	0.3
CHR–Chr Chs & Chs Cr	1	NR	570	677	0.3	0.5
CHR–Chs of Christ	3	434	400	490	0.2	0.4
Evan Free Ch	2	2,780	NR	2,780	1.2	2.2
FRND–Fr Gen Cf & Un Mtg	1	NR	44	52	0.0	0.0
HINDU–Post Ren	2	NR	NR	2,025	0.9	1.6
HINDU–Trad Temples	1	NR	NR	4,500	1.9	3.6
Jain	1	NR	NR	NR	-	-
Jehovah's Witness	2	NR	NR	NR	-	-
JUD–Reconst	1	272	348	940	0.4	0.8
JUD–Reform	1	20	36	97	0.0	0.1
LDS–L-D Saints	2	NR	NR	1,149	0.5	0.9
LUTH–E.L.C.A.	27	3,967	11,538	13,809	5.9	11.1
LUTH–Luth–MO Synod	2	97	177	211	0.1	0.2
MENN–Amish Undif	3	NR	201	436	0.2	0.4
MENN–CG in Cr (Menn)	1	NR	88	105	0.0	0.1
MENN–Mennonite USA	3	302	293	348	0.1	0.3
MENN–Ref Mennonite	1	NR	27	28	0.0	0.0
METH–AME	2	0	300	356	0.2	0.3
METH–AME Zion	2	30	160	190	0.1	0.2
METH–Un Methodist	49	6,746	15,350	19,511	8.3	15.7
METH–Wesleyan	3	214	240	278	0.1	0.2
Muslim Est	4	742	NR	2,326	1.0	1.9
Non-denom Chr Chs	27	5,533	5,655	7,075	3.0	5.7
ORTHE–Greek Orthodox	1	250	NR	1,000	0.4	0.8
ORTHE–Holy Orth in NA	2	97	NR	127	0.1	0.1
ORTHE–Orth Ch in Amer	1	96	NR	114	0.0	0.1
PENT–Assemb of God	8	3,958	4,902	5,637	2.4	4.5
PENT–Ch God (Cleve)	6	302	475	564	0.2	0.5
PENT–Ch of God Proph	1	NR	15	18	0.0	0.0
PENT–COGIC	1	0	50	59	0.0	0.0
PENT–Elim	1	NR	NR	NR	-	-
PENT–Un Pent Ch Intl	2	NR	NR	NR	-	-
PRES–Korean Pres Amer	1	NR	NR	NR	-	-
PRES–Orth Pres Ch	1	61	48	64	0.0	0.1
PRES–Presb Ch (USA)	15	2,053	5,080	6,033	2.6	4.9
PRES–Presb Ch Amer	3	510	496	660	0.3	0.5
Salvation Army	1	37	205	710	0.3	0.6
Sev Day Adv	2	76	133	153	0.1	0.1
Sikh	1	NR	NR	NR	-	-
Un Breth in Cr	3	486	582	415	0.2	0.3
Un C of Christ	8	704	1,916	2,275	1.0	1.8
Unit Univ	1	90	164	221	0.1	0.2
Unity Ch	1	NR	NR	NR	-	-
Zoroastrian	0	NR	NR	13	0.0	0.0
DAUPHIN	**364**	**35,413**	**59,694**	**128,347**	**47.9**	**100.0**
ANG/EPIS–Anglican NA	1	NR	NR	NR	-	-
ANG/EPIS–Episcopal	4	494	1,411	1,469	0.5	1.1
Bahá'í	1	NR	40	40	0.0	0.0
BAPT–Amer Bapt USA	5	1,162	2,051	2,486	0.9	1.9
BAPT–Converge/BGC	1	75	NR	90	0.0	0.1
BAPT–Ind Bapt Flwsp Intl	1	NR	NR	NR	-	-
BAPT–NBC USA	4	795	1,469	1,781	0.7	1.4
BAPT–So Bapt Conv	11	1,022	1,246	1,511	0.6	1.2
BRETH–Breth in Chr	7	NR	NR	NR	-	-
BRETH–Ch of Brethren	7	589	1,106	1,341	0.5	1.0
BUDD–Mahayana	1	NR	NR	102	0.0	0.1
BUDD–Vajrayana	1	NR	NR	456	0.2	0.4
Catholic	16	NR	NR	39,739	14.8	31.0
CGOD–Ch God (Ander)	1	60	NR	60	0.0	0.0
CGOD–Ches God-Gen Con	17	1,574	2,335	2,831	1.1	2.2
Ch Cr, Scientst	1	NR	NR	NR	-	-
Ch God (7th Day)	1	NR	NR	NR	-	-
Ch of Nazarene	3	282	344	401	0.1	0.3
Chr & Miss Al	5	562	536	814	0.3	0.6
CHR–Chs of Christ	2	190	170	245	0.1	0.2
CHR–Int Chs of Christ	1	NR	29	35	0.0	0.0
Evan Cong Ch	6	NR	838	1,016	0.4	0.8
Evan Cov Ch	1	105	195	136	0.1	0.1
Evan Free Ch	4	2,540	NR	2,540	0.9	2.0
FRND–Fr Gen Cf	1	NR	72	87	0.0	0.1
HINDU–I/A Temples	1	NR	NR	1,742	0.6	1.4
HINDU–Post Ren	2	NR	NR	35	0.0	0.0

Religious Group	Number of Congrega-tions	Number of Attendees	Number of Communicant, Confirmed, or Full Members	Adherents		
				Number of Adherents	% of Total Pop.	% of Total Adh.
Ind Fund Churches	2	NR	NR	NR	-	-
Jehovah's Witness	5	NR	NR	NR	-	-
JUD–Conserv	2	533	598	1,615	0.6	1.3
JUD–Orth	2	482	215	670	0.2	0.5
JUD–Reform	1	193	341	921	0.3	0.7
LDS–Comm of Christ	1	NR	161	161	0.1	0.1
LDS–L-D Saints	3	NR	NR	1,682	0.6	1.3
LUTH–Assoc Free Luth	1	NR	NR	NR	-	-
LUTH–E.L.C.A.	36	3,147	9,708	12,683	4.7	9.9
LUTH–Luth Cong Msn Chr	1	153	790	958	0.4	0.7
LUTH–Wisc Ev Luth Syn	1	51	101	117	0.0	0.1
MENN–Amish Undif	7	NR	348	862	0.3	0.7
MENN–Bible Flwshp	3	263	NR	355	0.1	0.3
MENN–Mennonite USA	4	175	151	183	0.1	0.1
METH–AME	8	405	1,500	1,818	0.7	1.4
METH–AME Zion	6	113	593	719	0.3	0.6
METH–C.M.E.	1	0	150	182	0.1	0.1
METH–Un Methodist	52	6,367	14,096	18,666	7.0	14.5
METH–Wesleyan	2	88	64	115	0.0	0.1
Metro Comm Ch	1	56	128	155	0.1	0.1
Muslim Est	4	772	NR	2,356	0.9	1.8
Non-denom Chr Chs	48	7,394	7,402	9,513	3.5	7.4
ORTHE–Bulgar Orth USA	1	15	NR	80	0.0	0.1
ORTHE–Orth Ch in Amer	2	164	NR	249	0.1	0.2
ORTHE–Serb Orth USA	1	43	NR	260	0.1	0.2
ORTHO–Coptic Orth Ch	1	80	NR	100	0.0	0.1
PENT–Assemb of God	8	1,124	563	1,422	0.5	1.1
PENT–Ch Lord Jesus Apos	1	NR	NR	NR	-	-
PENT–Ch of God Proph	1	NR	49	59	0.0	0.0
PENT–COGIC	9	275	1,620	1,964	0.7	1.5
PENT–Fire Bapt Hol Ch	1	NR	NR	NR	-	-
PENT–Full Gosp Bapt	1	NR	NR	NR	-	-
PENT–Int Foursq Gos	1	47	31	38	0.0	0.0
PENT–Intl Pent Holiness	3	197	217	263	0.1	0.2
PENT–United Holy Ch	1	NR	NR	NR	-	-
PRES–Orth Pres Ch	1	93	99	124	0.0	0.1
PRES–Presb Ch (USA)	9	1,266	3,615	4,382	1.6	3.4
PRES–Presb Ch Amer	2	382	494	601	0.2	0.5
Salvation Army	2	90	243	618	0.2	0.5
Sev Day Adv	6	486	845	972	0.4	0.8
Un Breth in Cr	1	181	201	154	0.1	0.1
Un C of Christ	14	1,055	3,104	3,763	1.4	2.9
Unit Univ	1	273	425	602	0.2	0.5
Zoroastrian	0	NR	NR	8	0.0	0.0
DELAWARE	**429**	**36,999**	**67,986**	**358,908**	**64.2**	**100.0**
ANG/EPIS–Anglican NA	4	NR	NR	NR	-	-
ANG/EPIS–Episcopal	27	2,881	8,568	10,507	1.9	2.9
Bahá'í	2	NR	141	141	0.0	0.0
BAPT–Alliance Bapt	1	NR	NR	NR	-	-
BAPT–Amer Bapt USA	24	3,745	6,745	8,178	1.5	2.3
BAPT–Asc Ref Bap Ch Am	1	NR	NR	NR	-	-
BAPT–Consrv Bapt	1	NR	NR	NR	-	-
BAPT–Ind Bapt Flwsp Intl	1	NR	NR	NR	-	-
BAPT–NBC USA	1	100	190	230	0.0	0.1
BAPT–Ref Bapt Ch	1	NR	NR	NR	-	-
BAPT–Reg Bapt Gen As	3	NR	NR	NR	-	-
BAPT–So Bapt Conv	10	1,109	1,466	1,777	0.3	0.5
BRETH–Ch of Brethren	1	18	43	52	0.0	0.0
BUDD–Mahayana	3	NR	NR	618	0.1	0.2
BUDD–Vajrayana	2	NR	NR	163	0.0	0.0
Calv Chpl	1	NR	NR	NR	-	-
Catholic	50	NR	NR	262,506	47.0	73.1
Ch Cr, Scientst	1	NR	NR	NR	-	-
Ch of Nazarene	4	218	306	761	0.1	0.2
Chr & Miss Al	2	135	139	204	0.0	0.1
CHR–Chr Ch (Disc)	1	0	108	131	0.0	0.0
CHR–Chr Chs & Chs Cr	1	NR	250	303	0.1	0.1
CHR–Chs of Christ	4	221	200	265	0.0	0.1
Christian Brethren	1	NR	NR	NR	-	-
CONG–Cong Chr, NA	1	NR	65	79	0.0	0.0
FRND–Evan Fr Ch Intl	1	130	45	55	0.0	0.0
FRND–Fr Gen Cf	15	NR	1,788	2,168	0.4	0.6
Ind Fund Churches	2	NR	NR	NR	-	-

NR–Not Reported - Represents no adherents reported. Percentages may not total 100 due to rounding.

Table 3: Religious Congregations by County and Group: 2010

Religious Group	Number of Congrega-tions	Number of Attendees	Number of Communicant, Confirmed, or Full Members	Adherents: Number of Adherents	Adherents: % of Total Pop.	Adherents: % of Total Adh.
Int Cou Comm Ch	1	NR	NR	NR	-	-
Jehovah's Witness	5	NR	NR	NR	-	-
JUD–Conserv	2	396	444	1,199	0.2	0.3
JUD–Orth	1	43	50	60	0.0	0.0
JUD–Reconst	1	150	192	518	0.1	0.1
JUD–Reform	1	284	501	1,353	0.2	0.4
LUTH–E.L.C.A.	21	1,887	4,762	6,823	1.2	1.9
LUTH–Luth-MO Synod	3	156	233	299	0.1	0.1
MENN–Bible Flwshp	1	234	NR	316	0.1	0.1
MENN–Mennonite USA	4	285	290	352	0.1	0.1
METH–AME	18	370	2,222	2,694	0.5	0.8
METH–AME Zion	2	0	250	303	0.1	0.1
METH–C.M.E.	5	0	1,025	1,243	0.2	0.3
METH–Un Methodist	39	3,370	9,991	12,838	2.3	3.6
METH–Wesleyan	2	278	362	362	0.1	0.1
Metro Comm Ch	1	28	41	50	0.0	0.0
Muslim Est	6	1,364	NR	4,565	0.8	1.3
Non-denom Chr Chs	52	10,915	13,850	14,909	2.7	4.2
ORTHE–Ant Orth of NA	1	24	NR	66	0.0	0.0
ORTHE–Greek Orthodox	3	1,300	NR	4,530	0.8	1.3
ORTHE–Orth Ch in Amer	1	180	NR	290	0.1	0.1
ORTHE–Rus Orth Moscow	2	24	NR	60	0.0	0.0
ORTHE–Ukrainian Orth	1	80	NR	150	0.0	0.0
PENT–Apos Faith Msn	1	NR	35	42	0.0	0.0
PENT–Assemb of God	7	650	274	974	0.2	0.3
PENT–Ch God (Cleve)	7	302	197	239	0.0	0.1
PENT–Ch Lord Jesus Apos	2	NR	NR	NR	-	-
PENT–COGIC	5	356	946	1,147	0.2	0.3
PENT–Full Gosp Bapt	3	NR	NR	NR	-	-
PENT–Int Foursq Gos	1	2	4	5	0.0	0.0
PENT–Un Pent Ch Intl	1	NR	NR	NR	-	-
PENT–United Holy Ch	3	NR	NR	NR	-	-
PENT–Vineyard	1	466	525	637	0.1	0.2
PRES–Korean Pres Amer	2	NR	NR	NR	-	-
PRES–Orth Pres Ch	1	40	23	37	0.0	0.0
PRES–Presb Ch (USA)	35	3,389	9,167	11,114	2.0	3.1
PRES–Presb Ch Amer	6	1,021	1,239	1,566	0.3	0.4
PRES–Ref Pres of NA	1	64	69	79	0.0	0.0
REF–Christian Ref	1	53	73	89	0.0	0.0
Salvation Army	2	68	118	560	0.1	0.2
Sev Day Adv	5	286	498	573	0.1	0.2
Sikh	1	NR	NR	NR	-	-
Tao	1	NR	NR	NR	-	-
Un C of Christ	3	140	277	336	0.1	0.1
Unit Univ	1	237	274	357	0.1	0.1
Zoroastrian	0	NR	NR	35	0.0	0.0
ELK	**46**	**1,636**	**4,693**	**28,351**	**88.7**	**100.0**
ANG/EPIS–Episcopal	2	41	117	121	0.4	0.4
Bahá'í	0	NR	4	4	0.0	0.0
BAPT–Amer Bapt USA	1	58	91	107	0.3	0.4
BAPT–So Bapt Conv	1	14	43	51	0.2	0.2
Catholic	8	NR	NR	22,476	70.4	79.3
Ch of Nazarene	1	35	36	41	0.1	0.1
Chr & Miss Al	1	131	112	248	0.8	0.9
CHR–Chr Chs & Chs Cr	1	NR	70	83	0.3	0.3
Evan Cov Ch	1	43	81	56	0.2	0.2
Jehovah's Witness	1	NR	NR	NR	-	-
LDS–L-D Saints	1	NR	NR	225	0.7	0.8
LUTH–E.L.C.A.	6	237	1,242	1,384	4.3	4.9
METH–Un Methodist	12	598	1,866	2,280	7.1	8.0
METH–Wesleyan	1	104	115	135	0.4	0.5
Non-denom Chr Chs	2	125	130	156	0.5	0.6
PENT–Assemb of God	1	83	37	100	0.3	0.4
PRES–Presb Ch (USA)	4	147	290	343	1.1	1.2
Salvation Army	1	20	31	35	0.1	0.1
Un C of Christ	1	0	428	506	1.6	1.8
ERIE	**312**	**23,932**	**37,707**	**158,280**	**56.4**	**100.0**
ANG/EPIS–Anglican NA	1	NR	NR	NR	-	-
ANG/EPIS–Episcopal	10	520	1,003	1,410	0.5	0.9
Bahá'í	0	NR	25	25	0.0	0.0
BAPT–Amer Bapt USA	10	1,078	2,065	2,494	0.9	1.6

Religious Group	Number of Congrega-tions	Number of Attendees	Number of Communicant, Confirmed, or Full Members	Adherents: Number of Adherents	Adherents: % of Total Pop.	Adherents: % of Total Adh.
BAPT–Converge/BGC	4	1,025	NR	1,230	0.4	0.8
BAPT–N Am Bapt Conf	1	NR	30	36	0.0	0.0
BAPT–Natl Mis Bapt Conv	2	100	200	242	0.1	0.2
BAPT–NBC USA	4	540	1,200	1,449	0.5	0.9
BAPT–Ref Bapt Ch	1	NR	NR	NR	-	-
BAPT–Reg Bapt Gen As	8	NR	NR	NR	-	-
BAPT–So Bapt Conv	4	332	314	379	0.1	0.2
BRETH–Ch of Brethren	1	0	156	188	0.1	0.1
BUDD–Mahayana	1	NR	NR	57	0.0	0.0
BUDD–Vajrayana	1	NR	NR	72	0.0	0.0
Catholic	40	NR	NR	93,998	33.5	59.4
CGOD–Ch God (Ander)	3	163	NR	163	0.1	0.1
Ch Cr, Scientst	2	NR	NR	NR	-	-
Ch of Nazarene	7	388	522	958	0.3	0.6
Chr & Miss Al	11	2,551	1,425	3,910	1.4	2.5
CHR–Chr Ch (Disc)	1	20	106	128	0.0	0.1
CHR–Chs of Christ	2	160	170	190	0.1	0.1
Evan Ch	1	NR	NR	NR	-	-
Evan Free Ch	1	100	NR	100	0.0	0.1
FRND–Fr Gen Cf	1	NR	0	0	0.0	0.0
Jehovah's Witness	11	NR	NR	NR	-	-
JUD–Conserv	1	39	44	119	0.0	0.1
JUD–Reform	1	101	178	481	0.2	0.3
LDS–Comm of Christ	1	NR	158	158	0.1	0.1
LDS–L-D Saints	3	NR	NR	1,525	0.5	1.0
LUTH–E.L.C.A.	22	1,810	5,266	7,595	2.7	4.8
LUTH–Luth-MO Synod	3	197	514	805	0.3	0.5
MENN–Amish Undif	1	NR	67	155	0.1	0.1
MENN–Mennonite USA	1	120	145	175	0.1	0.1
METH–A.W.M.C.	2	65	20	83	0.0	0.1
METH–AME	1	0	60	72	0.0	0.0
METH–AME Zion	2	100	247	298	0.1	0.2
METH–Free Methodist	2	13	15	15	0.0	0.0
METH–Un Methodist	44	4,209	11,498	15,448	5.5	9.8
Muslim Est	3	783	NR	1,826	0.7	1.2
New Apost Ch	1	NR	NR	NR	-	-
Non-denom Chr Chs	23	3,511	4,295	4,856	1.7	3.1
ORTHE–Carp Rus Orth	1	65	NR	100	0.0	0.1
ORTHE–Greek Orthodox	1	170	NR	300	0.1	0.2
ORTHE–Orth Ch in Amer	1	115	NR	130	0.0	0.1
ORTHE–Rus Orth Abroad	1	450	NR	150	0.1	0.1
ORTHE–Rus Orth Moscow	1	15	NR	25	0.0	0.0
ORTHE–Serb Orth USA	1	14	NR	60	0.0	0.0
ORTHO–Armen Ap Etchm	1	15	NR	50	0.0	0.0
PENT–Assemb of God	12	2,248	1,002	4,533	1.6	2.9
PENT–Ch God (Cleve)	3	297	585	706	0.3	0.4
PENT–Ch of God Proph	1	NR	36	43	0.0	0.0
PENT–COGIC	2	0	300	362	0.1	0.2
PENT–Full Gosp Bapt	5	NR	NR	NR	-	-
PENT–I F Chr Assmbl	1	NR	NR	NR	-	-
PENT–Intl Pent Holiness	5	300	494	597	0.2	0.4
PENT–Un Pent Ch Intl	2	NR	NR	NR	-	-
PRES–Korean Pres Amer	1	NR	NR	NR	-	-
PRES–Presb Ch (USA)	21	1,827	4,583	5,534	2.0	3.5
PRES–Presb Ch Amer	2	86	70	99	0.0	0.1
Salvation Army	2	116	252	4,176	1.5	2.6
Sev Day Adv	4	145	252	290	0.1	0.2
Un C of Christ	2	51	264	319	0.1	0.2
Unit Univ	2	93	146	166	0.1	0.1
Unity Ch	1	NR	NR	NR	-	-
FAYETTE	**264**	**12,963**	**26,910**	**60,518**	**44.3**	**100.0**
ANG/EPIS–Anglican NA	2	NR	NR	NR	-	-
Bahá'í	0	NR	8	8	0.0	0.0
BAPT–Amer Bapt Assn	1	NR	85	100	0.1	0.2
BAPT–Amer Bapt USA	12	1,052	2,396	2,823	2.1	4.7
BAPT–NBC USA	1	0	150	177	0.1	0.3
BAPT–Ref Bapt Ch	1	NR	NR	NR	-	-
BAPT–Reg Bapt Gen As	1	NR	NR	NR	-	-
BAPT–So Bapt Conv	4	172	203	239	0.2	0.4
BRETH–Brethren (Ash)	1	NR	80	94	0.1	0.2
BRETH–Ch of Brethren	13	422	996	1,173	0.9	1.9
BRETH–Grace Breth	1	NR	NR	NR	-	-
Catholic	28	NR	NR	24,544	18.0	40.6

NR–Not Reported   - Represents no adherents reported.   Percentages may not total 100 due to rounding.

Table 3: Religious Congregations by County and Group: 2010

Religious Group	Number of Congregations	Number of Attendees	Number of Communicant, Confirmed, or Full Members	Adherents: Number of Adherents	Adherents: % of Total Pop.	Adherents: % of Total Adh.
CGOD–Ch God (Ander)	1	120	NR	120	0.1	0.2
CGOD–Ches God-Gen Con	5	488	630	742	0.5	1.2
Ch of Nazarene	4	132	230	340	0.2	0.6
Chr & Miss Al	4	364	304	839	0.6	1.4
CHR–Chr Ch (Disc)	6	386	1,734	2,043	1.5	3.4
CHR–Chr Chs & Chs Cr	8	NR	1,093	1,288	0.9	2.1
CHR–Chs of Christ	2	188	163	239	0.2	0.4
CHR–Int Chs of Christ	1	NR	163	192	0.1	0.3
Evan Ch	2	NR	NR	NR	-	-
Jehovah's Witness	5	NR	NR	NR	-	-
JUD–Reform	1	12	22	59	0.0	0.1
LDS–Comm of Christ	1	NR	158	158	0.1	0.3
LDS–L-D Saints	1	NR	NR	397	0.3	0.7
LUTH–E.L.C.A.	7	521	1,968	3,086	2.3	5.1
MENN–Bruderhof Comm	2	534	255	434	0.3	0.7
MENN–Mennonite USA	1	45	55	65	0.0	0.1
METH–A.W.M.C.	2	45	27	86	0.1	0.1
METH–AME	6	15	540	636	0.5	1.1
METH–AME Zion	1	0	100	118	0.1	0.2
METH–Free Methodist	13	883	611	915	0.7	1.5
METH–Un Methodist	47	2,091	7,197	8,852	6.5	14.6
Muslim Est	1	260	NR	812	0.6	1.3
Non-denom Chr Chs	22	2,850	3,589	4,160	3.0	6.9
OCATH–Pol Natl Cath	1	NR	NR	NR	-	-
ORTHE–Ant Orth of NA	1	20	NR	41	0.0	0.1
ORTHE–Orth Ch in Amer	4	113	NR	283	0.2	0.5
ORTHE–Rus Orth Abroad	1	7	NR	20	0.0	0.0
PENT–Assemb of God	5	603	389	916	0.7	1.5
PENT–Ch God (Cleve)	5	329	567	668	0.5	1.1
PENT–Ch of God Proph	3	NR	51	60	0.0	0.1
PENT–Un Pent Ch Intl	2	NR	NR	NR	-	-
PRES–Presb Ch (USA)	30	1,176	2,812	3,313	2.4	5.5
Salvation Army	1	39	167	286	0.2	0.5
Sev Day Adv	3	96	167	192	0.1	0.3
FOREST	**19**	**697**	**998**	**2,521**	**32.7**	**100.0**
Catholic	2	NR	NR	485	6.3	19.2
CGOD–Ch God (Ander)	2	145	NR	145	1.9	5.8
Chr & Miss Al	1	47	30	82	1.1	3.3
LUTH–E.L.C.A.	1	40	110	140	1.8	5.6
MENN–Amish Undif	2	NR	59	152	2.0	6.0
METH–Free Methodist	1	8	13	13	0.2	0.5
METH–Un Methodist	5	285	629	1,286	16.7	51.0
Non-denom Chr Chs	2	95	65	119	1.5	4.7
PRES–Presb Ch (USA)	3	77	92	99	1.3	3.9
FRANKLIN	**238**	**19,948**	**31,747**	**51,903**	**34.7**	**100.0**
ANG/EPIS–Episcopal	4	164	382	559	0.4	1.1
Bahá'í	0	NR	7	7	0.0	0.0
BAPT–Amer Bapt Assn	1	NR	40	49	0.0	0.1
BAPT–Amer Bapt USA	1	69	50	61	0.0	0.1
BAPT–Asc Ref Bap Ch Am	1	NR	NR	NR	-	-
BAPT–Ref Bapt Ch	1	NR	NR	NR	-	-
BAPT–So Bapt Conv	5	244	412	505	0.3	1.0
BRETH–Breth in Chr	13	NR	NR	NR	-	-
BRETH–Brethren (Ash)	1	NR	80	98	0.1	0.2
BRETH–Ch of Brethren	11	1,062	1,332	1,632	1.1	3.1
BRETH–Grace Breth	4	NR	NR	NR	-	-
BRETH–Old Ord Rvr Br	3	NR	193	360	0.2	0.7
Catholic	6	NR	NR	10,259	6.9	19.8
CGOD–Ches God-Gen Con	6	1,240	1,079	1,322	0.9	2.5
Ch Cr, Scientst	1	NR	NR	NR	-	-
Ch of Nazarene	2	86	65	415	0.3	0.8
Chr & Miss Al	2	176	109	254	0.2	0.5
CHR–Chr Chs & Chs Cr	1	NR	70	86	0.1	0.2
CHR–Chs of Christ	1	50	40	55	0.0	0.1
Christian Brethren	1	NR	NR	NR	-	-
Evan Assoc RCC	2	NR	NR	NR	-	-
Evan Free Ch	2	160	NR	160	0.1	0.3
FRND–Fr Gen Cf	1	NR	34	42	0.0	0.1
Ind Fund Churches	1	NR	NR	NR	-	-
Jehovah's Witness	2	NR	NR	NR	-	-
LDS–L-D Saints	3	NR	NR	1,557	1.0	3.0
LUTH–E.L.C.A.	19	1,540	4,003	5,393	3.6	10.4
MENN–Amish Undif	8	NR	443	1,073	0.7	2.1
MENN–Cons Menn Conf	1	103	83	102	0.1	0.2
MENN–Menn Chr Fell	1	114	60	114	0.1	0.2
MENN–Mennonite USA	9	1,090	1,108	1,358	0.9	2.6
MENN–Ref Mennonite	1	NR	12	13	0.0	0.0
METH–AME	4	0	570	699	0.5	1.3
METH–AME Zion	1	0	150	184	0.1	0.4
METH–Un Methodist	33	2,970	5,998	7,671	5.1	14.8
Non-denom Chr Chs	28	3,487	4,806	5,118	3.4	9.9
ORTHE–Ant Orth of NA	1	90	NR	120	0.1	0.2
PENT–Assemb of God	11	1,288	824	2,117	1.4	4.1
PENT–Ch God (Cleve)	7	751	1,111	1,362	0.9	2.6
PENT–Int Foursq Gos	1	33	32	39	0.0	0.1
PENT–Un Pent Ch Intl	1	NR	NR	NR	-	-
PRES–Presb Ch (USA)	8	487	2,347	2,876	1.9	5.5
Salvation Army	1	119	126	214	0.1	0.4
Sev Day Adv	3	199	346	398	0.3	0.8
Un Breth in Cr	13	3,625	3,758	3,086	2.1	5.9
Un C of Christ	11	801	2,077	2,545	1.7	4.9
FULTON	**46**	**2,302**	**3,363**	**4,386**	**29.5**	**100.0**
BRETH–Ch of Brethren	3	135	203	247	1.7	5.6
Catholic	1	NR	NR	191	1.3	4.4
CGOD–Ches God-Gen Con	2	135	100	122	0.8	2.8
Ch of Nazarene	2	62	107	112	0.8	2.6
CONG–Cong Chr Add'l	3	NR	229	278	1.9	6.3
CONG–Consrv Cong Chr	1	70	91	111	0.7	2.5
LDS–L-D Saints	1	NR	NR	51	0.3	1.2
LUTH–E.L.C.A.	1	7	30	33	0.2	0.8
MENN–Mennonite USA	2	50	117	142	1.0	3.2
METH–AME	1	0	100	122	0.8	2.8
METH–Un Methodist	14	720	1,192	1,360	9.2	31.0
Non-denom Chr Chs	6	715	762	948	6.4	21.6
PENT–Assemb of God	2	124	51	209	1.4	4.8
PENT–Ch God (Cleve)	1	27	16	19	0.1	0.4
PRES–Presb Ch (USA)	4	194	255	310	2.1	7.1
Sev Day Adv	1	26	45	52	0.4	1.2
Un C of Christ	1	37	65	79	0.5	1.8
GREENE	**96**	**3,843**	**8,922**	**16,186**	**41.8**	**100.0**
ANG/EPIS–Anglican NA	1	NR	NR	NR	-	-
Bahá'í	0	NR	2	2	0.0	0.0
BAPT–Amer Bapt USA	10	488	1,270	1,494	3.9	9.2
BAPT–Reg Bapt Gen As	1	NR	NR	NR	-	-
BAPT–So Bapt Conv	4	230	312	367	0.9	2.3
Catholic	8	NR	NR	4,680	12.1	28.9
CGOD–Ches God-Gen Con	2	27	31	36	0.1	0.2
Ch of Nazarene	2	302	449	637	1.6	3.9
CHR–Chr Ch (Disc)	2	43	441	519	1.3	3.2
CHR–Chr Chs & Chs Cr	3	NR	356	419	1.1	2.6
CHR–Chs of Christ	4	100	100	125	0.3	0.8
Jehovah's Witness	2	NR	NR	NR	-	-
LDS–L-D Saints	1	NR	NR	165	0.4	1.0
LUTH–E.L.C.A.	1	38	95	150	0.4	0.9
METH–A.W.M.C.	1	28	12	31	0.1	0.2
METH–Free Methodist	1	41	29	41	0.1	0.3
METH–Un Methodist	31	1,047	3,465	4,137	10.7	25.6
Missionary Ch	2	80	49	80	0.2	0.5
New Apost Ch	1	NR	NR	NR	-	-
Non-denom Chr Chs	4	245	300	343	0.9	2.1
ORTHE–Serb Orth USA	1	25	NR	73	0.2	0.5
PENT–Assemb of God	3	577	539	1,197	3.1	7.4
PENT–Ch God (Cleve)	2	157	448	527	1.4	3.3
PENT–Ch of God Proph	1	NR	40	47	0.1	0.3
PRES–Presb Ch (USA)	7	284	600	706	1.8	4.4
PRES–Presb Ch Amer	1	131	384	410	1.1	2.5
HUNTINGDON	**131**	**6,568**	**10,847**	**16,974**	**37.0**	**100.0**
ANG/EPIS–Episcopal	1	61	153	153	0.3	0.9
Bahá'í	0	NR	10	10	0.0	0.1
BAPT–Amer Bapt USA	5	198	452	534	1.2	3.1
BRETH–Breth in Chr	2	NR	NR	NR	-	-

NR–Not Reported - Represents no adherents reported. Percentages may not total 100 due to rounding.

Table 3: Religious Congregations by County and Group: 2010

Religious Group	Number of Congrega-tions	Number of Attendees	Number of Communicant, Confirmed, or Full Members	Adherents: Number of Adherents	Adherents: % of Total Pop.	Adherents: % of Total Adh.
BRETH–Ch of Brethren	8	427	1,101	1,301	2.8	7.7
Catholic	4	NR	NR	2,572	5.6	15.2
CGOD–Ch God (Ander)	1	180	NR	180	0.4	1.1
CGOD–Ches God-Gen Con	2	40	25	30	0.1	0.2
Ch of Nazarene	4	284	259	424	0.9	2.5
Chr & Miss Al	3	338	255	642	1.4	3.8
CHR–Chs of Christ	2	62	60	74	0.2	0.4
CONG–Consrv Cong Chr	1	35	72	85	0.2	0.5
Evan Ch	2	NR	NR	NR	-	-
FRND–Fr Gen Cf	1	NR	4	5	0.0	0.0
Jehovah's Witness	1	NR	NR	NR	-	-
LDS–L-D Saints	1	NR	NR	296	0.6	1.7
LUTH–E.L.C.A.	7	274	748	846	1.8	5.0
MENN–Amish Undif	1	NR	55	124	0.3	0.7
MENN–Cons Menn Conf	1	33	18	21	0.0	0.1
MENN–Unaffil Amish-Menn	1	115	94	115	0.3	0.7
METH–AME	2	0	250	295	0.6	1.7
METH–Un Methodist	37	1,541	3,348	4,141	9.0	24.4
METH–Wesleyan	1	78	44	101	0.2	0.6
Non-denom Chr Chs	16	1,690	1,922	2,202	4.8	13.0
ORTHE–Carp Rus Orth	2	12	NR	20	0.0	0.1
PENT–Assemb of God	3	305	158	564	1.2	3.3
PENT–Ch God (Cleve)	1	115	197	233	0.5	1.4
PENT–Ch of God Proph	1	NR	37	44	0.1	0.3
PENT–Elim	1	NR	NR	NR	-	-
PRES–Presb Ch (USA)	13	555	991	1,171	2.6	6.9
Salvation Army	1	39	68	170	0.4	1.0
Un C of Christ	5	186	526	621	1.4	3.7
INDIANA	**214**	**11,092**	**19,374**	**41,605**	**46.8**	**100.0**
ANG/EPIS–Anglican NA	1	NR	NR	NR	-	-
ANG/EPIS–Episcopal	2	54	137	150	0.2	0.4
Bahá'í	0	NR	3	3	0.0	0.0
BAPT–Amer Bapt USA	5	200	467	546	0.6	1.3
BAPT–Consrv Bapt	1	NR	NR	NR	-	-
BAPT–Reg Bapt Gen As	1	NR	NR	NR	-	-
BAPT–So Bapt Conv	3	110	104	121	0.1	0.3
BRETH–Ch of Brethren	5	265	521	609	0.7	1.5
BRETH–Grace Breth	1	NR	NR	NR	-	-
BUDD–Vajrayana	1	NR	NR	71	0.1	0.2
Catholic	17	NR	NR	12,383	13.9	29.8
CGOD–Ch God (Ander)	4	194	NR	194	0.2	0.5
CGOD–Ches God-Gen Con	1	60	31	36	0.0	0.1
Ch of Nazarene	3	164	234	234	0.3	0.6
Chr & Miss Al	5	540	329	801	0.9	1.9
CHR–Chr Ch (Disc)	2	107	362	423	0.5	1.0
CHR–Chr Chs & Chs Cr	3	NR	170	199	0.2	0.5
CHR–Chs of Christ	5	332	337	472	0.5	1.1
Evan Free Ch	1	140	NR	140	0.2	0.3
FRND–Fr Gen Cf	1	NR	0	0	0.0	0.0
Ind Fund Churches	2	NR	NR	NR	-	-
Jehovah's Witness	2	NR	NR	NR	-	-
JUD–Reform	1	13	23	62	0.1	0.1
LDS–L-D Saints	1	NR	NR	304	0.3	0.7
LUTH–E.L.C.A.	12	698	2,280	3,327	3.7	8.0
LUTH–Nor Amer Luth C	2	NR	NR	NR	-	-
MENN–Amish Undif	17	NR	961	2,525	2.8	6.1
MENN–Menn Chr Fell	1	147	67	147	0.2	0.4
METH–A.W.M.C.	10	352	144	471	0.5	1.1
METH–AME Zion	1	0	150	175	0.2	0.4
METH–Evan Meth Ch	1	NR	NR	NR	-	-
METH–Free Methodist	2	85	84	86	0.1	0.2
METH–Un Methodist	34	2,334	6,212	8,307	9.3	20.0
METH–Wesleyan	2	163	119	212	0.2	0.5
Muslim Est	1	260	NR	812	0.9	2.0
Non-denom Chr Chs	21	2,272	2,717	3,196	3.6	7.7
ORTHE–Carp Rus Orth	2	60	NR	151	0.2	0.4
ORTHE–Orth Ch in Amer	2	29	NR	52	0.1	0.1
ORTHE–Rus Orth Abroad	1	55	NR	100	0.1	0.2
ORTHE–Ukrainian Orth	1	45	NR	120	0.1	0.3
PENT–Assemb of God	5	590	393	700	0.8	1.7
PENT–COGIC	1	100	50	58	0.1	0.1
PRES–Orth Pres Ch	1	41	36	46	0.1	0.1
PRES–Presb Ch (USA)	24	1,505	3,140	3,668	4.1	8.8

Religious Group	Number of Congrega-tions	Number of Attendees	Number of Communicant, Confirmed, or Full Members	Adherents: Number of Adherents	Adherents: % of Total Pop.	Adherents: % of Total Adh.
Salvation Army	1	30	82	431	0.5	1.0
Sev Day Adv	2	78	136	157	0.2	0.4
Un C of Christ	1	14	17	20	0.0	0.0
Unit Univ	1	55	68	91	0.1	0.2
Zoroastrian	0	NR	NR	5	0.0	0.0
JEFFERSON	**144**	**5,953**	**10,579**	**26,611**	**58.9**	**100.0**
ANG/EPIS–Episcopal	1	29	47	56	0.1	0.2
Bahá'í	0	NR	5	5	0.0	0.0
BAPT–Amer Bapt USA	3	163	337	403	0.9	1.5
BAPT–Consrv Bapt	2	NR	NR	NR	-	-
BAPT–So Bapt Conv	1	NR	NR	NR	-	-
Catholic	12	NR	NR	10,341	22.9	38.9
CGOD–Ch God (Ander)	3	723	NR	723	1.6	2.7
CGOD–Ches God-Gen Con	1	11	12	14	0.0	0.1
Ch of Nazarene	4	126	186	287	0.6	1.1
Chr & Miss Al	4	384	261	599	1.3	2.3
CHR–Chr Chs & Chs Cr	2	NR	175	209	0.5	0.8
CHR–Chs of Christ	4	221	201	272	0.6	1.0
CONG–Consrv Cong Chr	1	40	50	60	0.1	0.2
Jehovah's Witness	1	NR	NR	NR	-	-
LDS–L-D Saints	1	NR	NR	359	0.8	1.3
LUTH–E.L.C.A.	7	190	577	878	1.9	3.3
LUTH–Luth–MO Synod	1	20	30	30	0.1	0.1
MENN–Amish Undif	10	NR	430	1,129	2.5	4.2
MENN–Cons Menn Conf	1	0	6	7	0.0	0.0
METH–A.W.M.C.	1	42	7	42	0.1	0.2
METH–Free Methodist	3	35	37	39	0.1	0.1
METH–Un Methodist	49	2,173	5,139	7,083	15.7	26.6
Missionary Ch	1	46	29	46	0.1	0.2
Non-denom Chr Chs	10	790	955	1,055	2.3	4.0
PENT–Assemb of God	3	184	155	544	1.2	2.0
PENT–Ch God (Cleve)	1	58	43	51	0.1	0.2
PRES–Presb Ch (USA)	14	531	1,449	1,735	3.8	6.5
Salvation Army	1	39	137	272	0.6	1.0
Un C of Christ	2	148	311	372	0.8	1.4
JUNIATA	**68**	**4,015**	**6,755**	**11,153**	**45.3**	**100.0**
BAPT–Consrv Bapt	2	NR	NR	NR	-	-
BAPT–So Bapt Conv	1	140	116	143	0.6	1.3
BRETH–Breth in Chr	2	NR	NR	NR	-	-
BRETH–Ch of Brethren	4	287	349	429	1.7	3.8
Catholic	1	NR	NR	264	1.1	2.4
HINDU–I/A Temples	1	NR	NR	1,562	6.3	14.0
Jehovah's Witness	1	NR	NR	NR	-	-
JUD–Orth	1	133	50	185	0.8	1.7
LUTH–Ch of Luth Br	1	66	58	181	0.7	1.6
LUTH–E.L.C.A.	8	555	1,537	1,885	7.7	16.9
MENN–Amish Undif	7	NR	411	973	3.9	8.7
MENN–Beachy Amish-Menn	1	193	116	193	0.8	1.7
MENN–Mennonite USA	4	252	300	369	1.5	3.3
METH–Un Methodist	16	991	2,114	2,773	11.3	24.9
Non-denom Chr Chs	5	915	865	1,177	4.8	10.6
PENT–Assemb of God	1	35	35	35	0.1	0.3
PENT–Ch God (Cleve)	1	26	67	82	0.3	0.7
PENT–Ch of God Proph	1	NR	11	14	0.1	0.1
PRES–Presb Ch (USA)	7	343	560	688	2.8	6.2
Sev Day Adv	1	24	43	49	0.2	0.4
Un C of Christ	2	55	123	151	0.6	1.4
LACKAWANNA	**218**	**12,538**	**21,824**	**133,720**	**62.4**	**100.0**
ANG/EPIS–Anglican NA	1	NR	NR	NR	-	-
ANG/EPIS–Episcopal	6	347	728	1,375	0.6	1.0
Bahá'í	0	NR	7	7	0.0	0.0
BAPT–Amer Bapt USA	9	705	1,853	2,192	1.0	1.6
BAPT–Ref Bapt Ch	1	NR	NR	NR	-	-
BAPT–Reg Bapt Gen As	5	NR	NR	NR	-	-
BAPT–So Bapt Conv	3	315	74	88	0.0	0.1
BUDD–Mahayana	2	NR	NR	22	0.0	0.0
Catholic	54	NR	NR	96,140	44.8	71.9
CGOD–Ch God (Ander)	1	55	NR	55	0.0	0.0
Chr & Miss Al	2	76	61	131	0.1	0.1
CHR–Chr Ch (Disc)	1	0	68	80	0.0	0.1

NR–Not Reported - Represents no adherents reported. Percentages may not total 100 due to rounding.

Table 3: Religious Congregations by County and Group: 2010

Religious Group	Number of Congrega-tions	Number of Attendees	Number of Communicant, Confirmed, or Full Members	Adherents: Number of Adherents	Adherents: % of Total Pop.	Adherents: % of Total Adh.
CHR–Chr Chs & Chs Cr	1	NR	0	0	0.0	0.0
CHR–Chs of Christ	1	37	30	40	0.0	0.0
Evan Free Ch	1	200	NR	200	0.1	0.1
HINDU–I/A Temples	1	NR	NR	1,742	0.8	1.3
HINDU–Post Ren	1	NR	NR	77	0.0	0.1
Jehovah's Witness	2	NR	NR	NR	-	-
JUD–Conserv	1	175	196	529	0.2	0.4
JUD–Orth	3	666	250	925	0.4	0.7
JUD–Reform	1	96	170	459	0.2	0.3
LDS–Comm of Christ	1	NR	161	161	0.1	0.1
LDS–L-D Saints	1	NR	NR	788	0.4	0.6
LUTH–E.L.C.A.	5	319	1,111	1,331	0.6	1.0
LUTH–Luth–MO Synod	3	232	731	898	0.4	0.7
METH–AME	2	231	481	569	0.3	0.4
METH–Free Methodist	1	31	22	31	0.0	0.0
METH–Prim Meth Ch	5	NR	NR	NR	-	-
METH–Un Methodist	34	2,004	8,059	10,184	4.7	7.6
Non-denom Chr Chs	19	3,285	3,445	4,306	2.0	3.2
OCATH–Pol Natl Cath	4	NR	NR	NR	-	-
ORTHE–Carp Rus Orth	3	203	NR	500	0.2	0.4
ORTHE–Greek Orthodox	1	15	NR	70	0.0	0.1
ORTHE–Orth Ch in Amer	5	415	NR	746	0.3	0.6
ORTHE–Rus Orth Abroad	3	296	NR	730	0.3	0.5
ORTHE–Rus Orth Moscow	1	60	NR	150	0.1	0.1
ORTHE–Ukrainian Orth	2	140	NR	330	0.2	0.2
PENT–Assemb of God	7	1,321	971	4,768	2.2	3.6
PENT–Ch God (Cleve)	1	45	30	35	0.0	0.0
PENT–Elim	1	NR	NR	NR	-	-
PRES–As Ref Pres Ch	1	NR	44	52	0.0	0.0
PRES–Presb Ch (USA)	11	818	2,270	2,685	1.3	2.0
PRES–Presb Ch Amer	1	85	99	125	0.1	0.1
REF–Un Ref Chs N.A.	1	NR	NR	NR	-	-
Salvation Army	1	130	117	202	0.1	0.2
Sev Day Adv	1	58	101	116	0.1	0.1
Un C of Christ	6	178	745	881	0.4	0.7
LANCASTER	**810**	**90,478**	**134,524**	**255,121**	**49.1**	**100.0**
ANG/EPIS–Anglican NA	1	NR	NR	NR	-	-
ANG/EPIS–Episcopal	10	1,067	2,356	2,784	0.5	1.1
Bahá'í	1	NR	121	121	0.0	0.0
BAPT–Amer Bapt Assn	1	NR	70	87	0.0	0.0
BAPT–Amer Bapt USA	3	317	353	437	0.1	0.2
BAPT–Consrv Bapt	2	NR	NR	NR	-	-
BAPT–NBC USA	1	450	750	927	0.2	0.4
BAPT–Ref Bapt Ch	1	NR	NR	NR	-	-
BAPT–So Bapt Conv	17	835	1,452	1,796	0.3	0.7
BRETH–Breth in Chr	20	NR	NR	NR	-	-
BRETH–Ch of Brethren	27	4,758	7,252	8,968	1.7	3.5
BRETH–Grace Breth	8	NR	NR	NR	-	-
BRETH–Old Ord Rvr Br	1	NR	113	177	0.0	0.1
BRETH–United Zion Ch	7	NR	425	526	0.1	0.2
BUDD–Mahayana	1	NR	NR	505	0.1	0.2
BUDD–Vajrayana	1	NR	NR	14	0.0	0.0
Calv Chpl	1	NR	NR	NR	-	-
Catholic	20	NR	NR	51,292	9.9	20.1
CGOD–Ches God-Gen Con	21	2,077	2,428	3,002	0.6	1.2
Ch Cr, Scientst	1	NR	NR	NR	-	-
Ch of Nazarene	3	1,115	1,243	2,269	0.4	0.9
Chr & Miss Al	7	1,702	1,125	2,575	0.5	1.0
CHR–Chr Ch (Disc)	1	25	46	57	0.0	0.0
CHR–Chr Chs & Chs Cr	2	NR	530	655	0.1	0.3
CHR–Chs of Christ	3	195	206	278	0.1	0.1
Evan Assoc RCC	3	NR	NR	NR	-	-
Evan Cong Ch	27	NR	3,478	4,301	0.8	1.7
Evan Free Ch	4	1,210	NR	1,210	0.2	0.5
FRND–Consrv Yr Mtgs	1	NR	10	12	0.0	0.0
FRND–Fr Gen Cf	2	NR	206	255	0.0	0.1
FRND–Fr Gen Cf & Un Mtg	2	NR	79	98	0.0	0.0
Ind Fund Churches	8	NR	NR	NR	-	-
Int Cou Comm Ch	1	NR	NR	NR	-	-
Jehovah's Witness	6	NR	NR	NR	-	-
JUD–Conserv	1	113	127	343	0.1	0.1
JUD–Orth	1	266	100	370	0.1	0.1
JUD–Reform	1	189	334	902	0.2	0.4
LDS–L-D Saints	3	NR	NR	1,819	0.4	0.7
LUTH–E.L.C.A.	43	6,297	17,975	22,429	4.3	8.8
LUTH–Luth–MO Synod	2	175	302	389	0.1	0.2
LUTH–Nor Amer Luth C	2	NR	NR	NR	-	-
MENN–Amish Undif	164	NR	11,461	26,270	5.1	10.3
MENN–Beachy Amish-Menn	4	1,014	621	1,014	0.2	0.4
MENN–Bible Flwshp	4	985	NR	1,330	0.3	0.5
MENN–Mara Amish-Menn	2	409	235	409	0.1	0.2
MENN–Mennonite USA	91	10,835	12,312	15,225	2.9	6.0
MENN–Ref Mennonite	1	NR	76	84	0.0	0.0
MENN–Unaffil Amish-Menn	2	458	250	458	0.1	0.2
METH–AME	3	210	610	754	0.1	0.3
METH–Un Methodist	75	9,368	21,923	28,676	5.5	11.2
METH–Wesleyan	2	103	65	134	0.0	0.1
Metro Comm Ch	1	77	0	95	0.0	0.0
MJEW–Assoc Mes Cong	1	NR	NR	NR	-	-
MORAV–Morav Ch-North	2	332	853	987	0.2	0.4
Muslim Est	1	260	NR	812	0.2	0.3
New Apost Ch	1	NR	NR	NR	-	-
Non-denom Chr Chs	97	33,502	25,459	43,103	8.3	16.9
ORTHE–Greek Orthodox	1	500	NR	1,250	0.2	0.5
ORTHO–Coptic Orth Ch	1	210	NR	350	0.1	0.1
PENT–Assemb of God	14	2,966	2,030	3,831	0.7	1.5
PENT–Ch God (Cleve)	3	607	679	840	0.2	0.3
PENT–Ch Lord Jesus Apos	1	NR	NR	NR	-	-
PENT–COGIC	3	75	390	482	0.1	0.2
PENT–Elim	1	NR	NR	NR	-	-
PENT–Int Foursq Gos	1	20	22	27	0.0	0.0
PENT–Un Pent Ch Intl	1	NR	NR	NR	-	-
PENT–Vineyard	1	75	95	117	0.0	0.0
PRES–Korean Amer Pres	1	NR	NR	NR	-	-
PRES–Korean Pres Amer	1	NR	NR	NR	-	-
PRES–Presb Ch (USA)	16	2,290	5,213	6,446	1.2	2.5
PRES–Presb Ch Amer	7	2,116	2,287	2,749	0.5	1.1
REF–Can Amer Ref	1	NR	NR	NR	-	-
REF–Comm Ref Evan	1	NR	NR	NR	-	-
REF–Un Ref Chs N.A.	1	NR	NR	NR	-	-
Salvation Army	2	140	257	492	0.1	0.2
Sev Day Adv	5	314	547	629	0.1	0.2
Un C of Christ	28	2,601	7,528	9,309	1.8	3.6
Unit Univ	1	220	530	650	0.1	0.3
LAWRENCE	**164**	**11,084**	**20,154**	**53,495**	**58.7**	**100.0**
ANG/EPIS–Episcopal	1	90	145	146	0.2	0.3
Bahá'í	0	NR	15	15	0.0	0.0
BAPT–Amer Bapt USA	2	45	71	84	0.1	0.2
BAPT–Converge/BGC	1	400	NR	480	0.5	0.9
BAPT–NBC USA	1	50	65	77	0.1	0.1
Catholic	10	NR	NR	25,113	27.6	46.9
CGOD–Ch God (Ander)	2	230	NR	230	0.3	0.4
CGOD–Ches God-Gen Con	1	166	133	158	0.2	0.3
Ch of Nazarene	2	0	0	26	0.0	0.0
Chr & Miss Al	9	697	462	1,039	1.1	1.9
CHR–Chr Ch (Disc)	1	60	319	379	0.4	0.7
CHR–Chr Chs & Chs Cr	5	NR	419	498	0.5	0.9
CHR–Chs of Christ	1	25	20	30	0.0	0.1
Evan Cov Ch	1	75	110	98	0.1	0.2
Jehovah's Witness	2	NR	NR	NR	-	-
LDS–L-D Saints	1	NR	NR	327	0.4	0.6
LUTH–E.L.C.A.	4	254	989	1,333	1.5	2.5
LUTH–Luth–MO Synod	1	83	152	175	0.2	0.3
MENN–Amish Undif	10	NR	647	1,447	1.6	2.7
MENN–Mennonite USA	1	45	27	32	0.0	0.1
METH–A.W.M.C.	1	28	15	38	0.0	0.1
METH–AME	1	30	80	95	0.1	0.2
METH–AME Zion	1	80	150	178	0.2	0.3
METH–Evan Meth Ch	1	NR	NR	NR	-	-
METH–Free Methodist	3	181	137	198	0.2	0.4
METH–Un Methodist	16	957	3,133	4,232	4.6	7.9
METH–Wesleyan	1	87	64	113	0.1	0.2
Muslim Est	1	260	NR	812	0.9	1.5
Non-denom Chr Chs	18	2,820	4,526	4,647	5.1	8.7
OCATH–Pol Natl Cath	1	NR	NR	NR	-	-
ORTHE–Ant Orth of NA	1	157	NR	433	0.5	0.8

NR–Not Reported - Represents no adherents reported. Percentages may not total 100 due to rounding.

Table 3: Religious Congregations by County and Group: 2010

Religious Group	Number of Congrega-tions	Number of Attendees	Number of Communicant, Confirmed, or Full Members	Adherents		
				Number of Adherents	% of Total Pop.	% of Total Adh.
ORTHE–Carp Rus Orth	1	19	NR	31	0.0	0.1
ORTHE–Greek Orthodox	1	60	NR	150	0.2	0.3
ORTHE–Orth Ch in Amer	3	63	NR	107	0.1	0.2
ORTHE–Ukrainian Orth	1	18	NR	40	0.0	0.1
PENT–Assemb of God	5	537	355	967	1.1	1.8
PENT–Ch God (Cleve)	1	105	190	226	0.2	0.4
PENT–COGIC	3	170	326	388	0.4	0.7
PENT–I F Chr Assmbl	1	NR	NR	NR	-	-
PENT–Int Foursq Gos	1	32	24	29	0.0	0.1
PENT–Intl Pent Holiness	1	50	50	59	0.1	0.1
PENT–United Holy Ch	1	NR	NR	NR	-	-
PRES–Evan Presby Ch	1	NR	235	279	0.3	0.5
PRES–Orth Pres Ch	1	40	30	41	0.0	0.1
PRES–Presb Ch (USA)	35	2,667	6,572	7,816	8.6	14.6
PRES–Presb Ch Amer	2	249	262	375	0.4	0.7
PRES–Ref Pres of NA	1	52	66	74	0.1	0.1
Salvation Army	1	28	118	296	0.3	0.6
Sev Day Adv	1	32	55	63	0.1	0.1
Un Breth in Cr	2	142	192	121	0.1	0.2
LEBANON	**193**	**16,651**	**30,405**	**57,007**	**42.7**	**100.0**
ANG/EPIS–Episcopal	1	126	345	487	0.4	0.9
Bahá'í	0	NR	5	5	0.0	0.0
BAPT–Converge/BGC	1	75	NR	90	0.1	0.2
BAPT–So Bapt Conv	2	52	52	63	0.0	0.1
BRETH–Breth in Chr	2	NR	NR	NR	-	-
BRETH–Ch of Brethren	11	1,431	2,509	3,051	2.3	5.4
BRETH–Grace Breth	2	NR	NR	NR	-	-
BRETH–United Zion Ch	5	NR	160	195	0.1	0.3
Calv Chpl	1	NR	NR	NR	-	-
Catholic	8	NR	NR	12,218	9.1	21.4
Ch Christ Chr Union	1	NR	NR	NR	-	-
Ch of Nazarene	1	0	0	0	0.0	0.0
Chr & Miss Al	2	90	0	178	0.1	0.3
CHR–Chs of Christ	1	94	69	115	0.1	0.2
Evan Assoc RCC	1	NR	NR	NR	-	-
Evan Cong Ch	9	NR	1,376	1,673	1.3	2.9
Evan Free Ch	2	1,080	NR	1,080	0.8	1.9
FRND–Fr Gen Cf	1	NR	0	0	0.0	0.0
Ind Fund Churches	3	NR	NR	NR	-	-
Jehovah's Witness	2	NR	NR	NR	-	-
LDS–L-D Saints	1	NR	NR	477	0.4	0.8
LUTH–E.L.C.A.	18	1,754	5,591	7,958	6.0	14.0
LUTH–Nor Amer Luth C	4	NR	NR	NR	-	-
MENN–Amish Undif	6	NR	332	728	0.5	1.3
MENN–Bible Flwshp	1	270	NR	365	0.3	0.6
MENN–Mennonite USA	7	369	316	384	0.3	0.7
METH–AME	1	50	45	55	0.0	0.1
METH–Un Methodist	33	4,441	9,056	12,963	9.7	22.7
METH–Wesleyan	1	21	19	27	0.0	0.0
Missionary Ch	1	20	18	20	0.0	0.0
MORAV–Morav Ch-North	1	51	108	156	0.1	0.3
Muslim Est	1	260	NR	812	0.6	1.4
Non-denom Chr Chs	24	3,330	3,565	4,424	3.3	7.8
ORTHE–Serb Orth USA	1	20	NR	68	0.1	0.1
ORTHO–Coptic Orth Ch	1	85	NR	160	0.1	0.3
PENT–Assemb of God	4	518	175	1,112	0.8	2.0
PENT–Ch God (Cleve)	2	214	45	55	0.0	0.1
PRES–Korean Pres Amer	1	NR	NR	NR	-	-
PRES–Presb Ch (USA)	2	256	517	629	0.5	1.1
PRES–Presb Ch Amer	1	0	42	55	0.0	0.1
Salvation Army	1	48	40	92	0.1	0.2
Sev Day Adv	2	66	115	132	0.1	0.2
Un C of Christ	22	1,930	5,905	7,180	5.4	12.6
Unity Ch	1	NR	NR	NR	-	-
LEHIGH	**296**	**32,504**	**64,747**	**176,420**	**50.5**	**100.0**
ANG/EPIS–Episcopal	6	521	1,219	1,322	0.4	0.7
Bahá'í	0	NR	58	58	0.0	0.0
BAPT–Amer Bapt USA	3	360	538	656	0.2	0.4
BAPT–Consrv Bapt	2	NR	NR	NR	-	-
BAPT–NBC USA	1	400	400	488	0.1	0.3
BAPT–Ref Bapt Ch	1	NR	NR	NR	-	-
BAPT–So Bapt Conv	1	55	50	61	0.0	0.0
BRETH–Grace Breth	1	NR	NR	NR	-	-
BUDD–Mahayana	1	NR	NR	11	0.0	0.0
Catholic	27	NR	NR	68,213	19.5	38.7
CGOD–Ch God (Ander)	1	55	NR	55	0.0	0.0
Ch Cr, Scientst	1	NR	NR	NR	-	-
Ch of Nazarene	2	177	415	415	0.1	0.2
Chr & Miss Al	3	272	167	388	0.1	0.2
CHR–Chr Chs & Chs Cr	2	NR	113	138	0.0	0.1
CHR–Chs of Christ	1	65	80	100	0.0	0.1
Christian Brethren	1	NR	NR	NR	-	-
Evan Cong Ch	9	NR	1,428	1,741	0.5	1.0
Evan Free Ch	3	1,430	NR	1,430	0.4	0.8
HINDU–I/A Temples	2	NR	NR	10,862	3.1	6.2
HINDU–Post Ren	1	NR	NR	10	0.0	0.0
HINDU–Renaiss	1	NR	NR	12	0.0	0.0
HINDU–Trad Temples	1	NR	NR	300	0.1	0.2
Ind Fund Churches	1	NR	NR	NR	-	-
Jehovah's Witness	7	NR	NR	NR	-	-
JUD–Conserv	1	420	471	1,272	0.4	0.7
JUD–Orth	2	576	250	800	0.2	0.5
JUD–Reconst	1	44	56	151	0.0	0.1
JUD–Reform	1	248	438	1,183	0.3	0.7
LDS–L-D Saints	4	NR	NR	1,862	0.5	1.1
LUTH–E.L.C.A.	51	5,894	21,816	28,856	8.3	16.4
LUTH–Luth-MO Synod	1	102	127	185	0.1	0.1
MENN–Bible Flwshp	7	2,019	NR	2,726	0.8	1.5
MENN–Mennonite USA	4	159	214	261	0.1	0.1
METH–AME Zion	1	0	150	183	0.1	0.1
METH–C.M.E.	1	0	150	183	0.1	0.1
METH–Free Methodist	4	322	351	365	0.1	0.2
METH–Prim Meth Ch	1	NR	NR	NR	-	-
METH–Un Methodist	8	2,078	4,095	5,943	1.7	3.4
METH–Wesleyan	4	263	265	341	0.1	0.2
Metro Comm Ch	1	116	132	161	0.0	0.1
Missionary Ch	1	118	150	150	0.0	0.1
MORAV–Morav Ch-North	4	321	911	1,195	0.3	0.7
Muslim Est	4	1,044	NR	3,252	0.9	1.8
New Apost Ch	1	NR	NR	NR	-	-
Non-denom Chr Chs	36	6,732	7,377	8,939	2.6	5.1
ORTHE–Ant Orth of NA	2	420	NR	1,710	0.5	1.0
ORTHE–Carp Rus Orth	1	75	NR	150	0.0	0.1
ORTHE–Orth Ch in Amer	1	30	NR	65	0.0	0.0
ORTHE–Ukrainian Orth	1	180	NR	700	0.2	0.4
PENT–Assemb of God	6	1,123	432	1,486	0.4	0.8
PENT–Ch God (Cleve)	3	200	180	219	0.1	0.1
PENT–Ch of God by Faith	1	NR	NR	NR	-	-
PENT–Int Foursq Gos	1	27	31	38	0.0	0.0
PRES–Free Pres NA	1	NR	NR	NR	-	-
PRES–Orth Pres Ch	1	134	100	146	0.0	0.1
PRES–Presb Ch (USA)	6	1,232	3,115	3,797	1.1	2.2
PRES–Presb Ch Amer	3	385	272	351	0.1	0.2
Salvation Army	2	95	206	381	0.1	0.2
Sev Day Adv	3	364	633	728	0.2	0.4
Un C of Christ	46	4,448	18,357	22,378	6.4	12.7
Unity Ch	1	NR	NR	NR	-	-
Zoroastrian	0	NR	NR	3	0.0	0.0
LUZERNE	**355**	**17,134**	**34,770**	**189,155**	**58.9**	**100.0**
ANG/EPIS–Episcopal	10	549	1,237	1,755	0.5	0.9
Bahá'í	0	NR	26	26	0.0	0.0
BAPT–Amer Bapt USA	9	743	924	1,088	0.3	0.6
BAPT–Ref Bapt Ch	1	NR	NR	NR	-	-
BAPT–Reg Bapt Gen As	2	NR	NR	NR	-	-
BAPT–So Bapt Conv	3	225	447	526	0.2	0.3
BRETH–Breth in Chr	1	NR	NR	NR	-	-
Catholic	68	NR	NR	138,000	43.0	73.0
Ch of Nazarene	1	25	17	35	0.0	0.0
Chr & Miss Al	3	223	101	324	0.1	0.2
CHR–Chr Ch (Disc)	1	0	305	359	0.1	0.2
CHR–Chr Chs & Chs Cr	6	NR	1,005	1,184	0.4	0.6
CHR–Chs of Christ	4	147	125	191	0.1	0.1
CONG–Consrv Cong Chr	1	50	140	165	0.1	0.1
Evan Free Ch	1	260	NR	260	0.1	0.1

NR–Not Reported - Represents no adherents reported. Percentages may not total 100 due to rounding.

Table 3: Religious Congregations by County and Group: 2010

Religious Group	Number of Congregations	Number of Attendees	Number of Communicant, Confirmed, or Full Members	Adherents: Number of Adherents	Adherents: % of Total Pop.	Adherents: % of Total Adh.
FRND–Fr Gen Cf	1	NR	35	41	0.0	0.0
Ind Fund Churches	1	NR	NR	NR	-	-
Jehovah's Witness	6	NR	NR	NR	-	-
JUD–Conserv	2	345	387	1,045	0.3	0.6
JUD–Orth	2	691	260	960	0.3	0.5
JUD–Reform	2	103	181	489	0.2	0.3
LDS–L-D Saints	1	NR	NR	884	0.3	0.5
LUTH–E.L.C.A.	26	2,070	6,718	8,813	2.7	4.7
LUTH–Luth-MO Synod	4	295	866	1,111	0.3	0.6
MENN–Mennonite USA	2	85	94	111	0.0	0.1
METH–AME	1	0	100	118	0.0	0.1
METH–Free Methodist	5	193	206	231	0.1	0.1
METH–Prim Meth Ch	10	NR	NR	NR	-	-
METH–Un Methodist	55	2,886	11,373	13,647	4.3	7.2
Muslim Est	2	522	NR	1,626	0.5	0.9
Non-denom Chr Chs	31	2,961	3,323	4,046	1.3	2.1
OCATH–Pol Natl Cath	7	NR	NR	NR	-	-
ORTHE–Ant Orth of NA	1	110	NR	250	0.1	0.1
ORTHE–Carp Rus Orth	1	70	NR	127	0.0	0.1
ORTHE–Georgian Orth	1	20	NR	35	0.0	0.0
ORTHE–Greek Orthodox	2	150	NR	290	0.1	0.2
ORTHE–Orth Ch in Amer	6	415	NR	890	0.3	0.5
ORTHE–Rus Orth Moscow	1	60	NR	75	0.0	0.0
PENT–Assemb of God	12	1,640	994	3,150	1.0	1.7
PENT–Ch God (Cleve)	1	51	28	33	0.0	0.0
PENT–Ch of God Proph	1	NR	20	24	0.0	0.0
PENT–I F Chr Assmbl	1	NR	NR	NR	-	-
PENT–Int Foursq Gos	1	27	31	37	0.0	0.0
PENT–Pent Ch of God	1	70	NR	109	0.0	0.1
PENT–Un Pent Ch Intl	3	NR	NR	NR	-	-
PRES–AmPres	1	NR	NR	NR	-	-
PRES–Korean Pres Amer	1	NR	NR	NR	-	-
PRES–Presb Ch (USA)	23	957	2,360	2,780	0.9	1.5
PRES–Ref Pres of NA	1	40	26	39	0.0	0.0
Salvation Army	3	149	343	611	0.2	0.3
Sev Day Adv	6	158	274	315	0.1	0.2
Un C of Christ	17	787	2,760	3,251	1.0	1.7
Unit Univ	1	57	64	104	0.0	0.1
Unity Ch	1	NR	NR	NR	-	-
LYCOMING	**205**	**14,471**	**27,423**	**56,867**	**49.0**	**100.0**
ANG/EPIS–Episcopal	7	322	696	776	0.7	1.4
Bahá'í	0	NR	13	13	0.0	0.0
BAPT–Amer Bapt USA	11	779	1,695	2,015	1.7	3.5
BAPT–Consrv Bapt	1	NR	NR	NR	-	-
BAPT–Reg Bapt Gen As	1	NR	NR	NR	-	-
BAPT–So Bapt Conv	3	332	605	719	0.6	1.3
BRETH–Breth in Chr	1	NR	NR	NR	-	-
BUDD–Mahayana	1	NR	NR	11	0.0	0.0
Catholic	11	NR	NR	18,500	15.9	32.5
CGOD–Ch God (Ander)	1	200	NR	200	0.2	0.4
Ch of Nazarene	2	115	97	161	0.1	0.3
Chr & Miss Al	5	637	359	1,064	0.9	1.9
CHR–Chr Ch (Disc)	1	68	180	214	0.2	0.4
CHR–Chr Chs & Chs Cr	9	NR	1,295	1,539	1.3	2.7
CHR–Chs of Christ	1	42	30	59	0.1	0.1
Evan Free Ch	1	80	NR	80	0.1	0.1
FRND–Evan Fr Ch Intl	1	193	131	156	0.1	0.3
FRND–Fr Gen Cf	1	NR	24	29	0.0	0.1
Jehovah's Witness	3	NR	NR	NR	-	-
JUD–Reform	1	24	43	116	0.1	0.2
LDS–L-D Saints	1	NR	NR	639	0.6	1.1
LUTH–E.L.C.A.	19	1,469	5,425	7,023	6.0	12.3
LUTH–Luth Cong Msn Chr	1	155	319	379	0.3	0.7
MENN–Amish Undif	5	NR	232	620	0.5	1.1
MENN–Mennonite USA	3	307	161	191	0.2	0.3
METH–AME	1	0	150	178	0.2	0.3
METH–AME Zion	2	0	200	238	0.2	0.4
METH–Free Methodist	1	119	93	119	0.1	0.2
METH–Un Methodist	64	4,509	9,835	13,219	11.4	23.2
METH–Wesleyan	3	401	220	521	0.4	0.9
Muslim Est	1	260	NR	812	0.7	1.4
Non-denom Chr Chs	19	2,715	3,093	3,596	3.1	6.3
ORTHE–Orth Ch in Amer	1	78	NR	121	0.1	0.2
PENT–Assemb of God	5	484	293	819	0.7	1.4
PENT–Ch God (Cleve)	1	14	14	17	0.0	0.0
PENT–Un Pent Ch Intl	2	NR	NR	NR	-	-
PRES–Orth Pres Ch	1	182	178	220	0.2	0.4
PRES–Presb Ch (USA)	10	720	1,357	1,613	1.4	2.8
Salvation Army	1	52	205	325	0.3	0.6
Sev Day Adv	1	91	158	182	0.2	0.3
Un C of Christ	1	123	322	383	0.3	0.7
MCKEAN	**87**	**4,158**	**8,000**	**20,567**	**47.3**	**100.0**
ANG/EPIS–Episcopal	4	114	223	239	0.6	1.2
Bahá'í	0	NR	2	2	0.0	0.0
BAPT–Amer Bapt USA	3	183	488	580	1.3	2.8
BAPT–Reg Bapt Gen As	1	NR	NR	NR	-	-
BAPT–So Bapt Conv	1	70	180	214	0.5	1.0
Catholic	9	NR	NR	7,987	18.4	38.8
CGOD–Ch God (Ander)	2	315	NR	315	0.7	1.5
Ch of Nazarene	2	179	141	355	0.8	1.7
Chr & Miss Al	3	194	108	390	0.9	1.9
CHR–Chs of Christ	1	40	50	50	0.1	0.2
Evan Ch	2	NR	NR	NR	-	-
Evan Cov Ch	3	81	122	106	0.2	0.5
Jehovah's Witness	3	NR	NR	NR	-	-
JUD–Reform	1	17	30	81	0.2	0.4
LUTH–E.L.C.A.	7	327	1,082	1,307	3.0	6.4
LUTH–Luth-MO Synod	1	272	375	576	1.3	2.8
LUTH–Nor Amer Luth C	1	NR	NR	NR	-	-
MENN–Mennonite USA	1	50	33	39	0.1	0.2
METH–Free Methodist	6	173	101	173	0.4	0.8
METH–Un Methodist	17	1,116	3,547	4,497	10.3	21.9
METH–Wesleyan	2	70	89	91	0.2	0.4
Non-denom Chr Chs	6	380	322	475	1.1	2.3
PENT–Assemb of God	3	150	131	202	0.5	1.0
PENT–Elim	1	NR	NR	NR	-	-
PENT–Int Foursq Gos	1	60	96	114	0.3	0.6
PRES–Presb Ch (USA)	3	270	693	824	1.9	4.0
Salvation Army	1	37	83	1,830	4.2	8.9
Sev Day Adv	2	60	104	120	0.3	0.6
MERCER	**209**	**13,740**	**27,395**	**66,502**	**57.0**	**100.0**
ANG/EPIS–Episcopal	4	255	514	792	0.7	1.2
Bahá'í	0	NR	31	31	0.0	0.0
BAPT–Amer Bapt Assn	1	NR	30	36	0.0	0.1
BAPT–Amer Bapt USA	5	418	742	882	0.8	1.3
BAPT–NBC USA	1	150	225	267	0.2	0.4
BAPT–Prog NBC	2	0	300	357	0.3	0.5
BAPT–Reg Bapt Gen As	3	NR	NR	NR	-	-
BAPT–So Bapt Conv	4	143	174	207	0.2	0.3
Catholic	15	NR	NR	28,244	24.2	42.5
CGOD–Ch God (Ander)	5	599	NR	599	0.5	0.9
CGOD–Ches God-Gen Con	1	25	7	8	0.0	0.0
Ch Cr, Scientst	1	NR	NR	NR	-	-
Ch of Nazarene	7	409	504	795	0.7	1.2
Chr & Miss Al	5	1,209	535	1,511	1.3	2.3
CHR–Chr Ch (Disc)	2	70	366	435	0.4	0.7
CHR–Chr Chs & Chs Cr	2	NR	430	511	0.4	0.8
CHR–Chs of Christ	2	170	171	190	0.2	0.3
Evan Cong Ch	2	NR	154	183	0.2	0.3
Evan Free Ch	1	225	NR	225	0.2	0.3
Intl Fell Bible Ch	1	NR	NR	NR	-	-
Jehovah's Witness	4	NR	NR	NR	-	-
JUD–Reform	1	56	98	265	0.2	0.4
LDS–Comm of Christ	2	NR	316	316	0.3	0.5
LUTH–E.L.C.A.	5	521	1,983	2,367	2.0	3.6
LUTH–Luth-MO Synod	1	89	245	283	0.2	0.4
MENN–Amish Undif	19	NR	1,137	2,602	2.2	3.9
MENN–Menn Chr Fell	1	128	62	128	0.1	0.2
MENN–Unaffil Amish-Menn	1	17	11	17	0.0	0.0
METH–A.W.M.C.	5	141	81	181	0.2	0.3
METH–AME	1	80	150	178	0.2	0.3
METH–AME Zion	1	75	115	137	0.1	0.2
METH–Free Methodist	1	22	32	32	0.0	0.0
METH–Un Methodist	27	1,908	6,675	8,098	6.9	12.2

NR–Not Reported   - Represents no adherents reported.   Percentages may not total 100 due to rounding.

Table 3: Religious Congregations by County and Group: 2010

Religious Group	Number of Congrega-tions	Number of Attendees	Number of Communicant, Confirmed, or Full Members	Adherents: Number of Adherents	Adherents: % of Total Pop.	Adherents: % of Total Adh.
METH–Wesleyan	1	492	160	640	0.5	1.0
New Apost Ch	1	NR	NR	NR	-	-
Non-denom Chr Chs	14	2,045	2,839	3,090	2.6	4.6
ORTHE–Carp Rus Orth	2	158	NR	283	0.2	0.4
ORTHE–Greek Orthodox	1	50	NR	220	0.2	0.3
ORTHE–Orth Ch in Amer	1	60	NR	110	0.1	0.2
ORTHE–Serb Orth USA	1	36	NR	141	0.1	0.2
ORTHE–Ukrainian Orth	1	40	NR	175	0.2	0.3
PENT–Assemb of God	4	525	305	831	0.7	1.2
PENT–Ch of God Proph	1	NR	30	36	0.0	0.1
PENT–COGIC	1	125	175	208	0.2	0.3
PENT–Full Gosp Bapt	1	NR	NR	NR	-	-
PENT–I F Chr Assmbl	2	NR	NR	NR	-	-
PENT–Intl Pent Holiness	4	382	422	502	0.4	0.8
PENT–Un Pent Ch Intl	1	NR	NR	NR	-	-
PRES–As Ref Pres Ch	1	NR	37	44	0.0	0.1
PRES–Orth Pres Ch	1	168	145	194	0.2	0.3
PRES–Presb Ch (USA)	31	2,441	6,470	7,691	6.6	11.6
Salvation Army	2	147	327	802	0.7	1.2
Sev Day Adv	1	46	80	92	0.1	0.1
Un C of Christ	4	315	1,317	1,566	1.3	2.4
MIFFLIN	**115**	**7,891**	**14,661**	**22,162**	**47.5**	**100.0**
ANG/EPIS–Episcopal	1	46	70	144	0.3	0.6
Bahá'í	0	NR	1	1	0.0	0.0
BAPT–Amer Bapt USA	1	60	124	151	0.3	0.7
BRETH–Breth in Chr	5	NR	NR	NR	-	-
BRETH–Ch of Brethren	6	302	939	1,142	2.4	5.2
BRETH–Grace Breth	1	NR	NR	NR	-	-
Catholic	1	NR	NR	1,190	2.5	5.4
Ch of Nazarene	1	19	31	31	0.1	0.1
Chr & Miss Al	6	645	501	982	2.1	4.4
CHR–Chs of Christ	1	69	75	81	0.2	0.4
Jehovah's Witness	1	NR	NR	NR	-	-
LUTH–E.L.C.A.	8	576	2,041	2,905	6.2	13.1
MENN–Amish Undif	21	NR	1,334	2,899	6.2	13.1
MENN–Beachy Amish-Menn	2	428	268	428	0.9	1.9
MENN–CG in Cr (Menn)	2	NR	173	210	0.4	0.9
MENN–Cons Menn Conf	3	756	845	1,028	2.2	4.6
MENN–Menn Chr Fell	1	138	77	138	0.3	0.6
MENN–Mennonite USA	2	233	348	423	0.9	1.9
METH–AME	1	0	60	73	0.2	0.3
METH–Un Methodist	25	1,582	3,822	5,244	11.2	23.7
Non-denom Chr Chs	12	2,170	2,300	2,825	6.1	12.7
PENT–Assemb of God	1	188	126	219	0.5	1.0
PENT–Ch God (Cleve)	1	37	160	195	0.4	0.9
PENT–Elim	1	NR	NR	NR	-	-
PRES–Presb Ch (USA)	8	460	989	1,203	2.6	5.4
Salvation Army	1	102	144	369	0.8	1.7
Sev Day Adv	1	20	35	40	0.1	0.2
Un C of Christ	1	60	198	241	0.5	1.1
MONROE	**122**	**11,257**	**17,520**	**76,158**	**44.8**	**100.0**
ANG/EPIS–Episcopal	2	178	375	375	0.2	0.5
Bahá'í	0	NR	16	16	0.0	0.0
BAPT–Consrv Bapt	2	NR	NR	NR	-	-
BAPT–Ref Bapt Ch	1	NR	NR	NR	-	-
BAPT–So Bapt Conv	2	105	80	97	0.1	0.1
Calv Chpl	1	NR	NR	NR	-	-
Catholic	10	NR	NR	41,650	24.5	54.7
Ch Cr, Scientst	1	NR	NR	NR	-	-
Chr & Miss Al	2	136	169	187	0.1	0.2
CHR–Chs of Christ	1	60	50	70	0.0	0.1
Evan Cong Ch	1	NR	207	250	0.1	0.3
Evan Free Ch	1	50	NR	50	0.0	0.1
HINDU–Post Ren	1	NR	NR	25	0.0	0.0
HINDU–Trad Temples	2	NR	NR	1,333	0.8	1.8
Ind Fund Churches	1	NR	NR	NR	-	-
Intl Fell Bible Ch	1	NR	NR	NR	-	-
Jehovah's Witness	5	NR	NR	NR	-	-
JUD–Conserv	1	76	85	230	0.1	0.3
JUD–Reform	1	30	53	143	0.1	0.2
LDS–L-D Saints	1	NR	NR	798	0.5	1.0

Religious Group	Number of Congrega-tions	Number of Attendees	Number of Communicant, Confirmed, or Full Members	Adherents: Number of Adherents	Adherents: % of Total Pop.	Adherents: % of Total Adh.
LUTH–E.L.C.A.	11	1,297	4,060	5,738	3.4	7.5
LUTH–Luth–MO Synod	1	68	135	156	0.1	0.2
MENN–Bible Flwshp	2	218	NR	294	0.2	0.4
METH–Un Methodist	19	1,638	5,212	6,148	3.6	8.1
METH–Wesleyan	2	498	147	647	0.4	0.8
MORAV–Morav Ch-North	1	26	36	37	0.0	0.0
Muslim Est	1	260	NR	812	0.5	1.1
Non-denom Chr Chs	17	2,046	2,525	2,821	1.7	3.7
ORTHE–Greek Orthodox	1	100	NR	350	0.2	0.5
ORTHE–Orth Ch in Amer	1	80	NR	130	0.1	0.2
ORTHO–Coptic Orth Ch	1	50	NR	100	0.1	0.1
PENT–Assemb of God	5	2,712	1,054	9,587	5.6	12.6
PENT–Ch God (Cleve)	1	53	99	120	0.1	0.2
PRES–Korean Amer Pres	1	NR	NR	NR	-	-
PRES–Korean Pres Amer	1	NR	NR	NR	-	-
PRES–Orth Pres Ch	1	29	28	31	0.0	0.0
PRES–Presb Ch (USA)	6	567	1,010	1,220	0.7	1.6
REF–Ref Ch in Am	1	165	160	215	0.1	0.3
Salvation Army	1	111	253	432	0.3	0.6
Sev Day Adv	4	310	539	621	0.4	0.8
Un C of Christ	6	351	1,155	1,395	0.8	1.8
Unit Univ	1	43	72	80	0.0	0.1
MONTGOMERY	**633**	**75,167**	**134,705**	**508,577**	**63.6**	**100.0**
ANG/EPIS–Anglican NA	3	NR	NR	NR	-	-
ANG/EPIS–Episcopal	35	3,650	10,206	13,389	1.7	2.6
Bahá'í	1	NR	127	127	0.0	0.0
BAPT–Amer Bapt USA	29	4,622	9,596	11,617	1.5	2.3
BAPT–Consrv Bapt	2	NR	NR	NR	-	-
BAPT–NBC USA	2	800	1,500	1,816	0.2	0.4
BAPT–Prog NBC	1	75	100	121	0.0	0.0
BAPT–Ref Bapt Ch	2	NR	NR	NR	-	-
BAPT–Reg Bapt Gen As	2	NR	NR	NR	-	-
BAPT–So Bapt Conv	15	2,502	1,938	2,346	0.3	0.5
BRETH–Breth in Chr	5	NR	NR	NR	-	-
BRETH–Ch of Brethren	9	228	810	981	0.1	0.2
BRETH–Grace Breth	5	NR	NR	NR	-	-
BUDD–Mahayana	4	NR	NR	694	0.1	0.1
BUDD–Vajrayana	1	NR	NR	36	0.0	0.0
Calv Chpl	2	NR	NR	NR	-	-
Catholic	55	NR	NR	301,220	37.7	59.2
CGOD–Ch God (Ander)	2	35	NR	35	0.0	0.0
Ch Cr, Scientst	3	NR	NR	NR	-	-
Ch of Nazarene	6	1,605	1,410	3,409	0.4	0.7
Chr & Miss Al	2	82	26	159	0.0	0.0
CHR–Chr Ch (Disc)	1	0	66	80	0.0	0.0
CHR–Chr Chs & Chs Cr	1	NR	0	0	0.0	0.0
CHR–Chs of Christ	4	311	297	396	0.0	0.1
CHR–Int Chs of Christ	1	NR	631	764	0.1	0.2
Christian Brethren	2	NR	NR	NR	-	-
CONG–Consrv Cong Chr	2	210	567	686	0.1	0.1
Evan Cong Ch	4	NR	637	771	0.1	0.2
Evan Cov Ch	1	145	297	188	0.0	0.0
Evan Free Ch	2	65	NR	65	0.0	0.0
FRND–Fr Gen Cf	11	NR	1,167	1,413	0.2	0.3
HINDU–I/A Temples	1	NR	NR	1,742	0.2	0.3
HINDU–Post Ren	3	NR	NR	112	0.0	0.0
HINDU–Renaiss	1	NR	NR	12	0.0	0.0
HINDU–Trad Temples	2	NR	NR	115	0.0	0.0
Ind Fund Churches	1	NR	NR	NR	-	-
Jehovah's Witness	7	NR	NR	NR	-	-
JUD–Conserv	11	4,885	5,483	14,804	1.9	2.9
JUD–Orth	8	3,197	1,200	4,440	0.6	0.9
JUD–Reconst	1	172	220	594	0.1	0.1
JUD–Reform	9	3,010	5,309	14,334	1.8	2.8
LDS–L-D Saints	8	NR	NR	3,098	0.4	0.6
LUTH–E.L.C.A.	47	7,748	26,456	37,708	4.7	7.4
LUTH–Luth Ch-Am Asc	1	NR	NR	NR	-	-
LUTH–Luth–MO Synod	2	65	71	110	0.0	0.0
LUTH–Nor Amer Luth C	2	NR	NR	NR	-	-
LUTH–Wisc Ev Luth Syn	1	49	86	110	0.0	0.0
MENN–Bible Flwshp	6	788	NR	1,064	0.1	0.2
MENN–Mennonite USA	23	3,275	4,119	4,986	0.6	1.0
METH–AME	6	200	935	1,132	0.1	0.2

NR–Not Reported - Represents no adherents reported. Percentages may not total 100 due to rounding.

Table 3: Religious Congregations by County and Group: 2010

Religious Group	Number of Congrega-tions	Number of Attendees	Number of Communicant, Confirmed, or Full Members	Adherents		
				Number of Adherents	% of Total Pop.	% of Total Adh.
METH–Free Methodist	1	316	138	316	0.0	0.1
METH–Prim Meth Ch	2	NR	NR	NR	-	-
METH–Un Methodist	29	3,817	10,090	14,331	1.8	2.8
METH–Wesleyan	3	129	77	168	0.0	0.0
MJEW–Union Mes Cong	1	NR	NR	NR	-	-
Muslim Est	4	848	NR	3,252	0.4	0.6
New Apost Ch	2	NR	NR	NR	-	-
Non-denom Chr Chs	79	19,003	22,097	25,381	3.2	5.0
ORTHE–Ant Orth of NA	1	200	NR	400	0.1	0.1
ORTHE–Greek Orthodox	2	260	NR	770	0.1	0.2
ORTHE–Orth Ch in Amer	2	165	NR	275	0.0	0.1
ORTHO–Armen Ap Etchm	2	310	NR	1,000	0.1	0.2
ORTHO–Coptic Orth Ch	2	285	NR	500	0.1	0.1
PENT–Assemb of God	16	2,100	1,082	3,433	0.4	0.7
PENT–Ch God (Cleve)	3	166	179	217	0.0	0.0
PENT–COGIC	1	0	100	121	0.0	0.0
PENT–Fire Bapt Hol Ch	1	NR	NR	NR	-	-
PENT–Full Gosp Bapt	1	NR	NR	NR	-	-
PENT–Int Foursq Gos	1	38	26	31	0.0	0.0
PENT–Intl Pent Holiness	1	73	155	188	0.0	0.0
PENT–Un Pent Ch Intl	1	NR	NR	NR	-	-
PRES–Evan Presby Ch	1	NR	421	510	0.1	0.1
PRES–Kor Pres Abroad	4	NR	NR	NR	-	-
PRES–Korean Amer Pres	4	NR	NR	NR	-	-
PRES–Korean Pres Amer	14	NR	NR	NR	-	-
PRES–Orth Pres Ch	3	386	399	513	0.1	0.1
PRES–Presb Ch (USA)	29	3,387	10,530	12,748	1.6	2.5
PRES–Presb Ch Amer	15	2,083	2,371	2,919	0.4	0.6
PRES–Ref Pres of NA	1	52	34	53	0.0	0.0
REF–Christian Ref	2	33	52	63	0.0	0.0
REF–Ref Ch in Am	2	141	215	243	0.0	0.0
Salvation Army	2	57	193	389	0.0	0.1
Schwenkfelder	3	NR	2,177	2,635	0.3	0.5
Sev Day Adv	9	664	1,155	1,329	0.2	0.3
Un C of Christ	33	2,890	9,868	11,946	1.5	2.3
Unit Univ	1	45	92	113	0.0	0.0
Zoroastrian	0	NR	NR	59	0.0	0.0
MONTOUR	**32**	**1,540**	**3,892**	**7,949**	**43.5**	**100.0**
ANG/EPIS–Episcopal	2	57	104	141	0.8	1.8
BAPT–Amer Bapt USA	1	45	78	93	0.5	1.2
BAPT–Consrv Bapt	1	NR	NR	NR	-	-
BAPT–So Bapt Conv	1	65	85	101	0.6	1.3
Catholic	1	NR	NR	2,932	16.1	36.9
Ch of Nazarene	1	49	45	49	0.3	0.6
LUTH–E.L.C.A.	7	518	1,388	1,830	10.0	23.0
MENN–Amish Undif	4	NR	203	446	2.4	5.6
METH–Un Methodist	3	235	692	802	4.4	10.1
Non-denom Chr Chs	2	90	80	112	0.6	1.4
PENT–Un Pent Ch Intl	1	NR	NR	NR	-	-
PRES–Orth Pres Ch	1	0	0	0	0.0	0.0
PRES–Presb Ch (USA)	3	209	527	626	3.4	7.9
Sev Day Adv	1	45	78	90	0.5	1.1
Un C of Christ	3	227	612	727	4.0	9.1
NORTHAMPTON	**255**	**24,362**	**54,971**	**158,759**	**53.3**	**100.0**
ANG/EPIS–Episcopal	7	758	1,702	2,371	0.8	1.5
Bahá'í	2	NR	58	58	0.0	0.0
BAPT–Amer Bapt USA	3	430	755	904	0.3	0.6
BAPT–Consrv Bapt	1	NR	NR	NR	-	-
BAPT–N Am Bapt Conf	1	NR	842	1,008	0.3	0.6
BAPT–So Bapt Conv	4	209	192	230	0.1	0.1
BRETH–Ch of Brethren	1	52	48	57	0.0	0.0
BRETH–Grace Breth	1	NR	NR	NR	-	-
Calv Chpl	1	NR	NR	NR	-	-
Catholic	25	NR	NR	81,456	27.4	51.3
Ch of Nazarene	3	215	336	417	0.1	0.3
CHR–Chr Ch (Disc)	1	0	0	0	0.0	0.0
CHR–Chs of Christ	2	118	107	144	0.0	0.1
Evan Assoc RCC	1	NR	NR	NR	-	-
Evan Cong Ch	5	NR	893	1,069	0.4	0.7
Evan Free Ch	1	450	NR	450	0.2	0.3
FRND–Fr Gen Cf	1	NR	127	152	0.1	0.1

Religious Group	Number of Congrega-tions	Number of Attendees	Number of Communicant, Confirmed, or Full Members	Adherents		
				Number of Adherents	% of Total Pop.	% of Total Adh.
Jain	1	NR	NR	NR	-	-
Jehovah's Witness	7	NR	NR	NR	-	-
JUD–Conserv	2	284	319	861	0.3	0.5
JUD–Orth	1	0	50	0	0.0	0.0
JUD–Reconst	1	44	56	151	0.1	0.1
JUD–Reform	1	71	126	340	0.1	0.2
LDS–L-D Saints	1	NR	NR	701	0.2	0.4
LUTH–Ch of Luth Br	1	247	219	668	0.2	0.4
LUTH–E.L.C.A.	41	4,577	16,875	22,787	7.7	14.4
LUTH–Luth Cong Msn Chr	1	160	850	1,018	0.3	0.6
LUTH–Luth–MO Synod	3	258	779	980	0.3	0.6
MENN–Bible Flwshp	4	813	NR	1,098	0.4	0.7
MENN–Cons Menn Conf	1	155	132	158	0.1	0.1
MENN–Mennonite USA	3	171	143	171	0.1	0.1
METH–AME	1	0	60	72	0.0	0.0
METH–AME Zion	1	0	70	84	0.0	0.1
METH–Un Methodist	19	1,832	5,138	6,427	2.2	4.0
METH–Wesleyan	5	1,293	975	1,682	0.6	1.1
MORAV–Morav Ch-North	10	1,581	3,798	4,651	1.6	2.9
Muslim Est	1	130	NR	400	0.1	0.3
Non-denom Chr Chs	19	3,730	4,722	5,389	1.8	3.4
OCATH–Pol Natl Cath	1	NR	NR	NR	-	-
ORTHE–Greek Orthodox	2	360	NR	1,600	0.5	1.0
ORTHE–Orth Ch in Amer	1	120	NR	350	0.1	0.2
ORTHE–Ukrainian Orth	1	90	NR	250	0.1	0.2
ORTHO–Ethiopian Orth	1	NR	NR	NR	-	-
PENT–Assemb of God	8	1,116	354	1,600	0.5	1.0
PENT–Ch God (Cleve)	2	120	136	163	0.1	0.1
PENT–Ch of God by Faith	1	NR	NR	NR	-	-
PENT–Cong Hol Ch	1	39	35	42	0.0	0.0
PENT–Int Foursq Gos	1	52	3	4	0.0	0.0
PENT–Pent Ch of God	1	70	NR	109	0.0	0.1
PENT–Un Pent Ch Intl	1	NR	NR	NR	-	-
PRES–Orth Pres Ch	1	52	49	58	0.0	0.0
PRES–Presb Ch (USA)	8	1,670	3,843	4,601	1.5	2.9
PRES–Presb Ch Amer	1	0	0	0	0.0	0.0
REF–Hung Ref Add'l	1	NR	NR	NR	-	-
Salvation Army	4	121	220	857	0.3	0.5
Sev Day Adv	5	211	366	422	0.1	0.3
Un C of Christ	28	2,646	10,393	12,443	4.2	7.8
Unit Univ	1	117	200	302	0.1	0.2
Unity Ch	1	NR	NR	NR	-	-
Zoroastrian	0	NR	NR	4	0.0	0.0
NORTHUMBERLAND	**187**	**12,676**	**22,831**	**48,645**	**51.5**	**100.0**
ANG/EPIS–Episcopal	5	175	489	537	0.6	1.1
Bahá'í	0	NR	1	1	0.0	0.0
BAPT–Amer Bapt USA	3	261	477	565	0.6	1.2
BAPT–Consrv Bapt	2	NR	NR	NR	-	-
BAPT–Ref Bapt Ch	1	NR	NR	NR	-	-
Catholic	12	NR	NR	14,540	15.4	29.9
CGOD–Ches God-Gen Con	1	12	46	54	0.1	0.1
Ch Cr, Scientst	1	NR	NR	NR	-	-
Ch of Nazarene	2	675	516	691	0.7	1.4
Chr & Miss Al	3	539	395	878	0.9	1.8
Evan Assoc RCC	1	NR	NR	NR	-	-
Evan Cong Ch	5	NR	411	487	0.5	1.0
Evan Free Ch	2	275	NR	275	0.3	0.6
Ind Fund Churches	1	NR	NR	NR	-	-
Jehovah's Witness	3	NR	NR	NR	-	-
LDS–L-D Saints	2	NR	NR	900	1.0	1.9
LUTH–E.L.C.A.	32	2,064	5,918	7,945	8.4	16.3
LUTH–Luth Cong Msn Chr	2	78	570	675	0.7	1.4
LUTH–Luth–MO Synod	1	24	69	85	0.1	0.2
MENN–Amish Undif	5	NR	242	620	0.7	1.3
MENN–Bible Flwshp	3	507	NR	684	0.7	1.4
MENN–Mennonite USA	2	275	194	230	0.2	0.5
METH–AME	1	0	100	118	0.1	0.2
METH–Prim Meth Ch	2	NR	NR	NR	-	-
METH–Un Methodist	33	1,987	6,032	7,249	7.7	14.9
METH–Wesleyan	6	1,485	843	1,931	2.0	4.0
Muslim Est	2	522	NR	1,626	1.7	3.3
Non-denom Chr Chs	12	1,545	1,504	1,983	2.1	4.1
ORTHE–Orth Ch in Amer	1	40	NR	76	0.1	0.2

NR–Not Reported   - Represents no adherents reported.   Percentages may not total 100 due to rounding.

Table 3: Religious Congregations by County and Group: 2010

Religious Group	Number of Congrega-tions	Number of Attendees	Number of Communicant, Confirmed, or Full Members	Adherents		
				Number of Adherents	% of Total Pop.	% of Total Adh.
PENT–Assemb of God	4	254	189	569	0.6	1.2
PENT–Un Pent Ch Intl	2	NR	NR	NR	-	-
PRES–Presb Ch (USA)	9	619	1,083	1,282	1.4	2.6
Salvation Army	3	116	275	519	0.5	1.1
Sev Day Adv	2	56	99	113	0.1	0.2
Un C of Christ	20	1,101	3,274	3,877	4.1	8.0
Unit Univ	1	66	104	135	0.1	0.3
PERRY	**111**	**6,133**	**9,273**	**16,587**	**36.1**	**100.0**
ANG/EPIS–Episcopal	1	51	143	143	0.3	0.9
Bahá'í	0	NR	4	4	0.0	0.0
BAPT–Asc Ref Bap Ch Am	1	NR	NR	NR	-	-
BAPT–Consrv Bapt	1	NR	NR	NR	-	-
BAPT–Ref Bapt Ch	1	NR	NR	NR	-	-
BAPT–So Bapt Conv	1	8	12	15	0.0	0.1
BRETH–Breth in Chr	4	NR	NR	NR	-	-
BRETH–Ch of Brethren	2	134	151	183	0.4	1.1
BRETH–Grace Breth	1	NR	NR	NR	-	-
Catholic	3	NR	NR	2,000	4.4	12.1
CGOD–Ches God-Gen Con	10	592	714	864	1.9	5.2
Chr & Miss Al	2	217	123	306	0.7	1.8
CHR–Chs of Christ	1	10	10	10	0.0	0.1
Evan Assoc RCC	1	NR	NR	NR	-	-
Evan Free Ch	1	500	NR	500	1.1	3.0
Jehovah's Witness	1	NR	NR	NR	-	-
LDS–L-D Saints	1	NR	NR	342	0.7	2.1
LUTH–Assoc Free Luth	3	NR	NR	NR	-	-
LUTH–E.L.C.A.	12	613	1,649	2,587	5.6	15.6
MENN–Amish Undif	5	NR	232	528	1.1	3.2
METH–Un Methodist	28	1,675	3,461	4,984	10.8	30.0
METH–Wesleyan	1	46	39	60	0.1	0.4
Non-denom Chr Chs	10	913	833	1,149	2.5	6.9
PENT–Assemb of God	3	551	311	883	1.9	5.3
PENT–Ch God (Cleve)	1	26	29	35	0.1	0.2
PENT–Pent Ch of God	1	70	NR	109	0.2	0.7
PRES–Presb Ch (USA)	6	363	692	837	1.8	5.0
Sev Day Adv	1	36	63	72	0.2	0.4
Un C of Christ	8	328	807	976	2.1	5.9
PHILADELPHIA	**1,292**	**170,446**	**230,081**	**744,268**	**48.8**	**100.0**
ANG/EPIS–Anglican NA	3	NR	NR	NR	-	-
ANG/EPIS–Episcopal	49	4,245	10,299	12,273	0.8	1.6
Bahá'í	1	NR	360	360	0.0	0.0
BAPT–Amer Bapt USA	86	36,107	48,102	58,161	3.8	7.8
BAPT–Consrv Bapt	6	NR	NR	NR	-	-
BAPT–Converge/BGC	2	150	NR	180	0.0	0.0
BAPT–N Am Bapt Conf	4	NR	1,077	1,302	0.1	0.2
BAPT–Natl Mis Bapt Conv	2	0	300	363	0.0	0.0
BAPT–NBC Amer	5	660	910	1,100	0.1	0.1
BAPT–NBC USA	57	13,230	25,901	31,317	2.1	4.2
BAPT–Prog NBC	16	1,895	4,380	5,296	0.3	0.7
BAPT–Ref Bapt Ch	1	NR	NR	NR	-	-
BAPT–Reg Bapt Gen As	3	NR	NR	NR	-	-
BAPT–S-D Baptist Gen Con	1	37	53	64	0.0	0.0
BAPT–So Bapt Conv	128	22,865	27,314	33,026	2.2	4.4
BRETH–Breth in Chr	4	NR	NR	NR	-	-
BRETH–Ch of Brethren	2	35	118	143	0.0	0.0
BRETH–Grace Breth	4	NR	NR	NR	-	-
BUDD–Mahayana	14	NR	NR	9,426	0.6	1.3
BUDD–Theravada	6	NR	NR	2,182	0.1	0.3
BUDD–Vajrayana	4	NR	NR	602	0.0	0.1
Calv Chpl	4	NR	NR	NR	-	-
Catholic	114	NR	NR	378,561	24.8	50.9
CGOD–Ch God (Ander)	11	2,800	NR	2,800	0.2	0.4
CGOD–Ches God-Gen Con	1	9	0	0	0.0	0.0
Ch Cr, Scientist	3	NR	NR	NR	-	-
Ch God (7th Day)	1	NR	NR	NR	-	-
Ch of Nazarene	4	202	186	249	0.0	0.0
Chr & Miss Al	7	609	548	732	0.0	0.1
CHR–Chr Ch (Disc)	9	30	209	253	0.0	0.0
CHR–Chs of Christ	9	535	637	732	0.0	0.1
Christian Brethren	3	NR	NR	NR	-	-
CONG–Consrv Cong Chr	1	26	153	185	0.0	0.0
Evan Free Ch	1	144	NR	144	0.0	0.0
FRND–Evan Fr Ch Intl	1	120	65	79	0.0	0.0
FRND–Fr Gen Cf	8	NR	1,235	1,493	0.1	0.2
HINDU–I/A Temples	4	NR	NR	3,612	0.2	0.5
HINDU–Post Ren	3	NR	NR	50	0.0	0.0
HINDU–Renaiss	1	NR	NR	12	0.0	0.0
HINDU–Trad Temples	1	NR	NR	500	0.0	0.1
Jain	2	NR	NR	NR	-	-
Jehovah's Witness	25	NR	NR	NR	-	-
JUD–Conserv	3	1,102	1,237	3,340	0.2	0.4
JUD–Orth	18	6,660	2,500	9,250	0.6	1.2
JUD–Reconst	4	389	497	1,342	0.1	0.2
JUD–Reform	2	584	1,030	2,781	0.2	0.4
LDS–L-D Saints	9	NR	NR	6,803	0.4	0.9
LUTH–E.L.C.A.	40	2,629	7,055	9,135	0.6	1.2
LUTH–Luth Cong Msn Chr	2	278	1,280	1,548	0.1	0.2
LUTH–Luth-MO Synod	6	286	367	435	0.0	0.1
LUTH–Nor Amer Luth C	1	NR	NR	NR	-	-
MENN–Bible Flwshp	1	30	NR	41	0.0	0.0
MENN–Mennonite USA	10	645	657	794	0.1	0.1
METH–AME	29	3,572	7,630	9,226	0.6	1.2
METH–AME Zion	4	100	530	641	0.0	0.1
METH–C.M.E.	4	145	531	642	0.0	0.1
METH–Un Methodist	51	3,113	8,877	10,514	0.7	1.4
METH–Wesleyan	1	140	124	182	0.0	0.0
Metro Comm Ch	1	32	43	52	0.0	0.0
MORAV–Morav Ch-North	1	44	79	88	0.0	0.0
Muslim Est	40	12,363	NR	39,540	2.6	5.3
Nat Spirit Asso	2	NR	NR	NR	-	-
New Apost Ch	1	NR	NR	NR	-	-
Non-denom Chr Chs	179	32,332	43,622	48,950	3.2	6.6
OCATH–Pol Natl Cath	1	NR	NR	NR	-	-
ORTHE–Georgian Orth	1	55	NR	275	0.0	0.0
ORTHE–Greek Orthodox	2	250	NR	1,200	0.1	0.2
ORTHE–Macedonian Orth	1	6	NR	50	0.0	0.0
ORTHE–Orth Ch in Amer	5	520	NR	1,668	0.1	0.2
ORTHE–Romania Orth Ar	1	60	NR	400	0.0	0.1
ORTHE–Rus Orth Abroad	1	40	NR	75	0.0	0.0
ORTHE–Rus Orth Moscow	2	280	NR	1,400	0.1	0.2
ORTHE–Serb Orth USA	1	50	NR	350	0.0	0.0
ORTHE–Ukrainian Orth	2	190	NR	600	0.0	0.1
ORTHO–Armen Ap Cilic	1	200	NR	3,000	0.2	0.4
ORTHO–Eritrean Orth	1	25	NR	260	0.0	0.0
ORTHO–Malan Dioc Am	4	885	NR	1,440	0.1	0.2
ORTHO–Malan Syr Orth	2	295	NR	558	0.0	0.1
PENT–Assemb of God	23	2,308	2,154	3,675	0.2	0.5
PENT–Ch God (Cleve)	15	1,869	2,226	2,692	0.2	0.4
PENT–Ch Lord Jesus Apos	3	NR	NR	NR	-	-
PENT–Ch of God by Faith	1	NR	NR	NR	-	-
PENT–Ch of God Proph	6	NR	639	773	0.1	0.1
PENT–COGIC	23	3,353	6,766	8,181	0.5	1.1
PENT–Cong Hol Ch	1	39	35	42	0.0	0.0
PENT–Fire Bapt Hol Ch	6	NR	NR	NR	-	-
PENT–Full Gosp Bapt	8	NR	NR	NR	-	-
PENT–I F Chr Assmbl	1	NR	NR	NR	-	-
PENT–Int Foursq Gos	2	51	40	48	0.0	0.0
PENT–Intl Pent Holiness	1	68	87	105	0.0	0.0
PENT–Un Pent Ch Intl	2	NR	NR	NR	-	-
PENT–United Holy Ch	13	NR	NR	NR	-	-
PENT–Vineyard	1	143	215	260	0.0	0.0
PRES–Cumber Presb	1	NR	100	96	0.0	0.0
PRES–Korean Amer Pres	2	NR	NR	NR	-	-
PRES–Korean Pres Amer	1	NR	NR	NR	-	-
PRES–Orth Pres Ch	4	232	238	347	0.0	0.0
PRES–Presb Ch (USA)	52	2,655	5,635	6,813	0.4	0.9
PRES–Presb Ch Amer	18	3,233	4,274	5,362	0.4	0.7
REF–Christian Ref	7	347	254	307	0.0	0.0
Salvation Army	9	679	809	3,482	0.2	0.5
Schwenkfelder	1	NR	50	60	0.0	0.0
Sev Day Adv	22	2,802	4,872	5,604	0.4	0.8
Un Breth in Cr	2	0	0	0	0.0	0.0
Un C of Christ	18	1,308	3,180	3,845	0.3	0.5
Unit Univ	3	360	601	778	0.1	0.1
Unity Ch	1	NR	NR	NR	-	-

NR–Not Reported - Represents no adherents reported. Percentages may not total 100 due to rounding.

Table 3: Religious Congregations by County and Group: 2010

Religious Group	Number of Congregations	Number of Attendees	Number of Communicant, Confirmed, or Full Members	Adherents: Number of Adherents	Adherents: % of Total Pop.	Adherents: % of Total Adh.
Zoroastrian	0	NR	NR	21	0.0	0.0
PIKE	**37**	**2,068**	**3,105**	**17,388**	**30.3**	**100.0**
ANG/EPIS–Episcopal	1	101	211	223	0.4	1.3
Bahá'í	0	NR	4	4	0.0	0.0
BAPT–Asc Ref Bap Ch Am	1	NR	NR	NR	-	-
BAPT–Ref Bapt Ch	1	NR	NR	NR	-	-
Catholic	11	NR	NR	12,500	21.8	71.9
Chr & Miss Al	1	94	60	147	0.3	0.8
Evan Cong Ch	1	NR	48	58	0.1	0.3
Evan Cov Ch	1	103	100	134	0.2	0.8
Evan Free Ch	1	40	NR	40	0.1	0.2
Jehovah's Witness	1	NR	NR	NR	-	-
LUTH–E.L.C.A.	4	278	778	1,184	2.1	6.8
LUTH–Luth Ch-Am Asc	1	NR	NR	NR	-	-
LUTH–Luth–MO Synod	1	20	11	13	0.0	0.1
METH–Un Methodist	6	440	1,158	1,803	3.1	10.4
Non-denom Chr Chs	3	715	470	920	1.6	5.3
PENT–Assemb of God	1	35	20	39	0.1	0.2
PRES–Presb Ch (USA)	1	135	200	240	0.4	1.4
REF–Ref Ch in Am	1	107	45	83	0.1	0.5
POTTER	**48**	**2,067**	**3,206**	**6,300**	**36.1**	**100.0**
ANG/EPIS–Episcopal	2	64	94	141	0.8	2.2
BAPT–Amer Bapt USA	2	168	205	246	1.4	3.9
BAPT–Reg Bapt Gen As	3	NR	NR	NR	-	-
BAPT–S-D Baptist Gen Con	1	34	42	50	0.3	0.8
Catholic	5	NR	NR	1,876	10.7	29.8
Chr & Miss Al	3	316	203	536	3.1	8.5
CHR–Chs of Christ	1	2	2	25	0.1	0.4
LUTH–E.L.C.A.	2	73	439	534	3.1	8.5
MENN–Amish Undif	2	NR	77	275	1.6	4.4
MENN–Mennonite USA	1	15	20	24	0.1	0.4
METH–Free Methodist	3	115	106	125	0.7	2.0
METH–Un Methodist	12	363	911	1,168	6.7	18.5
METH–Wesleyan	1	35	29	46	0.3	0.7
Non-denom Chr Chs	5	750	842	975	5.6	15.5
PENT–Assemb of God	1	35	40	46	0.3	0.7
PENT–Elim	1	NR	NR	NR	-	-
PRES–Presb Ch (USA)	2	71	151	181	1.0	2.9
Sev Day Adv	1	26	45	52	0.3	0.8
SCHUYLKILL	**283**	**11,561**	**36,424**	**88,280**	**59.5**	**100.0**
ANG/EPIS–Episcopal	4	164	556	659	0.4	0.7
Bahá'í	0	NR	3	3	0.0	0.0
BAPT–Amer Bapt USA	4	112	224	264	0.2	0.3
BAPT–Ref Bapt Ch	1	NR	NR	NR	-	-
BAPT–So Bapt Conv	2	16	14	17	0.0	0.0
BRETH–Breth in Chr	1	NR	NR	NR	-	-
BRETH–Ch of Brethren	1	94	189	223	0.2	0.3
BRETH–Grace Breth	1	NR	NR	NR	-	-
Catholic	43	NR	NR	40,814	27.5	46.2
CGOD–Ches God-Gen Con	5	204	224	264	0.2	0.3
Ch Christ Chr Union	1	NR	NR	NR	-	-
Ch of Nazarene	2	172	272	275	0.2	0.3
CHR–Chr Chs & Chs Cr	1	NR	50	59	0.0	0.1
CHR–Chs of Christ	1	5	5	5	0.0	0.0
CONG–Consrv Cong Chr	1	37	105	124	0.1	0.1
Evan Assoc RCC	4	NR	NR	NR	-	-
Evan Cong Ch	14	NR	2,233	2,632	1.8	3.0
Evan Free Ch	4	286	NR	286	0.2	0.3
HINDU–I/A Temples	1	NR	NR	0	0.0	0.0
Ind Fund Churches	1	NR	NR	NR	-	-
Jehovah's Witness	6	NR	NR	NR	-	-
LDS–L-D Saints	2	NR	NR	527	0.4	0.6
LUTH–E.L.C.A.	47	3,405	15,596	19,236	13.0	21.8
MENN–Amish Undif	1	NR	28	69	0.0	0.1
MENN–Mennonite USA	3	121	109	128	0.1	0.1
METH–AME	1	0	150	177	0.1	0.2
METH–Prim Meth Ch	3	NR	NR	NR	-	-
METH–Un Methodist	44	1,720	5,919	7,345	5.0	8.3
METH–Wesleyan	3	199	160	258	0.2	0.3
Missionary Ch	1	35	20	35	0.0	0.0
Muslim Est	1	261	NR	812	0.5	0.9
Non-denom Chr Chs	13	1,383	1,555	1,837	1.2	2.1
OCATH–Pol Natl Cath	5	NR	NR	NR	-	-
ORTHE–Carp Rus Orth	1	150	NR	250	0.2	0.3
ORTHE–Orth Ch in Amer	5	234	NR	410	0.3	0.5
ORTHE–Ukrainian Orth	1	30	NR	75	0.1	0.1
PENT–Assemb of God	3	178	101	298	0.2	0.3
PENT–Int Foursq Gos	3	195	236	278	0.2	0.3
PENT–Un Pent Ch Intl	1	NR	NR	NR	-	-
PRES–Presb Ch (USA)	4	169	397	468	0.3	0.5
Salvation Army	2	74	159	879	0.6	1.0
Sev Day Adv	1	26	45	52	0.0	0.1
Un C of Christ	40	2,291	8,074	9,517	6.4	10.8
Zoroastrian	0	NR	NR	4	0.0	0.0
SNYDER	**89**	**6,109**	**11,149**	**16,842**	**42.4**	**100.0**
ANG/EPIS–Episcopal	1	32	59	87	0.2	0.5
Bahá'í	0	NR	3	3	0.0	0.0
BAPT–So Bapt Conv	3	115	71	86	0.2	0.5
BRETH–Ch of Brethren	1	34	116	140	0.4	0.8
Calv Chpl	1	NR	NR	NR	-	-
Catholic	1	NR	NR	1,899	4.8	11.3
Ch Christ Chr Union	1	NR	NR	NR	-	-
Ch of Nazarene	1	478	364	616	1.6	3.7
Chr & Miss Al	1	94	64	146	0.4	0.9
CHR–Chs of Christ	1	114	115	150	0.4	0.9
CONG–Consrv Cong Chr	1	75	178	215	0.5	1.3
Evan Assoc RCC	4	NR	NR	NR	-	-
Evan Free Ch	1	150	NR	150	0.4	0.9
Jehovah's Witness	1	NR	NR	NR	-	-
LUTH–E.L.C.A.	23	1,270	3,935	4,933	12.4	29.3
MENN–Amish Undif	2	NR	171	344	0.9	2.0
MENN–Beachy Amish-Menn	1	179	105	179	0.5	1.1
MENN–Cons Menn Conf	2	111	101	122	0.3	0.7
MENN–Mennonite USA	1	50	35	42	0.1	0.2
METH–A.W.M.C.	1	4	0	6	0.0	0.0
METH–Un Methodist	25	1,827	3,863	5,077	12.8	30.1
METH–Wesleyan	1	125	142	163	0.4	1.0
Non-denom Chr Chs	9	1,243	1,089	1,592	4.0	9.5
PENT–Ch of God Proph	1	NR	19	23	0.1	0.1
PENT–Un Pent Ch Intl	1	NR	NR	NR	-	-
Un C of Christ	4	208	719	868	2.2	5.2
Zoroastrian	0	NR	NR	1	0.0	0.0
SOMERSET	**209**	**11,902**	**26,625**	**45,952**	**59.1**	**100.0**
ANG/EPIS–Anglican NA	2	NR	NR	NR	-	-
ANG/EPIS–Episcopal	1	28	52	52	0.1	0.1
Bahá'í	0	NR	4	4	0.0	0.0
BAPT–Amer Bapt USA	1	14	37	43	0.1	0.1
BAPT–So Bapt Conv	1	40	14	16	0.0	0.0
BRETH–Brethren (Ash)	3	NR	240	281	0.4	0.6
BRETH–Ch of Brethren	24	1,462	3,734	4,370	5.6	9.5
BRETH–Grace Breth	2	NR	NR	NR	-	-
Catholic	15	NR	NR	10,298	13.2	22.4
CGOD–Ches God-Gen Con	4	384	475	556	0.7	1.2
Ch of Nazarene	5	185	341	356	0.5	0.8
Chr & Miss Al	5	839	625	1,371	1.8	3.0
CHR–Chr Chs & Chs Cr	6	NR	553	647	0.8	1.4
CHR–Chs of Christ	1	65	60	90	0.1	0.2
Jehovah's Witness	2	NR	NR	NR	-	-
LDS–L-D Saints	1	NR	NR	206	0.3	0.4
LUTH–E.L.C.A.	34	2,278	8,259	10,654	13.7	23.2
LUTH–Luth–MO Synod	2	103	140	158	0.2	0.3
LUTH–Nor Amer Luth C	1	NR	NR	NR	-	-
MENN–Amish Undif	7	NR	528	1,161	1.5	2.5
MENN–Beachy Amish-Menn	1	274	200	274	0.4	0.6
MENN–Cons Menn Conf	2	286	295	345	0.4	0.8
MENN–Menn Chr Fell	1	149	73	149	0.2	0.3
MENN–Mennonite USA	7	693	904	1,058	1.4	2.3
METH–Un Methodist	38	2,049	5,580	7,062	9.1	15.4
Muslim Est	1	260	NR	812	1.0	1.8
New Apost Ch	1	NR	NR	NR	-	-
Non-denom Chr Chs	6	720	870	962	1.2	2.1

NR–Not Reported   - Represents no adherents reported.   Percentages may not total 100 due to rounding.

Table 3: Religious Congregations by County and Group: 2010

Religious Group	Number of Congrega-tions	Number of Attendees	Number of Communicant, Confirmed, or Full Members	Adherents: Number of Adherents	Adherents: % of Total Pop.	Adherents: % of Total Adh.
ORTHE–Carp Rus Orth	3	155	NR	303	0.4	0.7
ORTHE–Orth Ch in Amer	2	40	NR	40	0.1	0.1
PENT–Assemb of God	6	450	314	772	1.0	1.7
PENT–Ch God (Cleve)	4	545	483	565	0.7	1.2
PENT–Un Pent Ch Intl	3	NR	NR	NR	-	-
PRES–Evan Presby Ch	1	NR	363	425	0.5	0.9
PRES–Orth Pres Ch	1	55	31	55	0.1	0.1
PRES–Presb Ch (USA)	2	68	131	153	0.2	0.3
Un C of Christ	13	760	2,319	2,714	3.5	5.9
SULLIVAN	**17**	**443**	**622**	**1,879**	**29.2**	**100.0**
BAPT–Amer Bapt USA	1	31	10	11	0.2	0.6
Catholic	4	NR	NR	1,000	15.6	53.2
FRND–Fr Gen Cf	1	NR	0	0	0.0	0.0
LUTH–E.L.C.A.	1	90	190	276	4.3	14.7
METH–Un Methodist	6	133	300	310	4.8	16.5
METH–Wesleyan	2	83	77	108	1.7	5.7
ORTHE–Orth Ch in Amer	1	16	NR	40	0.6	2.1
PENT–Assemb of God	1	90	45	134	2.1	7.1
SUSQUEHANNA	**84**	**3,145**	**6,260**	**13,776**	**31.8**	**100.0**
ANG/EPIS–Episcopal	4	133	202	250	0.6	1.8
Bahá'í	0	NR	5	5	0.0	0.0
BAPT–Amer Bapt USA	3	139	378	448	1.0	3.3
BAPT–Consrv Bapt	1	NR	NR	NR	-	-
BAPT–Reg Bapt Gen As	6	NR	NR	NR	-	-
Catholic	9	NR	NR	5,550	12.8	40.3
Chr & Miss Al	1	32	20	36	0.1	0.3
Evan Free Ch	1	190	NR	190	0.4	1.4
HINDU–Post Ren	1	NR	NR	54	0.1	0.4
Jehovah's Witness	1	NR	NR	NR	-	-
LDS–L-D Saints	2	NR	NR	412	1.0	3.0
LUTH–Luth–MO Synod	1	50	216	270	0.6	2.0
MENN–Mennonite USA	1	75	70	83	0.2	0.6
METH–Free Methodist	1	13	0	13	0.0	0.1
METH–Un Methodist	29	1,025	3,533	4,024	9.3	29.2
Non-denom Chr Chs	11	1,055	1,127	1,536	3.5	11.1
ORTHE–Orth Ch in Amer	2	50	NR	70	0.2	0.5
PRES–Presb Ch (USA)	7	262	380	450	1.0	3.3
Sev Day Adv	1	16	28	32	0.1	0.2
Un C of Christ	1	65	273	323	0.7	2.3
Unit Univ	1	40	28	30	0.1	0.2
TIOGA	**111**	**4,977**	**7,718**	**13,230**	**31.5**	**100.0**
ANG/EPIS–Episcopal	4	157	367	412	1.0	3.1
Bahá'í	0	NR	6	6	0.0	0.0
BAPT–Amer Bapt USA	9	550	1,141	1,345	3.2	10.2
BAPT–Reg Bapt Gen As	2	NR	NR	NR	-	-
BRETH–Breth in Chr	1	NR	NR	NR	-	-
Catholic	5	NR	NR	3,000	7.1	22.7
Chr & Miss Al	3	104	59	124	0.3	0.9
CHR–Chr Ch (Disc)	2	75	197	232	0.6	1.8
CHR–Chs of Christ	1	45	40	45	0.1	0.3
FRND–Fr Gen Cf	1	NR	33	39	0.1	0.3
Jehovah's Witness	3	NR	NR	NR	-	-
LDS–L-D Saints	1	NR	NR	259	0.6	2.0
LUTH–E.L.C.A.	5	146	401	479	1.1	3.6
LUTH–Luth–MO Synod	1	98	162	194	0.5	1.5
LUTH–Nor Amer Luth C	1	NR	NR	NR	-	-
MENN–Mennonite USA	2	80	70	83	0.2	0.6
METH–Free Methodist	2	50	18	50	0.1	0.4
METH–Un Methodist	32	1,248	2,619	3,533	8.4	26.7
METH–Wesleyan	2	187	143	243	0.6	1.8
Non-denom Chr Chs	15	1,425	1,541	1,810	4.3	13.7
PENT–Assemb of God	4	319	173	500	1.2	3.8
PENT–Elim	4	NR	NR	NR	-	-
PENT–Vineyard	1	100	150	177	0.4	1.3
PRES–Orth Pres Ch	1	10	10	10	0.0	0.1
PRES–Presb Ch (USA)	7	300	444	523	1.2	4.0
Sev Day Adv	2	83	144	166	0.4	1.3

Religious Group	Number of Congrega-tions	Number of Attendees	Number of Communicant, Confirmed, or Full Members	Adherents: Number of Adherents	Adherents: % of Total Pop.	Adherents: % of Total Adh.
UNION	**74**	**5,833**	**10,512**	**15,482**	**34.4**	**100.0**
ANG/EPIS–Episcopal	1	96	183	239	0.5	1.5
Bahá'í	0	NR	10	10	0.0	0.1
BAPT–Amer Bapt USA	2	130	409	476	1.1	3.1
BAPT–Reg Bapt Gen As	2	NR	NR	NR	-	-
BAPT–So Bapt Conv	2	325	271	315	0.7	2.0
BRETH–Ch of Brethren	1	267	261	304	0.7	2.0
Catholic	1	NR	NR	1,973	4.4	12.7
Ch Christ Chr Union	1	NR	NR	NR	-	-
Ch of Nazarene	1	310	404	588	1.3	3.8
Chr & Miss Al	2	327	180	445	1.0	2.9
FRND–Fr Gen Cf	1	NR	9	10	0.0	0.1
LUTH–Ch of Luth Br	1	50	53	116	0.3	0.7
LUTH–E.L.C.A.	9	945	2,449	3,258	7.2	21.0
MENN–Amish Undif	1	NR	31	73	0.2	0.5
MENN–Beachy Amish-Menn	2	220	125	220	0.5	1.4
MENN–CG in Cr (Menn)	1	NR	120	140	0.3	0.9
MENN–Mennonite USA	2	308	221	257	0.6	1.7
MENN–Unaffil Amish-Menn	1	86	46	86	0.2	0.6
METH–Un Methodist	15	787	1,976	2,603	5.8	16.8
Non-denom Chr Chs	10	1,005	1,220	1,338	3.0	8.6
PENT–Assemb of God	1	95	42	112	0.2	0.7
PENT–COGIC	1	0	150	175	0.4	1.1
PENT–Un Pent Ch Intl	1	NR	NR	NR	-	-
PRES–Orth Pres Ch	1	37	29	36	0.1	0.2
PRES–Presb Ch (USA)	3	304	654	761	1.7	4.9
Un C of Christ	10	541	1,639	1,908	4.2	12.3
Unit Univ	1	0	30	39	0.1	0.3
VENANGO	**138**	**8,061**	**14,577**	**28,868**	**52.5**	**100.0**
ANG/EPIS–Episcopal	2	133	287	287	0.5	1.0
BAPT–Amer Bapt USA	2	82	204	243	0.4	0.8
BAPT–Ind Bapt Flwsp Intl	2	NR	NR	NR	-	-
BAPT–Reg Bapt Gen As	1	NR	NR	NR	-	-
BAPT–So Bapt Conv	1	79	42	50	0.1	0.2
Catholic	7	NR	NR	9,096	16.5	31.5
CGOD–Ch God (Ander)	5	442	NR	442	0.8	1.5
CGOD–Ches God-Gen Con	4	199	302	360	0.7	1.2
Ch of Nazarene	3	280	328	595	1.1	2.1
Chr & Miss Al	2	180	99	296	0.5	1.0
CHR–Chs of Christ	1	20	12	27	0.0	0.1
Evan Cong Ch	2	NR	99	118	0.2	0.4
Jehovah's Witness	1	NR	NR	NR	-	-
LDS–L-D Saints	1	NR	NR	317	0.6	1.1
LUTH–E.L.C.A.	4	259	816	946	1.7	3.3
LUTH–Luth–MO Synod	1	36	83	91	0.2	0.3
MENN–Amish Undif	3	NR	157	332	0.6	1.2
METH–A.W.M.C.	3	168	91	230	0.4	0.8
METH–Free Methodist	4	158	74	178	0.3	0.6
METH–Un Methodist	46	2,891	7,566	9,933	18.1	34.4
Non-denom Chr Chs	16	1,658	2,171	2,347	4.3	8.1
PENT–Assemb of God	2	183	128	305	0.6	1.1
PENT–Ch of God Proph	1	NR	77	92	0.2	0.3
PENT–Full Gosp Bapt	1	NR	NR	NR	-	-
PENT–Int Foursq Gos	1	36	23	27	0.0	0.1
PRES–Orth Pres Ch	1	20	19	24	0.0	0.1
PRES–Presb Ch (USA)	15	625	1,477	1,761	3.2	6.1
Salvation Army	2	78	171	283	0.5	1.0
Sev Day Adv	2	28	49	57	0.1	0.2
Un Breth in Cr	2	506	302	431	0.8	1.5
WARREN	**83**	**4,921**	**9,304**	**19,668**	**47.0**	**100.0**
ANG/EPIS–Episcopal	2	115	220	231	0.6	1.2
Bahá'í	0	NR	10	10	0.0	0.1
BAPT–Amer Bapt USA	1	113	167	198	0.5	1.0
BAPT–Converge/BGC	1	75	NR	90	0.2	0.5
Calv Chpl	1	NR	NR	NR	-	-
Catholic	6	NR	NR	7,330	17.5	37.3
CGOD–Ch God (Ander)	1	100	NR	100	0.2	0.5
Ch Cr, Scientst	1	NR	NR	NR	-	-
Ch of Nazarene	1	310	422	422	1.0	2.1
Chr & Miss Al	1	155	129	282	0.7	1.4
CHR–Chs of Christ	1	52	48	62	0.1	0.3

NR–Not Reported   - Represents no adherents reported.   Percentages may not total 100 due to rounding.

Table 3: Religious Congregations by County and Group: 2010

Religious Group	Number of Congrega-tions	Number of Attendees	Number of Communicant, Confirmed, or Full Members	Adherents: Number of Adherents	Adherents: % of Total Pop.	Adherents: % of Total Adh.
CONG–Cong Chr Add'l	1	NR	81	96	0.2	0.5
CONG–Cong Chr, NA	1	NR	50	59	0.1	0.3
CONG–Consrv Cong Chr	2	159	107	127	0.3	0.6
Evan Cov Ch	3	293	280	381	0.9	1.9
Evan Free Ch	1	45	NR	45	0.1	0.2
Ind Fund Churches	1	NR	NR	NR	-	-
Jehovah's Witness	1	NR	NR	NR	-	-
LDS–L-D Saints	1	NR	NR	272	0.7	1.4
LUTH–E.L.C.A.	7	470	1,281	1,645	3.9	8.4
MENN–Amish Undif	7	NR	274	608	1.5	3.1
METH–A.W.M.C.	2	91	36	113	0.3	0.6
METH–Free Methodist	4	341	206	344	0.8	1.7
METH–Un Methodist	21	1,418	4,006	4,929	11.8	25.1
METH–Wesleyan	1	43	28	56	0.1	0.3
Non-denom Chr Chs	2	615	808	844	2.0	4.3
PENT–Assemb of God	1	35	21	49	0.1	0.2
PENT–Ch God (Cleve)	1	21	19	22	0.1	0.1
PENT–Elim	1	NR	NR	NR	-	-
PRES–Presb Ch (USA)	6	357	818	968	2.3	4.9
Salvation Army	1	55	157	225	0.5	1.1
Sev Day Adv	1	18	31	36	0.1	0.2
Un C of Christ	1	40	105	124	0.3	0.6
WASHINGTON	**280**	**19,848**	**37,197**	**103,519**	**49.8**	**100.0**
ANG/EPIS–Anglican NA	5	NR	NR	NR	-	-
ANG/EPIS–Episcopal	1	37	62	97	0.0	0.1
Bahá'í	0	NR	9	9	0.0	0.0
BAPT–Amer Bapt USA	11	900	1,686	1,995	1.0	1.9
BAPT–Consrv Bapt	3	NR	NR	NR	-	-
BAPT–Converge/BGC	1	75	NR	90	0.0	0.1
BAPT–NBC USA	3	160	350	414	0.2	0.4
BAPT–Reg Bapt Gen As	2	NR	NR	NR	-	-
BAPT–So Bapt Conv	9	695	903	1,068	0.5	1.0
BRETH–Brethren (Ash)	1	NR	80	95	0.0	0.1
BRETH–Ch of Brethren	1	0	30	35	0.0	0.0
BUDD–Mahayana	1	NR	NR	116	0.1	0.1
Calv Chpl	1	NR	NR	NR	-	-
Catholic	26	NR	NR	53,777	25.9	51.9
Ch of Nazarene	7	322	666	899	0.4	0.9
Chr & Miss Al	4	649	401	1,154	0.6	1.1
CHR–Chr Ch (Disc)	9	235	2,301	2,722	1.3	2.6
CHR–Chr Chs & Chs Cr	5	NR	535	633	0.3	0.6
CHR–Chs of Christ	6	431	420	625	0.3	0.6
Christian Brethren	1	NR	NR	NR	-	-
Evan Free Ch	1	150	NR	150	0.1	0.1
Jehovah's Witness	2	NR	NR	NR	-	-
JUD–Reform	1	12	21	57	0.0	0.1
LDS–Comm of Christ	1	NR	158	158	0.1	0.2
LDS–L-D Saints	2	NR	NR	1,119	0.5	1.1
LUTH–E.L.C.A.	8	578	1,662	2,185	1.1	2.1
LUTH–Luth–MO Synod	2	119	181	209	0.1	0.2
LUTH–Nor Amer Luth C	1	NR	NR	NR	-	-
MENN–Beachy Amish-Menn	1	89	45	89	0.0	0.1
METH–A.W.M.C.	1	26	0	52	0.0	0.1
METH–AME	5	0	550	651	0.3	0.6
METH–AME Zion	1	0	75	89	0.0	0.1
METH–Free Methodist	2	328	343	346	0.2	0.3
METH–Un Methodist	43	2,395	8,536	10,792	5.2	10.4
Non-denom Chr Chs	24	6,664	7,070	8,569	4.1	8.3
OCATH–Pol Natl Cath	2	NR	NR	NR	-	-
ORTHE–Carp Rus Orth	1	50	NR	72	0.0	0.1
ORTHE–Greek Orthodox	1	325	NR	800	0.4	0.8
ORTHE–Orth Ch in Amer	4	247	NR	376	0.2	0.4
ORTHE–Rus Orth Abroad	1	15	NR	27	0.0	0.0
PENT–Assemb of God	4	740	495	1,370	0.7	1.3
PENT–Ch God (Cleve)	1	95	187	221	0.1	0.2
PENT–Ch of God Proph	1	NR	40	47	0.0	0.0
PENT–COGIC	2	109	157	186	0.1	0.2
PENT–I F Chr Assmbl	4	NR	NR	NR	-	-
PENT–Intl Pent Holiness	1	70	80	95	0.0	0.1
PENT–Un Pent Ch Intl	2	NR	NR	NR	-	-
PENT–Vineyard	1	140	160	189	0.1	0.2
PRES–Evan Presby Ch	1	NR	450	532	0.3	0.5
PRES–Presb Ch (USA)	57	4,027	9,303	11,006	5.3	10.6

Religious Group	Number of Congrega-tions	Number of Attendees	Number of Communicant, Confirmed, or Full Members	Adherents: Number of Adherents	Adherents: % of Total Pop.	Adherents: % of Total Adh.
PRES–Presb Ch Amer	2	110	127	164	0.1	0.2
Salvation Army	1	21	55	171	0.1	0.2
Sev Day Adv	1	34	59	68	0.0	0.1
Sikh	1	NR	NR	NR	-	-
WAYNE	**81**	**3,481**	**7,602**	**27,244**	**51.6**	**100.0**
ANG/EPIS–Episcopal	3	146	292	337	0.6	1.2
BAPT–Amer Bapt USA	4	150	412	478	0.9	1.8
BAPT–So Bapt Conv	1	NR	NR	NR	-	-
Catholic	11	NR	NR	16,000	30.3	58.7
CHR–Chs of Christ	1	9	12	13	0.0	0.0
FRND–Fr Gen Cf	1	NR	0	0	0.0	0.0
HINDU–Post Ren	1	NR	NR	1,000	1.9	3.7
Ind Fund Churches	1	NR	NR	NR	-	-
Jehovah's Witness	4	NR	NR	NR	-	-
JUD–Reform	1	57	100	270	0.5	1.0
LDS–L-D Saints	1	NR	NR	352	0.7	1.3
LUTH–E.L.C.A.	3	255	1,109	1,669	3.2	6.1
METH–Free Methodist	4	367	230	385	0.7	1.4
METH–Un Methodist	28	1,028	3,830	4,534	8.6	16.6
MORAV–Morav Ch-North	1	62	86	119	0.2	0.4
Non-denom Chr Chs	6	660	713	905	1.7	3.3
ORTHE–Orth Ch in Amer	1	140	NR	200	0.4	0.7
PENT–Assemb of God	2	254	200	263	0.5	1.0
PRES–Presb Ch (USA)	5	321	543	629	1.2	2.3
REF–Ref Ch in U.S.	1	NR	20	27	0.1	0.1
Sev Day Adv	1	32	55	63	0.1	0.2
WESTMORELAND	**468**	**31,586**	**73,360**	**219,820**	**60.2**	**100.0**
ANG/EPIS–Anglican NA	4	NR	NR	NR	-	-
ANG/EPIS–Episcopal	4	165	339	393	0.1	0.2
Bahá'í	0	NR	24	24	0.0	0.0
BAPT–Amer Bapt USA	9	421	1,322	1,550	0.4	0.7
BAPT–Free Will Bapt	1	NR	67	79	0.0	0.0
BAPT–N Am Bapt Conf	1	NR	NR	NR	-	-
BAPT–NBC USA	1	85	100	117	0.0	0.1
BAPT–Ref Bapt Ch	1	NR	NR	NR	-	-
BAPT–Reg Bapt Gen As	2	NR	NR	NR	-	-
BAPT–So Bapt Conv	11	396	359	421	0.1	0.2
BRETH–Brethren (Ash)	4	NR	320	375	0.1	0.2
BRETH–Ch of Brethren	4	296	908	1,065	0.3	0.5
Calv Chpl	1	NR	NR	NR	-	-
Catholic	59	NR	NR	121,691	33.3	55.4
CGOD–Ch God (Ander)	5	475	NR	475	0.1	0.2
CGOD–Ches God-Gen Con	10	684	1,490	1,747	0.5	0.8
Ch Cr, Scientst	1	NR	NR	NR	-	-
Ch of Nazarene	6	203	372	544	0.1	0.2
Chr & Miss Al	12	1,997	996	3,011	0.8	1.4
CHR–Chr Ch (Disc)	2	201	615	721	0.2	0.3
CHR–Chr Chs & Chs Cr	9	NR	2,310	2,709	0.7	1.2
CHR–Chs of Christ	5	265	273	361	0.1	0.2
Christian Brethren	1	NR	NR	NR	-	-
CONG–Consrv Cong Chr	2	58	50	59	0.0	0.0
Evan Ch	1	NR	NR	NR	-	-
HINDU–Post Ren	1	NR	NR	76	0.0	0.0
Ind Fund Churches	1	NR	NR	NR	-	-
Jain	1	NR	NR	NR	-	-
Jehovah's Witness	8	NR	NR	NR	-	-
JUD–Reform	1	60	105	284	0.1	0.1
LDS–L-D Saints	1	NR	NR	646	0.2	0.3
LUTH–E.L.C.A.	44	4,010	15,175	20,600	5.6	9.4
LUTH–Evan Luth Syn	1	21	14	22	0.0	0.0
LUTH–Luth–MO Synod	3	188	437	473	0.1	0.2
LUTH–Nor Amer Luth C	2	NR	NR	NR	-	-
LUTH–Wisc Ev Luth Syn	1	43	73	78	0.0	0.0
MENN–Mennonite USA	2	97	170	199	0.1	0.1
METH–A.W.M.C.	2	26	26	16	0.0	0.0
METH–AME	6	51	566	664	0.2	0.3
METH–AME Zion	1	0	100	117	0.0	0.1
METH–Evan Meth Ch	1	NR	NR	NR	-	-
METH–Free Methodist	2	94	70	96	0.0	0.0
METH–Prim Meth Ch	2	NR	NR	NR	-	-
METH–Un Methodist	73	6,506	21,917	28,420	7.8	12.9

NR–Not Reported - Represents no adherents reported. Percentages may not total 100 due to rounding.

Table 3: Religious Congregations by County and Group: 2010

Religious Group	Number of Congrega-tions	Number of Attendees	Number of Communicant, Confirmed, or Full Members	Adherents		
				Number of Adherents	% of Total Pop.	% of Total Adh.
METH–Wesleyan	1	272	264	354	0.1	0.2
Non-denom Chr Chs	35	6,752	8,064	9,186	2.5	4.2
OCATH–Pol Natl Cath	1	NR	NR	NR	-	-
ORTHE–Ant Orth of NA	4	378	NR	1,086	0.3	0.5
ORTHE–Carp Rus Orth	3	98	NR	165	0.0	0.1
ORTHE–Greek Orthodox	3	155	NR	275	0.1	0.1
ORTHE–Orth Ch in Amer	3	115	NR	192	0.1	0.1
ORTHE–Serb Orth USA	1	34	NR	98	0.0	0.0
ORTHE–Ukrainian Orth	3	85	NR	220	0.1	0.1
PENT–Assemb of God	11	1,288	951	1,937	0.5	0.9
PENT–Assm God Intl F	1	NR	NR	NR	-	-
PENT–Ch God (Cleve)	1	66	59	69	0.0	0.0
PENT–COGIC	3	0	360	422	0.1	0.2
PENT–I F Chr Assmbl	1	NR	NR	NR	-	-
PENT–Intl Pent Holiness	4	345	338	396	0.1	0.2
PENT–Open Bible Std	1	100	NR	100	0.0	0.0
PENT–Un Pent Ch Intl	3	NR	NR	NR	-	-
PRES–Evan Presby Ch	2	NR	577	677	0.2	0.3
PRES–Presb Ch (USA)	39	3,804	10,434	12,236	3.4	5.6
PRES–Presb Ch Amer	5	518	706	950	0.3	0.4
PRES–Ref Pres of NA	1	35	36	49	0.0	0.0
REF–Hung Ref Add'l	1	NR	NR	NR	-	-
Salvation Army	5	172	499	1,005	0.3	0.5
Sev Day Adv	2	74	128	147	0.0	0.1
Un C of Christ	22	878	2,634	3,089	0.8	1.4
Unit Univ	3	75	112	130	0.0	0.1
Zoroastrian	0	NR	NR	4	0.0	0.0
WYOMING	**48**	**2,457**	**4,523**	**11,757**	**41.6**	**100.0**
ANG/EPIS–Episcopal	1	30	54	83	0.3	0.7
Bahá'í	0	NR	14	14	0.0	0.1
BAPT–Amer Bapt USA	1	45	201	240	0.8	2.0
BAPT–Reg Bapt Gen As	2	NR	NR	NR	-	-
BAPT–So Bapt Conv	1	50	70	83	0.3	0.7
Catholic	4	NR	NR	6,000	21.2	51.0
Ind Fund Churches	1	NR	NR	NR	-	-
Jehovah's Witness	1	NR	NR	NR	-	-
LDS–L-D Saints	1	NR	NR	156	0.6	1.3
LUTH–E.L.C.A.	1	20	88	88	0.3	0.7
LUTH–Luth-MO Synod	1	65	123	153	0.5	1.3
METH–Free Methodist	1	60	46	60	0.2	0.5
METH–Un Methodist	18	969	2,677	3,229	11.4	27.5
Non-denom Chr Chs	9	890	881	1,112	3.9	9.5
PENT–Assemb of God	3	201	194	333	1.2	2.8
PRES–Presb Ch (USA)	2	97	122	145	0.5	1.2
Sev Day Adv	1	30	53	61	0.2	0.5
YORK	**488**	**56,499**	**96,850**	**168,962**	**38.8**	**100.0**
ANG/EPIS–Episcopal	4	423	981	1,137	0.3	0.7
Bahá'í	0	NR	43	43	0.0	0.0
BAPT–Amer Bapt USA	2	469	343	418	0.1	0.2
BAPT–Consrv Bapt	1	NR	NR	NR	-	-
BAPT–NBC USA	2	150	350	426	0.1	0.3
BAPT–Ref Bapt Ch	1	NR	NR	NR	-	-
BAPT–Reg Bapt Gen As	1	NR	NR	NR	-	-
BAPT–So Bapt Conv	16	1,222	2,058	2,505	0.6	1.5
BRETH–Breth in Chr	8	NR	NR	NR	-	-
BRETH–Ch of Brethren	14	1,819	2,620	3,189	0.7	1.9
BRETH–Grace Breth	4	NR	NR	NR	-	-
BUDD–Mahayana	1	NR	NR	11	0.0	0.0
Calv Chpl	2	NR	NR	NR	-	-
Catholic	13	NR	NR	35,605	8.2	21.1
CGOD–Ches God-Gen Con	11	2,006	1,503	1,830	0.4	1.1
Ch Cr, Scientst	2	NR	NR	NR	-	-
Ch of Nazarene	4	1,848	1,583	2,156	0.5	1.3
Chr & Miss Al	8	1,174	690	1,604	0.4	0.9
CHR–Chr Chs & Chs Cr	1	NR	250	304	0.1	0.2
CHR–Chs of Christ	4	366	375	515	0.1	0.3
Christian Brethren	1	NR	NR	NR	-	-
Evan Assoc RCC	1	NR	NR	NR	-	-
Evan Cong Ch	5	NR	644	784	0.2	0.5
Evan Cov Ch	2	266	513	346	0.1	0.2
Evan Free Ch	3	340	NR	340	0.1	0.2

Religious Group	Number of Congrega-tions	Number of Attendees	Number of Communicant, Confirmed, or Full Members	Adherents		
				Number of Adherents	% of Total Pop.	% of Total Adh.
FRND–Fr Gen Cf & Un Mtg	2	NR	60	73	0.0	0.0
Ind Fund Churches	1	NR	NR	NR	-	-
Jehovah's Witness	11	NR	NR	NR	-	-
JUD–Conserv	1	14	16	43	0.0	0.0
JUD–Reform	1	143	252	680	0.2	0.4
LDS–Comm of Christ	1	NR	161	161	0.0	0.1
LDS–L-D Saints	5	NR	NR	2,677	0.6	1.6
LUTH–E.L.C.A.	65	7,650	22,963	30,170	6.9	17.9
LUTH–Luth Cong Msn Chr	3	534	2,015	2,453	0.6	1.5
LUTH–Luth-MO Synod	3	417	879	1,158	0.3	0.7
LUTH–Nor Amer Luth C	2	NR	NR	NR	-	-
MENN–Amish Undif	3	NR	85	266	0.1	0.2
MENN–Bible Flwshp	1	157	NR	212	0.0	0.1
MENN–Mennonite USA	1	110	92	112	0.0	0.1
METH–AME	1	80	125	152	0.0	0.1
METH–AME Zion	3	0	350	426	0.1	0.3
METH–Free Methodist	1	13	17	17	0.0	0.0
METH–Un Methodist	86	10,518	20,583	28,904	6.6	17.1
METH–Wesleyan	1	123	130	160	0.0	0.1
Missionary Ch	3	121	67	122	0.0	0.1
MORAV–Morav Ch-North	2	125	237	261	0.1	0.2
Muslim Est	1	261	NR	813	0.2	0.5
Non-denom Chr Chs	70	15,909	15,662	20,122	4.6	11.9
ORTHE–Ant Orth of NA	1	140	NR	250	0.1	0.1
ORTHE–Greek Orthodox	1	85	NR	150	0.0	0.1
PENT–Assemb of God	21	2,640	1,832	3,368	0.8	2.0
PENT–Ch God (Cleve)	6	612	1,286	1,565	0.4	0.9
PENT–Ch of God Proph	1	NR	54	66	0.0	0.0
PENT–COGIC	2	75	275	335	0.1	0.2
PENT–Elim	1	NR	NR	NR	-	-
PENT–Full Gosp Bapt	2	NR	NR	NR	-	-
PENT–Int Foursq Gos	3	180	288	351	0.1	0.2
PENT–Un Pent Ch Intl	2	NR	NR	NR	-	-
PRES–Evan Presby Ch	1	NR	97	118	0.0	0.1
PRES–Orth Pres Ch	1	36	55	80	0.0	0.0
PRES–Presb Ch (USA)	15	1,496	3,237	3,940	0.9	2.3
PRES–Presb Ch Amer	5	447	450	559	0.1	0.3
Salvation Army	2	128	287	1,904	0.4	1.1
Sev Day Adv	4	380	662	761	0.2	0.5
Un Breth in Cr	3	213	320	183	0.0	0.1
Un C of Christ	37	3,640	12,117	14,750	3.4	8.7
Unit Univ	1	169	243	387	0.1	0.2
RHODE ISLAND	**677**	**42,181**	**69,563**	**576,919**	**54.8**	**100.0**
BRISTOL	**25**	**1,321**	**3,213**	**41,626**	**83.5**	**100.0**
ANG/EPIS–Episcopal	3	406	1,174	1,201	2.4	2.9
Bahá'í	0	NR	11	11	0.0	0.0
BAPT–Amer Bapt USA	2	66	179	211	0.4	0.5
BAPT–Consrv Bapt	1	NR	NR	NR	-	-
Catholic	9	NR	NR	37,476	75.1	90.0
Jehovah's Witness	1	NR	NR	NR	-	-
JUD–Reform	1	99	174	470	0.9	1.1
LUTH–E.L.C.A.	1	140	307	428	0.9	1.0
METH–Un Methodist	2	90	403	599	1.2	1.4
PENT–Assemb of God	2	122	89	198	0.4	0.5
PRES–Presb Ch (USA)	1	54	99	117	0.2	0.3
Un C of Christ	2	344	777	915	1.8	2.2
KENT	**86**	**5,739**	**10,915**	**95,151**	**57.3**	**100.0**
ANG/EPIS–Episcopal	5	620	2,085	2,418	1.5	2.5
Bahá'í	1	NR	40	40	0.0	0.0
BAPT–Amer Bapt USA	11	793	1,914	2,263	1.4	2.4
BAPT–Consrv Bapt	3	NR	NR	NR	-	-
BAPT–So Bapt Conv	1	223	315	372	0.2	0.4
BUDD–Mahayana	2	NR	NR	113	0.1	0.1
Catholic	23	NR	NR	79,337	47.7	83.4
CHR–Chs of Christ	1	45	52	59	0.0	0.1
CONG–Cong Chr, NA	1	NR	25	30	0.0	0.0
CONG–Consrv Cong Chr	1	200	354	419	0.3	0.4
Evan Cov Ch	1	704	371	915	0.6	1.0
Jehovah's Witness	2	NR	NR	NR	-	-

NR–Not Reported - Represents no adherents reported. Percentages may not total 100 due to rounding.

Table 3: Religious Congregations by County and Group: 2010

Religious Group	Number of Congrega-tions	Number of Attendees	Number of Communicant, Confirmed, or Full Members	Adherents: Number of Adherents	Adherents: % of Total Pop.	Adherents: % of Total Adh.
JUD–Conserv	1	157	176	475	0.3	0.5
JUD–Orth	1	43	50	60	0.0	0.1
LDS–Comm of Christ	1	NR	102	102	0.1	0.1
LDS–L-D Saints	2	NR	NR	1,135	0.7	1.2
LUTH–E.L.C.A.	4	513	1,682	2,325	1.4	2.4
METH–Un Methodist	6	543	1,554	2,036	1.2	2.1
Non-denom Chr Chs	8	1,360	1,175	1,710	1.0	1.8
PENT–Assemb of God	3	161	133	243	0.1	0.3
PENT–Ch God (Cleve)	1	14	8	9	0.0	0.0
PRES–Pres Ref	1	NR	NR	NR	-	-
PRES–Presb Ch (USA)	2	134	533	630	0.4	0.7
PRES–Presb Ch Amer	1	65	36	59	0.0	0.1
Un C of Christ	2	65	128	151	0.1	0.2
Unit Univ	1	99	182	249	0.1	0.3
Zoroastrian	0	NR	NR	1	0.0	0.0
NEWPORT	**64**	**3,611**	**7,704**	**39,084**	**47.2**	**100.0**
ANG/EPIS–Episcopal	10	971	2,361	3,293	4.0	8.4
Bahá'í	0	NR	23	23	0.0	0.1
BAPT–Amer Bapt USA	4	350	1,101	1,292	1.6	3.3
BAPT–Consrv Bapt	1	NR	NR	NR	-	-
BAPT–So Bapt Conv	4	147	116	136	0.2	0.3
BUDD–Mahayana	1	NR	NR	102	0.1	0.3
Catholic	14	NR	NR	28,392	34.3	72.6
Ch Cr, Scientst	1	NR	NR	NR	-	-
CHR–Chs of Christ	1	35	30	35	0.0	0.1
CONG–Cong Chr Add'l	2	NR	863	1,013	1.2	2.6
FRND–Evan Fr Ch Intl	2	361	145	170	0.2	0.4
FRND–Fr Gen Cf & Un Mtg	1	NR	0	0	0.0	0.0
Jehovah's Witness	2	NR	NR	NR	-	-
JUD–Orth	1	122	140	170	0.2	0.4
JUD–Reform	1	12	22	59	0.1	0.2
LDS–Comm of Christ	1	NR	102	102	0.1	0.3
LDS–L-D Saints	1	NR	NR	428	0.5	1.1
LUTH–E.L.C.A.	1	102	264	360	0.4	0.9
METH–AME	1	0	100	117	0.1	0.3
METH–Un Methodist	3	238	811	906	1.1	2.3
Non-denom Chr Chs	3	631	720	789	1.0	2.0
ORTHE–Greek Orthodox	1	95	NR	300	0.4	0.8
PENT–Assemb of God	1	80	26	115	0.1	0.3
PENT–Un Pent Ch Intl	2	NR	NR	NR	-	-
PRES–Presb Ch (USA)	1	210	309	363	0.4	0.9
Salvation Army	1	21	60	277	0.3	0.7
Un C of Christ	2	105	300	352	0.4	0.9
Unit Univ	1	131	211	290	0.3	0.7
PROVIDENCE	**410**	**25,875**	**37,867**	**341,982**	**54.6**	**100.0**
ANG/EPIS–Episcopal	26	2,486	6,268	8,736	1.4	2.6
Bahá'í	1	NR	167	167	0.0	0.0
BAPT–Alliance Bapt	1	NR	NR	NR	-	-
BAPT–Amer Bapt USA	44	3,382	7,912	9,493	1.5	2.8
BAPT–Consrv Bapt	2	NR	NR	NR	-	-
BAPT–Converge/BGC	1	75	NR	90	0.0	0.0
BAPT–Ref Bapt Ch	1	NR	NR	NR	-	-
BAPT–Reg Bapt Gen As	1	NR	NR	NR	-	-
BAPT–So Bapt Conv	7	187	153	184	0.0	0.1
BUDD–Mahayana	5	NR	NR	487	0.1	0.1
BUDD–Theravada	4	NR	NR	1,487	0.2	0.4
BUDD–Vajrayana	3	NR	NR	116	0.0	0.0
Catholic	96	NR	NR	276,011	44.0	80.7
CGOD–Ch God (Ander)	1	110	NR	110	0.0	0.0
Ch Cr, Scientst	2	NR	NR	NR	-	-
Ch of Nazarene	6	510	571	653	0.1	0.2
Chr & Miss Al	3	392	385	551	0.1	0.2
CHR–Chr Chs & Chs Cr	3	NR	0	0	0.0	0.0
CHR–Chs of Christ	4	290	301	450	0.1	0.1
CONG–Consrv Cong Chr	1	90	114	137	0.0	0.0
Evan Cov Ch	3	149	216	193	0.0	0.1
FRND–Fr Gen Cf & Un Mtg	3	NR	263	316	0.1	0.1
HINDU–Post Ren	1	NR	NR	25	0.0	0.0
HINDU–Renaiss	1	NR	NR	84	0.0	0.0
Jehovah's Witness	6	NR	NR	NR	-	-
JUD–Conserv	3	977	1,096	2,959	0.5	0.9

Religious Group	Number of Congrega-tions	Number of Attendees	Number of Communicant, Confirmed, or Full Members	Adherents: Number of Adherents	Adherents: % of Total Pop.	Adherents: % of Total Adh.
JUD–Orth	6	972	400	1,350	0.2	0.4
JUD–Reform	2	693	1,223	3,302	0.5	1.0
LDS–L-D Saints	3	NR	NR	1,934	0.3	0.6
LUTH–Ch of Luth Br	1	47	30	82	0.0	0.0
LUTH–E.L.C.A.	5	380	998	1,292	0.2	0.4
LUTH–Luth–MO Synod	2	365	663	814	0.1	0.2
METH–AME	2	75	325	390	0.1	0.1
METH–AME Zion	2	0	250	300	0.0	0.1
METH–Free Methodist	1	348	159	348	0.1	0.1
METH–Prim Meth Ch	4	NR	NR	NR	-	-
METH–Un Methodist	9	720	2,289	2,528	0.4	0.7
Missionary Ch	1	15	14	15	0.0	0.0
Muslim Est	5	548	NR	1,244	0.2	0.4
New Apost Ch	1	NR	NR	NR	-	-
Non-denom Chr Chs	15	4,075	4,205	5,181	0.8	1.5
OCATH–Pol Natl Cath	2	NR	NR	NR	-	-
ORTHE–Ant Orth of NA	1	105	NR	450	0.1	0.1
ORTHE–Greek Orthodox	2	525	NR	2,325	0.4	0.7
ORTHE–Orth Ch in Amer	2	95	NR	525	0.1	0.2
ORTHE–Ukrainian Orth	1	80	NR	175	0.0	0.1
ORTHO–Armen Ap Cilic	1	200	NR	2,500	0.4	0.7
ORTHO–Armen Ap Etchm	1	175	NR	500	0.1	0.1
ORTHO–Coptic Orth Ch	1	275	NR	450	0.1	0.1
ORTHO–Syrian Orth Ch	1	80	NR	400	0.1	0.1
PENT–Assemb of God	20	2,571	1,561	3,463	0.6	1.0
PENT–Ch God (Cleve)	23	1,412	1,529	1,834	0.3	0.5
PENT–Ch Lord Jesus Apos	1	NR	NR	NR	-	-
PENT–Ch of God Proph	4	NR	121	145	0.0	0.0
PENT–COGIC	1	15	18	22	0.0	0.0
PENT–Full Gosp Bapt	2	NR	NR	NR	-	-
PENT–Int Foursq Gos	1	107	52	62	0.0	0.0
PENT–Un Pent Ch Intl	7	NR	NR	NR	-	-
PENT–United Holy Ch	1	NR	NR	NR	-	-
PRES–Presb Ch (USA)	3	218	373	448	0.1	0.1
PRES–Presb Ch Amer	1	145	167	206	0.0	0.1
PRES–Ref Pres of NA	1	40	30	50	0.0	0.0
REF–Christian Ref	1	NR	0	0	0.0	0.0
Salvation Army	3	154	340	563	0.1	0.2
Sev Day Adv	16	882	1,534	1,764	0.3	0.5
Un C of Christ	20	1,597	3,609	4,330	0.7	1.3
Unit Univ	5	313	531	730	0.1	0.2
Zoroastrian	0	NR	NR	11	0.0	0.0
WASHINGTON	**92**	**5,635**	**9,864**	**59,076**	**46.5**	**100.0**
ANG/EPIS–Episcopal	10	1,040	2,592	3,729	2.9	6.3
Bahá'í	0	NR	32	32	0.0	0.1
BAPT–Amer Bapt USA	14	746	1,672	1,961	1.5	3.3
BAPT–Consrv Bapt	1	NR	NR	NR	-	-
BAPT–Free Will Bapt	1	NR	101	118	0.1	0.2
BAPT–S-D Baptist Gen Con	4	87	246	289	0.2	0.5
BAPT–So Bapt Conv	3	135	323	379	0.3	0.6
BUDD–Mahayana	1	NR	NR	11	0.0	0.0
Calv Chpl	1	NR	NR	NR	-	-
Catholic	17	NR	NR	45,382	35.7	76.8
CGOD–Ch God (Ander)	1	55	NR	55	0.0	0.1
Ch Cr, Scientst	1	NR	NR	NR	-	-
Ch of Nazarene	1	15	31	40	0.0	0.1
CHR–Chs of Christ	1	85	68	100	0.1	0.2
Evan Free Ch	1	20	NR	20	0.0	0.0
FRND–Fr Gen Cf & Un Mtg	1	NR	65	76	0.1	0.1
Jehovah's Witness	3	NR	NR	NR	-	-
LDS–L-D Saints	1	NR	NR	336	0.3	0.6
LUTH–E.L.C.A.	2	355	585	856	0.7	1.4
LUTH–Luth–MO Synod	1	66	161	201	0.2	0.3
METH–Un Methodist	3	223	456	832	0.7	1.4
Muslim Est	1	40	NR	200	0.2	0.3
Non-denom Chr Chs	11	1,400	1,723	1,924	1.5	3.3
PENT–Assemb of God	5	483	236	647	0.5	1.1
PENT–Ch God (Cleve)	1	10	13	15	0.0	0.0
PRES–Presb Ch (USA)	2	303	470	551	0.4	0.9
Sev Day Adv	1	26	46	53	0.0	0.1
Un C of Christ	2	411	897	1,052	0.8	1.8
Unit Univ	1	135	147	217	0.2	0.4

NR–Not Reported - Represents no adherents reported. Percentages may not total 100 due to rounding.

Table 3: Religious Congregations by County and Group: 2010

Religious Group	Number of Congregations	Number of Attendees	Number of Communicant, Confirmed, or Full Members	Adherents: Number of Adherents	Adherents: % of Total Pop.	Adherents: % of Total Adh.
SOUTH CAROLINA	**8,051**	**867,878**	**1,782,676**	**2,413,443**	**52.2**	**100.0**
ABBEVILLE	**89**	**5,407**	**13,353**	**16,523**	**65.0**	**100.0**
ANG/EPIS–Episcopal	1	36	40	40	0.2	0.2
Bahá'í	0	NR	25	25	0.1	0.2
BAPT–So Bapt Conv	22	2,340	6,056	7,326	28.8	44.3
Catholic	1	NR	NR	121	0.5	0.7
CHR–Chs of Christ	4	406	530	733	2.9	4.4
MENN–Beachy Amish-Menn	1	219	133	219	0.9	1.3
METH–AME	21	110	2,468	2,985	11.7	18.1
METH–AME Zion	1	0	150	181	0.7	1.1
METH–C.M.E.	2	0	300	363	1.4	2.2
METH–Un Methodist	9	779	1,321	1,629	6.4	9.9
Non-denom Chr Chs	3	515	500	645	2.5	3.9
ORTHE–Greek Orthodox	1	60	NR	63	0.2	0.4
PENT–Assemb of God	2	93	72	96	0.4	0.6
PENT–Ch God (Cleve)	3	181	359	434	1.7	2.6
PENT–Ch of God Proph	1	NR	45	54	0.2	0.3
PENT–Cong Hol Ch	1	67	63	76	0.3	0.5
PENT–Fire Bapt Hol Ch	1	NR	NR	NR	-	-
PENT–Intl Pent Holiness	3	200	405	490	1.9	3.0
PRES–As Ref Pres Ch	3	NR	182	220	0.9	1.3
PRES–Presb Ch (USA)	7	300	525	635	2.5	3.8
PRES–Presb Ch Amer	2	101	179	188	0.7	1.1
AIKEN	**267**	**34,477**	**71,616**	**96,010**	**60.0**	**100.0**
ANG/EPIS–Anglican NA	1	NR	NR	NR	-	-
ANG/EPIS–Episcopal	5	589	1,241	1,372	0.9	1.4
Bahá'í	1	NR	73	73	0.0	0.1
BAPT–Free Will Bapt	1	NR	38	46	0.0	0.0
BAPT–Natl Mis Bapt Conv	5	270	693	842	0.5	0.9
BAPT–NBC USA	13	1,400	4,740	5,758	3.6	6.0
BAPT–So Bapt Conv	93	13,830	35,717	43,386	27.1	45.2
BRETH–Grace Breth	1	NR	NR	NR	-	-
Calv Chpl	1	NR	NR	NR	-	-
Catholic	4	NR	NR	8,400	5.2	8.7
CGOD–Ch God (Ander)	3	116	NR	116	0.1	0.1
Ch Cr, Scientst	1	NR	NR	NR	-	-
Ch of Nazarene	4	600	803	859	0.5	0.9
CHR–Chr Ch (Disc)	3	159	281	341	0.2	0.4
CHR–Chr Chs & Chs Cr	1	NR	40	49	0.0	0.1
CHR–Chs of Christ	10	579	564	754	0.5	0.8
FRND–Fr Gen Cf	1	NR	0	0	0.0	0.0
Jehovah's Witness	5	NR	NR	NR	-	-
JUD–Reform	1	42	74	200	0.1	0.2
LDS–L-D Saints	4	NR	NR	1,601	1.0	1.7
LUTH–E.L.C.A.	3	512	882	1,253	0.8	1.3
LUTH–Luth-MO Synod	1	68	128	137	0.1	0.1
MENN–Cons Menn Conf	1	34	19	23	0.0	0.0
METH–AME	2	0	200	243	0.2	0.3
METH–C.M.E.	1	40	75	91	0.1	0.1
METH–So Methodist	1	NR	NR	NR	-	-
METH–Un Methodist	18	2,218	6,031	6,898	4.3	7.2
Non-denom Chr Chs	30	9,570	12,157	13,892	8.7	14.5
ORTHE–Ant Orth of NA	1	16	NR	25	0.0	0.0
ORTHE–Orth Ch in Amer	2	56	NR	79	0.0	0.1
PENT–Apos Faith Msn	1	NR	35	43	0.0	0.0
PENT–Assemb of God	2	54	29	54	0.0	0.1
PENT–Ch God (Cleve)	15	1,622	2,809	3,412	2.1	3.6
PENT–Ch of God Proph	1	NR	11	13	0.0	0.0
PENT–COGIC	1	0	150	182	0.1	0.2
PENT–Cong Hol Ch	3	495	537	652	0.4	0.7
PENT–Fire Bapt Hol Ch	2	NR	NR	NR	-	-
PENT–Int Foursq Gos	1	18	18	22	0.0	0.0
PENT–Intl Pent Holiness	9	733	1,465	1,780	1.1	1.9
PENT–Un Pent Ch Intl	2	NR	NR	NR	-	-
PRES–Orth Pres Ch	1	41	45	61	0.0	0.1
PRES–Presb Ch (USA)	3	919	2,008	2,439	1.5	2.5
PRES–Presb Ch Amer	2	266	375	445	0.3	0.5
REF–Comm Ref Evan	1	NR	NR	NR	-	-
Salvation Army	1	50	90	132	0.1	0.1
Sev Day Adv	3	131	228	262	0.2	0.3
Unit Univ	1	49	60	75	0.0	0.1

Religious Group	Number of Congregations	Number of Attendees	Number of Communicant, Confirmed, or Full Members	Adherents: Number of Adherents	Adherents: % of Total Pop.	Adherents: % of Total Adh.
ALLENDALE	**30**	**984**	**3,621**	**4,379**	**42.0**	**100.0**
ANG/EPIS–Episcopal	1	15	23	24	0.2	0.5
Bahá'í	0	NR	20	20	0.2	0.5
BAPT–NBC USA	2	75	450	542	5.2	12.4
BAPT–So Bapt Conv	7	367	1,342	1,616	15.5	36.9
Catholic	1	NR	NR	115	1.1	2.6
CHR–Chr Ch (Disc)	4	101	182	219	2.1	5.0
LUTH–E.L.C.A.	2	65	120	148	1.4	3.4
METH–AME	2	0	300	361	3.5	8.2
METH–C.M.E.	2	0	300	361	3.5	8.2
METH–Un Methodist	5	191	664	701	6.7	16.0
Non-denom Chr Chs	1	150	150	188	1.8	4.3
PENT–Ch God (Cleve)	1	20	53	64	0.6	1.5
PENT–Ch Lord Jesus Apos	1	NR	NR	NR	-	-
PRES–Presb Ch (USA)	1	0	17	20	0.2	0.5
ANDERSON	**338**	**50,317**	**96,525**	**121,561**	**65.0**	**100.0**
ANG/EPIS–Episcopal	2	196	485	496	0.3	0.4
Bahá'í	1	NR	172	172	0.1	0.1
BAPT–Free Will Bapt	1	NR	38	47	0.0	0.0
BAPT–NBC USA	9	720	1,836	2,255	1.2	1.9
BAPT–Prog NBC	9	1,178	2,814	3,456	1.8	2.8
BAPT–So Bapt Conv	122	31,484	62,450	76,696	41.0	63.1
BRETH–Grace Breth	1	NR	NR	NR	-	-
BUDD–Vajrayana	1	NR	NR	16	0.0	0.0
Catholic	2	NR	NR	2,851	1.5	2.3
Ch of God Gen Conf	1	NR	20	25	0.0	0.0
Ch of Nazarene	1	33	0	33	0.0	0.0
CHR–Chs of Christ	3	110	118	138	0.1	0.1
HINDU–Post Ren	1	NR	NR	25	0.0	0.0
Jehovah's Witness	1	NR	NR	NR	-	-
LDS–L-D Saints	1	NR	NR	933	0.5	0.8
LUTH–E.L.C.A.	1	134	256	293	0.2	0.2
LUTH–Luth-MO Synod	1	67	137	166	0.1	0.1
METH–AME	7	200	1,220	1,498	0.8	1.2
METH–C.M.E.	4	0	550	675	0.4	0.6
METH–Un Methodist	37	2,813	6,799	7,766	4.2	6.4
METH–Wesleyan	6	323	359	420	0.2	0.3
Non-denom Chr Chs	33	5,935	6,982	7,839	4.2	6.4
ORTHE–Ant Orth of NA	1	35	NR	50	0.0	0.0
PENT–Assemb of God	7	757	336	930	0.5	0.8
PENT–Ch God (Cleve)	22	2,995	4,967	6,100	3.3	5.0
PENT–Ch of God Proph	12	NR	406	499	0.3	0.4
PENT–Fire Bapt Hol Ch	4	NR	NR	NR	-	-
PENT–Full Gosp Bapt	1	NR	NR	NR	-	-
PENT–Intl Pent Holiness	14	1,395	2,939	3,609	1.9	3.0
PENT–Un Pent Ch Intl	2	NR	NR	NR	-	-
PRES–As Ref Pres Ch	4	NR	215	264	0.1	0.2
PRES–Evan Presby Ch	1	NR	119	146	0.1	0.1
PRES–Presb Ch (USA)	18	1,325	2,622	3,220	1.7	2.6
PRES–Presb Ch Amer	3	450	407	549	0.3	0.5
Salvation Army	1	25	31	110	0.1	0.1
Sev Day Adv	2	142	247	284	0.2	0.2
Unity Ch	1	NR	NR	NR	-	-
BAMBERG	**56**	**2,396**	**5,766**	**6,581**	**41.2**	**100.0**
ANG/EPIS–Episcopal	2	36	74	81	0.5	1.2
Bahá'í	0	NR	97	97	0.6	1.5
BAPT–NBC USA	1	150	150	180	1.1	2.7
BAPT–So Bapt Conv	12	787	2,475	2,972	18.6	45.2
Ch of Nazarene	1	17	56	56	0.4	0.9
CHR–Chr Ch (Disc)	3	31	44	53	0.3	0.8
CHR–Chs of Christ	1	7	8	8	0.1	0.1
Jehovah's Witness	1	NR	NR	NR	-	-
LUTH–E.L.C.A.	2	50	51	60	0.4	0.9
METH–AME	1	0	100	120	0.8	1.8
METH–So Methodist	1	NR	NR	NR	-	-
METH–Un Methodist	17	860	1,960	2,076	13.0	31.5
Non-denom Chr Chs	2	225	300	338	2.1	5.1
PENT–Ch God (Cleve)	3	60	82	98	0.6	1.5
PENT–Ch of God Proph	2	NR	38	46	0.3	0.7
PENT–COGIC	1	0	60	72	0.5	1.1
PENT–Intl Pent Holiness	3	137	204	245	1.5	3.7

NR–Not Reported - Represents no adherents reported. Percentages may not total 100 due to rounding.

Table 3: Religious Congregations by County and Group: 2010

Religious Group	Number of Congregations	Number of Attendees	Number of Communicant, Confirmed, or Full Members	Adherents: Number of Adherents	Adherents: % of Total Pop.	Adherents: % of Total Adh.
PENT–Un Pent Ch Intl	1	NR	NR	NR	-	-
PRES–Presb Ch (USA)	1	14	29	35	0.2	0.5
Sev Day Adv	1	22	38	44	0.3	0.7
BARNWELL	**65**	**4,129**	**10,405**	**13,116**	**58.0**	**100.0**
ANG/EPIS–Episcopal	1	39	91	91	0.4	0.7
Bahá'í	0	NR	36	36	0.2	0.3
BAPT–NBC USA	3	155	266	331	1.5	2.5
BAPT–So Bapt Conv	28	2,346	7,415	9,228	40.8	70.4
Catholic	2	NR	NR	150	0.7	1.1
CGOD–Ch God (Ander)	1	18	NR	18	0.1	0.1
CHR–Chr Chs & Chs Cr	1	NR	80	100	0.4	0.8
CHR–Chs of Christ	3	200	220	255	1.1	1.9
Jehovah's Witness	2	NR	NR	NR	-	-
LDS–L-D Saints	1	NR	NR	233	1.0	1.8
MENN–Beachy Amish-Menn	1	66	41	66	0.3	0.5
METH–So Methodist	2	NR	NR	NR	-	-
METH–Un Methodist	5	287	952	1,001	4.4	7.6
Non-denom Chr Chs	3	295	330	369	1.6	2.8
PENT–Assemb of God	1	25	7	35	0.2	0.3
PENT–Ch God (Cleve)	3	104	156	194	0.9	1.5
PENT–COGIC	1	200	150	187	0.8	1.4
PENT–Intl Pent Holiness	3	384	398	495	2.2	3.8
PENT–Un Pent Ch Intl	1	NR	NR	NR	-	-
PRES–Presb Ch (USA)	3	10	263	327	1.4	2.5
BEAUFORT	**140**	**18,822**	**35,470**	**60,862**	**37.5**	**100.0**
ANG/EPIS–Anglican NA	1	NR	NR	NR	-	-
ANG/EPIS–Episcopal	4	2,173	4,414	5,091	3.1	8.4
Bahá'í	1	NR	448	448	0.3	0.7
BAPT–NBC USA	6	560	1,075	1,294	0.8	2.1
BAPT–So Bapt Conv	22	2,601	9,344	11,245	6.9	18.5
BUDD–Mahayana	2	NR	NR	21	0.0	0.0
Catholic	5	NR	NR	16,117	9.9	26.5
CGOD–Ches God-Gen Con	1	0	0	0	0.0	0.0
Ch Cr, Scientst	2	NR	NR	NR	-	-
Ch of Nazarene	1	78	52	124	0.1	0.2
CHR–Chr Ch (Disc)	3	190	360	433	0.3	0.7
CHR–Chr Chs & Chs Cr	2	NR	290	349	0.2	0.6
CHR–Chs of Christ	6	254	180	266	0.2	0.4
FRND–Fr Gen Cf	1	NR	0	0	0.0	0.0
Jehovah's Witness	4	NR	NR	NR	-	-
JUD–Conserv	1	61	68	184	0.1	0.3
JUD–Reform	1	104	183	494	0.3	0.8
LDS–L-D Saints	2	NR	NR	1,391	0.9	2.3
LUTH–E.L.C.A.	3	725	1,156	1,465	0.9	2.4
LUTH–Luth Cong Msn Chr	1	85	80	96	0.1	0.2
LUTH–Luth–MO Synod	1	110	129	137	0.1	0.2
METH–AME	9	175	1,155	1,390	0.9	2.3
METH–Un Methodist	9	1,281	2,790	3,297	2.0	5.4
METH–Wesleyan	1	35	14	46	0.0	0.1
Non-denom Chr Chs	21	5,853	7,559	8,503	5.2	14.0
ORTHE–Greek Orthodox	1	50	NR	140	0.1	0.2
PENT–Assemb of God	4	942	154	942	0.6	1.5
PENT–Ch God (Cleve)	2	453	796	958	0.6	1.6
PENT–Ch of God Proph	1	NR	8	10	0.0	0.0
PENT–COGIC	1	30	40	48	0.0	0.1
PENT–Int Foursq Gos	1	0	0	0	0.0	0.0
PENT–Un Pent Ch Intl	3	NR	NR	NR	-	-
PENT–Vineyard	1	150	180	217	0.1	0.4
PRES–Evan Presby Ch	1	NR	1	1	0.0	0.0
PRES–Presb Ch (USA)	6	2,162	4,002	4,816	3.0	7.9
PRES–Presb Ch Amer	2	380	380	490	0.3	0.8
Salvation Army	1	42	69	201	0.1	0.3
Sev Day Adv	3	208	362	417	0.3	0.7
Unit Univ	2	120	181	231	0.1	0.4
Unity Ch	1	NR	NR	NR	-	-
BERKELEY	**225**	**17,258**	**35,500**	**54,341**	**30.6**	**100.0**
ANG/EPIS–Anglican NA	17	NR	NR	NR	-	-
ANG/EPIS–Episcopal	5	243	346	438	0.2	0.8
Bahá'í	1	NR	317	317	0.2	0.6
BAPT–Free Will Bapt	2	NR	76	95	0.1	0.2
BAPT–Natl Mis Bapt Conv	2	11	161	201	0.1	0.4
BAPT–NBC USA	4	100	620	773	0.4	1.4
BAPT–Ref Bapt Ch	1	NR	NR	NR	-	-
BAPT–S-D Baptist Gen Con	1	NR	NR	NR	-	-
BAPT–So Bapt Conv	40	3,615	11,438	14,260	8.0	26.2
Calv Chpl	1	NR	NR	NR	-	-
Catholic	4	NR	NR	7,244	4.1	13.3
Ch of Nazarene	3	270	458	458	0.3	0.8
CHR–Chr Ch (Disc)	7	545	963	1,201	0.7	2.2
CHR–Chr Chs & Chs Cr	6	NR	793	989	0.6	1.8
CHR–Chs of Christ	3	252	189	269	0.2	0.5
HINDU–Trad Temples	1	NR	NR	1,033	0.6	1.9
Jehovah's Witness	2	NR	NR	NR	-	-
LDS–L-D Saints	1	NR	NR	557	0.3	1.0
LUTH–E.L.C.A.	3	346	777	1,147	0.6	2.1
METH–AME	22	770	3,815	4,756	2.7	8.8
METH–So Methodist	1	NR	NR	NR	-	-
METH–Un Methodist	32	2,633	5,758	6,531	3.7	12.0
MJEW–Union Mes Cong	1	NR	NR	NR	-	-
Muslim Est	1	134	NR	308	0.2	0.6
Non-denom Chr Chs	15	3,535	3,983	4,714	2.7	8.7
PENT–Assemb of God	3	2,470	1,587	3,780	2.1	7.0
PENT–Ch God (Cleve)	4	314	744	928	0.5	1.7
PENT–Ch Lord Jesus Apos	4	NR	NR	NR	-	-
PENT–Ch of God Proph	4	NR	158	197	0.1	0.4
PENT–COGIC	5	70	528	658	0.4	1.2
PENT–Int Foursq Gos	1	16	7	9	0.0	0.0
PENT–Intl Pent Holiness	19	1,147	1,512	1,885	1.1	3.5
PENT–Un Pent Ch Intl	1	NR	NR	NR	-	-
PENT–Vineyard	1	64	76	95	0.1	0.2
PRES–Presb Ch (USA)	4	465	825	1,029	0.6	1.9
PRES–Presb Ch Amer	1	200	268	353	0.2	0.6
Sev Day Adv	2	58	101	116	0.1	0.2
CALHOUN	**41**	**1,584**	**4,727**	**5,692**	**37.5**	**100.0**
ANG/EPIS–Episcopal	1	44	83	108	0.7	1.9
Bahá'í	0	NR	106	106	0.7	1.9
BAPT–So Bapt Conv	2	200	523	627	4.1	11.0
CGOD–Ch God (Ander)	1	45	NR	45	0.3	0.8
Jehovah's Witness	1	NR	NR	NR	-	-
LUTH–E.L.C.A.	4	262	464	558	3.7	9.8
METH–AME	14	134	2,010	2,411	15.9	42.4
METH–So Methodist	1	NR	NR	NR	-	-
METH–Un Methodist	9	423	1,021	1,191	7.8	20.9
Non-denom Chr Chs	3	340	340	426	2.8	7.5
PENT–Assemb of God	1	18	10	18	0.1	0.3
PENT–Ch God (Cleve)	1	45	55	66	0.4	1.2
PENT–Ch Lord Jesus Apos	1	NR	NR	NR	-	-
PENT–Intl Pent Holiness	1	35	60	72	0.5	1.3
PRES–Presb Ch Amer	1	38	55	64	0.4	1.1
CHARLESTON	**477**	**73,992**	**141,638**	**197,883**	**56.5**	**100.0**
ANG/EPIS–Anglican NA	15	NR	NR	NR	-	-
ANG/EPIS–Episcopal	22	5,617	14,188	14,957	4.3	7.6
Bahá'í	1	NR	676	676	0.2	0.3
BAPT–Consrv Bapt	1	NR	NR	NR	-	-
BAPT–Free Will Bapt	2	NR	76	91	0.0	0.0
BAPT–Natl Mis Bapt Conv	1	0	150	180	0.1	0.1
BAPT–NBC Amer	1	100	150	180	0.1	0.1
BAPT–NBC USA	15	4,125	8,620	10,326	2.9	5.2
BAPT–Prog NBC	4	130	510	611	0.2	0.3
BAPT–S-D Baptist Gen Con	1	NR	NR	NR	-	-
BAPT–So Bapt Conv	59	10,489	26,529	31,780	9.1	16.1
Calv Chpl	1	NR	NR	NR	-	-
Catholic	19	NR	NR	26,003	7.4	13.1
CGOD–Ch God (Ander)	1	0	NR	0	0.0	0.0
Ch Cr, Scientst	1	NR	NR	NR	-	-
Ch of Nazarene	3	269	397	469	0.1	0.2
Chr & Miss Al	1	NR	NR	NR	-	-
CHR–Chr Ch (Disc)	2	100	254	304	0.1	0.2
CHR–Chr Chs & Chs Cr	2	NR	22	26	0.0	0.0
CHR–Chs of Christ	8	1,089	1,289	1,549	0.4	0.8
FRND–Fr Gen Cf	1	NR	7	8	0.0	0.0

NR–Not Reported   - Represents no adherents reported.   Percentages may not total 100 due to rounding.

Table 3: Religious Congregations by County and Group: 2010

Religious Group	Number of Congrega-tions	Number of Attendees	Number of Communicant, Confirmed, or Full Members	Adherents		
				Number of Adherents	% of Total Pop.	% of Total Adh.
HINDU–Post Ren	1	NR	NR	77	0.0	0.0
Ind Fund Churches	1	NR	NR	NR	-	-
Jehovah's Witness	6	NR	NR	NR	-	-
JUD–Conserv	1	278	312	842	0.2	0.4
JUD–Orth	2	266	110	370	0.1	0.2
JUD–Reform	1	232	410	1,107	0.3	0.6
LDS–Comm of Christ	1	NR	118	118	0.0	0.1
LDS–L-D Saints	5	NR	NR	4,199	1.2	2.1
LUTH–E.L.C.A.	12	1,400	3,693	4,622	1.3	2.3
LUTH–Luth–MO Synod	2	166	168	211	0.1	0.1
METH–AME	68	6,695	20,720	24,821	7.1	12.5
METH–AME Zion	1	0	100	120	0.0	0.1
METH–C.M.E.	1	0	250	299	0.1	0.2
METH–So Methodist	4	NR	NR	NR	-	-
METH–Un Methodist	43	5,329	13,099	14,724	4.2	7.4
Metro Comm Ch	1	89	79	95	0.0	0.0
Muslim Est	3	402	NR	924	0.3	0.5
Non-denom Chr Chs	79	28,540	33,750	37,581	10.7	19.0
ORTHE–Greek Orthodox	1	250	NR	720	0.2	0.4
ORTHE–Orth Ch in Amer	1	75	NR	130	0.0	0.1
PENT–Assemb of God	9	770	516	1,137	0.3	0.6
PENT–Ch God (Cleve)	7	849	1,211	1,451	0.4	0.7
PENT–Ch Lord Jesus Apos	8	NR	NR	NR	-	-
PENT–Ch of God Proph	3	NR	91	109	0.0	0.1
PENT–COGIC	4	360	830	994	0.3	0.5
PENT–Intl Pent Holiness	7	471	659	789	0.2	0.4
PENT–Un Pent Asbl God	2	NR	NR	NR	-	-
PENT–Un Pent Ch Intl	3	NR	NR	NR	-	-
PRES–As Ref Pres Ch	1	NR	55	66	0.0	0.0
PRES–Kor Pres Abroad	1	NR	NR	NR	-	-
PRES–Presb Ch (USA)	23	4,273	9,998	11,977	3.4	6.1
PRES–Presb Ch Amer	4	311	301	372	0.1	0.2
Salvation Army	1	71	133	278	0.1	0.1
Sev Day Adv	5	846	1,472	1,693	0.5	0.9
Un C of Christ	2	232	436	522	0.1	0.3
Unit Univ	1	168	259	374	0.1	0.2
Unity Ch	1	NR	NR	NR	-	-
Zoroastrian	0	NR	NR	1	0.0	0.0
CHEROKEE	**112**	**11,482**	**26,585**	**34,565**	**62.5**	**100.0**
ANG/EPIS–Episcopal	1	58	109	109	0.2	0.3
Bahá'í	0	NR	53	53	0.1	0.2
BAPT–Alliance Bapt	1	NR	NR	NR	-	-
BAPT–Free Will Bapt	1	NR	38	47	0.1	0.1
BAPT–NBC USA	4	475	816	1,008	1.8	2.9
BAPT–Prog NBC	1	350	550	679	1.2	2.0
BAPT–So Bapt Conv	58	7,213	19,088	23,569	42.6	68.2
Catholic	1	NR	NR	1,100	2.0	3.2
CHR–Chs of Christ	1	22	22	28	0.1	0.1
Jehovah's Witness	1	NR	NR	NR	-	-
LDS–L-D Saints	1	NR	NR	591	1.1	1.7
LUTH–E.L.C.A.	1	6	11	11	0.0	0.0
LUTH–Luth Cong Msn Chr	1	85	140	173	0.3	0.5
METH–AME Zion	2	0	200	247	0.4	0.7
METH–C.M.E.	2	60	250	309	0.6	0.9
METH–Un Methodist	9	760	1,983	2,379	4.3	6.9
Non-denom Chr Chs	9	1,760	1,782	2,209	4.0	6.4
PENT–Assemb of God	1	47	33	110	0.2	0.3
PENT–Ch God (Cleve)	4	511	982	1,213	2.2	3.5
PENT–Ch of God Proph	1	NR	26	32	0.1	0.1
PENT–Fire Bapt Hol Ch	2	NR	NR	NR	-	-
PENT–Full Gosp Bapt	1	NR	NR	NR	-	-
PENT–Un Pent Ch Intl	1	NR	NR	NR	-	-
PRES–As Ref Pres Ch	1	NR	44	54	0.1	0.2
PRES–Evan Presby Ch	1	NR	52	64	0.1	0.2
PRES–Presb Ch (USA)	3	0	268	331	0.6	1.0
PRES–Presb Ch Amer	2	85	79	98	0.2	0.3
Salvation Army	1	50	59	151	0.3	0.4
CHESTER	**109**	**5,248**	**14,106**	**17,560**	**53.0**	**100.0**
ANG/EPIS–Episcopal	2	31	54	61	0.2	0.3
Bahá'í	0	NR	249	249	0.8	1.4
BAPT–Free Will Bapt	2	NR	76	93	0.3	0.5

Religious Group	Number of Congrega-tions	Number of Attendees	Number of Communicant, Confirmed, or Full Members	Adherents		
				Number of Adherents	% of Total Pop.	% of Total Adh.
BAPT–NBC Amer	1	0	0	0	0.0	0.0
BAPT–NBC USA	3	250	850	1,039	3.1	5.9
BAPT–So Bapt Conv	20	2,031	5,599	6,847	20.7	39.0
Catholic	2	NR	NR	174	0.5	1.0
Ch of Nazarene	2	222	343	467	1.4	2.7
CHR–Chs of Christ	1	8	10	10	0.0	0.1
Jehovah's Witness	1	NR	NR	NR	-	-
METH–AME Zion	24	390	2,949	3,606	10.9	20.5
METH–Un Methodist	15	610	1,404	1,643	5.0	9.4
Non-denom Chr Chs	7	755	600	965	2.9	5.5
PENT–Ch God (Cleve)	5	480	632	773	2.3	4.4
PENT–Ch of God Proph	1	NR	54	66	0.2	0.4
PENT–Intl Pent Holiness	2	49	88	108	0.3	0.6
PRES–As Ref Pres Ch	5	NR	355	434	1.3	2.5
PRES–Presb Ch (USA)	14	300	681	833	2.5	4.7
PRES–Presb Ch Amer	2	122	162	192	0.6	1.1
CHESTERFIELD	**145**	**7,599**	**18,656**	**23,277**	**49.8**	**100.0**
ANG/EPIS–Episcopal	1	66	116	120	0.3	0.5
Bahá'í	0	NR	212	212	0.5	0.9
BAPT–Free Will Bapt	1	NR	38	47	0.1	0.2
BAPT–Natl Mis Bapt Conv	2	0	300	369	0.8	1.6
BAPT–Prog NBC	2	0	150	184	0.4	0.8
BAPT–So Bapt Conv	54	3,887	9,302	11,433	24.5	49.1
Catholic	2	NR	NR	152	0.3	0.7
Ch of Nazarene	1	64	103	103	0.2	0.4
CHR–Chs of Christ	1	18	16	20	0.0	0.1
Jehovah's Witness	2	NR	NR	NR	-	-
LDS–L-D Saints	1	NR	NR	474	1.0	2.0
METH–AME	2	0	250	307	0.7	1.3
METH–AME Zion	13	240	1,874	2,303	4.9	9.9
METH–So Methodist	1	NR	NR	NR	-	-
METH–Un Methodist	30	1,409	3,626	4,181	8.9	18.0
Non-denom Chr Chs	5	425	350	544	1.2	2.3
PENT–Ch God (Cleve)	7	797	828	1,018	2.2	4.4
PENT–Ch of God Proph	3	NR	81	100	0.2	0.4
PENT–COGIC	1	0	150	184	0.4	0.8
PENT–Intl Pent Holiness	1	181	356	438	0.9	1.9
PRES–Presb Ch (USA)	12	416	769	945	2.0	4.1
PRES–Presb Ch Amer	1	65	81	81	0.2	0.3
Sev Day Adv	2	31	54	62	0.1	0.3
CLARENDON	**102**	**4,679**	**11,938**	**14,511**	**41.5**	**100.0**
ANG/EPIS–Episcopal	1	59	123	134	0.4	0.9
Bahá'í	0	NR	247	247	0.7	1.7
BAPT–Free Will Bapt	5	NR	190	228	0.7	1.6
BAPT–NBC USA	2	0	300	361	1.0	2.5
BAPT–So Bapt Conv	10	957	2,307	2,773	7.9	19.1
Catholic	2	NR	NR	360	1.0	2.5
CGOD–Ch God (Ander)	1	3	NR	3	0.0	0.0
CHR–Chs of Christ	1	63	62	70	0.2	0.5
Jehovah's Witness	2	NR	NR	NR	-	-
METH–AME	26	225	3,310	3,979	11.4	27.4
METH–So Methodist	2	NR	NR	NR	-	-
METH–Un Methodist	11	590	1,512	1,694	4.8	11.7
Non-denom Chr Chs	11	1,475	1,570	1,897	5.4	13.1
PENT–Assemb of God	1	25	20	32	0.1	0.2
PENT–Ch God (Cleve)	1	23	69	83	0.2	0.6
PENT–Ch of God by Faith	1	NR	NR	NR	-	-
PENT–Ch of God Proph	4	NR	139	167	0.5	1.2
PENT–Fire Bapt Hol Ch	3	NR	NR	NR	-	-
PENT–Intl Pent Holiness	6	408	461	554	1.6	3.8
PENT–Un Pent Ch Intl	1	NR	NR	NR	-	-
PRES–Presb Ch (USA)	7	551	1,095	1,316	3.8	9.1
PRES–Presb Ch Amer	3	255	455	523	1.5	3.6
Sev Day Adv	1	45	78	90	0.3	0.6
COLLETON	**131**	**6,774**	**16,838**	**20,999**	**54.0**	**100.0**
ANG/EPIS–Episcopal	2	89	221	228	0.6	1.1
Bahá'í	0	NR	455	455	1.2	2.2
BAPT–So Bapt Conv	27	2,095	6,539	8,036	20.7	38.3
Catholic	2	NR	NR	650	1.7	3.1
Ch of Nazarene	1	31	28	31	0.1	0.1

NR–Not Reported - Represents no adherents reported. Percentages may not total 100 due to rounding.

Table 3: Religious Congregations by County and Group: 2010

Religious Group	Number of Congrega-tions	Number of Attendees	Number of Communicant, Confirmed, or Full Members	Adherents		
				Number of Adherents	% of Total Pop.	% of Total Adh.
CHR–Chr Ch (Disc)	4	147	302	371	1.0	1.8
CHR–Chr Chs & Chs Cr	2	NR	152	187	0.5	0.9
CHR–Chs of Christ	2	62	53	62	0.2	0.3
Jehovah's Witness	1	NR	NR	NR	-	-
LDS–L-D Saints	1	NR	NR	332	0.9	1.6
LUTH–E.L.C.A.	1	53	156	184	0.5	0.9
METH–AME	14	200	2,100	2,581	6.6	12.3
METH–C.M.E.	3	0	350	430	1.1	2.0
METH–Un Methodist	34	1,575	3,628	3,819	9.8	18.2
Non-denom Chr Chs	14	1,963	1,945	2,464	6.3	11.7
PENT–Assemb of God	1	97	64	133	0.3	0.6
PENT–Ch God (Cleve)	1	161	238	292	0.8	1.4
PENT–Ch Lord Jesus Apos	8	NR	NR	NR	-	-
PENT–Ch of God Proph	3	NR	110	135	0.3	0.6
PENT–Intl Pent Holiness	3	142	166	204	0.5	1.0
PENT–Un Pent Asbl God	1	NR	NR	NR	-	-
PENT–Un Pent Ch Intl	2	NR	NR	NR	-	-
PRES–Presb Ch (USA)	3	151	316	388	1.0	1.8
Sev Day Adv	1	8	15	17	0.0	0.1
DARLINGTON	**145**	**10,528**	**25,891**	**32,187**	**46.9**	**100.0**
ANG/EPIS–Episcopal	2	181	302	313	0.5	1.0
Bahá'í	1	NR	1,198	1,198	1.7	3.7
BAPT–Free Will Bapt	6	NR	228	280	0.4	0.9
BAPT–NBC USA	11	670	1,960	2,407	3.5	7.5
BAPT–So Bapt Conv	31	3,316	10,144	12,455	18.1	38.7
Catholic	2	NR	NR	500	0.7	1.6
CGOD–Ch God (Ander)	5	312	NR	312	0.5	1.0
Ch of Nazarene	2	147	309	309	0.4	1.0
CHR–Chs of Christ	1	31	27	35	0.1	0.1
Jehovah's Witness	2	NR	NR	NR	-	-
LDS–L-D Saints	1	NR	NR	723	1.1	2.2
LUTH–E.L.C.A.	1	50	70	83	0.1	0.3
METH–AME	5	300	1,400	1,719	2.5	5.3
METH–So Methodist	4	NR	NR	NR	-	-
METH–Un Methodist	28	2,062	5,388	6,074	8.8	18.9
Non-denom Chr Chs	14	2,100	2,425	2,749	4.0	8.5
PENT–Assemb of God	1	30	18	44	0.1	0.1
PENT–Ch God (Cleve)	6	389	560	688	1.0	2.1
PENT–Ch of God Proph	3	NR	83	102	0.1	0.3
PENT–COGIC	1	75	85	104	0.2	0.3
PENT–Cong Hol Ch	1	11	10	12	0.0	0.0
PENT–Fire Bapt Hol Ch	2	NR	NR	NR	-	-
PENT–Intl Pent Holiness	6	312	401	492	0.7	1.5
PENT–Un Pent Asbl God	1	NR	NR	NR	-	-
PRES–Presb Ch (USA)	6	420	1,146	1,407	2.0	4.4
PRES–Presb Ch Amer	1	70	46	76	0.1	0.2
Sev Day Adv	1	52	91	105	0.2	0.3
DILLON	**88**	**6,081**	**15,138**	**18,319**	**57.1**	**100.0**
ANG/EPIS–Episcopal	1	22	48	51	0.2	0.3
Bahá'í	0	NR	1,155	1,155	3.6	6.3
BAPT–So Bapt Conv	25	2,646	6,242	7,862	24.5	42.9
Catholic	1	NR	NR	128	0.4	0.7
CHR–Chs of Christ	1	35	25	40	0.1	0.2
METH–AME	12	200	2,000	2,519	7.9	13.8
METH–AME Zion	1	0	100	126	0.4	0.7
METH–So Methodist	2	NR	NR	NR	-	-
METH–Un Methodist	17	921	2,115	2,221	6.9	12.1
Non-denom Chr Chs	5	850	930	1,126	3.5	6.1
PENT–Assemb of God	1	60	60	65	0.2	0.4
PENT–Ch God (Cleve)	6	815	1,554	1,957	6.1	10.7
PENT–Ch of God Proph	1	NR	6	8	0.0	0.0
PENT–COGIC	1	0	0	0	0.0	0.0
PENT–Cong Hol Ch	1	184	167	210	0.7	1.1
PENT–Intl Pent Holiness	3	148	133	168	0.5	0.9
PENT–United Holy Ch	1	NR	NR	NR	-	-
PRES–Presb Ch (USA)	6	80	254	320	1.0	1.7
PRES–Presb Ch Amer	2	110	332	343	1.1	1.9
Sev Day Adv	1	10	17	20	0.1	0.1
DORCHESTER	**166**	**17,802**	**38,119**	**56,226**	**41.2**	**100.0**
ANG/EPIS–Anglican NA	1	NR	NR	NR	-	-

Religious Group	Number of Congrega-tions	Number of Attendees	Number of Communicant, Confirmed, or Full Members	Adherents		
				Number of Adherents	% of Total Pop.	% of Total Adh.
ANG/EPIS–Episcopal	3	728	1,146	1,462	1.1	2.6
Bahá'í	0	NR	83	83	0.1	0.1
BAPT–NBC USA	4	315	899	1,135	0.8	2.0
BAPT–So Bapt Conv	34	5,435	13,034	16,454	12.0	29.3
BUDD–Vajrayana	1	NR	NR	14	0.0	0.0
Catholic	2	NR	NR	7,926	5.8	14.1
CGOD–Ch God (Ander)	2	267	NR	267	0.2	0.5
Chr & Miss Al	1	41	35	67	0.0	0.1
CHR–Chr Ch (Disc)	5	474	1,028	1,298	1.0	2.3
CHR–Chr Chs & Chs Cr	2	NR	198	250	0.2	0.4
CHR–Chs of Christ	3	626	599	743	0.5	1.3
Ind Fund Churches	1	NR	NR	NR	-	-
Jehovah's Witness	2	NR	NR	NR	-	-
LDS–L-D Saints	2	NR	NR	1,556	1.1	2.8
LUTH–E.L.C.A.	2	396	800	984	0.7	1.8
LUTH–Luth–MO Synod	1	112	206	267	0.2	0.5
LUTH–Wisc Ev Luth Syn	1	185	195	313	0.2	0.6
METH–AME	16	310	2,092	2,641	1.9	4.7
METH–AME Zion	1	0	150	189	0.1	0.3
METH–C.M.E.	1	500	600	757	0.6	1.3
METH–So Methodist	3	NR	NR	NR	-	-
METH–Un Methodist	31	3,575	10,376	11,705	8.6	20.8
New Apost Ch	1	NR	NR	NR	-	-
Non-denom Chr Chs	18	3,547	4,048	4,757	3.5	8.5
ORTHE–Rus Orth Abroad	1	35	NR	75	0.1	0.1
PENT–Ch God (Cleve)	7	349	472	596	0.4	1.1
PENT–Ch Lord Jesus Apos	2	NR	NR	NR	-	-
PENT–Ch of God Proph	2	NR	409	516	0.4	0.9
PENT–Fire Bapt Hol Ch	2	NR	NR	NR	-	-
PENT–Intl Pent Holiness	3	152	140	177	0.1	0.3
PENT–Un Pent Asbl God	3	NR	NR	NR	-	-
PENT–Un Pent Ch Intl	1	NR	NR	NR	-	-
PRES–As Ref Pres Ch	1	NR	63	80	0.1	0.1
PRES–Presb Ch (USA)	2	425	1,050	1,326	1.0	2.4
PRES–Presb Ch Amer	1	106	106	139	0.1	0.2
Sev Day Adv	3	224	390	449	0.3	0.8
EDGEFIELD	**46**	**2,896**	**7,297**	**10,434**	**38.7**	**100.0**
ANG/EPIS–Episcopal	1	49	93	106	0.4	1.0
Bahá'í	0	NR	36	36	0.1	0.3
BAPT–NBC USA	3	75	425	506	1.9	4.8
BAPT–So Bapt Conv	18	1,946	4,888	5,823	21.6	55.8
Catholic	2	NR	NR	1,830	6.8	17.5
CHR–Chs of Christ	1	16	7	7	0.0	0.1
Jehovah's Witness	1	NR	NR	NR	-	-
LUTH–E.L.C.A.	2	122	348	382	1.4	3.7
METH–AME	2	0	250	298	1.1	2.9
METH–Un Methodist	5	364	832	944	3.5	9.0
Non-denom Chr Chs	1	150	150	188	0.7	1.8
PENT–Ch God (Cleve)	2	63	117	139	0.5	1.3
PENT–Fire Bapt Hol Ch	2	NR	NR	NR	-	-
PENT–Intl Pent Holiness	2	72	90	107	0.4	1.0
PRES–As Ref Pres Ch	1	NR	0	0	0.0	0.0
PRES–Presb Ch (USA)	1	5	6	7	0.0	0.1
PRES–Presb Ch Amer	1	10	13	13	0.0	0.1
Sev Day Adv	1	24	42	48	0.2	0.5
FAIRFIELD	**83**	**4,230**	**11,195**	**13,817**	**57.7**	**100.0**
ANG/EPIS–Episcopal	3	99	257	263	1.1	1.9
Bahá'í	0	NR	94	94	0.4	0.7
BAPT–NBC USA	2	350	460	556	2.3	4.0
BAPT–Prog NBC	1	250	250	302	1.3	2.2
BAPT–So Bapt Conv	19	1,586	4,529	5,470	22.8	39.6
Catholic	1	NR	NR	105	0.4	0.8
CGOD–Ch God (Ander)	1	10	NR	10	0.0	0.1
Ch of Nazarene	1	186	324	324	1.4	2.3
CHR–Chs of Christ	1	60	50	75	0.3	0.5
Jehovah's Witness	1	NR	NR	NR	-	-
LDS–L-D Saints	1	NR	NR	467	1.9	3.4
METH–AME	14	0	1,710	2,065	8.6	14.9
METH–AME Zion	4	0	450	544	2.3	3.9
METH–Un Methodist	8	316	834	899	3.8	6.5
Non-denom Chr Chs	5	640	719	858	3.6	6.2

NR–Not Reported   - Represents no adherents reported.   Percentages may not total 100 due to rounding.

Table 3: Religious Congregations by County and Group: 2010

Religious Group	Number of Congrega-tions	Number of Attendees	Number of Communicant, Confirmed, or Full Members	Adherents		
				Number of Adherents	% of Total Pop.	% of Total Adh.
PENT–Assemb of God	1	41	35	46	0.2	0.3
PENT–Ch God (Cleve)	1	64	164	198	0.8	1.4
PENT–Ch of God Proph	2	NR	41	50	0.2	0.4
PENT–Intl Pent Holiness	1	31	107	129	0.5	0.9
PENT–Un Pent Ch Intl	1	NR	NR	NR	-	-
PRES–As Ref Pres Ch	2	NR	115	139	0.6	1.0
PRES–Presb Ch (USA)	8	250	520	628	2.6	4.5
PRES–Presb Ch Amer	5	347	536	595	2.5	4.3
FLORENCE	**302**	**26,666**	**57,754**	**75,363**	**55.1**	**100.0**
ANG/EPIS–Anglican NA	1	NR	NR	NR	-	-
ANG/EPIS–Episcopal	3	326	792	839	0.6	1.1
Bahá'í	1	NR	2,308	2,308	1.7	3.1
BAPT–Free Will Bapt	31	NR	1,178	1,456	1.1	1.9
BAPT–NBC USA	16	979	4,200	5,192	3.8	6.9
BAPT–Prog NBC	1	2,400	1,450	1,792	1.3	2.4
BAPT–S-D Baptist Gen Con	1	NR	NR	NR	-	-
BAPT–So Bapt Conv	54	6,554	17,444	21,564	15.8	28.6
Catholic	4	NR	NR	3,320	2.4	4.4
CGOD–Ch God (Ander)	3	160	NR	160	0.1	0.2
Ch of Nazarene	1	33	47	60	0.0	0.1
CHR–Chr Chs & Chs Cr	1	NR	45	56	0.0	0.1
CHR–Chs of Christ	9	421	432	543	0.4	0.7
Jehovah's Witness	2	NR	NR	NR	-	-
JUD–Reform	1	32	56	151	0.1	0.2
LDS–L-D Saints	1	NR	NR	1,163	0.8	1.5
LUTH–E.L.C.A.	2	264	344	574	0.4	0.8
LUTH–Luth–MO Synod	1	42	53	66	0.0	0.1
METH–AME	15	635	2,465	3,047	2.2	4.0
METH–C.M.E.	1	0	100	124	0.1	0.2
METH–So Methodist	2	NR	NR	NR	-	-
METH–Un Methodist	40	3,484	9,150	11,329	8.3	15.0
METH–Wesleyan	1	27	12	35	0.0	0.0
Muslim Est	2	174	NR	508	0.4	0.7
Non-denom Chr Chs	29	6,005	9,400	10,407	7.6	13.8
ORTHE–Greek Orthodox	1	115	NR	400	0.3	0.5
PENT–Apos Faith Msn	1	NR	35	43	0.0	0.1
PENT–Assemb of God	3	147	145	246	0.2	0.3
PENT–Ch God (Cleve)	10	956	1,552	1,919	1.4	2.5
PENT–Ch Lord Jesus Apos	1	NR	NR	NR	-	-
PENT–Ch of God by Faith	1	NR	NR	NR	-	-
PENT–Ch of God Proph	8	NR	243	300	0.2	0.4
PENT–COGIC	2	75	250	309	0.2	0.4
PENT–Intl Pent Holiness	33	2,691	3,358	4,151	3.0	5.5
PENT–Un Pent Ch Intl	1	NR	NR	NR	-	-
PRES–As Ref Pres Ch	1	NR	119	147	0.1	0.2
PRES–Evan Presby Ch	1	NR	397	491	0.4	0.7
PRES–Presb Ch (USA)	9	659	1,440	1,780	1.3	2.4
PRES–Presb Ch Amer	1	45	50	64	0.0	0.1
Salvation Army	1	82	64	100	0.1	0.1
Sev Day Adv	5	360	625	719	0.5	1.0
GEORGETOWN	**145**	**13,936**	**26,981**	**36,759**	**61.1**	**100.0**
ANG/EPIS–Anglican NA	2	NR	NR	NR	-	-
ANG/EPIS–Episcopal	3	547	978	1,303	2.2	3.5
Bahá'í	0	NR	626	626	1.0	1.7
BAPT–Free Will Bapt	2	NR	76	91	0.2	0.2
BAPT–Natl Mis Bapt Conv	2	0	300	359	0.6	1.0
BAPT–NBC Amer	4	425	1,000	1,196	2.0	3.3
BAPT–NBC USA	1	200	425	508	0.8	1.4
BAPT–So Bapt Conv	24	3,049	5,611	6,713	11.2	18.3
Catholic	3	NR	NR	3,990	6.6	10.9
CGOD–Ch God (Ander)	3	65	NR	65	0.1	0.2
Ch of Nazarene	1	13	0	13	0.0	0.0
CHR–Chr Ch (Disc)	1	19	27	32	0.1	0.1
CHR–Chs of Christ	3	360	354	463	0.8	1.3
Jehovah's Witness	2	NR	NR	NR	-	-
JUD–Reform	1	24	43	116	0.2	0.3
LDS–L-D Saints	1	NR	NR	244	0.4	0.7
LUTH–E.L.C.A.	3	492	889	1,008	1.7	2.7
METH–AME	31	2,022	5,475	6,551	10.9	17.8
METH–Un Methodist	10	1,873	5,177	5,914	9.8	16.1
Non-denom Chr Chs	15	2,110	2,095	2,692	4.5	7.3
PENT–Assemb of God	3	549	439	656	1.1	1.8
PENT–Ch God (Cleve)	3	337	644	771	1.3	2.1
PENT–Fire Bapt Hol Ch	1	NR	NR	NR	-	-
PENT–Intl Pent Holiness	15	1,019	1,401	1,676	2.8	4.6
PENT–Un Pent Ch Intl	1	NR	NR	NR	-	-
PRES–Presb Ch (USA)	5	732	1,276	1,527	2.5	4.2
PRES–Presb Ch Amer	1	40	51	52	0.1	0.1
Salvation Army	1	9	30	115	0.2	0.3
Sev Day Adv	2	16	29	33	0.1	0.1
Unit Univ	1	35	35	45	0.1	0.1
GREENVILLE	**629**	**115,368**	**194,153**	**271,911**	**60.3**	**100.0**
ANG/EPIS–Anglican NA	2	NR	NR	NR	-	-
ANG/EPIS–Episcopal	9	1,959	4,621	6,168	1.4	2.3
Bahá'í	2	NR	258	258	0.1	0.1
BAPT–Alliance Bapt	1	NR	NR	NR	-	-
BAPT–Amer Bapt Assn	2	NR	195	240	0.1	0.1
BAPT–Asc Ref Bap Ch Am	1	NR	NR	NR	-	-
BAPT–Free Will Bapt	4	NR	228	281	0.1	0.1
BAPT–Fund Bapt Flwsp	2	NR	NR	NR	-	-
BAPT–Ind Bapt Flwsp Intl	1	NR	NR	NR	-	-
BAPT–NBC Amer	1	225	250	308	0.1	0.1
BAPT–NBC USA	9	1,855	2,700	3,328	0.7	1.2
BAPT–NT Ind Bapt	1	NR	NR	NR	-	-
BAPT–Prog NBC	6	1,400	1,900	2,342	0.5	0.9
BAPT–Ref Bapt Ch	2	NR	NR	NR	-	-
BAPT–So Bapt Conv	208	38,285	82,650	101,887	22.6	37.5
BRETH–Ch of Brethren	1	42	60	74	0.0	0.0
Calv Chpl	3	NR	NR	NR	-	-
Catholic	8	NR	NR	25,417	5.6	9.3
CGOD–Ch God (Ander)	2	60	NR	60	0.0	0.0
Ch Cr, Scientist	1	NR	NR	NR	-	-
Ch of God Gen Conf	3	NR	303	374	0.1	0.1
Ch of Nazarene	3	706	1,142	1,645	0.4	0.6
Chr & Miss Al	3	481	160	625	0.1	0.2
CHR–Chr Ch (Disc)	1	42	97	120	0.0	0.0
CHR–Chr Chs & Chs Cr	2	NR	230	284	0.1	0.1
CHR–Chs of Christ	10	1,341	1,330	1,715	0.4	0.6
CHR–Int Chs of Christ	1	NR	40	49	0.0	0.0
Christian Brethren	1	NR	NR	NR	-	-
FRND–Consrv Yr Mtgs	1	NR	0	0	0.0	0.0
FRND–Fr Gen Cf	1	NR	6	7	0.0	0.0
HINDU–Post Ren	2	NR	NR	41	0.0	0.0
Jehovah's Witness	6	NR	NR	NR	-	-
JUD–Conserv	1	97	109	294	0.1	0.1
JUD–Reform	1	109	193	521	0.1	0.2
LDS–Comm of Christ	2	NR	236	236	0.1	0.1
LDS–L-D Saints	5	NR	NR	3,234	0.7	1.2
LUTH–Apostolic Luth	2	NR	NR	NR	-	-
LUTH–E.L.C.A.	6	1,218	2,635	3,400	0.8	1.3
LUTH–Luth–MO Synod	2	260	535	675	0.1	0.2
LUTH–Wisc Ev Luth Syn	1	124	148	201	0.0	0.1
METH–AME	2	400	750	925	0.2	0.3
METH–AME Zion	1	0	100	123	0.0	0.0
METH–C.M.E.	2	345	550	678	0.2	0.2
METH–So Methodist	1	NR	NR	NR	-	-
METH–Un Methodist	58	7,650	18,533	22,656	5.0	8.3
METH–Wesleyan	8	413	341	539	0.1	0.2
Metro Comm Ch	1	23	40	49	0.0	0.0
Muslim Est	2	268	NR	616	0.1	0.2
New Apost Ch	1	NR	NR	NR	-	-
Non-denom Chr Chs	96	24,349	28,984	34,893	7.7	12.8
ORTHE–Greek Orthodox	1	325	NR	1,440	0.3	0.5
ORTHE–Orth Ch in Amer	1	120	NR	175	0.0	0.1
ORTHO–Coptic Orth Ch	1	160	NR	315	0.1	0.1
PENT–Assemb of God	17	1,452	1,377	1,927	0.4	0.7
PENT–Ch God (Cleve)	29	4,767	8,971	11,059	2.5	4.1
PENT–Ch Lord Jesus Apos	1	NR	NR	NR	-	-
PENT–Ch of God Proph	10	NR	675	832	0.2	0.3
PENT–COGIC	1	40	40	49	0.0	0.0
PENT–Fire Bapt Hol Ch	4	NR	NR	NR	-	-
PENT–Full Gosp Bapt	1	NR	NR	NR	-	-
PENT–Intl Pent Holiness	14	17,953	19,227	23,702	5.3	8.7
PENT–Un Pent Asbl God	1	NR	NR	NR	-	-

NR–Not Reported - Represents no adherents reported. Percentages may not total 100 due to rounding.

Table 3: Religious Congregations by County and Group: 2010

Religious Group	Number of Congregations	Number of Attendees	Number of Communicant, Confirmed, or Full Members	Adherents: Number of Adherents	Adherents: % of Total Pop.	Adherents: % of Total Adh.
PENT–Un Pent Ch Intl	2	NR	NR	NR	-	-
PENT–Vineyard	2	87	77	95	0.0	0.0
PRES–As Ref Pres Ch	5	NR	609	751	0.2	0.3
PRES–Free Ch Scot	1	NR	NR	NR	-	-
PRES–Free Pres NA	2	NR	NR	NR	-	-
PRES–Orth Pres Ch	1	71	44	64	0.0	0.0
PRES–Presb Ch (USA)	19	4,708	9,572	11,800	2.6	4.3
PRES–Presb Ch Amer	16	3,325	3,210	4,120	0.9	1.5
PRES–Ref Pres GA	1	NR	NR	NR	-	-
REF–Comm Ref Evan	1	NR	NR	NR	-	-
Salvation Army	1	225	163	228	0.1	0.1
Sev Day Adv	3	318	552	635	0.1	0.2
Unit Univ	1	165	312	451	0.1	0.2
Unity Ch	1	NR	NR	NR	-	-
Zoroastrian	0	NR	NR	5	0.0	0.0
GREENWOOD	**156**	**14,416**	**33,626**	**43,314**	**62.2**	**100.0**
ANG/EPIS–Anglican NA	1	NR	NR	NR	-	-
ANG/EPIS–Episcopal	1	176	379	459	0.7	1.1
Bahá'í	0	NR	85	85	0.1	0.2
BAPT–Alliance Bapt	1	NR	NR	NR	-	-
BAPT–Free Will Bapt	1	NR	38	47	0.1	0.1
BAPT–NBC USA	9	325	1,625	1,990	2.9	4.6
BAPT–So Bapt Conv	29	6,094	14,996	18,365	26.4	42.4
Calv Chpl	1	NR	NR	NR	-	-
Catholic	1	NR	NR	2,010	2.9	4.6
Ch of Nazarene	1	144	138	159	0.2	0.4
CHR–Chr Chs & Chs Cr	1	NR	45	55	0.1	0.1
CHR–Chs of Christ	2	115	122	140	0.2	0.3
Jehovah's Witness	2	NR	NR	NR	-	-
LDS–L-D Saints	1	NR	NR	691	1.0	1.6
LUTH–E.L.C.A.	1	162	331	367	0.5	0.8
LUTH–Luth–MO Synod	1	15	22	25	0.0	0.1
METH–AME	19	35	2,096	2,567	3.7	5.9
METH–C.M.E.	2	0	300	367	0.5	0.8
METH–Un Methodist	23	2,004	5,215	5,999	8.6	13.9
METH–Wesleyan	1	41	35	53	0.1	0.1
Non-denom Chr Chs	13	2,110	2,525	2,759	4.0	6.4
PENT–Assemb of God	3	155	179	355	0.5	0.8
PENT–Ch God (Cleve)	7	570	1,383	1,694	2.4	3.9
PENT–Ch Lord Jesus Apos	1	NR	NR	NR	-	-
PENT–Ch of God Proph	4	NR	111	136	0.2	0.3
PENT–Cong Hol Ch	2	48	43	53	0.1	0.1
PENT–Fire Bapt Hol Ch	2	NR	NR	NR	-	-
PENT–Intl Pent Holiness	11	1,139	1,478	1,810	2.6	4.2
PENT–Un Pent Ch Intl	1	NR	NR	NR	-	-
PRES–As Ref Pres Ch	3	NR	208	255	0.4	0.6
PRES–Evan Presby Ch	1	NR	49	60	0.1	0.1
PRES–Presb Ch (USA)	6	928	1,782	2,182	3.1	5.0
PRES–Presb Ch Amer	1	180	166	235	0.3	0.5
Salvation Army	1	47	53	141	0.2	0.3
Sev Day Adv	2	128	222	255	0.4	0.6
HAMPTON	**79**	**3,924**	**9,515**	**11,767**	**55.8**	**100.0**
ANG/EPIS–Episcopal	2	34	49	50	0.2	0.4
Bahá'í	0	NR	58	58	0.3	0.5
BAPT–NBC USA	1	0	250	306	1.5	2.6
BAPT–So Bapt Conv	24	1,825	4,824	5,896	28.0	50.1
Catholic	1	NR	NR	84	0.4	0.7
CGOD–Ch God (Ander)	1	73	NR	73	0.3	0.6
CHR–Chr Ch (Disc)	4	237	709	867	4.1	7.4
CHR–Chr Chs & Chs Cr	1	NR	100	122	0.6	1.0
CHR–Chs of Christ	1	10	3	3	0.0	0.0
Jehovah's Witness	1	NR	NR	NR	-	-
METH–AME	7	80	847	1,035	4.9	8.8
METH–C.M.E.	6	120	630	770	3.7	6.5
METH–Un Methodist	9	256	606	694	3.3	5.9
Non-denom Chr Chs	8	1,050	1,060	1,320	6.3	11.2
PENT–Assemb of God	1	50	25	57	0.3	0.5
PENT–Ch God (Cleve)	2	92	114	139	0.7	1.2
PENT–Ch Lord Jesus Apos	2	NR	NR	NR	-	-
PENT–Ch of God Proph	3	NR	87	106	0.5	0.9
PENT–COGIC	1	35	50	61	0.3	0.5

Religious Group	Number of Congregations	Number of Attendees	Number of Communicant, Confirmed, or Full Members	Adherents: Number of Adherents	Adherents: % of Total Pop.	Adherents: % of Total Adh.
PENT–Un Pent Ch Intl	1	NR	NR	NR	-	-
PRES–Presb Ch (USA)	3	62	103	126	0.6	1.1
HORRY	**372**	**41,170**	**72,644**	**109,924**	**40.8**	**100.0**
ANG/EPIS–Anglican NA	1	NR	NR	NR	-	-
ANG/EPIS–Episcopal	4	1,079	1,662	2,092	0.8	1.9
Bahá'í	1	NR	892	892	0.3	0.8
BAPT–Free Will Bapt	15	NR	570	676	0.3	0.6
BAPT–Natl Mis Bapt Conv	7	0	1,050	1,245	0.5	1.1
BAPT–NBC USA	4	0	1,000	1,186	0.4	1.1
BAPT–Orig Free Will Bapt	2	180	246	292	0.1	0.3
BAPT–Prog NBC	2	350	650	771	0.3	0.7
BAPT–Ref Bapt Ch	1	NR	NR	NR	-	-
BAPT–So Bapt Conv	129	16,129	32,941	39,058	14.5	35.5
BUDD–Vajrayana	1	NR	NR	35	0.0	0.0
Calv Chpl	1	NR	NR	NR	-	-
Catholic	5	NR	NR	18,159	6.7	16.5
CGOD–Ch God (Ander)	2	190	NR	190	0.1	0.2
Ch Cr, Scientst	2	NR	NR	NR	-	-
Ch of Nazarene	2	69	132	133	0.0	0.1
Chr & Miss Al	1	40	0	55	0.0	0.1
CHR–Chr Ch (Disc)	1	0	0	0	0.0	0.0
CHR–Chr Chs & Chs Cr	4	NR	1,012	1,200	0.4	1.1
CHR–Chs of Christ	2	398	294	396	0.1	0.4
Christian Brethren	1	NR	NR	NR	-	-
Evan Free Ch	1	120	NR	120	0.0	0.1
FRND–Fr Gen Cf	1	NR	0	0	0.0	0.0
Jehovah's Witness	4	NR	NR	NR	-	-
JUD–Orth	2	72	70	100	0.0	0.1
LDS–L-D Saints	2	NR	NR	1,805	0.7	1.6
LUTH–E.L.C.A.	2	390	355	658	0.2	0.6
LUTH–Luth Cong Msn Chr	2	238	458	543	0.2	0.5
LUTH–Luth–MO Synod	2	416	359	417	0.2	0.4
LUTH–Wisc Ev Luth Syn	1	48	49	71	0.0	0.1
METH–AME	24	660	3,649	4,327	1.6	3.9
METH–C.M.E.	1	0	100	119	0.0	0.1
METH–Free Methodist	1	25	21	25	0.0	0.0
METH–So Methodist	3	NR	NR	NR	-	-
METH–Un Methodist	26	5,176	9,776	11,797	4.4	10.7
METH–Wesleyan	1	140	56	182	0.1	0.2
Missionary Ch	4	290	200	310	0.1	0.3
Muslim Est	1	134	NR	308	0.1	0.3
Non-denom Chr Chs	46	9,735	9,550	12,693	4.7	11.5
ORTHE–Ant Orth of NA	1	65	NR	115	0.0	0.1
ORTHE–Greek Orthodox	1	135	NR	600	0.2	0.5
ORTHO–Coptic Orth Ch	1	15	NR	15	0.0	0.0
PENT–Assemb of God	6	334	172	474	0.2	0.4
PENT–Ch God (Cleve)	10	1,062	1,227	1,455	0.5	1.3
PENT–COGIC	2	75	205	243	0.1	0.2
PENT–Elim	1	NR	NR	NR	-	-
PENT–Fire Bapt Hol Ch	1	NR	NR	NR	-	-
PENT–Intl Pent Holiness	14	803	986	1,169	0.4	1.1
PENT–Pent FW Bapt	2	NR	NR	NR	-	-
PENT–Un Pent Ch Intl	3	NR	NR	NR	-	-
PENT–United Holy Ch	1	NR	NR	NR	-	-
PENT–Vineyard	1	420	500	593	0.2	0.5
PRES–As Ref Pres Ch	1	NR	38	45	0.0	0.0
PRES–Evan Presby Ch	1	NR	226	268	0.1	0.2
PRES–Presb Ch (USA)	5	1,517	3,147	3,731	1.4	3.4
PRES–Presb Ch Amer	3	624	618	867	0.3	0.8
Salvation Army	1	55	110	114	0.0	0.1
Sev Day Adv	4	186	323	372	0.1	0.3
Unity Ch	1	NR	NR	NR	-	-
Zoroastrian	0	NR	NR	8	0.0	0.0
JASPER	**36**	**1,724**	**4,457**	**6,964**	**28.1**	**100.0**
ANG/EPIS–Episcopal	1	69	104	122	0.5	1.8
Bahá'í	0	NR	25	25	0.1	0.4
BAPT–So Bapt Conv	11	1,110	2,699	3,348	13.5	48.1
Catholic	2	NR	NR	956	3.9	13.7
CHR–Chs of Christ	1	15	9	9	0.0	0.1
LDS–L-D Saints	2	NR	NR	656	2.6	9.4
METH–AME	3	120	465	577	2.3	8.3

NR–Not Reported   - Represents no adherents reported.   Percentages may not total 100 due to rounding.

Table 3: Religious Congregations by County and Group: 2010

Religious Group	Number of Congrega-tions	Number of Attendees	Number of Communicant, Confirmed, or Full Members	Adherents		
				Number of Adherents	% of Total Pop.	% of Total Adh.
METH–Un Methodist	5	173	549	565	2.3	8.1
Missionary Ch	1	25	30	30	0.1	0.4
PENT–Assemb of God	1	78	85	85	0.3	1.2
PENT–Ch God (Cleve)	1	22	57	71	0.3	1.0
PENT–Ch of God Proph	3	NR	87	108	0.4	1.6
PENT–COGIC	1	0	150	186	0.8	2.7
PENT–Un Pent Ch Intl	1	NR	NR	NR	-	-
PRES–As Ref Pres Ch	1	NR	1	1	0.0	0.0
Sev Day Adv	2	112	196	225	0.9	3.2
KERSHAW	**131**	**11,617**	**24,516**	**32,782**	**53.1**	**100.0**
ANG/EPIS–Episcopal	1	152	391	506	0.8	1.5
Bahá'í	0	NR	81	81	0.1	0.2
BAPT–Free Will Bapt	1	NR	38	47	0.1	0.1
BAPT–NBC USA	2	125	500	617	1.0	1.9
BAPT–So Bapt Conv	46	5,738	13,707	16,903	27.4	51.6
Catholic	1	NR	NR	1,724	2.8	5.3
CGOD–Ch God (Ander)	3	287	NR	287	0.5	0.9
Ch of Nazarene	2	128	216	271	0.4	0.8
CHR–Chs of Christ	3	150	157	197	0.3	0.6
Jehovah's Witness	2	NR	NR	NR	-	-
LDS–L-D Saints	2	NR	NR	1,085	1.8	3.3
LUTH–E.L.C.A.	1	92	143	169	0.3	0.5
METH–AME	3	0	350	432	0.7	1.3
METH–AME Zion	7	120	873	1,077	1.7	3.3
METH–So Methodist	1	NR	NR	NR	-	-
METH–Un Methodist	22	1,506	3,571	3,899	6.3	11.9
Non-denom Chr Chs	9	1,194	1,353	1,568	2.5	4.8
PENT–Assemb of God	2	68	39	110	0.2	0.3
PENT–Ch God (Cleve)	6	861	1,191	1,469	2.4	4.5
PENT–Ch of God Proph	1	NR	30	37	0.1	0.1
PENT–COGIC	1	50	0	0	0.0	0.0
PENT–Cong Hol Ch	2	88	80	99	0.2	0.3
PENT–Intl Pent Holiness	3	534	700	863	1.4	2.6
PENT–Un Pent Ch Intl	1	NR	NR	NR	-	-
PRES–As Ref Pres Ch	1	NR	125	154	0.2	0.5
PRES–Presb Ch (USA)	6	457	854	1,053	1.7	3.2
Sev Day Adv	2	67	117	134	0.2	0.4
LANCASTER	**166**	**12,018**	**31,806**	**39,704**	**51.8**	**100.0**
ANG/EPIS–Episcopal	1	45	76	104	0.1	0.3
Bahá'í	0	NR	297	297	0.4	0.7
BAPT–Free Will Bapt	7	NR	266	325	0.4	0.8
BAPT–Natl Mis Bapt Conv	1	0	150	183	0.2	0.5
BAPT–NBC USA	1	200	500	611	0.8	1.5
BAPT–So Bapt Conv	61	7,146	18,735	22,909	29.9	57.7
Catholic	2	NR	NR	780	1.0	2.0
Ch of Nazarene	1	76	86	86	0.1	0.2
CHR–Chs of Christ	1	25	27	35	0.0	0.1
Jehovah's Witness	1	NR	NR	NR	-	-
LDS–L-D Saints	1	NR	NR	290	0.4	0.7
LUTH–E.L.C.A.	1	62	109	147	0.2	0.4
METH–AME	1	125	207	253	0.3	0.6
METH–AME Zion	24	315	3,203	3,917	5.1	9.9
METH–Un Methodist	20	1,750	4,681	5,453	7.1	13.7
Non-denom Chr Chs	13	1,350	1,350	1,695	2.2	4.3
PENT–Assemb of God	2	77	57	106	0.1	0.3
PENT–Ch God (Cleve)	4	168	278	340	0.4	0.9
PENT–Ch of God Proph	3	NR	112	137	0.2	0.3
PENT–Intl Pent Holiness	4	203	222	271	0.4	0.7
PENT–Un Pent Ch Intl	1	NR	NR	NR	-	-
PRES–As Ref Pres Ch	4	NR	547	669	0.9	1.7
PRES–Presb Ch (USA)	11	416	848	1,037	1.4	2.6
PRES–Presb Ch Amer	1	60	55	59	0.1	0.1
LAURENS	**173**	**12,672**	**33,207**	**40,559**	**61.0**	**100.0**
ANG/EPIS–Episcopal	2	77	168	195	0.3	0.5
Bahá'í	0	NR	45	45	0.1	0.1
BAPT–NBC USA	8	770	2,271	2,763	4.2	6.8
BAPT–Ref Bapt Ch	1	NR	NR	NR	-	-
BAPT–So Bapt Conv	65	7,426	21,110	25,681	38.6	63.3
Catholic	2	NR	NR	396	0.6	1.0
CGOD–Ch God (Ander)	1	35	NR	35	0.1	0.1

Religious Group	Number of Congrega-tions	Number of Attendees	Number of Communicant, Confirmed, or Full Members	Adherents		
				Number of Adherents	% of Total Pop.	% of Total Adh.
Ch of Nazarene	1	14	13	27	0.0	0.1
CHR–Chr Chs & Chs Cr	1	NR	0	0	0.0	0.0
CHR–Chs of Christ	2	75	61	78	0.1	0.2
Jehovah's Witness	2	NR	NR	NR	-	-
LUTH–E.L.C.A.	2	56	117	130	0.2	0.3
MENN–Beachy Amish-Menn	1	78	44	78	0.1	0.2
METH–AME	14	325	2,157	2,624	3.9	6.5
METH–So Methodist	1	NR	NR	NR	-	-
METH–Un Methodist	21	991	2,662	2,922	4.4	7.2
METH–Wesleyan	1	58	69	75	0.1	0.2
Non-denom Chr Chs	2	300	275	375	0.6	0.9
PENT–Assemb of God	3	180	162	187	0.3	0.5
PENT–Ch God (Cleve)	6	660	979	1,191	1.8	2.9
PENT–Ch of God Proph	3	NR	106	129	0.2	0.3
PENT–COGIC	1	0	0	0	0.0	0.0
PENT–Fire Bapt Hol Ch	1	NR	NR	NR	-	-
PENT–Intl Pent Holiness	7	486	823	1,001	1.5	2.5
PENT–Un Pent Ch Intl	1	NR	NR	NR	-	-
PRES–As Ref Pres Ch	2	NR	118	144	0.2	0.4
PRES–Presb Ch (USA)	16	840	1,606	1,954	2.9	4.8
PRES–Presb Ch Amer	5	277	379	481	0.7	1.2
Sev Day Adv	1	24	42	48	0.1	0.1
LEE	**46**	**2,082**	**5,524**	**6,450**	**33.6**	**100.0**
Bahá'í	0	NR	201	201	1.0	3.1
BAPT–So Bapt Conv	8	452	1,344	1,620	8.4	25.1
Ch of Nazarene	2	82	110	119	0.6	1.8
Chr & Miss Al	1	92	81	143	0.7	2.2
CHR–Chs of Christ	1	100	90	200	1.0	3.1
Jehovah's Witness	1	NR	NR	NR	-	-
METH–AME	9	130	1,300	1,567	8.2	24.3
METH–So Methodist	1	NR	NR	NR	-	-
METH–Un Methodist	11	767	1,786	1,839	9.6	28.5
Non-denom Chr Chs	4	245	235	306	1.6	4.7
PENT–Ch God (Cleve)	1	36	27	33	0.2	0.5
PENT–Ch of God by Faith	2	NR	NR	NR	-	-
PRES–Presb Ch (USA)	5	178	350	422	2.2	6.5
LEXINGTON	**307**	**44,645**	**90,108**	**126,818**	**48.3**	**100.0**
ANG/EPIS–Episcopal	4	811	1,781	2,384	0.9	1.9
Bahá'í	2	NR	299	299	0.1	0.2
BAPT–Amer Bapt Assn	1	NR	85	105	0.0	0.1
BAPT–Free Will Bapt	1	NR	38	47	0.0	0.0
BAPT–Natl Mis Bapt Conv	1	0	150	185	0.1	0.1
BAPT–NBC USA	2	175	400	493	0.2	0.4
BAPT–So Bapt Conv	73	13,695	34,037	41,969	16.0	33.1
Calv Chpl	2	NR	NR	NR	-	-
Catholic	3	NR	NR	5,739	2.2	4.5
CGOD–Ch God (Ander)	1	59	NR	59	0.0	0.0
Ch of Nazarene	6	555	989	1,296	0.5	1.0
CHR–Chr Chs & Chs Cr	1	NR	90	111	0.0	0.1
CHR–Chs of Christ	5	648	544	711	0.3	0.6
CHR–Int Chs of Christ	1	NR	374	461	0.2	0.4
HINDU–Trad Temples	1	NR	NR	1,500	0.6	1.2
Jehovah's Witness	4	NR	NR	NR	-	-
LDS–L-D Saints	6	NR	NR	2,634	1.0	2.1
LUTH–Ch Luth Conf	1	NR	NR	NR	-	-
LUTH–E.L.C.A.	38	5,329	12,167	16,502	6.3	13.0
LUTH–Luth–MO Synod	1	195	289	364	0.1	0.3
LUTH–Nor Amer Luth C	2	NR	NR	NR	-	-
METH–AME	18	960	2,919	3,599	1.4	2.8
METH–AME Zion	1	70	123	152	0.1	0.1
METH–C.M.E.	3	80	225	277	0.1	0.2
METH–So Methodist	4	NR	NR	NR	-	-
METH–Un Methodist	32	7,190	17,577	22,799	8.7	18.0
New Apost Ch	1	NR	NR	NR	-	-
Non-denom Chr Chs	34	7,132	7,322	9,169	3.5	7.2
ORTHE–Ant Orth of NA	1	22	NR	30	0.0	0.0
ORTHE–Orth Ch in Amer	1	100	NR	100	0.0	0.1
ORTHE–Rus Orth Abroad	1	45	NR	100	0.0	0.1
PENT–Assemb of God	6	1,767	1,163	4,156	1.6	3.3
PENT–Ch God (Cleve)	10	911	1,417	1,747	0.7	1.4
PENT–Ch Lord Jesus Apos	1	NR	NR	NR	-	-

NR–Not Reported - Represents no adherents reported. Percentages may not total 100 due to rounding.

Table 3: Religious Congregations by County and Group: 2010

Religious Group	Number of Congrega-tions	Number of Attendees	Number of Communicant, Confirmed, or Full Members	Adherents: Number of Adherents	Adherents: % of Total Pop.	Adherents: % of Total Adh.
PENT–Ch of God by Faith	1	NR	NR	NR	-	-
PENT–Ch of God Proph	2	NR	101	125	0.0	0.1
PENT–Cong Hol Ch	2	101	100	123	0.0	0.1
PENT–Fire Bapt Hol Ch	2	NR	NR	NR	-	-
PENT–Intl Pent Holiness	16	1,853	3,007	3,708	1.4	2.9
PENT–Un Pent Ch Intl	2	NR	NR	NR	-	-
PRES–As Ref Pres Ch	1	NR	73	90	0.0	0.1
PRES–Presb Ch (USA)	4	1,065	1,804	2,224	0.8	1.8
PRES–Presb Ch Amer	5	1,330	2,075	2,457	0.9	1.9
Sev Day Adv	3	552	959	1,103	0.4	0.9
MCCORMICK	**29**	**1,074**	**3,346**	**4,014**	**39.2**	**100.0**
ANG/EPIS–Anglican NA	1	NR	NR	NR	-	-
Bahá'í	0	NR	13	13	0.1	0.3
BAPT–NBC USA	1	75	75	84	0.8	2.1
BAPT–So Bapt Conv	7	458	1,162	1,301	12.7	32.4
Catholic	1	NR	NR	290	2.8	7.2
LUTH–E.L.C.A.	1	232	282	287	2.8	7.1
METH–AME	10	0	1,260	1,410	13.8	35.1
METH–Un Methodist	4	283	509	578	5.6	14.4
PENT–Fire Bapt Hol Ch	2	NR	NR	NR	-	-
PRES–As Ref Pres Ch	1	NR	14	16	0.2	0.4
PRES–Presb Ch (USA)	1	26	31	35	0.3	0.9
MARION	**80**	**5,790**	**14,924**	**18,145**	**54.9**	**100.0**
ANG/EPIS–Episcopal	1	23	32	34	0.1	0.2
Bahá'í	0	NR	1,806	1,806	5.5	10.0
BAPT–Free Will Bapt	3	NR	114	140	0.4	0.8
BAPT–NBC Amer	1	415	350	430	1.3	2.4
BAPT–NBC USA	2	1,100	1,351	1,659	5.0	9.1
BAPT–Prog NBC	1	200	300	368	1.1	2.0
BAPT–So Bapt Conv	18	1,668	5,000	6,140	18.6	33.8
Catholic	1	NR	NR	150	0.5	0.8
CHR–Chs of Christ	1	10	10	10	0.0	0.1
Jehovah's Witness	1	NR	NR	NR	-	-
LDS–L-D Saints	1	NR	NR	360	1.1	2.0
METH–AME	17	620	2,351	2,887	8.7	15.9
METH–So Methodist	4	NR	NR	NR	-	-
METH–Un Methodist	14	665	1,889	2,093	6.3	11.5
Non-denom Chr Chs	5	570	640	764	2.3	4.2
PENT–Ch God (Cleve)	3	245	361	443	1.3	2.4
PENT–Intl Pent Holiness	2	119	132	162	0.5	0.9
PENT–United Holy Ch	2	NR	NR	NR	-	-
PRES–Presb Ch (USA)	1	79	161	198	0.6	1.1
PRES–Presb Ch Amer	1	0	294	348	1.1	1.9
Sev Day Adv	1	76	133	153	0.5	0.8
MARLBORO	**80**	**4,335**	**9,310**	**10,817**	**37.4**	**100.0**
ANG/EPIS–Episcopal	1	37	61	77	0.3	0.7
Bahá'í	0	NR	242	242	0.8	2.2
BAPT–NBC Amer	1	0	110	132	0.5	1.2
BAPT–NBC USA	3	100	350	419	1.4	3.9
BAPT–So Bapt Conv	12	774	2,056	2,462	8.5	22.8
Catholic	1	NR	NR	50	0.2	0.5
CGOD–Ch God (Ander)	1	21	NR	21	0.1	0.2
Ch of Nazarene	2	66	136	136	0.5	1.3
CHR–Chs of Christ	1	35	35	40	0.1	0.4
METH–AME Zion	7	105	685	820	2.8	7.6
METH–Un Methodist	29	1,338	3,316	3,551	12.3	32.8
METH–Wesleyan	3	111	87	145	0.5	1.3
Non-denom Chr Chs	7	1,135	1,150	1,427	4.9	13.2
PENT–Ch God (Cleve)	5	271	583	698	2.4	6.5
PENT–Intl Pent Holiness	4	225	260	311	1.1	2.9
PRES–Presb Ch (USA)	3	117	239	286	1.0	2.6
NEWBERRY	**126**	**7,464**	**18,779**	**23,708**	**63.2**	**100.0**
ANG/EPIS–Episcopal	1	50	85	127	0.3	0.5
Bahá'í	0	NR	33	33	0.1	0.1
BAPT–NBC USA	2	0	300	365	1.0	1.5
BAPT–Prog NBC	1	0	0	0	0.0	0.0
BAPT–So Bapt Conv	23	1,712	4,560	5,546	14.8	23.4
Catholic	1	NR	NR	250	0.7	1.1
CGOD–Ch God (Ander)	1	28	NR	28	0.1	0.1
CHR–Chr Chs & Chs Cr	1	NR	20	24	0.1	0.1
Jehovah's Witness	1	NR	NR	NR	-	-
LDS–L-D Saints	1	NR	NR	421	1.1	1.8
LUTH–E.L.C.A.	26	2,401	5,207	6,608	17.6	27.9
LUTH–Nor Amer Luth C	1	NR	NR	NR	-	-
METH–AME	22	515	2,832	3,445	9.2	14.5
METH–AME Zion	5	0	600	730	1.9	3.1
METH–So Methodist	1	NR	NR	NR	-	-
METH–Un Methodist	16	1,276	3,061	3,603	9.6	15.2
METH–Wesleyan	1	57	57	74	0.2	0.3
Non-denom Chr Chs	3	450	450	564	1.5	2.4
PENT–Assemb of God	1	20	27	27	0.1	0.1
PENT–Ch God (Cleve)	3	198	250	304	0.8	1.3
PENT–Intl Pent Holiness	5	302	349	424	1.1	1.8
PENT–Un Pent Ch Intl	1	NR	NR	NR	-	-
PRES–As Ref Pres Ch	2	NR	168	204	0.5	0.9
PRES–Presb Ch (USA)	5	334	575	699	1.9	2.9
PRES–Presb Ch Amer	1	101	180	207	0.6	0.9
Unit Univ	1	20	25	25	0.1	0.1
OCONEE	**174**	**15,875**	**32,589**	**42,661**	**57.4**	**100.0**
ANG/EPIS–Anglican NA	1	NR	NR	NR	-	-
ANG/EPIS–Episcopal	1	81	195	195	0.3	0.5
Bahá'í	0	NR	19	19	0.0	0.0
BAPT–NBC USA	1	0	150	179	0.2	0.4
BAPT–Prog NBC	2	125	150	179	0.2	0.4
BAPT–So Bapt Conv	75	9,540	23,008	27,443	36.9	64.3
Catholic	2	NR	NR	2,491	3.4	5.8
Ch Cr, Scientst	1	NR	NR	NR	-	-
Ch of Nazarene	1	23	55	113	0.2	0.3
Chr & Miss Al	1	50	16	53	0.1	0.1
CHR–Chs of Christ	2	180	155	192	0.3	0.5
Jehovah's Witness	2	NR	NR	NR	-	-
LDS–L-D Saints	1	NR	NR	799	1.1	1.9
LUTH–E.L.C.A.	1	143	496	682	0.9	1.6
LUTH–Luth–MO Synod	1	191	312	365	0.5	0.9
METH–So Methodist	1	NR	NR	NR	-	-
METH–Un Methodist	14	857	2,058	2,269	3.1	5.3
METH–Wesleyan	7	399	456	519	0.7	1.2
Non-denom Chr Chs	16	1,602	1,549	2,011	2.7	4.7
PENT–Assemb of God	3	358	216	593	0.8	1.4
PENT–Ch God (Cleve)	17	1,442	2,146	2,560	3.4	6.0
PENT–Ch of God Proph	7	NR	281	335	0.5	0.8
PENT–Fire Bapt Hol Ch	1	NR	NR	NR	-	-
PENT–Full Gosp Bapt	1	NR	NR	NR	-	-
PENT–Intl Pent Holiness	1	89	120	143	0.2	0.3
PENT–Un Pent Ch Intl	1	NR	NR	NR	-	-
PRES–As Ref Pres Ch	1	NR	68	81	0.1	0.2
PRES–Presb Ch (USA)	6	460	713	850	1.1	2.0
PRES–Presb Ch Amer	2	145	129	141	0.2	0.3
Salvation Army	2	56	65	182	0.2	0.4
Sev Day Adv	2	134	232	267	0.4	0.6
ORANGEBURG	**236**	**17,966**	**43,933**	**54,908**	**59.4**	**100.0**
ANG/EPIS–Episcopal	3	193	466	500	0.5	0.9
Bahá'í	1	NR	543	543	0.6	1.0
BAPT–Free Will Bapt	2	NR	76	92	0.1	0.2
BAPT–Natl Mis Bapt Conv	2	0	300	365	0.4	0.7
BAPT–NBC USA	5	155	1,200	1,460	1.6	2.7
BAPT–So Bapt Conv	55	6,231	16,244	19,765	21.4	36.0
Catholic	3	NR	NR	1,125	1.2	2.0
CGOD–Ch God (Ander)	1	0	NR	0	0.0	0.0
Ch of Nazarene	2	215	306	400	0.4	0.7
CHR–Chr Ch (Disc)	2	386	942	1,146	1.2	2.1
CHR–Chr Chs & Chs Cr	1	NR	250	304	0.3	0.6
CHR–Chs of Christ	2	130	121	204	0.2	0.4
HINDU–Trad Temples	1	NR	NR	1,033	1.1	1.9
Jehovah's Witness	4	NR	NR	NR	-	-
LDS–L-D Saints	1	NR	NR	537	0.6	1.0
LUTH–E.L.C.A.	3	246	534	574	0.6	1.0
METH–AME	29	1,500	6,125	7,453	8.1	13.6
METH–AME Zion	1	0	100	122	0.1	0.2

NR–Not Reported   - Represents no adherents reported.   Percentages may not total 100 due to rounding.

Table 3: Religious Congregations by County and Group: 2010

Religious Group	Number of Congrega-tions	Number of Attendees	Number of Communicant, Confirmed, or Full Members	Adherents: Number of Adherents	Adherents: % of Total Pop.	Adherents: % of Total Adh.
METH–So Methodist	8	NR	NR	NR	-	-
METH–Un Methodist	49	4,324	11,500	12,384	13.4	22.6
Muslim Est	1	70	NR	200	0.2	0.4
Non-denom Chr Chs	28	3,060	3,025	3,887	4.2	7.1
PENT–Assemb of God	1	12	12	12	0.0	0.0
PENT–Ch God (Cleve)	10	457	626	762	0.8	1.4
PENT–Ch Lord Jesus Apos	4	NR	NR	NR	-	-
PENT–Ch of God by Faith	2	NR	NR	NR	-	-
PENT–Intl Pent Holiness	6	327	390	475	0.5	0.9
PENT–Un Pent Ch Intl	1	NR	NR	NR	-	-
PRES–Presb Ch (USA)	3	297	602	732	0.8	1.3
PRES–Presb Ch Amer	1	150	186	221	0.2	0.4
Salvation Army	1	21	52	229	0.2	0.4
Sev Day Adv	3	192	333	383	0.4	0.7
PICKENS	**194**	**25,594**	**46,915**	**60,188**	**50.5**	**100.0**
ANG/EPIS–Episcopal	2	302	553	667	0.6	1.1
Bahá'í	2	NR	114	114	0.1	0.2
BAPT–NBC USA	1	100	0	0	0.0	0.0
BAPT–Prog NBC	2	180	150	178	0.1	0.3
BAPT–Ref Bapt Ch	1	NR	NR	NR	-	-
BAPT–So Bapt Conv	75	14,258	29,458	34,915	29.3	58.0
Catholic	3	NR	NR	2,868	2.4	4.8
Ch of Nazarene	1	9	0	65	0.1	0.1
CHR–Chs of Christ	3	110	102	130	0.1	0.2
CHR–Int Chs of Christ	1	NR	44	52	0.0	0.1
FRND–Fr Gen Cf	1	NR	0	0	0.0	0.0
Jehovah's Witness	3	NR	NR	NR	-	-
LUTH–E.L.C.A.	3	260	569	677	0.6	1.1
LUTH–Luth Cong Msn Chr	1	40	60	71	0.1	0.1
METH–AME	1	0	100	119	0.1	0.2
METH–C.M.E.	1	0	150	178	0.1	0.3
METH–Un Methodist	20	1,941	4,749	5,928	5.0	9.8
METH–Wesleyan	11	1,382	1,321	1,798	1.5	3.0
Muslim Est	1	300	NR	700	0.6	1.2
Non-denom Chr Chs	14	2,880	2,825	3,710	3.1	6.2
PENT–Assemb of God	2	85	63	92	0.1	0.2
PENT–Ch God (Cleve)	17	1,311	2,223	2,635	2.2	4.4
PENT–Ch of God Proph	8	NR	375	444	0.4	0.7
PENT–Fire Bapt Hol Ch	3	NR	NR	NR	-	-
PENT–Int Foursq Gos	1	17	14	17	0.0	0.0
PENT–Intl Pent Holiness	3	484	880	1,043	0.9	1.7
PRES–Presb Ch (USA)	6	884	1,998	2,368	2.0	3.9
PRES–Presb Ch Amer	3	887	883	1,090	0.9	1.8
Salvation Army	1	12	32	32	0.0	0.1
Sev Day Adv	2	74	129	148	0.1	0.2
Unit Univ	1	78	123	149	0.1	0.2
RICHLAND	**458**	**71,918**	**137,913**	**197,190**	**51.3**	**100.0**
ANG/EPIS–Anglican NA	5	NR	NR	NR	-	-
ANG/EPIS–Episcopal	12	2,157	6,971	8,383	2.2	4.3
Bahá'í	2	NR	539	539	0.1	0.3
BAPT–Alliance Bapt	1	NR	NR	NR	-	-
BAPT–Amer Bapt USA	2	535	770	934	0.2	0.5
BAPT–Free Will Bapt	1	NR	38	46	0.0	0.0
BAPT–Natl Mis Bapt Conv	1	250	301	365	0.1	0.2
BAPT–NBC Amer	3	350	2,250	2,730	0.7	1.4
BAPT–NBC USA	6	1,425	3,065	3,719	1.0	1.9
BAPT–Prog NBC	6	3,150	7,775	9,434	2.5	4.8
BAPT–Reg Bapt Gen As	1	NR	NR	NR	-	-
BAPT–So Bapt Conv	90	17,523	39,279	47,659	12.4	24.2
BUDD–Mahayana	2	NR	NR	2,116	0.6	1.1
BUDD–Vajrayana	1	NR	NR	456	0.1	0.2
Calv Chpl	2	NR	NR	NR	-	-
Catholic	8	NR	NR	16,300	4.2	8.3
CGOD–Ch God (Ander)	2	105	NR	105	0.0	0.1
CGOD–Ches God-Gen Con	1	0	0	0	0.0	0.0
Ch Cr, Scientst	1	NR	NR	NR	-	-
Ch of Nazarene	4	768	1,053	1,068	0.3	0.5
Chr & Miss Al	3	1,140	629	1,377	0.4	0.7
CHR–Chr Ch (Disc)	3	96	170	206	0.1	0.1
CHR–Chr Chs & Chs Cr	2	NR	290	352	0.1	0.2
CHR–Chs of Christ	10	1,105	962	1,394	0.4	0.7

Religious Group	Number of Congrega-tions	Number of Attendees	Number of Communicant, Confirmed, or Full Members	Adherents: Number of Adherents	Adherents: % of Total Pop.	Adherents: % of Total Adh.
Evan Cov Ch	1	43	6	56	0.0	0.0
Evan Free Ch	1	50	NR	50	0.0	0.0
FRND–Fr Gen Cf	1	NR	17	21	0.0	0.0
HINDU–Post Ren	2	NR	NR	26	0.0	0.0
Intl Fell Bible Ch	1	NR	NR	NR	-	-
Jehovah's Witness	5	NR	NR	NR	-	-
JUD–Conserv	1	257	289	780	0.2	0.4
JUD–Orth	2	86	100	120	0.0	0.1
JUD–Reform	1	167	295	796	0.2	0.4
LDS–Comm of Christ	1	NR	118	118	0.0	0.1
LDS–L-D Saints	7	NR	NR	4,086	1.1	2.1
LUTH–E.L.C.A.	22	2,415	5,420	7,580	2.0	3.8
LUTH–Luth Cong Msn Chr	1	12	18	22	0.0	0.0
LUTH–Luth–MO Synod	1	72	76	88	0.0	0.0
LUTH–Wisc Ev Luth Syn	1	140	164	227	0.1	0.1
METH–AME	26	2,120	6,376	7,736	2.0	3.9
METH–AME Zion	3	225	900	1,092	0.3	0.6
METH–C.M.E.	3	150	624	757	0.2	0.4
METH–So Methodist	2	NR	NR	NR	-	-
METH–Un Methodist	41	6,098	17,446	20,690	5.4	10.5
METH–Wesleyan	2	110	12	143	0.0	0.1
Muslim Est	4	428	NR	846	0.2	0.4
Non-denom Chr Chs	72	20,806	21,657	28,006	7.3	14.2
ORTHE–Greek Orthodox	1	250	NR	700	0.2	0.4
PENT–Apos Faith Msn	1	NR	35	42	0.0	0.0
PENT–Assemb of God	10	1,023	690	1,372	0.4	0.7
PENT–Ch God (Cleve)	7	903	1,700	2,063	0.5	1.0
PENT–Ch Lord Jesus Apos	3	NR	NR	NR	-	-
PENT–Ch of God by Faith	1	NR	NR	NR	-	-
PENT–Ch of God Proph	2	NR	48	58	0.0	0.0
PENT–COGIC	5	1,200	2,200	2,669	0.7	1.4
PENT–Fire Bapt Hol Ch	2	NR	NR	NR	-	-
PENT–Int Foursq Gos	1	0	0	0	0.0	0.0
PENT–Intl Pent Holiness	6	374	557	676	0.2	0.3
PENT–Un Pent Ch Intl	1	NR	NR	NR	-	-
PRES–As Ref Pres Ch	7	NR	2,793	3,389	0.9	1.7
PRES–Bible Pres	1	NR	NR	NR	-	-
PRES–Free Pres NA	1	NR	NR	NR	-	-
PRES–Kor Pres Abroad	1	NR	NR	NR	-	-
PRES–Presb Ch (USA)	15	3,514	8,101	9,829	2.6	5.0
PRES–Presb Ch Amer	11	2,104	3,072	4,560	1.2	2.3
REF–Christian Ref	1	30	25	30	0.0	0.0
Salvation Army	2	116	135	225	0.1	0.1
Sev Day Adv	5	366	636	731	0.2	0.4
Sikh	1	NR	NR	NR	-	-
Un C of Christ	1	100	140	170	0.0	0.1
Unit Univ	1	155	171	251	0.1	0.1
Unity Ch	1	NR	NR	NR	-	-
Zoroastrian	0	NR	NR	2	0.0	0.0
SALUDA	**51**	**2,333**	**5,863**	**7,198**	**36.2**	**100.0**
Bahá'í	0	NR	36	36	0.2	0.5
BAPT–NBC USA	3	0	300	366	1.8	5.1
BAPT–So Bapt Conv	11	667	2,145	2,614	13.2	36.3
Catholic	1	NR	NR	300	1.5	4.2
LUTH–E.L.C.A.	6	263	550	651	3.3	9.0
METH–AME	2	0	200	244	1.2	3.4
METH–C.M.E.	2	0	300	366	1.8	5.1
METH–Un Methodist	10	666	1,502	1,615	8.1	22.4
Non-denom Chr Chs	3	195	205	246	1.2	3.4
PENT–Ch God (Cleve)	1	88	97	118	0.6	1.6
PENT–Cong Hol Ch	5	214	222	271	1.4	3.8
PENT–Fire Bapt Hol Ch	1	NR	NR	NR	-	-
PENT–Intl Pent Holiness	4	194	240	293	1.5	4.1
PRES–Presb Ch (USA)	1	30	37	45	0.2	0.6
Sev Day Adv	1	16	29	33	0.2	0.5
SPARTANBURG	**471**	**54,541**	**121,175**	**156,065**	**54.9**	**100.0**
ANG/EPIS–Anglican NA	4	NR	NR	NR	-	-
ANG/EPIS–Episcopal	6	828	2,427	2,557	0.9	1.6
Bahá'í	2	NR	201	201	0.1	0.1
BAPT–Free Will Bapt	14	NR	532	655	0.2	0.4
BAPT–Ind Bapt Flwsp Intl	3	NR	NR	NR	-	-

NR–Not Reported - Represents no adherents reported. Percentages may not total 100 due to rounding.

Table 3: Religious Congregations by County and Group: 2010

Religious Group	Number of Congregations	Number of Attendees	Number of Communicant, Confirmed, or Full Members	Adherents		
				Number of Adherents	% of Total Pop.	% of Total Adh.
BAPT–NBC USA	17	2,158	6,023	7,416	2.6	4.8
BAPT–Prog NBC	1	0	0	0	0.0	0.0
BAPT–So Bapt Conv	152	28,995	70,882	87,278	30.7	55.9
BUDD–Mahayana	1	NR	NR	11	0.0	0.0
BUDD–Theravada	2	NR	NR	695	0.2	0.4
Calv Chpl	1	NR	NR	NR	-	-
Catholic	2	NR	NR	5,311	1.9	3.4
CGOD–Ch God (Ander)	1	60	NR	60	0.0	0.0
Ch Cr, Scientst	1	NR	NR	NR	-	-
Ch of Nazarene	3	160	340	381	0.1	0.2
Chr & Miss Al	1	175	263	263	0.1	0.2
CHR–Chr Chs & Chs Cr	1	NR	60	74	0.0	0.0
CHR–Chs of Christ	6	769	742	948	0.3	0.6
FRND–Fr Gen Cf	1	NR	0	0	0.0	0.0
HINDU–Trad Temples	1	NR	NR	250	0.1	0.2
Jehovah's Witness	5	NR	NR	NR	-	-
JUD–Reform	1	67	118	319	0.1	0.2
LDS–L-D Saints	5	NR	NR	2,609	0.9	1.7
LUTH–E.L.C.A.	4	736	1,045	1,565	0.6	1.0
LUTH–Luth–MO Synod	1	45	70	85	0.0	0.1
METH–AME	4	60	375	462	0.2	0.3
METH–AME Zion	7	0	850	1,047	0.4	0.7
METH–C.M.E.	5	125	825	1,016	0.4	0.7
METH–Un Methodist	61	4,752	13,495	15,284	5.4	9.8
METH–Wesleyan	15	897	869	1,169	0.4	0.7
Muslim Est	1	50	NR	100	0.0	0.1
Non-denom Chr Chs	54	8,065	10,060	11,369	4.0	7.3
ORTHE–Greek Orthodox	1	120	NR	270	0.1	0.2
PENT–Assemb of God	7	983	850	1,068	0.4	0.7
PENT–Ch God (Cleve)	17	1,435	2,795	3,442	1.2	2.2
PENT–Ch of God Proph	8	NR	229	282	0.1	0.2
PENT–COGIC	2	60	200	246	0.1	0.2
PENT–Cong Hol Ch	1	39	35	43	0.0	0.0
PENT–Fire Bapt Hol Ch	5	NR	NR	NR	-	-
PENT–Full Gosp Bapt	2	NR	NR	NR	-	-
PENT–Int Foursq Gos	1	96	98	121	0.0	0.1
PENT–Intl Pent Holiness	6	609	660	813	0.3	0.5
PENT–Un Pent Ch Intl	5	NR	NR	NR	-	-
PRES–As Ref Pres Ch	2	NR	240	296	0.1	0.2
PRES–Presb Ch (USA)	15	1,805	4,748	5,846	2.1	3.7
PRES–Presb Ch Amer	10	689	849	1,005	0.4	0.6
Salvation Army	1	49	89	103	0.0	0.1
Sev Day Adv	4	610	1,061	1,221	0.4	0.8
Unit Univ	1	104	144	184	0.1	0.1
SUMTER	**215**	**22,161**	**45,442**	**60,153**	**56.0**	**100.0**
ANG/EPIS–Episcopal	5	351	815	1,020	0.9	1.7
Bahá'í	0	NR	388	388	0.4	0.6
BAPT–Free Will Bapt	1	NR	38	47	0.0	0.1
BAPT–Natl Mis Bapt Conv	1	0	150	187	0.2	0.3
BAPT–NBC USA	2	1,475	2,350	2,934	2.7	4.9
BAPT–Prog NBC	3	1,250	2,006	2,505	2.3	4.2
BAPT–So Bapt Conv	41	5,182	15,086	18,838	17.5	31.3
Catholic	2	NR	NR	1,942	1.8	3.2
CGOD–Ch God (Ander)	2	501	NR	501	0.5	0.8
Ch Cr, Scientst	1	NR	NR	NR	-	-
Ch of Nazarene	4	741	1,029	1,122	1.0	1.9
CHR–Chr Chs & Chs Cr	1	NR	100	125	0.1	0.2
CHR–Chs of Christ	4	375	380	423	0.4	0.7
FRND–Consrv Yr Mtgs	1	NR	0	0	0.0	0.0
Jehovah's Witness	7	NR	NR	NR	-	-
JUD–Reform	1	24	43	116	0.1	0.2
LDS–L-D Saints	1	NR	NR	1,203	1.1	2.0
LUTH–E.L.C.A.	1	130	2	290	0.3	0.5
LUTH–Nor Amer Luth C	1	NR	NR	NR	-	-
METH–AME	36	995	6,455	8,060	7.5	13.4
METH–AME Zion	1	0	100	125	0.1	0.2
METH–So Methodist	2	NR	NR	NR	-	-
METH–Un Methodist	26	2,615	6,447	7,201	6.7	12.0
Muslim Est	2	268	NR	616	0.6	1.0
Non-denom Chr Chs	25	5,105	5,343	6,478	6.0	10.8
PENT–Assemb of God	3	526	621	822	0.8	1.4
PENT–Ch God (Cleve)	2	903	730	912	0.8	1.5
PENT–Ch Lord Jesus Apos	1	NR	NR	NR	-	-
PENT–Ch of God by Faith	2	NR	NR	NR	-	-
PENT–Ch of God Proph	3	NR	100	125	0.1	0.2
PENT–COGIC	1	75	75	94	0.1	0.2
PENT–Fire Bapt Hol Ch	3	NR	NR	NR	-	-
PENT–Full Gosp Bapt	1	NR	NR	NR	-	-
PENT–Intl Pent Holiness	5	206	255	318	0.3	0.5
PENT–Un Pent Ch Intl	1	NR	NR	NR	-	-
PRES–As Ref Pres Ch	3	NR	153	191	0.2	0.3
PRES–Presb Ch (USA)	15	931	1,961	2,449	2.3	4.1
PRES–Presb Ch Amer	1	184	235	302	0.3	0.5
Salvation Army	1	61	123	293	0.3	0.5
Sev Day Adv	2	263	457	526	0.5	0.9
UNION	**91**	**6,734**	**19,409**	**23,397**	**80.8**	**100.0**
ANG/EPIS–Episcopal	1	23	50	53	0.2	0.2
Bahá'í	0	NR	37	37	0.1	0.2
BAPT–Amer Bapt Assn	2	NR	110	133	0.5	0.6
BAPT–Free Will Bapt	2	NR	76	92	0.3	0.4
BAPT–NBC USA	3	200	600	723	2.5	3.1
BAPT–Prog NBC	1	175	550	663	2.3	2.8
BAPT–So Bapt Conv	31	4,420	12,447	15,007	51.8	64.1
Catholic	1	NR	NR	50	0.2	0.2
CHR–Chs of Christ	2	120	131	144	0.5	0.6
LDS–L-D Saints	1	NR	NR	173	0.6	0.7
LUTH–E.L.C.A.	1	20	52	52	0.2	0.2
METH–AME	8	25	990	1,194	4.1	5.1
METH–AME Zion	6	0	700	844	2.9	3.6
METH–Un Methodist	14	909	2,441	2,718	9.4	11.6
Non-denom Chr Chs	3	460	435	575	2.0	2.5
PENT–Assemb of God	1	18	22	22	0.1	0.1
PENT–Ch God (Cleve)	3	154	354	427	1.5	1.8
PENT–Ch of God Proph	1	NR	9	11	0.0	0.0
PENT–Fire Bapt Hol Ch	1	NR	NR	NR	-	-
PENT–Full Gosp Bapt	1	NR	NR	NR	-	-
PENT–Int Foursq Gos	1	10	31	37	0.1	0.2
PENT–Un Pent Ch Intl	1	NR	NR	NR	-	-
PRES–Presb Ch (USA)	4	156	296	357	1.2	1.5
PRES–Presb Ch Amer	1	16	30	30	0.1	0.1
Sev Day Adv	1	28	48	55	0.2	0.2
WILLIAMSBURG	**123**	**7,000**	**18,540**	**21,535**	**62.6**	**100.0**
ANG/EPIS–Anglican NA	1	NR	NR	NR	-	-
ANG/EPIS–Episcopal	1	23	50	61	0.2	0.3
Bahá'í	1	NR	1,550	1,550	4.5	7.2
BAPT–Free Will Bapt	4	NR	152	185	0.5	0.9
BAPT–Natl Mis Bapt Conv	2	0	300	364	1.1	1.7
BAPT–NBC USA	1	25	50	61	0.2	0.3
BAPT–So Bapt Conv	9	598	1,931	2,345	6.8	10.9
Catholic	1	NR	NR	85	0.2	0.4
CHR–Chs of Christ	1	75	125	185	0.5	0.9
Jehovah's Witness	1	NR	NR	NR	-	-
METH–AME	25	1,095	4,495	5,459	15.9	25.3
METH–AME Zion	1	0	100	121	0.4	0.6
METH–So Methodist	1	NR	NR	NR	-	-
METH–Un Methodist	38	2,735	6,412	6,999	20.3	32.5
Non-denom Chr Chs	8	1,090	1,105	1,371	4.0	6.4
PENT–Apos Faith Msn	1	NR	35	43	0.1	0.2
PENT–Assemb of God	1	40	23	40	0.1	0.2
PENT–Ch God (Cleve)	3	182	230	279	0.8	1.3
PENT–Ch of God Proph	2	NR	108	131	0.4	0.6
PENT–COGIC	1	50	51	62	0.2	0.3
PENT–Fire Bapt Hol Ch	2	NR	NR	NR	-	-
PENT–Intl Pent Holiness	9	475	695	844	2.5	3.9
PRES–Presb Ch (USA)	4	231	471	572	1.7	2.7
PRES–Presb Ch Amer	4	255	437	525	1.5	2.4
Sev Day Adv	1	126	220	253	0.7	1.2
YORK	**326**	**38,170**	**75,863**	**112,306**	**49.7**	**100.0**
ANG/EPIS–Episcopal	4	405	1,055	1,174	0.5	1.0
Bahá'í	2	NR	1,111	1,111	0.5	1.0
BAPT–Amer Bapt Assn	1	NR	85	106	0.0	0.1
BAPT–Free Will Bapt	8	NR	456	569	0.3	0.5
BAPT–NBC USA	3	0	60	75	0.0	0.1

NR–Not Reported   - Represents no adherents reported.   Percentages may not total 100 due to rounding.

Table 3: Religious Congregations by County and Group: 2010

Religious Group	Number of Congrega-tions	Number of Attendees	Number of Communicant, Confirmed, or Full Members	Adherents: Number of Adherents	% of Total Pop.	% of Total Adh.
BAPT–Prog NBC	1	285	400	499	0.2	0.4
BAPT–So Bapt Conv	76	14,026	29,401	36,679	16.2	32.7
Calv Chpl	1	NR	NR	NR	-	-
Catholic	5	NR	NR	14,030	6.2	12.5
Ch of Nazarene	9	809	1,334	1,559	0.7	1.4
Chr & Miss Al	1	25	17	32	0.0	0.0
CHR–Chr Chs & Chs Cr	2	NR	210	262	0.1	0.2
CHR–Chs of Christ	4	553	500	594	0.3	0.5
Evan Free Ch	1	120	NR	120	0.1	0.1
Int Cou Comm Ch	1	NR	NR	NR	-	-
Jehovah's Witness	2	NR	NR	NR	-	-
LDS–L-D Saints	4	NR	NR	2,344	1.0	2.1
LUTH–E.L.C.A.	2	370	672	805	0.4	0.7
LUTH–Luth Cong Msn Chr	2	251	467	583	0.3	0.5
LUTH–Luth–MO Synod	1	25	27	36	0.0	0.0
METH–AME	1	0	150	187	0.1	0.2
METH–AME Zion	27	160	3,583	4,470	2.0	4.0
METH–Free Methodist	1	77	29	77	0.0	0.1
METH–Un Methodist	31	3,443	9,649	11,959	5.3	10.6
METH–Wesleyan	4	204	425	265	0.1	0.2
Muslim Est	3	303	NR	666	0.3	0.6
Non-denom Chr Chs	40	8,699	8,499	11,046	4.9	9.8
ORTHE–Orth Ch in Amer	1	15	NR	15	0.0	0.0
PENT–Assemb of God	7	1,132	645	1,777	0.8	1.6
PENT–Ch God (Cleve)	15	2,081	3,908	4,875	2.2	4.3
PENT–Ch of God Proph	5	NR	313	390	0.2	0.3
PENT–COGIC	2	0	300	374	0.2	0.3
PENT–Fire Bapt Hol Ch	4	NR	NR	NR	-	-
PENT–Int Foursq Gos	2	365	490	611	0.3	0.5
PENT–Intl Pent Holiness	5	291	509	635	0.3	0.6
PENT–Un Pent Ch Intl	1	NR	NR	NR	-	-
PRES–As Ref Pres Ch	12	NR	2,306	2,877	1.3	2.6
PRES–Evan Presby Ch	1	NR	45	56	0.0	0.0
PRES–Presb Ch (USA)	22	2,397	5,581	6,963	3.1	6.2
PRES–Presb Ch Amer	9	1,980	3,368	4,176	1.8	3.7
Sev Day Adv	3	154	268	309	0.1	0.3
SOUTH DAKOTA	**1,819**	**118,799**	**221,469**	**476,832**	**58.6**	**100.0**
AURORA	**12**	**548**	**1,274**	**2,676**	**98.7**	**100.0**
Bahá'í	0	NR	1	1	0.0	0.0
Catholic	3	NR	NR	1,227	45.3	45.9
LUTH–E.L.C.A.	3	158	397	445	16.4	16.6
LUTH–Luth–MO Synod	2	99	312	389	14.4	14.5
METH–Un Methodist	3	156	333	366	13.5	13.7
REF–Ref Ch in Am	1	135	231	248	9.2	9.3
BEADLE	**40**	**2,560**	**5,725**	**10,452**	**60.1**	**100.0**
ANG/EPIS–Episcopal	1	28	57	81	0.5	0.8
BAPT–Amer Bapt USA	1	220	302	370	2.1	3.5
BAPT–So Bapt Conv	3	73	103	126	0.7	1.2
Catholic	2	NR	NR	2,235	12.8	21.4
Ch of Nazarene	1	45	74	88	0.5	0.8
Chr & Miss Al	1	107	94	214	1.2	2.0
CHR–Chr Chs & Chs Cr	1	NR	250	306	1.8	2.9
CHR–Chs of Christ	1	27	28	30	0.2	0.3
Jehovah's Witness	1	NR	NR	NR	-	-
LDS–L-D Saints	1	NR	NR	223	1.3	2.1
LUTH–E.L.C.A.	2	336	1,036	1,319	7.6	12.6
LUTH–Luth Cong Msn Chr	1	67	80	98	0.6	0.9
LUTH–Luth–MO Synod	3	413	1,054	1,361	7.8	13.0
LUTH–Wisc Ev Luth Syn	1	25	30	33	0.2	0.3
MENN–Hutt Breth	2	NR	NR	NR	-	-
MENN–Menn Br US Conf	2	NR	423	519	3.0	5.0
METH–Un Methodist	4	583	1,088	1,625	9.3	15.5
METH–Wesleyan	1	37	24	48	0.3	0.5
Non-denom Chr Chs	1	55	52	69	0.4	0.7
PENT–Assemb of God	1	91	50	130	0.7	1.2
PENT–Open Bible Std	1	67	NR	67	0.4	0.6
PRES–Presb Ch (USA)	5	258	658	807	4.6	7.7
Salvation Army	1	15	43	366	2.1	3.5
Sev Day Adv	1	38	66	76	0.4	0.7

Religious Group	Number of Congrega-tions	Number of Attendees	Number of Communicant, Confirmed, or Full Members	Adherents: Number of Adherents	% of Total Pop.	% of Total Adh.
Un C of Christ	1	75	213	261	1.5	2.5
BENNETT	**8**	**165**	**415**	**1,472**	**42.9**	**100.0**
ANG/EPIS–Episcopal	1	26	85	220	6.4	14.9
Bahá'í	0	NR	122	122	3.6	8.3
Catholic	1	NR	NR	792	23.1	53.8
CGOD–Ch God (Ander)	1	25	NR	25	0.7	1.7
LDS–L-D Saints	1	NR	NR	42	1.2	2.9
LUTH–Wisc Ev Luth Syn	1	48	107	135	3.9	9.2
Non-denom Chr Chs	1	8	9	10	0.3	0.7
PRES–Presb Ch (USA)	2	58	92	126	3.7	8.6
BON HOMME	**26**	**1,015**	**2,429**	**5,254**	**74.3**	**100.0**
BAPT–N Am Bapt Conf	2	NR	285	333	4.7	6.3
Catholic	4	NR	NR	2,375	33.6	45.2
LUTH–E.L.C.A.	1	144	296	348	4.9	6.6
LUTH–Luth–MO Synod	4	205	421	566	8.0	10.8
MENN–Hutt Breth	3	NR	NR	NR	-	-
MENN–Mennonite USA	1	80	75	88	1.2	1.7
METH–Un Methodist	2	49	151	165	2.3	3.1
Non-denom Chr Chs	1	30	40	40	0.6	0.8
PRES–Presb Ch (USA)	5	121	296	346	4.9	6.6
REF–Ref Ch in Am	1	200	324	361	5.1	6.9
Un C of Christ	2	186	541	632	8.9	12.0
BROOKINGS	**56**	**4,839**	**8,613**	**16,939**	**53.0**	**100.0**
ANG/EPIS–Episcopal	1	54	120	126	0.4	0.7
Bahá'í	0	NR	6	6	0.0	0.0
BAPT–Amer Bapt USA	1	40	45	53	0.2	0.3
BAPT–Converge/BGC	1	75	NR	90	0.3	0.5
BAPT–NT Ind Bapt	3	NR	NR	NR	-	-
BAPT–So Bapt Conv	1	NR	NR	NR	-	-
BUDD–Mahayana	1	NR	NR	103	0.3	0.6
Catholic	5	NR	NR	4,844	15.2	28.6
CGOD–Ch God (Ander)	1	255	NR	255	0.8	1.5
Ch of Nazarene	1	0	0	0	0.0	0.0
CHR–Chr Chs & Chs Cr	2	NR	150	177	0.6	1.0
CHR–Chs of Christ	1	35	29	40	0.1	0.2
Jehovah's Witness	1	NR	NR	NR	-	-
LDS–L-D Saints	1	NR	NR	216	0.7	1.3
LUTH–Assoc Free Luth	1	NR	NR	NR	-	-
LUTH–E.L.C.A.	5	1,448	4,045	5,043	15.8	29.8
LUTH–Luth Cong Msn Chr	1	50	146	172	0.5	1.0
LUTH–Luth–MO Synod	4	343	661	884	2.8	5.2
LUTH–Wisc Ev Luth Syn	2	219	441	514	1.6	3.0
MENN–Hutt Breth	3	NR	NR	NR	-	-
METH–Un Methodist	5	450	1,198	1,220	3.8	7.2
METH–Wesleyan	1	848	312	1,102	3.4	6.5
Muslim Est	1	134	NR	308	1.0	1.8
Non-denom Chr Chs	3	289	340	382	1.2	2.3
PENT–Assemb of God	1	185	96	202	0.6	1.2
PENT–Un Pent Ch Intl	1	NR	NR	NR	-	-
PRES–Orth Pres Ch	1	24	37	43	0.1	0.3
PRES–Presb Ch (USA)	2	8	256	302	0.9	1.8
REF–Christian Ref	1	95	133	157	0.5	0.9
REF–Ref Ch in Am	2	206	354	412	1.3	2.4
Un C of Christ	2	81	244	288	0.9	1.7
BROWN	**74**	**5,684**	**12,821**	**28,151**	**77.1**	**100.0**
ANG/EPIS–Episcopal	1	43	84	130	0.4	0.5
Bahá'í	0	NR	7	7	0.0	0.0
BAPT–Amer Bapt USA	1	393	718	877	2.4	3.1
BAPT–N Am Bapt Conf	1	NR	181	221	0.6	0.8
BAPT–So Bapt Conv	1	35	35	43	0.1	0.2
Calv Chpl	1	NR	NR	NR	-	-
Catholic	6	NR	NR	8,543	23.4	30.3
Ch of Nazarene	1	45	39	80	0.2	0.3
Chr & Miss Al	4	192	110	291	0.8	1.0
CHR–Chs of Christ	1	20	22	25	0.1	0.1
Evan Free Ch	1	35	NR	35	0.1	0.1
FRND–Fr Gen Cf	1	NR	0	0	0.0	0.0
Jehovah's Witness	1	NR	NR	NR	-	-

NR–Not Reported - Represents no adherents reported. Percentages may not total 100 due to rounding.

Table 3: Religious Congregations by County and Group: 2010

Religious Group	Number of Congregations	Number of Attendees	Number of Communicant, Confirmed, or Full Members	Adherents: Number of Adherents	Adherents: % of Total Pop.	Adherents: % of Total Adh.
JUD–Conserv	1	8	9	24	0.1	0.1
LDS–L-D Saints	1	NR	NR	395	1.1	1.4
LUTH–Apostolic Luth	1	NR	NR	NR	-	-
LUTH–Ch Luth Conf	1	NR	NR	NR	-	-
LUTH–E.L.C.A.	8	1,854	5,387	7,571	20.7	26.9
LUTH–Luth Cong Msn Chr	3	121	219	267	0.7	0.9
LUTH–Luth–MO Synod	9	505	2,376	3,078	8.4	10.9
LUTH–Wisc Ev Luth Syn	1	194	333	435	1.2	1.5
MENN–Hutt Breth	4	NR	NR	NR	-	-
METH–Un Methodist	8	1,004	1,562	2,231	6.1	7.9
METH–Wesleyan	1	57	33	74	0.2	0.3
Non-denom Chr Chs	4	315	460	500	1.4	1.8
PENT–Assemb of God	2	478	156	664	1.8	2.4
PENT–Ch God (Cleve)	1	51	25	31	0.1	0.1
PENT–Un Pent Ch Intl	1	NR	NR	NR	-	-
PRES–Presb Ch (USA)	2	60	267	326	0.9	1.2
REF–Ref Ch in U.S.	1	NR	108	129	0.4	0.5
Salvation Army	1	24	62	1,414	3.9	5.0
Sev Day Adv	1	56	98	113	0.3	0.4
Un C of Christ	3	194	530	647	1.8	2.3
BRULE	**16**	**575**	**1,242**	**4,399**	**83.7**	**100.0**
ANG/EPIS–Episcopal	2	16	56	75	1.4	1.7
Bahá'í	0	NR	2	2	0.0	0.0
Catholic	3	NR	NR	2,676	50.9	60.8
Jehovah's Witness	1	NR	NR	NR	-	-
LUTH–Assoc Free Luth	2	NR	NR	NR	-	-
LUTH–E.L.C.A.	2	179	329	420	8.0	9.5
LUTH–Luth–MO Synod	1	150	404	521	9.9	11.8
MENN–Hutt Breth	1	NR	NR	NR	-	-
METH–Un Methodist	1	95	35	157	3.0	3.6
PENT–Assemb of God	1	35	25	65	1.2	1.5
PRES–Presb Ch (USA)	1	0	15	19	0.4	0.4
Un C of Christ	1	100	376	464	8.8	10.5
BUFFALO	**5**	**18**	**77**	**1,126**	**58.9**	**100.0**
ANG/EPIS–Episcopal	1	18	40	149	7.8	13.2
Bahá'í	0	NR	18	18	0.9	1.6
Catholic	2	NR	NR	787	41.2	69.9
LDS–L-D Saints	1	NR	NR	144	7.5	12.8
PRES–Presb Ch (USA)	1	0	19	28	1.5	2.5
BUTTE	**19**	**912**	**1,456**	**3,591**	**35.5**	**100.0**
ANG/EPIS–Episcopal	1	23	38	49	0.5	1.4
BAPT–Amer Bapt USA	1	45	150	186	1.8	5.2
BAPT–So Bapt Conv	2	51	42	52	0.5	1.4
Catholic	2	NR	NR	784	7.8	21.8
Jehovah's Witness	1	NR	NR	NR	-	-
LDS–L-D Saints	1	NR	NR	427	4.2	11.9
LUTH–E.L.C.A.	3	175	669	1,003	9.9	27.9
METH–Un Methodist	1	77	146	314	3.1	8.7
METH–Wesleyan	1	17	10	22	0.2	0.6
Non-denom Chr Chs	3	380	230	474	4.7	13.2
PENT–Assemb of God	1	20	8	24	0.2	0.7
PENT–Open Bible Std	1	54	NR	54	0.5	1.5
Un C of Christ	1	70	163	202	2.0	5.6
CAMPBELL	**8**	**247**	**681**	**970**	**66.2**	**100.0**
BAPT–N Am Bapt Conf	1	NR	135	154	10.5	15.9
Catholic	1	NR	NR	191	13.0	19.7
LUTH–E.L.C.A.	2	106	257	286	19.5	29.5
LUTH–Wisc Ev Luth Syn	1	17	50	51	3.5	5.3
PENT–Assemb of God	1	29	8	41	2.8	4.2
PRES–Presb Ch Amer	1	95	181	186	12.7	19.2
REF–Ref Ch in U.S.	1	NR	50	61	4.2	6.3
CHARLES MIX	**32**	**1,487**	**2,342**	**6,161**	**67.5**	**100.0**
ANG/EPIS–Episcopal	3	60	131	142	1.6	2.3
Bahá'í	0	NR	3	3	0.0	0.0
BAPT–Converge/BGC	1	75	NR	90	1.0	1.5
Catholic	6	NR	NR	2,788	30.5	45.3
Chr & Miss Al	1	96	60	175	1.9	2.8
LDS–L-D Saints	1	NR	NR	86	0.9	1.4
LUTH–Ch of Luth Br	1	34	30	47	0.5	0.8
LUTH–E.L.C.A.	1	40	106	123	1.3	2.0
LUTH–Luth Cong Msn Chr	1	188	402	520	5.7	8.4
LUTH–Luth–MO Synod	1	82	239	340	3.7	5.5
MENN–Hutt Breth	3	NR	NR	NR	-	-
METH–Un Methodist	2	132	293	417	4.6	6.8
METH–Wesleyan	1	13	2	17	0.2	0.3
Non-denom Chr Chs	1	45	45	56	0.6	0.9
PENT–Assemb of God	1	59	0	59	0.6	1.0
PRES–Presb Ch (USA)	4	132	334	432	4.7	7.0
REF–Christian Ref	1	225	289	374	4.1	6.1
REF–Ref Ch in Am	1	265	352	420	4.6	6.8
Sev Day Adv	1	6	10	12	0.1	0.2
Un C of Christ	1	35	46	60	0.7	1.0
CLARK	**24**	**760**	**1,766**	**2,660**	**72.1**	**100.0**
Catholic	1	NR	NR	439	11.9	16.5
LUTH–E.L.C.A.	7	366	933	1,183	32.1	44.5
LUTH–Wisc Ev Luth Syn	3	109	182	200	5.4	7.5
MENN–Hutt Breth	5	NR	NR	NR	-	-
METH–Un Methodist	3	114	364	447	12.1	16.8
PENT–Assemb of God	1	56	29	76	2.1	2.9
PRES–Presb Ch (USA)	2	60	116	142	3.8	5.3
Un C of Christ	2	55	142	173	4.7	6.5
CLAY	**24**	**1,257**	**2,834**	**7,434**	**53.6**	**100.0**
ANG/EPIS–Episcopal	1	32	112	117	0.8	1.6
Bahá'í	0	NR	10	10	0.1	0.1
BAPT–Amer Bapt USA	1	52	132	153	1.1	2.1
BAPT–So Bapt Conv	2	134	214	248	1.8	3.3
Catholic	3	NR	NR	3,515	25.4	47.3
Chr & Miss Al	1	124	60	162	1.2	2.2
CHR–Chs of Christ	1	15	15	20	0.1	0.3
LDS–L-D Saints	1	NR	NR	234	1.7	3.1
LUTH–E.L.C.A.	4	353	1,267	1,546	11.2	20.8
LUTH–Luth–MO Synod	1	69	100	117	0.8	1.6
METH–Un Methodist	3	123	300	416	3.0	5.6
PENT–Assemb of God	1	108	32	172	1.2	2.3
PENT–Open Bible Std	1	28	NR	28	0.2	0.4
REF–Ref Ch in U.S.	1	NR	22	35	0.3	0.5
Un C of Christ	2	209	564	655	4.7	8.8
Unit Univ	1	10	6	6	0.0	0.1
CODINGTON	**45**	**5,117**	**9,196**	**20,111**	**73.9**	**100.0**
ANG/EPIS–Episcopal	1	21	38	38	0.1	0.2
Bahá'í	0	NR	1	1	0.0	0.0
BAPT–Amer Bapt USA	1	124	264	328	1.2	1.6
BAPT–So Bapt Conv	1	25	53	66	0.2	0.3
Catholic	7	NR	NR	6,809	25.0	33.9
Chr & Miss Al	1	NR	NR	NR	-	-
CHR–Chr Chs & Chs Cr	1	NR	75	93	0.3	0.5
CHR–Chs of Christ	1	30	30	35	0.1	0.2
Evan Free Ch	1	310	NR	310	1.1	1.5
Jehovah's Witness	1	NR	NR	NR	-	-
LDS–L-D Saints	1	NR	NR	185	0.7	0.9
LUTH–Apostolic Luth	1	NR	NR	NR	-	-
LUTH–Assoc Free Luth	1	NR	NR	NR	-	-
LUTH–Ch Luth Conf	1	NR	NR	NR	-	-
LUTH–Ch of Luth Br	1	21	21	37	0.1	0.2
LUTH–E.L.C.A.	4	1,629	3,951	5,574	20.5	27.7
LUTH–Luth Cong Msn Chr	1	175	157	195	0.7	1.0
LUTH–Luth–MO Synod	1	153	411	539	2.0	2.7
LUTH–Wisc Ev Luth Syn	4	782	1,571	2,151	7.9	10.7
METH–Un Methodist	4	1,054	1,366	2,029	7.5	10.1
METH–Wesleyan	1	123	128	160	0.6	0.8
Non-denom Chr Chs	2	100	185	194	0.7	1.0
PENT–Assemb of God	1	120	55	166	0.6	0.8
PENT–Int Foursq Gos	1	255	427	531	2.0	2.6
PENT–Un Pent Ch Intl	1	NR	NR	NR	-	-
PRES–Presb Ch (USA)	1	20	27	34	0.1	0.2
REF–Ref Ch in U.S.	1	NR	19	25	0.1	0.1
Salvation Army	1	28	78	197	0.7	1.0

NR–Not Reported - Represents no adherents reported. Percentages may not total 100 due to rounding.

Table 3: Religious Congregations by County and Group: 2010

Religious Group	Number of Congrega-tions	Number of Attendees	Number of Communicant, Confirmed, or Full Members	Adherents: Number of Adherents	Adherents: % of Total Pop.	Adherents: % of Total Adh.
Sev Day Adv	1	45	78	90	0.3	0.4
Un C of Christ	1	102	261	324	1.2	1.6
CORSON	**29**	**266**	**610**	**2,372**	**58.6**	**100.0**
ANG/EPIS–Episcopal	5	69	110	333	8.2	14.0
Bahá'í	1	NR	62	62	1.5	2.6
BAPT–N Am Bapt Conf	1	NR	40	55	1.4	2.3
Catholic	10	NR	NR	1,018	25.1	42.9
LDS–L-D Saints	1	NR	NR	376	9.3	15.9
LUTH–E.L.C.A.	1	29	76	97	2.4	4.1
LUTH–Wisc Ev Luth Syn	2	43	63	69	1.7	2.9
PENT–Assemb of God	1	18	11	24	0.6	1.0
PENT–Ch God (Cleve)	1	66	1	1	0.0	0.0
PRES–Presb Ch (USA)	2	23	73	100	2.5	4.2
Un C of Christ	4	18	174	237	5.9	10.0
CUSTER	**23**	**885**	**1,839**	**2,784**	**33.9**	**100.0**
Bahá'í	0	NR	10	10	0.1	0.4
BAPT–So Bapt Conv	2	110	187	217	2.6	7.8
Catholic	3	NR	NR	368	4.5	13.2
CHR–Chs of Christ	2	23	22	25	0.3	0.9
Evan Free Ch	1	75	NR	75	0.9	2.7
Jehovah's Witness	1	NR	NR	NR	-	-
LUTH–E.L.C.A.	2	299	966	1,307	15.9	46.9
LUTH–Luth-MO Synod	1	79	141	182	2.2	6.5
LUTH–Wisc Ev Luth Syn	1	20	19	21	0.3	0.8
METH–Un Methodist	2	28	36	68	0.8	2.4
METH–Wesleyan	1	27	27	35	0.4	1.3
Non-denom Chr Chs	1	100	150	150	1.8	5.4
PENT–Vineyard	1	5	6	7	0.1	0.3
Sev Day Adv	3	12	20	23	0.3	0.8
Un C of Christ	2	107	255	296	3.6	10.6
DAVISON	**37**	**2,827**	**5,486**	**14,198**	**72.8**	**100.0**
ANG/EPIS–Episcopal	1	50	111	111	0.6	0.8
Bahá'í	0	NR	5	5	0.0	0.0
BAPT–Converge/BGC	1	75	NR	90	0.5	0.6
BAPT–So Bapt Conv	1	30	39	48	0.2	0.3
Catholic	4	NR	NR	6,054	31.0	42.6
Ch God (7th Day)	1	NR	NR	NR	-	-
Ch of Nazarene	1	111	227	232	1.2	1.6
CHR–Chs of Christ	1	10	9	14	0.1	0.1
Jehovah's Witness	1	NR	NR	NR	-	-
LDS–L-D Saints	1	NR	NR	174	0.9	1.2
LUTH–Assoc Free Luth	1	NR	NR	NR	-	-
LUTH–E.L.C.A.	4	631	1,890	2,526	13.0	17.8
LUTH–Luth Cong Msn Chr	1	157	542	665	3.4	4.7
LUTH–Luth-MO Synod	1	302	650	801	4.1	5.6
LUTH–Wisc Ev Luth Syn	1	31	58	67	0.3	0.5
MENN–Hutt Breth	3	NR	NR	NR	-	-
METH–Un Methodist	3	427	933	1,687	8.6	11.9
METH–Wesleyan	1	428	207	556	2.9	3.9
Non-denom Chr Chs	1	90	20	112	0.6	0.8
PENT–Assemb of God	1	52	33	97	0.5	0.7
PENT–Int Foursq Gos	1	34	35	43	0.2	0.3
PENT–Un Pent Ch Intl	1	NR	NR	NR	-	-
PRES–Presb Ch (USA)	1	43	77	94	0.5	0.7
REF–Ref Ch in Am	1	225	374	436	2.2	3.1
REF–Ref Ch in U.S.	1	NR	75	100	0.5	0.7
Salvation Army	1	54	67	122	0.6	0.9
Sev Day Adv	1	7	12	14	0.1	0.1
Un C of Christ	1	70	122	150	0.8	1.1
DAY	**28**	**967**	**2,278**	**4,880**	**85.5**	**100.0**
ANG/EPIS–Episcopal	2	42	64	277	4.9	5.7
BAPT–Amer Bapt USA	1	2	3	4	0.1	0.1
BAPT–So Bapt Conv	2	51	79	95	1.7	1.9
Catholic	4	NR	NR	1,808	31.7	37.0
LUTH–Assoc Free Luth	4	NR	NR	NR	-	-
LUTH–E.L.C.A.	7	595	1,509	1,907	33.4	39.1
LUTH–Luth Cong Msn Chr	2	30	128	153	2.7	3.1
LUTH–Luth-MO Synod	2	74	210	249	4.4	5.1
METH–Un Methodist	2	101	187	282	4.9	5.8
METH–Wesleyan	1	62	78	81	1.4	1.7
PRES–Presb Ch (USA)	1	10	20	24	0.4	0.5
DEUEL	**19**	**929**	**2,230**	**3,225**	**73.9**	**100.0**
BAPT–Converge/BGC	1	75	NR	90	2.1	2.8
Catholic	2	NR	NR	283	6.5	8.8
CHR–Chs of Christ	1	10	6	10	0.2	0.3
LUTH–Ch Luth Conf	1	NR	NR	NR	-	-
LUTH–Ch of Luth Br	1	46	25	78	1.8	2.4
LUTH–E.L.C.A.	6	403	1,288	1,557	35.7	48.3
LUTH–Wisc Ev Luth Syn	3	202	511	656	15.0	20.3
METH–Un Methodist	2	141	307	438	10.0	13.6
PRES–Presb Ch (USA)	1	27	45	55	1.3	1.7
Un C of Christ	1	25	48	58	1.3	1.8
DEWEY	**34**	**411**	**1,126**	**3,510**	**66.2**	**100.0**
ANG/EPIS–Episcopal	7	108	418	904	17.1	25.8
Bahá'í	0	NR	8	8	0.2	0.2
BAPT–Amer Bapt USA	1	11	27	37	0.7	1.1
BAPT–N Am Bapt Conf	1	NR	32	43	0.8	1.2
BAPT–So Bapt Conv	4	76	227	307	5.8	8.7
Catholic	6	NR	NR	1,201	22.7	34.2
LDS–L-D Saints	1	NR	NR	442	8.3	12.6
LUTH–Assoc Free Luth	1	NR	NR	NR	-	-
LUTH–E.L.C.A.	1	17	32	32	0.6	0.9
LUTH–Wisc Ev Luth Syn	1	28	34	39	0.7	1.1
METH–Un Methodist	1	17	29	29	0.5	0.8
METH–Wesleyan	1	30	0	39	0.7	1.1
Non-denom Chr Chs	1	30	30	38	0.7	1.1
PENT–Ch God (Cleve)	2	44	17	23	0.4	0.7
Un C of Christ	6	50	272	368	6.9	10.5
DOUGLAS	**18**	**1,265**	**2,038**	**2,861**	**95.3**	**100.0**
BAPT–Converge/BGC	1	75	NR	90	3.0	3.1
Catholic	1	NR	NR	308	10.3	10.8
LUTH–Assoc Free Luth	2	NR	NR	NR	-	-
LUTH–E.L.C.A.	2	183	443	559	18.6	19.5
LUTH–Luth Cong Msn Chr	1	76	132	158	5.3	5.5
LUTH–Luth-MO Synod	2	192	404	498	16.6	17.4
MENN–Hutt Breth	2	NR	NR	NR	-	-
REF–Christian Ref	3	385	574	687	22.9	24.0
REF–Ref Ch in Am	3	300	329	374	12.5	13.1
Un C of Christ	1	54	156	187	6.2	6.5
EDMUNDS	**20**	**645**	**1,043**	**2,912**	**71.5**	**100.0**
BAPT–Amer Bapt USA	1	57	58	70	1.7	2.4
Catholic	4	NR	NR	1,523	37.4	52.3
LUTH–Ch Luth Conf	2	NR	NR	NR	-	-
LUTH–E.L.C.A.	2	153	386	476	11.7	16.3
LUTH–Luth-MO Synod	1	15	26	48	1.2	1.6
LUTH–Wisc Ev Luth Syn	2	94	231	260	6.4	8.9
MENN–Hutt Breth	2	NR	NR	NR	-	-
METH–Wesleyan	1	206	115	268	6.6	9.2
PENT–Ch God (Cleve)	1	12	20	24	0.6	0.8
REF–Ref Ch in U.S.	1	NR	23	23	0.6	0.8
Sev Day Adv	1	28	49	56	1.4	1.9
Un C of Christ	2	80	135	164	4.0	5.6
FALL RIVER	**25**	**1,229**	**1,406**	**3,202**	**45.1**	**100.0**
ANG/EPIS–Episcopal	1	32	69	90	1.3	2.8
Bahá'í	0	NR	8	8	0.1	0.2
BAPT–Amer Bapt USA	1	155	44	51	0.7	1.6
BAPT–So Bapt Conv	2	45	72	84	1.2	2.6
Catholic	2	NR	NR	812	11.4	25.4
CHR–Chr Chs & Chs Cr	1	NR	50	58	0.8	1.8
CHR–Chs of Christ	1	26	15	27	0.4	0.8
Evan Free Ch	1	130	NR	130	1.8	4.1
Jehovah's Witness	1	NR	NR	NR	-	-
LDS–L-D Saints	1	NR	NR	274	3.9	8.6
LUTH–E.L.C.A.	2	135	245	326	4.6	10.2
LUTH–Luth-MO Synod	1	104	314	414	5.8	12.9

NR–Not Reported - Represents no adherents reported. Percentages may not total 100 due to rounding.

Table 3: Religious Congregations by County and Group: 2010

Religious Group	Number of Congregations	Number of Attendees	Number of Communicant, Confirmed, or Full Members	Adherents		
				Number of Adherents	% of Total Pop.	% of Total Adh.
LUTH–Wisc Ev Luth Syn	1	12	22	22	0.3	0.7
METH–Un Methodist	3	277	307	526	7.4	16.4
METH–Wesleyan	1	50	25	65	0.9	2.0
PENT–Assemb of God	2	65	37	85	1.2	2.7
PENT–Un Pent Ch Intl	1	NR	NR	NR	-	-
PRES–Presb Ch (USA)	1	96	53	62	0.9	1.9
Sev Day Adv	1	60	104	120	1.7	3.7
Un C of Christ	1	42	41	48	0.7	1.5
FAULK	**16**	**281**	**577**	**1,712**	**72.4**	**100.0**
Catholic	4	NR	NR	876	37.1	51.2
LUTH–Ch Luth Conf	1	NR	NR	NR	-	-
LUTH–E.L.C.A.	1	56	104	198	8.4	11.6
LUTH–Luth–MO Synod	3	78	173	198	8.4	11.6
MENN–Hutt Breth	4	NR	NR	NR	-	-
METH–Un Methodist	3	147	300	440	18.6	25.7
GRANT	**24**	**1,627**	**3,937**	**7,787**	**105.9**	**100.0**
ANG/EPIS–Episcopal	1	20	27	30	0.4	0.4
BAPT–N Am Bapt Conf	1	NR	111	134	1.8	1.7
Catholic	3	NR	NR	2,824	38.4	36.3
Evan Cov Ch	2	70	98	91	1.2	1.2
LUTH–E.L.C.A.	5	327	1,193	1,397	19.0	17.9
LUTH–Luth Cong Msn Chr	1	200	352	424	5.8	5.4
LUTH–Luth–MO Synod	3	339	1,064	1,368	18.6	17.6
LUTH–Wisc Ev Luth Syn	1	45	76	89	1.2	1.1
METH–Un Methodist	3	385	774	1,082	14.7	13.9
Non-denom Chr Chs	1	150	150	188	2.6	2.4
PENT–Assemb of God	1	58	42	97	1.3	1.2
REF–Ref Ch in Am	1	13	16	22	0.3	0.3
Un C of Christ	1	20	34	41	0.6	0.5
GREGORY	**24**	**856**	**1,674**	**3,024**	**70.8**	**100.0**
ANG/EPIS–Episcopal	3	36	73	88	2.1	2.9
Bahá'í	0	NR	1	1	0.0	0.0
BAPT–Amer Bapt USA	2	170	127	153	3.6	5.1
BAPT–So Bapt Conv	1	85	132	159	3.7	5.3
Catholic	4	NR	NR	1,107	25.9	36.6
Jehovah's Witness	1	NR	NR	NR	-	-
LUTH–Luth–MO Synod	2	149	397	447	10.5	14.8
LUTH–Wisc Ev Luth Syn	2	132	333	382	8.9	12.6
METH–Un Methodist	4	178	405	415	9.7	13.7
PENT–Assemb of God	1	11	10	37	0.9	1.2
PRES–Presb Ch (USA)	1	0	7	8	0.2	0.3
Un C of Christ	3	95	189	227	5.3	7.5
HAAKON	**12**	**282**	**445**	**1,625**	**83.9**	**100.0**
Catholic	3	NR	NR	668	34.5	41.1
Evan Free Ch	2	64	NR	64	3.3	3.9
LUTH–Luth Cong Msn Chr	2	85	221	268	13.8	16.5
LUTH–Luth–MO Synod	2	48	83	99	5.1	6.1
METH–Un Methodist	1	85	68	437	22.6	26.9
PENT–Open Bible Std	1	0	NR	0	0.0	0.0
PRES–Presb Ch (USA)	1	0	73	89	4.6	5.5
HAMLIN	**21**	**659**	**1,244**	**2,226**	**37.7**	**100.0**
BAPT–Converge/BGC	1	75	NR	90	1.5	4.0
Catholic	3	NR	NR	616	10.4	27.7
Evan Cov Ch	1	57	60	74	1.3	3.3
LUTH–Apostolic Luth	1	NR	NR	NR	-	-
LUTH–E.L.C.A.	2	195	513	646	10.9	29.0
LUTH–Nor Amer Luth C	4	NR	NR	NR	-	-
LUTH–Wisc Ev Luth Syn	2	42	88	88	1.5	4.0
MENN–Hutt Breth	2	NR	NR	NR	-	-
METH–Un Methodist	1	14	22	24	0.4	1.1
PRES–Presb Ch (USA)	1	76	201	265	4.5	11.9
REF–Ref Ch in Am	1	135	239	263	4.5	11.8
Un C of Christ	2	65	121	160	2.7	7.2
HAND	**13**	**443**	**912**	**2,295**	**66.9**	**100.0**
Bahá'í	0	NR	1	1	0.0	0.0

Religious Group	Number of Congregations	Number of Attendees	Number of Communicant, Confirmed, or Full Members	Adherents		
				Number of Adherents	% of Total Pop.	% of Total Adh.
BAPT–So Bapt Conv	1	36	49	58	1.7	2.5
Catholic	3	NR	NR	1,157	33.7	50.4
Ch of Nazarene	1	38	45	54	1.6	2.4
LDS–L-D Saints	1	NR	NR	45	1.3	2.0
LUTH–E.L.C.A.	1	106	359	421	12.3	18.3
MENN–Hutt Breth	1	NR	NR	NR	-	-
METH–Un Methodist	2	85	203	247	7.2	10.8
Non-denom Chr Chs	1	30	35	38	1.1	1.7
PENT–Assemb of God	1	25	17	33	1.0	1.4
PRES–Presb Ch (USA)	1	123	203	241	7.0	10.5
HANSON	**12**	**142**	**639**	**2,014**	**60.5**	**100.0**
BAPT–N Am Bapt Conf	1	NR	271	365	11.0	18.1
Catholic	4	NR	NR	1,184	35.5	58.8
LUTH–Luth–MO Synod	3	75	258	303	9.1	15.0
MENN–Hutt Breth	2	NR	NR	NR	-	-
METH–Un Methodist	1	47	78	119	3.6	5.9
PRES–Presb Ch (USA)	1	20	32	43	1.3	2.1
HARDING	**12**	**197**	**455**	**1,042**	**83.0**	**100.0**
Catholic	4	NR	NR	502	40.0	48.2
LUTH–Assoc Free Luth	1	NR	NR	NR	-	-
LUTH–E.L.C.A.	1	34	64	88	7.0	8.4
LUTH–Luth Cong Msn Chr	2	73	152	181	14.4	17.4
METH–Un Methodist	1	11	17	30	2.4	2.9
Non-denom Chr Chs	1	45	150	150	12.0	14.4
PENT–Assemb of God	1	16	9	16	1.3	1.5
Un C of Christ	1	18	63	75	6.0	7.2
HUGHES	**36**	**3,182**	**6,597**	**13,057**	**76.7**	**100.0**
ANG/EPIS–Episcopal	1	50	144	144	0.8	1.1
Bahá'í	0	NR	25	25	0.1	0.2
BAPT–Amer Bapt USA	2	122	280	343	2.0	2.6
BAPT–So Bapt Conv	2	72	281	344	2.0	2.6
BUDD–Mahayana	1	NR	NR	102	0.6	0.8
Catholic	3	NR	NR	2,822	16.6	21.6
Ch of Nazarene	1	42	26	77	0.5	0.6
CHR–Chs of Christ	1	70	70	118	0.7	0.9
Jehovah's Witness	1	NR	NR	NR	-	-
LDS–L-D Saints	1	NR	NR	283	1.7	2.2
LUTH–E.L.C.A.	2	470	1,792	3,190	18.7	24.4
LUTH–Luth–MO Synod	3	496	1,584	1,912	11.2	14.6
LUTH–Wisc Ev Luth Syn	1	47	73	95	0.6	0.7
METH–Un Methodist	4	395	823	1,218	7.2	9.3
METH–Wesleyan	2	75	14	97	0.6	0.7
Non-denom Chr Chs	4	739	535	1,019	6.0	7.8
PENT–Assemb of God	1	160	86	251	1.5	1.9
PENT–Un Pent Ch Intl	1	NR	NR	NR	-	-
PRES–Presb Ch (USA)	1	43	69	84	0.5	0.6
REF–Ref Ch in U.S.	1	NR	25	30	0.2	0.2
Sev Day Adv	2	301	524	602	3.5	4.6
Un C of Christ	1	100	246	301	1.8	2.3
HUTCHINSON	**36**	**2,194**	**4,298**	**6,418**	**87.4**	**100.0**
Bahá'í	0	NR	1	1	0.0	0.0
BAPT–N Am Bapt Conf	1	NR	56	68	0.9	1.1
Catholic	3	NR	NR	1,254	17.1	19.5
CONG–Consrv Cong Chr	1	175	276	335	4.6	5.2
Evan Assoc RCC	1	NR	NR	NR	-	-
LUTH–Assoc Free Luth	2	NR	NR	NR	-	-
LUTH–E.L.C.A.	2	142	303	403	5.5	6.3
LUTH–Luth Cong Msn Chr	2	105	390	473	6.4	7.4
LUTH–Luth–MO Synod	5	475	995	1,143	15.6	17.8
LUTH–Nor Amer Luth C	2	NR	NR	NR	-	-
MENN–Amish Undif	1	NR	13	31	0.4	0.5
MENN–Hutt Breth	3	NR	NR	NR	-	-
MENN–Menn Br US Conf	1	NR	98	119	1.6	1.9
MENN–Mennonite USA	4	732	1,137	1,378	18.8	21.5
METH–Un Methodist	2	47	107	107	1.5	1.7
Missionary Ch	1	59	63	63	0.9	1.0
PRES–Orth Pres Ch	1	50	96	115	1.6	1.8
REF–Christian Ref	1	136	228	276	3.8	4.3

NR–Not Reported - Represents no adherents reported. Percentages may not total 100 due to rounding.

Table 3: Religious Congregations by County and Group: 2010

Religious Group	Number of Congrega-tions	Number of Attendees	Number of Communicant, Confirmed, or Full Members	Adherents: Number of Adherents	Adherents: % of Total Pop.	Adherents: % of Total Adh.
REF–Ref Ch in U.S.	1	NR	156	181	2.5	2.8
Un Breth in Cr	1	13	0	12	0.2	0.2
Un C of Christ	1	260	379	459	6.3	7.2
HYDE	**7**	**189**	**605**	**2,032**	**143.1**	**100.0**
Catholic	3	NR	NR	1,245	87.7	61.3
CHR–Chr Chs & Chs Cr	1	NR	80	96	6.8	4.7
LUTH–E.L.C.A.	1	78	343	484	34.1	23.8
METH–Un Methodist	1	51	122	132	9.3	6.5
Non-denom Chr Chs	1	60	60	75	5.3	3.7
JACKSON	**10**	**124**	**423**	**1,752**	**57.8**	**100.0**
ANG/EPIS–Episcopal	1	13	20	92	3.0	5.3
Bahá'í	0	NR	66	66	2.2	3.8
Catholic	5	NR	NR	1,090	36.0	62.2
LUTH–E.L.C.A.	1	36	184	247	8.1	14.1
LUTH–Luth Cong Msn Chr	1	35	120	160	5.3	9.1
PENT–Assemb of God	1	28	0	53	1.7	3.0
PRES–Presb Ch (USA)	1	12	33	44	1.5	2.5
JERAULD	**12**	**469**	**897**	**1,420**	**68.6**	**100.0**
Bahá'í	0	NR	1	1	0.0	0.1
BAPT–N Am Bapt Conf	1	NR	95	115	5.6	8.1
Catholic	1	NR	NR	326	15.7	23.0
LUTH–E.L.C.A.	2	187	377	381	18.4	26.8
LUTH–Luth–MO Synod	1	27	72	87	4.2	6.1
MENN–Hutt Breth	1	NR	NR	NR	-	-
METH–Free Methodist	1	34	11	34	1.6	2.4
METH–Un Methodist	2	86	176	277	13.4	19.5
Un C of Christ	3	135	165	199	9.6	14.0
JONES	**8**	**145**	**362**	**509**	**50.6**	**100.0**
Bahá'í	0	NR	1	1	0.1	0.2
Catholic	2	NR	NR	46	4.6	9.0
Evan Free Ch	1	36	NR	36	3.6	7.1
LUTH–Luth–MO Synod	2	0	128	150	14.9	29.5
METH–Un Methodist	2	79	193	236	23.5	46.4
Non-denom Chr Chs	1	30	40	40	4.0	7.9
KINGSBURY	**30**	**1,025**	**3,027**	**4,746**	**92.2**	**100.0**
ANG/EPIS–Episcopal	1	5	20	20	0.4	0.4
Bahá'í	0	NR	1	1	0.0	0.0
BAPT–NT Ind Bapt	1	NR	NR	NR	-	-
Catholic	3	NR	NR	857	16.6	18.1
Chr & Miss Al	1	87	56	120	2.3	2.5
LUTH–Assoc Free Luth	1	NR	NR	NR	-	-
LUTH–E.L.C.A.	7	561	2,050	2,575	50.0	54.3
LUTH–Nor Amer Luth C	1	NR	NR	NR	-	-
MENN–CG in Cr (Menn)	1	NR	158	189	3.7	4.0
MENN–Hutt Breth	3	NR	NR	NR	-	-
METH–Un Methodist	5	179	387	570	11.1	12.0
Non-denom Chr Chs	1	40	50	50	1.0	1.1
PRES–Orth Pres Ch	1	20	37	44	0.9	0.9
PRES–Presb Ch (USA)	1	25	33	39	0.8	0.8
Un C of Christ	3	108	235	281	5.5	5.9
LAKE	**27**	**1,397**	**3,817**	**7,373**	**65.8**	**100.0**
ANG/EPIS–Episcopal	1	11	17	17	0.2	0.2
Bahá'í	0	NR	1	1	0.0	0.0
BAPT–Amer Bapt USA	1	33	48	58	0.5	0.8
BAPT–N Am Bapt Conf	1	NR	337	404	3.6	5.5
Catholic	2	NR	NR	2,049	18.3	27.8
Ch of Nazarene	1	45	71	71	0.6	1.0
LDS–L-D Saints	1	NR	NR	125	1.1	1.7
LUTH–Assoc Free Luth	1	NR	NR	NR	-	-
LUTH–E.L.C.A.	4	447	2,118	2,781	24.8	37.7
LUTH–Luth Ch-Am Asc	2	NR	NR	NR	-	-
LUTH–Luth–MO Synod	3	254	509	619	5.5	8.4
MENN–Hutt Breth	3	NR	NR	NR	-	-
METH–Un Methodist	2	224	469	635	5.7	8.6
METH–Wesleyan	1	241	10	313	2.8	4.2
PENT–Assemb of God	1	56	41	65	0.6	0.9
PRES–Presb Ch (USA)	2	51	134	161	1.4	2.2
Un C of Christ	1	35	62	74	0.7	1.0
LAWRENCE	**42**	**3,635**	**4,950**	**10,348**	**42.9**	**100.0**
ANG/EPIS–Episcopal	3	136	282	334	1.4	3.2
Bahá'í	0	NR	12	12	0.0	0.1
BAPT–Amer Bapt USA	1	97	78	92	0.4	0.9
BAPT–N Am Bapt Conf	1	NR	209	246	1.0	2.4
BAPT–So Bapt Conv	2	46	79	93	0.4	0.9
Catholic	3	NR	NR	2,153	8.9	20.8
Ch Cr, Scientst	1	NR	NR	NR	-	-
Ch of Nazarene	1	62	75	160	0.7	1.5
CHR–Chr Chs & Chs Cr	1	NR	150	177	0.7	1.7
CHR–Chs of Christ	2	129	141	154	0.6	1.5
Evan Free Ch	1	50	NR	50	0.2	0.5
Jehovah's Witness	1	NR	NR	NR	-	-
LUTH–E.L.C.A.	1	355	916	1,545	6.4	14.9
LUTH–Luth Cong Msn Chr	2	176	669	787	3.3	7.6
LUTH–Luth–MO Synod	2	222	491	581	2.4	5.6
LUTH–Nor Amer Luth C	2	NR	NR	NR	-	-
LUTH–Wisc Ev Luth Syn	1	62	112	143	0.6	1.4
METH–Un Methodist	3	329	568	948	3.9	9.2
METH–Wesleyan	1	1,064	168	1,383	5.7	13.4
Non-denom Chr Chs	2	295	335	369	1.5	3.6
PENT–Assemb of God	2	209	131	404	1.7	3.9
PENT–Int Foursq Gos	1	6	7	8	0.0	0.1
PENT–Open Bible Std	1	38	NR	38	0.2	0.4
PRES–Presb Ch (USA)	2	128	161	189	0.8	1.8
PRES–Presb Ch Amer	1	40	34	48	0.2	0.5
Salvation Army	1	10	23	75	0.3	0.7
Sev Day Adv	1	92	160	184	0.8	1.8
Un C of Christ	2	89	149	175	0.7	1.7
LINCOLN	**50**	**6,798**	**9,802**	**17,255**	**38.5**	**100.0**
BAPT–Converge/BGC	3	950	NR	1,140	2.5	6.6
BAPT–N Am Bapt Conf	1	NR	142	188	0.4	1.1
Catholic	4	NR	NR	1,706	3.8	9.9
Ch God (7th Day)	1	NR	NR	NR	-	-
Evan Free Ch	1	626	NR	626	1.4	3.6
LDS–Comm of Christ	1	NR	189	189	0.4	1.1
LUTH–Assoc Free Luth	2	NR	NR	NR	-	-
LUTH–E.L.C.A.	10	1,768	4,290	6,207	13.8	36.0
LUTH–Luth Cong Msn Chr	4	125	513	679	1.5	3.9
LUTH–Luth–MO Synod	2	415	650	884	2.0	5.1
LUTH–Nor Amer Luth C	1	NR	NR	NR	-	-
MENN–Menn Br US Conf	2	NR	111	147	0.3	0.9
METH–Un Methodist	2	340	677	938	2.1	5.4
METH–Wesleyan	1	533	230	693	1.5	4.0
Non-denom Chr Chs	1	65	150	150	0.3	0.9
PENT–Assemb of God	3	424	221	501	1.1	2.9
PRES–Presb Ch (USA)	1	22	24	32	0.1	0.2
PRES–Presb Ch Amer	2	270	516	602	1.3	3.5
REF–Christian Ref	1	86	58	77	0.2	0.4
REF–Ref Ch in Am	5	1,019	1,539	1,818	4.1	10.5
REF–Ref Ch in U.S.	1	NR	141	214	0.5	1.2
Un C of Christ	1	155	351	464	1.0	2.7
LYMAN	**16**	**302**	**603**	**3,736**	**99.5**	**100.0**
ANG/EPIS–Episcopal	1	23	46	337	9.0	9.0
Bahá'í	0	NR	11	11	0.3	0.3
Catholic	4	NR	NR	2,543	67.7	68.1
Ch of Nazarene	1	10	28	37	1.0	1.0
Evan Free Ch	1	50	NR	50	1.3	1.3
LUTH–E.L.C.A.	3	75	262	362	9.6	9.7
LUTH–Luth–MO Synod	2	37	72	72	1.9	1.9
METH–Un Methodist	3	75	184	250	6.7	6.7
PENT–Assemb of God	1	32	0	74	2.0	2.0
MCCOOK	**20**	**774**	**1,427**	**3,154**	**56.1**	**100.0**
Bahá'í	0	NR	1	1	0.0	0.0
BAPT–Converge/BGC	2	150	NR	180	3.2	5.7

NR–Not Reported - Represents no adherents reported. Percentages may not total 100 due to rounding.

Table 3: Religious Congregations by County and Group: 2010

Religious Group	Number of Congrega-tions	Number of Attendees	Number of Communicant, Confirmed, or Full Members	Adherents		
				Number of Adherents	% of Total Pop.	% of Total Adh.
Catholic	3	NR	NR	1,134	20.2	36.0
LUTH–E.L.C.A.	3	210	501	650	11.6	20.6
LUTH–Luth–MO Synod	3	185	403	537	9.6	17.0
MENN–Hutt Breth	2	NR	NR	NR	-	-
MENN–Mennonite USA	1	18	50	63	1.1	2.0
METH–Un Methodist	2	116	229	280	5.0	8.9
PRES–Orth Pres Ch	1	14	17	26	0.5	0.8
PRES–Presb Ch (USA)	3	81	226	283	5.0	9.0
MCPHERSON	**14**	**529**	**1,412**	**2,005**	**81.5**	**100.0**
BAPT–N Am Bapt Conf	1	NR	96	115	4.7	5.7
Catholic	2	NR	NR	351	14.3	17.5
Ch God (7th Day)	1	NR	NR	NR	-	-
LUTH–E.L.C.A.	3	283	739	822	33.4	41.0
LUTH–Luth Cong Msn Chr	1	25	65	78	3.2	3.9
LUTH–Luth–MO Synod	1	35	76	111	4.5	5.5
MENN–Hutt Breth	1	NR	NR	NR	-	-
METH–Un Methodist	2	145	192	257	10.5	12.8
REF–Ref Ch in U.S.	1	NR	153	162	6.6	8.1
Un C of Christ	1	41	91	109	4.4	5.4
MARSHALL	**22**	**900**	**2,257**	**3,740**	**80.3**	**100.0**
Bahá'í	0	NR	2	2	0.0	0.1
Catholic	4	NR	NR	852	18.3	22.8
Evan Free Ch	1	120	NR	120	2.6	3.2
LUTH–E.L.C.A.	5	205	623	813	17.5	21.7
LUTH–Luth Cong Msn Chr	3	327	963	1,154	24.8	30.9
LUTH–Luth–MO Synod	1	59	173	215	4.6	5.7
MENN–Hutt Breth	2	NR	NR	NR	-	-
METH–Un Methodist	1	45	118	136	2.9	3.6
PRES–Presb Ch (USA)	4	108	318	381	8.2	10.2
REF–Ref Ch in Am	1	36	60	67	1.4	1.8
MEADE	**40**	**1,828**	**3,055**	**6,487**	**25.5**	**100.0**
ANG/EPIS–Episcopal	1	21	30	102	0.4	1.6
Bahá'í	0	NR	12	12	0.0	0.2
BAPT–Amer Bapt USA	2	5	61	77	0.3	1.2
BAPT–So Bapt Conv	2	101	203	255	1.0	3.9
Catholic	7	NR	NR	1,988	7.8	30.6
CHR–Chr Chs & Chs Cr	2	NR	107	134	0.5	2.1
CHR–Chs of Christ	2	145	135	183	0.7	2.8
Evan Free Ch	1	150	NR	150	0.6	2.3
Jehovah's Witness	1	NR	NR	NR	-	-
LDS–L-D Saints	1	NR	NR	248	1.0	3.8
LUTH–Assoc Free Luth	1	NR	NR	NR	-	-
LUTH–E.L.C.A.	2	283	870	1,089	4.3	16.8
LUTH–Luth–MO Synod	2	170	328	425	1.7	6.6
LUTH–Wisc Ev Luth Syn	2	65	99	131	0.5	2.0
METH–Un Methodist	3	335	509	729	2.9	11.2
METH–Wesleyan	1	117	76	152	0.6	2.3
Non-denom Chr Chs	3	121	233	239	0.9	3.7
PENT–Assemb of God	1	32	30	65	0.3	1.0
PENT–Ch God (Cleve)	1	41	27	34	0.1	0.5
PENT–Open Bible Std	1	60	NR	60	0.2	0.9
PRES–Presb Ch (USA)	2	122	253	317	1.2	4.9
PRES–Presb Ch Amer	1	60	82	97	0.4	1.5
Unity Ch	1	NR	NR	NR	-	-
MELLETTE	**14**	**255**	**313**	**864**	**42.2**	**100.0**
ANG/EPIS–Episcopal	3	74	65	254	12.4	29.4
Bahá'í	0	NR	16	16	0.8	1.9
BAPT–Amer Bapt USA	1	9	7	9	0.4	1.0
Catholic	2	NR	NR	80	3.9	9.3
Ch of Nazarene	1	32	22	47	2.3	5.4
LDS–L-D Saints	1	NR	NR	87	4.2	10.1
LUTH–Ch Luth Conf	1	NR	NR	NR	-	-
LUTH–Luth–MO Synod	1	36	72	91	4.4	10.5
METH–Un Methodist	1	49	96	216	10.5	25.0
Non-denom Chr Chs	1	30	35	38	1.9	4.4
PENT–Assemb of God	1	6	0	7	0.3	0.8
PENT–Open Bible Std	1	19	NR	19	0.9	2.2

Religious Group	Number of Congrega-tions	Number of Attendees	Number of Communicant, Confirmed, or Full Members	Adherents		
				Number of Adherents	% of Total Pop.	% of Total Adh.
MINER	**13**	**510**	**1,132**	**2,143**	**89.7**	**100.0**
Bahá'í	0	NR	1	1	0.0	0.0
Catholic	1	NR	NR	674	28.2	31.5
LUTH–E.L.C.A.	6	271	614	820	34.3	38.3
LUTH–Luth–MO Synod	1	89	262	299	12.5	14.0
METH–Un Methodist	1	72	148	188	7.9	8.8
Non-denom Chr Chs	1	6	6	8	0.3	0.4
PENT–Assemb of God	1	22	9	41	1.7	1.9
PRES–Presb Ch (USA)	1	35	78	95	4.0	4.4
Un C of Christ	1	15	14	17	0.7	0.8
MINNEHAHA	**195**	**28,973**	**48,528**	**105,041**	**62.0**	**100.0**
ANG/EPIS–Episcopal	3	330	756	1,292	0.8	1.2
Bahá'í	1	NR	74	74	0.0	0.1
BAPT–Amer Bapt USA	7	865	1,882	2,346	1.4	2.2
BAPT–Converge/BGC	1	75	NR	90	0.1	0.1
BAPT–Ind Bapt Flwsp Intl	1	NR	NR	NR	-	-
BAPT–N Am Bapt Conf	5	NR	657	819	0.5	0.8
BAPT–So Bapt Conv	10	390	585	729	0.4	0.7
BUDD–Theravada	1	NR	NR	14	0.0	0.0
Calv Chpl	1	NR	NR	NR	-	-
Catholic	16	NR	NR	30,335	17.9	28.9
CGOD–Ch God (Ander)	1	155	NR	155	0.1	0.1
Ch of Nazarene	1	94	53	94	0.1	0.1
Chr & Miss Al	2	155	53	237	0.1	0.2
CHR–Chr Ch (Disc)	2	106	224	279	0.2	0.3
CHR–Chr Chs & Chs Cr	1	NR	185	231	0.1	0.2
CHR–Chs of Christ	3	232	204	270	0.2	0.3
Christian Brethren	1	NR	NR	NR	-	-
Evan Cov Ch	4	421	489	546	0.3	0.5
FRND–Consrv Yr Mtgs	1	NR	0	0	0.0	0.0
Grace Gosp Fel	1	NR	NR	NR	-	-
Jehovah's Witness	2	NR	NR	NR	-	-
JUD–Reform	1	37	65	176	0.1	0.2
LDS–L-D Saints	3	NR	NR	1,513	0.9	1.4
LUTH–Assoc Free Luth	1	NR	NR	NR	-	-
LUTH–Ch Luth Conf	1	NR	NR	NR	-	-
LUTH–E.L.C.A.	40	9,122	22,800	33,233	19.6	31.6
LUTH–Luth Cong Msn Chr	2	152	95	118	0.1	0.1
LUTH–Luth–MO Synod	9	1,550	2,791	3,617	2.1	3.4
LUTH–Nor Amer Luth C	1	NR	NR	NR	-	-
LUTH–Wisc Ev Luth Syn	2	410	761	999	0.6	1.0
MENN–Menn Br US Conf	1	NR	31	39	0.0	0.0
MENN–Mennonite USA	2	160	230	287	0.2	0.3
METH–Un Methodist	13	2,104	4,191	6,238	3.7	5.9
METH–Wesleyan	3	3,874	911	5,036	3.0	4.8
Muslim Est	3	298	NR	716	0.4	0.7
Non-denom Chr Chs	14	2,536	2,815	3,281	1.9	3.1
ORTHE–Greek Orthodox	1	60	NR	250	0.1	0.2
ORTHE–Holy Orth in NA	1	8	NR	10	0.0	0.0
PENT–Assemb of God	3	1,235	730	1,651	1.0	1.6
PENT–Ch God (Cleve)	1	0	0	0	0.0	0.0
PENT–Ch of God Proph	1	NR	26	32	0.0	0.0
PENT–COGIC	1	150	200	249	0.1	0.2
PENT–Un Pent Ch Intl	1	NR	NR	NR	-	-
PRES–Presb Ch (USA)	5	951	1,820	2,269	1.3	2.2
PRES–Presb Ch Amer	1	0	0	0	0.0	0.0
REF–Christian Ref	4	1,355	2,229	2,779	1.6	2.6
REF–Prot Ref Chs	1	48	32	53	0.0	0.1
REF–Ref Ch in Am	5	1,483	2,072	2,693	1.6	2.6
REF–Un Ref Chs N.A.	1	NR	NR	NR	-	-
Salvation Army	1	48	72	437	0.3	0.4
Sev Day Adv	1	166	289	332	0.2	0.3
Un C of Christ	5	341	1,130	1,409	0.8	1.3
Unit Univ	1	62	76	113	0.1	0.1
MOODY	**19**	**716**	**1,878**	**4,260**	**65.7**	**100.0**
ANG/EPIS–Episcopal	1	13	10	47	0.7	1.1
Bahá'í	0	NR	5	5	0.1	0.1
BAPT–Amer Bapt USA	1	77	149	186	2.9	4.4
Catholic	2	NR	NR	1,943	30.0	45.6
LUTH–E.L.C.A.	4	325	1,078	1,319	20.3	31.0
LUTH–Luth–MO Synod	1	25	41	41	0.6	1.0

NR–Not Reported   - Represents no adherents reported.   Percentages may not total 100 due to rounding.

Table 3: Religious Congregations by County and Group: 2010

Religious Group	Number of Congrega-tions	Number of Attendees	Number of Communicant, Confirmed, or Full Members	Adherents: Number of Adherents	Adherents: % of Total Pop.	Adherents: % of Total Adh.
LUTH–Wisc Ev Luth Syn	1	27	42	43	0.7	1.0
MENN–CG in Cr (Menn)	1	NR	59	74	1.1	1.7
MENN–Hutt Breth	1	NR	NR	NR	-	-
METH–Un Methodist	3	78	151	210	3.2	4.9
Non-denom Chr Chs	2	100	174	181	2.8	4.2
PRES–Presb Ch (USA)	2	71	169	211	3.3	5.0
PENNINGTON	**119**	**12,431**	**19,972**	**41,612**	**41.2**	**100.0**
ANG/EPIS–Episcopal	3	295	1,001	1,214	1.2	2.9
Bahá'í	1	NR	81	81	0.1	0.2
BAPT–Amer Bapt Assn	1	NR	85	106	0.1	0.3
BAPT–Amer Bapt USA	2	215	276	343	0.3	0.8
BAPT–N Am Bapt Conf	1	NR	415	515	0.5	1.2
BAPT–Ref Bapt Ch	1	NR	NR	NR	-	-
BAPT–Reg Bapt Gen As	1	NR	NR	NR	-	-
BAPT–So Bapt Conv	7	442	1,956	2,428	2.4	5.8
Calv Chpl	1	NR	NR	NR	-	-
Catholic	10	NR	NR	7,072	7.0	17.0
CGOD–Ch God (Ander)	1	24	NR	24	0.0	0.1
Ch Cr, Scientst	1	NR	NR	NR	-	-
Ch of Nazarene	1	107	80	195	0.2	0.5
Chr & Miss Al	1	50	39	77	0.1	0.2
CHR–Chr Chs & Chs Cr	1	NR	250	310	0.3	0.7
CHR–Chs of Christ	3	145	123	167	0.2	0.4
Evan Free Ch	3	1,165	NR	1,165	1.2	2.8
FRND–Fr Gen Cf	1	NR	0	0	0.0	0.0
Grace Gosp Fel	1	NR	NR	NR	-	-
HINDU–Post Ren	2	NR	NR	32	0.0	0.1
JUD–Reform	1	18	31	84	0.1	0.2
LDS–L-D Saints	5	NR	NR	3,208	3.2	7.7
LUTH–Ch Luth Conf	1	NR	NR	NR	-	-
LUTH–E.L.C.A.	8	1,889	5,206	7,135	7.1	17.1
LUTH–Luth–MO Synod	7	1,023	2,747	3,792	3.8	9.1
LUTH–Nor Amer Luth C	1	NR	NR	NR	-	-
LUTH–Wisc Ev Luth Syn	1	404	661	920	0.9	2.2
MENN–Menn Br US Conf	1	NR	101	125	0.1	0.3
METH–Free Methodist	2	39	47	47	0.0	0.1
METH–Un Methodist	7	1,218	2,113	3,394	3.4	8.2
METH–Wesleyan	6	1,035	369	1,346	1.3	3.2
Missionary Ch	1	0	0	0	0.0	0.0
Muslim Est	1	134	NR	308	0.3	0.7
Non-denom Chr Chs	9	699	879	1,012	1.0	2.4
ORTHE–Ant Orth of NA	1	27	NR	60	0.1	0.1
PENT–Assemb of God	4	820	395	1,456	1.4	3.5
PENT–Ch God (Cleve)	1	51	74	92	0.1	0.2
PENT–Ch of God Proph	1	NR	27	34	0.0	0.1
PENT–COGIC	1	100	150	186	0.2	0.4
PENT–Int Foursq Gos	1	413	315	391	0.4	0.9
PENT–Open Bible Std	2	953	NR	953	0.9	2.3
PENT–Un Pent Ch Intl	1	NR	NR	NR	-	-
PRES–Presb Ch (USA)	3	408	758	941	0.9	2.3
PRES–Presb Ch Amer	1	45	68	76	0.1	0.2
REF–Christian Ref	1	60	107	133	0.1	0.3
REF–Ref Ch in U.S.	1	NR	68	106	0.1	0.3
Salvation Army	1	31	46	268	0.3	0.6
Sev Day Adv	1	300	522	600	0.6	1.4
Un C of Christ	4	281	942	1,169	1.2	2.8
Unit Univ	1	40	40	47	0.0	0.1
PERKINS	**23**	**615**	**1,361**	**2,959**	**99.2**	**100.0**
Bahá'í	0	NR	1	1	0.0	0.0
BAPT–So Bapt Conv	1	30	30	36	1.2	1.2
Catholic	3	NR	NR	1,378	46.2	46.6
CHR–Chs of Christ	1	11	9	11	0.4	0.4
LUTH–Ch Luth Conf	1	NR	NR	NR	-	-
LUTH–E.L.C.A.	6	191	719	801	26.9	27.1
LUTH–Wisc Ev Luth Syn	1	34	58	65	2.2	2.2
METH–Wesleyan	1	49	40	64	2.1	2.2
Non-denom Chr Chs	1	35	42	44	1.5	1.5
PENT–Ch God (Cleve)	1	67	102	122	4.1	4.1
PRES–Presb Ch (USA)	2	89	179	213	7.1	7.2
PRES–Presb Ch Amer	1	75	51	69	2.3	2.3
REF–Christian Ref	1	30	62	74	2.5	2.5

Religious Group	Number of Congrega-tions	Number of Attendees	Number of Communicant, Confirmed, or Full Members	Adherents: Number of Adherents	Adherents: % of Total Pop.	Adherents: % of Total Adh.
Sev Day Adv	1	4	6	7	0.2	0.2
Un C of Christ	2	0	62	74	2.5	2.5
POTTER	**12**	**259**	**736**	**2,187**	**93.9**	**100.0**
ANG/EPIS–Episcopal	1	7	8	8	0.3	0.4
Catholic	2	NR	NR	1,245	53.5	56.9
LDS–L-D Saints	1	NR	NR	35	1.5	1.6
LUTH–Luth–MO Synod	2	98	236	285	12.2	13.0
MENN–Menn Br US Conf	1	NR	117	138	5.9	6.3
METH–Un Methodist	2	93	320	387	16.6	17.7
METH–Wesleyan	1	47	31	61	2.6	2.8
PENT–Ch God (Cleve)	1	6	11	13	0.6	0.6
Sev Day Adv	1	8	13	15	0.6	0.7
ROBERTS	**38**	**1,277**	**3,273**	**6,203**	**61.1**	**100.0**
ANG/EPIS–Episcopal	2	54	102	315	3.1	5.1
Bahá'í	0	NR	6	6	0.1	0.1
BAPT–So Bapt Conv	3	48	93	119	1.2	1.9
Catholic	5	NR	NR	1,575	15.5	25.4
Chr & Miss Al	3	91	60	120	1.2	1.9
Jehovah's Witness	1	NR	NR	NR	-	-
LDS–L-D Saints	1	NR	NR	157	1.5	2.5
LUTH–Assoc Free Luth	1	NR	NR	NR	-	-
LUTH–E.L.C.A.	9	614	1,906	2,441	24.1	39.4
LUTH–Luth–MO Synod	4	185	563	677	6.7	10.9
LUTH–Wisc Ev Luth Syn	1	30	62	87	0.9	1.4
MENN–Hutt Breth	1	NR	NR	NR	-	-
PENT–Assemb of God	1	150	74	186	1.8	3.0
PRES–Presb Ch (USA)	6	105	407	520	5.1	8.4
SANBORN	**8**	**153**	**301**	**1,550**	**65.8**	**100.0**
BAPT–So Bapt Conv	1	9	3	4	0.2	0.3
Catholic	2	NR	NR	1,189	50.5	76.7
CONG–Consrv Cong Chr	1	75	100	119	5.1	7.7
LUTH–E.L.C.A.	1	37	123	163	6.9	10.5
LUTH–Luth–MO Synod	1	12	15	15	0.6	1.0
MENN–Hutt Breth	1	NR	NR	NR	-	-
METH–Un Methodist	1	20	60	60	2.5	3.9
SHANNON	**25**	**513**	**1,299**	**4,013**	**29.5**	**100.0**
ANG/EPIS–Episcopal	6	108	380	882	6.5	22.0
Bahá'í	0	NR	187	187	1.4	4.7
BAPT–S-D Baptist Gen Con	1	NR	NR	NR	-	-
BAPT–So Bapt Conv	2	85	90	129	0.9	3.2
Catholic	5	NR	NR	1,918	14.1	47.8
CGOD–Ch God (Ander)	1	32	NR	32	0.2	0.8
Ch of Nazarene	2	39	18	119	0.9	3.0
LUTH–Wisc Ev Luth Syn	1	11	32	36	0.3	0.9
MENN–Menn Br US Conf	1	NR	0	0	0.0	0.0
Non-denom Chr Chs	2	185	300	338	2.5	8.4
PENT–Assemb of God	1	53	108	108	0.8	2.7
PRES–Presb Ch (USA)	3	0	184	264	1.9	6.6
SPINK	**27**	**1,712**	**2,037**	**4,618**	**72.0**	**100.0**
BAPT–So Bapt Conv	1	20	23	28	0.4	0.6
Catholic	6	NR	NR	2,152	33.5	46.6
LUTH–E.L.C.A.	1	142	398	495	7.7	10.7
LUTH–Luth–MO Synod	2	67	188	228	3.6	4.9
MENN–Hutt Breth	4	NR	NR	NR	-	-
METH–Un Methodist	6	366	771	922	14.4	20.0
METH–Wesleyan	1	53	63	69	1.1	1.5
Non-denom Chr Chs	1	30	30	38	0.6	0.8
PRES–Presb Ch (USA)	1	810	7	9	0.1	0.2
Sev Day Adv	1	22	39	45	0.7	1.0
Un C of Christ	3	202	518	632	9.9	13.7
STANLEY	**4**	**43**	**110**	**2,368**	**79.8**	**100.0**
ANG/EPIS–Episcopal	1	19	30	42	1.4	1.8
Bahá'í	0	NR	3	3	0.1	0.1
Catholic	1	NR	NR	2,205	74.3	93.1
LUTH–E.L.C.A.	1	12	36	68	2.3	2.9

NR–Not Reported   - Represents no adherents reported.   Percentages may not total 100 due to rounding.

Table 3: Religious Congregations by County and Group: 2010

Religious Group	Number of Congrega-tions	Number of Attendees	Number of Communicant, Confirmed, or Full Members	Adherents: Number of Adherents	Adherents: % of Total Pop.	Adherents: % of Total Adh.
LUTH–Luth Cong Msn Chr	1	12	41	50	1.7	2.1
SULLY	**6**	**101**	**397**	**774**	**56.4**	**100.0**
Bahá'í	0	NR	2	2	0.1	0.3
Catholic	1	NR	NR	315	22.9	40.7
LUTH–Luth-MO Synod	1	41	120	138	10.1	17.8
MENN–Menn Br US Conf	1	NR	30	36	2.6	4.7
METH–Un Methodist	2	60	108	118	8.6	15.2
PRES–Presb Ch (USA)	1	0	137	165	12.0	21.3
TODD	**18**	**246**	**436**	**2,856**	**29.7**	**100.0**
ANG/EPIS–Episcopal	5	83	108	733	7.6	25.7
Bahá'í	0	NR	197	197	2.0	6.9
Catholic	5	NR	NR	1,365	14.2	47.8
Ch of Nazarene	1	27	0	27	0.3	0.9
LDS–L-D Saints	1	NR	NR	314	3.3	11.0
LUTH–Ch Luth Conf	1	NR	NR	NR	-	-
LUTH–Wisc Ev Luth Syn	1	24	52	55	0.6	1.9
METH–Un Methodist	1	15	25	52	0.5	1.8
METH–Wesleyan	1	24	10	31	0.3	1.1
Non-denom Chr Chs	1	35	35	44	0.5	1.5
PENT–Assemb of God	1	38	9	38	0.4	1.3
TRIPP	**26**	**993**	**1,775**	**2,780**	**49.3**	**100.0**
ANG/EPIS–Episcopal	2	51	165	176	3.1	6.3
Bahá'í	0	NR	3	3	0.1	0.1
BAPT–Amer Bapt USA	2	55	63	76	1.3	2.7
BAPT–So Bapt Conv	1	10	8	10	0.2	0.4
Catholic	3	NR	NR	513	9.1	18.5
Ch of Nazarene	1	35	59	65	1.2	2.3
CHR–Chr Ch (Disc)	1	0	125	152	2.7	5.5
Evan Free Ch	1	30	NR	30	0.5	1.1
LDS–L-D Saints	1	NR	NR	96	1.7	3.5
LUTH–Luth-MO Synod	3	83	274	303	5.4	10.9
LUTH–Wisc Ev Luth Syn	3	216	435	508	9.0	18.3
METH–Un Methodist	2	274	468	485	8.6	17.4
PENT–Assemb of God	1	65	42	70	1.2	2.5
PENT–Pent Ch of God	1	70	NR	109	1.9	3.9
PRES–Orth Pres Ch	2	74	81	121	2.1	4.4
PRES–Presb Ch (USA)	1	20	35	42	0.7	1.5
Un C of Christ	1	10	17	21	0.4	0.8
TURNER	**36**	**1,705**	**3,688**	**5,471**	**65.5**	**100.0**
BAPT–Amer Bapt USA	2	207	358	437	5.2	8.0
BAPT–N Am Bapt Conf	1	NR	185	226	2.7	4.1
Catholic	4	NR	NR	865	10.4	15.8
CGOD–Ch God (Ander)	1	117	NR	117	1.4	2.1
Ch of Nazarene	1	20	23	40	0.5	0.7
LUTH–Assoc Free Luth	1	NR	NR	NR	-	-
LUTH–E.L.C.A.	6	519	1,271	1,626	19.5	29.7
LUTH–Luth-MO Synod	4	118	291	327	3.9	6.0
MENN–Fel Evg Bib Ch	1	48	30	48	0.6	0.9
METH–Un Methodist	4	111	216	219	2.6	4.0
PRES–Presb Ch (USA)	4	131	301	367	4.4	6.7
PRES–Presb Ch Amer	1	30	121	121	1.4	2.2
REF–Christian Ref	1	13	25	31	0.4	0.6
REF–Ref Ch in Am	3	325	718	868	10.4	15.9
Sev Day Adv	1	29	50	58	0.7	1.1
Un C of Christ	1	37	99	121	1.4	2.2
UNION	**32**	**1,842**	**3,200**	**9,228**	**64.1**	**100.0**
Bahá'í	0	NR	1	1	0.0	0.0
BAPT–Converge/BGC	3	225	NR	270	1.9	2.9
BAPT–So Bapt Conv	5	63	63	79	0.5	0.9
Catholic	4	NR	NR	4,474	31.1	48.5
Evan Cov Ch	1	100	66	130	0.9	1.4
Evan Free Ch	1	210	NR	210	1.5	2.3
LUTH–Assoc Free Luth	1	NR	NR	NR	-	-
LUTH–E.L.C.A.	6	546	2,130	2,741	19.0	29.7
LUTH–Luth-MO Synod	2	112	168	217	1.5	2.4
METH–Un Methodist	3	249	330	498	3.5	5.4
Non-denom Chr Chs	2	80	85	101	0.7	1.1
PENT–Assemb of God	1	52	23	88	0.6	1.0
Un C of Christ	3	205	334	419	2.9	4.5
WALWORTH	**28**	**1,312**	**2,801**	**4,455**	**81.9**	**100.0**
ANG/EPIS–Episcopal	1	23	36	59	1.1	1.3
Bahá'í	0	NR	14	14	0.3	0.3
BAPT–Amer Bapt USA	1	31	74	89	1.6	2.0
BAPT–So Bapt Conv	1	64	175	211	3.9	4.7
Catholic	2	NR	NR	948	17.4	21.3
Evan Free Ch	1	70	NR	70	1.3	1.6
Jehovah's Witness	1	NR	NR	NR	-	-
LUTH–E.L.C.A.	4	204	775	828	15.2	18.6
LUTH–Luth Cong Msn Chr	2	148	590	713	13.1	16.0
LUTH–Nor Amer Luth C	1	NR	NR	NR	-	-
LUTH–Wisc Ev Luth Syn	3	142	283	326	6.0	7.3
METH–Un Methodist	2	77	164	216	4.0	4.8
Non-denom Chr Chs	3	194	190	312	5.7	7.0
PENT–Assemb of God	1	29	29	100	1.8	2.2
PENT–Ch God (Cleve)	2	196	131	158	2.9	3.5
Sev Day Adv	1	6	11	13	0.2	0.3
Un C of Christ	2	128	329	398	7.3	8.9
YANKTON	**35**	**2,477**	**5,560**	**15,152**	**67.5**	**100.0**
ANG/EPIS–Episcopal	1	59	154	203	0.9	1.3
Bahá'í	0	NR	3	3	0.0	0.0
BAPT–Converge/BGC	1	400	NR	480	2.1	3.2
BAPT–So Bapt Conv	1	21	32	38	0.2	0.3
Catholic	5	NR	NR	7,392	32.9	48.8
CHR–Chr Chs & Chs Cr	1	NR	70	84	0.4	0.6
CHR–Chs of Christ	1	12	12	14	0.1	0.1
Jehovah's Witness	1	NR	NR	NR	-	-
LDS–L-D Saints	1	NR	NR	292	1.3	1.9
LUTH–Assoc Free Luth	1	NR	NR	NR	-	-
LUTH–E.L.C.A.	6	642	2,686	3,032	13.5	20.0
LUTH–Luth-MO Synod	2	429	1,023	1,319	5.9	8.7
LUTH–Nor Amer Luth C	1	NR	NR	NR	-	-
LUTH–Wisc Ev Luth Syn	2	34	56	71	0.3	0.5
MENN–Hutt Breth	1	NR	NR	NR	-	-
METH–Un Methodist	2	288	550	893	4.0	5.9
Non-denom Chr Chs	4	110	119	138	0.6	0.9
PENT–Assemb of God	1	182	167	395	1.8	2.6
REF–Ref Ch in Am	1	115	234	254	1.1	1.7
Sev Day Adv	1	23	40	46	0.2	0.3
Un C of Christ	1	162	414	498	2.2	3.3
ZIEBACH	**15**	**80**	**330**	**1,201**	**42.9**	**100.0**
ANG/EPIS–Episcopal	3	36	68	128	4.6	10.7
Bahá'í	0	NR	24	24	0.9	2.0
BAPT–So Bapt Conv	1	36	43	63	2.2	5.2
Catholic	5	NR	NR	515	18.4	42.9
CONG–Cong Chr Add'l	1	NR	28	41	1.5	3.4
LDS–L-D Saints	2	NR	NR	191	6.8	15.9
LUTH–Wisc Ev Luth Syn	1	8	16	18	0.6	1.5
Un C of Christ	2	0	151	221	7.9	18.4
TENNESSEE	**11,542**	**1,240,173**	**2,620,536**	**3,522,345**	**55.5**	**100.0**
ANDERSON	**129**	**13,681**	**36,393**	**49,351**	**65.7**	**100.0**
ANG/EPIS–Episcopal	2	257	590	729	1.0	1.5
Bahá'í	0	NR	12	12	0.0	0.0
BAPT–Alliance Bapt	1	NR	NR	NR	-	-
BAPT–Free Will Bapt	1	NR	96	115	0.2	0.2
BAPT–Natl Mis Bapt Conv	2	160	325	390	0.5	0.8
BAPT–NBC USA	1	250	250	300	0.4	0.6
BAPT–So Bapt Conv	49	6,514	23,578	28,284	37.6	57.3
Catholic	3	NR	NR	3,295	4.4	6.7
Ch Cr, Scientst	1	NR	NR	NR	-	-
Ch of Nazarene	1	176	415	415	0.6	0.8
Chr & Miss Al	1	31	48	131	0.2	0.3
CHR–Chr Chs & Chs Cr	2	NR	0	0	0.0	0.0
CHR–Chs of Christ	8	886	950	1,145	1.5	2.3

NR–Not Reported - Represents no adherents reported. Percentages may not total 100 due to rounding.

Table 3: Religious Congregations by County and Group: 2010

Religious Group	Number of Congrega-tions	Number of Attendees	Number of Communicant, Confirmed, or Full Members	Adherents: Number of Adherents	Adherents: % of Total Pop.	Adherents: % of Total Adh.
Evan Free Ch	2	160	NR	160	0.2	0.3
Int Cou Comm Ch	2	NR	NR	NR	-	-
Jehovah's Witness	2	NR	NR	NR	-	-
LDS–L-D Saints	2	NR	NR	1,099	1.5	2.2
LUTH–E.L.C.A.	1	175	338	375	0.5	0.8
LUTH–Luth-MO Synod	1	186	372	493	0.7	1.0
METH–AME Zion	1	0	100	120	0.2	0.2
METH–Un Methodist	14	1,614	4,290	5,817	7.7	11.8
METH–Wesleyan	1	79	72	103	0.1	0.2
Missionary Ch	1	0	0	0	0.0	0.0
Non-denom Chr Chs	11	1,614	1,724	2,057	2.7	4.2
ORTHE–Orth Ch in Amer	1	150	NR	280	0.4	0.6
PENT–Assemb of God	5	354	253	440	0.6	0.9
PENT–Ch God (Cleve)	3	692	2,039	2,446	3.3	5.0
PENT–Ch God Mtn Asm	3	NR	NR	NR	-	-
PENT–Ch of God Proph	1	NR	115	138	0.2	0.3
PENT–Un Pent Ch Intl	1	NR	NR	NR	-	-
PRES–Cumber Presb	1	NR	140	140	0.2	0.3
PRES–Presb Ch (USA)	1	97	249	299	0.4	0.6
PRES–Presb Ch Amer	1	140	148	183	0.2	0.4
Sev Day Adv	1	31	54	62	0.1	0.1
Unit Univ	1	115	235	323	0.4	0.7
BEDFORD	**102**	**8,717**	**14,903**	**20,125**	**44.7**	**100.0**
ANG/EPIS–Episcopal	1	37	82	82	0.2	0.4
Bahá'í	1	NR	20	20	0.0	0.1
BAPT–NBC USA	1	50	80	101	0.2	0.5
BAPT–So Bapt Conv	24	3,364	7,210	9,126	20.3	45.3
Catholic	1	NR	NR	900	2.0	4.5
CGOD–Ch God (Ander)	1	0	NR	0	0.0	0.0
Ch of Nazarene	4	365	508	817	1.8	4.1
CHR–Chr Ch (Disc)	1	0	410	519	1.2	2.6
CHR–Chr Chs & Chs Cr	1	NR	25	32	0.1	0.2
CHR–Chs of Christ	22	1,903	1,934	2,404	5.3	11.9
LDS–L-D Saints	1	NR	NR	355	0.8	1.8
LUTH–E.L.C.A.	2	46	79	85	0.2	0.4
METH–AME	3	0	400	506	1.1	2.5
METH–Un Methodist	17	1,007	2,012	2,425	5.4	12.0
Non-denom Chr Chs	10	1,470	1,555	1,928	4.3	9.6
PENT–Assemb of God	2	116	78	192	0.4	1.0
PENT–Ch God (Cleve)	2	137	133	168	0.4	0.8
PENT–Ch of God Proph	1	NR	32	41	0.1	0.2
PENT–COGIC	1	0	0	0	0.0	0.0
PENT–Un Pent Ch Intl	1	NR	NR	NR	-	-
PRES–Cumber Presb	2	NR	27	27	0.1	0.1
PRES–Presb Ch (USA)	2	192	267	338	0.8	1.7
Sev Day Adv	1	30	51	59	0.1	0.3
BENTON	**56**	**3,038**	**7,230**	**8,772**	**53.2**	**100.0**
Bahá'í	0	NR	1	1	0.0	0.0
BAPT–Natl Mis Bapt Conv	1	0	150	177	1.1	2.0
BAPT–So Bapt Conv	17	1,357	3,837	4,530	27.5	51.6
Catholic	1	NR	NR	212	1.3	2.4
Ch of Nazarene	1	33	30	41	0.2	0.5
CHR–Chs of Christ	7	501	615	776	4.7	8.8
Jehovah's Witness	1	NR	NR	NR	-	-
METH–C.M.E.	1	0	100	118	0.7	1.3
METH–Cong Meth	1	NR	57	67	0.4	0.8
METH–Un Methodist	14	653	1,405	1,572	9.5	17.9
Non-denom Chr Chs	1	150	150	188	1.1	2.1
PENT–Assemb of God	1	117	126	126	0.8	1.4
PENT–Ch God (Cleve)	2	203	568	671	4.1	7.6
PENT–Ch of God Proph	2	NR	104	123	0.7	1.4
PENT–Un Pent Ch Intl	3	NR	NR	NR	-	-
PRES–Cumber Presb	1	NR	40	116	0.7	1.3
PRES–Presb Ch (USA)	1	0	6	7	0.0	0.1
Sev Day Adv	1	24	41	47	0.3	0.5
BLEDSOE	**31**	**1,624**	**2,394**	**2,921**	**22.7**	**100.0**
Bahá'í	0	NR	2	2	0.0	0.1
BAPT–Free Will Bapt	1	NR	96	114	0.9	3.9
BAPT–So Bapt Conv	4	178	477	566	4.4	19.4
CHR–Chs of Christ	12	676	603	804	6.2	27.5

Religious Group	Number of Congrega-tions	Number of Attendees	Number of Communicant, Confirmed, or Full Members	Adherents: Number of Adherents	Adherents: % of Total Pop.	Adherents: % of Total Adh.
Jehovah's Witness	1	NR	NR	NR	-	-
METH–AME Zion	1	0	100	119	0.9	4.1
METH–Un Methodist	3	156	321	376	2.9	12.9
PENT–Ch God (Cleve)	7	564	668	793	6.2	27.1
PENT–Ch of God Proph	1	NR	40	47	0.4	1.6
Sev Day Adv	1	50	87	100	0.8	3.4
BLOUNT	**186**	**23,650**	**55,113**	**70,799**	**57.6**	**100.0**
ANG/EPIS–Episcopal	1	149	336	389	0.3	0.5
Bahá'í	0	NR	21	21	0.0	0.0
BAPT–Natl Mis Bapt Conv	1	0	150	181	0.1	0.3
BAPT–NBC USA	1	75	100	120	0.1	0.2
BAPT–Ref Bapt Ch	2	NR	NR	NR	-	-
BAPT–Reg Bapt Gen As	1	NR	NR	NR	-	-
BAPT–So Bapt Conv	80	11,544	35,332	42,527	34.6	60.1
Calv Chpl	1	NR	NR	NR	-	-
Catholic	3	NR	NR	3,221	2.6	4.5
CGOD–Ch God (Ander)	1	51	NR	51	0.0	0.1
Ch of Nazarene	2	82	162	165	0.1	0.2
CHR–Chr Chs & Chs Cr	7	NR	887	1,068	0.9	1.5
CHR–Chs of Christ	5	788	751	809	0.7	1.1
Evan Free Ch	2	215	NR	215	0.2	0.3
FRND–Fr Un Mtg	2	NR	50	60	0.0	0.1
Jehovah's Witness	3	NR	NR	NR	-	-
LDS–L-D Saints	1	NR	NR	730	0.6	1.0
LUTH–E.L.C.A.	1	195	337	533	0.4	0.8
LUTH–Luth-MO Synod	1	60	80	90	0.1	0.1
LUTH–Nor Amer Luth C	1	NR	NR	NR	-	-
METH–AME	1	45	96	116	0.1	0.2
METH–AME Zion	3	70	394	474	0.4	0.7
METH–Un Methodist	23	3,693	8,350	9,949	8.1	14.1
Non-denom Chr Chs	14	2,535	2,760	3,270	2.7	4.6
PENT–Assemb of God	4	348	137	405	0.3	0.6
PENT–Ch God (Cleve)	8	2,401	2,599	3,128	2.5	4.4
PENT–Un Pent Ch Intl	1	NR	NR	NR	-	-
PENT–Vineyard	1	350	450	542	0.4	0.8
PRES–Cum Pres Am	1	NR	NR	NR	-	-
PRES–Cumber Presb	2	NR	147	356	0.3	0.5
PRES–Orth Pres Ch	1	47	44	61	0.0	0.1
PRES–Presb Ch (USA)	7	686	1,500	1,805	1.5	2.5
PRES–Presb Ch Amer	2	127	148	184	0.1	0.3
Sev Day Adv	1	123	214	246	0.2	0.3
Unit Univ	1	66	68	83	0.1	0.1
BRADLEY	**179**	**22,236**	**47,422**	**59,798**	**60.4**	**100.0**
ANG/EPIS–Episcopal	1	149	461	461	0.5	0.8
Bahá'í	0	NR	4	4	0.0	0.0
BAPT–So Bapt Conv	61	9,222	23,206	28,233	28.5	47.2
Calv Chpl	1	NR	NR	NR	-	-
Catholic	1	NR	NR	1,863	1.9	3.1
Ch of Nazarene	2	110	148	219	0.2	0.4
CHR–Chr Ch (Disc)	1	60	125	152	0.2	0.3
CHR–Chr Chs & Chs Cr	2	NR	212	258	0.3	0.4
CHR–Chs of Christ	4	893	930	1,175	1.2	2.0
FRND–Fr Gen Cf	1	NR	0	0	0.0	0.0
Jehovah's Witness	1	NR	NR	NR	-	-
LDS–L-D Saints	1	NR	NR	506	0.5	0.8
LUTH–Luth-MO Synod	1	129	303	364	0.4	0.6
METH–AME Zion	2	0	200	243	0.2	0.4
METH–Un Methodist	20	1,632	4,187	5,027	5.1	8.4
Non-denom Chr Chs	20	2,380	2,820	3,179	3.2	5.3
PENT–Assemb of God	1	60	42	80	0.1	0.1
PENT–Ch God (Cleve)	29	6,131	10,466	12,733	12.9	21.3
PENT–Ch of God Proph	8	NR	1,348	1,640	1.7	2.7
PENT–COGIC	2	0	150	182	0.2	0.3
PENT–Orig Ch of God	1	NR	NR	NR	-	-
PENT–Pent Ch of God	1	70	NR	109	0.1	0.2
PENT–Un Pent Ch Intl	1	NR	NR	NR	-	-
PRES–Cum Pres Am	2	NR	NR	NR	-	-
PRES–Cumber Presb	5	NR	268	400	0.4	0.7
PRES–Presb Ch (USA)	2	138	296	360	0.4	0.6
PRES–Presb Ch Amer	1	0	62	87	0.1	0.1
Sev Day Adv	7	1,262	2,194	2,523	2.5	4.2

NR–Not Reported   - Represents no adherents reported.   Percentages may not total 100 due to rounding.

Table 3: Religious Congregations by County and Group: 2010

Religious Group	Number of Congregations	Number of Attendees	Number of Communicant, Confirmed, or Full Members	Adherents: Number of Adherents	Adherents: % of Total Pop.	Adherents: % of Total Adh.
CAMPBELL	**72**	**4,492**	**12,198**	**14,854**	**36.5**	**100.0**
ANG/EPIS–Episcopal	1	10	25	26	0.1	0.2
BAPT–Ind Bapt Flwsp Intl	1	NR	NR	NR	-	-
BAPT–Natl Mis Bapt Conv	2	0	300	361	0.9	2.4
BAPT–So Bapt Conv	30	2,399	7,961	9,575	23.5	64.5
Catholic	1	NR	NR	190	0.5	1.3
CHR–Chs of Christ	3	137	131	154	0.4	1.0
Jehovah's Witness	2	NR	NR	NR	-	-
LDS–L-D Saints	1	NR	NR	311	0.8	2.1
METH–AME Zion	1	0	100	120	0.3	0.8
METH–Un Methodist	7	384	956	1,081	2.7	7.3
METH–Wesleyan	1	15	18	20	0.0	0.1
Non-denom Chr Chs	7	655	921	932	2.3	6.3
PENT–Assemb of God	1	100	271	271	0.7	1.8
PENT–Ch God (Cleve)	7	625	1,216	1,463	3.6	9.8
PENT–Ch God Mtn Asm	4	NR	NR	NR	-	-
PRES–Presb Ch (USA)	1	54	103	124	0.3	0.8
Sev Day Adv	2	113	196	226	0.6	1.5
CANNON	**48**	**3,556**	**5,045**	**6,094**	**44.2**	**100.0**
BAPT–So Bapt Conv	12	1,056	2,355	2,834	20.5	46.5
CHR–Chs of Christ	23	1,938	1,767	2,276	16.5	37.3
Jehovah's Witness	1	NR	NR	NR	-	-
METH–Free Methodist	1	48	44	48	0.3	0.8
METH–Un Methodist	4	225	336	336	2.4	5.5
Non-denom Chr Chs	1	100	150	150	1.1	2.5
PENT–Assemb of God	1	75	80	80	0.6	1.3
PENT–Ch God (Cleve)	2	46	150	180	1.3	3.0
PENT–Un Pent Ch Intl	1	NR	NR	NR	-	-
PRES–Presb Ch (USA)	1	0	44	53	0.4	0.9
Sev Day Adv	1	68	119	137	1.0	2.2
CARROLL	**82**	**5,863**	**12,684**	**15,440**	**54.1**	**100.0**
Bahá'í	0	NR	1	1	0.0	0.0
BAPT–Natl Mis Bapt Conv	1	250	300	361	1.3	2.3
BAPT–So Bapt Conv	22	2,792	7,988	9,605	33.7	62.2
Catholic	1	NR	NR	69	0.2	0.4
CHR–Chs of Christ	16	1,810	1,732	2,190	7.7	14.2
MENN–Amish Undif	1	NR	67	150	0.5	1.0
METH–AME	1	0	100	120	0.4	0.8
METH–C.M.E.	1	0	100	120	0.4	0.8
METH–Cong Meth	1	NR	10	12	0.0	0.1
METH–Un Methodist	17	786	1,605	1,784	6.3	11.6
Non-denom Chr Chs	1	20	10	25	0.1	0.2
PENT–Ch God (Cleve)	1	20	88	106	0.4	0.7
PENT–Ch of God Proph	1	NR	31	37	0.1	0.2
PENT–Intl Pent Holiness	1	48	50	60	0.2	0.4
PENT–Un Pent Ch Intl	3	NR	NR	NR	-	-
PRES–Cum Pres Am	2	NR	NR	NR	-	-
PRES–Cumber Presb	7	NR	388	549	1.9	3.6
PRES–Presb Ch (USA)	4	61	82	99	0.3	0.6
Sev Day Adv	1	76	132	152	0.5	1.0
CARTER	**116**	**7,024**	**22,659**	**26,891**	**46.8**	**100.0**
ANG/EPIS–Episcopal	1	35	61	87	0.2	0.3
Bahá'í	0	NR	1	1	0.0	0.0
BAPT–Free Will Bapt	13	NR	1,248	1,475	2.6	5.5
BAPT–So Bapt Conv	42	4,231	13,945	16,485	28.7	61.3
Catholic	1	NR	NR	210	0.4	0.8
CGOD–Ch God (Ander)	2	50	NR	50	0.1	0.2
Ch of Nazarene	1	66	129	130	0.2	0.5
Chr & Miss Al	1	147	170	232	0.4	0.9
CHR–Chr Chs & Chs Cr	20	NR	2,735	3,233	5.6	12.0
CHR–Chs of Christ	4	640	585	705	1.2	2.6
Jehovah's Witness	1	NR	NR	NR	-	-
LUTH–Luth-MO Synod	1	33	52	58	0.1	0.2
METH–AME Zion	1	0	100	118	0.2	0.4
METH–Un Methodist	8	463	1,151	1,256	2.2	4.7
Non-denom Chr Chs	7	810	1,160	1,213	2.1	4.5
PENT–Assemb of God	1	65	34	102	0.2	0.4
PENT–Ch God (Cleve)	5	304	371	439	0.8	1.6
PENT–Ch of God Proph	1	NR	103	122	0.2	0.5

Religious Group	Number of Congregations	Number of Attendees	Number of Communicant, Confirmed, or Full Members	Adherents: Number of Adherents	Adherents: % of Total Pop.	Adherents: % of Total Adh.
PRES–Presb Ch (USA)	4	150	401	474	0.8	1.8
PRES–Presb Ch Amer	1	0	361	441	0.8	1.6
Sev Day Adv	1	30	52	60	0.1	0.2
CHEATHAM	**69**	**4,784**	**9,861**	**13,074**	**33.4**	**100.0**
Bahá'í	0	NR	7	7	0.0	0.1
BAPT–Amer Bapt Assn	1	NR	85	105	0.3	0.8
BAPT–Free Will Bapt	7	NR	672	827	2.1	6.3
BAPT–So Bapt Conv	13	1,694	5,032	6,196	15.8	47.4
Catholic	1	NR	NR	500	1.3	3.8
Ch of Nazarene	2	185	234	243	0.6	1.9
CHR–Chs of Christ	20	1,921	1,646	2,367	6.1	18.1
Jehovah's Witness	1	NR	NR	NR	-	-
METH–AME	2	16	170	209	0.5	1.6
METH–Un Methodist	11	535	1,551	1,917	4.9	14.7
Non-denom Chr Chs	2	150	210	212	0.5	1.6
PENT–Assemb of God	2	130	147	254	0.6	1.9
PENT–Ch God (Cleve)	1	55	25	31	0.1	0.2
PENT–Ch of God Proph	1	NR	34	42	0.1	0.3
PENT–Pent Ch of God	1	70	NR	109	0.3	0.8
PENT–Un Pent Ch Intl	2	NR	NR	NR	-	-
Sev Day Adv	2	28	48	55	0.1	0.4
CHESTER	**49**	**3,241**	**7,051**	**8,730**	**51.0**	**100.0**
Bahá'í	1	NR	20	20	0.1	0.2
BAPT–So Bapt Conv	13	1,175	3,722	4,508	26.3	51.6
CHR–Chs of Christ	9	1,543	1,355	1,849	10.8	21.2
Jehovah's Witness	1	NR	NR	NR	-	-
LDS–Comm of Christ	1	NR	156	156	0.9	1.8
METH–AME	1	0	100	121	0.7	1.4
METH–C.M.E.	6	0	600	727	4.2	8.3
METH–Un Methodist	9	314	757	869	5.1	10.0
Non-denom Chr Chs	1	120	150	150	0.9	1.7
PENT–Assemb of God	1	55	21	55	0.3	0.6
PENT–Ch God (Cleve)	1	9	108	131	0.8	1.5
PENT–Intl Pent Holiness	1	25	30	36	0.2	0.4
PENT–Un Pent Ch Intl	3	NR	NR	NR	-	-
PRES–Cumber Presb	1	NR	32	108	0.6	1.2
CLAIBORNE	**93**	**5,217**	**15,985**	**19,564**	**60.7**	**100.0**
Bahá'í	0	NR	1	1	0.0	0.0
BAPT–So Bapt Conv	68	4,483	14,686	17,421	54.1	89.0
Catholic	1	NR	NR	110	0.3	0.6
CHR–Chr Chs & Chs Cr	1	NR	80	95	0.3	0.5
CHR–Chs of Christ	2	97	79	117	0.4	0.6
Jehovah's Witness	1	NR	NR	NR	-	-
LDS–L-D Saints	1	NR	NR	451	1.4	2.3
LUTH–Luth-MO Synod	1	18	22	22	0.1	0.1
METH–Un Methodist	9	263	796	860	2.7	4.4
Non-denom Chr Chs	3	236	275	337	1.0	1.7
PENT–Assemb of God	1	63	23	83	0.3	0.4
PENT–Ch God (Cleve)	1	17	23	27	0.1	0.1
PENT–Ch God Mtn Asm	3	NR	NR	NR	-	-
PENT–Open Bible Std	1	40	NR	40	0.1	0.2
CLAY	**31**	**2,090**	**2,650**	**3,450**	**43.9**	**100.0**
BAPT–So Bapt Conv	4	370	1,196	1,424	18.1	41.3
Catholic	1	NR	NR	40	0.5	1.2
CGOD–Ch God (Ander)	1	56	NR	56	0.7	1.6
CHR–Chs of Christ	24	1,591	1,308	1,766	22.5	51.2
METH–Un Methodist	1	73	146	164	2.1	4.8
COCKE	**94**	**4,911**	**13,062**	**15,639**	**43.9**	**100.0**
ANG/EPIS–Episcopal	1	49	69	91	0.3	0.6
Bahá'í	0	NR	3	3	0.0	0.0
BAPT–Free Will Bapt	7	NR	672	805	2.3	5.1
BAPT–Natl Mis Bapt Conv	1	0	150	180	0.5	1.2
BAPT–So Bapt Conv	39	2,649	7,158	8,571	24.0	54.8
Catholic	1	NR	NR	240	0.7	1.5
CGOD–Ch God (Ander)	2	80	NR	80	0.2	0.5
Ch of Nazarene	1	38	34	93	0.3	0.6
CHR–Chr Chs & Chs Cr	4	NR	365	437	1.2	2.8

NR–Not Reported   - Represents no adherents reported.   Percentages may not total 100 due to rounding.

Table 3: Religious Congregations by County and Group: 2010

Religious Group	Number of Congrega-tions	Number of Attendees	Number of Communicant, Confirmed, or Full Members	Adherents: Number of Adherents	Adherents: % of Total Pop.	Adherents: % of Total Adh.
CHR–Chs of Christ	3	190	170	231	0.6	1.5
Jehovah's Witness	1	NR	NR	NR	-	-
LUTH–E.L.C.A.	3	152	264	313	0.9	2.0
METH–AME Zion	1	0	150	180	0.5	1.2
METH–Un Methodist	13	603	1,273	1,433	4.0	9.2
Non-denom Chr Chs	6	670	1,795	1,851	5.2	11.8
PENT–Ch God (Cleve)	7	382	745	892	2.5	5.7
PENT–Fire Bapt Hol Ch	1	NR	NR	NR	-	-
PRES–Presb Ch (USA)	1	0	53	63	0.2	0.4
PRES–Presb Ch Amer	1	45	69	70	0.2	0.4
Sev Day Adv	1	53	92	106	0.3	0.7
COFFEE	**112**	**11,111**	**20,842**	**27,532**	**52.1**	**100.0**
ANG/EPIS–Anglican NA	1	NR	NR	NR	-	-
ANG/EPIS–Episcopal	2	109	238	254	0.5	0.9
Bahá'í	0	NR	7	7	0.0	0.0
BAPT–Free Will Bapt	2	NR	192	236	0.4	0.9
BAPT–So Bapt Conv	22	4,008	9,784	12,048	22.8	43.8
Catholic	2	NR	NR	1,245	2.4	4.5
Ch Cr, Scientst	1	NR	NR	NR	-	-
Ch of Nazarene	5	256	339	500	0.9	1.8
CHR–Chr Ch (Disc)	1	201	490	603	1.1	2.2
CHR–Chs of Christ	30	3,053	2,847	3,762	7.1	13.7
Jehovah's Witness	1	NR	NR	NR	-	-
LDS–Comm of Christ	1	NR	156	156	0.3	0.6
LDS–L-D Saints	1	NR	NR	687	1.3	2.5
LUTH–E.L.C.A.	1	137	304	329	0.6	1.2
LUTH–Luth–MO Synod	1	151	257	277	0.5	1.0
METH–AME	1	60	90	111	0.2	0.4
METH–Un Methodist	15	1,359	3,440	4,011	7.6	14.6
Non-denom Chr Chs	8	1,090	1,345	1,513	2.9	5.5
PENT–Assemb of God	2	175	187	277	0.5	1.0
PENT–Ch God (Cleve)	2	173	265	326	0.6	1.2
PENT–Ch of God Proph	2	NR	52	64	0.1	0.2
PENT–COGIC	1	0	150	185	0.4	0.7
PENT–Un Pent Ch Intl	2	NR	NR	NR	-	-
PRES–Cumber Presb	3	NR	129	264	0.5	1.0
PRES–Presb Ch (USA)	2	156	318	392	0.7	1.4
PRES–Presb Ch Amer	1	79	77	91	0.2	0.3
Sev Day Adv	1	74	128	147	0.3	0.5
Unit Univ	1	30	47	47	0.1	0.2
CROCKETT	**61**	**5,327**	**8,507**	**10,307**	**70.7**	**100.0**
Bahá'í	0	NR	2	2	0.0	0.0
BAPT–NBC USA	1	0	150	185	1.3	1.8
BAPT–So Bapt Conv	18	1,446	4,662	5,760	39.5	55.9
CHR–Chr Ch (Disc)	2	0	381	471	3.2	4.6
CHR–Chr Chs & Chs Cr	2	NR	150	185	1.3	1.8
CHR–Chs of Christ	12	796	894	1,101	7.5	10.7
METH–C.M.E.	2	0	200	247	1.7	2.4
METH–Cong Meth	1	NR	58	72	0.5	0.7
METH–Un Methodist	11	641	1,382	1,502	10.3	14.6
Non-denom Chr Chs	1	100	150	150	1.0	1.5
PENT–Assemb of God	3	161	131	196	1.3	1.9
PENT–Ch God (Cleve)	2	83	144	178	1.2	1.7
PENT–Ch God Mtn Asm	1	NR	NR	NR	-	-
PENT–COGIC	2	2,100	180	222	1.5	2.2
PENT–Un Pent Ch Intl	1	NR	NR	NR	-	-
PRES–Cumber Presb	2	NR	23	36	0.2	0.3
CUMBERLAND	**113**	**10,827**	**20,645**	**27,869**	**49.7**	**100.0**
ANG/EPIS–Episcopal	1	55	145	195	0.3	0.7
Bahá'í	0	NR	4	4	0.0	0.0
BAPT–Free Will Bapt	2	NR	192	225	0.4	0.8
BAPT–Reg Bapt Gen As	1	NR	NR	NR	-	-
BAPT–So Bapt Conv	32	3,792	9,308	10,890	19.4	39.1
Calv Chpl	1	NR	NR	NR	-	-
Catholic	2	NR	NR	2,531	4.5	9.1
Ch of Nazarene	2	156	214	214	0.4	0.8
CHR–Chr Ch (Disc)	1	30	36	42	0.1	0.2
CHR–Chr Chs & Chs Cr	2	NR	195	228	0.4	0.8
CHR–Chs of Christ	14	1,310	1,217	1,541	2.7	5.5
CONG–Cong Chr, NA	1	NR	67	78	0.1	0.3

Religious Group	Number of Congrega-tions	Number of Attendees	Number of Communicant, Confirmed, or Full Members	Adherents: Number of Adherents	Adherents: % of Total Pop.	Adherents: % of Total Adh.
FRND–Fr Gen Cf	1	NR	9	11	0.0	0.0
Jehovah's Witness	1	NR	NR	NR	-	-
JUD–Reform	1	339	598	1,615	2.9	5.8
LDS–L-D Saints	1	NR	NR	591	1.1	2.1
LUTH–E.L.C.A.	1	250	397	397	0.7	1.4
LUTH–Luth–MO Synod	1	186	271	300	0.5	1.1
LUTH–Wisc Ev Luth Syn	1	71	84	86	0.2	0.3
MENN–Mara Amish-Menn	1	203	100	203	0.4	0.7
METH–Un Methodist	11	1,476	3,140	3,353	6.0	12.0
METH–Wesleyan	1	11	2	14	0.0	0.1
Non-denom Chr Chs	12	1,605	2,315	2,407	4.3	8.6
PENT–Assemb of God	2	277	360	506	0.9	1.8
PENT–Ch God (Cleve)	4	185	402	470	0.8	1.7
PENT–Ch of God Proph	6	NR	309	362	0.6	1.3
PENT–Cong Hol Ch	1	35	30	35	0.1	0.1
PENT–Pent Ch of God	1	70	NR	109	0.2	0.4
PENT–Un Pent Ch Intl	1	NR	NR	NR	-	-
PRES–Presb Ch (USA)	3	215	399	467	0.8	1.7
PRES–Presb Ch Amer	1	85	93	115	0.2	0.4
Sev Day Adv	1	178	309	355	0.6	1.3
Un C of Christ	2	298	449	525	0.9	1.9
DAVIDSON	**782**	**147,533**	**254,935**	**365,223**	**58.3**	**100.0**
ANG/EPIS–Anglican NA	3	NR	NR	NR	-	-
ANG/EPIS–Episcopal	14	3,027	7,683	9,133	1.5	2.5
Ap Chr Ch-Amer	1	24	12	24	0.0	0.0
Bahá'í	1	NR	751	751	0.1	0.2
BAPT–Alliance Bapt	1	NR	NR	NR	-	-
BAPT–Amer Bapt USA	2	350	590	715	0.1	0.2
BAPT–Free Will Bapt	16	NR	1,536	1,862	0.3	0.5
BAPT–Natl Mis Bapt Conv	7	80	1,075	1,303	0.2	0.4
BAPT–NBC Amer	10	2,195	4,325	5,243	0.8	1.4
BAPT–NBC USA	39	16,124	23,587	28,592	4.6	7.8
BAPT–Ref Bapt Ch	1	NR	NR	NR	-	-
BAPT–S-D Baptist Gen Con	1	25	17	21	0.0	0.0
BAPT–So Bapt Conv	153	20,930	73,005	88,496	14.1	24.2
BUDD–Mahayana	3	NR	NR	124	0.0	0.0
BUDD–Theravada	2	NR	NR	696	0.1	0.2
BUDD–Vajrayana	1	NR	NR	39	0.0	0.0
Calv Chpl	1	NR	NR	NR	-	-
Catholic	18	NR	NR	30,874	4.9	8.5
CGOD–Ch God (Ander)	1	319	NR	319	0.1	0.1
Ch Cr, Scientst	1	NR	NR	NR	-	-
Ch of God Gen Conf	1	NR	5	6	0.0	0.0
Ch of Nazarene	29	4,482	5,436	6,393	1.0	1.8
CHR–Chr Ch (Disc)	11	1,095	2,634	3,193	0.5	0.9
CHR–Chr Chs & Chs Cr	2	NR	950	1,152	0.2	0.3
CHR–Chs of Christ	99	26,472	27,433	35,421	5.7	9.7
CHR–Int Chs of Christ	1	NR	404	490	0.1	0.1
Christian Brethren	1	NR	NR	NR	-	-
Evan Free Ch	1	30	NR	30	0.0	0.0
FRND–Fr Gen Cf	1	NR	54	65	0.0	0.0
FRND–Fr Un Mtg	1	NR	0	0	0.0	0.0
HINDU–I/A Temples	2	NR	NR	1,980	0.3	0.5
HINDU–Trad Temples	1	NR	NR	1,033	0.2	0.3
Int Cou Comm Ch	1	NR	NR	NR	-	-
Jehovah's Witness	10	NR	NR	NR	-	-
JUD–Conserv	1	282	316	853	0.1	0.2
JUD–Orth	2	522	230	725	0.1	0.2
LDS–Comm of Christ	1	NR	156	156	0.0	0.0
LDS–L-D Saints	9	NR	NR	5,022	0.8	1.4
LUTH–E.L.C.A.	6	496	989	1,135	0.2	0.3
LUTH–Luth–MO Synod	7	818	1,255	1,641	0.3	0.4
LUTH–Wisc Ev Luth Syn	1	84	104	136	0.0	0.0
MENN–Mennonite USA	1	12	13	16	0.0	0.0
METH–AME	15	825	3,240	3,928	0.6	1.1
METH–C.M.E.	6	275	1,120	1,358	0.2	0.4
METH–So Methodist	4	NR	NR	NR	-	-
METH–Un Methodist	68	9,292	24,388	28,748	4.6	7.9
METH–Wesleyan	4	295	210	385	0.1	0.1
Muslim Est	11	1,840	NR	5,080	0.8	1.4
New Apost Ch	1	NR	NR	NR	-	-
Non-denom Chr Chs	74	29,755	36,695	41,423	6.6	11.3
ORTHE–Greek Orthodox	2	255	NR	655	0.1	0.2

NR–Not Reported - Represents no adherents reported. Percentages may not total 100 due to rounding.

Table 3: Religious Congregations by County and Group: 2010

Religious Group	Number of Congrega-tions	Number of Attendees	Number of Communicant, Confirmed, or Full Members	Adherents: Number of Adherents	Adherents: % of Total Pop.	Adherents: % of Total Adh.
ORTHE–Orth Ch in Amer	1	20	NR	65	0.0	0.0
ORTHE–Romania Orth Ar	1	25	NR	100	0.0	0.0
ORTHE–Serb Orth USA	1	50	NR	70	0.0	0.0
ORTHO–Armen Ap Etchm	1	65	NR	175	0.0	0.0
ORTHO–Coptic Orth Ch	4	1,900	NR	5,957	1.0	1.6
PENT–Assemb of God	23	7,766	6,728	12,035	1.9	3.3
PENT–Ch God (Cleve)	5	2,220	2,820	3,418	0.5	0.9
PENT–Ch Lord Jesus Apos	1	NR	NR	NR	-	-
PENT–Ch of God Proph	6	NR	216	262	0.0	0.1
PENT–COGIC	4	3,075	4,139	5,017	0.8	1.4
PENT–Fire Bapt Hol Ch	1	NR	NR	NR	-	-
PENT–Full Gosp Bapt	3	NR	NR	NR	-	-
PENT–Int Foursq Gos	1	60	90	109	0.0	0.0
PENT–Pent Ch of God	1	70	NR	109	0.0	0.0
PENT–Un Pent Ch Intl	10	NR	NR	NR	-	-
PRES–Cum Pres Am	1	NR	NR	NR	-	-
PRES–Cumber Presb	10	NR	1,066	2,471	0.4	0.7
PRES–Korean Pres Amer	1	NR	NR	NR	-	-
PRES–Presb Ch (USA)	23	3,226	10,104	12,248	2.0	3.4
PRES–Presb Ch Amer	7	4,673	4,155	5,189	0.8	1.4
REF–Christian Ref	1	71	130	158	0.0	0.0
Salvation Army	4	248	263	461	0.1	0.1
Sev Day Adv	13	3,452	6,003	6,904	1.1	1.9
Sikh	1	NR	NR	NR	-	-
Un C of Christ	4	391	525	636	0.1	0.2
Unit Univ	2	317	483	619	0.1	0.2
Unity Ch	2	NR	NR	NR	-	-
Zoroastrian	0	NR	NR	4	0.0	0.0
DECATUR	**53**	**2,737**	**5,515**	**6,567**	**55.9**	**100.0**
BAPT–So Bapt Conv	20	1,421	3,506	4,189	35.6	63.8
Catholic	1	NR	NR	88	0.7	1.3
CGOD–Ch God (Ander)	1	0	NR	0	0.0	0.0
CHR–Chs of Christ	5	364	380	459	3.9	7.0
METH–AME	2	25	130	155	1.3	2.4
METH–AME Zion	1	25	30	36	0.3	0.5
METH–Un Methodist	11	490	963	1,013	8.6	15.4
Non-denom Chr Chs	1	35	40	44	0.4	0.7
PENT–Assemb of God	1	227	211	227	1.9	3.5
PENT–Ch God (Cleve)	1	66	86	103	0.9	1.6
PENT–COGIC	1	60	50	60	0.5	0.9
PENT–Un Pent Ch Intl	5	NR	NR	NR	-	-
PRES–Cumber Presb	2	NR	76	144	1.2	2.2
Sev Day Adv	1	24	43	49	0.4	0.7
DEKALB	**66**	**3,327**	**7,389**	**9,755**	**52.1**	**100.0**
Bahá'í	0	NR	1	1	0.0	0.0
BAPT–Free Will Bapt	2	NR	192	233	1.2	2.4
BAPT–So Bapt Conv	22	1,599	4,517	5,486	29.3	56.2
BRETH–Breth in Chr	2	NR	NR	NR	-	-
Catholic	1	NR	NR	900	4.8	9.2
Ch of Nazarene	1	85	44	85	0.5	0.9
CHR–Chs of Christ	7	543	571	716	3.8	7.3
Jehovah's Witness	1	NR	NR	NR	-	-
METH–Cong Meth	1	NR	44	53	0.3	0.5
METH–Un Methodist	20	688	1,204	1,258	6.7	12.9
Non-denom Chr Chs	1	100	150	150	0.8	1.5
PENT–Assemb of God	2	100	95	166	0.9	1.7
PENT–Ch God (Cleve)	2	177	336	408	2.2	4.2
PENT–Un Pent Ch Intl	1	NR	NR	NR	-	-
PRES–Cumber Presb	2	NR	184	237	1.3	2.4
PRES–Presb Ch (USA)	1	35	51	62	0.3	0.6
DICKSON	**110**	**8,399**	**15,408**	**20,944**	**42.2**	**100.0**
ANG/EPIS–Episcopal	2	53	69	84	0.2	0.4
Bahá'í	0	NR	1	1	0.0	0.0
BAPT–Free Will Bapt	6	NR	576	713	1.4	3.4
BAPT–NT Ind Bapt	1	NR	NR	NR	-	-
BAPT–So Bapt Conv	15	2,571	6,384	7,899	15.9	37.7
Calv Chpl	1	NR	NR	NR	-	-
Catholic	1	NR	NR	800	1.6	3.8
Ch of Nazarene	2	243	419	595	1.2	2.8
CHR–Chs of Christ	29	3,177	3,247	4,229	8.5	20.2

Religious Group	Number of Congrega-tions	Number of Attendees	Number of Communicant, Confirmed, or Full Members	Adherents: Number of Adherents	Adherents: % of Total Pop.	Adherents: % of Total Adh.
Jehovah's Witness	1	NR	NR	NR	-	-
LDS–L-D Saints	2	NR	NR	841	1.7	4.0
LUTH–Luth–MO Synod	1	107	209	278	0.6	1.3
MENN–Beachy Amish-Menn	1	102	59	102	0.2	0.5
METH–AME	3	0	350	433	0.9	2.1
METH–Un Methodist	17	751	1,630	1,712	3.4	8.2
Non-denom Chr Chs	10	883	1,190	1,235	2.5	5.9
PENT–Assemb of God	1	352	0	424	0.9	2.0
PENT–Ch God (Cleve)	1	12	46	57	0.1	0.3
PENT–Ch of God Proph	7	NR	378	468	0.9	2.2
PENT–Full Gosp Bapt	1	NR	NR	NR	-	-
PENT–Un Pent Ch Intl	1	NR	NR	NR	-	-
PRES–Cumber Presb	3	NR	461	615	1.2	2.9
PRES–Presb Ch (USA)	2	12	206	255	0.5	1.2
PRES–Presb Ch Amer	1	60	50	50	0.1	0.2
Sev Day Adv	1	76	133	153	0.3	0.7
DYER	**104**	**7,107**	**16,742**	**21,599**	**56.3**	**100.0**
ANG/EPIS–Episcopal	1	55	186	186	0.5	0.9
BAPT–So Bapt Conv	30	2,807	8,944	11,013	28.7	51.0
Catholic	1	NR	NR	800	2.1	3.7
Ch of Nazarene	1	31	33	44	0.1	0.2
CHR–Chr Chs & Chs Cr	1	NR	233	287	0.7	1.3
CHR–Chs of Christ	19	1,802	1,661	2,057	5.4	9.5
Jehovah's Witness	1	NR	NR	NR	-	-
LDS–L-D Saints	1	NR	NR	238	0.6	1.1
LUTH–Luth–MO Synod	1	28	65	70	0.2	0.3
METH–AME	1	0	150	185	0.5	0.9
METH–C.M.E.	2	0	250	308	0.8	1.4
METH–Un Methodist	14	917	2,470	2,937	7.7	13.6
Non-denom Chr Chs	6	640	896	973	2.5	4.5
PENT–Assemb of God	3	375	354	437	1.1	2.0
PENT–Ch God (Cleve)	2	264	729	898	2.3	4.2
PENT–Ch of God Proph	2	NR	80	99	0.3	0.5
PENT–COGIC	1	40	50	62	0.2	0.3
PENT–Un Pent Ch Intl	4	NR	NR	NR	-	-
PRES–Cum Pres Am	3	NR	NR	NR	-	-
PRES–Cumber Presb	7	NR	455	779	2.0	3.6
PRES–Presb Ch (USA)	1	38	43	53	0.1	0.2
PRES–Presb Ch Amer	1	60	57	74	0.2	0.3
Sev Day Adv	1	50	86	99	0.3	0.5
FAYETTE	**80**	**3,985**	**10,074**	**13,554**	**35.3**	**100.0**
ANG/EPIS–Episcopal	2	52	87	87	0.2	0.6
Bahá'í	0	NR	100	100	0.3	0.7
BAPT–NBC USA	1	0	150	183	0.5	1.4
BAPT–So Bapt Conv	20	1,999	5,244	6,400	16.7	47.2
Catholic	1	NR	NR	900	2.3	6.6
Ch of Nazarene	1	0	0	0	0.0	0.0
CHR–Chr Ch (Disc)	1	30	46	56	0.1	0.4
CHR–Chs of Christ	6	375	406	499	1.3	3.7
Jehovah's Witness	1	NR	NR	NR	-	-
LDS–L-D Saints	1	NR	NR	358	0.9	2.6
LUTH–Luth–MO Synod	1	40	51	68	0.2	0.5
MENN–Mara Amish-Menn	1	114	79	114	0.3	0.8
MENN–Ref Mennonite	1	NR	6	8	0.0	0.1
METH–C.M.E.	10	45	1,230	1,501	3.9	11.1
METH–Un Methodist	14	616	1,267	1,502	3.9	11.1
Non-denom Chr Chs	1	260	410	410	1.1	3.0
PENT–Assemb of God	2	138	114	260	0.7	1.9
PENT–Ch God (Cleve)	1	56	116	142	0.4	1.0
PENT–COGIC	5	85	440	537	1.4	4.0
PENT–Full Gosp Bapt	1	NR	NR	NR	-	-
PENT–Un Pent Ch Intl	2	NR	NR	NR	-	-
PRES–Cumber Presb	2	NR	36	68	0.2	0.5
PRES–Presb Ch (USA)	3	85	194	237	0.6	1.7
PRES–Presb Ch Amer	1	80	80	103	0.3	0.8
Sev Day Adv	1	10	18	21	0.1	0.2
FENTRESS	**36**	**2,644**	**4,875**	**6,216**	**34.6**	**100.0**
BAPT–So Bapt Conv	8	1,022	2,241	2,723	15.2	43.8
Catholic	1	NR	NR	80	0.4	1.3
Ch Christ Chr Union	1	NR	NR	NR	-	-

NR–Not Reported - Represents no adherents reported. Percentages may not total 100 due to rounding.

Table 3: Religious Congregations by County and Group: 2010

Religious Group	Number of Congrega-tions	Number of Attendees	Number of Communicant, Confirmed, or Full Members	Adherents: Number of Adherents	Adherents: % of Total Pop.	Adherents: % of Total Adh.
Ch of Nazarene	2	169	164	199	1.1	3.2
CHR–Chs of Christ	2	155	145	191	1.1	3.1
Jehovah's Witness	1	NR	NR	NR	-	-
LDS–L-D Saints	1	NR	NR	346	1.9	5.6
METH–Un Methodist	9	329	870	898	5.0	14.4
METH–Wesleyan	3	99	31	129	0.7	2.1
Non-denom Chr Chs	3	475	600	638	3.6	10.3
PENT–Assemb of God	1	31	25	44	0.2	0.7
PENT–Ch God (Cleve)	1	267	582	707	3.9	11.4
PENT–Ch of God Proph	1	NR	5	6	0.0	0.1
PRES–Presb Ch (USA)	1	70	165	201	1.1	3.2
Sev Day Adv	1	27	47	54	0.3	0.9
FRANKLIN	**107**	**7,099**	**16,178**	**20,311**	**49.5**	**100.0**
ANG/EPIS–Anglican NA	1	NR	NR	NR	-	-
ANG/EPIS–Episcopal	6	289	564	676	1.6	3.3
Bahá'í	0	NR	4	4	0.0	0.0
BAPT–So Bapt Conv	25	2,674	7,980	9,580	23.3	47.2
Catholic	1	NR	NR	800	1.9	3.9
Ch of Nazarene	6	725	967	1,314	3.2	6.5
CHR–Chs of Christ	19	1,400	1,332	1,648	4.0	8.1
FRND–Fr Gen Cf	1	NR	0	0	0.0	0.0
Jehovah's Witness	2	NR	NR	NR	-	-
MENN–Beachy Amish-Menn	1	85	65	85	0.2	0.4
METH–AME	2	0	250	300	0.7	1.5
METH–Cong Meth	1	NR	35	42	0.1	0.2
METH–Un Methodist	10	880	2,426	2,670	6.5	13.1
Non-denom Chr Chs	7	565	725	768	1.9	3.8
PENT–Assemb of God	1	60	74	74	0.2	0.4
PENT–Ch God (Cleve)	5	340	419	503	1.2	2.5
PENT–Ch of God Proph	1	NR	5	6	0.0	0.0
PENT–COGIC	1	0	150	180	0.4	0.9
PENT–Un Pent Ch Intl	2	NR	NR	NR	-	-
PRES–Cum Pres Am	1	NR	NR	NR	-	-
PRES–Cumber Presb	9	NR	958	1,395	3.4	6.9
PRES–Presb Ch (USA)	2	0	50	60	0.1	0.3
Sev Day Adv	2	44	75	87	0.2	0.4
Un C of Christ	1	37	99	119	0.3	0.6
GIBSON	**182**	**11,362**	**26,880**	**33,997**	**68.4**	**100.0**
ANG/EPIS–Episcopal	1	22	43	43	0.1	0.1
Bahá'í	0	NR	5	5	0.0	0.0
BAPT–NBC USA	1	0	150	185	0.4	0.5
BAPT–So Bapt Conv	55	6,028	16,619	20,529	41.3	60.4
Catholic	2	NR	NR	540	1.1	1.6
CHR–Chr Ch (Disc)	1	70	201	248	0.5	0.7
CHR–Chs of Christ	26	2,310	2,385	2,686	5.4	7.9
Jehovah's Witness	4	NR	NR	NR	-	-
LDS–L-D Saints	1	NR	NR	205	0.4	0.6
LUTH–Assoc Free Luth	1	NR	NR	NR	-	-
MENN–Amish Undif	1	NR	24	85	0.2	0.3
MENN–Menn Chr Fell	1	176	91	176	0.4	0.5
METH–C.M.E.	13	135	1,438	1,776	3.6	5.2
METH–Un Methodist	26	1,286	2,928	3,442	6.9	10.1
Non-denom Chr Chs	5	365	505	519	1.0	1.5
PENT–Assemb of God	6	603	671	894	1.8	2.6
PENT–Ch God (Cleve)	4	176	263	325	0.7	1.0
PENT–Ch of God Proph	1	NR	10	12	0.0	0.0
PENT–Intl Pent Holiness	2	60	73	90	0.2	0.3
PENT–Un Pent Ch Intl	7	NR	NR	NR	-	-
PENT–Vineyard	1	117	138	170	0.3	0.5
PRES–Cum Pres Am	3	NR	NR	NR	-	-
PRES–Cumber Presb	17	NR	974	1,619	3.3	4.8
PRES–Evan Presby Ch	1	NR	100	124	0.2	0.4
PRES–Presb Ch (USA)	2	14	262	324	0.7	1.0
GILES	**115**	**6,825**	**15,856**	**19,676**	**66.7**	**100.0**
ANG/EPIS–Anglican NA	1	NR	NR	NR	-	-
ANG/EPIS–Episcopal	1	61	73	104	0.4	0.5
Bahá'í	0	NR	4	4	0.0	0.0
BAPT–Natl Mis Bapt Conv	1	0	150	180	0.6	0.9
BAPT–NBC USA	1	75	125	150	0.5	0.8
BAPT–So Bapt Conv	30	2,766	8,469	10,183	34.5	51.8

Religious Group	Number of Congrega-tions	Number of Attendees	Number of Communicant, Confirmed, or Full Members	Adherents: Number of Adherents	Adherents: % of Total Pop.	Adherents: % of Total Adh.
Catholic	1	NR	NR	400	1.4	2.0
CGOD–Ch God (Ander)	2	70	NR	70	0.2	0.4
CHR–Chs of Christ	24	2,050	2,003	2,683	9.1	13.6
Jehovah's Witness	1	NR	NR	NR	-	-
MENN–Amish Undif	0	NR	14	38	0.1	0.2
MENN–Mara Amish-Menn	1	96	41	96	0.3	0.5
METH–AME	9	20	978	1,176	4.0	6.0
METH–Un Methodist	26	1,051	2,721	3,082	10.5	15.7
Non-denom Chr Chs	3	230	335	338	1.1	1.7
PENT–Assemb of God	1	49	37	54	0.2	0.3
PENT–Ch God (Cleve)	1	162	397	477	1.6	2.4
PENT–Ch of God Proph	1	NR	54	65	0.2	0.3
PENT–Orig Ch of God	1	NR	NR	NR	-	-
PENT–Un Pent Ch Intl	1	NR	NR	NR	-	-
PRES–Cum Pres Am	1	NR	NR	NR	-	-
PRES–Cumber Presb	2	NR	80	133	0.5	0.7
PRES–Presb Ch (USA)	4	114	234	281	1.0	1.4
Sev Day Adv	2	81	141	162	0.5	0.8
GRAINGER	**60**	**3,609**	**9,994**	**11,966**	**52.8**	**100.0**
Bahá'í	0	NR	5	5	0.0	0.0
BAPT–Free Will Bapt	1	NR	96	115	0.5	1.0
BAPT–So Bapt Conv	43	3,143	8,982	10,804	47.7	90.3
Catholic	1	NR	NR	NR	-	-
CHR–Chs of Christ	1	40	24	28	0.1	0.2
Jehovah's Witness	1	NR	NR	NR	-	-
METH–Un Methodist	10	262	624	728	3.2	6.1
Non-denom Chr Chs	1	100	150	150	0.7	1.3
PENT–Ch God (Cleve)	2	64	113	136	0.6	1.1
GREENE	**188**	**11,183**	**25,094**	**33,460**	**48.6**	**100.0**
ANG/EPIS–Episcopal	1	87	170	219	0.3	0.7
Bahá'í	0	NR	2	2	0.0	0.0
BAPT–Free Will Bapt	24	NR	2,304	2,741	4.0	8.2
BAPT–Prim Bapt E Dst	2	50	178	212	0.3	0.6
BAPT–So Bapt Conv	25	3,162	9,550	11,362	16.5	34.0
BRETH–Ch of Brethren	1	50	87	104	0.2	0.3
Calv Chpl	1	NR	NR	NR	-	-
Catholic	1	NR	NR	1,094	1.6	3.3
CGOD–Ch God (Ander)	6	1,152	NR	1,152	1.7	3.4
Ch of Nazarene	1	86	68	135	0.2	0.4
CHR–Chr Chs & Chs Cr	3	NR	470	559	0.8	1.7
CHR–Chs of Christ	4	269	245	334	0.5	1.0
Jehovah's Witness	1	NR	NR	NR	-	-
LDS–L-D Saints	1	NR	NR	324	0.5	1.0
LUTH–E.L.C.A.	4	342	579	728	1.1	2.2
MENN–Mara Amish-Menn	1	155	73	155	0.2	0.5
METH–AME Zion	1	50	80	95	0.1	0.3
METH–Free Methodist	1	24	20	24	0.0	0.1
METH–Un Methodist	59	3,022	6,146	7,562	11.0	22.6
Non-denom Chr Chs	7	985	1,203	1,404	2.0	4.2
PENT–Assemb of God	3	272	148	306	0.4	0.9
PENT–Ch God (Cleve)	6	300	523	622	0.9	1.9
PENT–Ch of God Proph	1	NR	29	35	0.1	0.1
PENT–Intl Pent Holiness	3	197	715	851	1.2	2.5
PENT–Un Pent Ch Intl	2	NR	NR	NR	-	-
PRES–Cumber Presb	14	NR	789	1,430	2.1	4.3
PRES–Presb Ch (USA)	10	420	830	987	1.4	2.9
PRES–Presb Ch Amer	2	105	94	113	0.2	0.3
Sev Day Adv	3	455	791	910	1.3	2.7
GRUNDY	**47**	**1,990**	**3,362**	**4,330**	**31.6**	**100.0**
ANG/EPIS–Episcopal	2	42	156	156	1.1	3.6
Bahá'í	0	NR	3	3	0.0	0.1
BAPT–Free Will Bapt	1	NR	96	117	0.9	2.7
BAPT–So Bapt Conv	8	549	1,246	1,514	11.0	35.0
Ch of Nazarene	2	105	149	155	1.1	3.6
CHR–Chs of Christ	8	359	360	453	3.3	10.5
HINDU–Renaiss	1	NR	NR	12	0.1	0.3
Jehovah's Witness	1	NR	NR	NR	-	-
LDS–L-D Saints	1	NR	NR	373	2.7	8.6
METH–Cong Meth	2	NR	68	83	0.6	1.9
METH–Un Methodist	9	488	611	690	5.0	15.9

NR–Not Reported   - Represents no adherents reported.   Percentages may not total 100 due to rounding.

Table 3: Religious Congregations by County and Group: 2010

Religious Group	Number of Congrega-tions	Number of Attendees	Number of Communicant, Confirmed, or Full Members	Adherents: Number of Adherents	Adherents: % of Total Pop.	Adherents: % of Total Adh.
Non-denom Chr Chs	1	100	150	150	1.1	3.5
PENT–Ch God (Cleve)	4	256	305	371	2.7	8.6
PENT–Ch of God Proph	2	NR	53	64	0.5	1.5
PENT–Un Pent Ch Intl	1	NR	NR	NR	-	-
PRES–Cumber Presb	1	NR	7	7	0.1	0.2
Sev Day Adv	3	91	158	182	1.3	4.2
HAMBLEN	**119**	**11,658**	**31,514**	**41,616**	**66.5**	**100.0**
ANG/EPIS–Episcopal	1	145	285	442	0.7	1.1
Bahá'í	0	NR	16	16	0.0	0.0
BAPT–Free Will Bapt	4	NR	331	406	0.6	1.0
BAPT–Prim Bapt E Dst	2	50	177	217	0.3	0.5
BAPT–So Bapt Conv	49	7,085	21,947	26,890	43.0	64.6
Catholic	1	NR	NR	1,954	3.1	4.7
CGOD–Ch God (Ander)	2	40	NR	40	0.1	0.1
Ch of Nazarene	1	11	37	37	0.1	0.1
CHR–Chr Chs & Chs Cr	3	NR	335	410	0.7	1.0
CHR–Chs of Christ	1	145	150	180	0.3	0.4
Evan Free Ch	1	125	NR	125	0.2	0.3
Jehovah's Witness	1	NR	NR	NR	-	-
LDS–L-D Saints	2	NR	NR	994	1.6	2.4
LUTH–E.L.C.A.	1	66	198	200	0.3	0.5
LUTH–Luth–MO Synod	1	45	90	109	0.2	0.3
LUTH–Wisc Ev Luth Syn	1	10	12	15	0.0	0.0
METH–AME Zion	1	0	150	184	0.3	0.4
METH–Un Methodist	13	1,252	3,367	4,160	6.7	10.0
METH–Wesleyan	1	105	110	137	0.2	0.3
Non-denom Chr Chs	12	1,390	1,700	1,884	3.0	4.5
PENT–Assemb of God	1	34	25	46	0.1	0.1
PENT–Ch God (Cleve)	6	673	1,115	1,366	2.2	3.3
PENT–Ch of God Proph	1	NR	272	333	0.5	0.8
PENT–COGIC	1	35	100	123	0.2	0.3
PENT–Fire Bapt Hol Ch	1	NR	NR	NR	-	-
PENT–Intl Pent Holiness	2	95	120	147	0.2	0.4
PENT–Un Pent Ch Intl	1	NR	NR	NR	-	-
PRES–Cumber Presb	2	NR	151	206	0.3	0.5
PRES–Presb Ch (USA)	3	226	606	742	1.2	1.8
Sev Day Adv	3	126	220	253	0.4	0.6
HAMILTON	**527**	**73,501**	**155,512**	**202,960**	**60.3**	**100.0**
ANG/EPIS–Anglican NA	3	NR	NR	NR	-	-
ANG/EPIS–Episcopal	11	1,706	5,006	6,139	1.8	3.0
Bahá'í	1	NR	120	120	0.0	0.1
BAPT–Free Will Bapt	2	NR	192	230	0.1	0.1
BAPT–Ind Bapt Flwsp Intl	1	NR	NR	NR	-	-
BAPT–Natl Mis Bapt Conv	7	35	825	990	0.3	0.5
BAPT–NBC Amer	1	75	75	90	0.0	0.0
BAPT–NBC USA	19	2,400	6,760	8,112	2.4	4.0
BAPT–Prog NBC	1	0	150	180	0.1	0.1
BAPT–Ref Bapt Ch	2	NR	NR	NR	-	-
BAPT–So Bapt Conv	108	23,549	61,330	73,598	21.9	36.3
BUDD–Mahayana	1	NR	NR	28	0.0	0.0
Calv Chpl	3	NR	NR	NR	-	-
Catholic	6	NR	NR	12,685	3.8	6.3
CGOD–Ch God (Ander)	3	250	NR	250	0.1	0.1
Ch Cr, Scientst	1	NR	NR	NR	-	-
Ch God (7th Day)	1	NR	NR	NR	-	-
Ch of Nazarene	9	677	1,399	1,399	0.4	0.7
Chr & Miss Al	2	88	94	154	0.0	0.1
CHR–Chr Ch (Disc)	3	56	558	670	0.2	0.3
CHR–Chr Chs & Chs Cr	4	NR	600	720	0.2	0.4
CHR–Chs of Christ	34	5,437	5,601	6,763	2.0	3.3
CHR–Int Chs of Christ	1	NR	46	55	0.0	0.0
FRND–Fr Gen Cf	1	NR	31	37	0.0	0.0
HINDU–Post Ren	2	NR	NR	41	0.0	0.0
Jehovah's Witness	4	NR	NR	NR	-	-
JUD–Conserv	1	178	200	540	0.2	0.3
JUD–Orth	1	79	30	110	0.0	0.1
JUD–Reform	1	122	215	580	0.2	0.3
LDS–Comm of Christ	3	NR	468	468	0.1	0.2
LDS–L-D Saints	6	NR	NR	1,947	0.6	1.0
LUTH–E.L.C.A.	3	253	604	727	0.2	0.4
LUTH–Luth–MO Synod	5	599	947	1,208	0.4	0.6

Religious Group	Number of Congrega-tions	Number of Attendees	Number of Communicant, Confirmed, or Full Members	Adherents: Number of Adherents	Adherents: % of Total Pop.	Adherents: % of Total Adh.
LUTH–Nor Amer Luth C	1	NR	NR	NR	-	-
METH–AME	7	150	1,200	1,440	0.4	0.7
METH–AME Zion	8	75	1,140	1,368	0.4	0.7
METH–C.M.E.	3	70	330	396	0.1	0.2
METH–Un Methodist	39	7,285	19,369	22,312	6.6	11.0
METH–Wesleyan	2	103	51	134	0.0	0.1
Metro Comm Ch	1	40	22	26	0.0	0.0
Muslim Est	7	938	NR	2,156	0.6	1.1
Non-denom Chr Chs	62	11,085	15,107	16,086	4.8	7.9
ORTHE–Greek Orthodox	1	100	NR	225	0.1	0.1
ORTHE–Orth Ch in Amer	1	35	NR	72	0.0	0.0
ORTHO–Coptic Orth Ch	1	25	NR	70	0.0	0.0
ORTHO–Malan Dioc Am	1	7	NR	21	0.0	0.0
PENT–Assemb of God	8	609	556	873	0.3	0.4
PENT–Ch God (Cleve)	43	5,413	9,887	11,865	3.5	5.8
PENT–Ch of God Proph	7	NR	405	486	0.1	0.2
PENT–COGIC	10	534	1,624	1,949	0.6	1.0
PENT–Fire Bapt Hol Ch	2	NR	NR	NR	-	-
PENT–Full Gosp Bapt	1	NR	NR	NR	-	-
PENT–Intl Pent Holiness	1	49	39	47	0.0	0.0
PENT–Orig Ch of God	2	NR	NR	NR	-	-
PENT–Un Pent Ch Intl	3	NR	NR	NR	-	-
PENT–Vineyard	2	330	380	456	0.1	0.2
PRES–Cum Pres Am	4	NR	NR	NR	-	-
PRES–Cumber Presb	5	NR	693	1,209	0.4	0.6
PRES–Evan Presby Ch	4	NR	2,497	2,996	0.9	1.5
PRES–Orth Pres Ch	1	77	50	72	0.0	0.0
PRES–Presb Ch (USA)	9	716	1,555	1,866	0.6	0.9
PRES–Presb Ch Amer	12	4,720	5,760	7,130	2.1	3.5
Salvation Army	4	201	151	953	0.3	0.5
Sev Day Adv	20	5,255	9,136	10,510	3.1	5.2
Un C of Christ	1	68	170	204	0.1	0.1
Unit Univ	1	112	139	197	0.1	0.1
Unity Ch	2	NR	NR	NR	-	-
HANCOCK	**37**	**1,434**	**4,870**	**5,795**	**85.0**	**100.0**
BAPT–Prim Bapt E Dst	6	150	534	638	9.4	11.0
BAPT–So Bapt Conv	25	1,155	4,156	4,965	72.8	85.7
Catholic	1	NR	NR	4	0.1	0.1
CHR–Chs of Christ	1	15	12	16	0.2	0.3
Evan Cov Ch	1	15	41	20	0.3	0.3
METH–Un Methodist	2	99	120	144	2.1	2.5
PENT–Ch of God Proph	1	NR	7	8	0.1	0.1
HARDEMAN	**89**	**4,531**	**13,113**	**15,712**	**57.7**	**100.0**
ANG/EPIS–Episcopal	1	22	47	47	0.2	0.3
Bahá'í	0	NR	2	2	0.0	0.0
BAPT–Natl Mis Bapt Conv	1	0	150	179	0.7	1.1
BAPT–NBC USA	5	295	970	1,158	4.2	7.4
BAPT–So Bapt Conv	37	2,732	8,764	10,461	38.4	66.6
Catholic	1	NR	NR	125	0.5	0.8
CHR–Chs of Christ	11	712	656	859	3.2	5.5
Jehovah's Witness	1	NR	NR	NR	-	-
METH–AME	1	0	150	179	0.7	1.1
METH–C.M.E.	7	25	840	1,003	3.7	6.4
METH–Un Methodist	10	354	867	984	3.6	6.3
Non-denom Chr Chs	4	280	473	473	1.7	3.0
PENT–Ch God (Cleve)	1	26	52	62	0.2	0.4
PENT–COGIC	2	85	110	131	0.5	0.8
PENT–Un Pent Ch Intl	6	NR	NR	NR	-	-
PRES–Cumber Presb	1	NR	32	49	0.2	0.3
HARDIN	**79**	**5,685**	**11,766**	**14,898**	**57.2**	**100.0**
BAPT–Free Will Bapt	1	NR	96	115	0.4	0.8
BAPT–So Bapt Conv	23	2,848	6,851	8,189	31.5	55.0
Catholic	2	NR	NR	507	1.9	3.4
CGOD–Ch God (Ander)	1	0	NR	0	0.0	0.0
Ch of Nazarene	1	34	41	47	0.2	0.3
CHR–Chs of Christ	10	1,182	998	1,280	4.9	8.6
METH–AME	2	0	250	299	1.1	2.0
METH–C.M.E.	1	50	85	102	0.4	0.7
METH–Un Methodist	19	687	2,064	2,221	8.5	14.9
Non-denom Chr Chs	3	230	320	320	1.2	2.1

NR–Not Reported - Represents no adherents reported. Percentages may not total 100 due to rounding.

Table 3: Religious Congregations by County and Group: 2010

Religious Group	Number of Congrega-tions	Number of Attendees	Number of Communicant, Confirmed, or Full Members	Adherents: Number of Adherents	Adherents: % of Total Pop.	Adherents: % of Total Adh.
PENT–Assemb of God	3	308	107	437	1.7	2.9
PENT–Ch God (Cleve)	2	95	146	175	0.7	1.2
PENT–Ch of God Proph	1	NR	17	20	0.1	0.1
PENT–COGIC	1	0	150	179	0.7	1.2
PENT–Int Foursq Gos	1	41	78	93	0.4	0.6
PENT–Intl Pent Holiness	1	15	15	18	0.1	0.1
PENT–Pent Ch of God	1	70	NR	109	0.4	0.7
PENT–Un Pent Ch Intl	2	NR	NR	NR	-	-
PRES–Cumber Presb	2	NR	308	510	2.0	3.4
PRES–Presb Ch (USA)	1	0	23	27	0.1	0.2
Sev Day Adv	1	125	217	250	1.0	1.7
HAWKINS	**156**	**8,840**	**25,736**	**31,544**	**55.5**	**100.0**
ANG/EPIS–Episcopal	1	9	17	19	0.0	0.1
BAPT–Free Will Bapt	9	NR	820	989	1.7	3.1
BAPT–Natl Mis Bapt Conv	1	0	150	181	0.3	0.6
BAPT–Prim Bapt E Dst	9	225	800	964	1.7	3.1
BAPT–So Bapt Conv	71	5,868	18,763	22,619	39.8	71.7
BRETH–Ch of Brethren	2	0	45	54	0.1	0.2
Catholic	1	NR	NR	156	0.3	0.5
CGOD–Ch God (Ander)	1	38	NR	38	0.1	0.1
Ch of Nazarene	1	6	27	27	0.0	0.1
CHR–Chr Ch (Disc)	1	0	110	133	0.2	0.4
CHR–Chr Chs & Chs Cr	4	NR	98	118	0.2	0.4
CHR–Chs of Christ	2	88	58	75	0.1	0.2
Jehovah's Witness	1	NR	NR	NR	-	-
LDS–L-D Saints	1	NR	NR	248	0.4	0.8
METH–AME Zion	3	17	276	333	0.6	1.1
METH–Un Methodist	29	1,229	3,031	3,589	6.3	11.4
Non-denom Chr Chs	6	920	930	1,174	2.1	3.7
PENT–Assemb of God	2	150	60	168	0.3	0.5
PENT–Ch God (Cleve)	3	109	169	204	0.4	0.6
PENT–Ch of God Proph	1	NR	6	7	0.0	0.0
PENT–Intl Pent Holiness	1	25	35	42	0.1	0.1
PENT–Un Pent Ch Intl	1	NR	NR	NR	-	-
PRES–Presb Ch (USA)	4	100	243	293	0.5	0.9
Sev Day Adv	1	56	98	113	0.2	0.4
HAYWOOD	**58**	**2,974**	**8,643**	**10,674**	**56.8**	**100.0**
ANG/EPIS–Episcopal	1	9	28	28	0.1	0.3
Bahá'í	0	NR	32	32	0.2	0.3
BAPT–NBC USA	4	0	450	558	3.0	5.2
BAPT–So Bapt Conv	13	1,306	4,334	5,377	28.6	50.4
Catholic	1	NR	NR	232	1.2	2.2
Ch of Chr (Hol)	1	NR	NR	NR	-	-
CHR–Chs of Christ	4	315	290	379	2.0	3.6
Jehovah's Witness	1	NR	NR	NR	-	-
JUD–Reform	1	6	11	30	0.2	0.3
METH–C.M.E.	6	50	800	992	5.3	9.3
METH–Un Methodist	13	571	1,250	1,365	7.3	12.8
Non-denom Chr Chs	4	450	600	650	3.5	6.1
PENT–Assemb of God	1	45	91	91	0.5	0.9
PENT–Ch God (Cleve)	1	47	44	55	0.3	0.5
PENT–COGIC	5	175	560	695	3.7	6.5
PENT–Un Pent Ch Intl	1	NR	NR	NR	-	-
PRES–Presb Ch (USA)	1	0	153	190	1.0	1.8
HENDERSON	**65**	**5,118**	**10,388**	**13,034**	**46.9**	**100.0**
Bahá'í	0	NR	8	8	0.0	0.1
BAPT–So Bapt Conv	22	2,989	7,145	8,778	31.6	67.3
Catholic	1	NR	NR	140	0.5	1.1
CHR–Chr Chs & Chs Cr	1	NR	127	156	0.6	1.2
CHR–Chs of Christ	16	1,184	1,214	1,500	5.4	11.5
Jehovah's Witness	1	NR	NR	NR	-	-
METH–AME	1	0	100	123	0.4	0.9
METH–Un Methodist	11	589	1,176	1,470	5.3	11.3
Non-denom Chr Chs	2	200	270	275	1.0	2.1
PENT–Assemb of God	1	55	23	100	0.4	0.8
PENT–Ch God (Cleve)	1	71	59	72	0.3	0.6
PENT–COGIC	1	30	20	25	0.1	0.2
PENT–Un Pent Ch Intl	3	NR	NR	NR	-	-
PRES–Cumber Presb	3	NR	242	382	1.4	2.9
PRES–Presb Ch (USA)	1	0	4	5	0.0	0.0

Religious Group	Number of Congrega-tions	Number of Attendees	Number of Communicant, Confirmed, or Full Members	Adherents: Number of Adherents	Adherents: % of Total Pop.	Adherents: % of Total Adh.
HENRY	**104**	**7,185**	**15,859**	**20,761**	**64.2**	**100.0**
ANG/EPIS–Episcopal	1	52	102	102	0.3	0.5
Bahá'í	0	NR	2	2	0.0	0.0
BAPT–Natl Mis Bapt Conv	1	30	35	42	0.1	0.2
BAPT–NBC USA	1	75	150	180	0.6	0.9
BAPT–Prog NBC	1	0	150	180	0.6	0.9
BAPT–So Bapt Conv	34	3,643	10,139	12,173	37.7	58.6
Catholic	1	NR	NR	1,000	3.1	4.8
Ch of Nazarene	1	53	66	78	0.2	0.4
CHR–Chr Ch (Disc)	1	69	144	173	0.5	0.8
CHR–Chs of Christ	17	1,604	1,417	1,882	5.8	9.1
HINDU–Post Ren	1	NR	NR	77	0.2	0.4
Jehovah's Witness	1	NR	NR	NR	-	-
LDS–Comm of Christ	2	NR	312	312	1.0	1.5
LDS–L-D Saints	1	NR	NR	436	1.3	2.1
LUTH–Luth-MO Synod	1	48	65	110	0.3	0.5
MENN–Beachy Amish-Menn	1	98	54	98	0.3	0.5
MENN–Mara Amish-Menn	1	174	80	174	0.5	0.8
METH–AME	2	0	250	300	0.9	1.4
METH–C.M.E.	4	25	345	414	1.3	2.0
METH–Un Methodist	17	871	2,043	2,227	6.9	10.7
Non-denom Chr Chs	2	155	185	210	0.6	1.0
PENT–Assemb of God	1	15	20	23	0.1	0.1
PENT–Ch of God Proph	1	NR	67	80	0.2	0.4
PENT–COGIC	1	30	10	12	0.0	0.1
PENT–Pent Ch of God	2	140	NR	217	0.7	1.0
PENT–Un Pent Ch Intl	2	NR	NR	NR	-	-
PRES–Cum Pres Am	1	NR	NR	NR	-	-
PRES–Cumber Presb	2	NR	32	33	0.1	0.2
PRES–Presb Ch (USA)	1	59	114	137	0.4	0.7
PRES–Ref Pres US	1	NR	NR	NR	-	-
Sev Day Adv	1	44	77	89	0.3	0.4
HICKMAN	**78**	**4,597**	**7,607**	**9,389**	**38.0**	**100.0**
Bahá'í	0	NR	1	1	0.0	0.0
BAPT–Natl Mis Bapt Conv	1	0	150	181	0.7	1.9
BAPT–So Bapt Conv	18	1,184	2,911	3,506	14.2	37.3
Catholic	1	NR	NR	120	0.5	1.3
Ch of Nazarene	1	16	17	22	0.1	0.2
CHR–Chs of Christ	37	2,774	3,063	3,904	15.8	41.6
Jehovah's Witness	1	NR	NR	NR	-	-
METH–AME	1	0	100	120	0.5	1.3
METH–Un Methodist	11	407	998	1,075	4.4	11.4
Non-denom Chr Chs	2	116	166	170	0.7	1.8
PENT–Assemb of God	1	54	25	86	0.3	0.9
PENT–Ch of God Proph	1	NR	80	96	0.4	1.0
PENT–Un Pent Ch Intl	1	NR	NR	NR	-	-
PRES–Cumber Presb	1	NR	17	17	0.1	0.2
Sev Day Adv	1	46	79	91	0.4	1.0
HOUSTON	**30**	**1,364**	**2,864**	**3,633**	**43.1**	**100.0**
BAPT–So Bapt Conv	4	230	725	885	10.5	24.4
Catholic	1	NR	NR	150	1.8	4.1
Ch of Nazarene	2	317	516	652	7.7	17.9
CHR–Chs of Christ	1	70	60	85	1.0	2.3
METH–AME	1	0	150	183	2.2	5.0
METH–C.M.E.	2	0	250	305	3.6	8.4
METH–Un Methodist	10	382	659	703	8.3	19.4
Non-denom Chr Chs	1	150	200	200	2.4	5.5
PENT–Assemb of God	1	190	111	215	2.6	5.9
PENT–Ch of God Proph	1	NR	72	88	1.0	2.4
PENT–Intl Pent Holiness	1	25	25	31	0.4	0.9
PRES–Cumber Presb	5	NR	96	136	1.6	3.7
HUMPHREYS	**62**	**5,136**	**8,771**	**11,052**	**59.6**	**100.0**
ANG/EPIS–Episcopal	1	19	30	30	0.2	0.3
BAPT–Free Will Bapt	4	NR	384	464	2.5	4.2
BAPT–So Bapt Conv	10	679	2,432	2,937	15.8	26.6
Catholic	1	NR	NR	600	3.2	5.4
Ch of Nazarene	2	316	306	507	2.7	4.6
CHR–Chs of Christ	14	1,240	1,265	1,470	7.9	13.3
METH–AME	2	55	224	271	1.5	2.5

NR–Not Reported   - Represents no adherents reported.   Percentages may not total 100 due to rounding.

Table 3: Religious Congregations by County and Group: 2010

Religious Group	Number of Congrega-tions	Number of Attendees	Number of Communicant, Confirmed, or Full Members	Adherents: Number of Adherents	Adherents: % of Total Pop.	Adherents: % of Total Adh.
METH–Un Methodist	9	647	1,385	1,566	8.4	14.2
METH–Wesleyan	1	70	136	91	0.5	0.8
Non-denom Chr Chs	4	1,080	1,350	1,450	7.8	13.1
PENT–Assemb of God	2	64	51	93	0.5	0.8
PENT–Ch of God Proph	2	NR	44	53	0.3	0.5
PENT–Intl Pent Holiness	4	966	918	1,109	6.0	10.0
PENT–Un Pent Ch Intl	1	NR	NR	NR	-	-
PRES–Cumber Presb	4	NR	171	320	1.7	2.9
PRES–Presb Ch (USA)	1	0	75	91	0.5	0.8
JACKSON	**49**	**2,423**	**2,813**	**3,458**	**29.7**	**100.0**
Bahá'í	0	NR	5	5	0.0	0.1
BAPT–So Bapt Conv	4	198	498	588	5.1	17.0
CHR–Chs of Christ	32	1,905	1,662	2,205	18.9	63.8
Jehovah's Witness	2	NR	NR	NR	-	-
METH–Free Methodist	1	12	12	12	0.1	0.3
METH–Un Methodist	6	217	420	422	3.6	12.2
METH–Wesleyan	1	13	27	17	0.1	0.5
Non-denom Chr Chs	1	30	100	100	0.9	2.9
PENT–Assemb of God	1	17	20	28	0.2	0.8
PENT–Ch God (Cleve)	1	31	69	81	0.7	2.3
JEFFERSON	**111**	**8,846**	**22,490**	**27,585**	**53.7**	**100.0**
ANG/EPIS–Episcopal	1	6	12	12	0.0	0.0
Bahá'í	0	NR	4	4	0.0	0.0
BAPT–Free Will Bapt	4	NR	384	462	0.9	1.7
BAPT–Ind Bapt Flwsp Intl	1	NR	NR	NR	-	-
BAPT–Natl Mis Bapt Conv	1	0	150	180	0.4	0.7
BAPT–So Bapt Conv	43	5,492	15,418	18,531	36.0	67.2
BRETH–Ch of Brethren	1	38	125	150	0.3	0.5
Calv Chpl	1	NR	NR	NR	-	-
Catholic	1	NR	NR	698	1.4	2.5
CGOD–Ch God (Ander)	1	0	NR	0	0.0	0.0
CHR–Chr Chs & Chs Cr	2	NR	300	361	0.7	1.3
CHR–Chs of Christ	2	82	91	113	0.2	0.4
FRND–Fr Un Mtg	1	NR	27	32	0.1	0.1
Jehovah's Witness	1	NR	NR	NR	-	-
LUTH–E.L.C.A.	1	0	0	0	0.0	0.0
METH–AME Zion	3	30	270	325	0.6	1.2
METH–Un Methodist	24	1,538	3,354	3,950	7.7	14.3
Non-denom Chr Chs	6	930	1,045	1,187	2.3	4.3
PENT–Assemb of God	1	27	22	32	0.1	0.1
PENT–Ch God (Cleve)	8	523	706	849	1.7	3.1
PENT–Un Pent Ch Intl	1	NR	NR	NR	-	-
PRES–Cumber Presb	1	NR	15	18	0.0	0.1
PRES–Presb Ch (USA)	6	180	567	681	1.3	2.5
JOHNSON	**54**	**2,849**	**7,793**	**9,063**	**49.7**	**100.0**
Bahá'í	0	NR	1	1	0.0	0.0
BAPT–Free Will Bapt	3	NR	288	335	1.8	3.7
BAPT–So Bapt Conv	18	1,440	4,534	5,280	28.9	58.3
Catholic	1	NR	NR	110	0.6	1.2
CHR–Chr Chs & Chs Cr	8	NR	917	1,068	5.9	11.8
CHR–Chs of Christ	7	485	433	574	3.1	6.3
METH–Un Methodist	7	247	599	629	3.4	6.9
Non-denom Chr Chs	4	550	800	800	4.4	8.8
PENT–Assemb of God	1	9	0	9	0.0	0.1
PENT–Ch God (Cleve)	1	33	31	36	0.2	0.4
PRES–Presb Ch (USA)	3	45	120	140	0.8	1.5
Sev Day Adv	1	40	70	81	0.4	0.9
KNOX	**553**	**93,813**	**198,235**	**271,980**	**62.9**	**100.0**
ANG/EPIS–Anglican NA	2	NR	NR	NR	-	-
ANG/EPIS–Episcopal	8	1,568	3,523	4,368	1.0	1.6
Bahá'í	3	NR	164	164	0.0	0.1
BAPT–Amer Bapt Assn	1	NR	25	30	0.0	0.0
BAPT–Amer Bapt USA	1	150	250	301	0.1	0.1
BAPT–Free Will Bapt	7	NR	672	810	0.2	0.3
BAPT–Ind Bapt Flwsp Intl	1	NR	NR	NR	-	-
BAPT–Natl Mis Bapt Conv	5	490	1,180	1,423	0.3	0.5
BAPT–NBC USA	6	835	1,717	2,070	0.5	0.8
BAPT–Prog NBC	1	349	400	482	0.1	0.2

Religious Group	Number of Congrega-tions	Number of Attendees	Number of Communicant, Confirmed, or Full Members	Adherents: Number of Adherents	Adherents: % of Total Pop.	Adherents: % of Total Adh.
BAPT–So Bapt Conv	182	38,857	106,457	128,365	29.7	47.2
BRETH–Ch of Brethren	1	0	30	36	0.0	0.0
BUDD–Mahayana	1	NR	NR	11	0.0	0.0
Calv Chpl	1	NR	NR	NR	-	-
Catholic	7	NR	NR	21,988	5.1	8.1
CGOD–Ch God (Ander)	1	100	NR	100	0.0	0.0
Ch Cr, Scientst	1	NR	NR	NR	-	-
Ch of Nazarene	2	138	369	369	0.1	0.1
CHR–Chr Ch (Disc)	3	120	421	508	0.1	0.2
CHR–Chr Chs & Chs Cr	12	NR	1,738	2,096	0.5	0.8
CHR–Chs of Christ	19	3,134	3,053	3,995	0.9	1.5
CHR–Int Chs of Christ	1	NR	102	123	0.0	0.0
Evan Free Ch	1	3,000	NR	3,000	0.7	1.1
FRND–Fr Gen Cf	1	NR	55	66	0.0	0.0
FRND–Fr Un Mtg	1	NR	30	36	0.0	0.0
HINDU–Post Ren	2	NR	NR	70	0.0	0.0
Jehovah's Witness	5	NR	NR	NR	-	-
JUD–Conserv	1	180	202	545	0.1	0.2
JUD–Reform	1	126	223	602	0.1	0.2
LDS–Comm of Christ	1	NR	156	156	0.0	0.1
LDS–L-D Saints	9	NR	NR	3,850	0.9	1.4
LUTH–E.L.C.A.	5	982	1,792	2,169	0.5	0.8
LUTH–Luth-MO Synod	3	892	1,329	1,724	0.4	0.6
LUTH–Wisc Ev Luth Syn	1	80	91	131	0.0	0.0
MENN–Mennonite USA	2	58	59	71	0.0	0.0
METH–A.W.M.C.	2	34	9	38	0.0	0.0
METH–AME	2	281	540	651	0.2	0.2
METH–AME Zion	10	560	1,555	1,875	0.4	0.7
METH–C.M.E.	1	35	50	60	0.0	0.0
METH–Un Methodist	66	11,833	29,223	35,226	8.1	13.0
METH–Wesleyan	3	343	241	446	0.1	0.2
Metro Comm Ch	1	102	148	178	0.0	0.1
Missionary Ch	3	285	30	285	0.1	0.1
MJEW–Union Mes Cong	1	NR	NR	NR	-	-
Muslim Est	3	402	NR	924	0.2	0.3
New Apost Ch	1	NR	NR	NR	-	-
Non-denom Chr Chs	51	18,620	20,064	24,145	5.6	8.9
ORTHE–Greek Orthodox	1	150	NR	750	0.2	0.3
ORTHO–Coptic Orth Ch	1	30	NR	68	0.0	0.0
PENT–Assemb of God	10	1,425	1,852	2,358	0.5	0.9
PENT–Ch God (Cleve)	26	3,230	4,758	5,737	1.3	2.1
PENT–Ch Lord Jesus Apos	1	NR	NR	NR	-	-
PENT–Ch of God Proph	2	NR	222	268	0.1	0.1
PENT–COGIC	3	30	279	336	0.1	0.1
PENT–Fire Bapt Hol Ch	3	NR	NR	NR	-	-
PENT–Intl Pent Holiness	2	37	100	121	0.0	0.0
PENT–Un Pent Ch Intl	1	NR	NR	NR	-	-
PENT–Vineyard	1	40	50	60	0.0	0.0
PRES–Cumber Presb	7	NR	1,161	1,994	0.5	0.7
PRES–Evan Presby Ch	3	NR	3,516	4,240	1.0	1.6
PRES–Presb Ch (USA)	29	2,871	6,792	8,190	1.9	3.0
PRES–Presb Ch Amer	4	1,096	1,262	1,555	0.4	0.6
PRES–Ref Pres GA	1	NR	NR	NR	-	-
REF–Comm Ref Evan	1	NR	NR	NR	-	-
Salvation Army	1	89	152	170	0.0	0.1
Sev Day Adv	7	744	1,294	1,487	0.3	0.5
Sikh	1	NR	NR	NR	-	-
Un C of Christ	1	123	251	303	0.1	0.1
Unit Univ	2	394	648	850	0.2	0.3
Unity Ch	2	NR	NR	NR	-	-
Zoroastrian	0	NR	NR	6	0.0	0.0
LAKE	**24**	**1,037**	**3,452**	**3,935**	**50.2**	**100.0**
BAPT–So Bapt Conv	8	559	2,212	2,533	32.3	64.4
CHR–Chs of Christ	5	228	299	372	4.7	9.5
METH–C.M.E.	1	0	150	172	2.2	4.4
METH–Un Methodist	3	108	305	323	4.1	8.2
Non-denom Chr Chs	1	120	150	150	1.9	3.8
PENT–Ch God (Cleve)	1	10	118	135	1.7	3.4
PENT–Ch of God Proph	1	NR	49	56	0.7	1.4
PENT–COGIC	1	0	150	172	2.2	4.4
PENT–Un Pent Ch Intl	2	NR	NR	NR	-	-
PRES–Presb Ch (USA)	1	12	19	22	0.3	0.6

NR–Not Reported   - Represents no adherents reported.   Percentages may not total 100 due to rounding.

Table 3: Religious Congregations by County and Group: 2010

Religious Group	Number of Congregations	Number of Attendees	Number of Communicant, Confirmed, or Full Members	Adherents		
				Number of Adherents	% of Total Pop.	% of Total Adh.
LAUDERDALE	**80**	**4,219**	**10,621**	**13,147**	**47.3**	**100.0**
ANG/EPIS–Episcopal	1	25	31	48	0.2	0.4
Bahá'í	0	NR	2	2	0.0	0.0
BAPT–NBC USA	2	90	275	339	1.2	2.6
BAPT–So Bapt Conv	28	1,831	6,287	7,743	27.8	58.9
Catholic	1	NR	NR	34	0.1	0.3
CHR–Chr Ch (Disc)	1	0	0	0	0.0	0.0
CHR–Chs of Christ	8	390	390	498	1.8	3.8
Jehovah's Witness	1	NR	NR	NR	-	-
METH–C.M.E.	4	175	670	825	3.0	6.3
METH–Un Methodist	18	749	1,829	2,087	7.5	15.9
Non-denom Chr Chs	4	340	450	474	1.7	3.6
PENT–Assemb of God	6	438	328	635	2.3	4.8
PENT–Ch God (Cleve)	2	181	301	371	1.3	2.8
PENT–Un Pent Ch Intl	2	NR	NR	NR	-	-
PRES–Cumber Presb	1	NR	41	70	0.3	0.5
PRES–Presb Ch (USA)	1	0	17	21	0.1	0.2
LAWRENCE	**132**	**10,506**	**18,793**	**25,823**	**61.7**	**100.0**
ANG/EPIS–Anglican NA	1	NR	NR	NR	-	-
Bahá'í	0	NR	1	1	0.0	0.0
BAPT–Free Will Bapt	2	NR	192	238	0.6	0.9
BAPT–So Bapt Conv	36	4,553	10,322	12,808	30.6	49.6
Catholic	3	NR	NR	1,200	2.9	4.6
Ch of Nazarene	4	144	222	250	0.6	1.0
CHR–Chs of Christ	33	3,164	2,879	3,718	8.9	14.4
Jehovah's Witness	1	NR	NR	NR	-	-
LDS–L-D Saints	1	NR	NR	562	1.3	2.2
MENN–Amish Undif	10	NR	549	1,482	3.5	5.7
METH–Cong Meth	1	NR	26	32	0.1	0.1
METH–Un Methodist	20	1,217	2,662	2,969	7.1	11.5
Non-denom Chr Chs	8	705	850	939	2.2	3.6
PENT–Assemb of God	1	200	100	290	0.7	1.1
PENT–Ch God (Cleve)	5	401	710	881	2.1	3.4
PENT–Un Pent Ch Intl	2	NR	NR	NR	-	-
PRES–Cumber Presb	2	NR	65	203	0.5	0.8
PRES–Presb Ch (USA)	1	15	29	36	0.1	0.1
Sev Day Adv	1	107	186	214	0.5	0.8
LEWIS	**42**	**2,779**	**3,970**	**5,104**	**42.0**	**100.0**
Bahá'í	0	NR	1	1	0.0	0.0
BAPT–So Bapt Conv	6	637	1,556	1,899	15.6	37.2
Catholic	1	NR	NR	160	1.3	3.1
CHR–Chs of Christ	17	1,422	1,243	1,672	13.7	32.8
Jehovah's Witness	1	NR	NR	NR	-	-
MENN–Amish Undif	1	NR	29	77	0.6	1.5
METH–Un Methodist	7	281	613	628	5.2	12.3
Non-denom Chr Chs	2	350	400	462	3.8	9.1
PENT–Assemb of God	1	50	24	50	0.4	1.0
PENT–Ch God (Cleve)	1	15	28	34	0.3	0.7
PENT–Un Pent Ch Intl	3	NR	NR	NR	-	-
PRES–Cumber Presb	1	NR	35	74	0.6	1.4
Sev Day Adv	1	24	41	47	0.4	0.9
LINCOLN	**120**	**7,430**	**16,368**	**22,912**	**68.7**	**100.0**
ANG/EPIS–Episcopal	1	72	151	151	0.5	0.7
Bahá'í	0	NR	7	7	0.0	0.0
BAPT–Natl Mis Bapt Conv	2	0	300	366	1.1	1.6
BAPT–So Bapt Conv	33	3,482	10,058	12,279	36.8	53.6
Catholic	1	NR	NR	621	1.9	2.7
CGOD–Ch God (Ander)	3	99	NR	99	0.3	0.4
Ch of Nazarene	1	40	85	85	0.3	0.4
CHR–Chs of Christ	32	2,284	2,161	2,762	8.3	12.1
HINDU–I/A Temples	1	NR	NR	1,562	4.7	6.8
Jehovah's Witness	1	NR	NR	NR	-	-
LDS–L-D Saints	1	NR	NR	440	1.3	1.9
METH–AME	6	140	760	928	2.8	4.1
METH–Un Methodist	15	640	1,295	1,360	4.1	5.9
Non-denom Chr Chs	3	210	200	263	0.8	1.1
PENT–Assemb of God	1	151	94	151	0.5	0.7
PENT–Ch God (Cleve)	1	46	34	42	0.1	0.2
PENT–Intl Pent Holiness	1	53	102	125	0.4	0.5

Religious Group	Number of Congregations	Number of Attendees	Number of Communicant, Confirmed, or Full Members	Adherents		
				Number of Adherents	% of Total Pop.	% of Total Adh.
PENT–Un Pent Ch Intl	1	NR	NR	NR	-	-
PRES–As Ref Pres Ch	3	NR	389	475	1.4	2.1
PRES–Cumber Presb	9	NR	297	671	2.0	2.9
PRES–Presb Ch (USA)	3	159	342	418	1.3	1.8
Sev Day Adv	1	54	93	107	0.3	0.5
LOUDON	**100**	**10,092**	**22,431**	**31,124**	**64.1**	**100.0**
ANG/EPIS–Episcopal	1	89	148	154	0.3	0.5
Bahá'í	0	NR	8	8	0.0	0.0
BAPT–Free Will Bapt	2	NR	192	227	0.5	0.7
BAPT–Ind Bapt Flwsp Intl	1	NR	NR	NR	-	-
BAPT–So Bapt Conv	47	5,066	16,028	18,956	39.0	60.9
Catholic	1	NR	NR	1,678	3.5	5.4
CGOD–Ch God (Ander)	1	47	NR	47	0.1	0.2
Ch of Nazarene	3	159	214	354	0.7	1.1
CHR–Chr Chs & Chs Cr	1	NR	150	177	0.4	0.6
CHR–Chs of Christ	2	207	207	254	0.5	0.8
Evan Free Ch	1	1,800	NR	1,800	3.7	5.8
HINDU–Trad Temples	1	NR	NR	350	0.7	1.1
Int Cou Comm Ch	1	NR	NR	NR	-	-
Jehovah's Witness	1	NR	NR	NR	-	-
LDS–L-D Saints	1	NR	NR	298	0.6	1.0
LUTH–Luth–MO Synod	1	239	317	336	0.7	1.1
METH–AME Zion	1	0	100	118	0.2	0.4
METH–Un Methodist	14	967	2,401	3,081	6.3	9.9
Missionary Ch	1	0	0	0	0.0	0.0
Non-denom Chr Chs	4	290	370	413	0.9	1.3
PENT–Assemb of God	1	13	12	24	0.0	0.1
PENT–Ch God (Cleve)	5	767	1,437	1,700	3.5	5.5
PENT–Cong Hol Ch	1	100	80	95	0.2	0.3
PENT–Un Pent Ch Intl	1	NR	NR	NR	-	-
PENT–Vineyard	1	80	100	118	0.2	0.4
PRES–Cumber Presb	2	NR	269	469	1.0	1.5
PRES–Presb Ch (USA)	3	204	286	338	0.7	1.1
Sev Day Adv	1	64	112	129	0.3	0.4
MCMINN	**144**	**11,819**	**30,967**	**39,071**	**74.8**	**100.0**
ANG/EPIS–Episcopal	1	117	342	342	0.7	0.9
Bahá'í	0	NR	4	4	0.0	0.0
BAPT–So Bapt Conv	68	7,145	22,174	26,762	51.2	68.5
Catholic	1	NR	NR	986	1.9	2.5
CGOD–Ch God (Ander)	5	206	NR	206	0.4	0.5
Ch of Nazarene	2	119	161	306	0.6	0.8
CHR–Chr Chs & Chs Cr	3	NR	395	477	0.9	1.2
CHR–Chs of Christ	12	688	718	904	1.7	2.3
Jehovah's Witness	1	NR	NR	NR	-	-
LDS–L-D Saints	1	NR	NR	460	0.9	1.2
LUTH–Luth–MO Synod	1	83	138	149	0.3	0.4
METH–AME Zion	5	0	800	966	1.8	2.5
METH–Un Methodist	19	1,339	3,511	4,250	8.1	10.9
Non-denom Chr Chs	9	1,065	1,159	1,370	2.6	3.5
PENT–Assemb of God	1	20	18	30	0.1	0.1
PENT–Ch God (Cleve)	4	814	1,109	1,338	2.6	3.4
PENT–Ch of God Proph	2	NR	32	39	0.1	0.1
PENT–Intl Pent Holiness	1	15	15	18	0.0	0.0
PENT–Un Pent Ch Intl	2	NR	NR	NR	-	-
PENT–Vineyard	1	35	50	60	0.1	0.2
PRES–Cum Pres Am	1	NR	NR	NR	-	-
PRES–Presb Ch (USA)	3	99	213	257	0.5	0.7
Sev Day Adv	1	74	128	147	0.3	0.4
MCNAIRY	**93**	**4,876**	**11,238**	**13,991**	**53.7**	**100.0**
Bahá'í	0	NR	3	3	0.0	0.0
BAPT–Amer Bapt Assn	1	NR	85	103	0.4	0.7
BAPT–So Bapt Conv	29	2,877	7,334	8,927	34.2	63.8
Catholic	1	NR	NR	150	0.6	1.1
CHR–Chr Chs & Chs Cr	3	NR	310	377	1.4	2.7
CHR–Chs of Christ	18	1,242	1,214	1,607	6.2	11.5
Jehovah's Witness	1	NR	NR	NR	-	-
MENN–Amish Undif	1	NR	13	35	0.1	0.3
METH–Un Methodist	11	371	1,299	1,377	5.3	9.8
Non-denom Chr Chs	2	155	134	198	0.8	1.4
PENT–Ch God (Cleve)	2	60	209	254	1.0	1.8

NR–Not Reported - Represents no adherents reported. Percentages may not total 100 due to rounding.

Table 3: Religious Congregations by County and Group: 2010

Religious Group	Number of Congregations	Number of Attendees	Number of Communicant, Confirmed, or Full Members	Adherents: Number of Adherents	Adherents: % of Total Pop.	Adherents: % of Total Adh.
PENT–Ch of God Proph	4	NR	164	200	0.8	1.4
PENT–Pent Ch of God	1	70	NR	109	0.4	0.8
PENT–Un Pent Ch Intl	6	NR	NR	NR	-	-
PRES–Cumber Presb	5	NR	165	283	1.1	2.0
PRES–Presb Ch (USA)	6	47	214	260	1.0	1.9
Sev Day Adv	2	54	94	108	0.4	0.8
MACON	**37**	**2,944**	**4,380**	**5,770**	**25.9**	**100.0**
BAPT–So Bapt Conv	9	568	1,537	1,903	8.6	33.0
Catholic	1	NR	NR	400	1.8	6.9
CHR–Chs of Christ	10	1,220	1,239	1,594	7.2	27.6
Jehovah's Witness	1	NR	NR	NR	-	-
METH–AME	1	0	100	124	0.6	2.1
METH–Un Methodist	4	161	304	304	1.4	5.3
Non-denom Chr Chs	6	710	910	987	4.4	17.1
PENT–Assemb of God	1	45	34	146	0.7	2.5
PENT–Ch God (Cleve)	3	207	199	246	1.1	4.3
Sev Day Adv	1	33	57	66	0.3	1.1
MADISON	**191**	**21,723**	**49,149**	**64,402**	**65.5**	**100.0**
ANG/EPIS–Anglican NA	1	NR	NR	NR	-	-
ANG/EPIS–Episcopal	1	147	302	344	0.3	0.5
Bahá'í	0	NR	25	25	0.0	0.0
BAPT–Free Will Bapt	1	NR	96	118	0.1	0.2
BAPT–Natl Mis Bapt Conv	2	0	300	368	0.4	0.6
BAPT–NBC USA	8	525	1,200	1,474	1.5	2.3
BAPT–So Bapt Conv	50	8,681	24,588	30,200	30.7	46.9
BUDD–Mahayana	1	NR	NR	57	0.1	0.1
Catholic	1	NR	NR	3,500	3.6	5.4
Ch of Chr (Hol)	1	NR	NR	NR	-	-
Ch of Nazarene	1	70	67	86	0.1	0.1
CHR–Chr Ch (Disc)	1	0	0	0	0.0	0.0
CHR–Chr Chs & Chs Cr	1	NR	250	307	0.3	0.5
CHR–Chs of Christ	13	2,855	3,025	3,465	3.5	5.4
Jehovah's Witness	1	NR	NR	NR	-	-
JUD–Reform	1	15	26	70	0.1	0.1
LDS–L-D Saints	1	NR	NR	817	0.8	1.3
LUTH–Luth–MO Synod	1	87	165	199	0.2	0.3
METH–AME	2	0	200	246	0.3	0.4
METH–C.M.E.	17	178	2,072	2,545	2.6	4.0
METH–Un Methodist	32	2,710	7,851	9,335	9.5	14.5
Muslim Est	1	134	NR	308	0.3	0.5
Non-denom Chr Chs	21	4,375	5,900	6,464	6.6	10.0
PENT–Assemb of God	5	685	440	1,151	1.2	1.8
PENT–Ch God (Cleve)	5	195	286	351	0.4	0.5
PENT–Ch of God Proph	1	NR	12	15	0.0	0.0
PENT–COGIC	4	475	950	1,167	1.2	1.8
PENT–Un Pent Ch Intl	5	NR	NR	NR	-	-
PRES–Cum Pres Am	1	NR	NR	NR	-	-
PRES–Cumber Presb	3	NR	317	497	0.5	0.8
PRES–Evan Presby Ch	1	NR	2	2	0.0	0.0
PRES–Presb Ch (USA)	2	186	470	577	0.6	0.9
PRES–Presb Ch Amer	2	150	182	198	0.2	0.3
Salvation Army	1	50	67	106	0.1	0.2
Sev Day Adv	2	205	356	410	0.4	0.6
MARION	**75**	**3,747**	**8,016**	**10,102**	**35.8**	**100.0**
ANG/EPIS–Episcopal	2	75	136	168	0.6	1.7
Bahá'í	0	NR	2	2	0.0	0.0
BAPT–Free Will Bapt	1	NR	96	115	0.4	1.1
BAPT–So Bapt Conv	16	1,202	3,920	4,708	16.7	46.6
Catholic	2	NR	NR	200	0.7	2.0
Ch of Nazarene	3	126	217	237	0.8	2.3
CHR–Chs of Christ	11	759	653	820	2.9	8.1
Jehovah's Witness	1	NR	NR	NR	-	-
LDS–L-D Saints	1	NR	NR	227	0.8	2.2
METH–AME Zion	1	25	25	30	0.1	0.3
METH–Un Methodist	13	652	1,399	1,635	5.8	16.2
Non-denom Chr Chs	4	265	360	400	1.4	4.0
PENT–Ch God (Cleve)	9	581	973	1,169	4.1	11.6
PENT–Un Pent Ch Intl	1	NR	NR	NR	-	-
PRES–Cumber Presb	8	NR	128	268	0.9	2.7
PRES–Presb Ch Amer	1	0	0	0	0.0	0.0

Religious Group	Number of Congregations	Number of Attendees	Number of Communicant, Confirmed, or Full Members	Adherents: Number of Adherents	Adherents: % of Total Pop.	Adherents: % of Total Adh.
Sev Day Adv	1	62	107	123	0.4	1.2
MARSHALL	**86**	**7,077**	**12,936**	**17,395**	**56.8**	**100.0**
Bahá'í	0	NR	2	2	0.0	0.0
BAPT–Natl Mis Bapt Conv	1	0	150	185	0.6	1.1
BAPT–So Bapt Conv	22	2,917	7,508	9,272	30.3	53.3
Catholic	1	NR	NR	600	2.0	3.4
CGOD–Ch God (Ander)	2	465	NR	465	1.5	2.7
Ch of Nazarene	1	64	64	80	0.3	0.5
CHR–Chs of Christ	23	2,369	2,383	3,111	10.2	17.9
Jehovah's Witness	1	NR	NR	NR	-	-
METH–AME	2	0	300	370	1.2	2.1
METH–Un Methodist	13	587	1,438	1,783	5.8	10.3
Non-denom Chr Chs	3	300	450	450	1.5	2.6
PENT–Assemb of God	1	164	72	225	0.7	1.3
PENT–Ch God (Cleve)	2	52	70	86	0.3	0.5
PENT–Ch of God Proph	2	NR	84	104	0.3	0.6
PENT–Cong Hol Ch	1	20	10	12	0.0	0.1
PENT–Full Gosp Bapt	1	NR	NR	NR	-	-
PENT–Int Foursq Gos	1	27	44	54	0.2	0.3
PENT–Un Pent Ch Intl	1	NR	NR	NR	-	-
PRES–Cum Pres Am	1	NR	NR	NR	-	-
PRES–Cumber Presb	4	NR	172	363	1.2	2.1
PRES–Presb Ch (USA)	3	112	189	233	0.8	1.3
MAURY	**190**	**16,030**	**26,195**	**38,353**	**47.4**	**100.0**
ANG/EPIS–Episcopal	2	224	506	532	0.7	1.4
Bahá'í	0	NR	15	15	0.0	0.0
BAPT–Free Will Bapt	3	NR	288	356	0.4	0.9
BAPT–Natl Mis Bapt Conv	1	0	150	186	0.2	0.5
BAPT–NBC USA	3	110	580	717	0.9	1.9
BAPT–So Bapt Conv	32	2,639	6,665	8,244	10.2	21.5
Calv Chpl	2	NR	NR	NR	-	-
Catholic	2	NR	NR	3,900	4.8	10.2
Ch of Nazarene	5	913	1,058	1,250	1.5	3.3
CHR–Chr Chs & Chs Cr	2	NR	500	618	0.8	1.6
CHR–Chs of Christ	53	6,626	5,864	7,675	9.5	20.0
Jehovah's Witness	2	NR	NR	NR	-	-
LDS–L-D Saints	4	NR	NR	1,592	2.0	4.2
LUTH–E.L.C.A.	1	51	4	112	0.1	0.3
LUTH–Luth–MO Synod	1	105	144	172	0.2	0.4
LUTH–Wisc Ev Luth Syn	1	269	360	461	0.6	1.2
METH–AME	7	0	910	1,126	1.4	2.9
METH–Un Methodist	22	1,382	3,821	4,166	5.1	10.9
Muslim Est	1	134	NR	308	0.4	0.8
Non-denom Chr Chs	16	2,260	2,855	3,149	3.9	8.2
PENT–Assemb of God	3	480	162	598	0.7	1.6
PENT–Ch God (Cleve)	2	125	231	286	0.4	0.7
PENT–Ch Lord Jesus Apos	1	NR	NR	NR	-	-
PENT–Ch of God Proph	1	NR	155	192	0.2	0.5
PENT–Full Gosp Bapt	1	NR	NR	NR	-	-
PENT–Un Pent Ch Intl	1	NR	NR	NR	-	-
PRES–As Ref Pres Ch	1	NR	60	74	0.1	0.2
PRES–Cum Pres Am	1	NR	NR	NR	-	-
PRES–Cumber Presb	9	NR	536	950	1.2	2.5
PRES–Presb Ch (USA)	6	293	852	1,054	1.3	2.7
PRES–Presb Ch Amer	2	335	332	451	0.6	1.2
Sev Day Adv	2	84	147	169	0.2	0.4
MEIGS	**31**	**2,365**	**5,187**	**6,160**	**52.4**	**100.0**
BAPT–So Bapt Conv	12	1,246	3,370	4,043	34.4	65.6
CHR–Chs of Christ	2	53	52	62	0.5	1.0
Jehovah's Witness	1	NR	NR	NR	-	-
METH–Un Methodist	9	274	518	644	5.5	10.5
Non-denom Chr Chs	2	395	520	550	4.7	8.9
PENT–Ch God (Cleve)	3	263	494	593	5.0	9.6
Sev Day Adv	2	134	233	268	2.3	4.4
MONROE	**112**	**8,618**	**22,970**	**28,369**	**63.7**	**100.0**
Bahá'í	0	NR	1	1	0.0	0.0
BAPT–Free Will Bapt	2	NR	192	233	0.5	0.8
BAPT–So Bapt Conv	65	6,570	19,055	23,144	52.0	81.6

NR–Not Reported   - Represents no adherents reported.   Percentages may not total 100 due to rounding.

Table 3: Religious Congregations by County and Group: 2010

Religious Group	Number of Congrega-tions	Number of Attendees	Number of Communicant, Confirmed, or Full Members	Adherents: Number of Adherents	Adherents: % of Total Pop.	Adherents: % of Total Adh.
Calv Chpl	1	NR	NR	NR	-	-
Catholic	1	NR	NR	500	1.1	1.8
CGOD–Ch God (Ander)	1	58	NR	58	0.1	0.2
Ch of Nazarene	1	47	38	63	0.1	0.2
CHR–Chr Chs & Chs Cr	1	NR	30	36	0.1	0.1
CHR–Chs of Christ	2	120	113	145	0.3	0.5
FRND–Fr Un Mtg	2	NR	123	149	0.3	0.5
Jehovah's Witness	1	NR	NR	NR	-	-
LUTH–E.L.C.A.	1	30	35	51	0.1	0.2
METH–AME Zion	1	0	100	121	0.3	0.4
METH–Un Methodist	8	693	1,383	1,658	3.7	5.8
Non-denom Chr Chs	2	200	325	325	0.7	1.1
PENT–Assemb of God	3	256	393	441	1.0	1.6
PENT–Ch God (Cleve)	4	257	500	607	1.4	2.1
PENT–Ch of God Proph	1	NR	34	41	0.1	0.1
PENT–Intl Pent Holiness	1	10	10	12	0.0	0.0
PENT–Un Pent Ch Intl	1	NR	NR	NR	-	-
PRES–Cum Pres Am	2	NR	NR	NR	-	-
PRES–Cumber Presb	2	NR	53	77	0.2	0.3
PRES–Presb Ch (USA)	7	207	403	489	1.1	1.7
PRES–Presb Ch Amer	1	50	51	59	0.1	0.2
Un C of Christ	1	120	131	159	0.4	0.6
MONTGOMERY	**206**	**23,132**	**54,799**	**81,396**	**47.2**	**100.0**
ANG/EPIS–Episcopal	2	206	346	436	0.3	0.5
Bahá'í	0	NR	23	23	0.0	0.0
BAPT–Amer Bapt Assn	1	NR	125	161	0.1	0.2
BAPT–Free Will Bapt	6	NR	576	742	0.4	0.9
BAPT–NBC Amer	2	1,150	1,700	2,189	1.3	2.7
BAPT–NBC USA	1	150	300	386	0.2	0.5
BAPT–So Bapt Conv	46	8,830	29,398	37,853	22.0	46.5
BUDD–Mahayana	1	NR	NR	11	0.0	0.0
Calv Chpl	1	NR	NR	NR	-	-
Catholic	1	NR	NR	7,500	4.4	9.2
CGOD–Ch God (Ander)	3	75	NR	75	0.0	0.1
Ch of Nazarene	6	1,566	1,651	2,262	1.3	2.8
Chr & Miss Al	1	221	60	243	0.1	0.3
CHR–Chr Ch (Disc)	1	90	140	180	0.1	0.2
CHR–Chr Chs & Chs Cr	2	NR	240	309	0.2	0.4
CHR–Chs of Christ	14	1,683	1,875	2,556	1.5	3.1
FRND–Fr Gen Cf	1	NR	0	0	0.0	0.0
Ind Fund Churches	1	NR	NR	NR	-	-
Jain	1	NR	NR	NR	-	-
Jehovah's Witness	2	NR	NR	NR	-	-
LDS–Comm of Christ	1	NR	156	156	0.1	0.2
LDS–L-D Saints	5	NR	NR	3,433	2.0	4.2
LUTH–E.L.C.A.	1	78	172	206	0.1	0.3
LUTH–Luth-MO Synod	1	256	558	749	0.4	0.9
LUTH–Wisc Ev Luth Syn	1	186	304	445	0.3	0.5
MENN–Amish Undif	0	NR	2	11	0.0	0.0
METH–AME	6	0	800	1,030	0.6	1.3
METH–AME Zion	1	0	100	129	0.1	0.2
METH–C.M.E.	1	0	150	193	0.1	0.2
METH–Un Methodist	30	2,662	6,715	8,682	5.0	10.7
Muslim Est	1	134	NR	308	0.2	0.4
Non-denom Chr Chs	23	3,390	4,002	4,560	2.6	5.6
ORTHE–Orth Ch in Amer	1	20	NR	40	0.0	0.0
PENT–Assemb of God	5	1,235	2,157	2,266	1.3	2.8
PENT–Ch God (Cleve)	3	165	231	297	0.2	0.4
PENT–Ch of God Proph	4	NR	272	350	0.2	0.4
PENT–COGIC	3	12	170	219	0.1	0.3
PENT–Full Gosp Bapt	3	NR	NR	NR	-	-
PENT–Pent Ch of God	1	70	NR	109	0.1	0.1
PENT–Un Pent Ch Intl	5	NR	NR	NR	-	-
PENT–Vineyard	1	275	400	515	0.3	0.6
PRES–Cumber Presb	8	NR	563	724	0.4	0.9
PRES–Presb Ch (USA)	3	343	1,086	1,398	0.8	1.7
PRES–Presb Ch Amer	1	100	81	128	0.1	0.2
Salvation Army	1	22	49	50	0.0	0.1
Sev Day Adv	2	213	370	426	0.2	0.5
Unit Univ	1	0	27	42	0.0	0.1
Zoroastrian	0	NR	NR	4	0.0	0.0

Religious Group	Number of Congrega-tions	Number of Attendees	Number of Communicant, Confirmed, or Full Members	Adherents: Number of Adherents	Adherents: % of Total Pop.	Adherents: % of Total Adh.
MOORE	**17**	**945**	**1,896**	**2,206**	**34.7**	**100.0**
Bahá'í	0	NR	3	3	0.0	0.1
BAPT–So Bapt Conv	3	194	675	806	12.7	36.5
CHR–Chs of Christ	6	485	493	643	10.1	29.1
METH–AME	1	0	150	179	2.8	8.1
METH–Un Methodist	7	266	575	575	9.0	26.1
MORGAN	**44**	**2,844**	**7,703**	**9,339**	**42.5**	**100.0**
ANG/EPIS–Episcopal	1	32	41	44	0.2	0.5
Bahá'í	0	NR	1	1	0.0	0.0
BAPT–Natl Mis Bapt Conv	2	0	300	357	1.6	3.8
BAPT–So Bapt Conv	18	1,980	6,137	7,304	33.2	78.2
Catholic	1	NR	NR	56	0.3	0.6
Ch of Nazarene	2	73	68	132	0.6	1.4
CHR–Chs of Christ	2	86	80	104	0.5	1.1
Jehovah's Witness	1	NR	NR	NR	-	-
LUTH–Luth-MO Synod	1	156	248	315	1.4	3.4
MENN–Unaffil Amish-Menn	1	116	50	116	0.5	1.2
METH–Un Methodist	4	97	187	231	1.1	2.5
Non-denom Chr Chs	2	160	230	230	1.0	2.5
PENT–Ch God (Cleve)	1	21	30	36	0.2	0.4
PENT–Ch of God Proph	2	NR	95	113	0.5	1.2
PENT–Un Pent Ch Intl	1	NR	NR	NR	-	-
PRES–Cumber Presb	1	NR	53	86	0.4	0.9
PRES–Presb Ch (USA)	2	39	54	64	0.3	0.7
Sev Day Adv	1	60	104	120	0.5	1.3
Un C of Christ	1	24	25	30	0.1	0.3
OBION	**126**	**8,467**	**18,303**	**23,202**	**72.9**	**100.0**
ANG/EPIS–Episcopal	1	42	56	71	0.2	0.3
BAPT–NBC USA	1	130	180	218	0.7	0.9
BAPT–So Bapt Conv	32	4,226	11,004	13,331	41.9	57.5
Catholic	1	NR	NR	558	1.8	2.4
CGOD–Ch God (Ander)	1	30	NR	30	0.1	0.1
Ch of Chr (Hol)	1	NR	NR	NR	-	-
CHR–Chr Ch (Disc)	1	35	100	121	0.4	0.5
CHR–Chs of Christ	24	1,777	1,692	2,198	6.9	9.5
Ind Fund Churches	1	NR	NR	NR	-	-
Jehovah's Witness	1	NR	NR	NR	-	-
LUTH–Luth-MO Synod	1	45	83	99	0.3	0.4
LUTH–Wisc Ev Luth Syn	1	15	21	21	0.1	0.1
METH–AME	2	60	289	350	1.1	1.5
METH–C.M.E.	1	0	100	121	0.4	0.5
METH–Un Methodist	22	909	2,411	2,619	8.2	11.3
Non-denom Chr Chs	3	340	430	455	1.4	2.0
PENT–Assemb of God	6	409	197	509	1.6	2.2
PENT–Ch God (Cleve)	4	180	453	549	1.7	2.4
PENT–Ch of God Proph	2	NR	53	64	0.2	0.3
PENT–COGIC	2	125	550	666	2.1	2.9
PENT–Un Pent Ch Intl	1	NR	NR	NR	-	-
PRES–Cumber Presb	13	NR	539	1,040	3.3	4.5
PRES–Presb Ch (USA)	1	40	28	34	0.1	0.1
PRES–Presb Ch Amer	1	70	59	81	0.3	0.3
Sev Day Adv	2	34	58	67	0.2	0.3
OVERTON	**60**	**3,796**	**6,764**	**8,068**	**36.5**	**100.0**
BAPT–So Bapt Conv	12	1,026	2,745	3,347	15.2	41.5
CGOD–Ch God (Ander)	1	45	NR	45	0.2	0.6
CHR–Chr Ch (Disc)	2	55	449	548	2.5	6.8
CHR–Chr Chs & Chs Cr	1	NR	125	152	0.7	1.9
CHR–Chs of Christ	14	1,450	1,334	1,630	7.4	20.2
Jehovah's Witness	2	NR	NR	NR	-	-
METH–Un Methodist	15	787	1,490	1,553	7.0	19.2
METH–Wesleyan	1	6	11	8	0.0	0.1
Non-denom Chr Chs	2	245	275	306	1.4	3.8
PENT–Assemb of God	2	95	45	97	0.4	1.2
PENT–Ch God (Cleve)	2	87	158	193	0.9	2.4
PENT–Ch of God Proph	2	NR	43	52	0.2	0.6
PENT–Un Pent Ch Intl	1	NR	NR	NR	-	-
PRES–Cumber Presb	2	NR	17	49	0.2	0.6
PRES–Presb Ch (USA)	1	0	72	88	0.4	1.1

NR–Not Reported - Represents no adherents reported. Percentages may not total 100 due to rounding.

Table 3: Religious Congregations by County and Group: 2010

Religious Group	Number of Congregations	Number of Attendees	Number of Communicant, Confirmed, or Full Members	Adherents: Number of Adherents	Adherents: % of Total Pop.	Adherents: % of Total Adh.
PERRY	**24**	**1,292**	**2,508**	**3,347**	**42.3**	**100.0**
Bahá'í	0	NR	1	1	0.0	0.0
BAPT–So Bapt Conv	4	327	879	1,060	13.4	31.7
CHR–Chr Chs & Chs Cr	2	NR	355	428	5.4	12.8
CHR–Chs of Christ	8	630	545	735	9.3	22.0
LDS–L-D Saints	1	NR	NR	297	3.8	8.9
MENN–CG in Cr (Menn)	1	NR	103	124	1.6	3.7
METH–AME	1	0	100	121	1.5	3.6
METH–Un Methodist	4	113	318	334	4.2	10.0
PENT–Ch God (Cleve)	1	198	164	198	2.5	5.9
PENT–Un Pent Ch Intl	1	NR	NR	NR	-	-
Sev Day Adv	1	24	43	49	0.6	1.5
PICKETT	**14**	**552**	**1,746**	**2,095**	**41.3**	**100.0**
BAPT–Natl Mis Bapt Conv	1	0	150	177	3.5	8.4
BAPT–So Bapt Conv	4	324	903	1,068	21.0	51.0
Ch Christ Chr Union	1	NR	NR	NR	-	-
CHR–Chr Ch (Disc)	1	0	39	46	0.9	2.2
CHR–Chr Chs & Chs Cr	2	NR	398	471	9.3	22.5
CHR–Chs of Christ	3	130	110	156	3.1	7.4
METH–Un Methodist	2	98	146	177	3.5	8.4
POLK	**60**	**4,252**	**9,445**	**11,492**	**68.3**	**100.0**
ANG/EPIS–Episcopal	1	27	29	30	0.2	0.3
BAPT–Amer Bapt Assn	1	NR	0	0	0.0	0.0
BAPT–So Bapt Conv	40	3,475	7,877	9,468	56.3	82.4
Catholic	1	NR	NR	190	1.1	1.7
CHR–Chs of Christ	3	127	130	163	1.0	1.4
Jehovah's Witness	1	NR	NR	NR	-	-
METH–Un Methodist	3	171	454	536	3.2	4.7
Non-denom Chr Chs	2	180	260	275	1.6	2.4
PENT–Ch God (Cleve)	5	160	503	605	3.6	5.3
PENT–Ch of God Proph	1	NR	22	26	0.2	0.2
PRES–Presb Ch (USA)	1	52	65	78	0.5	0.7
Sev Day Adv	1	60	105	121	0.7	1.1
PUTNAM	**152**	**17,410**	**28,080**	**39,571**	**54.7**	**100.0**
ANG/EPIS–Episcopal	1	134	335	388	0.5	1.0
Bahá'í	0	NR	6	6	0.0	0.0
BAPT–Amer Bapt Assn	1	NR	85	102	0.1	0.3
BAPT–Free Will Bapt	9	NR	864	1,037	1.4	2.6
BAPT–Natl Mis Bapt Conv	1	0	150	180	0.2	0.5
BAPT–So Bapt Conv	39	6,869	12,856	15,436	21.3	39.0
BUDD–Vajrayana	1	NR	NR	39	0.1	0.1
Catholic	1	NR	NR	3,500	4.8	8.8
CGOD–Ch God (Ander)	4	334	NR	334	0.5	0.8
Ch Cr, Scientist	1	NR	NR	NR	-	-
Ch of Nazarene	2	234	474	597	0.8	1.5
CHR–Chr Chs & Chs Cr	2	NR	425	510	0.7	1.3
CHR–Chs of Christ	28	4,219	4,115	4,988	6.9	12.6
FRND–Fr Gen Cf	1	NR	3	4	0.0	0.0
Jehovah's Witness	1	NR	NR	NR	-	-
LDS–L-D Saints	2	NR	NR	1,168	1.6	3.0
LUTH–Luth–MO Synod	1	258	469	558	0.8	1.4
MENN–CG in Cr (Menn)	1	NR	88	106	0.1	0.3
METH–Un Methodist	13	1,133	3,181	3,693	5.1	9.3
METH–Wesleyan	2	68	37	89	0.1	0.2
Non-denom Chr Chs	10	1,110	1,320	1,447	2.0	3.7
PENT–Assemb of God	5	2,163	1,714	2,984	4.1	7.5
PENT–Ch God (Cleve)	7	248	348	418	0.6	1.1
PENT–Ch of God Proph	2	NR	61	73	0.1	0.2
PENT–Pent Ch of God	1	70	NR	109	0.2	0.3
PENT–Un Pent Ch Intl	1	NR	NR	NR	-	-
PRES–Cumber Presb	4	NR	699	786	1.1	2.0
PRES–Orth Pres Ch	1	33	19	24	0.0	0.1
PRES–Presb Ch (USA)	4	138	270	324	0.4	0.8
PRES–Presb Ch Amer	1	149	175	225	0.3	0.6
Sev Day Adv	3	200	347	399	0.6	1.0
Un C of Christ	1	50	39	47	0.1	0.1
Unity Ch	1	NR	NR	NR	-	-

Religious Group	Number of Congregations	Number of Attendees	Number of Communicant, Confirmed, or Full Members	Adherents: Number of Adherents	Adherents: % of Total Pop.	Adherents: % of Total Adh.
RHEA	**82**	**5,762**	**12,297**	**15,691**	**49.3**	**100.0**
ANG/EPIS–Episcopal	1	19	33	33	0.1	0.2
Bahá'í	0	NR	2	2	0.0	0.0
BAPT–Reg Bapt Gen As	1	NR	NR	NR	-	-
BAPT–So Bapt Conv	21	2,159	6,468	7,927	24.9	50.5
Catholic	1	NR	NR	400	1.3	2.5
Ch God (7th Day)	1	NR	NR	NR	-	-
CHR–Chr Chs & Chs Cr	1	NR	40	49	0.2	0.3
CHR–Chs of Christ	3	230	198	262	0.8	1.7
Ind Fund Churches	1	NR	NR	NR	-	-
Jehovah's Witness	1	NR	NR	NR	-	-
LDS–L-D Saints	1	NR	NR	173	0.5	1.1
LUTH–Luth–MO Synod	1	34	49	49	0.2	0.3
METH–AME Zion	3	0	300	368	1.2	2.3
METH–Un Methodist	13	784	1,806	2,347	7.4	15.0
Non-denom Chr Chs	8	1,100	1,168	1,382	4.3	8.8
PENT–Ch God (Cleve)	12	970	1,431	1,754	5.5	11.2
PENT–Ch of God Proph	2	NR	50	61	0.2	0.4
PENT–Int Foursq Gos	2	85	188	230	0.7	1.5
PENT–Un Pent Ch Intl	1	NR	NR	NR	-	-
PRES–Presb Ch (USA)	1	30	50	61	0.2	0.4
PRES–Presb Ch Amer	1	75	33	41	0.1	0.3
Sev Day Adv	6	276	481	552	1.7	3.5
ROANE	**124**	**9,574**	**28,886**	**34,385**	**63.5**	**100.0**
ANG/EPIS–Episcopal	1	33	86	86	0.2	0.3
Bahá'í	0	NR	6	6	0.0	0.0
BAPT–Free Will Bapt	1	NR	96	114	0.2	0.3
BAPT–Natl Mis Bapt Conv	1	0	150	178	0.3	0.5
BAPT–So Bapt Conv	44	4,532	17,362	20,603	38.0	59.9
Catholic	1	NR	NR	500	0.9	1.5
CHR–Chr Ch (Disc)	2	94	380	451	0.8	1.3
CHR–Chr Chs & Chs Cr	7	NR	515	611	1.1	1.8
CHR–Chs of Christ	7	550	600	778	1.4	2.3
Ind Fund Churches	1	NR	NR	NR	-	-
Jehovah's Witness	1	NR	NR	NR	-	-
LDS–L-D Saints	1	NR	NR	339	0.6	1.0
LUTH–Luth–MO Synod	1	64	172	208	0.4	0.6
METH–AME Zion	3	0	400	475	0.9	1.4
METH–Free Methodist	1	55	40	55	0.1	0.2
METH–Un Methodist	13	897	2,042	2,341	4.3	6.8
METH–Wesleyan	1	14	12	18	0.0	0.1
Non-denom Chr Chs	16	2,791	5,540	5,810	10.7	16.9
PENT–Ch God (Cleve)	4	200	417	495	0.9	1.4
PENT–Ch God Mtn Asm	3	NR	NR	NR	-	-
PENT–Ch of God Proph	3	NR	92	109	0.2	0.3
PENT–Int Foursq Gos	1	40	208	247	0.5	0.7
PENT–Un Pent Ch Intl	1	NR	NR	NR	-	-
PRES–Cumber Presb	2	NR	127	202	0.4	0.6
PRES–Presb Ch (USA)	4	156	427	507	0.9	1.5
PRES–Presb Ch Amer	1	54	51	65	0.1	0.2
Sev Day Adv	3	94	163	187	0.3	0.5
ROBERTSON	**124**	**13,864**	**27,470**	**35,142**	**53.0**	**100.0**
ANG/EPIS–Episcopal	1	19	19	19	0.0	0.1
Bahá'í	0	NR	1	1	0.0	0.0
BAPT–Free Will Bapt	5	NR	480	601	0.9	1.7
BAPT–Ind Bapt Flwsp Intl	1	NR	NR	NR	-	-
BAPT–NBC Amer	2	0	300	376	0.6	1.1
BAPT–So Bapt Conv	36	4,608	13,582	17,009	25.7	48.4
Catholic	1	NR	NR	900	1.4	2.6
Ch of Nazarene	4	236	153	326	0.5	0.9
CHR–Chr Ch (Disc)	1	0	104	130	0.2	0.4
CHR–Chs of Christ	14	2,036	2,117	2,639	4.0	7.5
Jehovah's Witness	1	NR	NR	NR	-	-
LUTH–Luth–MO Synod	1	43	40	40	0.1	0.1
METH–AME	1	75	125	157	0.2	0.4
METH–C.M.E.	2	65	215	269	0.4	0.8
METH–Un Methodist	21	1,570	3,647	4,362	6.6	12.4
Non-denom Chr Chs	14	3,520	4,100	4,674	7.1	13.3
PENT–Assemb of God	4	1,134	1,250	1,931	2.9	5.5
PENT–Assm God Intl F	1	NR	NR	NR	-	-
PENT–Ch God (Cleve)	1	44	114	143	0.2	0.4

NR–Not Reported - Represents no adherents reported. Percentages may not total 100 due to rounding.

Table 3: Religious Congregations by County and Group: 2010

Religious Group	Number of Congrega-tions	Number of Attendees	Number of Communicant, Confirmed, or Full Members	Adherents		
				Number of Adherents	% of Total Pop.	% of Total Adh.
PENT–Ch of God Proph	1	NR	61	76	0.1	0.2
PENT–Un Pent Ch Intl	3	NR	NR	NR	-	-
PRES–Cumber Presb	2	NR	192	353	0.5	1.0
PRES–Presb Ch (USA)	2	65	190	238	0.4	0.7
Sev Day Adv	5	449	780	898	1.4	2.6
RUTHERFORD	**275**	**42,841**	**71,633**	**100,847**	**38.4**	**100.0**
ANG/EPIS–Anglican NA	1	NR	NR	NR	-	-
ANG/EPIS–Episcopal	3	473	1,115	1,190	0.5	1.2
Bahá'í	2	NR	110	110	0.0	0.1
BAPT–Amer Bapt Assn	2	NR	120	151	0.1	0.1
BAPT–Free Will Bapt	3	NR	288	362	0.1	0.4
BAPT–Natl Mis Bapt Conv	1	0	150	189	0.1	0.2
BAPT–NBC USA	1	315	500	629	0.2	0.6
BAPT–So Bapt Conv	65	13,925	31,018	38,992	14.8	38.7
BUDD–Theravada	2	NR	NR	675	0.3	0.7
Calv Chpl	1	NR	NR	NR	-	-
Catholic	2	NR	NR	8,600	3.3	8.5
CGOD–Ch God (Ander)	3	180	NR	180	0.1	0.2
Ch Cr, Scientst	1	NR	NR	NR	-	-
Ch of Nazarene	3	251	478	502	0.2	0.5
CHR–Chr Ch (Disc)	1	78	163	205	0.1	0.2
CHR–Chr Chs & Chs Cr	2	NR	100	126	0.0	0.1
CHR–Chs of Christ	54	8,518	7,974	10,224	3.9	10.1
Christian Brethren	1	NR	NR	NR	-	-
FRND–Fr Gen Cf	1	NR	0	0	0.0	0.0
HINDU–I/A Temples	1	NR	NR	250	0.1	0.2
Jehovah's Witness	2	NR	NR	NR	-	-
LDS–L-D Saints	6	NR	NR	2,528	1.0	2.5
LUTH–E.L.C.A.	1	119	239	274	0.1	0.3
LUTH–Luth Cong Msn Chr	1	45	60	75	0.0	0.1
LUTH–Luth–MO Synod	1	164	372	489	0.2	0.5
LUTH–Wisc Ev Luth Syn	1	91	135	182	0.1	0.2
METH–AME	3	0	260	327	0.1	0.3
METH–C.M.E.	1	0	150	189	0.1	0.2
METH–Free Methodist	2	170	168	199	0.1	0.2
METH–Un Methodist	31	3,792	9,926	11,701	4.5	11.6
METH–Wesleyan	1	20	13	26	0.0	0.0
Muslim Est	1	350	NR	500	0.2	0.5
Non-denom Chr Chs	31	11,719	13,839	15,913	6.1	15.8
ORTHE–Ant Orth of NA	1	81	NR	90	0.0	0.1
PENT–Assemb of God	8	1,197	1,290	1,752	0.7	1.7
PENT–Ch God (Cleve)	4	203	474	596	0.2	0.6
PENT–Ch of God Proph	2	NR	82	103	0.0	0.1
PENT–COGIC	2	90	300	377	0.1	0.4
PENT–Full Gosp Bapt	2	NR	NR	NR	-	-
PENT–Un Pent Ch Intl	4	NR	NR	NR	-	-
PRES–Cumber Presb	7	NR	470	836	0.3	0.8
PRES–Presb Ch (USA)	6	551	1,139	1,432	0.5	1.4
PRES–Presb Ch Amer	1	164	179	238	0.1	0.2
Salvation Army	1	41	44	74	0.0	0.1
Sev Day Adv	3	244	425	489	0.2	0.5
Unit Univ	1	60	52	72	0.0	0.1
Unity Ch	1	NR	NR	NR	-	-
SCOTT	**29**	**2,265**	**5,301**	**6,419**	**28.9**	**100.0**
BAPT–Natl Mis Bapt Conv	2	0	175	217	1.0	3.4
BAPT–So Bapt Conv	13	1,247	3,543	4,401	19.8	68.6
Catholic	1	NR	NR	32	0.1	0.5
CHR–Chs of Christ	2	170	150	183	0.8	2.9
Jehovah's Witness	1	NR	NR	NR	-	-
METH–Un Methodist	1	80	220	238	1.1	3.7
Non-denom Chr Chs	4	630	975	987	4.4	15.4
PENT–Assemb of God	1	20	25	97	0.4	1.5
PENT–Ch God (Cleve)	1	72	83	103	0.5	1.6
PENT–Ch of God Proph	1	NR	29	36	0.2	0.6
PENT–Un Pent Ch Intl	1	NR	NR	NR	-	-
PRES–Presb Ch (USA)	1	46	101	125	0.6	1.9
SEQUATCHIE	**33**	**2,573**	**4,624**	**6,035**	**42.8**	**100.0**
Bahá'í	0	NR	2	2	0.0	0.0
BAPT–So Bapt Conv	8	1,000	2,168	2,646	18.8	43.8
Catholic	1	NR	NR	200	1.4	3.3

Religious Group	Number of Congrega-tions	Number of Attendees	Number of Communicant, Confirmed, or Full Members	Adherents		
				Number of Adherents	% of Total Pop.	% of Total Adh.
CHR–Chs of Christ	5	340	282	393	2.8	6.5
METH–Cong Meth	1	NR	23	28	0.2	0.5
METH–Un Methodist	2	272	597	826	5.9	13.7
Non-denom Chr Chs	1	101	101	126	0.9	2.1
PENT–Assemb of God	1	52	35	75	0.5	1.2
PENT–Ch God (Cleve)	10	682	1,102	1,345	9.5	22.3
PENT–Ch of God Proph	1	NR	54	66	0.5	1.1
PENT–Un Pent Ch Intl	1	NR	NR	NR	-	-
PRES–Cumber Presb	1	NR	40	75	0.5	1.2
Sev Day Adv	1	126	220	253	1.8	4.2
SEVIER	**147**	**16,286**	**34,066**	**46,589**	**51.8**	**100.0**
ANG/EPIS–Episcopal	3	154	293	302	0.3	0.6
Bahá'í	0	NR	17	17	0.0	0.0
BAPT–So Bapt Conv	67	8,057	23,830	28,609	31.8	61.4
Catholic	3	NR	NR	2,846	3.2	6.1
CGOD–Ch God (Ander)	1	23	NR	23	0.0	0.0
Ch of Nazarene	1	23	25	25	0.0	0.1
CHR–Chr Chs & Chs Cr	4	NR	750	900	1.0	1.9
CHR–Chs of Christ	8	718	442	568	0.6	1.2
FRND–Fr Gen Cf	1	NR	0	0	0.0	0.0
Jehovah's Witness	2	NR	NR	NR	-	-
LDS–L-D Saints	2	NR	NR	691	0.8	1.5
LUTH–E.L.C.A.	1	50	105	107	0.1	0.2
LUTH–Luth–MO Synod	2	111	178	204	0.2	0.4
METH–Un Methodist	21	1,931	3,750	4,374	4.9	9.4
Muslim Est	1	134	NR	308	0.3	0.7
Non-denom Chr Chs	14	3,239	2,187	4,291	4.8	9.2
PENT–Assemb of God	4	406	132	454	0.5	1.0
PENT–Ch God (Cleve)	6	1,001	1,897	2,277	2.5	4.9
PENT–Un Pent Ch Intl	1	NR	NR	NR	-	-
PRES–Presb Ch (USA)	3	66	129	155	0.2	0.3
PRES–Presb Ch Amer	1	300	204	292	0.3	0.6
Sev Day Adv	1	73	127	146	0.2	0.3
SHELBY	**1,026**	**171,135**	**413,405**	**588,132**	**63.4**	**100.0**
ANG/EPIS–Anglican NA	3	NR	NR	NR	-	-
ANG/EPIS–Episcopal	18	2,847	6,210	7,009	0.8	1.2
Bahá'í	1	NR	229	229	0.0	0.0
BAPT–Alliance Bapt	1	NR	NR	NR	-	-
BAPT–Amer Bapt Assn	1	NR	60	75	0.0	0.0
BAPT–Amer Bapt USA	6	555	2,178	2,728	0.3	0.5
BAPT–Free Will Bapt	2	NR	192	240	0.0	0.0
BAPT–Natl Mis Bapt Conv	15	600	2,600	3,256	0.4	0.6
BAPT–NBC Amer	8	850	1,626	2,037	0.2	0.3
BAPT–NBC USA	103	24,301	61,393	76,893	8.3	13.1
BAPT–Prog NBC	8	4,800	10,060	12,600	1.4	2.1
BAPT–Ref Bapt Ch	1	NR	NR	NR	-	-
BAPT–So Bapt Conv	155	30,398	109,578	137,244	14.8	23.3
BUDD–Mahayana	5	NR	NR	1,363	0.1	0.2
BUDD–Theravada	3	NR	NR	425	0.0	0.1
BUDD–Vajrayana	1	NR	NR	52	0.0	0.0
Calv Chpl	2	NR	NR	NR	-	-
Catholic	28	NR	NR	60,500	6.5	10.3
CGOD–Ch God (Ander)	6	54	NR	54	0.0	0.0
Ch Cr, Scientst	1	NR	NR	NR	-	-
Ch of Chr (Hol)	1	NR	NR	NR	-	-
Ch of Nazarene	19	1,313	2,270	2,302	0.2	0.4
Chr & Miss Al	1	12	11	12	0.0	0.0
CHR–Chr Ch (Disc)	18	2,993	25,095	31,431	3.4	5.3
CHR–Chr Chs & Chs Cr	3	NR	1,675	2,098	0.2	0.4
CHR–Chs of Christ	65	14,005	14,520	18,798	2.0	3.2
CHR–Int Chs of Christ	1	NR	77	96	0.0	0.0
Evan Free Ch	1	30	NR	30	0.0	0.0
FRND–Fr Gen Cf	1	NR	37	46	0.0	0.0
HINDU–I/A Temples	2	NR	NR	1,792	0.2	0.3
HINDU–Post Ren	2	NR	NR	41	0.0	0.0
HINDU–Trad Temples	1	NR	NR	3,000	0.3	0.5
Jain	1	NR	NR	NR	-	-
Jehovah's Witness	15	NR	NR	NR	-	-
JUD–Conserv	1	249	280	756	0.1	0.1
JUD–Orth	4	2,574	1,000	3,575	0.4	0.6
JUD–Reform	1	887	1,564	4,223	0.5	0.7

NR–Not Reported   - Represents no adherents reported.   Percentages may not total 100 due to rounding.

Table 3: Religious Congregations by County and Group: 2010

Religious Group	Number of Congrega-tions	Number of Attendees	Number of Communicant, Confirmed, or Full Members	Adherents		
				Number of Adherents	% of Total Pop.	% of Total Adh.
LDS–Comm of Christ	1	NR	156	156	0.0	0.0
LDS–L-D Saints	12	NR	NR	5,776	0.6	1.0
LUTH–E.L.C.A.	4	319	565	743	0.1	0.1
LUTH–Luth–MO Synod	10	1,638	2,926	3,422	0.4	0.6
LUTH–Nor Amer Luth C	1	NR	NR	NR	-	-
LUTH–Wisc Ev Luth Syn	1	80	124	159	0.0	0.0
METH–AME	27	375	3,380	4,233	0.5	0.7
METH–AME Zion	7	0	900	1,127	0.1	0.2
METH–C.M.E.	33	915	6,350	7,953	0.9	1.4
METH–Evan Meth Ch	1	NR	NR	NR	-	-
METH–So Methodist	1	NR	NR	NR	-	-
METH–Un Methodist	57	9,826	33,135	37,981	4.1	6.5
METH–Wesleyan	1	27	50	35	0.0	0.0
MJEW–Union Mes Cong	1	NR	NR	NR	-	-
Muslim Est	8	1,816	NR	4,468	0.5	0.8
New Apost Ch	1	NR	NR	NR	-	-
Non-denom Chr Chs	145	42,993	57,909	63,204	6.8	10.7
OCATH–Un Cath Ch	1	NR	NR	702	0.1	0.1
ORTHE–Ant Orth of NA	1	150	NR	300	0.0	0.1
ORTHE–Greek Orthodox	1	175	NR	550	0.1	0.1
ORTHE–Orth Ch in Amer	1	40	NR	125	0.0	0.0
ORTHO–Armen Ap Etchm	1	25	NR	50	0.0	0.0
ORTHO–Coptic Orth Ch	1	67	NR	100	0.0	0.0
ORTHO–Ethiopian Orth	1	NR	NR	NR	-	-
PENT–Assemb of God	15	3,815	6,108	7,246	0.8	1.2
PENT–Ch God (Cleve)	8	229	755	946	0.1	0.2
PENT–Ch Lord Jesus Apos	2	NR	NR	NR	-	-
PENT–Ch of God by Faith	2	NR	NR	NR	-	-
PENT–Ch of God Proph	3	NR	183	229	0.0	0.0
PENT–COGIC	83	14,139	34,168	42,795	4.6	7.3
PENT–Full Gosp Bapt	6	NR	NR	NR	-	-
PENT–Intl Pent Holiness	5	291	378	473	0.1	0.1
PENT–Un Pent Ch Intl	8	NR	NR	NR	-	-
PENT–Vineyard	1	43	58	73	0.0	0.0
PRES–As Ref Pres Ch	2	NR	114	143	0.0	0.0
PRES–Cumber Presb	10	NR	833	1,502	0.2	0.3
PRES–Evan Presby Ch	7	NR	11,156	13,973	1.5	2.4
PRES–Korean Pres Amer	4	NR	NR	NR	-	-
PRES–Orth Pres Ch	1	27	23	30	0.0	0.0
PRES–Presb Ch (USA)	19	3,219	5,808	7,274	0.8	1.2
PRES–Presb Ch Amer	6	1,760	2,860	3,592	0.4	0.6
Salvation Army	2	97	203	451	0.0	0.1
Sev Day Adv	9	1,987	3,456	3,974	0.4	0.7
Sikh	1	NR	NR	NR	-	-
Un C of Christ	3	342	621	778	0.1	0.1
Unit Univ	3	272	531	664	0.1	0.1
Unity Ch	3	NR	NR	NR	-	-
SMITH	**46**	**2,577**	**5,336**	**6,417**	**33.5**	**100.0**
Bahá'í	0	NR	1	1	0.0	0.0
BAPT–Free Will Bapt	1	NR	96	118	0.6	1.8
BAPT–So Bapt Conv	10	844	2,388	2,931	15.3	45.7
Ch of Nazarene	2	125	134	187	1.0	2.9
CHR–Chs of Christ	6	498	426	535	2.8	8.3
Jehovah's Witness	1	NR	NR	NR	-	-
METH–AME	2	0	250	307	1.6	4.8
METH–Un Methodist	14	542	1,169	1,256	6.6	19.6
Non-denom Chr Chs	3	375	375	468	2.4	7.3
PENT–Ch God (Cleve)	3	169	331	406	2.1	6.3
PENT–Ch of God Proph	2	NR	76	93	0.5	1.4
PRES–Cumber Presb	1	NR	48	67	0.3	1.0
Sev Day Adv	1	24	42	48	0.3	0.7
STEWART	**58**	**2,879**	**5,182**	**7,143**	**53.6**	**100.0**
BAPT–Free Will Bapt	5	NR	480	579	4.3	8.1
BAPT–So Bapt Conv	15	924	2,635	3,178	23.9	44.5
Catholic	1	NR	NR	220	1.7	3.1
CGOD–Ch God (Ander)	4	352	NR	352	2.6	4.9
Ch of Nazarene	2	89	177	189	1.4	2.6
CHR–Chr Ch (Disc)	1	0	0	0	0.0	0.0
CHR–Chs of Christ	9	429	364	501	3.8	7.0
Jehovah's Witness	1	NR	NR	NR	-	-
METH–Un Methodist	13	550	1,147	1,321	9.9	18.5
Non-denom Chr Chs	1	100	150	150	1.1	2.1
PENT–Assemb of God	2	295	205	375	2.8	5.2
PENT–Pent Ch of God	2	140	NR	217	1.6	3.0
PENT–Un Pent Ch Intl	1	NR	NR	NR	-	-
PRES–Cumber Presb	1	NR	24	61	0.5	0.9
SULLIVAN	**297**	**30,479**	**70,415**	**87,742**	**55.9**	**100.0**
ANG/EPIS–Episcopal	4	295	518	768	0.5	0.9
Bahá'í	0	NR	19	19	0.0	0.0
BAPT–Amer Bapt USA	1	140	350	414	0.3	0.5
BAPT–Asc Ref Bap Ch Am	1	NR	NR	NR	-	-
BAPT–Free Will Bapt	19	NR	1,560	1,847	1.2	2.1
BAPT–NBC USA	1	0	150	178	0.1	0.2
BAPT–Prim Bapt E Dst	6	150	533	631	0.4	0.7
BAPT–Ref Bapt Ch	2	NR	NR	NR	-	-
BAPT–So Bapt Conv	62	10,975	30,694	36,341	23.2	41.4
BRETH–Ch of Brethren	3	44	129	153	0.1	0.2
Catholic	1	NR	NR	2,245	1.4	2.6
CGOD–Ch God (Ander)	3	254	NR	254	0.2	0.3
Ch Cr, Scientist	1	NR	NR	NR	-	-
Ch God (7th Day)	1	NR	NR	NR	-	-
Ch of Nazarene	2	112	167	167	0.1	0.2
CHR–Chr Ch (Disc)	1	39	67	79	0.1	0.1
CHR–Chr Chs & Chs Cr	19	NR	4,446	5,264	3.4	6.0
CHR–Chs of Christ	5	493	439	568	0.4	0.6
Evan Free Ch	1	40	NR	40	0.0	0.0
HINDU–Trad Temples	1	NR	NR	100	0.1	0.1
Ind Fund Churches	1	NR	NR	NR	-	-
Jehovah's Witness	3	NR	NR	NR	-	-
JUD–Reform	1	29	52	140	0.1	0.2
LDS–L-D Saints	2	NR	NR	1,107	0.7	1.3
LUTH–E.L.C.A.	3	234	934	1,013	0.6	1.2
LUTH–Luth–MO Synod	2	91	129	162	0.1	0.2
METH–AME Zion	3	175	376	445	0.3	0.5
METH–Un Methodist	45	4,757	12,964	15,476	9.9	17.6
Non-denom Chr Chs	42	8,413	10,090	11,390	7.3	13.0
ORTHE–Greek Orthodox	1	30	NR	140	0.1	0.2
PENT–Assemb of God	7	779	627	1,137	0.7	1.3
PENT–Ch God (Cleve)	5	496	924	1,094	0.7	1.2
PENT–Ch of God Proph	2	NR	42	50	0.0	0.1
PENT–COGIC	1	0	150	178	0.1	0.2
PENT–Full Gosp Bapt	2	NR	NR	NR	-	-
PENT–Intl Pent Holiness	5	86	137	162	0.1	0.2
PENT–Un Pent Ch Intl	4	NR	NR	NR	-	-
PRES–Bible Pres	1	NR	NR	NR	-	-
PRES–Evan Presby Ch	1	NR	71	84	0.1	0.1
PRES–Presb Ch (USA)	20	1,620	3,240	3,836	2.4	4.4
PRES–Presb Ch Amer	7	843	950	1,130	0.7	1.3
Salvation Army	2	196	329	751	0.5	0.9
Sev Day Adv	3	188	328	377	0.2	0.4
Zoroastrian	0	NR	NR	2	0.0	0.0
SUMNER	**179**	**27,979**	**53,496**	**73,385**	**45.7**	**100.0**
ANG/EPIS–Anglican NA	1	NR	NR	NR	-	-
ANG/EPIS–Episcopal	2	140	268	323	0.2	0.4
Bahá'í	1	NR	48	48	0.0	0.1
BAPT–Free Will Bapt	3	NR	288	358	0.2	0.5
BAPT–Natl Mis Bapt Conv	2	0	150	186	0.1	0.3
BAPT–NBC USA	4	430	980	1,217	0.8	1.7
BAPT–So Bapt Conv	45	12,482	29,404	36,501	22.7	49.7
Catholic	2	NR	NR	5,500	3.4	7.5
Ch of Nazarene	6	1,313	1,322	1,566	1.0	2.1
CHR–Chs of Christ	32	5,036	5,145	6,631	4.1	9.0
Jehovah's Witness	2	NR	NR	NR	-	-
LDS–L-D Saints	2	NR	NR	1,223	0.8	1.7
LUTH–E.L.C.A.	1	215	504	569	0.4	0.8
LUTH–Luth–MO Synod	1	83	161	204	0.1	0.3
METH–AME	2	125	300	372	0.2	0.5
METH–Free Methodist	2	99	104	105	0.1	0.1
METH–Un Methodist	21	2,283	6,424	8,252	5.1	11.2
Muslim Est	1	134	NR	308	0.2	0.4
Non-denom Chr Chs	19	4,005	4,635	5,309	3.3	7.2
PENT–Assemb of God	5	419	303	609	0.4	0.8

NR–Not Reported   - Represents no adherents reported.   Percentages may not total 100 due to rounding.

Table 3: Religious Congregations by County and Group: 2010

Religious Group	Number of Congrega-tions	Number of Attendees	Number of Communicant, Confirmed, or Full Members	Adherents		
				Number of Adherents	% of Total Pop.	% of Total Adh.
PENT–Ch God (Cleve)	3	214	482	598	0.4	0.8
PENT–Ch of God Proph	5	NR	410	509	0.3	0.7
PENT–COGIC	1	0	150	186	0.1	0.3
PENT–Un Pent Ch Intl	2	NR	NR	NR	-	-
PRES–Cumber Presb	5	NR	376	386	0.2	0.5
PRES–Presb Ch (USA)	3	319	855	1,061	0.7	1.4
Sev Day Adv	6	682	1,187	1,364	0.8	1.9
TIPTON	**116**	**7,566**	**19,314**	**25,614**	**41.9**	**100.0**
ANG/EPIS–Episcopal	4	78	123	128	0.2	0.5
Bahá'í	0	NR	4	4	0.0	0.0
BAPT–Natl Mis Bapt Conv	6	280	550	692	1.1	2.7
BAPT–NBC USA	4	250	860	1,082	1.8	4.2
BAPT–Prog NBC	1	0	150	189	0.3	0.7
BAPT–So Bapt Conv	27	3,116	9,568	12,038	19.7	47.0
Catholic	1	NR	NR	450	0.7	1.8
Ch of Nazarene	2	89	140	140	0.2	0.5
CHR–Chr Chs & Chs Cr	1	NR	300	377	0.6	1.5
CHR–Chs of Christ	8	806	731	1,082	1.8	4.2
Jehovah's Witness	1	NR	NR	NR	-	-
LUTH–Luth-MO Synod	1	30	33	38	0.1	0.1
METH–AME	1	50	80	101	0.2	0.4
METH–C.M.E.	6	0	900	1,132	1.9	4.4
METH–Free Methodist	1	40	13	40	0.1	0.2
METH–Un Methodist	13	1,162	2,853	3,605	5.9	14.1
Non-denom Chr Chs	8	645	910	968	1.6	3.8
PENT–Assemb of God	10	905	608	1,462	2.4	5.7
PENT–Ch God (Cleve)	1	23	6	8	0.0	0.0
PENT–Pent Ch of God	1	70	NR	109	0.2	0.4
PENT–Un Pent Ch Intl	4	NR	NR	NR	-	-
PRES–As Ref Pres Ch	4	NR	299	376	0.6	1.5
PRES–Cumber Presb	4	NR	632	899	1.5	3.5
PRES–Evan Presby Ch	2	NR	169	213	0.3	0.8
PRES–Presb Ch (USA)	3	0	349	439	0.7	1.7
PRES–Presb Ch Amer	1	13	20	24	0.0	0.1
Sev Day Adv	1	9	16	18	0.0	0.1
TROUSDALE	**20**	**1,015**	**2,153**	**2,661**	**33.8**	**100.0**
BAPT–Asc Ref Bap Ch Am	1	NR	NR	NR	-	-
BAPT–NBC USA	1	125	250	306	3.9	11.5
BAPT–Ref Bapt Ch	1	NR	NR	NR	-	-
BAPT–So Bapt Conv	3	153	669	820	10.4	30.8
CHR–Chs of Christ	4	327	300	423	5.4	15.9
METH–AME	1	0	150	184	2.3	6.9
METH–Un Methodist	4	167	401	529	6.7	19.9
Non-denom Chr Chs	2	200	300	300	3.8	11.3
PENT–Ch God (Cleve)	1	43	49	60	0.8	2.3
PENT–Ch of God Proph	1	NR	20	25	0.3	0.9
PRES–Cumber Presb	1	NR	14	14	0.2	0.5
UNICOI	**44**	**2,143**	**7,153**	**8,446**	**46.1**	**100.0**
Bahá'í	0	NR	2	2	0.0	0.0
BAPT–Free Will Bapt	6	NR	576	683	3.7	8.1
BAPT–So Bapt Conv	13	893	3,848	4,563	24.9	54.0
BRETH–Ch of Brethren	1	0	67	79	0.4	0.9
CGOD–Ch God (Ander)	1	0	NR	0	0.0	0.0
Ch of Nazarene	1	21	43	43	0.2	0.5
CHR–Chr Chs & Chs Cr	5	NR	630	747	4.1	8.8
CHR–Chs of Christ	2	167	160	185	1.0	2.2
Jehovah's Witness	1	NR	NR	NR	-	-
METH–Un Methodist	4	343	841	946	5.2	11.2
Non-denom Chr Chs	2	225	220	281	1.5	3.3
PENT–Assemb of God	1	18	23	35	0.2	0.4
PENT–Ch God (Cleve)	3	238	258	306	1.7	3.6
PENT–Intl Pent Holiness	1	132	267	317	1.7	3.8
PRES–Presb Ch (USA)	3	106	218	259	1.4	3.1
UNION	**27**	**1,935**	**5,498**	**6,800**	**35.6**	**100.0**
Bahá'í	0	NR	3	3	0.0	0.0
BAPT–Free Will Bapt	1	NR	96	118	0.6	1.7
BAPT–So Bapt Conv	19	1,601	5,008	6,143	32.1	90.3
CHR–Chr Chs & Chs Cr	1	NR	22	27	0.1	0.4

Religious Group	Number of Congrega-tions	Number of Attendees	Number of Communicant, Confirmed, or Full Members	Adherents		
				Number of Adherents	% of Total Pop.	% of Total Adh.
CHR–Chs of Christ	1	40	40	48	0.3	0.7
METH–Un Methodist	3	102	133	181	0.9	2.7
Non-denom Chr Chs	1	100	70	125	0.7	1.8
PENT–Ch God (Cleve)	1	92	126	155	0.8	2.3
VAN BUREN	**23**	**1,026**	**1,417**	**1,729**	**31.2**	**100.0**
BAPT–So Bapt Conv	4	147	475	564	10.2	32.6
CHR–Chs of Christ	11	513	388	550	9.9	31.8
METH–Un Methodist	1	16	62	62	1.1	3.6
Non-denom Chr Chs	1	100	150	150	2.7	8.7
PENT–Ch God (Cleve)	3	210	230	273	4.9	15.8
PENT–Ch of God Proph	2	NR	43	51	0.9	2.9
Sev Day Adv	1	40	69	79	1.4	4.6
WARREN	**125**	**10,687**	**16,434**	**21,764**	**54.6**	**100.0**
ANG/EPIS–Episcopal	1	54	120	126	0.3	0.6
Bahá'í	0	NR	6	6	0.0	0.0
BAPT–Free Will Bapt	2	NR	192	237	0.6	1.1
BAPT–Natl Mis Bapt Conv	1	0	150	185	0.5	0.9
BAPT–So Bapt Conv	27	2,595	7,029	8,688	21.8	39.9
BRETH–Breth in Chr	1	NR	NR	NR	-	-
Catholic	1	NR	NR	500	1.3	2.3
CGOD–Ch God (Ander)	1	177	NR	177	0.4	0.8
Ch God (7th Day)	1	NR	NR	NR	-	-
CHR–Chs of Christ	43	4,754	4,593	5,787	14.5	26.6
HINDU–Post Ren	1	NR	NR	100	0.3	0.5
Jehovah's Witness	1	NR	NR	NR	-	-
LDS–L-D Saints	2	NR	NR	678	1.7	3.1
LUTH–Luth-MO Synod	1	55	54	66	0.2	0.3
MENN–Menn Chr Fell	1	48	21	48	0.1	0.2
METH–Free Methodist	1	23	35	35	0.1	0.2
METH–Un Methodist	9	717	1,265	1,388	3.5	6.4
Non-denom Chr Chs	9	1,620	1,720	2,028	5.1	9.3
PENT–Assemb of God	4	220	130	311	0.8	1.4
PENT–Ch God (Cleve)	4	270	389	481	1.2	2.2
PENT–Ch of God Proph	3	NR	173	214	0.5	1.0
PENT–Un Pent Ch Intl	1	NR	NR	NR	-	-
PRES–Cumber Presb	6	NR	258	356	0.9	1.6
PRES–Presb Ch (USA)	2	40	100	124	0.3	0.6
Sev Day Adv	2	114	199	229	0.6	1.1
WASHINGTON	**247**	**23,207**	**55,144**	**69,909**	**56.8**	**100.0**
ANG/EPIS–Anglican NA	1	NR	NR	NR	-	-
ANG/EPIS–Episcopal	2	182	549	549	0.4	0.8
Bahá'í	0	NR	12	12	0.0	0.0
BAPT–Free Will Bapt	20	NR	1,920	2,275	1.8	3.3
BAPT–NBC USA	1	280	350	415	0.3	0.6
BAPT–S-D Baptist Gen Con	1	13	10	12	0.0	0.0
BAPT–So Bapt Conv	53	8,072	22,024	26,096	21.2	37.3
BRETH–Ch of Brethren	7	235	565	669	0.5	1.0
BRETH–Grace Breth	1	NR	NR	NR	-	-
Calv Chpl	1	NR	NR	NR	-	-
Catholic	1	NR	NR	3,000	2.4	4.3
CGOD–Ch God (Ander)	4	137	NR	137	0.1	0.2
Ch Cr, Scientst	1	NR	NR	NR	-	-
Ch of Nazarene	2	13	62	62	0.1	0.1
Chr & Miss Al	1	117	73	168	0.1	0.2
CHR–Chr Ch (Disc)	1	0	163	193	0.2	0.3
CHR–Chr Chs & Chs Cr	25	NR	6,046	7,164	5.8	10.2
CHR–Chs of Christ	8	785	809	1,039	0.8	1.5
FRND–Fr Gen Cf	1	NR	7	8	0.0	0.0
Ind Fund Churches	1	NR	NR	NR	-	-
Jehovah's Witness	2	NR	NR	NR	-	-
LDS–L-D Saints	2	NR	NR	1,397	1.1	2.0
LUTH–E.L.C.A.	2	217	309	694	0.6	1.0
LUTH–Luth-MO Synod	1	80	184	216	0.2	0.3
LUTH–Wisc Ev Luth Syn	1	126	193	278	0.2	0.4
METH–AME Zion	2	0	200	237	0.2	0.3
METH–Un Methodist	31	3,475	8,299	9,673	7.9	13.8
Muslim Est	1	134	NR	308	0.3	0.4
Non-denom Chr Chs	27	6,553	9,243	9,995	8.1	14.3
ORTHE–Ant Orth of NA	1	35	NR	45	0.0	0.1
PENT–Assemb of God	5	358	335	429	0.3	0.6

NR–Not Reported - Represents no adherents reported. Percentages may not total 100 due to rounding.

Table 3: Religious Congregations by County and Group: 2010

Religious Group	Number of Congrega-tions	Number of Attendees	Number of Communicant, Confirmed, or Full Members	Adherents		
				Number of Adherents	% of Total Pop.	% of Total Adh.
PENT–Ch God (Cleve)	8	562	803	951	0.8	1.4
PENT–Ch of God Proph	1	NR	75	89	0.1	0.1
PENT–COGIC	2	89	71	84	0.1	0.1
PENT–Fire Bapt Hol Ch	1	NR	NR	NR	-	-
PENT–Intl Pent Holiness	1	25	25	30	0.0	0.0
PENT–Un Pent Ch Intl	2	NR	NR	NR	-	-
PRES–As Ref Pres Ch	1	NR	0	0	0.0	0.0
PRES–Cumber Presb	2	NR	68	78	0.1	0.1
PRES–Presb Ch (USA)	12	760	1,485	1,760	1.4	2.5
PRES–Presb Ch Amer	6	501	583	749	0.6	1.1
Salvation Army	1	68	72	356	0.3	0.5
Sev Day Adv	1	267	464	534	0.4	0.8
Unit Univ	1	123	145	207	0.2	0.3
Unity Ch	1	NR	NR	NR	-	-
WAYNE	**63**	**2,957**	**5,669**	**6,670**	**39.2**	**100.0**
Bahá'í	0	NR	4	4	0.0	0.1
BAPT–So Bapt Conv	21	1,233	3,222	3,770	22.1	56.5
Catholic	1	NR	NR	75	0.4	1.1
CHR–Chr Ch (Disc)	1	10	35	41	0.2	0.6
CHR–Chs of Christ	11	698	661	790	4.6	11.8
Jehovah's Witness	1	NR	NR	NR	-	-
METH–Un Methodist	17	638	1,075	1,221	7.2	18.3
Non-denom Chr Chs	1	100	140	140	0.8	2.1
PENT–Ch God (Cleve)	3	218	299	350	2.1	5.2
PENT–Ch of God Proph	1	NR	38	44	0.3	0.7
PENT–Intl Pent Holiness	2	30	26	30	0.2	0.4
PENT–Un Pent Ch Intl	1	NR	NR	NR	-	-
PRES–Cumber Presb	1	NR	51	68	0.4	1.0
PRES–Presb Ch (USA)	1	0	66	77	0.5	1.2
Sev Day Adv	1	30	52	60	0.4	0.9
WEAKLEY	**119**	**8,382**	**19,110**	**23,377**	**66.8**	**100.0**
BAPT–Natl Mis Bapt Conv	1	0	150	177	0.5	0.8
BAPT–So Bapt Conv	53	4,959	14,114	16,684	47.6	71.4
Catholic	1	NR	NR	245	0.7	1.0
CHR–Chr Chs & Chs Cr	1	NR	80	95	0.3	0.4
CHR–Chs of Christ	18	1,780	1,714	2,104	6.0	9.0
Jehovah's Witness	1	NR	NR	NR	-	-
MENN–Amish Undif	1	NR	17	70	0.2	0.3
METH–C.M.E.	1	0	100	118	0.3	0.5
METH–Un Methodist	21	891	1,960	2,184	6.2	9.3
Muslim Est	1	134	NR	308	0.9	1.3
Non-denom Chr Chs	3	450	450	564	1.6	2.4
PENT–Assemb of God	3	146	105	207	0.6	0.9
PENT–Ch God (Cleve)	1	22	26	31	0.1	0.1
PENT–Un Pent Ch Intl	3	NR	NR	NR	-	-
PRES–Cumber Presb	8	NR	228	394	1.1	1.7
PRES–Evan Presby Ch	1	NR	103	122	0.3	0.5
PRES–Presb Ch (USA)	1	0	63	74	0.2	0.3
WHITE	**89**	**6,750**	**9,800**	**12,054**	**46.6**	**100.0**
Bahá'í	0	NR	1	1	0.0	0.0
BAPT–Free Will Bapt	1	NR	96	116	0.4	1.0
BAPT–So Bapt Conv	16	1,663	3,873	4,681	18.1	38.8
BRETH–Breth in Chr	1	NR	NR	NR	-	-
Catholic	1	NR	NR	290	1.1	2.4
Ch of Nazarene	2	172	187	219	0.8	1.8
CHR–Chr Ch (Disc)	1	0	100	121	0.5	1.0
CHR–Chs of Christ	25	1,845	1,717	2,170	8.4	18.0
Jehovah's Witness	1	NR	NR	NR	-	-
MENN–Menn Chr Fell	1	217	97	217	0.8	1.8
METH–Un Methodist	15	1,239	1,418	1,450	5.6	12.0
Non-denom Chr Chs	7	960	990	1,202	4.7	10.0
PENT–Assemb of God	1	52	73	78	0.3	0.6
PENT–Ch God (Cleve)	8	602	1,083	1,309	5.1	10.9
PENT–Ch of God Proph	2	NR	61	74	0.3	0.6
PENT–Un Pent Ch Intl	1	NR	NR	NR	-	-
PRES–Cumber Presb	2	NR	14	17	0.1	0.1
PRES–Presb Ch (USA)	4	0	90	109	0.4	0.9

Religious Group	Number of Congrega-tions	Number of Attendees	Number of Communicant, Confirmed, or Full Members	Adherents		
				Number of Adherents	% of Total Pop.	% of Total Adh.
WILLIAMSON	**200**	**48,544**	**73,246**	**113,633**	**62.0**	**100.0**
ANG/EPIS–Anglican NA	1	NR	NR	NR	-	-
ANG/EPIS–Episcopal	3	648	1,823	2,517	1.4	2.2
Bahá'í	3	NR	114	114	0.1	0.1
BAPT–Free Will Bapt	2	NR	192	248	0.1	0.2
BAPT–Natl Mis Bapt Conv	1	0	150	194	0.1	0.2
BAPT–So Bapt Conv	40	16,285	23,196	29,927	16.3	26.3
Calv Chpl	3	NR	NR	NR	-	-
Catholic	3	NR	NR	16,836	9.2	14.8
Ch of Nazarene	6	692	886	894	0.5	0.8
Chr & Miss Al	1	70	37	88	0.0	0.1
CHR–Chr Chs & Chs Cr	3	NR	1,600	2,064	1.1	1.8
CHR–Chs of Christ	38	6,340	5,766	7,484	4.1	6.6
Jehovah's Witness	1	NR	NR	NR	-	-
JUD–Reform	1	257	454	1,226	0.7	1.1
LDS–L-D Saints	2	NR	NR	1,231	0.7	1.1
LUTH–E.L.C.A.	1	264	504	725	0.4	0.6
LUTH–Luth–MO Synod	1	117	150	194	0.1	0.2
METH–AME	1	0	100	129	0.1	0.1
METH–So Methodist	1	NR	NR	NR	-	-
METH–Un Methodist	24	5,531	15,405	20,828	11.4	18.3
Muslim Est	1	20	NR	100	0.1	0.1
Non-denom Chr Chs	28	14,620	16,560	18,934	10.3	16.7
ORTHE–Ant Orth of NA	1	171	NR	474	0.3	0.4
PENT–Assemb of God	4	319	190	381	0.2	0.3
PENT–Ch God (Cleve)	2	230	320	413	0.2	0.4
PENT–Ch of God Proph	1	NR	33	43	0.0	0.0
PENT–Int Foursq Gos	2	870	956	1,233	0.7	1.1
PENT–Un Pent Ch Intl	2	NR	NR	NR	-	-
PENT–Vineyard	1	150	165	213	0.1	0.2
PRES–Cumber Presb	8	NR	646	1,077	0.6	0.9
PRES–Presb Ch (USA)	7	795	1,914	2,469	1.3	2.2
PRES–Presb Ch Amer	3	1,003	1,804	3,274	1.8	2.9
REF–Comm Ref Evan	1	NR	NR	NR	-	-
Sev Day Adv	3	162	281	323	0.2	0.3
WILSON	**165**	**20,652**	**40,650**	**53,425**	**46.9**	**100.0**
ANG/EPIS–Episcopal	1	43	78	106	0.1	0.2
Bahá'í	1	NR	27	27	0.0	0.1
BAPT–Natl Mis Bapt Conv	4	100	600	744	0.7	1.4
BAPT–So Bapt Conv	48	8,661	22,573	28,003	24.6	52.4
Catholic	1	NR	NR	900	0.8	1.7
CGOD–Ch God (Ander)	1	0	NR	0	0.0	0.0
Ch of Nazarene	3	324	564	655	0.6	1.2
CHR–Chs of Christ	35	5,208	5,186	6,688	5.9	12.5
Evan Cov Ch	1	56	0	73	0.1	0.1
Jehovah's Witness	2	NR	NR	NR	-	-
LDS–L-D Saints	4	NR	NR	1,326	1.2	2.5
LUTH–E.L.C.A.	2	126	262	355	0.3	0.7
METH–AME	3	0	650	806	0.7	1.5
METH–C.M.E.	1	0	100	124	0.1	0.2
METH–Un Methodist	20	2,522	5,307	7,134	6.3	13.4
METH–Wesleyan	1	139	110	181	0.2	0.3
Non-denom Chr Chs	12	2,410	2,720	3,102	2.7	5.8
PENT–Assemb of God	3	433	401	607	0.5	1.1
PENT–Ch God (Cleve)	3	347	1,018	1,263	1.1	2.4
PENT–Ch of God Proph	2	NR	144	179	0.2	0.3
PENT–Full Gosp Bapt	2	NR	NR	NR	-	-
PENT–Un Pent Ch Intl	2	NR	NR	NR	-	-
PRES–Cumber Presb	7	NR	520	690	0.6	1.3
PRES–Presb Ch (USA)	3	138	200	248	0.2	0.5
PRES–Presb Ch Amer	1	90	94	104	0.1	0.2
Sev Day Adv	2	55	96	110	0.1	0.2
TEXAS	**27,848**	**3,509,943**	**6,708,243**	**14,083,008**	**56.0**	**100.0**
ANDERSON	**114**	**9,013**	**19,689**	**29,066**	**49.7**	**100.0**
ANG/EPIS–Episcopal	1	85	197	197	0.3	0.7
Bahá'í	0	NR	2	2	0.0	0.0
BAPT–Amer Bapt Assn	4	NR	360	425	0.7	1.5
BAPT–Ind Bapt Flwsp Intl	1	NR	NR	NR	-	-
BAPT–Natl Mis Bapt Conv	1	0	150	177	0.3	0.6

NR–Not Reported   - Represents no adherents reported.   Percentages may not total 100 due to rounding.

Table 3: Religious Congregations by County and Group: 2010

Religious Group	Number of Congrega-tions	Number of Attendees	Number of Communicant, Confirmed, or Full Members	Adherents		
				Number of Adherents	% of Total Pop.	% of Total Adh.
BAPT–NBC Amer	1	0	0	0	0.0	0.0
BAPT–So Bapt Conv	27	3,014	9,507	11,223	19.2	38.6
Catholic	2	NR	NR	4,476	7.7	15.4
Ch Cr, Scientst	1	NR	NR	NR	-	-
Ch of Nazarene	1	55	71	82	0.1	0.3
CHR–Chr Ch (Disc)	5	106	285	336	0.6	1.2
CHR–Chr Chs & Chs Cr	1	NR	38	45	0.1	0.2
CHR–Chs of Christ	12	1,154	1,235	1,487	2.5	5.1
Jehovah's Witness	1	NR	NR	NR	-	-
LDS–L-D Saints	1	NR	NR	363	0.6	1.2
LUTH–Luth–MO Synod	1	84	146	190	0.3	0.7
METH–AME	5	0	800	944	1.6	3.2
METH–Cong Meth	1	NR	NR	NR	-	-
METH–Un Methodist	8	564	1,584	1,753	3.0	6.0
Non-denom Chr Chs	16	2,550	3,650	4,107	7.0	14.1
PENT–Assemb of God	13	1,172	716	2,145	3.7	7.4
PENT–Ch God (Cleve)	1	70	506	597	1.0	2.1
PENT–Ch of God Proph	2	NR	64	76	0.1	0.3
PENT–COGIC	1	10	49	58	0.1	0.2
PENT–Un Pent Ch Intl	2	NR	NR	NR	-	-
PRES–Presb Ch (USA)	1	53	162	191	0.3	0.7
Sev Day Adv	4	96	167	192	0.3	0.7
ANDREWS	**29**	**1,783**	**4,685**	**8,793**	**59.5**	**100.0**
ANG/EPIS–Episcopal	1	4	3	3	0.0	0.0
BAPT–Amer Bapt Assn	1	NR	70	91	0.6	1.0
BAPT–So Bapt Conv	7	668	3,202	4,144	28.0	47.1
Catholic	1	NR	NR	2,100	14.2	23.9
Ch of Nazarene	1	20	37	57	0.4	0.6
CHR–Chr Ch (Disc)	1	0	4	5	0.0	0.1
CHR–Chs of Christ	2	285	343	463	3.1	5.3
Jehovah's Witness	1	NR	NR	NR	-	-
LDS–L-D Saints	1	NR	NR	121	0.8	1.4
LUTH–Luth–MO Synod	1	19	30	37	0.3	0.4
METH–Un Methodist	2	131	429	902	6.1	10.3
Non-denom Chr Chs	2	250	250	313	2.1	3.6
PENT–Assemb of God	4	348	213	422	2.9	4.8
PENT–Ch God (Cleve)	1	32	60	78	0.5	0.9
PENT–Un Pent Ch Intl	2	NR	NR	NR	-	-
PRES–Presb Ch (USA)	1	26	44	57	0.4	0.6
ANGELINA	**156**	**15,518**	**33,006**	**57,290**	**66.0**	**100.0**
ANG/EPIS–Episcopal	1	175	540	598	0.7	1.0
Bahá'í	0	NR	38	38	0.0	0.1
BAPT–Amer Bapt Assn	7	NR	810	1,025	1.2	1.8
BAPT–Natl Mis Bapt Conv	2	0	150	190	0.2	0.3
BAPT–NBC Amer	1	0	0	0	0.0	0.0
BAPT–NBC USA	2	750	825	1,044	1.2	1.8
BAPT–So Bapt Conv	42	5,505	18,985	24,025	27.7	41.9
Catholic	3	NR	NR	10,628	12.2	18.6
Ch Cr, Scientst	1	NR	NR	NR	-	-
Ch of Nazarene	1	138	226	280	0.3	0.5
CHR–Chr Ch (Disc)	1	196	606	767	0.9	1.3
CHR–Chs of Christ	15	1,486	1,542	2,113	2.4	3.7
Jehovah's Witness	2	NR	NR	NR	-	-
LDS–L-D Saints	2	NR	NR	621	0.7	1.1
LUTH–E.L.C.A.	1	67	102	126	0.1	0.2
LUTH–Luth–MO Synod	1	41	179	217	0.3	0.4
METH–C.M.E.	2	300	400	506	0.6	0.9
METH–Cong Meth	3	NR	68	86	0.1	0.2
METH–Un Methodist	16	1,113	3,489	4,139	4.8	7.2
Muslim Est	1	623	NR	2,541	2.9	4.4
Non-denom Chr Chs	18	2,335	2,600	3,053	3.5	5.3
ORTHO–Malan Dioc Am	1	11	NR	33	0.0	0.1
PENT–Assemb of God	10	2,380	1,869	3,785	4.4	6.6
PENT–COGIC	1	0	0	0	0.0	0.0
PENT–Pent Ch of God	2	140	NR	217	0.3	0.4
PENT–Un Pent Ch Intl	13	NR	NR	NR	-	-
PRES–Presb Ch (USA)	1	79	281	356	0.4	0.6
PRES–Presb Ch Amer	1	32	33	37	0.0	0.1
Salvation Army	1	58	112	694	0.8	1.2
Sev Day Adv	3	77	134	154	0.2	0.3
Unit Univ	1	12	17	17	0.0	0.0

Religious Group	Number of Congrega-tions	Number of Attendees	Number of Communicant, Confirmed, or Full Members	Adherents		
				Number of Adherents	% of Total Pop.	% of Total Adh.
ARANSAS	**29**	**2,513**	**4,896**	**10,400**	**44.9**	**100.0**
ANG/EPIS–Episcopal	1	125	210	335	1.4	3.2
BAPT–So Bapt Conv	8	1,159	2,949	3,449	14.9	33.2
Catholic	3	NR	NR	4,095	17.7	39.4
CGOD–Ch God (Ander)	1	40	NR	40	0.2	0.4
CHR–Chs of Christ	3	140	118	156	0.7	1.5
Jehovah's Witness	2	NR	NR	NR	-	-
LDS–L-D Saints	1	NR	NR	278	1.2	2.7
LUTH–E.L.C.A.	1	97	161	161	0.7	1.5
LUTH–Luth–MO Synod	1	75	81	94	0.4	0.9
METH–Un Methodist	1	247	504	738	3.2	7.1
Non-denom Chr Chs	2	300	450	450	1.9	4.3
PENT–Assemb of God	1	80	85	100	0.4	1.0
PENT–Pent Ch of God	1	70	NR	109	0.5	1.0
PENT–Un Pent Ch Intl	1	NR	NR	NR	-	-
PRES–Presb Ch (USA)	1	180	338	395	1.7	3.8
Unity Ch	1	NR	NR	NR	-	-
ARCHER	**23**	**1,125**	**3,968**	**5,868**	**64.8**	**100.0**
Bahá'í	0	NR	1	1	0.0	0.0
BAPT–So Bapt Conv	11	778	3,335	4,062	44.9	69.2
Catholic	3	NR	NR	1,018	11.2	17.3
CHR–Chr Ch (Disc)	1	26	63	77	0.9	1.3
CHR–Chs of Christ	3	112	123	139	1.5	2.4
METH–Un Methodist	3	119	371	412	4.6	7.0
PENT–Assemb of God	2	90	75	159	1.8	2.7
ARMSTRONG	**6**	**375**	**1,248**	**1,474**	**77.5**	**100.0**
BAPT–So Bapt Conv	2	73	711	846	44.5	57.4
CHR–Chs of Christ	1	60	50	65	3.4	4.4
METH–Un Methodist	2	92	337	375	19.7	25.4
Non-denom Chr Chs	1	150	150	188	9.9	12.8
ATASCOSA	**72**	**4,316**	**7,442**	**24,063**	**53.6**	**100.0**
ANG/EPIS–Episcopal	1	13	36	44	0.1	0.2
Bahá'í	0	NR	4	4	0.0	0.0
BAPT–So Bapt Conv	23	2,254	4,386	5,633	12.5	23.4
Catholic	10	NR	NR	13,637	30.4	56.7
CGOD–Ch God (Ander)	1	65	NR	65	0.1	0.3
Chr & Miss Al	1	12	0	12	0.0	0.0
CHR–Chs of Christ	6	397	474	612	1.4	2.5
Evan Free Ch	1	90	NR	90	0.2	0.4
Jehovah's Witness	3	NR	NR	NR	-	-
LDS–L-D Saints	1	NR	NR	690	1.5	2.9
LUTH–Assoc Free Luth	1	NR	NR	NR	-	-
LUTH–E.L.C.A.	1	70	346	469	1.0	1.9
METH–Un Methodist	6	383	919	1,316	2.9	5.5
Non-denom Chr Chs	7	680	980	992	2.2	4.1
PENT–Assemb of God	4	147	105	156	0.3	0.6
PENT–Ch God (Cleve)	2	54	49	63	0.1	0.3
PENT–Pent Ch of God	1	70	NR	109	0.2	0.5
PENT–Un Pent Ch Intl	1	NR	NR	NR	-	-
PRES–Presb Ch (USA)	1	25	46	59	0.1	0.2
Sev Day Adv	1	56	97	112	0.2	0.5
AUSTIN	**55**	**3,938**	**7,629**	**18,651**	**65.6**	**100.0**
ANG/EPIS–Anglican NA	1	NR	NR	NR	-	-
ANG/EPIS–Episcopal	2	97	170	176	0.6	0.9
Bahá'í	0	NR	4	4	0.0	0.0
BAPT–Natl Mis Bapt Conv	2	0	300	370	1.3	2.0
BAPT–So Bapt Conv	9	612	1,815	2,239	7.9	12.0
Catholic	5	NR	NR	8,333	29.3	44.7
Ch Cr, Scientst	1	NR	NR	NR	-	-
CHR–Chs of Christ	3	159	162	200	0.7	1.1
Jehovah's Witness	1	NR	NR	NR	-	-
LDS–L-D Saints	1	NR	NR	493	1.7	2.6
LUTH–E.L.C.A.	5	566	1,343	1,623	5.7	8.7
LUTH–Luth–MO Synod	2	194	536	680	2.4	3.6
METH–AME	4	80	525	648	2.3	3.5
METH–Un Methodist	8	655	1,682	2,006	7.1	10.8
MORAV–Unity Of Breth	2	NR	NR	NR	-	-
Non-denom Chr Chs	4	840	960	1,081	3.8	5.8

NR–Not Reported   - Represents no adherents reported.   Percentages may not total 100 due to rounding.

Table 3: Religious Congregations by County and Group: 2010

Religious Group	Number of Congrega-tions	Number of Attendees	Number of Communicant, Confirmed, or Full Members	Adherents: Number of Adherents	Adherents: % of Total Pop.	Adherents: % of Total Adh.
PENT–Assemb of God	1	650	100	650	2.3	3.5
PENT–Ch of God Proph	1	NR	5	6	0.0	0.0
PENT–Pent Ch of God	1	70	NR	109	0.4	0.6
PENT–Un Pent Ch Intl	1	NR	NR	NR	-	-
PRES–Presb Ch (USA)	1	15	27	33	0.1	0.2
BAILEY	**16**	**1,098**	**2,929**	**5,194**	**72.5**	**100.0**
ANG/EPIS–Anglican NA	1	NR	NR	NR	-	-
Bahá'í	0	NR	3	3	0.0	0.1
BAPT–Ind Bapt Flwsp Intl	1	NR	NR	NR	-	-
BAPT–So Bapt Conv	4	242	1,514	2,006	28.0	38.6
Catholic	1	NR	NR	1,432	20.0	27.6
CHR–Chs of Christ	2	283	339	380	5.3	7.3
METH–Un Methodist	2	128	450	585	8.2	11.3
Non-denom Chr Chs	3	325	530	588	8.2	11.3
PENT–Assemb of God	2	120	93	200	2.8	3.9
BANDERA	**37**	**2,782**	**5,290**	**9,168**	**44.8**	**100.0**
ANG/EPIS–Episcopal	1	45	150	150	0.7	1.6
Bahá'í	0	NR	7	7	0.0	0.1
BAPT–So Bapt Conv	11	710	1,849	2,156	10.5	23.5
BUDD–Theravada	1	NR	NR	375	1.8	4.1
Catholic	3	NR	NR	2,661	13.0	29.0
CHR–Chr Chs & Chs Cr	1	NR	150	175	0.9	1.9
CHR–Chs of Christ	4	280	287	351	1.7	3.8
Jehovah's Witness	1	NR	NR	NR	-	-
LDS–Comm of Christ	1	NR	110	110	0.5	1.2
LUTH–E.L.C.A.	1	87	225	252	1.2	2.7
METH–Un Methodist	3	417	952	1,132	5.5	12.3
Non-denom Chr Chs	8	1,141	1,436	1,623	7.9	17.7
PENT–Assemb of God	1	45	33	70	0.3	0.8
PRES–Presb Ch (USA)	1	57	91	106	0.5	1.2
BASTROP	**109**	**7,301**	**15,236**	**29,061**	**39.2**	**100.0**
ANG/EPIS–Episcopal	1	146	393	455	0.6	1.6
Ap Chr Ch-Amer	1	26	11	26	0.0	0.1
Bahá'í	0	NR	89	89	0.1	0.3
BAPT–Ind Bapt Flwsp Intl	1	NR	NR	NR	-	-
BAPT–Natl Mis Bapt Conv	1	0	150	188	0.3	0.6
BAPT–NBC Amer	1	150	350	439	0.6	1.5
BAPT–Ref Bapt Ch	1	NR	NR	NR	-	-
BAPT–So Bapt Conv	28	2,098	6,383	8,007	10.8	27.6
Calv Chpl	1	NR	NR	NR	-	-
Catholic	7	NR	NR	8,796	11.9	30.3
CGOD–Ch God (Ander)	2	76	NR	76	0.1	0.3
Ch God (7th Day)	1	NR	NR	NR	-	-
Ch of Nazarene	0	30	0	91	0.1	0.3
CHR–Chr Ch (Disc)	3	30	133	167	0.2	0.6
CHR–Chr Chs & Chs Cr	1	NR	26	33	0.0	0.1
CHR–Chs of Christ	7	518	512	659	0.9	2.3
Evan Free Ch	2	105	NR	105	0.1	0.4
Jehovah's Witness	1	NR	NR	NR	-	-
LDS–L-D Saints	1	NR	NR	798	1.1	2.7
LUTH–Assoc Free Luth	1	NR	NR	NR	-	-
LUTH–E.L.C.A.	5	274	496	822	1.1	2.8
LUTH–Luth Cong Msn Chr	2	73	52	65	0.1	0.2
LUTH–Luth–MO Synod	5	454	784	992	1.3	3.4
MENN–Beachy Amish-Menn	1	76	31	76	0.1	0.3
METH–AME	3	0	400	502	0.7	1.7
METH–Un Methodist	6	867	2,213	2,956	4.0	10.2
Non-denom Chr Chs	12	1,860	2,420	2,538	3.4	8.7
PENT–Assemb of God	3	210	121	256	0.3	0.9
PENT–Ch Lord Jesus Apos	1	NR	NR	NR	-	-
PENT–COGIC	1	0	150	188	0.3	0.6
PENT–Pent Ch of God	1	70	NR	109	0.1	0.4
PENT–Un Pent Ch Intl	2	NR	NR	NR	-	-
PRES–Presb Ch (USA)	3	94	272	341	0.5	1.2
Sev Day Adv	3	144	250	287	0.4	1.0
BAYLOR	**15**	**704**	**2,433**	**3,307**	**88.8**	**100.0**
BAPT–Ind Bapt Flwsp Intl	1	NR	NR	NR	-	-
BAPT–So Bapt Conv	5	269	1,703	2,039	54.7	61.7

Religious Group	Number of Congrega-tions	Number of Attendees	Number of Communicant, Confirmed, or Full Members	Adherents: Number of Adherents	Adherents: % of Total Pop.	Adherents: % of Total Adh.
Catholic	1	NR	NR	380	10.2	11.5
CHR–Chs of Christ	1	120	120	140	3.8	4.2
LDS–L-D Saints	1	NR	NR	61	1.6	1.8
LUTH–Luth–MO Synod	1	10	18	18	0.5	0.5
METH–Un Methodist	1	73	269	305	8.2	9.2
Non-denom Chr Chs	2	140	160	179	4.8	5.4
PENT–Assemb of God	1	30	50	50	1.3	1.5
PRES–Presb Ch (USA)	1	62	113	135	3.6	4.1
BEE	**52**	**2,492**	**5,307**	**22,994**	**72.2**	**100.0**
ANG/EPIS–Episcopal	1	51	93	140	0.4	0.6
Bahá'í	0	NR	1	1	0.0	0.0
BAPT–NBC USA	1	80	250	301	0.9	1.3
BAPT–So Bapt Conv	14	1,002	2,793	3,365	10.6	14.6
Catholic	7	NR	NR	16,118	50.6	70.1
CHR–Chr Ch (Disc)	2	48	101	122	0.4	0.5
CHR–Chs of Christ	2	120	145	151	0.5	0.7
Jehovah's Witness	2	NR	NR	NR	-	-
LDS–L-D Saints	1	NR	NR	386	1.2	1.7
LUTH–E.L.C.A.	2	98	229	270	0.8	1.2
MENN–Amish Undif	1	NR	20	52	0.2	0.2
METH–Un Methodist	5	233	591	707	2.2	3.1
Non-denom Chr Chs	6	585	739	791	2.5	3.4
PENT–Assemb of God	1	53	21	100	0.3	0.4
PENT–Ch God (Cleve)	1	47	78	94	0.3	0.4
PENT–Pent Ch of God	1	70	NR	109	0.3	0.5
PENT–Un Pent Ch Intl	1	NR	NR	NR	-	-
PRES–Presb Ch (USA)	1	46	146	176	0.6	0.8
PRES–Presb Ch Amer	1	21	39	40	0.1	0.2
Sev Day Adv	1	24	41	47	0.1	0.2
Un C of Christ	1	14	20	24	0.1	0.1
BELL	**316**	**41,499**	**86,225**	**146,711**	**47.3**	**100.0**
ANG/EPIS–Episcopal	4	457	1,294	1,366	0.4	0.9
Bahá'í	1	NR	331	331	0.1	0.2
BAPT–Amer Bapt Assn	1	NR	85	110	0.0	0.1
BAPT–Ind Bapt Flwsp Intl	1	NR	NR	NR	-	-
BAPT–NBC Amer	2	525	1,375	1,781	0.6	1.2
BAPT–NBC USA	2	80	400	518	0.2	0.4
BAPT–So Bapt Conv	92	10,776	39,204	50,789	16.4	34.6
BUDD–Mahayana	3	NR	NR	2,152	0.7	1.5
BUDD–Theravada	1	NR	NR	1,364	0.4	0.9
Calv Chpl	2	NR	NR	NR	-	-
Catholic	9	NR	NR	25,366	8.2	17.3
CGOD–Ch God (Ander)	1	40	NR	40	0.0	0.0
Ch of Nazarene	4	449	692	800	0.3	0.5
CHR–Chr Ch (Disc)	8	343	718	930	0.3	0.6
CHR–Chr Chs & Chs Cr	1	NR	44	57	0.0	0.0
CHR–Chs of Christ	20	3,294	3,436	4,465	1.4	3.0
CHR–Int Chs of Christ	1	NR	42	54	0.0	0.0
HINDU–Trad Temples	1	NR	NR	350	0.1	0.2
Jehovah's Witness	1	NR	NR	NR	-	-
LDS–L-D Saints	7	NR	NR	5,046	1.6	3.4
LUTH–E.L.C.A.	4	522	1,186	1,312	0.4	0.9
LUTH–Luth–MO Synod	3	207	1,283	1,800	0.6	1.2
LUTH–Wisc Ev Luth Syn	2	89	135	185	0.1	0.1
METH–AME	5	312	812	1,052	0.3	0.7
METH–Evan Meth Ch	1	NR	NR	NR	-	-
METH–Un Methodist	23	3,230	10,447	12,151	3.9	8.3
MORAV–Unity Of Breth	3	NR	NR	NR	-	-
Muslim Est	2	1,248	NR	5,084	1.6	3.5
New Apost Ch	1	NR	NR	NR	-	-
Non-denom Chr Chs	57	15,853	19,631	21,489	6.9	14.6
PENT–Assemb of God	13	1,598	1,301	3,000	1.0	2.0
PENT–Ch God (Cleve)	1	144	127	165	0.1	0.1
PENT–Ch Lord Jesus Apos	1	NR	NR	NR	-	-
PENT–COGIC	8	815	1,565	2,027	0.7	1.4
PENT–Full Gosp Bapt	1	NR	NR	NR	-	-
PENT–Pent Ch of God	3	210	NR	326	0.1	0.2
PENT–Un Pent Ch Intl	7	NR	NR	NR	-	-
PENT–Vineyard	1	90	125	162	0.1	0.1
PRES–Presb Ch (USA)	5	436	851	1,102	0.4	0.8
PRES–Presb Ch Amer	3	100	90	98	0.0	0.1

NR–Not Reported - Represents no adherents reported. Percentages may not total 100 due to rounding.

Table 3: Religious Congregations by County and Group: 2010

Religious Group	Number of Congrega-tions	Number of Attendees	Number of Communicant, Confirmed, or Full Members	Adherents: Number of Adherents	Adherents: % of Total Pop.	Adherents: % of Total Adh.
Salvation Army	3	215	196	247	0.1	0.2
Sev Day Adv	5	466	811	933	0.3	0.6
Unit Univ	1	0	44	59	0.0	0.0
Unity Ch	1	NR	NR	NR	-	-
BEXAR	**1,189**	**187,817**	**302,435**	**967,735**	**56.4**	**100.0**
ANG/EPIS–Anglican NA	3	NR	NR	NR	-	-
ANG/EPIS–Episcopal	19	3,297	7,043	11,006	0.6	1.1
Bahá'í	1	NR	678	678	0.0	0.1
BAPT–Alliance Bapt	1	NR	NR	NR	-	-
BAPT–Amer Bapt Assn	3	NR	187	237	0.0	0.0
BAPT–Amer Bapt USA	3	850	2,290	2,906	0.2	0.3
BAPT–Free Will Bapt	2	NR	104	132	0.0	0.0
BAPT–Ind Bapt Flwsp Intl	7	NR	NR	NR	-	-
BAPT–N Am Bapt Conf	1	NR	15	19	0.0	0.0
BAPT–Natl Mis Bapt Conv	2	0	300	381	0.0	0.0
BAPT–NBC Amer	8	1,450	2,461	3,123	0.2	0.3
BAPT–NBC USA	1	15	30	38	0.0	0.0
BAPT–Prog NBC	1	600	1,025	1,301	0.1	0.1
BAPT–Ref Bapt Ch	5	NR	NR	NR	-	-
BAPT–So Bapt Conv	279	33,732	91,714	116,389	6.8	12.0
BUDD–Mahayana	6	NR	NR	2,497	0.1	0.3
BUDD–Theravada	4	NR	NR	3,118	0.2	0.3
BUDD–Vajrayana	3	NR	NR	116	0.0	0.0
Calv Chpl	5	NR	NR	NR	-	-
Catholic	102	NR	NR	528,827	30.8	54.6
CGOD–Ch God (Ander)	5	345	NR	345	0.0	0.0
Ch Cr, Scientst	3	NR	NR	NR	-	-
Ch God (7th Day)	8	NR	NR	NR	-	-
Ch of Nazarene	21	1,517	2,011	2,727	0.2	0.3
Chr & Miss Al	1	47	32	52	0.0	0.0
CHR–Chr Ch (Disc)	12	959	1,598	2,028	0.1	0.2
CHR–Chr Chs & Chs Cr	10	NR	1,198	1,520	0.1	0.2
CHR–Chs of Christ	35	5,272	5,420	7,170	0.4	0.7
CHR–Int Chs of Christ	1	NR	380	482	0.0	0.0
Evan Free Ch	7	2,285	NR	2,285	0.1	0.2
FRND–Fr Gen Cf	1	NR	85	108	0.0	0.0
HINDU–I/A Temples	2	NR	NR	1,992	0.1	0.2
HINDU–Post Ren	4	NR	NR	130	0.0	0.0
HINDU–Trad Temples	1	NR	NR	2,000	0.1	0.2
Jehovah's Witness	33	NR	NR	NR	-	-
JUD–Conserv	1	403	452	1,220	0.1	0.1
JUD–Orth	2	842	350	1,170	0.1	0.1
JUD–Reconst	1	41	52	140	0.0	0.0
JUD–Reform	1	582	1,027	2,773	0.2	0.3
LDS–Comm of Christ	2	NR	241	241	0.0	0.0
LDS–L-D Saints	40	NR	NR	24,489	1.4	2.5
LUTH–E.L.C.A.	26	3,391	7,343	10,345	0.6	1.1
LUTH–Evan Luth Syn	1	43	44	75	0.0	0.0
LUTH–Luth–MO Synod	12	3,680	8,381	11,316	0.7	1.2
LUTH–Wisc Ev Luth Syn	2	305	454	627	0.0	0.1
MENN–Cons Menn Conf	2	25	69	88	0.0	0.0
MENN–Mennonite USA	2	70	46	58	0.0	0.0
METH–AME	12	795	1,860	2,360	0.1	0.2
METH–AME Zion	2	0	200	254	0.0	0.0
METH–C.M.E.	1	50	75	95	0.0	0.0
METH–Free Methodist	1	45	13	45	0.0	0.0
METH–Un Methodist	57	12,615	32,554	41,276	2.4	4.3
METH–Wesleyan	1	100	35	130	0.0	0.0
Metro Comm Ch	1	217	212	269	0.0	0.0
Missionary Ch	2	1,237	601	1,237	0.1	0.1
MJEW–Assoc Mes Cong	1	NR	NR	NR	-	-
MJEW–Union Mes Cong	1	NR	NR	NR	-	-
Muslim Est	9	5,017	NR	20,456	1.2	2.1
Nat Spirit Asso	1	NR	NR	NR	-	-
New Apost Ch	1	NR	NR	NR	-	-
Non-denom Chr Chs	204	82,586	105,579	113,976	6.6	11.8
OCATH–Pol Natl Cath	2	NR	NR	NR	-	-
ORTHE–Ant Orth of NA	1	60	NR	175	0.0	0.0
ORTHE–Greek Orthodox	1	190	NR	350	0.0	0.0
ORTHE–Orth Ch in Amer	2	92	NR	179	0.0	0.0
ORTHO–Armen Ap Etchm	1	40	NR	60	0.0	0.0
ORTHO–Coptic Orth Ch	1	100	NR	165	0.0	0.0
ORTHO–Malan Dioc Am	1	25	NR	75	0.0	0.0
PENT–Assemb of God	49	13,040	6,955	18,071	1.1	1.9
PENT–Ch God (Cleve)	19	3,392	2,875	3,649	0.2	0.4
PENT–Ch God Apos Fth	1	NR	NR	NR	-	-
PENT–Ch Lord Jesus Apos	3	NR	NR	NR	-	-
PENT–Ch of God Proph	3	NR	140	178	0.0	0.0
PENT–COGIC	11	320	1,110	1,409	0.1	0.1
PENT–Int Foursq Gos	14	883	916	1,162	0.1	0.1
PENT–Intl Pent Holiness	5	490	515	654	0.0	0.1
PENT–Pent Ch of God	1	70	NR	109	0.0	0.0
PENT–Un Pent Ch Intl	22	NR	NR	NR	-	-
PENT–Vineyard	2	111	133	169	0.0	0.0
PRES–Cum Pres Am	1	NR	NR	NR	-	-
PRES–Cumber Presb	2	NR	312	398	0.0	0.0
PRES–Evan Presby Ch	1	NR	122	155	0.0	0.0
PRES–Kor Pres Abroad	1	NR	NR	NR	-	-
PRES–Korean Pres Amer	1	NR	NR	NR	-	-
PRES–Orth Pres Ch	1	75	79	106	0.0	0.0
PRES–Presb Ch (USA)	26	3,535	8,336	10,579	0.6	1.1
PRES–Presb Ch Amer	3	567	688	898	0.1	0.1
REF–Christian Ref	1	265	151	192	0.0	0.0
REF–Comm Ref Evan	1	NR	NR	NR	-	-
Salvation Army	3	180	471	677	0.0	0.1
Sev Day Adv	15	1,603	2,788	3,206	0.2	0.3
Sikh	2	NR	NR	NR	-	-
Un C of Christ	3	116	266	338	0.0	0.0
Unit Univ	2	250	419	528	0.0	0.1
Unity Ch	1	NR	NR	NR	-	-
Zoroastrian	0	NR	NR	6	0.0	0.0
BLANCO	**19**	**1,174**	**2,853**	**4,381**	**41.7**	**100.0**
ANG/EPIS–Episcopal	2	82	153	179	1.7	4.1
Bahá'í	0	NR	7	7	0.1	0.2
BAPT–So Bapt Conv	2	226	1,069	1,282	12.2	29.3
Catholic	2	NR	NR	872	8.3	19.9
CHR–Chs of Christ	3	171	145	190	1.8	4.3
LUTH–E.L.C.A.	1	0	0	0	0.0	0.0
LUTH–Luth Cong Msn Chr	1	143	447	536	5.1	12.2
METH–Un Methodist	2	252	732	876	8.3	20.0
Non-denom Chr Chs	2	200	300	300	2.9	6.8
PENT–Assemb of God	1	30	0	30	0.3	0.7
PENT–Pent Ch of God	1	70	NR	109	1.0	2.5
PENT–Un Pent Ch Intl	2	NR	NR	NR	-	-
BORDEN	**4**	**56**	**383**	**449**	**70.0**	**100.0**
BAPT–So Bapt Conv	4	56	383	449	70.0	100.0
BOSQUE	**59**	**2,974**	**7,460**	**9,977**	**54.8**	**100.0**
ANG/EPIS–Anglican NA	1	NR	NR	NR	-	-
BAPT–So Bapt Conv	23	1,479	4,485	5,412	29.7	54.2
Catholic	2	NR	NR	1,005	5.5	10.1
CHR–Chs of Christ	7	377	354	483	2.7	4.8
LUTH–E.L.C.A.	4	295	791	925	5.1	9.3
LUTH–Luth–MO Synod	1	88	164	193	1.1	1.9
LUTH–Nor Amer Luth C	1	NR	NR	NR	-	-
METH–Un Methodist	8	383	1,083	1,275	7.0	12.8
Non-denom Chr Chs	3	180	260	260	1.4	2.6
PENT–Assemb of God	1	26	19	57	0.3	0.6
PENT–Un Pent Ch Intl	4	NR	NR	NR	-	-
PRES–Cum Pres Am	2	NR	NR	NR	-	-
PRES–Presb Ch (USA)	1	70	108	130	0.7	1.3
Un C of Christ	1	76	196	237	1.3	2.4
BOWIE	**198**	**16,779**	**42,699**	**56,686**	**61.2**	**100.0**
ANG/EPIS–Episcopal	2	267	471	614	0.7	1.1
Bahá'í	0	NR	44	44	0.0	0.1
BAPT–Amer Bapt Assn	13	NR	1,335	1,639	1.8	2.9
BAPT–Natl Mis Bapt Conv	2	0	300	368	0.4	0.6
BAPT–NBC USA	4	650	1,150	1,412	1.5	2.5
BAPT–So Bapt Conv	62	7,259	23,527	28,888	31.2	51.0
Calv Chpl	1	NR	NR	NR	-	-
Catholic	2	NR	NR	3,600	3.9	6.4
Ch of Nazarene	2	193	464	464	0.5	0.8

NR–Not Reported - Represents no adherents reported. Percentages may not total 100 due to rounding.

Table 3: Religious Congregations by County and Group: 2010

Religious Group	Number of Congregations	Number of Attendees	Number of Communicant, Confirmed, or Full Members	Adherents: Number of Adherents	Adherents: % of Total Pop.	Adherents: % of Total Adh.
CHR–Chr Ch (Disc)	4	175	495	608	0.7	1.1
CHR–Chr Chs & Chs Cr	4	NR	195	239	0.3	0.4
CHR–Chs of Christ	16	1,948	2,144	2,673	2.9	4.7
FRND–Fr Gen Cf	1	NR	19	23	0.0	0.0
Jehovah's Witness	3	NR	NR	NR	-	-
JUD–Reform	1	16	28	76	0.1	0.1
LDS–Comm of Christ	2	NR	162	162	0.2	0.3
LDS–L-D Saints	2	NR	NR	1,160	1.3	2.0
LUTH–E.L.C.A.	1	5	15	18	0.0	0.0
LUTH–Luth–MO Synod	1	120	302	424	0.5	0.7
METH–AME	2	0	250	307	0.3	0.5
METH–C.M.E.	4	0	695	853	0.9	1.5
METH–Cong Meth	1	NR	35	43	0.0	0.1
METH–Un Methodist	19	1,607	4,945	5,467	5.9	9.6
Non-denom Chr Chs	19	3,083	3,914	4,311	4.7	7.6
PENT–Assemb of God	6	850	452	1,116	1.2	2.0
PENT–Ch God (Cleve)	1	28	97	119	0.1	0.2
PENT–Ch of God Proph	2	NR	66	81	0.1	0.1
PENT–COGIC	6	135	680	835	0.9	1.5
PENT–Full Gosp Bapt	3	NR	NR	NR	-	-
PENT–Int Foursq Gos	1	21	16	20	0.0	0.0
PENT–Un Pent Ch Intl	3	NR	NR	NR	-	-
PRES–Evan Presby Ch	1	NR	89	109	0.1	0.2
PRES–Presb Ch (USA)	3	74	203	249	0.3	0.4
Salvation Army	1	56	98	180	0.2	0.3
Sev Day Adv	3	292	508	584	0.6	1.0
BRAZORIA	**315**	**41,871**	**94,375**	**178,462**	**57.0**	**100.0**
ANG/EPIS–Episcopal	6	646	1,406	1,720	0.5	1.0
Bahá'í	2	NR	63	63	0.0	0.0
BAPT–Amer Bapt Assn	4	NR	955	1,221	0.4	0.7
BAPT–So Bapt Conv	83	12,611	43,989	56,240	18.0	31.5
Catholic	12	NR	NR	50,863	16.2	28.5
Ch Cr, Scientst	1	NR	NR	NR	-	-
Ch God (7th Day)	1	NR	NR	NR	-	-
Ch of Nazarene	2	182	358	358	0.1	0.2
CHR–Chr Ch (Disc)	4	55	326	417	0.1	0.2
CHR–Chr Chs & Chs Cr	1	NR	5,000	6,393	2.0	3.6
CHR–Chs of Christ	26	2,430	2,509	3,243	1.0	1.8
Evan Free Ch	1	160	NR	160	0.1	0.1
FRND–Evan Fr Ch Intl	3	120	175	224	0.1	0.1
HINDU–I/A Temples	1	NR	NR	16	0.0	0.0
HINDU–Trad Temples	1	NR	NR	700	0.2	0.4
Jehovah's Witness	2	NR	NR	NR	-	-
LDS–Comm of Christ	1	NR	110	110	0.0	0.1
LDS–L-D Saints	8	NR	NR	3,770	1.2	2.1
LUTH–E.L.C.A.	6	585	1,477	1,803	0.6	1.0
LUTH–Luth–MO Synod	4	880	1,488	1,951	0.6	1.1
LUTH–Wisc Ev Luth Syn	1	20	33	45	0.0	0.0
METH–AME	9	105	887	1,134	0.4	0.6
METH–Un Methodist	19	3,072	9,405	11,793	3.8	6.6
Missionary Ch	1	30	45	45	0.0	0.0
Muslim Est	2	1,248	NR	5,084	1.6	2.8
Non-denom Chr Chs	44	14,443	20,380	22,303	7.1	12.5
PENT–Assemb of God	18	2,154	1,512	3,176	1.0	1.8
PENT–Ch God (Cleve)	1	10	30	38	0.0	0.0
PENT–Ch of God Proph	3	NR	96	123	0.0	0.1
PENT–COGIC	2	150	250	320	0.1	0.2
PENT–Full Gosp Bapt	2	NR	NR	NR	-	-
PENT–Int Foursq Gos	2	810	542	693	0.2	0.4
PENT–Intl Pent Holiness	5	745	795	1,016	0.3	0.6
PENT–Pent Ch of God	1	70	NR	109	0.0	0.1
PENT–Un Pent Ch Intl	17	NR	NR	NR	-	-
PENT–Vineyard	2	298	480	614	0.2	0.3
PRES–As Ref Pres Ch	1	NR	38	49	0.0	0.0
PRES–Presb Ch (USA)	10	799	1,659	2,121	0.7	1.2
PRES–Presb Ch Amer	1	108	124	173	0.1	0.1
Salvation Army	1	32	56	150	0.0	0.1
Sev Day Adv	3	108	187	215	0.1	0.1
Unity Ch	1	NR	NR	NR	-	-
Zoroastrian	0	NR	NR	9	0.0	0.0

Religious Group	Number of Congregations	Number of Attendees	Number of Communicant, Confirmed, or Full Members	Adherents: Number of Adherents	Adherents: % of Total Pop.	Adherents: % of Total Adh.
BRAZOS	**156**	**24,505**	**44,021**	**80,197**	**41.2**	**100.0**
ANG/EPIS–Episcopal	3	447	1,024	1,176	0.6	1.5
Bahá'í	2	NR	166	166	0.1	0.2
BAPT–Amer Bapt Assn	1	NR	0	0	0.0	0.0
BAPT–Free Will Bapt	3	NR	156	186	0.1	0.2
BAPT–Ind Bapt Flwsp Intl	1	NR	NR	NR	-	-
BAPT–Natl Mis Bapt Conv	3	0	300	359	0.2	0.4
BAPT–NBC USA	1	550	700	837	0.4	1.0
BAPT–So Bapt Conv	32	7,482	19,290	23,054	11.8	28.7
BUDD–Theravada	1	NR	NR	14	0.0	0.0
Calv Chpl	1	NR	NR	NR	-	-
Catholic	6	NR	NR	21,925	11.3	27.3
CGOD–Ch God (Ander)	1	50	NR	50	0.0	0.1
Ch Cr, Scientst	1	NR	NR	NR	-	-
Ch of Nazarene	1	122	150	150	0.1	0.2
CHR–Chr Ch (Disc)	1	65	169	202	0.1	0.3
CHR–Chr Chs & Chs Cr	1	NR	100	120	0.1	0.1
CHR–Chs of Christ	10	1,984	2,129	2,843	1.5	3.5
Evan Free Ch	2	230	NR	230	0.1	0.3
FRND–Fr Gen Cf	1	NR	3	4	0.0	0.0
HINDU–Post Ren	1	NR	NR	15	0.0	0.0
Jehovah's Witness	1	NR	NR	NR	-	-
JUD–Reform	1	33	58	157	0.1	0.2
LDS–L-D Saints	6	NR	NR	2,588	1.3	3.2
LUTH–E.L.C.A.	2	430	1,146	1,489	0.8	1.9
LUTH–Luth–MO Synod	2	606	891	1,239	0.6	1.5
LUTH–Wisc Ev Luth Syn	1	60	85	106	0.1	0.1
METH–AME	2	0	250	299	0.2	0.4
METH–Un Methodist	15	3,288	7,385	8,244	4.2	10.3
MORAV–Unity Of Breth	1	NR	NR	NR	-	-
Muslim Est	1	623	NR	2,541	1.3	3.2
Non-denom Chr Chs	22	6,877	7,562	8,896	4.6	11.1
ORTHE–Ant Orth of NA	1	25	NR	45	0.0	0.1
ORTHE–Rus Orth Abroad	1	17	NR	32	0.0	0.0
ORTHO–Coptic Orth Ch	1	10	NR	15	0.0	0.0
PENT–Assemb of God	4	408	447	615	0.3	0.8
PENT–COGIC	1	0	150	179	0.1	0.2
PENT–Intl Pent Holiness	1	170	120	143	0.1	0.2
PENT–Pent Ch of God	1	70	NR	109	0.1	0.1
PENT–Un Pent Ch Intl	5	NR	NR	NR	-	-
PENT–Vineyard	1	0	0	0	0.0	0.0
PRES–Korean Pres Amer	1	NR	NR	NR	-	-
PRES–Presb Ch (USA)	2	372	779	931	0.5	1.2
PRES–Presb Ch Amer	2	261	389	463	0.2	0.6
Salvation Army	1	16	23	117	0.1	0.1
Sev Day Adv	3	76	131	151	0.1	0.2
Un C of Christ	2	165	321	384	0.2	0.5
Unit Univ	1	68	97	117	0.1	0.1
Unity Ch	1	NR	NR	NR	-	-
Zoroastrian	0	NR	NR	6	0.0	0.0
BREWSTER	**24**	**728**	**1,756**	**4,283**	**46.4**	**100.0**
ANG/EPIS–Anglican NA	1	NR	NR	NR	-	-
Bahá'í	0	NR	16	16	0.2	0.4
BAPT–So Bapt Conv	6	294	1,164	1,387	15.0	32.4
Catholic	2	NR	NR	1,900	20.6	44.4
CHR–Chr Ch (Disc)	1	15	57	68	0.7	1.6
CHR–Chs of Christ	2	62	37	58	0.6	1.4
FRND–Fr Gen Cf	1	NR	4	5	0.1	0.1
Jehovah's Witness	1	NR	NR	NR	-	-
LDS–L-D Saints	1	NR	NR	210	2.3	4.9
LUTH–Luth–MO Synod	1	23	43	57	0.6	1.3
METH–Un Methodist	1	62	131	160	1.7	3.7
Non-denom Chr Chs	2	106	156	158	1.7	3.7
ORTHE–Orth Ch in Amer	1	15	NR	15	0.2	0.4
PENT–Assemb of God	2	78	49	125	1.4	2.9
PRES–Presb Ch (USA)	1	48	68	81	0.9	1.9
Unit Univ	1	25	31	43	0.5	1.0
BRISCOE	**10**	**499**	**1,165**	**1,550**	**94.7**	**100.0**
Bahá'í	0	NR	2	2	0.1	0.1
BAPT–So Bapt Conv	3	213	757	909	55.5	58.6
Catholic	2	NR	NR	155	9.5	10.0

NR–Not Reported   - Represents no adherents reported.   Percentages may not total 100 due to rounding.

Table 3: Religious Congregations by County and Group: 2010

Religious Group	Number of Congrega-tions	Number of Attendees	Number of Communicant, Confirmed, or Full Members	Adherents		
				Number of Adherents	% of Total Pop.	% of Total Adh.
CHR–Chs of Christ	3	188	159	208	12.7	13.4
METH–Un Methodist	2	98	247	276	16.9	17.8
BROOKS	**16**	**477**	**622**	**5,952**	**82.4**	**100.0**
BAPT–So Bapt Conv	4	105	203	259	3.6	4.4
BRETH–Ch of Brethren	1	0	19	24	0.3	0.4
Catholic	2	NR	NR	5,091	70.5	85.5
CGOD–Ch God (Ander)	1	10	NR	10	0.1	0.2
CHR–Chs of Christ	1	32	30	45	0.6	0.8
Jehovah's Witness	1	NR	NR	NR	-	-
METH–Un Methodist	1	38	70	116	1.6	1.9
Non-denom Chr Chs	1	200	175	250	3.5	4.2
PENT–Assemb of God	1	45	34	45	0.6	0.8
PENT–Intl Pent Holiness	1	6	7	9	0.1	0.2
PRES–Presb Ch (USA)	1	23	52	66	0.9	1.1
Sev Day Adv	1	18	32	37	0.5	0.6
BROWN	**96**	**8,867**	**22,509**	**30,211**	**79.3**	**100.0**
ANG/EPIS–Anglican NA	2	NR	NR	NR	-	-
Bahá'í	0	NR	2	2	0.0	0.0
BAPT–Amer Bapt Assn	1	NR	85	104	0.3	0.3
BAPT–Ind Bapt Flwsp Intl	2	NR	NR	NR	-	-
BAPT–So Bapt Conv	44	4,806	15,088	18,470	48.5	61.1
Catholic	1	NR	NR	2,500	6.6	8.3
Ch of Nazarene	1	12	38	38	0.1	0.1
CHR–Chr Ch (Disc)	1	62	206	252	0.7	0.8
CHR–Chs of Christ	13	1,291	1,521	1,856	4.9	6.1
Jehovah's Witness	2	NR	NR	NR	-	-
LDS–L-D Saints	1	NR	NR	456	1.2	1.5
LUTH–Luth–MO Synod	1	82	165	198	0.5	0.7
METH–AME	1	15	30	37	0.1	0.1
METH–Un Methodist	10	539	2,864	3,232	8.5	10.7
Non-denom Chr Chs	9	1,792	2,325	2,571	6.7	8.5
PENT–Assemb of God	2	55	44	108	0.3	0.4
PENT–Pent Ch of God	2	140	NR	217	0.6	0.7
PENT–Un Pent Ch Intl	1	NR	NR	NR	-	-
PRES–Presb Ch (USA)	1	51	102	125	0.3	0.4
Sev Day Adv	1	22	39	45	0.1	0.1
BURLESON	**39**	**1,781**	**4,720**	**8,088**	**47.1**	**100.0**
Bahá'í	0	NR	23	23	0.1	0.3
BAPT–So Bapt Conv	11	740	2,654	3,236	18.8	40.0
Catholic	3	NR	NR	2,144	12.5	26.5
CGOD–Ch God (Ander)	1	68	NR	68	0.4	0.8
CHR–Chr Ch (Disc)	1	0	58	71	0.4	0.9
CHR–Chs of Christ	4	140	167	218	1.3	2.7
Jehovah's Witness	1	NR	NR	NR	-	-
LDS–L-D Saints	1	NR	NR	39	0.2	0.5
LUTH–E.L.C.A.	2	207	515	631	3.7	7.8
LUTH–Luth–MO Synod	1	14	29	41	0.2	0.5
METH–AME	1	0	150	183	1.1	2.3
METH–Un Methodist	4	338	776	859	5.0	10.6
MORAV–Unity Of Breth	3	NR	NR	NR	-	-
PENT–Assemb of God	2	178	123	300	1.7	3.7
PENT–Un Pent Ch Intl	1	NR	NR	NR	-	-
PRES–Presb Ch (USA)	2	14	21	26	0.2	0.3
Un C of Christ	1	82	204	249	1.4	3.1
BURNET	**78**	**6,354**	**13,058**	**21,167**	**49.5**	**100.0**
ANG/EPIS–Episcopal	2	196	413	434	1.0	2.1
Bahá'í	0	NR	4	4	0.0	0.0
BAPT–Ind Bapt Flwsp Intl	3	NR	NR	NR	-	-
BAPT–Ref Bapt Ch	1	NR	NR	NR	-	-
BAPT–So Bapt Conv	18	1,579	5,620	6,837	16.0	32.3
Catholic	4	NR	NR	4,687	11.0	22.1
CHR–Chr Ch (Disc)	3	85	181	220	0.5	1.0
CHR–Chs of Christ	13	1,177	1,212	1,493	3.5	7.1
LDS–L-D Saints	1	NR	NR	734	1.7	3.5
LUTH–E.L.C.A.	3	339	642	860	2.0	4.1
LUTH–Wisc Ev Luth Syn	1	0	0	0	0.0	0.0
METH–AME	1	0	150	182	0.4	0.9
METH–Un Methodist	5	802	1,806	2,195	5.1	10.4

Religious Group	Number of Congrega-tions	Number of Attendees	Number of Communicant, Confirmed, or Full Members	Adherents		
				Number of Adherents	% of Total Pop.	% of Total Adh.
Non-denom Chr Chs	13	1,739	2,474	2,647	6.2	12.5
PENT–Assemb of God	2	336	169	336	0.8	1.6
PENT–Un Pent Ch Intl	3	NR	NR	NR	-	-
PRES–Cumber Presb	1	NR	88	177	0.4	0.8
PRES–Presb Ch (USA)	3	75	255	310	0.7	1.5
Sev Day Adv	1	26	44	51	0.1	0.2
CALDWELL	**63**	**3,812**	**8,115**	**16,296**	**42.8**	**100.0**
ANG/EPIS–Anglican NA	1	NR	NR	NR	-	-
ANG/EPIS–Episcopal	2	102	183	202	0.5	1.2
Bahá'í	0	NR	27	27	0.1	0.2
BAPT–NBC Amer	1	175	300	374	1.0	2.3
BAPT–So Bapt Conv	16	1,452	4,180	5,209	13.7	32.0
Catholic	3	NR	NR	5,894	15.5	36.2
CHR–Chr Ch (Disc)	2	91	190	237	0.6	1.5
CHR–Chs of Christ	3	218	217	268	0.7	1.6
Jehovah's Witness	2	NR	NR	NR	-	-
LUTH–E.L.C.A.	3	170	392	455	1.2	2.8
METH–AME	2	21	193	240	0.6	1.5
METH–Un Methodist	9	478	1,255	1,533	4.0	9.4
Non-denom Chr Chs	6	510	715	760	2.0	4.7
PENT–Assemb of God	3	322	154	495	1.3	3.0
PENT–COGIC	1	20	20	25	0.1	0.2
PENT–Pent Ch of God	2	140	NR	217	0.6	1.3
PENT–Un Pent Ch Intl	2	NR	NR	NR	-	-
PRES–Presb Ch (USA)	3	93	152	189	0.5	1.2
Un C of Christ	2	20	137	171	0.4	1.0
CALHOUN	**41**	**1,981**	**6,337**	**11,926**	**55.8**	**100.0**
ANG/EPIS–Episcopal	1	32	39	39	0.2	0.3
Bahá'í	0	NR	17	17	0.1	0.1
BAPT–So Bapt Conv	11	707	4,112	5,155	24.1	43.2
BUDD–Mahayana	1	NR	NR	536	2.5	4.5
Catholic	4	NR	NR	3,191	14.9	26.8
CHR–Chs of Christ	4	225	220	331	1.5	2.8
Jehovah's Witness	1	NR	NR	NR	-	-
LDS–L-D Saints	1	NR	NR	303	1.4	2.5
LUTH–E.L.C.A.	1	86	178	218	1.0	1.8
LUTH–Luth Cong Msn Chr	1	14	25	31	0.1	0.3
METH–Un Methodist	4	298	1,070	1,207	5.6	10.1
Non-denom Chr Chs	2	90	95	113	0.5	0.9
PENT–Assemb of God	6	470	449	619	2.9	5.2
PENT–Ch of God Proph	1	NR	14	18	0.1	0.2
PENT–Un Pent Ch Intl	1	NR	NR	NR	-	-
PRES–Presb Ch (USA)	2	59	118	148	0.7	1.2
CALLAHAN	**36**	**3,015**	**6,678**	**8,186**	**60.4**	**100.0**
BAPT–Ind Bapt Flwsp Intl	1	NR	NR	NR	-	-
BAPT–So Bapt Conv	14	1,276	4,266	5,207	38.4	63.6
Catholic	1	NR	NR	150	1.1	1.8
CHR–Chs of Christ	8	881	830	1,064	7.9	13.0
METH–Un Methodist	4	289	898	962	7.1	11.8
Non-denom Chr Chs	2	480	550	625	4.6	7.6
PENT–Assemb of God	1	42	32	53	0.4	0.6
PENT–Ch God (Cleve)	1	31	71	87	0.6	1.1
PENT–Un Pent Ch Intl	2	NR	NR	NR	-	-
PRES–Presb Ch (USA)	2	16	31	38	0.3	0.5
CAMERON	**328**	**31,984**	**42,595**	**202,006**	**49.7**	**100.0**
ANG/EPIS–Anglican NA	1	NR	NR	NR	-	-
ANG/EPIS–Episcopal	5	681	1,167	1,613	0.4	0.8
Bahá'í	2	NR	162	162	0.0	0.1
BAPT–Ind Bapt Flwsp Intl	2	NR	NR	NR	-	-
BAPT–So Bapt Conv	58	5,795	12,095	16,280	4.0	8.1
BUDD–Mahayana	1	NR	NR	11	0.0	0.0
Calv Chpl	1	NR	NR	NR	-	-
Catholic	38	NR	NR	137,889	33.9	68.3
CGOD–Ch God (Ander)	2	134	NR	134	0.0	0.1
Ch Cr, Scientst	1	NR	NR	NR	-	-
Ch God (7th Day)	2	NR	NR	NR	-	-
Ch of Nazarene	7	348	526	609	0.1	0.3
Chr & Miss Al	2	156	58	152	0.0	0.1

NR–Not Reported - Represents no adherents reported. Percentages may not total 100 due to rounding.

Table 3: Religious Congregations by County and Group: 2010

Religious Group	Number of Congrega-tions	Number of Attendees	Number of Communicant, Confirmed, or Full Members	Adherents		
				Number of Adherents	% of Total Pop.	% of Total Adh.
CHR–Chr Ch (Disc)	4	325	428	576	0.1	0.3
CHR–Chr Chs & Chs Cr	2	NR	750	1,010	0.2	0.5
CHR–Chs of Christ	17	1,271	1,205	1,691	0.4	0.8
Jehovah's Witness	13	NR	NR	NR	-	-
LDS–Comm of Christ	2	NR	262	262	0.1	0.1
LDS–L-D Saints	10	NR	NR	6,133	1.5	3.0
LUTH–Assoc Free Luth	1	NR	NR	NR	-	-
LUTH–E.L.C.A.	2	132	171	171	0.0	0.1
LUTH–Luth-MO Synod	6	772	995	1,298	0.3	0.6
MENN–Mennonite USA	3	170	245	330	0.1	0.2
METH–Un Methodist	12	1,491	2,854	3,627	0.9	1.8
Missionary Ch	5	330	175	330	0.1	0.2
Muslim Est	1	624	NR	2,542	0.6	1.3
New Apost Ch	1	NR	NR	NR	-	-
Non-denom Chr Chs	54	14,018	15,887	18,290	4.5	9.1
PENT–Assemb of God	32	3,620	2,770	5,281	1.3	2.6
PENT–Ch God (Cleve)	4	288	114	153	0.0	0.1
PENT–Ch God Apos Fth	1	NR	NR	NR	-	-
PENT–Ch of God Proph	1	NR	20	27	0.0	0.0
PENT–Intl Pent Holiness	7	565	465	626	0.2	0.3
PENT–Un Pent Ch Intl	5	NR	NR	NR	-	-
PENT–Vineyard	1	52	75	101	0.0	0.0
PRES–Evan Presby Ch	1	NR	38	51	0.0	0.0
PRES–Korean Pres Amer	1	NR	NR	NR	-	-
PRES–Presb Ch (USA)	9	507	944	1,271	0.3	0.6
PRES–Presb Ch Amer	1	65	50	66	0.0	0.0
Salvation Army	1	42	119	149	0.0	0.1
Sev Day Adv	7	583	1,015	1,166	0.3	0.6
Unit Univ	1	15	5	5	0.0	0.0
Unity Ch	1	NR	NR	NR	-	-
CAMP	**38**	**2,030**	**5,723**	**8,648**	**69.7**	**100.0**
ANG/EPIS–Episcopal	1	46	72	72	0.6	0.8
Bahá'í	0	NR	2	2	0.0	0.0
BAPT–Amer Bapt Assn	3	NR	255	323	2.6	3.7
BAPT–So Bapt Conv	11	1,085	3,177	4,023	32.4	46.5
Catholic	1	NR	NR	1,421	11.5	16.4
Ch of Nazarene	1	35	64	64	0.5	0.7
CHR–Chs of Christ	5	315	400	480	3.9	5.6
METH–AME	1	0	150	190	1.5	2.2
METH–C.M.E.	4	40	600	760	6.1	8.8
METH–Un Methodist	3	234	544	732	5.9	8.5
Non-denom Chr Chs	1	100	150	150	1.2	1.7
PENT–Assemb of God	2	115	62	119	1.0	1.4
PENT–Ch God (Cleve)	1	49	54	68	0.5	0.8
PENT–Ch of God Proph	1	NR	23	29	0.2	0.3
PENT–COGIC	1	0	150	190	1.5	2.2
PENT–Un Pent Ch Intl	1	NR	NR	NR	-	-
PRES–Presb Ch (USA)	1	11	20	25	0.2	0.3
CARSON	**19**	**1,024**	**3,445**	**4,801**	**77.7**	**100.0**
Bahá'í	0	NR	2	2	0.0	0.0
BAPT–So Bapt Conv	8	544	2,410	2,987	48.3	62.2
Catholic	3	NR	NR	628	10.2	13.1
CHR–Chs of Christ	3	215	215	253	4.1	5.3
METH–Un Methodist	3	220	799	882	14.3	18.4
Non-denom Chr Chs	1	15	19	19	0.3	0.4
PENT–Assemb of God	1	30	0	30	0.5	0.6
CASS	**111**	**6,211**	**18,171**	**23,282**	**76.4**	**100.0**
ANG/EPIS–Episcopal	1	13	22	38	0.1	0.2
Bahá'í	0	NR	9	9	0.0	0.0
BAPT–Amer Bapt Assn	9	NR	1,935	2,346	7.7	10.1
BAPT–Ind Bapt Flwsp Intl	1	NR	NR	NR	-	-
BAPT–NBC USA	2	160	300	364	1.2	1.6
BAPT–So Bapt Conv	45	3,757	10,998	13,334	43.8	57.3
Catholic	2	NR	NR	810	2.7	3.5
Ch of Nazarene	1	53	128	128	0.4	0.5
CHR–Chr Chs & Chs Cr	1	NR	65	79	0.3	0.3
CHR–Chs of Christ	4	370	377	503	1.7	2.2
Jehovah's Witness	1	NR	NR	NR	-	-
LDS–L-D Saints	1	NR	NR	387	1.3	1.7
LUTH–Luth-MO Synod	1	21	53	58	0.2	0.2
METH–C.M.E.	7	115	960	1,164	3.8	5.0
METH–Un Methodist	14	676	1,823	2,077	6.8	8.9
Non-denom Chr Chs	5	610	635	800	2.6	3.4
PENT–Assemb of God	5	323	179	357	1.2	1.5
PENT–Ch God (Cleve)	1	61	146	177	0.6	0.8
PENT–COGIC	4	0	450	546	1.8	2.3
PENT–Full Gosp Bapt	2	NR	NR	NR	-	-
PENT–Un Pent Ch Intl	1	NR	NR	NR	-	-
Sev Day Adv	3	52	91	105	0.3	0.5
CASTRO	**20**	**774**	**2,367**	**5,379**	**66.7**	**100.0**
BAPT–So Bapt Conv	8	303	1,512	2,004	24.9	37.3
Catholic	3	NR	NR	2,322	28.8	43.2
CHR–Chr Chs & Chs Cr	1	NR	20	27	0.3	0.5
CHR–Chs of Christ	3	205	289	367	4.6	6.8
METH–Un Methodist	2	106	392	452	5.6	8.4
Non-denom Chr Chs	1	75	125	125	1.6	2.3
PENT–Assemb of God	1	40	0	44	0.5	0.8
PENT–Intl Pent Holiness	1	45	29	38	0.5	0.7
CHAMBERS	**43**	**3,172**	**5,027**	**10,503**	**29.9**	**100.0**
ANG/EPIS–Episcopal	1	22	58	99	0.3	0.9
Bahá'í	0	NR	3	3	0.0	0.0
BAPT–Natl Mis Bapt Conv	1	20	0	0	0.0	0.0
BAPT–So Bapt Conv	11	1,189	2,074	2,644	7.5	25.2
Catholic	3	NR	NR	3,926	11.2	37.4
CHR–Chs of Christ	6	243	215	253	0.7	2.4
Jehovah's Witness	2	NR	NR	NR	-	-
LUTH–Luth-MO Synod	1	39	122	157	0.4	1.5
METH–Un Methodist	8	640	1,656	2,070	5.9	19.7
Non-denom Chr Chs	4	215	315	318	0.9	3.0
PENT–Assemb of God	4	804	584	1,033	2.9	9.8
PENT–Un Pent Ch Intl	2	NR	NR	NR	-	-
CHEROKEE	**127**	**6,940**	**16,684**	**29,483**	**58.0**	**100.0**
ANG/EPIS–Episcopal	1	37	59	59	0.1	0.2
Bahá'í	0	NR	6	6	0.0	0.0
BAPT–Amer Bapt Assn	8	NR	1,330	1,667	3.3	5.7
BAPT–Ind Bapt Flwsp Intl	1	NR	NR	NR	-	-
BAPT–So Bapt Conv	33	3,643	8,645	10,836	21.3	36.8
Catholic	4	NR	NR	8,917	17.5	30.2
Ch of Nazarene	3	168	251	315	0.6	1.1
CHR–Chr Ch (Disc)	5	14	238	298	0.6	1.0
CHR–Chs of Christ	12	837	862	1,077	2.1	3.7
Jehovah's Witness	2	NR	NR	NR	-	-
METH–AME	2	0	200	251	0.5	0.9
METH–C.M.E.	4	60	385	483	0.9	1.6
METH–Cong Meth	1	NR	27	34	0.1	0.1
METH–Un Methodist	18	802	2,013	2,255	4.4	7.6
Non-denom Chr Chs	10	874	1,952	1,995	3.9	6.8
ORTHE–Ant Orth of NA	1	17	NR	18	0.0	0.1
PENT–Assemb of God	7	288	178	470	0.9	1.6
PENT–Ch God (Cleve)	1	35	61	76	0.1	0.3
PENT–Ch of God Proph	1	NR	62	78	0.2	0.3
PENT–COGIC	1	0	150	188	0.4	0.6
PENT–Pent Ch of God	1	70	NR	109	0.2	0.4
PENT–Un Pent Ch Intl	3	NR	NR	NR	-	-
PRES–Cum Pres Am	4	NR	NR	NR	-	-
PRES–Cumber Presb	1	NR	56	100	0.2	0.3
PRES–Presb Ch (USA)	2	35	104	130	0.3	0.4
Sev Day Adv	1	60	105	121	0.2	0.4
CHILDRESS	**16**	**1,069**	**2,137**	**2,943**	**41.8**	**100.0**
Bahá'í	0	NR	1	1	0.0	0.0
BAPT–So Bapt Conv	4	465	945	1,135	16.1	38.6
Catholic	1	NR	NR	210	3.0	7.1
CHR–Chr Ch (Disc)	1	23	45	54	0.8	1.8
CHR–Chs of Christ	2	287	357	460	6.5	15.6
LUTH–Luth-MO Synod	1	6	6	6	0.1	0.2
METH–Un Methodist	1	156	576	664	9.4	22.6
Non-denom Chr Chs	1	10	10	12	0.2	0.4
PENT–Assemb of God	1	52	26	87	1.2	3.0

NR–Not Reported - Represents no adherents reported. Percentages may not total 100 due to rounding.

Table 3: Religious Congregations by County and Group: 2010

Religious Group	Number of Congrega-tions	Number of Attendees	Number of Communicant, Confirmed, or Full Members	Adherents: Number of Adherents	Adherents: % of Total Pop.	Adherents: % of Total Adh.
PENT–COGIC	1	0	150	180	2.6	6.1
PENT–Pent Ch of God	1	70	NR	109	1.5	3.7
PENT–Un Pent Ch Intl	1	NR	NR	NR	-	-
PRES–Presb Ch (USA)	1	0	21	25	0.4	0.8
CLAY	**26**	**1,802**	**4,948**	**6,307**	**58.7**	**100.0**
ANG/EPIS–Anglican NA	1	NR	NR	NR	-	-
Bahá'í	0	NR	2	2	0.0	0.0
BAPT–Free Will Bapt	1	NR	52	62	0.6	1.0
BAPT–So Bapt Conv	10	722	3,357	4,033	37.5	63.9
Catholic	1	NR	NR	180	1.7	2.9
CHR–Chr Ch (Disc)	1	0	108	130	1.2	2.1
CHR–Chs of Christ	4	305	315	394	3.7	6.2
METH–Un Methodist	5	210	521	594	5.5	9.4
Non-denom Chr Chs	1	400	400	500	4.7	7.9
PENT–Assemb of God	1	125	0	180	1.7	2.9
PENT–Ch God (Cleve)	1	40	193	232	2.2	3.7
COCHRAN	**15**	**693**	**1,286**	**2,307**	**73.8**	**100.0**
BAPT–So Bapt Conv	7	285	863	1,107	35.4	48.0
Catholic	1	NR	NR	621	19.9	26.9
CHR–Chs of Christ	3	210	198	257	8.2	11.1
METH–Un Methodist	1	43	121	155	5.0	6.7
PENT–Assemb of God	3	155	104	167	5.3	7.2
COKE	**13**	**629**	**1,662**	**2,328**	**70.1**	**100.0**
Bahá'í	0	NR	1	1	0.0	0.0
BAPT–So Bapt Conv	4	344	1,204	1,430	43.1	61.4
Catholic	2	NR	NR	300	9.0	12.9
CHR–Chs of Christ	3	158	169	217	6.5	9.3
METH–Un Methodist	2	89	268	342	10.3	14.7
PENT–Assemb of God	1	38	20	38	1.1	1.6
PENT–Un Pent Ch Intl	1	NR	NR	NR	-	-
COLEMAN	**46**	**1,689**	**4,412**	**5,798**	**65.2**	**100.0**
ANG/EPIS–Episcopal	1	29	60	60	0.7	1.0
BAPT–Ind Bapt Flwsp Intl	2	NR	NR	NR	-	-
BAPT–Ref Bapt Ch	1	NR	NR	NR	-	-
BAPT–So Bapt Conv	19	696	2,324	2,805	31.5	48.4
Catholic	1	NR	NR	700	7.9	12.1
Ch of Nazarene	1	17	29	29	0.3	0.5
CHR–Chr Ch (Disc)	1	20	137	165	1.9	2.8
CHR–Chs of Christ	5	354	472	573	6.4	9.9
METH–Un Methodist	7	192	658	712	8.0	12.3
Non-denom Chr Chs	3	340	630	630	7.1	10.9
PENT–Assemb of God	1	12	9	14	0.2	0.2
PENT–Un Pent Ch Intl	1	NR	NR	NR	-	-
PRES–Presb Ch (USA)	2	10	60	72	0.8	1.2
Sev Day Adv	1	19	33	38	0.4	0.7
COLLIN	**485**	**117,551**	**191,341**	**410,214**	**52.4**	**100.0**
ANG/EPIS–Anglican NA	3	NR	NR	NR	-	-
ANG/EPIS–Episcopal	5	791	1,212	1,486	0.2	0.4
Bahá'í	6	NR	868	868	0.1	0.2
BAPT–Amer Bapt Assn	2	NR	170	220	0.0	0.1
BAPT–Amer Bapt USA	1	75	175	226	0.0	0.1
BAPT–Free Will Bapt	1	NR	52	67	0.0	0.0
BAPT–Ind Bapt Flwsp Intl	2	NR	NR	NR	-	-
BAPT–Natl Mis Bapt Conv	1	60	70	90	0.0	0.0
BAPT–Ref Bapt Ch	1	NR	NR	NR	-	-
BAPT–So Bapt Conv	141	26,250	61,358	79,277	10.1	19.3
BUDD–Mahayana	1	NR	NR	102	0.0	0.0
Calv Chpl	2	NR	NR	NR	-	-
Catholic	8	NR	NR	111,182	14.2	27.1
Ch Cr, Scientst	1	NR	NR	NR	-	-
Ch of Nazarene	6	629	1,114	1,218	0.2	0.3
Chr & Miss Al	3	510	324	760	0.1	0.2
CHR–Chr Ch (Disc)	12	816	1,473	1,903	0.2	0.5
CHR–Chr Chs & Chs Cr	3	NR	590	762	0.1	0.2
CHR–Chs of Christ	27	4,412	3,723	5,543	0.7	1.4
Christian Brethren	1	NR	NR	NR	-	-
Evan Free Ch	2	680	NR	680	0.1	0.2

Religious Group	Number of Congrega-tions	Number of Attendees	Number of Communicant, Confirmed, or Full Members	Adherents: Number of Adherents	Adherents: % of Total Pop.	Adherents: % of Total Adh.
HINDU–I/A Temples	5	NR	NR	7,513	1.0	1.8
HINDU–Post Ren	2	NR	NR	41	0.0	0.0
HINDU–Trad Temples	3	NR	NR	7,100	0.9	1.7
Jehovah's Witness	8	NR	NR	NR	-	-
JUD–Conserv	1	367	412	1,112	0.1	0.3
JUD–Orth	2	173	200	240	0.0	0.1
JUD–Reform	1	105	186	502	0.1	0.1
LDS–Comm of Christ	1	NR	126	126	0.0	0.0
LDS–L-D Saints	32	NR	NR	13,461	1.7	3.3
LUTH–E.L.C.A.	5	1,126	1,840	2,363	0.3	0.6
LUTH–Luth Cong Msn Chr	1	45	29	37	0.0	0.0
LUTH–Luth-MO Synod	7	2,650	4,665	5,934	0.8	1.4
LUTH–Wisc Ev Luth Syn	1	121	164	219	0.0	0.1
METH–C.M.E.	2	100	300	388	0.0	0.1
METH–Un Methodist	28	12,894	32,869	49,441	6.3	12.1
METH–Wesleyan	3	670	197	871	0.1	0.2
Muslim Est	9	5,269	NR	22,994	2.9	5.6
New Apost Ch	1	NR	NR	NR	-	-
Non-denom Chr Chs	74	51,789	70,697	78,049	10.0	19.0
ORTHE–Orth Ch in Amer	1	120	NR	190	0.0	0.0
PENT–Assemb of God	20	4,947	3,051	8,060	1.0	2.0
PENT–Ch God (Cleve)	4	250	462	597	0.1	0.1
PENT–COGIC	5	83	415	536	0.1	0.1
PENT–Int Foursq Gos	1	43	49	63	0.0	0.0
PENT–Pent Ch of God	1	70	NR	109	0.0	0.0
PENT–Un Pent Ch Intl	13	NR	NR	NR	-	-
PRES–Korean Amer Pres	1	NR	NR	NR	-	-
PRES–Korean Pres Amer	1	NR	NR	NR	-	-
PRES–Presb Ch (USA)	8	829	2,392	3,091	0.4	0.8
PRES–Presb Ch Amer	5	529	585	892	0.1	0.2
PRES–Ref Pres GA	1	NR	NR	NR	-	-
REF–Ref Ch in Am	1	160	504	512	0.1	0.1
Salvation Army	3	423	162	162	0.0	0.0
Sev Day Adv	4	406	705	811	0.1	0.2
Unit Univ	1	159	202	300	0.0	0.1
Zoroastrian	0	NR	NR	116	0.0	0.0
COLLINGSWORTH	**16**	**780**	**2,308**	**3,190**	**104.4**	**100.0**
BAPT–Ind Bapt Flwsp Intl	1	NR	NR	NR	-	-
BAPT–So Bapt Conv	5	266	1,456	1,851	60.5	58.0
Catholic	1	NR	NR	150	4.9	4.7
Ch of Nazarene	2	131	167	233	7.6	7.3
CHR–Chr Chs & Chs Cr	1	NR	100	127	4.2	4.0
CHR–Chs of Christ	4	264	202	318	10.4	10.0
METH–Un Methodist	1	94	348	476	15.6	14.9
Non-denom Chr Chs	1	25	35	35	1.1	1.1
COLORADO	**48**	**1,839**	**4,916**	**12,401**	**59.4**	**100.0**
ANG/EPIS–Episcopal	2	54	112	201	1.0	1.6
Bahá'í	0	NR	2	2	0.0	0.0
BAPT–So Bapt Conv	8	404	1,627	1,988	9.5	16.0
Catholic	6	NR	NR	6,541	31.3	52.7
Ch of Nazarene	1	65	114	135	0.6	1.1
CHR–Chs of Christ	4	120	102	143	0.7	1.2
Jehovah's Witness	1	NR	NR	NR	-	-
LUTH–E.L.C.A.	4	322	890	1,055	5.1	8.5
METH–AME	1	20	45	55	0.3	0.4
METH–Un Methodist	7	326	875	954	4.6	7.7
Non-denom Chr Chs	4	227	335	337	1.6	2.7
PENT–Assemb of God	1	25	25	25	0.1	0.2
PENT–Ch God (Cleve)	2	145	187	229	1.1	1.8
PENT–Ch of God Proph	1	NR	4	5	0.0	0.0
PENT–COGIC	2	0	300	367	1.8	3.0
PENT–Un Pent Ch Intl	2	NR	NR	NR	-	-
PRES–Presb Ch (USA)	1	10	19	23	0.1	0.2
Un C of Christ	1	121	279	341	1.6	2.7
COMAL	**109**	**15,624**	**25,358**	**53,968**	**49.8**	**100.0**
ANG/EPIS–Anglican NA	2	NR	NR	NR	-	-
ANG/EPIS–Episcopal	2	232	455	479	0.4	0.9
Bahá'í	0	NR	24	24	0.0	0.0
BAPT–So Bapt Conv	21	4,608	7,963	9,706	8.9	18.0
BUDD–Mahayana	4	NR	NR	410	0.4	0.8

NR–Not Reported - Represents no adherents reported. Percentages may not total 100 due to rounding.

Table 3: Religious Congregations by County and Group: 2010

Religious Group	Number of Congregations	Number of Attendees	Number of Communicant, Confirmed, or Full Members	Adherents: Number of Adherents	Adherents: % of Total Pop.	Adherents: % of Total Adh.
Calv Chpl	1	NR	NR	NR	-	-
Catholic	7	NR	NR	17,828	16.4	33.0
Ch Cr, Scientst	1	NR	NR	NR	-	-
Ch of Nazarene	1	109	132	132	0.1	0.2
CHR–Chr Ch (Disc)	1	82	171	208	0.2	0.4
CHR–Chr Chs & Chs Cr	2	NR	310	378	0.3	0.7
CHR–Chs of Christ	7	782	788	980	0.9	1.8
Evan Assoc RCC	1	NR	NR	NR	-	-
Evan Free Ch	3	1,575	NR	1,575	1.5	2.9
Jehovah's Witness	3	NR	NR	NR	-	-
LDS–Comm of Christ	1	NR	110	110	0.1	0.2
LDS–L-D Saints	4	NR	NR	2,012	1.9	3.7
LUTH–E.L.C.A.	3	561	1,326	1,527	1.4	2.8
LUTH–Luth Cong Msn Chr	2	700	2,664	3,247	3.0	6.0
LUTH–Luth-MO Synod	1	373	577	607	0.6	1.1
METH–AME	1	0	150	183	0.2	0.3
METH–Un Methodist	5	1,476	3,630	5,650	5.2	10.5
METH–Wesleyan	1	211	142	274	0.3	0.5
Non-denom Chr Chs	14	3,610	4,763	5,719	5.3	10.6
ORTHE–Romania Orth Ar	1	30	NR	200	0.2	0.4
PENT–Assemb of God	3	197	113	201	0.2	0.4
PENT–Un Pent Ch Intl	6	NR	NR	NR	-	-
PENT–Vineyard	1	80	142	173	0.2	0.3
PRES–Presb Ch (USA)	4	574	1,324	1,614	1.5	3.0
PRES–Presb Ch Amer	1	287	356	476	0.4	0.9
Salvation Army	1	2	0	0	0.0	0.0
Sev Day Adv	1	36	63	72	0.1	0.1
Un C of Christ	1	52	82	100	0.1	0.2
Unit Univ	1	47	73	83	0.1	0.2
Unity Ch	1	NR	NR	NR	-	-
COMANCHE	**54**	**2,973**	**6,855**	**8,869**	**63.5**	**100.0**
ANG/EPIS–Anglican NA	1	NR	NR	NR	-	-
Bahá'í	0	NR	1	1	0.0	0.0
BAPT–Free Will Bapt	1	NR	52	64	0.5	0.7
BAPT–Ind Bapt Flwsp Intl	1	NR	NR	NR	-	-
BAPT–So Bapt Conv	23	1,925	4,830	5,929	42.4	66.9
Catholic	2	NR	NR	508	3.6	5.7
CHR–Chr Chs & Chs Cr	1	NR	42	52	0.4	0.6
CHR–Chs of Christ	9	435	443	528	3.8	6.0
Jehovah's Witness	1	NR	NR	NR	-	-
LDS–L-D Saints	1	NR	NR	67	0.5	0.8
LUTH–E.L.C.A.	1	19	32	56	0.4	0.6
METH–Cong Meth	1	NR	0	0	0.0	0.0
METH–Un Methodist	5	245	1,058	1,151	8.2	13.0
Non-denom Chr Chs	2	200	300	300	2.1	3.4
PENT–Assemb of God	2	79	97	104	0.7	1.2
PENT–Pent Ch of God	1	70	NR	109	0.8	1.2
PENT–Un Pent Ch Intl	2	NR	NR	NR	-	-
CONCHO	**15**	**307**	**511**	**997**	**24.4**	**100.0**
Bahá'í	0	NR	1	1	0.0	0.1
BAPT–So Bapt Conv	5	144	295	332	8.1	33.3
Catholic	3	NR	NR	400	9.8	40.1
CHR–Chs of Christ	2	56	52	64	1.6	6.4
Evan Free Ch	1	20	NR	20	0.5	2.0
LUTH–Luth-MO Synod	2	51	88	105	2.6	10.5
METH–Un Methodist	2	36	75	75	1.8	7.5
COOKE	**82**	**5,244**	**11,825**	**23,524**	**61.2**	**100.0**
ANG/EPIS–Anglican NA	1	NR	NR	NR	-	-
Bahá'í	0	NR	19	19	0.0	0.1
BAPT–Amer Bapt Assn	2	NR	170	211	0.5	0.9
BAPT–Ind Bapt Flwsp Intl	1	NR	NR	NR	-	-
BAPT–So Bapt Conv	31	2,570	6,005	7,448	19.4	31.7
Catholic	3	NR	NR	8,715	22.7	37.0
Ch Cr, Scientst	1	NR	NR	NR	-	-
Ch of Nazarene	2	75	118	148	0.4	0.6
CHR–Chr Ch (Disc)	1	119	243	301	0.8	1.3
CHR–Chr Chs & Chs Cr	1	NR	40	50	0.1	0.2
CHR–Chs of Christ	9	644	794	1,075	2.8	4.6
Jehovah's Witness	1	NR	NR	NR	-	-
LDS–L-D Saints	1	NR	NR	527	1.4	2.2
LUTH–Luth-MO Synod	1	80	134	151	0.4	0.6
METH–AME	1	0	100	124	0.3	0.5
METH–C.M.E.	1	0	150	186	0.5	0.8
METH–Un Methodist	8	657	1,386	1,699	4.4	7.2
Non-denom Chr Chs	7	650	2,110	2,130	5.5	9.1
PENT–Assemb of God	3	158	120	238	0.6	1.0
PENT–Ch God (Cleve)	1	43	79	98	0.3	0.4
PENT–Intl Pent Holiness	1	19	22	27	0.1	0.1
PENT–Un Pent Ch Intl	1	NR	NR	NR	-	-
PRES–Presb Ch (USA)	1	74	123	153	0.4	0.7
PRES–Presb Ch Amer	2	117	145	147	0.4	0.6
Sev Day Adv	1	38	67	77	0.2	0.3
CORYELL	**104**	**10,687**	**22,465**	**32,555**	**43.2**	**100.0**
ANG/EPIS–Episcopal	1	26	25	53	0.1	0.2
Bahá'í	0	NR	14	14	0.0	0.0
BAPT–Amer Bapt Assn	1	NR	85	110	0.1	0.3
BAPT–Ind Bapt Flwsp Intl	2	NR	NR	NR	-	-
BAPT–NBC Amer	1	80	125	162	0.2	0.5
BAPT–So Bapt Conv	44	3,695	10,803	13,963	18.5	42.9
Catholic	2	NR	NR	3,735	5.0	11.5
Ch of God Gen Conf	1	NR	50	65	0.1	0.2
Ch of Nazarene	2	111	176	227	0.3	0.7
CHR–Chr Ch (Disc)	1	15	102	132	0.2	0.4
CHR–Chr Chs & Chs Cr	1	NR	70	90	0.1	0.3
CHR–Chs of Christ	9	613	657	889	1.2	2.7
Jehovah's Witness	3	NR	NR	NR	-	-
LDS–L-D Saints	3	NR	NR	1,560	2.1	4.8
LUTH–E.L.C.A.	1	49	140	155	0.2	0.5
LUTH–Luth-MO Synod	3	364	584	731	1.0	2.2
METH–AME	1	0	100	129	0.2	0.4
METH–Evan Meth Ch	1	NR	NR	NR	-	-
METH–Un Methodist	8	747	2,456	3,019	4.0	9.3
Non-denom Chr Chs	10	4,640	6,540	6,600	8.8	20.3
PENT–Assemb of God	2	220	99	245	0.3	0.8
PENT–Ch God (Cleve)	1	32	137	177	0.2	0.5
PENT–Pent Ch of God	1	70	NR	109	0.1	0.3
PENT–Un Pent Ch Intl	2	NR	NR	NR	-	-
PRES–Presb Ch (USA)	2	25	188	243	0.3	0.7
Un C of Christ	1	0	114	147	0.2	0.5
COTTLE	**9**	**225**	**1,072**	**1,488**	**98.9**	**100.0**
BAPT–So Bapt Conv	2	94	833	1,018	67.6	68.4
Catholic	1	NR	NR	181	12.0	12.2
CHR–Chr Ch (Disc)	1	0	0	0	0.0	0.0
CHR–Chs of Christ	2	58	46	62	4.1	4.2
METH–Un Methodist	1	35	152	177	11.8	11.9
Non-denom Chr Chs	1	15	10	19	1.3	1.3
PENT–Assemb of God	1	23	31	31	2.1	2.1
CRANE	**10**	**365**	**1,277**	**2,357**	**53.9**	**100.0**
BAPT–Ind Bapt Flwsp Intl	1	NR	NR	NR	-	-
BAPT–So Bapt Conv	3	120	922	1,187	27.1	50.4
Catholic	1	NR	NR	750	17.1	31.8
CHR–Chs of Christ	2	103	103	132	3.0	5.6
METH–Un Methodist	1	62	172	188	4.3	8.0
Non-denom Chr Chs	1	80	80	100	2.3	4.2
PENT–Un Pent Ch Intl	1	NR	NR	NR	-	-
CROCKETT	**11**	**396**	**873**	**2,462**	**66.2**	**100.0**
BAPT–So Bapt Conv	3	160	486	612	16.5	24.9
Catholic	1	NR	NR	1,350	36.3	54.8
CHR–Chs of Christ	2	105	103	128	3.4	5.2
LUTH–Luth-MO Synod	1	5	7	8	0.2	0.3
METH–Un Methodist	1	53	221	262	7.0	10.6
PENT–Assemb of God	2	73	45	88	2.4	3.6
PENT–Ch of God Proph	1	NR	11	14	0.4	0.6
CROSBY	**25**	**1,092**	**2,570**	**5,132**	**84.7**	**100.0**
Bahá'í	0	NR	2	2	0.0	0.0
BAPT–So Bapt Conv	9	602	1,805	2,315	38.2	45.1
Catholic	3	NR	NR	1,826	30.1	35.6

NR–Not Reported - Represents no adherents reported. Percentages may not total 100 due to rounding.

Table 3: Religious Congregations by County and Group: 2010

Religious Group	Number of Congrega-tions	Number of Attendees	Number of Communicant, Confirmed, or Full Members	Adherents		
				Number of Adherents	% of Total Pop.	% of Total Adh.
CHR–Chs of Christ	6	245	273	356	5.9	6.9
METH–Un Methodist	4	120	417	498	8.2	9.7
PENT–Assemb of God	2	65	23	71	1.2	1.4
PENT–Intl Pent Holiness	1	60	50	64	1.1	1.2
CULBERSON	**9**	**234**	**419**	**1,467**	**61.2**	**100.0**
Bahá'í	0	NR	17	17	0.7	1.2
BAPT–So Bapt Conv	3	119	170	215	9.0	14.7
Catholic	1	NR	NR	950	39.6	64.8
CHR–Chs of Christ	2	41	100	126	5.3	8.6
METH–Un Methodist	1	23	45	59	2.5	4.0
PENT–Assemb of God	1	3	3	3	0.1	0.2
Sev Day Adv	1	48	84	97	4.0	6.6
DALLAM	**25**	**1,403**	**2,960**	**4,641**	**69.2**	**100.0**
ANG/EPIS–Episcopal	1	33	122	156	2.3	3.4
Bahá'í	0	NR	2	2	0.0	0.0
BAPT–So Bapt Conv	3	254	797	1,046	15.6	22.5
Catholic	2	NR	NR	760	11.3	16.4
CHR–Chr Chs & Chs Cr	1	NR	150	197	2.9	4.2
CHR–Chs of Christ	3	280	318	433	6.5	9.3
Jehovah's Witness	1	NR	NR	NR	-	-
LDS–L-D Saints	1	NR	NR	164	2.4	3.5
LUTH–Luth–MO Synod	1	28	104	142	2.1	3.1
MENN–CG in Cr (Menn)	2	NR	216	283	4.2	6.1
METH–Un Methodist	2	203	470	537	8.0	11.6
Non-denom Chr Chs	4	540	675	788	11.8	17.0
PENT–Assemb of God	1	16	15	22	0.3	0.5
PENT–Un Pent Ch Intl	1	NR	NR	NR	-	-
PRES–Presb Ch (USA)	1	19	38	50	0.7	1.1
Sev Day Adv	1	30	53	61	0.9	1.3
DALLAS	**2,336**	**388,437**	**690,451**	**1,455,158**	**61.4**	**100.0**
ANG/EPIS–Anglican NA	7	NR	NR	NR	-	-
ANG/EPIS–Episcopal	35	7,295	20,443	22,730	1.0	1.6
Bahá'í	11	NR	1,659	1,659	0.1	0.1
BAPT–Alliance Bapt	1	NR	NR	NR	-	-
BAPT–Amer Bapt Assn	10	NR	1,199	1,533	0.1	0.1
BAPT–Amer Bapt USA	5	311	993	1,269	0.1	0.1
BAPT–Free Will Bapt	1	NR	52	66	0.0	0.0
BAPT–Ind Bapt Flwsp Intl	19	NR	NR	NR	-	-
BAPT–N Am Bapt Conf	1	NR	105	134	0.0	0.0
BAPT–Natl Mis Bapt Conv	30	845	4,920	6,290	0.3	0.4
BAPT–NBC Amer	27	7,110	20,425	26,111	1.1	1.8
BAPT–NBC USA	13	5,670	7,976	10,196	0.4	0.7
BAPT–Ref Bapt Ch	2	NR	NR	NR	-	-
BAPT–So Bapt Conv	726	76,334	204,332	261,216	11.0	18.0
BUDD–Mahayana	18	NR	NR	11,185	0.5	0.8
BUDD–Theravada	5	NR	NR	1,196	0.1	0.1
BUDD–Vajrayana	3	NR	NR	165	0.0	0.0
Calv Chpl	3	NR	NR	NR	-	-
Catholic	56	NR	NR	446,996	18.9	30.7
CGOD–Ch God (Ander)	2	212	NR	212	0.0	0.0
Ch Cr, Scientst	7	NR	NR	NR	-	-
Ch God (7th Day)	6	NR	NR	NR	-	-
Ch of Nazarene	21	1,234	2,380	2,933	0.1	0.2
Chr & Miss Al	4	277	285	385	0.0	0.0
CHR–Chr Ch (Disc)	38	2,618	6,919	8,845	0.4	0.6
CHR–Chr Chs & Chs Cr	9	NR	5,485	7,012	0.3	0.5
CHR–Chs of Christ	103	28,424	31,887	41,160	1.7	2.8
CHR–Int Chs of Christ	1	NR	589	753	0.0	0.1
Christian Brethren	1	NR	NR	NR	-	-
Evan Cov Ch	2	79	142	103	0.0	0.0
Evan Free Ch	2	250	NR	250	0.0	0.0
FRND–Fr Gen Cf	1	NR	47	60	0.0	0.0
HINDU–I/A Temples	8	NR	NR	6,442	0.3	0.4
HINDU–Post Ren	5	NR	NR	183	0.0	0.0
HINDU–Renaiss	2	NR	NR	62	0.0	0.0
HINDU–Trad Temples	1	NR	NR	1,000	0.0	0.1
Jain	1	NR	NR	NR	-	-
Jehovah's Witness	18	NR	NR	NR	-	-
JUD–Conserv	2	1,487	1,669	4,506	0.2	0.3
JUD–Orth	9	2,448	1,000	3,400	0.1	0.2

Religious Group	Number of Congrega-tions	Number of Attendees	Number of Communicant, Confirmed, or Full Members	Adherents		
				Number of Adherents	% of Total Pop.	% of Total Adh.
JUD–Reform	4	1,914	3,375	9,112	0.4	0.6
LDS–Comm of Christ	4	NR	504	504	0.0	0.0
LDS–L-D Saints	39	NR	NR	21,953	0.9	1.5
LUTH–Ch Luth Conf	1	NR	NR	NR	-	-
LUTH–E.L.C.A.	22	3,433	6,440	8,026	0.3	0.6
LUTH–Luth Cong Msn Chr	1	100	415	531	0.0	0.0
LUTH–Luth–MO Synod	16	2,185	4,713	6,028	0.3	0.4
LUTH–Nor Amer Luth C	1	NR	NR	NR	-	-
LUTH–Wisc Ev Luth Syn	3	353	580	766	0.0	0.1
MENN–Mennonite USA	7	142	205	262	0.0	0.0
METH–AME	22	978	3,705	4,736	0.2	0.3
METH–AME Zion	2	80	250	320	0.0	0.0
METH–C.M.E.	14	3,950	9,025	11,537	0.5	0.8
METH–Cong Meth	6	NR	324	414	0.0	0.0
METH–Evan Meth Ch	2	NR	NR	NR	-	-
METH–Free Methodist	2	116	24	116	0.0	0.0
METH–So Methodist	1	NR	NR	NR	-	-
METH–Un Methodist	88	26,071	69,231	94,881	4.0	6.5
METH–Wesleyan	1	55	18	72	0.0	0.0
Metro Comm Ch	2	118	178	228	0.0	0.0
Missionary Ch	2	285	310	310	0.0	0.0
MJEW–Union Mes Cong	1	NR	NR	NR	-	-
Muslim Est	25	18,098	NR	84,256	3.6	5.8
New Apost Ch	1	NR	NR	NR	-	-
Non-denom Chr Chs	438	136,636	190,385	208,131	8.8	14.3
OCATH–Pol Natl Cath	1	NR	NR	NR	-	-
ORTHE–Ant Orth of NA	2	183	NR	492	0.0	0.0
ORTHE–Greek Orthodox	1	550	NR	4,000	0.2	0.3
ORTHE–Orth Ch in Amer	1	200	NR	600	0.0	0.0
ORTHE–Rus Orth Abroad	1	35	NR	175	0.0	0.0
ORTHE–Serb Orth USA	1	170	NR	280	0.0	0.0
ORTHO–Armen Ap Etchm	1	40	NR	100	0.0	0.0
ORTHO–Coptic Orth Ch	1	300	NR	650	0.0	0.0
ORTHO–Eritrean Orth	1	75	NR	650	0.0	0.0
ORTHO–Ethiopian Orth	2	NR	NR	NR	-	-
ORTHO–Malan Dioc Am	6	370	NR	1,110	0.0	0.1
ORTHO–Malan Syr Orth	2	400	NR	756	0.0	0.1
PENT–Assemb of God	96	27,754	31,398	49,796	2.1	3.4
PENT–Ch God (Cleve)	41	5,128	5,522	7,059	0.3	0.5
PENT–Ch God Apos Fth	1	NR	NR	NR	-	-
PENT–Ch of God Proph	5	NR	249	318	0.0	0.0
PENT–COGIC	52	3,710	8,324	10,641	0.4	0.7
PENT–Cong Hol Ch	11	429	385	492	0.0	0.0
PENT–Full Gosp Bapt	13	NR	NR	NR	-	-
PENT–Int Foursq Gos	7	354	645	825	0.0	0.1
PENT–Intl Pent Holiness	8	778	657	840	0.0	0.1
PENT–Open Bible Std	1	55	NR	55	0.0	0.0
PENT–Pent Ch of God	8	560	NR	870	0.0	0.1
PENT–Un Pent Ch Intl	22	NR	NR	NR	-	-
PENT–Vineyard	1	125	150	192	0.0	0.0
PRES–As Ref Pres Ch	1	NR	0	0	0.0	0.0
PRES–Cum Pres Am	1	NR	NR	NR	-	-
PRES–Cumber Presb	2	NR	246	334	0.0	0.0
PRES–Evan Presby Ch	1	NR	97	124	0.0	0.0
PRES–Kor Pres Abroad	1	NR	NR	NR	-	-
PRES–Korean Amer Pres	1	NR	NR	NR	-	-
PRES–Korean Pres Amer	1	NR	NR	NR	-	-
PRES–Orth Pres Ch	1	70	45	70	0.0	0.0
PRES–Presb Ch (USA)	41	7,040	18,974	24,256	1.0	1.7
PRES–Presb Ch Amer	14	2,383	4,558	6,071	0.3	0.4
PRES–Ref Pres Han	1	NR	NR	NR	-	-
REF–Christian Ref	2	90	40	51	0.0	0.0
REF–Hung Ref Add'l	1	NR	NR	NR	-	-
Salvation Army	6	458	930	4,670	0.2	0.3
Sev Day Adv	39	5,848	10,172	11,695	0.5	0.8
Sikh	4	NR	NR	NR	-	-
Un C of Christ	6	1,665	4,638	5,929	0.3	0.4
Unit Univ	3	559	1,232	1,655	0.1	0.1
Unity Ch	3	NR	NR	NR	-	-
Zoroastrian	0	NR	NR	167	0.0	0.0
DAWSON	**39**	**2,230**	**6,220**	**9,803**	**70.9**	**100.0**
Bahá'í	0	NR	6	6	0.0	0.1
BAPT–So Bapt Conv	13	1,091	4,460	5,529	40.0	56.4

NR–Not Reported   - Represents no adherents reported.   Percentages may not total 100 due to rounding.

Table 3: Religious Congregations by County and Group: 2010

Religious Group	Number of Congrega-tions	Number of Attendees	Number of Communicant, Confirmed, or Full Members	Adherents: Number of Adherents	Adherents: % of Total Pop.	Adherents: % of Total Adh.
Catholic	2	NR	NR	2,068	14.9	21.1
Ch of Nazarene	1	27	53	71	0.5	0.7
CHR–Chs of Christ	5	442	494	614	4.4	6.3
Jehovah's Witness	1	NR	NR	NR	-	-
LUTH–Luth–MO Synod	1	40	70	90	0.7	0.9
METH–Un Methodist	4	217	705	780	5.6	8.0
Non-denom Chr Chs	2	110	135	150	1.1	1.5
PENT–Assemb of God	6	199	139	299	2.2	3.1
PENT–COGIC	1	20	30	37	0.3	0.4
PENT–Int Foursq Gos	1	38	44	55	0.4	0.6
PENT–Un Pent Ch Intl	1	NR	NR	NR	-	-
PRES–Presb Ch (USA)	1	46	84	104	0.8	1.1
DEAF SMITH	**39**	**2,816**	**5,967**	**16,261**	**83.9**	**100.0**
ANG/EPIS–Episcopal	1	13	33	34	0.2	0.2
Bahá'í	0	NR	11	11	0.1	0.1
BAPT–Ind Bapt Flwsp Intl	1	NR	NR	NR	-	-
BAPT–So Bapt Conv	11	917	2,585	3,472	17.9	21.4
Catholic	2	NR	NR	8,330	43.0	51.2
Ch of Nazarene	2	323	568	875	4.5	5.4
CHR–Chs of Christ	4	264	319	385	2.0	2.4
Jehovah's Witness	1	NR	NR	NR	-	-
LDS–L-D Saints	1	NR	NR	322	1.7	2.0
LUTH–Luth–MO Synod	1	24	26	31	0.2	0.2
METH–Un Methodist	3	243	1,132	1,228	6.3	7.6
Non-denom Chr Chs	6	780	1,075	1,075	5.5	6.6
PENT–Assemb of God	3	155	52	290	1.5	1.8
PRES–Presb Ch (USA)	1	51	87	117	0.6	0.7
Sev Day Adv	2	46	79	91	0.5	0.6
DELTA	**24**	**1,255**	**2,677**	**3,358**	**64.2**	**100.0**
Bahá'í	0	NR	3	3	0.1	0.1
BAPT–Ind Bapt Flwsp Intl	1	NR	NR	NR	-	-
BAPT–So Bapt Conv	9	620	1,872	2,242	42.9	66.8
Catholic	1	NR	NR	46	0.9	1.4
CHR–Chs of Christ	2	75	69	92	1.8	2.7
METH–Un Methodist	4	166	368	421	8.0	12.5
Non-denom Chr Chs	3	204	254	280	5.4	8.3
PENT–Assemb of God	1	104	82	132	2.5	3.9
PENT–Pent Ch of God	1	70	NR	109	2.1	3.2
PENT–Un Pent Ch Intl	1	NR	NR	NR	-	-
Sev Day Adv	1	16	29	33	0.6	1.0
DENTON	**436**	**99,639**	**157,088**	**266,302**	**40.2**	**100.0**
ANG/EPIS–Anglican NA	2	NR	NR	NR	-	-
ANG/EPIS–Episcopal	6	1,555	3,199	3,858	0.6	1.4
Bahá'í	5	NR	372	372	0.1	0.1
BAPT–Amer Bapt Assn	3	NR	320	409	0.1	0.2
BAPT–Ind Bapt Flwsp Intl	10	NR	NR	NR	-	-
BAPT–N Am Bapt Conf	1	NR	32	41	0.0	0.0
BAPT–Natl Mis Bapt Conv	1	0	60	77	0.0	0.0
BAPT–NBC USA	1	0	115	147	0.0	0.1
BAPT–So Bapt Conv	126	47,473	88,410	112,973	17.0	42.4
Calv Chpl	2	NR	NR	NR	-	-
Catholic	8	NR	NR	44,615	6.7	16.8
Ch Cr, Scientst	1	NR	NR	NR	-	-
Ch of Nazarene	6	541	870	1,054	0.2	0.4
CHR–Chr Ch (Disc)	7	522	1,126	1,439	0.2	0.5
CHR–Chr Chs & Chs Cr	3	NR	1,125	1,438	0.2	0.5
CHR–Chs of Christ	28	4,594	4,974	6,194	0.9	2.3
Evan Cov Ch	2	246	275	319	0.0	0.1
Evan Free Ch	2	135	NR	135	0.0	0.1
HINDU–Post Ren	1	NR	NR	10	0.0	0.0
Jehovah's Witness	4	NR	NR	NR	-	-
JUD–Reform	1	82	145	392	0.1	0.1
LDS–L-D Saints	22	NR	NR	9,750	1.5	3.7
LUTH–E.L.C.A.	5	740	1,948	2,565	0.4	1.0
LUTH–Luth Cong Msn Chr	1	85	NR	NR	-	-
LUTH–Luth–MO Synod	5	2,013	3,222	4,141	0.6	1.6
LUTH–Wisc Ev Luth Syn	1	75	89	117	0.0	0.0
METH–AME	3	85	235	300	0.0	0.1
METH–C.M.E.	2	0	300	383	0.1	0.1
METH–Un Methodist	31	8,415	18,502	23,102	3.5	8.7
METH–Wesleyan	2	306	95	398	0.1	0.1
Metro Comm Ch	1	35	60	77	0.0	0.0
Muslim Est	4	1,932	NR	7,826	1.2	2.9
Non-denom Chr Chs	63	22,070	24,306	29,223	4.4	11.0
ORTHE–Orth Ch in Amer	1	70	NR	120	0.0	0.0
PENT–Assemb of God	30	5,848	2,768	8,413	1.3	3.2
PENT–Assm God Intl F	1	NR	NR	NR	-	-
PENT–Ch God (Cleve)	5	419	453	579	0.1	0.2
PENT–COGIC	1	275	350	447	0.1	0.2
PENT–Cong Hol Ch	2	78	70	89	0.0	0.0
PENT–Int Foursq Gos	1	15	23	29	0.0	0.0
PENT–Intl Pent Holiness	2	113	100	128	0.0	0.0
PENT–Pent Ch of God	3	210	NR	326	0.0	0.1
PENT–Un Pent Ch Intl	7	NR	NR	NR	-	-
PRES–Cumber Presb	1	NR	53	185	0.0	0.1
PRES–Presb Ch (USA)	5	589	1,461	1,867	0.3	0.7
PRES–Presb Ch Amer	5	277	478	643	0.1	0.2
Salvation Army	2	206	310	421	0.1	0.2
Sev Day Adv	5	345	600	690	0.1	0.3
Un C of Christ	1	70	338	432	0.1	0.2
Unit Univ	2	220	304	553	0.1	0.2
Unity Ch	1	NR	NR	NR	-	-
Zoroastrian	1	NR	NR	25	0.0	0.0
DEWITT	**46**	**1,608**	**4,230**	**10,319**	**51.3**	**100.0**
ANG/EPIS–Episcopal	1	31	97	97	0.5	0.9
Bahá'í	0	NR	4	4	0.0	0.0
BAPT–Free Will Bapt	1	NR	52	63	0.3	0.6
BAPT–So Bapt Conv	12	659	2,039	2,463	12.3	23.9
Catholic	8	NR	NR	5,079	25.3	49.2
CHR–Chs of Christ	2	95	100	105	0.5	1.0
Jehovah's Witness	1	NR	NR	NR	-	-
LDS–L-D Saints	1	NR	NR	250	1.2	2.4
LUTH–E.L.C.A.	5	333	1,132	1,162	5.8	11.3
LUTH–Nor Amer Luth C	2	NR	NR	NR	-	-
METH–Un Methodist	3	147	270	363	1.8	3.5
Non-denom Chr Chs	3	160	210	225	1.1	2.2
PENT–Assemb of God	2	50	63	81	0.4	0.8
PENT–Assm God Intl F	1	NR	NR	NR	-	-
PENT–Pent Ch of God	1	70	NR	109	0.5	1.1
PENT–Un Pent Ch Intl	1	NR	NR	NR	-	-
PRES–Presb Ch (USA)	2	63	263	318	1.6	3.1
DICKENS	**14**	**485**	**1,116**	**1,670**	**68.3**	**100.0**
BAPT–So Bapt Conv	4	156	746	883	36.1	52.9
Catholic	1	NR	NR	274	11.2	16.4
Ch of Nazarene	1	12	16	28	1.1	1.7
CHR–Chs of Christ	3	122	124	145	5.9	8.7
METH–Un Methodist	1	65	160	160	6.5	9.6
Non-denom Chr Chs	2	55	70	75	3.1	4.5
PENT–Assemb of God	2	75	0	105	4.3	6.3
DIMMIT	**19**	**410**	**941**	**10,588**	**105.9**	**100.0**
ANG/EPIS–Episcopal	1	13	23	49	0.5	0.5
BAPT–So Bapt Conv	5	204	653	848	8.5	8.0
Catholic	4	NR	NR	9,100	91.0	85.9
CHR–Chs of Christ	1	40	40	50	0.5	0.5
Jehovah's Witness	1	NR	NR	NR	-	-
LDS–L-D Saints	1	NR	NR	216	2.2	2.0
METH–Un Methodist	1	41	133	159	1.6	1.5
Non-denom Chr Chs	1	60	60	75	0.8	0.7
PENT–Assemb of God	2	45	20	77	0.8	0.7
PENT–Ch Lord Jesus Apos	1	NR	NR	NR	-	-
Sev Day Adv	1	7	12	14	0.1	0.1
DONLEY	**14**	**646**	**1,948**	**2,335**	**63.5**	**100.0**
ANG/EPIS–Episcopal	1	6	4	5	0.1	0.2
BAPT–So Bapt Conv	4	250	1,180	1,389	37.8	59.5
Catholic	1	NR	NR	90	2.4	3.9
Ch of Nazarene	1	45	87	87	2.4	3.7
CHR–Chs of Christ	2	192	207	241	6.6	10.3
Jehovah's Witness	1	NR	NR	NR	-	-

NR–Not Reported   - Represents no adherents reported.   Percentages may not total 100 due to rounding.

Table 3: Religious Congregations by County and Group: 2010

Religious Group	Number of Congregations	Number of Attendees	Number of Communicant, Confirmed, or Full Members	Adherents: Number of Adherents	Adherents: % of Total Pop.	Adherents: % of Total Adh.
METH–Un Methodist	1	79	417	418	11.4	17.9
PENT–Assemb of God	1	68	34	83	2.3	3.6
PENT–Un Pent Ch Intl	1	NR	NR	NR	-	-
PRES–Presb Ch (USA)	1	6	19	22	0.6	0.9
DUVAL	**18**	**368**	**1,192**	**8,341**	**70.8**	**100.0**
BAPT–So Bapt Conv	7	267	1,101	1,373	11.7	16.5
Catholic	7	NR	NR	6,800	57.7	81.5
CHR–Chs of Christ	1	20	15	23	0.2	0.3
METH–Un Methodist	2	49	73	113	1.0	1.4
PENT–Assemb of God	1	32	3	32	0.3	0.4
EASTLAND	**79**	**4,954**	**12,117**	**15,277**	**82.2**	**100.0**
ANG/EPIS–Anglican NA	1	NR	NR	NR	-	-
Bahá'í	0	NR	4	4	0.0	0.0
BAPT–Ind Bapt Flwsp Intl	2	NR	NR	NR	-	-
BAPT–So Bapt Conv	36	2,523	8,507	10,253	55.2	67.1
Catholic	3	NR	NR	475	2.6	3.1
Ch of Nazarene	1	93	94	145	0.8	0.9
CHR–Chr Ch (Disc)	1	0	80	96	0.5	0.6
CHR–Chs of Christ	10	1,028	1,143	1,450	7.8	9.5
Jehovah's Witness	1	NR	NR	NR	-	-
LDS–L-D Saints	1	NR	NR	222	1.2	1.5
LUTH–Luth-MO Synod	1	60	130	143	0.8	0.9
METH–Un Methodist	5	170	816	844	4.5	5.5
Non-denom Chr Chs	8	995	1,100	1,343	7.2	8.8
PENT–Assemb of God	1	45	30	48	0.3	0.3
PENT–Ch God (Cleve)	1	12	32	39	0.2	0.3
PENT–Ch of God Proph	1	NR	74	89	0.5	0.6
PENT–Un Pent Ch Intl	3	NR	NR	NR	-	-
PRES–Presb Ch (USA)	2	0	59	71	0.4	0.5
Sev Day Adv	1	28	48	55	0.3	0.4
ECTOR	**167**	**15,088**	**39,209**	**72,110**	**52.6**	**100.0**
ANG/EPIS–Anglican NA	1	NR	NR	NR	-	-
ANG/EPIS–Episcopal	3	227	450	641	0.5	0.9
Bahá'í	0	NR	38	38	0.0	0.1
BAPT–Amer Bapt Assn	2	NR	450	585	0.4	0.8
BAPT–Free Will Bapt	1	NR	52	68	0.0	0.1
BAPT–Ind Bapt Flwsp Intl	2	NR	NR	NR	-	-
BAPT–Natl Mis Bapt Conv	1	0	150	195	0.1	0.3
BAPT–So Bapt Conv	45	3,946	19,483	25,349	18.5	35.2
Catholic	7	NR	NR	21,600	15.8	30.0
CGOD–Ch God (Ander)	2	121	NR	121	0.1	0.2
Ch of Nazarene	3	167	337	417	0.3	0.6
CHR–Chr Ch (Disc)	2	185	437	569	0.4	0.8
CHR–Chr Chs & Chs Cr	4	NR	1,005	1,308	1.0	1.8
CHR–Chs of Christ	16	1,825	2,073	2,725	2.0	3.8
Jehovah's Witness	4	NR	NR	NR	-	-
JUD–Conserv	0	29	32	86	0.1	0.1
JUD–Reform	0	18	32	86	0.1	0.1
LDS–Comm of Christ	1	NR	61	61	0.0	0.1
LDS–L-D Saints	3	NR	NR	1,529	1.1	2.1
LUTH–E.L.C.A.	1	30	97	168	0.1	0.2
LUTH–Luth Cong Msn Chr	2	130	240	312	0.2	0.4
LUTH–Luth-MO Synod	2	124	265	291	0.2	0.4
METH–AME	1	0	150	195	0.1	0.3
METH–C.M.E.	1	0	150	195	0.1	0.3
METH–Evan Meth Ch	1	NR	NR	NR	-	-
METH–Un Methodist	8	687	2,007	2,370	1.7	3.3
Non-denom Chr Chs	27	6,295	9,715	10,002	7.3	13.9
ORTHE–Ant Orth of NA	1	25	NR	25	0.0	0.0
PENT–Assemb of God	10	558	300	956	0.7	1.3
PENT–Ch God (Cleve)	2	94	172	224	0.2	0.3
PENT–COGIC	1	0	150	195	0.1	0.3
PENT–Int Foursq Gos	2	58	89	116	0.1	0.2
PENT–Intl Pent Holiness	1	64	33	43	0.0	0.1
PENT–Un Pent Ch Intl	2	NR	NR	NR	-	-
PRES–Cumber Presb	1	NR	116	199	0.1	0.3
PRES–Presb Ch (USA)	2	234	680	885	0.6	1.2
Salvation Army	1	55	80	138	0.1	0.2
Sev Day Adv	2	204	355	408	0.3	0.6
Unit Univ	1	12	10	10	0.0	0.0
Unity Ch	1	NR	NR	NR	-	-
EDWARDS	**13**	**525**	**770**	**1,529**	**76.4**	**100.0**
BAPT–So Bapt Conv	4	180	301	357	17.8	23.3
Catholic	1	NR	NR	533	26.6	34.9
CHR–Chs of Christ	2	75	78	94	4.7	6.1
METH–Un Methodist	2	45	126	187	9.3	12.2
Non-denom Chr Chs	2	225	200	281	14.0	18.4
PENT–Un Pent Ch Intl	1	NR	NR	NR	-	-
PRES–Presb Ch (USA)	1	0	65	77	3.8	5.0
ELLIS	**225**	**26,594**	**46,417**	**77,746**	**52.0**	**100.0**
ANG/EPIS–Episcopal	2	164	457	457	0.3	0.6
Bahá'í	0	NR	204	204	0.1	0.3
BAPT–Ind Bapt Flwsp Intl	6	NR	NR	NR	-	-
BAPT–NBC USA	2	0	400	513	0.3	0.7
BAPT–So Bapt Conv	65	10,314	20,994	26,927	18.0	34.6
BUDD–Theravada	1	NR	NR	292	0.2	0.4
Catholic	4	NR	NR	17,381	11.6	22.4
Ch of Nazarene	3	533	209	822	0.5	1.1
CHR–Chr Ch (Disc)	6	67	296	380	0.3	0.5
CHR–Chs of Christ	17	2,700	2,969	3,862	2.6	5.0
Jehovah's Witness	3	NR	NR	NR	-	-
LDS–Comm of Christ	1	NR	126	126	0.1	0.2
LDS–L-D Saints	2	NR	NR	1,147	0.8	1.5
LUTH–E.L.C.A.	2	92	146	190	0.1	0.2
LUTH–Luth Cong Msn Chr	1	30	45	58	0.0	0.1
LUTH–Luth-MO Synod	1	121	214	287	0.2	0.4
METH–AME	6	10	518	664	0.4	0.9
METH–AME Zion	1	0	150	192	0.1	0.2
METH–C.M.E.	1	0	150	192	0.1	0.2
METH–Evan Meth Ch	1	NR	NR	NR	-	-
METH–Un Methodist	18	1,813	6,475	7,522	5.0	9.7
Non-denom Chr Chs	35	7,107	9,469	10,200	6.8	13.1
PENT–Assemb of God	18	2,414	1,204	2,858	1.9	3.7
PENT–Ch God (Cleve)	2	243	791	1,015	0.7	1.3
PENT–COGIC	3	20	354	454	0.3	0.6
PENT–Int Foursq Gos	2	217	193	248	0.2	0.3
PENT–Intl Pent Holiness	1	50	50	64	0.0	0.1
PENT–Pent Ch of God	3	210	NR	326	0.2	0.4
PENT–Un Pent Ch Intl	4	NR	NR	NR	-	-
PRES–Cumber Presb	1	NR	91	205	0.1	0.3
PRES–Presb Ch (USA)	6	237	508	652	0.4	0.8
Salvation Army	1	71	89	146	0.1	0.2
Sev Day Adv	6	181	315	362	0.2	0.5
EL PASO	**485**	**57,201**	**76,868**	**462,176**	**57.7**	**100.0**
ANG/EPIS–Anglican NA	1	NR	NR	NR	-	-
ANG/EPIS–Episcopal	5	302	638	698	0.1	0.2
Bahá'í	1	NR	425	425	0.1	0.1
BAPT–Ind Bapt Flwsp Intl	3	NR	NR	NR	-	-
BAPT–Natl Mis Bapt Conv	1	0	150	195	0.0	0.0
BAPT–NBC USA	1	0	0	0	0.0	0.0
BAPT–Prog NBC	1	200	300	390	0.0	0.1
BAPT–So Bapt Conv	129	10,199	20,351	26,448	3.3	5.7
BUDD–Mahayana	1	NR	NR	1,014	0.1	0.2
Calv Chpl	3	NR	NR	NR	-	-
Catholic	55	NR	NR	345,950	43.2	74.9
CGOD–Ch God (Ander)	1	25	NR	25	0.0	0.0
Ch Cr, Scientst	2	NR	NR	NR	-	-
Ch God (7th Day)	6	NR	NR	NR	-	-
Ch of Nazarene	10	462	822	1,221	0.2	0.3
Chr & Miss Al	3	272	195	374	0.0	0.1
CHR–Chr Ch (Disc)	5	255	525	682	0.1	0.1
CHR–Chr Chs & Chs Cr	4	NR	460	598	0.1	0.1
CHR–Chs of Christ	14	1,329	1,262	1,633	0.2	0.4
CHR–Int Chs of Christ	1	NR	94	122	0.0	0.0
Evan Free Ch	3	365	NR	365	0.0	0.1
FRND–Fr Gen Cf	1	NR	13	17	0.0	0.0
Jehovah's Witness	12	NR	NR	NR	-	-
JUD–Conserv	1	286	321	867	0.1	0.2
JUD–Orth	1	43	50	60	0.0	0.0
JUD–Reform	1	208	366	988	0.1	0.2

NR–Not Reported - Represents no adherents reported. Percentages may not total 100 due to rounding.

Table 3: Religious Congregations by County and Group: 2010

Religious Group	Number of Congrega-tions	Number of Attendees	Number of Communicant, Confirmed, or Full Members	Adherents: Number of Adherents	Adherents: % of Total Pop.	Adherents: % of Total Adh.
LDS–L-D Saints	17	NR	NR	12,549	1.6	2.7
LUTH–E.L.C.A.	5	406	571	854	0.1	0.2
LUTH–Luth Cong Msn Chr	1	17	34	44	0.0	0.0
LUTH–Luth–MO Synod	5	614	1,168	1,311	0.2	0.3
LUTH–Wisc Ev Luth Syn	2	235	318	420	0.1	0.1
MENN–Cons Menn Conf	1	25	14	18	0.0	0.0
METH–AME	1	35	50	65	0.0	0.0
METH–C.M.E.	1	0	100	130	0.0	0.0
METH–Un Methodist	19	2,538	4,408	6,424	0.8	1.4
Metro Comm Ch	1	46	43	56	0.0	0.0
Missionary Ch	1	0	0	0	0.0	0.0
Muslim Est	1	400	NR	700	0.1	0.2
New Apost Ch	1	NR	NR	NR	-	-
Non-denom Chr Chs	57	29,562	34,584	39,789	5.0	8.6
ORTHE–Ant Orth of NA	1	183	NR	507	0.1	0.1
ORTHE–Greek Orthodox	1	40	NR	65	0.0	0.0
ORTHO–Armen Ap Etchm	1	25	NR	75	0.0	0.0
PENT–Assemb of God	34	4,735	2,814	7,531	0.9	1.6
PENT–Ch God (Cleve)	5	312	356	463	0.1	0.1
PENT–Ch Lord Jesus Apos	1	NR	NR	NR	-	-
PENT–Ch of God Proph	7	NR	254	330	0.0	0.1
PENT–COGIC	5	180	710	923	0.1	0.2
PENT–Full Gosp Bapt	1	NR	NR	NR	-	-
PENT–Int Foursq Gos	2	258	349	454	0.1	0.1
PENT–Intl Pent Holiness	12	1,152	955	1,241	0.2	0.3
PENT–Un Pent Ch Intl	2	NR	NR	NR	-	-
PENT–Vineyard	3	352	440	572	0.1	0.1
PRES–Cumber Presb	2	NR	145	161	0.0	0.0
PRES–Korean Amer Pres	1	NR	NR	NR	-	-
PRES–Korean Pres Amer	1	NR	NR	NR	-	-
PRES–Presb Ch (USA)	8	509	1,025	1,332	0.2	0.3
PRES–Presb Ch Amer	2	110	87	97	0.0	0.0
REF–Christian Ref	3	260	76	99	0.0	0.0
Salvation Army	2	34	303	1,467	0.2	0.3
Sev Day Adv	8	1,136	1,975	2,273	0.3	0.5
Un C of Christ	2	51	63	82	0.0	0.0
Unit Univ	1	40	54	72	0.0	0.0
Unity Ch	1	NR	NR	NR	-	-
ERATH	**77**	**7,139**	**16,261**	**21,321**	**56.3**	**100.0**
ANG/EPIS–Anglican NA	1	NR	NR	NR	-	-
ANG/EPIS–Episcopal	1	80	203	226	0.6	1.1
Bahá'í	0	NR	8	8	0.0	0.0
BAPT–Ind Bapt Flwsp Intl	3	NR	NR	NR	-	-
BAPT–So Bapt Conv	29	4,491	11,273	13,612	35.9	63.8
Catholic	2	NR	NR	1,100	2.9	5.2
Ch of Nazarene	1	51	52	120	0.3	0.6
CHR–Chr Ch (Disc)	1	77	264	319	0.8	1.5
CHR–Chs of Christ	12	1,035	1,108	1,340	3.5	6.3
Jehovah's Witness	1	NR	NR	NR	-	-
LDS–L-D Saints	1	NR	NR	528	1.4	2.5
LUTH–Luth–MO Synod	1	113	184	256	0.7	1.2
METH–C.M.E.	1	0	100	121	0.3	0.6
METH–Cong Meth	1	NR	28	34	0.1	0.2
METH–Un Methodist	9	561	2,166	2,442	6.4	11.5
Non-denom Chr Chs	1	130	150	162	0.4	0.8
PENT–Assemb of God	5	398	424	690	1.8	3.2
PENT–Ch God (Cleve)	2	85	101	122	0.3	0.6
PENT–Un Pent Ch Intl	2	NR	NR	NR	-	-
PRES–Presb Ch (USA)	1	40	80	97	0.3	0.5
REF–Christian Ref	1	60	90	109	0.3	0.5
Sev Day Adv	1	18	30	35	0.1	0.2
FALLS	**55**	**2,296**	**5,247**	**8,440**	**47.2**	**100.0**
ANG/EPIS–Episcopal	1	27	58	61	0.3	0.7
Bahá'í	0	NR	3	3	0.0	0.0
BAPT–NBC Amer	1	0	150	180	1.0	2.1
BAPT–So Bapt Conv	16	1,118	2,796	3,353	18.8	39.7
Catholic	5	NR	NR	2,179	12.2	25.8
CHR–Chr Ch (Disc)	1	25	70	84	0.5	1.0
CHR–Chs of Christ	8	293	313	405	2.3	4.8
Jehovah's Witness	1	NR	NR	NR	-	-
LUTH–E.L.C.A.	1	52	103	112	0.6	1.3
LUTH–Luth–MO Synod	2	63	175	216	1.2	2.6
MENN–Beachy Amish-Menn	1	189	100	189	1.1	2.2
METH–AME	1	0	150	180	1.0	2.1
METH–Un Methodist	9	370	949	989	5.5	11.7
PENT–Assemb of God	2	75	46	88	0.5	1.0
PENT–COGIC	1	0	150	180	1.0	2.1
PENT–Un Pent Ch Intl	1	NR	NR	NR	-	-
PRES–Presb Ch (USA)	2	29	65	78	0.4	0.9
Un C of Christ	2	55	119	143	0.8	1.7
FANNIN	**114**	**5,953**	**16,222**	**21,084**	**62.2**	**100.0**
ANG/EPIS–Episcopal	1	28	49	49	0.1	0.2
Bahá'í	0	NR	2	2	0.0	0.0
BAPT–Ind Bapt Flwsp Intl	1	NR	NR	NR	-	-
BAPT–Natl Mis Bapt Conv	1	0	150	181	0.5	0.9
BAPT–Ref Bapt Ch	1	NR	NR	NR	-	-
BAPT–So Bapt Conv	43	3,294	11,700	14,091	41.5	66.8
Catholic	1	NR	NR	943	2.8	4.5
Ch of Nazarene	1	13	64	64	0.2	0.3
CHR–Chr Ch (Disc)	3	5	117	141	0.4	0.7
CHR–Chs of Christ	18	925	916	1,164	3.4	5.5
Jain	1	NR	NR	NR	-	-
Jehovah's Witness	1	NR	NR	NR	-	-
LDS–L-D Saints	1	NR	NR	341	1.0	1.6
LUTH–Luth–MO Synod	3	71	81	95	0.3	0.5
METH–AME	1	0	100	120	0.4	0.6
METH–C.M.E.	1	0	150	181	0.5	0.9
METH–Cong Meth	1	NR	51	61	0.2	0.3
METH–Un Methodist	17	608	1,412	1,704	5.0	8.1
Non-denom Chr Chs	5	535	535	700	2.1	3.3
PENT–Assemb of God	4	142	79	155	0.5	0.7
PENT–Ch God (Cleve)	2	241	421	507	1.5	2.4
PENT–COGIC	1	0	150	181	0.5	0.9
PENT–Pent Ch of God	1	70	NR	109	0.3	0.5
PENT–Un Pent Ch Intl	3	NR	NR	NR	-	-
PRES–Presb Ch (USA)	2	21	245	295	0.9	1.4
FAYETTE	**64**	**3,182**	**7,503**	**18,806**	**76.6**	**100.0**
ANG/EPIS–Episcopal	1	89	104	129	0.5	0.7
Bahá'í	0	NR	5	5	0.0	0.0
BAPT–Ind Bapt Flwsp Intl	1	NR	NR	NR	-	-
BAPT–So Bapt Conv	8	768	2,280	2,731	11.1	14.5
Catholic	14	NR	NR	9,555	38.9	50.8
CHR–Chs of Christ	4	192	204	267	1.1	1.4
JUD–Reform	1	17	30	81	0.3	0.4
LUTH–E.L.C.A.	10	632	1,868	2,446	10.0	13.0
LUTH–Luth–MO Synod	4	433	953	1,131	4.6	6.0
METH–AME	3	15	270	323	1.3	1.7
METH–Un Methodist	7	411	926	1,186	4.8	6.3
MORAV–Unity Of Breth	1	NR	NR	NR	-	-
Non-denom Chr Chs	4	435	600	600	2.4	3.2
PENT–Assemb of God	2	80	48	95	0.4	0.5
PENT–Un Pent Ch Intl	1	NR	NR	NR	-	-
PRES–Presb Ch (USA)	2	103	203	243	1.0	1.3
Sev Day Adv	1	7	12	14	0.1	0.1
FISHER	**17**	**764**	**2,708**	**3,653**	**91.9**	**100.0**
Bahá'í	0	NR	1	1	0.0	0.0
BAPT–So Bapt Conv	9	432	1,995	2,372	59.7	64.9
Catholic	2	NR	NR	449	11.3	12.3
CHR–Chs of Christ	2	190	212	260	6.5	7.1
METH–Un Methodist	3	105	441	501	12.6	13.7
PENT–Int Foursq Gos	1	37	59	70	1.8	1.9
FLOYD	**23**	**1,272**	**2,922**	**5,028**	**78.0**	**100.0**
BAPT–So Bapt Conv	9	614	1,407	1,808	28.0	36.0
Catholic	2	NR	NR	1,170	18.2	23.3
CHR–Chs of Christ	4	296	306	385	6.0	7.7
LUTH–E.L.C.A.	1	25	58	58	0.9	1.2
METH–Un Methodist	2	208	844	1,108	17.2	22.0
PENT–Assemb of God	3	111	127	267	4.1	5.3
PENT–COGIC	1	0	150	193	3.0	3.8

NR–Not Reported   - Represents no adherents reported.   Percentages may not total 100 due to rounding.

Table 3: Religious Congregations by County and Group: 2010

Religious Group	Number of Congrega-tions	Number of Attendees	Number of Communicant, Confirmed, or Full Members	Adherents: Number of Adherents	Adherents: % of Total Pop.	Adherents: % of Total Adh.
PENT–Intl Pent Holiness	1	18	30	39	0.6	0.8
FOARD	**9**	**373**	**1,109**	**1,392**	**104.2**	**100.0**
BAPT–So Bapt Conv	1	105	591	690	51.6	49.6
Catholic	1	NR	NR	32	2.4	2.3
CHR–Chr Chs & Chs Cr	1	NR	125	146	10.9	10.5
CHR–Chs of Christ	2	57	85	105	7.9	7.5
METH–Un Methodist	2	81	137	188	14.1	13.5
Non-denom Chr Chs	1	100	150	150	11.2	10.8
PENT–Assemb of God	1	30	21	81	6.1	5.8
FORT BEND	**347**	**56,506**	**88,214**	**236,412**	**40.4**	**100.0**
ANG/EPIS–Episcopal	5	605	934	1,079	0.2	0.5
Bahá'í	3	NR	271	271	0.0	0.1
BAPT–Amer Bapt Assn	1	NR	300	388	0.1	0.2
BAPT–Free Will Bapt	1	NR	52	67	0.0	0.0
BAPT–Ind Bapt Flwsp Intl	1	NR	NR	NR	-	-
BAPT–N Am Bapt Conf	1	NR	128	166	0.0	0.1
BAPT–Natl Mis Bapt Conv	2	0	300	388	0.1	0.2
BAPT–NBC Amer	1	75	75	97	0.0	0.0
BAPT–So Bapt Conv	97	16,365	33,161	42,941	7.3	18.2
BUDD–Mahayana	2	NR	NR	3,137	0.5	1.3
Catholic	12	NR	NR	81,096	13.9	34.3
CGOD–Ch God (Ander)	3	105	NR	105	0.0	0.0
Ch God (7th Day)	2	NR	NR	NR	-	-
Ch of Nazarene	2	124	135	153	0.0	0.1
Chr & Miss Al	1	70	60	70	0.0	0.0
CHR–Chr Ch (Disc)	3	0	30	39	0.0	0.0
CHR–Chr Chs & Chs Cr	3	NR	625	809	0.1	0.3
CHR–Chs of Christ	11	3,830	3,622	4,682	0.8	2.0
Evan Cov Ch	1	68	35	88	0.0	0.0
Evan Free Ch	2	275	NR	275	0.0	0.1
HINDU–I/A Temples	5	NR	NR	3,992	0.7	1.7
HINDU–Post Ren	1	NR	NR	16	0.0	0.0
HINDU–Trad Temples	2	NR	NR	2,540	0.4	1.1
Jehovah's Witness	6	NR	NR	NR	-	-
JUD–Orth	1	43	50	60	0.0	0.0
JUD–Reform	1	132	232	626	0.1	0.3
LDS–Comm of Christ	1	NR	110	110	0.0	0.0
LDS–L-D Saints	12	NR	NR	5,537	0.9	2.3
LUTH–E.L.C.A.	5	1,070	2,230	3,215	0.5	1.4
LUTH–Luth–MO Synod	5	484	1,025	1,280	0.2	0.5
LUTH–Nor Amer Luth C	3	NR	NR	NR	-	-
LUTH–Wisc Ev Luth Syn	1	89	108	156	0.0	0.1
METH–AME	6	320	1,150	1,489	0.3	0.6
METH–C.M.E.	1	0	100	129	0.0	0.1
METH–Free Methodist	4	293	288	360	0.1	0.2
METH–Un Methodist	18	8,492	20,206	34,341	5.9	14.5
MORAV–Unity Of Breth	1	NR	NR	NR	-	-
Muslim Est	7	4,368	NR	17,794	3.0	7.5
Non-denom Chr Chs	61	15,055	16,970	19,848	3.4	8.4
ORTHE–Ant Orth of NA	1	90	NR	150	0.0	0.1
ORTHO–Malan Dioc Am	1	185	NR	555	0.1	0.2
ORTHO–Syrian Orth Ch	1	43	NR	160	0.0	0.1
PENT–Assemb of God	13	1,303	937	1,614	0.3	0.7
PENT–Ch God (Cleve)	3	217	224	290	0.0	0.1
PENT–Ch of God Proph	1	NR	63	82	0.0	0.0
PENT–Full Gosp Bapt	1	NR	NR	NR	-	-
PENT–Int Foursq Gos	3	400	316	409	0.1	0.2
PENT–Un Pent Ch Intl	8	NR	NR	NR	-	-
PENT–Vineyard	1	764	1,228	1,590	0.3	0.7
PRES–Presb Ch (USA)	5	474	936	1,212	0.2	0.5
PRES–Presb Ch Amer	3	321	273	323	0.1	0.1
Sev Day Adv	7	447	777	894	0.2	0.4
Un C of Christ	3	339	1,184	1,533	0.3	0.6
Unit Univ	1	60	79	106	0.0	0.0
Zoroastrian	0	NR	NR	150	0.0	0.1
FRANKLIN	**23**	**1,492**	**3,068**	**4,381**	**41.3**	**100.0**
Bahá'í	0	NR	1	1	0.0	0.0
BAPT–Ind Bapt Flwsp Intl	2	NR	NR	NR	-	-
BAPT–NBC USA	1	25	150	185	1.7	4.2
BAPT–So Bapt Conv	8	680	1,533	1,895	17.9	43.3
Catholic	1	NR	NR	611	5.8	13.9
CHR–Chs of Christ	2	185	194	243	2.3	5.5
LUTH–Wisc Ev Luth Syn	1	59	67	79	0.7	1.8
METH–Un Methodist	1	237	640	756	7.1	17.3
Non-denom Chr Chs	2	230	265	300	2.8	6.8
PENT–Assemb of God	1	41	0	41	0.4	0.9
PENT–Ch of God Proph	1	NR	8	10	0.1	0.2
PENT–COGIC	2	35	210	260	2.5	5.9
PENT–Un Pent Ch Intl	1	NR	NR	NR	-	-
FREESTONE	**47**	**2,508**	**6,928**	**8,986**	**45.3**	**100.0**
Bahá'í	0	NR	1	1	0.0	0.0
BAPT–Ind Bapt Flwsp Intl	1	NR	NR	NR	-	-
BAPT–So Bapt Conv	15	1,337	4,201	5,121	25.8	57.0
Catholic	2	NR	NR	662	3.3	7.4
CHR–Chs of Christ	6	288	309	410	2.1	4.6
Jehovah's Witness	1	NR	NR	NR	-	-
LUTH–Luth–MO Synod	1	19	34	42	0.2	0.5
METH–AME	1	0	100	122	0.6	1.4
METH–Un Methodist	9	553	1,290	1,418	7.2	15.8
Non-denom Chr Chs	2	150	175	187	0.9	2.1
PENT–Assemb of God	2	78	62	102	0.5	1.1
PENT–COGIC	4	0	600	731	3.7	8.1
PENT–Un Pent Ch Intl	1	NR	NR	NR	-	-
PRES–Presb Ch (USA)	2	83	156	190	1.0	2.1
FRIO	**24**	**979**	**1,730**	**10,121**	**58.8**	**100.0**
BAPT–So Bapt Conv	7	463	876	1,082	6.3	10.7
Catholic	5	NR	NR	7,850	45.6	77.6
CHR–Chs of Christ	3	103	101	124	0.7	1.2
Jehovah's Witness	1	NR	NR	NR	-	-
LUTH–Luth–MO Synod	1	25	58	73	0.4	0.7
METH–Un Methodist	4	220	535	802	4.7	7.9
Non-denom Chr Chs	1	90	100	112	0.7	1.1
PENT–Assemb of God	1	60	60	60	0.3	0.6
PENT–Open Bible Std	1	18	NR	18	0.1	0.2
GAINES	**31**	**1,877**	**6,207**	**10,944**	**62.4**	**100.0**
Bahá'í	0	NR	1	1	0.0	0.0
BAPT–So Bapt Conv	12	823	4,904	6,772	38.6	61.9
Catholic	2	NR	NR	2,170	12.4	19.8
Ch of Nazarene	1	15	27	27	0.2	0.2
CHR–Chs of Christ	6	395	378	464	2.6	4.2
LDS–L-D Saints	1	NR	NR	121	0.7	1.1
METH–Un Methodist	2	139	387	435	2.5	4.0
Non-denom Chr Chs	1	150	150	188	1.1	1.7
PENT–Assemb of God	4	325	273	646	3.7	5.9
PENT–Un Pent Ch Intl	1	NR	NR	NR	-	-
PRES–Presb Ch (USA)	1	30	87	120	0.7	1.1
GALVESTON	**299**	**40,906**	**67,906**	**157,705**	**54.1**	**100.0**
ANG/EPIS–Episcopal	9	1,125	2,475	2,665	0.9	1.7
Bahá'í	1	NR	184	184	0.1	0.1
BAPT–Amer Bapt Assn	2	NR	267	332	0.1	0.2
BAPT–Ind Bapt Flwsp Intl	1	NR	NR	NR	-	-
BAPT–Natl Mis Bapt Conv	4	400	825	1,027	0.4	0.7
BAPT–NBC Amer	3	450	800	996	0.3	0.6
BAPT–NBC USA	1	0	130	162	0.1	0.1
BAPT–So Bapt Conv	74	11,147	25,207	31,381	10.8	19.9
BRETH–Breth in Chr	1	NR	NR	NR	-	-
BUDD–Mahayana	2	NR	NR	533	0.2	0.3
BUDD–Vajrayana	1	NR	NR	14	0.0	0.0
Calv Chpl	1	NR	NR	NR	-	-
Catholic	8	NR	NR	57,907	19.9	36.7
CGOD–Ch God (Ander)	3	12	NR	12	0.0	0.0
Ch Cr, Scientst	1	NR	NR	NR	-	-
Ch God (7th Day)	1	NR	NR	NR	-	-
Ch of Nazarene	1	54	139	139	0.0	0.1
CHR–Chr Ch (Disc)	3	40	85	106	0.0	0.1
CHR–Chr Chs & Chs Cr	4	NR	767	955	0.3	0.6
CHR–Chs of Christ	16	1,536	1,808	2,340	0.8	1.5
Evan Free Ch	4	575	NR	575	0.2	0.4

NR–Not Reported - Represents no adherents reported. Percentages may not total 100 due to rounding.

Table 3: Religious Congregations by County and Group: 2010

Religious Group	Number of Congregations	Number of Attendees	Number of Communicant, Confirmed, or Full Members	Adherents: Number of Adherents	Adherents: % of Total Pop.	Adherents: % of Total Adh.
FRND–Evan Fr Ch Intl	4	464	1,168	1,454	0.5	0.9
FRND–Fr Gen Cf	1	NR	10	12	0.0	0.0
HINDU–I/A Temples	1	NR	NR	238	0.1	0.2
HINDU–Post Ren	1	NR	NR	16	0.0	0.0
Jehovah's Witness	4	NR	NR	NR	-	-
JUD–Reform	1	64	113	305	0.1	0.2
LDS–L-D Saints	8	NR	NR	4,710	1.6	3.0
LUTH–E.L.C.A.	8	802	1,565	1,934	0.7	1.2
LUTH–Luth–MO Synod	3	572	988	1,244	0.4	0.8
METH–AME	4	422	1,061	1,321	0.5	0.8
METH–C.M.E.	2	0	300	373	0.1	0.2
METH–Un Methodist	21	3,947	10,257	12,858	4.4	8.2
Muslim Est	3	1,872	NR	7,626	2.6	4.8
New Apost Ch	1	NR	NR	NR	-	-
Non-denom Chr Chs	35	14,115	16,085	19,792	6.8	12.6
ORTHE–Greek Orthodox	2	90	NR	139	0.0	0.1
ORTHE–Serb Orth USA	1	163	NR	420	0.1	0.3
PENT–Assemb of God	18	1,673	994	2,371	0.8	1.5
PENT–Ch of God Proph	2	NR	84	105	0.0	0.1
PENT–COGIC	3	500	1,200	1,494	0.5	0.9
PENT–Int Foursq Gos	2	194	164	204	0.1	0.1
PENT–Intl Pent Holiness	2	90	74	92	0.0	0.1
PENT–Pent Ch of God	1	70	NR	109	0.0	0.1
PENT–Un Pent Ch Intl	13	NR	NR	NR	-	-
PENT–Vineyard	1	103	143	178	0.1	0.1
PRES–As Ref Pres Ch	1	NR	61	76	0.0	0.0
PRES–Presb Ch (USA)	8	117	641	798	0.3	0.5
Salvation Army	2	168	70	226	0.1	0.1
Sev Day Adv	3	90	157	180	0.1	0.1
Unit Univ	1	51	84	87	0.0	0.1
Unity Ch	1	NR	NR	NR	-	-
Zoroastrian	0	NR	NR	15	0.0	0.0
GARZA	**19**	**753**	**2,036**	**2,794**	**43.2**	**100.0**
BAPT–So Bapt Conv	6	270	1,099	1,291	20.0	46.2
Catholic	1	NR	NR	408	6.3	14.6
Ch of Nazarene	1	16	70	70	1.1	2.5
CHR–Chr Ch (Disc)	1	14	43	51	0.8	1.8
CHR–Chs of Christ	3	205	230	285	4.4	10.2
METH–Un Methodist	2	96	410	422	6.5	15.1
Non-denom Chr Chs	1	75	75	94	1.5	3.4
PENT–Assemb of God	1	45	17	65	1.0	2.3
PENT–Ch of God Proph	1	NR	18	21	0.3	0.8
PENT–Intl Pent Holiness	1	12	9	11	0.2	0.4
PRES–Presb Ch (USA)	1	20	65	76	1.2	2.7
GILLESPIE	**43**	**3,648**	**6,642**	**14,872**	**59.9**	**100.0**
ANG/EPIS–Episcopal	1	220	545	545	2.2	3.7
Bahá'í	0	NR	2	2	0.0	0.0
BAPT–So Bapt Conv	5	693	1,666	1,966	7.9	13.2
Catholic	4	NR	NR	6,448	26.0	43.4
CHR–Chr Ch (Disc)	1	0	15	18	0.1	0.1
CHR–Chs of Christ	1	175	150	175	0.7	1.2
Evan Free Ch	2	385	NR	385	1.6	2.6
Jehovah's Witness	2	NR	NR	NR	-	-
LDS–L-D Saints	1	NR	NR	258	1.0	1.7
LUTH–E.L.C.A.	6	681	1,755	2,034	8.2	13.7
LUTH–Luth Cong Msn Chr	1	95	NR	NR	-	-
LUTH–Luth–MO Synod	1	60	91	103	0.4	0.7
LUTH–Nor Amer Luth C	1	NR	NR	NR	-	-
LUTH–Wisc Ev Luth Syn	1	44	60	75	0.3	0.5
METH–Un Methodist	1	334	937	1,342	5.4	9.0
Non-denom Chr Chs	7	665	975	985	4.0	6.6
ORTHE–Ant Orth of NA	1	15	NR	25	0.1	0.2
PENT–Assemb of God	1	43	60	60	0.2	0.4
PENT–Intl Pent Holiness	1	40	40	47	0.2	0.3
PENT–Un Pent Ch Intl	1	NR	NR	NR	-	-
PRES–Presb Ch (USA)	2	132	230	271	1.1	1.8
Sev Day Adv	2	66	116	133	0.5	0.9
GLASSCOCK	**4**	**80**	**112**	**638**	**52.0**	**100.0**
BAPT–So Bapt Conv	1	30	46	58	4.7	9.1
Catholic	1	NR	NR	500	40.8	78.4

Religious Group	Number of Congregations	Number of Attendees	Number of Communicant, Confirmed, or Full Members	Adherents: Number of Adherents	Adherents: % of Total Pop.	Adherents: % of Total Adh.
CHR–Chs of Christ	1	40	29	43	3.5	6.7
METH–Un Methodist	1	10	37	37	3.0	5.8
GOLIAD	**21**	**756**	**1,833**	**4,466**	**61.9**	**100.0**
ANG/EPIS–Episcopal	1	11	19	21	0.3	0.5
Bahá'í	0	NR	3	3	0.0	0.1
BAPT–So Bapt Conv	6	290	742	891	12.4	20.0
Catholic	3	NR	NR	2,271	31.5	50.9
Ch Cr, Scientst	1	NR	NR	NR	-	-
CHR–Chs of Christ	1	80	78	92	1.3	2.1
LUTH–E.L.C.A.	3	163	486	572	7.9	12.8
LUTH–Luth Cong Msn Chr	1	75	232	279	3.9	6.2
LUTH–Nor Amer Luth C	1	NR	NR	NR	-	-
METH–Un Methodist	2	77	165	217	3.0	4.9
Non-denom Chr Chs	1	35	50	50	0.7	1.1
PRES–Presb Ch (USA)	1	25	58	70	1.0	1.6
GONZALES	**48**	**2,058**	**6,010**	**11,292**	**57.0**	**100.0**
ANG/EPIS–Episcopal	1	26	48	65	0.3	0.6
Bahá'í	0	NR	3	3	0.0	0.0
BAPT–So Bapt Conv	15	736	3,211	4,086	20.6	36.2
Catholic	5	NR	NR	3,144	15.9	27.8
CHR–Chs of Christ	2	65	74	92	0.5	0.8
Jehovah's Witness	1	NR	NR	NR	-	-
LDS–L-D Saints	1	NR	NR	510	2.6	4.5
LUTH–E.L.C.A.	1	91	255	364	1.8	3.2
METH–AME	3	0	300	382	1.9	3.4
METH–Un Methodist	8	519	1,336	1,636	8.3	14.5
Non-denom Chr Chs	4	460	510	650	3.3	5.8
PENT–Assemb of God	2	51	34	56	0.3	0.5
PENT–Ch God (Cleve)	1	15	25	32	0.2	0.3
PENT–Ch Lord Jesus Apos	1	NR	NR	NR	-	-
PRES–Presb Ch (USA)	3	95	214	272	1.4	2.4
GRAY	**54**	**4,598**	**14,043**	**20,285**	**90.0**	**100.0**
ANG/EPIS–Episcopal	1	62	105	222	1.0	1.1
Bahá'í	0	NR	9	9	0.0	0.0
BAPT–So Bapt Conv	12	1,637	8,975	11,127	49.4	54.9
Catholic	1	NR	NR	2,358	10.5	11.6
Ch of Nazarene	1	31	35	40	0.2	0.2
CHR–Chr Ch (Disc)	1	135	425	527	2.3	2.6
CHR–Chr Chs & Chs Cr	1	NR	75	93	0.4	0.5
CHR–Chs of Christ	7	603	763	932	4.1	4.6
Jehovah's Witness	1	NR	NR	NR	-	-
LDS–L-D Saints	1	NR	NR	414	1.8	2.0
LUTH–Luth–MO Synod	1	59	104	134	0.6	0.7
METH–C.M.E.	2	0	300	372	1.7	1.8
METH–Un Methodist	3	309	780	852	3.8	4.2
Non-denom Chr Chs	10	1,395	1,750	1,987	8.8	9.8
PENT–Assemb of God	3	143	110	220	1.0	1.1
PENT–Ch God (Cleve)	1	25	85	105	0.5	0.5
PENT–Ch of God Proph	1	NR	37	46	0.2	0.2
PENT–COGIC	1	0	150	186	0.8	0.9
PENT–Intl Pent Holiness	2	153	78	97	0.4	0.5
PENT–Un Pent Ch Intl	1	NR	NR	NR	-	-
PRES–Presb Ch (USA)	1	0	150	186	0.8	0.9
Salvation Army	1	20	66	325	1.4	1.6
Sev Day Adv	1	26	46	53	0.2	0.3
GRAYSON	**233**	**21,790**	**50,186**	**71,633**	**59.3**	**100.0**
ANG/EPIS–Anglican NA	1	NR	NR	NR	-	-
ANG/EPIS–Episcopal	3	243	438	443	0.4	0.6
Bahá'í	0	NR	44	44	0.0	0.1
BAPT–Amer Bapt Assn	7	NR	601	739	0.6	1.0
BAPT–Ind Bapt Flwsp Intl	5	NR	NR	NR	-	-
BAPT–NBC Amer	1	100	250	307	0.3	0.4
BAPT–So Bapt Conv	77	8,806	28,998	35,657	29.5	49.8
Catholic	4	NR	NR	5,952	4.9	8.3
Ch Cr, Scientst	1	NR	NR	NR	-	-
Ch of Nazarene	3	198	345	389	0.3	0.5
CHR–Chr Ch (Disc)	3	85	505	621	0.5	0.9
CHR–Chs of Christ	31	3,299	3,362	4,388	3.6	6.1

NR–Not Reported   - Represents no adherents reported.   Percentages may not total 100 due to rounding.

Table 3: Religious Congregations by County and Group: 2010

Religious Group	Number of Congregations	Number of Attendees	Number of Communicant, Confirmed, or Full Members	Adherents		
				Number of Adherents	% of Total Pop.	% of Total Adh.
Jehovah's Witness	1	NR	NR	NR	-	-
JUD–Reform	1	9	15	40	0.0	0.1
LDS–L-D Saints	2	NR	NR	1,174	1.0	1.6
LUTH–E.L.C.A.	1	115	182	203	0.2	0.3
LUTH–Luth-MO Synod	1	134	239	293	0.2	0.4
METH–AME	2	35	150	184	0.2	0.3
METH–C.M.E.	6	150	1,050	1,291	1.1	1.8
METH–Un Methodist	19	2,308	5,780	6,729	5.6	9.4
Muslim Est	1	623	NR	2,541	2.1	3.5
Non-denom Chr Chs	21	3,157	4,396	4,803	4.0	6.7
ORTHE–Orth Ch in Amer	1	40	NR	120	0.1	0.2
PENT–Assemb of God	10	1,386	1,419	2,482	2.1	3.5
PENT–Ch God (Cleve)	4	200	606	745	0.6	1.0
PENT–COGIC	5	100	486	598	0.5	0.8
PENT–Intl Pent Holiness	4	150	195	240	0.2	0.3
PENT–Pent Ch of God	2	140	NR	217	0.2	0.3
PENT–Un Pent Ch Intl	4	NR	NR	NR	-	-
PRES–Cumber Presb	2	NR	11	40	0.0	0.1
PRES–Presb Ch (USA)	7	355	870	1,070	0.9	1.5
Salvation Army	1	59	98	157	0.1	0.2
Sev Day Adv	1	60	105	121	0.1	0.2
Unit Univ	1	38	41	45	0.0	0.1
GREGG	**254**	**29,410**	**67,024**	**99,479**	**81.7**	**100.0**
ANG/EPIS–Episcopal	3	297	598	635	0.5	0.6
Bahá'í	0	NR	31	31	0.0	0.0
BAPT–Amer Bapt Assn	9	NR	1,155	1,444	1.2	1.5
BAPT–Ind Bapt Flwsp Intl	5	NR	NR	NR	-	-
BAPT–Natl Mis Bapt Conv	1	0	150	188	0.2	0.2
BAPT–NBC USA	6	740	2,150	2,688	2.2	2.7
BAPT–Ref Bapt Ch	1	NR	NR	NR	-	-
BAPT–So Bapt Conv	56	9,371	30,617	38,281	31.4	38.5
BRETH–Grace Breth	1	NR	NR	NR	-	-
Calv Chpl	1	NR	NR	NR	-	-
Catholic	4	NR	NR	15,271	12.5	15.4
CGOD–Ch God (Ander)	3	150	NR	150	0.1	0.2
Ch of Nazarene	4	300	424	790	0.6	0.8
Chr & Miss Al	1	127	66	145	0.1	0.1
CHR–Chr Ch (Disc)	7	473	1,498	1,873	1.5	1.9
CHR–Chr Chs & Chs Cr	1	NR	200	250	0.2	0.3
CHR–Chs of Christ	23	3,180	3,524	4,928	4.0	5.0
Jehovah's Witness	4	NR	NR	NR	-	-
JUD–Reform	1	12	21	57	0.0	0.1
LDS–Comm of Christ	1	NR	81	81	0.1	0.1
LDS–L-D Saints	4	NR	NR	1,621	1.3	1.6
LUTH–E.L.C.A.	1	157	370	443	0.4	0.4
LUTH–Luth-MO Synod	2	106	177	213	0.2	0.2
METH–AME	1	0	100	125	0.1	0.1
METH–C.M.E.	11	365	1,457	1,822	1.5	1.8
METH–Un Methodist	17	1,924	6,703	7,355	6.0	7.4
Metro Comm Ch	1	7	9	11	0.0	0.0
Non-denom Chr Chs	35	9,185	12,300	12,932	10.6	13.0
PENT–Assemb of God	13	1,535	804	2,072	1.7	2.1
PENT–Ch God (Cleve)	6	414	1,621	2,027	1.7	2.0
PENT–Ch of God Proph	2	NR	49	61	0.1	0.1
PENT–COGIC	4	28	525	656	0.5	0.7
PENT–Full Gosp Bapt	1	NR	NR	NR	-	-
PENT–Pent Ch of God	1	70	NR	109	0.1	0.1
PENT–Un Pent Ch Intl	7	NR	NR	NR	-	-
PRES–Cumber Presb	3	NR	185	414	0.3	0.4
PRES–Orth Pres Ch	1	48	35	45	0.0	0.0
PRES–Presb Ch (USA)	6	655	1,466	1,833	1.5	1.8
Salvation Army	1	64	127	227	0.2	0.2
Sev Day Adv	2	119	207	238	0.2	0.2
Un C of Christ	2	55	345	431	0.4	0.4
Unit Univ	1	28	29	32	0.0	0.0
GRIMES	**47**	**1,766**	**4,646**	**13,008**	**48.9**	**100.0**
ANG/EPIS–Episcopal	1	28	75	75	0.3	0.6
Bahá'í	0	NR	4	4	0.0	0.0
BAPT–Free Will Bapt	2	NR	104	126	0.5	1.0
BAPT–So Bapt Conv	13	792	2,786	3,369	12.7	25.9
Catholic	4	NR	NR	7,123	26.8	54.8

Religious Group	Number of Congregations	Number of Attendees	Number of Communicant, Confirmed, or Full Members	Adherents		
				Number of Adherents	% of Total Pop.	% of Total Adh.
CHR–Chs of Christ	5	127	69	126	0.5	1.0
HINDU–Trad Temples	1	NR	NR	140	0.5	1.1
Jehovah's Witness	2	NR	NR	NR	-	-
LDS–L-D Saints	1	NR	NR	154	0.6	1.2
LUTH–Luth-MO Synod	3	293	673	837	3.1	6.4
METH–Un Methodist	10	362	691	759	2.9	5.8
Non-denom Chr Chs	1	75	75	94	0.4	0.7
PENT–Un Pent Ch Intl	1	NR	NR	NR	-	-
PRES–Presb Ch (USA)	2	54	108	131	0.5	1.0
Sev Day Adv	1	35	61	70	0.3	0.5
GUADALUPE	**105**	**11,826**	**22,826**	**44,694**	**34.0**	**100.0**
ANG/EPIS–Anglican NA	1	NR	NR	NR	-	-
ANG/EPIS–Episcopal	1	159	321	559	0.4	1.3
Bahá'í	0	NR	39	39	0.0	0.1
BAPT–NBC Amer	1	0	150	190	0.1	0.4
BAPT–Ref Bapt Ch	1	NR	NR	NR	-	-
BAPT–So Bapt Conv	36	5,644	11,287	14,292	10.9	32.0
Catholic	4	NR	NR	15,094	11.5	33.8
CHR–Chs of Christ	5	275	295	350	0.3	0.8
Evan Assoc RCC	2	NR	NR	NR	-	-
Evan Free Ch	1	20	NR	20	0.0	0.0
Jehovah's Witness	1	NR	NR	NR	-	-
LDS–L-D Saints	1	NR	NR	809	0.6	1.8
LUTH–E.L.C.A.	4	442	1,613	1,998	1.5	4.5
LUTH–Luth Cong Msn Chr	1	219	900	1,140	0.9	2.6
LUTH–Luth-MO Synod	3	55	318	384	0.3	0.9
LUTH–Nor Amer Luth C	1	NR	NR	NR	-	-
METH–Un Methodist	6	877	2,555	3,167	2.4	7.1
Non-denom Chr Chs	21	3,019	3,695	4,210	3.2	9.4
PENT–Assemb of God	5	576	285	727	0.6	1.6
PENT–Ch Lord Jesus Apos	2	NR	NR	NR	-	-
PENT–Intl Pent Holiness	2	65	107	135	0.1	0.3
PENT–Un Pent Ch Intl	1	NR	NR	NR	-	-
PRES–Presb Ch (USA)	1	70	162	205	0.2	0.5
Sev Day Adv	2	78	136	156	0.1	0.3
Un C of Christ	2	327	963	1,219	0.9	2.7
HALE	**88**	**6,976**	**17,544**	**33,500**	**92.4**	**100.0**
ANG/EPIS–Episcopal	1	17	41	41	0.1	0.1
Bahá'í	0	NR	20	20	0.1	0.1
BAPT–Ind Bapt Flwsp Intl	1	NR	NR	NR	-	-
BAPT–So Bapt Conv	30	2,329	11,628	15,033	41.4	44.9
Catholic	5	NR	NR	9,094	25.1	27.1
Ch of Nazarene	4	111	139	229	0.6	0.7
CHR–Chr Ch (Disc)	1	0	0	0	0.0	0.0
CHR–Chs of Christ	10	1,274	1,220	1,656	4.6	4.9
Evan Free Ch	1	30	NR	30	0.1	0.1
Jehovah's Witness	2	NR	NR	NR	-	-
LDS–L-D Saints	2	NR	NR	514	1.4	1.5
LUTH–Luth-MO Synod	1	110	179	199	0.5	0.6
METH–Un Methodist	7	507	1,607	1,846	5.1	5.5
Non-denom Chr Chs	8	1,275	1,625	1,694	4.7	5.1
PENT–Assemb of God	5	871	452	2,207	6.1	6.6
PENT–Ch God (Cleve)	1	56	107	138	0.4	0.4
PENT–Intl Pent Holiness	4	195	200	259	0.7	0.8
PENT–Pent Ch of God	1	70	NR	109	0.3	0.3
PENT–Un Pent Ch Intl	1	NR	NR	NR	-	-
PRES–Presb Ch (USA)	1	75	182	235	0.6	0.7
Salvation Army	1	25	90	134	0.4	0.4
Sev Day Adv	1	31	54	62	0.2	0.2
HALL	**16**	**738**	**1,643**	**2,190**	**65.3**	**100.0**
Bahá'í	0	NR	1	1	0.0	0.0
BAPT–So Bapt Conv	5	276	871	1,084	32.3	49.5
Catholic	2	NR	NR	140	4.2	6.4
CHR–Chr Chs & Chs Cr	1	NR	30	37	1.1	1.7
CHR–Chs of Christ	2	205	200	301	9.0	13.7
METH–Un Methodist	3	114	343	418	12.5	19.1
Non-denom Chr Chs	1	100	150	150	4.5	6.8
PENT–Assemb of God	1	43	48	59	1.8	2.7
PENT–Un Pent Ch Intl	1	NR	NR	NR	-	-

NR–Not Reported   - Represents no adherents reported.   Percentages may not total 100 due to rounding.

Table 3: Religious Congregations by County and Group: 2010

Religious Group	Number of Congrega-tions	Number of Attendees	Number of Communicant, Confirmed, or Full Members	Adherents: Number of Adherents	Adherents: % of Total Pop.	Adherents: % of Total Adh.
HAMILTON	**29**	**1,699**	**3,912**	**5,009**	**58.8**	**100.0**
ANG/EPIS–Anglican NA	1	NR	NR	NR	-	-
ANG/EPIS–Episcopal	1	11	31	31	0.4	0.6
BAPT–So Bapt Conv	7	493	1,944	2,322	27.3	46.4
Catholic	1	NR	NR	190	2.2	3.8
CHR–Chs of Christ	4	427	364	534	6.3	10.7
Jehovah's Witness	1	NR	NR	NR	-	-
LUTH–E.L.C.A.	2	58	160	182	2.1	3.6
LUTH–Luth–MO Synod	2	200	440	623	7.3	12.4
METH–Un Methodist	3	116	531	543	6.4	10.8
Non-denom Chr Chs	3	275	375	394	4.6	7.9
PENT–Assemb of God	1	18	14	18	0.2	0.4
PENT–Pent Ch of God	1	70	NR	109	1.3	2.2
PRES–Presb Ch (USA)	1	20	34	41	0.5	0.8
Sev Day Adv	1	11	19	22	0.3	0.4
HANSFORD	**19**	**971**	**2,724**	**4,713**	**84.0**	**100.0**
BAPT–Ind Bapt Flwsp Intl	1	NR	NR	NR	-	-
BAPT–So Bapt Conv	4	330	1,324	1,732	30.9	36.7
Catholic	2	NR	NR	1,200	21.4	25.5
CHR–Chr Ch (Disc)	2	0	134	175	3.1	3.7
CHR–Chs of Christ	2	195	224	306	5.5	6.5
LUTH–E.L.C.A.	2	58	129	165	2.9	3.5
METH–Un Methodist	2	301	827	992	17.7	21.0
Non-denom Chr Chs	1	60	60	75	1.3	1.6
PENT–Assemb of God	1	22	20	60	1.1	1.3
PENT–Un Pent Ch Intl	1	NR	NR	NR	-	-
PRES–Presb Ch (USA)	1	5	6	8	0.1	0.2
HARDEMAN	**15**	**821**	**3,116**	**3,873**	**93.6**	**100.0**
Bahá'í	0	NR	3	3	0.1	0.1
BAPT–So Bapt Conv	5	317	2,076	2,561	61.9	66.1
Catholic	1	NR	NR	90	2.2	2.3
CHR–Chr Ch (Disc)	1	108	245	302	7.3	7.8
CHR–Chs of Christ	4	183	220	285	6.9	7.4
METH–Un Methodist	2	124	516	525	12.7	13.6
PENT–Assemb of God	1	79	38	85	2.1	2.2
PRES–Presb Ch (USA)	1	10	18	22	0.5	0.6
HARDIN	**99**	**7,477**	**20,099**	**29,882**	**54.7**	**100.0**
ANG/EPIS–Episcopal	1	55	124	240	0.4	0.8
Bahá'í	0	NR	3	3	0.0	0.0
BAPT–Amer Bapt Assn	2	NR	170	212	0.4	0.7
BAPT–Natl Mis Bapt Conv	1	0	150	187	0.3	0.6
BAPT–So Bapt Conv	34	3,796	14,104	17,626	32.3	59.0
Catholic	4	NR	NR	3,214	5.9	10.8
CHR–Chr Chs & Chs Cr	1	NR	60	75	0.1	0.3
CHR–Chs of Christ	6	513	440	591	1.1	2.0
Jehovah's Witness	3	NR	NR	NR	-	-
LDS–L-D Saints	1	NR	NR	849	1.6	2.8
METH–Un Methodist	6	614	2,011	2,925	5.4	9.8
Non-denom Chr Chs	12	1,475	2,079	2,193	4.0	7.3
PENT–Assemb of God	10	636	406	861	1.6	2.9
PENT–Ch God (Cleve)	1	88	149	186	0.3	0.6
PENT–Ch of God Proph	1	NR	26	32	0.1	0.1
PENT–COGIC	4	140	340	425	0.8	1.4
PENT–Pent Ch of God	2	140	NR	217	0.4	0.7
PENT–Un Pent Ch Intl	9	NR	NR	NR	-	-
PRES–Presb Ch (USA)	1	20	37	46	0.1	0.2
HARRIS	**3,031**	**632,063**	**1,152,306**	**2,389,775**	**58.4**	**100.0**
ANG/EPIS–Anglican NA	15	NR	NR	NR	-	-
ANG/EPIS–Episcopal	43	12,871	32,568	39,041	1.0	1.6
Bahá'í	7	NR	2,030	2,030	0.0	0.1
BAPT–Alliance Bapt	1	NR	NR	NR	-	-
BAPT–Amer Bapt Assn	17	NR	2,243	2,878	0.1	0.1
BAPT–Amer Bapt USA	3	130	1,063	1,364	0.0	0.1
BAPT–Converge/BGC	5	700	NR	840	0.0	0.0
BAPT–Free Will Bapt	4	NR	208	267	0.0	0.0
BAPT–Ind Bapt Flwsp Intl	10	NR	NR	NR	-	-
BAPT–Natl Mis Bapt Conv	51	1,850	8,948	11,483	0.3	0.5
BAPT–NBC Amer	39	6,995	14,475	18,575	0.5	0.8
BAPT–NBC USA	15	2,420	6,025	7,732	0.2	0.3
BAPT–Prog NBC	4	0	600	770	0.0	0.0
BAPT–Ref Bapt Ch	3	NR	NR	NR	-	-
BAPT–Reg Bapt Gen As	4	NR	NR	NR	-	-
BAPT–S-D Baptist Gen Con	2	25	52	67	0.0	0.0
BAPT–So Bapt Conv	811	181,241	451,788	579,759	14.2	24.3
BUDD–Mahayana	27	NR	NR	11,286	0.3	0.5
BUDD–Theravada	7	NR	NR	3,492	0.1	0.1
BUDD–Vajrayana	5	NR	NR	607	0.0	0.0
Calv Chpl	5	NR	NR	NR	-	-
Catholic	109	NR	NR	741,896	18.1	31.0
CGOD–Ch God (Ander)	17	987	NR	987	0.0	0.0
Ch Cr, Scientst	7	NR	NR	NR	-	-
Ch God (7th Day)	16	NR	NR	NR	-	-
Ch of Chr (Hol)	2	NR	NR	NR	-	-
Ch of Nazarene	21	2,878	4,445	5,504	0.1	0.2
Chr & Miss Al	9	736	672	1,124	0.0	0.0
CHR–Chr Ch (Disc)	21	1,764	4,399	5,645	0.1	0.2
CHR–Chr Chs & Chs Cr	15	NR	2,839	3,643	0.1	0.2
CHR–Chs of Christ	124	22,463	26,826	33,525	0.8	1.4
CHR–Int Chs of Christ	1	NR	532	683	0.0	0.0
Evan Cov Ch	3	262	208	340	0.0	0.0
Evan Free Ch	3	800	NR	800	0.0	0.0
FRND–Evan Fr Ch Intl	3	49	53	68	0.0	0.0
FRND–Fr Gen Cf	1	NR	224	287	0.0	0.0
HINDU–I/A Temples	8	NR	NR	3,855	0.1	0.2
HINDU–Post Ren	6	NR	NR	203	0.0	0.0
HINDU–Renaiss	2	NR	NR	24	0.0	0.0
HINDU–Trad Temples	5	NR	NR	5,729	0.1	0.2
Jain	2	NR	NR	NR	-	-
Jehovah's Witness	41	NR	NR	NR	-	-
JUD–Conserv	4	2,409	2,704	7,301	0.2	0.3
JUD–Orth	10	2,196	900	3,050	0.1	0.1
JUD–Reconst	1	38	48	130	0.0	0.0
JUD–Reform	6	2,379	4,195	11,326	0.3	0.5
LDS–Comm of Christ	5	NR	550	550	0.0	0.0
LDS–L-D Saints	77	NR	NR	44,472	1.1	1.9
LUTH–Assoc Free Luth	1	NR	NR	NR	-	-
LUTH–Ch Luth Conf	1	NR	NR	NR	-	-
LUTH–E.L.C.A.	33	4,563	9,213	11,828	0.3	0.5
LUTH–Luth–MO Synod	46	13,162	22,752	30,521	0.7	1.3
LUTH–Nor Amer Luth C	3	NR	NR	NR	-	-
LUTH–Wisc Ev Luth Syn	4	621	1,070	1,549	0.0	0.1
MENN–CG in Cr (Menn)	1	NR	7	9	0.0	0.0
MENN–Mennonite USA	3	60	107	137	0.0	0.0
METH–AME	20	1,330	4,299	5,517	0.1	0.2
METH–AME Zion	2	90	125	160	0.0	0.0
METH–C.M.E.	9	475	1,725	2,214	0.1	0.1
METH–Cong Meth	1	NR	8	10	0.0	0.0
METH–Free Methodist	2	28	90	90	0.0	0.0
METH–Un Methodist	124	45,028	132,177	182,624	4.5	7.6
Metro Comm Ch	1	519	644	826	0.0	0.0
Missionary Ch	6	321	167	321	0.0	0.0
MJEW–Union Mes Cong	1	NR	NR	NR	-	-
MORAV–Unity Of Breth	5	NR	NR	NR	-	-
Muslim Est	47	30,046	NR	117,148	2.9	4.9
Nat Spirit Asso	2	NR	NR	NR	-	-
New Apost Ch	3	NR	NR	NR	-	-
Non-denom Chr Chs	577	238,123	325,607	348,461	8.5	14.6
ORTHE–Ant Orth of NA	4	865	NR	2,249	0.1	0.1
ORTHE–Greek Orthodox	3	1,030	NR	5,550	0.1	0.2
ORTHE–Orth Ch in Amer	2	125	NR	650	0.0	0.0
ORTHE–Romania Orth Ar	1	50	NR	250	0.0	0.0
ORTHE–Rus Orth Abroad	4	215	NR	665	0.0	0.0
ORTHE–Serb Orth USA	1	130	NR	400	0.0	0.0
ORTHO–Armen Ap Etchm	1	85	NR	110	0.0	0.0
ORTHO–Coptic Orth Ch	3	780	NR	1,640	0.0	0.1
ORTHO–Eritrean Orth	1	25	NR	350	0.0	0.0
ORTHO–Ethiopian Orth	1	NR	NR	NR	-	-
ORTHO–Malan Dioc Am	2	190	NR	570	0.0	0.0
ORTHO–Malan Syr Orth	2	240	NR	450	0.0	0.0
PENT–Apos Faith Msn	2	NR	70	90	0.0	0.0
PENT–Assemb of God	88	19,076	16,023	30,491	0.7	1.3
PENT–Ch God (Cleve)	34	2,996	4,007	5,142	0.1	0.2

NR–Not Reported - Represents no adherents reported. Percentages may not total 100 due to rounding.

Table 3: Religious Congregations by County and Group: 2010

Religious Group	Number of Congrega-tions	Number of Attendees	Number of Communicant, Confirmed, or Full Members	Adherents: Number of Adherents	Adherents: % of Total Pop.	Adherents: % of Total Adh.
PENT–Ch Lord Jesus Apos	2	NR	NR	NR	-	-
PENT–Ch of God Proph	7	NR	380	488	0.0	0.0
PENT–COGIC	64	6,049	14,954	19,190	0.5	0.8
PENT–Cong Hol Ch	2	78	70	90	0.0	0.0
PENT–Full Gosp Bapt	5	NR	NR	NR	-	-
PENT–Int Foursq Gos	7	818	1,455	1,867	0.0	0.1
PENT–Intl Pent Holiness	9	840	900	1,155	0.0	0.0
PENT–Pent Ch of God	18	1,260	NR	1,957	0.0	0.1
PENT–Un Pent Ch Intl	99	NR	NR	NR	-	-
PENT–Vineyard	6	1,182	1,677	2,152	0.1	0.1
PRES–As Ref Pres Ch	2	NR	76	98	0.0	0.0
PRES–Cumber Presb	2	NR	214	419	0.0	0.0
PRES–Evan Presby Ch	4	NR	1,558	1,999	0.0	0.1
PRES–Korean Amer Pres	1	NR	NR	NR	-	-
PRES–Korean Pres Amer	1	NR	NR	NR	-	-
PRES–Orth Pres Ch	2	50	30	47	0.0	0.0
PRES–Presb Ch (USA)	49	8,127	27,241	34,957	0.9	1.5
PRES–Presb Ch Amer	15	1,662	1,984	2,735	0.1	0.1
REF–Christian Ref	3	443	456	585	0.0	0.0
REF–Comm Ref Evan	1	NR	NR	NR	-	-
REF–Hung Ref Add'l	1	NR	NR	NR	-	-
Salvation Army	6	572	656	3,681	0.1	0.2
Sev Day Adv	53	6,354	11,049	12,708	0.3	0.5
Sikh	11	NR	NR	NR	-	-
Tao	1	NR	NR	NR	-	-
Un C of Christ	11	566	1,779	2,283	0.1	0.1
Unit Univ	5	696	1,141	1,528	0.0	0.1
Unity Ch	5	NR	NR	NR	-	-
Zoroastrian	1	NR	NR	481	0.0	0.0
HARRISON	**141**	**9,105**	**28,404**	**38,852**	**59.2**	**100.0**
ANG/EPIS–Episcopal	2	197	398	398	0.6	1.0
Bahá'í	0	NR	95	95	0.1	0.2
BAPT–Amer Bapt Assn	2	NR	180	225	0.3	0.6
BAPT–Ind Bapt Flwsp Intl	2	NR	NR	NR	-	-
BAPT–Natl Mis Bapt Conv	2	30	200	250	0.4	0.6
BAPT–NBC Amer	1	50	50	63	0.1	0.2
BAPT–NBC USA	3	200	1,150	1,439	2.2	3.7
BAPT–So Bapt Conv	47	4,843	18,668	23,367	35.6	60.1
Catholic	3	NR	NR	3,641	5.5	9.4
Ch Cr, Scientst	1	NR	NR	NR	-	-
Ch of Nazarene	2	48	76	86	0.1	0.2
CHR–Chr Ch (Disc)	1	0	0	0	0.0	0.0
CHR–Chs of Christ	9	659	648	785	1.2	2.0
Jehovah's Witness	3	NR	NR	NR	-	-
LDS–L-D Saints	1	NR	NR	323	0.5	0.8
LUTH–E.L.C.A.	1	20	31	33	0.1	0.1
METH–AME	1	0	150	188	0.3	0.5
METH–C.M.E.	4	0	600	751	1.1	1.9
METH–Un Methodist	19	1,084	2,605	3,013	4.6	7.8
Non-denom Chr Chs	12	1,487	2,365	2,373	3.6	6.1
PENT–Assemb of God	5	253	123	299	0.5	0.8
PENT–Ch of God Proph	3	NR	50	63	0.1	0.2
PENT–COGIC	3	0	340	426	0.6	1.1
PENT–Full Gosp Bapt	2	NR	NR	NR	-	-
PENT–Pent Ch of God	1	70	NR	109	0.2	0.3
PENT–Un Pent Ch Intl	3	NR	NR	NR	-	-
PRES–Cumber Presb	1	NR	187	336	0.5	0.9
PRES–Evan Presby Ch	3	NR	214	268	0.4	0.7
PRES–Presb Ch (USA)	1	35	50	63	0.1	0.2
Sev Day Adv	3	129	224	258	0.4	0.7
HARTLEY	**9**	**507**	**1,385**	**1,814**	**29.9**	**100.0**
BAPT–So Bapt Conv	4	295	1,044	1,265	20.9	69.7
Ch of Nazarene	2	76	93	256	4.2	14.1
CHR–Chs of Christ	1	30	30	38	0.6	2.1
METH–Un Methodist	2	106	218	255	4.2	14.1
HASKELL	**30**	**1,320**	**4,586**	**6,056**	**102.7**	**100.0**
Bahá'í	0	NR	1	1	0.0	0.0
BAPT–Ind Bapt Flwsp Intl	1	NR	NR	NR	-	-
BAPT–So Bapt Conv	16	775	3,523	4,182	70.9	69.1
Catholic	1	NR	NR	577	9.8	9.5

Religious Group	Number of Congrega-tions	Number of Attendees	Number of Communicant, Confirmed, or Full Members	Adherents: Number of Adherents	Adherents: % of Total Pop.	Adherents: % of Total Adh.
CHR–Chr Chs & Chs Cr	1	NR	40	47	0.8	0.8
CHR–Chs of Christ	3	249	261	326	5.5	5.4
LUTH–E.L.C.A.	1	47	79	82	1.4	1.4
LUTH–Luth Cong Msn Chr	1	52	118	140	2.4	2.3
METH–Un Methodist	2	128	381	438	7.4	7.2
PENT–Assemb of God	1	30	35	87	1.5	1.4
PENT–Ch God (Cleve)	1	4	31	37	0.6	0.6
PENT–Int Foursq Gos	1	35	86	102	1.7	1.7
PRES–Presb Ch (USA)	1	0	31	37	0.6	0.6
HAYS	**124**	**16,255**	**27,357**	**76,673**	**48.8**	**100.0**
ANG/EPIS–Episcopal	4	609	1,199	1,514	1.0	2.0
Bahá'í	1	NR	112	112	0.1	0.1
BAPT–N Am Bapt Conf	1	NR	141	175	0.1	0.2
BAPT–NBC USA	1	0	150	186	0.1	0.2
BAPT–So Bapt Conv	34	4,375	9,986	12,371	7.9	16.1
Calv Chpl	1	NR	NR	NR	-	-
Catholic	8	NR	NR	36,801	23.4	48.0
Ch of Nazarene	1	42	43	43	0.0	0.1
CHR–Chr Ch (Disc)	2	120	340	421	0.3	0.5
CHR–Chs of Christ	7	890	854	1,050	0.7	1.4
Evan Free Ch	1	30	NR	30	0.0	0.0
HINDU–I/A Temples	2	NR	NR	1,264	0.8	1.6
Jehovah's Witness	2	NR	NR	NR	-	-
LDS–L-D Saints	5	NR	NR	2,256	1.4	2.9
LUTH–Ch of Luth Br	1	58	37	72	0.0	0.1
LUTH–E.L.C.A.	4	238	691	775	0.5	1.0
LUTH–Luth-MO Synod	2	122	213	276	0.2	0.4
METH–Free Methodist	1	430	315	430	0.3	0.6
METH–Un Methodist	8	1,773	4,607	6,263	4.0	8.2
Muslim Est	1	624	NR	2,542	1.6	3.3
Non-denom Chr Chs	15	5,921	7,358	8,243	5.2	10.8
ORTHE–Ant Orth of NA	1	50	NR	75	0.0	0.1
PENT–Assemb of God	5	237	115	313	0.2	0.4
PENT–Ch Lord Jesus Apos	1	NR	NR	NR	-	-
PENT–Ch of God Proph	1	NR	54	67	0.0	0.1
PENT–COGIC	1	100	100	124	0.1	0.2
PENT–Un Pent Ch Intl	4	NR	NR	NR	-	-
PRES–Presb Ch (USA)	4	376	675	836	0.5	1.1
PRES–Presb Ch Amer	1	73	69	81	0.1	0.1
Sev Day Adv	1	137	238	274	0.2	0.4
Unit Univ	1	50	60	75	0.0	0.1
Unity Ch	2	NR	NR	NR	-	-
Zoroastrian	0	NR	NR	4	0.0	0.0
HEMPHILL	**11**	**867**	**2,108**	**2,984**	**78.4**	**100.0**
BAPT–So Bapt Conv	2	122	908	1,183	31.1	39.6
Catholic	1	NR	NR	321	8.4	10.8
CHR–Chr Chs & Chs Cr	1	NR	150	195	5.1	6.5
CHR–Chs of Christ	1	180	160	175	4.6	5.9
METH–Un Methodist	1	170	339	429	11.3	14.4
Non-denom Chr Chs	1	150	250	250	6.6	8.4
PENT–Assemb of God	2	170	156	242	6.4	8.1
PENT–Un Pent Ch Intl	1	NR	NR	NR	-	-
PRES–Presb Ch (USA)	1	75	145	189	5.0	6.3
HENDERSON	**158**	**11,000**	**25,877**	**40,050**	**51.0**	**100.0**
ANG/EPIS–Anglican NA	1	NR	NR	NR	-	-
ANG/EPIS–Episcopal	1	41	74	74	0.1	0.2
Bahá'í	0	NR	4	4	0.0	0.0
BAPT–Amer Bapt Assn	2	NR	145	176	0.2	0.4
BAPT–Ind Bapt Flwsp Intl	1	NR	NR	NR	-	-
BAPT–So Bapt Conv	59	5,186	16,147	19,567	24.9	48.9
Catholic	4	NR	NR	8,560	10.9	21.4
CGOD–Ch God (Ander)	1	0	NR	0	0.0	0.0
Ch Cr, Scientst	1	NR	NR	NR	-	-
Ch of Nazarene	2	55	149	149	0.2	0.4
CHR–Chr Ch (Disc)	2	152	558	676	0.9	1.7
CHR–Chs of Christ	15	1,066	1,120	1,350	1.7	3.4
Jehovah's Witness	1	NR	NR	NR	-	-
LDS–L-D Saints	1	NR	NR	559	0.7	1.4
LUTH–Luth-MO Synod	2	185	313	374	0.5	0.9
METH–AME	4	0	550	666	0.8	1.7

NR–Not Reported - Represents no adherents reported. Percentages may not total 100 due to rounding.

Table 3: Religious Congregations by County and Group: 2010

Religious Group	Number of Congrega-tions	Number of Attendees	Number of Communicant, Confirmed, or Full Members	Adherents: Number of Adherents	Adherents: % of Total Pop.	Adherents: % of Total Adh.
METH–C.M.E.	1	0	150	182	0.2	0.5
METH–Un Methodist	19	1,151	2,396	2,644	3.4	6.6
Non-denom Chr Chs	16	1,930	2,630	2,840	3.6	7.1
PENT–Assemb of God	13	956	928	1,371	1.7	3.4
PENT–Ch God (Cleve)	2	142	85	103	0.1	0.3
PENT–COGIC	1	0	0	0	0.0	0.0
PENT–Intl Pent Holiness	1	75	75	91	0.1	0.2
PENT–Un Pent Ch Intl	5	NR	NR	NR	-	-
PRES–Presb Ch (USA)	1	0	447	542	0.7	1.4
Sev Day Adv	2	61	106	122	0.2	0.3
HIDALGO	**677**	**51,327**	**67,406**	**377,462**	**48.7**	**100.0**
ANG/EPIS–Episcopal	5	534	1,081	1,198	0.2	0.3
Bahá'í	2	NR	160	160	0.0	0.0
BAPT–Amer Bapt Assn	3	NR	255	350	0.0	0.1
BAPT–Consrv Bapt	1	NR	NR	NR	-	-
BAPT–Free Will Bapt	1	NR	52	71	0.0	0.0
BAPT–N Am Bapt Conf	1	NR	80	110	0.0	0.0
BAPT–So Bapt Conv	275	13,042	22,718	31,225	4.0	8.3
BRETH–Grace Breth	2	NR	NR	NR	-	-
Calv Chpl	1	NR	NR	NR	-	-
Catholic	56	NR	NR	269,071	34.7	71.3
CGOD–Ch God (Ander)	1	0	NR	0	0.0	0.0
Ch Cr, Scientst	2	NR	NR	NR	-	-
Ch God (7th Day)	3	NR	NR	NR	-	-
Ch of Nazarene	8	368	482	651	0.1	0.2
Chr & Miss Al	10	953	558	1,079	0.1	0.3
CHR–Chr Ch (Disc)	5	247	542	745	0.1	0.2
CHR–Chr Chs & Chs Cr	2	NR	200	275	0.0	0.1
CHR–Chs of Christ	18	1,526	1,261	1,767	0.2	0.5
CHR–Int Chs of Christ	1	NR	68	93	0.0	0.0
Evan Cov Ch	3	204	218	265	0.0	0.1
Evan Free Ch	1	120	NR	120	0.0	0.0
FRND–Fr Gen Cf	1	NR	27	37	0.0	0.0
Jehovah's Witness	17	NR	NR	NR	-	-
JUD–Reform	1	77	136	367	0.0	0.1
LDS–Comm of Christ	2	NR	241	241	0.0	0.1
LDS–L-D Saints	14	NR	NR	10,092	1.3	2.7
LUTH–Assoc Free Luth	1	NR	NR	NR	-	-
LUTH–Ch Luth Conf	1	NR	NR	NR	-	-
LUTH–E.L.C.A.	8	962	1,167	1,612	0.2	0.4
LUTH–Luth Cong Msn Chr	1	40	67	92	0.0	0.0
LUTH–Luth–MO Synod	4	634	1,122	1,354	0.2	0.4
LUTH–Wisc Ev Luth Syn	1	109	50	65	0.0	0.0
MENN–Menn Br US Conf	5	NR	156	214	0.0	0.1
MENN–Mennonite USA	1	35	32	44	0.0	0.0
METH–Free Methodist	1	54	83	83	0.0	0.0
METH–Un Methodist	23	2,774	7,341	9,527	1.2	2.5
Missionary Ch	2	95	71	101	0.0	0.0
Muslim Est	3	1,872	NR	7,626	1.0	2.0
Non-denom Chr Chs	68	16,156	17,415	22,052	2.8	5.8
ORTHE–Orth Ch in Amer	1	60	NR	160	0.0	0.0
PENT–Assemb of God	32	5,422	3,677	6,480	0.8	1.7
PENT–Ch God (Cleve)	4	119	113	155	0.0	0.0
PENT–Ch God Apos Fth	12	NR	NR	NR	-	-
PENT–Ch of God Proph	1	NR	5	7	0.0	0.0
PENT–Cong Hol Ch	9	351	315	433	0.1	0.1
PENT–Int Foursq Gos	1	63	57	78	0.0	0.0
PENT–Intl Pent Holiness	20	1,771	1,634	2,246	0.3	0.6
PENT–Pent Ch of God	1	70	NR	109	0.0	0.0
PENT–Un Pent Ch Intl	8	NR	NR	NR	-	-
PRES–Presb Ch (USA)	8	652	928	1,275	0.2	0.3
PRES–Presb Ch Amer	2	50	59	73	0.0	0.0
Salvation Army	2	189	252	253	0.0	0.1
Sev Day Adv	19	2,741	4,764	5,482	0.7	1.5
Unit Univ	1	37	19	24	0.0	0.0
Unity Ch	1	NR	NR	NR	-	-
HILL	**105**	**6,192**	**14,303**	**18,821**	**53.6**	**100.0**
ANG/EPIS–Anglican NA	2	NR	NR	NR	-	-
ANG/EPIS–Episcopal	1	13	15	16	0.0	0.1
Bahá'í	0	NR	26	26	0.1	0.1
BAPT–Amer Bapt Assn	2	NR	485	598	1.7	3.2
BAPT–Natl Mis Bapt Conv	2	120	450	555	1.6	2.9
BAPT–So Bapt Conv	34	2,762	7,800	9,618	27.4	51.1
Catholic	3	NR	NR	915	2.6	4.9
CGOD–Ch God (Ander)	1	60	NR	60	0.2	0.3
Ch of Nazarene	2	153	281	303	0.9	1.6
CHR–Chr Ch (Disc)	1	35	72	89	0.3	0.5
CHR–Chs of Christ	14	827	834	1,090	3.1	5.8
Jehovah's Witness	2	NR	NR	NR	-	-
LDS–L-D Saints	1	NR	NR	328	0.9	1.7
LUTH–E.L.C.A.	1	15	44	52	0.1	0.3
LUTH–Luth–MO Synod	2	172	449	461	1.3	2.4
LUTH–Wisc Ev Luth Syn	1	8	11	11	0.0	0.1
MENN–Unaffil Amish-Menn	1	139	62	139	0.4	0.7
METH–AME	3	0	350	432	1.2	2.3
METH–Un Methodist	9	468	1,706	1,925	5.5	10.2
Non-denom Chr Chs	9	740	1,120	1,176	3.4	6.2
PENT–Assemb of God	3	296	133	353	1.0	1.9
PENT–Int Foursq Gos	1	129	149	184	0.5	1.0
PENT–Pent Ch of God	1	70	NR	109	0.3	0.6
PENT–Un Pent Ch Intl	2	NR	NR	NR	-	-
PRES–Cumber Presb	2	NR	37	41	0.1	0.2
PRES–Presb Ch (USA)	3	155	228	281	0.8	1.5
Sev Day Adv	1	30	51	59	0.2	0.3
Unity Ch	1	NR	NR	NR	-	-
HOCKLEY	**55**	**3,352**	**10,745**	**17,442**	**76.0**	**100.0**
ANG/EPIS–Episcopal	1	12	16	16	0.1	0.1
BAPT–Amer Bapt Assn	1	NR	150	190	0.8	1.1
BAPT–So Bapt Conv	17	1,258	7,526	9,547	41.6	54.7
Catholic	5	NR	NR	3,882	16.9	22.3
Ch of Nazarene	2	33	64	92	0.4	0.5
CHR–Chs of Christ	13	1,021	1,000	1,298	5.7	7.4
Jehovah's Witness	1	NR	NR	NR	-	-
LUTH–E.L.C.A.	1	34	63	75	0.3	0.4
METH–Un Methodist	4	259	814	913	4.0	5.2
Non-denom Chr Chs	2	450	600	600	2.6	3.4
PENT–Assemb of God	2	219	142	360	1.6	2.1
PENT–Ch God (Cleve)	1	30	24	30	0.1	0.2
PENT–COGIC	1	0	150	190	0.8	1.1
PENT–Full Gosp Bapt	1	NR	NR	NR	-	-
PENT–Int Foursq Gos	1	36	74	94	0.4	0.5
PENT–Un Pent Ch Intl	1	NR	NR	NR	-	-
PRES–Evan Presby Ch	1	NR	122	155	0.7	0.9
HOOD	**67**	**10,506**	**20,107**	**29,107**	**56.9**	**100.0**
ANG/EPIS–Anglican NA	1	NR	NR	NR	-	-
ANG/EPIS–Episcopal	1	65	90	90	0.2	0.3
Bahá'í	0	NR	11	11	0.0	0.0
BAPT–Ind Bapt Flwsp Intl	1	NR	NR	NR	-	-
BAPT–So Bapt Conv	23	4,410	9,869	11,784	23.0	40.5
Catholic	1	NR	NR	3,450	6.7	11.9
Ch Cr, Scientst	1	NR	NR	NR	-	-
Ch of Nazarene	1	25	43	43	0.1	0.1
CHR–Chr Ch (Disc)	1	195	512	611	1.2	2.1
CHR–Chs of Christ	7	1,119	1,114	1,364	2.7	4.7
Jehovah's Witness	1	NR	NR	NR	-	-
LDS–L-D Saints	2	NR	NR	778	1.5	2.7
LUTH–E.L.C.A.	1	74	129	166	0.3	0.6
LUTH–Luth–MO Synod	1	133	150	227	0.4	0.8
METH–Un Methodist	6	1,182	3,650	5,365	10.5	18.4
Non-denom Chr Chs	12	2,800	3,550	3,936	7.7	13.5
PENT–Assemb of God	3	180	118	246	0.5	0.8
PENT–Ch God (Cleve)	1	103	416	497	1.0	1.7
PENT–Un Pent Ch Intl	1	NR	NR	NR	-	-
PRES–Presb Ch (USA)	1	160	350	418	0.8	1.4
Sev Day Adv	1	60	105	121	0.2	0.4
HOPKINS	**88**	**6,664**	**14,841**	**22,274**	**63.3**	**100.0**
ANG/EPIS–Episcopal	1	47	71	71	0.2	0.3
Bahá'í	0	NR	9	9	0.0	0.0
BAPT–NBC USA	1	250	500	622	1.8	2.8
BAPT–So Bapt Conv	32	3,005	8,712	10,834	30.8	48.6
Catholic	1	NR	NR	3,860	11.0	17.3

NR–Not Reported   - Represents no adherents reported.   Percentages may not total 100 due to rounding.

Table 3: Religious Congregations by County and Group: 2010

Religious Group	Number of Congrega-tions	Number of Attendees	Number of Communicant, Confirmed, or Full Members	Adherents: Number of Adherents	Adherents: % of Total Pop.	Adherents: % of Total Adh.
Ch of Nazarene	1	132	146	398	1.1	1.8
CHR–Chr Chs & Chs Cr	1	NR	70	87	0.2	0.4
CHR–Chs of Christ	9	804	937	1,119	3.2	5.0
Jehovah's Witness	2	NR	NR	NR	-	-
LDS–L-D Saints	1	NR	NR	319	0.9	1.4
LUTH–Luth–MO Synod	1	70	97	99	0.3	0.4
METH–C.M.E.	1	0	150	187	0.5	0.8
METH–Un Methodist	15	790	1,737	1,963	5.6	8.8
Non-denom Chr Chs	7	1,020	1,405	1,411	4.0	6.3
PENT–Assemb of God	5	318	279	372	1.1	1.7
PENT–Ch God (Cleve)	1	155	428	532	1.5	2.4
PENT–COGIC	1	30	150	187	0.5	0.8
PENT–Un Pent Ch Intl	2	NR	NR	NR	-	-
PRES–Cumber Presb	2	NR	28	55	0.2	0.2
PRES–Presb Ch (USA)	3	25	92	114	0.3	0.5
Sev Day Adv	1	18	30	35	0.1	0.2
HOUSTON	**87**	**4,083**	**9,296**	**12,561**	**52.9**	**100.0**
ANG/EPIS–Episcopal	1	10	22	25	0.1	0.2
Bahá'í	0	NR	2	2	0.0	0.0
BAPT–Amer Bapt Assn	2	NR	170	201	0.8	1.6
BAPT–NBC Amer	2	450	650	769	3.2	6.1
BAPT–So Bapt Conv	34	1,636	4,778	5,653	23.8	45.0
Catholic	1	NR	NR	1,411	5.9	11.2
CHR–Chr Ch (Disc)	2	23	112	133	0.6	1.1
CHR–Chs of Christ	9	513	477	641	2.7	5.1
Jehovah's Witness	1	NR	NR	NR	-	-
LDS–L-D Saints	1	NR	NR	143	0.6	1.1
LUTH–Luth–MO Synod	1	55	84	107	0.5	0.9
METH–AME	2	0	200	237	1.0	1.9
METH–C.M.E.	1	0	150	177	0.7	1.4
METH–Un Methodist	10	428	1,115	1,194	5.0	9.5
Non-denom Chr Chs	8	675	950	976	4.1	7.8
PENT–Assemb of God	4	208	129	351	1.5	2.8
PENT–Ch God (Cleve)	1	20	33	39	0.2	0.3
PENT–Ch of God Proph	1	NR	12	14	0.1	0.1
PENT–COGIC	2	0	300	355	1.5	2.8
PENT–Un Pent Ch Intl	3	NR	NR	NR	-	-
PRES–Presb Ch (USA)	1	65	112	133	0.6	1.1
HOWARD	**66**	**4,453**	**12,171**	**19,901**	**56.8**	**100.0**
ANG/EPIS–Episcopal	1	45	98	251	0.7	1.3
Bahá'í	0	NR	24	24	0.1	0.1
BAPT–Ind Bapt Flwsp Intl	1	NR	NR	NR	-	-
BAPT–So Bapt Conv	27	1,782	7,399	8,960	25.6	45.0
Catholic	2	NR	NR	4,500	12.9	22.6
CGOD–Ch God (Ander)	1	0	NR	0	0.0	0.0
Ch of Nazarene	2	127	238	243	0.7	1.2
CHR–Chr Ch (Disc)	1	75	116	140	0.4	0.7
CHR–Chs of Christ	8	768	906	1,064	3.0	5.3
Jehovah's Witness	1	NR	NR	NR	-	-
LDS–L-D Saints	1	NR	NR	383	1.1	1.9
LUTH–Luth–MO Synod	2	81	222	327	0.9	1.6
METH–AME	1	0	150	182	0.5	0.9
METH–Un Methodist	3	227	1,169	1,357	3.9	6.8
Non-denom Chr Chs	5	905	1,125	1,275	3.6	6.4
PENT–Assemb of God	2	185	0	225	0.6	1.1
PENT–Ch God (Cleve)	1	50	112	136	0.4	0.7
PENT–Ch of God Proph	1	NR	9	11	0.0	0.1
PENT–COGIC	1	0	150	182	0.5	0.9
PENT–Un Pent Ch Intl	1	NR	NR	NR	-	-
PRES–Presb Ch (USA)	2	70	242	293	0.8	1.5
Salvation Army	1	74	99	219	0.6	1.1
Sev Day Adv	1	64	112	129	0.4	0.6
HUDSPETH	**10**	**227**	**137**	**1,768**	**50.9**	**100.0**
Bahá'í	0	NR	2	2	0.1	0.1
BAPT–So Bapt Conv	4	60	84	108	3.1	6.1
Catholic	3	NR	NR	1,460	42.0	82.6
CHR–Chs of Christ	1	24	20	24	0.7	1.4
METH–Un Methodist	1	13	31	44	1.3	2.5
PENT–Assemb of God	1	130	0	130	3.7	7.4

Religious Group	Number of Congrega-tions	Number of Attendees	Number of Communicant, Confirmed, or Full Members	Adherents: Number of Adherents	Adherents: % of Total Pop.	Adherents: % of Total Adh.
HUNT	**188**	**15,780**	**32,767**	**43,877**	**50.9**	**100.0**
ANG/EPIS–Episcopal	2	90	183	315	0.4	0.7
Bahá'í	0	NR	127	127	0.1	0.3
BAPT–Amer Bapt Assn	1	NR	85	105	0.1	0.2
BAPT–Ind Bapt Flwsp Intl	1	NR	NR	NR	-	-
BAPT–Natl Mis Bapt Conv	1	0	150	186	0.2	0.4
BAPT–NBC USA	1	200	300	371	0.4	0.8
BAPT–So Bapt Conv	72	7,500	20,206	25,016	29.0	57.0
Catholic	3	NR	NR	2,361	2.7	5.4
Ch Cr, Scientst	1	NR	NR	NR	-	-
Ch of Nazarene	2	93	191	195	0.2	0.4
CHR–Chr Ch (Disc)	7	174	402	498	0.6	1.1
CHR–Chr Chs & Chs Cr	1	NR	80	99	0.1	0.2
CHR–Chs of Christ	20	1,690	1,925	2,407	2.8	5.5
Jehovah's Witness	2	NR	NR	NR	-	-
LDS–L-D Saints	1	NR	NR	825	1.0	1.9
LUTH–E.L.C.A.	1	53	81	98	0.1	0.2
LUTH–Luth–MO Synod	1	22	47	53	0.1	0.1
MENN–Unaffil Amish-Menn	1	52	20	52	0.1	0.1
METH–AME	1	25	70	87	0.1	0.2
METH–C.M.E.	4	13	465	576	0.7	1.3
METH–Cong Meth	1	NR	48	59	0.1	0.1
METH–Un Methodist	17	1,258	2,836	3,295	3.8	7.5
Muslim Est	1	50	NR	50	0.1	0.1
Non-denom Chr Chs	23	3,437	4,197	4,665	5.4	10.6
PENT–Assemb of God	7	517	304	873	1.0	2.0
PENT–Ch God (Cleve)	1	80	97	120	0.1	0.3
PENT–COGIC	3	60	360	446	0.5	1.0
PENT–Cong Hol Ch	1	39	35	43	0.0	0.1
PENT–Pent Ch of God	2	140	NR	217	0.3	0.5
PENT–Un Pent Ch Intl	2	NR	NR	NR	-	-
PRES–Presb Ch (USA)	3	189	391	484	0.6	1.1
PRES–Presb Ch Amer	1	18	29	33	0.0	0.1
Salvation Army	1	16	28	94	0.1	0.2
Sev Day Adv	2	64	110	127	0.1	0.3
HUTCHINSON	**58**	**4,292**	**11,169**	**15,161**	**68.4**	**100.0**
ANG/EPIS–Episcopal	1	14	17	18	0.1	0.1
Bahá'í	0	NR	4	4	0.0	0.0
BAPT–So Bapt Conv	11	1,219	6,626	8,317	37.5	54.9
Catholic	2	NR	NR	900	4.1	5.9
Ch of Nazarene	5	187	313	399	1.8	2.6
CHR–Chr Ch (Disc)	3	80	115	144	0.7	0.9
CHR–Chr Chs & Chs Cr	1	NR	50	63	0.3	0.4
CHR–Chs of Christ	6	818	917	1,122	5.1	7.4
Jehovah's Witness	1	NR	NR	NR	-	-
LDS–Comm of Christ	1	NR	61	61	0.3	0.4
LDS–L-D Saints	1	NR	NR	335	1.5	2.2
LUTH–Luth–MO Synod	2	60	105	106	0.5	0.7
METH–Un Methodist	5	305	1,092	1,203	5.4	7.9
Non-denom Chr Chs	8	1,200	1,403	1,610	7.3	10.6
PENT–Assemb of God	4	228	119	334	1.5	2.2
PENT–Ch God (Cleve)	1	43	191	240	1.1	1.6
PENT–Intl Pent Holiness	1	43	89	112	0.5	0.7
PENT–Pent Ch of God	1	70	NR	109	0.5	0.7
PENT–Un Pent Ch Intl	3	NR	NR	NR	-	-
PRES–Presb Ch (USA)	1	25	67	84	0.4	0.6
IRION	**6**	**217**	**584**	**1,209**	**75.6**	**100.0**
BAPT–So Bapt Conv	1	80	325	385	24.1	31.8
Catholic	1	NR	NR	500	31.3	41.4
CHR–Chr Ch (Disc)	1	16	16	19	1.2	1.6
CHR–Chs of Christ	1	35	30	38	2.4	3.1
METH–Un Methodist	2	86	213	267	16.7	22.1
JACK	**34**	**1,364**	**3,395**	**4,282**	**47.3**	**100.0**
ANG/EPIS–Anglican NA	1	NR	NR	NR	-	-
Bahá'í	0	NR	8	8	0.1	0.2
BAPT–Ind Bapt Flwsp Intl	2	NR	NR	NR	-	-
BAPT–So Bapt Conv	13	799	2,350	2,822	31.2	65.9
Catholic	1	NR	NR	158	1.7	3.7
CHR–Chr Ch (Disc)	1	50	172	207	2.3	4.8

NR–Not Reported - Represents no adherents reported. Percentages may not total 100 due to rounding.

Table 3: Religious Congregations by County and Group: 2010

Religious Group	Number of Congrega-tions	Number of Attendees	Number of Communicant, Confirmed, or Full Members	Adherents: Number of Adherents	Adherents: % of Total Pop.	Adherents: % of Total Adh.
CHR–Chs of Christ	4	221	241	268	3.0	6.3
METH–C.M.E.	1	0	100	120	1.3	2.8
METH–Un Methodist	4	115	325	392	4.3	9.2
Non-denom Chr Chs	1	30	35	38	0.4	0.9
PENT–Assemb of God	5	137	129	227	2.5	5.3
PRES–Presb Ch (USA)	1	12	35	42	0.5	1.0
JACKSON	**36**	**1,815**	**4,669**	**10,148**	**72.1**	**100.0**
ANG/EPIS–Episcopal	1	14	21	30	0.2	0.3
BAPT–So Bapt Conv	11	916	2,972	3,713	26.4	36.6
Catholic	4	NR	NR	4,127	29.3	40.7
CHR–Chs of Christ	6	292	316	404	2.9	4.0
Jehovah's Witness	1	NR	NR	NR	-	-
LUTH–E.L.C.A.	1	78	250	347	2.5	3.4
LUTH–Luth–MO Synod	1	61	179	233	1.7	2.3
LUTH–Wisc Ev Luth Syn	1	118	155	198	1.4	2.0
METH–Un Methodist	4	181	601	695	4.9	6.8
PENT–Assemb of God	1	45	61	150	1.1	1.5
PENT–Pent Ch of God	1	70	NR	109	0.8	1.1
PENT–Un Pent Ch Intl	3	NR	NR	NR	-	-
PRES–Presb Ch (USA)	1	40	114	142	1.0	1.4
JASPER	**85**	**6,042**	**17,306**	**23,988**	**67.2**	**100.0**
ANG/EPIS–Episcopal	1	20	28	32	0.1	0.1
Bahá'í	0	NR	9	9	0.0	0.0
BAPT–Amer Bapt Assn	5	NR	462	572	1.6	2.4
BAPT–Natl Mis Bapt Conv	1	0	150	186	0.5	0.8
BAPT–NBC USA	1	0	150	186	0.5	0.8
BAPT–So Bapt Conv	27	3,623	11,820	14,623	40.9	61.0
Catholic	3	NR	NR	1,912	5.4	8.0
Ch of Nazarene	1	22	32	101	0.3	0.4
CHR–Chs of Christ	6	682	1,045	1,187	3.3	4.9
Jehovah's Witness	1	NR	NR	NR	-	-
LDS–L-D Saints	2	NR	NR	682	1.9	2.8
LUTH–Luth–MO Synod	1	12	26	26	0.1	0.1
METH–C.M.E.	3	0	400	495	1.4	2.1
METH–Un Methodist	9	558	1,639	1,930	5.4	8.0
Non-denom Chr Chs	7	506	699	767	2.1	3.2
PENT–Assemb of God	7	557	463	806	2.3	3.4
PENT–Ch God (Cleve)	1	45	29	36	0.1	0.2
PENT–COGIC	2	0	330	408	1.1	1.7
PENT–Un Pent Ch Intl	6	NR	NR	NR	-	-
PRES–Presb Ch (USA)	1	17	24	30	0.1	0.1
JEFF DAVIS	**10**	**321**	**654**	**1,121**	**47.9**	**100.0**
Bahá'í	0	NR	1	1	0.0	0.1
BAPT–So Bapt Conv	4	136	341	389	16.6	34.7
Catholic	2	NR	NR	380	16.2	33.9
CHR–Chs of Christ	1	40	38	52	2.2	4.6
METH–Un Methodist	1	64	141	143	6.1	12.8
Non-denom Chr Chs	1	35	35	44	1.9	3.9
PRES–Presb Ch (USA)	1	46	98	112	4.8	10.0
JEFFERSON	**388**	**39,422**	**92,119**	**195,963**	**77.7**	**100.0**
ANG/EPIS–Episcopal	3	563	1,562	1,588	0.6	0.8
Bahá'í	0	NR	102	102	0.0	0.1
BAPT–Amer Bapt Assn	4	NR	470	576	0.2	0.3
BAPT–Ind Bapt Flwsp Intl	1	NR	NR	NR	-	-
BAPT–Natl Mis Bapt Conv	7	525	1,450	1,777	0.7	0.9
BAPT–NBC Amer	10	1,442	3,890	4,768	1.9	2.4
BAPT–NBC USA	18	3,890	9,174	11,245	4.5	5.7
BAPT–So Bapt Conv	97	9,502	35,471	43,479	17.2	22.2
BUDD–Mahayana	2	NR	NR	1,011	0.4	0.5
BUDD–Theravada	1	NR	NR	15	0.0	0.0
Calv Chpl	1	NR	NR	NR	-	-
Catholic	25	NR	NR	71,211	28.2	36.3
CGOD–Ch God (Ander)	2	108	NR	108	0.0	0.1
Ch Cr, Scientst	1	NR	NR	NR	-	-
Ch of Chr (Hol)	1	NR	NR	NR	-	-
Ch of Nazarene	3	190	417	580	0.2	0.3
CHR–Chr Ch (Disc)	5	291	767	940	0.4	0.5
CHR–Chr Chs & Chs Cr	2	NR	166	203	0.1	0.1

Religious Group	Number of Congrega-tions	Number of Attendees	Number of Communicant, Confirmed, or Full Members	Adherents: Number of Adherents	Adherents: % of Total Pop.	Adherents: % of Total Adh.
CHR–Chs of Christ	24	2,657	2,710	3,349	1.3	1.7
Evan Cov Ch	1	57	12	74	0.0	0.0
Evan Free Ch	1	270	NR	270	0.1	0.1
HINDU–I/A Temples	1	NR	NR	250	0.1	0.1
Jehovah's Witness	4	NR	NR	NR	-	-
JUD–Reform	1	65	115	310	0.1	0.2
LDS–Comm of Christ	1	NR	110	110	0.0	0.1
LDS–L-D Saints	7	NR	NR	2,149	0.9	1.1
LUTH–E.L.C.A.	2	109	320	371	0.1	0.2
LUTH–Luth–MO Synod	5	672	1,693	2,193	0.9	1.1
METH–AME	4	55	467	572	0.2	0.3
METH–C.M.E.	2	200	1,005	1,232	0.5	0.6
METH–Un Methodist	24	3,478	8,997	10,132	4.0	5.2
MORAV–Unity Of Breth	1	NR	NR	NR	-	-
Muslim Est	3	1,872	NR	7,626	3.0	3.9
Non-denom Chr Chs	62	10,295	17,205	17,859	7.1	9.1
ORTHE–Ant Orth of NA	1	126	NR	350	0.1	0.2
ORTHE–Greek Orthodox	1	15	NR	65	0.0	0.0
PENT–Assemb of God	15	1,639	1,757	2,495	1.0	1.3
PENT–Ch God (Cleve)	1	15	59	72	0.0	0.0
PENT–Ch Lord Jesus Apos	1	NR	NR	NR	-	-
PENT–COGIC	17	325	2,345	2,874	1.1	1.5
PENT–Un Pent Ch Intl	12	NR	NR	NR	-	-
PRES–Presb Ch (USA)	4	417	920	1,128	0.4	0.6
PRES–Presb Ch Amer	1	95	79	124	0.0	0.1
Salvation Army	2	200	269	4,071	1.6	2.1
Sev Day Adv	4	318	551	635	0.3	0.3
Un C of Christ	1	16	23	28	0.0	0.0
Unit Univ	1	15	13	19	0.0	0.0
Unity Ch	1	NR	NR	NR	-	-
Zoroastrian	0	NR	NR	2	0.0	0.0
JIM HOGG	**10**	**119**	**370**	**5,046**	**95.2**	**100.0**
ANG/EPIS–Episcopal	1	10	38	39	0.7	0.8
BAPT–So Bapt Conv	1	30	224	290	5.5	5.7
Catholic	4	NR	NR	4,600	86.8	91.2
CHR–Chs of Christ	2	37	27	36	0.7	0.7
Jehovah's Witness	1	NR	NR	NR	-	-
METH–Un Methodist	1	42	81	81	1.5	1.6
JIM WELLS	**53**	**2,420**	**6,822**	**26,717**	**65.4**	**100.0**
ANG/EPIS–Episcopal	1	29	54	54	0.1	0.2
Bahá'í	0	NR	20	20	0.0	0.1
BAPT–Natl Mis Bapt Conv	1	0	150	193	0.5	0.7
BAPT–So Bapt Conv	14	1,063	4,431	5,698	14.0	21.3
Catholic	9	NR	NR	17,258	42.3	64.6
CHR–Chr Ch (Disc)	1	0	54	69	0.2	0.3
CHR–Chs of Christ	3	165	245	280	0.7	1.0
Jehovah's Witness	1	NR	NR	NR	-	-
LDS–L-D Saints	1	NR	NR	583	1.4	2.2
LUTH–E.L.C.A.	1	0	0	0	0.0	0.0
LUTH–Luth Cong Msn Chr	2	197	568	730	1.8	2.7
METH–Un Methodist	3	160	443	534	1.3	2.0
Non-denom Chr Chs	6	444	510	589	1.4	2.2
ORTHO–Coptic Orth Ch	2	34	NR	37	0.1	0.1
PENT–Assemb of God	3	175	31	276	0.7	1.0
PENT–Un Pent Ch Intl	1	NR	NR	NR	-	-
PRES–Presb Ch (USA)	1	53	94	121	0.3	0.5
Sev Day Adv	2	44	76	87	0.2	0.3
Un C of Christ	1	56	146	188	0.5	0.7
JOHNSON	**194**	**23,351**	**50,685**	**68,100**	**45.1**	**100.0**
ANG/EPIS–Anglican NA	2	NR	NR	NR	-	-
Bahá'í	0	NR	44	44	0.0	0.1
BAPT–Ind Bapt Flwsp Intl	8	NR	NR	NR	-	-
BAPT–Natl Mis Bapt Conv	1	0	150	190	0.1	0.3
BAPT–NBC USA	1	0	150	190	0.1	0.3
BAPT–Ref Bapt Ch	1	NR	NR	NR	-	-
BAPT–So Bapt Conv	68	8,508	26,103	33,068	21.9	48.6
Calv Chpl	1	NR	NR	NR	-	-
Catholic	1	NR	NR	1,878	1.2	2.8
Ch God (7th Day)	1	NR	NR	NR	-	-
Ch of Nazarene	2	120	253	253	0.2	0.4

NR–Not Reported - Represents no adherents reported. Percentages may not total 100 due to rounding.

Table 3: Religious Congregations by County and Group: 2010

Religious Group	Number of Congrega-tions	Number of Attendees	Number of Communicant, Confirmed, or Full Members	Adherents: Number of Adherents	Adherents: % of Total Pop.	Adherents: % of Total Adh.
CHR–Chr Ch (Disc)	3	213	537	680	0.5	1.0
CHR–Chs of Christ	15	2,253	2,594	3,284	2.2	4.8
Jehovah's Witness	2	NR	NR	NR	-	-
LDS–Comm of Christ	1	NR	126	126	0.1	0.2
LDS–L-D Saints	3	NR	NR	1,844	1.2	2.7
LUTH–E.L.C.A.	1	30	82	107	0.1	0.2
LUTH–Luth–MO Synod	1	95	172	189	0.1	0.3
MENN–Unaffil Amish-Menn	1	76	43	76	0.1	0.1
METH–AME	2	0	200	253	0.2	0.4
METH–C.M.E.	1	0	150	190	0.1	0.3
METH–Un Methodist	12	1,468	5,220	6,555	4.3	9.6
Non-denom Chr Chs	27	4,058	5,479	5,877	3.9	8.6
PENT–Assemb of God	15	2,473	1,357	3,528	2.3	5.2
PENT–Ch God (Cleve)	3	71	197	250	0.2	0.4
PENT–Full Gosp Bapt	1	NR	NR	NR	-	-
PENT–Pent Ch of God	1	70	NR	109	0.1	0.2
PENT–Un Pent Ch Intl	2	NR	NR	NR	-	-
PRES–Cumber Presb	1	NR	925	1,434	1.0	2.1
PRES–Presb Ch (USA)	2	113	291	369	0.2	0.5
Sev Day Adv	14	3,803	6,612	7,606	5.0	11.2
JONES	**48**	**2,979**	**6,689**	**9,223**	**45.7**	**100.0**
Bahá'í	0	NR	3	3	0.0	0.0
BAPT–So Bapt Conv	17	1,270	4,296	4,994	24.7	54.1
Catholic	3	NR	NR	997	4.9	10.8
Ch of Nazarene	2	61	133	134	0.7	1.5
CHR–Chs of Christ	10	770	870	1,108	5.5	12.0
LUTH–E.L.C.A.	1	60	271	312	1.5	3.4
METH–AME	1	0	100	116	0.6	1.3
METH–Un Methodist	6	355	811	894	4.4	9.7
PENT–Assemb of God	3	367	30	462	2.3	5.0
PENT–Ch God (Cleve)	1	30	94	109	0.5	1.2
PENT–COGIC	1	15	20	23	0.1	0.2
PENT–Int Foursq Gos	1	31	27	31	0.2	0.3
PENT–Un Pent Ch Intl	1	NR	NR	NR	-	-
PRES–Presb Ch (USA)	1	20	34	40	0.2	0.4
KARNES	**40**	**1,246**	**3,055**	**8,185**	**55.2**	**100.0**
ANG/EPIS–Episcopal	1	11	14	14	0.1	0.2
Bahá'í	0	NR	1	1	0.0	0.0
BAPT–So Bapt Conv	14	559	1,912	2,263	15.3	27.6
Catholic	8	NR	NR	4,435	29.9	54.2
CHR–Chs of Christ	3	145	149	204	1.4	2.5
LUTH–E.L.C.A.	3	184	385	553	3.7	6.8
LUTH–Luth Cong Msn Chr	1	35	43	51	0.3	0.6
LUTH–Nor Amer Luth C	1	NR	NR	NR	-	-
METH–Un Methodist	3	132	312	327	2.2	4.0
Non-denom Chr Chs	1	90	150	150	1.0	1.8
PENT–Assemb of God	3	90	40	129	0.9	1.6
PENT–Un Pent Ch Intl	1	NR	NR	NR	-	-
PRES–Presb Ch (USA)	1	0	49	58	0.4	0.7
KAUFMAN	**144**	**16,793**	**32,294**	**49,198**	**47.6**	**100.0**
ANG/EPIS–Episcopal	3	211	282	340	0.3	0.7
Bahá'í	0	NR	96	96	0.1	0.2
BAPT–Amer Bapt Assn	1	NR	85	109	0.1	0.2
BAPT–Ind Bapt Flwsp Intl	4	NR	NR	NR	-	-
BAPT–Natl Mis Bapt Conv	2	0	300	386	0.4	0.8
BAPT–NBC Amer	2	105	160	206	0.2	0.4
BAPT–So Bapt Conv	41	8,523	20,660	26,582	25.7	54.0
BUDD–Theravada	1	NR	NR	267	0.3	0.5
Calv Chpl	1	NR	NR	NR	-	-
Catholic	3	NR	NR	6,064	5.9	12.3
Ch Cr, Scientst	1	NR	NR	NR	-	-
Ch of Nazarene	1	64	74	74	0.1	0.2
CHR–Chr Ch (Disc)	3	134	275	354	0.3	0.7
CHR–Chs of Christ	15	2,101	2,193	2,877	2.8	5.8
Jehovah's Witness	2	NR	NR	NR	-	-
LDS–L-D Saints	2	NR	NR	919	0.9	1.9
LUTH–Luth–MO Synod	1	60	57	81	0.1	0.2
METH–AME	4	0	450	579	0.6	1.2
METH–C.M.E.	1	0	100	129	0.1	0.3
METH–Un Methodist	12	1,154	2,593	3,439	3.3	7.0
Non-denom Chr Chs	16	2,998	3,330	4,095	4.0	8.3
ORTHE–Orth Ch in Amer	1	40	NR	43	0.0	0.1
PENT–Assemb of God	8	949	615	1,245	1.2	2.5
PENT–Ch God (Cleve)	1	50	50	64	0.1	0.1
PENT–Ch of God Proph	1	NR	23	30	0.0	0.1
PENT–COGIC	5	135	435	560	0.5	1.1
PENT–Cong Hol Ch	1	39	35	45	0.0	0.1
PENT–Full Gosp Bapt	2	NR	NR	NR	-	-
PENT–Int Foursq Gos	1	48	57	73	0.1	0.1
PENT–Intl Pent Holiness	1	60	60	77	0.1	0.2
PENT–Un Pent Ch Intl	2	NR	NR	NR	-	-
PRES–Presb Ch (USA)	4	100	327	421	0.4	0.9
Sev Day Adv	1	22	37	43	0.0	0.1
KENDALL	**39**	**3,991**	**8,325**	**17,148**	**51.3**	**100.0**
ANG/EPIS–Anglican NA	1	NR	NR	NR	-	-
ANG/EPIS–Episcopal	2	474	913	1,276	3.8	7.4
Bahá'í	0	NR	5	5	0.0	0.0
BAPT–So Bapt Conv	8	648	1,352	1,647	4.9	9.6
Catholic	3	NR	NR	5,980	17.9	34.9
CHR–Chs of Christ	1	190	205	248	0.7	1.4
Evan Free Ch	2	165	NR	165	0.5	1.0
Jehovah's Witness	1	NR	NR	NR	-	-
LDS–L-D Saints	2	NR	NR	1,141	3.4	6.7
LUTH–E.L.C.A.	2	70	242	266	0.8	1.6
LUTH–Luth Cong Msn Chr	1	469	1,425	1,735	5.2	10.1
LUTH–Luth–MO Synod	1	192	307	343	1.0	2.0
LUTH–Nor Amer Luth C	1	NR	NR	NR	-	-
METH–Un Methodist	2	708	2,409	2,629	7.9	15.3
Non-denom Chr Chs	6	650	970	988	3.0	5.8
PENT–Assemb of God	2	110	78	207	0.6	1.2
PENT–Un Pent Ch Intl	1	NR	NR	NR	-	-
PRES–Presb Ch (USA)	1	215	351	427	1.3	2.5
PRES–Presb Ch Amer	1	100	68	91	0.3	0.5
Unity Ch	1	NR	NR	NR	-	-
KENEDY	**2**	**NR**	**NR**	**125**	**30.0**	**100.0**
Catholic	2	NR	NR	125	30.0	100.0
KENT	**5**	**148**	**559**	**758**	**93.8**	**100.0**
BAPT–So Bapt Conv	1	40	439	529	65.5	69.8
Catholic	1	NR	NR	73	9.0	9.6
CHR–Chs of Christ	1	50	47	61	7.5	8.0
METH–Un Methodist	1	20	47	55	6.8	7.3
PENT–Assemb of God	1	38	26	40	5.0	5.3
KERR	**76**	**8,601**	**17,322**	**26,643**	**53.7**	**100.0**
ANG/EPIS–Anglican NA	1	NR	NR	NR	-	-
ANG/EPIS–Episcopal	1	305	966	999	2.0	3.7
Bahá'í	0	NR	26	26	0.1	0.1
BAPT–NBC Amer	1	0	350	413	0.8	1.6
BAPT–So Bapt Conv	15	1,605	5,369	6,334	12.8	23.8
Calv Chpl	1	NR	NR	NR	-	-
Catholic	1	NR	NR	5,354	10.8	20.1
Ch Cr, Scientst	1	NR	NR	NR	-	-
Ch of Nazarene	1	22	21	25	0.1	0.1
CHR–Chr Ch (Disc)	2	258	703	829	1.7	3.1
CHR–Chs of Christ	5	905	949	1,175	2.4	4.4
Evan Free Ch	1	75	NR	75	0.2	0.3
FRND–Fr Gen Cf	1	NR	17	20	0.0	0.1
Jehovah's Witness	3	NR	NR	NR	-	-
LDS–L-D Saints	1	NR	NR	744	1.5	2.8
LUTH–Luth Cong Msn Chr	1	226	570	672	1.4	2.5
LUTH–Luth–MO Synod	2	227	270	300	0.6	1.1
METH–Un Methodist	6	1,484	3,765	4,622	9.3	17.3
Non-denom Chr Chs	20	2,513	2,891	3,328	6.7	12.5
ORTHE–Orth Ch in Amer	1	5	NR	10	0.0	0.0
PENT–Assemb of God	3	285	240	329	0.7	1.2
PENT–Int Foursq Gos	1	100	174	205	0.4	0.8
PENT–Un Pent Ch Intl	1	NR	NR	NR	-	-
PRES–Presb Ch (USA)	2	450	799	943	1.9	3.5
Sev Day Adv	1	70	121	139	0.3	0.5

NR–Not Reported   - Represents no adherents reported.   Percentages may not total 100 due to rounding.

Table 3: Religious Congregations by County and Group: 2010

Religious Group	Number of Congrega-tions	Number of Attendees	Number of Communicant, Confirmed, or Full Members	Adherents: Number of Adherents	Adherents: % of Total Pop.	Adherents: % of Total Adh.
Unit Univ	2	71	91	101	0.2	0.4
Unity Ch	1	NR	NR	NR	-	-
KIMBLE	**16**	**688**	**2,004**	**3,154**	**68.5**	**100.0**
ANG/EPIS–Episcopal	1	31	57	105	2.3	3.3
BAPT–So Bapt Conv	3	199	1,117	1,317	28.6	41.8
Catholic	1	NR	NR	500	10.9	15.9
CHR–Chs of Christ	4	195	208	267	5.8	8.5
Jehovah's Witness	1	NR	NR	NR	-	-
METH–Un Methodist	2	150	304	621	13.5	19.7
Non-denom Chr Chs	2	113	175	175	3.8	5.5
PENT–Un Pent Ch Intl	1	NR	NR	NR	-	-
PRES–Presb Ch (USA)	1	0	143	169	3.7	5.4
KING	**4**	**185**	**961**	**1,133**	**396.2**	**100.0**
BAPT–So Bapt Conv	3	85	811	983	343.7	86.8
Non-denom Chr Chs	1	100	150	150	52.4	13.2
KINNEY	**11**	**433**	**728**	**2,347**	**65.2**	**100.0**
ANG/EPIS–Episcopal	1	10	35	35	1.0	1.5
Bahá'í	0	NR	2	2	0.1	0.1
BAPT–So Bapt Conv	4	166	380	444	12.3	18.9
Catholic	1	NR	NR	1,408	39.1	60.0
CHR–Chs of Christ	1	83	77	101	2.8	4.3
LUTH–E.L.C.A.	1	32	57	73	2.0	3.1
LUTH–Luth Cong Msn Chr	1	35	60	70	1.9	3.0
METH–Un Methodist	1	62	94	169	4.7	7.2
PENT–Assemb of God	1	45	23	45	1.3	1.9
KLEBERG	**46**	**2,956**	**4,963**	**21,536**	**67.2**	**100.0**
ANG/EPIS–Episcopal	1	98	176	177	0.6	0.8
Bahá'í	0	NR	12	12	0.0	0.1
BAPT–Natl Mis Bapt Conv	1	0	150	187	0.6	0.9
BAPT–So Bapt Conv	9	757	2,343	2,921	9.1	13.6
Catholic	9	NR	NR	11,798	36.8	54.8
CGOD–Ch God (Ander)	1	23	NR	23	0.1	0.1
Ch of Nazarene	2	35	24	56	0.2	0.3
CHR–Chr Ch (Disc)	1	53	107	133	0.4	0.6
CHR–Chs of Christ	1	150	194	238	0.7	1.1
Jehovah's Witness	1	NR	NR	NR	-	-
LDS–L-D Saints	1	NR	NR	628	2.0	2.9
LUTH–E.L.C.A.	1	38	36	55	0.2	0.3
LUTH–Luth–MO Synod	1	89	198	230	0.7	1.1
METH–AME	1	70	150	187	0.6	0.9
METH–Un Methodist	4	191	652	861	2.7	4.0
Muslim Est	1	623	NR	2,541	7.9	11.8
Non-denom Chr Chs	4	268	430	430	1.3	2.0
PENT–Assemb of God	2	475	279	795	2.5	3.7
PENT–Ch of God Proph	1	NR	12	15	0.0	0.1
PENT–Intl Pent Holiness	1	15	25	31	0.1	0.1
PENT–Un Pent Ch Intl	1	NR	NR	NR	-	-
PRES–Presb Ch (USA)	2	71	175	218	0.7	1.0
KNOX	**24**	**694**	**2,122**	**3,306**	**88.9**	**100.0**
BAPT–So Bapt Conv	9	332	1,257	1,568	42.2	47.4
Catholic	2	NR	NR	725	19.5	21.9
CHR–Chr Ch (Disc)	1	0	0	0	0.0	0.0
CHR–Chr Chs & Chs Cr	1	NR	90	112	3.0	3.4
CHR–Chs of Christ	5	153	187	211	5.7	6.4
METH–Un Methodist	4	144	400	452	12.2	13.7
PENT–Assemb of God	1	15	9	15	0.4	0.5
PENT–Int Foursq Gos	1	50	179	223	6.0	6.7
LAMAR	**129**	**9,159**	**20,882**	**28,822**	**57.9**	**100.0**
ANG/EPIS–Episcopal	1	95	197	245	0.5	0.9
Bahá'í	0	NR	9	9	0.0	0.0
BAPT–Amer Bapt Assn	2	NR	235	288	0.6	1.0
BAPT–Ind Bapt Flwsp Intl	1	NR	NR	NR	-	-
BAPT–NBC USA	1	101	500	614	1.2	2.1
BAPT–So Bapt Conv	43	3,424	10,414	12,781	25.7	44.3
Calv Chpl	1	NR	NR	NR	-	-
Catholic	1	NR	NR	2,467	5.0	8.6
Ch of Nazarene	2	63	106	147	0.3	0.5
CHR–Chr Ch (Disc)	3	90	337	414	0.8	1.4
CHR–Chs of Christ	13	1,524	1,675	2,174	4.4	7.5
Ind Fund Churches	1	NR	NR	NR	-	-
LDS–L-D Saints	1	NR	NR	642	1.3	2.2
LUTH–Luth–MO Synod	2	50	74	79	0.2	0.3
MENN–CG in Cr (Menn)	1	NR	55	68	0.1	0.2
METH–AME	1	0	100	123	0.2	0.4
METH–C.M.E.	1	10	10	12	0.0	0.0
METH–Un Methodist	13	795	2,231	2,635	5.3	9.1
Non-denom Chr Chs	16	1,400	1,880	2,016	4.0	7.0
PENT–Assemb of God	5	260	153	355	0.7	1.2
PENT–Ch God (Cleve)	8	1,017	2,313	2,839	5.7	9.9
PENT–COGIC	1	0	150	184	0.4	0.6
PENT–Full Gosp Bapt	2	NR	NR	NR	-	-
PENT–Pent Ch of God	2	140	NR	217	0.4	0.8
PENT–Un Pent Ch Intl	1	NR	NR	NR	-	-
PRES–Presb Ch (USA)	3	110	270	331	0.7	1.1
PRES–Presb Ch Amer	1	26	39	42	0.1	0.1
Salvation Army	1	31	94	94	0.2	0.3
Sev Day Adv	1	23	40	46	0.1	0.2
LAMB	**45**	**2,794**	**6,883**	**12,045**	**86.2**	**100.0**
BAPT–So Bapt Conv	15	1,184	4,629	5,982	42.8	49.7
Catholic	3	NR	NR	3,013	21.6	25.0
CHR–Chs of Christ	8	728	819	988	7.1	8.2
Jehovah's Witness	1	NR	NR	NR	-	-
LUTH–E.L.C.A.	1	15	37	39	0.3	0.3
LUTH–Luth–MO Synod	1	33	68	77	0.6	0.6
METH–Un Methodist	6	479	972	1,242	8.9	10.3
Non-denom Chr Chs	2	180	250	250	1.8	2.1
PENT–Assemb of God	2	58	42	259	1.9	2.2
PENT–Full Gosp Bapt	1	NR	NR	NR	-	-
PENT–Intl Pent Holiness	2	33	43	56	0.4	0.5
PENT–Pent Ch of God	1	70	NR	109	0.8	0.9
PENT–Un Pent Ch Intl	1	NR	NR	NR	-	-
PRES–Presb Ch (USA)	1	14	23	30	0.2	0.2
LAMPASAS	**39**	**2,907**	**4,771**	**6,141**	**31.2**	**100.0**
ANG/EPIS–Episcopal	1	60	91	143	0.7	2.3
Bahá'í	0	NR	6	6	0.0	0.1
BAPT–Ref Bapt Ch	1	NR	NR	NR	-	-
BAPT–So Bapt Conv	17	1,177	2,592	3,180	16.2	51.8
Catholic	1	NR	NR	346	1.8	5.6
CHR–Chr Ch (Disc)	1	43	112	137	0.7	2.2
CHR–Chs of Christ	5	456	491	608	3.1	9.9
Jehovah's Witness	1	NR	NR	NR	-	-
LUTH–Luth–MO Synod	1	50	189	203	1.0	3.3
METH–Un Methodist	2	69	137	160	0.8	2.6
Non-denom Chr Chs	5	893	1,003	1,154	5.9	18.8
PENT–Assemb of God	1	122	83	122	0.6	2.0
PENT–Un Pent Ch Intl	1	NR	NR	NR	-	-
PRES–Presb Ch (USA)	2	37	67	82	0.4	1.3
LA SALLE	**11**	**180**	**621**	**5,538**	**80.4**	**100.0**
ANG/EPIS–Episcopal	1	7	8	10	0.1	0.2
BAPT–So Bapt Conv	3	74	423	507	7.4	9.2
Catholic	2	NR	NR	4,800	69.7	86.7
Ch God (7th Day)	1	NR	NR	NR	-	-
CHR–Chs of Christ	1	45	35	50	0.7	0.9
METH–Un Methodist	1	54	150	165	2.4	3.0
PENT–Un Pent Ch Intl	1	NR	NR	NR	-	-
PRES–Presb Ch (USA)	1	0	5	6	0.1	0.1
LAVACA	**53**	**2,223**	**5,405**	**19,810**	**102.8**	**100.0**
ANG/EPIS–Episcopal	2	21	42	45	0.2	0.2
Bahá'í	0	NR	1	1	0.0	0.0
BAPT–NBC Amer	1	70	280	341	1.8	1.7
BAPT–So Bapt Conv	8	532	1,625	1,978	10.3	10.0
Catholic	8	NR	NR	12,798	66.4	64.6
CGOD–Ch God (Ander)	1	0	NR	0	0.0	0.0

NR–Not Reported - Represents no adherents reported. Percentages may not total 100 due to rounding.

Table 3: Religious Congregations by County and Group: 2010

Religious Group	Number of Congrega-tions	Number of Attendees	Number of Communicant, Confirmed, or Full Members	Adherents: Number of Adherents	Adherents: % of Total Pop.	Adherents: % of Total Adh.
CHR–Chs of Christ	4	242	170	268	1.4	1.4
Jehovah's Witness	1	NR	NR	NR	-	-
LDS–L-D Saints	1	NR	NR	545	2.8	2.8
LUTH–E.L.C.A.	4	249	538	627	3.3	3.2
LUTH–Luth Cong Msn Chr	2	291	1,137	1,384	7.2	7.0
LUTH–Nor Amer Luth C	1	NR	NR	NR	-	-
METH–AME	2	0	200	243	1.3	1.2
METH–Un Methodist	9	272	699	783	4.1	4.0
MORAV–Unity Of Breth	1	NR	NR	NR	-	-
Non-denom Chr Chs	5	415	580	594	3.1	3.0
PENT–Assemb of God	1	112	100	163	0.8	0.8
PENT–COGIC	1	5	10	12	0.1	0.1
PRES–Presb Ch (USA)	1	14	23	28	0.1	0.1
LEE	**35**	**2,863**	**6,615**	**10,021**	**60.3**	**100.0**
Bahá'í	0	NR	1	1	0.0	0.0
BAPT–So Bapt Conv	6	460	1,276	1,574	9.5	15.7
Catholic	3	NR	NR	1,764	10.6	17.6
CHR–Chr Ch (Disc)	1	49	104	128	0.8	1.3
CHR–Chr Chs & Chs Cr	1	NR	110	136	0.8	1.4
CHR–Chs of Christ	2	115	115	135	0.8	1.3
LUTH–E.L.C.A.	1	0	0	0	0.0	0.0
LUTH–Luth Cong Msn Chr	2	310	945	1,166	7.0	11.6
LUTH–Luth–MO Synod	7	1,391	2,783	3,469	20.9	34.6
METH–AME	3	0	350	432	2.6	4.3
METH–Un Methodist	3	153	526	638	3.8	6.4
MORAV–Unity Of Breth	1	NR	NR	NR	-	-
Non-denom Chr Chs	3	265	370	381	2.3	3.8
PENT–Assemb of God	1	120	35	197	1.2	2.0
PENT–Un Pent Ch Intl	1	NR	NR	NR	-	-
LEON	**57**	**2,358**	**6,592**	**10,224**	**60.9**	**100.0**
BAPT–So Bapt Conv	18	980	3,909	4,714	28.1	46.1
Catholic	3	NR	NR	2,302	13.7	22.5
CHR–Chr Ch (Disc)	1	0	0	0	0.0	0.0
CHR–Chs of Christ	7	360	362	476	2.8	4.7
Jehovah's Witness	1	NR	NR	NR	-	-
LUTH–Luth–MO Synod	1	60	103	125	0.7	1.2
METH–AME	5	0	500	603	3.6	5.9
METH–Un Methodist	9	307	852	941	5.6	9.2
Non-denom Chr Chs	5	425	600	612	3.6	6.0
PENT–Assemb of God	4	183	159	322	1.9	3.1
PENT–Ch God (Cleve)	1	20	96	116	0.7	1.1
PENT–COGIC	1	23	11	13	0.1	0.1
PENT–Un Pent Ch Intl	1	NR	NR	NR	-	-
LIBERTY	**121**	**9,603**	**24,361**	**39,096**	**51.7**	**100.0**
ANG/EPIS–Episcopal	1	71	111	114	0.2	0.3
Bahá'í	0	NR	15	15	0.0	0.0
BAPT–Amer Bapt Assn	3	NR	198	246	0.3	0.6
BAPT–So Bapt Conv	42	5,034	17,619	21,891	28.9	56.0
Catholic	7	NR	NR	7,524	9.9	19.2
CHR–Chs of Christ	10	674	789	928	1.2	2.4
Jehovah's Witness	2	NR	NR	NR	-	-
LDS–L-D Saints	2	NR	NR	1,291	1.7	3.3
LUTH–E.L.C.A.	1	17	93	123	0.2	0.3
LUTH–Luth–MO Synod	1	49	82	111	0.1	0.3
METH–AME	1	0	150	186	0.2	0.5
METH–Un Methodist	7	536	1,964	2,040	2.7	5.2
Missionary Ch	1	155	200	200	0.3	0.5
Non-denom Chr Chs	12	1,745	2,200	2,381	3.1	6.1
PENT–Assemb of God	13	1,061	615	1,326	1.8	3.4
PENT–Ch of God Proph	2	NR	76	94	0.1	0.2
PENT–COGIC	1	0	150	186	0.2	0.5
PENT–Pent Ch of God	3	210	NR	326	0.4	0.8
PENT–Un Pent Ch Intl	10	NR	NR	NR	-	-
PRES–Presb Ch (USA)	1	0	10	12	0.0	0.0
Sev Day Adv	1	51	89	102	0.1	0.3
LIMESTONE	**75**	**3,775**	**10,358**	**13,361**	**57.1**	**100.0**
ANG/EPIS–Episcopal	1	32	43	61	0.3	0.5
Bahá'í	0	NR	1	1	0.0	0.0

Religious Group	Number of Congrega-tions	Number of Attendees	Number of Communicant, Confirmed, or Full Members	Adherents: Number of Adherents	Adherents: % of Total Pop.	Adherents: % of Total Adh.
BAPT–Amer Bapt Assn	1	NR	248	303	1.3	2.3
BAPT–Natl Mis Bapt Conv	2	0	300	366	1.6	2.7
BAPT–So Bapt Conv	24	1,583	5,056	6,169	26.4	46.2
Catholic	1	NR	NR	865	3.7	6.5
Ch of Nazarene	1	61	0	61	0.3	0.5
CHR–Chr Ch (Disc)	1	0	0	0	0.0	0.0
CHR–Chs of Christ	11	533	619	751	3.2	5.6
Jehovah's Witness	1	NR	NR	NR	-	-
LDS–L-D Saints	1	NR	NR	253	1.1	1.9
LUTH–Luth–MO Synod	1	0	77	103	0.4	0.8
METH–AME	4	0	500	610	2.6	4.6
METH–Un Methodist	10	581	2,013	2,093	9.0	15.7
Non-denom Chr Chs	5	590	990	1,000	4.3	7.5
PENT–Assemb of God	5	265	262	312	1.3	2.3
PENT–Ch of God Proph	1	NR	18	22	0.1	0.2
PENT–COGIC	1	0	100	122	0.5	0.9
PENT–Pent Ch of God	1	70	NR	109	0.5	0.8
PENT–Un Pent Ch Intl	2	NR	NR	NR	-	-
PRES–Presb Ch (USA)	1	60	131	160	0.7	1.2
LIPSCOMB	**15**	**508**	**1,446**	**2,146**	**65.0**	**100.0**
BAPT–So Bapt Conv	4	168	636	805	24.4	37.5
Catholic	1	NR	NR	320	9.7	14.9
Ch of Nazarene	1	21	38	38	1.2	1.8
CHR–Chr Chs & Chs Cr	1	NR	120	152	4.6	7.1
CHR–Chs of Christ	1	18	16	22	0.7	1.0
CONG–Consrv Cong Chr	1	30	23	29	0.9	1.4
FRND–Evan Fr Ch Intl	1	55	78	99	3.0	4.6
LUTH–E.L.C.A.	1	36	92	122	3.7	5.7
METH–Un Methodist	3	120	343	459	13.9	21.4
Non-denom Chr Chs	1	60	100	100	3.0	4.7
LIVE OAK	**26**	**1,401**	**3,245**	**7,508**	**65.1**	**100.0**
ANG/EPIS–Episcopal	1	33	69	71	0.6	0.9
Bahá'í	0	NR	2	2	0.0	0.0
BAPT–So Bapt Conv	10	642	2,210	2,600	22.5	34.6
Catholic	3	NR	NR	3,354	29.1	44.7
CHR–Chs of Christ	4	225	232	351	3.0	4.7
Jehovah's Witness	1	NR	NR	NR	-	-
LUTH–Luth–MO Synod	1	15	13	17	0.1	0.2
LUTH–Nor Amer Luth C	1	NR	NR	NR	-	-
METH–Un Methodist	2	154	469	701	6.1	9.3
Non-denom Chr Chs	1	250	250	312	2.7	4.2
PENT–Assemb of God	1	82	0	100	0.9	1.3
PENT–Un Pent Ch Intl	1	NR	NR	NR	-	-
LLANO	**40**	**2,467**	**6,200**	**8,429**	**43.7**	**100.0**
ANG/EPIS–Episcopal	1	40	93	106	0.5	1.3
Bahá'í	0	NR	3	3	0.0	0.0
BAPT–Ind Bapt Flwsp Intl	1	NR	NR	NR	-	-
BAPT–So Bapt Conv	9	970	3,422	3,904	20.2	46.3
Calv Chpl	1	NR	NR	NR	-	-
Catholic	2	NR	NR	1,408	7.3	16.7
CHR–Chr Ch (Disc)	1	39	57	65	0.3	0.8
CHR–Chs of Christ	6	343	349	432	2.2	5.1
Jehovah's Witness	1	NR	NR	NR	-	-
LUTH–E.L.C.A.	2	101	215	254	1.3	3.0
LUTH–Luth–MO Synod	1	0	159	169	0.9	2.0
METH–Un Methodist	6	561	1,150	1,308	6.8	15.5
Non-denom Chr Chs	4	380	735	735	3.8	8.7
PENT–Assemb of God	1	23	0	25	0.1	0.3
PENT–Ch of God Proph	1	NR	4	5	0.0	0.1
PENT–Un Pent Ch Intl	2	NR	NR	NR	-	-
PRES–Presb Ch (USA)	1	10	13	15	0.1	0.2
LOVING	**1**	**5**	**NR**	**6**	**7.3**	**100.0**
Non-denom Chr Chs	1	5	NR	6	7.3	100.0
LUBBOCK	**340**	**46,982**	**93,027**	**160,539**	**57.6**	**100.0**
ANG/EPIS–Anglican NA	1	NR	NR	NR	-	-
ANG/EPIS–Episcopal	3	405	1,243	1,863	0.7	1.2
Bahá'í	1	NR	79	79	0.0	0.0

NR–Not Reported   - Represents no adherents reported.   Percentages may not total 100 due to rounding.

Table 3: Religious Congregations by County and Group: 2010

Religious Group	Number of Congrega-tions	Number of Attendees	Number of Communicant, Confirmed, or Full Members	Adherents		
				Number of Adherents	% of Total Pop.	% of Total Adh.
BAPT–Amer Bapt Assn	1	NR	460	570	0.2	0.4
BAPT–Free Will Bapt	2	NR	104	129	0.0	0.1
BAPT–Ind Bapt Flwsp Intl	1	NR	NR	NR	-	-
BAPT–Natl Mis Bapt Conv	1	0	150	186	0.1	0.1
BAPT–NBC USA	1	150	300	372	0.1	0.2
BAPT–So Bapt Conv	107	11,612	36,225	44,923	16.1	28.0
BUDD–Mahayana	1	NR	NR	103	0.0	0.1
Calv Chpl	1	NR	NR	NR	-	-
Catholic	17	NR	NR	36,239	13.0	22.6
Ch Cr, Scientst	2	NR	NR	NR	-	-
Ch God (7th Day)	1	NR	NR	NR	-	-
Ch of Nazarene	4	580	932	968	0.3	0.6
CHR–Chr Ch (Disc)	5	563	1,575	1,953	0.7	1.2
CHR–Chr Chs & Chs Cr	1	NR	750	930	0.3	0.6
CHR–Chs of Christ	31	8,253	9,074	11,994	4.3	7.5
CHR–Int Chs of Christ	1	NR	13	16	0.0	0.0
FRND–Fr Gen Cf	1	NR	26	32	0.0	0.0
FRND–Unaffl Mtgs	1	NR	NR	NR	-	-
HINDU–I/A Temples	1	NR	NR	1,742	0.6	1.1
Jain	1	NR	NR	NR	-	-
Jehovah's Witness	3	NR	NR	NR	-	-
JUD–Reform	1	48	85	230	0.1	0.1
LDS–Comm of Christ	1	NR	61	61	0.0	0.0
LDS–L-D Saints	8	NR	NR	3,872	1.4	2.4
LUTH–E.L.C.A.	4	161	366	428	0.2	0.3
LUTH–Luth–MO Synod	3	519	634	816	0.3	0.5
LUTH–Wisc Ev Luth Syn	1	35	58	69	0.0	0.0
METH–AME	2	106	336	417	0.1	0.3
METH–C.M.E.	1	0	150	186	0.1	0.1
METH–Evan Meth Ch	1	NR	NR	NR	-	-
METH–Un Methodist	23	4,303	15,293	17,821	6.4	11.1
Metro Comm Ch	1	83	91	113	0.0	0.1
Muslim Est	2	1,248	NR	5,084	1.8	3.2
Non-denom Chr Chs	47	14,750	19,515	20,817	7.5	13.0
ORTHE–Greek Orthodox	1	50	NR	175	0.1	0.1
ORTHO–Coptic Orth Ch	1	10	NR	33	0.0	0.0
PENT–Assemb of God	15	1,725	958	2,573	0.9	1.6
PENT–Ch God (Cleve)	3	135	414	513	0.2	0.3
PENT–Ch of God Proph	1	NR	4	5	0.0	0.0
PENT–COGIC	5	265	615	763	0.3	0.5
PENT–Full Gosp Bapt	4	NR	NR	NR	-	-
PENT–Int Foursq Gos	4	337	684	848	0.3	0.5
PENT–Intl Pent Holiness	7	310	392	486	0.2	0.3
PENT–Pent Ch of God	1	70	NR	109	0.0	0.1
PENT–Un Pent Ch Intl	1	NR	NR	NR	-	-
PRES–Cumber Presb	1	NR	115	204	0.1	0.1
PRES–Presb Ch (USA)	4	609	1,389	1,723	0.6	1.1
PRES–Presb Ch Amer	1	145	138	189	0.1	0.1
Salvation Army	1	121	147	147	0.1	0.1
Sev Day Adv	3	322	560	643	0.2	0.4
Un C of Christ	1	19	22	27	0.0	0.0
Unit Univ	1	48	69	77	0.0	0.0
Unity Ch	1	NR	NR	NR	-	-
Zoroastrian	0	NR	NR	11	0.0	0.0
LYNN	**23**	**1,051**	**2,853**	**4,885**	**82.6**	**100.0**
Bahá'í	0	NR	1	1	0.0	0.0
BAPT–So Bapt Conv	9	653	2,000	2,555	43.2	52.3
Catholic	3	NR	NR	1,266	21.4	25.9
Ch of Nazarene	1	39	65	100	1.7	2.0
CHR–Chs of Christ	4	137	138	183	3.1	3.7
LUTH–E.L.C.A.	1	27	71	91	1.5	1.9
LUTH–Luth–MO Synod	1	69	111	127	2.1	2.6
METH–Evan Meth Ch	1	NR	NR	NR	-	-
METH–Un Methodist	3	126	467	562	9.5	11.5
MCCULLOCH	**32**	**1,563**	**2,883**	**4,695**	**56.7**	**100.0**
ANG/EPIS–Episcopal	1	50	89	89	1.1	1.9
BAPT–Ind Bapt Flwsp Intl	1	NR	NR	NR	-	-
BAPT–So Bapt Conv	9	453	1,231	1,519	18.3	32.4
Catholic	2	NR	NR	1,100	13.3	23.4
CHR–Chr Ch (Disc)	1	35	131	162	2.0	3.5
CHR–Chs of Christ	4	248	204	310	3.7	6.6

Religious Group	Number of Congrega-tions	Number of Attendees	Number of Communicant, Confirmed, or Full Members	Adherents		
				Number of Adherents	% of Total Pop.	% of Total Adh.
Jehovah's Witness	1	NR	NR	NR	-	-
LDS–L-D Saints	1	NR	NR	116	1.4	2.5
LUTH–Luth–MO Synod	1	15	44	45	0.5	1.0
METH–Un Methodist	2	196	372	458	5.5	9.8
Non-denom Chr Chs	4	355	485	491	5.9	10.5
PENT–Assemb of God	2	53	45	58	0.7	1.2
PENT–Ch God (Cleve)	1	116	190	234	2.8	5.0
PENT–Un Pent Ch Intl	1	NR	NR	NR	-	-
PRES–Presb Ch (USA)	1	42	92	113	1.4	2.4
MCLENNAN	**378**	**38,637**	**87,530**	**231,825**	**98.7**	**100.0**
ANG/EPIS–Anglican NA	2	NR	NR	NR	-	-
ANG/EPIS–Episcopal	3	606	1,723	1,849	0.8	0.8
Bahá'í	0	NR	65	65	0.0	0.0
BAPT–Alliance Bapt	1	NR	NR	NR	-	-
BAPT–Amer Bapt Assn	2	NR	235	293	0.1	0.1
BAPT–Free Will Bapt	1	NR	52	65	0.0	0.0
BAPT–Ind Bapt Flwsp Intl	2	NR	NR	NR	-	-
BAPT–N Am Bapt Conf	2	NR	198	246	0.1	0.1
BAPT–Natl Mis Bapt Conv	1	0	150	187	0.1	0.1
BAPT–NBC Amer	3	550	1,000	1,245	0.5	0.5
BAPT–NBC USA	1	0	250	311	0.1	0.1
BAPT–So Bapt Conv	151	16,561	48,873	60,838	25.9	26.2
Calv Chpl	1	NR	NR	NR	-	-
Catholic	14	NR	NR	27,864	11.9	12.0
CGOD–Ch God (Ander)	1	14	NR	14	0.0	0.0
Ch Cr, Scientst	1	NR	NR	NR	-	-
Ch of Nazarene	2	179	442	442	0.2	0.2
Chr & Miss Al	1	118	101	150	0.1	0.1
CHR–Chr Ch (Disc)	5	285	740	921	0.4	0.4
CHR–Chs of Christ	26	2,670	2,836	4,004	1.7	1.7
Evan Assoc RCC	1	NR	NR	NR	-	-
Evan Free Ch	1	350	NR	350	0.1	0.2
Jehovah's Witness	2	NR	NR	NR	-	-
JUD–Conserv	1	70	79	213	0.1	0.1
JUD–Reform	1	56	98	265	0.1	0.1
LDS–Comm of Christ	1	NR	126	126	0.1	0.1
LDS–L-D Saints	4	NR	NR	2,053	0.9	0.9
LUTH–E.L.C.A.	5	458	1,290	1,495	0.6	0.6
LUTH–Luth–MO Synod	6	1,098	1,906	2,259	1.0	1.0
MENN–Mennonite USA	1	40	18	22	0.0	0.0
METH–AME	6	185	962	1,198	0.5	0.5
METH–C.M.E.	1	0	100	124	0.1	0.1
METH–Un Methodist	36	3,903	13,328	103,928	44.2	44.8
Metro Comm Ch	1	30	39	49	0.0	0.0
MORAV–Unity Of Breth	1	NR	NR	NR	-	-
Muslim Est	2	1,248	NR	5,084	2.2	2.2
Non-denom Chr Chs	40	6,734	9,366	9,570	4.1	4.1
ORTHE–Greek Orthodox	1	70	NR	160	0.1	0.1
PENT–Assemb of God	10	1,839	716	2,588	1.1	1.1
PENT–Ch of God Proph	1	NR	54	67	0.0	0.0
PENT–COGIC	5	200	635	790	0.3	0.3
PENT–Full Gosp Bapt	1	NR	NR	NR	-	-
PENT–Pent Ch of God	3	210	NR	326	0.1	0.1
PENT–Un Pent Ch Intl	8	NR	NR	NR	-	-
PRES–Cum Pres Am	3	NR	NR	NR	-	-
PRES–Presb Ch (USA)	4	345	890	1,108	0.5	0.5
PRES–Presb Ch Amer	1	275	212	258	0.1	0.1
Salvation Army	1	123	185	255	0.1	0.1
Sev Day Adv	4	202	351	404	0.2	0.2
Un C of Christ	4	158	443	551	0.2	0.2
Unit Univ	1	60	67	88	0.0	0.0
Unity Ch	1	NR	NR	NR	-	-
MCMULLEN	**2**	**22**	**185**	**433**	**61.2**	**100.0**
BAPT–So Bapt Conv	1	22	185	214	30.3	49.4
Catholic	1	NR	NR	219	31.0	50.6
MADISON	**36**	**2,130**	**4,814**	**7,353**	**53.8**	**100.0**
ANG/EPIS–Episcopal	1	17	23	23	0.2	0.3
BAPT–Free Will Bapt	1	NR	52	63	0.5	0.9
BAPT–NBC Amer	1	0	150	181	1.3	2.5
BAPT–So Bapt Conv	12	976	2,471	2,978	21.8	40.5

NR–Not Reported   - Represents no adherents reported.   Percentages may not total 100 due to rounding.

Table 3: Religious Congregations by County and Group: 2010

Religious Group	Number of Congrega-tions	Number of Attendees	Number of Communicant, Confirmed, or Full Members	Adherents: Number of Adherents	Adherents: % of Total Pop.	Adherents: % of Total Adh.
Catholic	1	NR	NR	1,426	10.4	19.4
CHR–Chs of Christ	11	688	778	964	7.1	13.1
Jehovah's Witness	1	NR	NR	NR	-	-
LDS–L-D Saints	1	NR	NR	283	2.1	3.8
LUTH–Luth–MO Synod	1	0	198	235	1.7	3.2
METH–Un Methodist	2	209	672	720	5.3	9.8
Non-denom Chr Chs	2	225	450	450	3.3	6.1
PENT–Assemb of God	1	15	20	30	0.2	0.4
PENT–Un Pent Ch Intl	1	NR	NR	NR	-	-
MARION	**32**	**1,125**	**2,764**	**3,639**	**34.5**	**100.0**
ANG/EPIS–Episcopal	1	18	20	21	0.2	0.6
Bahá'í	0	NR	4	4	0.0	0.1
BAPT–So Bapt Conv	9	380	1,414	1,652	15.7	45.4
Catholic	1	NR	NR	407	3.9	11.2
CHR–Chs of Christ	3	210	200	235	2.2	6.5
Jehovah's Witness	1	NR	NR	NR	-	-
METH–AME	1	0	100	117	1.1	3.2
METH–C.M.E.	1	0	150	175	1.7	4.8
METH–Un Methodist	7	227	389	430	4.1	11.8
PENT–Assemb of God	1	45	37	77	0.7	2.1
PENT–COGIC	1	5	7	8	0.1	0.2
PENT–Un Pent Ch Intl	2	NR	NR	NR	-	-
PRES–Cumber Presb	1	NR	26	34	0.3	0.9
Sev Day Adv	3	240	417	479	4.5	13.2
MARTIN	**13**	**652**	**1,667**	**3,043**	**63.4**	**100.0**
BAPT–So Bapt Conv	4	267	971	1,262	26.3	41.5
Catholic	2	NR	NR	1,000	20.8	32.9
CHR–Chs of Christ	4	194	190	229	4.8	7.5
LDS–Comm of Christ	1	NR	61	61	1.3	2.0
METH–Un Methodist	1	91	295	341	7.1	11.2
Non-denom Chr Chs	1	100	150	150	3.1	4.9
MASON	**13**	**940**	**1,918**	**2,853**	**71.1**	**100.0**
BAPT–So Bapt Conv	4	150	540	643	16.0	22.5
Catholic	1	NR	NR	553	13.8	19.4
CHR–Chs of Christ	1	125	138	142	3.5	5.0
LUTH–E.L.C.A.	1	129	372	432	10.8	15.1
METH–Un Methodist	2	228	563	688	17.1	24.1
Non-denom Chr Chs	3	300	305	375	9.3	13.1
PENT–Assemb of God	1	8	0	20	0.5	0.7
MATAGORDA	**86**	**4,379**	**11,247**	**22,247**	**60.6**	**100.0**
ANG/EPIS–Episcopal	3	169	397	500	1.4	2.2
Bahá'í	0	NR	4	4	0.0	0.0
BAPT–Ind Bapt Flwsp Intl	1	NR	NR	NR	-	-
BAPT–Natl Mis Bapt Conv	3	10	330	413	1.1	1.9
BAPT–So Bapt Conv	21	1,896	5,834	7,297	19.9	32.8
Catholic	7	NR	NR	8,143	22.2	36.6
Ch of Nazarene	1	28	67	67	0.2	0.3
CHR–Chr Ch (Disc)	4	159	219	274	0.7	1.2
CHR–Chs of Christ	5	428	539	648	1.8	2.9
Jehovah's Witness	3	NR	NR	NR	-	-
LDS–L-D Saints	1	NR	NR	394	1.1	1.8
LUTH–E.L.C.A.	1	66	199	244	0.7	1.1
LUTH–Luth–MO Synod	1	35	41	71	0.2	0.3
METH–AME	1	35	67	84	0.2	0.4
METH–C.M.E.	1	0	150	188	0.5	0.8
METH–Un Methodist	7	498	1,215	1,381	3.8	6.2
Non-denom Chr Chs	7	770	1,050	1,107	3.0	5.0
PENT–Assemb of God	1	80	60	87	0.2	0.4
PENT–Ch of God Proph	5	NR	197	246	0.7	1.1
PENT–COGIC	2	0	300	375	1.0	1.7
PENT–Intl Pent Holiness	2	60	70	88	0.2	0.4
PENT–Un Pent Ch Intl	4	NR	NR	NR	-	-
PENT–Vineyard	1	80	150	188	0.5	0.8
PRES–Presb Ch (USA)	4	65	358	448	1.2	2.0
MAVERICK	**46**	**2,607**	**3,484**	**18,687**	**34.4**	**100.0**
ANG/EPIS–Episcopal	1	110	189	189	0.3	1.0
Bahá'í	0	NR	29	29	0.1	0.2
BAPT–So Bapt Conv	7	372	447	601	1.1	3.2
Catholic	4	NR	NR	12,600	23.2	67.4
CGOD–Ch God (Ander)	1	199	NR	199	0.4	1.1
CHR–Chr Chs & Chs Cr	1	NR	80	108	0.2	0.6
CHR–Chs of Christ	2	115	116	147	0.3	0.8
Jehovah's Witness	1	NR	NR	NR	-	-
LDS–L-D Saints	2	NR	NR	1,261	2.3	6.7
LUTH–E.L.C.A.	1	140	11	325	0.6	1.7
METH–Cong Meth	9	NR	630	847	1.6	4.5
METH–Un Methodist	2	100	279	282	0.5	1.5
Non-denom Chr Chs	5	1,085	1,260	1,418	2.6	7.6
PENT–Assemb of God	4	282	240	328	0.6	1.8
PENT–Ch God (Cleve)	1	50	56	75	0.1	0.4
PENT–Ch Lord Jesus Apos	2	NR	NR	NR	-	-
PENT–Pent Ch of God	1	70	NR	109	0.2	0.6
PENT–Un Pent Ch Intl	1	NR	NR	NR	-	-
Sev Day Adv	1	84	147	169	0.3	0.9
MEDINA	**57**	**2,877**	**7,191**	**22,508**	**48.9**	**100.0**
ANG/EPIS–Episcopal	1	14	25	25	0.1	0.1
Bahá'í	0	NR	2	2	0.0	0.0
BAPT–Ind Bapt Flwsp Intl	1	NR	NR	NR	-	-
BAPT–Ref Bapt Ch	1	NR	NR	NR	-	-
BAPT–So Bapt Conv	15	1,315	3,845	4,782	10.4	21.2
Catholic	8	NR	NR	13,097	28.5	58.2
Ch of Nazarene	1	68	72	85	0.2	0.4
CHR–Chr Ch (Disc)	1	0	31	39	0.1	0.2
CHR–Chs of Christ	5	216	231	329	0.7	1.5
Jehovah's Witness	3	NR	NR	NR	-	-
LDS–L-D Saints	1	NR	NR	511	1.1	2.3
LUTH–E.L.C.A.	1	65	145	170	0.4	0.8
LUTH–Luth Cong Msn Chr	2	232	768	955	2.1	4.2
LUTH–Luth–MO Synod	1	54	91	114	0.2	0.5
METH–Un Methodist	5	520	1,542	1,861	4.0	8.3
Non-denom Chr Chs	5	282	337	386	0.8	1.7
PENT–Assemb of God	2	62	40	79	0.2	0.4
PENT–Ch God (Cleve)	1	25	19	24	0.1	0.1
PENT–Un Pent Ch Intl	2	NR	NR	NR	-	-
Sev Day Adv	1	24	43	49	0.1	0.2
MENARD	**10**	**281**	**587**	**1,165**	**52.0**	**100.0**
ANG/EPIS–Episcopal	2	19	40	40	1.8	3.4
BAPT–So Bapt Conv	2	60	103	121	5.4	10.4
Catholic	1	NR	NR	500	22.3	42.9
CHR–Chs of Christ	1	30	44	48	2.1	4.1
LUTH–Luth–MO Synod	1	29	33	38	1.7	3.3
METH–Un Methodist	1	43	190	236	10.5	20.3
Non-denom Chr Chs	1	100	150	150	6.7	12.9
PRES–Presb Ch (USA)	1	0	27	32	1.4	2.7
MIDLAND	**148**	**23,844**	**48,329**	**97,922**	**71.5**	**100.0**
ANG/EPIS–Anglican NA	2	NR	NR	NR	-	-
ANG/EPIS–Episcopal	3	183	496	608	0.4	0.6
Bahá'í	0	NR	24	24	0.0	0.0
BAPT–Amer Bapt Assn	1	NR	75	95	0.1	0.1
BAPT–Ind Bapt Flwsp Intl	3	NR	NR	NR	-	-
BAPT–Natl Mis Bapt Conv	2	0	300	382	0.3	0.4
BAPT–So Bapt Conv	34	6,032	22,189	28,250	20.6	28.8
BUDD–Vajrayana	1	NR	NR	35	0.0	0.0
Calv Chpl	2	NR	NR	NR	-	-
Catholic	4	NR	NR	30,700	22.4	31.4
CGOD–Ch God (Ander)	1	45	NR	45	0.0	0.0
Ch Cr, Scientst	1	NR	NR	NR	-	-
Ch God (7th Day)	2	NR	NR	NR	-	-
Ch of Nazarene	1	104	227	227	0.2	0.2
Chr & Miss Al	1	79	48	131	0.1	0.1
CHR–Chr Ch (Disc)	3	316	794	1,011	0.7	1.0
CHR–Chr Chs & Chs Cr	1	NR	150	191	0.1	0.2
CHR–Chs of Christ	14	3,013	3,563	4,667	3.4	4.8
HINDU–Trad Temples	1	NR	NR	500	0.4	0.5
Jehovah's Witness	2	NR	NR	NR	-	-
LDS–Comm of Christ	1	NR	61	61	0.0	0.1
LDS–L-D Saints	4	NR	NR	1,582	1.2	1.6

NR–Not Reported - Represents no adherents reported. Percentages may not total 100 due to rounding.

Table 3: Religious Congregations by County and Group: 2010

Religious Group	Number of Congrega-tions	Number of Attendees	Number of Communicant, Confirmed, or Full Members	Adherents		
				Number of Adherents	% of Total Pop.	% of Total Adh.
LUTH–E.L.C.A.	2	71	220	255	0.2	0.3
LUTH–Luth–MO Synod	2	254	512	619	0.5	0.6
LUTH–Wisc Ev Luth Syn	1	9	15	19	0.0	0.0
METH–AME	1	0	100	127	0.1	0.1
METH–C.M.E.	1	0	150	191	0.1	0.2
METH–Free Methodist	1	30	61	61	0.0	0.1
METH–Un Methodist	5	1,295	4,583	5,474	4.0	5.6
Muslim Est	2	1,248	NR	5,084	3.7	5.2
Non-denom Chr Chs	24	8,960	10,775	12,103	8.8	12.4
PENT–Assemb of God	6	906	678	1,190	0.9	1.2
PENT–Ch God (Cleve)	1	95	116	148	0.1	0.2
PENT–Ch of God Proph	1	NR	37	47	0.0	0.0
PENT–COGIC	3	150	550	700	0.5	0.7
PENT–Int Foursq Gos	2	78	92	117	0.1	0.1
PENT–Un Pent Ch Intl	3	NR	NR	NR	-	-
PENT–Vineyard	1	28	35	45	0.0	0.0
PRES–Presb Ch (USA)	3	663	1,992	2,536	1.9	2.6
PRES–Presb Ch Amer	1	40	43	63	0.0	0.1
Salvation Army	1	57	103	236	0.2	0.2
Sev Day Adv	2	164	284	327	0.2	0.3
Unit Univ	1	24	56	71	0.1	0.1
MILAM	**87**	**3,598**	**9,229**	**15,206**	**61.4**	**100.0**
ANG/EPIS–Episcopal	2	42	59	59	0.2	0.4
BAPT–Amer Bapt Assn	1	NR	150	187	0.8	1.2
BAPT–So Bapt Conv	25	1,467	3,819	4,766	19.3	31.3
Catholic	4	NR	NR	3,853	15.6	25.3
CHR–Chr Ch (Disc)	3	28	201	251	1.0	1.7
CHR–Chr Chs & Chs Cr	3	NR	340	424	1.7	2.8
CHR–Chs of Christ	13	613	669	800	3.2	5.3
Jehovah's Witness	1	NR	NR	NR	-	-
LDS–L-D Saints	1	NR	NR	187	0.8	1.2
LUTH–E.L.C.A.	3	177	452	525	2.1	3.5
LUTH–Luth–MO Synod	2	277	721	845	3.4	5.6
LUTH–Nor Amer Luth C	1	NR	NR	NR	-	-
METH–AME	5	0	550	686	2.8	4.5
METH–Un Methodist	10	507	1,603	1,862	7.5	12.2
MORAV–Unity Of Breth	1	NR	NR	NR	-	-
Non-denom Chr Chs	4	295	400	413	1.7	2.7
PENT–Assemb of God	4	132	112	157	0.6	1.0
PENT–Un Pent Ch Intl	1	NR	NR	NR	-	-
PRES–Presb Ch (USA)	3	60	153	191	0.8	1.3
MILLS	**20**	**1,170**	**3,057**	**4,138**	**83.8**	**100.0**
Bahá'í	0	NR	1	1	0.0	0.0
BAPT–So Bapt Conv	9	467	1,830	2,227	45.1	53.8
Catholic	1	NR	NR	415	8.4	10.0
CHR–Chs of Christ	3	332	328	403	8.2	9.7
LUTH–Luth Cong Msn Chr	1	78	368	448	9.1	10.8
METH–Cong Meth	1	NR	NR	NR	-	-
METH–Un Methodist	2	158	380	436	8.8	10.5
Non-denom Chr Chs	1	100	150	150	3.0	3.6
PENT–Assemb of God	1	35	0	58	1.2	1.4
PENT–Un Pent Ch Intl	1	NR	NR	NR	-	-
MITCHELL	**25**	**971**	**3,262**	**5,571**	**59.2**	**100.0**
ANG/EPIS–Episcopal	1	14	26	26	0.3	0.5
BAPT–So Bapt Conv	8	553	2,514	2,950	31.4	53.0
Catholic	2	NR	NR	1,650	17.5	29.6
CHR–Chr Ch (Disc)	1	18	22	26	0.3	0.5
CHR–Chs of Christ	4	147	224	284	3.0	5.1
Jehovah's Witness	2	NR	NR	NR	-	-
METH–Un Methodist	4	149	421	526	5.6	9.4
PENT–Assemb of God	1	75	26	75	0.8	1.3
PENT–Un Pent Ch Intl	1	NR	NR	NR	-	-
PRES–Presb Ch (USA)	1	15	29	34	0.4	0.6
MONTAGUE	**70**	**3,906**	**6,674**	**9,794**	**49.7**	**100.0**
ANG/EPIS–Anglican NA	1	NR	NR	NR	-	-
Bahá'í	0	NR	1	1	0.0	0.0
BAPT–Free Will Bapt	1	NR	52	63	0.3	0.6
BAPT–Ind Bapt Flwsp Intl	6	NR	NR	NR	-	-

Religious Group	Number of Congrega-tions	Number of Attendees	Number of Communicant, Confirmed, or Full Members	Adherents		
				Number of Adherents	% of Total Pop.	% of Total Adh.
BAPT–So Bapt Conv	20	1,591	3,755	4,575	23.2	46.7
BRETH–Ch of Brethren	0	0	77	94	0.5	1.0
Catholic	3	NR	NR	1,110	5.6	11.3
Ch of Nazarene	4	118	150	292	1.5	3.0
CHR–Chr Ch (Disc)	2	25	129	157	0.8	1.6
CHR–Chs of Christ	6	478	462	539	2.7	5.5
Jehovah's Witness	1	NR	NR	NR	-	-
LUTH–Luth–MO Synod	1	92	178	231	1.2	2.4
METH–Un Methodist	6	353	654	812	4.1	8.3
Non-denom Chr Chs	8	652	925	997	5.1	10.2
PENT–Assemb of God	4	310	143	421	2.1	4.3
PENT–Pent Ch of God	3	210	NR	326	1.7	3.3
PENT–Un Pent Ch Intl	1	NR	NR	NR	-	-
PRES–Presb Ch (USA)	2	45	92	112	0.6	1.1
Sev Day Adv	1	32	56	64	0.3	0.7
MONTGOMERY	**334**	**70,189**	**117,654**	**227,784**	**50.0**	**100.0**
ANG/EPIS–Anglican NA	1	NR	NR	NR	-	-
ANG/EPIS–Episcopal	2	633	1,690	1,690	0.4	0.7
Bahá'í	1	NR	141	141	0.0	0.1
BAPT–Amer Bapt Assn	4	NR	303	385	0.1	0.2
BAPT–Asc Ref Bap Ch Am	1	NR	NR	NR	-	-
BAPT–Free Will Bapt	3	NR	156	198	0.0	0.1
BAPT–Ind Bapt Flwsp Intl	1	NR	NR	NR	-	-
BAPT–Natl Mis Bapt Conv	2	20	180	229	0.1	0.1
BAPT–So Bapt Conv	116	35,833	68,084	86,620	19.0	38.0
BUDD–Mahayana	1	NR	NR	300	0.1	0.1
Calv Chpl	1	NR	NR	NR	-	-
Catholic	4	NR	NR	58,383	12.8	25.6
CGOD–Ch God (Ander)	1	0	NR	0	0.0	0.0
Ch Cr, Scientst	2	NR	NR	NR	-	-
Ch God (7th Day)	4	NR	NR	NR	-	-
Ch of Nazarene	4	335	510	611	0.1	0.3
CHR–Chr Ch (Disc)	2	297	488	621	0.1	0.3
CHR–Chr Chs & Chs Cr	1	NR	250	318	0.1	0.1
CHR–Chs of Christ	21	3,028	3,256	4,198	0.9	1.8
Grace Gosp Fel	1	NR	NR	NR	-	-
HINDU–I/A Temples	1	NR	NR	50	0.0	0.0
HINDU–Post Ren	1	NR	NR	25	0.0	0.0
HINDU–Trad Temples	1	NR	NR	450	0.1	0.2
Jehovah's Witness	5	NR	NR	NR	-	-
JUD–Orth	1	43	50	60	0.0	0.0
JUD–Reform	1	99	175	473	0.1	0.2
LDS–L-D Saints	15	NR	NR	6,220	1.4	2.7
LUTH–E.L.C.A.	5	902	1,953	2,502	0.5	1.1
LUTH–Luth–MO Synod	4	657	1,203	1,551	0.3	0.7
LUTH–Wisc Ev Luth Syn	2	197	284	451	0.1	0.2
METH–AME	1	0	100	127	0.0	0.1
METH–AME Zion	2	33	140	178	0.0	0.1
METH–C.M.E.	1	0	60	76	0.0	0.0
METH–Un Methodist	15	7,822	17,524	24,925	5.5	10.9
Muslim Est	4	2,496	NR	10,168	2.2	4.5
Non-denom Chr Chs	48	11,905	15,014	16,301	3.6	7.2
ORTHE–Orth Ch in Amer	1	40	NR	90	0.0	0.0
PENT–Assemb of God	20	4,248	2,714	6,054	1.3	2.7
PENT–Ch God (Cleve)	1	40	156	198	0.0	0.1
PENT–Ch God Apos Fth	1	NR	NR	NR	-	-
PENT–COGIC	4	10	470	598	0.1	0.3
PENT–Intl Pent Holiness	3	290	330	420	0.1	0.2
PENT–Pent Ch of God	1	70	NR	109	0.0	0.0
PENT–Un Pent Ch Intl	12	NR	NR	NR	-	-
PENT–Vineyard	1	221	289	368	0.1	0.2
PRES–Presb Ch (USA)	1	0	779	991	0.2	0.4
PRES–Presb Ch Amer	1	250	217	274	0.1	0.1
Salvation Army	1	55	66	132	0.0	0.1
Sev Day Adv	5	510	886	1,019	0.2	0.4
Unit Univ	1	155	186	274	0.1	0.1
Unity Ch	1	NR	NR	NR	-	-
Zoroastrian	0	NR	NR	6	0.0	0.0
MOORE	**50**	**4,485**	**6,992**	**13,403**	**61.2**	**100.0**
ANG/EPIS–Episcopal	1	15	29	29	0.1	0.2
Bahá'í	0	NR	9	9	0.0	0.1

NR–Not Reported - Represents no adherents reported. Percentages may not total 100 due to rounding.

Table 3: Religious Congregations by County and Group: 2010

Religious Group	Number of Congrega-tions	Number of Attendees	Number of Communicant, Confirmed, or Full Members	Adherents		
				Number of Adherents	% of Total Pop.	% of Total Adh.
BAPT–Ind Bapt Flwsp Intl	2	NR	NR	NR	-	-
BAPT–So Bapt Conv	10	1,007	3,703	4,941	22.6	36.9
Catholic	3	NR	NR	1,239	5.7	9.2
Ch of Nazarene	2	69	139	187	0.9	1.4
CHR–Chr Ch (Disc)	1	0	167	223	1.0	1.7
CHR–Chr Chs & Chs Cr	1	NR	60	80	0.4	0.6
CHR–Chs of Christ	6	620	676	870	4.0	6.5
Jehovah's Witness	1	NR	NR	NR	-	-
LDS–L-D Saints	1	NR	NR	286	1.3	2.1
LUTH–Luth–MO Synod	1	49	136	159	0.7	1.2
METH–Un Methodist	4	201	648	937	4.3	7.0
Muslim Est	2	1,248	NR	2,542	11.6	19.0
Non-denom Chr Chs	6	780	895	994	4.5	7.4
PENT–Assemb of God	6	363	244	526	2.4	3.9
PENT–Intl Pent Holiness	1	44	79	105	0.5	0.8
PENT–Un Pent Ch Intl	1	NR	NR	NR	-	-
PRES–Presb Ch (USA)	1	89	207	276	1.3	2.1
MORRIS	**45**	**1,815**	**6,150**	**8,191**	**63.3**	**100.0**
Bahá'í	0	NR	1	1	0.0	0.0
BAPT–Amer Bapt Assn	4	NR	325	394	3.0	4.8
BAPT–Ind Bapt Flwsp Intl	1	NR	NR	NR	-	-
BAPT–NBC USA	1	0	500	607	4.7	7.4
BAPT–So Bapt Conv	11	787	2,947	3,576	27.6	43.7
Catholic	1	NR	NR	703	5.4	8.6
CHR–Chr Chs & Chs Cr	2	NR	235	285	2.2	3.5
CHR–Chs of Christ	6	631	661	895	6.9	10.9
Jehovah's Witness	1	NR	NR	NR	-	-
METH–AME	1	0	150	182	1.4	2.2
METH–C.M.E.	1	0	150	182	1.4	2.2
METH–Cong Meth	2	NR	106	129	1.0	1.6
METH–Un Methodist	8	222	697	794	6.1	9.7
Non-denom Chr Chs	1	100	150	150	1.2	1.8
PENT–Assemb of God	2	75	67	100	0.8	1.2
PENT–COGIC	1	0	150	182	1.4	2.2
PENT–Un Pent Ch Intl	1	NR	NR	NR	-	-
PRES–Cumber Presb	1	NR	11	11	0.1	0.1
MOTLEY	**9**	**370**	**768**	**1,007**	**83.2**	**100.0**
BAPT–So Bapt Conv	2	88	443	533	44.0	52.9
Catholic	1	NR	NR	85	7.0	8.4
CHR–Chs of Christ	3	80	84	110	9.1	10.9
METH–Un Methodist	2	52	91	91	7.5	9.0
Non-denom Chr Chs	1	150	150	188	15.5	18.7
NACOGDOCHES	**122**	**8,792**	**20,814**	**33,265**	**51.6**	**100.0**
ANG/EPIS–Episcopal	1	136	308	383	0.6	1.2
Bahá'í	0	NR	46	46	0.1	0.1
BAPT–Alliance Bapt	1	NR	NR	NR	-	-
BAPT–Amer Bapt Assn	1	NR	150	184	0.3	0.6
BAPT–Free Will Bapt	2	NR	104	127	0.2	0.4
BAPT–Natl Mis Bapt Conv	1	55	134	164	0.3	0.5
BAPT–NBC Amer	1	0	75	92	0.1	0.3
BAPT–NBC USA	1	0	500	613	1.0	1.8
BAPT–So Bapt Conv	32	3,247	11,096	13,603	21.1	40.9
Catholic	5	NR	NR	6,411	9.9	19.3
CGOD–Ch God (Ander)	1	61	NR	61	0.1	0.2
Ch of Nazarene	1	186	291	312	0.5	0.9
CHR–Chr Ch (Disc)	2	346	666	816	1.3	2.5
CHR–Chs of Christ	13	1,084	1,049	1,319	2.0	4.0
Jehovah's Witness	1	NR	NR	NR	-	-
LDS–L-D Saints	2	NR	NR	824	1.3	2.5
LUTH–Luth–MO Synod	1	100	154	197	0.3	0.6
METH–C.M.E.	4	0	600	736	1.1	2.2
METH–Cong Meth	4	NR	407	499	0.8	1.5
METH–Un Methodist	13	751	1,791	1,907	3.0	5.7
Non-denom Chr Chs	9	1,730	1,715	2,250	3.5	6.8
PENT–Assemb of God	2	570	212	869	1.3	2.6
PENT–COGIC	7	200	790	968	1.5	2.9
PENT–Cong Hol Ch	1	39	35	43	0.1	0.1
PENT–Un Pent Ch Intl	8	NR	NR	NR	-	-
PENT–Vineyard	1	80	300	368	0.6	1.1
PRES–Cum Pres Am	1	NR	NR	NR	-	-
PRES–Presb Ch (USA)	2	161	310	380	0.6	1.1
REF–Comm Ref Evan	1	NR	NR	NR	-	-
Sev Day Adv	2	46	81	93	0.1	0.3
Unity Ch	1	NR	NR	NR	-	-
NAVARRO	**117**	**7,201**	**18,325**	**25,219**	**52.8**	**100.0**
ANG/EPIS–Episcopal	1	143	301	326	0.7	1.3
Bahá'í	0	NR	29	29	0.1	0.1
BAPT–Amer Bapt Assn	8	NR	813	1,027	2.2	4.1
BAPT–Ind Bapt Flwsp Intl	2	NR	NR	NR	-	-
BAPT–Natl Mis Bapt Conv	1	0	150	189	0.4	0.7
BAPT–NBC Amer	1	0	150	189	0.4	0.7
BAPT–NBC USA	1	0	150	189	0.4	0.7
BAPT–So Bapt Conv	34	3,044	8,837	11,161	23.4	44.3
Catholic	1	NR	NR	1,800	3.8	7.1
Ch of Nazarene	1	175	0	175	0.4	0.7
CHR–Chr Ch (Disc)	2	25	60	76	0.2	0.3
CHR–Chs of Christ	8	1,173	1,472	1,847	3.9	7.3
Evan Free Ch	1	100	NR	100	0.2	0.4
HINDU–Post Ren	1	NR	NR	16	0.0	0.1
Jehovah's Witness	1	NR	NR	NR	-	-
LDS–L-D Saints	1	NR	NR	405	0.8	1.6
LUTH–Luth–MO Synod	1	65	83	118	0.2	0.5
METH–AME	4	30	500	631	1.3	2.5
METH–Un Methodist	18	784	3,087	3,370	7.1	13.4
Non-denom Chr Chs	7	580	798	825	1.7	3.3
PENT–Assemb of God	5	288	124	305	0.6	1.2
PENT–Ch God (Cleve)	1	56	324	409	0.9	1.6
PENT–COGIC	3	60	560	707	1.5	2.8
PENT–Full Gosp Bapt	1	NR	NR	NR	-	-
PENT–Intl Pent Holiness	4	390	475	600	1.3	2.4
PENT–Pent Ch of God	2	140	NR	217	0.5	0.9
PENT–Un Pent Ch Intl	2	NR	NR	NR	-	-
PRES–Presb Ch (USA)	2	68	213	269	0.6	1.1
Salvation Army	1	16	89	112	0.2	0.4
Sev Day Adv	2	64	110	127	0.3	0.5
NEWTON	**40**	**1,366**	**3,624**	**5,057**	**35.0**	**100.0**
Bahá'í	0	NR	1	1	0.0	0.0
BAPT–NBC USA	1	0	0	0	0.0	0.0
BAPT–So Bapt Conv	8	692	1,870	2,262	15.7	44.7
BUDD–Mahayana	1	NR	NR	506	3.5	10.0
CGOD–Ch God (Ander)	3	70	NR	70	0.5	1.4
CHR–Chs of Christ	5	225	221	312	2.2	6.2
METH–C.M.E.	5	0	700	847	5.9	16.7
METH–Cong Meth	1	NR	31	38	0.3	0.8
METH–Un Methodist	3	88	215	249	1.7	4.9
Non-denom Chr Chs	3	200	260	274	1.9	5.4
PENT–Assemb of God	1	21	26	26	0.2	0.5
PENT–COGIC	2	0	300	363	2.5	7.2
PENT–Pent Ch of God	1	70	NR	109	0.8	2.2
PENT–Un Pent Ch Intl	6	NR	NR	NR	-	-
NOLAN	**45**	**2,362**	**6,941**	**10,503**	**69.0**	**100.0**
ANG/EPIS–Episcopal	1	15	34	34	0.2	0.3
Bahá'í	0	NR	10	10	0.1	0.1
BAPT–So Bapt Conv	13	1,040	4,453	5,587	36.7	53.2
Catholic	3	NR	NR	1,700	11.2	16.2
CHR–Chr Ch (Disc)	1	0	160	201	1.3	1.9
CHR–Chs of Christ	7	545	604	752	4.9	7.2
Jehovah's Witness	1	NR	NR	NR	-	-
LDS–L-D Saints	1	NR	NR	173	1.1	1.6
LUTH–E.L.C.A.	1	22	72	81	0.5	0.8
LUTH–Luth–MO Synod	1	30	78	85	0.6	0.8
METH–AME	1	0	100	125	0.8	1.2
METH–Evan Meth Ch	1	NR	NR	NR	-	-
METH–Un Methodist	4	239	838	972	6.4	9.3
New Apost Ch	1	NR	NR	NR	-	-
Non-denom Chr Chs	4	270	340	363	2.4	3.5
PENT–Assemb of God	2	110	22	132	0.9	1.3
PENT–Ch God (Cleve)	1	33	75	94	0.6	0.9
PENT–Ch of God Proph	1	NR	13	16	0.1	0.2
PRES–Presb Ch (USA)	1	58	142	178	1.2	1.7

NR–Not Reported - Represents no adherents reported. Percentages may not total 100 due to rounding.

Table 3: Religious Congregations by County and Group: 2010

Religious Group	Number of Congregations	Number of Attendees	Number of Communicant, Confirmed, or Full Members	Adherents		
				Number of Adherents	% of Total Pop.	% of Total Adh.
NUECES	**353**	**44,604**	**64,630**	**205,612**	**60.4**	**100.0**
ANG/EPIS–Anglican NA	1	NR	NR	NR	-	-
ANG/EPIS–Episcopal	7	964	1,926	2,568	0.8	1.2
Bahá'í	1	NR	228	228	0.1	0.1
BAPT–Ind Bapt Flwsp Intl	2	NR	NR	NR	-	-
BAPT–Natl Mis Bapt Conv	2	0	0	0	0.0	0.0
BAPT–NBC Amer	1	300	500	626	0.2	0.3
BAPT–Ref Bapt Ch	1	NR	NR	NR	-	-
BAPT–So Bapt Conv	101	18,552	28,919	36,207	10.6	17.6
BUDD–Vajrayana	1	NR	NR	56	0.0	0.0
Calv Chpl	1	NR	NR	NR	-	-
Catholic	38	NR	NR	111,687	32.8	54.3
CGOD–Ch God (Ander)	6	245	NR	245	0.1	0.1
Ch Cr, Scientist	1	NR	NR	NR	-	-
Ch God (7th Day)	2	NR	NR	NR	-	-
Ch of Nazarene	4	274	362	397	0.1	0.2
CHR–Chr Ch (Disc)	6	356	584	731	0.2	0.4
CHR–Chs of Christ	19	1,899	2,127	2,792	0.8	1.4
Evan Free Ch	1	250	NR	250	0.1	0.1
FRND–Fr Gen Cf	1	NR	15	19	0.0	0.0
HINDU–I/A Temples	2	NR	NR	1,992	0.6	1.0
HINDU–Trad Temples	1	NR	NR	500	0.1	0.2
Jehovah's Witness	10	NR	NR	NR	-	-
JUD–Reform	1	101	179	483	0.1	0.2
LDS–Comm of Christ	1	NR	110	110	0.0	0.1
LDS–L-D Saints	5	NR	NR	3,871	1.1	1.9
LUTH–Ch Luth Conf	1	NR	NR	NR	-	-
LUTH–E.L.C.A.	4	440	788	970	0.3	0.5
LUTH–Luth-MO Synod	6	567	1,408	1,821	0.5	0.9
LUTH–Nor Amer Luth C	1	NR	NR	NR	-	-
LUTH–Wisc Ev Luth Syn	1	60	122	160	0.0	0.1
MENN–Mennonite USA	1	30	54	68	0.0	0.0
METH–AME	2	70	210	263	0.1	0.1
METH–Free Methodist	2	49	25	49	0.0	0.0
METH–Un Methodist	17	2,541	6,320	7,707	2.3	3.7
Metro Comm Ch	1	40	62	78	0.0	0.0
Muslim Est	1	624	NR	2,542	0.7	1.2
New Apost Ch	1	NR	NR	NR	-	-
Non-denom Chr Chs	40	12,218	14,086	17,682	5.2	8.6
ORTHE–Greek Orthodox	1	125	NR	190	0.1	0.1
ORTHE–Serb Orth USA	1	30	NR	275	0.1	0.1
ORTHO–Syrian Orth Ch	1	40	NR	50	0.0	0.0
PENT–Assemb of God	17	2,143	2,671	4,360	1.3	2.1
PENT–Ch God (Cleve)	1	12	53	66	0.0	0.0
PENT–Ch Lord Jesus Apos	2	NR	NR	NR	-	-
PENT–Ch of God Proph	1	NR	46	58	0.0	0.0
PENT–COGIC	3	75	375	470	0.1	0.2
PENT–Int Foursq Gos	1	363	149	187	0.1	0.1
PENT–Intl Pent Holiness	3	370	515	645	0.2	0.3
PENT–Pent Ch of God	3	210	NR	326	0.1	0.2
PENT–Un Pent Ch Intl	5	NR	NR	NR	-	-
PRES–Presb Ch (USA)	10	897	1,804	2,259	0.7	1.1
PRES–Presb Ch Amer	2	125	163	163	0.0	0.1
PRES–Ref Pres US	1	NR	NR	NR	-	-
Salvation Army	1	188	106	1,610	0.5	0.8
Sev Day Adv	3	312	544	625	0.2	0.3
Un C of Christ	1	35	71	89	0.0	0.0
Unit Univ	1	99	108	137	0.0	0.1
Unity Ch	1	NR	NR	NR	-	-
OCHILTREE	**27**	**1,914**	**4,231**	**7,049**	**69.0**	**100.0**
ANG/EPIS–Episcopal	1	10	11	11	0.1	0.2
BAPT–So Bapt Conv	4	352	1,795	2,404	23.5	34.1
Catholic	1	NR	NR	1,680	16.4	23.8
Ch of Nazarene	1	10	28	36	0.4	0.5
CHR–Chr Ch (Disc)	1	85	219	293	2.9	4.2
CHR–Chr Chs & Chs Cr	1	NR	50	67	0.7	1.0
CHR–Chs of Christ	3	130	169	214	2.1	3.0
LDS–L-D Saints	1	NR	NR	99	1.0	1.4
LUTH–Luth-MO Synod	1	10	39	40	0.4	0.6
MENN–Mennonite USA	1	25	35	47	0.5	0.7
METH–Un Methodist	1	157	612	640	6.3	9.1
Non-denom Chr Chs	4	920	1,120	1,200	11.7	17.0
PENT–Assemb of God	2	100	48	177	1.7	2.5
PENT–Ch God (Cleve)	1	14	20	27	0.3	0.4
PENT–Int Foursq Gos	1	101	70	94	0.9	1.3
PENT–Un Pent Ch Intl	2	NR	NR	NR	-	-
PRES–Presb Ch (USA)	1	0	15	20	0.2	0.3
OLDHAM	**8**	**264**	**901**	**1,283**	**62.5**	**100.0**
BAPT–So Bapt Conv	2	97	646	821	40.0	64.0
Catholic	1	NR	NR	200	9.7	15.6
CHR–Chs of Christ	2	39	38	43	2.1	3.4
METH–Un Methodist	2	53	117	119	5.8	9.3
Non-denom Chr Chs	1	75	100	100	4.9	7.8
ORANGE	**130**	**11,021**	**31,484**	**51,091**	**62.4**	**100.0**
ANG/EPIS–Episcopal	1	54	104	104	0.1	0.2
Bahá'í	0	NR	16	16	0.0	0.0
BAPT–Amer Bapt Assn	1	NR	60	74	0.1	0.1
BAPT–Natl Mis Bapt Conv	1	0	150	185	0.2	0.4
BAPT–So Bapt Conv	40	5,345	22,923	28,284	34.6	55.4
Catholic	7	NR	NR	10,228	12.5	20.0
CGOD–Ch God (Ander)	1	30	NR	30	0.0	0.1
Ch of Nazarene	2	228	374	376	0.5	0.7
CHR–Chr Ch (Disc)	1	0	0	0	0.0	0.0
CHR–Chr Chs & Chs Cr	3	NR	235	290	0.4	0.6
CHR–Chs of Christ	11	730	794	1,003	1.2	2.0
Jehovah's Witness	3	NR	NR	NR	-	-
LDS–L-D Saints	5	NR	NR	2,090	2.6	4.1
LUTH–E.L.C.A.	2	86	162	204	0.2	0.4
LUTH–Luth-MO Synod	1	45	92	105	0.1	0.2
METH–C.M.E.	1	200	312	385	0.5	0.8
METH–Un Methodist	8	975	2,076	2,658	3.2	5.2
Non-denom Chr Chs	18	1,790	2,440	2,670	3.3	5.2
PENT–Assemb of God	6	1,160	929	1,384	1.7	2.7
PENT–Ch God (Cleve)	1	60	129	159	0.2	0.3
PENT–Ch of God Proph	1	NR	17	21	0.0	0.0
PENT–COGIC	1	115	225	278	0.3	0.5
PENT–Un Pent Ch Intl	10	NR	NR	NR	-	-
PRES–Presb Ch (USA)	3	150	290	358	0.4	0.7
Salvation Army	1	20	99	123	0.2	0.2
Sev Day Adv	1	33	57	66	0.1	0.1
PALO PINTO	**78**	**4,135**	**11,553**	**15,822**	**56.3**	**100.0**
ANG/EPIS–Anglican NA	2	NR	NR	NR	-	-
Bahá'í	0	NR	49	49	0.2	0.3
BAPT–Ind Bapt Flwsp Intl	2	NR	NR	NR	-	-
BAPT–So Bapt Conv	30	2,000	7,989	9,892	35.2	62.5
Catholic	3	NR	NR	1,152	4.1	7.3
Ch of Nazarene	1	21	39	49	0.2	0.3
CHR–Chr Ch (Disc)	1	68	164	203	0.7	1.3
CHR–Chs of Christ	10	740	908	1,123	4.0	7.1
Grace Gosp Fel	1	NR	NR	NR	-	-
Jehovah's Witness	1	NR	NR	NR	-	-
LDS–Comm of Christ	1	NR	126	126	0.4	0.8
LDS–L-D Saints	1	NR	NR	254	0.9	1.6
LUTH–Luth-MO Synod	1	58	108	129	0.5	0.8
METH–AME	1	0	150	186	0.7	1.2
METH–Un Methodist	8	352	879	1,121	4.0	7.1
Non-denom Chr Chs	7	397	540	571	2.0	3.6
PENT–Assemb of God	2	110	0	121	0.4	0.8
PENT–Ch God (Cleve)	1	238	441	546	1.9	3.5
PENT–Ch of God Proph	1	NR	39	48	0.2	0.3
PENT–Pent Ch of God	1	70	NR	109	0.4	0.7
PENT–Un Pent Ch Intl	1	NR	NR	NR	-	-
PRES–Presb Ch (USA)	1	35	42	52	0.2	0.3
Sev Day Adv	1	46	79	91	0.3	0.6
PANOLA	**71**	**3,199**	**8,727**	**11,628**	**48.9**	**100.0**
ANG/EPIS–Episcopal	1	20	42	42	0.2	0.4
Bahá'í	0	NR	8	8	0.0	0.1
BAPT–Amer Bapt Assn	12	NR	1,160	1,436	6.0	12.3
BAPT–Free Will Bapt	4	NR	208	257	1.1	2.2
BAPT–Natl Mis Bapt Conv	1	30	50	62	0.3	0.5

NR–Not Reported - Represents no adherents reported. Percentages may not total 100 due to rounding.

Table 3: Religious Congregations by County and Group: 2010

Religious Group	Number of Congrega-tions	Number of Attendees	Number of Communicant, Confirmed, or Full Members	Adherents: Number of Adherents	Adherents: % of Total Pop.	Adherents: % of Total Adh.
BAPT–NBC USA	1	90	20	25	0.1	0.2
BAPT–So Bapt Conv	16	1,136	3,368	4,168	17.5	35.8
Catholic	1	NR	NR	1,299	5.5	11.2
Ch of Nazarene	1	24	31	37	0.2	0.3
CHR–Chr Chs & Chs Cr	1	NR	90	111	0.5	1.0
CHR–Chs of Christ	3	230	240	287	1.2	2.5
Jehovah's Witness	1	NR	NR	NR	-	-
METH–C.M.E.	3	0	400	495	2.1	4.3
METH–Un Methodist	11	563	1,460	1,664	7.0	14.3
Non-denom Chr Chs	7	935	1,315	1,340	5.6	11.5
PENT–Assemb of God	3	155	311	367	1.5	3.2
PENT–Full Gosp Bapt	1	NR	NR	NR	-	-
PENT–Un Pent Ch Intl	2	NR	NR	NR	-	-
PRES–Cum Pres Am	1	NR	NR	NR	-	-
PRES–Presb Ch (USA)	1	16	24	30	0.1	0.3
PARKER	**167**	**22,748**	**48,271**	**64,563**	**55.2**	**100.0**
ANG/EPIS–Anglican NA	3	NR	NR	NR	-	-
ANG/EPIS–Episcopal	2	54	37	37	0.0	0.1
Bahá'í	0	NR	28	28	0.0	0.0
BAPT–Free Will Bapt	1	NR	52	64	0.1	0.1
BAPT–Ind Bapt Flwsp Intl	7	NR	NR	NR	-	-
BAPT–Ref Bapt Ch	1	NR	NR	NR	-	-
BAPT–So Bapt Conv	65	12,463	31,931	39,554	33.8	61.3
Calv Chpl	1	NR	NR	NR	-	-
Catholic	2	NR	NR	4,493	3.8	7.0
Ch of Nazarene	1	10	28	50	0.0	0.1
CHR–Chr Ch (Disc)	2	241	616	763	0.7	1.2
CHR–Chs of Christ	20	1,931	2,006	2,661	2.3	4.1
Jehovah's Witness	2	NR	NR	NR	-	-
LDS–L-D Saints	3	NR	NR	969	0.8	1.5
LUTH–E.L.C.A.	2	122	238	287	0.2	0.4
LUTH–Luth–MO Synod	1	108	236	302	0.3	0.5
METH–Un Methodist	15	1,783	5,855	6,575	5.6	10.2
Non-denom Chr Chs	19	4,725	5,341	6,246	5.3	9.7
PENT–Assemb of God	7	586	592	914	0.8	1.4
PENT–Ch God (Cleve)	4	308	583	722	0.6	1.1
PENT–Int Foursq Gos	1	70	58	72	0.1	0.1
PENT–Un Pent Ch Intl	1	NR	NR	NR	-	-
PRES–Cumber Presb	1	NR	30	40	0.0	0.1
PRES–Presb Ch (USA)	2	245	502	622	0.5	1.0
PRES–Presb Ch Amer	1	40	30	38	0.0	0.1
REF–Comm Ref Evan	1	NR	NR	NR	-	-
Sev Day Adv	2	62	108	124	0.1	0.2
Zoroastrian	0	NR	NR	2	0.0	0.0
PARMER	**29**	**1,920**	**4,819**	**7,869**	**76.6**	**100.0**
Bahá'í	0	NR	2	2	0.0	0.0
BAPT–So Bapt Conv	8	644	2,717	3,577	34.8	45.5
Catholic	2	NR	NR	1,700	16.6	21.6
CHR–Chs of Christ	6	456	504	566	5.5	7.2
Jehovah's Witness	1	NR	NR	NR	-	-
LUTH–Luth–MO Synod	1	76	138	194	1.9	2.5
MENN–CG in Cr (Menn)	1	NR	123	162	1.6	2.1
METH–Un Methodist	5	314	892	1,076	10.5	13.7
Non-denom Chr Chs	2	250	300	338	3.3	4.3
PENT–Assemb of God	1	95	60	145	1.4	1.8
PENT–Intl Pent Holiness	1	41	41	54	0.5	0.7
Un C of Christ	1	44	42	55	0.5	0.7
PECOS	**37**	**959**	**2,783**	**7,215**	**46.5**	**100.0**
ANG/EPIS–Episcopal	1	11	20	20	0.1	0.3
Bahá'í	0	NR	5	5	0.0	0.1
BAPT–So Bapt Conv	8	298	1,287	1,595	10.3	22.1
Catholic	6	NR	NR	3,700	23.9	51.3
CHR–Chr Ch (Disc)	1	30	123	152	1.0	2.1
CHR–Chr Chs & Chs Cr	1	NR	52	64	0.4	0.9
CHR–Chs of Christ	5	240	285	380	2.5	5.3
Jehovah's Witness	1	NR	NR	NR	-	-
LDS–L-D Saints	1	NR	NR	121	0.8	1.7
LUTH–Luth–MO Synod	1	6	9	9	0.1	0.1
MENN–CG in Cr (Menn)	1	NR	47	58	0.4	0.8
METH–Un Methodist	2	62	239	249	1.6	3.5
Non-denom Chr Chs	4	220	325	350	2.3	4.9
PENT–Assemb of God	3	52	56	97	0.6	1.3
PENT–Intl Pent Holiness	1	40	35	43	0.3	0.6
PRES–Presb Ch (USA)	1	0	300	372	2.4	5.2
POLK	**72**	**4,357**	**10,003**	**14,911**	**32.8**	**100.0**
ANG/EPIS–Episcopal	1	53	83	83	0.2	0.6
Bahá'í	0	NR	27	27	0.1	0.2
BAPT–Amer Bapt Assn	1	NR	150	179	0.4	1.2
BAPT–Ind Bapt Flwsp Intl	1	NR	NR	NR	-	-
BAPT–So Bapt Conv	17	1,431	5,074	6,056	13.3	40.6
Catholic	2	NR	NR	1,808	4.0	12.1
Ch of Nazarene	1	55	143	143	0.3	1.0
CHR–Chs of Christ	7	440	471	566	1.2	3.8
Jehovah's Witness	3	NR	NR	NR	-	-
LDS–Comm of Christ	1	NR	110	110	0.2	0.7
LDS–L-D Saints	1	NR	NR	616	1.4	4.1
LUTH–E.L.C.A.	1	28	38	49	0.1	0.3
LUTH–Luth–MO Synod	1	70	134	158	0.3	1.1
METH–Un Methodist	9	816	1,729	2,040	4.5	13.7
Non-denom Chr Chs	7	470	620	657	1.4	4.4
PENT–Assemb of God	6	672	497	1,314	2.9	8.8
PENT–Ch God (Cleve)	2	133	316	377	0.8	2.5
PENT–COGIC	3	30	340	406	0.9	2.7
PENT–Un Pent Ch Intl	5	NR	NR	NR	-	-
PRES–Presb Ch (USA)	2	147	249	297	0.7	2.0
Sev Day Adv	1	12	22	25	0.1	0.2
POTTER	**175**	**19,637**	**55,623**	**93,488**	**77.2**	**100.0**
ANG/EPIS–Episcopal	2	342	1,004	1,221	1.0	1.3
Bahá'í	1	NR	390	390	0.3	0.4
BAPT–Amer Bapt Assn	2	NR	150	193	0.2	0.2
BAPT–NBC USA	1	185	375	482	0.4	0.5
BAPT–So Bapt Conv	38	7,911	37,005	47,559	39.3	50.9
BUDD–Mahayana	3	NR	NR	1,048	0.9	1.1
BUDD–Theravada	1	NR	NR	300	0.2	0.3
Calv Chpl	1	NR	NR	NR	-	-
Catholic	10	NR	NR	15,904	13.1	17.0
Ch Cr, Scientst	1	NR	NR	NR	-	-
Ch of Nazarene	3	210	132	321	0.3	0.3
Chr & Miss Al	1	8	47	83	0.1	0.1
CHR–Chr Ch (Disc)	1	0	275	353	0.3	0.4
CHR–Chr Chs & Chs Cr	1	NR	0	0	0.0	0.0
CHR–Chs of Christ	15	2,359	2,581	3,396	2.8	3.6
CHR–Int Chs of Christ	1	NR	8	10	0.0	0.0
FRND–Fr Gen Cf	1	NR	0	0	0.0	0.0
Jehovah's Witness	2	NR	NR	NR	-	-
JUD–Reform	1	35	61	165	0.1	0.2
LDS–Comm of Christ	1	NR	61	61	0.1	0.1
LDS–L-D Saints	3	NR	NR	2,082	1.7	2.2
LUTH–Luth–MO Synod	2	253	605	804	0.7	0.9
METH–AME	1	0	100	129	0.1	0.1
METH–C.M.E.	1	0	100	129	0.1	0.1
METH–Un Methodist	9	1,150	3,629	4,074	3.4	4.4
METH–Wesleyan	1	80	30	104	0.1	0.1
Metro Comm Ch	1	38	58	75	0.1	0.1
Muslim Est	1	624	NR	2,542	2.1	2.7
Non-denom Chr Chs	28	3,135	4,149	4,494	3.7	4.8
ORTHE–Greek Orthodox	1	45	NR	80	0.1	0.1
PENT–Assemb of God	11	666	390	1,423	1.2	1.5
PENT–Ch of God Proph	1	NR	20	26	0.0	0.0
PENT–COGIC	7	140	925	1,189	1.0	1.3
PENT–Int Foursq Gos	1	34	39	50	0.0	0.1
PENT–Intl Pent Holiness	5	978	875	1,125	0.9	1.2
PENT–Pent Ch of God	3	210	NR	326	0.3	0.3
PENT–Un Pent Ch Intl	4	NR	NR	NR	-	-
PRES–Presb Ch (USA)	4	863	1,950	2,506	2.1	2.7
Salvation Army	1	69	138	239	0.2	0.3
Sev Day Adv	2	302	526	605	0.5	0.6
Unity Ch	1	NR	NR	NR	-	-
PRESIDIO	**20**	**450**	**666**	**4,004**	**51.2**	**100.0**
ANG/EPIS–Episcopal	1	36	132	132	1.7	3.3

NR–Not Reported - Represents no adherents reported. Percentages may not total 100 due to rounding.

Table 3: Religious Congregations by County and Group: 2010

Religious Group	Number of Congregations	Number of Attendees	Number of Communicant, Confirmed, or Full Members	Adherents		
				Number of Adherents	% of Total Pop.	% of Total Adh.
Bahá'í	0	NR	34	34	0.4	0.8
BAPT–So Bapt Conv	6	121	139	177	2.3	4.4
Catholic	5	NR	NR	3,200	40.9	79.9
CHR–Chr Chs & Chs Cr	1	NR	0	0	0.0	0.0
CHR–Chs of Christ	2	55	45	59	0.8	1.5
Jehovah's Witness	1	NR	NR	NR	-	-
METH–Un Methodist	1	18	81	86	1.1	2.1
Non-denom Chr Chs	1	200	200	250	3.2	6.2
PENT–Assemb of God	1	20	12	37	0.5	0.9
PRES–Presb Ch (USA)	1	0	23	29	0.4	0.7
RAINS	**26**	**1,721**	**3,182**	**4,387**	**40.2**	**100.0**
Bahá'í	0	NR	1	1	0.0	0.0
BAPT–Ind Bapt Flwsp Intl	1	NR	NR	NR	-	-
BAPT–So Bapt Conv	13	1,167	2,268	2,701	24.7	61.6
Catholic	1	NR	NR	621	5.7	14.2
CHR–Chs of Christ	3	189	189	239	2.2	5.4
METH–Un Methodist	2	88	221	252	2.3	5.7
Non-denom Chr Chs	2	60	190	194	1.8	4.4
PENT–Assemb of God	1	35	24	35	0.3	0.8
PENT–Ch God (Cleve)	2	182	289	344	3.2	7.8
PENT–Un Pent Ch Intl	1	NR	NR	NR	-	-
RANDALL	**100**	**31,040**	**56,304**	**70,770**	**58.6**	**100.0**
ANG/EPIS–Episcopal	1	15	23	23	0.0	0.0
Bahá'í	0	NR	19	19	0.0	0.0
BAPT–Amer Bapt Assn	1	NR	85	105	0.1	0.1
BAPT–Free Will Bapt	1	NR	52	65	0.1	0.1
BAPT–Ind Bapt Flwsp Intl	1	NR	NR	NR	-	-
BAPT–So Bapt Conv	24	5,363	19,334	23,988	19.9	33.9
Catholic	2	NR	NR	1,561	1.3	2.2
Ch of Nazarene	3	428	933	933	0.8	1.3
CHR–Chr Ch (Disc)	3	295	741	919	0.8	1.3
CHR–Chr Chs & Chs Cr	5	NR	1,723	2,138	1.8	3.0
CHR–Chs of Christ	7	1,892	2,098	2,701	2.2	3.8
Evan Free Ch	1	75	NR	75	0.1	0.1
Jehovah's Witness	2	NR	NR	NR	-	-
LDS–L-D Saints	2	NR	NR	909	0.8	1.3
LUTH–E.L.C.A.	1	147	257	295	0.2	0.4
LUTH–Luth-MO Synod	2	180	362	443	0.4	0.6
METH–Un Methodist	5	1,655	3,848	5,003	4.1	7.1
Muslim Est	1	624	NR	2,542	2.1	3.6
Non-denom Chr Chs	26	19,416	25,505	27,249	22.6	38.5
PENT–Assemb of God	3	367	343	611	0.5	0.9
PENT–Ch God (Cleve)	1	21	12	15	0.0	0.0
PENT–Int Foursq Gos	1	36	84	104	0.1	0.1
PENT–Un Pent Ch Intl	2	NR	NR	NR	-	-
PRES–Orth Pres Ch	1	68	57	85	0.1	0.1
PRES–Presb Ch (USA)	1	60	181	225	0.2	0.3
PRES–Presb Ch Amer	1	25	34	42	0.0	0.1
Sev Day Adv	1	289	503	578	0.5	0.8
Unit Univ	1	84	110	142	0.1	0.2
REAGAN	**10**	**593**	**1,253**	**2,887**	**85.7**	**100.0**
Bahá'í	0	NR	4	4	0.1	0.1
BAPT–So Bapt Conv	3	243	820	1,070	31.8	37.1
Catholic	1	NR	NR	1,100	32.7	38.1
CHR–Chs of Christ	1	150	150	191	5.7	6.6
LDS–L-D Saints	1	NR	NR	82	2.4	2.8
METH–Un Methodist	1	40	176	231	6.9	8.0
PENT–Assemb of God	2	160	103	209	6.2	7.2
PENT–Un Pent Ch Intl	1	NR	NR	NR	-	-
REAL	**11**	**616**	**1,215**	**2,274**	**68.7**	**100.0**
BAPT–So Bapt Conv	3	259	846	981	29.6	43.1
Catholic	2	NR	NR	739	22.3	32.5
CHR–Chs of Christ	4	195	176	230	7.0	10.1
METH–Un Methodist	1	92	193	215	6.5	9.5
PENT–Pent Ch of God	1	70	NR	109	3.3	4.8
RED RIVER	**59**	**1,740**	**5,215**	**6,553**	**51.0**	**100.0**
Bahá'í	0	NR	1	1	0.0	0.0

Religious Group	Number of Congregations	Number of Attendees	Number of Communicant, Confirmed, or Full Members	Adherents		
				Number of Adherents	% of Total Pop.	% of Total Adh.
BAPT–Amer Bapt Assn	9	NR	977	1,163	9.0	17.7
BAPT–So Bapt Conv	12	591	2,601	3,097	24.1	47.3
Catholic	1	NR	NR	92	0.7	1.4
CHR–Chr Ch (Disc)	2	12	30	36	0.3	0.5
CHR–Chs of Christ	7	276	269	325	2.5	5.0
Jehovah's Witness	1	NR	NR	NR	-	-
LUTH–Luth-MO Synod	1	20	26	26	0.2	0.4
MENN–CG in Cr (Menn)	1	NR	114	136	1.1	2.1
METH–Cong Meth	1	NR	46	55	0.4	0.8
METH–Un Methodist	12	512	932	1,126	8.8	17.2
Non-denom Chr Chs	1	25	40	40	0.3	0.6
PENT–Assemb of God	4	214	25	242	1.9	3.7
PENT–Ch God (Cleve)	2	31	38	45	0.3	0.7
PENT–Un Pent Ch Intl	1	NR	NR	NR	-	-
PRES–Cumber Presb	1	NR	8	40	0.3	0.6
PRES–Presb Ch (USA)	3	59	108	129	1.0	2.0
REEVES	**30**	**827**	**2,148**	**7,736**	**56.1**	**100.0**
ANG/EPIS–Episcopal	1	4	11	15	0.1	0.2
BAPT–So Bapt Conv	10	410	1,514	1,835	13.3	23.7
Catholic	4	NR	NR	4,800	34.8	62.0
CHR–Chr Ch (Disc)	1	30	125	152	1.1	2.0
CHR–Chs of Christ	3	140	170	251	1.8	3.2
Jehovah's Witness	1	NR	NR	NR	-	-
LDS–L-D Saints	1	NR	NR	170	1.2	2.2
METH–Un Methodist	3	49	130	141	1.0	1.8
Non-denom Chr Chs	1	70	35	88	0.6	1.1
PENT–Assemb of God	2	89	58	161	1.2	2.1
PENT–Un Pent Ch Intl	1	NR	NR	NR	-	-
PRES–Presb Ch (USA)	1	0	44	53	0.4	0.7
Sev Day Adv	1	35	61	70	0.5	0.9
REFUGIO	**34**	**874**	**2,755**	**5,754**	**77.9**	**100.0**
ANG/EPIS–Episcopal	1	9	16	27	0.4	0.5
Bahá'í	0	NR	3	3	0.0	0.1
BAPT–So Bapt Conv	9	390	1,841	2,250	30.5	39.1
Catholic	8	NR	NR	2,357	31.9	41.0
CHR–Chs of Christ	3	108	115	145	2.0	2.5
Jehovah's Witness	1	NR	NR	NR	-	-
LUTH–E.L.C.A.	1	39	105	137	1.9	2.4
LUTH–Luth Cong Msn Chr	1	25	84	103	1.4	1.8
LUTH–Luth-MO Synod	1	10	14	16	0.2	0.3
METH–Un Methodist	3	125	309	398	5.4	6.9
Non-denom Chr Chs	1	100	150	150	2.0	2.6
PENT–Assemb of God	1	23	0	24	0.3	0.4
PRES–Presb Ch (USA)	3	0	85	104	1.4	1.8
Un C of Christ	1	45	33	40	0.5	0.7
ROBERTS	**4**	**257**	**499**	**621**	**66.8**	**100.0**
BAPT–So Bapt Conv	1	98	243	308	33.2	49.6
CHR–Chr Ch (Disc)	1	34	74	94	10.1	15.1
CHR–Chs of Christ	1	65	65	83	8.9	13.4
METH–Un Methodist	1	60	117	136	14.6	21.9
ROBERTSON	**47**	**2,108**	**5,247**	**9,151**	**55.1**	**100.0**
ANG/EPIS–Episcopal	2	23	19	19	0.1	0.2
Bahá'í	0	NR	6	6	0.0	0.1
BAPT–So Bapt Conv	19	1,356	3,471	4,295	25.8	46.9
Catholic	3	NR	NR	2,722	16.4	29.7
CHR–Chs of Christ	4	310	349	415	2.5	4.5
LDS–Comm of Christ	1	NR	110	110	0.7	1.2
LDS–L-D Saints	1	NR	NR	92	0.6	1.0
METH–AME	1	0	150	186	1.1	2.0
METH–Un Methodist	10	329	750	874	5.3	9.6
Non-denom Chr Chs	1	90	225	225	1.4	2.5
PENT–Assemb of God	1	0	0	0	0.0	0.0
PENT–COGIC	1	0	150	186	1.1	2.0
PENT–Un Pent Ch Intl	2	NR	NR	NR	-	-
PRES–Presb Ch (USA)	1	0	17	21	0.1	0.2
ROCKWALL	**73**	**18,157**	**41,139**	**64,136**	**81.9**	**100.0**
ANG/EPIS–Anglican NA	1	NR	NR	NR	-	-

NR–Not Reported   - Represents no adherents reported.   Percentages may not total 100 due to rounding.

Table 3: Religious Congregations by County and Group: 2010

Religious Group	Number of Congrega-tions	Number of Attendees	Number of Communicant, Confirmed, or Full Members	Adherents: Number of Adherents	Adherents: % of Total Pop.	Adherents: % of Total Adh.
ANG/EPIS–Episcopal	1	163	356	411	0.5	0.6
Bahá'í	0	NR	37	37	0.0	0.1
BAPT–N Am Bapt Conf	1	NR	NR	NR	-	-
BAPT–So Bapt Conv	26	12,336	32,511	42,249	53.9	65.9
BUDD–Theravada	1	NR	NR	300	0.4	0.5
Calv Chpl	1	NR	NR	NR	-	-
Catholic	1	NR	NR	9,619	12.3	15.0
CHR–Chr Ch (Disc)	2	144	190	247	0.3	0.4
CHR–Chr Chs & Chs Cr	1	NR	100	130	0.2	0.2
CHR–Chs of Christ	3	732	713	788	1.0	1.2
Evan Free Ch	2	155	NR	155	0.2	0.2
LDS–L-D Saints	2	NR	NR	942	1.2	1.5
LUTH–E.L.C.A.	1	60	107	130	0.2	0.2
LUTH–Luth–MO Synod	1	230	512	613	0.8	1.0
METH–AME	2	100	260	338	0.4	0.5
METH–Free Methodist	1	54	56	56	0.1	0.1
METH–Un Methodist	4	1,319	3,102	4,162	5.3	6.5
Non-denom Chr Chs	10	1,230	1,550	1,700	2.2	2.7
PENT–Assemb of God	5	1,299	1,131	1,592	2.0	2.5
PENT–Ch God (Cleve)	3	228	205	266	0.3	0.4
PENT–Int Foursq Gos	1	14	11	14	0.0	0.0
PENT–Un Pent Ch Intl	1	NR	NR	NR	-	-
PRES–Presb Ch (USA)	1	93	298	387	0.5	0.6
PRES–Presb Ch Amer	1	0	0	0	0.0	0.0
RUNNELS	**41**	**1,636**	**5,042**	**9,335**	**88.9**	**100.0**
Bahá'í	0	NR	27	27	0.3	0.3
BAPT–So Bapt Conv	12	606	3,130	3,883	37.0	41.6
Catholic	5	NR	NR	3,200	30.5	34.3
CGOD–Ch God (Ander)	1	0	NR	0	0.0	0.0
CHR–Chr Ch (Disc)	1	60	108	134	1.3	1.4
CHR–Chs of Christ	7	377	390	458	4.4	4.9
Evan Assoc RCC	1	NR	NR	NR	-	-
Jehovah's Witness	1	NR	NR	NR	-	-
LUTH–E.L.C.A.	1	50	111	133	1.3	1.4
LUTH–Luth Cong Msn Chr	1	83	203	252	2.4	2.7
LUTH–Luth–MO Synod	1	5	10	10	0.1	0.1
METH–Un Methodist	4	205	729	833	7.9	8.9
Non-denom Chr Chs	3	172	192	215	2.0	2.3
PENT–Assemb of God	1	14	0	14	0.1	0.1
PENT–Ch God (Cleve)	1	19	33	41	0.4	0.4
PRES–Presb Ch (USA)	1	45	109	135	1.3	1.4
RUSK	**115**	**5,479**	**16,898**	**24,894**	**46.7**	**100.0**
ANG/EPIS–Episcopal	1	37	83	83	0.2	0.3
Bahá'í	0	NR	7	7	0.0	0.0
BAPT–Amer Bapt Assn	14	NR	2,617	3,188	6.0	12.8
BAPT–Free Will Bapt	3	NR	156	190	0.4	0.8
BAPT–So Bapt Conv	29	2,964	8,797	10,717	20.1	43.1
Catholic	3	NR	NR	3,458	6.5	13.9
Ch of Nazarene	2	88	203	358	0.7	1.4
CHR–Chr Ch (Disc)	4	92	127	155	0.3	0.6
CHR–Chs of Christ	8	566	621	771	1.4	3.1
LDS–L-D Saints	1	NR	NR	518	1.0	2.1
METH–C.M.E.	1	0	150	183	0.3	0.7
METH–Un Methodist	16	651	1,853	2,186	4.1	8.8
Non-denom Chr Chs	7	765	770	988	1.9	4.0
PENT–Assemb of God	4	228	70	338	0.6	1.4
PENT–Ch of God Proph	1	NR	17	21	0.0	0.1
PENT–COGIC	9	0	1,275	1,553	2.9	6.2
PENT–Un Pent Ch Intl	5	NR	NR	NR	-	-
PRES–Cum Pres Am	2	NR	NR	NR	-	-
PRES–Cumber Presb	1	NR	4	4	0.0	0.0
PRES–Presb Ch (USA)	2	50	82	100	0.2	0.4
Sev Day Adv	2	38	66	76	0.1	0.3
SABINE	**33**	**1,558**	**4,046**	**5,394**	**49.8**	**100.0**
Bahá'í	0	NR	1	1	0.0	0.0
BAPT–Amer Bapt Assn	4	NR	405	474	4.4	8.8
BAPT–So Bapt Conv	7	778	2,790	3,266	30.1	60.5
Catholic	1	NR	NR	367	3.4	6.8
CGOD–Ch God (Ander)	3	136	NR	136	1.3	2.5
CHR–Chs of Christ	4	205	205	272	2.5	5.0
LDS–L-D Saints	1	NR	NR	141	1.3	2.6
METH–Free Methodist	1	50	26	50	0.5	0.9
METH–Un Methodist	3	121	242	282	2.6	5.2
Non-denom Chr Chs	2	200	305	305	2.8	5.7
PENT–Assemb of God	2	50	42	65	0.6	1.2
PENT–Un Pent Ch Intl	4	NR	NR	NR	-	-
Sev Day Adv	1	18	30	35	0.3	0.6
SAN AUGUSTINE	**28**	**1,293**	**3,688**	**4,581**	**51.7**	**100.0**
ANG/EPIS–Episcopal	1	12	29	29	0.3	0.6
BAPT–Amer Bapt Assn	3	NR	285	339	3.8	7.4
BAPT–NBC USA	1	150	250	298	3.4	6.5
BAPT–So Bapt Conv	9	620	2,185	2,602	29.4	56.8
Catholic	1	NR	NR	183	2.1	4.0
Ch Cr, Scientst	1	NR	NR	NR	-	-
CHR–Chs of Christ	3	200	195	235	2.7	5.1
METH–C.M.E.	2	0	300	357	4.0	7.8
METH–Un Methodist	2	76	200	209	2.4	4.6
Non-denom Chr Chs	1	150	150	188	2.1	4.1
PENT–Assemb of God	1	45	32	67	0.8	1.5
PENT–Un Pent Ch Intl	2	NR	NR	NR	-	-
PRES–Presb Ch (USA)	1	40	62	74	0.8	1.6
SAN JACINTO	**39**	**1,696**	**4,483**	**6,384**	**24.2**	**100.0**
Bahá'í	0	NR	2	2	0.0	0.0
BAPT–Amer Bapt Assn	2	NR	585	714	2.7	11.2
BAPT–Natl Mis Bapt Conv	1	0	150	183	0.7	2.9
BAPT–So Bapt Conv	16	813	2,349	2,868	10.9	44.9
BUDD–Mahayana	1	NR	NR	500	1.9	7.8
Catholic	1	NR	NR	397	1.5	6.2
CHR–Chs of Christ	3	145	145	179	0.7	2.8
METH–AME	2	0	200	244	0.9	3.8
METH–Un Methodist	4	283	507	594	2.3	9.3
Non-denom Chr Chs	4	310	460	472	1.8	7.4
PENT–Assemb of God	2	45	50	79	0.3	1.2
PENT–COGIC	1	30	35	43	0.2	0.7
PENT–Pent Ch of God	1	70	NR	109	0.4	1.7
PENT–Un Pent Ch Intl	1	NR	NR	NR	-	-
SAN PATRICIO	**122**	**6,178**	**13,950**	**40,377**	**62.3**	**100.0**
ANG/EPIS–Episcopal	3	114	192	275	0.4	0.7
Bahá'í	0	NR	30	30	0.0	0.1
BAPT–Ind Bapt Flwsp Intl	1	NR	NR	NR	-	-
BAPT–Natl Mis Bapt Conv	1	0	150	191	0.3	0.5
BAPT–So Bapt Conv	31	2,054	7,725	9,843	15.2	24.4
BUDD–Theravada	1	NR	NR	375	0.6	0.9
Calv Chpl	1	NR	NR	NR	-	-
Catholic	14	NR	NR	21,024	32.4	52.1
Ch of Nazarene	1	47	40	71	0.1	0.2
CHR–Chr Ch (Disc)	2	69	122	155	0.2	0.4
CHR–Chr Chs & Chs Cr	1	NR	74	94	0.1	0.2
CHR–Chs of Christ	11	916	813	1,077	1.7	2.7
Jehovah's Witness	4	NR	NR	NR	-	-
LDS–L-D Saints	2	NR	NR	797	1.2	2.0
LUTH–E.L.C.A.	3	85	198	228	0.4	0.6
LUTH–Luth Cong Msn Chr	1	65	134	171	0.3	0.4
LUTH–Luth–MO Synod	3	94	120	131	0.2	0.3
LUTH–Nor Amer Luth C	1	NR	NR	NR	-	-
MENN–Mennonite USA	3	75	147	187	0.3	0.5
METH–Un Methodist	7	744	2,063	2,842	4.4	7.0
Non-denom Chr Chs	13	1,280	1,485	1,674	2.6	4.1
PENT–Assemb of God	7	348	256	483	0.7	1.2
PENT–COGIC	3	30	250	319	0.5	0.8
PENT–Intl Pent Holiness	2	85	47	60	0.1	0.1
PENT–Pent Ch of God	2	140	NR	217	0.3	0.5
PENT–Un Pent Ch Intl	1	NR	NR	NR	-	-
PRES–Presb Ch (USA)	3	32	104	133	0.2	0.3
SAN SABA	**24**	**1,108**	**2,789**	**3,953**	**64.5**	**100.0**
ANG/EPIS–Episcopal	1	13	30	32	0.5	0.8
Bahá'í	0	NR	3	3	0.0	0.1
BAPT–So Bapt Conv	9	679	2,190	2,591	42.3	65.5

NR–Not Reported - Represents no adherents reported. Percentages may not total 100 due to rounding.

Table 3: Religious Congregations by County and Group: 2010

Religious Group	Number of Congregations	Number of Attendees	Number of Communicant, Confirmed, or Full Members	Adherents: Number of Adherents	Adherents: % of Total Pop.	Adherents: % of Total Adh.
Catholic	1	NR	NR	623	10.2	15.8
CHR–Chr Ch (Disc)	1	25	40	47	0.8	1.2
CHR–Chs of Christ	6	217	251	302	4.9	7.6
METH–Un Methodist	2	86	147	207	3.4	5.2
PENT–Assemb of God	1	35	45	50	0.8	1.3
PENT–Un Pent Ch Intl	1	NR	NR	NR	-	-
PRES–Presb Ch (USA)	2	53	83	98	1.6	2.5
SCHLEICHER	**11**	**441**	**1,035**	**1,880**	**54.3**	**100.0**
BAPT–So Bapt Conv	4	235	658	889	25.7	47.3
Catholic	1	NR	NR	400	11.6	21.3
CHR–Chs of Christ	2	80	78	101	2.9	5.4
METH–Un Methodist	1	64	203	248	7.2	13.2
PENT–Assemb of God	2	62	11	127	3.7	6.8
PRES–Presb Ch (USA)	1	0	85	115	3.3	6.1
SCURRY	**44**	**2,680**	**6,991**	**11,051**	**65.3**	**100.0**
Bahá'í	0	NR	5	5	0.0	0.0
BAPT–Amer Bapt Assn	2	NR	235	293	1.7	2.7
BAPT–Ind Bapt Flwsp Intl	2	NR	NR	NR	-	-
BAPT–So Bapt Conv	11	1,241	4,371	5,446	32.2	49.3
Catholic	3	NR	NR	2,316	13.7	21.0
CGOD–Ch God (Ander)	1	48	NR	48	0.3	0.4
CHR–Chr Ch (Disc)	1	0	30	37	0.2	0.3
CHR–Chs of Christ	8	612	516	709	4.2	6.4
LDS–Comm of Christ	1	NR	61	61	0.4	0.6
LDS–L-D Saints	1	NR	NR	113	0.7	1.0
METH–AME	1	0	150	187	1.1	1.7
METH–Un Methodist	6	254	774	886	5.2	8.0
Non-denom Chr Chs	3	315	650	650	3.8	5.9
PENT–Assemb of God	2	190	120	202	1.2	1.8
PENT–Un Pent Ch Intl	1	NR	NR	NR	-	-
PRES–Presb Ch (USA)	1	20	79	98	0.6	0.9
SHACKELFORD	**19**	**757**	**2,108**	**2,782**	**82.4**	**100.0**
ANG/EPIS–Episcopal	1	14	16	17	0.5	0.6
BAPT–So Bapt Conv	7	260	1,343	1,645	48.7	59.1
Catholic	1	NR	NR	120	3.6	4.3
CHR–Chr Ch (Disc)	1	90	240	294	8.7	10.6
CHR–Chs of Christ	2	135	150	202	6.0	7.3
LUTH–Luth-MO Synod	1	32	74	88	2.6	3.2
METH–Un Methodist	2	65	116	144	4.3	5.2
PENT–Assemb of God	1	65	0	65	1.9	2.3
PENT–Un Pent Ch Intl	2	NR	NR	NR	-	-
PRES–Presb Ch (USA)	1	96	169	207	6.1	7.4
SHELBY	**94**	**2,915**	**10,050**	**13,699**	**53.8**	**100.0**
ANG/EPIS–Episcopal	1	15	25	25	0.1	0.2
Bahá'í	0	NR	4	4	0.0	0.0
BAPT–Amer Bapt Assn	19	NR	1,750	2,208	8.7	16.1
BAPT–Ind Bapt Flwsp Intl	1	NR	NR	NR	-	-
BAPT–Natl Mis Bapt Conv	2	0	300	379	1.5	2.8
BAPT–So Bapt Conv	17	1,420	4,890	6,170	24.2	45.0
Catholic	2	NR	NR	1,263	5.0	9.2
Ch of Nazarene	1	7	16	41	0.2	0.3
CHR–Chr Ch (Disc)	2	0	45	57	0.2	0.4
CHR–Chr Chs & Chs Cr	2	NR	180	227	0.9	1.7
CHR–Chs of Christ	10	445	532	637	2.5	4.6
Jehovah's Witness	2	NR	NR	NR	-	-
MENN–Unaffil Amish-Menn	1	42	23	42	0.2	0.3
METH–C.M.E.	3	0	450	568	2.2	4.1
METH–Cong Meth	2	NR	21	26	0.1	0.2
METH–Un Methodist	11	347	850	969	3.8	7.1
Non-denom Chr Chs	3	400	600	600	2.4	4.4
PENT–Assemb of God	4	239	191	265	1.0	1.9
PENT–COGIC	1	0	150	189	0.7	1.4
PENT–Un Pent Ch Intl	9	NR	NR	NR	-	-
PRES–Presb Ch (USA)	1	0	23	29	0.1	0.2
SHERMAN	**10**	**500**	**1,428**	**2,201**	**72.5**	**100.0**
BAPT–So Bapt Conv	3	190	851	1,089	35.9	49.5
Catholic	1	NR	NR	303	10.0	13.8
CHR–Chr Ch (Disc)	1	0	0	0	0.0	0.0
CHR–Chs of Christ	1	70	73	100	3.3	4.5
MENN–CG in Cr (Menn)	1	NR	70	90	3.0	4.1
METH–Un Methodist	1	105	366	465	15.3	21.1
PENT–Assemb of God	2	135	68	154	5.1	7.0
SMITH	**373**	**47,020**	**97,768**	**148,908**	**71.0**	**100.0**
ANG/EPIS–Anglican NA	2	NR	NR	NR	-	-
ANG/EPIS–Episcopal	4	534	1,523	1,875	0.9	1.3
Bahá'í	1	NR	69	69	0.0	0.0
BAPT–Amer Bapt Assn	4	NR	362	452	0.2	0.3
BAPT–Free Will Bapt	1	NR	52	65	0.0	0.0
BAPT–Ind Bapt Flwsp Intl	3	NR	NR	NR	-	-
BAPT–NBC Amer	1	0	0	0	0.0	0.0
BAPT–NBC USA	13	935	2,380	2,974	1.4	2.0
BAPT–So Bapt Conv	94	16,730	47,884	59,837	28.5	40.2
Calv Chpl	1	NR	NR	NR	-	-
Catholic	7	NR	NR	25,573	12.2	17.2
CGOD–Ch God (Ander)	1	30	NR	30	0.0	0.0
Ch Cr, Scientst	1	NR	NR	NR	-	-
Ch of Nazarene	4	323	640	662	0.3	0.4
CHR–Chr Ch (Disc)	4	430	1,048	1,310	0.6	0.9
CHR–Chr Chs & Chs Cr	1	NR	25	31	0.0	0.0
CHR–Chs of Christ	23	3,813	4,405	5,749	2.7	3.9
FRND–Fr Gen Cf	1	NR	0	0	0.0	0.0
Jehovah's Witness	6	NR	NR	NR	-	-
JUD–Conserv	1	32	36	97	0.0	0.1
JUD–Reform	1	40	70	189	0.1	0.1
LDS–Comm of Christ	1	NR	126	126	0.1	0.1
LDS–L-D Saints	6	NR	NR	2,326	1.1	1.6
LUTH–E.L.C.A.	2	235	382	464	0.2	0.3
LUTH–Luth Cong Msn Chr	1	22	28	35	0.0	0.0
LUTH–Luth-MO Synod	1	351	635	755	0.4	0.5
LUTH–Nor Amer Luth C	1	NR	NR	NR	-	-
METH–AME	2	0	200	250	0.1	0.2
METH–C.M.E.	14	310	1,843	2,303	1.1	1.5
METH–So Methodist	1	NR	NR	NR	-	-
METH–Un Methodist	30	3,870	9,011	10,825	5.2	7.3
MJEW–Union Mes Cong	1	NR	NR	NR	-	-
Muslim Est	1	300	NR	800	0.4	0.5
Non-denom Chr Chs	70	12,824	17,086	18,826	9.0	12.6
ORTHE–Ant Orth of NA	1	20	NR	40	0.0	0.0
ORTHE–Orth Ch in Amer	1	35	NR	45	0.0	0.0
PENT–Assemb of God	18	1,981	1,411	2,522	1.2	1.7
PENT–Ch God (Cleve)	5	1,930	3,598	4,496	2.1	3.0
PENT–Ch of God Proph	2	NR	31	39	0.0	0.0
PENT–COGIC	19	583	2,473	3,090	1.5	2.1
PENT–Int Foursq Gos	1	39	10	12	0.0	0.0
PENT–Intl Pent Holiness	1	150	150	187	0.1	0.1
PENT–Un Pent Ch Intl	5	NR	NR	NR	-	-
PENT–Vineyard	1	230	250	312	0.1	0.2
PRES–Cum Pres Am	2	NR	NR	NR	-	-
PRES–Orth Pres Ch	1	108	94	117	0.1	0.1
PRES–Presb Ch (USA)	4	381	842	1,052	0.5	0.7
PRES–Presb Ch Amer	1	145	177	202	0.1	0.1
Salvation Army	1	208	198	334	0.2	0.2
Sev Day Adv	3	406	706	812	0.4	0.5
Unit Univ	1	25	23	25	0.0	0.0
Unity Ch	1	NR	NR	NR	-	-
SOMERVELL	**19**	**1,184**	**2,706**	**3,482**	**41.0**	**100.0**
ANG/EPIS–Anglican NA	1	NR	NR	NR	-	-
Bahá'í	0	NR	1	1	0.0	0.0
BAPT–So Bapt Conv	8	637	1,551	1,921	22.6	55.2
Catholic	1	NR	NR	185	2.2	5.3
CHR–Chs of Christ	2	120	122	151	1.8	4.3
LUTH–Assoc Free Luth	1	NR	NR	NR	-	-
METH–Un Methodist	1	179	689	833	9.8	23.9
Non-denom Chr Chs	3	225	330	331	3.9	9.5
PENT–Assemb of God	1	23	13	60	0.7	1.7
PENT–Un Pent Ch Intl	1	NR	NR	NR	-	-

NR–Not Reported - Represents no adherents reported. Percentages may not total 100 due to rounding.

Table 3: Religious Congregations by County and Group: 2010

Religious Group	Number of Congrega-tions	Number of Attendees	Number of Communicant, Confirmed, or Full Members	Adherents		
				Number of Adherents	% of Total Pop.	% of Total Adh.
STARR	**47**	**1,487**	**2,076**	**30,462**	**50.0**	**100.0**
Bahá'í	0	NR	1	1	0.0	0.0
BAPT–N Am Bapt Conf	1	NR	21	28	0.0	0.1
BAPT–So Bapt Conv	11	558	732	990	1.6	3.2
Catholic	15	NR	NR	27,156	44.5	89.1
Chr & Miss Al	1	25	0	43	0.1	0.1
Jehovah's Witness	2	NR	NR	NR	-	-
LDS–L-D Saints	1	NR	NR	543	0.9	1.8
MENN–Menn Br US Conf	3	NR	140	189	0.3	0.6
METH–Un Methodist	2	93	361	394	0.6	1.3
Missionary Ch	1	85	45	85	0.1	0.3
Non-denom Chr Chs	2	275	450	450	0.7	1.5
PENT–Assemb of God	5	415	264	512	0.8	1.7
PENT–Un Pent Ch Intl	2	NR	NR	NR	-	-
Sev Day Adv	1	36	62	71	0.1	0.2
STEPHENS	**28**	**2,118**	**5,106**	**7,443**	**77.3**	**100.0**
ANG/EPIS–Anglican NA	1	NR	NR	NR	-	-
Bahá'í	0	NR	3	3	0.0	0.0
BAPT–So Bapt Conv	10	1,176	3,486	4,274	44.4	57.4
Catholic	1	NR	NR	1,200	12.5	16.1
Ch Cr, Scientst	1	NR	NR	NR	-	-
CHR–Chr Ch (Disc)	1	50	120	147	1.5	2.0
CHR–Chs of Christ	2	320	364	448	4.7	6.0
Jehovah's Witness	1	NR	NR	NR	-	-
METH–Un Methodist	3	168	572	683	7.1	9.2
Non-denom Chr Chs	4	305	395	431	4.5	5.8
PENT–Assemb of God	2	44	37	99	1.0	1.3
PENT–Un Pent Ch Intl	1	NR	NR	NR	-	-
PRES–Presb Ch (USA)	1	55	129	158	1.6	2.1
STERLING	**6**	**312**	**598**	**872**	**76.3**	**100.0**
Bahá'í	0	NR	7	7	0.6	0.8
BAPT–So Bapt Conv	3	132	271	337	29.5	38.6
Catholic	1	NR	NR	100	8.7	11.5
CHR–Chs of Christ	1	75	59	97	8.5	11.1
METH–Un Methodist	1	105	261	331	29.0	38.0
STONEWALL	**9**	**369**	**1,020**	**1,396**	**93.7**	**100.0**
BAPT–So Bapt Conv	4	176	654	794	53.3	56.9
Catholic	1	NR	NR	152	10.2	10.9
CHR–Chs of Christ	2	78	71	100	6.7	7.2
METH–Un Methodist	1	40	220	256	17.2	18.3
Non-denom Chr Chs	1	75	75	94	6.3	6.7
SUTTON	**12**	**674**	**1,587**	**3,118**	**75.5**	**100.0**
ANG/EPIS–Episcopal	1	54	145	177	4.3	5.7
Bahá'í	0	NR	22	22	0.5	0.7
BAPT–So Bapt Conv	3	252	785	994	24.1	31.9
Catholic	1	NR	NR	1,200	29.1	38.5
CHR–Chs of Christ	1	100	100	127	3.1	4.1
Jehovah's Witness	1	NR	NR	NR	-	-
LUTH–Luth-MO Synod	1	8	14	15	0.4	0.5
METH–Un Methodist	1	62	233	280	6.8	9.0
Non-denom Chr Chs	1	175	250	250	6.1	8.0
PENT–Assemb of God	1	3	0	5	0.1	0.2
PRES–Presb Ch (USA)	1	20	38	48	1.2	1.5
SWISHER	**31**	**1,430**	**4,318**	**6,091**	**77.6**	**100.0**
Bahá'í	0	NR	15	15	0.2	0.2
BAPT–So Bapt Conv	7	529	2,691	3,397	43.3	55.8
Catholic	3	NR	NR	545	6.9	8.9
CHR–Chr Ch (Disc)	1	20	68	86	1.1	1.4
CHR–Chs of Christ	5	343	341	444	5.7	7.3
LUTH–Assoc Free Luth	1	NR	NR	NR	-	-
METH–Un Methodist	5	286	832	1,013	12.9	16.6
Non-denom Chr Chs	1	30	35	38	0.5	0.6
PENT–Assemb of God	3	135	48	193	2.5	3.2
PENT–Ch God (Cleve)	1	40	30	38	0.5	0.6
PENT–COGIC	1	0	150	189	2.4	3.1
PENT–Un Pent Ch Intl	1	NR	NR	NR	-	-
PRES–Presb Ch (USA)	1	28	75	95	1.2	1.6
Sev Day Adv	1	19	33	38	0.5	0.6
TARRANT	**1,695**	**304,820**	**574,826**	**998,849**	**55.2**	**100.0**
ANG/EPIS–Anglican NA	23	NR	NR	NR	-	-
ANG/EPIS–Episcopal	13	1,706	4,391	5,585	0.3	0.6
Bahá'í	8	NR	841	841	0.0	0.1
BAPT–Alliance Bapt	1	NR	NR	NR	-	-
BAPT–Amer Bapt Assn	5	NR	510	654	0.0	0.1
BAPT–Amer Bapt USA	1	0	525	673	0.0	0.1
BAPT–Asc Ref Bap Ch Am	1	NR	NR	NR	-	-
BAPT–Converge/BGC	1	400	NR	480	0.0	0.0
BAPT–Free Will Bapt	2	NR	104	133	0.0	0.0
BAPT–Ind Bapt Flwsp Intl	45	NR	NR	NR	-	-
BAPT–Natl Mis Bapt Conv	8	550	1,200	1,539	0.1	0.2
BAPT–NBC Amer	13	2,625	8,600	11,030	0.6	1.1
BAPT–NBC USA	21	1,755	6,860	8,799	0.5	0.9
BAPT–Prog NBC	1	0	30	38	0.0	0.0
BAPT–Ref Bapt Ch	3	NR	NR	NR	-	-
BAPT–S-D Baptist Gen Con	1	8	NR	NR	-	-
BAPT–So Bapt Conv	564	102,357	244,660	313,798	17.3	31.4
BUDD–Mahayana	8	NR	NR	6,200	0.3	0.6
BUDD–Theravada	3	NR	NR	975	0.1	0.1
BUDD–Vajrayana	2	NR	NR	913	0.1	0.1
Calv Chpl	3	NR	NR	NR	-	-
Catholic	33	NR	NR	200,645	11.1	20.1
CGOD–Ch God (Ander)	2	76	NR	76	0.0	0.0
Ch Cr, Scientst	3	NR	NR	NR	-	-
Ch God (7th Day)	3	NR	NR	NR	-	-
Ch of Chr (Hol)	1	NR	NR	NR	-	-
Ch of Nazarene	27	2,727	3,714	5,733	0.3	0.6
Chr & Miss Al	7	468	400	741	0.0	0.1
CHR–Chr Ch (Disc)	23	2,802	10,963	14,061	0.8	1.4
CHR–Chr Chs & Chs Cr	3	NR	2,775	3,559	0.2	0.4
CHR–Chs of Christ	89	20,533	23,876	31,905	1.8	3.2
CHR–Int Chs of Christ	0	NR	294	377	0.0	0.0
Christian Brethren	1	NR	NR	NR	-	-
Evan Free Ch	3	265	NR	265	0.0	0.0
FRND–Fr Gen Cf	1	NR	48	62	0.0	0.0
Grace Gosp Fel	2	NR	NR	NR	-	-
HINDU–I/A Temples	1	NR	NR	250	0.0	0.0
HINDU–Post Ren	2	NR	NR	81	0.0	0.0
Jehovah's Witness	20	NR	NR	NR	-	-
JUD–Conserv	1	313	351	948	0.1	0.1
JUD–Orth	2	86	100	120	0.0	0.0
JUD–Reform	3	448	790	2,133	0.1	0.2
LDS–Comm of Christ	1	NR	126	126	0.0	0.0
LDS–L-D Saints	43	NR	NR	21,996	1.2	2.2
LUTH–E.L.C.A.	15	1,990	4,069	4,934	0.3	0.5
LUTH–Luth Cong Msn Chr	1	375	1,132	1,452	0.1	0.1
LUTH–Luth-MO Synod	15	4,371	6,923	8,591	0.5	0.9
LUTH–Nor Amer Luth C	1	NR	NR	NR	-	-
LUTH–Wisc Ev Luth Syn	4	280	406	546	0.0	0.1
METH–AME	11	333	1,980	2,540	0.1	0.3
METH–AME Zion	1	65	125	160	0.0	0.0
METH–C.M.E.	4	250	1,050	1,347	0.1	0.1
METH–Cong Meth	1	NR	NR	NR	-	-
METH–Evan Meth Ch	1	NR	NR	NR	-	-
METH–Free Methodist	1	260	65	260	0.0	0.0
METH–Un Methodist	76	23,132	86,337	106,504	5.9	10.7
METH–Wesleyan	1	55	0	72	0.0	0.0
Metro Comm Ch	2	142	169	217	0.0	0.0
Missionary Ch	1	460	0	460	0.0	0.0
Muslim Est	16	10,292	NR	40,046	2.2	4.0
Non-denom Chr Chs	286	100,593	124,867	142,517	7.9	14.3
ORTHE–Ant Orth of NA	1	165	NR	290	0.0	0.0
ORTHE–Greek Orthodox	2	195	NR	635	0.0	0.1
ORTHE–Orth Ch in Amer	2	147	NR	405	0.0	0.0
ORTHO–Coptic Orth Ch	2	500	NR	1,266	0.1	0.1
PENT–Apos Faith Msn	1	NR	35	45	0.0	0.0
PENT–Assemb of God	61	10,270	8,366	15,810	0.9	1.6
PENT–Ch God (Cleve)	19	1,700	3,215	4,124	0.2	0.4
PENT–Ch God Apos Fth	1	NR	NR	NR	-	-
PENT–Ch of God Proph	3	NR	126	162	0.0	0.0

NR–Not Reported - Represents no adherents reported. Percentages may not total 100 due to rounding.

Table 3: Religious Congregations by County and Group: 2010

Religious Group	Number of Congregations	Number of Attendees	Number of Communicant, Confirmed, or Full Members	Adherents: Number of Adherents	Adherents: % of Total Pop.	Adherents: % of Total Adh.
PENT–COGIC	36	1,853	6,403	8,212	0.5	0.8
PENT–Full Gosp Bapt	7	NR	NR	NR	-	-
PENT–Int Foursq Gos	6	529	682	875	0.0	0.1
PENT–Intl Pent Holiness	2	60	75	96	0.0	0.0
PENT–Open Bible Std	3	75	NR	75	0.0	0.0
PENT–Pent Ch of God	3	210	NR	326	0.0	0.0
PENT–Un Pent Ch Intl	24	NR	NR	NR	-	-
PENT–Vineyard	4	387	467	599	0.0	0.1
PRES–Cum Pres Am	1	NR	NR	NR	-	-
PRES–Cumber Presb	5	NR	484	713	0.0	0.1
PRES–Orth Pres Ch	3	134	144	182	0.0	0.0
PRES–Presb Ch (USA)	24	3,173	7,370	9,453	0.5	0.9
PRES–Presb Ch Amer	6	860	919	1,190	0.1	0.1
REF–Christian Ref	1	60	30	38	0.0	0.0
REF–Comm Ref Evan	1	NR	NR	NR	-	-
Salvation Army	4	258	356	705	0.0	0.1
Sev Day Adv	27	4,056	7,052	8,111	0.4	0.8
Sikh	2	NR	NR	NR	-	-
Un C of Christ	2	121	350	449	0.0	0.0
Unit Univ	4	350	471	649	0.0	0.1
Unity Ch	3	NR	NR	NR	-	-
Zoroastrian	0	NR	NR	57	0.0	0.0
TAYLOR	**212**	**29,984**	**62,909**	**87,067**	**66.2**	**100.0**
ANG/EPIS–Episcopal	2	273	1,000	1,258	1.0	1.4
Bahá'í	0	NR	54	54	0.0	0.1
BAPT–Amer Bapt Assn	2	NR	85	105	0.1	0.1
BAPT–Free Will Bapt	1	NR	52	64	0.0	0.1
BAPT–Ind Bapt Flwsp Intl	6	NR	NR	NR	-	-
BAPT–NBC USA	1	100	200	248	0.2	0.3
BAPT–Reg Bapt Gen As	1	NR	NR	NR	-	-
BAPT–So Bapt Conv	68	10,331	33,523	41,564	31.6	47.7
Catholic	5	NR	NR	7,600	5.8	8.7
Ch Cr, Scientst	1	NR	NR	NR	-	-
Ch of Nazarene	3	199	479	479	0.4	0.6
CHR–Chr Ch (Disc)	3	308	703	872	0.7	1.0
CHR–Chr Chs & Chs Cr	1	NR	80	99	0.1	0.1
CHR–Chs of Christ	36	8,939	9,278	11,305	8.6	13.0
Jehovah's Witness	1	NR	NR	NR	-	-
JUD–Reform	1	12	21	57	0.0	0.1
LDS–L-D Saints	3	NR	NR	1,711	1.3	2.0
LUTH–E.L.C.A.	1	75	415	562	0.4	0.6
LUTH–Luth-MO Synod	2	392	752	981	0.7	1.1
METH–AME	1	0	150	186	0.1	0.2
METH–C.M.E.	1	0	100	124	0.1	0.1
METH–Evan Meth Ch	1	NR	NR	NR	-	-
METH–Free Methodist	1	95	69	95	0.1	0.1
METH–Un Methodist	20	1,805	6,701	8,193	6.2	9.4
Metro Comm Ch	1	67	89	110	0.1	0.1
Non-denom Chr Chs	28	5,334	6,457	7,115	5.4	8.2
ORTHE–Ant Orth of NA	1	20	NR	42	0.0	0.0
PENT–Assemb of God	8	1,211	618	1,596	1.2	1.8
PENT–Ch God (Cleve)	1	26	150	186	0.1	0.2
PENT–Ch of God Proph	1	NR	15	19	0.0	0.0
PENT–Int Foursq Gos	2	116	178	221	0.2	0.3
PENT–Un Pent Ch Intl	1	NR	NR	NR	-	-
PRES–Orth Pres Ch	1	26	25	33	0.0	0.0
PRES–Presb Ch (USA)	2	347	1,285	1,593	1.2	1.8
Salvation Army	1	179	216	351	0.3	0.4
Sev Day Adv	1	114	199	229	0.2	0.3
Unit Univ	1	15	15	15	0.0	0.0
Unity Ch	1	NR	NR	NR	-	-
TERRELL	**8**	**139**	**521**	**1,079**	**109.7**	**100.0**
BAPT–So Bapt Conv	1	21	187	226	23.0	20.9
Catholic	1	NR	NR	500	50.8	46.3
CHR–Chs of Christ	1	40	37	48	4.9	4.4
METH–Un Methodist	3	28	109	109	11.1	10.1
Non-denom Chr Chs	1	50	150	150	15.2	13.9
PRES–Presb Ch (USA)	1	0	38	46	4.7	4.3
TERRY	**34**	**1,812**	**4,616**	**7,648**	**60.5**	**100.0**
ANG/EPIS–Episcopal	1	12	25	46	0.4	0.6

Religious Group	Number of Congregations	Number of Attendees	Number of Communicant, Confirmed, or Full Members	Adherents: Number of Adherents	Adherents: % of Total Pop.	Adherents: % of Total Adh.
Bahá'í	0	NR	5	5	0.0	0.1
BAPT–So Bapt Conv	13	801	2,401	3,028	23.9	39.6
Catholic	1	NR	NR	1,772	14.0	23.2
CHR–Chr Ch (Disc)	1	70	274	346	2.7	4.5
CHR–Chs of Christ	5	454	543	696	5.5	9.1
METH–Un Methodist	2	104	374	420	3.3	5.5
Non-denom Chr Chs	2	190	225	238	1.9	3.1
PENT–Assemb of God	4	133	52	193	1.5	2.5
PENT–Ch God (Cleve)	1	12	224	282	2.2	3.7
PENT–Ch of God Proph	1	NR	8	10	0.1	0.1
PENT–Int Foursq Gos	2	36	485	612	4.8	8.0
PENT–Un Pent Ch Intl	1	NR	NR	NR	-	-
THROCKMORTON	**10**	**406**	**1,286**	**1,628**	**99.2**	**100.0**
Bahá'í	0	NR	1	1	0.1	0.1
BAPT–So Bapt Conv	2	187	911	1,080	65.8	66.3
CHR–Chr Ch (Disc)	1	32	71	84	5.1	5.2
CHR–Chs of Christ	3	108	108	130	7.9	8.0
METH–Un Methodist	2	56	183	301	18.3	18.5
PENT–Assemb of God	1	20	10	30	1.8	1.8
PRES–Presb Ch (USA)	1	3	2	2	0.1	0.1
TITUS	**78**	**5,824**	**13,872**	**26,758**	**82.8**	**100.0**
ANG/EPIS–Episcopal	1	52	71	92	0.3	0.3
Bahá'í	0	NR	2	2	0.0	0.0
BAPT–Amer Bapt Assn	8	NR	950	1,248	3.9	4.7
BAPT–Ind Bapt Flwsp Intl	1	NR	NR	NR	-	-
BAPT–Natl Mis Bapt Conv	3	75	500	657	2.0	2.5
BAPT–Ref Bapt Ch	1	NR	NR	NR	-	-
BAPT–So Bapt Conv	17	2,729	8,150	10,705	33.1	40.0
Calv Chpl	1	NR	NR	NR	-	-
Catholic	1	NR	NR	8,173	25.3	30.5
Ch God (7th Day)	1	NR	NR	NR	-	-
Ch of Nazarene	2	93	143	162	0.5	0.6
CHR–Chr Ch (Disc)	1	0	87	114	0.4	0.4
CHR–Chs of Christ	8	981	886	1,097	3.4	4.1
Jehovah's Witness	1	NR	NR	NR	-	-
LDS–L-D Saints	1	NR	NR	521	1.6	1.9
LUTH–Luth-MO Synod	1	58	82	99	0.3	0.4
METH–AME	1	0	150	197	0.6	0.7
METH–C.M.E.	1	15	15	20	0.1	0.1
METH–Cong Meth	1	NR	18	24	0.1	0.1
METH–Un Methodist	6	407	1,027	1,124	3.5	4.2
Non-denom Chr Chs	7	600	825	862	2.7	3.2
PENT–Assemb of God	6	657	444	986	3.0	3.7
PENT–Ch of God Proph	3	NR	135	177	0.5	0.7
PENT–COGIC	2	45	100	131	0.4	0.5
PENT–Un Pent Ch Intl	1	NR	NR	NR	-	-
PRES–Presb Ch (USA)	1	75	223	293	0.9	1.1
Sev Day Adv	1	37	64	74	0.2	0.3
TOM GREEN	**144**	**17,581**	**38,915**	**66,473**	**60.3**	**100.0**
ANG/EPIS–Anglican NA	1	NR	NR	NR	-	-
ANG/EPIS–Episcopal	2	182	441	516	0.5	0.8
Bahá'í	0	NR	45	45	0.0	0.1
BAPT–Amer Bapt Assn	1	NR	85	104	0.1	0.2
BAPT–Ind Bapt Flwsp Intl	1	NR	NR	NR	-	-
BAPT–Natl Mis Bapt Conv	1	0	150	184	0.2	0.3
BAPT–Ref Bapt Ch	1	NR	NR	NR	-	-
BAPT–So Bapt Conv	37	6,656	22,667	27,862	25.3	41.9
Calv Chpl	1	NR	NR	NR	-	-
Catholic	9	NR	NR	16,000	14.5	24.1
Ch Cr, Scientst	1	NR	NR	NR	-	-
Ch of Nazarene	2	233	373	404	0.4	0.6
CHR–Chr Ch (Disc)	2	255	641	788	0.7	1.2
CHR–Chr Chs & Chs Cr	1	NR	320	393	0.4	0.6
CHR–Chs of Christ	13	1,978	2,132	2,948	2.7	4.4
Jehovah's Witness	1	NR	NR	NR	-	-
LDS–L-D Saints	4	NR	NR	1,912	1.7	2.9
LUTH–E.L.C.A.	2	151	171	194	0.2	0.3
LUTH–Luth-MO Synod	1	261	447	551	0.5	0.8
LUTH–Wisc Ev Luth Syn	1	6	11	11	0.0	0.0
METH–AME	1	35	40	49	0.0	0.1

NR–Not Reported - Represents no adherents reported. Percentages may not total 100 due to rounding.

Table 3: Religious Congregations by County and Group: 2010

Religious Group	Number of Congrega-tions	Number of Attendees	Number of Communicant, Confirmed, or Full Members	Adherents		
				Number of Adherents	% of Total Pop.	% of Total Adh.
METH–Un Methodist	11	1,469	3,432	4,182	3.8	6.3
MORAV–Unity Of Breth	1	NR	NR	NR	-	-
Non-denom Chr Chs	14	3,509	4,000	4,525	4.1	6.8
ORTHE–Greek Orthodox	1	30	NR	77	0.1	0.1
PENT–Assemb of God	12	1,764	1,322	2,055	1.9	3.1
PENT–Ch God (Cleve)	2	72	78	96	0.1	0.1
PENT–Ch Lord Jesus Apos	1	NR	NR	NR	-	-
PENT–COGIC	2	0	500	615	0.6	0.9
PENT–Int Foursq Gos	2	80	112	138	0.1	0.2
PENT–Pent Ch of God	3	210	NR	326	0.3	0.5
PENT–Un Pent Ch Intl	3	NR	NR	NR	-	-
PRES–Cum Pres Am	1	NR	NR	NR	-	-
PRES–Presb Ch (USA)	4	535	1,623	1,995	1.8	3.0
Salvation Army	1	48	139	289	0.3	0.4
Sev Day Adv	2	107	186	214	0.2	0.3
Unity Ch	1	NR	NR	NR	-	-
TRAVIS	**670**	**119,955**	**205,151**	**473,364**	**46.2**	**100.0**
ANG/EPIS–Anglican NA	4	NR	NR	NR	-	-
ANG/EPIS–Episcopal	19	4,485	12,664	14,526	1.4	3.1
Bahá'í	4	NR	875	875	0.1	0.2
BAPT–Alliance Bapt	2	NR	NR	NR	-	-
BAPT–Amer Bapt USA	1	150	475	588	0.1	0.1
BAPT–Ind Bapt Flwsp Intl	3	NR	NR	NR	-	-
BAPT–N Am Bapt Conf	1	NR	25	31	0.0	0.0
BAPT–Natl Mis Bapt Conv	1	350	350	433	0.0	0.1
BAPT–NBC Amer	5	4,200	11,300	13,994	1.4	3.0
BAPT–NBC USA	3	475	1,411	1,747	0.2	0.4
BAPT–Reg Bapt Gen As	1	NR	NR	NR	-	-
BAPT–So Bapt Conv	153	32,386	66,510	82,367	8.0	17.4
BUDD–Mahayana	8	NR	NR	5,730	0.6	1.2
BUDD–Theravada	2	NR	NR	1,378	0.1	0.3
BUDD–Vajrayana	7	NR	NR	875	0.1	0.2
Calv Chpl	3	NR	NR	NR	-	-
Catholic	30	NR	NR	177,192	17.3	37.4
CGOD–Ch God (Ander)	3	72	NR	72	0.0	0.0
Ch Cr, Scientst	3	NR	NR	NR	-	-
Ch God (7th Day)	4	NR	NR	NR	-	-
Ch of Nazarene	5	382	745	873	0.1	0.2
Chr & Miss Al	1	95	97	133	0.0	0.0
CHR–Chr Ch (Disc)	15	531	1,601	1,983	0.2	0.4
CHR–Chr Chs & Chs Cr	1	NR	400	495	0.0	0.1
CHR–Chs of Christ	29	4,931	4,832	6,525	0.6	1.4
CHR–Int Chs of Christ	1	NR	216	267	0.0	0.1
Christian Brethren	1	NR	NR	NR	-	-
Evan Free Ch	3	2,520	NR	2,520	0.2	0.5
FRND–Fr Gen Cf	1	NR	196	243	0.0	0.1
FRND–Unaffl Mtgs	1	NR	NR	NR	-	-
HINDU–I/A Temples	3	NR	NR	3,554	0.3	0.8
HINDU–Post Ren	6	NR	NR	232	0.0	0.0
HINDU–Renaiss	1	NR	NR	12	0.0	0.0
HINDU–Trad Temples	2	NR	NR	2,100	0.2	0.4
Jain	1	NR	NR	NR	-	-
Jehovah's Witness	9	NR	NR	NR	-	-
JUD–Conserv	1	508	570	1,539	0.2	0.3
JUD–Orth	2	180	100	250	0.0	0.1
JUD–Reconst	1	25	32	86	0.0	0.0
JUD–Reform	2	574	1,013	2,735	0.3	0.6
LDS–Comm of Christ	1	NR	110	110	0.0	0.0
LDS–L-D Saints	14	NR	NR	9,323	0.9	2.0
LUTH–E.L.C.A.	17	2,645	7,884	10,162	1.0	2.1
LUTH–Luth Cong Msn Chr	1	84	284	352	0.0	0.1
LUTH–Luth–MO Synod	14	3,789	7,112	9,314	0.9	2.0
LUTH–Wisc Ev Luth Syn	2	331	618	769	0.1	0.2
MENN–Mennonite USA	1	50	63	78	0.0	0.0
METH–AME	9	749	1,915	2,372	0.2	0.5
METH–C.M.E.	1	0	150	186	0.0	0.0
METH–Free Methodist	1	50	0	50	0.0	0.0
METH–Un Methodist	36	6,794	17,661	24,411	2.4	5.2
METH–Wesleyan	1	154	82	200	0.0	0.0
Metro Comm Ch	1	253	438	542	0.1	0.1
Missionary Ch	1	10	0	10	0.0	0.0
MJEW–Union Mes Cong	1	NR	NR	NR	-	-
MORAV–Unity Of Breth	1	NR	NR	NR	-	-
Muslim Est	5	3,120	NR	12,710	1.2	2.7
Nat Spirit Asso	1	NR	NR	NR	-	-
New Apost Ch	1	NR	NR	NR	-	-
Non-denom Chr Chs	81	37,150	44,247	49,980	4.9	10.6
ORTHE–Ant Orth of NA	1	215	NR	550	0.1	0.1
ORTHE–Greek Orthodox	1	200	NR	600	0.1	0.1
ORTHE–Rus Orth Abroad	1	23	NR	150	0.0	0.0
ORTHO–Armen Ap Etchm	1	35	NR	170	0.0	0.0
ORTHO–Ethiopian Orth	1	NR	NR	NR	-	-
ORTHO–Malan Syr Orth	1	30	NR	54	0.0	0.0
PENT–Assemb of God	29	3,870	3,924	6,277	0.6	1.3
PENT–Assm God Intl F	1	NR	NR	NR	-	-
PENT–Ch God (Cleve)	4	92	103	128	0.0	0.0
PENT–Ch Lord Jesus Apos	2	NR	NR	NR	-	-
PENT–COGIC	7	125	1,150	1,424	0.1	0.3
PENT–Int Foursq Gos	2	112	154	191	0.0	0.0
PENT–Intl Pent Holiness	10	1,060	1,240	1,536	0.1	0.3
PENT–Pent Ch of God	3	210	NR	326	0.0	0.1
PENT–Un Pent Ch Intl	21	NR	NR	NR	-	-
PENT–Vineyard	2	183	300	372	0.0	0.1
PRES–Cumber Presb	3	NR	539	645	0.1	0.1
PRES–Korean Pres Amer	1	NR	NR	NR	-	-
PRES–Orth Pres Ch	1	101	88	119	0.0	0.0
PRES–Presb Ch (USA)	18	3,663	9,133	11,310	1.1	2.4
PRES–Presb Ch Amer	4	1,120	1,456	1,808	0.2	0.4
REF–Christian Ref	1	95	67	83	0.0	0.0
Salvation Army	1	67	138	224	0.0	0.0
Sev Day Adv	7	1,024	1,780	2,047	0.2	0.4
Sikh	4	NR	NR	NR	-	-
Un C of Christ	3	319	484	599	0.1	0.1
Unit Univ	3	368	619	804	0.1	0.2
Unity Ch	3	NR	NR	NR	-	-
Zoroastrian	1	NR	NR	23	0.0	0.0
TRINITY	**48**	**2,576**	**7,400**	**9,623**	**66.0**	**100.0**
BAPT–Amer Bapt Assn	1	NR	85	101	0.7	1.0
BAPT–Natl Mis Bapt Conv	2	0	300	357	2.4	3.7
BAPT–So Bapt Conv	21	1,473	5,018	5,966	40.9	62.0
Catholic	1	NR	NR	973	6.7	10.1
CHR–Chs of Christ	7	310	298	370	2.5	3.8
METH–AME	1	0	100	119	0.8	1.2
METH–C.M.E.	1	0	150	178	1.2	1.8
METH–Cong Meth	2	NR	31	37	0.3	0.4
METH–Un Methodist	3	158	479	480	3.3	5.0
Non-denom Chr Chs	4	500	650	675	4.6	7.0
PENT–Assemb of God	2	95	81	120	0.8	1.2
PENT–Ch God (Cleve)	1	40	58	69	0.5	0.7
PENT–COGIC	1	0	150	178	1.2	1.8
PENT–Un Pent Ch Intl	1	NR	NR	NR	-	-
TYLER	**59**	**3,675**	**9,657**	**12,900**	**59.3**	**100.0**
ANG/EPIS–Episcopal	1	40	77	98	0.5	0.8
Bahá'í	0	NR	3	3	0.0	0.0
BAPT–Amer Bapt Assn	1	NR	85	100	0.5	0.8
BAPT–Natl Mis Bapt Conv	1	0	150	177	0.8	1.4
BAPT–So Bapt Conv	29	2,327	7,542	8,887	40.8	68.9
Catholic	1	NR	NR	950	4.4	7.4
CHR–Chs of Christ	4	200	208	252	1.2	2.0
LDS–L-D Saints	2	NR	NR	394	1.8	3.1
LUTH–Luth–MO Synod	1	26	42	52	0.2	0.4
METH–Un Methodist	4	217	519	612	2.8	4.7
Non-denom Chr Chs	3	275	425	425	2.0	3.3
PENT–Assemb of God	7	572	426	738	3.4	5.7
PENT–COGIC	1	0	150	177	0.8	1.4
PENT–Un Pent Ch Intl	3	NR	NR	NR	-	-
Sev Day Adv	1	18	30	35	0.2	0.3
UPSHUR	**83**	**5,816**	**11,569**	**19,134**	**48.7**	**100.0**
Bahá'í	0	NR	1	1	0.0	0.0
BAPT–Amer Bapt Assn	2	NR	300	370	0.9	1.9
BAPT–Natl Mis Bapt Conv	1	0	150	185	0.5	1.0
BAPT–NBC USA	1	0	60	74	0.2	0.4
BAPT–So Bapt Conv	30	3,058	7,693	9,489	24.1	49.6

NR–Not Reported - Represents no adherents reported. Percentages may not total 100 due to rounding.

Table 3: Religious Congregations by County and Group: 2010

Religious Group	Number of Congregations	Number of Attendees	Number of Communicant, Confirmed, or Full Members	Adherents: Number of Adherents	Adherents: % of Total Pop.	Adherents: % of Total Adh.
Catholic	2	NR	NR	743	1.9	3.9
Ch of Nazarene	1	76	143	185	0.5	1.0
CHR–Chr Ch (Disc)	1	0	0	0	0.0	0.0
CHR–Chs of Christ	15	882	945	1,245	3.2	6.5
Jehovah's Witness	3	NR	NR	NR	-	-
LDS–L-D Saints	3	NR	NR	1,504	3.8	7.9
METH–AME	1	0	150	185	0.5	1.0
METH–C.M.E.	3	50	350	432	1.1	2.3
METH–Un Methodist	7	429	968	1,091	2.8	5.7
Muslim Est	1	624	NR	2,542	6.5	13.3
Non-denom Chr Chs	6	550	655	743	1.9	3.9
PENT–Assemb of God	3	126	74	246	0.6	1.3
PENT–Ch God (Cleve)	1	21	80	99	0.3	0.5
PENT–Un Pent Ch Intl	2	NR	NR	NR	-	-
UPTON	**14**	**452**	**1,390**	**2,360**	**70.3**	**100.0**
BAPT–So Bapt Conv	4	186	961	1,225	36.5	51.9
Catholic	3	NR	NR	500	14.9	21.2
CHR–Chs of Christ	2	125	140	170	5.1	7.2
Jehovah's Witness	1	NR	NR	NR	-	-
METH–Un Methodist	2	89	251	375	11.2	15.9
PENT–Assemb of God	2	52	38	90	2.7	3.8
UVALDE	**52**	**3,205**	**6,584**	**20,591**	**78.0**	**100.0**
ANG/EPIS–Episcopal	2	100	191	286	1.1	1.4
Bahá'í	0	NR	44	44	0.2	0.2
BAPT–So Bapt Conv	11	799	2,857	3,682	13.9	17.9
Catholic	3	NR	NR	11,673	44.2	56.7
Ch of Nazarene	1	19	34	41	0.2	0.2
Chr & Miss Al	1	21	0	31	0.1	0.2
CHR–Chr Chs & Chs Cr	1	NR	110	142	0.5	0.7
CHR–Chs of Christ	8	499	691	829	3.1	4.0
Jehovah's Witness	1	NR	NR	NR	-	-
LDS–L-D Saints	1	NR	NR	454	1.7	2.2
LUTH–E.L.C.A.	1	48	110	131	0.5	0.6
LUTH–Luth–MO Synod	1	62	98	123	0.5	0.6
MENN–CG in Cr (Menn)	1	NR	74	95	0.4	0.5
METH–Un Methodist	5	474	1,189	1,478	5.6	7.2
Non-denom Chr Chs	8	695	965	979	3.7	4.8
PENT–Assemb of God	4	430	115	469	1.8	2.3
PENT–Un Pent Ch Intl	1	NR	NR	NR	-	-
PRES–Presb Ch (USA)	1	44	82	106	0.4	0.5
Sev Day Adv	1	14	24	28	0.1	0.1
VAL VERDE	**47**	**3,754**	**4,518**	**18,723**	**38.3**	**100.0**
ANG/EPIS–Episcopal	1	81	152	281	0.6	1.5
Bahá'í	0	NR	23	23	0.0	0.1
BAPT–So Bapt Conv	10	697	1,011	1,318	2.7	7.0
Catholic	5	NR	NR	11,188	22.9	59.8
CHR–Chr Ch (Disc)	1	0	0	0	0.0	0.0
CHR–Chr Chs & Chs Cr	1	NR	150	196	0.4	1.0
CHR–Chs of Christ	3	210	175	260	0.5	1.4
Jehovah's Witness	1	NR	NR	NR	-	-
LDS–L-D Saints	2	NR	NR	1,182	2.4	6.3
LUTH–Luth–MO Synod	1	33	51	51	0.1	0.3
METH–Un Methodist	2	183	646	909	1.9	4.9
Non-denom Chr Chs	8	1,470	1,740	1,962	4.0	10.5
PENT–Assemb of God	6	961	311	1,038	2.1	5.5
PENT–Ch Lord Jesus Apos	1	NR	NR	NR	-	-
PENT–Un Pent Ch Intl	1	NR	NR	NR	-	-
PRES–Presb Ch (USA)	1	35	112	146	0.3	0.8
Sev Day Adv	3	84	147	169	0.3	0.9
VAN ZANDT	**110**	**8,616**	**18,774**	**25,260**	**48.0**	**100.0**
Bahá'í	0	NR	15	15	0.0	0.1
BAPT–Asc Ref Bap Ch Am	1	NR	NR	NR	-	-
BAPT–Ind Bapt Flwsp Intl	3	NR	NR	NR	-	-
BAPT–Natl Mis Bapt Conv	1	64	100	122	0.2	0.5
BAPT–So Bapt Conv	42	4,291	11,403	13,942	26.5	55.2
Catholic	3	NR	NR	1,945	3.7	7.7
Ch of Nazarene	1	66	129	192	0.4	0.8
CHR–Chr Ch (Disc)	1	15	45	55	0.1	0.2
CHR–Chs of Christ	13	1,092	1,169	1,423	2.7	5.6
Jehovah's Witness	1	NR	NR	NR	-	-
LDS–L-D Saints	1	NR	NR	563	1.1	2.2
LUTH–E.L.C.A.	1	42	71	84	0.2	0.3
LUTH–Luth–MO Synod	1	50	54	60	0.1	0.2
METH–C.M.E.	4	20	485	593	1.1	2.3
METH–Un Methodist	12	996	2,661	3,064	5.8	12.1
Non-denom Chr Chs	13	1,513	1,851	2,045	3.9	8.1
PENT–Assemb of God	6	311	247	492	0.9	1.9
PENT–Ch God (Cleve)	2	109	439	537	1.0	2.1
PENT–Int Foursq Gos	1	35	82	100	0.2	0.4
PENT–Un Pent Ch Intl	2	NR	NR	NR	-	-
PRES–Presb Ch (USA)	1	12	23	28	0.1	0.1
VICTORIA	**106**	**11,890**	**25,896**	**65,456**	**75.4**	**100.0**
ANG/EPIS–Episcopal	2	293	634	726	0.8	1.1
Bahá'í	1	NR	48	48	0.1	0.1
BAPT–Free Will Bapt	1	NR	52	66	0.1	0.1
BAPT–Ind Bapt Flwsp Intl	1	NR	NR	NR	-	-
BAPT–NBC Amer	3	523	800	1,010	1.2	1.5
BAPT–So Bapt Conv	23	2,949	9,036	11,412	13.1	17.4
Catholic	8	NR	NR	31,313	36.1	47.8
CGOD–Ch God (Ander)	1	20	NR	20	0.0	0.0
Ch Cr, Scientst	1	NR	NR	NR	-	-
Ch of Nazarene	1	65	104	128	0.1	0.2
CHR–Chr Ch (Disc)	1	62	103	130	0.1	0.2
CHR–Chs of Christ	8	999	1,119	1,417	1.6	2.2
Jehovah's Witness	1	NR	NR	NR	-	-
JUD–Reform	1	13	23	62	0.1	0.1
LDS–L-D Saints	1	NR	NR	427	0.5	0.7
LUTH–E.L.C.A.	4	620	2,161	2,545	2.9	3.9
LUTH–Luth Cong Msn Chr	3	487	1,848	2,334	2.7	3.6
LUTH–Luth–MO Synod	2	262	771	853	1.0	1.3
LUTH–Nor Amer Luth C	1	NR	NR	NR	-	-
MENN–CG in Cr (Menn)	1	NR	37	47	0.1	0.1
METH–AME	3	0	300	379	0.4	0.6
METH–AME Zion	1	50	50	63	0.1	0.1
METH–Un Methodist	9	554	2,061	2,582	3.0	3.9
Muslim Est	1	624	NR	2,542	2.9	3.9
Non-denom Chr Chs	9	3,358	5,195	5,260	6.1	8.0
PENT–Assemb of God	5	535	595	772	0.9	1.2
PENT–Ch God (Cleve)	1	63	151	191	0.2	0.3
PENT–COGIC	1	75	50	63	0.1	0.1
PENT–Pent Ch of God	1	70	NR	109	0.1	0.2
PENT–Un Pent Ch Intl	2	NR	NR	NR	-	-
PRES–Presb Ch (USA)	3	80	469	592	0.7	0.9
PRES–Presb Ch Amer	1	50	54	59	0.1	0.1
Salvation Army	1	34	50	97	0.1	0.1
Sev Day Adv	1	92	160	184	0.2	0.3
Unit Univ	1	12	25	25	0.0	0.0
Unity Ch	1	NR	NR	NR	-	-
WALKER	**78**	**7,932**	**18,394**	**28,766**	**42.4**	**100.0**
ANG/EPIS–Episcopal	1	104	225	296	0.4	1.0
Bahá'í	0	NR	81	81	0.1	0.3
BAPT–Amer Bapt Assn	2	NR	111	127	0.2	0.4
BAPT–Free Will Bapt	1	NR	52	60	0.1	0.2
BAPT–Natl Mis Bapt Conv	2	0	300	344	0.5	1.2
BAPT–NBC Amer	1	35	50	57	0.1	0.2
BAPT–NBC USA	1	500	800	916	1.3	3.2
BAPT–So Bapt Conv	21	4,017	10,859	12,438	18.3	43.2
Catholic	2	NR	NR	6,217	9.2	21.6
CGOD–Ch God (Ander)	1	0	NR	0	0.0	0.0
Ch God (7th Day)	1	NR	NR	NR	-	-
Ch of Nazarene	1	55	50	84	0.1	0.3
CHR–Chr Ch (Disc)	1	100	219	251	0.4	0.9
CHR–Chs of Christ	7	728	733	994	1.5	3.5
Jehovah's Witness	1	NR	NR	NR	-	-
LDS–L-D Saints	3	NR	NR	701	1.0	2.4
LUTH–Luth–MO Synod	1	171	345	450	0.7	1.6
METH–AME	2	0	250	286	0.4	1.0
METH–Un Methodist	10	959	2,650	3,264	4.8	11.3
Non-denom Chr Chs	3	350	375	451	0.7	1.6

NR–Not Reported - Represents no adherents reported. Percentages may not total 100 due to rounding.

Table 3: Religious Congregations by County and Group: 2010

Religious Group	Number of Congrega-tions	Number of Attendees	Number of Communicant, Confirmed, or Full Members	Adherents		
				Number of Adherents	% of Total Pop.	% of Total Adh.
PENT–Assemb of God	4	545	286	594	0.9	2.1
PENT–COGIC	3	0	450	515	0.8	1.8
PENT–Un Pent Ch Intl	2	NR	NR	NR	-	-
PENT–Vineyard	1	65	80	92	0.1	0.3
PRES–Presb Ch (USA)	3	183	299	342	0.5	1.2
Sev Day Adv	2	80	140	161	0.2	0.6
Unit Univ	1	40	39	45	0.1	0.2
WALLER	**54**	**3,172**	**6,777**	**14,544**	**33.7**	**100.0**
ANG/EPIS–Episcopal	2	64	102	140	0.3	1.0
Bahá'í	0	NR	7	7	0.0	0.0
BAPT–So Bapt Conv	17	1,356	3,652	4,522	10.5	31.1
BUDD–Mahayana	1	NR	NR	500	1.2	3.4
Catholic	2	NR	NR	4,631	10.7	31.8
CHR–Chr Ch (Disc)	1	0	0	0	0.0	0.0
CHR–Chs of Christ	4	278	242	374	0.9	2.6
LDS–L-D Saints	2	NR	NR	761	1.8	5.2
LUTH–E.L.C.A.	2	169	465	616	1.4	4.2
LUTH–Luth-MO Synod	1	46	122	151	0.3	1.0
METH–AME	2	0	250	310	0.7	2.1
METH–C.M.E.	1	0	150	186	0.4	1.3
METH–Un Methodist	9	504	1,015	1,172	2.7	8.1
Non-denom Chr Chs	5	440	450	550	1.3	3.8
PENT–Assemb of God	2	315	172	438	1.0	3.0
PENT–COGIC	1	0	150	186	0.4	1.3
PENT–Un Pent Ch Intl	2	NR	NR	NR	-	-
WARD	**31**	**1,345**	**3,146**	**6,741**	**63.2**	**100.0**
ANG/EPIS–Episcopal	1	5	5	5	0.0	0.1
Bahá'í	0	NR	6	6	0.1	0.1
BAPT–Ind Bapt Flwsp Intl	1	NR	NR	NR	-	-
BAPT–So Bapt Conv	9	686	2,081	2,640	24.8	39.2
Catholic	3	NR	NR	2,525	23.7	37.5
CHR–Chr Ch (Disc)	1	30	60	76	0.7	1.1
CHR–Chr Chs & Chs Cr	1	NR	0	0	0.0	0.0
CHR–Chs of Christ	3	240	239	335	3.1	5.0
Jehovah's Witness	1	NR	NR	NR	-	-
LDS–L-D Saints	1	NR	NR	156	1.5	2.3
LUTH–Luth-MO Synod	1	14	44	64	0.6	0.9
METH–Un Methodist	3	96	532	591	5.5	8.8
Non-denom Chr Chs	1	100	100	125	1.2	1.9
PENT–Assemb of God	3	165	65	200	1.9	3.0
PENT–Un Pent Ch Intl	1	NR	NR	NR	-	-
PRES–Presb Ch (USA)	1	9	14	18	0.2	0.3
WASHINGTON	**72**	**7,003**	**13,753**	**23,310**	**69.1**	**100.0**
ANG/EPIS–Episcopal	1	137	192	216	0.6	0.9
Bahá'í	0	NR	4	4	0.0	0.0
BAPT–N Am Bapt Conf	1	NR	123	148	0.4	0.6
BAPT–Natl Mis Bapt Conv	1	0	150	181	0.5	0.8
BAPT–NBC Amer	1	0	75	90	0.3	0.4
BAPT–So Bapt Conv	16	2,123	3,230	3,888	11.5	16.7
Catholic	3	NR	NR	6,112	18.1	26.2
CGOD–Ch God (Ander)	2	252	NR	252	0.7	1.1
CHR–Chs of Christ	2	227	257	355	1.1	1.5
Evan Free Ch	1	90	NR	90	0.3	0.4
Jehovah's Witness	1	NR	NR	NR	-	-
LDS–L-D Saints	1	NR	NR	306	0.9	1.3
LUTH–E.L.C.A.	13	1,731	4,976	5,908	17.5	25.3
LUTH–Luth Cong Msn Chr	2	55	175	211	0.6	0.9
LUTH–Luth-MO Synod	2	405	855	1,001	3.0	4.3
LUTH–Nor Amer Luth C	1	NR	NR	NR	-	-
METH–AME	4	174	454	546	1.6	2.3
METH–Un Methodist	4	392	1,018	1,123	3.3	4.8
MORAV–Unity Of Breth	1	NR	NR	NR	-	-
Non-denom Chr Chs	5	644	665	806	2.4	3.5
ORTHE–Greek Orthodox	1	6	NR	6	0.0	0.0
PENT–Assemb of God	2	236	85	269	0.8	1.2
PENT–Un Pent Ch Intl	2	NR	NR	NR	-	-
PENT–Vineyard	1	116	233	280	0.8	1.2
PRES–Presb Ch (USA)	1	118	345	415	1.2	1.8
Un C of Christ	3	297	916	1,103	3.3	4.7

Religious Group	Number of Congrega-tions	Number of Attendees	Number of Communicant, Confirmed, or Full Members	Adherents		
				Number of Adherents	% of Total Pop.	% of Total Adh.
WEBB	**138**	**10,773**	**8,885**	**147,243**	**58.8**	**100.0**
ANG/EPIS–Episcopal	1	70	169	179	0.1	0.1
Bahá'í	0	NR	36	36	0.0	0.0
BAPT–So Bapt Conv	29	1,783	2,127	2,935	1.2	2.0
BUDD–Mahayana	1	NR	NR	102	0.0	0.1
Catholic	26	NR	NR	126,750	50.6	86.1
Ch Christ Chr Union	1	NR	NR	NR	-	-
Ch God (7th Day)	2	NR	NR	NR	-	-
Ch of Nazarene	2	46	120	120	0.0	0.1
CHR–Chr Ch (Disc)	1	30	45	62	0.0	0.0
CHR–Chs of Christ	5	163	125	232	0.1	0.2
Evan Free Ch	1	550	NR	550	0.2	0.4
Jehovah's Witness	5	NR	NR	NR	-	-
LDS–L-D Saints	4	NR	NR	3,436	1.4	2.3
LUTH–E.L.C.A.	2	267	28	267	0.1	0.2
LUTH–Luth-MO Synod	1	21	35	50	0.0	0.0
METH–Free Methodist	1	69	58	69	0.0	0.0
METH–Un Methodist	4	250	663	722	0.3	0.5
Muslim Est	1	624	NR	2,542	1.0	1.7
Non-denom Chr Chs	17	2,220	2,948	3,215	1.3	2.2
PENT–Assemb of God	15	4,098	1,425	4,581	1.8	3.1
PENT–Ch God (Cleve)	6	174	190	262	0.1	0.2
PENT–COGIC	1	0	150	207	0.1	0.1
PENT–Intl Pent Holiness	1	75	80	110	0.0	0.1
PENT–Un Pent Ch Intl	2	NR	NR	NR	-	-
PRES–Evan Presby Ch	1	NR	16	22	0.0	0.0
PRES–Presb Ch (USA)	1	0	90	124	0.0	0.1
PRES–Presb Ch Amer	2	0	0	0	0.0	0.0
Sev Day Adv	4	333	580	666	0.3	0.5
Sikh	1	NR	NR	NR	-	-
Zoroastrian	0	NR	NR	4	0.0	0.0
WHARTON	**84**	**5,372**	**12,112**	**33,492**	**81.1**	**100.0**
ANG/EPIS–Episcopal	1	94	171	197	0.5	0.6
Bahá'í	0	NR	22	22	0.1	0.1
BAPT–Natl Mis Bapt Conv	1	100	250	316	0.8	0.9
BAPT–NBC Amer	1	0	150	189	0.5	0.6
BAPT–So Bapt Conv	20	1,540	5,288	6,679	16.2	19.9
Catholic	10	NR	NR	18,110	43.9	54.1
CGOD–Ch God (Ander)	2	61	NR	61	0.1	0.2
CHR–Chr Ch (Disc)	1	70	150	189	0.5	0.6
CHR–Chs of Christ	4	378	425	530	1.3	1.6
Jehovah's Witness	2	NR	NR	NR	-	-
LDS–L-D Saints	1	NR	NR	312	0.8	0.9
LUTH–Assoc Free Luth	1	NR	NR	NR	-	-
LUTH–E.L.C.A.	3	227	643	783	1.9	2.3
LUTH–Luth Cong Msn Chr	1	55	192	243	0.6	0.7
LUTH–Luth-MO Synod	1	97	206	258	0.6	0.8
MENN–CG in Cr (Menn)	1	NR	95	120	0.3	0.4
METH–AME	2	0	200	253	0.6	0.8
METH–Free Methodist	1	50	44	50	0.1	0.1
METH–Un Methodist	9	504	1,658	1,837	4.5	5.5
Non-denom Chr Chs	10	1,790	1,845	2,277	5.5	6.8
PENT–Assemb of God	5	255	185	323	0.8	1.0
PENT–Ch of God Proph	1	NR	7	9	0.0	0.0
PENT–COGIC	3	25	325	411	1.0	1.2
PENT–Un Pent Ch Intl	1	NR	NR	NR	-	-
PRES–Presb Ch (USA)	2	126	256	323	0.8	1.0
WHEELER	**22**	**903**	**1,837**	**2,348**	**43.4**	**100.0**
ANG/EPIS–Episcopal	1	7	9	9	0.2	0.4
BAPT–So Bapt Conv	6	444	1,016	1,264	23.4	53.8
Catholic	2	NR	NR	75	1.4	3.2
CHR–Chs of Christ	3	230	227	295	5.5	12.6
Jehovah's Witness	1	NR	NR	NR	-	-
LUTH–Luth-MO Synod	1	18	40	47	0.9	2.0
METH–Un Methodist	5	179	520	616	11.4	26.2
PENT–Assemb of God	1	11	0	11	0.2	0.5
PENT–Ch God (Cleve)	1	14	25	31	0.6	1.3
PENT–Un Pent Ch Intl	1	NR	NR	NR	-	-

NR–Not Reported   - Represents no adherents reported.   Percentages may not total 100 due to rounding.

Table 3: Religious Congregations by County and Group: 2010

Religious Group	Number of Congregations	Number of Attendees	Number of Communicant, Confirmed, or Full Members	Adherents: Number of Adherents	Adherents: % of Total Pop.	Adherents: % of Total Adh.
WICHITA	**211**	**22,635**	**59,929**	**88,146**	**67.0**	**100.0**
ANG/EPIS–Anglican NA	3	NR	NR	NR	-	-
ANG/EPIS–Episcopal	3	66	83	90	0.1	0.1
Bahá'í	0	NR	76	76	0.1	0.1
BAPT–Amer Bapt Assn	2	NR	85	104	0.1	0.1
BAPT–Free Will Bapt	1	NR	52	64	0.0	0.1
BAPT–Ind Bapt Flwsp Intl	4	NR	NR	NR	-	-
BAPT–Natl Mis Bapt Conv	1	150	150	184	0.1	0.2
BAPT–NBC Amer	1	300	800	979	0.7	1.1
BAPT–NBC USA	3	390	616	754	0.6	0.9
BAPT–Prog NBC	1	0	150	184	0.1	0.2
BAPT–So Bapt Conv	49	7,897	35,207	43,080	32.8	48.9
BUDD–Mahayana	1	NR	NR	505	0.4	0.6
Catholic	7	NR	NR	11,699	8.9	13.3
Ch Cr, Scientst	1	NR	NR	NR	-	-
Ch of Nazarene	4	283	421	581	0.4	0.7
CHR–Chr Ch (Disc)	4	426	1,599	1,957	1.5	2.2
CHR–Chr Chs & Chs Cr	1	NR	150	184	0.1	0.2
CHR–Chs of Christ	17	2,320	2,828	3,528	2.7	4.0
Jehovah's Witness	3	NR	NR	NR	-	-
LDS–L-D Saints	2	NR	NR	1,791	1.4	2.0
LUTH–E.L.C.A.	2	150	280	372	0.3	0.4
LUTH–Luth–MO Synod	5	396	686	831	0.6	0.9
METH–AME	1	25	50	61	0.0	0.1
METH–C.M.E.	1	0	60	73	0.1	0.1
METH–Un Methodist	13	1,621	4,258	5,107	3.9	5.8
Metro Comm Ch	1	47	93	114	0.1	0.1
Muslim Est	1	60	NR	100	0.1	0.1
Non-denom Chr Chs	34	4,712	5,882	6,658	5.1	7.6
ORTHE–Ant Orth of NA	1	30	NR	69	0.1	0.1
ORTHE–Greek Orthodox	1	20	NR	75	0.1	0.1
PENT–Assemb of God	13	1,969	2,716	3,948	3.0	4.5
PENT–Ch God (Cleve)	4	471	1,206	1,476	1.1	1.7
PENT–Ch of God Proph	1	NR	36	44	0.0	0.0
PENT–COGIC	5	25	590	722	0.5	0.8
PENT–Int Foursq Gos	2	91	157	192	0.1	0.2
PENT–Intl Pent Holiness	2	243	113	138	0.1	0.2
PENT–Pent Ch of God	4	280	NR	435	0.3	0.5
PENT–Un Pent Ch Intl	5	NR	NR	NR	-	-
PRES–Orth Pres Ch	1	23	12	20	0.0	0.0
PRES–Presb Ch (USA)	4	465	1,279	1,565	1.2	1.8
Salvation Army	1	86	139	208	0.2	0.2
Sev Day Adv	1	89	155	178	0.1	0.2
WILBARGER	**39**	**3,078**	**8,799**	**11,194**	**82.7**	**100.0**
ANG/EPIS–Episcopal	1	13	17	17	0.1	0.2
Bahá'í	0	NR	27	27	0.2	0.2
BAPT–NBC Amer	1	100	225	279	2.1	2.5
BAPT–So Bapt Conv	12	1,630	5,956	7,392	54.6	66.0
Catholic	1	NR	NR	320	2.4	2.9
Ch Cr, Scientst	1	NR	NR	NR	-	-
CHR–Chr Ch (Disc)	1	0	0	0	0.0	0.0
CHR–Chs of Christ	6	396	450	591	4.4	5.3
LDS–L-D Saints	1	NR	NR	95	0.7	0.8
LUTH–E.L.C.A.	1	13	16	16	0.1	0.1
LUTH–Luth–MO Synod	3	249	603	727	5.4	6.5
METH–AME	1	0	150	186	1.4	1.7
METH–Un Methodist	3	218	594	643	4.8	5.7
Non-denom Chr Chs	2	190	310	310	2.3	2.8
PENT–Assemb of God	2	168	173	248	1.8	2.2
PENT–Ch God (Cleve)	1	21	95	118	0.9	1.1
PRES–Presb Ch (USA)	1	62	152	189	1.4	1.7
Sev Day Adv	1	18	31	36	0.3	0.3
WILLACY	**38**	**1,310**	**1,849**	**13,767**	**62.2**	**100.0**
ANG/EPIS–Episcopal	1	25	50	63	0.3	0.5
Bahá'í	0	NR	4	4	0.0	0.0
BAPT–So Bapt Conv	7	212	502	630	2.8	4.6
Catholic	6	NR	NR	11,010	49.7	80.0
CHR–Chr Ch (Disc)	1	0	0	0	0.0	0.0
CHR–Chs of Christ	1	38	47	62	0.3	0.5
Jehovah's Witness	1	NR	NR	NR	-	-
LDS–L-D Saints	1	NR	NR	333	1.5	2.4
LUTH–E.L.C.A.	1	71	68	85	0.4	0.6
LUTH–Luth–MO Synod	1	62	123	164	0.7	1.2
METH–Un Methodist	4	283	564	628	2.8	4.6
METH–Wesleyan	2	37	21	48	0.2	0.3
Non-denom Chr Chs	1	150	150	188	0.8	1.4
PENT–Assemb of God	4	263	95	279	1.3	2.0
PENT–Ch of God Proph	1	NR	33	41	0.2	0.3
PENT–Int Foursq Gos	1	27	12	15	0.1	0.1
PENT–Intl Pent Holiness	2	90	65	82	0.4	0.6
PENT–Un Pent Ch Intl	1	NR	NR	NR	-	-
PRES–Presb Ch (USA)	1	0	24	30	0.1	0.2
Sev Day Adv	1	52	91	105	0.5	0.8
WILLIAMSON	**300**	**39,980**	**75,253**	**158,412**	**37.5**	**100.0**
ANG/EPIS–Anglican NA	1	NR	NR	NR	-	-
ANG/EPIS–Episcopal	4	551	1,202	1,347	0.3	0.9
Bahá'í	5	NR	413	413	0.1	0.3
BAPT–Alliance Bapt	1	NR	NR	NR	-	-
BAPT–Amer Bapt Assn	1	NR	150	194	0.0	0.1
BAPT–Amer Bapt USA	1	42	113	146	0.0	0.1
BAPT–Free Will Bapt	1	NR	52	67	0.0	0.0
BAPT–Ind Bapt Flwsp Intl	2	NR	NR	NR	-	-
BAPT–NBC Amer	1	0	150	194	0.0	0.1
BAPT–NBC USA	1	60	100	130	0.0	0.1
BAPT–So Bapt Conv	65	10,542	25,955	33,635	8.0	21.2
BUDD–Mahayana	1	NR	NR	506	0.1	0.3
Calv Chpl	1	NR	NR	NR	-	-
Catholic	10	NR	NR	46,503	11.0	29.4
Ch Cr, Scientst	1	NR	NR	NR	-	-
Ch God (7th Day)	1	NR	NR	NR	-	-
Ch of Nazarene	2	432	692	692	0.2	0.4
CHR–Chr Ch (Disc)	3	150	427	553	0.1	0.3
CHR–Chr Chs & Chs Cr	4	NR	300	389	0.1	0.2
CHR–Chs of Christ	16	2,669	2,676	3,664	0.9	2.3
Evan Cov Ch	1	157	140	204	0.0	0.1
Evan Free Ch	4	366	NR	366	0.1	0.2
HINDU–I/A Temples	1	NR	NR	3,400	0.8	2.1
Jehovah's Witness	6	NR	NR	NR	-	-
LDS–Comm of Christ	1	NR	110	110	0.0	0.1
LDS–L-D Saints	16	NR	NR	7,445	1.8	4.7
LUTH–E.L.C.A.	8	1,099	2,695	3,403	0.8	2.1
LUTH–Luth Cong Msn Chr	4	410	1,590	2,060	0.5	1.3
LUTH–Luth–MO Synod	6	2,033	3,610	4,493	1.1	2.8
LUTH–Wisc Ev Luth Syn	2	118	132	185	0.0	0.1
METH–AME	3	0	350	454	0.1	0.3
METH–Un Methodist	22	4,262	15,829	20,065	4.7	12.7
Missionary Ch	1	20	0	20	0.0	0.0
MORAV–Unity Of Breth	2	NR	NR	NR	-	-
Muslim Est	3	1,548	NR	5,584	1.3	3.5
Non-denom Chr Chs	43	12,388	14,699	16,226	3.8	10.2
ORTHE–Ant Orth of NA	1	89	NR	246	0.1	0.2
ORTHE–Orth Ch in Amer	1	15	NR	30	0.0	0.0
ORTHE–Romania Orth Ar	1	25	NR	150	0.0	0.1
ORTHO–Coptic Orth Ch	1	55	NR	60	0.0	0.0
ORTHO–Malan Dioc Am	1	30	NR	90	0.0	0.1
PENT–Assemb of God	10	854	556	1,028	0.2	0.6
PENT–Ch God (Cleve)	2	103	79	102	0.0	0.1
PENT–COGIC	3	0	520	674	0.2	0.4
PENT–Cong Hol Ch	1	39	35	45	0.0	0.0
PENT–Intl Pent Holiness	2	175	170	220	0.1	0.1
PENT–Open Bible Std	1	0	NR	0	0.0	0.0
PENT–Pent Ch of God	1	70	NR	109	0.0	0.1
PENT–Un Pent Ch Intl	10	NR	NR	NR	-	-
PRES–Cumber Presb	1	NR	15	62	0.0	0.0
PRES–Presb Ch (USA)	6	562	1,032	1,337	0.3	0.8
PRES–Presb Ch Amer	1	65	46	70	0.0	0.0
REF–Christian Ref	1	350	200	259	0.1	0.2
Sev Day Adv	6	442	770	885	0.2	0.6
Un C of Christ	2	80	225	292	0.1	0.2
Unit Univ	2	179	220	296	0.1	0.2
Unity Ch	1	NR	NR	NR	-	-
Zoroastrian	0	NR	NR	9	0.0	0.0

NR–Not Reported   - Represents no adherents reported.   Percentages may not total 100 due to rounding.

Table 3: Religious Congregations by County and Group: 2010

Religious Group	Number of Congrega-tions	Number of Attendees	Number of Communicant, Confirmed, or Full Members	Adherents		
				Number of Adherents	% of Total Pop.	% of Total Adh.
WILSON	**44**	**3,371**	**5,977**	**19,673**	**45.8**	**100.0**
BAPT–Amer Bapt Assn	1	NR	85	106	0.2	0.5
BAPT–N Am Bapt Conf	1	NR	47	59	0.1	0.3
BAPT–So Bapt Conv	13	1,449	3,031	3,781	8.8	19.2
Catholic	5	NR	NR	12,088	28.2	61.4
CHR–Chs of Christ	5	298	310	424	1.0	2.2
Evan Free Ch	1	125	NR	125	0.3	0.6
Jehovah's Witness	2	NR	NR	NR	-	-
LUTH–E.L.C.A.	2	77	309	373	0.9	1.9
LUTH–Nor Amer Luth C	2	NR	NR	NR	-	-
METH–Un Methodist	4	568	1,384	1,531	3.6	7.8
Non-denom Chr Chs	3	525	575	656	1.5	3.3
PENT–Assemb of God	3	325	229	522	1.2	2.7
PENT–Un Pent Ch Intl	1	NR	NR	NR	-	-
Sev Day Adv	1	4	7	8	0.0	0.0
WINKLER	**21**	**583**	**2,647**	**5,234**	**73.6**	**100.0**
ANG/EPIS–Episcopal	1	5	12	14	0.2	0.3
Bahá'í	0	NR	1	1	0.0	0.0
BAPT–Free Will Bapt	1	NR	52	67	0.9	1.3
BAPT–So Bapt Conv	6	319	2,071	2,686	37.8	51.3
Catholic	1	NR	NR	1,875	26.4	35.8
CHR–Chr Ch (Disc)	1	0	35	45	0.6	0.9
CHR–Chs of Christ	3	95	109	137	1.9	2.6
LUTH–Luth–MO Synod	1	10	32	40	0.6	0.8
METH–Un Methodist	2	59	257	262	3.7	5.0
Non-denom Chr Chs	1	25	30	31	0.4	0.6
PENT–Assemb of God	1	18	5	20	0.3	0.4
PENT–Ch God (Cleve)	1	52	36	47	0.7	0.9
PENT–Ch of God Proph	1	NR	7	9	0.1	0.2
PENT–Un Pent Ch Intl	1	NR	NR	NR	-	-
WISE	**115**	**11,003**	**17,090**	**24,379**	**41.2**	**100.0**
ANG/EPIS–Anglican NA	1	NR	NR	NR	-	-
Bahá'í	0	NR	12	12	0.0	0.0
BAPT–Free Will Bapt	1	NR	52	65	0.1	0.3
BAPT–Ind Bapt Flwsp Intl	13	NR	NR	NR	-	-
BAPT–So Bapt Conv	44	4,775	8,963	11,197	18.9	45.9
Catholic	2	NR	NR	2,280	3.9	9.4
Ch of Nazarene	2	120	121	140	0.2	0.6
CHR–Chr Ch (Disc)	1	16	33	41	0.1	0.2
CHR–Chs of Christ	13	929	953	1,192	2.0	4.9
LDS–L-D Saints	1	NR	NR	554	0.9	2.3
LUTH–Luth–MO Synod	2	56	93	137	0.2	0.6
METH–Un Methodist	9	727	2,067	2,451	4.1	10.1
Non-denom Chr Chs	15	3,930	4,440	5,461	9.2	22.4
PENT–Assemb of God	6	310	280	538	0.9	2.2
PENT–Pent Ch of God	2	140	NR	217	0.4	0.9
PENT–Un Pent Ch Intl	1	NR	NR	NR	-	-
PRES–Cumber Presb	1	NR	12	12	0.0	0.0
PRES–Presb Ch (USA)	1	0	64	80	0.1	0.3
Zoroastrian	0	NR	NR	2	0.0	0.0
WOOD	**90**	**8,085**	**17,690**	**24,336**	**58.0**	**100.0**
ANG/EPIS–Episcopal	1	74	144	156	0.4	0.6
Bahá'í	0	NR	2	2	0.0	0.0
BAPT–So Bapt Conv	28	4,172	11,706	13,861	33.0	57.0
Catholic	3	NR	NR	2,684	6.4	11.0
Ch of Nazarene	2	73	103	126	0.3	0.5
CHR–Chr Ch (Disc)	4	192	341	404	1.0	1.7
CHR–Chs of Christ	10	754	740	939	2.2	3.9
Jehovah's Witness	2	NR	NR	NR	-	-
LDS–L-D Saints	1	NR	NR	443	1.1	1.8
METH–C.M.E.	2	0	250	296	0.7	1.2
METH–Un Methodist	14	962	2,165	2,367	5.6	9.7
Non-denom Chr Chs	7	1,155	1,255	1,519	3.6	6.2
PENT–Assemb of God	8	543	368	704	1.7	2.9
PENT–COGIC	3	0	450	533	1.3	2.2
PENT–Pent Ch of God	1	70	NR	109	0.3	0.4
PENT–Un Pent Ch Intl	2	NR	NR	NR	-	-
PRES–Presb Ch (USA)	1	28	58	69	0.2	0.3
Sev Day Adv	1	62	108	124	0.3	0.5

Religious Group	Number of Congrega-tions	Number of Attendees	Number of Communicant, Confirmed, or Full Members	Adherents		
				Number of Adherents	% of Total Pop.	% of Total Adh.
YOAKUM	**21**	**1,200**	**3,006**	**6,441**	**81.7**	**100.0**
Bahá'í	0	NR	1	1	0.0	0.0
BAPT–So Bapt Conv	8	635	2,094	2,789	35.4	43.3
Catholic	2	NR	NR	2,462	31.2	38.2
Ch of Nazarene	1	42	26	56	0.7	0.9
CHR–Chs of Christ	2	243	298	395	5.0	6.1
Jehovah's Witness	1	NR	NR	NR	-	-
METH–Un Methodist	2	135	492	571	7.2	8.9
Non-denom Chr Chs	1	20	30	30	0.4	0.5
PENT–Assemb of God	3	125	65	137	1.7	2.1
PENT–Un Pent Ch Intl	1	NR	NR	NR	-	-
YOUNG	**65**	**4,574**	**11,412**	**15,474**	**83.4**	**100.0**
ANG/EPIS–Anglican NA	1	NR	NR	NR	-	-
Bahá'í	0	NR	76	76	0.4	0.5
BAPT–Ind Bapt Flwsp Intl	3	NR	NR	NR	-	-
BAPT–So Bapt Conv	17	2,147	6,981	8,587	46.3	55.5
Catholic	2	NR	NR	950	5.1	6.1
Ch of Nazarene	1	25	33	110	0.6	0.7
CHR–Chr Ch (Disc)	2	0	75	92	0.5	0.6
CHR–Chs of Christ	9	659	818	956	5.2	6.2
Jehovah's Witness	1	NR	NR	NR	-	-
LDS–L-D Saints	1	NR	NR	290	1.6	1.9
LUTH–Luth–MO Synod	2	105	243	293	1.6	1.9
METH–Un Methodist	7	568	1,655	1,985	10.7	12.8
Non-denom Chr Chs	5	448	555	623	3.4	4.0
PENT–Assemb of God	5	306	280	425	2.3	2.7
PENT–Ch God (Cleve)	2	76	308	379	2.0	2.4
PENT–Ch God Apos Fth	1	NR	NR	NR	-	-
PENT–Pent Ch of God	2	140	NR	217	1.2	1.4
PENT–Un Pent Ch Intl	1	NR	NR	NR	-	-
PRES–Cumber Presb	1	NR	62	92	0.5	0.6
PRES–Presb Ch (USA)	1	82	294	362	2.0	2.3
Sev Day Adv	1	18	32	37	0.2	0.2
ZAPATA	**17**	**458**	**640**	**4,294**	**30.6**	**100.0**
Ap Chr Ch-Amer	1	20	14	20	0.1	0.5
BAPT–So Bapt Conv	3	132	335	458	3.3	10.7
Catholic	5	NR	NR	3,500	25.0	81.5
Ch Christ Chr Union	1	NR	NR	NR	-	-
CHR–Chs of Christ	1	100	50	62	0.4	1.4
Jehovah's Witness	1	NR	NR	NR	-	-
LUTH–Luth–MO Synod	1	22	16	16	0.1	0.4
METH–Un Methodist	1	54	60	60	0.4	1.4
Non-denom Chr Chs	2	110	130	138	1.0	3.2
Sev Day Adv	1	20	35	40	0.3	0.9
ZAVALA	**15**	**595**	**881**	**4,997**	**42.8**	**100.0**
Bahá'í	0	NR	2	2	0.0	0.0
BAPT–So Bapt Conv	4	124	316	416	3.6	8.3
Catholic	2	NR	NR	3,400	29.1	68.0
Ch God (7th Day)	1	NR	NR	NR	-	-
CHR–Chr Chs & Chs Cr	1	NR	35	46	0.4	0.9
CHR–Chs of Christ	1	8	5	10	0.1	0.2
METH–Un Methodist	2	56	220	240	2.1	4.8
Non-denom Chr Chs	2	189	210	248	2.1	5.0
PENT–Assemb of God	2	218	93	635	5.4	12.7
UTAH	**5,557**	**50,875**	**62,560**	**2,186,403**	**79.1**	**100.0**
BEAVER	**18**	**32**	**13**	**5,146**	**77.6**	**100.0**
Bahá'í	0	NR	1	1	0.0	0.0
BAPT–So Bapt Conv	1	20	12	16	0.2	0.3
Catholic	1	NR	NR	152	2.3	3.0
Chr & Miss Al	1	12	0	12	0.2	0.2
LDS–L-D Saints	15	NR	NR	4,965	74.9	96.5
BOX ELDER	**120**	**665**	**835**	**45,125**	**90.3**	**100.0**
ANG/EPIS–Episcopal	1	34	80	85	0.2	0.2
Bahá'í	0	NR	3	3	0.0	0.0

NR–Not Reported - Represents no adherents reported. Percentages may not total 100 due to rounding.

Table 3: Religious Congregations by County and Group: 2010

Religious Group	Number of Congrega-tions	Number of Attendees	Number of Communicant, Confirmed, or Full Members	Adherents		
				Number of Adherents	% of Total Pop.	% of Total Adh.
BAPT–So Bapt Conv	2	92	144	197	0.4	0.4
BUDD–Mahayana	1	NR	NR	1,250	2.5	2.8
Catholic	2	NR	NR	2,008	4.0	4.4
CHR–Chs of Christ	1	12	15	17	0.0	0.0
Jehovah's Witness	1	NR	NR	NR	-	-
LDS–L-D Saints	103	NR	NR	40,668	81.4	90.1
LUTH–Luth Cong Msn Chr	1	40	127	174	0.3	0.4
METH–Un Methodist	1	85	79	166	0.3	0.4
Non-denom Chr Chs	4	211	202	270	0.5	0.6
PENT–Assemb of God	1	97	63	120	0.2	0.3
PENT–Ch God (Cleve)	1	19	21	29	0.1	0.1
PRES–Presb Ch (USA)	1	75	101	138	0.3	0.3
CACHE	**312**	**1,865**	**1,780**	**98,851**	**87.7**	**100.0**
ANG/EPIS–Episcopal	1	114	190	319	0.3	0.3
Bahá'í	1	NR	44	44	0.0	0.0
BAPT–So Bapt Conv	4	280	321	432	0.4	0.4
Catholic	1	NR	NR	3,308	2.9	3.3
CHR–Chs of Christ	1	40	16	45	0.0	0.0
Evan Free Ch	1	75	NR	75	0.1	0.1
FRND–Fr Gen Cf	1	NR	22	30	0.0	0.0
HINDU–Post Ren	1	NR	NR	16	0.0	0.0
Jehovah's Witness	1	NR	NR	NR	-	-
LDS–L-D Saints	285	NR	NR	92,665	82.3	93.7
LUTH–E.L.C.A.	1	73	115	141	0.1	0.1
LUTH–Luth-MO Synod	1	80	89	111	0.1	0.1
Muslim Est	1	134	NR	308	0.3	0.3
Non-denom Chr Chs	4	315	385	419	0.4	0.4
PENT–Assemb of God	2	263	118	295	0.3	0.3
PENT–Ch God (Cleve)	2	136	75	101	0.1	0.1
PENT–Intl Pent Holiness	1	125	40	54	0.0	0.1
PRES–Presb Ch (USA)	1	159	262	353	0.3	0.4
Sev Day Adv	1	32	56	64	0.1	0.1
Unit Univ	1	39	47	71	0.1	0.1
CARBON	**54**	**886**	**953**	**17,110**	**79.9**	**100.0**
ANG/EPIS–Episcopal	1	56	114	128	0.6	0.7
Bahá'í	0	NR	3	3	0.0	0.0
BAPT–So Bapt Conv	3	70	142	180	0.8	1.1
Catholic	4	NR	NR	4,091	19.1	23.9
Chr & Miss Al	2	226	169	305	1.4	1.8
CHR–Chs of Christ	1	60	57	60	0.3	0.4
Jehovah's Witness	1	NR	NR	NR	-	-
LDS–L-D Saints	31	NR	NR	11,367	53.1	66.4
LUTH–E.L.C.A.	1	56	94	128	0.6	0.7
METH–Un Methodist	1	40	87	111	0.5	0.6
Non-denom Chr Chs	3	135	169	178	0.8	1.0
ORTHE–Greek Orthodox	1	75	NR	280	1.3	1.6
PENT–Assemb of God	1	25	0	25	0.1	0.1
PENT–Ch of God Proph	1	NR	24	30	0.1	0.2
PENT–Int Foursq Gos	1	47	50	64	0.3	0.4
PENT–Pent Ch of God	1	70	NR	109	0.5	0.6
Sev Day Adv	1	26	44	51	0.2	0.3
DAGGETT	**3**	**NR**	**NR**	**695**	**65.6**	**100.0**
LDS–L-D Saints	3	NR	NR	695	65.6	100.0
DAVIS	**599**	**4,371**	**4,814**	**252,450**	**82.4**	**100.0**
ANG/EPIS–Episcopal	2	104	281	286	0.1	0.1
Bahá'í	1	NR	75	75	0.0	0.0
BAPT–Amer Bapt Assn	1	NR	85	117	0.0	0.0
BAPT–Amer Bapt USA	2	193	313	432	0.1	0.2
BAPT–Consrv Bapt	1	NR	NR	NR	-	-
BAPT–Converge/BGC	1	75	NR	90	0.0	0.0
BAPT–NBC USA	1	60	145	200	0.1	0.1
BAPT–So Bapt Conv	7	762	1,606	2,219	0.7	0.9
BUDD–Mahayana	1	NR	NR	102	0.0	0.0
BUDD–Theravada	1	NR	NR	1,365	0.4	0.5
Calv Chpl	1	NR	NR	NR	-	-
Catholic	1	NR	NR	12,782	4.2	5.1
Ch of Nazarene	1	43	47	82	0.0	0.0
CHR–Chs of Christ	2	190	182	247	0.1	0.1
Evan Free Ch	1	210	NR	210	0.1	0.1
Jehovah's Witness	2	NR	NR	NR	-	-
LDS–L-D Saints	550	NR	NR	228,813	74.7	90.6
LUTH–E.L.C.A.	1	35	49	129	0.0	0.1
LUTH–Luth-MO Synod	2	66	243	328	0.1	0.1
LUTH–Wisc Ev Luth Syn	1	58	109	136	0.0	0.1
Muslim Est	1	30	NR	50	0.0	0.0
Non-denom Chr Chs	6	650	806	925	0.3	0.4
PENT–Assemb of God	5	1,520	561	3,315	1.1	1.3
PENT–Ch God (Cleve)	1	25	44	61	0.0	0.0
PENT–Int Foursq Gos	1	27	30	41	0.0	0.0
PENT–Pent Ch of God	1	70	NR	109	0.0	0.0
PENT–Un Pent Ch Intl	1	NR	NR	NR	-	-
PRES–Presb Ch (USA)	1	125	146	202	0.1	0.1
PRES–Presb Ch Amer	1	80	30	48	0.0	0.0
Un C of Christ	1	48	62	86	0.0	0.0
DUCHESNE	**42**	**309**	**411**	**14,528**	**78.1**	**100.0**
Bahá'í	0	NR	1	1	0.0	0.0
BAPT–So Bapt Conv	2	111	237	326	1.8	2.2
Catholic	1	NR	NR	268	1.4	1.8
Jehovah's Witness	1	NR	NR	NR	-	-
LDS–L-D Saints	33	NR	NR	13,676	73.5	94.1
LUTH–Luth-MO Synod	1	12	24	15	0.1	0.1
Non-denom Chr Chs	2	79	94	99	0.5	0.7
PENT–Assemb of God	1	92	42	125	0.7	0.9
PRES–Presb Ch (USA)	1	15	13	18	0.1	0.1
EMERY	**28**	**285**	**227**	**8,991**	**81.9**	**100.0**
BAPT–So Bapt Conv	2	35	77	103	0.9	1.1
Catholic	2	NR	NR	105	1.0	1.2
Evan Free Ch	1	150	NR	150	1.4	1.7
LDS–L-D Saints	22	NR	NR	8,483	77.3	94.3
Non-denom Chr Chs	1	100	150	150	1.4	1.7
GARFIELD	**17**	**39**	**20**	**3,856**	**74.6**	**100.0**
BAPT–So Bapt Conv	1	39	20	25	0.5	0.6
Catholic	1	NR	NR	50	1.0	1.3
LDS–L-D Saints	15	NR	NR	3,781	73.1	98.1
GRAND	**22**	**500**	**1,113**	**4,961**	**53.8**	**100.0**
ANG/EPIS–Episcopal	2	101	253	259	2.8	5.2
Bahá'í	0	NR	2	2	0.0	0.0
BAPT–Amer Bapt USA	1	140	234	285	3.1	5.7
BAPT–So Bapt Conv	1	60	416	506	5.5	10.2
Catholic	1	NR	NR	635	6.9	12.8
CHR–Chs of Christ	1	20	22	25	0.3	0.5
FRND–Fr Gen Cf	1	NR	9	11	0.1	0.2
HINDU–Post Ren	1	NR	NR	77	0.8	1.6
Jehovah's Witness	1	NR	NR	NR	-	-
LDS–L-D Saints	8	NR	NR	2,869	31.1	57.8
LUTH–Luth-MO Synod	1	18	28	32	0.3	0.6
Non-denom Chr Chs	1	70	50	88	1.0	1.8
PENT–Assemb of God	1	47	23	85	0.9	1.7
Sev Day Adv	2	44	76	87	0.9	1.8
IRON	**114**	**1,008**	**1,221**	**35,770**	**77.5**	**100.0**
ANG/EPIS–Episcopal	1	36	46	46	0.1	0.1
Bahá'í	0	NR	3	3	0.0	0.0
BAPT–Ind Bapt Flwsp Intl	1	NR	NR	NR	-	-
BAPT–So Bapt Conv	2	235	416	547	1.2	1.5
Calv Chpl	1	NR	NR	NR	-	-
Catholic	2	NR	NR	2,248	4.9	6.3
CHR–Chs of Christ	1	30	28	40	0.1	0.1
Jehovah's Witness	2	NR	NR	NR	-	-
LDS–L-D Saints	96	NR	NR	31,883	69.1	89.1
LUTH–Luth-MO Synod	1	0	57	77	0.2	0.2
Non-denom Chr Chs	3	300	270	375	0.8	1.0
PENT–Assemb of God	1	60	46	99	0.2	0.3
PENT–Int Foursq Gos	1	137	115	151	0.3	0.4
PRES–Presb Ch (USA)	1	162	157	206	0.4	0.6
Sev Day Adv	1	48	83	95	0.2	0.3

NR–Not Reported - Represents no adherents reported. Percentages may not total 100 due to rounding.

Table 3: Religious Congregations by County and Group: 2010

Religious Group	Number of Congrega-tions	Number of Attendees	Number of Communicant, Confirmed, or Full Members	Adherents		
				Number of Adherents	% of Total Pop.	% of Total Adh.
JUAB	**21**	**16**	**29**	**8,551**	**83.5**	**100.0**
Bahá'í	0	NR	1	1	0.0	0.0
Catholic	1	NR	NR	145	1.4	1.7
LDS–L-D Saints	19	NR	NR	8,373	81.7	97.9
METH–Un Methodist	1	16	28	32	0.3	0.4
KANE	**24**	**205**	**358**	**4,750**	**66.7**	**100.0**
Bahá'í	0	NR	2	2	0.0	0.0
BAPT–Consrv Bapt	1	NR	NR	NR	-	-
Catholic	2	NR	NR	242	3.4	5.1
CHR–Chr Ch (Disc)	1	20	40	49	0.7	1.0
Jehovah's Witness	2	NR	NR	NR	-	-
LDS–L-D Saints	12	NR	NR	4,117	57.8	86.7
LUTH–Luth–MO Synod	1	20	34	38	0.5	0.8
METH–Un Methodist	1	15	49	49	0.7	1.0
Non-denom Chr Chs	2	130	170	175	2.5	3.7
PRES–Presb Ch (USA)	1	20	8	10	0.1	0.2
Un C of Christ	1	0	55	68	1.0	1.4
MILLARD	**38**	**278**	**327**	**10,379**	**83.0**	**100.0**
Bahá'í	0	NR	2	2	0.0	0.0
BAPT–So Bapt Conv	1	10	15	20	0.2	0.2
Catholic	2	NR	NR	76	0.6	0.7
CHR–Chs of Christ	1	16	12	20	0.2	0.2
Evan Free Ch	1	25	NR	25	0.2	0.2
Jehovah's Witness	1	NR	NR	NR	-	-
LDS–L-D Saints	27	NR	NR	9,909	79.3	95.5
Non-denom Chr Chs	3	190	250	263	2.1	2.5
PENT–Int Foursq Gos	1	23	27	36	0.3	0.3
PRES–Presb Ch (USA)	1	14	21	28	0.2	0.3
MORGAN	**23**	**18**	**50**	**8,487**	**89.6**	**100.0**
BAPT–Amer Bapt USA	1	18	50	69	0.7	0.8
LDS–L-D Saints	22	NR	NR	8,418	88.9	99.2
PIUTE	**3**	**NR**	**NR**	**1,036**	**66.6**	**100.0**
LDS–L-D Saints	3	NR	NR	1,036	66.6	100.0
RICH	**6**	**NR**	**NR**	**1,992**	**88.0**	**100.0**
LDS–L-D Saints	6	NR	NR	1,992	88.0	100.0
SALT LAKE	**1,671**	**23,937**	**29,357**	**754,089**	**73.2**	**100.0**
ANG/EPIS–Episcopal	6	755	2,414	2,679	0.3	0.4
Bahá'í	11	NR	789	789	0.1	0.1
BAPT–Amer Bapt Assn	1	NR	85	111	0.0	0.0
BAPT–Amer Bapt USA	3	750	935	1,218	0.1	0.2
BAPT–Consrv Bapt	3	NR	NR	NR	-	-
BAPT–Converge/BGC	1	75	NR	90	0.0	0.0
BAPT–Free Will Bapt	1	NR	42	55	0.0	0.0
BAPT–Ind Bapt Flwsp Intl	1	NR	NR	NR	-	-
BAPT–NBC USA	1	500	400	521	0.1	0.1
BAPT–Reg Bapt Gen As	2	NR	NR	NR	-	-
BAPT–So Bapt Conv	22	2,238	3,863	5,032	0.5	0.7
BUDD–Mahayana	9	NR	NR	3,791	0.4	0.5
BUDD–Theravada	2	NR	NR	696	0.1	0.1
BUDD–Vajrayana	1	NR	NR	45	0.0	0.0
Calv Chpl	1	NR	NR	NR	-	-
Catholic	24	NR	NR	84,342	8.2	11.2
Ch Cr, Scientst	2	NR	NR	NR	-	-
Ch God (7th Day)	1	NR	NR	NR	-	-
Ch of Nazarene	4	171	195	330	0.0	0.0
Chr & Miss Al	4	212	95	323	0.0	0.0
CHR–Chr Ch (Disc)	2	210	463	603	0.1	0.1
CHR–Chr Chs & Chs Cr	2	NR	400	521	0.1	0.1
CHR–Chs of Christ	4	440	404	478	0.0	0.1
CHR–Int Chs of Christ	1	NR	30	39	0.0	0.0
CONG–Armen Evang Add'l	1	NR	NR	NR	-	-
CONG–Cong Chr, NA	1	NR	219	285	0.0	0.0
Evan Free Ch	3	620	NR	620	0.1	0.1
FRND–Fr Gen Cf	1	NR	25	33	0.0	0.0
HINDU–I/A Temples	1	NR	NR	250	0.0	0.0
HINDU–Post Ren	4	NR	NR	128	0.0	0.0
HINDU–Trad Temples	1	NR	NR	50	0.0	0.0
Ind Fund Churches	2	NR	NR	NR	-	-
Jehovah's Witness	5	NR	NR	NR	-	-
JUD–Conserv	0	105	118	317	0.0	0.0
JUD–Orth	2	72	75	100	0.0	0.0
JUD–Reconst	1	23	30	81	0.0	0.0
JUD–Reform	0	67	118	317	0.0	0.0
LDS–Comm of Christ	1	NR	128	128	0.0	0.0
LDS–L-D Saints	1,400	NR	NR	610,846	59.3	81.0
LUTH–E.L.C.A.	5	447	1,030	1,292	0.1	0.2
LUTH–Evan Luth Syn	1	46	88	147	0.0	0.0
LUTH–Luth Cong Msn Chr	1	500	1,396	1,818	0.2	0.2
LUTH–Luth–MO Synod	5	612	1,493	1,894	0.2	0.3
LUTH–Wisc Ev Luth Syn	1	177	239	348	0.0	0.0
MENN–Menn Br US Conf	3	NR	500	651	0.1	0.1
METH–AME	1	0	150	195	0.0	0.0
METH–Un Methodist	9	1,308	2,793	3,568	0.3	0.5
Muslim Est	6	1,270	NR	4,540	0.4	0.6
New Apost Ch	1	NR	NR	NR	-	-
Non-denom Chr Chs	26	4,289	3,462	5,635	0.5	0.7
ORTHE–Ant Orth of NA	1	92	NR	255	0.0	0.0
ORTHE–Greek Orthodox	2	800	NR	4,500	0.4	0.6
ORTHE–Holy Orth in NA	1	27	NR	35	0.0	0.0
ORTHE–Rus Orth Abroad	1	75	NR	250	0.0	0.0
ORTHE–Serb Orth USA	1	70	NR	300	0.0	0.0
ORTHO–Coptic Orth Ch	1	6	NR	12	0.0	0.0
PENT–Assemb of God	14	3,955	1,132	5,805	0.6	0.8
PENT–Ch God (Cleve)	2	20	20	26	0.0	0.0
PENT–Ch of God Proph	5	NR	147	191	0.0	0.0
PENT–COGIC	4	0	450	586	0.1	0.1
PENT–Int Foursq Gos	4	908	322	419	0.0	0.1
PENT–Intl Pent Holiness	1	20	40	52	0.0	0.0
PENT–Open Bible Std	1	25	NR	25	0.0	0.0
PENT–Un Pent Ch Intl	4	NR	NR	NR	-	-
PENT–Vineyard	4	319	340	443	0.0	0.1
PRES–Orth Pres Ch	1	51	57	80	0.0	0.0
PRES–Presb Ch (USA)	8	933	1,923	2,505	0.2	0.3
PRES–Presb Ch Amer	4	243	248	300	0.0	0.0
REF–Christian Ref	4	192	214	279	0.0	0.0
Salvation Army	2	72	187	248	0.0	0.0
Sev Day Adv	7	768	1,337	1,537	0.1	0.2
Sikh	2	NR	NR	NR	-	-
Un C of Christ	3	388	465	606	0.1	0.1
Unit Univ	2	86	496	727	0.1	0.1
Unity Ch	1	NR	NR	NR	-	-
Zoroastrian	0	NR	NR	2	0.0	0.0
SAN JUAN	**37**	**402**	**575**	**7,422**	**50.3**	**100.0**
ANG/EPIS–Episcopal	4	68	144	177	1.2	2.4
Bahá'í	0	NR	43	43	0.3	0.6
BAPT–So Bapt Conv	3	90	93	126	0.9	1.7
Catholic	2	NR	NR	177	1.2	2.4
CHR–Chs of Christ	2	31	16	34	0.2	0.5
LDS–L-D Saints	22	NR	NR	6,490	44.0	87.4
PENT–Assemb of God	1	38	0	42	0.3	0.6
PENT–Ch God (Cleve)	2	48	58	79	0.5	1.1
Sev Day Adv	1	127	221	254	1.7	3.4
SANPETE	**73**	**123**	**217**	**22,272**	**80.1**	**100.0**
Bahá'í	0	NR	1	1	0.0	0.0
BAPT–So Bapt Conv	2	18	37	48	0.2	0.2
Catholic	2	NR	NR	76	0.3	0.3
Jehovah's Witness	1	NR	NR	NR	-	-
LDS–L-D Saints	65	NR	NR	21,957	78.9	98.6
Non-denom Chr Chs	2	87	160	165	0.6	0.7
PRES–Presb Ch (USA)	1	18	19	25	0.1	0.1
SEVIER	**49**	**403**	**423**	**18,250**	**87.7**	**100.0**
Bahá'í	0	NR	2	2	0.0	0.0
BAPT–So Bapt Conv	3	74	71	94	0.5	0.5
Catholic	1	NR	NR	273	1.3	1.5
Jehovah's Witness	1	NR	NR	NR	-	-

NR–Not Reported   - Represents no adherents reported.   Percentages may not total 100 due to rounding.

Table 3: Religious Congregations by County and Group: 2010

Religious Group	Number of Congrega-tions	Number of Attendees	Number of Communicant, Confirmed, or Full Members	Adherents		
				Number of Adherents	% of Total Pop.	% of Total Adh.
LDS–L-D Saints	39	NR	NR	17,392	83.6	95.3
LUTH–Luth–MO Synod	1	22	30	44	0.2	0.2
Non-denom Chr Chs	2	170	240	240	1.2	1.3
PENT–Assemb of God	1	104	47	161	0.8	0.9
PRES–Presb Ch (USA)	1	33	33	44	0.2	0.2
SUMMIT	**45**	**1,297**	**1,267**	**20,907**	**57.6**	**100.0**
ANG/EPIS–Anglican NA	1	NR	NR	NR	-	-
ANG/EPIS–Episcopal	1	96	160	262	0.7	1.3
Bahá'í	0	NR	24	24	0.1	0.1
BAPT–So Bapt Conv	1	9	23	29	0.1	0.1
Catholic	1	NR	NR	5,279	14.5	25.2
Ch Cr, Scientst	1	NR	NR	NR	-	-
Evan Free Ch	1	520	NR	520	1.4	2.5
HINDU–Post Ren	1	NR	NR	10	0.0	0.0
JUD–Reform	1	149	263	710	2.0	3.4
LDS–L-D Saints	30	NR	NR	12,704	35.0	60.8
LUTH–E.L.C.A.	1	114	280	394	1.1	1.9
METH–Un Methodist	1	259	367	773	2.1	3.7
Non-denom Chr Chs	2	60	50	75	0.2	0.4
PENT–Vineyard	1	90	100	127	0.3	0.6
PRES–Presb Ch Amer	1	0	0	0	0.0	0.0
Unity Ch	1	NR	NR	NR	-	-
TOOELE	**106**	**834**	**1,028**	**51,144**	**87.8**	**100.0**
ANG/EPIS–Episcopal	1	25	92	92	0.2	0.2
Bahá'í	0	NR	7	7	0.0	0.0
BAPT–Consrv Bapt	1	NR	NR	NR	-	-
BAPT–So Bapt Conv	5	183	222	313	0.5	0.6
Catholic	2	NR	NR	10,706	18.4	20.9
CHR–Chs of Christ	1	37	35	52	0.1	0.1
Evan Free Ch	1	60	NR	60	0.1	0.1
Jehovah's Witness	1	NR	NR	NR	-	-
LDS–L-D Saints	87	NR	NR	38,888	66.8	76.0
LUTH–Luth Cong Msn Chr	1	50	92	130	0.2	0.3
LUTH–Luth–MO Synod	1	40	85	110	0.2	0.2
METH–Un Methodist	1	36	99	201	0.3	0.4
Non-denom Chr Chs	3	310	360	412	0.7	0.8
PENT–Assemb of God	1	93	36	173	0.3	0.3
UINTAH	**65**	**607**	**1,395**	**23,328**	**71.6**	**100.0**
ANG/EPIS–Episcopal	3	89	402	402	1.2	1.7
Bahá'í	0	NR	9	9	0.0	0.0
BAPT–Reg Bapt Gen As	1	NR	NR	NR	-	-
BAPT–So Bapt Conv	1	102	242	331	1.0	1.4
Calv Chpl	1	NR	NR	NR	-	-
Catholic	2	NR	NR	1,209	3.7	5.2
CHR–Chr Chs & Chs Cr	1	NR	176	241	0.7	1.0
CHR–Chs of Christ	1	30	30	35	0.1	0.2
Jehovah's Witness	1	NR	NR	NR	-	-
LDS–L-D Saints	47	NR	NR	20,349	62.4	87.2
LUTH–Luth–MO Synod	1	69	97	133	0.4	0.6
Non-denom Chr Chs	1	50	50	62	0.2	0.3
PENT–Assemb of God	2	148	320	361	1.1	1.5
PENT–Pent Ch of God	1	70	NR	109	0.3	0.5
Sev Day Adv	1	20	34	39	0.1	0.2
Un C of Christ	1	29	35	48	0.1	0.2
UTAH	**1,340**	**2,191**	**1,764**	**469,813**	**90.9**	**100.0**
ANG/EPIS–Episcopal	1	39	31	48	0.0	0.0
Bahá'í	0	NR	55	55	0.0	0.0
BAPT–Consrv Bapt	2	NR	NR	NR	-	-
BAPT–Reg Bapt Gen As	1	NR	NR	NR	-	-
BAPT–So Bapt Conv	3	152	222	312	0.1	0.1
BUDD–Mahayana	1	NR	NR	103	0.0	0.0
Calv Chpl	1	NR	NR	NR	-	-
Catholic	4	NR	NR	6,792	1.3	1.4
CHR–Chs of Christ	1	8	8	8	0.0	0.0
Evan Free Ch	1	800	NR	800	0.2	0.2
HINDU–I/A Temples	1	NR	NR	1,562	0.3	0.3
Jehovah's Witness	3	NR	NR	NR	-	-
LDS–Comm of Christ	1	NR	128	128	0.0	0.0

Religious Group	Number of Congrega-tions	Number of Attendees	Number of Communicant, Confirmed, or Full Members	Adherents		
				Number of Adherents	% of Total Pop.	% of Total Adh.
LDS–L-D Saints	1,297	NR	NR	457,999	88.7	97.5
LUTH–Luth–MO Synod	1	50	103	176	0.0	0.0
METH–Un Methodist	1	60	84	84	0.0	0.0
METH–Wesleyan	1	25	2	33	0.0	0.0
Non-denom Chr Chs	6	365	405	496	0.1	0.1
PENT–Assemb of God	4	327	90	367	0.1	0.1
PENT–Ch God (Cleve)	1	56	56	79	0.0	0.0
PENT–COGIC	1	0	150	211	0.0	0.0
PENT–Int Foursq Gos	1	48	50	70	0.0	0.0
PRES–Kor Pres Abroad	1	NR	NR	NR	-	-
PRES–Presb Ch (USA)	2	95	106	149	0.0	0.0
Sev Day Adv	2	100	173	199	0.0	0.0
Un C of Christ	2	66	101	142	0.0	0.0
WASATCH	**45**	**120**	**101**	**15,692**	**66.7**	**100.0**
Bahá'í	0	NR	2	2	0.0	0.0
BAPT–So Bapt Conv	2	70	64	88	0.4	0.6
Catholic	1	NR	NR	368	1.6	2.3
Evan Free Ch	1	0	NR	0	0.0	0.0
Jehovah's Witness	1	NR	NR	NR	-	-
LDS–L-D Saints	39	NR	NR	15,172	64.5	96.7
Non-denom Chr Chs	1	50	35	62	0.3	0.4
WASHINGTON	**276**	**2,344**	**3,576**	**104,505**	**75.7**	**100.0**
ANG/EPIS–Episcopal	2	164	272	283	0.2	0.3
Bahá'í	0	NR	16	16	0.0	0.0
BAPT–Consrv Bapt	1	NR	NR	NR	-	-
BAPT–Reg Bapt Gen As	1	NR	NR	NR	-	-
BAPT–So Bapt Conv	5	343	348	458	0.3	0.4
Calv Chpl	1	NR	NR	NR	-	-
Catholic	1	NR	NR	5,845	4.2	5.6
Ch Cr, Scientst	1	NR	NR	NR	-	-
CHR–Chs of Christ	1	35	33	40	0.0	0.0
Jehovah's Witness	1	NR	NR	NR	-	-
LDS–Comm of Christ	1	NR	159	159	0.1	0.2
LDS–L-D Saints	239	NR	NR	94,191	68.2	90.1
LUTH–E.L.C.A.	1	186	339	387	0.3	0.4
LUTH–Luth–MO Synod	2	152	255	303	0.2	0.3
MENN–Menn Br US Conf	1	NR	0	0	0.0	0.0
METH–Un Methodist	1	174	243	285	0.2	0.3
Non-denom Chr Chs	7	970	990	1,220	0.9	1.2
PENT–Assemb of God	1	90	0	125	0.1	0.1
PENT–Ch of God Proph	1	NR	12	16	0.0	0.0
PENT–COGIC	2	0	500	658	0.5	0.6
PENT–Int Foursq Gos	1	42	35	46	0.0	0.0
PENT–Un Pent Ch Intl	1	NR	NR	NR	-	-
PRES–Presb Ch (USA)	1	120	255	336	0.2	0.3
PRES–Presb Ch Amer	1	0	0	0	0.0	0.0
Sev Day Adv	1	68	119	137	0.1	0.1
Unity Ch	1	NR	NR	NR	-	-
WAYNE	**8**	**8**	**9**	**2,184**	**78.6**	**100.0**
Bahá'í	0	NR	1	1	0.0	0.0
BAPT–So Bapt Conv	1	8	8	10	0.4	0.5
Catholic	1	NR	NR	15	0.5	0.7
LDS–L-D Saints	6	NR	NR	2,158	77.7	98.8
WEBER	**398**	**8,132**	**10,697**	**174,119**	**75.3**	**100.0**
ANG/EPIS–Episcopal	1	105	258	341	0.1	0.2
Bahá'í	1	NR	43	43	0.0	0.0
BAPT–Amer Bapt USA	1	57	59	78	0.0	0.0
BAPT–Consrv Bapt	2	NR	NR	NR	-	-
BAPT–Free Will Bapt	1	NR	42	55	0.0	0.0
BAPT–Ind Bapt Flwsp Intl	1	NR	NR	NR	-	-
BAPT–NBC USA	1	150	225	296	0.1	0.2
BAPT–Ref Bapt Ch	1	NR	NR	NR	-	-
BAPT–So Bapt Conv	5	324	898	1,181	0.5	0.7
BUDD–Mahayana	1	NR	NR	1,250	0.5	0.7
Calv Chpl	1	NR	NR	NR	-	-
Catholic	6	NR	NR	18,933	8.2	10.9
Ch Cr, Scientst	1	NR	NR	NR	-	-
Chr & Miss Al	2	41	46	61	0.0	0.0

NR–Not Reported - Represents no adherents reported. Percentages may not total 100 due to rounding.

Table 3: Religious Congregations by County and Group: 2010

Religious Group	Number of Congrega-tions	Number of Attendees	Number of Communicant, Confirmed, or Full Members	Adherents: Number of Adherents	Adherents: % of Total Pop.	Adherents: % of Total Adh.
CHR–Chr Chs & Chs Cr	2	NR	185	243	0.1	0.1
CHR–Chs of Christ	1	28	31	34	0.0	0.0
Evan Free Ch	1	0	NR	0	0.0	0.0
Jehovah's Witness	2	NR	NR	NR	-	-
JUD–Reform	1	24	43	116	0.1	0.1
LDS–Comm of Christ	1	NR	128	128	0.1	0.1
LDS–L-D Saints	314	NR	NR	138,648	60.0	79.6
LUTH–E.L.C.A.	2	240	543	715	0.3	0.4
LUTH–Luth Cong Msn Chr	1	169	463	609	0.3	0.3
LUTH–Luth-MO Synod	1	265	543	809	0.3	0.5
METH–AME	1	0	150	197	0.1	0.1
METH–Un Methodist	2	294	502	887	0.4	0.5
Muslim Est	1	100	NR	100	0.0	0.1
Non-denom Chr Chs	10	3,390	3,460	4,271	1.8	2.5
ORTHE–Greek Orthodox	1	110	NR	350	0.2	0.2
PENT–Assemb of God	6	657	251	846	0.4	0.5
PENT–Ch God (Cleve)	5	1,100	1,018	1,339	0.6	0.8
PENT–Ch of God Proph	2	NR	112	147	0.1	0.1
PENT–COGIC	2	0	300	394	0.2	0.2
PENT–Int Foursq Gos	3	197	160	210	0.1	0.1
PENT–Pent Ch of God	2	140	NR	217	0.1	0.1
PENT–Un Pent Ch Intl	1	NR	NR	NR	-	-
PRES–Orth Pres Ch	1	31	0	0	0.0	0.0
PRES–Presb Ch (USA)	3	220	464	610	0.3	0.4
Salvation Army	1	53	38	136	0.1	0.1
Sev Day Adv	2	302	524	603	0.3	0.3
Sikh	1	NR	NR	NR	-	-
Un C of Christ	2	45	99	130	0.1	0.1
Unit Univ	1	90	112	142	0.1	0.1
VERMONT	**854**	**33,702**	**56,004**	**210,391**	**33.6**	**100.0**
ADDISON	**52**	**1,914**	**3,422**	**10,744**	**29.2**	**100.0**
ANG/EPIS–Episcopal	2	163	433	575	1.6	5.4
Bahá'í	0	NR	19	19	0.1	0.2
BAPT–Amer Bapt USA	5	336	514	604	1.6	5.6
BAPT–Consrv Bapt	1	NR	NR	NR	-	-
BAPT–So Bapt Conv	3	60	26	31	0.1	0.3
BUDD–Vajrayana	2	NR	NR	53	0.1	0.5
Catholic	6	NR	NR	5,892	16.0	54.8
Ch Cr, Scientst	1	NR	NR	NR	-	-
Ch of Nazarene	1	34	53	53	0.1	0.5
CHR–Chs of Christ	1	28	20	28	0.1	0.3
CONG–Cong Chr Add'l	1	NR	27	32	0.1	0.3
CONG–Consrv Cong Chr	1	70	52	61	0.2	0.6
FRND–Fr Gen Cf & Un Mtg	2	NR	45	53	0.1	0.5
Jehovah's Witness	1	NR	NR	NR	-	-
LDS–L-D Saints	1	NR	NR	251	0.7	2.3
METH–Un Methodist	9	264	906	1,363	3.7	12.7
Non-denom Chr Chs	1	45	45	56	0.2	0.5
PENT–Assemb of God	2	267	190	369	1.0	3.4
REF–Christian Ref	1	90	143	168	0.5	1.6
REF–Un Ref Chs N.A.	1	NR	NR	NR	-	-
Sev Day Adv	1	18	30	35	0.1	0.3
Un C of Christ	8	407	736	864	2.3	8.0
Unit Univ	1	132	183	237	0.6	2.2
BENNINGTON	**51**	**2,128**	**4,758**	**12,930**	**34.8**	**100.0**
ANG/EPIS–Episcopal	3	279	1,017	1,195	3.2	9.2
Bahá'í	0	NR	24	24	0.1	0.2
BAPT–Amer Bapt USA	5	267	921	1,084	2.9	8.4
BAPT–Consrv Bapt	1	NR	NR	NR	-	-
BAPT–So Bapt Conv	5	236	207	244	0.7	1.9
Catholic	8	NR	NR	6,742	18.2	52.1
Ch Cr, Scientst	1	NR	NR	NR	-	-
Chr & Miss Al	1	99	53	166	0.4	1.3
CHR–Chr Chs & Chs Cr	1	NR	50	59	0.2	0.5
CHR–Chs of Christ	1	35	24	40	0.1	0.3
CONG–Cong Chr Add'l	1	NR	45	53	0.1	0.4
CONG–Cong Chr, NA	2	NR	134	158	0.4	1.2
FRND–Fr Gen Cf & Un Mtg	1	NR	27	32	0.1	0.2
Jehovah's Witness	1	NR	NR	NR	-	-

Religious Group	Number of Congrega-tions	Number of Attendees	Number of Communicant, Confirmed, or Full Members	Adherents: Number of Adherents	Adherents: % of Total Pop.	Adherents: % of Total Adh.
JUD–Reconst	1	85	108	292	0.8	2.3
LDS–L-D Saints	1	NR	NR	302	0.8	2.3
LUTH–E.L.C.A.	1	25	43	52	0.1	0.4
METH–Un Methodist	7	150	621	730	2.0	5.6
Non-denom Chr Chs	2	330	330	412	1.1	3.2
Sev Day Adv	1	42	73	84	0.2	0.6
Un C of Christ	6	529	1,008	1,186	3.2	9.2
Unit Univ	1	51	73	75	0.2	0.6
CALEDONIA	**62**	**2,183**	**4,098**	**10,433**	**33.4**	**100.0**
ANG/EPIS–Episcopal	3	80	126	167	0.5	1.6
Bahá'í	0	NR	4	4	0.0	0.0
BAPT–Amer Bapt USA	5	190	661	790	2.5	7.6
BAPT–So Bapt Conv	6	258	194	232	0.7	2.2
BUDD–Vajrayana	4	NR	NR	335	1.1	3.2
Catholic	6	NR	NR	4,355	13.9	41.7
CONG–Cong Chr Add'l	1	NR	140	167	0.5	1.6
CONG–Cong Chr, NA	1	NR	170	203	0.7	1.9
FRND–Fr Gen Cf & Un Mtg	1	NR	0	0	0.0	0.0
Jehovah's Witness	2	NR	NR	NR	-	-
LDS–L-D Saints	1	NR	NR	392	1.3	3.8
METH–Un Methodist	8	357	1,113	1,423	4.6	13.6
Non-denom Chr Chs	5	821	655	1,076	3.4	10.3
PENT–Assemb of God	2	70	54	117	0.4	1.1
PENT–Un Pent Ch Intl	1	NR	NR	NR	-	-
PRES–Presb Ch (USA)	3	46	215	257	0.8	2.5
Sev Day Adv	1	32	55	63	0.2	0.6
Un C of Christ	10	323	672	803	2.6	7.7
Unit Univ	2	6	39	49	0.2	0.5
CHITTENDEN	**126**	**9,680**	**12,949**	**61,199**	**39.1**	**100.0**
ANG/EPIS–Anglican NA	1	NR	NR	NR	-	-
ANG/EPIS–Episcopal	6	587	1,154	1,674	1.1	2.7
Bahá'í	1	NR	79	79	0.1	0.1
BAPT–Amer Bapt USA	9	560	1,043	1,227	0.8	2.0
BAPT–Converge/BGC	2	475	NR	570	0.4	0.9
BAPT–So Bapt Conv	4	543	257	302	0.2	0.5
BUDD–Mahayana	5	NR	NR	148	0.1	0.2
BUDD–Vajrayana	1	NR	NR	52	0.0	0.1
Calv Chpl	1	NR	NR	NR	-	-
Catholic	19	NR	NR	39,143	25.0	64.0
Ch Cr, Scientst	1	NR	NR	NR	-	-
Ch of Nazarene	1	46	53	53	0.0	0.1
Chr & Miss Al	4	1,924	688	3,943	2.5	6.4
CHR–Chs of Christ	2	145	102	138	0.1	0.2
CHR–Int Chs of Christ	1	NR	21	25	0.0	0.0
CONG–Consrv Cong Chr	1	152	153	180	0.1	0.3
Evan Cov Ch	1	76	94	99	0.1	0.2
Evan Free Ch	1	80	NR	80	0.1	0.1
FRND–Fr Gen Cf & Un Mtg	2	NR	78	92	0.1	0.2
HINDU–Post Ren	2	NR	NR	102	0.1	0.2
Jehovah's Witness	1	NR	NR	NR	-	-
JUD–Conserv	1	282	317	856	0.5	1.4
JUD–Orth	1	43	50	60	0.0	0.1
JUD–Reform	1	117	206	556	0.4	0.9
LDS–L-D Saints	2	NR	NR	914	0.6	1.5
LUTH–E.L.C.A.	2	152	358	385	0.2	0.6
LUTH–Luth-MO Synod	1	134	284	354	0.2	0.6
METH–Free Methodist	1	0	0	0	0.0	0.0
METH–Un Methodist	12	737	2,185	2,597	1.7	4.2
Muslim Est	1	100	NR	300	0.2	0.5
Non-denom Chr Chs	12	1,410	1,855	2,074	1.3	3.4
ORTHE–Greek Orthodox	1	35	NR	100	0.1	0.2
PENT–Assemb of God	5	368	279	522	0.3	0.9
PENT–Un Pent Ch Intl	2	NR	NR	NR	-	-
PENT–Vineyard	1	17	23	27	0.0	0.0
PRES–Presb Ch (USA)	1	48	67	79	0.1	0.1
Salvation Army	1	44	73	185	0.1	0.3
Sev Day Adv	1	43	75	86	0.1	0.1
Un C of Christ	11	1,200	2,867	3,373	2.2	5.5
Unit Univ	2	362	588	824	0.5	1.3
Unity Ch	1	NR	NR	NR	-	-

NR–Not Reported   - Represents no adherents reported.   Percentages may not total 100 due to rounding.

Table 3: Religious Congregations by County and Group: 2010

Religious Group	Number of Congrega-tions	Number of Attendees	Number of Communicant, Confirmed, or Full Members	Adherents: Number of Adherents	Adherents: % of Total Pop.	Adherents: % of Total Adh.
ESSEX	**13**	**89**	**307**	**982**	**15.6**	**100.0**
ANG/EPIS–Episcopal	2	13	26	40	0.6	4.1
Bahá'í	0	NR	3	3	0.0	0.3
BRETH–Grace Breth	1	NR	NR	NR	-	-
Catholic	2	NR	NR	619	9.8	63.0
CONG–Cong Chr Add'l	1	NR	4	5	0.1	0.5
METH–Un Methodist	6	66	254	292	4.6	29.7
Un C of Christ	1	10	20	23	0.4	2.3
FRANKLIN	**54**	**1,667**	**2,917**	**20,701**	**43.4**	**100.0**
ANG/EPIS–Episcopal	5	143	373	454	1.0	2.2
Bahá'í	0	NR	6	6	0.0	0.0
BAPT–Amer Bapt USA	4	175	348	428	0.9	2.1
BAPT–So Bapt Conv	2	46	44	54	0.1	0.3
Catholic	15	NR	NR	16,526	34.6	79.8
Ch of Nazarene	1	21	35	46	0.1	0.2
CONG–Consrv Cong Chr	1	100	125	154	0.3	0.7
Jehovah's Witness	2	NR	NR	NR	-	-
LDS–L-D Saints	1	NR	NR	210	0.4	1.0
METH–Un Methodist	17	592	1,552	2,047	4.3	9.9
PENT–Assemb of God	2	421	249	542	1.1	2.6
PRES–Presb Ch Amer	1	48	48	66	0.1	0.3
Sev Day Adv	1	6	10	12	0.0	0.1
Un C of Christ	2	115	127	156	0.3	0.8
GRAND ISLE	**10**	**161**	**485**	**3,275**	**47.0**	**100.0**
ANG/EPIS–Episcopal	1	8	15	18	0.3	0.5
Bahá'í	0	NR	1	1	0.0	0.0
Catholic	5	NR	NR	2,609	37.4	79.7
METH–Un Methodist	3	79	278	423	6.1	12.9
Un C of Christ	1	74	191	224	3.2	6.8
LAMOILLE	**31**	**873**	**1,313**	**4,628**	**18.9**	**100.0**
ANG/EPIS–Episcopal	1	47	73	111	0.5	2.4
Bahá'í	0	NR	14	14	0.1	0.3
BAPT–So Bapt Conv	1	NR	NR	NR	-	-
BUDD–Mahayana	1	NR	NR	11	0.0	0.2
Catholic	7	NR	NR	2,339	9.6	50.5
Ch of Nazarene	3	271	266	649	2.7	14.0
Ind Fund Churches	1	NR	NR	NR	-	-
Jehovah's Witness	2	NR	NR	NR	-	-
LDS–L-D Saints	1	NR	NR	319	1.3	6.9
METH–Un Methodist	3	98	355	431	1.8	9.3
Non-denom Chr Chs	2	165	175	210	0.9	4.5
PENT–Assemb of God	1	50	19	50	0.2	1.1
Sev Day Adv	1	15	26	30	0.1	0.6
Un C of Christ	7	227	385	464	1.9	10.0
ORANGE	**51**	**1,437**	**2,390**	**4,145**	**14.3**	**100.0**
ANG/EPIS–Episcopal	2	74	159	188	0.6	4.5
Bahá'í	0	NR	17	17	0.1	0.4
BAPT–Amer Bapt USA	3	157	182	216	0.7	5.2
BAPT–Consrv Bapt	1	NR	NR	NR	-	-
BAPT–So Bapt Conv	3	121	178	211	0.7	5.1
Catholic	5	NR	NR	1,218	4.2	29.4
Ch Cr, Scientist	1	NR	NR	NR	-	-
Ch of Nazarene	1	0	27	27	0.1	0.7
CONG–Cong Chr Add'l	1	NR	15	18	0.1	0.4
Evan Free Ch	1	55	NR	55	0.2	1.3
FRND–Fr Gen Cf & Un Mtg	1	NR	0	0	0.0	0.0
METH–Un Methodist	7	219	387	484	1.7	11.7
PENT–Assemb of God	1	75	40	75	0.3	1.8
PENT–Un Pent Ch Intl	2	NR	NR	NR	-	-
PRES–Presb Ch (USA)	1	38	49	58	0.2	1.4
Sev Day Adv	2	35	61	70	0.2	1.7
Un C of Christ	18	649	1,248	1,479	5.1	35.7
Unit Univ	1	14	27	29	0.1	0.7
ORLEANS	**53**	**1,417**	**1,842**	**7,942**	**29.2**	**100.0**
ANG/EPIS–Episcopal	1	52	142	183	0.7	2.3
Bahá'í	0	NR	13	13	0.0	0.2
BAPT–Amer Bapt USA	1	45	50	60	0.2	0.8
Catholic	12	NR	NR	5,312	19.5	66.9
Ch Cr, Scientist	1	NR	NR	NR	-	-
Ch of Nazarene	2	80	52	163	0.6	2.1
CHR–Chs of Christ	1	25	17	30	0.1	0.4
CONG–Consrv Cong Chr	2	62	78	93	0.3	1.2
Evan Free Ch	1	90	NR	90	0.3	1.1
FRND–Fr Gen Cf & Un Mtg	2	NR	15	18	0.1	0.2
Ind Fund Churches	1	NR	NR	NR	-	-
Jehovah's Witness	1	NR	NR	NR	-	-
LDS–L-D Saints	1	NR	NR	281	1.0	3.5
METH–Un Methodist	7	216	396	397	1.5	5.0
Non-denom Chr Chs	3	171	181	227	0.8	2.9
PENT–Assemb of God	2	87	65	91	0.3	1.1
PENT–Ch God (Cleve)	1	134	58	69	0.3	0.9
PRES–Presb Ch (USA)	1	51	79	94	0.3	1.2
Sev Day Adv	1	30	51	59	0.2	0.7
Un C of Christ	11	354	616	733	2.7	9.2
Unit Univ	1	20	29	29	0.1	0.4
RUTLAND	**97**	**3,159**	**5,949**	**23,636**	**38.3**	**100.0**
ANG/EPIS–Anglican NA	1	NR	NR	NR	-	-
ANG/EPIS–Episcopal	6	222	474	666	1.1	2.8
Ap Chr Ch-Amer	1	30	10	30	0.0	0.1
Bahá'í	0	NR	19	19	0.0	0.1
BAPT–Amer Bapt Assn	1	NR	85	99	0.2	0.4
BAPT–Amer Bapt USA	5	163	837	978	1.6	4.1
BAPT–N Am Bapt Conf	1	NR	37	43	0.1	0.2
BAPT–Ref Bapt Ch	1	NR	NR	NR	-	-
BAPT–So Bapt Conv	5	206	189	221	0.4	0.9
Catholic	17	NR	NR	15,500	25.1	65.6
Ch Cr, Scientist	1	NR	NR	NR	-	-
Ch of Nazarene	1	24	15	42	0.1	0.2
Chr & Miss Al	1	69	50	137	0.2	0.6
CHR–Chr Chs & Chs Cr	2	NR	60	70	0.1	0.3
CHR–Chs of Christ	1	32	26	42	0.1	0.2
CONG–Cong Chr Add'l	1	NR	13	15	0.0	0.1
CONG–Consrv Cong Chr	1	18	55	64	0.1	0.3
FRND–Fr Gen Cf & Un Mtg	1	NR	11	13	0.0	0.1
Jehovah's Witness	1	NR	NR	NR	-	-
JUD–Conserv	1	50	56	151	0.2	0.6
LDS–L-D Saints	1	NR	NR	252	0.4	1.1
LUTH–E.L.C.A.	2	86	279	308	0.5	1.3
LUTH–Luth–MO Synod	1	20	32	34	0.1	0.1
METH–Un Methodist	10	321	818	1,056	1.7	4.5
METH–Wesleyan	2	90	38	118	0.2	0.5
Non-denom Chr Chs	10	861	925	1,213	2.0	5.1
ORTHE–Greek Orthodox	1	20	NR	85	0.1	0.4
PENT–Assemb of God	2	162	78	227	0.4	1.0
PENT–Ch God (Cleve)	1	10	7	8	0.0	0.0
PENT–I F Chr Assmbl	1	NR	NR	NR	-	-
PENT–Un Pent Ch Intl	1	NR	NR	NR	-	-
PRES–Presb Ch (USA)	1	61	42	49	0.1	0.2
Salvation Army	1	28	59	164	0.3	0.7
Sev Day Adv	1	38	65	75	0.1	0.3
Un C of Christ	12	585	1,591	1,859	3.0	7.9
Unit Univ	1	63	78	98	0.2	0.4
WASHINGTON	**89**	**3,381**	**5,646**	**20,984**	**35.2**	**100.0**
ANG/EPIS–Episcopal	4	187	409	499	0.8	2.4
Bahá'í	0	NR	37	37	0.1	0.2
BAPT–Amer Bapt USA	3	84	126	149	0.3	0.7
BAPT–So Bapt Conv	6	275	227	269	0.5	1.3
BUDD–Vajrayana	2	NR	NR	89	0.1	0.4
Catholic	9	NR	NR	12,800	21.5	61.0
Ch Cr, Scientist	1	NR	NR	NR	-	-
Chr & Miss Al	3	215	185	394	0.7	1.9
CHR–Chs of Christ	1	25	33	43	0.1	0.2
CONG–Cong Chr Add'l	1	NR	17	20	0.0	0.1
Evan Free Ch	2	263	NR	263	0.4	1.3
FRND–Fr Gen Cf & Un Mtg	1	NR	25	30	0.1	0.1
HINDU–Post Ren	1	NR	NR	54	0.1	0.3
Jehovah's Witness	2	NR	NR	NR	-	-

NR–Not Reported - Represents no adherents reported. Percentages may not total 100 due to rounding.

Table 3: Religious Congregations by County and Group: 2010

Religious Group	Number of Congrega-tions	Number of Attendees	Number of Communicant, Confirmed, or Full Members	Adherents		
				Number of Adherents	% of Total Pop.	% of Total Adh.
LDS–L-D Saints	1	NR	NR	521	0.9	2.5
LUTH–E.L.C.A.	1	38	85	114	0.2	0.5
LUTH–Luth-MO Synod	1	60	109	109	0.2	0.5
LUTH–Wisc Ev Luth Syn	1	39	56	69	0.1	0.3
METH–Un Methodist	14	448	1,808	2,265	3.8	10.8
METH–Wesleyan	1	20	13	26	0.0	0.1
New Apost Ch	1	NR	NR	NR	-	-
Non-denom Chr Chs	6	390	432	595	1.0	2.8
ORTHE–Orth Ch in Amer	1	30	NR	50	0.1	0.2
PENT–Assemb of God	1	43	32	60	0.1	0.3
PENT–Ch of God Proph	2	NR	48	57	0.1	0.3
PENT–COGIC	1	30	30	36	0.1	0.2
PENT–Un Pent Ch Intl	1	NR	NR	NR	-	-
PRES–Orth Pres Ch	1	71	70	95	0.2	0.5
PRES–Presb Ch (USA)	2	70	159	188	0.3	0.9
Salvation Army	1	37	64	92	0.2	0.4
Sev Day Adv	1	95	165	190	0.3	0.9
Un C of Christ	12	645	1,221	1,446	2.4	6.9
Unit Univ	4	316	295	424	0.7	2.0
WINDHAM	**71**	**2,322**	**3,924**	**13,838**	**31.1**	**100.0**
ANG/EPIS–Episcopal	3	199	333	407	0.9	2.9
Bahá'í	1	NR	72	72	0.2	0.5
BAPT–Amer Bapt USA	13	395	884	1,038	2.3	7.5
BAPT–Consrv Bapt	1	NR	NR	NR	-	-
BUDD–Mahayana	3	NR	NR	32	0.1	0.2
BUDD–Vajrayana	3	NR	NR	131	0.3	0.9
Calv Chpl	1	NR	NR	NR	-	-
Catholic	8	NR	NR	8,753	19.7	63.3
Ch Cr, Scientst	1	NR	NR	NR	-	-
Chr & Miss Al	1	48	42	64	0.1	0.5
CHR–Chs of Christ	1	84	61	105	0.2	0.8
CONG–Cong Chr Add'l	1	NR	26	31	0.1	0.2
CONG–Consrv Cong Chr	1	40	55	65	0.1	0.5
FRND–Fr Gen Cf & Un Mtg	1	NR	92	108	0.2	0.8
Jehovah's Witness	1	NR	NR	NR	-	-
JUD–Reform	1	59	104	281	0.6	2.0
LUTH–E.L.C.A.	1	42	112	112	0.3	0.8
METH–Un Methodist	2	71	120	154	0.3	1.1
Non-denom Chr Chs	4	405	395	507	1.1	3.7
PENT–Assemb of God	2	100	41	105	0.2	0.8
Sev Day Adv	2	90	156	180	0.4	1.3
Tao	1	NR	NR	NR	-	-
Un C of Christ	17	724	1,330	1,562	3.5	11.3
Unit Univ	1	65	101	131	0.3	0.9
WINDSOR	**94**	**3,291**	**6,004**	**14,954**	**26.4**	**100.0**
ANG/EPIS–Anglican NA	1	NR	NR	NR	-	-
ANG/EPIS–Episcopal	8	333	764	822	1.5	5.5
Bahá'í	0	NR	37	37	0.1	0.2
BAPT–Amer Bapt USA	4	251	515	604	1.1	4.0
BAPT–So Bapt Conv	3	205	261	306	0.5	2.0
BUDD–Mahayana	2	NR	NR	22	0.0	0.1
BUDD–Vajrayana	1	NR	NR	53	0.1	0.4
Catholic	10	NR	NR	6,485	11.4	43.4
Ch Cr, Scientst	2	NR	NR	NR	-	-
CHR–Chs of Christ	2	150	186	225	0.4	1.5
CONG–Cong Chr Add'l	1	NR	5	6	0.0	0.0
CONG–Consrv Cong Chr	1	40	70	82	0.1	0.5
Evan Free Ch	2	120	NR	120	0.2	0.8
FRND–Fr Gen Cf & Un Mtg	1	NR	0	0	0.0	0.0
HINDU–Post Ren	1	NR	NR	16	0.0	0.1
Jehovah's Witness	1	NR	NR	NR	-	-
JUD–Reform	1	51	90	243	0.4	1.6
LDS–L-D Saints	2	NR	NR	942	1.7	6.3
MENN–Mennonite USA	2	95	98	115	0.2	0.8
METH–Un Methodist	12	322	837	1,048	1.8	7.0
Non-denom Chr Chs	5	440	550	619	1.1	4.1
ORTHE–Orth Ch in Amer	1	25	NR	55	0.1	0.4
PENT–Assemb of God	3	105	79	172	0.3	1.2
PENT–Int Foursq Gos	1	86	84	99	0.2	0.7
Sev Day Adv	1	6	10	12	0.0	0.1
Un C of Christ	19	773	1,893	2,220	3.9	14.8

Religious Group	Number of Congrega-tions	Number of Attendees	Number of Communicant, Confirmed, or Full Members	Adherents		
				Number of Adherents	% of Total Pop.	% of Total Adh.
Unit Univ	7	289	525	651	1.1	4.4
VIRGINIA	**10,088**	**1,094,227**	**2,067,179**	**3,586,592**	**44.8**	**100.0**
ACCOMACK	**96**	**4,672**	**11,241**	**13,974**	**42.1**	**100.0**
ANG/EPIS–Episcopal	4	133	248	301	0.9	2.2
Bahá'í	0	NR	21	21	0.1	0.2
BAPT–So Bapt Conv	18	1,494	3,219	3,846	11.6	27.5
BRETH–Breth in Chr	1	NR	NR	NR	-	-
Catholic	2	NR	NR	817	2.5	5.8
Ch of Nazarene	1	30	35	35	0.1	0.3
CHR–Chs of Christ	2	50	71	94	0.3	0.7
Jehovah's Witness	1	NR	NR	NR	-	-
LDS–L-D Saints	1	NR	NR	205	0.6	1.5
LUTH–Luth-MO Synod	1	14	10	10	0.0	0.1
METH–AME	6	0	750	896	2.7	6.4
METH–Un Methodist	43	2,113	5,661	6,284	18.9	45.0
METH–Wesleyan	1	19	17	25	0.1	0.2
Non-denom Chr Chs	4	455	550	626	1.9	4.5
PENT–Assemb of God	1	30	13	44	0.1	0.3
PENT–Ch God (Cleve)	2	210	436	521	1.6	3.7
PENT–Un Pent Ch Intl	1	NR	NR	NR	-	-
PRES–Presb Ch (USA)	5	98	164	196	0.6	1.4
PRES–Presb Ch Amer	1	0	0	0	0.0	0.0
Sev Day Adv	1	26	46	53	0.2	0.4
ALBEMARLE	**108**	**10,181**	**18,030**	**24,809**	**25.1**	**100.0**
ANG/EPIS–Anglican NA	2	NR	NR	NR	-	-
ANG/EPIS–Episcopal	11	1,670	3,573	4,360	4.4	17.6
Bahá'í	1	NR	68	68	0.1	0.3
BAPT–So Bapt Conv	29	2,851	4,776	5,722	5.8	23.1
BRETH–Ch of Brethren	5	67	407	488	0.5	2.0
BUDD–Mahayana	1	NR	NR	11	0.0	0.0
BUDD–Vajrayana	1	NR	NR	36	0.0	0.1
Catholic	1	NR	NR	166	0.2	0.7
Ch of Nazarene	1	148	136	195	0.2	0.8
Chr & Miss Al	1	25	16	40	0.0	0.2
CHR–Chr Ch (Disc)	1	65	160	192	0.2	0.8
CHR–Chr Chs & Chs Cr	1	NR	500	599	0.6	2.4
CHR–Chs of Christ	2	137	136	208	0.2	0.8
HINDU–Post Ren	1	NR	NR	25	0.0	0.1
Jehovah's Witness	1	NR	NR	NR	-	-
LDS–L-D Saints	4	NR	NR	2,222	2.2	9.0
LUTH–E.L.C.A.	1	200	281	346	0.3	1.4
MENN–Mennonite USA	1	6	17	20	0.0	0.1
METH–Un Methodist	15	1,079	3,047	3,865	3.9	15.6
METH–Wesleyan	1	40	47	52	0.1	0.2
Non-denom Chr Chs	7	1,045	1,270	1,350	1.4	5.4
PENT–Assemb of God	2	440	164	530	0.5	2.1
PENT–Ch God (Cleve)	2	538	875	1,048	1.1	4.2
PENT–Ch Lord Jesus Apos	1	NR	NR	NR	-	-
PENT–Intl Pent Holiness	1	30	40	48	0.0	0.2
PENT–Un Pent Ch Intl	1	NR	NR	NR	-	-
PENT–Vineyard	1	40	50	60	0.1	0.2
PRES–Evan Presby Ch	1	NR	89	107	0.1	0.4
PRES–Orth Pres Ch	1	38	40	59	0.1	0.2
PRES–Presb Ch (USA)	6	405	758	908	0.9	3.7
PRES–Presb Ch Amer	2	1,357	1,580	2,084	2.1	8.4
Sikh	1	NR	NR	NR	-	-
Unity Ch	1	NR	NR	NR	-	-
ALEXANDRIA (CITY)	**95**	**13,025**	**30,483**	**63,951**	**45.7**	**100.0**
ANG/EPIS–Anglican NA	1	NR	NR	NR	-	-
ANG/EPIS–Episcopal	8	1,888	7,437	8,139	5.8	12.7
Bahá'í	1	NR	140	140	0.1	0.2
BAPT–Amer Bapt USA	3	55	900	1,051	0.8	1.6
BAPT–NBC USA	4	2,350	4,785	5,587	4.0	8.7
BAPT–Prog NBC	1	0	150	175	0.1	0.3
BAPT–Reg Bapt Gen As	1	NR	NR	NR	-	-
BAPT–So Bapt Conv	9	1,444	4,857	5,671	4.1	8.9
BRETH–Grace Breth	1	NR	NR	NR	-	-

NR–Not Reported   - Represents no adherents reported.   Percentages may not total 100 due to rounding.

Table 3: Religious Congregations by County and Group: 2010

Religious Group	Number of Congrega- tions	Number of Attendees	Number of Communicant, Confirmed, or Full Members	Adherents		
				Number of Adherents	% of Total Pop.	% of Total Adh.
BUDD–Mahayana	2	NR	NR	152	0.1	0.2
BUDD–Vajrayana	1	NR	NR	41	0.0	0.1
Catholic	4	NR	NR	18,596	13.3	29.1
Ch Cr, Scientst	1	NR	NR	NR	-	-
Ch of Nazarene	2	84	91	205	0.1	0.3
CHR–Chr Ch (Disc)	1	70	152	177	0.1	0.3
CHR–Chs of Christ	2	150	109	145	0.1	0.2
HINDU–Post Ren	1	NR	NR	25	0.0	0.0
Jehovah's Witness	2	NR	NR	NR	-	-
JUD–Conserv	1	440	494	1,334	1.0	2.1
JUD–Orth	1	43	50	60	0.0	0.1
JUD–Reform	1	367	648	1,750	1.3	2.7
LDS–L-D Saints	4	NR	NR	2,929	2.1	4.6
LUTH–E.L.C.A.	1	176	313	440	0.3	0.7
LUTH–Luth–MO Synod	1	148	236	301	0.2	0.5
METH–AME Zion	1	0	100	117	0.1	0.2
METH–C.M.E.	1	150	300	350	0.3	0.5
METH–Free Methodist	1	93	77	93	0.1	0.1
METH–Un Methodist	8	1,061	3,359	4,671	3.3	7.3
METH–Wesleyan	1	350	301	455	0.3	0.7
Muslim Est	1	792	NR	3,436	2.5	5.4
New Apost Ch	1	NR	NR	NR	-	-
Non-denom Chr Chs	3	396	416	508	0.4	0.8
ORTHE–Orth Ch in Amer	1	100	NR	400	0.3	0.6
ORTHO–Ethiopian Orth	1	NR	NR	NR	-	-
PENT–Assemb of God	1	465	161	600	0.4	0.9
PENT–Ch God (Cleve)	2	125	579	676	0.5	1.1
PENT–Ch Lord Jesus Apos	1	NR	NR	NR	-	-
PENT–COGIC	2	0	500	584	0.4	0.9
PENT–Full Gosp Bapt	1	NR	NR	NR	-	-
PENT–Int Foursq Gos	1	33	50	58	0.0	0.1
PENT–United Holy Ch	1	NR	NR	NR	-	-
PRES–Korean Pres Amer	1	NR	NR	NR	-	-
PRES–Presb Ch (USA)	4	792	2,137	2,495	1.8	3.9
PRES–Presb Ch Amer	2	473	433	617	0.4	1.0
Salvation Army	2	180	318	362	0.3	0.6
Sev Day Adv	3	800	1,390	1,599	1.1	2.5
Unity Ch	1	NR	NR	NR	-	-
Zoroastrian	0	NR	NR	12	0.0	0.0
ALLEGHANY	**40**	**1,899**	**4,795**	**5,614**	**34.5**	**100.0**
ANG/EPIS–Episcopal	1	11	17	25	0.2	0.4
BAPT–So Bapt Conv	5	358	1,488	1,766	10.9	31.5
BRETH–Ch of Brethren	1	22	26	31	0.2	0.6
Catholic	1	NR	NR	111	0.7	2.0
Ch of Nazarene	1	47	64	85	0.5	1.5
CHR–Chr Ch (Disc)	1	26	162	192	1.2	3.4
CHR–Chr Chs & Chs Cr	1	NR	65	77	0.5	1.4
Jehovah's Witness	1	NR	NR	NR	-	-
METH–Un Methodist	14	501	1,673	1,712	10.5	30.5
Non-denom Chr Chs	4	520	600	688	4.2	12.3
PENT–Assemb of God	2	101	94	208	1.3	3.7
PENT–Ch of God Proph	1	NR	45	53	0.3	0.9
PENT–COGIC	1	50	70	83	0.5	1.5
PRES–Presb Ch (USA)	6	263	491	583	3.6	10.4
AMELIA	**31**	**1,804**	**3,644**	**4,583**	**36.1**	**100.0**
ANG/EPIS–Episcopal	1	40	75	75	0.6	1.6
Bahá'í	0	NR	5	5	0.0	0.1
BAPT–So Bapt Conv	9	924	2,015	2,433	19.2	53.1
Catholic	1	NR	NR	218	1.7	4.8
CHR–Chr Ch (Disc)	1	0	11	13	0.1	0.3
Jehovah's Witness	1	NR	NR	NR	-	-
LUTH–Luth–MO Synod	1	23	41	45	0.4	1.0
METH–Un Methodist	7	282	711	812	6.4	17.7
Non-denom Chr Chs	1	190	170	238	1.9	5.2
PENT–Ch God (Cleve)	1	80	99	120	0.9	2.6
PENT–Ch of God by Faith	1	NR	NR	NR	-	-
PENT–Int Foursq Gos	1	161	298	360	2.8	7.9
PRES–Presb Ch (USA)	6	104	219	264	2.1	5.8
AMHERST	**61**	**5,143**	**10,909**	**13,339**	**41.2**	**100.0**
ANG/EPIS–Episcopal	4	98	147	259	0.8	1.9

Religious Group	Number of Congrega- tions	Number of Attendees	Number of Communicant, Confirmed, or Full Members	Adherents		
				Number of Adherents	% of Total Pop.	% of Total Adh.
Bahá'í	0	NR	4	4	0.0	0.0
BAPT–So Bapt Conv	18	2,155	4,884	5,811	18.0	43.6
BRETH–Ch of Brethren	1	44	146	174	0.5	1.3
Calv Chpl	1	NR	NR	NR	-	-
Catholic	1	NR	NR	184	0.6	1.4
Ch of Nazarene	1	33	57	89	0.3	0.7
CHR–Chr Ch (Disc)	1	60	242	288	0.9	2.2
CHR–Chr Chs & Chs Cr	1	NR	447	532	1.6	4.0
Jehovah's Witness	1	NR	NR	NR	-	-
METH–Un Methodist	12	512	1,916	2,427	7.5	18.2
Non-denom Chr Chs	14	2,005	2,390	2,767	8.6	20.7
PENT–Ch God (Cleve)	1	100	150	178	0.6	1.3
PENT–Intl Pent Holiness	1	15	61	73	0.2	0.5
PRES–Presb Ch (USA)	4	121	465	553	1.7	4.1
APPOMATTOX	**34**	**1,862**	**4,638**	**5,613**	**37.5**	**100.0**
ANG/EPIS–Anglican NA	1	NR	NR	NR	-	-
ANG/EPIS–Episcopal	1	32	64	64	0.4	1.1
Bahá'í	0	NR	3	3	0.0	0.1
BAPT–So Bapt Conv	8	843	2,491	3,002	20.0	53.5
Catholic	1	NR	NR	155	1.0	2.8
METH–Un Methodist	8	523	1,337	1,492	10.0	26.6
Non-denom Chr Chs	2	160	185	200	1.3	3.6
PENT–Assemb of God	1	28	0	28	0.2	0.5
PENT–Ch God (Cleve)	1	31	26	31	0.2	0.6
PENT–Ch of God Proph	1	NR	36	43	0.3	0.8
PENT–Intl Pent Holiness	3	112	213	257	1.7	4.6
PRES–Presb Ch (USA)	6	102	229	276	1.8	4.9
Sev Day Adv	1	31	54	62	0.4	1.1
ARLINGTON	**113**	**12,493**	**23,339**	**64,834**	**31.2**	**100.0**
ANG/EPIS–Anglican NA	2	NR	NR	NR	-	-
ANG/EPIS–Episcopal	9	1,371	3,520	4,113	2.0	6.3
Bahá'í	1	NR	150	150	0.1	0.2
BAPT–Amer Bapt USA	3	585	990	1,138	0.5	1.8
BAPT–Free Will Bapt	1	NR	52	60	0.0	0.1
BAPT–NBC USA	2	1,500	3,300	3,792	1.8	5.8
BAPT–Prog NBC	2	225	310	356	0.2	0.5
BAPT–S-D Baptist Gen Con	1	90	70	80	0.0	0.1
BAPT–So Bapt Conv	19	1,159	2,398	2,756	1.3	4.3
BRETH–Ch of Brethren	1	49	99	114	0.1	0.2
Catholic	7	NR	NR	30,311	14.6	46.8
CGOD–Ch God (Ander)	2	99	NR	99	0.0	0.2
Ch Cr, Scientst	1	NR	NR	NR	-	-
Ch of Nazarene	1	38	46	58	0.0	0.1
Chr & Miss Al	1	31	30	39	0.0	0.1
CHR–Chr Ch (Disc)	1	0	0	0	0.0	0.0
CHR–Chs of Christ	2	238	220	274	0.1	0.4
Christian Brethren	1	NR	NR	NR	-	-
Int Cou Comm Ch	1	NR	NR	NR	-	-
Jehovah's Witness	1	NR	NR	NR	-	-
JUD–Conserv	1	158	177	478	0.2	0.7
LDS–L-D Saints	4	NR	NR	1,733	0.8	2.7
LUTH–E.L.C.A.	3	390	878	1,142	0.6	1.8
LUTH–Luth–MO Synod	1	230	353	595	0.3	0.9
METH–AME Zion	3	150	325	373	0.2	0.6
METH–Un Methodist	12	1,433	4,756	6,323	3.0	9.8
Muslim Est	1	792	NR	3,436	1.7	5.3
Non-denom Chr Chs	8	1,880	1,922	2,353	1.1	3.6
PENT–Assemb of God	5	312	281	637	0.3	1.0
PRES–Presb Ch (USA)	6	637	1,355	1,557	0.7	2.4
PRES–Presb Ch Amer	2	192	193	260	0.1	0.4
Salvation Army	2	107	264	379	0.2	0.6
Sev Day Adv	2	116	201	231	0.1	0.4
Un C of Christ	2	212	561	645	0.3	1.0
Unit Univ	1	499	888	1,337	0.6	2.1
Unity Ch	1	NR	NR	NR	-	-
Zoroastrian	0	NR	NR	15	0.0	0.0
AUGUSTA	**129**	**11,100**	**22,519**	**28,087**	**38.1**	**100.0**
Bahá'í	0	NR	21	21	0.0	0.1
BAPT–NBC USA	1	60	60	72	0.1	0.3
BAPT–Ref Bapt Ch	1	NR	NR	NR	-	-

NR–Not Reported - Represents no adherents reported. Percentages may not total 100 due to rounding.

Table 3: Religious Congregations by County and Group: 2010

Religious Group	Number of Congrega-tions	Number of Attendees	Number of Communicant, Confirmed, or Full Members	Adherents: Number of Adherents	Adherents: % of Total Pop.	Adherents: % of Total Adh.
BAPT–So Bapt Conv	12	1,340	2,796	3,333	4.5	11.9
BRETH–Ch of Brethren	19	1,098	3,319	3,957	5.4	14.1
Calv Chpl	1	NR	NR	NR	-	-
Ch of Nazarene	3	609	911	1,565	2.1	5.6
CHR–Chr Ch (Disc)	1	0	21	25	0.0	0.1
CHR–Chr Chs & Chs Cr	2	NR	623	743	1.0	2.6
CHR–Chs of Christ	1	50	40	55	0.1	0.2
LUTH–E.L.C.A.	10	494	1,008	1,132	1.5	4.0
MENN–Beachy Amish-Menn	1	199	130	199	0.3	0.7
MENN–Ber Amish-Menn	1	17	9	17	0.0	0.1
MENN–Mennonite USA	4	419	391	466	0.6	1.7
METH–Un Methodist	28	2,368	6,336	8,133	11.0	29.0
Non-denom Chr Chs	8	1,485	1,825	2,121	2.9	7.6
ORTHE–Rus Orth Abroad	1	40	NR	60	0.1	0.2
PENT–Assemb of God	1	275	185	411	0.6	1.5
PENT–Ch God (Cleve)	3	156	134	160	0.2	0.6
PENT–Ch of God Proph	2	NR	68	81	0.1	0.3
PENT–Int Foursq Gos	2	502	748	892	1.2	3.2
PENT–Pent Ch of God	1	70	NR	109	0.1	0.4
PENT–Un Pent Ch Intl	1	NR	NR	NR	-	-
PRES–As Ref Pres Ch	1	NR	196	234	0.3	0.8
PRES–Presb Ch (USA)	19	1,288	2,998	3,574	4.8	12.7
PRES–Presb Ch Amer	1	165	139	193	0.3	0.7
Un Breth in Cr	2	437	425	372	0.5	1.3
Un C of Christ	2	28	136	162	0.2	0.6
BATH	**18**	**715**	**2,208**	**2,465**	**52.1**	**100.0**
ANG/EPIS–Episcopal	1	37	89	90	1.9	3.7
Bahá'í	0	NR	1	1	0.0	0.0
BAPT–So Bapt Conv	2	60	267	303	6.4	12.3
BRETH–Ch of Brethren	1	0	139	158	3.3	6.4
Catholic	1	NR	NR	35	0.7	1.4
CHR–Chr Chs & Chs Cr	1	NR	80	91	1.9	3.7
METH–Un Methodist	5	196	598	605	12.8	24.5
Non-denom Chr Chs	1	80	80	100	2.1	4.1
PENT–Intl Pent Holiness	1	177	588	667	14.1	27.1
PRES–Presb Ch (USA)	5	165	366	415	8.8	16.8
BEDFORD	**106**	**11,027**	**22,288**	**28,006**	**40.8**	**100.0**
ANG/EPIS–Episcopal	4	544	530	550	0.8	2.0
Bahá'í	0	NR	13	13	0.0	0.0
BAPT–Free Will Bapt	2	NR	104	125	0.2	0.4
BAPT–So Bapt Conv	35	4,272	11,204	13,422	19.5	47.9
BRETH–Ch of Brethren	3	109	182	218	0.3	0.8
Catholic	2	NR	NR	2,119	3.1	7.6
CGOD–Ch God (Ander)	2	70	NR	70	0.1	0.2
Ch of Nazarene	1	60	33	60	0.1	0.2
Chr & Miss Al	1	50	32	70	0.1	0.2
CHR–Chr Chs & Chs Cr	2	NR	460	551	0.8	2.0
METH–Un Methodist	29	1,494	3,503	3,990	5.8	14.2
METH–Wesleyan	1	236	222	307	0.4	1.1
Non-denom Chr Chs	9	3,640	5,110	5,398	7.9	19.3
PENT–Assemb of God	1	70	35	85	0.1	0.3
PENT–Ch God (Cleve)	2	115	290	347	0.5	1.2
PENT–Ch of God Proph	1	NR	17	20	0.0	0.1
PENT–Intl Pent Holiness	2	52	80	96	0.1	0.3
PRES–Presb Ch (USA)	7	289	427	512	0.7	1.8
PRES–Presb Ch Amer	1	0	0	0	0.0	0.0
Sev Day Adv	1	26	46	53	0.1	0.2
BEDFORD (CITY)	**20**	**1,455**	**3,873**	**4,828**	**77.6**	**100.0**
ANG/EPIS–Episcopal	1	18	15	18	0.3	0.4
Bahá'í	0	NR	7	7	0.1	0.1
BAPT–Amer Bapt USA	1	50	100	119	1.9	2.5
BAPT–Free Will Bapt	1	NR	52	62	1.0	1.3
BAPT–So Bapt Conv	4	382	1,360	1,621	26.1	33.6
CHR–Chr Ch (Disc)	1	84	270	322	5.2	6.7
CHR–Chs of Christ	2	53	43	67	1.1	1.4
LDS–L-D Saints	1	NR	NR	332	5.3	6.9
METH–Un Methodist	3	275	996	1,116	17.9	23.1
Non-denom Chr Chs	4	455	780	847	13.6	17.5
PENT–Assemb of God	1	35	19	42	0.7	0.9
PRES–Presb Ch (USA)	1	103	231	275	4.4	5.7
BLAND	**34**	**894**	**1,870**	**2,099**	**30.8**	**100.0**
BAPT–So Bapt Conv	2	58	249	287	4.2	13.7
CHR–Chr Ch (Disc)	1	0	0	0	0.0	0.0
CHR–Chr Chs & Chs Cr	4	NR	168	194	2.8	9.2
LUTH–E.L.C.A.	3	75	55	66	1.0	3.1
METH–AME Zion	1	0	100	115	1.7	5.5
METH–Free Methodist	1	68	71	71	1.0	3.4
METH–Un Methodist	14	505	906	995	14.6	47.4
PENT–Ch God (Cleve)	3	117	158	182	2.7	8.7
PENT–Ch of God Proph	1	NR	25	29	0.4	1.4
PENT–Intl Pent Holiness	2	40	83	96	1.4	4.6
PRES–Presb Ch (USA)	1	24	43	50	0.7	2.4
Sev Day Adv	1	7	12	14	0.2	0.7
BOTETOURT	**80**	**5,416**	**12,284**	**15,553**	**46.9**	**100.0**
ANG/EPIS–Anglican NA	1	NR	NR	NR	-	-
ANG/EPIS–Episcopal	2	84	131	134	0.4	0.9
Bahá'í	0	NR	7	7	0.0	0.0
BAPT–Reg Bapt Gen As	1	NR	NR	NR	-	-
BAPT–So Bapt Conv	22	2,896	7,439	8,936	27.0	57.5
BRETH–Breth in Chr	1	NR	NR	NR	-	-
BRETH–Ch of Brethren	11	522	1,240	1,489	4.5	9.6
Catholic	1	NR	NR	807	2.4	5.2
CGOD–Ch God (Ander)	1	0	NR	0	0.0	0.0
CHR–Chr Chs & Chs Cr	1	NR	46	55	0.2	0.4
Jehovah's Witness	2	NR	NR	NR	-	-
LUTH–E.L.C.A.	3	103	162	176	0.5	1.1
METH–Un Methodist	12	597	1,514	1,924	5.8	12.4
METH–Wesleyan	1	41	17	53	0.2	0.3
Non-denom Chr Chs	9	843	1,040	1,129	3.4	7.3
PENT–Assemb of God	2	56	50	76	0.2	0.5
PENT–Ch God (Cleve)	1	21	57	68	0.2	0.4
PENT–Ch of God Proph	1	NR	24	29	0.1	0.2
PENT–COGIC	1	0	0	0	0.0	0.0
PRES–As Ref Pres Ch	1	NR	122	147	0.4	0.9
PRES–Presb Ch (USA)	6	253	435	523	1.6	3.4
BRISTOL (CITY)	**56**	**6,447**	**11,471**	**16,420**	**92.1**	**100.0**
ANG/EPIS–Episcopal	1	91	265	269	1.5	1.6
Bahá'í	0	NR	40	40	0.2	0.2
BAPT–Free Will Bapt	2	NR	192	230	1.3	1.4
BAPT–So Bapt Conv	10	1,063	3,032	3,627	20.3	22.1
Catholic	1	NR	NR	1,679	9.4	10.2
CGOD–Ch God (Ander)	1	85	NR	85	0.5	0.5
Ch of Nazarene	2	48	36	49	0.3	0.3
CHR–Chr Chs & Chs Cr	3	NR	350	419	2.3	2.6
CHR–Chs of Christ	2	295	320	380	2.1	2.3
LDS–L-D Saints	1	NR	NR	1,079	6.0	6.6
LUTH–E.L.C.A.	1	75	60	137	0.8	0.8
METH–AME Zion	1	0	100	120	0.7	0.7
METH–Un Methodist	7	691	2,303	2,633	14.8	16.0
Non-denom Chr Chs	11	3,340	3,760	4,269	23.9	26.0
ORTHE–Rus Orth Abroad	1	20	NR	40	0.2	0.2
PENT–Assemb of God	1	125	83	250	1.4	1.5
PENT–Ch God (Cleve)	2	194	261	312	1.7	1.9
PENT–Ch of God Proph	1	NR	3	4	0.0	0.0
PENT–Fire Bapt Hol Ch	1	NR	NR	NR	-	-
PENT–Intl Pent Holiness	2	68	83	99	0.6	0.6
PENT–Un Pent Ch Intl	1	NR	NR	NR	-	-
PRES–Presb Ch (USA)	3	338	559	669	3.8	4.1
PRES–Presb Ch Amer	1	14	24	30	0.2	0.2
BRUNSWICK	**56**	**2,534**	**6,093**	**7,518**	**43.1**	**100.0**
ANG/EPIS–Episcopal	4	115	170	235	1.3	3.1
Bahá'í	0	NR	3	3	0.0	0.0
BAPT–So Bapt Conv	10	783	1,901	2,220	12.7	29.5
Catholic	1	NR	NR	185	1.1	2.5
Ch of Chr (Hol)	1	NR	NR	NR	-	-
CHR–Chr Ch (Disc)	2	78	172	201	1.2	2.7
CHR–Chr Chs & Chs Cr	1	NR	300	350	2.0	4.7
LDS–L-D Saints	1	NR	NR	158	0.9	2.1
METH–AME Zion	4	0	400	467	2.7	6.2

NR–Not Reported - Represents no adherents reported. Percentages may not total 100 due to rounding.

Table 3: Religious Congregations by County and Group: 2010

Religious Group	Number of Congrega-tions	Number of Attendees	Number of Communicant, Confirmed, or Full Members	Adherents		
				Number of Adherents	% of Total Pop.	% of Total Adh.
METH–Un Methodist	18	576	1,921	2,084	12.0	27.7
Non-denom Chr Chs	4	665	950	988	5.7	13.1
PENT–Assemb of God	2	196	176	401	2.3	5.3
PENT–Ch Lord Jesus Apos	3	NR	NR	NR	-	-
PENT–COGIC	1	0	0	0	0.0	0.0
PENT–Pent Ch of God	1	70	NR	109	0.6	1.4
PRES–Presb Ch (USA)	3	51	100	117	0.7	1.6
BUCHANAN	**42**	**1,847**	**4,735**	**5,694**	**23.6**	**100.0**
BAPT–Amer Bapt USA	1	75	100	116	0.5	2.0
BAPT–Free Will Bapt	1	NR	52	60	0.2	1.1
BAPT–So Bapt Conv	8	657	2,309	2,682	11.1	47.1
Catholic	1	NR	NR	21	0.1	0.4
CHR–Chr Chs & Chs Cr	10	NR	985	1,144	4.7	20.1
CHR–Chs of Christ	4	190	168	212	0.9	3.7
METH–Un Methodist	5	161	350	364	1.5	6.4
Non-denom Chr Chs	2	175	180	219	0.9	3.8
PENT–Assemb of God	2	380	258	380	1.6	6.7
PENT–Ch God (Cleve)	2	16	123	143	0.6	2.5
PENT–Pent Ch of God	1	70	NR	109	0.5	1.9
PRES–Presb Ch (USA)	5	123	210	244	1.0	4.3
BUCKINGHAM	**36**	**1,329**	**2,502**	**3,465**	**20.2**	**100.0**
ANG/EPIS–Episcopal	1	9	16	17	0.1	0.5
Bahá'í	0	NR	5	5	0.0	0.1
BAPT–So Bapt Conv	9	481	1,303	1,525	8.9	44.0
Catholic	1	NR	NR	34	0.2	1.0
Ch of Nazarene	1	25	20	65	0.4	1.9
HINDU–Renaiss	2	NR	NR	312	1.8	9.0
LDS–L-D Saints	1	NR	NR	190	1.1	5.5
MENN–Beachy Amish-Menn	1	43	25	43	0.3	1.2
METH–Un Methodist	10	256	487	580	3.4	16.7
METH–Wesleyan	1	48	65	62	0.4	1.8
Non-denom Chr Chs	3	240	340	350	2.0	10.1
PENT–Ch Lord Jesus Apos	1	NR	NR	NR	-	-
PENT–Intl Pent Holiness	2	140	111	130	0.8	3.8
PRES–Presb Ch (USA)	3	87	130	152	0.9	4.4
BUENA VISTA (CITY)	**23**	**1,199**	**2,478**	**4,435**	**66.7**	**100.0**
ANG/EPIS–Episcopal	1	16	18	29	0.4	0.7
BAPT–So Bapt Conv	1	132	436	525	7.9	11.8
BRETH–Grace Breth	1	NR	NR	NR	-	-
LDS–L-D Saints	7	NR	NR	1,499	22.5	33.8
METH–Un Methodist	3	92	308	365	5.5	8.2
Non-denom Chr Chs	4	491	616	701	10.5	15.8
PENT–Ch of God Proph	1	NR	56	67	1.0	1.5
PENT–Intl Pent Holiness	2	278	701	844	12.7	19.0
PRES–Presb Ch (USA)	2	96	179	216	3.2	4.9
Sev Day Adv	1	94	164	189	2.8	4.3
CAMPBELL	**98**	**8,842**	**17,688**	**22,334**	**40.7**	**100.0**
ANG/EPIS–Anglican NA	1	NR	NR	NR	-	-
ANG/EPIS–Episcopal	1	20	49	52	0.1	0.2
Bahá'í	0	NR	3	3	0.0	0.0
BAPT–So Bapt Conv	34	4,494	9,287	11,108	20.3	49.7
CHR–Chr Chs & Chs Cr	1	NR	235	281	0.5	1.3
Evan Free Ch	1	825	NR	825	1.5	3.7
Jehovah's Witness	2	NR	NR	NR	-	-
METH–C.M.E.	1	0	150	179	0.3	0.8
METH–Un Methodist	24	1,880	5,018	6,435	11.7	28.8
METH–Wesleyan	2	44	71	57	0.1	0.3
Muslim Est	1	35	NR	150	0.3	0.7
New Apost Ch	1	NR	NR	NR	-	-
Non-denom Chr Chs	9	826	1,155	1,188	2.2	5.3
PENT–Assemb of God	1	75	64	75	0.1	0.3
PENT–Ch God (Cleve)	1	21	50	60	0.1	0.3
PENT–Ch Lord Jesus Apos	1	NR	NR	NR	-	-
PENT–Ch of God Proph	4	NR	366	438	0.8	2.0
PENT–COGIC	2	25	210	251	0.5	1.1
PENT–Intl Pent Holiness	4	189	257	307	0.6	1.4
PRES–Presb Ch (USA)	7	408	773	925	1.7	4.1

Religious Group	Number of Congrega-tions	Number of Attendees	Number of Communicant, Confirmed, or Full Members	Adherents		
				Number of Adherents	% of Total Pop.	% of Total Adh.
CAROLINE	**37**	**2,888**	**7,067**	**9,601**	**33.6**	**100.0**
ANG/EPIS–Episcopal	2	87	180	180	0.6	1.9
Bahá'í	0	NR	1	1	0.0	0.0
BAPT–NBC Amer	1	0	100	123	0.4	1.3
BAPT–Prog NBC	1	300	525	648	2.3	6.7
BAPT–So Bapt Conv	16	1,717	4,854	5,990	21.0	62.4
Catholic	1	NR	NR	771	2.7	8.0
CHR–Chr Ch (Disc)	1	14	32	39	0.1	0.4
Jehovah's Witness	1	NR	NR	NR	-	-
METH–Un Methodist	7	552	1,094	1,536	5.4	16.0
Non-denom Chr Chs	3	188	238	260	0.9	2.7
PENT–Ch Lord Jesus Apos	1	NR	NR	NR	-	-
PENT–United Holy Ch	1	NR	NR	NR	-	-
PRES–Korean Amer Pres	1	NR	NR	NR	-	-
PRES–Presb Ch (USA)	1	30	43	53	0.2	0.6
CARROLL	**74**	**4,601**	**8,533**	**10,470**	**34.9**	**100.0**
Bahá'í	0	NR	1	1	0.0	0.0
BAPT–So Bapt Conv	22	2,137	4,490	5,330	17.7	50.9
BRETH–Breth in Chr	1	NR	NR	NR	-	-
BRETH–Ch of Brethren	2	166	231	274	0.9	2.6
Catholic	1	NR	NR	257	0.9	2.5
CHR–Chr Ch (Disc)	4	103	287	341	1.1	3.3
CHR–Chr Chs & Chs Cr	1	NR	100	119	0.4	1.1
CHR–Chs of Christ	4	249	235	293	1.0	2.8
FRND–Fr Un Mtg	2	NR	25	30	0.1	0.3
LUTH–E.L.C.A.	1	54	100	110	0.4	1.1
METH–Un Methodist	13	847	1,773	2,107	7.0	20.1
METH–Wesleyan	1	14	18	18	0.1	0.2
MORAV–Morav Ch-South	2	116	107	135	0.4	1.3
Non-denom Chr Chs	5	327	284	408	1.4	3.9
PENT–Ch God (Cleve)	2	40	96	114	0.4	1.1
PENT–Ch of God Proph	1	NR	17	20	0.1	0.2
PENT–Intl Pent Holiness	5	278	374	444	1.5	4.2
PENT–United Holy Ch	1	NR	NR	NR	-	-
PRES–Presb Ch (USA)	5	270	381	452	1.5	4.3
Un C of Christ	1	0	14	17	0.1	0.2
CHARLES CITY	**9**	**797**	**3,013**	**3,540**	**48.8**	**100.0**
ANG/EPIS–Episcopal	1	68	200	272	3.7	7.7
BAPT–Amer Bapt USA	2	247	600	693	9.6	19.6
BAPT–NBC USA	1	0	100	116	1.6	3.3
BAPT–So Bapt Conv	3	419	2,000	2,312	31.9	65.3
METH–Un Methodist	1	60	110	144	2.0	4.1
PRES–Presb Ch (USA)	1	3	3	3	0.0	0.1
CHARLOTTE	**48**	**2,603**	**4,756**	**7,721**	**61.3**	**100.0**
ANG/EPIS–Episcopal	1	6	7	7	0.1	0.1
BAPT–So Bapt Conv	14	1,113	2,567	3,100	24.6	40.2
CHR–Chr Chs & Chs Cr	2	NR	372	449	3.6	5.8
Jehovah's Witness	2	NR	NR	NR	-	-
LDS–L-D Saints	1	NR	NR	332	2.6	4.3
MENN–Amish Undif	1	NR	60	157	1.2	2.0
METH–Evan Meth Ch	1	NR	NR	NR	-	-
METH–Un Methodist	12	402	1,192	1,293	10.3	16.7
Muslim Est	1	792	NR	1,718	13.7	22.3
Non-denom Chr Chs	1	90	100	112	0.9	1.5
PRES–Presb Ch (USA)	12	200	458	553	4.4	7.2
CHARLOTTESVILLE (CITY)	**71**	**8,060**	**16,713**	**35,467**	**81.6**	**100.0**
ANG/EPIS–Episcopal	3	482	1,066	1,901	4.4	5.4
Bahá'í	1	NR	47	47	0.1	0.1
BAPT–Amer Bapt USA	1	53	48	54	0.1	0.2
BAPT–Free Will Bapt	1	NR	52	59	0.1	0.2
BAPT–NBC USA	1	0	150	170	0.4	0.5
BAPT–Ref Bapt Ch	1	NR	NR	NR	-	-
BAPT–So Bapt Conv	13	2,350	5,978	6,781	15.6	19.1
BUDD–Mahayana	1	NR	NR	103	0.2	0.3
BUDD–Vajrayana	2	NR	NR	504	1.2	1.4
Calv Chpl	1	NR	NR	NR	-	-
Catholic	3	NR	NR	10,777	24.8	30.4
Ch Cr, Scientst	1	NR	NR	NR	-	-

NR–Not Reported   - Represents no adherents reported.   Percentages may not total 100 due to rounding.

Table 3: Religious Congregations by County and Group: 2010

Religious Group	Number of Congrega-tions	Number of Attendees	Number of Communicant, Confirmed, or Full Members	Adherents		
				Number of Adherents	% of Total Pop.	% of Total Adh.
Ch of Nazarene	1	130	197	213	0.5	0.6
CHR–Chr Chs & Chs Cr	3	NR	910	1,032	2.4	2.9
CHR–Int Chs of Christ	1	NR	80	91	0.2	0.3
FRND–Fr Gen Cf & Un Mtg	1	NR	138	157	0.4	0.4
Jehovah's Witness	1	NR	NR	NR	-	-
LUTH–E.L.C.A.	1	107	203	270	0.6	0.8
LUTH–Luth–MO Synod	1	122	230	306	0.7	0.9
MENN–Mennonite USA	1	65	53	60	0.1	0.2
METH–Un Methodist	3	543	1,998	2,507	5.8	7.1
METH–Wesleyan	1	61	30	79	0.2	0.2
Muslim Est	1	792	NR	3,436	7.9	9.7
Non-denom Chr Chs	11	1,652	1,950	2,250	5.2	6.3
ORTHE–Greek Orthodox	1	75	NR	340	0.8	1.0
ORTHE–Ukrainian Orth	1	40	NR	120	0.3	0.3
PENT–Ch God (Cleve)	1	48	93	105	0.2	0.3
PENT–COGIC	2	0	300	340	0.8	1.0
PENT–Int Foursq Gos	1	55	34	39	0.1	0.1
PENT–Intl Pent Holiness	1	15	13	15	0.0	0.0
PRES–Korean Pres Amer	1	NR	NR	NR	-	-
PRES–Presb Ch (USA)	3	912	2,169	2,460	5.7	6.9
Salvation Army	1	27	127	162	0.4	0.5
Sev Day Adv	2	130	227	261	0.6	0.7
Un C of Christ	1	90	204	231	0.5	0.7
Unit Univ	1	311	416	597	1.4	1.7
CHESAPEAKE (CITY)	**204**	**28,539**	**53,564**	**85,878**	**38.6**	**100.0**
ANG/EPIS–Anglican NA	1	NR	NR	NR	-	-
ANG/EPIS–Episcopal	2	218	595	831	0.4	1.0
Bahá'í	1	NR	45	45	0.0	0.1
BAPT–Alliance Bapt	1	NR	NR	NR	-	-
BAPT–Amer Bapt USA	1	65	85	105	0.0	0.1
BAPT–Free Will Bapt	2	NR	104	129	0.1	0.2
BAPT–Fund Bapt Flwsp	1	NR	NR	NR	-	-
BAPT–NBC USA	1	1,900	2,500	3,102	1.4	3.6
BAPT–So Bapt Conv	39	7,799	19,237	23,872	10.7	27.8
Catholic	5	NR	NR	13,212	5.9	15.4
Ch of Nazarene	1	63	127	127	0.1	0.1
CHR–Chr Ch (Disc)	2	36	83	103	0.0	0.1
CHR–Chr Chs & Chs Cr	10	NR	1,495	1,855	0.8	2.2
CHR–Chs of Christ	4	415	375	510	0.2	0.6
CONG–Consrv Cong Chr	1	70	140	174	0.1	0.2
Evan Free Ch	1	100	NR	100	0.0	0.1
HINDU–Trad Temples	1	NR	NR	400	0.2	0.5
Jehovah's Witness	5	NR	NR	NR	-	-
LDS–L-D Saints	5	NR	NR	2,627	1.2	3.1
LUTH–E.L.C.A.	1	95	115	125	0.1	0.1
LUTH–Luth Cong Msn Chr	1	220	398	494	0.2	0.6
LUTH–Luth–MO Synod	2	104	100	127	0.1	0.1
LUTH–Wisc Ev Luth Syn	1	216	302	398	0.2	0.5
MENN–Cons Menn Conf	1	50	34	42	0.0	0.0
MENN–Mennonite USA	1	151	311	386	0.2	0.4
METH–AME	8	115	1,175	1,458	0.7	1.7
METH–AME Zion	5	100	700	869	0.4	1.0
METH–Evan Meth Ch	1	NR	NR	NR	-	-
METH–Un Methodist	16	2,728	9,260	11,724	5.3	13.7
METH–Wesleyan	1	71	0	92	0.0	0.1
Muslim Est	1	792	NR	3,436	1.5	4.0
Non-denom Chr Chs	42	9,081	11,108	12,417	5.6	14.5
ORTHE–Orth Ch in Amer	1	40	NR	100	0.0	0.1
ORTHE–Rus Orth Abroad	1	23	NR	42	0.0	0.0
PENT–Assemb of God	4	896	410	977	0.4	1.1
PENT–Ch God (Cleve)	3	532	722	896	0.4	1.0
PENT–COGIC	4	415	1,030	1,278	0.6	1.5
PENT–Int Foursq Gos	2	277	51	63	0.0	0.1
PENT–Intl Pent Holiness	5	609	521	647	0.3	0.8
PENT–Pent FW Bapt	1	NR	NR	NR	-	-
PENT–Un Pent Ch Intl	2	NR	NR	NR	-	-
PENT–United Holy Ch	2	NR	NR	NR	-	-
PENT–Vineyard	1	93	93	115	0.1	0.1
PRES–Presb Ch (USA)	3	725	1,501	1,863	0.8	2.2
PRES–Presb Ch Amer	1	0	0	0	0.0	0.0
Sev Day Adv	5	250	433	499	0.2	0.6
Un C of Christ	3	290	514	638	0.3	0.7
Unity Ch	1	NR	NR	NR	-	-

Religious Group	Number of Congrega-tions	Number of Attendees	Number of Communicant, Confirmed, or Full Members	Adherents		
				Number of Adherents	% of Total Pop.	% of Total Adh.
CHESTERFIELD	**262**	**35,229**	**67,224**	**122,814**	**38.8**	**100.0**
ANG/EPIS–Anglican NA	3	NR	NR	NR	-	-
ANG/EPIS–Episcopal	8	1,093	2,855	3,339	1.1	2.7
Bahá'í	1	NR	98	98	0.0	0.1
BAPT–Alliance Bapt	1	NR	NR	NR	-	-
BAPT–Amer Bapt USA	1	312	442	550	0.2	0.4
BAPT–Free Will Bapt	1	NR	52	65	0.0	0.1
BAPT–Ref Bapt Ch	1	NR	NR	NR	-	-
BAPT–Reg Bapt Gen As	1	NR	NR	NR	-	-
BAPT–So Bapt Conv	67	9,927	22,162	27,556	8.7	22.4
BRETH–Ch of Brethren	1	22	47	58	0.0	0.0
BRETH–Grace Breth	1	NR	NR	NR	-	-
BUDD–Mahayana	2	NR	NR	83	0.0	0.1
Calv Chpl	1	NR	NR	NR	-	-
Catholic	5	NR	NR	22,861	7.2	18.6
Ch God (7th Day)	1	NR	NR	NR	-	-
Ch of Nazarene	5	1,434	1,245	3,424	1.1	2.8
Chr & Miss Al	2	64	58	93	0.0	0.1
CHR–Chr Ch (Disc)	1	192	456	567	0.2	0.5
CHR–Chr Chs & Chs Cr	4	NR	1,411	1,754	0.6	1.4
CHR–Chs of Christ	5	418	363	494	0.2	0.4
CHR–Int Chs of Christ	1	NR	197	245	0.1	0.2
FRND–Fr Gen Cf & Un Mtg	1	NR	68	85	0.0	0.1
HINDU–I/A Temples	1	NR	NR	1,742	0.6	1.4
Jehovah's Witness	3	NR	NR	NR	-	-
LDS–Comm of Christ	1	NR	137	137	0.0	0.1
LDS–L-D Saints	8	NR	NR	3,667	1.2	3.0
LUTH–E.L.C.A.	1	114	359	424	0.1	0.3
LUTH–Luth–MO Synod	3	764	1,312	1,452	0.5	1.2
LUTH–Wisc Ev Luth Syn	1	68	106	145	0.0	0.1
METH–AME Zion	1	0	150	187	0.1	0.2
METH–Un Methodist	23	5,437	17,808	22,376	7.1	18.2
Muslim Est	2	1,592	NR	7,436	2.4	6.1
New Apost Ch	1	NR	NR	NR	-	-
Non-denom Chr Chs	38	6,140	7,186	8,555	2.7	7.0
ORTHE–Orth Ch in Amer	1	53	NR	103	0.0	0.1
PENT–Assemb of God	7	2,061	641	2,753	0.9	2.2
PENT–Ch God (Cleve)	6	1,240	2,348	2,919	0.9	2.4
PENT–Ch Lord Jesus Apos	5	NR	NR	NR	-	-
PENT–Ch of God Proph	3	NR	206	256	0.1	0.2
PENT–COGIC	1	0	60	75	0.0	0.1
PENT–Cong Hol Ch	1	39	35	44	0.0	0.0
PENT–Full Gosp Bapt	1	NR	NR	NR	-	-
PENT–Intl Pent Holiness	7	487	368	458	0.1	0.4
PENT–Un Pent Ch Intl	3	NR	NR	NR	-	-
PRES–Bible Pres	1	NR	NR	NR	-	-
PRES–Korean Amer Pres	1	NR	NR	NR	-	-
PRES–Presb Ch (USA)	13	2,418	5,312	6,605	2.1	5.4
PRES–Presb Ch Amer	5	1,133	1,325	1,713	0.5	1.4
Sev Day Adv	2	180	314	361	0.1	0.3
Sikh	4	NR	NR	NR	-	-
Un C of Christ	2	41	103	128	0.0	0.1
Unity Ch	1	NR	NR	NR	-	-
Zoroastrian	1	NR	NR	6	0.0	0.0
CLARKE	**28**	**1,890**	**3,860**	**5,594**	**39.9**	**100.0**
ANG/EPIS–Episcopal	5	218	391	613	4.4	11.0
Bahá'í	0	NR	4	4	0.0	0.1
BAPT–Amer Bapt USA	1	90	125	150	1.1	2.7
BAPT–Fund Bapt Flwsp	1	NR	NR	NR	-	-
BAPT–So Bapt Conv	4	288	584	702	5.0	12.5
Catholic	1	NR	NR	449	3.2	8.0
LDS–L-D Saints	1	NR	NR	431	3.1	7.7
METH–Un Methodist	8	500	1,639	1,985	14.1	35.5
Non-denom Chr Chs	4	450	600	638	4.5	11.4
PENT–Intl Pent Holiness	1	231	350	421	3.0	7.5
PRES–Presb Ch (USA)	2	113	167	201	1.4	3.6
COLONIAL HEIGHTS (CITY)	**27**	**5,351**	**12,792**	**19,200**	**110.3**	**100.0**
ANG/EPIS–Episcopal	1	81	211	333	1.9	1.7
Bahá'í	0	NR	1	1	0.0	0.0
BAPT–So Bapt Conv	7	3,320	9,076	10,915	62.7	56.8
Catholic	1	NR	NR	2,880	16.5	15.0

NR–Not Reported   - Represents no adherents reported.   Percentages may not total 100 due to rounding.

Table 3: Religious Congregations by County and Group: 2010

Religious Group	Number of Congrega-tions	Number of Attendees	Number of Communicant, Confirmed, or Full Members	Adherents		
				Number of Adherents	% of Total Pop.	% of Total Adh.
Ch of Nazarene	2	79	103	145	0.8	0.8
CHR–Chr Ch (Disc)	1	55	137	165	0.9	0.9
CHR–Chs of Christ	2	165	183	217	1.2	1.1
LDS–L-D Saints	2	NR	NR	1,066	6.1	5.6
METH–Un Methodist	2	430	1,680	1,816	10.4	9.5
Non-denom Chr Chs	5	840	1,112	1,200	6.9	6.3
PENT–Assemb of God	1	304	158	304	1.7	1.6
PENT–Ch God (Cleve)	1	26	39	47	0.3	0.2
PENT–Ch Lord Jesus Apos	1	NR	NR	NR	-	-
PRES–Presb Ch (USA)	1	51	92	111	0.6	0.6
COVINGTON (CITY)	**38**	**2,113**	**5,131**	**6,763**	**113.5**	**100.0**
ANG/EPIS–Episcopal	1	33	44	44	0.7	0.7
BAPT–Amer Bapt USA	1	105	185	220	3.7	3.3
BAPT–So Bapt Conv	2	123	543	647	10.9	9.6
BRETH–Grace Breth	1	NR	NR	NR	-	-
Catholic	1	NR	NR	141	2.4	2.1
CHR–Chr Ch (Disc)	1	54	130	155	2.6	2.3
CHR–Chr Chs & Chs Cr	2	NR	438	522	8.8	7.7
CHR–Chs of Christ	1	60	50	82	1.4	1.2
Ind Fund Churches	1	NR	NR	NR	-	-
Jehovah's Witness	1	NR	NR	NR	-	-
LDS–L-D Saints	1	NR	NR	300	5.0	4.4
METH–Un Methodist	5	429	1,247	1,735	29.1	25.7
METH–Wesleyan	1	24	33	31	0.5	0.5
Non-denom Chr Chs	4	665	915	1,021	17.1	15.1
PENT–Ch God (Cleve)	1	19	25	30	0.5	0.4
PENT–Ch of God Proph	4	NR	153	182	3.1	2.7
PENT–COGIC	2	125	330	393	6.6	5.8
PENT–Int Foursq Gos	1	183	161	192	3.2	2.8
PENT–Intl Pent Holiness	1	70	152	181	3.0	2.7
PRES–As Ref Pres Ch	2	NR	165	197	3.3	2.9
PRES–Evan Presby Ch	1	NR	27	32	0.5	0.5
PRES–Presb Ch (USA)	2	189	447	533	8.9	7.9
Salvation Army	1	34	86	125	2.1	1.8
CRAIG	**14**	**315**	**1,947**	**2,369**	**45.6**	**100.0**
Bahá'í	0	NR	3	3	0.1	0.1
BAPT–So Bapt Conv	1	75	160	190	3.7	8.0
Catholic	1	NR	NR	64	1.2	2.7
CHR–Chr Ch (Disc)	2	25	132	157	3.0	6.6
CHR–Chr Chs & Chs Cr	4	NR	1,151	1,369	26.4	57.8
CHR–Chs of Christ	1	18	19	20	0.4	0.8
METH–Un Methodist	3	137	349	404	7.8	17.1
Non-denom Chr Chs	1	60	60	75	1.4	3.2
PENT–Ch of God Proph	1	NR	73	87	1.7	3.7
CULPEPER	**67**	**5,632**	**9,574**	**16,830**	**36.0**	**100.0**
ANG/EPIS–Episcopal	4	229	515	573	1.2	3.4
Bahá'í	0	NR	26	26	0.1	0.2
BAPT–Amer Bapt USA	1	85	210	263	0.6	1.6
BAPT–So Bapt Conv	21	1,655	3,782	4,739	10.2	28.2
Calv Chpl	1	NR	NR	NR	-	-
Catholic	1	NR	NR	2,655	5.7	15.8
Ch of Nazarene	1	61	40	254	0.5	1.5
Chr & Miss Al	1	30	21	41	0.1	0.2
CHR–Chr Chs & Chs Cr	1	NR	19	24	0.1	0.1
CHR–Chs of Christ	1	58	56	69	0.1	0.4
Ind Fund Churches	1	NR	NR	NR	-	-
Jehovah's Witness	2	NR	NR	NR	-	-
LDS–L-D Saints	2	NR	NR	867	1.9	5.2
LUTH–E.L.C.A.	1	88	156	217	0.5	1.3
LUTH–Nor Amer Luth C	1	NR	NR	NR	-	-
METH–Free Methodist	1	70	31	70	0.1	0.4
METH–Un Methodist	6	645	1,725	2,311	4.9	13.7
Non-denom Chr Chs	10	1,755	1,910	2,474	5.3	14.7
PENT–Assemb of God	2	447	274	1,245	2.7	7.4
PENT–Assm God Intl F	1	NR	NR	NR	-	-
PENT–Ch God (Cleve)	1	23	17	21	0.0	0.1
PENT–Un Pent Ch Intl	1	NR	NR	NR	-	-
PRES–Presb Ch (USA)	2	272	575	720	1.5	4.3
PRES–Presb Ch Amer	1	100	19	33	0.1	0.2
Sev Day Adv	3	114	198	228	0.5	1.4

Religious Group	Number of Congrega-tions	Number of Attendees	Number of Communicant, Confirmed, or Full Members	Adherents		
				Number of Adherents	% of Total Pop.	% of Total Adh.
CUMBERLAND	**18**	**1,272**	**2,102**	**2,806**	**27.9**	**100.0**
ANG/EPIS–Episcopal	1	18	39	40	0.4	1.4
Bahá'í	0	NR	8	8	0.1	0.3
BAPT–So Bapt Conv	7	491	1,220	1,474	14.7	52.5
METH–Un Methodist	5	166	357	361	3.6	12.9
Non-denom Chr Chs	1	110	60	138	1.4	4.9
PENT–Assemb of God	1	460	265	600	6.0	21.4
PENT–Ch God (Cleve)	1	27	19	23	0.2	0.8
PRES–Presb Ch (USA)	2	0	134	162	1.6	5.8
DANVILLE (CITY)	**100**	**11,064**	**20,677**	**30,886**	**71.7**	**100.0**
Bahá'í	0	NR	10	10	0.0	0.0
BAPT–NBC USA	1	100	150	180	0.4	0.6
BAPT–So Bapt Conv	17	2,375	7,838	9,420	21.9	30.5
BUDD–Mahayana	1	NR	NR	11	0.0	0.0
Catholic	1	NR	NR	2,504	5.8	8.1
CHR–Chr Ch (Disc)	1	0	99	119	0.3	0.4
CHR–Chr Chs & Chs Cr	2	NR	205	246	0.6	0.8
CHR–Chs of Christ	2	115	140	168	0.4	0.5
FRND–Evan Fr Ch Intl	1	52	25	30	0.1	0.1
Jehovah's Witness	1	NR	NR	NR	-	-
JUD–Reform	1	18	32	86	0.2	0.3
LDS–L-D Saints	1	NR	NR	614	1.4	2.0
LUTH–E.L.C.A.	1	94	294	319	0.7	1.0
LUTH–Luth–MO Synod	1	48	175	219	0.5	0.7
METH–AME	1	22	40	48	0.1	0.2
METH–AME Zion	1	20	50	60	0.1	0.2
METH–Un Methodist	9	952	2,849	3,157	7.3	10.2
METH–Wesleyan	1	36	29	47	0.1	0.2
Muslim Est	1	792	NR	3,436	8.0	11.1
Non-denom Chr Chs	29	4,236	5,117	5,732	13.3	18.6
ORTHE–Greek Orthodox	1	40	NR	72	0.2	0.2
PENT–Assemb of God	1	70	30	105	0.2	0.3
PENT–Ch God (Cleve)	4	883	1,437	1,727	4.0	5.6
PENT–Ch Lord Jesus Apos	1	NR	NR	NR	-	-
PENT–Ch of God Proph	2	NR	72	87	0.2	0.3
PENT–COGIC	1	0	150	180	0.4	0.6
PENT–Full Gosp Bapt	2	NR	NR	NR	-	-
PENT–Int Foursq Gos	1	341	107	129	0.3	0.4
PENT–Intl Pent Holiness	5	441	743	893	2.1	2.9
PENT–Un Pent Ch Intl	1	NR	NR	NR	-	-
PENT–United Holy Ch	1	NR	NR	NR	-	-
PRES–Presb Ch (USA)	4	171	629	756	1.8	2.4
Salvation Army	1	38	75	92	0.2	0.3
Sev Day Adv	2	220	381	439	1.0	1.4
DICKENSON	**23**	**770**	**1,808**	**2,116**	**13.3**	**100.0**
BAPT–So Bapt Conv	4	240	646	771	4.8	36.4
BRETH–Ch of Brethren	3	40	169	202	1.3	9.5
Catholic	1	NR	NR	38	0.2	1.8
CHR–Chr Chs & Chs Cr	2	NR	125	149	0.9	7.0
CHR–Chs of Christ	1	67	54	70	0.4	3.3
Jehovah's Witness	1	NR	NR	NR	-	-
METH–AME Zion	1	0	100	119	0.7	5.6
METH–Un Methodist	2	116	251	252	1.6	11.9
Non-denom Chr Chs	3	175	255	281	1.8	13.3
PENT–Ch of God Proph	1	NR	33	39	0.2	1.8
PRES–Presb Ch Amer	4	132	175	195	1.2	9.2
DINWIDDIE	**45**	**3,135**	**6,242**	**7,471**	**26.7**	**100.0**
ANG/EPIS–Episcopal	2	31	66	80	0.3	1.1
Bahá'í	0	NR	2	2	0.0	0.0
BAPT–Amer Bapt USA	1	325	350	421	1.5	5.6
BAPT–So Bapt Conv	9	963	2,022	2,432	8.7	32.6
Catholic	1	NR	NR	186	0.7	2.5
Ch of Nazarene	1	29	51	63	0.2	0.8
CHR–Chr Ch (Disc)	2	53	165	198	0.7	2.7
CHR–Chs of Christ	1	90	100	125	0.4	1.7
MENN–Beachy Amish-Menn	1	29	9	29	0.1	0.4
METH–AME Zion	1	0	100	120	0.4	1.6
METH–Un Methodist	15	843	2,348	2,640	9.4	35.3
Non-denom Chr Chs	4	530	725	737	2.6	9.9

NR–Not Reported - Represents no adherents reported. Percentages may not total 100 due to rounding.

Table 3: Religious Congregations by County and Group: 2010

Religious Group	Number of Congrega-tions	Number of Attendees	Number of Communicant, Confirmed, or Full Members	Adherents: Number of Adherents	Adherents: % of Total Pop.	Adherents: % of Total Adh.
PENT–Assemb of God	2	160	123	222	0.8	3.0
PENT–Full Gosp Bapt	1	NR	NR	NR	-	-
PENT–Intl Pent Holiness	1	10	25	30	0.1	0.4
PRES–Presb Ch (USA)	2	52	121	146	0.5	2.0
Sev Day Adv	1	20	35	40	0.1	0.5
EMPORIA (CITY)	**19**	**1,942**	**2,356**	**4,484**	**75.7**	**100.0**
ANG/EPIS–Anglican NA	1	NR	NR	NR	-	-
Bahá'í	0	NR	2	2	0.0	0.0
BAPT–So Bapt Conv	1	91	462	580	9.8	12.9
Catholic	1	NR	NR	91	1.5	2.0
CHR–Chs of Christ	1	32	25	35	0.6	0.8
METH–AME Zion	1	0	100	125	2.1	2.8
METH–Un Methodist	2	149	541	620	10.5	13.8
Muslim Est	1	792	NR	1,718	29.0	38.3
Non-denom Chr Chs	9	766	1,076	1,096	18.5	24.4
PENT–Assemb of God	1	80	41	80	1.3	1.8
PRES–Presb Ch (USA)	1	32	109	137	2.3	3.1
ESSEX	**26**	**1,385**	**3,153**	**4,601**	**41.3**	**100.0**
ANG/EPIS–Episcopal	4	159	489	542	4.9	11.8
BAPT–So Bapt Conv	9	692	1,575	1,882	16.9	40.9
Catholic	1	NR	NR	600	5.4	13.0
CHR–Chr Ch (Disc)	1	0	0	0	0.0	0.0
LDS–L-D Saints	1	NR	NR	301	2.7	6.5
METH–Un Methodist	5	250	639	726	6.5	15.8
Non-denom Chr Chs	1	60	125	125	1.1	2.7
PENT–Assemb of God	1	50	29	80	0.7	1.7
PENT–Ch God (Cleve)	1	57	93	111	1.0	2.4
Sev Day Adv	2	117	203	234	2.1	5.1
FAIRFAX	**627**	**106,008**	**165,090**	**486,358**	**45.0**	**100.0**
ANG/EPIS–Anglican NA	3	NR	NR	NR	-	-
ANG/EPIS–Episcopal	29	5,074	12,210	17,421	1.6	3.6
Bahá'í	11	NR	1,344	1,344	0.1	0.3
BAPT–Alliance Bapt	3	NR	NR	NR	-	-
BAPT–Amer Bapt USA	5	851	2,388	2,941	0.3	0.6
BAPT–Converge/BGC	1	75	NR	90	0.0	0.0
BAPT–Ind Bapt Flwsp Intl	1	NR	NR	NR	-	-
BAPT–NBC Amer	1	80	175	216	0.0	0.0
BAPT–Prog NBC	1	85	250	308	0.0	0.1
BAPT–Reg Bapt Gen As	1	NR	NR	NR	-	-
BAPT–So Bapt Conv	100	14,005	27,302	33,623	3.1	6.9
BRETH–Ch of Brethren	2	144	304	374	0.0	0.1
BUDD–Mahayana	16	NR	NR	9,990	0.9	2.1
BUDD–Theravada	2	NR	NR	666	0.1	0.1
BUDD–Vajrayana	2	NR	NR	242	0.0	0.0
Calv Chpl	3	NR	NR	NR	-	-
Catholic	29	NR	NR	184,183	17.0	37.9
Ch Cr, Scientst	5	NR	NR	NR	-	-
Ch God (7th Day)	1	NR	NR	NR	-	-
Ch of God Gen Conf	1	NR	8	10	0.0	0.0
Ch of Nazarene	5	280	635	866	0.1	0.2
Chr & Miss Al	9	679	714	789	0.1	0.2
CHR–Chr Ch (Disc)	5	442	1,309	1,612	0.1	0.3
CHR–Chr Chs & Chs Cr	9	NR	1,823	2,245	0.2	0.5
CHR–Chs of Christ	7	845	729	997	0.1	0.2
Evan Cov Ch	1	38	91	49	0.0	0.0
Evan Free Ch	1	250	NR	250	0.0	0.1
FRND–Fr Gen Cf & Un Mtg	3	NR	459	565	0.1	0.1
HINDU–I/A Temples	3	NR	NR	738	0.1	0.2
HINDU–Post Ren	7	NR	NR	244	0.0	0.1
HINDU–Renaiss	1	NR	NR	12	0.0	0.0
HINDU–Trad Temples	2	NR	NR	4,500	0.4	0.9
Int Cou Comm Ch	1	NR	NR	NR	-	-
Jain	1	NR	NR	NR	-	-
Jehovah's Witness	3	NR	NR	NR	-	-
JUD–Conserv	1	378	424	1,145	0.1	0.2
JUD–Orth	2	86	100	120	0.0	0.0
JUD–Reconst	1	29	37	100	0.0	0.0
JUD–Reform	4	791	1,395	3,767	0.3	0.8
LDS–Comm of Christ	1	NR	137	137	0.0	0.0
LDS–L-D Saints	30	NR	NR	16,497	1.5	3.4
LUTH–E.L.C.A.	17	3,576	8,972	11,919	1.1	2.5
LUTH–Luth–MO Synod	7	1,794	3,211	4,424	0.4	0.9
LUTH–Wisc Ev Luth Syn	1	301	423	584	0.1	0.1
MENN–Mennonite USA	3	84	89	110	0.0	0.0
METH–AME	2	0	250	308	0.0	0.1
METH–AME Zion	2	0	250	308	0.0	0.1
METH–Un Methodist	51	11,863	34,858	52,643	4.9	10.8
METH–Wesleyan	2	73	90	95	0.0	0.0
MJEW–Union Mes Cong	1	NR	NR	NR	-	-
Muslim Est	16	14,441	NR	50,108	4.6	10.3
Non-denom Chr Chs	55	31,900	38,455	41,344	3.8	8.5
ORTHE–Ant Orth of NA	1	70	NR	150	0.0	0.0
ORTHE–Greek Orthodox	1	700	NR	3,500	0.3	0.7
ORTHE–Orth Ch in Amer	5	283	NR	859	0.1	0.2
ORTHO–Syrian Orth Ch	1	75	NR	185	0.0	0.0
PENT–Assemb of God	17	3,167	3,603	5,157	0.5	1.1
PENT–Ch God (Cleve)	8	335	457	563	0.1	0.1
PENT–Ch of God Proph	2	NR	266	328	0.0	0.1
PENT–COGIC	2	0	300	369	0.0	0.1
PENT–Full Gosp Bapt	1	NR	NR	NR	-	-
PENT–Int Foursq Gos	1	472	283	349	0.0	0.1
PENT–Intl Pent Holiness	1	300	250	308	0.0	0.1
PENT–Open Bible Std	1	70	NR	70	0.0	0.0
PENT–Pent FW Bapt	1	NR	NR	NR	-	-
PENT–Un Pent Ch Intl	2	NR	NR	NR	-	-
PRES–As Ref Pres Ch	2	NR	38	47	0.0	0.0
PRES–Evan Presby Ch	3	NR	511	629	0.1	0.1
PRES–Kor Pres Abroad	3	NR	NR	NR	-	-
PRES–Korean Amer Pres	11	NR	NR	NR	-	-
PRES–Korean Pres Amer	19	NR	NR	NR	-	-
PRES–Orth Pres Ch	1	236	220	326	0.0	0.1
PRES–Presb Ch (USA)	27	4,766	9,509	11,711	1.1	2.4
PRES–Presb Ch Amer	16	4,367	5,445	6,447	0.6	1.3
REF–Christian Ref	1	92	155	191	0.0	0.0
Salvation Army	1	53	152	241	0.0	0.0
Sev Day Adv	13	1,508	2,624	3,016	0.3	0.6
Sikh	3	NR	NR	NR	-	-
Un C of Christ	5	480	1,391	1,713	0.2	0.4
Unit Univ	4	870	1,454	2,161	0.2	0.4
Unity Ch	3	NR	NR	NR	-	-
Zoroastrian	0	NR	NR	154	0.0	0.0
FAIRFAX (CITY)	**44**	**8,321**	**9,468**	**27,537**	**122.0**	**100.0**
ANG/EPIS–Anglican NA	4	NR	NR	NR	-	-
Bahá'í	1	NR	31	31	0.1	0.1
BAPT–Natl Mis Bapt Conv	1	0	150	178	0.8	0.6
BAPT–So Bapt Conv	3	300	387	460	2.0	1.7
BUDD–Mahayana	1	NR	NR	300	1.3	1.1
Catholic	1	NR	NR	9,953	44.1	36.1
CGOD–Ch God (Ander)	1	1,651	NR	1,651	7.3	6.0
Ch Cr, Scientst	1	NR	NR	NR	-	-
CHR–Chr Ch (Disc)	1	0	100	119	0.5	0.4
CHR–Chs of Christ	1	960	910	1,408	6.2	5.1
CHR–Int Chs of Christ	1	NR	306	364	1.6	1.3
Evan Free Ch	1	240	NR	240	1.1	0.9
HINDU–Post Ren	2	NR	NR	35	0.2	0.1
HINDU–Trad Temples	1	NR	NR	100	0.4	0.4
Jehovah's Witness	1	NR	NR	NR	-	-
JUD–Conserv	1	552	619	1,671	7.4	6.1
JUD–Orth	2	72	75	100	0.4	0.4
LUTH–Ch Luth Conf	1	NR	NR	NR	-	-
LUTH–E.L.C.A.	1	100	326	386	1.7	1.4
MENN–Mennonite USA	1	47	22	26	0.1	0.1
METH–Un Methodist	1	413	2,252	2,691	11.9	9.8
METH–Wesleyan	1	44	41	57	0.3	0.2
Metro Comm Ch	1	74	108	128	0.6	0.5
Non-denom Chr Chs	8	2,665	3,310	3,648	16.2	13.2
ORTHO–Coptic Orth Ch	1	875	NR	3,000	13.3	10.9
PRES–Kor Pres Abroad	1	NR	NR	NR	-	-
PRES–Presb Ch (USA)	1	249	694	826	3.7	3.0
PRES–Presb Ch Amer	1	0	0	0	0.0	0.0
Sev Day Adv	1	79	137	158	0.7	0.6
Sikh	1	NR	NR	NR	-	-
Zoroastrian	0	NR	NR	7	0.0	0.0

NR–Not Reported   - Represents no adherents reported.   Percentages may not total 100 due to rounding.

Table 3: Religious Congregations by County and Group: 2010

Religious Group	Number of Congrega-tions	Number of Attendees	Number of Communicant, Confirmed, or Full Members	Adherents: Number of Adherents	Adherents: % of Total Pop.	Adherents: % of Total Adh.
FALLS CHURCH (CITY)	**21**	**3,033**	**6,700**	**17,240**	**139.8**	**100.0**
ANG/EPIS–Anglican NA	1	NR	NR	NR	-	-
ANG/EPIS–Episcopal	2	108	203	221	1.8	1.3
Bahá'í	1	NR	29	29	0.2	0.2
BAPT–Amer Bapt USA	3	538	979	1,205	9.8	7.0
BAPT–So Bapt Conv	2	657	2,113	2,600	21.1	15.1
BUDD–Mahayana	1	NR	NR	102	0.8	0.6
Catholic	1	NR	NR	6,332	51.3	36.7
Ch of Nazarene	1	150	82	170	1.4	1.0
HINDU–Post Ren	1	NR	NR	16	0.1	0.1
JUD–Reform	1	843	1,487	4,015	32.6	23.3
METH–Un Methodist	3	315	1,020	1,600	13.0	9.3
Nat Spirit Asso	1	NR	NR	NR	-	-
PRES–Presb Ch (USA)	1	250	488	601	4.9	3.5
Sev Day Adv	2	172	299	344	2.8	2.0
Zoroastrian	0	NR	NR	5	0.0	0.0
FAUQUIER	**101**	**9,406**	**16,918**	**29,384**	**45.1**	**100.0**
ANG/EPIS–Anglican NA	1	NR	NR	NR	-	-
ANG/EPIS–Episcopal	9	910	2,065	2,516	3.9	8.6
Bahá'í	0	NR	12	12	0.0	0.0
BAPT–Free Will Bapt	1	NR	52	64	0.1	0.2
BAPT–Prog NBC	1	100	180	222	0.3	0.8
BAPT–Ref Bapt Ch	1	NR	NR	NR	-	-
BAPT–So Bapt Conv	22	1,625	4,144	5,121	7.9	17.4
BRETH–Ch of Brethren	1	0	152	188	0.3	0.6
BUDD–Theravada	1	NR	NR	300	0.5	1.0
Catholic	1	NR	NR	6,600	10.1	22.5
Ch Cr, Scientst	1	NR	NR	NR	-	-
CHR–Chr Chs & Chs Cr	2	NR	70	87	0.1	0.3
CHR–Chs of Christ	1	147	165	223	0.3	0.8
Evan Free Ch	2	525	NR	525	0.8	1.8
Int Cou Comm Ch	1	NR	NR	NR	-	-
Jehovah's Witness	1	NR	NR	NR	-	-
LDS–L-D Saints	2	NR	NR	1,095	1.7	3.7
LUTH–E.L.C.A.	2	267	679	829	1.3	2.8
LUTH–Nor Amer Luth C	1	NR	NR	NR	-	-
MENN–Beachy Amish-Menn	1	84	50	84	0.1	0.3
MENN–Cons Menn Conf	1	130	41	51	0.1	0.2
MENN–Unaffil Amish-Menn	1	38	31	38	0.1	0.1
METH–Un Methodist	20	1,500	4,249	4,874	7.5	16.6
METH–Wesleyan	1	241	125	313	0.5	1.1
Non-denom Chr Chs	11	2,565	3,685	3,949	6.1	13.4
ORTHE–Ant Orth of NA	1	50	NR	80	0.1	0.3
ORTHE–Holy Orth in NA	2	27	NR	35	0.1	0.1
PENT–Assemb of God	5	680	308	1,067	1.6	3.6
PRES–Orth Pres Ch	1	25	14	22	0.0	0.1
PRES–Presb Ch (USA)	3	306	649	802	1.2	2.7
PRES–Presb Ch Amer	1	125	141	163	0.2	0.6
Sev Day Adv	2	61	106	122	0.2	0.4
Zoroastrian	0	NR	NR	2	0.0	0.0
FLOYD	**53**	**2,478**	**4,271**	**5,444**	**35.6**	**100.0**
Bahá'í	0	NR	4	4	0.0	0.1
BAPT–So Bapt Conv	5	429	954	1,146	7.5	21.1
BRETH–Ch of Brethren	13	806	1,573	1,889	12.4	34.7
Catholic	1	NR	NR	53	0.3	1.0
Ch of Nazarene	1	26	31	73	0.5	1.3
CHR–Chr Ch (Disc)	2	0	50	60	0.4	1.1
CHR–Chs of Christ	1	45	42	54	0.4	1.0
FRND–Fr Gen Cf & Un Mtg	1	NR	20	24	0.2	0.4
Jehovah's Witness	2	NR	NR	NR	-	-
LDS–L-D Saints	1	NR	NR	152	1.0	2.8
LUTH–E.L.C.A.	2	73	134	215	1.4	3.9
METH–Un Methodist	9	364	663	829	5.4	15.2
Non-denom Chr Chs	4	247	292	335	2.2	6.2
PENT–Assemb of God	1	23	15	26	0.2	0.5
PENT–Ch God (Cleve)	3	272	236	283	1.9	5.2
PENT–Intl Pent Holiness	1	6	17	20	0.1	0.4
PRES–Presb Ch (USA)	3	124	181	217	1.4	4.0
PRES–Presb Ch Amer	1	55	44	47	0.3	0.9
REF–Fed Ref Ch	1	NR	NR	NR	-	-
Sev Day Adv	1	8	15	17	0.1	0.3
FLUVANNA	**26**	**1,656**	**3,907**	**5,645**	**22.0**	**100.0**
ANG/EPIS–Episcopal	2	50	89	89	0.3	1.6
Bahá'í	0	NR	7	7	0.0	0.1
BAPT–So Bapt Conv	7	639	1,767	2,146	8.4	38.0
Calv Chpl	1	NR	NR	NR	-	-
Catholic	1	NR	NR	1,070	4.2	19.0
CHR–Chr Chs & Chs Cr	1	NR	330	401	1.6	7.1
Jehovah's Witness	1	NR	NR	NR	-	-
LUTH–E.L.C.A.	1	83	136	150	0.6	2.7
METH–Un Methodist	8	391	1,040	1,127	4.4	20.0
Non-denom Chr Chs	2	465	500	606	2.4	10.7
ORTHE–Bulgar Orth USA	1	3	NR	3	0.0	0.1
PRES–Presb Ch (USA)	1	25	38	46	0.2	0.8
FRANKLIN	**105**	**9,915**	**19,323**	**24,209**	**43.1**	**100.0**
ANG/EPIS–Episcopal	2	114	260	260	0.5	1.1
Bahá'í	0	NR	8	8	0.0	0.0
BAPT–Amer Bapt USA	3	105	216	257	0.5	1.1
BAPT–Ref Bapt Ch	1	NR	NR	NR	-	-
BAPT–So Bapt Conv	26	4,011	9,117	10,831	19.3	44.7
BRETH–Ch of Brethren	15	1,067	2,059	2,446	4.4	10.1
Catholic	1	NR	NR	559	1.0	2.3
CGOD–Ch God (Ander)	1	30	NR	30	0.1	0.1
CHR–Chr Ch (Disc)	4	125	770	915	1.6	3.8
CHR–Chr Chs & Chs Cr	2	NR	185	220	0.4	0.9
CHR–Chs of Christ	1	45	35	54	0.1	0.2
Jehovah's Witness	1	NR	NR	NR	-	-
LDS–L-D Saints	1	NR	NR	323	0.6	1.3
LUTH–E.L.C.A.	1	339	215	256	0.5	1.1
METH–AME	1	0	100	119	0.2	0.5
METH–Un Methodist	23	1,440	3,488	4,294	7.6	17.7
Non-denom Chr Chs	7	1,482	1,632	1,934	3.4	8.0
PENT–Assemb of God	5	334	219	495	0.9	2.0
PENT–Ch God (Cleve)	2	248	338	402	0.7	1.7
PENT–Ch Lord Jesus Apos	1	NR	NR	NR	-	-
PENT–Ch of God Proph	1	NR	20	24	0.0	0.1
PENT–Intl Pent Holiness	2	142	102	121	0.2	0.5
PRES–Presb Ch (USA)	3	383	473	562	1.0	2.3
Sev Day Adv	1	50	86	99	0.2	0.4
FRANKLIN (CITY)	**23**	**1,486**	**3,684**	**5,105**	**59.5**	**100.0**
ANG/EPIS–Episcopal	1	82	259	281	3.3	5.5
Bahá'í	0	NR	10	10	0.1	0.2
BAPT–NBC Amer	1	185	350	432	5.0	8.5
BAPT–NBC USA	1	0	500	617	7.2	12.1
BAPT–So Bapt Conv	2	130	208	257	3.0	5.0
Catholic	1	NR	NR	344	4.0	6.7
Jehovah's Witness	1	NR	NR	NR	-	-
LDS–L-D Saints	1	NR	NR	331	3.9	6.5
METH–AME	1	0	150	185	2.2	3.6
METH–AME Zion	2	40	210	259	3.0	5.1
METH–Un Methodist	1	132	524	755	8.8	14.8
Non-denom Chr Chs	7	680	935	975	11.4	19.1
PENT–Ch God (Cleve)	1	28	115	142	1.7	2.8
PRES–Presb Ch (USA)	1	50	81	100	1.2	2.0
Sev Day Adv	1	34	60	69	0.8	1.4
Un C of Christ	1	125	282	348	4.1	6.8
FREDERICK	**100**	**11,247**	**17,215**	**25,979**	**33.2**	**100.0**
ANG/EPIS–Anglican NA	1	NR	NR	NR	-	-
ANG/EPIS–Episcopal	1	98	230	246	0.3	0.9
Bahá'í	1	NR	31	31	0.0	0.1
BAPT–Amer Bapt Assn	1	NR	75	93	0.1	0.4
BAPT–Free Will Bapt	1	NR	52	64	0.1	0.2
BAPT–So Bapt Conv	8	1,022	1,504	1,859	2.4	7.2
BRETH–Ch of Brethren	3	193	352	435	0.6	1.7
BRETH–Grace Breth	2	NR	NR	NR	-	-
Ch of Nazarene	1	407	228	415	0.5	1.6
CHR–Chr Ch (Disc)	2	29	92	114	0.1	0.4
CHR–Chr Chs & Chs Cr	5	NR	1,650	2,040	2.6	7.9
FRND–Fr Gen Cf & Un Mtg	1	NR	96	119	0.2	0.5
Grace Gosp Fel	1	NR	NR	NR	-	-

NR–Not Reported - Represents no adherents reported. Percentages may not total 100 due to rounding.

Table 3: Religious Congregations by County and Group: 2010

Religious Group	Number of Congrega-tions	Number of Attendees	Number of Communicant, Confirmed, or Full Members	Adherents		
				Number of Adherents	% of Total Pop.	% of Total Adh.
LDS–L-D Saints	1	NR	NR	503	0.6	1.9
LUTH–E.L.C.A.	4	377	644	848	1.1	3.3
LUTH–Luth-MO Synod	1	99	195	235	0.3	0.9
MENN–Mennonite USA	1	68	81	100	0.1	0.4
METH–Un Methodist	31	2,199	5,535	7,055	9.0	27.2
Muslim Est	1	792	NR	3,436	4.4	13.2
Non-denom Chr Chs	10	2,748	2,810	3,494	4.5	13.4
PENT–Assemb of God	5	681	367	822	1.0	3.2
PENT–Ch God (Cleve)	1	1,751	1,865	2,306	2.9	8.9
PENT–Intl Pent Holiness	1	61	127	157	0.2	0.6
PENT–Un Pent Ch Intl	1	NR	NR	NR	-	-
PRES–Presb Ch (USA)	10	480	906	1,120	1.4	4.3
Salvation Army	2	123	227	264	0.3	1.0
Un Breth in Cr	1	27	0	23	0.0	0.1
Unit Univ	1	92	148	200	0.3	0.8
Unity Ch	1	NR	NR	NR	-	-
FREDERICKSBURG (CITY)	**75**	**14,829**	**28,861**	**46,741**	**192.5**	**100.0**
ANG/EPIS–Episcopal	2	604	1,536	2,015	8.3	4.3
Bahá'í	0	NR	24	24	0.1	0.1
BAPT–Amer Bapt USA	1	158	220	262	1.1	0.6
BAPT–Prog NBC	1	325	601	716	2.9	1.5
BAPT–So Bapt Conv	10	3,986	11,172	13,304	54.8	28.5
Catholic	1	NR	NR	12,785	52.6	27.4
CGOD–Ch God (Ander)	2	105	NR	105	0.4	0.2
Ch Cr, Scientst	1	NR	NR	NR	-	-
Chr & Miss Al	1	38	0	45	0.2	0.1
CHR–Chr Chs & Chs Cr	1	NR	0	0	0.0	0.0
CHR–Chs of Christ	1	150	160	190	0.8	0.4
Evan Free Ch	1	35	NR	35	0.1	0.1
JUD–Reform	1	62	109	294	1.2	0.6
LUTH–E.L.C.A.	1	203	548	703	2.9	1.5
METH–Un Methodist	2	796	2,695	3,297	13.6	7.1
METH–Wesleyan	2	142	211	185	0.8	0.4
Metro Comm Ch	1	16	25	30	0.1	0.1
MJEW–Union Mes Cong	1	NR	NR	NR	-	-
Non-denom Chr Chs	34	6,865	9,551	10,101	41.6	21.6
PENT–Assemb of God	1	184	116	255	1.0	0.5
PENT–Ch God (Cleve)	1	155	235	280	1.2	0.6
PENT–Ch of God Proph	1	NR	11	13	0.1	0.0
PENT–Intl Pent Holiness	1	25	18	21	0.1	0.0
PENT–Vineyard	1	153	89	106	0.4	0.2
PRES–Presb Ch (USA)	2	426	1,022	1,217	5.0	2.6
PRES–Presb Ch Amer	1	217	206	286	1.2	0.6
Salvation Army	1	68	135	226	0.9	0.5
Un C of Christ	1	25	23	27	0.1	0.1
Unit Univ	1	91	154	219	0.9	0.5
GALAX (CITY)	**30**	**2,496**	**4,558**	**5,410**	**76.8**	**100.0**
ANG/EPIS–Episcopal	1	39	71	84	1.2	1.6
Bahá'í	0	NR	1	1	0.0	0.0
BAPT–So Bapt Conv	3	299	568	683	9.7	12.6
CHR–Chr Ch (Disc)	1	71	310	373	5.3	6.9
CHR–Chr Chs & Chs Cr	2	NR	90	108	1.5	2.0
Jehovah's Witness	1	NR	NR	NR	-	-
LUTH–E.L.C.A.	1	0	0	0	0.0	0.0
METH–Un Methodist	8	517	1,214	1,458	20.7	27.0
METH–Wesleyan	1	67	91	87	1.2	1.6
Non-denom Chr Chs	4	625	790	838	11.9	15.5
PENT–Assemb of God	1	153	140	242	3.4	4.5
PENT–Ch God (Cleve)	2	509	705	848	12.0	15.7
PENT–Ch of God Proph	1	NR	130	156	2.2	2.9
PENT–Intl Pent Holiness	1	66	89	107	1.5	2.0
PENT–United Holy Ch	1	NR	NR	NR	-	-
PRES–Presb Ch (USA)	1	70	220	265	3.8	4.9
Sev Day Adv	1	80	139	160	2.3	3.0
GILES	**71**	**2,939**	**6,932**	**8,664**	**50.1**	**100.0**
ANG/EPIS–Episcopal	1	36	59	65	0.4	0.8
Bahá'í	0	NR	1	1	0.0	0.0
BAPT–So Bapt Conv	8	402	1,009	1,210	7.0	14.0
BRETH–Ch of Brethren	1	10	21	25	0.1	0.3
Catholic	1	NR	NR	97	0.6	1.1

Religious Group	Number of Congrega-tions	Number of Attendees	Number of Communicant, Confirmed, or Full Members	Adherents		
				Number of Adherents	% of Total Pop.	% of Total Adh.
CGOD–Ch God (Ander)	1	16	NR	16	0.1	0.2
CHR–Chr Ch (Disc)	7	93	479	574	3.3	6.6
CHR–Chr Chs & Chs Cr	4	NR	380	456	2.6	5.3
CHR–Chs of Christ	2	36	36	51	0.3	0.6
Jehovah's Witness	1	NR	NR	NR	-	-
LDS–L-D Saints	1	NR	NR	527	3.0	6.1
LUTH–E.L.C.A.	1	22	40	47	0.3	0.5
MENN–Amish Undif	1	NR	47	120	0.7	1.4
METH–A.W.M.C.	1	24	9	39	0.2	0.5
METH–Un Methodist	23	1,004	2,620	2,977	17.2	34.4
Non-denom Chr Chs	3	862	1,500	1,532	8.9	17.7
PENT–Assemb of God	2	101	57	120	0.7	1.4
PENT–Ch God (Cleve)	1	24	25	30	0.2	0.3
PENT–Ch God Mtn Asm	1	NR	NR	NR	-	-
PENT–Ch of God Proph	2	NR	116	139	0.8	1.6
PENT–COGIC	1	0	150	180	1.0	2.1
PENT–Cong Hol Ch	1	39	35	42	0.2	0.5
PENT–Intl Pent Holiness	4	217	249	299	1.7	3.5
PRES–Presb Ch (USA)	2	33	65	78	0.5	0.9
Sev Day Adv	1	20	34	39	0.2	0.5
GLOUCESTER	**47**	**4,801**	**11,053**	**15,228**	**41.3**	**100.0**
ANG/EPIS–Episcopal	2	229	588	733	2.0	4.8
Bahá'í	0	NR	6	6	0.0	0.0
BAPT–NBC USA	1	50	100	119	0.3	0.8
BAPT–So Bapt Conv	14	2,002	5,545	6,609	17.9	43.4
Calv Chpl	1	NR	NR	NR	-	-
Catholic	1	NR	NR	1,160	3.1	7.6
CHR–Chr Chs & Chs Cr	1	NR	85	101	0.3	0.7
CHR–Chs of Christ	1	84	75	100	0.3	0.7
CONG–Consrv Cong Chr	1	103	156	186	0.5	1.2
FRND–Evan Fr Ch Intl	2	46	28	33	0.1	0.2
Jehovah's Witness	1	NR	NR	NR	-	-
LDS–L-D Saints	1	NR	NR	482	1.3	3.2
LUTH–E.L.C.A.	1	59	165	203	0.6	1.3
METH–Un Methodist	9	932	2,694	3,220	8.7	21.1
Non-denom Chr Chs	5	365	480	509	1.4	3.3
PENT–Assemb of God	1	260	270	742	2.0	4.9
PENT–Ch God (Cleve)	2	415	345	411	1.1	2.7
PRES–Presb Ch (USA)	2	237	483	576	1.6	3.8
Sev Day Adv	1	19	33	38	0.1	0.2
GOOCHLAND	**36**	**3,785**	**8,204**	**14,306**	**65.9**	**100.0**
ANG/EPIS–Episcopal	4	457	2,276	2,794	12.9	19.5
Bahá'í	0	NR	5	5	0.0	0.0
BAPT–Amer Bapt USA	1	244	414	489	2.3	3.4
BAPT–So Bapt Conv	15	1,315	3,558	4,206	19.4	29.4
Catholic	2	NR	NR	971	4.5	6.8
Ch of Nazarene	1	98	107	153	0.7	1.1
CHR–Chr Ch (Disc)	1	75	214	253	1.2	1.8
CHR–Chr Chs & Chs Cr	1	NR	236	279	1.3	2.0
Jehovah's Witness	1	NR	NR	NR	-	-
METH–Un Methodist	3	313	882	976	4.5	6.8
Muslim Est	1	792	NR	3,436	15.8	24.0
Non-denom Chr Chs	1	80	80	100	0.5	0.7
PENT–Assemb of God	2	186	67	212	1.0	1.5
PENT–Intl Pent Holiness	1	60	54	64	0.3	0.4
PRES–Presb Ch (USA)	2	165	311	368	1.7	2.6
GRAYSON	**58**	**2,716**	**6,281**	**7,285**	**46.9**	**100.0**
Bahá'í	0	NR	1	1	0.0	0.0
BAPT–So Bapt Conv	17	1,348	3,467	4,028	25.9	55.3
CHR–Chs of Christ	4	130	97	136	0.9	1.9
LUTH–E.L.C.A.	1	26	41	52	0.3	0.7
METH–Un Methodist	27	907	2,054	2,369	15.3	32.5
Non-denom Chr Chs	2	100	180	188	1.2	2.6
PENT–Ch God (Cleve)	1	21	89	103	0.7	1.4
PENT–Ch of God Proph	2	NR	120	139	0.9	1.9
PENT–Intl Pent Holiness	3	184	194	225	1.4	3.1
PRES–Presb Ch (USA)	1	0	38	44	0.3	0.6

NR–Not Reported - Represents no adherents reported. Percentages may not total 100 due to rounding.

Table 3: Religious Congregations by County and Group: 2010

Religious Group	Number of Congrega-tions	Number of Attendees	Number of Communicant, Confirmed, or Full Members	Adherents		
				Number of Adherents	% of Total Pop.	% of Total Adh.
GREENE	**26**	**1,670**	**2,625**	**3,552**	**19.3**	**100.0**
ANG/EPIS–Episcopal	1	65	92	116	0.6	3.3
Bahá'í	0	NR	5	5	0.0	0.1
BAPT–So Bapt Conv	7	393	899	1,121	6.1	31.6
BRETH–Ch of Brethren	4	141	244	304	1.7	8.6
Calv Chpl	1	NR	NR	NR	-	-
Catholic	1	NR	NR	239	1.3	6.7
Jehovah's Witness	1	NR	NR	NR	-	-
MENN–Beachy Amish-Menn	1	167	105	167	0.9	4.7
METH–Un Methodist	6	311	634	862	4.7	24.3
Non-denom Chr Chs	2	295	375	400	2.2	11.3
PENT–Ch God (Cleve)	1	215	164	205	1.1	5.8
PRES–Presb Ch (USA)	1	83	107	133	0.7	3.7
GREENSVILLE	**26**	**759**	**2,421**	**2,731**	**22.3**	**100.0**
ANG/EPIS–Anglican NA	1	NR	NR	NR	-	-
ANG/EPIS–Episcopal	1	12	52	53	0.4	1.9
BAPT–NBC USA	2	0	300	342	2.8	12.5
BAPT–So Bapt Conv	7	355	1,302	1,486	12.1	54.4
CGOD–Ch God (Ander)	1	0	NR	0	0.0	0.0
CHR–Chr Ch (Disc)	1	0	0	0	0.0	0.0
CHR–Chr Chs & Chs Cr	1	NR	60	68	0.6	2.5
Jehovah's Witness	2	NR	NR	NR	-	-
LUTH–Luth–MO Synod	1	66	126	151	1.2	5.5
METH–Un Methodist	4	83	290	298	2.4	10.9
PENT–COGIC	3	200	200	228	1.9	8.3
PRES–Presb Ch (USA)	1	17	46	53	0.4	1.9
Sev Day Adv	1	26	45	52	0.4	1.9
HALIFAX	**111**	**7,465**	**17,731**	**24,727**	**68.2**	**100.0**
ANG/EPIS–Episcopal	3	142	187	259	0.7	1.0
Bahá'í	0	NR	2	2	0.0	0.0
BAPT–Prog NBC	1	0	150	180	0.5	0.7
BAPT–So Bapt Conv	44	3,719	11,312	13,561	37.4	54.8
Catholic	1	NR	NR	214	0.6	0.9
CHR–Chr Chs & Chs Cr	1	NR	0	0	0.0	0.0
CHR–Chs of Christ	1	35	34	40	0.1	0.2
Jehovah's Witness	1	NR	NR	NR	-	-
MENN–Amish Undif	1	NR	64	205	0.6	0.8
METH–AME	3	0	350	420	1.2	1.7
METH–C.M.E.	3	230	410	492	1.4	2.0
METH–Un Methodist	17	730	2,397	2,668	7.4	10.8
Muslim Est	1	792	NR	3,436	9.5	13.9
Non-denom Chr Chs	8	830	1,069	1,122	3.1	4.5
PENT–Assemb of God	1	15	0	26	0.1	0.1
PENT–Ch God (Cleve)	3	208	559	670	1.8	2.7
PENT–Ch of God Proph	1	NR	63	76	0.2	0.3
PENT–Cong Hol Ch	5	180	133	159	0.4	0.6
PENT–Int Foursq Gos	1	164	83	100	0.3	0.4
PENT–Intl Pent Holiness	2	38	81	97	0.3	0.4
PENT–Un Pent Ch Intl	1	NR	NR	NR	-	-
PRES–Presb Ch (USA)	9	335	692	830	2.3	3.4
Sev Day Adv	2	47	82	94	0.3	0.4
Un C of Christ	1	0	63	76	0.2	0.3
HAMPTON (CITY)	**145**	**24,564**	**41,300**	**64,677**	**47.1**	**100.0**
ANG/EPIS–Episcopal	4	483	1,160	1,373	1.0	2.1
Bahá'í	0	NR	47	47	0.0	0.1
BAPT–Amer Bapt USA	5	1,272	2,476	2,997	2.2	4.6
BAPT–Free Will Bapt	1	NR	52	63	0.0	0.1
BAPT–NBC Amer	1	700	850	1,029	0.7	1.6
BAPT–NBC USA	3	800	1,300	1,573	1.1	2.4
BAPT–Ref Bapt Ch	1	NR	NR	NR	-	-
BAPT–So Bapt Conv	20	5,221	12,991	15,724	11.4	24.3
Catholic	6	NR	NR	5,428	3.9	8.4
CGOD–Ch God (Ander)	2	135	NR	135	0.1	0.2
Ch Cr, Scientst	1	NR	NR	NR	-	-
Ch of Chr (Hol)	1	NR	NR	NR	-	-
Ch of Nazarene	3	182	166	312	0.2	0.5
CHR–Chr Ch (Disc)	2	135	296	358	0.3	0.6
CHR–Chr Chs & Chs Cr	2	NR	475	575	0.4	0.9
CHR–Chs of Christ	2	127	117	152	0.1	0.2
FRND–Evan Fr Ch Intl	1	149	86	104	0.1	0.2
Jehovah's Witness	3	NR	NR	NR	-	-
JUD–Conserv	1	190	213	575	0.4	0.9
LDS–L-D Saints	2	NR	NR	1,177	0.9	1.8
LUTH–E.L.C.A.	2	298	713	912	0.7	1.4
LUTH–Luth Ch-Am Asc	1	NR	NR	NR	-	-
LUTH–Luth–MO Synod	1	97	72	121	0.1	0.2
MENN–Mennonite USA	1	700	1,914	2,317	1.7	3.6
METH–AME	1	250	525	635	0.5	1.0
METH–AME Zion	1	0	100	121	0.1	0.2
METH–C.M.E.	2	0	200	242	0.2	0.4
METH–Un Methodist	12	1,375	4,886	5,943	4.3	9.2
Muslim Est	2	1,584	NR	6,872	5.0	10.6
Non-denom Chr Chs	33	5,100	6,504	7,180	5.2	11.1
ORTHO–Coptic Orth Ch	1	95	NR	180	0.1	0.3
PENT–Assemb of God	4	3,623	2,739	4,392	3.2	6.8
PENT–Ch God (Cleve)	3	387	451	546	0.4	0.8
PENT–COGIC	4	415	725	878	0.6	1.4
PENT–Elim	1	NR	NR	NR	-	-
PENT–Full Gosp Bapt	1	NR	NR	NR	-	-
PENT–Intl Pent Holiness	3	218	166	201	0.1	0.3
PRES–Evan Presby Ch	1	NR	62	75	0.1	0.1
PRES–Presb Ch (USA)	4	343	753	911	0.7	1.4
PRES–Presb Ch Amer	1	210	243	317	0.2	0.5
Salvation Army	1	34	87	120	0.1	0.2
Sev Day Adv	3	328	570	655	0.5	1.0
Un C of Christ	1	113	361	437	0.3	0.7
HANOVER	**117**	**14,259**	**32,614**	**48,936**	**49.0**	**100.0**
ANG/EPIS–Episcopal	9	631	1,559	2,350	2.4	4.8
Bahá'í	1	NR	22	22	0.0	0.0
BAPT–NBC USA	2	550	925	1,136	1.1	2.3
BAPT–So Bapt Conv	29	6,476	14,280	17,534	17.6	35.8
BUDD–Theravada	1	NR	NR	395	0.4	0.8
BUDD–Vajrayana	1	NR	NR	72	0.1	0.1
Calv Chpl	1	NR	NR	NR	-	-
Catholic	2	NR	NR	5,183	5.2	10.6
Ch of Nazarene	2	245	315	625	0.6	1.3
CHR–Chr Ch (Disc)	6	294	1,294	1,589	1.6	3.2
CHR–Chr Chs & Chs Cr	7	NR	3,389	4,161	4.2	8.5
CHR–Chs of Christ	1	150	150	200	0.2	0.4
FRND–Evan Fr Ch Intl	1	179	155	190	0.2	0.4
FRND–Fr Gen Cf & Un Mtg	1	NR	0	0	0.0	0.0
Jehovah's Witness	2	NR	NR	NR	-	-
LDS–L-D Saints	3	NR	NR	1,808	1.8	3.7
LUTH–E.L.C.A.	1	93	190	225	0.2	0.5
LUTH–Luth–MO Synod	2	99	235	258	0.3	0.5
METH–Un Methodist	16	1,859	5,529	7,409	7.4	15.1
METH–Wesleyan	1	77	38	100	0.1	0.2
Non-denom Chr Chs	8	880	1,015	1,162	1.2	2.4
ORTHE–Orth Ch in Amer	1	15	NR	30	0.0	0.1
PENT–Assemb of God	2	1,113	945	1,315	1.3	2.7
PENT–Ch God (Cleve)	1	208	309	379	0.4	0.8
PENT–Pent FW Bapt	1	NR	NR	NR	-	-
PENT–Un Pent Ch Intl	3	NR	NR	NR	-	-
PENT–Vineyard	1	83	70	86	0.1	0.2
PRES–Presb Ch (USA)	7	793	1,501	1,843	1.8	3.8
PRES–Presb Ch Amer	2	195	170	243	0.2	0.5
Sev Day Adv	1	203	353	406	0.4	0.8
Unit Univ	1	116	170	215	0.2	0.4
HARRISONBURG (CITY)	**67**	**9,429**	**13,953**	**24,834**	**50.8**	**100.0**
ANG/EPIS–Episcopal	2	240	512	520	1.1	2.1
Bahá'í	1	NR	34	34	0.1	0.1
BAPT–Amer Bapt USA	1	145	200	228	0.5	0.9
BAPT–Free Will Bapt	1	NR	52	59	0.1	0.2
BAPT–So Bapt Conv	7	1,459	1,750	1,992	4.1	8.0
BRETH–Brethren (Ash)	1	NR	80	91	0.2	0.4
Catholic	1	NR	NR	4,565	9.3	18.4
CHR–Chr Chs & Chs Cr	2	NR	220	250	0.5	1.0
CHR–Chs of Christ	2	90	82	105	0.2	0.4
Jehovah's Witness	1	NR	NR	NR	-	-
JUD–Reform	1	40	71	192	0.4	0.8

NR–Not Reported - Represents no adherents reported. Percentages may not total 100 due to rounding.

Table 3: Religious Congregations by County and Group: 2010

Religious Group	Number of Congrega-tions	Number of Attendees	Number of Communicant, Confirmed, or Full Members	Adherents: Number of Adherents	Adherents: % of Total Pop.	Adherents: % of Total Adh.
LDS–L-D Saints	3	NR	NR	1,030	2.1	4.1
LUTH–E.L.C.A.	1	538	1,008	1,191	2.4	4.8
MENN–Mennonite USA	8	1,771	1,906	2,170	4.4	8.7
METH–AME	1	0	150	171	0.3	0.7
METH–Free Methodist	1	154	87	154	0.3	0.6
METH–Un Methodist	5	610	2,344	2,592	5.3	10.4
Muslim Est	1	792	NR	3,436	7.0	13.8
Non-denom Chr Chs	13	2,450	3,034	3,278	6.7	13.2
PENT–Assemb of God	1	50	20	50	0.1	0.2
PENT–Ch God (Cleve)	2	86	402	458	0.9	1.8
PENT–Ch of God Proph	1	NR	80	91	0.2	0.4
PENT–Intl Pent Holiness	2	231	377	429	0.9	1.7
PENT–Un Pent Ch Intl	1	NR	NR	NR	-	-
PRES–Presb Ch (USA)	2	588	1,224	1,393	2.8	5.6
PRES–Presb Ch Amer	1	0	0	0	0.0	0.0
Salvation Army	1	72	138	154	0.3	0.6
Sev Day Adv	1	56	98	113	0.2	0.5
Un Breth in Cr	1	17	20	15	0.0	0.1
Un C of Christ	1	40	64	73	0.1	0.3
HENRICO	**229**	**49,721**	**99,611**	**156,372**	**50.9**	**100.0**
ANG/EPIS–Anglican NA	1	NR	NR	NR	-	-
ANG/EPIS–Episcopal	10	1,838	5,625	7,002	2.3	4.5
Bahá'í	1	NR	88	88	0.0	0.1
BAPT–Amer Bapt USA	4	1,140	2,310	2,841	0.9	1.8
BAPT–Free Will Bapt	2	NR	104	128	0.0	0.1
BAPT–NBC Amer	1	0	150	185	0.1	0.1
BAPT–NBC USA	1	0	150	185	0.1	0.1
BAPT–Reg Bapt Gen As	1	NR	NR	NR	-	-
BAPT–So Bapt Conv	62	15,795	45,412	55,858	18.2	35.7
BRETH–Ch of Brethren	1	65	163	200	0.1	0.1
BUDD–Mahayana	1	NR	NR	536	0.2	0.3
Catholic	6	NR	NR	17,097	5.6	10.9
Ch Cr, Scientst	1	NR	NR	NR	-	-
Ch God (7th Day)	1	NR	NR	NR	-	-
Ch of Nazarene	3	152	157	303	0.1	0.2
Chr & Miss Al	2	126	130	197	0.1	0.1
CHR–Chr Ch (Disc)	3	168	549	675	0.2	0.4
CHR–Chr Chs & Chs Cr	7	NR	1,140	1,402	0.5	0.9
CHR–Chs of Christ	2	480	420	510	0.2	0.3
Evan Free Ch	1	70	NR	70	0.0	0.0
FRND–Evan Fr Ch Intl	1	32	38	47	0.0	0.0
HINDU–I/A Temples	1	NR	NR	17	0.0	0.0
HINDU–Post Ren	2	NR	NR	26	0.0	0.0
Jehovah's Witness	3	NR	NR	NR	-	-
LDS–L-D Saints	4	NR	NR	2,213	0.7	1.4
LUTH–E.L.C.A.	2	532	1,221	1,559	0.5	1.0
LUTH–Luth–MO Synod	1	373	815	1,014	0.3	0.6
MENN–Mennonite USA	1	100	82	101	0.0	0.1
METH–Un Methodist	22	4,079	14,777	18,078	5.9	11.6
METH–Wesleyan	1	18	18	23	0.0	0.0
Muslim Est	4	3,168	NR	13,744	4.5	8.8
Non-denom Chr Chs	35	13,926	17,637	18,749	6.1	12.0
ORTHE–Holy Orth in NA	1	35	NR	45	0.0	0.0
ORTHO–Armen Ap Etchm	1	45	NR	90	0.0	0.1
PENT–Assemb of God	5	3,635	1,717	4,754	1.5	3.0
PENT–Ch God (Cleve)	3	301	586	721	0.2	0.5
PENT–Ch Lord Jesus Apos	6	NR	NR	NR	-	-
PENT–Int Foursq Gos	1	133	105	129	0.0	0.1
PENT–Intl Pent Holiness	2	175	164	202	0.1	0.1
PENT–United Holy Ch	1	NR	NR	NR	-	-
PRES–Evan Presby Ch	1	NR	406	499	0.2	0.3
PRES–Presb Ch (USA)	15	2,391	4,591	5,647	1.8	3.6
PRES–Presb Ch Amer	1	730	683	1,008	0.3	0.6
Sev Day Adv	4	214	373	429	0.1	0.3
HENRY	**119**	**9,229**	**21,826**	**26,006**	**48.0**	**100.0**
ANG/EPIS–Episcopal	1	139	323	323	0.6	1.2
Bahá'í	0	NR	3	3	0.0	0.0
BAPT–Free Will Bapt	2	NR	104	123	0.2	0.5
BAPT–Natl Mis Bapt Conv	1	0	150	178	0.3	0.7
BAPT–NBC USA	1	0	350	414	0.8	1.6
BAPT–Prog NBC	1	0	150	178	0.3	0.7

Religious Group	Number of Congrega-tions	Number of Attendees	Number of Communicant, Confirmed, or Full Members	Adherents: Number of Adherents	Adherents: % of Total Pop.	Adherents: % of Total Adh.
BAPT–So Bapt Conv	31	3,362	10,282	12,176	22.5	46.8
BRETH–Ch of Brethren	4	403	612	725	1.3	2.8
CHR–Chr Ch (Disc)	3	40	225	266	0.5	1.0
CHR–Chr Chs & Chs Cr	5	NR	1,402	1,660	3.1	6.4
CHR–Chs of Christ	6	287	279	339	0.6	1.3
FRND–Evan Fr Ch Intl	2	240	133	157	0.3	0.6
LDS–L-D Saints	1	NR	NR	484	0.9	1.9
METH–AME	1	0	100	118	0.2	0.5
METH–Un Methodist	13	537	1,680	1,900	3.5	7.3
METH–Wesleyan	1	50	40	65	0.1	0.2
Non-denom Chr Chs	25	3,075	3,773	4,191	7.7	16.1
PENT–Assemb of God	2	128	67	156	0.3	0.6
PENT–Ch God (Cleve)	4	248	664	786	1.5	3.0
PENT–Ch Lord Jesus Apos	2	NR	NR	NR	-	-
PENT–Ch of God Proph	2	NR	227	269	0.5	1.0
PENT–Intl Pent Holiness	6	527	704	834	1.5	3.2
PENT–United Holy Ch	2	NR	NR	NR	-	-
PRES–Presb Ch (USA)	3	193	558	661	1.2	2.5
HIGHLAND	**20**	**606**	**1,194**	**1,412**	**60.8**	**100.0**
ANG/EPIS–Episcopal	1	15	26	26	1.1	1.8
Bahá'í	0	NR	8	8	0.3	0.6
BAPT–So Bapt Conv	1	50	118	132	5.7	9.3
BRETH–Ch of Brethren	2	32	56	63	2.7	4.5
FRND–Unaffl Mtgs	1	NR	NR	NR	-	-
METH–Un Methodist	9	219	558	709	30.5	50.2
Non-denom Chr Chs	1	175	200	219	9.4	15.5
PENT–Ch of God Proph	1	NR	32	36	1.6	2.5
PRES–Presb Ch (USA)	4	115	196	219	9.4	15.5
HOPEWELL (CITY)	**44**	**3,793**	**8,837**	**11,599**	**51.3**	**100.0**
ANG/EPIS–Episcopal	1	68	180	185	0.8	1.6
Bahá'í	0	NR	4	4	0.0	0.0
BAPT–Amer Bapt USA	1	175	500	624	2.8	5.4
BAPT–So Bapt Conv	5	631	3,105	3,873	17.1	33.4
BRETH–Ch of Brethren	1	16	56	70	0.3	0.6
Catholic	1	NR	NR	930	4.1	8.0
Ch of Nazarene	1	30	119	119	0.5	1.0
CHR–Chr Ch (Disc)	1	62	334	417	1.8	3.6
CHR–Chr Chs & Chs Cr	1	NR	65	81	0.4	0.7
CHR–Chs of Christ	2	445	461	530	2.3	4.6
LUTH–Luth–MO Synod	1	75	116	153	0.7	1.3
METH–Un Methodist	2	286	958	1,037	4.6	8.9
New Apost Ch	1	NR	NR	NR	-	-
Non-denom Chr Chs	8	975	1,565	1,626	7.2	14.0
ORTHE–Greek Orthodox	1	75	NR	120	0.5	1.0
PENT–Assemb of God	2	131	15	133	0.6	1.1
PENT–Ch God (Cleve)	2	212	288	359	1.6	3.1
PENT–Ch Lord Jesus Apos	2	NR	NR	NR	-	-
PENT–Ch of God Proph	1	NR	26	32	0.1	0.3
PENT–Intl Pent Holiness	4	204	386	481	2.1	4.1
PRES–Presb Ch (USA)	2	106	198	247	1.1	2.1
PRES–Presb Ch Amer	2	223	294	370	1.6	3.2
Sev Day Adv	1	24	42	48	0.2	0.4
Un C of Christ	1	55	125	156	0.7	1.3
Zoroastrian	0	NR	NR	4	0.0	0.0
ISLE OF WIGHT	**58**	**3,858**	**9,736**	**13,954**	**39.6**	**100.0**
ANG/EPIS–Episcopal	1	82	151	198	0.6	1.4
Bahá'í	0	NR	20	20	0.1	0.1
BAPT–Amer Bapt USA	1	235	471	566	1.6	4.1
BAPT–Free Will Bapt	1	NR	52	63	0.2	0.5
BAPT–NBC USA	1	60	100	120	0.3	0.9
BAPT–So Bapt Conv	10	1,140	3,179	3,822	10.8	27.4
BUDD–Theravada	1	NR	NR	1,364	3.9	9.8
Catholic	1	NR	NR	778	2.2	5.6
Ch of Nazarene	1	25	95	95	0.3	0.7
CHR–Chr Chs & Chs Cr	1	NR	90	108	0.3	0.8
CHR–Chs of Christ	1	46	30	50	0.1	0.4
FRND–Evan Fr Ch Intl	1	23	15	18	0.1	0.1
Jehovah's Witness	1	NR	NR	NR	-	-
LDS–L-D Saints	1	NR	NR	207	0.6	1.5
METH–AME	7	135	1,086	1,306	3.7	9.4

NR–Not Reported - Represents no adherents reported. Percentages may not total 100 due to rounding.

Table 3: Religious Congregations by County and Group: 2010

Religious Group	Number of Congregations	Number of Attendees	Number of Communicant, Confirmed, or Full Members	Adherents: Number of Adherents	Adherents: % of Total Pop.	Adherents: % of Total Adh.
METH–AME Zion	1	50	105	126	0.4	0.9
METH–Un Methodist	7	646	1,869	2,283	6.5	16.4
Non-denom Chr Chs	6	685	910	944	2.7	6.8
PENT–Assemb of God	2	193	199	250	0.7	1.8
PENT–Ch God (Cleve)	2	147	206	248	0.7	1.8
PENT–Ch of God Proph	1	NR	54	65	0.2	0.5
PENT–COGIC	1	0	150	180	0.5	1.3
PENT–Vineyard	1	75	130	156	0.4	1.1
PRES–Presb Ch (USA)	1	58	130	156	0.4	1.1
PRES–Presb Ch Amer	1	0	0	0	0.0	0.0
Sev Day Adv	1	41	71	82	0.2	0.6
Un C of Christ	5	217	623	749	2.1	5.4
JAMES CITY	**43**	**6,488**	**9,217**	**26,384**	**39.4**	**100.0**
ANG/EPIS–Anglican NA	2	NR	NR	NR	-	-
ANG/EPIS–Episcopal	2	528	1,079	1,466	2.2	5.6
Bahá'í	0	NR	14	14	0.0	0.1
BAPT–Amer Bapt USA	2	678	845	1,006	1.5	3.8
BAPT–NBC USA	1	200	250	298	0.4	1.1
BAPT–Prog NBC	1	0	150	179	0.3	0.7
BAPT–So Bapt Conv	3	605	1,418	1,688	2.5	6.4
Calv Chpl	1	NR	NR	NR	-	-
Catholic	2	NR	NR	10,601	15.8	40.2
CHR–Chr Ch (Disc)	1	135	580	690	1.0	2.6
CHR–Chr Chs & Chs Cr	1	NR	0	0	0.0	0.0
Jehovah's Witness	1	NR	NR	NR	-	-
LDS–L-D Saints	2	NR	NR	891	1.3	3.4
LUTH–E.L.C.A.	1	75	156	198	0.3	0.8
LUTH–Luth-MO Synod	1	492	702	922	1.4	3.5
MENN–Mennonite USA	1	65	75	89	0.1	0.3
METH–Un Methodist	3	677	1,098	1,421	2.1	5.4
METH–Wesleyan	1	148	87	192	0.3	0.7
Muslim Est	1	792	NR	3,436	5.1	13.0
Non-denom Chr Chs	1	140	150	175	0.3	0.7
PENT–Assemb of God	4	874	1,087	1,222	1.8	4.6
PENT–Ch Lord Jesus Apos	1	NR	NR	NR	-	-
PENT–Elim	1	NR	NR	NR	-	-
PENT–Intl Pent Holiness	2	151	176	210	0.3	0.8
PRES–Presb Ch (USA)	2	230	446	531	0.8	2.0
PRES–Presb Ch Amer	1	327	300	368	0.5	1.4
Salvation Army	1	17	37	106	0.2	0.4
Sev Day Adv	2	175	304	350	0.5	1.3
Unit Univ	1	179	263	331	0.5	1.3
KING AND QUEEN	**17**	**631**	**1,813**	**2,186**	**31.5**	**100.0**
ANG/EPIS–Episcopal	1	5	6	6	0.1	0.3
Bahá'í	0	NR	1	1	0.0	0.0
BAPT–So Bapt Conv	9	444	1,369	1,625	23.4	74.3
CHR–Chr Ch (Disc)	1	40	92	109	1.6	5.0
FRND–Fr Gen Cf & Un Mtg	1	NR	0	0	0.0	0.0
Jehovah's Witness	1	NR	NR	NR	-	-
METH–Un Methodist	3	107	325	403	5.8	18.4
PENT–Assemb of God	1	35	20	42	0.6	1.9
KING GEORGE	**29**	**2,518**	**5,144**	**7,774**	**33.0**	**100.0**
ANG/EPIS–Episcopal	3	148	184	194	0.8	2.5
Bahá'í	0	NR	5	5	0.0	0.1
BAPT–Amer Bapt USA	1	175	400	511	2.2	6.6
BAPT–So Bapt Conv	10	1,030	2,785	3,556	15.1	45.7
Catholic	1	NR	NR	825	3.5	10.6
CHR–Chs of Christ	1	42	40	53	0.2	0.7
Jehovah's Witness	1	NR	NR	NR	-	-
LDS–L-D Saints	1	NR	NR	269	1.1	3.5
LUTH–Luth-MO Synod	1	131	237	298	1.3	3.8
METH–Un Methodist	3	259	784	1,227	5.2	15.8
Non-denom Chr Chs	3	405	510	531	2.3	6.8
PENT–Assemb of God	1	20	0	30	0.1	0.4
PENT–Ch God (Cleve)	1	208	120	153	0.6	2.0
PENT–Un Pent Ch Intl	1	NR	NR	NR	-	-
PRES–Presb Ch Amer	1	100	79	122	0.5	1.6

Religious Group	Number of Congregations	Number of Attendees	Number of Communicant, Confirmed, or Full Members	Adherents: Number of Adherents	Adherents: % of Total Pop.	Adherents: % of Total Adh.
KING WILLIAM	**31**	**1,911**	**4,927**	**6,828**	**42.8**	**100.0**
ANG/EPIS–Episcopal	3	115	227	280	1.8	4.1
Bahá'í	0	NR	8	8	0.1	0.1
BAPT–NBC USA	1	300	450	556	3.5	8.1
BAPT–Prog NBC	1	0	150	185	1.2	2.7
BAPT–So Bapt Conv	10	676	2,408	2,973	18.7	43.5
Catholic	1	NR	NR	569	3.6	8.3
Ch of Nazarene	1	37	46	123	0.8	1.8
CHR–Chr Ch (Disc)	1	30	107	132	0.8	1.9
CHR–Chr Chs & Chs Cr	2	NR	280	346	2.2	5.1
METH–A.W.M.C.	1	20	0	18	0.1	0.3
METH–Un Methodist	3	208	644	893	5.6	13.1
Non-denom Chr Chs	4	410	460	563	3.5	8.2
PENT–Ch God (Cleve)	1	68	51	63	0.4	0.9
PRES–Presb Ch (USA)	2	47	96	119	0.7	1.7
LANCASTER	**33**	**2,070**	**4,878**	**7,219**	**63.4**	**100.0**
ANG/EPIS–Episcopal	3	330	587	697	6.1	9.7
Bahá'í	0	NR	5	5	0.0	0.1
BAPT–So Bapt Conv	11	727	2,269	2,585	22.7	35.8
Catholic	1	NR	NR	1,352	11.9	18.7
Ch Cr, Scientst	1	NR	NR	NR	-	-
Ch of Nazarene	1	250	222	492	4.3	6.8
FRND–Unaffl Mtgs	1	NR	NR	NR	-	-
Jehovah's Witness	1	NR	NR	NR	-	-
LDS–L-D Saints	1	NR	NR	130	1.1	1.8
LUTH–E.L.C.A.	1	40	54	54	0.5	0.7
METH–Un Methodist	7	383	1,129	1,212	10.6	16.8
PRES–Presb Ch (USA)	3	268	499	568	5.0	7.9
Sev Day Adv	1	34	60	69	0.6	1.0
Unit Univ	1	38	53	55	0.5	0.8
LEE	**109**	**3,427**	**11,709**	**14,003**	**54.7**	**100.0**
Bahá'í	0	NR	13	13	0.1	0.1
BAPT–Free Will Bapt	4	NR	208	246	1.0	1.8
BAPT–Natl Mis Bapt Conv	2	0	300	355	1.4	2.5
BAPT–Prim Bapt E Dst	11	275	978	1,159	4.5	8.3
BAPT–So Bapt Conv	41	2,052	7,568	8,967	35.0	64.0
BRETH–Ch of Brethren	1	30	45	53	0.2	0.4
Catholic	1	NR	NR	59	0.2	0.4
Ch God (7th Day)	1	NR	NR	NR	-	-
CHR–Chr Chs & Chs Cr	7	NR	332	393	1.5	2.8
CHR–Chs of Christ	2	35	26	36	0.1	0.3
Jehovah's Witness	1	NR	NR	NR	-	-
MENN–Amish Undif	1	NR	24	65	0.3	0.5
MENN–Mara Amish-Menn	1	75	29	75	0.3	0.5
METH–AME Zion	1	0	100	118	0.5	0.8
METH–Un Methodist	21	610	1,474	1,723	6.7	12.3
PENT–Assemb of God	1	17	0	20	0.1	0.1
PENT–Ch God (Cleve)	5	236	412	488	1.9	3.5
PENT–Ch God Mtn Asm	2	NR	NR	NR	-	-
PENT–Ch of God Proph	4	NR	64	76	0.3	0.5
PENT–Cong Hol Ch	1	39	35	41	0.2	0.3
Sev Day Adv	1	58	101	116	0.5	0.8
LEXINGTON (CITY)	**28**	**1,572**	**3,623**	**5,341**	**75.8**	**100.0**
Bahá'í	0	NR	2	2	0.0	0.0
BAPT–So Bapt Conv	3	213	749	814	11.6	15.2
Catholic	1	NR	NR	831	11.8	15.6
CHR–Chs of Christ	1	30	25	30	0.4	0.6
Jehovah's Witness	2	NR	NR	NR	-	-
LDS–L-D Saints	1	NR	NR	381	5.4	7.1
LUTH–E.L.C.A.	1	37	58	73	1.0	1.4
METH–Un Methodist	2	276	545	670	9.5	12.5
Non-denom Chr Chs	3	450	577	602	8.5	11.3
PENT–Assemb of God	1	90	44	152	2.2	2.8
PENT–Ch God (Cleve)	1	25	36	39	0.6	0.7
PENT–Ch of God Proph	1	NR	6	7	0.1	0.1
PENT–COGIC	2	0	300	326	4.6	6.1
PENT–Full Gosp Bapt	1	NR	NR	NR	-	-
PENT–Int Foursq Gos	1	69	87	95	1.3	1.8
PENT–Intl Pent Holiness	2	107	142	154	2.2	2.9

NR–Not Reported   - Represents no adherents reported.   Percentages may not total 100 due to rounding.

Table 3: Religious Congregations by County and Group: 2010

Religious Group	Number of Congregations	Number of Attendees	Number of Communicant, Confirmed, or Full Members	Adherents: Number of Adherents	Adherents: % of Total Pop.	Adherents: % of Total Adh.
PENT–Un Pent Ch Intl	1	NR	NR	NR	-	-
PRES–As Ref Pres Ch	2	NR	231	251	3.6	4.7
PRES–Presb Ch (USA)	1	0	605	657	9.3	12.3
PRES–Presb Ch Amer	1	275	216	256	3.6	4.8
Zoroastrian	0	NR	NR	1	0.0	0.0
LOUDOUN	**176**	**22,914**	**30,070**	**119,821**	**38.4**	**100.0**
ANG/EPIS–Anglican NA	4	NR	NR	NR	-	-
ANG/EPIS–Episcopal	8	1,612	3,671	3,980	1.3	3.3
Bahá'í	2	NR	485	485	0.2	0.4
BAPT–So Bapt Conv	21	2,610	3,096	4,109	1.3	3.4
BUDD–Theravada	1	NR	NR	375	0.1	0.3
Calv Chpl	1	NR	NR	NR	-	-
Catholic	6	NR	NR	45,687	14.6	38.1
Ch Cr, Scientst	1	NR	NR	NR	-	-
Ch of Nazarene	4	404	394	656	0.2	0.5
Chr & Miss Al	2	208	243	252	0.1	0.2
CHR–Chr Chs & Chs Cr	1	NR	0	0	0.0	0.0
CHR–Chs of Christ	2	140	113	163	0.1	0.1
FRND–Fr Gen Cf & Un Mtg	1	NR	192	255	0.1	0.2
HINDU–I/A Temples	1	NR	NR	250	0.1	0.2
HINDU–Post Ren	4	NR	NR	55	0.0	0.0
Jehovah's Witness	3	NR	NR	NR	-	-
JUD–Conserv	1	123	138	373	0.1	0.3
JUD–Reform	1	85	150	405	0.1	0.3
LDS–L-D Saints	11	NR	NR	4,611	1.5	3.8
LUTH–E.L.C.A.	6	672	2,062	2,419	0.8	2.0
LUTH–Luth–MO Synod	2	509	604	1,043	0.3	0.9
LUTH–Wisc Ev Luth Syn	1	25	24	30	0.0	0.0
METH–AME	1	0	150	199	0.1	0.2
METH–Un Methodist	27	3,345	7,964	13,129	4.2	11.0
Muslim Est	2	3,292	NR	27,436	8.8	22.9
Non-denom Chr Chs	20	6,838	7,445	8,765	2.8	7.3
ORTHO–Coptic Orth Ch	1	125	NR	200	0.1	0.2
ORTHO–Malan Dioc Am	1	60	NR	100	0.0	0.1
PENT–Assemb of God	6	790	488	987	0.3	0.8
PENT–Ch God (Cleve)	2	18	29	38	0.0	0.0
PENT–Full Gosp Bapt	1	NR	NR	NR	-	-
PENT–Int Pent C Chr	2	40	4	105	0.0	0.1
PENT–Intl Pent Holiness	1	50	35	46	0.0	0.0
PENT–Un Pent Ch Intl	3	NR	NR	NR	-	-
PRES–Korean Amer Pres	1	NR	NR	NR	-	-
PRES–Orth Pres Ch	3	259	248	347	0.1	0.3
PRES–Presb Ch (USA)	7	946	1,648	2,187	0.7	1.8
PRES–Presb Ch Amer	4	425	292	350	0.1	0.3
Salvation Army	1	22	83	101	0.0	0.1
Sev Day Adv	3	161	280	322	0.1	0.3
Sikh	1	NR	NR	NR	-	-
Un C of Christ	2	25	83	110	0.0	0.1
Unit Univ	2	130	149	234	0.1	0.2
Unity Ch	1	NR	NR	NR	-	-
Zoroastrian	0	NR	NR	17	0.0	0.0
LOUISA	**56**	**2,829**	**7,298**	**10,060**	**30.3**	**100.0**
ANG/EPIS–Episcopal	2	109	214	278	0.8	2.8
Bahá'í	0	NR	3	3	0.0	0.0
BAPT–Free Will Bapt	1	NR	52	63	0.2	0.6
BAPT–So Bapt Conv	21	1,300	3,792	4,564	13.8	45.4
Calv Chpl	1	NR	NR	NR	-	-
Catholic	2	NR	NR	941	2.8	9.4
Ch of Nazarene	1	34	66	74	0.2	0.7
CHR–Chr Ch (Disc)	7	155	595	716	2.2	7.1
CHR–Chr Chs & Chs Cr	1	NR	288	347	1.0	3.4
FRND–Fr Gen Cf & Un Mtg	1	NR	0	0	0.0	0.0
Jehovah's Witness	1	NR	NR	NR	-	-
LDS–L-D Saints	1	NR	NR	283	0.9	2.8
METH–Un Methodist	8	691	1,470	1,936	5.8	19.2
Non-denom Chr Chs	6	437	710	725	2.2	7.2
PENT–Ch Lord Jesus Apos	1	NR	NR	NR	-	-
PRES–Presb Ch (USA)	2	103	108	130	0.4	1.3
LUNENBURG	**28**	**893**	**3,218**	**3,716**	**28.8**	**100.0**
ANG/EPIS–Episcopal	2	46	94	107	0.8	2.9
Bahá'í	0	NR	4	4	0.0	0.1
BAPT–NBC USA	1	6	6	7	0.1	0.2
BAPT–So Bapt Conv	3	215	848	997	7.7	26.8
Ch of Nazarene	1	65	138	138	1.1	3.7
CHR–Chr Ch (Disc)	2	101	312	367	2.8	9.9
CHR–Chr Chs & Chs Cr	2	NR	125	147	1.1	4.0
METH–AME	1	0	150	176	1.4	4.7
METH–AME Zion	3	0	350	411	3.2	11.1
METH–Un Methodist	6	246	699	839	6.5	22.6
Non-denom Chr Chs	2	145	335	338	2.6	9.1
PENT–Ch God (Cleve)	1	36	52	61	0.5	1.6
PENT–Ch of God Proph	1	NR	32	38	0.3	1.0
PRES–Evan Presby Ch	1	NR	23	27	0.2	0.7
PRES–Presb Ch (USA)	2	33	50	59	0.5	1.6
LYNCHBURG (CITY)	**136**	**33,525**	**54,469**	**72,781**	**96.3**	**100.0**
ANG/EPIS–Anglican NA	2	NR	NR	NR	-	-
ANG/EPIS–Episcopal	3	596	1,840	1,975	2.6	2.7
Bahá'í	0	NR	18	18	0.0	0.0
BAPT–Alliance Bapt	1	NR	NR	NR	-	-
BAPT–Amer Bapt USA	1	150	454	536	0.7	0.7
BAPT–NBC Amer	1	30	45	53	0.1	0.1
BAPT–So Bapt Conv	20	15,199	25,464	30,070	39.8	41.3
BRETH–Ch of Brethren	1	38	95	112	0.1	0.2
Calv Chpl	1	NR	NR	NR	-	-
Catholic	2	NR	NR	3,994	5.3	5.5
CGOD–Ch God (Ander)	2	125	NR	125	0.2	0.2
Ch Cr, Scientst	1	NR	NR	NR	-	-
Ch of Nazarene	1	376	578	725	1.0	1.0
Chr & Miss Al	1	70	18	58	0.1	0.1
CHR–Chr Ch (Disc)	7	575	1,660	1,960	2.6	2.7
CHR–Chr Chs & Chs Cr	1	NR	90	106	0.1	0.1
CHR–Chs of Christ	2	120	110	155	0.2	0.2
FRND–Fr Gen Cf & Un Mtg	1	NR	0	0	0.0	0.0
Jehovah's Witness	1	NR	NR	NR	-	-
JUD–Reform	1	46	81	219	0.3	0.3
LDS–L-D Saints	3	NR	NR	1,250	1.7	1.7
LUTH–E.L.C.A.	2	528	1,062	1,413	1.9	1.9
LUTH–Luth–MO Synod	1	65	44	70	0.1	0.1
METH–Free Methodist	1	37	35	37	0.0	0.1
METH–Un Methodist	18	1,626	5,235	6,090	8.1	8.4
METH–Wesleyan	1	113	47	147	0.2	0.2
Muslim Est	1	792	NR	3,436	4.5	4.7
Non-denom Chr Chs	26	7,554	9,899	10,775	14.3	14.8
ORTHE–Ant Orth of NA	1	30	NR	50	0.1	0.1
ORTHE–Greek Orthodox	1	35	NR	50	0.1	0.1
PENT–Assemb of God	2	155	50	254	0.3	0.3
PENT–Ch God (Cleve)	1	87	63	74	0.1	0.1
PENT–Ch of God Proph	1	NR	137	162	0.2	0.2
PENT–COGIC	2	400	575	679	0.9	0.9
PENT–Elim	1	NR	NR	NR	-	-
PENT–Int Foursq Gos	1	34	47	56	0.1	0.1
PENT–Intl Pent Holiness	7	3,117	3,242	3,828	5.1	5.3
PENT–Un Pent Ch Intl	1	NR	NR	NR	-	-
PENT–United Holy Ch	1	NR	NR	NR	-	-
PRES–Evan Presby Ch	1	NR	775	915	1.2	1.3
PRES–Orth Pres Ch	1	85	72	102	0.1	0.1
PRES–Presb Ch (USA)	4	543	1,689	1,995	2.6	2.7
PRES–Presb Ch Amer	1	486	262	365	0.5	0.5
REF–Comm Ref Evan	1	NR	NR	NR	-	-
Salvation Army	1	89	167	190	0.3	0.3
Sev Day Adv	2	272	473	544	0.7	0.7
Un C of Christ	1	40	23	27	0.0	0.0
Unit Univ	1	112	119	166	0.2	0.2
Unity Ch	1	NR	NR	NR	-	-
MADISON	**36**	**1,770**	**3,577**	**5,032**	**37.8**	**100.0**
ANG/EPIS–Episcopal	1	87	150	171	1.3	3.4
Bahá'í	0	NR	4	4	0.0	0.1
BAPT–Free Will Bapt	1	NR	52	63	0.5	1.3
BAPT–So Bapt Conv	6	382	942	1,133	8.5	22.5
BRETH–Ch of Brethren	1	42	60	72	0.5	1.4
Catholic	1	NR	NR	337	2.5	6.7

NR–Not Reported - Represents no adherents reported. Percentages may not total 100 due to rounding.

Table 3: Religious Congregations by County and Group: 2010

Religious Group	Number of Congrega-tions	Number of Attendees	Number of Communicant, Confirmed, or Full Members	Adherents		
				Number of Adherents	% of Total Pop.	% of Total Adh.
CHR–Chr Ch (Disc)	2	85	237	285	2.1	5.7
FRND–Fr Gen Cf & Un Mtg	1	NR	0	0	0.0	0.0
HINDU–I/A Temples	1	NR	NR	500	3.8	9.9
LUTH–E.L.C.A.	2	66	237	237	1.8	4.7
MENN–Beachy Amish-Menn	2	256	171	256	1.9	5.1
METH–Un Methodist	10	314	940	1,032	7.8	20.5
Non-denom Chr Chs	5	477	533	643	4.8	12.8
PENT–Ch God (Cleve)	1	28	26	31	0.2	0.6
PRES–Presb Ch (USA)	1	0	168	202	1.5	4.0
Sev Day Adv	1	33	57	66	0.5	1.3
MANASSAS (CITY)	**40**	**7,526**	**13,423**	**48,956**	**129.4**	**100.0**
ANG/EPIS–Episcopal	1	282	1,138	1,138	3.0	2.3
Bahá'í	0	NR	22	22	0.1	0.0
BAPT–Amer Bapt USA	1	425	863	1,112	2.9	2.3
BAPT–Prog NBC	1	250	500	644	1.7	1.3
BAPT–Reg Bapt Gen As	1	NR	NR	NR	-	-
BAPT–So Bapt Conv	3	550	687	885	2.3	1.8
BRETH–Ch of Brethren	1	185	373	480	1.3	1.0
Catholic	3	NR	NR	27,114	71.7	55.4
Ch of Nazarene	1	65	0	65	0.2	0.1
Evan Free Ch	1	250	NR	250	0.7	0.5
LDS–L-D Saints	4	NR	NR	2,010	5.3	4.1
LUTH–E.L.C.A.	1	194	724	966	2.6	2.0
METH–AME	1	250	700	902	2.4	1.8
METH–Un Methodist	2	1,028	4,179	5,053	13.4	10.3
METH–Wesleyan	1	85	17	111	0.3	0.2
Muslim Est	1	792	NR	3,436	9.1	7.0
Non-denom Chr Chs	8	2,694	3,450	3,630	9.6	7.4
ORTHE–Carp Rus Orth	1	75	NR	150	0.4	0.3
PENT–Assemb of God	1	90	122	122	0.3	0.2
PENT–Ch God (Cleve)	1	160	310	399	1.1	0.8
PENT–Ch of God Proph	2	NR	67	86	0.2	0.2
PENT–COGIC	1	0	0	0	0.0	0.0
PENT–Intl Pent Holiness	1	32	18	23	0.1	0.0
PENT–Un Pent Ch Intl	1	NR	NR	NR	-	-
Unit Univ	1	119	253	347	0.9	0.7
Zoroastrian	0	NR	NR	11	0.0	0.0
MANASSAS PARK (CITY)	**11**	**1,925**	**2,801**	**4,060**	**28.4**	**100.0**
Bahá'í	0	NR	3	3	0.0	0.1
LDS–L-D Saints	2	NR	NR	919	6.4	22.6
Non-denom Chr Chs	8	1,879	2,749	3,074	21.5	75.7
PENT–Ch God (Cleve)	1	46	49	64	0.4	1.6
MARTINSVILLE (CITY)	**67**	**4,270**	**8,589**	**10,984**	**79.5**	**100.0**
ANG/EPIS–Episcopal	1	32	27	27	0.2	0.2
Bahá'í	0	NR	4	4	0.0	0.0
BAPT–Alliance Bapt	1	NR	NR	NR	-	-
BAPT–Amer Bapt USA	1	0	0	0	0.0	0.0
BAPT–NBC USA	1	175	200	240	1.7	2.2
BAPT–So Bapt Conv	5	393	1,403	1,681	12.2	15.3
Catholic	1	NR	NR	650	4.7	5.9
CGOD–Ch God (Ander)	1	40	NR	40	0.3	0.4
CHR–Chr Ch (Disc)	12	253	1,222	1,464	10.6	13.3
CHR–Chr Chs & Chs Cr	3	NR	614	736	5.3	6.7
CHR–Chs of Christ	1	70	60	75	0.5	0.7
FRND–Evan Fr Ch Intl	2	92	35	42	0.3	0.4
Jehovah's Witness	2	NR	NR	NR	-	-
LUTH–E.L.C.A.	1	33	66	72	0.5	0.7
METH–AME	2	0	300	359	2.6	3.3
METH–Un Methodist	2	280	999	1,110	8.0	10.1
METH–Wesleyan	2	141	108	183	1.3	1.7
Non-denom Chr Chs	14	1,605	2,030	2,315	16.7	21.1
PENT–Assemb of God	1	125	102	300	2.2	2.7
PENT–Ch God (Cleve)	1	545	747	895	6.5	8.1
PENT–Intl Pent Holiness	2	123	126	151	1.1	1.4
PENT–United Holy Ch	3	NR	NR	NR	-	-
PRES–Presb Ch (USA)	2	118	174	208	1.5	1.9
PRES–Presb Ch Amer	1	46	34	42	0.3	0.4
Salvation Army	1	53	84	99	0.7	0.9
Sev Day Adv	4	146	254	291	2.1	2.6
MATHEWS	**25**	**2,036**	**3,767**	**4,823**	**53.7**	**100.0**
ANG/EPIS–Episcopal	1	122	242	246	2.7	5.1
BAPT–Asc Ref Bap Ch Am	1	NR	NR	NR	-	-
BAPT–Ref Bapt Ch	1	NR	NR	NR	-	-
BAPT–So Bapt Conv	6	325	1,009	1,163	13.0	24.1
Catholic	1	NR	NR	263	2.9	5.5
Ch of Nazarene	1	69	62	168	1.9	3.5
CHR–Chr Ch (Disc)	1	0	88	101	1.1	2.1
FRND–Evan Fr Ch Intl	1	18	12	14	0.2	0.3
METH–Un Methodist	10	602	1,554	1,718	19.1	35.6
Non-denom Chr Chs	2	900	800	1,150	12.8	23.8
MECKLENBURG	**92**	**4,621**	**12,127**	**14,710**	**44.9**	**100.0**
ANG/EPIS–Episcopal	8	200	344	362	1.1	2.5
Bahá'í	0	NR	22	22	0.1	0.1
BAPT–Ind Bapt Flwsp Intl	1	NR	NR	NR	-	-
BAPT–So Bapt Conv	31	2,241	7,356	8,630	26.4	58.7
Catholic	2	NR	NR	534	1.6	3.6
CHR–Chr Ch (Disc)	1	0	0	0	0.0	0.0
CHR–Chr Chs & Chs Cr	2	NR	140	164	0.5	1.1
CHR–Chs of Christ	1	7	7	7	0.0	0.0
METH–AME	1	0	100	117	0.4	0.8
METH–C.M.E.	1	0	100	117	0.4	0.8
METH–Un Methodist	21	848	2,384	2,682	8.2	18.2
Non-denom Chr Chs	8	830	985	1,137	3.5	7.7
PENT–Assemb of God	1	21	15	41	0.1	0.3
PENT–Ch God (Cleve)	2	158	240	282	0.9	1.9
PENT–Ch of God Proph	1	NR	14	16	0.0	0.1
PENT–Pent Ch of God	1	70	NR	109	0.3	0.7
PENT–United Holy Ch	2	NR	NR	NR	-	-
PRES–Presb Ch (USA)	4	123	248	291	0.9	2.0
Sev Day Adv	2	58	101	116	0.4	0.8
Un C of Christ	2	65	71	83	0.3	0.6
MIDDLESEX	**19**	**1,160**	**3,469**	**4,363**	**39.8**	**100.0**
ANG/EPIS–Episcopal	1	85	183	183	1.7	4.2
Bahá'í	0	NR	2	2	0.0	0.0
BAPT–Prog NBC	1	0	150	170	1.6	3.9
BAPT–So Bapt Conv	7	525	1,435	1,630	14.9	37.4
Catholic	1	NR	NR	341	3.1	7.8
CHR–Chr Ch (Disc)	1	0	288	327	3.0	7.5
METH–Un Methodist	4	340	1,142	1,409	12.9	32.3
METH–Wesleyan	2	73	70	95	0.9	2.2
Non-denom Chr Chs	1	100	150	150	1.4	3.4
PENT–Intl Pent Holiness	1	37	49	56	0.5	1.3
MONTGOMERY	**145**	**13,536**	**21,168**	**33,479**	**35.5**	**100.0**
ANG/EPIS–Anglican NA	2	NR	NR	NR	-	-
ANG/EPIS–Episcopal	2	220	557	827	0.9	2.5
Bahá'í	1	NR	37	37	0.0	0.1
BAPT–Alliance Bapt	1	NR	NR	NR	-	-
BAPT–Ref Bapt Ch	1	NR	NR	NR	-	-
BAPT–So Bapt Conv	17	3,016	4,938	5,644	6.0	16.9
BRETH–Ch of Brethren	4	113	275	314	0.3	0.9
BRETH–Grace Breth	1	NR	NR	NR	-	-
Catholic	3	NR	NR	3,249	3.4	9.7
CGOD–Ch God (Ander)	3	207	NR	207	0.2	0.6
Ch Cr, Scientst	1	NR	NR	NR	-	-
Ch of Nazarene	1	44	50	50	0.1	0.1
CHR–Chr Ch (Disc)	3	186	480	549	0.6	1.6
CHR–Chr Chs & Chs Cr	5	NR	993	1,135	1.2	3.4
CHR–Chs of Christ	4	378	384	453	0.5	1.4
FRND–Fr Gen Cf & Un Mtg	1	NR	33	38	0.0	0.1
HINDU–Post Ren	1	NR	NR	16	0.0	0.0
Ind Fund Churches	1	NR	NR	NR	-	-
Jehovah's Witness	1	NR	NR	NR	-	-
LDS–L-D Saints	3	NR	NR	1,092	1.2	3.3
LUTH–E.L.C.A.	5	447	793	1,159	1.2	3.5
MENN–Mennonite USA	1	50	35	40	0.0	0.1
METH–AME	1	40	50	57	0.1	0.2
METH–Un Methodist	20	1,837	4,743	5,824	6.2	17.4
METH–Wesleyan	4	203	256	265	0.3	0.8

NR–Not Reported   - Represents no adherents reported.   Percentages may not total 100 due to rounding.

Table 3: Religious Congregations by County and Group: 2010

Religious Group	Number of Congrega-tions	Number of Attendees	Number of Communicant, Confirmed, or Full Members	Adherents: Number of Adherents	Adherents: % of Total Pop.	Adherents: % of Total Adh.
Muslim Est	2	942	NR	3,686	3.9	11.0
Non-denom Chr Chs	17	2,850	3,300	3,774	4.0	11.3
PENT–Assemb of God	2	75	35	100	0.1	0.3
PENT–Ch God (Cleve)	3	318	428	489	0.5	1.5
PENT–Ch of God Proph	1	NR	28	32	0.0	0.1
PENT–Cong Hol Ch	4	185	86	98	0.1	0.3
PENT–Int Foursq Gos	1	118	162	185	0.2	0.6
PENT–Intl Pent Holiness	15	1,388	2,016	2,304	2.4	6.9
PENT–United Holy Ch	2	NR	NR	NR	-	-
PRES–As Ref Pres Ch	1	NR	94	107	0.1	0.3
PRES–Presb Ch (USA)	4	437	851	973	1.0	2.9
PRES–Presb Ch Amer	1	247	190	245	0.3	0.7
Salvation Army	1	19	58	89	0.1	0.3
Sev Day Adv	1	39	68	78	0.1	0.2
Un C of Christ	1	35	69	79	0.1	0.2
Unit Univ	1	142	159	284	0.3	0.8
Unity Ch	1	NR	NR	NR	-	-
NELSON	**45**	**1,886**	**5,771**	**7,721**	**51.4**	**100.0**
ANG/EPIS–Episcopal	3	64	61	78	0.5	1.0
Bahá'í	0	NR	3	3	0.0	0.0
BAPT–So Bapt Conv	18	1,104	3,749	4,402	29.3	57.0
BRETH–Ch of Brethren	1	30	84	99	0.7	1.3
BUDD–Vajrayana	1	NR	NR	428	2.8	5.5
Catholic	1	NR	NR	607	4.0	7.9
CHR–Chr Ch (Disc)	3	0	0	0	0.0	0.0
CHR–Chs of Christ	1	30	25	34	0.2	0.4
METH–AME Zion	2	0	250	294	2.0	3.8
METH–Un Methodist	6	326	985	1,080	7.2	14.0
Non-denom Chr Chs	2	125	165	169	1.1	2.2
PENT–Ch God (Cleve)	2	55	88	103	0.7	1.3
PENT–Intl Pent Holiness	2	34	51	60	0.4	0.8
PRES–Presb Ch (USA)	3	118	310	364	2.4	4.7
NEW KENT	**19**	**2,083**	**4,208**	**5,606**	**30.4**	**100.0**
ANG/EPIS–Episcopal	1	94	252	286	1.6	5.1
Bahá'í	0	NR	4	4	0.0	0.1
BAPT–So Bapt Conv	9	1,037	2,201	2,636	14.3	47.0
Catholic	1	NR	NR	477	2.6	8.5
METH–Un Methodist	3	299	935	1,194	6.5	21.3
Non-denom Chr Chs	3	395	600	600	3.3	10.7
PENT–Assemb of God	1	150	0	150	0.8	2.7
PRES–Presb Ch (USA)	1	108	216	259	1.4	4.6
NEWPORT NEWS (CITY)	**164**	**20,908**	**40,953**	**67,384**	**37.3**	**100.0**
ANG/EPIS–Anglican NA	1	NR	NR	NR	-	-
ANG/EPIS–Episcopal	5	525	1,688	1,788	1.0	2.7
Bahá'í	1	NR	43	43	0.0	0.1
BAPT–Amer Bapt USA	5	2,045	3,522	4,349	2.4	6.5
BAPT–NBC Amer	1	200	200	247	0.1	0.4
BAPT–NBC USA	2	725	1,175	1,451	0.8	2.2
BAPT–Reg Bapt Gen As	1	NR	NR	NR	-	-
BAPT–So Bapt Conv	32	3,956	10,346	12,777	7.1	19.0
BRETH–Ch of Brethren	1	59	162	200	0.1	0.3
BUDD–Mahayana	1	NR	NR	102	0.1	0.2
Calv Chpl	1	NR	NR	NR	-	-
Catholic	3	NR	NR	8,954	5.0	13.3
CGOD–Ch God (Ander)	2	45	NR	45	0.0	0.1
Ch of Chr (Hol)	1	NR	NR	NR	-	-
Ch of Nazarene	1	50	70	70	0.0	0.1
CHR–Chr Ch (Disc)	2	70	236	291	0.2	0.4
CHR–Chr Chs & Chs Cr	3	NR	1,000	1,235	0.7	1.8
CHR–Chs of Christ	3	450	405	591	0.3	0.9
CHR–Int Chs of Christ	0	NR	323	399	0.2	0.6
FRND–Evan Fr Ch Intl	1	51	37	46	0.0	0.1
HINDU–I/A Temples	1	NR	NR	1,742	1.0	2.6
Ind Fund Churches	1	NR	NR	NR	-	-
Jehovah's Witness	1	NR	NR	NR	-	-
JUD–Orth	1	22	20	30	0.0	0.0
JUD–Reform	1	83	147	397	0.2	0.6
LDS–L-D Saints	5	NR	NR	2,515	1.4	3.7
LUTH–E.L.C.A.	2	233	522	579	0.3	0.9
LUTH–Luth–MO Synod	1	279	519	621	0.3	0.9

Religious Group	Number of Congrega-tions	Number of Attendees	Number of Communicant, Confirmed, or Full Members	Adherents: Number of Adherents	Adherents: % of Total Pop.	Adherents: % of Total Adh.
MENN–Mennonite USA	3	230	335	414	0.2	0.6
METH–AME	1	125	200	247	0.1	0.4
METH–AME Zion	2	250	662	818	0.5	1.2
METH–Un Methodist	11	1,319	5,159	6,282	3.5	9.3
METH–Wesleyan	1	82	92	107	0.1	0.2
Muslim Est	1	792	NR	3,436	1.9	5.1
New Apost Ch	1	NR	NR	NR	-	-
Non-denom Chr Chs	31	5,300	7,472	7,812	4.3	11.6
ORTHE–Greek Orthodox	1	300	NR	1,500	0.8	2.2
PENT–Assemb of God	4	372	244	467	0.3	0.7
PENT–Ch God (Cleve)	2	1,714	2,238	2,764	1.5	4.1
PENT–Ch of God Proph	2	NR	213	263	0.1	0.4
PENT–COGIC	1	0	0	0	0.0	0.0
PENT–Full Gosp Bapt	2	NR	NR	NR	-	-
PENT–Intl Pent Holiness	2	85	109	135	0.1	0.2
PENT–Un Pent Ch Intl	2	NR	NR	NR	-	-
PENT–United Holy Ch	1	NR	NR	NR	-	-
PRES–Presb Ch (USA)	7	759	2,176	2,687	1.5	4.0
PRES–Presb Ch Amer	1	80	47	52	0.0	0.1
REF–Comm Ref Evan	1	NR	NR	NR	-	-
Sev Day Adv	3	420	729	839	0.5	1.2
Un C of Christ	3	157	724	894	0.5	1.3
Unit Univ	1	130	138	195	0.1	0.3
NORFOLK (CITY)	**268**	**41,413**	**66,608**	**110,587**	**45.5**	**100.0**
ANG/EPIS–Anglican NA	1	NR	NR	NR	-	-
ANG/EPIS–Episcopal	10	1,607	4,023	4,780	2.0	4.3
Bahá'í	1	NR	137	137	0.1	0.1
BAPT–Amer Bapt USA	10	2,960	6,820	8,183	3.4	7.4
BAPT–Consrv Bapt	1	NR	NR	NR	-	-
BAPT–Free Will Bapt	2	NR	104	125	0.1	0.1
BAPT–NBC Amer	1	500	700	840	0.3	0.8
BAPT–NBC USA	7	3,105	4,450	5,339	2.2	4.8
BAPT–So Bapt Conv	31	4,657	12,844	15,410	6.3	13.9
BRETH–Grace Breth	1	NR	NR	NR	-	-
BUDD–Mahayana	2	NR	NR	114	0.0	0.1
Catholic	7	NR	NR	11,457	4.7	10.4
CGOD–Ch God (Ander)	2	120	NR	120	0.0	0.1
Ch of Chr (Hol)	2	NR	NR	NR	-	-
Ch of Nazarene	2	51	54	80	0.0	0.1
CHR–Chr Ch (Disc)	7	0	0	0	0.0	0.0
CHR–Chr Chs & Chs Cr	1	NR	200	240	0.1	0.2
CHR–Chs of Christ	2	395	413	500	0.2	0.5
Christian Brethren	1	NR	NR	NR	-	-
FRND–Fr Gen Cf & Un Mtg	1	NR	0	0	0.0	0.0
Jehovah's Witness	4	NR	NR	NR	-	-
JUD–Conserv	2	722	810	2,187	0.9	2.0
JUD–Orth	1	324	125	450	0.2	0.4
JUD–Reform	1	336	593	1,601	0.7	1.4
LDS–L-D Saints	3	NR	NR	3,198	1.3	2.9
LUTH–E.L.C.A.	3	488	893	1,374	0.6	1.2
LUTH–Luth–MO Synod	3	196	358	408	0.2	0.4
MENN–Mennonite USA	1	15	9	11	0.0	0.0
METH–AME	4	450	1,650	1,980	0.8	1.8
METH–AME Zion	5	255	1,035	1,242	0.5	1.1
METH–C.M.E.	1	150	350	420	0.2	0.4
METH–Un Methodist	16	1,408	4,442	5,362	2.2	4.8
Metro Comm Ch	1	51	78	96	0.0	0.1
MJEW–Union Mes Cong	1	NR	NR	NR	-	-
Muslim Est	3	2,376	NR	10,308	4.2	9.3
Nat Spirit Asso	1	NR	NR	NR	-	-
New Apost Ch	1	NR	NR	NR	-	-
Non-denom Chr Chs	57	14,875	16,354	19,593	8.1	17.7
ORTHE–Carp Rus Orth	1	12	NR	35	0.0	0.0
ORTHE–Greek Orthodox	1	350	NR	2,100	0.9	1.9
ORTHE–Romania Orth Ar	1	50	NR	150	0.1	0.1
PENT–Assemb of God	5	765	567	1,268	0.5	1.1
PENT–Ch God (Cleve)	4	605	744	893	0.4	0.8
PENT–COGIC	12	876	1,820	2,184	0.9	2.0
PENT–Full Gosp Bapt	1	NR	NR	NR	-	-
PENT–Intl Pent Holiness	2	561	592	710	0.3	0.6
PENT–Pent FW Bapt	2	NR	NR	NR	-	-
PENT–Un Pent Ch Intl	2	NR	NR	NR	-	-
PENT–United Holy Ch	7	NR	NR	NR	-	-

NR–Not Reported   - Represents no adherents reported.   Percentages may not total 100 due to rounding.

Table 3: Religious Congregations by County and Group: 2010

Religious Group	Number of Congrega-tions	Number of Attendees	Number of Communicant, Confirmed, or Full Members	Adherents: Number of Adherents	Adherents: % of Total Pop.	Adherents: % of Total Adh.
PRES–Presb Ch (USA)	16	1,563	3,635	4,361	1.8	3.9
PRES–Presb Ch Amer	4	529	571	772	0.3	0.7
REF–Christian Ref	1	43	49	59	0.0	0.1
Salvation Army	1	114	480	481	0.2	0.4
Sev Day Adv	2	465	808	930	0.4	0.8
Un C of Christ	5	275	667	800	0.3	0.7
Unit Univ	1	164	233	289	0.1	0.3
NORTHAMPTON	**36**	**1,555**	**4,173**	**5,337**	**43.1**	**100.0**
ANG/EPIS–Anglican NA	1	NR	NR	NR	-	-
ANG/EPIS–Episcopal	3	130	231	297	2.4	5.6
Bahá'í	0	NR	4	4	0.0	0.1
BAPT–So Bapt Conv	9	661	1,282	1,516	12.2	28.4
Catholic	1	NR	NR	362	2.9	6.8
CGOD–Ch God (Ander)	1	18	NR	18	0.1	0.3
Ch of Nazarene	1	14	24	25	0.2	0.5
Jehovah's Witness	1	NR	NR	NR	-	-
METH–AME	7	55	910	1,076	8.7	20.2
METH–Un Methodist	9	592	1,577	1,870	15.1	35.0
PENT–Un Pent Ch Intl	1	NR	NR	NR	-	-
PRES–Presb Ch (USA)	1	47	78	92	0.7	1.7
Sev Day Adv	1	38	67	77	0.6	1.4
NORTHUMBERLAND	**34**	**1,898**	**4,277**	**4,930**	**40.0**	**100.0**
ANG/EPIS–Anglican NA	1	NR	NR	NR	-	-
ANG/EPIS–Episcopal	3	188	320	345	2.8	7.0
Bahá'í	0	NR	2	2	0.0	0.0
BAPT–Amer Bapt USA	1	125	225	257	2.1	5.2
BAPT–So Bapt Conv	11	584	1,615	1,846	15.0	37.4
CGOD–Ch God (Ander)	1	55	NR	55	0.4	1.1
Jehovah's Witness	2	NR	NR	NR	-	-
LUTH–Luth–MO Synod	1	64	73	80	0.6	1.6
METH–Un Methodist	11	602	1,677	1,967	16.0	39.9
Non-denom Chr Chs	3	280	365	378	3.1	7.7
NORTON (CITY)	**12**	**235**	**1,363**	**1,842**	**46.5**	**100.0**
Bahá'í	0	NR	2	2	0.1	0.1
BAPT–Free Will Bapt	4	NR	208	249	6.3	13.5
BAPT–So Bapt Conv	1	75	733	878	22.2	47.7
Catholic	1	NR	NR	149	3.8	8.1
CGOD–Ch God (Ander)	1	60	NR	60	1.5	3.3
CHR–Chr Chs & Chs Cr	1	NR	140	168	4.2	9.1
METH–AME Zion	1	0	100	120	3.0	6.5
PENT–Ch God (Cleve)	1	50	70	84	2.1	4.6
PENT–Intl Pent Holiness	1	50	74	89	2.2	4.8
PRES–Presb Ch (USA)	1	0	36	43	1.1	2.3
NOTTOWAY	**44**	**2,145**	**5,100**	**6,561**	**41.4**	**100.0**
ANG/EPIS–Episcopal	1	37	80	89	0.6	1.4
BAPT–Free Will Bapt	1	NR	52	62	0.4	0.9
BAPT–So Bapt Conv	6	463	1,613	1,919	12.1	29.2
Catholic	1	NR	NR	140	0.9	2.1
Ch of Nazarene	1	90	120	127	0.8	1.9
CHR–Chr Ch (Disc)	2	20	107	127	0.8	1.9
CHR–Chs of Christ	1	35	30	40	0.3	0.6
Jehovah's Witness	1	NR	NR	NR	-	-
LDS–L-D Saints	2	NR	NR	447	2.8	6.8
METH–AME Zion	2	0	200	238	1.5	3.6
METH–Un Methodist	7	388	1,261	1,461	9.2	22.3
METH–Wesleyan	1	48	32	62	0.4	0.9
Non-denom Chr Chs	7	725	940	1,006	6.3	15.3
PENT–Assemb of God	1	45	27	87	0.5	1.3
PENT–Ch God (Cleve)	1	30	107	127	0.8	1.9
PENT–Ch Lord Jesus Apos	1	NR	NR	NR	-	-
PENT–Ch of God Proph	1	NR	78	93	0.6	1.4
PENT–Intl Pent Holiness	1	60	25	30	0.2	0.5
PRES–Presb Ch (USA)	4	154	341	406	2.6	6.2
Sev Day Adv	2	50	87	100	0.6	1.5
ORANGE	**56**	**4,740**	**9,383**	**11,947**	**35.7**	**100.0**
ANG/EPIS–Anglican NA	1	NR	NR	NR	-	-
ANG/EPIS–Episcopal	2	152	423	423	1.3	3.5

Religious Group	Number of Congrega-tions	Number of Attendees	Number of Communicant, Confirmed, or Full Members	Adherents: Number of Adherents	Adherents: % of Total Pop.	Adherents: % of Total Adh.
Bahá'í	0	NR	17	17	0.1	0.1
BAPT–Free Will Bapt	1	NR	52	63	0.2	0.5
BAPT–NBC USA	1	150	200	242	0.7	2.0
BAPT–So Bapt Conv	17	1,924	4,727	5,729	17.1	48.0
BRETH–Ch of Brethren	1	0	25	30	0.1	0.3
Catholic	1	NR	NR	513	1.5	4.3
Ch of Nazarene	1	32	84	84	0.3	0.7
CHR–Chr Ch (Disc)	1	25	83	101	0.3	0.8
CHR–Chr Chs & Chs Cr	1	NR	100	121	0.4	1.0
CHR–Chs of Christ	1	25	19	25	0.1	0.2
HINDU–Post Ren	1	NR	NR	25	0.1	0.2
Jehovah's Witness	2	NR	NR	NR	-	-
LUTH–E.L.C.A.	1	31	73	77	0.2	0.6
METH–Un Methodist	6	402	1,054	1,248	3.7	10.4
Non-denom Chr Chs	10	1,487	1,814	1,966	5.9	16.5
PENT–Assemb of God	1	150	60	500	1.5	4.2
PENT–Ch God (Cleve)	1	93	119	144	0.4	1.2
PENT–Intl Pent Holiness	2	76	171	207	0.6	1.7
PRES–Presb Ch (USA)	2	129	250	303	0.9	2.5
Sev Day Adv	2	64	112	129	0.4	1.1
PAGE	**55**	**2,991**	**6,143**	**8,162**	**33.9**	**100.0**
ANG/EPIS–Episcopal	3	76	190	215	0.9	2.6
Bahá'í	0	NR	4	4	0.0	0.0
BAPT–Amer Bapt USA	2	29	101	121	0.5	1.5
BAPT–So Bapt Conv	3	480	873	1,044	4.3	12.8
BRETH–Ch of Brethren	6	330	598	715	3.0	8.8
BUDD–Vajrayana	2	NR	NR	41	0.2	0.5
Catholic	1	NR	NR	350	1.5	4.3
CHR–Chr Ch (Disc)	2	65	402	481	2.0	5.9
CHR–Chs of Christ	2	64	74	87	0.4	1.1
CONG–Consrv Cong Chr	1	55	77	92	0.4	1.1
Jehovah's Witness	1	NR	NR	NR	-	-
LDS–L-D Saints	1	NR	NR	130	0.5	1.6
LUTH–E.L.C.A.	8	446	1,102	1,438	6.0	17.6
MENN–Mennonite USA	1	35	40	48	0.2	0.6
METH–Un Methodist	8	453	1,330	1,687	7.0	20.7
Non-denom Chr Chs	3	280	450	450	1.9	5.5
PENT–Assemb of God	4	254	123	342	1.4	4.2
PENT–Intl Pent Holiness	3	217	425	508	2.1	6.2
PENT–Un Pent Ch Intl	1	NR	NR	NR	-	-
Sev Day Adv	2	182	316	364	1.5	4.5
Un C of Christ	1	25	38	45	0.2	0.6
PATRICK	**70**	**3,445**	**6,506**	**7,822**	**42.3**	**100.0**
BAPT–Amer Bapt Assn	1	NR	85	99	0.5	1.3
BAPT–Natl Mis Bapt Conv	1	0	150	176	1.0	2.3
BAPT–So Bapt Conv	12	884	2,048	2,396	13.0	30.6
BRETH–Ch of Brethren	2	185	361	422	2.3	5.4
Catholic	1	NR	NR	47	0.3	0.6
CHR–Chr Ch (Disc)	4	0	40	47	0.3	0.6
CHR–Chr Chs & Chs Cr	2	NR	225	263	1.4	3.4
CHR–Chs of Christ	3	135	123	158	0.9	2.0
LDS–L-D Saints	1	NR	NR	115	0.6	1.5
METH–Un Methodist	13	644	1,113	1,361	7.4	17.4
METH–Wesleyan	3	133	169	173	0.9	2.2
MORAV–Morav Ch-South	1	65	70	84	0.5	1.1
Non-denom Chr Chs	4	380	430	501	2.7	6.4
PENT–Ch God (Cleve)	2	212	339	397	2.1	5.1
PENT–Ch of God Proph	3	NR	123	144	0.8	1.8
PENT–Intl Pent Holiness	9	674	832	973	5.3	12.4
PRES–Evan Presby Ch	1	NR	122	143	0.8	1.8
PRES–Presb Ch (USA)	6	115	246	288	1.6	3.7
Sev Day Adv	1	18	30	35	0.2	0.4
PETERSBURG (CITY)	**80**	**9,768**	**18,592**	**26,073**	**80.4**	**100.0**
ANG/EPIS–Episcopal	4	320	666	970	3.0	3.7
Bahá'í	0	NR	24	24	0.1	0.1
BAPT–Amer Bapt USA	4	1,728	2,994	3,568	11.0	13.7
BAPT–Natl Mis Bapt Conv	1	0	150	179	0.6	0.7
BAPT–NBC USA	4	2,100	3,650	4,349	13.4	16.7
BAPT–So Bapt Conv	7	590	2,322	2,767	8.5	10.6
Catholic	1	NR	NR	939	2.9	3.6

NR–Not Reported - Represents no adherents reported. Percentages may not total 100 due to rounding.

Table 3: Religious Congregations by County and Group: 2010

Religious Group	Number of Congregations	Number of Attendees	Number of Communicant, Confirmed, or Full Members	Adherents: Number of Adherents	Adherents: % of Total Pop.	Adherents: % of Total Adh.
CHR–Chr Ch (Disc)	1	45	112	133	0.4	0.5
CHR–Chs of Christ	2	60	68	90	0.3	0.3
Jehovah's Witness	1	NR	NR	NR	-	-
LDS–L-D Saints	1	NR	NR	484	1.5	1.9
LUTH–E.L.C.A.	1	75	75	140	0.4	0.5
METH–A.W.M.C.	1	0	3	0	0.0	0.0
METH–AME Zion	2	75	300	357	1.1	1.4
METH–Un Methodist	3	159	592	629	1.9	2.4
Muslim Est	1	792	NR	3,436	10.6	13.2
Non-denom Chr Chs	27	3,011	6,333	6,403	19.8	24.6
PENT–Assemb of God	1	85	40	120	0.4	0.5
PENT–Ch Lord Jesus Apos	8	NR	NR	NR	-	-
PENT–COGIC	1	100	140	167	0.5	0.6
PENT–Intl Pent Holiness	1	140	170	203	0.6	0.8
PRES–Presb Ch (USA)	4	174	377	449	1.4	1.7
Salvation Army	1	15	69	79	0.2	0.3
Sev Day Adv	2	234	407	468	1.4	1.8
Un C of Christ	1	65	100	119	0.4	0.5
PITTSYLVANIA	**125**	**7,881**	**19,693**	**23,318**	**36.7**	**100.0**
ANG/EPIS–Episcopal	6	231	541	592	0.9	2.5
BAPT–Natl Mis Bapt Conv	2	0	300	358	0.6	1.5
BAPT–So Bapt Conv	39	4,688	11,638	13,873	21.8	59.5
BRETH–Ch of Brethren	3	81	298	355	0.6	1.5
Catholic	1	NR	NR	0	0.0	0.0
Ch of Nazarene	1	26	76	84	0.1	0.4
CHR–Chr Ch (Disc)	4	35	218	260	0.4	1.1
CHR–Chr Chs & Chs Cr	8	NR	1,046	1,247	2.0	5.3
FRND–Evan Fr Ch Intl	1	23	37	44	0.1	0.2
Jehovah's Witness	2	NR	NR	NR	-	-
LDS–L-D Saints	1	NR	NR	132	0.2	0.6
METH–AME	1	20	20	24	0.0	0.1
METH–Evan Meth Ch	1	NR	NR	NR	-	-
METH–Un Methodist	28	1,259	3,246	3,658	5.8	15.7
Non-denom Chr Chs	7	770	990	1,126	1.8	4.8
PENT–Assemb of God	1	30	21	60	0.1	0.3
PENT–Ch of God Proph	3	NR	139	166	0.3	0.7
PENT–Intl Pent Holiness	10	595	827	986	1.6	4.2
PENT–United Holy Ch	2	NR	NR	NR	-	-
PRES–Presb Ch (USA)	4	123	296	353	0.6	1.5
POQUOSON (CITY)	**10**	**1,002**	**4,309**	**5,011**	**41.2**	**100.0**
Bahá'í	0	NR	2	2	0.0	0.0
BAPT–So Bapt Conv	3	412	1,535	1,852	15.2	37.0
LDS–Comm of Christ	1	NR	137	137	1.1	2.7
METH–Un Methodist	2	466	2,550	2,848	23.4	56.8
PENT–Assemb of God	1	124	85	172	1.4	3.4
PENT–Un Pent Ch Intl	1	NR	NR	NR	-	-
PRES–Bible Pres	1	NR	NR	NR	-	-
PRES–Presb Ch Amer	1	0	0	0	0.0	0.0
PORTSMOUTH (CITY)	**118**	**14,737**	**30,493**	**42,889**	**44.9**	**100.0**
ANG/EPIS–Episcopal	5	360	750	945	1.0	2.2
Bahá'í	0	NR	17	17	0.0	0.0
BAPT–Amer Bapt USA	4	1,575	2,550	3,137	3.3	7.3
BAPT–NBC USA	1	0	150	185	0.2	0.4
BAPT–So Bapt Conv	24	2,469	8,669	10,665	11.2	24.9
Catholic	3	NR	NR	3,558	3.7	8.3
Ch Cr, Scientst	1	NR	NR	NR	-	-
Ch of Chr (Hol)	2	NR	NR	NR	-	-
Ch of Nazarene	1	61	74	92	0.1	0.2
Chr & Miss Al	2	217	210	368	0.4	0.9
CHR–Chr Ch (Disc)	2	115	365	449	0.5	1.0
CHR–Chr Chs & Chs Cr	3	NR	675	830	0.9	1.9
CHR–Chs of Christ	2	125	110	122	0.1	0.3
FRND–Evan Fr Ch Intl	1	49	40	49	0.1	0.1
Jehovah's Witness	2	NR	NR	NR	-	-
JUD–Reform	1	47	83	224	0.2	0.5
LDS–Comm of Christ	1	NR	137	137	0.1	0.3
LUTH–E.L.C.A.	3	165	471	597	0.6	1.4
LUTH–Luth-MO Synod	1	35	58	73	0.1	0.2
METH–AME	2	250	550	677	0.7	1.6
METH–AME Zion	2	86	317	390	0.4	0.9
METH–Un Methodist	10	805	3,458	4,037	4.2	9.4
Muslim Est	1	792	NR	3,436	3.6	8.0
Non-denom Chr Chs	23	6,258	9,034	9,350	9.8	21.8
PENT–Assemb of God	2	225	104	291	0.3	0.7
PENT–Ch of God Proph	1	NR	34	42	0.0	0.1
PENT–COGIC	3	200	800	984	1.0	2.3
PENT–Intl Pent Holiness	2	70	159	196	0.2	0.5
PENT–Un Pent Ch Intl	1	NR	NR	NR	-	-
PENT–United Holy Ch	2	NR	NR	NR	-	-
PRES–Presb Ch (USA)	5	447	920	1,132	1.2	2.6
Salvation Army	1	61	144	165	0.2	0.4
Sev Day Adv	1	104	180	207	0.2	0.5
Un C of Christ	3	221	434	534	0.6	1.2
POWHATAN	**33**	**4,155**	**6,346**	**9,478**	**33.8**	**100.0**
ANG/EPIS–Episcopal	2	128	265	329	1.2	3.5
Bahá'í	0	NR	1	1	0.0	0.0
BAPT–So Bapt Conv	8	2,227	3,388	4,065	14.5	42.9
Catholic	1	NR	NR	1,434	5.1	15.1
CHR–Chs of Christ	1	40	35	50	0.2	0.5
Jehovah's Witness	1	NR	NR	NR	-	-
LDS–L-D Saints	1	NR	NR	331	1.2	3.5
MENN–Mennonite USA	1	98	129	155	0.6	1.6
METH–Un Methodist	2	208	742	1,080	3.9	11.4
Non-denom Chr Chs	10	1,030	1,295	1,443	5.1	15.2
PENT–Assemb of God	1	44	35	44	0.2	0.5
PENT–Ch God (Cleve)	1	282	307	368	1.3	3.9
PENT–Int Foursq Gos	1	42	42	50	0.2	0.5
PRES–Presb Ch (USA)	2	56	107	128	0.5	1.4
PRES–Presb Ch Amer	1	0	0	0	0.0	0.0
PRINCE EDWARD	**44**	**1,855**	**4,496**	**6,058**	**25.9**	**100.0**
ANG/EPIS–Episcopal	1	94	164	222	1.0	3.7
Bahá'í	0	NR	53	53	0.2	0.9
BAPT–So Bapt Conv	6	460	1,425	1,641	7.0	27.1
Calv Chpl	1	NR	NR	NR	-	-
Catholic	2	NR	NR	699	3.0	11.5
Ch of Nazarene	1	0	0	0	0.0	0.0
CHR–Chr Ch (Disc)	1	40	95	109	0.5	1.8
CHR–Chr Chs & Chs Cr	1	NR	100	115	0.5	1.9
CHR–Chs of Christ	1	75	63	100	0.4	1.7
FRND–Fr Gen Cf & Un Mtg	1	NR	9	10	0.0	0.2
Jehovah's Witness	2	NR	NR	NR	-	-
LUTH–Luth-MO Synod	3	124	170	198	0.8	3.3
MENN–Cons Menn Conf	1	63	53	61	0.3	1.0
METH–AME	2	0	250	288	1.2	4.8
METH–Un Methodist	8	437	1,153	1,512	6.5	25.0
Non-denom Chr Chs	3	245	370	370	1.6	6.1
PENT–Ch God (Cleve)	1	12	16	18	0.1	0.3
PENT–Un Pent Ch Intl	1	NR	NR	NR	-	-
PRES–Presb Ch (USA)	6	239	459	529	2.3	8.7
Sev Day Adv	2	66	116	133	0.6	2.2
PRINCE GEORGE	**32**	**6,501**	**8,769**	**12,042**	**33.7**	**100.0**
ANG/EPIS–Episcopal	2	62	119	122	0.3	1.0
Bahá'í	0	NR	14	14	0.0	0.1
BAPT–So Bapt Conv	9	792	1,432	1,729	4.8	14.4
BRETH–Ch of Brethren	1	20	48	58	0.2	0.5
Catholic	1	NR	NR	1,252	3.5	10.4
CONG–Consrv Cong Chr	1	32	63	76	0.2	0.6
Jehovah's Witness	1	NR	NR	NR	-	-
LDS–L-D Saints	2	NR	NR	658	1.8	5.5
METH–Un Methodist	7	489	1,296	1,643	4.6	13.6
Non-denom Chr Chs	4	4,950	5,550	6,200	17.4	51.5
PENT–Full Gosp Bapt	1	NR	NR	NR	-	-
PRES–Presb Ch (USA)	2	104	167	202	0.6	1.7
PRES–Presb Ch Amer	1	52	80	88	0.2	0.7
PRINCE WILLIAM	**198**	**30,646**	**44,792**	**145,168**	**36.1**	**100.0**
ANG/EPIS–Anglican NA	6	NR	NR	NR	-	-
ANG/EPIS–Episcopal	1	65	71	79	0.0	0.1
Bahá'í	2	NR	158	158	0.0	0.1

NR–Not Reported - Represents no adherents reported. Percentages may not total 100 due to rounding.

Table 3: Religious Congregations by County and Group: 2010

Religious Group	Number of Congregations	Number of Attendees	Number of Communicant, Confirmed, or Full Members	Adherents		
				Number of Adherents	% of Total Pop.	% of Total Adh.
BAPT–Alliance Bapt	2	NR	NR	NR	-	-
BAPT–Amer Bapt Assn	1	NR	75	97	0.0	0.1
BAPT–Amer Bapt USA	1	75	100	129	0.0	0.1
BAPT–Converge/BGC	1	75	NR	90	0.0	0.1
BAPT–Free Will Bapt	2	NR	104	135	0.0	0.1
BAPT–NBC USA	3	2,450	4,900	6,344	1.6	4.4
BAPT–Ref Bapt Ch	2	NR	NR	NR	-	-
BAPT–So Bapt Conv	33	4,481	7,523	9,740	2.4	6.7
BRETH–Ch of Brethren	2	110	385	498	0.1	0.3
BUDD–Mahayana	2	NR	NR	1,011	0.3	0.7
BUDD–Theravada	1	NR	NR	396	0.1	0.3
Calv Chpl	1	NR	NR	NR	-	-
Catholic	6	NR	NR	59,551	14.8	41.0
CGOD–Ch God (Ander)	1	0	NR	0	0.0	0.0
CGOD–Ches God-Gen Con	1	62	56	72	0.0	0.0
Ch Cr, Scientst	1	NR	NR	NR	-	-
Ch of Nazarene	2	410	387	425	0.1	0.3
Chr & Miss Al	1	NR	NR	NR	-	-
CHR–Chr Chs & Chs Cr	1	NR	120	155	0.0	0.1
CHR–Chs of Christ	4	578	611	791	0.2	0.5
JUD–Reform	1	44	78	211	0.1	0.1
LDS–L-D Saints	10	NR	NR	3,949	1.0	2.7
LUTH–E.L.C.A.	6	802	2,210	2,987	0.7	2.1
LUTH–Luth-MO Synod	3	309	658	808	0.2	0.6
LUTH–Wisc Ev Luth Syn	2	172	318	416	0.1	0.3
METH–AME	2	0	200	259	0.1	0.2
METH–AME Zion	1	0	100	129	0.0	0.1
METH–Un Methodist	13	2,497	8,883	12,689	3.2	8.7
Muslim Est	5	3,368	NR	17,480	4.3	12.0
Non-denom Chr Chs	23	7,060	9,734	10,543	2.6	7.3
PENT–Assemb of God	13	4,714	2,319	8,756	2.2	6.0
PENT–Ch God (Cleve)	6	557	994	1,287	0.3	0.9
PENT–COGIC	1	0	150	194	0.0	0.1
PENT–Full Gosp Bapt	3	NR	NR	NR	-	-
PENT–Open Bible Std	1	15	NR	15	0.0	0.0
PENT–Pent FW Bapt	1	NR	NR	NR	-	-
PENT–Un Pent Ch Intl	3	NR	NR	NR	-	-
PENT–Vineyard	2	290	319	413	0.1	0.3
PRES–Evan Presby Ch	1	NR	41	53	0.0	0.0
PRES–Korean Amer Pres	2	NR	NR	NR	-	-
PRES–Korean Pres Amer	1	NR	NR	NR	-	-
PRES–Presb Ch (USA)	6	1,155	2,132	2,760	0.7	1.9
PRES–Presb Ch Amer	3	366	400	516	0.1	0.4
PRES–Ref Pres Han	1	NR	NR	NR	-	-
Salvation Army	1	17	71	75	0.0	0.1
Sev Day Adv	10	974	1,695	1,948	0.5	1.3
Zoroastrian	0	NR	NR	9	0.0	0.0
PULASKI	**91**	**5,951**	**12,013**	**14,283**	**41.0**	**100.0**
ANG/EPIS–Episcopal	1	26	56	83	0.2	0.6
Bahá'í	0	NR	3	3	0.0	0.0
BAPT–Ref Bapt Ch	1	NR	NR	NR	-	-
BAPT–So Bapt Conv	11	1,143	2,957	3,467	9.9	24.3
BRETH–Breth in Chr	1	NR	NR	NR	-	-
BRETH–Ch of Brethren	2	74	139	163	0.5	1.1
Catholic	1	NR	NR	81	0.2	0.6
CGOD–Ch God (Ander)	1	61	NR	61	0.2	0.4
Ch of Nazarene	2	53	55	80	0.2	0.6
CHR–Chr Ch (Disc)	4	147	260	305	0.9	2.1
CHR–Chr Chs & Chs Cr	2	NR	440	516	1.5	3.6
CHR–Chs of Christ	1	40	47	52	0.1	0.4
Jehovah's Witness	1	NR	NR	NR	-	-
LUTH–E.L.C.A.	1	62	172	216	0.6	1.5
METH–Un Methodist	22	1,262	3,187	3,583	10.3	25.1
Non-denom Chr Chs	3	500	725	750	2.2	5.3
PENT–Assemb of God	3	364	277	432	1.2	3.0
PENT–Ch God (Cleve)	5	850	1,261	1,479	4.2	10.4
PENT–Ch of God Proph	4	NR	113	132	0.4	0.9
PENT–COGIC	1	0	150	176	0.5	1.2
PENT–Int Pent C Chr	1	30	NR	50	0.1	0.4
PENT–Intl Pent Holiness	9	689	1,187	1,392	4.0	9.7
PENT–Orig Ch of God	1	NR	NR	NR	-	-
PENT–Pent Ch of God	1	70	NR	109	0.3	0.8
PENT–United Holy Ch	2	NR	NR	NR	-	-
PRES–Presb Ch (USA)	6	304	658	771	2.2	5.4
PRES–Presb Ch Amer	2	232	250	295	0.8	2.1
PRES–Ref Pres GA	1	NR	NR	NR	-	-
Sev Day Adv	1	44	76	87	0.2	0.6
RADFORD (CITY)	**34**	**3,184**	**5,198**	**6,112**	**37.3**	**100.0**
ANG/EPIS–Episcopal	1	67	142	252	1.5	4.1
Bahá'í	0	NR	3	3	0.0	0.0
BAPT–So Bapt Conv	1	180	530	591	3.6	9.7
BRETH–Grace Breth	1	NR	NR	NR	-	-
CHR–Chr Ch (Disc)	2	125	436	486	3.0	8.0
CHR–Chs of Christ	1	95	75	105	0.6	1.7
Evan Free Ch	1	100	NR	100	0.6	1.6
Jehovah's Witness	1	NR	NR	NR	-	-
LUTH–E.L.C.A.	1	23	65	65	0.4	1.1
METH–Un Methodist	5	565	1,233	1,452	8.8	23.8
METH–Wesleyan	1	68	37	88	0.5	1.4
Non-denom Chr Chs	4	704	809	880	5.4	14.4
PENT–Assemb of God	1	10	5	11	0.1	0.2
PENT–Ch God (Cleve)	3	287	582	649	4.0	10.6
PENT–Ch of God Proph	1	NR	46	51	0.3	0.8
PENT–COGIC	1	125	150	167	1.0	2.7
PENT–Cong Hol Ch	1	15	8	9	0.1	0.1
PENT–Int Foursq Gos	1	260	121	135	0.8	2.2
PENT–Intl Pent Holiness	4	407	657	733	4.5	12.0
PRES–Presb Ch (USA)	2	118	238	265	1.6	4.3
Sev Day Adv	1	35	61	70	0.4	1.1
RAPPAHANNOCK	**18**	**961**	**1,863**	**2,658**	**36.1**	**100.0**
ANG/EPIS–Episcopal	1	98	201	216	2.9	8.1
Bahá'í	0	NR	3	3	0.0	0.1
BAPT–So Bapt Conv	7	515	894	1,048	14.2	39.4
Catholic	1	NR	NR	401	5.4	15.1
METH–Un Methodist	4	159	561	718	9.7	27.0
Non-denom Chr Chs	3	129	174	184	2.5	6.9
PENT–Assemb of God	1	60	30	88	1.2	3.3
Unit Univ	1	NR	NR	NR	-	-
RICHMOND	**24**	**1,522**	**4,195**	**4,873**	**52.7**	**100.0**
ANG/EPIS–Episcopal	2	59	83	180	1.9	3.7
BAPT–So Bapt Conv	10	846	2,197	2,525	27.3	51.8
CHR–Chr Ch (Disc)	1	0	93	107	1.2	2.2
CHR–Chr Chs & Chs Cr	2	NR	400	460	5.0	9.4
METH–Un Methodist	3	150	526	665	7.2	13.6
Non-denom Chr Chs	3	320	625	625	6.8	12.8
PENT–Ch God (Cleve)	1	66	90	103	1.1	2.1
PRES–Presb Ch (USA)	1	45	119	137	1.5	2.8
Sev Day Adv	1	36	62	71	0.8	1.5
RICHMOND (CITY)	**275**	**55,059**	**100,918**	**152,613**	**74.7**	**100.0**
ANG/EPIS–Episcopal	12	2,924	8,786	11,153	5.5	7.3
Bahá'í	1	NR	167	167	0.1	0.1
BAPT–Alliance Bapt	4	NR	NR	NR	-	-
BAPT–Amer Bapt USA	24	8,122	17,545	20,628	10.1	13.5
BAPT–NBC USA	14	8,525	12,350	14,520	7.1	9.5
BAPT–Prog NBC	3	915	1,300	1,528	0.7	1.0
BAPT–So Bapt Conv	40	6,826	19,740	23,209	11.4	15.2
BUDD–Mahayana	1	NR	NR	102	0.0	0.1
BUDD–Vajrayana	1	NR	NR	36	0.0	0.0
Catholic	10	NR	NR	18,540	9.1	12.1
CGOD–Ch God (Ander)	2	100	NR	100	0.0	0.1
Ch Cr, Scientst	1	NR	NR	NR	-	-
Ch of Chr (Hol)	1	NR	NR	NR	-	-
Ch of Nazarene	1	207	470	470	0.2	0.3
CHR–Chr Ch (Disc)	4	207	809	951	0.5	0.6
CHR–Chs of Christ	4	441	426	557	0.3	0.4
FRND–Fr Gen Cf & Un Mtg	1	NR	192	226	0.1	0.1
HINDU–Post Ren	2	NR	NR	35	0.0	0.0
HINDU–Renaiss	1	NR	NR	12	0.0	0.0
HINDU–Trad Temples	1	NR	NR	1,000	0.5	0.7
Jehovah's Witness	4	NR	NR	NR	-	-
JUD–Conserv	2	471	529	1,428	0.7	0.9

NR–Not Reported - Represents no adherents reported. Percentages may not total 100 due to rounding.

Table 3: Religious Congregations by County and Group: 2010

Religious Group	Number of Congrega-tions	Number of Attendees	Number of Communicant, Confirmed, or Full Members	Adherents		
				Number of Adherents	% of Total Pop.	% of Total Adh.
JUD–Orth	3	504	250	700	0.3	0.5
JUD–Reform	2	535	944	2,549	1.2	1.7
LDS–L-D Saints	3	NR	NR	1,320	0.6	0.9
LUTH–E.L.C.A.	3	499	1,303	1,514	0.7	1.0
LUTH–Luth-MO Synod	2	112	480	635	0.3	0.4
METH–AME	2	275	500	588	0.3	0.4
METH–AME Zion	3	250	450	529	0.3	0.3
METH–C.M.E.	1	120	472	555	0.3	0.4
METH–Un Methodist	14	1,802	6,226	7,877	3.9	5.2
METH–Wesleyan	1	27	51	35	0.0	0.0
Metro Comm Ch	1	103	120	141	0.1	0.1
MJEW–Union Mes Cong	1	NR	NR	NR	-	-
Muslim Est	3	1,654	NR	6,992	3.4	4.6
Non-denom Chr Chs	51	14,869	17,439	19,821	9.7	13.0
ORTHE–Greek Orthodox	1	350	NR	1,600	0.8	1.0
ORTHO–Coptic Orth Ch	1	300	NR	430	0.2	0.3
PENT–Apos Faith Msn	1	NR	35	41	0.0	0.0
PENT–Assemb of God	2	565	352	879	0.4	0.6
PENT–Ch Lord Jesus Apos	4	NR	NR	NR	-	-
PENT–Ch of God Proph	1	NR	54	63	0.0	0.0
PENT–COGIC	7	1,192	3,080	3,621	1.8	2.4
PENT–Fire Bapt Hol Ch	1	NR	NR	NR	-	-
PENT–Full Gosp Bapt	3	NR	NR	NR	-	-
PENT–Intl Pent Holiness	1	45	111	131	0.1	0.1
PENT–United Holy Ch	6	NR	NR	NR	-	-
PENT–Vineyard	1	51	75	88	0.0	0.1
PRES–Presb Ch (USA)	12	1,626	4,142	4,870	2.4	3.2
PRES–Presb Ch Amer	2	243	246	315	0.2	0.2
Salvation Army	2	81	201	201	0.1	0.1
Sev Day Adv	3	723	1,258	1,446	0.7	0.9
Un C of Christ	1	110	236	277	0.1	0.2
Unit Univ	1	285	579	733	0.4	0.5
Unity Ch	1	NR	NR	NR	-	-
ROANOKE	**102**	**12,105**	**24,596**	**35,637**	**38.6**	**100.0**
ANG/EPIS–Anglican NA	2	NR	NR	NR	-	-
Bahá'í	1	NR	35	35	0.0	0.1
BAPT–NBC USA	1	0	0	0	0.0	0.0
BAPT–So Bapt Conv	24	4,727	9,964	11,880	12.9	33.3
BRETH–Breth in Chr	2	NR	NR	NR	-	-
BRETH–Ch of Brethren	7	463	853	1,017	1.1	2.9
BRETH–Grace Breth	1	NR	NR	NR	-	-
Catholic	1	NR	NR	3,536	3.8	9.9
Ch of Nazarene	2	73	145	145	0.2	0.4
Chr & Miss Al	1	186	124	268	0.3	0.8
CHR–Chr Ch (Disc)	1	30	59	70	0.1	0.2
CHR–Chr Chs & Chs Cr	3	NR	370	441	0.5	1.2
CHR–Chs of Christ	3	174	169	200	0.2	0.6
HINDU–Trad Temples	1	NR	NR	150	0.2	0.4
LDS–L-D Saints	4	NR	NR	1,561	1.7	4.4
LUTH–E.L.C.A.	2	193	383	573	0.6	1.6
LUTH–Luth Cong Msn Chr	1	580	1,100	1,312	1.4	3.7
LUTH–Luth-MO Synod	1	89	221	276	0.3	0.8
LUTH–Wisc Ev Luth Syn	1	55	74	74	0.1	0.2
METH–AME	1	0	91	109	0.1	0.3
METH–Un Methodist	11	1,587	5,287	6,512	7.0	18.3
METH–Wesleyan	2	170	242	221	0.2	0.6
Non-denom Chr Chs	11	2,286	2,761	3,405	3.7	9.6
PENT–Assemb of God	4	380	320	857	0.9	2.4
PENT–Ch God (Cleve)	4	556	1,389	1,656	1.8	4.6
PENT–Int Foursq Gos	1	101	140	167	0.2	0.5
PENT–Pent Ch of God	1	70	NR	109	0.1	0.3
PENT–Un Pent Ch Intl	1	NR	NR	NR	-	-
PRES–Orth Pres Ch	1	36	24	28	0.0	0.1
PRES–Presb Ch (USA)	3	75	518	618	0.7	1.7
PRES–Presb Ch Amer	1	166	140	200	0.2	0.6
Sev Day Adv	1	108	187	215	0.2	0.6
Unity Ch	1	NR	NR	NR	-	-
Zoroastrian	0	NR	NR	2	0.0	0.0
ROANOKE (CITY)	**184**	**23,419**	**48,287**	**71,413**	**73.6**	**100.0**
ANG/EPIS–Anglican NA	1	NR	NR	NR	-	-
ANG/EPIS–Episcopal	4	775	2,284	2,334	2.4	3.3
Bahá'í	1	NR	130	130	0.1	0.2
BAPT–Alliance Bapt	1	NR	NR	NR	-	-
BAPT–Amer Bapt USA	2	350	741	897	0.9	1.3
BAPT–Converge/BGC	1	75	NR	90	0.1	0.1
BAPT–Free Will Bapt	1	NR	52	63	0.1	0.1
BAPT–Ind Bapt Flwsp Intl	1	NR	NR	NR	-	-
BAPT–NBC USA	5	1,015	1,625	1,966	2.0	2.8
BAPT–So Bapt Conv	28	5,407	17,075	20,660	21.3	28.9
BRETH–Ch of Brethren	7	614	1,338	1,619	1.7	2.3
BRETH–Grace Breth	4	NR	NR	NR	-	-
BUDD–Mahayana	1	NR	NR	11	0.0	0.0
BUDD–Vajrayana	1	NR	NR	456	0.5	0.6
Calv Chpl	1	NR	NR	NR	-	-
Catholic	3	NR	NR	5,367	5.5	7.5
CGOD–Ch God (Ander)	2	177	NR	177	0.2	0.2
Ch Cr, Scientst	1	NR	NR	NR	-	-
Ch of Nazarene	4	710	881	1,417	1.5	2.0
CHR–Chr Ch (Disc)	6	734	1,901	2,300	2.4	3.2
CHR–Chr Chs & Chs Cr	3	NR	765	926	1.0	1.3
CHR–Chs of Christ	3	125	118	147	0.2	0.2
FRND–Fr Gen Cf & Un Mtg	1	NR	22	27	0.0	0.0
Jehovah's Witness	2	NR	NR	NR	-	-
JUD–Conserv	1	119	133	359	0.4	0.5
JUD–Reform	1	100	176	475	0.5	0.7
LUTH–E.L.C.A.	3	403	990	1,168	1.2	1.6
METH–AME	3	130	350	423	0.4	0.6
METH–AME Zion	2	110	150	181	0.2	0.3
METH–Un Methodist	12	1,497	5,134	6,167	6.4	8.6
METH–Wesleyan	5	1,433	1,578	1,863	1.9	2.6
Metro Comm Ch	1	75	118	143	0.1	0.2
Muslim Est	2	1,584	NR	6,872	7.1	9.6
Non-denom Chr Chs	34	4,166	5,411	5,861	6.0	8.2
ORTHE–Greek Orthodox	1	130	NR	275	0.3	0.4
ORTHO–Coptic Orth Ch	1	80	NR	100	0.1	0.1
ORTHO–Syrian Orth Ch	1	50	NR	150	0.2	0.2
PENT–Assemb of God	1	13	15	24	0.0	0.0
PENT–Ch God (Cleve)	1	34	83	100	0.1	0.1
PENT–Ch Lord Jesus Apos	2	NR	NR	NR	-	-
PENT–Ch of God Proph	3	NR	287	347	0.4	0.5
PENT–COGIC	4	600	710	859	0.9	1.2
PENT–Full Gosp Bapt	1	NR	NR	NR	-	-
PENT–Intl Pent Holiness	2	819	1,061	1,284	1.3	1.8
PENT–United Holy Ch	2	NR	NR	NR	-	-
PRES–As Ref Pres Ch	1	NR	35	42	0.0	0.1
PRES–Evan Presby Ch	1	NR	30	36	0.0	0.1
PRES–Presb Ch (USA)	8	1,447	3,905	4,725	4.9	6.6
PRES–Presb Ch Amer	1	100	148	163	0.2	0.2
Salvation Army	1	153	295	317	0.3	0.4
Sev Day Adv	4	301	523	602	0.6	0.8
Unit Univ	1	93	223	290	0.3	0.4
ROCKBRIDGE	**46**	**2,408**	**5,640**	**6,579**	**29.5**	**100.0**
ANG/EPIS–Episcopal	2	239	403	435	2.0	6.6
Bahá'í	0	NR	7	7	0.0	0.1
BAPT–So Bapt Conv	8	681	2,031	2,371	10.6	36.0
BRETH–Ch of Brethren	2	60	223	260	1.2	4.0
BUDD–Vajrayana	1	NR	NR	71	0.3	1.1
Ch of Nazarene	1	23	0	23	0.1	0.3
FRND–Fr Gen Cf & Un Mtg	1	NR	42	49	0.2	0.7
Jehovah's Witness	1	NR	NR	NR	-	-
LUTH–E.L.C.A.	2	46	116	133	0.6	2.0
METH–Un Methodist	7	254	678	756	3.4	11.5
Non-denom Chr Chs	2	180	250	250	1.1	3.8
PENT–Assemb of God	1	40	20	40	0.2	0.6
PENT–Ch of God Proph	1	NR	29	34	0.2	0.5
PENT–Intl Pent Holiness	2	205	298	348	1.6	5.3
PRES–As Ref Pres Ch	2	NR	51	60	0.3	0.9
PRES–Presb Ch (USA)	13	680	1,492	1,742	7.8	26.5
ROCKINGHAM	**160**	**13,411**	**24,550**	**31,261**	**41.0**	**100.0**
ANG/EPIS–Episcopal	2	61	99	99	0.1	0.3
Bahá'í	0	NR	21	21	0.0	0.1
BAPT–Converge/BGC	1	75	NR	90	0.1	0.3

NR–Not Reported - Represents no adherents reported. Percentages may not total 100 due to rounding.

Table 3: Religious Congregations by County and Group: 2010

Religious Group	Number of Congrega-tions	Number of Attendees	Number of Communicant, Confirmed, or Full Members	Adherents: Number of Adherents	% of Total Pop.	% of Total Adh.
BAPT–Free Will Bapt	2	NR	104	127	0.2	0.4
BAPT–So Bapt Conv	6	487	1,380	1,686	2.2	5.4
BRETH–Brethren (Ash)	2	NR	530	648	0.8	2.1
BRETH–Ch of Brethren	27	2,766	5,340	6,525	8.6	20.9
Catholic	1	NR	NR	171	0.2	0.5
Ch of Nazarene	4	1,473	1,709	2,378	3.1	7.6
CHR–Chr Chs & Chs Cr	1	NR	120	147	0.2	0.5
CHR–Chs of Christ	2	55	41	62	0.1	0.2
Evan Assoc RCC	2	NR	NR	NR	-	-
FRND–Consrv Yr Mtgs	1	NR	50	61	0.1	0.2
FRND–Fr Gen Cf & Un Mtg	1	NR	38	46	0.1	0.1
Jehovah's Witness	1	NR	NR	NR	-	-
LUTH–E.L.C.A.	7	304	638	793	1.0	2.5
MENN–CG in Cr (Menn)	1	NR	21	26	0.0	0.1
MENN–Mennonite USA	20	1,602	1,704	2,082	2.7	6.7
METH–Un Methodist	36	2,697	7,181	9,367	12.3	30.0
Non-denom Chr Chs	10	1,320	1,575	1,924	2.5	6.2
PENT–Assemb of God	2	277	183	495	0.6	1.6
PENT–Ch God (Cleve)	3	86	174	213	0.3	0.7
PENT–Ch of God Proph	1	NR	33	40	0.1	0.1
PENT–Int Pent C Chr	1	40	50	50	0.1	0.2
PENT–Intl Pent Holiness	3	141	216	264	0.3	0.8
PRES–Evan Presby Ch	1	NR	191	233	0.3	0.7
PRES–Presb Ch (USA)	6	687	1,145	1,399	1.8	4.5
PRES–Presb Ch Amer	1	913	902	1,096	1.4	3.5
REF–Fed Ref Ch	1	NR	NR	NR	-	-
Sev Day Adv	2	76	132	152	0.2	0.5
Un Breth in Cr	1	68	155	58	0.1	0.2
Un C of Christ	10	218	745	910	1.2	2.9
Unit Univ	1	65	73	98	0.1	0.3
RUSSELL	**70**	**3,491**	**7,503**	**8,936**	**30.9**	**100.0**
Bahá'í	0	NR	2	2	0.0	0.0
BAPT–Free Will Bapt	2	NR	104	123	0.4	1.4
BAPT–So Bapt Conv	27	1,671	4,514	5,341	18.5	59.8
Catholic	1	NR	NR	84	0.3	0.9
CHR–Chr Ch (Disc)	1	0	0	0	0.0	0.0
CHR–Chr Chs & Chs Cr	1	NR	0	0	0.0	0.0
CHR–Chs of Christ	1	98	91	119	0.4	1.3
Jehovah's Witness	1	NR	NR	NR	-	-
LDS–L-D Saints	1	NR	NR	51	0.2	0.6
METH–AME Zion	2	0	200	237	0.8	2.7
METH–Un Methodist	16	498	1,170	1,244	4.3	13.9
Non-denom Chr Chs	6	814	904	1,094	3.8	12.2
PENT–Assemb of God	2	75	55	93	0.3	1.0
PENT–Ch God (Cleve)	4	210	322	381	1.3	4.3
PENT–Intl Pent Holiness	2	72	42	50	0.2	0.6
PRES–Presb Ch (USA)	3	53	99	117	0.4	1.3
SALEM (CITY)	**53**	**6,028**	**13,015**	**17,627**	**71.1**	**100.0**
ANG/EPIS–Episcopal	1	154	444	454	1.8	2.6
Bahá'í	0	NR	9	9	0.0	0.1
BAPT–Amer Bapt USA	1	464	353	415	1.7	2.4
BAPT–NBC USA	1	35	60	70	0.3	0.4
BAPT–So Bapt Conv	7	1,380	3,861	4,534	18.3	25.7
BRETH–Ch of Brethren	1	24	25	29	0.1	0.2
Catholic	1	NR	NR	1,223	4.9	6.9
CGOD–Ch God (Ander)	1	65	NR	65	0.3	0.4
Ch of Nazarene	1	87	80	87	0.4	0.5
CHR–Chr Ch (Disc)	2	211	686	806	3.2	4.6
CHR–Chr Chs & Chs Cr	1	NR	350	411	1.7	2.3
CHR–Chs of Christ	1	200	188	237	1.0	1.3
CHR–Int Chs of Christ	1	NR	117	137	0.6	0.8
Jehovah's Witness	1	NR	NR	NR	-	-
LDS–L-D Saints	2	NR	NR	1,606	6.5	9.1
LUTH–E.L.C.A.	2	219	402	542	2.2	3.1
METH–Evan Meth Ch	1	NR	NR	NR	-	-
METH–Un Methodist	3	560	2,323	2,372	9.6	13.5
METH–Wesleyan	2	192	232	250	1.0	1.4
Non-denom Chr Chs	8	1,280	1,700	1,770	7.1	10.0
ORTHE–Bulgar Orth USA	1	20	NR	30	0.1	0.2
PENT–Assemb of God	1	55	68	95	0.4	0.5
PENT–Ch God (Cleve)	2	94	350	411	1.7	2.3
PENT–Ch Lord Jesus Apos	1	NR	NR	NR	-	-
PENT–Ch of God Proph	2	NR	74	87	0.4	0.5
PENT–Cong Hol Ch	1	25	25	29	0.1	0.2
PENT–Int Foursq Gos	1	40	47	55	0.2	0.3
PENT–Intl Pent Holiness	2	720	950	1,116	4.5	6.3
PENT–Un Pent Ch Intl	1	NR	NR	NR	-	-
PRES–Presb Ch (USA)	2	180	631	741	3.0	4.2
Sev Day Adv	1	23	40	46	0.2	0.3
SCOTT	**71**	**3,167**	**8,226**	**9,790**	**42.2**	**100.0**
Bahá'í	0	NR	1	1	0.0	0.0
BAPT–Free Will Bapt	10	NR	520	609	2.6	6.2
BAPT–Prim Bapt E Dst	8	200	708	830	3.6	8.5
BAPT–So Bapt Conv	17	1,401	4,248	4,979	21.5	50.9
Catholic	2	NR	NR	82	0.4	0.8
CHR–Chr Chs & Chs Cr	1	NR	20	23	0.1	0.2
CHR–Chs of Christ	1	28	50	65	0.3	0.7
Evan Cov Ch	1	34	42	44	0.2	0.4
Jehovah's Witness	1	NR	NR	NR	-	-
METH–Un Methodist	25	1,230	2,358	2,818	12.2	28.8
Non-denom Chr Chs	1	100	100	125	0.5	1.3
PENT–Assemb of God	1	45	35	45	0.2	0.5
PENT–Ch God (Cleve)	1	94	106	124	0.5	1.3
PENT–Un Pent Ch Intl	1	NR	NR	NR	-	-
PRES–Presb Ch (USA)	1	35	38	45	0.2	0.5
SHENANDOAH	**113**	**6,460**	**14,949**	**19,454**	**46.3**	**100.0**
ANG/EPIS–Episcopal	3	253	179	191	0.5	1.0
Bahá'í	0	NR	9	9	0.0	0.0
BAPT–So Bapt Conv	2	463	865	1,039	2.5	5.3
BRETH–Brethren (Ash)	5	NR	400	481	1.1	2.5
BRETH–Ch of Brethren	13	675	1,811	2,176	5.2	11.2
Catholic	2	NR	NR	1,374	3.3	7.1
Ch of God Gen Conf	1	NR	24	29	0.1	0.1
Ch of Nazarene	1	0	34	34	0.1	0.2
CHR–Chr Ch (Disc)	8	327	1,428	1,716	4.1	8.8
CHR–Chs of Christ	1	32	31	35	0.1	0.2
Jehovah's Witness	1	NR	NR	NR	-	-
LDS–L-D Saints	1	NR	NR	336	0.8	1.7
LUTH–E.L.C.A.	24	1,291	3,442	4,090	9.7	21.0
LUTH–Nor Amer Luth C	1	NR	NR	NR	-	-
MENN–Mennonite USA	1	20	12	14	0.0	0.1
METH–Un Methodist	21	1,296	3,481	4,086	9.7	21.0
Non-denom Chr Chs	9	1,015	1,140	1,331	3.2	6.8
PENT–Assemb of God	2	72	45	98	0.2	0.5
PENT–Ch God (Cleve)	1	50	85	102	0.2	0.5
PRES–Korean Pres Amer	1	NR	NR	NR	-	-
PRES–Presb Ch (USA)	2	195	405	487	1.2	2.5
PRES–Presb Ch Amer	1	0	0	0	0.0	0.0
REF–Comm Ref Evan	1	NR	NR	NR	-	-
Sev Day Adv	3	520	905	1,041	2.5	5.4
Un C of Christ	8	251	653	785	1.9	4.0
SMYTH	**91**	**4,413**	**9,411**	**12,436**	**38.6**	**100.0**
ANG/EPIS–Episcopal	2	64	87	102	0.3	0.8
Bahá'í	0	NR	3	3	0.0	0.0
BAPT–Free Will Bapt	5	NR	260	309	1.0	2.5
BAPT–So Bapt Conv	12	1,220	3,612	4,289	13.3	34.5
BRETH–Ch of Brethren	2	0	91	108	0.3	0.9
Catholic	1	NR	NR	238	0.7	1.9
CGOD–Ch God (Ander)	7	581	NR	581	1.8	4.7
Ch of Nazarene	3	93	140	151	0.5	1.2
CHR–Chr Chs & Chs Cr	5	NR	624	741	2.3	6.0
CHR–Chs of Christ	1	44	43	48	0.1	0.4
Jehovah's Witness	1	NR	NR	NR	-	-
LDS–L-D Saints	1	NR	NR	356	1.1	2.9
LUTH–E.L.C.A.	3	170	616	700	2.2	5.6
METH–Un Methodist	27	992	2,332	2,946	9.1	23.7
Non-denom Chr Chs	4	500	570	625	1.9	5.0
PENT–Assemb of God	1	14	10	16	0.0	0.1
PENT–Ch God (Cleve)	4	377	360	427	1.3	3.4
PENT–Ch of God Proph	3	NR	85	101	0.3	0.8
PENT–Intl Pent Holiness	1	12	12	14	0.0	0.1

NR–Not Reported   - Represents no adherents reported.   Percentages may not total 100 due to rounding.

Table 3: Religious Congregations by County and Group: 2010

Religious Group	Number of Congregations	Number of Attendees	Number of Communicant, Confirmed, or Full Members	Adherents: Number of Adherents	Adherents: % of Total Pop.	Adherents: % of Total Adh.
PRES–Orth Pres Ch	1	65	65	88	0.3	0.7
PRES–Presb Ch (USA)	6	247	441	524	1.6	4.2
Sev Day Adv	1	34	60	69	0.2	0.6
SOUTHAMPTON	**40**	**2,085**	**6,212**	**7,312**	**39.4**	**100.0**
ANG/EPIS–Episcopal	1	20	26	36	0.2	0.5
Bahá'í	0	NR	65	65	0.4	0.9
BAPT–NBC USA	1	0	0	0	0.0	0.0
BAPT–So Bapt Conv	13	1,348	3,894	4,620	24.9	63.2
CGOD–Ch God (Ander)	1	20	NR	20	0.1	0.3
FRND–Fr Un Mtg	2	NR	141	167	0.9	2.3
LUTH–E.L.C.A.	1	16	24	29	0.2	0.4
METH–AME Zion	5	85	525	623	3.4	8.5
METH–Un Methodist	12	421	1,255	1,455	7.8	19.9
Non-denom Chr Chs	2	140	200	200	1.1	2.7
PENT–United Holy Ch	1	NR	NR	NR	-	-
Un C of Christ	1	35	82	97	0.5	1.3
SPOTSYLVANIA	**81**	**10,360**	**14,912**	**47,114**	**38.5**	**100.0**
ANG/EPIS–Anglican NA	2	NR	NR	NR	-	-
ANG/EPIS–Episcopal	2	231	570	706	0.6	1.5
Bahá'í	1	NR	27	27	0.0	0.1
BAPT–Amer Bapt Assn	1	NR	80	101	0.1	0.2
BAPT–Free Will Bapt	1	NR	52	66	0.1	0.1
BAPT–Ind Bapt Flwsp Intl	2	NR	NR	NR	-	-
BAPT–So Bapt Conv	24	3,144	6,722	8,497	6.9	18.0
BUDD–Theravada	1	NR	NR	300	0.2	0.6
Calv Chpl	1	NR	NR	NR	-	-
Catholic	3	NR	NR	9,627	7.9	20.4
CGOD–Ch God (Ander)	1	90	NR	90	0.1	0.2
Ch of Nazarene	1	1,869	953	11,885	9.7	25.2
CHR–Chr Chs & Chs Cr	2	NR	195	246	0.2	0.5
CHR–Chs of Christ	1	125	95	140	0.1	0.3
Jehovah's Witness	2	NR	NR	NR	-	-
LDS–L-D Saints	5	NR	NR	2,513	2.1	5.3
LUTH–E.L.C.A.	2	370	672	920	0.8	2.0
LUTH–Luth Cong Msn Chr	1	NR	NR	NR	-	-
LUTH–Luth-MO Synod	1	372	495	845	0.7	1.8
METH–Un Methodist	9	876	2,348	3,562	2.9	7.6
Muslim Est	1	792	NR	3,436	2.8	7.3
Non-denom Chr Chs	2	185	200	231	0.2	0.5
ORTHE–Greek Orthodox	1	90	NR	225	0.2	0.5
PENT–Assemb of God	2	675	222	874	0.7	1.9
PENT–Ch God (Cleve)	1	397	467	590	0.5	1.3
PENT–Un Pent Ch Intl	1	NR	NR	NR	-	-
PRES–Evan Presby Ch	1	NR	50	63	0.1	0.1
PRES–Orth Pres Ch	1	81	88	110	0.1	0.2
PRES–Presb Ch (USA)	2	413	765	967	0.8	2.1
PRES–Presb Ch Amer	2	318	334	429	0.4	0.9
Sev Day Adv	3	332	577	664	0.5	1.4
Unity Ch	1	NR	NR	NR	-	-
STAFFORD	**95**	**10,232**	**20,372**	**34,247**	**26.6**	**100.0**
ANG/EPIS–Episcopal	1	209	767	1,098	0.9	3.2
Bahá'í	1	NR	35	35	0.0	0.1
BAPT–Amer Bapt USA	2	90	480	610	0.5	1.8
BAPT–Converge/BGC	1	75	NR	90	0.1	0.3
BAPT–Prog NBC	1	75	80	102	0.1	0.3
BAPT–So Bapt Conv	25	3,949	9,045	11,498	8.9	33.6
BRETH–Ch of Brethren	1	125	163	207	0.2	0.6
Calv Chpl	2	NR	NR	NR	-	-
Catholic	1	NR	NR	6,288	4.9	18.4
Ch of Nazarene	1	33	45	166	0.1	0.5
CHR–Chr Chs & Chs Cr	1	NR	250	318	0.2	0.9
CHR–Chs of Christ	3	180	139	216	0.2	0.6
CHR–Int Chs of Christ	1	NR	142	181	0.1	0.5
Jehovah's Witness	1	NR	NR	NR	-	-
LDS–L-D Saints	6	NR	NR	1,937	1.5	5.7
LUTH–E.L.C.A.	1	224	629	897	0.7	2.6
LUTH–Luth-MO Synod	1	115	146	189	0.1	0.6
METH–AME	2	0	200	254	0.2	0.7
METH–So Methodist	1	NR	NR	NR	-	-
METH–Un Methodist	8	1,701	3,726	4,503	3.5	13.1

Religious Group	Number of Congregations	Number of Attendees	Number of Communicant, Confirmed, or Full Members	Adherents: Number of Adherents	Adherents: % of Total Pop.	Adherents: % of Total Adh.
Non-denom Chr Chs	18	2,705	3,263	3,788	2.9	11.1
ORTHE–Orth Ch in Amer	1	35	NR	50	0.0	0.1
PENT–Assemb of God	3	210	116	355	0.3	1.0
PENT–Ch God (Cleve)	1	74	259	329	0.3	1.0
PENT–Ch Lord Jesus Apos	1	NR	NR	NR	-	-
PENT–Ch of God Proph	2	NR	212	269	0.2	0.8
PENT–Int Foursq Gos	1	33	12	15	0.0	0.0
PENT–Pent FW Bapt	1	NR	NR	NR	-	-
PENT–Un Pent Ch Intl	2	NR	NR	NR	-	-
PRES–Presb Ch (USA)	2	219	469	596	0.5	1.7
PRES–Presb Ch Amer	1	110	72	110	0.1	0.3
Sev Day Adv	1	70	122	140	0.1	0.4
Zoroastrian	0	NR	NR	6	0.0	0.0
STAUNTON (CITY)	**66**	**5,932**	**10,878**	**15,812**	**66.6**	**100.0**
ANG/EPIS–Anglican NA	1	NR	NR	NR	-	-
ANG/EPIS–Episcopal	3	304	647	749	3.2	4.7
Bahá'í	1	NR	26	26	0.1	0.2
BAPT–Ref Bapt Ch	1	NR	NR	NR	-	-
BAPT–So Bapt Conv	4	1,100	2,339	2,751	11.6	17.4
Catholic	1	NR	NR	1,535	6.5	9.7
CGOD–Ch God (Ander)	1	97	NR	97	0.4	0.6
Ch of Nazarene	1	39	104	104	0.4	0.7
Chr & Miss Al	1	245	143	415	1.7	2.6
CHR–Chr Chs & Chs Cr	1	NR	90	106	0.4	0.7
CHR–Chs of Christ	1	18	15	20	0.1	0.1
FRND–Fr Gen Cf & Un Mtg	1	NR	0	0	0.0	0.0
Jehovah's Witness	1	NR	NR	NR	-	-
JUD–Reform	1	24	42	113	0.5	0.7
LDS–L-D Saints	1	NR	NR	361	1.5	2.3
LUTH–E.L.C.A.	2	96	214	284	1.2	1.8
MENN–Mennonite USA	1	36	26	31	0.1	0.2
METH–AME	1	70	88	104	0.4	0.7
METH–Un Methodist	11	853	2,842	3,204	13.5	20.3
METH–Wesleyan	1	101	94	131	0.6	0.8
Non-denom Chr Chs	6	1,190	1,330	1,513	6.4	9.6
OCATH–Un Cath Ch	1	NR	NR	702	3.0	4.4
PENT–Assemb of God	1	110	60	153	0.6	1.0
PENT–Ch God (Cleve)	2	114	195	229	1.0	1.4
PENT–Ch of God Proph	1	NR	14	16	0.1	0.1
PENT–COGIC	1	25	50	59	0.2	0.4
PENT–Intl Pent Holiness	2	41	57	67	0.3	0.4
PENT–Pent Ch of God	1	70	NR	109	0.5	0.7
PENT–Un Pent Ch Intl	1	NR	NR	NR	-	-
PRES–Orth Pres Ch	1	50	46	62	0.3	0.4
PRES–Presb Ch (USA)	6	676	1,337	1,573	6.6	9.9
PRES–Presb Ch Amer	1	70	66	86	0.4	0.5
Salvation Army	1	64	153	177	0.7	1.1
Sev Day Adv	3	501	872	1,002	4.2	6.3
Sikh	1	NR	NR	NR	-	-
Un Breth in Cr	1	38	28	33	0.1	0.2
SUFFOLK (CITY)	**89**	**9,746**	**21,545**	**27,532**	**32.5**	**100.0**
ANG/EPIS–Episcopal	4	222	422	646	0.8	2.3
Bahá'í	0	NR	324	324	0.4	1.2
BAPT–Asc Ref Bap Ch Am	1	NR	NR	NR	-	-
BAPT–Free Will Bapt	1	NR	52	65	0.1	0.2
BAPT–Natl Mis Bapt Conv	1	70	185	232	0.3	0.8
BAPT–NBC USA	1	0	470	589	0.7	2.1
BAPT–So Bapt Conv	13	2,357	6,092	7,631	9.0	27.7
Calv Chpl	1	NR	NR	NR	-	-
Catholic	1	NR	NR	819	1.0	3.0
CGOD–Ch God (Ander)	1	0	NR	0	0.0	0.0
CHR–Chr Chs & Chs Cr	1	NR	130	163	0.2	0.6
CHR–Chs of Christ	1	85	79	103	0.1	0.4
CONG–Consrv Cong Chr	1	90	442	554	0.7	2.0
FRND–Fr Un Mtg	1	NR	47	59	0.1	0.2
Jehovah's Witness	2	NR	NR	NR	-	-
LDS–L-D Saints	1	NR	NR	516	0.6	1.9
LUTH–E.L.C.A.	1	159	184	232	0.3	0.8
METH–AME	1	180	230	288	0.3	1.0
METH–AME Zion	1	0	150	188	0.2	0.7
METH–Un Methodist	10	1,071	3,118	3,861	4.6	14.0

NR–Not Reported - Represents no adherents reported. Percentages may not total 100 due to rounding.

Table 3: Religious Congregations by County and Group: 2010

Religious Group	Number of Congrega-tions	Number of Attendees	Number of Communicant, Confirmed, or Full Members	Adherents		
				Number of Adherents	% of Total Pop.	% of Total Adh.
Non-denom Chr Chs	18	3,165	5,347	5,556	6.6	20.2
ORTHO–Coptic Orth Ch	1	125	NR	240	0.3	0.9
PENT–Assemb of God	1	61	45	135	0.2	0.5
PENT–Ch God (Cleve)	1	69	131	164	0.2	0.6
PENT–Ch of God Proph	2	NR	108	135	0.2	0.5
PENT–COGIC	4	250	520	651	0.8	2.4
PENT–Intl Pent Holiness	2	135	203	254	0.3	0.9
PENT–Un Pent Ch Intl	1	NR	NR	NR	-	-
PENT–United Holy Ch	2	NR	NR	NR	-	-
PRES–Presb Ch (USA)	2	296	615	770	0.9	2.8
PRES–Presb Ch Amer	1	964	1,158	1,492	1.8	5.4
Salvation Army	1	75	87	106	0.1	0.4
Sev Day Adv	1	32	55	63	0.1	0.2
Un C of Christ	8	340	1,351	1,692	2.0	6.1
Zoroastrian	0	NR	NR	4	0.0	0.0
SURRY	**23**	**854**	**2,066**	**2,406**	**34.1**	**100.0**
ANG/EPIS–Episcopal	1	20	26	55	0.8	2.3
Bahá'í	0	NR	1	1	0.0	0.0
BAPT–So Bapt Conv	8	506	1,060	1,253	17.8	52.1
CONG–Cong Chr Add'l	2	NR	38	45	0.6	1.9
METH–AME	2	0	250	296	4.2	12.3
METH–AME Zion	1	0	100	118	1.7	4.9
METH–Un Methodist	6	168	364	393	5.6	16.3
Non-denom Chr Chs	2	160	210	225	3.2	9.4
Un C of Christ	1	0	17	20	0.3	0.8
SUSSEX	**28**	**1,559**	**3,719**	**4,429**	**36.6**	**100.0**
ANG/EPIS–Episcopal	1	20	25	28	0.2	0.6
BAPT–Amer Bapt USA	1	520	461	528	4.4	11.9
BAPT–So Bapt Conv	7	330	1,053	1,206	10.0	27.2
Catholic	1	NR	NR	45	0.4	1.0
CONG–Cong Chr Add'l	1	NR	157	180	1.5	4.1
Jehovah's Witness	1	NR	NR	NR	-	-
LDS–L-D Saints	1	NR	NR	128	1.1	2.9
METH–AME Zion	2	40	270	309	2.6	7.0
METH–Un Methodist	6	335	1,067	1,273	10.5	28.7
Non-denom Chr Chs	3	216	370	370	3.1	8.4
Sev Day Adv	1	46	80	92	0.8	2.1
Un C of Christ	3	52	236	270	2.2	6.1
TAZEWELL	**141**	**6,099**	**12,514**	**17,015**	**37.7**	**100.0**
ANG/EPIS–Episcopal	4	76	171	204	0.5	1.2
Bahá'í	0	NR	8	8	0.0	0.0
BAPT–NBC USA	1	30	45	53	0.1	0.3
BAPT–So Bapt Conv	15	1,474	3,351	3,961	8.8	23.3
Catholic	3	NR	NR	214	0.5	1.3
CGOD–Ch God (Ander)	3	16	NR	16	0.0	0.1
CHR–Chr Ch (Disc)	8	84	479	566	1.3	3.3
CHR–Chr Chs & Chs Cr	8	NR	895	1,058	2.3	6.2
CHR–Chs of Christ	7	237	202	266	0.6	1.6
Jehovah's Witness	3	NR	NR	NR	-	-
LDS–L-D Saints	2	NR	NR	938	2.1	5.5
LUTH–E.L.C.A.	1	16	26	29	0.1	0.2
METH–A.W.M.C.	1	8	6	12	0.0	0.1
METH–Un Methodist	37	1,660	3,958	4,610	10.2	27.1
METH–Wesleyan	1	20	43	26	0.1	0.2
Non-denom Chr Chs	7	523	565	679	1.5	4.0
PENT–Assemb of God	12	801	397	1,564	3.5	9.2
PENT–Ch God (Cleve)	8	454	812	960	2.1	5.6
PENT–Ch of God Proph	3	NR	66	78	0.2	0.5
PENT–Intl Pent Holiness	5	434	692	818	1.8	4.8
PENT–Un Pent Ch Intl	1	NR	NR	NR	-	-
PRES–Presb Ch (USA)	8	193	695	822	1.8	4.8
PRES–Presb Ch Amer	1	65	89	117	0.3	0.7
PRES–Ref Pres US	1	NR	NR	NR	-	-
Sev Day Adv	1	8	14	16	0.0	0.1
VIRGINIA BEACH (CITY)	**265**	**46,502**	**87,984**	**164,875**	**37.6**	**100.0**
ANG/EPIS–Episcopal	11	1,987	4,109	5,960	1.4	3.6
Bahá'í	1	NR	147	147	0.0	0.1
BAPT–Amer Bapt USA	1	1,150	1,530	1,876	0.4	1.1

Religious Group	Number of Congrega-tions	Number of Attendees	Number of Communicant, Confirmed, or Full Members	Adherents		
				Number of Adherents	% of Total Pop.	% of Total Adh.
BAPT–Asc Ref Bap Ch Am	1	NR	NR	NR	-	-
BAPT–Free Will Bapt	3	NR	156	191	0.0	0.1
BAPT–Fund Bapt Flwsp	1	NR	NR	NR	-	-
BAPT–NBC USA	5	1,375	2,300	2,820	0.6	1.7
BAPT–Ref Bapt Ch	1	NR	NR	NR	-	-
BAPT–So Bapt Conv	36	7,002	17,515	21,474	4.9	13.0
BRETH–Ch of Brethren	1	0	97	119	0.0	0.1
BRETH–Grace Breth	1	NR	NR	NR	-	-
BUDD–Mahayana	6	NR	NR	4,582	1.0	2.8
BUDD–Vajrayana	2	NR	NR	62	0.0	0.0
Calv Chpl	2	NR	NR	NR	-	-
Catholic	11	NR	NR	47,025	10.7	28.5
CGOD–Ch God (Ander)	1	165	NR	165	0.0	0.1
Ch Cr, Scientst	1	NR	NR	NR	-	-
Ch of Nazarene	2	264	473	473	0.1	0.3
Chr & Miss Al	1	37	17	39	0.0	0.0
CHR–Chr Ch (Disc)	3	155	307	376	0.1	0.2
CHR–Chr Chs & Chs Cr	8	NR	2,480	3,041	0.7	1.8
CHR–Chs of Christ	5	470	500	612	0.1	0.4
CHR–Int Chs of Christ	1	NR	323	396	0.1	0.2
FRND–Consrv Yr Mtgs	1	NR	128	157	0.0	0.1
FRND–Evan Fr Ch Intl	1	90	55	67	0.0	0.0
HINDU–Post Ren	2	NR	NR	50	0.0	0.0
Jehovah's Witness	3	NR	NR	NR	-	-
JUD–Conserv	2	211	237	640	0.1	0.4
JUD–Reform	1	101	178	481	0.1	0.3
LDS–L-D Saints	6	NR	NR	3,319	0.8	2.0
LUTH–E.L.C.A.	4	794	1,417	1,966	0.4	1.2
LUTH–Luth–MO Synod	2	491	799	1,024	0.2	0.6
MENN–Beachy Amish-Menn	1	93	55	93	0.0	0.1
METH–AME	6	175	975	1,195	0.3	0.7
METH–AME Zion	1	0	100	123	0.0	0.1
METH–Un Methodist	22	4,740	14,319	17,614	4.0	10.7
METH–Wesleyan	1	48	16	62	0.0	0.0
Muslim Est	1	792	NR	3,436	0.8	2.1
Non-denom Chr Chs	52	19,910	28,630	30,620	7.0	18.6
ORTHE–Greek Orthodox	1	190	NR	840	0.2	0.5
PENT–Assemb of God	6	490	319	629	0.1	0.4
PENT–Ch God (Cleve)	8	1,445	2,121	2,600	0.6	1.6
PENT–Ch of God Proph	1	NR	54	66	0.0	0.0
PENT–Full Gosp Bapt	1	NR	NR	NR	-	-
PENT–Int Pent C Chr	1	46	38	90	0.0	0.1
PENT–Intl Pent Holiness	4	634	510	625	0.1	0.4
PENT–Un Pent Ch Intl	2	NR	NR	NR	-	-
PENT–Vineyard	3	1,055	1,515	1,857	0.4	1.1
PRES–Evan Presby Ch	1	NR	1,247	1,529	0.3	0.9
PRES–Korean Amer Pres	1	NR	NR	NR	-	-
PRES–Presb Ch (USA)	10	1,619	3,861	4,734	1.1	2.9
PRES–Presb Ch Amer	4	504	631	706	0.2	0.4
Sev Day Adv	3	124	217	249	0.1	0.2
Un C of Christ	6	345	608	745	0.2	0.5
Unity Ch	2	NR	NR	NR	-	-
WARREN	**48**	**3,307**	**6,696**	**12,326**	**32.8**	**100.0**
ANG/EPIS–Episcopal	1	110	221	329	0.9	2.7
Bahá'í	0	NR	3	3	0.0	0.0
BAPT–Alliance Bapt	1	NR	NR	NR	-	-
BAPT–Amer Bapt USA	1	122	594	728	1.9	5.9
BAPT–So Bapt Conv	5	385	1,115	1,367	3.6	11.1
BRETH–Ch of Brethren	1	115	246	302	0.8	2.5
Catholic	1	NR	NR	2,597	6.9	21.1
Ch of God Gen Conf	2	NR	90	110	0.3	0.9
Ch of Nazarene	1	65	67	67	0.2	0.5
CHR–Chr Chs & Chs Cr	1	NR	0	0	0.0	0.0
CHR–Chs of Christ	1	75	70	91	0.2	0.7
HINDU–Post Ren	1	NR	NR	10	0.0	0.1
HINDU–Renaiss	1	NR	NR	12	0.0	0.1
Jehovah's Witness	1	NR	NR	NR	-	-
LDS–L-D Saints	1	NR	NR	549	1.5	4.5
LUTH–E.L.C.A.	1	51	103	121	0.3	1.0
METH–C.M.E.	1	0	100	123	0.3	1.0
METH–Un Methodist	10	790	2,196	3,137	8.3	25.5
Non-denom Chr Chs	7	1,050	1,035	1,338	3.6	10.9
PENT–Assemb of God	3	256	144	580	1.5	4.7

NR–Not Reported - Represents no adherents reported. Percentages may not total 100 due to rounding.

Table 3: Religious Congregations by County and Group: 2010

Religious Group	Number of Congrega-tions	Number of Attendees	Number of Communicant, Confirmed, or Full Members	Adherents: Number of Adherents	Adherents: % of Total Pop.	Adherents: % of Total Adh.
PENT–Ch God (Cleve)	1	88	200	245	0.7	2.0
PRES–Presb Ch (USA)	3	154	312	382	1.0	3.1
Salvation Army	1	20	63	70	0.2	0.6
Sev Day Adv	1	26	45	52	0.1	0.4
Un C of Christ	1	0	92	113	0.3	0.9
WASHINGTON	**123**	**12,482**	**20,182**	**23,590**	**43.0**	**100.0**
ANG/EPIS–Episcopal	1	76	141	141	0.3	0.6
Bahá'í	0	NR	19	19	0.0	0.1
BAPT–Free Will Bapt	1	NR	52	61	0.1	0.3
BAPT–Natl Mis Bapt Conv	1	45	65	76	0.1	0.3
BAPT–So Bapt Conv	20	4,227	6,703	7,878	14.4	33.4
BRETH–Ch of Brethren	1	22	22	26	0.0	0.1
Catholic	1	NR	NR	360	0.7	1.5
CGOD–Ch God (Ander)	2	136	NR	136	0.2	0.6
Ch of Nazarene	1	64	131	131	0.2	0.6
CHR–Chr Chs & Chs Cr	8	NR	709	833	1.5	3.5
CHR–Chs of Christ	5	229	224	302	0.6	1.3
FRND–Fr Gen Cf & Un Mtg	1	NR	1	1	0.0	0.0
Jehovah's Witness	1	NR	NR	NR	-	-
LUTH–E.L.C.A.	3	90	302	352	0.6	1.5
METH–AME Zion	1	0	100	118	0.2	0.5
METH–Un Methodist	34	1,827	4,036	4,634	8.4	19.6
Non-denom Chr Chs	13	4,540	5,508	5,944	10.8	25.2
PENT–Assemb of God	2	120	91	147	0.3	0.6
PENT–Ch God (Cleve)	4	260	388	456	0.8	1.9
PENT–Ch of God Proph	2	NR	42	49	0.1	0.2
PENT–Intl Pent Holiness	2	157	290	341	0.6	1.4
PENT–Un Pent Ch Intl	2	NR	NR	NR	-	-
PRES–Evan Presby Ch	1	NR	71	83	0.2	0.4
PRES–Presb Ch (USA)	11	512	1,069	1,256	2.3	5.3
PRES–Presb Ch Amer	2	100	103	110	0.2	0.5
REF–Comm Ref Evan	1	NR	NR	NR	-	-
Sev Day Adv	1	42	72	83	0.2	0.4
Unit Univ	1	35	43	53	0.1	0.2
WAYNESBORO (CITY)	**53**	**4,536**	**8,711**	**13,229**	**63.0**	**100.0**
ANG/EPIS–Episcopal	1	135	242	392	1.9	3.0
Bahá'í	0	NR	8	8	0.0	0.1
BAPT–So Bapt Conv	4	742	1,523	1,875	8.9	14.2
Calv Chpl	1	NR	NR	NR	-	-
Catholic	1	NR	NR	1,638	7.8	12.4
Ch Cr, Scientst	1	NR	NR	NR	-	-
CHR–Chr Chs & Chs Cr	3	NR	653	804	3.8	6.1
CHR–Chs of Christ	1	205	145	338	1.6	2.6
Jehovah's Witness	2	NR	NR	NR	-	-
LDS–L-D Saints	1	NR	NR	728	3.5	5.5
LUTH–E.L.C.A.	1	143	424	509	2.4	3.8
LUTH–Luth–MO Synod	1	150	424	436	2.1	3.3
MENN–Mennonite USA	2	287	330	406	1.9	3.1
METH–Free Methodist	1	150	107	150	0.7	1.1
METH–Un Methodist	11	774	1,993	2,297	10.9	17.4
METH–Wesleyan	1	15	24	20	0.1	0.2
Non-denom Chr Chs	6	600	650	749	3.6	5.7
PENT–Assemb of God	1	200	0	200	1.0	1.5
PENT–Ch God (Cleve)	2	98	339	417	2.0	3.2
PENT–Ch of God Proph	1	NR	21	26	0.1	0.2
PENT–COGIC	1	0	150	185	0.9	1.4
PENT–Intl Pent Holiness	1	55	25	31	0.1	0.2
PENT–Un Pent Ch Intl	1	NR	NR	NR	-	-
PRES–Presb Ch (USA)	4	629	1,074	1,323	6.3	10.0
Salvation Army	1	26	84	99	0.5	0.7
Sev Day Adv	2	200	348	401	1.9	3.0
Unit Univ	1	127	147	197	0.9	1.5
WESTMORELAND	**30**	**1,700**	**4,545**	**7,154**	**41.0**	**100.0**
ANG/EPIS–Episcopal	5	230	581	809	4.6	11.3
Bahá'í	0	NR	6	6	0.0	0.1
BAPT–So Bapt Conv	7	634	2,168	2,552	14.6	35.7
Catholic	2	NR	NR	1,727	9.9	24.1
Jehovah's Witness	2	NR	NR	NR	-	-
METH–Un Methodist	10	401	1,337	1,482	8.5	20.7
Non-denom Chr Chs	3	360	420	486	2.8	6.8

Religious Group	Number of Congrega-tions	Number of Attendees	Number of Communicant, Confirmed, or Full Members	Adherents: Number of Adherents	Adherents: % of Total Pop.	Adherents: % of Total Adh.
PENT–Assemb of God	1	75	33	92	0.5	1.3
WILLIAMSBURG (CITY)	**19**	**6,696**	**9,871**	**12,100**	**86.0**	**100.0**
ANG/EPIS–Episcopal	1	610	1,955	1,955	13.9	16.2
Bahá'í	0	NR	10	10	0.1	0.1
BAPT–Alliance Bapt	1	NR	NR	NR	-	-
BAPT–So Bapt Conv	2	206	183	198	1.4	1.6
Ch Cr, Scientst	1	NR	NR	NR	-	-
CHR–Chs of Christ	1	155	135	175	1.2	1.4
FRND–Fr Gen Cf & Un Mtg	1	NR	23	25	0.2	0.2
LUTH–E.L.C.A.	1	222	441	500	3.6	4.1
METH–Un Methodist	1	640	2,089	2,258	16.1	18.7
Non-denom Chr Chs	9	4,347	3,622	5,446	38.7	45.0
PRES–Presb Ch (USA)	1	516	1,413	1,533	10.9	12.7
WINCHESTER (CITY)	**54**	**4,941**	**9,744**	**22,012**	**84.0**	**100.0**
ANG/EPIS–Anglican NA	1	NR	NR	NR	-	-
ANG/EPIS–Episcopal	1	233	563	621	2.4	2.8
Bahá'í	0	NR	14	14	0.1	0.1
BAPT–So Bapt Conv	4	431	1,079	1,310	5.0	6.0
BRETH–Brethren (Ash)	1	NR	450	546	2.1	2.5
BRETH–Grace Breth	1	NR	NR	NR	-	-
Calv Chpl	1	NR	NR	NR	-	-
Catholic	1	NR	NR	7,630	29.1	34.7
Chr & Miss Al	2	142	103	209	0.8	0.9
CHR–Chr Ch (Disc)	1	123	334	405	1.5	1.8
CHR–Chs of Christ	1	140	100	180	0.7	0.8
CONG–Cong Chr, NA	1	NR	44	53	0.2	0.2
Evan Assoc RCC	1	NR	NR	NR	-	-
JUD–Reform	1	52	91	246	0.9	1.1
LDS–L-D Saints	3	NR	NR	1,076	4.1	4.9
LUTH–E.L.C.A.	2	299	690	849	3.2	3.9
LUTH–Nor Amer Luth C	1	NR	NR	NR	-	-
LUTH–Wisc Ev Luth Syn	1	53	65	87	0.3	0.4
METH–AME	1	75	150	182	0.7	0.8
METH–C.M.E.	2	0	300	364	1.4	1.7
METH–Un Methodist	8	1,042	2,779	3,571	13.6	16.2
METH–Wesleyan	1	13	14	17	0.1	0.1
Muslim Est	1	20	NR	100	0.4	0.5
Non-denom Chr Chs	5	730	820	933	3.6	4.2
ORTHE–Greek Orthodox	1	70	NR	150	0.6	0.7
PENT–Assemb of God	2	575	387	1,200	4.6	5.5
PENT–COGIC	1	0	150	182	0.7	0.8
PENT–Int Foursq Gos	1	55	13	16	0.1	0.1
PENT–Pent Ch of God	1	70	NR	109	0.4	0.5
PRES–Presb Ch (USA)	2	502	1,106	1,343	5.1	6.1
PRES–Presb Ch Amer	1	125	117	181	0.7	0.8
Sev Day Adv	2	154	269	309	1.2	1.4
Un C of Christ	1	37	106	129	0.5	0.6
WISE	**106**	**4,369**	**9,423**	**12,186**	**29.4**	**100.0**
ANG/EPIS–Episcopal	3	65	135	142	0.3	1.2
Bahá'í	0	NR	3	3	0.0	0.0
BAPT–Free Will Bapt	17	NR	928	1,103	2.7	9.1
BAPT–Prim Bapt E Dst	2	50	178	212	0.5	1.7
BAPT–So Bapt Conv	22	1,599	3,964	4,712	11.4	38.7
Catholic	3	NR	NR	140	0.3	1.1
CGOD–Ch God (Ander)	2	155	NR	155	0.4	1.3
CHR–Chr Chs & Chs Cr	2	NR	175	208	0.5	1.7
CHR–Chs of Christ	3	105	113	144	0.3	1.2
Ind Fund Churches	1	NR	NR	NR	-	-
Jehovah's Witness	1	NR	NR	NR	-	-
LDS–L-D Saints	1	NR	NR	368	0.9	3.0
LUTH–E.L.C.A.	1	30	50	70	0.2	0.6
METH–AME Zion	1	0	100	119	0.3	1.0
METH–Un Methodist	17	722	1,712	1,958	4.7	16.1
Non-denom Chr Chs	7	820	930	1,063	2.6	8.7
PENT–Assemb of God	6	588	431	952	2.3	7.8
PENT–Ch God (Cleve)	4	155	232	276	0.7	2.3
PENT–Ch of God Proph	6	NR	190	226	0.5	1.9
PENT–Un Pent Ch Intl	1	NR	NR	NR	-	-
PRES–Presb Ch (USA)	5	55	240	285	0.7	2.3
PRES–Presb Ch Amer	1	25	42	50	0.1	0.4

NR–Not Reported   - Represents no adherents reported.   Percentages may not total 100 due to rounding.

Table 3: Religious Congregations by County and Group: 2010

Religious Group	Number of Congrega-tions	Number of Attendees	Number of Communicant, Confirmed, or Full Members	Adherents		
				Number of Adherents	% of Total Pop.	% of Total Adh.
WYTHE	**118**	**6,328**	**11,494**	**14,685**	**50.2**	**100.0**
ANG/EPIS–Episcopal	1	78	214	221	0.8	1.5
Bahá'í	0	NR	1	1	0.0	0.0
BAPT–So Bapt Conv	4	593	1,027	1,221	4.2	8.3
Catholic	1	NR	NR	299	1.0	2.0
CGOD–Ch God (Ander)	2	110	NR	110	0.4	0.7
Ch Christ Chr Union	1	NR	NR	NR	-	-
CHR–Chr Ch (Disc)	3	109	322	383	1.3	2.6
CHR–Chr Chs & Chs Cr	1	NR	85	101	0.3	0.7
CHR–Chs of Christ	3	125	119	160	0.5	1.1
Jehovah's Witness	1	NR	NR	NR	-	-
LDS–L-D Saints	1	NR	NR	547	1.9	3.7
LUTH–E.L.C.A.	10	368	671	900	3.1	6.1
LUTH–Luth Cong Msn Chr	1	50	153	182	0.6	1.2
MENN–Beachy Amish-Menn	1	146	60	146	0.5	1.0
METH–AME	1	0	100	119	0.4	0.8
METH–Un Methodist	39	1,427	3,655	4,113	14.1	28.0
Non-denom Chr Chs	6	895	950	1,127	3.9	7.7
PENT–Assemb of God	3	138	60	210	0.7	1.4
PENT–Ch God (Cleve)	9	827	1,207	1,436	4.9	9.8
PENT–Ch of God Proph	6	NR	221	263	0.9	1.8
PENT–Intl Pent Holiness	18	1,243	2,275	2,706	9.3	18.4
PENT–Orig Ch of God	1	NR	NR	NR	-	-
PRES–Presb Ch (USA)	3	153	259	308	1.1	2.1
PRES–Ref Pres US	1	NR	NR	NR	-	-
Sev Day Adv	1	66	115	132	0.5	0.9
YORK	**48**	**7,515**	**16,772**	**24,873**	**38.0**	**100.0**
ANG/EPIS–Anglican NA	1	NR	NR	NR	-	-
ANG/EPIS–Episcopal	2	360	751	876	1.3	3.5
Bahá'í	0	NR	15	15	0.0	0.1
BAPT–Free Will Bapt	1	NR	52	64	0.1	0.3
BAPT–So Bapt Conv	11	3,584	6,276	7,782	11.9	31.3
Catholic	2	NR	NR	3,511	5.4	14.1
CHR–Chr Ch (Disc)	1	0	372	461	0.7	1.9
CHR–Chr Chs & Chs Cr	3	NR	1,575	1,953	3.0	7.9
Jehovah's Witness	2	NR	NR	NR	-	-
LDS–L-D Saints	1	NR	NR	414	0.6	1.7
LUTH–E.L.C.A.	1	260	913	1,120	1.7	4.5
LUTH–Wisc Ev Luth Syn	1	65	95	124	0.2	0.5
METH–Un Methodist	4	944	3,749	4,502	6.9	18.1
MJEW–Assoc Mes Cong	1	NR	NR	NR	-	-
Non-denom Chr Chs	7	1,365	1,400	1,781	2.7	7.2
ORTHE–Ant Orth of NA	1	55	NR	100	0.2	0.4
ORTHO–Armen Ap Etchm	1	45	NR	120	0.2	0.5
ORTHO–Malan Syr Orth	1	30	NR	54	0.1	0.2
PENT–Assemb of God	1	80	47	103	0.2	0.4
PENT–Ch God (Cleve)	1	75	277	343	0.5	1.4
PENT–Intl Pent Holiness	1	8	10	12	0.0	0.0
PENT–Vineyard	1	34	62	77	0.1	0.3
PRES–Korean Amer Pres	1	NR	NR	NR	-	-
PRES–Presb Ch (USA)	2	610	1,178	1,461	2.2	5.9
WASHINGTON	**6,114**	**650,432**	**835,492**	**2,328,005**	**34.6**	**100.0**
ADAMS	**42**	**1,693**	**2,509**	**8,011**	**42.8**	**100.0**
ANG/EPIS–Episcopal	1	3	5	5	0.0	0.1
Bahá'í	0	NR	3	3	0.0	0.0
BAPT–Reg Bapt Gen As	1	NR	NR	NR	-	-
BAPT–So Bapt Conv	2	34	60	83	0.4	1.0
Catholic	4	NR	NR	2,024	10.8	25.3
Ch of Nazarene	2	343	243	481	2.6	6.0
CHR–Chr Ch (Disc)	1	0	43	59	0.3	0.7
CHR–Chs of Christ	1	15	19	27	0.1	0.3
Jehovah's Witness	1	NR	NR	NR	-	-
LDS–L-D Saints	9	NR	NR	2,245	12.0	28.0
LUTH–E.L.C.A.	3	156	671	797	4.3	9.9
MENN–Hutt Breth	1	NR	NR	NR	-	-
MENN–Mennonite USA	1	44	141	194	1.0	2.4
METH–Un Methodist	1	55	199	237	1.3	3.0
Non-denom Chr Chs	1	30	30	38	0.2	0.5
PENT–Assemb of God	3	362	268	728	3.9	9.1

Religious Group	Number of Congrega-tions	Number of Attendees	Number of Communicant, Confirmed, or Full Members	Adherents		
				Number of Adherents	% of Total Pop.	% of Total Adh.
PENT–Int Foursq Gos	2	99	106	146	0.8	1.8
PENT–Intl Pent Holiness	2	259	190	262	1.4	3.3
PRES–Presb Ch (USA)	2	108	191	263	1.4	3.3
Sev Day Adv	3	126	220	253	1.4	3.2
Un C of Christ	1	59	120	166	0.9	2.1
ASOTIN	**34**	**1,596**	**2,621**	**7,437**	**34.4**	**100.0**
Bahá'í	0	NR	21	21	0.1	0.3
BAPT–Amer Bapt Assn	1	NR	85	102	0.5	1.4
BAPT–Natl Mis Bapt Conv	1	0	150	180	0.8	2.4
BAPT–Ref Bapt Ch	1	NR	NR	NR	-	-
BAPT–Reg Bapt Gen As	1	NR	NR	NR	-	-
BAPT–So Bapt Conv	2	108	268	322	1.5	4.3
Catholic	1	NR	NR	2,529	11.7	34.0
CGOD–Ch God (Ander)	1	57	NR	57	0.3	0.8
CHR–Chr Ch (Disc)	1	83	172	207	1.0	2.8
CHR–Chs of Christ	1	20	19	24	0.1	0.3
Jehovah's Witness	1	NR	NR	NR	-	-
LDS–Comm of Christ	1	NR	128	128	0.6	1.7
LDS–L-D Saints	2	NR	NR	1,457	6.7	19.6
LUTH–Ch Luth Conf	1	NR	NR	NR	-	-
LUTH–E.L.C.A.	1	104	224	274	1.3	3.7
METH–Free Methodist	1	56	49	56	0.3	0.8
METH–Un Methodist	3	150	299	380	1.8	5.1
METH–Wesleyan	1	94	70	122	0.6	1.6
Non-denom Chr Chs	4	277	357	384	1.8	5.2
PENT–Assemb of God	2	94	0	162	0.7	2.2
PENT–Int Foursq Gos	2	149	238	286	1.3	3.8
PENT–Pent Ch of God	1	70	NR	109	0.5	1.5
PRES–Presb Ch (USA)	2	181	275	331	1.5	4.5
Sev Day Adv	2	153	266	306	1.4	4.1
BENTON	**162**	**15,105**	**24,421**	**73,805**	**42.1**	**100.0**
ANG/EPIS–Anglican NA	2	NR	NR	NR	-	-
ANG/EPIS–Episcopal	3	253	754	861	0.5	1.2
Bahá'í	2	NR	94	94	0.1	0.1
BAPT–Amer Bapt USA	2	172	385	487	0.3	0.7
BAPT–Consrv Bapt	3	NR	NR	NR	-	-
BAPT–Free Will Bapt	1	NR	41	52	0.0	0.1
BAPT–Reg Bapt Gen As	2	NR	NR	NR	-	-
BAPT–So Bapt Conv	13	1,170	2,504	3,170	1.8	4.3
BRETH–Grace Breth	1	NR	NR	NR	-	-
BUDD–Theravada	2	NR	NR	675	0.4	0.9
Calv Chpl	1	NR	NR	NR	-	-
Catholic	5	NR	NR	26,500	15.1	35.9
CGOD–Ch God (Ander)	1	592	NR	592	0.3	0.8
Ch of Nazarene	6	634	879	918	0.5	1.2
Chr & Miss Al	2	250	186	381	0.2	0.5
CHR–Chr Ch (Disc)	2	169	793	1,004	0.6	1.4
CHR–Chs of Christ	6	466	520	686	0.4	0.9
Evan Free Ch	1	35	NR	35	0.0	0.0
HINDU–Post Ren	1	NR	NR	16	0.0	0.0
Jehovah's Witness	4	NR	NR	NR	-	-
JUD–Conserv	1	45	51	138	0.1	0.2
LDS–Comm of Christ	1	NR	128	128	0.1	0.2
LDS–L-D Saints	31	NR	NR	14,294	8.2	19.4
LUTH–E.L.C.A.	2	334	1,050	1,247	0.7	1.7
LUTH–Luth Cong Msn Chr	1	421	1,191	1,508	0.9	2.0
LUTH–Luth–MO Synod	4	555	1,142	1,399	0.8	1.9
LUTH–Wisc Ev Luth Syn	1	109	214	279	0.2	0.4
METH–Un Methodist	8	1,078	2,413	4,330	2.5	5.9
Metro Comm Ch	1	27	30	38	0.0	0.1
Muslim Est	1	80	NR	800	0.5	1.1
Non-denom Chr Chs	14	5,390	7,905	8,198	4.7	11.1
PENT–Assemb of God	8	847	363	1,253	0.7	1.7
PENT–Ch God (Cleve)	3	117	156	197	0.1	0.3
PENT–Ch of God Proph	1	NR	53	67	0.0	0.1
PENT–Int Foursq Gos	2	238	284	359	0.2	0.5
PENT–Intl Pent Holiness	1	43	25	32	0.0	0.0
PENT–Un Pent Ch Intl	2	NR	NR	NR	-	-
PRES–Orth Pres Ch	1	47	44	57	0.0	0.1
PRES–Presb Ch (USA)	8	1,037	1,652	2,091	1.2	2.8
REF–Christian Ref	1	111	75	95	0.1	0.1

NR–Not Reported - Represents no adherents reported. Percentages may not total 100 due to rounding.

Table 3: Religious Congregations by County and Group: 2010

Religious Group	Number of Congrega-tions	Number of Attendees	Number of Communicant, Confirmed, or Full Members	Adherents: Number of Adherents	Adherents: % of Total Pop.	Adherents: % of Total Adh.
REF–Comm Ref Evan	1	NR	NR	NR	-	-
REF–Un Ref Chs N.A.	1	NR	NR	NR	-	-
Salvation Army	2	195	317	461	0.3	0.6
Sev Day Adv	5	602	1,046	1,204	0.7	1.6
Un C of Christ	1	88	126	159	0.1	0.2
CHELAN	**96**	**10,786**	**13,674**	**34,779**	**48.0**	**100.0**
ANG/EPIS–Anglican NA	1	NR	NR	NR	-	-
ANG/EPIS–Episcopal	3	119	254	268	0.4	0.8
Bahá'í	1	NR	55	55	0.1	0.2
BAPT–Amer Bapt USA	2	153	204	252	0.3	0.7
BAPT–Consrv Bapt	1	NR	NR	NR	-	-
BAPT–Reg Bapt Gen As	1	NR	NR	NR	-	-
BAPT–So Bapt Conv	3	186	848	1,048	1.4	3.0
BRETH–Ch of Brethren	2	107	234	289	0.4	0.8
Catholic	3	NR	NR	13,500	18.6	38.8
Ch Cr, Scientst	1	NR	NR	NR	-	-
Ch of Nazarene	4	572	567	1,233	1.7	3.5
Chr & Miss Al	1	NR	NR	NR	-	-
CHR–Chr Ch (Disc)	2	20	37	46	0.1	0.1
CHR–Chs of Christ	2	263	295	338	0.5	1.0
Evan Ch	2	NR	NR	NR	-	-
Evan Cov Ch	1	243	83	316	0.4	0.9
Evan Free Ch	1	135	NR	135	0.2	0.4
FRND–Evan Fr Ch Intl	1	27	50	62	0.1	0.2
FRND–Indep Yr Mtgs	1	NR	0	0	0.0	0.0
Grace Gosp Fel	1	NR	NR	NR	-	-
Ind Fund Churches	1	NR	NR	NR	-	-
Jehovah's Witness	2	NR	NR	NR	-	-
LDS–L-D Saints	7	NR	NR	2,777	3.8	8.0
LUTH–E.L.C.A.	5	554	907	1,118	1.5	3.2
LUTH–Luth–MO Synod	1	119	265	336	0.5	1.0
METH–Free Methodist	1	1,057	656	1,057	1.5	3.0
METH–Un Methodist	6	675	1,541	2,204	3.0	6.3
Non-denom Chr Chs	11	3,366	4,586	4,776	6.6	13.7
PENT–Assemb of God	6	1,092	443	1,583	2.2	4.6
PENT–Ch God (Cleve)	1	14	21	26	0.0	0.1
PENT–Int Foursq Gos	7	898	879	1,086	1.5	3.1
PENT–Un Pent Ch Intl	1	NR	NR	NR	-	-
PRES–Presb Ch (USA)	3	486	613	758	1.0	2.2
REF–Comm Ref Evan	1	NR	NR	NR	-	-
Salvation Army	1	31	61	260	0.4	0.7
Sev Day Adv	5	516	897	1,031	1.4	3.0
Un C of Christ	2	78	67	83	0.1	0.2
Unit Univ	1	75	111	142	0.2	0.4
CLALLAM	**94**	**6,595**	**9,824**	**20,906**	**29.3**	**100.0**
ANG/EPIS–Anglican NA	1	NR	NR	NR	-	-
ANG/EPIS–Episcopal	2	277	454	495	0.7	2.4
Bahá'í	3	NR	161	161	0.2	0.8
BAPT–Amer Bapt USA	1	95	135	156	0.2	0.7
BAPT–Converge/BGC	1	75	NR	90	0.1	0.4
BAPT–Reg Bapt Gen As	1	NR	NR	NR	-	-
BAPT–So Bapt Conv	2	129	516	598	0.8	2.9
BUDD–Vajrayana	1	NR	NR	37	0.1	0.2
Calv Chpl	3	NR	NR	NR	-	-
Catholic	4	NR	NR	4,581	6.4	21.9
CGOD–Ch God (Ander)	2	200	NR	200	0.3	1.0
Ch Cr, Scientst	1	NR	NR	NR	-	-
Ch of Nazarene	3	98	126	154	0.2	0.7
Chr & Miss Al	1	125	113	238	0.3	1.1
CHR–Chr Ch (Disc)	1	56	60	70	0.1	0.3
CHR–Chs of Christ	3	113	120	145	0.2	0.7
FRND–Evan Fr Ch Intl	1	106	76	88	0.1	0.4
Ind Fund Churches	3	NR	NR	NR	-	-
Jehovah's Witness	3	NR	NR	NR	-	-
JUD–Reform	1	25	44	119	0.2	0.6
LDS–L-D Saints	7	NR	NR	3,102	4.3	14.8
LUTH–E.L.C.A.	3	317	789	913	1.3	4.4
LUTH–Luth–MO Synod	3	316	630	759	1.1	3.6
METH–Free Methodist	1	45	37	45	0.1	0.2
METH–Un Methodist	2	313	790	1,054	1.5	5.0
Non-denom Chr Chs	10	2,170	3,125	3,314	4.6	15.9
PENT–Apos Faith Msn	2	NR	70	81	0.1	0.4
PENT–Assemb of God	8	879	504	1,968	2.8	9.4
PENT–Ch God (Cleve)	1	4	5	6	0.0	0.0
PENT–Int Foursq Gos	3	443	219	254	0.4	1.2
PENT–Open Bible Std	1	25	NR	25	0.0	0.1
PENT–Un Pent Ch Intl	1	NR	NR	NR	-	-
PENT–Vineyard	2	170	205	238	0.3	1.1
PRES–Evan Presby Ch	1	NR	673	780	1.1	3.7
PRES–Orth Pres Ch	1	27	24	31	0.0	0.1
PRES–Presb Ch (USA)	3	196	275	319	0.4	1.5
Salvation Army	1	23	48	177	0.2	0.8
Sev Day Adv	3	306	533	612	0.9	2.9
Un C of Christ	1	12	24	28	0.0	0.1
Unit Univ	1	50	68	68	0.1	0.3
Unity Ch	1	NR	NR	NR	-	-
CLARK	**300**	**45,460**	**54,024**	**120,961**	**28.4**	**100.0**
ANG/EPIS–Episcopal	5	614	1,125	1,255	0.3	1.0
Bahá'í	5	NR	304	304	0.1	0.3
BAPT–Amer Bapt Assn	1	NR	35	44	0.0	0.0
BAPT–Amer Bapt USA	2	130	110	138	0.0	0.1
BAPT–Consrv Bapt	9	NR	NR	NR	-	-
BAPT–Converge/BGC	3	950	NR	1,140	0.3	0.9
BAPT–N Am Bapt Conf	2	NR	311	391	0.1	0.3
BAPT–NBC USA	1	0	150	189	0.0	0.2
BAPT–Reg Bapt Gen As	1	NR	NR	NR	-	-
BAPT–So Bapt Conv	22	2,052	2,838	3,567	0.8	2.9
BUDD–Mahayana	1	NR	NR	11	0.0	0.0
Calv Chpl	4	NR	NR	NR	-	-
Catholic	9	NR	NR	26,886	6.3	22.2
CGOD–Ch God (Ander)	3	1,366	NR	1,366	0.3	1.1
Ch Cr, Scientst	2	NR	NR	NR	-	-
Ch of Nazarene	12	2,100	2,520	3,190	0.7	2.6
Chr & Miss Al	3	718	251	1,082	0.3	0.9
CHR–Chr Ch (Disc)	2	100	186	234	0.1	0.2
CHR–Chr Chs & Chs Cr	4	NR	490	616	0.1	0.5
CHR–Chs of Christ	6	730	754	895	0.2	0.7
Evan Ch	3	NR	NR	NR	-	-
Evan Cov Ch	1	73	63	95	0.0	0.1
Evan Free Ch	6	846	NR	846	0.2	0.7
FRND–Evan Fr Ch Intl	5	523	496	623	0.1	0.5
Ind Fund Churches	1	NR	NR	NR	-	-
Jehovah's Witness	7	NR	NR	NR	-	-
JUD–Orth	1	43	50	60	0.0	0.0
JUD–Reform	1	63	111	300	0.1	0.2
LDS–Comm of Christ	3	NR	501	501	0.1	0.4
LDS–L-D Saints	37	NR	NR	20,793	4.9	17.2
LUTH–Apostolic Luth	3	NR	NR	NR	-	-
LUTH–E.L.C.A.	10	1,691	3,635	4,827	1.1	4.0
LUTH–Luth Ch-Am Asc	1	NR	NR	NR	-	-
LUTH–Luth–MO Synod	7	1,168	1,849	2,624	0.6	2.2
LUTH–Wisc Ev Luth Syn	1	80	146	176	0.0	0.1
MENN–Menn Br US Conf	5	NR	1,925	2,419	0.6	2.0
METH–AME Zion	1	0	150	189	0.0	0.2
METH–Evan Meth Ch	1	NR	NR	NR	-	-
METH–Un Methodist	10	1,277	2,704	3,439	0.8	2.8
METH–Wesleyan	2	100	80	130	0.0	0.1
Metro Comm Ch	1	19	24	30	0.0	0.0
Missionary Ch	1	15	20	20	0.0	0.0
Muslim Est	1	134	NR	308	0.1	0.3
Non-denom Chr Chs	41	23,225	24,580	30,026	7.1	24.8
ORTHE–Orth Ch in Amer	1	25	NR	61	0.0	0.1
PENT–Assemb of God	9	1,691	749	2,052	0.5	1.7
PENT–Ch God (Cleve)	1	25	32	40	0.0	0.0
PENT–Ch of God Proph	2	NR	189	238	0.1	0.2
PENT–Int Foursq Gos	9	1,517	1,094	1,375	0.3	1.1
PENT–Open Bible Std	2	185	NR	185	0.0	0.2
PENT–Pent Ch of God	1	70	NR	109	0.0	0.1
PENT–Un Pent Ch Intl	4	NR	NR	NR	-	-
PENT–Vineyard	1	195	275	346	0.1	0.3
PRES–Kor Pres Abroad	1	NR	NR	NR	-	-
PRES–Presb Ch (USA)	6	1,055	1,946	2,446	0.6	2.0
PRES–Presb Ch Amer	1	205	227	295	0.1	0.2
REF–Christian Ref	1	20	0	0	0.0	0.0

NR–Not Reported - Represents no adherents reported. Percentages may not total 100 due to rounding.

Table 3: Religious Congregations by County and Group: 2010

Religious Group	Number of Congrega-tions	Number of Attendees	Number of Communicant, Confirmed, or Full Members	Adherents: Number of Adherents	Adherents: % of Total Pop.	Adherents: % of Total Adh.
Salvation Army	2	106	181	503	0.1	0.4
Sev Day Adv	9	2,010	3,495	4,020	0.9	3.3
Un C of Christ	1	132	210	264	0.1	0.2
Unit Univ	1	207	218	313	0.1	0.3
Unity Ch	1	NR	NR	NR	-	-
COLUMBIA	**14**	**285**	**567**	**1,099**	**26.9**	**100.0**
ANG/EPIS–Episcopal	1	16	18	18	0.4	1.6
Bahá'í	0	NR	9	9	0.2	0.8
BAPT–Consrv Bapt	1	NR	NR	NR	-	-
Catholic	1	NR	NR	74	1.8	6.7
Ch of Nazarene	1	22	27	48	1.2	4.4
CHR–Chr Chs & Chs Cr	1	NR	140	165	4.0	15.0
LDS–L-D Saints	1	NR	NR	286	7.0	26.0
LUTH–Apostolic Luth	1	NR	NR	NR	-	-
LUTH–Luth–MO Synod	1	0	126	144	3.5	13.1
METH–Un Methodist	1	30	54	54	1.3	4.9
Non-denom Chr Chs	1	45	25	56	1.4	5.1
PENT–Assemb of God	1	30	0	30	0.7	2.7
Sev Day Adv	1	46	80	92	2.3	8.4
Un Breth in Cr	1	56	24	48	1.2	4.4
Un C of Christ	1	40	64	75	1.8	6.8
COWLITZ	**118**	**10,175**	**16,279**	**35,680**	**34.8**	**100.0**
ANG/EPIS–Anglican NA	1	NR	NR	NR	-	-
ANG/EPIS–Episcopal	2	135	251	448	0.4	1.3
Bahá'í	2	NR	126	126	0.1	0.4
BAPT–Amer Bapt Assn	1	NR	85	104	0.1	0.3
BAPT–Amer Bapt USA	2	385	378	463	0.5	1.3
BAPT–Consrv Bapt	4	NR	NR	NR	-	-
BAPT–So Bapt Conv	10	1,278	3,919	4,805	4.7	13.5
Calv Chpl	3	NR	NR	NR	-	-
Catholic	5	NR	NR	9,294	9.1	26.0
CGOD–Ch God (Ander)	1	40	NR	40	0.0	0.1
Ch Cr, Scientist	1	NR	NR	NR	-	-
Ch of Nazarene	5	544	682	862	0.8	2.4
Chr & Miss Al	1	226	106	326	0.3	0.9
CHR–Chr Ch (Disc)	1	30	68	83	0.1	0.2
CHR–Chr Chs & Chs Cr	2	NR	310	380	0.4	1.1
CHR–Chs of Christ	3	130	111	138	0.1	0.4
Evan Free Ch	1	50	NR	50	0.0	0.1
FRND–Evan Fr Ch Intl	1	76	83	102	0.1	0.3
Jehovah's Witness	5	NR	NR	NR	-	-
LDS–Comm of Christ	1	NR	167	167	0.2	0.5
LDS–L-D Saints	7	NR	NR	4,513	4.4	12.6
LUTH–Ch of Luth Br	1	43	40	69	0.1	0.2
LUTH–E.L.C.A.	5	407	631	1,117	1.1	3.1
LUTH–Luth Cong Msn Chr	1	231	1,192	1,462	1.4	4.1
LUTH–Luth–MO Synod	1	74	182	202	0.2	0.6
METH–Free Methodist	1	132	62	132	0.1	0.4
METH–Un Methodist	4	257	714	993	1.0	2.8
Non-denom Chr Chs	22	3,638	4,249	5,056	4.9	14.2
ORTHE–Orth Ch in Amer	1	10	NR	20	0.0	0.1
PENT–Assemb of God	7	1,013	400	1,570	1.5	4.4
PENT–Ch God (Cleve)	3	519	621	761	0.7	2.1
PENT–Ch of God Proph	1	NR	27	33	0.0	0.1
PENT–Int Foursq Gos	2	131	321	394	0.4	1.1
PENT–Un Pent Ch Intl	1	NR	NR	NR	-	-
PRES–Presb Ch (USA)	3	105	290	356	0.3	1.0
Salvation Army	1	31	64	233	0.2	0.7
Sev Day Adv	5	690	1,200	1,381	1.3	3.9
DOUGLAS	**46**	**2,650**	**4,034**	**14,214**	**37.0**	**100.0**
Bahá'í	0	NR	11	11	0.0	0.1
BAPT–Amer Bapt Assn	1	NR	35	44	0.1	0.3
BAPT–Amer Bapt USA	1	81	214	271	0.7	1.9
BAPT–Consrv Bapt	1	NR	NR	NR	-	-
BAPT–Converge/BGC	1	75	NR	90	0.2	0.6
BAPT–Reg Bapt Gen As	1	NR	NR	NR	-	-
BAPT–So Bapt Conv	2	472	649	821	2.1	5.8
Calv Chpl	1	NR	NR	NR	-	-
Catholic	4	NR	NR	8,000	20.8	56.3
CGOD–Ch God (Ander)	1	65	NR	65	0.2	0.5

Religious Group	Number of Congrega-tions	Number of Attendees	Number of Communicant, Confirmed, or Full Members	Adherents: Number of Adherents	Adherents: % of Total Pop.	Adherents: % of Total Adh.
Ch of God Gen Conf	2	NR	80	101	0.3	0.7
Ch of Nazarene	1	37	24	95	0.2	0.7
CHR–Chr Ch (Disc)	1	81	206	260	0.7	1.8
Ind Fund Churches	1	NR	NR	NR	-	-
Jehovah's Witness	1	NR	NR	NR	-	-
LDS–Comm of Christ	1	NR	167	167	0.4	1.2
LDS–L-D Saints	3	NR	NR	797	2.1	5.6
LUTH–E.L.C.A.	1	101	227	286	0.7	2.0
LUTH–Luth Cong Msn Chr	1	65	NR	NR	-	-
LUTH–Luth–MO Synod	1	137	231	272	0.7	1.9
LUTH–Wisc Ev Luth Syn	2	64	118	139	0.4	1.0
METH–Free Methodist	1	179	107	179	0.5	1.3
METH–Un Methodist	2	161	225	425	1.1	3.0
Non-denom Chr Chs	3	350	510	510	1.3	3.6
PENT–Assemb of God	2	215	138	258	0.7	1.8
PENT–Ch God (Cleve)	1	31	348	440	1.1	3.1
PENT–Int Foursq Gos	2	29	33	42	0.1	0.3
PENT–Pent Ch of God	1	70	NR	109	0.3	0.8
PENT–Un Pent Ch Intl	1	NR	NR	NR	-	-
PRES–Presb Ch (USA)	3	103	130	164	0.4	1.2
Sev Day Adv	2	334	581	668	1.7	4.7
FERRY	**19**	**328**	**396**	**2,005**	**26.6**	**100.0**
ANG/EPIS–Episcopal	1	7	9	9	0.1	0.4
Bahá'í	0	NR	6	6	0.1	0.3
BAPT–Reg Bapt Gen As	1	NR	NR	NR	-	-
Catholic	4	NR	NR	1,173	15.5	58.5
Ch of Nazarene	1	36	30	50	0.7	2.5
Jehovah's Witness	1	NR	NR	NR	-	-
LDS–L-D Saints	1	NR	NR	296	3.9	14.8
LUTH–Luth–MO Synod	1	32	34	47	0.6	2.3
Non-denom Chr Chs	1	40	30	50	0.7	2.5
PENT–Assemb of God	2	28	15	59	0.8	2.9
PENT–Intl Pent Holiness	1	25	25	29	0.4	1.4
PRES–Presb Ch (USA)	2	40	40	47	0.6	2.3
Sev Day Adv	3	120	207	239	3.2	11.9
FRANKLIN	**82**	**5,409**	**8,913**	**27,509**	**35.2**	**100.0**
Bahá'í	1	NR	37	37	0.0	0.1
BAPT–Amer Bapt USA	1	0	80	111	0.1	0.4
BAPT–Reg Bapt Gen As	2	NR	NR	NR	-	-
BAPT–So Bapt Conv	6	140	323	447	0.6	1.6
Catholic	3	NR	NR	7,478	9.6	27.2
Ch Cr, Scientest	1	NR	NR	NR	-	-
Ch of Nazarene	2	206	280	342	0.4	1.2
CHR–Chr Ch (Disc)	1	0	0	0	0.0	0.0
CHR–Chr Chs & Chs Cr	1	NR	300	415	0.5	1.5
CHR–Chs of Christ	2	123	128	183	0.2	0.7
Evan Cov Ch	1	85	128	110	0.1	0.4
Jehovah's Witness	1	NR	NR	NR	-	-
LDS–L-D Saints	19	NR	NR	7,338	9.4	26.7
LUTH–Apostolic Luth	1	NR	NR	NR	-	-
LUTH–E.L.C.A.	3	142	361	477	0.6	1.7
LUTH–Luth–MO Synod	2	92	141	170	0.2	0.6
MENN–CG in Cr (Menn)	1	NR	118	163	0.2	0.6
METH–C.M.E.	1	0	150	207	0.3	0.8
METH–Un Methodist	4	208	465	624	0.8	2.3
Non-denom Chr Chs	8	2,315	4,265	4,344	5.6	15.8
ORTHE–Greek Orthodox	1	25	NR	162	0.2	0.6
PENT–Assemb of God	9	1,343	724	3,150	4.0	11.5
PENT–Ch God (Cleve)	2	122	381	527	0.7	1.9
PENT–Ch of God Proph	2	NR	37	51	0.1	0.2
PENT–Un Pent Ch Intl	1	NR	NR	NR	-	-
Sev Day Adv	4	518	901	1,036	1.3	3.8
Un C of Christ	1	40	34	47	0.1	0.2
Unit Univ	1	50	60	90	0.1	0.3
GARFIELD	**5**	**109**	**508**	**1,361**	**60.1**	**100.0**
ANG/EPIS–Episcopal	1	18	48	48	2.1	3.5
Bahá'í	0	NR	2	2	0.1	0.1
Catholic	1	NR	NR	777	34.3	57.1
Ch of Nazarene	1	61	91	91	4.0	6.7
CHR–Chr Chs & Chs Cr	1	NR	185	216	9.5	15.9

NR–Not Reported - Represents no adherents reported. Percentages may not total 100 due to rounding.

Table 3: Religious Congregations by County and Group: 2010

Religious Group	Number of Congregations	Number of Attendees	Number of Communicant, Confirmed, or Full Members	Adherents		
				Number of Adherents	% of Total Pop.	% of Total Adh.
METH–Un Methodist	1	30	182	227	10.0	16.7
GRANT	**131**	**6,911**	**8,390**	**34,708**	**38.9**	**100.0**
ANG/EPIS–Episcopal	3	65	179	199	0.2	0.6
Bahá'í	0	NR	22	22	0.0	0.1
BAPT–Consrv Bapt	1	NR	NR	NR	-	-
BAPT–Converge/BGC	1	75	NR	90	0.1	0.3
BAPT–Natl Mis Bapt Conv	1	30	40	53	0.1	0.2
BAPT–Reg Bapt Gen As	3	NR	NR	NR	-	-
BAPT–So Bapt Conv	6	197	719	946	1.1	2.7
Calv Chpl	1	NR	NR	NR	-	-
Catholic	9	NR	NR	14,500	16.3	41.8
CGOD–Ch God (Ander)	1	85	NR	85	0.1	0.2
Ch of Nazarene	5	259	320	459	0.5	1.3
Chr & Miss Al	1	728	358	1,337	1.5	3.9
CHR–Chr Ch (Disc)	1	32	68	90	0.1	0.3
CHR–Chs of Christ	3	168	171	220	0.2	0.6
CONG–Cong Chr, NA	1	NR	137	180	0.2	0.5
Evan Free Ch	1	82	NR	82	0.1	0.2
FRND–Evan Fr Ch Intl	1	7	34	45	0.1	0.1
Jehovah's Witness	4	NR	NR	NR	-	-
LDS–L-D Saints	19	NR	NR	7,562	8.5	21.8
LUTH–E.L.C.A.	4	246	941	1,269	1.4	3.7
LUTH–Luth–MO Synod	6	202	343	409	0.5	1.2
MENN–Hutt Breth	2	NR	NR	NR	-	-
MENN–Mennonite USA	1	25	64	84	0.1	0.2
METH–Evan Meth Ch	1	NR	NR	NR	-	-
METH–Free Methodist	3	447	178	447	0.5	1.3
METH–Un Methodist	5	217	562	662	0.7	1.9
Missionary Ch	1	40	24	40	0.0	0.1
Non-denom Chr Chs	8	915	1,077	1,271	1.4	3.7
PENT–Assemb of God	12	1,138	817	1,682	1.9	4.8
PENT–Ch of God Proph	2	NR	67	88	0.1	0.3
PENT–Int Foursq Gos	5	578	559	736	0.8	2.1
PENT–Intl Pent Holiness	2	120	64	84	0.1	0.2
PENT–Un Pent Ch Intl	1	NR	NR	NR	-	-
PRES–Evan Presby Ch	1	NR	144	190	0.2	0.5
PRES–Presb Ch (USA)	7	825	779	1,025	1.2	3.0
REF–Christian Ref	2	64	86	113	0.1	0.3
Sev Day Adv	5	352	612	705	0.8	2.0
Un C of Christ	1	14	25	33	0.0	0.1
GRAYS HARBOR	**105**	**5,339**	**7,375**	**21,650**	**29.7**	**100.0**
ANG/EPIS–Episcopal	4	173	470	478	0.7	2.2
Bahá'í	1	NR	63	63	0.1	0.3
BAPT–Amer Bapt USA	1	54	123	147	0.2	0.7
BAPT–Consrv Bapt	2	NR	NR	NR	-	-
BAPT–Converge/BGC	3	225	NR	270	0.4	1.2
BAPT–So Bapt Conv	5	432	465	556	0.8	2.6
Calv Chpl	2	NR	NR	NR	-	-
Catholic	8	NR	NR	7,602	10.4	35.1
CGOD–Ch God (Ander)	3	220	NR	220	0.3	1.0
Ch Cr, Scientst	1	NR	NR	NR	-	-
Ch of Nazarene	1	48	75	95	0.1	0.4
Chr & Miss Al	2	128	76	180	0.2	0.8
CHR–Chr Ch (Disc)	1	50	80	96	0.1	0.4
CHR–Chs of Christ	3	95	95	128	0.2	0.6
Evan Cov Ch	1	27	18	35	0.0	0.2
Ind Fund Churches	1	NR	NR	NR	-	-
Jehovah's Witness	4	NR	NR	NR	-	-
JUD–Reform	1	5	8	22	0.0	0.1
LDS–Comm of Christ	1	NR	167	167	0.2	0.8
LDS–L-D Saints	6	NR	NR	3,254	4.5	15.0
LUTH–E.L.C.A.	5	325	1,063	1,370	1.9	6.3
LUTH–Luth–MO Synod	1	130	405	800	1.1	3.7
METH–Free Methodist	1	57	40	57	0.1	0.3
METH–Un Methodist	9	318	793	981	1.3	4.5
Non-denom Chr Chs	14	1,440	2,028	2,226	3.1	10.3
PENT–Assemb of God	10	838	605	1,674	2.3	7.7
PENT–Int Foursq Gos	1	187	124	148	0.2	0.7
PENT–Open Bible Std	1	102	NR	102	0.1	0.5
PENT–Pent Ch of God	1	70	NR	109	0.1	0.5
PENT–Un Pent Ch Intl	2	NR	NR	NR	-	-
PRES–Korean Pres Amer	1	NR	NR	NR	-	-
PRES–Presb Ch (USA)	5	222	323	387	0.5	1.8
Salvation Army	1	21	54	138	0.2	0.6
Sev Day Adv	2	172	300	345	0.5	1.6
ISLAND	**70**	**6,982**	**9,746**	**18,261**	**23.3**	**100.0**
ANG/EPIS–Anglican NA	1	NR	NR	NR	-	-
ANG/EPIS–Episcopal	3	256	394	415	0.5	2.3
Bahá'í	1	NR	74	74	0.1	0.4
BAPT–Converge/BGC	1	75	NR	90	0.1	0.5
BAPT–Ref Bapt Ch	1	NR	NR	NR	-	-
BAPT–So Bapt Conv	3	215	1,106	1,316	1.7	7.2
BUDD–Mahayana	2	NR	NR	28	0.0	0.2
Calv Chpl	3	NR	NR	NR	-	-
Catholic	3	NR	NR	2,962	3.8	16.2
Ch Cr, Scientst	2	NR	NR	NR	-	-
Ch of Nazarene	1	226	377	377	0.5	2.1
Chr & Miss Al	1	240	149	388	0.5	2.1
CHR–Chs of Christ	2	142	110	199	0.3	1.1
Evan Free Ch	1	180	NR	180	0.2	1.0
FRND–Indep Yr Mtgs	1	NR	0	0	0.0	0.0
Ind Fund Churches	1	NR	NR	NR	-	-
Jehovah's Witness	3	NR	NR	NR	-	-
LDS–L-D Saints	4	NR	NR	2,335	3.0	12.8
LUTH–E.L.C.A.	4	900	1,965	2,594	3.3	14.2
LUTH–Luth–MO Synod	1	74	164	179	0.2	1.0
METH–Un Methodist	3	491	863	1,455	1.9	8.0
Non-denom Chr Chs	10	2,136	2,650	2,876	3.7	15.7
PENT–Assemb of God	4	462	264	816	1.0	4.5
PENT–Int Foursq Gos	4	772	568	676	0.9	3.7
PENT–Un Pent Ch Intl	1	NR	NR	NR	-	-
PENT–Vineyard	1	28	11	13	0.0	0.1
PRES–Orth Pres Ch	1	68	67	96	0.1	0.5
PRES–Presb Ch (USA)	2	168	224	266	0.3	1.5
REF–Christian Ref	1	100	158	188	0.2	1.0
REF–Ref Ch in Am	1	313	390	477	0.6	2.6
Sev Day Adv	1	76	132	152	0.2	0.8
Unit Univ	1	60	80	109	0.1	0.6
Unity Ch	1	NR	NR	NR	-	-
JEFFERSON	**42**	**2,159**	**3,419**	**7,474**	**25.0**	**100.0**
ANG/EPIS–Episcopal	1	114	290	313	1.0	4.2
Bahá'í	2	NR	48	48	0.2	0.6
BAPT–Amer Bapt USA	1	70	104	117	0.4	1.6
BAPT–So Bapt Conv	3	257	869	976	3.3	13.1
BUDD–Vajrayana	1	NR	NR	45	0.2	0.6
Catholic	1	NR	NR	1,786	6.0	23.9
Ch Cr, Scientst	1	NR	NR	NR	-	-
CHR–Chs of Christ	2	70	67	93	0.3	1.2
Evan Free Ch	1	85	NR	85	0.3	1.1
FRND–Indep Yr Mtgs	1	NR	29	33	0.1	0.4
HINDU–Post Ren	1	NR	NR	77	0.3	1.0
HINDU–Renaiss	1	NR	NR	12	0.0	0.2
Ind Fund Churches	1	NR	NR	NR	-	-
Jehovah's Witness	2	NR	NR	NR	-	-
LDS–L-D Saints	2	NR	NR	876	2.9	11.7
LUTH–E.L.C.A.	2	67	146	148	0.5	2.0
LUTH–Luth Cong Msn Chr	1	213	367	412	1.4	5.5
METH–Evan Meth Ch	1	NR	NR	NR	-	-
METH–Un Methodist	2	130	239	367	1.2	4.9
Non-denom Chr Chs	3	280	270	375	1.3	5.0
ORTHE–Orth Ch in Amer	1	47	NR	100	0.3	1.3
PENT–Assemb of God	4	304	165	598	2.0	8.0
PENT–Int Foursq Gos	1	36	30	34	0.1	0.5
PRES–Presb Ch (USA)	2	181	332	373	1.2	5.0
Sev Day Adv	2	87	152	174	0.6	2.3
Unit Univ	1	218	311	432	1.4	5.8
Unity Ch	1	NR	NR	NR	-	-
KING	**1,459**	**191,946**	**249,556**	**726,669**	**37.6**	**100.0**
ANG/EPIS–Anglican NA	4	NR	NR	NR	-	-
ANG/EPIS–Episcopal	35	4,494	11,687	14,971	0.8	2.1
Bahá'í	22	NR	2,946	2,946	0.2	0.4

NR–Not Reported   - Represents no adherents reported.   Percentages may not total 100 due to rounding.

Table 3: Religious Congregations by County and Group: 2010

Religious Group	Number of Congregations	Number of Attendees	Number of Communicant, Confirmed, or Full Members	Adherents: Number of Adherents	Adherents: % of Total Pop.	Adherents: % of Total Adh.
BAPT–Amer Bapt Assn	2	NR	185	222	0.0	0.0
BAPT–Amer Bapt USA	42	5,809	10,440	12,531	0.6	1.7
BAPT–Asc Ref Bap Ch Am	1	NR	NR	NR	-	-
BAPT–Consrv Bapt	11	NR	NR	NR	-	-
BAPT–Converge/BGC	22	3,825	NR	4,590	0.2	0.6
BAPT–Free Will Bapt	1	NR	41	49	0.0	0.0
BAPT–Ind Bapt Flwsp Intl	2	NR	NR	NR	-	-
BAPT–N Am Bapt Conf	3	NR	152	182	0.0	0.0
BAPT–Natl Mis Bapt Conv	2	150	400	480	0.0	0.1
BAPT–NBC USA	1	0	500	600	0.0	0.1
BAPT–Ref Bapt Ch	4	NR	NR	NR	-	-
BAPT–Reg Bapt Gen As	9	NR	NR	NR	-	-
BAPT–S-D Baptist Gen Con	1	51	54	65	0.0	0.0
BAPT–So Bapt Conv	55	5,352	5,577	6,694	0.3	0.9
BRETH–Ch of Brethren	3	132	181	217	0.0	0.0
BRETH–Grace Breth	1	NR	NR	NR	-	-
BUDD–Mahayana	39	NR	NR	18,185	0.9	2.5
BUDD–Theravada	7	NR	NR	4,495	0.2	0.6
BUDD–Vajrayana	17	NR	NR	1,195	0.1	0.2
Calv Chpl	7	NR	NR	NR	-	-
Catholic	71	NR	NR	278,340	14.4	38.3
CGOD–Ch God (Ander)	7	395	NR	395	0.0	0.1
Ch Cr, Scientst	16	NR	NR	NR	-	-
Ch of Nazarene	29	2,636	3,663	4,540	0.2	0.6
Chr & Miss Al	26	2,626	2,527	3,897	0.2	0.5
CHR–Chr Ch (Disc)	12	558	1,516	1,820	0.1	0.3
CHR–Chr Chs & Chs Cr	14	NR	7,275	8,732	0.5	1.2
CHR–Chs of Christ	29	2,975	2,702	3,618	0.2	0.5
CHR–Int Chs of Christ	1	NR	524	629	0.0	0.1
Christian Brethren	3	NR	NR	NR	-	-
CONG–Cong Chr, NA	1	NR	30	36	0.0	0.0
Evan Ch	3	NR	NR	NR	-	-
Evan Cov Ch	19	4,082	2,896	5,307	0.3	0.7
Evan Free Ch	7	1,170	NR	1,170	0.1	0.2
FRND–Evan Fr Ch Intl	2	85	171	205	0.0	0.0
FRND–Indep Yr Mtgs	6	NR	282	338	0.0	0.0
Grace Gosp Fel	2	NR	NR	NR	-	-
HINDU–I/A Temples	8	NR	NR	3,263	0.2	0.4
HINDU–Post Ren	15	NR	NR	478	0.0	0.1
HINDU–Renaiss	3	NR	NR	472	0.0	0.1
HINDU–Trad Temples	1	NR	NR	150	0.0	0.0
Ind Fund Churches	4	NR	NR	NR	-	-
Jehovah's Witness	26	NR	NR	NR	-	-
JUD–Conserv	2	1,026	1,151	3,108	0.2	0.4
JUD–Orth	8	1,872	800	2,600	0.1	0.4
JUD–Reconst	1	33	42	113	0.0	0.0
JUD–Reform	6	1,912	3,372	9,104	0.5	1.3
LDS–Comm of Christ	5	NR	835	835	0.0	0.1
LDS–L-D Saints	110	NR	NR	56,985	3.0	7.8
LUTH–Apostolic Luth	1	NR	NR	NR	-	-
LUTH–Assoc Free Luth	1	NR	NR	NR	-	-
LUTH–Ch of Luth Br	2	145	151	270	0.0	0.0
LUTH–E.L.C.A.	68	8,565	19,808	25,789	1.3	3.5
LUTH–Luth Cong Msn Chr	4	441	1,192	1,431	0.1	0.2
LUTH–Luth–MO Synod	29	3,403	6,634	8,690	0.4	1.2
LUTH–Nor Amer Luth C	1	NR	NR	NR	-	-
LUTH–Wisc Ev Luth Syn	6	566	847	1,091	0.1	0.2
MENN–Menn Br US Conf	5	NR	480	576	0.0	0.1
MENN–Mennonite USA	2	150	157	188	0.0	0.0
METH–AME	4	680	1,750	2,101	0.1	0.3
METH–AME Zion	3	0	260	312	0.0	0.0
METH–C.M.E.	2	30	150	180	0.0	0.0
METH–Evan Meth Ch	1	NR	NR	NR	-	-
METH–Free Methodist	13	3,422	2,468	3,715	0.2	0.5
METH–Un Methodist	50	5,863	13,579	18,161	0.9	2.5
Metro Comm Ch	1	30	41	49	0.0	0.0
Missionary Ch	2	13	0	13	0.0	0.0
MJEW–Union Mes Cong	1	NR	NR	NR	-	-
Muslim Est	21	3,067	NR	12,288	0.6	1.7
Nat Spirit Asso	1	NR	NR	NR	-	-
New Apost Ch	2	NR	NR	NR	-	-
Non-denom Chr Chs	159	70,834	82,584	95,218	4.9	13.1
ORTHE–Greek Orthodox	3	600	NR	4,765	0.2	0.7
ORTHE–Holy Orth in NA	1	100	NR	130	0.0	0.0

Religious Group	Number of Congregations	Number of Attendees	Number of Communicant, Confirmed, or Full Members	Adherents: Number of Adherents	Adherents: % of Total Pop.	Adherents: % of Total Adh.
ORTHE–Orth Ch in Amer	3	345	NR	995	0.1	0.1
ORTHE–Pal/Jor Orth	1	30	NR	125	0.0	0.0
ORTHE–Rus Orth Abroad	2	125	NR	365	0.0	0.1
ORTHE–Serb Orth USA	1	70	NR	1,500	0.1	0.2
ORTHE–Ukrainian Orth	1	45	NR	150	0.0	0.0
ORTHO–Armen Ap Etchm	1	125	NR	2,500	0.1	0.3
ORTHO–Coptic Orth Ch	1	170	NR	180	0.0	0.0
ORTHO–Eritrean Orth	3	700	NR	1,400	0.1	0.2
ORTHO–Ethiopian Orth	1	NR	NR	NR	-	-
ORTHO–Malan Dioc Am	1	25	NR	75	0.0	0.0
ORTHO–Malan Syr Orth	1	40	NR	72	0.0	0.0
PENT–Apos Faith Msn	1	NR	35	42	0.0	0.0
PENT–Assemb of God	63	16,541	7,672	25,937	1.3	3.6
PENT–Ch God (Cleve)	10	448	603	724	0.0	0.1
PENT–Ch of God Proph	3	NR	123	148	0.0	0.0
PENT–COGIC	12	1,334	2,797	3,357	0.2	0.5
PENT–Int Foursq Gos	38	7,114	6,071	7,287	0.4	1.0
PENT–Open Bible Std	1	70	NR	70	0.0	0.0
PENT–Pent Ch of God	1	70	NR	109	0.0	0.0
PENT–Un Pent Ch Intl	9	NR	NR	NR	-	-
PENT–Vineyard	4	526	695	834	0.0	0.1
PRES–Evan Presby Ch	1	NR	621	745	0.0	0.1
PRES–Kor Pres Abroad	2	NR	NR	NR	-	-
PRES–Korean Amer Pres	6	NR	NR	NR	-	-
PRES–Korean Pres Amer	8	NR	NR	NR	-	-
PRES–Orth Pres Ch	1	176	147	216	0.0	0.0
PRES–Presb Ch (USA)	54	14,687	20,752	24,909	1.3	3.4
PRES–Presb Ch Amer	13	1,249	1,320	1,555	0.1	0.2
PRES–Ref Pres of NA	1	65	71	83	0.0	0.0
REF–Christian Ref	12	866	966	1,159	0.1	0.2
REF–Comm Ref Evan	1	NR	NR	NR	-	-
REF–Ref Ch in Am	2	170	201	265	0.0	0.0
Salvation Army	5	344	468	2,762	0.1	0.4
Sev Day Adv	34	5,574	9,693	11,148	0.6	1.5
Sikh	3	NR	NR	NR	-	-
Swedenborgian	1	NR	NR	NR	-	-
Tao	1	NR	NR	NR	-	-
Un C of Christ	32	2,375	4,946	5,937	0.3	0.8
Unit Univ	8	1,570	2,325	3,475	0.2	0.5
Unity Ch	4	NR	NR	NR	-	-
Zoroastrian	1	NR	NR	21	0.0	0.0
KITSAP	**207**	**24,331**	**27,063**	**66,031**	**26.3**	**100.0**
ANG/EPIS–Anglican NA	2	NR	NR	NR	-	-
ANG/EPIS–Episcopal	6	660	1,547	2,359	0.9	3.6
Bahá'í	5	NR	205	205	0.1	0.3
BAPT–Amer Bapt Assn	1	NR	85	102	0.0	0.2
BAPT–Amer Bapt USA	7	366	773	931	0.4	1.4
BAPT–Converge/BGC	2	150	NR	180	0.1	0.3
BAPT–Ind Bapt Flwsp Intl	1	NR	NR	NR	-	-
BAPT–N Am Bapt Conf	1	NR	86	104	0.0	0.2
BAPT–Ref Bapt Ch	1	NR	NR	NR	-	-
BAPT–Reg Bapt Gen As	2	NR	NR	NR	-	-
BAPT–So Bapt Conv	5	448	851	1,025	0.4	1.6
BUDD–Mahayana	3	NR	NR	88	0.0	0.1
Calv Chpl	3	NR	NR	NR	-	-
Catholic	5	NR	NR	8,572	3.4	13.0
CGOD–Ch God (Ander)	2	75	NR	75	0.0	0.1
Ch Cr, Scientst	2	NR	NR	NR	-	-
Ch of Nazarene	3	415	619	716	0.3	1.1
Chr & Miss Al	6	535	380	899	0.4	1.4
CHR–Chr Ch (Disc)	1	77	191	230	0.1	0.3
CHR–Chr Chs & Chs Cr	3	NR	750	904	0.4	1.4
CHR–Chs of Christ	4	691	529	816	0.3	1.2
Evan Cov Ch	2	140	73	182	0.1	0.3
Evan Free Ch	2	625	NR	625	0.2	0.9
Grace Gosp Fel	1	NR	NR	NR	-	-
HINDU–Post Ren	1	NR	NR	25	0.0	0.0
Ind Fund Churches	5	NR	NR	NR	-	-
Jehovah's Witness	5	NR	NR	NR	-	-
JUD–Reform	2	74	130	351	0.1	0.5
LDS–Comm of Christ	1	NR	167	167	0.1	0.3
LDS–L-D Saints	19	NR	NR	11,093	4.4	16.8
LUTH–E.L.C.A.	10	1,599	2,304	4,185	1.7	6.3

NR–Not Reported - Represents no adherents reported. Percentages may not total 100 due to rounding.

Table 3: Religious Congregations by County and Group: 2010

Religious Group	Number of Congrega-tions	Number of Attendees	Number of Communicant, Confirmed, or Full Members	Adherents: Number of Adherents	Adherents: % of Total Pop.	Adherents: % of Total Adh.
LUTH–Evan Luth Syn	1	240	383	564	0.2	0.9
LUTH–Luth Ch-Am Asc	1	NR	NR	NR	-	-
LUTH–Luth Cong Msn Chr	1	310	484	583	0.2	0.9
LUTH–Luth–MO Synod	4	472	807	1,060	0.4	1.6
LUTH–Wisc Ev Luth Syn	1	189	270	338	0.1	0.5
METH–AME	1	0	70	84	0.0	0.1
METH–Un Methodist	8	653	1,368	1,853	0.7	2.8
Missionary Ch	1	15	25	25	0.0	0.0
Non-denom Chr Chs	34	8,176	8,763	10,519	4.2	15.9
ORTHE–Orth Ch in Amer	2	77	NR	140	0.1	0.2
PENT–Assemb of God	12	5,265	2,208	12,199	4.9	18.5
PENT–Ch of God Proph	1	NR	54	65	0.0	0.1
PENT–Int Foursq Gos	4	936	768	925	0.4	1.4
PENT–Un Pent Ch Intl	5	NR	NR	NR	-	-
PRES–Presb Ch (USA)	5	871	1,316	1,585	0.6	2.4
PRES–Presb Ch Amer	2	313	286	310	0.1	0.5
REF–Christian Ref	1	65	50	60	0.0	0.1
Salvation Army	1	39	61	141	0.1	0.2
Sev Day Adv	3	478	832	956	0.4	1.4
Un C of Christ	2	150	283	341	0.1	0.5
Unit Univ	2	227	345	448	0.2	0.7
Unity Ch	2	NR	NR	NR	-	-
Zoroastrian	0	NR	NR	1	0.0	0.0
KITTITAS	**49**	**2,788**	**2,962**	**11,546**	**28.2**	**100.0**
ANG/EPIS–Episcopal	2	83	240	248	0.6	2.1
Bahá'í	0	NR	35	35	0.1	0.3
BAPT–Amer Bapt USA	3	173	163	190	0.5	1.6
BAPT–Consrv Bapt	1	NR	NR	NR	-	-
BAPT–So Bapt Conv	2	184	268	312	0.8	2.7
Calv Chpl	1	NR	NR	NR	-	-
Catholic	3	NR	NR	4,800	11.7	41.6
CGOD–Ch God (Ander)	1	0	NR	0	0.0	0.0
Ch of Nazarene	2	83	113	159	0.4	1.4
Chr & Miss Al	2	809	387	1,740	4.3	15.1
CHR–Chr Chs & Chs Cr	1	NR	80	93	0.2	0.8
CHR–Chs of Christ	1	55	51	67	0.2	0.6
FRND–Indep Yr Mtgs	1	NR	0	0	0.0	0.0
Jehovah's Witness	3	NR	NR	NR	-	-
LDS–Comm of Christ	1	NR	167	167	0.4	1.4
LDS–L-D Saints	5	NR	NR	1,702	4.2	14.7
LUTH–E.L.C.A.	1	149	365	441	1.1	3.8
LUTH–Wisc Ev Luth Syn	2	34	89	91	0.2	0.8
METH–Un Methodist	1	53	70	70	0.2	0.6
Non-denom Chr Chs	4	129	150	168	0.4	1.5
PENT–Assemb of God	3	300	118	468	1.1	4.1
PENT–Int Foursq Gos	2	255	125	146	0.4	1.3
PENT–Un Pent Ch Intl	1	NR	NR	NR	-	-
PRES–Presb Ch (USA)	3	343	341	397	1.0	3.4
Sev Day Adv	2	92	159	183	0.4	1.6
Unit Univ	1	46	41	69	0.2	0.6
KLICKITAT	**38**	**1,416**	**1,880**	**5,916**	**29.1**	**100.0**
Bahá'í	1	NR	36	36	0.2	0.6
BAPT–Consrv Bapt	2	NR	NR	NR	-	-
BAPT–So Bapt Conv	3	123	311	373	1.8	6.3
BRETH–Grace Breth	1	NR	NR	NR	-	-
Catholic	2	NR	NR	2,200	10.8	37.2
CGOD–Ch God (Ander)	1	52	NR	52	0.3	0.9
Ch of Nazarene	2	112	167	202	1.0	3.4
CHR–Chr Chs & Chs Cr	1	NR	25	30	0.1	0.5
CHR–Chs of Christ	3	150	125	156	0.8	2.6
LDS–L-D Saints	2	NR	NR	945	4.7	16.0
LUTH–Apostolic Luth	1	NR	NR	NR	-	-
LUTH–E.L.C.A.	1	44	125	142	0.7	2.4
LUTH–Luth–MO Synod	2	41	103	114	0.6	1.9
METH–Un Methodist	3	118	237	296	1.5	5.0
Non-denom Chr Chs	3	160	115	199	1.0	3.4
ORTHE–Greek Orthodox	1	35	NR	55	0.3	0.9
PENT–Assemb of God	2	240	128	522	2.6	8.8
PRES–Presb Ch (USA)	3	103	104	125	0.6	2.1
Sev Day Adv	3	189	328	378	1.9	6.4
Un C of Christ	1	49	76	91	0.4	1.5

Religious Group	Number of Congrega-tions	Number of Attendees	Number of Communicant, Confirmed, or Full Members	Adherents: Number of Adherents	Adherents: % of Total Pop.	Adherents: % of Total Adh.
LEWIS	**112**	**7,876**	**9,178**	**28,321**	**37.5**	**100.0**
ANG/EPIS–Episcopal	1	55	158	158	0.2	0.6
Bahá'í	0	NR	47	47	0.1	0.2
BAPT–Amer Bapt USA	2	195	294	356	0.5	1.3
BAPT–Consrv Bapt	1	NR	NR	NR	-	-
BAPT–So Bapt Conv	5	447	1,117	1,353	1.8	4.8
BRETH–Ch of Brethren	2	10	93	113	0.1	0.4
BUDD–Theravada	1	NR	NR	266	0.4	0.9
BUDD–Vajrayana	1	NR	NR	20	0.0	0.1
Calv Chpl	1	NR	NR	NR	-	-
Catholic	9	NR	NR	8,102	10.7	28.6
CGOD–Ch God (Ander)	3	735	NR	735	1.0	2.6
Ch Cr, Scientst	1	NR	NR	NR	-	-
Ch of Nazarene	2	341	362	653	0.9	2.3
CHR–Chr Chs & Chs Cr	2	NR	300	363	0.5	1.3
CHR–Chs of Christ	2	100	120	140	0.2	0.5
Evan Ch	1	NR	NR	NR	-	-
Evan Free Ch	1	70	NR	70	0.1	0.2
Jehovah's Witness	5	NR	NR	NR	-	-
LDS–L-D Saints	7	NR	NR	4,304	5.7	15.2
LUTH–E.L.C.A.	4	404	906	1,229	1.6	4.3
LUTH–Luth–MO Synod	1	131	248	353	0.5	1.2
METH–Free Methodist	1	260	205	260	0.3	0.9
METH–Un Methodist	7	331	928	1,170	1.6	4.1
Non-denom Chr Chs	14	1,460	1,525	1,957	2.6	6.9
OCATH–Pol Natl Cath	1	NR	NR	NR	-	-
PENT–Apos Faith Msn	1	NR	35	42	0.1	0.1
PENT–Assemb of God	16	1,841	900	4,097	5.4	14.5
PENT–Ch God (Cleve)	1	10	62	75	0.1	0.3
PENT–Int Foursq Gos	3	257	324	392	0.5	1.4
PENT–Open Bible Std	1	85	NR	85	0.1	0.3
PENT–Pent Ch of God	1	70	NR	109	0.1	0.4
PRES–Presb Ch (USA)	6	507	585	708	0.9	2.5
Salvation Army	1	35	44	100	0.1	0.4
Sev Day Adv	6	532	925	1,064	1.4	3.8
Unity Ch	1	NR	NR	NR	-	-
LINCOLN	**35**	**1,208**	**2,345**	**4,403**	**41.7**	**100.0**
Bahá'í	0	NR	8	8	0.1	0.2
Catholic	6	NR	NR	1,018	9.6	23.1
Ch of Nazarene	2	95	85	141	1.3	3.2
CHR–Chr Ch (Disc)	1	40	162	195	1.8	4.4
FRND–Evan Fr Ch Intl	1	NR	0	0	0.0	0.0
Jehovah's Witness	1	NR	NR	NR	-	-
LDS–L-D Saints	1	NR	NR	215	2.0	4.9
LUTH–E.L.C.A.	5	218	583	897	8.5	20.4
LUTH–Luth Cong Msn Chr	1	65	333	402	3.8	9.1
LUTH–Luth–MO Synod	1	43	72	90	0.9	2.0
MENN–Hutt Breth	2	NR	NR	NR	-	-
METH–Un Methodist	4	141	291	348	3.3	7.9
Non-denom Chr Chs	2	190	170	237	2.2	5.4
PENT–Assemb of God	1	55	0	80	0.8	1.8
PENT–Int Foursq Gos	2	74	104	126	1.2	2.9
PRES–Presb Ch (USA)	4	261	492	594	5.6	13.5
Sev Day Adv	1	26	45	52	0.5	1.2
MASON	**48**	**2,946**	**4,244**	**16,947**	**27.9**	**100.0**
ANG/EPIS–Episcopal	4	124	182	208	0.3	1.2
Bahá'í	1	NR	51	51	0.1	0.3
BAPT–Amer Bapt USA	2	231	578	685	1.1	4.0
BAPT–Consrv Bapt	2	NR	NR	NR	-	-
BAPT–So Bapt Conv	1	60	75	89	0.1	0.5
BUDD–Mahayana	1	NR	NR	11	0.0	0.1
Calv Chpl	1	NR	NR	NR	-	-
Catholic	2	NR	NR	8,536	14.1	50.4
CGOD–Ch God (Ander)	1	45	NR	45	0.1	0.3
Ch of Nazarene	1	56	113	113	0.2	0.7
Chr & Miss Al	1	55	32	123	0.2	0.7
CHR–Chr Chs & Chs Cr	1	NR	275	326	0.5	1.9
CHR–Chs of Christ	1	53	43	53	0.1	0.3
Ind Fund Churches	1	NR	NR	NR	-	-
Jehovah's Witness	2	NR	NR	NR	-	-
LDS–L-D Saints	4	NR	NR	2,587	4.3	15.3

NR–Not Reported   - Represents no adherents reported.   Percentages may not total 100 due to rounding.

Table 3: Religious Congregations by County and Group: 2010

Religious Group	Number of Congrega-tions	Number of Attendees	Number of Communicant, Confirmed, or Full Members	Adherents		
				Number of Adherents	% of Total Pop.	% of Total Adh.
LUTH–E.L.C.A.	3	407	718	834	1.4	4.9
LUTH–Luth Cong Msn Chr	1	93	113	134	0.2	0.8
LUTH–Luth–MO Synod	1	121	197	315	0.5	1.9
METH–Un Methodist	2	220	380	452	0.7	2.7
Non-denom Chr Chs	6	585	538	819	1.3	4.8
PENT–Assemb of God	4	421	273	775	1.3	4.6
PENT–Ch God (Cleve)	1	74	53	63	0.1	0.4
PENT–Int Foursq Gos	1	59	131	155	0.3	0.9
PRES–Presb Ch (USA)	1	184	216	256	0.4	1.5
Sev Day Adv	2	158	276	317	0.5	1.9
OKANOGAN	**86**	**4,270**	**4,070**	**13,257**	**32.2**	**100.0**
ANG/EPIS–Episcopal	3	58	154	172	0.4	1.3
Bahá'í	0	NR	50	50	0.1	0.4
BAPT–Amer Bapt Assn	1	NR	50	61	0.1	0.5
BAPT–Converge/BGC	3	950	NR	1,140	2.8	8.6
BAPT–N Am Bapt Conf	1	NR	14	17	0.0	0.1
BAPT–So Bapt Conv	3	131	309	377	0.9	2.8
BRETH–Ch of Brethren	2	0	89	109	0.3	0.8
BUDD–Vajrayana	2	NR	NR	229	0.6	1.7
Calv Chpl	2	NR	NR	NR	-	-
Catholic	7	NR	NR	4,627	11.3	34.9
Ch of Nazarene	1	45	43	70	0.2	0.5
Chr & Miss Al	2	82	37	138	0.3	1.0
CHR–Chs of Christ	4	116	107	154	0.4	1.2
Evan Cov Ch	1	110	95	143	0.3	1.1
Ind Fund Churches	1	NR	NR	NR	-	-
Jehovah's Witness	3	NR	NR	NR	-	-
LDS–Comm of Christ	1	NR	167	167	0.4	1.3
LDS–L-D Saints	4	NR	NR	1,153	2.8	8.7
LUTH–Luth–MO Synod	5	159	249	292	0.7	2.2
LUTH–Wisc Ev Luth Syn	2	48	102	119	0.3	0.9
MENN–CG in Cr (Menn)	1	NR	60	73	0.2	0.6
METH–Free Methodist	3	529	305	529	1.3	4.0
METH–Un Methodist	7	336	500	978	2.4	7.4
Non-denom Chr Chs	4	250	225	312	0.8	2.4
PENT–Assemb of God	8	520	351	647	1.6	4.9
PENT–COGIC	1	0	150	183	0.4	1.4
PENT–Int Foursq Gos	2	79	63	77	0.2	0.6
PENT–Pent Ch of God	3	210	NR	326	0.8	2.5
PRES–Presb Ch (USA)	3	236	261	319	0.8	2.4
Sev Day Adv	5	374	650	747	1.8	5.6
Un C of Christ	1	37	39	48	0.1	0.4
PACIFIC	**42**	**1,368**	**2,004**	**6,308**	**30.2**	**100.0**
ANG/EPIS–Episcopal	2	46	78	78	0.4	1.2
Bahá'í	0	NR	15	15	0.1	0.2
BAPT–Amer Bapt USA	1	104	111	128	0.6	2.0
BAPT–Consrv Bapt	1	NR	NR	NR	-	-
BAPT–So Bapt Conv	1	27	NR	NR	-	-
Calv Chpl	1	NR	NR	NR	-	-
Catholic	2	NR	NR	2,728	13.0	43.2
Ch of Nazarene	2	47	45	61	0.3	1.0
CHR–Chs of Christ	1	15	10	12	0.1	0.2
FRND–Evan Fr Ch Intl	1	NR	0	0	0.0	0.0
FRND–Indep Yr Mtgs	1	NR	0	0	0.0	0.0
Jehovah's Witness	2	NR	NR	NR	-	-
LDS–L-D Saints	2	NR	NR	806	3.9	12.8
LUTH–E.L.C.A.	4	226	456	596	2.8	9.4
LUTH–Luth Cong Msn Chr	1	35	191	220	1.1	3.5
LUTH–Luth–MO Synod	1	29	60	60	0.3	1.0
METH–Un Methodist	5	183	445	519	2.5	8.2
METH–Wesleyan	1	14	9	18	0.1	0.3
Non-denom Chr Chs	3	165	150	205	1.0	3.2
PENT–Assemb of God	4	344	191	473	2.3	7.5
PENT–Pent Ch of God	1	70	NR	109	0.5	1.7
PRES–Presb Ch (USA)	2	0	144	166	0.8	2.6
Sev Day Adv	2	43	75	86	0.4	1.4
Un C of Christ	1	20	24	28	0.1	0.4
PEND OREILLE	**24**	**880**	**1,372**	**2,395**	**18.4**	**100.0**
Bahá'í	0	NR	3	3	0.0	0.1
BAPT–So Bapt Conv	2	99	131	156	1.2	6.5

Religious Group	Number of Congrega-tions	Number of Attendees	Number of Communicant, Confirmed, or Full Members	Adherents		
				Number of Adherents	% of Total Pop.	% of Total Adh.
BUDD–Vajrayana	1	NR	NR	78	0.6	3.3
Catholic	5	NR	NR	653	5.0	27.3
CHR–Chs of Christ	1	20	20	20	0.2	0.8
CONG–Consrv Cong Chr	1	15	28	33	0.3	1.4
Jehovah's Witness	1	NR	NR	NR	-	-
LDS–L-D Saints	1	NR	NR	112	0.9	4.7
LUTH–E.L.C.A.	1	124	300	318	2.4	13.3
MENN–Mennonite USA	1	53	53	63	0.5	2.6
Non-denom Chr Chs	2	200	300	300	2.3	12.5
PENT–Assemb of God	2	93	61	105	0.8	4.4
PRES–Presb Ch (USA)	1	0	15	18	0.1	0.8
Sev Day Adv	3	190	330	380	2.9	15.9
Un C of Christ	2	86	131	156	1.2	6.5
PIERCE	**644**	**84,210**	**108,753**	**280,373**	**35.3**	**100.0**
ANG/EPIS–Anglican NA	3	NR	NR	NR	-	-
ANG/EPIS–Episcopal	10	1,008	2,075	2,509	0.3	0.9
Bahá'í	8	NR	679	679	0.1	0.2
BAPT–Amer Bapt USA	15	1,824	3,053	3,781	0.5	1.3
BAPT–Asc Ref Bap Ch Am	1	NR	NR	NR	-	-
BAPT–Consrv Bapt	8	NR	NR	NR	-	-
BAPT–Converge/BGC	6	1,500	NR	1,800	0.2	0.6
BAPT–Ind Bapt Flwsp Intl	3	NR	NR	NR	-	-
BAPT–N Am Bapt Conf	5	NR	681	843	0.1	0.3
BAPT–NBC Amer	1	112	140	173	0.0	0.1
BAPT–NBC USA	3	510	1,100	1,362	0.2	0.5
BAPT–Ref Bapt Ch	2	NR	NR	NR	-	-
BAPT–Reg Bapt Gen As	10	NR	NR	NR	-	-
BAPT–So Bapt Conv	34	4,514	8,098	10,030	1.3	3.6
BRETH–Ch of Brethren	1	0	26	32	0.0	0.0
BUDD–Mahayana	7	NR	NR	5,967	0.8	2.1
BUDD–Theravada	5	NR	NR	7,582	1.0	2.7
Calv Chpl	4	NR	NR	NR	-	-
Catholic	26	NR	NR	69,558	8.7	24.8
CGOD–Ch God (Ander)	4	255	NR	255	0.0	0.1
Ch Cr, Scientst	4	NR	NR	NR	-	-
Ch God (7th Day)	1	NR	NR	NR	-	-
Ch of Nazarene	12	2,000	2,523	2,931	0.4	1.0
Chr & Miss Al	9	2,598	1,476	2,760	0.3	1.0
CHR–Chr Ch (Disc)	7	391	885	1,096	0.1	0.4
CHR–Chr Chs & Chs Cr	10	NR	1,860	2,304	0.3	0.8
CHR–Chs of Christ	13	1,253	1,265	1,661	0.2	0.6
CHR–Int Chs of Christ	1	NR	155	192	0.0	0.1
CONG–Cong Chr, NA	1	NR	141	175	0.0	0.1
Evan Ch	1	NR	NR	NR	-	-
Evan Cov Ch	8	1,265	1,211	1,644	0.2	0.6
Evan Free Ch	5	455	NR	455	0.1	0.2
FRND–Evan Fr Ch Intl	2	45	108	134	0.0	0.0
FRND–Indep Yr Mtgs	2	NR	39	48	0.0	0.0
HINDU–Post Ren	1	NR	NR	77	0.0	0.0
Ind Fund Churches	3	NR	NR	NR	-	-
Jehovah's Witness	19	NR	NR	NR	-	-
JUD–Orth	1	43	50	60	0.0	0.0
JUD–Reform	1	154	271	732	0.1	0.3
LDS–Comm of Christ	2	NR	334	334	0.0	0.1
LDS–L-D Saints	52	NR	NR	33,152	4.2	11.8
LUTH–Assoc Free Luth	1	NR	NR	NR	-	-
LUTH–Ch Luth Conf	1	NR	NR	NR	-	-
LUTH–Cons Luth Assn	1	NR	NR	NR	-	-
LUTH–E.L.C.A.	28	4,574	8,550	12,653	1.6	4.5
LUTH–Evan Luth Syn	2	223	476	640	0.1	0.2
LUTH–Luth Cong Msn Chr	2	185	NR	NR	-	-
LUTH–Luth–MO Synod	12	1,846	3,120	4,936	0.6	1.8
LUTH–Wisc Ev Luth Syn	2	295	447	558	0.1	0.2
MENN–Menn Br US Conf	3	NR	2,399	2,971	0.4	1.1
METH–AME	1	0	100	124	0.0	0.0
METH–C.M.E.	3	0	450	557	0.1	0.2
METH–Free Methodist	1	48	31	48	0.0	0.0
METH–Un Methodist	26	1,950	3,995	5,303	0.7	1.9
Metro Comm Ch	1	82	33	41	0.0	0.0
Missionary Ch	1	11	8	11	0.0	0.0
Muslim Est	2	268	NR	616	0.1	0.2
Nat Spirit Asso	2	NR	NR	NR	-	-
New Apost Ch	1	NR	NR	NR	-	-

NR–Not Reported - Represents no adherents reported. Percentages may not total 100 due to rounding.

Table 3: Religious Congregations by County and Group: 2010

Religious Group	Number of Congregations	Number of Attendees	Number of Communicant, Confirmed, or Full Members	Adherents: Number of Adherents	Adherents: % of Total Pop.	Adherents: % of Total Adh.
Non-denom Chr Chs	99	32,454	40,293	46,741	5.9	16.7
ORTHE–Greek Orthodox	1	100	NR	350	0.0	0.1
ORTHE–Holy Orth in NA	1	15	NR	20	0.0	0.0
ORTHE–Orth Ch in Amer	1	120	NR	180	0.0	0.1
ORTHO–Coptic Orth Ch	1	15	NR	55	0.0	0.0
PENT–Apos Faith Msn	1	NR	35	43	0.0	0.0
PENT–Assemb of God	25	8,759	3,270	27,374	3.4	9.8
PENT–Ch God (Cleve)	2	134	81	100	0.0	0.0
PENT–Ch of God by Faith	4	NR	NR	NR	-	-
PENT–Ch of God Proph	2	NR	102	126	0.0	0.0
PENT–COGIC	9	1,115	2,100	2,601	0.3	0.9
PENT–Int Foursq Gos	16	5,546	4,845	6,001	0.8	2.1
PENT–Open Bible Std	6	624	NR	624	0.1	0.2
PENT–Pent Ch of God	1	70	NR	109	0.0	0.0
PENT–Un Pent Ch Intl	6	NR	NR	NR	-	-
PENT–Vineyard	1	70	80	99	0.0	0.0
PRES–Bible Pres	1	NR	NR	NR	-	-
PRES–Evan Presby Ch	1	NR	42	52	0.0	0.0
PRES–Kor Pres Abroad	2	NR	NR	NR	-	-
PRES–Korean Amer Pres	2	NR	NR	NR	-	-
PRES–Korean Pres Amer	2	NR	NR	NR	-	-
PRES–Presb Ch (USA)	27	4,401	7,094	8,787	1.1	3.1
PRES–Presb Ch Amer	3	559	484	687	0.1	0.2
REF–Christian Ref	3	370	438	543	0.1	0.2
Salvation Army	2	131	185	537	0.1	0.2
Sev Day Adv	14	1,900	3,305	3,800	0.5	1.4
Tao	1	NR	NR	NR	-	-
Un C of Christ	6	251	414	513	0.1	0.2
Unit Univ	1	167	206	247	0.0	0.1
Unity Ch	2	NR	NR	NR	-	-
SAN JUAN	**27**	**974**	**1,247**	**4,845**	**30.7**	**100.0**
ANG/EPIS–Episcopal	3	203	416	459	2.9	9.5
Bahá'í	0	NR	30	30	0.2	0.6
BUDD–Mahayana	1	NR	NR	11	0.1	0.2
Calv Chpl	1	NR	NR	NR	-	-
Catholic	3	NR	NR	3,017	19.1	62.3
Ch Cr, Scientst	1	NR	NR	NR	-	-
FRND–Indep Yr Mtgs	3	NR	0	0	0.0	0.0
Jehovah's Witness	3	NR	NR	NR	-	-
LDS–L-D Saints	1	NR	NR	323	2.0	6.7
LUTH–E.L.C.A.	1	60	70	71	0.5	1.5
LUTH–Luth Cong Msn Chr	1	NR	NR	NR	-	-
Non-denom Chr Chs	4	455	435	568	3.6	11.7
PENT–Assemb of God	1	23	0	31	0.2	0.6
PRES–Presb Ch (USA)	1	153	166	187	1.2	3.9
Sev Day Adv	2	68	118	136	0.9	2.8
Unit Univ	1	12	12	12	0.1	0.2
SKAGIT	**136**	**13,361**	**15,566**	**46,497**	**39.8**	**100.0**
ANG/EPIS–Anglican NA	2	NR	NR	NR	-	-
ANG/EPIS–Episcopal	3	142	257	257	0.2	0.6
Bahá'í	2	NR	132	132	0.1	0.3
BAPT–Amer Bapt USA	3	452	803	980	0.8	2.1
BAPT–Consrv Bapt	1	NR	NR	NR	-	-
BAPT–Converge/BGC	1	800	NR	960	0.8	2.1
BAPT–Reg Bapt Gen As	1	NR	NR	NR	-	-
BAPT–So Bapt Conv	7	482	1,103	1,347	1.2	2.9
BUDD–Mahayana	1	NR	NR	11	0.0	0.0
Calv Chpl	1	NR	NR	NR	-	-
Catholic	7	NR	NR	19,177	16.4	41.2
Ch Cr, Scientst	1	NR	NR	NR	-	-
Ch of Nazarene	3	161	195	251	0.2	0.5
Chr & Miss Al	1	48	35	65	0.1	0.1
CHR–Chr Ch (Disc)	1	30	76	93	0.1	0.2
CHR–Chr Chs & Chs Cr	3	NR	333	407	0.3	0.9
CHR–Chs of Christ	4	285	253	336	0.3	0.7
Evan Cov Ch	3	999	661	1,299	1.1	2.8
FRND–Evan Fr Ch Intl	2	55	0	0	0.0	0.0
HINDU–Renaiss	1	NR	NR	12	0.0	0.0
Jehovah's Witness	5	NR	NR	NR	-	-
LDS–Comm of Christ	1	NR	167	167	0.1	0.4
LDS–L-D Saints	6	NR	NR	3,870	3.3	8.3
LUTH–Assoc Free Luth	1	NR	NR	NR	-	-
LUTH–Ch of Luth Br	1	15	15	68	0.1	0.1
LUTH–E.L.C.A.	10	1,083	2,729	3,958	3.4	8.5
LUTH–Evan Luth Syn	1	34	48	74	0.1	0.2
LUTH–Luth–MO Synod	1	111	161	181	0.2	0.4
METH–Free Methodist	3	409	169	409	0.3	0.9
METH–Un Methodist	7	574	1,745	1,930	1.7	4.2
Non-denom Chr Chs	17	4,511	3,841	5,766	4.9	12.4
PENT–Assemb of God	11	1,366	484	1,838	1.6	4.0
PENT–Ch God (Cleve)	1	7	16	20	0.0	0.0
PENT–Ch of God Proph	1	NR	48	59	0.1	0.1
PENT–Int Foursq Gos	2	142	56	68	0.1	0.1
PENT–Un Pent Ch Intl	2	NR	NR	NR	-	-
PRES–Orth Pres Ch	1	82	63	98	0.1	0.2
PRES–Presb Ch (USA)	4	348	470	574	0.5	1.2
REF–Christian Ref	4	549	527	643	0.6	1.4
REF–Un Ref Chs N.A.	1	NR	NR	NR	-	-
Salvation Army	1	25	20	99	0.1	0.2
Sev Day Adv	3	550	956	1,099	0.9	2.4
Un C of Christ	2	61	141	172	0.1	0.4
Unit Univ	1	40	62	77	0.1	0.2
Unity Ch	1	NR	NR	NR	-	-
SKAMANIA	**15**	**473**	**472**	**1,881**	**17.0**	**100.0**
Bahá'í	0	NR	5	5	0.0	0.3
BAPT–Consrv Bapt	1	NR	NR	NR	-	-
Catholic	1	NR	NR	625	5.6	33.2
Ch of Nazarene	2	103	169	309	2.8	16.4
CHR–Chs of Christ	1	30	23	45	0.4	2.4
Ind Fund Churches	2	NR	NR	NR	-	-
Jehovah's Witness	1	NR	NR	NR	-	-
LDS–L-D Saints	1	NR	NR	409	3.7	21.7
LUTH–E.L.C.A.	1	50	73	80	0.7	4.3
METH–Un Methodist	1	17	34	83	0.8	4.4
Non-denom Chr Chs	2	100	120	125	1.1	6.6
PENT–Open Bible Std	1	145	NR	145	1.3	7.7
Sev Day Adv	1	28	48	55	0.5	2.9
SNOHOMISH	**514**	**59,352**	**71,126**	**219,008**	**30.7**	**100.0**
ANG/EPIS–Anglican NA	2	NR	NR	NR	-	-
ANG/EPIS–Episcopal	7	504	1,099	1,232	0.2	0.6
Bahá'í	9	NR	662	662	0.1	0.3
BAPT–Amer Bapt USA	9	790	1,405	1,728	0.2	0.8
BAPT–Consrv Bapt	4	NR	NR	NR	-	-
BAPT–Converge/BGC	11	1,150	NR	1,380	0.2	0.6
BAPT–Ind Bapt Flwsp Intl	1	NR	NR	NR	-	-
BAPT–N Am Bapt Conf	3	NR	210	258	0.0	0.1
BAPT–Ref Bapt Ch	1	NR	NR	NR	-	-
BAPT–Reg Bapt Gen As	5	NR	NR	NR	-	-
BAPT–So Bapt Conv	33	2,057	1,944	2,391	0.3	1.1
BRETH–Grace Breth	1	NR	NR	NR	-	-
BUDD–Mahayana	3	NR	NR	710	0.1	0.3
BUDD–Theravada	2	NR	NR	686	0.1	0.3
BUDD–Vajrayana	1	NR	NR	46	0.0	0.0
Calv Chpl	6	NR	NR	NR	-	-
Catholic	16	NR	NR	75,393	10.6	34.4
CGOD–Ch God (Ander)	3	112	NR	112	0.0	0.1
Ch Cr, Scientst	2	NR	NR	NR	-	-
Ch of Nazarene	14	3,316	3,113	8,494	1.2	3.9
Chr & Miss Al	13	1,499	1,099	3,612	0.5	1.6
CHR–Chr Ch (Disc)	2	62	88	108	0.0	0.0
CHR–Chr Chs & Chs Cr	7	NR	3,385	4,163	0.6	1.9
CHR–Chs of Christ	8	579	508	669	0.1	0.3
CONG–Cong Chr, NA	1	NR	75	92	0.0	0.0
CONG–Consrv Cong Chr	1	20	15	18	0.0	0.0
Evan Ch	1	NR	NR	NR	-	-
Evan Cov Ch	4	274	337	356	0.0	0.2
Evan Free Ch	4	330	NR	330	0.0	0.2
FRND–Indep Yr Mtgs	2	NR	0	0	0.0	0.0
HINDU–Post Ren	2	NR	NR	35	0.0	0.0
HINDU–Renaiss	1	NR	NR	12	0.0	0.0
HINDU–Trad Temples	1	NR	NR	5,000	0.7	2.3
Ind Fund Churches	4	NR	NR	NR	-	-

NR–Not Reported   - Represents no adherents reported.   Percentages may not total 100 due to rounding.

Table 3: Religious Congregations by County and Group: 2010

Religious Group	Number of Congregations	Number of Attendees	Number of Communicant, Confirmed, or Full Members	Adherents: Number of Adherents	Adherents: % of Total Pop.	Adherents: % of Total Adh.
Jehovah's Witness	14	NR	NR	NR	-	-
JUD–Orth	1	43	50	60	0.0	0.0
JUD–Reform	1	67	119	321	0.0	0.1
LDS–Comm of Christ	1	NR	167	167	0.0	0.1
LDS–L-D Saints	41	NR	NR	22,684	3.2	10.4
LUTH–Assoc Free Luth	3	NR	NR	NR	-	-
LUTH–Ch Luth Conf	1	NR	NR	NR	-	-
LUTH–Ch of Luth Br	5	663	470	1,170	0.2	0.5
LUTH–E.L.C.A.	24	3,374	7,838	10,527	1.5	4.8
LUTH–Luth Cong Msn Chr	1	235	1,103	1,357	0.2	0.6
LUTH–Luth–MO Synod	11	1,075	1,814	2,282	0.3	1.0
LUTH–Nor Amer Luth C	1	NR	NR	NR	-	-
LUTH–Wisc Ev Luth Syn	2	130	190	245	0.0	0.1
MENN–Menn Br US Conf	3	NR	308	379	0.1	0.2
METH–AME	1	30	30	37	0.0	0.0
METH–Free Methodist	7	1,475	888	1,516	0.2	0.7
METH–Un Methodist	12	1,199	3,717	5,392	0.8	2.5
Muslim Est	5	936	NR	3,232	0.5	1.5
Non-denom Chr Chs	62	21,400	24,710	30,177	4.2	13.8
ORTHE–Ant Orth of NA	3	321	NR	433	0.1	0.2
ORTHE–Holy Orth in NA	1	8	NR	10	0.0	0.0
ORTHO–Coptic Orth Ch	1	300	NR	1,500	0.2	0.7
ORTHO–Ethiopian Orth	1	NR	NR	NR	-	-
PENT–Assemb of God	33	6,560	3,117	14,041	2.0	6.4
PENT–Ch God (Cleve)	2	69	127	156	0.0	0.1
PENT–Ch of God Proph	3	NR	91	112	0.0	0.1
PENT–COGIC	3	180	300	369	0.1	0.2
PENT–Int Foursq Gos	20	5,484	5,440	6,691	0.9	3.1
PENT–Open Bible Std	3	277	NR	277	0.0	0.1
PENT–Un Pent Ch Intl	4	NR	NR	NR	-	-
PENT–Vineyard	3	285	378	465	0.1	0.2
PRES–Bible Pres	1	NR	NR	NR	-	-
PRES–Kor Pres Abroad	4	NR	NR	NR	-	-
PRES–Korean Amer Pres	1	NR	NR	NR	-	-
PRES–Korean Pres Amer	6	NR	NR	NR	-	-
PRES–Orth Pres Ch	3	255	210	311	0.0	0.1
PRES–Presb Ch (USA)	9	1,211	1,722	2,118	0.3	1.0
PRES–Presb Ch Amer	2	190	220	259	0.0	0.1
REF–Christian Ref	5	575	643	791	0.1	0.4
REF–Comm Ref Evan	1	NR	NR	NR	-	-
REF–Ref Ch in Am	2	206	198	290	0.0	0.1
Salvation Army	1	37	48	261	0.0	0.1
Sev Day Adv	14	1,540	2,681	3,081	0.4	1.4
Shinto	1	NR	NR	NR	-	-
Sikh	1	NR	NR	NR	-	-
Un C of Christ	2	110	126	155	0.0	0.1
Unit Univ	2	424	481	650	0.1	0.3
Unity Ch	2	NR	NR	NR	-	-
Zoroastrian	0	NR	NR	5	0.0	0.0
SPOKANE	**416**	**46,808**	**63,174**	**174,289**	**37.0**	**100.0**
ANG/EPIS–Anglican NA	1	NR	NR	NR	-	-
ANG/EPIS–Episcopal	7	694	2,142	2,350	0.5	1.3
Bahá'í	3	NR	248	248	0.1	0.1
BAPT–Amer Bapt Assn	2	NR	205	250	0.1	0.1
BAPT–Amer Bapt USA	8	586	563	686	0.1	0.4
BAPT–Consrv Bapt	3	NR	NR	NR	-	-
BAPT–Converge/BGC	1	800	NR	960	0.2	0.6
BAPT–Ind Bapt Flwsp Intl	1	NR	NR	NR	-	-
BAPT–N Am Bapt Conf	1	NR	NR	NR	-	-
BAPT–Reg Bapt Gen As	2	NR	NR	NR	-	-
BAPT–So Bapt Conv	19	2,168	3,953	4,815	1.0	2.8
BUDD–Mahayana	5	NR	NR	3,354	0.7	1.9
BUDD–Vajrayana	1	NR	NR	20	0.0	0.0
Calv Chpl	3	NR	NR	NR	-	-
Catholic	27	NR	NR	61,575	13.1	35.3
CGOD–Ch God (Ander)	2	350	NR	350	0.1	0.2
Ch Cr, Scientst	2	NR	NR	NR	-	-
Ch God (7th Day)	1	NR	NR	NR	-	-
Ch of Nazarene	9	1,852	2,585	2,785	0.6	1.6
Chr & Miss Al	3	382	217	564	0.1	0.3
CHR–Chr Ch (Disc)	5	275	625	761	0.2	0.4
CHR–Chr Chs & Chs Cr	4	NR	680	828	0.2	0.5
CHR–Chs of Christ	6	555	563	708	0.2	0.4
CHR–Int Chs of Christ	1	NR	125	152	0.0	0.1
CONG–Cong Chr, NA	1	NR	44	54	0.0	0.0
CONG–Consrv Cong Chr	1	50	54	66	0.0	0.0
Evan Ch	2	NR	NR	NR	-	-
Evan Cov Ch	2	112	97	145	0.0	0.1
Evan Free Ch	4	354	NR	354	0.1	0.2
FRND–Evan Fr Ch Intl	1	52	73	89	0.0	0.1
Grace Gosp Fel	1	NR	NR	NR	-	-
HINDU–Post Ren	2	NR	NR	41	0.0	0.0
HINDU–Renaiss	1	NR	NR	12	0.0	0.0
Ind Fund Churches	1	NR	NR	NR	-	-
Intl Fell Bible Ch	1	NR	NR	NR	-	-
Jehovah's Witness	11	NR	NR	NR	-	-
JUD–Conserv	1	184	206	556	0.1	0.3
JUD–Orth	1	43	50	60	0.0	0.0
JUD–Reform	1	36	63	170	0.0	0.1
LDS–Comm of Christ	1	NR	128	128	0.0	0.1
LDS–L-D Saints	48	NR	NR	24,246	5.1	13.9
LUTH–Ch Luth Conf	2	NR	NR	NR	-	-
LUTH–E.L.C.A.	19	2,347	6,677	8,966	1.9	5.1
LUTH–Luth Cong Msn Chr	1	22	28	34	0.0	0.0
LUTH–Luth–MO Synod	9	1,296	3,161	4,190	0.9	2.4
LUTH–Wisc Ev Luth Syn	1	109	203	255	0.1	0.1
MENN–Menn Br US Conf	2	NR	1,251	1,524	0.3	0.9
MENN–Mennonite USA	1	25	17	21	0.0	0.0
METH–AME	1	250	350	426	0.1	0.2
METH–Free Methodist	4	915	590	915	0.2	0.5
METH–Un Methodist	17	1,194	2,928	3,815	0.8	2.2
METH–Wesleyan	1	88	37	114	0.0	0.1
Metro Comm Ch	1	32	40	49	0.0	0.0
MJEW–Union Mes Cong	1	NR	NR	NR	-	-
Muslim Est	1	134	NR	308	0.1	0.2
New Apost Ch	1	NR	NR	NR	-	-
Non-denom Chr Chs	70	15,350	17,362	20,462	4.3	11.7
ORTHE–Ant Orth of NA	2	136	NR	314	0.1	0.2
ORTHE–Greek Orthodox	1	95	NR	440	0.1	0.3
PENT–Assemb of God	16	3,048	1,644	4,599	1.0	2.6
PENT–Ch God (Cleve)	1	54	50	61	0.0	0.0
PENT–COGIC	3	0	210	256	0.1	0.1
PENT–Int Foursq Gos	7	5,822	6,260	7,624	1.6	4.4
PENT–Open Bible Std	5	1,312	NR	1,312	0.3	0.8
PENT–Un Pent Ch Intl	4	NR	NR	NR	-	-
PRES–Presb Ch (USA)	18	3,086	4,922	5,995	1.3	3.4
PRES–Ref Pres Han	1	NR	NR	NR	-	-
REF–Christian Ref	2	201	168	205	0.0	0.1
REF–Comm Ref Evan	1	NR	NR	NR	-	-
REF–Prot Ref Chs	1	28	17	33	0.0	0.0
Salvation Army	1	152	207	861	0.2	0.5
Sev Day Adv	15	2,070	3,600	4,141	0.9	2.4
Sikh	1	NR	NR	NR	-	-
Un C of Christ	5	309	463	564	0.1	0.3
Unit Univ	1	240	368	478	0.1	0.3
Unity Ch	2	NR	NR	NR	-	-
STEVENS	**71**	**3,700**	**3,896**	**11,731**	**26.9**	**100.0**
ANG/EPIS–Episcopal	1	14	19	19	0.0	0.2
Bahá'í	0	NR	31	31	0.1	0.3
BAPT–Reg Bapt Gen As	1	NR	NR	NR	-	-
BAPT–So Bapt Conv	4	139	152	184	0.4	1.6
Calv Chpl	1	NR	NR	NR	-	-
Catholic	10	NR	NR	3,974	9.1	33.9
CGOD–Ch God (Ander)	1	22	NR	22	0.1	0.2
Ch of Nazarene	2	158	140	224	0.5	1.9
CHR–Chr Chs & Chs Cr	1	NR	131	159	0.4	1.4
CHR–Chs of Christ	1	30	50	50	0.1	0.4
Evan Free Ch	2	260	NR	260	0.6	2.2
Jehovah's Witness	2	NR	NR	NR	-	-
LDS–L-D Saints	4	NR	NR	1,829	4.2	15.6
LUTH–E.L.C.A.	2	156	352	509	1.2	4.3
METH–Free Methodist	2	232	91	232	0.5	2.0
METH–Un Methodist	1	111	262	342	0.8	2.9
Non-denom Chr Chs	14	1,240	1,320	1,680	3.9	14.3
PENT–Assemb of God	8	671	345	1,008	2.3	8.6
PENT–Open Bible Std	1	18	NR	18	0.0	0.2

NR–Not Reported - Represents no adherents reported. Percentages may not total 100 due to rounding.

Table 3: Religious Congregations by County and Group: 2010

Religious Group	Number of Congrega-tions	Number of Attendees	Number of Communicant, Confirmed, or Full Members	Adherents		
				Number of Adherents	% of Total Pop.	% of Total Adh.
PENT–Un Pent Ch Intl	1	NR	NR	NR	-	-
PENT–Vineyard	1	140	200	242	0.6	2.1
PRES–Orth Pres Ch	1	21	12	27	0.1	0.2
PRES–Presb Ch (USA)	2	23	25	30	0.1	0.3
REF–Comm Ref Evan	1	NR	NR	NR	-	-
Sev Day Adv	4	348	606	697	1.6	5.9
Un C of Christ	2	117	160	194	0.4	1.7
Unity Ch	1	NR	NR	NR	-	-
THURSTON	**206**	**23,634**	**27,196**	**72,938**	**28.9**	**100.0**
ANG/EPIS–Anglican NA	2	NR	NR	NR	-	-
ANG/EPIS–Episcopal	3	423	941	1,009	0.4	1.4
Bahá'í	5	NR	217	217	0.1	0.3
BAPT–Amer Bapt Assn	2	NR	235	285	0.1	0.4
BAPT–Amer Bapt USA	2	557	862	1,045	0.4	1.4
BAPT–Consrv Bapt	2	NR	NR	NR	-	-
BAPT–Converge/BGC	4	1,025	NR	1,230	0.5	1.7
BAPT–N Am Bapt Conf	1	NR	84	102	0.0	0.1
BAPT–Reg Bapt Gen As	3	NR	NR	NR	-	-
BAPT–So Bapt Conv	7	475	1,006	1,220	0.5	1.7
BRETH–Ch of Brethren	1	38	73	89	0.0	0.1
BUDD–Mahayana	2	NR	NR	517	0.2	0.7
BUDD–Theravada	1	NR	NR	1,007	0.4	1.4
BUDD–Vajrayana	3	NR	NR	921	0.4	1.3
Calv Chpl	2	NR	NR	NR	-	-
Catholic	8	NR	NR	18,526	7.3	25.4
CGOD–Ch God (Ander)	2	267	NR	267	0.1	0.4
Ch Cr, Scientst	1	NR	NR	NR	-	-
Ch of Nazarene	3	1,262	1,667	3,060	1.2	4.2
Chr & Miss Al	3	100	71	118	0.0	0.2
CHR–Chr Ch (Disc)	2	98	248	301	0.1	0.4
CHR–Chr Chs & Chs Cr	3	NR	481	583	0.2	0.8
CHR–Chs of Christ	5	285	292	389	0.2	0.5
Evan Cov Ch	3	1,118	717	1,454	0.6	2.0
Evan Free Ch	1	150	NR	150	0.1	0.2
FRND–Fr Gen Cf	1	NR	61	74	0.0	0.1
FRND–Indep Yr Mtgs	1	NR	61	74	0.0	0.1
HINDU–Post Ren	1	NR	NR	77	0.0	0.1
Int Cou Comm Ch	1	NR	NR	NR	-	-
Jehovah's Witness	9	NR	NR	NR	-	-
JUD–Conserv	1	18	20	54	0.0	0.1
JUD–Orth	1	43	50	60	0.0	0.1
JUD–Reconst	1	166	212	572	0.2	0.8
LDS–Comm of Christ	1	NR	167	167	0.1	0.2
LDS–L-D Saints	18	NR	NR	10,774	4.3	14.8
LUTH–Ch of Luth Br	1	90	69	147	0.1	0.2
LUTH–E.L.C.A.	6	1,092	2,457	3,254	1.3	4.5
LUTH–Evan Luth Syn	1	45	55	69	0.0	0.1
LUTH–Luth Cong Msn Chr	2	198	581	704	0.3	1.0
LUTH–Luth–MO Synod	2	300	471	584	0.2	0.8
LUTH–Wisc Ev Luth Syn	1	64	99	134	0.1	0.2
METH–Free Methodist	2	223	106	223	0.1	0.3
METH–Un Methodist	7	746	1,983	3,266	1.3	4.5
Muslim Est	2	268	NR	616	0.2	0.8
New Apost Ch	1	NR	NR	NR	-	-
Non-denom Chr Chs	25	6,851	8,905	9,643	3.8	13.2
ORTHE–Ant Orth of NA	1	35	NR	110	0.0	0.2
PENT–Assemb of God	14	2,798	1,134	4,960	2.0	6.8
PENT–Ch God (Cleve)	2	173	301	365	0.1	0.5
PENT–Ch of God Proph	1	NR	23	28	0.0	0.0
PENT–Int Foursq Gos	7	2,397	544	660	0.3	0.9
PENT–Pent Ch of God	1	70	NR	109	0.0	0.1
PENT–Un Pent Ch Intl	2	NR	NR	NR	-	-
PRES–Bible Pres	1	NR	NR	NR	-	-
PRES–Korean Pres Amer	1	NR	NR	NR	-	-
PRES–Orth Pres Ch	1	88	62	97	0.0	0.1
PRES–Presb Ch (USA)	6	727	985	1,194	0.5	1.6
PRES–Presb Ch Amer	1	0	0	0	0.0	0.0
REF–Christian Ref	1	209	167	202	0.1	0.3
Salvation Army	1	42	80	211	0.1	0.3
Sev Day Adv	5	694	1,208	1,388	0.6	1.9
Un C of Christ	2	252	231	280	0.1	0.4
Unit Univ	2	247	270	350	0.1	0.5
Unity Ch	1	NR	NR	NR	-	-

Religious Group	Number of Congrega-tions	Number of Attendees	Number of Communicant, Confirmed, or Full Members	Adherents		
				Number of Adherents	% of Total Pop.	% of Total Adh.
Zoroastrian	0	NR	NR	2	0.0	0.0
WAHKIAKUM	**13**	**418**	**683**	**1,202**	**30.2**	**100.0**
ANG/EPIS–Episcopal	1	19	44	44	1.1	3.7
Bahá'í	0	NR	3	3	0.1	0.2
Catholic	1	NR	NR	90	2.3	7.5
Chr & Miss Al	1	65	71	96	2.4	8.0
Ind Fund Churches	1	NR	NR	NR	-	-
LDS–L-D Saints	1	NR	NR	212	5.3	17.6
LUTH–E.L.C.A.	1	55	120	161	4.0	13.4
LUTH–Luth Cong Msn Chr	1	55	161	186	4.7	15.5
METH–Un Methodist	2	35	75	105	2.6	8.7
Non-denom Chr Chs	1	90	100	112	2.8	9.3
PENT–Assemb of God	1	55	38	111	2.8	9.2
Sev Day Adv	1	26	45	52	1.3	4.3
Un C of Christ	1	18	26	30	0.8	2.5
WALLA WALLA	**75**	**7,798**	**10,846**	**23,768**	**40.4**	**100.0**
ANG/EPIS–Episcopal	1	115	300	509	0.9	2.1
Bahá'í	1	NR	71	71	0.1	0.3
BAPT–Amer Bapt Assn	1	NR	85	103	0.2	0.4
BAPT–Consrv Bapt	1	NR	NR	NR	-	-
BAPT–Reg Bapt Gen As	1	NR	NR	NR	-	-
BAPT–So Bapt Conv	3	120	154	186	0.3	0.8
Catholic	5	NR	NR	6,630	11.3	27.9
CGOD–Ch God (Ander)	1	300	NR	300	0.5	1.3
Ch Cr, Scientst	1	NR	NR	NR	-	-
Ch God (7th Day)	1	NR	NR	NR	-	-
Ch of Nazarene	2	207	200	257	0.4	1.1
Chr & Miss Al	1	75	43	101	0.2	0.4
CHR–Chr Ch (Disc)	2	125	198	239	0.4	1.0
CHR–Chs of Christ	2	110	90	130	0.2	0.5
FRND–Indep Yr Mtgs	1	NR	5	6	0.0	0.0
Jehovah's Witness	1	NR	NR	NR	-	-
JUD–Reform	1	20	35	94	0.2	0.4
LDS–Comm of Christ	1	NR	128	128	0.2	0.5
LDS–L-D Saints	6	NR	NR	2,468	4.2	10.4
LUTH–E.L.C.A.	1	122	300	385	0.7	1.6
LUTH–Luth Cong Msn Chr	1	110	162	196	0.3	0.8
LUTH–Luth–MO Synod	1	43	102	125	0.2	0.5
METH–Free Methodist	1	66	40	66	0.1	0.3
METH–Un Methodist	2	235	618	975	1.7	4.1
Non-denom Chr Chs	9	1,185	1,263	1,492	2.5	6.3
ORTHE–Rus Orth Abroad	1	125	NR	160	0.3	0.7
PENT–Assemb of God	4	320	222	1,027	1.7	4.3
PENT–COGIC	1	0	60	72	0.1	0.3
PENT–Int Foursq Gos	2	142	60	72	0.1	0.3
PENT–Pent Ch of God	2	140	NR	217	0.4	0.9
PENT–Un Pent Ch Intl	1	NR	NR	NR	-	-
PRES–Presb Ch (USA)	4	732	710	857	1.5	3.6
PRES–Presb Ch Amer	1	61	42	43	0.1	0.2
Sev Day Adv	9	3,360	5,844	6,721	11.4	28.3
Un C of Christ	1	85	114	138	0.2	0.6
Unity Ch	1	NR	NR	NR	-	-
WHATCOM	**185**	**23,310**	**28,372**	**58,182**	**28.9**	**100.0**
ANG/EPIS–Anglican NA	1	NR	NR	NR	-	-
ANG/EPIS–Episcopal	2	297	1,126	1,131	0.6	1.9
Bahá'í	3	NR	306	306	0.2	0.5
BAPT–Amer Bapt USA	4	342	400	476	0.2	0.8
BAPT–Converge/BGC	2	150	NR	180	0.1	0.3
BAPT–Reg Bapt Gen As	5	NR	NR	NR	-	-
BAPT–So Bapt Conv	4	266	235	280	0.1	0.5
BUDD–Mahayana	3	NR	NR	1,009	0.5	1.7
BUDD–Vajrayana	2	NR	NR	509	0.3	0.9
Calv Chpl	2	NR	NR	NR	-	-
Catholic	6	NR	NR	13,397	6.7	23.0
CGOD–Ch God (Ander)	2	1,890	NR	1,890	0.9	3.2
Ch Cr, Scientst	1	NR	NR	NR	-	-
Ch of Nazarene	3	107	173	173	0.1	0.3
Chr & Miss Al	3	313	170	513	0.3	0.9
CHR–Chr Ch (Disc)	1	85	255	304	0.2	0.5
CHR–Chs of Christ	3	255	257	317	0.2	0.5

NR–Not Reported - Represents no adherents reported. Percentages may not total 100 due to rounding.

Table 3: Religious Congregations by County and Group: 2010

Religious Group	Number of Congregations	Number of Attendees	Number of Communicant, Confirmed, or Full Members	Adherents: Number of Adherents	Adherents: % of Total Pop.	Adherents: % of Total Adh.
CHR–Int Chs of Christ	1	NR	21	25	0.0	0.0
Evan Cov Ch	2	354	237	461	0.2	0.8
Evan Free Ch	1	135	NR	135	0.1	0.2
FRND–Indep Yr Mtgs	1	NR	38	45	0.0	0.1
HINDU–Post Ren	1	NR	NR	77	0.0	0.1
Ind Fund Churches	3	NR	NR	NR	-	-
Jehovah's Witness	6	NR	NR	NR	-	-
JUD–Orth	1	43	50	60	0.0	0.1
JUD–Reform	1	126	222	599	0.3	1.0
LDS–L-D Saints	10	NR	NR	5,438	2.7	9.3
LUTH–Assoc Free Luth	1	NR	NR	NR	-	-
LUTH–Ch of Luth Br	2	180	68	134	0.1	0.2
LUTH–E.L.C.A.	11	889	2,106	2,639	1.3	4.5
LUTH–Luth-MO Synod	3	494	827	1,055	0.5	1.8
MENN–Menn Br US Conf	4	NR	798	950	0.5	1.6
METH–Free Methodist	1	90	50	90	0.0	0.2
METH–Un Methodist	7	414	877	1,098	0.5	1.9
Muslim Est	1	134	NR	308	0.2	0.5
Non-denom Chr Chs	28	9,730	11,180	12,357	6.1	21.2
ORTHE–Ant Orth of NA	1	110	NR	125	0.1	0.2
ORTHE–Greek Orthodox	1	55	NR	245	0.1	0.4
PENT–Assemb of God	7	1,409	752	2,082	1.0	3.6
PENT–Int Foursq Gos	1	65	52	62	0.0	0.1
PRES–Presb Ch (USA)	6	878	823	980	0.5	1.7
PRES–Presb Ch Amer	1	0	0	0	0.0	0.0
REF–Can Amer Ref	1	NR	NR	NR	-	-
REF–Christian Ref	14	2,566	3,431	4,087	2.0	7.0
REF–Prot Ref Chs	1	74	48	84	0.0	0.1
REF–Ref Ch in Am	3	800	1,346	1,467	0.7	2.5
REF–Un Ref Chs N.A.	2	NR	NR	NR	-	-
Salvation Army	1	66	118	247	0.1	0.4
Sev Day Adv	6	360	625	720	0.4	1.2
Sikh	1	NR	NR	NR	-	-
Un C of Christ	4	442	1,443	1,719	0.9	3.0
Unit Univ	2	191	338	408	0.2	0.7
Unity Ch	1	NR	NR	NR	-	-
WHITMAN	**74**	**4,588**	**5,326**	**13,442**	**30.0**	**100.0**
ANG/EPIS–Episcopal	2	94	129	204	0.5	1.5
Bahá'í	1	NR	58	58	0.1	0.4
BAPT–Amer Bapt USA	3	282	355	402	0.9	3.0
BAPT–N Am Bapt Conf	1	NR	208	235	0.5	1.7
BAPT–So Bapt Conv	4	644	570	645	1.4	4.8
BUDD–Mahayana	1	NR	NR	102	0.2	0.8
Calv Chpl	1	NR	NR	NR	-	-
Catholic	9	NR	NR	3,628	8.1	27.0
Ch of Nazarene	3	100	102	133	0.3	1.0
CHR–Chr Ch (Disc)	1	8	18	20	0.0	0.1
CHR–Chr Chs & Chs Cr	1	NR	150	170	0.4	1.3
CHR–Chs of Christ	1	65	55	80	0.2	0.6
CONG–Consrv Cong Chr	1	30	30	34	0.1	0.3
Evan Free Ch	2	380	NR	380	0.8	2.8
FRND–Indep Yr Mtgs	1	NR	14	16	0.0	0.1
Ind Fund Churches	2	NR	NR	NR	-	-
Jehovah's Witness	1	NR	NR	NR	-	-
LDS–Comm of Christ	1	NR	128	128	0.3	1.0
LDS–L-D Saints	5	NR	NR	1,792	4.0	13.3
LUTH–E.L.C.A.	3	208	365	661	1.5	4.9
LUTH–Luth Cong Msn Chr	1	25	142	161	0.4	1.2
LUTH–Luth-MO Synod	1	195	217	242	0.5	1.8
LUTH–Wisc Ev Luth Syn	1	15	17	17	0.0	0.1
METH–Un Methodist	6	275	576	809	1.8	6.0
Muslim Est	1	134	NR	308	0.7	2.3
Non-denom Chr Chs	7	1,265	1,220	1,583	3.5	11.8
PENT–Assemb of God	5	501	208	766	1.7	5.7
PENT–Int Foursq Gos	1	73	132	149	0.3	1.1
PRES–Presb Ch (USA)	1	57	93	105	0.2	0.8
Sev Day Adv	3	94	162	187	0.4	1.4
Un C of Christ	3	143	377	427	1.0	3.2
YAKIMA	**278**	**21,195**	**27,461**	**108,196**	**44.5**	**100.0**
ANG/EPIS–Anglican NA	1	NR	NR	NR	-	-
ANG/EPIS–Episcopal	4	202	268	681	0.3	0.6
Bahá'í	3	NR	213	213	0.1	0.2
BAPT–Amer Bapt USA	5	367	440	577	0.2	0.5
BAPT–Consrv Bapt	4	NR	NR	NR	-	-
BAPT–Reg Bapt Gen As	1	NR	NR	NR	-	-
BAPT–S-D Baptist Gen Con	1	22	29	38	0.0	0.0
BAPT–So Bapt Conv	9	512	1,168	1,533	0.6	1.4
BRETH–Ch of Brethren	1	12	4	5	0.0	0.0
BRETH–Grace Breth	7	NR	NR	NR	-	-
BUDD–Mahayana	1	NR	NR	1,250	0.5	1.2
Calv Chpl	2	NR	NR	NR	-	-
Catholic	16	NR	NR	59,500	24.5	55.0
CGOD–Ch God (Ander)	4	105	NR	105	0.0	0.1
Ch Cr, Scientst	2	NR	NR	NR	-	-
Ch of Nazarene	12	1,594	2,345	2,810	1.2	2.6
Chr & Miss Al	2	217	152	285	0.1	0.3
CHR–Chr Ch (Disc)	4	120	290	381	0.2	0.4
CHR–Chr Chs & Chs Cr	2	NR	120	157	0.1	0.1
CHR–Chs of Christ	9	603	599	736	0.3	0.7
Evan Ch	1	NR	NR	NR	-	-
Evan Cov Ch	2	366	372	476	0.2	0.4
FRND–Indep Yr Mtgs	1	NR	0	0	0.0	0.0
Ind Fund Churches	2	NR	NR	NR	-	-
Jehovah's Witness	7	NR	NR	NR	-	-
JUD–Reform	1	29	51	138	0.1	0.1
LDS–Comm of Christ	2	NR	334	334	0.1	0.3
LDS–L-D Saints	17	NR	NR	8,243	3.4	7.6
LUTH–E.L.C.A.	7	509	1,452	1,823	0.7	1.7
LUTH–Luth-MO Synod	4	389	742	897	0.4	0.8
LUTH–Wisc Ev Luth Syn	3	230	364	445	0.2	0.4
METH–AME	1	0	150	197	0.1	0.2
METH–Free Methodist	2	81	62	81	0.0	0.1
METH–Un Methodist	8	403	1,451	2,219	0.9	2.1
METH–Wesleyan	1	66	63	86	0.0	0.1
Metro Comm Ch	1	9	20	26	0.0	0.0
Missionary Ch	2	149	99	159	0.1	0.1
Muslim Est	1	134	NR	308	0.1	0.3
Non-denom Chr Chs	23	3,799	4,529	5,300	2.2	4.9
ORTHE–Ant Orth of NA	1	175	NR	250	0.1	0.2
PENT–Apos Faith Msn	1	NR	35	46	0.0	0.0
PENT–Assemb of God	15	2,466	1,239	4,282	1.8	4.0
PENT–Ch God (Cleve)	6	823	989	1,298	0.5	1.2
PENT–Ch of God Proph	2	NR	81	106	0.0	0.1
PENT–COGIC	1	0	0	0	0.0	0.0
PENT–Int Foursq Gos	12	2,271	2,212	2,903	1.2	2.7
PENT–Intl Pent Holiness	14	988	591	776	0.3	0.7
PENT–Open Bible Std	1	275	NR	275	0.1	0.3
PENT–Pent Ch of God	4	280	NR	435	0.2	0.4
PENT–Un Pent Ch Intl	5	NR	NR	NR	-	-
PENT–Vineyard	1	237	350	459	0.2	0.4
PRES–Kor Pres Abroad	1	NR	NR	NR	-	-
PRES–Korean Pres Amer	1	NR	NR	NR	-	-
PRES–Presb Ch (USA)	9	1,268	2,112	2,772	1.1	2.6
REF–Christian Ref	5	491	1,075	1,411	0.6	1.3
REF–Ref Ch in Am	1	109	197	236	0.1	0.2
REF–Un Ref Chs N.A.	1	NR	NR	NR	-	-
Salvation Army	2	86	202	399	0.2	0.4
Sev Day Adv	16	1,669	2,903	3,338	1.4	3.1
Un C of Christ	1	70	66	87	0.0	0.1
Unit Univ	1	69	92	120	0.0	0.1
Unity Ch	1	NR	NR	NR	-	-
WEST VIRGINIA	**4,413**	**240,457**	**428,729**	**658,313**	**35.5**	**100.0**
BARBOUR	**65**	**2,074**	**3,131**	**4,534**	**27.3**	**100.0**
BAPT–Amer Bapt USA	4	177	403	482	2.9	10.6
BAPT–So Bapt Conv	2	98	182	218	1.3	4.8
BRETH–Ch of Brethren	3	42	156	187	1.1	4.1
Catholic	2	NR	NR	203	1.2	4.5
Ch of Nazarene	3	125	167	304	1.8	6.7
Chr & Miss Al	1	75	37	126	0.8	2.8
CHR–Chs of Christ	6	310	329	381	2.3	8.4
Jehovah's Witness	1	NR	NR	NR	-	-

NR–Not Reported - Represents no adherents reported. Percentages may not total 100 due to rounding.

Table 3: Religious Congregations by County and Group: 2010

Religious Group	Number of Congrega-tions	Number of Attendees	Number of Communicant, Confirmed, or Full Members	Adherents: Number of Adherents	Adherents: % of Total Pop.	Adherents: % of Total Adh.
LDS–L-D Saints	1	NR	NR	225	1.4	5.0
MENN–Mennonite USA	2	46	61	73	0.4	1.6
METH–A.W.M.C.	1	4	4	4	0.0	0.1
METH–Un Methodist	29	621	1,221	1,490	9.0	32.9
Non-denom Chr Chs	4	390	495	533	3.2	11.8
PENT–Ch God (Cleve)	1	15	32	38	0.2	0.8
PENT–Pent Ch of God	2	140	NR	217	1.3	4.8
PENT–Un Pent Ch Intl	1	NR	NR	NR	-	-
PRES–Presb Ch (USA)	2	31	44	53	0.3	1.2
BERKELEY	**118**	**9,789**	**18,667**	**32,298**	**31.0**	**100.0**
ANG/EPIS–Episcopal	2	128	238	340	0.3	1.1
Bahá'í	1	NR	15	15	0.0	0.0
BAPT–Amer Bapt Assn	3	NR	770	959	0.9	3.0
BAPT–Free Will Bapt	2	NR	86	107	0.1	0.3
BAPT–Prog NBC	1	0	350	436	0.4	1.3
BAPT–So Bapt Conv	11	1,567	2,867	3,570	3.4	11.1
BRETH–Breth in Chr	1	NR	NR	NR	-	-
BRETH–Ch of Brethren	5	197	794	989	0.9	3.1
BRETH–Grace Breth	1	NR	NR	NR	-	-
Catholic	3	NR	NR	7,008	6.7	21.7
CGOD–Ch God (Ander)	2	65	NR	65	0.1	0.2
Ch of Nazarene	1	65	48	65	0.1	0.2
Chr & Miss Al	1	181	81	181	0.2	0.6
CHR–Chr Ch (Disc)	1	83	425	529	0.5	1.6
CHR–Chr Chs & Chs Cr	5	NR	475	591	0.6	1.8
CHR–Chs of Christ	1	150	105	130	0.1	0.4
Jehovah's Witness	1	NR	NR	NR	-	-
LDS–Comm of Christ	1	NR	137	137	0.1	0.4
LDS–L-D Saints	3	NR	NR	1,736	1.7	5.4
LUTH–E.L.C.A.	2	265	1,151	1,585	1.5	4.9
METH–Un Methodist	27	2,258	6,068	6,686	6.4	20.7
METH–Wesleyan	1	44	43	57	0.1	0.2
New Apost Ch	1	NR	NR	NR	-	-
Non-denom Chr Chs	14	2,589	2,580	3,238	3.1	10.0
PENT–Assemb of God	5	819	518	1,253	1.2	3.9
PENT–Assm God Intl F	1	NR	NR	NR	-	-
PENT–Ch God (Cleve)	2	251	259	322	0.3	1.0
PENT–Ch of God Proph	1	NR	14	17	0.0	0.1
PENT–Int Foursq Gos	1	33	58	72	0.1	0.2
PENT–Int Pent C Chr	1	30	4	80	0.1	0.2
PENT–Pent Ch of God	1	70	NR	109	0.1	0.3
PENT–Un Pent Ch Intl	1	NR	NR	NR	-	-
PRES–Presb Ch (USA)	9	503	776	966	0.9	3.0
PRES–Presb Ch Amer	1	100	124	153	0.1	0.5
Salvation Army	1	62	109	235	0.2	0.7
Sev Day Adv	2	272	474	545	0.5	1.7
Un C of Christ	1	57	98	122	0.1	0.4
BOONE	**68**	**2,805**	**4,298**	**5,759**	**23.4**	**100.0**
Bahá'í	0	NR	2	2	0.0	0.0
BAPT–Amer Bapt USA	4	288	931	1,131	4.6	19.6
BAPT–Free Will Bapt	1	NR	43	52	0.2	0.9
BAPT–Natl Mis Bapt Conv	2	0	300	365	1.5	6.3
BAPT–So Bapt Conv	3	59	252	306	1.2	5.3
Catholic	2	NR	NR	132	0.5	2.3
CGOD–Ch God (Ander)	1	20	NR	20	0.1	0.3
Ch of Nazarene	3	80	115	176	0.7	3.1
CHR–Chs of Christ	18	838	819	987	4.0	17.1
Jehovah's Witness	2	NR	NR	NR	-	-
METH–AME	1	0	100	122	0.5	2.1
METH–Un Methodist	9	402	660	784	3.2	13.6
METH–Wesleyan	2	28	15	37	0.2	0.6
Muslim Est	1	134	NR	308	1.3	5.3
Non-denom Chr Chs	4	640	640	801	3.3	13.9
PENT–Assemb of God	2	37	18	46	0.2	0.8
PENT–Ch God (Cleve)	7	250	313	380	1.5	6.6
PENT–Ch of God Proph	2	NR	26	32	0.1	0.6
PRES–Presb Ch (USA)	4	29	64	78	0.3	1.4
BRAXTON	**55**	**2,085**	**3,222**	**4,380**	**30.2**	**100.0**
Bahá'í	0	NR	1	1	0.0	0.0
BAPT–Amer Bapt USA	9	1,137	1,879	2,229	15.3	50.9
BAPT–So Bapt Conv	3	84	194	230	1.6	5.3
Catholic	1	NR	NR	143	1.0	3.3
Chr & Miss Al	1	11	11	17	0.1	0.4
CHR–Chs of Christ	1	55	42	53	0.4	1.2
Jehovah's Witness	1	NR	NR	NR	-	-
LDS–L-D Saints	1	NR	NR	276	1.9	6.3
METH–Un Methodist	32	576	890	1,089	7.5	24.9
Non-denom Chr Chs	1	50	60	62	0.4	1.4
PENT–Ch God (Cleve)	2	62	71	84	0.6	1.9
PENT–Pent Ch of God	1	70	NR	109	0.8	2.5
PRES–Presb Ch (USA)	1	28	52	62	0.4	1.4
Sev Day Adv	1	12	22	25	0.2	0.6
BROOKE	**46**	**2,094**	**4,821**	**8,578**	**35.6**	**100.0**
ANG/EPIS–Episcopal	3	90	140	173	0.7	2.0
Bahá'í	0	NR	1	1	0.0	0.0
BAPT–Amer Bapt USA	1	110	186	217	0.9	2.5
BAPT–So Bapt Conv	5	295	533	621	2.6	7.2
Catholic	3	NR	NR	2,940	12.2	34.3
CGOD–Ch God (Ander)	2	90	NR	90	0.4	1.0
CGOD–Ches God-Gen Con	1	45	44	51	0.2	0.6
Ch of Nazarene	6	461	926	1,025	4.3	11.9
CHR–Chr Ch (Disc)	3	100	549	640	2.7	7.5
CHR–Chr Chs & Chs Cr	3	NR	430	501	2.1	5.8
CHR–Chs of Christ	2	93	91	106	0.4	1.2
LDS–Comm of Christ	2	NR	236	236	1.0	2.8
METH–AME	1	20	30	35	0.1	0.4
METH–Free Methodist	1	192	277	277	1.2	3.2
METH–Un Methodist	6	323	980	1,142	4.7	13.3
PENT–Assemb of God	1	60	35	100	0.4	1.2
PENT–Ch God (Cleve)	1	97	126	147	0.6	1.7
PENT–I F Chr Assmbl	1	NR	NR	NR	-	-
PENT–Un Pent Ch Intl	1	NR	NR	NR	-	-
PRES–Presb Ch (USA)	3	118	237	276	1.1	3.2
CABELL	**156**	**15,181**	**28,046**	**37,771**	**39.2**	**100.0**
ANG/EPIS–Anglican NA	1	NR	NR	NR	-	-
ANG/EPIS–Episcopal	3	283	755	755	0.8	2.0
Bahá'í	0	NR	30	30	0.0	0.1
BAPT–Amer Bapt USA	16	2,613	6,326	7,475	7.8	19.8
BAPT–Free Will Bapt	8	NR	344	406	0.4	1.1
BAPT–NBC USA	1	0	0	0	0.0	0.0
BAPT–Prog NBC	1	180	150	177	0.2	0.5
BAPT–Ref Bapt Ch	1	NR	NR	NR	-	-
BAPT–So Bapt Conv	5	526	816	964	1.0	2.6
BUDD–Mahayana	1	NR	NR	11	0.0	0.0
Catholic	5	NR	NR	3,052	3.2	8.1
CGOD–Ch God (Ander)	1	176	NR	176	0.2	0.5
Ch Cr, Scientst	1	NR	NR	NR	-	-
Ch of Nazarene	3	356	345	619	0.6	1.6
Chr & Miss Al	1	60	0	60	0.1	0.2
CHR–Chr Ch (Disc)	2	215	572	676	0.7	1.8
CHR–Chr Chs & Chs Cr	6	NR	796	941	1.0	2.5
CHR–Chs of Christ	7	743	740	860	0.9	2.3
Jehovah's Witness	3	NR	NR	NR	-	-
JUD–Conserv	0	51	57	154	0.2	0.4
JUD–Reform	0	32	57	154	0.2	0.4
LDS–L-D Saints	3	NR	NR	1,347	1.4	3.6
LUTH–E.L.C.A.	2	156	935	948	1.0	2.5
LUTH–Luth-MO Synod	1	0	66	84	0.1	0.2
METH–AME	1	80	201	238	0.2	0.6
METH–Free Methodist	3	60	72	79	0.1	0.2
METH–Un Methodist	28	2,337	5,419	6,872	7.1	18.2
METH–Wesleyan	2	141	99	183	0.2	0.5
Muslim Est	1	40	NR	60	0.1	0.2
Non-denom Chr Chs	20	5,655	8,255	8,565	8.9	22.7
ORTHE–Ant Orth of NA	1	65	NR	150	0.2	0.4
ORTHE–Greek Orthodox	1	65	NR	105	0.1	0.3
PENT–Assemb of God	1	104	77	240	0.2	0.6
PENT–Ch God (Cleve)	2	244	134	158	0.2	0.4
PENT–Ch of God Proph	2	NR	57	67	0.1	0.2
PENT–Intl Pent Holiness	1	10	56	66	0.1	0.2
PENT–Pent Ch of God	1	70	NR	109	0.1	0.3

NR–Not Reported   - Represents no adherents reported.   Percentages may not total 100 due to rounding.

Table 3: Religious Congregations by County and Group: 2010

Religious Group	Number of Congrega-tions	Number of Attendees	Number of Communicant, Confirmed, or Full Members	Adherents: Number of Adherents	Adherents: % of Total Pop.	Adherents: % of Total Adh.
PENT–Un Pent Ch Intl	4	NR	NR	NR	-	-
PENT–United Holy Ch	1	NR	NR	NR	-	-
PRES–Orth Pres Ch	1	0	0	0	0.0	0.0
PRES–Presb Ch (USA)	8	709	1,323	1,563	1.6	4.1
PRES–Presb Ch Amer	1	75	63	79	0.1	0.2
Sev Day Adv	2	84	146	168	0.2	0.4
Un C of Christ	1	51	140	165	0.2	0.4
Unit Univ	1	0	15	15	0.0	0.0
Unity Ch	1	NR	NR	NR	-	-
CALHOUN	**23**	**845**	**1,518**	**1,798**	**23.6**	**100.0**
Bahá'í	0	NR	5	5	0.1	0.3
BAPT–Amer Bapt USA	5	218	536	630	8.3	35.0
BAPT–So Bapt Conv	3	97	308	362	4.7	20.1
CHR–Chs of Christ	1	20	19	24	0.3	1.3
METH–Un Methodist	12	320	440	539	7.1	30.0
Non-denom Chr Chs	2	190	210	238	3.1	13.2
CLAY	**31**	**1,053**	**2,066**	**2,576**	**27.4**	**100.0**
Bahá'í	0	NR	2	2	0.0	0.1
BAPT–Amer Bapt USA	9	423	875	1,069	11.4	41.5
BAPT–Free Will Bapt	2	NR	86	105	1.1	4.1
BAPT–Natl Mis Bapt Conv	3	150	505	617	6.6	24.0
BAPT–So Bapt Conv	1	45	69	84	0.9	3.3
Catholic	1	NR	NR	66	0.7	2.6
Ch of Nazarene	1	43	75	91	1.0	3.5
METH–Un Methodist	9	55	109	121	1.3	4.7
Non-denom Chr Chs	4	337	345	421	4.5	16.3
PENT–United Holy Ch	1	NR	NR	NR	-	-
DODDRIDGE	**27**	**990**	**1,792**	**2,167**	**26.4**	**100.0**
Bahá'í	0	NR	1	1	0.0	0.0
BAPT–Amer Bapt USA	5	210	475	555	6.8	25.6
BAPT–S-D Baptist Gen Con	1	15	23	27	0.3	1.2
BAPT–So Bapt Conv	3	263	367	429	5.2	19.8
Catholic	1	NR	NR	40	0.5	1.8
CHR–Chr Chs & Chs Cr	2	NR	225	263	3.2	12.1
CHR–Chs of Christ	1	30	35	40	0.5	1.8
LUTH–E.L.C.A.	1	22	101	144	1.8	6.6
METH–A.W.M.C.	1	19	10	21	0.3	1.0
METH–Un Methodist	9	281	410	464	5.7	21.4
Non-denom Chr Chs	1	60	60	75	0.9	3.5
PENT–Assemb of God	1	55	49	66	0.8	3.0
PENT–Ch God (Cleve)	1	35	36	42	0.5	1.9
FAYETTE	**136**	**5,964**	**10,901**	**15,085**	**32.8**	**100.0**
ANG/EPIS–Episcopal	3	59	182	172	0.4	1.1
Bahá'í	0	NR	22	22	0.0	0.1
BAPT–Amer Bapt USA	24	1,909	4,078	4,846	10.5	32.1
BAPT–Free Will Bapt	6	NR	258	307	0.7	2.0
BAPT–NBC USA	1	45	45	53	0.1	0.4
BAPT–Reg Bapt Gen As	1	NR	NR	NR	-	-
BAPT–So Bapt Conv	7	426	1,075	1,278	2.8	8.5
BRETH–Brethren (Ash)	1	NR	80	95	0.2	0.6
BRETH–Ch of Brethren	1	46	47	56	0.1	0.4
Catholic	3	NR	NR	1,593	3.5	10.6
CGOD–Ch God (Ander)	8	428	NR	428	0.9	2.8
CGOD–Ches God-Gen Con	1	45	57	68	0.1	0.5
Ch of Nazarene	1	177	304	430	0.9	2.9
Chr & Miss Al	1	27	23	64	0.1	0.4
CHR–Chr Ch (Disc)	1	0	0	0	0.0	0.0
CHR–Chr Chs & Chs Cr	2	NR	130	154	0.3	1.0
CHR–Chs of Christ	5	162	115	152	0.3	1.0
Jehovah's Witness	2	NR	NR	NR	-	-
METH–Un Methodist	30	855	1,671	1,975	4.3	13.1
METH–Wesleyan	2	70	44	91	0.2	0.6
Non-denom Chr Chs	9	850	1,040	1,162	2.5	7.7
PENT–Assemb of God	4	145	113	218	0.5	1.4
PENT–Ch God (Cleve)	6	431	1,006	1,196	2.6	7.9
PENT–Ch of God Proph	1	NR	7	8	0.0	0.1
PENT–COGIC	1	0	150	178	0.4	1.2
PENT–Intl Pent Holiness	2	131	166	197	0.4	1.3
PENT–Orig Ch of God	1	NR	NR	NR	-	-
PENT–Un Pent Ch Intl	4	NR	NR	NR	-	-
PRES–Presb Ch (USA)	8	158	288	342	0.7	2.3
GILMER	**33**	**894**	**1,990**	**2,397**	**27.6**	**100.0**
ANG/EPIS–Episcopal	1	4	7	13	0.1	0.5
BAPT–Amer Bapt USA	7	486	1,297	1,460	16.8	60.9
BAPT–So Bapt Conv	1	60	63	71	0.8	3.0
BRETH–Ch of Brethren	1	0	5	6	0.1	0.3
Catholic	1	NR	NR	97	1.1	4.0
Chr & Miss Al	1	20	0	30	0.3	1.3
CHR–Chs of Christ	3	93	101	114	1.3	4.8
Jehovah's Witness	1	NR	NR	NR	-	-
METH–Un Methodist	13	151	328	404	4.6	16.9
Non-denom Chr Chs	1	70	100	100	1.2	4.2
PENT–Ch of God Proph	1	NR	44	50	0.6	2.1
PRES–Presb Ch (USA)	1	0	28	32	0.4	1.3
Sev Day Adv	1	10	17	20	0.2	0.8
GRANT	**44**	**2,312**	**3,606**	**5,173**	**43.3**	**100.0**
BAPT–Amer Bapt USA	6	350	747	893	7.5	17.3
BAPT–So Bapt Conv	2	65	123	147	1.2	2.8
BRETH–Ch of Brethren	9	596	867	1,036	8.7	20.0
Catholic	1	NR	NR	158	1.3	3.1
CHR–Chs of Christ	1	20	20	25	0.2	0.5
LDS–L-D Saints	1	NR	NR	425	3.6	8.2
LUTH–E.L.C.A.	1	52	79	87	0.7	1.7
METH–Un Methodist	13	436	931	1,111	9.3	21.5
Non-denom Chr Chs	1	100	150	150	1.3	2.9
PENT–Assemb of God	4	391	156	504	4.2	9.7
PENT–Ch God (Cleve)	3	224	336	402	3.4	7.8
PRES–Presb Ch (USA)	2	78	197	235	2.0	4.5
GREENBRIER	**123**	**5,990**	**10,950**	**14,628**	**41.2**	**100.0**
ANG/EPIS–Episcopal	3	119	264	302	0.9	2.1
Bahá'í	0	NR	7	7	0.0	0.0
BAPT–Amer Bapt USA	16	867	2,443	2,883	8.1	19.7
BAPT–Free Will Bapt	2	NR	86	101	0.3	0.7
BAPT–NBC USA	1	70	133	157	0.4	1.1
BAPT–So Bapt Conv	3	237	432	510	1.4	3.5
Catholic	4	NR	NR	776	2.2	5.3
CGOD–Ch God (Ander)	4	193	NR	193	0.5	1.3
Ch of Nazarene	2	100	141	150	0.4	1.0
CHR–Chr Chs & Chs Cr	1	NR	0	0	0.0	0.0
CHR–Chs of Christ	3	142	143	175	0.5	1.2
Jehovah's Witness	2	NR	NR	NR	-	-
LDS–L-D Saints	1	NR	NR	451	1.3	3.1
MENN–Unaffil Amish-Menn	1	13	10	13	0.0	0.1
METH–Un Methodist	36	1,383	3,042	3,944	11.1	27.0
Non-denom Chr Chs	9	1,393	1,880	2,007	5.7	13.7
PENT–Assemb of God	3	39	31	50	0.1	0.3
PENT–Ch God (Cleve)	8	531	692	817	2.3	5.6
PENT–COGIC	1	0	150	177	0.5	1.2
PENT–Int Pent C Chr	1	18	9	20	0.1	0.1
PENT–Intl Pent Holiness	7	263	345	407	1.1	2.8
PENT–Open Bible Std	1	35	NR	35	0.1	0.2
PENT–Pent Ch of God	1	70	NR	109	0.3	0.7
PRES–As Ref Pres Ch	1	NR	39	46	0.1	0.3
PRES–Presb Ch (USA)	10	462	1,007	1,188	3.3	8.1
Sev Day Adv	2	55	96	110	0.3	0.8
HAMPSHIRE	**67**	**2,480**	**4,732**	**7,078**	**29.5**	**100.0**
ANG/EPIS–Episcopal	1	17	34	37	0.2	0.5
Bahá'í	0	NR	1	1	0.0	0.0
BAPT–Amer Bapt USA	3	179	301	361	1.5	5.1
BAPT–So Bapt Conv	3	194	257	308	1.3	4.4
BRETH–Ch of Brethren	5	253	622	746	3.1	10.5
BUDD–Theravada	1	NR	NR	300	1.3	4.2
Catholic	1	NR	NR	496	2.1	7.0
CGOD–Ch God (Ander)	1	17	NR	17	0.1	0.2
Ch of Nazarene	1	35	27	35	0.1	0.5
Chr & Miss Al	1	NR	NR	NR	-	-

NR–Not Reported - Represents no adherents reported. Percentages may not total 100 due to rounding.

Table 3: Religious Congregations by County and Group: 2010

Religious Group	Number of Congrega-tions	Number of Attendees	Number of Communicant, Confirmed, or Full Members	Adherents		
				Number of Adherents	% of Total Pop.	% of Total Adh.
CHR–Chr Chs & Chs Cr	6	NR	752	902	3.8	12.7
CHR–Chs of Christ	1	42	37	45	0.2	0.6
Jehovah's Witness	1	NR	NR	NR	-	-
LDS–L-D Saints	1	NR	NR	256	1.1	3.6
MENN–Beachy Amish-Menn	1	79	36	79	0.3	1.1
METH–Un Methodist	20	558	1,396	1,589	6.6	22.4
Non-denom Chr Chs	4	265	300	331	1.4	4.7
PENT–Assemb of God	7	626	394	887	3.7	12.5
PENT–Ch God (Cleve)	1	25	144	173	0.7	2.4
PENT–Int Foursq Gos	1	26	30	36	0.2	0.5
PENT–Un Pent Ch Intl	1	NR	NR	NR	-	-
PRES–Presb Ch (USA)	4	144	206	247	1.0	3.5
Sev Day Adv	1	20	36	41	0.2	0.6
Un C of Christ	1	0	159	191	0.8	2.7
HANCOCK	**59**	**3,280**	**6,853**	**16,630**	**54.2**	**100.0**
Bahá'í	0	NR	1	1	0.0	0.0
BAPT–Amer Bapt USA	2	225	802	947	3.1	5.7
BAPT–So Bapt Conv	3	74	222	262	0.9	1.6
Catholic	6	NR	NR	7,780	25.4	46.8
Ch of Nazarene	5	467	843	850	2.8	5.1
Chr & Miss Al	1	40	44	72	0.2	0.4
CHR–Chr Ch (Disc)	1	72	240	283	0.9	1.7
CHR–Chr Chs & Chs Cr	4	NR	615	726	2.4	4.4
CHR–Chs of Christ	4	675	775	932	3.0	5.6
Jehovah's Witness	1	NR	NR	NR	-	-
LUTH–E.L.C.A.	2	63	222	283	0.9	1.7
METH–AME	1	0	100	118	0.4	0.7
METH–Free Methodist	2	102	66	102	0.3	0.6
METH–Un Methodist	7	383	1,104	1,446	4.7	8.7
METH–Wesleyan	1	83	93	108	0.4	0.6
Non-denom Chr Chs	3	295	475	519	1.7	3.1
ORTHE–Greek Orthodox	1	100	NR	500	1.6	3.0
ORTHE–Orth Ch in Amer	1	35	NR	63	0.2	0.4
PENT–Assemb of God	1	229	224	330	1.1	2.0
PENT–Ch God (Cleve)	2	72	194	229	0.7	1.4
PENT–Un Pent Ch Intl	1	NR	NR	NR	-	-
PRES–As Ref Pres Ch	1	NR	0	0	0.0	0.0
PRES–Presb Ch (USA)	7	279	677	799	2.6	4.8
Salvation Army	1	64	117	229	0.7	1.4
Sev Day Adv	1	22	39	45	0.1	0.3
Zoroastrian	0	NR	NR	6	0.0	0.0
HARDY	**58**	**2,403**	**4,677**	**6,001**	**42.8**	**100.0**
ANG/EPIS–Episcopal	1	22	32	32	0.2	0.5
BAPT–So Bapt Conv	3	128	291	348	2.5	5.8
BRETH–Brethren (Ash)	1	NR	80	96	0.7	1.6
BRETH–Ch of Brethren	10	260	1,409	1,684	12.0	28.1
Catholic	1	NR	NR	153	1.1	2.5
CHR–Chr Chs & Chs Cr	1	NR	65	78	0.6	1.3
CHR–Chs of Christ	1	67	56	75	0.5	1.2
Jehovah's Witness	3	NR	NR	NR	-	-
LUTH–E.L.C.A.	6	111	297	405	2.9	6.7
MENN–Mennonite USA	1	14	15	18	0.1	0.3
METH–Un Methodist	15	636	1,130	1,325	9.4	22.1
Non-denom Chr Chs	5	525	580	690	4.9	11.5
PENT–Assemb of God	4	346	218	497	3.5	8.3
PENT–Ch God (Cleve)	1	126	132	158	1.1	2.6
PENT–Un Pent Ch Intl	1	NR	NR	NR	-	-
PRES–Presb Ch (USA)	3	141	325	388	2.8	6.5
Sev Day Adv	1	27	47	54	0.4	0.9
HARRISON	**158**	**10,909**	**19,113**	**34,866**	**50.5**	**100.0**
ANG/EPIS–Episcopal	2	71	142	144	0.2	0.4
Bahá'í	0	NR	4	4	0.0	0.0
BAPT–Amer Bapt USA	28	2,139	5,016	6,015	8.7	17.3
BAPT–Free Will Bapt	1	NR	43	52	0.1	0.1
BAPT–NBC USA	1	0	60	72	0.1	0.2
BAPT–Reg Bapt Gen As	1	NR	NR	NR	-	-
BAPT–S-D Baptist Gen Con	2	103	215	258	0.4	0.7
BAPT–So Bapt Conv	4	252	663	795	1.2	2.3
Catholic	7	NR	NR	8,647	12.5	24.8
CGOD–Ch God (Ander)	2	70	NR	70	0.1	0.2

Religious Group	Number of Congrega-tions	Number of Attendees	Number of Communicant, Confirmed, or Full Members	Adherents		
				Number of Adherents	% of Total Pop.	% of Total Adh.
Ch Cr, Scientst	1	NR	NR	NR	-	-
Ch of Nazarene	2	120	119	272	0.4	0.8
Chr & Miss Al	1	36	30	59	0.1	0.2
CHR–Chr Ch (Disc)	3	72	163	195	0.3	0.6
CHR–Chs of Christ	8	477	459	580	0.8	1.7
Jehovah's Witness	1	NR	NR	NR	-	-
LDS–L-D Saints	1	NR	NR	757	1.1	2.2
LUTH–E.L.C.A.	1	112	296	340	0.5	1.0
METH–A.W.M.C.	1	62	15	97	0.1	0.3
METH–AME	1	0	100	120	0.2	0.3
METH–Free Methodist	2	63	72	75	0.1	0.2
METH–Un Methodist	55	2,797	6,734	9,194	13.3	26.4
Muslim Est	1	134	NR	308	0.4	0.9
Non-denom Chr Chs	16	3,465	3,545	4,440	6.4	12.7
ORTHE–Greek Orthodox	1	25	NR	110	0.2	0.3
PENT–Assemb of God	3	438	340	724	1.0	2.1
PENT–Ch God (Cleve)	3	131	468	561	0.8	1.6
PENT–I F Chr Assmbl	1	NR	NR	NR	-	-
PENT–Pent Ch of God	1	70	NR	109	0.2	0.3
PENT–Un Pent Ch Intl	1	NR	NR	NR	-	-
PRES–Presb Ch (USA)	4	172	462	554	0.8	1.6
Salvation Army	1	56	90	225	0.3	0.6
Sev Day Adv	1	44	77	89	0.1	0.3
JACKSON	**62**	**4,214**	**6,924**	**8,966**	**30.7**	**100.0**
ANG/EPIS–Episcopal	2	35	58	58	0.2	0.6
Bahá'í	0	NR	5	5	0.0	0.1
BAPT–Amer Bapt USA	9	805	1,531	1,843	6.3	20.6
BAPT–Free Will Bapt	1	NR	43	52	0.2	0.6
BAPT–So Bapt Conv	2	187	441	531	1.8	5.9
Catholic	1	NR	NR	267	0.9	3.0
CGOD–Ch God (Ander)	1	30	NR	30	0.1	0.3
Ch of Nazarene	2	173	237	378	1.3	4.2
CHR–Chr Ch (Disc)	1	0	0	0	0.0	0.0
CHR–Chr Chs & Chs Cr	1	NR	150	181	0.6	2.0
CHR–Chs of Christ	6	345	321	405	1.4	4.5
Jehovah's Witness	1	NR	NR	NR	-	-
LDS–L-D Saints	1	NR	NR	247	0.8	2.8
LUTH–E.L.C.A.	1	12	19	19	0.1	0.2
METH–Un Methodist	20	940	2,023	2,566	8.8	28.6
Non-denom Chr Chs	6	1,385	1,799	2,014	6.9	22.5
PENT–Assemb of God	1	25	18	35	0.1	0.4
PENT–Ch God (Cleve)	2	206	163	196	0.7	2.2
PENT–Un Pent Ch Intl	1	NR	NR	NR	-	-
PRES–Presb Ch (USA)	2	57	91	110	0.4	1.2
Sev Day Adv	1	14	25	29	0.1	0.3
JEFFERSON	**73**	**5,214**	**9,295**	**17,554**	**32.8**	**100.0**
ANG/EPIS–Episcopal	7	362	940	1,059	2.0	6.0
Bahá'í	1	NR	29	29	0.1	0.2
BAPT–Amer Bapt Assn	1	NR	85	104	0.2	0.6
BAPT–Amer Bapt USA	1	60	120	147	0.3	0.8
BAPT–Free Will Bapt	1	NR	43	53	0.1	0.3
BAPT–Reg Bapt Gen As	1	NR	NR	NR	-	-
BAPT–So Bapt Conv	8	1,183	1,906	2,340	4.4	13.3
Catholic	2	NR	NR	4,679	8.7	26.7
Ch Cr, Scientst	1	NR	NR	NR	-	-
CHR–Chr Chs & Chs Cr	1	NR	50	61	0.1	0.3
CHR–Chs of Christ	1	65	54	87	0.2	0.5
FRND–Fr Gen Cf & Un Mtg	1	NR	0	0	0.0	0.0
Jehovah's Witness	1	NR	NR	NR	-	-
LDS–L-D Saints	2	NR	NR	700	1.3	4.0
LUTH–E.L.C.A.	4	212	527	1,156	2.2	6.6
METH–AME	2	0	250	307	0.6	1.7
METH–Un Methodist	17	1,351	3,488	3,809	7.1	21.7
Non-denom Chr Chs	4	850	570	1,088	2.0	6.2
PENT–Assemb of God	4	235	70	470	0.9	2.7
PENT–Ch God (Cleve)	2	191	178	219	0.4	1.2
PENT–Int Foursq Gos	1	176	104	128	0.2	0.7
PENT–Int Pent C Chr	2	75	33	85	0.2	0.5
PRES–Presb Ch (USA)	5	333	658	808	1.5	4.6
Sev Day Adv	1	60	105	121	0.2	0.7
Un C of Christ	2	61	85	104	0.2	0.6

NR–Not Reported   - Represents no adherents reported.   Percentages may not total 100 due to rounding.

Table 3: Religious Congregations by County and Group: 2010

Religious Group	Number of Congrega-tions	Number of Attendees	Number of Communicant, Confirmed, or Full Members	Adherents		
				Number of Adherents	% of Total Pop.	% of Total Adh.
KANAWHA	**368**	**31,011**	**49,445**	**72,386**	**37.5**	**100.0**
ANG/EPIS–Episcopal	5	495	1,227	1,385	0.7	1.9
Bahá'í	1	NR	156	156	0.1	0.2
BAPT–Amer Bapt USA	34	3,948	8,843	10,514	5.4	14.5
BAPT–Free Will Bapt	14	NR	602	716	0.4	1.0
BAPT–NBC USA	7	1,220	2,330	2,770	1.4	3.8
BAPT–Reg Bapt Gen As	2	NR	NR	NR	-	-
BAPT–So Bapt Conv	16	1,297	2,591	3,081	1.6	4.3
Catholic	11	NR	NR	7,331	3.8	10.1
CGOD–Ch God (Ander)	18	971	NR	971	0.5	1.3
CGOD–Ches God-Gen Con	3	88	97	115	0.1	0.2
Ch Cr, Scientst	1	NR	NR	NR	-	-
Ch of Nazarene	38	2,737	4,230	5,393	2.8	7.5
Chr & Miss Al	1	32	19	39	0.0	0.1
CHR–Chr Ch (Disc)	2	107	334	397	0.2	0.5
CHR–Chr Chs & Chs Cr	4	NR	855	1,017	0.5	1.4
CHR–Chs of Christ	23	1,512	1,485	1,838	1.0	2.5
FRND–Fr Gen Cf	1	NR	3	4	0.0	0.0
HINDU–Post Ren	1	NR	NR	16	0.0	0.0
Jehovah's Witness	2	NR	NR	NR	-	-
JUD–Reform	1	70	124	335	0.2	0.5
LDS–L-D Saints	2	NR	NR	1,349	0.7	1.9
LUTH–E.L.C.A.	2	139	568	636	0.3	0.9
LUTH–Luth-MO Synod	1	110	111	144	0.1	0.2
LUTH–Nor Amer Luth C	1	NR	NR	NR	-	-
METH–AME	2	25	140	166	0.1	0.2
METH–Un Methodist	49	3,582	8,391	10,546	5.5	14.6
METH–Wesleyan	4	180	100	235	0.1	0.3
Metro Comm Ch	1	16	23	27	0.0	0.0
Non-denom Chr Chs	40	10,512	11,093	13,578	7.0	18.8
ORTHE–Ant Orth of NA	1	400	NR	1,021	0.5	1.4
ORTHE–Greek Orthodox	1	35	NR	115	0.1	0.2
PENT–Assemb of God	13	826	518	1,539	0.8	2.1
PENT–Ch God (Cleve)	11	377	771	917	0.5	1.3
PENT–Ch of God Proph	6	NR	104	124	0.1	0.2
PENT–COGIC	2	100	150	178	0.1	0.2
PENT–Intl Pent Holiness	4	184	219	260	0.1	0.4
PENT–Pent Ch of God	1	70	NR	109	0.1	0.2
PENT–Un Pent Ch Intl	9	NR	NR	NR	-	-
PENT–United Holy Ch	1	NR	NR	NR	-	-
PRES–Evan Presby Ch	1	NR	146	174	0.1	0.2
PRES–Presb Ch (USA)	20	1,363	3,426	4,074	2.1	5.6
PRES–Presb Ch Amer	5	244	283	311	0.2	0.4
Salvation Army	2	98	117	312	0.2	0.4
Sev Day Adv	2	164	286	329	0.2	0.5
Unit Univ	1	109	103	159	0.1	0.2
Unity Ch	1	NR	NR	NR	-	-
Zoroastrian	0	NR	NR	5	0.0	0.0
LEWIS	**53**	**1,859**	**3,276**	**5,246**	**32.0**	**100.0**
ANG/EPIS–Episcopal	1	44	196	196	1.2	3.7
Bahá'í	0	NR	1	1	0.0	0.0
BAPT–Amer Bapt USA	6	310	581	689	4.2	13.1
BAPT–So Bapt Conv	4	258	156	185	1.1	3.5
Catholic	2	NR	NR	1,044	6.4	19.9
CGOD–Ch God (Ander)	1	0	NR	0	0.0	0.0
Ch of Nazarene	1	24	35	99	0.6	1.9
CHR–Chs of Christ	1	45	40	60	0.4	1.1
METH–Evan Meth Ch	1	NR	NR	NR	-	-
METH–Un Methodist	31	937	1,983	2,419	14.8	46.1
Non-denom Chr Chs	1	60	40	75	0.5	1.4
PENT–Assemb of God	1	140	73	275	1.7	5.2
PENT–Ch God (Cleve)	1	41	145	172	1.1	3.3
PENT–Un Pent Ch Intl	1	NR	NR	NR	-	-
PRES–Presb Ch (USA)	1	0	26	31	0.2	0.6
LINCOLN	**57**	**1,672**	**3,542**	**4,382**	**20.2**	**100.0**
Bahá'í	0	NR	3	3	0.0	0.1
BAPT–Amer Bapt USA	10	508	1,188	1,437	6.6	32.8
BAPT–Free Will Bapt	17	NR	731	884	4.1	20.2
BAPT–So Bapt Conv	3	115	284	343	1.6	7.8
CGOD–Ch God (Ander)	1	100	NR	100	0.5	2.3
Ch of Nazarene	1	10	15	15	0.1	0.3
CHR–Chs of Christ	10	455	405	529	2.4	12.1
METH–Un Methodist	10	184	406	481	2.2	11.0
Non-denom Chr Chs	1	130	170	170	0.8	3.9
PENT–Assemb of God	1	22	30	45	0.2	1.0
PENT–Ch God (Cleve)	3	148	310	375	1.7	8.6
LOGAN	**100**	**2,774**	**6,364**	**8,369**	**22.8**	**100.0**
ANG/EPIS–Episcopal	1	22	34	35	0.1	0.4
Bahá'í	0	NR	2	2	0.0	0.0
BAPT–Amer Bapt USA	5	170	206	243	0.7	2.9
BAPT–Free Will Bapt	34	NR	1,462	1,727	4.7	20.6
BAPT–NBC USA	1	0	150	177	0.5	2.1
BAPT–So Bapt Conv	4	100	165	195	0.5	2.3
Catholic	3	NR	NR	400	1.1	4.8
Ch of Nazarene	2	135	395	397	1.1	4.7
CHR–Chr Ch (Disc)	1	85	240	284	0.8	3.4
CHR–Chr Chs & Chs Cr	4	NR	170	201	0.5	2.4
CHR–Chs of Christ	8	360	344	416	1.1	5.0
LDS–L-D Saints	1	NR	NR	333	0.9	4.0
METH–AME	1	0	150	177	0.5	2.1
METH–Un Methodist	7	298	634	766	2.1	9.2
Non-denom Chr Chs	4	460	469	592	1.6	7.1
PENT–Assemb of God	2	74	27	87	0.2	1.0
PENT–Ch God (Cleve)	15	983	1,663	1,964	5.3	23.5
PENT–Ch of God Proph	2	NR	54	64	0.2	0.8
PENT–Un Pent Ch Intl	1	NR	NR	NR	-	-
PRES–Presb Ch (USA)	2	62	117	138	0.4	1.6
Salvation Army	1	7	51	135	0.4	1.6
Sev Day Adv	1	18	31	36	0.1	0.4
MCDOWELL	**97**	**1,817**	**3,278**	**4,833**	**21.9**	**100.0**
Bahá'í	0	NR	5	5	0.0	0.1
BAPT–Amer Bapt USA	3	92	121	143	0.6	3.0
BAPT–Free Will Bapt	1	NR	43	51	0.2	1.1
BAPT–NBC USA	1	0	150	177	0.8	3.7
BAPT–So Bapt Conv	4	91	157	185	0.8	3.8
Catholic	4	NR	NR	313	1.4	6.5
CGOD–Ch God (Ander)	3	38	NR	38	0.2	0.8
Ch of Nazarene	1	69	56	69	0.3	1.4
CHR–Chr Chs & Chs Cr	5	NR	30	35	0.2	0.7
CHR–Chs of Christ	5	143	123	163	0.7	3.4
Jehovah's Witness	1	NR	NR	NR	-	-
LDS–L-D Saints	1	NR	NR	466	2.1	9.6
METH–AME	3	0	300	354	1.6	7.3
METH–Un Methodist	21	282	630	688	3.1	14.2
Non-denom Chr Chs	4	295	445	456	2.1	9.4
PENT–Assemb of God	5	139	121	287	1.3	5.9
PENT–Ch God (Cleve)	11	316	604	713	3.2	14.8
PENT–Ch Lord Jesus Apos	4	NR	NR	NR	-	-
PENT–Intl Pent Holiness	12	251	387	457	2.1	9.5
PENT–Pent Ch of God	1	70	NR	109	0.5	2.3
PENT–United Holy Ch	3	NR	NR	NR	-	-
PRES–Presb Ch (USA)	3	11	70	83	0.4	1.7
Sev Day Adv	1	20	36	41	0.2	0.8
MARION	**141**	**8,169**	**13,169**	**25,478**	**45.2**	**100.0**
ANG/EPIS–Episcopal	1	54	163	163	0.3	0.6
Bahá'í	0	NR	1	1	0.0	0.0
BAPT–Amer Bapt USA	17	899	2,715	3,208	5.7	12.6
BAPT–NBC USA	2	0	650	768	1.4	3.0
BAPT–Reg Bapt Gen As	2	NR	NR	NR	-	-
BAPT–So Bapt Conv	2	21	55	65	0.1	0.3
BRETH–Ch of Brethren	1	15	16	19	0.0	0.1
Catholic	7	NR	NR	5,819	10.3	22.8
Ch of Nazarene	3	356	407	545	1.0	2.1
Chr & Miss Al	1	80	35	102	0.2	0.4
CHR–Chr Ch (Disc)	3	90	476	562	1.0	2.2
CHR–Chs of Christ	16	1,394	1,395	1,806	3.2	7.1
Jehovah's Witness	1	NR	NR	NR	-	-
LDS–L-D Saints	2	NR	NR	872	1.5	3.4
LUTH–E.L.C.A.	1	87	286	502	0.9	2.0
METH–A.W.M.C.	1	17	12	26	0.0	0.1
METH–Free Methodist	4	256	116	256	0.5	1.0

NR–Not Reported - Represents no adherents reported. Percentages may not total 100 due to rounding.

Table 3: Religious Congregations by County and Group: 2010

Religious Group	Number of Congrega-tions	Number of Attendees	Number of Communicant, Confirmed, or Full Members	Adherents		
				Number of Adherents	% of Total Pop.	% of Total Adh.
METH–Un Methodist	48	2,048	4,323	5,621	10.0	22.1
METH–Wesleyan	1	18	8	23	0.0	0.1
Non-denom Chr Chs	10	1,433	1,138	1,922	3.4	7.5
ORTHE–Serb Orth USA	1	10	NR	25	0.0	0.1
PENT–Assemb of God	3	1,035	639	2,308	4.1	9.1
PENT–Ch God (Cleve)	3	25	64	76	0.1	0.3
PENT–Ch of God Proph	3	NR	114	135	0.2	0.5
PENT–I F Chr Assmbl	1	NR	NR	NR	-	-
PENT–Int Foursq Gos	1	131	204	241	0.4	0.9
PENT–Un Pent Ch Intl	1	NR	NR	NR	-	-
PRES–Presb Ch (USA)	3	126	244	288	0.5	1.1
PRES–Presb Ch Amer	1	40	49	57	0.1	0.2
Sev Day Adv	1	34	59	68	0.1	0.3
MARSHALL	**74**	**3,412**	**6,896**	**14,186**	**42.8**	**100.0**
ANG/EPIS–Episcopal	1	43	119	119	0.4	0.8
Bahá'í	0	NR	3	3	0.0	0.0
BAPT–Amer Bapt USA	1	16	101	120	0.4	0.8
BAPT–Reg Bapt Gen As	1	NR	NR	NR	-	-
BAPT–So Bapt Conv	2	104	146	173	0.5	1.2
BRETH–Brethren (Ash)	1	NR	80	95	0.3	0.7
Catholic	6	NR	NR	4,040	12.2	28.5
CGOD–Ch God (Ander)	2	264	NR	264	0.8	1.9
CGOD–Ches God-Gen Con	1	74	75	89	0.3	0.6
Ch God (7th Day)	1	NR	NR	NR	-	-
Ch of Nazarene	2	123	190	268	0.8	1.9
CHR–Chr Ch (Disc)	7	282	1,100	1,303	3.9	9.2
CHR–Chr Chs & Chs Cr	1	NR	71	84	0.3	0.6
CHR–Chs of Christ	7	645	648	852	2.6	6.0
HINDU–I/A Temples	1	NR	NR	1,562	4.7	11.0
Jehovah's Witness	1	NR	NR	NR	-	-
JUD–Orth	1	43	50	60	0.2	0.4
LDS–Comm of Christ	1	NR	118	118	0.4	0.8
LUTH–E.L.C.A.	2	57	274	321	1.0	2.3
METH–AME	1	0	100	118	0.4	0.8
METH–Un Methodist	19	1,001	2,683	3,282	9.9	23.1
Non-denom Chr Chs	3	350	500	500	1.5	3.5
ORTHE–Orth Ch in Amer	1	18	NR	22	0.1	0.2
PENT–Assemb of God	1	40	35	40	0.1	0.3
PENT–Ch God (Cleve)	1	97	179	212	0.6	1.5
PENT–Int Foursq Gos	1	30	46	55	0.2	0.4
PENT–Un Pent Ch Intl	1	NR	NR	NR	-	-
PRES–Presb Ch (USA)	6	213	334	396	1.2	2.8
Salvation Army	1	12	44	90	0.3	0.6
MASON	**56**	**2,368**	**4,654**	**6,316**	**23.1**	**100.0**
ANG/EPIS–Episcopal	1	58	80	109	0.4	1.7
BAPT–Amer Bapt USA	5	346	1,124	1,349	4.9	21.4
BAPT–Reg Bapt Gen As	1	NR	NR	NR	-	-
BAPT–So Bapt Conv	3	297	610	732	2.7	11.6
Catholic	1	NR	NR	171	0.6	2.7
CGOD–Ch God (Ander)	2	221	NR	221	0.8	3.5
Ch of Nazarene	1	97	155	155	0.6	2.5
CHR–Chs of Christ	4	230	253	347	1.3	5.5
Jehovah's Witness	1	NR	NR	NR	-	-
LUTH–E.L.C.A.	3	75	138	177	0.6	2.8
LUTH–Nor Amer Luth C	1	NR	NR	NR	-	-
MENN–Amish Undif	1	NR	32	100	0.4	1.6
METH–A.W.M.C.	1	26	0	26	0.1	0.4
METH–Un Methodist	23	787	1,896	2,512	9.2	39.8
Non-denom Chr Chs	2	130	180	180	0.7	2.8
PENT–Assemb of God	1	14	4	20	0.1	0.3
PENT–Ch of God Proph	1	NR	19	23	0.1	0.4
PENT–Un Pent Ch Intl	2	NR	NR	NR	-	-
PRES–Presb Ch (USA)	1	65	124	149	0.5	2.4
Sev Day Adv	1	22	39	45	0.2	0.7
MERCER	**166**	**9,553**	**20,053**	**25,920**	**41.6**	**100.0**
ANG/EPIS–Episcopal	2	78	211	291	0.5	1.1
Bahá'í	0	NR	102	102	0.2	0.4
BAPT–Amer Bapt USA	3	111	194	230	0.4	0.9
BAPT–Free Will Bapt	5	NR	215	255	0.4	1.0
BAPT–Ref Bapt Ch	1	NR	NR	NR	-	-
BAPT–So Bapt Conv	25	1,975	5,601	6,649	10.7	25.7
BRETH–Ch of Brethren	2	35	59	70	0.1	0.3
Calv Chpl	1	NR	NR	NR	-	-
Catholic	2	NR	NR	1,560	2.5	6.0
CGOD–Ch God (Ander)	6	348	NR	348	0.6	1.3
Ch Cr, Scientst	1	NR	NR	NR	-	-
Ch of Nazarene	3	219	428	432	0.7	1.7
CHR–Chr Ch (Disc)	3	159	633	751	1.2	2.9
CHR–Chr Chs & Chs Cr	13	NR	1,186	1,408	2.3	5.4
CHR–Chs of Christ	3	245	236	299	0.5	1.2
Jehovah's Witness	2	NR	NR	NR	-	-
JUD–Reform	1	16	28	76	0.1	0.3
LUTH–E.L.C.A.	1	45	188	229	0.4	0.9
METH–A.W.M.C.	1	14	0	12	0.0	0.0
METH–AME Zion	1	40	80	95	0.2	0.4
METH–Free Methodist	1	23	25	25	0.0	0.1
METH–Un Methodist	36	1,594	3,854	4,560	7.3	17.6
METH–Wesleyan	2	38	29	50	0.1	0.2
Muslim Est	1	134	NR	308	0.5	1.2
Non-denom Chr Chs	10	2,135	3,090	3,277	5.3	12.6
ORTHE–Carp Rus Orth	1	50	NR	76	0.1	0.3
PENT–Assemb of God	2	181	82	234	0.4	0.9
PENT–Ch God (Cleve)	9	1,343	1,688	2,004	3.2	7.7
PENT–Ch of God Proph	1	NR	22	26	0.0	0.1
PENT–Intl Pent Holiness	11	396	982	1,166	1.9	4.5
PENT–United Holy Ch	6	NR	NR	NR	-	-
PRES–Evan Presby Ch	1	NR	336	399	0.6	1.5
PRES–Presb Ch (USA)	6	205	524	622	1.0	2.4
Salvation Army	2	77	99	181	0.3	0.7
Sev Day Adv	1	92	161	185	0.3	0.7
MINERAL	**86**	**4,125**	**7,973**	**11,576**	**41.0**	**100.0**
ANG/EPIS–Episcopal	1	36	64	67	0.2	0.6
BAPT–Reg Bapt Gen As	1	NR	NR	NR	-	-
BAPT–So Bapt Conv	9	355	978	1,162	4.1	10.0
BRETH–Ch of Brethren	7	418	811	963	3.4	8.3
Catholic	3	NR	NR	1,347	4.8	11.6
CHR–Chr Chs & Chs Cr	1	NR	35	42	0.1	0.4
CHR–Chs of Christ	1	25	28	35	0.1	0.3
Grace Gosp Fel	1	NR	NR	NR	-	-
LDS–L-D Saints	1	NR	NR	46	0.2	0.4
LUTH–E.L.C.A.	1	55	376	397	1.4	3.4
METH–A.W.M.C.	1	69	0	72	0.3	0.6
METH–Un Methodist	29	1,250	3,233	4,327	15.3	37.4
Non-denom Chr Chs	9	810	795	1,051	3.7	9.1
PENT–Assemb of God	6	484	361	640	2.3	5.5
PENT–Assm God Intl F	1	NR	NR	NR	-	-
PENT–Ch God (Cleve)	5	133	442	525	1.9	4.5
PENT–COGIC	1	0	150	178	0.6	1.5
PENT–Intl Pent Holiness	2	171	228	271	1.0	2.3
PENT–Un Pent Ch Intl	2	NR	NR	NR	-	-
PRES–Presb Ch (USA)	3	152	262	311	1.1	2.7
Un Breth in Cr	1	167	210	142	0.5	1.2
MINGO	**79**	**3,112**	**5,859**	**7,576**	**28.2**	**100.0**
ANG/EPIS–Episcopal	1	21	43	43	0.2	0.6
Bahá'í	0	NR	1	1	0.0	0.0
BAPT–Amer Bapt USA	4	291	659	794	3.0	10.5
BAPT–Free Will Bapt	15	NR	645	777	2.9	10.3
BAPT–Natl Mis Bapt Conv	1	0	150	181	0.7	2.4
BAPT–NBC USA	1	40	50	60	0.2	0.8
BAPT–So Bapt Conv	6	276	1,114	1,342	5.0	17.7
Catholic	1	NR	NR	265	1.0	3.5
CHR–Chr Ch (Disc)	1	0	0	0	0.0	0.0
CHR–Chr Chs & Chs Cr	3	NR	110	133	0.5	1.8
CHR–Chs of Christ	8	308	285	347	1.3	4.6
Jehovah's Witness	1	NR	NR	NR	-	-
METH–AME	1	0	100	120	0.4	1.6
METH–Un Methodist	5	125	437	483	1.8	6.4
METH–Wesleyan	1	22	18	29	0.1	0.4
Non-denom Chr Chs	6	495	550	669	2.5	8.8
PENT–Assemb of God	7	416	252	593	2.2	7.8
PENT–Ch God (Cleve)	11	1,022	1,285	1,548	5.8	20.4

NR–Not Reported   - Represents no adherents reported.   Percentages may not total 100 due to rounding.

Table 3: Religious Congregations by County and Group: 2010

Religious Group	Number of Congrega-tions	Number of Attendees	Number of Communicant, Confirmed, or Full Members	Adherents		
				Number of Adherents	% of Total Pop.	% of Total Adh.
PENT–Ch Lord Jesus Apos	1	NR	NR	NR	-	-
PENT–Un Pent Ch Intl	1	NR	NR	NR	-	-
PENT–United Holy Ch	1	NR	NR	NR	-	-
PRES–Presb Ch (USA)	2	84	139	167	0.6	2.2
Sev Day Adv	1	12	21	24	0.1	0.3
MONONGALIA	**134**	**8,836**	**12,840**	**26,802**	**27.9**	**100.0**
ANG/EPIS–Episcopal	2	173	448	493	0.5	1.8
Bahá'í	0	NR	32	32	0.0	0.1
BAPT–Amer Bapt Assn	1	NR	85	97	0.1	0.4
BAPT–Amer Bapt USA	7	391	1,418	1,618	1.7	6.0
BAPT–Fund Bapt Flwsp	1	NR	NR	NR	-	-
BAPT–So Bapt Conv	5	290	329	375	0.4	1.4
BRETH–Ch of Brethren	1	45	65	74	0.1	0.3
Calv Chpl	1	NR	NR	NR	-	-
Catholic	5	NR	NR	7,831	8.1	29.2
CGOD–Ch God (Ander)	2	59	NR	59	0.1	0.2
Ch Cr, Scientst	1	NR	NR	NR	-	-
Ch of Nazarene	3	257	258	410	0.4	1.5
Chr & Miss Al	4	625	354	939	1.0	3.5
CHR–Chr Ch (Disc)	1	45	300	342	0.4	1.3
CHR–Chs of Christ	5	405	386	527	0.5	2.0
FRND–Fr Gen Cf	1	NR	17	19	0.0	0.1
HINDU–Post Ren	1	NR	NR	10	0.0	0.0
Jain	1	NR	NR	NR	-	-
Jehovah's Witness	1	NR	NR	NR	-	-
JUD–Reform	1	54	96	259	0.3	1.0
LDS–L-D Saints	3	NR	NR	1,175	1.2	4.4
LUTH–E.L.C.A.	1	90	1	681	0.7	2.5
MENN–Bruderhof Comm	1	32	6	17	0.0	0.1
MENN–Mennonite USA	1	50	95	108	0.1	0.4
METH–AME	1	55	70	80	0.1	0.3
METH–Evan Meth Ch	2	NR	NR	NR	-	-
METH–Free Methodist	2	49	54	54	0.1	0.2
METH–Un Methodist	46	2,112	4,601	5,701	5.9	21.3
METH–Wesleyan	1	110	11	143	0.1	0.5
Muslim Est	1	134	NR	308	0.3	1.1
Non-denom Chr Chs	7	3,095	3,305	3,893	4.0	14.5
ORTHE–Carp Rus Orth	1	43	NR	70	0.1	0.3
ORTHE–Greek Orthodox	1	35	NR	160	0.2	0.6
PENT–Assemb of God	3	258	152	327	0.3	1.2
PENT–Ch God (Cleve)	2	85	126	144	0.1	0.5
PENT–Ch God Mtn Asm	1	NR	NR	NR	-	-
PENT–Ch of God Proph	1	NR	5	6	0.0	0.0
PENT–I F Chr Assmbl	1	NR	NR	NR	-	-
PENT–Int Foursq Gos	1	36	27	31	0.0	0.1
PENT–Un Pent Ch Intl	3	NR	NR	NR	-	-
PRES–Orth Pres Ch	1	72	63	78	0.1	0.3
PRES–Presb Ch (USA)	4	138	370	422	0.4	1.6
PRES–Presb Ch Amer	1	0	0	0	0.0	0.0
REF–Comm Ref Evan	1	NR	NR	NR	-	-
Salvation Army	1	32	71	205	0.2	0.8
Sev Day Adv	1	35	61	70	0.1	0.3
Unit Univ	1	31	34	44	0.0	0.2
MONROE	**60**	**2,035**	**3,928**	**4,882**	**36.2**	**100.0**
ANG/EPIS–Episcopal	1	24	40	46	0.3	0.9
Bahá'í	0	NR	2	2	0.0	0.0
BAPT–Amer Bapt USA	4	182	456	543	4.0	11.1
BAPT–Free Will Bapt	2	NR	86	102	0.8	2.1
BAPT–So Bapt Conv	5	289	574	684	5.1	14.0
BRETH–Ch of Brethren	1	54	164	195	1.4	4.0
CGOD–Ch God (Ander)	1	12	NR	12	0.1	0.2
Ch of Nazarene	2	43	70	70	0.5	1.4
CHR–Chr Ch (Disc)	1	0	0	0	0.0	0.0
CHR–Chr Chs & Chs Cr	4	NR	395	470	3.5	9.6
CHR–Chs of Christ	1	12	14	14	0.1	0.3
LDS–L-D Saints	1	NR	NR	150	1.1	3.1
MENN–Menn Chr Fell	1	60	37	60	0.4	1.2
METH–Un Methodist	19	690	1,239	1,464	10.8	30.0
Non-denom Chr Chs	4	360	345	454	3.4	9.3
PENT–Ch God (Cleve)	2	141	191	227	1.7	4.6
PENT–Ch of God Proph	1	NR	9	11	0.1	0.2
PENT–Int Pent C Chr	2	24	25	43	0.3	0.9
PENT–Intl Pent Holiness	1	74	98	117	0.9	2.4
PRES–As Ref Pres Ch	1	NR	27	32	0.2	0.7
PRES–Presb Ch (USA)	6	70	156	186	1.4	3.8
MORGAN	**36**	**1,896**	**3,262**	**4,593**	**26.2**	**100.0**
ANG/EPIS–Episcopal	1	35	72	86	0.5	1.9
Bahá'í	0	NR	7	7	0.0	0.2
BAPT–So Bapt Conv	3	149	167	197	1.1	4.3
Catholic	1	NR	NR	715	4.1	15.6
Ch of Nazarene	1	50	28	50	0.3	1.1
CHR–Chr Ch (Disc)	1	48	143	169	1.0	3.7
CHR–Chr Chs & Chs Cr	1	NR	100	118	0.7	2.6
CHR–Chs of Christ	2	144	153	177	1.0	3.9
Jehovah's Witness	1	NR	NR	NR	-	-
METH–Un Methodist	17	918	2,086	2,274	13.0	49.5
Non-denom Chr Chs	2	138	88	172	1.0	3.7
PENT–Assemb of God	3	247	155	321	1.8	7.0
PENT–Intl Pent Holiness	1	20	20	24	0.1	0.5
PRES–Presb Ch (USA)	1	75	117	138	0.8	3.0
Sev Day Adv	1	72	126	145	0.8	3.2
NICHOLAS	**89**	**3,223**	**6,900**	**8,635**	**32.9**	**100.0**
ANG/EPIS–Episcopal	1	14	38	43	0.2	0.5
Bahá'í	0	NR	1	1	0.0	0.0
BAPT–Amer Bapt USA	13	881	2,407	2,864	10.9	33.2
BAPT–Free Will Bapt	7	NR	301	358	1.4	4.1
BAPT–So Bapt Conv	5	418	853	1,015	3.9	11.8
Catholic	2	NR	NR	440	1.7	5.1
CGOD–Ch God (Ander)	4	135	NR	135	0.5	1.6
Ch of Nazarene	5	65	145	175	0.7	2.0
CHR–Chr Chs & Chs Cr	1	NR	40	48	0.2	0.6
CHR–Chs of Christ	2	62	55	72	0.3	0.8
Jehovah's Witness	2	NR	NR	NR	-	-
METH–Un Methodist	30	770	1,804	2,064	7.9	23.9
Non-denom Chr Chs	6	420	520	598	2.3	6.9
PENT–Assemb of God	1	200	252	252	1.0	2.9
PENT–Ch God (Cleve)	2	122	230	274	1.0	3.2
PENT–Ch of God Proph	1	NR	14	17	0.1	0.2
PENT–Un Pent Ch Intl	2	NR	NR	NR	-	-
PRES–Presb Ch (USA)	2	52	105	125	0.5	1.4
Salvation Army	1	14	14	15	0.1	0.2
Sev Day Adv	2	70	121	139	0.5	1.6
OHIO	**77**	**4,596**	**10,339**	**28,045**	**63.1**	**100.0**
ANG/EPIS–Episcopal	4	209	485	646	1.5	2.3
Bahá'í	0	NR	14	14	0.0	0.0
BAPT–Amer Bapt USA	2	123	293	342	0.8	1.2
BAPT–Ind Bapt Flwsp Intl	1	NR	NR	NR	-	-
BAPT–NBC USA	1	75	100	117	0.3	0.4
BAPT–So Bapt Conv	2	188	240	281	0.6	1.0
Catholic	9	NR	NR	13,134	29.6	46.8
CGOD–Ch God (Ander)	2	55	NR	55	0.1	0.2
Chr & Miss Al	1	35	32	52	0.1	0.2
CHR–Chr Ch (Disc)	2	144	493	576	1.3	2.1
CHR–Chr Chs & Chs Cr	4	NR	525	614	1.4	2.2
CHR–Chs of Christ	1	190	190	225	0.5	0.8
Evan Assoc RCC	1	NR	NR	NR	-	-
HINDU–I/A Temples	1	NR	NR	129	0.3	0.5
JUD–Reform	1	41	73	197	0.4	0.7
LDS–Comm of Christ	1	NR	118	118	0.3	0.4
LDS–L-D Saints	1	NR	NR	849	1.9	3.0
LUTH–E.L.C.A.	7	472	2,113	2,910	6.5	10.4
METH–AME	1	0	100	117	0.3	0.4
METH–Un Methodist	13	834	2,631	3,356	7.6	12.0
Muslim Est	1	134	NR	308	0.7	1.1
Non-denom Chr Chs	5	375	575	581	1.3	2.1
ORTHE–Greek Orthodox	1	120	NR	180	0.4	0.6
PENT–Assemb of God	2	230	187	319	0.7	1.1
PENT–Ch God (Cleve)	1	71	47	55	0.1	0.2
PENT–Open Bible Std	1	100	NR	100	0.2	0.4
PENT–Un Pent Ch Intl	1	NR	NR	NR	-	-
PENT–Vineyard	1	673	1,050	1,227	2.8	4.4

NR–Not Reported   - Represents no adherents reported.   Percentages may not total 100 due to rounding.

Table 3: Religious Congregations by County and Group: 2010

Religious Group	Number of Congrega-tions	Number of Attendees	Number of Communicant, Confirmed, or Full Members	Adherents: Number of Adherents	Adherents: % of Total Pop.	Adherents: % of Total Adh.
PRES–Presb Ch (USA)	7	431	932	1,089	2.5	3.9
Salvation Army	1	61	80	384	0.9	1.4
Sev Day Adv	1	35	61	70	0.2	0.2
PENDLETON	**51**	**1,496**	**2,949**	**4,002**	**52.0**	**100.0**
BAPT–Free Will Bapt	1	NR	43	50	0.6	1.2
BAPT–So Bapt Conv	4	349	654	765	9.9	19.1
BRETH–Ch of Brethren	7	152	416	486	6.3	12.1
Catholic	1	NR	NR	109	1.4	2.7
CHR–Chr Chs & Chs Cr	1	NR	50	58	0.8	1.4
CHR–Chs of Christ	1	9	10	10	0.1	0.2
Jehovah's Witness	1	NR	NR	NR	-	-
LDS–L-D Saints	1	NR	NR	235	3.1	5.9
LUTH–E.L.C.A.	5	141	280	318	4.1	7.9
METH–AME	1	0	100	117	1.5	2.9
METH–Un Methodist	18	441	833	1,162	15.1	29.0
Non-denom Chr Chs	1	170	200	212	2.8	5.3
PENT–Assemb of God	1	40	27	88	1.1	2.2
PENT–Ch God (Cleve)	1	35	41	48	0.6	1.2
PENT–Un Pent Ch Intl	1	NR	NR	NR	-	-
PRES–Presb Ch (USA)	5	143	267	312	4.1	7.8
Sev Day Adv	1	16	28	32	0.4	0.8
PLEASANTS	**32**	**1,085**	**2,031**	**2,551**	**33.5**	**100.0**
ANG/EPIS–Episcopal	1	15	23	27	0.4	1.1
BAPT–Amer Bapt USA	3	307	663	778	10.2	30.5
BAPT–Free Will Bapt	2	NR	86	101	1.3	4.0
BAPT–So Bapt Conv	2	29	34	40	0.5	1.6
Catholic	1	NR	NR	165	2.2	6.5
Ch of Nazarene	1	49	60	85	1.1	3.3
CHR–Chs of Christ	6	329	349	400	5.3	15.7
METH–Un Methodist	12	266	682	793	10.4	31.1
Non-denom Chr Chs	1	60	60	75	1.0	2.9
PENT–Intl Pent Holiness	1	12	50	59	0.8	2.3
PENT–Un Pent Ch Intl	1	NR	NR	NR	-	-
PRES–Presb Ch (USA)	1	18	24	28	0.4	1.1
POCAHONTAS	**50**	**1,239**	**2,112**	**2,688**	**30.8**	**100.0**
ANG/EPIS–Episcopal	2	29	21	24	0.3	0.9
Bahá'í	0	NR	1	1	0.0	0.0
BAPT–So Bapt Conv	5	226	651	754	8.6	28.1
BRETH–Ch of Brethren	4	180	205	238	2.7	8.9
Catholic	2	NR	NR	115	1.3	4.3
Ch of Nazarene	2	73	121	121	1.4	4.5
CHR–Chs of Christ	2	40	32	52	0.6	1.9
Jehovah's Witness	1	NR	NR	NR	-	-
METH–Un Methodist	21	378	676	891	10.2	33.1
Non-denom Chr Chs	2	70	70	88	1.0	3.3
PENT–Assemb of God	1	45	26	45	0.5	1.7
PENT–Ch God (Cleve)	1	15	48	56	0.6	2.1
PRES–Presb Ch (USA)	6	176	249	289	3.3	10.8
Sev Day Adv	1	7	12	14	0.2	0.5
PRESTON	**106**	**3,094**	**5,374**	**8,794**	**26.2**	**100.0**
ANG/EPIS–Episcopal	1	19	16	33	0.1	0.4
Bahá'í	0	NR	1	1	0.0	0.0
BAPT–Amer Bapt USA	6	251	425	499	1.5	5.7
BAPT–So Bapt Conv	2	55	280	329	1.0	3.7
BRETH–Brethren (Ash)	1	NR	80	94	0.3	1.1
BRETH–Ch of Brethren	10	221	486	571	1.7	6.5
Catholic	5	NR	NR	1,349	4.0	15.3
Ch of Nazarene	4	269	372	404	1.2	4.6
CHR–Chs of Christ	3	93	84	110	0.3	1.3
Jehovah's Witness	2	NR	NR	NR	-	-
LDS–L-D Saints	1	NR	NR	365	1.1	4.2
LUTH–E.L.C.A.	1	37	159	202	0.6	2.3
METH–A.W.M.C.	1	10	9	15	0.0	0.2
METH–Evan Meth Ch	1	NR	NR	NR	-	-
METH–Free Methodist	1	23	18	23	0.1	0.3
METH–Un Methodist	50	1,445	2,854	3,873	11.6	44.0
METH–Wesleyan	2	73	70	95	0.3	1.1
Non-denom Chr Chs	1	80	80	100	0.3	1.1

Religious Group	Number of Congrega-tions	Number of Attendees	Number of Communicant, Confirmed, or Full Members	Adherents: Number of Adherents	Adherents: % of Total Pop.	Adherents: % of Total Adh.
PENT–Assemb of God	5	172	102	235	0.7	2.7
PENT–Ch God (Cleve)	1	24	24	28	0.1	0.3
PENT–Intl Pent Holiness	1	81	110	129	0.4	1.5
PENT–Un Pent Ch Intl	2	NR	NR	NR	-	-
PRES–Presb Ch (USA)	3	65	145	170	0.5	1.9
Sev Day Adv	1	16	29	33	0.1	0.4
Un Breth in Cr	1	160	30	136	0.4	1.5
PUTNAM	**74**	**8,274**	**12,037**	**17,905**	**32.3**	**100.0**
ANG/EPIS–Episcopal	1	86	265	292	0.5	1.6
Bahá'í	0	NR	7	7	0.0	0.0
BAPT–Amer Bapt USA	6	1,560	3,394	4,155	7.5	23.2
BAPT–Free Will Bapt	2	NR	86	105	0.2	0.6
BAPT–So Bapt Conv	4	388	704	862	1.6	4.8
Catholic	2	NR	NR	1,176	2.1	6.6
CGOD–Ch God (Ander)	4	572	NR	572	1.0	3.2
Ch of Nazarene	5	712	902	1,466	2.6	8.2
Chr & Miss Al	1	52	38	83	0.1	0.5
CHR–Chr Chs & Chs Cr	1	NR	50	61	0.1	0.3
CHR–Chs of Christ	7	555	514	697	1.3	3.9
Evan Free Ch	1	35	NR	35	0.1	0.2
HINDU–Post Ren	1	NR	NR	16	0.0	0.1
Jehovah's Witness	1	NR	NR	NR	-	-
LDS–L-D Saints	1	NR	NR	541	1.0	3.0
LUTH–E.L.C.A.	1	43	72	123	0.2	0.7
METH–Un Methodist	11	1,323	2,697	3,719	6.7	20.8
Non-denom Chr Chs	11	2,295	2,516	2,968	5.3	16.6
PENT–Assemb of God	2	73	45	90	0.2	0.5
PENT–Ch God (Cleve)	1	28	35	43	0.1	0.2
PENT–Int Foursq Gos	1	0	0	0	0.0	0.0
PENT–Un Pent Ch Intl	2	NR	NR	NR	-	-
PENT–Vineyard	1	100	125	153	0.3	0.9
PRES–Presb Ch (USA)	5	235	455	557	1.0	3.1
PRES–Presb Ch Amer	2	217	132	184	0.3	1.0
RALEIGH	**146**	**9,778**	**17,421**	**24,166**	**30.6**	**100.0**
ANG/EPIS–Episcopal	1	45	205	231	0.3	1.0
Bahá'í	0	NR	29	29	0.0	0.1
BAPT–Amer Bapt USA	5	585	2,193	2,619	3.3	10.8
BAPT–Consrv Bapt	1	NR	NR	NR	-	-
BAPT–Free Will Bapt	15	NR	645	770	1.0	3.2
BAPT–Natl Mis Bapt Conv	3	0	300	358	0.5	1.5
BAPT–NBC USA	4	235	680	812	1.0	3.4
BAPT–Reg Bapt Gen As	1	NR	NR	NR	-	-
BAPT–So Bapt Conv	8	758	1,387	1,656	2.1	6.9
BRETH–Ch of Brethren	1	35	89	106	0.1	0.4
Calv Chpl	1	NR	NR	NR	-	-
Catholic	1	NR	NR	1,688	2.1	7.0
CGOD–Ch God (Ander)	3	362	NR	362	0.5	1.5
Ch of Nazarene	1	103	222	290	0.4	1.2
CHR–Chr Ch (Disc)	1	85	295	352	0.4	1.5
CHR–Chr Chs & Chs Cr	3	NR	699	835	1.1	3.5
CHR–Chs of Christ	8	322	308	389	0.5	1.6
Ind Fund Churches	1	NR	NR	NR	-	-
Jehovah's Witness	1	NR	NR	NR	-	-
JUD–Reform	1	19	34	92	0.1	0.4
LDS–L-D Saints	1	NR	NR	593	0.8	2.5
LUTH–E.L.C.A.	1	48	95	112	0.1	0.5
METH–AME	3	0	350	418	0.5	1.7
METH–Free Methodist	1	44	44	44	0.1	0.2
METH–Un Methodist	16	849	1,836	2,307	2.9	9.5
Muslim Est	1	134	NR	308	0.4	1.3
Non-denom Chr Chs	23	3,563	4,043	4,660	5.9	19.3
ORTHE–Ant Orth of NA	1	45	NR	64	0.1	0.3
PENT–Assemb of God	4	384	770	897	1.1	3.7
PENT–Ch God (Cleve)	15	1,502	2,287	2,731	3.5	11.3
PENT–Ch of God Proph	2	NR	31	37	0.0	0.2
PENT–Intl Pent Holiness	3	115	208	248	0.3	1.0
PENT–Pent Ch of God	3	210	NR	326	0.4	1.3
PENT–Un Pent Ch Intl	1	NR	NR	NR	-	-
PENT–United Holy Ch	1	NR	NR	NR	-	-
PRES–Presb Ch (USA)	6	173	453	541	0.7	2.2
Salvation Army	1	60	49	94	0.1	0.4

NR–Not Reported   - Represents no adherents reported.   Percentages may not total 100 due to rounding.

Table 3: Religious Congregations by County and Group: 2010

Religious Group	Number of Congregations	Number of Attendees	Number of Communicant, Confirmed, or Full Members	Adherents		
				Number of Adherents	% of Total Pop.	% of Total Adh.
Sev Day Adv	2	85	148	170	0.2	0.7
Unit Univ	1	17	21	27	0.0	0.1
RANDOLPH	**80**	**3,558**	**6,933**	**11,009**	**37.4**	**100.0**
ANG/EPIS–Episcopal	1	21	50	78	0.3	0.7
BAPT–Amer Bapt USA	2	300	1,116	1,308	4.4	11.9
BAPT–Reg Bapt Gen As	2	NR	NR	NR	-	-
BAPT–So Bapt Conv	2	61	223	261	0.9	2.4
BRETH–Ch of Brethren	5	113	179	210	0.7	1.9
Catholic	5	NR	NR	1,168	4.0	10.6
Ch of Nazarene	2	237	456	722	2.5	6.6
Chr & Miss Al	1	117	38	162	0.6	1.5
CHR–Chr Chs & Chs Cr	2	NR	300	352	1.2	3.2
CHR–Chs of Christ	2	95	97	125	0.4	1.1
Jehovah's Witness	1	NR	NR	NR	-	-
LDS–L-D Saints	1	NR	NR	768	2.6	7.0
LUTH–E.L.C.A.	1	21	109	166	0.6	1.5
MENN–Mennonite USA	1	15	5	6	0.0	0.1
METH–AME	1	0	100	117	0.4	1.1
METH–Un Methodist	25	1,028	2,390	3,187	10.8	28.9
Non-denom Chr Chs	5	640	645	799	2.7	7.3
PENT–Assemb of God	3	180	129	298	1.0	2.7
PENT–Ch God (Cleve)	3	377	513	601	2.0	5.5
PENT–Ch of God Proph	1	NR	22	26	0.1	0.2
PENT–Intl Pent Holiness	3	100	60	70	0.2	0.6
PENT–Un Pent Ch Intl	1	NR	NR	NR	-	-
PRES–Presb Ch (USA)	9	207	420	492	1.7	4.5
Sev Day Adv	1	46	81	93	0.3	0.8
RITCHIE	**49**	**1,565**	**2,996**	**3,865**	**37.0**	**100.0**
BAPT–Amer Bapt USA	7	321	843	1,003	9.6	26.0
BAPT–Free Will Bapt	1	NR	43	51	0.5	1.3
BAPT–NBC USA	1	0	150	178	1.7	4.6
Catholic	1	NR	NR	97	0.9	2.5
Ch of Nazarene	1	35	36	36	0.3	0.9
CHR–Chs of Christ	8	354	416	464	4.4	12.0
Jehovah's Witness	1	NR	NR	NR	-	-
LDS–Comm of Christ	1	NR	118	118	1.1	3.1
LDS–L-D Saints	1	NR	NR	150	1.4	3.9
METH–Un Methodist	19	508	1,036	1,283	12.3	33.2
PENT–Assemb of God	1	210	147	240	2.3	6.2
PENT–Ch God (Cleve)	3	84	131	156	1.5	4.0
PENT–Un Pent Ch Intl	2	NR	NR	NR	-	-
PRES–Presb Ch (USA)	1	20	19	23	0.2	0.6
Sev Day Adv	1	33	57	66	0.6	1.7
ROANE	**43**	**1,221**	**2,357**	**3,187**	**21.4**	**100.0**
Bahá'í	0	NR	1	1	0.0	0.0
BAPT–Amer Bapt USA	10	490	1,137	1,369	9.2	43.0
BAPT–Free Will Bapt	1	NR	43	52	0.3	1.6
Catholic	1	NR	NR	160	1.1	5.0
Ch of Nazarene	1	81	100	141	0.9	4.4
CHR–Chs of Christ	2	50	49	58	0.4	1.8
Jehovah's Witness	1	NR	NR	NR	-	-
LDS–L-D Saints	1	NR	NR	217	1.5	6.8
METH–Un Methodist	19	403	599	712	4.8	22.3
Non-denom Chr Chs	2	112	170	170	1.1	5.3
PENT–COGIC	1	0	150	181	1.2	5.7
PENT–Intl Pent Holiness	1	34	24	29	0.2	0.9
PENT–Un Pent Ch Intl	1	NR	NR	NR	-	-
PRES–Presb Ch (USA)	1	12	16	19	0.1	0.6
Sev Day Adv	1	39	68	78	0.5	2.4
SUMMERS	**34**	**1,147**	**1,865**	**2,432**	**17.5**	**100.0**
ANG/EPIS–Episcopal	1	16	41	41	0.3	1.7
Bahá'í	0	NR	2	2	0.0	0.1
BAPT–Amer Bapt USA	1	75	72	83	0.6	3.4
BAPT–Natl Mis Bapt Conv	1	50	0	0	0.0	0.0
BAPT–So Bapt Conv	4	285	490	565	4.1	23.2
Catholic	1	NR	NR	165	1.2	6.8
Ch of Nazarene	1	55	33	55	0.4	2.3
CHR–Chr Chs & Chs Cr	1	NR	75	87	0.6	3.6

Religious Group	Number of Congregations	Number of Attendees	Number of Communicant, Confirmed, or Full Members	Adherents		
				Number of Adherents	% of Total Pop.	% of Total Adh.
CHR–Chs of Christ	3	96	92	114	0.8	4.7
Jehovah's Witness	1	NR	NR	NR	-	-
MENN–Amish Undif	1	NR	27	79	0.6	3.2
METH–C.M.E.	1	0	100	115	0.8	4.7
METH–Un Methodist	11	273	581	698	5.0	28.7
Non-denom Chr Chs	3	227	227	284	2.0	11.7
PENT–Ch God (Cleve)	1	40	85	98	0.7	4.0
PRES–Presb Ch (USA)	2	30	40	46	0.3	1.9
Sev Day Adv	1	0	0	0	0.0	0.0
TAYLOR	**46**	**1,959**	**3,440**	**4,848**	**28.7**	**100.0**
ANG/EPIS–Episcopal	1	9	16	16	0.1	0.3
BAPT–Amer Bapt USA	8	496	941	1,123	6.6	23.2
BAPT–So Bapt Conv	1	37	200	239	1.4	4.9
BRETH–Grace Breth	2	NR	NR	NR	-	-
Catholic	1	NR	NR	395	2.3	8.1
Ch of Nazarene	2	139	243	304	1.8	6.3
CHR–Chr Ch (Disc)	1	25	90	107	0.6	2.2
CHR–Chs of Christ	2	125	110	149	0.9	3.1
Jehovah's Witness	1	NR	NR	NR	-	-
LUTH–E.L.C.A.	1	42	49	59	0.3	1.2
METH–A.W.M.C.	1	93	29	93	0.6	1.9
METH–Evan Meth Ch	1	NR	NR	NR	-	-
METH–Un Methodist	16	498	1,274	1,643	9.7	33.9
Non-denom Chr Chs	3	330	320	413	2.4	8.5
PENT–Assemb of God	2	55	27	73	0.4	1.5
PRES–Presb Ch (USA)	1	41	23	27	0.2	0.6
Salvation Army	1	33	56	136	0.8	2.8
Sev Day Adv	1	36	62	71	0.4	1.5
TUCKER	**39**	**1,478**	**2,010**	**3,076**	**43.1**	**100.0**
Bahá'í	0	NR	1	1	0.0	0.0
BAPT–So Bapt Conv	1	56	37	43	0.6	1.4
BRETH–Ch of Brethren	2	41	51	59	0.8	1.9
Catholic	2	NR	NR	463	6.5	15.1
Ch of Nazarene	1	46	80	80	1.1	2.6
CHR–Chs of Christ	1	15	12	18	0.3	0.6
LUTH–E.L.C.A.	1	25	117	123	1.7	4.0
METH–Free Methodist	1	28	26	28	0.4	0.9
METH–Un Methodist	19	680	1,122	1,395	19.5	45.4
Non-denom Chr Chs	2	160	220	222	3.1	7.2
PENT–Assemb of God	1	48	19	48	0.7	1.6
PENT–Ch God (Cleve)	3	199	227	265	3.7	8.6
PENT–Pent Ch of God	2	140	NR	217	3.0	7.1
PRES–Presb Ch (USA)	2	18	61	71	1.0	2.3
Sev Day Adv	1	22	37	43	0.6	1.4
TYLER	**35**	**1,132**	**1,718**	**2,442**	**26.5**	**100.0**
ANG/EPIS–Episcopal	1	11	21	21	0.2	0.9
Bahá'í	0	NR	1	1	0.0	0.0
BAPT–Amer Bapt USA	1	29	204	242	2.6	9.9
BAPT–So Bapt Conv	2	94	201	238	2.6	9.7
Catholic	2	NR	NR	122	1.3	5.0
Ch of Nazarene	1	65	105	159	1.7	6.5
CHR–Chr Ch (Disc)	1	0	0	0	0.0	0.0
CHR–Chs of Christ	14	440	409	581	6.3	23.8
METH–Un Methodist	11	404	741	926	10.1	37.9
PENT–Pent Ch of God	1	70	NR	109	1.2	4.5
PRES–Presb Ch (USA)	1	19	36	43	0.5	1.8
UPSHUR	**77**	**2,809**	**4,727**	**7,200**	**29.7**	**100.0**
ANG/EPIS–Episcopal	1	18	28	28	0.1	0.4
Bahá'í	0	NR	2	2	0.0	0.0
BAPT–Amer Bapt USA	6	365	917	1,088	4.5	15.1
BAPT–Reg Bapt Gen As	1	NR	NR	NR	-	-
BAPT–So Bapt Conv	2	76	110	131	0.5	1.8
BRETH–Ch of Brethren	2	10	27	32	0.1	0.4
Catholic	1	NR	NR	573	2.4	8.0
Ch of Nazarene	1	28	49	49	0.2	0.7
Chr & Miss Al	1	139	68	226	0.9	3.1
CHR–Chs of Christ	3	92	88	106	0.4	1.5
FRND–Fr Gen Cf	1	NR	0	0	0.0	0.0

NR–Not Reported   - Represents no adherents reported.   Percentages may not total 100 due to rounding.

Table 3: Religious Congregations by County and Group: 2010

Religious Group	Number of Congregations	Number of Attendees	Number of Communicant, Confirmed, or Full Members	Adherents: Number of Adherents	Adherents: % of Total Pop.	Adherents: % of Total Adh.
Jehovah's Witness	1	NR	NR	NR	-	-
LDS–L-D Saints	1	NR	NR	625	2.6	8.7
METH–A.W.M.C.	1	7	0	7	0.0	0.1
METH–Un Methodist	46	1,173	2,521	3,071	12.7	42.7
Non-denom Chr Chs	3	550	640	740	3.1	10.3
PENT–Assemb of God	1	81	44	141	0.6	2.0
PENT–Ch God (Cleve)	1	104	83	98	0.4	1.4
PENT–Pent Ch of God	1	70	NR	109	0.4	1.5
PENT–Un Pent Ch Intl	1	NR	NR	NR	-	-
PRES–Presb Ch (USA)	1	30	36	43	0.2	0.6
Sev Day Adv	1	66	114	131	0.5	1.8
WAYNE	**86**	**4,846**	**9,854**	**12,384**	**29.2**	**100.0**
Bahá'í	0	NR	2	2	0.0	0.0
BAPT–Amer Bapt USA	11	963	2,077	2,505	5.9	20.2
BAPT–Free Will Bapt	18	NR	957	1,154	2.7	9.3
BAPT–So Bapt Conv	8	1,297	2,941	3,548	8.4	28.6
Catholic	1	NR	NR	89	0.2	0.7
CGOD–Ch God (Ander)	2	95	NR	95	0.2	0.8
CHR–Chr Ch (Disc)	1	60	108	130	0.3	1.0
CHR–Chr Chs & Chs Cr	1	NR	150	181	0.4	1.5
CHR–Chs of Christ	12	776	725	922	2.2	7.4
CONG–Cong Chr, NA	1	NR	25	30	0.1	0.2
METH–Un Methodist	12	664	1,570	2,060	4.8	16.6
Non-denom Chr Chs	3	210	275	300	0.7	2.4
ORTHE–Rus Orth Abroad	3	100	NR	115	0.3	0.9
PENT–Ch God (Cleve)	8	508	827	998	2.3	8.1
PENT–Int Pent C Chr	1	33	31	45	0.1	0.4
PENT–Un Pent Ch Intl	1	NR	NR	NR	-	-
PRES–Presb Ch (USA)	2	67	95	115	0.3	0.9
Salvation Army	1	73	71	95	0.2	0.8
WEBSTER	**25**	**733**	**1,171**	**1,932**	**21.1**	**100.0**
BAPT–Amer Bapt USA	3	93	278	330	3.6	17.1
BAPT–So Bapt Conv	2	41	153	182	2.0	9.4
Catholic	1	NR	NR	76	0.8	3.9
Jehovah's Witness	1	NR	NR	NR	-	-
LDS–L-D Saints	1	NR	NR	305	3.3	15.8
METH–Un Methodist	9	145	311	369	4.0	19.1
Non-denom Chr Chs	2	195	195	244	2.7	12.6
PENT–Assemb of God	1	88	68	121	1.3	6.3
PENT–Ch God (Cleve)	1	42	79	94	1.0	4.9
PENT–Pent Ch of God	1	70	NR	109	1.2	5.6
PENT–Un Pent Ch Intl	1	NR	NR	NR	-	-
PRES–Presb Ch (USA)	1	43	58	69	0.8	3.6
Sev Day Adv	1	16	29	33	0.4	1.7
WETZEL	**70**	**2,952**	**5,214**	**7,742**	**46.7**	**100.0**
ANG/EPIS–Episcopal	1	18	62	62	0.4	0.8
Ap Chr Ch-Amer	1	0	0	0	0.0	0.0
Bahá'í	0	NR	5	5	0.0	0.1
BAPT–Amer Bapt USA	4	218	471	558	3.4	7.2
BAPT–Reg Bapt Gen As	3	NR	NR	NR	-	-
BAPT–So Bapt Conv	2	46	274	325	2.0	4.2
Catholic	2	NR	NR	664	4.0	8.6
CGOD–Ch God (Ander)	2	128	NR	128	0.8	1.7
Ch of Nazarene	2	121	208	358	2.2	4.6
CHR–Chr Ch (Disc)	1	138	384	455	2.7	5.9
CHR–Chr Chs & Chs Cr	3	NR	510	604	3.6	7.8
CHR–Chs of Christ	22	1,290	1,262	1,580	9.5	20.4
Jehovah's Witness	1	NR	NR	NR	-	-
LDS–L-D Saints	1	NR	NR	363	2.2	4.7
LUTH–E.L.C.A.	1	28	82	94	0.6	1.2
METH–Un Methodist	14	495	1,471	1,862	11.2	24.1
METH–Wesleyan	1	25	16	33	0.2	0.4
Non-denom Chr Chs	2	120	160	175	1.1	2.3
PENT–Ch God (Cleve)	2	177	193	229	1.4	3.0
PENT–Intl Pent Holiness	1	28	35	41	0.2	0.5
PENT–Pent Ch of God	1	70	NR	109	0.7	1.4
PENT–Un Pent Ch Intl	1	NR	NR	NR	-	-
PRES–Presb Ch (USA)	1	25	54	64	0.4	0.8
PRES–Presb Ch Amer	1	25	27	33	0.2	0.4
WIRT	**19**	**574**	**1,317**	**1,621**	**28.4**	**100.0**
Bahá'í	0	NR	1	1	0.0	0.1
BAPT–Amer Bapt USA	5	258	712	845	14.8	52.1
BAPT–So Bapt Conv	1	95	126	150	2.6	9.3
Catholic	1	NR	NR	61	1.1	3.8
Ch of Nazarene	1	43	101	102	1.8	6.3
CHR–Chs of Christ	1	25	24	28	0.5	1.7
MENN–Amish Undif	1	NR	14	38	0.7	2.3
METH–Un Methodist	7	153	322	376	6.6	23.2
PENT–Un Pent Ch Intl	1	NR	NR	NR	-	-
PRES–Presb Ch (USA)	1	0	17	20	0.3	1.2
WOOD	**184**	**16,545**	**27,438**	**39,519**	**45.4**	**100.0**
ANG/EPIS–Anglican NA	1	NR	NR	NR	-	-
ANG/EPIS–Episcopal	3	223	654	849	1.0	2.1
Bahá'í	0	NR	11	11	0.0	0.0
BAPT–Amer Bapt USA	22	4,098	7,452	8,937	10.3	22.6
BAPT–Free Will Bapt	2	NR	86	103	0.1	0.3
BAPT–Reg Bapt Gen As	1	NR	NR	NR	-	-
BAPT–So Bapt Conv	6	710	1,854	2,224	2.6	5.6
BRETH–Grace Breth	1	NR	NR	NR	-	-
Catholic	4	NR	NR	4,444	5.1	11.2
CGOD–Ch God (Ander)	1	210	NR	210	0.2	0.5
Ch God (7th Day)	1	NR	NR	NR	-	-
Ch of Nazarene	4	522	869	1,255	1.4	3.2
CHR–Chr Ch (Disc)	2	67	170	204	0.2	0.5
CHR–Chr Chs & Chs Cr	3	NR	151	181	0.2	0.5
CHR–Chs of Christ	21	2,744	2,929	3,431	3.9	8.7
Jehovah's Witness	2	NR	NR	NR	-	-
JUD–Reform	1	11	19	51	0.1	0.1
LDS–Comm of Christ	1	NR	118	118	0.1	0.3
LDS–L-D Saints	1	NR	NR	888	1.0	2.2
LUTH–E.L.C.A.	2	234	606	792	0.9	2.0
LUTH–Luth-MO Synod	1	86	112	142	0.2	0.4
METH–AME	1	15	20	24	0.0	0.1
METH–Evan Meth Ch	2	NR	NR	NR	-	-
METH–Un Methodist	60	3,594	7,009	8,821	10.1	22.3
METH–Wesleyan	5	172	106	225	0.3	0.6
Non-denom Chr Chs	16	2,930	3,300	3,914	4.5	9.9
PENT–Assemb of God	3	272	179	481	0.6	1.2
PENT–Ch God (Cleve)	5	290	833	999	1.1	2.5
PENT–Un Pent Ch Intl	3	NR	NR	NR	-	-
PRES–Presb Ch (USA)	5	193	631	757	0.9	1.9
Salvation Army	1	58	126	225	0.3	0.6
Sev Day Adv	3	116	203	233	0.3	0.6
WYOMING	**92**	**3,938**	**7,385**	**9,486**	**39.9**	**100.0**
ANG/EPIS–Episcopal	1	9	20	20	0.1	0.2
BAPT–Amer Bapt USA	18	1,075	2,898	3,474	14.6	36.6
BAPT–Free Will Bapt	13	NR	559	670	2.8	7.1
BAPT–Natl Mis Bapt Conv	1	0	150	180	0.8	1.9
BAPT–So Bapt Conv	6	212	404	484	2.0	5.1
Catholic	2	NR	NR	130	0.5	1.4
CGOD–Ch God (Ander)	3	30	NR	30	0.1	0.3
Ch of Nazarene	2	44	205	205	0.9	2.2
CHR–Chs of Christ	2	50	42	55	0.2	0.6
Jehovah's Witness	1	NR	NR	NR	-	-
METH–Un Methodist	11	238	596	687	2.9	7.2
METH–Wesleyan	1	30	16	39	0.2	0.4
Non-denom Chr Chs	10	985	965	1,239	5.2	13.1
PENT–Assemb of God	1	8	5	9	0.0	0.1
PENT–Ch God (Cleve)	11	606	807	968	4.1	10.2
PENT–Ch of God Proph	1	NR	35	42	0.2	0.4
PENT–Intl Pent Holiness	2	328	614	736	3.1	7.8
PENT–Pent Ch of God	4	280	NR	435	1.8	4.6
PRES–Presb Ch (USA)	2	43	69	83	0.3	0.9
WISCONSIN	**6,078**	**611,541**	**1,126,174**	**3,047,442**	**53.6**	**100.0**
ADAMS	**21**	**739**	**1,736**	**4,339**	**20.8**	**100.0**
Bahá'í	0	NR	3	3	0.0	0.1

NR–Not Reported   - Represents no adherents reported.   Percentages may not total 100 due to rounding.

Table 3: Religious Congregations by County and Group: 2010

Religious Group	Number of Congrega-tions	Number of Attendees	Number of Communicant, Confirmed, or Full Members	Adherents		
				Number of Adherents	% of Total Pop.	% of Total Adh.
BAPT–Reg Bapt Gen As	1	NR	NR	NR	-	-
Catholic	2	NR	NR	1,700	8.1	39.2
CHR–Chs of Christ	1	7	7	7	0.0	0.2
CONG–Cong Chr, NA	2	NR	77	88	0.4	2.0
Grace Gosp Fel	1	NR	NR	NR	-	-
Jehovah's Witness	1	NR	NR	NR	-	-
LDS–L-D Saints	1	NR	NR	286	1.4	6.6
LUTH–E.L.C.A.	4	244	825	1,259	6.0	29.0
LUTH–Luth–MO Synod	3	136	439	558	2.7	12.9
METH–Un Methodist	2	74	116	130	0.6	3.0
PENT–Assemb of God	2	262	239	274	1.3	6.3
Un C of Christ	1	16	30	34	0.2	0.8
ASHLAND	**37**	**1,660**	**3,516**	**9,997**	**61.9**	**100.0**
ANG/EPIS–Episcopal	1	16	77	77	0.5	0.8
Bahá'í	0	NR	5	5	0.0	0.1
BAPT–Converge/BGC	1	75	NR	90	0.6	0.9
Catholic	8	NR	NR	4,952	30.6	49.5
CHR–Chs of Christ	1	12	12	15	0.1	0.2
Evan Cov Ch	1	22	17	29	0.2	0.3
FRND–Fr Gen Cf	1	NR	3	4	0.0	0.0
Jehovah's Witness	2	NR	NR	NR	-	-
LDS–L-D Saints	1	NR	NR	270	1.7	2.7
LUTH–E.L.C.A.	2	177	619	954	5.9	9.5
LUTH–Luth–MO Synod	5	570	1,698	2,157	13.4	21.6
LUTH–Wisc Ev Luth Syn	1	20	41	48	0.3	0.5
METH–Un Methodist	3	104	150	210	1.3	2.1
Non-denom Chr Chs	1	40	65	65	0.4	0.7
PENT–Assemb of God	2	125	57	167	1.0	1.7
PENT–Un Pent Ch Intl	1	NR	NR	NR	-	-
PRES–Presb Ch (USA)	1	147	418	509	3.2	5.1
Sev Day Adv	1	31	54	62	0.4	0.6
Un C of Christ	3	253	266	324	2.0	3.2
Unit Univ	1	68	34	59	0.4	0.6
BARRON	**81**	**6,125**	**12,685**	**26,014**	**56.7**	**100.0**
ANG/EPIS–Episcopal	1	38	79	80	0.2	0.3
Bahá'í	0	NR	7	7	0.0	0.0
BAPT–Converge/BGC	1	75	NR	90	0.2	0.3
BAPT–Ref Bapt Ch	1	NR	NR	NR	-	-
BAPT–Reg Bapt Gen As	3	NR	NR	NR	-	-
BAPT–So Bapt Conv	1	47	56	67	0.1	0.3
Catholic	8	NR	NR	7,764	16.9	29.8
Chr & Miss Al	1	55	26	55	0.1	0.2
CHR–Chs of Christ	1	25	27	31	0.1	0.1
Evan Cov Ch	1	65	63	84	0.2	0.3
Evan Free Ch	2	615	NR	615	1.3	2.4
Jehovah's Witness	1	NR	NR	NR	-	-
LDS–Comm of Christ	1	NR	138	138	0.3	0.5
LDS–L-D Saints	1	NR	NR	430	0.9	1.7
LUTH–Assoc Free Luth	2	NR	NR	NR	-	-
LUTH–E.L.C.A.	16	1,840	6,706	8,479	18.5	32.6
LUTH–Luth Cong Msn Chr	1	71	204	245	0.5	0.9
LUTH–Luth–MO Synod	8	726	1,870	2,215	4.8	8.5
LUTH–Wisc Ev Luth Syn	2	145	245	280	0.6	1.1
MENN–Amish Undif	1	NR	31	115	0.3	0.4
MENN–CG in Cr (Menn)	3	NR	393	473	1.0	1.8
METH–Free Methodist	1	22	0	22	0.0	0.1
METH–Un Methodist	8	561	1,357	1,938	4.2	7.4
METH–Wesleyan	2	607	141	789	1.7	3.0
Muslim Est	1	134	NR	308	0.7	1.2
Non-denom Chr Chs	5	575	580	719	1.6	2.8
PENT–Assemb of God	3	154	41	215	0.5	0.8
PENT–Ch God (Cleve)	1	15	16	19	0.0	0.1
PENT–Int Foursq Gos	1	135	232	279	0.6	1.1
PRES–Presb Ch (USA)	1	110	284	342	0.7	1.3
Sev Day Adv	1	90	156	179	0.4	0.7
Unit Univ	1	20	33	36	0.1	0.1
BAYFIELD	**35**	**1,210**	**1,512**	**6,204**	**41.3**	**100.0**
ANG/EPIS–Episcopal	1	9	5	5	0.0	0.1
Bahá'í	0	NR	1	1	0.0	0.0
BAPT–Converge/BGC	3	225	NR	270	1.8	4.4

Religious Group	Number of Congrega-tions	Number of Attendees	Number of Communicant, Confirmed, or Full Members	Adherents		
				Number of Adherents	% of Total Pop.	% of Total Adh.
Catholic	10	NR	NR	3,109	20.7	50.1
Chr & Miss Al	1	69	28	89	0.6	1.4
Evan Free Ch	1	110	NR	110	0.7	1.8
Jehovah's Witness	1	NR	NR	NR	-	-
LUTH–Assoc Free Luth	1	NR	NR	NR	-	-
LUTH–E.L.C.A.	7	377	788	1,645	11.0	26.5
LUTH–Luth–MO Synod	1	38	115	121	0.8	2.0
METH–Un Methodist	2	72	82	168	1.1	2.7
Non-denom Chr Chs	1	35	20	44	0.3	0.7
PENT–Assemb of God	2	123	105	213	1.4	3.4
PRES–Presb Ch (USA)	2	62	180	210	1.4	3.4
Un C of Christ	2	90	188	219	1.5	3.5
BROWN	**167**	**23,365**	**40,404**	**166,233**	**67.0**	**100.0**
ANG/EPIS–Episcopal	4	331	880	1,438	0.6	0.9
Bahá'í	1	NR	79	79	0.0	0.0
BAPT–Amer Bapt USA	1	92	134	166	0.1	0.1
BAPT–Converge/BGC	2	150	NR	180	0.1	0.1
BAPT–Free Will Bapt	1	NR	92	114	0.0	0.1
BAPT–Reg Bapt Gen As	1	NR	NR	NR	-	-
BAPT–So Bapt Conv	5	786	903	1,120	0.5	0.7
BUDD–Mahayana	1	NR	NR	27	0.0	0.0
Calv Chpl	1	NR	NR	NR	-	-
Catholic	35	NR	NR	110,123	44.4	66.2
Ch Cr, Scientst	1	NR	NR	NR	-	-
Ch of Nazarene	1	56	38	56	0.0	0.0
Chr & Miss Al	2	295	497	557	0.2	0.3
CHR–Chr Chs & Chs Cr	1	NR	175	217	0.1	0.1
CHR–Chs of Christ	2	98	95	133	0.1	0.1
CONG–Cong Chr, NA	1	NR	222	275	0.1	0.2
Evan Cov Ch	1	38	37	49	0.0	0.0
Evan Free Ch	1	1,500	NR	1,500	0.6	0.9
FRND–Fr Gen Cf	1	NR	10	12	0.0	0.0
Jehovah's Witness	3	NR	NR	NR	-	-
JUD–Conserv	1	61	68	184	0.1	0.1
LDS–L-D Saints	3	NR	NR	1,177	0.5	0.7
LUTH–E.L.C.A.	14	3,198	8,958	12,493	5.0	7.5
LUTH–Evan Luth Syn	1	105	169	206	0.1	0.1
LUTH–Luth–MO Synod	11	3,030	6,599	8,720	3.5	5.2
LUTH–Wisc Ev Luth Syn	14	3,211	5,059	6,635	2.7	4.0
METH–Un Methodist	9	1,345	2,928	3,953	1.6	2.4
Metro Comm Ch	1	15	17	21	0.0	0.0
MORAV–Morav Ch-North	1	73	251	319	0.1	0.2
Muslim Est	1	134	NR	308	0.1	0.2
Non-denom Chr Chs	17	6,201	9,505	10,013	4.0	6.0
ORTHE–Orth Ch in Amer	1	60	NR	100	0.0	0.1
PENT–Assemb of God	7	1,003	618	1,283	0.5	0.8
PENT–Ch God (Cleve)	1	28	49	61	0.0	0.0
PENT–Un Pent Ch Intl	3	NR	NR	NR	-	-
PENT–Vineyard	1	130	175	217	0.1	0.1
PRES–Orth Pres Ch	1	139	155	241	0.1	0.1
PRES–Presb Ch (USA)	5	319	867	1,075	0.4	0.6
PRES–Presb Ch Amer	1	0	0	0	0.0	0.0
Salvation Army	1	74	120	1,095	0.4	0.7
Sev Day Adv	3	380	660	759	0.3	0.5
Un C of Christ	3	448	959	1,189	0.5	0.7
Unit Univ	1	65	85	138	0.1	0.1
BUFFALO	**35**	**1,409**	**4,013**	**8,769**	**64.5**	**100.0**
Bahá'í	0	NR	1	1	0.0	0.0
BAPT–Converge/BGC	1	75	NR	90	0.7	1.0
Catholic	4	NR	NR	3,100	22.8	35.4
CHR–Chs of Christ	1	13	12	18	0.1	0.2
Evan Cov Ch	1	22	24	29	0.2	0.3
Jehovah's Witness	2	NR	NR	NR	-	-
LUTH–E.L.C.A.	7	516	1,727	2,747	20.2	31.3
LUTH–Luth–MO Synod	4	145	572	704	5.2	8.0
LUTH–Wisc Ev Luth Syn	5	233	713	841	6.2	9.6
MENN–Amish Undif	1	NR	65	167	1.2	1.9
METH–Un Methodist	4	150	388	481	3.5	5.5
Non-denom Chr Chs	2	135	180	194	1.4	2.2
Un C of Christ	3	120	331	397	2.9	4.5

NR–Not Reported - Represents no adherents reported. Percentages may not total 100 due to rounding.

Table 3: Religious Congregations by County and Group: 2010

Religious Group	Number of Congregations	Number of Attendees	Number of Communicant, Confirmed, or Full Members	Adherents: Number of Adherents	Adherents: % of Total Pop.	Adherents: % of Total Adh.
BURNETT	**32**	**2,167**	**2,776**	**5,372**	**34.8**	**100.0**
Bahá'í	0	NR	1	1	0.0	0.0
BAPT–Converge/BGC	3	550	NR	660	4.3	12.3
BAPT–So Bapt Conv	1	75	NR	NR	-	-
Catholic	4	NR	NR	1,181	7.6	22.0
Ch of Nazarene	1	20	24	24	0.2	0.4
CHR–Chs of Christ	1	45	40	55	0.4	1.0
Evan Cov Ch	2	91	137	119	0.8	2.2
Evan Free Ch	1	110	NR	110	0.7	2.0
Jehovah's Witness	1	NR	NR	NR	-	-
LUTH–E.L.C.A.	8	754	1,888	2,215	14.3	41.2
LUTH–Luth–MO Synod	2	71	137	151	1.0	2.8
METH–Un Methodist	5	234	421	614	4.0	11.4
METH–Wesleyan	1	32	18	42	0.3	0.8
Non-denom Chr Chs	1	60	60	75	0.5	1.4
PENT–Assemb of God	1	125	50	125	0.8	2.3
CALUMET	**31**	**2,894**	**5,599**	**22,604**	**46.2**	**100.0**
Bahá'í	0	NR	4	4	0.0	0.0
Calv Chpl	1	NR	NR	NR	-	-
Catholic	7	NR	NR	15,168	31.0	67.1
Chr & Miss Al	1	172	167	292	0.6	1.3
LDS–L-D Saints	1	NR	NR	79	0.2	0.3
LUTH–Ch of Luth Br	1	70	46	100	0.2	0.4
LUTH–E.L.C.A.	1	70	293	300	0.6	1.3
LUTH–Luth–MO Synod	6	914	2,022	2,563	5.2	11.3
LUTH–Wisc Ev Luth Syn	3	1,005	1,492	1,975	4.0	8.7
MENN–Amish Undif	1	NR	36	89	0.2	0.4
METH–Un Methodist	4	233	529	707	1.4	3.1
Non-denom Chr Chs	1	100	84	125	0.3	0.6
PENT–Assemb of God	1	35	25	64	0.1	0.3
Un C of Christ	3	295	901	1,138	2.3	5.0
CHIPPEWA	**87**	**5,302**	**10,477**	**29,361**	**47.0**	**100.0**
ANG/EPIS–Episcopal	2	44	71	104	0.2	0.4
Bahá'í	0	NR	15	15	0.0	0.1
BAPT–Consrv Bapt	2	NR	NR	NR	-	-
BAPT–S-D Baptist Gen Con	1	55	53	65	0.1	0.2
BAPT–So Bapt Conv	2	85	145	177	0.3	0.6
BRETH–Ch of Brethren	1	0	21	26	0.0	0.1
Catholic	12	NR	NR	14,850	23.8	50.6
Chr & Miss Al	1	59	29	109	0.2	0.4
CHR–Chr Chs & Chs Cr	4	NR	314	384	0.6	1.3
Evan Free Ch	1	200	NR	200	0.3	0.7
Grace Gosp Fel	1	NR	NR	NR	-	-
Ind Fund Churches	1	NR	NR	NR	-	-
Jehovah's Witness	3	NR	NR	NR	-	-
LDS–L-D Saints	1	NR	NR	186	0.3	0.6
LUTH–E.L.C.A.	12	1,655	4,239	5,563	8.9	18.9
LUTH–Evan Luth Syn	1	46	73	82	0.1	0.3
LUTH–Luth Ch-Am Asc	1	NR	NR	NR	-	-
LUTH–Luth Cong Msn Chr	1	88	100	122	0.2	0.4
LUTH–Luth–MO Synod	5	573	1,434	1,847	3.0	6.3
LUTH–Wisc Ev Luth Syn	4	362	859	1,024	1.6	3.5
MENN–Amish Undif	4	NR	174	478	0.8	1.6
METH–Un Methodist	10	542	1,184	1,695	2.7	5.8
Non-denom Chr Chs	7	1,140	1,130	1,467	2.4	5.0
ORTHE–Orth Ch in Amer	1	25	NR	25	0.0	0.1
PENT–Assemb of God	3	160	82	230	0.4	0.8
PENT–Open Bible Std	1	35	NR	35	0.1	0.1
PENT–Vineyard	1	31	41	50	0.1	0.2
PRES–Presb Ch (USA)	2	120	270	330	0.5	1.1
Un C of Christ	2	82	243	297	0.5	1.0
CLARK	**80**	**3,209**	**7,131**	**20,117**	**58.0**	**100.0**
ANG/EPIS–Episcopal	1	24	27	27	0.1	0.1
Bahá'í	0	NR	7	7	0.0	0.0
BAPT–NT Ind Bapt	1	NR	NR	NR	-	-
Catholic	9	NR	NR	9,535	27.5	47.4
Chr & Miss Al	2	178	92	205	0.6	1.0
Evan Free Ch	1	150	NR	150	0.4	0.7
Ind Fund Churches	1	NR	NR	NR	-	-
Jehovah's Witness	5	NR	NR	NR	-	-
LUTH–E.L.C.A.	7	540	1,732	2,281	6.6	11.3
LUTH–Luth–MO Synod	8	837	1,915	2,459	7.1	12.2
LUTH–Wisc Ev Luth Syn	3	326	737	891	2.6	4.4
MENN–Amish Undif	15	NR	772	1,986	5.7	9.9
METH–Un Methodist	10	199	451	577	1.7	2.9
Non-denom Chr Chs	5	405	430	531	1.5	2.6
PENT–Assemb of God	3	200	82	326	0.9	1.6
PENT–Un Pent Ch Intl	1	NR	NR	NR	-	-
PRES–Presb Ch (USA)	1	43	106	137	0.4	0.7
Sev Day Adv	1	23	40	46	0.1	0.2
Un C of Christ	6	284	740	959	2.8	4.8
COLUMBIA	**90**	**7,446**	**14,624**	**31,383**	**55.2**	**100.0**
ANG/EPIS–Episcopal	1	27	53	73	0.1	0.2
Bahá'í	0	NR	9	9	0.0	0.0
BAPT–Amer Bapt USA	2	103	133	162	0.3	0.5
BAPT–Converge/BGC	1	75	NR	90	0.2	0.3
BAPT–NT Ind Bapt	1	NR	NR	NR	-	-
BAPT–S-D Baptist Gen Con	1	30	25	30	0.1	0.1
BAPT–So Bapt Conv	1	180	48	58	0.1	0.2
Catholic	9	NR	NR	11,473	20.2	36.6
Ch of Nazarene	1	37	35	37	0.1	0.1
Evan Free Ch	2	280	NR	280	0.5	0.9
Ind Fund Churches	4	NR	NR	NR	-	-
Jehovah's Witness	3	NR	NR	NR	-	-
LUTH–E.L.C.A.	9	1,175	3,280	4,490	7.9	14.3
LUTH–Evan Luth Syn	2	46	115	123	0.2	0.4
LUTH–Luth–MO Synod	3	854	2,233	2,976	5.2	9.5
LUTH–Wisc Ev Luth Syn	8	1,097	2,687	3,362	5.9	10.7
MENN–Amish Undif	4	NR	185	450	0.8	1.4
METH–Un Methodist	9	847	2,134	2,881	5.1	9.2
METH–Wesleyan	1	48	27	62	0.1	0.2
Non-denom Chr Chs	6	915	727	1,194	2.1	3.8
PENT–Assemb of God	4	324	214	477	0.8	1.5
PENT–Un Pent Ch Intl	1	NR	NR	NR	-	-
PRES–Presb Ch (USA)	10	549	1,105	1,345	2.4	4.3
PRES–Presb Ch Amer	1	175	129	129	0.2	0.4
REF–Ref Ch in Am	1	200	482	503	0.9	1.6
Sev Day Adv	3	361	628	722	1.3	2.3
Un C of Christ	2	123	375	457	0.8	1.5
CRAWFORD	**38**	**1,378**	**3,122**	**9,385**	**56.4**	**100.0**
ANG/EPIS–Episcopal	1	21	26	28	0.2	0.3
Bahá'í	0	NR	1	1	0.0	0.0
Catholic	7	NR	NR	5,150	30.9	54.9
CHR–Chr Chs & Chs Cr	2	NR	140	168	1.0	1.8
CONG–Cong Chr, NA	1	NR	17	20	0.1	0.2
Evan Free Ch	1	130	NR	130	0.8	1.4
FRND–Fr Gen Cf	1	NR	21	25	0.2	0.3
LDS–Comm of Christ	1	NR	138	138	0.8	1.5
LDS–L-D Saints	1	NR	NR	98	0.6	1.0
LUTH–E.L.C.A.	7	486	1,668	1,899	11.4	20.2
LUTH–Luth Cong Msn Chr	1	43	182	218	1.3	2.3
LUTH–Wisc Ev Luth Syn	1	69	121	158	0.9	1.7
MENN–Amish Undif	0	NR	15	51	0.3	0.5
METH–Un Methodist	8	308	467	847	5.1	9.0
METH–Wesleyan	1	40	17	52	0.3	0.6
Non-denom Chr Chs	1	170	150	212	1.3	2.3
PENT–Int Foursq Gos	1	95	133	159	1.0	1.7
PENT–Un Pent Ch Intl	1	NR	NR	NR	-	-
Sev Day Adv	1	10	18	21	0.1	0.2
Un C of Christ	1	6	8	10	0.1	0.1
DANE	**351**	**41,948**	**74,355**	**224,083**	**45.9**	**100.0**
ANG/EPIS–Anglican NA	1	NR	NR	NR	-	-
ANG/EPIS–Episcopal	5	589	1,380	1,402	0.3	0.6
Bahá'í	2	NR	282	282	0.1	0.1
BAPT–Alliance Bapt	1	NR	NR	NR	-	-
BAPT–Amer Bapt USA	3	1,690	3,115	3,755	0.8	1.7
BAPT–Consrv Bapt	1	NR	NR	NR	-	-
BAPT–Converge/BGC	4	625	NR	750	0.2	0.3
BAPT–Free Will Bapt	1	NR	32	39	0.0	0.0

NR–Not Reported - Represents no adherents reported. Percentages may not total 100 due to rounding.

Table 3: Religious Congregations by County and Group: 2010

Religious Group	Number of Congrega-tions	Number of Attendees	Number of Communicant, Confirmed, or Full Members	Adherents		
				Number of Adherents	% of Total Pop.	% of Total Adh.
BAPT–NBC USA	1	210	275	332	0.1	0.1
BAPT–Ref Bapt Ch	1	NR	NR	NR	-	-
BAPT–Reg Bapt Gen As	2	NR	NR	NR	-	-
BAPT–S-D Baptist Gen Con	2	13	36	43	0.0	0.0
BAPT–So Bapt Conv	8	408	530	639	0.1	0.3
BUDD–Mahayana	5	NR	NR	361	0.1	0.2
BUDD–Theravada	2	NR	NR	410	0.1	0.2
BUDD–Vajrayana	4	NR	NR	562	0.1	0.3
Calv Chpl	1	NR	NR	NR	-	-
Catholic	34	NR	NR	106,036	21.7	47.3
CGOD–Ch God (Ander)	1	8	NR	8	0.0	0.0
Ch Cr, Scientst	1	NR	NR	NR	-	-
Ch of Nazarene	2	87	160	160	0.0	0.1
Chr & Miss Al	2	212	220	411	0.1	0.2
CHR–Chr Chs & Chs Cr	3	NR	90	109	0.0	0.0
CHR–Chs of Christ	3	140	135	188	0.0	0.1
CHR–Int Chs of Christ	1	NR	118	142	0.0	0.1
CONG–Cong Chr, NA	1	NR	95	115	0.0	0.1
Evan Cov Ch	2	45	102	58	0.0	0.0
Evan Free Ch	8	6,075	NR	6,075	1.2	2.7
FRND–Consrv Yr Mtgs	1	NR	8	10	0.0	0.0
FRND–Fr Gen Cf	2	NR	309	373	0.1	0.2
Grace Gosp Fel	1	NR	NR	NR	-	-
HINDU–Post Ren	2	NR	NR	130	0.0	0.1
HINDU–Trad Temples	2	NR	NR	475	0.1	0.2
Ind Fund Churches	2	NR	NR	NR	-	-
Jehovah's Witness	7	NR	NR	NR	-	-
JUD–Conserv	1	246	276	745	0.2	0.3
JUD–Orth	1	43	50	60	0.0	0.0
JUD–Reconst	1	69	88	238	0.0	0.1
JUD–Reform	1	376	663	1,790	0.4	0.8
LDS–Comm of Christ	1	NR	138	138	0.0	0.1
LDS–L-D Saints	8	NR	NR	2,832	0.6	1.3
LUTH–Ch Luth Conf	2	NR	NR	NR	-	-
LUTH–E.L.C.A.	48	10,932	33,939	48,620	10.0	21.7
LUTH–Evan Luth Syn	6	833	1,632	2,031	0.4	0.9
LUTH–Luth Cong Msn Chr	1	192	291	351	0.1	0.2
LUTH–Luth–MO Synod	12	1,635	2,923	3,921	0.8	1.7
LUTH–Wisc Ev Luth Syn	11	2,261	3,245	4,214	0.9	1.9
MENN–Mennonite USA	1	102	150	181	0.0	0.1
METH–AME	2	195	280	338	0.1	0.2
METH–Free Methodist	2	164	22	164	0.0	0.1
METH–Un Methodist	25	3,177	6,531	9,753	2.0	4.4
METH–Wesleyan	1	56	23	73	0.0	0.0
MJEW–Union Mes Cong	1	NR	NR	NR	-	-
MORAV–Morav Ch-North	3	148	345	411	0.1	0.2
Muslim Est	3	388	NR	2,616	0.5	1.2
New Apost Ch	1	NR	NR	NR	-	-
Non-denom Chr Chs	35	5,826	5,864	7,448	1.5	3.3
ORTHE–Ant Orth of NA	1	120	NR	165	0.0	0.1
ORTHE–Greek Orthodox	1	100	NR	220	0.0	0.1
ORTHE–Serb Orth USA	1	10	NR	25	0.0	0.0
ORTHO–Coptic Orth Ch	1	28	NR	35	0.0	0.0
PENT–Apos Faith Msn	1	NR	35	42	0.0	0.0
PENT–Assemb of God	9	832	423	1,233	0.3	0.6
PENT–COGIC	1	0	90	109	0.0	0.0
PENT–Int Foursq Gos	3	153	186	224	0.0	0.1
PENT–Un Pent Ch Intl	2	NR	NR	NR	-	-
PENT–United Holy Ch	1	NR	NR	NR	-	-
PENT–Vineyard	2	93	130	157	0.0	0.1
PRES–Orth Pres Ch	1	58	39	50	0.0	0.0
PRES–Presb Ch (USA)	10	1,205	3,039	3,664	0.8	1.6
PRES–Presb Ch Amer	3	65	75	83	0.0	0.0
REF–Christian Ref	2	230	270	326	0.1	0.1
Salvation Army	2	122	122	736	0.2	0.3
Sev Day Adv	3	430	749	861	0.2	0.4
Sikh	1	NR	NR	NR	-	-
Un C of Christ	15	1,622	4,176	5,035	1.0	2.2
Unit Univ	3	135	1,674	2,328	0.5	1.0
Unity Ch	2	NR	NR	NR	-	-
Zoroastrian	0	NR	NR	1	0.0	0.0
DODGE	**109**	**11,906**	**24,547**	**44,822**	**50.5**	**100.0**
ANG/EPIS–Episcopal	2	67	88	118	0.1	0.3
Bahá'í	0	NR	32	32	0.0	0.1
BAPT–Converge/BGC	1	75	NR	90	0.1	0.2
BAPT–NT Ind Bapt	1	NR	NR	NR	-	-
Catholic	13	NR	NR	13,437	15.1	30.0
Chr & Miss Al	2	417	215	630	0.7	1.4
CHR–Chs of Christ	2	42	28	41	0.0	0.1
Evan Free Ch	2	380	NR	380	0.4	0.8
Jehovah's Witness	1	NR	NR	NR	-	-
LDS–L-D Saints	1	NR	NR	233	0.3	0.5
LUTH–E.L.C.A.	10	1,276	4,821	6,249	7.0	13.9
LUTH–Luth–MO Synod	12	1,860	4,640	5,629	6.3	12.6
LUTH–Nor Amer Luth C	2	NR	NR	NR	-	-
LUTH–Wisc Ev Luth Syn	22	3,353	7,173	8,897	10.0	19.8
METH–Un Methodist	7	745	1,711	2,151	2.4	4.8
Non-denom Chr Chs	3	375	395	469	0.5	1.0
PENT–Assemb of God	2	245	147	360	0.4	0.8
PENT–Assm God Intl F	1	NR	NR	NR	-	-
PENT–Int Foursq Gos	1	14	5	6	0.0	0.0
PENT–Un Pent Ch Intl	1	NR	NR	NR	-	-
PRES–Presb Ch (USA)	3	197	548	658	0.7	1.5
REF–Christian Ref	8	1,290	1,663	1,997	2.2	4.5
REF–Prot Ref Chs	1	189	122	214	0.2	0.5
REF–Ref Ch in Am	5	1,156	2,338	2,487	2.8	5.5
Sev Day Adv	1	22	38	44	0.0	0.1
Un C of Christ	5	203	583	700	0.8	1.6
DOOR	**53**	**4,284**	**7,674**	**19,261**	**69.3**	**100.0**
ANG/EPIS–Episcopal	4	203	188	213	0.8	1.1
Bahá'í	0	NR	30	30	0.1	0.2
BAPT–Converge/BGC	3	225	NR	270	1.0	1.4
Catholic	6	NR	NR	9,325	33.6	48.4
Ch Cr, Scientst	1	NR	NR	NR	-	-
Evan Free Ch	1	90	NR	90	0.3	0.5
FRND–Fr Un Mtg	1	NR	13	15	0.1	0.1
Jehovah's Witness	1	NR	NR	NR	-	-
LDS–L-D Saints	1	NR	NR	126	0.5	0.7
LUTH–E.L.C.A.	7	1,135	2,567	2,982	10.7	15.5
LUTH–Luth Cong Msn Chr	1	60	245	283	1.0	1.5
LUTH–Luth–MO Synod	2	228	396	503	1.8	2.6
LUTH–Wisc Ev Luth Syn	7	960	2,133	2,646	9.5	13.7
METH–Un Methodist	4	322	599	834	3.0	4.3
MORAV–Morav Ch-North	3	349	773	872	3.1	4.5
Non-denom Chr Chs	6	405	370	533	1.9	2.8
PENT–Assemb of God	1	125	48	186	0.7	1.0
Sev Day Adv	2	24	42	49	0.2	0.3
Un C of Christ	1	78	179	207	0.7	1.1
Unit Univ	1	80	91	97	0.3	0.5
DOUGLAS	**55**	**3,678**	**5,748**	**21,420**	**48.5**	**100.0**
ANG/EPIS–Episcopal	1	25	50	50	0.1	0.2
Bahá'í	0	NR	14	14	0.0	0.1
BAPT–Converge/BGC	3	225	NR	270	0.6	1.3
BAPT–So Bapt Conv	1	38	50	60	0.1	0.3
Calv Chpl	1	NR	NR	NR	-	-
Catholic	8	NR	NR	11,104	25.1	51.8
Chr & Miss Al	1	78	47	120	0.3	0.6
CHR–Chs of Christ	1	15	11	16	0.0	0.1
CONG–Consrv Cong Chr	1	45	55	66	0.1	0.3
Evan Cov Ch	3	596	311	775	1.8	3.6
Evan Free Ch	2	210	NR	210	0.5	1.0
Jehovah's Witness	2	NR	NR	NR	-	-
LUTH–Assoc Free Luth	1	NR	NR	NR	-	-
LUTH–E.L.C.A.	8	839	2,723	4,187	9.5	19.5
LUTH–Luth–MO Synod	2	74	434	468	1.1	2.2
METH–Un Methodist	1	156	282	473	1.1	2.2
METH–Wesleyan	2	149	144	194	0.4	0.9
Non-denom Chr Chs	5	430	593	606	1.4	2.8
PENT–Assemb of God	2	259	124	444	1.0	2.1
PENT–Un Pent Ch Intl	1	NR	NR	NR	-	-
PENT–Vineyard	1	107	210	252	0.6	1.2
PRES–Presb Ch (USA)	6	260	484	580	1.3	2.7
Salvation Army	1	138	156	1,462	3.3	6.8
Sev Day Adv	1	34	60	69	0.2	0.3

NR–Not Reported   - Represents no adherents reported.   Percentages may not total 100 due to rounding.

Table 3: Religious Congregations by County and Group: 2010

Religious Group	Number of Congrega-tions	Number of Attendees	Number of Communicant, Confirmed, or Full Members	Adherents: Number of Adherents	Adherents: % of Total Pop.	Adherents: % of Total Adh.
DUNN	**74**	**5,228**	**11,576**	**21,146**	**48.2**	**100.0**
ANG/EPIS–Episcopal	1	44	90	90	0.2	0.4
Bahá'í	0	NR	18	18	0.0	0.1
BAPT–Converge/BGC	1	75	NR	90	0.2	0.4
BAPT–NT Ind Bapt	1	NR	NR	NR	-	-
BAPT–Reg Bapt Gen As	2	NR	NR	NR	-	-
BUDD–Mahayana	1	NR	NR	10	0.0	0.0
BUDD–Vajrayana	2	NR	NR	107	0.2	0.5
Calv Chpl	1	NR	NR	NR	-	-
Catholic	5	NR	NR	4,422	10.1	20.9
Ch of Nazarene	3	166	189	251	0.6	1.2
Chr & Miss Al	2	570	484	787	1.8	3.7
Evan Cov Ch	1	450	159	585	1.3	2.8
Evan Free Ch	1	60	NR	60	0.1	0.3
FRND–Fr Gen Cf	1	NR	6	7	0.0	0.0
Jehovah's Witness	1	NR	NR	NR	-	-
LDS–L-D Saints	1	NR	NR	320	0.7	1.5
LUTH–Assoc Free Luth	1	NR	NR	NR	-	-
LUTH–Ch of Luth Br	2	124	71	199	0.5	0.9
LUTH–E.L.C.A.	17	1,668	6,744	9,106	20.8	43.1
LUTH–Evan Luth Syn	1	38	87	0	0.0	0.0
LUTH–Luth-MO Synod	4	138	379	421	1.0	2.0
LUTH–Nor Amer Luth C	1	NR	NR	NR	-	-
LUTH–Wisc Ev Luth Syn	4	467	1,088	1,277	2.9	6.0
MENN–Mennonite USA	1	NR	NR	NR	-	-
METH–Un Methodist	11	487	1,234	1,768	4.0	8.4
Non-denom Chr Chs	3	690	420	862	2.0	4.1
PENT–Assemb of God	1	50	35	90	0.2	0.4
PENT–Un Pent Ch Intl	1	NR	NR	NR	-	-
Sev Day Adv	1	50	87	100	0.2	0.5
Un C of Christ	1	137	463	551	1.3	2.6
Unit Univ	1	14	22	25	0.1	0.1
EAU CLAIRE	**109**	**13,131**	**27,485**	**55,646**	**56.4**	**100.0**
ANG/EPIS–Episcopal	1	112	450	473	0.5	0.9
Bahá'í	1	NR	58	58	0.1	0.1
BAPT–Amer Bapt USA	1	45	92	110	0.1	0.2
BAPT–Consrv Bapt	1	NR	NR	NR	-	-
BAPT–Converge/BGC	4	300	NR	360	0.4	0.6
BAPT–So Bapt Conv	2	1,365	240	287	0.3	0.5
BUDD–Vajrayana	2	NR	NR	73	0.1	0.1
Catholic	10	NR	NR	16,240	16.4	29.2
Ch Cr, Scientst	1	NR	NR	NR	-	-
Ch of Nazarene	1	46	55	55	0.1	0.1
Chr & Miss Al	1	152	196	206	0.2	0.4
CHR–Chr Chs & Chs Cr	1	NR	0	0	0.0	0.0
CHR–Chs of Christ	2	65	56	80	0.1	0.1
CHR–Int Chs of Christ	1	NR	33	39	0.0	0.1
Evan Free Ch	2	195	NR	195	0.2	0.4
FRND–Fr Gen Cf	1	NR	16	19	0.0	0.0
Jehovah's Witness	1	NR	NR	NR	-	-
JUD–Conserv	1	35	39	105	0.1	0.2
LDS–Comm of Christ	1	NR	138	138	0.1	0.2
LDS–L-D Saints	1	NR	NR	703	0.7	1.3
LUTH–Ch Luth Conf	2	NR	NR	NR	-	-
LUTH–Ch of Luth Br	1	647	351	1,391	1.4	2.5
LUTH–E.L.C.A.	14	3,240	11,432	15,067	15.3	27.1
LUTH–Evan Luth Syn	3	271	590	708	0.7	1.3
LUTH–Luth Cong Msn Chr	2	500	2,810	3,355	3.4	6.0
LUTH–Luth-MO Synod	11	2,205	5,442	6,953	7.0	12.5
LUTH–Wisc Ev Luth Syn	1	431	517	757	0.8	1.4
MENN–Amish Undif	6	NR	294	794	0.8	1.4
METH–Un Methodist	7	596	1,400	2,177	2.2	3.9
METH–Wesleyan	1	280	183	364	0.4	0.7
Muslim Est	2	164	NR	418	0.4	0.8
Non-denom Chr Chs	8	1,245	1,121	1,557	1.6	2.8
PENT–Assemb of God	4	590	414	969	1.0	1.7
PENT–Un Pent Ch Intl	2	NR	NR	NR	-	-
PRES–Presb Ch (USA)	2	121	275	328	0.3	0.6
Salvation Army	1	19	21	129	0.1	0.2
Sev Day Adv	1	122	211	243	0.2	0.4
Un C of Christ	3	278	876	1,046	1.1	1.9
Unit Univ	1	107	175	249	0.3	0.4
Unity Ch	1	NR	NR	NR	-	-
FLORENCE	**9**	**665**	**273**	**1,847**	**41.8**	**100.0**
BAPT–Converge/BGC	1	400	NR	480	10.9	26.0
Catholic	3	NR	NR	939	21.2	50.8
LUTH–E.L.C.A.	1	51	76	108	2.4	5.8
LUTH–Wisc Ev Luth Syn	2	104	166	175	4.0	9.5
PENT–Pent Ch of God	1	70	NR	109	2.5	5.9
PRES–Presb Ch (USA)	1	40	31	36	0.8	1.9
FOND DU LAC	**98**	**11,359**	**19,047**	**58,230**	**57.3**	**100.0**
ANG/EPIS–Episcopal	2	156	278	288	0.3	0.5
Bahá'í	1	NR	78	78	0.1	0.1
BAPT–Amer Bapt USA	2	113	217	262	0.3	0.4
BAPT–Converge/BGC	3	950	NR	1,140	1.1	2.0
BAPT–Reg Bapt Gen As	1	NR	NR	NR	-	-
Catholic	15	NR	NR	29,714	29.2	51.0
Ch Cr, Scientst	1	NR	NR	NR	-	-
Ch of Nazarene	1	0	0	0	0.0	0.0
Chr & Miss Al	1	55	24	77	0.1	0.1
CHR–Chs of Christ	1	10	19	23	0.0	0.0
Evan Free Ch	3	729	NR	729	0.7	1.3
Ind Fund Churches	1	NR	NR	NR	-	-
Jehovah's Witness	1	NR	NR	NR	-	-
LDS–L-D Saints	1	NR	NR	293	0.3	0.5
LUTH–Ch Luth Conf	1	NR	NR	NR	-	-
LUTH–E.L.C.A.	8	1,344	3,334	4,381	4.3	7.5
LUTH–Luth-MO Synod	3	637	1,744	2,350	2.3	4.0
LUTH–Wisc Ev Luth Syn	13	3,585	6,383	7,979	7.9	13.7
MENN–Amish Undif	0	NR	7	23	0.0	0.0
METH–Un Methodist	9	730	1,624	2,665	2.6	4.6
Non-denom Chr Chs	6	700	795	924	0.9	1.6
ORTHE–Greek Orthodox	1	45	NR	220	0.2	0.4
PENT–Assemb of God	3	305	175	393	0.4	0.7
PENT–Ch God (Cleve)	1	296	192	232	0.2	0.4
PENT–Un Pent Ch Intl	2	NR	NR	NR	-	-
PRES–Presb Ch (USA)	1	225	519	627	0.6	1.1
REF–Christian Ref	1	35	0	0	0.0	0.0
REF–Ref Ch in Am	2	520	1,180	1,335	1.3	2.3
REF–Un Ref Chs N.A.	1	NR	NR	NR	-	-
Salvation Army	1	49	58	1,564	1.5	2.7
Sev Day Adv	1	12	20	23	0.0	0.0
Un C of Christ	8	792	2,301	2,781	2.7	4.8
Unit Univ	2	71	99	129	0.1	0.2
FOREST	**23**	**686**	**1,125**	**4,384**	**47.1**	**100.0**
Bahá'í	0	NR	2	2	0.0	0.0
BAPT–Reg Bapt Gen As	1	NR	NR	NR	-	-
Catholic	5	NR	NR	2,984	32.1	68.1
Ch of Nazarene	1	5	15	29	0.3	0.7
CHR–Chs of Christ	1	27	22	37	0.4	0.8
CONG–Consrv Cong Chr	1	163	109	130	1.4	3.0
Jehovah's Witness	3	NR	NR	NR	-	-
LUTH–Luth-MO Synod	2	95	179	224	2.4	5.1
LUTH–Wisc Ev Luth Syn	3	132	387	473	5.1	10.8
METH–Un Methodist	2	115	131	162	1.7	3.7
Non-denom Chr Chs	1	65	60	81	0.9	1.8
PENT–Ch God (Cleve)	1	29	133	158	1.7	3.6
PRES–Presb Ch (USA)	2	55	87	104	1.1	2.4
GRANT	**103**	**4,134**	**7,572**	**33,092**	**64.6**	**100.0**
ANG/EPIS–Episcopal	1	22	41	49	0.1	0.1
Bahá'í	0	NR	4	4	0.0	0.0
BAPT–Consrv Bapt	1	NR	NR	NR	-	-
BAPT–So Bapt Conv	2	105	97	116	0.2	0.4
Catholic	19	NR	NR	20,489	40.0	61.9
Chr & Miss Al	1	157	48	279	0.5	0.8
CHR–Chs of Christ	1	18	17	22	0.0	0.1
CONG–Cong Chr, NA	3	NR	297	355	0.7	1.1
CONG–Consrv Cong Chr	1	20	60	72	0.1	0.2
Evan Free Ch	2	395	NR	395	0.8	1.2
Ind Fund Churches	2	NR	NR	NR	-	-

NR–Not Reported   - Represents no adherents reported.   Percentages may not total 100 due to rounding.

Table 3: Religious Congregations by County and Group: 2010

Religious Group	Number of Congregations	Number of Attendees	Number of Communicant, Confirmed, or Full Members	Adherents		
				Number of Adherents	% of Total Pop.	% of Total Adh.
Jehovah's Witness	2	NR	NR	NR	-	-
LDS–Comm of Christ	1	NR	138	138	0.3	0.4
LDS–L-D Saints	1	NR	NR	244	0.5	0.7
LUTH–Assoc Free Luth	1	NR	NR	NR	-	-
LUTH–E.L.C.A.	10	815	2,377	3,589	7.0	10.8
LUTH–Luth-MO Synod	3	96	169	192	0.4	0.6
LUTH–Wisc Ev Luth Syn	2	121	157	208	0.4	0.6
MENN–Amish Undif	5	NR	247	756	1.5	2.3
MENN–Tamp Amish-Menn	1	140	83	140	0.3	0.4
METH–Free Methodist	2	205	181	212	0.4	0.6
METH–Prim Meth Ch	3	NR	NR	NR	-	-
METH–Un Methodist	19	1,031	2,390	4,011	7.8	12.1
Non-denom Chr Chs	5	445	477	606	1.2	1.8
ORTHE–Rus Orth Abroad	1	17	NR	30	0.1	0.1
PENT–Assemb of God	4	209	72	331	0.6	1.0
PRES–Presb Ch (USA)	2	129	272	325	0.6	1.0
Sev Day Adv	2	36	62	71	0.1	0.2
Un C of Christ	6	173	383	458	0.9	1.4
GREEN	**47**	**3,368**	**6,628**	**15,416**	**41.8**	**100.0**
ANG/EPIS–Episcopal	1	10	12	12	0.0	0.1
Bahá'í	0	NR	7	7	0.0	0.0
BUDD–Mahayana	1	NR	NR	20	0.1	0.1
Catholic	4	NR	NR	6,560	17.8	42.6
Ch Cr, Scientst	1	NR	NR	NR	-	-
Ch of Nazarene	2	61	56	103	0.3	0.7
CHR–Chs of Christ	1	60	45	60	0.2	0.4
Evan Free Ch	1	100	NR	100	0.3	0.6
Jehovah's Witness	2	NR	NR	NR	-	-
LDS–L-D Saints	1	NR	NR	85	0.2	0.6
LUTH–Assoc Free Luth	1	NR	NR	NR	-	-
LUTH–E.L.C.A.	6	427	1,621	1,875	5.1	12.2
LUTH–Wisc Ev Luth Syn	2	131	278	327	0.9	2.1
MENN–Amish Undif	1	NR	34	75	0.2	0.5
METH–Un Methodist	7	726	1,369	1,858	5.0	12.1
New Apost Ch	1	NR	NR	NR	-	-
Non-denom Chr Chs	6	835	647	1,044	2.8	6.8
PENT–Assemb of God	1	150	0	150	0.4	1.0
PENT–Un Pent Ch Intl	1	NR	NR	NR	-	-
PRES–Presb Ch (USA)	1	70	160	197	0.5	1.3
Sev Day Adv	1	32	55	63	0.2	0.4
Un C of Christ	5	766	2,344	2,880	7.8	18.7
GREEN LAKE	**41**	**2,861**	**5,522**	**12,945**	**67.9**	**100.0**
Bahá'í	0	NR	8	8	0.0	0.1
BAPT–Amer Bapt USA	2	172	411	501	2.6	3.9
BAPT–Reg Bapt Gen As	1	NR	NR	NR	-	-
Catholic	4	NR	NR	5,290	27.8	40.9
CONG–Cong Chr, NA	1	NR	35	43	0.2	0.3
Evan Free Ch	1	330	NR	330	1.7	2.5
Ind Fund Churches	2	NR	NR	NR	-	-
Jehovah's Witness	1	NR	NR	NR	-	-
LUTH–Ch Luth Conf	1	NR	NR	NR	-	-
LUTH–E.L.C.A.	1	275	821	964	5.1	7.4
LUTH–Luth-MO Synod	4	498	948	1,173	6.2	9.1
LUTH–Wisc Ev Luth Syn	8	939	2,099	2,498	13.1	19.3
MENN–Amish Undif	5	NR	286	812	4.3	6.3
METH–Un Methodist	5	267	476	691	3.6	5.3
Non-denom Chr Chs	2	100	87	125	0.7	1.0
PENT–Assemb of God	1	118	59	154	0.8	1.2
Un C of Christ	2	162	292	356	1.9	2.8
IOWA	**45**	**1,584**	**3,526**	**11,601**	**49.0**	**100.0**
ANG/EPIS–Episcopal	1	20	36	40	0.2	0.3
Bahá'í	0	NR	1	1	0.0	0.0
BAPT–Converge/BGC	1	75	NR	90	0.4	0.8
BUDD–Vajrayana	1	NR	NR	27	0.1	0.2
Catholic	8	NR	NR	6,632	28.0	57.2
Evan Free Ch	1	60	NR	60	0.3	0.5
FRND–Fr Gen Cf	1	NR	0	0	0.0	0.0
Ind Fund Churches	2	NR	NR	NR	-	-
LUTH–Assoc Free Luth	1	NR	NR	NR	-	-
LUTH–E.L.C.A.	8	648	1,698	2,303	9.7	19.9

Religious Group	Number of Congregations	Number of Attendees	Number of Communicant, Confirmed, or Full Members	Adherents		
				Number of Adherents	% of Total Pop.	% of Total Adh.
LUTH–Luth-MO Synod	1	34	74	95	0.4	0.8
LUTH–Wisc Ev Luth Syn	1	27	65	80	0.3	0.7
MENN–Amish Undif	0	NR	2	6	0.0	0.1
METH–Prim Meth Ch	1	NR	NR	NR	-	-
METH–Un Methodist	9	325	814	1,173	5.0	10.1
Non-denom Chr Chs	4	220	245	363	1.5	3.1
PENT–Un Pent Ch Intl	1	NR	NR	NR	-	-
PRES–Presb Ch (USA)	1	22	51	63	0.3	0.5
Un C of Christ	3	153	540	668	2.8	5.8
IRON	**12**	**375**	**425**	**2,742**	**46.3**	**100.0**
Catholic	3	NR	NR	2,173	36.7	79.2
Ch of Nazarene	1	14	17	21	0.4	0.8
Ind Fund Churches	1	NR	NR	NR	-	-
LUTH–Luth-MO Synod	1	32	46	46	0.8	1.7
LUTH–Wisc Ev Luth Syn	2	76	118	133	2.2	4.9
METH–Un Methodist	1	56	60	114	1.9	4.2
Non-denom Chr Chs	1	150	125	188	3.2	6.9
PRES–Presb Ch (USA)	2	47	59	67	1.1	2.4
JACKSON	**40**	**2,242**	**5,212**	**9,164**	**44.8**	**100.0**
Bahá'í	0	NR	1	1	0.0	0.0
BAPT–Converge/BGC	1	75	NR	90	0.4	1.0
Catholic	3	NR	NR	1,440	7.0	15.7
Chr & Miss Al	1	64	28	104	0.5	1.1
CHR–Chr Chs & Chs Cr	1	NR	51	62	0.3	0.7
CHR–Chs of Christ	1	52	70	102	0.5	1.1
Evan Free Ch	1	55	NR	55	0.3	0.6
Jehovah's Witness	1	NR	NR	NR	-	-
LUTH–Ch Luth Conf	1	NR	NR	NR	-	-
LUTH–E.L.C.A.	9	686	2,356	3,083	15.1	33.6
LUTH–Luth-MO Synod	2	141	409	527	2.6	5.8
LUTH–Wisc Ev Luth Syn	3	564	921	1,203	5.9	13.1
MENN–Amish Undif	4	NR	184	509	2.5	5.6
METH–Un Methodist	6	332	821	1,379	6.7	15.0
Non-denom Chr Chs	2	74	67	92	0.4	1.0
PENT–Assemb of God	2	164	95	264	1.3	2.9
PRES–Presb Ch (USA)	1	35	90	109	0.5	1.2
Un C of Christ	1	0	119	144	0.7	1.6
JEFFERSON	**98**	**12,837**	**25,895**	**52,947**	**63.3**	**100.0**
ANG/EPIS–Episcopal	2	82	195	260	0.3	0.5
Bahá'í	0	NR	25	25	0.0	0.0
BAPT–Amer Bapt USA	1	25	33	40	0.0	0.1
BAPT–Converge/BGC	2	150	NR	180	0.2	0.3
BAPT–Fund Bapt Flwsp	1	NR	NR	NR	-	-
BAPT–N Am Bapt Conf	1	NR	124	152	0.2	0.3
BAPT–NT Ind Bapt	2	NR	NR	NR	-	-
BAPT–So Bapt Conv	1	22	55	67	0.1	0.1
Catholic	10	NR	NR	18,637	22.3	35.2
Ch Cr, Scientst	1	NR	NR	NR	-	-
Jehovah's Witness	3	NR	NR	NR	-	-
LDS–L-D Saints	1	NR	NR	339	0.4	0.6
LUTH–E.L.C.A.	9	1,526	4,909	6,586	7.9	12.4
LUTH–Luth Cong Msn Chr	1	340	750	917	1.1	1.7
LUTH–Luth-MO Synod	6	728	1,214	1,670	2.0	3.2
LUTH–Nor Amer Luth C	1	NR	NR	NR	-	-
LUTH–Wisc Ev Luth Syn	18	6,230	12,722	16,006	19.1	30.2
METH–Un Methodist	12	677	1,712	2,377	2.8	4.5
MORAV–Morav Ch-North	4	361	1,064	1,270	1.5	2.4
Non-denom Chr Chs	10	2,085	1,685	2,631	3.1	5.0
PENT–Assemb of God	2	103	47	138	0.2	0.3
PENT–Un Pent Ch Intl	2	NR	NR	NR	-	-
PRES–Presb Ch (USA)	1	35	33	40	0.0	0.1
Sev Day Adv	3	78	135	155	0.2	0.3
Un C of Christ	4	395	1,192	1,457	1.7	2.8
JUNEAU	**40**	**2,409**	**5,418**	**12,417**	**46.6**	**100.0**
ANG/EPIS–Episcopal	1	9	11	11	0.0	0.1
Bahá'í	0	NR	5	5	0.0	0.0
BAPT–Amer Bapt USA	1	25	30	36	0.1	0.3
BAPT–Converge/BGC	1	75	NR	90	0.3	0.7

NR–Not Reported - Represents no adherents reported. Percentages may not total 100 due to rounding.

Table 3: Religious Congregations by County and Group: 2010

Religious Group	Number of Congregations	Number of Attendees	Number of Communicant, Confirmed, or Full Members	Adherents: Number of Adherents	Adherents: % of Total Pop.	Adherents: % of Total Adh.
Catholic	7	NR	NR	5,280	19.8	42.5
Ch of Nazarene	1	46	65	87	0.3	0.7
Jehovah's Witness	1	NR	NR	NR	-	-
LUTH–E.L.C.A.	8	586	2,021	2,592	9.7	20.9
LUTH–Luth–MO Synod	3	143	464	554	2.1	4.5
LUTH–Wisc Ev Luth Syn	5	595	1,644	1,993	7.5	16.1
METH–Un Methodist	6	367	633	963	3.6	7.8
METH–Wesleyan	1	98	63	127	0.5	1.0
Non-denom Chr Chs	2	350	350	437	1.6	3.5
PENT–Assemb of God	1	85	55	150	0.6	1.2
PENT–Ch of God Proph	1	NR	35	42	0.2	0.3
PRES–Presb Ch (USA)	1	30	42	50	0.2	0.4
KENOSHA	**114**	**12,085**	**17,456**	**62,000**	**37.3**	**100.0**
ANG/EPIS–Anglican NA	1	NR	NR	NR	-	-
ANG/EPIS–Episcopal	2	129	388	534	0.3	0.9
Bahá'í	1	NR	42	42	0.0	0.1
BAPT–Amer Bapt USA	2	109	156	194	0.1	0.3
BAPT–Consrv Bapt	1	NR	NR	NR	-	-
BAPT–Converge/BGC	2	150	NR	180	0.1	0.3
BAPT–N Am Bapt Conf	2	NR	870	1,083	0.7	1.7
BAPT–Reg Bapt Gen As	1	NR	NR	NR	-	-
BAPT–So Bapt Conv	6	522	943	1,174	0.7	1.9
Catholic	14	NR	NR	35,008	21.0	56.5
Ch of Nazarene	2	95	117	119	0.1	0.2
CHR–Chr Chs & Chs Cr	1	NR	0	0	0.0	0.0
CHR–Chs of Christ	3	394	528	637	0.4	1.0
CONG–Cong Chr, NA	2	NR	167	208	0.1	0.3
Evan Free Ch	2	890	NR	890	0.5	1.4
FRND–Fr Gen Cf	1	NR	8	10	0.0	0.0
Jehovah's Witness	2	NR	NR	NR	-	-
JUD–Orth	1	43	50	60	0.0	0.1
JUD–Reform	1	61	107	289	0.2	0.5
LDS–L-D Saints	2	NR	NR	814	0.5	1.3
LUTH–E.L.C.A.	10	1,559	4,749	5,955	3.6	9.6
LUTH–Luth–MO Synod	4	402	617	829	0.5	1.3
LUTH–Wisc Ev Luth Syn	8	1,358	2,849	3,601	2.2	5.8
METH–AME	1	50	100	124	0.1	0.2
METH–Un Methodist	9	706	1,263	2,022	1.2	3.3
Muslim Est	1	134	NR	308	0.2	0.5
New Apost Ch	1	NR	NR	NR	-	-
Non-denom Chr Chs	11	1,960	2,436	2,727	1.6	4.4
ORTHE–Greek Orthodox	1	400	NR	200	0.1	0.3
ORTHE–Orth Ch in Amer	1	45	NR	100	0.1	0.2
PENT–Assemb of God	2	2,360	843	2,998	1.8	4.8
PENT–Ch God (Cleve)	1	100	112	139	0.1	0.2
PENT–COGIC	1	0	60	75	0.0	0.1
PENT–Full Gosp Bapt	1	NR	NR	NR	-	-
PENT–Int Foursq Gos	1	24	28	35	0.0	0.1
PENT–Pent Ch of God	1	70	NR	109	0.1	0.2
PENT–Un Pent Ch Intl	1	NR	NR	NR	-	-
PRES–Presb Ch (USA)	1	163	269	335	0.2	0.5
REF–Christian Ref	1	108	209	260	0.2	0.4
Salvation Army	1	27	19	300	0.2	0.5
Sev Day Adv	3	51	89	102	0.1	0.2
Un C of Christ	2	120	335	417	0.3	0.7
Unit Univ	1	55	102	122	0.1	0.2
Unity Ch	1	NR	NR	NR	-	-
KEWAUNEE	**23**	**1,583**	**2,989**	**14,534**	**70.6**	**100.0**
ANG/EPIS–Episcopal	1	18	26	27	0.1	0.2
Bahá'í	0	NR	8	8	0.0	0.1
BAPT–Converge/BGC	1	75	NR	90	0.4	0.6
Catholic	7	NR	NR	10,606	51.6	73.0
CONG–Cong Chr, NA	1	NR	134	163	0.8	1.1
Jehovah's Witness	1	NR	NR	NR	-	-
LUTH–E.L.C.A.	1	102	218	318	1.5	2.2
LUTH–Luth–MO Synod	3	612	1,053	1,356	6.6	9.3
LUTH–Wisc Ev Luth Syn	3	581	1,308	1,622	7.9	11.2
METH–Un Methodist	2	65	113	155	0.8	1.1
Non-denom Chr Chs	2	95	100	119	0.6	0.8
PENT–Assemb of God	1	35	29	70	0.3	0.5
LA CROSSE	**111**	**13,698**	**27,261**	**67,392**	**58.8**	**100.0**
ANG/EPIS–Episcopal	1	138	348	354	0.3	0.5
Bahá'í	0	NR	21	21	0.0	0.0
BAPT–Amer Bapt USA	1	41	52	62	0.1	0.1
BAPT–Converge/BGC	1	75	NR	90	0.1	0.1
BAPT–N Am Bapt Conf	1	NR	48	57	0.0	0.1
BAPT–So Bapt Conv	2	119	138	165	0.1	0.2
BUDD–Vajrayana	1	NR	NR	14	0.0	0.0
Catholic	12	NR	NR	28,200	24.6	41.8
Ch Cr, Scientst	1	NR	NR	NR	-	-
Ch of Nazarene	1	47	34	96	0.1	0.1
Chr & Miss Al	2	305	274	444	0.4	0.7
CHR–Chr Chs & Chs Cr	3	NR	315	377	0.3	0.6
CHR–Chs of Christ	1	75	55	95	0.1	0.1
Evan Free Ch	4	2,385	NR	2,385	2.1	3.5
FRND–Fr Gen Cf	1	NR	0	0	0.0	0.0
Jehovah's Witness	1	NR	NR	NR	-	-
JUD–Conserv	1	34	38	103	0.1	0.2
LDS–Comm of Christ	1	NR	138	138	0.1	0.2
LDS–L-D Saints	1	NR	NR	792	0.7	1.2
LUTH–Assoc Free Luth	1	NR	NR	NR	-	-
LUTH–Ch Luth Conf	1	NR	NR	NR	-	-
LUTH–E.L.C.A.	16	3,318	11,931	15,888	13.9	23.6
LUTH–Luth Cong Msn Chr	2	389	970	1,160	1.0	1.7
LUTH–Luth–MO Synod	3	383	759	1,027	0.9	1.5
LUTH–Nor Amer Luth C	1	NR	NR	NR	-	-
LUTH–Wisc Ev Luth Syn	10	2,630	6,065	7,672	6.7	11.4
MENN–Amish Undif	1	NR	17	41	0.0	0.1
METH–Un Methodist	5	513	1,351	1,785	1.6	2.6
METH–Wesleyan	1	202	141	263	0.2	0.4
Muslim Est	1	134	NR	308	0.3	0.5
Non-denom Chr Chs	11	1,490	1,745	2,012	1.8	3.0
ORTHE–Ant Orth of NA	1	30	NR	100	0.1	0.1
PENT–Assemb of God	2	216	132	286	0.2	0.4
PENT–Int Foursq Gos	1	20	12	14	0.0	0.0
PENT–Un Pent Ch Intl	2	NR	NR	NR	-	-
PENT–Vineyard	1	58	70	84	0.1	0.1
PRES–Presb Ch (USA)	6	558	1,273	1,522	1.3	2.3
PRES–Presb Ch Amer	1	80	99	128	0.1	0.2
Salvation Army	1	37	19	251	0.2	0.4
Sev Day Adv	2	100	175	201	0.2	0.3
Un C of Christ	3	233	949	1,135	1.0	1.7
Unit Univ	1	88	92	122	0.1	0.2
Unity Ch	1	NR	NR	NR	-	-
LAFAYETTE	**53**	**1,638**	**4,174**	**11,546**	**68.6**	**100.0**
BAPT–Converge/BGC	1	75	NR	90	0.5	0.8
Catholic	13	NR	NR	5,916	35.1	51.2
Evan Free Ch	2	130	NR	130	0.8	1.1
Jehovah's Witness	1	NR	NR	NR	-	-
LUTH–Assoc Free Luth	1	NR	NR	NR	-	-
LUTH–E.L.C.A.	11	698	2,536	3,055	18.1	26.5
LUTH–Luth Cong Msn Chr	2	NR	NR	NR	-	-
MENN–Amish Undif	3	NR	130	441	2.6	3.8
MENN–Tamp Amish-Menn	1	67	44	67	0.4	0.6
METH–Prim Meth Ch	5	NR	NR	NR	-	-
METH–Un Methodist	9	364	917	1,239	7.4	10.7
Non-denom Chr Chs	2	200	300	300	1.8	2.6
Un C of Christ	2	104	247	308	1.8	2.7
LANGLADE	**39**	**2,445**	**4,208**	**13,072**	**65.4**	**100.0**
ANG/EPIS–Episcopal	1	15	42	42	0.2	0.3
Bahá'í	0	NR	3	3	0.0	0.0
BAPT–Amer Bapt USA	1	35	42	50	0.3	0.4
Catholic	7	NR	NR	7,164	35.9	54.8
Ch of Nazarene	1	22	31	116	0.6	0.9
CHR–Chs of Christ	1	46	37	50	0.3	0.4
Evan Free Ch	1	179	NR	179	0.9	1.4
Jehovah's Witness	1	NR	NR	NR	-	-
LDS–L-D Saints	1	NR	NR	171	0.9	1.3
LUTH–E.L.C.A.	3	252	676	830	4.2	6.3
LUTH–Luth–MO Synod	6	954	2,000	2,420	12.1	18.5
LUTH–Wisc Ev Luth Syn	1	125	155	221	1.1	1.7

NR–Not Reported - Represents no adherents reported. Percentages may not total 100 due to rounding.

Table 3: Religious Congregations by County and Group: 2010

Religious Group	Number of Congrega-tions	Number of Attendees	Number of Communicant, Confirmed, or Full Members	Adherents		
				Number of Adherents	% of Total Pop.	% of Total Adh.
METH–Un Methodist	1	85	227	329	1.6	2.5
Non-denom Chr Chs	4	250	187	313	1.6	2.4
PENT–Assemb of God	2	135	61	300	1.5	2.3
PENT–Ch God (Cleve)	1	93	274	325	1.6	2.5
PENT–COGIC	1	50	50	59	0.3	0.5
PENT–Un Pent Ch Intl	1	NR	NR	NR	-	-
PRES–Presb Ch (USA)	1	14	16	19	0.1	0.1
Sev Day Adv	1	26	45	52	0.3	0.4
Un C of Christ	3	164	362	429	2.1	3.3
LINCOLN	**47**	**4,594**	**9,297**	**19,054**	**66.3**	**100.0**
ANG/EPIS–Episcopal	2	33	52	52	0.2	0.3
Bahá'í	0	NR	6	6	0.0	0.0
BAPT–Converge/BGC	1	400	NR	480	1.7	2.5
BAPT–Reg Bapt Gen As	1	NR	NR	NR	-	-
Catholic	4	NR	NR	6,201	21.6	32.5
Ch Cr, Scientst	1	NR	NR	NR	-	-
CONG–Cong Chr, NA	1	NR	71	84	0.3	0.4
FRND–Fr Gen Cf	1	NR	16	19	0.1	0.1
Ind Fund Churches	1	NR	NR	NR	-	-
Jehovah's Witness	1	NR	NR	NR	-	-
LUTH–E.L.C.A.	3	598	2,028	2,939	10.2	15.4
LUTH–Luth–MO Synod	9	1,746	4,586	5,711	19.9	30.0
LUTH–Wisc Ev Luth Syn	2	307	463	553	1.9	2.9
METH–Un Methodist	4	205	396	762	2.7	4.0
Non-denom Chr Chs	6	485	355	612	2.1	3.2
PENT–Assemb of God	1	68	61	121	0.4	0.6
PENT–Ch God (Cleve)	1	40	29	34	0.1	0.2
PENT–Un Pent Ch Intl	1	NR	NR	NR	-	-
PENT–Vineyard	1	227	390	464	1.6	2.4
PRES–Presb Ch (USA)	2	34	54	64	0.2	0.3
PRES–Presb Ch Amer	1	147	217	272	0.9	1.4
Sev Day Adv	2	25	43	50	0.2	0.3
Un C of Christ	1	279	530	630	2.2	3.3
MANITOWOC	**81**	**8,855**	**16,648**	**57,839**	**71.0**	**100.0**
ANG/EPIS–Episcopal	1	63	128	128	0.2	0.2
Bahá'í	0	NR	22	22	0.0	0.0
BAPT–Reg Bapt Gen As	1	NR	NR	NR	-	-
BAPT–So Bapt Conv	1	3	10	12	0.0	0.0
Calv Chpl	1	NR	NR	NR	-	-
Catholic	14	NR	NR	35,564	43.7	61.5
Chr & Miss Al	3	404	495	684	0.8	1.2
CHR–Chs of Christ	1	40	28	49	0.1	0.1
Evan Free Ch	2	1,240	NR	1,240	1.5	2.1
Jehovah's Witness	3	NR	NR	NR	-	-
LDS–L-D Saints	1	NR	NR	237	0.3	0.4
LUTH–E.L.C.A.	4	797	3,039	3,493	4.3	6.0
LUTH–Luth–MO Synod	2	340	936	1,159	1.4	2.0
LUTH–Wisc Ev Luth Syn	19	3,931	7,927	9,664	11.9	16.7
MENN–Amish Undif	1	NR	16	45	0.1	0.1
METH–Un Methodist	7	520	605	1,004	1.2	1.7
Non-denom Chr Chs	5	187	185	234	0.3	0.4
PENT–Assemb of God	2	246	127	571	0.7	1.0
PENT–Intl Pent Holiness	1	11	15	18	0.0	0.0
PENT–Un Pent Ch Intl	1	NR	NR	NR	-	-
PRES–Presb Ch (USA)	3	141	341	410	0.5	0.7
REF–Ref Ch in U.S.	1	NR	196	222	0.3	0.4
Salvation Army	1	45	67	67	0.1	0.1
Un C of Christ	6	887	2,511	3,016	3.7	5.2
MARATHON	**149**	**15,077**	**31,335**	**86,961**	**64.9**	**100.0**
ANG/EPIS–Episcopal	2	94	200	257	0.2	0.3
Bahá'í	0	NR	26	26	0.0	0.0
BAPT–Converge/BGC	3	225	NR	270	0.2	0.3
BAPT–So Bapt Conv	1	16	23	28	0.0	0.0
Calv Chpl	1	NR	NR	NR	-	-
Catholic	24	NR	NR	41,260	30.8	47.4
Ch Cr, Scientst	1	NR	NR	NR	-	-
Ch of Nazarene	1	26	29	41	0.0	0.0
Chr & Miss Al	2	613	750	1,078	0.8	1.2
CHR–Chs of Christ	2	95	68	95	0.1	0.1
Evan Free Ch	3	1,275	NR	1,275	1.0	1.5
Ind Fund Churches	2	NR	NR	NR	-	-
Jehovah's Witness	4	NR	NR	NR	-	-
JUD–Reform	1	49	86	232	0.2	0.3
LDS–L-D Saints	1	NR	NR	574	0.4	0.7
LUTH–E.L.C.A.	21	3,219	10,386	13,918	10.4	16.0
LUTH–Evan Luth Syn	1	27	50	61	0.0	0.1
LUTH–Luth Cong Msn Chr	3	169	159	196	0.1	0.2
LUTH–Luth–MO Synod	16	2,796	8,917	11,495	8.6	13.2
LUTH–Wisc Ev Luth Syn	17	1,842	3,642	4,424	3.3	5.1
MENN–Amish Undif	3	NR	122	371	0.3	0.4
METH–Un Methodist	8	853	1,633	2,854	2.1	3.3
New Apost Ch	1	NR	NR	NR	-	-
Non-denom Chr Chs	9	1,361	1,062	1,763	1.3	2.0
OCATH–Pol Natl Cath	1	NR	NR	NR	-	-
ORTHE–Rus Orth Abroad	1	12	NR	40	0.0	0.0
PENT–Assemb of God	6	898	545	1,516	1.1	1.7
PENT–Assm God Intl F	1	NR	NR	NR	-	-
PENT–Int Foursq Gos	1	79	58	71	0.1	0.1
PENT–Un Pent Ch Intl	1	NR	NR	NR	-	-
PRES–Presb Ch (USA)	2	406	992	1,220	0.9	1.4
REF–Ref Ch in Am	1	187	408	422	0.3	0.5
Salvation Army	1	23	60	820	0.6	0.9
Sev Day Adv	1	91	158	182	0.1	0.2
Un C of Christ	5	602	1,714	2,108	1.6	2.4
Unit Univ	1	119	247	364	0.3	0.4
MARINETTE	**67**	**4,230**	**7,264**	**20,125**	**48.2**	**100.0**
ANG/EPIS–Episcopal	1	64	99	131	0.3	0.7
Bahá'í	0	NR	1	1	0.0	0.0
BAPT–Converge/BGC	1	400	NR	480	1.1	2.4
Catholic	10	NR	NR	10,053	24.1	50.0
Ch Cr, Scientst	1	NR	NR	NR	-	-
CHR–Chs of Christ	1	5	5	5	0.0	0.0
Evan Cov Ch	1	0	0	0	0.0	0.0
Jehovah's Witness	3	NR	NR	NR	-	-
LUTH–E.L.C.A.	7	586	1,954	2,361	5.7	11.7
LUTH–Evan Luth Syn	1	100	162	185	0.4	0.9
LUTH–Luth Ch-Am Asc	1	NR	NR	NR	-	-
LUTH–Luth–MO Synod	1	104	214	277	0.7	1.4
LUTH–Wisc Ev Luth Syn	6	947	2,532	3,111	7.5	15.5
METH–Un Methodist	5	206	558	729	1.7	3.6
Non-denom Chr Chs	12	942	909	1,207	2.9	6.0
PENT–Assemb of God	6	573	219	759	1.8	3.8
PENT–Un Pent Ch Intl	1	NR	NR	NR	-	-
PRES–Presb Ch (USA)	6	222	473	559	1.3	2.8
Salvation Army	1	26	20	129	0.3	0.6
Sev Day Adv	1	26	45	52	0.1	0.3
Un C of Christ	1	29	73	86	0.2	0.4
MARQUETTE	**33**	**1,950**	**3,575**	**7,386**	**47.9**	**100.0**
Bahá'í	0	NR	2	2	0.0	0.0
Catholic	4	NR	NR	2,567	16.7	34.8
Evan Free Ch	1	165	NR	165	1.1	2.2
Ind Fund Churches	2	NR	NR	NR	-	-
LUTH–E.L.C.A.	1	55	119	144	0.9	1.9
LUTH–Luth–MO Synod	7	529	1,233	1,535	10.0	20.8
LUTH–Wisc Ev Luth Syn	2	315	704	863	5.6	11.7
MENN–Amish Undif	1	NR	89	244	1.6	3.3
METH–Un Methodist	6	330	670	990	6.4	13.4
Non-denom Chr Chs	4	400	480	550	3.6	7.4
PRES–Presb Ch (USA)	3	80	136	161	1.0	2.2
Sev Day Adv	1	46	81	93	0.6	1.3
Un C of Christ	1	30	61	72	0.5	1.0
MENOMINEE	**4**	**65**	**20**	**2,993**	**70.7**	**100.0**
Bahá'í	0	NR	1	1	0.0	0.0
Catholic	2	NR	NR	2,850	67.3	95.2
PENT–Assemb of God	1	38	0	98	2.3	3.3
PRES–Orth Pres Ch	1	27	19	44	1.0	1.5
MILWAUKEE	**744**	**94,162**	**162,149**	**439,526**	**46.4**	**100.0**
ANG/EPIS–Episcopal	13	1,198	3,116	3,606	0.4	0.8

NR–Not Reported - Represents no adherents reported. Percentages may not total 100 due to rounding.

Table 3: Religious Congregations by County and Group: 2010

Religious Group	Number of Congregations	Number of Attendees	Number of Communicant, Confirmed, or Full Members	Adherents: Number of Adherents	Adherents: % of Total Pop.	Adherents: % of Total Adh.
Bahá'í	3	NR	452	452	0.0	0.1
BAPT–Amer Bapt USA	23	3,482	5,692	7,066	0.7	1.6
BAPT–Converge/BGC	5	375	NR	450	0.0	0.1
BAPT–Natl Mis Bapt Conv	10	200	1,950	2,421	0.3	0.6
BAPT–NBC Amer	1	300	600	745	0.1	0.2
BAPT–NBC USA	27	5,152	14,602	18,127	1.9	4.1
BAPT–NT Ind Bapt	1	NR	NR	NR	-	-
BAPT–Prog NBC	1	0	150	186	0.0	0.0
BAPT–Ref Bapt Ch	1	NR	NR	NR	-	-
BAPT–So Bapt Conv	32	3,764	9,764	12,121	1.3	2.8
BUDD–Mahayana	5	NR	NR	1,799	0.2	0.4
BUDD–Theravada	1	NR	NR	300	0.0	0.1
BUDD–Vajrayana	4	NR	NR	114	0.0	0.0
Calv Chpl	1	NR	NR	NR	-	-
Catholic	80	NR	NR	199,153	21.0	45.3
CGOD–Ch God (Ander)	5	369	NR	369	0.0	0.1
Ch Cr, Scientst	5	NR	NR	NR	-	-
Ch of Nazarene	1	32	24	32	0.0	0.0
Chr & Miss Al	7	983	2,299	2,542	0.3	0.6
CHR–Chr Ch (Disc)	1	92	49	61	0.0	0.0
CHR–Chs of Christ	10	1,352	1,557	2,253	0.2	0.5
CHR–Int Chs of Christ	1	NR	222	276	0.0	0.1
CONG–Cong Chr, NA	4	NR	1,753	2,176	0.2	0.5
Evan Ch	1	NR	NR	NR	-	-
Evan Cov Ch	2	130	80	169	0.0	0.0
Evan Free Ch	3	555	NR	555	0.1	0.1
FRND–Fr Gen Cf	1	NR	124	154	0.0	0.0
Grace Gosp Fel	1	NR	NR	NR	-	-
HINDU–Post Ren	2	NR	NR	41	0.0	0.0
Ind Fund Churches	1	NR	NR	NR	-	-
Int Cou Comm Ch	1	NR	NR	NR	-	-
Jehovah's Witness	9	NR	NR	NR	-	-
JUD–Conserv	1	340	382	1,031	0.1	0.2
JUD–Orth	6	886	400	1,230	0.1	0.3
JUD–Reform	3	1,118	1,971	5,322	0.6	1.2
LDS–Comm of Christ	1	NR	138	138	0.0	0.0
LDS–L-D Saints	8	NR	NR	4,135	0.4	0.9
LUTH–Ch Luth Conf	1	NR	NR	NR	-	-
LUTH–E.L.C.A.	50	7,330	17,116	23,043	2.4	5.2
LUTH–Luth-MO Synod	44	9,435	21,293	28,274	3.0	6.4
LUTH–Wisc Ev Luth Syn	45	8,801	16,415	20,416	2.2	4.6
MENN–Mennonite USA	1	33	25	31	0.0	0.0
METH–AME	7	685	1,650	2,048	0.2	0.5
METH–AME Zion	1	0	100	124	0.0	0.0
METH–C.M.E.	7	512	2,208	2,741	0.3	0.6
METH–Un Methodist	25	2,755	5,362	7,840	0.8	1.8
METH–Wesleyan	4	238	101	310	0.0	0.1
Metro Comm Ch	1	41	34	42	0.0	0.0
Muslim Est	8	2,938	NR	9,156	1.0	2.1
New Apost Ch	1	NR	NR	NR	-	-
Non-denom Chr Chs	126	22,629	29,199	32,340	3.4	7.4
OCATH–Pol Natl Cath	3	NR	NR	NR	-	-
ORTHE–Greek Orthodox	2	700	NR	3,220	0.3	0.7
ORTHE–Orth Ch in Amer	1	75	NR	110	0.0	0.0
ORTHE–Rus Orth Abroad	1	150	NR	700	0.1	0.2
ORTHE–Serb Orth USA	2	1,560	NR	4,500	0.5	1.0
ORTHE–Ukrainian Orth	1	35	NR	100	0.0	0.0
ORTHO–Armen Ap Etchm	1	65	NR	250	0.0	0.1
ORTHO–Coptic Orth Ch	1	190	NR	200	0.0	0.0
PENT–Assemb of God	20	5,285	3,638	10,960	1.2	2.5
PENT–Ch God (Cleve)	5	103	134	166	0.0	0.0
PENT–Ch Lord Jesus Apos	1	NR	NR	NR	-	-
PENT–Ch of God Proph	1	NR	28	35	0.0	0.0
PENT–COGIC	28	5,131	9,820	12,191	1.3	2.8
PENT–Full Gosp Bapt	10	NR	NR	NR	-	-
PENT–Un Pent Ch Intl	10	NR	NR	NR	-	-
PENT–United Holy Ch	3	NR	NR	NR	-	-
PENT–Vineyard	1	95	150	186	0.0	0.0
PRES–Presb Ch (USA)	14	1,324	2,845	3,532	0.4	0.8
PRES–Presb Ch Amer	1	0	10	12	0.0	0.0
REF–Christian Ref	1	80	35	43	0.0	0.0
REF–Ref Ch in Am	3	252	403	531	0.1	0.1
Salvation Army	4	358	319	2,187	0.2	0.5
Sev Day Adv	10	1,286	2,235	2,571	0.3	0.6

Religious Group	Number of Congregations	Number of Attendees	Number of Communicant, Confirmed, or Full Members	Adherents: Number of Adherents	Adherents: % of Total Pop.	Adherents: % of Total Adh.
Sikh	1	NR	NR	NR	-	-
Un C of Christ	12	1,301	2,901	3,601	0.4	0.8
Unit Univ	2	447	803	1,041	0.1	0.2
Unity Ch	2	NR	NR	NR	-	-
Zoroastrian	0	NR	NR	1	0.0	0.0
MONROE	**75**	**4,859**	**8,931**	**22,932**	**51.3**	**100.0**
ANG/EPIS–Episcopal	2	90	163	204	0.5	0.9
Bahá'í	0	NR	5	5	0.0	0.0
BAPT–Amer Bapt USA	1	150	181	227	0.5	1.0
BAPT–NT Ind Bapt	1	NR	NR	NR	-	-
BAPT–So Bapt Conv	2	95	75	94	0.2	0.4
Catholic	10	NR	NR	9,250	20.7	40.3
Ch of Nazarene	2	128	113	155	0.3	0.7
CHR–Chs of Christ	1	60	48	65	0.1	0.3
CONG–Consrv Cong Chr	2	120	157	197	0.4	0.9
Evan Free Ch	4	672	NR	672	1.5	2.9
Jehovah's Witness	3	NR	NR	NR	-	-
LDS–L-D Saints	1	NR	NR	299	0.7	1.3
LUTH–E.L.C.A.	10	679	1,786	2,297	5.1	10.0
LUTH–Luth Cong Msn Chr	1	265	1,013	1,270	2.8	5.5
LUTH–Luth-MO Synod	1	158	366	470	1.1	2.0
LUTH–Wisc Ev Luth Syn	7	1,183	2,530	3,102	6.9	13.5
MENN–Amish Undif	11	NR	573	1,627	3.6	7.1
METH–Un Methodist	5	377	901	1,155	2.6	5.0
Non-denom Chr Chs	3	305	281	382	0.9	1.7
PENT–Assemb of God	3	384	177	767	1.7	3.3
PENT–Un Pent Ch Intl	1	NR	NR	NR	-	-
Sev Day Adv	2	58	100	115	0.3	0.5
Un C of Christ	2	135	462	579	1.3	2.5
OCONTO	**50**	**3,288**	**7,671**	**18,036**	**47.9**	**100.0**
Bahá'í	0	NR	1	1	0.0	0.0
BAPT–So Bapt Conv	1	NR	NR	NR	-	-
Catholic	8	NR	NR	7,931	21.1	44.0
Ch Cr, Scientst	1	NR	NR	NR	-	-
Chr & Miss Al	3	329	142	477	1.3	2.6
CHR–Chr Chs & Chs Cr	2	NR	125	150	0.4	0.8
Jehovah's Witness	1	NR	NR	NR	-	-
LUTH–E.L.C.A.	4	577	1,732	2,236	5.9	12.4
LUTH–Luth Cong Msn Chr	2	341	1,505	1,805	4.8	10.0
LUTH–Luth-MO Synod	10	885	2,461	2,961	7.9	16.4
LUTH–Wisc Ev Luth Syn	5	271	576	659	1.7	3.7
METH–Un Methodist	5	190	423	808	2.1	4.5
Non-denom Chr Chs	3	240	240	325	0.9	1.8
PENT–Assemb of God	2	240	135	293	0.8	1.6
PRES–Presb Ch (USA)	2	133	189	227	0.6	1.3
Sev Day Adv	1	82	142	163	0.4	0.9
ONEIDA	**56**	**4,509**	**7,194**	**20,613**	**57.3**	**100.0**
ANG/EPIS–Episcopal	2	140	219	247	0.7	1.2
Bahá'í	0	NR	15	15	0.0	0.1
BAPT–Converge/BGC	1	75	NR	90	0.3	0.4
BAPT–NT Ind Bapt	1	NR	NR	NR	-	-
BAPT–Ref Bapt Ch	1	NR	NR	NR	-	-
BAPT–Reg Bapt Gen As	1	NR	NR	NR	-	-
BUDD–Mahayana	1	NR	NR	28	0.1	0.1
Catholic	6	NR	NR	10,327	28.7	50.1
Ch Cr, Scientst	1	NR	NR	NR	-	-
CHR–Chs of Christ	2	75	59	73	0.2	0.4
Evan Free Ch	3	610	NR	610	1.7	3.0
Jehovah's Witness	2	NR	NR	NR	-	-
LDS–L-D Saints	1	NR	NR	341	0.9	1.7
LUTH–E.L.C.A.	5	919	2,130	2,703	7.5	13.1
LUTH–Luth-MO Synod	5	335	688	771	2.1	3.7
LUTH–Wisc Ev Luth Syn	4	640	1,605	1,828	5.1	8.9
METH–Un Methodist	2	332	693	1,057	2.9	5.1
Non-denom Chr Chs	6	565	387	707	2.0	3.4
ORTHE–Orth Ch in Amer	1	10	NR	16	0.0	0.1
PENT–Assemb of God	1	120	71	168	0.5	0.8
PENT–Ch God (Cleve)	1	18	30	35	0.1	0.2
PENT–Int Foursq Gos	1	190	393	454	1.3	2.2
PENT–Pent Ch of God	1	70	NR	109	0.3	0.5

NR–Not Reported - Represents no adherents reported. Percentages may not total 100 due to rounding.

Table 3: Religious Congregations by County and Group: 2010

Religious Group	Number of Congrega-tions	Number of Attendees	Number of Communicant, Confirmed, or Full Members	Adherents		
				Number of Adherents	% of Total Pop.	% of Total Adh.
PENT–Un Pent Ch Intl	1	NR	NR	NR	-	-
PENT–Vineyard	1	70	110	127	0.4	0.6
Sev Day Adv	2	90	156	179	0.5	0.9
Un C of Christ	2	200	560	647	1.8	3.1
Unit Univ	1	50	78	81	0.2	0.4
OUTAGAMIE	**139**	**21,781**	**39,329**	**129,228**	**73.1**	**100.0**
ANG/EPIS–Episcopal	1	125	325	646	0.4	0.5
Bahá'í	1	NR	68	68	0.0	0.1
BAPT–Converge/BGC	3	225	NR	270	0.2	0.2
BAPT–Ind Bapt Flwsp Intl	1	NR	NR	NR	-	-
BAPT–Reg Bapt Gen As	2	NR	NR	NR	-	-
BAPT–S-D Baptist Gen Con	1	7	8	10	0.0	0.0
BAPT–So Bapt Conv	6	323	529	655	0.4	0.5
BUDD–Mahayana	2	NR	NR	39	0.0	0.0
Calv Chpl	1	NR	NR	NR	-	-
Catholic	23	NR	NR	72,014	40.8	55.7
Ch Cr, Scientst	1	NR	NR	NR	-	-
Ch of Nazarene	1	0	43	43	0.0	0.0
Chr & Miss Al	2	3,222	1,391	3,765	2.1	2.9
CHR–Chr Chs & Chs Cr	1	NR	200	248	0.1	0.2
CHR–Chs of Christ	2	165	162	202	0.1	0.2
CHR–Int Chs of Christ	1	NR	36	45	0.0	0.0
CONG–Consrv Cong Chr	1	80	97	120	0.1	0.1
Evan Free Ch	2	300	NR	300	0.2	0.2
Jehovah's Witness	1	NR	NR	NR	-	-
JUD–Conserv	1	45	51	138	0.1	0.1
LDS–L-D Saints	3	NR	NR	1,186	0.7	0.9
LUTH–E.L.C.A.	10	3,592	10,498	14,329	8.1	11.1
LUTH–Luth Ch-Am Asc	1	NR	NR	NR	-	-
LUTH–Luth–MO Synod	6	2,373	6,528	8,831	5.0	6.8
LUTH–Nor Amer Luth C	1	NR	NR	NR	-	-
LUTH–Wisc Ev Luth Syn	18	5,689	10,069	12,851	7.3	9.9
METH–Un Methodist	9	1,241	2,657	3,924	2.2	3.0
MORAV–Morav Ch-North	1	71	184	221	0.1	0.2
Muslim Est	1	134	NR	308	0.2	0.2
New Apost Ch	1	NR	NR	NR	-	-
Non-denom Chr Chs	13	1,930	2,172	2,560	1.4	2.0
ORTHE–Greek Orthodox	1	50	NR	215	0.1	0.2
ORTHE–Rus Orth Abroad	1	3	NR	9	0.0	0.0
PENT–Assemb of God	6	666	382	1,115	0.6	0.9
PENT–Un Pent Ch Intl	1	NR	NR	NR	-	-
PRES–Presb Ch (USA)	2	175	438	543	0.3	0.4
REF–Christian Ref	1	80	117	145	0.1	0.1
Salvation Army	1	72	83	287	0.2	0.2
Un C of Christ	6	859	2,620	3,245	1.8	2.5
Unit Univ	1	354	671	896	0.5	0.7
Unity Ch	1	NR	NR	NR	-	-
OZAUKEE	**70**	**10,405**	**18,702**	**54,896**	**63.5**	**100.0**
ANG/EPIS–Episcopal	2	166	322	446	0.5	0.8
Bahá'í	1	NR	55	55	0.1	0.1
BAPT–Converge/BGC	2	150	NR	180	0.2	0.3
BAPT–Reg Bapt Gen As	1	NR	NR	NR	-	-
Catholic	8	NR	NR	28,644	33.2	52.2
Ch Cr, Scientst	1	NR	NR	NR	-	-
Chr & Miss Al	2	489	237	1,061	1.2	1.9
CONG–Cong Chr, NA	1	NR	200	242	0.3	0.4
Evan Free Ch	2	480	NR	480	0.6	0.9
HINDU–Post Ren	1	NR	NR	77	0.1	0.1
Ind Fund Churches	1	NR	NR	NR	-	-
Jehovah's Witness	2	NR	NR	NR	-	-
JUD–Orth	2	306	150	425	0.5	0.8
JUD–Reconst	1	78	100	270	0.3	0.5
LDS–L-D Saints	1	NR	NR	172	0.2	0.3
LUTH–E.L.C.A.	10	1,583	3,935	5,094	5.9	9.3
LUTH–Luth–MO Synod	7	2,979	6,709	8,464	9.8	15.4
LUTH–Wisc Ev Luth Syn	7	1,162	2,155	2,702	3.1	4.9
METH–Un Methodist	3	437	927	1,154	1.3	2.1
Non-denom Chr Chs	4	615	490	794	0.9	1.4
ORTHE–Ant Orth of NA	1	130	NR	250	0.3	0.5
PENT–Assemb of God	3	329	169	424	0.5	0.8
PENT–Vineyard	1	200	300	364	0.4	0.7

Religious Group	Number of Congrega-tions	Number of Attendees	Number of Communicant, Confirmed, or Full Members	Adherents		
				Number of Adherents	% of Total Pop.	% of Total Adh.
PRES–Orth Pres Ch	1	0	0	0	0.0	0.0
PRES–Presb Ch (USA)	1	764	1,481	1,795	2.1	3.3
Un C of Christ	3	537	1,285	1,558	1.8	2.8
Unit Univ	1	0	187	245	0.3	0.4
PEPIN	**20**	**596**	**1,979**	**4,661**	**62.4**	**100.0**
Bahá'í	0	NR	2	2	0.0	0.0
Catholic	3	NR	NR	2,180	29.2	46.8
Evan Cov Ch	2	83	97	108	1.4	2.3
Evan Free Ch	1	45	NR	45	0.6	1.0
LDS–Comm of Christ	1	NR	138	138	1.8	3.0
LUTH–E.L.C.A.	4	236	1,273	1,449	19.4	31.1
LUTH–Luth–MO Synod	1	51	98	125	1.7	2.7
MENN–Amish Undif	2	NR	68	187	2.5	4.0
METH–Un Methodist	3	128	233	324	4.3	7.0
PENT–Assemb of God	1	20	13	37	0.5	0.8
PENT–Un Pent Ch Intl	1	NR	NR	NR	-	-
Sev Day Adv	1	33	57	66	0.9	1.4
PIERCE	**57**	**4,526**	**9,053**	**19,518**	**47.6**	**100.0**
Bahá'í	0	NR	14	14	0.0	0.1
BAPT–Converge/BGC	1	400	NR	480	1.2	2.5
Catholic	6	NR	NR	6,790	16.6	34.8
CONG–Consrv Cong Chr	1	65	130	157	0.4	0.8
Evan Cov Ch	3	490	438	637	1.6	3.3
Evan Free Ch	1	50	NR	50	0.1	0.3
Jehovah's Witness	1	NR	NR	NR	-	-
LUTH–E.L.C.A.	13	1,520	4,856	6,776	16.5	34.7
LUTH–Luth–MO Synod	2	204	391	565	1.4	2.9
LUTH–Wisc Ev Luth Syn	2	90	321	361	0.9	1.8
METH–Un Methodist	10	346	956	1,305	3.2	6.7
Non-denom Chr Chs	8	683	762	855	2.1	4.4
PENT–Assemb of God	1	170	60	170	0.4	0.9
PENT–Un Pent Ch Intl	1	NR	NR	NR	-	-
PRES–Presb Ch (USA)	2	48	87	105	0.3	0.5
Un C of Christ	4	399	938	1,130	2.8	5.8
Unit Univ	1	61	100	123	0.3	0.6
POLK	**85**	**6,107**	**11,518**	**20,937**	**47.4**	**100.0**
ANG/EPIS–Episcopal	1	12	22	29	0.1	0.1
Bahá'í	0	NR	4	4	0.0	0.0
BAPT–Consrv Bapt	1	NR	NR	NR	-	-
BAPT–Converge/BGC	6	450	NR	540	1.2	2.6
BAPT–NT Ind Bapt	1	NR	NR	NR	-	-
BUDD–Mahayana	1	NR	NR	11	0.0	0.1
Catholic	5	NR	NR	3,716	8.4	17.7
Ch of Nazarene	1	16	59	59	0.1	0.3
Chr & Miss Al	2	573	255	840	1.9	4.0
Evan Cov Ch	1	124	181	161	0.4	0.8
Evan Free Ch	3	482	NR	482	1.1	2.3
FRND–Fr Gen Cf	1	NR	4	5	0.0	0.0
Jehovah's Witness	2	NR	NR	NR	-	-
LUTH–Assoc Free Luth	1	NR	NR	NR	-	-
LUTH–E.L.C.A.	25	2,149	6,436	9,120	20.6	43.6
LUTH–Luth Ch-Am Asc	1	NR	NR	NR	-	-
LUTH–Luth Cong Msn Chr	4	350	1,104	1,342	3.0	6.4
LUTH–Luth–MO Synod	5	344	663	794	1.8	3.8
LUTH–Wisc Ev Luth Syn	6	499	1,296	1,534	3.5	7.3
METH–Un Methodist	8	347	664	1,009	2.3	4.8
Non-denom Chr Chs	2	245	230	306	0.7	1.5
ORTHE–Orth Ch in Amer	1	75	NR	130	0.3	0.6
PENT–Assemb of God	2	125	34	177	0.4	0.8
PENT–Int Foursq Gos	1	43	49	60	0.1	0.3
PRES–Presb Ch (USA)	1	56	98	119	0.3	0.6
Sev Day Adv	2	92	161	185	0.4	0.9
Un C of Christ	1	125	258	314	0.7	1.5
PORTAGE	**74**	**5,639**	**8,278**	**40,989**	**58.5**	**100.0**
ANG/EPIS–Episcopal	2	73	174	199	0.3	0.5
Bahá'í	0	NR	29	29	0.0	0.1
BAPT–Converge/BGC	1	75	NR	90	0.1	0.2
BAPT–Reg Bapt Gen As	2	NR	NR	NR	-	-

NR–Not Reported   - Represents no adherents reported.   Percentages may not total 100 due to rounding.

Table 3: Religious Congregations by County and Group: 2010

Religious Group	Number of Congrega-tions	Number of Attendees	Number of Communicant, Confirmed, or Full Members	Adherents		
				Number of Adherents	% of Total Pop.	% of Total Adh.
BAPT–So Bapt Conv	3	110	68	81	0.1	0.2
BUDD–Theravada	1	NR	NR	15	0.0	0.0
BUDD–Vajrayana	1	NR	NR	13	0.0	0.0
Catholic	16	NR	NR	28,520	40.7	69.6
Ch Cr, Scientst	1	NR	NR	NR	-	-
Chr & Miss Al	1	91	146	153	0.2	0.4
CHR–Chs of Christ	3	113	98	124	0.2	0.3
Evan Free Ch	3	1,494	NR	1,494	2.1	3.6
FRND–Fr Gen Cf	1	NR	7	8	0.0	0.0
Ind Fund Churches	1	NR	NR	NR	-	-
Jehovah's Witness	1	NR	NR	NR	-	-
LDS–L-D Saints	1	NR	NR	290	0.4	0.7
LUTH–E.L.C.A.	7	922	2,940	3,907	5.6	9.5
LUTH–Evan Luth Syn	1	11	24	27	0.0	0.1
LUTH–Luth-MO Synod	5	812	1,752	2,223	3.2	5.4
LUTH–Wisc Ev Luth Syn	1	177	359	444	0.6	1.1
MENN–Amish Undif	0	NR	6	14	0.0	0.0
METH–Un Methodist	5	368	925	1,109	1.6	2.7
Non-denom Chr Chs	7	815	990	1,093	1.6	2.7
PENT–Assemb of God	2	315	177	471	0.7	1.1
PENT–Un Pent Ch Intl	1	NR	NR	NR	-	-
PRES–Presb Ch (USA)	1	99	259	308	0.4	0.8
Salvation Army	1	7	0	0	0.0	0.0
Sev Day Adv	3	88	153	176	0.3	0.4
Un C of Christ	1	44	131	156	0.2	0.4
Unit Univ	1	25	40	45	0.1	0.1
PRICE	**35**	**1,346**	**2,568**	**8,174**	**57.7**	**100.0**
ANG/EPIS–Episcopal	2	21	20	20	0.1	0.2
Bahá'í	0	NR	3	3	0.0	0.0
BAPT–Converge/BGC	4	300	NR	360	2.5	4.4
BAPT–Reg Bapt Gen As	1	NR	NR	NR	-	-
Catholic	5	NR	NR	4,502	31.8	55.1
Evan Cov Ch	1	26	36	34	0.2	0.4
Jehovah's Witness	1	NR	NR	NR	-	-
LUTH–E.L.C.A.	3	176	706	865	6.1	10.6
LUTH–Luth-MO Synod	4	277	920	1,235	8.7	15.1
LUTH–Nor Amer Luth C	2	NR	NR	NR	-	-
LUTH–Wisc Ev Luth Syn	2	62	112	138	1.0	1.7
METH–Un Methodist	1	38	93	127	0.9	1.6
Non-denom Chr Chs	4	230	255	302	2.1	3.7
PENT–Assemb of God	1	85	51	155	1.1	1.9
PENT–Un Pent Ch Intl	1	NR	NR	NR	-	-
PRES–Presb Ch (USA)	1	48	139	162	1.1	2.0
Un C of Christ	2	83	233	271	1.9	3.3
RACINE	**177**	**17,686**	**33,106**	**91,876**	**47.0**	**100.0**
ANG/EPIS–Episcopal	4	307	519	744	0.4	0.8
Bahá'í	1	NR	51	51	0.0	0.1
BAPT–Amer Bapt USA	4	255	1,695	2,094	1.1	2.3
BAPT–Converge/BGC	1	75	NR	90	0.0	0.1
BAPT–N Am Bapt Conf	2	NR	1,057	1,306	0.7	1.4
BAPT–Natl Mis Bapt Conv	1	0	150	185	0.1	0.2
BAPT–NBC USA	3	625	1,200	1,482	0.8	1.6
BAPT–Prog NBC	1	0	150	185	0.1	0.2
BAPT–Reg Bapt Gen As	3	NR	NR	NR	-	-
BAPT–So Bapt Conv	2	89	160	198	0.1	0.2
BRETH–Breth in Chr	1	NR	NR	NR	-	-
Calv Chpl	1	NR	NR	NR	-	-
Catholic	21	NR	NR	43,335	22.2	47.2
CGOD–Ch God (Ander)	2	85	NR	85	0.0	0.1
Ch Cr, Scientst	2	NR	NR	NR	-	-
Ch of Nazarene	3	220	469	492	0.3	0.5
CHR–Chr Chs & Chs Cr	1	NR	53	65	0.0	0.1
CHR–Chs of Christ	3	355	378	476	0.2	0.5
CONG–Cong Chr, NA	2	NR	162	200	0.1	0.2
Evan Free Ch	3	306	NR	306	0.2	0.3
Ind Fund Churches	2	NR	NR	NR	-	-
Jehovah's Witness	4	NR	NR	NR	-	-
LDS–L-D Saints	1	NR	NR	445	0.2	0.5
LUTH–E.L.C.A.	18	3,333	8,878	12,194	6.2	13.3
LUTH–Luth-MO Synod	15	2,372	5,090	6,648	3.4	7.2
LUTH–Wisc Ev Luth Syn	7	1,541	3,077	3,919	2.0	4.3
METH–AME	1	300	400	494	0.3	0.5
METH–C.M.E.	1	0	100	124	0.1	0.1
METH–Un Methodist	13	1,696	2,910	4,368	2.2	4.8
Muslim Est	1	134	NR	308	0.2	0.3
Non-denom Chr Chs	18	3,200	3,016	4,080	2.1	4.4
ORTHE–Greek Orthodox	1	150	NR	800	0.4	0.9
ORTHE–Serb Orth USA	2	219	NR	535	0.3	0.6
ORTHO–Armen Ap Cilic	1	60	NR	400	0.2	0.4
ORTHO–Armen Ap Etchm	1	115	NR	285	0.1	0.3
PENT–Assemb of God	4	550	344	761	0.4	0.8
PENT–Ch God (Cleve)	2	33	45	56	0.0	0.1
PENT–Ch of God Proph	1	NR	5	6	0.0	0.0
PENT–COGIC	4	350	850	1,050	0.5	1.1
PENT–Full Gosp Bapt	1	NR	NR	NR	-	-
PENT–Pent Ch of God	1	70	NR	109	0.1	0.1
PENT–Un Pent Ch Intl	2	NR	NR	NR	-	-
PENT–United Holy Ch	2	NR	NR	NR	-	-
PRES–Presb Ch (USA)	3	340	694	857	0.4	0.9
REF–Christian Ref	1	250	331	409	0.2	0.4
REF–Ref Ch in Am	1	63	102	122	0.1	0.1
Salvation Army	1	52	51	1,185	0.6	1.3
Sev Day Adv	3	186	324	373	0.2	0.4
Un C of Christ	3	183	522	645	0.3	0.7
Unit Univ	1	172	323	409	0.2	0.4
RICHLAND	**36**	**1,522**	**2,824**	**6,536**	**36.3**	**100.0**
ANG/EPIS–Episcopal	1	25	60	65	0.4	1.0
Bahá'í	0	NR	2	2	0.0	0.0
BAPT–Amer Bapt USA	1	40	98	119	0.7	1.8
BAPT–So Bapt Conv	1	23	6	7	0.0	0.1
Catholic	4	NR	NR	2,330	12.9	35.6
Ch of Nazarene	1	119	161	177	1.0	2.7
CHR–Chr Chs & Chs Cr	1	NR	0	0	0.0	0.0
CONG–Cong Chr, NA	1	NR	115	140	0.8	2.1
Evan Free Ch	1	158	NR	158	0.9	2.4
FRND–Fr Gen Cf	1	NR	0	0	0.0	0.0
Jehovah's Witness	1	NR	NR	NR	-	-
LDS–L-D Saints	1	NR	NR	63	0.3	1.0
LUTH–E.L.C.A.	3	238	911	1,126	6.2	17.2
LUTH–Luth-MO Synod	2	35	53	60	0.3	0.9
MENN–Amish Undif	2	NR	94	275	1.5	4.2
METH–Free Methodist	1	79	99	99	0.5	1.5
METH–Un Methodist	6	321	692	1,213	6.7	18.6
METH–Wesleyan	1	42	37	55	0.3	0.8
Non-denom Chr Chs	2	320	315	400	2.2	6.1
PENT–Apos Faith Msn	1	NR	35	43	0.2	0.7
PENT–Assemb of God	1	50	23	60	0.3	0.9
PENT–Un Pent Ch Intl	1	NR	NR	NR	-	-
PRES–Presb Ch (USA)	1	22	35	43	0.2	0.7
Sev Day Adv	1	50	88	101	0.6	1.5
ROCK	**157**	**16,563**	**35,123**	**75,831**	**47.3**	**100.0**
ANG/EPIS–Episcopal	2	138	377	415	0.3	0.5
Bahá'í	2	NR	105	105	0.1	0.1
BAPT–Amer Bapt Assn	1	NR	85	105	0.1	0.1
BAPT–Amer Bapt USA	3	311	542	670	0.4	0.9
BAPT–Converge/BGC	3	550	NR	660	0.4	0.9
BAPT–NBC USA	1	350	500	619	0.4	0.8
BAPT–NT Ind Bapt	1	NR	NR	NR	-	-
BAPT–S-D Baptist Gen Con	1	217	183	226	0.1	0.3
Catholic	12	NR	NR	27,158	16.9	35.8
Ch Cr, Scientst	1	NR	NR	NR	-	-
Ch of God Gen Conf	1	NR	17	21	0.0	0.0
Ch of Nazarene	1	26	89	89	0.1	0.1
Chr & Miss Al	1	47	0	53	0.0	0.1
CHR–Chr Ch (Disc)	1	45	109	135	0.1	0.2
CHR–Chr Chs & Chs Cr	3	NR	2,050	2,536	1.6	3.3
CHR–Chs of Christ	1	61	52	80	0.0	0.1
CONG–Cong Chr, NA	4	NR	596	737	0.5	1.0
Evan Cov Ch	1	75	67	98	0.1	0.1
Evan Free Ch	4	566	NR	566	0.4	0.7
FRND–Fr Gen Cf	1	NR	17	21	0.0	0.0
Grace Gosp Fel	1	NR	NR	NR	-	-

NR–Not Reported   - Represents no adherents reported.   Percentages may not total 100 due to rounding.

Table 3: Religious Congregations by County and Group: 2010

Religious Group	Number of Congregations	Number of Attendees	Number of Communicant, Confirmed, or Full Members	Adherents: Number of Adherents	Adherents: % of Total Pop.	Adherents: % of Total Adh.
Jehovah's Witness	4	NR	NR	NR	-	-
JUD–Reform	1	20	36	97	0.1	0.1
LDS–Comm of Christ	1	NR	138	138	0.1	0.2
LDS–L-D Saints	2	NR	NR	987	0.6	1.3
LUTH–Assoc Free Luth	1	NR	NR	NR	-	-
LUTH–E.L.C.A.	16	2,749	11,310	15,204	9.5	20.0
LUTH–Luth–MO Synod	11	1,817	4,761	6,041	3.8	8.0
LUTH–Wisc Ev Luth Syn	4	673	1,408	1,758	1.1	2.3
MENN–Amish Undif	0	NR	25	57	0.0	0.1
METH–AME	1	0	100	124	0.1	0.2
METH–C.M.E.	2	0	160	198	0.1	0.3
METH–Free Methodist	2	246	172	246	0.2	0.3
METH–Prim Meth Ch	2	NR	NR	NR	-	-
METH–Un Methodist	8	1,161	2,744	3,800	2.4	5.0
METH–Wesleyan	1	49	41	64	0.0	0.1
Missionary Ch	2	69	25	69	0.0	0.1
Muslim Est	1	15	NR	20	0.0	0.0
New Apost Ch	1	NR	NR	NR	-	-
Non-denom Chr Chs	19	4,902	5,615	6,558	4.1	8.6
PENT–Assemb of God	5	962	403	1,692	1.1	2.2
PENT–Ch God (Cleve)	1	133	211	261	0.2	0.3
PENT–Ch of God Proph	1	NR	52	64	0.0	0.1
PENT–Int Foursq Gos	1	8	9	11	0.0	0.0
PENT–Intl Pent Holiness	1	20	20	25	0.0	0.0
PENT–Open Bible Std	1	50	NR	50	0.0	0.1
PENT–Un Pent Ch Intl	2	NR	NR	NR	-	-
PRES–Cov Ref Pres	1	NR	NR	NR	-	-
PRES–Orth Pres Ch	1	83	93	140	0.1	0.2
PRES–Presb Ch (USA)	6	449	1,128	1,395	0.9	1.8
REF–Ref Ch in Am	1	80	156	163	0.1	0.2
Salvation Army	2	66	113	401	0.3	0.5
Sev Day Adv	3	153	266	306	0.2	0.4
Un C of Christ	6	472	1,348	1,668	1.0	2.2
RUSK	**44**	**1,261**	**3,212**	**7,506**	**50.9**	**100.0**
ANG/EPIS–Episcopal	1	13	54	54	0.4	0.7
Bahá'í	0	NR	1	1	0.0	0.0
BAPT–Converge/BGC	1	75	NR	90	0.6	1.2
BAPT–Reg Bapt Gen As	1	NR	NR	NR	-	-
Catholic	8	NR	NR	3,256	22.1	43.4
CHR–Chr Chs & Chs Cr	2	NR	309	371	2.5	4.9
Grace Gosp Fel	2	NR	NR	NR	-	-
Ind Fund Churches	1	NR	NR	NR	-	-
Jehovah's Witness	1	NR	NR	NR	-	-
LUTH–E.L.C.A.	5	285	1,134	1,457	9.9	19.4
LUTH–Luth–MO Synod	2	149	721	849	5.8	11.3
LUTH–Nor Amer Luth C	3	NR	NR	NR	-	-
LUTH–Wisc Ev Luth Syn	1	27	43	48	0.3	0.6
MENN–Amish Undif	1	NR	45	93	0.6	1.2
MENN–Mennonite USA	1	50	60	72	0.5	1.0
METH–Un Methodist	4	103	233	371	2.5	4.9
Non-denom Chr Chs	3	295	350	400	2.7	5.3
PENT–Assemb of God	3	164	114	267	1.8	3.6
PENT–Un Pent Ch Intl	1	NR	NR	NR	-	-
Un C of Christ	3	100	148	177	1.2	2.4
ST. CROIX	**78**	**7,395**	**15,271**	**42,581**	**50.5**	**100.0**
ANG/EPIS–Anglican NA	1	NR	NR	NR	-	-
ANG/EPIS–Episcopal	2	92	189	211	0.3	0.5
Bahá'í	0	NR	3	3	0.0	0.0
BAPT–Amer Bapt USA	1	91	200	254	0.3	0.6
BAPT–Consrv Bapt	1	NR	NR	NR	-	-
BAPT–Converge/BGC	4	1,025	NR	1,230	1.5	2.9
BAPT–NT Ind Bapt	2	NR	NR	NR	-	-
Catholic	9	NR	NR	18,471	21.9	43.4
CHR–Chs of Christ	1	33	22	41	0.0	0.1
CONG–Consrv Cong Chr	1	0	0	0	0.0	0.0
Evan Cov Ch	1	63	47	82	0.1	0.2
Jehovah's Witness	3	NR	NR	NR	-	-
LDS–L-D Saints	2	NR	NR	534	0.6	1.3
LUTH–Assoc Free Luth	1	NR	NR	NR	-	-
LUTH–E.L.C.A.	14	2,386	7,434	11,519	13.7	27.1
LUTH–Luth Cong Msn Chr	1	300	1,039	1,321	1.6	3.1

Religious Group	Number of Congregations	Number of Attendees	Number of Communicant, Confirmed, or Full Members	Adherents: Number of Adherents	Adherents: % of Total Pop.	Adherents: % of Total Adh.
LUTH–Luth–MO Synod	5	1,085	2,789	4,006	4.7	9.4
LUTH–Wisc Ev Luth Syn	3	339	482	623	0.7	1.5
METH–Un Methodist	8	559	1,182	1,679	2.0	3.9
Non-denom Chr Chs	4	410	510	550	0.7	1.3
PENT–Assemb of God	3	320	105	484	0.6	1.1
PENT–Int Foursq Gos	1	35	60	76	0.1	0.2
PENT–Un Pent Ch Intl	2	NR	NR	NR	-	-
PRES–Orth Pres Ch	1	73	53	88	0.1	0.2
PRES–Presb Ch (USA)	2	181	348	442	0.5	1.0
REF–Christian Ref	1	140	140	178	0.2	0.4
REF–Ref Ch in Am	1	130	317	348	0.4	0.8
Sev Day Adv	1	23	40	46	0.1	0.1
Un C of Christ	2	110	311	395	0.5	0.9
SAUK	**81**	**5,999**	**13,400**	**31,295**	**50.5**	**100.0**
ANG/EPIS–Episcopal	2	118	193	193	0.3	0.6
Bahá'í	0	NR	13	13	0.0	0.0
BAPT–Amer Bapt Assn	1	NR	65	80	0.1	0.3
BAPT–N Am Bapt Conf	1	NR	53	65	0.1	0.2
BAPT–So Bapt Conv	1	265	194	237	0.4	0.8
Catholic	8	NR	NR	12,618	20.4	40.3
CGOD–Ch God (Ander)	2	123	NR	123	0.2	0.4
Ch of Nazarene	1	64	78	150	0.2	0.5
CHR–Chs of Christ	1	8	8	8	0.0	0.0
CONG–Cong Chr, NA	1	NR	80	98	0.2	0.3
Evan Free Ch	2	285	NR	285	0.5	0.9
FRND–Fr Un Mtg	1	NR	64	78	0.1	0.2
Jehovah's Witness	1	NR	NR	NR	-	-
LDS–L-D Saints	1	NR	NR	360	0.6	1.2
LUTH–E.L.C.A.	8	1,339	4,696	6,417	10.4	20.5
LUTH–Luth–MO Synod	6	602	1,678	2,169	3.5	6.9
LUTH–Wisc Ev Luth Syn	7	774	1,872	2,322	3.7	7.4
MENN–Amish Undif	5	NR	261	631	1.0	2.0
METH–Un Methodist	13	981	1,997	2,726	4.4	8.7
Non-denom Chr Chs	7	746	850	957	1.5	3.1
PENT–Assemb of God	3	210	106	313	0.5	1.0
PRES–Orth Pres Ch	1	57	50	69	0.1	0.2
PRES–Presb Ch (USA)	3	150	408	499	0.8	1.6
Sev Day Adv	2	44	77	89	0.1	0.3
Un C of Christ	2	210	598	732	1.2	2.3
Unit Univ	1	23	59	63	0.1	0.2
SAWYER	**37**	**1,987**	**2,665**	**7,613**	**46.0**	**100.0**
ANG/EPIS–Episcopal	1	67	95	176	1.1	2.3
Bahá'í	0	NR	3	3	0.0	0.0
BAPT–Converge/BGC	1	75	NR	90	0.5	1.2
BAPT–Reg Bapt Gen As	1	NR	NR	NR	-	-
Catholic	6	NR	NR	3,747	22.6	49.2
CHR–Chs of Christ	1	15	10	18	0.1	0.2
CONG–Cong Chr, NA	1	NR	66	78	0.5	1.0
Evan Free Ch	2	80	NR	80	0.5	1.1
Jehovah's Witness	1	NR	NR	NR	-	-
LDS–L-D Saints	1	NR	NR	133	0.8	1.7
LUTH–E.L.C.A.	4	328	833	998	6.0	13.1
LUTH–Luth Cong Msn Chr	1	170	376	446	2.7	5.9
LUTH–Luth–MO Synod	1	81	142	153	0.9	2.0
LUTH–Wisc Ev Luth Syn	1	62	97	117	0.7	1.5
MENN–Mennonite USA	2	61	32	38	0.2	0.5
METH–Un Methodist	2	114	175	264	1.6	3.5
METH–Wesleyan	2	651	501	846	5.1	11.1
Non-denom Chr Chs	2	185	250	256	1.5	3.4
PENT–Assemb of God	2	62	12	85	0.5	1.1
PENT–Int Foursq Gos	1	0	0	0	0.0	0.0
PRES–Presb Ch (USA)	3	20	44	52	0.3	0.7
Sev Day Adv	1	16	29	33	0.2	0.4
SHAWANO	**81**	**5,293**	**12,718**	**23,809**	**56.8**	**100.0**
ANG/EPIS–Episcopal	1	32	49	49	0.1	0.2
Bahá'í	0	NR	7	7	0.0	0.0
BAPT–Converge/BGC	1	75	NR	90	0.2	0.4
BAPT–So Bapt Conv	3	62	60	73	0.2	0.3
Catholic	11	NR	NR	6,930	16.5	29.1
Ch of Nazarene	1	103	160	182	0.4	0.8

NR–Not Reported   - Represents no adherents reported.   Percentages may not total 100 due to rounding.

Table 3: Religious Congregations by County and Group: 2010

Religious Group	Number of Congrega-tions	Number of Attendees	Number of Communicant, Confirmed, or Full Members	Adherents: Number of Adherents	Adherents: % of Total Pop.	Adherents: % of Total Adh.
FRND–Fr Gen Cf	1	NR	0	0	0.0	0.0
Grace Gosp Fel	1	NR	NR	NR	-	-
Ind Fund Churches	1	NR	NR	NR	-	-
Jehovah's Witness	1	NR	NR	NR	-	-
LDS–L-D Saints	2	NR	NR	520	1.2	2.2
LUTH–E.L.C.A.	12	853	2,417	3,418	8.1	14.4
LUTH–Evan Luth Syn	1	94	161	194	0.5	0.8
LUTH–Luth Cong Msn Chr	1	75	147	178	0.4	0.7
LUTH–Luth–MO Synod	19	2,732	7,355	8,919	21.3	37.5
LUTH–Nor Amer Luth C	2	NR	NR	NR	-	-
LUTH–Wisc Ev Luth Syn	3	293	603	682	1.6	2.9
MENN–Amish Undif	2	NR	137	307	0.7	1.3
METH–Un Methodist	5	241	443	588	1.4	2.5
Non-denom Chr Chs	3	170	215	238	0.6	1.0
OCATH–Pol Natl Cath	1	NR	NR	NR	-	-
PENT–Assemb of God	2	197	115	401	1.0	1.7
PENT–Un Pent Ch Intl	1	NR	NR	NR	-	-
PRES–Orth Pres Ch	1	26	36	52	0.1	0.2
PRES–Presb Ch (USA)	2	137	275	333	0.8	1.4
Sev Day Adv	1	20	36	41	0.1	0.2
Un C of Christ	2	183	502	607	1.4	2.5
SHEBOYGAN	**134**	**18,452**	**33,285**	**68,389**	**59.2**	**100.0**
ANG/EPIS–Anglican NA	1	NR	NR	NR	-	-
ANG/EPIS–Episcopal	3	238	385	420	0.4	0.6
Bahá'í	0	NR	36	36	0.0	0.1
BAPT–Amer Bapt USA	1	37	57	70	0.1	0.1
BAPT–Converge/BGC	2	150	NR	180	0.2	0.3
BAPT–N Am Bapt Conf	1	NR	97	119	0.1	0.2
BAPT–So Bapt Conv	1	48	52	64	0.1	0.1
BUDD–Mahayana	1	NR	NR	28	0.0	0.0
BUDD–Vajrayana	1	NR	NR	53	0.0	0.1
Catholic	11	NR	NR	24,036	20.8	35.1
Ch Cr, Scientist	1	NR	NR	NR	-	-
Chr & Miss Al	4	866	625	1,252	1.1	1.8
CHR–Chs of Christ	2	125	118	153	0.1	0.2
CONG–Consrv Cong Chr	2	100	278	340	0.3	0.5
Evan Cov Ch	1	256	395	333	0.3	0.5
Evan Free Ch	1	950	NR	950	0.8	1.4
Ind Fund Churches	2	NR	NR	NR	-	-
Jehovah's Witness	1	NR	NR	NR	-	-
LDS–L-D Saints	1	NR	NR	497	0.4	0.7
LUTH–E.L.C.A.	6	1,050	2,998	3,846	3.3	5.6
LUTH–Luth–MO Synod	24	4,142	10,906	13,624	11.8	19.9
LUTH–Wisc Ev Luth Syn	3	561	1,015	1,310	1.1	1.9
MENN–Amish Undif	0	NR	2	3	0.0	0.0
METH–Un Methodist	7	670	1,453	1,795	1.6	2.6
Muslim Est	1	40	NR	70	0.1	0.1
Non-denom Chr Chs	8	1,218	1,311	1,623	1.4	2.4
ORTHE–Greek Orthodox	1	35	NR	145	0.1	0.2
PENT–Assemb of God	5	1,202	361	2,086	1.8	3.1
PENT–Intl Pent Holiness	1	38	68	83	0.1	0.1
PENT–Un Pent Ch Intl	1	NR	NR	NR	-	-
PRES–Evan Presby Ch	1	NR	65	79	0.1	0.1
PRES–Orth Pres Ch	3	572	724	927	0.8	1.4
PRES–Presb Ch (USA)	2	259	407	498	0.4	0.7
PRES–Ref Pres GA	1	NR	NR	NR	-	-
REF–Christian Ref	4	910	1,315	1,608	1.4	2.4
REF–Heritage Ref	1	NR	9	11	0.0	0.0
REF–Ref Ch in Am	8	2,819	5,048	5,276	4.6	7.7
Salvation Army	1	55	124	239	0.2	0.3
Sev Day Adv	2	100	173	199	0.2	0.3
Un C of Christ	16	2,011	5,263	6,434	5.6	9.4
Unity Ch	1	NR	NR	NR	-	-
Zoroastrian	0	NR	NR	2	0.0	0.0
TAYLOR	**37**	**1,836**	**5,020**	**15,363**	**74.3**	**100.0**
Bahá'í	0	NR	1	1	0.0	0.0
BAPT–Converge/BGC	1	75	NR	90	0.4	0.6
Catholic	7	NR	NR	8,417	40.7	54.8
LUTH–E.L.C.A.	5	433	1,618	2,039	9.9	13.3
LUTH–Luth–MO Synod	3	196	743	964	4.7	6.3
LUTH–Wisc Ev Luth Syn	5	642	1,809	2,303	11.1	15.0

Religious Group	Number of Congrega-tions	Number of Attendees	Number of Communicant, Confirmed, or Full Members	Adherents: Number of Adherents	Adherents: % of Total Pop.	Adherents: % of Total Adh.
MENN–Amish Undif	5	NR	223	502	2.4	3.3
METH–Un Methodist	2	87	236	383	1.9	2.5
Non-denom Chr Chs	3	262	195	328	1.6	2.1
OCATH–Pol Natl Cath	1	NR	NR	NR	-	-
ORTHE–Orth Ch in Amer	1	40	NR	70	0.3	0.5
PENT–Assemb of God	1	26	15	44	0.2	0.3
PENT–Un Pent Ch Intl	1	NR	NR	NR	-	-
PRES–Presb Ch (USA)	1	30	59	73	0.4	0.5
Un C of Christ	1	45	121	149	0.7	1.0
TREMPEALEAU	**53**	**2,988**	**10,940**	**21,219**	**73.6**	**100.0**
Bahá'í	0	NR	10	10	0.0	0.0
BAPT–Consrv Bapt	1	NR	NR	NR	-	-
Catholic	8	NR	NR	7,700	26.7	36.3
Ch of Nazarene	1	24	10	32	0.1	0.2
Jehovah's Witness	2	NR	NR	NR	-	-
LUTH–E.L.C.A.	24	2,134	8,940	10,847	37.6	51.1
LUTH–Luth–MO Synod	3	212	650	784	2.7	3.7
LUTH–Wisc Ev Luth Syn	2	147	172	236	0.8	1.1
MENN–Amish Undif	2	NR	148	351	1.2	1.7
METH–Un Methodist	2	97	167	257	0.9	1.2
Non-denom Chr Chs	4	158	240	250	0.9	1.2
PENT–Assemb of God	2	27	20	35	0.1	0.2
PRES–Presb Ch (USA)	1	130	335	412	1.4	1.9
Un C of Christ	1	59	248	305	1.1	1.4
VERNON	**83**	**4,010**	**10,570**	**18,315**	**61.5**	**100.0**
Bahá'í	0	NR	6	6	0.0	0.0
BAPT–Amer Bapt USA	1	5	6	8	0.0	0.0
Catholic	4	NR	NR	3,060	10.3	16.7
Ch of Nazarene	1	12	31	31	0.1	0.2
CHR–Chr Chs & Chs Cr	3	NR	145	182	0.6	1.0
CONG–Consrv Cong Chr	1	190	361	454	1.5	2.5
Evan Free Ch	1	130	NR	130	0.4	0.7
FRND–Fr Gen Cf	1	NR	0	0	0.0	0.0
Jehovah's Witness	2	NR	NR	NR	-	-
LDS–L-D Saints	1	NR	NR	109	0.4	0.6
LUTH–Ch of Luth Br	1	94	45	120	0.4	0.7
LUTH–E.L.C.A.	15	1,318	5,515	6,735	22.6	36.8
LUTH–Luth Cong Msn Chr	2	120	304	383	1.3	2.1
LUTH–Wisc Ev Luth Syn	7	609	1,186	1,402	4.7	7.7
MENN–Amish Undif	20	NR	1,001	2,786	9.4	15.2
MENN–CG in Cr (Menn)	1	NR	6	8	0.0	0.0
METH–Free Methodist	1	85	57	85	0.3	0.5
METH–Un Methodist	9	476	924	1,533	5.1	8.4
METH–Wesleyan	4	340	331	442	1.5	2.4
Non-denom Chr Chs	7	590	617	766	2.6	4.2
PENT–Assemb of God	1	41	35	75	0.3	0.4
VILAS	**37**	**2,340**	**3,950**	**7,696**	**35.9**	**100.0**
ANG/EPIS–Anglican NA	1	NR	NR	NR	-	-
ANG/EPIS–Episcopal	1	26	0	0	0.0	0.0
Bahá'í	0	NR	53	53	0.2	0.7
BAPT–Reg Bapt Gen As	1	NR	NR	NR	-	-
BAPT–So Bapt Conv	1	20	8	9	0.0	0.1
Catholic	8	NR	NR	2,923	13.6	38.0
Evan Cov Ch	1	98	189	127	0.6	1.7
Evan Free Ch	1	150	NR	150	0.7	1.9
Ind Fund Churches	1	NR	NR	NR	-	-
Jehovah's Witness	1	NR	NR	NR	-	-
LUTH–E.L.C.A.	4	339	828	926	4.3	12.0
LUTH–Luth–MO Synod	2	252	724	851	4.0	11.1
LUTH–Wisc Ev Luth Syn	3	330	566	676	3.2	8.8
Non-denom Chr Chs	4	530	452	662	3.1	8.6
PENT–Assemb of God	1	40	30	55	0.3	0.7
PRES–Presb Ch (USA)	2	198	336	386	1.8	5.0
Sev Day Adv	1	40	69	79	0.4	1.0
Un C of Christ	4	317	695	799	3.7	10.4
WALWORTH	**105**	**11,137**	**17,337**	**44,588**	**43.6**	**100.0**
ANG/EPIS–Episcopal	4	188	346	370	0.4	0.8
Bahá'í	0	NR	46	46	0.0	0.1

NR–Not Reported - Represents no adherents reported. Percentages may not total 100 due to rounding.

Table 3: Religious Congregations by County and Group: 2010

Religious Group	Number of Congregations	Number of Attendees	Number of Communicant, Confirmed, or Full Members	Adherents: Number of Adherents	Adherents: % of Total Pop.	Adherents: % of Total Adh.
BAPT–Amer Bapt USA	3	127	273	333	0.3	0.7
BAPT–Converge/BGC	3	550	NR	660	0.6	1.5
BAPT–Reg Bapt Gen As	1	NR	NR	NR	-	-
BUDD–Vajrayana	1	NR	NR	14	0.0	0.0
Catholic	8	NR	NR	19,868	19.4	44.6
Ch Cr, Scientst	1	NR	NR	NR	-	-
CHR–Chs of Christ	1	45	40	54	0.1	0.1
CONG–Cong Chr, NA	1	NR	30	37	0.0	0.1
Evan Cov Ch	2	187	255	243	0.2	0.5
Evan Free Ch	4	1,945	NR	1,945	1.9	4.4
Grace Gosp Fel	1	NR	NR	NR	-	-
Ind Fund Churches	1	NR	NR	NR	-	-
Jehovah's Witness	1	NR	NR	NR	-	-
LDS–L-D Saints	1	NR	NR	498	0.5	1.1
LUTH–E.L.C.A.	8	1,416	4,468	5,277	5.2	11.8
LUTH–Luth Cong Msn Chr	2	511	1,054	1,286	1.3	2.9
LUTH–Luth-MO Synod	6	780	2,059	2,915	2.9	6.5
LUTH–Wisc Ev Luth Syn	5	884	1,769	2,286	2.2	5.1
METH–AME	1	0	100	122	0.1	0.3
METH–Un Methodist	13	871	1,783	2,284	2.2	5.1
Non-denom Chr Chs	18	2,330	2,600	3,132	3.1	7.0
PENT–Assemb of God	4	194	96	264	0.3	0.6
PENT–Un Pent Ch Intl	1	NR	NR	NR	-	-
PRES–Presb Ch (USA)	1	110	230	281	0.3	0.6
REF–Christian Ref	1	240	469	572	0.6	1.3
REF–Ref Ch in Am	1	67	64	91	0.1	0.2
Sev Day Adv	1	47	82	94	0.1	0.2
Un C of Christ	9	625	1,549	1,890	1.8	4.2
Unit Univ	1	20	24	26	0.0	0.1
WASHBURN	**38**	**2,768**	**4,314**	**8,123**	**51.1**	**100.0**
ANG/EPIS–Episcopal	2	50	75	75	0.5	0.9
Bahá'í	0	NR	2	2	0.0	0.0
BAPT–So Bapt Conv	1	1	2	2	0.0	0.0
Catholic	5	NR	NR	2,317	14.6	28.5
Ch of Nazarene	1	48	56	77	0.5	0.9
Chr & Miss Al	1	71	38	121	0.8	1.5
CHR–Chr Chs & Chs Cr	1	NR	25	30	0.2	0.4
Jehovah's Witness	1	NR	NR	NR	-	-
LUTH–E.L.C.A.	5	574	1,671	1,924	12.1	23.7
LUTH–Luth Cong Msn Chr	2	190	452	534	3.4	6.6
LUTH–Luth-MO Synod	2	198	441	502	3.2	6.2
LUTH–Wisc Ev Luth Syn	1	91	152	190	1.2	2.3
METH–Un Methodist	4	227	537	663	4.2	8.2
METH–Wesleyan	2	460	206	598	3.8	7.4
Non-denom Chr Chs	6	805	592	1,007	6.3	12.4
PENT–Assemb of God	1	21	18	25	0.2	0.3
PENT–Un Pent Ch Intl	1	NR	NR	NR	-	-
Sev Day Adv	1	6	10	12	0.1	0.1
Un C of Christ	1	26	37	44	0.3	0.5
WASHINGTON	**100**	**15,627**	**24,781**	**77,163**	**58.5**	**100.0**
ANG/EPIS–Episcopal	2	151	320	380	0.3	0.5
Bahá'í	0	NR	38	38	0.0	0.0
BAPT–Converge/BGC	1	75	NR	90	0.1	0.1
BAPT–NT Ind Bapt	1	NR	NR	NR	-	-
Catholic	13	NR	NR	39,943	30.3	51.8
Ch Cr, Scientst	1	NR	NR	NR	-	-
Ch of Nazarene	1	18	20	46	0.0	0.1
Chr & Miss Al	2	744	364	1,099	0.8	1.4
CHR–Chs of Christ	1	30	25	35	0.0	0.0
CONG–Cong Chr, NA	1	NR	50	62	0.0	0.1
CONG–Consrv Cong Chr	1	88	47	58	0.0	0.1
Grace Gosp Fel	1	NR	NR	NR	-	-
HINDU–Post Ren	1	NR	NR	25	0.0	0.0
Ind Fund Churches	1	NR	NR	NR	-	-
Jehovah's Witness	3	NR	NR	NR	-	-
JUD–Reform	1	7	13	35	0.0	0.0
LDS–L-D Saints	1	NR	NR	431	0.3	0.6
LUTH–E.L.C.A.	7	1,388	3,677	5,315	4.0	6.9
LUTH–Evan Luth Syn	1	196	346	429	0.3	0.6
LUTH–Luth Cong Msn Chr	1	352	756	931	0.7	1.2
LUTH–Luth-MO Synod	7	2,247	4,576	6,157	4.7	8.0

Religious Group	Number of Congregations	Number of Attendees	Number of Communicant, Confirmed, or Full Members	Adherents: Number of Adherents	Adherents: % of Total Pop.	Adherents: % of Total Adh.
LUTH–Wisc Ev Luth Syn	13	3,954	7,269	9,376	7.1	12.2
METH–Un Methodist	3	853	1,698	2,349	1.8	3.0
Non-denom Chr Chs	12	3,115	2,785	3,970	3.0	5.1
ORTHE–Orth Ch in Amer	1	12	NR	28	0.0	0.0
PENT–Assemb of God	3	1,091	316	3,312	2.5	4.3
PENT–Un Pent Ch Intl	3	NR	NR	NR	-	-
PRES–Presb Ch (USA)	2	129	147	181	0.1	0.2
REF–Ref Ch in Am	1	45	69	81	0.1	0.1
Un C of Christ	14	1,132	2,265	2,789	2.1	3.6
Zoroastrian	0	NR	NR	3	0.0	0.0
WAUKESHA	**272**	**53,631**	**81,933**	**234,739**	**60.2**	**100.0**
ANG/EPIS–Anglican NA	1	NR	NR	NR	-	-
ANG/EPIS–Episcopal	12	807	1,679	1,740	0.4	0.7
Bahá'í	3	NR	194	194	0.0	0.1
BAPT–Amer Bapt USA	4	163	338	412	0.1	0.2
BAPT–Converge/BGC	2	2,075	NR	2,490	0.6	1.1
BAPT–N Am Bapt Conf	2	NR	372	454	0.1	0.2
BAPT–NT Ind Bapt	1	NR	NR	NR	-	-
BAPT–Reg Bapt Gen As	4	NR	NR	NR	-	-
BAPT–So Bapt Conv	1	68	57	70	0.0	0.0
BRETH–Breth in Chr	1	NR	NR	NR	-	-
BUDD–Theravada	2	NR	NR	675	0.2	0.3
Catholic	28	NR	NR	115,008	29.5	49.0
Ch Cr, Scientst	4	NR	NR	NR	-	-
Ch of Nazarene	2	52	121	225	0.1	0.1
Chr & Miss Al	2	1,516	722	3,298	0.8	1.4
CHR–Chr Chs & Chs Cr	2	NR	1,120	1,366	0.4	0.6
CHR–Chs of Christ	1	60	52	65	0.0	0.0
CONG–Cong Chr, NA	3	NR	307	374	0.1	0.2
Evan Free Ch	2	838	NR	838	0.2	0.4
FRND–Fr Gen Cf	1	NR	7	9	0.0	0.0
Grace Gosp Fel	1	NR	NR	NR	-	-
HINDU–I/A Temples	1	NR	NR	16	0.0	0.0
HINDU–Post Ren	1	NR	NR	10	0.0	0.0
HINDU–Trad Temples	1	NR	NR	6,000	1.5	2.6
Ind Fund Churches	4	NR	NR	NR	-	-
Jain	1	NR	NR	NR	-	-
Jehovah's Witness	7	NR	NR	NR	-	-
JUD–Reform	1	72	127	343	0.1	0.1
LDS–L-D Saints	4	NR	NR	1,645	0.4	0.7
LUTH–Assoc Free Luth	2	NR	NR	NR	-	-
LUTH–E.L.C.A.	28	6,789	18,470	24,007	6.2	10.2
LUTH–Evan Luth Syn	1	267	377	485	0.1	0.2
LUTH–Luth Cong Msn Chr	2	NR	NR	NR	-	-
LUTH–Luth-MO Synod	19	6,762	12,950	17,337	4.4	7.4
LUTH–Nor Amer Luth C	1	NR	NR	NR	-	-
LUTH–Wisc Ev Luth Syn	18	7,596	12,381	15,533	4.0	6.6
MENN–Mennonite USA	1	5	25	30	0.0	0.0
METH–Free Methodist	1	65	80	80	0.0	0.0
METH–Un Methodist	14	1,970	4,362	6,131	1.6	2.6
METH–Wesleyan	3	257	124	334	0.1	0.1
Non-denom Chr Chs	34	18,374	19,068	23,000	5.9	9.8
PENT–Assemb of God	5	2,442	1,730	3,426	0.9	1.5
PENT–Ch God (Cleve)	1	26	27	33	0.0	0.0
PENT–Un Pent Ch Intl	5	NR	NR	NR	-	-
PRES–Evan Presby Ch	1	NR	185	226	0.1	0.1
PRES–Orth Pres Ch	2	205	247	332	0.1	0.1
PRES–Presb Ch (USA)	12	675	1,507	1,838	0.5	0.8
PRES–Presb Ch Amer	2	273	236	322	0.1	0.1
REF–Christian Ref	1	404	735	896	0.2	0.4
REF–Ref Ch in Am	1	33	47	57	0.0	0.0
Salvation Army	1	33	48	121	0.0	0.1
Sev Day Adv	2	138	240	276	0.1	0.1
Sikh	1	NR	NR	NR	-	-
Un C of Christ	12	1,286	3,351	4,086	1.0	1.7
Unit Univ	3	380	647	944	0.2	0.4
Zoroastrian	0	NR	NR	13	0.0	0.0
WAUPACA	**90**	**9,301**	**20,325**	**34,034**	**64.9**	**100.0**
ANG/EPIS–Episcopal	2	163	297	374	0.7	1.1
Bahá'í	0	NR	9	9	0.0	0.0
BAPT–Converge/BGC	1	75	NR	90	0.2	0.3

NR–Not Reported - Represents no adherents reported. Percentages may not total 100 due to rounding.

Table 3: Religious Congregations by County and Group: 2010

Religious Group	Number of Congrega-tions	Number of Attendees	Number of Communicant, Confirmed, or Full Members	Adherents: Number of Adherents	Adherents: % of Total Pop.	Adherents: % of Total Adh.
BAPT–So Bapt Conv	3	95	87	105	0.2	0.3
Calv Chpl	1	NR	NR	NR	-	-
Catholic	7	NR	NR	6,932	13.2	20.4
Ch of Nazarene	1	4	5	13	0.0	0.0
CHR–Chr Chs & Chs Cr	1	NR	50	60	0.1	0.2
CHR–Chs of Christ	5	236	205	266	0.5	0.8
Evan Free Ch	2	724	NR	724	1.4	2.1
Jehovah's Witness	3	NR	NR	NR	-	-
LUTH–E.L.C.A.	5	1,052	3,562	4,969	9.5	14.6
LUTH–Evan Luth Syn	1	35	47	60	0.1	0.2
LUTH–Luth Cong Msn Chr	14	1,435	4,339	5,221	10.0	15.3
LUTH–Luth–MO Synod	12	1,622	4,277	5,250	10.0	15.4
LUTH–Wisc Ev Luth Syn	6	1,959	4,608	5,628	10.7	16.5
MENN–Amish Undif	3	NR	73	192	0.4	0.6
METH–Un Methodist	8	644	1,280	1,857	3.5	5.5
Non-denom Chr Chs	5	591	596	740	1.4	2.2
PENT–Assemb of God	4	356	230	752	1.4	2.2
PENT–Un Pent Ch Intl	2	NR	NR	NR	-	-
PRES–Presb Ch (USA)	1	67	107	129	0.2	0.4
Sev Day Adv	1	26	44	51	0.1	0.1
Un C of Christ	2	217	509	612	1.2	1.8
WAUSHARA	**41**	**2,260**	**4,085**	**12,445**	**50.8**	**100.0**
Bahá'í	0	NR	3	3	0.0	0.0
BAPT–NT Ind Bapt	1	NR	NR	NR	-	-
BAPT–Reg Bapt Gen As	1	NR	NR	NR	-	-
Calv Chpl	1	NR	NR	NR	-	-
Catholic	4	NR	NR	6,687	27.3	53.7
CHR–Chs of Christ	1	15	15	18	0.1	0.1
CONG–Consrv Cong Chr	1	36	37	43	0.2	0.3
Evan Free Ch	1	350	NR	350	1.4	2.8
Jehovah's Witness	1	NR	NR	NR	-	-
LUTH–E.L.C.A.	8	574	1,826	2,185	8.9	17.6
LUTH–Luth–MO Synod	5	287	614	742	3.0	6.0
LUTH–Wisc Ev Luth Syn	2	281	450	556	2.3	4.5
MENN–Amish Undif	3	NR	121	336	1.4	2.7
METH–Un Methodist	5	320	579	893	3.6	7.2
METH–Wesleyan	1	53	47	69	0.3	0.6
Non-denom Chr Chs	1	65	60	81	0.3	0.7
PENT–Assemb of God	2	178	139	255	1.0	2.0
PRES–Presb Ch (USA)	1	34	52	61	0.2	0.5
Un C of Christ	2	67	142	166	0.7	1.3
WINNEBAGO	**130**	**18,188**	**32,507**	**82,833**	**49.6**	**100.0**
ANG/EPIS–Episcopal	2	303	1,111	1,150	0.7	1.4
Bahá'í	1	NR	71	71	0.0	0.1
BAPT–Amer Bapt USA	1	60	121	145	0.1	0.2
BAPT–Converge/BGC	1	800	NR	960	0.6	1.2
BAPT–Reg Bapt Gen As	1	NR	NR	NR	-	-
BAPT–So Bapt Conv	2	49	59	71	0.0	0.1
BUDD–Mahayana	2	NR	NR	55	0.0	0.1
Catholic	11	NR	NR	36,514	21.9	44.1
Ch Cr, Scientst	1	NR	NR	NR	-	-
Ch of Nazarene	1	18	30	30	0.0	0.0
Chr & Miss Al	1	75	117	134	0.1	0.2
CHR–Chr Chs & Chs Cr	1	NR	70	84	0.1	0.1
CHR–Chs of Christ	1	80	68	100	0.1	0.1
CONG–Cong Chr, NA	1	NR	314	377	0.2	0.5
CONG–Consrv Cong Chr	2	315	334	401	0.2	0.5
Evan Free Ch	1	85	NR	85	0.1	0.1
FRND–Fr Gen Cf	2	NR	14	17	0.0	0.0
Grace Gosp Fel	1	NR	NR	NR	-	-
Jehovah's Witness	2	NR	NR	NR	-	-
LDS–L-D Saints	3	NR	NR	925	0.6	1.1
LUTH–E.L.C.A.	18	3,176	10,359	12,866	7.7	15.5
LUTH–Evan Luth Syn	1	21	37	42	0.0	0.1
LUTH–Luth Cong Msn Chr	1	180	698	837	0.5	1.0
LUTH–Luth–MO Synod	7	1,746	3,639	4,798	2.9	5.8
LUTH–Nor Amer Luth C	1	NR	NR	NR	-	-
LUTH–Wisc Ev Luth Syn	16	2,957	6,791	8,469	5.1	10.2
METH–Un Methodist	7	914	1,796	2,578	1.5	3.1
Muslim Est	1	134	NR	308	0.2	0.4
Non-denom Chr Chs	14	5,365	3,100	6,786	4.1	8.2
PENT–Assemb of God	3	254	112	360	0.2	0.4
PENT–Int Foursq Gos	2	108	62	74	0.0	0.1
PENT–Pent Ch of God	1	70	NR	109	0.1	0.1
PENT–Un Pent Ch Intl	4	NR	NR	NR	-	-
PRES–Korean Pres Amer	1	NR	NR	NR	-	-
PRES–Orth Pres Ch	1	71	59	99	0.1	0.1
PRES–Presb Ch (USA)	5	565	1,547	1,855	1.1	2.2
Salvation Army	1	44	44	202	0.1	0.2
Sev Day Adv	1	148	258	297	0.2	0.4
Un C of Christ	7	650	1,696	2,034	1.2	2.5
WOOD	**100**	**8,260**	**17,586**	**52,135**	**69.7**	**100.0**
ANG/EPIS–Episcopal	2	70	100	138	0.2	0.3
Bahá'í	0	NR	17	17	0.0	0.0
BAPT–Amer Bapt USA	1	42	70	84	0.1	0.2
BAPT–Converge/BGC	1	75	NR	90	0.1	0.2
BAPT–NT Ind Bapt	2	NR	NR	NR	-	-
BAPT–Ref Bapt Ch	1	NR	NR	NR	-	-
BAPT–Reg Bapt Gen As	1	NR	NR	NR	-	-
BAPT–So Bapt Conv	1	15	8	10	0.0	0.0
Calv Chpl	1	NR	NR	NR	-	-
Catholic	18	NR	NR	27,050	36.2	51.9
Ch of Nazarene	1	0	26	26	0.0	0.0
Chr & Miss Al	1	194	95	325	0.4	0.6
CHR–Chs of Christ	3	140	117	151	0.2	0.3
Evan Free Ch	3	588	NR	588	0.8	1.1
Ind Fund Churches	1	NR	NR	NR	-	-
Jehovah's Witness	2	NR	NR	NR	-	-
LDS–L-D Saints	2	NR	NR	637	0.9	1.2
LUTH–E.L.C.A.	6	1,060	3,670	4,320	5.8	8.3
LUTH–Luth–MO Synod	15	2,938	8,340	10,791	14.4	20.7
LUTH–Wisc Ev Luth Syn	2	346	1,120	1,387	1.9	2.7
MENN–Amish Undif	3	NR	53	143	0.2	0.3
METH–Un Methodist	3	233	573	775	1.0	1.5
METH–Wesleyan	1	89	41	116	0.2	0.2
MORAV–Morav Ch-North	5	180	452	547	0.7	1.0
Muslim Est	1	134	NR	308	0.4	0.6
Non-denom Chr Chs	6	625	635	782	1.0	1.5
PENT–Assemb of God	1	665	267	1,451	1.9	2.8
PENT–Ch of God Proph	1	NR	20	24	0.0	0.0
PENT–Un Pent Ch Intl	2	NR	NR	NR	-	-
PRES–Presb Ch (USA)	2	159	398	480	0.6	0.9
REF–Christian Ref	1	50	50	60	0.1	0.1
REF–Ref Ch in Am	1	98	149	185	0.2	0.4
Sev Day Adv	3	192	333	383	0.5	0.7
Un C of Christ	5	358	1,041	1,256	1.7	2.4
Unit Univ	1	9	11	11	0.0	0.0
WYOMING	**948**	**43,712**	**69,169**	**223,074**	**39.6**	**100.0**
ALBANY	**53**	**3,090**	**3,997**	**13,072**	**36.0**	**100.0**
ANG/EPIS–Episcopal	1	119	198	286	0.8	2.2
Bahá'í	0	NR	29	29	0.1	0.2
BAPT–Amer Bapt Assn	1	NR	85	98	0.3	0.7
BAPT–Amer Bapt USA	1	59	350	403	1.1	3.1
BAPT–Consrv Bapt	1	NR	NR	NR	-	-
BAPT–So Bapt Conv	5	561	460	530	1.5	4.1
BUDD–Mahayana	1	NR	NR	11	0.0	0.1
BUDD–Vajrayana	2	NR	NR	105	0.3	0.8
Calv Chpl	1	NR	NR	NR	-	-
Catholic	2	NR	NR	4,627	12.7	35.4
Ch of Nazarene	1	47	62	62	0.2	0.5
CHR–Chr Ch (Disc)	1	150	356	410	1.1	3.1
CHR–Chr Chs & Chs Cr	1	NR	110	127	0.3	1.0
CHR–Chs of Christ	1	135	115	159	0.4	1.2
Evan Free Ch	1	375	NR	375	1.0	2.9
FRND–Fr Gen Cf	1	NR	9	10	0.0	0.1
Grace Gosp Fel	1	NR	NR	NR	-	-
JUD–Reform	1	27	47	127	0.3	1.0
LDS–Comm of Christ	1	NR	128	128	0.4	1.0
LDS–L-D Saints	9	NR	NR	2,803	7.7	21.4
LUTH–E.L.C.A.	1	173	323	400	1.1	3.1

NR–Not Reported   - Represents no adherents reported.   Percentages may not total 100 due to rounding.

Table 3: Religious Congregations by County and Group: 2010

Religious Group	Number of Congrega-tions	Number of Attendees	Number of Communicant, Confirmed, or Full Members	Adherents		
				Number of Adherents	% of Total Pop.	% of Total Adh.
LUTH–Luth-MO Synod	2	161	308	358	1.0	2.7
METH–Un Methodist	1	156	434	530	1.5	4.1
Muslim Est	1	134	NR	308	0.8	2.4
Non-denom Chr Chs	4	290	330	388	1.1	3.0
PENT–Assemb of God	3	84	62	112	0.3	0.9
PENT–Int Foursq Gos	1	345	107	123	0.3	0.9
PENT–Un Pent Ch Intl	1	NR	NR	NR	-	-
PRES–Presb Ch (USA)	2	143	302	348	1.0	2.7
PRES–Ref Pres of NA	1	25	12	20	0.1	0.2
Sev Day Adv	1	44	77	89	0.2	0.7
Un C of Christ	1	23	41	47	0.1	0.4
Unit Univ	1	39	52	59	0.2	0.5
BIG HORN	**36**	**659**	**1,039**	**5,747**	**49.3**	**100.0**
ANG/EPIS–Episcopal	1	23	70	78	0.7	1.4
BAPT–Amer Bapt USA	1	21	15	19	0.2	0.3
BAPT–Consrv Bapt	1	NR	NR	NR	-	-
BAPT–So Bapt Conv	2	52	76	94	0.8	1.6
Catholic	3	NR	NR	458	3.9	8.0
Chr & Miss Al	1	61	42	90	0.8	1.6
LDS–L-D Saints	13	NR	NR	3,901	33.4	67.9
LUTH–E.L.C.A.	1	22	67	80	0.7	1.4
LUTH–Luth-MO Synod	3	150	302	388	3.3	6.8
METH–Un Methodist	4	97	157	259	2.2	4.5
Non-denom Chr Chs	2	165	165	206	1.8	3.6
PENT–Assemb of God	1	15	25	25	0.2	0.4
PENT–Ch of God Proph	1	NR	54	67	0.6	1.2
PRES–Presb Ch (USA)	2	53	66	82	0.7	1.4
CAMPBELL	**43**	**3,089**	**6,297**	**16,240**	**35.2**	**100.0**
ANG/EPIS–Episcopal	2	73	86	172	0.4	1.1
Bahá'í	0	NR	5	5	0.0	0.0
BAPT–Amer Bapt Assn	1	NR	85	110	0.2	0.7
BAPT–Amer Bapt USA	1	82	233	301	0.7	1.9
BAPT–Natl Mis Bapt Conv	1	10	12	15	0.0	0.1
BAPT–So Bapt Conv	5	487	1,467	1,893	4.1	11.7
Catholic	2	NR	NR	5,217	11.3	32.1
Ch of Nazarene	1	34	40	40	0.1	0.2
Chr & Miss Al	1	95	40	162	0.4	1.0
CHR–Chr Chs & Chs Cr	1	NR	113	146	0.3	0.9
CHR–Chs of Christ	2	83	82	96	0.2	0.6
Evan Ch	1	NR	NR	NR	-	-
Evan Free Ch	1	125	NR	125	0.3	0.8
LDS–L-D Saints	6	NR	NR	2,247	4.9	13.8
LUTH–E.L.C.A.	1	167	1,064	1,064	2.3	6.6
LUTH–Luth Ch-Am Asc	1	NR	NR	NR	-	-
LUTH–Luth-MO Synod	1	192	899	1,257	2.7	7.7
LUTH–Wisc Ev Luth Syn	1	61	95	125	0.3	0.8
METH–Un Methodist	1	86	283	523	1.1	3.2
METH–Wesleyan	1	502	154	653	1.4	4.0
Non-denom Chr Chs	2	385	775	775	1.7	4.8
ORTHE–Ant Orth of NA	1	18	NR	40	0.1	0.2
PENT–Assemb of God	2	337	140	351	0.8	2.2
PENT–Ch God (Cleve)	1	29	26	34	0.1	0.2
PENT–Ch of God Proph	1	NR	4	5	0.0	0.0
PENT–Int Foursq Gos	1	152	210	271	0.6	1.7
PENT–Un Pent Ch Intl	1	NR	NR	NR	-	-
PENT–Vineyard	1	65	100	129	0.3	0.8
PRES–Presb Ch (USA)	1	44	276	356	0.8	2.2
Sev Day Adv	1	62	108	124	0.3	0.8
Zoroastrian	0	NR	NR	4	0.0	0.0
CARBON	**45**	**1,024**	**1,711**	**5,715**	**36.0**	**100.0**
ANG/EPIS–Episcopal	5	64	176	249	1.6	4.4
Bahá'í	0	NR	7	7	0.0	0.1
BAPT–Amer Bapt USA	1	40	33	41	0.3	0.7
BAPT–So Bapt Conv	6	141	321	395	2.5	6.9
Calv Chpl	1	NR	NR	NR	-	-
Catholic	5	NR	NR	1,663	10.5	29.1
Ch of Nazarene	1	20	35	56	0.4	1.0
Chr & Miss Al	1	77	43	114	0.7	2.0
CHR–Chs of Christ	3	70	56	100	0.6	1.7
Jehovah's Witness	1	NR	NR	NR	-	-

Religious Group	Number of Congrega-tions	Number of Attendees	Number of Communicant, Confirmed, or Full Members	Adherents		
				Number of Adherents	% of Total Pop.	% of Total Adh.
LDS–L-D Saints	5	NR	NR	1,538	9.7	26.9
LUTH–Luth-MO Synod	3	97	209	250	1.6	4.4
METH–Un Methodist	2	87	365	509	3.2	8.9
Non-denom Chr Chs	3	145	145	181	1.1	3.2
PENT–Assemb of God	3	146	94	335	2.1	5.9
PENT–Un Pent Ch Intl	1	NR	NR	NR	-	-
PRES–Presb Ch (USA)	3	119	195	240	1.5	4.2
Sev Day Adv	1	18	32	37	0.2	0.6
CONVERSE	**25**	**997**	**1,485**	**3,870**	**28.0**	**100.0**
ANG/EPIS–Episcopal	2	46	172	237	1.7	6.1
Bahá'í	0	NR	3	3	0.0	0.1
BAPT–Amer Bapt USA	2	103	152	189	1.4	4.9
BAPT–Consrv Bapt	1	NR	NR	NR	-	-
BAPT–So Bapt Conv	2	142	255	317	2.3	8.2
Catholic	2	NR	NR	1,044	7.5	27.0
CHR–Chs of Christ	2	58	44	69	0.5	1.8
Jehovah's Witness	1	NR	NR	NR	-	-
LDS–L-D Saints	2	NR	NR	723	5.2	18.7
LUTH–Luth-MO Synod	2	105	152	194	1.4	5.0
METH–Un Methodist	1	60	202	272	2.0	7.0
Non-denom Chr Chs	3	290	245	363	2.6	9.4
PENT–Assemb of God	2	118	66	220	1.6	5.7
PENT–Un Pent Ch Intl	1	NR	NR	NR	-	-
Sev Day Adv	1	13	23	26	0.2	0.7
Un C of Christ	1	62	171	213	1.5	5.5
CROOK	**19**	**483**	**969**	**1,867**	**26.4**	**100.0**
ANG/EPIS–Episcopal	1	15	30	31	0.4	1.7
Bahá'í	0	NR	2	2	0.0	0.1
BAPT–So Bapt Conv	2	73	155	190	2.7	10.2
Catholic	3	NR	NR	374	5.3	20.0
CHR–Chs of Christ	1	40	38	45	0.6	2.4
LDS–Comm of Christ	1	NR	128	128	1.8	6.9
LDS–L-D Saints	2	NR	NR	299	4.2	16.0
LUTH–Luth-MO Synod	2	76	108	126	1.8	6.7
METH–Un Methodist	1	63	224	288	4.1	15.4
Non-denom Chr Chs	2	80	91	121	1.7	6.5
PENT–Assemb of God	1	40	19	51	0.7	2.7
PENT–Vineyard	1	30	65	80	1.1	4.3
PRES–Presb Ch (USA)	1	58	96	117	1.7	6.3
Sev Day Adv	1	8	13	15	0.2	0.8
FREMONT	**88**	**3,229**	**4,501**	**13,193**	**32.9**	**100.0**
ANG/EPIS–Episcopal	7	161	456	772	1.9	5.9
Bahá'í	0	NR	40	40	0.1	0.3
BAPT–Amer Bapt USA	1	86	108	135	0.3	1.0
BAPT–Consrv Bapt	2	NR	NR	NR	-	-
BAPT–So Bapt Conv	9	400	671	840	2.1	6.4
Catholic	10	NR	NR	3,047	7.6	23.1
CGOD–Ch God (Ander)	2	45	NR	45	0.1	0.3
Ch of Nazarene	4	214	244	327	0.8	2.5
Chr & Miss Al	2	203	100	367	0.9	2.8
CHR–Chr Chs & Chs Cr	3	NR	120	150	0.4	1.1
CHR–Chs of Christ	3	177	144	198	0.5	1.5
Evan Free Ch	1	195	NR	195	0.5	1.5
FRND–Fr Gen Cf	1	NR	7	9	0.0	0.1
Jehovah's Witness	2	NR	NR	NR	-	-
LDS–L-D Saints	10	NR	NR	3,618	9.0	27.4
LUTH–E.L.C.A.	2	125	296	343	0.9	2.6
LUTH–Luth-MO Synod	3	302	744	952	2.4	7.2
METH–Un Methodist	3	356	662	877	2.2	6.6
Non-denom Chr Chs	6	375	315	471	1.2	3.6
PENT–Assemb of God	5	225	178	317	0.8	2.4
PENT–Cong Hol Ch	2	78	70	88	0.2	0.7
PENT–Int Foursq Gos	2	45	56	70	0.2	0.5
PENT–Un Pent Ch Intl	2	NR	NR	NR	-	-
PRES–Presb Ch (USA)	2	43	66	83	0.2	0.6
PRES–Presb Ch Amer	1	145	131	142	0.4	1.1
Sev Day Adv	3	54	93	107	0.3	0.8

NR–Not Reported - Represents no adherents reported. Percentages may not total 100 due to rounding.

Table 3: Religious Congregations by County and Group: 2010

Religious Group	Number of Congrega-tions	Number of Attendees	Number of Communicant, Confirmed, or Full Members	Adherents: Number of Adherents	Adherents: % of Total Pop.	Adherents: % of Total Adh.
GOSHEN	**22**	**810**	**1,635**	**4,083**	**30.8**	**100.0**
ANG/EPIS–Episcopal	1	41	176	218	1.6	5.3
Bahá'í	0	NR	8	8	0.1	0.2
BAPT–Amer Bapt USA	1	65	128	151	1.1	3.7
BAPT–Converge/BGC	2	150	NR	180	1.4	4.4
BAPT–So Bapt Conv	2	10	9	11	0.1	0.3
Catholic	1	NR	NR	1,403	10.6	34.4
Ch of Nazarene	1	26	23	30	0.2	0.7
CHR–Chr Chs & Chs Cr	3	NR	123	145	1.1	3.6
Jehovah's Witness	1	NR	NR	NR	-	-
LDS–L-D Saints	1	NR	NR	495	3.7	12.1
LUTH–Luth–MO Synod	1	108	370	446	3.4	10.9
METH–Un Methodist	1	80	214	309	2.3	7.6
Non-denom Chr Chs	2	95	115	121	0.9	3.0
PENT–Assemb of God	1	29	23	40	0.3	1.0
PRES–Presb Ch (USA)	3	176	395	467	3.5	11.4
Sev Day Adv	1	30	51	59	0.4	1.4
HOT SPRINGS	**13**	**473**	**783**	**2,021**	**42.0**	**100.0**
ANG/EPIS–Episcopal	1	44	130	130	2.7	6.4
Bahá'í	0	NR	1	1	0.0	0.0
BAPT–Consrv Bapt	1	NR	NR	NR	-	-
BAPT–So Bapt Conv	2	173	304	360	7.5	17.8
Catholic	1	NR	NR	431	9.0	21.3
CHR–Chs of Christ	1	15	20	26	0.5	1.3
Evan Free Ch	1	0	NR	0	0.0	0.0
LDS–L-D Saints	1	NR	NR	551	11.5	27.3
LUTH–Luth–MO Synod	1	40	92	109	2.3	5.4
METH–Un Methodist	1	129	97	239	5.0	11.8
Non-denom Chr Chs	1	50	49	62	1.3	3.1
PENT–Assemb of God	1	22	25	35	0.7	1.7
PRES–Presb Ch (USA)	1	0	65	77	1.6	3.8
JOHNSON	**22**	**941**	**1,431**	**3,785**	**44.2**	**100.0**
ANG/EPIS–Episcopal	2	85	237	385	4.5	10.2
Bahá'í	0	NR	3	3	0.0	0.1
BAPT–Consrv Bapt	1	NR	NR	NR	-	-
BAPT–So Bapt Conv	2	135	255	308	3.6	8.1
Calv Chpl	1	NR	NR	NR	-	-
Catholic	2	NR	NR	1,199	14.0	31.7
CHR–Chs of Christ	1	25	23	29	0.3	0.8
Jehovah's Witness	1	NR	NR	NR	-	-
LDS–L-D Saints	1	NR	NR	437	5.1	11.5
LUTH–E.L.C.A.	1	70	250	275	3.2	7.3
LUTH–Luth–MO Synod	1	57	106	159	1.9	4.2
METH–Un Methodist	2	62	138	189	2.2	5.0
METH–Wesleyan	1	233	100	303	3.5	8.0
Non-denom Chr Chs	2	108	170	172	2.0	4.5
PENT–Assemb of God	1	120	71	234	2.7	6.2
PENT–Un Pent Ch Intl	1	NR	NR	NR	-	-
Sev Day Adv	1	19	33	38	0.4	1.0
Un C of Christ	1	27	45	54	0.6	1.4
LARAMIE	**107**	**7,316**	**12,264**	**36,606**	**39.9**	**100.0**
ANG/EPIS–Anglican NA	2	NR	NR	NR	-	-
ANG/EPIS–Episcopal	2	208	420	435	0.5	1.2
Bahá'í	0	NR	37	37	0.0	0.1
BAPT–Amer Bapt Assn	1	NR	150	186	0.2	0.5
BAPT–Amer Bapt USA	2	285	476	590	0.6	1.6
BAPT–Consrv Bapt	2	NR	NR	NR	-	-
BAPT–Converge/BGC	3	950	NR	1,140	1.2	3.1
BAPT–Free Will Bapt	1	NR	10	12	0.0	0.0
BAPT–Ind Bapt Flwsp Intl	1	NR	NR	NR	-	-
BAPT–NBC USA	1	0	0	0	0.0	0.0
BAPT–So Bapt Conv	11	550	2,508	3,109	3.4	8.5
BRETH–Brethren (Ash)	1	NR	80	99	0.1	0.3
Calv Chpl	1	NR	NR	NR	-	-
Catholic	6	NR	NR	13,821	15.1	37.8
Ch Cr, Scientst	1	NR	NR	NR	-	-
Ch of Nazarene	1	92	121	149	0.2	0.4
Chr & Miss Al	1	161	100	240	0.3	0.7
CHR–Chr Ch (Disc)	1	118	504	625	0.7	1.7
CHR–Chr Chs & Chs Cr	1	NR	360	446	0.5	1.2
CHR–Chs of Christ	2	255	233	295	0.3	0.8
Evan Ch	1	NR	NR	NR	-	-
Evan Free Ch	1	330	NR	330	0.4	0.9
FRND–Fr Gen Cf	1	NR	2	2	0.0	0.0
HINDU–Post Ren	1	NR	NR	76	0.1	0.2
Jehovah's Witness	1	NR	NR	NR	-	-
LDS–Comm of Christ	1	NR	128	128	0.1	0.3
LDS–L-D Saints	9	NR	NR	4,456	4.9	12.2
LUTH–Ch Luth Conf	1	NR	NR	NR	-	-
LUTH–E.L.C.A.	3	339	1,047	1,242	1.4	3.4
LUTH–Luth–MO Synod	5	514	1,168	1,519	1.7	4.1
LUTH–Wisc Ev Luth Syn	1	99	153	209	0.2	0.6
METH–AME	1	45	75	93	0.1	0.3
METH–Un Methodist	8	739	1,702	2,436	2.7	6.7
Muslim Est	2	169	NR	408	0.4	1.1
Non-denom Chr Chs	11	1,001	1,266	1,362	1.5	3.7
ORTHE–Greek Orthodox	1	100	NR	315	0.3	0.9
PENT–Assemb of God	4	611	368	888	1.0	2.4
PENT–Ch God (Cleve)	1	10	13	16	0.0	0.0
PENT–COGIC	2	30	40	50	0.1	0.1
PENT–Open Bible Std	1	25	NR	25	0.0	0.1
PENT–Un Pent Ch Intl	1	NR	NR	NR	-	-
PENT–Vineyard	1	95	135	167	0.2	0.5
PRES–Presb Ch (USA)	4	279	698	865	0.9	2.4
PRES–Presb Ch Amer	1	85	76	105	0.1	0.3
Salvation Army	1	52	118	377	0.4	1.0
Sev Day Adv	1	80	140	161	0.2	0.4
Unit Univ	1	94	136	192	0.2	0.5
LINCOLN	**50**	**796**	**845**	**11,412**	**63.0**	**100.0**
ANG/EPIS–Episcopal	2	19	63	63	0.3	0.6
Bahá'í	2	NR	43	43	0.2	0.4
BAPT–So Bapt Conv	4	111	122	156	0.9	1.4
Catholic	4	NR	NR	596	3.3	5.2
Evan Free Ch	1	60	NR	60	0.3	0.5
Jehovah's Witness	2	NR	NR	NR	-	-
LDS–L-D Saints	23	NR	NR	9,556	52.8	83.7
LUTH–E.L.C.A.	1	45	66	66	0.4	0.6
LUTH–Luth–MO Synod	2	54	107	161	0.9	1.4
METH–Un Methodist	1	26	52	83	0.5	0.7
Non-denom Chr Chs	4	375	360	472	2.6	4.1
PENT–Assemb of God	2	60	0	115	0.6	1.0
PENT–Un Pent Ch Intl	1	NR	NR	NR	-	-
PRES–Presb Ch (USA)	1	46	32	41	0.2	0.4
NATRONA	**80**	**7,346**	**9,708**	**27,780**	**36.8**	**100.0**
ANG/EPIS–Anglican NA	1	NR	NR	NR	-	-
ANG/EPIS–Episcopal	2	155	449	609	0.8	2.2
Bahá'í	1	NR	48	48	0.1	0.2
BAPT–Amer Bapt USA	2	211	315	387	0.5	1.4
BAPT–Ref Bapt Ch	1	NR	NR	NR	-	-
BAPT–So Bapt Conv	11	949	1,990	2,446	3.2	8.8
Calv Chpl	1	NR	NR	NR	-	-
Catholic	3	NR	NR	7,824	10.4	28.2
CGOD–Ch God (Ander)	1	1,800	NR	1,800	2.4	6.5
Ch of Nazarene	1	158	209	303	0.4	1.1
Chr & Miss Al	1	109	49	166	0.2	0.6
CHR–Chr Ch (Disc)	1	133	400	492	0.7	1.8
CHR–Chr Chs & Chs Cr	3	NR	295	363	0.5	1.3
CHR–Chs of Christ	2	182	151	185	0.2	0.7
Evan Free Ch	1	220	NR	220	0.3	0.8
Jehovah's Witness	1	NR	NR	NR	-	-
LDS–Comm of Christ	1	NR	128	128	0.2	0.5
LDS–L-D Saints	9	NR	NR	4,809	6.4	17.3
LUTH–E.L.C.A.	4	396	800	1,362	1.8	4.9
LUTH–Luth–MO Synod	2	308	612	776	1.0	2.8
LUTH–Nor Amer Luth C	1	NR	NR	NR	-	-
LUTH–Wisc Ev Luth Syn	1	39	63	69	0.1	0.2
METH–AME	1	0	100	123	0.2	0.4
METH–Un Methodist	3	387	1,162	1,692	2.2	6.1
Non-denom Chr Chs	12	1,427	1,755	1,926	2.6	6.9
ORTHE–Greek Orthodox	1	55	NR	235	0.3	0.8

NR–Not Reported   - Represents no adherents reported.   Percentages may not total 100 due to rounding.

Table 3: Religious Congregations by County and Group: 2010

Religious Group	Number of Congrega-tions	Number of Attendees	Number of Communicant, Confirmed, or Full Members	Adherents		
				Number of Adherents	% of Total Pop.	% of Total Adh.
PENT–Assemb of God	2	286	147	445	0.6	1.6
PENT–Ch of God Proph	1	NR	33	41	0.1	0.1
PENT–Int Foursq Gos	1	50	16	20	0.0	0.1
PENT–Un Pent Ch Intl	1	NR	NR	NR	-	-
PRES–Presb Ch (USA)	3	250	525	645	0.9	2.3
Salvation Army	1	20	110	255	0.3	0.9
Sev Day Adv	1	146	253	291	0.4	1.0
Un C of Christ	1	40	64	79	0.1	0.3
Unit Univ	1	25	34	41	0.1	0.1
NIOBRARA	**11**	**305**	**392**	**743**	**29.9**	**100.0**
ANG/EPIS–Episcopal	1	16	50	50	2.0	6.7
Bahá'í	0	NR	1	1	0.0	0.1
BAPT–Amer Bapt USA	1	58	70	82	3.3	11.0
BAPT–So Bapt Conv	1	22	12	14	0.6	1.9
Catholic	1	NR	NR	105	4.2	14.1
Chr & Miss Al	3	124	90	194	7.8	26.1
CHR–Chr Chs & Chs Cr	1	NR	25	29	1.2	3.9
LDS–L-D Saints	1	NR	NR	84	3.4	11.3
LUTH–Luth-MO Synod	1	70	135	164	6.6	22.1
PENT–Assemb of God	1	15	9	20	0.8	2.7
PARK	**63**	**3,037**	**4,247**	**12,431**	**44.1**	**100.0**
ANG/EPIS–Anglican NA	1	NR	NR	NR	-	-
ANG/EPIS–Episcopal	3	180	591	708	2.5	5.7
Bahá'í	0	NR	16	16	0.1	0.1
BAPT–Consrv Bapt	2	NR	NR	NR	-	-
BAPT–NT Ind Bapt	1	NR	NR	NR	-	-
BAPT–Ref Bapt Ch	1	NR	NR	NR	-	-
BAPT–So Bapt Conv	5	202	349	416	1.5	3.3
Catholic	4	NR	NR	2,985	10.6	24.0
CGOD–Ch God (Ander)	2	65	NR	65	0.2	0.5
Ch Cr, Scientst	1	NR	NR	NR	-	-
Ch of Nazarene	2	81	83	131	0.5	1.1
Chr & Miss Al	1	321	136	642	2.3	5.2
CHR–Chr Chs & Chs Cr	1	NR	0	0	0.0	0.0
CHR–Chs of Christ	2	156	139	171	0.6	1.4
Evan Free Ch	1	100	NR	100	0.4	0.8
Jehovah's Witness	3	NR	NR	NR	-	-
LDS–L-D Saints	9	NR	NR	3,180	11.3	25.6
LUTH–E.L.C.A.	2	146	375	458	1.6	3.7
LUTH–Luth Cong Msn Chr	1	NR	NR	NR	-	-
LUTH–Luth-MO Synod	2	269	527	681	2.4	5.5
METH–Un Methodist	2	242	519	774	2.7	6.2
Non-denom Chr Chs	7	625	675	823	2.9	6.6
PENT–Assemb of God	2	270	28	319	1.1	2.6
PENT–Ch of God Proph	1	NR	32	38	0.1	0.3
PENT–Int Foursq Gos	1	69	52	62	0.2	0.5
PENT–Un Pent Ch Intl	2	NR	NR	NR	-	-
PRES–Presb Ch (USA)	2	276	665	792	2.8	6.4
Sev Day Adv	2	35	60	70	0.2	0.6
PLATTE	**26**	**788**	**1,542**	**3,210**	**37.0**	**100.0**
ANG/EPIS–Episcopal	3	56	153	220	2.5	6.9
Bahá'í	0	NR	2	2	0.0	0.1
BAPT–Consrv Bapt	1	NR	NR	NR	-	-
BAPT–Converge/BGC	1	75	NR	90	1.0	2.8
BAPT–NT Ind Bapt	1	NR	NR	NR	-	-
BAPT–So Bapt Conv	2	107	443	522	6.0	16.3
Catholic	4	NR	NR	779	9.0	24.3
Ch of Nazarene	1	9	22	22	0.3	0.7
CHR–Chr Chs & Chs Cr	1	NR	125	147	1.7	4.6
Jehovah's Witness	1	NR	NR	NR	-	-
LDS–L-D Saints	1	NR	NR	308	3.6	9.6
LUTH–E.L.C.A.	1	60	168	181	2.1	5.6
LUTH–Luth-MO Synod	1	50	125	163	1.9	5.1
METH–A.W.M.C.	1	14	0	18	0.2	0.6
METH–Un Methodist	2	75	147	195	2.2	6.1
Non-denom Chr Chs	1	185	89	231	2.7	7.2
PENT–Assemb of God	1	44	24	45	0.5	1.4
PRES–Presb Ch (USA)	1	46	67	79	0.9	2.5
Sev Day Adv	1	10	18	21	0.2	0.7
Un C of Christ	1	57	159	187	2.2	5.8

Religious Group	Number of Congrega-tions	Number of Attendees	Number of Communicant, Confirmed, or Full Members	Adherents		
				Number of Adherents	% of Total Pop.	% of Total Adh.
SHERIDAN	**51**	**2,616**	**5,158**	**12,581**	**43.2**	**100.0**
ANG/EPIS–Anglican NA	1	NR	NR	NR	-	-
ANG/EPIS–Episcopal	1	191	935	935	3.2	7.4
Bahá'í	0	NR	12	12	0.0	0.1
BAPT–Consrv Bapt	1	NR	NR	NR	-	-
BAPT–So Bapt Conv	5	195	335	405	1.4	3.2
Catholic	4	NR	NR	4,222	14.5	33.6
Ch Cr, Scientst	1	NR	NR	NR	-	-
Ch of Nazarene	1	72	75	116	0.4	0.9
Chr & Miss Al	1	68	18	93	0.3	0.7
CHR–Chr Ch (Disc)	1	103	175	211	0.7	1.7
CHR–Chs of Christ	4	98	88	107	0.4	0.9
Evan Ch	1	NR	NR	NR	-	-
FRND–Fr Gen Cf	1	NR	4	5	0.0	0.0
FRND–Indep Yr Mtgs	1	NR	4	5	0.0	0.0
Jehovah's Witness	1	NR	NR	NR	-	-
LDS–L-D Saints	5	NR	NR	1,452	5.0	11.5
LUTH–E.L.C.A.	1	159	776	1,296	4.5	10.3
LUTH–Luth-MO Synod	1	165	545	766	2.6	6.1
LUTH–Wisc Ev Luth Syn	1	20	22	26	0.1	0.2
METH–Un Methodist	1	122	229	301	1.0	2.4
METH–Wesleyan	1	237	108	308	1.1	2.4
Non-denom Chr Chs	6	680	810	887	3.0	7.1
PENT–Assemb of God	1	43	24	92	0.3	0.7
PENT–Ch of God Proph	1	NR	160	193	0.7	1.5
PENT–Int Foursq Gos	1	55	211	255	0.9	2.0
PENT–Pent Ch of God	1	70	NR	109	0.4	0.9
PENT–Un Pent Ch Intl	1	NR	NR	NR	-	-
PRES–Presb Ch (USA)	1	168	370	447	1.5	3.6
PRES–Presb Ch Amer	1	37	16	26	0.1	0.2
Salvation Army	1	20	57	99	0.3	0.8
Sev Day Adv	1	48	83	95	0.3	0.8
Un C of Christ	1	25	55	66	0.2	0.5
Unit Univ	1	40	46	52	0.2	0.4
SUBLETTE	**18**	**459**	**871**	**3,406**	**33.2**	**100.0**
ANG/EPIS–Episcopal	2	67	201	310	3.0	9.1
Bahá'í	0	NR	1	1	0.0	0.0
BAPT–So Bapt Conv	2	95	173	212	2.1	6.2
Catholic	2	NR	NR	844	8.2	24.8
CHR–Chs of Christ	1	20	19	24	0.2	0.7
CONG–Cong Chr, NA	1	NR	20	25	0.2	0.7
Jehovah's Witness	1	NR	NR	NR	-	-
LDS–L-D Saints	2	NR	NR	1,407	13.7	41.3
LUTH–Luth-MO Synod	2	46	132	221	2.2	6.5
Non-denom Chr Chs	3	180	252	267	2.6	7.8
PENT–Assemb of God	1	8	4	10	0.1	0.3
Un C of Christ	1	43	69	85	0.8	2.5
SWEETWATER	**66**	**2,140**	**4,341**	**20,905**	**47.7**	**100.0**
ANG/EPIS–Episcopal	2	65	201	209	0.5	1.0
Bahá'í	0	NR	21	21	0.0	0.1
BAPT–Amer Bapt USA	1	40	40	51	0.1	0.2
BAPT–So Bapt Conv	12	553	1,882	2,409	5.5	11.5
Calv Chpl	1	NR	NR	NR	-	-
Catholic	5	NR	NR	7,007	16.0	33.5
Ch of Nazarene	1	36	37	50	0.1	0.2
Chr & Miss Al	1	66	57	129	0.3	0.6
CHR–Chr Chs & Chs Cr	1	NR	81	104	0.2	0.5
CHR–Chs of Christ	4	181	153	196	0.4	0.9
Evan Free Ch	1	33	NR	33	0.1	0.2
Jehovah's Witness	2	NR	NR	NR	-	-
LDS–L-D Saints	15	NR	NR	7,972	18.2	38.1
LUTH–E.L.C.A.	1	40	163	208	0.5	1.0
LUTH–Luth-MO Synod	2	137	263	341	0.8	1.6
METH–Un Methodist	2	132	340	496	1.1	2.4
Non-denom Chr Chs	6	505	625	663	1.5	3.2
ORTHE–Greek Orthodox	1	45	NR	195	0.4	0.9
PENT–Assemb of God	2	188	71	303	0.7	1.4
PENT–Un Pent Ch Intl	2	NR	NR	NR	-	-
REF–Ref Ch in U.S.	1	NR	38	53	0.1	0.3
Sev Day Adv	1	30	53	61	0.1	0.3
Un C of Christ	2	89	316	404	0.9	1.9

NR–Not Reported - Represents no adherents reported. Percentages may not total 100 due to rounding.

Table 3: Religious Congregations by County and Group: 2010

Religious Group	Number of Congregations	Number of Attendees	Number of Communicant, Confirmed, or Full Members	Adherents: Number of Adherents	Adherents: % of Total Pop.	Adherents: % of Total Adh.
TETON	**20**	**1,621**	**2,402**	**5,544**	**26.0**	**100.0**
ANG/EPIS–Episcopal	1	257	903	903	4.2	16.3
Bahá'í	0	NR	3	3	0.0	0.1
BAPT–Amer Bapt USA	1	330	250	295	1.4	5.3
BAPT–So Bapt Conv	2	33	31	37	0.2	0.7
BUDD–Mahayana	1	NR	NR	11	0.1	0.2
Catholic	1	NR	NR	1,397	6.6	25.2
Ch Cr, Scientst	1	NR	NR	NR	-	-
CHR–Chs of Christ	1	60	42	67	0.3	1.2
FRND–Fr Gen Cf	1	NR	3	4	0.0	0.1
Jehovah's Witness	1	NR	NR	NR	-	-
LDS–L-D Saints	3	NR	NR	1,418	6.7	25.6
LUTH–E.L.C.A.	1	93	151	212	1.0	3.8
LUTH–Luth–MO Synod	1	31	57	57	0.3	1.0
Non-denom Chr Chs	3	560	610	725	3.4	13.1
PRES–Presb Ch (USA)	1	253	344	406	1.9	7.3
Sev Day Adv	1	4	8	9	0.0	0.2
UINTA	**47**	**978**	**1,286**	**12,815**	**60.7**	**100.0**
ANG/EPIS–Episcopal	2	48	92	163	0.8	1.3
Bahá'í	0	NR	2	2	0.0	0.0
BAPT–Amer Bapt USA	1	10	20	26	0.1	0.2
BAPT–So Bapt Conv	4	180	396	519	2.5	4.0
Catholic	2	NR	NR	803	3.8	6.3
Ch of Nazarene	1	22	21	41	0.2	0.3
Chr & Miss Al	1	168	95	267	1.3	2.1
CHR–Chs of Christ	1	28	26	34	0.2	0.3
Jehovah's Witness	1	NR	NR	NR	-	-
LDS–L-D Saints	22	NR	NR	10,064	47.7	78.5
LUTH–E.L.C.A.	1	39	79	100	0.5	0.8
LUTH–Luth–MO Synod	2	24	82	120	0.6	0.9
Non-denom Chr Chs	4	265	270	331	1.6	2.6
PENT–Assemb of God	2	98	45	138	0.7	1.1
PENT–Un Pent Ch Intl	1	NR	NR	NR	-	-
PRES–Presb Ch (USA)	2	96	158	207	1.0	1.6
WASHAKIE	**25**	**923**	**1,538**	**4,026**	**47.2**	**100.0**
ANG/EPIS–Episcopal	1	27	71	93	1.1	2.3
Bahá'í	0	NR	1	1	0.0	0.0
BAPT–So Bapt Conv	3	250	466	581	6.8	14.4
Catholic	1	NR	NR	809	9.5	20.1
CGOD–Ch God (Ander)	1	120	NR	120	1.4	3.0
CHR–Chs of Christ	1	92	98	136	1.6	3.4
Jehovah's Witness	1	NR	NR	NR	-	-
LDS–L-D Saints	3	NR	NR	1,129	13.2	28.0
LUTH–E.L.C.A.	1	53	238	254	3.0	6.3
LUTH–Luth–MO Synod	1	46	110	136	1.6	3.4
MENN–CG in Cr (Menn)	1	NR	8	10	0.1	0.2
METH–Un Methodist	2	105	237	314	3.7	7.8
PENT–Assemb of God	3	113	84	168	2.0	4.2
PENT–Ch of God Proph	1	NR	32	40	0.5	1.0
PENT–Int Foursq Gos	1	41	47	59	0.7	1.5
PENT–Un Pent Ch Intl	1	NR	NR	NR	-	-
PRES–Presb Ch (USA)	1	36	77	96	1.1	2.4
Sev Day Adv	2	40	69	80	0.9	2.0
WESTON	**18**	**592**	**727**	**2,022**	**28.1**	**100.0**
ANG/EPIS–Episcopal	1	12	23	23	0.3	1.1
Bahá'í	0	NR	5	5	0.1	0.2
BAPT–So Bapt Conv	1	40	40	48	0.7	2.4
Catholic	2	NR	NR	567	7.9	28.0
CHR–Chr Chs & Chs Cr	1	NR	20	24	0.3	1.2
CHR–Chs of Christ	1	19	15	20	0.3	1.0
Evan Free Ch	1	80	NR	80	1.1	4.0
Jehovah's Witness	1	NR	NR	NR	-	-
LDS–L-D Saints	1	NR	NR	357	5.0	17.7
LUTH–Nor Amer Luth C	1	NR	NR	NR	-	-
METH–Un Methodist	2	115	349	482	6.7	23.8
Non-denom Chr Chs	1	150	150	188	2.6	9.3
PENT–Assemb of God	2	115	63	156	2.2	7.7
PENT–Int Foursq Gos	1	34	15	18	0.2	0.9
Sev Day Adv	2	27	47	54	0.7	2.7

NR–Not Reported - Represents no adherents reported. Percentages may not total 100 due to rounding.

Table 4: Religious Congregations by Metropolitan Size and Group: 2010

Religious Group	Total Adherents	Percent of Adherents in Metro/Micropolitan Size of:					Percent of Adherents Outside Metro/Micro Areas	Percent of Congregations Outside Metro/Micro Areas
		5,000,000 or More	1,000,000 to 4,999,999	250,000 to 999,999	Less Than 250,000	Micro-politan Area		
TOTAL U.S. POPULATION	**308,745,538**	**24.6**	**29.5**	**20.9**	**8.7**	**10.0**	**6.3**	
TOTAL ADHERENTS	**150,686,156**	**26.4**	**27.8**	**20.6**	**8.7**	**10.0**	**6.5**	**15.6**
Amana Ch Soc	433	0.0	0.0	0.0	0.0	0.0	100.0	100.0
ANG/EPIS–Anglican NA	NR	NR	NR	NR	NR	NR	NR	4.8
ANG/EPIS–Episcopal	1,951,907	28.0	30.5	22.4	7.3	8.1	3.7	13.3
Ap Chr Ch-Amer	23,309	4.2	8.4	39.7	9.5	17.2	21.0	25.0
Bahá'í	171,449	23.7	29.8	19.3	9.7	10.3	7.2	1.8
BAPT–Alliance Bapt	NR	NR	NR	NR	NR	NR	NR	1.6
BAPT–Amer Bapt Assn	203,374	7.3	7.4	26.3	14.5	20.8	23.7	24.5
BAPT–Amer Bapt USA	1,560,572	30.5	30.8	16.2	6.4	9.8	6.4	12.9
BAPT–Asc Ref Bap Ch Am	NR	NR	NR	NR	NR	NR	NR	9.0
BAPT–Consrv Bapt	NR	NR	NR	NR	NR	NR	NR	9.9
BAPT–Converge/BGC	260,100	18.4	45.8	13.1	7.4	9.0	6.3	11.7
BAPT–Enterprise Bapt Assoc	NR	NR	NR	NR	NR	NR	NR	50.9
BAPT–Free Will Bapt	217,560	1.5	14.6	22.9	11.6	21.0	28.3	28.9
BAPT–Fund Bapt Flwsp	NR	NR	NR	NR	NR	NR	NR	0.0
BAPT–Ind Bapt Flwsp Intl	NR	NR	NR	NR	NR	NR	NR	13.3
BAPT–N Am Bapt Conf	57,219	13.2	40.2	13.6	13.6	8.0	11.5	19.3
BAPT–Natl Mis Bapt Conv	261,873	20.1	27.7	16.6	8.7	15.3	11.5	13.2
BAPT–NBC Amer	304,414	30.1	36.9	21.2	5.9	3.8	2.1	4.2
BAPT–NBC USA	1,881,341	26.1	32.6	23.6	7.9	7.0	2.7	5.5
BAPT–NT Ind Bapt	NR	NR	NR	NR	NR	NR	NR	25.0
BAPT–Orig Free Will Bapt	36,823	0.0	13.6	4.9	25.8	38.1	17.6	17.6
BAPT–Prim Bapt E Dst	6,046	0.0	0.0	45.4	3.6	5.3	45.7	45.6
BAPT–Prog NBC	203,732	38.6	36.8	16.4	4.6	2.5	1.2	2.6
BAPT–Ref Bapt Ch	NR	NR	NR	NR	NR	NR	NR	4.2
BAPT–Reg Bapt Gen As	NR	NR	NR	NR	NR	NR	NR	15.5
BAPT–S-D Baptist Gen Con	5,168	19.0	19.5	18.4	24.5	7.8	10.7	10.4
BAPT–So Bapt Conv	19,896,975	16.5	19.0	21.3	12.5	17.2	13.5	19.9
BRETH–Breth in Chr	NR	NR	NR	NR	NR	NR	NR	10.2
BRETH–Brethren (Ash)	13,260	2.9	10.9	19.2	27.3	29.5	10.2	12.4
BRETH–Ch of Brethren	146,588	8.1	6.5	27.6	20.8	21.8	15.3	21.0
BRETH–Grace Breth	NR	NR	NR	NR	NR	NR	NR	6.8
BRETH–Old Ord Rvr Br	619	0.0	0.0	40.9	0.0	58.2	1.0	16.7
BRETH–United Zion Ch	721	0.0	0.0	73.0	27.0	0.0	0.0	0.0
BUDD–Mahayana	732,783	37.1	39.0	15.0	1.9	6.8	0.4	2.1
BUDD–Theravada	203,900	28.4	42.8	24.7	1.9	1.9	0.3	0.5

NR–Not Reported Percentages may not total 100 due to rounding.

Table 4: Religious Congregations by Metropolitan Size and Group: 2010

Religious Group	Total Adherents	Percent of Adherents in Metro/Micropolitan Size of:					Percent of Adherents Outside Metro/Micro Area	Percent of Congregations Outside Metro/Micro Area
		5,000,000 or More	1,000,000 to 4,999,999	250,000 to 999,999	Less Than 250,000	Micro-politan Area		
BUDD–Vajrayana	55,000	25.8	28.7	25.5	8.0	4.7	7.2	6.5
Calv Chpl	NR	NR	NR	NR	NR	NR	NR	5.7
Catholic	58,928,987	35.0	30.1	19.1	6.2	6.2	3.3	17.4
CGOD–Ch God (Ander)	225,753	10.1	29.7	20.7	14.6	17.4	7.4	14.4
CGOD–Ches God-Gen Con	39,331	1.4	10.1	44.0	10.8	26.5	7.2	12.4
Ch Christ Chr Union	NR	NR	NR	NR	NR	NR	NR	24.7
Ch Cr, Scientst	NR	NR	NR	NR	NR	NR	NR	4.9
Ch God (7th Day)	NR	NR	NR	NR	NR	NR	NR	5.5
Ch of Chr (Hol)	NR	NR	NR	NR	NR	NR	NR	8.7
Ch of God Gen Conf	3,842	8.4	9.1	47.7	11.2	16.5	7.1	15.5
Ch of Nazarene	893,649	12.8	27.2	23.9	12.3	15.6	8.2	14.2
Chr & Miss Al	428,721	16.9	29.3	25.5	12.2	11.4	4.8	7.9
CHR–Chr Ch (Disc)	785,776	10.8	28.8	19.3	11.4	17.7	12.0	17.0
CHR–Chr Chs & Chs Cr	1,453,160	9.1	31.5	19.1	12.9	15.9	11.5	22.3
CHR–Chs of Christ	1,584,162	15.6	23.4	18.0	12.9	17.1	13.1	23.5
CHR–Int Chs of Christ	42,106	45.8	32.4	18.2	3.3	0.2	0.0	0.0
Christian Brethren	NR	NR	NR	NR	NR	NR	NR	1.1
Christian Un	NR	NR	NR	NR	NR	NR	NR	37.5
CONG–Armen Evang Add'l	NR	NR	NR	NR	NR	NR	NR	0.0
CONG–Cong Chr Add'l	8,410	5.5	36.5	14.9	3.6	14.8	24.8	23.8
CONG–Cong Chr, NA	66,749	13.5	34.5	21.2	9.1	13.4	8.2	14.8
CONG–Consrv Cong Chr	50,707	12.8	37.5	14.8	8.5	14.1	12.2	18.2
CONG–Midw Cong Chr Fel	1,213	0.0	0.0	0.0	12.4	44.0	43.6	40.0
Evan Assoc RCC	NR	NR	NR	NR	NR	NR	NR	7.5
Evan Ch	NR	NR	NR	NR	NR	NR	NR	18.8
Evan Cong Ch	20,592	5.1	0.0	65.4	8.1	19.4	1.9	3.8
Evan Cov Ch	228,365	12.6	55.3	16.2	5.3	6.4	4.3	11.5
Evan Free Ch	357,186	14.5	30.0	24.5	10.7	12.5	7.8	16.9
FRND–Central Yr Mtg	290	0.0	36.2	7.6	7.6	8.3	40.3	37.5
FRND–Consrv Yr Mtgs	1,976	0.0	13.4	35.7	19.6	15.6	15.6	17.5
FRND–Evan Fr Ch Intl	34,565	19.9	25.6	24.4	7.3	10.5	12.3	16.0
FRND–Fr Gen Cf	22,192	58.6	12.8	17.7	4.6	5.4	0.9	6.3
FRND–Fr Gen Cf & Un Mtg	15,436	36.9	28.4	12.3	9.7	8.4	4.3	12.5
FRND–Fr Un Mtg	24,826	1.8	12.7	33.2	12.1	24.2	16.0	20.2
FRND–Indep Yr Mtgs	2,850	10.2	48.0	26.5	8.7	5.4	1.2	9.5
FRND–Unaffl Mtgs	NR	NR	NR	NR	NR	NR	NR	23.1
Grace Gosp Fel	NR	NR	NR	NR	NR	NR	NR	12.5
HINDU–I/A Temples	304,150	40.0	36.1	19.3	1.5	1.5	1.4	1.5

NR–Not Reported   Percentages may not total 100 due to rounding.

Table 4: Religious Congregations by Metropolitan Size and Group: 2010

Religious Group	Total Adherents	Percent of Adherents in Metro/Micropolitan Size of:					Percent of Adherents Outside Metro/Micro Areas	Percent of Congregations Outside Metro/Micro Areas
		5,000,000 or More	1,000,000 to 4,999,999	250,000 to 999,999	Less Than 250,000	Micro-politan Area		
HINDU–Post Ren	36,720	25.6	30.3	27.8	6.2	5.4	4.7	2.1
HINDU–Renaiss	24,202	10.1	75.8	0.7	1.4	3.3	8.8	7.3
HINDU–Trad Temples	276,114	36.4	46.3	14.6	0.6	1.5	0.4	1.2
Ind Fund Churches	NR	NR	NR	NR	NR	NR	NR	14.5
Int Cou Comm Ch	NR	NR	NR	NR	NR	NR	NR	3.2
Intl Fell Bible Ch	NR	NR	NR	NR	NR	NR	NR	7.4
Jain	NR	NR	NR	NR	NR	NR	NR	0.0
Jehovah's Witness	NR	NR	NR	NR	NR	NR	NR	15.5
JUD–Conserv	501,776	54.2	30.0	14.0	1.3	0.4	0.1	0.3
JUD–Orth	947,020	82.6	12.0	4.8	0.1	0.0	0.4	0.7
JUD–Reconst	41,436	54.9	26.4	14.7	1.3	2.7	0.0	0.0
JUD–Reform	766,352	44.5	35.8	14.7	3.3	1.3	0.4	1.7
LDS–Comm of Christ	123,189	5.5	32.7	19.1	13.0	14.0	15.8	17.7
LDS–L-D Saints	6,144,582	10.0	33.3	28.1	11.3	11.6	5.6	7.9
LUTH–Apostolic Luth	NR	NR	NR	NR	NR	NR	NR	21.2
LUTH–Assoc Free Luth	NR	NR	NR	NR	NR	NR	NR	38.0
LUTH–Ch Luth Conf	NR	NR	NR	NR	NR	NR	NR	21.5
LUTH–Ch of Luth Br	26,695	11.0	16.4	7.2	24.3	27.0	14.0	23.8
LUTH–Cons Luth Assn	NR	NR	NR	NR	NR	NR	NR	0.0
LUTH–E.L.C.A.	4,181,219	12.1	24.4	20.6	13.3	16.0	13.6	20.1
LUTH–Evan Luth Syn	19,291	3.4	19.6	20.9	26.0	13.4	16.7	24.0
LUTH–Luth Ch-Am Asc	NR	NR	NR	NR	NR	NR	NR	28.6
LUTH–Luth Cong Msn Chr	310,185	8.7	31.5	15.0	10.9	16.0	17.8	28.7
LUTH–Luth–MO Synod	2,270,921	13.3	29.4	16.7	13.3	13.7	13.6	21.6
LUTH–Nor Amer Luth C	NR	NR	NR	NR	NR	NR	NR	22.3
LUTH–Wisc Ev Luth Syn	382,883	5.6	26.8	11.8	21.4	21.5	13.0	18.3
MENN–Amb Amish-Menn	677	0.0	0.0	0.0	0.0	18.8	81.2	83.3
MENN–Amish Undif	241,356	1.3	5.1	19.1	6.9	33.2	34.4	37.1
MENN–Beachy Amish-Menn	12,311	0.7	12.0	13.0	10.3	32.7	31.3	29.9
MENN–Ber Amish-Menn	914	0.0	0.0	0.0	3.3	16.3	80.4	63.6
MENN–Bible Flwshp	13,653	23.9	0.0	64.1	3.5	8.5	0.0	0.0
MENN–Bruderhof Comm	1,813	0.6	25.2	23.7	38.9	0.0	11.7	7.7
MENN–CG in Cr (Menn)	18,440	0.1	4.1	14.6	2.3	28.1	50.8	49.7
MENN–Cons Menn Conf	14,284	1.0	9.2	12.4	11.3	33.5	32.5	34.3
MENN–Fel Evg Bib Ch	2,121	0.0	0.0	52.5	2.3	6.8	38.4	57.9
MENN–Fel Evg Ch	9,193	0.8	5.8	72.7	7.2	9.8	3.8	8.7
MENN–Hutt Breth	NR	NR	NR	NR	NR	NR	NR	71.1
MENN–Mara Amish-Menn	1,548	3.6	7.4	26.4	12.1	34.4	16.1	25.0

NR–Not Reported   Percentages may not total 100 due to rounding.

Table 4: Religious Congregations by Metropolitan Size and Group: 2010

Religious Group	Total Adherents	Percent of Adherents in Metro/Micropolitan Size of:					Percent of Adherents Outside Metro/Micro Area	Percent of Congregations Outside Metro/Micro Area
		5,000,000 or More	1,000,000 to 4,999,999	250,000 to 999,999	Less Than 250,000	Micro-politan Area		
MENN–Menn Br US Conf	41,928	3.6	37.2	36.3	4.4	8.1	10.4	13.2
MENN–Menn Chr Fell	2,629	0.0	3.5	9.6	9.7	37.2	39.9	37.5
MENN–Mennonite USA	127,363	15.3	9.1	30.3	16.0	14.9	14.3	14.4
MENN–Midw Bchy Am-Menn	747	0.0	0.0	15.0	0.0	50.5	34.5	33.3
MENN–Ref Mennonite	275	0.0	2.9	46.9	12.0	27.3	10.9	11.1
MENN–Tamp Amish-Menn	3,342	0.0	0.0	28.4	0.0	30.3	41.2	68.8
MENN–Unaffil Amish-Menn	3,224	5.5	0.0	26.0	6.3	35.6	26.7	30.3
METH–A.W.M.C.	4,031	0.0	20.0	18.0	6.0	46.5	9.6	10.1
METH–AME	1,009,682	27.8	22.5	19.4	7.9	12.3	10.0	16.4
METH–AME Zion	301,005	13.9	27.3	22.7	5.4	20.0	10.7	13.5
METH–C.M.E.	290,601	16.8	24.1	19.1	11.6	13.6	14.9	20.5
METH–Cong Meth	14,837	37.9	0.2	8.5	8.7	23.1	21.7	39.9
METH–Evan Meth Ch	NR	NR	NR	NR	NR	NR	NR	13.4
METH–Free Methodist	107,271	11.3	31.4	20.4	11.7	16.2	9.0	14.0
METH–Prim Meth Ch	NR	NR	NR	NR	NR	NR	NR	7.5
METH–So Methodist	NR	NR	NR	NR	NR	NR	NR	19.0
METH–Un Methodist	9,948,221	16.6	21.6	23.0	12.3	15.3	11.1	23.5
METH–Wesleyan	250,051	11.6	17.9	27.0	14.2	20.2	9.2	15.1
Metro Comm Ch	17,600	28.3	39.8	25.9	4.2	1.9	0.0	0.0
Missionary Ch	63,775	16.0	17.1	36.0	14.1	11.3	5.5	9.2
MJEW–Assoc Mes Cong	NR	NR	NR	NR	NR	NR	NR	0.0
MJEW–Union Mes Cong	NR	NR	NR	NR	NR	NR	NR	1.5
MORAV–Morav Ch-AK	2,649	0.0	0.0	4.0	0.0	0.0	96.0	95.7
MORAV–Morav Ch-North	20,286	20.5	4.5	41.0	7.3	19.0	7.7	7.1
MORAV–Morav Ch-South	15,737	6.3	8.0	81.3	0.0	3.1	1.4	5.4
MORAV–Unity Of Breth	NR	NR	NR	NR	NR	NR	NR	14.8
Muslim Est	2,600,082	56.2	24.3	12.0	4.8	2.0	0.6	0.8
Nat Spirit Asso	NR	NR	NR	NR	NR	NR	NR	3.6
New Apost Ch	NR	NR	NR	NR	NR	NR	NR	4.1
Non-denom Chr Chs	12,241,329	26.1	31.9	22.2	8.5	7.8	3.5	8.3
OCATH–Pol Natl Cath	NR	NR	NR	NR	NR	NR	NR	1.7
OCATH–Un Cath Ch	7,019	0.0	50.0	20.0	0.0	30.0	0.0	0.0
ORTHE–Alban Orth Dio	700	50.0	50.0	0.0	0.0	0.0	0.0	0.0
ORTHE–Ant Orth of NA	74,527	29.0	40.0	24.6	4.0	2.0	0.4	2.4
ORTHE–Bulgar Orth USA	2,212	23.7	52.6	22.4	0.1	1.1	0.0	0.0
ORTHE–Carp Rus Orth	10,457	28.1	15.1	38.0	7.9	10.4	0.5	2.5
ORTHE–Georgian Orth	920	85.3	10.9	3.8	0.0	0.0	0.0	0.0
ORTHE–Greek Orthodox	476,878	42.4	36.0	17.9	2.7	0.9	0.1	1.5

NR–Not Reported Percentages may not total 100 due to rounding.

Table 4: Religious Congregations by Metropolitan Size and Group: 2010

Religious Group	Total Adherents	Percent of Adherents in Metro/Micropolitan Size of:					Percent of Adherents Outside Metro/Micro Areas	Percent of Congregations Outside Metro/Micro Areas
		5,000,000 or More	1,000,000 to 4,999,999	250,000 to 999,999	Less Than 250,000	Micro-politan Area		
ORTHE–Holy Orth in NA	2,212	16.0	66.7	10.0	2.3	5.0	0.0	0.0
ORTHE–Macedonian Orth	15,513	56.1	38.4	5.4	0.0	0.0	0.0	0.0
ORTHE–Orth Ch in Amer	84,928	27.8	31.5	20.2	3.4	5.1	12.1	15.1
ORTHE–Pal/Jor Orth	6,775	3.7	73.8	22.5	0.0	0.0	0.0	0.0
ORTHE–Romania Orth Ar	11,203	50.3	43.3	6.5	0.0	0.0	0.0	0.0
ORTHE–Rus Orth Abroad	27,677	41.5	41.9	12.0	2.6	1.8	0.2	1.4
ORTHE–Rus Orth Moscow	12,377	78.6	12.7	7.8	0.8	0.0	0.1	3.1
ORTHE–Serb Orth USA	68,760	39.0	47.1	10.2	2.8	0.5	0.3	3.0
ORTHE–Ukrainian Orth	22,362	47.7	31.6	15.3	3.0	2.1	0.3	2.0
ORTHO–Armen Ap Cilic	30,530	63.2	28.3	7.2	1.3	0.0	0.0	0.0
ORTHO–Armen Ap Etchm	64,545	43.1	41.0	14.1	1.8	0.0	0.0	0.0
ORTHO–Coptic Orth Ch	92,191	58.2	34.4	6.9	0.3	0.2	0.0	0.0
ORTHO–Eritrean Orth	12,685	43.5	56.1	0.4	0.0	0.0	0.0	0.0
ORTHO–Ethiopian Orth	NR	NR	NR	NR	NR	NR	NR	0.0
ORTHO–Malan Dioc Am	16,952	83.9	14.3	1.6	0.0	0.2	0.0	0.0
ORTHO–Malan Syr Orth	6,426	77.3	21.3	1.4	0.0	0.0	0.0	0.0
ORTHO–Syrian Orth Ch	15,705	64.5	30.8	3.2	1.5	0.0	0.0	0.0
PENT–Apos Faith Msn	3,119	20.8	38.6	15.3	13.3	7.9	4.1	5.9
PENT–Assemb of God	2,944,887	18.9	29.3	24.7	9.8	11.0	6.3	16.2
PENT–Assm God Intl F	NR	NR	NR	NR	NR	NR	NR	11.1
PENT–Ch God (Cleve)	1,109,992	17.7	21.3	20.8	12.5	17.5	10.3	16.4
PENT–Ch God Apos Fth	NR	NR	NR	NR	NR	NR	NR	23.6
PENT–Ch God Mtn Asm	NR	NR	NR	NR	NR	NR	NR	21.8
PENT–Ch Lord Jesus Apos	NR	NR	NR	NR	NR	NR	NR	5.3
PENT–Ch of God by Faith	NR	NR	NR	NR	NR	NR	NR	11.1
PENT–Ch of God Proph	98,407	19.0	22.4	21.8	10.8	14.9	11.1	15.5
PENT–COGIC	624,419	23.7	36.6	19.6	7.8	7.3	4.9	6.9
PENT–Cong Hol Ch	15,193	19.6	4.3	14.6	25.1	17.2	19.2	17.3
PENT–Elim	NR	NR	NR	NR	NR	NR	NR	10.7
PENT–Fire Bapt Hol Ch	NR	NR	NR	NR	NR	NR	NR	9.3
PENT–Full Gosp Bapt	NR	NR	NR	NR	NR	NR	NR	2.9
PENT–I F Chr Assmbl	NR	NR	NR	NR	NR	NR	NR	0.0
PENT–Int Foursq Gos	321,763	23.2	28.7	26.7	8.5	10.0	2.9	5.5
PENT–Int Pent C Chr	3,756	14.9	9.6	27.0	8.5	22.7	17.3	21.0
PENT–Intl Pent Holiness	289,475	10.4	14.9	37.3	11.8	13.7	11.9	17.6
PENT–Open Bible Std	22,659	13.4	20.9	28.8	19.4	11.6	5.9	9.6
PENT–Orig Ch of God	NR	NR	NR	NR	NR	NR	NR	46.2
PENT–Pent Ch of God	125,030	9.5	16.1	24.9	13.6	19.6	16.4	17.1

NR–Not Reported   Percentages may not total 100 due to rounding.

Table 4: Religious Congregations by Metropolitan Size and Group: 2010

Religious Group	Total Adherents	Percent of Adherents in Metro/Micropolitan Size of: 5,000,000 or More	1,000,000 to 4,999,999	250,000 to 999,999	Less Than 250,000	Micro-politan Area	Percent of Adherents Outside Metro/Micro Area	Percent of Congregations Outside Metro/Micro Area
PENT–Pent FW Bapt	NR	NR	NR	NR	NR	NR	NR	30.4
PENT–Un Pent Asbl God	NR	NR	NR	NR	NR	NR	NR	0.0
PENT–Un Pent Ch Intl	NR	NR	NR	NR	NR	NR	NR	17.5
PENT–United Holy Ch	NR	NR	NR	NR	NR	NR	NR	9.5
PENT–Vineyard	220,941	18.2	43.6	19.5	10.6	6.4	1.8	4.0
Pillar of Fire	2,100	73.8	26.2	0.0	0.0	0.0	0.0	0.0
PRES–AmPres	NR	NR	NR	NR	NR	NR	NR	0.0
PRES–As Ref Pres Ch	31,978	13.4	27.7	30.1	4.1	17.5	7.2	11.4
PRES–Bible Pres	NR	NR	NR	NR	NR	NR	NR	5.0
PRES–Cov Ref Pres	NR	NR	NR	NR	NR	NR	NR	0.0
PRES–Cum Pres Am	NR	NR	NR	NR	NR	NR	NR	15.0
PRES–Cumber Presb	66,960	6.2	21.4	16.3	8.7	29.7	17.7	27.1
PRES–Evan Presby Ch	129,636	8.1	53.0	23.9	6.4	7.3	1.3	6.5
PRES–Free Ch Scot	NR	NR	NR	NR	NR	NR	NR	0.0
PRES–Free Pres NA	NR	NR	NR	NR	NR	NR	NR	0.0
PRES–Kor Pres Abroad	NR	NR	NR	NR	NR	NR	NR	0.0
PRES–Korean Amer Pres	NR	NR	NR	NR	NR	NR	NR	0.0
PRES–Korean Pres Amer	NR	NR	NR	NR	NR	NR	NR	0.5
PRES–Orth Pres Ch	28,559	24.3	27.8	24.9	13.4	6.7	3.0	6.6
PRES–Pres Ref	NR	NR	NR	NR	NR	NR	NR	0.0
PRES–Presb Ch (USA)	2,451,980	21.1	30.5	22.1	8.7	11.4	6.1	16.6
PRES–Presb Ch Amer	341,431	24.9	30.5	26.7	8.2	6.5	3.3	7.7
PRES–Ref Pres GA	NR	NR	NR	NR	NR	NR	NR	0.0
PRES–Ref Pres Han	NR	NR	NR	NR	NR	NR	NR	0.0
PRES–Ref Pres of NA	5,983	7.1	40.1	18.0	19.3	7.7	7.8	13.0
PRES–Ref Pres US	NR	NR	NR	NR	NR	NR	NR	11.1
REF–Can Amer Ref	NR	NR	NR	NR	NR	NR	NR	0.0
REF–Christian Ref	224,003	18.4	9.7	44.9	7.8	9.9	9.2	8.9
REF–Comm Ref Evan	NR	NR	NR	NR	NR	NR	NR	12.3
REF–Fed Ref Ch	NR	NR	NR	NR	NR	NR	NR	14.3
REF–Free Ref NA	NR	NR	NR	NR	NR	NR	NR	0.0
REF–Heritage Ref	804	14.3	0.0	69.8	1.4	2.7	11.8	20.0
REF–Hung Ref Add'l	NR	NR	NR	NR	NR	NR	NR	0.0
REF–Prot Ref Chs	7,323	11.8	3.3	67.5	1.9	2.9	12.6	14.3
REF–Ref Ch in Am	295,120	27.6	8.5	30.5	11.3	11.8	10.2	11.2
REF–Ref Ch in U.S.	3,923	2.4	18.7	19.0	11.3	28.0	20.6	20.9
REF–Un Ref Chs N.A.	NR	NR	NR	NR	NR	NR	NR	9.5
Salvation Army	379,031	16.4	25.8	23.4	18.8	14.8	0.9	2.1

NR–Not Reported   Percentages may not total 100 due to rounding.

Table 4: Religious Congregations by Metropolitan Size and Group: 2010

Religious Group	Total Adherents	Percent of Adherents in Metro/Micropolitan Size of:					Percent of Adherents Outside Metro/Micro Areas	Percent of Congregations Outside Metro/Micro Areas
		5,000,000 or More	1,000,000 to 4,999,999	250,000 to 999,999	Less Than 250,000	Micro-politan Area		
Schwenkfelder	2,695	100.0	0.0	0.0	0.0	0.0	0.0	0.0
Sev Day Adv	1,194,996	29.1	29.2	21.1	8.3	8.2	4.1	11.9
Shinto	NR	NR	NR	NR	NR	NR	NR	0.0
Sikh	NR	NR	NR	NR	NR	NR	NR	0.0
Swedenborgian	NR	NR	NR	NR	NR	NR	NR	2.9
Tao	NR	NR	NR	NR	NR	NR	NR	7.0
Un Breth in Cr	18,259	0.7	6.2	31.6	8.7	38.4	14.4	20.2
Un C of Christ	1,284,296	13.9	28.4	28.1	8.9	13.5	7.2	13.8
Unit Univ	211,606	19.6	39.1	24.6	9.6	5.6	1.5	5.1
Unity Ch	NR	NR	NR	NR	NR	NR	NR	2.2
Zoroastrian	6,558	58.2	30.0	9.7	1.4	0.5	0.1	0.0

NR–Not Reported   Percentages may not total 100 due to rounding.

This page intentionally left blank.

Appendix A
Religious Groups: Definitions, Procedures, and Comments

African Methodist Episcopal Church [METH–AME]
See Appendix C: African American Bodies

African Methodist Episcopal Zion Church [METH–AME Zion]
See Appendix C: African American Bodies

Albanian Orthodox Diocese of America [ORTHE–Alban Orth Dio]
Contact person(s): His Grace Bishop Ilia (Katre); Alexei Krindatch
Date of statistics: December 2010
Definition of congregations: Parish (i.e. permanent local place of worship which is lead by ordained priest)
Definition of attendees: Average number of persons (including children) who attend Liturgy (main weekly worship service) on a typical (not festive) Sunday.
Definition of adherents: Total number of persons participating in the life of a parish (congregation): counting adults and children, regular and occasional attendees, paid stewards and persons who do not contribute financially.
Dual affiliation: No

Allegheny Wesleyan Methodist Connection [METH–A.W.M.C.]
Contact person(s): James Kunselman
Date of statistics: December 2010
Definition of congregations: Groups of persons who meet together for worship
Definition of attendees: Average of Sunday morning attendance
Definition of members: Full membership
Definition of adherents: Those whose names are on the attendance roll
Dual affiliation: No

Alliance of Baptists [BAPT–Alliance Bapt]
See Appendix K: On-line Listings

Amana Church Society [Amana Ch Soc]
Date of statistics: Dec. 6, 2011
Definition of members: Reported in phone conversation with June Pasco, researcher for the study.

Ambassadors Amish-Mennonite [MENN–Amb Amish-Menn]
See Appendix D: Amish Groups

American Association of Lutheran Churches [LUTH–Luth Ch-Am Asc]
See Appendix K: On-line Listings
Comments on the accuracy of statistics: This group reports 26,537 members in the *Yearbook.*

American Baptist Association [BAPT–Amer Bapt Assn]
Contact person(s): Russell P. Baker
Comments on the accuracy of statistics: This group reports 65,000 members in the *Yearbook.*

American Baptist Churches in the USA [BAPT–Amer Bapt USA]
Contact person(s): Maureen Morrissey

American Carpatho-Russian Orthodox Diocese [ORTHE–Carp Rus Orth]
Contact person(s): Very Rev. Protopresbyter Frank Miloro; Alexei Krindatch
Date of statistics: December 2010
Definition of congregations: Parish (i.e. permanent local place of worship which is lead by ordained priest)
Definition of attendees: Average number of persons (including children) who attend Liturgy (main weekly worship service) on a typical (not festive) Sunday.
Definition of adherents: Total number of persons participating in the life of a parish (congregation): counting adults and children, regular and occasional attendees, paid stewards and persons who do not contribute financially.
Dual affiliation: No

American Presbyterian Church [PRES–AmPres]
See Appendix K: On-line Listings

Amish Groups, undifferentiated [MENN–Amish Undif]
See Appendix D: Amish Groups

Anglican Church in North America [ANG/EPIS–Anglican NA]
See Appendix K: On-line Listings
Definition of congregations: Parishes listed on their website, which may include congregations still associated with and reported by the Episcopal Church.
Comments on the accuracy of statistics: This group reports 100,000 members in the *Yearbook.*

Antiochian Orthodox Christian Archdiocese of North America [ORTHE–Ant Orth of NA]
Contact person(s): Fr. George Kevorkian; Alexei Krindatch
Date of statistics: December 2010
Definition of congregations: Parish (i.e. permanent local place of worship which is lead by ordained priest)
Definition of attendees: Average number of persons (including children) who attend Liturgy (main weekly worship service) on a typical (not festive) Sunday.
Definition of adherents: Total number of persons participating in the life of a parish (congregation): counting adults and children, regular and occasional attendees, paid stewards and persons who do not contribute financially.
Dual affiliation: No

Appendix A / Religious Groups: Definitions, Procedures, and Comments

Apostolic Christian Church of America, Inc. [Ap Chr Ch-Amer]
See Appendix K: On-line Listings

Apostolic Faith Mission of Portland, OR [PENT–Apos Faith Msn]
Contact person(s): Alicia Parker; Darrel Lee
Date of statistics: December 2, 2011
Definition of adherents: This is an estimate.
Dual affiliation: No

Apostolic Lutheran Church of America [LUTH–Apostolic Luth]
See Appendix K: On-line Listings

Armenian Apostolic Church of America (Catholicosate of Cilicia) [ORTHO–Armen Ap Cilic]
Contact person(s): Vazken Chougassian; Alexei Krindatch
Date of statistics: December 2010
Definition of congregations: Parish (i.e. permanent local place of worship which is lead by ordained priest)
Definition of attendees: Average number of persons (including children) who attend Liturgy (main weekly worship service) on a typical (not festive) Sunday.
Definition of adherents: Total number of persons participating in the life of a parish (congregation): counting adults and children, regular and occasional attendees, paid stewards and persons who do not contribute financially.
Dual affiliation: No

Armenian Church of North America (Catholicosate of Etchmiadzin) [ORTHO–Armen Ap Etchm]
Contact person(s): Christopher Zakian; Alexei Krindatch
Date of statistics: December 2010
Definition of congregations: Parish (i.e. permanent local place of worship which is lead by ordained priest)
Definition of attendees: Average number of persons (including children) who attend Liturgy (main weekly worship service) on a typical (not festive) Sunday.
Definition of adherents: Total number of persons participating in the life of a parish (congregation): counting adults and children, regular and occasional attendees, paid stewards and persons who do not contribute financially.
Dual affiliation: No

Armenian Evangelical Churches (Additional) [CONG–Armen Evang Add'l]
Contact person(s): Richard H. Taylor
Date of statistics: December 2010
Definition of congregations: Those listed on the aeuna.org website that are not part of another denomination.
Comments on the accuracy of statistics: The Armenian Evangelical Union of North America is a union of Armenian Protestant churches and mission fellowships in three western hemisphere nations. Most of these are full members of other denominations. This list indicates additional churches and mission fellowships in the United States, not part of another denomination. The website aeuna.org in December, 2010 listed a total of 29 churches and two mission fellowships. 23 churches and the two mission fellowships are in the United States. Ten of the churches (IL-1; MA-3; MI-1; NH-1; NY-2; PA-1; RI-1) are members of the United Church of Christ. One church (NJ) is a member of the Presbyterian Church (USA). One church (CA) is a member of the Evangelical Presbyterian Church. One church (CA) is a member of the Church of the Nazarene. The remaining ten congregations and two mission fellowships are counted here.

Assemblies of God [PENT–Assemb of God]
Contact person(s): Sherri Doty
Date of statistics: December 31, 2010
Definition of congregations: Officially chartered church
Definition of attendees: Attendance of each week's services divided by the number of weeks in the year (usually 52). EXCEPTION CLAUSE: When extreme weather, major epidemic or similar disaster beyond the control of the church causes cancellation or drastic reduction in attendance, such weeks may be omitted in figuring weekly averages.
Definition of members: All whom local church considers members, regardless of age.
Definition of adherents: Total number of persons who consider a local AG church their home church whether or not they are enrolled as members. All ages including children are included.
Comments on the RCMS estimating procedure for adherents: NA; we are submitting total adherents.
Dual affiliation: No
Comments on the accuracy of statistics: Data are self-reported by churches and are likely to include some errors.

Assemblies of God International Fellowship [PENT–Assm God Intl F]
See Appendix K: On-line Listings

Associate Reformed Presbyterian Church [PRES–As Ref Pres Ch]
Contact person(s): Leland R. Beaudrot
Definition of congregations: Local churches
Definition of attendees: We do not track attendees at this level
Definition of members: Active communicant (full) members
Definition of adherents: We do not track adherents at this level
Comments on the RCMS estimating procedure for adherents: Seems good to me

Association of Free Lutheran Congregations [LUTH–Assoc Free Luth]
See Appendix K: On-line Listings
Comments on the accuracy of statistics: This group reports 43,360 members in the *Yearbook*.

Association of Messianic Congregations [MJEW–Assoc Mes Cong]
See Appendix K: On-line Listings

Association of Reformed Baptist Churches of America [BAPT–Asc Ref Bap Ch Am]
Published directory

Bahá'í [Bahá'í]
Contact person(s): Robert Stockman, Thomas Ralya

Date of statistics: July 2011
Definition of congregations: Bahá'í communities are organized on a "parish" type system whereby all Bahá'ís located in a civil jurisdiction are considered members of the same community.
Definition of members: Person joining Bahá'í community
Definition of adherents: Use membership data
Dual affiliation: No.

Beachy Amish-Mennonite Churches [MENN–Beachy Amish-Menn]
See Appendix D: Amish Groups

Berea Amish-Mennonite [MENN–Ber Amish-Menn]
See Appendix D: Amish Groups

Bible Fellowship Church [MENN–Bible Flwshp]
Contact person(s): David Allen; Ronald Kohl
Date of statistics: 2010
Definition of congregations: An incorporated church, or a group going through the process of becoming a particular church within the Bible Fellowship Church.
Definition of attendees: The total number of worshipers each week added up for the year, then divided by the number of weeks per year.
Definition of members: Those who give evidence of personal salvation, have been baptized, and have been accepted as members within a Bible Fellowship Church Congregation.
Dual affiliation: No

Bible Presbyterian Church (General Synod) [PRES–Bible Pres]
See Appendix K: On-line Listings

Brethren Church (Ashland, Ohio) [BRETH–Brethren (Ash)]
Contact person(s): Paula Strickland
Date of statistics: Dec. 8, 2011
Definition of congregations: Churches
Definition of attendees: Regular attendance, 3 time per month.
Definition of members: Typically no children. Most 15+ included in membership.
Dual affiliation: No

Brethren In Christ Church [BRETH–Breth in Chr]
Contact person(s): Pam Arnold; Warren L. Hoffman
Date of statistics: 2009
Definition of congregations: Officially launched or adopted; recognized by conference, per Manual Document of Government.
Definition of attendees: Tracked instead of membership at some churches.
Definition of members: Members take vows, are baptized in a church, no specific age, but membership is most likely at 16+ years old.
Dual affiliation: Yes. Related to the Mennonite Church, MCC member, attends Mennonite World Conference
Comments on the accuracy of statistics: This group reports 20,739 members in the *Yearbook*.

Bruderhof Communities, Inc. [MENN–Bruderhof Comm]
Contact person(s): Johann Huleatt
Date of statistics: Dec. 1, 2011
Definition of attendees: Daily
Definition of members: Adult Christian Baptism
Dual affiliation: No
Comments on the accuracy of statistics: 100% accurate and up-to-date.

Bulgarian Eastern Orthodox Diocese of the USA, Canada and Australia [ORTHE–Bulgar Orth USA]
Contact person(s): Metropolitan Joseph (Blagoev); Alexei Krindatch
Date of statistics: December 2010
Definition of congregations: Parish (i.e. permanent local place of worship which is lead by ordained priest)
Definition of attendees: Average number of persons (including children) who attend Liturgy (main weekly worship service) on a typical (not festive) Sunday.
Definition of adherents: Total number of persons participating in the life of a parish (congregation): counting adults and children, regular and occasional attendees, paid stewards and persons who do not contribute financially.
Dual affiliation: No

Calvary Chapel Fellowship Churches [Calv Chpl]
See Appendix K: On-line Listings

Canadian and American Reformed Churches [REF–Can Amer Ref]
See Appendix K: On-line Listings

Catholic Church [Catholic]
Contact person(s): Clifford Grammich
Date of statistics: 2010
Definition of congregations: Parish churches, mission churches, and some limited locations with regularly scheduled weekend Masses that may be considered regularly meeting Catholic congregations equivalent to other congregations in this study.
Definition of adherents: "Adherents" are generally equivalent to the number of baptized Catholic individuals known to each parish or mission church. For the 2010 study, each diocese was asked to provide, by parish or mission, their number of registered households, registered individuals, infant baptisms within the past year, deaths within the past year, and weekly attendance. This was part of an effort to provide a more congregational-based definition comparable to those of other religious bodies in the study. Put another way, the number of "adherents" is roughly equivalent to those who are known in some way to each parish or mission.
Comments on the accuracy of the statistics: Altogether, this work enumerated nearly 59 million Catholics known in some way to each parish or mission in the United States. This number is substantially below two common measures of the Catholic population in the United States.

First, as indicated in the introduction of this work, survey statistics indicate that more than 75 million persons in the United States may identify themselves as Catholic. Yet a large proportion of this population rarely or never attends religious services. As earlier noted, the General Social Survey of the National Opinion Research Center for 2010 indicates that 25.2 percent of the population claims to be Catholic, but only 20.2 percent of the population claims both to be Catholic and to attend religious services at least once yearly, and that only 15.4 percent of the population claims both to be Catholic and to attend religious services more than once yearly. Multiplying these percentages by the U.S. population in 2010 of more than 308 million indicates that there are nearly 78 million Catholics in the United States, but only 62 million who attend religious services at least once yearly, and less than 48 million who attend more than once yearly. Put another way, the count presented in this work of persons known to parishes or missions, nearly 59 million, is reasonably close to the population of 62 million that both claims to be Catholic and to attend religious services at least once yearly.

Second, *The Official Catholic Directory* (OCD) for 2010 indicated a Catholic population of 68,503,456. Yet there is reason to believe that the means used to generate the OCD number varies by diocese, with some dioceses relying on survey estimates of the Catholic population rather than parish-level statistics.

Variations in reporting and accuracy by diocese were also evident in the data received for this work. We received attendance statistics for less than half of the churches. We received registration statistics and baptism and death statistics for most churches, but many did not provide all these statistics, while some provided more than we requested. Accuracy will very likely vary the amount of time and care each parish and diocese puts into gathering and reporting statistics—and the time and care appears to vary substantially.

The adherent statistics as reported do reflect in most locations the number of Catholics calculated through a method developed by the Catholic Research Forum "based upon Canon Law and assum[ing] the definition of a Catholic as someone who is linked with the Catholic community through baptism and Catholic burial. The basis of the methodology is the computation of: 1) the percentage of babies born who receive Catholic baptism; 2) the percentage of people who die who receive Catholic funerals; and 3) an average of the baptism and funeral statistics." For more on this method, see Michael Cieslak, "Being Creative: Diverse Approaches to Estimating Catholics," paper presented to the annual meeting of the Religious Research Association, St. Louis, Missouri, October 1995. For more on varying methods for enumerating Catholic populations and their implications, see Clifford Grammich, "How Many Catholics? A Comparison of Methods for Estimating Catholic Populations," paper presented to the annual meeting of the Religious Research Association, Louisville, Kentucky, October 2008.

Central Yearly Meeting of Friends [FRND–Central Yr Mtg]

Contact person(s): Richard H. Taylor
Date of statistics: August 2011
Definition of congregations: Churches and church extension
Definition of attendees: Average Attendance
Definition of members: Members
Comments on the RCMS estimating procedure for adherents: This provides for children. However, since average attendance surpasses membership, many adherents are probably not included.
Dual affiliation: No
Comments on the accuracy of statistics: Current

Christian and Missionary Alliance [Chr & Miss Al]

Contact person(s): Julianne Connon
Date of statistics: December 31, 2010
Definition of congregations: These are churches that are accredited, affiliated, and developing churches with the C&MA. This does not include church plants.
Definition of attendees: The average number of people that attend the main worship services.
Definition of members: Members are adults who have completed a membership class, confessed Jesus Christ as Savior and Lord, and signed the C&MA application of membership.
Definition of adherents: Adherents are members and non-members who regularly attend the church's worship services and consider the church to be their church. This includes children, youth, and adults.
Dual affiliation: Unkown. We do have churches that we consider to be affiliated but we have no way of knowing if they are affiliated with any other organizations. They are required to do an Annual Report just like our other churches.
Comments on the accuracy of statistics: The totals of membership, total inclusive membership, and attendance change all the time based on information we receive throughout the year from our churches and districts. These numbers do not necessarily match our "published" numbers.

Christian Brethren [Christian Brethren]

See Appendix K: On-line Listings
Comments on the accuracy of statistics: This group reports 86,000 members in the *Yearbook.*

Christian Church (Disciples of Christ) [CHR–Chr Ch (Disc)]

Contact person(s): Howard Bowers
Date of statistics: December 31, 2010
Definition of congregations: Number of congregation officially recognized as of December 31, 2010.
Definition of attendees: Average attendance (per week) reported by congregations. Those congregations that have not reported in the past three reporting cycles are not estimated. Those that have reported within the last three reporting cycles are estimated at the last reported level.
Definition of members: Persons who are baptized and considered members by the local congregation.
Definition of adherents: No definition. There is no estimate made of the congregation's non-member participants either child or adult.
Comments on the RCMS estimating procedure for adherents: The

procedure seems like a viable method for estimating the adherents.

Dual affiliation: Yes. About 1% of our congregation have dual affiliation. That is usually with the American Baptist, Church of the Brethern, Presbyterian, United Church of Christ and United Methodist.

Comments on the accuracy of statistics: Reports rely upon a key responder. In most cases the key responder is the pastor who may have a vested interest in the figures reported.

Christian Churches and Churches of Christ [CHR–Chr Chs & Chs Cr]

Contact person(s): Larry Collins

Comments on the accuracy of statistics: Data compiled from the 2011 Directory of the Ministry.

Christian Methodist Episcopal Church [METH–C.M.E.]

See Appendix C: African American Bodies

Christian Reformed Church in North America [REF–Christian Ref]

Contact person(s): Nancy Haynes

Christian Union [Christian Un]

Contact person(s): Jim Eschenbrenner

Definition of congregations: Local gathering recognized by "district" officials.

Definition of members: Christian Union does not have a history of collecting data from churches.

Comments on the accuracy of statistics: This group reports 4,500 members in the *Yearbook*.

Church of Christ (Holiness), U.S.A [Ch of Chr (Hol)]

Contact person(s): Joseph Campbell; Sheila Bingham

Date of statistics: July 2010

Definition of congregations: Each local church is counted as a congregation

Comments on the accuracy of statistics: This group reports 10,460 members in the *Yearbook*.

Church of Christ, Scientist [Ch Cr, Scientst]

Contact person(s): Debbi Lawrence

Date of statistics: Dec. 15, 2011

Definition of congregations: Includes Authorized branches Churches of Christ, Scientist, and Christian Science Societies, formed in accordance with the Church Manual of The First Church of Christ, Scientist, in Boston, MA (c1895).

Definition of members: Membership numbers in The First Church of Christ, Scientist, in Boston, MA are not public. Article VIII, Section 28 of the Church Manual "Numbering the People," states the following directive in regards to releasing membership numbers: "Christian Scientists shall not report for publication the number of the members of The Mother Church, nor that of the branch churches. According to the Scripture they shall turn away from personality and numbering the people."

Dual affiliation: No

Church of God (Anderson, Indiana) [CGOD–Ch God (Ander)]

Contact person(s): Robert Edwards

Church of God (Cleveland, Tennessee) [PENT–Ch God (Cleve)]

Contact person(s): Sharon Adkins; Julian Robinson; Lynn Stone

See Appendix K: On-line Listings

Church of God (Seventh Day) [Ch God (7th Day)]

Contact person(s): Whaid Rose

Date of statistics: Dec. 31, 2010

Definition of congregations: Those listed in our Directory of Ministers & Churches, which is updated monthly.

Dual affiliation: Unknown

Comments on the accuracy of statistics: I have been working for over 2 years on a membership update, and have found many errors, areas where we do not have all the data imputed into our data base. I have often needed long time members to submit copies of membership certificates. We are hoping accuracy will increase in the next 2 years as this project continues.

Comments on the accuracy of statistics: This group reports 11,000 members in the *Yearbook*.

Church of God by Faith, Inc. [PENT–Ch of God by Faith]

See Appendix K: On-line Listings

Comments on the accuracy of statistics: This group reports 35,000 members in the *Yearbook*.

Church of God General Conference [Ch of God Gen Conf]

Contact person(s): David Krogh

Date of statistics: Dec. 31, 2010

Definition of congregations: A group of people who meet weekly for worship that have applied for and been granted membership in our association of churches by the Board of Directors.

Definition of members: Baptized and active in the church by attending at least 13 Sundays per year and make periodic financial contributions.

Comments on the RCMS estimating procedure for adherents: Your procedure is acceptable.

Dual affiliation: No

Comments on the accuracy of statistics: A statistical form is mailed to each church requesting information for the previous year. This form must be returned in order for a church to have delegate representation at our annual summer Conference. When a church does not return the form, information from the previous year is used as an estimate for the current year.

Church of God in Christ [PENT–COGIC]

See Appendix C: African American Bodies

Church of God in Christ, Mennonite [MENN–CG in Cr (Menn)]

Contact person(s): Dale Koehn

Church of God of Prophecy [PENT–Ch of God Proph]

Contact person(s): Shaun McKinley

Date of statistics: August 2010

Definition of congregations: An organized local church, does not include churches that are designated as "mission" status due to being newly planted.
Definition of attendees: Not reported
Definition of members: Number of members reported by local churches as having accepted our "membership covenant." Does not include regular attendees who have not accepted church membership covenant.
Definition of adherents: To be estimated using the RCMS standard formula.
Comments on the RCMS estimating procedure for adherents: Acceptable
Dual affiliation: No
Comments on the accuracy of statistics: Reporting is mandatory but not heavily enforced. We do strive to maintain accurate records but cannot verify the accuracy of the report.

Church of God of the Apostolic Faith, Inc. [PENT–Ch God Apos Fth]
See Appendix K: On-line Listings

Church of God, Mountain Assembly, Inc. [PENT–Ch God Mtn Asm]
Contact person(s): James Kilgore
Comments on the accuracy of statistics: This group reports 7,000 members in the *Yearbook.*

Church of Jesus Christ of Latter-day Saints [LDS–L-D Saints]
Contact person(s): Cliff Higbee; Glen Buckner
Date of statistics: Year-end 2010
Definition of congregations: Total wards and branches in the United States
Definition of adherents: Total members, including children of record, in the United States
Dual affiliation: No

Church of Our Lord Jesus Christ of the Apostolic Faith, Inc. [PENT–Ch Lord Jesus Apos]
See Appendix K: On-line Listings

Church of the Brethren [BRETH–Ch of Brethren]
Contact person(s): Jean Clements

Church of the Lutheran Brethren of America [LUTH–Ch of Luth Br]
Contact person(s): Barb Walswick

Church of the Lutheran Confession [LUTH–Ch Luth Conf]
See Appendix K: On-line Listings
Comments on the accuracy of statistics: This group reports 6,175 members in the *Yearbook.*

Church of the Nazarene [Ch of Nazarene]
Contact person(s): Dale Jones
Date of statistics: September 30, 2010
Definition of congregations: All organized churches plus those not yet organized reporting statistics.
Definition of attendees: Average weekly attendance at worship services during the prior year. This usually includes children and workers in nurseries or other specialized ministries conducted at the same time as the worship service. When multiple services are held, the totals from all services would typically be included.
Definition of members: Full members received into local congregations. All members of the Church of the Nazarene are members of a local congregation.
Definition of adherents: The larger of full and associate members, responsibility list (those involved in Sunday School or other discipleship ministries), average weekly attendance in discipleship activities, or average weekly worship attendance.
Dual affiliation: No
Comments on the accuracy of statistics: High participation rates (over 98% annually) and double-checked by district personnel.

Church of the United Brethren in Christ [Un Breth in Cr]
Contact person(s): Cathy Reich
Date of statistics: December 8, 2011
Definition of congregations: Every congregation in the USA which agrees to sign a covenant.
Definition of attendees: The number of attendees at the major weekend services, combined.
Definition of members: The congregation keeps a listing of all adults who become full members.
Definition of adherents: I could recommend adherents to be same number as attendees at 85% to account for visitors, etc.
Dual affiliation: No
Comments on the accuracy of statistics: We have submitted all figures and data as reported to us. There were some not reported at all, therefore no figures given.

Churches of Christ [CHR–Chs of Christ]
Contact person(s): Carl Royster

Churches of Christ in Christian Union [Ch Christ Chr Union]
See Appendix K: On-line Listings
Comments on the accuracy of statistics: This group reports 10,645 members in the *Yearbook.*

Churches of God, General Conference [CGOD–Ches God-Gen Con]
Contact person(s): Candice Shoemaker

Communion of Reformed Evangelical Churches [REF–Comm Ref Evan]
See Appendix K: On-line Listings

Community of Christ [LDS–Comm of Christ]
Contact person(s): Christi Duke

Congregational Christian Churches, Additional (not part of any national CCC body) [CONG–Cong Chr Add'l]
Contact person(s): Richard H. Taylor
Date of statistics: Dec. 31, 2010
Definition of congregations: Churches are a "local continuing body of believers which is a congregation of the universal Church of Christ." (Report on the Commission on the Study of the Congregational Christian Churches, 1956)
Definition of members: Total membership

Comments on the RCMS estimating procedure for adherents: This is consistent with past reports.

Dual affiliation: Yes. These churches are affiliated with Associations and Conferences of the United Church of Christ, but are not part of any national Congregational Christian body.

The Constitution of the United Church of Christ provides that local Conferences and Associations may remain in fellowship with Congregational Christian Churches not part of the United Church of Christ. Their statistics are to be kept separately. As of December 31, 2010, twenty-one of the Conferences of the United Church Conferences took advantage of this clause for 95 congregations. These are included in two categories: "Schedule I" churches (which "have not voted" or have "voted to abstain from voting" on whether to join the United Church) and "Schedule II" churches (which have "voted not to be a part" of the United Church). Of the 95 congregations, 28 have a primary national relationship with the National Association of Congregational Christian Churches or the Conservative Congregational Christian Conference, and are not reported here. An additional four congregations are inactive (having a legal existance, but not holding regular worship services) are also not shown here. This leaves the 63 congregations shown here. Of the reported churches one is dually aligned to the American Baptist Churches and one to the Evangelical Covenant Church. One is federated to an American Baptist Church and another one is federated to a United Methodist Church.

Comments on the accuracy of statistics: Most are current or very recent reports. One church did not report membership. About ten churches (notably in IN, IA, and PA) reported very old data.

Congregational Holiness Church [PENT–Cong Hol Ch]

Contact person(s): Lynn Carnes

Congregational Methodist Church [METH–Cong Meth]

Contact person(s): Janet Woods

Date of statistics: December 31, 2010

Definition of congregations: Number of churches who meet each week for worship.

Definition of attendees: Average morning worship (separate from Sunday School) is reported annually to their annual conferences and to our head General Conference.

Definition of members: Age 16+, Full Member; Below 16, Junior Member

Dual affiliation: No

Comments on the accuracy of statistics: Not all of our churches report so these figures are based solely on the number who did report; 149 of 178 churches reported.

Conservative Baptist Association of America [BAPT–Consrv Bapt]

Published Directory

Comments on the accuracy of statistics: This group reports 200,000 members in the *Yearbook*.

Conservative Congregational Christian Conference [CONG–Consrv Cong Chr]

Contact person(s): Richard H. Taylor

Date of statistics: Dec. 31, 2010

Definition of congregations: "Member churches" or "churches in development"

Definition of attendees: AM attendance

Definition of members: Church membership

Comments on the RCMS estimating procedure for adherents: This has been the normal format for reported Conservative Conference data. However, the strong average attendance in most congregations suggests many adult adherents not included in these numbers.

Dual affiliation: Yes. Limited. United Church of Christ; National Association of Congregational Christian Churches.

Comments on the accuracy of statistics: 223 of 293 reported full member churches are current year membership reports. Seventy churches (23.8%) are picked up from previous year's reports. Average attendance for two congregations was estimated using the national denominational percentage of members. No membership or attendance figures provided for churches in development.

Conservative Judaism [JUD–Conserv]

See Appendix H: Jewish Groups

Conservative Lutheran Association [LUTH–Cons Luth Assn]

See Appendix K: On-line Listings

Comments on the accuracy of statistics: This group reports 1,338 members in the *Yearbook*.

Conservative Mennonite Conference [MENN–Cons Menn Conf]

Contact person(s): Delores Yoder

Date of statistics: September 2010

Definition of congregations: Established, organized churches church plants are not included.

Definition of attendees: includes children, counted each Sunday by local churches.

Definition of members: Most churches have an official membership roll that tracks additions and subtractions

Definition of adherents: Those who attend regularly, but have not formally committed themselves through membership.

Dual affiliation: Yes. Maple Grove Mennonite, Hartville, Ohio; Lowville Mennonite and Pine Grove Mennonite, New York, and Faith Community, El Dorado, Arkansas share their affiliation with Mennonite Church USA

Comments on the accuracy of statistics: Each September we send out a letter with our current information asking the churches to update their information. These are used for our data. These figures are adjusted to represent 100%.

Conservative Yearly Meetings of Friends [FRND–Consrv Yr Mtgs]

Contact person(s): Richard H. Taylor

Date of statistics: Iowa and Ohio: 2010; North Carolina: 2011

Definition of congregations: Meetings, churches, and worship groups.

Definition of attendees: N/A
Definition of members: Members.
Definition of adherents: N/A
Comments on the RCMS estimating procedure for adherents: This has been the normal format for reporting Quaker data. However, some Conservative meetings may include younger children in their membership figures. While this would contradict the use of this formula, its use is counter-balanced by another fact. Since nearly a quarter of reported Conservative meetings do not report any membership the adherents must be significantly higher than reported members. This formula does maintain consistency of reporting and perhaps balances out two contradictory tendencies.
Dual affiliation: Yes. Four local meetings in North Carolina (with 286 members) are dually aligned to a Friends General Conference Fellowship.
Comments on the accuracy of statistics: Member data is collected by Yearly Meetings and varies in the items collected. Nine of 40 local meetings (22.5%) are worship groups, preparatory meetings, etc. that do not report members and are shown with "zero" members. Often key members of these groups belong to other local meetings. Other times these groups are not fully organized.
See Appendix F: Friends

Convention of Original Free Will Baptists [BAPT–Orig Free Will Bapt]
Contact person(s): Buddy Sasser
Date of statistics: Dec. 7, 2011
Definition of congregations: By church name
Definition of attendees: Sunday morning attendance
Definition of members: Full members
Definition of adherents: All attenders
Dual affiliation: No

Converge Worldwide/Baptist General Conference [BAPT–Converge/BGC]
Contact person(s): Peg Windmiller
Date of statistics: 2010
Definition of congregations: Any church or church plant recognized by one of the 11 Converge Worldwide/BGC Regions of the US
Definition of attendees: Average Sunday Attendance
Definition of adherents: Estimated using attendance * 1.2
Dual affiliation: Yes. About 25 are affiliated with Vision 360

Coptic Orthodox Church [ORTHO–Coptic Orth Ch]
Contact person(s): His Grace Bishop David; Alexei Krindatch
Date of statistics: December 2010
Definition of congregations: : Parish (i.e. permanent local place of worship which is lead by ordained priest)
Definition of attendees: Average number of persons (including children) who attend Liturgy (main weekly worship service) on a typical (not festive) Sunday.
Definition of adherents: Total number of persons participating in the life of a parish (congregation): counting adults and children, regular and occasional attendees, paid stewards and persons who do not contribute financially
Dual affiliation: No

Covenant Reformed Presbyterian Church [PRES–Cov Ref Pres]
See Appendix K: On-line Listings
Comments on the accuracy of statistics: This group reports 300 members in the *Yearbook*.

Cumberland Presbyterian Church [PRES–Cumber Presb]
Contact person(s): Michael Sharpe
Date of statistics: Dec. 31, 2010
Definition of congregations: Consists of professing Christians, together with their baptized children, who covenant with each other to meet regularly to worship God and study the Word of God, join together in a common witness to the gospel, and engage in good works to which Christians are called, and who have adopted a certain form of government.
Definition of attendees: Not available
Definition of members: Persons who have confessed Jesus Christ as Lord and Savior, entered into the church covenant, and received the sacrament of baptism.
Dual affiliation: Yes. We have 12 congregations that are union congregations with the Presbyterian Church USA. These congregations hold dual membership in each denomination, usually reporting stats (1/2 to each denomination).
Comments on the accuracy of statistics: See reporting form sent to each congregation yearly.

Cumberland Presbyterian Church in America [PRES–Cum Pres Am]
See Appendix K: On-line Listings
Comments on the accuracy of statistics: This group reports 15,142 members in the *Yearbook*.

Elim Fellowship [PENT–Elim]
See Appendix K: On-line Listings

Enterprise Baptists Association [BAPT–Enterprise Bapt Assoc]
See Appendix K: On-line Listings

Episcopal Church [ANG/EPIS–Episcopal]
Contact person(s): Kirk Hadaway

Eritrean Orthodox [ORTHO–Eritrean Orth]
Contact person(s): Rev. Fr. Michael Yohannes; Alexei Krindatch
Date of statistics: December 2011
Definition of congregations: Parish (i.e. permanent local place of worship which is lead by ordained priest)
Definition of attendees: Average number of persons (including children) who attend Liturgy (main weekly worship service) on a typical (not festive) Sunday.
Definition of adherents: Total number of persons participating in the life of a parish (congregation): counting adults and children, regular and occasional attendees, paid stewards and persons who do not contribute financially.
Dual affiliation: No

Ethiopian Orthodox [ORTHO–Ethiopian Orth]

Contact person(s): His Grace Bishop Melchizedek; Alexei Krindatch

Date of statistics: December 2011

Definition of congregations: Parish (i.e. permanent local place of worship which is lead by ordained priest)

Dual affiliation: No

Evangelical Association of Reformed, and Congregational Christian Churches [Evan Assoc RCC]

See Appendix K: On-line Listings

Evangelical Church [Evan Ch]

See Appendix K: On-line Listings

Comments on the accuracy of statistics: This group reports 12,430 members in the *Yearbook.*

Evangelical Congregational Church [Evan Cong Ch]

Contact person(s): Brenda Long

Evangelical Covenant Church [Evan Cov Ch]

Contact person(s): David Olson; Fredrik Wall

Date of statistics: 2010

Definition of congregations: Worship group; officially affiliated and self-supporting with pastor.

Definition of members: Received as members via official process of Local Church; some include children, some don't. On average, children 13+ can be members.

Definition of adherents: Regular participants in the life of the church.

Comments on the RCMS estimating procedure for adherents: Our analysis of churches in our denomination suggests that there is a multiplication factor of 1.3 to get to a best estimate of adherents. The analysis is based on research done by Dave Olson.

Dual affiliation: No

Comments on the accuracy of statistics: To find our statistical data for attendance we have determined that the month of November is the most accurate month in order to see over or underestimate attendance because of holidays, etc. We are sampling 5 weekends and take out high and low data and do an average of the remaining three. We still do a manual control of the outcome and communicate back to churches and our local conferences should the data not seem to be representative based on prior year's numbers. Membership data is collected as a yearend number from another statistical report sent to our churches.

Evangelical Free Church of America [Evan Free Ch]

Contact person(s): Lisa Theurer

Evangelical Friends Church International [FRND–Evan Fr Ch Intl]

Contact person(s): Richard H. Taylor

Date of statistics: Data from four regions is from their 2010 meetings. Southwest data is from December 2005. Alaska details were estimated from incomplete 2007 data. Information on Hispanic congregations has been enhanced through the use of the Hispanic Friends website www.institutualma.org/directorio/ in 2011.

Definition of congregations: Meetings, churches, and worship groups.

Definition of attendees: Sunday AM.

Definition of members: Members

Definition of adherents: N/A

Comments on the RCMS estimating procedure for adherents: This has been the normal way for reporting Friends data. However, some churches do include minor children in their membership. Nevertheless, with Evangelical Friends attendance so outstripping membership, it is clear that this formula undercounts Evangelical Friends total adherents.

Dual affiliation: Yes. One Kansas church reported with 443 members is dually aligned to the Friends United Meeting.

Comments on the accuracy of statistics: Member data is collected by the Regions and Yearly Meetings and varies in content. 40 local churches out of 306 total (13.1%) are mission points, new starts, worship groups, etc. that do not report members and are shown with "zero" members. Often key members of these groups belong to other local meetings. Other times these groups are not fully organized.

See Appendix F: Friends

Evangelical Lutheran Church in America [LUTH–E.L.C.A.]

Contact person(s): Deborah Myers

Date of statistics: August 30, 2011

Definition of congregations: Those that have incorporated and have been received onto the roster of the Synod (territory) in which they are located.

Definition of attendees: The number of people worshiping weekly at all regularly held worship services: i.e. Sunday, Saturday and a mid-week service if it is held throughout the year (not just during Lent).

Definition of members: The ELCA begins communion for 5th graders. Confirmation takes place a few years after communion.

Definition of adherents: The ELCA counts all baptized members when determining its membership. Confirmed members would be a subset of baptized. Confirmed members is: 3,444,021 and baptized is: 4,543,037.

Dual affiliation: No

Comments on the accuracy of statistics: We rely on our congregations to file reports annually to obtain the data. Not all congregations file. For those that do not file, their data is carried over from the last year filed on record and is included in our numbers.

Evangelical Lutheran Synod [LUTH–Evan Luth Syn]

Contact person(s): Elsa Ferkenstad

Date of statistics: December 31, 2010

Definition of congregations: Incorporated congregations accepted into membership in the synod.

Definition of attendees: Average total attendance for weekend (i.e., if the congregation has two identical Sunday services, it is the attendance at both services).

Definition of members: Members who have completed confirmation

instruction.
Definition of adherents: Baptized members of congregations.
Dual affiliation: No
Comments on the accuracy of statistics: Statistics are reported to synod office by local pastors. Every effort is made to receive updated information each year. However, there is occasionally data for a particular church that is carried over from the previous year because a current report was not available.

Evangelical Methodist Church [METH–Evan Meth Ch]
See Appendix K: On-line Listings
Comments on the accuracy of statistics: This group reports 8,615 members in the *Yearbook*.

Evangelical Presbyterian Church [PRES–Evan Presby Ch]
Contact person(s): Annette Minard
Date of statistics: December 31, 2010
Definition of congregations: Organized bodies of faith formally recognized by our Presbyteries as qualified particular or mission churches.
Definition of attendees: Average weekly worship attendance (both adults and children) in primary (Saturday night/Sunday morning) worship services. This figure does not include additional Sunday night or Wednesday services unless that is the time of primary worship.
Definition of members: Membership formally recognized by church, usually ages 12 or older (not baptized children).
Definition of adherents: Members plus baptized rolls (children)
Dual affiliation: No

Federation of Reformed Churches [REF–Fed Ref Ch]
See Appendix K: On-line Listings

Fellowship of Evangelical Bible Churches [MENN–Fel Evg Bib Ch]
Contact person(s): Paul A. Boecker
Date of statistics: November 22, 2011
Definition of members: Most 14+, no definitive age for Baptism, usually Jr. High, most members adults
Dual affiliation: No

Fellowship of Evangelical Churches [MENN–Fel Evg Ch]
Contact person(s): Lynette Augsburger

Foursquare Gospel, International Church of the [PENT–Int Foursq Gos]
Contact person(s): Wanda Brackett

Free Church of Scotland (Continuing) [PRES–Free Ch Scot]
See Appendix K: On-line Listings

Free Methodist Church of North America [METH–Free Methodist]
Contact person(s): Kelly Sheads

Free Presbyterian Church of North America [PRES–Free Pres NA]
See Appendix K: On-line Listings

Free Reformed Church of North America [REF–Free Ref NA]
See Appendix K: On-line Listings

Free Will Baptists, National Association of [BAPT–Free Will Bapt]
Contact person(s): Keith Burden, Dari Goodfellow, Ryan Lewis

Friends General Conference [FRND–Fr Gen Cf]
Contact person(s): Richard H. Taylor
Date of statistics: See Accuracy section below
Definition of congregations: Meetings, churches, and worship groups.
Definition of attendees: Only two of the Yearly Meetings or Fellowship publish attendance records, so it is not shown in the main lists. (See comments under adherent formula.)
Definition of members: Includes "non-resident," "youth," "teens," and other designations.
Definition of adherents: N/A
Comments on the RCMS estimating procedure for adherents: This has been the normal procedure for Friends data. Some local meetings may include children in member figures, but there is no uniform policy. There is other data that may suggest General Conference adherents. Four Yearly Meetings report a figure roughly equivalent to adherents. Intermountain with 983 members (not including 25 in the Wyoming group) reports a total of 1,589 as "number in meetings, including worship groups." Ohio Valley with (rounded for dual meetings) 769 members reports an additional 143 "non-member attendees." Southern Appalachian with 594 members reports 1,142 "total individuals." Southeastern with 501 members reports 903 "total persons." Average attendance data is also available for two Yearly Meetings. Reported attendance as a percentage of membership for each of these is 74.6% for Lake Erie; and 45.8% for Ohio Valley, an average of 66.9% for these two Yearly Meetings. Since, also, the data collected includes many local meetings not reporting any membership the total General Conference adherent number must be higher than reported. It must be concluded that this formula undercounts General Conference adherents.
Dual affiliation: Yes. For the extensive dual alignment with the Friends United Meeting see the separate entry for "Friends General Conference and Friends United Meeting, dually aligned meetings." In addition there are the following dual alignments. Four meetings in North Carolina with 286 members are dually aligned to the Friends – Conservative. Five meetings, (California: 2 with 92 members; Idaho 1 with no member report; Washington 1 with 61 members; and Wyoming 1 with 4 members) are dually aligned with one of the Independent Yearly Meetings.
Comments on the accuracy of statistics: Member data is collected by the Yearly Meetings and varies in dating and items collected. 103 local meetings out of 382 total (27.0%) are worship groups, preparatory meetings, etc. that do not report members and are shown with "zero" members. Often key members of these groups belong to other local meetings. Some others of these groups are not fully organized. The Wyoming group of five local communities mentioned above is affiliated directly to the General Conference and to one General Conference Yearly Meeting. Two other meetings (one in North Carolina and one in

Wisconsin) each belong to two General Conference Yearly Meetings. These duplications have been removed in the figures reported.Data for five Yearly Meetings is from their 2010 meetings. Northern Yearly Meeting is also from their 2010 report, but many local memberships were estimated from other data in written reports. Southeastern is from its 2011 report, Ohio Valley the 2009 report, and South Central its 2007 report. Surveys conducted in 2011 were used to assemble member data shown for the Piedmont Fellowship (very incomplete), and for meetings directly affiliated to the General Conference. Alaska Conference details were estimated from partial 2010 data. When data for dually aligned meetings is not available from a General Conference source, but was available from their dual source, it is inserted.

See Appendix F: Friends

Friends General Conference and Friends United Meeting, dually aligned meetings [FRND–Fr Gen Cf & Un Mtg]

Contact person(s): Richard H. Taylor

Date of statistics: Canadian: 2008; others: 2010

Definition of congregations: Meetings, churches, and worship groups.

Definition of attendees: Only the New England Yearly Meeting reported average attendance, and not for all meetings. Therefore that data is not shown in the main lists. For meetings reporting it, the attendance as a percentage of membership is 46.6%.

Definition of adherents: N/A

Comments on the RCMS estimating procedure for adherents: This has been the normal format for Quaker reporting. But some local meetings/churches may include younger children in their member totals. For comparison to the formula, the New England Yearly Meeting (the only one here to do so) specifically reports 3,964 members and an additional 1,167 “average number of active attendees (non-members).” Thus non-members make up a significant proportion of New England Yearly Meeting attendees. Since the over all data collected includes many local meetings not reporting any membership the adherent number over all must be higher than reported. It must be concluded that this formula undercounts dual General Conference and United Meeting adherents.

Dual affiliation: Yes. This grouping are dual congregations to General Conference and United Meeting, in addition to those reported separately. This group has not been counted in either of the other groups in the various lists.

See Appendix F: Friends

Friends United Meeting [FRND–Fr Un Mtg]

Contact person(s): Richard H. Taylor

Date of statistics: Western: 2011; Indiana: 2009; others:2010

Definition of congregations: Meetings, churches, and worship groups.

Definition of attendees: Only four of the seven Yearly Meetings included here reported attendance figures, so it is not shown in the main lists. Reported attendance as a percentage of membership is 101.8% for the Indiana Yearly Meeting, 56.6% for the Iowa Yearly Meeting, 63.6% for the North Carolina Meeting, and 43.2% for the Western Yearly Meeting. this gives an overall percentage of 65.9% for those Meetings collecting this data.

Definition of members: Members.

Definition of adherents: N/A

Comments on the RCMS estimating procedure for adherents: This has been the format historically used for Quaker data. Most United Meeting churches/meetings probably separate younger children from full members. However, there is no uniform rule about excluding younger children from membership reports. Nevertheless this is probably a useful format for most member-reported churches/meetings. The presence of some local churches/meetings not reporting any membership suggests that the adherent number might be higher than reported. In addition, because the percentage of attendees, where known, compared to membership is higher than in many denominational groups, it must be concluded that this formula further undercounts United Meeting adherents.

Dual affiliation: Yes. For the extensive dual alignment with the Friends General Conference see the separate entry "Friends General Conference and Friends United Meeting, dually aligned meetings."

In addition one church in Kansas with 437 members is also dually aligned to the Evangelical Friends International. Also one Indiana church is federated to groups affiliated with the Presbyterian Church (USA), United Methodist Church, and Christian Church (Disciples of Christ).

Comments on the accuracy of statistics: Member data is collected by the Yearly Meetings and varies in dating and items collected. 28 local meetings out of 258 total (10.9%) are shown with “zero” members. The majority of these are a group of regular meetings in the North Carolina Yearly Meeting with no current reports. The few others are a mix of worship groups, preparatory meetings, etc. that do not report members. Often key members of these types of gropus belong to other local meetings. Other times these groups are not fully organized.

See Appendix F: Friends

Full Gospel Baptist Church Fellowship [PENT–Full Gosp Bapt]

See Appendix K: On-line Listings

Fundamental Baptist Fellowship [BAPT–Fund Bapt Flwsp]

Published directory

General Association of Regular Baptist Churches [BAPT–Reg Bapt Gen As]

Published directory

Comments on the accuracy of statistics: This group reports 135,815 members in the *Yearbook.*

Georgian Orthodox Parishes in the United States [ORTHE–Georgian Orth]

Contact person(s): Alexei Krindatch
Date of statistics: December 2010
Definition of congregations: Parish (i.e. permanent local place of worship which is lead by ordained priest)
Definition of attendees: Average number of persons (including children) who attend Liturgy (main weekly worship service) on a typical (not festive) Sunday.
Definition of adherents: Total number of persons participating in the life of a parish (congregation): counting adults and children, regular and occasional attendees, paid stewards and persons who do not contribute financially.
Dual affiliation: No

Grace Brethren Churches, Fellowship of [BRETH–Grace Breth]
See Appendix K: On-line Listings
Comments on the accuracy of statistics: This group reports 30,371 members in the *Yearbook.*

Grace Gospel Fellowship [Grace Gosp Fel]
Contact person(s): Cynthia Carmichael; Frosty Hansen
Definition of congregations: They sign a form, agree with doctrine and constitution, sign and return. No financial support required.
Definition of members: No children. 18+, but most older; some in college.
Comments on the accuracy of statistics: This group reports 5,000 members in the *Yearbook.*

Greek Orthodox Archdiocese of America [ORTHE–Greek Orthodox]
Contact person(s): His Grace Bishop Andonios; Alexei Krindatch
Date of statistics: December 2010
Definition of congregations: Total number of persons participating in the life of a parish (congregation): counting adults and children, regular and occasional attendees, paid stewards and persons who do not contribute financially.
Definition of attendees: Average number of persons (including children) who attend Liturgy (main weekly worship service) on a typical (not festive) Sunday.
Definition of members: : Total number of persons participating in the life of a parish (congregation): counting adults and children, regular and occasional attendees, paid stewards and persons who do not contribute financially.
Dual affiliation: No

Heritage Reformed Churches [REF–Heritage Ref]
Contact person(s): Ann Dykema
Date of statistics: December 2011
Definition of congregations: Organized church with elders and deacons, under the rule of the Senate, subscribe to beliefs.
Definition of attendees: N/A
Definition of members: Full time members who take classes and do public confession, usually over 18yrs old.
Dual affiliation: Yes. Have the highest level of interaction with: Free Reformed Churches of North America. Exchange pastors, and share events.

Hindu Post Renaissance [HINDU–Post Ren]
See Appendix G: Hindu Groups

Hindu Renaissance [HINDU–Renaiss]
See Appendix G: Hindu Groups

Holy Orthodox Church in North America [ORTHE–Holy Orth in NA]
Contact person(s): His Grace Bishop Demetrius; Alexei Krindatch
Date of statistics: December 2010
Definition of congregations: Parish (i.e. permanent local place of worship which is lead by ordained priest)
Definition of attendees: Average number of persons (including children) who attend Liturgy (main weekly worship service) on a typical (not festive) Sunday.
Definition of adherents: Total number of persons participating in the life of a parish (congregation): counting adults and children, regular and occasional attendees, paid stewards and persons who do not contribute financially.
Dual affiliation: No

Hungarian Reformed Churches (Additional) [REF–Hung Ref Add'l]
Definition of congregations: The Hungarian Reformed Federation of America is a service and fellowship organization serving Hungarian (Magyar) Reformed congregations in several denominations. In December, 2010 its website (www.hrfa.org) listed 65 congregations. Thirty of these are members of the United Church of Christ (CA – 2; CT – 3; FL – 1; IL – 1; IN – 1; MI – 2; NJ – 4; NY – 2; OH – 8; PA – 6). Four are members of the Presbyterian Church (USA) (NJ – 2; OH – 1; PA – 1). One church (VA) is a member of the Reformed Presbyterian Church, Hanover Presbytery. The thirty remaining congregations are shown here.
See Appendix K: On-line Listings

Hutterian Brethren [MENN–Hutt Breth]
See Appendix K: On-line Listings
Comments on the accuracy of statistics: This group reports 42,800 members in the *Yearbook.*

Independent Baptist Fellowship International [BAPT–Ind Bapt Flwsp Intl]
Published directory

Independent Fundamental Churches of America [Ind Fund Churches]
Contact person(s): Tom Olson
Comments on the accuracy of statistics: This group reports 69,857 members in the *Yearbook.*

Independent Yearly Meetings of Friends [FRND–Indep Yr Mtgs]
Contact person(s): Richard H. Taylor
Date of statistics: North Pacific: 2011; Pacific: 2010
Definition of congregations: Meetings, churches, and worship groups.
Definition of attendees: N/A
Definition of members: Members
Definition of adherents: N/A
Comments on the RCMS estimating procedure for adherents: This

has been the usual format for reporting Quaker data. It does account for children. The Pacific Yearly Meeting specifically does not include younger children in its reported membership, so this formula is helpful in that regard. However, because the data provided includes so many meetings not reporting any membership, even with this formula, there is probably a significant undercount for adherents in Independent Yearly Meetings.

Dual affiliation: Yes. Five meetings (CA 2 with 92 members; ID 1 with no members reported; WA 1 with 61 members; and WY 1 with 4 members) are dually aligned to the Friends General Conference.

Comments on the accuracy of statistics: 35 local meetings out of 95 total (36.8%) are worship groups, preparatory meetings, etc. that do not report members and are shown with "zero" members. Often key members of these groups belong to other meetings. Other times these are not fully organized.

See Appendix F: Friends

Indian-American Hindu Temple Associations [HINDU–I/A Temples]

See Appendix G: Hindu Groups

International Churches of Christ [CHR–Int Chs of Christ]

Contact person(s): Kelcy Hahn

Definition of congregations: Each congregation is under its own leadership, but may be comprised of many smaller groups spread over an area that seldom meet together in one location. In general (but not always) International Churches of Christ have only one congregation per city, and the entire metropolitan area will be considered a "city." So, for example, there is one ICOC in Los Angeles, but it meets separately on multiple campuses.

Definition of attendees: not collected

Definition of members: International Churches of Christ define members as baptized, adult (including older teenage) believers who take an active part in the church's activities. Those who no longer attend or move to another city are not counted as members.

Definition of adherents: Not counted separately, but children of members attend regularly, and are not included in membership.

Comments on the RCMS estimating procedure for adherents: Yes, the described procedure is reasonably accurate for the ICOC.

Dual affiliation: No

International Council of Community Churches [Int Cou Comm Ch]

Contact person(s): Donald Ashmall

Comments on the accuracy of statistics: This group reports 250,000 members in the *Yearbook*.

International Fellowship of Bible Churches [Intl Fell Bible Ch]

See Appendix K: On-line Listings

International Fellowship of Christian Assemblies [PENT–I F Chr Assmbl]

Contact person(s): Michael Player; Christine Marini

Comments on the accuracy of statistics: This group reports 7,150 members in the *Yearbook*.

International Pentecostal Church of Christ [PENT–Int Pent C Chr]

Contact person(s): Patty Howard

Date of statistics: 2011

Definition of attendees: Highest reported attendance from either Sunday School or Morning Worship ServicesHighest reported attendance from either Sunday School or Morning Worship Services

Definition of members: Confirmed members

Definition of adherents: Inclusive members

International Pentecostal Holiness Church [PENT–Intl Pent Holiness]

Contact person(s): Damaris Cabrera; Ron Carpenter

Date of statistics: 2011

Definition of congregations: Pentecostal Holiness Church and Full Gospel Charismatic Church

Definition of attendees: Membership attendance, Sunday worship; statistics are by District.

Definition of members: 258,000 is with children 14+

Dual affiliation: No

Jain [Jain]

See Appendix K: On-line Listings

Jehovah's Witnesses [Jehovah's Witness]

See Appendix B: Address Lists

Comments on the accuracy of statistics: This group reports 974,719 members in the *Yearbook*.

Korean Presbyterian Church Abroad [PRES–Kor Pres Abroad]

See Appendix K: On-line Listings

Korean Presbyterian Church in America [PRES–Korean Pres Amer]

Published directory

Korean-American Presbyterian Church [PRES–Korean Amer Pres]

Contact person(s): David Kong

Date of statistics: November 19, 2011

Dual affiliation: No

Lutheran Church—Missouri Synod [LUTH–Luth–MO Synod]

Contact person(s): Ryan Curnutt

Date of statistics: December 31, 2010

Definition of congregations: Individual congregations which have formally joined the LCMS.

Definition of attendees: Congregation's reported weekly average attendance in worship.

Definition of members: Number of confirmed members.

Definition of adherents: Number of baptized members.

Dual affiliation: No

Lutheran Congregations in Mission for Christ [LUTH–Luth Cong Msn Chr]

See Appendix K: On-line Listings

Macedonian Orthodox Church: American Diocese [ORTHE–Macedonian Orth]

Contact person(s): Tome Stamatov; Alexei Krindatch

Date of statistics: December 2010
Definition of congregations: Parish (i.e. permanent local place of worship which is lead by ordained priest)
Definition of attendees: Average number of persons (including children) who attend Liturgy (main weekly worship service) on a typical (not festive) Sunday.
Definition of adherents: Total number of persons participating in the life of a parish (congregation): counting adults and children, regular and occasional attendees, paid stewards and persons who do not contribute financially.
Dual affiliation: No

Mahayana Buddhism [BUDD–Mahayana]
See Appendix E: Buddhist Groups

Malankara Archdiocese of the Syrian Orthodox Church in North America [ORTHO–Malan Syr Orth]
Contact person(s): Archbishop Mor Titus Yeldho; Alexei Krindatch
Date of statistics: December 2010
Definition of congregations: Parish (i.e. permanent local place of worship which is lead by ordained priest)
Definition of attendees: Average number of persons (including children) who attend Liturgy (main weekly worship service) on a typical (not festive) Sunday.
Definition of adherents: Total number of persons participating in the life of a parish (congregation): counting adults and children, regular and occasional attendees, paid stewards and persons who do not contribute financially.
Dual affiliation: No

Malankara Orthodox Syrian Church [ORTHO–Malan Dioc Am]
Contact person(s): Metropolitan Zachariah Mar Nicholovos; Alexei Krindatch
Date of statistics: December 2010
Definition of congregations: Parish (i.e. permanent local place of worship which is lead by ordained priest)
Definition of attendees: Average number of persons (including children) who attend Liturgy (main weekly worship service) on a typical (not festive) Sunday.
Definition of adherents: Total number of persons participating in the life of a parish (congregation): counting adults and children, regular and occasional attendees, paid stewards and persons who do not contribute financially.
Dual affiliation: No

Maranatha Amish-Mennonite [MENN–Mara Amish-Menn]
See Appendix D: Amish Groups

Mennonite Christian Fellowship [MENN–Menn Chr Fell]
See Appendix D: Amish Groups

Mennonite Church USA [MENN–Mennonite USA]
Contact person(s): Nancy Kauffmann
Date of statistics: November 11, 2011
Definition of congregations: A faith community who holds to Anabaptist theology as expressed in The Confession of Faith from a Mennonite Perspective.
Definition of attendees: Unable to give figures, but would define this as the total number of people whether members, attenders, visitors on a Sunday morning.
Definition of members: Persons who are baptized into the Mennonite Church (baptism and joining a local congregation are held together) and individuals who have transferred their membership from another Mennonite congregation or faith tradition into a local Mennonite congregation. They would identify with The Confession of Faith from a Mennonite Perspective.
Definition of adherents: Do not have that information available.
Comments on the RCMS estimating procedure for adherents: We would be fine with your procedure for estimating total adherents.
Dual affiliation: No. We would have a number of pastors of groups who are a part of the Emergent Church movement who have asked to have a more formal relationship with MC USA. We would hold their credentials but their group would not have formally joined.
Comments on the accuracy of statistics: We recently transferred to a new data system (2010). We are in the process of working on clean up and checking information. This report is 90% plus accurate at this point.

Metropolitan Community Churches, Universal Fellowship of [Metro Comm Ch]
Contact person(s): Barbara Crabtree
Date of statistics: December 2010
Definition of congregations: Bodies that have met the criteria, as established by the Council of Elders and approved by the Governing Board, for affiliation and recognition as "church".
Definition of attendees: Total reported attendance divided by number of weeks in which congregation held at least 1 worship service.
Definition of members: As defined by local church bylaws, articles of incorporation and/or governing documents.
Definition of adherents: No data
Comments on the RCMS estimating procedure for adherents: We believe that the procedure described in the Instructions will result in a significant underestimate of the number of total adherents. At issue is the fact that a number of our churches are now streaming their worship services live, and their (informal) reporting of that indicates they have a significant number of remote participants. An additional point of awareness; we do have a relatively specific ministry to and among the LGBT population and that population is much more widely distributed than are our "brick & mortar" churches, and we're keenly aware that our current methods of tracking impact are distinctly inadequate for "the digital world."
Dual affiliation: Yes. 2 of 150 congregations reporting are known to maintain affiliation with another group.

Midwest Beachy Amish-Mennonite [MENN–Midw Bchy Am-Menn]
See Appendix D: Amish Groups

Midwest Congregational Christian Fellowship [CONG–Midw Cong Chr Fel]
Contact person(s): Richard H. Taylor
Date of statistics: August 31, 2008
Definition of congregations: Churches
Definition of attendees: Average Attendance
Definition of members: Total Members
Definition of adherents: N/A
Comments on the RCMS estimating procedure for adherents: This does account for children. However, since Midwest Fellowship attendance outstrips membership, the total adherents estimated is probably too low.
Dual affiliation: No
Comments on the accuracy of statistics: 23 of 25 churches and 22 of 25 attendance is as of the collection date. The other numbers were inserted from earlier reports.

Missionary Church [Missionary Ch]
Contact person(s): Bob Ransom
Date of statistics: December 31, 2010
Definition of congregations: 15 or more members
Definition of attendees: Weekly, main worship service
Definition of members: Age 16 or older
Dual affiliation: No

Moravian Church in America—Alaska Province [MORAV–Morav Ch-AK]
Contact person(s): Mike Riess

Moravian Church in America—Northern Province [MORAV–Morav Ch-North]
Contact person(s): Mike Riess

Moravian Church in America—Southern Province [MORAV–Morav Ch-South]
Contact person(s): Mike Riess

Muslim Estimate [Muslim Est]
See Appendix I: Muslim Estimate

National Association of Congregational Christian Churches [CONG–Cong Chr, NA]
Contact person(s): Thomas Richard; Richard Taylor
Date of statistics: Late 2010 and early 2011, most recent fiscal year
Definition of congregations: Full member churches. "Churches which have officially voted to join the Association and have been received by vote of an annual meetings."
Definition of members: "Total Active Members"
Comments on the RCMS estimating procedure for adherents: This has been the traditional method used for NACCC data.
Dual affiliation: Yes. Dual align limited but includes some large congregations. Also a few federated churches. With United Church of Christ; Conservative Congregational Christian Conference; Evangelical Association of Reformed and Congregational Christian Churches; and American Baptist Churches.
Comments on the accuracy of statistics: 377 churches are from current data. Twenty churches are from earlier data. Three are estimated from other sources.

National Baptist Convention of America, Inc. [BAPT–NBC Amer]
See Appendix C: African American Bodies

National Baptist Convention, USA, Inc. [BAPT–NBC USA]
See Appendix C: African American Bodies

National Missionary Baptist Convention, Inc. [BAPT–Natl Mis Bapt Conv]
See Appendix C: African American Bodies

National Spiritualist Association of Churches [Nat Spirit Asso]
See Appendix K: On-line Listings
Comments on the accuracy of statistics: This group reports 3,530 members in the *Yearbook*.

New Apostolic Church of North America, National Organization of the [New Apost Ch]
Contact person(s): Stefan Heinzelman; Allison Swierk
Comments on the accuracy of statistics: This group reports 41,863 members in the *Yearbook*.

New Testament Association of Independent Baptist Churches [BAPT–NT Ind Bapt]
Published directory

Non-denominational Christian Churches [Non-denom Chr Chs]
See Appendix J: Non-denominational Christian Churches

North American Baptist Conference [BAPT–N Am Bapt Conf]
Published directory

North American Lutheran Church [LUTH–Nor Amer Luth C]
See Appendix K: On-line Listings

Old Order River Brethren [BRETH–Old Ord Rvr Br]
Contact person(s): Stephen Scott
Date of statistics: December 31, 2010
Definition of members: Baptized Members
Definition of adherents: Dependent non-member children, regular non-member visitors, and members.
Dual affiliation: No
Comments on the accuracy of statistics: Exact counts from church directory which is regularly updated.

Open Bible Standard Churches, Inc. [PENT–Open Bible Std]
Contact person(s): Linda Dixon; Jeff Farmer

(Original) Church of God [PENT–Orig Ch of God]
See Appendix K: On-line Listings

Orthodox Church in America [ORTHE–Orth Ch in Amer]
Contact person(s): Very Rev. John A. Jillions; Alexei Krindatch
Date of statistics: December 2010
Definition of congregations: Parish (i.e. permanent local place of

worship which is lead by ordained priest)

Definition of attendees: Average number of persons (including children) who attend Liturgy (main weekly worship service) on a typical (not festive) Sunday.

Definition of adherents: Total number of persons participating in the life of a parish (congregation): counting adults and children, regular and occasional attendees, paid stewards and persons who do not contribute financially.

Dual affiliation: No

Orthodox Judaism [JUD–Orth]

See Appendix H: Jewish Groups

Orthodox Presbyterian Church [PRES–Orth Pres Ch]

Contact person(s): George R. Cottenden; Luke Brown

Date of statistics: End of Year 2010

Definition of congregations: Comprised of 265 organized churches and 55 unorganized mission works.

Definition of attendees: Weekly average morning worship attendance in November 2010.

Definition of members: Includes 21,390 communicant members and 489 ministers.

Definition of adherents: Total of 21,390 communicant members, 489 ministers, and 7,572 baptized children (non-communicants).

Comments on the RCMS estimating procedure for adherents: Our 2010 statistics are based on reports received from congregations comprising 98 percent of the total church membership.

Dual affiliation: No

Patriarchal Parishes of the Russian Orthodox Church in the USA [ORTHE–Rus Orth Moscow]

Contact person(s): His Eminence Archbishop Justinian (Ovchinnikov); Alexei Krindatch

Date of statistics: December 2010

Definition of congregations: Parish (i.e. permanent local place of worship which is lead by ordained priest)

Definition of attendees: Average number of persons (including children) who attend Liturgy (main weekly worship service) on a typical (not festive) Sunday.

Definition of adherents: : Total number of persons participating in the life of a parish (congregation): counting adults and children, regular and occasional attendees, paid stewards and persons who do not contribute financially.

Dual affiliation: No

Pentecostal Church of God [PENT–Pent Ch of God]

Contact person(s): Kimberly Ming

Date of statistics: June 2011

Definition of congregations: Those who attend services on a regular basis – Sun. AM worship

Definition of members: Member numbers include children 16+ and in some church 18+ is required.

Dual affiliation: No

Pentecostal Fire-Baptized Holiness Church [PENT–Fire Bapt Hol Ch]

See Appendix K: On-line Listings

Comments on the accuracy of statistics: This group reports 223 members in the *Yearbook.*

Pentecostal Free Will Baptist Church, Inc. [PENT–Pent FW Bapt]

See Appendix K: On-line Listings

Comments on the accuracy of statistics: This group reports 16,000 members in the *Yearbook.*

Pillar of Fire [Pillar of Fire]

Contact person(s): Joe Gross

Polish National Catholic Church [OCATH–Pol Natl Cath]

See Appendix K: On-line Listings

Presbyterian Church (U.S.A.) [PRES–Presb Ch (USA)]

Contact person(s): Kris Valerius

Presbyterian Church in America [PRES–Presb Ch Amer]

Contact person(s): Susan Cullen; Roy Taylor

Presbyterian Reformed Church [PRES–Pres Ref]

See Appendix K: On-line Listings

Primitive Baptists, Eastern District Association of [BAPT–Prim Bapt E Dst]

Contact person(s): Danny Lawson

Definition of congregations: Number of churches. This includes 57 churches in 4 states, TN, VA, OH, KY. There are 22 in VA, 24 in TN, 7 in KY and 4 in OH.

Definition of attendees: This number is not known, these are small country churches so attendance varies but would average 20 - 25 or so.

Definition of members: Total Church membership is 5,065, this includes everyone who has been saved and joined the church, it does not account for those not attending services, etc. Only the individual churches can answer this question, the association does not have a record of this information.

Primitive Methodist Church in the USA [METH–Prim Meth Ch]

See Appendix K: On-line Listings

Comments on the accuracy of statistics: This group reports 6,588 members in the *Yearbook.*

Progressive National Baptist Convention, Inc. [BAPT–Prog NBC]

See Appendix C: African American Bodies

Protestant Reformed Churches in America [REF–Prot Ref Chs]

Contact person(s): Don Doezema

Reconstructionist Judaism [JUD–Reconst]

See Appendix H: Jewish Groups

Reform Judaism [JUD–Reform]

See Appendix H: Jewish Groups

Reformed Baptist Churches [BAPT–Ref Bapt Ch]

See Appendix K: On-line Listings

Reformed Church in America [REF–Ref Ch in Am]
Contact person(s): Meredith Nieuwsma
Date of statistics: Calendar year 2010
Definition of congregations: Organized RCA churches (this excludes new church starts that have not officially organized).
Definition of attendees: The average number of worshippers each Sunday as reported by the individual church.
Definition of members: "Members" are all confessing members (those who have received Christian baptism and have been received by the board of elders through profession of faith, reaffirmation of faith, or presentation of a satisfactory certificate of transfer of membership from another Christian church), baptized members (those who have received Christian baptism but who have not been received by the board of elders as confessing members), and inactive members (those who have been removed by the board of elders from the confessing membership list).
Definition of adherents: "Adherents" are those who participate in the life, work, and worship of the church, whether a member or not.
Dual affiliation: Yes. The RCA has 17 organized congregations that are union or federated congregations. Union congregations are churches that have dual affiliation with the RCA and either the Christian Reformed Church in North America, the Presbyterian Church (USA), the United Church of Christ, or the Advent Lutheran Church. A Federated congregation is a church that has at least dual denominational affiliation with a variety of other protestant denominations.

Reformed Church in the United States [REF–Ref Ch in U.S.]
Contact person(s): Pastor Fagrey

Reformed Mennonite Church [MENN–Ref Mennonite]
Contact person(s): Glenn M. Gross

Reformed Presbyterian Church General Assembly [PRES–Ref Pres GA]
See Appendix K: On-line Listings

Reformed Presbyterian Church Hanover Presbytery [PRES–Ref Pres Han]
See Appendix K: On-line Listings

Reformed Presbyterian Church in the United States [PRES–Ref Pres US]
See Appendix K: On-line Listings

Reformed Presbyterian Church of North America [PRES–Ref Pres of NA]
Contact person(s): Thomas G. Reid
Date of statistics: December 31, 2010
Definition of congregations: Number of congregations
Definition of attendees: Average attendance for the year 2010
Definition of members: Full (someone who is both baptized and communicant) membership
Definition of adherents: Total (someone who is baptized and communicant OR who is only baptized) membership for December 31, 2010. Note: we baptize infants.

Romanian Orthodox Archdiocese in Americas [ORTHE–Romania Orth Ar]
Contact person(s): His Eminence Archbishop Nicolae (Condrea); Alexei Krindatch
Date of statistics: December 2010
Definition of congregations: Parish (i.e. permanent local place of worship which is lead by ordained priest)
Definition of attendees: Average number of persons (including children) who attend Liturgy (main weekly worship service) on a typical (not festive) Sunday.
Definition of adherents: Total number of persons participating in the life of a parish (congregation): counting adults and children, regular and occasional attendees, paid stewards and persons who do not contribute financially.
Dual affiliation: No

Russian Orthodox Church Outside of Russia [ORTHE–Rus Orth Abroad]
Contact person(s): His Grace Bishop Jerome of Manhattan; Alexei Krindatch
Date of statistics: December 2010
Definition of congregations: Parish (i.e. permanent local place of worship which is lead by ordained priest)
Definition of attendees: Average number of persons (including children) who attend Liturgy (main weekly worship service) on a typical (not festive) Sunday.
Definition of adherents: : Total number of persons participating in the life of a parish (congregation): counting adults and children, regular and occasional attendees, paid stewards and persons who do not contribute financially.
Dual affiliation: No

Salvation Army [Salvation Army]
Contact person(s): Sylvia Kirkland

Schwenkfelder Church [Schwenkfelder]
Contact person(s): David W. Luz
Date of statistics: Dec. 31, 2010
Dual Affiliation: Yes. One church (Olivet) is jointly affiliated with the United Church of Christ.

Serbian Orthodox Church in North America [ORTHE–Serb Orth USA]
Contact person(s): His Grace Bishop Maxim; Alexei Krindatch
Date of statistics: December 2010
Definition of congregations: Parish (i.e. permanent local place of worship which is lead by ordained priest)
Definition of attendees: Average number of persons (including children) who attend Liturgy (main weekly worship service) on a typical (not festive) Sunday.
Definition of adherents: Total number of persons participating in the life of a parish (congregation): counting adults and children, regular and occasional attendees, paid stewards and persons who do not contribute financially.
Dual affiliation: No

Seventh Day Baptist General Conference, USA and Canada (BAPT–S-D Baptist Gen Con)
Contact person(s): Rob Appel

Seventh-day Adventist Church [Sev Day Adv]
Contact person(s): Monte Sahlin

Shinto [Shinto]
See Appendix K: On-line Listings

Sikh [Sikh]
See Appendix K: On-line Listings

Southern Baptist Convention [BAPT–So Bapt Conv]
Contact person(s): Richie Stanley
Date of statistics: 2010
Definition of congregations: Southern Baptists have 2 categories of congregations. Churches have been constituted and are (theoretically) self-supporting. Church-type missions are typically newer, have not constituted as a church, and are likely receiving assistance from a sponsoring church. The distinction between these 2 categories continues to blur over time. In previous decades the SBC data provided to RCMS included churches only. For the 2010 data it seems more appropriate to include church-type missions also. The 50,816 SBC congregations for 2010 include 45,768 churches and 5,048 church-type missions.
Definition of attendees: Average number of persons in the primary worship service(s) of the congregation.
Definition of members: Total membership of the congregation.
Comments on the RCMS estimating procedure for adherents: The RCMS estimation procedure for calculating adherents is acceptable.
Dual affiliation: Yes. It would not be unusual for African American Southern Baptist congregations to also be affiliated with one of the traditionally African American Baptist denominations. There are about 3,500 African American Southern Baptist congregations.
Comments on the accuracy of statistics: We did our best!

Southern Methodist Church [METH–So Methodist]
Contact person(s): John Hucks
Definition of members: Some children are reflected in membership numbers because membership is offered to all ages. But the minimum voting age for members is 18, more or less.
Dual affiliation: No
Comments on the accuracy of statistics: This group reports 5,000 members in the *Yearbook*.

Swedenborgian Church [Swedenborgian]
Contact person(s): Renee Hellenbrecht
Date of statistics: December 31, 2010
Definition of congregations: Groups that have been recognized as member societies by one of our regional associations.
Definition of members: Full members are 18 years of age as of December 31 of the reporting year, and have been confirmed into membership by their respective congregations. (Congregations may have their own membership requirements.)
Definition of adherents: We do not track this data. We only ask that active and inactive full members (i.e., those that have been confirmed into membership) be reported. Some groups will include associate members, child members, friends, etc. when reporting, but we do not track these, and, again, not everyone submits these.
Dual affiliation: No
Comments on the accuracy of statistics: This group reports 1,521 members in the *Yearbook*.

Syriac Orthodox Church of Antioch [ORTHO–Syrian Orth Ch]
Contact person(s): Metropolitan Mor Cyril Aphrem Karim; Alexei Krindatch
Date of statistics: December 2010
Definition of congregations: Parish (i.e. permanent local place of worship which is lead by ordained priest)
Definition of attendees: Average number of persons (including children) who attend Liturgy (main weekly worship service) on a typical (not festive) Sunday.
Definition of adherents: Total number of persons participating in the life of a parish (congregation): counting adults and children, regular and occasional attendees, paid stewards and persons who do not contribute financially.
Dual affiliation: No

Tampico Amish-Mennonite [MENN–Tamp Amish-Menn]
See Appendix D: Amish Groups

Tao [Tao]
See Appendix K: On-line Listings

Theravada Buddhism [BUDD–Theravada]
See Appendix E: Buddhist Groups

Traditional Hindu Temples [HINDU–Trad Temples]
See Appendix G: Hindu Groups

U.S. Mennonite Brethren [MENN–Menn Br US Conf]
Contact person(s): Donna Sullivan

Ukrainian Orthodox Church of the USA [ORTHE–Ukrainian Orth]
Contact person(s): Anthony Sharba; Alexei Krindatch
Date of statistics: December 2010
Definition of congregations: Parish (i.e. permanent local place of worship which is lead by ordained priest)
Definition of attendees: Average number of persons (including children) who attend Liturgy (main weekly worship service) on a typical (not festive) Sunday.
Definition of adherents: Total number of persons participating in the life of a parish (congregation): counting adults and children, regular and occasional attendees, paid stewards and persons who do not contribute financially.
Dual affiliation: No

Unaffiliated Conservative Amish-Mennonite Church [MENN–Unaffil Amish-Menn]

See Appendix D: Amish Groups

Unaffiliated Friends Meetings [FRND–Unaffl Mtgs]

Contact person(s): Richard H. Taylor

See Appendix F: Friends

Union of Messianic Jewish Congregations [MJEW–Union Mes Cong]

See Appendix K: On-line Listings

Unitarian Universalist Association of Congregations [Unit Univ]

Contact person(s): Michelle Rediker

Date of statistics: February 28, 2011

Definition of congregations: Please see the following pages:
http://www.uua.org/uuagovernance/bylaws/ruleiii/7096.shtml
http://www.uua.org/uuarelations/
Emerging congregations are not included in UUA statistics.

Definition of attendees: Please see the following page:
http://www.uua.org/directory/data/faq/certifyingmembership/20576.shtml

Definition of members: The definition of a "Certified Member" is up to individual congregations, according to their bylaws. Most congregations define members as those who would be eligible to vote in a congregational meeting, in other words, the "voting members."

Definition of adherents: The UUA does not track the number of Adherents, but we do calculate, annually, the number of Certified Members + Religious Education Enrollees. That was used as the number of Adherents for this exercise. "Adherents" may not, however, include family members who occasionally or even regularly attend services but are not "registered," paying/supporting members of a congregation. If an individual, a partner or spouse in this instance, is not a registered, voting, or supporting member of a congregation, they would not be included in the Certified Member tally, and therefore not counted as an "adherent."

Dual affiliation: Yes. There were 23 multi-denominational congregations that certified during this certification period. Multi-denominational congregations hold membership in more than one denomination; the United Church of Christ is a common example. Only the Unitarian Universalist members of such congregations are counted for Certified Members.

Comments on the accuracy of statistics: The data provided was derived from data collected during the UUA Certification period, then stored as a static numbers collectively known as the "Annual Report of Membership" statistics.

UUA Annual Report of Membership Production Notes, 3/4/2011

1. Beginning in 2010, annual totals are computed for the twelve months ending the last day of February. The 2010 Annual Report of Membership issued on March 1, 2010, for example, is based on data reported by congregations during March 2009 through February 2010. (GA Certification closes on February 1, and the extra month allows late-comers to be accounted for, data to be examined and cleaned up, totals to be double-checked, reports to be formatted, etc.).

2. If a congregation leaves the Association during a report year, its numbers are not included in that year's report. For example, if a congregation leaves the UUA in September 2010, its numbers will not be included in the 2011 Annual Report of Membership published on 3/1/11 and based on numbers reported during March 2010 through February 2011.

3. When a congregation reports more than once during a report year the latest number is used.

4. For the 2010 Annual Report, all prior years were restated so they would be consistent with tabulation based on the last day of February. In future Annual Reports, data already reported in a previous year WILL NOT CHANGE IN SUBSEQUENT YEARS. That is, for each new report year, that year's data will be appended to the Report. Previous years' data will not be recomputed each year as it was prior to 2010. Changes made retroactively will not be reflected in future Annual Reports.

5. Canadian congregations who left the UUA to join the CUC several years ago are omitted from the tabulations altogether.

6. Numbers reported by each congregation are included in the Annual Report of Membership whether they are considered "certified" or not. Congregations report membership numbers throughout the year, not just during "certification" between 11/15 and 2/1, the period for GA delegate purposes. Also, congregations may not achieve "certification" for a variety of reasons, including failing to meet financial criteria. We count the numbers they report anyway, since this is a report about how many people are Uus, not how many Uus qualify to be represented at GA. So this report is not "Certified Membership"; merely "Membership".

7. This report will not match numbers published elsewhere. Changes are made and approved throughout the year that affect totals shown on the website, in the Directory, as part of ad hoc data requests, etc. This report is a static "snapshot" of a point in time (i.e. March 1), and historic data will not vary from year to year, even if the underlying historic data indeed changes.

8. This report may not match the "Certified members" report shown online as this includes counts that are not "certified."

9. When a congregation does not report membership during the report year, the last reported number is used for subsequent years.

United Catholic Church, Inc. [OCATH–Un Cath Ch]

See Appendix K: On-line Listings

United Church of Christ [Un C of Christ]

Contact person(s): Destiny Hisey

Date of statistics: December 31, 2010

Definition of congregations: We rely on our congregations to file reports annually to obtain the data. Not all congregations file. For those that do not file, their data is carried over from the last year filed on record and is included in our numbers.

Definition of attendees: Reported by local congregations as average weekly attendance in worship service.

Definition of members: In accordance with the custom and usage of a Local Church, persons become members by (a) baptism and either confirmation or profession of faith in Jesus Christ as Lord and Savior; (b) reaffirmation or reprofession of faith; or (c) letter of transfer or certification from other Christian churches. All persons who are or shall become members of a Local Church of the United Church of Christ are thereby members of the United Church of Christ. – Constitution paragraphs 11 & 12

Comments on the RCMS estimating procedure for adherents: Procedure is acceptable

Dual affiliation: Yes. There are 232 United Church of Christ congregations dually aligned with other denominational groups and 163 federated with other denominational groups. The four most common denomination groups to which UCC church relate are Baptist bodies (primarily American Baptist Churches), the Christian Church (Disciples of Christ), the United Methodist Church and the Presbyterian Church, USA.

Comments on the accuracy of statistics: A new data warehouse was developed and used for the 2010 data collection. Unfortunately, we are currently unable to determine our response rate for the 2010 data collection period. Previous year's response rate of congregations to the annual statistical report has been between 66% and 69%. There is nothing to indicate the 2010 data collection response was any different. For congregations that did not report, the most recently reported data was used.

United Holy Church of America, Inc. [PENT–United Holy Ch]

See Appendix K: On-line Listings

United Methodist Church [METH–Un Methodist]

Contact person(s): Laura Chambers

Date of statistics: December 31, 2010

Definition of congregations: "The local church is a connectional society of persons who have been baptized, have professed their faith in Christ, and have assumed the vows of membership in The United Methodist Church. They gather in fellowship to hear the Word of God, receive the sacraments, praise and worship the triune God, and carry forward the work that Christ has committed to his church" (Paragraph 203, the 2008 Book of Discipline). Number of congregations includes organized (chartered) churches with membership.

Definition of attendees: "Average combined attendance at all services held on a weekly basis as the primary opportunity for worship" (Table 1 of the Local Church Report to the Annual Conference).

Definition of members: "The professing membership of a local United Methodist church shall include all baptized people who have come into membership by profession of faith through appropriate services of the baptismal covenant in the ritual or by transfer from other churches" (Paragraph 215.2, the 2008 Book of Discipline).

Definition of adherents: Total includes full (professing) members, baptized members and constituent members. "The baptized membership of a local United Methodist church shall include baptized all baptized people who have received Christian baptism in the local congregation or elsewhere, or whose membership has been transferred to the United Methodist church subsequent to baptism in some other congregation" (Paragraph 215.1, the 2008 Book of Discipline). "Constituent members include all unbaptized children, church school members, and others who are not members of the church but are in a relationship with the congregation and for whom the local church has pastoral responsibility" (Table 1 of the Local Church Report to the Annual Conference).

Dual affiliation: Possible. "Ecumenical shared ministries are ecumenical congregations formed by a local United Methodist church and one or more local congregations of other Christian traditions. Forms of ecumenical shared ministries include: (a) a federated church, in which one congregation is related to two or more denominations, with persons choosing to hold membership in one or the other of the denominations; (b) a union church, in which a congregation with one unified membership roll is related to two denominations; (c) a merged church, in which two or more congregations of different denominations from one congregation that related to only one of the constituent denominations; (d) a yoked parish, in which congregations of different denominations share a pastor" (Paragraph 208, the 2008 Book of Discipline). Congregations are instructed to only report their United Methodist membership to this office.

United Pentecostal Church International [PENT–Un Pent Ch Intl]

Contact person(s): Diana Dunlap; Jerry Jones

Date of statistics: November 29, 2011

Definition of congregations: churches pastored by a licensed UPCI minister

Definition of attendees: n/a

Dual affiliation: No

Comments on the accuracy of statistics: This group reports 800,000 members in the *Yearbook*.

United Pentecostal Council of the Assemblies of God [PENT–Un Pent Asbl God]

See Appendix K: On-line Listings

United Reformed Churches in North America [REF–Un Ref Chs N.A.]

See Appendix K: On-line Listings

United Zion Church [BRETH–United Zion Ch]

Contact person(s): Charles Brown

Definition of congregations: Separate churches.

Definition of members: Baptized members over the age of 16

Unity Churches, Association of [Unity Ch]

Contact person(s): Young Bae

Unity of the Brethren [MORAV–Unity Of Breth]

See Appendix K: On-line Listings

Comments on the accuracy of statistics: This group reports 3,090 members in the *Yearbook*.

Vajrayana Buddhism [BUDD–Vajrayana]

See Appendix E: Buddhist Groups

Vicariate for the Palestinian/Jordanian Orthodox Christian Communities [ORTHE–Pal/Jor Orth]

Contact person(s): George Jweinat; Alexei Krindatch
Date of statistics: December 2010
Definition of congregations: Parish (i.e. permanent local place of worship which is lead by ordained priest)
Definition of attendees: Average number of persons (including children) who attend Liturgy (main weekly worship service) on a typical (not festive) Sunday.
Definition of adherents: Total number of persons participating in the life of a parish (congregation): counting adults and children, regular and occasional attendees, paid stewards and persons who do not contribute financially.
Dual affiliation: No

Vineyard USA [PENT–Vineyard]

Contact person(s): Pam Trautmann; Berten Waggoner
Date of statistics: 12/31/2010
Definition of congregations: active churches year end 2010
Definition of attendees: weekly attendance numbers divided by number of active churches year end 2010
Definition of members: total number of members
Definition of adherents: total number of weekly attendance, including children
Dual affiliation: No
Comments on the accuracy of statistics: Annual online census completed by local churches – some answers are estimated, information is automatically entered into national database (not manually)

Wesleyan Church [METH–Wesleyan]

Contact person(s): Ronald Kelly; Ronald McClung
Date of statistics: August 31, 2010
Definition of congregations: All developing and established churches; does not include missions.
Definition of attendees: Total number present at all primary worship services.
Definition of members: All covenant members of the church, those who agree to abide by the covenant membership commitments.
Definition of adherents: Thirty percent more than the average attendance. This is the rule of thumb accepted in some church growth circles, considering that 30 percent more than the average attendance are absent each Sunday, due to illness, travel, etc.
Dual affiliation: No
Comments on the accuracy of statistics: These statistics are taken from the annual statistical reports submitted by local congregations and districts.

Wisconsin Evangelical Lutheran Synod [LUTH–Wisc Ev Luth Syn]

Contact person(s): Jan Lampe
Date of statistics: December 31, 2010
Definition of congregations: Established congregations who support the work of the Wisconsin Evangelical Lutheran Synod (WELS)
Definition of attendees: Combined totals of Average Worship Attendance submitted by WELS congregations
Definition of members: Members who have been confirmed or profess the beliefs of the WELS and have been accepted as communicants within a WELS congregation
Definition of adherents: Members who have been baptized or are communicants in the WELS
Dual affiliation: No
Comments on the accuracy of statistics: Verification of submitted statistics per each WELS church can be found at https://connect.wels.net. Click on Synod Administration/ then Ministry of Christian Giving/ on the left hand column WELS Statistical Report/ scroll down to Congregational Statistics and choose Details – Excel Sheet

Zoroastrian [Zoroastrian]

See Appendix K: On-line Listings

Appendix B
Address Lists

Companies wishing to market to religious congregations often purchase mailing lists. Such address lists are a possible source for locating religious congregations. In addition to mailing addresses, these lists often contain indications of congregational size, with membership and attendance figures included. The Operations Committee explored this possibility for the 2010 religion census.

Two of the first denominations to report data were the Churches of Christ and the Church of the Nazarene. In comparing their 2010 denominational reports to those obtained through the mailing lists, it appeared that a majority of each group's churches was included in the address listing. Approximately 54% of Churches of Christ were included and 77% of Churches of the Nazarene. Respectively, 80% and 93% of their membership was accounted for from the address lists, and 65% and 87% of their reported attendance figures.

(Part of the difficulty for non-denominational data collectors is determining which denomination a church belongs to. Denominations with similar names, such as Churches of Christ, United Church of Christ, Christian Churches and Churches of Christ, and Churches of Christ in Christian Union, are especially difficult to categorize well. This may help to explain why the address list count for Churches of Christ is less complete than for the Church of the Nazarene with a relatively unique name.)

The Operations Committee determined that the address lists would not be used when denominational sources were available. However, nine large religious bodies had traditionally not supplied information for previous studies, so the address lists could be used to provide some information for these groups.

	Reported in *Yearbook**	
Group	**Congregations**	**Membership**
African Methodist Episcopal Church	4,174	2,500,000
African Methodist Episcopal Zion Church	3,310	1,443,405
Christian Methodist Episcopal Church	3,500	850,000
Church of God in Christ	15,300	5,499,875
Jehovah's Witnesses	10,883	974,719
National Baptist Convention of America, Inc.	2,500	3,500,000
National Baptist Convention, USA, Inc.	33,000	8,200,000
National Missionary Baptist Convention, Inc.	Unknown	2,500,000
Progressive National Baptist Convention, Inc.	2,000	2,500,000

* *Yearbook of American and Canadian Churches: 2010*

All but one of these groups historically focuses on African American congregations, and Appendix C will explain further data collection efforts for those denominations.

The address list information for Jehovah's Witnesses was known to be incomplete. Only 5,769 Kingdom Hall locations were given out of 10,883 reported by the group. The Operations Committee determined that membership and attendance sizes were especially inadequate. Fewer than 10,000 attendees were included on the address list. Well over half the congregations on the list were assigned a membership of exactly 350.

Efforts were made to obtain further information directly from the denominational offices, but these were unsuccessful. It was decided to list the known locations in the book with no other information included.

Appendix C
African American Church Bodies

Traditionally, church bodies focused on the African American population have been less focused on gathering statistics than those groups largely composed of European Americans. This has made it difficult for such groups to take part in religion censuses focused on congregational location and size.

For the 2010 religion census, the Operations Committee obtained mailing lists for the eight largest historically African American denominations:

African Methodist Episcopal Church
African Methodist Episcopal Zion Church
Christian Methodist Episcopal Church
Church of God in Christ
National Baptist Convention of America, Inc.
National Baptist Convention, USA, Inc.
National Missionary Baptist Convention, Inc.
Progressive National Baptist Convention, Inc.

(See Appendix B for further information on such address lists.)

Based on the reported membership sizes included on the address lists, less than 50% of any group's churches or members were able to be identified. Still, the available locations did represent nearly four million people associated with specific religious congregations, so the Operations Committee decided to include this information in the 2010 religion census if no better information could be obtained.

Further efforts were made to gather denominational statistics. The preliminary results were shared with the groups, but none of the denominations was able to supply further details. However, three groups did have on-line church locators, so additional congregation locations were identified for the African Methodist Episcopal Church, African Methodist Episcopal Church Zion, and Christian Methodist Episcopal Church. For each congregation located in this way, a membership of 100 was assigned. This represented the modal size of Protestant churches that were reported to the data collection office.

For the African Methodist Episcopal Church, this yielded approximately the correct number of congregations, though the membership figures are only about one-third of their official reports. For other groups, the church counts range from 11% to 50% of reported numbers, and membership figures are from 7% to 28% of the reported amounts.

An adherent formula was used to account for children likely to be associated with each church in addition to adult members. The result is 4,877,067 adherents identified as part of eight historically African American denominations in the United States in 2010.

Additionally, three smaller church bodies that had on-line directories available are described as predominantly African American: Church of Our Lord Jesus Christ of the Apostolic Faith, Inc.; Cumberland Presbyterian Church in America; and United Holy Church of America, Inc. No adherent information was available, so only the locations are included in this study.

	Reported in Yearbook*		Reported in Religion Census	
Group	**Congregations**	**Membership**	**Congregations**	**Members**
African Methodist Episcopal Church	4,174	2,500,000	4,256	827,663
African Methodist Episcopal Zion Church	3,310	1,443,405	1,657	246,285
Christian Methodist Episcopal Church	3,500	850,000	1,462	236,242
Church of God in Christ	15,300	5,499,875	2,966	506,106
National Baptist Convention of America, Inc.	2,500	3,500,000	575	246,044
National Baptist Convention, USA, Inc.	33,000	8,200,000	3,536	1,535,087
National Missionary Baptist Convention, Inc.	Unknown	2,500,000	1,283	213,275
Progressive National Baptist Convention, Inc.	2,000	2,500,000	390	167,286

* *Yearbook of American and Canadian Churches: 2010*

Appendix D
Amish Groups

[Editor's note: Two sets of Amish data were collected in separate studies. Each of the methodologies is described below.]

Amish Religious Membership Count

The purpose of this project is to obtain a county based count of membership in the religious sect known as the Amish. This group consists of a number of different affiliations or fellowships, ranging from groups who resist almost all forms of modern technology to more progressive groups who increasingly embrace contemporary forms of technology. However, what all the variations on the Amish have in common are historical roots which go back to a specific offshoot of the Protestant Reformation in Zurich, Switzerland that also spawned other unique Anabaptist groups who practice only adult baptism, such as the Mennonites and the Hutterites, and a reliance on horsepower for local travel and farm work.

Two dimensions of the Amish subculture help facilitate my ability to conduct a county by county census of Amish religious membership. First, the Amish maintain a small scale to their social organization. For example, church districts (of which there are now over 1,750) are subdivided into separate districts if the number of households exceeds 45, and new church elders (bishop, minister, deacon) are nominated and selected by lottery from among the male members. This form of social organization reflects the strong community orientation of the Amish sect, which also means that it is nearly impossible for an adult, baptized member to be inactive (i.e., nominal membership) for any period of time without pressure and ensuing sanctions (including shunning and excommunication) from their church group (with exception for illness or other forms of incapacitation). Hence, a count of adult, baptized Amish members is 99 percent identical with active involvement or religiosity.

Second, the extended family is important to the Amish as a form of social capital. It is not unusual for grandparents and elderly aunts and uncles to live next door to, or as an extension of the same house. Abandonment of spouse is forbidden and subject to excommunication of the guilty party, divorce is likewise proscribed, and remarriage of widows and widowers, even among surviving spouses in their 60's and 70's is frequent. Unmarried, baptized adults will live at the same place where they were raised, or in a home nearby. Elderly couples and singles are considered to form a separate household and will be listed as such in Amish directories and other information sources from which this census of church membership will be derived. As a result, the average number of baptized adult members per household is nearly two (preliminary results indicate an average of 1.9 – see narrative on data entry below). If specific information about adult members is not available for an Amish church district, then knowledge of the number of households will allow for a reasonably accurate estimate.

Beyond these two advantages, however, the remainder of the task is not so simple, as information for various communities varies in its completeness and recency. Three concurrent activities took place during the period, July 1 – December 31, 2009 to establish a firm database for counts and reliably valid estimates of Amish religious membership.

First, the names and approximate locations of all existing Amish settlements (their name for a community) were identified and verified. Using a list published in July, 2008 by Pathway Publishers (Amish Communities Across North America), reports from an Amish-based newspaper known as The Diary, and two visits to the Heritage Historical Library (HHL) in Aylmer, Ontario, a master list of slightly over 400 settlements has been developed. This task is complicated by two things. (1) over the past 19 years, about 12 new settlements are founded annually, or one per month. Finding reports from members of already established communities in The Diary about extended family, neighbors, and friends who may be moving to a new community, plus the report of migration of households at the front end of this same monthly publication, helps identify most of the possible start-ups, and of communities that occasionally become extinct (about 3 per year). These new places are then confirmed during visits to HHL files, and these same files at HHL are used to locate other start-ups that may not appear in the reporter's notes from various established communities in The Diary. Of particular importance to county-based estimates of Amish religious membership is that since 1990, over 150 counties (mostly in various Midwestern states) are first-time hosts for new Amish settlements. (2) Places names can be confusing relative to location. For example, there are two places in Pennsylvania with the unusual name of "Glen Campbell." One of those was the location of a start-up community in 2007. Perusing road atlases, detailed topographic maps from the DeLorme company, and computer searches are useful for identifying exact locations within counties, and if either new or previously established communities straddle county lines and therefore are multi-county. Although tedious, it will be possible to specify which households live on either side of a county line.

Second, as many Amish directories as possible have been identified. For a significant share of Amish communities, a directory is published that lists all households within each church district of a community (the majority of Amish communities have only one church district, although there are many well-known, large communities, with the largest containing nearly 220 church districts). By household, directory information typically includes an address, the names and birth dates of the husband and wife, plus the birth dates and names of all their children. Adult children who have married and started their own families are included, but given a code (such as the letter "B" or "C", depending on the directory), to indicate that they have now formed their own household and no longer live at home. Many directories also report the husband's (i.e., "breadwinner's") occupation, listing the occupation of baptized women only if they are single and live as adults independently of their parents, in which case they compose a single person household. Some baptized men, who are bachelors, will also be listed as a single person household. Regardless of marital status, in the vast majority of cases, all adult children can be found listed as baptized members of the community where they grew up, or of another community to which they moved (with their spouse).

Usually, a member of the Amish community takes on the mantle of compiling and publishing the information, and then advertises its availability for purchase. In larger communities, a local printing company (often Amish owned) coordinates receipt and compilation of the information from reporters of each church district. These directories are mostly meant for Amish readers, however, they are frequently advertised through publications like The Diary, and a large collection of them are available at HHL, hence, access through direct purchase or through trips to Aylmer is possible. At this point, I have purchased 32 directories with information on over 200 communities (some directories list all communities in a state), and now rely on HHL as a supplemental source.

Third, appropriate data for a count of religious membership have been entered into an excel spreadsheet. The first column includes the name of the community/name of church district, and the date of publication or year of reference the data designates. The second column includes the name of the state. The third column is a household number, which will be used to establish metrics related to mean/median size, variance, standard deviation and standard error of the mean for church district size. The fourth column is a numerical value indicating the number of adult members in each household, which is "2" for 95 percent plus of all households. Most of the remainder are single person households, which means someone who is never/not yet married but lives independently, plus widows and widowers who have not yet remarried. On rare occasion, several unmarried brothers and sisters are listed as a single household. The fifth column designates the number of children still living at home, and the sixth column indicates the number of adult children who are baptized Amish and who have set up an independent household, whether married or single. This information will be used to develop a measure of the number of adult, baptized members from which estimates to mostly smaller communities for which there are no directories can be estimated (in combination with statistics on the average size of a church district).

Since directories are published on an occasional basis, few correspond to either the 2009 or 2010 calendar year. Hence, it will be necessary to enter data from both recent and older directories for the same community so that a projection of membership growth can be established.

Supplementing this task, but performing another function as well, is the development of a second excel file. From numerous settlements in the December through March issues of The Diary is information about "community statistics." Generally, a community report will describe the number of church districts, number of households, and the number of parochial schools. Most of these "community statistics" reports are for the smaller and newer communities for which there are no published directories. Although this represents a small share of the Amish population (and of baptized, adult members), they represents a majority of Amish communities and of counties where the Amish can be found. A new excel database will be developed that lists community statistics, year by year, going back to December, 1999 – March, 2000 for as many communities as possible. From these statistics, estimates of church district size can be developed and then compared to information from the directories for the more established communities. This will allow for a weighted estimate of the number of households, adjusted for the age of the community (or possibly, separate estimates for smaller and newer communities) for those remaining communities for which neither a directory or a report in The Diary is available.

Finally, once the excel spreadsheet information is completely compiled, statistical estimates of each of the 400 plus settlements can begin. Concurrent with this effort will be the extensive use of maps to specify the apportionment of membership for settlements that overlap county boundaries (and in the case of at least three settlements, state boundaries).

Submitted by: Joseph F. Donnermeyer
[Donnermeyer's tally is listed as Amish Groups, undifferentiated in the 2010 U.S. Religion Census, part of the Mennonite family of church bodies.]

Amish-Mennonite Religious Counts

A related group of denominations is known as Amish-Mennonite. Cory Anderson of Newcomerstown, Ohio, used much the same methodology as that of Joe Donnermeyer. These are his comments on the methods used for Amish-Mennonite bodies:

> Because the Amish Mennonites have meeting houses 99% of the time, . . . all households will be counted as residents of that county. . . . The work will consist of collecting data from four directories, categorizing churches correctly, and extracting and calculating the requested data.
>
> The categorization is going to be based off the past three years of field work I've been conducting, whereby I've been able to categorize each church in this complex, highly autonomous movement of "Amish Mennonites."

Anderson was able to provide information on eight groups, all included in the Mennonite family listings in the *2010 U.S. Religion Census*: Ambassadors Amish-Mennonite; Beachy Amish-Mennonite; Berea Amish-Mennonite; Maranatha Amish-Mennonite; Mennonite Christian Fellowship; Midwest Beachy Amish-Mennonite; Tampico Amish-Mennonite; Unaffiliated Amish-Mennonite.

Appendix E
Buddhist Groups

In 2009, The Institute for the Study of American Religion (ISAR) was asked to do a census of the American Buddhist Community, the first such attempt to do an assessment of the number of individuals who are affiliated with the burgeoning and now highly visible Buddhist religious facilities that have since 1965 appeared in every state of the Union. Responsibility for overseeing this project was accepted by Dr. J. Gordon Melton, ISAR's director, with the work on the census carried out by the ISAR staff. The effort was funded by a grant from the John Templeton Foundation through a request by the American Religion Data Archive (ARDA) based at Pennsylvania State University.

American Buddhism burgeoned following the changes of the immigration laws relative to Asia in 1965. From relatively few centers based in the Chinese- and Japanese American communities, the whole spectrum of Buddhist organized life appeared through the 1970s and 1980s and has continued to grow as organizations from Eastern, Southeastern, and Southern Asia moved to establish centers to serve their members who had become residents of the United States. Simultaneously, a host of new American-based organizations were formed to serve non-Asians who had converted to the different forms of Buddhism. That process was accelerated by the high levels of sympathy found among non-Asian Americans for the plight of the Tibetan exiles who left their country following its annexation by the Peoples Republic of China and the special consideration given to Vietnamese who left their country after the end of the Vietnamese War.

As Buddhism emerged in strength in the United States, it was divided by language, ethnicity, and variant emphases in belief and practice. Buddhism has commonly been seen to exist in three major forms—Theravada (the dominant form in Sri Lanka, Myanmar, Thailand, Laos, and Cambodia), Mahayana (the dominant form in China, Hong Kong, Taiwan, Japan, Korea, and Vietnam), and Vajrayana, which some consider another form of Mahayana (the dominant form in Tibet, Nepal, Bhutan, and Mongolia). Both Theravada and Mahayana have spawned a meditative form which emphasizes the practice of meditation and the de-emphasis on theology. The Theravada form is termed Vipassana and the Mahayana form is known as Chan (China), Zen (Japan), or Son (Korea). That being said, a classification system of Buddhist groups can be created as follows:

- Theravada
  - Burmese
  - Cambodian
  - Laotian
  - Sri Lankan
  - Thai
- Mahayana
  - Chinese
  - Japanese
    - Nichiren
    - Shin
    - Shingon
    - Tendai
  - Zen
  - Korean
  - Vietnamese
- Vrajayana
  - Bhutan
  - Nepal
  - Mongolian
  - Tibetan

Estimates of the Buddhist population of the United States have varied, with some long-term knowledgeable observers estimating it to be as high as 3.5 million and most recently as high as 5 to 6 million. Polling has revealed much lower figures, the 2008 report of the Pew Forum, for example, suggesting that Buddhism had the allegiance of some 0.7 percent of the population, roughly a little more than two million followers. This ISAR approaches the problem in a different way as it focuses on reported membership and constituency of Buddhist groups. All of the known Buddhist groups in America were contacted by mail with telephone follow-ups with requests for information. Where information was not forthcoming, visits were made to multiple local centers of groups to establish an average size of local centers and an estimate made based on those observations and reports.

As a whole, Buddhist groups are just beginning to make counts of membership and support, part of a larger transition process to adapting to the volunteerism of American religious life. Of the major world religions, Buddhism has most clearly adapted itself to the denominational pattern of religions that tends to emerge in free societies, especially to the lack of any social assigning of religious status at the time of birth.

Theravada

Theravada Buddhism has been built immigration from Southeastern Asia, and the large communities of Sri Lankans, Thais, Cambodians, and Laotians have created national networks of temples. While spread around the nation, including the South, these temples are concentrated in urban/suburban areas along the West Coast and in the Washington-New York Corridor. These temples show a pattern of development over the last generation as new temples are formed by small groups of committed believers who meet in borrowed or rented facilities while land is secured and permanent temple facilities constructed. While such temples are commonly designed to serve the larger population of Asian Americans, a relatively small percentage (20 to 25 percent) constitutes the active membership.

The influence of Theravada Buddhism has been extended by the popularity of the Vipassana or Insight meditation movement, the primary form of Theravada to which non-Asian believers adhere. Vipassana is practiced by hundreds of small sitting groups, many of which are part of one of half a dozen loosely affiliated networks, others independent and unconnected, and in a constant state of flux. As with other forms of meditation, Vipassana is taught in classes somewhat separated from its Buddhist religious roots. Those who master the technique may or may not continue the practice afterwards and may or may not integrate that practice into a more complete Buddhist life or self identify as a Buddhist.

Mahayana

The oldest segment of the American Buddhism is the Japanese American Buddhist community which dates to the formation of temples by immigrant workers in the 1880s in what is now the state of Hawaii. Prior to World War I, groups representing the major branches of Japanese Buddhism—Jodo Shinshu, Nichiren, Shingon, Zen—were formed, which the Honpa Hongwanji group of the Jodo Shinshu (represented by two organization, The Buddhist Churches of America and the Honpa Hongwanji Mission of Hawaii) becoming the largest. Hawaii would become the only state with a Buddhist majority.

In the 1970s, the balance within the Buddhist community was upset by the radical growth of the Nichiren Shoshu through its educational arm, the Soka Gakkai. In the 1990s, the older temple-based Nichiren Shoshu organization and the Soka Gakkai separated, and the Soka Gakkai emerged as the singled largest Buddhist group in the United States (and a number of other Western countries). It currently reports more than 300,000 members, most non-Asians. It is the only Buddhist group with more than a quarter of a million members and one of only two with as many as a 100,000 members.

During the decade after World War II, Zen Buddhism emerged as a popular movement in the counter culture and has continued to expand steadily over the last six decades. The community is based in more than fifty Zen organizations in which relatively small local Zen centers (zendos) associate. Many Zen sitting groups meet regularly in borrowed or rented facilities. Though even the largest of Zen organization count their adherents in the thousands, the accumulated numbers of Zen adherents reach above a hundred thousand.

The next largest groups of Mahayana adherents come for Vietnam. The Vietnamese Buddhist community began with a single temple with a Vietnamese priest and a group of non-Asian followers in Los Angeles, but grew rapidly after the Vietnamese war. The immigrant community, concentrated in orange County, California, began to build temples in the 1980s and has emerged as the second largest segment of the Buddhist community. The network of more than 150 Vietnamese temples now has more than 100,000 adherents. A similar but smaller number of Korean temples associated with the Chogye order (the largest Korean Buddhist organization) also exists. Also, within the Vietnamese community, the monk Thich Nhat Hahn became a celebrity from his opposition to the Vietnam War, and after leaving huis home country attracted a large international community around him and his teachings. In the United States more than 300 centers (almost all small sitting groups meeting in a member's home) has emerged.

Chinese Americans, most of whom have come to the United States from Taiwan and Hong Kong with smaller groups from Southeast Asia, form the largest body of Asian Americans. Like other Asian groups, the largest block of Chinese Americans appear to be unattached religiously or in Christians churches.[1] Yiguandao, a new religious movement that originated in China in the nineteenth century, the largest religious group in Taiwan is also significantly under-represented within the Chinese American community. That being said, the half-dozen larger Taiwanese Buddhist groups such as the Buddhist Compassion Tzu Chi Association, Foguanshan, Dharma Drum Mountain, True Buddha School, Chuan Tai, and the Amitabha Buddhist Societies have built national followings, and represent a significant portion of the current American Buddhist community.

Vajrayana

The Vajrayana community is represented internationally by Japanese Shingon (12 million), Tibetan (7 million), and lesser numbers of believers in Bhutan, Nepal, Mongolia and China, In the United States, the first (and for many decades the only) Vajrayana temples were several Shingon temples established in Hawaii and California. Then in the early 1960s, a small group of Mongolians migrated to the United States and established a temple in Howell, New Jersey. By this time, however, massive sympathy had been created for the plight of the tens of thousands of Tibetans who had left their country and resettled in northern India and Nepal. Tibetan lamas began arriving in the United states for extended visits in the 1970s and slowly began to settle permanently, especially after the Dalai Lama open an office for his Government-in-Exile in New York City.

Today, the Tibetan Buddhist community in America is significantly different from other Buddhist groups. Unlike the Vietnamese or Japanese, there is not a large community of Tibetans residing in the United States. Thus, the American Tibetan Buddhist community is built around more than sixty distinct organizations each of which is made up of non-Asian Buddhist converts and usually led by one or a few Tibetan teachers, though increasingly non-Asian teachers are gradually emerging. Each of the four larger Tibetan Schools (Gelugpa, Kagyupa, Nyingmapa, and Sakyapa) has established an American headquarters and created a network of small centers around the nation. The largest network is an independent Kagyu group established by Trungpa Rinpoche, the first lama to settle permanently in the United States.[2] That network, Shambhala International, is now headquartered in Canada.

The larger Tibetan groups have established temples and monastic centers, but the great majority of 600+ Tibetan Buddhist groups are small meditation and study groups that gather in borrowed and rented facilities. (There are also several Chinese Vajrayana temple associations, the largest being the Taiwanese-based True Buddha School, which has a half-dozen American temples.)

1: The larger estimates of Buddhism in the United States are grounded in the belief that the great majority of Asian Americans from predominantly Buddhist countries are themselves Buddhists, but it appears that such belief is groundless, and that only 20 to 25 percent of the Chinese, Vietnamese and Southeast Asian American communities adhere to Buddhism even nominally.

2: Relative to membership, the largest Tibetan Buddhist group appears to be the New Kadampa Tradition which has developed a national following and now reports more than 20,000 members.

The Tibetan groups also manifest a common organizational pattern into which many Asian American Buddhist groups fall. Most American Tibetan groups exist as the United States outpost of an international movement whose headquarters is located in Asia (or in a few cases in Europe). As such, the American branch is a minority segment of the group's international membership. Often, there is only one American center in a much larger international association.

A Growing Community

The Buddhist community exists on a growing trajectory, with tens of thousands of adherents coming into the country from Asia annually, and thousands of Americans turning to Buddhism especially in its Zen, Vipassana, and Tibetan forms.

Counting the number of Buddhists is complicated by the fact that few of the 200+ Buddhist temple networks and organizations make or keep records of membership. Thus almost all reported numbers are estimates. Many of the American based movements remain quite fluid, and the number of informal sitting groups for Buddhist meditation unknown. Some 200 Zen and Vipassana sitting groups meet weekly in the churches of the Unitarian Universalists with many members also being counted at members of the local congregation. No count has been made of the membership of the larger Asian American temple associations though visits to a selection of temples has yielded an average count on membership and constituency. Those numbers are somewhat distorted by the phenomenon of multiple temple attendance by many adherents. Special events by different temples in urban areas with more than one temple of the same group will attract the people from other temples and people who are not temple members but who will attend events at different temples during the year. This reported constituency numbers are increased by double counting.

That being said, an estimate on membership/constituency can be made:

Theravada	187,700
Vietnamese Mahayana	151,000
Japanese Mahayana	120,000
Soka Gakkai	286,516
Japanese Zen[3]	17,770
Chinese	129,850
Other Mahayana	30,000
Vajrayana	55,000
Total	971,766

Thus the number of visible practicing Buddhists (including the nominally practicing) is about 900,000, or slightly less than half who identify themselves as Buddhists in the polls and far less than some of the recent estimates made by observers of the Buddhist community. Even with this sweep of the Buddhist community based on records accumulated over the last 40 years has most likely missed a few centers and organizations, but those missed have been accounted for by a somewhat liberal estimate of membership for many of the groups found. Thus it is believed that the number presented is as accurate a count as can at present be made, and provides a foundation upon which future research on the American Buddhist community can proceed.

Submitted by: J. Gordon Melton

Editor's note: J. Gordon Melton provided the Religion Census data collection office a list of 215 Buddhist groups with 2,854 locations. In most cases, a total number of persons associated with each group were included. The number of persons associated with specific locations was often available. For groups or locations without identified totals, estimates were made based upon similar groups or locations. After these allocations, the total numbers of adherents reported in the earlier tables may differ slightly from the figures originally reported in the accompanying text.

3: The Pew survey indicates a much larger number of Zen adherents, but these seem to include not just the Japanese Zen practitioners, but also the Son and the larger numbers of Chan practitioners who most often describe their practice as Zen to outsiders.

Appendix F
Friends

Data from local meetings and churches within the Society of Friends (Quakers) is shown in this study in eight "family groups." Many Friends have worked for years for the unity of their movements. But there are also theological and practical differences within the community. The Friends community has evolved in the last sixty years with many new unifications and divisions.

Friends' data was combined in the 1971, 1980, and 2000 studies. Member and adherent data in the 2000 was estimated for local situations by a division of national totals.

The current study more closely resembles the 1952 and 1990 studies that were also broken down by family group. The 1952 study did not include two groups. The 1990 study combined the Central Yearly Meeting with the Alaska Yearly Meeting as "Independent Evangelical." The latter has since become part of the Evangelical Friends Church. The 1990 study also divided local unaffiliated meetings. Some with a more conservative stance were reported with the Independent Evangelical group, while others with a more liberal stance or unprogrammed meeting style were reported with the "Independent" Yearly Meetings. Since assignments of unaffiliated meetings to other groupings may be prejudicial, all unaffiliated meetings are listed together in the current study.

Friends' member and adherent data is collected by regional Yearly Meetings. Even for those that belong to larger fellowships, date, definitions, and type of data collected may vary among Yearly Meetings. Many local worship meetings may be "preparatory meetings" or worship groups that meet regularly, but have no formal organization or may have their member data joined to other local groups. This accounts for large number of meetings or churches reported with "zero" members.

Four Yearly Meetings and several local meetings belong to both the Friends General Conference and the Friends United Meeting. Because of this significant dual affiliation, these churches and meetings are shown as a separate family group. To determine total congregations and adherents for either the General Conference or the United Meeting it is necessary to combine the data for the individual group with that for the dual group.

For those desiring to see a comparative picture of the entire Friends community, one should combine all eight family groups. (This total does include a handful of additional dual affiliations that are noted in the discussions for each family group in Appendix A.)

Thanks are extended to the Friends World Committee for Consultation – Section of the Americas, and to officers of many Yearly Meetings for generous help in compiling this information.

Appendix G
Hindu Groups

In 2009, The Institute for the Study of American Religion (ISAR) was asked to do a census of the American Hindu Community, the first such attempt to count to do an assessment of the number of individuals who are affiliated with the burgeoning and now highly visible Hindu religious facilities that have since 1965 appeared in every state of the Union. Responsibility for overseeing this project was accepted by Dr. Constance Jones, a sociologist and professor at the California Institute of Integral Studies in San Francisco, with the work on the census carried out by the ISAR staff. The effort was funded by a grant from the John Templeton Foundation through a request by the American Religion Data Archive (ARDA) based at Pennsylvania State University.

Preliminary Considerations: The term "Hinduism" is among the most contested in the field of religious studies. It arose as a designation of the various religious strains that were found by Westerners on the Indian Subcontinent in the eighteenth century. The term has been met with a range of acceptance by the modern Hindu community but has come to be used by most Indians in the modern West to apply to that range of religions currents that originated on the Indian subcontinent, apart from the three large strains whose adherents have come to be seen as constituting separate religious communities—Jainism, Hinduism, and Sikhism. The Hindu community is tied together by its use of a number of ancient holy texts (most notably the Vedas, the Upanishads, the Mahabharata, the Puranas, etc.), acknowledgement of a number of deities discussed in these texts, and the creation of temples at which rituals are performed and holy days observed.

There being no body which regularly collects data on Hindu religious groups, ISAR originally planned to gather the basic data by mail. As the original mailings met with an almost universal lack of response, that plan was scrapped and replaced with an effort to phone each groups and interview a local representative. Thus, in 2009 a list of all the known Hindu temples (some 450) in the United States was compiled and beginning in January 2010, an attempt was made to call each local temple and interview the president, a priest serving the temple, or local knowledgeable board member. That process continued through the fall. In the process of contacting the temples, several hundred additional temples were discovered and a picture of the overall organization of the community as of the fall of 2010 emerged. That overall organization is presented below.

It is to be noted that most temples do not make or keep counts on their membership (with many having no formal membership) nor on the larger community of support (constituency). Temples regularly reported membership as a range (200 to 500) and often as family units (100 to 150 families), with an understanding that the average size of a family unit was four. For most temples, membership consisted of those individuals or families who regularly supported the temples by their time, attendance, and gifts, but overwhelmingly, the temple served a far larger group of worshippers and attendees who might only be seen a couple of times a year at the most important holy days. Phone calls to the local temples were supplements to on site visits made by Drs. Jones and Melton and members of the ISAR staff to verify information received over the phone and gain some firsthand understanding of the situations in which such observations were made. On site visits were made to multiple locations in southern California, the San Francisco Bay Area, Chicago, Washington, DC, Atlanta, Houston, Dallas, and Austin.

The Structure of the American Hindu Community

The American Hindu community can be divided into four basic groupings. First, the largest number of believers are associated with the approximately 260 traditional Hindu temples which have been established by first and second generation Hindus who have migrated to the United states since the change of the immigration laws in 1965. The initial temple was established in Flushing, Long Island, new York in the 1970s. Since that time as populations of Indian American have emerged in the major urban centers, a growing number of temples have been organized. Such temples are locally owned and maintained and organizationally autonomous. Each temple follows one of the major traditions (or sampradaya) of Hindu religion based on the worship of specific deities—Vaisnava, based on the worship of Vishnu (whose most popular incarnations were as Venkateswara and Krishna); Saivite, based on the worship of Shiva and his family—Ganesh, Muragan, Lakshmi; and the Goddess who is worshipped primarily as Durga, Kali, and/or Devi.

Because the initial temples in a particular location will attempt to serve the entire Indian American community, a new phenomena has emerged in the West, the mixed tradition temple. The Mixed tradition temple will generally have either a form of Vishnu or Shiva at its central altar, but also include murtis (statues) of Durga and other deities in side altars, more or less prominently displayed. In smaller communities, the side altars may include a murti of the popular guru (teacher) Sai Baba of Shirdi, the main teacher of the Jain religion Mahavira, and on rare occasion a murti of Nanak (the founder of the sikh faith) or Buddha. In larger temples, the initial temple become the central structure of a temple complex which has it develops will house separate temples for the different sampradayas.

Over the years the Hindu community has given birth to a variety of movements within the main sampradayas which now exists and sub-traditions organized around a particular teacher (and/or lineage of teachers) and one or more distinctive ideas. These movements have produced temples representing these various sub-traditions which differ from the more traditional community-based temples primarily by their being associated with other temples of the tradition. Typical of these sub-traditions are the temples of the Swaminarayan movement. Swaminarayan Hindus are distinctive in that they feel that the prominent nineteenth-century Gujarati teacher Swaminarayan (1781-1830) was an incarnation of the deity Krishna. Based in Gujarat, the movement has followed a lineage of teachers that is traced to Swaminarayan. That lineage has diverged over the years, and several distinctive lineages have emerged, each of which is now the center of separate Swaminarayan groups. Currently, no less that eight such groups exist in the United States. The largest of these groups, the Bochasanwasi Shri Akshar Purushottam Swaminarayan Sanstha or BAPS, has emerged as the largest Hindu group in America. It has attained some added prominence by its construction of large temple complexes in Atlanta, Houston and Chicago (with additional such temples to be completed in the near future). Approximately two thirds of the Hindu temples now found in the United States are related to the approximately 40 particular sub-traditions that have been identified.

Third, the nineteenth century in Indian history was marked a great revival of Hinduism, in part spurred by the challenge of the growth of Christianity during the Colonial era. This revival gave birth to a number of new forms of Hinduism that collectively began known as the Hindu Renaissance. Renaissance groups were known for their emphasis on Hindu philosophy and their downplaying of temple worship and devotion to particular deities. The Renaissance gave birth to a number of new religious traditions, which through the twentieth century led to multiple competing organizations (comparable to Christian denominations). Hinduism was initially introduced to the west by several representatives of the Hindu Renaissance who were born in India in the late nineteenth century (most notably Swami Vivekananda and Swami Yogananda) and perpetuated by several representative twentieth century figures—Ramana Maharshi, Swami Sivananda and Swami Muktananda). The effort begun by these five figures have led directly to no less than 40 Hindu groups now existing in the United States.

Fourth, In the middle- and late-twentieth century, a number of gurus/teachers, whose perspectives draw heavily on Renaissance themes mixed in various ways with more traditional forms of Hinduism, have appeared in the West, especially since the 1960s. These new forms of the Hindu tradition are most often built around a single Hindu teacher and his/her lineage and local centers are organizationally tied together. These groups generally keep the renaissance emphasis on Hindu philosophy, an emphasis on practice of a particular form(s) of devotion, and the central role of the guru or teacher as a conduit of spiritual wisdom. In the 1980s, a set of American-born gurus, continuing the lineage of an Indian teacher began to appear as founders of new movements. The number of American-born gurus (of non-Indian ethnicity) has continued to grow.

More than 40 new post-Renaissance movements have emerged in America in the last generation.

Toward a Demographic Assessment of the American Hindu Community

Moving to a count of the number of Hindus in America is a multi-layered problem. Quite visible are those individuals who participate with some regularity (weekly, monthly) in one of the several hundred Hindu temples or organizations. Secondly, there is a much larger group that more occasionally visit a Hindu temple/group for special events or holy day celebrations, who identify with the temple/group visited and to some extent support it financially. Finally, there those who think of themselves as Hindus (especially if they have to choose between religious communities with which to identify), but who for various reasons are not active in anyway in supporting the visible Hindu community. It is this latter groups that is usually reached by polling on American religious preferences and in recent polls that number has been assessed at approximately two million. On one border, this latter group of inactive self-identified Hindus fades into the community of secular Indian Americans who at present profess no religious faith though they may hold some personal spiritual ideals. This largest group of "Hindus" become somewhat visible during Divali, a Hindu holy day that has become a widely celebrated and secularized national Indian holiday that nevertheless retains much of its religious flavor (much as Christmas has become in the larger Christian culture).

This report is, however, primarily concerned with the first two groups who manifest some active relationship to a Hindu temple or group. Of the 258 traditional Hindu temples in America, 241 have reported membership figures totaling 249,097. This represents a core number of active adherents plus the larger community envisioned as being served by the temple. In addition, we asked each temple the number of people who attended the largest event (holy day) in the last year. As a whole, that number was lower than the reported membership. If the 17 non-reporting temples are taken as a group to be somewhat equal in size to the reporting temples, with an average membership of 1,033, an estimated 19,276 members can be added. Thus a total number of 268,364 adherents can be seen to attend and support the 258 traditional temples in the United States. That represents approximately 15 percent of the total number of people who self-identify as Hindus in the United States.

The various temples associations formed by those temples from the various sub-traditions of the Hindu faith present a more complicated situation. The largest temples are associated with the single largest association, the Bochasanwasi Shri Akshar Purushottam Swaminarayan Sanstha (BAPS). It reports some 25,000 affiliated families, or roughly 100,000 members in its 57 temples. Its larger temples have become popular and well-advertised tourist attractions that are visited by thousands of pilgrims and hundreds of thousands of visitors annually. Apart from it, however, the association temples appear to fall into the same range of membership and constituencies manifest by the traditional community-based temples.

There are approximately 400 association-based temples and the associated smaller centers that have yet to evolve into a temple. Of the 41 temple associations, 25 have reported their membership:

All World Gayatri Pariwar	10	8,000
Shri Surya Narayan Mandir	2	350
Congress of Arya Samajs in North America	26	1,200
American Sevashram Sangha of NA (BSSNA)	7	2,000
ISKCON (Int. Society of Krishna Consciousness)	47	75,000
Global Organization for Divinity (G.O.D.)	11	200
VRINDA/ Vrindavan Institute for Vaisnava Culture and Studies	2	50
Sai Baba of Shirdi Temple	21	20,000
Sant Shri Asarmaji Ashram	20	5,000
Bochasanwasi Shri Akshar Purushottam Swaminarayan Sanstha (BAPS)	57	100,000
Anoopam Mission	1	10,000
Laxmi Narayan Dev (Spiritual organization)/ LNSO, Vadtal Temple	5	14,000
Maningar Shree Swaminarayan Gadi Sansthan (MSSGS)	1	2,000
Original Shree Swaminarayan Sampraday (Under Shree Nar Narayan Dev Gadi)	19	7,000
Shree Swaminarayan Gurukul, USA	1	5,000
Swaminarayan Mandir Vasna Sanstha (SMVS)	2	2,000
Yogi Divine Society/Illinois HQ/Waukegan Mandir	2	300
Yogi Divine Society/Hari Dham/Hindu Swami Narayan Temple + Cultural Center	2	5,000
Datta Yoga Centers USA	3	3,000
Five Fold Path Inc./Agnihortra Worldwide	1	500
Nithyananda Vedic Temples/Life Bliss Foundation	7	3,000
Sadhu Vaswami Centers	11	6,500
The Sambodh Society	1	700
Veerashaiva Samaja of North America	14	2,000

Together they account for 169 of the 400 temples and have a reported 183,000 members

Among those associations that have not reported their membership, there are 54 centers reported as temples and 177 centers reported as a more informal group (satsang, chapter, center etc.) If we assume that the association temples average the same a the traditional community based temple, or approximately 1000 members and that the chapters and satsangs are smaller, around 250, we account for an additional 98,000 adherents.[1] The temple associations thus account for an additional 282,000 Hindu adherents.

The 40 groups of the Hindu Renaissance associations present a more complicated problem of assessment. While a few of the older groups (the Vedanta Societies and the Self-Realization Fellowship) have an old and established membership and constituency, as a whole they have been reluctant to publish any membership figures. Most of the newer groups will publish lists of local affiliated centers but either refuse to count members or offer any assessment on the number of members. Many operate without any formal membership at all, though they have a core of dedicated supporters who attend regularly scheduled events. While almost all the groups have a permanent worship center attached to their headquarters, and many affiliated groups have similar facilities, the majority of groups affiliated with the Renaissance organizations meet informally in borrowed or rented facilities and have a minimal visibility in the communities in which they meet.

It has been observed that such informal groups while on occasion growing larger, will overwhelming be in the 5 to 25 range in size, averaging about a dozen. At the same time, none of the groups have the large constituencies manifest in the traditional Hindu tenmples whose relatively small facilities can often accommodate a worshipping community in the thousands.

1: We believe this to be a generous figure, but one that can become a future beginning point for further research.

Based upon that observation, some estimate of the total membership/ constituency of the Renaissance groups can be made.

As of 2010 it is estimated that the total number of adherents of the 40 groups can be set at approximately 20,000.

The last set of groups, the Post-renaissance Guru Groups are the hardest to deal with. Most have no membership figures to offer and many operate as non-membership organizations. Though a few are large international organizations with 100 or more affiliated groups in the United States. At the other extreme, some or relatively new and have but a single center of activity. A few are large internationally, but have only one or two centers within the United States.

The largest of the post-Renaissance groups are the group built around the work of Mata Amritanandmayi (with 110 centers); the International Sai Organization headed by Satya Sai Baba (with 225 centers); Sahaja Yoga headed by Shri Mataji Nirmala Devi (with 125 centers); and the movement founded by the late Sri Chinmoy (which declined participation in this survey). Each is an international movements with many centers in the United States. While these movements have many centers, each center is relatively small. They may be as small as 3 to 5 people and rarely more than 25, with 10 to 15 an average size.

Those group with but a single center, while a few may have more, generally have from 50 to 100 participants, though many more may be correspondents. Groups meeting in borrowed or rented facilities generally average about a dozen (5 to 25) participants. Based upon these assumptions, we can reach a total estimate of 35000 participants in the Post-Renaissance groups.

Summary

	No. of Centers	Members/Participants
Traditional temples	248	268,000
Temple Associations	400	282,000
Renaissance groups	292	20,000
Post renaissance Groups	650	35,000

Adding all the figures proposed above together, we reach an estimated 606,000 active participating Hindus[2] in the United States as of the end of 2010. It is also difficult to assess from our present state of knowledge as to the percentage of Indian Americans included in the count. The first two groups of temples almost totally consist of Indian Americans, though a number of Westerners are to be found in a few groups such as the International Society for Krishna Consciousness. The two latter groupings are predominantly made up of Western converts, but several of the movements, including the International Sai Organization, have received an influx of Indian members in the last few decades.

Submitted by: Constance A. Jones and J. Gordon Melton

2: It is noted that one movement about which only partial material has been received, and whose complete figures might measurable effect the total is the Global Country of World Peace, better known as the TM (Transcendental Meditation) movements, but it is extremely difficult to assess at present due to its rapidly changing organization in the wake of its founders' death.

Editor's note: Constance A. Jones and J. Gordon Melton provided the Religion Census data collection office a list of 127 Hindu groups with 1,625 locations. In most cases, a total number of persons associated with each group were included. The number of persons associated with specific locations was often available. For groups or locations without identified totals, estimates were made based upon similar groups or locations. After these allocations, the total numbers of adherents reported in the earlier tables may differ slightly from the figures originally reported in the accompanying text.

Appendix H
Jewish Groups

The information we supplied on Jewish congregations consists of the following estimates, calculated by denomination and by county:

- Number of synagogues
- Number of members
- Number of adherents
- Number of worshipers

Synagogue Counts Derived from Three Congregational Roof Organizations

The congregational arms of the Conservative (United Synagogue for Conservative Judaism), Reconstructionist (Jewish Reconstructionist Federation) and Reform (Union for Reform Judaism) movements provided us with lists of their synagogues and exact membership totals (or estimates) for each congregation.

Not included in the synagogue counts or membership totals are the small number of synagogues that call themselves Conservative, Reconstructionist or Reform but are not affiliates of their respective national congregational arms.

A few congregations have affiliations with more than one movement. In those cases, each movement was given .5 of that congregation in the "Synagogue" column, and 50% of the membership units.

Diverse Ways of Counting the Orthodox Congregations

For Orthodox synagogues, the main national congregational body, the Union of Orthodox Jewish Congregations (Orthodox Union, or "OU"), provided us with a list of their synagogues and membership totals. In addition, the website for the National Council of Young Israel lists the names and locations of all Young Israel congregations, an additional source of Orthodox congregations.

Chabad is a Hasidic sect which fields about 1,500 outreach emissaries worldwide with the vast majority in the US. Its national website, provides a detailed listing of every Chabad-run outreach endeavor. We examined the website for each individual Chabad to determine if religious worship services take place on a regularly scheduled basis in that location.

In addition, we consulted the website of every Jewish Federation in the United States to check for other Orthodox congregations not otherwise found. Finally, we consulted a variety of other local and national websites catering to the Orthodox community to locate Hasidic, Syrian, Persian, Yemenite, Sephardic, Mizrachi and other Orthodox congregations that are either independent of the OU or are affiliated with the more traditionally oriented Agudath Israel (which does not have a website)

Not included in these Orthodox synagogue totals are afternoon-only worship services that meet in offices; yeshivas; Kollels (institutions of full-time study of sacred text); or worship services that meet in a home solely on a Friday night or a Saturday night.

Finally, the overall synagogue totals do not include worship services that occur on college campus Hillels or Chabad.

"Membership Units" or Households: Preliminary to Counting Adherents

Jewish congregations and their denominational roof bodies enumerate their adherents in terms of "membership units," or households who are dues-paying members of congregations. Almost all congregations rely upon annual membership dues for financial sustainability. We first determined number of membership units and then proceeded to estimate adherents.

Members of Three Denominations from National Roof Organizations

Member unit figures or estimates for Reform, Reconstructionist and Conservative congregations were provided by the national movements as noted above. While counting membership in these three denominations was relatively straightforward, enumerating the Orthodox proved far more complex and challenging.

Orthodox Complexities

In some counties, those with very few Orthodox congregations, we were able to gather and rely upon published membership figures for Orthodox congregations.

In counties with larger numbers of Orthodox congregations, membership information was generally insufficient. In these counties, we used published Jewish population estimates from recently conducted local Jewish community studies sponsored by local Jewish federations to arrive at estimated Orthodox membership totals. Some population studies provide estimates of the number of members of Orthodox congregations by county. Where such estimates were not available, we drew upon the estimated number of Orthodox households in any given county to estimate the number of congregationally affiliated membership units. In so doing, we estimated that 90% of the Orthodox households were members of Orthodox congregations, consistent with figures observed in several local population studies.

In a few self-contained Orthodox communities such as Kiryas Joel in Orange County, NY, we used 2010 US Census data were used to arrive at membership, adherent and worshipper figures.

In computing Orthodox membership figures, member information for most Chabad congregations was unavailable, so we used a figure of 50 members per Chabad, an estimate that is complicated by the overlap of worshippers at Chabad services with other nearby congregations, and by the non-uniformity and irregularity in attendance.

From Members to Adherents

As noted, Jewish congregations record their size in terms of "member units," or entire households who pay membership dues. To calculate the number of adherents, for each Jewish denomination we multiplied the number of its households by the mean number of its household members (Jewish or not) derived from the 2001 National Jewish Population Survey. We focused upon respondents who identified with a given denomination and reported membership in a congregation, aware that a small number of congregants belong to congregations whose denominational identity differs from their own.

Average household size by Jewish denomination by geographic location

Jewish Denomination	*New York 8-county area (5 boroughs of New York City, Nassau, Suffolk and Westchester)*	*Rest of US*
Orthodox	4.0	3.7
Conservative	2.6	2.7
Reform	2.6	2.7
Reconstructionist	2.6	2.7

We noted significant-enough differences between means for the New York eight-county area and the rest of the country to warrant treating New York separately. Hence, we applied mean scores specific to the eight-county New York area, as provided by the 2011 Jewish Community Study of New York. These differed from those applied to other parts of the US. Illustrative and relevant means are provided below:

Outside the New York 8-county area, in selected other counties with high concentrations of Orthodox Jews, we also assigned a mean household size of 4.0. In a few other instances of heavy Orthodox concentration, such as in Kiryas Joel (Orange County, NY), where 2010 US Census data provided even higher household sizes, those were used.

From Adherents to Worshipers

We used the 2001 National Jewish Population Survey as well to derive the denominationally specific number of worshippers, drawing upon responses to questions on frequency of religious service attendance. We calculated the average number of weekly services attended per year and applied the mean to its number of total adherents of all ages. The result yielded an estimate of the average numbers of worshippers attending services on any week, by denomination as recorded below.

Average number of worshippers per week by denomination

Jewish Denomination	*Proportion of Adherents Attending Synagogue in a Given Week*
Orthodox	.71
Conservative	.33
Reform	.21
Reconstructionist	.29

Acknowledgments

We gratefully acknowledge the following individuals for their assistance: Rabbi Steven Wernick, Faye Gingold and Marty Kunoff (United Synagogue of Conservative Judaism); Rabbi Joel Baker (Pacific Southwest Region of United Synagogue); Rabbi Daniel Freelander and Carole Goldberg (Union for Reform Judaism); Dan Hazony and Rabbi Judah Isaacs (Orthodox Union); Rabbis Amy Small and Shawn Zevit (Jewish Reconstructionist Federation); Adina Frydman (UJA-Federation of New York) and Ron Miller (North American Jewish Data Bank.

Submitted by: Jonathon Ament and Steven M. Cohen

Appendix I

Muslim Estimate

The following proposal was accepted by the Operations Committee and formed the basis of the Muslim Estimate in the *2010 U.S. Religion Census.*

Proposed Mosque and Muslim Count
Lead Researcher: Ihsan Bagby

Objective: Provide a county level count of all masjids in the United States and obtain a count of adherents and attendance at these masjids.

Participating People/Organizations:

Ihsan Bagby, Professor, University of Kentucky
Riad Ali, President of MuslimGuide.com
Larry Mamiya, Professor, Vassar College
Dave Roozen, Director, Hartford Institute for Religion Research
Rich Houseal, Association of Statisticians of American Religious Bodies
Louay Safi, Executive Director, ISNA Leadership Training Center
Yaser Tabbara, Director of Chapter Development, CAIR

Definition of Congregation: U.S. Religion Census will aggregate to the county level the number of Masjids, defined as (1) a Muslim association/organization, that (2) holds Jum'ah Prayer and that (3) organizes other Islamic activities.

Definition of Adherent: U.S. Religion Census will aggregate to the county level the number of adherents as defined by survey question 6: "Approximately how many Muslims are associated in any way with the religious life of your masjid? Please include adults and children, as well as both regular and irregular participants."

Definition of Attendance: U.S. Religion Census will aggregate to the county level an average attendance as defined by survey question 2: "At a typical Jum'ah Prayer, what is the total attendance—including men, women and children?"

After this proposal was accepted, Bagby outlined the following procedures:

An initial masjid was compiled from four sources, three of them being online sources of information on mosques: (1) the masjid list from the 2000 Masjid Study, (2) Muslim Guide, (3) Islamic Finder, and (4) Salatomatic. Local Muslims were contacted to verify information on existing mosques and identify mosques not on our list. Most local Muslims were representatives of local CAIR chapters. The Islamic Shura Council of Southern California also helped us. In New York City, the Center for American Muslim Research and Information helped. Based on these efforts we identified a little over 1,900 masjids.

From this list we sampled 727 mosques, using a stratified sample based on zip codes. A first-class letter was sent to masjids asking them to participate in the study. Only about 10 masjids responded. Interviewers conducted a phone interview with masjid leaders. A masjid leader was defined as (1) the Imam or President of the mosque or (2) a member of the Mosque's Board. About 9 interviewers were hired at different times to conduct the telephone interviews.

Interviewers were asked to modify the existing masjid list as they sought to locate masjid leaders. Through this process the original list was expanded to its final number of 2,106 mosques.

Estimating Adherents and Attendance to the County Level:

Bagby was able to supply location information for every masjid in the United States to the U.S. Religion Census data collection office. He used the survey information to estimate a total Muslim population within each state. The U.S. Religion Census staff then used Bagby's state figures to estimate adherents and attendance for each mosque. For surveyed masjids, the reported adherent and attendance counts were used. For those not surveyed, the remaining state Muslim counts were assigned proportionately, with larger estimates for those masjids within larger metropolitan areas. Totals were then aggregated to the county level.

Appendix J
Non-denominational Christian Churches

Over the past several years, the primary researcher has been collecting nondenominational church lists found on the Internet. To this list were added eight additional listings of non-denominational congregations, house churches, megachurches, and independent networks of churches that were collected on the web and privately during 2009/10. Additionally three purchased mailing lists of independent and non-denominational Christian congregations were added to the database. After all these lists were merged together, the database was then screened for duplicates, incorrect entries, and non church listings.

Following this effort, a team of 6 temporary staff persons spent over 1,000 hours culling the web to attempt to verify the status of these congregations. Every church in the database was looked up on Google and in the online Yellow Pages to confirm if it existed and if it was independent/non-denominational. Every church was also emailed and/or called in order to confirm further their independent/non-denominational status, their membership and their attendance. Additionally, one of the staff members spoke Spanish and established contact with the obviously Hispanic/Latino churches in the listing. Approximately 30% responded to the request and verified their information. While engaged in this research, the staff found additional church lists from the websites of newspapers, towns and counties that added new independent and non-denominational churches. They then attempted to confirm the information on these churches using the above method.

The end result was a database that contained over 50,000 potential entries. Over 15,000 were removed due to uncertainty about their existence, size, non-denominational status or being a part of the Vineyard Christian Fellowship or Calvary Chapel Networks (which are listed separately in the U.S. Religion Census). The resulting 35,496 congregations are the best estimate of the independent and non-denominational churches in the U.S.

Even given these efforts, the primary researcher is certain that the current listing is not entirely accurate. The independent status or exact size of many churches could not be confirmed. Additionally, we found that when we checked several cities approximately 9 months later, quite a few of the previously confirmed congregations had already closed. Non-denominational and independent congregations are a very fluid grouping of churches. Additionally some of the non-denominational churches listed might be affiliated with a denomination but did not indicate it on their website, in their published material or even after we contacted them.

Submitted by: Scott Thumma

Appendix K
On-line Listings

Many religious groups now provide on-line locators for the benefit of those looking for one of their congregations. Rarely, these include membership or attendance information as well. The Operations Committee preferred to obtain information directly from a religious body, but opted to use these on-line listings when such direct information was unavailable.

Church locations for sixty-eight groups were obtained from such on-line listings. Three groups provided on-line attendance information for each congregation, and four were able to provide membership or adherent numbers. For those without actual adherent counts, membership figures were used to provide adherent estimates by adding an appropriate number to account for children who might be associated with the congregations as well.

Ideally, these locations would have been obtained in 2010, but most were instead gathered at the end of the data collection process. Since this represents over twenty thousand congregations, the Operations Committee had hoped to receive the information from other sources. The month of data collection is shown in the accompanying table.

Group	Date	Congregations
African Methodist Episcopal Church	January, 2012	4,256
African Methodist Episcopal Zion Church	January, 2012	1,657
Alliance of Baptists	January, 2012	124
American Association of Lutheran Churches	February, 2012	70
American Presbyterian Church	July, 2011	3
Anglican Church in North America	February, 2012	913
Apostolic Christian Church of America, Inc.	January, 2012	88
Apostolic Lutheran Church of America	Fall, 2011	52
Assemblies of God International Fellowship	February, 2012	18
Association of Free Lutheran Congregations	February, 2012	276
Association of Messianic Congregations	January, 2012	12
Bible Presbyterian Church (General Synod)	Summer, 2011	20
Brethren In Christ Church	January, 2012	256
Calvary Chapel Fellowship Churches	January, 2012	1,136
Canadian and American Reformed Churches	July, 2011	4
Christian Brethren	January, 2012	183
Christian Methodist Episcopal Church	January, 2012	1,462
Church of Christ (Holiness), U.S.A	January, 2012	172
Church of God by Faith, Inc.	January, 2012	162
Church of God of the Apostolic Faith, Inc.	February, 2012	55
Church of Our Lord Jesus Christ of the Apostolic Faith, Inc.	February, 2012	454
Church of the Lutheran Confession	October, 2011	79
Churches of Christ in Christian Union	August, 2011	194
Communion of Reformed Evangelical Churches	November, 2011	73
Conservative Lutheran Association	August, 2011	4
Covenant Reformed Presbyterian Church	January, 2012	3
Cumberland Presbyterian Church in America	July, 2011	107
Elim Fellowship	January, 2012	103
Enterprise Baptists Association	February, 2012	55
Evangelical Association of Reformed, and Congregational Christian Churches	July, 2011	67
Evangelical Church	January, 2012	128
Evangelical Methodist Church	February, 2012	97
Federation of Reformed Churches	July, 2011	7
Free Church of Scotland (Continuing)	July, 2011	5
Free Presbyterian Church of North America	July, 2011	14
Free Reformed Church of North America	July, 2011	2
Full Gospel Baptist Church Fellowship	February, 2012	699
Grace Brethren Churches, Fellowship of	January, 2012	266
Hutterian Brethren	February, 2012	135
International Fellowship of Bible Churches	February, 2012	27
Jain	February, 2012	71
Korean Presbyterian Church Abroad	January, 2012	193
Lutheran Congregations in Mission for Christ	February, 2012	673
National Spiritualist Association of Churches	January, 2012	84
North American Lutheran Church	February, 2012	305
(Original) Church of God	February, 2012	13
Pentecostal Fire-Baptized Holiness Church	February, 2012	216
Pentecostal Free Will Baptist Church, Inc.	January, 2012	148
Polish National Catholic Church	August, 2011	119
Presbyterian Reformed Church	July, 2011	4
Primitive Baptists, Eastern District Association of	February, 2012	57
Primitive Methodist Church in the USA	January, 2012	67
Reformed Baptist Churches	February, 2012	353
Reformed Presbyterian Church General Assembly	July, 2011	9
Reformed Presbyterian Church Hanover Presbytery	July, 2011	8
Reformed Presbyterian Church in the United States	July, 2011	9

Appendix K / On-line Listings

Group	Date	Congregations
Shinto	February, 2012	5
Sikh	February, 2012	246
Swedenborgian Church	August, 2011	34
Tao	February, 2012	43
Union of Messianic Jewish Congregations	January, 2012	65
United Catholic Church, Inc.	February, 2012	10
United Holy Church of America, Inc.	February, 2012	369
United Pentecostal Church International	January, 2012	4,062
United Pentecostal Council of the Assemblies of God	February, 2012	25
United Reformed Churches in North America	January, 2012	74
Unity of the Brethren	August, 2011	27
Zoroastrian	June, 2010	33

The discrepancy between web lists and denominational reports has been covered for three of these groups in Appendix C. The remaining groups may have more than 1.4 million members, based on figures reported in published reports or on-line. Their combined reported congregation count of 14,913 is about 11% more than the on-line listing of 13,385.

This page intentionally left blank.

This page intentionally left blank.

This page intentionally left blank.

This page intentionally left blank.

African Methodist Episcopal Church
Adherents as a Percentage of Total Population, 2010

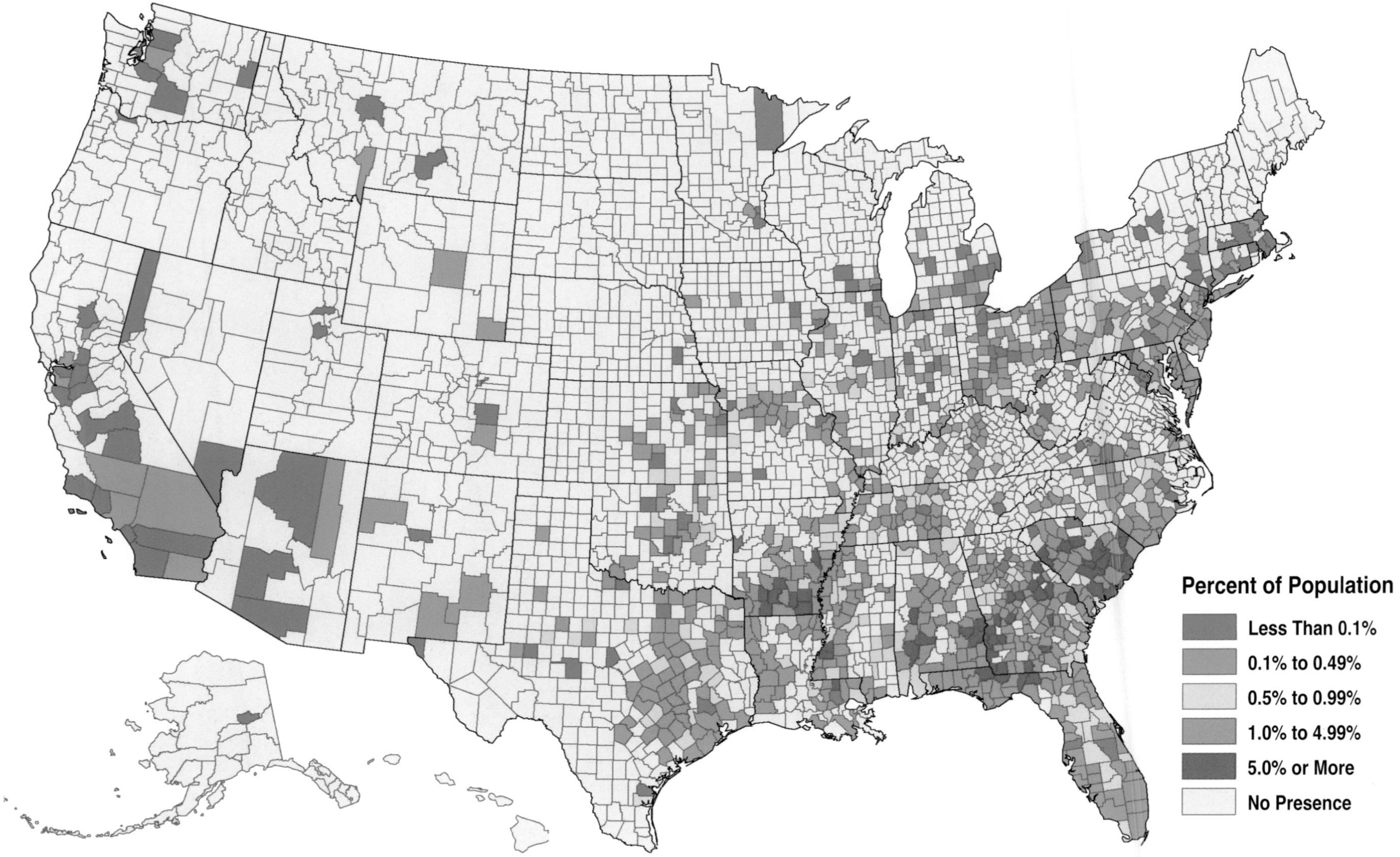

4,256 congregatoins and 1,009,682 adherents were reported in 1,044 counties.
Note: Totals are incomplete; see Appendix C.

American Baptist Churches in the USA

Adherents as a Percentage of Total Population, 2010

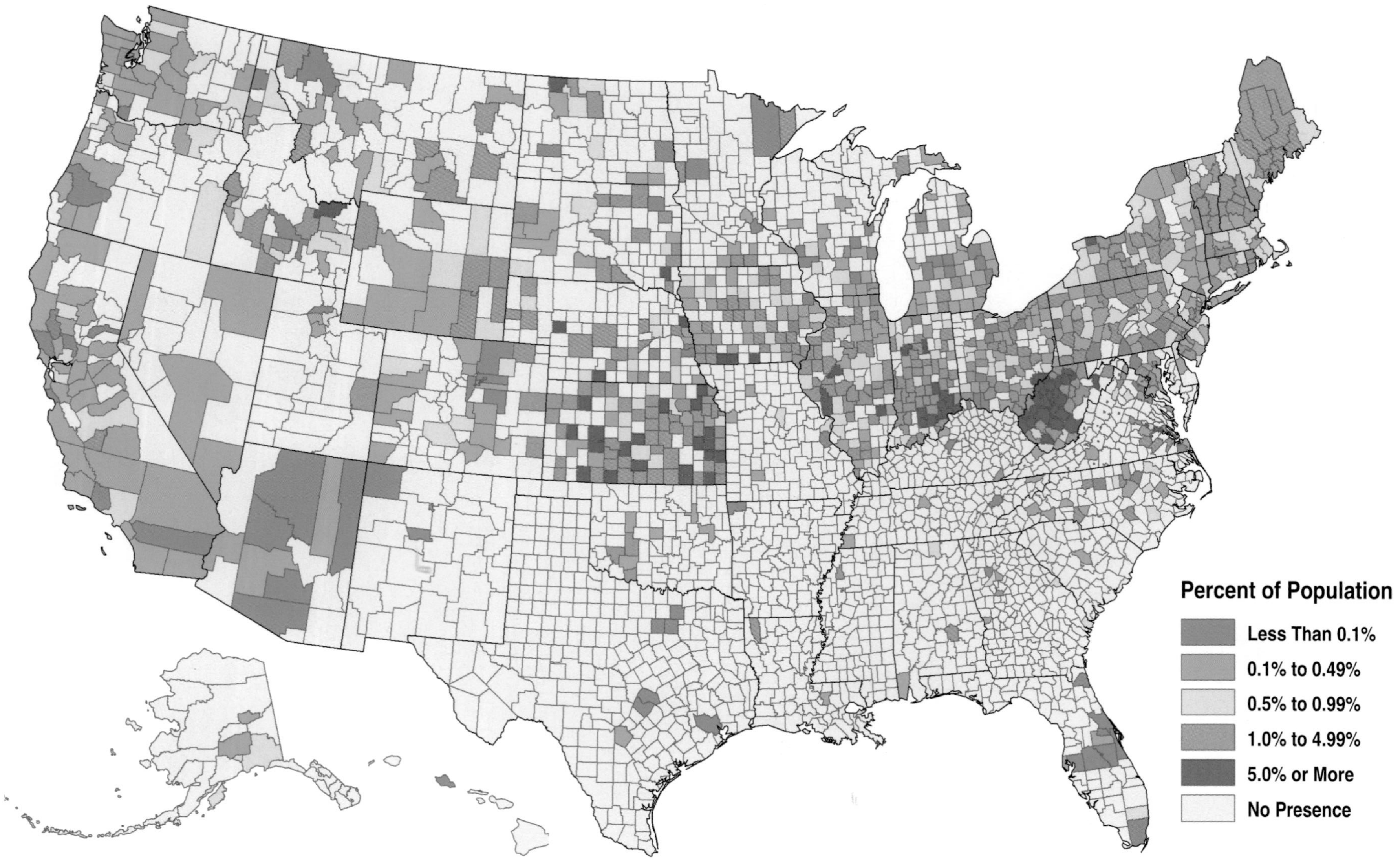

5,243 congregations and 1,560,572 adherents were reported in 1,051 counties.

Created by Research Services using ESRI ArcMap 10.0

Assemblies of God

Adherents as a Percentage of Total Population, 2010

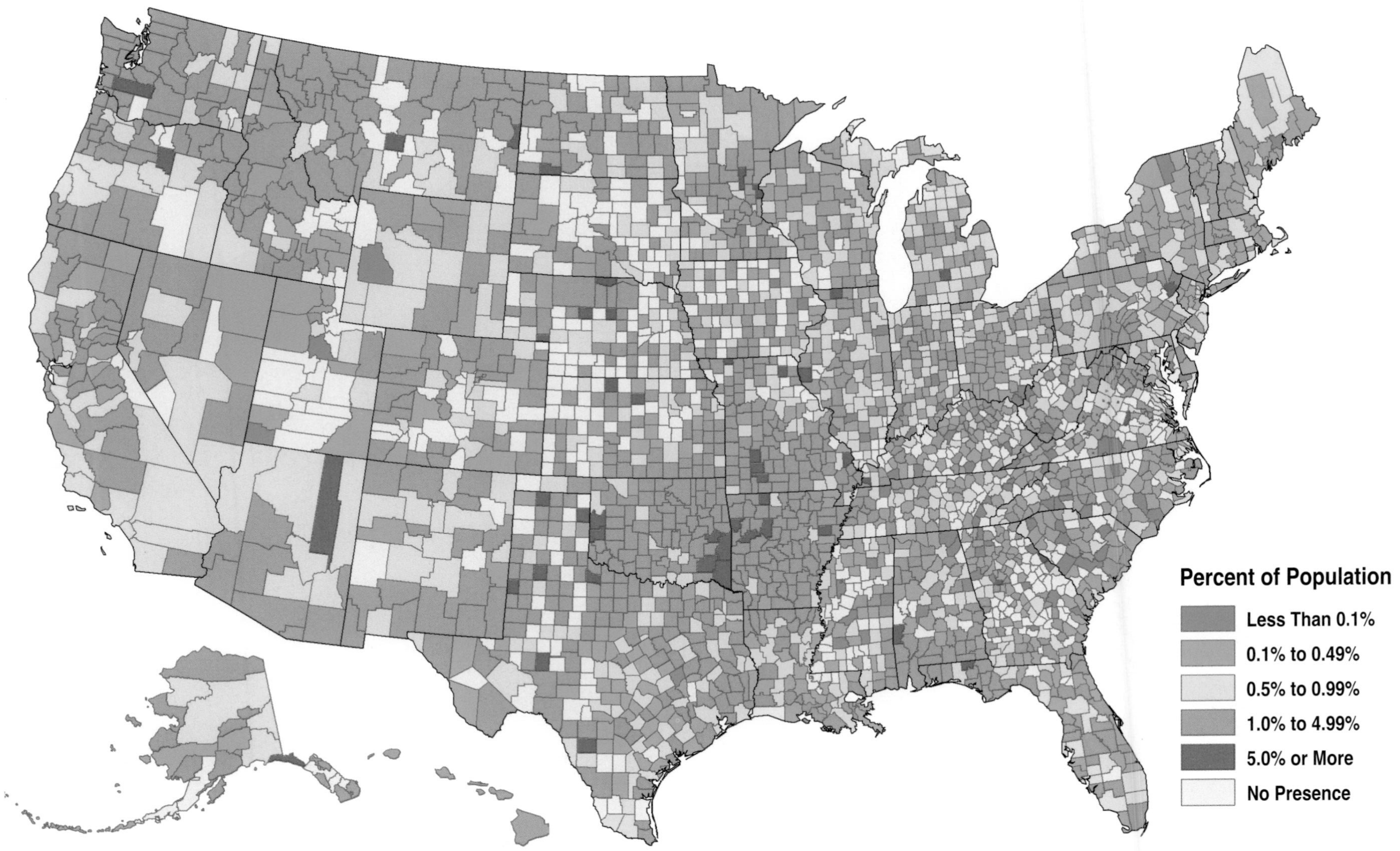

12,258 congregations and 2,944,887 adherents were reported in 2,563 counties.

Created by Research Services using ESRI ArcMap 10.0

Catholic Church

Adherents as a Percentage of Total Population, 2010

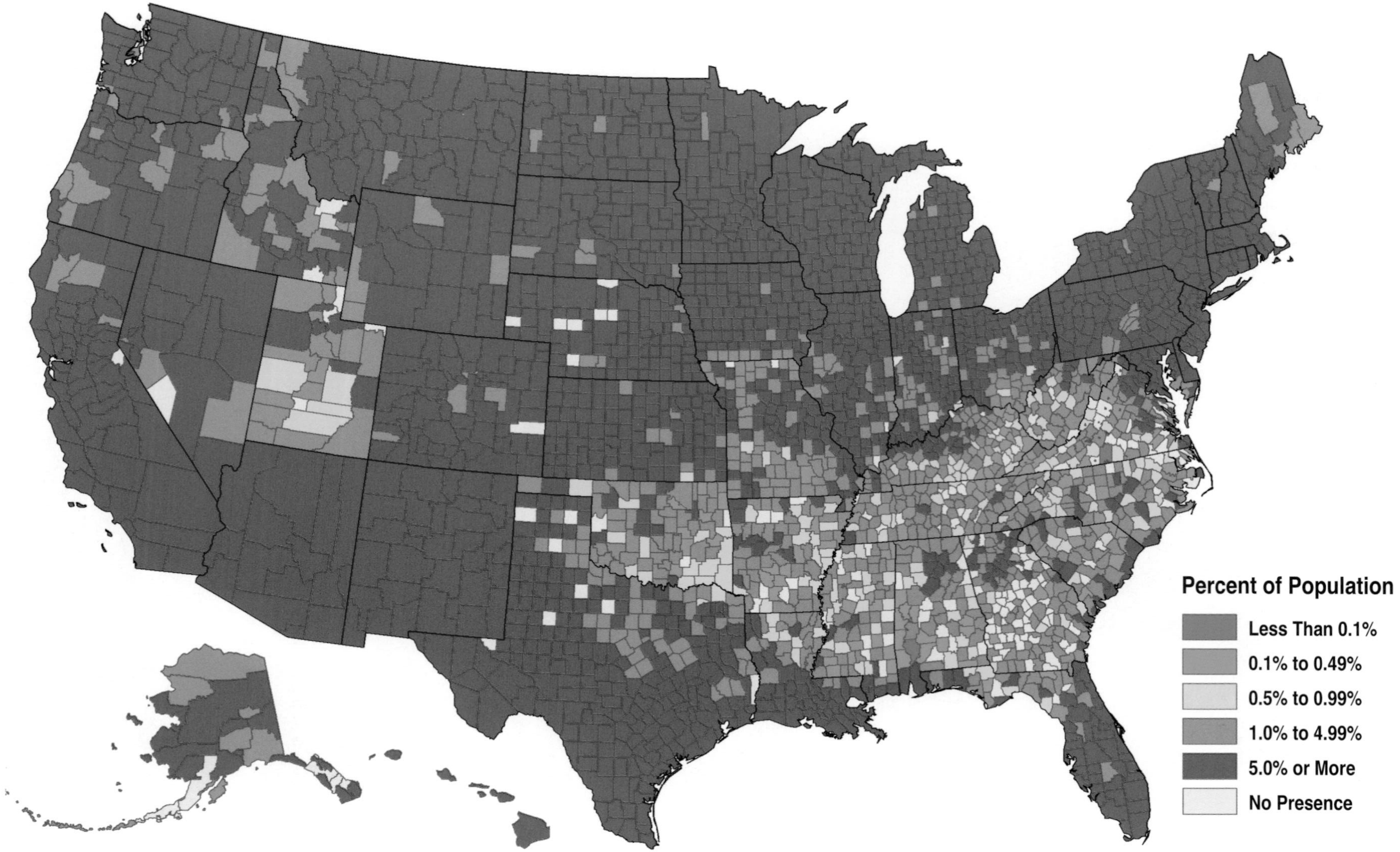

20,589 congregations and 58,928,987 adherents were reported in 2,960 counties.

Created by Research Services using ESRI ArcMap 10.0

Christian Churches and Churches of Christ

Adherents as a Percentage of Total Population, 2010

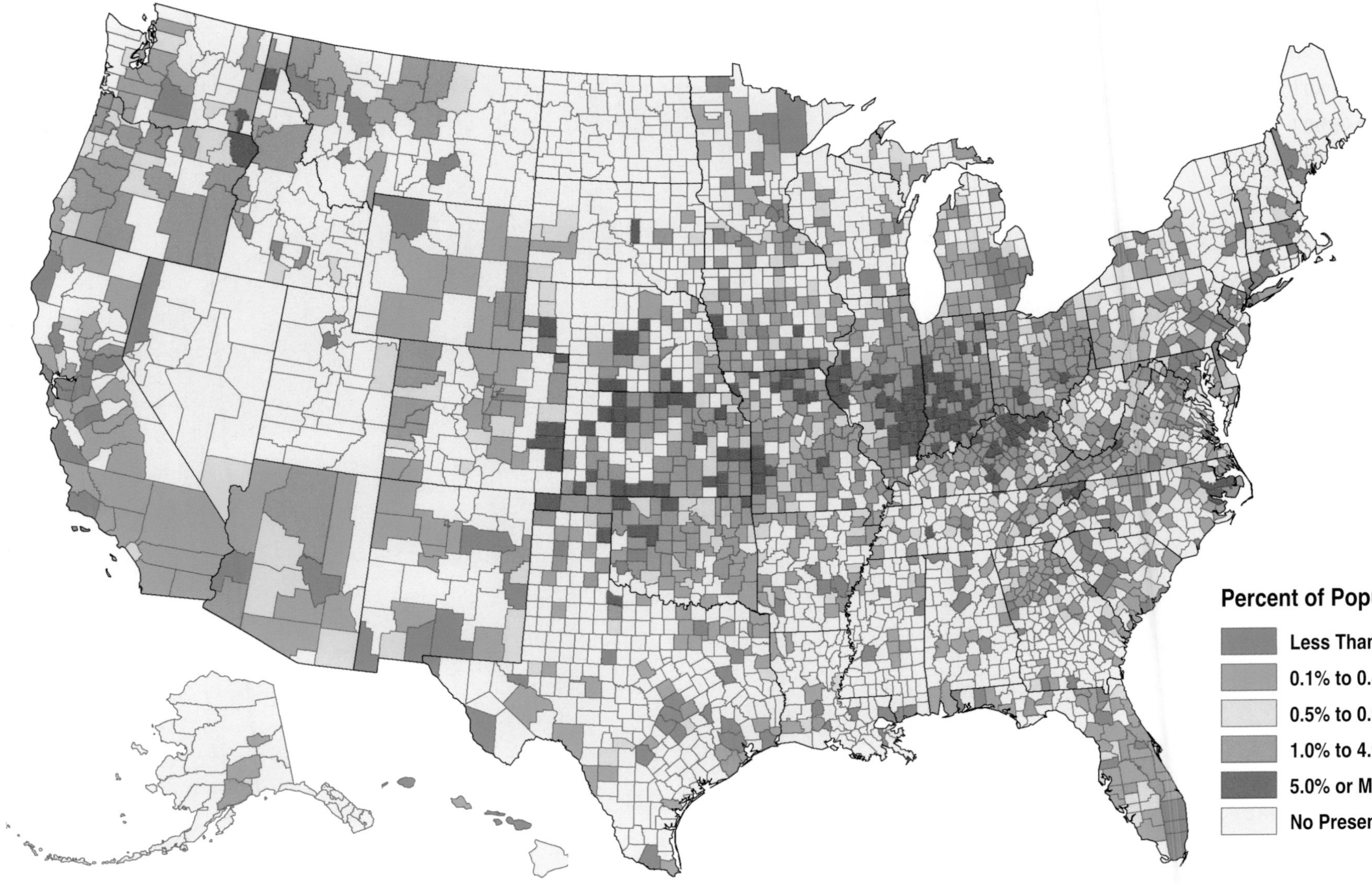

5,293 congregations and 1,453,160 adherents were reported in 1,580 counties.

Church of God (Cleveland, Tennessee)
Adherents as a Percentage of Total Population, 2010

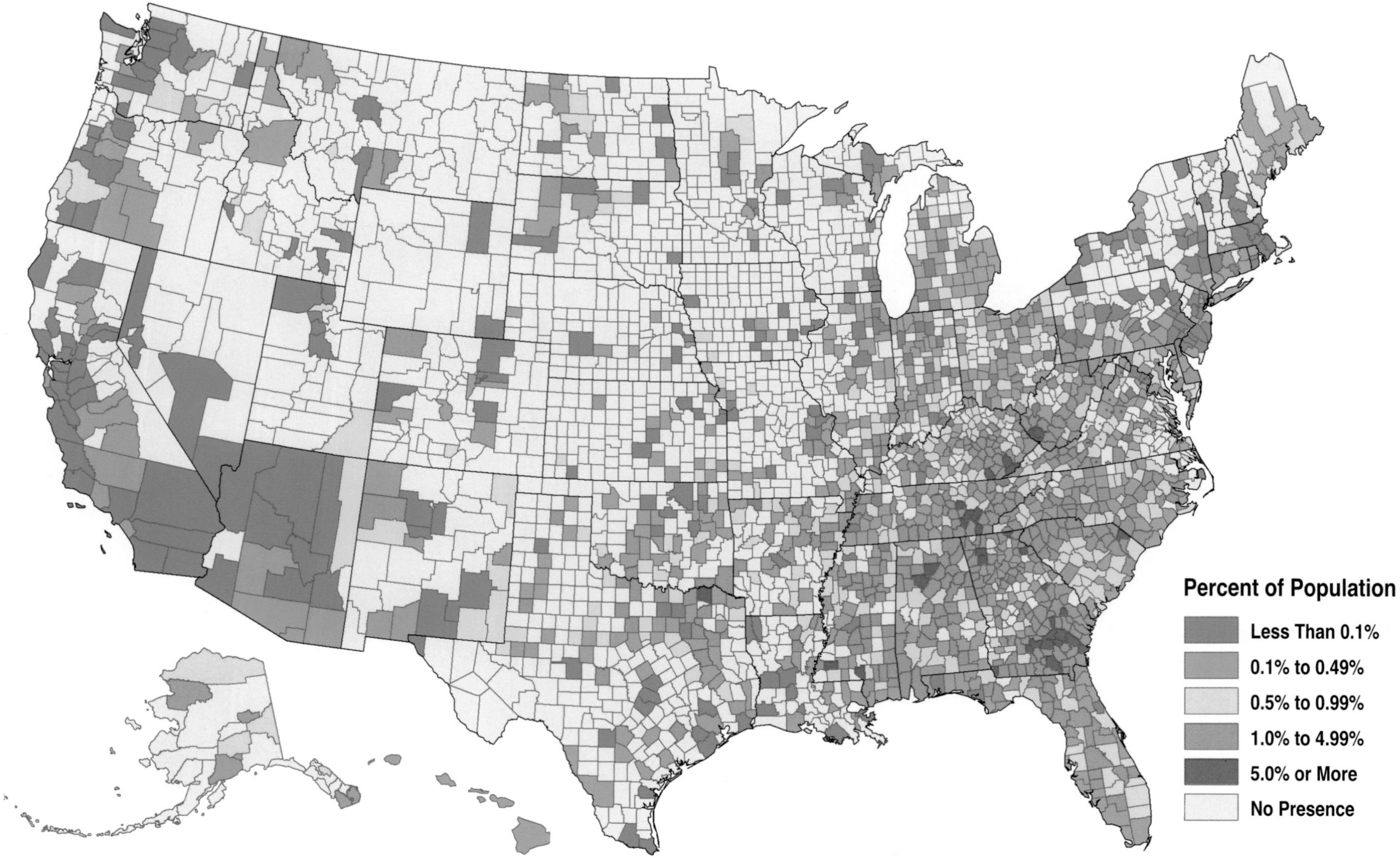

6,100 congregations and 1,109,992 adherents were reported in 1,598 counties.

Church of Jesus Christ of Latter-day Saints

Adherents as a Percentage of Total Population, 2010

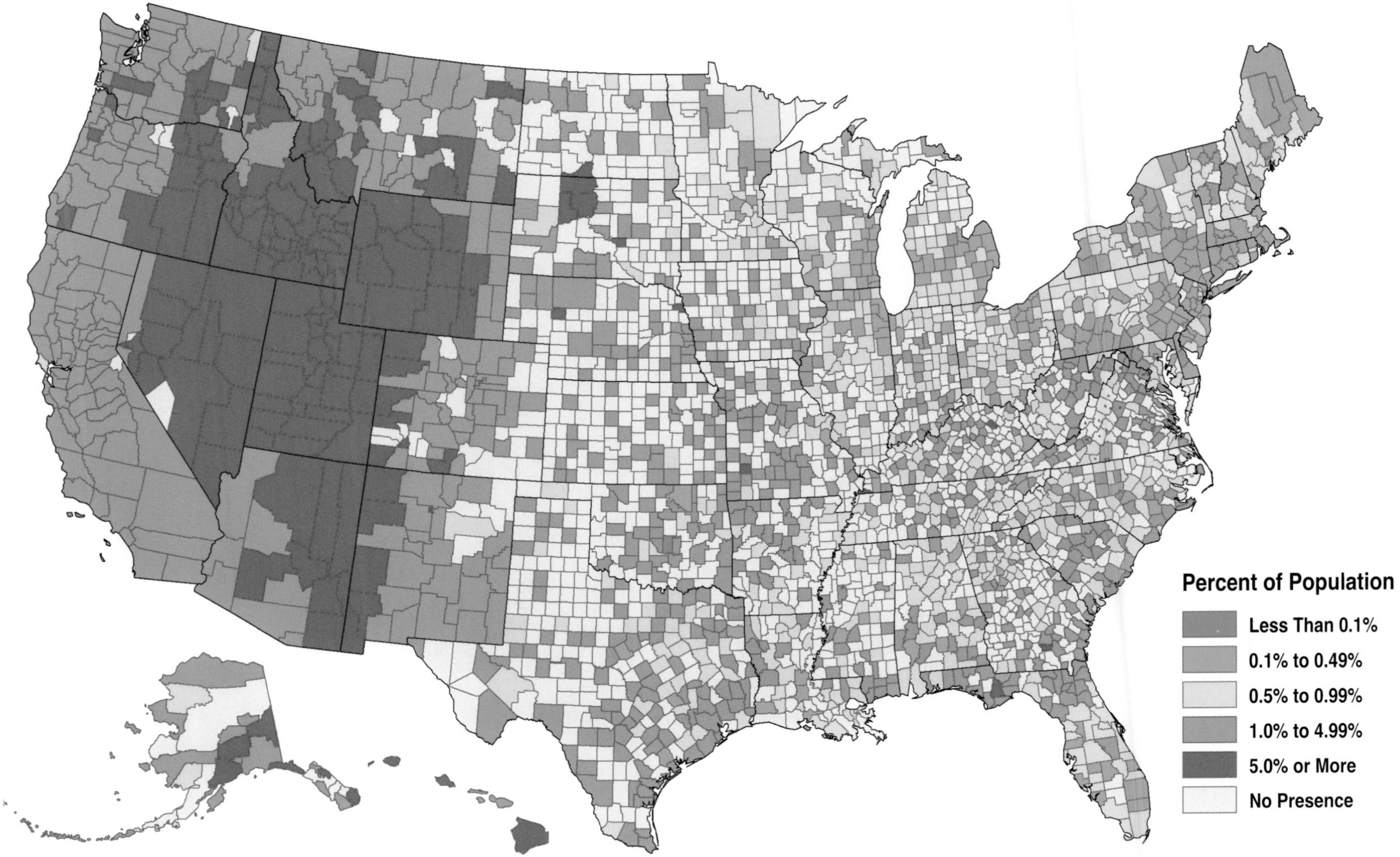

13,601 congregations and 6,144,582 adherents were reported in 1,873 counties.

Church of the Nazarene

Adherents as a Percentage of Total Population, 2010

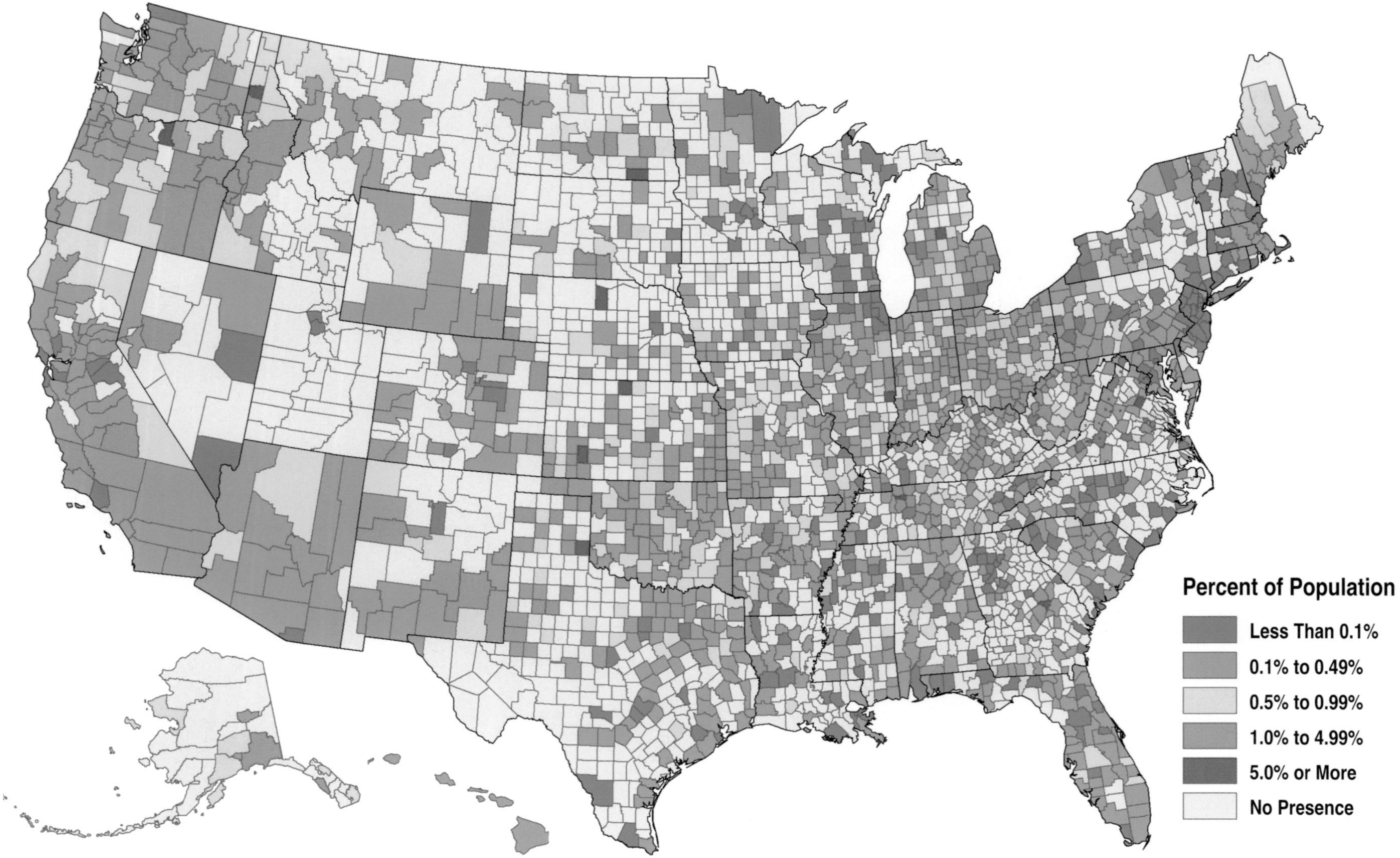

5,056 congregations and 893,649 adherents were reported in 1,766 counties.

Churches of Christ

Adherents as a Percentage of Total Population, 2010

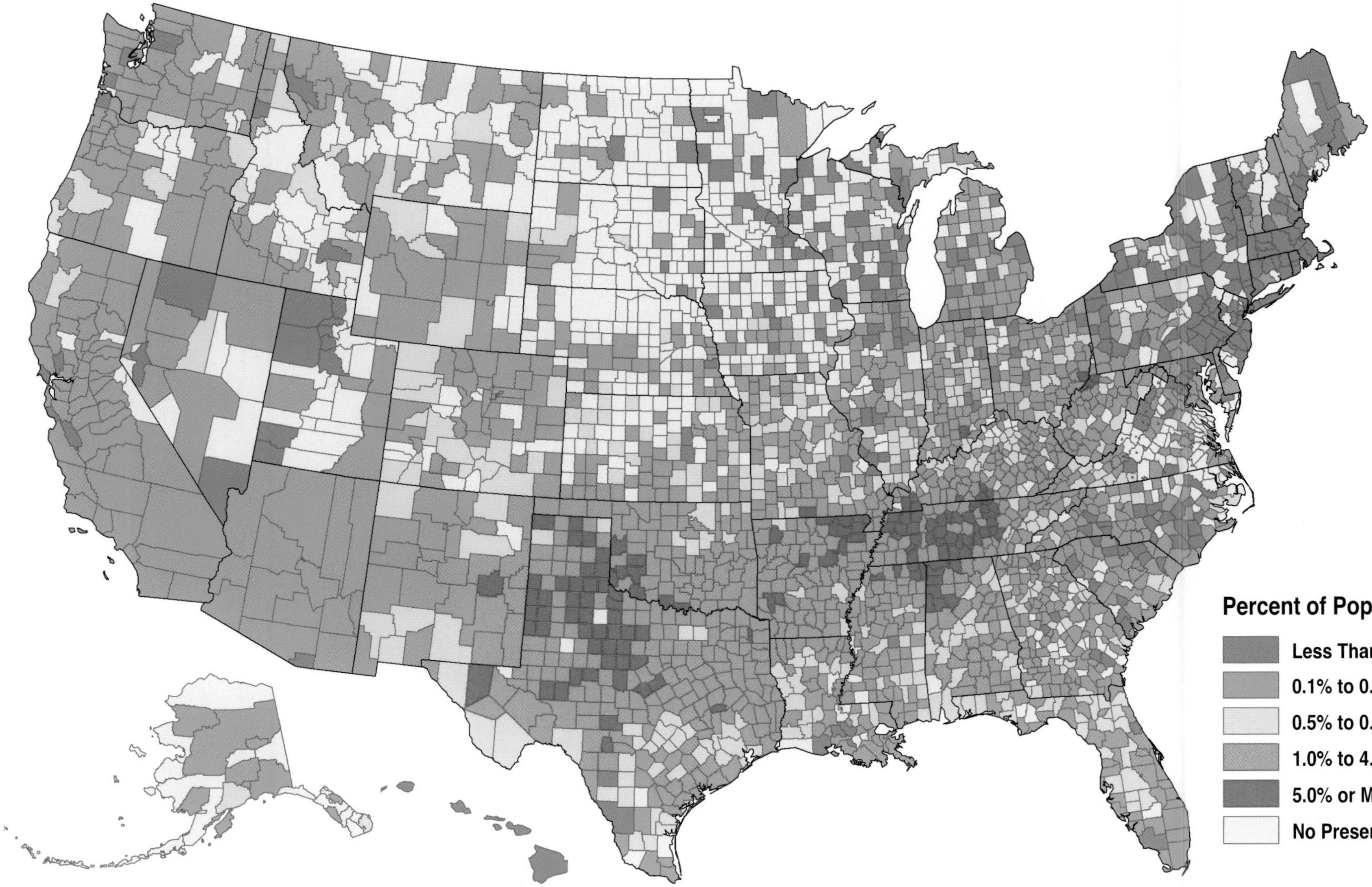

Percent of Population

- Less Than 0.1%
- 0.1% to 0.49%
- 0.5% to 0.99%
- 1.0% to 4.99%
- 5.0% or More
- No Presence

12,584 congregations and 1,584,162 adherents were reported in 2,427 counties.

Episcopal Church

Adherents as a Percentage of Total Population, 2010

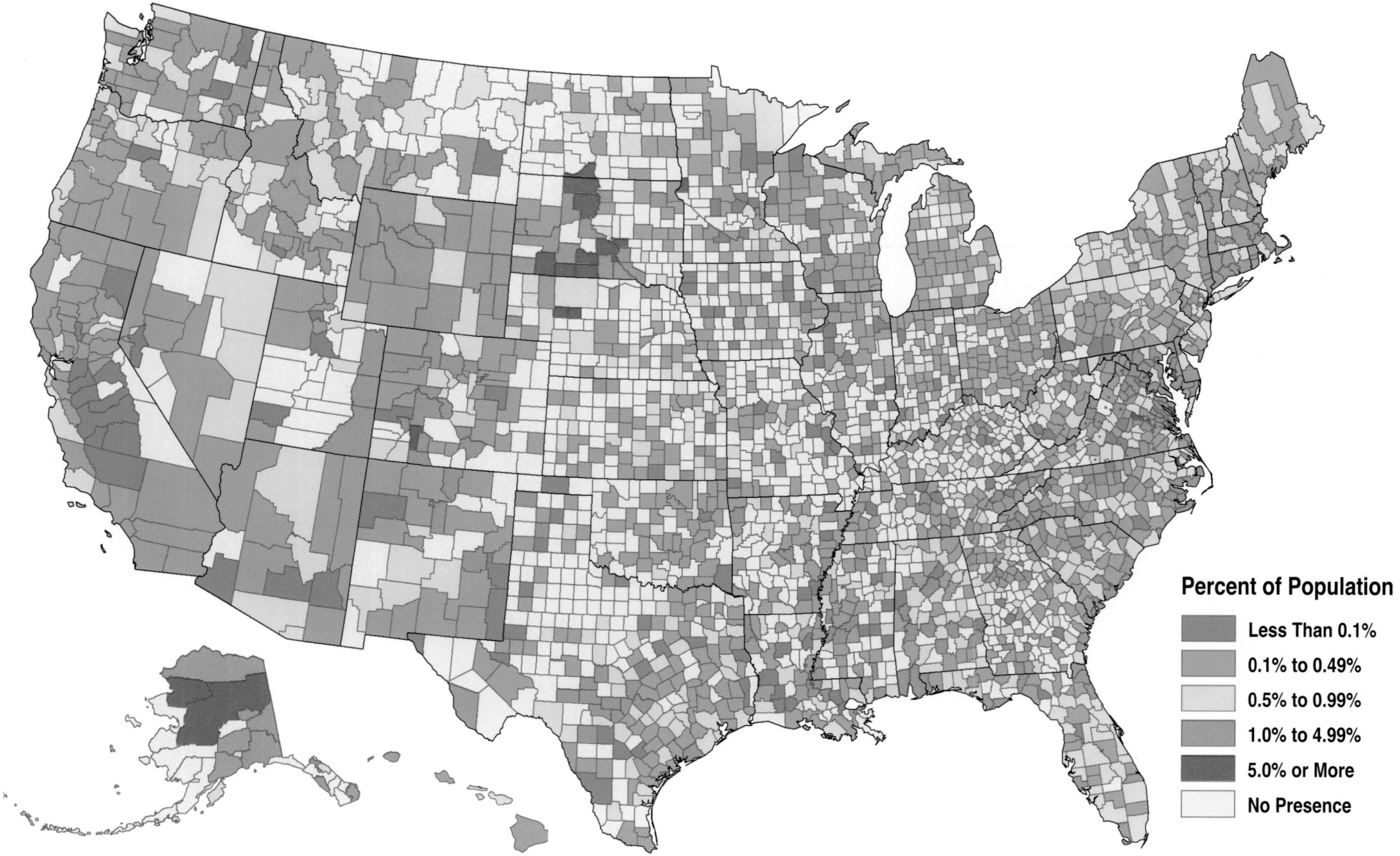

6,794 congregations and 1,951,907 adherents were reported in 2,049 counties.

Evangelical Lutheran Church in America
Adherents as a Percentage of Total Population, 2010

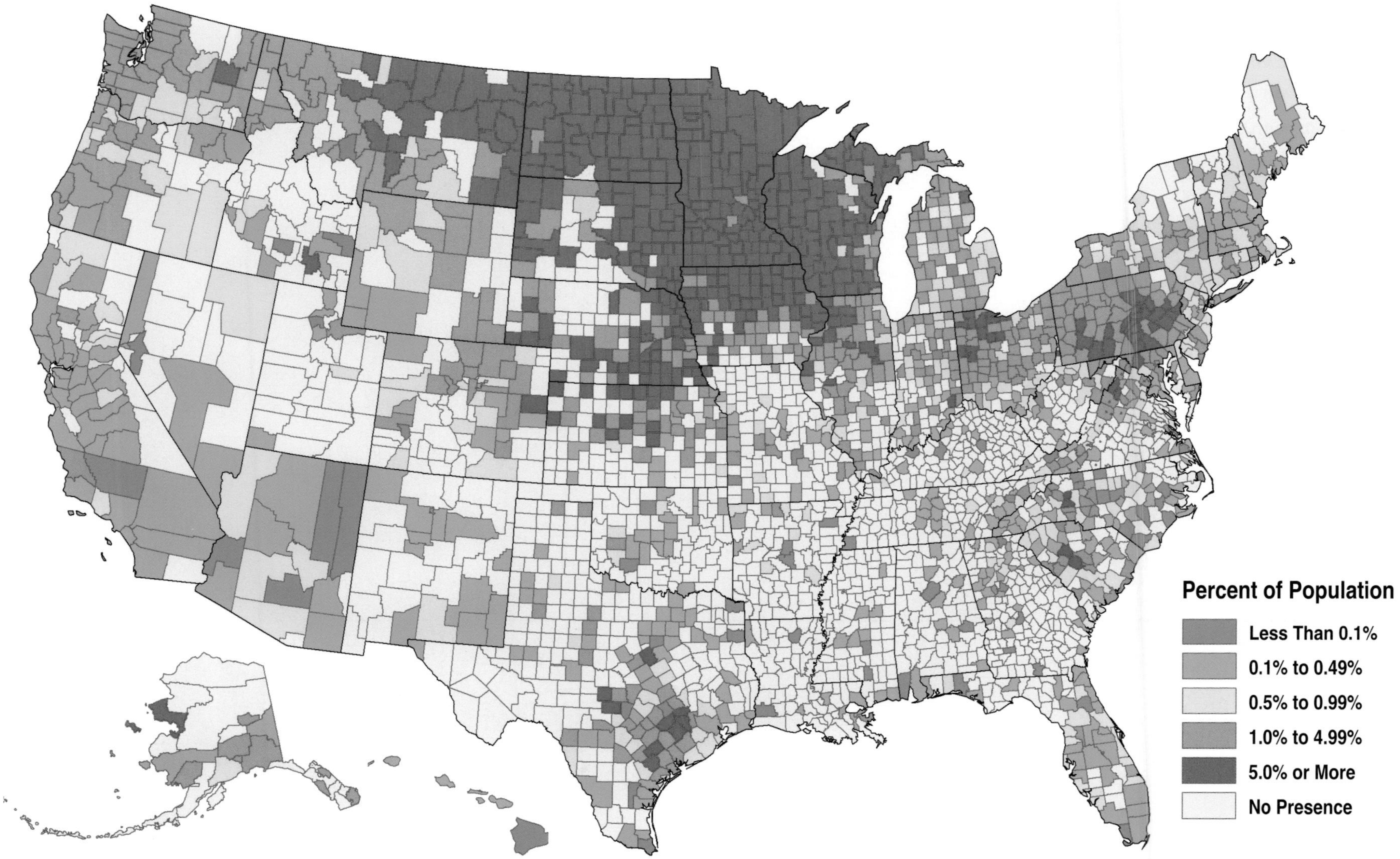

9,846 congregations and 4,181,219 adherents were reported in 1,739 counties.

Created by Research Services using ESRI ArcMap 10.0

Lutheran Church—Missouri Synod

Adherents as a Percentage of Total Population, 2010

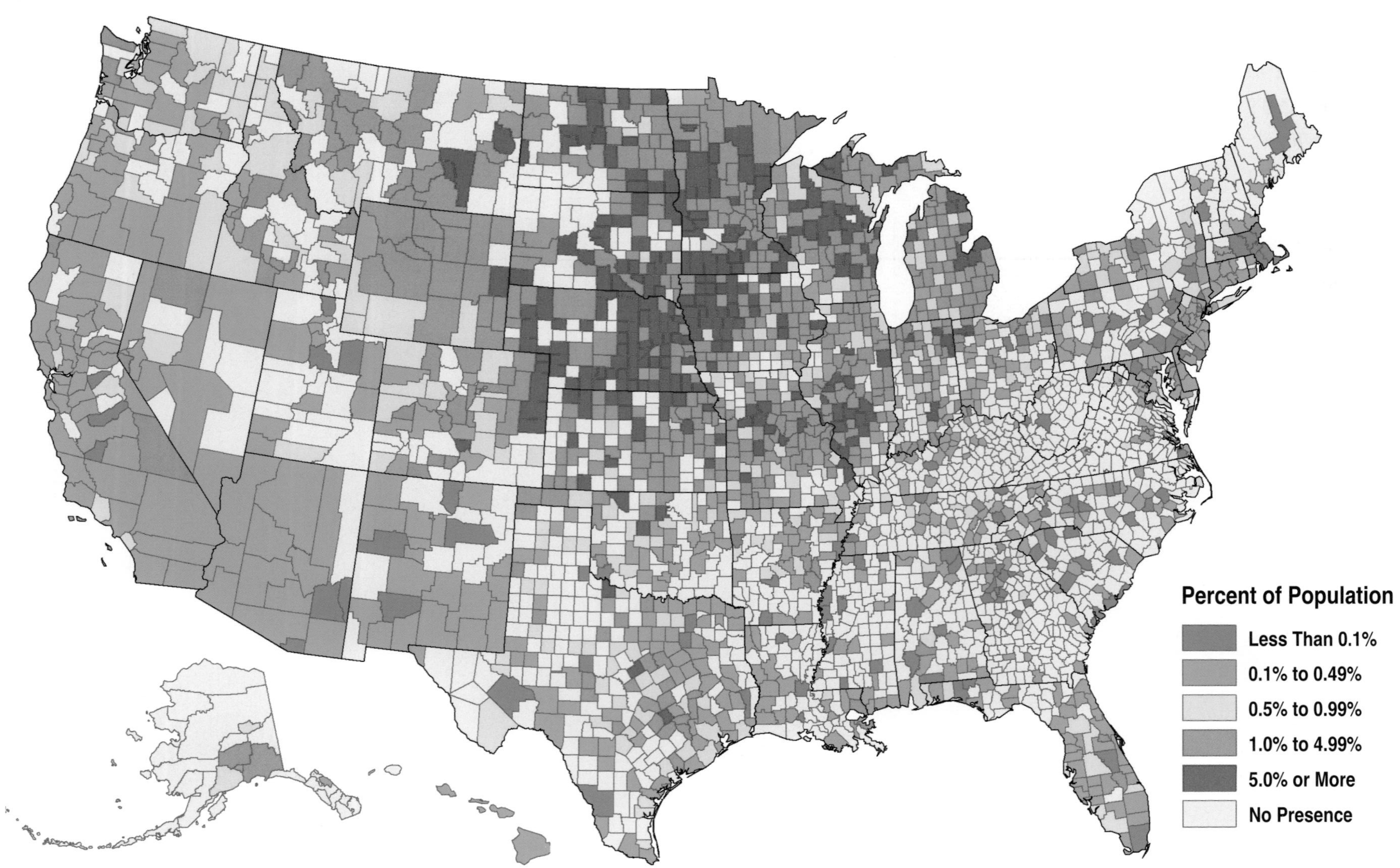

6,040 congregations and 2,270,921 adherents were reported in 1,804 counties.

Muslim Estimate

Adherents as a Percentage of Total Population, 2010

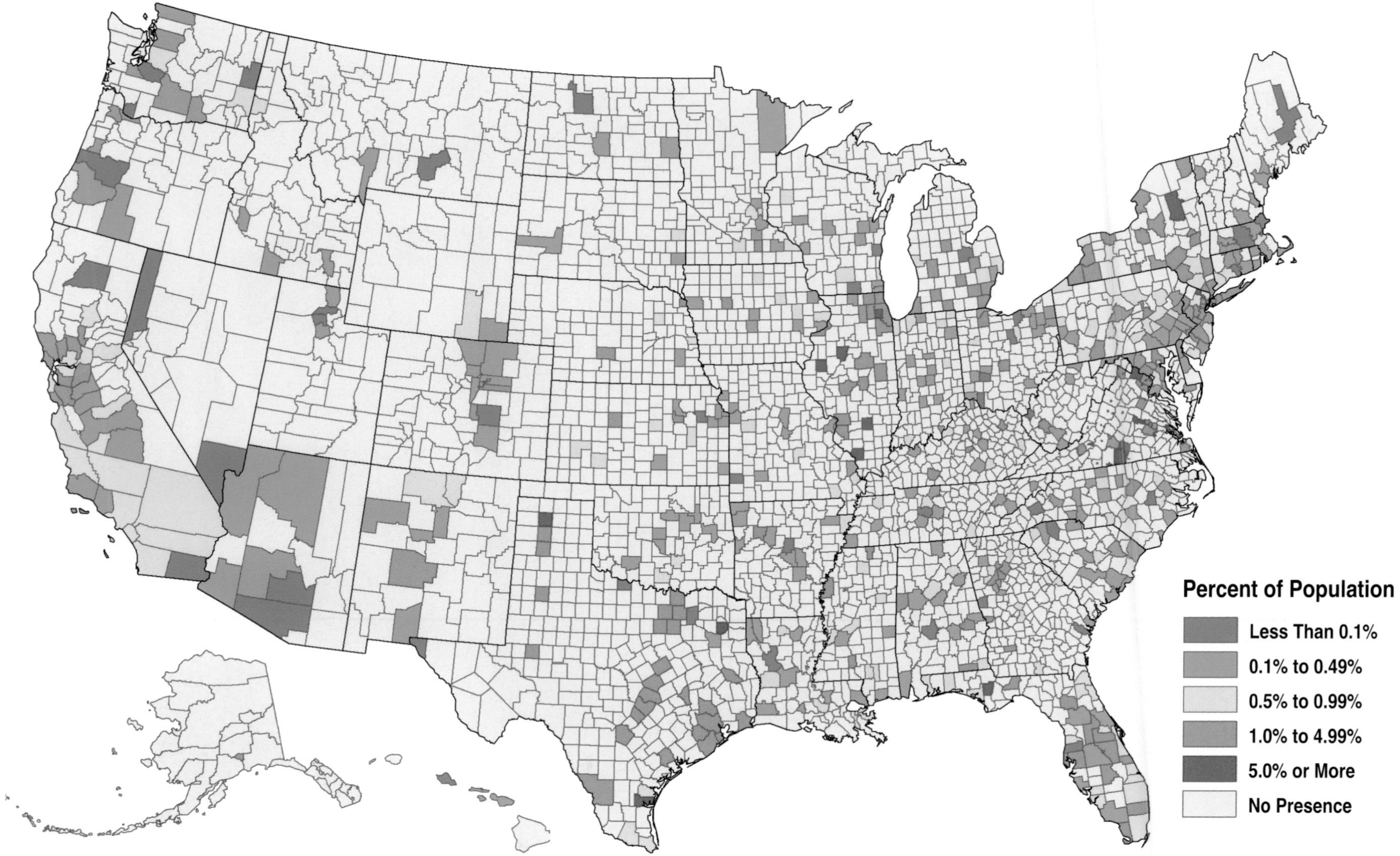

2,106 congregations and 2,600,082 adherents were reported in 592 counties.

Created by Research Services using ESRI ArcMap 10.0

National Baptist Convention, USA, Inc.
Adherents as a Percentage of Total Population, 2010

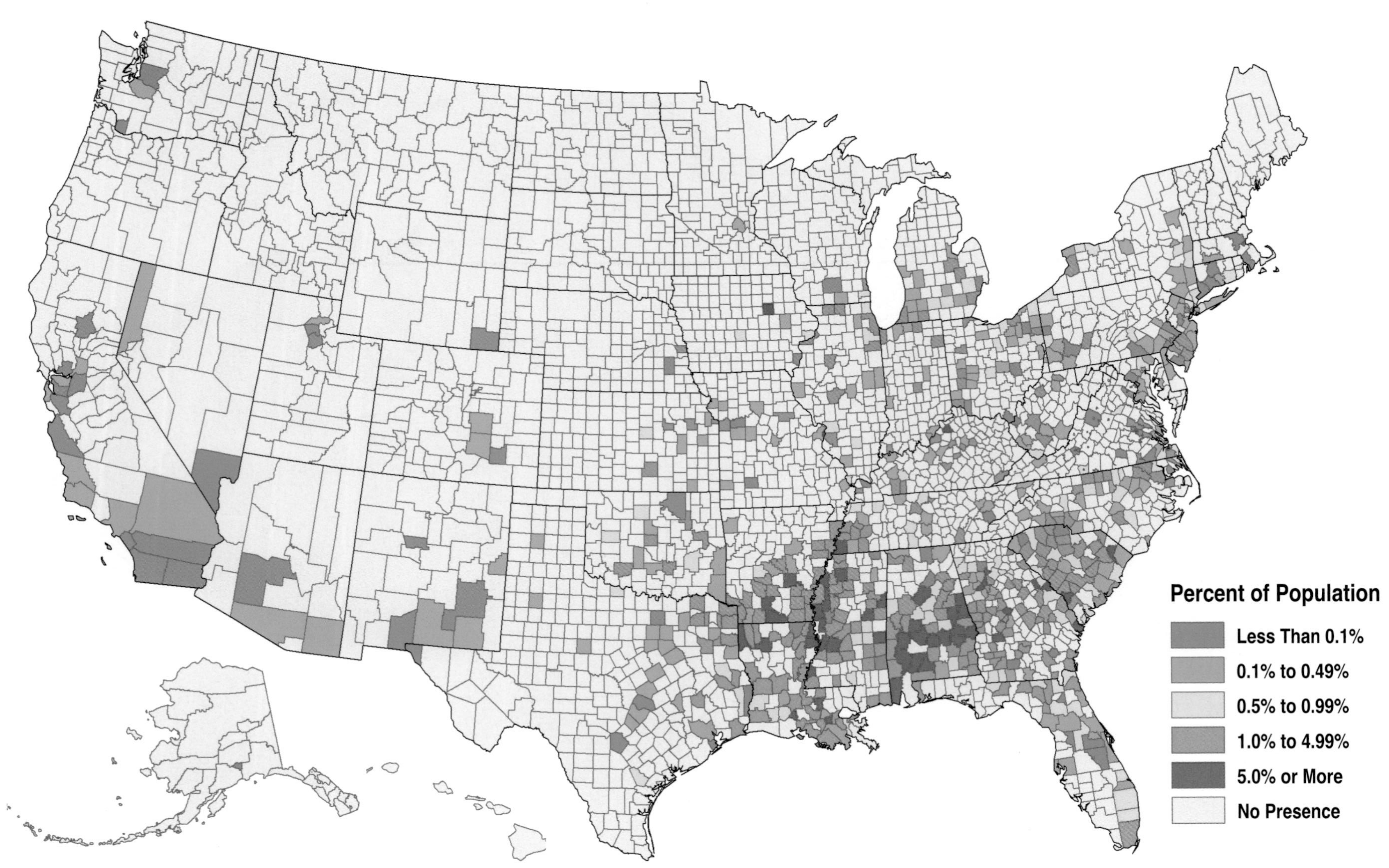

3,536 congregations and 1,881,341 adherents were reported in 722 counties.
Note: Totals are incomplete; see Appendix C.

Non-denominational Christian Churches

Adherents as a Percentage of Total Population, 2010

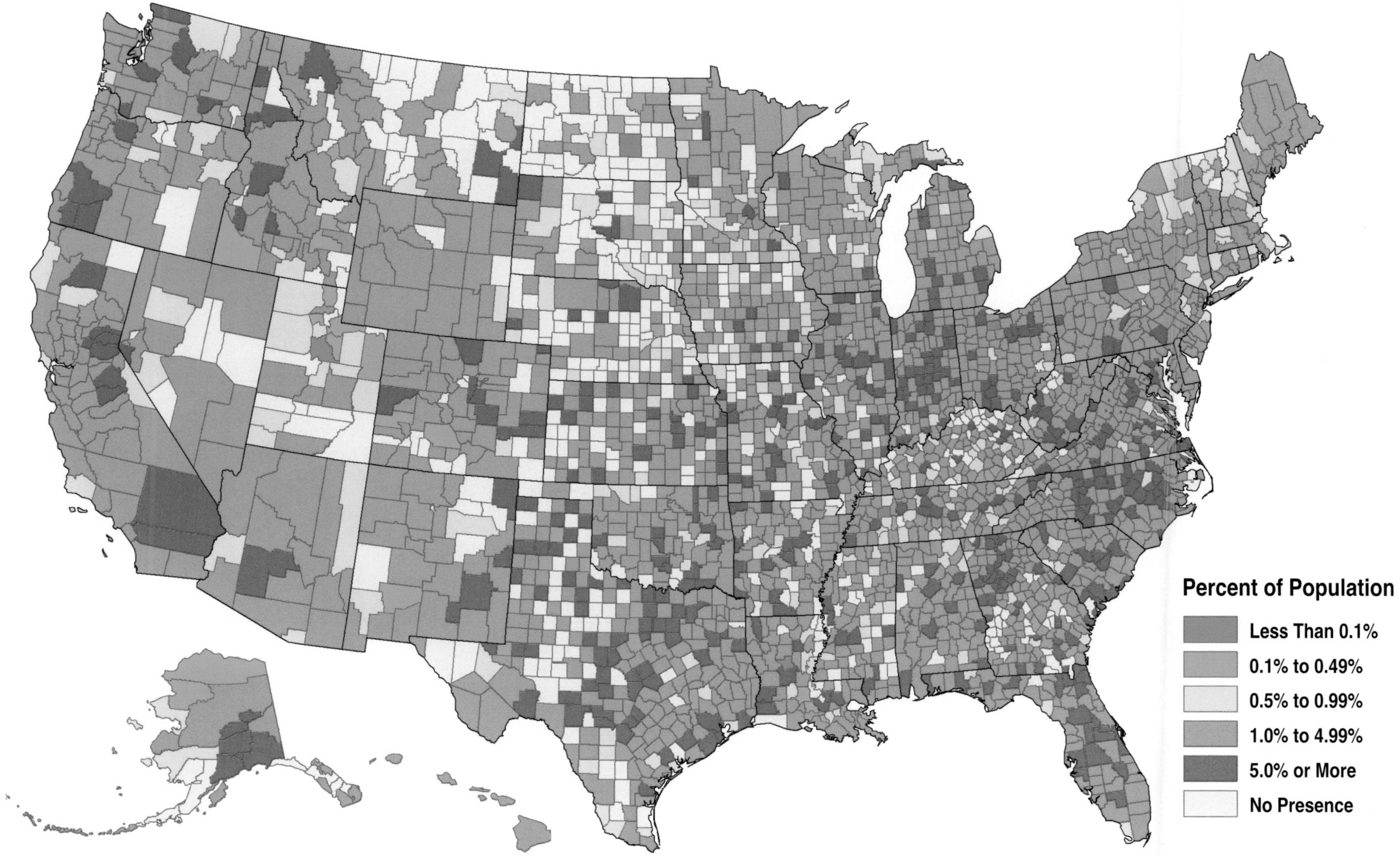

35,496 congregations and 12,241,329 adherents were reported in 2,665 counties.

Presbyterian Church (U.S.A.)

Adherents as a Percentage of Total Population, 2010

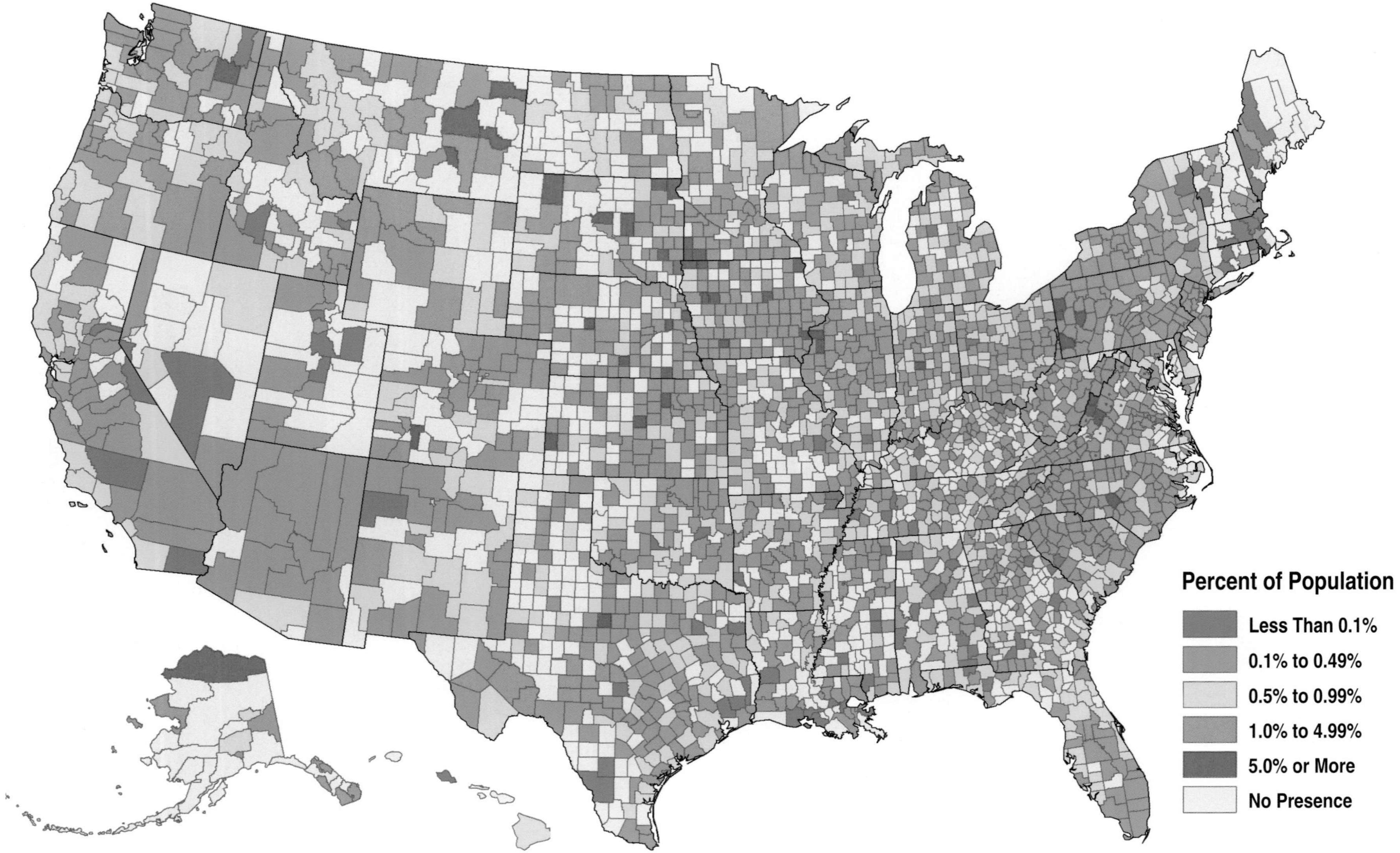

10,487 congregations and 2,451,980 adherents were reported in 2,358 counties.

Created by Research Services using ESRI ArcMap 10.0

Seventh-day Adventist Church

Adherents as a Percentage of Total Population, 2010

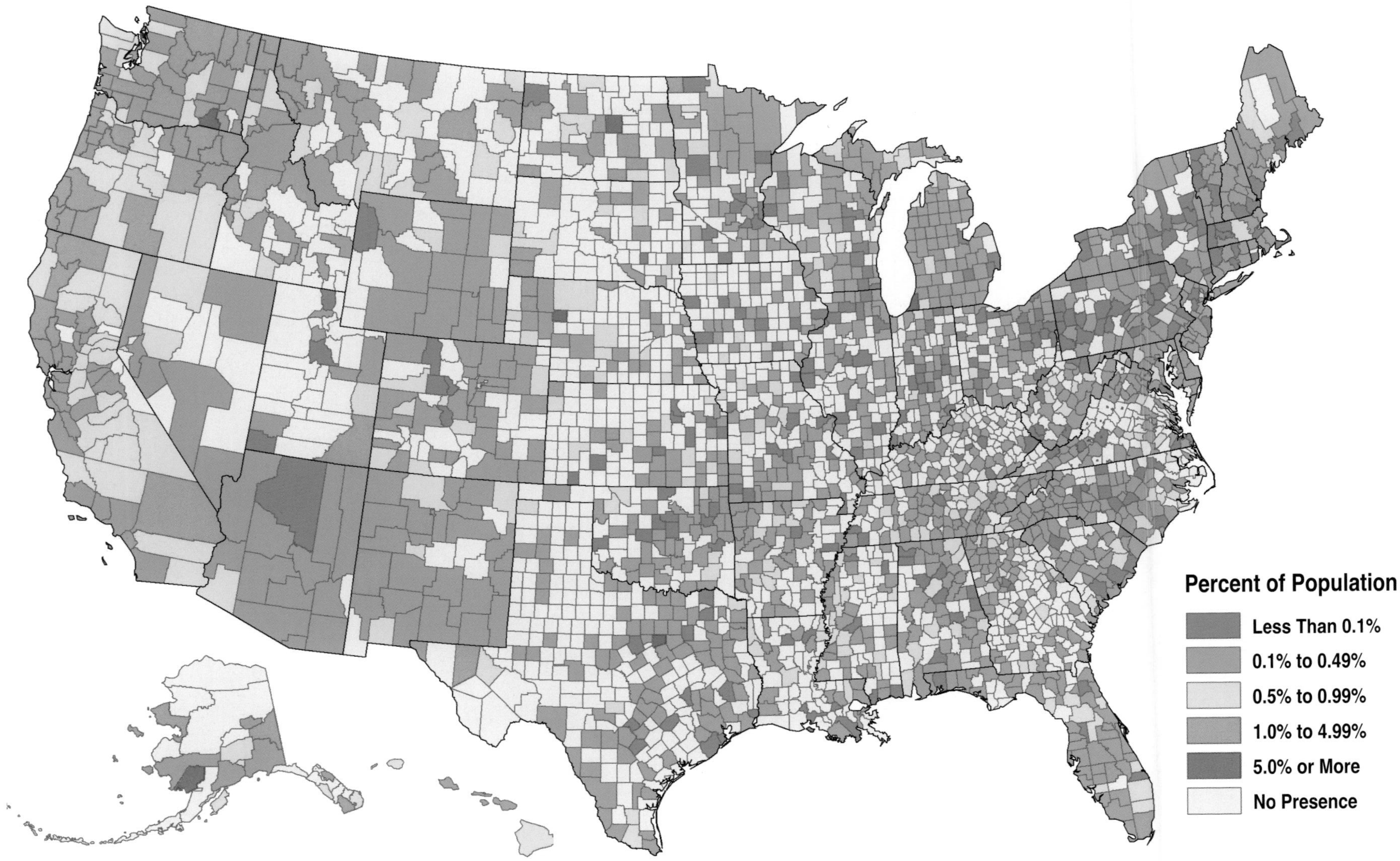

5,665 congregations and 1,194,996 adherents were reported in 1,827 counties.

Created by Research Services using ESRI ArcMap 10.0

Southern Baptist Convention

Adherents as a Percentage of Total Population, 2010

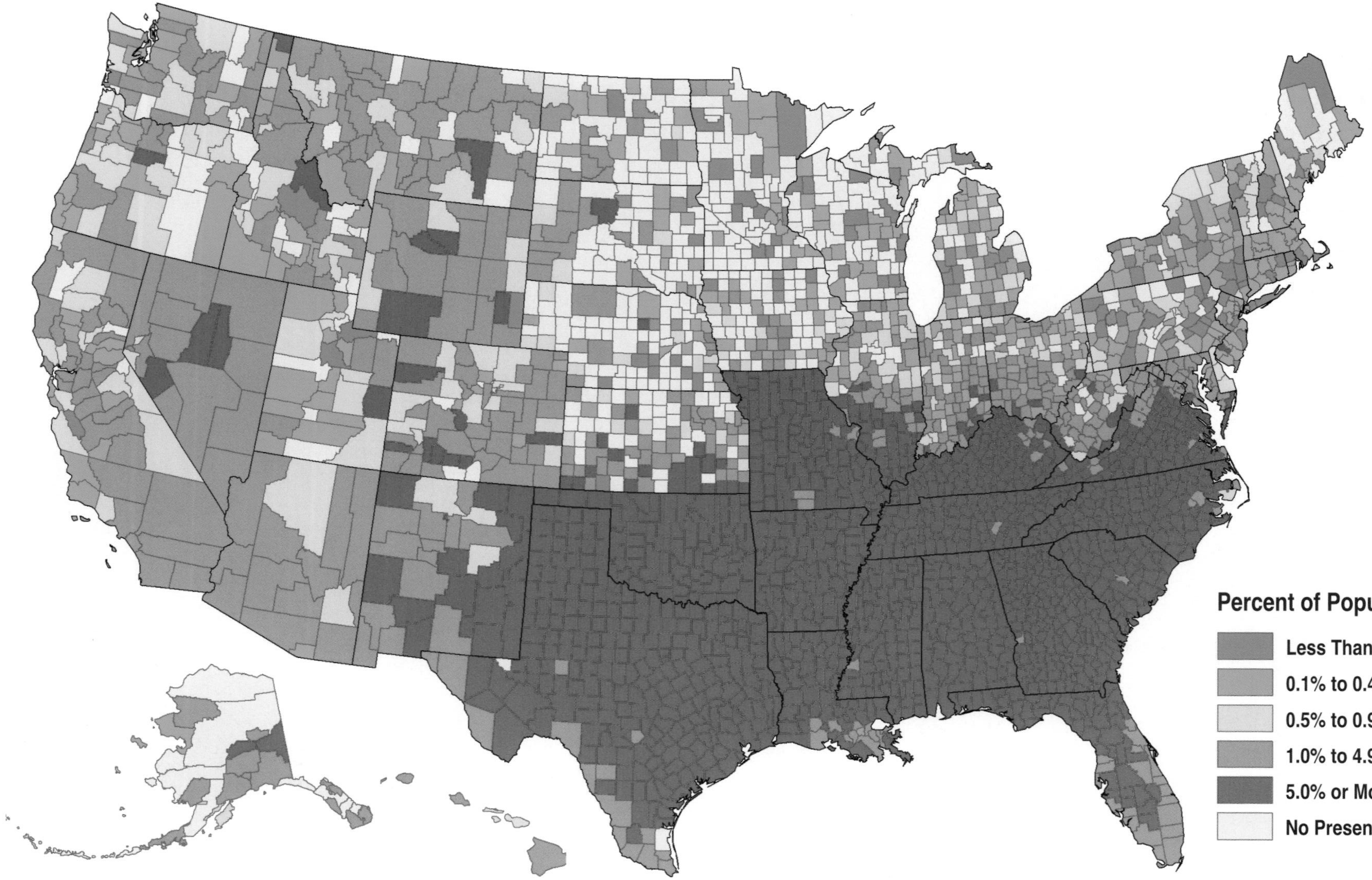

50,816 congregations and 19,896,975 adherents were reported in 2,702 counties.

Created by Research Services using ESRI ArcMap 10.0

United Church of Christ
Adherents as a Percentage of Total Population, 2010

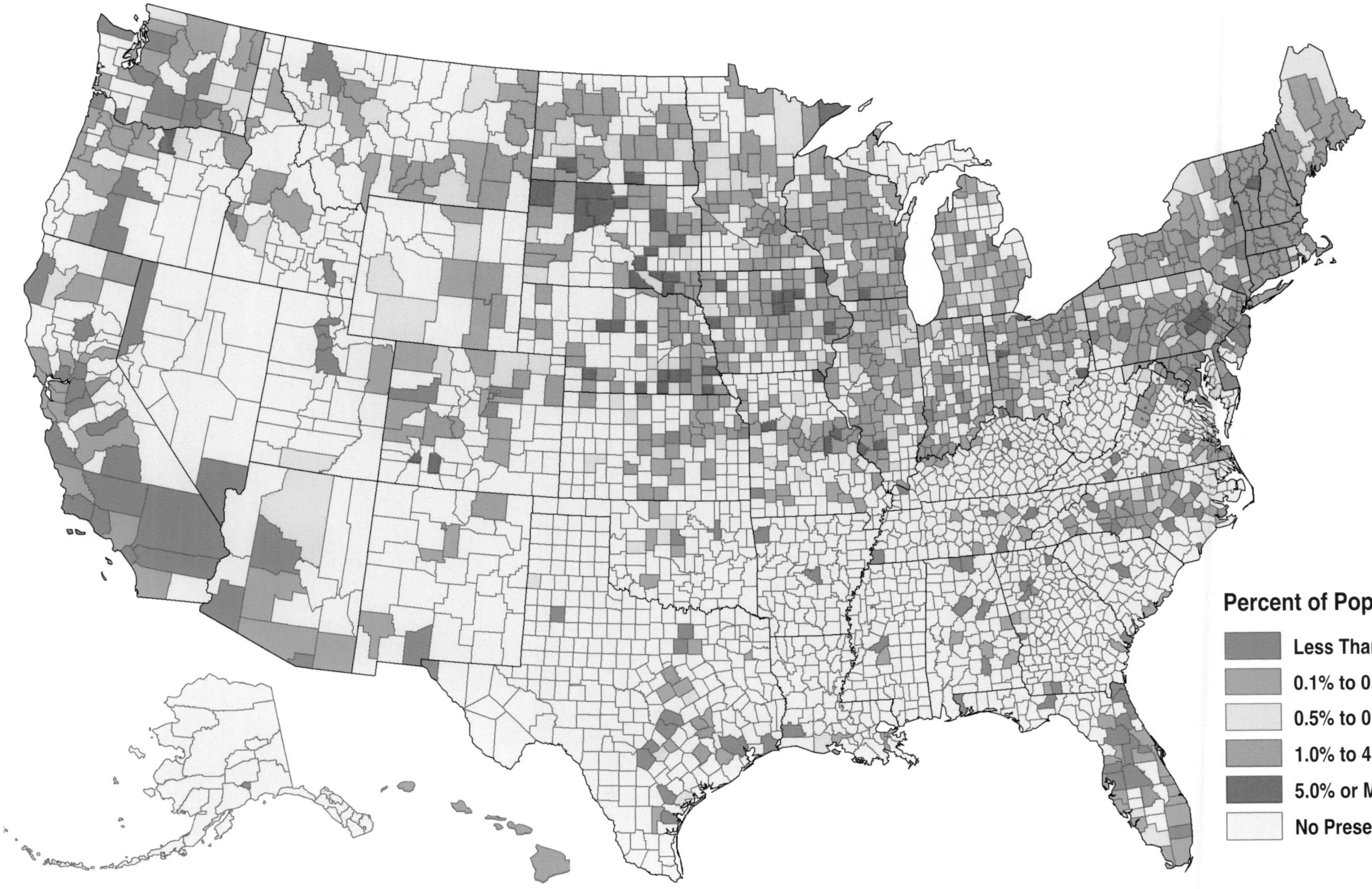

5,225 congregations and 1,284,296 adherents were reported in 1,168 counties.

Created by Research Services using ESRI ArcMap 10.0

United Methodist Church

Adherents as a Percentage of Total Population, 2010

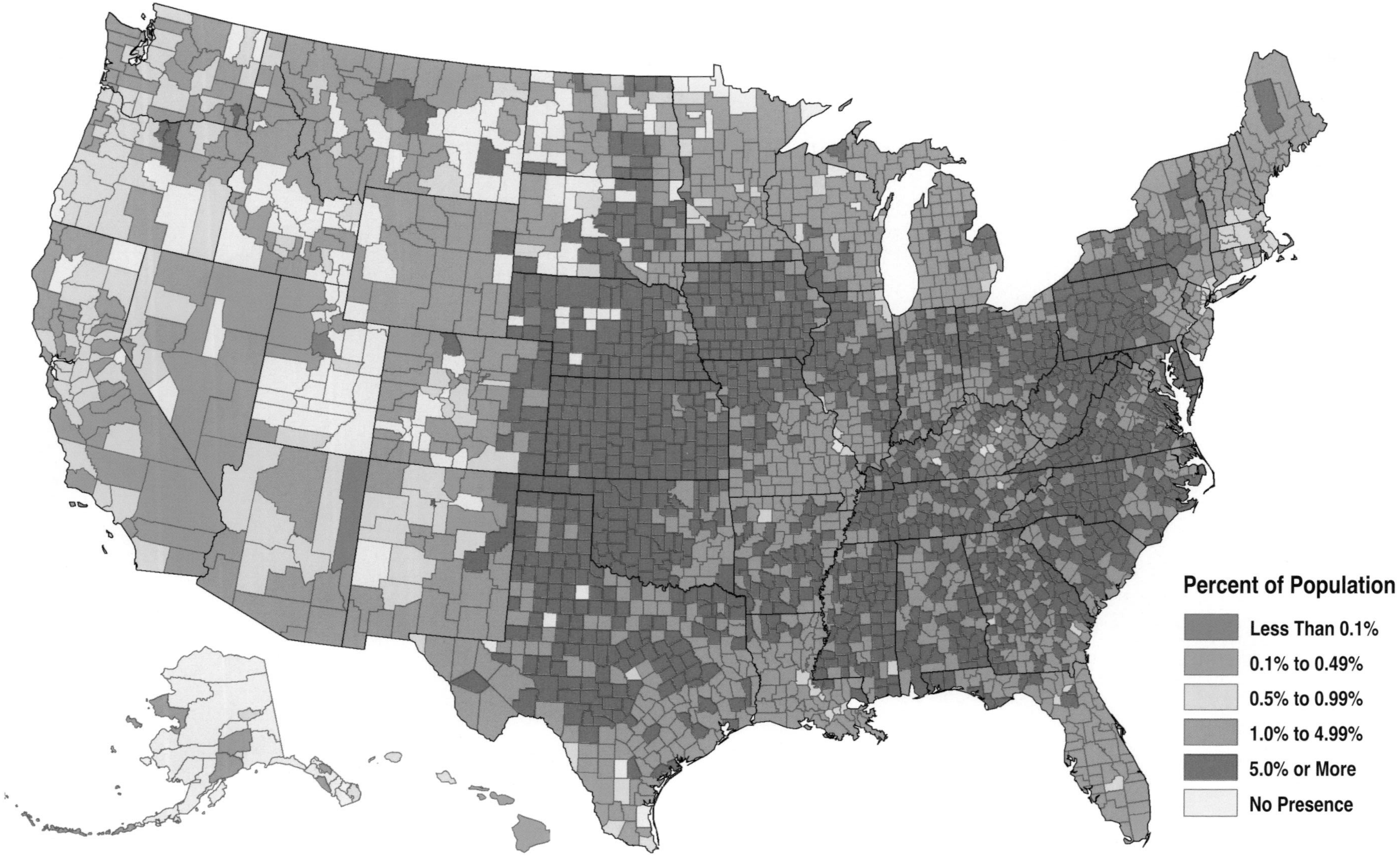

33,323 congregations and 9,948,221 adherents were reported in 2,991 counties.

Jewish Groups

Adherents as a Percentage of Total Population, 2010

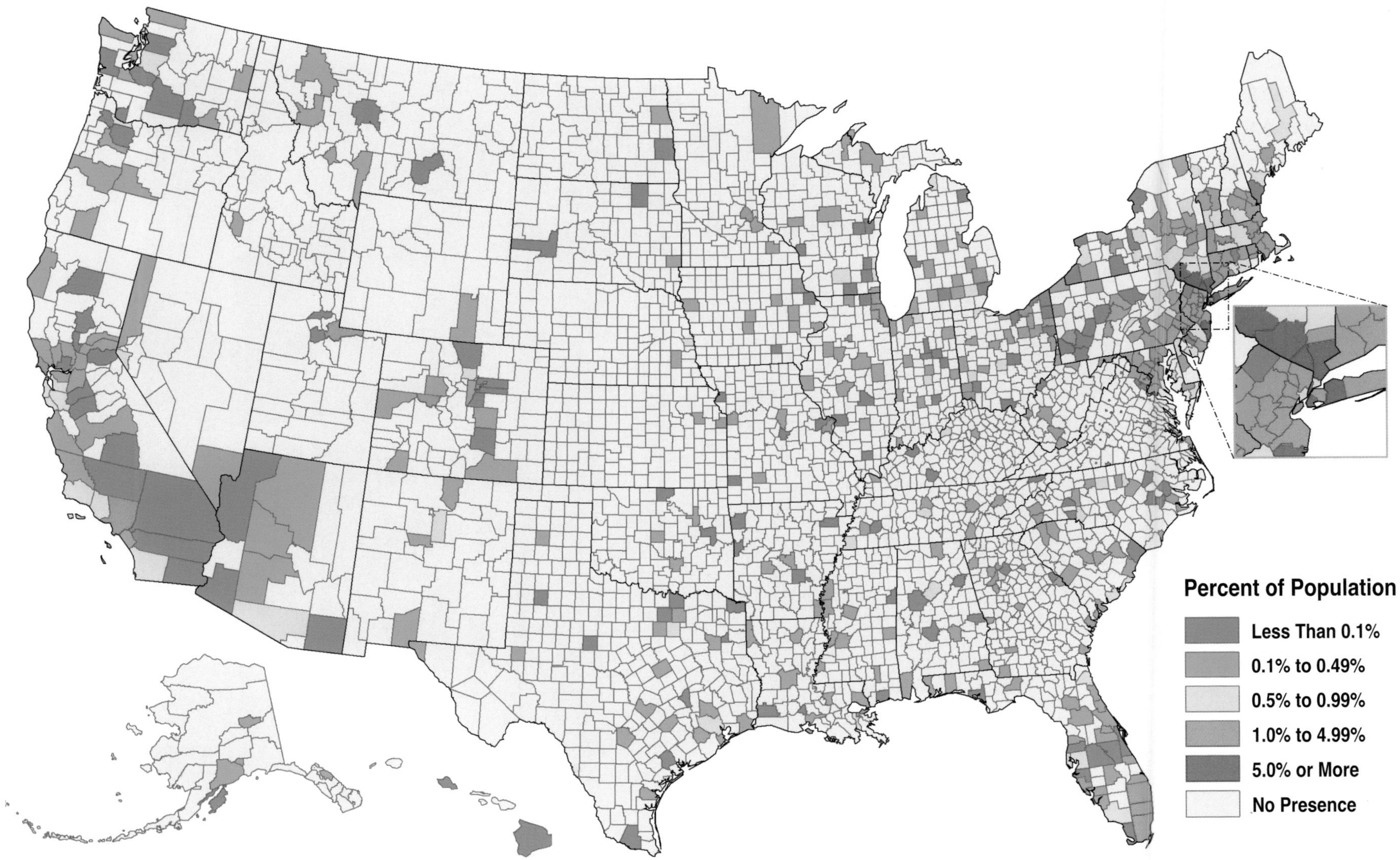

3,464 congregations and 2,256,584 adherents were reported in 548 counties.

Created by Research Services using ESRI ArcMap 10.0

Eastern Orthodox Churches

Adherents as a Percentage of Total Population, 2010

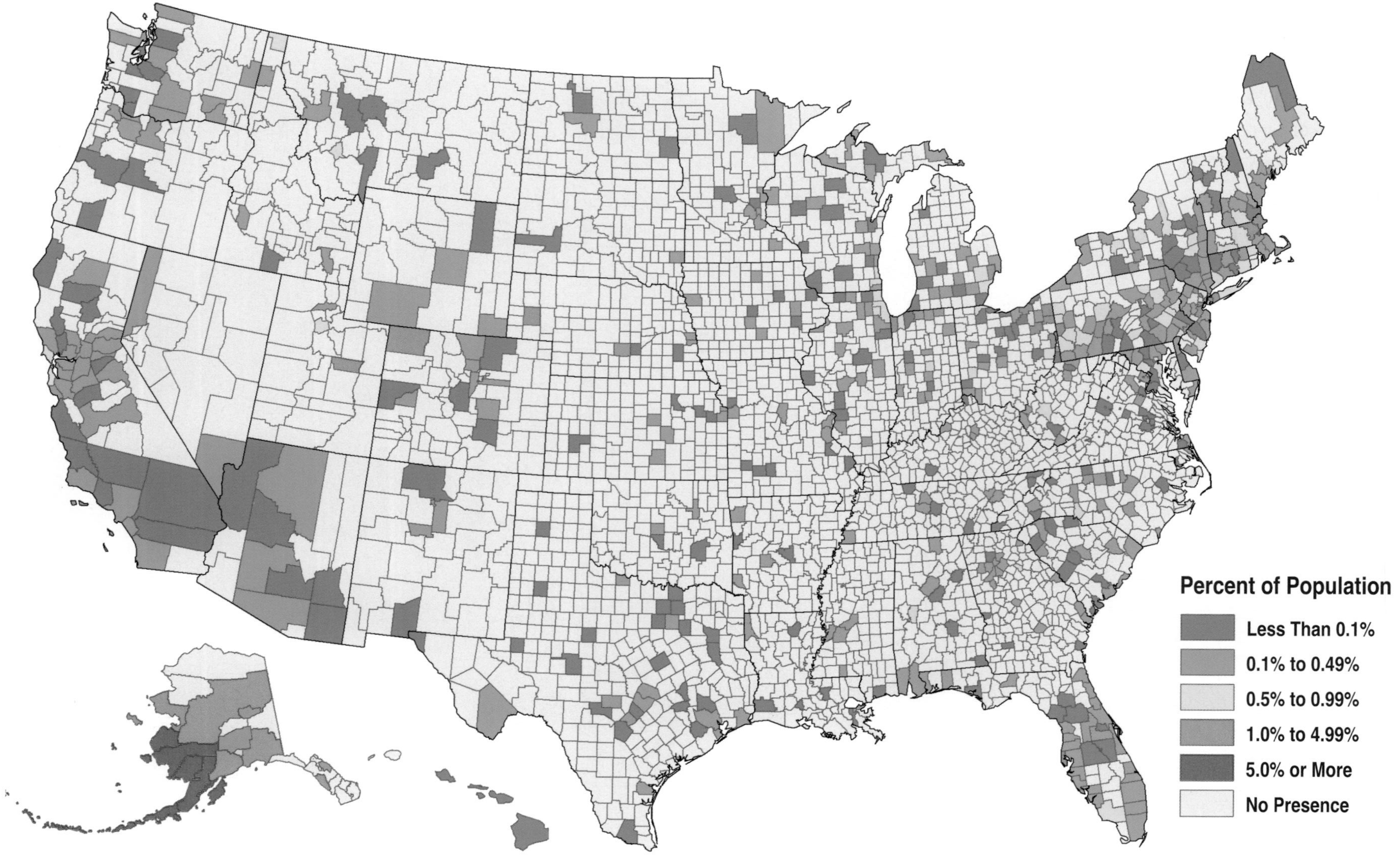

1,984 congregations and 817,501 adherents were reported in 629 counties.

Created by Research Services using ESRI ArcMap 10.0

Oriental Orthodox Churches

Adherents as a Percentage of Total Population, 2010

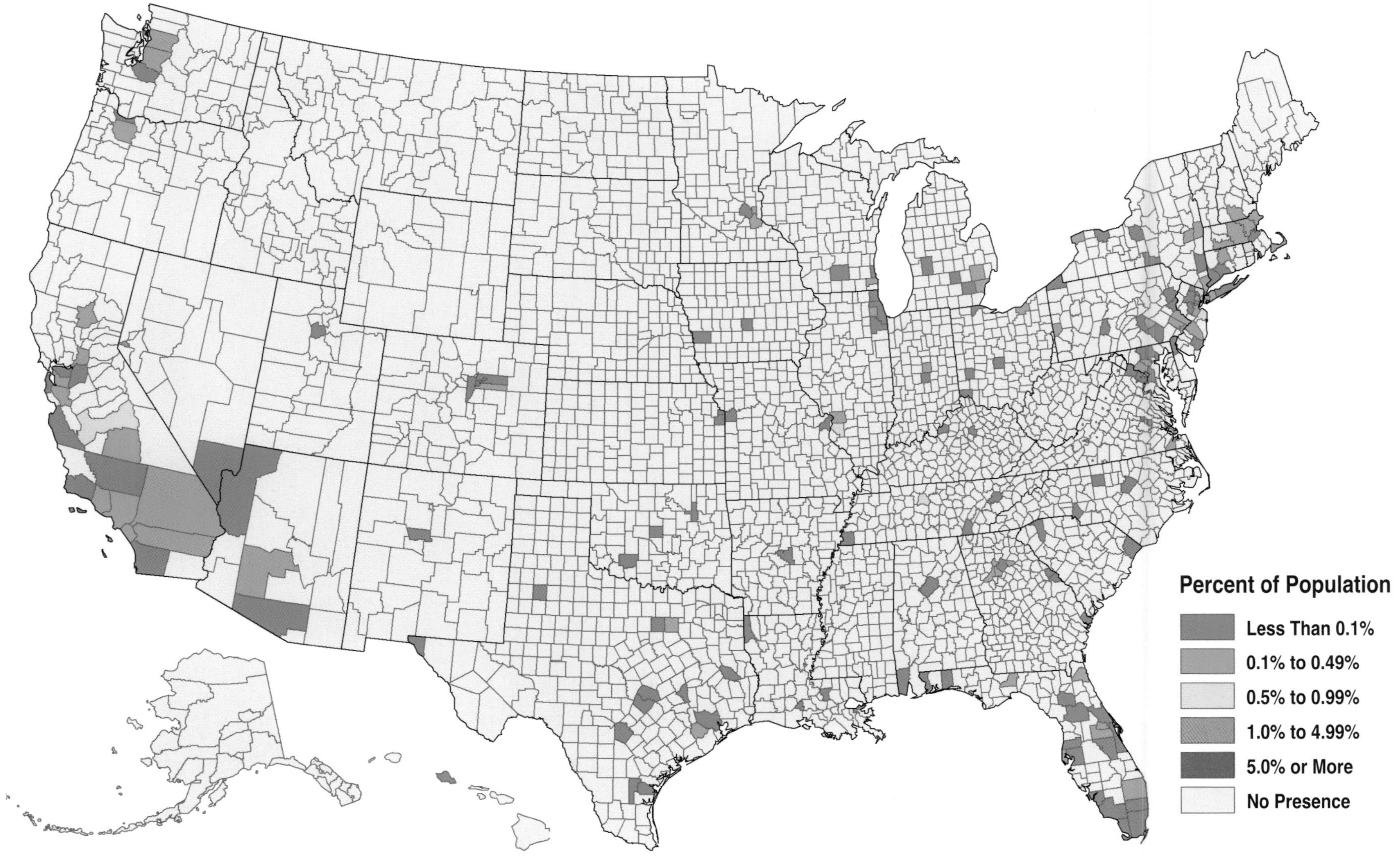

567 congregations and 239,034 adherents were reported in 194 counties.

Created by Research Services using ESRI ArcMap 10.0

Largest Participating Eastern Religion

Group with the Largest Number of Adherents by County, 2010

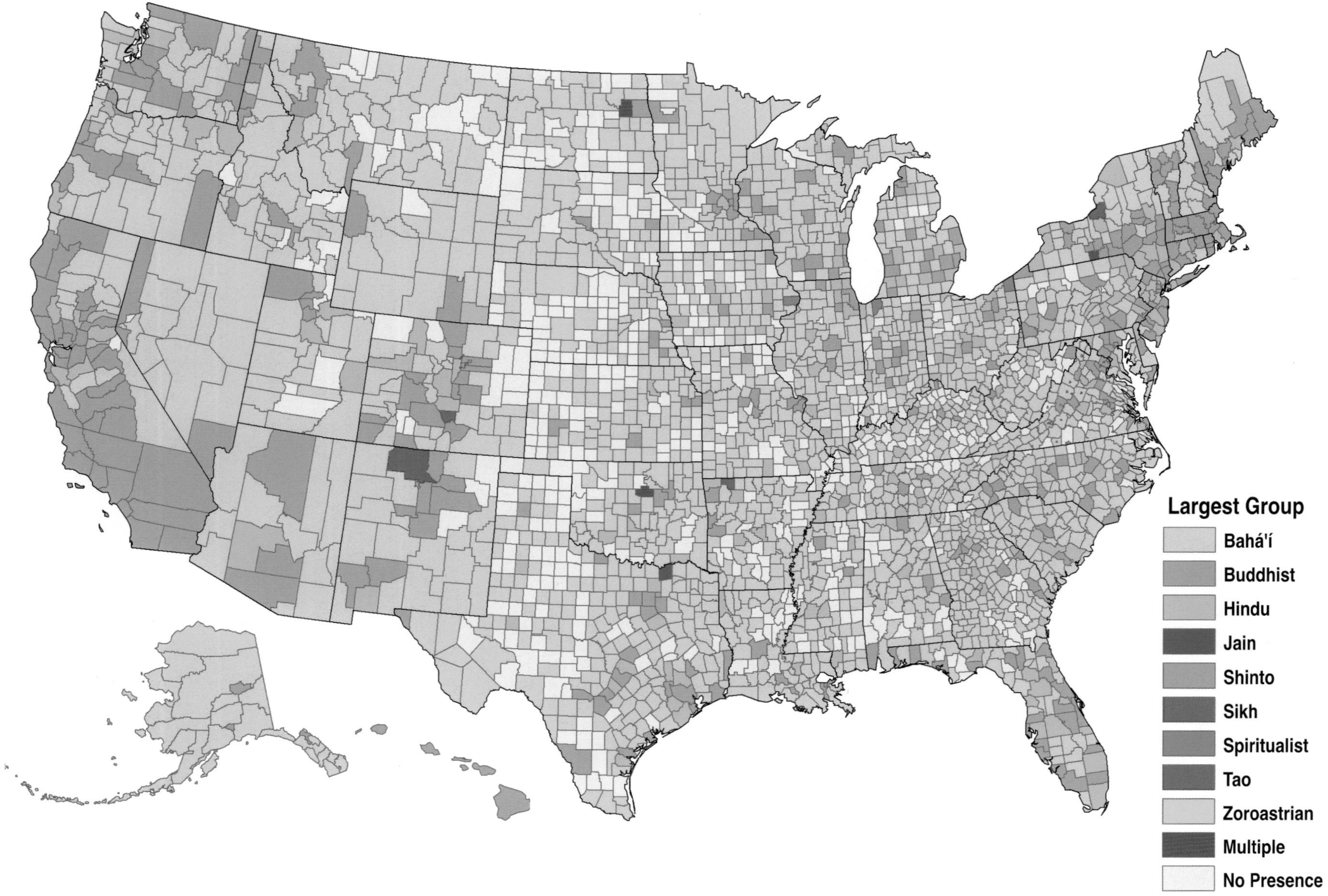

Created by Research Services using ESRI ArcMap 10.0

Largest Participating Religious Group

Group with the Largest Number of Adherents by County, 2010

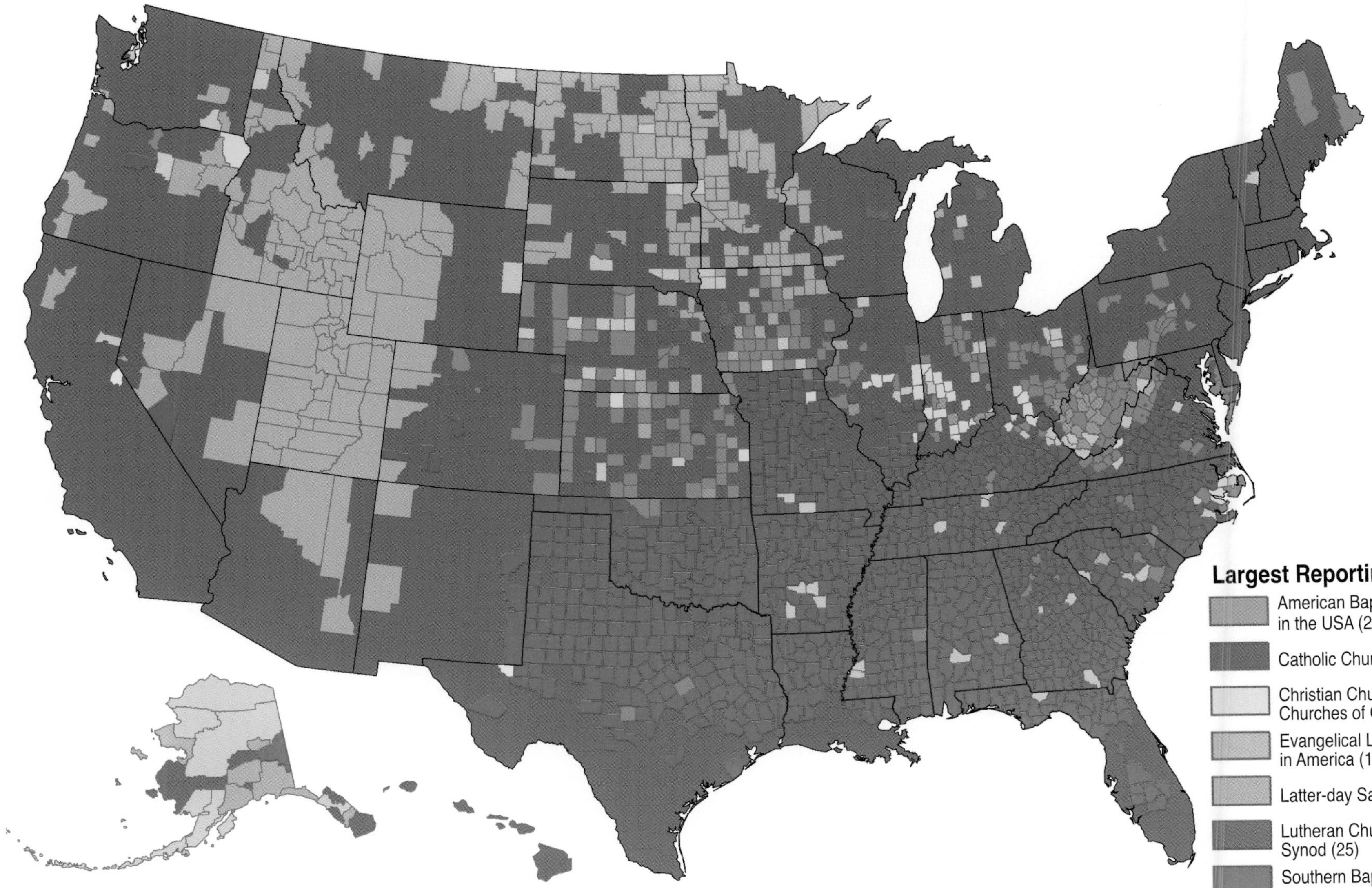

Largest Reporting Group

- American Baptist Churches in the USA (26 counties)
- Catholic Church (1,231)
- Christian Churches & Churches of Christ (33)
- Evangelical Lutheran Church in America (155)
- Latter-day Saints (115)
- Lutheran Church—Missouri Synod (25)
- Southern Baptist Convention (1,217)
- United Methodist Church (244)
- Other* (95)
- None Reported (2)

The "Other" category includes 34 groups with less than 10 counties each. Also shown as "Other" is Traverse County, Minnesota, with an equal number of Catholic Church adherents and Lutheran Church—Missouri Synod adherents.

Created by Research Services using ESRI ArcMap 10.0

Largest Participating Protestant Christian Group

Group with the Largest Number of Adherents by County, 2010

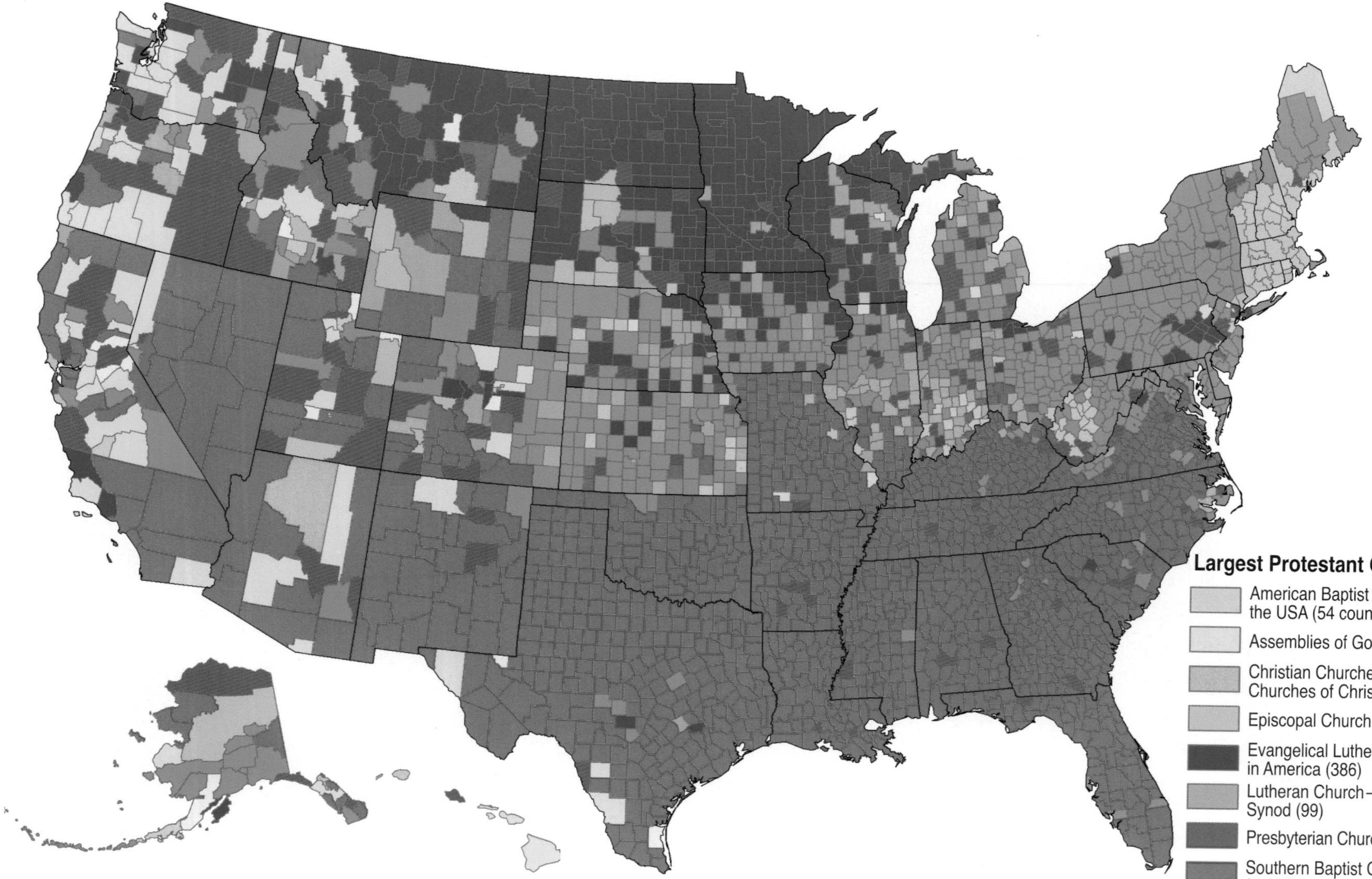

Largest Protestant Group

- American Baptist Churches in the USA (54 counties)
- Assemblies of God (77)
- Christian Churches and Churches of Christ (57)
- Episcopal Church (36)
- Evangelical Lutheran Church in America (386)
- Lutheran Church—Missouri Synod (99)
- Presbyterian Church (USA) (23)
- Southern Baptist Convention (1,513)
- United Church of Christ (44)
- United Methodist Church (641)
- *Other (204)
- None Reported (9)

* The "Other" category includes 37 groups with less than 20 counties each. Six of these had at least 10 counties where each was the largest group: Lutheran Congregations in Mission for Christ (16 counties), Wisconsin Evangelical Lutheran Synod (16), Church of the Nazarene (15), Amish Groups, undifferentiated (13), National Baptist Convention, USA, Inc. (12), and African Methodist Episcopal Church (10).

Created by Research Services using ESRI ArcMap 10.0

Religious Diversity in the United States, 2010

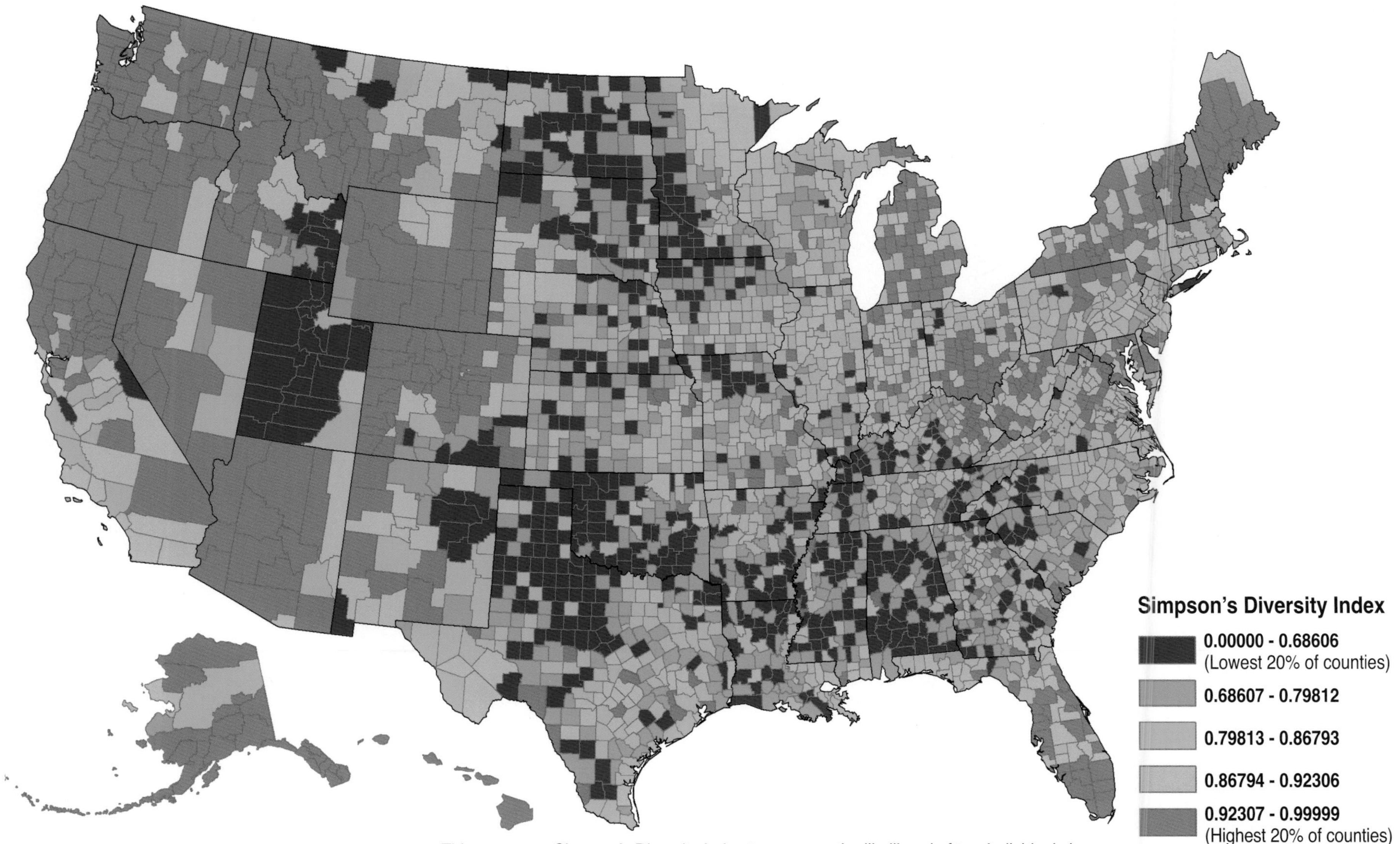

This map uses Simpson's Diversity Index to measure the likelihood of two individuals in the same county belonging to different religious groups based on the following groupings: Latter-day Saints, Catholic, Protestant, Other Christian (primarily Orthodox Christian churches), Islam, Jewish, or Other Religions. The high proportion of Protestants in the central states and the high proportion of Latter-day Saints in the mountain west create areas of low religious diversity. Greater diversity is found where many groups are at least moderately large, such as in many western states or northern New England.

Created by Research Services using ESRI ArcMap 10.0

Key to Cartograms

Same Color Scheme Used in All Cartograms

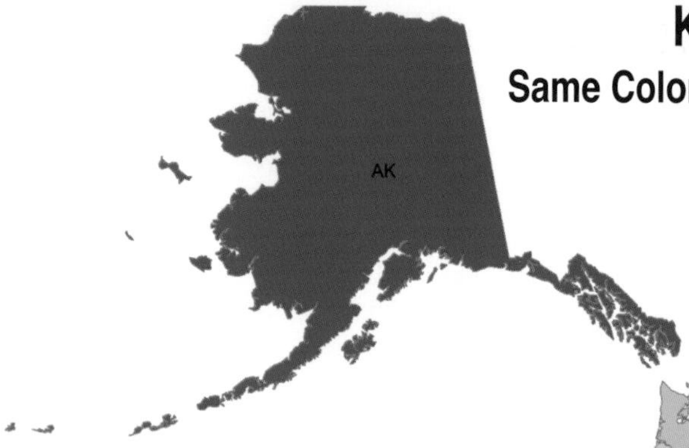

Cartograms resize each state proportionately based upon a comparable variable. This map is sized according to area, the "normal" map view. Other maps in this section are re-sized according to the number of adherents of various religious groups, as reported for that state in the *2010 U.S. Religion Census: Religious Congregations & Membership Study*. To facilitate comparisons, the color scheme remains consistent throughout the series.

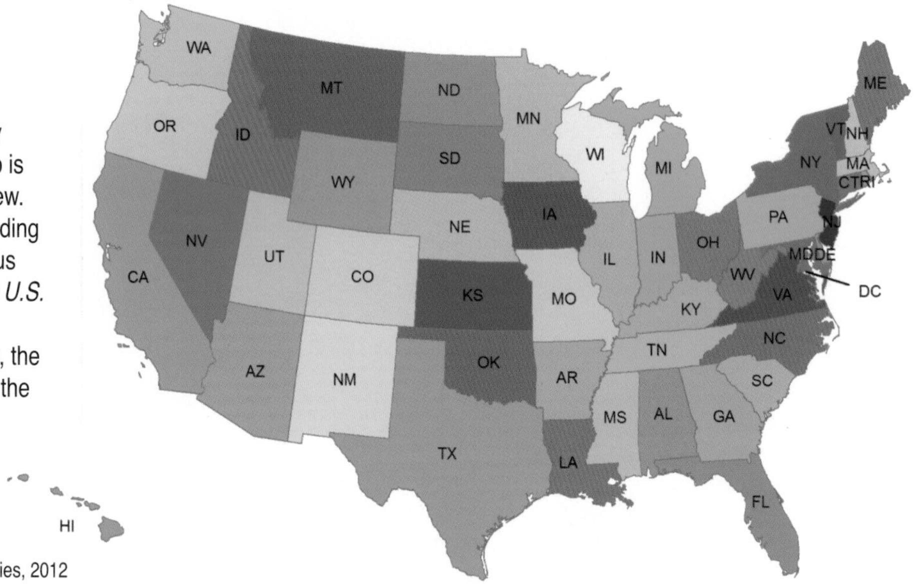

Created by Research Services using ESRI ArcMap 10.0

Total Religious Adherent, 2010

Cartogram Showing Total Adherents for 236 Religious Groups

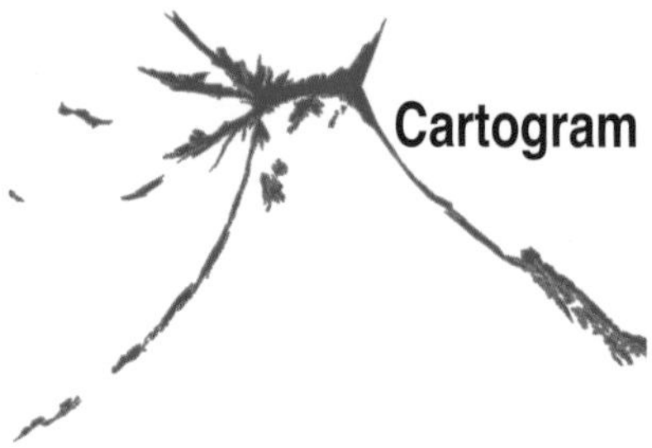

States are resized proportionately based upon the total number of adherents reported for 236 religious groups in each state in the *2010 U.S. Religion Census: Religious Congregations & Membership Study*.

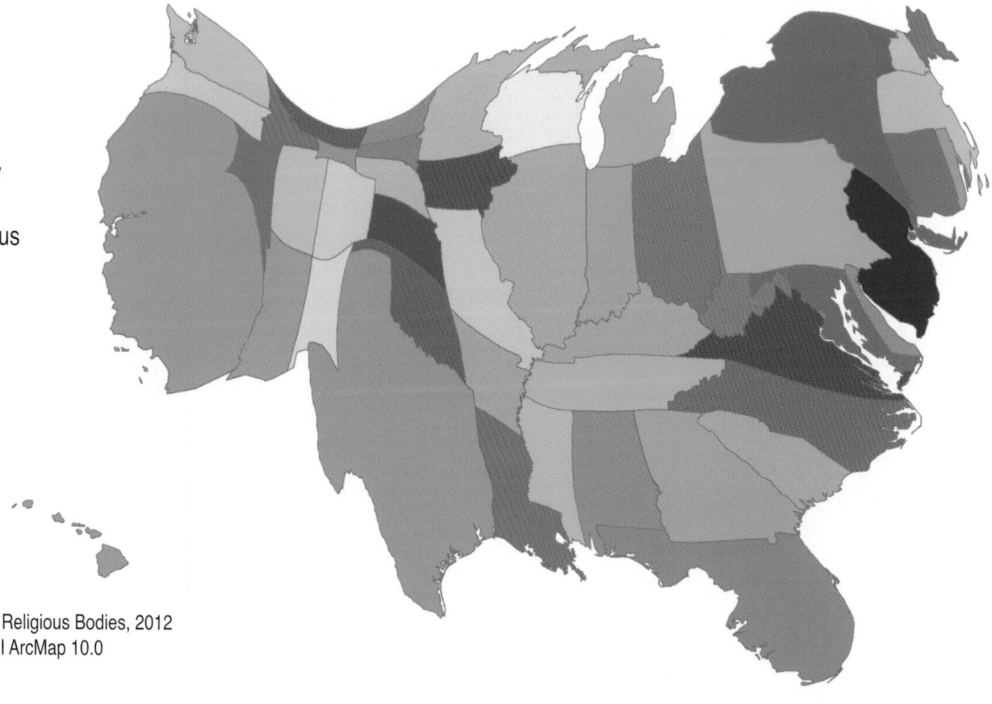

Created by Research Services using ESRI ArcMap 10.0

Church of Jesus Christ of Latter-day Saints, 2010
Cartogram of Adherents

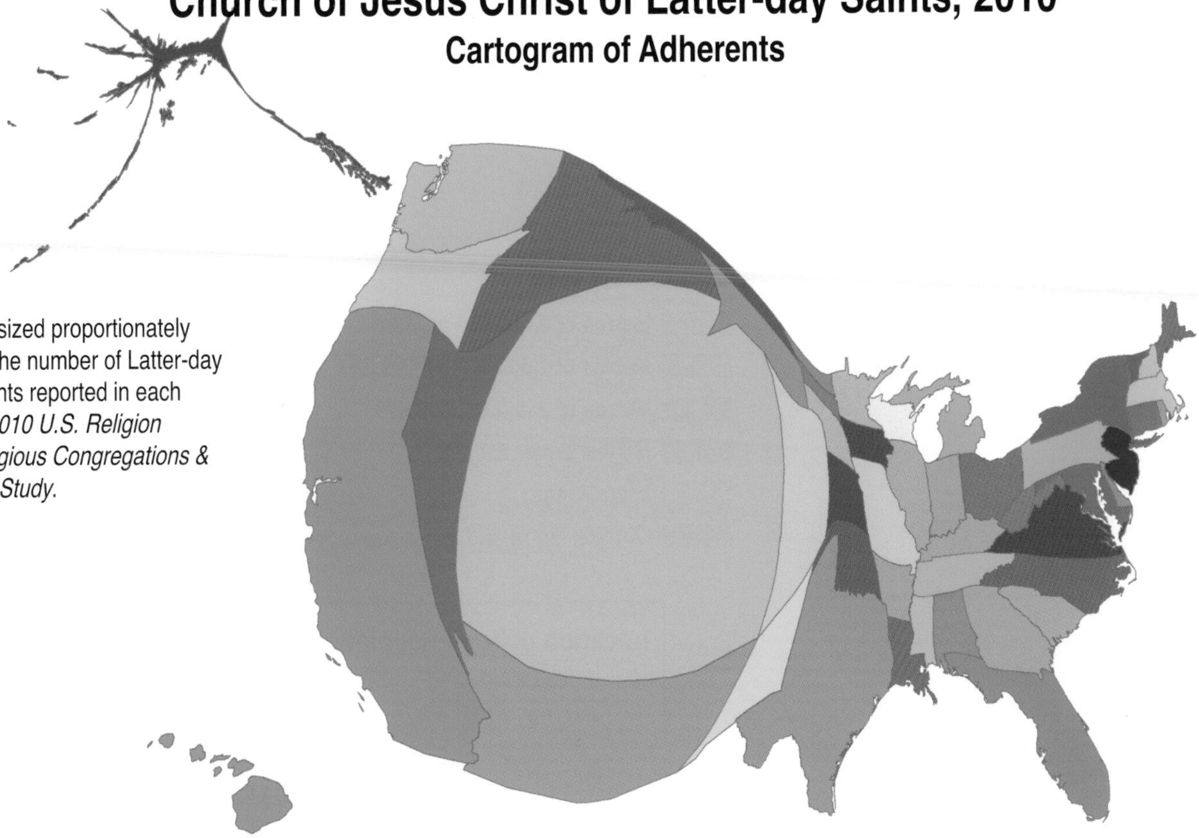

States are resized proportionately based upon the number of Latter-day Saint adherents reported in each state in the *2010 U.S. Religion Census: Religious Congregations & Membership Study.*

Created by Research Services using ESRI ArcMap 10.0

Southern Baptist Convention, 2010
Cartogram of Adherents

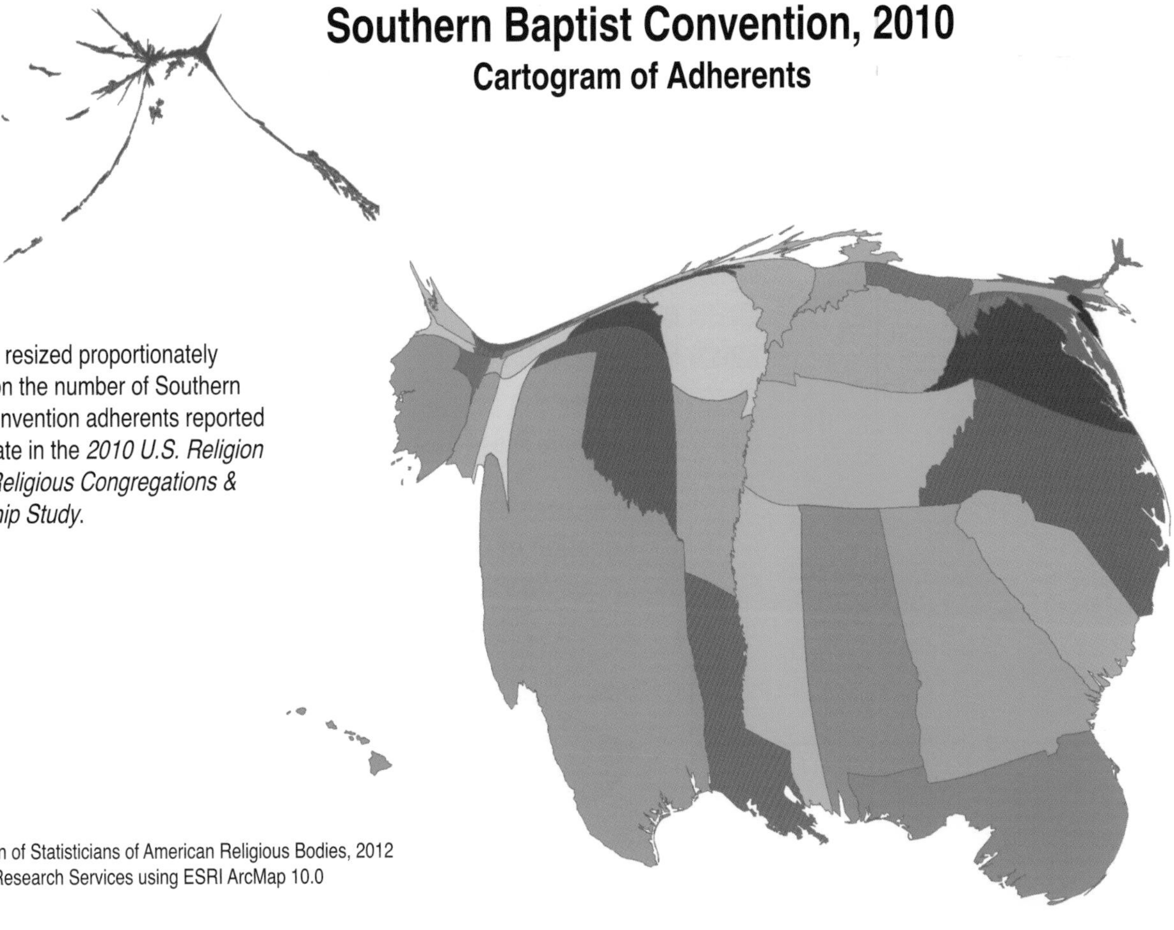

States are resized proportionately based upon the number of Southern Baptist Convention adherents reported in each state in the *2010 U.S. Religion Census: Religious Congregations & Membership Study.*

Created by Research Services using ESRI ArcMap 10.0

Distribution of Adherents and Congregations
Based on Metropolitan and Micropolitan Definitions, 2010

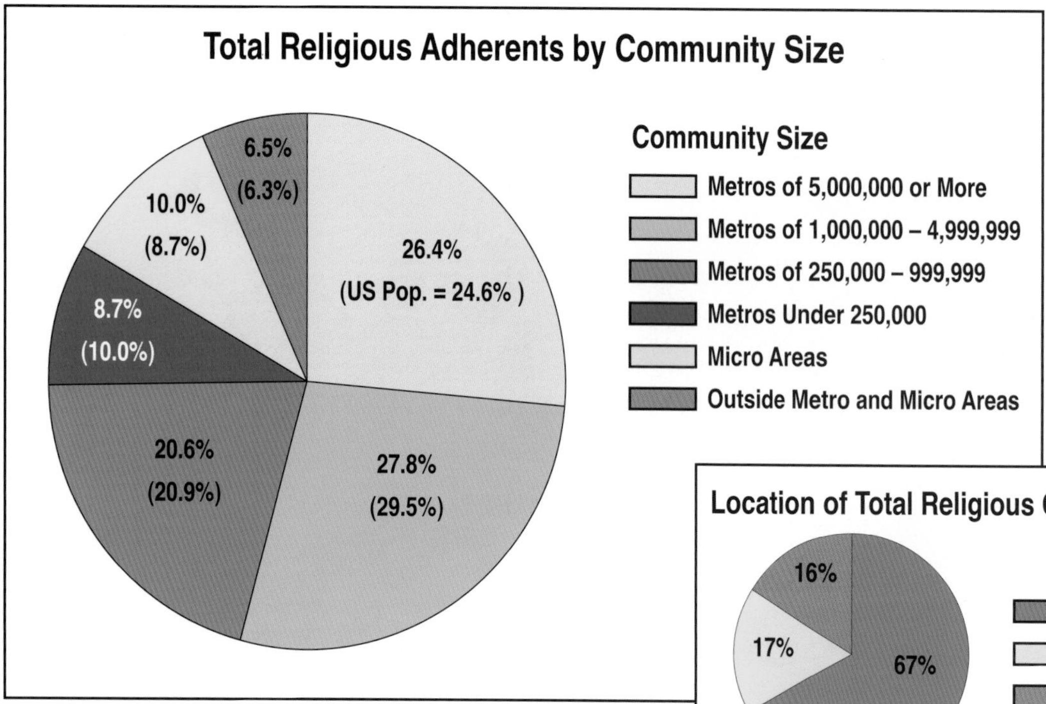

The United States government defines both metropolitan and micropolitan areas for statistical purposes. Broadly, a metropolitan area is composed of counties associated with an urban core of at least 50,000 people. At the time of the 2010 Census, metropolitan areas ranged in size from Carson City's 55,274 to New York City's 18,897,109. Micropolitan areas are composed of counties associated with smaller urban cores still having at least 10,000 people. Many counties are not associated with either metropolitan or micropolitan areas.

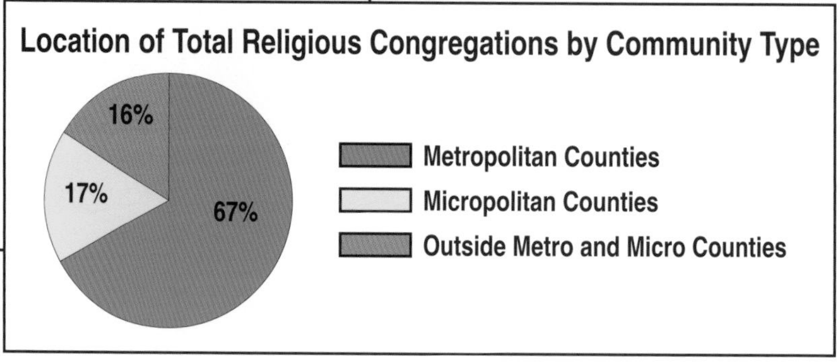

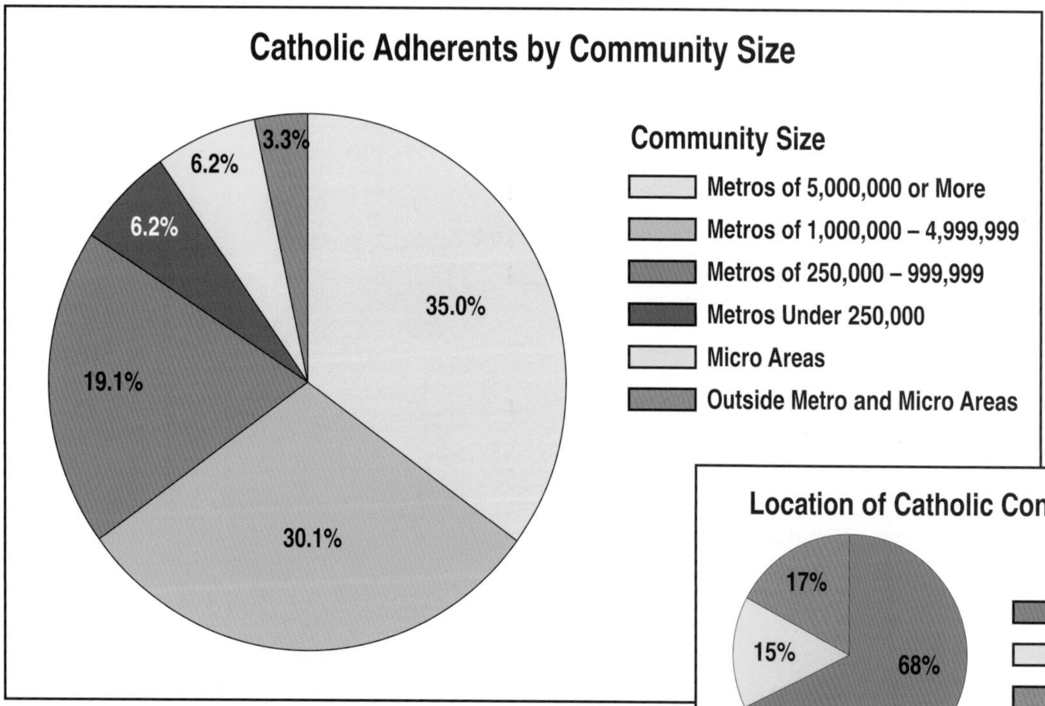

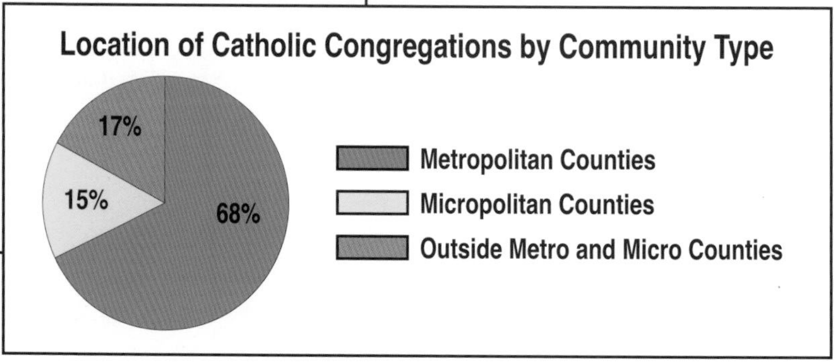

Distribution of Adherents and Congregations
Based on Metropolitan and Micropolitan Definitions, 2010

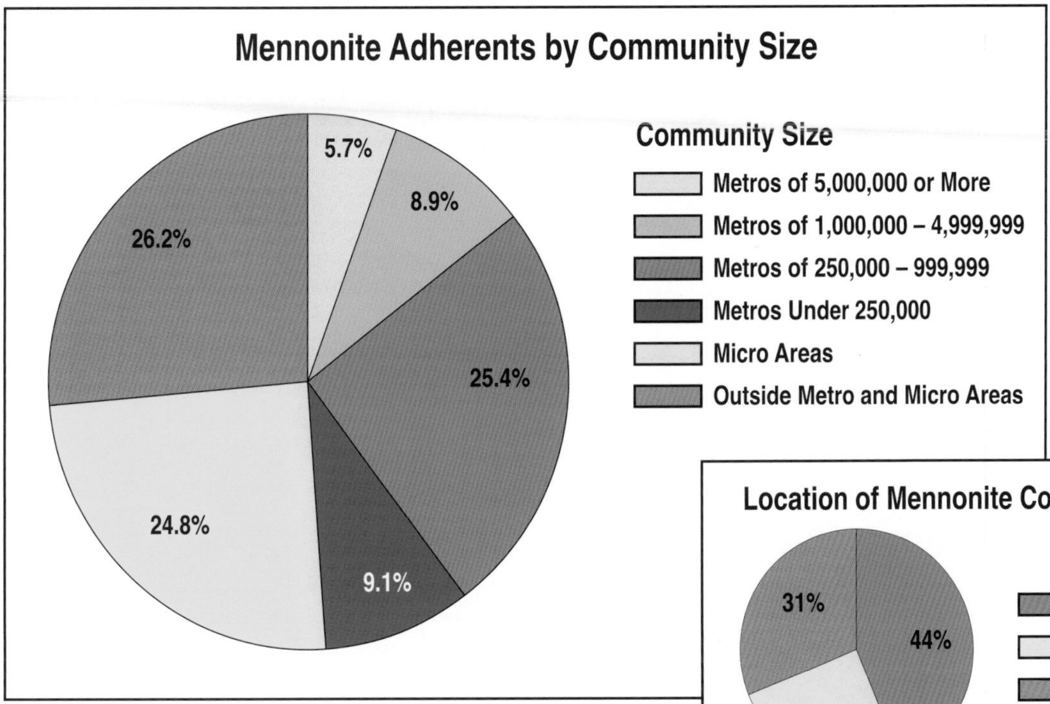

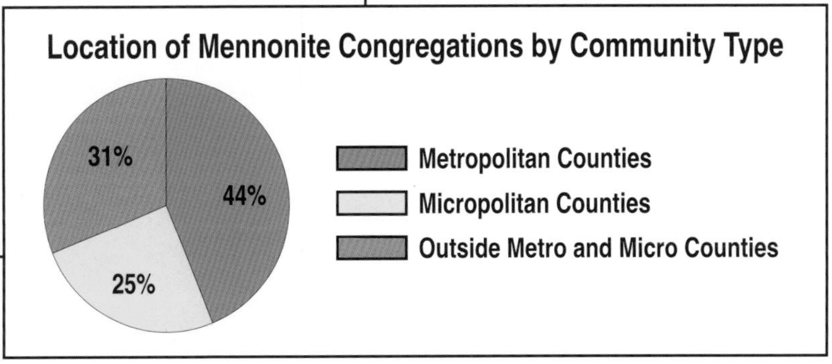

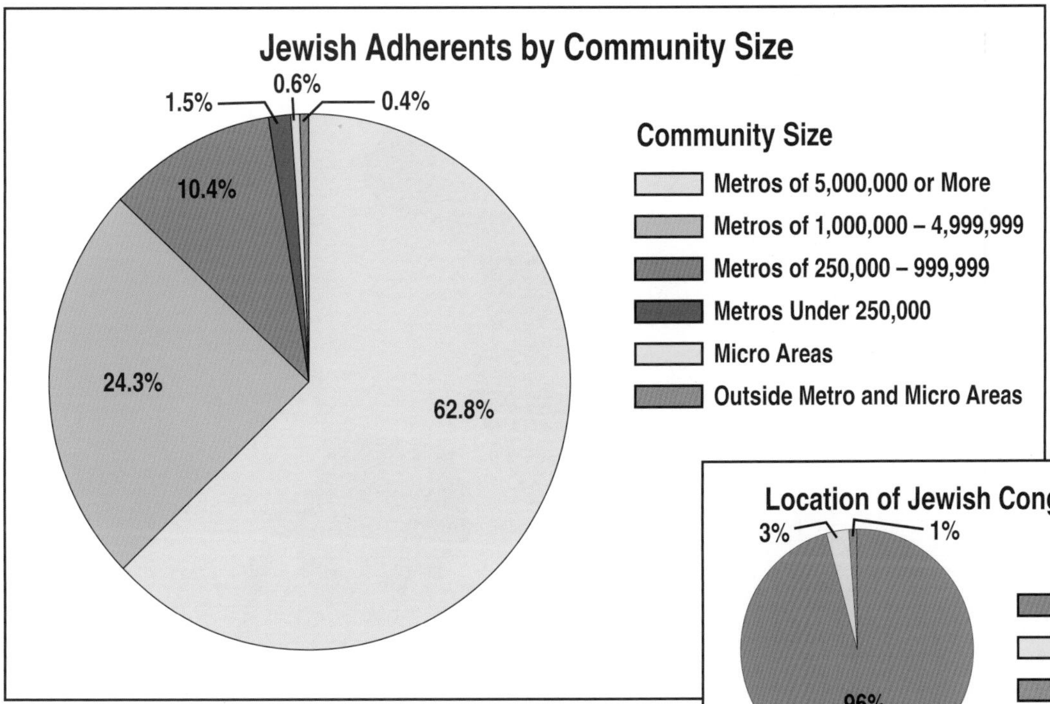

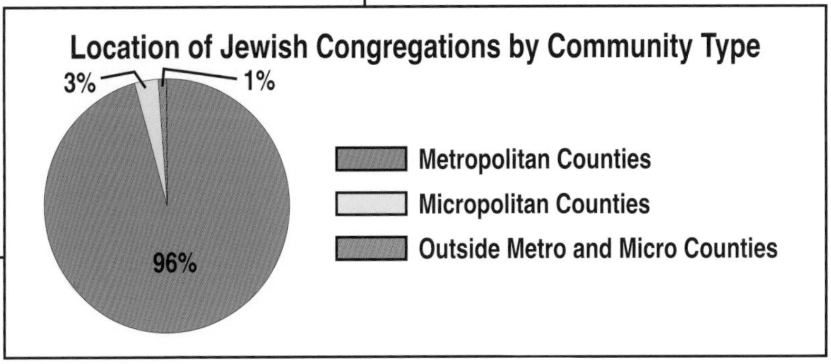

Percent of the Population Claimed by 236 Participating Religious Groups

Adherents as a Percentage of Total Population, 2010

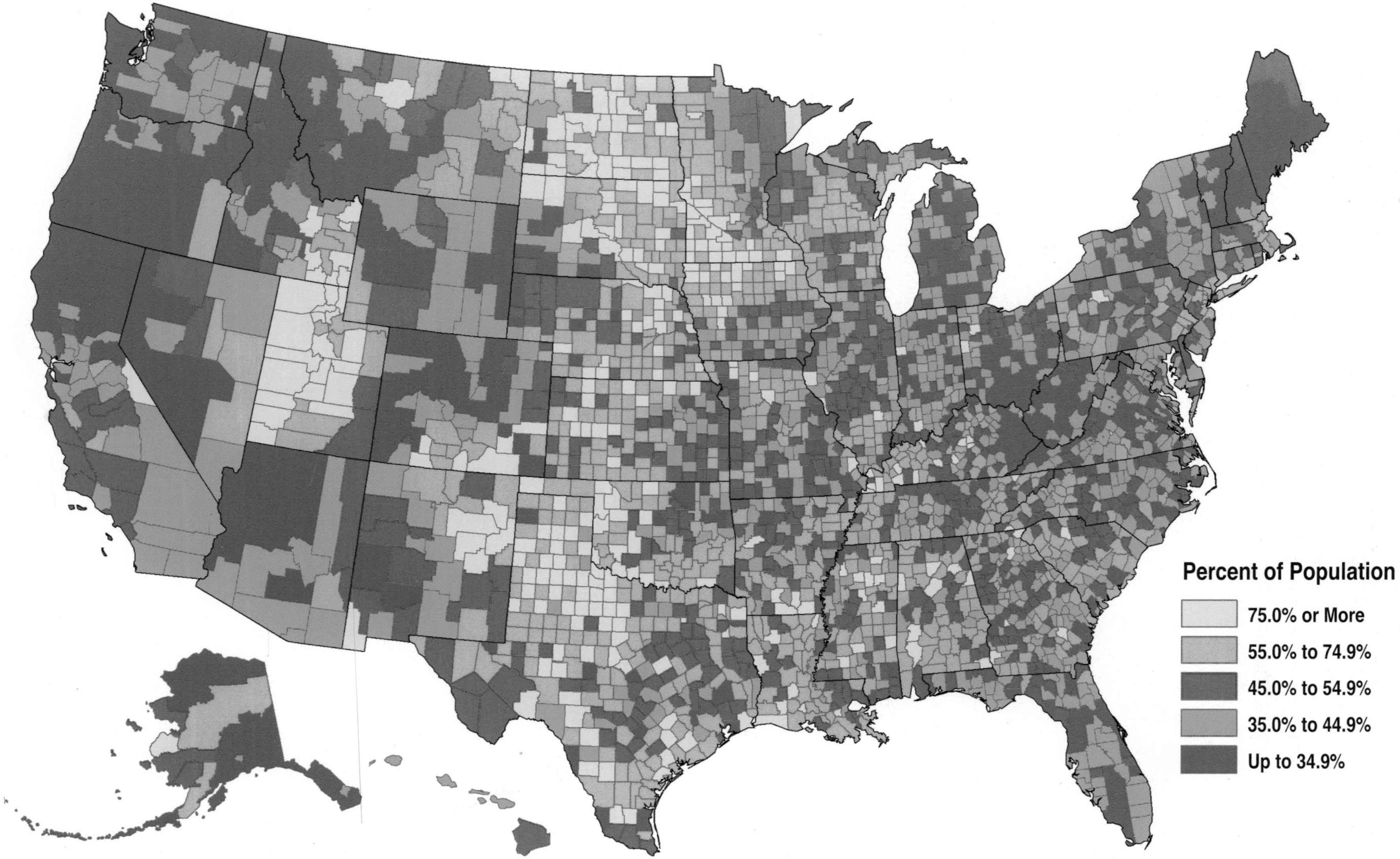

Created by Research Services using ESRI ArcMap 10.0